The HarperCollins
STUDY BIBLE

The HarperCollins
STUDY BIBLE

Fully Revised and Updated

NEW REVISED STANDARD VERSION

With the Apocryphal/Deuterocanonical Books

Student Edition

General Editor, Revised Edition
HAROLD W. ATTRIDGE

General Editor, Original Edition
WAYNE A. MEEKS

ASSOCIATE EDITORS

Jouette M. Bassler

Werner E. Lemke

Susan Niditch

Eileen M. Schuller

With the Society of Biblical Literature

HarperOne
A Division of HarperCollinsPublishers

Contents

Names and Order of the Books of the Old and New
Testaments with the Apocryphal/Deuterocanonical Books   *vi*

Alphabetical List of the Books of the New Revised Standard
Version (Including the Apocryphal/Deuterocanonical Books)   *viii*

Editorial Board   *ix*

Contributors   *x*

Introduction to the *HarperCollins Study Bible*   *xiii*

To the Reader   *xxi*

Abbreviations   *xxvii*

List of Illustrations, Maps, and Tables   *xxix*

Names and Order of Books of the Bible
in Several Traditions   *xxxi*

Time Line   *xxxiv*

Strategies for Reading Scripture   *xxxix*

Israelite Religion   *xliv*

The Greco-Roman Context of the New Testament   *xlix*

The Bible and Archaeology   *lvii*

Archaeology and the New Testament   *lxii*

The Hebrew Scriptures/The Old Testament   *1*

The Apocryphal/Deuterocanonical Books   1289

The New Testament   1651

Index to Color Maps   2121

Color Maps follow the last page of text

Names and Order of the Books of the Old and New Testaments with the Apocryphal/Deuterocanonical Books

The Old Testament with the Apocryphal/Deuterocanonical Books

THE HEBREW SCRIPTURES

Genesis, 3   Exodus, 83   Leviticus, 150   Numbers, 194   Deuteronomy, 255

Joshua, 310   Judges, 346   Ruth, 382

1 Samuel (1 Kingdoms in Greek), 389   2 Samuel (2 Kingdoms in Greek), 435

1 Kings (3 Kingdoms in Greek), 474   2 Kings (4 Kingdoms in Greek), 519

1 Chronicles (1 Paralipomenon in Greek), 560   2 Chronicles (2 Paralipomenon in Greek), 599

Ezra, 646   Nehemiah (2 Esdras in Greek), 663   Esther, 680

Job, 692   Psalms, 732   Proverbs, 849   Ecclesiastes, 890   Song of Solomon, 903

Isaiah, 912   Jeremiah, 998   Lamentations, 1085   Ezekiel, 1096

Daniel, 1168   Hosea, 1193   Joel, 1209   Amos, 1216   Obadiah, 1229

Jonah, 1233   Micah, 1238   Nahum, 1249   Habakkuk, 1254   Zephaniah, 1259

Haggai, 1265   Zechariah, 1269   Malachi, 1284

The Apocryphal/Deuterocanonical Books

THE APOCRYPHAL/DEUTEROCANONICAL BOOKS are listed here in four groupings.

(a) Books and Additions to Esther and Daniel that are in the Roman Catholic, Greek, and Slavonic Bibles:

Tobit, 1293   Judith, 1313

The Additions to the Book of Esther (with a translation of the entire Greek text of Esther), 1333

Wisdom of Solomon, 1348   Ecclesiasticus, or the Wisdom of Jesus Son of Sirach, 1378

Baruch, 1452   The Letter of Jeremiah (= Baruch ch. 6), 1460

The Additions to the Book of Daniel:

The Prayer of Azariah and the Song of the Three Jews, 1466   Susanna, 1470

Bel and the Dragon, 1474

1 Maccabees, 1477   2 Maccabees, 1519

(b) Books in the Greek and Slavonic Bibles; not in the Roman Catholic canon:

1 Esdras (= 2 Esdras in Slavonic, = 3 Esdras in Vulgate Appendix), 1548

Prayer of Manasseh (in Vulgate Appendix), 1568

Psalm 151 (following Psalm 150 in the Greek Bible), 1571   3 Maccabees, 1573

(c) In the Slavonic Bible and in the Latin Vulgate Appendix:

2 Esdras (= 3 Esdras in Slavonic, = 4 Esdras in Vulgate Appendix), *1588*

(Note: In the Latin Vulgate, Ezra–Nehemiah = 1 and 2 Esdras.)

(d) In an Appendix to the Greek Bible:

4 Maccabees, *1629*

The New Testament

Matthew, *1665*   Mark, *1722*   Luke, *1759*   John, *1814*

Acts of the Apostles, *1855*   Romans, *1909*

1 Corinthians, *1932*   2 Corinthians, *1956*   Galatians, *1972*

Ephesians, *1982*   Philippians, *1991*   Colossians, *1998*

1 Thessalonians, *2005*   2 Thessalonians, *2011*   1 Timothy, *2015*

2 Timothy, *2023*   Titus, *2028*   Philemon, *2032*   Hebrews, *2035*

James, *2052*   1 Peter, *2059*   2 Peter, *2067*

1 John, *2072*   2 John, *2079*   3 John, *2081*

Jude, *2083*   Revelation, *2086*

Alphabetical List of the Books of the New Revised Stand Version
(Including the Apocryphal/Deuterocanonical Books)

Acts of the Apostles, *1855*

Amos, *1216*

Baruch, *1452*

Bel and the Dragon, *1474*

1 Chronicles, *560*

2 Chronicles, *599*

Colossians, *1998*

1 Corinthians, *1932*

2 Corinthians, *1956*

Daniel, *1168*

Deuteronomy, *255*

Ecclesiastes, *890*

Ephesians, *1982*

1 Esdras, *1548*

2 Esdras, *1588*

Esther, *680*

Esther with the Additions, *1333*

Exodus, *83*

Ezekiel, *1096*

Ezra, *646*

Galatians, *1972*

Genesis, *3*

Habakkuk, *1254*

Haggai, *1265*

Hebrews, *2035*

Hosea, *1193*

Isaiah, *912*

James, *2052*

Jeremiah, *998*

Job, *692*

Joel, *1209*

John, *1814*

1 John, *2072*

2 John, *2079*

3 John, *2081*

Jonah, *1233*

Joshua, *310*

Jude, *2083*

Judges, *346*

Judith, *1313*

1 Kings, *474*

2 Kings, *519*

Lamentations, *1085*

Letter of Jeremiah, *1460*

Leviticus, *150*

Luke, *1759*

1 Maccabees, *1477*

2 Maccabees, *1519*

3 Maccabees, *1573*

4 Maccabees, *1629*

Malachi, *1284*

Mark, *1722*

Matthew, *1665*

Micah, *1238*

Nahum, *1249*

Nehemiah, *663*

Numbers, *194*

Obadiah, *1229*

1 Peter, *2059*

2 Peter, *2067*

Philemon, *2032*

Philippians, *1991*

Prayer of Azariah and
  the Song of the Three Jews, *1466*

Prayer of Manasseh, *1568*

Proverbs, *849*

Psalm 151, *1571*

Psalms, *732*

Revelation, *2086*

Romans, *1909*

Ruth, *382*

1 Samuel, *389*

2 Samuel, *435*

Sirach (Ecclesiasticus), *1378*

Song of Solomon, *903*

Susanna, *1470*

1 Thessalonians, *2005*

2 Thessalonians, *2011*

1 Timothy, *2015*

2 Timothy, *2023*

Titus, *2028*

Tobit, *1293*

Wisdom of Solomon, *1348*

Zechariah, *1269*

Zephaniah, *1259*

Editorial Board

Contributors

Paul J. Achtemeier, Th.D. Professor Emeritus of Biblical Interpretation; Union Theological Seminary and Presbyterian School of Christian Education; Richmond, Virginia; *1 Peter*

James S. Ackerman, Th.D. Professor of Religious Studies; Indiana University; Bloomington, Indiana; *Jonah*

Harold W. Attridge, Ph.D. Dean and Lillian Claus Professor of New Testament; Yale University Divinity School; New Haven, Connecticut; *John, Philemon, Hebrews, 1, 2, 3 John*

David E. Aune, Ph.D. Professor, Department of Theology; University of Notre Dame; Notre Dame, Indiana; *The Greco-Roman Context of the New Testament, Revelation*

David L. Balch, Ph.D. Professor of New Testament; Brite Divinity School; Texas Christian University; Fort Worth, Texas; *1 Peter*

John Barton, D.Phil., D.Litt. Oriel and Laing Professor of the Interpretation of Holy Scripture; University of Oxford, Oriel College; Oxford, England; *Strategies for Reading Scripture*

Jouette M. Bassler, Ph.D. Professor of New Testament; Perkins School of Theology; Southern Methodist University; Dallas, Texas; *2 Thessalonians, 1, 2 Timothy, Titus*

Richard J. Bauckham, Ph.D. Professor of New Testament; St. Mary's College; University of St. Andrews; St. Andrews, Scotland; *2 Peter, Jude*

Ehud Ben Zvi, Ph.D. Professor of Religious Studies; University of Alberta; Edmonton, Alberta, Canada; *Obadiah*

Adele Berlin, Ph.D. Robert H. Smith Professor of Hebrew Bible; University of Maryland; College Park, Maryland; *Ruth*

C. Clifton Black, Ph.D. Otto A. Piper Professor of Biblical Theology; Princeton Theological Seminary; Princeton, New Jersey; *Mark*

†Robert G. Boling, Ph.D. *Joshua, Judges*

Roger S. Boraas, Ph.D. Elkins Park, Pennsylvania; *Consultant for Maps*

Claudia V. Camp, Ph.D. Professor of Religion; Texas Christian University; Fort Worth, Texas; *Proverbs*

Richard J. Clifford, Ph.D. Professor of Old Testament; Weston Jesuit School of Theology; Cambridge, Massachusetts; *Letter of Jeremiah*

David J. A. Clines, M.A. Emeritus Professor of Biblical Studies; University of Sheffield; Sheffield, England; *Ezra, Nehemiah, 1 Esdras*

John J. Collins, Ph.D. Holmes Professor of Old Testament Criticism and Interpretation; Yale University Divinity School; New Haven, Connecticut; *Daniel, Judith, 3 Maccabees*

Stephen L. Cook, Ph.D. Associate Professor Old Testament; Virginia Theological Seminary; Alexandria, Virginia; *Hosea*

Toni Craven, Ph.D. I. Wylie and Elizabeth Briscoe Professor of Hebrew Bible; Brite Divinity School; Texas Christian University; Fort Worth, Texas; *Judith*

Sidnie White Crawford, Ph.D. Professor of Hebrew Bible; University of Nebraska at Lincoln; Lincoln, Nebraska; *Esther, Additions to Esther*

James L. Crenshaw, Ph.D. Robert L. Flowers Professor of Old Testament; The Divinity School; Duke University; Durham, North Carolina; *Job*

J. Andrew Dearman, Ph.D. Professor of Old Testament; Austin Presbyterian Theological Seminary; Austin, Texas; *Amos*

Carol J. Dempsey, Ph.D. Associate Professor of Theology; University of Portland; Portland, Oregon; *Micah*

Dennis C. Duling, Ph.D. Professor of Religious Studies; Canisius College; Buffalo, New York; *Matthew*

John T. Fitzgerald, Ph.D. Associate Professor of New Testament; University of Miami; Coral Gables, Florida; *2 Corinthians*

Carole R. Fontaine, Ph.D. Taylor Professor of Biblical Theology and History; Andover-Newton Theological School; Newton Centre, Massachusetts; *Proverbs*

Michael V. Fox, Ph.D. Jay C. and Ruth Halls-Bascom Professor of Hebrew; University of Wisconsin; Madison, Wisconsin; *Song of Solomon*

Victor Paul Furnish, Ph.D. University Distinguished Professor Emeritus of New Testament; Perkins School of Theology; Southern Methodist University; Dallas, Texas; *1 Corinthians*

Beverly Roberts Gaventa, Ph.D. Helen H. P. Manson Professor of New Testament Literature and Exegesis; Princeton Theological Seminary; Princeton, New Jersey; *Acts*

Jeffrey C. Geoghegan, Ph.D. Assistant Professor of Theology; Boston College; Boston, Massachusetts; *Letter of Jeremiah*

Edward L. Greenstein, Ph.D. Professor of Bible; Tel Aviv University; Tel Aviv, Israel; *Exodus*

Jo Ann Hackett, Ph.D. Professor of the Practice of Biblical Hebrew and Northwest Semitic Epigraphy; Harvard University; Cambridge, Massachusetts; *Numbers*

Daniel J. Harrington, Ph.D. Professor of New Testament; Weston Jesuit School of Theology; Cambridge, Massachusetts; *1, 2 Maccabees*

Richard B. Hays, Ph.D. George Washington Ivey Professor of New Testament; The Divinity School; Duke University; Durham, North Carolina; *Galatians*

Ronald Hendel, Ph.D. Professor of Hebrew Bible; University of California at Berkeley; Berkeley, California; *Israelite Religion, Genesis*

Richard A. Henshaw, Ph.D. Professor Emeritus of Old Testament; Colgate Rochester Crozer Divinity School; Rochester, New York; *Joel, Obadiah*

Ronald F. Hock, Ph.D. Professor of Religion; University of Southern California; Los Angeles, California; *Philippians, Philemon*

W. Lee Humphreys, Ph.D. Emeritus Professor of Religious Studies; University of Tennessee; Knoxville, Tennessee; *Esther, Esther with the Additions*

Leander E. Keck, Ph.D. Winkley Emeritus Professor of Biblical Theology; Yale University Divinity School; New Haven, Connecticut; *Romans*

Philip J. King, S.T.D. Professor Emeritus of Biblical Studies; Boston College; Chestnut Hill, Massachusetts; *Micah*

Ralph W. Klein, Th.D. Christ Seminary–Seminex Professor of Old Testament; Lutheran School of Theology at Chicago; Chicago, Illinois; *1, 2 Chronicles*

Edgar M. Krentz, Ph.D. Christ Seminary–Seminex Professor of New Testament, Emeritus; Lutheran School of Theology at Chicago; Chicago, Illinois; *1 Thessalonians*

Sophie Laws, B.Litt., M.A. Oxon. Professor of History and Religion; Regent's College; London, England; *James*

Werner E. Lemke, Th.D. Baptist Missionary Training School Professor Emeritus of Biblical Interpretation; Colgate Rochester Crozer Divinity School; Rochester, New York; *Lamentations*

S. Dean McBride Jr., Ph.D. Cyrus H. McCormick Professor of Hebrew and Old Testament Interpretation; Union Theological Seminary and Presbyterian School of Christian Education; Richmond, Virginia; *Deuteronomy*

P. Kyle McCarter Jr., Ph.D. William Foxwell Albright Professor of Ancient Near Eastern Studies; Johns Hopkins University; Baltimore, Maryland; *1, 2 Samuel*

Burton L. Mack, Ph.D. Emeritus Professor of New Testament; Claremont School of Theology; Claremont, California; *Sirach*

Christopher R. Matthews, Ph.D. Adjunct Assistant Professor of New Testament; Weston Jesuit School of Theology; Cambridge, Massachusetts; *Luke*

James Luther Mays, Ph.D. Cyrus McCormick Professor Emeritus of Hebrew and Old Testament Interpretation; Union Theological Seminary and Presbyterian School of Christian Education; Richmond, Virginia; *Hosea*

Eric M. Meyers, Ph.D. Bernice and Morton Lerner Professor of Judaic Studies; Duke University; Durham, North Carolina; *The Bible and Archaeology*

Jacob Milgrom, D.H.L. Emeritus Professor of Hebrew and Bible; University of California at Berkeley; Berkeley, California; *Leviticus*

Patrick D. Miller, Ph.D. Charles T. Haley Professor of Old Testament Theology Emeritus; Princeton Theological Seminary; Princeton, New Jersey; *Psalms*

Pamela J. Milne, Ph.D. Professor of Religious Studies; University of Windsor; Windsor, Ontario, Canada; *Daniel*

Richard D. Nelson, Ph.D. W. J. A. Power Professor of Biblical Hebrew and Old Testament;

Interpretation; Perkins School of Theology; Southern Methodist University; Dallas, Texas; *Joshua, Judges*

Carol A. Newsom, Ph.D. Charles Howard Candler Professor of Old Testament; Candler School of Theology; Emory University; Atlanta, Georgia; *Baruch*

George W. E. Nickelsburg, Th.D. Emeritus Professor of New Testament and Early Judaism; University of Iowa; Iowa City, Iowa; *Tobit*

Kathleen O'Connor, Ph.D. William Marcellus McPheeters Professor of Old Testament; Columbia Theological Seminary; Decatur, Georgia; *Lamentations*

Leo G. Perdue, Ph.D. Professor of Hebrew Bible; Brite Divinity School; Texas Christian University; Fort Worth, Texas; *Jeremiah*

David L. Petersen, Ph.D. Professor of Old Testament; Candler School of Theology; Emory University; Atlanta, Georgia; *Ezekiel*

David K. Rensberger, Ph.D. Professor of New Testament; Interdenominational Theological Center; Atlanta, Georgia; *John, 1, 2, 3 John*

Kent Harold Richards, Ph.D. Professor of Old Testament, Executive Director; Society of Biblical Literature; Atlanta, Georgia; *Ecclesiastes, Nahum, Habakkuk, Zephaniah*

J. J. M. Roberts, Ph.D. William Henry Green Professor of Old Testament Literature Emeritus; Princeton Theological Seminary; Princeton, New Jersey; *Isaiah*

Joel W. Rosenberg *Genesis, first edition*

J. Paul Sampley, Ph.D. Professor of New Testament; Boston University; Boston, Massachusetts; *Ephesians, Colossians*

James A. Sanders, Ph.D. Emeritus Professor of Biblical Studies; Claremont School of Theology; Claremont, California; *Prayer of Manasseh, Psalm 151*

Michael E. Stone, Ph.D., D. Litt. Gail Levin De Nur Professor of Comparative Religion; Hebrew University of Jerusalem; Jerusalem, Israel; *2 Esdras*

Marvin A. Sweeney, Ph.D. Professor of Hebrew Bible; Claremont School of Theology; Claremont, California; *Joel*

David L. Tiede, Ph.D. Bernhard M. Christensen Professor in Religion; Augsburg College; Minneapolis, Minnesota; *Luke*

Thomas H. Tobin, Ph.D. Professor of Theology; Loyola University of Chicago; Chicago, Illinois; *Wisdom of Solomon, 4 Maccabees*

W. Sibley Towner, Ph.D. Professor Emeritus of Biblical Interpretation; Union Theological Seminary and Presbyterian School of Christian Education; Richmond, Virginia; *Haggai, Zechariah, Malachi*

Gene M. Tucker, Ph.D. Emeritus Professor of Old Testament; Candler School of Theology; Emory University; Atlanta, Georgia; *Amos*

Raymond C. Van Leeuwen, Ph.D. Professor of Biblical Studies; Eastern University; St. Davids, Pennsylvania; *Ecclesiastes*

Lawrence Wills, Th.D. Ethelbert Talbot Professor of Biblical Studies; Episcopal Divinity School; Cambridge, Massachusetts; *Prayer of Azariah and the Song of the Three Jews, Susanna, Bel and the Dragon*

Robert R. Wilson, Ph.D. Hoober Professor of Religious Studies and Professor of Old Testament; Yale University Divinity School; New Haven, Connecticut; *1, 2 Kings, Jeremiah*

Walter T. Wilson, Ph.D. Associate Professor of New Testament; Candler School of Theology; Emory University; Atlanta, Georgia; *James*

David Winston, Ph.D. Professor Emeritus of Hellenistic and Judaic Studies; Graduate Theological Union; Berkeley, California; *Wisdom of Solomon*

Benjamin G. Wright III, Ph.D. Professor of the History of Christianity; Lehigh University; Bethlehem, Pennsylvania; *Sirach, 2 Esdras*

Adela Yarbro Collins, Ph.D. Buckingham Professor of New Testament Criticism and Interpretation; Yale University Divinity School; New Haven, Connecticut; *Mark*

Jürgen Zangenberg, Ph.D. Professor, Faculty of Theological Studies; University of Leiden; Leiden, The Netherlands; *Archaeology and the New Testament*

John Leinenweber Research Associate; Yale University Divinity School; *Editorial assistant, revised edition*

Lindsay A. Lingo Publications Staff; Society of Biblical Literature; *Editorial assistant, revised edition*

Introduction to the HarperCollins Study Bible

WAYNE A. MEEKS

THE BIBLE IS THE MOST FAMILIAR BOOK in the English-speaking world; certainly it is the one most often published and most widely owned. Yet many a serious reader has found it one of the strangest of books. This paradox arises from factors in the book's history as well as from dimensions of our own history that have shaped the expectations with which we begin to read.

Enabling the Reader to Read

The most elementary of the obstacles standing in the way of reading the Bible is that its component parts were originally written in languages most of us do not know. Reading must therefore begin with a translation. The New Revised Standard Version stands in a tradition, many centuries old, of translating the Bible so that ordinary people can understand it when it is read aloud in worship gatherings or when they study it for themselves. More immediately, the NRSV stands in a direct succession from the King James Version of 1611 (as Professor Metzger explains in the Translation Committee's preface, pp. xxi–xxv). The NRSV is one among a large number of recent translations of the whole or parts of the Bible that together give to the present generation of English readers an unprecedented variety of fresh renderings of the original languages. All these are informed by significant advances in historical, archaeological, and linguistic knowledge that have occurred in recent decades.

The NRSV is selected for this *HarperCollins Study Bible* for several reasons, of which two are most significant. First, the declared intention of the Translation Committee to produce a translation "as literal as possible" makes this version well adapted for study. For example, careful reading is enhanced when we can observe such things as the recurrence of certain key words; if these are rendered into our language with some consistency, the task is obviously easier. Second, the NRSV was designed to be as inclusive as possible, in two different senses. It includes the most complete range of biblical books representing the several differing canons of scripture (about which more will be said below) than any other English version. In addition, it avoids language that might inappropriately suggest limits of gender.

Yet even the most excellent translation from the Hebrew, Aramaic, and Greek texts cannot by itself completely remove the strangeness that many modern readers sense when they encounter the Bible. It is, after all, an ancient book. Indeed, it is a collection—no, several collections—of books that were formed and written in cultures distant from our own not only in time and space but also in character. Indeed, what is required of us as readers is rather to enter, through these texts, into another world of meaning. Only when we have sensed the peculiarity and integrity of that other world can we build a bridge of understanding between it and our own. The introductions and notes accompanying the text in the *HarperCollins Study Bible* are designed to provide readers with information that will make it easier to use this excellent translation for the deeper kind of translation readers must make for themselves: the actual encounter with the multiple worlds of meaning that these texts can reveal.

With the aim of removing as many obstacles as possible between readers and the text, the notes in this volume provide several kinds of information. First, they point to characteristics of the language that are significant for meaning. These include the biblical writers' choice of words, the formal patterns of speech, the styles and genres of ancient literature that appear in the texts, and the rhetorical strategies—familiar to ancient readers but foreign to us—adopted by the writers. Second, the notes contain facts about historical events alluded to in the texts or underlying their message. Many of these facts have come to light through modern archaeological discoveries and the analysis of ancient inscriptions and other material evidence. Comparisons and contrasts between the biblical writings and other writings from around the same time and from the same part of the world also help to place them in their historical context. Third, the notes call attention to echoes between different texts of scripture. Sometimes these are direct quotations or paraphrases of earlier texts by later ones. At other times, they represent parallel formulations of common traditions or retellings of familiar stories in new settings. Fourth, the notes sometimes illuminate ambiguities in the text, multiple possibilities that the original languages leave open but that cannot be directly expressed by a single English translation.

One Book or Many?

Anyone who looks carefully at the Bible will be struck by the immense variety of its contents. Here we have prose and poetry, expansive narratives and short stories, legal codes embedded in historical reports, hymns and prayers, quoted archival documents, quasi-mythic accounts of things that happened "in the beginning" or in God's court in heaven, collections of proverbs, maxims, aphorisms, and riddles, letters to various groups, and reports of mysterious revelations interpreted by heavenly figures. This variety accounts for some of the richness that generations of readers have found within its pages, but it also causes much of the puzzlement even the most devoted readers often feel. How did it come about that so many different kinds of writing have been brought together into one book?

This is a question that has preoccupied many modern scholars. They have sought to answer it by investigating the history of the Bible itself. The very word "Bible" is derived from a plural Greek word, *ta biblia*, "the little scrolls." A Christian term, the latter refers to the separate rolls of leather or papyrus on which the sacred writings, like other literary works in antiquity, were ordinarily written. The physical limits of the roll meant that many rolls were required for the writings that had come to be held sacred in the Jewish and Christian communities. Sometimes a long document had to be divided into two scrolls, such as the books of Samuel and Kings or the Gospel of Luke and the Acts of the Apostles. As early as the second century, Christians began to use instead the relatively new form of the codex, very much like our modern books. This made it possible actually to put all the sacred writings into one large manuscript, but the name *ta biblia* somehow stuck.

The individual books that make up our Bible were written over a period of more than a thousand years. During that time the people of Israel underwent many changes, even deep transformations, in their national life and culture. Their patterns of government, their cultic and legal organization, and their relationships to neighboring peoples and to the great empires of the ancient Mesopotamian and Mediterranean regions all changed. Those changes go far to account for the variety we see in content, language, and style of the biblical books.

Critical Study of the Old Testament

Several major narrative complexes within the Bible extend across several books. These have been the focus of especially intense research in the attempt to understand how these books came to have the form in which we know them. The first of these complexes is the Pentateuch (so called from a Greek word meaning "Five Scrolls"): Genesis, Exodus, Leviticus, Numbers, and Deuteronomy. These five books constitute the Torah (Hebrew for "teaching") in the Hebrew scriptures. Some scholars have preferred to speak of a Tetrateuch ("Four Scrolls"), taking Deuteronomy to be the foundation and introduction for the second great narrative. That second narrative, comprising the books of Joshua, Judges, Samuel, and Kings, is called the Deuteronomistic History because its understanding of the Mosaic covenant and Israel's obligations under it are those expounded in Deuteronomy. The history of Israel's national life down to the Babylonian exile is explained and judged according to the degree to which each generation, particularly the monarchs of Israel and of the divided kingdoms of Israel and Judah, abided by the laws of Deuteronomy.

The third major composition presents the same history related in the Deuteronomistic account, although from a quite different point of view, and extends it to include the restoration of Israel as a subject people under the Persian Empire. This composition comprises the books of 1 and 2 Chronicles, Ezra, and Nehemiah. Its unknown author is often called "the Chronicler," though we cannot be certain that a single person was responsible for the composition.

In addition to the three major narrative complexes, some scholars have isolated smaller compositions, such as the cycle of Joseph stories (Gen 37–50) and the narrative of the succession to David's throne (2 Sam 9–1 Kings 2), that may have existed on their own before being woven into the larger narratives.

The history of the biblical writings is further complicated by the fact that some of these books speak of still earlier times, before any of them were written. What were the sources for the pictures of the ancient days that these writers passed on? Some of the writings refer explicitly to other books or archives; others show less direct evidence of predecessors who told or sang the stories and codes and prayers that are now included in the larger literary frameworks.

In the eighteenth and nineteenth centuries, scholars began by trying to detect in the existing narratives differences in style, language, or ideas that might indicate "seams" in the text, where older documents had been inserted or where two older versions of one story or two different sets of similar rules had been joined together. The most famous and controversial of the hypotheses that emerged was a reconstruction of four extended sources that, its advocates proposed, had been brought together over a period of centuries and through several distinct stages of editing, or "redaction," to produce the Pentateuch (or, in other versions of the theory, the Tetrateuch [Genesis–Numbers] or the Hexateuch [Genesis–Joshua]). Beginning with the observations that some passages used almost exclusively the name represented by the Hebrew letters *YHWH* to speak of God, while others used mostly a common Semitic word for a divine being, but in its plural form, *'Elohim,* these scholars guessed that these passages had originally belonged to separate documents. These hypothetical documents, which also differed in other characteristics of both style and content, were accordingly labeled "J" for "Yahwist" (because *j* in German and neo-Latin is pronounced like the Hebrew *y*) and "E" for "Elohist." A later source, called "D" by the scholars, was identified with an early version of the book of Deuteronomy. The fourth and latest document, thought to serve as the framework for the final stage of editing the whole Pentateuch, was intensely concerned with cultic matters, especially rules for priests and the temple, so it was called "P" for "Priestly."

This "Documentary Hypothesis," first associated especially with the name of the German Protestant scholar Julius Wellhausen, came to dominate much of OT scholarship in Europe, Britain, and America in the early twentieth century. In some circles great ingenuity was exercised in trying to assign each verse, or even parts of verses, to one or another of the hypothetical sources or to the "redactors" who put them together. The very complexity of the results aroused skepticism in other quarters, and many scholars came to feel that the documentary analysts were not taking sufficient account of two other factors affecting the formation of the biblical books: the importance of oral transmission and memory in ancient societies; and the stylistic conventions and inventions of ancient writers, which were in many ways quite different from the expectations of modern print-based intellectual culture.

The response to the first of these concerns was the attempt to investigate characteristics of oral folklore that might be comparable to the lore of ancient Israel lying behind the written documents we possess. By studying the particular patterns of speech often repeated in various texts and by comparing these with similar patterns found in neighboring cultures, "form critics" undertook to discover the typical settings in the life of the community in which each "form" or pattern was characteristically used. By further analyzing variations in that form in other texts, they tried further to reconstruct a "history of forms" or "history of traditions." For example, one might seek to show how a maxim or a style of address first used in village courts under local elders could later have affected central legal codes and, again, how it might have become a metaphor in prophetic speech to describe God's "case" against the whole people.

Some of the form critics were satisfied to describe small, individual units of tradition they thought were eventually embedded in the literary compositions of the Bible. Others, however, were interested in the process of oral composition, as seen, for example, in the sagas of the Old Norse and Icelandic peoples or in the lengthy tales sung by skilled reciters in some parts of the modern Balkans and Africa. For some, it seemed plausible that the supposed "documents" of the Pentateuch had been rather the orally transmitted traditions of different groups within the people Israel. There also seemed no good reason to suppose that the oral culture of such groups would have disappeared once their traditions were put into writing. Oral recitation would have continued to affect the way writers remembered and copied documents.

Furthermore, many readers felt that the attempts to distinguish separate sources and the early, analytic kind of form criticism tended to dissolve the larger units of the text into unrelated fragments. They sensed that these results obscured the unique literary qualities of the final compositions, for some of these qualities are produced by the interplay between just those "doublets" and dissonant elements that had set the critics looking for earlier sources of embedded forms. Both within the guild of biblical scholars and from literary critics outside it, there has come in recent decades a new attention to the rhetorical and literary qualities of the biblical books and larger compositions as we have received them.

Critical Study of the New Testament

The NT contains no narrative of the length and scope of those of the OT, but the four Gospels and the Acts of the Apostles present problems that are in some ways analogous to the OT compositions. The methods by which scholars have tried to solve them have been, in part, similar. Scholars of the nineteenth century attempted to solve the "synoptic problem"—why Matthew, Mark, and Luke are in some places similar to the point of identical wording, while in other respects they differ substantially—by discovering what sources each Gospel writer used. The hypothesis that emerged as the dominant explanation was called the "Two-Source Hypothesis." According to it, Matthew and Luke independently used the earlier Gospel of Mark, keeping almost entirely to its narrative outline but adjusting its style to their own somewhat more literary tastes and adding to it large blocks of material they had from other sources. Among these other sources was one that Matthew and Luke had in common (the second of the "two sources"), from which they drew the sayings of Jesus that were not found in Mark. Conventionally, this hypothetical second source has been called "Q," presumably from the German word *Quelle*, "source."

The Two-Source Hypothesis is still taken as the working hypothesis by most critical scholars of the NT, though everyone acknowledges that it does not explain all the peculiarities of the relationships among the first three Gospels. Attempts to revive earlier hypotheses, such as the proposal that Matthew wrote first, Luke adapted Matthew's Gospel, and Mark excerpted rather idiosyncratically from both, have not won wide acceptance. Also unconvincing have been the many attempts to fine-tune the Two-Source Hypothesis by adding yet other hypothetical sources. The remaining problems with the hypothesis are better solved by considering the impact of oral tradition, on the one hand, and the skill and freedom of the Gospel writers, on the other.

Form criticism too was employed by students of the NT in attempts to reconstruct the process by which the stories about Jesus and the sayings attributed to him were shaped, transmitted, and modified by their uses in the life of the early Christian communities. Applied to the Letters of the NT, similar techniques isolated some passages that seemed to be excerpts from liturgical poetry or from simple creeds or confessional formulas.

In NT scholarship too there have been reactions against what many have come to see as an overemphasis on the hypothetical prehistory of writings to the neglect of the rhetorical and literary qualities of the books as we have them. Many recent commentators have emphasized the role of the Gospel writers as authors, fully in command of whatever sources they used and creating from them coherent literary wholes. Others have warned against forcing these ancient writings into modern categories by imposing on them literary theories derived from the study of the modern novel or modern poetry. At the same time, extensive study of ancient genres of writing and patterns of rhetoric has provided sturdier models with which to compare the biblical documents.

Biblical Scholarship Today

The issues mentioned in this brief survey are only examples of the issues raised in the several phases of modern critical study of the Bible. Historical and literary studies have affected our understanding of the other parts of the Bible as well, raising analogous problems. Some of the issues are discussed in the introductions and notes to individual books.

The present moment in scholarly investigation of the Bible is a time when many different methods are in use. That diversity of method is reflected to some extent in the notes in this study Bible. The scholar chosen to annotate each book is an expert on that particular document and may emphasize the results of one or another method that seems most useful in understanding that book. Characteristic of the best scholarship is a healthy degree of self-criticism and skepticism about any rigid hypotheses. All our annotators, even when they differ from one another on theoretical matters, have in common a primary focus on the text. Their notes are designed to help readers make sense of that text, in its parts and as a whole.

Some questions raised by material in the Bible, however, cannot be answered on the basis of our present knowledge. For example, despite the impressive results and continuing discoveries of archaeology in the Middle East, some places mentioned in the Bible cannot be located with certainty on a modern map. Some discrepancies in chronology cannot be resolved. In a few instances where experts differ on such matters, we have allowed inconsistencies between one scholar's notes and another's to stand, as a reminder that our knowledge of the ancient world remains imperfect.

Bibles and Their Communities

Despite the Bible's diversity, most readers do feel that as a *whole* it somehow makes sense. There is an odd concentricity about its diverse stories and its various genres. The tensions within it are held within some common framework. In some more than trivial way, "the Bible" is one book.

Yet our perception of the Bible's unity may obscure a complicated reality. If one asks a reader exactly what gives the Bible its oneness and wholeness, the answer will depend in part on the religious community to which that reader belongs. Our notes try to come to terms with the fact that we have, so to speak, at least two Bibles between the same covers: a Jewish Bible and a Christian Bible. This is not a superficial difference. It is not merely that the Christian Bible adds a New Testament and therefore calls the Jewish scriptures "the Old Testament." The Jewish scriptures are not the same as the OT. The order is different (see the table on p. xxxi). The text has been transmitted by different means and with different approaches to establishing authoritative readings. For example, the Bible of most of the early Christians was the Septuagint. Even the list of books included has differed.

More important than these external differences, however, is the different sense of the whole that is engendered when, on the one hand, we read the Torah, the Prophets, and the Writings of the Hebrew Bible as complete in themselves, the foundation of the life of Israel through the ages, or when, on the other hand, we read them as open toward a future that was "fulfilled" in the events of the NT and still awaits an "end." In the latter case, the Christian Bible presents us with a single narrative line that unites all the diverse episodes and different kinds of writing into a sweeping epic, almost a giant novel claiming to embrace the entire story of humanity. It begins "in the beginning," treats of God electing a special people, recounts their disobedience, punishment, and hope, declares the story's climax in the appearance of God's Son, and looks to a final "coming."

When read independently of the Christian additions and Christian habits of reading, the unity of the Hebrew scriptures looks quite different. They do not have a single plot or a single center, but many. The many voices that speak are not united in a single hope, nor do they point to a single future. Their unity lies rather in a continuous counterpoint. The multiple plots of the narratives move forward with odd echoes of the past, repetitions and rehearsals, reminders and foreshadowings. The wisdom gathered and cultivated by professional elites and servants of kings rubs against the sensibilities of peasants. Codes from the time when "there was no king in Israel" stand beside laws of monarchy and laws of a temple state. Prophets name the injustice done to the common poor by petty local tyrants and perceive in the march of great empires the chastening hand of God. The people Israel sings in the manifold occasions of its national and cultic life, and it sings the complaints, fears, and hopes of its individuals. All this variety, and more, is woven together by complex threads, but its rhythms are quite different from the dominant pulse of the Christian Bible.

The overall arrangement of the NRSV is that of Protestant Bibles, because that is the arrangement that has dominated the public use of the Bible in English-speaking countries since the seventeenth century. The NRSV has, however, included the books that are variously called apocryphal or deuterocanonical and are found in the Bible used by one or more of the Roman Catholic, Greek, and Slavonic churches. In this respect the NRSV is the most inclusive English version now commonly available. (For the several canons, see the tables on pp. xxxi–xxxiii as well as the introductions to the books of the Apocrypha.) Readers thus have in hand not merely two Bibles, the Jewish and the Christian, but *several* Bibles that have spoken and continue to speak to historically diverse Jewish and Christian communities.

The Society of Biblical Literature

The editors and annotators who have worked together to produce the *HarperCollins Study Bible* themselves exemplify the diversity of confessional traditions for which the Bible is foundational. What unites them, however, is the tradition of historical, critical, and open scholarship that has been fostered for more than a century by the Society of Biblical Literature, the sponsor of the present project.

The Society of Biblical Literature and Exegesis was founded in 1880 and is one of the oldest learned societies in the United States. Its purpose is to stimulate the critical investigation of classical biblical literatures, together with other related literatures, by the exchange of scholarly research both in published form and in public forum. It has at present over seven thousand members from more than eighty countries.

The *HarperCollins Study Bible* is one of a series of publishing projects undertaken by the SBL in conjunction with HarperCollins. Others include *HarperCollins Bible Dictionary, HarperCollins Bible Commentary,* and *HarperCollins Bible Pronunciation Guide.* Users of the *HarperCollins Study Bible* who wish to pursue their studies further will find more detailed information on many biblical topics in the articles of those companion volumes. All of these joint projects represent the commitment of the Society to share the results of scholarly research with a wide public who are interested in the Bible and the religious traditions associated with it.

On the Revised Edition

The present revised edition of the HarperCollins Study Bible has updated and expanded the annotations with the latest perspectives on the biblical text derived from historical, archaeological, and literary sources. The notes also provide more complete information on the ways in which various biblical books echo other parts of scripture. A series of introductory essays offer reflections about the contexts within which biblical books are currently read.

To the Reader

THIS PREFACE IS ADDRESSED TO YOU by the Committee of translators, who wish to explain, as briefly as possible, the origin and character of our work. The publication of our revision is yet another step in the long, continual process of making the Bible available in the form of the English language that is most widely current in our day. To summarize in a single sentence: the New Revised Standard Version of the Bible is an authorized revision of the Revised Standard Version, published in 1952, which was a revision of the American Standard Version, published in 1901, which, in turn, embodied earlier revisions of the King James Version, published in 1611.

In the course of time, the King James Version came to be regarded as the "Authorized Version." With good reason it has been termed "the noblest monument of English prose," and it has entered, as no other book has, into the making of the personal character and the public institutions of the English-speaking peoples. We owe to it an incalculable debt.

Yet the King James Version has serious defects. By the middle of the nineteenth century, the development of biblical studies and the discovery of many biblical manuscripts more ancient than those on which the King James Version was based made it apparent that these defects were so many as to call for revision. The task was begun, by authority of the Church of England, in 1870. The (British) Revised Version of the Bible was published in 1881–85; and the American Standard Version, its variant embodying the preferences of the American scholars associated with the work, was published, as was mentioned above, in 1901. In 1928 the copyright of the latter was acquired by the International Council of Religious Education and thus passed into the ownership of the churches of the United States and Canada that were associated in this council through their boards of education and publication.

The Council appointed a committee of scholars to have charge of the text of the American Standard Version and to undertake inquiry concerning the need for further revision. After studying the questions of whether revision should be undertaken and, if so, what its nature and extent should be, in 1937 the Council authorized a revision. The scholars who served as members of the Committee worked in two sections, one dealing with the OT and one with the NT. In 1946 the Revised Standard Version of the NT was published. The publication of the Revised Standard Version of the Bible, containing the OT and NT, took place on September 30, 1952. A translation of the Apocryphal/Deuterocanonical Books of the OT followed in 1957. In 1977 this collection was issued in an expanded edition containing three additional texts received by Eastern Orthodox communions (3 and 4 Maccabees and Psalm 151). Thereafter the Revised Standard Version gained the distinction of being officially authorized for use by all major Christian churches: Protestant, Anglican, Roman Catholic, and Eastern Orthodox.

The Revised Standard Version Bible Committee is a continuing body, comprising about thirty members, both men and women. Ecumenical in representation, it includes scholars affiliated with various Protestant denominations as well as several Roman Catholic members, an Eastern Orthodox member, and a Jewish member who serves in the OT section. For a period of time the Committee included several members from Canada and from England.

Because no translation of the Bible is perfect or acceptable to all groups of readers, and because discoveries of older manuscripts and further investigation of linguistic features of the text continue to become available, renderings of the Bible have proliferated. During the years following the publication of the Revised Standard Version, twenty-six other English translations and revisions of the Bible were produced by committees and by individual scholars—not to mention twenty-five other translations and revisions of the NT alone. One of the latter was the second edition of the RSV NT, issued in 1971, twenty-five years after its initial publication.

Following the publication of the RSV OT in 1952, significant advances were made in the discovery and interpretation of documents in Semitic languages related to Hebrew. In addition to the information that had become available in the late 1940s from the Dead Sea texts of Isaiah and Habakkuk, subsequent acquisitions from the same area brought to light many other early copies of all the books of the Hebrew scriptures (except Esther), though most of these copies are fragmentary. During the same period early Greek manuscript copies of books of the NT also became available.

In order to take these discoveries into account, along with recent studies of documents in Semitic languages related to Hebrew, in 1974 the Policies Committee of the Revised Standard Version, which is a standing committee of the National Council of the Churches of Christ in the U.S.A., authorized the preparation of a revision of the entire RSV Bible.

For the OT the Committee has made use of the *Biblia Hebraica Stuttgartensia* (1977; ed. sec. emendata, 1983). This is an edition of the Hebrew and Aramaic text as current early in the Christian era and fixed by Jewish scholars (the "Masoretes") of the sixth to the ninth centuries. The vowel signs, which were added by the Masoretes, are accepted in the main, but where a more probable and convincing reading can be obtained by assuming different vowels, this has been done. No notes are given in such cases, because the vowel points are less ancient and reliable than the consonants. When an alternative reading given by the Masoretes is translated in a footnote, it is identified by the words "Another reading is."

Departures from the consonantal text of the best manuscripts have been made only where it seems clear that errors in copying had been made before the text was standardized. Most of the corrections adopted are based on the ancient versions (translations into Greek, Aramaic, Syriac, and Latin), which were made prior to the time of the work of the Masoretes and which therefore may reflect earlier forms of the Hebrew text. In such instances a footnote specifies the version or versions from which the correction has been derived and also gives a translation of the Masoretic Text. Where it was deemed appropriate to do so, information is supplied in footnotes from subsidiary Jewish traditions concerning other textual readings (the *Tiqqune Sopherim*, "emendations of the scribes"). These are identified in the footnotes as "Ancient Heb tradition."

Occasionally it is evident that the text has suffered in transmission and that none of the versions provides a satisfactory restoration. Here we can only follow the best judgment of competent scholars as to the most probable reconstruction of the original text. Such reconstructions are indicated in footnotes by the abbreviation Cn ("Correction"), and a translation of the Masoretic Text is added.

For the Apocryphal/Deuterocanonical Books of the OT the Committee has made use of a number of texts. For most of these books the basic Greek text from which the present translation was made is the edition of the Septuagint prepared by Alfred Rahlfs and published by the Württemberg Bible Society (Stuttgart, 1935). For several of the books the more recently published individual volumes of the Göttingen Septuagint project were utilized. For the book of Tobit it was decided to follow the form of the Greek text found in Codex Sinaiticus (supported as it is by evidence from Qumran); where this text is defective, it was supplemented and corrected by other Greek manuscripts. For the three Additions to Daniel (namely, Susanna, the Prayer of Azariah and the Song of the Three Jews, and Bel and the Dragon) the Committee continued to use the Greek version attributed to Theodotion (the so-called Theodotion-Daniel). In translating Ecclesiasticus (Sirach), although constant reference was made to the Hebrew fragments of a large portion of this book (those discovered at Qumran and Masada as well as those recovered from the Cairo Geniza), the Committee generally followed the Greek text (including verse numbers) published by Joseph Ziegler in the Göttingen Septuagint (1965). But in many places the Committee has translated the Hebrew text when this provides a reading that is clearly superior to the Greek; the Syriac and Latin versions were also consulted throughout and occasionally adopted. The basic text adopted in rendering 2 Esdras is the Latin version given in *Biblia Sacra,* edited by Robert Weber (Stuttgart, 1971). This was supplemented by consulting the Latin text as edited by R. L. Bensly (1895) and by Bruno Violet (1910) as well as by taking into account the several Oriental versions of 2 Esdras, namely, the Syriac, Ethiopic, Arabic (two forms, referred to as Arabic 1 and Arabic 2), Armenian, and Georgian versions. Finally, since the Additions to the Book of Esther are disjointed and quite unintelligible as they stand in most editions of the Apocrypha, we have provided them with their original context by translating the whole of the Greek version of Esther from Robert Hanhart's Göttingen edition (1983).

For the NT the Committee has based its work on the most recent edition of *The Greek New Testament,* prepared by an interconfessional and international committee and published by the United Bible Societies (1966; 3d ed. corrected, 1983; information concerning changes to be introduced into the critical apparatus of the forthcoming 4th edition was available to the Committee). As in that edition, double brackets are used to enclose a few passages that are generally regarded to be later additions to the text, but that we have retained because of their evident antiquity and their importance in the textual tradition. Only in very rare instances have we replaced the text or the punctuation of the Bible Societies' edition by an alternative that seemed to us to be superior. Here and there in the footnotes the phrase "Other ancient authorities read" identifies alternative readings preserved by Greek manuscripts and early versions. In both OT and NT, alternative renderings of the text are indicated by the word "Or."

As for the style of English adopted for the present revision, among the mandates given to the Committee in 1980 by the Division of Education and Ministry of the National Council of Churches of Christ (which now holds the copyright of the RSV Bible) was the directive to continue in the tradition of the King James Bible, but to introduce such changes as are warranted on the basis of accuracy, clarity, euphony, and current English usage. Within the constraints set by the original texts and by the mandates of the Division, the Committee has followed the maxim "As literal as possible, as free as necessary." As a consequence, the New Revised Standard Version (NRSV) remains essentially a literal translation. Paraphrastic renderings have been adopted only sparingly, and then chiefly to compensate for a deficiency in the English language—the lack of a common-gender third-person singular pronoun.

During the almost half a century since the publication of the RSV, many in the churches have become sensitive to the danger of linguistic sexism arising from the inherent bias of the English language toward the masculine gender, a bias that in the case of the Bible has often restricted or obscured the meaning of the original text. The mandates from the Division specified that, in references to men and women, masculine-oriented language should be eliminated as far as this can be done without altering passages that reflect the historical situation of ancient patriarchal culture. As can be appreciated, more than once the Committee found that the several mandates stood in tension and even in conflict. The various concerns had to be balanced case by case in order to provide a faithful and acceptable rendering without using contrived English. Only very occasionally has the pronoun "he" or "him" been retained in passages where the reference may have been to a woman as well as to a man, for example, in several legal texts in Leviticus and Deuteronomy. In such instances of formal, legal language, the options of either putting the passage in the plural or of introducing additional nouns to avoid masculine pronouns in English seemed to the Committee to obscure the historic structure and literary character of the original. In the vast majority of cases, however, inclusiveness has been attained by simple rephrasing or by introducing plural forms when this does not distort the meaning of the passage. Of course, in narrative and in parable no attempt was made to generalize the sex of individual persons.

Another aspect of style will be detected by readers who compare the more stately English rendering of the OT with the less formal rendering adopted for the NT. For example, the traditional distinction between "shall" and "will" in English has been retained in the OT as appropriate in rendering a document that embodies what may be termed the classic form of Hebrew, while in the NT the abandonment of such distinctions in the usage of the future tense in English reflects the more colloquial nature of the Koine Greek used by most NT authors except when they are quoting the OT.

Careful readers will notice that here and there in the OT the word LORD (or in certain cases GOD) is printed in capital letters. This represents the traditional manner in English versions of rendering the divine name, the "Tetragrammaton" (see the text notes on Exodus 3.14–15), following the precedent of the ancient Greek and Latin translators and the long-established practice in the reading of the Hebrew scriptures in the synagogue. Although it is almost if not quite certain that the name was originally pronounced "Yahweh," this pronunciation was not indicated when the Masoretes added vowel sounds to the consonantal Hebrew text. To the four consonants YHWH of the divine name, which had come to be regarded as too sacred to be pronounced, they attached vowel signs indicating that in its place should be read the Hebrew word *Adonai,* meaning "Lord" (or *Elohim,* meaning "God"). Ancient Greek translators employed the word *Kyrios* ("Lord") for the name. The Vulgate likewise used the Latin word *Dominus* ("Lord"). The form "Jehovah" is of late medieval origin; it is a combination of the consonants of the divine name and the vowels attached to it by the Masoretes but belonging to an entirely different word. Although the American Standard Version (1901) had used "Jehovah" to render the Tetragrammaton (the sound of *y* being represented by *j* and the sound of *w* by *v,* as in Latin), for two reasons the Committees that produced the RSV and the NRSV returned to the more familiar usage of the King James Version. (1) The word "Jehovah" does not accurately represent any form of the divine name ever used in Hebrew. (2) The use of any proper name for the one and only God, as though there were other gods from whom the true God had to be distinguished, began to be discontinued in Judaism before the Christian era and is inappropriate for the universal faith of the Christian church.

It will be seen that in the Psalms and in other prayers addressed to God the archaic second-person singular pronouns ("thee, thou, thine") and verb forms ("art, hast, hadst") are no longer used. Although some readers may regret this change, it should be pointed out that in the original languages neither the OT nor the NT makes any linguistic distinction between addressing a human being and addressing the deity. Furthermore, in the tradition of the King James Version one will not expect to find the use of capital letters for pronouns that refer to the deity—such capitalization is an unnecessary innovation that has only recently been introduced into a few English translations of the Bible. Finally, we have left to the discretion of the licensed publishers such matters as section headings, cross-references, and clues to the pronunciation of proper names.

This new version seeks to preserve all that is best in the English Bible as it has been known and used through the years. It is intended for use in public reading and congregational worship as well as in private study, instruction, and meditation. We have resisted the temptation to introduce terms and phrases that merely reflect current moods, and have tried to put the message of the scriptures in simple, enduring words and expressions that are worthy to stand in the great tradition of the King James Bible and its predecessors.

In traditional Judaism and Christianity, the Bible has been more than a historical document to be preserved or a classic of literature to be cherished and admired; it is recognized as the unique record of God's dealings with people over the ages. The OT sets forth the call of a special people to enter into covenant relation with the God of justice and steadfast love and to bring God's law to the nations. The NT records the life and work of Jesus Christ, the one in whom "the Word became flesh," as well as describes the rise and spread of the early Christian church. The Bible carries its full message not to those who regard it simply as a noble literary heritage of the past or who wish to use it to enhance political purposes and advance otherwise desirable goals, but to all persons and communities who read it so that they may discern and understand what God is saying to them. That message must not be disguised in phrases that are no longer clear or hidden under words that have changed or lost their meaning; it must be presented in language that is direct and plain and meaningful to people today. It is the hope and prayer of the translators that this version of the Bible may continue to hold a large place in congregational life and to speak to all readers, young and old alike, helping them to understand and believe and respond to its message.

For the Committee,
Bruce M. Metzger

Abbreviations

The following abbreviations are used for the books of the Bible:

OLD TESTAMENT

Gen	Genesis	2 Chr	2 Chronicles	Dan	Daniel
Ex.	Exodus	Ezra	Ezra	Hos	Hosea
Lev	Leviticus	Neh	Nehemiah	Joel	Joel
Num	Numbers	Esth	Esther	Am	Amos
Deut	Deuteronomy	Job	Job	Ob	Obadiah
Josh	Joshua	Ps(s)	Psalms	Jon	Jonah
Judg	Judges	Prov	Proverbs	Mic	Micah
Ruth	Ruth	Eccl	Ecclesiastes	Nah	Nahum
1 Sam	1 Samuel	Song	Song of Solomon	Hab	Habakkuk
2 Sam	2 Samuel	Isa	Isaiah	Zeph	Zephaniah
1 Kings	1 Kings	Jer	Jeremiah	Hag	Haggai
2 Kings	2 Kings	Lam	Lamentations	Zech	Zechariah
1 Chr	1 Chronicles	Ezek	Ezekiel	Mal	Malachi

APOCRYPHAL/DEUTEROCANONICAL BOOKS

Tob	Tobit	Let Jer	Letter of Jeremiah	2 Macc	2 Maccabees
Jdt	Judith	Pr Azar	Prayer of Azariah and	1 Esd	1 Esdras
Add Esth	Additions to Esther		the Song of the Three Jews	Pr Man	Prayer of Manasseh
Wis	Wisdom of Solomon	Sus	Susanna	3 Macc	3 Maccabees
Sir	Sirach (Ecclesiasticus)	Bel	Bel and the Dragon	2 Esd	2 Esdras
Bar	Baruch	1 Macc	1 Maccabees	4 Macc	4 Maccabees

NEW TESTAMENT

Mt	Matthew	Eph	Ephesians	Heb	Hebrews
Mk	Mark	Phil	Philippians	Jas	James
Lk	Luke	Col	Colossians	1 Pet	1 Peter
Jn	John	1 Thess	1 Thessalonians	2 Pet	2 Peter
Acts	Acts of the Apostles	2 Thess	2 Thessalonians	1 Jn	1 John
Rom	Romans	1 Tim	1 Timothy	2 Jn	2 John
1 Cor	1 Corinthians	2 Tim	2 Timothy	3 Jn	3 John
2 Cor	2 Corinthians	Titus	Titus	Jude	Jude
Gal	Galatians	Philem	Philemon	Rev	Revelation

Abbreviations used in the text notes to the books of the OT:

Ant.	Josephus, *Antiquities of the Jews*
Aram	Aramaic
Ch(s)	Chapter(s)
Cn	Correction; made where the text has suffered in transmission and the versions provide no satisfactory restoration, but where the Standard Bible Committee agrees with the judgment of competent scholars as to the most probable reconstruction of the original text.
Gk	Septuagint, Greek version of the OT
Heb	Hebrew of the consonantal Masoretic Text of the OT
Josephus	Flavius Josephus (Jewish historian, ca. 37–95 CE)

Macc.	The book(s) of the Maccabees
Ms(s)	Manuscript(s)
MT	The Hebrew of the pointed Masoretic Text of the OT
OL	Old Latin
Q Ms(s)	Manuscript(s) found at Qumran by the Dead Sea
Sam	Samaritan Hebrew text of the OT
Syr	Syriac Version of the OT
Syr H	Syriac Version of Origen's Hexapla
Tg	Targum
Vg	Vulgate, Latin Version of the OT

Abbreviations used in the study notes:

ch(s).	chapter(s)
v(v).	verse(s)
OT	Old Testament
NT	New Testament
BCE	Before the Common Era
CE	Common Era

List of Illustrations, Maps, and Tables

Before Genesis	Names and Order of Books of the Bible in Several Traditions	*xxxi*
	Jewish Bibles	*xxxi*
	Protestant Bibles	*xxxi*
	Orthodox Bibles	*xxxii*
	Catholic Bibles	*xxxiii*
Exodus	Asiatic Captives Making Bricks	*92*
	Geography of the Exodus and Numbers Narratives (map)	*106*
	Court of the Tabernacle	*131*
Numbers	Geography of Israel's Migration into Canaan (map)	*195*
	The Land of Canaan (map)	*219*
Joshua	The Conquest of Canaan (map)	*318*
1 Samuel	The Kingdom of Saul (map)	*408*
1 Kings	Solomon's Twelve Administrative Districts (map)	*483*
	Solomon's Temple (floor plan)	*488*
	Solomon's Temple	*489*
	Chronology of the Kings of the Divided Monarchy	*500*
2 Kings	The Assyrian Empire and the Conquest of the West (map)	*542*
Before Tobit	Apocryphal/Deuterocanonical Books in Various Bibles	*1291*
	Designations for Books Associated with Ezra and Nehemiah	*1291*
1 Maccabees	Division of Alexander's Empire (map)	*1477*
	The Maccabees: A Family Tree	*1479*
	A Family Tree of Seleucid Rulers in the Maccabean Period	*1481*
1 Esdras	The Relation of 1 Esdras to Other Biblical Books	*1549*
Before Matthew	A Table of Parallel Passages in the Four Gospels	*1653*
Matthew	The Herods: A Simplified Family Tree	*1672*
	Galilee at the Time of Jesus (map)	*1675*
John	Jewish Festivals in the Gospel of John	*1820*
Acts	The Fulfillment of Acts 1.8 in the Following Narrative	*1859*
	Early Spread of Christianity (map)	*1872*
	Early Expansion of Christianity into Asia Minor (map)	*1877*
	Cyprus, Pamphylia, and Pisidia (map)	*1880*
	The Aegean (map)	*1886*
Before Romans	Possible Chronology of the Pauline Letters	*1908*
1 Corinthians	Rome's Aegean Provinces (map)	*1933*
Colossians	Western Asia Minor (map)	*2001*
1 Thessalonians	Macedonia (map)	*2006*

1 Timothy	The Eastern Mediterranean (map)	2016
1 Peter	Asia Minor (map)	2060
Revelation	Western Asia Minor and the Aegean (map)	2088
	Alternate Ways of Counting the Roman Emperors Signified in Rev 17.10–11	2107
After Revelation	Quotations of the Jewish Scriptures in the New Testament	2115

COLOR MAPS SECTION AT THE END OF THIS VOLUME

Map 1   Physical Map of the Land of Israel and Surrounding Area in Biblical Times

Map 2   The Ancient World in the Late Bronze Age

Map 3   Settlement in Canaan and the Tribal Areas

Map 4   The Empire of David and Solomon

Map 5   The Kingdoms of Israel and Judah

Map 6   The Assyrian Empire

Map 7   Judah After the Fall of Israel

Map 8   Great Empires of the Sixth Century BCE

Map 9   Israel Under Persian Rule (After the Return from Exile)

Map 10   The Empire of Alexander

Map 11   Israel's Boundary Under the Maccabees

Map 12   The Roman World

Map 13   Judea, Samaria, and Surrounding Areas in New Testament Times

Map 14   Jerusalem of David and Solomon

Map 15   Jerusalem After the Exile

Map 16   Jerusalem in Jesus' Time

Map 17   The Eastern Mediterranean World at the Time of the New Testament (First Century CE)

Map 18   Archaeological Sites in Israel and Jordan

Names and Order of Books of the Bible
in Several Traditions

Jewish Bibles

Jewish Bibles include the books of the Hebrew scriptures (Tanak). Most modern editions present the twenty-four books (counting the Twelve Prophets as one book) in the following order:

TORAH	PROPHETS				WRITINGS
Genesis	Joshua				Psalms
Exodus	Judges				Proverbs
Leviticus	Samuel (1 & 2)				Job
Numbers	Kings (1 & 2)				Song of Solomon
Deuteronomy	Isaiah				Ruth
	Jeremiah				Lamentations
	Ezekiel				Ecclesiastes
	The Twelve:				Esther
	Hosea	Obadiah	Nahum	Haggai	Daniel
	Joel	Jonah	Habakkuk	Zechariah	Ezra-Nehemiah
	Amos	Micah	Zephaniah	Malachi	Chronicles (1 & 2)

Protestant Bibles

Protestant Bibles include the books of the Hebrew scriptures (also known as the OT) and the books of the NT. The OT is arranged in thirty-nine books (counting 1 and 2 Samuel, 1 and 2 Kings, 1 and 2 Chronicles, each of the Twelve Prophets, and Ezra and Nehemiah as separate books). Some Protestant Bibles include the Apocrypha—those books of the Catholic OT not found in Jewish Bibles—but as a distinct section.

OLD TESTAMENT

Genesis	1 Samuel	Esther	Lamentations	Micah
Exodus	2 Samuel	Job	Ezekiel	Nahum
Leviticus	1 Kings	Psalms	Daniel	Habakkuk
Numbers	2 Kings	Proverbs	Hosea	Zephaniah
Deuteronomy	1 Chronicles	Ecclesiastes	Joel	Haggai
Joshua	2 Chronicles	Song of Solomon	Amos	Zechariah
Judges	Ezra	Isaiah	Obadiah	Malachi
Ruth	Nehemiah	Jeremiah	Jonah	

NEW TESTAMENT

Matthew	2 Corinthians	1 Timothy	2 Peter
Mark	Galatians	2 Timothy	1 John
Luke	Ephesians	Titus	2 John
John	Philippians	Philemon	3 John
Acts	Colossians	Hebrews	Jude
Romans	1 Thessalonians	James	Revelation
1 Corinthians	2 Thessalonians	1 Peter	

Orthodox Bibles

Bibles of the Orthodox churches consist of the OT and the NT. The OT contains, in addition to all the books of the Jewish Bible (as translated into Greek in the Septuagint), Tobit, Judith, 1, 2, and 3 Maccabees (with 4 Maccabees as an appendix), the Wisdom of Solomon, Sirach, Baruch, the Letter of Jeremiah, 1 Esdras, the Prayer of Manasseh, and Psalm 151. The book of Esther includes the six additions to Esther, and the book of Daniel includes the Prayer of Azariah and the Song of the Three Jews, Susanna, and Bel and the Dragon. Slavonic Bibles of the Russian Orthodox church also include 3 Esdras. The order of books varies somewhat in different editions.

OLD TESTAMENT

Genesis	Tobit	Nahum
Exodus	1 Maccabees	Habakkuk
Leviticus	2 Maccabees	Zephaniah
Numbers	3 Maccabees	Haggai
Deuteronomy	Psalms (with Psalm 151)	Zechariah
Joshua	Prayer of Manasseh	Malachi
Judges	Job	Isaiah
Ruth	Proverbs	Jeremiah
1 Kingdoms (1 Samuel)	Ecclesiastes	Baruch
2 Kingdoms (2 Samuel)	Song of Solomon	Lamentations
3 Kingdoms (1 Kings)	Wisdom of Solomon	Letter of Jeremiah
4 Kingdoms (2 Kings)	Sirach	Ezekiel
1 Chronicles	Hosea	Daniel (including the Prayer of
2 Chronicles	Amos	Azariah and the Song of the
1 Esdras	Micah	Three Jews, Susanna, Bel and
2 Esdras (Ezra, Nehemiah)	Joel	the Dragon)
Esther (with the Additions)	Obadiah	(4 Maccabees in appendix)
Judith	Jonah	

NEW TESTAMENT

Matthew	Ephesians	Hebrews
Mark	Philippians	James
Luke	Colossians	1 Peter
John	1 Thessalonians	2 Peter
Acts	2 Thessalonians	1 John
Romans	1 Timothy	2 John
1 Corinthians	2 Timothy	3 John
2 Corinthians	Titus	Jude
Galatians	Philemon	Revelation

Catholic Bibles

Catholic Bibles include forty-six books in the OT (as listed by the Council of Trent in 1546) and the books of the NT. The OT includes the following books not found in Jewish Bibles: Tobit, Judith, 1 and 2 Maccabees, the Wisdom of Solomon, Sirach, and Baruch with the Letter of Jeremiah. The book of Esther includes the six additions to Esther, and the book of Daniel includes the Prayer of Azariah and the Song of the Three Jews, Susanna, and Bel and the Dragon.

OLD TESTAMENT

Genesis	Judith	Daniel
Exodus	Esther (with the Additions)	Prayer of Azariah and the Song
Leviticus	1 Maccabees	of the Three Jews
Numbers	2 Maccabees	Susanna
Deuteronomy	Job	Bel and the Dragon
Joshua	Psalms	Hosea
Judges	Proverbs	Joel
Ruth	Ecclesiastes	Amos
1 Samuel	Song of Solomon	Obadiah
2 Samuel	Wisdom of Solomon	Jonah
1 Kings	Sirach	Micah
2 Kings	Isaiah	Nahum
1 Chronicles	Jeremiah	Habakkuk
2 Chronicles	Lamentations	Zephaniah
Ezra	Baruch	Haggai
Nehemiah	Letter of Jeremiah	Zechariah
Tobit	Ezekiel	Malachi

NEW TESTAMENT

Matthew	Ephesians	Hebrews
Mark	Philippians	James
Luke	Colossians	1 Peter
John	1 Thessalonians	2 Peter
Acts	2 Thessalonians	1 John
Romans	1 Timothy	2 John
1 Corinthians	2 Timothy	3 John
2 Corinthians	Titus	Jude
Galatians	Philemon	Revelation

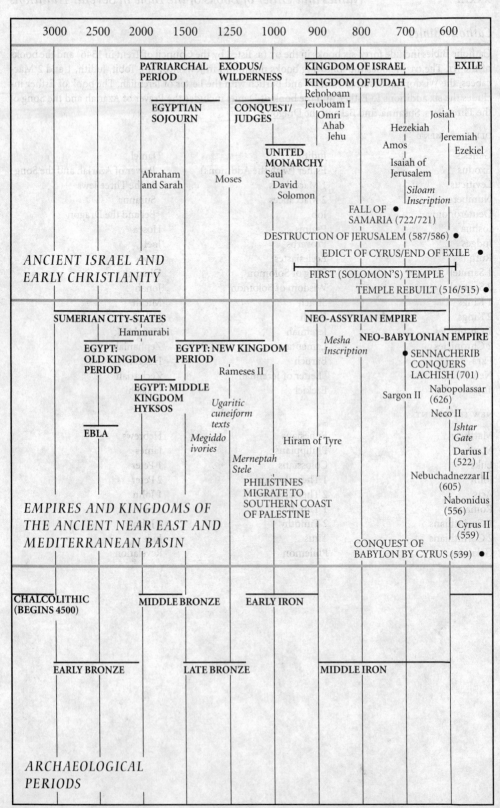

400	300	200	150	100	50	BCE	CE	50	100	150

PERSIAN PERIOD
(BEGINS 539)

HELLENISTIC PERIOD

REVOLT AGAINST ROME

MACCABEAN PERIOD
Judas Maccabeus

ROMAN RULE IN PALESTINE

Jesus

Mark

Ezra
Nehemiah

Herod
the Great

Matthew
Luke
John

Peter
Paul

1 Thessalonians
Romans

SECOND TEMPLE PERIOD

HEROD'S TEMPLE

PERSIAN EMPIRE (BEGINS 550)

ROMAN EMPIRE

Alexander
the Great

Augustus

Tiberius

Antiochus IV
(Epiphanes)

Claudius

Vespasian

Nero

●
ALEXANDRIA
FOUNDED
(EGYPT, 332)

Arch of Titus
in Rome

● ROMAN DESTRUCTION
OF JERUSALEM (70)

LATE IRON

NOTE: *The period of time between vertical bars increases at*
intervals from right to left; this allows a wide range of events
to be shown across the breadth of two pages.

The HarperCollins
STUDY BIBLE

Strategies for Reading Scripture

JOHN BARTON

AMONG THE MANY WAYS people have approached the Bible down through the ages, two are likely to be encountered by readers of this book. They may be called the canonical and critical approaches.

Canonical Reading

A CANONICAL APPROACH TO READING SCRIPTURE is essentially the way most Christians usually understand the task if they are not involved in technical biblical study, but in recent years it has also been promoted by an influential movement within biblical scholarship. It begins from the conviction that the Bible is the Word of God to the church and that the meanings to be found in it flow from this. The scriptures, it is believed, are not simply a collection of ancient books that happen to have come together to form a corpus, but a carefully selected range of works in which the church has encountered a communication from God. This is very obviously true of the writings of the NT, which are the primary witness to the events of the life, death, and resurrection of Jesus of Nazareth and the beginnings of the Christian church, which revered him as its founder; these include the very early testimony of the apostles, above all perhaps of the apostle Paul. It is also true of the OT, in which the God whom Jesus worshiped is encountered throughout the history of ancient Israel, witnessed to by prophets, priests, and sages, and described by historians and psalmists. In these works the word of life is to be found, and reading them is thus not at all the same kind of experience as reading any other books, not even other religious texts. It calls for a particular mental attitude and for a number of presuppositions about what will be found in the text. We may mention five of these.

First, we should read the Bible in the expectation that what we find there will be *true*. For some Christians, especially on the more conservative and evangelical wings of the churches, the truth that is looked for is literal and historical truth, so that whatever the biblical text affirms is taken to be factually accurate. For many who do not subscribe to this position it remains the case that the Bible is to be read as true rather than as false. The truth it contains may sometimes be poetic or symbolic truth rather than factual truth, but it is not an option to suggest that anything in the Bible is an expression of error. Even if, for example, the author of Gen 1–2 did not accurately express the length of time it took God to create the universe, it is unacceptable to say that he was therefore simply mistaken about the events he describes: at some level what he wrote is true. Many Christians will say that although the idea of creation in six days is not factually accurate, the intention of showing that God is the creator remains, and this is indeed a profound truth. It would be wrong for Christians to read Gen 1–2 looking for fundamental error in what it is trying to tell us.

Second, scripture is to be read as *relevant*. Even where Paul is discussing an issue that arose in the early church but does not arise in the same form today (e.g., whether to eat meat that has been sacrificed to false gods, as in 1 Cor 8, 10), this does not mean that the text in question has nothing to say to us. It is our task as readers of scripture to discern what God is saying to us through the inclusion of such passages in the Bible. Because the Bible is canonical, i.e., authoritative, it does not have passages that were once relevant but are so no longer: all that is written is there for *our* instruction (1 Cor 10.11). So it is not an option, when faced with a puzzling or difficult text, to say that it simply has nothing to say to us today. The fact that it was included in the scriptures means that it is eternally relevant to Christian believers.

Third, everything in the Bible is *important* and *profound*. There is no triviality in scripture, nothing that should be read as superficial or insignificant—in a way this is close to the previous point about its relevance. The Bible is a book of divine wisdom, and it does not contain any unimportant texts. This can be difficult for readers who are likely to feel that some parts of scripture are more important than others. For example, most Protestants, at least, make much more of Romans than they do of 2 John or Jude, especially since it was Romans, with its doctrine of justification by faith, that lay at the root of much of the Reformation. But strictly speaking there is no hierarchy within scripture: everything is inspired by God and therefore everything is important, even if in practice we may at times concentrate more on some books than on others. We are not at liberty, for example, to regard the historical narrations in the OT as mere historical records devoid of spiritual significance: they are all deep texts with profound meanings.

Fourth, scripture is *self-consistent*. Christian readers must not play one part of the Bible off against another. If there appear to be contradictions between two texts, more careful reading is required to show that they really cohere. A classic case of this would be the apparent discord between Paul and James over the question of works. On the face of it Paul denies that human beings are made righteous by good works, whereas James affirms that good works are essential— indeed, that faith apart from good works is empty and false. Some Christians have argued that this difference is irreconcilable, and Martin Luther famously proposed to exclude James from the Bible as worthless. But for Christians following a canonical approach this is not an option. They are obliged to find ways of showing that Paul and James are not really at odds, but teach messages that, though different in emphasis, are ultimately compatible. In a way, the self-consistency of scripture is already implied by saying that it is true, since two messages that are incompatible cannot both be true. Because scripture speaks with a single voice, we can always elucidate obscure passages from more transparent ones.

The first four preconditions of Bible reading according to a canonical perspective are shared by all Christians. The fifth is more obvious in a Catholic context, though it has parallels in the Protestant world. The Bible is to be read *so as to conform to the teachings of the church*. Catholics will normally say, for example, that where the NT appears to speak of Jesus' brothers and sisters, the words "brother" and "sister" must refer to more distant relatives, because Jesus cannot have had literal brothers and sisters if, as the church teaches, his mother remained forever a virgin. At most they could be half siblings from a previous marriage of Joseph. Protestants usually do not follow this line of reasoning since they typically do not believe in the perpetual virginity of Mary, but on other matters they may well stress that the Bible is to be read and received within the teaching of the church. Like early Christian writers, they generally say that the Bible's meaning depends on consonance with the church's "rule of faith." If our reading of the biblical text conflicts with basic Christian belief, we can be sure we have misread the text. When we read some of the prophets, we may feel that we are hearing about a God of vindictiveness rather than of love, but that must be a mistake since the God we worship is indeed a loving God; we must read the prophets in the light of that belief, even if they portray God's love as "tough love."

Critical Reading

THE TRADITION CALLED BIBLICAL CRITICISM developed in significant ways in contrast to the kind of religiously committed approach to the Bible just described, though it has often been practiced by people who are equally committed Christians. It has the following features.

First, it approaches the biblical text from a *literary* rather than a religious perspective. Another way of putting this is to say that it treats the Bible as a text first, and only secondarily as a holy or inspired collection of writings. It seeks to inquire into the meaning of this text in the same way that one might inquire into the meaning of any other text. (A technical way of putting this is that it does not believe in a "special hermeneutic" for reading the Bible). This has two important additional aspects.

On the one hand, it is concerned to discover *what kind of text* each biblical book is. Reading prophecy is not the same kind of activity as reading poetry; reading historical narrative not the same kind of thing as reading law. The Gospels and the Letters of Paul belong to different literary types. One cannot legitimately treat all these different works as though they were cut from the same cloth. If we want to know how we ought to live, we will not learn this from a psalm or an OT narrative in the same way we might learn it from one of Paul's ethical instructions or advice given in Proverbs. The various kinds of literature in the Bible cannot simply be added together to make a single work. The Bible is, as often said, a library of books rather than one book, books of many different types with different claims to inform readers.

On the other hand, criticism is also concerned with the question of *when each book was written.* This is not because it regards books as limited to the period they come from. Clearly, this is not the case for major literary works—no one thinks that Shakespeare was important only to the Elizabethan age and has nothing to say to us! But taking account of context is important for discovering what the text means. Words and phrases can change their meaning over time, and we need to know the historical context of expressions before we can know what they truly mean. Further, the whole meaning of an extended line of thought may make sense only once we can establish its original historical context. To return to Paul's discussion of meat sacrificed to false gods: we cannot understand this at all without some idea of the historical circumstances in which Paul lived and worked. Often (as perhaps in this case) we can work out a good deal of this from the text itself, but sometimes we need more information. We cannot begin to apply the text to our own situation until we know enough about its original one to know whether there really are parallels, and the general principle that "scripture is always relevant" is not enough to guarantee this.

Second, critical reading brackets the question of the truth of a text until it has established what the text means. Rather than believing that we can know the meaning of the text by approaching it with the correct predispositions and presuppositions, biblical critics think that the meaning emerges from reading the text cold, without a prior commitment to its truth or a ready-made framework (such as the church's faith) within which it is read. Critics think of this as showing the text more *respect* than a committed reading, because it does not limit what the text might mean on the basis of an already existing theory about what this meaning is bound to be. Bracketing the question of truth does not mean being indifferent to the text's truth claims; a sound method requires seeing the question of meaning as coming first and the question of truth second. This stance has consequences that a canonical approach regards as undesirable. For example, it makes it impossible to be sure in advance that two biblical books are not inconsistent. A critical reading of Paul and James might result in the conclusion that they really are incompatible, which would have considerable consequences for claims about the inspiration and authority of scripture.

As practiced over the last few hundred years, biblical criticism has resulted in some very radical conclusions about the books of the Bible. It has suggested not only that some books are inconsistent with other books, but that some are even inconsistent within themselves—in some cases to such an extent that it is hard to believe they were originally single works. "Source criticism" has refined this discovery and argued that we can, in some cases, reconstruct the raw materials from which certain books (especially the Pentateuch and the Gospels) were composed. Other types of criticism have studied the way in which different sources have been woven together to make the finished books we now have, an approach generally called "redaction criticism." Critical scholars have also reconstructed the history of ancient Israel and of the early church using the biblical text and other ancient evidence and have sometimes produced a story strongly different from the one the Bible itself tells. Nowhere, perhaps, does this affect believers more than in the case of the figure of Jesus: the "quest of the historical Jesus" has had many phases since the nineteenth century and has resulted in pictures of Jesus very different from what emerges from an uncritical reading of the Gospels. For example, most critical scholars refuse to harmonize the account in the Synoptic Gospels (Matthew, Mark, and Luke) with that of John, regarding them as two strikingly variant versions of the story of Jesus.

But critical study is not defined by its results, whether radical or conservative. What characterizes it is its approach: an open, rational approach that treats the biblical texts like any other books from the ancient world. Many believers feel that this rational approach is at odds with a recognition of the Bible as special; yet it is hard to see how someone who habitually reads books in such a critical way can simply switch off this approach when the Bible is the book being read, and in practice biblical criticism is probably here to stay, whether one likes it or not. Can anything be said to reconcile the two approaches and reduce the area of conflict?

A Compromise?

AT THE THEORETICAL LEVEL it is hard to see how there can be any compromise between critical and canonical readings. They have diametrically opposed starting points: one begins with the church's perception of the Bible as holy scripture; the other treats the Bible like any other book. Yet at a practical level people who practice these two approaches can in fact talk to each other. Some critical scholars come to very conservative conclusions that are not far from those reached by canonical readers even though they start from different places. Conversely, people who read the Bible with a sense of its special character and inspiration still have to ask about where and when its books were written unless they treat it in a completely two-dimensional way. All readers, whatever their attitude, need to know the situation Paul faced in Corinth, when the prophets lived and in what sort of society they prophesied, and how the Pentateuch came to be put together. There is thus quite a lot of common ground between the two approaches described rather starkly above.

The majority of critics do not deny the assumption that the Bible is important and profound; most of them would not bother to study it if they thought it trivial or insignificant. They maintain, however, that certain texts can, on examination, turn out to be less important than others. For such critics this is an empirical question rather than one that can be settled before reading begins. For a critic, only texts that might in principle turn out to be trivial can in fact prove to be important, for otherwise importance is being attributed rather than discovered. More critical readers are always worried that more canonical readers bring meaning to the text rather than finding it there and thus constrain the text to bear meanings that may not really be in it. Yet when confronted with this contrast, most people who read the text as holy scripture would also say that they are on a quest to understand it: they are not deliberately trying to make it mean what they already believe on other grounds.

Thus in practice there is a large area in which Bible readers of all sorts can agree on what they find when they read scripture. Many of both persuasions find there a message both important in itself and relevant in ever new situations and believe that they are in touch with truth. Users of either camp should find in this study Bible material to help them.

Israelite Religion

RONALD HENDEL

THE PEOPLE OF ANCIENT ISRAEL lived in a world of ancient and powerful civilizations, each of which had elaborate religious systems. Israelite religion emerged in an ancient Near Eastern matrix and changed and evolved over many centuries. This essay will address some of the major themes in Israelite religion from its hazy origins in the beginning of the Iron Age (ca. 1200 BCE) through the crystallization of the Bible as a sacred text during the Second Temple period (ca. 530 BCE–70 CE).

God and the Gods

BY A REMARKABLE ACT of theological reduction, the complex divine hierarchy of prior polytheistic religion was transformed into the authority of a sole high god in classical Israelite religion. YHWH (the name of Israel's deity, probably pronounced "Yahweh," translated "the LORD" in the NRSV) was not, however, the only god in Israelite religion. Like a king in his court, Yahweh was served by lesser deities, variously called "the sons of God," "the host of heaven," and similar titles. This "host" sometimes fought battles of holy war (see the battle of Jericho, where Joshua meets the divine "commander of the army of the LORD," Josh 5.13–15) and were also represented as stars ("the stars fought from heaven," Judg 5.20; also Job 38.7). These lesser deities attend Yahweh in heaven, as in the prophet Micaiah's vision: "I saw the LORD sitting on his throne, with all the host of heaven standing beside him" (1 Kings 22.19). Another category of divine beings consists of messenger gods or angels. The angels carry Yahweh's messages to earth, as illustrated by Jacob's dream vision in which "the angels of God were ascending and descending" on the celestial staircase that links heaven and earth (Gen 28.12). In late biblical books, the sons of God and the angels merge into a single category and proliferate; in Daniel's vision of the heavenly court, "a thousand thousands served him" (Dan 7.10).

The tripartite hierarchy of the divine world—Yahweh, the sons of God or heavenly host, and the angels—derives from the earlier structure of Canaanite religion. According to the texts from Ugarit (ca. 1200 BCE) and other Canaanite sources, the high god of the Canaanite pantheon was El (whose name means "God"), and his wife, the mother of the gods, was Asherah. The other gods of the pantheon are collectively called "the children of El" and are subordinate to El's authority, although some are prominent deities. A third category consists of servants and messenger gods. Israelite religion, however, differs from this earlier structure in significant ways. On the level of high god, El seems to have merged with Yahweh, who absorbs El's name and has many of his attributes. Asherah in Israelite religion becomes the name of a sacred pole or tree in local Yahwistic shrines, although there are hints in some texts that she was worshiped as a goddess in some times and places. The second tier of deities, "the children of El" (*bn 'il*), is equivalent in name to "the sons of God" (*bene ha'elohim*), but in Israelite religion this group has been demoted to a class of relatively powerless beings (but see Gen 6.1–4; Deut 32.8). Yahweh replaces or absorbs the functions of the major gods of the pantheon; hence like El he is the beneficent patriarch and judge; like Baal he is the Divine Warrior; and like Asherah and her daughters he dispenses the "blessings of the breasts and of the womb" (Gen 49.25). In these respects, Israelite religion is a transformation of its ancient West Semitic forebears.

Early biblical texts seem to acknowledge that gods of other nations exist (see Deut 32.8). The nations each have their own god, but Yahweh is Israel's god. This seems to be the earliest sense of the first commandment, "You shall have no other gods before me" (Ex 20.3). Yahweh is Israel's high god, who delivered his people from slavery and oppression, and he is entitled to Israel's exclusive worship and loyalty. Other national gods exist, but Yahweh is Israel's god and is the greatest god. This type of worship is sometimes called monolotry (the worship of one god without denying the existence of others) or henotheism (belief in one god without denying the existence of others). A more thoroughgoing monotheism, which denies the existence of other gods, is a product of the prophetic and Deuteronomistic critique that developed during the eighth through the sixth centuries BCE.

Humans and God

IN THE PRIESTLY CREATION ACCOUNT of Gen 1, God creates humans "in the image of God," a phrase that conveys an exalted status for humans akin to that of the king in other Near Eastern cultures. As God's earthly image, humans are collectively to rule the earth and all of its creatures (Gen 1.26–28). Humans—male and female—are godlike mediators between God and the world. To be created in "the image of God" also implies a spiritual, moral, or intellectual component that transcends ordinary creaturely existence. Humans are more than animals but less than gods and are the pinnacle of creation (see also Ps 8.4–9).

A less exalted status is given to humans in the Yahwistic (denoted J) creation myth in the garden of Eden (Gen 2.4–3.24). There the first human is created as a laborer in the Garden "to till it and keep it" (Gen 2.15). This status is similar to that in older Mesopotamian creation myths, in which humans are created to be the laborers of the gods. In the course of the garden of Eden story, the humans become "like God, knowing good and evil" (Gen 3.5, 22), gaining a godlike aspect comparable to the lofty status of humans in Gen 1. In this story the desire to be godlike leads to higher knowledge and self-awareness, but also leads to pain, suffering, hard labor, and consciousness of death, i.e., the ordinary fare of human existence. Unlike the original situation in paradise, the human world is limited by pain and mortality, but it is also enriched by a godlike "knowledge of good and evil." This divine quality includes moral discernment and sexual maturity ("they knew that they were naked," Gen 3.7; "the man knew his wife," Gen 4.1). Human existence contrasts with the perfection of paradise or divine existence, yet humans have some degree of divinity or likeness to divinity.

Humans, however, also have a propensity toward evil. This flaw gives rise to various problems and solutions. In Gen 6, God responds to the collective problem of human evil by sending the flood. In both the Yahwistic and Priestly versions of the flood story (edited together in Gen 6–9),

God saves the sole righteous man and begins a new era of human existence. This new era, according to the Priestly version, is distinguished by the first laws and covenant (Gen 9.1–17), establishing clear limits to human violence, particularly the slaughter of animals and murder. The Noachian covenant and its laws, which apply to all earthly creatures, are a first step toward the great promulgation of laws and covenant to Israel at Mount Sinai. In the Yahwistic version of the flood human evil is not decisively controlled; rather, Yahweh resigns himself to the persistence of human evil, promising that despite their corrupt nature he will never again destroy humans (Gen 8.21). In the Yahwistic narrative the problem of evil is relieved by Yahweh's compassion for humans and later by his election of Abraham, who will teach justice and righteousness to his children and through whom all the earth's peoples will be blessed (Gen 12.1–3; 18.19).

The human propensity for evil creates the need for religion, which, through stories, rites, and laws, teaches morality, regulates behavior, and restores a beneficial relationship with God and the cosmos. People—including Israelites and foreigners—can choose to disobey the religious norms, in which case God will send destruction (e.g., Sodom and Gomorrah, Gen 19). But there remains a mutuality of interest in the continuance of human existence: God desires justice and morality, and from Israel he also desires worship; in return he grants his blessing. God and humans are linked in a relationship of mutual benefit regulated by a divinely sanctioned cosmic order. In situations in which this cosmic order has been disrupted or destroyed, God's relationship with Israel, or with humans generally, becomes a critical problem, as in the story of the flood and Jeremiah's prediction of destruction at the hands of Babylon (Jer 21.8-10).

Varieties of Religion

THE WORSHIP OF GOD took different forms in various social contexts in ancient Israel. The most notable distinction is between family religion and state religion. In the domestic domain of family religion, portrayed most directly in the patriarchal narratives, Yahweh is "the god of the father" who provides blessings of offspring, abundance, healing, and protection for members of a household or lineage. The worship of "the god of the father" and the reverence for the lineage ancestors were complementary features of family religion. Problems of infertility (e.g., Sarah, Rebekah, Rachel), marriage (e.g., Isaac, Jacob), inheritance (e.g., Ishmael and Isaac, Jacob and Esau), family strife (e.g., Jacob and Laban, Joseph and his brothers), and famine (e.g., Abraham, Isaac, Jacob) are occasions when family religion becomes prominent in these stories and in Israelite domestic life.

The worship of gods other than Yahweh is occasionally attested in domestic contexts in the biblical text, such as the family worship of the Queen of Heaven (probably a local form of Ishtar or Astarte; Jer 7.17–18; 44.15–25); women planting ritual gardens and mourning for Adonis, Tammuz, or Baal (Isa 17.10–11; Ezek 8.14; Zech 12.11); and the offering of incense to the host of heaven on rooftops (Jer 19.13; Zeph 1.5). The latter, at least, is the worship of Yahweh's heavenly entourage. It is possible that family religion also included a ritual of passing children through fire as a rite of initiation or redemption, perhaps called a *molech* (or *mulk*) offering or an offering to the god Molech (e.g., Deut 18.10; 2 Kings 23.10). This may have been a symbolic attenuation of an older rite of child sacrifice. Many of the practices of family religion were deplored by various biblical writers (e.g., Deut 18.9–11), and they were officially prohibited by King Josiah (2 Kings 23).

State religion, which descended from the pre-state tribal religion, was rooted in the public structures of political authority. In the early period, tribal and pan-tribal identity was activated most directly during pilgrimage festivals and military crises. For example, the Song of Deborah

(Judg 5) describes the call of the tribes to war (not all of them come) and depicts Yahweh as the mighty Divine Warrior and savior of the tribal confederation. The Song of the Sea (Ex 15), perhaps originally recited at tribal festivals, describes Yahweh as the mighty warrior and national savior in his triumph over Pharaoh's army at the exodus and his delivery of his people to the promised land. Jerusalem became the royal capital and the center of the state religion for the Southern Kingdom, Judah, and Dan and Bethel were the official state shrines for the Northern Kingdom, Israel. State religion regulated the system of sacrifices offered at the central shrines, which supported the guild of official priests. The king was the patron of the state religion, which in turn provided the charter for his sacral authority. The king maintained the temple (or, in the Northern Kingdom, the official shrines), appointed the chief priests, and at times presided over the sacrificial ceremonies (e.g., 1 Kings 8.62–66). The Jerusalem temple and the dynasty of Davidic kings were symbolically linked, as illustrated by the proximity and names of the two institutions: the temple was the "house of Yahweh" (*bet yhwh*), which stood next to the somewhat larger palace of the royal dynasty, the "house of David" (*bet david*). The centralization of worship at the temple, promulgated by kings Hezekiah and Josiah, concentrated the sacrificial tribute in Jerusalem and exalted and extended the authority of the royal house.

It is useful to distinguish a third type or level of religious worship, local religion, which mediated between family and state religion. Regional shrines served local families and lineages, functioning as a unifying feature in Israelite society. There is evidence that Yahweh was worshiped in various local manifestations: he was invoked in blessings as "Yahweh of Samaria" and "Yahweh of Teman" in eighth-century inscriptions from Kuntillet ʿAjrud, and Absalom speaks of going to Hebron to pay his vow to Yahweh (2 Sam 15.7). These local manifestations of Yahweh were no doubt conceived of as the same god, but worshiped with local variations and accents. The local shrines—and the local priests who earned their living by the sacrifices offered there—were anathematized by the prophets and Deuteronomy. In some respects state religion was a version of local religion writ large, because Yahweh in Zion is a local manifestation of Yahweh who becomes the authorized state god, a jealous god inimical to the local cults.

The Prophetic Critique

THE RELIGIOUS CRITIQUES of the classical prophets (eighth through the sixth centuries BCE) effected significant shifts in the structures of belief and practice in Israelite religion. Many aspects of traditional religious practice, such as sacrifice, worship at local sacred sites, and the use of various types of religious iconography, came under attack. Veneration of other divine beings, including Yahweh's entourage, the heavenly host, was defined as sacrilege. Political institutions such as kingship and the ruling elite came under attack. The classical prophets regarded Israelite society—particularly the ruling classes—as ethically corrupt, and the major religious institutions and traditions were part of the problem. Hence these institutions were defined as empty and abhorred by Yahweh.

The critique of traditional religious symbols and practices is exemplified in Jeremiah's temple sermon: "Thus says the LORD of hosts, the God of Israel: Amend your ways and your doings, and let me dwell with you in this place. Do not trust in these deceptive words: 'This is the temple of the LORD, the temple of the LORD, the temple of the LORD.' . . . You are trusting in deceptive words to no avail" (Jer 7.3–8). In a situation in which the people are morally corrupt, even the temple—the religious institution par excellence—is devoid of value. In the absence of ethical behavior, all religious symbols and rituals are vacant.

As part of the prophets' religious critique, the divine realm is reconceived such that Yahweh becomes the sole high god of all the nations. Rather than being the best of gods, as in older texts, Yahweh is the only god: "The LORD is the true God; he is the living God and the everlasting King" (Jer 10.10). The gods of other nations are mere illusions. Second Isaiah (Isa 40–55) makes this point in the exilic oracles: "I am God, and there is no other; I am God, and there is no one like me" (Isa 46.9). In this new conception of God, the former anthropomorphic traits are purged: God is beyond human imagination, omniscient, and omnipresent. The prophetic critique produced the classical monotheism of Judaism, Christianity, and Islam.

The Scripturalization of Religion

DURING THE PREEXILIC PERIOD, religious knowledge circulated orally, particularly in the rites and festivals of family, local, and state religion. Elders, priests, and prophets were the primary religious authorities. Toward the end of the monarchical period a shift begins to occur in the locus of religious knowledge from oral tradition to the written word. 2 Kings 22 describes the discovery in the Jerusalem temple of "the book of the law" (*sefer hatorah,* probably an early version of the book of Deuteronomy) that authorizes King Josiah's religious reforms. Deut 17.18–20 instructs the king to read a scroll that is "a copy of this law" throughout his days to ensure his just rule. In these scenes the authority of the written word begins to take the place of the prophets and priests—the latter are limited to copying the scroll or pronouncing on its authenticity. The image of God's word as a textual product is vividly portrayed in the initiatory vision of the prophet Ezekiel, who becomes a prophet when God commands him to swallow a scroll: "I ate it; and in my mouth it was as sweet as honey" (Ezek 3.3). God's word has become a text, which the prophet recites to the people.

Henceforth the history of Israelite religion is inseparable from the history of the text and its interpretation. The canonical moment for this history, according to the biblical portrayal, is Ezra's reading of "the book of the law of Moses" (*sefer torah moshe,* an early version of the Pentateuch, i.e., the first five books of the Bible) accompanied by learned men who "helped the people to understand the law" (Neh 8.1–7). The function of religious specialists was now to read and interpret the authoritative text to discern the true meaning of God's textualized word. A striking example of the new concept of divine revelation during the Second Temple period 539 BCE–70 CE is Daniel's vision in Dan 9, in which the pious Daniel reads the book of Jeremiah to learn when the redemption of Jerusalem will occur; then he prays, mourns, and fasts. The angel Gabriel arrives from heaven to reveal the scriptural secrets: "Daniel, I have now come out to give you wisdom and understanding" (Dan 9.22). God's word is contained in a text, but it takes further divine revelation to understand its true meaning.

Once religion becomes textualized, each community needs a divinely inspired or authorized interpreter or class of interpreters to discern the scriptural secrets. The Teacher of Righteousness at Qumran and Jesus of Nazareth are prominent examples of inspired teachers of scriptural secrets during the latter part of the Second Temple period. New institutions arose, such as the Pharisees and rabbis, whose authority was rooted in their ability to interpret scripture. Commentary became the major vehicle for religious discourse. In Christianity "the Word became flesh and lived among us" (Jn 1.14), but its gospel was also a text, and Christianity preserved its Jewish origins as a scriptural religion. By the end of the Second Temple period, Israelite religion had been transformed into a plurality of cultures of interpretation, including Essenes, Pharisees, Samaritans, and various types of Christians.

The Greco-Roman Context of the New Testament

DAVID E. AUNE

THE HYPHENATED ADJECTIVE "GRECO-ROMAN" reflects the convergence of two great political and cultural empires that together exercised a profound effect on Western civilization and on Christianity. The older centered in Greece and Macedonia and under Alexander the Great (356–323 BCE) eventually came to control not only the lands bordering the eastern Mediterranean, but also much of central Asia. The younger, centered in the Italian peninsula and the regions surrounding the western Mediterranean, eventually took over a good deal of the empire conquered by Alexander. Each culture contributed important components to the Greco-Roman mix: the Romans contributed political organization, administrative skill, a sophisticated legal system, a nearly invincible army, and expert engineering; the Greeks contributed the liberal arts: philosophy, history, literature, oratory, art, and music.

Since the Greeks' own self-designation was "Hellenes," Greek culture from its prehistoric beginnings to the death of Alexander is generally referred to as "Hellenic," a term describing the period before the Greeks developed any more comprehensive form of political union than the independent city-state (*polis*) and the league of relatively independent city-states. "Hellenism" as the designation for a historical era was coined by the great historian J. G. Droysen (1808–84) to describe the mixture of Greek and oriental culture that paved the way for Christianity. The term "Hellenism" has thus come to characterize the dominative interaction of Greek culture with other indigenous cultures of the ancient world during the period between Alexander and Cleopatra. The Hellenistic period (323–31 BCE), then, is conventionally regarded as beginning with the politically significant event of the death of Alexander the Great, though of course the phenomenon of hellenization predated that event. Alexander's death was quickly followed by the fragmentation of his vast empire into a number of major and minor Hellenistic monarchies.

The Greco-Roman period, also referred to as the period of Roman Hellenism, began when the Hellenistic period ended, in 31 BCE. In that year, Octavian's admiral Agrippa defeated Mark Antony in a decisive sea battle near Actium, Greece, on September 2. This was followed by the suicides of Mark Antony and Cleopatra VII (the last pharaoh of the thirty-second dynasty) in Alexandria in 30. The year 31 BCE is the date of an important symbolic political event, but cannot be considered in itself a culturally significant event, given the continued dominance of Hellenism during the Roman period.

Alexander and the Hellenistic Monarchies

THE TRANSITION FROM THE HELLENIC to the Hellenistic period began when Alexander III, who became king of Macedon when his father, Philip II, was assassinated in 336 BCE, determined to invade the sprawling but well-organized Persian Empire in retaliation for the destructive invasions of Ionia, Greece, and Macedonia by the Persian kings Darius I and his son Xerxes I a century and a half earlier. In 334 Alexander crossed the Hellespont into Persian-controlled Asia Minor with a force of at least thirty thousand foot soldiers and five thousand cavalry and a retinue of hired philosophers and historians. Using the superior Macedonian phalanx formation and a Greek fleet, Alexander routed the Persian forces and their Greek mercenaries at the Granicus River, near the site of Troy, in June 334. Proceeding south along the coast of Asia Minor, he freed Greek cities from tyrants and oligarchies sponsored by Persia, established democracies, giving each city its own laws, and abolished the hated Persian tribute. He also besieged, captured, and punished cities that resisted.

Turning inland, he went northeast to Gordium (where he cut the famous Gordian knot with a sword), then southeast to Issus, where he defeated a large Persian force under Darius in October 333 (Callisthenes in Polybius 12.17–22). Marching south along the coast of Palestine, he besieged the recalcitrant island city of Tyre (January–July 332), which fell after seven months (Arrian 2.16–24). After besieging and conquering Gaza, he entered Egypt, which he liberated from Persian domination. On November 14, 332, he became pharaoh of Egypt, traditionally regarded as an incarnation of Amon-Ra. According to Callisthenes, the oracle of Apollo at Didyma affirmed Alexander's descent from Zeus (Strabo 17.1.43), and the prophet of Ammon at the Oasis of Siwah reportedly addressed Alexander as the son of Zeus (Plutarch, *Alexander* 27.5–11); thereafter he began to designate himself as Zeus-Ammon (following the traditional Greek interpretation of foreign cults that equated Amon-Ra with Zeus).

Alexander next met and decisively defeated Darius III and the Persian forces at Gaugamela on October 1, 331, near the Tigris River (Diodorus Siculus 17.61). He then assumed the Persian royal title *Shahanshah* ("King of kings") and proceeded to Babylon and Susa, both of which surrendered immediately. In January 330, Alexander looted and destroyed Persepolis (in southern Iran), the immensely wealthy capital of the Persian Empire (Diodorus 17.70.1–73.2).

Alexander then set out to conquer central Asia, convinced that India was the last eastern region before the world-encircling ocean. An increasing number of Persians were incorporated into Alexander's army because of the continuing need for reinforcements due to casualties and desertions (according to Arrian 7.7, thirty thousand young Persian soldiers joined Alexander's army following the mutiny at Opis in 327 BCE). Eventually thousands of Indians became part of his force as well. The cavalry (comprised of both Macedonians and Greeks) was a key part of Alexander's force, and Persians were not integrated into it until ca. 328 BCE (Arrian 4.17.3).

When Alexander died on June 10, 323, he had been on the march for eleven years, covered more than twenty thousand miles, and dealt with many mutinies and revolts, yet he had cobbled together a vast empire of about 2.1 million square miles; he had forever changed the political and cultural climate of the lands clustered around the eastern Mediterranean east to central Asia. Alexander founded a number of cities (the number is often exaggerated; Plutarch claims he founded seventy [*On the Fortune of Alexander* 328e]), at least seventeen of which are reliably attested, though little or nothing is known about most of them, and only three or four can be identified with modern localities. His foundations, invariably named Alexandria, were strategically located near large, rich oases close to existing Persian centers. These foundations were part of a deliberate colonization program; each city was populated by natives ("barbarians") from the surrounding area (including some nomads) together with Greek or Macedonian settlers. Many of these were Greek veterans and Macedonian soldiers, who had completed their tour of duty; the "barbarians" were never integrated into city life as equals with the Greeks and Macedonians. Contrary to a widespread and ancient notion, popularized in Plutarch's *On the Fortune of Alexander,* Alexander did not intend the adoption of Greek culture as a tool for improving the native population. Alexandria in Egypt was the most famous of these foundations and was the farthest west; the foundation farthest east was Alexandria Eschate, a frontier city on the Jaxartes River (the modern Syr Darya in Uzbekistan). In Alexander's lifetime new foundations were ruled by governors appointed by him and subject to him (or his satraps) and were unlike the democratically constituted Greek cities he had liberated.

The enormous Macedonian-Iranian empire forged by Alexander fell apart shortly after his unexpected death of natural causes in 323 BCE. The internecine conflicts that erupted among powerful members of Alexander's court were temporarily resolved at the battle of Ipsus in 301, as a result of which Alexander's empire was carved into three spheres of influence. The political turmoil in the ancient Near East during the third and second centuries BCE is presented from a Jewish perspective in the apocalyptic visions of Dan 11.1–12.13.

Antigonus I Monophthalmos, "the One-eyed" (382–301 BCE), one of Alexander's generals, took control of Greece, Macedonia, and eventually Asia Minor and declared himself king in 306. He was killed at the decisive battle of Ipsus in 301, but his dynasty survived intact until 168. This Antigonid dynasty was involved in a series of unlucky Macedonian wars with Rome and finally came to an end with the defeat of Perseus (212–166 BCE), the last Antigonid, at the Battle of Pydna (June 22, 168), when Macedonia came under Roman rule.

Egypt and Palestine came under the control of Ptolemy Lagus (ca. 364–282 BCE), one of Alexander's generals, who was initially appointed governor of Egypt after Alexander's death by Perdiccas, his vizier. He became pharaoh of Egypt in 305 BCE, taking the Egyptian throne name Meryamun Setepenre ("Beloved of Amun, Chosen of Re"); he was also known as Ptolemy I Soter. Ptolemy Lagus had kidnapped the body of Alexander from Damascus in 322, when it was en route to Aegae in Macedonia, and interred it in Alexandria, Egypt, in order to give his claim legitimacy. Ptolemy I Soter was the founder of the thirty-second pharaonic dynasty, which lasted until the death of Cleopatra VII in 30 BCE.

Seleucus I Nicator (358–281 BCE), another of Alexander's generals, established his control over Babylon, including all of Mesopotamia and the regions east to Afghanistan, in 312, the foundation date of the Seleucid Empire. The Seleucid kingdom began as the largest of the three major Hellenistic monarchies, and its disparate population included the largest number of peoples and languages. At its greatest extent, from western Anatolia to Afghanistan, it comprised about 1.3 million square miles of territory. Allied with Lysimachus, Seleucus I defeated Antigonus I at the battle of Ipsus in 301 BCE, taking over northern Syria and eastern Anatolia. The Seleucids followed Alexander's example by founding Hellenistic cities, particularly in Asia Minor and Syria, each an island of Greek culture in a barbarian sea. The Seleucid Empire had two capitals, both Seleucid foundations, Antioch on the Orontes in Syria and Seleucia in Mesopotamia. Smaller Hellenistic monarchies were formed when local rulers broke away from Seleucid control, including the Attalid dynasty of Pergamum as well as Bithynia, Pontus, and Cappadocia. The Seleucids had a series of conflicts with Rome during the third and second centuries BCE but always came out second best. One of the more ambitious of the Seleucids, Antiochus IV Epiphanes (175–165 BCE), was turned back from invading Alexandria by the Roman governor Popilius Laenas. By 100, the Seleucid "Empire" had collapsed and consisted only of Antioch and a few Syrian cities, and the brief attempt at restoration by Antiochus XIII in 69 was embroiled in civil war. Pompey the Great ended the dynasty when he made Syria a Roman province in 63 BCE.

Roman Conquest of the Mediterranean

THE COMPLEX HISTORIES of each of the three major Hellenistic kingdoms is a story of intermittent conflict with Roman interests in the eastern Mediterranean that ended with the subjugation of all of them by Rome. Rome had gained complete political and economic control of the western Mediterranean by defeating its chief rival, Carthage, originally a Phoenician colony and the greatest naval power in the Mediterranean, in the Second Punic War (218–202 BCE). Eventually Rome permanently eliminated the economic competition of Carthage by completely destroying the North African city at the end of the Third Punic War (149–146). Rome had made a practice of forging mutual alliances with many Greek cities in the east, and when they were threatened by one or another of the Hellenistic kingdoms, they turned to Rome for help. For this reason, Rome turned eastward to halt the expansionist policies of Philip V of Macedonia (reigned 221–179), who was defeated in 197 BCE at Cynocephalae in Thessaly by the Roman general Titus Flamininus. By the mid-second century, cities of the Achaean League were trying to stop Roman expansion in Greece. Corinth, one of these cities, was punished with complete destruction in 146 (Polybius 28.3–11); replaced more than a century later by Julius Caesar with a Roman colony in 44 BCE, it became the capital of the province of Achaea in 27. By the time Paul arrived in Corinth in 51 CE (Acts 18.1–17), the city was more Roman than Greek and had been completely rebuilt.

Rome had gradually organized the Mediterranean world into two types of provinces. Imperial provinces were controlled directly by the emperor through a praetor who headed the locally stationed Roman legion. Senatorial provinces were under the formal control of the Roman Senate and governed by proconsuls (former consuls or praetors). The power of provincial proconsuls was enormous, and they were frequently corrupt. The number of provinces increased over the years as Rome annexed more territory, turned regions nominally ruled by client kings into provinces, and subdivided larger provinces for more effective management. At the end of the Roman Republic (ca. 29 CE), there were fifteen Republican provinces; when Augustus died in 14 CE, there were thirty-one Roman provinces; by 120, the number had grown to forty-nine. When Herod Archelaus was deposed in 6 CE, Judea temporarily became a Roman province governed by a series of equestrian prefects, including Pontius Pilatus (ca. 26–37 CE), who was appointed by Tiberius but eventually recalled for incompetence.

The Spread of Koine Greek

ALEXANDER, LIKE HIS FATHER, PHILIP II, made Attic Greek, the dialect of Athens, the official language of his court and his diplomatic correspondence. A form of the language that developed after that time became known as Koine ("common"), or Hellenistic, Greek. The Greeks in

Alexander's army and navy were drawn from all over the Greek world (Quintus Curtius Rufus 5.39; Diodorus Siculus 17.17.3), and Koine Greek became their common dialect. Because Greek language and culture were thought superior to indigenous languages and cultures, Koine quickly became the spoken and written language of the ruling elite as well as of upwardly mobile natives. Following the death of Alexander in 323 BCE, Koine Greek became the official language of the three major Hellenistic kingdoms.

Two languages were used in the administration of the sixteen eastern Roman provinces, Latin and Greek. Latin was the language of administration; it was used for communication between the central government and Roman magistrates, between Roman magistrates and Roman colonies, and when Roman citizens were involved. The language of the native population was nearly always Greek. The language of the NT is Koine Greek, though different linguistic registers are evident. The Gospels of Mark and John belong to the lowest level, Luke-Acts to an intermediate level, and Hebrews and 1 Peter to the highest level.

Religion

THROUGHOUT THE FIRST CENTURY CE, Greek religion and culture dominated the eastern Mediterranean, with the exception of such cultural islands as Roman colonies (e.g., Corinth in Achaia, founded in 44 BCE; Patra in Achaia, founded in 14; Philippi in Macedonia, founded in 42; Berytus in Syria, modern Beirut, founded in 15). Greek religion had changed very little over the centuries, with each city carefully preserving its own distinctive traditions (Pausanias describes the great variety of Greek religious practices in the second century CE). An exception was the innovative development of Hellenistic ruler cults beginning in the late fourth century BCE.

Greek religion took three main forms: public cults fostered by the Greek cities and largely restricted to citizens; private cults practiced by associations with limited membership (including mystery cults); and domestic cults practiced by Greek families in the privacy of their homes. Greek public cults were highly visible and part of the public space of each city. Athens, one of the wealthiest Greek cities, had a stunning acropolis studded with important temples dominated by the Parthenon, dedicated to Athena, the city's patron deity. Temples, shrines, statues, and altars permeated public spaces. Paul was reportedly distressed because the city was so full of idols (Acts 17.16), and he was probably reacting as many other visitors had when he told a group of Athenians how extremely religious they were in every way (Acts 17.22).

Greek cults were not based on a set of coherent doctrines (like early Christianity), but rather on the careful observance of such traditional rituals as processions, feasts, prayers, libations, and sacrifices. As in Judaism (and Islam), orthopraxy was valued over orthodoxy. Greek cults had little interest in ethics unless cultic issues were involved, e.g., the impurity resulting from homicide; it was the philosophical schools (see below) that were primarily concerned with the moral life. The primary object of such public cults was the fostering of proper relationships with the gods to ensure the well-being of the city, protection from war and disease, and the prosperity that resulted from good harvests and successful commerce. Traditional Greek gods were neither omnipotent nor omniscient; they did not create the cosmos but were thought to have come into being after the cosmos. The sun, moon, and stars (part of the cosmos) were therefore called "eternals," and Olympian deities (e.g., Zeus, Hera, Poseidon) and the chthonic or earth deities (e.g., Dionysius, Demeter) were designated "immortals"; both were separated by a great gulf from humans, who were "mortals." Though gods were more powerful than mortals, both gods and humans were thought to be subject to *moira,* or "fate." During the Hellenistic period the traditional Greek distinction between mortal and immortal became blurred; this was encouraged by myths of humans who became immortal and the availability of immortality through some "mystery religions."

Though Rome was a single city-state that became the political seat and administrative center of an enormous empire centered on the Mediterranean, native Roman religious cults and cultic practices had very little influence on non-Romans, with the noteworthy exception of Roman ruler cults in the Greek East. The development of the ruler cult of Alexander the Great in the Greek world, followed by the cults devoted to subsequent Hellenistic kings and queens, appears to have been a functional adjustment to the political reality that cities were no longer independent, but required a type of cult appropriate to their new subordinate status. In the tradition of Alexander, Hellenistic ruler cults (with priests, processions, sacrifices, and games) were established to honor powerful Greek rulers and benefactors, such as Lysander of Sparta and Dion of Syracuse. Greek cities typically received privileges, benefactions, and financial aid from those whom they honored with cults (a *quid pro quo* based on the patron-client social relationship). Cities normally took the initiative in founding ruler cults, which were integral to the public affairs of each city-state. Since the Ptolemaic dynasty constituted the thirty-second pharaonic dynasty, each Ptolemaic pharaoh could claim to be an incarnation of Amon-Ra. After the death of Ptolemy I (ca. 280 BCE), his son and successor, Ptolemy II Philadelphos, arranged the formal deification of his father as well as his mother, Berenike, as *theoi soteres,* "savior gods." In the 270s, Ptolemy II and his wife Arsinoe II were officially deified while yet living as *theoi adelphoi,* "sibling gods," and were offered divine worship in the shrine of Alexander the Great. After Ptolemy II, each successive Ptolemaic king and queen was deified upon accession and worshiped as part of the royal household.

The ruler cults of the Hellenistic kings were antecedents of the Roman imperial cult. Beginning in the third century BCE the Greek cities sometimes devoted cults to the Roman magistrates who governed them. Octavian arranged for the official deification of Julius Caesar by the Roman Senate on January 1, 42 BCE. Thereafter, Octavian, as Caesar Augustus, assumed the official title *divi filius* ("son of the god [Julius Caesar]"), though he discouraged worship both at home and in the provinces. The deified Julius Caesar and the other emperors deified upon death by official acts of the Roman Senate became parts of the official pantheon of the Roman people, though the imperial cult was more important in the provinces than in Rome itself. In Roman Asia the imperial cult provided a ritual presence for a physically absent emperor. In the traditional form of the imperial cult, the emperor was worshiped as a god only after his death and apotheosis. In the imperial cults in Anatolia, the divinized emperor was usually associated with other, more traditional gods such as Dea Roma or various groups of Olympian deities. The divinization of human rulers finds an echo in the story of the acclamation of Herod Agrippa as a god by the people of Tyre and Sidon and his subsequent death because of hubris (Acts 12.20–23).

Three main types of voluntary Greek private associations (*thiasoi* or *collegia*) existed, each of which had a greater or lesser cultic component: professional corporations or guilds (e.g., fishermen, fruit growers, shipowners, and silversmiths; cf. Acts 19.23–41); funerary societies (*collegia tenuiorum*); and religious or cult societies (*collegia sodalicia*), centering on the worship of a deity. The last category includes "mystery religions," a general term for a variety of ancient private cults that shared several features. The term "mystery" is related to a Greek term meaning "initiate," and "mystery" itself means "ritual of initiation," referring to the secret initiation rites at the center of such cults. The mystery religions did not enter suddenly into the Mediterranean world during the Hellenistic period, though the period of their greatest popularity appears to have been the first through the third centuries CE. Little is known about them, but they seem to have consisted of three interrelated features: *dromena*, "things acted out," i.e., the enactment of the cult myth; *legomena*, "things spoken," i.e., the oral presentation of the cult myth; and *deiknoumena*, "things shown," i.e., the ritual presentation of symbolic objects to the initiate. Initiates who experienced the central mystery ritual became convinced that they would enjoy *soteria* ("salvation"), health and prosperity in this life as well as a blissful afterlife. Mystery religions were once thought to focus on a divinity that represented the annual decay and renewal of vegetation through his or her death and restoration to life, but in recent years the great diversity among those cults formerly lumped together as "mystery cults" has become increasingly apparent.

More than a century ago, German scholars associated with the Göttingen-based "history of religions school" argued that early Christian sacramentalism (particularly the baptismal experience of sharing the death and resurrection of Christ reflected in Rom 6) was dependent on the Hellenistic mystery cults, with their focus on a dying and rising god with whom initiates identified and through whom they received salvation. It now appears that the mystery cults had no standard theology centering on the promise of immortality through ritually sharing the death-and-resurrection experience of the cult deity, nor is the view that the mysteries offered immortality through the ritual identification of the initiate with such a deity verified by the surviving evidence about the significance of such mystery initiations.

Philosophy

DURING THE HELLENISTIC PERIOD, the most important philosophical schools in the Greek world were no longer Plato's Academy or Aristotle's Peripatetic tradition, but rather the three Hellenistic philosophical traditions of Stoicism, Epicureanism, and Skepticism. Cynicism, a countercultural movement that fostered no school tradition, ran a distant fourth. The philosophical schools of the classical period (ca. 480–323 BCE) typically organized their dialectical efforts into three areas, physics, logic, and ethics; the main Hellenistic philosophical traditions, however, tended to focus on logical arguments in pursuit of *eudaimonia*, "the happy life" or "the flourishing life." During the Hellenistic and Greco-Roman periods, therefore, philosophy was thought of not as an abstract intellectual exercise but rather as therapy for the soul in which the philosopher played the role of a moral physician.

Early Christianity and early Judaism regarded conformity to moral norms as a primary expression of faithfulness and obedience to God, but there were no counterparts to ethical monotheism in the public cults of the Greek world. Emphasis on individual happiness was in part the result of the decline of the Greek city-state through subordination to Hellenistic monarchies and Roman imperialism, resulting in a growing stress on the role and importance of the individual in society.

Epicurus (341–270 BCE) moved to Athens in 307, where he bought a house with a garden; there he and his school lived a secluded life in order to avoid the negative influences of city life. Though they had the reputation of being hedonists, they actually pursued a spartan standard of living. The limit of pleasure for Epicureans was the absence of pain, and seeking more pleasure only served to introduce the pain of unsatisfied desire. Since pleasures of the soul were preferable to pleasures of the body, the greatest pleasure was a life of philosophical contemplation. For Epicureans, the universe existed only out of chance. They thought the gods were uninterested in the human world, as they enjoyed their own perfectly blessed life; thus humans were free from the irrational and superstitious fear of the supernatural. The private life of Epicureans ensured that their influence on Hellenistic and Greco-Roman culture was minimal.

Zeno (335–263 BCE), the founder of Stoicism, arrived in Athens in 313 and began teaching in the Agora in the Painted Porch (*stoa poikile*), from which the school derived its name. Stoicism was perhaps the most influential philosophical school in the Hellenistic world, surviving in modified form into late antiquity. When Paul arrived in Athens in the mid-first century CE, he found Epicurean and Stoic philosophers arguing their views in the Agora (Acts 17.18). For Stoics, philosophy is not a pastime but a way of life, and the goal of the good life produces *eudaimonia,* or "happiness." The good is achieved by "living in agreement with nature." Virtue alone is adequate for happiness, and nothing but virtue is good. All emotions (the primary emotions are appetite and fear) are bad, and Stoics must be "apathetic," i.e., not allow emotions to rule reason. Emotions are not experienced by the ideal sage (one who had attained moral and intellectual perfection). Stoic ethics emphasized self-sufficiency (*autarkeia*) and obedience to the dictates of reason.

Elements of these major intellectual traditions appear within the NT and became more influential as Christianity became more assimilated to the culture of the Greco-Roman world.

The Bible and Archaeology

ERIC M. MEYERS

THE STUDY OF THE RELATIONSHIP between the Bible and archaeology has traditionally been identified with the field of biblical archaeology, a discipline that goes back over a century and a half to the time when the West began to rediscover its rich cultural legacy in the ancient Near East. Adventurers, explorers, clergymen, and biblical scholars in the nineteenth century set out to recover the larger setting of the world of the Bible in a charged atmosphere of scientific rationalism that had been created as a result of the forces unleashed in the Enlightenment. Napoleon Bonaparte's expedition to conquer Egypt in 1798 was accompanied by a Commission of Arts and Science, a group of scientists and orientalists who would study the land and its linguistic heritage along with all its material aspects. Their work was the trigger that inaugurated a new era of discovery and study of the Old World that was to dominate Western circles till today. Interest in Mesopotamia soon followed, and at the beginning of the nineteenth century in Ottoman Palestine, an English explorer and geographer, Edward Daniel Clarke, set out to identify the major sites of the Bible. A student of Clarke, Jean Louis Burckhardt, soon followed his teacher's lead in his exploration of Transjordan and Palestine and was the first to identify Petra.

The two Americans who came after and who inaugurated a project of systematic exploration of biblical sites were Edward Robinson, professor of Old Testament at Andover Theological Seminary in Massachusetts, later at Union Theological Seminary in New York, and Eli Smith, a young missionary from Beirut who possessed the necessary linguistic abilities to navigate through the Holy Land. Robinson and Smith set out in 1838 to follow the route of the exodus from Egypt. They realized their goal of producing a scientific geography of biblical lands but also professed a profound belief in the historicity of the Bible and looked upon their explorations as part pilgrimage and part science. This mixture of faith and scientific inquiry characterized the beginning of an era of continuous study of the Holy Land; this has carried forward through the twentieth into the twenty-first century and is part of the mixed legacy of this extraordinary era. The publication of their work, *Biblical Researches in Palestine* (London, 1841), marked the end of the era of missionaries and pilgrims and the beginning of biblical archaeology as a subject of intellectual pursuit.

Among the first expeditions to follow Robinson and Smith was the Lynch Expedition, sent by the U.S. Navy to explore the Jordan Valley and Dead Sea region in 1849. In 1865 the British established the Palestine Exploration Fund (PEF), which served as the vehicle for the first full survey of

Palestine conducted by royal engineers Charles Warren and Charles Wilson in 1872–78 and 1881. One of the primary purposes of the PEF was to illustrate the Bible. The American Palestine Exploration Society, a forerunner of the American Schools of Oriental Research (ASOR), was established during this period (1870–84) for the purpose of "the illustration and defense of the Bible." The marriage between the Bible and archaeology, therefore, was very much a part of the formative period in which Americans and British cemented their ties to the Holy Land through exploration, research, and ultimately excavation of biblical sites. All this occurred at a time when higher criticism of the Bible was gaining new visibility, best signified by the publication of the English edition of Julius Wellhausen's *Prolegomenon to the History of Ancient Israel* (Edinburgh, 1885).

The first "modern" scientific excavation of a biblical site in Palestine came at the end of the nineteenth century. In 1890 Sir Flinders Petrie led an expedition to Tell el-Hesi to determine for the PEF the extent of Egyptian influence in Palestine. An American, Frederick Bliss, joined Petrie there in 1894. Petrie is credited with establishing the fundamentals of stratigraphic archaeology and the typological analysis of pottery, which he separated by period. In making judgments about the peoples associated with the various stratified layers, however, Petrie became associated with the eugenics movement of Francis Galton; this association influenced racial thinking about Near Eastern archaeology until the 1940s in a most negative way.

The establishment of the American Schools of Oriental Research in Jerusalem in 1900 was a watershed event that led to some of the most important archaeological developments of the twentieth century. These included excavations, historical and linguistic research relating to the biblical world, the discovery of the Dead Sea Scrolls, and ultimately the geographical broadening of the horizon of research and the construction of centers in Baghdad, Amman, and Nicosia. The suggestion for establishing such an institution in Palestine came from J. Henry Thayer, professor of New Testament at Harvard University and president of the Society of Biblical Literature (SBL), in 1895. Thayer referred his idea to a committee, which published a circular to solicit support for the project. In that document the committee expressed the rationale for the school in this way: "The object of the school would be to afford graduates of American theological seminaries, and other similarly qualified persons, opportunity to prosecute biblical and linguistic investigations under more favorable conditions than can be secured at a distance from the Holy Land;. . . to gather material for the illustration of the biblical narratives; to settle doubtful points in biblical topography; to identify historic localities; to explore and, if possible, excavate, sacred sites." * This document illustrates well the strong dedication to recovering biblical history typical at the turn of the twentieth century. In their disregard for the nonbiblical aspects of Near Eastern culture the founding fathers betray their Western bias, which was subsequently modified by the organizing committee of universities and seminaries that constituted ASOR's first academic consortium.

Although the focus on the Bible dominated American and British interest in recovering the archaeological heritage of Palestine and neighboring lands when ASOR set down its first institutional roots in the Holy Land, the oversight committee eventually extended ASOR's interests and purview to the rest of the Levant and the greater Near East to include "nonbiblical cultures." In the early part of the twentieth century the SBL published ASOR's research that was clearly biblical in focus, and the Archaeological Institute of America (AIA) the nonbiblical material. The relationship between the Bible and archaeology at that time was thus very much

---

* Philip J. King, *American Archaeology in the Mideast: A History of the American Schools of Oriental Research* (Winona Lake, IN: Eisenbrauns, 1983), 26.

framed as a dialogue between societies, one focused on the biblical heritage (SBL), the other on the classical heritage (AIA) but with an openness to the archaeology of the ancient Near East. With the publication of the first *Bulletin of the America Schools of Oriental Research* (*BASOR*) in 1920, ASOR at least in theory allowed the possibility of bringing the two worlds of the Bible and archaeology together within a single society as well as of bridging the gulf that separated the archaeology of the Near East from the world of classical archaeology. These developments illustrate how biblical studies and the study of ancient Near Eastern civilizations, as well as classical culture to a lesser degree, were linked together early in the history of scholarship in the field.

World War I delayed progress in fieldwork in Palestine, since the Jerusalem School was closed from 1916 to 1918. It also delayed the arrival of W. F. Albright, who was to have such a determinative influence on the history of the discipline. Albright came to Jerusalem as Thayer Fellow in 1920 and stayed for a decade of work that included excavation, exploration, and teaching in the field of archaeology and biblical studies with a great emphasis on the linguistic heritage of the ancient Near East. His excavations included Tell el-Ful, the palace of King Saul at Gibeah, and Tell Beit Mirsim, which he identified as the biblical Debir. There he established the basic pottery typology for Palestinian archaeology that was standard till the 1970s. He also conducted excavations at Bethel and Beth Zur during the period when he split his year between Jerusalem and Baltimore, where he was head of Johns Hopkins Oriental Seminary from 1929 till 1958.

Albright arrived at the Jerusalem School the year that *BASOR* was established, and he was its editor from 1930 to 1968. In the pages of the *Bulletin* can be found the core of his scholarly agenda, namely, support for the basic historical reliability of the Bible, which he believed was reflected in its narratives, language, and accurate references to aspects of everyday life. In his fieldwork Albright adopted the best of the stratigraphic method and recording system developed by George Reisner and Clarence Fisher at the Harvard excavations at Samaria (1908–10) and combined it with his own emphasis on ceramic typology to develop his own approach to field methodology. His most eminent follower was G. Ernest Wright, though Yigael Yadin, Israel's most famous archaeologist, often cited Albright as his intellectual mentor and as the "father of biblical archaeology."

Albright's fieldwork during the 1920s and 1930s led him to ever more positive assessments of the role of archaeology in supporting the Bible. In the second half of his career he interpreted many of the results of his own and others' work as supporting the historicity of the patriarchal narratives. In no small measure Albright's zeal for the patriarchs derived from his disdain for Wellhausen and his followers, who emphasized the exile and its aftermath as the most formative period in Israel's history. Albright first summarized these views in 1932 in his *The Archeology of Palestine and the Bible*. His positivistic views on the historicity of the patriarchs dominated American scholarship into the 1960s.

George Ernest Wright carried Albright's achievements forward, especially in respect to the biblical theology movement then popular in America. In presenting the theological underpinnings of what was basically Albright's scientific construct, Wright was the last in a long tradition of making biblical archaeology a respected scientific inquiry. The field was more or less what Albright had also called "Palestinian archaeology," albeit tied closely to biblical theology. With respect to encouraging new excavations, training new students, and embracing the "new archaeology" of the 1960s and 1970s, Wright succeeded to an unprecedented degree, and this success had an impact on an entire new generation of scholars and teachers.

Wright's excavations at Shechem (1956–69) laid the groundwork for the future work of many who would continue in the Albright/Wright tradition (e.g., Bull, Campbell, Calloway, Dever, Holiday, Lance, Seger, Toombs). By beginning the excavations at Gezer with Nelson Glueck in 1964, Wright made it possible for those of the next generation to begin their own independent work. The foremost among them, William Dever, soon took over the Gezer operations and became the main advocate for changing the name of the discipline to "Syro-Palestinian archaeology." Dever's hope was that by changing its name the field could sever its ties with theology, thereby delegitimizing any theological claims over archaeological data. He also hoped that changing the name from "biblical archaeology" would leave open a way for genuine dialogue between the science of archaeology and the sophisticated field of biblical studies. Dever believed that the conservative theological tendency of the field of biblical archaeology to support the historical veracity of the Bible would be diminished if archaeologists and biblical scholars could do their work separately and at the conclusion of their discrete investigations compare results on issues of joint interest.

While debates about the definition of the field progressed, the opinion of specialists on several key issues was changing. By the mid-1970s support for the historicity of the patriarchal age was fast declining, and soon after there was a growing consensus that the period of the Israelite conquest and settlement, a major pillar of Wright's biblical archaeology, was far more complicated than anyone had anticipated and that the historicity of the exodus itself was now open to serious debate.

Dever's sustained critique resulted in a reevaluation of where the field was going and allowed for a more inclusive Near Eastern archaeology to evolve during a period of growing political tension. The broadening of the discipline to include new interpretive frameworks as well as new methodologies taken from anthropology also permitted new types of field archaeologists to pursue their interests without having to deal with the questions of most interest to biblical studies. In the areas of prehistory, Islamic archaeology, and the archaeology of Jordan and Syria, for example, such a development was most welcome and had the immediate effect of encouraging many newcomers to enter the field, now conceived of as "Near Eastern archaeology." That is not to say that the biblical archaeology movement had peaked or would disappear, but it had moved on in ways more congenial to the academic and intellectual atmosphere of the end of the twentieth century.

When viewed in historical perspective, the maximalist/minimalist debate about the implications of archaeological findings for the history of Israel that emerged in the 1990s was a natural outgrowth of the ongoing tension between archaeologists who had long been working in Palestine and Israel and biblical scholars. Since the time of Wellhausen biblical scholars had been trying to reconcile the large historical gap that separated the probable editing and redaction of the Hebrew Bible, which occurred during the exile or later during the Persian or Hellenistic period, from the period when Israelite remains from the Iron Age were documented in the material record. Moreover, archaeological surveys and analysis of excavations that could provide information about the critical transition between the Late Bronze Age and the Iron Age, the thirteenth–twelfth century BCE, seemed not to support the existence of a new people arriving from Egypt or Mesopotamia, who within several centuries were able to establish a new kingdom in the form of the United Monarchy. Instead, the data seemed to indicate that Israel had emerged from indigenous groups in the central hill country somewhat later than what is indicated in the biblical narrative.

Arguments over dating tenth-century material, pottery in particular, led to a bitter dispute over whether there was a United Monarchy and whether Jerusalem had developed into an urban center before the eighth century. In this aspect of the debate the minimalists, largely based in England and Europe, were indirectly supported by the pioneering work of Israel Finkelstein of Tel Aviv University, who questioned whether key archaeological data used to support the existence of a strong centralized kingdom were correctly dated, data from such sites as Beersheba, Dan, Hazor, Gezer, Jerusalem, and Megiddo. Finkelstein's views have been overwhelmingly rejected by the archaeological community, which still supports the position, based on ceramic dating, that monumental remains compatible with a United Monarchy were constructed in the tenth and ninth centuries. Ceramic typology and the interpretation and dating of such remains have become the central issues dividing the archaeological camps, while biblical scholars have differed on the implications of a late editing of the Bible and have debated whether a fictional narrative would or would not be possible in the later periods.

For all those who study the Bible seriously, the harshness of the debates and the attendant publicity have created confusion. To say that the older Albright/Wright positivist stance has collapsed is an understatement. What in fact can be said of the situation at the beginning of the twentieth-first century is this: there is no longer a consensus on the history of ancient Israel either from biblical scholarship or from archaeology. A new synthesis is in the making, one that will be significantly different from the one that dominated in American circles for most of the twentieth century.

Just as the old consensus regarding how to reconstruct ancient Israel has fallen, so too has the consensus on how to pursue the field of Syro-Palestinian archaeology. The quest to recover ancient Israel through archaeology and the critical use of the Hebrew Bible has for decades now been cast in socio-historical terms. Syro-Palestinian archaeology, however, has not kept pace with current trends in world archaeology or historical research. Understanding the Bible is no longer an appropriate focus for archaeological research in the Near East. A number of new trends in field excavation can be noted: a shift away from excavating large, spectacular sites in favor of smaller sites without known literary pedigree, allowing scholars to reconstruct the lives of nonelite, ordinary people; greater use of ethnographic and environmental data in reconstructing ancient societies; and greater care in recording the mundane objects of daily living to enable more precise study of households and gender roles of antiquity. This new approach, attempting to broaden and deepen the investigator's ability to appreciate an ancient culture, has been called "socio-archaeology" by Eric and Carol Meyers. William Dever, in reacting to recent developments, has called for what he labels "contextual archaeology." Dever has also called upon archaeologists to take the biblical record seriously and to use it critically, while at the same time being concerned with religious and social history. In making these suggestions Dever hopes to keep alive the "biblical archaeology" movement in a new form while being faithful to its distinguished record of achievement.

Perhaps all this is asking too much of archaeologists who simply want to work in Syro-Palestine or the Levant. Not everyone can be a good biblical scholar and an excellent field archaeologist at the same time. Whatever may be the resolution of the more than century-old debate concerning the proper relationship between archaeology and the Bible, each discipline quite certainly needs the other. A more constructive and positive discourse between the two fields will have to emerge if a new consensus about ancient Israel's complex social history is to be forged.

Archaeology and the New Testament

JÜRGEN ZANGENBERG

SINCE FOR CHRISTIANS THE NT forms an integral part of the Bible, and since the groups behind the NT did not live in a world consisting only of texts and ideas, but one that also contained pots, jars, houses, and temples, archaeology is a natural partner for any research on the NT and early Christianity.

Inventing a New Discipline

THE GREAT MAJORITY OF NT SCHOLARS have always had a keen interest in the results of archaeological work and have used whatever elements of material culture were available to them to explain realia and describe locations, habits, and practices mentioned in the NT text. One source for such data, of course, was the series of ongoing explorations in Palestine. The scope of these expeditions was quite broad. Much of the early work followed a rather general "biblical" agenda to locate sites, reconstruct the history of particular regions through historical geography, find new epigraphical sources, and describe architectural remains from various periods irrespective of their connection to either the OT or the NT. In that regard NT research benefited equally from the efforts of great pioneers such as Robinson, Schick, Warren and Conder, Vincent and Abel, Clermont-Ganneau, Reisner and Fisher, Smith, Dalman, Alt, and Albright. Not surprisingly, Jerusalem provided enough material to engage scholars from many different fields—excavations in the City of David (Bliss and Dickie, Warren, Macalister and Duncan, Weill) and around the Temple Mount (Warren, Robinson), explorations in the Old City to locate sites mentioned by Josephus and prominent in the passion narratives (Schick, Dalman, Mauss, Vincent), and the quest for the magnificent Constantinian buildings mentioned by Eusebius (Coüasnon, Vincent)—though other sites like Samaria, with its Israelite and Herodian monuments, attracted equal attention (Reisner and Fisher). Other scholars went to the field to explore sites directly relevant to the NT or early Christianity (e.g., early Franciscan archaeologists in Jerusalem and Capernaum) or worked in regions prominent in NT or early Christian tradition (Kohl and Watzinger's synagogue survey in Galilee and southern Syria). Even though many of these activities had an overt confessional or national agenda in the increasing competition of Western nations before World War I, these early explorations laid the foundations for a critical understanding of one key region for early Christian history until in the 1950s and 1960s Israeli archaeologists ushered in a new era of systematic archaeological exploration.

At about the time archaeological work in Palestine began, European scholars turned to Asia Minor, the second key region of early Christianity. Schliemann's discoveries in Troy in the 1870s—a sensational success in correlating ancient texts with the archaeology of a site redis-covered by reading Homeric epics with a keen eye for local geography and a vivid imagina-tion—were only the start of a series of highly prestigious expeditions sponsored by Western powers to the west coast of Turkey and Greece (e.g., Austria in Ephesus, Germany in Olympia and Pergamon, France in Delphi, Britain in Athens and many sites in Anatolia, the United States in Corinth and Sardis). Given the apparent success of biblically inspired archaeology in Palestine in locating sites, substantiating biblical history, and supporting plausible reconstruc-tions of the life and ministry of Jesus, it was only a small step to take on the life and ministry of Paul and contextualize the earliest Christian communities mentioned in his Letters, Revelation, and Acts. Like Palestine, Asia Minor had a century-long history of Christian life and culture, which only waited to be freed from oblivion.

Since direct OT connections were virtually nonexistent in Asia Minor (apart from the Hittite culture, whose exploration started in 1906 when Winckler and Makridi excavated Bogazköy), research in Asia Minor and Greece opened up new perspectives by emphasizing the classical Greco-Roman (or "Hellenistic" according to a new term coined by Droysen) heritage of early Christianity. A prominent example of this kind of pioneering work was done by William M. Ramsay (1851–1939). Ramsey deliberately concentrated on the unknown inland regions of Asia Minor, especially Phrygia, through which he traveled systematically during several long journeys between 1881 and 1914, collecting a tremendous amount of data that flowed into sev-eral monumental works still indispensable today. By analyzing the language and contents of thousands of newly found inscriptions (the most famous perhaps being the epitaph of Abercius), mapping sites (especially famous is the rediscovery of the land of the Montanists), and drawing conclusions about historical geography and local infrastructure in antiquity, Ramsay was able to bring back to life an entire region once deeply rooted in Christianity. A whole new branch of "biblical archaeology" developed outside of Palestine and was, at least ini-tially, entirely devoted to the NT and the early Christian heritage. A great advantage possessed by scholars working at sites in Asia Minor or Greece was that they had enjoyed a sound classical education enabling them to record and discuss all traces of ancient culture they happened upon in a region that was still quite inaccessible to Westerners.

On the other hand, still only few genuine NT scholars personally went into the field to *gener-ate* the data they were using. Neither did many NT scholars enter into a systematic dialogue with professional archaeologists in order to reflect on methods of interpreting material culture and to correlate their results with textual sources.

Only when NT scholars became not simply recipients but producers of prime data and part-ners in dialogue should one speak of NT archaeology. In this respect NT archaeology is a fairly re-cent development, even though it continued a much older impulse. Two factors were decisive in producing this development. First, NT studies, like many fields in the humanities including ar-chaeology, underwent a profound diversification and professionalization in the late 1960s and 1970s. NT scholarship benefited from extending its methodological spectrum beyond philology and from enhancing its available data through collaboration with neighboring disciplines. This "sociological turn" broke the ground for a new interest in questions of social setting, group for-mation processes, religious rituals, patterns of everyday life, and modes of enculturation of early

Christian communities, thereby allowing an increasingly creative and *comprehensive* dialogue with the social sciences and with professional archaeology. In this way NT scholarship used archaeology to fulfill its theological and historical task of interpreting the NT contextually and of better understanding the historical, social, and religious formation of early Christianity.

The second decisive impulse came from Judaic studies that, since the early twentieth century, have collected a huge wealth of data on Jewish material culture and everyday life from the vast literary tradition (Krauss). Other scholars systematically researched particular regions (Büchler, Galilee), events (Tcherikover), and art (Goodenough). They programmatically included evidence from epigraphy and—if available—archaeology. Especially prominent with regard to archaeology were the discovery of a synagogue and early house church in Dura Europos (Cumont, Kraeling, Rostovtzeff), the excavations of a synagogue in Bet Alfa (Sukenik), and explorations in the necropolis at Bet Shearim (Maisler, Lifshitz, and Schwabe) as well as the find of the century, Qumran. As scholars became increasingly aware of Judaism's diversity not only in matters of theology, but also in art and everyday life, they realized the role of regional factors in the expression of Judaism. Debates about "sectarian" versus "normative" Judaism (Goodenough) were also affected by such regional expressions. Scholars also became aware of the manifold connections between Jewish culture and the wider Hellenistic world.

Significant new developments occurred after the foundation of the State of Israel when Jewish scholars made every effort to excavate systematically and independently the material roots of their culture in their new homeland. Only then was it possible to confront ideas about Jewish religion and identity drawn from literature with an ever increasing wave of evidence from actual settlement contexts. Much of the data recovered in large-scale, often highly publicized excavations had immediate relevance for NT scholars, including Yadin's excavations in Masada, the exploration of the Dead Sea caves, Qumran, and the Jewish Quarter in Jerusalem, and the study of synagogue architecture, even though many of these expeditions only had a peripheral interest in the NT itself. If NT research wanted to keep pace with these rapid developments, more professionalization was required as well as the willingness to engage in international and interdisciplinary cooperation. Owing to the long and uninterrupted history of Jewish-Christian dialogue, ample material resources, and the accommodating diversity of institutional settings in which NT research was conducted in the United States, the leading projects were and to an extent still are sponsored by U.S. academic institutions.

In the 1970s, a pioneering and especially fruitful example of cooperation was launched between scholars of Judaic, NT, and religious studies. In the Meiron project, Meyers, Strange, Groh, and their colleagues, beginning from the premise that the early, formative phase of Christianity in the Galilee was paralleled by similar trends in the formation of Jewish communities, developed a concrete research plan with objectives applicable to actual fieldwork. Their systematic survey of the Galilee for traces of synagogues and excavations at exemplary sites produced the first "hard" data about rural life in a region extremely important for Judaism and Christianity. They also fully acknowledged the importance of regional factors for understanding Jewish and Christian culture. Their work produced many groundbreaking results regarding synagogue architecture (Meiron, Gush Halav, Nabratein), the interaction between Jewish and Hellenistic cultures, and many important details of regional material culture, such as ceramic typology. That such an integrative approach inspired further studies in related fields of Jesus research, regional history, Galilean Judaism, and rabbinic history is significant.

The Profile of an Interdisciplinary Discipline

FOR VARIOUS REASONS ARCHAEOLOGICAL RESEARCH on the NT has its own profile. First, the texts and traditions contained in the NT are extremely diverse. Backgrounds range from Aramaic-speaking Jewish Palestine to Syria, Asia Minor, Greece, and Rome with their Greek-speaking Jewish diaspora communities and multiple forms of indigenous Greek and Roman paganism. Such diversity precludes the possibility of conceiving of NT archaeology as a simple continuation or special case of traditional "biblical" or "Syro-Palestinian" archaeology. Since the composition of the canon of the NT followed criteria that are nonarchaeological, the themes and regions on the agenda for NT archaeology are somewhat arbitrary and artificial, representing a diverse segment of ancient culture. With its wide geographical and cultural outlook NT archaeology is inevitably a more interdisciplinary and cooperative endeavor than classical biblical archaeology with its mainly Palestinian/Near Eastern perspective. Since the cultural profile of a site being excavated dictates the forms of research and cooperation, so that a team working in Ostia may be confronted with quite different material than another team excavating in Galilean Tiberias, the contours of "NT archaeology" are much less clear-cut than traditional biblical or Syro-Palestinian archaeology.

Second, "NT archaeology" is almost a contradiction in itself, because the literature to which the designation refers covers only a relatively short period of time, about a hundred years, a period far too brief for the kinds of long-term analysis common in archaeology. Moreover, archaeological relics of persons or events mentioned in the NT are notoriously scarce, with the exception of members of the upper classes like Pilate, Gallio, and Caiaphas, who is possibly mentioned on an ossuary, a box for the reburial of bones. Although they need to be analyzed by acknowledged methods and integrated into our reconstructions of the history of nascent Christianity if proven genuine, archaeological relics of such figures cannot constitute the main occupation of the discipline. Hence, NT archaeology is also not to be concerned primarily with the analysis of particular events. In the earliest period of their movement, Christian groups did not produce group-specific elements of material culture but used what their surrounding cultures had available, thereby making it virtually impossible to identify their presence in the material record. The impact of the intellectual impulses triggered by Christianity on material culture becomes apparent only in the late second century CE and matures during the age of Constantine. To follow those trends considerably expands the traditional boundaries of NT studies as an academic discipline. Moreover, the cultural impulses and milieus that created the world of the NT are treated by Judaic or classical studies. Therefore, NT archaeologists are necessarily eclectic.

Since the NT represents a segment of ancient culture that is quantitatively too small and chronologically too short to produce its own identifiable material remains, NT archaeology does not operate diachronically, by tracing cultural trajectories or general social and religious developments, but rather regionally, concentrating on reconstructing as accurately as possible the concrete cultural circumstances of a given place at a given time in its dynamic interaction. It thus enables us to contextualize the early Christian traditions and texts pertinent to specific places such as Galilee, Corinth, Ephesus, and Rome. Of special interest are factors of natural and human-made conditions of living; questions of religious, ethnic, and social identity formation, represented by such things as synagogues, temples, purity-related artifacts and structures, burial places and practices, and village structures; and questions of cultural influence and exchange. Insights gained from these fields can be integrated into more general studies of Christian identity formation and history. That NT archaeology naturally overlaps with much research conducted in the neighboring disciplines of classics and Judaic studies is to be expected.

Needless to say, despite its methodological flexibility and diversification and despite its concern with a textual corpus normative for many people, NT archaeology works strictly according to the methods of its discipline. Fieldwork, documentation, and modes of interpretation in NT archaeology differ in no way from similar proceedings in archaeology in general. There can and should be no *archaeologia sacra* (sacred archaeology)! Archaeology will neither prove nor disprove faith claims, nor be subject to them. Reservations about the critical and sometimes deconstructive potential of archaeology are as unjustified as those about other critical scholarly disciplines. What counts in, for instance, determining the authenticity of some artifact will be arguments that are comprehensible by those familiar with archaeological method.

The Future of a Successful Discipline

OUR UNDERSTANDING OF THE NT is notably different today from what it would be without the interdisciplinary efforts of archaeologists and textual scholars. Archaeological work relative to the NT underscores its intimate connectedness to the ancient world, to Judaism in particular. Archaeological work on the NT and early Christianity also emphasizes the diversity of ways in which new faith came to expression and the complexity of the processes of enculturation and identity formation. Therefore, that many elements of the diverse world of ancient Judaism and Greco-Roman culture are reflected in the NT is not surprising.

Despite all progress and success, however, few people doubt that the situation of the discipline today is complex and sometimes confusing. On the one hand, we are in the privileged position of having a wealth of data available that no earlier period has enjoyed. NT scholars fruitfully cooperate with archaeologists in projects all around the ancient Mediterranean, producing data that refine our picture of early Christianity and our understanding of the NT. Places like Jerusalem, Tiberias, Sepphoris, Hippos, Jewish and early Christian Rome, Ostia, Corinth, Athens, Philippi, Pergamon, Ephesus, Miletus, Sagalassos, Sardis, and many more are under exploration, as well as regions like the Dead Sea area, Galilee, Samaria, Troas, Galatia, and Phrygia.

NT studies in general are also experiencing methodological experimentation. Historical research into the context of the original communities vies with linguistic, intertextual, and literary approaches to the text that often emphasize the subjective role of readers of the texts in construing their meaning. Yet even these approaches are not in principle "ahistorical," since context does not only involve texts, but the entire social and spatial circumstances of living interpreters. Debates similar to those in NT circles about how to read a text rage in archaeological circles about the conditions of "reading archaeological remains as expressions of past and present culture." The debates present an opportunity for both disciplines to continue dialogue and benefit from mutual inspiration and criticism, just as transcending traditional lines of disciplines in the 1960s and 1970s brought innovation and progress to the study of the NT.

Archaeology, as a disciplined way of treating contextual and diachronic factors in the production of culture, will continue to be an essential partner for NT scholars.

THE HEBREW SCRIPTURES

Commonly Called

THE OLD TESTAMENT

NEW REVISED STANDARD VERSION

GENESIS

THE BOOK OF GENESIS derives its name from the Greek translation of 2.4 and 5.1, "This is the book of the origin of (*biblos geneseos*)." In Jewish tradition the book is called *Bereshit*, after the first word of the book, which means "in the beginning of." Both names accurately convey the content of the book—it tells of the origins of the cosmos, humankind, and the ancestors of Israel. The origins of the cosmos and humans are recounted in the primeval narratives (chs. 1–11) and the origins of Israel's ancestors in the patriarchal narratives (chs. 12–50). In the ancient world as in the modern, the era of origins has a special authority—its formative events set the rules and conditions for all subsequent developments. As a book of origins, Genesis partakes of the sacredness and authority of this era and has served as a foundation for thought, belief, and action for millennia.

The Genesis of Genesis

ACCORDING TO JEWISH AND CHRISTIAN TRADITION, the book of Genesis was dictated by God to Moses, but this belief is not found in the Hebrew Bible. (It seems to be first attested in the book of *Jubilees* and in the Dead Sea Scrolls from about the second century BCE.) Commentators have long noted that several points in Genesis indicate the narrator lived well after Moses, at a time when the Canaanites had disappeared from the promised land (12.6) and when kings ruled over Israel (36.31; 49.10). Modern archaeological and historical discoveries confirm this general picture: the constellation of peoples, places, and religious practices and the language of Genesis indicate that the book was primarily composed and compiled during the centuries of monarchical rule and immediately thereafter, roughly from the tenth through the sixth centuries BCE.

Biblical scholarship has identified three major literary sources that were edited together to form the book of Genesis called the Yahwist (J), Elohist (E), and Priestly (P) sources. The first two (often called "old epic" sources) reflect the predominance in certain narratives of forms of the divine name, Yahweh (Jahweh in German, hence J) and Elohim. The P source reflects concerns of the Priestly writers most evident in the book of Leviticus. There are also a few texts that belong to none of these sources (including chs. 14, 15, 24, and 49). The literary sources drew on traditional oral lore as well as written records and were engaged in preserving and revising Israel's traditions of the past. This is the standard model of the composition of Genesis, and although various scholars have proposed modifications, it remains the most coherent explanation of the evidence.

The editor (or editors) who wove the literary sources together created a text with an abundance of meaning, combining the different theologies, philosophical perspectives, and literary styles of the sources into a work of great power and complexity. The editors were not embarrassed by the duplications of particular episodes (e.g., the different creation accounts in 1.1–2.3 and 2.4–25, the two flood stories in chs. 6–9, the three wife-sister stories in 12.10–20; 20; and 26.1–11, and the multiple accounts of Jacob's change of name to Israel and the founding of Bethel in 28.10–22; 32.22–32; and 35.9–15), but, rather, valued the preservation of different traditions. One result of this complexity is that Genesis is a layered "mosaic" of meanings that is richer than any of the sources alone. Yet its lucid and tersely evocative narrative style generally allows readers to pass untroubled over its internal compositional seams.

Science, History, and Genesis

GENESIS IS NOT A SCIENTIFIC OR HISTORICAL TEXTBOOK in the modern sense. Rather, it is a narration of ancient Israel's traditions and concepts of the past—a mixture of myths and legends, cultural memories, revisions of tradition, and literary brilliance. It is a complex portrait of the past that encodes the values of biblical religion and creates a rich array of perspectives on the world.

There are authentic historical memories in the book, but most of the historical details reflect the period when Israel was an established nation. The older memories include the rise of urban civilization in the land of Sumer (10.8–12; 11.1–9), the region of Haran as an ancient tribal homeland (12.4; 24; 27.43), Semitic rulers and officials in Egypt (ch. 41), and the worship of the high god named El in pre-Israelite times (17.1). These and other old memories are mingled with more recent memories, such as relations with Israel's neighbors, including Aram, Philistia, Edom, Ammon, and Moab, which arose at roughly the same time as Israel. The portrayal of the natural world in Genesis also belongs to the worldview of its time—a geocentric universe with light and the earth created before the sun, and with the stars, sun, and moon attached to the surface of the dome of heaven (ch. 1); the first woman fashioned from the first man's rib (2.21–22); the rainbow as God's huge weapon set in the clouds (9.13); and the desolate landscape of the Dead Sea (including the pillar that was once Lot's wife) as the result of ancient transgressions (ch. 19). These and other details reflect ancient lore about life, the earth, and the universe.

It is somewhat unfair to note the scientific inadequacies of Genesis, since it was not written to be a work of modern science. We need to learn to read Genesis as a book that speaks strongly to modern readers, but we need to read it on its terms, recognize its ancient voice, and not superimpose on it our own. It is a book of memories—of marvels and miracles, imperfect saints and holy sinners, a beneficent and often inscrutable God, and promises that bind the past to the present and the future. It tells us where we came from, not in the sense that the book is historically accurate, but in the sense that the book itself is our historical root. [RONALD HENDEL]

Six Days of Creation and the Sabbath

1 In the beginning when God created*ᵃ* the heavens and the earth, ²the earth was a formless void and darkness covered the face of the deep, while a wind from God*ᵇ* swept over the face of the waters. ³Then God said, "Let there be light"; and there was light. ⁴And God saw that the light was good; and God separated the light from the darkness. ⁵God called the light Day, and the darkness he called Night. And there was evening and there was morning, the first day.

6 And God said, "Let there be a dome in the midst of the waters, and let it separate the waters from the waters." ⁷So God made the dome and separated the waters that were under the dome from the waters that were above the dome. And it was so. ⁸God called the dome Sky. And there was evening and there was morning, the second day.

9 And God said, "Let the waters under the sky be gathered together into one place, and let the dry land appear." And it was so. ¹⁰God called the dry land Earth, and the waters that

---

a Or *when God began to create* or *In the beginning God created*
b Or *while the spirit of God* or *while a mighty wind*

1.1–11.32 The primeval narratives of chs. 1–11 present a universal backdrop to the stories of Israel's past. In both the P and J versions (see Introduction), an idyllic beginning is sullied by human transgression. In the P version God counters these transgressions with the flood, marking the beginning of a new era of creation, which is protected by the covenant with Noah. The J version presents a narrative cycle of transgressions and divine responses, of which the flood is one instance, which collectively build up the conditions and problems of the present world. The primeval era is a time of corruption and curses, but it is also a time when the world is formed to be good (P) and when humans experience an enlargement of capacities from an innocent, animal-like existence to the broadened, godlike consciousness of "knowing good and evil" (J). But human autonomy is tainted by a tendency toward violence and evil, which entails conflicts with God and the cosmic order. These stories sketch the origins, growth, and limits of the human situation in the world and the moral problems that create the need for an enduring solution, providing the background for God's call and covenant with Abraham. **1.1–2.3** The P account of creation is a magnificent and terse portrayal of God's transcendent power and the intricate order with which he created the cosmos. The seven-day structure highlights the sacred time of the sabbath, which is later revealed to Moses at Mount Sinai as a "sign" of God's covenant with Israel (Ex 31.12–17). There is a symmetrical relation between the creations of the first three days (light; sky; division of waters; land and plants) and those of the next three days (heavenly lights; water and sky animals; land animals and humans, with plants as food) that highlights the uniqueness of the seventh day (cessation of work). On the first three days God creates the major domains of the cosmos by creating new things and using them to separate the primeval materials of chaos. On the second three days God populates these cosmic domains and empowers his new creations to govern and fill these domains. The last creation, humans, are to rule the earth and its creatures as the earthly representative ("image") of God. The harmonious order of creation is characterized by the themes of separation, blessing, and goodness. **1.1** *In the beginning when God created,* or "When God began to create." The grammar of this temporal clause was clarified by the medieval Jewish commentator Rashi, who noted that the Hebrew word for "beginning" (*reshit*) requires a dependent relation—it is the "beginning *of*" something— and can be followed by a verb. The traditional rendering, "In the beginning, God created," dates to the Hellenistic period (as in the Septuagint), when these details of classical Hebrew grammar had been forgotten. The idea of *creatio ex nihilo* (Latin, "creation out of nothing") is dependent on the later rendering. In the original grammar, creation is a process of ordering and separation that begins with preexisting chaotic matter. **1.2** This disjunctive clause portrays the primordial state as a dark, watery chaos, an image similar to the primordial state in Egyptian, Mesopotamian, and Greek traditions. Unlike these other traditions, the chaos here is not a god or gods, but mere matter. The *wind from God* is the only divine substance and seems to indicate the incipient ordering of this chaos (cf. the role of God's *wind* in initiating the reversal of watery chaos in 8.1). **1.3–5** *Light,* the first creation, created by God's effective word in a marvelously terse and sublime utterance. Creation by word is celebrated in Ps 33.6. The separate existence of light from the sun is implied in Job 38.19 and in other ancient Near Eastern creation accounts. The separation of light and darkness initiates the theme of creation by separation. Time begins with the first procession of day and night. **1.4** *God saw that . . . was good,* a refrain occurring seven times (also vv. 10, 12, 18, 21, 25, 31), a number representing wholeness and corresponding to the seven-day structure of creation. **1.6–8** *Dome,* made of hard material (the Hebrew word means "hammered out") that shines like ice or crystal (Ezek 1.22). The dome's separation of the waters is later reversed in the flood when the windows in the dome are opened (7.11). **1.9–10** The Septuagint, supported partially by a Qumran biblical fragment (4QGenᵏ), preserves a sentence after v. 9 that was lost by scribal error in the traditional Hebrew text: "And the waters under the sky gathered together into their gathering place, and the dry land appeared." The separation of the terrestrial waters and

were gathered together he called Seas. And God saw that it was good. 11Then God said, "Let the earth put forth vegetation: plants yielding seed, and fruit trees of every kind on earth that bear fruit with the seed in it." And it was so. 12The earth brought forth vegetation: plants yielding seed of every kind, and trees of every kind bearing fruit with the seed in it. And God saw that it was good. 13And there was evening and there was morning, the third day.

14 And God said, "Let there be lights in the dome of the sky to separate the day from the night; and let them be for signs and for seasons and for days and years, 15and let them be lights in the dome of the sky to give light upon the earth." And it was so. 16God made the two great lights—the greater light to rule the day and the lesser light to rule the night—and the stars. 17God set them in the dome of the sky to give light upon the earth, 18to rule over the day and over the night, and to separate the light from the darkness. And God saw that it was good. 19And there was evening and there was morning, the fourth day.

20 And God said, "Let the waters bring forth swarms of living creatures, and let birds fly above the earth across the dome of the sky." 21So God created the great sea monsters and every living creature that moves, of every kind, with which the waters swarm, and every winged bird of every kind. And God saw that it was good. 22God blessed them, saying, "Be fruitful and multiply and fill the waters in the seas, and let birds multiply on the earth." 23And there was evening and there was morning, the fifth day.

24 And God said, "Let the earth bring forth living creatures of every kind: cattle and creeping things and wild animals of the earth of every kind." And it was so. 25God made the wild animals of the earth of every kind, and the cattle of every kind, and everything that creeps upon the ground of every kind. And God saw that it was good.

26 Then God said, "Let us make humankind*a* in our image, according to our likeness; and let them have dominion over the fish of the sea, and over the birds of the air, and over the cattle, and over all the wild animals of the earth,*b* and over every creeping thing that creeps upon the earth."

27   So God created humankind*a* in his image,
      in the image of God he created them;*c*
      male and female he created them.

_____

a Heb *adam*   *b* Syr: Heb *and over all the earth*   *c* Heb *him*

the dry land and their naming as *Seas* and *Earth* completes the transformation of primordial matter into beneficial cosmic domains ready to support life. **1.11–13** God's command for the earth to bring forth *vegetation* initiates the process of life on earth, which will be self-sustaining. Hence the emphasis on *seed* and *every kind*—the vegetation will propagate its kind on the earth through its seed, continuing the task of creation, comparable to the later fruitfulness of animals and humans. **1.14–19** The heavenly bodies do not create light but rather govern the light (which was created on the first day) and the alternation of day and night (which had begun on the first day). Their purpose is regulatory and calendrical. The designation of the sun and the moon as the *greater light* and the *lesser light* (v. 16) seems to emphasize that they are merely lights and not independent gods. As material objects set into the dome of the sky, the sun, moon, and stars may have been conceived of as holes or membranes channeling various amounts of heavenly light. **1.20–23** *Great sea monsters*, included among the water and sky animals, which populate the domains created on the second day. According to other biblical texts, God defeated these monsters in battle in primeval times (Ps 74.13; Isa 51.9) or will defeat them again in the future (Isa 27.1). These biblical traditions are rooted in older Near Eastern traditions. The reference here seems to refute these older traditions—God established his authority over the sea monsters by creating them, not by engaging them in battle. The dragons matter are just another type of sea creature, not independent deities. They, along with the other water and sky creatures, are declared to be *good* (v. 21) and given a blessing of fertility in order to continue the task of creation (by procreation) and fill their respective cosmic domains. **1.26–28** Humans are God's last and climactic work of creation. The style of the text briefly verges on poetry, indicating a dramatic high point. *Let us . . . our image.* The plural seems to refer to the lesser deities of the divine assembly described in other biblical texts (e.g., 1 Kings 22.19–22; Isa 6; Job 1–2). In the accomplishment of this utterance, however, God acts alone (*God created humankind in his image*, v. 27). The reference to the divine assembly seems to acknowledge its presence but discounts its active participation in creation. It also complicates the idea of the image in which humans are made. The concept of being made according to the *image of God* (or the gods) has various overlapping implications—humans in some way look like God/gods; humans collectively represent God on earth; and humans are like God/gods with respect to moral, spiritual, political, or other qualities. The immediate implication of this concept in God's speech is that humans are appointed to rule over the earth and its creatures. This ruling function is related to the ancient Near Eastern concept of the king as the image of

28God blessed them, and God said to them, "Be fruitful and multiply, and fill the earth and subdue it; and have dominion over the fish of the sea and over the birds of the air and over every living thing that moves upon the earth." 29God said, "See, I have given you every plant yielding seed that is upon the face of all the earth, and every tree with seed in its fruit; you shall have them for food. 30And to every beast of the earth, and to every bird of the air, and to everything that creeps on the earth, everything that has the breath of life, I have given every green plant for food." And it was so. 31God saw everything that he had made, and indeed, it was very good. And there was evening and there was morning, the sixth day.

2 Thus the heavens and the earth were finished, and all their multitude. 2And on the seventh day God finished the work that he had done, and he rested on the seventh day from all the work that he had done. 3So God blessed the seventh day and hallowed it, because on it God rested from all the work that he had done in creation.

4 These are the generations of the heavens and the earth when they were created.

Another Account of the Creation

In the day that the LORD*a* God made the earth and the heavens, 5when no plant of the field was yet in the earth and no herb of the field had yet sprung up—for the LORD God had not caused it to rain upon the earth, and there was no one to till the ground; 6but a stream would rise from the earth, and water the whole face of the ground— 7then the LORD God formed man from the dust of the ground,*b* and

a Heb YHWH, as in other places where "LORD" is spelled with capital letters (see also Exod 3.14-15 with notes).   b Or formed a man (Heb adam) of dust from the ground (Heb adamah)

the high god on earth, a concept that is democratized here. The implication that creation in the image of God entails male and female seems to be connected with the following blessing to be fruitful and multiply (v. 28); i.e., procreation (as the human mode of creation) is part of what makes humans correspond to the image of God. This is a dense and multivalent notion characterizing different aspects of human qualities and duties. **1.29–30** God grants the vegetation (created on the third day) to the humans and land animals as food. This rule of vegetarianism is later altered in the Noachian covenant when God allows humans to eat animal meat in addition to vegetation (9.3–4). The killing of animals for meat and the resulting bloodshed seem to be included in the violence that precipitated the flood (6.11–13). **1.31** It was very good. The last and most emphatic instance of the sevenfold refrain (see note on 1.4) seals the moral and functional harmony of creation. The goodness of creation is fragile, however. In the light of later transgressions by all flesh, God sees that the earth is corrupt (6.12), a verse that echoes and reverses this one and results in God's decision to undo the created order with a flood. **2.1–3** God . . . hallowed it. The seventh day, when God rests from his work of creation, is the first sacred thing. The implications of this sacred day are later revealed when the sabbath command is given to Israel (Ex 20.8–11; 31.12–17). The sabbath commemorates God's rest, functions as a "sign" of the covenant, and allows Israel to be refreshed by its sacred time. This particular Israelite practice is "hidden" in the structure of creation.

2.4–3.24 The garden of Eden story, from the J source, begins with an account of creation (2.4–25), which sets the stage for the story of human disobedience and expulsion (3.1–24). The J creation account differs in many ways from the P account (1.1–2.3). The sequence of creations is man, garden, animals, woman, which differs in tone and detail from the grand sequence of creation in P. The J story is earthy and folkloristic and is focused on the characters and their moral and psychological dilemmas. It is not a complete account of creation, but provides only as much as is necessary for the ensuing plot. God is now named YHWH (probably to be vocalized Yahweh) God, rendered LORD God, and is a more anthropomorphic and fallible God than in P. (Note his unsuccessful experiment in creating animals to be the man's "helping partner" in 2.18–20 and his humanlike afternoon stroll in the Garden in 3.8.) The story explores the complexity of the human condition as rooted in primeval events and transgressions and the beneficent and troubled relationship between humans and God. It is a story of paradise and why we are no longer in it. **2.4–5** The J account of creation begins like the P account, with a temporal clause followed by a description of the primeval chaos. The earth and the heavens, the reverse of the P order (1.1), perhaps showing J's more earth-centered perspective in contrast to P's cosmic scope. The primeval chaos in J is a picture of a barren landscape—no plants, no rain, and no one to till the ground. This picture of lack will be filled in by the following acts of creation. No one to till the ground has a Hebrew wordplay between one, lit. "man" ('adam), and ground ('adamah), anticipating a key thematic relationship in the story. **2.4** These are the generations (also These are the descendants, This is the story), a structuring refrain inserted in Genesis by an editor that occurs ten times: five times in the primeval narratives (also 5.1; 6.9; 10.1; 11.10) and five times (with one duplication) in the patriarchal narratives (11.27; 25.12, 19; 36.1, 9; 37.2). It was probably adapted from the opening line of the book of generations (or list of the descendants) in 5.1. This refrain emphasizes the idea that the past is conceived as a genealogy, which provides continuity for past events. The garden of Eden story is therefore the next link in the genealogy of

breathed into his nostrils the breath of life; and the man became a living being. 8And the LORD God planted a garden in Eden, in the east; and there he put the man whom he had formed. 9Out of the ground the LORD God made to grow every tree that is pleasant to the sight and good for food, the tree of life also in the midst of the garden, and the tree of the knowledge of good and evil.

10 A river flows out of Eden to water the garden, and from there it divides and becomes four branches. 11The name of the first is Pishon; it is the one that flows around the whole land of Havilah, where there is gold; 12and the gold of that land is good; bdellium and onyx stone are there. 13The name of the second river is Gihon; it is the one that flows around the whole land of Cush. 14The name of the third river is Tigris, which flows east of Assyria. And the fourth river is the Euphrates.

15 The LORD God took the man and put him in the garden of Eden to till it and keep it.

16And the LORD God commanded the man, "You may freely eat of every tree of the garden; 17but of the tree of the knowledge of good and evil you shall not eat, for in the day that you eat of it you shall die."

18 Then the LORD God said, "It is not good that the man should be alone; I will make him a helper as his partner." 19So out of the ground the LORD God formed every animal of the field and every bird of the air, and brought them to the man to see what he would call them; and whatever the man called every living creature, that was its name. 20The man gave names to all cattle, and to the birds of the air, and to every animal of the field; but for the man*a* there was not found a helper as his partner. 21So the LORD God caused a deep sleep to fall upon the man, and he slept; then he took one of his ribs and closed up its place with flesh. 22And the rib that the LORD God had

_____

a Or for Adam

---

the past. **2.6** The primeval *stream* seems to anticipate the rivers of Eden in vv. 10–14. **2.7** The creation of man differs in many respects from the parallel in 1.26–28. Here the man has a more humble origin—he is formed *from the dust of the ground,* rather than created in the image of God. *Formed* suggests an act of physical molding, as a potter forms clay. The earthy quality of man anticipates both his role in working the ground and his mortality (*return to the ground,* 3.19). The *breath of life* that God breathes into his nose is the divine life-breath, and humans are alive as long as they breathe. Man consists of a "soft" duality of flesh and life-breath. At death the life-breath returns to God and the flesh returns to earth; hence human destiny is already implied or anticipated in the creation of man. The first man stands for humankind in general and is also a solitary male, though his gender is not prominent until the creation of his helper-partner, woman. *Man* (*'adam*) can be a collective plural or a single creature, a semantic range that is central to the story. Paul in 1 Cor 15.45 uses this verse in his explanation of resurrection, comparing the initial gift of life with its counterpart in the end time. **2.8–9** *Eden* means "abundance, plenty, fullness," often referring to abundance of food, as there is in the garden of Eden. For the magnificent trees of Eden, see Ezek 31.8–9. The fruits of the *tree of life* and the *tree of the knowledge of good and evil* are in some sense divine food, since they impart immortality and divine knowledge. Similar divine food is known from Mesopotamia (e.g., the food and water of life from the myth of Adapa) and Greece (the food of the immortals, nectar and ambrosia). The *knowledge of good and evil,* an ambiguous and suggestive phrase encompassing moral, spiritual, and physical (sexual) knowledge. The image of the *tree of life* appears in Rev 22.2 in a vision of paradise restored. **2.10–14** The four branches of the river of paradise water the whole earth—four represents wholeness. Only the *Tigris* and *Euphrates* are known rivers. This geographical aside lends a sense of realism to the story, but it is also deliberately opaque about Eden's location. An old tradition about the gods' sacred preserve at the Cedar Forest (as in the Gilgamesh Epic) or at the source of the two rivers in Canaanite religion may lie behind this mythic geography. **2.15–17** The man's task as gardener in Eden is comparable to humankind's task of doing the work of the gods in Mesopotamian creation myths. Later the man's task will be intensified to hard agricultural labor (3.17–19). Only the fruit of the *tree of the knowledge of good and evil* is prohibited to man, not the fruit of the tree of life, perhaps indicating that man had a chance at immortality while he lived in the Garden. The prohibition naturally anticipates that it will be violated later in the story. The threatened penalty of death for eating the fruit will not be carried out, probably due to God's compassion for his fallible creature. **2.18–23** God's perception of the man's incompleteness without a *helper as his partner,* or "helping partner" (vv. 18, 20), shows compassion and wisdom, but his plan is not immediately successful. The animals are like man as living creatures, but they are also unlike him. The man *gave names* to them (v. 20), indicating his superiority in language and authority. The man also names the *Woman* (v. 23), which may suggest his authority over her, but this aspect of their relationship is muted until the woman's punishment. *Bone of my bones and flesh of my flesh,* a literal description and also a metaphorical expression of kinship (see 29.14). *Woman* (Hebrew *'ishah*), so called because she is taken from the *man* (*'ish*); these are the

taken from the man he made into a woman and brought her to the man. 23Then the man said,

"This at last is bone of my bones
and flesh of my flesh;
this one shall be called Woman,*a*
for out of Man*b* this one was taken."

24Therefore a man leaves his father and his mother and clings to his wife, and they become one flesh. 25And the man and his wife were both naked, and were not ashamed.

The First Sin and Its Punishment

3 Now the serpent was more crafty than any other wild animal that the LORD God had made. He said to the woman, "Did God say, 'You shall not eat from any tree in the garden'?" 2The woman said to the serpent, "We may eat of the fruit of the trees in the garden; 3but God said, 'You shall not eat of the fruit of the tree that is in the middle of the garden, nor shall you touch it, or you shall die.' " 4But the serpent said to the woman, "You will not die; 5for God knows that when you eat of it your eyes will be opened, and you will be like God,*c* knowing good and evil." 6So when the woman saw that the tree was good for food, and that it was a delight to the eyes, and that the tree was to be desired to make one wise, she took of its fruit and ate; and she also gave some to her husband, who was with her, and he ate. 7Then the eyes of both were opened, and they knew that they were naked; and they sewed fig leaves together and made loincloths for themselves.

8 They heard the sound of the LORD God walking in the garden at the time of the evening breeze, and the man and his wife hid themselves from the presence of the LORD God among the trees of the garden. 9But the LORD God called to the man, and said to him, "Where are you?" 10He said, "I heard the sound of you in the garden, and I was afraid, because I was naked; and I hid myself." 11He said, "Who told you that you were naked? Have you eaten from the tree of which I commanded you not to eat?" 12The man said, "The woman whom you gave to be with me, she gave me fruit from the tree, and I ate." 13Then the LORD God said to the woman, "What is this that you have done?" The woman said, "The serpent tricked me, and I ate." 14The LORD God said to the serpent,

---

a Heb *ishshah* *b* Heb *ish* *c* Or *gods*

---

first explicitly gendered terms applied to the humans. **2.24–25** The creation of the woman from the body of the man provides the motive for sexuality as a way to reverse this primal separation and return to a unity of *one flesh.* This event provides a charter for marriage wherein the man travels to his bride's home to negotiate the marriage contract and celebrate the wedding. This etiology for the human condition also anticipates the future sexuality of the first couple, deliberately called *the man and his wife,* though at present they are unaware of their sexual nature in spite of being *naked* (Hebrew *'arumim;* see note on 3.1–5). **3.1–24** Creation is complicated by the snake's deception, the humans' disobedience, and God's punishment and exile of the humans. Painful labor and mortality are the human lot, but humans also gain the knowledge of good and evil, which makes them in some sense *like God* (v. 5). The exile from paradise, accompanied by the awakening of shame, sexuality, and a deeper consciousness and spirit, is in some sense the original passage from childhood to adulthood. **3.1– 5** The serpent (or snake) is *more crafty* ('*arum,* v. 1, a wordplay on '*arumim* in 2.25) than the other animals, which indicates that he too is an animal, not a demon or devil. A parallel is the snake in the Gilgamesh Epic who steals the plant of rejuvenation (and therefore sheds his skin). The snake in Eden is a trickster figure who is more clever than the other animals, can speak (like humans), and knows about divine things. He bridges the boundaries between animals, humans, and God and effectively elicits the woman's desire to break the boundary between humans and God, to *be like God* (v. 5). The exchange between the snake and the woman is a masterpiece of ambiguity and half-truths. **3.6** The woman's desire is physical, aesthetic, and intellectual. She is the focus of the story as she exercises her will, while the man is her passive cohort, described as *her husband, who was with her.* The woman's command over the man will be reversed in v. 16, the curse of (and justification for) male authority. **3.7** As the serpent had predicted, *the eyes of both were opened,* but what they see is an ironic surprise—their nakedness, of which they are now ashamed (cf. 2.25). The wordplay of *naked* ('*arumim*) and *crafty* ('*arum*) in v. 1 echoes here. Complicating the meaning of the knowledge gained is God's later admission that *the man has become like one of us, knowing good and evil* (v. 22). In some manner, consciousness of nakedness and sexuality is part of the knowledge that makes one like God (or gods). This moment is also the origin of clothing, which signals the beginning of the passage from nature to culture. **3.8–13** God's stroll in the Garden turns into a series of interrogations and admissions of guilt. The humans (who are hiding) are fearful and alienated from God. The man confesses, blames the woman, and pointedly extends the blame to God since God *gave* her *to be with* him (v. 12). The woman similarly confesses and passes blame to the snake. The snake is not given a chance to speak, perhaps because he can twist language too effectively. **3.14–19** God's punishments reverse the order of

"Because you have done this,
  cursed are you among all animals
  and among all wild creatures;
upon your belly you shall go,
  and dust you shall eat
  all the days of your life.
15 I will put enmity between you and the
      woman,
  and between your offspring and hers;
he will strike your head,
  and you will strike his heel."
16 To the woman he said,
"I will greatly increase your pangs in
      childbearing;
  in pain you shall bring forth children,
yet your desire shall be for your husband,
  and he shall rule over you."
17 And to the man*a* he said,
"Because you have listened to the voice of
      your wife,
  and have eaten of the tree
about which I commanded you,
  'You shall not eat of it,'
cursed is the ground because of you;
  in toil you shall eat of it all the days of
      your life;
18 thorns and thistles it shall bring forth for
      you;
  and you shall eat the plants of the field.

19 By the sweat of your face
  you shall eat bread
until you return to the ground,
  for out of it you were taken;
you are dust,
  and to dust you shall return."

20 The man named his wife Eve,*b* because she was the mother of all living. 21 And the Lord God made garments of skins for the man*c* and for his wife, and clothed them.

22 Then the Lord God said, "See, the man has become like one of us, knowing good and evil; and now, he might reach out his hand and take also from the tree of life, and eat, and live forever"— 23 therefore the Lord God sent him forth from the garden of Eden, to till the ground from which he was taken. 24 He drove out the man; and at the east of the garden of Eden he placed the cherubim, and a sword flaming and turning to guard the way to the tree of life.

Cain Murders Abel

4 Now the man knew his wife Eve, and she conceived and bore Cain, saying, "I have produced*d* a man with the help of the Lord."

---

a Or *to Adam* *b* In Heb *Eve* resembles the word for *living*
c Or *for Adam* *d* The verb in Heb resembles the word for *Cain*

---

the interrogation. They also reverse the conditions that led to the humans' transgression. The snake will henceforth be humbled and alienated from the woman and her descendants. This explains why snakes crawl on their belly and why humans have an innate revulsion to them. The woman is punished with painful labor in childbirth, which seems to be a negative correlate to the discovery of sexuality. She is also cursed with male authority, which reverses her previous command over the man. The man (Hebrew *'adam*) is now punished with painful labor on the unfruitful ground (*'adamah*) for food, reversing his previous easy relationship with the fruit and ground of Eden. Moreover, the man is told that he will *return to the ground* (*'adamah*, v. 19). Man seems to have been made mortal (*from the dust of the ground,* 2.7), but henceforth he will be conscious of his mortality, another addition to his self-knowledge. **3.20–21** The passage to the harsh life of human culture is somewhat relieved by the naming of Eve (lit., "life") and God's gracious act of clothing the couple. God's anger has turned into solicitude for the humans, and the leather clothes he provides are more durable than the fig-leaf loincloths that the humans had previously made. The name of Eve and her description as the *mother of all living* may be related to similar names and epithets of older Near Eastern goddesses. **3.22–24** The humans are cast out of the Garden, not directly be-

cause of their disobedience, but so that they cannot also eat of the tree of life. If they had both divine knowledge *and* immortality, they would complete the transition to deities. God *drove out the man* (including the woman by association) to make permanent the separation between divine and human. *Us.* See note on 1.26–28. *Cherubim,* mixed, liminal creatures combining human, animal, and bird traits who guard the threshold of the Garden; they are related to the Egyptian sphinx and the Mesopotamian *karibu. A sword flaming and turning,* another mysterious weapon or creature guarding the threshold. The eastern entrance, the cherubim, and the sacred trees suggest an analogy with the Jerusalem temple, which had similar architectural and iconographic features as well as a limitation on access into it.
4.1–16 The next generation resumes the themes of transgression, this time the first murder and exile. Many verbal echoes link this J story with the garden of Eden story. The conflict between brothers and the favor shown to the younger are themes that recur in later stories (chs. 21, 25, 27, 37, 48). There is also an ethnographic dimension to the story: Cain (*qayin*) is the ancestor of the Kenites (*qeni*), a little-known ethnic group who may at one time have been itinerant metalworkers. God (now called YHWH, rendered Lord) is mysterious, just, and compassionate. **4.1–2** *Knew,* a eu-

²Next she bore his brother Abel. Now Abel was a keeper of sheep, and Cain a tiller of the ground. ³In the course of time Cain brought to the Lord an offering of the fruit of the ground, ⁴and Abel for his part brought of the firstlings of his flock, their fat portions. And the Lord had regard for Abel and his offering, ⁵but for Cain and his offering he had no regard. So Cain was very angry, and his countenance fell. ⁶The Lord said to Cain, "Why are you angry, and why has your countenance fallen? ⁷If you do well, will you not be accepted? And if you do not do well, sin is lurking at the door; its desire is for you, but you must master it."

8 Cain said to his brother Abel, "Let us go out to the field."ᵃ And when they were in the field, Cain rose up against his brother Abel, and killed him. ⁹Then the Lord said to Cain, "Where is your brother Abel?" He said, "I do not know; am I my brother's keeper?" ¹⁰And the Lord said, "What have you done? Listen; your brother's blood is crying out to me from the ground! ¹¹And now you are cursed from the ground, which has opened its mouth to receive your brother's blood from your hand. ¹²When you till the ground, it will no longer yield to you its strength; you will be a fugitive and a wanderer on the earth." ¹³Cain said to the Lord, "My punishment is greater than I can bear! ¹⁴Today you have driven me away from the soil, and I shall be hidden from your face; I shall be a fugitive and a wanderer on the earth, and anyone who meets me may kill me." ¹⁵Then the Lord said to him, "Not so!ᵇ Whoever kills Cain will suffer a sevenfold vengeance." And the Lord put a mark on Cain, so that no one who came upon him would kill him. ¹⁶Then Cain went away from the presence of the Lord, and settled in the land of Nod,ᶜ east of Eden.

Beginnings of Civilization

17 Cain knew his wife, and she conceived and bore Enoch; and he built a city, and named it Enoch after his son Enoch. ¹⁸To Enoch was born Irad; and Irad was the father of Mehujael,

---

a Sam Gk Syr Compare Vg: MT lacks *Let us go out to the field* b Gk Syr Vg: Heb *Therefore* c That is *Wandering*

---

phemism for "had sex with," echoing the implicit relationship between sexuality and knowledge in the garden of Eden story. The first sexual act seems to occur outside of the Garden, though this is not entirely clear. The name *Cain* (*qayin*) is given a folk etymology from *I have produced* (*qaniti*). Linguistically, Cain means "metalworker." In many traditional societies metalworkers belong to marginal ethnic groups and are looked upon with suspicion and disdain. Here Cain is initially *a tiller of the ground*, like his father, continuing the troubled relationship between man (*'adam*) and the ground (*'adamah;* see notes on 2.4–5; 3.14–19). Abel's name is not explained, but in Hebrew means "emptiness, transitoriness," which aptly describes the fate of Abel. The younger son is often *a keeper of sheep* (e.g., David), which has less prestige than farming. The focus on the two brothers proceeds in chiastic order: Cain, Abel; Abel, Cain; Cain, Abel; Abel, Cain (vv. 1–5), stylistically highlighting the issue of fraternal rivalry. **4.3–5** The only obvious difference between the value of the two sacrifices is that Abel offers the *firstlings*, in contrast to Cain who offers the *fruit* (not the first fruit). This difference also highlights the issue of the honor of the firstborn son, who should have priority, though the younger son is favored here. God's preference is not just for Abel's offering but for *Abel and his offering* in contrast to *Cain and his offering*. **4.6–7** God's speech to Cain has verbal echoes of his punishment of Eve (2.16), suggesting a similar nexus of temptation, sin, and punishment. Sin is an interior disposition (described as an evil inclination in 6.5), personified here as a ravenous beast or demon, which the individual can and must control. This divine instruction has profound moral and psychological insight, describing a world of individual responsibility and dark instincts, but it is lost on Cain. **4.6** Cain's fallen *countenance* (lit. "face") anticipates his later exile from the presence of God's *face* (v. 14). **4.8** Cain's speech to Abel maneuvers the unsuspecting brother to the *field,* away from human habitation, where he is most vulnerable to violence (see Deut 22.25–27). The stylistic repetition of *brother* (six times in vv. 8–11) highlights the enormity of Cain's fratricide. **4.9–12** *Where is your brother . . . , What have you done . . . , cursed from the ground,* echoes of God's interrogation and punishment of Adam and Eve (2.9–19). The curse of Cain *from the ground* (*'adamah*) is an intensification of the curse in 2.17 and means that Cain can no longer till the ground, since he polluted it with his brother's blood. Cain's plan to murder Abel where no one could hear his cry is foiled by Abel's blood *crying out . . . from the ground* (v. 10). Hence God is both witness and judge. *A fugitive and a wanderer* (v. 12). The punishment of exile from human culture is an alternative to capital punishment when murder of kin is the offense (cf. 2 Sam 14). **4.13–16** *Anyone . . . may kill me.* Away from human habitation and the protection of his kin, Cain is vulnerable to violence and murder. Ironically, Cain uses this problem in his plea for mercy, a mercy he did not show his brother. God grants this mercy by applying a visible *mark on Cain* similar to the brand that identifies the owner of a slave. **4.17–26** The lineage of Cain takes a curious turn, attributing to Cain and his descendants the origin of various arts of civilization: cities, herding, music, and (as Cain's name foreshadows; see notes on 4.1–16; 4.1–2) metalwork-

and Mehujael the father of Methushael, and Methushael the father of Lamech. [19]Lamech took two wives; the name of the one was Adah, and the name of the other Zillah. [20]Adah bore Jabal; he was the ancestor of those who live in tents and have livestock. [21]His brother's name was Jubal; he was the ancestor of all those who play the lyre and pipe. [22]Zillah bore Tubal-cain, who made all kinds of bronze and iron tools. The sister of Tubal-cain was Naamah.

23 Lamech said to his wives:

"Adah and Zillah, hear my voice;
     you wives of Lamech, listen to what I
        say:
I have killed a man for wounding me,
     a young man for striking me.
24   If Cain is avenged sevenfold,
        truly Lamech seventy-sevenfold."

25 Adam knew his wife again, and she bore a son and named him Seth, for she said, "God has appointed[a] for me another child instead of Abel, because Cain killed him." [26]To Seth also a son was born, and he named him Enosh. At that time people began to invoke the name of the Lord.

Adam's Descendants to Noah and His Sons

5 This is the list of the descendants of Adam. When God created humankind,[b] he made them[c] in the likeness of God. [2]Male and female he created them, and he blessed them and named them "Humankind"[b] when they were created.

3 When Adam had lived one hundred thirty years, he became the father of a son in his likeness, according to his image, and named him Seth. [4]The days of Adam after he became the father of Seth were eight hundred years; and he had other sons and daughters. [5]Thus all the days that Adam lived were nine hundred thirty years; and he died.

6 When Seth had lived one hundred five years, he became the father of Enosh. [7]Seth lived after the birth of Enosh eight hundred seven years, and had other sons and daughters. [8]Thus all the days of Seth were nine hundred twelve years; and he died.

9 When Enosh had lived ninety years, he became the father of Kenan. [10]Enosh lived after the birth of Kenan eight hundred fifteen years, and had other sons and daughters. [11]Thus all the days of Enosh were nine hundred five years; and he died.

12 When Kenan had lived seventy years, he became the father of Mahalalel. [13]Kenan lived after the birth of Mahalalel eight hundred and forty years, and had other sons and daughters. [14]Thus all the days of Kenan were nine hundred and ten years; and he died.

15 When Mahalalel had lived sixty-five

---

a The verb in Heb resembles the word for *Seth*   *b* Heb *adam*
c Heb *him*

---

ing. But the wickedness of Lamech continues Cain's evil legacy. The birth of Seth to Adam and Eve provides a new younger son who takes the place of Abel and restores the proper lineage for the future humanity. The goodness of this line is indicated by the beginning of the worship of "the Lord" in v. 26, perhaps initiated by Seth's son Enosh. Many of the names in the Cainite lineage (J) are paralleled in the Sethite lineage in ch. 5 (P), suggesting that the two lineages may descend from oral variants. The association of the arts of civilization with the Cainites may suggest that civilization is tainted with evil, but this is not clear. Traditions of culture heroes who lived before the flood are found in neighboring cultures (Mesopotamia, Phoenicia, Greece).

5.1–32 The genealogy from Adam to Noah is from the P source and may have been drawn from a separate document called "the book of the generations of Adam" (*the list of the descendants of Adam*, 5.1), which continues in 11.10–32. The antediluvian genealogy seems to be related to the J genealogy of Cain in 4.17–26, perhaps originally as an oral variant. The P list traces the lineage through Seth and makes no mention of Cain and Abel. After Seth and Enosh, the list closely parallels the Cainite genealogy: cf. Kenan, Cain; Mahalalel, Mehujael; Jared, Irad; Enoch, Enoch; Methuselah, Methushael; and Lamech, Lamech. The long lives of the patriarchs before the flood (ten generations) are a sign of the greatness of the ancestors and their distance from the present era. A similar concept is found in Mesopotamian king lists, where the kings before the flood (usually seven to ten kings) lived for tens of thousands of years. **5.1–3** The beginning of the genealogy repeats the language of God's creation of humans in 1.26–28. The semantic range of the word *'adam*, "man," is exploited in these verses to refer to the collective, *humankind*, and to the name of the first man, *Adam*. (This is the first clear use of Adam as a proper name.) The repetition of the statement that God created humans *in the likeness of God* (v. 1) is complicated by the following statement that Adam fathered *a son in his likeness, according to his image* (v. 3). The latter seems to have a physical and visual sense— Seth looked like Adam. The language may be deliberately ambiguous or ironic. **5.4** *He had other sons and daughters,* a statement, repeated for each generation (e.g., vv. 7, 9, 13), accounting for the increase in the population before the flood, while keeping the focus

years, he became the father of Jared. [16]Mahalalel lived after the birth of Jared eight hundred thirty years, and had other sons and daughters. [17]Thus all the days of Mahalalel were eight hundred ninety-five years; and he died.

18 When Jared had lived one hundred sixty-two years he became the father of Enoch. [19]Jared lived after the birth of Enoch eight hundred years, and had other sons and daughters. [20]Thus all the days of Jared were nine hundred sixty-two years; and he died.

21 When Enoch had lived sixty-five years, he became the father of Methuselah. [22]Enoch walked with God after the birth of Methuselah three hundred years, and had other sons and daughters. [23]Thus all the days of Enoch were three hundred sixty-five years. [24]Enoch walked with God; then he was no more, because God took him.

25 When Methuselah had lived one hundred eighty-seven years, he became the father of Lamech. [26]Methuselah lived after the birth of Lamech seven hundred eighty-two years, and had other sons and daughters. [27]Thus all the days of Methuselah were nine hundred sixty-nine years; and he died.

28 When Lamech had lived one hundred

eighty-two years, he became the father of a son; [29]he named him Noah, saying, "Out of the ground that the LORD has cursed this one shall bring us relief from our work and from the toil of our hands." [30]Lamech lived after the birth of Noah five hundred ninety-five years, and had other sons and daughters. [31]Thus all the days of Lamech were seven hundred seventy-seven years; and he died.

32 After Noah was five hundred years old, Noah became the father of Shem, Ham, and Japheth.

The Wickedness of Humankind

6 When people began to multiply on the face of the ground, and daughters were born to them, [2]the sons of God saw that they were fair; and they took wives for themselves of all that they chose. [3]Then the LORD said, "My spirit shall not abide[a] in mortals forever, for they are flesh; their days shall be one hundred twenty years." [4]The Nephilim were on the earth in those days—and also afterward— when the sons of God went in to the daughters of humans, who bore children to them. These

---

a Meaning of Heb uncertain

---

on the main patrilineal sequence. (Only the firstborn sons are named, not wives or siblings.) **5.21– 24** Enoch's description differs from the others. After the birth of his firstborn son is added *Enoch walked with God* (v. 22), indicating piety and righteousness and placing him in the same category as Noah (6.9). Instead of the usual death formula, it is said Enoch . . . *was no more, because God took him* (v. 24). The end of Enoch's life is mysterious and gave rise to much speculation in the vast Enochic literature of the Second Temple period. Enoch's life span of 365 years, much shorter than the other antediluvians, suggests a connection with calendrical speculation. **5.27** The life span of Methuselah makes him the longest-lived of the antediluvians and places his death in the year of the flood. The Samaritan Pentateuch and the Septuagint give different numbers for his life span and those of the other antediluvians. **5.28–29** In a brief inset from the J source, Lamech derives the name *Noah* from the word *relief* and foretells that Noah will relieve the harshness of human toil, referring to the curse on the ground in 3.17. This seems to be fulfilled in God's promise after the flood to *never again curse the ground* (8.21) and may also be fulfilled in a different way with Noah's invention of wine (9.20). **6.1–4** The strange account of the *sons of God* who marry and have sons with the *daughters of humans* is another instance of transgression of the boundaries between human and divine

(like the garden of Eden and the Tower of Babel stories). This time, however, the transgression is initiated by the divine beings. *Sons of God* are elsewhere in the Hebrew Bible members of God's divine entourage (see Deut 32.8; Job 1.6; 2.1; Pss 29.1; 89.7) who were even present at creation (Job 38.7). In Canaanite mythology, all of the gods in the pantheon, under the authority (and parentage) of El, were called the *banu ili,* "children/sons of El/God." The attraction of male gods to human women has numerous parallels in Greek mythology. It seems that an older traditional story has been truncated by J to serve as another step in the spread of the chaos and transgression that gave rise to the flood. **6.3** God's response to the breach of boundaries between divine and human is to restrict the human life span to 120 years. (Moses, as the ideal man, lives exactly 120 years.) Presumably this relates to the potentially huge life spans of the offspring of gods and humans. **6.4** *Nephilim,* lit. "fallen ones," a name for the offspring of the sons of God and daughters of humans; they are further identified as *the heroes . . . of old, warriors of renown.* We are not told what their heroic deeds were. They were on the earth *also afterward,* referring to Num 13.33, where the Nephilim are the giant aboriginal inhabitants of Canaan. These two traditions about the Nephilim—before the flood and before the conquest—may have originally been oral variants. The idea that there were giants in antiquity may have been

were the heroes that were of old, warriors of renown.

5 The LORD saw that the wickedness of humankind was great in the earth, and that every inclination of the thoughts of their hearts was only evil continually. 6 And the LORD was sorry that he had made humankind on the earth, and it grieved him to his heart. 7 So the LORD said, "I will blot out from the earth the human beings I have created—people together with animals and creeping things and birds of the air, for I am sorry that I have made them." 8 But Noah found favor in the sight of the LORD.

Noah Pleases God

9 These are the descendants of Noah. Noah was a righteous man, blameless in his generation; Noah walked with God. 10 And Noah had three sons, Shem, Ham, and Japheth.

11 Now the earth was corrupt in God's sight, and the earth was filled with violence. 12 And God saw that the earth was corrupt; for all flesh had corrupted its ways upon the earth. 13 And God said to Noah, "I have determined to make an end of all flesh, for the earth is filled with violence because of them; now I am going to destroy them along with the earth. 14 Make yourself an ark of cypress*a* wood; make rooms in the ark, and cover it inside and out with pitch. 15 This is how you are to make it: the length of the ark three hundred cubits, its width fifty cubits, and its height thirty cubits. 16 Make a roof*b* for the ark, and finish it to a cubit above; and put the door of the ark in its side; make it with lower, second, and third decks. 17 For my part, I am going to bring a flood of waters on the earth, to destroy from under heaven all flesh in which is the breath of life; everything that is on the earth shall die. 18 But I will establish my covenant with you; and you shall come into the ark, you, your sons, your wife, and your sons' wives with you. 19 And of every living thing, of all flesh, you shall bring two of every kind into the ark, to keep them alive with you; they shall be male and female. 20 Of the birds according to their kinds, and of the animals according to their kinds, of every creeping thing of the

a Meaning of Heb uncertain   *b* Or *window*

spurred by the gigantic ruins of Middle Bronze Age fortifications, which would have been prominent in the Israelite landscape.

6.5–9.17 The flood story is an amalgam of two texts, the J version (6.5–8; 7.1–5, 7–10, 12, 16b–17, 22–23; 8.2b–3a, 6–12, 13b, 20–22) and the P version (6.9–22; 7.6, 11, 13–16a, 18–21, 24; 8.1–2a, 3b–5, 13a, 14–19; 9.1–17), along with some editorial passages that harmonize the two texts (in 6.7; 7.3, 8–9, 23). In both versions, God decides to send the flood to destroy life, because humans are perpetually evil (J) and have corrupted the earth (P). Yet he chooses to save Noah, the righteous man, along with his family and the seed of all animals on a huge boat. After the flood, God vows never again to send a flood, in spite of continuing human evil (J), and institutes the Noachian covenant (P). The biblical flood stories are related to the older Mesopotamian flood tradition (in Atrahasis and Gilgamesh tablet 11), in which the destroyer god (Enlil) and the savior god (Enki) are two different gods in conflict. In biblical monotheism, one God combines these two impulses, and the moral conflict is transposed from the divine realm to the relationship between God and humans and the problem of human immorality. **6.5–8** *Every inclination . . . was only evil continually,* the reason for the flood, which is unchanged at the end of the flood (8.21) and reveals a darkly pessimistic (or realistic) analysis of human nature. Equally striking is God's sorrow at having made humans, an anthropomorphic touch characteristic of J's portrayal of God. *Noah found favor,* a wordplay on Noah (*nch*) and "favor" (*chn*), indicating that God's favor (graciousness) will counterbalance his sorrow. **6.9–13** The righteousness of Noah contrasts with the wickedness of his generation, which has corrupted the earth. The repetition of verbs for corruption (including *to destroy,* v. 13) emphasize the scope of cosmic corruption and the necessity of cosmic destruction. In line with P's concern for purity, the flood serves as God's agent to cleanse the earth of its corruption. **6.14–16** The ark is a huge boat, roughly 450 feet long, 75 feet wide, and 45 feet high (a *cubit* is about 18 inches). It is possible that there is a relationship to the dimensions of the tabernacle courtyard (see Ex 27), which has the same width but one-third the length and height. The Hebrew word for *ark* (*tebah*) occurs elsewhere only in the story of baby Moses, who is placed in a pitch-coated "basket" (*tebah*) that carries him to safety on the water (Ex 2.3). **6.18** The Noachian *covenant* is given in (see note on) 9.8–17. It is the first of a series of covenants in P that progress from the universal to the particular: the Noachian covenant with all creatures; the Abrahamic covenant with the chosen people, Israel (ch. 17); the Mosaic covenant, which resumes the Abrahamic (see Ex 6.4; 31.16–17); and the priestly covenant with the Aaronite priests (Num 25.10–13). **6.19–20** In the P version, *two of every kind* are taken on the ark to preserve life. In contrast, J has *seven pairs* of all clean animals and *a pair* of all unclean animals (7.2–3). The reason for this difference is that the J version (like the older Mesopotamian versions) has a sacrifice after the flood (8.20), which requires extra clean animals. In P there is no sacrifice until the establishment of the tabernacle, the sacrificial laws,

ground according to its kind, two of every kind shall come in to you, to keep them alive. [21]Also take with you every kind of food that is eaten, and store it up; and it shall serve as food for you and for them." [22]Noah did this; he did all that God commanded him.

The Great Flood

7 Then the LORD said to Noah, "Go into the ark, you and all your household, for I have seen that you alone are righteous before me in this generation. [2]Take with you seven pairs of all clean animals, the male and its mate; and a pair of the animals that are not clean, the male and its mate; [3]and seven pairs of the birds of the air also, male and female, to keep their kind alive on the face of all the earth. [4]For in seven days I will send rain on the earth for forty days and forty nights; and every living thing that I have made I will blot out from the face of the ground." [5]And Noah did all that the LORD had commanded him.

6 Noah was six hundred years old when the flood of waters came on the earth. [7]And Noah with his sons and his wife and his sons' wives went into the ark to escape the waters of the flood. [8]Of clean animals, and of animals that are not clean, and of birds, and of everything that creeps on the ground, [9]two and two, male and female, went into the ark with Noah, as God had commanded Noah. [10]And after seven days the waters of the flood came on the earth.

11 In the six hundredth year of Noah's life, in the second month, on the seventeenth day of the month, on that day all the fountains of the great deep burst forth, and the windows of the heavens were opened. [12]The rain fell on the earth forty days and forty nights. [13]On the very same day Noah with his sons, Shem and Ham and Japheth, and Noah's wife and the three wives of his sons entered the ark, [14]they and every wild animal of every kind, and all domestic animals of every kind, and every creeping thing that creeps on the earth, and every bird of every kind—every bird, every winged creature. [15]They went into the ark with Noah, two and two of all flesh in which there was the breath of life. [16]And those that entered, male and female of all flesh, went in as God had commanded him; and the LORD shut him in.

17 The flood continued forty days on the earth; and the waters increased, and bore up the ark, and it rose high above the earth. [18]The waters swelled and increased greatly on the earth; and the ark floated on the face of the waters. [19]The waters swelled so mightily on the earth that all the high mountains under the whole heaven were covered; [20]the waters swelled above the mountains, covering them fifteen cubits deep. [21]And all flesh died that moved on the earth, birds, domestic animals, wild animals, all swarming creatures that swarm on the earth, and all human beings; [22]everything on dry land in whose nostrils was the breath of life died. [23]He blotted out every living thing that was on the face of the ground, human beings and animals and creeping things and birds of the air; they were blotted out from the earth. Only Noah was left, and those that were with him in the ark. [24]And the waters swelled on the earth for one hundred fifty days.

The Flood Subsides

8 But God remembered Noah and all the wild animals and all the domestic animals that were with him in the ark. And God made a wind blow over the earth, and the waters subsided; [2]the fountains of the deep and the windows of the heavens were closed, the rain from the heavens was restrained, [3]and the waters gradually receded from the earth. At the end of one hundred fifty days the waters had abated; [4]and in the seventh month, on the seventeenth day of the month, the ark came to

---

and the priestly office (Lev 1–9). **7.4** In the J version, God sends the flood as *rain . . . for forty days and forty nights* (also v. 12). In contrast, the P flood is a cosmic upsurge that comes on the earth *for one hundred fifty days* (v. 24), after which it takes even more time to subside (8.3–5). The P version characteristically portrays the flood on a grander scale than J. In the Mesopotamian versions the flood is on the earth for seven days. **7.11** In the P version, God opens the *fountains of the great deep* and the *windows of the heavens* in order to inundate the earth with the cosmic waters below the

ocean and above the dome of the sky. This returns the earth to a state of watery chaos like the one before God separated the waters (1.6–7). The flood in P is a reversal of creation. *Great deep* (or "great ocean") deliberately evokes the primeval *deep* of 1.2.

8.1 *God remembered Noah*, the turning point of the P story, which highlights the importance of memory in biblical religion. See also 9.15–16; 19.29; Ex 2.24. God's memory is salvific, yielding beneficent deeds that fulfill his promises. The image of God making *a wind blow over the earth* (which is covered by the cos-

rest on the mountains of Ararat. [5]The waters continued to abate until the tenth month; in the tenth month, on the first day of the month, the tops of the mountains appeared.

6 At the end of forty days Noah opened the window of the ark that he had made [7]and sent out the raven; and it went to and fro until the waters were dried up from the earth. [8]Then he sent out the dove from him, to see if the waters had subsided from the face of the ground; [9]but the dove found no place to set its foot, and it returned to him to the ark, for the waters were still on the face of the whole earth. So he put out his hand and took it and brought it into the ark with him. [10]He waited another seven days, and again he sent out the dove from the ark; [11]and the dove came back to him in the evening, and there in its beak was a freshly plucked olive leaf; so Noah knew that the waters had subsided from the earth. [12]Then he waited another seven days, and sent out the dove; and it did not return to him any more.

13 In the six hundred first year, in the first month, on the first day of the month, the waters were dried up from the earth; and Noah removed the covering of the ark, and looked, and saw that the face of the ground was drying. [14]In the second month, on the twenty-seventh day of the month, the earth was dry. [15]Then God said to Noah, [16]"Go out of the ark, you and your wife, and your sons and your sons' wives with you. [17]Bring out with you every living thing that is with you of all flesh—birds and animals and every creeping thing that creeps on the earth—so that they may abound on the earth, and be fruitful and multiply on the earth." [18]So Noah went out with his sons and his wife and his sons' wives. [19]And every animal, every creeping thing, and every bird, everything that moves on the earth, went out of the ark by families.

God's Promise to Noah

20 Then Noah built an altar to the LORD, and took of every clean animal and of every clean bird, and offered burnt offerings on the altar. [21]And when the LORD smelled the pleasing odor, the LORD said in his heart, "I will never again curse the ground because of humankind, for the inclination of the human heart is evil from youth; nor will I ever again destroy every living creature as I have done.
[22] As long as the earth endures,
     seedtime and harvest, cold and heat,
     summer and winter, day and night,
     shall not cease."

The Covenant with Noah

9 God blessed Noah and his sons, and said to them, "Be fruitful and multiply, and fill the earth. [2]The fear and dread of you shall rest on every animal of the earth, and on every bird of the air, on everything that creeps on the ground, and on all the fish of the sea; into your hand they are delivered. [3]Every moving thing that lives shall be food for you; and just as I gave you the green plants, I give you everything. [4]Only, you shall not eat flesh with its

---

mic waters) recalls the primordial situation of 1.2. Creation is about to begin again. **8.4** *Mountains of Ararat,* in Turkish Kurdistan (ancient Urartu), the tallest mountains in the Near East and hence the appropriate place for the ark to come to rest. In Mesopotamian traditions, the flood hero's boat comes to rest on Mount Nimush, in Iraqi Kurdistan, the tallest mountain in Mesopotamia. **8.6–12** The sending of the birds is paralleled in the Mesopotamian flood story in Gilgamesh tablet 11, where the flood hero sends a sequence of three birds, a dove, a swallow, and a raven. The use of birds to scout for land is also common maritime practice. Noah's sending the dove three times, with seven days between, serves stylistically to express the passage of time and Noah's watchful expectation. **8.13** The drying of the waters on *the first month, on the first day of the month* suggests the beginning of a new era analogous to the first day of creation in ch. 1 and the inauguration of the tabernacle (Ex 40.2, 17). In the P calendar, the first month was in the spring. **8.17** God's blessing for all creatures to *abound . . . be fruitful and*

multiply echoes his blessing in 1.22, 28. With the departure from the ark, the history of life begins again. **8.20–22** Noah's offering of sacrifices at the end of the flood reestablishes the relationship between humans and God. Although human predilection for evil has not changed (cf. 6.5), God's compassion toward humans overcomes his anger and regret. His pledge never to destroy all life again reaches a dramatic climax in the poetry of v. 22. The eternal rhythms of time are colored as human time, beginning with *seedtime and harvest.* The Mesopotamian flood hero similarly offers a sacrifice after the flood, which reestablishes the reciprocity between gods and humans.

9.1–7 *Be fruitful and multiply,* blessing repeated in vv. 1, 7 signaling the beginning of the new era after the flood in P (cf. 1.28). Between these blessings God gives the first laws, which are designed to control the violence that corrupted the earth before the flood (see 6.11–12). Humans are henceforth allowed to eat animal flesh, with the condition that they do not eat *its life, that is, its blood* (v. 4; cf. Lev 17.11; Deut 12.23),

life, that is, its blood. 5For your own lifeblood I will surely require a reckoning: from every animal I will require it and from human beings, each one for the blood of another, I will require a reckoning for human life.

6 Whoever sheds the blood of a human,
      by a human shall that person's blood
        be shed;
    for in his own image
      God made humankind.

7And you, be fruitful and multiply, abound on the earth and multiply in it."

8 Then God said to Noah and to his sons with him, 9"As for me, I am establishing my covenant with you and your descendants after you, 10and with every living creature that is with you, the birds, the domestic animals, and every animal of the earth with you, as many as came out of the ark.a 11I establish my covenant with you, that never again shall all flesh be cut off by the waters of a flood, and never again shall there be a flood to destroy the earth." 12God said, "This is the sign of the covenant that I make between me and you and every living creature that is with you, for all future generations: 13I have set my bow in the clouds, and it shall be a sign of the covenant between me and the earth. 14When I bring clouds over the earth and the bow is seen in the clouds, 15I will remember my covenant that is between me and you and every living creature of all flesh; and the waters shall never again become a flood to destroy all flesh. 16When the bow is in the clouds, I will see it

and remember the everlasting covenant between God and every living creature of all flesh that is on the earth." 17God said to Noah, "This is the sign of the covenant that I have established between me and all flesh that is on the earth."

Noah and His Sons

18 The sons of Noah who went out of the ark were Shem, Ham, and Japheth. Ham was the father of Canaan. 19These three were the sons of Noah; and from these the whole earth was peopled.

20 Noah, a man of the soil, was the first to plant a vineyard. 21He drank some of the wine and became drunk, and he lay uncovered in his tent. 22And Ham, the father of Canaan, saw the nakedness of his father, and told his two brothers outside. 23Then Shem and Japheth took a garment, laid it on both their shoulders, and walked backward and covered the nakedness of their father; their faces were turned away, and they did not see their father's nakedness. 24When Noah awoke from his wine and knew what his youngest son had done to him, 25he said,

    "Cursed be Canaan;
      lowest of slaves shall he be to his
        brothers."

26He also said,

    "Blessed by the LORD my God be Shem;
      and let Canaan be his slave.

_____
a Gk: Heb adds every animal of the earth

since the lifeblood belongs to God. The killing of humans is also prohibited, on penalty of death, since humans are made in the image of God. **9.8–17** The formal grant of the covenant between God and all creatures, framed by the phrases *I am establishing my covenant* (v. 9) and *the covenant that I have established* (v. 17). The covenant is essentially a promise that the flood will never recur and confirms the eternal bond between God and his creatures. *Sign of the covenant* (v. 12), the rainbow, a visual reminder for God. *Set my bow in the clouds* (v. 13). The setting aside of God's weapon of war conveys a sense of the cessation of destruction. Circumcision will be the sign of the Abrahamic covenant (17.11), and the sabbath will be the sign of the Mosaic covenant (Ex 31.16–17). See also notes on 6.18; 8.1. **9.18–27** The story of the curse of Canaan, from the J source, has an ethnographic meaning, describing the Canaanites as cursed for their ancestor's transgression. Hence the Canaanites are destined to be slaves. The story justifies Israel's later conquest of Canaan. The story also concerns proper filial duties toward the father, exemplified by Shem

and Japheth, and describes the origin of wine. **9.20–21** Noah resumes the relationship between man (*'adam*) and the soil (*'adamah*) by inventing viticulture (see also notes on 2.4–5; 4.1–2; 3.14–19). This may be part of his destiny to *bring . . . relief from work* (5.29). Elsewhere wine is described as a boon that "cheers gods and mortals" (Judg 9.13), but here it leads to drunkenness, which here and elsewhere is associated with nakedness (see Hab 2.15). **9.22–24** For a son to see his father drunk and naked and to leave him in that state is a dereliction of filial duty. Ham's guilt is compounded by his telling his brothers. The brothers perform their proper filial duty by covering Noah without looking at his nakedness. Although the shame of seeing his father's nakedness is clear, the text also hints that sexual transgression (homosexual incest?) may have been involved, since when he woke Noah *knew what his youngest son had done to him*. This hint may anticipate the licentiousness of Canaanites in biblical tradition (e.g., ch. 19). **9.25–27** Noah's curse is on Canaan, not his father Ham, because of the ethnographic import of the story. The blessings and curses

27 May God make space for[a] Japheth,
    and let him live in the tents of Shem;
    and let Canaan be his slave."

28 After the flood Noah lived three hundred fifty years. 29 All the days of Noah were nine hundred fifty years; and he died.

Nations Descended from Noah

10 These are the descendants of Noah's sons, Shem, Ham, and Japheth; children were born to them after the flood.

2 The descendants of Japheth: Gomer, Magog, Madai, Javan, Tubal, Meshech, and Tiras. 3 The descendants of Gomer: Ashkenaz, Riphath, and Togarmah. 4 The descendants of Javan: Elishah, Tarshish, Kittim, and Rodanim.[b] 5 From these the coastland peoples spread. These are the descendants of Japheth[c] in their lands, with their own language, by their families, in their nations.

6 The descendants of Ham: Cush, Egypt, Put, and Canaan. 7 The descendants of Cush: Seba, Havilah, Sabtah, Raamah, and Sabteca. The descendants of Raamah: Sheba and Dedan. 8 Cush became the father of Nimrod; he was the first on earth to become a mighty warrior. 9 He was a mighty hunter before the LORD; therefore it is said, "Like Nimrod a mighty hunter before the LORD." 10 The beginning of his kingdom was Babel, Erech, and Accad, all of them in the land of Shinar. 11 From that land he went into Assyria, and built Nineveh, Rehoboth-ir, Calah, and 12 Resen between Nineveh and Calah; that is the great city. 13 Egypt became the father of Ludim, Anamim, Lehabim, Naphtuhim, 14 Pathrusim, Casluhim, and Caphtorim, from which the Philistines come.[d]

15 Canaan became the father of Sidon his firstborn, and Heth, 16 and the Jebusites, the Amorites, the Girgashites, 17 the Hivites, the Arkites, the Sinites, 18 the Arvadites, the Zemarites, and the Hamathites. Afterward the families of the Canaanites spread abroad. 19 And the territory of the Canaanites extended from Sidon, in the direction of Gerar, as far as Gaza, and in the direction of Sodom, Gomorrah, Admah, and Zeboiim, as far as Lasha. 20 These are the descendants of Ham, by their families, their languages, their lands, and their nations.

21 To Shem also, the father of all the chil-

---

a Heb *yapht,* a play on *Japheth* *b* Heb Mss Sam Gk See 1 Chr 1.7: MT *Dodanim* *c* Compare verses 20, 31. Heb lacks *These are the descendants of Japheth* *d* Cn: Heb *Casluhim, from which the Philistines come, and Caphtorim*

---

on the different lineages of Noah anticipate the spread of nations in chs. 10–11 and the blessings and curses in the promise to Abraham (12.2–3).

10.1–32 The Table of Nations, a genealogical map of the nations descended from Noah and his three sons. It proceeds from Noah's youngest son, Japheth, to his oldest, Shem, and Shem's line continues in 11.10–26 with the descent of Abram. The table is primarily a P text into which some J sequences have been appended (Hamites in vv. 8–19; Shemites in vv. 24–30). The grouping of the three branches of nations is primarily geographical: the Japhethites are to the north and west of Israel; the Hamites are to the south (but also include Canaan, which perhaps recalls that it was once a province of the Egyptian empire); and the Shemites are to the east. There are some exceptions to this rule, e.g., *Lud/Ludim* (Lydia) is a Hamite in J (v. 13), a Shemite in P (v. 22), and should be a Japhethite by its geographical location. The Arabian peoples (e.g., *Seba/Sheba* and *Havilah*) are Hamite in P (v. 7), but Shemite in J (v. 28–29). There are no "racial" characteristics for any of the three groups. **10.2–5** *Japheth,* a name probably related to Greek *Iapetos,* a Titan who was the grandfather of Deucalion, the Greek flood hero. His descendants are primarily peoples of Asia Minor and the Mediterranean, include *Gomer* (Cimmerians), *Magog* (probably a region of Lydia, whose king, Gog [Greek Gyges], is an enemy in Ezek 38–39), *Javan* (Ionia), *Ashkenaz* (Scythia; in medieval Hebrew the word was reused to refer to Germany and later denoted the Jews of central and eastern Europe), *Elishah* and *Kittim* (both names for Cyprus), *Tarshish* (Tarsus), and *Rodanim* (Rhodes). **10.6–7** The descendants of *Ham* (which means "hot" in Hebrew) are primarily peoples of North Africa and Arabia, including *Cush* (Nubia), *Egypt,* and *Put* (Libya). *Cush* is the father of Arabian peoples, including *Sheba,* whose queen visits Solomon in 1 Kings 10. *Canaan* is a son of *Ham,* perhaps because of its historical ties with Egypt. **10.8–19** The J list of Hamites consists of the children of *Cush, Egypt,* and *Canaan. Cush,* the father of *Nimrod,* may serve here as a homonym for the Kassites, who ruled Mesopotamia in the mid- to late second millennium. The children of Egypt include *Caphtorim* (Crete), which had close trade relations with Egypt. The children and territory of *Canaan* include *Sidon* (referring to the Phoenicians), the *Jebusites* (of Jerusalem; see 2 Sam 5.6), and the cities of *Sodom* and *Gomorrah* (see ch. 19). **10.8–12** The brief legend of *Nimrod* provides an epitome of Mesopotamian history up to the time of the Assyrian Empire (with its great capital of *Nineveh*). The name *Nimrod* is probably a distortion of Ninurta, a Mesopotamian god of kingship and the hunt, who was a patron god of the Assyrian kings. **10.21–31** The descendants of *Shem* (which means "name, fame") include many peoples of

dren of Eber, the elder brother of Japheth, children were born. 22The descendants of Shem: Elam, Asshur, Arpachshad, Lud, and Aram. 23The descendants of Aram: Uz, Hul, Gether, and Mash. 24Arpachshad became the father of Shelah; and Shelah became the father of Eber. 25To Eber were born two sons: the name of the one was Peleg,ᵃ for in his days the earth was divided, and his brother's name was Joktan. 26Joktan became the father of Almodad, Sheleph, Hazarmaveth, Jerah, 27Hadoram, Uzal, Diklah, 28Obal, Abimael, Sheba, 29Ophir, Havilah, and Jobab; all these were the descendants of Joktan. 30The territory in which they lived extended from Mesha in the direction of Sephar, the hill country of the east. 31These are the descendants of Shem, by their families, their languages, their lands, and their nations.

32 These are the families of Noah's sons, according to their genealogies, in their nations; and from these the nations spread abroad on the earth after the flood.

The Tower of Babel

11 Now the whole earth had one language and the same words. 2And as they migrated from the east,ᵇ they came upon a plain in the land of Shinar and settled there. 3And they said to one another, "Come, let us make bricks, and burn them thoroughly." And they had brick for stone, and bitumen for mortar. 4Then they said, "Come, let us build ourselves a city, and a tower with its top in the heavens, and let us make a name for ourselves; otherwise we shall be scattered abroad upon the face of the whole earth." 5The LORD came down to see the city and the tower, which mortals had built. 6And the LORD said, "Look, they are one people, and they have all one language; and this is only the beginning of what they will do; nothing that they propose to do will now be impossible for them. 7Come, let us go down, and confuse their language there, so that they will not understand one another's speech." 8So the LORD scattered them abroad from there over the face of all the earth, and they left off building the city. 9Therefore it was called Babel, because there the LORD confusedᶜ the language of all the earth; and from there the LORD scattered them abroad over the face of all the earth.

Descendants of Shem

10 These are the descendants of Shem. When Shem was one hundred years old, he became the father of Arpachshad two years after the

---

ᵃ That is *Division*   ᵇ Or *migrated eastward*   ᶜ Heb *balal*, meaning *to confuse*

---

the Near East (western Asia), excluding Canaan. *Eber,* the eponymous ancestor of the Hebrews. His name may refer to his geographical location "on the other side of the (Euphrates) river" (*'eber hannahar*), perhaps referring to the patriarchal homeland. **11.1–9** The Tower of Babel story (J) is the last tale in the primeval narratives of human hubris and its consequences and also serves to mock the pretensions of the contemporary imperial power of Mesopotamia. As in the garden of Eden story, humans attempt to cross the boundary between human and divine and are thrown back permanently into the human world. The diversity of languages and nations become limiting conditions of human existence. As a story about language and power, it employs language artfully to express and undermine the human pretensions to power. The two parts of the story have a series of verbal echoes and reversals, creating a dramatic symmetry. Vv. 1–4 describe the humans' actions; vv. 5–9 describe God's response. The story is built on the following symmetrical pattern: A *the whole earth had one language* (v. 1), B *they said to one another* (v. 3), C *Come, let us make* (*nlbnh*) *bricks* (v. 3), D *let us build ourselves* (v. 4), E *a city, and a tower* (v. 4), E′ *the city and the tower* (v. 5), D′ *which mortals had built* (v. 5), C′ *Come, let us go down, and confuse* (*nblh*; v. 7), B′ *they will not* understand one another's speech (v. 7), A′ the language of all the earth (v. 9). **11.2** Land of Shinar, southern Mesopotamia or Babylonia, the ancient land of Sumer; see 10.10. **11.4** A tower with its top in the heavens, probably a Mesopotamian temple tower, or ziggurat, but here taken as an unauthorized incursion into God's domain. The humans' fear that they will be *scattered abroad upon . . . the whole earth* ironically comes to pass as a consequence of their deeds in v. 8. The desire of the men of Babel to *make a name* for themselves (which equals fame and renown) comes to naught with anonymous infamy, but the ruined city gets a name in v. 9. The desire for a name anticipates God's promise of a great name to Abraham (12.2), who serves as a counterpoint to the men of Babel. **11.9** *Babel* (Babylon), so named because it is the place of *balal*, Hebrew, "confusion." Babylon was one of the most famous cities of antiquity, but it is mocked here as a ruined site of ancient hubris, transgression, and confusion. **11.10–26** The genealogy of Shem continues the "book of the generations of Adam" (5.1–32 + 9.28–29) and also resumes the Shemite genealogy of 10.21–23 (all P). It provides a transition to the story of Abraham, who is born to *Terah* in v. 26. Abraham is the tenth generation in this list. The age of the postdiluvian patriarchs gradually shortens from Shem

flood; [11]and Shem lived after the birth of Arpachshad five hundred years, and had other sons and daughters.

12 When Arpachshad had lived thirty-five years, he became the father of Shelah; [13]and Arpachshad lived after the birth of Shelah four hundred three years, and had other sons and daughters.

14 When Shelah had lived thirty years, he became the father of Eber; [15]and Shelah lived after the birth of Eber four hundred three years, and had other sons and daughters.

16 When Eber had lived thirty-four years, he became the father of Peleg; [17]and Eber lived after the birth of Peleg four hundred thirty years, and had other sons and daughters.

18 When Peleg had lived thirty years, he became the father of Reu; [19]and Peleg lived after the birth of Reu two hundred nine years, and had other sons and daughters.

20 When Reu had lived thirty-two years, he became the father of Serug; [21]and Reu lived after the birth of Serug two hundred seven years, and had other sons and daughters.

22 When Serug had lived thirty years, he became the father of Nahor; [23]and Serug lived after the birth of Nahor two hundred years, and had other sons and daughters.

24 When Nahor had lived twenty-nine years, he became the father of Terah; [25]and Nahor lived after the birth of Terah one hundred nineteen years, and had other sons and daughters.

26 When Terah had lived seventy years, he became the father of Abram, Nahor, and Haran.

Descendants of Terah

27 Now these are the descendants of Terah. Terah was the father of Abram, Nahor, and Haran; and Haran was the father of Lot. [28]Haran died before his father Terah in the land of his birth, in Ur of the Chaldeans. [29]Abram and Nahor took wives; the name of Abram's wife was Sarai, and the name of Nahor's wife was Milcah. She was the daughter of Haran the father of Milcah and Iscah. [30]Now Sarai was barren; she had no child.

31 Terah took his son Abram and his grandson Lot son of Haran, and his daughter-in-law Sarai, his son Abram's wife, and they went out together from Ur of the Chaldeans to go into the land of Canaan; but when they came to Haran, they settled there. [32]The days of Terah were two hundred five years; and Terah died in Haran.

The Call of Abram

12 Now the LORD said to Abram, "Go from your country and your kindred and your father's house to the land that I will show you. [2]I will make of you a great nation, and I will bless you, and make your name great, so that you will be a blessing. [3]I will bless those who bless you, and the one who curses you I will curse; and in you all the families of the earth shall be blessed." [a]

4 So Abram went, as the LORD had told him; and Lot went with him. Abram was seventy-five years old when he departed from Haran.

_____

a Or by you all the families of the earth shall bless themselves

(600 years) to Abraham (175 years; see 25.7). Some members of this genealogy (Serug, Nahor, and Terah) are known as place-names in the region of Haran, the patriarchal homeland (see v. 31). **11.26** The vertical genealogy from Shem to Terah branches into three sons, Abram, Nahor, and Haran, just as the vertical genealogy from Adam to Noah branched into three sons, Shem, Ham, and Japheth, in 5.32. _Abram_ means "the father is exalted," highlighting Abraham's role as father and patriarch. God changes _Abram_ to _Abraham_ in 17.5. **11.27–32** _These are the descendants_, a genealogical rubric that begins the Abraham story (see note on 2.4). _Lot_, Abram's nephew, will accompany Abram to Canaan and become the ancestor of the Moabites and Ammonites (19.37–38). _Nahor_, Abram's brother, will dwell in Haran and become father of the Aramean peoples, including his son, Bethuel, father of Laban and Rebekah (22.20–24; 24.10). _Sarai_ means "princess," but her origins are not given. God changes _Sarai_ to _Sarah_

in 17.15. The migration of Terah's family from _Ur of the Chaldeans_ in southern Mesopotamia to _Haran_ in the middle Euphrates region occurs only in the P source, which perhaps joined together two traditions about Abram's origin. _Chaldeans_, an Aramean people who become prominent in southern Mesopotamia beginning in the eighth century BCE, in southern Mesopotamia. **11.30** The notice that _Sarai . . . had no child_ is an anticipatory announcement of the central problem of the Abraham narrative, which will come to the foreground in gradual stages after God's promise that Abram will be father of _a great nation_ in 12.2.

12.1–9 The call of Abram (largely J), with its fivefold repetition of _bless/blessing_, effectively reverses the accumulation of curses and punishments of the primeval narratives. Henceforth in Abram _all the families of the earth shall be blessed_ (v. 3). The standard for this blessing seems to be the degree to which the families of the earth bless Abraham and the _great nation_ (v. 2) that

5Abram took his wife Sarai and his brother's son Lot, and all the possessions that they had gathered, and the persons whom they had acquired in Haran; and they set forth to go to the land of Canaan. When they had come to the land of Canaan, 6Abram passed through the land to the place at Shechem, to the oak*a* of Moreh. At that time the Canaanites were in the land. 7Then the LORD appeared to Abram, and said, "To your offspring*b* I will give this land." So he built there an altar to the LORD, who had appeared to him. 8From there he moved on to the hill country on the east of Bethel, and pitched his tent, with Bethel on the west and Ai on the east; and there he built an altar to the LORD and invoked the name of the LORD. 9And Abram journeyed on by stages toward the Negeb.

Abram and Sarai in Egypt

10 Now there was a famine in the land. So Abram went down to Egypt to reside there as an alien, for the famine was severe in the land. 11When he was about to enter Egypt, he said to his wife Sarai, "I know well that you are a woman beautiful in appearance; 12and when the Egyptians see you, they will say, 'This is his wife'; then they will kill me, but they will let you live. 13Say you are my sister, so that it may go well with me because of you, and that my life may be spared on your account." 14When Abram entered Egypt the Egyptians saw that the woman was very beautiful. 15When the officials of Pharaoh saw her, they praised her to Pharaoh. And the woman was taken into Pharaoh's house. 16And for her sake he dealt well with Abram; and he had sheep, oxen, male donkeys, male and female slaves, female donkeys, and camels.

17 But the LORD afflicted Pharaoh and his house with great plagues because of Sarai, Abram's wife. 18So Pharaoh called Abram, and said, "What is this you have done to me? Why did you not tell me that she was your wife? 19Why did you say, 'She is my sister,' so that I took her for my wife? Now then, here is your wife, take her, and be gone." 20And Pharaoh gave his men orders concerning him; and they set him on the way, with his wife and all that he had.

Abram and Lot Separate

13 So Abram went up from Egypt, he and his wife, and all that he had, and Lot with him, into the Negeb.

2 Now Abram was very rich in livestock, in

_____
a Or terebinth *b* Heb seed

descends from him, Israel: God's blessing goes to *those who bless* them and God's curse to *the one who curses* them (v. 3). The call of Abram thus serves as a turning point in the moral history of humanity. The promises to Abram include blessing, a great name (fame, renown), numerous descendants who will become a great nation, and land. The promise of land is given in v. 7, when Abram reaches *the land that* God *will show* him (v. 1; a phrase ominously echoed in 22.2). God (or his angel) reiterates the patriarchal promises several times in the Abraham narrative (13.14–17; 15.5; 22.17–18) and later grants them to Isaac (26.2–5) and Jacob (28.13–15; cf. 32.12; 35.11–12; 46.2–4). The book of Kings depicts the promises as fulfilled during Solomon's glorious reign (1 Kings 4.20–21), though Genesis is never so specific. Heb 11.8 finds in Abraham's call a model of faith. **12.4** Abram's righteousness and faithfulness are shown by his simple response: *So Abram went, as the LORD had told him.* Lot accompanies him, perhaps as a presumptive heir, since Sarai is barren. **12.6–7** God's first revelation to Abram is at *Shechem,* later site of the all-Israel covenant ceremony in Josh 24. *Oak of Moreh* (or "oak of the Teacher"), a sacred tree where Jacob later buries the household gods of his family (35.4) and where Joshua erects a standing stone (Josh 24.26). Abram founds this sacred shrine by building an altar there. He also founds shrines at or near Bethel and Ai (v. 8), Hebron (13.18), Beer-sheba (21.33), and Moriah (22.14). *At that time the Canaanites were in the land,* an aside that serves as a backdrop to God's promise of the land to Abram's offspring. It also betrays the post-Mosaic chronological perspective of the biblical narrator, as the medieval commentator Ibn Ezra hinted, calling it "a great secret." **12.10–20** The story of the matriarch in danger occurs in three varying forms: here with Abram and Sarai in Egypt (J); in ch. 20 with Abraham and Sarah in Gerar (E); and in 26.6–11 with Isaac and Rebekah in Gerar (J). Each story expresses a threat to the promise of progeny that is narrowly averted. In each the patriarch uses the ruse that the woman is really his sister, so that he will not be killed because of her beauty. This version also has a number of features that foreshadow the exodus: famine in the land, descent into Egypt, Sarai being taken into Pharaoh's house, the great plagues with which God afflicts Pharaoh's house in order to release her, and the acquisition of wealth (see Ex 12.35–36). Abram's character is resourceful yet somewhat problematic—note that when Pharaoh castigates Abram for his duplicity, he offers no reply (cf. 20.11–13).

13.1–18 Although Abram's nephew Lot is his only eligible heir, the two now separate because their great possessions lead to strife. The moral qualities of the

silver, and in gold. ³He journeyed on by stages from the Negeb as far as Bethel, to the place where his tent had been at the beginning, between Bethel and Ai, ⁴to the place where he had made an altar at the first; and there Abram called on the name of the LORD. ⁵Now Lot, who went with Abram, also had flocks and herds and tents, ⁶so that the land could not support both of them living together; for their possessions were so great that they could not live together, ⁷and there was strife between the herders of Abram's livestock and the herders of Lot's livestock. At that time the Canaanites and the Perizzites lived in the land.

8 Then Abram said to Lot, "Let there be no strife between you and me, and between your herders and my herders; for we are kindred. ⁹Is not the whole land before you? Separate yourself from me. If you take the left hand, then I will go to the right; or if you take the right hand, then I will go to the left." ¹⁰Lot looked about him, and saw that the plain of the Jordan was well watered everywhere like the garden of the LORD, like the land of Egypt, in the direction of Zoar; this was before the LORD had destroyed Sodom and Gomorrah. ¹¹So Lot chose for himself all the plain of the

Jordan, and Lot journeyed eastward; thus they separated from each other. ¹²Abram settled in the land of Canaan, while Lot settled among the cities of the Plain and moved his tent as far as Sodom. ¹³Now the people of Sodom were wicked, great sinners against the LORD.

14 The LORD said to Abram, after Lot had separated from him, "Raise your eyes now, and look from the place where you are, northward and southward and eastward and westward; ¹⁵for all the land that you see I will give to you and to your offspring[a] forever. ¹⁶I will make your offspring like the dust of the earth; so that if one can count the dust of the earth, your offspring also can be counted. ¹⁷Rise up, walk through the length and the breadth of the land, for I will give it to you." ¹⁸So Abram moved his tent, and came and settled by the oaks[b] of Mamre, which are at Hebron; and there he built an altar to the LORD.

Lot's Captivity and Rescue

14 In the days of King Amraphel of Shinar, King Arioch of Ellasar, King Chedorlaomer of Elam, and King Tidal of Goiim,

a Heb *seed*   b Or *terebinths*

---

two are subtly contrasted: Abram is wise and magnanimous, offering Lot the first choice of land. Lot is implicitly disrespectful by taking the choice rather than yielding it to his elder. Lot pays for his disrespect by choosing the region of Sodom and Gomorrah, which will later become desolate. Abram takes the remaining portion, the *land of Canaan,* which God confirms as the land of the promise. **13.7** *At that time the Canaanites . . . lived in the land,* an aside that recalls 12.6 and serves as a backdrop to the issue of the inheritance of the land, which is now potentially endangered by the strife between Lot and Abram. **13.10, 13** The comparison of the lush Jordan plain with the *garden of the LORD* (a synonym for the garden of Eden; see Ezek 28.13) and the *land of Egypt* evokes two fertile lands that are also places of transgression. *This was before . . . Sodom and Gomorrah, the people of Sodom . . . against the LORD,* notices indicating the dark side of this land and pointing forward to ch. 19. **13.14–17** God reiterates his promise of land and offspring (cf. 12.1–3, 7), adding the intensifying word *forever* (v. 15). That Abram's offspring will be *like the dust of the earth,* numerous and uncountable, recurs in the promise to Jacob (28.14). This image alternates with *the stars of heaven* (15.5; 26.4) and *the sand of the sea* (32.12; 22.17 combines *stars* and *sand*). **13.18** Abram settles at Hebron, which later becomes the chief city of Judah; there David is first crowned king (2 Sam 2.1–4; 5.1–5). Abram builds an altar by the *oaks of Mamre,* which

may be sacred trees; cf. 12.6–7. The region from Shechem to Hebron was the principle area of Israelite settlement; hence Abram is a cultural and religious founder for all Israel.

14.1–24 The account of Abram's rescue of Lot from the army of four eastern kings has a different character from the other Abraham narratives and cannot be identified with any of the pentateuchal sources. The first part (vv. 1–9) imitates the style of a royal annal or inscription, including the apparently concocted names of various kings and countries. The second part (vv. 13–16) portrays Abram as a mighty sheik with a sizable army of retainers, able to conquer foreign armies in order to rescue his nephew. The third part (vv. 17–24) portrays the aftermath of Abram's victory—Abram's nobility and his blessing by a foreign priest-king. This story gives an indication of the different types of traditions about Abraham that circulated in ancient Israel. In Genesis it continues the Abram-Lot cycle begun in ch. 13 and shows Abram's care for Lot, which will recur in the story of the destruction of Sodom in chs. 18–19 (see 19.29). **14.1** The names and countries of the four eastern kings are a pastiche of real and fictional names. *Shinar* (Babylonia) and *Elam* are real places, *Ellasar* is unknown, and *Goiim* means "nations." *Amraphel* sounds like a Semitic name, *Arioch* like a Hurrian name, *Chedorlaomer* like an Elamite name, and *Tidal* like a Hittite name, but there are no historical people or kings with which these can be

2these kings made war with King Bera of Sodom, King Birsha of Gomorrah, King Shinab of Admah, King Shemeber of Zeboiim, and the king of Bela (that is, Zoar). 3All these joined forces in the Valley of Siddim (that is, the Dead Sea).ᵃ 4Twelve years they had served Chedorlaomer, but in the thirteenth year they rebelled. 5In the fourteenth year Chedorlaomer and the kings who were with him came and subdued the Rephaim in Ashteroth-karnaim, the Zuzim in Ham, the Emim in Shaveh-kiriathaim, 6and the Horites in the hill country of Seir as far as El-paran on the edge of the wilderness; 7then they turned back and came to En-mishpat (that is, Kadesh), and subdued all the country of the Amalekites, and also the Amorites who lived in Hazazontamar. 8Then the king of Sodom, the king of Gomorrah, the king of Admah, the king of Zeboiim, and the king of Bela (that is, Zoar) went out, and they joined battle in the Valley of Siddim 9with King Chedorlaomer of Elam, King Tidal of Goiim, King Amraphel of Shinar, and King Arioch of Ellasar, four kings against five. 10Now the Valley of Siddim was full of bitumen pits; and as the kings of Sodom and Gomorrah fled, some fell into them, and the rest fled to the hill country. 11So the enemy took all the goods of Sodom and Gomorrah, and all their provisions, and went their way; 12they also took Lot, the son of Abram's brother, who lived in Sodom, and his goods, and departed.

13 Then one who had escaped came and told Abram the Hebrew, who was living by the oaksᵇ of Mamre the Amorite, brother of Eshcol and of Aner; these were allies of Abram. 14When Abram heard that his nephew had been taken captive, he led forth his trained men, born in his house, three hundred eighteen of them, and went in pursuit as far as Dan. 15He divided his forces against them by night, he and his servants, and routed them and pursued them to Hobah, north of Damascus. 16Then he brought back all the goods, and also brought back his nephew Lot with his goods, and the women and the people.

Abram Blessed by Melchizedek

17 After his return from the defeat of Chedorlaomer and the kings who were with him, the king of Sodom went out to meet him at the Valley of Shaveh (that is, the King's Valley). 18And King Melchizedek of Salem brought out bread and wine; he was priest of God Most High.ᶜ 19He blessed him and said,
"Blessed be Abram by God Most High,ᶜ
    maker of heaven and earth;
20 and blessed be God Most High,ᶜ
    who has delivered your enemies into
        your hand!"
And Abram gave him one-tenth of everything. 21Then the king of Sodom said to Abram, "Give me the persons, but take the goods for yourself." 22But Abram said to the king of Sodom, "I have sworn to the LORD, God Most High,ᶜ maker of heaven and earth, 23that I would not take a thread or a sandal-thong or

---

a Heb Salt Sea   b Or terebinths   c Heb El Elyon

---

identified. This is a learned exercise in invented history. **14.2** The kings of the cities of the Plain are also invented. *Bera,* "in evil," and *Birsha,* "in wickedness," appropriate names for the kings of Sodom and Gomorrah. **14.5–7** The kings of the east defeat the aboriginal inhabitants of Canaan, who are elsewhere depicted as giants: the *Rephaim, Zuzim (Zamzummim), Emim, Horites,* and *Amorites;* cf. 15.19–21; Num 13.32–33; Deut 2.10–12, 20–23; Am 2.9. **14.12–13** The mention of Lot breaks the annalistic style and returns the focus to the patriarchal family. *Hebrew,* an ethnic term usually used by foreigners or when speaking to or about foreigners (e.g., 39.14; 40.15; Ex 1.19; 1 Sam 4.6; Jon 1.9). The usage here is unusual. *Mamre,* here a native Amorite; he and his brothers are *allies* (lit. "lords of the covenant") of Abram (cf. 13.18). This association with Amorites is also unusual. **14.14–15** The details of Abram's battle with the kings of the east emphasize his skill and military prowess—with only 318 men he defeated the great eastern alliance, pursuing them all the way to Syria. **14.17** The king of Sodom meets the victorious Abram at a place identified as the *King's Valley* next to Jerusalem (see 2 Sam 18.18). This encounter resumes in v. 21, after Abram's meeting with the king of Jerusalem. **14.18–20** *Salem,* a short form of Jerusalem (see Ps 76.2). Its king and priest, Melchizedek (which means "my king is righteousness"), bestows on Abram the blessing of *God Most High, maker of heaven and earth.* This is an expansion of a traditional West Semitic divine title, "God, maker of earth," known from various inscriptions (including a Hebrew text from Jerusalem). Abram equates *God Most High (El Elyon)* with Yahweh in v. 22. The blessing on Abram creates a patriarchal link with Jerusalem and its cult (including the payment of a tithe to its priests), which are in some sense legitimized by this association. Ps 110.4 applies Melchizedek's combination of royal and priestly authority to the Jerusalem king, suggesting that Melchizedek played a symbolic role in Israel's royal ideology. **14.21–24** Abram's graciousness to the

anything that is yours, so that you might not say, 'I have made Abram rich.' 24I will take nothing but what the young men have eaten, and the share of the men who went with me— Aner, Eshcol, and Mamre. Let them take their share."

God's Covenant with Abram

15 After these things the word of the LORD came to Abram in a vision, "Do not be afraid, Abram, I am your shield; your reward shall be very great." 2But Abram said, "O Lord GOD, what will you give me, for I continue childless, and the heir of my house is Eliezer of Damascus?"*a* 3And Abram said, "You have given me no offspring, and so a slave born in my house is to be my heir." 4But the word of the LORD came to him, "This man shall not be your heir; no one but your very own issue shall be your heir." 5He brought him outside and said, "Look toward heaven and count the stars, if you are able to count them." Then he said to him, "So shall your descendants be." 6And he believed the LORD; and the LORD*b* reckoned it to him as righteousness.

7 Then he said to him, "I am the LORD who brought you from Ur of the Chaldeans, to give you this land to possess." 8But he said, "O Lord GOD, how am I to know that I shall possess it?" 9He said to him, "Bring me a heifer three years old, a female goat three years old, a ram three years old, a turtledove, and a young pigeon." 10He brought him all these and cut them in two, laying each half over against the other; but he did not cut the birds in two. 11And when birds of prey came down on the carcasses, Abram drove them away.

12 As the sun was going down, a deep sleep fell upon Abram, and a deep and terrifying darkness descended upon him. 13Then the LORD*b* said to Abram, "Know this for certain, that your offspring shall be aliens in a land that is not theirs, and shall be slaves there, and they shall be oppressed for four hundred years; 14but I will bring judgment on the nation that they serve, and afterward they shall come out with great possessions. 15As for yourself, you shall go to your ancestors in peace; you shall be buried in a good old age. 16And they shall come back here in the fourth generation; for the iniquity of the Amorites is not yet complete."

---

a Meaning of Heb uncertain   *b* Heb *he*

---

king of Sodom and his refusal to enrich himself presents him as an honorable and eloquent leader, to whom the kings and peoples of Canaan are indebted.

15.1–21 This chapter returns to the theme of the promises. In the first part (vv. 1–6), Abram expresses doubt about the promise of offspring and, when reassured, shows his trust in God, and in the second part (vv. 7–21) he expresses doubt about the promise of the land, and God makes a covenant that guarantees its fulfillment. The two parts have different styles and different settings (in v. 5 it is night since the stars are visible; in v. 12 *the sun was going down*), and neither can be assigned to the major pentateuchal sources. The two scenes are, however, complementary and are presented as a two-part revelatory encounter that confirms and adds detail to the promises. **15.1–6** *Eliezer of Damascus,* not mentioned elsewhere, although an unnamed servant of Abraham plays a major role in ch. 24. V. 3 appears to be an explication of obscure terms in v. 2. God's promise that Abram's *very own issue* shall be his *heir* (v. 4) leaves open the identity of the mother (cf. 18.10) and sets the stage for the conflict between Sarah and Hagar. Bringing Abram outside to *count the stars* (v. 5) provides a vivid symbolic action accompanying the verbal promise comparable to the covenant ceremony in the second part of the chapter. Abram's response—*he believed the LORD* (v. 6)—means that he trusts God and his promise. It is not faith without evidence, but rather faith that takes God's word as sufficient. The theme of Abram's *righteousness* (v. 6) recurs

in 18.19. Paul in Rom 4.3; Gal 3.6 uses this passage as a basis for his understanding of the importance of faith. Jas 2.23 makes different use of the text. **15.7** God's self-identification to Abram echoes the beginning of the Decalogue (Ex 20.2) with *Ur of the Chaldeans* in the place of Egypt. This allusion anticipates God's foretelling of the Egyptian bondage and the exodus in vv. 13–16. **15.9–12, 17** The ceremonial splitting of animals is an old West Semitic rite that seals oaths or covenants. Jeremiah refers to a covenant ceremony that involves splitting a calf in half and passing between its parts (Jer 34.18–21). The symbolism of this act seems to be that the party passing between the parts will die (like the animal) if it breaks its oath. In the covenant ceremony in ch. 15, God is the party affirming the covenant, and *the smoking fire pot and a flaming torch* that mysteriously pass *between* the *pieces* (v. 17) are his symbols. These two items may be small-scale allusions to God's pillar of smoke and pillar of fire (e.g., Ex 13.21–22). The *birds of prey* that attack the pieces (v. 11) and the *terrifying darkness* (v. 12) that descends upon Abram set a fearful mood for the prophecy of Egyptian bondage that follows. **15.13–16** The prediction of the Egyptian oppression and the exodus is the only explicit mention in Genesis (but see note on 12.10–20). *Four hundred years,* roughly equal to the 430 years in Ex 12.40. The return *in the fourth generation* corresponds to the four generations from Levi to Moses in Ex 6.16–20. *Iniquity of the Amorites,* apparently their worship of other gods and idolatry (see Ex

17 When the sun had gone down and it was dark, a smoking fire pot and a flaming torch passed between these pieces. 18On that day the LORD made a covenant with Abram, saying, "To your descendants I give this land, from the river of Egypt to the great river, the river Euphrates, 19the land of the Kenites, the Kenizzites, the Kadmonites, 20the Hittites, the Perizzites, the Rephaim, 21the Amorites, the Canaanites, the Girgashites, and the Jebusites."

The Birth of Ishmael

16 Now Sarai, Abram's wife, bore him no children. She had an Egyptian slave-girl whose name was Hagar, 2and Sarai said to Abram, "You see that the LORD has prevented me from bearing children; go in to my slave-girl; it may be that I shall obtain children by her." And Abram listened to the voice of Sarai. 3So, after Abram had lived ten years in the land of Canaan, Sarai, Abram's wife, took Hagar the Egyptian, her slave-girl, and gave her to her husband Abram as a wife. 4He went in to Hagar, and she conceived; and when she saw that she had conceived, she looked with contempt on her mistress. 5Then Sarai said to Abram, "May the wrong done to me be on you! I gave my slave-girl to your embrace, and when she saw that she had conceived, she looked on me with contempt. May the LORD judge between you and me!" 6But Abram said to Sarai, "Your slave-girl is in your power; do to her as you please." Then Sarai dealt harshly with her, and she ran away from her.

7 The angel of the LORD found her by a spring of water in the wilderness, the spring on the way to Shur. 8And he said, "Hagar, slave-girl of Sarai, where have you come from and where are you going?" She said, "I am running away from my mistress Sarai." 9The angel of the LORD said to her, "Return to your mistress, and submit to her." 10The angel of the LORD also said to her, "I will so greatly multiply your offspring that they cannot be counted for multitude." 11And the angel of the LORD said to her,

"Now you have conceived and shall bear a
        son;
    you shall call him Ishmael,[a]

a That is God hears

23.23–33), which is punishable up to the fourth generation (see Ex 20.5). The return of Israel to the promised land will entail the destruction of the Amorites. **15.18–21** The boundaries of the promised land, from *the river of Egypt* (the Nile) to *the great river* (the Euphrates), is a maximal interpretation of earlier descriptions (see Num 34.1–12; Deut 11.24; 1 Kings 4.21; 8.65). The parallelism of the two rivers is a descriptive figure and does not reflect Israel's boundaries at any period. The list of ten peoples of the promised land expands the standard list of six or seven peoples (e.g., Ex 3.8; Deut 7.1; Josh 9.1; Judg 3.5) with three alliterative peoples (*Kenites, Kenizzites, Kadmonites*) and the *Rephaim* (cf. 14.5).

16.1–16 The story of the expulsion of Hagar is told twice, here by the J (vv. 1–2, 4–14) and P sources (vv. 3, 15–16) and in 21.8–21 by the E source. In both Hagar incurs Sarai's wrath, is expelled with the approval of Abram, and is rescued by an angel, who conveys the divine promise that Ishmael's descendants will become a mighty nation. This is an ethnographic story about the ancestry of the Arab peoples, collectively called the Ishmaelites (see 25.12–18). The Arabs are culturally distinct, yet part of Israel's family tree, and receive a version of the patriarchal blessing. In this story Sarai shows herself to be a dominant figure in the domestic domain, zealously protecting her honor and authority, while Hagar is a sympathetic and suffering figure, to whom God gives aid and an annunciation of her child's birth and destiny. Paul in Gal 4.21–31 uses the story of Hagar as a polemical allegory. **16.1–2** The initial situation echoes the problem first stated in 11.30, Sarai's barrenness, and also announces that Sarai will be a major figure in this story. *An Egyptian,* probably from the westernmost territory of the Arab tribes in the wilderness of Shur (see 16.7; 25.18), in the desert of north Sinai opposite Egypt. *Hagar* means "city, province, region" in old Arabic. Hagarite tribes (and Ishmaelites) are also located in Transjordan (see Ps 83.6; 1 Chr 5.10). Sarai takes the initiative by assigning her slave-girl to be a surrogate mother, in accordance with ancient Near Eastern custom (see also 30.3, 9). Abram's response, here and later (see v. 6) acknowledges Sarai's authority in domestic affairs. **16.4–6** *She looked with contempt on her mistress,* better "her mistress was lowered in her eyes." Hagar's inner response reverses the normal hierarchy of slave-girl and mistress. This enrages Sarai, who demands justice from Abram for the *wrong* (or "violence, injustice") done to her. Abram grants Sarai unrestricted power over Hagar, in spite of the moral problem of exposing the pregnant slave-girl to her mistress's wrath (cf. 21.11). Sarai's oppression of her Egyptian slave, who then flees toward Egypt, ironically reverses the exodus theme. **16.7–12** God's angel grants Hagar the patriarchal promise of descendants so abundant *that they cannot be counted* (v. 10; cf. the promise to Abram in 13.16; 15.5). The angel's announcement of the future child's name and destiny is also similar to the announcements given to Abraham (17.19; 18.10) and Rebekah (25.23). *Ishmael* (lit. "God has heard"), so named because God *has given heed to* (lit. "heard") Hagar's *affliction.* The

for the LORD has given heed to your
affliction.

12 He shall be a wild ass of a man,
   with his hand against everyone,
    and everyone's hand against him;
   and he shall live at odds with all his kin."
13So she named the LORD who spoke to her,
"You are El-roi";ᵃ for she said, "Have I really
seen God and remained alive after seeing
him?"ᵇ 14Therefore the well was called Beer-
lahai-roi;ᶜ it lies between Kadesh and Bered.

15 Hagar bore Abram a son; and Abram
named his son, whom Hagar bore, Ishmael.
16Abram was eighty-six years old when Hagar
bore himᵈ Ishmael.

The Sign of the Covenant

17 When Abram was ninety-nine years
old, the LORD appeared to Abram, and
said to him, "I am God Almighty;ᵉ walk before
me, and be blameless. 2And I will make my
covenant between me and you, and will make
you exceedingly numerous." 3Then Abram fell
on his face; and God said to him, 4"As for me,
this is my covenant with you: You shall be the
ancestor of a multitude of nations. 5No longer
shall your name be Abram,ᶠ but your name

shall be Abraham;ᵍ for I have made you the ancestor of a multitude of nations. 6I will make
you exceedingly fruitful; and I will make nations of you, and kings shall come from you. 7I
will establish my covenant between me and
you, and your offspring after you throughout
their generations, for an everlasting covenant,
to be God to you and to your offspringʰ after
you. 8And I will give to you, and to your offspring after you, the land where you are now
an alien, all the land of Canaan, for a perpetual
holding; and I will be their God."

9 God said to Abraham, "As for you, you
shall keep my covenant, you and your offspring after you throughout their generations.
10This is my covenant, which you shall keep,
between me and you and your offspring after
you: Every male among you shall be circumcised. 11You shall circumcise the flesh of your
foreskins, and it shall be a sign of the covenant
between me and you. 12Throughout your generations every male among you shall be cir-

---

a Perhaps God of seeing or God who sees   b Meaning of Heb
uncertain   c That is the Well of the Living One who sees me
d Heb Abram   e Traditional rendering of Heb El Shaddai
f That is exalted ancestor   g Here taken to mean ancestor of a
multitude   h Heb seed

---

name highlights God's compassion for Hagar, probably because he has saved her life, but this is tempered
by the command to return to Sarai and submit to her
(v. 9). The description of Ishmael as a wild ass of a man
(v. 12), in conflict with all, describes the fierce independence and warrior ethos of the Arab peoples of antiquity. 16.13–14 A difficult sequence that connects
the divine revelation to Hagar with the place-name
Beer-lahai-roi. The LORD who spoke to her. Hagar identifies the angel as God himself. The angel is in some respects a manifestation of God; cf. Ex 23.20–21. Those
who see God and live have special status (see also
32.30; Ex 33.20; Judg 6.22; 13.22), though the text is
suspect at this point. 16.15–16 The brief P version of
the story (along with v. 3). In this version there is a
concern for chronology, and Abraham names the son.
The placement of these verses here returns the focus to
Abraham.
   17.1–27 The covenant with Abraham is the second
of the great covenants in the P source, after the covenant with Noah (9.8–17; see note on 6.18). Here the
covenantal focus narrows from all creatures to the patriarchal line from which Israel will come. The Abrahamic covenant includes the promises of land, abundant offspring, and a great nation, and its visible sign is
circumcision (cf. the rainbow; see note on 9.8–17). In
some respects the P covenant with Abraham is parallel
to the J promises to Abram (12.1–3, 7) and to the covenant with Abram in ch. 15 (source unknown). 17.1–
2 Ninety-nine years old. Abram's advanced age pro-

vides a backdrop for his incredulous reaction to God's
promise of a son to him and Sarah in v. 17. El Shaddai
probably means "God, the Mountain One," referring
to his dwelling place on a holy mountain (for
Horeb/Sinai, see Ex 3.1; 19; for Zion, see Ps 48). God's
revelation of this name to Abraham will be superseded
by his revelation of the name Yahweh to Moses in the
next covenant (Ex 6.3; see note on 6.18). Walk before
me, and be blameless. The Abrahamic covenant is conditioned on Abraham's virtue. 17.3–8 Abram's name
change to Abraham is part of his passage to a new
covenantal identity, as is Sarai's name change in v. 15.
God explains that Abraham means ancestor (lit. "father") of a multitude, which creatively links Abraham
(a dialectal variant of Abram) to the Hebrew words for
"father" ('ab), and "multitude" (hamon). The promise
to make Abraham exceedingly fruitful (v. 6) recalls the
blessing to Noah (9.1, 7) and the first humans (1.28).
The nations and kings descended from Abraham include the dynasties of Israel, Ishmael, and Edom (for
the kings of Edom, see 36.31–39). Although the Abrahamic covenant is conditioned on Abraham's virtue, it
is an everlasting covenant (v. 7), and the promised land
will be a perpetual holding (v. 8). In the historical context of the P source, which may have included the
Babylonian exile, this is an expression of great trust
and hope. 17.9–14 Circumcision is the sign of the covenant (v. 11; cf. the rainbow in 9.12, 17 and the sabbath
in Ex 31.12–17). This symbolic mark of the male
member is probably related to the blessing to be ex-

cumcised when he is eight days old, including the slave born in your house and the one bought with your money from any foreigner who is not of your offspring. 13 Both the slave born in your house and the one bought with your money must be circumcised. So shall my covenant be in your flesh an everlasting covenant. 14 Any uncircumcised male who is not circumcised in the flesh of his foreskin shall be cut off from his people; he has broken my covenant."

15 God said to Abraham, "As for Sarai your wife, you shall not call her Sarai, but Sarah shall be her name. 16 I will bless her, and moreover I will give you a son by her. I will bless her, and she shall give rise to nations; kings of peoples shall come from her." 17 Then Abraham fell on his face and laughed, and said to himself, "Can a child be born to a man who is a hundred years old? Can Sarah, who is ninety years old, bear a child?" 18 And Abraham said to God, "O that Ishmael might live in your sight!" 19 God said, "No, but your wife Sarah shall bear you a son, and you shall name him Isaac.*ᵃ* I will establish my covenant with him as an everlasting covenant for his offspring after him. 20 As for Ishmael, I have heard you; I will bless him and make him fruitful and exceedingly numerous; he shall be the father of twelve princes, and I will make him a great nation. 21 But my covenant I will establish with Isaac, whom Sarah shall bear to you at this season next year." 22 And when he had finished talking with him, God went up from Abraham.

23 Then Abraham took his son Ishmael and all the slaves born in his house or bought with his money, every male among the men of Abraham's house, and he circumcised the flesh of their foreskins that very day, as God had said to him. 24 Abraham was ninety-nine years old when he was circumcised in the flesh of his foreskin. 25 And his son Ishmael was thirteen years old when he was circumcised in the flesh of his foreskin. 26 That very day Abraham and his son Ishmael were circumcised; 27 and all the men of his house, slaves born in the house and those bought with money from a foreigner, were circumcised with him.

A Son Promised to Abraham and Sarah

18 The Lᴏʀᴅ appeared to Abraham*ᵇ* by the oaks*ᶜ* of Mamre, as he sat at the entrance of his tent in the heat of the day. 2 He looked up and saw three men standing near him. When he saw them, he ran from the tent entrance to meet them, and bowed down to the ground. 3 He said, "My lord, if I find favor with you, do not pass by your servant. 4 Let a little water be brought, and wash your feet, and rest yourselves under the tree. 5 Let me bring a little bread, that you may refresh yourselves, and after that you may pass on—since you have come to your servant." So they said, "Do as you have said." 6 And Abraham hastened into the tent to Sarah, and said, "Make ready quickly three measures*ᵈ* of choice flour,

---

a That is *he laughs*   *b* Heb *him*   *c* Or *terebinths*   *d* Heb *seahs*

---

ceedingly fruitful in v. 6 and functions as a male rite of passage into the covenant. In a patriarchal and patrilineal society such as ancient Israel, this sign covers each household, including women. *Eight days old.* The timing of the ceremony allows for the mother's presence, for she is now ritually clean (Lev 12.2–3). **17.15–22** Sarai's name change signals her new destiny as the mother of the promised child and as the mother of kings. *Sarah,* a dialectal variant of *Sarai,* means "princess." *Ninety years old* (v. 17). Her advanced age highlights the miracle of this promise. Abraham uncharacteristically *laughed* at this promise, which provides the motive for the child's name, *Isaac,* which means "he laughed." In the J version of the promise of the child, it is Sarah who laughs (18.12). Abraham understandably assumes that God is referring to Ishmael as his heir, but God clarifies that Isaac will be the heir of the covenant. Because of Abraham's concern, God grants Ishmael his own patriarchal blessing: abundant offspring, *twelve princes* (v. 20; see 25.12–16), and a great nation. **18.1–15** The J version of the divine announcement

that Sarah will bear Abraham's child (cf. the P version in ch. 17). It is a turning point in the narrative, solving the problem of Sarah's barrenness and Abraham's need for an heir. The story also highlights Abraham's virtue and hospitality, providing a foil for the story of Lot and the angels in ch. 19. **18.1–3** In v. 1 *the* Lᴏʀᴅ *appeared to Abraham,* but in v. 2 Abraham *looked up and saw three men.* This initial ambiguity is resolved as we understand later that God is accompanied by two angels (e.g., 19.1). The point here is that Abraham thinks they are men, while we know otherwise. This dual perspective on the identity of the visitors is also sounded in v. 3, where Abraham addresses them as *My lord,* which in the Hebrew is the plural form ("lords"), also the standard form for addressing God. **18.3–8** *Ran* (vv. 2, 7), *hastened* (vv. 6–7), indications of Abraham's great hospitality and generosity toward the strangers. *A little water, a little bread.* Abraham's humble offer turns into a magnificent feast: *cakes* of *choice flour* rather than bread, *curds and milk* rather than water, and *a calf, tender and good* (vv. 6–8). Finally, he honors the strangers by standing while they eat (v. 8).

knead it, and make cakes." 7Abraham ran to the herd, and took a calf, tender and good, and gave it to the servant, who hastened to prepare it. 8Then he took curds and milk and the calf that he had prepared, and set it before them; and he stood by them under the tree while they ate.

9 They said to him, "Where is your wife Sarah?" And he said, "There, in the tent." 10Then one said, "I will surely return to you in due season, and your wife Sarah shall have a son." And Sarah was listening at the tent entrance behind him. 11Now Abraham and Sarah were old, advanced in age; it had ceased to be with Sarah after the manner of women. 12So Sarah laughed to herself, saying, "After I have grown old, and my husband is old, shall I have pleasure?" 13The LORD said to Abraham, "Why did Sarah laugh, and say, 'Shall I indeed bear a child, now that I am old?' 14Is anything too wonderful for the LORD? At the set time I will return to you, in due season, and Sarah shall have a son." 15But Sarah denied, saying, "I did not laugh"; for she was afraid. He said, "Oh yes, you did laugh."

Judgment Pronounced on Sodom

16 Then the men set out from there, and they looked toward Sodom; and Abraham went with them to set them on their way. 17The LORD said, "Shall I hide from Abraham what I am about to do, 18seeing that Abraham shall become a great and mighty nation, and all the nations of the earth shall be blessed in him?ª 19No, for I have chosenᵇ him, that he may charge his children and his household after him to keep the way of the LORD by doing righteousness and justice; so that the LORD may bring about for Abraham what he has promised him." 20Then the LORD said, "How great is the outcry against Sodom and Gomorrah and how very grave their sin! 21I must go down and see whether they have done altogether according to the outcry that has come to me; and if not, I will know."

22 So the men turned from there, and went toward Sodom, while Abraham remained standing before the LORD.ᶜ 23Then Abraham came near and said, "Will you indeed sweep away the righteous with the wicked? 24Suppose there are fifty righteous within the city; will you then sweep away the place and not forgive it for the fifty righteous who are in it? 25Far be it from you to do such a thing, to slay the righteous with the wicked, so that the righteous fare as the wicked! Far be that from you! Shall not the Judge of all the earth do what is just?" 26And the LORD said, "If I find at Sodom fifty righteous in the city, I will forgive the whole place for their sake." 27Abraham answered, "Let me take it upon myself to speak to

a Or and all the nations of the earth shall bless themselves by him
b Heb known   c Another ancient tradition reads while the LORD remained standing before Abraham

---

18.9–15 God's announcement that Sarah will *have a son* is followed by the scene of Sarah's laughter and God's response (cf. Abraham's laughter in 17.17). The repetition of *laugh(ed)* (four times, vv. 12, 13, 15) motivates the name of Isaac (from the root "to laugh"). This is itself a comical scene, as Sarah is listening in on the conversation between Abraham and his guests and doesn't realize that God is also listening in on her. Her denial of the possibility of postmenopausal *pleasure* (v. 12; better "fruitfulness, abundance," i.e., pregnancy) is met by God's affirmation of his wondrous powers, which signals that this will be a miraculous birth. God also shows great tact, omitting Sarah's remark *my husband is old* (v. 12) when he repeats her words to Abraham. Sarah's denial of her laughter is met by God's denial of her denial, which is both dramatic and humorous. **18.16–33** From the J source, the dispute over the fate of Sodom shows the great moral virtue of Abraham and affirms God's choice of him as Israel's patriarch. Interestingly, God also shows himself to be amenable to moral instruction. Abraham's greatness consists of being willing to contend with God about moral principles, and, remarkably, he prevails (contrast the book of Job). In some respects this scene is God's test of Abraham, which Abraham passes magnificently. **18.17–21** God's inner monologue announces the theme of *doing righteousness and justice* (v. 19), which is Abraham's task as the chosen patriarch and which Abraham must teach his descendants. The investigation and punishment of Sodom and Gomorrah also concerns this issue; hence God decides to confide in Abraham. *Outcry* (v. 20), a call for justice. The appropriate punishment for the cities' injustice is not stated, but Abraham assumes that it is destruction of the cities (as the angels state in 19.13). God is deliberately silent about his plan, since he wants to see what Abraham has to say. **18.22–33** While the angels go off to investigate, Abraham stands alone with God and has the courage to speak. With great diplomacy and humility, he argues that God must be just (v. 23), and even more that God must be merciful (v. 24). When God grants Abraham's plea (v. 26), Abraham presses his advantage and in a remarkable rhetorical exchange talks God down from fifty righteous to ten (v. 32). There is an element of humor in the Middle Eastern custom of haggling, here not over the price of goods, but the proper balance of justice and mercy and the fate of Sodom. As it happens, Abraham prevails in es-

the Lord, I who am but dust and ashes. 28Suppose five of the fifty righteous are lacking? Will you destroy the whole city for lack of five?" And he said, "I will not destroy it if I find forty-five there." 29Again he spoke to him, "Suppose forty are found there." He answered, "For the sake of forty I will not do it." 30Then he said, "Oh do not let the Lord be angry if I speak. Suppose thirty are found there." He answered, "I will not do it, if I find thirty there." 31He said, "Let me take it upon myself to speak to the Lord. Suppose twenty are found there." He answered, "For the sake of twenty I will not destroy it." 32Then he said, "Oh do not let the Lord be angry if I speak just once more. Suppose ten are found there." He answered, "For the sake of ten I will not destroy it." 33And the LORD went his way, when he had finished speaking to Abraham; and Abraham returned to his place.

The Depravity of Sodom

19 The two angels came to Sodom in the evening, and Lot was sitting in the gateway of Sodom. When Lot saw them, he rose to meet them, and bowed down with his face to the ground. 2He said, "Please, my lords, turn aside to your servant's house and spend the night, and wash your feet; then you can rise early and go on your way." They said, "No; we will spend the night in the square." 3But he urged them strongly; so they turned aside to him and entered his house; and he made them a feast, and baked unleavened bread, and they ate. 4But before they lay down, the men of the city, the men of Sodom, both young and old, all the people to the last man, surrounded the house; 5and they called to Lot, "Where are the men who came to you tonight? Bring them out to us, so that we may know them." 6Lot went out of the door to the men, shut the door after him, 7and said, "I beg you, my brothers, do not act so wickedly. 8Look, I have two daughters who have not known a man; let me bring them out to you, and do to them as you please; only do nothing to these men, for they have come under the shelter of my roof." 9But they replied, "Stand back!" And they said, "This fellow came here as an alien, and he would play the judge! Now we will deal worse with you than with them." Then they pressed hard against the man Lot, and came near the door to break it down. 10But the men inside reached out their hands and brought Lot into the house with them, and shut the door. 11And they struck with blindness the men who were at the door of the house, both small and great, so that they were unable to find the door.

Sodom and Gomorrah Destroyed

12 Then the men said to Lot, "Have you anyone else here? Sons-in-law, sons, daughters, or

---

tablishing the right moral principle, but God still destroys the cities, since of all its inhabitants only Lot and his immediate family are not wicked.

19.1–38 The story of the destruction of Sodom and Gomorrah (mainly J, with a P coda in v. 29) has three sections: the angel's investigation of the wickedness of Sodom and the righteousness of Lot (vv. 1–11); the escape of Lot's family and the destruction of the cities (vv. 12–29); and the birth of Lot's sons (vv. 30–38). In each part Lot's righteousness with respect to the men of Sodom is tempered by his moral weakness with respect to Abraham, a theme that resumes from ch. 13. This situation justifies Lot's deliverance from destruction and his lesser genealogical position as the (somewhat scandalous) ancestor of Moab and Ammon. **19.1–3** Lot's hospitality to the strangers, although genuine, is not as gracious as Abraham's in the previous chapter (18.1–8). Whereas Abraham *ran . . . to meet them,* Lot *rose to meet them.* Whereas Abraham served *cakes* of *choice flour,* Lot served *unleavened bread.* Whereas Abraham *stood by them . . . while they ate,* at Lot's feast they ate together: *and they ate.* These are subtle denigrations of Lot by comparison with Abraham. **19.4–5** The wickedness of Sodom consists of the shameful behavior of the men toward strangers.

Rather than exhibiting hospitality and protection, as does Lot, the men of the city seek to sexually assault them (v. 5). Homosexual rape is a strategy of humiliation. This shameful behavior toward the strangers is exhibited by all the men of the city (v. 4). There are no innocents among them, in contrast to Lot. **19.6–8** Lot's response is to maintain his honor as host by protecting the strangers and to offer his virgin daughters as surrogate victims for the men's sexual assault. His response shows that the men's wickedness is not homosexuality as such, since the daughters are offered as suitable surrogates; their wickedness is sexual violence (gang rape) as the inverse of hospitality and protection. Lot's offer of his daughters for gang rape is, however, also immoral and impugns his honor as a father. He later pays the price for this shameful offer when his daughters serially rape him (vv. 31–36). **19.9–11** The wicked men threaten to sexually assault Lot (v. 9), though it is unclear whether sexual assault or murder is intended. The angels now extend their protection to Lot, rescuing him and blinding the wicked men in return for his attempt to protect them. **19.12–23** Lot is ineffectual and rather comic as he fails to convince his prospective sons-in-law to flee (v. 14). He hesitates to leave himself, so that the angels seize him

anyone you have in the city—bring them out of the place. [13] For we are about to destroy this place, because the outcry against its people has become great before the LORD, and the LORD has sent us to destroy it." [14] So Lot went out and said to his sons-in-law, who were to marry his daughters, "Up, get out of this place; for the LORD is about to destroy the city." But he seemed to his sons-in-law to be jesting.

15 When morning dawned, the angels urged Lot, saying, "Get up, take your wife and your two daughters who are here, or else you will be consumed in the punishment of the city." [16] But he lingered; so the men seized him and his wife and his two daughters by the hand, the LORD being merciful to him, and they brought him out and left him outside the city. [17] When they had brought them outside, they[a] said, "Flee for your life; do not look back or stop anywhere in the Plain; flee to the hills, or else you will be consumed." [18] And Lot said to them, "Oh, no, my lords; [19] your servant has found favor with you, and you have shown me great kindness in saving my life; but I cannot flee to the hills, for fear the disaster will overtake me and I die. [20] Look, that city is near enough to flee to, and it is a little one. Let me escape there—is it not a little one?—and my life will be saved!" [21] He said to him, "Very well, I grant you this favor too, and will not overthrow the city of which you have spoken. [22] Hurry, escape there, for I can do nothing until you arrive there." Therefore the city was called Zoar.[b] [23] The sun had risen on the earth when Lot came to Zoar.

24 Then the LORD rained on Sodom and Gomorrah sulfur and fire from the LORD out of heaven; [25] and he overthrew those cities, and all the Plain, and all the inhabitants of the cities, and what grew on the ground. [26] But Lot's wife, behind him, looked back, and she became a pillar of salt.

27 Abraham went early in the morning to the place where he had stood before the LORD; [28] and he looked down toward Sodom and Gomorrah and toward all the land of the Plain and saw the smoke of the land going up like the smoke of a furnace.

29 So it was that, when God destroyed the cities of the Plain, God remembered Abraham, and sent Lot out of the midst of the overthrow, when he overthrew the cities in which Lot had settled.

The Shameful Origin of Moab and Ammon

30 Now Lot went up out of Zoar and settled in the hills with his two daughters, for he was afraid to stay in Zoar; so he lived in a cave with his two daughters. [31] And the firstborn said to the younger, "Our father is old, and there is not a man on earth to come in to us after the manner of all the world. [32] Come, let us make our father drink wine, and we will lie with him, so that we may preserve offspring through our father." [33] So they made their father drink wine that night; and the firstborn

a Gk Syr Vg: Heb *he*   b That is *Little*

---

and his family and drag them out of the city (v. 16). He also resists the angels' instructions to flee to the hills and pleads for a closer refuge, the little city of *Zoar* (which means "little," vv. 20, 22). Though Lot is a buffoon, his wife is even worse off, for she cannot resist a peek at the cities' destruction in spite of the angels' command *not to look back*. For this tragic flaw, she becomes a part of the landscape of the Dead Sea region, *a pillar of salt* (v. 26). This brief notice accounts for a particularly strange geological formation, which in turn serves as a memorial for Lot's wife and a visual sign of the story. **19.27–29** The scene shifts to Abraham's perspective on the hills above the plain, recalling Abraham's effort to save the city on behalf of its innocents. In v. 29, a P coda to the J story, the scene shifts to God's perspective. Because *God remembered Abraham*, he saved Lot in the midst of destruction, clarifying the larger picture of what happened. **19.30–38** The aftermath of the great destruction, with the story of Lot and his two daughters, thematically echoes the aftermath of the flood, with the story of Noah

and his three sons (9.18–27). In both the father becomes drunk and is the object of (sexual?) transgression by his offspring, resulting in a shameful ancestry for Israel's neighbors (Canaan, Moab, and Ammon). These are ethnographic stories that cast aspersions on Israel's cultural rivals while acknowledging a kinship between them. Lot's daughters are well-intentioned, aiming to engender *offspring through* their *father,* since they think there are no men left to impregnate them (v. 32). Their justification for engaging in sex with their father happens to be wrong, since only the cities of the plain were destroyed, but they do not know this. Lot is also relatively innocent, since he is drunk and unconscious during the sexual act (v. 35). Nonetheless, he is culpable for having offered his daughters previously for gang rape, and now he receives poetic justice, measure for measure, as his daughters rape him. The offspring of Lot and his daughters have names that betray their shameful origins: *Moab* is a play on *me'ab,* "from the father," and *Ben-ammi* means "son of my kinsman" (vv. 37–38).

went in, and lay with her father; he did not know when she lay down or when she rose. 34On the next day, the firstborn said to the younger, "Look, I lay last night with my father; let us make him drink wine tonight also; then you go in and lie with him, so that we may preserve offspring through our father." 35So they made their father drink wine that night also; and the younger rose, and lay with him; and he did not know when she lay down or when she rose. 36Thus both the daughters of Lot became pregnant by their father. 37The firstborn bore a son, and named him Moab; he is the ancestor of the Moabites to this day. 38The younger also bore a son and named him Ben-ammi; he is the ancestor of the Ammonites to this day.

Abraham and Sarah at Gerar

20 From there Abraham journeyed toward the region of the Negeb, and settled between Kadesh and Shur. While residing in Gerar as an alien, 2Abraham said of his wife Sarah, "She is my sister." And King Abimelech of Gerar sent and took Sarah. 3But God came to Abimelech in a dream by night, and said to him, "You are about to die because of the woman whom you have taken; for she is a married woman." 4Now Abimelech had not approached her; so he said, "Lord, will you destroy an innocent people? 5Did he not himself say to me, 'She is my sister'? And she herself said, 'He is my brother.' I did this in the integrity of my heart and the innocence of my hands." 6Then God said to him in the dream,

"Yes, I know that you did this in the integrity of your heart; furthermore it was I who kept you from sinning against me. Therefore I did not let you touch her. 7Now then, return the man's wife; for he is a prophet, and he will pray for you and you shall live. But if you do not restore her, know that you shall surely die, you and all that are yours."

8 So Abimelech rose early in the morning, and called all his servants and told them all these things; and the men were very much afraid. 9Then Abimelech called Abraham, and said to him, "What have you done to us? How have I sinned against you, that you have brought such great guilt on me and my kingdom? You have done things to me that ought not to be done." 10And Abimelech said to Abraham, "What were you thinking of, that you did this thing?" 11Abraham said, "I did it because I thought, There is no fear of God at all in this place, and they will kill me because of my wife. 12Besides, she is indeed my sister, the daughter of my father but not the daughter of my mother; and she became my wife. 13And when God caused me to wander from my father's house, I said to her, 'This is the kindness you must do me: at every place to which we come, say of me, He is my brother.' " 14Then Abimelech took sheep and oxen, and male and female slaves, and gave them to Abraham, and restored his wife Sarah to him. 15Abimelech said, "My land is before you; settle where it pleases you." 16To Sarah he said, "Look, I have given your brother a thousand

---

20.1–18 The first continuous story from the E source, a version of the matriarch in danger. As in the J version in (see note on) 12.10–20, the couple are Abraham and Sarah, and as in the J story in 26.6–11, the couple journey to Gerar, ruled by King Abimelech. In each story, the patriarch attempts to save his life by claiming that his beautiful wife is really his sister. The E version interposes God's presence throughout the story and maintains Abraham's and Sarah's virtue. As in the other versions, the foreign king is noble and resents Abraham's ruse. Here Abraham's piety justifies his actions, and God is firmly in control. Note that in the other sources Sarah is already an old woman (17.17, P; 18.12, J), but in this chapter she is still beautiful and desirable. **20.3–7** God reveals himself in a dream (v. 3; cf. 28.12), threatens Abimelech with death if he does not return Abraham's wife, and reveals that he has been monitoring and controlling events (v. 6). God has maintained Sarah's virtue and Abimelech's innocence. God further reveals that Abraham is a prophet, with the power of intercessory prayer (v. 7).

The reason for his prophetic prayer is delayed until v. 17, where we are told retrospectively that God had afflicted Abimelech and his household. **20.8–10** Abimelech eloquently upbraids Abraham (cf. 12.18–19; 26.10), showing himself to be a righteous man in spite of Abraham's fears (v. 11). Abraham is initially silent and only replies after Abimelech's second speech. Things . . . that ought not to be done, later applied to the rape of Dinah (34.7). **20.11–13** Abraham maintains his integrity by comparable eloquence, justifying his actions by his pious expectation (v. 11). Moreover, he covers his ruse by explaining that it was not a lie: she is indeed his sister because they are related (v. 12). His conduct toward Sarah was also respectful (v. 13). **20.14–18** Abimelech responds to Abraham's eloquent speech by restoring Sarah, enriching Abraham, inviting him to settle in his land, and paying restitution. In turn, Abraham prays for God to heal Abimelech and his house, fulfilling his role as prophet (v. 7). God's healing allows them to have children, suggesting retrospectively that Abimelech had been afflicted with im-

pieces of silver; it is your exoneration before all who are with you; you are completely vindicated." 17Then Abraham prayed to God; and God healed Abimelech, and also healed his wife and female slaves so that they bore children. 18For the LORD had closed fast all the wombs of the house of Abimelech because of Sarah, Abraham's wife.

The Birth of Isaac

21 The LORD dealt with Sarah as he had said, and the LORD did for Sarah as he had promised. 2Sarah conceived and bore Abraham a son in his old age, at the time of which God had spoken to him. 3Abraham gave the name Isaac to his son whom Sarah bore him. 4And Abraham circumcised his son Isaac when he was eight days old, as God had commanded him. 5Abraham was a hundred years old when his son Isaac was born to him. 6Now Sarah said, "God has brought laughter for me; everyone who hears will laugh with me." 7And she said, "Who would ever have said to Abraham that Sarah would nurse children? Yet I have borne him a son in his old age."

Hagar and Ishmael Sent Away

8 The child grew, and was weaned; and Abraham made a great feast on the day that Isaac was weaned. 9But Sarah saw the son of Hagar the Egyptian, whom she had borne to Abraham, playing with her son Isaac.ᵃ 10So she said

to Abraham, "Cast out this slave woman with her son; for the son of this slave woman shall not inherit along with my son Isaac." 11The matter was very distressing to Abraham on account of his son. 12But God said to Abraham, "Do not be distressed because of the boy and because of your slave woman; whatever Sarah says to you, do as she tells you, for it is through Isaac that offspring shall be named for you. 13As for the son of the slave woman, I will make a nation of him also, because he is your offspring." 14So Abraham rose early in the morning, and took bread and a skin of water, and gave it to Hagar, putting it on her shoulder, along with the child, and sent her away. And she departed, and wandered about in the wilderness of Beer-sheba.

15 When the water in the skin was gone, she cast the child under one of the bushes. 16Then she went and sat down opposite him a good way off, about the distance of a bowshot; for she said, "Do not let me look on the death of the child." And as she sat opposite him, she lifted up her voice and wept. 17And God heard the voice of the boy; and the angel of God called to Hagar from heaven, and said to her, "What troubles you, Hagar? Do not be afraid; for God has heard the voice of the boy where he is. 18Come, lift up the boy and hold him fast with your hand, for I will make a great nation

---

a Gk Vg: Heb lacks *with her son Isaac*

---

potence (tactfully described by God in v. 6). V. 18 is a gloss that clarifies the women's affliction and its connection to Sarah's abduction.

21.1–7 The birth of Isaac is a turning point in the Abraham narrative, a first step in the fulfillment of the patriarchal promises. This section is an amalgam of J (vv. 1a, 2a), P (vv. 1b, 2b–5), and E (vv. 6–7). The P section emphasizes the child's circumcision (see 17.12), and the E section highlights Sarah's surprise and the theme word *laughter,* for Isaac's name means "laughter, play."

21.8–21 The story of the expulsion of Hagar is the E counterpart to the J story in ch. 16. In both, Sarah's wrath is kindled against Hagar, who flees or is expelled and is then met by an angel, who grants a patriarchal promise to her child. In this story, Abraham's virtue is maintained in spite of his acquiescence in Sarah's treatment of Hagar (cf. the E portrait of Abraham in ch. 20). In this story, as in ch. 16, Hagar and Ishmael are portrayed as sympathetic figures, ancestors of the Arab tribes of the Sinai and Arabian deserts. Note that in P Ishmael is already a teenager (17.25), but in this story he is still a child (see vv. 14–15). **21.8–10** On the day when Isaac is ceremonially separated from his

mother's breast, Sarah sees Ishmael *playing* (or perhaps better "laughing"), which is the theme word of Isaac's name (see v. 6). Sarah identifies Ishmael not by his proper name, but as *the son of Hagar the Egyptian, whom she had borne to Abraham.* Her perception of this child "Isaac-ing" on the day of Isaac's weaning brings forth her rage and fear that this child will supplant Isaac, and she seeks Abraham's permission to expel them. **21.11–14** In contrast to ch. 16, where Sarai was the dominant figure and Abram merely obedient, here the matter is *very distressing* to Abraham (v. 11), and God intervenes to give him counsel. God reveals that Abraham's promised seed will come *through Isaac* (v. 12), though both sons will become nations. By this, God promises that Ishmael will survive the expulsion. Abraham's wordless provisioning of Hagar (v. 14) anticipates the description of his own journey with Isaac in 22.3, both journeys that seem to be death marches for his sons. Note that Ishmael is a small child, riding on his mother's shoulder. **21.15–21** Hagar's grief at the impending death of her child is finely drawn. Her desire not to *look on* her child's death and her sitting away from him *about the distance of a bowshot* (v. 16) are turned about when *God opened*

of him." 19Then God opened her eyes and she saw a well of water. She went, and filled the skin with water, and gave the boy a drink.

20 God was with the boy, and he grew up; he lived in the wilderness, and became an expert with the bow. 21He lived in the wilderness of Paran; and his mother got a wife for him from the land of Egypt.

Abraham and Abimelech Make a Covenant

22 At that time Abimelech, with Phicol the commander of his army, said to Abraham, "God is with you in all that you do; 23now therefore swear to me here by God that you will not deal falsely with me or with my offspring or with my posterity, but as I have dealt loyally with you, you will deal with me and with the land where you have resided as an alien." 24And Abraham said, "I swear it."

25 When Abraham complained to Abimelech about a well of water that Abimelech's servants had seized, 26Abimelech said, "I do not know who has done this; you did not tell me, and I have not heard of it until today." 27So Abraham took sheep and oxen and gave them to Abimelech, and the two men made a

covenant. 28Abraham set apart seven ewe lambs of the flock. 29And Abimelech said to Abraham, "What is the meaning of these seven ewe lambs that you have set apart?" 30He said, "These seven ewe lambs you shall accept from my hand, in order that you may be a witness for me that I dug this well." 31Therefore that place was called Beer-sheba;*a* because there both of them swore an oath. 32When they had made a covenant at Beer-sheba, Abimelech, with Phicol the commander of his army, left and returned to the land of the Philistines. 33Abraham*b* planted a tamarisk tree in Beer-sheba, and called there on the name of the LORD, the Everlasting God.*c* 34And Abraham resided as an alien many days in the land of the Philistines.

The Command to Sacrifice Isaac

22 After these things God tested Abraham. He said to him, "Abraham!" And he said, "Here I am." 2He said, "Take your son, your only son Isaac, whom you love, and go to the land of Moriah, and offer him there as a

---

a That is *Well of seven* or *Well of the oath* *b* Heb *He* *c* Or *the* LORD, *El Olam*

---

her eyes and she saw a well of water (v. 19) and the child becomes an expert with the bow (v. 20). Further, her loud weeping (v. 16) is met, with a shift to Ishmael's voice, when God heard the voice of the boy (v. 17). God's response also fulfills Ishmael's name, which means "God has heard." The moment when the angel of God called to Hagar from heaven echoes the parallel moment in the next story (22.11), saving the life of Isaac. God's promise to make a great nation of Ishmael (v. 18) echoes the promise to Abraham (12.2). In all of these echoes, Ishmael is truly Abraham's son, even though his descendants are a different nation. **21.22–34** The E story (with perhaps some admixture of J) of the founding of Beer-sheba (cf. the J story of Isaac in 26.12–33). Abraham, a resident alien in the rural hinterlands ruled by Gerar (see 20.15), prospers since God is with him in all that he does (v. 22). A dispute over ownership of a well is resolved by a covenant with King Abimelech, in which Abraham exchanges livestock for rights to the well. The oath and the seven ewe lambs are linked to the name of Beer-sheba, which means "well of the seven" or "well of the oath." This story affirms Israel's ancient rights to the land. **21.33–34** Abraham plants a tamarisk tree to mark the sacred place where he called . . . on the name of the LORD. Sacred trees often mark local Israelite shrines, e.g., the oak of Moreh at Shechem, where Abraham builds an altar (12.6–7). The Everlasting God (El Olam), probably an old epithet of the Canaanite high god El here applied to

Yahweh. Cf. the other El epithets in the Abraham narrative: El Elyon (14.22), El-roi (16.13), El Shaddai (17.1).

22.1–19 The story of the near sacrifice of Isaac shows Abraham's astonishing faith and obedience to God, which are his great virtues in this E story. (Cf. his virtue of arguing with God over moral principles in 18.16–33, from the J source.) The practice of child sacrifice is known from the West Semitic world, usually occurring only in times of crisis (see 2 Kings 3.27). All firstborn sons belong to God (see Ex 22.29), but they may be redeemed by offering a sheep (Ex 34.20), as ultimately happens in this story (v. 13). Abraham's willingness to sacrifice his son is conceivable in this context but still requires an absolutely unconditional trust in God's word. The enormity of this trust is emphasized by the diction of the story, in which the key words father and son echo prominently, and by its placement immediately after the banishment of Ishmael, leaving no heir other than Isaac. **22.1** God tested Abraham. This provides an interpretive frame for the story, with the command as a test of Abraham's trust in God rather than an actual killing. (Cf. the test of Job's trust in God in Job 1–2.) "Abraham!" "Here I am." This initial dialogue is repeated with rising tension in v. 7 (with Isaac) and v. 11 (with the angel). **22.2** An ascending sequence that moves from the general (your son) to the particular (your only son Isaac) to the emotional (whom you love) has an intensifying effect. Isaac is Abraham's only son now that Ishmael is gone, and the

burnt offering on one of the mountains that I shall show you." ³So Abraham rose early in the morning, saddled his donkey, and took two of his young men with him, and his son Isaac; he cut the wood for the burnt offering, and set out and went to the place in the distance that God had shown him. ⁴On the third day Abraham looked up and saw the place far away. ⁵Then Abraham said to his young men, "Stay here with the donkey; the boy and I will go over there; we will worship, and then we will come back to you." ⁶Abraham took the wood of the burnt offering and laid it on his son Isaac, and he himself carried the fire and the knife. So the two of them walked on together. ⁷Isaac said to his father Abraham, "Father!" And he said, "Here I am, my son." He said, "The fire and the wood are here, but where is the lamb for a burnt offering?" ⁸Abraham said, "God himself will provide the lamb for a burnt offering, my son." So the two of them walked on together.

9 When they came to the place that God had shown him, Abraham built an altar there and laid the wood in order. He bound his son Isaac, and laid him on the altar, on top of the wood. ¹⁰Then Abraham reached out his hand and took the knife to kill*ᵃ* his son. ¹¹But the angel of the LORD called to him from heaven, and said, "Abraham, Abraham!" And he said, "Here I am." ¹²He said, "Do not lay your hand on the boy or do anything to him; for now I know that you fear God, since you have not withheld your son, your only son, from me." ¹³And Abraham looked up and saw a ram, caught in a thicket by its horns. Abraham went and took the ram and offered it up as a burnt offering instead of his son. ¹⁴So Abraham called that place "The LORD will provide";ᵇ as it is said to this day, "On the mount of the LORD it shall be provided."ᶜ

15 The angel of the LORD called to Abraham a second time from heaven, ¹⁶and said, "By myself I have sworn, says the LORD: Because you have done this, and have not withheld your son, your only son, ¹⁷I will indeed bless you, and I will make your offspring as numerous as the stars of heaven and as the sand that is on the seashore. And your offspring shall possess the gate of their enemies, ¹⁸and by your offspring shall all the nations of the earth gain blessing for themselves, because you have obeyed my voice." ¹⁹So Abraham returned to his young men, and they arose and went together to Beer-sheba; and Abraham lived at Beer-sheba.

The Children of Nahor

20 Now after these things it was told Abraham, "Milcah also has borne children, to your

---

a Or *to slaughter*   *b* Or *will see;* Heb traditionally transliterated *Jehovah Jireh*   *c* Or *he shall be seen*

---

promise depends on him. But Abraham's love for his son is more important still. Note how the diction evokes Abraham's interior life without describing it explicitly. The mountain in the *land of Moriah,* later identified as the Temple Mount in Jerusalem (2 Chr 3.1). Land *that I shall show you,* an echo of the call of Abraham in 12.1. **22.5** *We will worship, and . . . come back to you.* Abraham's words seem to be deceptive speech masking his plan to sacrifice Isaac, yet his words come true. There is irony in the equivalence between Abraham's attempt at concealment and what comes to pass. This points to the complex relations between human plans and God's plan (cf. 50.20) and makes Abraham an unself-conscious prophet (cf. 20.7). **22.6–8** *The two . . . walked on together* (v. 6, repeated in v. 8). The focus narrows to the father and son. The sole dialogue between the two repeats the words *father* and *my son* (twice each), subtly expressing their emotional bond. Isaac's innocent question receives Abraham's ambiguous answer that *God himself will provide the lamb.* As with Abraham's words in v. 5, these words spoken as an apparent attempt to shield Isaac from the truth in fact come true. **22.9–10** The action slows to show each of Abraham's actions as he carefully prepares to sacrifice his son. The clinical precision of the details is heartrending and builds tremendous suspense. Abraham's first action leads to the traditional Jewish designation of the passage as the Aqedah, or Binding of Isaac. **22.11–14** The last-second intervention of the angel saves the day and confirms that Abraham has passed the test. To *fear God* (v. 12) implies obedience, piety, and righteousness (cf. 20.11; Ex 1.21). The *ram* is lexically a type of sheep or lamb, fulfilling Abraham's words in v. 8 and motivating the name of the place, *the LORD will provide* (which is also a play on the name *Moriah,* v. 2). *The mount of the LORD* either implies or is later understood as a reference to the Temple Mount in Jerusalem (see note on 22.2). In Heb 11.17–19 the episode is used as a testimony to belief in resurrection. **22.15–19** The second speech of the angel, probably an editorial addition to the E story, reconfirms the patriarchal promises to Abraham in elaborate form (cf. 12.2; 13.16; 15.5). *Abraham returned* (v. 19), without mention of Isaac, turns the focus back to Abraham, as in the story's beginning (v. 1). **22.20–24** In this J addition, Abraham's brother, Nahor (11.27), is father to twelve sons, eight from his wife and four from his concubine. The number of his sons echoes the number of Ishmael's (25.13–16) and, more important, Jacob's. Nahor's sons are

brother Nahor: 21Uz the firstborn, Buz his brother, Kemuel the father of Aram, 22Chesed, Hazo, Pildash, Jidlaph, and Bethuel." 23Bethuel became the father of Rebekah. These eight Milcah bore to Nahor, Abraham's brother. 24Moreover, his concubine, whose name was Reumah, bore Tebah, Gaham, Tahash, and Maacah.

Sarah's Death and Burial

23 Sarah lived one hundred twenty-seven years; this was the length of Sarah's life. 2And Sarah died at Kiriath-arba (that is, Hebron) in the land of Canaan; and Abraham went in to mourn for Sarah and to weep for her. 3Abraham rose up from beside his dead, and said to the Hittites, 4"I am a stranger and an alien residing among you; give me property among you for a burying place, so that I may bury my dead out of my sight." 5The Hittites answered Abraham, 6"Hear us, my lord; you are a mighty prince among us. Bury your dead in the choicest of our burial places; none of us will withhold from you any burial ground for burying your dead." 7Abraham rose and bowed to the Hittites, the people of the land. 8He said to them, "If you are willing that I should bury my dead out of my sight, hear me, and entreat for me Ephron son of Zohar, 9so that he may give me the cave of Machpelah, which he owns; it is at the end of his field. For the full price let him give it to me in your presence as a possession for a burying place." 10Now Ephron was sitting among the Hittites; and Ephron the Hittite answered Abraham in

the hearing of the Hittites, of all who went in at the gate of his city, 11"No, my lord, hear me; I give you the field, and I give you the cave that is in it; in the presence of my people I give it to you; bury your dead." 12Then Abraham bowed down before the people of the land. 13He said to Ephron in the hearing of the people of the land, "If you only will listen to me! I will give the price of the field; accept it from me, so that I may bury my dead there." 14Ephron answered Abraham, 15"My lord, listen to me; a piece of land worth four hundred shekels of silver—what is that between you and me? Bury your dead." 16Abraham agreed with Ephron; and Abraham weighed out for Ephron the silver that he had named in the hearing of the Hittites, four hundred shekels of silver, according to the weights current among the merchants.

17 So the field of Ephron in Machpelah, which was to the east of Mamre, the field with the cave that was in it and all the trees that were in the field, throughout its whole area, passed 18to Abraham as a possession in the presence of the Hittites, in the presence of all who went in at the gate of his city. 19After this, Abraham buried Sarah his wife in the cave of the field of Machpelah facing Mamre (that is, Hebron) in the land of Canaan. 20The field and the cave that is in it passed from the Hittites into Abraham's possession as a burying place.

The Marriage of Isaac and Rebekah

24 Now Abraham was old, well advanced in years; and the LORD had blessed

---

mostly the names of Aramean tribes or places, including his grandson *Aram* (v. 21). *Bethuel* is identified as the *father of Rebekah*, providing genealogical background for ch. 24.

23.1–20 The Abraham narrative winds down with the purchase of the cave at Machpelah, near Hebron, where Sarah and Abraham (25.9) will be buried. This P text establishes another link between the ancestors and the promise of the land. The next two generations of patriarchs and matriarchs (Isaac, Rebekah, Jacob, and Leah) will also be buried here. **23.2** *Kiriath-arba, Hebron, Canaan,* place-names that raise the theme of God's promise of the land of Canaan to Abraham's descendants. His purchase of the family tomb is a first step in the fulfillment of this promise and marks the land with a prominent memorial to the dead ancestors. For Hebron, see note on 13.18. **23.3** *Hittites,* one of the indigenous peoples of Canaan (see 10.15, which names their putative ancestor Heth; 15.20; 27.46; Ezek 16.3). They are what historians call Neo-Hittites to

distinguish them from the Indo-European Hittite people of Anatolia, who formed a great empire in the second millennium BCE. The best-known member of this ethnic group is Bathsheba's husband, Uriah the Hittite (2 Sam 11.3). **23.4–9** As a resident alien, Abraham owns no land to bury his dead. In diplomatic language the Hittites offer him the use of *the choicest of* their *burial places* (v. 6), which indicates a reluctance to sell or grant Abraham his own property. Abraham presses his case for ownership, offering to pay *full price* for the *cave of Machpelah* (v. 9), i.e., without bargaining over the (usually inflated) asking price. **23.10–16** Ephron the Hittite and Abraham engage in an elaborate and deferential dialogue that results in the sale of the cave and field for an exorbitant price that Abraham willingly pays. Ephron's initial offer to give it as a gift (v. 11) is a rhetorical gesture of honor and generosity, which Abraham knows not to take seriously and which Ephron undermines with his inflated price.

24.1–67 Abraham sends his servant to his kinfolk in

Abraham in all things. ²Abraham said to his servant, the oldest of his house, who had charge of all that he had, "Put your hand under my thigh ³and I will make you swear by the LORD, the God of heaven and earth, that you will not get a wife for my son from the daughters of the Canaanites, among whom I live, ⁴but will go to my country and to my kindred and get a wife for my son Isaac." ⁵The servant said to him, "Perhaps the woman may not be willing to follow me to this land; must I then take your son back to the land from which you came?" ⁶Abraham said to him, "See to it that you do not take my son back there. ⁷The LORD, the God of heaven, who took me from my father's house and from the land of my birth, and who spoke to me and swore to me, 'To your offspring I will give this land,' he will send his angel before you, and you shall take a wife for my son from there. ⁸But if the woman is not willing to follow you, then you will be free from this oath of mine; only you must not take my son back there." ⁹So the servant put his hand under the thigh of Abraham his master and swore to him concerning this matter.

10 Then the servant took ten of his master's camels and departed, taking all kinds of choice gifts from his master; and he set out and went to Aram-naharaim, to the city of Nahor. ¹¹He made the camels kneel down outside the city by the well of water; it was toward evening, the time when women go out to draw water. ¹²And he said, "O LORD, God of my master Abraham, please grant me success today and show steadfast love to my master Abraham. ¹³I am standing here by the spring of water, and the daughters of the townspeople are coming out to draw water. ¹⁴Let the girl to whom I shall say, 'Please offer your jar that I may drink,' and who shall say, 'Drink, and I will water your camels'—let her be the one whom you have appointed for your servant Isaac. By this I shall know that you have shown steadfast love to my master."

15 Before he had finished speaking, there was Rebekah, who was born to Bethuel son of Milcah, the wife of Nahor, Abraham's brother, coming out with her water jar on her shoulder. ¹⁶The girl was very fair to look upon, a virgin, whom no man had known. She went down to the spring, filled her jar, and came up. ¹⁷Then the servant ran to meet her and said, "Please let me sip a little water from your jar." ¹⁸"Drink, my lord," she said, and quickly lowered her jar upon her hand and gave him a drink. ¹⁹When she had finished giving him a drink, she said, "I will draw for your camels also, until they have finished drinking." ²⁰So she quickly emptied her jar into the trough and ran again to the well to draw, and she drew for all his camels. ²¹The man gazed at her in si-

---

Haran (see 11.31) to acquire a wife for Isaac. This story emphasizes the importance of marrying within the patriarchal lineage and the taboo against marrying a Canaanite woman (see similarly for the next generation, 27.46–28.9). This story, which is probably a post-exilic composition or expansion, proceeds at a leisurely pace (it is the longest chapter in Genesis) and focuses on God's guidance of events for the benefit of Abraham and his heirs. **24.1–9** *Abraham was . . . advanced in years,* the reason for the urgency to find a wife for Isaac. We learn retrospectively that Isaac has been deeply affected by his mother's death (24.67), and Abraham turns to *his servant* for aid. The unnamed servant is Abraham's chief steward (v. 2) and may be the same character as Eliezer of Damascus, mentioned in 15.2. *Put your hand under my thigh,* a ritual component of the servant's oath that seems to signify (either literally or by proximity) Abraham's reproductive organ, an appropriate source of authority for the patriarch (cf. 47.29). *He will send his angel before you* (v. 7), an assurance that indicates Abraham's status as a prophet (20.7) and God's predestination of a positive outcome. *God of heaven* (v. 7), a divine title common in postexilic writings (e.g., Jon 1.9; 2 Chr 36.23; Neh 1.4; and often in the Aramaic of Ezra and Daniel).

24.10–14 The detail that *the servant took ten . . . camels* provides the vehicle through which the servant will know God's choice: the girl who offers to *water* the *camels* (v. 14). This is an offer of extraordinary hospitality and labor (cf. Abraham's hospitality in 18.1–8). *City of Nahor,* Haran (see 11.31; 28.2). *Aram-naharaim* means "Aram of the two rivers," referring to the region from the great bend of the upper Euphrates to the Habur River, in which Haran is located. The meeting of the future wife at the well (v. 11) echoes similar scenes in the stories of Jacob (29.1–14) and Moses (Ex 2.15–22). In Middle Eastern tribal societies, the well is one of the few places where a man can meet an unmarried woman. The servant's plan relies on God's manipulation of events for the sake of his *steadfast love* (Hebrew *chesed,* v. 14) for Abraham (this theme word also appears in vv.12, 27, 49). **24.15–21** *Before he had finished speaking.* The servant's prayer is immediately fulfilled in spectacular fashion. Rebekah is fit in terms of kinship (she is Isaac's second cousin on his father's side), physical beauty (*very fair*), and marriageability (*a virgin,* v. 16). There is suspense as she initially says *Drink, my lord* (v. 18) without mentioning the camels. Only after he has finished does she offer to water the camels, emphatically showing her hospitality and passing the

lence to learn whether or not the LORD had made his journey successful.

22 When the camels had finished drinking, the man took a gold nose-ring weighing a half shekel, and two bracelets for her arms weighing ten gold shekels, 23and said, "Tell me whose daughter you are. Is there room in your father's house for us to spend the night?" 24She said to him, "I am the daughter of Bethuel son of Milcah, whom she bore to Nahor." 25She added, "We have plenty of straw and fodder and a place to spend the night." 26The man bowed his head and worshiped the LORD 27and said, "Blessed be the LORD, the God of my master Abraham, who has not forsaken his steadfast love and his faithfulness toward my master. As for me, the LORD has led me on the way to the house of my master's kin."

28 Then the girl ran and told her mother's household about these things. 29Rebekah had a brother whose name was Laban; and Laban ran out to the man, to the spring. 30As soon as he had seen the nose-ring, and the bracelets on his sister's arms, and when he heard the words of his sister Rebekah, "Thus the man spoke to me," he went to the man; and there he was, standing by the camels at the spring. 31He said, "Come in, O blessed of the LORD. Why do you stand outside when I have prepared the house and a place for the camels?" 32So the man came into the house; and Laban unloaded the camels, and gave him straw and fodder for the camels, and water to wash his feet and the feet of the men who were with him. 33Then food was set before him to eat; but he said, "I will not eat until I have told my errand." He said, "Speak on."

34 So he said, "I am Abraham's servant. 35The LORD has greatly blessed my master, and he has become wealthy; he has given him flocks and herds, silver and gold, male and female slaves, camels and donkeys. 36And Sarah my master's wife bore a son to my master when she was old; and he has given him all that he has. 37My master made me swear, saying, 'You shall not take a wife for my son from the daughters of the Canaanites, in whose land I live; 38but you shall go to my father's house, to my kindred, and get a wife for my son.' 39I said to my master, 'Perhaps the woman will not follow me.' 40But he said to me, 'The LORD, before whom I walk, will send his angel with you and make your way successful. You shall get a wife for my son from my kindred, from my father's house. 41Then you will be free from my oath, when you come to my kindred; even if they will not give her to you, you will be free from my oath.'

42 "I came today to the spring, and said, 'O LORD, the God of my master Abraham, if now you will only make successful the way I am going! 43I am standing here by the spring of water; let the young woman who comes out to draw, to whom I shall say, "Please give me a little water from your jar to drink," 44and who will say to me, "Drink, and I will draw for your camels also"—let her be the woman whom the LORD has appointed for my master's son.'

45 "Before I had finished speaking in my heart, there was Rebekah coming out with her water jar on her shoulder; and she went down to the spring, and drew. I said to her, 'Please let me drink.' 46She quickly let down her jar from her shoulder, and said, 'Drink, and I will also water your camels.' So I drank, and she also watered the camels. 47Then I asked her, 'Whose daughter are you?' She said, 'The daughter of Bethuel, Nahor's son, whom Milcah bore to him.' So I put the ring on her nose, and the bracelets on her arms. 48Then I bowed my head and worshiped the LORD, and blessed the LORD, the God of my master Abraham, who had led me by the right way to obtain the daughter of my master's kinsman for his son. 49Now then, if you will deal loyally and truly with my master, tell me; and if not, tell me, so that I may turn either to the right hand or to the left."

50 Then Laban and Bethuel answered, "The thing comes from the LORD; we cannot speak

---

test of recognition. Her haste in watering the camels (v. 20) is reminiscent of Abraham's haste in tending to his visitors in 18.1–8. **24.22** The servant's gifts show Abraham's wealth and, subsequently, Laban's greed. Laban's hospitality (in contrast to Rebekah's) seems to be activated by seeing the gifts (v. 30). This aspect of Laban's character will later come into play in his dealings with Jacob (29.27; 31.7, 14–15, 41). **24.24** Rebekah modestly identifies herself not by her name, but by her father and paternal grandparents. This expresses her intuitive sense of the importance of the patriarchal lineage and her identity as the divinely chosen bride for Isaac. **24.41** The servant strategically rephrases Abraham's statement for Laban's benefit, from *if the woman is not willing to follow you* (v. 8) to *if they will not give her to you* (v. 41). The deciding agent is now the family (and its male heads), not the woman. As it happens, the male heads of household (Laban

to you anything bad or good. 51Look, Rebekah is before you, take her and go, and let her be the wife of your master's son, as the LORD has spoken."

52 When Abraham's servant heard their words, he bowed himself to the ground before the LORD. 53And the servant brought out jewelry of silver and of gold, and garments, and gave them to Rebekah; he also gave to her brother and to her mother costly ornaments. 54Then he and the men who were with him ate and drank, and they spent the night there. When they rose in the morning, he said, "Send me back to my master." 55Her brother and her mother said, "Let the girl remain with us a while, at least ten days; after that she may go." 56But he said to them, "Do not delay me, since the LORD has made my journey successful; let me go that I may go to my master." 57They said, "We will call the girl, and ask her." 58And they called Rebekah, and said to her, "Will you go with this man?" She said, "I will." 59So they sent away their sister Rebekah and her nurse along with Abraham's servant and his men. 60And they blessed Rebekah and said to her,

"May you, our sister, become
     thousands of myriads;
may your offspring gain possession
     of the gates of their foes."

61Then Rebekah and her maids rose up, mounted the camels, and followed the man; thus the servant took Rebekah, and went his way.

62 Now Isaac had come from[a] Beer-lahai-roi, and was settled in the Negeb. 63Isaac went out in the evening to walk[b] in the field; and looking up, he saw camels coming. 64And Rebekah looked up, and when she saw Isaac, she slipped quickly from the camel, 65and said to the servant, "Who is the man over there, walking in the field to meet us?" The servant said, "It is my master." So she took her veil and covered herself. 66And the servant told Isaac all the things that he had done. 67Then Isaac brought her into his mother Sarah's tent. He took Rebekah, and she became his wife; and he loved her. So Isaac was comforted after his mother's death.

Abraham Marries Keturah

25 Abraham took another wife, whose name was Keturah. 2She bore him Zimran, Jokshan, Medan, Midian, Ishbak, and Shuah. 3Jokshan was the father of Sheba and Dedan. The sons of Dedan were Asshurim, Letushim, and Leummim. 4The sons of Midian were Ephah, Epher, Hanoch, Abida, and Eldaah. All these were the children of Keturah. 5Abraham gave all he had to Isaac. 6But to the

---

a Syr Tg: Heb *from coming to*   *b* Meaning of Heb word is uncertain

and Bethuel, v. 50) and Rebekah (v. 58) give their assent. **24.50** *Bethuel,* Rebekah's father, appears only here. Elsewhere in the story Rebekah's brother, *Laban,* acts as the responsible male of the family. **24.53** The gifts bestowed here seem to be the bride-price for Rebekah; cf. Jacob's labor as his bride-price for Rachel (29.20, 30). **24.60** The family's blessing on Rebekah echoes the diction of the angel's blessing on Abraham in 22.17. This characterizes her, once again, as Abrahamic in virtue and blessing and signals the appropriateness (and providential nature) of her selection as Isaac's wife. **24.62–67** The scene shifts to Isaac's perspective as he strolls aimlessly in the field. He looks up and sees camels, but Rebekah sees him. She veils herself, an enticing form of concealment, as a marriageable woman before a marriageable man. Isaac is a passive figure and needs to be instructed by the servant. Thereupon his fixation on his mother is redirected toward Rebekah, with whom he falls in love.

25.1–34 This chapter ends the Abraham narrative, telling of his death and his various lines of descendants. The chapter begins retrospectively, with the previously unmentioned wife, Keturah, and their offspring (vv. 1–6, J), followed by a brief description of Abraham's death and burial (vv. 7–11, P). A list of the descendants of Hagar follows (vv. 12–18, J), balancing the list of the descendants of Keturah. With the non-chosen lines complete down to the next two or three generations, the text returns to its chronological place after the death of Abraham to follow the chosen line, the children of Isaac and Rebekah (vv. 19–34, predominately J). **25.1–6** The descendants of Abraham from his wife Keturah are names of places or tribes in Arabia. Keturah's name means "incense," which seems to refer to the incense trade from southern Arabia. *Midian,* the region in northwest Arabia where Moses flees and settles (Ex 2.15–22). *Sheba,* the wealthy southern Arabian kingdom whose queen visits Solomon (1 Kings 10.1–13). The genealogical split between the children of Hagar and the children of Keturah distinguishes the Arabs of the Syrian and Sinai deserts (the Ishmaelites), who were primarily pastoralists, from the peoples of the Arabian peninsula, in whose southern regions were settled nations wealthy from trade in incense, spices, and gold. This J text has an interesting genealogical variation: here Sheba is the son of Jokshan (v. 3), who is Abraham's son, whereas in a J portion of the Table of Nations, Sheba is the son of Joktan (10.27–28), son of Eber. **25.6** *Concubines,* in the plural, is puzzling. Perhaps it refers to both Keturah

sons of his concubines Abraham gave gifts, while he was still living, and he sent them away from his son Isaac, eastward to the east country.

The Death of Abraham

7 This is the length of Abraham's life, one hundred seventy-five years. 8Abraham breathed his last and died in a good old age, an old man and full of years, and was gathered to his people. 9His sons Isaac and Ishmael buried him in the cave of Machpelah, in the field of Ephron son of Zohar the Hittite, east of Mamre, 10the field that Abraham purchased from the Hittites. There Abraham was buried, with his wife Sarah. 11After the death of Abraham God blessed his son Isaac. And Isaac settled at Beer-lahai-roi.

Ishmael's Descendants

12 These are the descendants of Ishmael, Abraham's son, whom Hagar the Egyptian, Sarah's slave-girl, bore to Abraham. 13These are the names of the sons of Ishmael, named in the order of their birth: Nebaioth, the first-born of Ishmael; and Kedar, Adbeel, Mibsam, 14Mishma, Dumah, Massa, 15Hadad, Tema, Jetur, Naphish, and Kedemah. 16These are the sons of Ishmael and these are their names, by their villages and by their encampments, twelve princes according to their tribes.

17(This is the length of the life of Ishmael, one hundred thirty-seven years; he breathed his last and died, and was gathered to his people.) 18They settled from Havilah to Shur, which is opposite Egypt in the direction of Assyria; he settled down*a* alongside of*b* all his people.

The Birth and Youth of Esau and Jacob

19 These are the descendants of Isaac, Abraham's son: Abraham was the father of Isaac, 20and Isaac was forty years old when he married Rebekah, daughter of Bethuel the Aramean of Paddan-aram, sister of Laban the Aramean. 21Isaac prayed to the LORD for his wife, because she was barren; and the LORD granted his prayer, and his wife Rebekah conceived. 22The children struggled together within her; and she said, "If it is to be this way, why do I live?"*c* So she went to inquire of the LORD. 23And the LORD said to her,

"Two nations are in your womb,
    and two peoples born of you shall be
        divided;
the one shall be stronger than the other,
    the elder shall serve the younger."

24When her time to give birth was at hand, there were twins in her womb. 25The first

---

a Heb *he fell*   *b* Or *down in opposition to*   *c* Syr: Meaning of Heb uncertain

---

and Hagar, who are each also referred to as Abraham's *wife* (v. 1; 16.3). Note that Abraham gives *gifts* to all his children, even those who are not of the chosen line. This expresses a positive view of the Arab peoples, who are fully children of Abraham. **25.7–11** A brief and dignified notice, from the P source, of the death of Abraham and his burial in the cave of Machpelah. Isaac and Ishmael are briefly rejoined at their father's burial, some time after the death of Sarah. At Abraham's death, the patriarchal blessing passes to Isaac (v. 11). **25.12–18** Like Nahor (22.20–24) and Jacob, Ishmael has twelve sons. *Havilah to . . . Assyria* (v. 18), the Sinai and Syrian deserts. *Princes according to their tribes,* living in *villages and . . . encampments,* a nice description of the lives and political structures of the Arab peoples on the fringes of the desert living a life similar to the later bedouin. **25.19–28** The Jacob story extends from 25.19 to 37.1. As in the uncertainty over Abraham's heir, there is conflict and rivalry over who will be Isaac's heir. In the birth story of the twins, the theme of the barren wife is quickly resolved and the focus turns to the rivalry between Jacob and Esau, which begins already in the womb. An oracle from God announces that the outcome of the rivalry is foreseen, with the genealogy branching into two nations. **25.19–20** The Jacob story begins with the formula

These are the descendants (see note on 2.4). Genealogical details follow in this brief summary from the P source. *Paddan-aram* (perhaps "plain, or road, of Aram"), either the region of Aram-naharaim (24.10) or the city of Haran. **25.21** In the space of one verse the theme of the barren wife is raised and resolved, presenting an analogy to the situation of Abraham and Sarah (18.9–15; and later to Jacob and Rachel, 29.31; 30.22–24), but quickly moving on. *The LORD granted his prayer* shows that the conception is miraculous (as with Abraham and Sarah) and marks the offspring as special. **25.22–23** It is now Rebekah's turn to seek God's help, as the successful conception becomes a difficult pregnancy. *The children struggled together within her* announces the theme of the struggle between Jacob and Esau, which will be a major theme of the Jacob story. The goal of the struggle is not yet clear but is hinted at in God's oracle: *the elder shall serve the younger.* The brothers seem already to be struggling over who will have priority, i.e., who will be the first-born. The method of Rebekah's inquiry is obscure, but God's response sketches the future of the children to be born—they will be *two nations*—much like the angelic oracle forecasting the prenatal Ishmael's future (16.10–12). The ascent of the younger son is a repeated theme in Genesis (Isaac, Jacob, Joseph,

came out red, all his body like a hairy mantle; so they named him Esau. [26]Afterward his brother came out, with his hand gripping Esau's heel; so he was named Jacob.[a] Isaac was sixty years old when she bore them.

27 When the boys grew up, Esau was a skillful hunter, a man of the field, while Jacob was a quiet man, living in tents. [28]Isaac loved Esau, because he was fond of game; but Rebekah loved Jacob.

Esau Sells His Birthright

29 Once when Jacob was cooking a stew, Esau came in from the field, and he was famished. [30]Esau said to Jacob, "Let me eat some of that red stuff, for I am famished!" (Therefore he

was called Edom.[b]) [31]Jacob said, "First sell me your birthright." [32]Esau said, "I am about to die; of what use is a birthright to me?" [33]Jacob said, "Swear to me first."[c] So he swore to him, and sold his birthright to Jacob. [34]Then Jacob gave Esau bread and lentil stew, and he ate and drank, and rose and went his way. Thus Esau despised his birthright.

Isaac and Abimelech

26 Now there was a famine in the land, besides the former famine that had occurred in the days of Abraham. And Isaac

---

a That is *He takes by the heel* or *He supplants*   *b* That is *Red*
c Heb *today*

Ephraim, even Abel) and later (David). **25.24–27** The birth and youth of the twins show many of their defining traits. *Red* (Hebrew *'admoni*) signals Esau's ancestry of Edom (a wordplay made explicit in v. 30). *Hairy* (*se'ar*) echoes the word Seir, a region in Edom, and loosely motivates the name *Esau*. The mention of Esau's hairiness also sets the stage for its prominence in the deception of Isaac in ch. 27. The red and hairy body of Esau also anticipate his character as *a skillful hunter, a man of the field* (v. 27). All of these traits describe Esau as a man of nature who operates in the wild as a skilled predator. His animal-like instincts and lack of intelligence are treated in the following story. *A quiet man, living in tents.* Jacob is a man of the domestic domain, a man of culture. *Gripping Esau's heel.* Jacob seems to be trying to pull Esau back so that he can be the firstborn, showing his ability to scheme and plan (cf. the birth of the twins Perez and Zerah, 38.27–30); this act foreshadows his more successful attempts to supplant his brother. *Heel* (*'aqev*) is the motivation for the name Jacob (*ya'aqov*). Jacob's smooth skin, in contrast to Esau's hairiness, is not mentioned until 27.11, when it becomes central to the plot. **25.28** The opposition between the brothers is compounded by an opposition between the parents. *Fond of game.* Isaac's preference for wild food motivates his love for Esau and anticipates the role of this cuisine in ch. 27. In his filial preference, Isaac is ruled by his belly (like Esau in v. 30). *Rebekah loved Jacob.* No reason given for her preference—a mother's love needs no motive. And yet she knows that Jacob will prevail (see v. 23), and she operates and wields authority in the domestic domain that Jacob inhabits (*living in tents*, v. 27). Note that Jacob, in this respect, is allied with the feminine: he is his mother's boy (see 27.5–17). The alliances of the parents with the two sons provide background for the events of ch. 27. **25.29–34** The first story of Jacob's ascent over Esau shows their contrasting traits. In this story Jacob gains Esau's *birthright* (*bekorah*), his rights as the firstborn son. In ch. 27 Jacob gains Esau's *blessing* (*berakah*), which also belongs to the firstborn son. These two stories are complementary (and are both

from the J source), hinging on the wordplay of *bekorah* and *berakah* (see 27.36) and binding both Esau and Isaac to Jacob's ascent. The dubious means of Jacob's victories are qualified by his (and his mother's) charms as a trickster. As the underdog, he resorts to trickery and wiles to defeat his big brother, who is stronger but not wiser. **25.29–30** The brothers are in their respective domains: domestic Jacob is preparing a *stew*, and Esau has returned from the wilds, having failed in his attempt to kill wild game (to the potential disappointment of his father). Esau is inarticulate, referring to the stew as *that red stuff* (lit. "this red red," *ha'adom ha'adom hazzeh*), which also signifies his name *Edom. Let me eat*, lit. "feed me," perhaps with the connotation of feeding animals. **25.30–33** *Sell me your birthright.* Jacob poses an outrageous price for a bowl of stew. Esau fails to respond to the invitation to barter, claiming that he is *about to die*, when in fact he is merely very hungry. As a man of nature, Esau thinks with his belly, not his brain. As a knowledgeable (and manipulative) man of culture, Jacob seals the trade with a legally binding oath. **25.34** *Ate, drank, rose, went.* A quick series of verbs shows Esau as a man of action, unaware of the implications of his actions. *Despised his birthright.* Esau failed to value his birthright, treated it badly, and perhaps deserved to have lost it. Cf. Heb 12.16.

26.1–33 A brief cycle of stories about Isaac and Rebekah in Gerar, from the J source. These are the only stories in which Isaac has the major rather than a supporting role. A number of features—famine in the land, residence at Gerar under King Abimelech, the "wife-sister" motif, acquisition of wealth, conflict over wells, and the founding of Beer-sheba—are paralleled by the E stories of Abraham in 20.1–18; 21.22–34. Interestingly, these stories show no awareness of Isaac's sons, Esau and Jacob, and seem loosely connected chronologically to their context. Their focus on Isaac provides a transition to the more consequential story of Isaac's old age in ch. 27 and provides separation between Jacob's acquisition of the birthright (from Esau) and blessing (from Isaac). **26.1** *Former famine . . .*

went to Gerar, to King Abimelech of the Philistines. 2The LORD appeared to Isaac[a] and
said, "Do not go down to Egypt; settle in the
land that I shall show you. 3Reside in this land
as an alien, and I will be with you, and will
bless you; for to you and to your descendants I
will give all these lands, and I will fulfill the
oath that I swore to your father Abraham. 4I
will make your offspring as numerous as the
stars of heaven, and will give to your offspring
all these lands; and all the nations of the earth
shall gain blessing for themselves through
your offspring, 5because Abraham obeyed my
voice and kept my charge, my commandments, my statutes, and my laws."

6 So Isaac settled in Gerar. 7When the men
of the place asked him about his wife, he said,
"She is my sister"; for he was afraid to say, "My
wife," thinking, "or else the men of the place
might kill me for the sake of Rebekah, because
she is attractive in appearance." 8When Isaac
had been there a long time, King Abimelech of
the Philistines looked out of a window and
saw him fondling his wife Rebekah. 9So Abimelech called for Isaac, and said, "So she is your
wife! Why then did you say, 'She is my sister'?"
Isaac said to him, "Because I thought I might
die because of her." 10Abimelech said, "What is
this you have done to us? One of the people
might easily have lain with your wife, and you
would have brought guilt upon us." 11So
Abimelech warned all the people, saying,
"Whoever touches this man or his wife shall
be put to death."

12 Isaac sowed seed in that land, and in the
same year reaped a hundredfold. The LORD
blessed him, 13and the man became rich; he
prospered more and more until he became
very wealthy. 14He had possessions of flocks
and herds, and a great household, so that the
Philistines envied him. 15(Now the Philistines
had stopped up and filled with earth all the
wells that his father's servants had dug in the
days of his father Abraham.) 16And Abimelech
said to Isaac, "Go away from us; you have become too powerful for us."

17 So Isaac departed from there and camped
in the valley of Gerar and settled there. 18Isaac
dug again the wells of water that had been dug
in the days of his father Abraham; for the Philistines had stopped them up after the death of
Abraham; and he gave them the names that his
father had given them. 19But when Isaac's servants dug in the valley and found there a well of
spring water, 20the herders of Gerar quarreled
with Isaac's herders, saying, "The water is ours."
So he called the well Esek,[b] because they contended with him. 21Then they dug another
well, and they quarreled over that one also; so
he called it Sitnah.[c] 22He moved from there and
dug another well, and they did not quarrel over
it; so he called it Rehoboth,[d] saying, "Now the
LORD has made room for us, and we shall be
fruitful in the land."

23 From there he went up to Beer-sheba.
24And that very night the LORD appeared to
him and said, "I am the God of your father

---

a Heb *him* *b* That is *Contention* *c* That is *Enmity* *d* That
is *Broad places* or *Room*

Abraham. See 12.10. Isaac is in some sense recapitulating events of his father's life. Isaac's journey to *Gerar,
to King Abimelech,* is parallel to the E story of Abraham
and Sarah in ch. 20. In these stories, the patriarch and
matriarch journey to a foreign land and claim that the
beautiful wife is really the patriarch's sister, with similar outcomes (see also note on 12.10–20). **26.2–5** God
reveals himself to Isaac, as he had done often to Abraham, gives him instructions, and grants him his blessing. Vv. 3b–5 are later expansions on the initial blessing, providing Isaac with the patriarchal promises of
land, offspring, and blessings. This expansion is based
on the second angelic speech to Abraham in 22.15–18
and alludes to Abraham's obedience in that chapter.
Obeyed my voice (v. 5). Cf. 22.18. **26.6–11** This variation of the story of the matriarch in danger differs
from the others in that the beautiful matriarch is not
taken into the king's harem (cf. 12.10–20, J; 20.1–18,
E). It also has a moment of comedy when Abimelech
sees Isaac *fondling his wife Rebekah.* The Hebrew is

yitschaq metsacheq, "Isaac playing" (with his wife Rebekah), which is a play on Isaac's name, here with a
sexual connotation. This kind of "play" reveals the
truth to the perceptive king. As with the pharaoh in
12.10–20 and with his double, King Abimelech of
Gerar, in 20.1–18, Abimelech is justly offended by the
patriarch's ruse, questions him, and protects the wife.
Since he did not take the wife, he does not enrich the
patriarch in bride-price or recompense. **26.12–33** *The
LORD blessed him.* Isaac gains wealth as promised in v.
3. His wealth provokes a separation from Abimelech
reminiscent of the separation of Abram and Lot
(13.1–12). The conflict with the Philistines over wells
recalls Abraham's conflict with the Philistines over the
well of Beer-sheba (21.25, E). The story of the *oath* and
covenant (v. 28) between Isaac and the Philistines
(*Abimelech, Ahuzzath,* and *Phicol,* v. 26) is parallel to
the story with Abraham and the same Philistines
(Abimelech and Phicol) in 21.22–34 (E). Both stories
conclude with the founding of Beer-sheba, meaning

Abraham; do not be afraid, for I am with you and will bless you and make your offspring numerous for my servant Abraham's sake." ²⁵So he built an altar there, called on the name of the LORD, and pitched his tent there. And there Isaac's servants dug a well.

26 Then Abimelech went to him from Gerar, with Ahuzzath his adviser and Phicol the commander of his army. ²⁷Isaac said to them, "Why have you come to me, seeing that you hate me and have sent me away from you?" ²⁸They said, "We see plainly that the LORD has been with you; so we say, let there be an oath between you and us, and let us make a covenant with you ²⁹so that you will do us no harm, just as we have not touched you and have done to you nothing but good and have sent you away in peace. You are now the blessed of the LORD." ³⁰So he made them a feast, and they ate and drank. ³¹In the morning they rose early and exchanged oaths; and Isaac set them on their way, and they departed from him in peace. ³²That same day Isaac's servants came and told him about the well that they had dug, and said to him, "We have found water!" ³³He called it Shibah;ᵃ therefore the name of the city is Beer-shebaᵇ to this day.

Esau's Hittite Wives

34 When Esau was forty years old, he married Judith daughter of Beeri the Hittite, and Base-math daughter of Elon the Hittite; ³⁵and they made life bitter for Isaac and Rebekah.

Isaac Blesses Jacob

27 When Isaac was old and his eyes were dim so that he could not see, he called his elder son Esau and said to him, "My son"; and he answered, "Here I am." ²He said, "See, I am old; I do not know the day of my death. ³Now then, take your weapons, your quiver and your bow, and go out to the field, and hunt game for me. ⁴Then prepare for me savory food, such as I like, and bring it to me to eat, so that I may bless you before I die."

5 Now Rebekah was listening when Isaac spoke to his son Esau. So when Esau went to the field to hunt for game and bring it, ⁶Rebekah said to her son Jacob, "I heard your father say to your brother Esau, ⁷'Bring me game, and prepare for me savory food to eat, that I may bless you before the LORD before I die.' ⁸Now therefore, my son, obey my word as I command you. ⁹Go to the flock, and get me two choice kids, so that I may prepare from them savory food for your father, such as he likes; ¹⁰and you shall take it to your father to eat, so that he may bless you before he dies." ¹¹But Jacob said to his mother Rebekah, "Look,

---

a A word resembling the word for *oath*   *b* That is *Well of the oath* or *Well of seven*

"well of the oath" (cf. v. 33; 21.31). **26.34–35** In pointed contrast to his father Isaac, who at forty years of age married Rebekah, daughter of the appropriate patriarchal lineage (25.20), Esau at forty marries two women of Hittite families, natives of the land of Canaan (see note on 23.3; cf. the names of Esau's wives in 36.2). These marriages make life *bitter* for Isaac and Rebekah, since they violate the family code (see 24.3). This notice, from the P source, continues in 27.46–28.5, with Isaac and Rebekah's insistence that Jacob return to the patriarchal homeland to take a proper wife. These P texts form a frame around the J story that follows and provide a parallel motive for his journey to Haran.

27.1–45 The story of Jacob's deception of Isaac (J) is one of the most dramatic and suspenseful in all the Bible. Although we only see the actions and words, the characters' inner dispositions are palpable: Jacob's fear, Rebekah's determination, Isaac's indecision, Esau's grief. This story complements Jacob's acquisition of Esau's *birthright* (*bekorah*, 25.29–34) by having Isaac grant him the *blessing* (*berakah*) of the firstborn son (see v. 36). In contrast to the story of the birthright, Esau in this story is portrayed in a sympathetic light as a brother wronged. The blessings of the two brothers anticipate that they will be two nations, corresponding to the divine oracle in 25.23. In her decisive role Rebekah acts out her love for Jacob (25.28) and also brings to pass the divine oracle in 25.23. Jacob's success in gaining the blessing by deception is balanced by the price he pays later in the corresponding deceptions played on him in 29.23–27; 37.32–35. **27.1–4** Isaac's blindness provides the key condition for the deception by Jacob and Rebekah and sets the stage for his tests of Jacob's identity through his other senses: hearing, touch, and smell. His request to Esau, pointedly identified as *his elder son Esau* (v. 1), has elements of high and low drama. His closeness to death and desire to pass along the patriarchal blessing are very serious, but his request for game (v. 4) recalls his appetite-driven reason for loving Esau (25.28). *So that I may bless you* (v. 4) suggests that this meal has a ritual or sacred quality. **27.5–10** Like Sarah in 18.10, *Rebekah was listening* to the conversation. Rebekah's plan to outfox Isaac and Esau on behalf of the son she loves (25.28) depends on her expertise in the domestic domain. Just as Rebekah substitutes domestic animals for wild game (v. 9), so she will substitute Jacob, the domestic son, for Esau. Rebekah is here the trickster, exercising her domestic authority, culinary skills, and intelligence to win her

my brother Esau is a hairy man, and I am a man of smooth skin. [12]Perhaps my father will feel me, and I shall seem to be mocking him, and bring a curse on myself and not a blessing." [13]His mother said to him, "Let your curse be on me, my son; only obey my word, and go, get them for me." [14]So he went and got them and brought them to his mother; and his mother prepared savory food, such as his father loved. [15]Then Rebekah took the best garments of her elder son Esau, which were with her in the house, and put them on her younger son Jacob; [16]and she put the skins of the kids on his hands and on the smooth part of his neck. [17]Then she handed the savory food, and the bread that she had prepared, to her son Jacob.

18 So he went in to his father, and said, "My father"; and he said, "Here I am; who are you, my son?" [19]Jacob said to his father, "I am Esau your firstborn. I have done as you told me; now sit up and eat of my game, so that you may bless me." [20]But Isaac said to his son, "How is it that you have found it so quickly, my son?" He answered, "Because the LORD your God granted me success." [21]Then Isaac said to Jacob, "Come near, that I may feel you, my son, to know whether you are really my son Esau or not." [22]So Jacob went up to his father Isaac, who felt him and said, "The voice is Jacob's voice, but the hands are the hands of Esau." [23]He did not recognize him, because his hands were hairy like his brother Esau's hands; so he blessed him. [24]He said, "Are you really my son Esau?" He answered, "I am." [25]Then he said,

"Bring it to me, that I may eat of my son's game and bless you." So he brought it to him, and he ate; and he brought him wine, and he drank. [26]Then his father Isaac said to him, "Come near and kiss me, my son." [27]So he came near and kissed him; and he smelled the smell of his garments, and blessed him, and said,

"Ah, the smell of my son
    is like the smell of a field that the LORD
        has blessed.
[28] May God give you of the dew of heaven,
        and of the fatness of the earth,
        and plenty of grain and wine.
[29] Let peoples serve you,
        and nations bow down to you.
    Be lord over your brothers,
        and may your mother's sons bow down
            to you.
    Cursed be everyone who curses you,
        and blessed be everyone who blesses
            you!"

Esau's Lost Blessing

30 As soon as Isaac had finished blessing Jacob, when Jacob had scarcely gone out from the presence of his father Isaac, his brother Esau came in from his hunting. [31]He also prepared savory food, and brought it to his father. And he said to his father, "Let my father sit up and eat of his son's game, so that you may bless me." [32]His father Isaac said to him, "Who are you?" He answered, "I am your firstborn son, Esau." [33]Then Isaac trembled violently, and said, "Who was it then that hunted game and

---

preferred son the blessing. **27.11–13** Jacob's reservation, based on the tactile contrast between a *hairy man* and a *man of smooth skin,* is overruled by his mother. The danger of Isaac's *curse,* rather than his *blessing,* hangs over the subsequent scene. Although Isaac never pronounces a curse, Rebekah does pay a price when she later commands Jacob to flee (v. 43), and there is no mention of her ever seeing him again. **27.15–16** Rebekah uses her domestic intelligence to solve the problem Jacob raised in vv. 11–12. She clothes him in the *garments of her elder son Esau,* and on the smooth skin still uncovered she puts the skins of the domestic kids. The disguise of the domestic son as his wild brother is now complete. Note that, in recompense, Jacob will later be deceived by the garment of his beloved son (37.32–33). **27.18–27** The scene of deception is fraught with suspense. Isaac's suspicion seems to be aroused immediately, and each exchange holds the chance of discovery, bringing the father's curse. Although Isaac recognizes *Jacob's voice* (v. 22), he is deceived by his senses of taste, touch, and smell, as Rebekah had planned, and *so he blessed him* (v. 23).

My/his father, my/his son, key words in this scene (occurring four and eight times, respectively), highlighting the drama and disruption of this father-son relationship. Jacob's response to his father's suspicion about the speedy success of the hunt is ironic: *because the LORD your God granted me success* (v. 20). This is a deceptive reply, since Rebekah was responsible for the quickness of the meal, but it is also true, since God had predicted Jacob's ascent (25.23). **27.27–29** *Like . . . a field . . . blessed.* Jacob goes from smelling as though he had been blessed to actually being blessed by the words of vv. 28–29, as the patriarchal blessing invokes the glorious fertility of the land (cf. the poetry of Jacob's blessing on Joseph in 49.25). The blessing of rule over other nations, in particular *over your brothers,* corresponds closely to God's prediction in 25.23. *Brothers, mother's sons.* The plural is probably a poetic formula; cf. 49.8. The invocation of curses and blessings echoes the promises to Abraham (12.3). **27.31–38** The dialogue between Isaac and Esau in vv. 31–33 almost exactly repeats the exchange between Jacob and Isaac in vv. 18–19, but now the sequence in v. 32 has a radically

brought it to me, and I ate it all*a* before you came, and I have blessed him?—yes, and blessed he shall be!" 34When Esau heard his father's words, he cried out with an exceedingly great and bitter cry, and said to his father, "Bless me, me also, father!" 35But he said, "Your brother came deceitfully, and he has taken away your blessing." 36Esau said, "Is he not rightly named Jacob?*b* For he has supplanted me these two times. He took away my birthright; and look, now he has taken away my blessing." Then he said, "Have you not reserved a blessing for me?" 37Isaac answered Esau, "I have already made him your lord, and I have given him all his brothers as servants, and with grain and wine I have sustained him. What then can I do for you, my son?" 38Esau said to his father, "Have you only one blessing, father? Bless me, me also, father!" And Esau lifted up his voice and wept.

39 Then his father Isaac answered him:
"See, away from*c* the fatness of the earth
    shall your home be,
  and away from*d* the dew of heaven on
    high.
40 By your sword you shall live,
  and you shall serve your brother;
but when you break loose,*e*
  you shall break his yoke from your
    neck."

Jacob Escapes Esau's Fury

41 Now Esau hated Jacob because of the blessing with which his father had blessed him, and

Esau said to himself, "The days of mourning for my father are approaching; then I will kill my brother Jacob." 42But the words of her elder son Esau were told to Rebekah; so she sent and called her younger son Jacob and said to him, "Your brother Esau is consoling himself by planning to kill you. 43Now therefore, my son, obey my voice; flee at once to my brother Laban in Haran, 44and stay with him a while, until your brother's fury turns away— 45until your brother's anger against you turns away, and he forgets what you have done to him; then I will send, and bring you back from there. Why should I lose both of you in one day?"

46 Then Rebekah said to Isaac, "I am weary of my life because of the Hittite women. If Jacob marries one of the Hittite women such as these, one of the women of the land, what good will my life be to me?"

28 Then Isaac called Jacob and blessed him, and charged him, "You shall not marry one of the Canaanite women. 2Go at once to Paddan-aram to the house of Bethuel, your mother's father; and take as wife from there one of the daughters of Laban, your mother's brother. 3May God Almighty*f* bless you and make you fruitful and numerous, that you may become a company of peoples. 4May he give to you the blessing of Abraham, to you and to your offspring with you, so that you

---

a Cn: Heb *of all*   *b* That is *He supplants* or *He takes by the heel*
c Or *See, of*   *d* Or *and of*   *e* Meaning of Heb uncertain
f Traditional rendering of Heb *El Shaddai*

---

different tone as the truth begins to sink in. Isaac's violent trembling and Esau's *exceedingly great and bitter cry* (v. 34) bring pathos to this tragic scene, turning our sympathy toward the defeated father and son. Esau's speech, including his repeated desperate plea for a blessing (vv. 34, 38), highlights Jacob's duplicity and Esau's dawning understanding. Esau observes astutely, *Is he not rightly named Jacob* (i.e., supplanter)? (v. 36). In defeat, Esau gains a new awareness, which perhaps foreshadows his dignity and eloquence when he meets Jacob in ch. 33. **27.39–40** Isaac's equivocal pronouncement is more a curse than a blessing, locating Esau away from fertility and under Jacob's rule, the inverse of Jacob's blessing. Like Ishmael (16.12), his life will be violent. *You shall break his yoke from your neck.* This ray of hope probably refers to Edom's successful revolt against Judah in the mid-ninth century BCE after a period of Judean hegemony (2 Kings 8.20–22). **27.41–45** Esau's plan to kill Jacob (cf. Cain and Abel, 4.1–16) is foiled by Rebekah's superior intelligence. She commands Jacob once again (v. 43; cf. v. 8) to flee to the patriarchal homeland until Esau's wrath abates.

Her plan is once again successful, but Jacob's absence will last for twenty years (31.38). Her plan, moreover, saves the lives of both sons, since Esau would have been executed as a murderer, and she does not want to lose *both . . . in one day* (v. 45). **27.46–28.9** This P section continues from 26.34–35 about Esau's marriages to Hittite (i.e., Canaanite) women. Here Rebekah gives voice to her bitterness over these marriages and fears that Jacob will also marry a Hittite woman. In response, Isaac sends Jacob to the patriarchal homeland to marry a proper wife (cf. 24.3–4). Isaac also takes this opportunity to grant Jacob the patriarchal blessing, *the blessing of Abraham* (28.3–4). This P account is an alternative to the J story of ch. 27, providing Jacob with Isaac's blessing without any duplicity or conflict. Esau has apparently forfeited the blessing because of his marriages with the Hittite women. This text also serves well as a frame to the J story. When read after Rebekah's speech to Jacob in 27.42–45, Rebekah's lament to Isaac serves as an effective cover story, a way to make Isaac assent to Jacob's flight to Haran. **28.3** On *God Almighty* (*El Shaddai*) and the patriarchal blessing

may take possession of the land where you now live as an alien—land that God gave to Abraham." [5]Thus Isaac sent Jacob away; and he went to Paddan-aram, to Laban son of Bethuel the Aramean, the brother of Rebekah, Jacob's and Esau's mother.

Esau Marries Ishmael's Daughter

6 Now Esau saw that Isaac had blessed Jacob and sent him away to Paddan-aram to take a wife from there, and that as he blessed him he charged him, "You shall not marry one of the Canaanite women," [7]and that Jacob had obeyed his father and his mother and gone to Paddan-aram. [8]So when Esau saw that the Canaanite women did not please his father Isaac, [9]Esau went to Ishmael and took Mahalath daughter of Abraham's son Ishmael, and sister of Nebaioth, to be his wife in addition to the wives he had.

Jacob's Dream at Bethel

10 Jacob left Beer-sheba and went toward Haran. [11]He came to a certain place and stayed there for the night, because the sun had set. Taking one of the stones of the place, he put it under his head and lay down in that place. [12]And he dreamed that there was a ladder[a] set up on the earth, the top of it reaching to heaven; and the angels of God were ascending and descending on it. [13]And the LORD stood beside him[b] and said, "I am the LORD, the God of Abraham your father and the God of Isaac; the land on which you lie I will give to you and to your offspring; [14]and your offspring shall be like the dust of the earth, and you shall spread abroad to the west and to the east and to the north and to the south; and all the families of the earth shall be blessed[c] in you and in your offspring. [15]Know that I am with you and will keep you wherever you go, and will bring you back to this land; for I will not leave you until I have done what I have promised you." [16]Then Jacob woke from his sleep and said, "Surely the LORD is in this place—and I did not know it!" [17]And he was afraid, and said, "How awesome is this place! This is none other than the house of God, and this is the gate of heaven."

18 So Jacob rose early in the morning, and he took the stone that he had put under his

---

a Or stairway or ramp   b Or stood above it   c Or shall bless themselves

---

in the P narrative, see 17.1–8. **28.6–9** Esau responds by marrying a daughter of Ishmael, who is within the patriarchal lineage. But Ishmael, like Esau, has an equivocal status, since he is the father of a foreign people. Moreover, Esau marries this woman in addition to his other wives, so he remains guilty for his marriages to the Hittite women. This is a weak response to the larger problem of Isaac blessing Jacob. Note how the P story reconfigures the rivalry over the patriarchal blessing: Esau is the guilty party, Isaac's dignity is intact, and Jacob and Rebekah are wholly innocent.

28.10–22 Jacob's first encounter with God confirms his status as the chosen patriarch. It occurs during his journey away from home and is the origin of the sanctuary at Bethel (Hebrew, "house of God"). On his return journey home, Jacob has a corresponding encounter with God that is the origin of the sanctuary at Penuel ("presence of God"; see 32.22–32). The encounter at Bethel is mostly from the E source (vv. 11–12, 17–18, 20–22) with some portions from a parallel story in the J source (vv. 10, 13–16, 19). Note that both versions are concerned with God's protection of Jacob during his journey—in J as part of God's promise (v. 15) and in E as part of Jacob's vow (vv. 20–21). **28.11** Place (Hebrew maqom, repeated three times) can also mean "shrine," a fruitful ambiguity here. The setting at night has an aura of mystery and corresponds to the later divine encounter in 32.22–33. The odd detail of Jacob laying his head on one of the stones of the place becomes clearer in retrospect—the stone

signifies sacred space (v. 22), and sleeping on it induces a revelatory dream. **28.12** Ladder (or "stairway"), a cosmic passageway between heaven and earth whose earthly terminus is sacred space. A similar "stairway of heaven" that the gods traverse is known from Mesopotamian texts. Mesopotamian temple towers (ziggurats) are also described as linking heaven and earth (cf. 11.4), showing that earthly shrines could be conceived of as a cosmic axis, like Bethel. **28.13–15** The dream vision is expanded by a divine revelation from the J source. God appears to Jacob while he is sleeping and grants him the patriarchal promises (see 12.2; 13.14). This gives God's confirmation to the blessing that Isaac had previously given him. I am . . . you go. God's assurance adds a key dimension to the story: at Jacob's most vulnerable moment, fleeing from home to a foreign land, he gains a divine protector and discovers his destiny. **28.16–17** These verses are a mixture of J (v. 16) and E (v. 17), giving Jacob's parallel responses to the divine encounter. In both versions, Jacob is astonished and awed. His recognition that the place is the house of God (bet 'elohim) motivates the name of the place as Bethel (bet 'el, "house of God"). Jacob names the place in each source: v. 19 (J); 35.7 (E); 35.15 (P). **28.18–22** Jacob ritually marks the sacred place by setting up and anointing a sacred pillar. Such pillars are symbols at many Israelite shrines, such as Shechem (Josh 24.26), Gilgal (Josh 4.20), and Sinai (Ex 24.4). Vows are typically made at shrines (e.g., Hannah in 1 Sam 1.11), and Jacob makes a vow to

head and set it up for a pillar and poured oil on the top of it. [19]He called that place Bethel;[a] but the name of the city was Luz at the first. [20]Then Jacob made a vow, saying, "If God will be with me, and will keep me in this way that I go, and will give me bread to eat and clothing to wear, [21]so that I come again to my father's house in peace, then the LORD shall be my God, [22]and this stone, which I have set up for a pillar, shall be God's house; and of all that you give me I will surely give one-tenth to you."

Jacob Meets Rachel

29 Then Jacob went on his journey, and came to the land of the people of the east. [2]As he looked, he saw a well in the field and three flocks of sheep lying there beside it; for out of that well the flocks were watered. The stone on the well's mouth was large, [3]and when all the flocks were gathered there, the shepherds would roll the stone from the mouth of the well, and water the sheep, and put the stone back in its place on the mouth of the well.

4 Jacob said to them, "My brothers, where do you come from?" They said, "We are from Haran." [5]He said to them, "Do you know Laban son of Nahor?" They said, "We do." [6]He said to them, "Is it well with him?" "Yes," they replied, "and here is his daughter Rachel, coming with the sheep." [7]He said, "Look, it is still broad daylight; it is not time for the animals to

be gathered together. Water the sheep, and go, pasture them." [8]But they said, "We cannot until all the flocks are gathered together, and the stone is rolled from the mouth of the well; then we water the sheep."

9 While he was still speaking with them, Rachel came with her father's sheep; for she kept them. [10]Now when Jacob saw Rachel, the daughter of his mother's brother Laban, and the sheep of his mother's brother Laban, Jacob went up and rolled the stone from the well's mouth, and watered the flock of his mother's brother Laban. [11]Then Jacob kissed Rachel, and wept aloud. [12]And Jacob told Rachel that he was her father's kinsman, and that he was Rebekah's son; and she ran and told her father.

13 When Laban heard the news about his sister's son Jacob, he ran to meet him; he embraced him and kissed him, and brought him to his house. Jacob[b] told Laban all these things, [14]and Laban said to him, "Surely you are my bone and my flesh!" And he stayed with him a month.

Jacob Marries Laban's Daughters

15 Then Laban said to Jacob, "Because you are my kinsman, should you therefore serve me for nothing? Tell me, what shall your wages be?" [16]Now Laban had two daughters; the

---

a That is *House of God*   *b* Heb *He*

God, promising worship, establishment of a shrine at Bethel, and tithing if God will be with him and keep him (note the similar wording to God's promise in v. 15). Jacob's hope that God will protect him will be fulfilled, and Jacob will return to Bethel in 35.1–7 (E).
29.1–14 In this J account Jacob meets his future wife at the well near Haran. This episode echoes similar ones in ch. 24 (Isaac and Rebekah) and Ex 2.15–21 (Moses and Zipporah). Like Moses, Jacob performs a heroic deed for his future wife, rolling away the huge stone over the well's mouth to water her flocks (v. 10). This act portrays Jacob as physically strong (cf. 32.22–32) and as an agent of fertility, a role he masters at Haran. There is a dense repetition of kinship language in this passage, emphasizing Jacob's journey to his patriarchal kin and the likelihood of a proper marriage. Kinship words—*brothers, son, daughter, father, mother, sister*—occur often after v. 4, and *his mother's brother Laban* occurs three times in v. 10, *when Jacob saw Rachel*. The encounters of Jacob with his kin are sealed by kisses, hugs, and weeping (vv. 11, 13). *My bone and my flesh* stresses the importance of the kinship bond (cf. 2.24). **29.12** *Her father's kinsman.* Jacob and Rachel are related on their father's side (through Abraham and

Nahor). *Rebekah's son.* They are also related on his mother's side. *Rebekah, she ran,* a combination of terms that recalls Rebekah's virtuous haste in 24.28. **29.15–30** As J continues, the happy union of kin is complicated by Jacob's betrothal to Rachel, the younger of Laban's two daughters. The issues of the rights of the firstborn, trickery between father and son, divisions in who loves whom, and even the ability to see echo the story of the deception of Isaac in ch. 27. This time the roles are reversed, and Jacob becomes the trickster tricked, paying a price for his previous deeds. Jacob is deceived by his father-in-law into marrying the firstborn daughter, because he cannot see who she is during the night (v. 25). This is poetic justice for Jacob's deception in ch. 27. *This is not done . . . giving the younger before the firstborn* (v. 26). Laban's resonant reply to Jacob upon his discovery of the deception makes the relationship between the two deceptions clear. Laban prevails by marrying off both daughters to Jacob, the firstborn and then the younger, and receiving fourteen years' labor for the bride-price, twice what Jacob had bargained for. **29.16–18** The issue of the rights of the firstborn is introduced by the aside about Laban's daughters with the contrast of

name of the elder was Leah, and the name of the younger was Rachel. ¹⁷Leah's eyes were lovely,ᵃ and Rachel was graceful and beautiful. ¹⁸Jacob loved Rachel; so he said, "I will serve you seven years for your younger daughter Rachel." ¹⁹Laban said, "It is better that I give her to you than that I should give her to any other man; stay with me." ²⁰So Jacob served seven years for Rachel, and they seemed to him but a few days because of the love he had for her.

21 Then Jacob said to Laban, "Give me my wife that I may go in to her, for my time is completed." ²²So Laban gathered together all the people of the place, and made a feast. ²³But in the evening he took his daughter Leah and brought her to Jacob; and he went in to her. ²⁴(Laban gave his maid Zilpah to his daughter Leah to be her maid.) ²⁵When morning came, it was Leah! And Jacob said to Laban, "What is this you have done to me? Did I not serve with you for Rachel? Why then have you deceived me?" ²⁶Laban said, "This is not done in our country—giving the younger before the first-born. ²⁷Complete the week of this one, and we will give you the other also in return for serving me another seven years." ²⁸Jacob did so, and completed her week; then Laban gave him his daughter Rachel as a wife. ²⁹(Laban gave his maid Bilhah to his daughter Rachel to be her maid.) ³⁰So Jacob went in to Rachel also, and he loved Rachel more than Leah. He served Labanᵇ for another seven years.

31 When the LORD saw that Leah was unloved, he opened her womb; but Rachel was barren. ³²Leah conceived and bore a son, and she named him Reuben;ᶜ for she said, "Because the LORD has looked on my affliction; surely now my husband will love me." ³³She conceived again and bore a son, and said, "Because the LORD has heardᵈ that I am hated, he has given me this son also"; and she named him Simeon. ³⁴Again she conceived and bore a son, and said, "Now this time my husband will be joinedᵉ to me, because I have borne him three sons"; therefore he was named Levi. ³⁵She conceived again and bore a son, and said, "This time I will praiseᶠ the LORD"; therefore she named him Judah; then she ceased bearing.

30 When Rachel saw that she bore Jacob no children, she envied her sister; and she said to Jacob, "Give me children, or I shall die!" ²Jacob became very angry with Rachel and said, "Am I in the place of God, who has withheld from you the fruit of the womb?" ³Then she said, "Here is my maid Bilhah; go in to her, that she may bear upon my knees and that I too may have children through her." ⁴So she gave him her maid Bilhah as a wife; and Jacob went in to her. ⁵And Bilhah conceived and bore Jacob a son. ⁶Then Rachel said, "God

---

ᵃ Meaning of Heb uncertain ᵇ Heb *him* ᶜ That is *See, a son* ᵈ Heb *shama* ᵉ Heb *lawah* ᶠ Heb *hodah*

---

elder and *younger*. The physical contrast between the two daughters brings up the issue of sight: Leah's eyes were *lovely*, or perhaps "weak," but Rachel was *graceful and beautiful*, like Sarah (12.11) and Rebekah (24.16; 26.7). *Jacob loved Rachel*, echoing Isaac's love for Rebekah (24.67). **29.20** The depth of Jacob's love for Rachel makes the seven years of labor seem *but a few days*. This is a rare expression of romantic love in the Bible (outside of the Song of Solomon) and its intensity will extend to her children, Joseph and Benjamin, after Rachel's death. **29.30** *He loved Rachel more than Leah*, an ominous statement leading to God's response in v. 31 and the intense rivalry between the two wives.

29.31–30.24 The birth of Jacob's twelve children in Haran (eleven sons and one daughter; another son is born in 35.16–18) is colored by the barrenness of Rachel and the rivalry of the wives, recalling the relationship of Sarah and Hagar (chs. 16, 21). Like Abraham, Jacob is a rather passive figure in this domestic tale (though he is obviously fertile). The women are the major agents, conceiving, naming the children, and even negotiating over Jacob's services. The names of the sons—the tribes of Israel—are all motivated by the mother's state of mind, and the naming speeches spin elaborate wordplays to anchor the names. Only the daughter, Dinah (who is not a tribe), does not receive a naming speech. The overall movement is determined by God's agency in opening wombs (29.31; 30.22). This text is mostly E, with J sections in 29.31–35; 30.24. **29.31–35** As a consequence of Jacob's preference for Rachel over Leah (v. 30), God opens Leah's womb and not Rachel's. As with Sarah and Rebekah, the wives' barrenness is a preexisting condition, motivating God's intervention. By withholding his grant of fertility to Rachel until 30.22, God causes the unloved wife to bear Jacob's firstborn son. This is recompense to Leah, the senior wife, who deserves Jacob's love. Leah's naming speeches highlight her grief at being unloved, with a moment of divine praise at the birth of her fourth son, Judah, ancestor of the Davidic kings. **30.1–8** Rachel's envy of Leah recalls Sarah's responses to Hagar's pregnancy and child (16.5; 21.10), in which the husband bears the brunt of the wife's anger. Unlike Abraham, Jacob angrily rebuffs his wife and points to God's agency (cf. Joseph's calmer response to his brothers in 50.19). Rachel adopts Sarah's strategy of granting her husband her handmaid as a surrogate wife. *That she may bear upon my knees*, either a legal

has judged me, and has also heard my voice and given me a son"; therefore she named him Dan.[a] [7]Rachel's maid Bilhah conceived again and bore Jacob a second son. [8]Then Rachel said, "With mighty wrestlings I have wrestled[b] with my sister, and have prevailed"; so she named him Naphtali.

9 When Leah saw that she had ceased bearing children, she took her maid Zilpah and gave her to Jacob as a wife. [10]Then Leah's maid Zilpah bore Jacob a son. [11]And Leah said, "Good fortune!" so she named him Gad.[c] [12]Leah's maid Zilpah bore Jacob a second son. [13]And Leah said, "Happy am I! For the women will call me happy"; so she named him Asher.[d]

14 In the days of wheat harvest Reuben went and found mandrakes in the field, and brought them to his mother Leah. Then Rachel said to Leah, "Please give me some of your son's mandrakes." [15]But she said to her, "Is it a small matter that you have taken away my husband? Would you take away my son's mandrakes also?" Rachel said, "Then he may lie with you tonight for your son's mandrakes." [16]When Jacob came from the field in the evening, Leah went out to meet him, and said, "You must come in to me; for I have hired you with my son's mandrakes." So he lay with her that night. [17]And God heeded Leah, and she conceived and bore Jacob a fifth son. [18]Leah said, "God has given me my hire[e] because I gave my maid to my husband"; so she named

him Issachar. [19]And Leah conceived again, and she bore Jacob a sixth son. [20]Then Leah said, "God has endowed me with a good dowry; now my husband will honor[f] me, because I have borne him six sons"; so she named him Zebulun. [21]Afterwards she bore a daughter, and named her Dinah.

22 Then God remembered Rachel, and God heeded her and opened her womb. [23]She conceived and bore a son, and said, "God has taken away my reproach"; [24]and she named him Joseph,[g] saying, "May the LORD add to me another son!"

Jacob Prospers at Laban's Expense

25 When Rachel had borne Joseph, Jacob said to Laban, "Send me away, that I may go to my own home and country. [26]Give me my wives and my children for whom I have served you, and let me go; for you know very well the service I have given you." [27]But Laban said to him, "If you will allow me to say so, I have learned by divination that the LORD has blessed me because of you; [28]name your wages, and I will give it." [29]Jacob said to him, "You yourself know how I have served you, and how your cattle have fared with me. [30]For you had little before I came, and it has increased abundantly; and the LORD has blessed

a That is He judged   b Heb niphtal   c That is Fortune   d That is Happy   e Heb sakar   f Heb zabal   g That is He adds

idiom or an actual ritual signifying that the baby will be Rachel's legal child. Her naming speeches for Dan (v. 6) and Naphtali (v. 8) express her thanks to God and her rivalry with Leah. **30.14–21** The rivalry between Rachel and Leah erupts into a direct confrontation when Reuben discovers some mandrakes, a plant often thought to have aphrodisiac and fertility properties (see Song 7.13). Rachel strikes a slightly comical bargain—Jacob's services in exchange for the mandrakes—and pays the price when Leah conceives yet again. God heeded Leah and not the mandrakes. After the births of Issachar and Zebulun, with appropriate naming speeches, Leah bears a daughter, and names her Dinah (v. 21). Dinah, Leah's seventh and last child, figures prominently in ch. 34. The absence of a naming speech or a motive for her name is curious, perhaps indicating the lesser family status of daughters, which precludes her ancestry of a tribe. **30.22–24** God remembered Rachel, as he had remembered Noah and Abraham previously (8.1; 19.29). God's act of remembering generally entails salvific actions, so God heeded her and opened her womb, as he had previously done twice for Leah (29.31; 30.17). Rachel's firstborn son, Joseph, is now Jacob's youngest son, but he will be

Jacob's favorite (37.3). Joseph receives two naming speeches, one from E (v. 23) and one from J (v. 24), expressing Rachel's thanks and relief and her prayer for another son, which will be fulfilled, but tragically, since she will die in childbirth (35.16–19). **30.25–43** Jacob gains wealth at Laban's expense. The conflict between Jacob and Laban takes a new turn as Laban, the trickster in 29.23–27, tries to trick Jacob again, but is himself tricked. Jacob regains his status as the triumphant trickster, this time in wholly justified fashion. Jacob's acquisition of wealth is due to his own ingenuity and God's blessing, casting him as the appropriate heir to Abraham and Isaac (see 13.2; 26.12–13). Jacob's ability to manipulate the multiplication of flocks also shows him to be a master of fertility, as befits the father of twelve tribes. This story is primarily from the J source, with perhaps v. 40 from the E source; note that the E source in 31.10–12 gives a slightly different account of events. **30.25–28** Send me away. Jacob's plea indicates that his service to Laban is not yet complete (but see 31.41). Laban's greed is not sated, since he has learned by divination that the LORD has blessed him because of Jacob (cf. Joseph's divination in 44.15). He refuses to release Jacob, but relents

you wherever I turned. But now when shall I provide for my own household also?" 31He said, "What shall I give you?" Jacob said, "You shall not give me anything; if you will do this for me, I will again feed your flock and keep it: 32let me pass through all your flock today, removing from it every speckled and spotted sheep and every black lamb, and the spotted and speckled among the goats; and such shall be my wages. 33So my honesty will answer for me later, when you come to look into my wages with you. Every one that is not speckled and spotted among the goats and black among the lambs, if found with me, shall be counted stolen." 34Laban said, "Good! Let it be as you have said." 35But that day Laban removed the male goats that were striped and spotted, and all the female goats that were speckled and spotted, every one that had white on it, and every lamb that was black, and put them in charge of his sons; 36and he set a distance of three days' journey between himself and Jacob, while Jacob was pasturing the rest of Laban's flock.

37 Then Jacob took fresh rods of poplar and almond and plane, and peeled white streaks in them, exposing the white of the rods. 38He set the rods that he had peeled in front of the flocks in the troughs, that is, the watering places, where the flocks came to drink. And since they bred when they came to drink, 39the flocks bred in front of the rods, and so the flocks produced young that were striped, speckled, and spotted. 40Jacob separated the lambs, and set the faces of the flocks toward the striped and the completely black animals in the flock of Laban; and he put his own droves apart, and did not put them with Laban's flock. 41Whenever the stronger of the flock were breeding, Jacob laid the rods in the troughs before the eyes of the flock, that they might breed among the rods, 42but for the feebler of the flock he did not lay them there; so the feebler were Laban's, and the stronger Jacob's. 43Thus the man grew exceedingly rich, and had large flocks, and male and female slaves, and camels and donkeys.

Jacob Flees with Family and Flocks

31 Now Jacob heard that the sons of Laban were saying, "Jacob has taken all that was our father's; he has gained all this wealth from what belonged to our father." 2And Jacob saw that Laban did not regard him as favorably as he did before. 3Then the LORD said to Jacob, "Return to the land of your ancestors and to your kindred, and I will be with you." 4So Jacob sent and called Rachel and Leah into the field where his flock was, 5and said to them, "I see that your father does not regard me as favorably as he did before. But the God of my father has been with me. 6You know that I have served your father with all my strength; 7yet your father has cheated me

somewhat by asking Jacob to name his terms. **30.30–36** Jacob desires to *provide for* his *own household also,* and so agrees to continue keeping Laban's flock on the condition that he will receive as wages the sheep and goats that are discolored (*speckled, spotted,* or *striped*) and the *black lambs* (vv. 32, 35). According to this arrangement, Laban (whose name means "white") retains the white sheep and the black goats (which are their normal colors). But Laban cheats Jacob by removing all the discolored sheep and goats and black lambs to his sons' care, so that Jacob has no flock and no wages. **30.37–43** Jacob turns the tables on Laban by breeding discolored animals from Laban's flock using sympathetic magic: the animals that see discolored rods of wood while breeding will bear discolored offspring. (*White streaks,* an echo of Laban's name; see note on 30.30–36.) Moreover, Jacob only does this for the strong animals; the weaker ones he lets breed normally. As a result, *the feebler were Laban's, and the stronger Jacob's* (v. 42). Thus Jacob tricks Laban, who had tried once again to trick him, and acquires great wealth. **31.1–55** The beginning of Jacob's journey home completes the Jacob-Laban conflict as Jacob flees from Laban and then is caught, and the two finally reconcile. (Note that the end of the journey, in ch. 33, will complete the Jacob-Esau conflict.) In his flight from Laban, reminiscent of his initial flight from Esau, Jacob is still to some extent a trickster, since he leaves without Laban's knowledge (v. 20). Rachel becomes a trickster, stealing the household gods (v. 19, 34–35). The conflict, culminating in a covenant of peace between Jacob and Laban, has resonances of the national conflicts between Israel and Aram. This is primarily an E chapter, with interpolated J passages in vv. 3 (cf. v. 13), 17, and portions of 43–55 and a P text in v. 18. **31.1–16** Jacob's flight is motivated by fear of retribution by Laban and his sons and by God's instruction to return home (v. 13, similarly v. 3). Most of this section is Jacob's speech to Rachel and Leah, seeking their approval. Jacob justifies his acquisition of Laban's wealth on account of his own labor (v. 6), Laban's deceit (v. 7), and God's recompense (v. 9). Throughout his speech he credits God, and he finally relates the dream revelation from God to flee. God's self-revelation that he is the *God of Bethel* and his reference to Jacob's *vow* (v. 13; see 28.20–22) confirm that God has been protecting Jacob, as Jacob had said previously (v. 5), and im-

and changed my wages ten times, but God did not permit him to harm me. 8If he said, 'The speckled shall be your wages,' then all the flock bore speckled; and if he said, 'The striped shall be your wages,' then all the flock bore striped. 9Thus God has taken away the livestock of your father, and given them to me.

10 "During the mating of the flock I once had a dream in which I looked up and saw that the male goats that leaped upon the flock were striped, speckled, and mottled. 11Then the angel of God said to me in the dream, 'Jacob,' and I said, 'Here I am!' 12And he said, 'Look up and see that all the goats that leap on the flock are striped, speckled, and mottled; for I have seen all that Laban is doing to you. 13I am the God of Bethel,*a* where you anointed a pillar and made a vow to me. Now leave this land at once and return to the land of your birth.' " 14Then Rachel and Leah answered him, "Is there any portion or inheritance left to us in our father's house? 15Are we not regarded by him as foreigners? For he has sold us, and he has been using up the money given for us. 16All the property that God has taken away from our father belongs to us and to our children; now then, do whatever God has said to you."

17 So Jacob arose, and set his children and his wives on camels; 18and he drove away all his livestock, all the property that he had gained, the livestock in his possession that he had acquired in Paddan-aram, to go to his father Isaac in the land of Canaan.

19 Now Laban had gone to shear his sheep, and Rachel stole her father's household gods. 20And Jacob deceived Laban the Aramean, in that he did not tell him that he intended to flee. 21So he fled with all that he had; starting out he crossed the Euphrates,*b* and set his face toward the hill country of Gilead.

Laban Overtakes Jacob

22 On the third day Laban was told that Jacob had fled. 23So he took his kinsfolk with him and pursued him for seven days until he caught up with him in the hill country of Gilead. 24But God came to Laban the Aramean in a dream by night, and said to him, "Take heed that you say not a word to Jacob, either good or bad."

25 Laban overtook Jacob. Now Jacob had pitched his tent in the hill country, and Laban with his kinsfolk camped in the hill country of Gilead. 26Laban said to Jacob, "What have you done? You have deceived me, and carried away my daughters like captives of the sword. 27Why did you flee secretly and deceive me and not tell me? I would have sent you away with mirth and songs, with tambourine and lyre. 28And why did you not permit me to kiss my sons and my daughters farewell? What you have done is foolish. 29It is in my power to do you harm; but the God of your father spoke to me last night, saying, 'Take heed that you speak to Jacob neither good nor bad.' 30Even though you had to go because you longed greatly for your father's house, why did you steal my gods?" 31Jacob answered Laban, "Because I was afraid, for I thought that you would take your daughters from me by force. 32But anyone with whom you find your gods shall not live. In the presence of our kinsfolk, point out what I have that is yours, and take

a Cn: Meaning of Heb uncertain   *b* Heb *the river*

plies that God will bring him home safely. After this compelling speech, the wives eloquently express their own anger at Laban and give Jacob their assent (v. 16). **31.19–20** *Rachel stole, Jacob deceived.* Jacob and Rachel are portrayed as parallel tricksters, but Jacob does not know about Rachel's theft (see v. 32). *Household gods,* statues of gods or deified ancestors whose possession is a ritual symbol of the family blessing; they should be inherited by Laban's firstborn son. Rachel's theft of the symbols of Laban's patriarchal blessing thus creates a thematic parallel with Jacob's theft of Isaac's patriarchal blessing (ch. 27). *Deceived Laban,* lit. "stole the heart of Laban"; there is a wordplay on "heart" (Hebrew *leb*) and Laban. *Laban the Aramean* suggests that Laban's ethnic identity as a foreign people will become relevant (see v. 24). **31.22–42** Laban and his kin menacingly pursue and confront Jacob at

Gilead, where their covenant and separation will be marked (v. 47). But God warns Laban not to harm Jacob (v. 29). Laban rebukes Jacob, claiming disingenuously that he would have had a festive farewell, then turns to the matter of the stolen household gods. When Laban fails to find them, Jacob rebukes him and in an eloquent speech sums up his grievances at Laban's hands. **31.23–24** *Kinsfolk . . . pursued . . . seven days,* a picture of a quasi-military campaign. This image, in combination with the setting of *the hill country of Gilead* and God's warning to *Laban the Aramean,* create a connection with the historical conflict between Israel and Aram. The region of Gilead (in Transjordan) was contested by Israel and Aram in the ninth century BCE (see 2 Kings 6–13), and the encounter of Laban and Jacob resonates with this historical conflict. **31.32** Jacob's oath to Laban (v. 32) is based on his not

it." Now Jacob did not know that Rachel had stolen the gods. [a]

33 So Laban went into Jacob's tent, and into Leah's tent, and into the tent of the two maids, but he did not find them. And he went out of Leah's tent, and entered Rachel's. 34Now Rachel had taken the household gods and put them in the camel's saddle, and sat on them. Laban felt all about in the tent, but did not find them. 35And she said to her father, "Let not my lord be angry that I cannot rise before you, for the way of women is upon me." So he searched, but did not find the household gods.

36 Then Jacob became angry, and upbraided Laban. Jacob said to Laban, "What is my offense? What is my sin, that you have hotly pursued me? 37Although you have felt about through all my goods, what have you found of all your household goods? Set it here before my kinsfolk and your kinsfolk, so that they may decide between us two. 38These twenty years I have been with you; your ewes and your female goats have not miscarried, and I have not eaten the rams of your flocks. 39That which was torn by wild beasts I did not bring to you; I bore the loss of it myself; of my hand you required it, whether stolen by day or stolen by night. 40It was like this with me: by day the heat consumed me, and the cold by night, and my sleep fled from my eyes. 41These twenty years I have been in your house; I served you fourteen years for your two daughters, and six years for your flock, and you have changed my wages ten times. 42If the God of

my father, the God of Abraham and the Fear [b] of Isaac, had not been on my side, surely now you would have sent me away empty-handed. God saw my affliction and the labor of my hands, and rebuked you last night."

Laban and Jacob Make a Covenant

43 Then Laban answered and said to Jacob, "The daughters are my daughters, the children are my children, the flocks are my flocks, and all that you see is mine. But what can I do today about these daughters of mine, or about their children whom they have borne? 44Come now, let us make a covenant, you and I; and let it be a witness between you and me." 45So Jacob took a stone, and set it up as a pillar. 46And Jacob said to his kinsfolk, "Gather stones," and they took stones, and made a heap; and they ate there by the heap. 47Laban called it Jegar-sahadutha: [c] but Jacob called it Galeed. [d] 48Laban said, "This heap is a witness between you and me today." Therefore he called it Galeed, [e] 49and the pillar [e] Mizpah, [f] for he said, "The LORD watch between you and me, when we are absent one from the other. 50If you ill-treat my daughters, or if you take wives in addition to my daughters, though no one else is with us, remember that God is witness between you and me."

51 Then Laban said to Jacob, "See this heap and see the pillar, which I have set between

---

a Heb them b Meaning of Heb uncertain c In Aramaic The heap of witness d In Hebrew The heap of witness e Compare Sam: MT lacks the pillar f That is Watchpost

---

knowing *that Rachel had stolen the gods.* Laban does not find the gods, but Rachel dies shortly after the return to Canaan (35.19), perhaps in tragic fulfillment of Jacob's oath. **31.34–35** The scene of Laban's search of the tents is suspenseful and comical. In Rachel's tent—domestic space, a woman's space—Laban is completely outwitted. Laban feels all about (cf. Isaac feeling Jacob in 27.21–22), but he cannot feel the saddlebag because of Rachel's ruse. The father loses the symbols of the family blessing because of his daughter's ruse, confirming Rachel as a trickster and Jacob's true counterpart. There is further irony, since Rachel, Leah, and Jacob have indeed inherited Laban's wealth, but due to the agency of God, not Laban's household gods (see vv. 5, 16). **31.43–55** The covenant of peace between Laban and Jacob is woven together from E and J passages that have been carefully harmonized. Note that two symbols of the covenant are erected: a pillar (v. 45) and a heap of stones (v. 46). There are two meals (vv. 46, 54). There are two names of the place: Galeed (a variation on Gilead) and Mizpah (vv. 47–

49). Laban makes two speeches announcing the stipulations of the covenant: in one Jacob is to treat Laban's daughters well and take no other wives, and *God is witness* (vv. 48–50, mostly E); and in the other neither party will pass beyond the covenant marker, and God is invoked *to judge between* them (vv. 51–54, mostly J). Both of Laban's speeches to Jacob are eloquent and noble, and his last gestures, kissing and blessing his grandchildren and daughters, rehabilitate his character and provide a proper reconciliation. **31.45–49** The stone pillar recalls the pillar that Jacob set up at Bethel (28.18). Stone pillars mark sacred space, boundaries, and other places of memory (such as tombs; see 35.20). Here the stone pillar and the heap of stones memorialize the covenant with Laban and mark the boundary between Israel and Aram. The stone pillar (Hebrew *mazzevah*) motivates the name of the place as *Mizpah*, "watchpost," and the pile of stones motivates the name of the place as *Galeed* (Gilead), taken to mean "the heap of witness." The bilingual naming of *Galeed* in v. 47, in Aramaic by Laban and in Hebrew by

you and me. ⁵²This heap is a witness, and the pillar is a witness, that I will not pass beyond this heap to you, and you will not pass beyond this heap and this pillar to me, for harm. ⁵³May the God of Abraham and the God of Nahor"—the God of their father—"judge between us." So Jacob swore by the Fear*ᵃ* of his father Isaac, ⁵⁴and Jacob offered a sacrifice on the height and called his kinsfolk to eat bread; and they ate bread and tarried all night in the hill country.

⁵⁵*ᵇ* Early in the morning Laban rose up, and kissed his grandchildren and his daughters and blessed them; then he departed and returned home.

32 Jacob went on his way and the angels of God met him; ²and when Jacob saw them he said, "This is God's camp!" So he called that place Mahanaim.*ᶜ*

Jacob Sends Presents to Appease Esau

3 Jacob sent messengers before him to his brother Esau in the land of Seir, the country of Edom, ⁴instructing them, "Thus you shall say to my lord Esau: Thus says your servant Jacob, 'I have lived with Laban as an alien, and stayed until now; ⁵and I have oxen, donkeys, flocks,

male and female slaves; and I have sent to tell my lord, in order that I may find favor in your sight.' "

6 The messengers returned to Jacob, saying, "We came to your brother Esau, and he is coming to meet you, and four hundred men are with him." ⁷Then Jacob was greatly afraid and distressed; and he divided the people that were with him, and the flocks and herds and camels, into two companies, ⁸thinking, "If Esau comes to the one company and destroys it, then the company that is left will escape."

9 And Jacob said, "O God of my father Abraham and God of my father Isaac, O LORD who said to me, 'Return to your country and to your kindred, and I will do you good,' ¹⁰I am not worthy of the least of all the steadfast love and all the faithfulness that you have shown to your servant, for with only my staff I crossed this Jordan; and now I have become two companies. ¹¹Deliver me, please, from the hand of my brother, from the hand of Esau, for I am afraid of him; he may come and kill us all, the mothers with the children. ¹²Yet you

---

a Meaning of Heb uncertain   *b* Ch 32.1 in Heb   *c* Here taken to mean *Two camps*

Jacob, highlights the resonance of this treaty as one between Aram and Israel. **31.53** *The God of Abraham and the God of Nahor.* It is not clear whether Laban's invocation refers to one god or two. Normally in such treaties one invokes the gods of both parties as judges or witnesses. *The God of their father,* probably an explanatory gloss to indicate one god. *The Fear of his father Isaac,* an expansion of the divine epithet *the Fear of Isaac* (see v. 42), equivalent to *the God of Abraham* (as in v. 42). This unusual epithet seems to refer to the religious awe or fear of being in God's presence. Note the expression *fear of God* (with a different Hebrew word for "fear") to denote religious devotion and virtue (20.11; 22.12). **32.1–2** In this brief report from E, Jacob's angelic encounter has resonances that point backward and forward. He encounters the *angels of God* during both journeys (see 28.12). His naming speech, *This is God's camp* (Hebrew *machaneh*), motivating the place-name *Mahanaim,* also recalls his naming speech at Bethel (*bet 'el,* 28.17). Jacob's angelic encounter also points forward to his sending of *messengers* (*mal'akim,* the same word for "angels") in v. 3 and to his encounter with a divine being (vv. 22–32). *Mahanaim* (lit. "two camps") anticipates Jacob's division of his retinue into *two companies* ("two camps") in vv. 7–8, 10. **32.3–21** Jacob prepares to meet Esau, fearing that Esau will attack him. In the J version (vv. 3–13a) he prepares by dividing his retinue into two camps, hoping that in case of attack one *will escape* (v. 8) and prays to God to

deliver him. In the E text (vv. 13b–21) he prepares a gift of livestock, hoping to *appease* Esau (v. 20). The two versions complement each other and provide an ironic backdrop to the dangerous encounter that occurs next—not with Esau (who turns out not to be menacing at all), but with God. **32.3–4** Esau now lives *in the land of Seir, the country of Edom,* as the earlier story foretold by the indicative words, *hairy* (25.25; 27.11) and *red* (25.25, 30; see note on 25.24–27). Although Esau is *his brother,* Jacob delicately addresses him as *my lord Esau* and refers to himself as *your servant Jacob.* He continues to use these terms when they meet in 33.4–16 (*my lord,* five times; *your servant,* twice). This locution reverses the relationship foretold in Isaac's blessing: Jacob will *be lord over* his brother (27.29) and Esau *shall serve* his brother (27.40). Jacob is attempting to mollify Esau by his deliberate use of language. **32.6** That Esau *is coming to meet* Jacob is a natural response to Jacob's message. That *four hundred men are with him* raises the likelihood that Esau is coming to exact revenge, echoing the pursuit of Jacob by Laban and his kin (31.23) and recalling Esau's intention to kill Jacob (27.41). **32.9–13** Jacob's eloquent prayer recalls, at the beginning and end, God's promises in 31.3 and 28.13–15. Jacob's humility (v. 10) sounds a new note in his character, though self-abasement is a normal part of such discourse; cf. 47.9. His emotional appeal to the death of *mothers* and *children* (v. 11) is capped by his reference to God's promise of many descendants (v. 12), which yields a compelling

have said, 'I will surely do you good, and make your offspring as the sand of the sea, which cannot be counted because of their number.' "

13 So he spent that night there, and from what he had with him he took a present for his brother Esau, [14]two hundred female goats and twenty male goats, two hundred ewes and twenty rams, [15]thirty milch camels and their colts, forty cows and ten bulls, twenty female donkeys and ten male donkeys. [16]These he delivered into the hand of his servants, every drove by itself, and said to his servants, "Pass on ahead of me, and put a space between drove and drove." [17]He instructed the foremost, "When Esau my brother meets you, and asks you, 'To whom do you belong? Where are you going? And whose are these ahead of you?' [18]then you shall say, 'They belong to your servant Jacob; they are a present sent to my lord Esau; and moreover he is behind us.' " [19]He likewise instructed the second and the third and all who followed the droves, "You shall say the same thing to Esau when you meet him, [20]and you shall say, 'Moreover your servant Jacob is behind us.' " For he thought, "I may appease him with the present that goes ahead of me, and afterwards I shall see his face; perhaps he will accept me." [21]So the present passed on ahead of him; and he himself spent that night in the camp.

Jacob Wrestles at Peniel

22 The same night he got up and took his two wives, his two maids, and his eleven children, and crossed the ford of the Jabbok. [23]He took them and sent them across the stream, and likewise everything that he had. [24]Jacob was left alone; and a man wrestled with him until daybreak. [25]When the man saw that he did not prevail against Jacob, he struck him on the hip socket; and Jacob's hip was put out of joint as he wrestled with him. [26]Then he said, "Let me go, for the day is breaking." But Jacob said, "I will not let you go, unless you bless me." [27]So he said to him, "What is your name?" And he said, "Jacob." [28]Then the man[a] said, "You shall no longer be called Jacob, but Israel,[b] for you have striven with God and with humans,[c] and have prevailed." [29]Then Jacob asked him, "Please tell me your name." But he said, "Why is it that you ask my name?" And there he blessed him. [30]So Jacob called the place Peniel,[d] saying, "For I have seen God face to face,

---

a Heb *he*   b That is *The one who strives with God* or *God strives*   c Or *with divine and human beings*   d That is *The face of God*

---

case for deliverance. His spending the night (v. 13a, J) is resumed in v. 22. Note the doublet in the E version (v. 21). **32.13–21** Jacob will offer his *present* (*minchah*, v. 13) to Esau in 33.10. The spacing of the groups of livestock will allow ample time for Esau's anger to abate before he sees Jacob. *Afterwards I shall see his face* (*panav*, v. 20), ironic anticipation of Jacob seeing God's face at Penuel (lit. "face of God"). While the *present* (*minchah*) passes ahead, Jacob sleeps at the *camp* (*machaneh*, v. 21). **32.22–32** Jacob's encounter with a mysterious divine being at Penuel is a counterpart to his encounter with God or angels of God at Bethel (28.10–22). Through this symbolic and dangerous rite of passage, the patriarch becomes the eponymous ancestor of Israel, a name that commemorates his successful strivings with God and humans. In this story Jacob-Israel also becomes a symbol—he epitomizes the people Israel, who perennially strive with God and others, survive, and prevail. The tone of the story is deliberately ambiguous and mysterious. It is primarily an E story, with a J text in v. 22. **32.22–24** The strangeness of the story begins with the disconcerting doublet of vv. 22 (J) and 23 (E). In one Jacob crosses the river with his family, but in the other Jacob remains behind. It is the middle of the night (as in Jacob's divine encounter at Bethel), and *Jacob was left alone*. The strangeness continues with the abrupt assault. The identity of the man is not given; even the type of being is unknown

(Hebrew '*ish, man*, can refer to a human or a deity). *Wrestled* (*ye'abeq*) completes a three-way wordplay with Jacob's name (*ya'aqov*) and the name of the river Jabbok (*yabboq*), as if the mysterious encounter emerges from Jacob's being in this place. *Until daybreak* anticipates the mysterious request in v. 26. **32.25–30** Jacob is injured, but he refuses to relent unless he receives a blessing (v. 26). By this request Jacob reveals his recognition that his mysterious assailant is a deity. The request echoes his earlier successful attempts to gain the firstborn's blessing. *Let me go . . . day is breaking.* Perhaps angels have a duty to be present in heaven at dawn, or perhaps the nighttime is generally a dangerous time when divine spirits may attack. Jacob gives his name and receives a new one, but the deity will not disclose his own name (cf. Judg 13.17–18). The meaning of Jacob's new name, *Israel*, is explained as *you have striven* (*sarita*) *with God* ('*elohim*) *and with humans, and have prevailed*, referring to Jacob's victory over Esau, Isaac, Laban, and now God (or alternately, "gods"). It is unclear whether the divine being is an angel of God or God himself, since angels can speak in God's name. Jacob's response of naming the place *Peniel/Penuel* (vv. 30–31; both mean "face of God"), since he saw God *face to face* (v. 30), points to God himself, but the story and its language are ambiguous (note that the divine adversary is explicitly an "angel" in Hos 12.4). On the idea that no one can see God's face and

and yet my life is preserved." 31The sun rose upon him as he passed Penuel, limping because of his hip. 32Therefore to this day the Israelites do not eat the thigh muscle that is on the hip socket, because he struck Jacob on the hip socket at the thigh muscle.

Jacob and Esau Meet

33 Now Jacob looked up and saw Esau coming, and four hundred men with him. So he divided the children among Leah and Rachel and the two maids. 2He put the maids with their children in front, then Leah with her children, and Rachel and Joseph last of all. 3He himself went on ahead of them, bowing himself to the ground seven times, until he came near his brother.

4 But Esau ran to meet him, and embraced him, and fell on his neck and kissed him, and they wept. 5When Esau looked up and saw the women and children, he said, "Who are these with you?" Jacob said, "The children whom God has graciously given your servant." 6Then the maids drew near, they and their children, and bowed down; 7Leah likewise and her children drew near and bowed down; and finally Joseph and Rachel drew near, and they bowed down. 8Esau said, "What do you mean by all this company that I met?" Jacob answered, "To find favor with my lord." 9But Esau said, "I have enough, my brother; keep what you have

for yourself." 10Jacob said, "No, please; if I find favor with you, then accept my present from my hand; for truly to see your face is like seeing the face of God—since you have received me with such favor. 11Please accept my gift that is brought to you, because God has dealt graciously with me, and because I have everything I want." So he urged him, and he took it.

12 Then Esau said, "Let us journey on our way, and I will go alongside you." 13But Jacob said to him, "My lord knows that the children are frail and that the flocks and herds, which are nursing, are a care to me; and if they are overdriven for one day, all the flocks will die. 14Let my lord pass on ahead of his servant, and I will lead on slowly, according to the pace of the cattle that are before me and according to the pace of the children, until I come to my lord in Seir." 15So Esau said, "Let me leave with you some of the people who are with me." But he said, "Why should my lord be so kind to me?" 16So Esau returned that day on his way to Seir. 17But Jacob journeyed to Succoth,a and built himself a house, and made booths for his cattle; therefore the place is called Succoth.

Jacob Reaches Shechem

18 Jacob came safely to the city of Shechem, which is in the land of Canaan, on his way

_____
a That is Booths

live, see Ex 33.20, Isa 6.5; this idea applies also to angels in Judg 6.22–23; 13.22. **32.31–32** *The sun rose upon him,* signaling a new beginning and new life after Jacob's potentially deadly encounter. *Limping* (see v. 25). Jacob is both blessed and damaged by his divine encounter. An aside derives the dietary prohibition of the *thigh muscle* (the Hebrew phrase is obscure) as a commemoration of Jacob's injury. *Therefore to this day the Israelites.* The shift to the present joins the sacred past to the present as a charter and justification and discloses the Israelites (lit. "the sons of Israel") as the promised descendants of the patriarch Israel.

33.1–17 In the final encounter of his journey home, Jacob meets Esau and the two are reconciled. Jacob is consistently suspicious of Esau's intentions, but Esau shows himself to be gracious and noble, harboring no hostility. *My lord, your servant.* See note on 32.3–4. At the end, ever the trickster, Jacob parts from Esau with deceptive excuses, rather than journeying on with him. This text is primarily J, with some interpolations from E (e.g., in vv. 10–11). **33.1–3** Jacob's defensive strategy on seeing Esau with *four hundred men* is to divide the women and children into three groups (cf. 32.7), from least to most valuable. His preference for *Rachel and Joseph,* placing them *last of all,* recalls the

reason for his wives' rivalry in chs. 29–30 and anticipates the conflict between Joseph and his brothers. Jacob's *bowing himself to the ground* is intended to placate Esau's wrath and neatly reverses the blessing of 27.29. **33.4** Esau's running to meet Jacob is possibly the feared violent attack, but instead there is a traditional joyous greeting of kin (see 29.11, 13). Instead of an attack, the brothers are reconciled. **33.8–9** Jacob hopes *to find favor with* Esau, apparently by offering all his possessions as a gift. But Esau shows that he harbors no ill will, replying that he has *enough.* In this exchange, Esau shows virtue and eloquence and apparently has prospered in spite of the loss of his blessing. **33.10** *To see your face . . . face of God,* high praise and also ironic, since Jacob has just *seen God face to face* the night before (32.30). And in both meetings, to Jacob's relief, his life was preserved (32.30). **33.11** *My gift,* better "my blessing" (Hebrew *birkati*). Jacob rhetorically offers to return the blessing to Esau. The gift may be the flocks and herds of 32.13–15. **33.12–17** Jacob remains unsure of Esau's intentions and gives deceptive excuses not to travel to Seir with him. Instead, Jacob journeys toward Canaan and stays for a time at Succoth, east of the Jordan River, so called because he built booths (*sukkot*) there. **33.18–20** A brief passage from E

from Paddan-aram; and he camped before the city. 19And from the sons of Hamor, Shechem's father, he bought for one hundred pieces of money[a] the plot of land on which he had pitched his tent. 20There he erected an altar and called it El-Elohe-Israel.[b]

The Rape of Dinah

34 Now Dinah the daughter of Leah, whom she had borne to Jacob, went out to visit the women of the region. 2When Shechem son of Hamor the Hivite, prince of the region, saw her, he seized her and lay with her by force. 3And his soul was drawn to Dinah daughter of Jacob; he loved the girl, and spoke tenderly to her. 4So Shechem spoke to his father Hamor, saying, "Get me this girl to be my wife."

5 Now Jacob heard that Shechem[c] had defiled his daughter Dinah; but his sons were with his cattle in the field, so Jacob held his peace until they came. 6And Hamor the father of Shechem went out to Jacob to speak with him, 7just as the sons of Jacob came in from the field. When they heard of it, the men were indignant and very angry, because he had committed an outrage in Israel by lying with Jacob's daughter, for such a thing ought not to be done.

8 But Hamor spoke with them, saying, "The heart of my son Shechem longs for your daughter; please give her to him in marriage. 9Make marriages with us; give your daughters to us, and take our daughters for yourselves. 10You shall live with us; and the land shall be open to you; live and trade in it, and get property in it." 11Shechem also said to her father and to her brothers, "Let me find favor with you, and whatever you say to me I will give. 12Put the marriage present and gift as high as you like, and I will give whatever you ask me; only give me the girl to be my wife."

13 The sons of Jacob answered Shechem and his father Hamor deceitfully, because he had defiled their sister Dinah. 14They said to them, "We cannot do this thing, to give our sister to one who is uncircumcised, for that

a Heb one hundred qesitah   b That is God, the God of Israel
c Heb he

describing Jacob's arrival at Shechem and his purchase of a plot of land there, where he founds a shrine to *El-Elohe-Israel* ("El, the God of Israel"). Shechem was an important Israelite shrine (see Josh 24). This El epithet is comparable to *El Elyon* (14.19), *El Shaddai* (17.1), *El Olam* (21.33), and *El-bethel* (35.7), all of which seem to identify El (the old Canaanite high god) with the God of Israel. The brief reference to *Paddan-aram* is from the P source.

34.1–31 With Jacob's return to Canaan the stories turn to conflicts involving Jacob's children. In this story Jacob's children are grown, and Jacob becomes the aging patriarch whose authority is waning. The story of Dinah concerns the proper relations between the children of Israel and the native inhabitants of Canaan and involves honor, sex, violence, and moral breaches within Israel's family. Dinah's role is as daughter, sister, sexual victim, and potential bride, but she only briefly has volition of her own; generally her role is in relation to the men of the story. Of her later life we are not told. This is a J story, in which the characters are enmeshed in moral ambiguities of their own making. **34.1** *The daughter of Leah . . . Jacob.* Dinah's introduction places her in the context of women, marriage, and offspring and also signals the responsibility of Jacob and her nearest brothers, the sons of Leah (including Simeon and Levi), to protect her. *Women of the region,* lit. "daughters of the land." Easy commerce between the daughter of Leah and the daughters of the land is potentially dangerous, because daughters have brothers. **34.2–4** *Shechem,* the name of the city and of its prince. The Hivites are one of the peoples of Ca-

naan (10.17), whom the Israelites are later admonished not to marry and to utterly destroy (Deut 7.1–3). Perhaps because he is a Canaanite, Shechem rapes Dinah *by force,* yet he also falls in love with her and speaks *tenderly to her*—a remarkable turn from a violent rapist to a sympathetic figure. Dinah is now referred to as *daughter of Jacob,* raising the issue of her father's response to rape or betrothal, but as a dishonored daughter Dinah has no active voice in the issue. **34.5–8** Surprisingly, Jacob is silent and waits for his sons' reaction. Although Dinah has been *defiled* by the rape, in theory her honor and the family's honor can be restored if the man marries her (Deut 22.28–29), though this is complicated by his identity as a Hivite (see note on 34.2–4). The sons are *indignant and very angry,* not seeing the complexity of the situation, only the dishonor. *Committed an outrage in Israel* emphasizes the contrast between Israel, still a nascent nation, and the Canaanite/Hivite world of its neighbors. **34.8–12** *Hamor*'s name ("donkey") may refer to the old Canaanite practice of sealing a treaty with a donkey sacrifice. He offers a treaty here to intermarry and share the land. This would efface the independent identity of Israel, leading to its absorption into Canaan. It also violates the commandment not to enter into a covenant with the Canaanites (Ex 23.32). Shechem increases the offer to include any bride-price. **34.13–17** Jacob's sons, showing their true inheritance, answer *deceitfully* (cf. Jacob in 27.35). Now the sons are tricksters, proposing circumcision as their condition. This painful operation (for an adult) is poetic justice for Shechem's violent act of rape and will dis-

would be a disgrace to us. 15Only on this condition will we consent to you: that you will become as we are and every male among you be circumcised. 16Then we will give our daughters to you, and we will take your daughters for ourselves, and we will live among you and become one people. 17But if you will not listen to us and be circumcised, then we will take our daughter and be gone."

18 Their words pleased Hamor and Hamor's son Shechem. 19And the young man did not delay to do the thing, because he was delighted with Jacob's daughter. Now he was the most honored of all his family. 20So Hamor and his son Shechem came to the gate of their city and spoke to the men of their city, saying, 21"These people are friendly with us; let them live in the land and trade in it, for the land is large enough for them; let us take their daughters in marriage, and let us give them our daughters. 22Only on this condition will they agree to live among us, to become one people: that every male among us be circumcised as they are circumcised. 23Will not their livestock, their property, and all their animals be ours? Only let us agree with them, and they will live among us." 24And all who went out of the city gate heeded Hamor and his son Shechem; and every male was circumcised, all who went out of the gate of his city.

Dinah's Brothers Avenge Their Sister

25 On the third day, when they were still in pain, two of the sons of Jacob, Simeon and Levi, Dinah's brothers, took their swords and came against the city unawares, and killed all the males. 26They killed Hamor and his son Shechem with the sword, and took Dinah out of Shechem's house, and went away. 27And the other sons of Jacob came upon the slain, and plundered the city, because their sister had been defiled. 28They took their flocks and their herds, their donkeys, and whatever was in the city and in the field. 29All their wealth, all their little ones and their wives, all that was in the houses, they captured and made their prey. 30Then Jacob said to Simeon and Levi, "You have brought trouble on me by making me odious to the inhabitants of the land, the Canaanites and the Perizzites; my numbers are few, and if they gather themselves against me and attack me, I shall be destroyed, both I and my household." 31But they said, "Should our sister be treated like a whore?"

Jacob Returns to Bethel

35 God said to Jacob, "Arise, go up to Bethel, and settle there. Make an altar there to the God who appeared to you when you fled from your brother Esau." 2So Jacob said to his household and to all who were with him, "Put away the foreign gods that are among you, and purify yourselves, and change your clothes; 3then come, let us go up to Bethel, that I may make an altar there to the God who answered me in the day of my distress and has been with me wherever I have gone." 4So they gave to Jacob all the foreign gods that they had, and the rings that were in their ears; and Jacob hid them under the oak that was near Shechem.

5 As they journeyed, a terror from God fell

comfit the Shechemite males for several days. **34.25–31** *Dinah's brothers.* Simeon and Levi are Leah's children and as such are responsible for their sister. They exact revenge, taking advantage of the men's incapacity owing to the circumcision, and rescue Dinah (who is curiously in *Shechem's house,* v. 26). The brothers despoil the city. This brutality serves to restore the family's honor, but is unwise, as Jacob angrily points out. The brothers' crude justice prevails, but Simeon and Levi pay the price when Jacob curses them on his deathbed (49.7). Hence the tribe of Simeon was absorbed into Judah, and Levi, the priestly tribe, was scattered throughout Israel.

35.1–29 The last chapter of the Jacob story tells of his return to Bethel and is punctuated by three deaths (Deborah, Rachel, and Isaac) and one birth (Benjamin). The death of Isaac is the formal end of this part of the patriarchal narratives, and the birth of Benjamin points toward the next section, the Joseph story.

This chapter is composed of E and P texts, with one passage from J (vv. 21–22a). **35.1–15** Jacob's return to Bethel is told in two versions, E (vv. 1–8) and P (vv. 9–15). The E story refers to the earlier revelation at Bethel (28.10–22) and provides a fulfillment of his vow made there. The P story provides Jacob with the patriarchal blessing and the change of name from Jacob to Israel (cf. 32.28, E). Both stories conclude with Jacob naming the place Bethel or El-bethel (vv. 7, 15). **35.1–4** God calls Jacob to move from Shechem to Bethel to fulfill his vow (see 28.20–22). Since God has done his part (*has been with me,* v. 3; cf. 28.20), Jacob prepares his family for the worship of God alone by casting off foreign gods and purifying them for worship (cf. Ex 19.10–11; Josh 24.23, the latter also at Shechem). The earrings are buried with the statues of foreign gods, presumably because they could be used to make more such statues (as Ex 32.2; Judg 8.24). The *oak that was near Shechem,* the sacred tree where

upon the cities all around them, so that no one pursued them. 6Jacob came to Luz (that is, Bethel), which is in the land of Canaan, he and all the people who were with him, 7and there he built an altar and called the place El-bethel,*a* because it was there that God had revealed himself to him when he fled from his brother. 8And Deborah, Rebekah's nurse, died, and she was buried under an oak below Bethel. So it was called Allon-bacuth.*b*

9 God appeared to Jacob again when he came from Paddan-aram, and he blessed him. 10God said to him, "Your name is Jacob; no longer shall you be called Jacob, but Israel shall be your name." So he was called Israel. 11God said to him, "I am God Almighty:*c* be fruitful and multiply; a nation and a company of nations shall come from you, and kings shall spring from you. 12The land that I gave to Abraham and Isaac I will give to you, and I will give the land to your offspring after you." 13Then God went up from him at the place where he had spoken with him. 14Jacob set up a pillar in the place where he had spoken with him, a pillar of stone; and he poured out a drink offering on it, and poured oil on it. 15So Jacob called the place where God had spoken with him Bethel.

The Birth of Benjamin and the Death of Rachel

16 Then they journeyed from Bethel; and when they were still some distance from Ephrath, Rachel was in childbirth, and she had hard labor. 17When she was in her hard labor, the midwife said to her, "Do not be afraid; for now you will have another son." 18As her soul was departing (for she died), she named him Ben-oni;*d* but his father called him Benjamin.*e* 19So Rachel died, and she was buried on the way to Ephrath (that is, Bethlehem), 20and Jacob set up a pillar at her grave; it is the pillar of Rachel's tomb, which is there to this day. 21Israel journeyed on, and pitched his tent beyond the tower of Eder.

22 While Israel lived in that land, Reuben

---

a That is *God of Bethel* *b* That is *Oak of weeping* *c* Traditional rendering of Heb *El Shaddai* *d* That is *Son of my sorrow* *e* That is *Son of the right hand* or *Son of the South*

Abram built an altar in 12.6–7 (J) and where the covenant ceremony occurs in Josh 24.26. **35.5** *Terror from God* anticipates the divine fear that protects the Israelites on their journey to the promised land (Ex 15.16; 23.27; Josh 1.9). This detail presupposes a version of the conflict with the people of Shechem like that in ch. 34 (J). **35.6–7** *Luz,* the older name of the site, which Jacob now names *El-bethel,* "El of Bethel" or "God of Bethel." Cf. the naming of Bethel in J (28.19) and P (35.15). The altar and the naming complete the shrine, which Jacob had vowed would be *God's house* (*bet 'elohim,* 28.22) if God would return him in peace. **35.8** The death of *Deborah, Rebekah's nurse* (who suckled her as an infant), is a curious detail. Rebekah's nurse accompanies Rebekah to Canaan (24.59), but is unnamed. Rebekah's own death is never mentioned. The death of the old nursemaid, associated with Jacob's mother as a baby, foreshadows the death of Rachel, Jacob's beloved wife, in childbirth. Her monument, the *oak of weeping,* also foreshadows Rachel's tomb and memorial pillar (35.20). **35.9–15** The P version of God's revelation to Jacob and the establishment of the shrine of Bethel echoes many features of the revelation to Abram in 17.1–8 (P). God changes the patriarch's name from Jacob to Israel (as he changed Abram to Abraham, 17.5), reveals his divine name as *El Shaddai* (as in 17.1), and gives the patriarchal promises of fruitfulness, nations, kings, and land (see 17.6–8). Unlike the parallels in 28.10–20; 32.22–32, there are no angelic visions or vows or dangerous encounters, merely God's direct revelation and speech to his chosen patriarch. The placement of the P version after the J and E stories makes it a serious and emphatic reiteration of the divine promises and blessings. The erection of the pillar and the naming of Bethel (cf. 28.18–19; 35.7) also serve to highlight the association of Jacob as the founder of this important shrine. Interestingly, this is the only local shrine that has a foundation legend in P. **35.16–20** Benjamin is the only child of Jacob born in the land of Canaan, in his own tribal territory, but Benjamin's birth is tragically colored by the death of his mother in childbirth. The simultaneous birth of Benjamin and death of Rachel set the stage for Jacob's deep attachment to Rachel's sons, Joseph and Benjamin, in the Joseph story. As Rachel was the beloved wife (see 29.20, 30), so her sons will be the beloved sons. But here the grief belongs to Rachel, as she dies with the birth name, *Son of my sorrow* (v. 18), on her lips. This is an E passage (cf. 48.7, P). Jacob's erection of a *pillar* as Rachel's memorial recalls the sacred pillar at Bethel (28.18, E) and the huge stone that he moved for Rachel when they first met (29.10, J). **35.19** According to 1 Sam 10.2 (cf. Jer 31.14), Rachel's tomb is in the territory of Benjamin, north of Jerusalem. This fits the location *on the way to Ephrath* from Bethel. The territory of the Judahite clan of Ephrath extended to Kiriath-jearim, on the border between Benjamin and Judah, northwest of Jerusalem (Josh 9.17; 1 Chr 2.50). The scribal gloss situating Rachel's tomb in *Bethlehem* is probably a confusion based on the close association of Ephrath with the city of Bethlehem, south of Jerusalem, famous as the birthplace of David (see Mic 5.2). **35.21–22a** This brief passage from the J source tells of Jacob (now usually called

went and lay with Bilhah his father's concubine; and Israel heard of it.

Now the sons of Jacob were twelve. 23The sons of Leah: Reuben (Jacob's firstborn), Simeon, Levi, Judah, Issachar, and Zebulun. 24The sons of Rachel: Joseph and Benjamin. 25The sons of Bilhah, Rachel's maid: Dan and Naphtali. 26The sons of Zilpah, Leah's maid: Gad and Asher. These were the sons of Jacob who were born to him in Paddan-aram.

The Death of Isaac

27 Jacob came to his father Isaac at Mamre, or Kiriath-arba (that is, Hebron), where Abraham and Isaac had resided as aliens. 28Now the days of Isaac were one hundred eighty years. 29And Isaac breathed his last; he died and was gathered to his people, old and full of days; and his sons Esau and Jacob buried him.

Esau's Descendants

36 These are the descendants of Esau (that is, Edom). 2Esau took his wives from the Canaanites: Adah daughter of Elon the Hittite, Oholibamah daughter of Anah son*a* of Zibeon the Hivite, 3and Basemath, Ishmael's daughter, sister of Nebaioth. 4Adah bore Eliphaz to Esau; Basemath bore Reuel; 5and Oholibamah bore Jeush, Jalam, and Korah. These are the sons of Esau who were born to him in the land of Canaan.

6 Then Esau took his wives, his sons, his daughters, and all the members of his household, his cattle, all his livestock, and all the property he had acquired in the land of Ca-

naan; and he moved to a land some distance from his brother Jacob. 7For their possessions were too great for them to live together; the land where they were staying could not support them because of their livestock. 8So Esau settled in the hill country of Seir; Esau is Edom.

9 These are the descendants of Esau, ancestor of the Edomites, in the hill country of Seir. 10These are the names of Esau's sons: Eliphaz son of Adah the wife of Esau; Reuel, the son of Esau's wife Basemath. 11The sons of Eliphaz were Teman, Omar, Zepho, Gatam, and Kenaz. 12(Timna was a concubine of Eliphaz, Esau's son; she bore Amalek to Eliphaz.) These were the sons of Adah, Esau's wife. 13These were the sons of Reuel: Nahath, Zerah, Shammah, and Mizzah. These were the sons of Esau's wife, Basemath. 14These were the sons of Esau's wife Oholibamah, daughter of Anah son*b* of Zibeon: she bore to Esau Jeush, Jalam, and Korah.

Clans and Kings of Edom

15 These are the clans*c* of the sons of Esau. The sons of Eliphaz the firstborn of Esau: the clans*c* Teman, Omar, Zepho, Kenaz, 16Korah, Gatam, and Amalek; these are the clans*c* of Eliphaz in the land of Edom; they are the sons of Adah. 17These are the sons of Esau's son Reuel: the clans*c* Nahath, Zerah, Shammah, and Mizzah; these are the clans*c* of Reuel in the land of

---

a Sam Gk Syr: Heb *daughter*   *b* Gk Syr: Heb *daughter*
c Or *chiefs*

Israel in J) journeying to an unknown location (*tower of Eder* means "Tower of the Flocks"), where his firstborn son, Reuben, has sex with Bilhah, *and Israel heard of it.* The J narrative seems be truncated here. This episode is referred to in 49.4 as the reason for Reuben's loss of the status of the firstborn son. Having sex with a father's concubine(s) is an act of rebellion in 2 Sam 16.21–22; 1 Kings 2.17–24. This transgression explains why the tribe of Reuben disappeared (see Deut 33.6). **35.22b–29** This passage from the P source concludes the Jacob narrative by listing Jacob's twelve sons and briefly describing Isaac's death. Interestingly, Benjamin is grouped with the other sons as having been *born to him in Paddan-aram* (i.e., Haran, v. 26); cf. 35.16–18. The death of Isaac echoes the peaceful scene of Abraham's death, which has the same phrases in different order: *breathed his last, old and full (of days), gathered to his people* (25.7–10). Like Abraham, Isaac is buried by his two sons, a picture of family peace and solidarity.

36.1–43 Like the end of the Abraham narrative, the text lists the descendants of the son whose story will no longer be followed, Ishmael (25.12–18) and Esau (here). This chapter seems to have been compiled from several texts by the P source, with overlaps and inconsistencies among them. **36.2** The names and origins of Esau's wives are slightly different than in 26.34; 28.9 (both P). **36.6–8** The peaceful parting of Esau and Jacob is reminiscent of the parting of Abraham and Lot in ch. 13. The wording of v. 7 echoes 13.6 (P). This parting presumes that the two brothers lived side by side in Hebron for a time as adults, and it provides the motive for Esau's settlement in Edom. Note that in P the brothers' relationship is entirely amicable. **36.9–19** The list of Esau's *descendants* in vv. 9–14 and the list of his *clans* in vv. 15–19 consist of the same names with some slight variations, e.g., *Eliphaz* has six sons in vv. 11–12 but seven sons in vv. 15–16. *Kenaz* (vv. 11, 15), Esau's grandson, is elsewhere a Judahite clan to which Caleb and Othniel belong (Num 32.12; Judg

Edom; they are the sons of Esau's wife Basemath. [18]These are the sons of Esau's wife Oholibamah: the clans*a* Jeush, Jalam, and Korah; these are the clans*a* born of Esau's wife Oholibamah, the daughter of Anah. [19]These are the sons of Esau (that is, Edom), and these are their clans.*a*

20 These are the sons of Seir the Horite, the inhabitants of the land: Lotan, Shobal, Zibeon, Anah, [21]Dishon, Ezer, and Dishan; these are the clans*a* of the Horites, the sons of Seir in the land of Edom. [22]The sons of Lotan were Hori and Heman; and Lotan's sister was Timna. [23]These are the sons of Shobal: Alvan, Manahath, Ebal, Shepho, and Onam. [24]These are the sons of Zibeon: Aiah and Anah; he is the Anah who found the springs*b* in the wilderness, as he pastured the donkeys of his father Zibeon. [25]These are the children of Anah: Dishon and Oholibamah daughter of Anah. [26]These are the sons of Dishon: Hemdan, Eshban, Ithran, and Cheran. [27]These are the sons of Ezer: Bilhan, Zaavan, and Akan. [28]These are the sons of Dishan: Uz and Aran. [29]These are the clans*a* of the Horites: the clans*a* Lotan, Shobal, Zibeon, Anah, [30]Dishon, Ezer, and Dishan; these are the clans*a* of the Horites, clan by clan*c* in the land of Seir.

31 These are the kings who reigned in the land of Edom, before any king reigned over the Israelites. [32]Bela son of Beor reigned in Edom, the name of his city being Dinhabah.

[33]Bela died, and Jobab son of Zerah of Bozrah succeeded him as king. [34]Jobab died, and Husham of the land of the Temanites succeeded him as king. [35]Husham died, and Hadad son of Bedad, who defeated Midian in the country of Moab, succeeded him as king, the name of his city being Avith. [36]Hadad died, and Samlah of Masrekah succeeded him as king. [37]Samlah died, and Shaul of Rehoboth on the Euphrates succeeded him as king. [38]Shaul died, and Baal-hanan son of Achbor succeeded him as king. [39]Baal-hanan son of Achbor died, and Hadar succeeded him as king, the name of his city being Pau; his wife's name was Mehetabel, the daughter of Matred, daughter of Me-zahab.

40 These are the names of the clans*a* of Esau, according to their families and their localities by their names: the clans*a* Timna, Alvah, Jetheth, [41]Oholibamah, Elah, Pinon, [42]Kenaz, Teman, Mibzar, [43]Magdiel, and Iram; these are the clans*a* of Edom (that is, Esau, the father of Edom), according to their settlements in the land that they held.

Joseph Dreams of Greatness

37 Jacob settled in the land where his father had lived as an alien, the land of Canaan. [2]This is the story of the family of Jacob.

_____

a Or *chiefs*   *b* Meaning of Heb uncertain   *c* Or *chief by chief*

3.9). *Amalek,* also Esau's grandson (vv. 12, 16); see Ex 17.8–16. **36.20** *Seir,* here the ancestor of the people of Seir/Edom. His granddaughter is *Oholibamah* (v. 18), Esau's wife. *Horites,* the indigenous people of Edom; see 14.6. **36.28** *Uz,* in Edom, the home of Job. **36.31–39** The Edomite king list states that Edom had kings before Israel, indicating that the list was written well after the beginning of the Israelite monarchy. Each Edomite king seems to be from a different city, raising the possibility that this list places in chronological order local kings who may have ruled different regions of Edom at various times. **36.40–43** This list of the clans of Edom differs from the list in vv. 15–19.

37.1–50.26 The last section of Genesis is the Joseph story, which tells of further conflicts within Jacob's family and of its migration to Egypt. This story completes the patriarchal narratives and serves as a bridge to the story of the exodus. The rivalry among Jacob's sons echoes the rivalries in previous patriarchal generations, but there are a number of unique features in the Joseph story. It is a single elaborate narration, unlike the episodic and self-contained quality of the previous stories. (The exception is ch. 38, the story of Judah and Tamar.) There is only one direct divine revelation, to Israel at Beer-sheba (46.1–4); otherwise God never speaks or appears. Yet God is guiding events, as Joseph reveals in speeches to his brothers in 45.5–8; 50.20. The length of the Joseph story may be related to its nonsacral content, as the story focuses on the exploration of character and motive and the themes of knowledge, wisdom, and reconciliation. The J, E, and P sources are recognizable at various points in the Joseph story, although it is difficult consistently to distinguish between J and E. The name *Israel* is an indication of the J source, although the name *Jacob* also occurs in J. **37.1–11** The story opens with a picture of a pampered son who attracts the hatred of his brothers. Joseph tattles on his brothers, is openly favored by their father, and dreams of dominance over them all. A number of details prepare for later developments of plot and theme, including the enmity of the brothers, Joseph's dreams as divine prophecy, clothing (Joseph's *long robe,* v. 3) as a symbol of identity, and the question of knowledge (Jacob *kept the matter in mind,* v. 11). Vv. 1–2a belong to the P source; vv. 2b–4 are from the J source; and vv. 5–11 are mostly from the E source, though they may also include J material. **37.1–2a** The P introduction to the Joseph story.

Joseph, being seventeen years old, was shepherding the flock with his brothers; he was a helper to the sons of Bilhah and Zilpah, his father's wives; and Joseph brought a bad report of them to their father. 3Now Israel loved Joseph more than any other of his children, because he was the son of his old age; and he had made him a long robe with sleeves.*a* 4But when his brothers saw that their father loved him more than all his brothers, they hated him, and could not speak peaceably to him.

5 Once Joseph had a dream, and when he told it to his brothers, they hated him even more. 6He said to them, "Listen to this dream that I dreamed. 7There we were, binding sheaves in the field. Suddenly my sheaf rose and stood upright; then your sheaves gathered around it, and bowed down to my sheaf." 8His brothers said to him, "Are you indeed to reign over us? Are you indeed to have dominion over us?" So they hated him even more because of his dreams and his words.

9 He had another dream, and told it to his brothers, saying, "Look, I have had another dream: the sun, the moon, and eleven stars were bowing down to me." 10But when he told it to his father and to his brothers, his father rebuked him, and said to him, "What kind of dream is this that you have had? Shall we indeed come, I and your mother and your brothers, and bow to the ground before you?" 11So his brothers were jealous of him, but his father kept the matter in mind.

Joseph Is Sold by His Brothers

12 Now his brothers went to pasture their father's flock near Shechem. 13And Israel said to Joseph, "Are not your brothers pasturing the flock at Shechem? Come, I will send you to them." He answered, "Here I am." 14So he said to him, "Go now, see if it is well with your brothers and with the flock; and bring word back to me." So he sent him from the valley of Hebron.

He came to Shechem, 15and a man found him wandering in the fields; the man asked him, "What are you seeking?" 16"I am seeking

---

a Traditional rendering (compare Gk): *a coat of many colors;* meaning of Heb uncertain

---

This is the story of the family of Jacob, better "These are the descendants of Jacob," follows the pattern of the beginnings of the Abraham and Jacob stories (11.27; 25.19; see note on 2.4), placing the emphasis on the genealogical progression of the stories. **37.2b** *Seventeen.* Joseph is mature, but not yet an adult. The wordplay between *shepherding* (ro'eh) and the *bad* (ra'ah) *report* highlights the troubling situation of Joseph, allied with his brothers yet informing on them. That he is with the *sons of Bilhah and Zilpah* suggests tension with the sons of Leah, who are the older sons. **37.3** *Israel loved Joseph more* ominously echoes 29.30. Israel's favoritism leads to crises in both cases. *Old age,* the reason for Israel's preference for Joseph and also a suggestion that Israel is in his dotage; cf. 27.1. *A long robe with sleeves* (or *coat of many colors*), a fine robe such as princesses wear (see 2 Sam 13.18) and a symbol of Israel's love. The symbolism of this robe will play an important role in the encounter between Joseph and his brothers in vv. 23, 31–34. **37.4** The story turns to the perspective of the brothers, who are resentful of Joseph and angry: *their father loved him,* but *they hated him.* Their inability to *speak peaceably* (shalom) *to him* will echo in Joseph's journey to *see if it is well* (shalom) with them (v. 14), which will escalate into violence. **37.5–11** Joseph's two dreams anticipate the two pairs of dreams on which his fate will turn in chs. 40–41. When he provocatively tells his brothers, *they hated him even more* (yosifu), a play on the name *Joseph* (yosef), which is emphasized by repetition (vv. 5, 8). The dream of sheaves of grain bowing down is fulfilled when the brothers bow to him in 42.6, seeking grain.

The significance of the second dream, with the same theme, is elucidated by Jacob's later wisdom in dream interpretation: the doubling of the dream means that *the thing is fixed by God* (41.32). The brothers' questions (v. 8) are ironic, since they are rhetorical questions meant in anger, but will indeed come true. The brothers are unaware of the truth of such dreams and were *jealous* of Joseph, but with greater wisdom his father *kept the matter in mind* (v. 11). **37.10** The mention of Joseph's *mother,* symbolized by the moon in his dream, suggests that Rachel is still alive (cf. 35.19), although she does not appear elsewhere in the story. **37.12–36** The brothers' enmity leads to an improvised plan to murder Joseph. The responsible older brother (Reuben in E, Judah in J) dissuades the brothers, anticipating their later protection of Benjamin (Reuben in 42.37; Judah in 44.18–34). The scene ends with Joseph's transport to Egypt as a slave and the brothers' deception of Jacob. This key section is a careful combination of J (vv. 12–18, 23b, 25b–27, 28b, 31–35) and E (vv. 19–23a, 24–25a, 28ac, 29–30, 36). **37.12–14** The location of the brothers at Shechem recalls the deception and violence perpetrated by the brothers at Shechem in ch. 34. Now they are inflamed by shame caused by their brother rather than their sister. Israel naively sends Joseph to *see if it is well* (shalom) with the brothers and flocks and to *bring word back,* recalling Joseph's habit of bringing back *bad report* (v. 2) and the brothers' lack of *shalom* toward Joseph (see note on 3.4). *Here I am.* Joseph's willingness to comply (cf. 22.1) displays similar naïveté under the circumstances. **37.15–18** The meeting with the helpful stranger at

my brothers," he said; "tell me, please, where they are pasturing the flock." 17The man said, "They have gone away, for I heard them say, 'Let us go to Dothan.'" So Joseph went after his brothers, and found them at Dothan. 18They saw him from a distance, and before he came near to them, they conspired to kill him. 19They said to one another, "Here comes this dreamer. 20Come now, let us kill him and throw him into one of the pits; then we shall say that a wild animal has devoured him, and we shall see what will become of his dreams." 21But when Reuben heard it, he delivered him out of their hands, saying, "Let us not take his life." 22Reuben said to them, "Shed no blood; throw him into this pit here in the wilderness, but lay no hand on him"—that he might rescue him out of their hand and restore him to his father. 23So when Joseph came to his brothers, they stripped him of his robe, the long robe with sleeves*a* that he wore; 24and they took him and threw him into a pit. The pit was empty; there was no water in it.

25 Then they sat down to eat; and looking up they saw a caravan of Ishmaelites coming from Gilead, with their camels carrying gum, balm, and resin, on their way to carry it down to Egypt. 26Then Judah said to his brothers, "What profit is it if we kill our brother and conceal his blood? 27Come, let us sell him to the Ishmaelites, and not lay our hands on him, for he is our brother, our own flesh." And his brothers agreed. 28When some Midianite traders passed by, they drew Joseph up, lifting him out of the pit, and sold him to the Ishmaelites for twenty pieces of silver. And they took Joseph to Egypt.

29 When Reuben returned to the pit and saw that Joseph was not in the pit, he tore his clothes. 30He returned to his brothers, and said, "The boy is gone; and I, where can I turn?" 31Then they took Joseph's robe, slaughtered a goat, and dipped the robe in the blood. 32They had the long robe with sleeves*a* taken to their father, and they said, "This we have found; see now whether it is your son's robe or not." 33He recognized it, and said, "It is my son's robe! A wild animal has devoured him; Joseph is without doubt torn to pieces." 34Then Jacob tore his garments, and put sackcloth on his loins, and mourned for his son many days. 35All his sons and all his daughters

_____
a See note on 37.3

Shechem delays the dangerous encounter with his brothers and perhaps provides a foil to their uncaring response: *they conspired to kill him* (v. 18). **37.19–20** *This dreamer*, lit. "this master of dreams." The brothers use this term with disdain, not knowing that Joseph will indeed become a master of dreams. *We shall see . . . his dreams,* a deeply ironic mocking boast, since their plan sets into motion the chain of events that will make his dreams come true. **37.21–22** Reuben, as the oldest son, has the authority to influence his brothers but does not openly overrule them. His suggestion to throw Joseph in a *pit* still condemns Joseph to death, although he secretly plans to rescue him. His plan is accepted because it achieves the same end, Joseph's death, without the taint of murder. **37.23** Stripping Joseph's robe strips him symbolically of his identity as the beloved son. Stripping off and putting on clothing will mark each of Joseph's passages of identity: from beloved son to slave, from slave to prisoner, and from prisoner to vizier (see 39.12–18; 41.14, 42). **37.24–25a** Being thrown into a *pit* (Hebrew *bor*) is a symbolic death; this word occurs in poetry to refer to the underworld (e.g., Isa 14.15; Pss 28.1; 30.3). This descent into a symbolic death will recur when Joseph is cast into a *dungeon* (*bor*) in 40.15; 41.14. The absence of water in the pit means that Joseph will not drown. Later the brothers reveal with guilty conscience that he pleaded with them, but they would not listen (42.21). That the brothers *sat down to eat* shows remarkable callousness. **37.25b–27** In the J version, the brothers' plan to kill Joseph is altered by Judah, who argues for selling him to the Ishmaelites. This rids them of Joseph without the stain of bloodshed, especially from a family member (*our own flesh,* v. 26), and gains the brothers some *profit.* Judah saves Joseph's life, but his motives are less than honorable. **37.28** The J text reads: *His brothers agreed* (v. 27) *and sold him to the Ishmaelites for twenty pieces of silver.* This is the price for a male slave under twenty years old (see Lev 27.5). The E text reads: *When some Midianite traders passed by, they drew Joseph up, lifting him out of the pit. . . . And they took Joseph to Egypt.* The Midianites apparently come by while the brothers are busy eating (v. 25). The two versions are skillfully woven together, with each text preserved intact. The composite text yields the curious impression that the Midianites sold Joseph to the Ishmaelites, although the E version continues: *the Midianites had sold him in Egypt to Potiphar* (v. 36). **37.29–30** Reuben's response, tearing his clothes in grief, parallels Jacob's grief in v. 34 (J). **37.31–35** The conclusion in the J version is the brothers' deception of Jacob, echoing the terms of Jacob's deception of his father in ch. 27. Both involve a brother's fine clothes, the slaughtering of a goat, and an old father. In both the father recognizes his son, but falsely. (Note the tragic irony of the inference that Joseph is *torn to pieces,* v. 33.) The older brothers deceive their father, and Jacob, the younger son, grieves for his

sought to comfort him; but he refused to be comforted, and said, "No, I shall go down to Sheol to my son, mourning." Thus his father bewailed him. 36Meanwhile the Midianites had sold him in Egypt to Potiphar, one of Pharaoh's officials, the captain of the guard.

Judah and Tamar

38 It happened at that time that Judah went down from his brothers and settled near a certain Adullamite whose name was Hirah. 2There Judah saw the daughter of a certain Canaanite whose name was Shua; he married her and went in to her. 3She conceived and bore a son; and he named him Er. 4Again she conceived and bore a son whom she named Onan. 5Yet again she bore a son, and she named him Shelah. She*a* was in Chezib when she bore him. 6Judah took a wife for Er his firstborn; her name was Tamar. 7But Er, Judah's firstborn, was wicked in the sight of the LORD, and the LORD put him to death. 8Then Judah said to Onan, "Go in to your brother's wife and perform the duty of a brother-in-law to her; raise up offspring for your brother." 9But since Onan knew that the offspring would not be his, he spilled his semen on the ground whenever he went in to his brother's wife, so that he would not give offspring to his brother. 10What he did was displeasing in the sight of the LORD, and he put him to death also. 11Then Judah said to his daughter-in-law Tamar, "Remain a widow in your father's house until my son Shelah grows up"—for he feared that he too would die, like his brothers. So Tamar went to live in her father's house.

12 In course of time the wife of Judah, Shua's daughter, died; when Judah's time of mourning was over,*b* he went up to Timnah to his sheepshearers, he and his friend Hirah the Adullamite. 13When Tamar was told, "Your father-in-law is going up to Timnah to shear his sheep," 14she put off her widow's garments, put on a veil, wrapped herself up, and sat down at the entrance to Enaim, which is on the road to Timnah. She saw that Shelah was grown up, yet she had not been given to him in marriage. 15When Judah saw her, he thought her to be a prostitute, for she had covered her

a Gk: Heb *He*   *b* Heb *when Judah was comforted*

younger son. Jacob's false recognition is a measure of poetic justice for his deception of Isaac and anticipates the key moments of recognition to come in 38.25–26; 42.7–8. **37.36** *Potiphar . . . guard.* See note on 39.1.

38.1–30 Joseph's plight is interrupted by a story about Judah and his family (from the J source), in which themes of knowledge, deception, and recognition continue to reverberate. Judah's previous duplicity toward his brother and father are repaid by his daughter-in-law Tamar's deception of him, crowned by a moment of recognition (v. 26), when he perceives his iniquity and reforms himself (see Judah's exemplary behavior thereafter in the Joseph story). Tamar is a successful matriarch and trickster (echoing the qualities of Jacob, Rebekah, and Rachel) who preserves the tribe of Judah. The story ends with a glimpse of the ancestry of David and a resumption of the theme of strife between brothers. Among the story's remarkable features is the heroic prominence of a righteous foreign woman in contrast to the usually dangerous foreign woman, exemplified by Potiphar's wife in ch. 39. **38.1–6** Judah's marriage to a Canaanite woman is not seen as problematic in the story, nor is the arranged marriage of his firstborn son to Tamar. The J source differs from 24.3 and the P source (27.46–28.2) in this attitude. Judah's three sons' names have a folkloric quality: *Er* is a wordplay on "evil" (see note on 38.7), *Onan* sounds like "sorrow, trouble, wickedness" (see *'oni* in 35.18), and *Shelah* can mean "request, something asked for," each an appropriate name for the character. **38.7** The name *Er* (*'er*) and his moral quality, *wicked,* better "evil" (*ra'*), are anagrams. God *put him to death* because of his intrinsic evil, but no one else knows why he died. **38.8–10** Judah's instruction to Onan in v. 8 is a way of providing an heir for the dead husband (see Deut 25.5–10). Onan's evil is his refusal to perform this sexual and familial duty, so God rightly *put him to death also.* In the *sight of the LORD,* to which we are given partial access, both brothers are rightly put to death, but the other characters cannot see this. **38.11** Judah fears that Shelah will die too, if he performs the still unfulfilled duty of the brother-in-law. Judah deceives Tamar by seeming to promise Shelah's services when he *grows up,* when in fact he is expelling her from his household to *her father's house.* Tamar is pointedly called *his daughter-in-law Tamar* at the moment when Judah violates his legal responsibilities toward her. He instructs her to *remain a widow,* outside of his care. Tamar is deceived, unaware of Judah's intentions. **38.12–14** The tables turn when Tamar recognizes the truth some time later and plans a counter-deception. *Entrance to Enaim,* lit. "opening of the eyes," an apt setting for her dawning perception. Her change of clothes, from widow's garb to a prostitute's, reverses her situation from a dependent figure to an active agent, a woman empowered to negotiate with men about sex. This is her ruse to enforce the *duty of a brother-in-law* (v. 8), which now falls to the next closest male kin, not Shelah but Judah himself. **38.15–19** *Judah saw her.* Judah sees falsely, however, deceived by Tamar's disguise, and has sex with her. *Signet, cord, staff,* tokens of Judah's identity (v. 18). By taking his in-

face. [16]He went over to her at the roadside, and said, "Come, let me come in to you," for he did not know that she was his daughter-in-law. She said, "What will you give me, that you may come in to me?" [17]He answered, "I will send you a kid from the flock." And she said, "Only if you give me a pledge, until you send it." [18]He said, "What pledge shall I give you?" She replied, "Your signet and your cord, and the staff that is in your hand." So he gave them to her, and went in to her, and she conceived by him. [19]Then she got up and went away, and taking off her veil she put on the garments of her widowhood.

20 When Judah sent the kid by his friend the Adullamite, to recover the pledge from the woman, he could not find her. [21]He asked the townspeople, "Where is the temple prostitute who was at Enaim by the wayside?" But they said, "No prostitute has been here." [22]So he returned to Judah, and said, "I have not found her; moreover the townspeople said, 'No prostitute has been here.' " [23]Judah replied, "Let her keep the things as her own, otherwise we will be laughed at; you see, I sent this kid, and you could not find her."

24 About three months later Judah was told, "Your daughter-in-law Tamar has played the whore; moreover she is pregnant as a result of whoredom." And Judah said, "Bring her out, and let her be burned." [25]As she was being brought out, she sent word to her father-in-law, "It was the owner of these who made me pregnant." And she said, "Take note, please, whose these are, the signet and the cord and the staff." [26]Then Judah acknowledged them and said, "She is more in the right than I, since I did not give her to my son Shelah." And he did not lie with her again.

27 When the time of her delivery came, there were twins in her womb. [28]While she was in labor, one put out a hand; and the midwife took and bound on his hand a crimson thread, saying, "This one came out first." [29]But just then he drew back his hand, and out came his brother; and she said, "What a breach you have made for yourself!" Therefore he was named Perez.[a] [30]Afterward his brother came out with the crimson thread on his hand; and he was named Zerah.[b]

Joseph and Potiphar's Wife

39 Now Joseph was taken down to Egypt, and Potiphar, an officer of Pharaoh, the captain of the guard, an Egyptian, bought him from the Ishmaelites who had brought him down there. [2]The LORD was with Joseph, and he became a successful man; he was in the house of his Egyptian master. [3]His master saw that the LORD was with him, and that the LORD

a That is A breach   b That is Brightness; perhaps alluding to the crimson thread

---

signia, Tamar symbolically assumes his role as head of the lineage and tribe of Judah, and she ensures its proper continuance. Judah, unknowing, fulfills his duty (v. 18; cf. his instruction in v. 8). Having achieved her goal, Tamar puts back on the garments of her widowhood (v. 19). 38.20–23 Temple prostitute, probably a polite euphemism for prostitute. Judah cannot pay his debt, because Tamar is no longer there. No prostitute has been here is literally true. Judah remains deceived and fears being laughed at, which is ironic in light of what is to come. 38.24–26 Tamar has played the whore, an accusation that is true in its way, and as a type of adultery it warrants the death penalty for both parties (see Deut 22.22). But Tamar's defense rests in her possession of Judah's insignia, which he recognizes, in diction that echoes Jacob's recognition of Joseph's robe (37.32–33). Daughter-in-law, father-in-law. The repetition of kinship terms highlights the significance of this relationship in the recognition scene. Judah now sees rightly and understands the justice of Tamar's actions (v. 26). He did not lie with her again. Judah resumes his proper role as father-in-law. 38.27–30 The story concludes with the birth of twins, echoing the birth of Jacob and Esau (25.21–26). These brothers too are struggling in the womb over who will be the firstborn, and Perez prevails over Zerah (both are clans of Judah in Num 26.19–22). Perez will be David's ancestor (see Ruth 4.18–22), ending the story with a hint of future glory.

39.1–23 The Joseph story resumes with Joseph a slave in Egypt, foreshadowing his family's later fate. In his master's house he shows his virtue by resisting the advances of his master's wife, but falls victim to her false accusation. The beginning and end of the chapter relate with similar diction Joseph's rise to success as second in command in his two domains (his master's house and prison) because the LORD was with Joseph (v. 2; cf. v. 21). His twofold ascent in this chapter anticipates his final ascent in Pharaoh's court (ch. 41). This is a J chapter; note that the Ishmaelites had brought him down there (v. 1), resuming from 37.25b–27, 28b. 39.1 Potiphar . . . guard, probably an editorial expansion harmonizing the J story with the previous E text (37.36) and creating a resumptive repetition around the story of Judah and Tamar in ch. 38. Elsewhere in the story Joseph's owner is referred to as his Egyptian master (v. 2) or his master (e.g., v. 3). 39.2–6 The LORD was with Joseph (v. 2), as he had previously been with Jacob (28.15). The LORD blessed the Egyptian's house for Joseph's sake (v. 5), as he had previously blessed Laban

caused all that he did to prosper in his hands. ⁴So Joseph found favor in his sight and attended him; he made him overseer of his house and put him in charge of all that he had. ⁵From the time that he made him overseer in his house and over all that he had, the LORD blessed the Egyptian's house for Joseph's sake; the blessing of the LORD was on all that he had, in house and field. ⁶So he left all that he had in Joseph's charge; and, with him there, he had no concern for anything but the food that he ate.

Now Joseph was handsome and good-looking. ⁷And after a time his master's wife cast her eyes on Joseph and said, "Lie with me." ⁸But he refused and said to his master's wife, "Look, with me here, my master has no concern about anything in the house, and he has put everything that he has in my hand. ⁹He is not greater in this house than I am, nor has he kept back anything from me except yourself, because you are his wife. How then could I do this great wickedness, and sin against God?" ¹⁰And although she spoke to Joseph day after day, he would not consent to lie beside her or to be with her. ¹¹One day, however, when he went into the house to do his work, and while no one else was in the house, ¹²she caught hold of his garment, saying, "Lie with me!" But he left his garment in her hand, and fled and ran outside. ¹³When she saw that he had left his garment in her hand and had fled outside, ¹⁴she called out to the members of her household and said to them, "See, my husband*a* has brought among

us a Hebrew to insult us! He came in to me to lie with me, and I cried out with a loud voice; ¹⁵and when he heard me raise my voice and cry out, he left his garment beside me, and fled outside." ¹⁶Then she kept his garment by her until his master came home, ¹⁷and she told him the same story, saying, "The Hebrew servant, whom you have brought among us, came in to me to insult me; ¹⁸but as soon as I raised my voice and cried out, he left his garment beside me, and fled outside."

19 When his master heard the words that his wife spoke to him, saying, "This is the way your servant treated me," he became enraged. ²⁰And Joseph's master took him and put him into the prison, the place where the king's prisoners were confined; he remained there in prison. ²¹But the LORD was with Joseph and showed him steadfast love; he gave him favor in the sight of the chief jailer. ²²The chief jailer committed to Joseph's care all the prisoners who were in the prison, and whatever was done there, he was the one who did it. ²³The chief jailer paid no heed to anything that was in Joseph's care, because the LORD was with him; and whatever he did, the LORD made it prosper.

The Dreams of Two Prisoners

40 Some time after this, the cupbearer of the king of Egypt and his baker of-

a Heb *he*

---

because of Jacob (30.27–30). The theme of divine care for the family of Israel, stemming from the patriarchal promises, is central to the Joseph story, and here it is first openly signaled. Corresponding to these notices, Joseph now shows himself worthy of divine favor. This is a dual causality: Joseph's success is due to God's favor but also depends on his own exercise of wisdom, such as he shows in this chapter. *Found favor in his* master's *sight* (v. 4) is echoed at the end of the chapter by *favor in the sight of the chief jailer* (v. 21). *Left all . . . in Joseph's charge* (*charge*, lit. "hand"; cf. v. 22), all except his wife, as Joseph notes in vv. 8–9. **39.6–12** *Handsome and good-looking*, a repetition of adjectives for emphasis; cf. 29.17. This rare description of physical characteristics sets the stage for trouble with Joseph's *master's wife*. She flaunts her authority over him with a terse command, *Lie with me* (v. 7). Joseph shows his virtue and wisdom and his vulnerable position with an eloquent reply, laying out the moral issues and his responsibility to his master and to God. As a dangerous and lustful foreign woman (cf. the adulterous foreign woman in Prov 5, 7), she is uninterested in moral discourse and subsequently repeats her blunt

command (v. 12). **39.12–19** The wife's stripping Joseph of his garment, which she will use as a prop in her false accusation to Joseph's master, echoes the brothers' stripping of Joseph's robe, which they use as a prop to deceive Joseph's father (37.23, 32). The master's wife now shows her eloquence: she garners her household's support by blaming her *husband* for bringing in a *Hebrew to insult* them, but blames the *Hebrew servant* for insulting her when speaking to her husband (v. 17). *Insult* can have a sexual nuance, which is brought out in the speech to her husband by the phrase *came in to me*. Her use of suggestive language to describe the attempted rape has its desired effect: the master becomes enraged (v. 19). **39.20–23** Joseph's passage from slavery to prison echoes his previous passage from beloved son to slave. Yet, as before, *the LORD was with Joseph* (v. 21). The chapter ends as it began, with a description of Joseph's ascent in his new domain. *The place where the king's prisoners were confined* (v. 20), an editorial expansion harmonizing the J text with the E story that follows in ch. 40.

40.1–23 While in prison Joseph shows another kind of wisdom by interpreting dreams. This is God-given

fended their lord the king of Egypt. ²Pharaoh was angry with his two officers, the chief cupbearer and the chief baker, ³and he put them in custody in the house of the captain of the guard, in the prison where Joseph was confined. ⁴The captain of the guard charged Joseph with them, and he waited on them; and they continued for some time in custody. ⁵One night they both dreamed—the cupbearer and the baker of the king of Egypt, who were confined in the prison—each his own dream, and each dream with its own meaning. ⁶When Joseph came to them in the morning, he saw that they were troubled. ⁷So he asked Pharaoh's officers, who were with him in custody in his master's house, "Why are your faces downcast today?" ⁸They said to him, "We have had dreams, and there is no one to interpret them." And Joseph said to them, "Do not interpretations belong to God? Please tell them to me."

9 So the chief cupbearer told his dream to Joseph, and said to him, "In my dream there was a vine before me, ¹⁰and on the vine there were three branches. As soon as it budded, its blossoms came out and the clusters ripened into grapes. ¹¹Pharaoh's cup was in my hand; and I took the grapes and pressed them into Pharaoh's cup, and placed the cup in Pharaoh's hand." ¹²Then Joseph said to him, "This is its interpretation: the three branches are three days; ¹³within three days Pharaoh will lift up your head and restore you to your office; and you shall place Pharaoh's cup in his hand, just as you used to do when you were his cupbearer. ¹⁴But remember me when it is well with you; please do me the kindness to make mention of me to Pharaoh, and so get me out of this place. ¹⁵For in fact I was stolen out of the land of the Hebrews; and here also I have done nothing that they should have put me into the dungeon."

16 When the chief baker saw that the interpretation was favorable, he said to Joseph, "I also had a dream: there were three cake baskets on my head, ¹⁷and in the uppermost basket there were all sorts of baked food for Pharaoh, but the birds were eating it out of the basket on my head." ¹⁸And Joseph answered, "This is its interpretation: the three baskets are three days; ¹⁹within three days Pharaoh will lift up your head—from you!—and hang you on a pole; and the birds will eat the flesh from you."

20 On the third day, which was Pharaoh's birthday, he made a feast for all his servants, and lifted up the head of the chief cupbearer and the head of the chief baker among his servants. ²¹He restored the chief cupbearer to his cupbearing, and he placed the cup in Pharaoh's hand; ²²but the chief baker he hanged, just as Joseph had interpreted to them. ²³Yet the chief cupbearer did not remember Joseph, but forgot him.

Joseph Interprets Pharaoh's Dream

41 After two whole years, Pharaoh dreamed that he was standing by the Nile, ²and there came up out of the Nile seven

---

wisdom, since *interpretations belong to God* (v. 8). The two dreams in this chapter are the second in a series of double dreams; they are preceded by Joseph's in 37.5–9 and followed by Pharaoh's in 41.1–7. In this chapter Joseph turns from a dreamer to a dream interpreter, a gift that will occasion his final ascent in the next chapter. Chs. 40–41 are from the E source. **40.5** *Each dream with its own meaning.* The two dreams, although they seem similar, will have quite different interpretations. **40.8** The officers, unaware of Joseph's ability, say *there is no one to interpret* the dreams. Joseph shows that one doesn't need to be an Egyptian magician or wise man (see 41.8) to interpret dreams, since *interpretations belong to God.* This is both a critique of professional and foreign seers and a pious statement of trust in God. Like his forebear Abraham (20.7), Joseph is a kind of prophet, discerning and mediating God's will through dream interpretation. **40.9–13** The cupbearer's dream is favorable: he sees himself placing the *cup in Pharaoh's hand. Pharaoh will lift up your head* means restoration for the cupbearer, but will have a different

meaning for the next dream. **40.14–15** Joseph's plea to the cupbearer to *remember* him will be forgotten (v. 23) until the cupbearer finally remembers two years later (41.1, 9). Joseph's description of his past (*stolen,* v. 15) refers to the version of events in (see note on) 37.28. *Dungeon* also recalls his past, when his brothers threw him into a pit (see note on 37.24–25). **40.16–19** Against the baker's expectation, his dream is not favorable: birds are eating the Pharaoh's food. *Pharaoh will lift your head* (cf. v. 13) now has a literal rather than metaphorical meaning. Joseph's interpretive speech is itself allusive and dramatic. **40.23** The cupbearer *did not remember Joseph,* a fault he will remedy when Pharaoh dreams his dreams (41.9). Themes of remembering and forgetting circulate throughout the Joseph story (see 37.11; 41.51; 42.9).

41.1–57 Because of his wisdom in dream interpretation and his practical wisdom, Joseph ascends to become governor of Egypt, second only to Pharaoh. His rise in this domain echoes his previous ascents in Potiphar's house and in prison. The twin dreams of Phar-

sleek and fat cows, and they grazed in the reed grass. ³Then seven other cows, ugly and thin, came up out of the Nile after them, and stood by the other cows on the bank of the Nile. ⁴The ugly and thin cows ate up the seven sleek and fat cows. And Pharaoh awoke. ⁵Then he fell asleep and dreamed a second time; seven ears of grain, plump and good, were growing on one stalk. ⁶Then seven ears, thin and blighted by the east wind, sprouted after them. ⁷The thin ears swallowed up the seven plump and full ears. Pharaoh awoke, and it was a dream. ⁸In the morning his spirit was troubled; so he sent and called for all the magicians of Egypt and all its wise men. Pharaoh told them his dreams, but there was no one who could interpret them to Pharaoh.

9 Then the chief cupbearer said to Pharaoh, "I remember my faults today. ¹⁰Once Pharaoh was angry with his servants, and put me and the chief baker in custody in the house of the captain of the guard. ¹¹We dreamed on the same night, he and I, each having a dream with its own meaning. ¹²A young Hebrew was there with us, a servant of the captain of the guard. When we told him, he interpreted our dreams to us, giving an interpretation to each according to his dream. ¹³As he interpreted to us, so it turned out; I was restored to my office, and the baker was hanged."

14 Then Pharaoh sent for Joseph, and he was hurriedly brought out of the dungeon.

When he had shaved himself and changed his clothes, he came in before Pharaoh. ¹⁵And Pharaoh said to Joseph, "I have had a dream, and there is no one who can interpret it. I have heard it said of you that when you hear a dream you can interpret it." ¹⁶Joseph answered Pharaoh, "It is not I; God will give Pharaoh a favorable answer." ¹⁷Then Pharaoh said to Joseph, "In my dream I was standing on the banks of the Nile; ¹⁸and seven cows, fat and sleek, came up out of the Nile and fed in the reed grass. ¹⁹Then seven other cows came up after them, poor, very ugly, and thin. Never had I seen such ugly ones in all the land of Egypt. ²⁰The thin and ugly cows ate up the first seven fat cows, ²¹but when they had eaten them no one would have known that they had done so, for they were still as ugly as before. Then I awoke. ²²I fell asleep a second time[a] and I saw in my dream seven ears of grain, full and good, growing on one stalk, ²³and seven ears, withered, thin, and blighted by the east wind, sprouting after them; ²⁴and the thin ears swallowed up the seven good ears. But when I told it to the magicians, there was no one who could explain it to me."

25 Then Joseph said to Pharaoh, "Pharaoh's dreams are one and the same; God has revealed to Pharaoh what he is about to do. ²⁶The seven good cows are seven years, and

---

a Gk Syr Vg: Heb lacks *I fell asleep a second time*

---

aoh are the third in a sequence of double dreams, after Joseph's twin dreams and the two dreams of the prisoners. Like Joseph's the two dreams have the same meaning, and like the prisoners' they encompass good fortune and bad. Joseph's change of identity is accompanied by changes of clothes (vv. 14, 42), recalling his earlier transitions, and he also gains a new name, a wife, and sons. Joseph's piety and wisdom are amply rewarded, and his misfortune turns to good, with the result that he can preserve life in Egypt. This chapter, a sequel to ch. 40, is an E text, with some J and P expansions in the second half. **41.1–4** After being forgotten for two years, Joseph gets his main chance, because Pharaoh has two dreams. *Seven sleek and fat cows* emerging from the *Nile*, the source of Egyptian fertility, is a rich symbol of fertility. Seven *ugly and thin* cows eating the fat cows is a vivid and paradoxical image of famine, since, as Pharaoh later explains, the thin cows that ate the fat cows remained unchanged, *as ugly as before* (v. 21). Seven years of famine is a traditional motif, as in the Canaanite Epic of Aqhat. **41.8** *Troubled* echoes the condition of the cupbearer and baker (40.6) and brings to mind Joseph's role in interpreting their dreams. The inability of *all the magi-*

cians and *wise men* to interpret the dreams also recalls Joseph's remark to the prisoners about interpretations belonging to God (40.8), which he will reiterate to Pharaoh in v. 16. This scene forms the background for the dream story in Dan 2. **41.9** *I remember my faults.* The cupbearer's act of remembering Joseph, piously expressed, is a turning point in the story. **41.14** *Brought out of the dungeon,* lit. "pit" (*bor;* see note on 37.24–25). This is Joseph's symbolic ascent from death, in his case a kind of social death, recalling the language of the psalms of lament and thanksgiving (see, e.g., Ps 30.1–3). He will now be restored to the status of free person and will rise, as he has previously, to the status of second in command. His symbolic passage to a new status is accompanied by shaving and a change of clothes, recalling the symbolism of clothing that accompanied his downward passages (37.23; 39.12) and anticipating his ultimate finery in v. 42. **41.16** Joseph's protestation shows his wisdom, piety, and humility, which make him the apt instrument for God's interpretation. **41.25–36** Joseph's speech to Pharaoh is twofold. In the first part, the interpretation (vv. 25–32), Joseph discerns God's plan through the coded symbolism of the dream. The *doubling of Pharaoh's*

the seven good ears are seven years; the dreams are one. 27The seven lean and ugly cows that came up after them are seven years, as are the seven empty ears blighted by the east wind. They are seven years of famine. 28It is as I told Pharaoh; God has shown to Pharaoh what he is about to do. 29There will come seven years of great plenty throughout all the land of Egypt. 30After them there will arise seven years of famine, and all the plenty will be forgotten in the land of Egypt; the famine will consume the land. 31The plenty will no longer be known in the land because of the famine that will follow, for it will be very grievous. 32And the doubling of Pharaoh's dream means that the thing is fixed by God, and God will shortly bring it about. 33Now therefore let Pharaoh select a man who is discerning and wise, and set him over the land of Egypt. 34Let Pharaoh proceed to appoint overseers over the land, and take one-fifth of the produce of the land of Egypt during the seven plenteous years. 35Let them gather all the food of these good years that are coming, and lay up grain under the authority of Pharaoh for food in the cities, and let them keep it. 36That food shall be a reserve for the land against the seven years of famine that are to befall the land of Egypt, so that the land may not perish through the famine."

Joseph's Rise to Power

37 The proposal pleased Pharaoh and all his servants. 38Pharaoh said to his servants, "Can we find anyone else like this—one in whom is the spirit of God?" 39So Pharaoh said to Joseph, "Since God has shown you all this, there is no one so discerning and wise as you. 40You shall be over my house, and all my people shall order themselves as you command; only with regard to the throne will I be greater than you." 41And Pharaoh said to Joseph, "See, I have set you over all the land of Egypt." 42Removing his signet ring from his hand, Pharaoh put it on Joseph's hand; he arrayed him in garments of fine linen, and put a gold chain around his neck. 43He had him ride in the chariot of his second-in-command; and they cried out in front of him, "Bow the knee!"a Thus he set him over all the land of Egypt. 44Moreover Pharaoh said to Joseph, "I am Pharaoh, and without your consent no one shall lift up hand or foot in all the land of Egypt." 45Pharaoh gave Joseph the name Zaphenath-paneah; and he gave him Asenath daughter of Potiphera, priest of On, as his wife. Thus Joseph gained authority over the land of Egypt.

46 Joseph was thirty years old when he entered the service of Pharaoh king of Egypt. And Joseph went out from the presence of Pharaoh, and went through all the land of Egypt. 47During the seven plenteous years the earth produced abundantly. 48He gathered up all the food of the seven years when there was plentyb in the land of Egypt, and stored up food in the cities; he stored up in every city the food from the fields around it. 49So Joseph stored up grain in such abundance—like the sand of the sea—that he stopped measuring it; it was beyond measure.

50 Before the years of famine came, Joseph had two sons, whom Asenath daughter of Potiphera, priest of On, bore to him. 51Joseph named the firstborn Manasseh,c "For," he said,

---

a *Abrek*, apparently an Egyptian word similar in sound to the Hebrew word meaning *to kneel* b Sam Gk: MT *the seven years that were* c That is *Making to forget*

---

dream is part of the code, meaning that the plan is *fixed by God* and imminent (v. 32). The second part of the speech (vv. 33–36) shows Joseph's own practical wisdom. On the basis of his knowledge of God's plan he formulates a human plan, showing great insight and organizational planning. His advice to Pharaoh to *select a man who is discerning and wise* (v. 33) is followed by a plan that is discerning and wise, making Pharaoh's choice an easy one. **41.37–44** Pharaoh shows his own wisdom by appointing Joseph governor of the land. The mention of God in his praise of Joseph shows Pharaoh's own piety. *God* may be an ecumenical term here (and perhaps in vv. 14–32; 39.9; 40.8, all spoken by Joseph) that does not make a distinction between Joseph's and Pharaoh's god, or it may imply Pharaoh's recognition of Joseph's God. *Only with re-*

gard . . . greater than you. Pharaoh's statement to Joseph is breathtaking for a former slave and prisoner. Joseph's sumptuous new garb as Pharaoh's favored one recalls and transcends the fine robe he wore as Israel's favorite son (37.3). This is Joseph's last change of clothes in the story. **41.45** Joseph's new name also signals his new ascent in status; its meaning is obscure, but has to do with "life" (Egyptian *ankh*). His new father-in-law, *Potiphera*, curiously echoes his former master *Potiphar* of 37.36; 39.1. Joseph's marriage to an Egyptian woman, *Asenath*, seems to carry no sense of impropriety. **41.49** The simile for the abundance of grain that Joseph stored up, *like the sand of the sea*, recalls the patriarchal promise of many descendants (22.17; 32.12) and anticipates that this act will save the lives of the children of Israel. **41.51–52** The naming

"God has made me forget all my hardship and all my father's house." 52 The second he named Ephraim,*a* "For God has made me fruitful in the land of my misfortunes."

53 The seven years of plenty that prevailed in the land of Egypt came to an end; 54 and the seven years of famine began to come, just as Joseph had said. There was famine in every country, but throughout the land of Egypt there was bread. 55 When all the land of Egypt was famished, the people cried to Pharaoh for bread. Pharaoh said to all the Egyptians, "Go to Joseph; what he says to you, do." 56 And since the famine had spread over all the land, Joseph opened all the storehouses,*b* and sold to the Egyptians, for the famine was severe in the land of Egypt. 57 Moreover, all the world came to Joseph in Egypt to buy grain, because the famine became severe throughout the world.

Joseph's Brothers Go to Egypt

42 When Jacob learned that there was grain in Egypt, he said to his sons, "Why do you keep looking at one another? 2 I have heard," he said, "that there is grain in Egypt; go down and buy grain for us there, that we may live and not die." 3 So ten of Joseph's brothers went down to buy grain in Egypt. 4 But Jacob did not send Joseph's brother Benjamin with his brothers, for he feared that harm might come to him. 5 Thus the sons of Israel were among the other people who came to buy grain, for the famine had reached the land of Canaan.

6 Now Joseph was governor over the land; it was he who sold to all the people of the land. And Joseph's brothers came and bowed themselves before him with their faces to the ground. 7 When Joseph saw his brothers, he recognized them, but he treated them like strangers and spoke harshly to them. "Where do you come from?" he said. They said, "From the land of Canaan, to buy food." 8 Although Joseph had recognized his brothers, they did not recognize him. 9 Joseph also remembered the dreams that he had dreamed about them. He said to them, "You are spies; you have come to see the nakedness of the land!" 10 They said to him, "No, my lord; your servants have come to buy food. 11 We are all sons of one man; we are honest men; your servants have never been spies." 12 But he said to them, "No, you have come to see the nakedness of the land!" 13 They said, "We, your servants, are twelve brothers, the sons of a certain man in the land of Ca-

a From a Hebrew word meaning *to be fruitful*   *b* Gk Vg Compare Syr: Heb *opened all that was in* (or, *among*) *them*

---

speeches for Joseph's sons, Manasseh and Ephraim, are the only glimpse of Joseph's inner dispositions (cf. Leah and Rachel in chs. 29–30). *My father's house* and *fruitful in the land* anticipate the turn of focus to his family coming to Egypt for grain. **41.57** *All the world,* a broad frame that will narrow to a single family for the rest of the story.

42.1–38 The focus turns to Joseph's family and the reunion of Joseph and his brothers. In this new situation Joseph is their superior, as predicted in his dreams. He recognizes them but conceals his identity and devises a deceptive scheme to test their loyalty to their youngest brother, Benjamin. This is the brothers' punishment for their evil treatment of Joseph, but also provides an opportunity for redemption if they protect rather than abandon Benjamin. Jacob, however, is still grief-stricken and will not let Benjamin go. This chapter is primarily E, with portions of the J version of the brothers' journey in vv. 5–6a, 26–28, 38. **42.4** Jacob will not send Benjamin, fearing harm. Since Benjamin is Rachel's only remaining child and Joseph's brother, he is now the focus of Jacob's love. Jacob's preference for and overprotection of Benjamin suggest that the brothers would now be jealous of Benjamin, as they were of Joseph (37.4, 11). **42.6–9** The brothers bow before Joseph, unknowingly fulfilling Joseph's dreams (37.7, 9). Joseph *recognized them,* but *treated them like* strangers (which uses the same Hebrew root as *recognized*), a wordplay that highlights the themes of recognition and deception that have colored the story throughout. Joseph *remembered the dreams,* highlighting his role as master of dreams (37.19) and adding to what Joseph recognizes and the brothers do not. The contrast in knowledge between Joseph and his brothers will continue to reverberate, adding various ironies, until Joseph reveals his identity to them in 45.3. **42.9–11** *You are spies.* Joseph asserts his power over his brothers and threatens death, perhaps ironically alluding to his own tragic journey to spy on them (37.14). This accusation elicits a claim of innocence, but Joseph knows the truth: they have never been *spies,* but they are not *honest men* (v. 11). The brothers' references to Joseph as *my lord* (v. 10) and to themselves as *your servants* (three times in vv. 10–13) highlight the fulfillment of Joseph's dreams and recall the brothers' rebuke in 37.8. **42.12–13** The second exchange of accusation and defense elicits the brothers' self-identification as *twelve brothers,* which requires an explanation of the two missing brothers. Joseph uses their first piece of information, about Benjamin, for his test in order to see if the brothers have repented of the second, the fate of the other brother. *One is no more.* The truth of this statement is both less and more than the brothers know, since they know that they are culpable

naan; the youngest, however, is now with our father, and one is no more." 14But Joseph said to them, "It is just as I have said to you; you are spies! 15Here is how you shall be tested: as Pharaoh lives, you shall not leave this place unless your youngest brother comes here! 16Let one of you go and bring your brother, while the rest of you remain in prison, in order that your words may be tested, whether there is truth in you; or else, as Pharaoh lives, surely you are spies." 17And he put them all together in prison for three days.

18 On the third day Joseph said to them, "Do this and you will live, for I fear God: 19if you are honest men, let one of your brothers stay here where you are imprisoned. The rest of you shall go and carry grain for the famine of your households, 20and bring your youngest brother to me. Thus your words will be verified, and you shall not die." And they agreed to do so. 21They said to one another, "Alas, we are paying the penalty for what we did to our brother; we saw his anguish when he pleaded with us, but we would not listen. That is why this anguish has come upon us." 22Then Reuben answered them, "Did I not tell you not to wrong the boy? But you would not listen. So now there comes a reckoning for his blood." 23They did not know that Joseph understood them, since he spoke with them through an interpreter. 24He turned away from them and wept; then he returned and spoke to them. And he picked out Simeon and had him bound before their eyes. 25Joseph then gave orders to fill their bags with grain, to return every man's money to his sack, and to give them provisions for their journey. This was done for them.

Joseph's Brothers Return to Canaan

26 They loaded their donkeys with their grain, and departed. 27When one of them opened his sack to give his donkey fodder at the lodging place, he saw his money at the top of the sack. 28He said to his brothers, "My money has been put back; here it is in my sack!" At this they lost heart and turned trembling to one another, saying, "What is this that God has done to us?"

29 When they came to their father Jacob in the land of Canaan, they told him all that had happened to them, saying, 30"The man, the lord of the land, spoke harshly to us, and charged us with spying on the land. 31But we said to him, 'We are honest men, we are not spies. 32We are twelve brothers, sons of our father; one is no more, and the youngest is now with our father in the land of Canaan.' 33Then the man, the lord of the land, said to us, 'By this I shall know that you are honest men: leave one of your brothers with me, take grain for the famine of your households, and go your way. 34Bring your youngest brother to me, and I shall know that you are not spies but honest men. Then I will release your brother to you, and you may trade in the land.' "

35 As they were emptying their sacks, there in each one's sack was his bag of money. When they and their father saw their bundles of money, they were dismayed. 36And their father Jacob said to them, "I am the one you have bereaved of children: Joseph is no more,

---

(a guilt that will haunt them in vv. 21–22) and since Joseph is in fact standing before them. **42.14–16** Joseph's third repetition of the accusation includes a test. *Whether there is truth in you.* The truth Joseph is seeking requires the brothers to go get Benjamin. They think this is to test whether they have lied about having a brother, but Joseph plans to test whether they will abandon their brother once he is in Egypt. This is a deeper test of the *truth* (*'emet,* also meaning "faithfulness, reliability") *in* them. **42.17** *Put them all together* (Hebrew *ye'esof*), a wordplay on *Joseph,* alluding to Joseph's own time in prison. The brothers' incarceration is a measure of justice for Joseph's long imprisonment. **42.18–24** Joseph shows a measure of mercy (because he fears God; cf. 22.12) by retaining only one brother in prison instead of all but one (see v. 16), but forces the brothers to return home having abandoned yet another brother. They correctly perceive that they are *paying the penalty* for what they did to their brother (v.

21), but they do not know the whole truth, that Joseph is meting out the penalty for what they did. Moreover, they do not know that Joseph understands them when they speak among themselves (an interpreter was used earlier), adding another level of contrasting knowledge between Joseph and his brothers. Since he understands their speech, he now also understands their confession of guilt. For the first but not the last time, Joseph weeps (see 45.1, 14; 46.29), showing his feelings for his kin. Yet he persists in the test, choosing Simeon as hostage after Reuben's remark in v. 22 indicating Reuben's innocence. **42.25** Joseph's order *to return every man's money to his sack* raises the stakes of the test, since when the brothers return to Egypt they may be accused of theft. Joseph will repeat this trick with the addition of a silver cup for Benjamin in 44.1–2. **42.26–27** The J version of the discovery of the money, referred to again in 43.21; cf. the E version of the discovery in v. 35. The two discoveries add suspense and

and Simeon is no more, and now you would take Benjamin. All this has happened to me!" 37 Then Reuben said to his father, "You may kill my two sons if I do not bring him back to you. Put him in my hands, and I will bring him back to you." 38 But he said, "My son shall not go down with you, for his brother is dead, and he alone is left. If harm should come to him on the journey that you are to make, you would bring down my gray hairs with sorrow to Sheol."

The Brothers Come Again, Bringing Benjamin

43 Now the famine was severe in the land. 2 And when they had eaten up the grain that they had brought from Egypt, their father said to them, "Go again, buy us a little more food." 3 But Judah said to him, "The man solemnly warned us, saying, 'You shall not see my face unless your brother is with you.' 4 If you will send our brother with us, we will go down and buy you food; 5 but if you will not send him, we will not go down, for the man said to us, 'You shall not see my face, unless your brother is with you.'" 6 Israel said, "Why did you treat me so badly as to tell the man that you had another brother?" 7 They replied,

"The man questioned us carefully about ourselves and our kindred, saying, 'Is your father still alive? Have you another brother?' What we told him was in answer to these questions. Could we in any way know that he would say, 'Bring your brother down'?" 8 Then Judah said to his father Israel, "Send the boy with me, and let us be on our way, so that we may live and not die—you and we and also our little ones. 9 I myself will be surety for him; you can hold me accountable for him. If I do not bring him back to you and set him before you, then let me bear the blame forever. 10 If we had not delayed, we would now have returned twice."

11 Then their father Israel said to them, "If it must be so, then do this: take some of the choice fruits of the land in your bags, and carry them down as a present to the man—a little balm and a little honey, gum, resin, pistachio nuts, and almonds. 12 Take double the money with you. Carry back with you the money that was returned in the top of your sacks; perhaps it was an oversight. 13 Take your brother also, and be on your way again to the man; 14 may God Almighty[a] grant you mercy before the man, so that he may send back your

a Traditional rendering of Heb El Shaddai

---

magnify the brothers' mounting fear. **42.36–37** Jacob's response is to emphasize their guilt, assume the worst, and indulge in self-pity. *Joseph is no more* puts a name to the brother's reticent description *one is no more* (vv. 13, 32). Jacob prematurely includes Simeon in the same category (v. 34) and refuses to let them take Benjamin. Jacob is here a tragic and pathetic figure. Reuben's response, to pledge his own sons as a guarantee for his protection of Benjamin, is heroic and confirms his righteous role in the E version (see 37.22; 42.22). The E story stops here until Joseph's self-revelation in ch. 45. In the J version, Judah will be the guarantor of Benjamin's safety (43.9; 44.18–34). **42.38** The J story resumes with the father's grief (cf. the E version in v. 36). Jacob, a pitiable old man, is unwilling to let Benjamin *go down* with the brothers, lest that *bring him down . . . to Sheol.* One descent entails the other. Jacob's speech echoes his earlier grief at his loss of Joseph (37.35). Note that the return to Egypt is less pressing since the J version seems to lack the detail of Simeon's imprisonment (cf. v. 36).

43.1–34 The brothers travel to Egypt a second time, this time with Benjamin, and are welcomed warmly. Joseph continues to conceal his identity. This is a J section, and Judah, the leader of the brothers, eloquently convinces Israel to allow Benjamin to accompany them. At the feast, Benjamin is lavished with a greater portion than his brothers, signaling Joseph's love for

him and, potentially, his brothers' jealousy. **43.1** An echo of 12.10, when the famine in Abraham's day caused him to journey to Egypt and settle there as a resident alien. Abraham's descent to Egypt foreshadows the descent of Israel's family. **43.3–7** Judah recounts Joseph's words to them in Egypt, including his poignant inquiries (v. 7). These are recalled by Joseph in vv. 27–29; the full conversation is recalled by Judah in 44.19–23. (Cf. the different dialogue in the E version, 42.7–20.) Joseph's interrogation of the brothers highlights his anxious emotions, of which the brothers are naturally oblivious. **43.8–10** Judah's firmness toward his father shows his quality of leadership. As often in the biblical narrative, there is twofold causality in which the hero's resolve and God's plan intertwine. Judah pledges himself as *surety* for Benjamin; cf. Reuben's pledge of his sons in the E version (42.37). **43.11–15** The brothers' journey to Egypt with their youngest brother and various natural products, including *a little balm . . . gum, resin,* echoes the Ishmaelite caravan carrying *gum, balm, and resin* (37.25) that transported Joseph to Egypt. This journey is a consequence of and atonement for the brothers' involvement in the previous journey. They also carry back *the money that was returned in the top of* their sacks (see 42.27), which adds a degree of suspense to their return. **43.14** An editorial expansion harmonizing the J story with the imprisonment of Simeon in E and using

other brother and Benjamin. As for me, if I am bereaved of my children, I am bereaved." 15So the men took the present, and they took double the money with them, as well as Benjamin. Then they went on their way down to Egypt, and stood before Joseph.

16 When Joseph saw Benjamin with them, he said to the steward of his house, "Bring the men into the house, and slaughter an animal and make ready, for the men are to dine with me at noon." 17The man did as Joseph said, and brought the men to Joseph's house. 18Now the men were afraid because they were brought to Joseph's house, and they said, "It is because of the money, replaced in our sacks the first time, that we have been brought in, so that he may have an opportunity to fall upon us, to make slaves of us and take our donkeys." 19So they went up to the steward of Joseph's house and spoke with him at the entrance to the house. 20They said, "Oh, my lord, we came down the first time to buy food; 21and when we came to the lodging place we opened our sacks, and there was each one's money in the top of his sack, our money in full weight. So we have brought it back with us. 22Moreover we have brought down with us additional money to buy food. We do not know who put our money in our sacks." 23He replied, "Rest assured, do not be afraid; your God and the God of your father must have put treasure in your sacks for you; I received your money." Then he brought Simeon out to them. 24When the steward[a] had brought the men into Joseph's house, and given them water, and they had washed their feet, and when he had given their donkeys fodder, 25they made the present ready for Joseph's coming at noon, for they had heard that they would dine there.

26 When Joseph came home, they brought him the present that they had carried into the house, and bowed to the ground before him. 27He inquired about their welfare, and said, "Is your father well, the old man of whom you spoke? Is he still alive?" 28They said, "Your servant our father is well; he is still alive." And they bowed their heads and did obeisance. 29Then he looked up and saw his brother Benjamin, his mother's son, and said, "Is this your youngest brother, of whom you spoke to me? God be gracious to you, my son!" 30With that, Joseph hurried out, because he was overcome with affection for his brother, and he was about to weep. So he went into a private room and wept there. 31Then he washed his face and came out; and controlling himself he said, "Serve the meal." 32They served him by himself, and them by themselves, and the Egyptians who ate with him by themselves, because the Egyptians could not eat with the Hebrews, for that is an abomination to the Egyptians. 33When they were seated before him, the firstborn according to his birthright and the youngest according to his youth, the men looked at one another in amazement. 34Portions were taken to them from Joseph's table, but Benjamin's portion was five times as much as any of theirs. So they drank and were merry with him.

___
a Heb the man

the divine title God Almighty (El Shaddai), which is elsewhere found in the P source (17.1). **43.16–23** Because of the possible charge of theft on account of the returned money, the brothers were afraid (v. 18). Their fear is unfounded this time, but anticipates the next time, when Benjamin will be implicated (44.1–17). Joseph is playing on their fears as part of the test. The steward, who had probably planted the money (see 44.1), gives a theological explanation by attributing matters to God (v. 23). This answer, even if insincere, rightly raises the theme of divine providence. The last part of v. 23, concerning Simeon, is probably an editorial harmonization (see v. 14). **43.26–31** The brothers bow to Joseph twice more, recalling his two dreams (37.5–11). Joseph inquires about their welfare (shalom), which in a sense completes his interrupted journey to see if it is well (shalom) with his brothers (37.14), but in totally changed circumstances. His twofold inquiry about their father shows us Joseph's intense concern for

him (v. 27). The dramatic sight of Benjamin, pointedly referred to as his brother Benjamin, his mother's son, causes Joseph to be overcome with affection (v. 30), a rare direct description of inner emotions. Joseph the trickster almost loses his disguise, but he manages to control himself. **43.32–34** At the meal Joseph eats separately from his brothers and the Egyptians, signifying his liminal status between identities. Disguised from his kin, he is a Hebrew who rules over Egyptians, but one with whom the Egyptians cannot eat. (Cf. the Egyptian abhorrence of shepherds, 46.34.) The brothers' astonishment at the correct seating order, from firstborn to youngest, shows again the crossed perspectives. Joseph is knowledgeable and the brothers deceived; Joseph is again toying with them. The youngest has the most lavish portion, recalling Joseph's previous status within the family, which might kindle the jealousy of the older brothers. But the brothers drank and were merry (v. 34), with no hint of resentment.

Joseph Detains Benjamin

44 Then he commanded the steward of his house, "Fill the men's sacks with food, as much as they can carry, and put each man's money in the top of his sack. ²Put my cup, the silver cup, in the top of the sack of the youngest, with his money for the grain." And he did as Joseph told him. ³As soon as the morning was light, the men were sent away with their donkeys. ⁴When they had gone only a short distance from the city, Joseph said to his steward, "Go, follow after the men; and when you overtake them, say to them, 'Why have you returned evil for good? Why have you stolen my silver cup?ᵃ ⁵Is it not from this that my lord drinks? Does he not indeed use it for divination? You have done wrong in doing this.'"

6 When he overtook them, he repeated these words to them. ⁷They said to him, "Why does my lord speak such words as these? Far be it from your servants that they should do such a thing! ⁸Look, the money that we found at the top of our sacks, we brought back to you from the land of Canaan; why then would we steal silver or gold from your lord's house? ⁹Should it be found with any one of your servants, let him die; moreover the rest of us will become my lord's slaves." ¹⁰He said, "Even so; in accordance with your words, let it be: he with

whom it is found shall become my slave, but the rest of you shall go free." ¹¹Then each one quickly lowered his sack to the ground, and each opened his sack. ¹²He searched, beginning with the eldest and ending with the youngest; and the cup was found in Benjamin's sack. ¹³At this they tore their clothes. Then each one loaded his donkey, and they returned to the city.

14 Judah and his brothers came to Joseph's house while he was still there; and they fell to the ground before him. ¹⁵Joseph said to them, "What deed is this that you have done? Do you not know that one such as I can practice divination?" ¹⁶And Judah said, "What can we say to my lord? What can we speak? How can we clear ourselves? God has found out the guilt of your servants; here we are then, my lord's slaves, both we and also the one in whose possession the cup has been found." ¹⁷But he said, "Far be it from me that I should do so! Only the one in whose possession the cup was found shall be my slave; but as for you, go up in peace to your father."

Judah Pleads for Benjamin's Release

18 Then Judah stepped up to him and said, "O my lord, let your servant please speak a word in my lord's ears, and do not be angry

ᵃ Gk Compare Vg: Heb lacks *Why have you stolen my silver cup?*

44.1–34 Joseph's test of his brothers comes to a climax in this J section when Joseph's cup is discovered in Benjamin's sack, marking Benjamin for slavery. Judah's eloquent plea to Joseph, his offer to take Benjamin's place, and his fear for their father's suffering demonstrate that the brothers will not again abandon a brother to slavery and inflict grief on their father. The brothers are tested by a potential reprise of their former crime, and they pass the test. 44.2 *My cup, the silver cup,* the cup that Joseph uses for drinking and divination (v. 5). This bait, along with the *money* (lit. "silver") placed in their sacks, recalls the *twenty pieces of silver* for which the brothers sold Joseph (37.28). Will they abandon Benjamin for the sake of this silver? 44.9–10 The brothers' vow echoes Jacob's vow when Rachel stole Laban's family gods (31.32). They are similarly unaware that one of them (Rachel's son) has the missing item. The steward lightens their vow to slavery for the one *with whom it is found.* Note that this description doesn't say that he stole the cup, merely that it is in his possession. Note that the steward is the one who put it there. 44.12–13 The steward's search, *eldest* to *youngest,* creates suspense and echoes the happier situation of the previous day's feast, when they were arranged from the *firstborn* to the *youngest* (43.33).

Tore their clothes. Their response to the discovery of the cup and the imminent loss of Benjamin directly echoes Jacob's response to the loss of Joseph (37.34), a gesture of mourning. Their grief is poetic justice for the grief they caused their father. 44.14–17 *Do you not know . . . I can practice divination?* Ironic, since Joseph does not need divination to know that the brothers have possession of his divination cup. *God has found out the guilt.* Similarly ironic, since their guilt does not concern the cup, but their sale of Joseph into slavery. Judah's offer for all the brothers to be slaves (v. 16) is a first step of atonement for abandoning Joseph to slavery. Joseph's response, that he will keep Benjamin and the others shall go . . . *in peace* (v. 17), seems to require a repetition of their abandonment of Joseph. 44.18–34 Judah's eloquent and heartfelt reply removes any doubt as to the brothers' moral rehabilitation as he rehearses the history and the reasons why they cannot abandon Benjamin. Use of *your servant(s)* twelve times and *my lord* seven times highlights that the brothers—and also Israel—are already Joseph's slaves (*servant,* Hebrew *'eved,* also means "slave"), perhaps a reminder of Joseph's dreams. 44.18 The preface to Judah's speech echoes the preface to Abraham's potent speech to God in 18.23 (the same Hebrew verbs are

with your servant; for you are like Pharaoh himself. 19My lord asked his servants, saying, 'Have you a father or a brother?' 20And we said to my lord, 'We have a father, an old man, and a young brother, the child of his old age. His brother is dead; he alone is left of his mother's children, and his father loves him.' 21Then you said to your servants, 'Bring him down to me, so that I may set my eyes on him.' 22We said to my lord, 'The boy cannot leave his father, for if he should leave his father, his father would die.' 23Then you said to your servants, 'Unless your youngest brother comes down with you, you shall see my face no more.' 24When we went back to your servant my father we told him the words of my lord. 25And when our father said, 'Go again, buy us a little food,' 26we said, 'We cannot go down. Only if our youngest brother goes with us, will we go down; for we cannot see the man's face unless our youngest brother is with us.' 27Then your servant my father said to us, 'You know that my wife bore me two sons; 28one left me, and I said, Surely he has been torn to pieces; and I have never seen him since. 29If you take this one also from me, and harm comes to him, you will bring down my gray hairs in sorrow to Sheol.' 30Now therefore, when I come to your servant my father and the boy is not with us, then, as his life is bound up in the boy's life, 31when he sees that the boy is not with us, he

will die; and your servants will bring down the gray hairs of your servant our father with sorrow to Sheol. 32For your servant became surety for the boy to my father, saying, 'If I do not bring him back to you, then I will bear the blame in the sight of my father all my life.' 33Now therefore, please let your servant remain as a slave to my lord in place of the boy; and let the boy go back with his brothers. 34For how can I go back to my father if the boy is not with me? I fear to see the suffering that would come upon my father."

Joseph Reveals Himself to His Brothers

45 Then Joseph could no longer control himself before all those who stood by him, and he cried out, "Send everyone away from me." So no one stayed with him when Joseph made himself known to his brothers. 2And he wept so loudly that the Egyptians heard it, and the household of Pharaoh heard it. 3Joseph said to his brothers, "I am Joseph. Is my father still alive?" But his brothers could not answer him, so dismayed were they at his presence.

4 Then Joseph said to his brothers, "Come closer to me." And they came closer. He said, "I am your brother, Joseph, whom you sold into Egypt. 5And now do not be distressed, or angry with yourselves, because you sold me here; for God sent me before you to preserve

used in both). This echo emphasizes Judah's courage and conviction. **44.20** *Child of his old age . . . his father loves him.* Judah's description of Benjamin evokes the earlier situation of Joseph (37.3), but now there is no jealousy or sibling rivalry, only compassion. **44.22–34** Judah's several descriptions of Israel's frailty and possible death build upon one another to produce an image of the intense suffering that would result from the loss of Benjamin; see vv. 22, 29–31, 34. **44.33–34** Judah revises his insistence that all the brothers remain as slaves (v. 16) and offers himself in Benjamin's place; the boy is to *go back.* This reverses the earlier situation in which Judah sold his brother into slavery and went back himself, in deceit, to his father. *How can I go back to my father?* better "How can I go up to my father?" The directional sense of "go up" contrasts with *bring down:* how can Judah "go up" to his father, knowing that it will *bring down* his father *to Sheol* (v. 31)? In the sense of his speech, Judah is offering his own life to save his father's life.

45.1–28 Overcome by emotion, Joseph reveals his identity to his brothers. His role as interpreter then comes to a climax as he interprets the meaning of their mutual travails, discerning in these events God's plan of deliverance. Joseph shows his wisdom by further

implementing God's plan and instructing his family to settle in Egypt. The chapter is capped by the brothers' return to Canaan and Jacob's emotional response when he learns that his son is still alive. This chapter is a composite of J and E; the J source is dominant in vv. 1–4 and the E source thereafter, but parallel verses are interwoven throughout. **45.1** Joseph's loss of self-control and his loud weeping echo his first two encounters with his brothers in Egypt (42.24; 43.30–31), particularly when they came with Benjamin, when he left the room to weep and compose himself. Now he sends the Egyptians out of the room, weeps, and makes himself known to his brothers. The themes of knowledge, recognition, and deception will now be resolved. **45.3–4** Joseph reveals his identity twice, perhaps an editorial amalgam of the sources (E in v. 3; J in v. 4). As the text stands, the brothers are *so dismayed* that he dramatically calls them *closer* (echoing Judah's approach in 44.18) and announces himself again, adding ominously *whom you sold into Egypt.* The brothers' dismay is compounded by fear for their lives, since Joseph is in a position to exact justice for their crime. **45.5–8** In the moment of resolution, Joseph shows his wisdom, compassion, and insight into God's plan, interpreting for the brothers the meaning of their mutual history.

life. 6For the famine has been in the land these two years; and there are five more years in which there will be neither plowing nor harvest. 7God sent me before you to preserve for you a remnant on earth, and to keep alive for you many survivors. 8So it was not you who sent me here, but God; he has made me a father to Pharaoh, and lord of all his house and ruler over all the land of Egypt. 9Hurry and go up to my father and say to him, 'Thus says your son Joseph, God has made me lord of all Egypt; come down to me, do not delay. 10You shall settle in the land of Goshen, and you shall be near me, you and your children and your children's children, as well as your flocks, your herds, and all that you have. 11I will provide for you there—since there are five more years of famine to come—so that you and your household, and all that you have, will not come to poverty.' 12And now your eyes and the eyes of my brother Benjamin see that it is my own mouth that speaks to you. 13You must tell my father how greatly I am honored in Egypt, and all that you have seen. Hurry and bring my father down here." 14Then he fell upon his brother Benjamin's neck and wept, while Benjamin wept upon his neck. 15And he kissed all his brothers and wept upon them; and after that his brothers talked with him.

16 When the report was heard in Pharaoh's house, "Joseph's brothers have come," Pharaoh and his servants were pleased. 17Pharaoh said to Joseph, "Say to your brothers, 'Do this: load your animals and go back to the land of Canaan. 18Take your father and your households and come to me, so that I may give you the best of the land of Egypt, and you may enjoy the fat of the land.' 19You are further charged to say, 'Do this: take wagons from the land of Egypt for your little ones and for your wives, and bring your father, and come. 20Give no thought to your possessions, for the best of all the land of Egypt is yours.' "

21 The sons of Israel did so. Joseph gave them wagons according to the instruction of Pharaoh, and he gave them provisions for the journey. 22To each one of them he gave a set of garments; but to Benjamin he gave three hundred pieces of silver and five sets of garments. 23To his father he sent the following: ten donkeys loaded with the good things of Egypt, and ten female donkeys loaded with grain, bread, and provision for his father on the journey. 24Then he sent his brothers on their way, and as they were leaving he said to them, "Do not quarrel[a] along the way."

25 So they went up out of Egypt and came to their father Jacob in the land of Canaan. 26And they told him, "Joseph is still alive! He is even ruler over all the land of Egypt." He was stunned; he could not believe them. 27But when they told him all the words of Joseph that he had said to them, and when he saw the wagons that Joseph had sent to carry him, the spirit of their father Jacob revived. 28Israel said, "Enough! My son Joseph is still alive. I must go and see him before I die."

Jacob Brings His Whole Family to Egypt

46 When Israel set out on his journey with all that he had and came to Beersheba, he offered sacrifices to the God of his

a Or be agitated

Events have a double agency, with God's plan containing and guiding human intentions. The brothers *sold* Joseph in Egypt, but *God sent* him *before* them with the divine plan *to preserve life*. *God sent me before you*, repeated three times in vv. 5–8 (with identical wording in vv. 5, 7), highlights the divine agency behind events. By his interpretive gift, Joseph reestablishes peace among the brothers. **45.9** *Go up to my father* and *come down to me* revise the symbolic contrast of going up and coming down in Judah's speech (see note on 44.33–34). Now their father will *come down* to Joseph rather than to Sheol. **45.14–15** After Joseph's speech, the brothers hug, kiss, and weep, recalling the emotional reunion of Jacob and Esau (33.4). Joseph hugs Benjamin first, signaling their special bond. At last, calmed of their fears, the brothers *talked with him*. **45.16–20** Joseph's instructions are seconded by Pharaoh, who extends great generosity to Joseph's family,

granting them *the best of the land of Egypt* (vv. 18, 20). Pharaoh's beneficence contrasts with the actions of his later successor "who did not know Joseph" (Ex 1.8). **45.22–24** The gift of new garments again signals an ascent in status (cf. 41.42). Joseph's greater gift to Benjamin recalls Israel's favoritism of Joseph, expressed by his special *long robe* (37.3). But now the brothers are reconciled. As a gentle reminder of their past, Joseph cautions them not to *quarrel along the way*. **45.26–28** *Joseph is still alive!* The brothers' first words to Jacob echo Joseph's first words to them after his self-revelation, *Is my father still alive?* (v. 3). After initially being *stunned* (better "numb"), Jacob's spirit *revived* (lit, "came alive," v. 27). The news that Joseph is alive brings Jacob, in a sense, back to life. Israel dramatizes this point and makes Joseph's instructions his own by saying *I must go and see him before I die* (v. 28). **46.1–27** The focus turns back to Jacob as his family

father Isaac. 2God spoke to Israel in visions of the night, and said, "Jacob, Jacob." And he said, "Here I am." 3Then he said, "I am God,[a] the God of your father; do not be afraid to go down to Egypt, for I will make of you a great nation there. 4I myself will go down with you to Egypt, and I will also bring you up again; and Joseph's own hand shall close your eyes."

5 Then Jacob set out from Beer-sheba; and the sons of Israel carried their father Jacob, their little ones, and their wives, in the wagons that Pharaoh had sent to carry him. 6They also took their livestock and the goods that they had acquired in the land of Canaan, and they came into Egypt, Jacob and all his offspring with him, 7his sons, and his sons' sons with him, his daughters, and his sons' daughters; all his offspring he brought with him into Egypt.

8 Now these are the names of the Israelites, Jacob and his offspring, who came to Egypt. Reuben, Jacob's firstborn, 9and the children of Reuben: Hanoch, Pallu, Hezron, and Carmi. 10The children of Simeon: Jemuel, Jamin, Ohad, Jachin, Zohar, and Shaul,[b] the son of a Canaanite woman. 11The children of Levi: Gershon, Kohath, and Merari. 12The children of Judah: Er, Onan, Shelah, Perez, and Zerah (but Er and Onan died in the land of Canaan); and the children of Perez were Hezron and Hamul. 13The children of Issachar: Tola, Puvah, Jashub,[c] and Shimron. 14The children of Zebulun: Sered, Elon, and Jahleel 15(these are the sons of Leah, whom she bore to Jacob in Paddan-aram, together with his daughter Dinah; in all his sons and his daughters numbered thirty-three). 16The children of Gad: Ziphion, Haggi, Shuni, Ezbon, Eri, Arodi, and Areli. 17The children of Asher: Imnah, Ishvah, Ishvi, Beriah, and their sister Serah. The chil-

dren of Beriah: Heber and Malchiel 18(these are the children of Zilpah, whom Laban gave to his daughter Leah; and these she bore to Jacob—sixteen persons). 19The children of Jacob's wife Rachel: Joseph and Benjamin. 20To Joseph in the land of Egypt were born Manasseh and Ephraim, whom Asenath daughter of Potiphera, priest of On, bore to him. 21The children of Benjamin: Bela, Becher, Ashbel, Gera, Naaman, Ehi, Rosh, Muppim, Huppim, and Ard 22(these are the children of Rachel, who were born to Jacob—fourteen persons in all). 23The children of Dan: Hashum.[d] 24The children of Naphtali: Jahzeel, Guni, Jezer, and Shillem 25(these are the children of Bilhah, whom Laban gave to his daughter Rachel, and these she bore to Jacob—seven persons in all). 26All the persons belonging to Jacob who came into Egypt, who were his own offspring, not including the wives of his sons, were sixty-six persons in all. 27The children of Joseph, who were born to him in Egypt, were two; all the persons of the house of Jacob who came into Egypt were seventy.

Jacob Settles in Goshen

28 Israel[e] sent Judah ahead to Joseph to lead the way before him into Goshen. When they came to the land of Goshen, 29Joseph made ready his chariot and went up to meet his father Israel in Goshen. He presented himself to him, fell on his neck, and wept on his neck a good while. 30Israel said to Joseph, "I can die now, having seen for myself that you are still alive." 31Joseph said to his brothers and to his father's household, "I will go up and tell Phar-

---

[a] Heb *the God*　[b] Or *Saul*　[c] Compare Sam Gk Num 26.24; 1 Chr 7.1: MT *Iob*　[d] Gk: Heb *Hushim*　[e] Heb *He*

---

moves to Egypt. With the conflict between Joseph and his brothers now resolved, the Joseph story gradually comes to a close and prepares for the story of the exodus. This chapter consists of a combination of J and E in vv. 1–7, and a P genealogy in vv. 8–27. **46.1–4** At the altar that Isaac had built in Beer-sheba (see 26.25), God reveals himself to Jacob for the last time and outlines the future. *Bring you up again* has a double meaning. God will bring Jacob up to Canaan to be buried by Joseph (50.1–14), and God will bring the Israelites up from Egypt in the exodus. **46.8–27** The list of Jacob and his descendants who came to Egypt interrupts the action and adds a degree of grandeur to the journey. *Seventy*, a number representing wholeness (cf. Ex 15.27; 24.1; Judg 1.7; 8.30; 2 Kings 10.1). The list was originally a separate document that has been adapted

to its context here. An editorial comment in v. 26 observes that only sixty-six of Jacob's family *came into Egypt*, excluding Er and Onan, who *died in the land of Canaan* (v. 12), and Manasseh and Ephraim, who were born *in the land of Egypt* (v. 20). Joseph's status in this list is, however, obscure, since he is in Egypt, but seems to be included among the sixty-six. These problems are simplified in Ex 1.5, which states that "the total number of people born to Jacob was seventy" and that "Joseph was already in Egypt." **46.28–47.12** The journey resumes with the arrival in Egypt, Jacob's joyous reunion with Joseph, and the audience with Pharaoh. The first part (46.28–47.4, 6b) is from the J source; the second part (47.5–6a, 7–12) is from P. **46.29–30** *I can die now*. The reunion of Jacob and Joseph is sealed by the father's tragicomic remark,

aoh, and will say to him, 'My brothers and my father's household, who were in the land of Canaan, have come to me. ³²The men are shepherds, for they have been keepers of livestock; and they have brought their flocks, and their herds, and all that they have.' ³³When Pharaoh calls you, and says, 'What is your occupation?' ³⁴you shall say, 'Your servants have been keepers of livestock from our youth even until now, both we and our ancestors'—in order that you may settle in the land of Goshen, because all shepherds are abhorrent to the Egyptians."

47 So Joseph went and told Pharaoh, "My father and my brothers, with their flocks and herds and all that they possess, have come from the land of Canaan; they are now in the land of Goshen." ²From among his brothers he took five men and presented them to Pharaoh. ³Pharaoh said to his brothers, "What is your occupation?" And they said to Pharaoh, "Your servants are shepherds, as our ancestors were." ⁴They said to Pharaoh, "We have come to reside as aliens in the land; for there is no pasture for your servants' flocks because the famine is severe in the land of Canaan. Now, we ask you, let your servants settle in the land of Goshen." ⁵Then Pharaoh said to Joseph, "Your father and your brothers have come to you. ⁶The land of Egypt is before you; settle your father and your brothers in the best part of the land; let them live in the land of Goshen; and if you know that there are capable men among them, put them in charge of my livestock."

7 Then Joseph brought in his father Jacob, and presented him before Pharaoh, and Jacob blessed Pharaoh. ⁸Pharaoh said to Jacob, "How many are the years of your life?" ⁹Jacob said to Pharaoh, "The years of my earthly sojourn are one hundred thirty; few and hard have been the years of my life. They do not compare with the years of the life of my ancestors during their long sojourn." ¹⁰Then Jacob blessed Pharaoh, and went out from the presence of Pharaoh. ¹¹Joseph settled his father and his brothers, and granted them a holding in the land of Egypt, in the best part of the land, in the land of Rameses, as Pharaoh had instructed. ¹²And Joseph provided his father, his brothers, and all his father's household with food, according to the number of their dependents.

The Famine in Egypt

13 Now there was no food in all the land, for the famine was very severe. The land of Egypt and the land of Canaan languished because of the famine. ¹⁴Joseph collected all the money to be found in the land of Egypt and in the land of Canaan, in exchange for the grain that they bought; and Joseph brought the money into Pharaoh's house. ¹⁵When the money from the land of Egypt and from the land of Canaan was spent, all the Egyptians came to Joseph, and said, "Give us food! Why should we die before your eyes? For our money is gone." ¹⁶And Joseph answered, "Give me your livestock, and I will give you food in exchange for your livestock, if your money is gone." ¹⁷So they brought their livestock to Joseph; and Joseph gave them food in exchange for the horses, the flocks, the herds, and the donkeys. That year he supplied them with food in exchange for all their livestock. ¹⁸When that year was ended, they came to him the following year, and said to him, "We can not hide from my lord that our money is all spent; and the herds of cattle are my lord's. There is nothing left in the sight of my lord but our bodies and our lands. ¹⁹Shall we die before your eyes, both we and our land? Buy us and our land in

---

recalling 45.28 and his earlier cries of dying in 37.35; 42.38. **46.33–47.6** Joseph counsels a final deception so that the family *may settle in the land of Goshen.* It is not clear why he says *shepherds are abhorrent to the Egyptians* (46.34). Curiously, the brothers disregard Joseph's counsel and tell the truth, and Pharaoh lets them *live in the land of Goshen* (47.6). **47.5–12** In the P version Pharaoh speaks to Joseph, telling him to settle his family in the *best part of the land* (v. 6). Preoccupied with his mortality, as ever, Jacob states that his years have been *few and hard* (v. 9), but he manages to impress with his longevity and ancestry. *Jacob blessed Pharaoh* in greeting and farewell (v. 7), a gesture that also conveys a sense of Jacob's superiority over Pharaoh. *Land of Rameses,* the P equivalent of the *land of Goshen;* it foreshadows the time when the Israelite slaves will build the city of Rameses (Ex 1.11). **47.13–26** This unusual section tells of Joseph's brutal strategy during the seven years of famine, following his preparations during the seven years of plenty (41.47–49). Joseph first acquires for Pharaoh all the money in Egypt and Canaan. Then he acquires all the Egyptians' livestock and land and even the Egyptians themselves as slaves. This section may explain why all of Egypt was regarded as Pharaoh's personal property, with special provision for the priests. The source(s) of this section

exchange for food. We with our land will become slaves to Pharaoh; just give us seed, so that we may live and not die, and that the land may not become desolate."

20 So Joseph bought all the land of Egypt for Pharaoh. All the Egyptians sold their fields, because the famine was severe upon them; and the land became Pharaoh's. 21As for the people, he made slaves of them*a* from one end of Egypt to the other. 22Only the land of the priests he did not buy; for the priests had a fixed allowance from Pharaoh, and lived on the allowance that Pharaoh gave them; therefore they did not sell their land. 23Then Joseph said to the people, "Now that I have this day bought you and your land for Pharaoh, here is seed for you; sow the land. 24And at the harvests you shall give one-fifth to Pharaoh, and four-fifths shall be your own, as seed for the field and as food for yourselves and your households, and as food for your little ones." 25They said, "You have saved our lives; may it please my lord, we will be slaves to Pharaoh." 26So Joseph made it a statute concerning the land of Egypt, and it stands to this day, that Pharaoh should have the fifth. The land of the priests alone did not become Pharaoh's.

The Last Days of Jacob

27 Thus Israel settled in the land of Egypt, in the region of Goshen; and they gained possessions in it, and were fruitful and multiplied exceedingly. 28Jacob lived in the land of Egypt seventeen years; so the days of Jacob, the years of his life, were one hundred forty-seven years.

29 When the time of Israel's death drew near, he called his son Joseph and said to him, "If I have found favor with you, put your hand under my thigh and promise to deal loyally and truly with me. Do not bury me in Egypt. 30When I lie down with my ancestors, carry me out of Egypt and bury me in their burial place." He answered, "I will do as you have said." 31And he said, "Swear to me"; and he swore to him. Then Israel bowed himself on the head of his bed.

Jacob Blesses Joseph's Sons

48 After this Joseph was told, "Your father is ill." So he took with him his two sons, Manasseh and Ephraim. 2When Jacob was told, "Your son Joseph has come to you," he*b* summoned his strength and sat up in bed. 3And Jacob said to Joseph, "God Almighty*c* appeared to me at Luz in the land of Canaan, and he blessed me, 4and said to me, 'I am going to make you fruitful and increase your numbers; I will make of you a company of peoples, and will give this land to your offspring after you for a perpetual holding.' 5Therefore your two sons, who were born to

---

a Sam Gk Compare Vg: MT *He removed them to the cities*
b Heb *Israel*   *c* Traditional rendering of Heb *El Shaddai*

---

are difficult to identify. There is perhaps some irony or poetic justice in Joseph's enslavement of all the Egyptians before Pharaoh enslaves all the Israelites. **47.27–31** Having declared his readiness to die (46.30), Israel's last days are at hand. On his deathbed he will bless Joseph's sons (ch. 48) and give his last words to his sons (ch. 49). Here he pledges Joseph to bury him in the patriarchal tomb in Canaan. This is a J section, with a P text in vv. 27–28. **47.27–28** The P summary of Israel's settlement in Egypt evokes God's blessing to *be fruitful and multiply,* which punctuates the Genesis narrative; it was granted to the first couple, then Noah, Abraham, and Jacob (1.28; 9.1, 7; 17.6; 35.11). This blessing is now fulfilled for Israel in Egypt, as the people *were fruitful and multiplied exceedingly.* But this happy situation will turn problematic shortly (Ex 1.12). On Jacob's life span, cf. Isaac's and Abraham's in 35.28; 25.7. **47.29–31** The image of Jacob, old and near death, recalls his father, Isaac, in 27.2, ready to grant his blessing to his firstborn son, and his grandfather, Abraham, in 24.1, who tells his servant to follow his wishes (24.2). Jacob's wish to be buried with his *ancestors* has extra resonance by these echoes of his ancestors in their final days. The image of Israel bow-

ing *on the head of his bed* indicates his physical frailty; cf. David on his deathbed (1 Kings 1.47).

48.1–22 On his deathbed Jacob plays one last trick, elevating Joseph's younger son, Ephraim, over his firstborn, Manasseh. By doing this, Jacob tricks Joseph much as he had earlier deceived Isaac by elevating himself over Esau in ch. 27. Yet Jacob is also changed: he tricks his son because he can now foresee the future, in which Ephraim is the greater tribe (v. 19). Jacob's deathbed ability to foretell the future will continue in his last words in ch. 49. This chapter is primarily a composite of E (vv. 1–2a, 8–9, 10b–12, 15–16, 21–22) and J (vv. 2b, 10a, 13–14, 17–20), with a P version in vv. 3–7. Note that Jacob is blind in the J version (see v. 10a), like Isaac in 27.1, but he can see in the E version (see vv. 8, 11). **48.3–7** Jacob refers to the divine revelation and blessings given to him at Bethel (35.9–15, P). *God Almighty* (*El Shaddai*). See 35.11; 17.1. Jacob adopts Joseph's two sons, Ephraim and Manasseh, as his own sons, so that they can be tribes in their own right, yet with close affinity to each other. See, e.g., Num 1.10, which lists Ephraim and Manasseh as "the sons of Joseph" and also as separate tribes. The reference to Rachel's death, recalled with some emotion,

you in the land of Egypt before I came to you in Egypt, are now mine; Ephraim and Manasseh shall be mine, just as Reuben and Simeon are. 6As for the offspring born to you after them, they shall be yours. They shall be recorded under the names of their brothers with regard to their inheritance. 7For when I came from Paddan, Rachel, alas, died in the land of Canaan on the way, while there was still some distance to go to Ephrath; and I buried her there on the way to Ephrath" (that is, Bethlehem).

8 When Israel saw Joseph's sons, he said, "Who are these?" 9Joseph said to his father, "They are my sons, whom God has given me here." And he said, "Bring them to me, please, that I may bless them." 10Now the eyes of Israel were dim with age, and he could not see well. So Joseph brought them near him; and he kissed them and embraced them. 11Israel said to Joseph, "I did not expect to see your face; and here God has let me see your children also." 12Then Joseph removed them from his father's knees,ᵃ and he bowed himself with his face to the earth. 13Joseph took them both, Ephraim in his right hand toward Israel's left, and Manasseh in his left hand toward Israel's right, and brought them near him. 14But Israel stretched out his right hand and laid it on the head of Ephraim, who was the younger, and his left hand on the head of Manasseh, crossing his hands, for Manasseh was the firstborn. 15He blessed Joseph, and said,

"The God before whom my ancestors
Abraham and Isaac walked,
the God who has been my shepherd all
my life to this day,

16   the angel who has redeemed me from all
harm, bless the boys;
and in them let my name be perpetuated,
and the name of my ancestors
Abraham and Isaac;
and let them grow into a multitude on
the earth."

17 When Joseph saw that his father laid his right hand on the head of Ephraim, it displeased him; so he took his father's hand, to remove it from Ephraim's head to Manasseh's head. 18Joseph said to his father, "Not so, my father! Since this one is the firstborn, put your right hand on his head." 19But his father refused, and said, "I know, my son, I know; he also shall become a people, and he also shall be great. Nevertheless his younger brother shall be greater than he, and his offspring shall become a multitude of nations." 20So he blessed them that day, saying,

"By youᵇ Israel will invoke blessings,
saying,
'God make youᵇ like Ephraim and like
Manasseh.' "

So he put Ephraim ahead of Manasseh. 21Then Israel said to Joseph, "I am about to die, but God will be with you and will bring you again to the land of your ancestors. 22I now give to you one portionᶜ more than to your brothers, the portionᶜ that I took from the hand of the Amorites with my sword and with my bow."

ᵃ Heb *from his knees*   ᵇ *you* here is singular in Heb
ᶜ Or *mountain slope* (Heb *shekem*, a play on the name of the town and district of Shechem)

---

may imply that they are now adopted sons of Jacob and Rachel. The children's order—Ephraim and Manasseh—may imply that Ephraim is already the firstborn in P. **48.8–9, 10b–12, 15–16** The E version of the blessing of Ephraim and Manasseh follows from v. 2. In the final text, Israel's question *Who are these?* in v. 8 sounds jarring after his adoption of the boys in vv. 5–6, as if he were slipping into senility. In this version, Israel hugs and kisses the boys, as one does when meeting or reuniting with kin (see 45.14–15; 46.29), speaks warmly to Joseph, and grants the boys a gracious and poetic blessing. The resonance of this tender scene is dissipated in the composite text. **48.10a, 13–14, 17–20** In the J version Israel is once again a trickster, but now he is also a seer. The description in v. 10a is an echo of Isaac's blindness in 27.1. In that scene Jacob tricked his blind father, but now Jacob, the blind father, will trick his son. He does this by *crossing his hands* (v.

14), so that his right hand is on Ephraim, the younger. Joseph is *displeased* (lit. "it was evil in his eyes"), but Israel calms him by prophesying the greatness of both sons, though the *younger brother shall be greater* (v. 19). The ascent of the younger mirrors Jacob's ascent to his current role as wise patriarch of a great people. **48.21–22** In the E version Israel also becomes a seer, foretelling that God will be with Joseph and bring him again to the land of his ancestors, as God had been with Jacob and brought him back to his father's house (28.20–21; 35.3). This prophecy is fulfilled when Joseph's bones are buried in Shechem (Josh 24.32). The *portion* (Hebrew *shekem*) that Israel grants Joseph is an allusion to Shechem, site of Joseph's grave and the most prominent city in Ephraim. Israel's recollection that he took it in battle from the Amorites presumes a story that is somewhat different from the one in ch. 34 (J), where the city is Hivite and taken by Jacob's sons.

Jacob's Last Words to His Sons

49 Then Jacob called his sons, and said: "Gather around, that I may tell you what will happen to you in days to come.

2 Assemble and hear, O sons of Jacob;
   listen to Israel your father.

3 Reuben, you are my firstborn,
   my might and the first fruits of my
      vigor,
   excelling in rank and excelling in
      power.
4 Unstable as water, you shall no longer excel
   because you went up onto your father's
      bed;
   then you defiled it—you *a* went up onto
      my couch!

5 Simeon and Levi are brothers;
   weapons of violence are their swords.
6 May I never come into their council;
   may I not be joined to their company—
   for in their anger they killed men,
   and at their whim they hamstrung oxen.
7 Cursed be their anger, for it is fierce,
   and their wrath, for it is cruel!
   I will divide them in Jacob,
   and scatter them in Israel.

8 Judah, your brothers shall praise you;
   your hand shall be on the neck of your
      enemies;

your father's sons shall bow down
   before you.
9 Judah is a lion's whelp;
   from the prey, my son, you have gone
      up.
   He crouches down, he stretches out like a
      lion,
   like a lioness—who dares rouse him
      up?
10 The scepter shall not depart from Judah,
   nor the ruler's staff from between his
      feet,
   until tribute comes to him; *b*
   and the obedience of the peoples is his.
11 Binding his foal to the vine
   and his donkey's colt to the choice
      vine,
   he washes his garments in wine
   and his robe in the blood of grapes;
12 his eyes are darker than wine,
   and his teeth whiter than milk.

13 Zebulun shall settle at the shore of the
      sea;
   he shall be a haven for ships,
   and his border shall be at Sidon.

14 Issachar is a strong donkey,
   lying down between the sheepfolds;
15 he saw that a resting place was good,

---

a Gk Syr Tg: Heb *he*   *b* Or *until Shiloh comes* or *until he comes to Shiloh* or (with Syr) *until he comes to whom it belongs*

49.1–28 Jacob's last words continue his prophetic foresight. These prophecies are a collection of old poetic tribal blessings and curses similar to those in Moses' blessings in Deut 33. Genesis ends with Jacob's final blessings and death, just as the Pentateuch ends with Moses' blessings and death. In these sayings the future of Jacob's sons is that of the tribes descended from them. They look forward to the settlement in the land, the disappearance of some tribes, the ascent of kingship in Judah, and the prosperity of Joseph. With their archaic linguistic features, these poetic tribal sayings are probably the oldest verses in Genesis. **49.3–4** Reuben seems to be blessed, but is cursed, because he *went up onto* his *father's bed*. In the J source, this allusion occasions the brief account of Reuben sleeping with Bilhah (35.22). The tribe of Reuben diminished (see Deut 33.6) and eventually disappeared; some of its clans were absorbed into Judah. **49.5–7** Simeon and Levi are *cursed* because *in their anger they killed men.* In the J source this allusion leads to the story of the massacre of the men of Shechem, for which Jacob rebukes them (34.25–31). Simeon eventually disappeared as a tribe, some of its clans were absorbed into

Judah, and Levi was scattered throughout Israel as the landless tribe of priests. **49.8–12** The blessing withheld from the three oldest sons now comes to Judah. *Praise,* Hebrew *yodu,* a play on Judah (v. 8). Like Jacob, Judah is blessed with authority over his brothers (v. 8; cf. 27.29). This blessing points forward to King David, from the tribe of Judah. *The scepter shall not depart from Judah,* an explicit reference to the Davidic dynasty. Judah's blessing of power and wealth is rivaled only by Joseph's blessing of might and fertility (vv. 22–26). From the time of King David, Judah was the prominent tribe in the south; the Joseph tribes were always the prominent tribes in the north. *Binding his foal to the vine, washes his garments in wine,* lovely images that highlight the superabundance of agricultural wealth; Judah can treat vines like ordinary trees and wine like water because he has so much. **49.13** The saying for Zebulun is neither a blessing nor a curse, but a description of his maritime activity, in which he profits from proximity to the Phoenician port of Sidon. Note that in Josh 19.10–15 Zebulun seems to be landlocked, suggesting a historical shift in boundaries. **49.14–15** Issachar's name is taken to mean "hired

and that the land was pleasant;
    so he bowed his shoulder to the burden,
    and became a slave at forced labor.

16 Dan shall judge his people
    as one of the tribes of Israel.
17 Dan shall be a snake by the roadside,
    a viper along the path,
    that bites the horse's heels
    so that its rider falls backward.

18 I wait for your salvation, O LORD.

19 Gad shall be raided by raiders,
    but he shall raid at their heels.

20 Asher's[a] food shall be rich,
    and he shall provide royal delicacies.

21 Naphtali is a doe let loose
    that bears lovely fawns.[b]

22 Joseph is a fruitful bough,
    a fruitful bough by a spring;
    his branches run over the wall.[c]
23 The archers fiercely attacked him;
    they shot at him and pressed him hard.
24 Yet his bow remained taut,
    and his arms[d] were made agile
    by the hands of the Mighty One of Jacob,
    by the name of the Shepherd, the Rock
        of Israel,

25 by the God of your father, who will help
        you,
    by the Almighty[e] who will bless you
    with blessings of heaven above,
    blessings of the deep that lies beneath,
    blessings of the breasts and of the
        womb.
26 The blessings of your father
    are stronger than the blessings of the
        eternal mountains,
    the bounties[f] of the everlasting hills;
    may they be on the head of Joseph,
    on the brow of him who was set apart
        from his brothers.

27 Benjamin is a ravenous wolf,
    in the morning devouring the prey,
    and at evening dividing the spoil."

28 All these are the twelve tribes of Israel,
and this is what their father said to them when
he blessed them, blessing each one of them
with a suitable blessing.

Jacob's Death and Burial

29 Then he charged them, saying to them, "I
am about to be gathered to my people. Bury
me with my ancestors—in the cave in the field

---

a Gk Vg Syr: Heb *From Asher*   b Or *that gives beautiful words*
c Meaning of Heb uncertain   d Heb *the arms of his hands*
e Traditional rendering of Heb *Shaddai*   f Cn Compare Gk:
Heb *of my progenitors to the boundaries*

---

man," leading to his description as a *slave at forced labor* in spite of his lovely land. **49.16–17** Dan means "judge," so he *shall judge his people*. But he will also be fierce like a snake (cf. the lion metaphor for Dan in Deut 33.22). **49.18** An interpolation in the style of Psalms (cf. Ps 119.166). **49.19** An elaborate play on the name of Gad, taken to mean "raiding group." *Heels,* an echo of the saying for Dan (v. 17). **49.22–26** Although some words and phrases are obscure, Joseph is blessed with fertility and greatness. The attack by *the archers,* in which Joseph remains resolute, perhaps resonates with the hostility of his brothers in the Joseph story. The repetition of *bless* and *blessings* (six times in vv. 25–26) creates a dense poetic texture in which God's blessings of fertility emanate from the cosmic domains (*heaven, the deep, mountains, hills*) and the female body (*breasts, womb*) onto Joseph's *head,* crowning him with blessings. The numerous titles of God also make Joseph's blessing a powerful one. **49.27** *Ravenous wolf.* The metaphor of Benjamin as a fierce fighter is similar to the animal metaphors in several of the other tribal sayings (Judah, Issachar, Dan, Naphtali, possibly Joseph); see also the animal metaphors in the tribal blessings of Deut 33. **49.28** The prose frame clarifies

that the sons addressed are the *twelve tribes of Israel.* The sayings describe the tribal polity of Israel and give focus to the patriarchal promise of a great people. This concluding sentence also somewhat misleadingly characterizes all the tribal sayings as blessings.

49.29–50.14 Jacob's death and burial are narrated in two versions, P (49.29–33, 50.12–13) and J (50.1–11, 14), which have been neatly combined. The P version refers to the patriarchal burial cave at Machpelah (see ch. 23), while the J version seems to imply that Jacob was buried east of the Jordan River (50.11), similar to Moses (Deut 34.6). With Jacob's death and burial, the end of Genesis is near. **49.29–33** *Gathered to my people.* Jacob's prediction in v. 29 is fulfilled in v. 33, creating an envelope structure to his final speech. This expression is both a euphemism for death and a literal description of burial in the ancestral grave. As the last burial in the cave of Machpelah, he will join most of the other patriarchs and matriarchs, with the exception of Rachel (see 48.7). This is the first time we learn that Isaac, Rebekah, and Leah were buried at Machpelah; hence Jacob's speech serves as a coda to their deaths and burials as well. *He drew up his feet into the bed* (v. 33) probably comes from the J source, conclud-

of Ephron the Hittite, 30in the cave in the field at Machpelah, near Mamre, in the land of Canaan, in the field that Abraham bought from Ephron the Hittite as a burial site. 31There Abraham and his wife Sarah were buried; there Isaac and his wife Rebekah were buried; and there I buried Leah— 32the field and the cave that is in it were purchased from the Hittites." 33When Jacob ended his charge to his sons, he drew up his feet into the bed, breathed his last, and was gathered to his people.

50 Then Joseph threw himself on his father's face and wept over him and kissed him. 2Joseph commanded the physicians in his service to embalm his father. So the physicians embalmed Israel; 3they spent forty days in doing this, for that is the time required for embalming. And the Egyptians wept for him seventy days.

4 When the days of weeping for him were past, Joseph addressed the household of Pharaoh, "If now I have found favor with you, please speak to Pharaoh as follows: 5My father made me swear an oath; he said, 'I am about to die. In the tomb that I hewed out for myself in the land of Canaan, there you shall bury me.' Now therefore let me go up, so that I may bury my father; then I will return." 6Pharaoh answered, "Go up, and bury your father, as he made you swear to do."

7 So Joseph went up to bury his father. With him went up all the servants of Pharaoh, the elders of his household, and all the elders of the land of Egypt, 8as well as all the household of Joseph, his brothers, and his father's household. Only their children, their flocks, and their herds were left in the land of Goshen. 9Both chariots and charioteers went up with him. It was a very great company. 10When they came to the threshing floor of Atad, which is beyond the Jordan, they held there a very great and sorrowful lamentation; and he observed a time of mourning for his father seven days. 11When the Canaanite inhabitants of the land saw the mourning on the threshing floor of Atad, they said, "This is a grievous mourning on the part of the Egyptians." Therefore the place was named Abel-mizraim;[a] it is beyond the Jordan. 12Thus his sons did for him as he had instructed them. 13They carried him to the land of Canaan and buried him in the cave of the field at Machpelah, the field near Mamre, which Abraham bought as a burial site from Ephron the Hittite. 14After he had buried his father, Joseph returned to Egypt with his brothers and all who had gone up with him to bury his father.

Joseph Forgives His Brothers

15 Realizing that their father was dead, Joseph's brothers said, "What if Joseph still bears a grudge against us and pays us back in full for all the wrong that we did to him?" 16So they approached[b] Joseph, saying, "Your father gave this instruction before he died, 17'Say to Joseph: I beg you, forgive the crime of your brothers and the wrong they did in harming you.' Now therefore please forgive the crime of the servants of the God of your father." Joseph wept when they spoke to him. 18Then his brothers also wept,[c] fell down before him, and said, "We are here as your slaves." 19But Joseph said to them, "Do not be afraid! Am I in the

a That is mourning (or meadow) of Egypt   b Gk Syr: Heb they commanded   c Cn: Heb also came

ing the deathbed scene of blessings that began in 48.2b. **50.1–11** Great mourning and ceremony follow Israel's death. He was mourned by *Joseph* (v. 1), the *Egyptians* (v. 3), and a *very great company* of Egyptians and Israelites (v. 9). Perhaps curiously, Joseph has his father *embalmed*, or mummified in the Egyptian manner, which took *forty days* (vv. 2–3). All of this emphasizes Joseph's high status among the Egyptians and conveys collective respect for the passing of his father. The lamentations of the Egyptians and the cooperation of Pharaoh present a strong contrast to the relationship between Egypt and Israel to come. **50.5** *Tomb that I hewed out for myself*, obscure. Israel's request to be buried there is parallel to his request in the P source to be buried in the cave of Machpelah (49.29–32), but the two may not be identical. Note that the seven-day lamentation for Israel takes place in Transjordan (vv.

10–11). There may have been more than one tradition for the site of Jacob's tomb. **50.15–21** The focus returns to Joseph and his brothers, and in a coda to the Joseph story the brothers fear yet again that Joseph will exact revenge. They attempt a final deception—a deathbed appeal for clemency by their father. Joseph reiterates his wise perception of the divine plan that brought them all to Egypt (see 45.5–8) and assures their safety. This scene is from the E source. **50.17–18** Joseph and his brothers weep, but for different reasons. Joseph weeps because the brothers still do not understand. The brothers weep because they fear that Joseph will now execute revenge. The brothers fall down before him and offer themselves as his slaves, recalling Joseph's dreams in 37.5–9. Only with Joseph's eloquent reiteration of God's plan are they reassured that Joseph has forgiven them, because God is the

place of God? 20Even though you intended to do harm to me, God intended it for good, in order to preserve a numerous people, as he is doing today. 21So have no fear; I myself will provide for you and your little ones." In this way he reassured them, speaking kindly to them.

Joseph's Last Days and Death

22 So Joseph remained in Egypt, he and his father's household; and Joseph lived one hundred ten years. 23Joseph saw Ephraim's children of the third generation; the children of Machir son of Manasseh were also born on Joseph's knees.

24 Then Joseph said to his brothers, "I am about to die; but God will surely come to you, and bring you up out of this land to the land that he swore to Abraham, to Isaac, and to Jacob." 25So Joseph made the Israelites swear, saying, "When God comes to you, you shall carry up my bones from here." 26And Joseph died, being one hundred ten years old; he was embalmed and placed in a coffin in Egypt.

---

deeper agent of events. **50.19–20** Joseph's command to his brothers to not be afraid is given twice (vv. 19, 21) surrounding his explanation of God's plan. *Am I in the place of God?* echoes Jacob's angry retort to Rachel in 30.2, but now in a compassionate voice. *You intended to do harm* (lit. "evil"), *God intended it for good*, a pointed antithesis in which there is a clear sense that God's intentions shaped their intentions (cf. 20.5–6) and hence the brothers are forgiven. But the brothers' fear is not entirely unfounded, for they ought to be responsible in some fashion for their intentions. This moral problem lingers in the background of this encounter. **50.22–26** The description of Joseph's final days and death echoes the lengthier portrayal of Jacob's last days. Like his father, he lives a long and full life, on his deathbed foretells Israel's future, and is embalmed in Egypt, with an oath to be buried in the promised land. V. 22 is from the P source, and the rest is from the E source. **50.22–23** The P statement of Joseph's residence in Egypt and life span echoes the similar statement for Jacob prior to his death (47.28, P). These statements compress a considerable passage of time into a brief text. V. 23 (E) similarly describes Joseph's long and full life, but does so with the familial image of Joseph seeing his great-grandchildren by both sons. This familial image highlights the importance and blessing of offspring, ending Genesis with an image of the ancestral promise in full bloom. **50.24** Like his father, Joseph foresees the future on the eve of his death. He foretells God's plan in the exodus and the return to the promised land, but makes no mention of the enslavement in Egypt. This provides a transition to the book of Exodus, without revealing to his brothers the dangers to come. Heb 11.22 cites the episode as an example of faith. **50.25** The oath to carry Joseph's bones is fulfilled in Ex 13.19 and he is finally buried in the promised land (at Shechem) in Josh 24.32. Joseph's last request thus looks forward to the exodus and the return to Canaan. **50.26** The second mention of Joseph's life span (here from E) echoes the statement in v. 22 (P), creating an envelope structure around Joseph's death. His embalming echoes Jacob's (50.2–3), but he lacks the lengthy period of mourning, the journey, and the burial. These await the fulfillment of his prophecy of exodus and return. *Coffin* (Hebrew *'aron*), the same word used for the *ark* of the covenant (e.g., Ex 25.16), perhaps a brief allusion to another key aspect of the exodus-Sinai story. *In Egypt,* an apt hinge between the books of Genesis and Exodus.

EXODUS

Name and Content

THE NAME EXODUS, DERIVED FROM GREEK, refers to the first of the two central narrative events in the book—the liberation of the Israelites from Egyptian bondage (chs. 1–15). The other event, the Lord's covenant-forging revelation to Israel at Mount Sinai (chs. 19–24), and the laws and instructions that ensue from it complete the book.

The book's Hebrew name, "These are the names," derives from the first words of the text's prologue (1.1–7), which harks back to and abridges the genealogy in Gen 46.8–27. In one sense Exodus directly continues the story of Jacob's clan in Egypt (Gen 37–50). The Lord is said to rescue Israel on account of his covenant with its ancestors (2.24; cf. 3.6, 15–16; 4.5; 6.2–4). In another sense, Exodus is a distinct book, relating the story of Israel's formation as a people and its covenant with God. The second part of the story is dependent on the first: by redeeming the Israelite slaves from Egypt, the Lord earns the right to "enslave" them to himself (Lev 25.42, 55) by binding them to the covenant obligations.

Biblical Context

COVENANT LAW ISSUING IMMEDIATELY or indirectly from the Sinai event makes up most of what follows Exodus in the Pentateuch. Moses has the people recommit themselves to the covenant before he dies (Deut 29–30). In the next generation the Israelites twice reaffirm the covenant (Josh 4–5, 24), an act that will be expressly repeated only centuries later (2 Kings 22–23) and again after the Babylonian exile (Neh 8–10). Precedent for renewing, or restoring, the covenant is set within Exodus itself, following the golden calf incident (ch. 34).

Although biblical tradition links the exodus with a (geographically unspecified) covenant (e.g., Deut 4.45; 6.21–25; 29.25; 1 Kings 8.9, 21; Jer 11.2–4, 6–7; 31.32; 34.13), it is the exodus itself that chiefly exercises the biblical memory. Within the Pentateuch, or Torah, the recent exodus provides a motive for worshiping the Lord (e.g., Ex 20.2; 29.46; Lev 26.13; Deut 6.12; 13.6–10; cf. Josh 24.17) and observing the law (e.g., Lev 11.45; 22.32–33; Num 15.41; Deut 5.15; 8.11–14; 29.2), especially those precepts protecting the disadvantaged (e.g., Lev 19.35; 25.38, 42, 55), because the experience of slavery is meant to instill empathy for them (e.g., Ex 23.9; Lev 19.34; Deut 10.19; 15.15; 16.12; 24.22; and see Jer 34.13–14).

Moreover, the rescue of Israel from Egypt serves as a paradigm of divine saving power, within the Torah (e.g., Lev 26.24–25; Num 23.22; 24.8; Deut 6.21–22; 20.1; 26.8) as well as among the prophets (e.g., Isa 11.16; 51.10; Jer 16.14–15; 23.7–8; 32.20–21; Am 2.10; 9.7; Mic 6.4; 7.15; cf. also Dan 9.15) and psalmists (e.g., Pss 77; 78; 81; 105; 106; 136). God is repeatedly implored to arise and save Israel from its present distress as God had in the past, in the exodus. Future redemptions of Israel may be typologically conceived as reiterations of the exodus, as the foundational narrative of the Torah is transformed from a one-time event to a recurring one (or myth; e.g., Isa 51.10–11). Nevertheless, even as the exodus may serve as myth, it does not lose its historical character. Unlike the Sinai revelation, the exodus event functions in the Bible as a point of chronological reference (e.g., Num 1.1; 9.1; Deut 9.7; Judg 19.30; 1 Sam 8.8; 2 Sam 7.6; 1 Kings 6.1; 8.16; 2 Kings 21.15; Jer 7.25).

Historical Context

THE PRESENT TEXT SEEMS TO INCORPORATE a variety of once independent sources (e.g., 4.24–26; 15.1–18; 20.2–17; chs. 21–23). The narratives of complaint during the wilderness trek (15.22–17.7) overlap with stories in Numbers; the plagues narrative (chs. 7–11) and Passover passage (ch. 12) manifest the kinds of duplication and dissonance that suggest the presence of different traditions. Details of the narrative often conflict or make little sense; for example, though the Israelites are said to live apart in Goshen (e.g., Gen 47.1–6; Ex 8.22; 9.26), they borrow valuable objects from their Egyptian neighbors (3.21–22) and the Lord must pass over Israelite homes to strike Egyptian households in the tenth plague (12.12–13). Comparison of Exodus with folklore and myth suggests the story is already the stuff of legend. Historical reconstruction is accordingly obstructed by a centuries-long process of literary formation that can hardly be retraced.

Nevertheless, the sojourn of Israelites in Egypt, plagues, and crossing the sea and wilderness are traditions on which diverse biblical sources inside and outside the Torah agree. External considerations lead many to place the historical exodus in the late thirteenth century BCE during the long reign of Rameses II, when numbers of Western Semites are known to have inhabited the Nile Delta and when conflicts with foreign labor are reported. But there is no archaeological record of the exodus in Egypt, and historical references in Exodus are slim, vague, or problematic. On the other hand, a relatively large number of Egyptian personal names are found within the tribe of Levi (e.g., Moses, Aaron, Miriam, Merari, Putiel, Phinehas, Hophni). There is therefore a basis to surmise that ancestors of some Israelites, and particularly those associated with the priestly tribe, came out of Egypt. [EDWARD L. GREENSTEIN]

1 These are the names of the sons of Israel who came to Egypt with Jacob, each with his household: ²Reuben, Simeon, Levi, and Judah, ³Issachar, Zebulun, and Benjamin, ⁴Dan and Naphtali, Gad and Asher. ⁵The total number of people born to Jacob was seventy. Joseph was already in Egypt. ⁶Then Joseph died, and all his brothers, and that whole generation. ⁷But the Israelites were fruitful and prolific; they multiplied and grew exceedingly strong, so that the land was filled with them.

The Israelites Are Oppressed

8 Now a new king arose over Egypt, who did not know Joseph. ⁹He said to his people, "Look, the Israelite people are more numerous and more powerful than we. ¹⁰Come, let us deal shrewdly with them, or they will increase and, in the event of war, join our enemies and fight against us and escape from the land." ¹¹Therefore they set taskmasters over them to oppress them with forced labor. They

built supply cities, Pithom and Rameses, for Pharaoh. 12But the more they were oppressed, the more they multiplied and spread, so that the Egyptians came to dread the Israelites. 13The Egyptians became ruthless in imposing tasks on the Israelites, 14and made their lives bitter with hard service in mortar and brick and in every kind of field labor. They were ruthless in all the tasks that they imposed on them.

15 The king of Egypt said to the Hebrew midwives, one of whom was named Shiphrah and the other Puah, 16"When you act as midwives to the Hebrew women, and see them on the birthstool, if it is a boy, kill him; but if it is a girl, she shall live." 17But the midwives feared God; they did not do as the king of Egypt commanded them, but they let the boys live. 18So the king of Egypt summoned the midwives and said to them, "Why have you done this, and allowed the boys to live?" 19The midwives said to Pharaoh, "Because the Hebrew women are not like the Egyptian women; for they are vigorous and give birth before the

---

1.1–7 The prologue returns to a point prior to the conclusion of Genesis (see Introduction). The story of the Israelite population explosion in Egypt fulfills the Lord's promise of numerous progeny to the patriarchs (Gen 13.16; 15.5; 22.17; 26.4; 32.13). **1.1** *Israel*, the patriarch Jacob (Gen 32.29; 35.10). **1.2–4** The list of Jacob's sons separates the sons of his wives, Leah and Rachel, from those of his concubines, Bilhah and Zilpah. Daughter Dinah (Gen 30.21; 34) is, like other women, omitted in this enumeration. **1.5** *Born to Jacob*, lit. "coming out of Jacob's thigh," which was impaired (Gen 32.26, 32). *Seventy*, counting only Jacob's sons and grandsons, a very close approximation. **1.6** *Joseph*'s death and mummification conclude Genesis. *Generation*, the unit of patriarchal periodization; cf. note on 12.40. **1.7** *Israelites*, lit. "the sons of Israel" (cf. v. 1), but here referring to the "children of Israel" as a people. *Fruitful and . . . multiplied*. See Gen 47.27; cf. Gen 1.28; 9.1, 7; 17.6, 20. *Prolific*. The unusual Hebrew term (cf. Gen 9.7) connotes the proliferation of animals (e.g., Gen 1.21; Ex 8.3). Israel's populousness motivates the pharaoh's attempts at genocide.

1.8–22 The episode of the midwives recalls such fairy tales as "Snow White": a monarch orders a servant of the opposite sex to murder a child of the monarch's sex who is feared as a threat to the throne. **1.8** The *new king* seems to initiate a new policy toward the Asian foreigners, but *did not know* might mean "did not care about" (the same Hebrew verb is translated *took notice* in 2.25). The king remains anonymous, although many identify him with Rameses II (ca. 1290–1224 BCE) on the basis of v. 11 and the mention of "Israel" within Canaan on a monument of the succeeding pharaoh, Merneptah (ca. 1224–1204). **1.9** *The Israelite people*, in contrast to *his* (the king's) *people. Numerous . . . powerful*, in Hebrew cognate to the verbs rendered *multiplied* and *grew . . . strong* in v. 7; both terms may refer to strength in numbers (cf., e.g., Num 32.1; Deut 26.5; Joel 1.6). The assertion that Israel outnumbers Egypt is surely hyperbolic. **1.10** *Shrewdly*, lit. "wisely"—an earlier pharaoh had called Joseph incomparably "wise" (Gen 41.39); the king may resent Egypt's debt to Joseph. *Join*, the same Hebrew verb (*nosaf*) as the name Joseph (*yosef*). *Escape*, lit. "go up," more aptly referring to taking control ("rising over") rather than leaving. Letters from Egypt's agents in Canaan to pharaohs of the four-

teenth century BCE at el-Amarna complain of landless "Apiru" joining forces with rebellious towns. Scholars have suggested a link between these landless folk and the "Hebrews," a term that may be related to "Apiru." **1.11** *They set*. The king's people cooperate. *Taskmasters*, lit. "officers of the corvée" (cf. 1 Kings 5.13–14). *To oppress*, used prophetically of the Egyptian bondage (Gen 15.13) and of Sarai's affliction of Hagar (Gen 16.6, 9, 11). *Pithom*, Egyptian *Per-Atum*, "House of (the sun god) Atum," and *Rameses*, "(House of) Rameses," sites in the region presumably inhabited by the Israelites in the eastern Nile Delta, the latter possibly Qantir, but also possibly a first-millennium BCE city. *Pharaoh*, Egyptian *Per-'o*, "Great House," used to refer to the king of Egypt as though it were a proper name. **1.12** *They were oppressed*, lit. "they (namely, the Egyptians) oppressed him (namely, the Israelite people)," emphasizing the Egyptians' role. *The more they multiplied*. The Hebrew, *ken yirbeh*, mocks the pharaoh's words in v. 10, *pen yirbeh, or* ("lest") *they will increase. Spread*, the same Hebrew verb rendered "grew . . . rich" in Gen 30.43; Israel's proliferation in the face of Pharaoh's measures echoes Jacob's increase despite Laban's scheme. The Hebrew verb, which means lit. "to explode," sounds like a contraction of *were fruitful and prolific* (v. 7), an ironic reversal of the pharaoh's plan to contain Hebrew reproduction. *Came to dread*. Cf. Num 22.3. **1.13** More precisely "The Egyptians made the Israelites work to the point of collapse," a practice explicitly forbidden in Lev 25.43, 46; this is repeated in v. 14. **1.14** *Made . . . bitter*. See 12.8. *Mortar*, more likely "bitumen" as in another text tradition; the Hebrew words are spelled the same but vocalized differently (cf. Gen 11.3). *Field labor*, including digging irrigation canals (see Deut 11.10). **1.15** *Hebrew midwives*. Despite the Semitic names of the midwives, the Hebrew may be interpreted as "midwives of the Hebrews," i.e., Egyptian women serving the Israelites. Unlike the pharaoh, these heroic women are named. **1.16** *Birthstool*, a distinctively Egyptian device. In ancient Israel ethnicity was patrilineal, so that eliminating the males suffices to wipe out the people. **1.17** For the motif of a Gentile acknowledging Israel's God, see 18.1–12; Gen 14.18–20; Num 24.1; Josh 2.10–11; 2 Kings 5.15; Jon 1.16. The midwives precede both Israel and Egypt in recognizing Israel's national God as the true one. **1.19** *Vigorous*, lit. "lively," probably

midwife comes to them." ²⁰So God dealt well with the midwives; and the people multiplied and became very strong. ²¹And because the midwives feared God, he gave them families. ²²Then Pharaoh commanded all his people, "Every boy that is born to the Hebrews*ᵃ* you shall throw into the Nile, but you shall let every girl live."

Birth and Youth of Moses

2 Now a man from the house of Levi went and married a Levite woman. ²The woman conceived and bore a son; and when she saw that he was a fine baby, she hid him three months. ³When she could hide him no longer she got a papyrus basket for him, and plastered it with bitumen and pitch; she put the child in it and placed it among the reeds on the bank of the river. ⁴His sister stood at a distance, to see what would happen to him.

5 The daughter of Pharaoh came down to bathe at the river, while her attendants walked beside the river. She saw the basket among the reeds and sent her maid to bring it. ⁶When she opened it, she saw the child. He was crying, and she took pity on him. "This must be one of the Hebrews' children," she said. ⁷Then his sister said to Pharaoh's daughter, "Shall I go and get you a nurse from the Hebrew women to nurse the child for you?" ⁸Pharaoh's daughter said to her, "Yes." So the girl went and called the child's mother. ⁹Pharaoh's daughter said to her, "Take this child and nurse it for me, and I will give you your wages." So the woman took the child and nursed it. ¹⁰When the child grew up, she brought him to Pharaoh's daughter, and she took him as her son. She named him Moses,ᵇ "because," she said, "I drew him out"ᶜ of the water."

Moses Flees to Midian

11 One day, after Moses had grown up, he went out to his people and saw their forced labor. He saw an Egyptian beating a Hebrew, one of his kinsfolk. ¹²He looked this way and that, and seeing no one he killed the Egyptian and hid him in the sand. ¹³When he went out

---

a Sam Gk Tg: Heb lacks *to the Hebrews*   *b* Heb *Mosheh*
c Heb *mashah*

"quick." **1.20** *Multiplied and became . . . strong,* the same verbs as in vv. 7, 9; see note on 1.9. **1.21** *Families,* lit. "house(hold)s." **1.22** *All his people,* and not only the midwives (see note on 1.15). Since all Egyptians are involved in the genocide, all Egyptian households will suffer the plagues (chs. 7–12). *Every boy.* See v. 16. *Nile,* Hebrew *ye'or,* "river" in Egyptian.
2.1–10 The story of Moses' exposure and miraculous survival resembles diverse folktales of a hero's birth, especially the legend of Sargon of Akkad (probably from the late eighth century BCE). **2.1** The parents are unnamed as in folktales; they are identified as Amram and Jochebed in 6.20. *A Levite woman,* or, since in 6.20 Amram marries *his father's sister,* "a daughter of (the tribal namesake) Levi." Moses' levitical pedigree is emphasized; cf. 6.14–27. **2.2** *That he was . . . fine,* the same phrase rendered "that it was good" in the creation story (e.g., Gen 1.10, 12, 18). *Baby,* not in the Hebrew. **2.3** *Papyrus,* a seaworthy material (cf. Isa 18.2). *Basket,* used only here and of Noah's ark (e.g., Gen 6.14), another rudderless box under the deity's protection. The Hebrew terms for *papyrus, basket,* and *reeds* are Egyptian loanwords. *Plastered,* from the same Hebrew root as "bitumen" (see note on 1.14); different from the term rendered "pitch" (Gen 6.14). *The river,* lit. "the Nile"; cf. 1.22. **2.4** *His sister* is unnamed, but later identified with Miriam, who is introduced as Aaron's sister in 15.20 and cited as Moses' sister in Num 26.59. *Stood,* more precisely "stationed herself." *Would happen,* lit. "would be done." **2.5** *The daughter of Pharaoh* too is unnamed. *The river,* both times lit. "the Nile"; see note on 2.3.

2.6 *He was crying,* rather "and here: a lad crying," indicating that that is what she saw. *Children,* lit. "boys." Although "boy" in Hebrew is a generic term for "child," she seems to recognize him as a boy. The daughter's compassion contrasts with her father's brutality. **2.8** *Girl,* one who is past puberty (cf. Gen 24.43; Isa 7.14). **2.9** *Take,* better "take away," echoing "Go!" (rendered *Yes*) in v. 8. **2.10** *She took him as her son,* lit. "he became a son to her," an idiom indicating adoption. *Moses* in Hebrew means "the one who draws out," not, as the punning princess implies, the one she has drawn out. The name may derive from Egyptian "child of" (e.g., Thutmose) and/or be related to the levitical clan of Mushites (e.g., 6.19; Num 3.20, 33; 26.58).
2.11–22 Moses' flight prior to a comeback as national deliverer parallels the stories of Jacob (Gen 27–33), Jephthah (Judg 11), and David (e.g., 1 Sam 20), as well as the extrabiblical stories of the Egyptian Sinuhe and the Syrian Idrimi (fifteenth century BCE). The flight eastward and dispute with the Hebrews anticipates the exodus and later confrontations (15.22–17.7; Num 11; 14; 16). The episode at the well in Midian (vv. 15–21) evokes a traditional motif (Gen 24; 29); the present version highlights Moses' role as savior (v. 17). **2.11** *One day,* rather "in those days" of oppression. *His people,* lit. "his brothers," the same word translated *his kinsfolk* in the next sentence; Moses seems to identify with the Israelites. *Their forced labor.* See 1.11. *Beating.* The retributive plagues use the same Hebrew verb (translated *strike;* e.g., 3.20; 7.17, 20, 25; 8.16–17; 9.15; 12.12–13, 29). **2.12** *Killed,* lit. "struck," the same Hebrew word translated *beating* in v. 11. *Hid,* buried in

the next day, he saw two Hebrews fighting; and he said to the one who was in the wrong, "Why do you strike your fellow Hebrew?" 14He answered, "Who made you a ruler and judge over us? Do you mean to kill me as you killed the Egyptian?" Then Moses was afraid and thought, "Surely the thing is known." 15When Pharaoh heard of it, he sought to kill Moses.

But Moses fled from Pharaoh. He settled in the land of Midian, and sat down by a well. 16The priest of Midian had seven daughters. They came to draw water, and filled the troughs to water their father's flock. 17But some shepherds came and drove them away. Moses got up and came to their defense and watered their flock. 18When they returned to their father Reuel, he said, "How is it that you have come back so soon today?" 19They said, "An Egyptian helped us against the shepherds; he even drew water for us and watered the flock." 20He said to his daughters, "Where is he? Why did you leave the man? Invite him to

break bread." 21Moses agreed to stay with the man, and he gave Moses his daughter Zipporah in marriage. 22She bore a son, and he named him Gershom; for he said, "I have been an alien*a* residing in a foreign land."

23 After a long time the king of Egypt died. The Israelites groaned under their slavery, and cried out. Out of the slavery their cry for help rose up to God. 24God heard their groaning, and God remembered his covenant with Abraham, Isaac, and Jacob. 25God looked upon the Israelites, and God took notice of them.

Moses at the Burning Bush

3 Moses was keeping the flock of his father-in-law Jethro, the priest of Midian; he led his flock beyond the wilderness, and came to Horeb, the mountain of God. 2There the angel of the LORD appeared to him in a flame of fire

a Heb ger

---

the ground, a different Hebrew word from that translated *hid/hide* in vv. 2–3. **2.13** *Strike,* the same Hebrew word translated *beat* in v. 11 and *kill* in v. 12. **2.14** *Kill,* not the Hebrew term translated *strike* in vv. 11–13. *Surely,* contrary to what I thought (e.g., Gen 28.16). **2.15** *Kill,* the verb used in v. 14. *Midian.* The Midianites, described in Gen 25.2 as nomadic offspring of Abraham and Keturah, range from the Sinai Peninsula to northern Arabia. **2.16** *Priest,* probably a position of leadership, like Moses' later role. *Seven,* a round number, characteristic of folktales. **2.17** *Came to their defense,* rendered *saved* in 14.30, foreshadows the rescue of Israel. **2.18** *Reuel,* meaning "Friend of God" in Hebrew, is of the same root as *fellow* (v. 13) and echoes the Hebrew *ro'eh,* "shepherd" (v. 17). Different traditions name him Jethro (e.g., 3.1; 18.1) and Hobab (Num 10.29, where he is Reuel's son); in Judg 4.11 he is a Kenite, traced to the nomadic Cain (Gen 4.12, 14); concerning the hypothesis of diverse sources, see note on 4.2–5. **2.19** *Egyptian.* Raised in Pharaoh's household, Moses still looks Egyptian. *Drew water.* Moses' generosity recalls Rebekah's (Gen 24.19). **2.21** *In marriage,* lit. "as a wife," added to the Hebrew text on the basis of some versions. There is a parallel in the Egyptian tale of Sinuhe. **2.22** *Gershom,* interpreted by wordplay here and in 18.3 as *ger-sham,* Hebrew, "an alien there," referring to Midian or possibly Egypt; the letters of the name also echo *drove them away* (v. 17). **2.23–25** God's renewed attention to the Israelites' plight is conditioned by the covenant with Israel's ancestors. **2.23** *A long time,* lit. "in those many days" of Moses' exile and/or Israel's oppression; see v. 11. *The king of Egypt died.* The stage is set for Moses' return; see 4.19. *Slavery,* the term rendered *tasks* and *service* in 1.13–14, a reference more to hard labor than to slavery

per se. *Cried out,* supplication, not merely an outcry (e.g., Judg 3.9; 1 Sam 7.9; Ps 107.13; Jer 11.11–12; Jon 1.5); the plea is not directed to the Lord (cf. 14.10). **2.24** *Groaning,* the sound of the oppressed (see Judg 2.18). *Remembered.* Hebrew does not distinguish "to remember" from "to pay mind to," which seems more apt in context. *Abraham.* Cf. Gen 17.7–8. *Isaac.* Cf. Gen 17.19, 21. *Jacob.* Cf. Gen 35.11–12; 46.3–4. **2.25** *Looked upon,* in the sense of "took note." *Took notice.* See note on 1.8.

3.1–12 The commissioning of Moses begins with a numinous experience, appropriate to the wonder-working task that awaits him. **3.1** *Moses was,* lit. "Now Moses, he was," indicating that the ensuing episode takes place simultaneously with the preceding (2.23–25). *Keeping,* from the same Hebrew root as *shepherd* (2.17), a distinctively Hebrew occupation (Gen 46.32–34; 47.3–4). Moses' future role is betokened: "shepherd" is a metaphor for leader (see Num 27.17; 2 Sam 5.2; Jer 22.22; Ezek 34.2); David too was a shepherd (2 Sam 7.8). *Jethro.* See note on 2.18. *He led,* apparently intentionally; see note on 4.18–20. *Beyond.* The odd Hebrew has "behind." *Horeb,* the name of Mount Sinai in a tradition ascribed by scholars to the putative Elohist and Deuteronomic sources, i.e., to traditions in Genesis, Exodus, and Deuteronomy (e.g., 17.6; 33.6; Deut 1.2, 6). *Mountain of God,* the narrator's anticipation or a hint of Moses' knowledge prior to the revelation to follow that it was a holy mountain; see note on 4.18–20. **3.2** *Fire,* a conventional medium of the divine presence (e.g., Gen 15.17; Judg 13.20); fire will surround the deity in the revelation at Mount Sinai (19.18). *A bush,* in Hebrew "the bush," another hint that the site was known to be sacred. The Hebrew term for "bush," *seneh,* suggests the mountain's name, Sinai,

out of a bush; he looked, and the bush was blazing, yet it was not consumed. ³Then Moses said, "I must turn aside and look at this great sight, and see why the bush is not burned up." ⁴When the LORD saw that he had turned aside to see, God called to him out of the bush, "Moses, Moses!" And he said, "Here I am." ⁵Then he said, "Come no closer! Remove the sandals from your feet, for the place on which you are standing is holy ground." ⁶He said further, "I am the God of your father, the God of Abraham, the God of Isaac, and the God of Jacob." And Moses hid his face, for he was afraid to look at God.

7 Then the LORD said, "I have observed the misery of my people who are in Egypt; I have heard their cry on account of their taskmasters. Indeed, I know their sufferings, ⁸and I have come down to deliver them from the Egyptians, and to bring them up out of that land to a good and broad land, a land flowing with milk and honey, to the country of the Canaanites, the Hittites, the Amorites, the Perizzites, the Hivites, and the Jebusites. ⁹The cry of the Israelites has now come to me; I have

also seen how the Egyptians oppress them. ¹⁰So come, I will send you to Pharaoh to bring my people, the Israelites, out of Egypt." ¹¹But Moses said to God, "Who am I that I should go to Pharaoh, and bring the Israelites out of Egypt?" ¹²He said, "I will be with you; and this shall be the sign for you that it is I who sent you: when you have brought the people out of Egypt, you shall worship God on this mountain."

The Divine Name Revealed

13 But Moses said to God, "If I come to the Israelites and say to them, 'The God of your ancestors has sent me to you,' and they ask me, 'What is his name?' what shall I say to them?" ¹⁴God said to Moses, "I AM WHO I AM."ᵃ He said further, "Thus you shall say to the Israelites, 'I AM has sent me to you.' " ¹⁵God also said to Moses, "Thus you shall say to the Israelites, 'The LORD,ᵇ the God of your ancestors, the

---

a Or I AM WHAT I AM or I WILL BE WHAT I WILL BE
b The word "LORD" when spelled with capital letters stands for the divine name, YHWH, which is here connected with the verb hayah, "to be"

Yahweh's original location according to Deut 33.2; Judg 5.5 and site of the Lord's appearance before all Israel (chs. 19–20). **3.3** Physical attraction, here visual stimulation, is typical of the numinous experience. *Is not burned up,* rather "does not burn." **3.4** *The LORD.* Although it was an *angel* that appeared in v. 2, there is no substantive difference between the deity and his agents. *Moses, Moses!* Doubling the name may serve to reassure that it is not mirage (cf. Gen 22.11; 1 Sam 3.10). *Here I am,* an obliging gesture on Moses' part (e.g., Gen 22.1; 1 Sam 3.4). **3.5** *No closer.* Cf. 19.12, 21–24. *Remove . . . holy ground.* Cf. Josh 5.15. **3.6** *God of . . . Jacob.* Cf. 2.24. *Hid his face,* a phrase elsewhere used mostly of God's shutting out human affairs, e.g., Deut 31.17–18; Ps 44.24; Isa 8.17; Ezek 39.23–24. *Afraid to look.* Gazing directly into the deity's face is said to be fatal (see 33.20; cf. Isa 6.5), but seeing an angel or a mitigated divine vision does no harm; see Gen 32.30; Ex 24.11; 33.23; Judg 6.22–23; 13.22–23; cf. Ex. 33.11. Fear, along with fascination (v. 3), characterizes the numinous experience. **3.7–9** An elaboration of 2.23–25. **3.7** *Observed,* the same Hebrew term rendered *looked upon* (2.25), *looked/look* (3.2–3), and *saw* (3.4). *Misery,* or "affliction," cognate to *oppress* (1.11). *Their cry,* "outcry," connoting moral outrage (e.g., Gen 18.21; Isa 5.7). *Sufferings,* physical pain (e.g., Isa 53.4; Jer 20.15; 51.8). **3.8** *Have come down,* from God's abode in the sky (e.g., 19.11, 20; Gen 11.5; 18.21; 28.13; Ps 18.7–20). *Milk and honey,* the first instance of this cliché for the land of Israel (e.g., 13.5; 33.3; Lev 20.24; Num 13.27; Deut 6.3). *Canaanites . . . Jebusites,* six of the indigenous Canaanite peoples, recapitulated in v.

17. Gen 15.19–21 lists ten, but not the Hivites. *Hittites,* a people originally from Asia Minor who populated Canaan beginning about 1400 BCE. *Amorites,* a generic term for Western Semites. *Jebusites,* inhabitants of Jerusalem, conquered by David (2 Sam 5.6–7). **3.9** *Seen,* the same Hebrew term rendered *observed* in v. 7. *Oppress,* different from the term in 1.11–12; used twice in the Hebrew phrasing, it has the root sense of "press"; cf. 22.20; 23.9. **3.10** *So.* The Hebrew is stronger: "Now then." *Send.* This verb defines the prophet's role as a messenger from God. *Pharaoh.* Moses may not know the pharaoh; the one he knew has died (2.23; see note on 4.18–20). *Bring . . . out,* the causative verb "to have them go out," the etymology of "exodus," a theme word of the narrative and a term by which the delivering Lord will be identified (e.g., 6.6–7; 20.2). **3.11** A pragmatic concern or a display of Moses' famed modesty (Num 12.3). Moses plays the reluctant prophet (cf. Judg 6.15; Isa 6.8; Jer 1). **3.12** The deity echoes Moses' language. Although not reflected in the English, the Hebrew particle "that, indeed" is used twice by Moses in v. 11 and twice by God in this verse. *Sign,* a key term throughout this and the ensuing narrative. Signs authenticate those who perform them and demonstrate the Lord's power.

3.13–22 The Lord is revealed as the God of Israel's ancestors, and the exodus is previewed. **3.13** *Ask,* the same Hebrew verb rendered *say* here twice. **3.14** *I AM WHO I AM,* on the basis of 33.19 (*I will be gracious to whom I will be gracious . . .*), "I will be whatever I will be." The name puns on the divine name Yahweh and in the present context would seem to connote "being

God of Abraham, the God of Isaac, and the God of Jacob, has sent me to you':

This is my name forever,
and this my title for all generations.

16Go and assemble the elders of Israel, and say to them, 'The LORD, the God of your ancestors, the God of Abraham, of Isaac, and of Jacob, has appeared to me, saying: I have given heed to you and to what has been done to you in Egypt. 17I declare that I will bring you up out of the misery of Egypt, to the land of the Canaanites, the Hittites, the Amorites, the Perizzites, the Hivites, and the Jebusites, a land flowing with milk and honey.' 18They will listen to your voice; and you and the elders of Israel shall go to the king of Egypt and say to him, 'The LORD, the God of the Hebrews, has met with us; let us now go a three days' journey into the wilderness, so that we may sacrifice to the LORD our God.' 19I know, however, that the king of Egypt will not let you go unless compelled by a mighty hand.*a* 20So I will stretch out my hand and strike Egypt with all my wonders that I will perform in it; after that he will let you go. 21I will bring this people into such favor with the Egyptians that, when

you go, you will not go empty-handed; 22each woman shall ask her neighbor and any woman living in the neighbor's house for jewelry of silver and of gold, and clothing, and you shall put them on your sons and on your daughters; and so you shall plunder the Egyptians."

Moses' Miraculous Power

4 Then Moses answered, "But suppose they do not believe me or listen to me, but say, 'The LORD did not appear to you.' " 2The LORD said to him, "What is that in your hand?" He said, "A staff." 3And he said, "Throw it on the ground." So he threw the staff on the ground, and it became a snake; and Moses drew back from it. 4Then the LORD said to Moses, "Reach out your hand, and seize it by the tail"—so he reached out his hand and grasped it, and it became a staff in his hand— 5"so that they may believe that the LORD, the God of their ancestors, the God of Abraham, the God of Isaac, and the God of Jacob, has appeared to you."

6 Again, the LORD said to him, "Put your hand inside your cloak." He put his hand into

a Gk Vg: Heb *no, not by a mighty hand*

there" for Moses and the Israelites. The mystery in which the Lord surrounds his name may be of a piece with the coy refusals of divine beings to reveal their names in Gen 32.29; Judg 13.17–18. **3.15** The speech is punctuated by a couplet in parallelism, adding drama and/or solemnity. *My title,* the name by which I shall be invoked or memorialized; cf. 20.24, where *cause my name to be remembered* uses the same Hebrew root; cf. 23.13. **3.16** Moses will convince his people only after the Lord has performed wonders. **3.18** The ruse will not fool Pharaoh (5.1–4; 8.21–24; 10.8–11). *Sacrifice.* The term in Hebrew connotes slaughtering an animal, part of which is offered to the deity; it lacks the English word's connotation of surrender. **3.19** *Let . . . go,* not the same Hebrew verb as in v. 20 and in the recurrent liberation formula usually rendered *let go* (e.g., 4.23; 5.1; 7.16). The latter are from the root "to send." *Compelled,* added for clarity. *Mighty hand.* The difficult, textually uncertain Hebrew leaves open whether God will force Pharaoh's hand (cf. 13.9) or whether Pharaoh will force Israel out (cf. 6.1). **3.20** *Stretch out . . . hand,* lit. "send (the) hand," an idiom for inflicting harm (e.g., 1 Sam 22.17; Esth 2.21). *Strike,* translated *beat* in (see note on) 2.11. *Wonders,* a term used within the exodus story only here and in 34.10 but commonly in later texts referring to the exodus (e.g., Judg 6.13; Pss 78.4, 11; 106.22; Mic 7.15). *Let you go.* See note on 3.19. **3.21** The Israelites will not leave *empty-handed,* the way Jacob (Israel) left Laban (Gen 31.42); when the Israelites become autonomous, they must not "release" their slaves (Deut 15.13) or worship God (23.15;

34.20; Deut 16.16) empty-handed. Cf. Gen 15.14. **3.22** *Plunder,* lit. "stripping," divine compensation for Egypt's exploitation of the Hebrews; cf. Gen 12.16; 20.14–16. The "borrowing" is effected in 12.35–36, echoing the terms of vv. 21–22 here but in reverse (chiastic) order, indicating completion of the thematic unit (see notes on 4.30–31; 6.26–27; 17.7). Later Jewish traditions suggest that the women do the borrowing because they want to dress their children in the Egyptians' clothes and jewels.

4.1–17 Moses suggests two further impediments: credibility (vv. 1–9) and problematic speech (vv. 10–16). **4.1** *They,* the elders (3.16). *Believe,* in the sense of trust (19.9); cf. 14.31; in v. 5 below *believe* in the sense of "accept as true" is more apt. **4.2–5** Some explain the wondrous signs naturalistically, pointing here to the fact that some snakes stiffen when one grasps their tails. V. 2 makes clear that the snake began as Moses' staff. The deity's power is demonstrated by producing the fantastic from the ordinary. Moses will use none of the three signs to convince the Israelites; Aaron will turn the staff into a "serpent" (a different word in the Hebrew) in an attempt to persuade Pharaoh (7.8–13). On account of discrepancies like this (different word, actor, story line) some scholars suppose that the text is woven from different sources; others do not expect the text to be consistent or smooth. **4.3** *Drew back,* lit. "fled" (14.27). Gen 3.15 posits a normal human phobia of snakes. **4.4** *Reach out,* lit. "send" (see note on 3.20). **4.5** Cf. 3.16. **4.6–9** The third sign anticipates the first plague (7.14–25). In view of this, the second sign,

his cloak; and when he took it out, his hand was leprous,^a as white as snow. ⁷Then God said, "Put your hand back into your cloak"— so he put his hand back into his cloak, and when he took it out, it was restored like the rest of his body— ⁸"If they will not believe you or heed the first sign, they may believe the second sign. ⁹If they will not believe even these two signs or heed you, you shall take some water from the Nile and pour it on the dry ground; and the water that you shall take from the Nile will become blood on the dry ground."

10 But Moses said to the LORD, "O my Lord, I have never been eloquent, neither in the past nor even now that you have spoken to your servant; but I am slow of speech and slow of tongue." ¹¹Then the LORD said to him, "Who gives speech to mortals? Who makes them mute or deaf, seeing or blind? Is it not I, the LORD? ¹²Now go, and I will be with your mouth and teach you what you are to speak." ¹³But he said, "O my Lord, please send someone else." ¹⁴Then the anger of the LORD was kindled against Moses and he said, "What of your brother Aaron the Levite? I know that he can speak fluently; even now he is coming out to meet you, and when he sees you his heart will be glad. ¹⁵You shall speak to him and put the words in his mouth; and I will be with your mouth and with his mouth, and will teach you what you shall do. ¹⁶He indeed shall speak for you to the people; he shall serve as a mouth for you, and you shall serve as God for him. ¹⁷Take in your hand this staff, with which you shall perform the signs."

Moses Returns to Egypt

18 Moses went back to his father-in-law Jethro and said to him, "Please let me go back to my kindred in Egypt and see whether they are still living." And Jethro said to Moses, "Go in peace." ¹⁹The LORD said to Moses in Midian, "Go back to Egypt; for all those who were seeking your life are dead." ²⁰So Moses took his wife and his sons, put them on a donkey, and went back to the land of Egypt; and Moses carried the staff of God in his hand.

21 And the LORD said to Moses, "When you go back to Egypt, see that you perform before

a A term for several skin diseases; precise meaning uncertain

---

which is never used, may anticipate the plague of boils (9.8–12); and the first may suggest the plague of frogs, which is initiated by stretching the staff over Egypt's waterways (8.5–6). **4.7** *Rest of his body,* lit. "his flesh." **4.9** *Dry ground* anticipates the Israelites' crossing the sea on dry ground (14.22). **4.10** *Eloquent,* lit. "a man of words," of the same Hebrew root as *spoken. Slow of speech,* lit. "heavy of mouth." *Slow of tongue,* lit. "heavy of tongue"; see 6.12, 30. "Heavy" in various forms will figure throughout the plagues and exodus narrative (see, e.g., 5.9; notes on 4.21; 9.3; 10.14; 14.4; 14.25). Moses' "heavy" speech may entail a physical impediment (so comparative evidence) or an inability to wax eloquent in Egyptian (see Ezek 3.6, where foreign speech is indicated); in this story, however, Egyptians speak Hebrew (see 2.10). **4.11** *Speech,* lit. "a mouth"; Moses, whose mouth will be accompanied by Aaron's (vv. 12, 15), will put the necessary words into Aaron's mouth (v. 15). Prophecy consists of the deity's very words (e.g., Deut 18.18; Jer 1.9; Ezek 2.7–3.3; 3.4, 10). **4.13** *Someone else,* rather "whomever you will send," a construction resembling *I AM WHO I AM* in 3.14. **4.14** *Speak fluently.* Cf. the historical role of the Levites as transmitters of divine instructions (Deut 33.10); cf. 18.15, where Moses the Levite functions as an oracle. **4.15–16** Aaron will play the role of oracle (*mouth*) to Moses' role as God, the source of revelation; see 7.1, where the analogy is: Moses is to Aaron as God is to a prophet. For God as an oracular source, see 18.15; 21.6; 22.7.
4.18–31 The anticipation of the tenth plague—

slaying Egypt's firstborn (v. 23)—provides background to the assault on Moses or his firstborn (vv. 24–26). The perilous meeting with the Lord en route to Egypt contrasts with Aaron's meeting Moses (v. 27): the return to Egypt is hazardous; the journey away is smooth; cf. Deut 17.16. **4.18–20** In v. 19 the Lord orders Moses back to Egypt as though the preceding dialogue has not taken place; it implies that Moses' reluctance to return stems from the same fear that led to his flight (2.15). The language of 3.1 suggests that Moses has gone to the mountain for a purpose. Vv. 18–20 may reflect a different tradition from 3.1–4.17, one in which Moses, like other fugitive heroes (see note on 2.11–22), goes to Sinai/Horeb seeking an oracle to learn if it is safe to go home to Egypt and see his kin (4.18). **4.18** *Jethro.* The Hebrew has the variant "Jether"; see note on 2.18. *Kindred,* lit. "brothers"; see note on 2.11. **4.19** See 2.23. **4.20** *Sons.* The birth of only one of Moses' sons has been reported (2.22); see 18.2–6. Apart from the episode in vv. 24–26, Moses' Midianite family plays no role in the exodus story. *Staff of God,* apparently the wondrous one given to him, or magically transformed, by the deity (v. 17). **4.21** *Wonders,* better "signs" (so too 7.3, 9; 11.9–10), synonymous with the Hebrew word translated *sign* in 4.8–9, 30, not the same as *wonders* in 3.20, a word from a different Hebrew root. *Your power,* lit. "your hand"; the three signs given in vv. 2–9 are all indeed performed by one hand. *Harden his heart.* In 3.19 the Lord says that Pharaoh will be stubborn, but here the Lord claims responsibility for "stiffening" the Egyptian's

Pharaoh all the wonders that I have put in your power; but I will harden his heart, so that he will not let the people go. 22 Then you shall say to Pharaoh, 'Thus says the LORD: Israel is my firstborn son. 23 I said to you, "Let my son go that he may worship me." But you refused to let him go; now I will kill your firstborn son.' "

24 On the way, at a place where they spent the night, the LORD met him and tried to kill him. 25 But Zipporah took a flint and cut off her son's foreskin, and touched Moses'[a] feet with it, and said, "Truly you are a bridegroom of blood to me!" 26 So he let him alone. It was then she said, "A bridegroom of blood by circumcision."

27 The LORD said to Aaron, "Go into the wilderness to meet Moses." So he went; and he met him at the mountain of God and kissed him. 28 Moses told Aaron all the words of the LORD with which he had sent him, and all the signs with which he had charged him. 29 Then Moses and Aaron went and assembled all the elders of the Israelites. 30 Aaron spoke all the words that the LORD had spoken to Moses, and performed the signs in the sight of the people. 31 The people believed; and when they heard that the LORD had given heed to the Israelites and that he had seen their misery, they bowed down and worshiped.

Bricks without Straw

5 Afterward Moses and Aaron went to Pharaoh and said, "Thus says the LORD, the God of Israel, 'Let my people go, so that they may celebrate a festival to me in the wilderness.' " 2 But Pharaoh said, "Who is the LORD, that I should heed him and let Israel go? I do not know the LORD, and I will not let Israel go." 3 Then they said, "The God of the Hebrews has revealed himself to us; let us go a three days' journey into the wilderness to sac-

a Heb his

will; as the story unfolds Pharaoh's heart will "stiffen" or "grow heavy" (see note on 4.10) by Pharaoh's own will (7.13–14, 22–23; 8.15, 19, 32; 9.7, 34–35) or it will be stiffened, made heavy, or hardened by the Lord (9.12; 10.1, 20, 27; 11.10; 14.8). The hardening prolongs the plagues and ensures that Egypt will suffer the punishment it deserves and witness the Lord's power; see note on 1.22; cf. 7.3–5; 14.4. **4.22–23** The metaphor of Israel's election as the Lord's *firstborn son* (see Jer 31.9; Hos 11.1) lends the tenth plague a quality of poetic justice. *Worship,* the same Hebrew verb as "to serve, work, act-as-a-slave" (see note on 2.23); the Hebrews are to be the Lord's servants, not Pharaoh's (cf. Lev 25.42, 55). **4.24–26** The unmotivated divine assault is made even stranger by its ambiguous use of pronouns: it remains unclear whether Moses or his son is the victim. The juxtaposition with Pharaoh's *firstborn son* (v. 23) suggests that Moses' son may be the one at risk. The episode runs against the larger narrative sequence in which Moses has two sons (4.20; 18.2–6). The seeming obstruction of Moses' divine mission by God recalls a similar about-face in the commission of Balaam (Num 22). **4.24** *At a place . . . night.* The laconic Hebrew has only "at-the-lodging-place" (*bammalon*). *Tried,* the same Hebrew verb used of "seeking" Moses' death in v. 19. **4.25** In the context of Exodus the ritual blood produced by the circumcision protects against destructive divine power, like the blood of the paschal lamb (12.7, 12–13, 21–27). *Zipporah,* a priest's daughter, may be acquainted with ritual procedures. *Flint,* sharpened stone used in circumcision; e.g., Josh 5.2–3. *Cut off,* not the Hebrew term "to circumcise." *Moses' feet,* lit. "his feet" (see text note a), possibly a euphemism for the genitals (e.g., 2 Kings 18.27; Isa 6.2; 7.20), Moses' or his son's. *Bridegroom,*

either Moses (since among certain Semites a bridegroom was circumcised by his father-in-law; the Hebrew term for "father-in-law" means "one who circumcises") or his son (since among some Semites a boy undergoing circumcision is called a bridegroom). **4.26** *He,* the Lord. *Let him alone,* more precisely "let him loose." *A bridegroom . . . circumcision,* an apparent byword, the meaning of which, like the historical sense of the episode, has been lost. **4.27** *He met him.* See note on 4.18–31. *Mountain of God,* Sinai/Horeb (see note on 3.1). *Kissed him* evokes Gen 33.4; 45.14–15. **4.29** According to the instructions in 3.16. **4.30–31** Aaron's role (v. 30) answers to Moses' fourth objection (vv. 10–17), and the people's acceptance (v. 31) obviates the need for the signs provided in response to Moses' objection in vv. 1–9. The reverse (chiastic) sequence closes the passage; cf. note on 3.22. **4.31** *People,* not only the elders (v. 29). *Worshiped,* lit. "prostrated themselves," signifying obedience to God (see 12.27).

5.1–6.1 Pharaoh reacts to Moses and Aaron by making matters worse, vindicating the Lord's prediction (3.19) and further justifying the plagues. **5.1** *Moses and Aaron.* The elders are not included as the Lord ordained (3.18). *The LORD,* the first time in this story that the Lord's name is announced in Egypt; cf. v. 23. *Celebrate a festival,* one verb in Hebrew; the Hebrew cognate noun *chag* (cf. Arabic *haj*) denotes a pilgrimage. They do not yet ask for three days' leave (as in 3.18; 5.3). **5.2** *Who is the LORD,* an echo of what Moses said in 3.11. *Heed him,* lit. "listen to his voice," an echo of what Moses said in 4.1. *I do not know.* Cf. 1.8. To know the Lord is a main theme of the succeeding narrative (e.g., 7.5, 17; 8.10; 9.14; 14.18). **5.3** A recapitulation of 3.18 with the addition *or* ("lest") *he will fall . . . sword,* an ironic hint of the plagues that will

Asiatic captives making bricks under Thutmose III, ruler of Egypt in the fifteenth century BCE, for the temple of Amon at Thebes. Line drawing of an illustration from the tomb of Rekhmara. (From S. R. Driver, *The Book of Exodus*.)

rifice to the LORD our God, or he will fall upon us with pestilence or sword." 4But the king of Egypt said to them, "Moses and Aaron, why are you taking the people away from their work? Get to your labors!" 5Pharaoh continued, "Now they are more numerous than the people of the land*a* and yet you want them to stop working!" 6That same day Pharaoh commanded the taskmasters of the people, as well as their supervisors, 7"You shall no longer give the people straw to make bricks, as before; let them go and gather straw for themselves. 8But you shall require of them the same quantity of bricks as they have made previously; do not diminish it, for they are lazy; that is why they cry, 'Let us go and offer sacrifice to our God.' 9Let heavier work be laid on them; then they will labor at it and pay no attention to deceptive words."

10 So the taskmasters and the supervisors of the people went out and said to the people, "Thus says Pharaoh, 'I will not give you straw. 11Go and get straw yourselves, wherever you can find it; but your work will not be lessened in the least.' " 12So the people scattered throughout the land of Egypt, to gather stubble for straw. 13The taskmasters were urgent, saying, "Complete your work, the same daily assignment as when you were given straw." 14And the supervisors of the Israelites, whom Pharaoh's taskmasters had set over them, were beaten, and were asked, "Why did you not fin-

---

a Sam: Heb *The people of the land are now many*

beset Egypt; *pestilence* is used of the fifth plague (9.3); *sword* foreshadows the quasi-battle at the sea (see 15.9). **5.4** *King of Egypt.* By avoiding "Pharaoh" here a pun in Hebrew is averted on the verb *taking . . . away from. Labors,* imposed in 1.11. **5.5** *More numerous.* See 1.9. *You want them to stop,* lit. "you are stopping them." The Hebrew verb translated *stop* is the root of "sabbath" (see note on 16.23); the Lord, in contrast to Pharaoh, ordains a weekly break from labor (see Deut

5.12–15). **5.6** *Taskmasters,* lit. "oppressors," used in 3.7 and below in vv. 10, 13, 14; not the term rendered *taskmasters* in 1.11. Egyptian art depicts laborers being overseen, and sometimes beaten, by rod-wielding taskmasters. *Supervisors,* apparently Israelites (see v. 14). **5.7** *As before.* Only brick making was assigned in 1.14. **5.9** *Deceptive words,* rather "lies," that the Hebrews' God has appeared to Moses. **5.11** *Lessened,* translated *diminish* in v. 8. *Your work . . . in the least,* lit.

ish the required quantity of bricks yesterday and today, as you did before?"

15 Then the Israelite supervisors came to Pharaoh and cried, "Why do you treat your servants like this? 16No straw is given to your servants, yet they say to us, 'Make bricks!' Look how your servants are beaten! You are unjust to your own people."[a] 17He said, "You are lazy, lazy; that is why you say, 'Let us go and sacrifice to the LORD.' 18Go now, and work; for no straw shall be given you, but you shall still deliver the same number of bricks." 19The Israelite supervisors saw that they were in trouble when they were told, "You shall not lessen your daily number of bricks." 20As they left Pharaoh, they came upon Moses and Aaron who were waiting to meet them. 21They said to them, "The LORD look upon you and judge! You have brought us into bad odor with Pharaoh and his officials, and have put a sword in their hand to kill us."

22 Then Moses turned again to the LORD and said, "O LORD, why have you mistreated this people? Why did you ever send me? 23Since I first came to Pharaoh to speak in your name, he has mistreated this people, and you have done nothing at all to deliver your people."

Israel's Deliverance Assured

6 Then the LORD said to Moses, "Now you shall see what I will do to Pharaoh: Indeed, by a mighty hand he will let them go; by a mighty hand he will drive them out of his land."

2 God also spoke to Moses and said to him: "I am the LORD. 3I appeared to Abraham, Isaac, and Jacob as God Almighty,[b] but by my name 'The LORD'[c] I did not make myself known to them. 4I also established my covenant with them, to give them the land of Canaan, the land in which they resided as aliens. 5I have also heard the groaning of the Israelites whom the Egyptians are holding as slaves, and I have remembered my covenant. 6Say therefore to the Israelites, 'I am the LORD, and I will free you from the burdens of the Egyptians and deliver you from slavery to them. I will redeem you with an outstretched arm and with mighty acts of judgment. 7I will take you as my people, and I will be your God. You shall know that I am the LORD your God, who has freed you from the burdens of the Egyptians. 8I will bring you into the land that I swore to give to Abraham, Isaac, and Jacob; I will give it to you for a possession. I am the LORD.' " 9Moses told this to the Israelites; but they would not listen to Moses, because of their broken spirit and their cruel slavery.

10 Then the LORD spoke to Moses, 11"Go and tell Pharaoh king of Egypt to let the Israelites go out of his land." 12But Moses spoke to the LORD, "The Israelites have not listened to me; how then shall Pharaoh listen to me, poor speaker that I am?"[d] 13Thus the LORD spoke to

---

a Gk Compare Syr Vg: Heb *beaten, and the sin of your people*
b Traditional rendering of Heb *El Shaddai*   c Heb *YHWH*; see note at 3.15   d Heb *me? I am uncircumcised of lips*

"not a thing will be removed from your work." **5.14** *Were beaten.* Cf. 2.11. **5.15** *Cried* connotes complaining, as in 14.15 and perhaps 5.8. *Servants,* the same term as that for the slaves they oversee. **5.16** *You are unjust,* rather "you sin against," as in 9.27. **5.17** Cf. v. 8. **5.19** *Trouble,* lit. "bad, evil." **5.21** *You have brought us into bad odor with Pharaoh,* lit. "You have made our smell stink in the eyes of Pharaoh." Bad odor will attend the first two plagues (see 7.21; 8.10). **5.22** *Turned again,* returned to Mount Sinai. *Mistreated,* of the same Hebrew root as the word translated *trouble* in v. 19. **5.23** *Your name* and *your people* stress the Lord's responsibility and evoke Moses' diffidence at the burning bush (chs. 3–4); cf. 32.7, 11. **6.1** *Mighty hand.* Cf. 3.19–20.

6.2–13 Cf. the parallel passage, chs. 3–4, which scholars trace to a different tradition. In context, the present passage presupposes the Israelites' discouragement after the initial confrontation with Pharaoh (v. 9), and the divine charge to go to Pharaoh (v. 11) is a reassurance. **6.2** *Also,* not in the Hebrew. **6.3** *Almighty.* Etymologically the name suggests "One of the Mountain," appropriate for a deity who reveals himself on

Horeb/Sinai; cf. Gen 17.1; 28.3; 35.11. *The LORD.* Abraham, Isaac, and Jacob each use this name (Gen 12.8; 26.22; 32.10); the present passage seems to know a different tradition. **6.4** *Resided as aliens.* In this context merely "resided" might be more accurate (cf. Gen 26.3). The verse echoes Gen 17.7–8. **6.5** This verse echoes 2.24. **6.6** *Free.* See 3.10, where the same Hebrew verb is rendered *bring . . . out.* The Hebrew word translated *burdens* is rendered *forced labor* in 1.11; 2.11 and *labors* in 5.4. *Redeem* connotes the ransom of indentured kin; cf. Lev 25.47–49. **6.7** *Know.* See note on 5.2. The relationship between God and Israel is expressed in terms of legal adoption (cf., e.g., 2.10; 2 Sam 7.14) and/or matrimony (cf., e.g., Lev 26.12). **6.8** *Bring you,* like a bride into a new home (cf., e.g., Deut 21.10–12). *I swore,* expressed idiomatically in Hebrew by a gesture of oath taking, "I have raised my hand" (e.g., Deut 32.40). **6.9** *Broken spirit,* lit. "shortness of breath," frustration perhaps. *Cruel slavery,* the same phrase translated *hard service* in 1.14. **6.11** *Tell,* the substance of the preceding revelation. *To let,* rather "so that he (Pharaoh) will let." **6.12** *Poor speaker.* See note on 4.10. **6.13** *Aaron.* Cf. 4.14.

Moses and Aaron, and gave them orders regarding the Israelites and Pharaoh king of Egypt, charging them to free the Israelites from the land of Egypt.

The Genealogy of Moses and Aaron

14 The following are the heads of their ancestral houses: the sons of Reuben, the firstborn of Israel: Hanoch, Pallu, Hezron, and Carmi; these are the families of Reuben. 15The sons of Simeon: Jemuel, Jamin, Ohad, Jachin, Zohar, and Shaul,*a* the son of a Canaanite woman; these are the families of Simeon. 16The following are the names of the sons of Levi according to their genealogies: Gershon,*b* Kohath, and Merari, and the length of Levi's life was one hundred thirty-seven years. 17The sons of Gershon:*b* Libni and Shimei, by their families. 18The sons of Kohath: Amram, Izhar, Hebron, and Uzziel, and the length of Kohath's life was one hundred thirty-three years. 19The sons of Merari: Mahli and Mushi. These are the families of the Levites according to their genealogies. 20Amram married Jochebed his father's sister and she bore him Aaron and Moses, and the length of Amram's life was one hundred thirty-seven years. 21The sons of Izhar: Korah, Nepheg, and Zichri. 22The sons of Uzziel: Mishael, Elzaphan, and Sithri. 23Aaron married Elisheba, daughter of Amminadab and sister of Nahshon, and she bore him Nadab, Abihu, Eleazar, and Ithamar. 24The sons of Korah: Assir, Elkanah, and Abiasaph; these are the families of the Korahites. 25Aaron's son Eleazar married one of the daughters of Putiel, and she bore him Phinehas. These are the heads of the ancestral houses of the Levites by their families.

26 It was this same Aaron and Moses to whom the LORD said, "Bring the Israelites out of the land of Egypt, company by company." 27It was they who spoke to Pharaoh king of Egypt to bring the Israelites out of Egypt, the same Moses and Aaron.

Moses and Aaron Obey God's Commands

28 On the day when the LORD spoke to Moses in the land of Egypt, 29he said to him, "I am the LORD; tell Pharaoh king of Egypt all that I am speaking to you." 30But Moses said in the LORD's presence, "Since I am a poor speaker,*c* why would Pharaoh listen to me?"

7 The LORD said to Moses, "See, I have made you like God to Pharaoh, and your brother Aaron shall be your prophet. 2You shall speak all that I command you, and your brother Aaron shall tell Pharaoh to let the Israelites go out of his land. 3But I will harden Pharaoh's heart, and I will multiply my signs and wonders in the land of Egypt. 4When Pharaoh does not listen to you, I will lay my hand upon Egypt and bring my people the Israelites, company by company, out of the land of Egypt by great acts of judgment. 5The Egyptians shall know that I am the LORD, when I stretch out my hand against Egypt and

---

a Or *Saul*   *b* Also spelled *Gershom*; see 2.22   *c* Heb *am uncircumcised of lips*; see 6.12

6.14–27 The narrative is interrupted by a genealogy that places Moses and Aaron within the lineage of the Israelite tribes and among the various levitical clans. Vv. 26–27 repeat the contents of vv. 10–13 and resume the narrative. The genealogy breaks off after Levi, giving the impression that the text is excerpted from a fuller list, such as Gen 46.8–27. See the more ramified genealogy in Num 26. **6.14** *Ancestral houses*, lit. "fathers' houses," a technical term for tribal divisions. **6.16** *Merari*, an Egyptian name. *One hundred thirty-seven*. The limit of 120 years (Gen 6.3) only applies from Moses' generation on. **6.20** *Father's sister*. See note on 2.1. This is incest according to Lev 18.12. Heroes' births are often marked by the illicit; cf. the birth of Isaac from a brother and half-sister (Gen 20.12), David from a Moabite (Ruth), and Solomon from the once adulterous couple David and Bathsheba. *Aaron and Moses*. Some versions add here "and Miriam their sister" (see Num 26.59). **6.23** *Elisheba*, "Elizabeth" in the Greek version. *Amminadab*, clan head of Judah (Num 1.7). *Sister of Nahshon*. An unmarried woman is sometimes identified by her eldest brother, who may play a role in arranging her marriage (see Gen 24); cf. Ex 15.20; Gen 25.20; 28.9. *Nahshon* is the military chieftain of Judah (Num 2.3). *Nadab . . . Ithamar,* the Hebrew couples "Nadab and Abihu" and "Eleazar and Ithamar"; the older pair will die (Lev 10.1–5) and the younger will succeed to priestly leadership; cf. note on 7.7. **6.24** *Korah*, rebel (Num 16) and namesake of the Second Temple gatekeepers (1 Chr 9.19). **6.25** *Putiel*, an Egyptian name; cf. Potiphar (Gen 39.1), Potiphera (Gen 41.45). *Phinehas*, an Egyptian name. **6.26–27** The resumptive unit begins with the sequence *Aaron and Moses* and ends chiastically with *Moses and Aaron*. **6.26** *Company*, in a military sense (see Num 2); see 12.41; cf. 7.4; 12.51; 13.18.

6.28–7.7 A recapitulation of earlier passages, underscoring the fact that when Moses and Aaron address Pharaoh, they represent the Lord. **6.30** An echo of 6.12. **7.1–2** An echo of 4.16. **7.2** An echo of 6.11. **7.3–5** An echo of 3.19–20; 4.21. **7.3** *Wonders* anticipates vv. 8–13. **7.4** *Great acts of judgment* echoes 6.6; cf. 12.12. **7.5** *Shall know* echoes 6.7 and anticipates v. 17. *Stretch out my hand* (see note on 3.20) echoes 6.6 and

bring the Israelites out from among them." 6Moses and Aaron did so; they did just as the LORD commanded them. 7Moses was eighty years old and Aaron eighty-three when they spoke to Pharaoh.

Aaron's Miraculous Rod

8 The LORD said to Moses and Aaron, 9"When Pharaoh says to you, 'Perform a wonder,' then you shall say to Aaron, 'Take your staff and throw it down before Pharaoh, and it will become a snake.'" 10So Moses and Aaron went to Pharaoh and did as the LORD had commanded; Aaron threw down his staff before Pharaoh and his officials, and it became a snake. 11Then Pharaoh summoned the wise men and the sorcerers; and they also, the magicians of Egypt, did the same by their secret arts. 12Each one threw down his staff, and they became snakes; but Aaron's staff swallowed up theirs. 13Still Pharaoh's heart was hardened, and he would not listen to them, as the LORD had said.

The First Plague: Water Turned to Blood

14 Then the LORD said to Moses, "Pharaoh's heart is hardened; he refuses to let the people go. 15Go to Pharaoh in the morning, as he is going out to the water; stand by at the river bank to meet him, and take in your hand the staff that was turned into a snake. 16Say to him, 'The LORD, the God of the Hebrews, sent me to you to say, "Let my people go, so that they may worship me in the wilderness." But until now you have not listened. 17Thus says the LORD, "By this you shall know that I am the LORD." See, with the staff that is in my hand I will strike the water that is in the Nile, and it shall be turned to blood. 18The fish in the river shall die, the river itself shall stink, and the Egyptians shall be unable to drink water from the Nile.'" 19The LORD said to Moses, "Say to Aaron, 'Take your staff and stretch out your hand over the waters of Egypt—over its rivers, its canals, and its ponds, and all its pools of water—so that they may become blood; and there shall be blood throughout the whole land of Egypt, even in vessels of wood and in vessels of stone.'"

20 Moses and Aaron did just as the LORD commanded. In the sight of Pharaoh and of his officials he lifted up the staff and struck the water in the river, and all the water in the river was turned into blood, 21and the fish in the river died. The river stank so that the Egyptians could not drink its water, and there was blood throughout the whole land of Egypt. 22But the magicians of Egypt did the same by their secret arts; so Pharaoh's heart remained hardened, and he would not listen to them, as the LORD had said. 23Pharaoh turned and went into his house, and he did not take even this to heart. 24And all the Egyptians had to dig along the Nile for water to drink, for they could not drink the water of the river.

25 Seven days passed after the LORD had struck the Nile.

---

anticipates the first three plagues (see 7.19; 8.5–6, 16–17). **7.7** In traditional literature and regularly in the narrative traditions of the Hebrew Bible, the older brother is subordinated to the younger. **7.8–13** See note on 4.2. Here, as in the first three plagues, Aaron performs the signs with his own staff and Pharaoh, not Israel, is the object. **7.9** *Snake.* See note on 4.2–5; in Ezek 29.3; 32.2 the term is used to describe a pharaoh as a "dragon." **7.11** *Magicians.* The Hebrew is a loanword from Egyptian, where it refers to a type of priest; the term is used in the Pentateuch only of Egyptians. **7.12** *Swallowed.* Cf. 15.12. The one staff swallowing the many recalls the dreams Egypt's magicians could not interpret (Gen 41.1–7). The magicians' competition with Aaron here and in the first three plagues prefigures the contest between the Lord and Pharaoh. **7.13** *Hardened,* "stiffened"; see note on 4.21.

7.14–12.32 The ten plagues appear to comprise different traditions; Pss 78; 105 count no more than eight. Here they are arranged in three sets of three plus a climactic tenth. Although some see the plagues as a plausible series of natural disasters, the narrative distinguishes their incredible, unprecedented (9.18, 24; 10.6, 14; 11.6) character; the tenth admits of no "natural" explanation. **7.14–25** Afflicting Egypt's deified life source recalls the genocide at the Nile (1.22). **7.14** *Hardened,* lit. "heavy"; see note on 4.21. **7.15** Each set of three plagues begins with Moses alone confronting Pharaoh in the morning (cf. 8.20; 9.13). Moses' concern in 3.11 was for naught. *Turned* anticipates the coming plague (see vv. 17, 20). *Snake,* the term used in 4.3. **7.16** An allusion to 5.1–4. **7.17** *Know.* See note on 5.2. *It,* the water. **7.18** *Shall stink.* Cf. 5.21. **7.19** *Canals,* plural of the same word translated "Nile." *Pools of water,* a term used in Gen 1.10, suggesting perhaps that the plagues, like the flood, reverse the order of creation. *Vessels,* added for clarity. The fact that water found apart from the river turned to blood differentiates the plague from a "natural" disaster of the Nile. **7.20** *Struck.* See note on 2.11. **7.20–21** *The river,* in Hebrew refers to "the Nile." **7.22** Where the *magicians* found water to turn to blood is not explained. *Hardened,* "stiffened." See note on 4.21. The sentence repeats v. 13 verbatim, lending coherence to the narrative. **7.23** *Turned,* did an about-face. **7.25** *Seven days,* a round number. The unusual

The Second Plague: Frogs

8 [a] Then the LORD said to Moses, "Go to Pharaoh and say to him, 'Thus says the LORD: Let my people go, so that they may worship me. [2]If you refuse to let them go, I will plague your whole country with frogs. [3]The river shall swarm with frogs; they shall come up into your palace, into your bedchamber and your bed, and into the houses of your officials and of your people,[b] and into your ovens and your kneading bowls. [4]The frogs shall come up on you and on your people and on all your officials.'" [5][c]And the LORD said to Moses, "Say to Aaron, 'Stretch out your hand with your staff over the rivers, the canals, and the pools, and make frogs come up on the land of Egypt.'" [6]So Aaron stretched out his hand over the waters of Egypt; and the frogs came up and covered the land of Egypt. [7]But the magicians did the same by their secret arts, and brought frogs up on the land of Egypt.

[8]Then Pharaoh called Moses and Aaron, and said, "Pray to the LORD to take away the frogs from me and my people, and I will let the people go to sacrifice to the LORD." [9]Moses said to Pharaoh, "Kindly tell me when I am to pray for you and for your officials and for your people, that the frogs may be removed from you and your houses and be left only in the Nile." [10]And he said, "Tomorrow." Moses said, "As you say! So that you may know that there is no one like the LORD our God, [11]the frogs shall leave you and your houses and your officials and your people; they shall be left only in the Nile." [12]Then Moses and Aaron went out from Pharaoh; and Moses cried out to the LORD concerning the frogs that he had brought upon Pharaoh.[d] [13]And the LORD did as Moses requested: the frogs died in the houses, the courtyards, and the fields. [14]And they gathered them together in heaps, and the land stank. [15]But when Pharaoh saw that there was a respite, he hardened his heart, and would not listen to them, just as the LORD had said.

The Third Plague: Gnats

[16]Then the LORD said to Moses, "Say to Aaron, 'Stretch out your staff and strike the dust of the earth, so that it may become gnats throughout the whole land of Egypt.'" [17]And they did so; Aaron stretched out his hand with his staff and struck the dust of the earth, and gnats came on humans and animals alike; all the dust of the earth turned into gnats throughout the whole land of Egypt. [18]The magicians tried to produce gnats by their secret arts, but they could not. There were gnats on both humans and animals. [19]And the magicians said to Pharaoh, "This is the finger of God!" But Pharaoh's heart was hardened, and he would not listen to them, just as the LORD had said.

---

a Ch 7.26 in Heb   *b* Gk: Heb *upon your people*   *c* Ch 8.1 in Heb   *d* Or *frogs, as he had agreed with Pharaoh*

---

waiting period allows the Nile to return to normal and serve as the source of the next plague (see 8.3). *Struck.* See v. 20.

8.1–15 The first of four plagues connected with animals is remarkable for its extent. The magicians can produce frogs, ironically compounding the plague, but they cannot remove them. **8.1** Cf. 7.16. **8.3** *The river,* "the Nile." *Swarm.* Cf. Gen 1.20; see note on Ex 1.7, in whose light the plague is poetic justice. *Kneading bowls.* The first plague made it impossible to drink, the second to bake bread. **8.5** *Stretch out,* an echo of 7.19; see note on 7.5. **8.6** *Covered,* a motif recurring in the plagues of hail, locusts, and darkness. **8.8** Recalling 7.22, one is surprised that now *Pharaoh* calls *Moses and Aaron. Pray,* entreat. *From me.* The plague was directed at Pharaoh first (vv. 3–4). **8.9** *That the frogs may be removed.* In Hebrew the verb is active, "to cut off the frogs." **8.10** *Know.* See 7.17; Moses is "calling the shot" to demonstrate that the plague is directed by Yahweh. **8.12** *Cried out,* used in 14.15; 15.25 as well as in 3.7; 12.30. **8.13** *Died in,* in Hebrew "died from," meaning that the frogs in these areas died; for a similar usage, see 9.6–7. **8.14** *They,* the Egyptians. **8.15** *Hardened,* "made heavy"; see note on 4.21. **8.16–19** The term *gnats,* or mosquitoes, which are indigenous to Egypt, has also been interpreted as "lice," which are not. The last plague in each set of three is narrated briefly; there is no encounter with Pharaoh and no mention of removing the pest. **8.17** *Animals.* As in the flood story of Gen 6–9, animals are innocent victims, here afflicted to punish the Egyptians. *All the dust . . . into gnats,* an impossible, therefore amazing, feat; cf. 7.19. **8.18** See v. 7. **8.19** *This is . . . God.* To acknowledge God's power was an explicit purpose of the preceding two plagues (7.17; 8.10). *Hardened,* "stiffened." See note on 4.21. **8.20–32** The Hebrew word translated *flies* occurs only in connection with this plague and is not precisely defined. It may derive from the sense of "swarm"; Jewish tradition interprets "wild animals." The word resembles the word for "locusts" (eighth plague) and the sense of "fly" suits Ps 78.45. **8.20** *Morning.* See note on

The Fourth Plague: Flies

20 Then the LORD said to Moses, "Rise early in the morning and present yourself before Pharaoh, as he goes out to the water, and say to him, 'Thus says the LORD: Let my people go, so that they may worship me. 21For if you will not let my people go, I will send swarms of flies on you, your officials, and your people, and into your houses; and the houses of the Egyptians shall be filled with swarms of flies; so also the land where they live. 22But on that day I will set apart the land of Goshen, where my people live, so that no swarms of flies shall be there, that you may know that I the LORD am in this land. 23Thus I will make a distinction[a] between my people and your people. This sign shall appear tomorrow.'" 24The LORD did so, and great swarms of flies came into the house of Pharaoh and into his officials' houses; in all of Egypt the land was ruined because of the flies.

25 Then Pharaoh summoned Moses and Aaron, and said, "Go, sacrifice to your God within the land." 26But Moses said, "It would not be right to do so; for the sacrifices that we offer to the LORD our God are offensive to the Egyptians. If we offer in the sight of the Egyptians sacrifices that are offensive to them, will they not stone us? 27We must go a three days' journey into the wilderness and sacrifice to the LORD our God as he commands us." 28So

Pharaoh said, "I will let you go to sacrifice to the LORD your God in the wilderness, provided you do not go very far away. Pray for me." 29Then Moses said, "As soon as I leave you, I will pray to the LORD that the swarms of flies may depart tomorrow from Pharaoh, from his officials, and from his people; only do not let Pharaoh again deal falsely by not letting the people go to sacrifice to the LORD."

30 So Moses went out from Pharaoh and prayed to the LORD. 31And the LORD did as Moses asked: he removed the swarms of flies from Pharaoh, from his officials, and from his people; not one remained. 32But Pharaoh hardened his heart this time also, and would not let the people go.

The Fifth Plague: Livestock Diseased

9 Then the LORD said to Moses, "Go to Pharaoh, and say to him, 'Thus says the LORD, the God of the Hebrews: Let my people go, so that they may worship me. 2For if you refuse to let them go and still hold them, 3the hand of the LORD will strike with a deadly pestilence your livestock in the field: the horses, the donkeys, the camels, the herds, and the flocks. 4But the LORD will make a distinction between the livestock of Israel and the livestock of Egypt, so that nothing shall die of all that belongs to the Israelites.'" 5The LORD

---

a Gk Vg: Heb *will set redemption*

7.15. *Present yourself,* "position yourself," as in 2.4; 7.15, in which the term is translated with the verb "to stand." **8.21** This verse is an echo of vv. 3–4, forging coherence with the second plague. *Flies.* See note on 8.20–32. *Send.* The Hebrew term is of the same root as *let . . . go.* *Filled,* a verbal link with the first plague, rendered *passed* in 7.25. **8.22** *Set apart.* As in the fifth (9.4), seventh (9.26), ninth (10.23), and tenth (11.7; 12.23) plagues the Israelites are miraculously spared; see also note on 14.1–31. Segregating the Hebrews, by which Egypt had asserted its superiority (Gen 43.32; 46.34), is turned to Israel's advantage. *Goshen.* See Gen 45.10; the name may derive from Arabs who spread into Egypt in the seventh century BCE. *Know.* See note on 8.19. *In this land,* lit. "in the midst of the land." **8.23** *Sign,* as in 4.8–9. *Tomorrow* recalls 8.10. **8.24** *The LORD* effects this plague without the intermediation of Moses or Aaron. *Great swarms of flies,* lit. "a heavy swarm-of-flies"; see note on 4.10. *Ruined* evokes "corrupt" and "destroy," from the same Hebrew root in Gen 6.11–13. **8.25–27** Cf. 5.3. **8.26** The Hebrew terms for *right* and *so* play on the same root. *Offensive,* an "abomination." See note on 8.22. Egypt abominates Israelite sheepherding (Gen 46.34), and Israel would offer sheep to its God; cf. 12.3–

5. **8.29** *Tomorrow,* emphasized in the Hebrew. *Only,* rendered *provided* in v. 28; Moses' reply plays on Pharaoh's rhetoric. *Deal falsely,* play a dirty trick (e.g., Gen 31.7). **8.31** *Removed,* lit. "caused to depart," the Hebrew root used in v. 29 and of the removal of the frogs in vv. 9–11. *Remained,* another verbal link with the second plague (translated *be left* in v. 9). **8.32** *Hardened,* "made heavy" (see 8.15).

9.1–7 The affliction of Egypt's animals, anticipated in the third plague (see note on 8.17), is resumed in the sixth (vv. 9–10), seventh (9.19–22, 25), and tenth (11.5; 12.29) plagues. The Israelites' livestock is spared and will accompany them out of Egypt (10.26; 12.32, 38). Pestilence becomes a curse for the Israelites to shun (Lev 26.25; Deut 28.21). **9.1** The freedom refrain (7.16; 8.1, 20). **9.2** *Hold,* the Hebrew root of *hardened* in 7.13, 22; 8.19 (see note on 4.21). **9.3** *The LORD,* as in the preceding plague (see note on 8.24). *Strike with a deadly pestilence,* lit. "will be there . . . , a very heavy pestilence." "Will-be-there" is of the same root as the divine name (see note on 3.14); on "heavy," see note on 4.10. *Camels,* an anachronism; camels weren't used in Israel in substantial numbers until ca. 600 BCE and in Egypt even later. **9.4** *Distinction,* as in the preceding

set a time, saying, "Tomorrow the LORD will do this thing in the land." 6And on the next day the LORD did so; all the livestock of the Egyptians died, but of the livestock of the Israelites not one died. 7Pharaoh inquired and found that not one of the livestock of the Israelites was dead. But the heart of Pharaoh was hardened, and he would not let the people go.

The Sixth Plague: Boils

8 Then the LORD said to Moses and Aaron, "Take handfuls of soot from the kiln, and let Moses throw it in the air in the sight of Pharaoh. 9It shall become fine dust all over the land of Egypt, and shall cause festering boils on humans and animals throughout the whole land of Egypt." 10So they took soot from the kiln, and stood before Pharaoh, and Moses threw it in the air, and it caused festering boils on humans and animals. 11The magicians could not stand before Moses because of the boils, for the boils afflicted the magicians as well as all the Egyptians. 12But the LORD hardened the heart of Pharaoh, and he would not listen to them, just as the LORD had spoken to Moses.

The Seventh Plague: Thunder and Hail

13 Then the LORD said to Moses, "Rise up early in the morning and present yourself before Pharaoh, and say to him, 'Thus says the LORD, the God of the Hebrews: Let my people go, so that they may worship me. 14For this time I will send all my plagues upon you yourself, and upon your officials, and upon your people, so that you may know that there is no one like me in all the earth. 15For by now I could have stretched out my hand and struck you and your people with pestilence, and you would have been cut off from the earth. 16But this is why I have let you live: to show you my power, and to make my name resound through all the earth. 17You are still exalting yourself against my people, and will not let them go. 18Tomorrow at this time I will cause the heaviest hail to fall that has ever fallen in Egypt from the day it was founded until now. 19Send, therefore, and have your livestock and everything that you have in the open field brought to a secure place; every human or animal that is in the open field and is not brought under shelter will die when the hail comes down upon them.' " 20Those officials of Pharaoh who feared the word of the LORD hurried their slaves and livestock off to a secure place. 21Those who did not regard the word of the LORD left their slaves and livestock in the open field.

22 The LORD said to Moses, "Stretch out your hand toward heaven so that hail may fall on the whole land of Egypt, on humans and

---

plague (8.22–23). **9.5** See 8.10, 23. *Thing,* Hebrew *davar,* also used in *nothing* (v. 4) and in the phrase translated *did so* (v. 6), a play on *pestilence* (Hebrew *dever*) in v. 3. **9.6** *All the livestock,* a detail that, like *all the water* in 7.20, is inconsistent with what follows; some of Egypt's livestock will be explicitly affected by the sixth (9.10), seventh (9.19–21), and tenth (11.5; 12.29) plagues. **9.7** *Inquired,* lit. "sent," an ironic play in Hebrew on the cognate *let go* (v. 1). *Was hardened,* lit. "became heavy" (see 8.15, 32).

9.8–12 See note on 8.16–19; Pharaoh is not addressed, but he is to witness the transformation of soot into boils. Boils is the first plague to affect humans directly; the "boils of Egypt" is a curse (Deut 28.27). **9.8** The Hebrew terms for *handfuls* and *soot* form a wordplay. *Moses.* Moses and Aaron collect the soot, but only Moses effects the plague by throwing the soot. **9.8, 10** *In the air,* lit. "heavenward." **9.11** The *magicians,* who increasingly fail, are not only beaten but ridiculed. *Could not,* a motif; cf. 7.18 (*be unable*); 7.21, 24; 8.18. **9.12** *Hardened,* lit. "stiffened"; this is the first time the Lord brings on Pharaoh's stubbornness; see note on 4.21.

9.13–35 The first in the third set of plagues (see note on 7.15) is drawn out. Moses explains the reason for prolonging the plagues (vv. 14–16). The hail is ex-

traordinary for its combination with fire, its unprecedented extent (vv. 18, 23–24), and the exemption of the Israelites (v. 26). Pharaoh's temporary surrender (v. 27) is an anticlimax. **9.13** *Present yourself.* See note on 8.20. The rest of the verse echoes 9.1. **9.14** *All my plagues.* This is curious; perhaps it refers to the severity of the plague, or *this time* refers to the set of three plagues. *There is no one like me.* The claim carries greater conviction following the utter defeat of the magicians. **9.15** *Stretched,* rendered *send* in v. 14; cf. note on 3.20. *Struck.* See note on 2.11. Until now only the cattle have been afflicted with *pestilence* (v. 3). **9.16** *To make . . . resound,* lit. "to tell"; cf. 10.2; 12.27–28; 13.8; cf. Ps 78.1–6. **9.17** *Exalting,* elevating (see Prov 4.8). **9.18** *Tomorrow.* See 8.10. *Heaviest hail,* a close echo in Hebrew of "a very heavy pestilence" (see note on 9.3). *Has ever fallen.* See note on 7.14–12.32. **9.19** *Send,* proclaim through messengers. *Livestock.* According to v. 6, all the livestock of the Egyptians died in the fifth plague; see note on 9.6. The plague is directed against life supports, not life itself. **9.20** *Officials.* See 7.10. *A secure place,* rather *shelter* (v. 19). **9.21** Egypt's willfulness is ultimately responsible for its catastrophic fate; see note on 1.22. **9.22** *Stretch.* See note on 7.5. *Toward heaven,* a link with vv. 8, 10. *Whole land . . . on humans and animals* seems disso-

animals and all the plants of the field in the land of Egypt." 23Then Moses stretched out his staff toward heaven, and the LORD sent thunder and hail, and fire came down on the earth. And the LORD rained hail on the land of Egypt; 24there was hail with fire flashing continually in the midst of it, such heavy hail as had never fallen in all the land of Egypt since it became a nation. 25The hail struck down everything that was in the open field throughout all the land of Egypt, both human and animal; the hail also struck down all the plants of the field, and shattered every tree in the field. 26Only in the land of Goshen, where the Israelites were, there was no hail.

27 Then Pharaoh summoned Moses and Aaron, and said to them, "This time I have sinned; the LORD is in the right, and I and my people are in the wrong. 28Pray to the LORD! Enough of God's thunder and hail! I will let you go; you need stay no longer." 29Moses said to him, "As soon as I have gone out of the city, I will stretch out my hands to the LORD; the thunder will cease, and there will be no more hail, so that you may know that the earth is the LORD's. 30But as for you and your officials, I know that you do not yet fear the LORD God." 31(Now the flax and the barley were ruined, for the barley was in the ear and the flax was in bud. 32But the wheat and the spelt were not ruined, for they are late in coming up.) 33So Moses left Pharaoh, went out of the city, and stretched out his hands to the LORD; then the thunder and the hail ceased, and the rain no longer poured down on the earth. 34But when Pharaoh saw that the rain and the hail and the thunder had ceased, he sinned once more and hardened his heart, he and his officials. 35So the heart of Pharaoh was hardened, and he would not let the Israelites go, just as the LORD had spoken through Moses.

The Eighth Plague: Locusts

10 Then the LORD said to Moses, "Go to Pharaoh; for I have hardened his heart and the heart of his officials, in order that I may show these signs of mine among them, 2and that you may tell your children and grandchildren how I have made fools of the Egyptians and what signs I have done among them—so that you may know that I am the LORD."

3 So Moses and Aaron went to Pharaoh, and said to him, "Thus says the LORD, the God of the Hebrews, 'How long will you refuse to humble yourself before me? Let my people go, so that they may worship me. 4For if you refuse to let my people go, tomorrow I will bring locusts into your country. 5They shall cover the surface of the land, so that no one

---

nant with vv. 20–21; for consistency one assumes that the persons and livestock of the God-fearing are excepted. *Plants of the field,* also in v. 25, evokes Gen 2.5; see note on 7.19. **9.23** Extending the arm (v. 22) and extending the *staff* are viewed as the same act, as in 10.12–13; 14.16, 21. *Thunder* (lit. "sounds") and *fire* anticipate the Sinai revelation (19.16, 18). The combination of *heaven, fire,* and *rained* recalls the destruction of Sodom and Gomorrah (Gen 19.24). **9.24** *Flashing,* elsewhere only in Ezek 1.4. *Such heavy hail,* an echo of *no one like me* (v. 14); the incomparable deity effects unprecedented phenomena; cf. also v. 18. **9.25** *Struck ... shattered,* parallelism (see note on 3.15); cf. Ps 29.5. **9.26** See note on 8.22. **9.27** *Summoned,* lit. "sent and called for," using the Hebrew rendered *send* in v. 19. *In the right,* legal terminology (e.g., Deut 25.1) suggesting the Lord's superiority is proved by the evidence of the plagues. *In the right* and *in the wrong* also connote the "righteous" and "wicked," again evoking Sodom and Gomorrah (see note on 9.23; cf. Gen 18.23). **9.28** *Pray.* Cf. 8.28. *Enough,* lit. "it is (too) great"; cf. 1.9, where *more numerous* is lit. "too great." *God's thunder,* idiomatic for "very great thunder." **9.29** *Out of the city,* an indication of leaving the royal precincts or possibly a suggestion that the Lord may be contacted only outside the pagan site. *Stretch,* or "spread," a gesture of prayer (e.g., 1 Kings 8.22; Isa 1.15). *You may know* echoes v. 14. **9.30** Moses explains why he needed to provide additional proof that God is the supreme power by predicting the end of the plague. **9.31–32** Some crops had to survive to serve as fodder for the locusts in the next plague (10.5, 12, 15). **9.33** *Stretched.* See note on 9.29. *Rain,* not mentioned except in *cause ... to fall* (v. 18). **9.34** *Sinned.* See v. 27. *Hardened,* "made heavy" (see note on 4.21). **9.35** *Hardened,* "stiffened" by itself (see note on 4.21).

10.1–20 The locusts devour the remaining vegetation and cover the land (vv. 5, 15), providing a transition from the devastation of crops by hail to the darkness that follows. For the first time Pharaoh is pressured to release the Hebrews (v. 7), anticipating the tenth plague (12.33). Locusts are a curse (Deut 28.38); cf. note on 9.8–12. **10.1** *Hardened,* "made heavy," as in 9.34. **10.2** *Tell.* See note on 9.16. **10.3** *How long,* a rhetorical addition to the formula in 9.13. *Humble yourself,* the same Hebrew root translated *oppress* in 1.11–12; Pharaoh must receive poetic justice. **10.4** An echo of 8.2. *Tomorrow.* See 8.10. **10.5** The imagery is elaborated in Joel 1; cf. Judg 6.5; 7.12. Here human and animal life are only indirectly affected, as the severest plague is saved for last. *Cover the surface.*

will be able to see the land. They shall devour the last remnant left you after the hail, and they shall devour every tree of yours that grows in the field. 6 They shall fill your houses, and the houses of all your officials and of all the Egyptians—something that neither your parents nor your grandparents have seen, from the day they came on earth to this day.' " Then he turned and went out from Pharaoh.

7 Pharaoh's officials said to him, "How long shall this fellow be a snare to us? Let the people go, so that they may worship the LORD their God; do you not yet understand that Egypt is ruined?" 8 So Moses and Aaron were brought back to Pharaoh, and he said to them, "Go, worship the LORD your God! But which ones are to go?" 9 Moses said, "We will go with our young and our old; we will go with our sons and daughters and with our flocks and herds, because we have the LORD's festival to celebrate." 10 He said to them, "The LORD indeed will be with you, if ever I let your little ones go with you! Plainly, you have some evil purpose in mind. 11 No, never! Your men may go and worship the LORD, for that is what you are asking." And they were driven out from Pharaoh's presence.

12 Then the LORD said to Moses, "Stretch out your hand over the land of Egypt, so that the locusts may come upon it and eat every plant in the land, all that the hail has left." 13 So Moses stretched out his staff over the land of

Egypt, and the LORD brought an east wind upon the land all that day and all that night; when morning came, the east wind had brought the locusts. 14 The locusts came upon all the land of Egypt and settled on the whole country of Egypt, such a dense swarm of locusts as had never been before, nor ever shall be again. 15 They covered the surface of the whole land, so that the land was black; and they ate all the plants in the land and all the fruit of the trees that the hail had left; nothing green was left, no tree, no plant in the field, in all the land of Egypt. 16 Pharaoh hurriedly summoned Moses and Aaron and said, "I have sinned against the LORD your God, and against you. 17 Do forgive my sin just this once, and pray to the LORD your God that at the least he remove this deadly thing from me." 18 So he went out from Pharaoh and prayed to the LORD. 19 The LORD changed the wind into a very strong west wind, which lifted the locusts and drove them into the Red Sea;[a] not a single locust was left in all the country of Egypt. 20 But the LORD hardened Pharaoh's heart, and he would not let the Israelites go.

The Ninth Plague: Darkness

21 Then the LORD said to Moses, "Stretch out your hand toward heaven so that there may be darkness over the land of Egypt, a darkness that

---

a Or Sea of Reeds

Cf. Num 22.5, 11. *Remnant.* See note on 9.31–32. **10.6** Another echo of the frog plague (8.3–6), whose relative harmlessness contrasts with the severity of the locust plague. *Turned,* "faced" away, foreshadowing vv. 28–29. **10.7** *How long* echoes v. 3. *This fellow,* lit. "this" (see note on 32.1). *Snare.* Cf., e.g., 23.33; 34.12; Deut 7.16. *People.* The Hebrew has "persons," not the collective term "people." *Ruined,* not the Hebrew term so translated in 8.24. **10.8** In contrast to 8.8 and v. 16 below, Pharaoh does not directly summon *Moses and Aaron. Which ones.* Pharaoh is prepared to make a concession as in 8.25–28, but again with restrictions. **10.9** *Festival to celebrate.* See note on 5.1. **10.10** *Evil* may pun in Hebrew on the name of the Egyptian god Ra (Re). **10.11** *No, never,* or "No indeed," echoing *indeed* in v. 10. *Men,* as in 23.17; 34.23; Deut 16.16. *They were driven,* lit. "he drove them"; some versions read "they drove them." *Presence,* "face," again (see note on 10.6) foreshadowing vv. 28–29. **10.12** *Stretch,* as in 9.22; see note on 7.5. **10.13** *Staff.* See note on 9.23. *East wind,* an anticipation of 14.21. Locust swarms more typically enter Egypt from the south. *All that night,* "all night," exactly as in 14.21. **10.14** *Dense swarm,* lit. "very heavy"; see note on 4.10. **10.15** *Covered.* See note

on 10.5. *The land was black,* or "and the land became dark," anticipating the plague of darkness (vv. 21–22). *All the plants,* inconsistent with the Israelites' use of herbs and hyssop (12.8, 22) unless Goshen is spared. **10.16** *Hurriedly* foreshadows 12.33. *Summoned.* See note on 10.8. *I have sinned.* Pharaoh has said this before (9.27). **10.17** *Pray* as in 8.8, 28; 9.28. *Deadly thing,* lit. "death," hyperbole here but foreshadowing the tenth plague. **10.19** *West wind,* lit. "sea wind," an Israelite perspective since the Mediterranean lies west of Israel; cf. note on 26.18. References to "sea," *wind,* and *Red Sea* anticipate 14.21–28. *Drove . . . into,* not toward but lit. "into," different from *driven out* in v. 11; cf. Joel 2.20. *Red Sea,* the "Sea of Reeds," possibly one of the lagoons along the Mediterranean coast of the Sinai Peninsula (see note on 14.2), but also possibly the Bitter Lakes, farther south. Few of the geographical sites in the Exodus narrative can be identified, and it is possible the Red Sea (Gulf of Suez) is meant; although unrealistic here, it may have been adopted to present a later Israelite audience with a well-known body of water. *Not a single . . . was left,* the same Hebrew phrase rendered *not one remained* in 8.31, an anticipation of 14.28. **10.20** *Hardened,* "stiffened," as in 9.35.

can be felt." 22So Moses stretched out his hand toward heaven, and there was dense darkness in all the land of Egypt for three days. 23People could not see one another, and for three days they could not move from where they were; but all the Israelites had light where they lived. 24Then Pharaoh summoned Moses, and said, "Go, worship the LORD. Only your flocks and your herds shall remain behind. Even your children may go with you." 25But Moses said, "You must also let us have sacrifices and burnt offerings to sacrifice to the LORD our God. 26Our livestock also must go with us; not a hoof shall be left behind, for we must choose some of them for the worship of the LORD our God, and we will not know what to use to worship the LORD until we arrive there." 27But the LORD hardened Pharaoh's heart, and he was unwilling to let them go. 28Then Pharaoh said to him, "Get away from me! Take care that you do not see my face again, for on the day you see my face you shall die." 29Moses said, "Just as you say! I will never see your face again."

Warning of the Final Plague

11 The LORD said to Moses, "I will bring one more plague upon Pharaoh and upon Egypt; afterwards he will let you go from here; indeed, when he lets you go, he will drive you away. 2Tell the people that every man is to ask his neighbor and every woman is to ask her neighbor for objects of silver and gold." 3The LORD gave the people favor in the sight of the Egyptians. Moreover, Moses himself was a man of great importance in the land of Egypt, in the sight of Pharaoh's officials and in the sight of the people.

4 Moses said, "Thus says the LORD: About midnight I will go out through Egypt. 5Every firstborn in the land of Egypt shall die, from the firstborn of Pharaoh who sits on his throne to the firstborn of the female slave who is behind the handmill, and all the firstborn of the livestock. 6Then there will be a loud cry throughout the whole land of Egypt, such as has never been or will ever be again. 7But not a dog shall growl at any of the Israelites—not at people, not at animals—so that you may know that the LORD makes a distinction between Egypt and Israel. 8Then all these officials of yours shall come down to me, and bow low to me, saying, 'Leave us, you and all the people who follow you.' After that I will leave." And in hot anger he left Pharaoh.

10.21–29 Because light symbolizes freedom (e.g., Isa 9.1; Lam 3.1–2, where darkness and "oppression" are juxtaposed), the plague of darkness gives Egypt a taste of enslavement (see v. 23) and Israel a foretaste of liberation. The darkness also foreshadows the tenth plague (see 12.29). Cf. Deut 28.29. 10.21 Stretch, as in v. 12; see note on 7.5. That the darkness can be felt distinguishes it from ordinary darkness. 10.22 Three days, the only notice of a plague's duration since 7.25, forming a frame around the first nine plagues. 10.23 The Israelites had light. See note on 8.22. 10.24 Pharaoh reverses himself (see v. 10). 10.25 Let us have, lit. "give into our hands"; Pharaoh must contribute toward, and not merely tolerate, Israelite cult sacrifices, slaughtered animals that are partly burned on the altar and partly eaten by the worshiper. 10.26 What to use, or "how." 10.27 Hardened, "stiffened," as in v. 20. 10.28 Take care, be on your guard. 10.29 It was Pharaoh who summoned Moses in the eighth and ninth plagues; and he will summon Moses and Aaron after the tenth (12.31). Moses defies Pharaoh's warning (11.8).
  11.1–10 The tenth plague has been adumbrated since 4.22–23. In light of 13.1–2, another purpose to slaying both human and animal (v. 5) firstborns is suggested: the Lord exercises his right to collect, as it were, all firstborn males. 11.1 The Hebrew term translated plague is from the root "touch" and connotes disease; it is different from the word also translated plagues in 9.14 and strike in 12.23. "Touch" figured in 4.25, just after the firstborn plague was first revealed. Upon,

against. Afterwards, as predicted in 3.20. Drive you away. The Hebrew adds "completely"; others interpret "as he would divorce a bride." 11.2 Predicted in 3.22 (see note there). Tell, lit. "say now in the ears of." Objects . . . gold. 3.22; 12.35 also mention clothing, which term is also found here in some versions. 11.3 That the people found favor is predicted in 3.21. Man . . . importance, ironic (see 10.28–29). Again (see 10.7) Pharaoh's underlings arrive at the truth before he does. 11.4 It is surprising, in view of 10.28–29 and the omission of any reference to Pharaoh here, that this speech is addressed to Pharaoh in person (see v. 8). Midnight, an hour associated with death (Job 34.20; cf. Gen 32.23–25; Ex 4.24). Go out, the verb denoting "exodus" (see note on 3.10). 11.5 Firstborn, i.e., "firstborn male"; see note on 13.1–2. Female slave. Egypt had other than Hebrew slaves. Handmill, a stationary horizontal round stone with a mobile upper grinding stone; using it was the most menial chore (Isa 47.1–2). The livestock were all said to have perished (see note on 9.6). 11.6 Cry, poetic justice; see note on 3.7. Never been. See note on 7.14–12.32. Will . . . again echoes never . . . again in 10.28–29. 11.7 Growl, lit. "chop with the tongue," hence "bark"; cf. Josh 10.21. While Egypt is beset by unprecedented screams, Israel will not be disturbed by so much as a barking dog. Distinction. Cf. distinction in 9.4, set apart in 8.22; see note on 8.22. 11.8 Officials, lit. "servants," who will now "serve" the Lord. In Hebrew "these" and "to me" sound alike, reinforcing the sense that Pharaoh's courtiers will render

9 The LORD said to Moses, "Pharaoh will not listen to you, in order that my wonders may be multiplied in the land of Egypt." 10Moses and Aaron performed all these wonders before Pharaoh; but the LORD hardened Pharaoh's heart, and he did not let the people of Israel go out of his land.

The First Passover Instituted

12 The LORD said to Moses and Aaron in the land of Egypt: 2This month shall mark for you the beginning of months; it shall be the first month of the year for you. 3Tell the whole congregation of Israel that on the tenth of this month they are to take a lamb for each family, a lamb for each household. 4If a household is too small for a whole lamb, it shall join its closest neighbor in obtaining one; the lamb shall be divided in proportion to the number of people who eat of it. 5Your lamb shall be without blemish, a year-old male; you may take it from the sheep or from the goats. 6You shall keep it until the fourteenth day of this month; then the whole assembled congregation of Israel shall slaughter it at twilight. 7They shall take some of the blood and put it on the two doorposts and the lintel of the houses in which they eat it. 8They shall eat the lamb that same night; they shall eat it roasted over the fire with unleavened bread and bitter herbs. 9Do not eat any of it raw or boiled in water, but roasted over the fire, with its head, legs, and inner organs. 10You shall let none of it remain until the morning; anything that remains until the morning you shall burn. 11This is how you shall eat it: your loins girded, your sandals on your feet, and your staff in your hand; and you shall eat it hurriedly. It is the passover of the LORD. 12For I will pass through the land of Egypt that night, and I will strike down every firstborn in the land of Egypt, both human beings and animals; on all the gods of

---

homage to God. *Left Pharaoh.* See note on 11.4. **11.9** The plagues narrative pauses, echoing the story's beginning (7.3–4). **11.10** *Hardened.* See note on 4.21.
12.1–28 Although the Passover ceremony may have its origins in a spring fertility rite, it serves two functions here: the immediate one of warding off the plague (vv. 7, 13, 22–23) and the perennial one of commemorating the exodus redemption (vv. 14, 24–27). The weeklong Festival of Unleavened Bread (vv. 14–20), which immediately follows (Lev 23.5–6; Num 28.16–17) and coalesces with Passover (Deut 16.1–8; but see Ex 23.15; 34.18), is not celebrated before leaving Egypt, but is ordained here, as it too comes to commemorate the exodus (vv. 15–20; 13.3–10). **12.1** *Egypt.* The Egyptian Passover is distinguished from the perennial one (vv. 17, 20). Deut 16.1–8 centralizes the rite at a single shrine (cf. 2 Kings 23.21–23). **12.2** The Bible's cultic calendar begins with the exodus season. The Priestly term *first month* (Lev 23.5; Num 28.16) is Abib (Hebrew "new ear of grain") elsewhere in the Pentateuch (Ex 13.4; 23.15; 34.18; Deut 16.1) and Nisan (from Babylonian) in postexilic books (Neh 2.1; Esth 3.7). The agricultural calendar begins with the seventh month; see 23.17 and the tenth-century BCE Gezer inscription, which lists agricultural tasks by month. *Mark,* lit. "be." *Beginning,* lit. "head," cognate to *first.* **12.3** *Israel* has not expressly heard from Moses and Aaron since 6.12; its cooperation now reflects the impact of the Lord's wonders. The *tenth* day of the seventh month is the Day of Atonement (Lev 23.27). *Family,* lit. "house of fathers," a tribal division (see note on 6.14). **12.4** *It shall join … in obtaining,* lit. "he and his neighbor closest to his house will take." *The lamb … eat of it,* "according to the number of persons, each by how much he eats, you shall divide the lamb." **12.5** *Without blemish,* a stipula-

tion for all sacrificial offerings (e.g., Lev 1.3, 10). *A year-old male,* a typical sacrificial offering (e.g., Num 28.3; 29.2). **12.6** The *fourteenth,* the full moon, a propitious time when the night is brightest; see also Lev 23.34. *The whole assembled congregation,* or "the entire assembly," which does not imply that everyone performed the rite together. *Twilight,* lit. "between the two settings," apparently between sunset and the last of the residual light in the sky. **12.7** See note on 4.25. By performing this apotropaic ritual Israel is again "set apart" from Egypt (11.7). *They eat,* lit. "they shall eat." **12.8** *Same night.* See Num 9.12; Deut 16.4. The sacred meal may also serve to protect the household. *Roasted.* See note on 12.9. *Unleavened bread,* minimally cooked, biscuitlike "matsah" bread used generally in ritual offerings (e.g., Lev 2.4–5; 6.9); leavening further removes the flour from its natural, created state. See the symbolic interpretation in vv. 33–34. *Bitter herbs.* The species is uncertain, but see 1.14. The three components of the offering signify a complete meal. **12.9** The prohibition against eating the offering *raw* or *boiled* means that it must be *roasted,* which ensures that the blood, the protective element, is removed. Blood, the symbol of life (Gen 9.4; Lev 17.11, 14), is divine property and must be returned to the deity whenever meat is eaten (Lev 17.3–6; Deut 12.16); cf. Deut 16.7, which is harmonized in 2 Chr 35.13. *With its … organs,* in contradistinction to the wholly burnt offering (Lev 1.8–9). **12.10** *Let none of it remain,* lest it be profaned; cf. 23.18; Lev 7.15; see notes on 12.8; 10.19. **12.11** *Passover.* The name of the offering and its festival are related to the cognate verb *pass over* in vv. 13, 23, 27. Alternatively, the verb may mean "to protect." **12.12** *Pass through,* not pass over (see note on 13.5). *Strike.* See note on 2.11. *Firstborn.* See note on 13.1–2. *Gods.* See Num 33.4. By causing so severe a catastro-

Egypt I will execute judgments: I am the LORD. [13]The blood shall be a sign for you on the houses where you live: when I see the blood, I will pass over you, and no plague shall destroy you when I strike the land of Egypt.

14 This day shall be a day of remembrance for you. You shall celebrate it as a festival to the LORD; throughout your generations you shall observe it as a perpetual ordinance. [15]Seven days you shall eat unleavened bread; on the first day you shall remove leaven from your houses, for whoever eats leavened bread from the first day until the seventh day shall be cut off from Israel. [16]On the first day you shall hold a solemn assembly, and on the seventh day a solemn assembly; no work shall be done on those days; only what everyone must eat, that alone may be prepared by you. [17]You shall observe the festival of unleavened bread, for on this very day I brought your companies out of the land of Egypt: you shall observe this day throughout your generations as a perpetual ordinance. [18]In the first month, from the evening of the fourteenth day until the evening of the twenty-first day, you shall eat unleavened bread. [19]For seven days no leaven shall be found in your houses; for whoever eats what is leavened shall be cut off from the congregation of Israel, whether an alien or a native of the land. [20]You shall eat nothing leavened; in all your settlements you shall eat unleavened bread.

21 Then Moses called all the elders of Israel and said to them, "Go, select lambs for your families, and slaughter the passover lamb. [22]Take a bunch of hyssop, dip it in the blood that is in the basin, and touch the lintel and the two doorposts with the blood in the basin. None of you shall go outside the door of your house until morning. [23]For the LORD will pass through to strike down the Egyptians; when he sees the blood on the lintel and on the two doorposts, the LORD will pass over that door and will not allow the destroyer to enter your houses to strike you down. [24]You shall observe this rite as a perpetual ordinance for you and your children. [25]When you come to the land that the LORD will give you, as he has promised, you shall keep this observance. [26]And when your children ask you, 'What do you mean by this observance?' [27]you shall say, 'It is the passover sacrifice to the LORD, for he passed over the houses of the Israelites in Egypt, when he struck down the Egyptians but spared our houses.' " And the people bowed down and worshiped.

28 The Israelites went and did just as the LORD had commanded Moses and Aaron.

---

phe in Egypt, the Lord, who has sought acknowledgment among the Egyptians (see 9.14; cf. note on 5.2), defeats Egypt's gods, who, like Pharaoh's magicians (see notes on 7.12; 9.11), prove powerless. Deities other than the Lord are assumed to exist, even if they are ineffectual; cf. 15.11. **12.13** *No plague shall destroy,* rather "no plague will be a destroyer," the demonic agent that brings death ("ravager" in Isa 54.16), distinguished from the deity in v. 23. **12.14** *Celebrate . . . festival.* See note on 5.1. *Perpetual.* See note on 12.1; cf. v. 17. **12.15** See note on 12.1–28. *Remove,* lit. "cause to stop" (see note on 5.5). *Cut off,* a punishment imposed in the Priestly Torah literature primarily for serious ritual infractions (e.g., Lev 17.4); because it contrasts with capital punishment (31.14), it may entail divine retribution for transgressions that escape human detection. **12.16** See Lev 23.7–8; Num 28.18, 25. *Assembly,* or "convocation." The preparation of food for immediate consumption is permitted during the festival but prohibited on the sabbath (16.23; 35.3). **12.17** *I brought.* The Passover in Egypt is seen as past. *Companies.* See note on 6.26. **12.18** *Until,* up to the eve of the twenty-first if the festivals of Passover and Unleavened Bread have coalesced (see note on 12.1–28), up through the eve of the twenty-first if the festivals are discrete. **12.19** Cf. v. 15. *Alien.* Aliens who reside among the Israelites by dint of marriage or another circumstance and are circumcised (v. 48) are enjoined to observe most laws (so v. 49) and are protected from abuse (e.g., 22.20–22). **12.20** *Settlements* refers to Israel's future circumstances, as in v. 17. **12.21–28** An elaboration of the laws in vv. 1–13. The Festival of Unleavened Bread, which does not take place the night of the plague, is omitted. **12.21** *Moses.* Cf. v. 28, which includes Aaron. *Lambs,* rather "small cattle," sheep or goats; see v. 5. *Families,* not the term used in v. 3. *Select lambs.* The instruction presupposes that the ritual is already familiar; the term *passover* is introduced in v. 11 only after the offering has been described. **12.22** *Hyssop,* a brushlike plant of uncertain identity, used also in purification rites (e.g., Lev 14.4, 6; Num 19.6). *Basin,* to collect the blood of the Passover animal. *Touch.* Cf. 4.25. *None . . . go outside.* The phrasing, absent from the foregoing instructions, suggests the protective function of the ritual; see notes on 12.8; 12.42; see also v. 46. **12.23** *Pass through.* See note on 12.12. *Strike down,* or "afflict with plague" (twice), cognate to *plague* (v. 13). *The destroyer.* See note on 12.13. **12.24** *Rite,* lit. "word," command. **12.25** Cf., e.g., 3.8, 17; 6.8–9. The topic of rites to be observed once Israel is settled in Canaan is resumed in 13.5. **12.26** See note on 9.16. **12.27** *Struck down.* See note on 12.23. *Worshiped.* See note on 4.31. **12.28** *Aaron.* See note on 12.21.

The Tenth Plague: Death of the Firstborn

29 At midnight the LORD struck down all the firstborn in the land of Egypt, from the first-born of Pharaoh who sat on his throne to the firstborn of the prisoner who was in the dungeon, and all the firstborn of the livestock. [30]Pharaoh arose in the night, he and all his officials and all the Egyptians; and there was a loud cry in Egypt, for there was not a house without someone dead. [31]Then he summoned Moses and Aaron in the night, and said, "Rise up, go away from my people, both you and the Israelites! Go, worship the LORD, as you said. [32]Take your flocks and your herds, as you said, and be gone. And bring a blessing on me too!"

The Exodus: From Rameses to Succoth

33 The Egyptians urged the people to hasten their departure from the land, for they said, "We shall all be dead." [34]So the people took their dough before it was leavened, with their kneading bowls wrapped up in their cloaks on their shoulders. [35]The Israelites had done as Moses told them; they had asked the Egyptians for jewelry of silver and gold, and for clothing, [36]and the LORD had given the people favor in the sight of the Egyptians, so that they let them have what they asked. And so they plundered the Egyptians.

37 The Israelites journeyed from Rameses to Succoth, about six hundred thousand men on foot, besides children. [38]A mixed crowd also went up with them, and livestock in great numbers, both flocks and herds. [39]They baked unleavened cakes of the dough that they had brought out of Egypt; it was not leavened, because they were driven out of Egypt and could not wait, nor had they prepared any provisions for themselves.

40 The time that the Israelites had lived in Egypt was four hundred thirty years. [41]At the end of four hundred thirty years, on that very day, all the companies of the LORD went out from the land of Egypt. [42]That was for the LORD a night of vigil, to bring them out of the land of Egypt. That same night is a vigil to be kept for the LORD by all the Israelites throughout their generations.

Directions for the Passover

43 The LORD said to Moses and Aaron: This is the ordinance for the passover: no foreigner shall eat of it, [44]but any slave who has been purchased may eat of it after he has been circumcised; [45]no bound or hired servant may eat of it. [46]It shall be eaten in one house; you shall not take any of the animal outside the house, and you shall not break any of its bones. [47]The whole congregation of Israel shall celebrate it. [48]If an alien who resides with you wants to celebrate the passover to the LORD, all his males shall be circumcised; then he may draw near to celebrate it; he shall be re-

---

12.29–30 The fulfillment of 11.4–6, with some variations; cf. note on 11.1–10. **12.29** *Prisoner,* more severe than the image in 11.5. *Dungeon,* lit. "pit," alluding perhaps to Gen 41.14. **12.30** *Arose,* aroused by the outcry. **12.31** *Summoned.* See note on 10.29. Pharaoh's implicit surrender to the Lord is a reversal (see 5.2). **12.32** Pharaoh reverses his refusal in 10.24. *Bring a blessing on me too,* "bless me too" when you worship the Lord. **12.33** *Egyptians.* Cf. 10.7. *Urged,* ironically another rendering of the Hebrew verb used of "stiffening" Pharaoh's heart in 14.4, 8 ("hardened"; see note on 4.21). *Hasten.* See note on 10.16. *All.* They fear the tenth plague is not the last. **12.34** *Leavened,* a symbolic interpretation of v. 8 (cf. v. 11) and of the Festival of Unleavened Bread; see v. 39. *Kneading bowls,* an echo of 8.3 (7.28 in Hebrew). **12.35** *Told them.* It has not been reported that Moses gave the instruction to ask for jewelry and clothing, although he was so ordered (3.21–22; 11.2–3). *Clothing,* the *cloaks* of v. 34. *Plundered.* See note on 3.22. **12.37** *Rameses.* See 1.11. *Succoth,* hebraization ("Booths") of an Egyptian site (*Th-k-w*) in the area of Wadi Tumilat, east of Pithom (see 1.11). Num 33.4 adds a macabre detail. *Six hundred thousand.* 603,550 in Num 1.46, excluding 8,580 Levite men (Num 4.48). Counting women, children, and the elderly, the total would well exceed 2 million; a large army comprised perhaps 20,000 soldiers. **12.38** *Mixed,* intermarried (Neh 13.3); see Num 11.4; cf. Lev 24.10. The Hebrew term recalls the fourth plague's flies. *Great numbers,* "very heavy" (see note on 4.10). **12.39** See note on 12.34. **12.40** *Four hundred thirty.* It is 400 years in Gen 15.13. Gen 15.16 predicts four generations (160 years), a count that conforms to 6.16–20, in which Moses is the fourth generation in Egypt. **12.41** *Companies.* See note on 6.26. **12.42** If the *vigil* is Israel's and not the Lord's (the Hebrew is ambiguous), a protective function for the Passover rite is again suggested (see notes on 12.8; 12.22; see also v. 46).

12.43–49 A resumption of the instructions for the Passover night ritual (vv. 1–13, 21–27); cf. v. 19. Since vv. 14, 28 seem to close the preceding units, the present passage appears to be a codicil. See also Num 9.1–14. **12.43** *Foreigner,* not *alien* (vv. 19, 48–49). **12.44** *Purchased.* The Hebrew adds "for silver" (cf. Gen 37.28). **12.45** *Bound . . . servant,* more likely a transient "resident"; cf. a similar distinction in Lev 22.10–11. **12.46** *Outside.* See note on 12.22. *Bones.* See Num 9.12; cf. Jn 19.36. **12.48** *Alien.* See note on 12.19. *All his*

garded as a native of the land. But no uncircumcised person shall eat of it; 49there shall be one law for the native and for the alien who resides among you.

50 All the Israelites did just as the LORD had commanded Moses and Aaron. 51That very day the LORD brought the Israelites out of the land of Egypt, company by company.

13 The LORD said to Moses: 2Consecrate to me all the firstborn; whatever is the first to open the womb among the Israelites, of human beings and animals, is mine.

The Festival of Unleavened Bread

3 Moses said to the people, "Remember this day on which you came out of Egypt, out of the house of slavery, because the LORD brought you out from there by strength of hand; no leavened bread shall be eaten. 4Today, in the month of Abib, you are going out. 5When the LORD brings you into the land of the Canaanites, the Hittites, the Amorites, the Hivites, and the Jebusites, which he swore to your ancestors to give you, a land flowing with milk and honey, you shall keep this observance in this month. 6Seven days you shall eat unleavened bread, and on the seventh day there shall be a festival to the LORD. 7Unleavened bread shall be eaten for seven days; no leavened bread shall be seen in your possession, and no leaven shall be seen among you in

all your territory. 8You shall tell your child on that day, 'It is because of what the LORD did for me when I came out of Egypt.' 9It shall serve for you as a sign on your hand and as a reminder on your forehead, so that the teaching of the LORD may be on your lips; for with a strong hand the LORD brought you out of Egypt. 10You shall keep this ordinance at its proper time from year to year.

The Consecration of the Firstborn

11 "When the LORD has brought you into the land of the Canaanites, as he swore to you and your ancestors, and has given it to you, 12you shall set apart to the LORD all that first opens the womb. All the firstborn of your livestock that are males shall be the LORD's. 13But every firstborn donkey you shall redeem with a sheep; if you do not redeem it, you must break its neck. Every firstborn male among your children you shall redeem. 14When in the future your child asks you, 'What does this mean?' you shall answer, 'By strength of hand the LORD brought us out of Egypt, from the house of slavery. 15When Pharaoh stubbornly refused to let us go, the LORD killed all the firstborn in the land of Egypt, from human firstborn to the firstborn of animals. Therefore I sacrifice to the LORD every male that first opens the womb, but every firstborn of my sons I redeem.' 16It shall serve as a sign on your

---

males . . . circumcised, like Abraham and the males of his household (Gen 17.10–14, 23–27). **12.49** *Law,* lit. "instruction" (Hebrew *torah*). Cf. Lev 24.22. **12.51** A repetition of v. 41, enclosing the codicil. *Company.* See note on 6.26. **13.1–2** The law to consecrate Israel's human and animal firstborn is juxtaposed with the slaying of Egypt's firstborn, as in 34.18–20; Deut 15.19–16.8; see note on 11.1–10. It is assumed on the basis of vv. 12, 15 and all parallel passages that only males are meant (cf. 11.5; 12.29). The elaboration in vv. 11–26 is paralleled by 34.19–20; Num 18.15–18. The parallel law in 22.29–30 does not elaborate a method of consecration. Cf. the practices in Num 18; Deut 15.19–23 (which does not relate to firstborn humans) and the motive in Num 3.11–13, 41, 45; 8.17. **13.3–10** Cf. 12.14–20; differences suggest diverse traditions. **13.3** Cf. 12.14. *House of slavery.* Cf. 20.2. *Strength of hand.* See vv. 9, 14, 16; cf. *mighty hand* (6.1, from the same root) and 3.19. *No leavened bread.* Cf. 12.15. **13.4** *Abib.* See note on 12.2. **13.5** Cf. 3.17; see note on 12.25. **13.6** *Seventh day.* See 12.16. **13.7** In Hebrew *in your possession* and *among you* are expressed identically, creating a parallelism (see note on 3.15). **13.8** Cf. 12.26. **13.9** *Hand, forehead,* places where people would string identifying seals or ornaments; as in

v. 16 a metaphor for a reminder (cf. Deut 6.8; Song 8.6). **13.11–16** An elaboration of vv. 1–2. Firstborn redemption, like the Feast of Unleavened Bread (v. 6), is to be interpreted to the next generations in connection with the exodus (v. 14). The theme of redemption links this chapter with Passover. The paschal offering defends against harm (see notes on 12.1–28; 12.8; 12.11; 12.22; 12.42); the similar but more general Islamic sacrifice called *fidya,* cognate to Hebrew *padah,* "redeem" (vv. 13, 15) substitutes an animal for a person whose life is threatened. Redemption has an overtone of protection. **13.11** Cf. v. 5. **13.12** *Males.* See note on 13.1–2. **13.13** The *donkey* is ritually tainted (Lev 11.3); the *sheep* is pure. *Break its neck,* to kill the animal without ritually slaughtering it since it is tainted; the animal is rightfully God's and may not be used. Lev 27.27 stipulates that the tainted animal must be redeemed at 120 percent its value, which favors the priests, who suffer a loss here because a sheep is worth less than a donkey. *Children,* lit. "sons" (see note on 13.1–2). *Redeem.* The sum is not fixed; Num 18.16 specifies 5 shekels. **13.14** Cf. v. 8. *Strength of hand.* Cf. vv. 3, 9, 16. **13.15** *Stubbornly refused,* lit. "made hard" (see note on 4.21). *Therefore,* a formula introducing an explanation of origins (etiology). *Sacrifice.* See note on

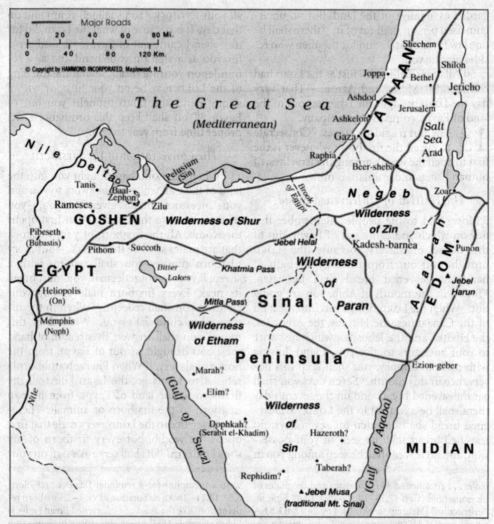

The geographical setting of the narratives in Exodus and Numbers.

hand and as an emblem[a] on your forehead that by strength of hand the LORD brought us out of Egypt."

The Pillars of Cloud and Fire

17 When Pharaoh let the people go, God did not lead them by way of the land of the Philistines, although that was nearer; for God thought, "If the people face war, they may change their minds and return to Egypt." [18]So God led the people by the roundabout way of the wilderness toward the Red Sea.[b] The Israelites went up out of the land of Egypt prepared for battle. [19]And Moses took with him the bones of Joseph who had required a

solemn oath of the Israelites, saying, "God will surely take notice of you, and then you must carry my bones with you from here." [20]They set out from Succoth, and camped at Etham, on the edge of the wilderness. [21]The LORD went in front of them in a pillar of cloud by day, to lead them along the way, and in a pillar of fire by night, to give them light, so that they might travel by day and by night. [22]Neither the pillar of cloud by day nor the pillar of fire by night left its place in front of the people.

---

a Or as a frontlet; meaning of Heb uncertain   b Or Sea of Reeds

Crossing the Red Sea

14 Then the LORD said to Moses: ²Tell the Israelites to turn back and camp in front of Pi-hahiroth, between Migdol and the sea, in front of Baal-zephon; you shall camp opposite it, by the sea. ³Pharaoh will say of the Israelites, "They are wandering aimlessly in the land; the wilderness has closed in on them." ⁴I will harden Pharaoh's heart, and he will pursue them, so that I will gain glory for myself over Pharaoh and all his army; and the Egyptians shall know that I am the LORD. And they did so.

5 When the king of Egypt was told that the people had fled, the minds of Pharaoh and his officials were changed toward the people, and they said, "What have we done, letting Israel leave our service?" ⁶So he had his chariot made ready, and took his army with him; ⁷he took six hundred picked chariots and all the other chariots of Egypt with officers over all of them. ⁸The LORD hardened the heart of Pharaoh king of Egypt and he pursued the Israelites, who were going out boldly. ⁹The Egyptians pursued them, all Pharaoh's horses and chariots, his chariot drivers and his army; they overtook them camped by the sea, by Pi-hahiroth, in front of Baal-zephon.

10 As Pharaoh drew near, the Israelites looked back, and there were the Egyptians advancing on them. In great fear the Israelites cried out to the LORD. ¹¹They said to Moses, "Was it because there were no graves in Egypt that you have taken us away to die in the wilderness? What have you done to us, bringing us out of Egypt? ¹²Is this not the very thing we told you in Egypt, 'Let us alone and let us serve the Egyptians'? For it would have been better for us to serve the Egyptians than to die in the wilderness." ¹³But Moses said to the people, "Do not be afraid, stand firm, and see the deliverance that the LORD will accomplish for you today; for the Egyptians whom you see today you shall

---

3.18. *Every male,* of the pure animals (see v. 13). **13.16** *Emblem,* a pendant or headband, interpreted in Judaism as phylacteries; see note on 13.9. **13.17** *Philistines,* apparently anachronistic; the Philistines would only have begun to settle the coast of Canaan at the time of the exodus; yet a Philistine presence there is taken for granted (see 15.14; cf. Gen 21.34; 26.1). *Thought,* lit. "said"; the apprehension anticipates 14.10–11. *Change their minds,* or "repent," a pun in Hebrew on *lead them.* From a historical perspective, the northern route out of Egypt was heavily fortified and therefore impassable. **13.18** *Led . . . roundabout,* lit. "had go around" (Hebrew *wayyasev*) plays on "Sea of Reeds" (*yam suf*); see note on 10.19. *Prepared for battle,* or "armed" (Judg 7.11). **13.19** See Gen 50.25. **13.20** *Succoth.* See note on 12.37, whose narrative is resumed here. *Etham.* The site is uncertain; Num 33.8 places the Etham wilderness on the far side of the water Israel will cross; see 14.2. **13.21** The Lord, depicted as a storm god (see chs. 15, 19), radiates light from within a cover of cloud (cf. Ps 18.9–13). The two pillars are one (see 14.24): by day only the cloud is visible, by night only the light; cf. 24.15–17; 40.34–38.

14.1–31 Following the pattern of contrasts developed through the plagues (see note on 8.22), Israel, whose sons had been marked for drowning by Pharaoh (1.22), is kept alive on dry land as Egypt is dealt a death blow in the water (vv. 27–30). **14.2** *Turn back.* Although the Israelites seem to have reached beyond the sea (see 13.20), they are instructed to double back in order to bait and entrap the Egyptians. *Pi-hahiroth,* possibly a temple site in the region of Succoth (13.20). *Migdol,* "Tower" in Hebrew, probably a fortification against Assyria north of the Bitter Lakes built in the seventh century BCE (cf. Jer 44.1). If *Baal-zephon* is the Zeus Casius temple that juts into Lake Sarbonis, the other sites too are located along the northern Sinai coast, and Lake Sarbonis is the *sea.* *Baal* is the Canaanite storm god; "Zaphon" is known as his home on the north Syrian coast, probably Mount Casius. **14.3** *Closed in on,* or "enclosed" (cf. Josh 6.1). **14.4** *Harden,* "stiffen" (see note on 4.21), a strong link with the plagues narratives. *Gain glory for myself,* lit. "prove heavy"; see v. 18; note on 4.10. *Know.* See note on 5.2; cf. also Josh 4.24. **14.5** *The people . . . fled,* as if Egypt had not pressed them to leave (12.31–33); or it has dawned on the Egyptians that the Israelites had left for more than three days (5.3). **14.6** *He had . . . made ready,* lit. "he (himself) harnessed"; see also note on 14.25. *Army,* lit. "people" (cf. Num 21.23); Pharaoh musters his "people" to head off the fleeing Hebrew *people* (v. 5). *With him,* Hebrew *'immo,* a wordplay on "his people (*'ammo*)." **14.7** *Officers,* not the *officials* of v. 5 but military captains. **14.8** *Hardened.* See v. 4. *Boldly,* lit. "with hand (held) high," defiantly (Num 15.30); see Num 33.3. **14.9** In the Hebrew *all Pharaoh's horses . . . army* is placed awkwardly following *camped by the sea;* similar phrases read smoothly in v. 23. On the anachronistic use of cavalry, see note on 15.1. **14.10** *Pharaoh.* The king is in focus even though the entire army is in pursuit; cf. v. 6. *There were,* "here: . . .*"; see note on 2.6. *Advancing.* In the Hebrew the verb is singular, suggesting that the Egyptian army is perceived as a single horde. *In great fear.* Cf. Moses' reply in v. 13. *Cried out to the LORD.* Cf. 2.23, where the prayer is undirected, and 5.15, where appeal is made to Pharaoh. **14.11–12** *Egypt* is used five times in two verses. **14.11** Cf. Num 11.18–20; 14.2–4. **14.12** *The very thing,* not exactly; see 5.20–21. **14.13** *Deliverance,* in Hebrew cognate to *came to their defense* in 2.17 and

never see again. ¹⁴The LORD will fight for you, and you have only to keep still."

15 Then the LORD said to Moses, "Why do you cry out to me? Tell the Israelites to go forward. ¹⁶But you lift up your staff, and stretch out your hand over the sea and divide it, that the Israelites may go into the sea on dry ground. ¹⁷Then I will harden the hearts of the Egyptians so that they will go in after them; and so I will gain glory for myself over Pharaoh and all his army, his chariots, and his chariot drivers. ¹⁸And the Egyptians shall know that I am the LORD, when I have gained glory for myself over Pharaoh, his chariots, and his chariot drivers."

19 The angel of God who was going before the Israelite army moved and went behind them; and the pillar of cloud moved from in front of them and took its place behind them. ²⁰It came between the army of Egypt and the army of Israel. And so the cloud was there with the darkness, and it lit up the night; one did not come near the other all night.

21 Then Moses stretched out his hand over the sea. The LORD drove the sea back by a strong east wind all night, and turned the sea into dry land; and the waters were divided. ²²The Israelites went into the sea on dry ground, the waters forming a wall for them on

their right and on their left. ²³The Egyptians pursued, and went into the sea after them, all of Pharaoh's horses, chariots, and chariot drivers. ²⁴At the morning watch the LORD in the pillar of fire and cloud looked down upon the Egyptian army, and threw the Egyptian army into panic. ²⁵He clogged*ᵃ* their chariot wheels so that they turned with difficulty. The Egyptians said, "Let us flee from the Israelites, for the LORD is fighting for them against Egypt."

The Pursuers Drowned

26 Then the LORD said to Moses, "Stretch out your hand over the sea, so that the water may come back upon the Egyptians, upon their chariots and chariot drivers." ²⁷So Moses stretched out his hand over the sea, and at dawn the sea returned to its normal depth. As the Egyptians fled before it, the LORD tossed the Egyptians into the sea. ²⁸The waters returned and covered the chariots and the chariot drivers, the entire army of Pharaoh that had followed them into the sea; not one of them remained. ²⁹But the Israelites walked on dry ground through the sea, the waters forming a wall for them on their right and on their left.

30 Thus the LORD saved Israel that day from

---

a Sam Gk Syr: MT *removed*

---

saved in 14.30; it anticipates 15.2, where it is rendered *salvation. Never see again* echoes 10.28–29. **14.14** *Will fight* anticipates the cognate *warrior* in 15.3. God's fighting on Israel's behalf (see Deut 1.30; 3.22; 20.4) is developed in Joshua (10.14, 42; 23.3, 10). **14.15** It is presupposed that, beside responding to the people's complaint (vv. 13–14), Moses appealed to the Lord, as in 5.22–23. **14.16** *Staff* (see note on 7.8–13) and *stretch out your hand* (see note on 7.5) recall the plagues (e.g., 10.12–13). *Divide.* Splitting the sea evokes an Israelite creation myth in which the Lord cuts through the primeval sea monster (Isa 51.9; Job 26.13); Isa 51.10 in fact compares the exodus to creation. The nature myth in which the Lord cleaves the hostile sea monster, a tale shared with other Near Eastern cultures, is here transformed into a historical drama in which the Lord divides an inanimate sea and slays his enemies in it. *Dry ground,* an allusion to a version of the creation myth in which the Lord dries up the primeval sea (Ps 74.13–15; Isa 50.2; 51.10; Nah 1.4). **14.17** *Gain glory.* See note on 14.4. **14.19** *Angel,* a divine manifestation in the cloud and fire, *the LORD* in v. 24; see note on 3.4. *Army,* lit. "camp" here and in vv. 20, 24. **14.20** *It . . . it,* apparently the angel. The divine presence, glowing within the cloud, blocks the oncoming Egyptians; see note on 13.21; cf. Josh 24.7. *One . . . the other,* the Israelite and Egyptian camps. **14.21** See

note on 14.16. *Strong* anticipates *my strength* in 15.2. *East wind.* See 10.13. *Dry land,* different from the Hebrew term rendered *dry ground* in vv. 16, 22; used in Gen 7.22; Josh 3.17; 4.18. **14.23** The Hebrew defers *into the sea* to the verse's end. **14.24** *The LORD.* See note on 14.19. *Looked down.* The Lord's radiant face, no longer veiled by cloud, "panics" the Egyptians, who recognize him (v. 25). Mesopotamian kings boasted that the mere sight of their divine auras would terrify the enemy. **14.25** *Clogged,* lit. "removed" or "turned aside." Greek and other manuscript traditions read lit. "he bound," thus having the Lord mirror Pharaoh, who "binds" or "harnesses," preparing his chariot in v. 6 (see note on 14.6). *Difficulty,* lit. "heaviness"; in vv. 4, 17 the Lord says he will "prove heavy" for Pharaoh's army (see note on 14.4). *Fighting.* See note on 14.14. **14.27** *Normal depth,* lit. "full strength." *Egyptians.* This word, lit. "Egypt," which occurs twice mid-verse, is enclosed by *sea,* twice before and once after, as the Egyptians are enveloped by the water. **14.28** *Not one . . . remained,* an echo of the plagues (see note on 10.19). **14.29** *Walked.* The Hebrew syntax may be better understood as "had walked"; see v. 22, whose echo here frames the episode of drowning; the frame highlights Israel's salvation. **14.30** *Saved.* See note on 14.13. *From the Egyptians,* lit. "from Egypt's hand," contrasting with the Lord's marvelous "hand," rendered *work* in v.

the Egyptians; and Israel saw the Egyptians dead on the seashore. [31]Israel saw the great work that the LORD did against the Egyptians. So the people feared the LORD and believed in the LORD and in his servant Moses.

The Song of Moses

15 Then Moses and the Israelites sang this song to the LORD:
"I will sing to the LORD, for he has triumphed gloriously;
　horse and rider he has thrown into the sea.
2 　The LORD is my strength and my might,[a]
　　and he has become my salvation;
this is my God, and I will praise him,
　my father's God, and I will exalt him.
3 　The LORD is a warrior;
　　the LORD is his name.

4 　"Pharaoh's chariots and his army he cast into the sea;
　his picked officers were sunk in the Red Sea.[b]
5 　The floods covered them;
　　they went down into the depths like a stone.
6 　Your right hand, O LORD, glorious in power—

your right hand, O LORD, shattered the enemy.
7 　In the greatness of your majesty you overthrew your adversaries;
you sent out your fury, it consumed them like stubble.
8 　At the blast of your nostrils the waters piled up,
　the floods stood up in a heap;
　the deeps congealed in the heart of the sea.
9 　The enemy said, 'I will pursue, I will overtake,
　I will divide the spoil, my desire shall have its fill of them.
　I will draw my sword, my hand shall destroy them.'
10 　You blew with your wind, the sea covered them;
　they sank like lead in the mighty waters.

11 　"Who is like you, O LORD, among the gods?
　Who is like you, majestic in holiness,
　awesome in splendor, doing wonders?
12 　You stretched out your right hand,
　the earth swallowed them.

---

a Or *song*　*b* Or *Sea of Reeds*

---

31. **14.31** *The Egyptians,* lit. "Egypt," referring perhaps to the wonders the Lord performed there. *Believed.* See note on 4.1.
15.1–19 The song of Moses proper, vv. 1b–18, written in "high," archaic Hebrew verse, extensively using parallelism, expresses Israel's trust (14.31; cf. Ps 106.12). Although the song refers to the events related in ch. 14, it does not narrate them in sequence and the descriptions do not entirely match. **15.1** *Moses.* See note on 15.21. *Israelites.* Since the song is formulated in the first-person singular, perhaps Moses sings a line and the Israelites respond antiphonally. *I will sing,* or "let me sing." The Hebrew rendered *triumphed gloriously* is used elsewhere of the sea's excrescence (e.g., Ps 89.9) and of human arrogance (e.g., Isa 2.12); the basic sense is "to be high," a polar contrast to the Egyptians (see vv. 5, 10). *Horse.* Egyptian reliefs and paintings of the late second millennium BCE show horses pulling chariots but not being ridden. Biblical texts of the eighth century BCE (e.g., Isa 31.1) know of Egyptians traveling on horseback. *Rider,* lit. "its rider." *Thrown,* ironically homonymous with "high" in "high hand" (see note on 14.8). **15.2** *The LORD,* the short name "Yah," placed at the end of the clause in Hebrew, meaning that the Israelites declare that "Yah"—and no other—is their God; see v. 11. *Salvation.* See note on 14.13. *Praise,* lit. "enshrine." *My father's God.* Cf. 3.15–

16. *Exalt,* cognate to "high" in (see note on) 14.8. **15.3** *Warrior,* lit. "man of war," typical of a storm god (see notes on 9.23; 13.21); cf. Ps 24.8. *Name.* See 3.13–15; 6.3. **15.4** The language recalls 14.7. *Red Sea.* See note on 10.19. **15.5** This verse chronologically follows vv. 8–10. *Floods,* plural of "the deep" (Gen 1.2). **15.7** *Majesty;* in Hebrew cognate to *triumphed* (v. 1). The first clause of this verse forms the third line of the distinctively Canaanite "staircase" parallelism begun in v. 6; other "staircases" are vv. 11, 16b–17a. Staircases have a retarding, focusing effect. **15.8** The mobile is turned stationary. *Nostrils.* Cf. Ps 18.8; cf. also Ex 14.21; Deut 11.4. *Floods* denotes "flow," a different Hebrew term from that translated *floods* in v. 5. In Hebrew this clause alliterates. *Heap,* used nearly always of water; cf. *wall* in 14.22, 29. *Deeps,* rendered *floods* in v. 5. *The sea,* or "Sea," a name of the Canaanite sea god; see note on 14.16. **15.9** The first five Hebrew words (through *spoil*) alliterate. *Destroy,* lit. "dispossess," an intention at cross-purposes with the Lord's (see v. 17). **15.10** *Blew,* a rare verb in Hebrew. *Sank,* a different Hebrew verb from that translated *sunk* in v. 4, echoing *depths* in v. 5. *Lead.* Cf. *stone* in v. 5. *Mighty,* in Hebrew cognate to *glorious* in v. 6. **15.11** The second praise in direct address, also a "staircase" parallelism (see note on 15.7). *Gods.* See note on 12.12; cf. 2 Sam 7.22–23; Ps 86.8–10. *Majestic,* rendered *glorious* in v. 6, a repeti-

13 "In your steadfast love you led the people
   whom you redeemed;
   you guided them by your strength to
   your holy abode.
14 The peoples heard, they trembled;
   pangs seized the inhabitants of
   Philistia.
15 Then the chiefs of Edom were dismayed;
   trembling seized the leaders of Moab;
   all the inhabitants of Canaan melted
   away.
16 Terror and dread fell upon them;
   by the might of your arm, they became
   still as a stone
   until your people, O LORD, passed by,
   until the people whom you acquired
   passed by.
17 You brought them in and planted them
   on the mountain of your own
   possession,
   the place, O LORD, that you made your
   abode,
   the sanctuary, O LORD, that your hands
   have established.
18 The LORD will reign forever and ever."
19 When the horses of Pharaoh with his

chariots and his chariot drivers went into the
sea, the LORD brought back the waters of the
sea upon them; but the Israelites walked
through the sea on dry ground.

The Song of Miriam

20 Then the prophet Miriam, Aaron's sister,
took a tambourine in her hand; and all the
women went out after her with tambourines
and with dancing. 21 And Miriam sang to
them:
   "Sing to the LORD, for he has triumphed
   gloriously;
   horse and rider he has thrown into the
   sea."

Bitter Water Made Sweet

22 Then Moses ordered Israel to set out from
the Red Sea,ᵃ and they went into the wilderness of Shur. They went three days in the
wilderness and found no water. 23 When they
came to Marah, they could not drink the water
of Marah because it was bitter. That is why it
was called Marah.ᵇ 24 And the people com-

_____

a Or Sea of Reeds   b That is Bitterness

tion enhancing coherence. *In holiness*, or "among the
holy ones" (so too in Ps 68.17 and perhaps 16.24).
15.12 *Stretched*. See note on 14.16. *Right hand*. See v. 6.
Earth, probably connoting the netherworld (e.g., Eccl
3.21; Isa 14.12), whose *swallow* (Num 16.32) is figurative of burial; cf. Isa 5.14 and the voracious appetite of
the Canaanite death god Mot (Hab 2.5). **15.13** The
song turns to the Lord's guidance of Israel to its land,
using pastoral language: *led, abode* (lit. "pasture") as in
Ps 23.2–3. *Steadfast love*, used of covenantal as well as
personal devotion. *Redeemed*. See note on 6.6. *Strength*
recalls v. 2, lending coherence. *Abode*, in Hebrew cognate to *exalt* (v. 2), the land of Israel (see v. 17). **15.14–
16** Anachronistic anticipation of the reaction in the
east to the news of Egypt's destruction; cf. 18.1; Josh
2.9–11; but see note on 15.15. **15.14** *Philistia*. See note
on 13.17. **15.15** The widespread dread suggested here
(cf. Josh 9.9–10) is contradicted by the succeeding
narrative; neither the Edomites (Num 20.14–21), the
southern Canaanites (Num 21.1), nor the Amorites
(Num 21.21–23) are intimidated by Israel; Moab conspires with Midian to defeat Israel by magic (Num
22.2–7). The terminology *chiefs*, lit. "bulls," and *leaders*, lit. "rams," reflects ancient Canaanite usage.
15.16 Ps 105.38 attributes the same *dread* to the post-
plague Egyptians. *As a stone*. The simile's repetition
(see v. 5) links the second part of the song with the
first. The Israelites *passed by* the peoples situated en
route to Canaan (cf. Deut 29.16). *Acquired*. "Created"
is more in keeping with archaic usage (e.g., Gen 14.19,
22; Deut 32.6; Pss 74.2; 78.54; 139.13; Prov 8.22).

15.17 *Mountain of . . . possession*, an archaic expression
referring either anachronistically to Mount Zion or to
hilly Canaan (e.g., Deut 3.25). *Abode*, not the same Hebrew word as that rendered *abode* in v. 13 but cognate
to *established* here. *Sanctuary*, the Jerusalem temple or
a holy abode in general (cf. Ps 78.54). When Israel
takes possession, the land becomes Israel's holy (designated) place (Ps 114.2). **15.18** Proclaiming the deity
king is customary in Near Eastern creation myths; cf.,
e.g., Deut 33.5; Ps 29.10. **15.19** This verse recapitulates
and resumes the narrative in 14.27–29.

15.20 *Prophet*, Miriam, so called only here; cf. Num
12.1–9; see Mic 6.4. *Miriam*. See note on 2.4. *Aaron's
sister*. See note on 6.23; she conspires with Aaron in
Num 12. *Tambourine*. Archaeological finds depict a
hand drum without jingles. *Dancing*, a form of (not
only female) religious praise; e.g., 32.19; Judg 21.21;
2 Sam 6.5; Pss 149.3; 150.4. **15.21** The victory song
typically belongs to women (see Judg 11.34; 1 Sam
18.6–7); Miriam and her cohort may in an earlier tradition have initiated the song; note the exhortation
sing in contrast to "let me sing" in v. 1; but in the present context the women answer the men. **15.22–27** In
parallel episodes in Numbers, Israel is punished for its
complaints. **15.22** *Shur*, the site of an oasis (see Gen
16.7), located between the Negeb and Egypt (Gen
20.1). **15.23** *Marah*, often identified with Hawwarah,
the site of a bitter spring down the eastern coast of the
Gulf of Suez. Alternatively, a site along the heavily
saline Bitter Lakes. **15.24** *Complained*, the key verb in
virtually all the complaint episodes. **15.25** *Showed*, un-

plained against Moses, saying, "What shall we drink?" 25He cried out to the LORD; and the LORD showed him a piece of wood;*a* he threw it into the water, and the water became sweet.

There the LORD*b* made for them a statute and an ordinance and there he put them to the test. 26He said, "If you will listen carefully to the voice of the LORD your God, and do what is right in his sight, and give heed to his commandments and keep all his statutes, I will not bring upon you any of the diseases that I brought upon the Egyptians; for I am the LORD who heals you."

27 Then they came to Elim, where there were twelve springs of water and seventy palm trees; and they camped there by the water.

Bread from Heaven

16 The whole congregation of the Israelites set out from Elim; and Israel came to the wilderness of Sin, which is between Elim and Sinai, on the fifteenth day of the second month after they had departed from the land of Egypt. 2The whole congregation of the Israelites complained against Moses and Aaron in the wilderness. 3The Israelites said to them, "If only we had died by the hand of the LORD in the land of Egypt, when we sat by the fleshpots and ate our fill of bread; for you have brought us out into this wilderness to kill this whole assembly with hunger."

4 Then the LORD said to Moses, "I am going to rain bread from heaven for you, and each day the people shall go out and gather enough for that day. In that way I will test them, whether they will follow my instruction or not. 5On the sixth day, when they prepare what they bring in, it will be twice as much as they gather on other days." 6So Moses and Aaron said to all the Israelites, "In the evening you shall know that it was the LORD who brought you out of the land of Egypt, 7and in the morning you shall see the glory of the LORD, because he has heard your complaining against the LORD. For what are we, that you complain against us?" 8And Moses said, "When the LORD gives you meat to eat in the evening and your fill of bread in the morning, because the LORD has heard the complaining that you utter against him—what are we? Your complaining is not against us but against the LORD."

9 Then Moses said to Aaron, "Say to the whole congregation of the Israelites, 'Draw near to the LORD, for he has heard your complaining.' " 10And as Aaron spoke to the whole congregation of the Israelites, they looked toward the wilderness, and the glory of the LORD appeared in the cloud. 11The LORD spoke to Moses and said, 12"I have heard the complaining of the Israelites; say to them, 'At twilight you shall eat meat, and in the morning you shall have your fill of bread; then you shall know that I am the LORD your God.' "

---

a Or *a tree*   *b* Heb *he*

---

usual usage of "to instruct" ("teach" in Deut 33.10), punning on the soundalike "Marah" and on *statute . . . ordinance,* synonyms of the Hebrew cognate *torah,* "instruction." The reference of *statute . . . ordinance* is unclear; see 16.4. *He put them.* The Hebrew has the ambiguous "he put him to the test"; Israel may be testing God's reliability too (cf. 17.2). **15.26** *Diseases,* not necessarily the plagues; Egypt is also otherwise portrayed as a diseased land (e.g., Deut 7.15). *Heals,* used of purifying water in a similar miracle tale ("made . . . wholesome" in 2 Kings 2.21–22), making the analogy plain: I can cure you as I cured the water—if you obey me. **15.27** *Elim,* often identified with Wadi Gharandel, south of Hawwarah (see note on 15.23). The round numbers set a legendary tone.

16.1–36 In the parallel episode in Num 11, God produces the quails only after the manna fails to suffice. **16.1** *The whole . . . came,* lit. "They set out from Elim, and the whole congregation came," an irregular variant on the typical travel formula (see Num 33). *Sin,* of uncertain identification, similar to *Sinai. Second month.* They have traveled exactly one month (see 12.6, 17–18), and this is the seventh stop (see 12.37; 13.20; 14.9; 15.22, 23, 27) and the third complaint (see 14.11; 15.24). *Departed,* the theme word "exodus" (see note on 3.10). **16.2** *Aaron.* In 15.24 the people *complained* against Moses alone. *In the wilderness,* superfluous information, suggesting perhaps that the wilderness is a factor (see v. 3). **16.3** Cf. 14.11; Num 20.3–5. **16.4** *Rain.* Cf. the hail the Lord "rained down" on Egypt (rendered *cause . . . to fall* in 9.18). *Test.* Cf. 15.25–26; Deut 8.16. *Instruction,* Hebrew *torah;* see note on 15.25. **16.5** *Prepare,* in the sense of "set aside" (e.g., 23.20; Josh 4.3) or "measure" ("calculate" in Deut 19.3) as in v. 18. *Twice as much,* so that one portion can be saved for the sabbath, on which gathering is forbidden (Num 15.32–36); see vv. 22–30. **16.6–7** There is no mention of quail, as in v. 13. *Know.* See note on 5.2; cf. v. 12. *Glory,* the divine aura (e.g., v. 10; 24.16; 33.18–23; 40.34–35; see notes on 13.21; 14.24), lit. "heaviness" (see note on 4.10). *We,* an unusual Hebrew form, repeated in v. 8. **16.8** *Meat,* quail (v. 13). *Bread,* manna (vv. 13–15). **16.9** *To the LORD,* lit. "before the LORD," perhaps an anachronistic reference to the tabernacle; cf. vv. 33–34. **16.10** Cf. Num 16.42. **16.12** *Twilight* evokes Passover (12.6). *Know.* See v. 6; note on 5.2.

13 In the evening quails came up and covered the camp; and in the morning there was a layer of dew around the camp. 14When the layer of dew lifted, there on the surface of the wilderness was a fine flaky substance, as fine as frost on the ground. 15When the Israelites saw it, they said to one another, "What is it?"*a* For they did not know what it was. Moses said to them, "It is the bread that the LORD has given you to eat. 16This is what the LORD has commanded: 'Gather as much of it as each of you needs, an omer to a person according to the number of persons, all providing for those in their own tents.' " 17The Israelites did so, some gathering more, some less. 18But when they measured it with an omer, those who gathered much had nothing over, and those who gathered little had no shortage; they gathered as much as each of them needed. 19And Moses said to them, "Let no one leave any of it over until morning." 20But they did not listen to Moses; some left part of it until morning, and it bred worms and became foul. And Moses was angry with them. 21Morning by morning they gathered it, as much as each needed; but when the sun grew hot, it melted.

22 On the sixth day they gathered twice as much food, two omers apiece. When all the leaders of the congregation came and told Moses, 23he said to them, "This is what the LORD has commanded: 'Tomorrow is a day of solemn rest, a holy sabbath to the LORD; bake what you want to bake and boil what you want

to boil, and all that is left over put aside to be kept until morning.' " 24So they put it aside until morning, as Moses commanded them; and it did not become foul, and there were no worms in it. 25Moses said, "Eat it today, for today is a sabbath to the LORD; today you will not find it in the field. 26Six days you shall gather it; but on the seventh day, which is a sabbath, there will be none."

27 On the seventh day some of the people went out to gather, and they found none. 28The LORD said to Moses, "How long will you refuse to keep my commandments and instructions? 29See! The LORD has given you the sabbath, therefore on the sixth day he gives you food for two days; each of you stay where you are; do not leave your place on the seventh day." 30So the people rested on the seventh day.

31 The house of Israel called it manna; it was like coriander seed, white, and the taste of it was like wafers made with honey. 32Moses said, "This is what the LORD has commanded: 'Let an omer of it be kept throughout your generations, in order that they may see the food with which I fed you in the wilderness, when I brought you out of the land of Egypt.' " 33And Moses said to Aaron, "Take a jar, and put an omer of manna in it, and place it before the LORD, to be kept throughout your generations." 34As the LORD commanded Moses, so Aaron placed it before the cov-

a Or "It is manna" (Heb man hu, see verse 31)

16.13 Cf. Num 11.31–32. Quails migrate across the Red Sea to Europe in the spring, landing for rest at night. **16.14** *Lifted,* rendered *came up* in v. 13. *Flaky substance,* an unusual word in Hebrew, possibly related to "sherd" in Aramaic. **16.15** *What is it,* unusual dialectal language, a popular etymology of *manna* (v. 31). *What it was,* the Hebrew equivalent of *what it is.* **16.16** *Each of you,* lit. "(each) man"; apparently the head of each household collected for his family. *Needs,* in Hebrew "eats," another (see note on 16.11) evocation of the Passover (see note on 12.4). *Omer.* See v. 36. *A person,* lit. *a head* as in 38.26. *All,* lit. "(each) man." **16.18** *No shortage,* quoted in 2 Cor 8.15. *Needed,* lit. "eats"; each took the quantity appropriate to his family size. **16.19** *Leave . . . over,* another evocation of Passover (rendered *let . . . remain* in 12.10). **16.20** *Bred,* a unique Hebrew verb meaning "to crawl with," cognate to *worms* in v. 24. *Foul,* rendered *stank* in 7.21. *Was angry.* The root meaning is "to foam (at the mouth)." **16.21** *Each needed.* See note on 16.16. **16.22** *Twice as much.* See note on 16.5. *Leaders,* lit. the "elevated," tribal chiefs (Num 8). **16.23** *Commanded,* lit. "spoken," rendered "meant" in Lev 10.3, where it

likewise introduces an explanation of the mysterious. *Day of solemn rest,* lit., "a (time of) cessation (from work)," cognate to *sabbath* (*rested* in v. 30; Gen 2.2–3). Cooking is forbidden on the sabbath (cf. 35.3). *To be kept,* another evocation of the Passover (12.6). **16.24** See note on 16.20. **16.26** God, like Israel, ceases to labor on the sabbath (Gen 2.2–3); the formula anticipates 20.9–10. **16.27** *Some,* lit. "they." *You,* plural. *Instructions.* See v. 4. **16.29** *Stay . . . do not leave.* The positive-negative combination typifies laws contrary to natural inclination, e.g., Deut 9.7; 15.7–8, 12–13. Jewish law interprets this to prohibit travel on the sabbath. **16.31** *House of Israel,* a rare usage, elsewhere in Exodus only in 40.38, possibly evoking the Passover again (12.3–4, 27). *Manna.* See note on 16.15. *Coriander.* Cf. Num 11.7. *Made with,* or dipped in (the Hebrew is elliptical). *Honey.* See Num 11.7. **16.32** *An omer,* lit. "an omerful." See v. 16. *Be kept.* See note on 16.23; cf. the commemorative aspect of Passover (12.24–27). **16.33** *To Aaron* anticipates his priestly function; see note on 19.22. *Before the LORD.* See note on 16.9. **16.34** *Covenant,* the two stone tablets (25.16) or (metonymically) the ark (30.36), which would be

enant,[a] for safekeeping. 35The Israelites ate manna forty years, until they came to a habitable land; they ate manna, until they came to the border of the land of Canaan. 36An omer is a tenth of an ephah.

Water from the Rock

17 From the wilderness of Sin the whole congregation of the Israelites journeyed by stages, as the LORD commanded. They camped at Rephidim, but there was no water for the people to drink. 2The people quarreled with Moses, and said, "Give us water to drink." Moses said to them, "Why do you quarrel with me? Why do you test the LORD?" 3But the people thirsted there for water; and the people complained against Moses and said, "Why did you bring us out of Egypt, to kill us and our children and livestock with thirst?" 4So Moses cried out to the LORD, "What shall I do with this people? They are almost ready to stone me." 5The LORD said to Moses, "Go on ahead of the people, and take some of the elders of Israel with you; take in your hand the staff with which you struck the Nile, and go. 6I will be standing there in front of you on the rock at Horeb. Strike the rock, and water will come out of it, so that the people may drink." Moses did so, in the sight of the elders of Israel. 7He called the place Massah[b] and Meribah,[c] because the Israelites quarreled and tested the LORD, saying, "Is the LORD among us or not?"

Amalek Attacks Israel and Is Defeated

8 Then Amalek came and fought with Israel at Rephidim. 9Moses said to Joshua, "Choose some men for us and go out, fight with Amalek. Tomorrow I will stand on the top of the hill with the staff of God in my hand." 10So Joshua did as Moses told him, and fought with Amalek, while Moses, Aaron, and Hur went up to the top of the hill. 11Whenever Moses held up his hand, Israel prevailed; and whenever he lowered his hand, Amalek prevailed. 12But Moses' hands grew weary; so they took a stone and put it under him, and he sat on it. Aaron and Hur held up his hands, one on one side, and the other on the other side; so his hands

---

a Or *treaty* or *testimony*; Heb *eduth*   *b* That is *Test*   *c* That is *Quarrel*

---

anachronistic; but see note on 17.4–6. *For safekeeping,* rendered *to be kept* in vv. 23, 32. **16.35** A retrospective comment. *Canaan.* Cf. Josh 5.12. **16.36** An explanation called for by the fact that elsewhere in the Torah an *omer* is a sheaf of grain, not a measure, and that elsewhere a tenth of an ephah is an *issaron* (*one-tenth* in 29.40). An *ephah* is 22 liters.

17.1–7 Another version of the incident appears in Num 20.2–13. **17.1** *Stages,* journey stops; cf. Num 33.1. *There was no water . . . to drink.* Hebrew syntax favors "there was not (enough) water for the people to drink." **17.2** *Quarreled,* not *complained* (as in v. 3; see note on 15.24); the term is one root of the site's new compound name (v. 7; Num 20.3, 13). *Moses.* In 16.2; Num 20.2 Aaron too is addressed. *Test,* an echo of the two preceding episodes (15.25–26; 16.4) and root of the site's new name (v. 7), but not reflected in Num 20. The two verbs are arranged in parallel clauses (see note on 3.15). **17.3** See note on 16.3. Although some versions read *us . . . our,* the traditional Hebrew text has the more personal "me . . . my." **17.4** *Cried,* as in 14.15; 15.25. In contrast to Num 20.6, there is no shrine here at which to seek divine counsel. *Stone.* See 1 Sam 30.6. **17.5** *Struck the Nile,* and removed drinkable water from Egypt (7.21, 24). Num 20.8 lacks such a reference, perhaps on account of its magical aspect. **17.6** *I,* the Lord, visibly (see note on 13.21; see also Gen 18.22). *Horeb.* See note on 3.1. According to 19.1–2; Num 33.15, Sinai is the next journey stop. *Strike.* In Num 20.8 Moses and Aaron are to "command" the rock, making the same point that the Lord is responsi-

ble for the water but without manifesting the Lord's presence there physically. **17.7** *Massah and Meribah.* Only the latter name is used in Num 20.13. Deut 33.8–9 pairs the two names in reference to an opaque episode in which the Levites proved loyal to God in time of rebellion (cf. 32.25–28); *Massah* alone occurs in Deut 6.16; 9.22. A chiastic parallelism (*Test, Quarrel* [see text notes *b* and *c*], *quarrel, test*) closes the unit (see note on 3.22). *Among us.* See v. 6.

17.8–15 Typically, as in Assyrian annals and Xenophon's *Anabasis,* a raggedy group on march is attacked by marauders. In the light of the preceding episode, the unmotivated attack may be a fight over water rights; but cf. Deut 25.7–9; 1 Sam 30.1–20. **17.8** *Amalek,* an Edomite tribe (Gen 36.12), said to dwell in the Negeb (Num 13.29). *Rephidim.* See v. 1; note on 17.6. **17.9** *Joshua,* Moses' field commander, mentioned without his patronym, "son of Nun," as if he were already introduced; he is described elsewhere as Moses' young assistant (e.g., 33.11) and made his successor in Num 27. The name in Hebrew means "The LORD saves" (cf. Ex 2.17, which uses the same verb; see note on 2.17). *Staff.* See v. 5. **17.10** *Hur,* apparently a notable of the tribe of Judah, grandfather of the artisan Bezalel (31.2), paired here and in 24.14 with *Aaron,* who married Judean nobility (6.23); cf. note on 31.2. **17.11** The raised arms symbolize power and inspire morale. It is unclear whether Moses is holding up the staff (v. 9); cf. Josh 8.18–19. *Prevailed,* or "proved strong," unrelated to the term rendered "prevailed" in Gen 32.28. **17.12** *Weary,* lit. "heavy" (see

were steady until the sun set. ¹³And Joshua defeated Amalek and his people with the sword.

14 Then the LORD said to Moses, "Write this as a reminder in a book and recite it in the hearing of Joshua: I will utterly blot out the remembrance of Amalek from under heaven." ¹⁵And Moses built an altar and called it, The LORD is my banner. ¹⁶He said, "A hand upon the banner of the LORD!ᵃ The LORD will have war with Amalek from generation to generation."

Jethro's Advice

18 Jethro, the priest of Midian, Moses' father-in-law, heard of all that God had done for Moses and for his people Israel, how the LORD had brought Israel out of Egypt. ²After Moses had sent away his wife Zipporah, his father-in-law Jethro took her back, ³along with her two sons. The name of the one was Gershom (for he said, "I have been an alienᵇ in a foreign land"), ⁴and the name of the other, Eliezerᶜ (for he said, "The God of my father

was my help, and delivered me from the sword of Pharaoh"). ⁵Jethro, Moses' father-in-law, came into the wilderness where Moses was encamped at the mountain of God, bringing Moses' sons and wife to him. ⁶He sent word to Moses, "I, your father-in-law Jethro, am coming to you, with your wife and her two sons." ⁷Moses went out to meet his father-in-law; he bowed down and kissed him; each asked after the other's welfare, and they went into the tent. ⁸Then Moses told his father-in-law all that the LORD had done to Pharaoh and to the Egyptians for Israel's sake, all the hardship that had beset them on the way, and how the LORD had delivered them. ⁹Jethro rejoiced for all the good that the LORD had done to Israel, in delivering them from the Egyptians.

10 Jethro said, "Blessed be the LORD, who has delivered you from the Egyptians and from Pharaoh. ¹¹Now I know that the LORD is

a Cn: Meaning of Heb uncertain   *b* Heb *ger*   *c* Heb *Eli,* my God; *ezer,* help

---

note on 14.24). *Steady,* in Hebrew cognate to *believed* in 14.31. **17.13** *Defeated,* lit. "weakened," here antonymous to *steady* (v. 12); the Samaritan version adds "and smote." *Sword.* See 13.18. **17.14** *Reminder.* Cf. 16.32–33. *Book,* any document (see note on 17.16); this is the first text Moses is told to write. *Remembrance,* judging by curses typical of ancient royal inscriptions a reference to posterity as well to the name *Amalek;* cf. Deut 25.17–19. King Saul is ordered to obliterate the Amalekites (1 Sam 15.2–3), but fails (see 2 Sam 1.1–10; Esth 3.1). **17.15** *Altar,* for commemoration, not necessarily thanksgiving (e.g., Judg 6.24). *Banner,* a Hebrew term from a root similar to *test* (v. 2). **17.16** *Hand upon,* or "monument to" (e.g., 1 Sam 15.12), perhaps a stele on which he wrote the inscription. *Banner.* The translation assumes a scribal error; the Hebrew and ancient versions have "seat," referring perhaps to the stone on which Moses sat, hands raised (v. 12). The utterance is often understood as an oath gesture. *The LORD,* "Yah" (see note on 15.2). *Generation,* see Num 14.43–45; Judg 3.13; 6.3; 1 Sam 30.1–2.

18.1–27 Although Moses' establishment of a judicial system appears to precede the legislation that follows, v. 5 places it at what seems to be Sinai, where the Israelites are reported to arrive in 19.1–2. To the juxtaposition of the Midianite priest Jethro and the Amalekites here, cf. the conjunction of Midian and Amalek in Judg 6.3, 33; 7.12. The chapter is marked by uncommon usages of biblical language: *sent away* (v. 2), *rejoiced* (v. 9), *wear . . . out* (v. 18), *teach* (v. 20), *look for* (v. 21), and the forms of *them* (v. 20) and *decided* (v. 26); some linguistic features are shared by 20.22–23.33. **18.1** *Jethro.* See note on 2.18. *Heard.* Cf. 15.14; see note on 1.17. **18.2–4** A comment resolving the

contradiction between vv. 5–6 and (see note on) 4.20. **18.2** *Sent away,* in Deut 24.1 a term for divorce. **18.3** *Gershom.* See note on 2.22. **18.4** *Father.* See 3.6. *Help.* Cf. Gen 49.25. *Pharaoh.* See 2.15; 4.19. **18.5** *Bringing,* added in English to smooth the syntax; the verse reads lit. "Jethro, Moses' father-in-law, and his sons and his wife, came . . ." *Mountain of God.* See 3.1; note on 18.1–27. **18.6** *Sent word,* in Hebrew "said," but see v. 7. *With . . . sons.* In Hebrew the phrase sounds tacked on. **18.7** No reference is made here or below to Moses' wife and sons; cf. note on 4.20. Unlike Genesis, Exodus through Deuteronomy concerns the entire people and not families per se. *Bowed down and kissed.* Cf., e.g., Gen 33.4–7; 2 Sam 14.33. *Tent,* presumably Jethro's. **18.8** *Told,* as in 10.2 (*tell*). *Egyptians.* See note on 14.31. *For Israel's sake,* rather "about" (Gen 21.25) or "on account of" (Gen 21.11) "Israel." *Hardship,* in Hebrew cognate to *unable* (7.18), rendered "adversity" in Num 20.14. *On the way.* See 15.22–17.16. **18.9** *Good,* acts of good. *To,* for. *From the Egyptians,* lit. "from the hand of Egypt," somewhat echoing v. 4; see note on 18.10. **18.10** *Blessed be the LORD.* Cf. Gen 14.20; see note on 1.17. *Delivered,* the verb used in vv. 4, 8–9, not the one translated "delivered" in Gen 14.20. *From . . . Pharaoh,* lit. "from the hand of Egypt and from the hand of Pharaoh," echoing (see note on) 14.30. **18.11** *I know.* Cf. 5.2. *Gods.* See note on 15.11. *From the Egyptians,* lit. "from under the hand of Egypt," an idiom for overturning foreign rule (e.g., 2 Kings 8.20; 13.5). The transposed clause (see text note *a*) may well belong in v. 10: Jethro celebrates the divine deliverance expansively. *Dealt arrogantly with,* or "acted with malice against," or "acted with malice against" (see, e.g., 1.10), in Hebrew cognate to *willfully attacks* in 21.14 and alluded to in Neh 9.10.

greater than all gods, because he delivered the people from the Egyptians,ᵃ when they dealt arrogantly with them." 12And Jethro, Moses' father-in-law, brought a burnt offering and sacrifices to God; and Aaron came with all the elders of Israel to eat bread with Moses' father-in-law in the presence of God.

13 The next day Moses sat as judge for the people, while the people stood around him from morning until evening. 14When Moses' father-in-law saw all that he was doing for the people, he said, "What is this that you are doing for the people? Why do you sit alone, while all the people stand around you from morning until evening?" 15Moses said to his father-in-law, "Because the people come to me to inquire of God. 16When they have a dispute, they come to me and I decide between one person and another, and I make known to them the statutes and instructions of God." 17Moses' father-in-law said to him, "What you are doing is not good. 18You will surely wear yourself out, both you and these people with you. For the task is too heavy for you; you cannot do it alone. 19Now listen to me. I will give you counsel, and God be with you! You should represent the people before God, and you should bring their cases before God; 20teach them the statutes and instructions and make known to them the way they are to go and the things they are to do. 21You should also look for able men among all the people, men who fear God, are trustworthy, and hate dishonest gain; set such men over them as officers over thousands, hundreds, fifties, and tens. 22Let them sit as judges for the people at all times; let them bring every important case to you, but decide every minor case themselves. So it will be easier for you, and they will bear the burden with you. 23If you do this, and God so commands you, then you will be able to endure, and all these people will go to their home in peace."

24 So Moses listened to his father-in-law and did all that he had said. 25Moses chose able men from all Israel and appointed them as heads over the people, as officers over thousands, hundreds, fifties, and tens. 26And they judged the people at all times; hard cases they brought to Moses, but any minor case they decided themselves. 27Then Moses let his father-in-law depart, and he went off to his own country.

ᵃ The clause *because . . . Egyptians* has been transposed from verse 10

18.12 *Burnt offering,* one wholly incinerated on an altar (20.24). *Sacrifices.* See note on 10.25. *Bread,* in the sense of "food" (Lev 3.11). The homage ritual often entails a meal shared by the deity and worshiper (e.g., 24.11; 32.6) just as ancient pacts were often so sealed (e.g., Gen 26.30). *In the presence of God,* in front of the mountain (v. 5). **18.13–16** Moses legislates ad hoc, case by case, in advance of the code that will issue from the Sinai revelation (chs. 20–23). **18.13** *Sat,* according to ancient custom (e.g., Judg 4.5), illustrated already in Ugaritic epic (mid-second millennium BCE). **18.14** *This,* Hebrew "this thing (lit. word)," a pun on *dispute* (v. 16). **18.15** *To inquire of God,* to seek an oracle (cf., e.g., Gen 25.22; see notes on 4.14; 4.15–16; 4.18–20); used of seeking prophetic oracles (e.g., 1 Sam 9.9; 2 Kings 8.8; Ezek 20.1) and later of scriptural exegesis (Ezra 7.10). **18.16** *Dispute,* a legal case (v. 19), lit. "a word." *They come,* in Hebrew "he (the people, v. 15) comes" or "it (the case) comes"; 22.9 favors the latter. *Person,* lit. "man"; it is unclear whether a woman could personally initiate or appear in a litigation. *Another,* lit. "his fellow." *Instructions.* See note on 16.4. The Hebrew cognate verb is used of priestly "instruction" or "teaching" (e.g., Deut 17.10; 33.10). **18.17–23** In Deut 1.9–18 Moses credits himself with setting up the judicial system. **18.17** *What,* Hebrew "the thing" (see note on 18.14). **18.18** *Wear . . . out,* the less common form of the Hebrew verbal root, punning on the verbs "to be foolhardy" (e.g., Deut 32.6; 1 Sam 25.25) and "to con-

found" (e.g., Gen 11.7, 9). *Task,* lit. "thing" (see note on 18.14). *Alone,* the same word rendered "all by myself" in Deut 1.12. **18.19** *Counsel.* See Num 10.29–32. *God,* the oracle (see note on 18.15), punning in Hebrew on *God be with you. Cases,* another pun (see note on 18.16) since an oracle "speaks" (see notes on 4.14; 4.15–16). Typically (cf. Abigail, 1 Sam 25.2, 25) Jethro's wisdom is demonstrated by his wit. **18.20** *Teach* connotes illumining and admonishing. *The way.* Israel's actual way in the wilderness is attributed to Jethro's eyes (Num 10.31). *Things,* lit. "acts." **18.21** Cf. Deut 1.13. *You should also,* or "You yourself." *Look for,* and find (cf. the use of "see," rendered "provide" in Gen 22.8; 1 Sam 16.1), elsewhere "to prophesy" and therefore perhaps another pun (see note on 18.19). *Able.* Other nuances are "worthy" (1 Kings 1.42) and "valiant" (1 Sam 14.52). *Dishonest gain.* Cf. 23.6–8. *Officers,* elsewhere used militarily; the judicial levels and divisions seem artificial. **18.22** *Sit as judges,* lit. "judge," but see vv. 13–14. *You.* Under the monarchy the king acts as chief judge (e.g., 2 Sam 15.2; 1 Kings 3.16–28). *Decide,* "judge." *Easier,* lit. "lighter," the antithesis of *heavy* (v. 18). **18.23** *This.* See note on 18.14. *And God so commands you,* or "when the oracle directs you." *Endure,* lit. "stand," punning perhaps on *sat/sit* (vv. 13–14). *Home,* lit. "place." **18.24** *Listened.* See v. 19. **18.26** *Brought . . . decided,* "would bring . . . would judge" (see note on 18.22). **18.27** *Let . . . depart,* the same Hebrew verb rendered *let . . . go* in the liberation formula (see note on 3.19).

The Israelites Reach Mount Sinai

19 On the third new moon after the Israelites had gone out of the land of Egypt, on that very day, they came into the wilderness of Sinai. ²They had journeyed from Rephidim, entered the wilderness of Sinai, and camped in the wilderness; Israel camped there in front of the mountain. ³Then Moses went up to God; the LORD called to him from the mountain, saying, "Thus you shall say to the house of Jacob, and tell the Israelites: ⁴You have seen what I did to the Egyptians, and how I bore you on eagles' wings and brought you to myself. ⁵Now therefore, if you obey my voice and keep my covenant, you shall be my treasured possession out of all the peoples. Indeed, the whole earth is mine, ⁶but you shall be for me a priestly kingdom and a holy nation. These are the words that you shall speak to the Israelites."

7 So Moses came, summoned the elders of the people, and set before them all these words that the LORD had commanded him. ⁸The people all answered as one: "Everything that the LORD has spoken we will do." Moses reported the words of the people to the LORD. ⁹Then the LORD said to Moses, "I am going to come to you in a dense cloud, in order that the people may hear when I speak with you and so trust you ever after."

The People Consecrated

When Moses had told the words of the people to the LORD, ¹⁰the LORD said to Moses: "Go to the people and consecrate them today and tomorrow. Have them wash their clothes ¹¹and prepare for the third day, because on the third day the LORD will come down upon Mount Sinai in the sight of all the people. ¹²You shall set limits for the people all around, saying, 'Be careful not to go up the mountain or to touch the edge of it. Any who touch the mountain shall be put to death. ¹³No hand shall touch them, but they shall be stoned or shot with arrows;ᵃ whether animal or human being, they shall not live.' When the trumpet sounds a long blast, they may go up on the mountain." ¹⁴So Moses went down from the mountain to the people. He consecrated the people, and

a Heb lacks *with arrows*

19.1–24.18 The Sinai revelation, in which context the Ten Commandments (34.28) and the Book of the Covenant (24.7) are presented, is comprised of several units beginning with 19.1–9. The arrangement of diverse sections seems to conclude at 24.18. The laws are surrounded by a covenant framework (19.3–6; 24.1–14) to which the people commit themselves (19.7–25; 24.3–8). Israel remains encamped at Sinai until Num 10.11–12 (second year, second month, twentieth day). Moses' repeated trips up and down the mountain together with his exclusive admission to the divine presence (cf. 3.5) strengthen his image as divine mediator. **19.1** The *Sinai* Peninsula contains a large mountainous center; several peaks have been proposed for Mount Sinai, and one in the south-central peninsula (e.g., Jebel Musa, Jebel Serbal) would be most consistent with earlier locations on the route (see 15.23, 27). On the chronology, see Introduction; note on 18.1–27. **19.2** *Had journeyed.* The Hebrew means only "journeyed"; v. 2 chronologically precedes v. 1, making v. 1 look like an overview. **19.3** *Then Moses went.* Hebrew syntax favors "Moses had gone." It is unclear in what manifestation the Lord addresses Moses; he is said to descend onto the mountain only on the *third day* (vv. 16–20). *Thus . . . Israelites,* expressed in parallelism (see note on 3.15). **19.4** *You have seen,* a motif phrase unifying the larger passage (see 20.22; 20.18, where *witnessed* is lit. "seen"); in Deut 4.12, 15 the aural experience is favored. *Eagles' wings.* Cf. Deut 32.11. **19.5** *Treasured.* For the literal root of the

metaphor see 1 Chr 29.3; cf. Deut 7.6; 14.2; 26.18–19; Ps 135.4. *Indeed,* or "because"; the Lord has the right to covenant with any people he wants; see Deut 10.14–15. **19.6** *But,* not expressed in Hebrew. *Priestly.* Israel, exposed to the divine presence at Sinai, is meant to maintain a degree of holiness higher than that of other nations just as priests observe more stringent purity rules than other Israelites; see v. 10. Isa 61.6 uses a similar metaphor of restored Judah, and 1 Pet 2.5, 9; Rev 1.6 apply it to the Christian community. **19.7** *Elders.* Cf., e.g., 3.16; 4.29; 12.21. Typically the Torah does not report that the elders fulfill the mediating function. **19.9** *Hear,* that the Lord speaks directly to Moses; the people do not seem to discern the words themselves; see 20.18–21; cf. Deut 4.10, 12; 5.22; see note on 19.25. *Trust.* Cf. 14.31. *When . . . had,* not expressed in Hebrew. Syntactically the phrase, "Moses told the words . . . to the LORD," which seems to duplicate v. 8b, may belong to what precedes rather than to what follows. **19.10** *Consecrate,* by rituals of purification and avoidance of defilement (see v. 15); the people must be in a priestly state for the divine encounter (cf. 28.41); cf., e.g., 1 Sam 16.5. *Clothes.* See Num 8.21. **19.11** *Third day.* Priests undergo a seven-day rite (29.35). *Sight.* See note on 19.4. **19.12** *Limits,* physical boundaries (Deut 20.14). *Edge,* even the edge. **19.13** *No hand shall touch* lest the executioner become contaminated or transgress the limit. *Stoned or shot,* from outside the limit. Vv. 22, 24 describe direct extermination by God, whose holy presence will tolerate no

they washed their clothes. 15And he said to the people, "Prepare for the third day; do not go near a woman."

16 On the morning of the third day there was thunder and lightning, as well as a thick cloud on the mountain, and a blast of a trumpet so loud that all the people who were in the camp trembled. 17Moses brought the people out of the camp to meet God. They took their stand at the foot of the mountain. 18Now Mount Sinai was wrapped in smoke, because the LORD had descended upon it in fire; the smoke went up like the smoke of a kiln, while the whole mountain shook violently. 19As the blast of the trumpet grew louder and louder, Moses would speak and God would answer him in thunder. 20When the LORD descended upon Mount Sinai, to the top of the mountain, the LORD summoned Moses to the top of the mountain, and Moses went up. 21Then the LORD said to Moses, "Go down and warn the people not to break through to the LORD to look; otherwise many of them will perish. 22Even the priests who approach the LORD must consecrate themselves or the LORD will break out against them." 23Moses said to the LORD, "The people are not permitted to come

up to Mount Sinai; for you yourself warned us, saying, 'Set limits around the mountain and keep it holy.' " 24The LORD said to him, "Go down, and come up bringing Aaron with you; but do not let either the priests or the people break through to come up to the LORD; otherwise he will break out against them." 25So Moses went down to the people and told them.

The Ten Commandments

20 Then God spoke all these words: 2 I am the LORD your God, who brought you out of the land of Egypt, out of the house of slavery; 3you shall have no other gods before*a* me.

4 You shall not make for yourself an idol, whether in the form of anything that is in heaven above, or that is on the earth beneath, or that is in the water under the earth. 5You shall not bow down to them or worship them; for I the LORD your God am a jealous God, punishing children for the iniquity of parents, to the third and the fourth generation of those who reject me, 6but showing steadfast love to

_____
a Or besides

contact with the impure, even impure animals. *Trumpet,* ram's horn, used for signaling (Josh 6.5). **19.15** *The third day,* lit. "three days." *Do not go near a woman.* The sexual act ritually defiled one for a day (Deut 23.10–11); cf. 1 Sam 21.4; only adult males are addressed. **19.16–24** The Lord (Yahweh) is described in the conventional imagery of a Canaanite storm god, as in ch. 15 and Pss 18; 29; 68. **19.16** *Morning,* more precisely "daybreak." *Thick,* lit. "heavy." *Trumpet,* the more common term, not the one so translated in v. 13. The storm god is a warrior (see 15.3), and the trumpet signals battle (Num 10.9); cf. Zech 9.14. *So . . . that,* not in the Hebrew. **19.18** *Wrapped in smoke,* lit. "all smoking." *Shook,* the same Hebrew term rendered *trembled* in v. 16. In Ugaritic epic and Pss 18.7; 68.8 the earth quakes at the storm god's appearance. **19.19** *Thunder,* different in form from *thunder* in v. 16, more probably "(human) voice" (see 33.11; 1 Sam 3.4–8). **19.20** *When,* not in the Hebrew, added because v. 18 already reports the Lord's descent; but *The* LORD *summoned . . . Moses went up* seems prior to v. 19. **19.21** *To look,* at odds with 20.18–21; Deut 5.5, 25–27. *Otherwise,* lit. "and (as a result)." *Perish,* lit. "fall" (32.28) through a divine outburst (see vv. 22, 24; 2 Sam 6.6–8). **19.22** *Priests,* anachronistic since the priests are not yet commissioned (Lev 8–9). *Break out,* not the Hebrew word for *break through* in vv. 21, 24, but the root rendered *break out* in v. 24 and "burst forth" in 2 Sam 6.8; see note on 19.13. The divine presence neutralizes any encroachment; cf. also Lev 10.1–5.

19.23 *Limits.* See note on 19.12. **19.24** A repetition of vv. 21–22, adding an order to *bring Aaron,* vaguely anticipating 24.1. *Break out.* See note on 19.22. **19.25** *Told them,* rather "said to them," apparently governing 20.1–17. Moses seems to relate the laws to the people (see note on 19.9).

20.1–17 The Decalogue comprises a core of ten rules (lit. *words,* 34.28), essentially prohibitions, addressed to the individual, with no penalties and few details spelled out. Nine of the rules appear variously elsewhere in the Torah, and the core Decalogue is elaborated differently in Deut 5.6–21. Prophets hold Israel accountable for the rules (e.g., Jer 7.9; 29.23; Ezek 18.5–18; 22.6–12; Hos 4.2), and psalms allude to them (e.g., Pss 50.16–19; 81.9–10); see also Mk 10.19; Lk 18.20; Rom 13.9. The severity of the commandments is such that violation of most of them is elsewhere said to be punishable by death. The Decalogue may have served as a creed, as it did later in Judaism and Christianity. The text of the Decalogue will be inscribed by God (31.18; 32.16) and placed in the ark of the covenant (Deut 10.1–5; cf. Ex 25.16, 22). **20.2** A prologue. **20.3** The first rule; cf. 23.24; 34.14; Deut 6.13. *Gods.* See note on 12.12. **20.4–6** Cf. v. 23; 34.17; Lev 19.4; 26.1; Deut 4.15–20. **20.4** *Water under the earth,* the subterranean ocean (e.g., Gen 49.25; Ps 24.2). For the division heaven-earth-water, cf. Gen 1. The tabernacle's iconography depicts creatures not of this world; see note on 25.18. **20.5** *Worship.* See note on 4.22–23. *Jealous.* The Hebrew term also connotes zeal (e.g.,

the thousandth generation[a] of those who love me and keep my commandments.

7 You shall not make wrongful use of the name of the LORD your God, for the LORD will not acquit anyone who misuses his name.

8 Remember the sabbath day, and keep it holy. 9Six days you shall labor and do all your work. 10But the seventh day is a sabbath to the LORD your God; you shall not do any work— you, your son or your daughter, your male or female slave, your livestock, or the alien resident in your towns. 11For in six days the LORD made heaven and earth, the sea, and all that is in them, but rested the seventh day; therefore the LORD blessed the sabbath day and consecrated it.

12 Honor your father and your mother, so that your days may be long in the land that the LORD your God is giving you.

13 You shall not murder.[b]

14 You shall not commit adultery.

15 You shall not steal.

16 You shall not bear false witness against your neighbor.

17 You shall not covet your neighbor's house; you shall not covet your neighbor's wife, or male or female slave, or ox, or donkey, or anything that belongs to your neighbor.

18 When all the people witnessed the thunder and lightning, the sound of the trumpet, and the mountain smoking, they were afraid[c] and trembled and stood at a distance, 19and said to Moses, "You speak to us, and we will listen; but do not let God speak to us, or we will die." 20Moses said to the people, "Do not be afraid; for God has come only to test you and to put the fear of him upon you so that you do not sin." 21Then the people stood at a distance, while Moses drew near to the thick darkness where God was.

---

a Or to thousands   b Or kill   c Sam Gk Syr Vg: MT they saw

Num 25.11); cf. Deut 4.24; 6.15. *Punishing . . . parents,* lit. "accounting the sins of the fathers to the sons" (cf. 34.7); that God punishes vicariously is denied by Jer 31.29–30; Ezek 18. In contrast to other ancient Near Eastern legislation, vicarious punishment is prohibited in criminal matters (Deut 24.16); but see Josh 7.24; 2 Kings 9.26. *Reject,* lit. "hate." **20.6** *Steadfast love.* See note on 15.13; see also Deut 7.9. *Thousandth generation.* See Deut 7.9. **20.7** *Make wrongful use,* particularly in an oath (Lev 6.3; 19.12; Ps 24.4), in which the deity's name is typically invoked (Deut 6.13; 10.20; cf., e.g., Gen 14.22; 24.3). *Acquit,* rendered *clear . . . the guilty* in 34.7. *Misuses,* the same Hebrew term rendered *make wrongful use of.* For a thematic link between this commandment and the preceding two, see 23.13. **20.8–11** Cf. 23.12; 31.12–17; 34.21; 35.1–3; Lev 23.3; Jer 17.19–27. **20.8** *Remember.* See note on 2.24; in Deut 5.12, "observe" (or "keep"). *Sabbath.* See note on 16.23. Mesopotamians sought to avoid evil spirits on the seventh, fourteenth, twenty-first, and twenty-eighth days of the (lunar) month; the Torah's proscriptions of fire and work/movement outdoors on the sabbath are consonant with an original motive to avoid danger. *Keep . . . holy,* "hallow" in Gen 2.3 and *consecrate* in v. 11; by observing the sabbath one does what God does. **20.10** Major textual versions add "on it" after *do. Livestock.* Deut 5.14 adds here "or your ox or your donkey" and at the end "so that your . . . slave may rest as well as you" in accordance with the motive there. *Alien resident.* See Introduction. *Towns,* lit. "city gates," a locution characteristic of Deut (e.g., 12.12, 18). **20.11** *Therefore.* Cf. Gen 2.3; Ex 23.12; Deut 5.15. **20.12** Cf. Lev 19.3; Prov 19.26; 28.24; elsewhere this commandment is formulated as a prohibition (Ex 21.15, 17; Lev 20.9; Deut 27.16; and see Deut 21.18–21); for linking the positive and negative formulations,

see Mt 15.4. Honoring parents serves as a metaphor for the covenant between God and Israel (e.g., Deut 32.16–21; Isa 1.2; Mal 1.6). *Long,* an expression characteristic of Deuteronomy (e.g., 4.40; 22.6–7). **20.13** *Murder.* Cf. 21.12; Lev 24.17; Num 35.30–34; Deut 19.11–13; see Gen 9.5–6. **20.14** Since men may be polygamous, adultery is intercourse between a married woman and any man but her husband; cf. Lev 18.20; 20.10; Deut 22.22; also cf. Num 5.11–31. For adultery as a metaphor for apostasy, see, e.g., Hos 1–3; Mal 2.13–16. In some versions this commandment precedes v. 13. **20.15** Cf. 22.1–12; Lev 19.11. *Steal,* possibly referring to kidnapping (21.16; Deut 24.7; cf. Gen 40.15). **20.16** Witnesses not only testify but bring charges (e.g., Deut 19.15–19; 1 Kings 21.13). Cf. Ex 23.1; Num 35.30; Deut 19.16–21; Prov 6.19; 14.5, 25; 19.5, 9. **20.17** *Covet,* to the point of theft (see 34.24; Deut 7.25; Josh 7.21; Mic 2.2; cf. 2 Sam 11; 1 Kings 21, although the term *covet* is not employed there). *House,* household, including the wife, whom Deut 5.21 separates as an individual. **20.18–21** A different perspective from that of 19.16–23; cf. Deut 5.5, 22–27. The passage serves to incorporate the succeeding laws into the Sinai revelation. **20.18** *Witnessed.* See note on 19.4. The paradoxical "seeing" *the thunder* lends mystique to the revelation. *Lightning,* lit. "torches," not the Hebrew term so translated in 19.16. *Trembled,* different from the term used in 19.16, but the same as the term translated "shook" in Isa 7.2. **20.19** *And we will listen,* rather "so that we may listen/hear." *Or we will die,* "lest we die"; cf. Deut 4.33; 5.23–26. **20.20** *Test.* Cf. 16.4; Judg 2.22–23. **20.21** *Thick darkness,* or "fog" (e.g., Ps 18.10), synonymous with *cloud* (19.9, 16). References to Moses' approach to God here and in 24.2, where *come near* is the same as *drew near* here, frame the corpus of law that follows.

The Law concerning the Altar

22 The LORD said to Moses: Thus you shall say to the Israelites: "You have seen for yourselves that I spoke with you from heaven. 23 You shall not make gods of silver alongside me, nor shall you make for yourselves gods of gold. 24 You need make for me only an altar of earth and sacrifice on it your burnt offerings and your offerings of well-being, your sheep and your oxen; in every place where I cause my name to be remembered I will come to you and bless you. 25 But if you make for me an altar of stone, do not build it of hewn stones; for if you use a chisel upon it you profane it. 26 You shall not go up by steps to my altar, so that your nakedness may not be exposed on it."

The Law concerning Slaves

21 These are the ordinances that you shall set before them:

2 When you buy a male Hebrew slave, he shall serve six years, but in the seventh he shall go out a free person, without debt. 3 If he comes in single, he shall go out single; if he comes in married, then his wife shall go out with him. 4 If his master gives him a wife and she bears him sons or daughters, the wife and her children shall be her master's and he shall go out alone. 5 But if the slave declares, "I love my master, my wife, and my children; I will not go out a free person," 6 then his master shall bring him before God.[a] He shall be brought to the door or the doorpost; and his master shall pierce his ear with an awl; and he shall serve him for life.

7 When a man sells his daughter as a slave, she shall not go out as the male slaves do. 8 If she does not please her master, who designated her for himself, then he shall let her be redeemed; he shall have no right to sell her to a

_____

a Or to the judges

20.22–23.33 The so-called Book of the Covenant (see 24.7) is generally regarded as the oldest legislation in the Bible, dating perhaps to premonarchical times. Parallels to Mesopotamian law abound, and subsequent biblical texts may be taken to repeat and revise the law found here. Sections of ritual and civil/criminal law alternate. The archaic language has some features in common with ch. 18 (see note on 18.1–27). 20.22–26 The laws of worship elaborate the second commandment (vv. 4–6), adding positive injunctions to the commandment's prohibitions. 20.22 Seen, a link to the preceding section (see note on 19.4). With you, in tension with 20.18–21 (see note there). 20.23 Silver... gold is an ancient and common word pair in parallelism (see note on 3.15). 20.24 Altar of earth. Such a primitive altar was found at Mari, a northwest Mesopotamian city of the eighteenth century BCE with a West Semitic population; see 2 Kings 5.17; cf. 27.1–8; 1 Kings 8.64. Sacrifice. See note on 3.18. Burnt offerings. See note on 18.12. Well-being, or "goodwill," for propitiation; cf. Lev 3.1–16; 7.11–18. Every place. Many local altars are implied; cf., e.g., Judg 6.24; 1 Sam 14.35; contrast Deut 12.5–14, which is taken to originate centuries later. On the altar God is remembered (see note on 17.15) or invoked (as in 23.13; see note on 3.15). 20.25 Stone. See Deut 27.5–6; Josh 8.30–31; 1 Kings 18.31–32; 1 Macc 4.47; cf. Judg 13.19; 1 Sam 6.14; 1 Kings 1.9. Early Israelite religion favors the natural; cf. note on 12.8; cf. 27.1–8. Use, in a sweeping motion. Chisel, a cutting tool (or weapon) specified as iron in Deut 27.5; Josh 8.31. Metal tools taint the sanctuary (1 Kings 6.7). 20.26 Steps. Cf. Ezek 43.17; the eighth-century BCE altar at Dan too was reached by steps. Nakedness. Cf. 28.42. It is implied that sacrificers—who are not necessarily priests—wear full-length garments, like God (Isa 6.1); cf. 28.42. Cultic practices had no sex-

ual aspect in Israelite religion; accordingly, women did not serve in the cult, to avoid the aspect of a sexual relationship to the Lord, who is conceived as male.

21.1–22.17 Civil and criminal laws mostly formulated casuistically ("When/if . . . then . . .") in the fashion of other ancient Near Eastern collections. 21.2–11 Laws involving slavery, a prominent theme of the exodus (see Introduction) and in the prologue to the Decalogue (20.2). 21.1 These, "And these"; the succeeding laws are attached to the foregoing. 21.2 Buy. The law is seller-oriented; Lev 25.39 and Deut 15.12 focus on the slave. Male. Deut 15.12–17 treats the female as an individual. Seventh. Cf. Lev 25.40. Without debt, "gratis" ("for nothing" in Gen 29.15); see v. 11; note on 3.21. 21.3 Married, lit. "master of a woman." The provisions in vv. 3–5 are irrelevant to Deut 15.12–17 (see note on 21.2). 21.5 Master. Cf. Deut 15.16. 21.6 God, the household gods, an oracle (see note on 4.15–16), or the local shrine; omitted in Deut 15.17. Door, of the master's house. Pierce his ear. The wound disappears, but the blood on the doorpost signifies the permanent attachment of the person to the household. For life. Slavery of Israelites is a vocation, taken on to repay debts (see v. 7; 22.3; Lev 25.39; 2 Kings 4.1; Neh 5.4–5); foreign slaves are permanent (Lev 25.44–46). 21.7 Daughter. The Code of Hammurabi sets a three-year term on family members sold to repay a debt. Israelite sons, who could also be sold (see note on 21.6), seem to go free after six years (v. 2) since the present law deals only with the contingencies of selling a daughter. No such situation is treated in Deut 15.12–17. Lev 25.41 treats indentured children the same as parents. Slave, a term designating a woman often purchased for concubinage ("slave woman" in Gen 21.10–13; Judg 9.18; 19.19, where the translation omits "slave" before "woman"). 21.8 Designated her, as a con-

foreign people, since he has dealt unfairly with her. ⁹If he designates her for his son, he shall deal with her as with a daughter. ¹⁰If he takes another wife to himself, he shall not diminish the food, clothing, or marital rights of the first wife.ᵃ ¹¹And if he does not do these three things for her, she shall go out without debt, without payment of money.

The Law concerning Violence

12 Whoever strikes a person mortally shall be put to death. ¹³If it was not premeditated, but came about by an act of God, then I will appoint for you a place to which the killer may flee. ¹⁴But if someone willfully attacks and kills another by treachery, you shall take the killer from my altar for execution.

15 Whoever strikes father or mother shall be put to death.

16 Whoever kidnaps a person, whether that person has been sold or is still held in possession, shall be put to death.

17 Whoever curses father or mother shall be put to death.

18 When individuals quarrel and one strikes the other with a stone or fist so that the injured party, though not dead, is confined to bed, ¹⁹but recovers and walks around outside with the help of a staff, then the assailant shall be free of liability, except to pay for the loss of time, and to arrange for full recovery.

20 When a slaveowner strikes a male or female slave with a rod and the slave dies immediately, the owner shall be punished. ²¹But if the slave survives a day or two, there is no punishment; for the slave is the owner's property.

22 When people who are fighting injure a pregnant woman so that there is a miscarriage, and yet no further harm follows, the one responsible shall be fined what the woman's husband demands, paying as much as the judges determine. ²³If any harm follows, then you shall give life for life, ²⁴eye for eye, tooth for tooth, hand for hand, foot for foot, ²⁵burn for burn, wound for wound, stripe for stripe.

26 When a slaveowner strikes the eye of a

_____

a Heb *of her*

cubine (see note on 21.7); cf. Lev 19.20. *Foreign people,* or "another clan" than hers (taking *people* in its archaic sense); redemption is the clan's duty (see Ruth 3.13, where "act as next-of-kin" translates the verb elsewhere rendered "redeem," and Ezek 11.15, where Hebrew "people of your redemption" denotes kin; cf. Lev 25.25). *Dealt unfairly,* rather "broken faith" (e.g., Jer 3.20), reneged. **21.9** *As with a daughter,* more precisely "according to the rule of (free) daughters." **21.10–11** These verses resume the situation of v. 8. **21.10** *Wife.* The Hebrew has "another (female)," probably a concubine. *Food,* lit. "meat." *Marital rights,* the traditional conjugal understanding. Etymology and Islamic parallels favor "lodging"; Mesopotamian parallels favor "(cosmetic) oil" (cf. Hos 2.8). **21.11** *Without debt.* See note on 21.2.

21.12–17 Capital crimes corresponding to rules on murder, honoring parents, and theft in the Decalogue (20.12–15; see notes there). **21.12** *Put to death,* by the "avenger of blood" (Num 35.19, 21; Deut 19.12; 2 Sam 14.11). Hittite laws (see note on 3.8) provide for compensation. **21.13** *Not premeditated,* lit. "If he did not lie in ambush"; cf. Num 35.20. Num 35.11, 15; Deut 19.4 are less graphic. *Act of God.* For illustrations, see Num 35.22–23; Deut 19.5. *A place,* elaborated as the six cities of refuge (Num 35.9–28; Deut 19.1–13; Josh 20). **21.14** *Willfully attacks.* See note on 18.11. *Altar.* See 1 Kings 1.50–53; 2.28–34. The altar, like the cities of refuge (see note on 21.13), apparently protects accidental slayers. **21.15** *Strikes,* less than fatally (cf. v. 12). The Code of Hammurabi prescribes cutting off the hand. **21.16** *Kidnaps,* the same Hebrew term rendered *steal* in 20.15. *Person.* Deut 24.7 and ancient transla-

tions of the present verse indicate that an Israelite is meant. *Sold,* as a slave (e.g., Gen 37.27–28, 36; Joel 3.6). *Death,* the punishment also in the Code of Hammurabi; Hittite laws (see note on 3.8) penalize economically. **21.17** *Curses,* rejects the authority of or denounces (cf. 2 Sam 16.5–8), in Hebrew cognate to "dishonors" (Deut 27.16); cf. Lev 20.9; Deut 21.18–21; Prov 20.20. Various ancient Near Eastern laws punish rejection of parents with disinheritance or enslavement.

21.18–27 A resumption of the topic of vv. 12–14, treating less than fatal "striking" of persons by persons. **21.18** *Injured party,* supplied for clarity. *Not dead.* If death is caused, the culprit presumably seeks asylum (v. 13); other ancient Near Eastern codes fix a fine. *Is confined,* lit. "falls." **21.19** *But,* lit. "if he." *Recovers,* lit. "gets up." *To pay,* lit. "he must pay." *Loss of time,* unemployment compensation. *Recovery,* lit. "healing." **21.20** *Slaveowner,* lit. "a man," but a woman too might abuse her slave (e.g., Gen 16.6). *A . . . slave,* "his (own) . . . slave." *Punished,* lit. "avenged," by the victim's kin or another party (see Num 35.16–19). **21.21** *Survives,* lit. "stands." *Property.* Owners have the right to discipline a slave through beating, so long as they stop short of manslaughter. **21.22** *Harm,* to the woman. *Demands,* rendered *imposes* in v. 30. Vv. 12–14 do not apply because the fetus is legally not a person. **21.23** *Life for life,* life of the perpetrator for the life of the woman. The Code of Hammurabi requires the life of the perpetrator's daughter; biblical law opposes vicarious punishment (see note on 20.5). **21.24** *Eye.* Cf. Lev 24.19–21; Deut 19.21. Unlike other ancient Near Eastern codes, biblical law puts no price on limbs as it puts none on

male or female slave, destroying it, the owner shall let the slave go, a free person, to compensate for the eye. ²⁷If the owner knocks out a tooth of a male or female slave, the slave shall be let go, a free person, to compensate for the tooth.

Laws concerning Property

28 When an ox gores a man or a woman to death, the ox shall be stoned, and its flesh shall not be eaten; but the owner of the ox shall not be liable. ²⁹If the ox has been accustomed to gore in the past, and its owner has been warned but has not restrained it, and it kills a man or a woman, the ox shall be stoned, and its owner also shall be put to death. ³⁰If a ransom is imposed on the owner, then the owner shall pay whatever is imposed for the redemption of the victim's life. ³¹If it gores a boy or a girl, the owner shall be dealt with according to this same rule. ³²If the ox gores a male or female slave, the owner shall pay to the slaveowner thirty shekels of silver, and the ox shall be stoned.

33 If someone leaves a pit open, or digs a pit and does not cover it, and an ox or a donkey falls into it, ³⁴the owner of the pit shall make restitution, giving money to its owner, but keeping the dead animal.

35 If someone's ox hurts the ox of another, so that it dies, then they shall sell the live ox and divide the price of it; and the dead animal they shall also divide. ³⁶But if it was known that the ox was accustomed to gore in the past, and its owner has not restrained it, the owner shall restore ox for ox, but keep the dead animal.

Laws of Restitution

22 ᵃ When someone steals an ox or a sheep, and slaughters it or sells it, the thief shall pay five oxen for an ox, and four sheep for a sheep. ᵇ The thief shall make restitution, but if unable to do so, shall be sold for the theft. ⁴When the animal, whether ox or donkey or sheep, is found alive in the thief's possession, the thief shall pay double.

2ᶜ If a thief is found breaking in, and is beaten to death, no bloodguilt is incurred; ³but if it happens after sunrise, bloodguilt is incurred.

5 When someone causes a field or vineyard to be grazed over, or lets livestock loose to graze in someone else's field, restitution shall be made from the best in the owner's field or vineyard.

6 When fire breaks out and catches in thorns so that the stacked grain or the standing grain or the field is consumed, the one who started the fire shall make full restitution.

7 When someone delivers to a neighbor money or goods for safekeeping, and they are stolen from the neighbor's house, then the thief, if caught, shall pay double. ⁸If the thief is

---

a Ch 21.37 in Heb   *b* Verses 2, 3, and 4 rearranged thus: 3b, 4, 2, 3a   *c* Ch 22.1 in Heb

---

life (Num 35.31). **21.26** *Slaveowner.* See note on 21.20. *A . . . slave,* "his (own) . . . slave." *Free person.* Cf. v. 2. Ancient Near Eastern codes generally penalize economically. **21.28–36** Personal injuries caused by animals or negligence. **21.28** *Stoned.* See Gen 9.5. *Not be eaten,* because the animal is not properly slaughtered (22.31; Lev 17; Deut 12.15–16) and/or because it is polluted by bloodguilt (cf. Deut 21.1–9). **21.29** *Death,* in theory (see v. 30); the Code of Hammurabi imposes a fine and in no case has the animal killed. **21.30** *Ransom.* Compensation is allowed, contra Num 35.31, because this is not premeditated murder. *Imposed,* by the victim's kin. **21.31** *A boy or a girl,* lit. "a son . . . or a daughter." Vicarious punishment (see note on 21.23) is ruled out; in the Code of Hammurabi if a builder's faulty work kills a citizen's child, his own child is executed. **21.32** *Thirty.* Cf. Gen 37.28. **21.34** *Keeping,* for its hide and for food if Lev 17.15; Deut 14.21 do not yet hold. **21.35** *Divide,* lit. "halve." **21.36** *If it was known,* "If he (the owner) was informed." *Restore,* "pay." *Keep.* See note on 21.34.
22.1 *Oxen,* any "large cattle." *Five . . . and four,* ten

and six in Hittite laws (see note on 3.8); cf 2 Sam 12.6. *Sheep,* any "small cattle." *Make restitution,* "pay" restitution plus the fine. *Unable to do so,* lit. "he doesn't have it." *Sold.* See note on 21.6. Hammurabi's laws would have the insolvent thief executed. **22.4** *Double,* restitution plus fine; cf. vv. 7, 9. **22.2** *Breaking in.* The Hebrew root means "to dig"; "digging" is figurative for "in the act"; cf. Job 24.16. *Is beaten to death,* rather "is struck and dies." *Bloodguilt,* "blood" (plural) criminally spilled; cf. Gen 4.10. *Incurred.* Mesopotamian, Greek, and Roman law similarly allow for defense against thieves. **22.3** *After sunrise,* lit. "the sun shone on him"; the thief is caught sometime after the crime, which is typically perpetrated at night (see Job 24.14–17). *Bloodguilt is incurred,* because the slaying is premeditated. **22.5** *Restitution . . . vineyard,* or "(the perpetrator) shall pay the best (highest potential yield) of (the owner's) field or vineyard." **22.6** *Thorns,* used to hedge a field (Sir 28.24), removed to this day by burning. *Started the fire,* in Hebrew plays on *causes . . . to be grazed* (v. 5); it is a case of negligence. *Restitution,* according to the principle in v. 5. **22.7–15** On the safekeeping and use of another's property. **22.7** *Goods,* "uten-

not caught, the owner of the house shall be brought before God,[a] to determine whether or not the owner had laid hands on the neighbor's goods.

9 In any case of disputed ownership involving ox, donkey, sheep, clothing, or any other loss, of which one party says, "This is mine," the case of both parties shall come before God;[a] the one whom God condemns[b] shall pay double to the other.

10 When someone delivers to another a donkey, ox, sheep, or any other animal for safekeeping, and it dies or is injured or is carried off, without anyone seeing it, [11]an oath before the Lord shall decide between the two of them that the one has not laid hands on the property of the other; the owner shall accept the oath, and no restitution shall be made. [12]But if it was stolen, restitution shall be made to its owner. [13]If it was mangled by beasts, let it be brought as evidence; restitution shall not be made for the mangled remains.

14 When someone borrows an animal from another and it is injured or dies, the owner not being present, full restitution shall be made. [15]If the owner was present, there shall be no restitution; if it was hired, only the hiring fee is due.

Social and Religious Laws

16 When a man seduces a virgin who is not engaged to be married, and lies with her, he shall give the bride-price for her and make her his wife. [17]But if her father refuses to give her to him, he shall pay an amount equal to the bride-price for virgins.

18 You shall not permit a female sorcerer to live.

19 Whoever lies with an animal shall be put to death.

20 Whoever sacrifices to any god, other than the Lord alone, shall be devoted to destruction.

21 You shall not wrong or oppress a resident alien, for you were aliens in the land of Egypt. [22]You shall not abuse any widow or orphan. [23]If you do abuse them, when they cry out to me, I will surely heed their cry; [24]my wrath will burn, and I will kill you with the sword, and your wives shall become widows and your children orphans.

25 If you lend money to my people, to the poor among you, you shall not deal with them as a creditor; you shall not exact interest from

a Or *before the judges*   *b* Or *the judges condemn*

---

sils." *Double,* as in v. 4. **22.8** *Be brought,* rather "approach." *God,* an oracle (see note on 21.6). *To determine,* not in the Hebrew; rather, the householder swears (the words rendered *whether or not* are an oath formula) "he did not lay a hand . . ." *Goods,* meaning *property* as in v. 11, not *goods* as in v. 7. **22.9** *God.* See note on 22.8; cf. 1 Kings 8.31–32. *Condemns,* or "declares to be in the wrong" (as in Deut 25.1). *Double,* as in v. 4. The Code of Hammurabi condemns the culprit to death. **22.10** *Carried off.* Cf. Job 1.14–17. **22.11** *Before the Lord,* or "(taking) the Lord's (name)" (see note on 21.6); cf. 1 Kings 2.43. *That,* the oath formula (see note on 22.8), taken by the safekeeper. *No restitution shall be made,* "(one) does not pay" restitution plus fine (see v. 9). **22.12** *Restitution shall be made,* because the safekeeper's negligence, spelled out in Hammurabi's laws, is assumed. **22.13** *Evidence.* Cf. 1 Sam 17.34–35; Am 3.12. *Restitution . . . remains.* In Gen 31.39 Jacob goes beyond the law. **22.14** *An animal,* not in the Hebrew; any borrowed property may be meant. *Injured,* "broken," referring to an animal or object. **22.15** *If the owner was present.* The owner could have prevented a mishap as well as the borrower. *It,* the object or animal. *The hiring fee is due* because the renter paid for a sound implement or animal. **22.16** *A virgin,* a young woman. *Is not,* more precisely "has never been." *Bride-price.* Cf. Gen 24.12; 1 Sam 18.25. Deut 22.29 specifies 50 shekels. Cf. Deut 22.23–27 (rape).

22.17 *If her father refuses.* Deut 22.29 excludes the circumstance so that the girl's marriage is guaranteed. *For virgins.* Cf. the legal principle implied in (see note on) 22.5. **22.18–22** These laws are formulated apodictically (*you shall/shall not*) like the Ten Commandments. **22.18** *Female sorcerer,* from the Hebrew for "to cast a spell," singled out perhaps for her popularity (cf. 1 Sam 28; Ezek 13.17–23); for the popularity of sorcery generally, see, e.g., 2 Kings 23.24; Isa 3.2–3. The Torah abominates any form of divine manipulation other than a direct approach to the Lord; cf. Lev 19.26, 31; 20.6, 27; Deut 18.9–14. **22.19** Cf. Lev 18.23; 20.15–16; Deut 27.21. **22.20** *Devoted* to destruction, placed under ban; see Deut 13.12–17; cf. Lev 27.28–29; Josh 6.21; 7; Judg 21.5–11; 1 Sam 15.1–9. **22.21** *Oppress.* See 3.9; cf. 23.9. *Aliens.* See Introduction. **22.22** *Abuse.* See 1.11–12. *Orphan.* Protecting the "fatherless," along with the indigent *widow,* is an express duty of ancient Near Eastern monarchs as well as the Lord (e.g., Deut 10.18; Ps 68.5); cf., e.g., Deut 24.17; Isa 1.17; Jer 7.6; 22.3; Zech 7.10. **22.23** *Cry.* See 3.7. **22.24** *Sword,* in war (cf. Isa 9.11–17). *Wives.* Men are addressed (see note on 19.15). The grim poetic justice underscores the idea that Israel was liberated for the purpose of establishing a just society. **22.25** *People,* Israel. Cf. Lev 25.36–37; Deut 23.19–20; Ps 15.5; Prov 28.8; Ezek 18.8, 13, 17. **22.26–27** Cf. Deut 24.6, 10–13; Ezek 18.12, 16; 33.15. **22.26** *Cloak.* Cf. Am 2.8. An Israelite letter from the

them. 26If you take your neighbor's cloak in pawn, you shall restore it before the sun goes down; 27for it may be your neighbor's only clothing to use as cover; in what else shall that person sleep? And if your neighbor cries out to me, I will listen, for I am compassionate.

28 You shall not revile God, or curse a leader of your people.

29 You shall not delay to make offerings from the fullness of your harvest and from the outflow of your presses. *a*

The firstborn of your sons you shall give to me. 30You shall do the same with your oxen and with your sheep: seven days it shall remain with its mother; on the eighth day you shall give it to me.

31 You shall be people consecrated to me; therefore you shall not eat any meat that is mangled by beasts in the field; you shall throw it to the dogs.

Justice for All

23 You shall not spread a false report. You shall not join hands with the wicked to act as a malicious witness. 2You shall not follow a majority in wrongdoing; when you bear witness in a lawsuit, you shall not side with the majority so as to pervert justice; 3nor shall you be partial to the poor in a lawsuit.

4 When you come upon your enemy's ox or donkey going astray, you shall bring it back.

5 When you see the donkey of one who hates you lying under its burden and you would hold back from setting it free, you must help to set it free. *a*

6 You shall not pervert the justice due to your poor in their lawsuits. 7Keep far from a false charge, and do not kill the innocent and those in the right, for I will not acquit the guilty. 8You shall take no bribe, for a bribe blinds the officials, and subverts the cause of those who are in the right.

9 You shall not oppress a resident alien; you know the heart of an alien, for you were aliens in the land of Egypt.

Sabbatical Year and Sabbath

10 For six years you shall sow your land and gather in its yield; 11but the seventh year you shall let it rest and lie fallow, so that the poor of your people may eat; and what they leave the wild animals may eat. You shall do the same with your vineyard, and with your olive orchard.

12 Six days you shall do your work, but on the seventh day you shall rest, so that your ox and your donkey may have relief, and your homeborn slave and the resident alien may be refreshed. 13Be attentive to all that I have said to you. Do not invoke the names of other gods; do not let them be heard on your lips.

The Annual Festivals

14 Three times in the year you shall hold a festival for me. 15You shall observe the festival of

_____
a Meaning of Heb uncertain

seventh century BCE complains that a laborer's garment was seized for unsatisfactory work. **22.27** *For ... cover,* lit. "for it is his only covering, it is his cloak for his skin." Cf. Job 22.6; 24.7. *Compassionate* anticipates 34.6 (rendered *gracious* there). **22.28** *Revile,* rather "curse," as in Lev 24.11–16, 23; cf. 1 Kings 21.13; Job 2.9–10; Isa 8.21. *Leader.* See note on 16.22; cf. 2 Sam 16.5–13. Quoted in Acts 23.5. **22.29** *Offerings,* added in translation, inferred from such passages as Num 18.11–12, 26–30; Deut 26.1–15; the juxtaposition with the firstborn law suggests first fruits (23.19) are meant, but tithes (Num 18.21–32; Deut 14.22–29) too may be intended. *Firstborn.* See note on 13.1–2. **22.30** *On the eighth day,* following a seven-day period for overcoming the ritual pollution that accompanies birth (Lev 12.2–3); see Lev 22.27; cf. Ex 29.35–37. **22.31** *Consecrated,* or "who are holy," as in Lev 19.2, a similar context. *Mangled.* See note on 21.28.

23.1–3 Laws addressed to potential witnesses. **23.1** *False.* Cf. (and see note on) 20.16; Lev 19.16; Deut 5.20. *Malicious.* See Pss 27.12; 35.11. The penalty would seem to be as in Deut 19.18–19 (and in the Code of Hammurabi). **23.3** *Partial.* See Deut 16.19. *To the poor,* in light of Lev 19.15; Deut 1.17, and esp. v. 6 below, "(even) to the poor," for whom sympathy is natural (for the style see v. 4). **23.4** *Your enemy's,* "(even) your enemy's" (see note on 23.3), anyone's; cf. Deut 22.1–3. On overcoming hatred, cf. Lev 19.17–18. **23.5** *One who hates,* a poetic synonym of *enemy* (e.g., Ps 21.8). *Setting it free,* or "unloading it"; cf. Deut 22.4, where loading or "lifting up," a more demanding activity, is called for. **23.6–9** These verses resume vv. 1–3 and address judges. **23.6** See note on 23.3; cf. Ps 82.3–4; Isa 10.2; Jer 5.28; Am 2.6–7; 5.12. **23.7** *False charge.* Cf. v. 1. *Kill,* by erroneous condemnation; cf. Ps 94.6–7. *Acquit,* "declare in the right" (as in Deut 25.1); cf. Ex 34.7. **23.8** See Deut 1.17; 16.19; 27.25; cf. Ps 26.9–10; Prov 17.23; Isa 1.23; 5.23; Ezek 22.12; Mic 3.11. **23.9** See 22.21; Introduction. **23.10–11** Cf. the cultic emphasis of Lev 25.1–7, 20–22 and the socioeconomic emphasis of Deut 15. **23.12** *Refreshed,* like the Lord after creation (31.17). See note on 20.8–11; cf. the motive in 23.11; Deut 5.14–15. **23.13** *Invoke* may be taken to elaborate 20.3; cf. Josh 23.7; Hos 2.17; Zech 13.2. The repetitive, impressionistic style called "parallelism" brings the section to closure. **23.14–17** On the

unleavened bread; as I commanded you, you shall eat unleavened bread for seven days at the appointed time in the month of Abib, for in it you came out of Egypt.

No one shall appear before me empty-handed.

16 You shall observe the festival of harvest, of the first fruits of your labor, of what you sow in the field. You shall observe the festival of ingathering at the end of the year, when you gather in from the field the fruit of your labor. [17]Three times in the year all your males shall appear before the Lord GoD.

18 You shall not offer the blood of my sacrifice with anything leavened, or let the fat of my festival remain until the morning.

19 The choicest of the first fruits of your ground you shall bring into the house of the LORD your God.

You shall not boil a kid in its mother's milk.

The Conquest of Canaan Promised

20 I am going to send an angel in front of you, to guard you on the way and to bring you to the place that I have prepared. [21]Be attentive to him and listen to his voice; do not rebel against him, for he will not pardon your transgression; for my name is in him.

22 But if you listen attentively to his voice and do all that I say, then I will be an enemy to your enemies and a foe to your foes.

23 When my angel goes in front of you, and brings you to the Amorites, the Hittites, the Perizzites, the Canaanites, the Hivites, and the Jebusites, and I blot them out, [24]you shall not bow down to their gods, or worship them, or follow their practices, but you shall utterly demolish them and break their pillars in pieces. [25]You shall worship the LORD your God, and I[a] will bless your bread and your water; and I will take sickness away from among you. [26]No one shall miscarry or be barren in your land; I will fulfill the number of your days. [27]I will send my terror in front of you, and will throw into confusion all the people against whom you shall come, and I will make all your enemies

***

a Gk Vg: Heb *he*

calendar, see note on 12.2. **23.14** *Hold a festival.* See note on 5.1. **23.15** *Commanded.* See 12.14–20; 13.3–10. The Passover offering, a home ritual (see 12.1–11), is not mentioned here (see note on 12.1–28). *Abib.* See note on 12.2. *Appear before me,* lit. "see my face," an idiom meaning "to worship," devolving from the practice of seeing a god's image in a shrine (e.g., Ps 42.2; Isa 1.12). *Empty-handed.* See note on 3.21. **23.16** *Festival of harvest,* the Festival of Weeks (34.22; Num 28.26; Deut 16.10; cf. Lev 23.15), so named for its timing seven weeks after Passover (Lev 23.15; Deut 16.9). *First fruits.* The first produce of each crop, like human and animal firstborn (see note on 13.1–2), is rendered to God; cf. v. 19. Deut 26.1–11 does not connect first fruits with a particular festival. The crop is elsewhere described as *wheat* (34.22), "new grain" (Lev 23.16; Num 28.26), and "standing grain" (Deut 16.9). *Festival of ingathering,* the Festival of Booths (Lev 23.34; Deut 16.13). The Priestly traditions reflected in Lev 23.34; Num 29.12 date it to the fifteenth day of the seventh month. *Fruit of your labor.* See Deut 16.13. **23.17** *Males.* See note on 10.11. *Appear before,* "see the face of" (see note on 23.15). *Lord,* rendered *master* in 21.4–6, implying the Israelites are the Lord's servants (Lev 25.55). GoD, the name Yahweh, elsewhere rendered LORD. **23.18** *Leavened,* in light of 34.25; Deut 16.3–4, an addendum to v. 15. *Fat,* the hard, inedible coating of the entrails, burned into smoke (e.g., 29.12; Lev 3.5) and savored by God, signifying acceptance (e.g., Gen 8.21; Lev 26.31). *Until the morning.* See note on 12.10. **23.19** *Choicest,* rendered *best* in 34.26; an addendum to v. 16. The amount depends on individual ability (Deut 16.17). *House,* a temple such as that at Shiloh

(Judg 18.31; 1 Sam 1.17) or Jerusalem (1 Kings 8.10). *You shall not . . . milk.* Mixing death with a life fluid is ritually polluting (cf. loss of blood or semen from a reproductive organ, Lev 12; 15). The context here and in 34.26 is opaque, but in Deut 14.21 the law occurs among eating regulations.

23.20–33 Biblical law is presented through the analogy of ancient Near Eastern treaty conditions that an overlord (the Lord) imposes on a vassal (Israel). Such treaties conclude with curses to befall the vassal should it disobey. Blessings and curses conclude legislation in Lev 26; Deut 28. Here they are intermixed with commands because the legislation does not end but resumes with cultic law. The passage is elaborated in Deut 7.12–26. **23.20** *Angel.* Cf. 14.19; see Josh 5.13–15; Judg 2.1–5. **23.21** *Name,* a concretization of the deity; e.g., Deut 12.5, 11; Pss 20.1; 54.1. **23.22** *Foe,* Hebrew *tsar,* perhaps a play on "Egypt" (*mitsrayim*). Cf. Lev 26.7–8; Deut 28.7. The last two clauses are parallel (see note on 3.15). **23.23** *Jebusites.* Cf. 3.17; Josh 3.10; 24.11. *Blot . . . out,* as Pharaoh has been (the same Hebrew verb rendered *cut off* in 9.15). **23.24** *Bow down . . . worship.* Cf. 20.5; Deut 28.14. *Pillars,* steles, representing deities, on which libations are poured, well attested archaeologically in Canaan; cf. 34.13; Deut 12.3. Israelite pillars are eventually forbidden (Lev 26.1; Deut 16.22; 2 Kings 18.4; 23.14). **23.25** *Bread.* Cf. Lev 26.5, 26. *Sickness,* such as God brought upon Egypt (the same Hebrew word translated *diseases* in 15.26); cf. Lev 26.16; Deut 28.21–22, 58–61. **23.26** Cf. Lev 26.9; Deut 28.4, 11; also cf. Lev 26.22 ("bereave" is the same Hebrew verb as *miscarry* here); Deut 28.18, 63. **23.27** *Terror.* Cf. 15.14–16; see note on 14.24. *Throw*

turn their backs to you. 28 And I will send the pestilence*a* in front of you, which shall drive out the Hivites, the Canaanites, and the Hittites from before you. 29 I will not drive them out from before you in one year, or the land would become desolate and the wild animals would multiply against you. 30 Little by little I will drive them out from before you, until you have increased and possess the land. 31 I will set your borders from the Red Sea*b* to the sea of the Philistines, and from the wilderness to the Euphrates; for I will hand over to you the inhabitants of the land, and you shall drive them out before you. 32 You shall make no covenant with them and their gods. 33 They shall not live in your land, or they will make you sin against me; for if you worship their gods, it will surely be a snare to you.

The Blood of the Covenant

24 Then he said to Moses, "Come up to the LORD, you and Aaron, Nadab, and Abihu, and seventy of the elders of Israel, and worship at a distance. 2 Moses alone shall come near the LORD; but the others shall not come near, and the people shall not come up with him."

3 Moses came and told the people all the words of the LORD and all the ordinances; and all the people answered with one voice, and said, "All the words that the LORD has spoken we will do." 4 And Moses wrote down all the words of the LORD. He rose early in the morning, and built an altar at the foot of the mountain, and set up twelve pillars, corresponding to the twelve tribes of Israel. 5 He sent young men of the people of Israel, who offered burnt offerings and sacrificed oxen as offerings of well-being to the LORD. 6 Moses took half of the blood and put it in basins, and half of the blood he dashed against the altar. 7 Then he took the book of the covenant, and read it in the hearing of the people; and they said, "All that the LORD has spoken we will do, and we will be obedient." 8 Moses took the blood and dashed it on the people, and said, "See the blood of the covenant that the LORD has made with you in accordance with all these words."

On the Mountain with God

9 Then Moses and Aaron, Nadab, and Abihu, and seventy of the elders of Israel went up, 10 and they saw the God of Israel. Under his

a Or *hornets*: Meaning of Heb uncertain *b* Or *Sea of Reeds*

---

into confusion, as the Lord has done to Egypt (14.24, where *threw . . . into panic* is the same verb); cf. Josh 10.10; also cf. Lev 26.36–37; Deut 28.20, 28–29. *Turn their backs,* as Israel must do when it is punished (Josh 7.8, 12); cf. Lev 26.7–8; Deut 28.7; 28.25. **23.28** *Pestilence,* Hebrew *tsir'ah,* personified angel of destruction as in v. 20 and like "the destroyer" of (see note on) 12.13; in Hebrew it echoes *foe* in v. 22; cf. Deut 7.20; Josh 24.12. *Hivites . . . Hittites,* a list abridged from v. 23. **23.29** *In one year,* as in Josh 10–11, but gradually as in Josh 13; Judg 1. *Wild animals.* Cf. Lev 26.22; Lam 5.18. **23.30** *Increased,* as you began to do in Egypt (1.7, 12). *Possess,* inherit (e.g., Josh 14.1); cf. Josh 13.6–7. **23.31** *Sea of the Philistines,* the Mediterranean ("Western Sea" in Deut 11.24; "Great Sea" in Josh 1.4). *Wilderness,* the Negeb (cf. Deut 11.24; Josh 1.4). *Euphrates,* lit. "the river" (see Deut 11.24). Cf. the extent of Solomon's kingdom (1 Kings 4.21). **23.32–33** These verses are elaborated in 34.11–16; cf. Josh 23.12–13; Judg 2.2–3; and note the Gibeonites' trick in Josh 9. **23.33** *A snare,* eventually leading to disaster; cf. Judg 8.27; 1 Sam 18.21.

24.1–8 Ritual ratification of the covenant (cf. note on 19.1–9), an apparent but imprecise sequel to 19.24 (see 20.21). **24.1** *To Moses.* Cf. the address to all Israel (20.22). *To the LORD.* The Lord refers to himself in the third person as in 19.24. *Nadab, and Abihu.* Cf. 6.23. *Seventy,* a full complement (cf. 1.5). Cf. Num 11.16–17, 24–25. *Elders.* Cf. 19.7. *Worship,* lit. "bow down." *At a distance.* Cf. 20.18, 21. **24.3** *Came,* presumably prior to fulfilling the command in vv. 1–2; see note on 24.9–11. *Ordinances,* in 20.23–23.19. *Do.* Cf. v. 7; 19.8; see note on 19.1–9. The repetition of *all* suggests completion. **24.4** *Wrote down.* Cf. 17.14. The *book* (v. 7), presumably parchment since stone is not specified (as in v. 12; 31.18), may be understood to be deposited in the ark (25.16, 21) as was customary with treaty documents. *Pillars,* as witnesses (Gen 31.44–48; Josh 24.26–27); cf. note on 23.24. **24.5** *Young men,* acting as cultic assistants prior to the establishment of the hereditary priesthood (cf. 1 Sam 2.11–18). *Oxen,* rather "bulls"; the term occurs at the end of the sentence in the Hebrew, meaning that both types of offering consist of bulls. *Well-being.* See note on 20.24. The people eat the flesh of this offering (see Lev 3) so that both parties partake. **24.6** The Hebrew term translated *basins* here is never used of implements in priestly practices. *Altar,* the Lord's surrogate in the ceremony. **24.7** *Read it.* Cf. Deut 31.9–13; 2 Kings 23.1–3; Neh 8.1–8. *Be obedient,* rendered *listen* in 20.19. **24.8** *People,* or the pillars (v. 4) as their surrogates. Dashing blood, elsewhere an instrument of purification and atonement, on the two parties signifies somehow that the onus is on both; cf. Heb 9.18–22. There is a possible parallel in a periodic ceremony at Emar, in eastern Syria, in the mid-second millennium BCE. **24.9–11** A

feet there was something like a pavement of sapphire stone, like the very heaven for clearness. [11]God[a] did not lay his hand on the chief men of the people of Israel; also they beheld God, and they ate and drank.

12 The LORD said to Moses, "Come up to me on the mountain, and wait there; and I will give you the tablets of stone, with the law and the commandment, which I have written for their instruction." [13]So Moses set out with his assistant Joshua, and Moses went up into the mountain of God. [14]To the elders he had said, "Wait here for us, until we come to you again; for Aaron and Hur are with you; whoever has a dispute may go to them."

15 Then Moses went up on the mountain, and the cloud covered the mountain. [16]The glory of the LORD settled on Mount Sinai, and the cloud covered it for six days; on the seventh day he called to Moses out of the cloud. [17]Now the appearance of the glory of the LORD was like a devouring fire on the top of the mountain in the sight of the people of Israel. [18]Moses entered the cloud, and went up on the mountain. Moses was on the mountain for forty days and forty nights.

Offerings for the Tabernacle

25 The LORD said to Moses: [2]Tell the Israelites to take for me an offering; from all whose hearts prompt them to give you shall receive the offering for me. [3]This is the offering that you shall receive from them: gold, silver, and bronze, [4]blue, purple, and crimson yarns and fine linen, goats' hair, [5]tanned rams' skins, fine leather,[b] acacia wood, [6]oil for the lamps, spices for the anointing oil and for the fragrant incense, [7]onyx stones and gems to be set in the ephod and for the breastpiece. [8]And have them make me a sanctuary, so that I may dwell among them. [9]In accordance with all that I show you concerning the pattern of the tabernacle and of all its furniture, so you shall make it.

The Ark of the Covenant

10 They shall make an ark of acacia wood; it shall be two and a half cubits long, a cubit and a half wide, and a cubit and a half high. [11]You shall overlay it with pure gold, inside and out-

a Heb He b Meaning of Heb uncertain

resumption of vv. 1–2. **24.10** *Saw.* See note on 19.4. *Something like,* more precisely "like the construction of" (e.g., Ezek 1.16). *Sapphire,* as in Ezek 1.26–28. God's upper body is not directly perceived (cf. 33.20). **24.11** *Lay his hand.* The command in vv. 1–2 supersedes 19.24. *Chief men,* presumably the *elders* (v. 9). *Beheld,* elsewhere used of prophetic visions (e.g., Isa 1.1). *Ate and drank.* See note on 18.12. **24.12–18** Since Moses is already on the mountain, this resumes v. 8 or takes place after the others mentioned in v. 9 descend (see v. 14). **24.12** *Wait,* lit. "be," the root of God's name (see note on 3.14). *And I will,* rather "so that I may." *Tablets of stone.* Cf. 31.18; 34.1; Deut 4.13; called "tablets of the covenant" in Deut 9.9. *Law* (Hebrew *torah*) is cognate to the verb translated *instruction;* see note on 18.16. **24.13** *Joshua.* See note on 17.9. Joshua appears to station himself partway up the mountain (cf. 32.17). *Mountain of God.* See 3.1. **24.14** *Wait here.* See Gen 22.5. The vagueness sets the stage for 32.1. *Hur.* See note on 17.10; Hur fulfills Moses' judicial duties (18.26) along with Aaron. *Dispute.* See note on 18.16. **24.15–16** These verses anticipate 40.34–35. **24.15** *Cloud.* Cf. 19.9, 16; 20.21. **24.16** *Glory.* See note on 16.6–7. *Settled,* rendered *dwell* in 25.8, used of making the divine presence, in whatever form, immanent. *Six days,* double the period the people underwent sanctification merely to witness the divine presence (see 19.11). **24.17** *Devouring fire.* Cf. Isa 30.30; Ezek 1.4; note on 13.21. **24.18** *Forty,* a stereotypical number indicating a full period; cf. 34.28; Deut 9.9–11, 18, 25.

25.1–31.18 Moses learns how to set up a mobile dwelling (tabernacle) for the deity in the midst of the Israelite camp and to establish its priesthood. The dwelling serves as a shrine for worship and as an oracular source (29.43–44), the tent of meeting (27.21); cf. note on 33.7. The construction of the dwelling follows the golden calf incident (ch. 32) and consequent renewal of the covenant (chs. 33–34). It is uncertain whether the tabernacle described here corresponds to any historical edifice. **25.2** *Offering,* from the Hebrew for "to raise," unrelated to the term for sacrificial offerings, a "donation" (Num 15.19–21; Deut 12.6, 11, 17) to the priests and cult. *You,* plural, Israel at large. **25.3** *Gold . . . bronze.* Like descriptions of the tabernacle and its paraphernalia generally, the three metals are presented in descending order of value. The holier the object (the more immediately it impinges upon the divine presence), the more valuable the materials of which it is made. **25.4** *Blue, purple,* dyes fit for royalty (Esth 1.6; 8.15), taken from the sea (Ezek 27.7), a staple of Canaanite industry. *Fine linen,* an Egyptian export (Ezek 27.7), worn by nobility (Gen 41.42). **25.5** *Tanned,* lit. "reddened." *Fine leather,* cognate to Akkadian (Mesopotamian Semitic) "dyed sheep/goat leather." *Acacia,* found locally. **25.6** *Oil,* of olives (27.20). *Spices.* See 30.23–38. *Incense.* See 30.34–38. **25.7** *Onyx.* Cf. Gen 2.12; Ezek 28.13. *Ephod.* See 28.6–14. *Breastpiece.* See 28.15–30. **25.8** Cf. 29.43–46. **25.9** *Pattern,* structural design, from the Hebrew "to build." Ascribing a temple's blueprint to its god is attested too in Mesopotamia and Egypt. **25.10–22** That

side you shall overlay it, and you shall make a molding of gold upon it all around. 12You shall cast four rings of gold for it and put them on its four feet, two rings on the one side of it, and two rings on the other side. 13You shall make poles of acacia wood, and overlay them with gold. 14And you shall put the poles into the rings on the sides of the ark, by which to carry the ark. 15The poles shall remain in the rings of the ark; they shall not be taken from it. 16You shall put into the ark the covenant*a* that I shall give you.

17 Then you shall make a mercy seat*b* of pure gold; two cubits and a half shall be its length, and a cubit and a half its width. 18You shall make two cherubim of gold; you shall make them of hammered work, at the two ends of the mercy seat.*c* 19Make one cherub at the one end, and one cherub at the other; of one piece with the mercy seat*c* you shall make the cherubim at its two ends. 20The cherubim shall spread out their wings above, overshadowing the mercy seat*c* with their wings. They shall face one to another; the faces of the cherubim shall be turned toward the mercy seat.*c* 21You shall put the mercy seat*c* on the top of the ark; and in the ark you shall put the covenant*a* that I shall give you. 22There I will meet with you, and from above the mercy seat,*c* from between the two cherubim that are on the ark of the covenant,*a* I will deliver to you all my commands for the Israelites.

The Table for the Bread of the Presence

23 You shall make a table of acacia wood, two cubits long, one cubit wide, and a cubit and a half high. 24You shall overlay it with pure gold, and make a molding of gold around it. 25You shall make around it a rim a handbreadth wide, and a molding of gold around the rim. 26You shall make for it four rings of gold, and fasten the rings to the four corners at its four legs. 27The rings that hold the poles used for carrying the table shall be close to the rim. 28You shall make the poles of acacia wood, and overlay them with gold, and the table shall be carried with these. 29You shall make its plates and dishes for incense, and its flagons and bowls with which to pour drink offerings; you shall make them of pure gold. 30And you shall set the bread of the Presence on the table before me always.

The Lampstand

31 You shall make a lampstand of pure gold. The base and the shaft of the lampstand shall be made of hammered work; its cups, its calyxes, and its petals shall be of one piece with it; 32and there shall be six branches going out of its sides, three branches of the lampstand out of one side of it and three branches of the

a Or *treaty,* or *testimony;* Heb *eduth* *b* Or *a cover* *c* Or *the cover*

---

the Lord sits between and above two cherubim in the manner of ancient Near Eastern kings indicates that the ark is the divine throne or its footstool; cf. Ps 99.1. **25.10** *Ark,* lit. "box, chest," not the Hebrew term translated "ark" in Gen 6.14 (see note on 2.3). **25.11** *Molding,* an ornamented ridge. **25.12** *Feet,* bottom corners. *Side,* the shorter side, so that the divine presence always faces forward; the poles, which are never removed (v. 15), are perpendicular to the ark's length (cf. 1 Kings 8.8). **25.15** Once the tablets of the covenant (vv. 16, 21) are deposited in it (40.20), the ark itself becomes too holy to handle (see 2 Sam 6.6–7). **25.16** *Covenant,* the Ten Commandments (31.18). **25.17** *Pure gold,* solid gold, not plated like the rest of the ark, because God sits directly above it (cf. note on 25.3). **25.18** *Cherubim,* winged sphinxes with the body of a bull or lion and a human head; representations of these creatures are abundant in the archaeological evidence. Cf. Ezek 1; 10; 41.18–20; cf. the size and position of the cherubim in 1 Kings 6.23–28. These hybrid creatures represent the various animal powers over which God has control; cf. Gen 3.24; Ps 18.10. **25.20** *Spread,* to support the divine presence; cf. Ezek

1.11. *Overshadowing,* "screening over," so that the entire divine presence is seated above the lid (mercy seat). **25.22** *Meet.* See note on 25.1–31.18. *I will . . . commands,* lit. "I will speak with you all I will command you"; cf. Num 7.89. **25.23** For the *table's* placement, see 26.35. **25.25** *Rim,* more precisely "frame"; the area between it and the molding above it gives a sunken look, described by the historian Josephus and depicted on the Arch of Titus (70 CE). **25.27** *That hold the poles,* lit. "for houses for the poles," a rhyming phrase in Hebrew. **25.29** *For incense,* added in translation, assuming that this is the purpose of the dishes (cf. Lev 24.7). *With which,* or "into which." *To pour,* or "can be poured"; in fact no liquid is poured into or out of these (cf. 30.9). *Drink offerings,* added in translation. **25.30** *Bread,* laid out for presentation but consumed by the priests (Lev 24.5–9; 1 Sam 21.1–6). Since the deity does not eat or drink, setting the table is a show of hospitality. *Presence,* lit. "face" (cf. note on 23.15). *Always,* rather "regularly" (as in 27.20), every sabbath (Lev 24.8; 1 Chr 9.32). **25.31** For the placement of the *lampstand,* see 26.35. *Pure,* solid. *Calyxes,* "capitals" in Am 9.1. *Petals,* "flowers." **25.32** *Branches,*

lampstand out of the other side of it; 33three cups shaped like almond blossoms, each with calyx and petals, on one branch, and three cups shaped like almond blossoms, each with calyx and petals, on the other branch—so for the six branches going out of the lampstand. 34On the lampstand itself there shall be four cups shaped like almond blossoms, each with its calyxes and petals. 35There shall be a calyx of one piece with it under the first pair of branches, a calyx of one piece with it under the next pair of branches, and a calyx of one piece with it under the last pair of branches—so for the six branches that go out of the lampstand. 36Their calyxes and their branches shall be of one piece with it, the whole of it one hammered piece of pure gold. 37You shall make the seven lamps for it; and the lamps shall be set up so as to give light on the space in front of it. 38Its snuffers and trays shall be of pure gold. 39It, and all these utensils, shall be made from a talent of pure gold. 40And see that you make them according to the pattern for them, which is being shown you on the mountain.

The Tabernacle

26 Moreover you shall make the tabernacle with ten curtains of fine twisted linen, and blue, purple, and crimson yarns; you shall make them with cherubim skillfully worked into them. 2The length of each curtain shall be twenty-eight cubits, and the width of each curtain four cubits; all the curtains shall be of the same size. 3Five curtains shall be joined to one another; and the other five curtains shall be joined to one another. 4You shall make loops of blue on the edge of the outermost curtain in the first set; and likewise you shall make loops on the edge of the outermost curtain in the second set. 5You shall make fifty loops on the one curtain, and you shall make fifty loops on the edge of the curtain that is in the second set; the loops shall be opposite one another. 6You shall make fifty clasps of gold, and join the curtains to one another with the clasps, so that the tabernacle may be one whole.

7 You shall also make curtains of goats' hair for a tent over the tabernacle; you shall make eleven curtains. 8The length of each curtain shall be thirty cubits, and the width of each curtain four cubits; the eleven curtains shall be of the same size. 9You shall join five curtains by themselves, and six curtains by themselves, and the sixth curtain you shall double over at the front of the tent. 10You shall make fifty loops on the edge of the curtain that is outermost in one set, and fifty loops on the edge of the curtain that is outermost in the second set.

11 You shall make fifty clasps of bronze, and put the clasps into the loops, and join the tent together, so that it may be one whole. 12The part that remains of the curtains of the tent, the half curtain that remains, shall hang over the back of the tabernacle. 13The cubit on the one side, and the cubit on the other side, of what remains in the length of the curtains of the tent, shall hang over the sides of the tabernacle, on this side and that side, to cover it. 14You shall make for the tent a covering of tanned rams' skins and an outer covering of fine leather.[a]

The Framework

15 You shall make upright frames of acacia wood for the tabernacle. 16Ten cubits shall be the length of a frame, and a cubit and a half the

_____
a Meaning of Heb uncertain

translated *shaft* in v. 31. **25.34** *Itself,* the center shaft. **25.37** *Shall be set,* lit. "he (Aaron) shall set," every evening (30.8), treating the deity like a royal guest. **25.38** *Snuffers,* "tongs" for adjusting the wicks and removing their charred remains. **25.39** *Talent,* an "ingot" weighing 3,000 shekels.

26.1–14 Four layers cover the frame of the tabernacle, the "dwelling" proper (not including the courtyard and its altar). **26.1** *Ten.* Segmenting the curtain facilitates transport. *Curtains,* to be laid over the top of the structure along the shorter side. *Cherubim.* See note on 25.18. The design of the bottommost curtain is visible only on the inside. *Skillfully worked into them,* lit. "the work of a designer" (cf. 35.32), woven in.

26.2 *Twenty-eight.* This decorative curtain is a cubit off the ground on both ends. *Four,* making the total length of all ten 40, covering the 30-cubit length of the tabernacle and overlapping the front and back (vv. 12–13). **26.4** *Set,* in Hebrew cognate to *join* in v. 3. **26.6** *Whole,* added in translation. **26.7** The *goats' hair* was woven into a heavy cloth, a practice still current among Bedouin. *Tent,* a cover for the curtain beneath. *Eleven.* The extra length (cf. v. 1) makes a portal (v. 9). **26.11** *Bronze.* See note on 25.3. **26.12** *Part,* more precisely "extension," cognate to *hang over.* **26.14** *Fine leather.* See note on 25.6. The two outer layers are weatherproofing. **26.15** *Upright frames,* "planks," which, placed side by side, form the 10-by-30-cubit

width of each frame. ¹⁷There shall be two pegs in each frame to fit the frames together; you shall make these for all the frames of the tabernacle. ¹⁸You shall make the frames for the tabernacle: twenty frames for the south side; ¹⁹and you shall make forty bases of silver under the twenty frames, two bases under the first frame for its two pegs, and two bases under the next frame for its two pegs; ²⁰and for the second side of the tabernacle, on the north side twenty frames, ²¹and their forty bases of silver, two bases under the first frame, and two bases under the next frame; ²²and for the rear of the tabernacle westward you shall make six frames. ²³You shall make two frames for corners of the tabernacle in the rear; ²⁴they shall be separate beneath, but joined at the top, at the first ring; it shall be the same with both of them; they shall form the two corners. ²⁵And so there shall be eight frames, with their bases of silver, sixteen bases; two bases under the first frame, and two bases under the next frame.

26 You shall make bars of acacia wood, five for the frames of the one side of the tabernacle, ²⁷and five bars for the frames of the other side of the tabernacle, and five bars for the frames of the side of the tabernacle at the rear westward. ²⁸The middle bar, halfway up the frames, shall pass through from end to end. ²⁹You shall overlay the frames with gold, and shall make their rings of gold to hold the bars; and you shall overlay the bars with gold. ³⁰Then you shall erect the tabernacle according to the plan for it that you were shown on the mountain.

The Curtain

31 You shall make a curtain of blue, purple, and crimson yarns, and of fine twisted linen; it shall be made with cherubim skillfully worked into it. ³²You shall hang it on four pillars of acacia overlaid with gold, which have hooks of gold and rest on four bases of silver. ³³You shall hang the curtain under the clasps, and bring the ark of the covenant* in there, within the curtain; and the curtain shall separate for you the holy place from the most holy. ³⁴You shall put the mercy seat* on the ark of the covenant* in the most holy place. ³⁵You shall set the table outside the curtain, and the lampstand on the south side of the tabernacle opposite the table; and you shall put the table on the north side.

36 You shall make a screen for the entrance of the tent, of blue, purple, and crimson yarns, and of fine twisted linen, embroidered with needlework. ³⁷You shall make for the screen five pillars of acacia, and overlay them with gold; their hooks shall be of gold, and you shall cast five bases of bronze for them.

The Altar of Burnt Offering

27 You shall make the altar of acacia wood, five cubits long and five cubits wide; the altar shall be square, and it shall be three cubits high. ²You shall make horns for it on its four corners; its horns shall be of one

a Or *treaty*, or *testimony*; Heb *eduth*   *b* Or *the cover*

---

structure. **26.17** *Pegs*, tenons on the bottom edge to be inserted into the bases (v. 19). *To fit the frames together*, rather "each (peg) parallel to the other," perpendicular to the bottom edge of the plank. **26.18** *South*, lit. "toward the Negeb, southward," an orientation assuming a setting in the land of Israel. **26.19** *Bases*, sockets. *Silver*. See note on 25.3. **26.22** *Westward*, lit. "toward the (Mediterranean) sea"; see notes on 26.18; 10.19. **26.23** *Corners*, to enclose the open space left by the six planks in the rear, which cover only 9 cubits of the length. **26.24** *Separate*, rather "congruent" ("twinned"); the spaces on each side of the rear planks are to be symmetrical. *But joined*, rather "and identically (in the same pattern) will they end" (a Hebrew play on "congruent"). *First ring*, or "one ring," a single band holding the planks together around the top of the perimeter. **26.25** *Eight*, the six planks plus the two corners. **26.26** *Bars*, to stabilize the planks in the middle. *Side*, "flank," different from *side* in vv. 18, 20. **26.28** *Halfway up*, "in the middle" (cognate to *middle*). *Pass through*, cognate to *bar*. The other bars, surely to be arranged in

parallel above and below the middle, do not extend all the way across. **26.30** *Plan*, rendered *ordinance* in 21.1 and "rule" in (see note on) 21.9. Cf. 25.40. **26.31** *Curtain*, close in sound to *mercy seat* (25.17), referred to in v. 34. *Cherubim*. Cf. 26.1. *Skillfully worked*. See note on 26.1. The curtain matches the draped walls and ceiling of the *most holy place* (v. 34). **26.32** The construction is the same as the tabernacle framework. **26.33** *Under the clasps*, i.e., under the ceiling drape; see 26.6. **26.34** *Most holy place*, "holy of holies," the 10-cubit cube on the western end of the tabernacle proper, where the divine presence rests. Symmetry of space signifies holiness; cf. 27.1. **26.36** *Embroidered*, not woven in like the curtain (v. 31) since it is farther from the divine presence.

27.1–8 The courtyard altar, the altar of burnt offering (38.1), is bronze (cf. 30.3; note on 25.3); also cf. 20.24–25. **27.1** *Square*. See note on 26.34; the *altar* is called *most holy* (29.37). **27.2** *Horns*, a symbol of God (cf. Num 23.22 and note that the Canaanite god Baal is depicted with horns on his helmet) or the animals of-

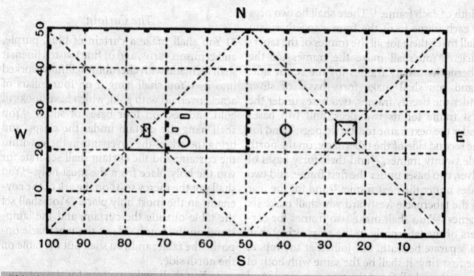

This plan approximates the court of the tabernacle as it is described in Exodus 27. The 50-by-100-cubit rectangular court, a topless tent, surrounds the tabernacle in its western half and the bronze courtyard altar, the altar of burnt offering, in its eastern half. (From S. R. Driver, *The Book of Exodus*.)

piece with it, and you shall overlay it with bronze. ³You shall make pots for it to receive its ashes, and shovels and basins and forks and firepans; you shall make all its utensils of bronze. ⁴You shall also make for it a grating, a network of bronze; and on the net you shall make four bronze rings at its four corners. ⁵You shall set it under the ledge of the altar so that the net shall extend halfway down the altar. ⁶You shall make poles for the altar, poles of acacia wood, and overlay them with bronze; ⁷the poles shall be put through the rings, so that the poles shall be on the two sides of the altar when it is carried. ⁸You shall make it hollow, with boards. They shall be made just as you were shown on the mountain.

The Court and Its Hangings

9 You shall make the court of the tabernacle. On the south side the court shall have hangings of fine twisted linen one hundred cubits long for that side; ¹⁰its twenty pillars and their

twenty bases shall be of bronze, but the hooks of the pillars and their bands shall be of silver. ¹¹Likewise for its length on the north side there shall be hangings one hundred cubits long, their pillars twenty and their bases twenty, of bronze, but the hooks of the pillars and their bands shall be of silver. ¹²For the width of the court on the west side there shall be fifty cubits of hangings, with ten pillars and ten bases. ¹³The width of the court on the front to the east shall be fifty cubits. ¹⁴There shall be fifteen cubits of hangings on the one side, with three pillars and three bases. ¹⁵There shall be fifteen cubits of hangings on the other side, with three pillars and three bases. ¹⁶For the gate of the court there shall be a screen twenty cubits long, of blue, purple, and crimson yarns, and of fine twisted linen, embroidered with needlework; it shall have four pillars and with them four bases. ¹⁷All the pillars around the court shall be banded with silver; their hooks shall be of silver, and their

---

fered; cf. 1 Kings 1.50–53; 2.28–34. Stone altars with "horns" at the four corners have been excavated at several Israelite sites. **27.4** *Grating*, to support the ledge (v. 5), on which the officiating priests presumably stood. **27.5** *Down*, lit. "up" from the ground. **27.8** *Boards*, panels, the same word translated *tablets* (e.g., 24.12). *Shown.* Cf. 25.40; 26.30. **27.9–19** The 50-by-100-cubit rectangular court, a topless tent, surrounds the tabernacle in its western half and the bronze altar in its east-

ern half; it is assumed that the ark and altar were situated at the centers of their respective squares, in which case the eastern edge of the tabernacle proper lies on the line that bisects the court's length. **27.10** *Bases*, sockets. *Hooks*, for holding the hangings. *Bands*, decoration encircling the pillars; see v. 17; 38.17, which also mentions capitals. **27.13** Oriented eastward, the tabernacle fills with sunlight in the morning. **27.16** The *gate* stands in front of an open entryway in the middle of

bases of bronze. [18] The length of the court shall be one hundred cubits, the width fifty, and the height five cubits, with hangings of fine twisted linen and bases of bronze. [19] All the utensils of the tabernacle for every use, and all its pegs and all the pegs of the court, shall be of bronze.

The Oil for the Lamp

20 You shall further command the Israelites to bring you pure oil of beaten olives for the light, so that a lamp may be set up to burn regularly. [21] In the tent of meeting, outside the curtain that is before the covenant,[a] Aaron and his sons shall tend it from evening to morning before the LORD. It shall be a perpetual ordinance to be observed throughout their generations by the Israelites.

Vestments for the Priesthood

28 Then bring near to you your brother Aaron, and his sons with him, from among the Israelites, to serve me as priests— Aaron and Aaron's sons, Nadab and Abihu, Eleazar and Ithamar. [2] You shall make sacred vestments for the glorious adornment of your brother Aaron. [3] And you shall speak to all who have ability, whom I have endowed with skill, that they make Aaron's vestments to consecrate him for my priesthood. [4] These are the vestments that they shall make: a breastpiece, an ephod, a robe, a checkered tunic, a turban, and a sash. When they make these sacred vestments for your brother Aaron and his sons to serve me as priests, [5] they shall use gold, blue, purple, and crimson yarns, and fine linen.

The Ephod

6 They shall make the ephod of gold, of blue, purple, and crimson yarns, and of fine twisted linen, skillfully worked. [7] It shall have two shoulder-pieces attached to its two edges, so that it may be joined together. [8] The decorated band on it shall be of the same workmanship and materials, of gold, of blue, purple, and crimson yarns, and of fine twisted linen. [9] You shall take two onyx stones, and engrave on them the names of the sons of Israel, [10] six of their names on the one stone, and the names of the remaining six on the other stone, in the order of their birth. [11] As a gem-cutter engraves signets, so you shall engrave the two stones with the names of the sons of Israel; you shall mount them in settings of gold filigree. [12] You shall set the two stones on the shoulder-pieces of the ephod, as stones of remembrance for the sons of Israel; and Aaron shall bear their names before the LORD on his two shoulders for remembrance. [13] You shall make settings of gold filigree, [14] and two chains of pure gold, twisted like cords; and you shall attach the corded chains to the settings.

The Breastplate

15 You shall make a breastpiece of judgment, in skilled work; you shall make it in the style of

a Or treaty, or testimony; Heb eduth

---

the eastern edge. *Screen,* like the one in 26.36 but narrower. **27.19** *Use,* a term for cultic "service" (cognate to *worship* in 4.23). *Pegs,* tent pins whose cords (35.18) stabilize the pillars. **27.20** *To burn,* not in the Hebrew. *Regularly,* every evening (v. 21). The instructions return to service within the tabernacle itself. **27.21** *Tent of meeting,* the tabernacle proper (see note on 25.1– 31.18). *Covenant,* elliptical for *ark of the covenant* (25.22). *Aaron and his sons,* whoever of Aaron's lineage is the chief priest at the time (see Lev 24.3). *Tend,* lit. "arrange," fill the lamp every evening with enough fuel to burn till daybreak (cf. 1 Sam 3.3). *Perpetual,* and not the one time implied by 25.1–7. *To be observed,* added for clarity.

28.1–43 The description up to v. 40 concerns the vestments worn only by the chief priest (Aaron) and only when officiating inside the tabernacle. **28.1** Cf. 6.23. **28.3** *To all who have ability,* lit. "to all wise of heart," cognate to *skill. To consecrate.* See 29.5–6; Lev 8.6–13. *For my priesthood,* meaning *to serve me as priest* (vv. 1, 4). **28.4** *Checkered,* or "fringed," cognate to

filigree (e.g., v. 11). **28.6** *Ephod,* a long vest (1 Sam 2.18; 2 Sam 6.14) made of the same materials as the curtain (26.31), open at the bottom and fastened at the top; it is possibly derived from the questionable cult object of the same name (e.g., Judg 8.27; 17.5; 1 Sam 21.9; Hos 3.4) used as an oracle (1 Sam 23.9–12; 30.7–8). **28.7** *Attached,* permanently (sewn on). The Hebrew is unclear; *to its two edges* may modify *it may be joined,* i.e., it is to be fastened at the top corner edges, on the shoulders. **28.8** *Decorated band,* a girdle around the middle, perhaps more precisely "the band of the vest." *Decorated* is a play on *skillfully worked* (v. 6); *band* is cognate to *ephod* (v. 6). **28.10** *In the order of their birth* (see Gen 29–30; 35), or "according to their lineages," in order by mother (cf. Gen 46; Num 1). **28.12** *Remembrance,* to call Israel, the covenant partner the priest represents, to the Lord's attention; cf. v. 29; 2.24; 30.16; Num 10.10; 31.54. **28.13** *Settings,* in the shoulderpieces of the ephod (v. 7). **28.14** *Chains,* to attach the breastpiece (vv. 22–28) to the ephod. **28.15** *Breastpiece,* or "pouch." *Judgment,* in the sense of divine mes-

the ephod; of gold, of blue and purple and crimson yarns, and of fine twisted linen you shall make it. [16]It shall be square and doubled, a span in length and a span in width. [17]You shall set in it four rows of stones. A row of carnelian,[a] chrysolite, and emerald shall be the first row; [18]and the second row a turquoise, a sapphire,[b] and a moonstone; [19]and the third row a jacinth, an agate, and an amethyst; [20]and the fourth row a beryl, an onyx, and a jasper; they shall be set in gold filigree. [21]There shall be twelve stones with names corresponding to the names of the sons of Israel; they shall be like signets, each engraved with its name, for the twelve tribes. [22]You shall make for the breastpiece chains of pure gold, twisted like cords; [23]and you shall make for the breastpiece two rings of gold, and put the two rings on the two edges of the breastpiece. [24]You shall put the two cords of gold in the two rings at the edges of the breastpiece; [25]the two ends of the two cords you shall attach to the two settings, and so attach it in front to the shoulder-pieces of the ephod. [26]You shall make two rings of gold, and put them at the two ends of the breastpiece, on its inside edge next to the ephod. [27]You shall make two rings of gold, and attach them in front to the lower part of the two shoulder-pieces of the ephod, at its joining above the decorated band of the ephod. [28]The breastpiece shall be bound by its rings to the rings of the ephod with a blue cord, so that it may lie on the decorated band of the ephod, and so that the breastpiece shall

not come loose from the ephod. [29]So Aaron shall bear the names of the sons of Israel in the breastpiece of judgment on his heart when he goes into the holy place, for a continual remembrance before the LORD. [30]In the breastpiece of judgment you shall put the Urim and the Thummim, and they shall be on Aaron's heart when he goes in before the LORD; thus Aaron shall bear the judgment of the Israelites on his heart before the LORD continually.

Other Priestly Vestments

31 You shall make the robe of the ephod all of blue. [32]It shall have an opening for the head in the middle of it, with a woven binding around the opening, like the opening in a coat of mail,[c] so that it may not be torn. [33]On its lower hem you shall make pomegranates of blue, purple, and crimson yarns, all around the lower hem, with bells of gold between them all around— [34]a golden bell and a pomegranate alternating all around the lower hem of the robe. [35]Aaron shall wear it when he ministers, and its sound shall be heard when he goes into the holy place before the LORD, and when he comes out, so that he may not die.

36 You shall make a rosette of pure gold, and engrave on it, like the engraving of a signet, "Holy to the LORD." [37]You shall fasten it on the turban with a blue cord; it shall be on the front of the turban. [38]It shall be on Aaron's

a The identity of several of these stones is uncertain   b Or lapis lazuli   c Meaning of Heb uncertain

---

sages (cf. 22.9) mediated by the Urim and Thummim (v. 30; see note on 28.30). **28.16** *Square.* Cf. 27.1. *Doubled,* to form the pouch (see note on 28.15). **28.17** *In it.* The Hebrew adds "settings of stone." *Stones.* The gems in all but row three (v. 19) are said by Ezekiel (28.13) to adorn "Eden, the garden of God" (cf. Gen 2.12) and the king of Tyre; cf. Rev 21.19–20. **28.23** *On the . . . edges,* at the shoulders (cf. note on 28.7). **28.25** *Settings.* See v. 13. *In front,* more precisely "opposite the face (front)"; the *ephod* will double under (v. 26). **28.26** *On . . . ephod,* more precisely "on its lip (hemmed edge) (running) along the ephod on the inside." **28.27** See notes on 28.7; 28.8. **28.28** *Bound,* linked. *Blue.* See note on 25.4; cf. Num 15.38. *Lie on,* more precisely "be (right) over." **28.29** *In,* or "on." *Holy place,* the outer part of the tabernacle proper, location of the lampstand and table. *Continual,* rendered *regularly* in 27.20. *Remembrance.* Cf. v. 12. **28.30** *Urim and Thummim,* according to comparative evidence, light and dark stones extracted from the pouch for the purposes of divination (see 1 Sam 14.41; cf. Num 27.21;

Deut 33.8; 1 Sam 28.6; Ezra 2.63). *Bear the judgment,* carry the divining medium (cf. note on 28.15). **28.31** The *robe* is worn underneath the ephod; it is woven (39.22). *All,* or "of one piece of," in Hebrew plays on the sound of *blue.* *Blue.* See note on 25.4. **28.33** *Hem,* of fine twisted linen (39.24). *Pomegranates,* a common decorative pattern; cf. the almond blossoms in 25.33–34. **28.34** *Alternating,* lit. "a golden bell and a pomegranate," which rhyme in Hebrew, creating euphony; the rhythmic and sound patterns that adorn the descriptions are lost in translation. **28.35** The *sound* of the bells shows courtesy to the deity, who, like a monarch, may not be approached without announcement; cf. note on 25.10–22. *So that he may not die,* an admonition accompanying various cultic instructions (e.g., 30.20, 21; Lev 8.35; 10.9). **28.36** *Rosette,* lit. "flower," but more probably "shiny plate" (some Hebrew verbs for sprouting denote shining too) on which an inscription could be engraved; cf. 39.30. *Holy to,* or "sacred property of" (singular in Hebrew of *sacred donations* in v. 38). **28.37** *Blue cord.* Cf.

forehead, and Aaron shall take on himself any guilt incurred in the holy offering that the Israelites consecrate as their sacred donations; it shall always be on his forehead, in order that they may find favor before the LORD.

39 You shall make the checkered tunic of fine linen, and you shall make a turban of fine linen, and you shall make a sash embroidered with needlework.

40 For Aaron's sons you shall make tunics and sashes and headdresses; you shall make them for their glorious adornment. 41You shall put them on your brother Aaron, and on his sons with him, and shall anoint them and ordain them and consecrate them, so that they may serve me as priests. 42You shall make for them linen undergarments to cover their naked flesh; they shall reach from the hips to the thighs; 43Aaron and his sons shall wear them when they go into the tent of meeting, or when they come near the altar to minister in the holy place; or they will bring guilt on themselves and die. This shall be a perpetual ordinance for him and for his descendants after him.

The Ordination of the Priests

29 Now this is what you shall do to them to consecrate them, so that they may serve me as priests. Take one young bull and two rams without blemish, 2and unleavened bread, unleavened cakes mixed with oil, and unleavened wafers spread with oil. You shall

make them of choice wheat flour. 3You shall put them in one basket and bring them in the basket, and bring the bull and the two rams. 4You shall bring Aaron and his sons to the entrance of the tent of meeting, and wash them with water. 5Then you shall take the vestments, and put on Aaron the tunic and the robe of the ephod, and the ephod, and the breastpiece, and gird him with the decorated band of the ephod; 6and you shall set the turban on his head, and put the holy diadem on the turban. 7You shall take the anointing oil, and pour it on his head and anoint him. 8Then you shall bring his sons, and put tunics on them, 9and you shall gird them with sashes[a] and tie headdresses on them; and the priesthood shall be theirs by a perpetual ordinance. You shall then ordain Aaron and his sons.

10 You shall bring the bull in front of the tent of meeting. Aaron and his sons shall lay their hands on the head of the bull, 11and you shall slaughter the bull before the LORD, at the entrance of the tent of meeting, 12and shall take some of the blood of the bull and put it on the horns of the altar with your finger, and all the rest of the blood you shall pour out at the base of the altar. 13You shall take all the fat that covers the entrails, and the appendage of the liver, and the two kidneys with the fat that is on them, and turn them into smoke on the altar. 14But the flesh of the bull, and its skin,

a Gk: Heb sashes, Aaron and his sons

---

v. 28. **28.38** *On,* or "above, over." *Incurred.* Cf. Lev 22.3, 9, 15–16. The head-plate may act like a lightning rod, mitigating divine reaction against unwitting desecrations (cf. notes on 19.13; 19.21). *Always,* regularly (27.20), when he enters the *holy place* (v. 35). *They,* the sacred donations (cf., e.g., Lev 22.20). **28.39** *Checkered.* See note on 28.4. *Tunic,* woven of one cloth (39.27). *Turban,* worn by at least one Judean king (Ezek 21.26). *Sash,* worn by nobility (Isa 22.21). *With needlework,* added for clarity. The *sash* exhibits the royal hues that adorn the chief priest's vestments; see 39.29. **28.40** The *headdresses* are apparently wound on like a turban into a conical shape. See 29.9, where the headdresses are *tied* or lit. "wound" on. *Glorious adornment.* Cf. v. 2. **28.41** *Ordain,* lit. "fill the hands" ("mandate"). The verse previews ch. 29. **28.42** *Undergarments,* drawers; see note on 20.26. **28.43** *Tent of meeting.* See note on 27.21. *Holy place,* here the tabernacle and its court, where the altar stands (e.g., 36.1). *Die.* See note on 28.35.

29.1–35 The ordination procedure includes washing, investiture, and anointing (vv. 4–9), purification

(vv. 10–14), propitiation (vv. 15–18), ordination (vv. 19–21), and homage (vv. 22–27). The ordination is performed in Lev 8–9. **29.1** *You,* Moses (25.1). *Them,* Aaron and his sons (28.43). *Without blemish,* lit. "whole." **29.2** *Unleavened.* See note on 12.8. *Cakes . . . wafers.* Cf. Lev 2.4. *Spread,* elsewhere translated "anointed" (e.g., 29.36). **29.3** *In,* "on," suggesting an open basket or tray. *Bring,* "bring near," used of cultic offerings and approaching the deity, often repeated in this section. **29.5** *Vestments.* See ch. 28. The *undergarments* (28.42) are not mentioned because the priests put them on alone. *Gird,* in Hebrew cognate to *ephod.* **29.6** *Diadem,* the rosette (28.36), also used of a royal crown (e.g., 2 Sam 1.10). **29.7** *Anointing oil.* See 30.22–33. Anointing, performed also on kings, signifies luxury and privilege (cf., e.g., Ps 23.5; Eccl 9.8). **29.9** *Ordain.* See note on 28.41. **29.10** *Lay their hands,* to signify it is theirs (e.g., Lev 1.4); cf. Lev 4.4. **29.12** *The rest of,* added for clarity. **29.13** *Fat.* See note on 23.18. **29.14** *Outside the camp,* because the offering pollutes; cf. Num 19. *Sin offering,* or "purification offering" (from the verb "cleanse," Lev 14.52). Its purpose is to

and its dung, you shall burn with fire outside the camp; it is a sin offering.

15 Then you shall take one of the rams, and Aaron and his sons shall lay their hands on the head of the ram, 16and you shall slaughter the ram, and shall take its blood and dash it against all sides of the altar. 17Then you shall cut the ram into its parts, and wash its entrails and its legs, and put them with its parts and its head, 18and turn the whole ram into smoke on the altar; it is a burnt offering to the LORD; it is a pleasing odor, an offering by fire to the LORD.

19 You shall take the other ram; and Aaron and his sons shall lay their hands on the head of the ram, 20and you shall slaughter the ram, and take some of its blood and put it on the lobe of Aaron's right ear and on the lobes of the right ears of his sons, and on the thumbs of their right hands, and on the big toes of their right feet, and dash the rest of the blood against all sides of the altar. 21Then you shall take some of the blood that is on the altar, and some of the anointing oil, and sprinkle it on Aaron and his vestments and on his sons and his sons' vestments with him; then he and his vestments shall be holy, as well as his sons and his sons' vestments.

22 You shall also take the fat of the ram, the fat tail, the fat that covers the entrails, the appendage of the liver, the two kidneys with the fat that is on them, and the right thigh (for it is a ram of ordination), 23and one loaf of bread, one cake of bread made with oil, and one wafer, out of the basket of unleavened bread that is before the LORD; 24and you shall place all these on the palms of Aaron and on the palms of his sons, and raise them as an elevation offering before the LORD. 25Then you

shall take them from their hands, and turn them into smoke on the altar on top of the burnt offering of pleasing odor before the LORD; it is an offering by fire to the LORD.

26 You shall take the breast of the ram of Aaron's ordination and raise it as an elevation offering before the LORD; and it shall be your portion. 27You shall consecrate the breast that was raised as an elevation offering and the thigh that was raised as an elevation offering from the ram of ordination, from that which belonged to Aaron and his sons. 28These things shall be a perpetual ordinance for Aaron and his sons from the Israelites, for this is an offering; and it shall be an offering by the Israelites from their sacrifice of offerings of well-being, their offering to the LORD.

29 The sacred vestments of Aaron shall be passed on to his sons after him; they shall be anointed in them and ordained in them. 30The son who is priest in his place shall wear them seven days, when he comes into the tent of meeting to minister in the holy place.

31 You shall take the ram of ordination, and boil its flesh in a holy place; 32and Aaron and his sons shall eat the flesh of the ram and the bread that is in the basket, at the entrance of the tent of meeting. 33They themselves shall eat the food by which atonement is made, to ordain and consecrate them, but no one else shall eat of them, because they are holy. 34If any of the flesh for the ordination, or of the bread, remains until the morning, then you shall burn the remainder with fire; it shall not be eaten, because it is holy.

35 Thus you shall do to Aaron and to his sons, just as I have commanded you; through seven days you shall ordain them. 36Also every day you shall offer a bull as a sin offering for

---

remove ritual pollution and transform to a state of purity, a prerequisite to approaching God (cf. note on 19.10); it is used of purifying the altar in vv. 36–37. **29.16** *Dashing* the blood signifies its return to God (cf. Lev 17.6, 11). **29.17** *Parts*, in Hebrew cognate to *cut*; cf. Lev 1.6. *With*, rather "on top of." **29.18** *Odor*. See note on 23.18. **29.19–28** The ordination rite adapts the well-being offering (Lev 3). **29.20** *Blood*, a divine substance (cf. Lev 17.11) and therefore an agent of purification and safeguard against ritual pollution (see v. 21). Cf. Lev 14.14. *The rest of*, added for clarity. **29.22** *Fat tail*, part of the fat (Lev 3.9). *Right thigh*, ordinarily eaten by the priests (Lev 7.32–33), here served to God; the offering symbolizes a meal (see v. 25). **29.23** *Loaf*, more precisely "a (flat) round." **29.24** *Raise*, in Hebrew cognate to *elevation;* on the significance of

the presentation, cf. note on 25.30. *Before the* LORD, in front of the tent of meeting (v. 4). **29.26** *You*, Moses, who partakes of the offering since he functions here as priest; cf. Lev 7.30–31. **29.27** *Consecrate*, render as cultic property. The second occurrence of *elevation offering* in this verse translates a generic Hebrew term for cultic donations (see note on 25.2), rendered *offering* in v. 28. The first occurrence translates a different Hebrew word, also in v. 26. **29.28** *Perpetual*. See Lev 7.28–36; Num 18.8, 18–19. **29.29** See Num 20.26. **29.30** *Seven days*. See vv. 35–37. *When he comes*, rather "who will come," in apposition to *priest*. **29.31** A resumption of v. 27. **29.33** *No one else*, an outsider (Num 1.51; 3.10, 38; 16.40; 18.4, 7) or nonpriest, here applied to any but the chief priests (as in Num 16.40). **29.34** *Holy*, rendered *sacred donations* in 28.38.

atonement. Also you shall offer a sin offering for the altar, when you make atonement for it, and shall anoint it, to consecrate it. 37Seven days you shall make atonement for the altar, and consecrate it, and the altar shall be most holy; whatever touches the altar shall become holy.

The Daily Offerings

38 Now this is what you shall offer on the altar: two lambs a year old regularly each day. 39One lamb you shall offer in the morning, and the other lamb you shall offer in the evening; 40and with the first lamb one-tenth of a measure of choice flour mixed with one-fourth of a hin of beaten oil, and one-fourth of a hin of wine for a drink offering. 41And the other lamb you shall offer in the evening, and shall offer with it a grain offering and its drink offering, as in the morning, for a pleasing odor, an offering by fire to the LORD. 42It shall be a regular burnt offering throughout your generations at the entrance of the tent of meeting before the LORD, where I will meet with you, to speak to you there. 43I will meet with the Israelites there, and it shall be sanctified by my glory; 44I will consecrate the tent of meeting and the altar; Aaron also and his sons I will consecrate, to serve me as priests. 45I will dwell among the Israelites, and I will be their God. 46And they shall know that I am the LORD their God, who brought them out of the land of Egypt that I might dwell among them; I am the LORD their God.

The Altar of Incense

30 You shall make an altar on which to offer incense; you shall make it of aca-

cia wood. 2It shall be one cubit long, and one cubit wide; it shall be square, and shall be two cubits high; its horns shall be of one piece with it. 3You shall overlay it with pure gold, its top, and its sides all around and its horns; and you shall make for it a molding of gold all around. 4And you shall make two golden rings for it; under its molding on two opposite sides of it you shall make them, and they shall hold the poles with which to carry it. 5You shall make the poles of acacia wood, and overlay them with gold. 6You shall place it in front of the curtain that is above the ark of the covenant,[a] in front of the mercy seat[b] that is over the covenant,[a] where I will meet with you. 7Aaron shall offer fragrant incense on it; every morning when he dresses the lamps he shall offer it, 8and when Aaron sets up the lamps in the evening, he shall offer it, a regular incense offering before the LORD throughout your generations. 9You shall not offer unholy incense on it, or a burnt offering, or a grain offering; and you shall not pour a drink offering on it. 10Once a year Aaron shall perform the rite of atonement on its horns. Throughout your generations he shall perform the atonement for it once a year with the blood of the atoning sin offering. It is most holy to the LORD.

The Half Shekel for the Sanctuary

11 The LORD spoke to Moses: 12When you take a census of the Israelites to register them, at registration all of them shall give a ransom for their lives to the LORD, so that no plague may come upon them for being registered. 13This is what each one who is registered shall give: half

---

a Or *treaty,* or *testimony;* Heb *eduth*   *b* Or *the cover*

29.36 *Sin offering.* See note on 29.14. *Atonement,* in the sense of expurgating ritual pollution, such as that of the altar; cf. Lev 16. **29.37** *Seven days.* Cf. Ezek 43.26. *Most holy,* "holy of holies"; cf. 40.10. *Holy,* cultic property (a noun); see note on 29.34; cf. Num 16.37–39. **29.38–42** A digression on the use of the *altar;* cf. Num 28.3–6. **29.39** *In the evening,* rather *at twilight,* as translated in 12.6. **29.40** *A measure,* an ephah (see note on 16.36). *Hin,* one-sixth of a bath, the liquid equivalent of an ephah. **29.42** *Meet.* See note on 25.1–31.18. **29.43** *Glory.* See note on 16.6–7. **29.45** *Dwell.* See note on 25.1–31.18. **29.46** *Know.* Cf. note on 5.2; cf. 20.2.

30.1–5 The incense altar is constructed like that of the courtyard, but it is of more precious material since it will stand in the "holy place"; cf. note on 27.1–8. **30.1** *Offer,* in Hebrew cognate to *incense,* lit. "(aro-

matic) smoke." **30.4** *On two opposite sides,* lit. "on its two flanks, on its two sides." **30.6** *It,* the altar (v. 1). *Above,* rather "over" (see 26.31–33; 35.12). *Meet.* See 25.21–22. **30.7** *Offer,* burn (see note on v. 1). *Every morning,* lit. "in the morning, in the morning." *Dresses,* or cleans. **30.8** *Sets up.* Cf. 27.21. *In the evening.* See note on 29.39. **30.9** *Unholy,* lit. "alien"; cf. Lev 10.1; see note on 29.33. **30.10** *Once a year,* presumably on the Day of Atonement, although this rite is not specified in Lev 16. *Atonement.* See note on 29.36. *Most holy.* See note on 29.37. **30.11–16** The levy gives the Israelites a share in the tabernacle and protects them against the demonic attack that a head count attracts; cf. 2 Sam 24; also cf. the harmless military census in Num 1. For the use of the levy, see 38.25–28; cf. 2 Chr 24.4–10; Mt 17.24. **30.12** *Take a census,* lit. "raise the head" (see Num 1.2). *Register,* rendered "take a census" in 2 Sam

a shekel according to the shekel of the sanctuary (the shekel is twenty gerahs), half a shekel as an offering to the LORD. [14]Each one who is registered, from twenty years old and upward, shall give the LORD's offering. [15]The rich shall not give more, and the poor shall not give less, than the half shekel, when you bring this offering to the LORD to make atonement for your lives. [16]You shall take the atonement money from the Israelites and shall designate it for the service of the tent of meeting; before the LORD it will be a reminder to the Israelites of the ransom given for your lives.

The Bronze Basin

17 The LORD spoke to Moses: [18]You shall make a bronze basin with a bronze stand for washing. You shall put it between the tent of meeting and the altar, and you shall put water in it; [19]with the water[a] Aaron and his sons shall wash their hands and their feet. [20]When they go into the tent of meeting, or when they come near the altar to minister, to make an offering by fire to the LORD, they shall wash with water, so that they may not die. [21]They shall wash their hands and their feet, so that they may not die: it shall be a perpetual ordinance for them, for him and for his descendants throughout their generations.

The Anointing Oil and Incense

22 The LORD spoke to Moses: [23]Take the finest spices: of liquid myrrh five hundred shekels, and of sweet-smelling cinnamon half as much, that is, two hundred fifty, and two hundred fifty of aromatic cane, [24]and five hundred of cas-

sia—measured by the sanctuary shekel—and a hin of olive oil; [25]and you shall make of these a sacred anointing oil blended as by the perfumer; it shall be a holy anointing oil. [26]With it you shall anoint the tent of meeting and the ark of the covenant,[b] [27]and the table and all its utensils, and the lampstand and its utensils, and the altar of incense, [28]and the altar of burnt offering with all its utensils, and the basin with its stand; [29]you shall consecrate them, so that they may be most holy; whatever touches them will become holy. [30]You shall anoint Aaron and his sons, and consecrate them, in order that they may serve me as priests. [31]You shall say to the Israelites, "This shall be my holy anointing oil throughout your generations. [32]It shall not be used in any ordinary anointing of the body, and you shall make no other like it in composition; it is holy, and it shall be holy to you. [33]Whoever compounds any like it or whoever puts any of it on an unqualified person shall be cut off from the people."

34 The LORD said to Moses: Take sweet spices, stacte, and onycha, and galbanum, sweet spices with pure frankincense (an equal part of each), [35]and make an incense blended as by the perfumer, seasoned with salt, pure and holy; [36]and you shall beat some of it into powder, and put part of it before the covenant[b] in the tent of meeting where I shall meet with you; it shall be for you most holy. [37]When you make incense according to this composition, you shall not make it for yourselves; it shall be regarded by you as holy to the

---

a Heb *it*   *b* Or *treaty*, or *testimony*; Heb *eduth*

24.2. *Plague*, the Hebrew term also rendered *plague* in 12.13 but not the one rendered "pestilence" in 2 Sam 24.15. **30.13** *Each one*, only males (cf. Num 1.2). *Twenty gerahs*. Cf. Lev 27.25; Num 3.47; 18.16. *Offering*. See note on 25.2. **30.14** *Twenty*. Cf. Num 1.3. **30.15** *To make atonement*, "ransom," in Hebrew cognate to *ransom* in v. 12; the same phrase is translated *ransom* in (see note on) 30.16. **30.16** *To the Israelites*, rather "of the Israelites." *Before the LORD*. See note on 28.12. *Of the ransom . . . lives*, rather "to ransom your lives." **30.18** *Basin*, or "laver," a different Hebrew term from the one so rendered in 24.6; the term is used in 1 Kings 7.38, where, unlike here, dimensions are given. **30.19** *With the water*, rather "from it," from the basin. **30.20** *Die*. See note on 28.35. **30.21** A parallelism effects closure (cf. note on 23.13). **30.22–38** For the actual anointing, see Lev 8.10–12. **30.23** *Finest spices*. Cf. Song 4.14. *Liquid*, or "solidified" (resinous), contrasting with the flowing state described in Song 5.5, 13.

Aromatic, cognate to *spice* and *sweet-smelling*. **30.24** *Hin*. See note on 29.40. **30.25** *Blended as by the perfumer*. The Hebrew plies the same root three ways. *Holy*, the same Hebrew term rendered *sacred*; see also v. 32. **30.29** *Holy*. See note on 29.37. **30.30** *And his sons*. 29.7, 29 direct only that Aaron and his vestments be anointed; to resolve the discrepancy, cf. note on 27.21. **30.31** Cf. 1 Chr 9.30. **30.32** *It shall not . . . body*, lit. "On (ordinary) human flesh it shall not be poured." **30.33** *Compounds*, in Hebrew cognate to *blend*, rendered *perfumer* in v. 25. *Unqualified person*. See note on 30.9 (where the term is translated *unholy*). *Cut off*. See note on 12.15. **30.34** *Sweet spices*, a different Hebrew term from (aromatic) *spices* in v. 23 and *fragrant* (spices) in 25.6. *An equal part of each*, lit. "part like part shall it be." **30.35** *Make*, lit. "make of them." *Blended*. Cf. v. 25. *Seasoned with salt*, rather "salted." *Pure*, ritually pure (not as in v. 34, which uses a different term). *Holy*. See note on 29.37. **30.36** *Part*, the same Hebrew term

LORD. [38]Whoever makes any like it to use as perfume shall be cut off from the people.

Bezalel and Oholiab

31 The LORD spoke to Moses: [2]See, I have called by name Bezalel son of Uri son of Hur, of the tribe of Judah: [3]and I have filled him with divine spirit,[a] with ability, intelligence, and knowledge in every kind of craft, [4]to devise artistic designs, to work in gold, silver, and bronze, [5]in cutting stones for setting, and in carving wood, in every kind of craft. [6]Moreover, I have appointed with him Oholiab son of Ahisamach, of the tribe of Dan; and I have given skill to all the skillful, so that they may make all that I have commanded you: [7]the tent of meeting, and the ark of the covenant,[b] and the mercy seat[c] that is on it, and all the furnishings of the tent, [8]the table and its utensils, and the pure lampstand with all its utensils, and the altar of incense, [9]and the altar of burnt offering with all its utensils, and the basin with its stand, [10]and the finely worked vestments, the holy vestments for the priest Aaron and the vestments of his sons, for their service as priests, [11]and the anointing oil and the fragrant incense for the holy place. They shall do just as I have commanded you.

The Sabbath Law

12 The LORD said to Moses: [13]You yourself are to speak to the Israelites: "You shall keep my sabbaths, for this is a sign between me and you throughout your generations, given in order that you may know that I, the LORD, sanctify you. [14]You shall keep the sabbath, because it is holy for you; everyone who profanes it shall be put to death; whoever does any work on it shall be cut off from among the people. [15]Six days shall work be done, but the seventh day is a sabbath of solemn rest, holy to the LORD; whoever does any work on the sabbath day shall be put to death. [16]Therefore the Israelites shall keep the sabbath, observing the sabbath throughout their generations, as a perpetual covenant. [17]It is a sign forever between me and the people of Israel that in six days the LORD made heaven and earth, and on the seventh day he rested, and was refreshed."

The Two Tablets of the Covenant

18 When God[d] finished speaking with Moses on Mount Sinai, he gave him the two tablets of the covenant,[b] tablets of stone, written with the finger of God.

The Golden Calf

32 When the people saw that Moses delayed to come down from the mountain, the people gathered around Aaron, and said to him, "Come, make gods for us, who shall go before us; as for this Moses, the man who brought us up out of the land of Egypt,

---

a Or *with the spirit of God*   *b* Or *treaty,* or *testimony;* Heb *eduth*   *c* Or *the cover*   *d* Heb *he*

---

rendered *some. Covenant.* See note on 27.21. **30.38** *To use as perfume,* lit. "to smell by it." *Cut off.* Cf. v. 33.

31.1–11 The primary role of a Judahite versus the secondary role of a Danite in constructing the tabernacle presages the superiority of the Jerusalem temple of Solomon (of Judah; 1 Kings 6); cf. note on 32.1–35. The passage is reprised in 35.30–36.1. **31.2** *Called by name,* idiomatic for "designated" (e.g., Isa 43.1). *Bezalel* in Hebrew means "In-the-Shade (Protection)-of-God." *Hur.* See note on 17.10. Hur, Uri, and Bezalel are descendants of the Judahite Caleb (Num 13.6) in 1 Chr 2.18–20. **31.3** *Divine spirit.* Cf. Gen 41.38. *Craft,* rendered *work* in 20.9. **31.4** *Devise,* in Hebrew cognate to *designs.* **31.5** *Setting.* Cf., e.g., 25.7. *Carving,* the same word rendered *cutting. In.* The Hebrew adds "doing," which is assonant with *setting.* **31.6** *Oholiab* in Hebrew means "My-Tent-Is-the-Father (God)." *Skill to all the skillful,* lit. "wisdom in the heart of every wise of heart"; cf. note on 28.3. **31.7** *Furnishings,* rendered *utensils* in vv. 8–9. **31.10** *Finely worked,* some ancient manuscript traditions read "service," of a root similar to *to minister* (e.g., 30.20). **31.12–17** The sacred time of the sabbath is analogous to the sacred space of the tabernacle; see Lev 19.30; cf. Ex 39.32; 40.34; Gen 2.1–2; also cf. Ex 39.43; Gen 2.3. See also Ex 16.22–26; 20.8–11; 23.12; 34.21; 35.2–3. **31.13** *You yourself,* a rhetorical indication of a new topic (27.20; 28.1; 30.23), not an emphasis on Moses' personal performance. *Keep.* See note on 20.8, where the term is translated *remember;* cf. Lev 19.3, 30. *Sign.* Cf. Gen 9.12–13; 17.11. *Know.* Cf. 29.46; see Ezek 20.12. **31.14** *Holy.* See note on 29.37. *Profanes,* used of the sanctuary (e.g., Lev 21.12, 23; Ezek 23.39) as well as the sabbath (e.g., Ezek 20.13). *Put to death,* by the community; cf. Num 15.32–36. *Work.* Cf. 20.9. *Cut off.* See note on 12.15. **31.15** *Solemn rest.* See note on 16.23. **31.17** *Rested.* Cf. Gen 2.2. *Refreshed.* Cf. 23.12. **31.18** *He gave him.* In Hebrew the phrase prominently begins the verse. *Tablets.* See 24.12.

32.1–35 Making the golden calf violates 20.4, 23; cf. King Jeroboam's calves (1 Kings 12.25–33; see note on 32.4), which functioned historically not as idols but as pedestals for the deity (like the cherubim; see note on 25.18), but which are viewed as idolatrous in 2 Kings 17.16; Hos 8.4–6; 10.5–6; 13.2. Cf. the variations in

we do not know what has become of him." ²Aaron said to them, "Take off the gold rings that are on the ears of your wives, your sons, and your daughters, and bring them to me." ³So all the people took off the gold rings from their ears, and brought them to Aaron. ⁴He took the gold from them, formed it in a mold,ᵃ and cast an image of a calf; and they said, "These are your gods, O Israel, who brought you up out of the land of Egypt!" ⁵When Aaron saw this, he built an altar before it; and Aaron made proclamation and said, "Tomorrow shall be a festival to the LORD." ⁶They rose early the next day, and offered burnt offerings and brought sacrifices of well-being; and the people sat down to eat and drink, and rose up to revel.

7 The LORD said to Moses, "Go down at once! Your people, whom you brought up out of the land of Egypt, have acted perversely; ⁸they have been quick to turn aside from the way that I commanded them; they have cast for themselves an image of a calf, and have worshiped it and sacrificed to it, and said, 'These are your gods, O Israel, who brought you up out of the land of Egypt!' " ⁹The LORD said to Moses, "I have seen this people, how stiff-necked they are. ¹⁰Now let me alone, so that my wrath may burn hot against them and I may consume them; and of you I will make a great nation."

11 But Moses implored the LORD his God, and said, "O LORD, why does your wrath burn hot against your people, whom you brought out of the land of Egypt with great power and with a mighty hand? ¹²Why should the Egyptians say, 'It was with evil intent that he brought them out to kill them in the mountains, and to consume them from the face of the earth'? Turn from your fierce wrath; change your mind and do not bring disaster on your people. ¹³Remember Abraham, Isaac, and Israel, your servants, how you swore to them by your own self, saying to them, 'I will multiply your descendants like the stars of heaven, and all this land that I have promised I will give to your descendants, and they shall inherit it forever.' " ¹⁴And the LORD changed his mind about the disaster that he planned to bring on his people.

15 Then Moses turned and went down from the mountain, carrying the two tablets of the covenantᵇ in his hands, tablets that were written on both sides, written on the front and on the back. ¹⁶The tablets were the work of God, and the writing was the writing of God, engraved upon the tablets. ¹⁷When Joshua heard the noise of the people as they shouted, he said to Moses, "There is a noise of war in the camp." ¹⁸But he said,

"It is not the sound made by victors,
    or the sound made by losers;
    it is the sound of revelers that I hear."

¹⁹As soon as he came near the camp and saw the calf and the dancing, Moses' anger burned

---

ᵃ Or *fashioned it with a graving tool*; Meaning of Heb uncertain
ᵇ Or *treaty*, or *testimony*; Heb *eduth*

Deut 9.8–21, 25–29; also Neh 9.16–18. **32.1** *Delayed.* Readers know Moses will be on the mountain forty days (24.18), but the Israelites do not. *Around,* rather "against" (e.g., Num 16.3). *Aaron.* See 24.14. *Gods,* or "a god." *This,* an expression of contempt (e.g., 1 Sam 10.27; 21.15). *The man,* or "this man Moses." **32.2** *Rings,* associated in Gen 35.4 with foreign gods that must be suppressed at Bethel, one of Jeroboam's cult sites (see note on 32.1–35). **32.4** *Image.* "Molten" is connoted. *Calf,* or young bull (cf. Ps 106.19–20, where the word translated "ox" means "bull"), an image applied to leading Canaanite gods; but see note on 32.1–35. *These.* The plural pronoun, which is more appropriate in 1 Kings 12.28 (a verse in which the words are virtually identical to this one), evokes Jeroboam's calves; cf. Neh 9.18. **32.5** *Saw.* Cf. v. 1. *Altar.* Cf. the legitimate altar (27.1–8). *It,* the calf (v. 4). *Festival.* Cf. 23.14–17. **32.6** *Revel.* Cf. v. 19; the verb has sexual overtones ("fondling" in Gen 26.8). The ritual seems to parody 24.5, 11; see also note on 32.8. **32.7** *Go down,* counterposed to v. 1. *Your . . . you.* The Lord follows suit in disavowing the people; cf., e.g., 20.2; 29.46. *Per-* versely, translated "corrupt" in Gen 6.11–12; "dealt falsely" in Deut 32.5a. **32.8** *Worshiped.* Cf. 24.1; see note on 4.31. *These.* See note on 32.4. **32.9** *Seen.* Cf. v. 5. *Stiff-necked,* like an unresponsive draft animal (cf. Num 22.23). **32.10** *Consume,* in the sense of "put to an end," perhaps a pun in Hebrew on "devour" (Deut 4.24). *Great nation.* See Gen 12.2; cf. Num 14.12. Moses responds in v. 32. **32.11** *Your people.* Cf. v. 7; 33.13. **32.12** *Egyptians.* Cf. Num 14.13–16. *Mountains.* See note on 19.1. *Consume.* See note on 32.10. *Fierce,* burning (vv. 10–11). *Change your mind,* in Hebrew a pun on *let me alone* (v. 10); cf. Jon 3.9–10. *Disaster,* the same term rendered *evil intent.* **32.13** *Israel,* not *Jacob* as in 2.24, reiterating the bond between the people and its namesake. *Swore.* See Gen 22.16–17. *Forever.* See Gen 17.7–8. **32.14** *His people.* See v. 11. **32.15** *Turned,* "about-faced" (see note on 32.11). *Carrying,* not in the Hebrew. *Hands,* "hand" in Hebrew. **32.17** *Joshua.* See note on 24.13. *Noise,* rendered *sound* in v. 18. *As they shouted,* in Hebrew a pun on *with evil intent* (v. 12). **32.18** *Made by victors,* more precisely "of singing triumph," as in 15.1–18. *Made by losers,* more precisely

hot, and he threw the tablets from his hands and broke them at the foot of the mountain. 20He took the calf that they had made, burned it with fire, ground it to powder, scattered it on the water, and made the Israelites drink it.

21 Moses said to Aaron, "What did this people do to you that you have brought so great a sin upon them?" 22And Aaron said, "Do not let the anger of my lord burn hot; you know the people, that they are bent on evil. 23They said to me, 'Make us gods, who shall go before us; as for this Moses, the man who brought us up out of the land of Egypt, we do not know what has become of him.' 24So I said to them, 'Whoever has gold, take it off'; so they gave it to me, and I threw it into the fire, and out came this calf!"

25 When Moses saw that the people were running wild (for Aaron had let them run wild, to the derision of their enemies), 26then Moses stood in the gate of the camp, and said, "Who is on the LORD's side? Come to me!" And all the sons of Levi gathered around him. 27He said to them, "Thus says the LORD, the God of Israel, 'Put your sword on your side, each of you! Go back and forth from gate to gate throughout the camp, and each of you kill your brother, your friend, and your neighbor.'" 28The sons of Levi did as Moses commanded, and about three thousand of the people fell on that day. 29Moses said, "Today you have ordained yourselves[a] for the service of the LORD, each one at the cost of a son or a brother, and so have brought a blessing on yourselves this day."

30 On the next day Moses said to the peo-ple, "You have sinned a great sin. But now I will go up to the LORD; perhaps I can make atonement for your sin." 31So Moses returned to the LORD and said, "Alas, this people has sinned a great sin; they have made for themselves gods of gold. 32But now, if you will only forgive their sin—but if not, blot me out of the book that you have written." 33But the LORD said to Moses, "Whoever has sinned against me I will blot out of my book. 34But now go, lead the people to the place about which I have spoken to you; see, my angel shall go in front of you. Nevertheless, when the day comes for punishment, I will punish them for their sin."

35 Then the LORD sent a plague on the people, because they made the calf—the one that Aaron made.

The Command to Leave Sinai

33 The LORD said to Moses, "Go, leave this place, you and the people whom you have brought up out of the land of Egypt, and go to the land of which I swore to Abraham, Isaac, and Jacob, saying, 'To your descendants I will give it.' 2I will send an angel before you, and I will drive out the Canaanites, the Amorites, the Hittites, the Perizzites, the Hivites, and the Jebusites. 3Go up to a land flowing with milk and honey; but I will not go up among you, or I would consume you on the way, for you are a stiff-necked people."

4 When the people heard these harsh words, they mourned, and no one put on ornaments. 5For the LORD had said to Moses,

---

a Gk Vg Compare Tg: Heb *Today ordain yourselves*

"of singing defeat." *Revelers,* "singing" (the same Hebrew verb as in 15.21; Isa 27.2). **32.19** *Dancing,* as in 15.20. *Anger.* Cf. Num 20.10–11. *Burned hot.* Cf. vv. 10–11. **32.20** *Drink it,* a detail that goes beyond Deut 9.21; cf. Num 5.24. The calf is annihilated like a god in Ugaritic myth. **32.22** *Aaron* echoes Moses in v. 11. *Bent on evil.* The soundalike *running wild* (v. 25) is read here by another version. **32.23** Cf. v. 1. **32.24** *Threw* echoes Moses' action in v. 19; cf. v. 4. In Deut 9.20 Moses prays for Aaron's life. **32.25** *Let them run wild.* The Hebrew (*pera'o*) puns on "Pharaoh" and perhaps "Peor" (Num 25); see note on 32.28. **32.26** *Gate,* the place of assembly (e.g., Gen 23.10; Ruth 4.1). *Camp.* Cf. 19.2; see also Num 2. *On the LORD's side,* lit. "for the LORD." *Levi.* The Levites are subordinated to Aaron narratively in Num 16–18; cf. Deut 10.8–9; they are first consecrated for cultic service in Num 8. **32.27** *Neighbor,* or "relative"; cf. Deut 33.9. **32.28** Cf. Num 25.6–12. **32.29** *Ordained.* See note on 28.41. *For*

the service of, Hebrew "for," as in v. 26 (see note on 32.26). *So have brought,* rather "so that he (the LORD) will bring." **32.30** *Great sin.* Cf. v. 21. **32.31** *Returned,* ironic for Moses, who had begged the Lord to *turn* (same Hebrew verb, v. 12). *Gods.* See note on 32.1. **32.32** *Book.* See note on 17.14. That the names of those who are to live is recorded on high is an ancient Near Eastern tradition; cf. Ps 69.28; Isa 4.3; Mal 3.16; also cf. Num 11.15. **32.34** *Lead,* a play in Hebrew on *let me alone* (v. 10). *Angel.* See 32.2. *For punishment;* lit. "of my accounting" (cf. 20.5). **32.35** *Plague.* See note on 30.12; the plague may result from the account in v. 20.

33.1 *Leave,* lit. "go up" (cf. 32.7). *You.* Cf. 32.7. *Jacob.* See note on 32.13. **33.2** *Angel.* Cf. 23.20. *Drive out.* Cf. 23.28; 34.11. **33.3** *Milk and honey.* Cf. 3.8. *I will not.* See vv. 16–17. *Or,* "lest," an anticipation of rebellions to come (e.g., Num 11; 14). *Consume.* See note on 32.10. **33.4** *Harsh,* or "disastrous" (see 32.12). *Ornaments.* Cf. Jdt 10.1–4. In contrast to vv. 5–6, here the people take

"Say to the Israelites, 'You are a stiff-necked people; if for a single moment I should go up among you, I would consume you. So now take off your ornaments, and I will decide what to do to you.' " 6Therefore the Israelites stripped themselves of their ornaments, from Mount Horeb onward.

The Tent outside the Camp

7 Now Moses used to take the tent and pitch it outside the camp, far off from the camp; he called it the tent of meeting. And everyone who sought the LORD would go out to the tent of meeting, which was outside the camp. 8Whenever Moses went out to the tent, all the people would rise and stand, each of them, at the entrance of their tents and watch Moses until he had gone into the tent. 9When Moses entered the tent, the pillar of cloud would descend and stand at the entrance of the tent, and the LORD would speak with Moses. 10When all the people saw the pillar of cloud standing at the entrance of the tent, all the people would rise and bow down, all of them, at the entrance of their tent. 11Thus the LORD used to speak to Moses face to face, as one speaks to a friend. Then he would return to the camp; but his young assistant, Joshua son of Nun, would not leave the tent.

Moses' Intercession

12 Moses said to the LORD, "See, you have said to me, 'Bring up this people'; but you have not let me know whom you will send with me. Yet you have said, 'I know you by name, and you have also found favor in my sight.' 13Now if I have found favor in your sight, show me your ways, so that I may know you and find favor in your sight. Consider too that this nation is your people." 14He said, "My presence will go with you, and I will give you rest." 15And he said to him, "If your presence will not go, do not carry us up from here. 16For how shall it be known that I have found favor in your sight, I and your people, unless you go with us? In this way, we shall be distinct, I and your people, from every people on the face of the earth."

17 The LORD said to Moses, "I will do the very thing that you have asked; for you have found favor in my sight, and I know you by name." 18Moses said, "Show me your glory, I pray." 19And he said, "I will make all my goodness pass before you, and will proclaim before you the name, 'The LORD';a and I will be gracious to whom I will be gracious, and will show mercy on whom I will show mercy. 20But," he said, "you cannot see my face; for no one shall see me and live." 21And the LORD continued, "See, there is a place by me where you shall stand on the rock; 22and while my glory passes by I will put you in a cleft of the rock, and I will cover you with my hand until I have passed by; 23then I will take away my hand, and you shall see my back; but my face shall not be seen."

a Heb YHWH; see note at 3.15

---

the initiative. **33.5** *For the* LORD *had said,* lit. "The LORD said," which would seem to precede v. 4. *And I will decide,* lit. "so that I will know," in Hebrew a pun on *ornaments.* **33.6** *Horeb.* See note on 3.1. **33.7** *Pitch it.* The Hebrew adds "for himself." Moses pitches the tent to administer the oracle (see v. 9; cf. note on 25.1–31.18). This *tent of meeting* is the precursor of the tabernacle, also called the tent of meeting (e.g., 27.21), which will be located at the center of the camp (Num 2.2). The *tent* cannot be situated in the camp until the camp can be cleansed of ritual pollution through appropriate cultic activity (cf. Num 5.1–4). **33.9** *Cloud.* See notes on 13.21; 24.15; cf. 40.34–38; Num 11.25; 12.5; Deut 31.15. *Entrance.* Cf. 25.22. **33.11** *Face to face,* figurative for immediate contact (see vv. 20–23); cf. Num 12.8 (lit. "mouth to mouth"); Deut 34.10. *Joshua.* See note on 17.9. **33.12–23** Note the key words *see, face* (cf. v. 11), and *know.* **33.12** *See,* responding to vv. 1–3. *Whom.* In light of v. 2, Moses would be asking for the angel's name (see Gen 32.29; Judg 13.17–18; cf.

3.13). *Know,* lit. "have known," an idiom for "to elect" (Jer 1.5; Hos 13.5). Moses anticipates the Lord (v. 17). **33.13** *Show me,* lit. "let me know." *Ways.* See v. 19; 34.6–7; cf. Ps 103.7–18. *Consider,* rendered *see* in v. 12. *Your,* responding to v. 1; cf. 32.11. **33.14** *Presence,* lit. "face" (also v. 15), replying to vv. 2–3 and anticipating 34.9. *Go.* Cf. 32.1. *Give you rest,* a play in Hebrew on *lead* (32.34) and referring to the settlement of Israel in Canaan (see Deut 3.20; 12.10; Josh 22.4). **33.15** *Carry . . . up,* rendered *bring up* in v. 12. **33.16** *Be distinct.* See note on 11.7; cf. Deut 7.6. **33.17** *Know.* See note on 33.12. **33.18** *Show me,* lit. "let me see." *Glory.* See note on 16.6–7. **33.19** *Goodness,* or "splendor" ("fair" in Hos 10.11). *LORD.* See note on 3.14. *Gracious,* in Hebrew cognate to *favor* (vv. 12, 13, 16, 17). Cf. 34.6. **33.20** See note on 3.6. **33.21** *See,* lit. "here." *Place.* Cf. 3.5. *Stand.* See note on 2.4. The Hebrew term is rendered *present yourself* in 34.2. *Rock.* Cf. 17.6. **33.22** *Passed.* See 1 Kings 19.11–12. **33.23** For the effect, see 34.29.

Moses Makes New Tablets

34 The LORD said to Moses, "Cut two tablets of stone like the former ones, and I will write on the tablets the words that were on the former tablets, which you broke. ²Be ready in the morning, and come up in the morning to Mount Sinai and present yourself there to me, on the top of the mountain. ³No one shall come up with you, and do not let anyone be seen throughout all the mountain; and do not let flocks or herds graze in front of that mountain." ⁴So Moses cut two tablets of stone like the former ones; and he rose early in the morning and went up on Mount Sinai, as the LORD had commanded him, and took in his hand the two tablets of stone. ⁵The LORD descended in the cloud and stood with him there, and proclaimed the name, "The LORD." *a* ⁶The LORD passed before him, and proclaimed,

"The LORD, the LORD,
a God merciful and gracious,
slow to anger,
and abounding in steadfast love and
         faithfulness,
7 keeping steadfast love for the thousandth
         generation, *b*
forgiving iniquity and transgression and
         sin,
yet by no means clearing the guilty,
but visiting the iniquity of the parents
upon the children
and the children's children,
to the third and the fourth generation."

⁸And Moses quickly bowed his head toward the earth, and worshiped. ⁹He said, "If now I have found favor in your sight, O Lord, I pray, let the Lord go with us. Although this is a stiff-necked people, pardon our iniquity and our sin, and take us for your inheritance."

The Covenant Renewed

10 He said: I hereby make a covenant. Before all your people I will perform marvels, such as have not been performed in all the earth or in any nation; and all the people among whom you live shall see the work of the LORD; for it is an awesome thing that I will do with you.

11 Observe what I command you today. See, I will drive out before you the Amorites, the Canaanites, the Hittites, the Perizzites, the Hivites, and the Jebusites. ¹²Take care not to make a covenant with the inhabitants of the land to which you are going, or it will become a snare among you. ¹³You shall tear down their altars, break their pillars, and cut down their sacred poles *c* ¹⁴(for you shall worship no other god, because the LORD, whose name is Jealous, is a jealous God). ¹⁵You shall not make a covenant with the inhabitants of the land, for when they prostitute themselves to their gods and sacrifice to their gods, someone among them will invite you, and you will eat of the sacrifice. ¹⁶And you will take wives from among their daughters for your sons, and their daughters who prostitute themselves to their gods will make your sons also prostitute themselves to their gods.

17 You shall not make cast idols.

18 You shall keep the festival of unleavened bread. Seven days you shall eat unleavened bread, as I commanded you, at the time ap-

a Heb YHWH; see note at 3.15   *b* Or *for thousands*
c Heb *Asherim*

34.1–8 Following the pardon of the people's apostasy, the Lord dispenses another covenant-forging revelation. **34.1** *Cut.* Cf. v. 28. *I will write.* Cf. v. 28; see Deut 10.1–2, 4. **34.2** *Be ready* and *morning* evoke the Sinai revelation (see 19.11, 15, 16; the Hebrew term rendered *prepare* there is the same one rendered *ready* here). *Top.* Cf. 19.20. **34.3** *No one.* Cf. 24.2, 12; 19.24. *Be seen.* Cf. 19.12–13, 21–24. **34.5** *The cloud,* lit. "a cloud"; cf. 19.9, 16; 24.15; see note on 13.21. *Stood.* See note on 33.21. *Proclaimed,* or "invoked" (e.g., Gen 12.8), the subject being Moses; cf. 33.19. **34.6–7** See notes on 20.5; 20.6; 20.7. Variants are found in Num 14.18; Neh 9.17; Pss 86.15; 103.8; 145.8; Jer 32.18; Joel 2.13; Jon 4.2; Nah 1.3, but these variants tend to focus on the divine compassion and omit the retribution. **34.8** *Toward the earth.* Bowing the head "to the ground" was a conventional gesture of homage and is depicted in ancient art. **34.9** See note on 33.14. **34.10–26** In view of Israel's cultic deviance in the golden calf incident (ch. 32), a reiteration of some fundamental ritual laws. **34.10** *Marvels,* translated *wonders* in 3.20 and similar to the term rendered *set apart* in 8.22. *Performed,* rather "created"; cf. Num 16.30; Deut 4.32–34. **34.11** Cf. 23.28; 33.2. **34.12** Cf. 23.32–33. **34.13** *Pillars.* Cf. 23.24. *Sacred poles,* stylized trees (Deut 16.21); the Hebrew term for them, *asherim,* is cognate with Asherah, the Canaanite mother goddess (cf. Judg 6.25); cf. Deut 7.5; 12.3. **34.14** *Jealous,* perhaps a play on the Lord's name, Yahweh, whose root can mean "crave" (Prov 10.3). Cf. 20.3, 5. **34.15** *Prostitute themselves.* See Num 25.1–2; cf. Lev 17.7; 20.5–6; Deut 31.16; Judg 2.17; 8.33. **34.16** Cf. Judg 3.6. **34.17** Cf. 20.4, 23; Lev 19.4. **34.18** In contrast to 23.12–15, the *festival of unleavened bread* is mentioned here before the sabbath and is

pointed in the month of Abib; for in the month of Abib you came out from Egypt.

19 All that first opens the womb is mine, all your male[a] livestock, the firstborn of cow and sheep. 20 The firstborn of a donkey you shall redeem with a lamb, or if you will not redeem it you shall break its neck. All the firstborn of your sons you shall redeem.

No one shall appear before me empty-handed.

21 Six days you shall work, but on the seventh day you shall rest; even in plowing time and in harvest time you shall rest. 22 You shall observe the festival of weeks, the first fruits of wheat harvest, and the festival of ingathering at the turn of the year. 23 Three times in the year all your males shall appear before the LORD God, the God of Israel. 24 For I will cast out nations before you, and enlarge your borders; no one shall covet your land when you go up to appear before the LORD your God three times in the year.

25 You shall not offer the blood of my sacrifice with leaven, and the sacrifice of the festival of the passover shall not be left until the morning.

26 The best of the first fruits of your ground you shall bring to the house of the LORD your God.

You shall not boil a kid in its mother's milk.

27 The LORD said to Moses: Write these words; in accordance with these words I have made a covenant with you and with Israel. 28 He was there with the LORD forty days and forty nights; he neither ate bread nor drank water. And he wrote on the tablets the words of the covenant, the ten commandments.[b]

The Shining Face of Moses

29 Moses came down from Mount Sinai. As he came down from the mountain with the two tablets of the covenant[c] in his hand, Moses did not know that the skin of his face shone because he had been talking with God. 30 When Aaron and all the Israelites saw Moses, the skin of his face was shining, and they were afraid to come near him. 31 But Moses called to them; and Aaron and all the leaders of the congregation returned to him, and Moses spoke with them. 32 Afterward all the Israelites came near, and he gave them in commandment all that the LORD had spoken with him on Mount Sinai. 33 When Moses had finished speaking with them, he put a veil on his face; 34 but whenever Moses went in before the LORD to speak with him, he would take the veil off, until he came out; and when he came out, and told the Israelites what he had been commanded, 35 the Israelites would see the face of Moses, that the skin of his face was shining; and Moses would put the veil on his face again, until he went in to speak with him.

Sabbath Regulations

35 Moses assembled all the congregation of the Israelites and said to them: These are the things that the LORD has commanded you to do:

2 Six days shall work be done, but on the seventh day you shall have a holy sabbath of solemn rest to the LORD; whoever does any

---

a Gk Theodotion Vg Tg: Meaning of Heb uncertain
b Heb words c Or treaty, or testimony; Heb eduth

---

separated from the other two pilgrimages, perhaps by virtue of its immediate connection to the exodus. **34.19–20** Cf. 13.12–13. *No one . . . empty-handed* pertains to the preceding law (v. 18; see 23.15); in ch. 13 too the law about the firstborn is juxtaposed with the Festival of Unleavened Bread. **34.21** Cf. 23.12. **34.22–23** Cf. 23.16–17. For the name *festival of weeks,* see Deut 16.9–10. **34.22** *Turn,* lit. "(completed) circuit." **34.24** *Cast out,* lit. "dispossess" (Deut 9.5); cf. 23.23, 27–31; Deut 4.38 (where "driving out" translates the same verb). *Enlarge.* Cf. Deut 12.20 (where "territory" translates the same word as *borders* here). *Covet.* See note on 20.17; cf. the allaying of fear in 23.29–30. *Go up,* an anticipation of the Jerusalem temple (e.g., 1 Kings 12.27). **34.25–26** Cf. 23.18–19. **34.27** *These words,* vv. 11–26. **34.28** *Forty.* Cf. 24.18. Here a second forty-day period is indicated; cf. Deut 10.10. *Neither ate . . . water.* Cf. Deut 9.9, 18; a semidivine state is sug-

gested. *Wrote.* See note on 34.1. *Commandments.* See v. 1. **34.29** *Moses came,* rather, "As Moses came." *Shone,* in Hebrew cognate to "rays" (Hab 3.4); see notes on 13.21; 14.24. *God,* lit. "him," some of whose radiance was imparted to Moses (see 33.17–23). **34.30** *They were afraid,* because Moses looked like a god; see v. 20; cf. 14.24. **34.31** *Returned,* rather "turned." **34.33** *Veil.* Cf. the cloud covering the deity's glory (e.g., 24.16). **34.34** *Before the LORD,* into the tent of meeting; see 33.7; Num 7.89.

35.1–3 Moses begins his instructions to the Israelites with the last matter in which he was instructed before descending the mountain (31.12–17); in this way the preceding topic of building the tabernacle (chs. 25–31) is resumed in what follows (chs. 35–40). The preparations for and construction of the tabernacle repeat the language of the instructions nearly verbatim, though with several ellipses. **35.2** Cf. 31.15.

work on it shall be put to death. ³You shall kindle no fire in all your dwellings on the sabbath day.

Preparations for Making the Tabernacle

4 Moses said to all the congregation of the Israelites: This is the thing that the LORD has commanded: ⁵Take from among you an offering to the LORD; let whoever is of a generous heart bring the LORD's offering: gold, silver, and bronze; ⁶blue, purple, and crimson yarns, and fine linen; goats' hair, ⁷tanned rams' skins, and fine leather;ᵃ acacia wood, ⁸oil for the light, spices for the anointing oil and for the fragrant incense, ⁹and onyx stones and gems to be set in the ephod and the breastpiece.

10 All who are skillful among you shall come and make all that the LORD has commanded: the tabernacle, ¹¹its tent and its covering, its clasps and its frames, its bars, its pillars, and its bases; ¹²the ark with its poles, the mercy seat,ᵇ and the curtain for the screen; ¹³the table with its poles and all its utensils, and the bread of the Presence; ¹⁴the lampstand also for the light, with its utensils and its lamps, and the oil for the light; ¹⁵and the altar of incense, with its poles, and the anointing oil and the fragrant incense, and the screen for the entrance, the entrance of the tabernacle; ¹⁶the altar of burnt offering, with its grating of bronze, its poles, and all its utensils, the basin with its stand; ¹⁷the hangings of the court, its pillars and its bases, and the screen for the gate of the court; ¹⁸the pegs of the tabernacle and the pegs of the court, and their cords; ¹⁹the finely worked vestments for ministering in the holy place, the holy vestments for the priest Aaron, and the vestments of his sons, for their service as priests.

Offerings for the Tabernacle

20 Then all the congregation of the Israelites withdrew from the presence of Moses. ²¹And they came, everyone whose heart was stirred, and everyone whose spirit was willing, and brought the LORD's offering to be used for the tent of meeting, and for all its service, and for the sacred vestments. ²²So they came, both men and women; all who were of a willing heart brought brooches and earrings and signet rings and pendants, all sorts of gold objects, everyone bringing an offering of gold to the LORD. ²³And everyone who possessed blue or purple or crimson yarn or fine linen or goats' hair or tanned rams' skins or fine leather,ᵃ brought them. ²⁴Everyone who could make an offering of silver or bronze brought it as the LORD's offering; and everyone who possessed acacia wood of any use in the work, brought it. ²⁵All the skillful women spun with their hands, and brought what they had spun in blue and purple and crimson yarns and fine linen; ²⁶all the women whose hearts moved them to use their skill spun the goats' hair. ²⁷And the leaders brought onyx stones and gems to be set in the ephod and the breastpiece, ²⁸and spices and oil for the light, and for the anointing oil, and for the fragrant incense. ²⁹All the Israelite men and women whose hearts made them willing to bring anything for the work that the LORD had commanded by Moses to be done, brought it as a freewill offering to the LORD.

Bezalel and Oholiab

30 Then Moses said to the Israelites: See, the LORD has called by name Bezalel son of Uri son of Hur, of the tribe of Judah; ³¹he has filled him with divine spirit,ᶜ with skill, intelligence, and knowledge in every kind of craft, ³²to devise artistic designs, to work in gold, silver, and bronze, ³³in cutting stones for setting, and in carving wood, in every kind of craft. ³⁴And he has inspired him to teach, both him and Oholiab son of Ahisamach, of the tribe of

---

ᵃ Meaning of Heb uncertain ᵇ Or *the cover* ᶜ Or *the spirit of God*

35.3 Cf. 16.23; see note on 20.8. 35.4–9 Cf. 25.2–7. The tabernacle's purpose (see 25.8; 29.45–46) is omitted. 35.10–19 An expansive parallel to 31.6–11; the list is pervaded by rhythmic repetition, assonance, and rhyme (cf. note on 28.34). The description moves from the holy of holies to the tabernacle proper to the court, each closed on the east by a screen (vv. 12, 10, 17). 35.10 *Skillful.* See note on 28.3. 35.12 *Curtain for the screen*, called a *screen* only here; cf. 26.31–33, where no screen is mentioned, but see 40.3 for an association between the terms *screen* and *curtain*. 35.14 *Also*, not in the Hebrew. 35.20–29 The overwhelming response (see also 36.3–7) redeems the people's contributions to the illicit cult (32.2–3). Cf. 2 Chr 24.4–14. 35.20 *The presence of,* or "attendance upon." 35.22 *Earrings.* Cf. 32.2–3. *Offering*, rendered *elevation offering* in 29.27, here in a general sense (as in 38.24). 35.23 *Fine leather.* See note on 25.5. 35.30–33 Cf. 31.1–5. 35.34–35 A more elaborate version of 31.6, adding notably *to teach* the artisans.

Dan. 35He has filled them with skill to do every kind of work done by an artisan or by a designer or by an embroiderer in blue, purple, and crimson yarns, and in fine linen, or by a weaver—by any sort of artisan or skilled designer.

36 Bezalel and Oholiab and every skillful one to whom the LORD has given skill and understanding to know how to do any work in the construction of the sanctuary shall work in accordance with all that the LORD has commanded.

2 Moses then called Bezalel and Oholiab and every skillful one to whom the LORD had given skill, everyone whose heart was stirred to come to do the work; 3and they received from Moses all the freewill offerings that the Israelites had brought for doing the work on the sanctuary. They still kept bringing him freewill offerings every morning, 4so that all the artisans who were doing every sort of task on the sanctuary came, each from the task being performed, 5and said to Moses, "The people are bringing much more than enough for doing the work that the LORD has commanded us to do." 6So Moses gave command, and word was proclaimed throughout the camp: "No man or woman is to make anything else as an offering for the sanctuary." So the people were restrained from bringing; 7for what they had already brought was more than enough to do all the work.

Construction of the Tabernacle

8 All those with skill among the workers made the tabernacle with ten curtains; they were made of fine twisted linen, and blue, purple, and crimson yarns, with cherubim skillfully worked into them. 9The length of each curtain was twenty-eight cubits, and the width of each curtain four cubits; all the curtains were of the same size.

10 He joined five curtains to one another, and the other five curtains he joined to one another. 11He made loops of blue on the edge of the outermost curtain of the first set; likewise he made them on the edge of the outermost curtain of the second set; 12he made fifty loops on the one curtain, and he made fifty loops on the edge of the curtain that was in the second set; the loops were opposite one another. 13And he made fifty clasps of gold, and joined the curtains one to the other with clasps; so the tabernacle was one whole.

14 He also made curtains of goats' hair for a tent over the tabernacle; he made eleven curtains. 15The length of each curtain was thirty cubits, and the width of each curtain four cubits; the eleven curtains were of the same size. 16He joined five curtains by themselves, and six curtains by themselves. 17He made fifty loops on the edge of the outermost curtain of the one set, and fifty loops on the edge of the other connecting curtain. 18He made fifty clasps of bronze to join the tent together so that it might be one whole. 19And he made for the tent a covering of tanned rams' skins and an outer covering of fine leather.[a]

20 Then he made the upright frames for the tabernacle of acacia wood. 21Ten cubits was the length of a frame, and a cubit and a half the width of each frame. 22Each frame had two pegs for fitting together; he did this for all the frames of the tabernacle. 23The frames for the tabernacle he made in this way: twenty frames for the south side; 24and he made forty bases of silver under the twenty frames, two bases under the first frame for its two pegs, and two bases under the next frame for its two pegs. 25For the second side of the tabernacle, on the north side, he made twenty frames 26and their forty bases of silver, two bases under the first frame and two bases under the next frame. 27For the rear of the tabernacle westward he made six frames. 28He made two frames for corners of the tabernacle in the rear. 29They were separate beneath, but joined at the top, at the first ring; he made two of them in this way, for the two corners. 30There were eight frames with their bases of silver: sixteen bases, under every frame two bases.

31 He made bars of acacia wood, five for the frames of the one side of the tabernacle, 32and five bars for the frames of the other side of the tabernacle, and five bars for the frames of the tabernacle at the rear westward. 33He made the middle bar to pass through from end to end halfway up the frames. 34And he overlaid the frames with gold, and made rings of gold for them to hold the bars, and overlaid the bars with gold.

35 He made the curtain of blue, purple, and crimson yarns, and fine twisted linen, with cherubim skillfully worked into it. 36For it he made four pillars of acacia, and overlaid them with gold; their hooks were of gold, and he

a Meaning of Heb uncertain

cast for them four bases of silver. [37]He also made a screen for the entrance to the tent, of blue, purple, and crimson yarns, and fine twisted linen, embroidered with needlework; [38]and its five pillars with their hooks. He overlaid their capitals and their bases with gold, but their five bases were of bronze.

Making the Ark of the Covenant

37 Bezalel made the ark of acacia wood; it was two and a half cubits long, a cubit and a half wide, and a cubit and a half high. [2]He overlaid it with pure gold inside and outside, and made a molding of gold around it. [3]He cast for it four rings of gold for its four feet, two rings on its one side and two rings on its other side. [4]He made poles of acacia wood, and overlaid them with gold, [5]and put the poles into the rings on the sides of the ark, to carry the ark. [6]He made a mercy seat[a] of pure gold; two cubits and a half was its length, and a cubit and a half its width. [7]He made two cherubim of hammered gold; at the two ends of the mercy seat[b] he made them, [8]one cherub at the one end, and one cherub at the other end; of one piece with the mercy seat[b] he made the cherubim at its two ends. [9]The cherubim spread out their wings above, overshadowing the mercy seat[b] with their wings. They faced one another; the faces of the cherubim were turned toward the mercy seat.[b]

Making the Table for the Bread of the Presence

10 He also made the table of acacia wood, two cubits long, one cubit wide, and a cubit and a half high. [11]He overlaid it with pure gold, and made a molding of gold around it. [12]He made around it a rim a handbreadth wide, and made a molding of gold around the rim. [13]He cast for it four rings of gold, and fastened the rings to the four corners at its four legs. [14]The rings that held the poles used for carrying the table were close to the rim. [15]He made the poles of acacia wood to carry the table, and overlaid them with gold. [16]And he made the vessels of pure gold that were to be on the table, its plates and dishes for incense, and its bowls and flagons with which to pour drink offerings.

Making the Lampstand

17 He also made the lampstand of pure gold. The base and the shaft of the lampstand were made of hammered work; its cups, its calyxes, and its petals were of one piece with it. [18]There were six branches going out of its sides, three branches of the lampstand out of one side of it and three branches of the lampstand out of the other side of it; [19]three cups shaped like almond blossoms, each with calyx and petals, on one branch, and three cups shaped like almond blossoms, each with calyx and petals, on the other branch—so for the six branches going out of the lampstand. [20]On the lampstand itself there were four cups shaped like almond blossoms, each with its calyxes and petals. [21]There was a calyx of one piece with it under the first pair of branches, a calyx of one piece with it under the next pair of branches, and a calyx of one piece with it under the last pair of branches. [22]Their calyxes and their branches were of one piece with it, the whole of it one hammered piece of pure gold. [23]He made its seven lamps and its snuffers and its trays of pure gold. [24]He made it and all its utensils of a talent of pure gold.

Making the Altar of Incense

25 He made the altar of incense of acacia wood, one cubit long, and one cubit wide; it was square, and was two cubits high; its horns

---

a Or a cover b Or the cover

36.1 In the construction of, rather "in connection with the service (i.e., sacrificial cult)" (see 39.40); cf. note on 27.19. **36.2** Come, "come near" (see note on 29.3). **36.3** Received, "took." Freewill offering, rather an offering (as in v. 6). Doing the work, or "the work of the service" (see note on 36.1). **36.4** Task, rendered work in vv. 1–2. **36.5–7** The people bring too much; Pharaoh had complained they were doing too little for him (5.4–9).

36.8–39.31 Unlike the instructions, which tend to treat the holiest objects first, the construction follows a practical sequence in which the holiest objects are not made until their protective surroundings are. Portions of the instructions that deal with the use of the ritual paraphernalia are typically omitted. **36.8–19** Cf. 26.1–14. **36.10** He, Bezalel (35.30–35; cf. 37.1). **36.20–34** Cf. 26.15–29. The command to erect the tabernacle (26.30) is fulfilled not here but in 40.17–19. Most other details of setting up parts of the tabernacle are altogether omitted. **36.35–38** Cf. 26.31–32, 36–37.

37.1–9 Cf. 25.10–14, 17–20. **37.1** Bezalel, Moses according to Deut 10.3, 5. **37.10–16** Cf. 25.23–29. **37.17–24** Cf. 25.31–39.

were of one piece with it. 26He overlaid it with pure gold, its top, and its sides all around, and its horns; and he made for it a molding of gold all around, 27and made two golden rings for it under its molding, on two opposite sides of it, to hold the poles with which to carry it. 28And he made the poles of acacia wood, and overlaid them with gold.

Making the Anointing Oil and the Incense

29 He made the holy anointing oil also, and the pure fragrant incense, blended as by the perfumer.

Making the Altar of Burnt Offering

38 He made the altar of burnt offering also of acacia wood; it was five cubits long, and five cubits wide; it was square, and three cubits high. 2He made horns for it on its four corners; its horns were of one piece with it, and he overlaid it with bronze. 3He made all the utensils of the altar, the pots, the shovels, the basins, the forks, and the firepans: all its utensils he made of bronze. 4He made for the altar a grating, a network of bronze, under its ledge, extending halfway down. 5He cast four rings on the four corners of the bronze grating to hold the poles; 6he made the poles of acacia wood, and overlaid them with bronze. 7And he put the poles through the rings on the sides of the altar, to carry it with them; he made it hollow, with boards.

8 He made the basin of bronze with its stand of bronze, from the mirrors of the women who served at the entrance to the tent of meeting.

Making the Court of the Tabernacle

9 He made the court; for the south side the hangings of the court were of fine twisted linen, one hundred cubits long; 10its twenty pillars and their twenty bases were of bronze, but the hooks of the pillars and their bands were of silver. 11For the north side there were hangings one hundred cubits long; its twenty pillars and their twenty bases were of bronze, but the hooks of the pillars and their bands were of silver. 12For the west side there were hangings fifty cubits long, with ten pillars and ten bases; the hooks of the pillars and their bands were of silver. 13And for the front to the east, fifty cubits. 14The hangings for one side of the gate were fifteen cubits, with three pil-

lars and three bases. 15And so for the other side; on each side of the gate of the court were hangings of fifteen cubits, with three pillars and three bases. 16All the hangings around the court were of fine twisted linen. 17The bases for the pillars were of bronze, but the hooks of the pillars and their bands were of silver; the overlaying of their capitals was also of silver, and all the pillars of the court were banded with silver. 18The screen for the entrance to the court was embroidered with needlework in blue, purple, and crimson yarns and fine twisted linen. It was twenty cubits long and, along the width of it, five cubits high, corresponding to the hangings of the court. 19There were four pillars; their four bases were of bronze, their hooks of silver, and the overlaying of their capitals and their bands of silver. 20All the pegs for the tabernacle and for the court all around were of bronze.

Materials of the Tabernacle

21 These are the records of the tabernacle, the tabernacle of the covenant,*a* which were drawn up at the commandment of Moses, the work of the Levites being under the direction of Ithamar son of the priest Aaron. 22Bezalel son of Uri son of Hur, of the tribe of Judah, made all that the LORD commanded Moses; 23and with him was Oholiab son of Ahisamach, of the tribe of Dan, engraver, designer, and embroiderer in blue, purple, and crimson yarns, and in fine linen.

24 All the gold that was used for the work, in all the construction of the sanctuary, the gold from the offering, was twenty-nine talents and seven hundred thirty shekels, measured by the sanctuary shekel. 25The silver from those of the congregation who were counted was one hundred talents and one thousand seven hundred seventy-five shekels, measured by the sanctuary shekel; 26a beka a head (that is, half a shekel, measured by the sanctuary shekel), for everyone who was counted in the census, from twenty years old and upward, for six hundred three thousand, five hundred fifty men. 27The hundred talents of silver were for casting the bases of the sanctuary, and the bases of the curtain; one hundred bases for the hundred talents, a talent for a base. 28Of the thousand seven hundred sev-

---

a Or *treaty*, or *testimony*; Heb *eduth*

enty-five shekels he made hooks for the pillars, and overlaid their capitals and made bands for them. 29The bronze that was contributed was seventy talents, and two thousand four hundred shekels; 30with it he made the bases for the entrance of the tent of meeting, the bronze altar and the bronze grating for it and all the utensils of the altar, 31the bases all around the court, and the bases of the gate of the court, all the pegs of the tabernacle, and all the pegs around the court.

Making the Vestments for the Priesthood

39 Of the blue, purple, and crimson yarns they made finely worked vestments, for ministering in the holy place; they made the sacred vestments for Aaron; as the LORD had commanded Moses.

2 He made the ephod of gold, of blue, purple, and crimson yarns, and of fine twisted linen. 3Gold leaf was hammered out and cut into threads to work into the blue, purple, and crimson yarns and into the fine twisted linen, in skilled design. 4They made for the ephod shoulder-pieces, joined to it at its two edges. 5The decorated band on it was of the same materials and workmanship, of gold, of blue, purple, and crimson yarns, and of fine twisted linen; as the LORD had commanded Moses.

6 The onyx stones were prepared, enclosed in settings of gold filigree and engraved like the engravings of a signet, according to the names of the sons of Israel. 7He set them on the shoulder-pieces of the ephod, to be stones of remembrance for the sons of Israel; as the LORD had commanded Moses.

8 He made the breastpiece, in skilled work, like the work of the ephod, of gold, of blue, purple, and crimson yarns, and of fine twisted linen. 9It was square; the breastpiece was made double, a span in length and a span in width when doubled. 10They set in it four rows of stones. A row of carnelian,*a* chrysolite, and emerald was the first row; 11and the second row, a turquoise, a sapphire,*b* and a moonstone; 12and the third row, a jacinth, an agate, and an amethyst; 13and the fourth row, a beryl, an onyx, and a jasper; they were enclosed in settings of gold filigree. 14There were twelve stones with names corresponding to the names of the sons of Israel; they were like signets, each engraved with its name, for the twelve tribes. 15They made on the breastpiece chains of pure gold, twisted like cords; 16and they made two settings of gold filigree and two gold rings, and put the two rings on the two edges of the breastpiece; 17and they put the two cords of gold in the two rings at the edges of the breastpiece. 18Two ends of the two cords they had attached to the two settings of filigree; in this way they attached it in front to the shoulder-pieces of the ephod. 19Then they made two rings of gold, and put them at the two ends of the breastpiece, on its inside edge next to the ephod. 20They made two rings of gold, and attached them in front to the lower part of the two shoulder-pieces of the ephod, at its joining above the decorated band of the ephod. 21They bound the breastpiece by its rings to the rings of the ephod with a blue

---

a The identification of several of these stones is uncertain
b Or *lapis lazuli*

37.25–28 Cf. 30.1–5. 37.29 A summary of 30.22–25, 34–35. 38.1–7 Cf. 27.1–8. 38.1 *Altar of burnt offering*, in contradistinction to the altar of incense (37.25–28). 38.2 *He*, Bezalel, but Eleazar according to Num 16.38–39. 38.8 *Basin of bronze.* Cf. 30.18. *From the mirrors . . . tent of meeting* provides new information, possibly alluding to a lost episode similar to the one in 1 Sam 2.22 in which the women who served were made to surrender their mirrors on account of sexual misconduct; for ritual paraphernalia melted down and reused as a cautionary reminder of misdeeds, see Num 16.36–40. The reference is out of place here since the tent has not yet been erected. 38.9–20 Cf. 27.9–19. 38.21–31 The inventory of metals presupposes the census that is prescribed in 30.12–16 but performed only in Num 1, dated a month later than the erection of the tabernacle (cf. 40.17; Num 1.1). 38.21 *Records*, rather "tally" (rendered *counted*, *census* in vv. 25–26). *Drawn up*, rather

"counted." *Levites*, anachronistic (see Num 3.5–13). *Ithamar.* Cf. Num 4.33; the death of Aaron's older sons (Lev 10.1–2) seems to be assumed. 38.22–23 Cf. 31.2–6; 35.30–35. 38.24 *Talents.* See note on 25.39. 38.25 There is also freely donated silver (25.2–3; 35.5, 24). 38.26 *Beka*, the term found as a label on excavated weights of that size. *Census.* Cf. Num 1.45–46. 38.30 The *basin* is omitted; see v. 8.

39.1–31 Cf. ch. 28. 39.1 *Of the blue . . . yarns* harks back to 38.23 (accordingly the use here of *they*, Bezalel and Oholiab), but *fine linen* is omitted. *As the LORD*, a sevenfold refrain in the passage, recalling the seven-day structure of Gen 1.1–2.4. 39.2 *He*, Bezalel (37.1). 39.3 *Gold leaf*, an additional detail. *Was hammered out*, rather "they hammered out," the volunteers (36.2, 4), who apparently also made the curtains, screen, and hangings (26.1–14, 31, 36; 27.9–15) that are omitted from the account; cf. v. 42.

cord, so that it should lie on the decorated band of the ephod, and that the breastpiece should not come loose from the ephod; as the LORD had commanded Moses.

22 He also made the robe of the ephod woven all of blue yarn; 23and the opening of the robe in the middle of it was like the opening in a coat of mail,[a] with a binding around the opening, so that it might not be torn. 24On the lower hem of the robe they made pomegranates of blue, purple, and crimson yarns, and of fine twisted linen. 25They also made bells of pure gold, and put the bells between the pomegranates on the lower hem of the robe all around, between the pomegranates; 26a bell and a pomegranate, a bell and a pomegranate all around on the lower hem of the robe for ministering; as the LORD had commanded Moses.

27 They also made the tunics, woven of fine linen, for Aaron and his sons, 28and the turban of fine linen, and the headdresses of fine linen, and the linen undergarments of fine twisted linen, 29and the sash of fine twisted linen, and of blue, purple, and crimson yarns, embroidered with needlework; as the LORD had commanded Moses.

30 They made the rosette of the holy diadem of pure gold, and wrote on it an inscription, like the engraving of a signet, "Holy to the LORD." 31They tied to it a blue cord, to fasten it on the turban above; as the LORD had commanded Moses.

The Work Completed

32 In this way all the work of the tabernacle of the tent of meeting was finished; the Israelites had done everything just as the LORD had commanded Moses. 33Then they brought the tabernacle to Moses, the tent and all its utensils, its hooks, its frames, its bars, its pillars, and its bases; 34the covering of tanned rams' skins and the covering of fine leather,[a] and the curtain for the screen; 35the ark of the covenant[b] with its poles and the mercy seat;[c] 36the table with all its utensils, and the bread of the Presence; 37the pure lampstand with its lamps set on it and all its utensils, and the oil for the light; 38the golden altar, the anointing oil and the fragrant incense, and the screen for the entrance of the tent; 39the bronze altar, and its grating of bronze, its poles, and all its utensils; the basin with its stand; 40the hangings of the court, its pillars, and its bases, and the screen for the gate of the court, its cords, and its pegs; and all the utensils for the service of the tabernacle, for the tent of meeting; 41the finely worked vestments for ministering in the holy place, the sacred vestments for the priest Aaron, and the vestments of his sons to serve as priests. 42The Israelites had done all of the work just as the LORD had commanded Moses. 43When Moses saw that they had done all the work just as the LORD had commanded, he blessed them.

The Tabernacle Erected and Its Equipment Installed

40 The LORD spoke to Moses: 2On the first day of the first month you shall set up the tabernacle of the tent of meeting. 3You shall put in it the ark of the covenant,[b] and you shall screen the ark with the curtain. 4You shall bring in the table, and arrange its setting; and you shall bring in the lampstand, and set up its lamps. 5You shall put the golden altar for incense before the ark of the covenant,[b] and set up the screen for the entrance of the tabernacle. 6You shall set the altar of burnt offering before the entrance of the tabernacle of the tent of meeting, 7and place the basin between the tent of meeting and the altar, and put water in it. 8You shall set up the court all around, and hang up the screen for the gate of the court. 9Then you shall take the anointing oil, and anoint the tabernacle and all that is in it, and consecrate it and all its furniture, so that it shall become holy. 10You shall also anoint the altar of burnt offering and all its

a Meaning of Heb uncertain   b Or treaty, or testimony; Heb eduth   c Or the cover

---

39.30 Diadem. Cf. 29.6. **39.32** In this way, not in the Hebrew. Finished. Cf. Gen 2.1; also cf. Ex 40.33; Gen 2.2; see note on 39.43. Near Eastern myth, e.g., the Babylonian Enuma Elish, associates temple building with creation; see note on 40.2. **39.33–41** Cf. 35.11–19. **39.42** Israelites. See note on 39.3. Work connotes service in maintaining the cultic or religious life of the community (see note on 36.1), different from the term translated work in v. 43. **39.43** Work, as in Gen 2.2–3. Blessed. Cf. Gen 2.3.

40.2 First month, the new year according to the rhythms of the ritual life of the community; see 12.2; note on 39.32. The new year, temple (or tabernacle) building, and creation are associated in the Israelite worldview. Cf. v. 17. You. See 25.9. **40.3** Screen. Cf. 35.12. **40.4** Setting. See 25.29–30. **40.5** Before, but out-

utensils, and consecrate the altar, so that the altar shall be most holy. ¹¹You shall also anoint the basin with its stand, and consecrate it. ¹²Then you shall bring Aaron and his sons to the entrance of the tent of meeting, and shall wash them with water, ¹³and put on Aaron the sacred vestments, and you shall anoint him and consecrate him, so that he may serve me as priest. ¹⁴You shall bring his sons also and put tunics on them, ¹⁵and anoint them, as you anointed their father, that they may serve me as priests: and their anointing shall admit them to a perpetual priesthood throughout all generations to come.

16 Moses did everything just as the LORD had commanded him. ¹⁷In the first month in the second year, on the first day of the month, the tabernacle was set up. ¹⁸Moses set up the tabernacle; he laid its bases, and set up its frames, and put in its poles, and raised up its pillars; ¹⁹and he spread the tent over the tabernacle, and put the covering of the tent over it; as the LORD had commanded Moses. ²⁰He took the covenant*a* and put it into the ark, and put the poles on the ark, and set the mercy seat*b* above the ark; ²¹and he brought the ark into the tabernacle, and set up the curtain for screening, and screened the ark of the covenant;*a* as the LORD had commanded Moses. ²²He put the table in the tent of meeting, on the north side of the tabernacle, outside the curtain, ²³and set the bread in order on it before the LORD; as the LORD had commanded Moses. ²⁴He put the lampstand in the tent of meeting, opposite the table on the south side of the tabernacle, ²⁵and set up the lamps before the LORD; as the LORD had commanded Moses. ²⁶He put the golden altar in

the tent of meeting before the curtain, ²⁷and offered fragrant incense on it; as the LORD had commanded Moses. ²⁸He also put in place the screen for the entrance of the tabernacle. ²⁹He set the altar of burnt offering at the entrance of the tabernacle of the tent of meeting, and offered on it the burnt offering and the grain offering as the LORD had commanded Moses. ³⁰He set the basin between the tent of meeting and the altar, and put water in it for washing, ³¹with which Moses and Aaron and his sons washed their hands and their feet. ³²When they went into the tent of meeting, and when they approached the altar, they washed; as the LORD had commanded Moses. ³³He set up the court around the tabernacle and the altar, and put up the screen at the gate of the court. So Moses finished the work.

The Cloud and the Glory

34 Then the cloud covered the tent of meeting, and the glory of the LORD filled the tabernacle. ³⁵Moses was not able to enter the tent of meeting because the cloud settled upon it, and the glory of the LORD filled the tabernacle. ³⁶Whenever the cloud was taken up from the tabernacle, the Israelites would set out on each stage of their journey; ³⁷but if the cloud was not taken up, then they did not set out until the day that it was taken up. ³⁸For the cloud of the LORD was on the tabernacle by day, and fire was in the cloud*c* by night, before the eyes of all the house of Israel at each stage of their journey.

---

a Or *treaty,* or *testimony;* Heb *eduth*   *b* Or *the cover*
c Heb *it*

---

side the curtain (see 30.6). **40.9** *Furniture,* translated *utensils* in v. 10. *Holy.* See note on 29.37. **40.10** *Most holy.* See note on 29.37. **40.12** *Bring.* See note on 29.3; see also v. 14. **40.15** *Perpetual.* Cf. 29.9; Num 25.11–13. **40.17** See note on 40.2. **40.18** *Moses.* Cf. v. 2. **40.19** *Tent.* See 26.7, 11. *Covering.* See 26.14. **40.20** *Poles.* See note on 25.12. *Above,* rather "on top of" (25.21). **40.22** *Tent of meeting.* See note on 27.21. **40.27** *Offered.* See note on 30.1. **40.28** *For the entrance,* aligned with but at some remove (see note on 27.9–19). **40.29** *Burnt offering.* See 28.38–39. *Grain offering.* See 28.40. Mention of the offerings provides a transition to Leviticus, which begins with the burnt offering (ch. 1) and grain offering (ch. 2). **40.31** *Washed,* or "would wash."

40.32 *Went . . . approached . . . washed.* In the Hebrew the tense is not past but present, describing ongoing activity and interrupting the investiture and anointing ceremony (vv. 13–15), which is resumed in Lev 8. **40.33** *Finished.* See note on 39.32. **40.34–38** The descent of the divine presence into the "dwelling" (*tabernacle*) parallels the *settling* (same Hebrew verb) of the Lord atop Mount Sinai (24.15–16). **40.34** *Cloud.* See note on 13.21. *Glory.* See note on 16.6–7; cf. 24.16–17. **40.35** Cf. 1 Kings 8.10–11. **40.36–38** An institutionalization of the *pillars* in 13.21–22; cf. Num 9.15–23. **40.38** *At each stage . . . journey,* lit. "in each of their journeys"; cf. Num 10.11–36. God's presence will accompany the Israelites as promised (e.g., 33.14).

LEVITICUS

THE BOOK OF LEVITICUS is more aptly described by its tannaitic, or early rabbinic, name, *Torat Kohanim*, the "Priests' Manual." It is thematically an independent entity. Priestly material in the book of Exodus describes the construction of the Israelite cultic implements (the sacred religious objects used in ritual—the tabernacle, its contents, and the priestly vestments); in Leviticus this static picture is converted into scenes from the living cult. The book of Numbers, which follows, concentrates on the cultic laws of the camp in motion. Since the transport of the sacred paraphernalia and their protection against encroachment by impurity is the function of the Levites, it is no accident that all the cultic laws pertaining to the Levites are in Numbers, and none are in Leviticus.

The Priesthood

ALTHOUGH THE PRIESTS' MANUAL focuses on the priesthood, few laws are reserved for priests alone (Lev 8–10; 16.1–28; 21.1–22.16). Their role is defined in pedagogic terms: to teach the distinctions "between the holy and the common, and between the unclean and the clean" (10.10 [cf. 14.57]; 15.31). They must do this because Israel's moral sins and physical impurities are leading to the pollution of the sanctuary and the expulsion of Israel from its land. The priests, then, are charged with a double task: to instruct Israel not to cause defilement and to purge the sanctuary whenever it is defiled. Leviticus, however, is not simply a collection of rituals. On the contrary, the ethical element fuses with and even informs the ritual, so that one may seek a moral basis behind each ritual act.

Israel's priests were not an insular elite. They were military chaplains, accompanying Israel's armies in distant and dangerous battlefields (Num 31.6). They were called outside the sanctuary and, indeed, outside the settlements to quarantine and certify carriers of scale disease (Lev 14.2). The responsibility of the priesthood for the welfare of all Israel is nowhere better exemplified than in the relationship of priests and laity in the sacrificial service. The preliminary rites with the sacrificial animal are performed by the offerer: hand leaning, slaughtering, flaying, quartering, and washing (1.1–9). The priest takes over at the altar and continues the sacrificial ritual in silence. By virtue of his sacred status, the priest acts as the offerer's (silent) intermediary before God. But he is more than a mere technician. In effect, he is the cultic counterpart of the prophet. Both represent the Israelites before God. Both intercede on their behalf, one through ritual, the other through prayer. The welfare of Israel depends on both a Moses and an Aaron.

Ideas of Holiness and Pollution According to P and H

THE BOOK OF LEVITICUS comprises two priestly sources, known as P (Priestly Code) and H (Holiness Code). They are not homogeneous; each betrays the work of schools. For example, two P strata are discernible in ch. 11 (a later P stratum in vv. 24–38, 47), as are two H strata in ch. 23 (a later H stratum in vv. 2–3, 39–43). Whether material belongs to P or H can be determined by two criteria: ideology and terminology.

The most important ideological distinction between the two codes rests in their contrasting concepts of holiness. For P, spatial holiness is limited to the sanctuary; for H, it is coextensive with the promised land. As for the holiness of persons, P restricts it to priests and Nazirites (cf. Num 6.5–8); H extends it to all of Israel. This expansion follows logically from H's doctrine of spatial holiness: since the land is holy, all who reside on it are to keep it that way. All adult Israelites are enjoined to attain holiness by observing God's commandments, and even resident aliens must heed the prohibitive commandments, the violation of which threatens to pollute the land for all (e.g., 18.26).

P's doctrine of holiness is static; H's is dynamic. P constricts holiness to the sanctuary and its priests, assiduously avoiding the root of the word "holy" even in describing the Levites. Although H concedes that only priests are innately holy, it repeatedly calls upon Israel to strive for holiness. The dynamic quality of H's concept is highlighted by the term "sanctify," used to describe the holiness of the laity and the priesthood. Sanctification is an ongoing process for priests (21.8, 15, 23; 22.9, 16) as well as for all Israelites (21.8; 22.32). The holiness of the priests and Israelites expands or contracts in proportion to their adherence to God's commandments.

The converse, the doctrine of pollution, also varies sharply. P holds that the sanctuary is polluted by Israel's moral and ritual violations (4.2) committed anywhere in the camp (but not outside) and that this pollution can and must be effaced by the violator's purification offering and, if committed deliberately, by priestly sacrifice and confession (16.3–22). H, however, concentrates instead on the polluting effects of Israel's violations of the covenant (26.15), for example, incest (18; 20.11–24), idolatry (20.1–6), and depriving the land of its sabbaths (26.34–35). Pollution for H is nonritualistic, as shown by its metaphoric usage (e.g., 18.20, 24; 19.31) and by the fact that the polluted land cannot be expiated by ritual. Violations irrevocably lead to the expulsion of its inhabitants (18.24–29; 20.22).

The distinctive vocabularies of P and H emerge in their use of homonyms and synonyms. For example, in P *shiqqets* means "defile (by ingestion)" (translated "unclean" in 11.8) and *timmē'* means "defile (by contact)" (translated "detestable" in 11.11), whereas in H they are used interchangeably (20.25). P's term for "law" or "statute" is always given in the feminine form *chuqqah, chuqqot* (e.g., 10.9), whereas H also resorts to masculine *choq, chuqqim* (e.g., 26.46). The term "commit sacrilege" in P is *ma'al* (translated "commit a trespass" in 6.2), and in H is *chillel* (translated "profaned" in 19.8). The pervasive intrusion of H characteristics into the P text points to the strong possibility that H is not only subsequent to P, but is also P's redactor.

Structure

GENERALLY, THE BOOK OF LEVITICUS divides into the main P text (chs. 1–16), comprising descriptions of the sacrificial system, the inaugural service at the sanctuary, and the laws of impurities; the H text (chs. 17–26); and a section on commutation of gifts to the sanctuary (ch. 27).

[JACOB MILGROM]

The Burnt Offering

1 The LORD summoned Moses and spoke to him from the tent of meeting, saying: 2 Speak to the people of Israel and say to them: When any of you bring an offering of livestock to the LORD, you shall bring your offering from the herd or from the flock.

3 If the offering is a burnt offering from the herd, you shall offer a male without blemish; you shall bring it to the entrance of the tent of meeting, for acceptance in your behalf before the LORD. 4 You shall lay your hand on the head of the burnt offering, and it shall be acceptable in your behalf as atonement for you.

5 The bull shall be slaughtered before the LORD; and Aaron's sons the priests shall offer the blood, dashing the blood against all sides of the altar that is at the entrance of the tent of meeting. 6 The burnt offering shall be flayed and cut up into its parts. 7 The sons of the priest Aaron shall put fire on the altar and arrange wood on the fire. 8 Aaron's sons the priests shall arrange the parts, with the head and the suet, on the wood that is on the fire on the altar; 9 but its entrails and its legs shall be washed with water. Then the priest shall turn the whole into smoke on the altar as a burnt offering, an offering by fire of pleasing odor to the LORD.

1.1–7.38 The sacrificial system. Sacrifice is a flexible symbol that conveys a variety of possible meanings. The quintessential sacrificial act is the transference of property from the profane to the sacred realm, in other words, a gift to the deity. That this notion is also basic to Israelite sacrifice is demonstrated by fundamental sacrificial terms that connote a gift, such as *mattanah* (23.38), *minchah* (rendered *grain offering* in 2.1), and *'isheh*, "food-gift" (rendered *an offering by fire* in 1.9). It explains why game and fish were unacceptable as sacrifices: "I will not offer burnt offerings to the LORD my God that cost me nothing" (2 Sam 24.24). To date, however, no single theory can encompass the sacrificial system of any society, even the most primitive. In chs. 1–5 the sacrifices are characterized by donor: chs. 1–3 speak of sacrifices brought spontaneously (burnt, cereal, well-being); chs. 4–5, of sacrifices required for expiation (purification and reparation). Chs. 6–7 regroup these sacrifices in order of their sanctity. The common denominator of the sacrifices discussed in these chapters is that they arise in answer to an unpredictable religious or emotional need and are thereby set apart from the sacrifices of the public feasts and fasts that are fixed by the calendar (chs. 9, 16, 23; cf. Num 28–29).

1.1–17 The burnt offering is the only sacrifice that is entirely consumed on the altar (cf. Deut 33.10; 1 Sam 7.9). Vv. 3–5 summarize the major concepts of the sacrificial system: imposition of hands, acceptance, expiation, slaughter, blood manipulation, and entrance to the tent of meeting. The donor is an active participant in the ritual. The burnt offering must be an unblemished male animal from an eligible species of livestock or birds. It is probably the oldest and most popular sacrifice (*Tosefta Zebachim* 13.1). Its function here is expiatory (v. 4; cf. 9.7; 14.20; Job 1.5; 42.8) and finds parallels in Ugaritic texts found at Ras Shamra on the coast of Syria dating to the middle of the second millennium BCE, but in H (see Introduction), the burnt offering by an individual marks a joyous occasion (cf. 22.17–21; Num 15.1–11). **1.2** *Any of you.* The text can be read "any person among you," thereby explaining the third person in the Hebrew of vv. 2, 3, 4, 10, translated by the second person in the NRSV.

1.3 *Without blemish.* The significance of this requirement is vividly underscored by the prophet: "When you offer blind animals in sacrifice, is that not wrong? And when you offer those that are lame or sick, is that not wrong? Try presenting that to your governor; will he be pleased with you or show you favor? says the LORD of hosts" (Mal 1.8). *Tent of meeting,* a term referring to the wilderness sanctuary, also called the tabernacle, which was contained within a collapsible and portable tent and itself contained an incense altar, a table for the bread of Presence, a lampstand, and, separated from these sacred objects by a curtain, the ark of the covenant (Ex 25.10–40). Its name is derived from its function; see Ex 29.42–43. The tent of meeting was surrounded by a fenced courtyard. The whole courtyard from its entrance to the entrance of the tent was accessible to the lay offerer and was where he performed the preliminary sacrificial rites (see Introduction). **1.4** *Lay your hand* (cf. 3.2, 8, 12; 4.4, 15, 24), lit. "lean your hand." This rite required pressure. Its purpose is to signify ownership, so that the benefits of the sacrifice will accrue to the donor. Hand leaning was not required whenever the offering could be carried by hand—cases where ownership was obvious—such as the burnt offering of birds, the grain offering, and the reparation-offering money (e.g., 5.14–6.7). *Acceptable in your behalf.* If the offering is unblemished it will be acceptable on the offerer's behalf, but "if you present a lame or sick one—it does not matter! Just offer it to your governor: will he accept you?" (Mal 1.13, alternate translation). From this citation we can derive two things. First, to be acceptable to God (or the governor) the sacrifice must be unblemished. Just as a king expects perfection in his gifts, so does the divine King of kings. Second, the function of the burnt offering here is to elicit the favor of the deity. *Atonement.* Originally the burnt offering may have been the only expiatory sacrifice. However, once the exclusively expiatory purification and reparation offerings came into being (see chs. 4–5), the sole expiatory function remaining for the burnt offering was to atone for neglected performative commandments or sinful thoughts (see Job 1.5). Thus the erstwhile sinner would be granted "at-

10 If your gift for a burnt offering is from the flock, from the sheep or goats, your offering shall be a male without blemish. ¹¹It shall be slaughtered on the north side of the altar before the LORD, and Aaron's sons the priests shall dash its blood against all sides of the altar. ¹²It shall be cut up into its parts, with its head and its suet, and the priest shall arrange them on the wood that is on the fire on the altar; ¹³but the entrails and the legs shall be washed with water. Then the priest shall offer the whole and turn it into smoke on the altar; it is a burnt offering, an offering by fire of pleasing odor to the LORD.

14 If your offering to the LORD is a burnt offering of birds, you shall choose your offering from turtledoves or pigeons. ¹⁵The priest shall bring it to the altar and wring off its head, and turn it into smoke on the altar; and its blood shall be drained out against the side of the altar. ¹⁶He shall remove its crop with its contents[a] and throw it at the east side of the altar, in the place for ashes. ¹⁷He shall tear it open by its wings without severing it. Then the priest shall turn it into smoke on the altar, on the wood that is on the fire; it is a burnt offering, an offering by fire of pleasing odor to the LORD.

Grain Offerings

2 When anyone presents a grain offering to the LORD, the offering shall be of choice flour; the worshiper shall pour oil on it, and put frankincense on it, ²and bring it to Aaron's sons the priests. After taking from it a handful of the choice flour and oil, with all its frankincense, the priest shall turn this token portion into smoke on the altar, an offering by fire of pleasing odor to the LORD. ³And what is left of the grain offering shall be for Aaron and his sons, a most holy part of the offerings by fire to the LORD.

4 When you present a grain offering baked in the oven, it shall be of choice flour: unleavened cakes mixed with oil, or unleavened wafers spread with oil. ⁵If your offering is grain prepared on a griddle, it shall be of choice flour mixed with oil, unleavened; ⁶break it in pieces, and pour oil on it; it is a grain offering. ⁷If your offering is grain prepared in a pan, it shall be made of choice flour in oil. ⁸You shall bring to the LORD the grain offering that is prepared in any of these ways; and when it is presented to the priest, he shall take it to the altar. ⁹The priest shall remove from the grain offering its token portion and turn this into smoke on the altar, an offering by fire of pleasing odor to the LORD. ¹⁰And what is left of the grain offering shall be for Aaron and his sons; it is a most holy part of the offerings by fire to the LORD.

---

a Meaning of Heb uncertain

---

one-ment" with the Lord. **1.9** *Turn . . . into smoke.* This term is carefully distinguished from "burn," the normal term for nonsacrificial incineration, to indicate that the offering is not destroyed but transformed into smoke so that it can ascend to heaven above, the dwelling place of God. *An offering by fire* (cf 1.13, 17; 2.3, 10), more accurately "a food gift." **1.16** *Crop with its contents,* or "crissum by its feathers." The waste material inside the bird is removed by cutting around and pulling its tail.

2.1–16 In nonpriestly texts the term "grain offering" connotes a present made to secure goodwill (e.g., Gen 32.13–21) or a tribute brought by subjects to their overlords, both human (Judg 3.15–18) and divine. This sacrifice may be brought in either animal or vegetable form (Gen 4.3; 1 Sam 2.17). In P, however (see Introduction), it is exclusively grain, semolina (Lev 2.1–3), semolina cakes (2.4–10), or roasted grain (2.14–16). Because leaven and honey (fruit syrup) ferment and salt preserves, the first two are forbidden, and salt is required on the altar (2.11–13). Leaven, however, is permitted as a first-fruit offering to the priest (23.17; 2 Chr 31.5). The restriction to grain emphasizes that people's tribute to God should be from the fruits of their labors on the soil. As in other ancient Near Eastern cultures, the burnt offering could appease the deity's anger. Because grain was abundant and cheap, it became the poor person's burnt offering (Philo, *On the Special Laws* 1.271; *Leviticus Rabbah* 8.4). **2.1** *Choice flour,* more specifically "semolina," or coarsely ground flour that remains after the fine flour has been extracted from the wheat (cf. *Mishnah Avot* 5.15). *Frankincense,* a fragrant and costly gum-resin tapped from three species of the Boswellia tree native only to southern Arabia (see Jer 6.20) and Somaliland. It was also the main ingredient in the incense burned on the incense altar (Ex 30.7–8, 34–36). **2.2** *Token portion.* The entire grain offering should go up in smoke, but only a portion does, *pars pro toto.* **2.3** *Most holy* defines the burnt, grain, purification, and reparation offerings (6.17, 25; 7.6), as distinct from the rest of the offerings designated by the term "holy," namely, the well-being offering, the devoted thing, and the first of animals, fruits, and processed foods (Num 18.12–19). **2.4–10** Four different preparations of the grain offering are here included: oven-baked (two varieties), griddle-toasted, and pan-fried. Their common denominator is that they are all cooked, unleavened semolina. Frankincense is not required for these cooked grain offerings, possibly as a deliberate conces-

11 No grain offering that you bring to the LORD shall be made with leaven, for you must not turn any leaven or honey into smoke as an offering by fire to the LORD. 12You may bring them to the LORD as an offering of choice products, but they shall not be offered on the altar for a pleasing odor. 13You shall not omit from your grain offerings the salt of the covenant with your God; with all your offerings you shall offer salt.

14 If you bring a grain offering of first fruits to the LORD, you shall bring as the grain offering of your first fruits coarse new grain from fresh ears, parched with fire. 15You shall add oil to it and lay frankincense on it; it is a grain offering. 16And the priest shall turn a token portion of it into smoke—some of the coarse grain and oil with all its frankincense; it is an offering by fire to the LORD.

Offerings of Well-Being

3 If the offering is a sacrifice of well-being, if you offer an animal of the herd, whether male or female, you shall offer one without blemish before the LORD. 2You shall lay your hand on the head of the offering and slaughter it at the entrance of the tent of meeting; and Aaron's sons the priests shall dash the blood against all sides of the altar. 3You shall offer from the sacrifice of well-being, as an offering by fire to the LORD, the fat that covers the entrails and all the fat that is around the entrails; 4the two kidneys with the fat that is on them at the loins, and the appendage of the liver, which he shall remove with the kidneys. 5Then Aaron's sons shall turn these into smoke on the altar, with the burnt offering that is on the wood on the fire, as an offering by fire of pleasing odor to the LORD.

6 If your offering for a sacrifice of well-being to the LORD is from the flock, male or female, you shall offer one without blemish. 7If you present a sheep as your offering, you shall bring it before the LORD 8and lay your hand on the head of the offering. It shall be slaughtered before the tent of meeting, and Aaron's sons shall dash its blood against all sides of the altar. 9You shall present its fat from the sacrifice of well-being, as an offering by fire to the LORD: the whole broad tail, which shall be removed close to the backbone, the fat that covers the entrails, and all the fat that is around the entrails; 10the two kidneys with the fat that is on them at the loins, and the appendage of the liver, which you shall remove with the kidneys. 11Then the priest shall turn these into

sion to the poor. **2.10** This verse stands in flat contradiction to 7.9, which assigns the cooked grain offering to the officiating priest. This may reflect different sanctuary traditions: the officiating priest was recompensed at the small, local sanctuary, whereas the priestly corps distributed the perquisites equitably at the Jerusalem temple (see also 7.31–33). **2.11** *Leaven* is the arch-symbol of fermentation, deterioration, and death and hence taboo on the altar of blessing and life. Wine, the epitome of fermentation, is never burned on the altar hearth, but is poured on the altar base, so the prohibition against *turning . . . into smoke* any fermented substance has not been transgressed. The *honey* mentioned here is fruit honey (see 2 Chr 31.5). The stereotypical metaphor for Canaan, "a land flowing with milk and honey," must intend fruit honey, because Canaan from time immemorial was known for its abundant fruits, especially dates, figs, and grapes. **2.12** *An offering of choice products,* or "a first-processed offering." The gift of the first fruits is due not only from the first-ripe crops but also from certain foods processed from these crops, namely, grain, new wine (must), new (olive) oil, fruit syrup, leavened food, and meal dough. **2.13** *Salt of the covenant.* Since salt was the preservative par excellence in antiquity, it made the ideal symbol for the perdurability of a covenant, and it is likely that salt played a prominent role at the solemn meal that sealed a covenant in the ancient Near East. **2.14** *First fruits* refers to barley, which Arab peasants

roast to this day, but not to wheat because of its flat taste (note the absence of the term "semolina"). It may refer to the offering originally required of each Israelite barley grower (see 23.10–11). *Coarse new grain from fresh ears,* more specifically "milky grain, groats of the first ear." Hebrew *'abib,* "milky grain," represents the intermediate (milky) stage between mere stalks and fully ripe grain; Hebrew *geres* (rabbinic *gerisim*) means "groats"; and *karmel* refers to the grain, namely, the "fresh ear" (cf. 2 Kings 4.42).

3.1–17 The well-being offering never serves as expiation (but cf. ch. 17). Its basic function is simply to permit the consumption of meat. The motivation was usually spontaneous and occasioned by a sense of elation. The rules are similar to those of the burnt offering except that the victims may be female, but not birds. Also, being of lesser sanctity, its portions are assigned to the donor as well as to God. The choicest internal fats (suet) are turned to smoke. **3.1** *You* (and throughout the chapter), lit. "he"/"him." *Without blemish.* See 1.3. **3.3** *Fat* (and throughout the chapter), more specifically "suet," referring to the layer of fat beneath the surface of the animal's skin and around its organs, which can be peeled off, in contrast to the fat that is inextricably entwined in the musculature. **3.4** *Kidneys,* frequently associated with the heart as the seat of thoughts, emotions, and life; like the blood, the proverbial life force, they must be returned to their creator. *Appendage,* i.e., the caudate lobe of the liver.

smoke on the altar as a food offering by fire to the LORD.

12 If your offering is a goat, you shall bring it before the LORD [13]and lay your hand on its head; it shall be slaughtered before the tent of meeting; and the sons of Aaron shall dash its blood against all sides of the altar. [14]You shall present as your offering from it, as an offering by fire to the LORD, the fat that covers the entrails, and all the fat that is around the entrails; [15]the two kidneys with the fat that is on them at the loins, and the appendage of the liver, which you shall remove with the kidneys. [16]Then the priest shall turn these into smoke on the altar as a food offering by fire for a pleasing odor.

All fat is the LORD's. [17]It shall be a perpetual statute throughout your generations, in all your settlements: you must not eat any fat or any blood.

Sin Offerings

4 The LORD spoke to Moses, saying, [2]Speak to the people of Israel, saying: When any-one sins unintentionally in any of the LORD's commandments about things not to be done, and does any one of them:

3 If it is the anointed priest who sins, thus bringing guilt on the people, he shall offer for the sin that he has committed a bull of the herd without blemish as a sin offering to the LORD. [4]He shall bring the bull to the entrance of the tent of meeting before the LORD and lay his hand on the head of the bull; the bull shall be slaughtered before the LORD. [5]The anointed priest shall take some of the blood of the bull and bring it into the tent of meeting. [6]The priest shall dip his finger in the blood and sprinkle some of the blood seven times before the LORD in front of the curtain of the sanctuary. [7]The priest shall put some of the blood on the horns of the altar of fragrant incense that is in the tent of meeting before the LORD; and the rest of the blood of the bull he shall pour out at the base of the altar of burnt offering, which is at the entrance of the tent of meeting. [8]He shall remove all the fat from the bull of sin offering: the fat that covers the en-

---

3.9 *Backbone,* rather the "sacrum," the lowest part of the spine closest to the broad tail. **3.16** *All fat is the LORD's.* Hence all sacrificial meat must initially be brought to the altar. Together with v. 17, this phrase is probably an H supplement (see Introduction).
4.1–35 The purpose of the purification offering (not properly *sin offering*) is to remove the impurity inflicted upon the sanctuary by the inadvertent violation of prohibitions. The brazen violation of these laws is punishable by death through divine agency (Num 15.27–31). Such serious violations include defilement of holy days (e.g., the Day of Atonement, Lev 23.29–30), contamination of sacred objects (7.20–21), prohibited ritual acts (17.3–4, 8–9), and illicit sex (18.29). The greater the sin, the deeper the penetration into the sanctuary compound and the more extensive the purification required (cf. vv. 3–21, 22–35; see note on 16.1–34). **4.2** *Any of the LORD's commandments,* including ethical ones (e.g., 19.11–18). The fusion of ethics and ritual is not an innovation of Israelite law. It is to be found in the earliest documents of the ancient Near East. Hence in pagan cultures too the violation of ethical as well as ritual norms can enrage the gods. But it is in Israel alone that both norms are tied to the purification offering and its central message: that the violation of ethics and/or ritual leads to the pollution of the sanctuary and its national consequence, the abandonment of the entire community of Israel by its God. Israel's neighbors also held to, indeed were obsessed by, a fear that their temples would be defiled and the concomitant need to purify them. But the source of this defilement, in their system, was not human beings but demons, and the plethora of incantations, unc-

tions, and rituals for the purification of temples was directed toward eliminating or warding off this supernal evil. Israel's priesthood, as reflected in this sacrificial ritual, gave a national dimension to ethics, making ethical behavior an indispensable factor in determining Israel's destiny. **4.3** *Anointed priest,* the title of the high priest in preexilic times. *Guilt on,* more accurately "harm to," the consequential meaning of the Hebrew noun *'asham,* "guilt" (cf. Gen 26.10; Jer 51.5b). **4.6** *Sprinkle . . . seven times.* Sevenfold sprinkling is attested for the blood of the purification offering (4.6, 17; 16.14, 15, 19; Num 19.4), for the oil and mixture of blood and water used in the purification of the healed leper (Lev 14.7, 16, 27, 51), and for anointing oil on the altar (8.11). In this chapter the blood of the purification offering acts as a ritual detergent purging the sanctuary of Israel's impurities. Seven is the number of completion and occurs frequently in the cultic calendar: seventh day (sabbath), seventh week (Pentecost), seventh month (Tishri), seventh year (sabbatical), and forty-ninth (seven times seven) year (jubilee). Even the magical use of seven is attested in the Bible: Balaam requires seven altars, seven bulls, and seven rams for his divination (Num 23.1); Job's friends require the same number of sacrifices (Job 42.8); Naaman bathes seven times in the Jordan (2 Kings 5.10, 14); Elijah's servant scans the skies seven times for signs of rain (1 Kings 18.43); Joshua's armies circuit Jericho seven times on the seventh day (Josh 6.15). **4.7** *Horns.* The altar's horns are right-angle tetrahedra projecting from the four corners and are of one piece with the altar (Ex 27.2; 30.2), as illustrated by archaeological finds from Megiddo and Beer-sheba. Their daubing

trails and all the fat that is around the entrails; [9]the two kidneys with the fat that is on them at the loins; and the appendage of the liver, which he shall remove with the kidneys, [10]just as these are removed from the ox of the sacrifice of well-being. The priest shall turn them into smoke upon the altar of burnt offering. [11]But the skin of the bull and all its flesh, as well as its head, its legs, its entrails, and its dung— [12]all the rest of the bull—he shall carry out to a clean place outside the camp, to the ash heap, and shall burn it on a wood fire; at the ash heap it shall be burned.

13 If the whole congregation of Israel errs unintentionally and the matter escapes the notice of the assembly, and they do any one of the things that by the LORD's commandments ought not to be done and incur guilt; [14]when the sin that they have committed becomes known, the assembly shall offer a bull of the herd for a sin offering and bring it before the tent of meeting. [15]The elders of the congregation shall lay their hands on the head of the bull before the LORD, and the bull shall be slaughtered before the LORD. [16]The anointed priest shall bring some of the blood of the bull into the tent of meeting, [17]and the priest shall dip his finger in the blood and sprinkle it seven times before the LORD, in front of the curtain. [18]He shall put some of the blood on the horns of the altar that is before the LORD in the tent of meeting; and the rest of the blood he shall pour out at the base of the altar of burnt offering that is at the entrance of the tent of meeting. [19]He shall remove all its fat and turn it into smoke on the altar. [20]He shall do with the bull just as is done with the bull of sin offering; he shall do the same with this. The priest shall make atonement for them, and they shall be forgiven. [21]He shall carry the bull outside the camp, and burn it as he burned the first bull; it is the sin offering for the assembly.

22 When a ruler sins, doing unintentionally any one of all the things that by commandments of the LORD his God ought not to be done and incurs guilt, [23]once the sin that he has committed is made known to him, he shall bring as his offering a male goat without blemish. [24]He shall lay his hand on the head of the goat; it shall be slaughtered at the spot where the burnt offering is slaughtered before the LORD; it is a sin offering. [25]The priest shall take some of the blood of the sin offering with his finger and put it on the horns of the altar of burnt offering, and pour out the rest of its blood at the base of the altar of burnt offering. [26]All its fat he shall turn into smoke on the altar, like the fat of the sacrifice of well-being. Thus the priest shall make atonement on his behalf for his sin, and he shall be forgiven.

27 If anyone of the ordinary people among you sins unintentionally in doing any one of the things that by the LORD's commandments ought not to be done and incurs guilt, [28]when the sin that you have committed is made known to you, you shall bring a female goat without blemish as your offering, for the sin that you have committed. [29]You shall lay your hand on the head of the sin offering; and the sin offering shall be slaughtered at the place of the burnt offering. [30]The priest shall take some of its blood with his finger and put it on the horns of the altar of burnt offering, and he shall pour out the rest of its blood at the base of the altar. [31]He shall remove all its fat, as the fat is removed from the offering of well-being, and the priest shall turn it into smoke on the altar for a pleasing odor to the LORD. Thus the priest shall make atonement on your behalf, and you shall be forgiven.

32 If the offering you bring as a sin offering

---

with the purification blood meant the purgation of the entire altar by the principle of *pars pro toto*. **4.12** *Clean place.* Though the sacrificial carcass has symbolically absorbed the sanctuary's impurities, it is still sacred and must be treated as such. *Ash heap.* That there actually existed a special dump for the sacrificial ashes outside Solomon's temple is shown by Jer 31.40 and by the discovery of a huge ash dump just north of ancient Jerusalem at the Mandelbaum Gate (the former passageway between East and West Jerusalem) consisting exclusively of remains of animal flesh, bones, and teeth. **4.13–21** This passage forms a single case with vv. 1–12. The high priest has erred in judgment, causing the people who follow his ruling also to err (v. 3). Because both errors comprise inadvertent violations of prohibitive commandments (vv. 2, 13) that pollute the shrine, each party is responsible for purging the shrine with the blood of a similar sacrifice, a purification-offering bull. **4.13** *Incur guilt.* The nuance is to feel guilt (see vv. 22, 27), the psychological component of the verb *'asham* (cf. 5.2–5, 17; 6.4a). **4.15** *Elders* act on behalf of the congregation (9.1; see Ex 3.16; 4.29; 12.21; 17.6; 18.12; 24.9). **4.20** *Sin offering,* i.e., the "purification offering." *And,* better "so that." Only God determines the efficacy of sacrifice. **4.22** *A ruler,* more specifically "a (tribal) chieftain."

is a sheep, you shall bring a female without blemish. 33You shall lay your hand on the head of the sin offering; and it shall be slaughtered as a sin offering at the spot where the burnt offering is slaughtered. 34The priest shall take some of the blood of the sin offering with his finger and put it on the horns of the altar of burnt offering, and pour out the rest of its blood at the base of the altar. 35You shall remove all its fat, as the fat of the sheep is removed from the sacrifice of well-being, and the priest shall turn it into smoke on the altar, with the offerings by fire to the LORD. Thus the priest shall make atonement on your behalf for the sin that you have committed, and you shall be forgiven.

5 When any of you sin in that you have heard a public adjuration to testify and— though able to testify as one who has seen or learned of the matter—do not speak up, you are subject to punishment. 2Or when any of you touch any unclean thing—whether the carcass of an unclean beast or the carcass of unclean livestock or the carcass of an unclean swarming thing—and are unaware of it, you have become unclean, and are guilty. 3Or when you touch human uncleanness—any uncleanness by which one can become unclean—and are unaware of it, when you come to know it, you shall be guilty. 4Or when any of you utter aloud a rash oath for a bad or a good purpose, whatever people utter in an oath, and are unaware of it, when you come to know it, you shall in any of these be guilty. 5When you realize your guilt in any of these, you shall confess the sin that you have committed. 6And you shall bring to the LORD, as your penalty for the sin that you have committed, a female

from the flock, a sheep or a goat, as a sin offering; and the priest shall make atonement on your behalf for your sin.

7 But if you cannot afford a sheep, you shall bring to the LORD, as your penalty for the sin that you have committed, two turtledoves or two pigeons, one for a sin offering and the other for a burnt offering. 8You shall bring them to the priest, who shall offer first the one for the sin offering, wringing its head at the nape without severing it. 9He shall sprinkle some of the blood of the sin offering on the side of the altar, while the rest of the blood shall be drained out at the base of the altar; it is a sin offering. 10And the second he shall offer for a burnt offering according to the regulation. Thus the priest shall make atonement on your behalf for the sin that you have committed, and you shall be forgiven.

11 But if you cannot afford two turtledoves or two pigeons, you shall bring as your offering for the sin that you have committed one-tenth of an ephah of choice flour for a sin offering; you shall not put oil on it or lay frankincense on it, for it is a sin offering. 12You shall bring it to the priest, and the priest shall scoop up a handful of it as its memorial portion, and turn this into smoke on the altar, with the offerings by fire to the LORD; it is a sin offering. 13Thus the priest shall make atonement on your behalf for whichever of these sins you have committed, and you shall be forgiven. Like the grain offering, the rest shall be for the priest.

Offerings with Restitution

14 The LORD spoke to Moses, saying: 15When any of you commit a trespass and sin uninten-

---

5.1–13 Rabbinic tradition distinguishes between the purification offering of ch. 4 and that of 5.1–13, calling the latter "the scaled offering" because it is geared not to status but to the financial means of the offender. This separate offering probably arises from the failure or inability to cleanse impurity immediately upon its incurrence. 5.1 *Any of you.* See 1.2. *Public adjuration,* lit. "imprecation." Thus Micah is induced by his mother's imprecation to confess that he had stolen her silver (Judg 17.1–5). A striking parallel to this case is cited in Prov 29.24, which might be translated "He who shares with a thief is his own enemy; he hears the imprecation and does not testify." 5.2–4 *Are unaware of it.* The fact escapes him, i.e., he has perhaps repressed the matter. *You have become unclean . . . you come to know it* might be translated "though he has become unclean . . . though he has

known it," i.e., he knows he did wrong before amnesia set in and prolonged his impure state. *Are guilty . . . shall be guilty,* feels guilt (see 4.13). 5.5 *Confess.* The Septuagint translates "declare," i.e., articulate the confession, as distinct from the silent "confession" mandated for the inadvertent wrongdoer. Confession must be verbalized because it is the act that counts, not just the intention. By the same token, neither can mere thought bear consequences. For a curse to incur penalty, it must be pronounced and the name of God articulated (see 24.16). Confession is never required for inadvertences, only for deliberate sins (5.1–4; 16.21; 26.40; Num 5.6–7). Confession converts deliberate sins into inadvertences, thereby qualifying them for sacrificial expiation (see 6.1–7). 5.14–6.7 The reparation offering is prescribed for trespass upon divine or human property, the latter

tionally in any of the holy things of the LORD, you shall bring, as your guilt offering to the LORD, a ram without blemish from the flock, convertible into silver by the sanctuary shekel; it is a guilt offering. ¹⁶And you shall make restitution for the holy thing in which you were remiss, and shall add one-fifth to it and give it to the priest. The priest shall make atonement on your behalf with the ram of the guilt offering, and you shall be forgiven.

17 If any of you sin without knowing it, doing any of the things that by the LORD's commandments ought not to be done, you have incurred guilt, and are subject to punishment. ¹⁸You shall bring to the priest a ram without blemish from the flock, or the equivalent, as a guilt offering; and the priest shall make atonement on your behalf for the error that you committed unintentionally, and you shall be forgiven. ¹⁹It is a guilt offering; you have incurred guilt before the LORD.

6 ᵃ The LORD spoke to Moses, saying: ²When any of you sin and commit a trespass against the LORD by deceiving a neighbor in a matter of a deposit or a pledge, or by robbery, or if you have defrauded a neighbor, ³or have found something lost and lied about it—if you swear falsely regarding any of the various things that one may do and sin thereby— ⁴when you have sinned and realize your guilt, and would restore what you took by robbery or by fraud or the deposit that was committed to you, or the lost thing that you found, ⁵or

anything else about which you have sworn falsely, you shall repay the principal amount and shall add one-fifth to it. You shall pay it to its owner when you realize your guilt. ⁶And you shall bring to the priest, as your guilt offering to the LORD, a ram without blemish from the flock, or its equivalent, for a guilt offering. ⁷The priest shall make atonement on your behalf before the LORD, and you shall be forgiven for any of the things that one may do and incur guilt thereby.

Instructions concerning Sacrifices

8ᵇ The LORD spoke to Moses, saying: ⁹Command Aaron and his sons, saying: This is the ritual of the burnt offering. The burnt offering itself shall remain on the hearth upon the altar all night until the morning, while the fire on the altar shall be kept burning. ¹⁰The priest shall put on his linen vestments after putting on his linen undergarments next to his body; and he shall take up the ashes to which the fire has reduced the burnt offering on the altar, and place them beside the altar. ¹¹Then he shall take off his vestments and put on other garments, and carry the ashes out to a clean place outside the camp. ¹²The fire on the altar shall be kept burning; it shall not go out. Every morning the priest shall add wood to it, lay out the burnt offering on it, and turn into smoke the fat pieces of the offerings of well-

---

a Ch 5.20 in Heb *b* Ch 6.1 in Heb

---

through the use of a false oath. The sin to which it relates is desecration: the sacred objects (*holy things*) or the name of God have become desanctified (as opposed to cases of the purification offering in ch. 4, where the sin is contamination of sacred objects). Sins brazenly committed against God (i.e., a lying oath) can be commuted retroactively to inadvertent sins by subsequent repentance. **5.14–16** Reparation offerings for malevolent sacrilege against sacred objects. **5.15** *Trespass*, more accurately "sacrilege," the legal term for the wrong that is redressed by the reparation offering. *Convertible into silver.* The priest charges the supplicant the amount of the desecrated sacred object plus the amount needed to purchase the requisite reparation animal. *Guilt offering*, better "reparation offering." God must be compensated for the desecrated sacred object. **5.16** *And give it to the priest*, or "when he gives it to the priest." **5.17–19** Reparation for suspected trespass against sacred objects. **5.17** *You have incurred guilt.* He feels guilt (cf. 4.13), though he only suspects he has sinned. **5.18** *The equivalent*, its assessment in sanctuary-weighed silver. **6.2** *Deposit.* The neighbor was entrusted with the safekeeping of an ob-

ject. *A pledge*, probably an investment. **6.2, 4** *Defrauded*, better "withheld from." The specific case is withholding wages from an employee (19.13). **6.6** *Equivalent.* See note on 5.18.

6.8–7.38 Supplementary instructions for sacrifices. Since the well-being offering is eaten chiefly by the donor, the rules pertain mainly to him (7.11–34, esp. 23, 29). Otherwise they are the concerns of the officiating priest. The subjects are the altar fire (6.8–13); the manner and place for eating the grain offering (6.14–18); the daily grain offering of the high priest and the voluntary one of the ordinary priest (6.19–23); safeguards in sacrificing the purification offering (6.24–30); the ritual for the reparation offering (7.1–7, missing in ch. 5); the priestly share in the burnt and cereal offerings (7.8–10); the types of well-being offering and their taboos (7.11–21); the prohibition against eating suet and blood (7.22–27); the priestly share of the well-being offering, set aside by the donor (7.28–36); and the summation (7.37–38). **6.10** *Body*, a euphemism for genitals. **6.11** *Other garments.* These must be nonsacral, profane clothes, as the priest was forbidden to wear his priestly vestments outside the

being. 13A perpetual fire shall be kept burning on the altar; it shall not go out.

14 This is the ritual of the grain offering: The sons of Aaron shall offer it before the LORD, in front of the altar. 15They shall take from it a handful of the choice flour and oil of the grain offering, with all the frankincense that is on the offering, and they shall turn its memorial portion into smoke on the altar as a pleasing odor to the LORD. 16Aaron and his sons shall eat what is left of it; it shall be eaten as unleavened cakes in a holy place; in the court of the tent of meeting they shall eat it. 17It shall not be baked with leaven. I have given it as their portion of my offerings by fire; it is most holy, like the sin offering and the guilt offering. 18Every male among the descendants of Aaron shall eat of it, as their perpetual due throughout your generations, from the LORD's offerings by fire; anything that touches them shall become holy.

19 The LORD spoke to Moses, saying: 20This is the offering that Aaron and his sons shall offer to the LORD on the day when he is anointed: one-tenth of an ephah of choice flour as a regular offering, half of it in the morning and half in the evening. 21It shall be made with oil on a griddle; you shall bring it well soaked, as a grain offering of baked*a* pieces, and you shall present it as a pleasing odor to the LORD. 22And so the priest, anointed from among Aaron's descendants as a successor, shall prepare it; it is the LORD's—a perpetual due—to be turned entirely into smoke. 23Every grain offering of a priest shall be wholly burned; it shall not be eaten.

24 The LORD spoke to Moses, saying: 25Speak to Aaron and his sons, saying: This is the ritual of the sin offering. The sin offering shall be slaughtered before the LORD at the spot where the burnt offering is slaughtered; it is

most holy. 26The priest who offers it as a sin offering shall eat of it; it shall be eaten in a holy place, in the court of the tent of meeting. 27Whatever touches its flesh shall become holy; and when any of its blood is spattered on a garment, you shall wash the bespattered part in a holy place. 28An earthen vessel in which it was boiled shall be broken; but if it is boiled in a bronze vessel, that shall be scoured and rinsed in water. 29Every male among the priests shall eat of it; it is most holy. 30But no sin offering shall be eaten from which any blood is brought into the tent of meeting for atonement in the holy place; it shall be burned with fire.

7 This is the ritual of the guilt offering. It is most holy; 2at the spot where the burnt offering is slaughtered, they shall slaughter the guilt offering, and its blood shall be dashed against all sides of the altar. 3All its fat shall be offered: the broad tail, the fat that covers the entrails, 4the two kidneys with the fat that is on them at the loins, and the appendage of the liver, which shall be removed with the kidneys. 5The priest shall turn them into smoke on the altar as an offering by fire to the LORD; it is a guilt offering. 6Every male among the priests shall eat of it; it shall be eaten in a holy place; it is most holy.

7 The guilt offering is like the sin offering, there is the same ritual for them; the priest who makes atonement with it shall have it. 8So, too, the priest who offers anyone's burnt offering shall keep the skin of the burnt offering that he has offered. 9And every grain offering baked in the oven, and all that is prepared in a pan or on a griddle, shall belong to the priest who offers it. 10But every other grain offering, mixed with oil or dry, shall belong to all the sons of Aaron equally.

----

a Meaning of Heb uncertain

----

sanctuary (see Ezek 44.19). **6.13** *A perpetual fire.* The sacrifices offered up at the inauguration of the public cult were consumed miraculously by a divine fire (9.24), and it is this fire that is not allowed to die out, so that all subsequent sacrifices might claim divine acceptance (see Philo, *On the Special Laws* 1.286). **6.14** *The grain offering,* the raw type described in 2.1–3. **6.18** *Anything,* but not anyone. The priestly legists have limited what is subject to contagion to things. **6.20** *On the day,* or "from the time." The high priest's grain offering is sacrificed every day. **6.27–30** Paradoxically, the purification offering, though it is most holy, pollutes objects that it contacts because it ab-

sorbs the impurities it purges. If, however, it purges severe impurity, i.e., one that polluted the shrine, it must be eliminated by burning. **7.1–6** Since one liable for a reparation offering was expected to bring its monetary equivalent to the sanctuary (5.15), the procedure for the sacrifice is given here in the administrative unit addressed to the priests (6.8–7.38) rather than in the didactic order addressed to the laity (1.1–6.7). Once the lay offerer purchases the requisite reparation animal from the priest, the latter makes certain that the proper sacrificial procedure is followed. **7.7–10** The priestly prebends belong to the officiating priest. The sole exception is the raw grain offering, which is di-

Further Instructions

11 This is the ritual of the sacrifice of the offering of well-being that one may offer to the LORD. 12If you offer it for thanksgiving, you shall offer with the thank offering unleavened cakes mixed with oil, unleavened wafers spread with oil, and cakes of choice flour well soaked in oil. 13With your thanksgiving sacrifice of well-being you shall bring your offering with cakes of leavened bread. 14From this you shall offer one cake from each offering, as a gift to the LORD; it shall belong to the priest who dashes the blood of the offering of well-being. 15And the flesh of your thanksgiving sacrifice of well-being shall be eaten on the day it is offered; you shall not leave any of it until morning. 16But if the sacrifice you offer is a votive offering or a freewill offering, it shall be eaten on the day that you offer your sacrifice, and what is left of it shall be eaten the next day; 17but what is left of the flesh of the sacrifice shall be burned up on the third day. 18If any of the flesh of your sacrifice of well-being is eaten on the third day, it shall not be acceptable, nor shall it be credited to the one who offers it; it shall be an abomination, and the one who eats of it shall incur guilt.

19 Flesh that touches any unclean thing shall not be eaten; it shall be burned up. As for other flesh, all who are clean may eat such flesh. 20But those who eat flesh from the LORD's sacrifice of well-being while in a state of uncleanness shall be cut off from their kin. 21When any one of you touches any unclean thing—human uncleanness or an unclean animal or any unclean creature—and then eats flesh from the LORD's sacrifice of well-being, you shall be cut off from your kin.

22 The LORD spoke to Moses, saying: 23Speak to the people of Israel, saying: You shall eat no fat of ox or sheep or goat. 24The fat of an animal that died or was torn by wild animals may be put to any other use, but you must not eat it. 25If any one of you eats the fat from an animal of which an offering by fire may be made to the LORD, you who eat it shall be cut off from your kin. 26You must not eat any blood whatever, either of bird or of animal, in any of your settlements. 27Any one of you who eats any blood shall be cut off from your kin.

28 The LORD spoke to Moses, saying: 29Speak to the people of Israel, saying: Any one of you who would offer to the LORD your sacrifice of well-being must yourself bring to the LORD your offering from your sacrifice of well-being. 30Your own hands shall bring the LORD's offering by fire; you shall bring the fat with the breast, so that the breast may be raised as an elevation offering before the LORD. 31The priest shall turn the fat into smoke on the altar, but the breast shall belong to Aaron and his sons. 32And the right thigh from your sacrifices of well-being you shall give to the priest as an offering; 33the one among the sons of Aaron who offers the blood and fat of the offering of well-being shall have the right thigh for a portion. 34For I have taken the breast of the elevation offering, and

---

vided equally among all the priests, a development that probably reflects the Jerusalem temple and its large priestly corps (see also vv. 31–33). **7.11** *That one . . . LORD,* an admission that it is permitted to eat the meat of pure, nonsacrificial animals. **7.12–21** *You.* All second-person pronouns here and in vv. 28–32 are actually third person in the Hebrew. **7.13, 15** *Thanksgiving sacrifice of well-being.* P's conflation of two sacrifices, the thanksgiving offering and the well-being offering, which H treats as distinct sacrifices (22.21, 29). On P and H, see Introduction. **7.16** *Votive offering,* brought following the successful fulfillment of a vow (e.g., 2 Sam 15.7–8; Prov 7.14). *Freewill offering,* brought as the spontaneous by-product of one's happiness, whatever its cause (e.g., Num 15.3, 8; Ezek 46.12). **7.18** *It shall not be acceptable.* The sacrifice retains its holiness until the time of its elimination. **7.20, 21, 25** *Cut off from their/your kin,* extermination of the line by God. In consonance with the sacrificial system, which clearly recognizes the principle of intention

(chs. 4–5), it must be assumed that if any impure person inadvertently, not deliberately, eats sacred food, his wrong will be expiated by a purification offering. **7.21** *Unclean creature,* any of the eight quadrupeds singled out in 11.29–31 whose contact is defiling. **7.22–27** This passage differs from the rest of the chapter by employing the second person in the Hebrew rather than the third. Furthermore, the banning of the suet of all sacrificial animals differs from P, which allows for profane slaughter, and is a telltale sign of H (cf. 3.16–17; 17.3–5). On P and H, see Introduction. **7.28–32** *You.* See note on 7.12–21. **7.30** The *elevation offering* transfers the object from the offerer to the deity (represented by the priest). Thus the hands of both the offerer and the priest are placed under the offering in the performance of this rite. **7.31–33** The breast belongs to the entire priestly corps, whereas the right thigh is awarded the officiating priest, the latter prebend probably reflecting the older custom prevailing in any of the small sanctuaries attended by a single

the thigh that is offered, from the people of Israel, from their sacrifices of well-being, and have given them to Aaron the priest and to his sons, as a perpetual due from the people of Israel. 35This is the portion allotted to Aaron and to his sons from the offerings made by fire to the LORD, once they have been brought forward to serve the LORD as priests; 36these the LORD commanded to be given them, when he anointed them, as a perpetual due from the people of Israel throughout their generations.

37 This is the ritual of the burnt offering, the grain offering, the sin offering, the guilt offering, the offering of ordination, and the sacrifice of well-being, 38which the LORD commanded Moses on Mount Sinai, when he commanded the people of Israel to bring their offerings to the LORD, in the wilderness of Sinai.

The Rites of Ordination

8 The LORD spoke to Moses, saying: 2Take Aaron and his sons with him, the vestments, the anointing oil, the bull of sin offering, the two rams, and the basket of unleavened bread; 3and assemble the whole congregation at the entrance of the tent of meeting. 4And Moses did as the LORD commanded him. When the congregation was assembled at the entrance of the tent of meeting, 5Moses said to the congregation, "This is what the LORD has commanded to be done."

6 Then Moses brought Aaron and his sons forward, and washed them with water. 7He put the tunic on him, fastened the sash around him, clothed him with the robe, and put the ephod on him. He then put the decorated band of the ephod around him, tying the ephod to him with it. 8He placed the breastpiece on him, and in the breastpiece he put the Urim and the Thummim. 9And he set the turban on his head, and on the turban, in front, he set the golden ornament, the holy crown, as the LORD commanded Moses.

10 Then Moses took the anointing oil and anointed the tabernacle and all that was in it, and consecrated them. 11He sprinkled some of it on the altar seven times, and anointed the altar and all its utensils, and the basin and its base, to consecrate them. 12He poured some of the anointing oil on Aaron's head and anointed him, to consecrate him. 13And Moses brought forward Aaron's sons, and clothed them with tunics, and fastened sashes around them, and tied headdresses on them, as the LORD commanded Moses.

14 He led forward the bull of sin offering; and Aaron and his sons laid their hands upon the head of the bull of sin offering, 15and it was slaughtered. Moses took the blood and with his finger put some on each of the horns of the altar, purifying the altar; then he poured out the blood at the base of the altar. Thus he consecrated it, to make atonement for it. 16Moses took all the fat that was around the entrails, and the appendage of the liver, and the two kidneys with their fat, and turned

---

priestly family (e.g., Shiloh). **7.37** *The offering of ordination.* The mention of this offering before the *sacrifice of well-being* suggests that a section based on Ex 29 originally preceded 7.11.

8.1–10.20 In chs. 8–10, which follow logically and chronologically upon Ex 35–40, the priests are inducted into service after the priestly vestments and the tabernacle are completed. It is not Aaron, however, but Moses who dominates the scene. He conducts the inaugural service, consecrates the priests, and apportions all tasks, while Aaron is clearly answerable to him (see 10.16–20). Strikingly, the Priestly document insists upon the superiority of prophet over priest.

8.1–36 *To ordain you* (v. 33), lit. "to fill your hands." In scripture this phrase is used exclusively for the consecration of priests (Ex 32.29; Judg 17.5, 12; 1 Kings 13.33), but in other ancient Near Eastern texts it refers to the distribution of booty. Thus, the Hebrew idiom indicates that installation rites officially entitle the priests to their share of the revenues and sacrifices brought to the sanctuary. *As the LORD commanded Moses* concludes each phase of the consecration ceremony, a reminder that this chapter is a repetition of

the instructions in Ex 29. **8.7** *Ephod,* a garment, shaped like an apron, covering the loins and suspended from two shoulder-pieces (Ex 28.6–14). It must be distinguished from the linen ephod attributed in nonpriestly sources to the ordinary priest (1 Sam 2.18; 22.18; 2 Sam 6.14) and from the oracular ephod (1 Sam 23.6, 9; Hos 3.4). **8.8** *The Urim and the Thummim,* a form of oracle placed inside the pocket-shaped breastpiece worn by the high priest on his chest. Their shape and function are still undetermined. **8.9** *Ornament.* The Hebrew word means "flower." Possibly it took the shape of a plate (so the Septuagint) containing a floral decoration. The plate was suspended from the high priest's turban by a blue cord. Because of its inscription "Holy to the LORD" (Ex 28.36), it had the power to "take on . . . any guilt incurred in the holy offering that the Israelites consecrate as their sacred donations" (Ex 28.38). In other words, any inadvertent impurity or imperfection in the offerings to the sanctuary would be expiated by the plate. **8.10** *Anointing oil.* For consecration see vv. 10–13, 30; Ex 30.23–24. *Tabernacle.* See note on 1.3. **8.11** *Sprinkled . . . seven.* See note on 4.6. **8.16** *Turned . . . into smoke.* See note on

them into smoke on the altar. 17But the bull itself, its skin and flesh and its dung, he burned with fire outside the camp, as the LORD commanded Moses.

18 Then he brought forward the ram of burnt offering. Aaron and his sons laid their hands on the head of the ram, 19and it was slaughtered. Moses dashed the blood against all sides of the altar. 20The ram was cut into its parts, and Moses turned into smoke the head and the parts and the suet. 21And after the entrails and the legs were washed with water, Moses turned into smoke the whole ram on the altar; it was a burnt offering for a pleasing odor, an offering by fire to the LORD, as the LORD commanded Moses.

22 Then he brought forward the second ram, the ram of ordination. Aaron and his sons laid their hands on the head of the ram, 23and it was slaughtered. Moses took some of its blood and put it on the lobe of Aaron's right ear and on the thumb of his right hand and on the big toe of his right foot. 24After Aaron's sons were brought forward, Moses put some of the blood on the lobes of their right ears and on the thumbs of their right hands and on the big toes of their right feet; and Moses dashed the rest of the blood against all sides of the altar. 25He took the fat—the broad tail, all the fat that was around the entrails, the appendage of the liver, and the two kidneys with their fat—and the right thigh. 26From the basket of unleavened bread that was before the LORD, he took one cake of unleavened bread, one cake of bread with oil, and one wafer, and placed them on the fat and on the right thigh. 27He placed all these on the palms of Aaron and on the palms of his sons, and raised them as an elevation offering before the LORD. 28Then Moses took them from their hands and turned them into smoke on the altar with the burnt offering. This was an ordination offering for a pleasing odor, an offering by fire to the LORD. 29Moses took the breast and raised it as an elevation offering before the LORD; it was Moses' portion of the ram of ordination, as the LORD commanded Moses.

30 Then Moses took some of the anointing oil and some of the blood that was on the altar and sprinkled them on Aaron and his vestments, and also on his sons and their vestments. Thus he consecrated Aaron and his vestments, and also his sons and their vestments.

31 And Moses said to Aaron and his sons, "Boil the flesh at the entrance of the tent of meeting, and eat it there with the bread that is in the basket of ordination offerings, as I was commanded, 'Aaron and his sons shall eat it'; 32and what remains of the flesh and the bread you shall burn with fire. 33You shall not go outside the entrance of the tent of meeting for seven days, until the day when your period of ordination is completed. For it will take seven days to ordain you; 34as has been done today, the LORD has commanded to be done to make atonement for you. 35You shall remain at the entrance of the tent of meeting day and night for seven days, keeping the LORD's charge so that you do not die; for so I am commanded." 36Aaron and his sons did all the things that the LORD commanded through Moses.

1.9. **8.23–24** In the ancient Near East, incantations recited during the ritual smearing of persons, statues of gods, and buildings testify that its purpose is purificatory and apotropaic: to wipe off and ward off the incursions of menacing forces. Always it is the vulnerable parts of bodies (extremities) and structures (corners, entrances) that are smeared with magical substances. **8.27** *Elevation offering.* See 7.30. Because the right thigh is given directly by its offerer to the officiating priest without the benefit of a ritual (7.32–33), it is imperative that it undergo the rite of elevation to indicate that it no longer belongs to the offerer, but now belongs to God and must be offered up on the altar. **8.28** *Ordination offering.* In 7.30, this sacrifice stands between the most holy offerings (burnt, grain, purification, reparation) and holy offerings (wellbeing). Like the most holy offerings, it is eaten only by male priests in the sanctuary court (v. 31; cf. 6.16, 26; 7.6); the priestly prebends of the well-being offering may be eaten by the priest's family at any pure place. Of the three kinds of well-being offering (7.11–16), it resembles most the thanksgiving offering in that it is also accompanied by bread offerings (v. 2; cf. Ex 29.2; Lev 7.12) and is consumed on the same day. It is a transitional offering and corresponds with the transitional nature of its offerers, the priestly consecrands, who are passing from the realm of the profane to the realm of the sacred. **8.29** Moses receives the breast as his prebend (from God but not from the offerers, the priests), but not the thigh, lest that make him in the people's eyes a priest (see 7.34). **8.30** Whereas the blood daubing is for purification (vv. 23–24), the blood sprinkling is for consecration (16.19). **8.33, 35** The seven-day priestly consecration is a rite of passage from the profane to the sacred sphere, a liminal state fraught with peril for initiates.

Aaron's Priesthood Inaugurated

9 On the eighth day Moses summoned Aaron and his sons and the elders of Israel. 2He said to Aaron, "Take a bull calf for a sin offering and a ram for a burnt offering, without blemish, and offer them before the LORD. 3And say to the people of Israel, 'Take a male goat for a sin offering; a calf and a lamb, yearlings without blemish, for a burnt offering; 4and an ox and a ram for an offering of well-being to sacrifice before the LORD; and a grain offering mixed with oil. For today the LORD will appear to you.'" 5They brought what Moses commanded to the front of the tent of meeting; and the whole congregation drew near and stood before the LORD. 6And Moses said, "This is the thing that the LORD commanded you to do, so that the glory of the LORD may appear to you." 7Then Moses said to Aaron, "Draw near to the altar and sacrifice your sin offering and your burnt offering, and make atonement for yourself and for the people; and sacrifice the offering of the people, and make atonement for them; as the LORD has commanded."

8 Aaron drew near to the altar, and slaughtered the calf of the sin offering, which was for himself. 9The sons of Aaron presented the blood to him, and he dipped his finger in the blood and put it on the horns of the altar; and the rest of the blood he poured out at the base of the altar. 10But the fat, the kidneys, and the appendage of the liver from the sin offering he turned into smoke on the altar, as the LORD commanded Moses; 11and the flesh and the skin he burned with fire outside the camp.

12 Then he slaughtered the burnt offering. Aaron's sons brought him the blood, and he dashed it against all sides of the altar. 13And they brought him the burnt offering piece by piece, and the head, which he turned into smoke on the altar. 14He washed the entrails and the legs and, with the burnt offering, turned them into smoke on the altar.

15 Next he presented the people's offering. He took the goat of the sin offering that was for the people, and slaughtered it, and presented it as a sin offering like the first one. 16He presented the burnt offering, and sacrificed it according to regulation. 17He presented the grain offering, and, taking a handful of it, he turned it into smoke on the altar, in addition to the burnt offering of the morning.

18 He slaughtered the ox and the ram as a sacrifice of well-being for the people. Aaron's sons brought him the blood, which he dashed against all sides of the altar, 19and the fat of the ox and of the ram—the broad tail, the fat that covers the entrails, the two kidneys and the fat on them,*a* and the appendage of the liver. 20They first laid the fat on the breasts, and the fat was turned into smoke on the altar; 21and the breasts and the right thigh Aaron raised as an elevation offering before the LORD, as Moses had commanded.

22 Aaron lifted his hands toward the people and blessed them; and he came down after sacrificing the sin offering, the burnt offering, and the offering of well-being. 23Moses and Aaron entered the tent of meeting, and then came out and blessed the people; and the glory

---

a Gk: Heb *the broad tail, and that which covers, and the kidneys*

9.1–24 On the eighth day following the week of consecration, the priests begin their official duties. They offer up special sacrifices for the people *that the glory of the LORD may appear* (9.6; also 9.4, 9.23). Indeed, the whole purpose of the sacrificial system is revelation, the assurance that God is with his people. However, God's presence is never assumed to be a co-efficient of the ritual performed; it is always viewed as an act of his grace. **9.2** *Sin offering*, more accurately "purification offering"; see note on 4.1–35. **9.6** The *glory (kavod)*, in the encased fire-cloud, presumably brightens as a signal to Moses whenever God desires an audience with him (Num 16.42–44) or when Moses (with Aaron) seeks divine counsel (Num 20.6–7) before it condenses between the outspread wings of the cherubim in the adytum (the innermost part of the tabernacle). Otherwise the *kavod*, encased in cloud, remains suspended above the tabernacle so that it is visible to all of Israel at night (Ex 40.38; Num 9.15). Here, uniquely at the inauguration of the public cult in the tabernacle, the *kavod* separates itself from its nebulous encasement in order to consume the sacrifices in the sight of all of Israel (see also vv. 23–24). **9.9** *Horns*. See note on 4.7. **9.10** *Turned into smoke*. See note on 1.9. **9.12** *Burnt offering*. See note on 1.1–17. **9.17** *Grain offering*. See note on 2.1–16. *Burnt offering of the morning*. See Ex 29.38–42. **9.18** *Sacrifice of well-being*. See note on 3.1–17. **9.21** *Elevation offering*. See 7.30. **9.22** *Blessed them*, probably with the priestly blessing of Num 6.24–26. *He came down*. Presumably the blessing was recited from the top of the altar. **9.23** *The glory . . . appeared*, in the form of fire. Israel will be guided in the wilderness not by God's voiced commands but by his visible presence, a cloud-encased fire (Ex 40.38) identified with God's "glory" (Ex 24.17; Ezek 1.27–28; 2 Chr

of the LORD appeared to all the people. 24Fire came out from the LORD and consumed the burnt offering and the fat on the altar; and when all the people saw it, they shouted and fell on their faces.

Nadab and Abihu

10 Now Aaron's sons, Nadab and Abihu, each took his censer, put fire in it, and laid incense on it; and they offered unholy fire before the LORD, such as he had not commanded them. 2And fire came out from the presence of the LORD and consumed them, and they died before the LORD. 3Then Moses said to Aaron, "This is what the LORD meant when he said,

'Through those who are near me
    I will show myself holy,
and before all the people
    I will be glorified.' "
And Aaron was silent.

4 Moses summoned Mishael and Elzaphan, sons of Uzziel the uncle of Aaron, and said to them, "Come forward, and carry your kinsmen away from the front of the sanctuary to a place outside the camp." 5They came forward and carried them by their tunics out of the camp, as Moses had ordered. 6And Moses said to Aaron and to his sons Eleazar and Ithamar, "Do not dishevel your hair, and do not tear your vestments, or you will die and wrath will strike all the congregation; but your kindred, the whole house of Israel, may mourn the burning that the LORD has sent. 7You shall not go outside the entrance of the tent of meeting, or you will die; for the anointing oil of the LORD is on you." And they did as Moses had ordered.

8 And the LORD spoke to Aaron: 9Drink no wine or strong drink, neither you nor your sons, when you enter the tent of meeting, that you may not die; it is a statute forever throughout your generations. 10You are to distinguish between the holy and the common, and between the unclean and the clean; 11and you are to teach the people of Israel all the statutes that the LORD has spoken to them through Moses.

12 Moses spoke to Aaron and to his remaining sons, Eleazar and Ithamar: Take the grain offering that is left from the LORD's offerings by fire, and eat it unleavened beside the altar, for it is most holy; 13you shall eat it in a holy place, because it is your due and your sons' due, from the offerings by fire to the LORD; for so I am commanded. 14But the breast that is

7.3). **9.24** *Fire . . . LORD,* presumably from the adytum, where God's "glory" rested between the outspread wings of the cherubim flanking the ark (Ex 25.22). The theophany functioned to legitimize the Aaronite priesthood.

10.1–20 Ch. 10 continues the material from ch. 9. Grain and well-being offerings are eaten by the priests in accordance with the injunctions of 6.16; 7.28–34. But the procedure for the purification offering is switched from the individual to the communal form: the disposal of blood (9.9; 10.18) has been carried out in accordance with 4.30, but not the disposal of the flesh (10.18), which follows 4.12 rather than 6.26. The death of Nadab and Abihu has intervened. Aaron follows the more stringent procedure of destroying rather than eating the sacrificial meat because it has been doubly polluted by the sin and death of his sons. **10.1** *Unholy fire,* "unauthorized coals" (cf. Num 16.37, 40). **10.2** *And fire . . . the LORD,* a measure-for-measure principle: those who sinned by fire are punished by fire. **10.3** *What the LORD meant when he said,* more accurately "what the LORD has decreed, saying" (see Gen 24.51). *Those who are near me,* i.e., the priests (Ezek 42.13, translated "who approach"). The greater responsibility of the priests is evidenced in the rules dealing with the crime of encroaching upon the sacred spaces and objects (Num 18.1, 3, 7). The penalty is that of Nadab and Abihu—death by divine agency. The Lord becomes sanctified and glorified through pun-ishment (see Ezek 28.22). *And Aaron was silent,* contrasting starkly with the people's shouting moments earlier (9.24). **10.4** *Mishael and Elzaphan* are Levites, not priests, hence permitted to come in contact with the dead. **10.6** *Dishevel . . . vestments,* signs of mourning (e.g., Gen 37.29, 34; Lev 13.45). Although Eleazar and Ithamar, the surviving sons of Aaron, were permitted to mourn their brothers (21.1–3), they were on duty, assisting their father in the performance of the sacrifices (9.9, 12, 18) and had yet to eat the sacred meat (10.17). Moreover, they were anointed, in contrast to their priestly successors (Ex 40.15). Hence they were forbidden to mourn as their father was (21.10–11), because *the anointing oil of the LORD* was on them (v. 7). **10.9** *Strong drink,* probably "ale." The existence of a beer industry in Israel is attested by the prevalence of beer jugs in archaeological excavations. *Enter the tent of meeting,* also forbidden to a priest if he was improperly washed (Ex 30.20), physically blemished (Lev 21.23), or improperly dressed (Ex 28.43). **10.10** Teaching these distinctions is essential to the priestly function (see Ezek 44.21–23). **10.11** *To them,* to Israel, not to the priests. The priests carry no new instruction; they transmit the old, the teaching imparted to Israel through the mediation of Moses. This may be a telltale sign of H (see Introduction). **10.12** *Grain offering.* See note on 2.1–16. *Most holy.* See 2.3. **10.13** *Holy place.* See 6.16. **10.14** *Offerings of well-being.* See note on

elevated and the thigh that is raised, you and your sons and daughters as well may eat in any clean place; for they have been assigned to you and your children from the sacrifices of the offerings of well-being of the people of Israel. 15 The thigh that is raised and the breast that is elevated they shall bring, together with the offerings by fire of the fat, to raise for an elevation offering before the LORD; they are to be your due and that of your children forever, as the LORD has commanded.

16 Then Moses made inquiry about the goat of the sin offering, and—it had already been burned! He was angry with Eleazar and Ithamar, Aaron's remaining sons, and said, 17 "Why did you not eat the sin offering in the sacred area? For it is most holy, and God[a] has given it to you that you may remove the guilt of the congregation, to make atonement on their behalf before the LORD. 18 Its blood was not brought into the inner part of the sanctuary. You should certainly have eaten it in the sanctuary, as I commanded." 19 And Aaron spoke to Moses, "See, today they offered their sin offering and their burnt offering before the LORD; and yet such things as these have befallen me! If I had eaten the sin offering today, would it have been agreeable to the LORD?" 20 And when Moses heard that, he agreed.

Clean and Unclean Foods

11 The LORD spoke to Moses and Aaron, saying to them: 2 Speak to the people of Israel, saying:

From among all the land animals, these are the creatures that you may eat. 3 Any animal that has divided hoofs and is cleft-footed and chews the cud—such you may eat. 4 But among those that chew the cud or have divided hoofs, you shall not eat the following: the camel, for even though it chews the cud, it does not have divided hoofs; it is unclean for you. 5 The rock badger, for even though it chews the cud, it does not have divided hoofs; it is unclean for you. 6 The hare, for even though it chews the cud, it does not have di-

a Heb he

3.1–12. **10.15** *Elevation offering.* See 7.30. **10.16** *Sin offering,* better "purification offering." See note on 4.1–35. *He,* Moses. The purification offering, whose blood is daubed on the horns of the outer altar (4.25, 30, 34) but not brought inside the tent of meeting (6.30), must be eaten by the officiating priest (6.26), namely, Aaron, and what he cannot finish must be eaten by the rest of the priestly cadre (6.29), namely, his remaining sons, Eleazar and Ithamar. Moses may have become angry because the reluctance of the priests to eat this sacrifice would engender the suspicion that they were afraid of the harm that might befall them if they ate the impurity-laden meat, a belief that was current in Israel's contemporary world but that the Priestly source (P) assiduously attempted to eradicate. **10.17** *Remove the guilt,* remove the iniquity by ingesting the purificatory offering. This sacrifice is the analogic counterpart to the high priest's golden plate (8.9). Just as the latter symbolically draws to itself all the impurities of Israel's sacred offerings (Ex 28.38), so the former, by the blood manipulation, draws out the pollution of the sanctuary caused by Israel's impurities and iniquities (see notes on 4.1–35; 16.1–34). **10.18** In accordance with 6.26, 30. **10.19** Aaron's excuse; see note on 10.1–20. **10.20** That the ministrations of Aaron and his sons require the approval not only of God but also of Moses strikingly proves that the Priestly source (P) acknowledges the superiority of the prophet (Moses) over the priest (Aaron).

11.1–16.34 Laws dealing with four sources of impurity: carcasses (ch. 11), childbirth (ch. 12), scale disease (chs. 13–14), and genital discharges (ch. 15). (A fifth source, the corpse, is dealt with in Num 19.) The common denominator of these impurity sources is that they stand for death. Blood and semen represent the forces of life and their loss, death. The wasting of the body characteristic of scale disease symbolizes the death process (cf. Num 12.12) as much as the loss of blood and semen. Carcasses and corpses obviously are the epitome of death and therefore of impurity. Since impurity and holiness are semantic opposites, it is incumbent upon Israel to prevent impurity or at least to control its occurrence, lest it impinge upon the sanctuary, the realm of the holy God.

11.1–23 Clean and unclean foods. **11.1–8** Cf. vv. 3–4 with Deut 14.4–6, where the permitted land animals are named. The classification is the result not of empirical medical knowledge but of the universal need to classify phenomena by establishing beneficent and destructive categories. Above all, the function of the following list of forbidden and defiling quadruped carcasses (vv. 4–8, 24–31) is to limit consumption to the three domestic animals permitted on the altar (i.e., God's table): cattle, sheep, and goats. **11.2** *Land animals,* i.e., quadrupeds. **11.3** *Divided hoofs,* rather "hoofs." Israel's access is thus limited to the main domestic species—cattle, sheep, and goats (plus several wild but virtually unobtainable animals, Deut 14.4–5). *Chews the cud* excludes the pig (v. 7), regarded as an abomination particularly because it was revered in chthonic cults that penetrated into Israel as late as the sixth century BCE, arousing the wrath of prophet and priest alike (Isa 66.3, 17; cf. 65.4–5). **11.5–6** The *rock badger* and *hare* are not true ruminants, but the sideward movement of their jaws gives them the appearance of one. Their habit of chewing their food twice

vided hoofs; it is unclean for you. 7 The pig, for even though it has divided hoofs and is cleft-footed, it does not chew the cud; it is unclean for you. 8 Of their flesh you shall not eat, and their carcasses you shall not touch; they are unclean for you.

9 These you may eat, of all that are in the waters. Everything in the waters that has fins and scales, whether in the seas or in the streams—such you may eat. 10 But anything in the seas or the streams that does not have fins and scales, of the swarming creatures in the waters and among all the other living creatures that are in the waters—they are detestable to you 11 and detestable they shall remain. Of their flesh you shall not eat, and their carcasses you shall regard as detestable. 12 Everything in the waters that does not have fins and scales is detestable to you.

13 These you shall regard as detestable among the birds. They shall not be eaten; they are an abomination: the eagle, the vulture, the osprey, 14 the buzzard, the kite of any kind; 15 every raven of any kind; 16 the ostrich, the nighthawk, the sea gull, the hawk of any kind; 17 the little owl, the cormorant, the great owl, 18 the water hen, the desert owl,[a] the carrion vulture, 19 the stork, the heron of any kind, the hoopoe, and the bat.[b]

20 All winged insects that walk upon all fours are detestable to you. 21 But among the winged insects that walk on all fours you may eat those that have jointed legs above their feet, with which to leap on the ground. 22 Of them you may eat: the locust according to its kind, the bald locust according to its kind, the cricket according to its kind, and the grass-hopper according to its kind. 23 But all other winged insects that have four feet are detestable to you.

Unclean Animals

24 By these you shall become unclean; whoever touches the carcass of any of them shall be unclean until the evening, 25 and whoever carries any part of the carcass of any of them shall wash his clothes and be unclean until the evening. 26 Every animal that has divided hoofs but is not cleft-footed or does not chew the cud is unclean for you; everyone who touches one of them shall be unclean. 27 All that walk on their paws, among the animals that walk on all fours, are unclean for you; whoever touches the carcass of any of them shall be unclean until the evening, 28 and the one who carries the carcass shall wash his clothes and be unclean until the evening; they are unclean for you.

29 These are unclean for you among the creatures that swarm upon the earth: the weasel, the mouse, the great lizard according to its kind, 30 the gecko, the land crocodile, the lizard, the sand lizard, and the chameleon. 31 These are unclean for you among all that swarm; whoever touches one of them when they are dead shall be unclean until the evening. 32 And anything upon which any of them falls when they are dead shall be unclean, whether an article of wood or cloth or skin or sacking, any article that is used for any purpose; it shall be dipped into water, and it

---

a Or pelican b Identification of several of the birds in verses 13-19 is uncertain

---

also creates the impression that they are incessantly chewing food. **11.9–12** That neither prohibited nor permitted fish are enumerated (either here or in Deut 14.9) may be explained by the relatively limited variety of species of sea life in the Mediterranean prior to the construction of the Suez Canal. Fish—alone among the creatures—were not named by Adam (Gen 2.19–20). **11.13–19** No criteria are stated for *birds*. The fact that only impure birds are enumerated implies that the species of pure birds are innumerable (*Sipre Deuteronomy* 103). **11.20–23** *Winged insects*. The reason for exempting locusts is not clear. It may be related to Israel's pastoral life in its presettlement period, when the community subsisted on its herds as well as on the sporadic visits of locusts, just as Bedouin do to this day (cf. Mt 3.4; Mk 1.6).
11.24–40 Impurity by contact with carcasses. This section is an insertion from another source, since it interrupts the fourfold classification (11.46) of creatures that may not be eaten. Nonporous articles polluted by cadavers of the species listed in vv. 29–30 must be washed, but contaminated earthenware (porous and absorbent, 6.28) may never be reused. Food and seed grain are immune to impurity except when moist, since water is an impurity carrier. Only the carcasses of quadrupeds and eight reptiles contaminate by touch; all others contaminate by ingestion. **11.24** *Unclean until the evening*. Bathing is presumed, but impurity also needs time to dissipate completely, until evening in the case of minor impurities. **11.25** *Wash his clothes*. Bathing is presumed. **11.29–30** These eight named land swarmers differ from the rest of their kind (vv. 41–43) in that they contaminate not only by ingestion but also by touch (v. 31), a characteristic they share with the impure quadrupeds (vv. 8, 24–28). These eight would com-

skin and the hair in it is yellow and thin, the priest shall pronounce him unclean; it is an itch, a leprous[a] disease of the head or the beard. 31If the priest examines the itching disease, and it appears no deeper than the skin and there is no black hair in it, the priest shall confine the person with the itching disease for seven days. 32On the seventh day the priest shall examine the itch; if the itch has not spread, and there is no yellow hair in it, and the itch appears to be no deeper than the skin, 33he shall shave, but the itch he shall not shave. The priest shall confine the person with the itch for seven days more. 34On the seventh day the priest shall examine the itch; if the itch has not spread in the skin and it appears to be no deeper than the skin, the priest shall pronounce him clean. He shall wash his clothes and be clean. 35But if the itch spreads in the skin after he was pronounced clean, 36the priest shall examine him. If the itch has spread in the skin, the priest need not seek for the yellow hair; he is unclean. 37But if in his eyes the itch is checked, and black hair has grown in it, the itch is healed, he is clean; and the priest shall pronounce him clean.

38 When a man or a woman has spots on the skin of the body, white spots, 39the priest shall make an examination, and if the spots on the skin of the body are of a dull white, it is a rash that has broken out on the skin; he is clean.

40 If anyone loses the hair from his head, he is bald but he is clean. 41If he loses the hair from his forehead and temples, he has baldness of the forehead but he is clean. 42But if there is on the bald head or the bald forehead a reddish-white diseased spot, it is a leprous[a] disease breaking out on his bald head or his bald forehead. 43The priest shall examine him; if the diseased swelling is reddish-white on his bald head or on his bald forehead, which resembles a leprous[a] disease in the skin of the body, 44he is leprous,[a] he is unclean. The priest shall pronounce him unclean; the disease is on his head.

45 The person who has the leprous[a] disease shall wear torn clothes and let the hair of his head be disheveled; and he shall cover his upper lip and cry out, "Unclean, unclean." 46He shall remain unclean as long as he has the disease; he is unclean. He shall live alone; his dwelling shall be outside the camp.

47 Concerning clothing: when a leprous[a] disease appears in it, in woolen or linen cloth, 48in warp or woof of linen or wool, or in a skin or in anything made of skin, 49if the disease shows greenish or reddish in the garment, whether in warp or woof or in skin or in anything made of skin, it is a leprous[a] disease and shall be shown to the priest. 50The priest shall examine the disease, and put the diseased article aside for seven days. 51He shall examine the disease on the seventh day. If the disease has spread in the cloth, in warp or woof, or in the skin, whatever be the use of the skin, this is a spreading leprous[a] disease; it is unclean. 52He shall burn the clothing, whether diseased in warp or woof, woolen or linen, or anything of skin, for it is a spreading leprous[a] disease; it shall be burned in fire.

_____

a A term for several skin diseases; precise meaning uncertain.

dated once she is completely healed (see expressly 14.19). **12.7** *Flow*, lit. "source."

13.1–14.57 The priest is instructed to identify and isolate those afflicted with scale disease, traditionally but not properly translated "leprosy" (Hansen's disease). It is mainly a noncontagious condition, probably vitiligo or, less likely, psoriasis. (Regarding these examples of scale disease as ritually contaminating, see note on 11.1–16.34.) Scaling is the common denominator of all the skin ailments described in ch. 13, as follows: boils (vv. 18–23); burns (vv. 24–28); scalls, i.e., infection of the hairy parts of the head (vv. 29–37); tetters and normal baldness (pure manifestations; vv. 38–41); and impure baldness (vv. 42–44). The comportment of certified scale-disease carriers is described in 13.45–46 and their purificatory rites in 14.1–20. Lev 13.47–59 describes the deterioration of garments probably because of mildew or fungus, and 14.33–53 describes the infection of houses because of the spread of saltpeter or moss, in which case quarantine procedures are also enforced. Unusual considerations for property are reflected in 14.36: the priest clears the house prior to his inspection so that the contents will not be condemned with the house. The priest is not a physician; his rituals commence only after the disease has passed. Both disease and healing stem from the one God. Chs. 13–14 are summarized in 14.54–57. **13.2** *A swelling . . . spot.* A preferable translation might be "a discoloration or a scab or a shining mark." Vv. 2–8 deal with shining marks and vv. 9–17 with discolorations. Nonspreading scabs are not impure (vv. 7–8). **13.3** *Leprous disease,* rather "scale disease" (so throughout; see note on 13.1–14.57). **13.43** *Diseased swelling,* or "discolored affliction." **13.45** The certified scale-diseased person adopts the manner of a mourner. **13.51** *Spreading,* a malignant disease (also 14.44).

53 If the priest makes an examination, and the disease has not spread in the clothing, in warp or woof or in anything of skin, 54the priest shall command them to wash the article in which the disease appears, and he shall put it aside seven days more. 55The priest shall examine the diseased article after it has been washed. If the diseased spot has not changed color, though the disease has not spread, it is unclean; you shall burn it in fire, whether the leprous*a* spot is on the inside or on the outside.

56 If the priest makes an examination, and the disease has abated after it is washed, he shall tear the spot out of the cloth, in warp or woof, or out of skin. 57If it appears again in the garment, in warp or woof, or in anything of skin, it is spreading; you shall burn with fire that in which the disease appears. 58But the cloth, warp or woof, or anything of skin from which the disease disappears when you have washed it, shall then be washed a second time, and it shall be clean.

59 This is the ritual for a leprous*a* disease in a cloth of wool or linen, either in warp or woof, or in anything of skin, to decide whether it is clean or unclean.

Purification of Lepers and Leprous Houses

14 The LORD spoke to Moses, saying: 2This shall be the ritual for the leprous*a* person at the time of his cleansing:

He shall be brought to the priest; 3the priest shall go out of the camp, and the priest shall make an examination. If the disease is healed in the leprous*a* person, 4the priest shall command that two living clean birds and cedarwood and crimson yarn and hyssop be brought for the one who is to be cleansed. 5The priest shall command that one of the birds be slaughtered over fresh water in an earthen vessel. 6He shall take the living bird with the cedarwood and the crimson yarn and the hyssop, and dip them and the living bird in the blood of the bird that was slaughtered over the fresh water. 7He shall sprinkle it seven times upon the one who is to be cleansed of the leprous*a* disease; then he shall pronounce him clean, and he shall let the living bird go into the open field. 8The one who is to be cleansed shall wash his clothes, and shave off all his hair, and bathe himself in water, and he shall be clean. After that he shall come into the camp, but shall live outside his tent seven days. 9On the seventh day he shall shave all his hair: of head, beard, eyebrows; he shall shave all his hair. Then he shall wash his clothes, and bathe his body in water, and he shall be clean.

10 On the eighth day he shall take two male lambs without blemish, and one ewe lamb in its first year without blemish, and a grain offering of three-tenths of an ephah of choice flour mixed with oil, and one log*b* of oil. 11The priest who cleanses shall set the person to be cleansed, along with these things, before the LORD, at the entrance of the tent of meeting. 12The priest shall take one of the lambs, and offer it as a guilt offering, along with the log*b* of oil, and raise them as an elevation offering before the LORD. 13He shall slaughter the lamb in the place where the sin offering and the burnt offering are slaughtered in the holy place; for the guilt offering, like the sin offering, belongs to the priest: it is most holy. 14The priest shall take some of the blood of the guilt offering and put it on the lobe of the right ear of the one to be cleansed, and on the thumb of the right hand, and on the big toe of the right foot. 15The priest shall take some of the log*b* of oil and pour it into the palm of his own left hand, 16and dip his right finger in the oil that is in his left hand and sprinkle some oil with his finger seven times before the LORD. 17Some of the oil that remains in his hand the priest shall put on the lobe of the right ear of the one to be cleansed, and on the thumb of the right hand, and on the big toe of the right foot, on top of the blood of the guilt offering. 18The rest of the oil that is in the priest's hand he shall put on the head of the one to be cleansed. Then the priest shall make atonement on his behalf before the LORD: 19the priest shall offer the sin offering, to make atonement for the one to be cleansed from his uncleanness. Afterward he shall slaughter the burnt offering; 20and the priest shall offer the burnt offering and the grain offering on the altar. Thus the priest shall make atonement on his behalf and he shall be clean.

21 But if he is poor and cannot afford so much, he shall take one male lamb for a guilt offering to be elevated, to make atonement on his behalf, and one-tenth of an ephah of

---

a A term for several skin diseases; precise meaning uncertain
b A liquid measure

choice flour mixed with oil for a grain offering and a log*a* of oil; 22also two turtledoves or two pigeons, such as he can afford, one for a sin offering and the other for a burnt offering. 23On the eighth day he shall bring them for his cleansing to the priest, to the entrance of the tent of meeting, before the Lord; 24and the priest shall take the lamb of the guilt offering and the log*a* of oil, and the priest shall raise them as an elevation offering before the Lord. 25The priest shall slaughter the lamb of the guilt offering and shall take some of the blood of the guilt offering, and put it on the lobe of the right ear of the one to be cleansed, and on the thumb of the right hand, and on the big toe of the right foot. 26The priest shall pour some of the oil into the palm of his own left hand, 27and shall sprinkle with his right finger some of the oil that is in his left hand seven times before the Lord. 28The priest shall put some of the oil that is in his hand on the lobe of the right ear of the one to be cleansed, and on the thumb of the right hand, and the big toe of the right foot, where the blood of the guilt offering was placed. 29The rest of the oil that is in the priest's hand he shall put on the head of the one to be cleansed, to make atonement on his behalf before the Lord. 30And he shall offer, of the turtledoves or pigeons such as he can afford, 31one*b* for a sin offering and the other for a burnt offering, along with a grain offering; and the priest shall make atonement before the Lord on behalf of the one being cleansed. 32This is the ritual for the one who has a leprous*c* disease, who cannot afford the offerings for his cleansing.

33 The Lord spoke to Moses and Aaron, saying:

34 When you come into the land of Canaan, which I give you for a possession, and I put a leprous*c* disease in a house in the land of your possession, 35the owner of the house shall come and tell the priest, saying, "There seems to me to be some sort of disease in my house." 36The priest shall command that they empty the house before the priest goes to examine the disease, or all that is in the house will become unclean; and afterward the priest shall go in to inspect the house. 37He shall examine the disease; if the disease is in the walls of the house with greenish or reddish spots, and if it appears to be deeper than the surface, 38the priest shall go outside to the door of the house and shut up the house seven days. 39The priest shall come again on the seventh day and make an inspection; if the disease has spread in the walls of the house, 40the priest shall command that the stones in which the disease appears be taken out and thrown into an unclean place outside the city. 41He shall have the inside of the house scraped thoroughly, and the plaster that is scraped off shall be dumped in an unclean place outside the city. 42They shall take other stones and put them in the place of those stones, and take other plaster and plaster the house.

43 If the disease breaks out again in the house, after he has taken out the stones and scraped the house and plastered it, 44the priest shall go and make inspection; if the disease has spread in the house, it is a spreading leprous*c* disease in the house; it is unclean. 45He shall have the house torn down, its stones and timber and all the plaster of the house, and taken outside the city to an unclean place. 46All who enter the house while it is shut up

---

a A liquid measure   *b* Gk Syr: Heb *afford,* 31*such as he can afford, one*   *c* A term for several skin diseases; precise meaning uncertain

---

14.1–32 Three separate purificatory ceremonies are required for a healed scale-diseased person: for the first day (vv. 2–8; also invoked for houses, vv. 48–53), for the seventh day (v. 9), and for the eighth day (vv. 10–32). They constitute a rite of passage whereby the person is successively reintegrated into the community. **14.2** *He shall . . . priest,* preferably "When it is reported to the priest," in view of the subsequent statement *the priest shall go out of the camp.* **14.4–8** The living bird, dipped in the blood of the slain bird, carries off enough ritual impurity to allow the erstwhile "leper" to reenter the camp after he shaves and bathes but not to reenter his (or any) tent lest he contaminate it (see 14.46). **14.9** After his second shaving and ablution on the seventh day, he resumes normal intercourse with family. **14.10–20** The final stage of his purification takes place the following day when he brings a reparation offering for having possibly desecrated a sacred object or space (see 5.17–19), the blood of which together with sanctified oil is smeared on his extremities to purify him (see 8.30); a purification offering (not properly *sin offering*) for having contaminated the sanctuary by his impurity (see esp. v. 19); and a burnt offering and a grain offering to expiate for neglected performative commandments or sinful thoughts (see 1.4). **14.16** *Seven times before the Lord,* to consecrate the oil (see 4.6). **14.36** Persons and objects that were in the house prior to its quarantine by the priest are declared pure. **14.46** *All who enter* points to the extraordinary power of the fungous house to

shall be unclean until the evening; 47and all who sleep in the house shall wash their clothes; and all who eat in the house shall wash their clothes.

48 If the priest comes and makes an inspection, and the disease has not spread in the house after the house was plastered, the priest shall pronounce the house clean; the disease is healed. 49For the cleansing of the house he shall take two birds, with cedarwood and crimson yarn and hyssop, 50and shall slaughter one of the birds over fresh water in an earthen vessel, 51and shall take the cedarwood and the hyssop and the crimson yarn, along with the living bird, and dip them in the blood of the slaughtered bird and the fresh water, and sprinkle the house seven times. 52Thus he shall cleanse the house with the blood of the bird, and with the fresh water, and with the living bird, and with the cedarwood and hyssop and crimson yarn; 53and he shall let the living bird go out of the city into the open field; so he shall make atonement for the house, and it shall be clean.

54 This is the ritual for any leprous*a* disease: for an itch, 55for leprous*a* diseases in clothing and houses, 56and for a swelling or an eruption or a spot, 57to determine when it is unclean and when it is clean. This is the ritual for leprous*a* diseases.

Concerning Bodily Discharges

15 The LORD spoke to Moses and Aaron, saying: 2Speak to the people of Israel and say to them:

When any man has a discharge from his member,*b* his discharge makes him ceremonially unclean. 3The uncleanness of his discharge is this: whether his member*b* flows with his discharge, or his member*b* is stopped from discharging, it is uncleanness for him. 4Every bed on which the one with the discharge lies shall be unclean; and everything on which he sits shall be unclean. 5Anyone who touches his bed shall wash his clothes, and bathe in water, and be unclean until the evening. 6All who sit on anything on which the one with the discharge has sat shall wash their clothes, and bathe in water, and be unclean until the evening. 7All who touch the body of the one with the discharge shall wash their clothes, and bathe in water, and be unclean until the evening. 8If the one with the discharge spits on persons who are clean, then they shall wash their clothes, and bathe in water, and be unclean until the evening. 9Any saddle on which the one with the discharge rides shall be unclean. 10All who touch anything that was under him shall be unclean until the evening, and all who carry such a thing shall wash their clothes, and bathe in water, and be unclean until the evening. 11All those whom the one with the discharge touches without his having rinsed his hands in water shall wash their clothes, and bathe in water, and be unclean until the evening. 12Any earthen vessel that the one with the discharge touches shall be broken; and every vessel of wood shall be rinsed in water.

13 When the one with a discharge is cleansed of his discharge, he shall count seven days for his cleansing; he shall wash his clothes and bathe his body in fresh water, and he shall

a A term for several skin diseases; precise meaning uncertain
b Heb *flesh*

---

contaminate by overhang, i.e., to contaminate anyone under its roof, proof that scale disease (and all severe impurities) emits a miasma that contaminates the sanctuary at a distance and, in the case of scale disease and corpse contamination (see Num 19.14), defiles persons and objects inside a house. **14.49–52** For the cleansing of the house only the first-day rite for scale disease (vv. 4–8) is required, since the impurity generated by the house is not strong enough to contaminate the sanctuary from afar.

15.1–33 Ch. 15 is composed of two sections: natural discharges of men and women (vv. 16–18, 19–24, respectively), an impurity removed simply by bathing, and pathological discharges (vv. 2–15, 25–30, respectively), which require sacrificial expiation. The eighth-day ritual for the latter, as for the scale-diseased person, is a rite of passage from death to life.

15.2 *Discharge*, an abnormal one, usually but not exclusively identified with gonorrhea. **15.3** The loss of semen and genital blood (vv. 19–30) generates impurity since it represents the loss of life and hence is opposed to the Lord, the source of holiness and life (see note on 11.1–16.34). **15.5** This extra-strength impurity, affecting persons and objects at a second (even a third, v. 23) remove, is limited to objects directly underneath those having genital discharges. **15.11** *Rinsed his hands.* Whoever takes this precaution may touch persons and objects. Thus he may live at home, a far-reaching leniency. **15.12** See 11.33. **15.13** *Fresh water.* Fresh, lit. "living," water is also required in two other cases: corpse contamination (Num 19.17) and scale disease (Lev 14.5–6, 50–52). Together with genital discharges they comprise all the sources of severe impurity (lasting seven days or more). Since impurity is

be clean. ¹⁴On the eighth day he shall take two turtledoves or two pigeons and come before the LORD to the entrance of the tent of meeting and give them to the priest. ¹⁵The priest shall offer them, one for a sin offering and the other for a burnt offering; and the priest shall make atonement on his behalf before the LORD for his discharge.

16 If a man has an emission of semen, he shall bathe his whole body in water, and be unclean until the evening. ¹⁷Everything made of cloth or of skin on which the semen falls shall be washed with water, and be unclean until the evening. ¹⁸If a man lies with a woman and has an emission of semen, both of them shall bathe in water, and be unclean until the evening.

19 When a woman has a discharge of blood that is her regular discharge from her body, she shall be in her impurity for seven days, and whoever touches her shall be unclean until the evening. ²⁰Everything upon which she lies during her impurity shall be unclean; everything also upon which she sits shall be unclean. ²¹Whoever touches her bed shall wash his clothes, and bathe in water, and be unclean until the evening. ²²Whoever touches anything upon which she sits shall wash his clothes, and bathe in water, and be unclean until the evening; ²³whether it is the bed or anything upon which she sits, when he touches it he shall be unclean until the evening. ²⁴If any man lies with her, and her impurity falls on him, he shall be unclean

seven days; and every bed on which he lies shall be unclean.

25 If a woman has a discharge of blood for many days, not at the time of her impurity, or if she has a discharge beyond the time of her impurity, all the days of the discharge she shall continue in uncleanness; as in the days of her impurity, she shall be unclean. ²⁶Every bed on which she lies during all the days of her discharge shall be treated as the bed of her impurity; and everything on which she sits shall be unclean, as in the uncleanness of her impurity. ²⁷Whoever touches these things shall be unclean, and shall wash his clothes, and bathe in water, and be unclean until the evening. ²⁸If she is cleansed of her discharge, she shall count seven days, and after that she shall be clean. ²⁹On the eighth day she shall take two turtledoves or two pigeons and bring them to the priest at the entrance of the tent of meeting. ³⁰The priest shall offer one for a sin offering and the other for a burnt offering; and the priest shall make atonement on her behalf before the LORD for her unclean discharge.

31 Thus you shall keep the people of Israel separate from their uncleanness, so that they do not die in their uncleanness by defiling my tabernacle that is in their midst.

32 This is the ritual for those who have a discharge: for him who has an emission of semen, becoming unclean thereby, ³³for her who is in the infirmity of her period, for anyone, male or female, who has a discharge, and for the man who lies with a woman who is unclean.

---

symbolic of death, its antidote is that which fosters life. **15.15** *Sin offering,* more accurately "purification offering" (see note on 4.1–35), for having polluted the sanctuary with his impurity. The function of the *burnt offering* here is to provide adequate substance for the altar, since the meat is assigned to the officiating priest (6.26). So too must every other purification-offering bird be accompanied by a burnt-offering bird (5.7; 12.8; 14.30–31). **15.16** Natural emissions of semen, as opposed to pathological ones, constitute only a minor impurity of one day's duration. **15.18** In many ancient cultures sexual intercourse disqualified a person from participating in religious ritual. The rite frequently prescribed for purification from sexual impurity is bathing, but the Bible uniquely adds one stipulation: for the impurity to be completely eliminated one must wait until evening (see 11.24). One can understand that seminal emissions, being a total loss of life-giving fluids, were regarded as impure, but what of the emission in conjugal union, the act of procreation? Obviously, the priestly legists were aware of the fact that it is the rare seed that results in procreation; mostly it is

wasted. **15.19** Laundering and bathing at the end of seven days must be presumed. **15.19–23** The menstruant is not banished but remains at home. She may prepare meals and perform her household chores. The family, in turn, has to avoid lying in her bed, sitting in her chair, or touching her. **15.23** *The bed or anything,* more precisely "on the bed or on anything." An object can be contaminated at a third remove provided it is in unbroken contact with the menstruant. **15.24** *If any man . . . on him* may be translated "if any man lies with her, her impurity will fall upon him," implying that copulation may have been a deliberate act, punishable by excision (20.18). The severe, seven-day impurity may be due to the loss of both life-giving semen and genital blood. **15.25** *The days of her impurity,* lit. "the days of her menstrual impurity," a reference to vv. 20, 22. **15.27** *These things.* Possibly with Septuagint read "her," in conformance with the law concerning men's discharge (v. 7). **15.30** See v. 15. **15.31** *Defiling my tabernacle.* Severe impurity incurred anywhere in the community will pollute the sanctuary. For this spatial notion of impurity, see chs. 4 and 16.

The Day of Atonement

16 The LORD spoke to Moses after the death of the two sons of Aaron, when they drew near before the LORD and died. ²The LORD said to Moses:

Tell your brother Aaron not to come just at any time into the sanctuary inside the curtain before the mercy seat*a* that is upon the ark, or he will die; for I appear in the cloud upon the mercy seat.*a* ³Thus shall Aaron come into the holy place: with a young bull for a sin offering and a ram for a burnt offering. ⁴He shall put on the holy linen tunic, and shall have the linen undergarments next to his body, fasten the linen sash, and wear the linen turban; these are the holy vestments. He shall bathe his body in water, and then put them on. ⁵He shall take from the congregation of the people of Israel two male goats for a sin offering, and one ram for a burnt offering.

6 Aaron shall offer the bull as a sin offering for himself, and shall make atonement for himself and for his house. ⁷He shall take the two goats and set them before the LORD at the entrance of the tent of meeting; ⁸and Aaron shall cast lots on the two goats, one lot for the LORD and the other lot for Azazel.*b* ⁹Aaron shall present the goat on which the lot fell for the LORD, and offer it as a sin offering; ¹⁰but the goat on which the lot fell for Azazel*b* shall be presented alive before the LORD to make atonement over it, that it may be sent away into the wilderness to Azazel.*b*

11 Aaron shall present the bull as a sin offering for himself, and shall make atonement for himself and for his house; he shall slaughter the bull as a sin offering for himself. ¹²He shall take a censer full of coals of fire from the altar before the LORD, and two handfuls of crushed sweet incense, and he shall bring it inside the curtain ¹³and put the incense on the fire before the LORD, that the cloud of the incense may cover the mercy seat*a* that is upon the covenant,*c* or he will die. ¹⁴He shall take some of the blood of the bull, and sprinkle it with his finger on the front of the mercy seat,*a* and before the mercy seat*a* he shall sprinkle the blood with his finger seven times.

---

a Or *the cover*   *b* Traditionally rendered *a scapegoat*
c Or *treaty,* or *testament*; Heb *eduth*

16.1–34 The annual Day of Atonement for the sanctuary and people. According to v. 1, ch. 16 follows upon ch. 10. Thus, chs. 11–15 are an insert listing the specific impurities that will contaminate the sanctuary (15.31) for which the purification ritual of ch. 16 is mandated. The impurities of the sanctuary are eliminated by purification offerings (16.16–19). The iniquities of the people are eliminated by the confession of the high priest over the dispatched goat while the people fast (vv. 21–22, 29–31). The text strongly suggests that the original form of the purgation rite described in vv. 2–28 was an emergency measure invoked by the high priest whenever he felt that the entire sanctuary had to be purged. It is the appendix, vv. 29–34, that fixes this rite as an annual observance. That it comprises an appendix is ascertained by the change of person (direct address to Israel); the fact that not Aaron but his descendants are officiating (v. 32); a change in terminology (e.g., the adytum is now called "the holiest part of the sanctuary"; see v. 33); the fact that only here is the date specified at the end (vv. 29, 34), whereas all other festival prescriptions begin with the date; and the unexpected inclusion of resident aliens, its first occurrence in the book of Leviticus. All seventeen subsequent attestations in chs. 17–24 are, by common scholarly consent, attributed to H (see Introduction). **16.1** *Drew near before,* better "encroached upon." **16.2** *In the cloud,* by means of the screen of incense raised by the high priest (v. 13). **16.2–3** *Sanctuary/holy place,* the adytum, innermost part of the tabernacle. *Sin offering,* better "purification offering" (see note on 4.1–35). **16.4** The high priest donned linen garments perhaps because entering the adytum was equivalent to being admitted to the heavenly council, whose members, the angels, were also dressed in linen (Ezek 9.2–3, 11; 10.2; Dan 10.5) **16.6** *Offer,* lit. "bring forward," as in v. 11, *present.* **16.8** *Azazel,* probably the name of a demon who has been stripped of his alleged powers by the priestly legists. No longer a personality but just a name, he designates the place to which Israel's impurities and sins are banished. **16.10** *To make atonement over it,* by the confession of Israel's sins (v. 21). **16.11** The high priest must purge the sanctuary of the impurities he and his fellow priests have caused before he is eligible to do the same for the people. **16.12–13** If the purpose of the incense is to raise a cloud of smoke that screens the high priest's view of the ark, how could it be that he lights the incense only *after* he enters the adytum? The clue to the solution is supplied by the fact that the lit incense by itself does not produce a cloud of smoke. Thus another smoke-raising ingredient has to be added to the incense and it, not the incense, was ignited by the high priest before he entered the adytum and ignited the incense. The incense, then, would have functioned to placate God for the high priest's presumption in entering before his presence. *The covenant,* short for "the ark of the covenant." **16.14** *On the front of,* lit. "on the surface of . . . the east side." Since the high priest could not see the ark cover, he merely threw the drop of blood toward it but made sure it landed on its east side, namely, before it. Thus symbol-

15 He shall slaughter the goat of the sin offering that is for the people and bring its blood inside the curtain, and do with its blood as he did with the blood of the bull, sprinkling it upon the mercy seat[a] and before the mercy seat.[a] 16Thus he shall make atonement for the sanctuary, because of the uncleannesses of the people of Israel, and because of their transgressions, all their sins; and so he shall do for the tent of meeting, which remains with them in the midst of their uncleannesses. 17No one shall be in the tent of meeting from the time he enters to make atonement in the sanctuary until he comes out and has made atonement for himself and for his house and for all the assembly of Israel. 18Then he shall go out to the altar that is before the LORD and make atonement on its behalf, and shall take some of the blood of the bull and of the blood of the goat, and put it on each of the horns of the altar. 19He shall sprinkle some of the blood on it with his finger seven times, and cleanse it and hallow it from the uncleannesses of the people of Israel.

20 When he has finished atoning for the holy place and the tent of meeting and the altar, he shall present the live goat. 21Then Aaron shall lay both his hands on the head of the live goat, and confess over it all the iniquities of the people of Israel, and all their transgressions, all their sins, putting them on the head of the goat, and sending it away into the wilderness by means of someone designated for the task.[b] 22The goat shall bear on itself all their iniquities to a barren region; and the goat shall be set free in the wilderness.

23 Then Aaron shall enter the tent of meeting, and shall take off the linen vestments that he put on when he went into the holy place, and shall leave them there. 24He shall bathe his body in water in a holy place, and put on his vestments; then he shall come out and offer his burnt offering and the burnt offering of the people, making atonement for himself and for the people. 25The fat of the sin offering he shall turn into smoke on the altar. 26The one who sets the goat free for Azazel[c] shall wash his clothes and bathe his body in water, and afterward may come into the camp. 27The bull of the sin offering and the goat of the sin offering, whose blood was brought in to make atonement in the holy place, shall be taken outside the camp; their skin and their flesh and their dung shall be consumed in fire. 28The one who burns them shall wash his clothes and bathe his body in water, and afterward may come into the camp.

29 This shall be a statute to you forever: In the seventh month, on the tenth day of the month, you shall deny yourselves,[d] and shall do no work, neither the citizen nor the alien who resides among you. 30For on this day atonement shall be made for you, to cleanse you; from all your sins you shall be clean before the LORD. 31It is a sabbath of complete rest to you, and you shall deny yourselves;[d] it is a statute forever. 32The priest who is anointed and consecrated as priest in his father's place shall make atonement, wearing the linen vestments, the holy vestments. 33He shall make

a Or *the cover*   b Meaning of Heb uncertain   c Traditionally rendered *a scapegoat*   d Or *shall fast*

---

ically the ark was purged, as was the entire adytum, by the sevenfold blood sprinkling on the adytum floor. **16.16** *Make . . . sanctuary,* purge the adytum. *Transgressions.* In the Priestly theology it is the transgressions, the willful, brazen impurities committed by the people, that have penetrated into the adytum, requiring its purgation by the high priest on the annual Day of Atonement. *So he . . . meeting.* The purgation rite of 4.6–7, 17–18 is presumed. The tent of meeting here refers to the outer room, the shrine. **16.18** *On its behalf,* better "upon it." Purification-offering blood is put directly on the sacrificial altar (see Ex 29.36). **16.18–19** The daubing of the blood on the altar purifies it (see 4.7, 25; 8.15); the sprinkling rite sanctifies it (see 8.11). **16.21** *Lay,* lit. "lean" (see note on 1.4). *Both his hands,* an act of transference (as in 24.14), in contrast with sacrificial, one-handed hand leaning, an act of ownership (1.4). *Iniquities.* Whereas the blood rites in the sanctuary purge it of Israel's impurities (*uncleannesses,* v. 16), the hand leaning of the confession over the live goat purges the people of their sins by transferring them to the head of the goat and dispatching it into the wilderness. *Confess.* Confession is required only for brazen, presumptuous sins (5.5; 26.40; Num 5.7). **16.22** *And.* Translate "when" and connect with v. 23 to avoid a redundancy with v. 21b. **16.23** *Leave them there,* because they contracted the extreme sanctity of the adytum. **16.24** *His vestments,* i.e., the ornate ones he always wore while officiating at the altar (8.6–9). **16.26–28** The handlers of the slain and live purification offerings are contaminated, but not the high priest, who is immune to impurity while officiating. **16.29** *Deny yourselves.* "Afflict yourselves, from food, drink, and from enjoying bathing, and from anointing, and from sexual intercourse" (*Targum Pseudo-Jonathan*). **16.29–31** See also 23.26–32. **16.32** *Priest in his father's place.* In contrast to vv. 2–28, which speak solely of Aaron, this verse focuses

atonement for the sanctuary, and he shall make atonement for the tent of meeting and for the altar, and he shall make atonement for the priests and for all the people of the assembly. 34This shall be an everlasting statute for you, to make atonement for the people of Israel once in the year for all their sins. And Moses did as the LORD had commanded him.

The Slaughtering of Animals

17 The LORD spoke to Moses: 2 Speak to Aaron and his sons and to all the people of Israel and say to them: This is what the LORD has commanded. 3If anyone of the house of Israel slaughters an ox or a lamb or a goat in the camp, or slaughters it outside the camp, 4and does not bring it to the entrance of the tent of meeting, to present it as an offering to the LORD before the tabernacle of the LORD, he shall be held guilty of bloodshed; he has shed blood, and he shall be cut off from the people. 5This is in order that the people of Israel may bring their sacrifices that they offer in the open field, that they may bring them to the LORD, to the priest at the entrance of the tent of meeting, and offer them as sacrifices of well-being to the LORD. 6The priest shall dash the blood against the altar of the LORD at the entrance of the tent of meeting, and turn the fat into smoke as a pleasing odor to the LORD, 7so that they may no longer offer their sacrifices for goat-demons, to whom they prostitute themselves. This shall be a statute forever to them throughout their generations.

8 And say to them further: Anyone of the house of Israel or of the aliens who reside among them who offers a burnt offering or sacrifice, 9and does not bring it to the entrance of the tent of meeting, to sacrifice it to the LORD, shall be cut off from the people.

Eating Blood Prohibited

10 If anyone of the house of Israel or of the aliens who reside among them eats any blood, I will set my face against that person who eats blood, and will cut that person off from the people. 11For the life of the flesh is in the blood; and I have given it to you for making atonement for your lives on the altar; for, as

---

on his successors. **16.33** *The sanctuary,* rather "the holiest part of the sanctuary," i.e., the adytum.

17.1–26.46 The Holiness source (H). The remainder of the book of Leviticus (excluding ch. 27), it is often held, consists largely of an independent code in which moral and ritual laws alternate, motivated by holiness. This, however, is questionable. Ch. 17, the alleged beginning of the code, is connected thematically and verbally with the preceding chapters. Chs. 25–26, which are often alleged to be the conclusion, form an independent scroll, to judge from the unique vocabulary (e.g., 25.18–19; 26.5), theme (25.8–13; 26.34–35, 43), and redaction (25.1; 26.46). Nonetheless, much of the language and some ideas in chs. 17–26 differ from the first part of Leviticus. For a fuller discussion of H and of the relationship between P and H, see the Introduction.

17.1–16 Whoever kills a sacrificial animal outside the sanctuary is guilty of murder (17.3–4). Sacrifice to goat-demons or "satyrs" is thus abolished (17.5–9), and expiation for killing the animal is assured through a ritual by which its lifeblood is returned to its creator, either upon the altar (17.10–12) or by being drained and covered by earth in the case of game animals (17.13–14; cf. Deut 12.16). V. 11 has nothing to do with the expiation of sin in general. **17.3–7** No common slaughter. **17.3** *Outside the camp,* but within easy access of the sanctuary. **17.4** *Guilty of bloodshed,* a capital crime. *Cut off from the people,* i.e., extinction of his line by divine agency, a capital punishment (see 7.20). **17.5** *In the open field,* for chthonic worship (see v. 7). *Sacrifices . . . LORD.* Henceforth, common slaughter is strictly forbidden. Meat for the table must initially be a sacrifice. **17.7** *Goat-demons.* It is possible that the demon Azazel (the first element of which means "goat"; see 16.8) was also a satyr. *Prostitute themselves,* a metaphor for idolatry (Ex 34.15–16; Lev 20.5, 6; Deut 31.16). **17.8–9** No sacrifices to other gods. **17.8** If *aliens* wish to have meat, they need not bring their animals to the sanctuary (a performative commandment), but they are forbidden to worship other gods (a prohibitive commandment). *Burnt offering or sacrifice.* The latter refers to the well-being (including the thanksgiving) offering. Thus, the purification and reparation offerings are excluded, possibly a reflex of the popular religion, which knew only the burnt offering as the exclusive expiatory sacrifice (see also 22.17–21). **17.10–12** Blood of animals may not be ingested. Both animals and people have a *nefesh* (Hebrew), "soul." *Nefesh* refers to the life essence of both human and beast as distinct from the body. It is the part of the person or animal that does not disintegrate into dust, but departs the body (see "as her *nefesh* was departing," Gen 35.18). It is presumed that the *nefesh* is contained in the blood. Vv. 11–12 are an aside to Moses; only the law is given to Israel, not its rationale. **17.10** *Aliens* are forbidden to ingest blood, a prohibitive commandment. *Eats,* proof that the blood is ingested in the course of eating meat. **17.11** *To you,* to Israel, but not to aliens who may slaughter animals at home. *For making atonement,* or "to ransom" (see Ex 30.12, 15, 16). Animal slaughter is murder except at the authorized altar, where the offered blood ransoms the donor's life. *As life . . . atonement,* or "it is the blood

life, it is the blood that makes atonement.
12Therefore I have said to the people of Israel:
No person among you shall eat blood, nor
shall any alien who resides among you eat
blood. 13And anyone of the people of Israel, or
of the aliens who reside among them, who
hunts down an animal or bird that may be
eaten shall pour out its blood and cover it with
earth.

14 For the life of every creature—its blood is
its life; therefore I have said to the people of Israel: You shall not eat the blood of any creature,
for the life of every creature is its blood; whoever
eats it shall be cut off. 15All persons, citizens or
aliens, who eat what dies of itself or what has
been torn by wild animals, shall wash their
clothes, and bathe themselves in water, and be
unclean until the evening; then they shall be
clean. 16But if they do not wash themselves or
bathe their body, they shall bear their guilt.

Sexual Relations

18 The LORD spoke to Moses, saying:
2 Speak to the people of Israel and say
to them: I am the LORD your God. 3You shall
not do as they do in the land of Egypt, where
you lived, and you shall not do as they do in
the land of Canaan, to which I am bringing
you. You shall not follow their statutes. 4My
ordinances you shall observe and my statutes
you shall keep, following them: I am the LORD
your God. 5You shall keep my statutes and my
ordinances; by doing so one shall live: I am the
LORD.

6 None of you shall approach anyone near
of kin to uncover nakedness: I am the LORD.
7You shall not uncover the nakedness of your
father, which is the nakedness of your mother;
she is your mother, you shall not uncover her
nakedness. 8You shall not uncover the naked-

---

that ransoms by means of life." **17.13–14** The blood of
game may not be ingested. Assumed is the knowledge
of 11.13–19, 24–28. **17.13** *Cover it with earth,* so that
the blood will not be used in chthonic worship (e.g.,
for divination) but returned to God, who endowed animals as well as humans with *nefesh* (Hebrew), "life,
soul." **17.14** The third aside to Moses providing ratio-
nales for required actions (in addition to vv. 5–7, 11–
12), virtually repeating vv. 10–11a. **17.15–16** Eating of
a carcass requires purification. **17.15** Lest they pollute
the land, *aliens* must also purify themselves after eating of a carcass. **17.16** *Guilt,* or "punishment." If their
impurity is prolonged, leading to the pollution of the
sanctuary, they will be punished by the excision of
their line (see 5.1–13).

18.1–20.27 On being holy. Chs. 18–20 are thematically united: ch. 20 prescribes the penalties for the illicit relations and homicidal cult practices proscribed
in ch. 18 (20.1–5) and for violating the ban on magic
put into effect in 19.31 (20.6). Moreover, the entire
unit is framed by a single goal: separation of the Israelites from the Canaanites, who are portrayed as engaging in idolatrous and immoral practices, which pollute
the divinely chosen land (18.3; 18.24–30; 20.22–24).
The arrangement of Ezek 22 contains a mixture of ethical and ritual sins based solely on these chapters, indicating that their written formulation is preexilic.

The key word in this section is *holy.* This word clusters in the food prohibitions (11.44–47; 20.23–26)
and significantly in only one other context, the rules
concerning the priesthood, 21.6–8. The priesthood,
Israel, and humankind form three rings of decreasing
holiness about the center, God. Ideally, all Israel shall
be "a priestly kingdom and a holy nation" (Ex 19.6). If
Israel is to attain its higher level of holiness, it must
abide by a more rigid code of behavior than that practiced by other nations, just as the priests live by more
stringent standards than common Israelites. Holiness,

then, implies separation and is so defined in 20.26. The
positive aspect of holiness is discussed in ch. 19.

18.1–30 The list of prohibitions is framed by passages (vv. 1–5, 24–30) castigating the sexual mores of
the Egyptians and the Canaanites. Israel is charged
with an exacting code of family purity whose violation
means death (20.10–16). Only the Holiness source
(H) proclaims the sanctity of the land of Canaan;
hence both Israelites and resident strangers are responsible for maintaining its sanctity (18.26–27; 20.2;
24.22). The moral justification for its conquest
(18.27–28; 20.22) is also a warning: if guilty of the
same infractions, Israel too will be *vomited out.* **18.2** *I
am the LORD your God,* or "I the LORD am your God."
Hence, you must follow my laws. **18.3** *Egypt* and *Canaan* are accused by biblical authors of consan-
guineous, incestuous, promiscuous, and homosexual
unions (Gen 9.22; 19.5; 34.2; 39.7; Ezek 16.26; 23.3,
20). **18.5** *I am the LORD,* or "I the LORD," i.e., "I the
LORD have spoken," equivalent to the prophetic "says
the LORD" (e.g., Am 2.16; 3.15).

18.6–23. Forbidden sexual relations. The major purpose of most of these rules is to protect the unmarried
woman from falling prey to the avaricious males in her
family. The basic sociological unit in Israel was the "father's house." It included three to five generations consisting of fifty to a hundred people living in close proximity. **18.6** *Approach,* a euphemism for "have sex with."
Near of kin, lit. "flesh of his flesh," i.e., the nearest kin,
one's mother, sister, and daughter, the last two otherwise missing in this list. *Uncover nakedness,* another euphemism for having sex with, given here in this initial
law for emphasis. **18.7** *The nakedness of your father,* i.e.,
your father's exclusive possession (18.20.11; 20.11; Deut
22.30; cf. Lev 20.20, 21). The same expression is found
in the enigmatic case of Noah's nakedness (Gen 9.22–
23), implying that Ham had sex with his mother, an incestuous union that produced their son Canaan.

ness of your father's wife; it is the nakedness of your father. ⁹You shall not uncover the nakedness of your sister, your father's daughter or your mother's daughter, whether born at home or born abroad. ¹⁰You shall not uncover the nakedness of your son's daughter or of your daughter's daughter, for their nakedness is your own nakedness. ¹¹You shall not uncover the nakedness of your father's wife's daughter, begotten by your father, since she is your sister. ¹²You shall not uncover the nakedness of your father's sister; she is your father's flesh. ¹³You shall not uncover the nakedness of your mother's sister, for she is your mother's flesh. ¹⁴You shall not uncover the nakedness of your father's brother, that is, you shall not approach his wife; she is your aunt. ¹⁵You shall not uncover the nakedness of your daughter-in-law: she is your son's wife; you shall not uncover her nakedness. ¹⁶You shall not uncover the nakedness of your brother's wife; it is your brother's nakedness. ¹⁷You shall not uncover the nakedness of a woman and her daughter, and you shall not take*a* her son's daughter or her daughter's daughter to uncover her nakedness; they are your*b* flesh; it is depravity. ¹⁸And you shall not take*a* a woman as a rival to her sister, uncovering her nakedness while her sister is still alive.

19 You shall not approach a woman to uncover her nakedness while she is in her menstrual uncleanness. ²⁰You shall not have sexual relations with your kinsman's wife, and defile yourself with her. ²¹You shall not give any of your offspring to sacrifice them*c* to Molech, and so profane the name of your God: I am the LORD. ²²You shall not lie with a male as with a woman; it is an abomination. ²³You shall not have sexual relations with any animal and defile yourself with it, nor shall any woman give herself to an animal to have sexual relations with it: it is perversion.

24 Do not defile yourselves in any of these ways, for by all these practices the nations I am casting out before you have defiled themselves. ²⁵Thus the land became defiled; and I punished it for its iniquity, and the land vomited out its inhabitants. ²⁶But you shall keep my statutes and my ordinances and commit none of these abominations, either the citizen or the alien who resides among you ²⁷(for the inhabitants of the land, who were before you, committed all of these abominations, and the land became defiled); ²⁸otherwise the land will vomit you out for defiling it, as it vomited out the nation that was before you. ²⁹For whoever commits any of these abominations shall be cut off from their people. ³⁰So keep my charge not to commit any of these abominations that were done before you, and not to defile yourselves by them: I am the LORD your God.

Ritual and Moral Holiness

19 The LORD spoke to Moses, saying: 2 Speak to all the congregation of the people of Israel and say to them: You shall be

a Or *marry*   *b* Gk: Heb lacks *your*   *c* Heb *to pass them over*

18.9 *Born at home . . . abroad,* whether she belongs to your kin group or another kin group; i.e., even if your half sister is totally unrelated to you by blood, she is forbidden. But see Gen 20.12, in which Abraham married his half sister. **18.11** *Begotten by your father,* rather "of your father's kin." But if she belongs to a different kin group, marriage is permissible. **18.12** Amram married Jochebed, his paternal aunt (they were the parents of Aaron and Moses), despite this prohibition. Reflecting sensitivity to this discrepancy, the Septuagint in Ex 6.20 reads "the daughter of his father's brother," i.e., his cousin. Perhaps for this reason the birth of Moses is attributed to anonymous Levite parents (Ex 2.1). **18.15** Judah married his daughter-in-law, Tamar, despite this prohibition—an early form of levirate marriage (cf. Gen 38; Deut 25.5–10). **18.16** Ostensibly, the verse is opposed to the institution of levirate marriage (Deut 25.5–10; see Lev 20.21). **18.18** Despite this prohibition, Jacob married two sisters, Rachel and Leah, while both were alive (Gen 29.15–30). The obvious answer to all four above-mentioned marital discrepancies

with vv. 9, 12, 18 is that they occurred before the Sinaitic law code became operative. **18.20** *Kinsman's,* rather "neighbor's" (cf. Ezek 18.6, 15). **18.21** *Give . . . offspring to sacrifice.* See 2 Kings 23.10; cf. Deut 12.31; 2 Kings 16.3; Jer 7.31; 19.5; 32.35. *Molech* may stand for *melek,* "king (of the underworld)," who was probably identified by his worshipers with Israel's God (cf. Jer 7.31; 19.5). If it were another god, the sacrifice would have been condemned as murder. See also note on 20.2. *Profane the name of your God,* since the rite is dedicated to him. **18.23** Different species should be kept apart, following God's example at creation (Gen 1); see also Lev 19.19. **18.25** Moral sins pollute the earth, e.g., those of Adam and Eve (Gen 3.17), Cain (4.10–12), and Noah's generation (8.21). Here, however, the pollution is confined to the land of Canaan (Ezek 36.17; see Num 35.33; Deut 21.23; Jer 2.7). Therein lies the theological basis of the concept of the holy land, namely, that all who reside on this land, including all aliens, must observe God's prohibitive commandments (see 17.8, 10; esp. 24.16). **19.1–37** For Israel, "holy" means more than that

holy, for I the LORD your God am holy. ³You shall each revere your mother and father, and you shall keep my sabbaths: I am the LORD your God. ⁴Do not turn to idols or make cast images for yourselves: I am the LORD your God.

5 When you offer a sacrifice of well-being to the LORD, offer it in such a way that it is acceptable in your behalf. ⁶It shall be eaten on the same day you offer it, or on the next day; and anything left over until the third day shall be consumed in fire. ⁷If it is eaten at all on the third day, it is an abomination; it will not be acceptable. ⁸All who eat it shall be subject to punishment, because they have profaned what is holy to the LORD; and any such person shall be cut off from the people.

9 When you reap the harvest of your land, you shall not reap to the very edges of your field, or gather the gleanings of your harvest. ¹⁰You shall not strip your vineyard bare, or gather the fallen grapes of your vineyard; you shall leave them for the poor and the alien: I am the LORD your God.

11 You shall not steal; you shall not deal falsely; and you shall not lie to one another. ¹²And you shall not swear falsely by my name, profaning the name of your God: I am the LORD.

13 You shall not defraud your neighbor; you shall not steal; and you shall not keep for yourself the wages of a laborer until morning. ¹⁴You shall not revile the deaf or put a stumbling block before the blind; you shall fear your God: I am the LORD.

15 You shall not render an unjust judgment; you shall not be partial to the poor or defer to the great: with justice you shall judge your neighbor. ¹⁶You shall not go around as a slanderer[a] among your people, and you shall not profit by the blood[b] of your neighbor: I am the LORD.

17 You shall not hate in your heart anyone of your kin; you shall reprove your neighbor, or you will incur guilt yourself. ¹⁸You shall not take vengeance or bear a grudge against any of your people, but you shall love your neighbor as yourself: I am the LORD.

19 You shall keep my statutes. You shall not let your animals breed with a different kind; you shall not sow your field with two kinds of seed; nor shall you put on a garment made of two different materials.

20 If a man has sexual relations with a woman who is a slave, designated for another man but not ransomed or given her freedom, an inquiry shall be held. They shall not be put to death, since she has not been freed; ²¹but he shall bring a guilt offering for himself to the LORD, at the entrance of the tent of meeting, a ram as guilt offering. ²²And the priest shall make atonement for him with the ram of guilt offering before the LORD for his sin that he committed; and the sin he committed shall be forgiven him.

23 When you come into the land and plant all kinds of trees for food, then you shall re-

---

a Meaning of Heb uncertain   b Heb stand against the blood

---

which is unapproachable. It becomes a positive concept, an inspiration and a goal associated with God's nature and his desire for humans to be holy: *You shall be holy; for I . . . am holy* (v. 2). That which humans are not and can never fully be, but which they are commanded to emulate and approximate is what the Bible calls "holy." Holiness means *imitatio Dei*—the life of godliness. How can human beings imitate God? The answer of Lev 19 is given in a series of ethical and ritual commands, above which soars the commandment to love all persons (v. 18), including aliens (v. 34). Such love must be concretely expressed in deeds: equality in civil justice (24:22; Num 35.15), free loans (Lev 25.35–38; Deut 10.18; 23.20), and free gleanings (Lev 19.9–10). **19.5–8** Here the well-being sacrifice is limited to the freewill and votive offerings, in contrast to 7.11–16, which includes the thanksgiving offering. **19.10** The widow and orphan fall under the category of the *poor.* The poor, however, do not appear as a separate category in the humanitarian legislation of Deuteronomy, which instead ordains for them loans (Deut 15.7–11); i.e., they can work off their debt, something that widows and orphans cannot. *I am the LORD your God,* "for the LORD pleads their cause and despoils of life those who despoil them" (Prov 22.23). **19.11** *Deal falsely,* e.g., deny you possessed your neighbor's property (6.2). **19.13** *Steal,* rather "rob" (cf. v. 11). **19.16** *Profit,* lit. "stand," i.e., don't stand idly by when your fellow is in danger. **19.17** *Guilt,* i.e., "punishment." *Yourself,* more accurately "because of him," i.e., you are likely to take action against him that may be sinful. **19.18** *Love,* reach out, befriend. Love here is not an emotion. *Neighbor,* i.e., an Israelite (cf. v. 34). *As yourself,* i.e., as you love yourself, or "who is like you," since he or she is also created by God. **19.19** *Two kinds of seed, two different materials.* See Deut 22.9. God separated everything according to its species (Gen 1). The human world should mirror the natural world. Israel, therefore, may not mix with other nations, but be holy, set apart for God. **19.20–22** A marginal case. Though not guilty before humans (not adulterous), he is guilty before God; hence he brings a reparation offering.

gard their fruit as forbidden;[a] three years it shall be forbidden[b] to you, it must not be eaten. 24In the fourth year all their fruit shall be set apart for rejoicing in the LORD. 25But in the fifth year you may eat of their fruit, that their yield may be increased for you: I am the LORD your God.

26 You shall not eat anything with its blood. You shall not practice augury or witchcraft. 27You shall not round off the hair on your temples or mar the edges of your beard. 28You shall not make any gashes in your flesh for the dead or tattoo any marks upon you: I am the LORD.

29 Do not profane your daughter by making her a prostitute, that the land not become prostituted and full of depravity. 30You shall keep my sabbaths and reverence my sanctuary: I am the LORD.

31 Do not turn to mediums or wizards; do not seek them out, to be defiled by them: I am the LORD your God.

32 You shall rise before the aged, and defer to the old; and you shall fear your God: I am the LORD.

33 When an alien resides with you in your land, you shall not oppress the alien. 34The alien who resides with you shall be to you as the citizen among you; you shall love the alien as yourself, for you were aliens in the land of Egypt: I am the LORD your God.

35 You shall not cheat in measuring length, weight, or quantity. 36You shall have honest balances, honest weights, an honest ephah, and an honest hin: I am the LORD your God, who brought you out of the land of Egypt. 37You shall keep all my statutes and all my ordinances, and observe them: I am the LORD.

Penalties for Violations of Holiness

20 The LORD spoke to Moses, saying: 2Say further to the people of Israel:

Any of the people of Israel, or of the aliens who reside in Israel, who give any of their offspring to Molech shall be put to death; the people of the land shall stone them to death. 3I myself will set my face against them, and will cut them off from the people, because they have given of their offspring to Molech, defiling my sanctuary and profaning my holy name. 4And if the people of the land should ever close their eyes to them, when they give of their offspring to Molech, and do not put them to death, 5I myself will set my face against them and against their family, and will cut them off from among their people, them and all who follow them in prostituting themselves to Molech.

6 If any turn to mediums and wizards, prostituting themselves to them, I will set my

---

a Heb as their uncircumcision   b Heb uncircumcision

19.24 Set apart . . . in the LORD, lit. "holy . . . before the LORD," i.e., at the sanctuary. 19.26 With, lit. "over," a chthonic rite for the purpose of consulting the dead spirits (see v. 31; 17.5–7, 13–14; 20.6; 1 Sam 14.32–35). Instead, the blood should be offered on the altar (17.3–4, 11). 19.27–28 Pagan mourning rites. 19.31 Mediums, or "ancestral spirits" (see v. 26; 20.27). 19.33 Oppress, or "cheat." 19.34 The summit of biblical ethics.

20.1–27 The penalties for illicit sexual relations are graded according to their severity: vv. 10–16, death by humans; vv. 17–19, death by God; vv. 20–21, childlessness. Of illicit worship of God, only Molech worship and oracles through mediums are singled out, the former because of its monstrousness and the latter because of its prevalence (Deut 18.9–12; 1 Sam 28.9; Isa 8.19). The absence of the lofty pronouncements of ch. 19 from this list is mute evidence that ethics are really unenforceable. 20.2 Since aliens reside in the Lord's land, they are required to observe all the prohibitive commandments (see 17.8, 10). The Molech cult is expressly mentioned in 18.21; 20.2–5; 2 Kings 23.10; Jer 32.35 and alluded to in Isa 57.9; Jer 7.31; 19.5. Though the Leviticus texts use the ambiguous verbs "give" and "pass over" (alternate translation of "give" in 18.21),

other references explicitly use the verb "burn" (Jer 7.31; 19.5; cf. 32.35; Isa 30.33). The reason this prohibition is set among the sexual offenses (note the sexual imagery in v. 5) is that it (and, indeed, all idolatry) was regarded as spiritual adultery (Ex 34.15–16; cf. Jer 3). Molech is probably identical with the Canaanite god mlk, who in Akkadian sources is called Malik and is equated with the underworld god Nergal. The sacrifices to Molech were offered in the Valley of Hinnom, just outside Jerusalem (2 Kings 23.10; cf. Jer 7.31; 32.35). 20.3 Defiling my sanctuary. Since Molech worship was practiced just beneath the Temple Mount in the Valley of Hinnom (Jer 32.35), it was feasible to worship at both sites the same day (Ezek 23.32–39), an indication that its devotees felt that its worship was compatible with the worship of and, indeed, demanded by the Lord. 20.5 Them, i.e., the Molech worshipers. Their family. The family may have protected them. 20.5–6 People, better "(deceased) kin." The Lord imposes a measure-for-measure punishment: he cuts off from ancestral spirits the one who tries to placate them. 20.6 It is no accident that this prohibition against turning to mediums and wizards (for the purpose of consulting the ancestral spirits; see 19.26) is cojoined with the Molech prohibition. Both are di-

face against them, and will cut them off from the people. ⁷Consecrate yourselves therefore, and be holy; for I am the LORD your God. ⁸Keep my statutes, and observe them; I am the LORD; I sanctify you. ⁹All who curse father or mother shall be put to death; having cursed father or mother, their blood is upon them.

10 If a man commits adultery with the wife of*[a] his neighbor, both the adulterer and the adulteress shall be put to death. ¹¹The man who lies with his father's wife has uncovered his father's nakedness; both of them shall be put to death; their blood is upon them. ¹²If a man lies with his daughter-in-law, both of them shall be put to death; they have committed perversion, their blood is upon them. ¹³If a man lies with a male as with a woman, both of them have committed an abomination; they shall be put to death; their blood is upon them. ¹⁴If a man takes a wife and her mother also, it is depravity; they shall be burned to death, both he and they, that there may be no depravity among you. ¹⁵If a man has sexual relations with an animal, he shall be put to death; and you shall kill the animal. ¹⁶If a woman approaches any animal and has sexual relations with it, you shall kill the woman and the animal; they shall be put to death, their blood is upon them.

17 If a man takes his sister, a daughter of his father or a daughter of his mother, and sees her nakedness, and she sees his nakedness, it is a disgrace, and they shall be cut off in the sight of their people; he has uncovered his sister's nakedness, he shall be subject to punishment. ¹⁸If a man lies with a woman having her sickness and uncovers her nakedness, he has laid bare her flow and she has laid bare her flow of blood; both of them shall be cut off from their people. ¹⁹You shall not uncover the nakedness of your mother's sister or of your father's sister, for that is to lay bare one's own flesh; they shall be subject to punishment. ²⁰If a man lies with his uncle's wife, he has uncovered his uncle's nakedness; they shall be subject to punishment; they shall die childless. ²¹If a man takes his brother's wife, it is impurity; he has uncovered his brother's nakedness; they shall be childless.

22 You shall keep all my statutes and all my ordinances, and observe them, so that the land to which I bring you to settle in may not vomit you out. ²³You shall not follow the practices of the nation that I am driving out before you. Because they did all these things, I abhorred them. ²⁴But I have said to you: You shall inherit their land, and I will give it to you to possess, a land flowing with milk and honey. I am the LORD your God; I have separated you from the peoples. ²⁵You shall therefore make a distinction between the clean animal and the unclean, and between the unclean bird and the clean; you shall not bring abomination on yourselves by animal or by bird or by anything with which the ground teems, which I have set apart for you to hold unclean. ²⁶You shall be

a Heb repeats *if a man commits adultery with the wife of*

rected against chthonic worship, which especially prevailed in Judah at the end of the eighth and beginning of the seventh century BCE. The Judean kings of this period, Ahaz and Manasseh, are accused of practicing Molech worship (2 Kings 16.3; 21.6), and Isaiah (eighth century) reports the resort to mediums and wizards (19.3 explicitly mentions its goal: "[to] consult . . . the spirits of the dead")—further indication that the Holiness source (H) originates from this period. **20.8** *I am the* LORD; *I sanctify you,* or "I, the LORD, sanctify you." Israel acquires holiness by observing the commandments (22.32; cf. Ex 31.13; Ezek 20.12; 37.28). **20.9** *Curse,* perhaps "insult, dishonor" (see Ex 21.17; Prov 20.20; Mt 15.4; Mk 7.10). *Their blood is upon them,* i.e., their executioner need not fear that their blood will be "on his head" (see Josh 2.14; 2 Sam 1.16; 1 Kings 2.37), namely, that God will hold him responsible for spilling their blood. **20.10** *If a man . . . neighbor.* The specification "his neighbor" limits the penalty to Israelites. Though adultery is listed last among the illicit heterosexual relations (18.20), it is first when it comes to these penalties since it concerns not only private morality but the stability and welfare of the community. **20.11** *His father's wife.* His mother is assumed (18.7–8). **20.12** See 18.15. **20.13** See 18.22. **20.14** *Takes,* in marriage or by common consent. See 18.17. **20.15–16** See 18.23. **20.15** *Kill the animal,* which has also sinned (cf. Ex 21.28–29). **20.17** See 18.9. *Sees her nakedness . . . sees his nakedness,* a willful act. *Subject to punishment,* probably excision. **20.18** *Sickness,* not just menstruation but any genital flow (15.25, 33), an expansion of 18.19. **20.19** See 18.12–13. *One's own flesh,* actually "the flesh of one's flesh." **20.20** See 18.14. **20.21** A rejection of the levirate (Deut 25.5), whereby the name of the deceased husband is preserved through the progeny born of his wife and his brother. *Childless.* Once again, the divine measure-for-measure punishment is manifest: his wish to have a child from his brother's widow will be denied. **20.24** *Honey,* date syrup (Deut 8.8). **20.25** Making distinctions between the animals that form one's diet teaches one to make distinctions in

holy to me; for I the LORD am holy, and I have separated you from the other peoples to be mine.

27 A man or a woman who is a medium or a wizard shall be put to death; they shall be stoned to death, their blood is upon them.

The Holiness of Priests

21 The LORD said to Moses: Speak to the priests, the sons of Aaron, and say to them:

No one shall defile himself for a dead person among his relatives, 2except for his nearest kin: his mother, his father, his son, his daughter, his brother; 3likewise, for a virgin sister, close to him because she has had no husband, he may defile himself for her. 4But he shall not defile himself as a husband among his people and so profane himself. 5They shall not make bald spots upon their heads, or shave off the edges of their beards, or make any gashes in their flesh. 6They shall be holy to their God, and not profane the name of their God; for they offer the LORD's offerings by fire, the food of their God; therefore they shall be holy. 7They shall not marry a prostitute or a woman who has been defiled; neither shall they marry a woman divorced from her husband. For they are holy to their God, 8and you shall treat

them as holy, since they offer the food of your God; they shall be holy to you, for I the LORD, I who sanctify you, am holy. 9When the daughter of a priest profanes herself through prostitution, she profanes her father; she shall be burned to death.

10 The priest who is exalted above his fellows, on whose head the anointing oil has been poured and who has been consecrated to wear the vestments, shall not dishevel his hair, nor tear his vestments. 11He shall not go where there is a dead body; he shall not defile himself even for his father or mother. 12He shall not go outside the sanctuary and thus profane the sanctuary of his God; for the consecration of the anointing oil of his God is upon him: I am the LORD. 13He shall marry only a woman who is a virgin. 14A widow, or a divorced woman, or a woman who has been defiled, a prostitute, these he shall not marry. He shall marry a virgin of his own kin, 15that he may not profane his offspring among his kin; for I am the LORD; I sanctify him.

16 The LORD spoke to Moses, saying: 17Speak to Aaron and say: No one of your offspring throughout their generations who has a blemish may approach to offer the food of his God. 18For no one who has a blemish shall draw near, one who is blind or lame, or

---

human contact. **20.27** *Is a medium,* lit. "has inside him an ancestral spirit." An appendix. Whereas those who consult mediums are punished by God (v. 6), the mediums themselves are put to death by people. **21.1–22.33** Restrictions are placed upon the priests to guard against moral and ritual defilement, which might entail dire consequences for them and the people (22.9, 15–16; cf. 4.3; 15.31). Disqualifications of sacrifices are also enumerated (22.21–24). Ritual impurity stems from these sources: certain scale diseases (see chs. 13–14), genital fluxes, both male and female (see ch. 15), and carcasses (see ch. 11) or corpses (Num 19, a knowledge of which is presumed here). Contamination by corpses is the most severe of the ritual impurities because a person becomes contaminated merely by being under the same roof as a corpse (Num 19.14) and because the impurity lasts for seven days (Num 19.14, 16) and can only be eliminated by the unique rite of being aspersed with the ashes of a red cow (Num 19.17–19). There is no prohibition against coming in contact with a corpse (it is assumed that one may, and indeed should, bury the dead). The only restriction is that the purificatory rite may not be overlooked or even delayed (Num 19.13, 19). This allowance, however, does not hold for a priest. He is holy, and the contact between holiness and impurity not only is forbidden; it is lethal (see 7.20–21; 22.9). Thus, the

permission given to priests to bury their closest blood relatives (their nuclear family; 21.1–4) constitutes a concession. **21.4** *People,* rather "kin" (see 20.5–6), implying that the priest may not defile himself for the burial of his wife or any of her relatives. If, however, the words *as a husband* are deleted (a possible dittography of the following word), then the prohibition repeats and forms an *inclusio* with v. 1, a structure repeated in vv. 17b, 21 (in an *inclusio,* the beginning and end repeat each other, thereby signaling a structural unit). **21.5** These mourning rites are also forbidden to Israelites (19.27–28). **21.7** *Woman . . . defiled,* probably raped, which carries no stigma for her if she is the daughter of a layman (Deut 22.28–29; cf. Lev 21.9). *Divorced,* but not a widow; the criterion is reputation. **21.8** *Treat them as holy,* by seeing to it that your daughters qualify as their wives (vv. 7, 9). *Sanctify you.* One may read "sanctify them" with Septuagint, the Samaritan Pentateuch, and a Dead Sea Scroll fragment of Leviticus written in the old Hebrew alphabet (11QpaleoLev). **21.9** *She profanes her father,* just as a wife's character reflects on her husband (v. 7). **21.10** *The priest . . . his fellows,* i.e., the high priest, may not engage even in permitted mourning rites. **21.11** Sight of a corpse also contaminates a high priest. **21.12** He may not leave the sanctuary to follow the bier (see 10.7). **21.13** Since he is appointed during the lifetime of his

one who has a mutilated face or a limb too long, [19]or one who has a broken foot or a broken hand, [20]or a hunchback, or a dwarf, or a man with a blemish in his eyes or an itching disease or scabs or crushed testicles. [21]No descendant of Aaron the priest who has a blemish shall come near to offer the LORD's offerings by fire; since he has a blemish, he shall not come near to offer the food of his God. [22]He may eat the food of his God, of the most holy as well as of the holy. [23]But he shall not come near the curtain or approach the altar, because he has a blemish, that he may not profane my sanctuaries; for I am the LORD; I sanctify them. [24]Thus Moses spoke to Aaron and to his sons and to all the people of Israel.

The Use of Holy Offerings

22 The LORD spoke to Moses, saying: [2]Direct Aaron and his sons to deal carefully with the sacred donations of the people of Israel, which they dedicate to me, so that they may not profane my holy name; I am the LORD. [3]Say to them: If anyone among all your offspring throughout your generations comes near the sacred donations, which the people of Israel dedicate to the LORD, while he is in a state of uncleanness, that person shall be cut off from my presence: I am the LORD. [4]No one of Aaron's offspring who has a leprous[a] disease or suffers a discharge may eat of the sacred donations until he is clean. Whoever touches anything made unclean by a corpse or a man who has had an emission of semen, [5]and whoever touches any swarming thing by which he may be made unclean or any human being by whom he may be made unclean— whatever his uncleanness may be— [6]the person who touches any such shall be unclean until evening and shall not eat of the sacred donations unless he has washed his body in water. [7]When the sun sets he shall be clean; and afterward he may eat of the sacred donations, for they are his food. [8]That which died or was torn by wild animals he shall not eat, becoming unclean by it: I am the LORD. [9]They shall keep my charge, so that they may not incur guilt and die in the sanctuary[b] for having profaned it: I am the LORD; I sanctify them.

10 No lay person shall eat of the sacred donations. No bound or hired servant of the priest shall eat of the sacred donations; [11]but if a priest acquires anyone by purchase, the person may eat of them; and those that are born in his house may eat of his food. [12]If a priest's daughter marries a layman, she shall not eat of the offering of the sacred donations; [13]but if a priest's daughter is widowed or divorced, without offspring, and returns to her father's house, as in her youth, she may eat of her father's food. No lay person shall eat of it. [14]If a man eats of the sacred donation unintentionally, he shall add one-fifth of its value to it, and give the sacred donation to the priest. [15]No one shall profane the sacred donations of the people of Israel, which they offer to the LORD, [16]causing them to bear guilt requiring a guilt offering, by eating their sacred donations: for I am the LORD; I sanctify them.

Acceptable Offerings

17 The LORD spoke to Moses, saying: [18]Speak to Aaron and his sons and all the people of Israel and say to them: When anyone of the house of Israel or of the aliens residing in Israel presents an offering, whether in payment of a vow or as a freewill offering that is offered to the LORD as a burnt offering, [19]to be accept-

---

a A term for several skin diseases; precise meaning uncertain
b Vg: Heb incur guilt for it and die in it

---

father (6.22; 16.32), he could be young and unmarried. **21.17, 21** Approach . . . come near, more precisely "qualify." **21.23** Near the curtain, i.e., officiate, the prerogative only of the high priest. My sanctuaries, literally, "my holy things." I sanctify them. Though the priests are invariably holy, their sanctity is enhanced by their observance of these prohibitions. **22.2** Deal carefully with, lit. "separate themselves from" (see Num 6.3; Ezek 14.7). Sacred donations include all the sacrifices and offerings to the sanctuary, both the less holy (e.g., the well-being offering, v. 21) and the most holy (e.g., the purification offering, 6.25), from which the priest receives stipulated prebends (see 6.25; 7.31–32) and which he would defile if he ate them in a state of impu-

rity (vv. 4–8). **22.3** Comes near, or "encroaches upon." **22.4** Has . . . discharge. See chs. 13–15. The third source of contamination, the corpse, is assumed. Anything, more accurately "anyone" (similarly "it" in Num 19.22 should read "him"). **22.6–7** Washed . . . When, rather "first washed . . . Then when." For they are his food, a concession. Note that Ezek 44.26 requires more rigorous purification. **22.8** Not forbidden to laypersons (17.15). **22.9** Keep my charge, i.e., "observe my prohibitions." Incur guilt . . . profaned it, more precisely, "incur punishment and die for it, having profaned it (the prohibition)." **22.10** Bound or hired servant, a resident laborer. **22.15** No one, i.e., no priest. **22.16** Guilt requiring a guilt offering, a penalty of reparation. **22.18** Payment

able in your behalf it shall be a male without blemish, of the cattle or the sheep or the goats. 20You shall not offer anything that has a blemish, for it will not be acceptable in your behalf.

21 When anyone offers a sacrifice of well-being to the LORD, in fulfillment of a vow or as a freewill offering, from the herd or from the flock, to be acceptable it must be perfect; there shall be no blemish in it. 22Anything blind, or injured, or maimed, or having a discharge or an itch or scabs—these you shall not offer to the LORD or put any of them on the altar as offerings by fire to the LORD. 23An ox or a lamb that has a limb too long or too short you may present for a freewill offering; but it will not be accepted for a vow. 24Any animal that has its testicles bruised or crushed or torn or cut, you shall not offer to the LORD; such you shall not do within your land, 25nor shall you accept any such animals from a foreigner to offer as food to your God; since they are mutilated, with a blemish in them, they shall not be accepted in your behalf.

26 The LORD spoke to Moses, saying: 27When an ox or a sheep or a goat is born, it shall remain seven days with its mother, and from the eighth day on it shall be acceptable as the LORD's offering by fire. 28But you shall not slaughter, from the herd or the flock, an animal with its young on the same day. 29When you sacrifice a thanksgiving offering to the LORD, you shall sacrifice it so that it may be acceptable in your behalf. 30It shall be eaten on the same day; you shall not leave any of it until morning: I am the LORD.

31 Thus you shall keep my commandments and observe them: I am the LORD. 32You shall not profane my holy name, that I may be sanctified among the people of Israel: I am the LORD; I sanctify you, 33I who brought you out of the land of Egypt to be your God: I am the LORD.

Appointed Festivals

23 The LORD spoke to Moses, saying: 2Speak to the people of Israel and say to them: These are the appointed festivals of the LORD that you shall proclaim as holy convocations, my appointed festivals.

The Sabbath, Passover, and Unleavened Bread

3 Six days shall work be done; but the seventh day is a sabbath of complete rest, a holy convocation; you shall do no work: it is a sabbath to the LORD throughout your settlements.

4 These are the appointed festivals of the LORD, the holy convocations, which you shall celebrate at the time appointed for them. 5In the first month, on the fourteenth day of the month, at twilight,*a* there shall be a passover offering to the LORD, 6and on the fifteenth day of the same month is the festival of unleavened bread to the LORD; seven days you shall eat unleavened bread. 7On the first day you shall have a holy convocation; you shall not work at your occupations. 8For seven days you

---

a Heb *between the two evenings*

... *freewill offering.* See 7.16. **22.21–24** The defects that disqualify animals from the altar closely resemble those that disqualify priests from officiating at it (21.16–23). **22.21** *In fulfillment of a,* or "for an explicit." **22.28** *An animal,* i.e., a mother. **22.29** *Thanksgiving offering.* In H this offering is not a well-being offering (v. 21; 19.5; cf. 7.11–15 [P]; on H and P, see Introduction). **22.32** *I sanctify you,* namely, Israel (see v. 33). However, Israel is not innately holy as are the priests (21.7); Israel is enjoined to strive for a holy life by obeying the Lord's commandments (v. 31; see note on 19.1–37).

23.1–44 H's listing of the festivals is distinguished from the old epic (JE) tradition (Ex 23.14–17; 34.21–23; see Introduction to Genesis) and the Deuteronomic influence (Deut 16; see Introduction to Deuteronomy) by emphasis on natural and agricultural data. Because Lev 23 addresses laypeople like farmers, rather than priests, the New Moon Festival is omitted (on this day the Israelites have no special duties or prohibitions). Indeed, with the exception of vv. 13, 18–20, all requirements of the priestly, public cult

are ignored, and only the offerings of individual farmers are enumerated. Center stage is occupied by the people. Israel is responsible for maintaining the *public* cult. To be sure, H, no differently from P, presumes that sacrificial service is conducted exclusively by priests. Maintenance of the public cult, however, and presumably supervision over the priestly order are ultimately the people's responsibility. **23.3** This verse dealing with the sabbath is a later interpolation, possibly from exilic times, since it mentions no sacrifices. Its incongruity in this chapter is emphasized by the fact that the sabbath is not an appointed festival (v. 2) and that the original beginning of this chapter is clearly v. 4. **23.5–8** Passover and the Festival of Unleavened Bread were originally discrete festivals. The Passover was observed at home (Ex 12) and the pilgrimage to the local sanctuary took place on the seventh day (Ex 13.6). When worship was centralized, the Passover sacrifice was observed at the Jerusalem temple and the pilgrimage was transferred to the first day, thus amalgamating the two festivals (Deut 16.1–8).

shall present the LORD's offerings by fire; on the seventh day there shall be a holy convocation: you shall not work at your occupations.

The Offering of First Fruits

9 The LORD spoke to Moses: 10Speak to the people of Israel and say to them: When you enter the land that I am giving you and you reap its harvest, you shall bring the sheaf of the first fruits of your harvest to the priest. 11He shall raise the sheaf before the LORD, that you may find acceptance; on the day after the sabbath the priest shall raise it. 12On the day when you raise the sheaf, you shall offer a lamb a year old, without blemish, as a burnt offering to the LORD. 13And the grain offering with it shall be two-tenths of an ephah of choice flour mixed with oil, an offering by fire of pleasing odor to the LORD; and the drink offering with it shall be of wine, one-fourth of a hin. 14You shall eat no bread or parched grain or fresh ears until that very day, until you have brought the offering of your God: it is a statute forever throughout your generations in all your settlements.

The Festival of Weeks

15 And from the day after the sabbath, from the day on which you bring the sheaf of the elevation offering, you shall count off seven weeks; they shall be complete. 16You shall count until the day after the seventh sabbath, fifty days; then you shall present an offering of new grain to the LORD. 17You shall bring from your settlements two loaves of bread as an elevation offering, each made of two-tenths of an ephah; they shall be of choice flour, baked with leaven, as first fruits to the LORD. 18You shall present with the bread seven lambs a year old without blemish, one young bull, and two rams; they shall be a burnt offering to the LORD, along with their grain offering and their drink offerings, an offering by fire of pleasing odor to the LORD. 19You shall also offer one male goat for a sin offering, and two male lambs a year old as a sacrifice of well-being. 20The priest shall raise them with the bread of the first fruits as an elevation offering before the LORD, together with the two lambs; they shall be holy to the LORD for the priest. 21On that same day you shall make proclamation; you shall hold a holy convocation; you shall not work at your occupations. This is a statute forever in all your settlements throughout your generations.

22 When you reap the harvest of your land, you shall not reap to the very edges of your field, or gather the gleanings of your harvest; you shall leave them for the poor and for the alien: I am the LORD your God.

The Festival of Trumpets

23 The LORD spoke to Moses, saying: 24Speak to the people of Israel, saying: In the seventh month, on the first day of the month, you shall observe a day of complete rest, a holy convocation commemorated with trumpet blasts. 25You shall not work at your occupations; and you shall present the LORD's offering by fire.

The Day of Atonement

26 The LORD spoke to Moses, saying: 27Now, the tenth day of this seventh month is the day of atonement; it shall be a holy convocation for you: you shall deny yourselves[a] and present the LORD's offering by fire; 28and you shall do no work during that entire day; for it is a day of atonement, to make atonement on your behalf before the LORD your God. 29For anyone who does not practice self-denial[b] during that entire day shall be cut off from the

a Or shall fast   b Or does not fast

23.8 The LORD's offerings, enumerated in Num 28.16–25. 23.10 Sheaf, or "armful." First fruits of your harvest, i.e., barley. See 2.14. 23.11 That you . . . acceptance, so that the Lord will bless your crop. The day after the sabbath. Three opinions about the day were recorded in Second Temple times—the day after the Passover, Nisan 16 (Pharisees); the Sunday falling during the festival (Sadducees); and the Sunday after the festival (Qumran)—creating confusion about when to celebrate the Festival of Weeks. This phrase (also in v. 15) is probably a gloss, and originally each farmer brought the first grain offering whenever it ripened. 23.15 Seven weeks, lit. "seven sabbaths," i.e., seven weeks, each ending with the sabbath. 23.16 New grain, i.e., wheat. 23.18–19 The sacrifices are enumerated since they differ slightly from those specified in Num 28.26–31. 23.22 Closing statement for both the barley and wheat harvests (cf. 19.9–10). 23.24, 39 Complete rest, not complete, since only occupational work is forbidden (v. 25). Trumpet, rather "horn" (Hebrew shofar; cf. Ps. 81.3). Its use marks the beginning of the old, agricultural calendar when the fates of humans and nature (i.e., adequate rain) were decided. 23.25 LORD's offering, prescribed in Num 29.1–6. 23.27 LORD's offering, prescribed in Num 29.7–11. 23.28 Prescriptions for the day of atonement are given in 16.1–28. 23.29 Self-denial. See 16.29.

people. 30And anyone who does any work during that entire day, such a one I will destroy from the midst of the people. 31You shall do no work: it is a statute forever throughout your generations in all your settlements. 32It shall be to you a sabbath of complete rest, and you shall deny yourselves;*a* on the ninth day of the month at evening, from evening to evening you shall keep your sabbath.

The Festival of Booths

33 The LORD spoke to Moses, saying: 34Speak to the people of Israel, saying: On the fifteenth day of this seventh month, and lasting seven days, there shall be the festival of booths*b* to the LORD. 35The first day shall be a holy convocation; you shall not work at your occupations. 36Seven days you shall present the LORD's offerings by fire; on the eighth day you shall observe a holy convocation and present the LORD's offerings by fire; it is a solemn assembly; you shall not work at your occupations.

37 These are the appointed festivals of the LORD, which you shall celebrate as times of holy convocation, for presenting to the LORD offerings by fire—burnt offerings and grain offerings, sacrifices and drink offerings, each on its proper day— 38apart from the sabbaths of the LORD, and apart from your gifts, and apart from all your votive offerings, and apart from all your freewill offerings, which you give to the LORD.

39 Now, the fifteenth day of the seventh month, when you have gathered in the produce of the land, you shall keep the festival of the LORD, lasting seven days; a complete rest on the first day, and a complete rest on the eighth day. 40On the first day you shall take the fruit of majestic*c* trees, branches of palm trees, boughs of leafy trees, and willows of the brook; and you shall rejoice before the LORD your God for seven days. 41You shall keep it as a festival to the LORD seven days in the year; you shall keep it in the seventh month as a statute forever throughout your generations. 42You shall live in booths for seven days; all that are citizens in Israel shall live in booths, 43so that your generations may know that I made the people of Israel live in booths when I brought them out of the land of Egypt: I am the LORD your God.

44 Thus Moses declared to the people of Israel the appointed festivals of the LORD.

The Lamp

24 The LORD spoke to Moses, saying: 2Command the people of Israel to bring you pure oil of beaten olives for the lamp, that a light may be kept burning regularly. 3Aaron shall set it up in the tent of meeting, outside the curtain of the covenant,*d* to burn from evening to morning before the LORD regularly; it shall be a statute forever throughout your generations. 4He shall set up the lamps on the lampstand of pure gold*e* before the LORD regularly.

The Bread for the Tabernacle

5 You shall take choice flour, and bake twelve loaves of it; two-tenths of an ephah shall be in each loaf. 6You shall place them in two rows, six in a row, on the table of pure gold.*f* 7You shall put pure frankincense with each row, to be a token offering for the bread, as an offering

---

a Or *shall fast*   *b* Or *tabernacles*: Heb *succoth*   *c* Meaning of Heb uncertain   *d* Or *treaty*, or *testament*; Heb *eduth*   *e* Heb *pure lampstand*   *f* Heb *pure table*

23.30 *I will destroy.* Work, a public act, is a worse violation than eating, a private act, evoking God's immediate retribution. **23.36** LORD's *offerings,* prescribed in Num 29.12–34, 35–38. The *solemn assembly,* the purpose of which is to pray for rain, is an important function of all the festivals of the seventh month (cf. Joel 2.15). **23.38** *Apart from the sabbaths*—proof that the prescription for the sabbath (vv. 2b–3) was not originally part of this chapter. **23.40** *Fruit of majestic trees,* traditionally, the citron. *Leafy trees,* identified with the myrtle. *Seven days,* to be spent at the sanctuary. **23.42** Possibly the *booths* were to accommodate the vast number of pilgrims at the sanctuary (cf. Hos 12.9). *Citizens,* but not aliens, who are not bound by performative commandments. **23.43** *Booths* (Hebrew

sukkot), possibly a topographical name referring to the first station in the wilderness after the exodus (Ex 12.37; Num 33.5).

24.1–23 Instructions on the lamp, the bread, and blasphemy. **24.1–4** The lamp oil. Since the lampstand stood inside the sanctuary, its greater sanctity required the use of pure oil and also required it to be lighted by the high priest (Ex 30.7; Num 8.1–4; "sons" in Ex 27.21 is a probable error). **24.2** *For the lamp, that a light,* or "for lighting, so that a lamp." **24.3** *Curtain of the covenant,* short for "curtain that is over the ark of the covenant" (Ex 30.6). **24.5–9** The bread of the Presence. **24.5** Moses provides the loaves the first time; thereafter, they are provided by the Israelites (v. 8). **24.6** *Rows,* i.e., piles. **24.7** The *token offering* is always

by fire to the LORD. [8]Every sabbath day Aaron shall set them in order before the LORD regularly as a commitment of the people of Israel, as a covenant forever. [9]They shall be for Aaron and his descendants, who shall eat them in a holy place, for they are most holy portions for him from the offerings by fire to the LORD, a perpetual due.

Blasphemy and Its Punishment

10 A man whose mother was an Israelite and whose father was an Egyptian came out among the people of Israel; and the Israelite woman's son and a certain Israelite began fighting in the camp. [11]The Israelite woman's son blasphemed the Name in a curse. And they brought him to Moses—now his mother's name was Shelomith, daughter of Dibri, of the tribe of Dan— [12]and they put him in custody, until the decision of the LORD should be made clear to them.

13 The LORD said to Moses, saying: [14]Take the blasphemer outside the camp; and let all who were within hearing lay their hands on his head, and let the whole congregation stone him. [15]And speak to the people of Israel, saying: Anyone who curses God shall bear the sin. [16]One who blasphemes the name of the LORD shall be put to death; the whole congregation shall stone the blasphemer. Aliens as well as citizens, when they blaspheme the Name, shall be put to death. [17]Anyone who kills a human being shall be put to death. [18]Anyone who kills an animal shall make restitution for it, life for life. [19]Anyone who maims another shall suffer the same injury in return: [20]fracture for fracture, eye for eye, tooth for tooth; the injury inflicted is the injury to be suffered. [21]One who kills an animal shall make restitution for it; but one who kills a human being shall be put to death. [22]You shall have one law for the alien and for the citizen: for I am the LORD your God. [23]Moses spoke thus to the people of Israel; and they took the blasphemer outside the camp, and stoned him to death. The people of Israel did as the LORD had commanded Moses.

The Sabbatical Year

25 The LORD spoke to Moses on Mount Sinai, saying: [2]Speak to the people of Israel and say to them: When you enter the land that I am giving you, the land shall observe a sabbath for the LORD. [3]Six years you shall sow your field, and six years you shall prune your vineyard, and gather in their yield; [4]but in the seventh year there shall be a sabbath of complete rest for the land, a sabbath for the LORD: you shall not sow your field or prune your vineyard. [5]You shall not reap the

offered up with part of the grain offering (2.9), but here, since none of the bread goes on the altar, the text must state that the token offering comprises solely the frankincense. **24.8** *Every sabbath day* Aaron should remove the old loaves and set up the new. **24.10–14, 23** The law of blasphemy. Blasphemy means more than speaking contemptuously of God, for which there is no stated penalty (Ex 22.28). It must involve the additional offense of uttering the sacred name of God, the Tetragrammaton (YHWH), and it is the combination of the two (24.15–16) that warrants the death penalty. The Tetragrammaton's power affects not only the speaker but the hearers; their contamination is literally transferred back to the blasphemer by the ritual of the imposition of hands. **24.11** *The Name*, a circumlocution for the divine name. **24.14** The purpose of the hand leaning (see note on 1.4) was to transfer the pollution generated by the blasphemy back to its source. **24.15–22** An appendix of civil-damage laws. The extension of *lex talionis* (Latin, "law of retaliation," Ex 21.23–25; Deut 19.21) to the stranger is one of the great moral achievements of the legislation preserved in Leviticus. Every distinction is eradicated, not only between the powerful and the helpless, but even between the Israelite and the non-Israelite. The interpolation of these civil statutes, with their emphasis upon the resident

alien, is due to the legal status of the half-Israelite offender. **24.15–16** One who *curses God*, in secret, will be punished by God; one who *blasphemes*, in public, will be punished by human agency. **24.16** *Aliens*, thereby including the blasphemer of vv. 10–11, the son of a non-Israelite father. **24.18** *Life for life* perhaps originally began the talion formula of v. 20. **24.21** A repetition of vv. 17–18 for the sake of an envelope structure.

25.1–55 Each seventh year is a sabbath of liberating respite for Hebrew slaves (Ex 21.2–6; Deut 15.12–18) and the land (Ex 23.10–11). In H (see Introduction), this "full" sabbatical is reserved for the jubilee, whereas the seventh-year sabbatical applies only to the land. These two laws are not in conflict. Exodus refers to members of a landless class who voluntarily sell themselves into slavery. Lev 25 deals with impoverished landed Israelites who are free to sell themselves as slaves but who may not be treated as slaves and who return to their land at the jubilee or when they are redeemed (vv. 39–42). Deuteronomy extends the sabbatical release to debtors (Deut 15.1–11). **25.1** *Mount Sinai* forms an *inclusio* with 26.46, indicating that originally chs. 25–26 formed a separate scroll. **25.2** *The land . . . sabbath.* All who reside on it, including aliens, must observe it. **25.3–5, 11** *Sow . . . reap*, proof that the sabbatical and jubilee years begin in the

aftergrowth of your harvest or gather the grapes of your unpruned vine: it shall be a year of complete rest for the land. 6You may eat what the land yields during its sabbath— you, your male and female slaves, your hired and your bound laborers who live with you; 7for your livestock also, and for the wild animals in your land all its yield shall be for food.

The Year of Jubilee

8 You shall count off seven weeks[a] of years, seven times seven years, so that the period of seven weeks of years gives forty-nine years. 9Then you shall have the trumpet sounded loud; on the tenth day of the seventh month— on the day of atonement—you shall have the trumpet sounded throughout all your land. 10And you shall hallow the fiftieth year and you shall proclaim liberty throughout the land to all its inhabitants. It shall be a jubilee for you: you shall return, every one of you, to your property and every one of you to your family. 11That fiftieth year shall be a jubilee for you: you shall not sow, or reap the aftergrowth, or harvest the unpruned vines. 12For it is a jubilee; it shall be holy to you: you shall eat only what the field itself produces.

13 In this year of jubilee you shall return, every one of you, to your property. 14When you make a sale to your neighbor or buy from your neighbor, you shall not cheat one another. 15When you buy from your neighbor, you shall pay only for the number of years since the jubilee; the seller shall charge you only for the remaining crop years. 16If the years are more, you shall increase the price, and if the years are fewer, you shall diminish

the price; for it is a certain number of harvests that are being sold to you. 17You shall not cheat one another, but you shall fear your God; for I am the LORD your God.

18 You shall observe my statutes and faithfully keep my ordinances, so that you may live on the land securely. 19The land will yield its fruit, and you will eat your fill and live on it securely. 20Should you ask, "What shall we eat in the seventh year, if we may not sow or gather in our crop?" 21I will order my blessing for you in the sixth year, so that it will yield a crop for three years. 22When you sow in the eighth year, you will be eating from the old crop; until the ninth year, when its produce comes in, you shall eat the old. 23The land shall not be sold in perpetuity, for the land is mine; with me you are but aliens and tenants. 24Throughout the land that you hold, you shall provide for the redemption of the land.

25 If anyone of your kin falls into difficulty and sells a piece of property, then the next of kin shall come and redeem what the relative has sold. 26If the person has no one to redeem it, but then prospers and finds sufficient means to do so, 27the years since its sale shall be computed and the difference shall be refunded to the person to whom it was sold, and the property shall be returned. 28But if there are not sufficient means to recover it, what was sold shall remain with the purchaser until the year of jubilee; in the jubilee it shall be released, and the property shall be returned.

29 If anyone sells a dwelling house in a

---

a Or sabbaths

---

fall. **25.6** This verse alters Ex 23.11 by denying the sabbatical aftergrowth to the poor and endowing it to the owner and his household. H (see Introduction) makes other, ongoing provisions for the poor (19.9–10; 23.20). **25.10** *Liberty.* Hebrew *deror* is related to Akkadian *duraru*, which could also entail the emancipation of indentured slaves, the return of confiscated land, and the cancellation of debts. However, it was episodic, occasionally proclaimed upon the ascension of the Mesopotamian king to the throne. Also its purpose was strictly economic, to relieve the plight of the poor, whereas in Israel its goal was social as well, to preserve the clan structure by restoring its landholdings. *For you,* not for the land or for the release of alien slaves (vv. 45–46). Note that the term "sabbath" is absent in the jubilee provisions. **25.15** *Pay,* i.e., deduct. **25.20–22** The sixth to ninth years, mentioned here, are reckoned by the spring calendar. Hence the sabbat-

ical and succeeding jubilee years, which follow the fall calendar, must begin in the fall of the sixth and seventh years and terminate in the spring of the seventh and eighth years, respectively. Thus, what is sown in the eighth year will be reaped in the ninth, and the harvest of the sixth year must therefore last three years. **25.23** *In perpetuity,* Hebrew *tsemitut,* related to the Akkadian verb *tsamatu,* "financially hand over (real estate)"; i.e., neither the seller nor his heirs may ever revoke the sale. **25.25–55** Four cases of worsening impoverishment: selling part of the land, depending upon an Israelite (probably a kinsman) for support, selling oneself as a resident laborer to an Israelite (probably a kinsman), and selling oneself as a slave to a resident alien. **25.25** Since the purpose of the jubilee is to preserve the clan holdings, the redeemer (a close kinsman) probably keeps the land until the jubilee (as shown by v. 33 below) as compensation for his pur-

walled city, it may be redeemed until a year has elapsed since its sale; the right of redemption shall be one year. 30If it is not redeemed before a full year has elapsed, a house that is in a walled city shall pass in perpetuity to the purchaser, throughout the generations; it shall not be released in the jubilee. 31But houses in villages that have no walls around them shall be classed as open country; they may be redeemed, and they shall be released in the jubilee. 32As for the cities of the Levites, the Levites shall forever have the right of redemption of the houses in the cities belonging to them. 33Such property as may be redeemed from the Levites—houses sold in a city belonging to them—shall be released in the jubilee; because the houses in the cities of the Levites are their possession among the people of Israel. 34But the open land around their cities may not be sold; for that is their possession for all time.

35 If any of your kin fall into difficulty and become dependent on you,*a* you shall support them; they shall live with you as though resident aliens. 36Do not take interest in advance or otherwise make a profit from them, but fear your God; let them live with you. 37You shall not lend them your money at interest taken in advance, or provide them food at a profit. 38I am the LORD your God, who brought you out of the land of Egypt, to give you the land of Canaan, to be your God.

39 If any who are dependent on you become so impoverished that they sell themselves to you, you shall not make them serve as slaves. 40They shall remain with you as hired or bound laborers. They shall serve with you until the year of the jubilee. 41Then they and their children with them shall be free from your authority; they shall go back to their own family and return to their ancestral property. 42For they are my servants, whom I brought out of the land of Egypt; they shall not be sold as slaves are sold. 43You shall not rule over them with harshness, but shall fear your God.

44As for the male and female slaves whom you may have, it is from the nations around you that you may acquire male and female slaves. 45You may also acquire them from among the aliens residing with you, and from their families that are with you, who have been born in your land; and they may be your property. 46You may keep them as a possession for your children after you, for them to inherit as property. These you may treat as slaves, but as for your fellow Israelites, no one shall rule over the other with harshness.

47 If resident aliens among you prosper, and if any of your kin fall into difficulty with one of them and sell themselves to an alien, or to a branch of the alien's family, 48after they have sold themselves they shall have the right of redemption; one of their brothers may redeem them, 49or their uncle or their uncle's son may redeem them, or anyone of their family who is of their own flesh may redeem them; or if they prosper they may redeem themselves. 50They shall compute with the purchaser the total from the year when they sold themselves to the alien until the jubilee year; the price of the sale shall be applied to the number of years: the time they were with the owner shall be rated as the time of a hired laborer. 51If many years remain, they shall pay for their redemption in proportion to the purchase price; 52and if few years remain until the jubilee year, they shall compute thus: according to the years involved they shall make payment for their redemption. 53As a laborer hired by the year they shall be under the alien's authority, who shall not, however, rule with harshness over them in your sight. 54And if they have not been redeemed in any of these ways, they and their children with them shall go free in the jubilee year. 55For to me the people of Israel are servants; they are my servants whom I brought out from the land of Egypt: I am the LORD your God.

_____
a Meaning of Heb uncertain

chase. **25.29–34** Unwalled (Canaanite) cities, not having been allocated to the tribal clans, are not subject to the jubilee. Redemption and jubilee, however, apply to the allocated cities of the Levites. **25.33** The first half of this verse reads better as "Whoever of the Levites redeems the house, which was sold in the city of his possession [so Septuagint], must be released in the jubilee." **25.36** _Otherwise make a profit,_ rather "accrued interest." **25.37** _A profit,_ or "accrued interest." **25.39–**

43 If the debtor still cannot repay his loan and otherwise cannot support himself and his family, he and they enter the household of the creditor. He no longer enjoys the usufruct of his forfeited land. Nonetheless, his status is not that of a slave but that of a resident hireling; he receives wages, all of which pay off his debt and status. **25.40** _Or bound,_ rather "resident." **25.42** _My servants,_ not yours. The heart of this chapter; cf. also v. 55.

Rewards for Obedience

26 You shall make for yourselves no idols and erect no carved images or pillars, and you shall not place figured stones in your land, to worship at them; for I am the LORD your God. [2]You shall keep my sabbaths and reverence my sanctuary: I am the LORD.

3 If you follow my statutes and keep my commandments and observe them faithfully, [4]I will give you your rains in their season, and the land shall yield its produce, and the trees of the field shall yield their fruit. [5]Your threshing shall overtake the vintage, and the vintage shall overtake the sowing; you shall eat your bread to the full, and live securely in your land. [6]And I will grant peace in the land, and you shall lie down, and no one shall make you afraid; I will remove dangerous animals from the land, and no sword shall go through your land. [7]You shall give chase to your enemies, and they shall fall before you by the sword. [8]Five of you shall give chase to a hundred, and a hundred of you shall give chase to ten thousand; your enemies shall fall before you by the sword. [9]I will look with favor upon you and make you fruitful and multiply you; and I will maintain my covenant with you. [10]You shall eat old grain long stored, and you shall have to clear out the old to make way for the new. [11]I will place my dwelling in your midst, and I shall not abhor you. [12]And I will walk among you, and will be your God, and you shall be my people. [13]I am the LORD your God who brought you out of the land of Egypt, to be their slaves no more; I have broken the bars of your yoke and made you walk erect.

Penalties for Disobedience

14 But if you will not obey me, and do not observe all these commandments, [15]if you spurn my statutes, and abhor my ordinances, so that you will not observe all my commandments, and you break my covenant, [16]I in turn will do this to you: I will bring terror on you; consumption and fever that waste the eyes and cause life to pine away. You shall sow your seed in vain, for your enemies shall eat it. [17]I will set my face against you, and you shall be struck down by your enemies; your foes shall rule over you, and you shall flee though no one pursues you. [18]And if in spite of this you will not obey me, I will continue to punish you sevenfold for your sins. [19]I will break your proud glory, and I will make your sky like iron and your earth like copper. [20]Your strength shall be spent to no purpose: your land shall not yield its produce, and the trees of the land shall not yield their fruit.

21 If you continue hostile to me, and will not obey me, I will continue to plague you sevenfold for your sins. [22]I will let loose wild animals against you, and they shall bereave you of your children and destroy your livestock; they shall make you few in number, and your roads shall be deserted.

23 If in spite of these punishments you have not turned back to me, but continue hostile to me, [24]then I too will continue hostile to you: I myself will strike you sevenfold for your sins. [25]I will bring the sword against you, executing vengeance for the covenant; and if you withdraw within your cities, I will send pestilence among you, and you shall be delivered into enemy hands. [26]When I break your staff of bread, ten women shall bake your bread in a single oven, and they shall dole out your bread by weight; and though you eat, you shall not be satisfied.

27 But if, despite this, you disobey me, and continue hostile to me, [28]I will continue hostile to you in fury; I in turn will punish you myself sevenfold for your sins. [29]You shall eat the flesh of your sons, and you shall eat the

---

26.1–46 The threat of total destruction and exile appears in three other books of the Bible: Deuteronomy, Jeremiah, and Ezekiel (whose eschatology is largely based on Lev 26). These books also share with this chapter a view that cultic transgressions alone, as here defined, cause the nation's collapse; idolatry (26.1) and the neglect of the sabbatical system (26.2, 34–35) are specified here. Since the events in chs. 25–26 are attributed to Israel's sojourn at Mount Sinai (25.1; 26.46), these may well constitute the text of the Sinaitic covenant according to the Holiness source. **26.1** *Carved images* even of Israel's God (Ex 20.4, 23).

Pillars. This prohibition was originally restricted to worship of foreign gods (Ex 23.24), but beginning with Hezekiah and Josiah, kings of the eighth and seventh centuries BCE, respectively, it was extended to include Israel's God (Deut 16.22). *At,* rather "on." For similar language, see Gen 47.31. **26.2** *Sabbaths,* i.e., the weekly sabbaths (19.3, 30), which may account for the inclusion of vv. 1–2 in this chapter to remind readers that neglecting not only the sabbatical year (vv. 34–35) but also the sabbath day accounts for Israel's exile. **26.3–13** The conditionality of the blessing is also found in ancient Near Eastern treaties. **26.14–39** Comparable

flesh of your daughters. 30I will destroy your high places and cut down your incense altars; I will heap your carcasses on the carcasses of your idols. I will abhor you. 31I will lay your cities waste, will make your sanctuaries desolate, and I will not smell your pleasing odors. 32I will devastate the land, so that your enemies who come to settle in it shall be appalled at it. 33And you I will scatter among the nations, and I will unsheathe the sword against you; your land shall be a desolation, and your cities a waste.

34 Then the land shall enjoy*ᵃ* its sabbath years as long as it lies desolate, while you are in the land of your enemies; then the land shall rest, and enjoy*ᵃ* its sabbath years. 35As long as it lies desolate, it shall have the rest it did not have on your sabbaths when you were living on it. 36And as for those of you who survive, I will send faintness into their hearts in the lands of their enemies; the sound of a driven leaf shall put them to flight, and they shall flee as one flees from the sword, and they shall fall though no one pursues. 37They shall stumble over one another, as if to escape a sword, though no one pursues; and you shall have no power to stand against your enemies. 38You shall perish among the nations, and the land of your enemies shall devour you. 39And those of you who survive shall languish in the land of your enemies because of their iniquities; also they shall languish because of the iniquities of their ancestors.

40 But if they confess their iniquity and the iniquity of their ancestors, in that they committed treachery against me and, moreover, that they continued hostile to me— 41so that I, in turn, continued hostile to them and brought them into the land of their enemies; if then their uncircumcised heart is humbled and they make amends for their iniquity, 42then will I remember my covenant with Jacob; I will remember also my covenant with Isaac and also my covenant with Abraham, and I will remember the land. 43For the land shall be deserted by them, and enjoy*ᵃ* its sabbath years by lying desolate without them, while they shall make amends for their iniquity, because they dared to spurn my ordinances, and they abhorred my statutes. 44Yet for all that, when they are in the land of their enemies, I will not spurn them, or abhor them so as to destroy them utterly and break my covenant with them; for I am the LORD their God; 45but I will remember in their favor the covenant with their ancestors whom I brought out of the land of Egypt in the sight of the nations, to be their God: I am the LORD.

46 These are the statutes and ordinances and laws that the LORD established between himself and the people of Israel on Mount Sinai through Moses.

Votive Offerings

27 The LORD spoke to Moses, saying: 2Speak to the people of Israel and say

---

a Or *make up for*

---

curses are appended to ancient Near Eastern treaties. **26.31** *Sanctuaries,* the multiple sanctuaries throughout the land before Hezekiah's reform. **26.34** *Sabbath years* refers to the sabbaticals, but not the jubilees, since the term "sabbath" is inappropriate for the jubilee. **26.40–45** Remorse and the recall of the covenant. Vv. 40–41a constitute Israel's confession that it committed sacrilege and stubbornly resisted God, and consequently God brought the people into exile. Vv. 41b–45 constitute God's response: if Israel truly humbles itself and accepts (the justice of) its punishment, then God will remember the covenant and, as soon as the land has made up its neglected sabbaticals, will restore Israel to the land. The importance of this concession should not be underestimated. It approximates and perhaps influences the prophetic doctrine of repentance, which not only suspends the sacrificial requirements but eliminates them entirely.

27.1–34 An appendix closely associated with ch. 25 by its theme, the redemption of dedications (not votive offerings). It is organized as follows: (1) Redemp-

tion does not apply to humans since only their value, not their person, may be dedicated (vv. 1–28; but cf. v. 29). (2) Only impure animals may be redeemed; offerable ones must be sacrificed (vv. 9–13). (3) All land is redeemable because land is unofferable (vv. 14–19, 22–25); only *cherem* (Hebrew, "devoted") dedications (man, animal, or land, vv. 20–21, 28–29) may not be redeemed. (4) Firstlings (vv. 26–27) must be sacrificed unless they are defective or impure, in which case they are redeemed or sold. (5) Offerable crop tithe is redeemable; offerable animal tithe is unredeemable (vv. 30–33). One postulate explains these gradations: offerable animals are irredeemable because they must be sacrificed, whereas nonofferable animals and other "holy things" (see 5.14–6.7) are redeemable unless they are *cherem* (see note on 27.28–29). When male and female valuations are compared, the results show that women, as a class, must have been considered an indispensable and powerful element in the Israelite labor force. **27.1–8** The values in this section probably prevailed in the slave markets. Note that the price of a

to them: When a person makes an explicit vow to the LORD concerning the equivalent for a human being, ³the equivalent for a male shall be: from twenty to sixty years of age the equivalent shall be fifty shekels of silver by the sanctuary shekel. ⁴If the person is a female, the equivalent is thirty shekels. ⁵If the age is from five to twenty years of age, the equivalent is twenty shekels for a male and ten shekels for a female. ⁶If the age is from one month to five years, the equivalent for a male is five shekels of silver, and for a female the equivalent is three shekels of silver. ⁷And if the person is sixty years old or over, then the equivalent for a male is fifteen shekels, and for a female ten shekels. ⁸If any cannot afford the equivalent, they shall be brought before the priest and the priest shall assess them; the priest shall assess them according to what each one making a vow can afford.

9 If it concerns an animal that may be brought as an offering to the LORD, any such that may be given to the LORD shall be holy. ¹⁰Another shall not be exchanged or substituted for it, either good for bad or bad for good; and if one animal is substituted for another, both that one and its substitute shall be holy. ¹¹If it concerns any unclean animal that may not be brought as an offering to the LORD, the animal shall be presented before the priest. ¹²The priest shall assess it: whether good or bad, according to the assessment of the priest, so it shall be. ¹³But if it is to be redeemed, one-fifth must be added to the assessment.

14 If a person consecrates a house to the LORD, the priest shall assess it: whether good or bad, as the priest assesses it, so it shall stand. ¹⁵And if the one who consecrates the house wishes to redeem it, one-fifth shall be added to its assessed value, and it shall revert to the original owner.

16 If a person consecrates to the LORD any inherited landholding, its assessment shall be in accordance with its seed requirements: fifty shekels of silver to a homer of barley seed. ¹⁷If the person consecrates the field as of the year of jubilee, that assessment shall stand; ¹⁸but if the field is consecrated after the jubilee, the priest shall compute the price for it according to the years that remain until the year of jubilee, and the assessment shall be reduced. ¹⁹And if the one who consecrates the field wishes to redeem it, then one-fifth shall be added to its assessed value, and it shall revert to the original owner; ²⁰but if the field is not redeemed, or if it has been sold to someone else, it shall no longer be redeemable. ²¹But when the field is released in the jubilee, it shall be holy to the LORD as a devoted field; it becomes the priest's holding. ²²If someone consecrates to the LORD a field that has been purchased, which is not a part of the inherited landholding, ²³the priest shall compute for it the proportionate assessment up to the year of jubilee, and the assessment shall be paid as of that day, a sacred donation to the LORD. ²⁴In the year of jubilee the field shall return to the one from whom it was bought, whose holding the land is. ²⁵All assessments shall be by the sanctuary shekel: twenty gerahs shall make a shekel.

26 A firstling of animals, however, which as a firstling belongs to the LORD, cannot be consecrated by anyone; whether ox or sheep, it is the LORD's. ²⁷If it is an unclean animal, it shall be ransomed at its assessment, with one-fifth added; if it is not redeemed, it shall be sold at its assessment.

28 Nothing that a person owns that has been devoted to destruction for the LORD, be it human or animal, or inherited landholding, may be sold or redeemed; every devoted thing is most holy to the LORD. ²⁹No human beings who have been devoted to destruction can be ransomed; they shall be put to death.

30 All tithes from the land, whether the seed from the ground or the fruit from the tree, are the LORD's; they are holy to the LORD. ³¹If persons wish to redeem any of their tithes, they must add one-fifth to them. ³²All tithes of

---

male infant (v. 6) above the age of one month corresponds with the redemption price of a male firstborn (Num 3.47; 18.16) and that the priest is enjoined to adjust the price according to the economic conditions of the vower (v. 8). **27.13** *If it is . . . redeemed.* This rule applies only to the owner, but the sanctuary may sell it to anyone else for the assessment price (v. 27). **27.20** *Has,* rather "had." The owner dedicated his field after he sold it. **27.21** *Devoted field,* i.e., *cherem* dedications are irredeemable. **27.28–29** *Devoted to destruction,* more precisely "totally dedicated," the distinction being that *cherem* (Hebrew, "devoted") animals and lands become the permanent property of the sanctuary, whereas *cherem* persons—probably prisoners of war resulting from *cherem* vows taken against an enemy (e.g., Num 21.1–3; 1 Sam 15.3, 33)—must be

herd and flock, every tenth one that passes under the shepherd's staff, shall be holy to the Lord. 33Let no one inquire whether it is good or bad, or make substitution for it; if one makes substitution for it, then both it and the substitute shall be holy and cannot be redeemed.

34 These are the commandments that the Lord gave to Moses for the people of Israel on Mount Sinai.

---

destroyed. **27.30** These tithes differ from those of Num 18.21 (P) and Deut 14.22–29 in that they are assigned to the sanctuary; those in Numbers belong to the Levites and those in Deuteronomy to the owner.

27.32 The only recorded instance of the animal tithe is during the reign of Hezekiah (2 Chr 31.6), an indication that H formed the basis of Hezekiah's reform. (On P and H, see Introduction.)

NUMBERS

NUMBERS IS THE FOURTH BOOK of the Bible and therefore the fourth in the Pentateuch ("five scrolls"), or Torah, as the first five books are known collectively. Numbers takes its English name from *Arithmoi,* the title of the book in the ancient Greek translation called the Septuagint, begun in the third century BCE. In Hebrew the book is called *Bemidbar,* "In the wilderness," a word in the first verse of the book and perhaps a more appropriate title given its contents. The book of Numbers begins with the Israelites encamped in the wilderness of Sinai and spans the forty years of the wilderness wanderings. It ends with the people on the east side of the Jordan River, in the "plains of Moab," poised for the conquest of Canaan. Lack of faith (chs. 13–14) leads to the almost complete destruction of the exodus generation, which is to be replaced by a new generation born in the wilderness and looking forward to Canaan rather than backward to Egypt.

Structure and Sources

THE STRUCTURE OF THE BOOK follows the geographical sequence of the account as well as the change in generations over the forty years of wandering. Geographically, Numbers can be divided into three fairly neat sections: in the wilderness of Sinai, 1.1–10.10; the march through the wilderness to Transjordan, 10.11–22.1; and in the plains of Moab, 22.2–36.13. The book is also, however, divided into two sections by the two military censuses in chs. 1 and 26, which represent the doubting exodus generation and the new generation that takes its place. These two censuses, as well as several other counting episodes, have led to the impression that "numbers" are the principal topic of the book; hence its title in the Septuagint.

Modern scholars believe that the material in the Pentateuch, and therefore in the book of Numbers, was brought together from several sources. It is useful to consider two broad types of sources evident in the book of Numbers: material called "Priestly," because of its interest in cultic matters pertaining to religious ritual and genealogy, and material drawn from "old epic" sources, which has a lexical and stylistic consistency with similar material elsewhere in the Pentateuch (see Introduction to Genesis). Both Priestly and epic sections preserve ancient traditions, but most modern scholars suggest that the history of the Israelites before their settlement in Canaan was more complicated than the picture in Numbers of the twelve-tribe march from the exodus to the conquest. The biblical traditions themselves contain some ambiguity

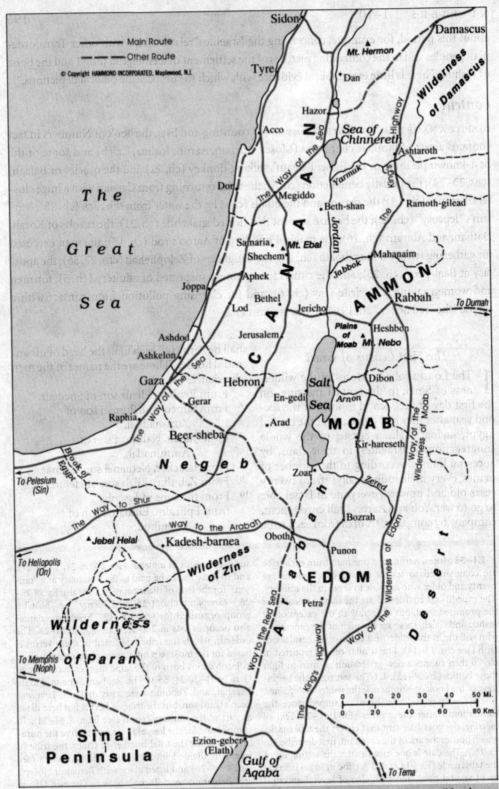

Main Route ———
Other Route – – – –

© Copyright HAMMOND INCORPORATED, Maplewood, N.J.

Sidon

Damascus

Mt. Hermon

Wilderness of Damascus

Tyre

Dan

Hazor

Sea of Chinnereth

Acco

Ashtaroth

The Great Sea

Dor

Way of the Sea

Megiddo

Beth-shan

Ramoth-gilead

Yarmuk

King's Highway

Jordan

AMMON

Samaria
Shechem

Mt. Ebal

Mahanaim

Jabbok

Aphek

Joppa

Bethel

Lod

Jericho

Rabbah

To Dumah

Ashdod

Jerusalem

Heshbon

Plains of Moab

Mt. Nebo

Ashkelon

Gaza

The Way of the Sea

Hebron

Salt Sea

Dibon

Gerar

En-gedi

Arnon

MOAB

Raphia

The Way to Shur

Arad

Kir-hareseth

Zered

Way of the Wilderness of Moab

Beer-sheba

Negeb

Zoar

To Pelesium (Sin)

Brook of Egypt

Way to the Arabah

Bozrah

Desert

Jebel Helal

Kadesh-barnea

Oboth

Punon

Way of the Wilderness of Edom

To Heliopolis (On)

Wilderness of Zin

EDOM

Wilderness of Paran

Petra

The King's Highway

To Memphis (Noph)

Way of the Red Sea

Arabah

0   10   20   30   40   50 Mi.

0 20 40 60 80 Km.

Sinai Peninsula

Ezion-geber (Elath)

Gulf of Aqaba

To Tema

The major places and routes that figure in the narratives of Israel's migration into Canaan (Numbers, Joshua, and Judges).

about this period, for example, concerning the Israelites' relationships with other Transjordanian peoples and in the contrasting pictures of the settlement that emerge in Judg 1 and the book of Joshua. There is little extrabiblical evidence with which to compare the biblical depictions.

Content

DESPITE A NAME THAT INDICATES a passion for counting and lists, the book of Numbers in fact contains a cast of familiar characters (Moses, Miriam, Aaron, Joshua, Caleb) and some of the best-known passages in the Bible: Balaam's talking donkey (ch. 22) and the oracles of Balaam (chs. 23–24); the priestly benediction (ch. 6); the spies returning from Canaan with a huge cluster of grapes (ch. 13); the manna and the quails (ch. 11); the water from the rock (ch. 20); Miriam's "leprosy" (ch. 12); the bronze serpent that healed snakebite (ch. 21); the revolts of Korah, Dathan, and Abiram (ch. 16); the magical budding of Aaron's rod (ch. 17); the man executed for gathering sticks on the sabbath (ch. 15); the daughters of Zelophehad (chs. 27, 36); the apostasy at Baal-peor (ch. 25); and the rituals for a woman suspected of adultery (ch. 5), for men and women taking a Nazirite vow (ch. 6), and for cleansing pollution from contact with a corpse (the "red heifer," ch. 19). [JO ANN HACKETT]

The First Census of Israel

1 The LORD spoke to Moses in the wilderness of Sinai, in the tent of meeting, on the first day of the second month, in the second year after they had come out of the land of Egypt, saying: ²Take a census of the whole congregation of Israelites, in their clans, by ancestral houses, according to the number of names, every male individually; ³from twenty years old and upward, everyone in Israel able to go to war. You and Aaron shall enroll them, company by company. ⁴A man from each tribe shall be with you, each man the head of his ancestral house. ⁵These are the names of the men who shall assist you:

From Reuben, Elizur son of Shedeur.
6 From Simeon, Shelumiel son of Zurishaddai.
7 From Judah, Nahshon son of Amminadab.
8 From Issachar, Nethanel son of Zuar.
9 From Zebulun, Eliab son of Helon.
10 From the sons of Joseph:
from Ephraim, Elishama son of Ammihud;

1.1–54 Moses, Aaron, and one man from each tribe are commanded to take a census of all males age twenty and older who are able to serve in the military. The expeditions envisioned are the battles to conquer the promised land, but in fact, with the exception of Joshua and Caleb, these are the men of the generation who will die in the wilderness because of their lack of faith (see chs. 13–14). The similar census reported in ch. 26 then counts a new generation of men to fight those battles (26.64–65). **1.1** The setting of the beginning of the book of Numbers is the *wilderness of Sinai,* where the Israelites have been encamped since the third month after the exodus (Ex 19.1–2). *Tent of meeting,* the goat-hair tent that covers the tabernacle, which houses the ark of the covenant, first described in Ex 26.7. The date is one month after the setting up of the tabernacle (Ex 40.17). **1.2** A tribe in Israel is made up of several *clans,* and each clan of several *ancestral houses.* Each individual male counted is to be identified by ancestral house and clan within each tribe. **1.3** Ex 30.11–12 reports the belief that a military census could result in a plague (see 2 Sam 24; 1 Chr 21), and so a tax was to be paid to the sanctuary as a "ransom" for the lives of those counted. (See also Ex 38.25–28.) *Company,* also translated "army" or "host," a group organized for war. **1.5–15** These same names also occur in lists in 2.3–31; 7.12–83; 10.14–28. The order in which the tribes are listed in these verses is based for the most part on subgroupings characterized as Jacob's sons born of the same mother, according to Gen 29.31–30.24; 35.16–18. Reuben, Simeon, Judah, Issachar, and Zebulun were sons of Leah. Levi was Leah's third son, but the tribe of Levi is not here listed as part of the military census (see Num 1.47–54). To compensate for the loss of Levi and preserve the number twelve for the total number of tribes, the tribe of Joseph is divided into Ephraim and Manasseh (see Gen 48.8–20) and listed along with Benjamin. Joseph and Benjamin were Rachel's sons in Genesis. Of the final four tribes, Dan and Naphtali were the sons of Rachel's maid Bilhah, and Gad and Asher were the sons of Leah's maid Zilpah. (Naphtali and Asher have

from Manasseh, Gamaliel son of
   Pedahzur.
11   From Benjamin, Abidan son of Gideoni.
12   From Dan, Ahiezer son of Ammishaddai.
13   From Asher, Pagiel son of Ochran.
14   From Gad, Eliasaph son of Deuel.
15   From Naphtali, Ahira son of Enan.
16These were the ones chosen from the congregation, the leaders of their ancestral tribes, the heads of the divisions of Israel.

17 Moses and Aaron took these men who had been designated by name, 18and on the first day of the second month they assembled the whole congregation together. They registered themselves in their clans, by their ancestral houses, according to the number of names from twenty years old and upward, individually, 19as the LORD commanded Moses. So he enrolled them in the wilderness of Sinai.

20 The descendants of Reuben, Israel's firstborn, their lineage, in their clans, by their ancestral houses, according to the number of names, individually, every male from twenty years old and upward, everyone able to go to war: 21those enrolled of the tribe of Reuben were forty-six thousand five hundred.

22 The descendants of Simeon, their lineage, in their clans, by their ancestral houses, those of them that were numbered, according to the number of names, individually, every male from twenty years old and upward, everyone able to go to war: 23those enrolled of the tribe of Simeon were fifty-nine thousand three hundred.

24 The descendants of Gad, their lineage, in their clans, by their ancestral houses, according to the number of the names, from twenty years old and upward, everyone able to go to war: 25those enrolled of the tribe of Gad were forty-five thousand six hundred fifty.

26 The descendants of Judah, their lineage, in their clans, by their ancestral houses, according to the number of names, from twenty years old and upward, everyone able to go to war: 27those enrolled of the tribe of Judah were seventy-four thousand six hundred.

28 The descendants of Issachar, their lineage, in their clans, by their ancestral houses, according to the number of names, from twenty years old and upward, everyone able to go to war: 29those enrolled of the tribe of Issachar were fifty-four thousand four hundred.

30 The descendants of Zebulun, their lineage, in their clans, by their ancestral houses, according to the number of names, from twenty years old and upward, everyone able to go to war: 31those enrolled of the tribe of Zebulun were fifty-seven thousand four hundred.

32 The descendants of Joseph, namely, the descendants of Ephraim, their lineage, in their clans, by their ancestral houses, according to the number of names, from twenty years old and upward, everyone able to go to war: 33those enrolled of the tribe of Ephraim were forty thousand five hundred.

34 The descendants of Manasseh, their lineage, in their clans, by their ancestral houses, according to the number of names, from twenty years old and upward, everyone able to go to war: 35those enrolled of the tribe of Manasseh were thirty-two thousand two hundred.

36 The descendants of Benjamin, their lineage, in their clans, by their ancestral houses, according to the number of names, from twenty years old and upward, everyone able to go to war: 37those enrolled of the tribe of Benjamin were thirty-five thousand four hundred.

38 The descendants of Dan, their lineage, in their clans, by their ancestral houses, according to the number of names, from twenty years old and upward, everyone able to go to war: 39those enrolled of the tribe of Dan were sixty-two thousand seven hundred.

40 The descendants of Asher, their lineage, in their clans, by their ancestral houses, according to the number of names, from twenty years old and upward, everyone able to go to war: 41those enrolled of the tribe of Asher were forty-one thousand five hundred.

42 The descendants of Naphtali, their lineage, in their clans, by their ancestral houses, according to the number of names, from twenty years old and upward, everyone able to go to war: 43those enrolled of the tribe of

---

switched positions in the list here.) **1.17–46** The tribes are listed in the same order as in vv. 5–15, except that Gad has shifted position. Gad occupies the third slot in this list, right after Reuben and Simeon. This shift seems to be based on Gad's position in the arrange-ment of tribes in the camp described in ch. 2. There Gad is joined with Simeon and Reuben on the south side (see 2.10–16). The total of 603,550 military men (v. 46) has seemed unrealistically high to commentators, as has the similar number, 601,730, in the second

Naphtali were fifty-three thousand four hundred.

44 These are those who were enrolled, whom Moses and Aaron enrolled with the help of the leaders of Israel, twelve men, each representing his ancestral house. 45So the whole number of the Israelites, by their ancestral houses, from twenty years old and upward, everyone able to go to war in Israel— 46their whole number was six hundred three thousand five hundred fifty. 47The Levites, however, were not numbered by their ancestral tribe along with them.

48 The LORD had said to Moses: 49Only the tribe of Levi you shall not enroll, and you shall not take a census of them with the other Israelites. 50Rather you shall appoint the Levites over the tabernacle of the covenant,ᵃ and over all its equipment, and over all that belongs to it; they are to carry the tabernacle and all its equipment, and they shall tend it, and shall camp around the tabernacle. 51When the tabernacle is to set out, the Levites shall take it down; and when the tabernacle is to be pitched, the Levites shall set it up. And any outsider who comes near shall be put to death. 52The other Israelites shall camp in their respective regimental camps, by companies; 53but the Levites shall camp around the tabernacle of the covenant,ᵃ that there may be no wrath on the congregation of the Israelites; and the Levites shall perform the guard duty of the tabernacle of the covenant.ᵃ 54The Isra-

elites did so; they did just as the LORD commanded Moses.

The Order of Encampment and Marching

2 The LORD spoke to Moses and Aaron, saying: 2The Israelites shall camp each in their respective regiments, under ensigns by their ancestral houses; they shall camp facing the tent of meeting on every side. 3Those to camp on the east side toward the sunrise shall be of the regimental encampment of Judah by companies. The leader of the people of Judah shall be Nahshon son of Amminadab, 4with a company as enrolled of seventy-four thousand six hundred. 5Those to camp next to him shall be the tribe of Issachar. The leader of the Issacharites shall be Nethanel son of Zuar, 6with a company as enrolled of fifty-four thousand four hundred. 7Then the tribe of Zebulun: The leader of the Zebulunites shall be Eliab son of Helon, 8with a company as enrolled of fifty-seven thousand four hundred. 9The total enrollment of the camp of Judah, by companies, is one hundred eighty-six thousand four hundred. They shall set out first on the march.

10 On the south side shall be the regimental encampment of Reuben by companies. The leader of the Reubenites shall be Elizur son of Shedeur, 11with a company as enrolled of forty-six thousand five hundred. 12And those

---

ᵃ Or treaty, or testimony; Heb eduth

---

census in ch. 26 (v. 51). **1.47–54** The tribe of Levi is to be considered separately from the "landed" tribes and dedicated entirely to service at the tabernacle (see also, e.g., Deut 10.8–9; 12.12; Josh 13.14, 33). Levi is left out of the tribal list in the poem in Judg 5. **1.50, 53** The tabernacle is called *tabernacle of the covenant* elsewhere only in Ex 38.21; Num 10.11. **1.51** *Outsider*, here anyone who is not a Levite (see also 3.10, 38; 18.7; cf. 16.40). **1.52** The word translated *regiment* probably originally referred to a standard or banner that was used to mark a military unit and then was extended to denote the unit itself, as here (cf. the translation, *standard*, of the same word in 10.14, 18, 22, 25). In fifth-century BCE texts from the Jewish colony at Elephantine in Egypt, this word can even represent a larger legal entity that includes the families of military men. **1.53** The *wrath* of the Lord would be brought on any nonlevitical trespasser who came into contact with the tabernacle. The Levites are literally its guards. **2.1–34** The tabernacle within the tent of meeting stands at the center of the camp in this description (cf. Ex 33.7–11, where the tent is set up outside the camp). At each of the cardinal points around the tent are three

tribes, separated from the tent by Levites (v. 17; 1.52–53). Each group of three is arranged in a camp named for the dominant tribe of the three. The order in which they camp is also the order in which they march, the tribes on the east leading the march. The sequence in which the tribes are named in this chapter is based on the genealogically organized list in 1.5–15 with minor changes; see vv. 3–9, 10–16. The leaders are those in the lists in 1.5–15; 7.12–83; 10.14–28. **2.2** *Ensigns*, or "signs," here suggests that each ancestral house had its own symbol that could be displayed. **2.3–9** Judah is the preeminent tribe in this scheme: it is the first tribe listed on the east side of the tabernacle and so leads the march. Judah takes with it Issachar and Zebulun from the list in ch. 1 to make up the *camp of Judah* (v. 9). **2.10–16** The tribes on the south side are next, headed by Reuben, the traditional firstborn. Since Judah is now at the head of the entire list, the *camp of Reuben* (v. 16) includes Gad in the position Judah held in the list in ch. 1. Gad is the tribe to be moved up either because Reuben and Gad are associated as Transjordanian tribes or because the earlier tribes have all been "Leah" tribes (see 1.5–15) and Gad is the firstborn of

to camp next to him shall be the tribe of Simeon. The leader of the Simeonites shall be Shelumiel son of Zurishaddai, 13with a company as enrolled of fifty-nine thousand three hundred. 14Then the tribe of Gad: The leader of the Gadites shall be Eliasaph son of Reuel, 15with a company as enrolled of forty-five thousand six hundred fifty. 16The total enrollment of the camp of Reuben, by companies, is one hundred fifty-one thousand four hundred fifty. They shall set out second.

17 The tent of meeting, with the camp of the Levites, shall set out in the center of the camps; they shall set out just as they camp, each in position, by their regiments.

18 On the west side shall be the regimental encampment of Ephraim by companies. The leader of the people of Ephraim shall be Elishama son of Ammihud, 19with a company as enrolled of forty thousand five hundred. 20Next to him shall be the tribe of Manasseh. The leader of the people of Manasseh shall be Gamaliel son of Pedahzur, 21with a company as enrolled of thirty-two thousand two hundred. 22Then the tribe of Benjamin: The leader of the Benjaminites shall be Abidan son of Gideoni, 23with a company as enrolled of thirty-five thousand four hundred. 24The total enrollment of the camp of Ephraim, by companies, is one hundred eight thousand one hundred. They shall set out third on the march.

25 On the north side shall be the regimental encampment of Dan by companies. The leader of the Danites shall be Ahiezer son of Ammishaddai, 26with a company as enrolled of sixty-two thousand seven hundred. 27Those to camp next to him shall be the tribe of Asher. The leader of the Asherites shall be Pagiel son of Ochran, 28with a company as enrolled of forty-one thousand five hundred. 29Then the tribe of Naphtali: The leader of the

Naphtalites shall be Ahira son of Enan, 30with a company as enrolled of fifty-three thousand four hundred. 31The total enrollment of the camp of Dan is one hundred fifty-seven thousand six hundred. They shall set out last, by companies.[a]

32 This was the enrollment of the Israelites by their ancestral houses; the total enrollment in the camps by their companies was six hundred three thousand five hundred fifty. 33Just as the LORD had commanded Moses, the Levites were not enrolled among the other Israelites.

34 The Israelites did just as the LORD had commanded Moses: They camped by regiments, and they set out the same way, everyone by clans, according to ancestral houses.

The Sons of Aaron

3 This is the lineage of Aaron and Moses at the time when the LORD spoke with Moses on Mount Sinai. 2These are the names of the sons of Aaron: Nadab the firstborn, and Abihu, Eleazar, and Ithamar; 3these are the names of the sons of Aaron, the anointed priests, whom he ordained to minister as priests. 4Nadab and Abihu died before the LORD when they offered unholy fire before the LORD in the wilderness of Sinai, and they had no children. Eleazar and Ithamar served as priests in the lifetime of their father Aaron.

The Duties of the Levites

5 Then the LORD spoke to Moses, saying: 6Bring the tribe of Levi near, and set them before Aaron the priest, so that they may assist him. 7They shall perform duties for him and for the whole congregation in front of the tent of meeting, doing service at the tabernacle; 8they shall be in charge of all the furnishings

---

a Compare verses 9, 16, 24: Heb by their regiments

Leah's maid Zilpah (Gen 30.9–11). **2.14** For *Reuel,* read "Deuel," following 1.14 and several ancient manuscripts. **2.18–24** Ephraim heads the western camp because in Genesis he became the dominant son of Jacob's favorite son, Joseph (Gen 48.13–20). **2.25– 31** Dan is first in the northern camp because he was the eldest son born to a concubine of Jacob (Bilhah, Gen 30.1–6). **2.33** See 1.48–49.

3.1–51 The duties, arrangement, and numbers of the tribe of Levi. **3.1** *Aaron* is listed before *Moses* here because Aaron is the firstborn. This verse is set at *Mount Sinai* (cf. 1.1; 3.14), when Nadab and Abihu

were alive (see v. 4). In reverting to Mount Sinai for a few verses, the narrative implies that the information in vv. 5–13 was already understood at the time the rest of the activity in this chapter takes place. **3.2** See also Ex 6.23. **3.3** *He.* It was Moses who ordained the sons of Aaron (Lev 8.30; see also Ex 29.21; 30.30; 40.12–15; cf. Lev 8.12). **3.4** See Lev 10.1–2. **3.5–10** A distinction is made between Aaron and his descendants (the anointed priests) and the rest of the tribe of Levi, to which both Aaron and Moses belong. The rest of the Levites will *assist* (v. 6) Aaron and his descendants. **3.7–8** One of the *duties* of the Levites is to guard the

of the tent of meeting, and attend to the duties for the Israelites as they do service at the tabernacle. 9You shall give the Levites to Aaron and his descendants; they are unreservedly given to him from among the Israelites. 10But you shall make a register of Aaron and his descendants; it is they who shall attend to the priesthood, and any outsider who comes near shall be put to death.

11 Then the LORD spoke to Moses, saying: 12I hereby accept the Levites from among the Israelites as substitutes for all the firstborn that open the womb among the Israelites. The Levites shall be mine, 13for all the firstborn are mine; when I killed all the firstborn in the land of Egypt, I consecrated for my own all the firstborn in Israel, both human and animal; they shall be mine. I am the LORD.

A Census of the Levites

14 Then the LORD spoke to Moses in the wilderness of Sinai, saying: 15Enroll the Levites by ancestral houses and by clans. You shall enroll every male from a month old and upward. 16So Moses enrolled them according to the word of the LORD, as he was commanded. 17The following were the sons of Levi, by their names: Gershon, Kohath, and Merari. 18These are the names of the sons of Gershon by their clans: Libni and Shimei. 19The sons of Kohath by their clans: Amram,

Izhar, Hebron, and Uzziel. 20The sons of Merari by their clans: Mahli and Mushi. These are the clans of the Levites, by their ancestral houses.

21 To Gershon belonged the clan of the Libnites and the clan of the Shimeites; these were the clans of the Gershonites. 22Their enrollment, counting all the males from a month old and upward, was seven thousand five hundred. 23The clans of the Gershonites were to camp behind the tabernacle on the west, 24with Eliasaph son of Lael as head of the ancestral house of the Gershonites. 25The responsibility of the sons of Gershon in the tent of meeting was to be the tabernacle, the tent with its covering, the screen for the entrance of the tent of meeting, 26the hangings of the court, the screen for the entrance of the court that is around the tabernacle and the altar, and its cords—all the service pertaining to these.

27 To Kohath belonged the clan of the Amramites, the clan of the Izharites, the clan of the Hebronites, and the clan of the Uzzielites; these are the clans of the Kohathites. 28Counting all the males, from a month old and upward, there were eight thousand six hundred, attending to the duties of the sanctuary. 29The clans of the Kohathites were to camp on the south side of the tabernacle, 30with Elizaphan son of Uzziel as head of the ancestral house of the clans of the Kohathites. 31Their responsi-

---

tabernacle from intrusion. **3.9** Instead of *to him,* several manuscripts have "to me," as in 8.16; see also 3.12; 18.6. **3.10** *Outsider.* See 1.51. **3.11–13** See 8.16–18. **3.12** Earlier laws had required that human *firstborn* (males are usually specified) be consecrated to the Lord (to a life of religious service), redeemed, or perhaps even sacrificed, presumably to ensure continued fertility (see Ex 13.2, 11–15; 22.29b–30; 34.19–20; see also Num 18.15).

3.14–39 Census of the Levites and recording of their duties. **3.14** This verse returns to the narrative's present time and place, in the *wilderness of Sinai.* **3.15–16** Cf. 1.47–49. The prohibition apparently does not extend to a separate census of the Levites. **3.15** *By ancestral houses and by clans.* Note the reverse order in 1.2 and throughout ch. 1. Unlike the earlier military census, which counted males twenty and older, this census of the Levites counts *every male from a month old and upward,* because they will be substitutes for Israelite firstborn males a month old and upward (vv. 40–41). One month seems to be the age at which personhood was believed to begin; see Lev 27.6. **3.17–20** See Gen 46.11; Ex 6.16–19. **3.21–39** The levitical clans are to encamp between the tabernacle and the Israelites on three sides of the tabernacle and are given the respon-

sibility to protect and to transport the tabernacle and its accessories, including the tent of meeting. **3.21–26** The first levitical clan discussed is the Gershonites; see v. 17. **3.23, 25–26** The *Gershonites* encamp on the *west* side of the tabernacle and have custody over the accessories made of fabric (see also 4.25–26): the *tabernacle,* the innermost tent housing the ark, made of blue (or violet), purple, and crimson linen curtains with a cherubim design (Ex 26.1); the *tent* of meeting, made of goat-hair curtains (Ex 26.7), and its ram-skin and leather *covering* (Ex 26.14); the linen *screen* for the entrance to the tent (Ex 26.36); the linen *hangings* for the court surrounding the tabernacle (Ex 27.9); and the linen *screen* for the entrance to the court (Ex 27.16) and its *cords* (Ex 39.40). **3.27–32** *Kohathites.* See v. 17. **3.28** *Eight thousand six hundred.* The Septuagint has "eight thousand three hundred," which accords with the total of twenty-two thousand reported in v. 39. The difference between the Hebrew words for "six" and "three" is only one consonant. **3.29, 31** The Kohathites camp on the *south side* of the tabernacle and have custody over the most sacred items: the *ark* itself (Ex 25.10–22) and its immediate surroundings—the *table* that holds the bread of the Presence (Ex 25.23–30; 35.13; 39.36); the *lampstand* (Ex 25.31–40); the two

bility was to be the ark, the table, the lamp-stand, the altars, the vessels of the sanctuary with which the priests minister, and the screen—all the service pertaining to these. 32 Eleazar son of Aaron the priest was to be chief over the leaders of the Levites, and to have oversight of those who had charge of the sanctuary.

33 To Merari belonged the clan of the Mahlites and the clan of the Mushites: these are the clans of Merari. 34 Their enrollment, counting all the males from a month old and upward, was six thousand two hundred. 35 The head of the ancestral house of the clans of Merari was Zuriel son of Abihail; they were to camp on the north side of the tabernacle. 36 The responsibility assigned to the sons of Merari was to be the frames of the tabernacle, the bars, the pillars, the bases, and all their accessories—all the service pertaining to these; 37 also the pillars of the court all around, with their bases and pegs and cords.

38 Those who were to camp in front of the tabernacle on the east—in front of the tent of meeting toward the east—were Moses and Aaron and Aaron's sons, having charge of the rites within the sanctuary, whatever had to be done for the Israelites; and any outsider who came near was to be put to death. 39 The total enrollment of the Levites whom Moses and Aaron enrolled at the commandment of the LORD, by their clans, all the males from a month old and upward, was twenty-two thousand.

The Redemption of the Firstborn

40 Then the LORD said to Moses: Enroll all the firstborn males of the Israelites, from a month old and upward, and count their names. 41 But you shall accept the Levites for me—I am the LORD—as substitutes for all the firstborn among the Israelites, and the livestock of the Levites as substitutes for all the firstborn among the livestock of the Israelites. 42 So Moses enrolled all the firstborn among the Israelites, as the LORD commanded him. 43 The total enrollment, all the firstborn males from a month old and upward, counting the number of names, was twenty-two thousand two hundred seventy-three.

44 Then the LORD spoke to Moses, saying: 45 Accept the Levites as substitutes for all the firstborn among the Israelites, and the livestock of the Levites as substitutes for their livestock; and the Levites shall be mine. I am the LORD. 46 As the price of redemption of the two hundred seventy-three of the firstborn of the Israelites, over and above the number of the Levites, 47 you shall accept five shekels apiece, reckoning by the shekel of the sanctuary, a shekel of twenty gerahs. 48 Give to Aaron and his sons the money by which the excess number of them is redeemed. 49 So Moses took the redemption money from those who were over and above those redeemed by the Levites; 50 from the firstborn of the Israelites he took the money, one thousand three hundred sixty-five shekels, reckoned by the shekel of the

---

horned *altars,* one covered with bronze in the court (Ex 27.1–8) and one covered with gold for burning incense (Ex 30.1–10); the *vessels of the sanctuary,* also translated "utensils" (e.g., Ex 27.19; 30.17–21, 26–29; 37.16; 38.3), enumerated in Num 4.5–15; and the *screen* (not one of the screens in vv. 25–26, but rather the curtain that sets off the holiest portion of the tabernacle, otherwise always called the "curtain," the "screening curtain," the "curtain for the screen," or the "curtain for screening," e.g., Ex 26.31–35; 35.12; 39.34; 40.21). **3.32** *Eleazar* (see also 4.16), like Aaron and Moses, is a Kohathite (Ex 6.16, 18, 20, 23). **3.33–37** Merarites; see v. 17. **3.35–36** The Merarites camp on the *north side* of the tabernacle and have custody over the supporting structure of the tabernacle, i.e., the wooden *frames, bars, pillars,* silver *bases,* and *accessories* (Ex 26.15–30; 35.10–11; 39.33; 40.18; see also Num 4.31), and of the surrounding court, its wooden *pillars,* its bronze *bases* and *pegs,* and its *cords* (Ex 27.10–19; 35.17–18; 39.40). **3.38** The preeminent position to the *east* of the tabernacle is taken by Moses, Aaron, and the descendants of Aaron, set apart from

the other Levites (see 3.5–10). *Outsider.* See 1.51. **3.39** *Twenty-two thousand.* The numbers in the text actually total twenty-two thousand, three hundred; see 3.28.

3.40–51 The Levites are substitutes for firstborn males (3.14–15). **3.41** Even the Levites' *livestock* are substituted for the livestock of the firstborn (see also v. 45, but cf. 18.17). **3.43** The number of firstborn males (22,273) is very low compared to the census numbers reported in 1.17–46. **3.46–48** Since each Levite could redeem only one firstborn male, a ransom of *five shekels* each had to be paid for the 273 above and beyond the number of Levites (unless that number should actually be 300 higher; see vv. 28, 39). Archaeological evidence suggests that the shekel in ancient Israel weighed about 11.4 grams, though it is possible that there were two systems at work simultaneously, as in ancient Mesopotamia, and that the *shekel of the sanctuary* (v. 47) was heavier than the common shekel (see also the "shekels by the king's weight" in 2 Sam 14.26). **3.49–50** The ransom money will be paid by the firstborn (v. 50) or by a portion of them (v. 49).

sanctuary; ⁵¹and Moses gave the redemption money to Aaron and his sons, according to the word of the LORD, as the LORD had commanded Moses.

The Kohathites

4 The LORD spoke to Moses and Aaron, saying: ²Take a census of the Kohathites separate from the other Levites, by their clans and their ancestral houses, ³from thirty years old up to fifty years old, all who qualify to do work relating to the tent of meeting. ⁴The service of the Kohathites relating to the tent of meeting concerns the most holy things.

5 When the camp is to set out, Aaron and his sons shall go in and take down the screening curtain, and cover the ark of the covenant ᵃ with it; ⁶then they shall put on it a covering of fine leather, ᵇ and spread over that a cloth all of blue, and shall put its poles in place. ⁷Over the table of the bread of the Presence they shall spread a blue cloth, and put on it the plates, the dishes for incense, the bowls, and the flagons for the drink offering; the regular bread also shall be on it; ⁸then they shall spread over them a crimson cloth, and cover it with a covering of fine leather, ᵇ and shall put its poles in place. ⁹They shall take a blue cloth, and cover the lampstand for the light, with its lamps, its snuffers, its trays, and all the vessels for oil with which it is supplied; ¹⁰and they shall put it with all its utensils in a covering of fine leather, ᵇ and put it on the carrying frame. ¹¹Over the golden altar they shall spread a blue cloth, and cover it with a covering of fine leather, ᵇ and shall put its poles in place; ¹²and they shall take all the utensils of the service that are used in the sanctuary, and put them in a blue cloth, and cover them with a covering of fine leather, ᵇ and put them on the carrying

frame. ¹³They shall take away the ashes from the altar, and spread a purple cloth over it; ¹⁴and they shall put on it all the utensils of the altar, which are used for the service there, the firepans, the forks, the shovels, and the basins, all the utensils of the altar; and they shall spread on it a covering of fine leather, ᵇ and shall put its poles in place. ¹⁵When Aaron and his sons have finished covering the sanctuary and all the furnishings of the sanctuary, as the camp sets out, after that the Kohathites shall come to carry these, but they must not touch the holy things, or they will die. These are the things of the tent of meeting that the Kohathites are to carry.

16 Eleazar son of Aaron the priest shall have charge of the oil for the light, the fragrant incense, the regular grain offering, and the anointing oil, the oversight of all the tabernacle and all that is in it, in the sanctuary and in its utensils.

17 Then the LORD spoke to Moses and Aaron, saying: ¹⁸You must not let the tribe of the clans of the Kohathites be destroyed from among the Levites. ¹⁹This is how you must deal with them in order that they may live and not die when they come near to the most holy things: Aaron and his sons shall go in and assign each to a particular task or burden. ²⁰But the Kohathites ᶜ must not go in to look on the holy things even for a moment; otherwise they will die.

The Gershonites and Merarites

21 Then the LORD spoke to Moses, saying: ²²Take a census of the Gershonites also, by their ancestral houses and by their clans;

ᵃ Or treaty, or testimony; Heb eduth   ᵇ Meaning of Heb uncertain   ᶜ Heb they

---

4.1–49 The second levitical census, to determine the number of Levites between the ages of thirty and fifty, the years during which they are qualified to perform their priestly duties (but cf. 8.24–26). **4.2–4** In 3.14–37 Gershon was counted first because Gershon is the "firstborn" (3.17, 21–26). Here, the Kohathites are counted first and are singled out *from the other Levites* because they have custody over *the most holy things* (v. 4; see also 3.31). **4.5–14** The most holy things are prepared for the march by Aaron and his sons. **4.5** *Screening curtain.* See note on 3.29, 31. **4.6** The *poles* for carrying the ark (Ex 25.13–15). **4.7** *Table of the bread of the Presence.* See note on 3.29, 31. The *plates . . . drink offering.* See Ex 25.29; 37.16. The *regular bread* is the bread that is continually on the table (Ex 25.30; Lev

24.5–9). **4.8** *Poles,* for carrying the table (Ex 25.28). **4.9** *Lampstand.* See 3.31. **4.11** *Golden altar,* for burning incense. See note on 3.29, 31 (its *poles,* Ex 30.4–5). **4.12** The *utensils of the service that are used in the sanctuary* are those that are used inside the tent itself and are most sacred (see 3.31). The *blue* (or violet) *cloth* and *fine leather* indicate the very sacred status of these items, which are placed within the tent while the camp is at rest. **4.13–14** The *altar* here is the bronze altar for sacrifice in the court that surrounds the tabernacle (see note on 3.29, 31) with its *utensils* (Ex 27.3) and its *poles* (Ex 27.6–7). **4.15** *Or they will die.* See Ex 19.20–24 (cf. Ex 19.12–13); 1 Sam 6.19 (Hebrew in text note b); 2 Sam 6.6–15. **4.16** See 3.32. **4.19** *Burden,* i.e., that which he is to transport. **4.21–28** The census of the

23from thirty years old up to fifty years old you shall enroll them, all who qualify to do work in the tent of meeting. 24This is the service of the clans of the Gershonites, in serving and bearing burdens: 25They shall carry the curtains of the tabernacle, and the tent of meeting with its covering, and the outer covering of fine leather*a* that is on top of it, and the screen for the entrance of the tent of meeting, 26and the hangings of the court, and the screen for the entrance of the gate of the court that is around the tabernacle and the altar, and their cords, and all the equipment for their service; and they shall do all that needs to be done with regard to them. 27All the service of the Gershonites shall be at the command of Aaron and his sons, in all that they are to carry, and in all that they have to do; and you shall assign to their charge all that they are to carry. 28This is the service of the clans of the Gershonites relating to the tent of meeting, and their responsibilities are to be under the oversight of Ithamar son of Aaron the priest.

29 As for the Merarites, you shall enroll them by their clans and their ancestral houses; 30from thirty years old up to fifty years old you shall enroll them, everyone who qualifies to do the work of the tent of meeting. 31This is what they are charged to carry, as the whole of their service in the tent of meeting: the frames of the tabernacle, with its bars, pillars, and bases, 32and the pillars of the court all around with their bases, pegs, and cords, with all their equipment and all their related service; and you shall assign by name the objects that they are required to carry. 33This is the service of the clans of the Merarites, the whole of their service relating to the tent of meeting, under the hand of Ithamar son of Aaron the priest.

Census of the Levites

34 So Moses and Aaron and the leaders of the congregation enrolled the Kohathites, by their clans and their ancestral houses, 35from thirty years old up to fifty years old, everyone who qualified for work relating to the tent of meeting; 36and their enrollment by clans was two thousand seven hundred fifty. 37This was the enrollment of the clans of the Kohathites, all who served at the tent of meeting, whom Moses and Aaron enrolled according to the commandment of the LORD by Moses.

38 The enrollment of the Gershonites, by their clans and their ancestral houses, 39from thirty years old up to fifty years old, everyone who qualified for work relating to the tent of meeting— 40their enrollment by their clans and their ancestral houses was two thousand six hundred thirty. 41This was the enrollment of the clans of the Gershonites, all who served at the tent of meeting, whom Moses and Aaron enrolled according to the commandment of the LORD.

42 The enrollment of the clans of the Merarites, by their clans and their ancestral houses, 43from thirty years old up to fifty years old, everyone who qualified for work relating to the tent of meeting— 44their enrollment by their clans was three thousand two hundred. 45This is the enrollment of the clans of the Merarites, whom Moses and Aaron enrolled according to the commandment of the LORD by Moses.

46 All those who were enrolled of the Levites, whom Moses and Aaron and the leaders of Israel enrolled, by their clans and their ancestral houses, 47from thirty years old up to fifty years old, everyone who qualified to do the work of service and the work of bearing burdens relating to the tent of meeting, 48their enrollment was eight thousand five hundred eighty. 49According to the commandment of the LORD through Moses they were appointed to their several tasks of serving or carrying; thus they were enrolled by him, as the LORD commanded Moses.

Unclean Persons

5 The LORD spoke to Moses, saying: 2Command the Israelites to put out of the camp everyone who is leprous,*b* or has a discharge, and everyone who is unclean through contact

---

a Meaning of Heb uncertain   *b* A term for several skin diseases; precise meaning uncertain

---

Gershonites aged thirty to fifty and the items they are to transport; see 3.21–26. **4.28** As Eleazar is supervisor for the Kohathites and any work having to do with the tabernacle itself, Aaron's other living son, *Ithamar* (see 3.1–4), is responsible for the Gershonites and the Merarites (v. 33) and the rest of the levitical service. **4.29–33** The census of the Merarites aged thirty to fifty and the items they are to transport; see 3.33–37. **4.33** See v. 28. **4.36, 40, 44, 48** The numbers here refer only to male Levites aged thirty to fifty; cf. 3.22, 28, 34, 39.

5.1–4 The entire encampment is treated as sacred because of the presence of the tabernacle, the place, the Lord says, *where I dwell among them* (v. 3). Any impurity, therefore, that is "contagious" must be kept

with a corpse; ³you shall put out both male and female, putting them outside the camp; they must not defile their camp, where I dwell among them. ⁴The Israelites did so, putting them outside the camp; as the LORD had spoken to Moses, so the Israelites did.

Confession and Restitution

5 The LORD spoke to Moses, saying: ⁶Speak to the Israelites: When a man or a woman wrongs another, breaking faith with the LORD, that person incurs guilt ⁷and shall confess the sin that has been committed. The person shall make full restitution for the wrong, adding one-fifth to it, and giving it to the one who was wronged. ⁸If the injured party has no next of kin to whom restitution may be made for the wrong, the restitution for wrong shall go to the LORD for the priest, in addition to the ram of atonement with which atonement is made for the guilty party. ⁹Among all the sacred donations of the Israelites, every gift that they bring to the priest shall be his. ¹⁰The sacred donations of all are their own; whatever anyone gives to the priest shall be his.

Concerning an Unfaithful Wife

11 The LORD spoke to Moses, saying: ¹²Speak to the Israelites and say to them: If any man's wife goes astray and is unfaithful to him, ¹³if a man has had intercourse with her but it is hidden from her husband, so that she is undetected though she has defiled herself, and there is no witness against her since she was not caught in the act; ¹⁴if a spirit of jealousy comes on him, and he is jealous of his wife who has defiled herself; or if a spirit of jealousy comes on him, and he is jealous of his wife, though she has not defiled herself; ¹⁵then the man shall bring his wife to the priest. And he shall bring the offering required for her, one-tenth of an ephah of barley flour. He shall pour no oil on it and put no frankincense on it, for it is a grain offering of jealousy, a grain offering of remembrance, bringing iniquity to remembrance.

16 Then the priest shall bring her near, and set her before the LORD; ¹⁷the priest shall take holy water in an earthen vessel, and take some of the dust that is on the floor of the tabernacle and put it into the water. ¹⁸The priest shall set the woman before the LORD, dishevel the woman's hair, and place in her hands the grain offering of remembrance, which is the grain offering of jealousy. In his own hand the priest shall have the water of bitterness that brings the curse. ¹⁹Then the priest shall make her take an oath, saying, "If no man has lain with you, if you have not turned aside to uncleanness while under your husband's authority, be immune to this water of bitterness that brings the curse. ²⁰But if you have gone astray while under your husband's authority, if you have defiled yourself and some man other than your husband has had intercourse with you," ²¹—let the priest make the woman take the oath of the curse and say to the woman—"the LORD make you an execration and an oath

outside the camp. Here the possibility of contagion comes from people ritually "unclean" because of a skin condition (Lev 13, esp. vv. 45–46), because of a bodily discharge (presumably, as in Lev 15, from the genitalia), or because of contact with a corpse (see Num 19.11–20). **5.5–8** A supplement to Lev 6.1–7 for the case in which the injured party has died and there is no next of kin. **5.8** *Next of kin*, lit. "redeemer." See Lev 25.25–26, 48–49; Num 35.12. *Ram of atonement*. See Lev 6.6–7. **5.9–10** An instruction allowing Israelites to earmark their donations for individual priests (see Lev 7.7–9, 14, 32–33; cf. 7.10, 31). **5.11–31** The instruction for a woman who is suspected of adultery. **5.12–14** Vv. 12–13 describe a wife who has in fact committed adultery, although there is no proof available. *Is unfaithful to him* uses the same Hebrew phrase as *breaking faith with the LORD* in v. 6. V. 14 describes a husband who is jealous without knowing whether his wife has in fact committed adultery. This instruction, then, concerns two types of cases in which a woman's guilt or innocence cannot be proven by the usual means. **5.15** An *ephah* is estimated to be around 15 liters, or about half a bushel. *Oil* and *frankincense* (or oil alone, Lev 2.4–7; 14.10, 21; Num 6.15) were usually poured on a grain offering, and the grain is usually choice wheat flour, not barley flour (Lev 2.1; 6.14–15; cf. Lev 5.11). **5.16** *Before the LORD*, probably before the altar of burnt offering in the court surrounding the tabernacle (see note on 3.29, 31; 1 Kings 8.31–32). **5.17** *Holy water*. See Ex 30.17–21, 28–29. An *earthen vessel* can be broken after use so that its contents do not pollute or endanger (see Lev 6.24–28; 11.33; 14.5, 50; 15.12). *Dust . . . tabernacle* is presumably thought to be powerful because of its association with the tabernacle. **5.18** *Dishevel the woman's hair*, a sign of mourning in Lev 10.6; 21.10, and of uncleanness because of skin disease in Lev 13.45. **5.19–22** The woman suspected of adultery must take an oath that she has not been unfaithful (see Ex 22.10–11). It is on the basis of this oath that the ordeal in vv. 23–28 operates. If she has sworn falsely, the *water of bitterness* (v. 19) will have an immediate negative effect on her body; if what she has sworn is the truth, there will be no effect. **5.21** *The LORD make . . . your people*. See Job

among your people, when the LORD makes your uterus drop, your womb discharge; 22now may this water that brings the curse enter your bowels and make your womb discharge, your uterus drop!" And the woman shall say, "Amen. Amen."

23 Then the priest shall put these curses in writing, and wash them off into the water of bitterness. 24He shall make the woman drink the water of bitterness that brings the curse, and the water that brings the curse shall enter her and cause bitter pain. 25The priest shall take the grain offering of jealousy out of the woman's hand, and shall elevate the grain offering before the LORD and bring it to the altar; 26and the priest shall take a handful of the grain offering, as its memorial portion, and turn it into smoke on the altar, and afterward shall make the woman drink the water. 27When he has made her drink the water, then, if she has defiled herself and has been unfaithful to her husband, the water that brings the curse shall enter into her and cause bitter pain, and her womb shall discharge, her uterus drop, and the woman shall become an execration among her people. 28But if the woman has not defiled herself and is clean, then she shall be immune and be able to conceive children.

29 This is the law in cases of jealousy, when a wife, while under her husband's authority, goes astray and defiles herself, 30or when a spirit of jealousy comes on a man and he is jealous of his wife; then he shall set the woman before the LORD, and the priest shall apply this entire law to her. 31The man shall be free from iniquity, but the woman shall bear her iniquity.

The Nazirites

6 The LORD spoke to Moses, saying: 2Speak to the Israelites and say to them: When either men or women make a special vow, the vow of a nazirite,[a] to separate themselves to the LORD, 3they shall separate themselves from wine and strong drink; they shall drink no wine vinegar or other vinegar, and shall not drink any grape juice or eat grapes, fresh or dried. 4All their days as nazirites[b] they shall eat nothing that is produced by the grapevine, not even the seeds or the skins.

5 All the days of their nazirite vow no razor shall come upon the head; until the time is completed for which they separate themselves to the LORD, they shall be holy; they shall let the locks of the head grow long.

6 All the days that they separate themselves to the LORD they shall not go near a corpse. 7Even if their father or mother, brother or sister, should die, they may not defile themselves; because their consecration to God is upon the head. 8All their days as nazirites[b] they are holy to the LORD.

9 If someone dies very suddenly nearby, defiling the consecrated head, then they shall

---

a That is *one separated* or *one consecrated*   *b* That is *those separated* or *those consecrated*

30.9; Jer 29.21–23. *Uterus drop, womb discharge.* The symptoms the woman is warned of seem to describe a prolapsed uterus. **5.22** *"Amen, amen"* signals the woman's acceptance of the consequences of a false oath, the equivalent of taking an oath that she has not committed adultery. A guilty woman would hesitate to take the oath. See also Deut 27.15–26; Neh 5.13. **5.23–28** The ordeal. The *water of bitterness* (vv. 23–24) will test the truth of the woman's oath. **5.23** The priest writes on something that would allow the writing to dissolve in water. The water then carries the force of the curse. See Jer 51.59–64; Ezek 3.1–4. **5.24** The *bitterness* is etymologized as causing *bitter (pain)*, presumably to a guilty woman only. (See Ex 32.20, 35.) V. 24 (perhaps vv. 23–24) is anticipatory, as the entire procedure is spelled out in vv. 25–27. **5.25** On elevating the guilt offering, see Lev 14.12, 21, 24. **5.26** For a *handful of the grain offering* as a *memorial portion*, see Lev 2.2, 9, 16 (there translated "token portion"). **5.28** The punishment for the one who swears falsely is a condition that precludes bearing children. **5.31** The husband will not be punished for putting even an innocent wife through the oath and ordeal; it is his right to ask for the procedure. The wife's punishment or lack of it will depend on the outcome of the ordeal.

6.1–21 The temporary Nazirite vow. **6.2** For women's vows, see also 30.3–16. On the Nazirite, see also Judg 13.2–14; 16.4–31; 1 Sam 1.11; Am 2.11–12. **6.3–4** Nazirites must abstain from all products of the vine; cf. the Rechabites (Jer 35; 2 Kings 10.15–28). *Other vinegar,* lit. "vinegar from (any) intoxicant." Even Samson's pregnant mother was to abstain from intoxicants and other grape products (Judg 13.4, 7, 14). See also 1 Sam 1.11; Am 2.11–12. *All their days as nazirites* (vv. 4, 5, 6, 8, 12), instructions for a temporary naziriteship, unlike Samson's and Samuel's, which were lifelong. **6.5** *Locks . . . grow long.* The Nazirites' uncut hair was their most important feature. See vv. 7, 9, 18 and the story of Samson's naziriteship (Judg 13.5; 16.4–31). (See also Lev 25.5, 11, where the unpruned vine is called in Hebrew *nazir.*) **6.6–7** Like the high priest, Nazirites were to avoid contact with a corpse, even of a close member of the family (see Lev 21.10–11; cf. vv. 1–3). **6.9–12** Acci-

shave the head on the day of their cleansing; on the seventh day they shall shave it. 10On the eighth day they shall bring two turtledoves or two young pigeons to the priest at the entrance of the tent of meeting, 11and the priest shall offer one as a sin offering and the other as a burnt offering, and make atonement for them, because they incurred guilt by reason of the corpse. They shall sanctify the head that same day, 12and separate themselves to the LORD for their days as nazirites,ᵃ and bring a male lamb a year old as a guilt offering. The former time shall be void, because the consecrated head was defiled.

13 This is the law for the naziritesᵃ when the time of their consecration has been completed: they shall be brought to the entrance of the tent of meeting, 14and they shall offer their gift to the LORD, one male lamb a year old without blemish as a burnt offering, one ewe lamb a year old without blemish as a sin offering, one ram without blemish as an offering of well-being, 15and a basket of unleavened bread, cakes of choice flour mixed with oil and unleavened wafers spread with oil, with their grain offering and their drink offerings. 16The priest shall present them before the LORD and offer their sin offering and burnt offering, 17and shall offer the ram as a sacrifice of well-being to the LORD, with the basket of unleavened bread; the priest also shall make the accompanying grain offering and drink offering. 18Then the naziritesᵃ shall shave the consecrated head at the entrance of the tent of meeting, and shall take the hair from the consecrated head and put it on the fire under the sacrifice of well-being. 19The priest shall take the shoulder of the ram, when it is boiled, and one unleavened cake out of the basket, and one unleavened wafer, and shall put them in the palms of the nazirites,ᵃ after they have shaved the consecrated head. 20Then the priest shall elevate them as an elevation offering before the LORD; they are a holy portion for the priest, together with the breast that is elevated and the thigh that is offered. After that the naziritesᵃ may drink wine.

21 This is the law for the naziritesᵃ who take a vow. Their offering to the LORD must be in accordance with the naziriteᵇ vow, apart from what else they can afford. In accordance with whatever vow they take, so they shall do, following the law for their consecration.

The Priestly Benediction

22 The LORD spoke to Moses, saying: 23Speak to Aaron and his sons, saying, Thus you shall bless the Israelites: You shall say to them,
24 The LORD bless you and keep you;
25 the LORD make his face to shine upon
          you, and be gracious to you;
26 the LORD lift up his countenance upon
          you, and give you peace.
27 So they shall put my name on the Israelites, and I will bless them.

ᵃ That is those separated or those consecrated   ᵇ That is one separated or one consecrated

---

dental contact with a corpse requires purification and rededication. **6.9** *Suddenly* implies there was no time for the Nazirite to avoid contact. *Seventh day.* See 19.11–12, 19. **6.10–12** Even priests who were contaminated by contact with a corpse were not required to undergo such a purification (see 19.11–12; cf. Ezek 44.25–27; see Lev 12.6–8; 14.10–32; 15.13–15, 28–30 for similar purification rituals). *Sanctify the head,* in preparation for a new vow of naziriteship, beginning the period of separation over again (v. 12). **6.13–20** The instruction for the ritual upon the completion of the Nazirite vow. **6.14–17** Regulations for the *burnt offering* are in Lev 1, for the *sin offering* in Lev 4.1–5.13, for the *offering of well-being* in Lev 3, and for the *grain offering* in Lev 2. For *drink offerings,* see Ex 29.40; 30.9; Lev 23.13. The extent of the ritual indicates the seriousness of the transformation from a state of consecration back to a mundane life. **6.18** The sacrifice of hair is not uncommon among the world's religions. Here the hair must be burned, *put on the fire,* because it is holy (see Lev 7.16–17; 19.5–8). **6.20** See Ex 29.26–28; Lev 7.32–34; 10.14–15. **6.22–27** The ancient and lovely priestly benediction that appears here need not be connected with its immediate context; it is in general a function of the priesthood to bless the worshiping community; see Lev 9.22–23; Deut 10.8; 21.5; 2 Chr 30.27; Ps 118.26. **6.24–26** Portions of this blessing appear on two tiny silver scroll amulets found in a tomb in Jerusalem from the seventh or sixth century BCE. **6.25** The *shining* face of the Lord is a sign of protection (Pss 4.6; 31.16; 44.3; 80.3; 89.15; cf. Deut 31.17–18). **6.26** The lifting up of the Lord's *countenance* is a sign of favor; the Hebrew is similar in Gen 19.21; 32.20; Job 42.8–9; Mal 1.8–9. *Peace,* i.e., well-being, wholeness. **6.27** Putting the Lord's name on the Israelites implies ownership; see Deut 12.5; 28.10; Jer 7.10–11; 14.9. This command may have been taken literally, i.e., by wearing the name of God as part of an amulet (see note on 6.24–26).

Offerings of the Leaders

7 On the day when Moses had finished setting up the tabernacle, and had anointed and consecrated it with all its furnishings, and had anointed and consecrated the altar with all its utensils, ²the leaders of Israel, heads of their ancestral houses, the leaders of the tribes, who were over those who were enrolled, made offerings. ³They brought their offerings before the LORD, six covered wagons and twelve oxen, a wagon for every two of the leaders, and for each one an ox; they presented them before the tabernacle. ⁴Then the LORD said to Moses: ⁵Accept these from them, that they may be used in doing the service of the tent of meeting, and give them to the Levites, to each according to his service. ⁶So Moses took the wagons and the oxen, and gave them to the Levites. ⁷Two wagons and four oxen he gave to the Gershonites, according to their service; ⁸and four wagons and eight oxen he gave to the Merarites, according to their service, under the direction of Ithamar son of Aaron the priest. ⁹But to the Kohathites he gave none, because they were charged with the care of the holy things that had to be carried on the shoulders.

10 The leaders also presented offerings for the dedication of the altar at the time when it was anointed; the leaders presented their offering before the altar. ¹¹The LORD said to Moses: They shall present their offerings, one leader each day, for the dedication of the altar.

12 The one who presented his offering the first day was Nahshon son of Amminadab, of the tribe of Judah; ¹³his offering was one silver plate weighing one hundred thirty shekels, one silver basin weighing seventy shekels, according to the shekel of the sanctuary, both of them full of choice flour mixed with oil for a grain offering; ¹⁴one golden dish weighing ten shekels, full of incense; ¹⁵one young bull, one ram, one male lamb a year old, for a burnt offering; ¹⁶one male goat for a sin offering;

¹⁷and for the sacrifice of well-being, two oxen, five rams, five male goats, and five male lambs a year old. This was the offering of Nahshon son of Amminadab.

18 On the second day Nethanel son of Zuar, the leader of Issachar, presented an offering; ¹⁹he presented for his offering one silver plate weighing one hundred thirty shekels, one silver basin weighing seventy shekels, according to the shekel of the sanctuary, both of them full of choice flour mixed with oil for a grain offering; ²⁰one golden dish weighing ten shekels, full of incense; ²¹one young bull, one ram, one male lamb a year old, as a burnt offering; ²²one male goat as a sin offering; ²³and for the sacrifice of well-being, two oxen, five rams, five male goats, and five male lambs a year old. This was the offering of Nethanel son of Zuar.

24 On the third day Eliab son of Helon, the leader of the Zebulunites: ²⁵his offering was one silver plate weighing one hundred thirty shekels, one silver basin weighing seventy shekels, according to the shekel of the sanctuary, both of them full of choice flour mixed with oil for a grain offering; ²⁶one golden dish weighing ten shekels, full of incense; ²⁷one young bull, one ram, one male lamb a year old, for a burnt offering; ²⁸one male goat for a sin offering; ²⁹and for the sacrifice of well-being, two oxen, five rams, five male goats, and five male lambs a year old. This was the offering of Eliab son of Helon.

30 On the fourth day Elizur son of Shedeur, the leader of the Reubenites: ³¹his offering was one silver plate weighing one hundred thirty shekels, one silver basin weighing seventy shekels, according to the shekel of the sanctuary, both of them full of choice flour mixed with oil for a grain offering; ³²one golden dish weighing ten shekels, full of incense; ³³one young bull, one ram, one male lamb a year old, for a burnt offering; ³⁴one male goat for a sin offering; ³⁵and for the sacrifice of well-being, two oxen, five rams, five male goats, and

---

7.1–9 *On the day.* Even though set one month earlier than the beginning of the book of Numbers (v. 1; see Ex 40.17; cf. Num 1.1), this description of the gifts offered presumes the information presented just prior to this section: the *wagons* and *oxen* are given to transport the sanctuary items assigned to the Levites in chs. 3–4, except for the items the Kohathites were to carry on their shoulders. The Merarites are given twice as many oxen and wagons as the Gershonites, since transporting the supporting structure of the tabernacle is more burdensome than transporting its various cloth items; see 3.23, 25–26, 35–37. **7.10** See vv. 1, 4–9. **7.12–83** The leaders are those in 1.5–15; 2.3–31; 10.14–28, presented in the order of the list in 2.3–31. The dedication offerings are the same from each tribe. **7.13** *Shekel of the sanctuary.* See note on 3.46–48. **7.17** *Oxen* here does not indicate castrated bulls, but simply male bovines. Castrated animals would not

five male lambs a year old. This was the offering of Elizur son of Shedeur.

36 On the fifth day Shelumiel son of Zurishaddai, the leader of the Simeonites: 37his offering was one silver plate weighing one hundred thirty shekels, one silver basin weighing seventy shekels, according to the shekel of the sanctuary, both of them full of choice flour mixed with oil for a grain offering; 38one golden dish weighing ten shekels, full of incense; 39one young bull, one ram, one male lamb a year old, for a burnt offering; 40one male goat for a sin offering; 41and for the sacrifice of well-being, two oxen, five rams, five male goats, and five male lambs a year old. This was the offering of Shelumiel son of Zurishaddai.

42 On the sixth day Eliasaph son of Deuel, the leader of the Gadites: 43his offering was one silver plate weighing one hundred thirty shekels, one silver basin weighing seventy shekels, according to the shekel of the sanctuary, both of them full of choice flour mixed with oil for a grain offering; 44one golden dish weighing ten shekels, full of incense; 45one young bull, one ram, one male lamb a year old, for a burnt offering; 46one male goat for a sin offering; 47and for the sacrifice of well-being, two oxen, five rams, five male goats, and five male lambs a year old. This was the offering of Eliasaph son of Deuel.

48 On the seventh day Elishama son of Ammihud, the leader of the Ephraimites: 49his offering was one silver plate weighing one hundred thirty shekels, one silver basin weighing seventy shekels, according to the shekel of the sanctuary, both of them full of choice flour mixed with oil for a grain offering; 50one golden dish weighing ten shekels, full of incense; 51one young bull, one ram, one male lamb a year old, for a burnt offering; 52one male goat for a sin offering; 53and for the sacrifice of well-being, two oxen, five rams, five male goats, and five male lambs a year old. This was the offering of Elishama son of Ammihud.

54 On the eighth day Gamaliel son of Pedahzur, the leader of the Manassites: 55his offering was one silver plate weighing one hundred thirty shekels, one silver basin weighing seventy shekels, according to the shekel of the sanctuary, both of them full of choice flour mixed with oil for a grain offering; 56one golden dish weighing ten shekels, full of incense; 57one young bull, one ram, one male lamb a year old, for a burnt offering; 58one male goat for a sin offering; 59and for the sacrifice of well-being, two oxen, five rams, five male goats, and five male lambs a year old. This was the offering of Gamaliel son of Pedahzur.

60 On the ninth day Abidan son of Gideoni, the leader of the Benjaminites: 61his offering was one silver plate weighing one hundred thirty shekels, one silver basin weighing seventy shekels, according to the shekel of the sanctuary, both of them full of choice flour mixed with oil for a grain offering; 62one golden dish weighing ten shekels, full of incense; 63one young bull, one ram, one male lamb a year old, for a burnt offering; 64one male goat for a sin offering; 65and for the sacrifice of well-being, two oxen, five rams, five male goats, and five male lambs a year old. This was the offering of Abidan son of Gideoni.

66 On the tenth day Ahiezer son of Ammishaddai, the leader of the Danites: 67his offering was one silver plate weighing one hundred thirty shekels, one silver basin weighing seventy shekels, according to the shekel of the sanctuary, both of them full of choice flour mixed with oil for a grain offering; 68one golden dish weighing ten shekels, full of incense; 69one young bull, one ram, one male lamb a year old, for a burnt offering; 70one male goat for a sin offering; 71and for the sacrifice of well-being, two oxen, five rams, five male goats, and five male lambs a year old. This was the offering of Ahiezer son of Ammishaddai.

72 On the eleventh day Pagiel son of Ochran, the leader of the Asherites: 73his offering was one silver plate weighing one hundred thirty shekels, one silver basin weighing seventy shekels, according to the shekel of the sanctuary, both of them full of choice flour mixed with oil for a grain offering; 74one golden dish weighing ten shekels, full of incense; 75one young bull, one ram, one male lamb a year old, for a burnt offering; 76one male goat for a sin offering; 77and for the sacrifice of well-being, two oxen, five rams, five male goats, and five male lambs a year old. This was the offering of Pagiel son of Ochran.

78 On the twelfth day Ahira son of Enan, the leader of the Naphtalites: 79his offering was one silver plate weighing one hundred

thirty shekels, one silver basin weighing seventy shekels, according to the shekel of the sanctuary, both of them full of choice flour mixed with oil for a grain offering; 80one golden dish weighing ten shekels, full of incense; 81one young bull, one ram, one male lamb a year old, for a burnt offering; 82one male goat for a sin offering; 83and for the sacrifice of well-being, two oxen, five rams, five male goats, and five male lambs a year old. This was the offering of Ahira son of Enan.

84 This was the dedication offering for the altar, at the time when it was anointed, from the leaders of Israel: twelve silver plates, twelve silver basins, twelve golden dishes, 85each silver plate weighing one hundred thirty shekels and each basin seventy, all the silver of the vessels two thousand four hundred shekels according to the shekel of the sanctuary, 86the twelve golden dishes, full of incense, weighing ten shekels apiece according to the shekel of the sanctuary, all the gold of the dishes being one hundred twenty shekels; 87all the livestock for the burnt offering twelve bulls, twelve rams, twelve male lambs a year old, with their grain offering; and twelve male goats for a sin offering; 88and all the livestock for the sacrifice of well-being twenty-four bulls, the rams sixty, the male goats sixty, the male lambs a year old sixty. This was the dedication offering for the altar, after it was anointed.

89 When Moses went into the tent of meeting to speak with the LORD,*a* he would hear the voice speaking to him from above the mercy seat*b* that was on the ark of the covenant*c* from between the two cherubim; thus it spoke to him.

The Seven Lamps

8 The LORD spoke to Moses, saying: 2Speak to Aaron and say to him: When you set up the lamps, the seven lamps shall give light in front of the lampstand. 3Aaron did so; he set up its lamps to give light in front of the lampstand, as the LORD had commanded Moses. 4Now this was how the lampstand was made, out of hammered work of gold. From its base to its flowers, it was hammered work; according to the pattern that the LORD had shown Moses, so he made the lampstand.

Consecration and Service of the Levites

5 The LORD spoke to Moses, saying: 6Take the Levites from among the Israelites and cleanse them. 7Thus you shall do to them, to cleanse them: sprinkle the water of purification on them, have them shave their whole body with a razor and wash their clothes, and so cleanse themselves. 8Then let them take a young bull and its grain offering of choice flour mixed with oil, and you shall take another young bull for a sin offering. 9You shall bring the Levites before the tent of meeting, and assemble the

---

a Heb *him*   *b* Or *the cover*   *c* Or *treaty*, or *testimony*; Heb *eduth*

---

have been considered suitable for sacrifice. **7.84,88** See vv. 1, 4–9. **7.89** This short notice has no obvious connection with what precedes or follows, except that it concerns the sanctuary. The *mercy seat* with the two cherubim is the cover of the ark, and it is from above the mercy seat, between the *cherubim*, that the Lord promises to meet with Moses (Ex 25.17–22; 30.6, 36). In 1 Chr 28.2 the ark is called God's "footstool" (see also Pss 99.5; 132.7), and the Lord is said to be enthroned upon the cherubim (1 Sam 4.4; 2 Sam 6.2; 2 Kings 19.15; 1 Chr 13.6; Pss 80.1; 99.1). Such a throne for a deity is also known from Canaanite iconography. **8.1** The setting is presumably still that of Ex 40.17 (see Num 7.1–9). **8.2–4** *In front of.* That the lamps should throw light forward (northward) toward the ark, the incense altar, and the table of the bread of the Presence was specified in the command to build the lampstand in Ex 25.31–40 (see v. 37), but not in the report of its construction in Ex 37.17–24. See also Ex 27.20–21; 30.7–8; Lev 24.4; 1 Sam 3.3. *Pattern.* See Ex 25.9, 40.

8.5–26 The Levites (presumably those twenty-five and older; see vv. 24–26) are purified by cleansing and sacrifice so that they will be in an appropriate state to handle the sanctuary items (v. 15). Cf. the anointing and ordination of the priests in Ex 29; Lev 8. **8.6–7** *From among the Israelites.* See 1.48–54; 3.11–13. *Cleanse,* i.e., make ritually "clean." *Water of purification.* See also 19.9, 17–19, 21; 31.23; the water for cleansing would seem to be the same as the water of purification (see also Ezek 36.25), but it is not the *holy water* for the priests mentioned in 5.17. In 8.7, *purification* (or "purification offering") is the same Hebrew word generally translated "sin" (or "sin offering"). *Have them . . . razor,* lit. "make a razor pass over their entire body" (cf. 6.9). Then they are to *wash their clothes* and presumably themselves (see Lev 13.29–34; 14.8–9; Num 19.19). See also Lev 8; 11; 16; 17 for various rituals involving washing of clothes or persons. **8.8** The first *young bull* is to be a burnt offering; see v. 12. **8.9–11** *Before the LORD,* i.e., at the entrance to the tent (cf., e.g., Ex 29.11, 42; Num 16.16–18). The laying

whole congregation of the Israelites. [10]When you bring the Levites before the LORD, the Israelites shall lay their hands on the Levites, [11]and Aaron shall present the Levites before the LORD as an elevation offering from the Israelites, that they may do the service of the LORD. [12]The Levites shall lay their hands on the heads of the bulls, and he shall offer the one for a sin offering and the other for a burnt offering to the LORD, to make atonement for the Levites. [13]Then you shall have the Levites stand before Aaron and his sons, and you shall present them as an elevation offering to the LORD.

14 Thus you shall separate the Levites from among the other Israelites, and the Levites shall be mine. [15]Thereafter the Levites may go in to do service at the tent of meeting, once you have cleansed them and presented them as an elevation offering. [16]For they are unreservedly given to me from among the Israelites; I have taken them for myself, in place of all that open the womb, the firstborn of all the Israelites. [17]For all the firstborn among the Israelites are mine, both human and animal. On the day that I struck down all the firstborn in the land of Egypt I consecrated them for myself, [18]but I have taken the Levites in place of all the firstborn among the Israelites. [19]Moreover, I have given the Levites as a gift to Aaron and his sons from among the Israelites, to do the service for the Israelites at the tent of meeting, and to make atonement for the Israelites, in order that there may be no plague among the Israelites for coming too close to the sanctuary.

20 Moses and Aaron and the whole congregation of the Israelites did with the Levites accordingly; the Israelites did with the Levites just as the LORD had commanded Moses con-

cerning them. [21]The Levites purified themselves from sin and washed their clothes; then Aaron presented them as an elevation offering before the LORD, and Aaron made atonement for them to cleanse them. [22]Thereafter the Levites went in to do their service in the tent of meeting in attendance on Aaron and his sons. As the LORD had commanded Moses concerning the Levites, so they did with them.

23 The LORD spoke to Moses, saying: [24]This applies to the Levites: from twenty-five years old and upward they shall begin to do duty in the service of the tent of meeting; [25]and from the age of fifty years they shall retire from the duty of the service and serve no more. [26]They may assist their brothers in the tent of meeting in carrying out their duties, but they shall perform no service. Thus you shall do with the Levites in assigning their duties.

The Passover at Sinai

9 The LORD spoke to Moses in the wilderness of Sinai, in the first month of the second year after they had come out of the land of Egypt, saying: [2]Let the Israelites keep the passover at its appointed time. [3]On the fourteenth day of this month, at twilight,[a] you shall keep it at its appointed time; according to all its statutes and all its regulations you shall keep it. [4]So Moses told the Israelites that they should keep the passover. [5]They kept the passover in the first month, on the fourteenth day of the month, at twilight,[a] in the wilderness of Sinai. Just as the LORD had commanded Moses, so the Israelites did. [6]Now there were certain people who were unclean through touching a corpse, so that they could not keep the passover on that day. They came

---

[a] Heb *between the two evenings*

on of *hands* identifies the sacrificer with the sacrificial victim (Lev 1.4; see also Num 8.12). The Levites have become the sacrifice, i.e., they have been dedicated to the Lord and serve as Israel's representatives in the sanctuary. **8.12** The Levites offer a sin offering and a burnt offering to atone for any possible sin (Lev 1.4; 4.20); see v. 15. **8.14** See vv. 6–7. **8.16–18** See 3.11–13. **8.19** *As a gift to Aaron and his sons.* See 3.5–9. Because the Levites stood between the Israelites and the sanctuary, the Israelites were less likely to trespass in dangerous proximity to the sanctuary; see 1.51–53; 2.17. **8.23–26** On the age limits for levitical duty, cf. 4.3, 23, 30. Num 8 liberalizes the age limits, and other writings expand them even more (see 1 Chr 23.3, 24, 27; 2 Chr 31.17; Ezra 3.8). The differences are presumably due to

variations over time in the numbers and duties of the Levites; an upper age limit is more appropriate for those doing heavy work such as transporting (Num 3–4); in v. 26 Levites over fifty could still assist in the tent of meeting. When the tabernacle was stationary within the temple (see 1 Kings 8.1–13), no such duties would fall to the Levites. Differences in lower age limits may be due to changing numbers of available Levite males (see Ezra 2.1–2, 40; Neh 7.6–7, 43).

9.1–5 The Passover is kept in the wilderness of Sinai. This second Passover is celebrated immediately before the people set out on a march, as was the first (Ex 12–13). **9.1** One month before the date in 1.1; see 7.1–9. **9.2–4** See Ex 12.1–27, 43–49. **9.6** *Unclean . . . corpse.* See 19.11–20; also 5.2. *Aaron* seems to be an

before Moses and Aaron on that day, [7]and said to him, "Although we are unclean through touching a corpse, why must we be kept from presenting the LORD's offering at its appointed time among the Israelites?" [8]Moses spoke to them, "Wait, so that I may hear what the LORD will command concerning you."

9 The LORD spoke to Moses, saying: [10]Speak to the Israelites, saying: Anyone of you or your descendants who is unclean through touching a corpse, or is away on a journey, shall still keep the passover to the LORD. [11]In the second month on the fourteenth day, at twilight,[a] they shall keep it; they shall eat it with unleavened bread and bitter herbs. [12]They shall leave none of it until morning, nor break a bone of it; according to all the statute for the passover they shall keep it. [13]But anyone who is clean and is not on a journey, and yet refrains from keeping the passover, shall be cut off from the people for not presenting the LORD's offering at its appointed time; such a one shall bear the consequences for the sin. [14]Any alien residing among you who wishes to keep the passover to the LORD shall do so according to the statute of the passover and according to its regulation; you shall have one statute for both the resident alien and the native.

The Cloud and the Fire

15 On the day the tabernacle was set up, the cloud covered the tabernacle, the tent of the covenant;[b] and from evening until morning it was over the tabernacle, having the appearance of fire. [16]It was always so: the cloud covered it by day[c] and the appearance of fire by night. [17]Whenever the cloud lifted from over the tent, then the Israelites would set out; and in the place where the cloud settled down, there the Israelites would camp. [18]At the command of the LORD the Israelites would set out, and at the command of the LORD they would camp. As long as the cloud rested over the tabernacle, they would remain in camp. [19]Even when the cloud continued over the tabernacle many days, the Israelites would keep the charge of the LORD, and would not set out. [20]Sometimes the cloud would remain a few days over the tabernacle, and according to the command of the LORD they would remain in camp; then according to the command of the LORD they would set out. [21]Sometimes the cloud would remain from evening until morning; and when the cloud lifted in the morning, they would set out, or if it continued for a day and a night, when the cloud lifted they would set out. [22]Whether it was two days, or a month, or a longer time, that the cloud continued over the tabernacle, resting upon it, the Israelites would remain in camp and would not set out; but when it lifted they would set out. [23]At the command of the LORD they would camp, and at the command of the LORD they would set out. They kept the charge of the LORD, at the command of the LORD by Moses.

---

a Heb between the two evenings   b Or treaty, or testimony; Heb eduth   c Gk Syr Vg: Heb lacks by day

---

addition here; the rest of the narrative involves only Moses. **9.10** Unclean . . . corpse. See 9.6. Being away on a journey was not part of the original question and seems to assume a settled life in Canaan (note the phrase or your descendants). **9.11** Supplemental instructions adapt the older regulations to unaddressed circumstances (see also 2 Chr 30.1–3, 15). **9.12** See Ex 12.10, 46; see also Ex 29.34; Lev 7.15; 22.29–30. **9.13** Commentators are divided on whether the phrase cut off from the people means the guilty person is killed or his family line is cut off, but most agree the phrase implies punishment by divine rather than human agency. For a clearer case, see 15.30–31. **9.14** The resident alien is not a native Israelite, but rather someone who has taken up permanent residence among the Israelites and finds protection in that community. Resident aliens, in contrast to foreigners passing through or living only temporarily in the Israelite community (Ex 12.43), were allowed to participate in the Passover as long as their males were circumcised (Ex 12.48–49), but they were not punished for not participating as native Israelites would be (Num 9.13). **9.15–23** The setting of these verses is the march from the wilderness of Sinai, although the beginning of the march is not reported until 10.11. **9.15–16** Day . . . was set up. On the date, see v. 1. The cloud . . . covenant. Among earlier mentions of the cloud, see Ex 13.21–22, where the cloud and the fire are described separately, the cloud by day and the fire by night; see other variations in Ex 16.10; 24.15–18; 33.9–10; 40.34–38; Lev 16.2. See also Ex 14.19, 24; Num 14.14; Deut 31.15; Neh 9.12, 19. The fire that is in the cloud in some descriptions has been associated with the "glory" of the Lord, and such descriptions have led commentators to describe this "glory" cloud as a kind of glowing aura, like the "radiance" of Mesopotamian gods (see, e.g., Ex 16.10; 24.16–18; also 40.34–35; Num 16.42; Ezek 1.28; 10.4). **9.16** Cf. Pss 78.14; 105.39. **9.17–23** See, e.g., Ex 40.36–37; Num 10.11–13. **9.17** Settled down, lit. "tabernacled." Presumably the cloud stopped at the point where the tabernacle was to be set up, determining, then, the position of the rest of the camp (ch. 2).

The Silver Trumpets

10 The LORD spoke to Moses, saying: ²Make two silver trumpets; you shall make them of hammered work; and you shall use them for summoning the congregation, and for breaking camp. ³When both are blown, the whole congregation shall assemble before you at the entrance of the tent of meeting. ⁴But if only one is blown, then the leaders, the heads of the tribes of Israel, shall assemble before you. ⁵When you blow an alarm, the camps on the east side shall set out; ⁶when you blow a second alarm, the camps on the south side shall set out. An alarm is to be blown whenever they are to set out. ⁷But when the assembly is to be gathered, you shall blow, but you shall not sound an alarm. ⁸The sons of Aaron, the priests, shall blow the trumpets; this shall be a perpetual institution for you throughout your generations. ⁹When you go to war in your land against the adversary who oppresses you, you shall sound an alarm with the trumpets, so that you may be remembered before the LORD your God and be saved from your enemies. ¹⁰Also on your days of rejoicing, at your appointed festivals, and at the beginnings of your months, you shall blow the trumpets over your burnt offerings and over your sacrifices of well-being; they shall serve as a reminder on your behalf before the LORD your God: I am the LORD your God.

Departure from Sinai

11 In the second year, in the second month, on the twentieth day of the month, the cloud lifted from over the tabernacle of the covenant.^a ¹²Then the Israelites set out by stages from the wilderness of Sinai, and the cloud settled down in the wilderness of Paran. ¹³They set out for the first time at the command of the LORD by Moses. ¹⁴The standard of the camp of Judah set out first, company by company, and over the whole company was Nahshon son of Amminadab. ¹⁵Over the company of the tribe of Issachar was Nethanel son of Zuar; ¹⁶and over the company of the tribe of Zebulun was Eliab son of Helon.

17 Then the tabernacle was taken down, and the Gershonites and the Merarites, who carried the tabernacle, set out. ¹⁸Next the standard of the camp of Reuben set out, company by company; and over the whole company was Elizur son of Shedeur. ¹⁹Over the company of the tribe of Simeon was Shelumiel son of Zurishaddai, ²⁰and over the company of the tribe of Gad was Eliasaph son of Deuel.

---

a Or *treaty*, or *testimony*; Heb *eduth*

10.1–10 Moses is to make two silver trumpets to be used during the march from the wilderness of Sinai. **10.2** Several Hebrew words are translated *trumpets*. The trumpets in this narrative are made of metal, not animal horns, and are used almost entirely for sacred and not secular purposes. They are blown by priests (see v. 8). According to Josephus and as depicted on later coins, they were slender with a wide mouth and about one foot long. **10.4** *The leaders . . . Israel.* See 1.16. **10.5–7** Many commentators suggest that an *alarm* is a series of short blasts, as distinguished from a *blow*, a long blast (v. 7). The Hebrew word translated *alarm* here is commonly a battle cry (e.g., v. 9; 31.6; Josh 6.5, 20; 2 Chr 13.12–16), but can also be a shout for joy (e.g., 2 Sam 6.15; Ps 33.3). Presumably an alarm is blown for the tribes on the west and north as well (so the Septuagint). **10.8** On these particular trumpets as instruments of the *priests*, see note on 10.2. **10.10** *Days of rejoicing*, e.g., the coronation of King Joash (2 Kings 11.14) or the laying of the foundation of the Second Temple (Ezra 3.10). *Appointed festivals.* See Num 28–29; Lev 23. *Beginnings of your months.* See Num 28.11–15. **10.11–22.1** The march from the wilderness of Sinai to Transjordan. **10.11–36** Cf. Deut 1.6–8. **10.11–12** *Second year . . . month.* The date is nineteen days after the census in 1.1 and eleven months and nineteen days after the Israelites arrived at the wilderness of Sinai (Ex 19.1). *Cloud.* See 9.15–23. For the *stages* of their journey, see also 33.1–49. In the first stage, the people move from the wilderness of Sinai to the wilderness of Paran (see also 11.3, 35; 12.16). Paran seems to refer to the entire area of the northern Sinai between Egypt and Midian (1 Kings 11.18). **10.14–28** For the order of the march, see ch. 2. Positions of the levitical families during the march are not quite symmetrically assigned. Those who are *over the company* parallel the lists of leaders in 1.5–15; 2.3–31; 7.12–83. For the *standard* of a tribe (vv. 14, 18, 22, 25), see 1.52. There are three tribes for each standard as there are three tribes for each "regimental encampment" in ch. 2. A regimental encampment consists of the tribes who camp under the same standard. *Company by company.* See 1.3. **10.17** The Gershonites and Merarites presumably also took down the parts of the tabernacle that they transported on wagons (7.1–9) and put the structure up again when the people camped (see 10.21). The descendants of Aaron pack up the most sacred items of the tabernacle structure for the Kohathites to carry (v. 21 here; 3.31–32; 4.5–20), and the dismantling of the rest is perhaps implied in 4.27–28, 32b–33. For the items that the Gershonites and Merarites transport, see 3.25–26, 36–37; 4.24–26,

21 Then the Kohathites, who carried the holy things, set out; and the tabernacle was set up before their arrival. 22Next the standard of the Ephraimite camp set out, company by company, and over the whole company was Elishama son of Ammihud. 23Over the company of the tribe of Manasseh was Gamaliel son of Pedahzur, 24and over the company of the tribe of Benjamin was Abidan son of Gideoni.

25 Then the standard of the camp of Dan, acting as the rear guard of all the camps, set out, company by company, and over the whole company was Ahiezer son of Ammishaddai. 26Over the company of the tribe of Asher was Pagiel son of Ochran, 27and over the company of the tribe of Naphtali was Ahira son of Enan. 28This was the order of march of the Israelites, company by company, when they set out.

29 Moses said to Hobab son of Reuel the Midianite, Moses' father-in-law, "We are setting out for the place of which the LORD said, 'I will give it to you'; come with us, and we will treat you well; for the LORD has promised good to Israel." 30But he said to him, "I will not go, but I will go back to my own land and to my kindred." 31He said, "Do not leave us, for you know where we should camp in the wilderness, and you will serve as eyes for us. 32Moreover, if you go with us, whatever good the LORD does for us, the same we will do for you."

33 So they set out from the mount of the LORD three days' journey with the ark of the covenant of the LORD going before them three days' journey, to seek out a resting place for them, 34the cloud of the LORD being over them by day when they set out from the camp.

35 Whenever the ark set out, Moses would say,

"Arise, O LORD, let your enemies be
      scattered,
    and your foes flee before you."
36And whenever it came to rest, he would say,
    "Return, O LORD of the ten thousand
      thousands of Israel." [a]

Complaining in the Desert

11 Now when the people complained in the hearing of the LORD about their misfortunes, the LORD heard it and his anger was kindled. Then the fire of the LORD burned against them, and consumed some outlying parts of the camp. 2But the people cried out to Moses; and Moses prayed to the LORD, and the

a Meaning of Heb uncertain

31–32a. **10.21** See 10.17. **10.25** *Rear guard,* lit. "gatherer"; see also Josh 6.9, 13; Isa 52.12. **10.29–36** At this point old epic materials return, interrupting the so-called Priestly materials (see Introduction) that have been the source of the narrative since Ex 35. **10.29–32** *Hobab . . . Moses' father-in-law,* is persuaded to accompany the people on their march. Elsewhere called Jethro (Ex 3.1; 4.18; 18.1–12) or even Reuel (Ex 2.18), Hobab is mentioned again in Judg 4.11 and in the Septuagint in Judg 1.16. Moses is frequently associated with Midianites or with the related Kenites, and his father-in-law is a priest of the Lord (Ex 2.16) even before Moses' encounter with the deity at the burning bush (Ex 3). Moses' and Israel's relations with Midianites or Kenites are sometimes described positively (Ex 2.11–22; 3.1–6; 4.18–20; 18; Judg 1.16; 4.11; 1 Sam 15.6; 27.8–12; 30.26–31), but sometimes a tradition of animosity against Midian is evident (Num 22.4, 7; 25; 31; Josh 13.21–23; Judg 6–8; Ps 83.9; Isa 9.4; 10.26). **10.33–34** *Mount of the LORD.* See Deut 1.6. For the *cloud* that was over the people by day, see 9.15–23. That the ark went before them *three days' journey* makes little sense; the temporal phrase is perhaps repeated mistakenly from earlier in the verse. Cf. Josh 3.1–4. **10.35–36** Two very short pieces that appear to be ancient battle cries. *"Arise, O LORD"* and *"Return, O LORD"* imply that the ark represents the presence of the Lord among the people (see 7.89; 14.44; Ex 25.10–22; 1 Sam 4.1–7.2; 2 Sam 6.1–19; 2 Chr 6.41; Pss 68.1;

132.8). In Hebrew manuscripts, this two-verse portion is set off by an inverted Hebrew letter *nun* at the beginning and end, indicating that ancient Jewish tradition considered these verses special in some way and took pains to mark them as such.

11.1–35 The stories in ch. 11 appear to be a doublet of the set of incidents in Ex 15.22–16.36. In each case there is a three-day march (Ex 15.22; Num 10.33), a set of complaints (Ex 15.24; 16.2–3; Num 11.1, 4, 10), and the provision of manna and quails for the people to eat (Ex 16.4, 13–15, 31–36; Num 11.7–9, 31–32). **11.1–3** A schematic story of complaint. This is the first appearance in Numbers of the common motif of the people's complaining because of the hardship of their life in the desert. They long for the settled life of Egypt and regret that they left what was familiar to make the dangerous trek through the unknown. Typically they complain and are punished by the Lord. In some of the stories, Moses intercedes with the Lord on behalf of the people, and in some the name of the place where the complaining happens is etymologized with reference to some incident or element within the story. Such stories begin in Ex 14.10; 15.24; 16.2; 17.2; (32.1); Num 11.1; 11.4; 14.1; 16.41; 20.3; 21.4. (See also Pss 78.15–31; 106.13–15.) **11.1** The *misfortunes* mentioned here are unspecified. *Fire of the LORD* is probably lightning (see Ex 9.23–24; 19.18; 2 Kings 1.9–14). **11.2** Moses *prayed* for the people, suggesting the prophet's role as intercessor. Complaint stories often

fire abated. [3]So that place was called Taberah,[a] because the fire of the LORD burned against them.

4 The rabble among them had a strong craving; and the Israelites also wept again, and said, "If only we had meat to eat! [5]We remember the fish we used to eat in Egypt for nothing, the cucumbers, the melons, the leeks, the onions, and the garlic; [6]but now our strength is dried up, and there is nothing at all but this manna to look at."

7 Now the manna was like coriander seed, and its color was like the color of gum resin. [8]The people went around and gathered it, ground it in mills or beat it in mortars, then boiled it in pots and made cakes of it; and the taste of it was like the taste of cakes baked with oil. [9]When the dew fell on the camp in the night, the manna would fall with it.

10 Moses heard the people weeping throughout their families, all at the entrances of their tents. Then the LORD became very angry, and Moses was displeased. [11]So Moses said to the LORD, "Why have you treated your servant so badly? Why have I not found favor in your sight, that you lay the burden of all this people on me? [12]Did I conceive all this people? Did I give birth to them, that you should say to me, 'Carry them in your bosom, as a nurse carries a sucking child, to the land that you promised on oath to their ancestors'? [13]Where am I to get meat to give to all this people? For they come weeping to me and say, 'Give us meat to eat!' [14]I am not able to carry all this people alone, for they are too heavy for me. [15]If this is the way you are going to treat me, put me to death at once—if I have found favor in your sight—and do not let me see my misery."

The Seventy Elders

16 So the LORD said to Moses, "Gather for me seventy of the elders of Israel, whom you know to be the elders of the people and officers over them; bring them to the tent of meeting, and have them take their place there with you. [17]I will come down and talk with you there; and I will take some of the spirit that is on you and put it on them; and they shall bear the burden of the people along with you so that you will not bear it all by yourself. [18]And say to the people: Consecrate yourselves for tomorrow, and you shall eat meat; for you have wailed in the hearing of the LORD, saying, 'If only we had meat to eat!

a That is Burning

include some intercession by Moses; see also in vv. 10–15. **11.3** Fire of the LORD. See v. 1. Taberah, presumably a place in the wilderness of Paran (see 10.11–12; Deut 9.22; cf. Num 33.16–17). **11.4–9** Another complaint, this time first voiced by the rabble (v. 4). **11.4** The word for rabble, lit. "a collection," occurs only here and is often interpreted to mean a mixed group of people, i.e., non-Israelites who were attached to the people (see Ex 12.38; Lev 24.10). This verse is evidence of a tradition that the Israelites did not have animals with them on the march; cf. Ex 10.24–26; 12.32, 38; 17.3; 34.3; Num 14.33; 32.1. **11.5** The foods listed here are typical in Egypt. Note that none is precisely "meat"; in fact, most are vegetables. **11.6–9** Manna. See Ex 16.14–21, 31. **11.8** Cakes baked with oil, a loose translation (see Ex 16.31), lit. "cream of oil," perhaps rich or choice cream. **11.10–15** In a very unusual passage, Moses, like the people, complains of his lot and says he would prefer death to a continuation of the current situation. Moses' complaint is that the Lord has not been responsible in caring for the Israelites, even though their situation is a result of the Lord's previous activity and promises; he feels caught in the middle between a complaining throng and an unconcerned deity (see v. 14). Moses' role as intercessor is not unusual (see v. 3; 14.13–19; 16.22; 21.7; see also Abraham in Gen 18.22–32), but in several instances his pleas are rather extended and in some of these, as here, he is sur-

prisingly indignant about his own role (see Ex 17.2–4; 32.11–14, 30–32; 33.12–16; cf. Ex 14.15–18, which seems to be a response to such an outcry, now lost). **11.12** The use of an extra Hebrew pronoun I twice lends emphasis to Moses' implication here that it was indeed the Lord who conceived and gave birth to Israel. (It is used again in v. 14.) The female imagery used here of the Lord and of Moses (he has been designated Israel's wet nurse) is unusual, but not unique (see Deut 32.18; also Isa 42.14; 66.13). Carry them in your bosom, a wet nurse's activity (see Isa 40.11 for the same image as a description of a shepherd with lambs). **11.14** Cf. Ex 18.17–18. **11.15** See Ex 32.32.

11.16–17 See a similar solution in Ex 18.13–26. **11.16** Seventy of the elders. See also Ex 24.1, 9. In the old epic traditions represented here (see Introduction) the tent of meeting is outside the camp (see vv. 26, 30), as in Ex 33.7–11 (note Joshua's role there also); Num 12.4; 19.1–4; it is said to be pitched quite simply, by Moses himself (Ex 33.7). The tradition that reports the tent outside the camp presents it as the site where anyone can obtain an oracle from the Lord (Ex 33.7) as Miriam and Aaron do in 12.4–9. **11.17** I will . . . there. See 7.89. Leaders and prophets are commonly perceived to possess a special spirit (see, e.g., 24.2–3; Judg 3.10; Ezek 2.2), and that spirit can be passed to others (Num 11.24–29; 1 Sam 10.5–10; 19.18–24; 2 Kings 2.9–15). **11.18** Consecrate yourselves, implying an up-

Surely it was better for us in Egypt.' Therefore the LORD will give you meat, and you shall eat. [19]You shall eat not only one day, or two days, or five days, or ten days, or twenty days, [20]but for a whole month—until it comes out of your nostrils and becomes loathsome to you—because you have rejected the LORD who is among you, and have wailed before him, saying, 'Why did we ever leave Egypt?' " [21]But Moses said, "The people I am with number six hundred thousand on foot; and you say, 'I will give them meat, that they may eat for a whole month'! [22]Are there enough flocks and herds to slaughter for them? Are there enough fish in the sea to catch for them?" [23]The LORD said to Moses, "Is the LORD's power limited?[a] Now you shall see whether my word will come true for you or not."

24 So Moses went out and told the people the words of the LORD; and he gathered seventy elders of the people, and placed them all around the tent. [25]Then the LORD came down in the cloud and spoke to him, and took some of the spirit that was on him and put it on the seventy elders; and when the spirit rested upon them, they prophesied. But they did not do so again.

26 Two men remained in the camp, one named Eldad, and the other named Medad, and the spirit rested on them; they were among those registered, but they had not gone out to the tent, and so they prophesied in the camp. [27]And a young man ran and told Moses, "Eldad and Medad are prophesying in the camp." [28]And Joshua son of Nun, the assistant of Moses, one of his chosen men,[b] said, "My lord Moses, stop them!" [29]But Moses said to him, "Are you jealous for my sake? Would that all the LORD's people were prophets, and that the LORD would put his spirit on them!" [30]And Moses and the elders of Israel returned to the camp.

The Quails

31 Then a wind went out from the LORD, and it brought quails from the sea and let them fall beside the camp, about a day's journey on this side and a day's journey on the other side, all around the camp, about two cubits deep on the ground. [32]So the people worked all that day and night and all the next day, gathering the quails; the least anyone gathered was ten homers; and they spread them out for themselves all around the camp. [33]But while the meat was still between their teeth, before it was consumed, the anger of the LORD was kindled against the people, and the LORD struck the people with a very great plague. [34]So that place was called Kibroth-hattaavah,[c] because there they buried the people who had the craving. [35]From Kibroth-hattaavah the people journeyed to Hazeroth.

Aaron and Miriam Jealous of Moses

12 While they were at Hazeroth, Miriam and Aaron spoke against Moses because of the Cushite woman whom he had

---

a Heb LORD's hand too short?   b Or of Moses from his youth
c That is Graves of craving

---

coming encounter with the divine or the sacred. **11.20** See 14.27; 1 Sam 8.7; 10.19. **11.21** The *six hundred thousand on foot* are the soldiers (see Ex 12.37; cf. Num 1.46). **11.23** *LORD's power limited.* See text note *a.* See Isa 50.2; 59.1 for the same image. **11.24–30** See 11.17. **11.25** The prophesying was a temporary condition and not a permanent occupation. **11.26, 30** The tent of meeting is outside the camp.

11.31–34 This section returns to the topic of vv. 18–24a; see Ps 105.40. **11.31** *Wind* provides a verbal connection with the preceding section because "wind" and "spirit" are the same word in Hebrew. *Quails.* See Ex 16.13. *Two cubits,* about one yard. **11.32** A *homer* is between 4 and 5 bushels. They *spread out* the quails to dry and preserve them. **11.33** On the Lord's anger resulting in a plague, see Ex 9.15; Lev 26.21; Num 12.9–10; 14.11–12, 36–37; 16.45–46; 21.5–6 (serpents); 25.1–9, 18; Deut 28.15, 27; 1 Sam 4.5–8; 2 Sam 24.10–17; 1 Chr 21.1–17; Jer 14.10–12. **11.34** The mention of *craving* here forms an *inclusio* with v. 4, in which the

rabble had a strong craving (in an *inclusio,* the beginning and end repeat each other, thereby signaling a structural unit). Taken literally, the use of this phrase suggests that only the rabble were affected by the plague. **11.35** The next stage on the journey. *Kibroth-hattaavah.* See 33.16–17; Deut 9.22. *Hazeroth.* See Num 12.1, 16; 33.17–18; Deut 1.1; cf. Num 10.11–12.

12.1 *Hazeroth.* See 11.35. *Miriam and Aaron* are Moses' sister and brother (Ex 4.14; 15.20). *A Cushite woman.* Cush often refers to Ethiopia in the Bible, and the Septuagint translates "Ethiopian" here. It is often thought, then, that this story contrasts Moses' dark-skinned wife with Miriam, who is *as white as snow* in v. 10, presumably referring to white scales or blemishes from her skin disease. (The disease is not necessarily leprosy, and the word "white" is not in the Hebrew; see note on 12.10.) There is also a place called Cush in northern Arabia, however, and, given Hab 3.7, where "Cushan" is used in parallel with Midian, it can also be the north Arabian Cush that is referred to here. Thus

married (for he had indeed married a Cushite woman); 2and they said, "Has the LORD spoken only through Moses? Has he not spoken through us also?" And the LORD heard it. 3Now the man Moses was very humble,*a* more so than anyone else on the face of the earth. 4Suddenly the LORD said to Moses, Aaron, and Miriam, "Come out, you three, to the tent of meeting." So the three of them came out. 5Then the LORD came down in a pillar of cloud, and stood at the entrance of the tent, and called Aaron and Miriam; and they both came forward. 6And he said, "Hear my words:

When there are prophets among you,
    I the LORD make myself known to
        them in visions;
    I speak to them in dreams.
7 Not so with my servant Moses;
        he is entrusted with all my house.
8 With him I speak face to face— clearly,
        not in riddles;
    and he beholds the form of the LORD.

Why then were you not afraid to speak against my servant Moses?" 9And the anger of the LORD was kindled against them, and he departed.

10 When the cloud went away from over the tent, Miriam had become leprous,*b* as white as snow. And Aaron turned towards Miriam and saw that she was leprous. 11Then Aaron said to Moses, "Oh, my lord, do not punish us*c* for a sin that we have so foolishly committed. 12Do not let her be like one stillborn, whose flesh is half consumed when it comes out of its mother's womb." 13And Moses cried to the LORD, "O God, please heal her." 14But the LORD said to Moses, "If her father had but spit in her face, would she not bear her shame for seven days? Let her be shut out of the camp for seven days, and after that she may be brought in again." 15So Miriam was shut out of the camp for seven days; and the people did not set out on the march until Miriam had been brought in again. 16After that the people set out from Hazeroth, and camped in the wilderness of Paran.

Spies Sent into Canaan

13 The LORD said to Moses, 2"Send men to spy out the land of Canaan, which I am giving to the Israelites; from each of their ancestral tribes you shall send a man, every one a leader among them." 3So Moses sent them from the wilderness of Paran, according to the command of the LORD, all of them lead-

---

a Or *devout* *b* A term for several skin diseases; precise meaning uncertain *c* Heb *do not lay sin upon us*

---

the Cushite woman would be Moses' wife Zipporah, a Midianite (Ex 2.15–21; 3.1; Num 10.29), more specifically a member of the Midianite subgroup the Kenites (Judg 1.16; 4.11). **12.2** In this verse Miriam and Aaron offer a different reason for their speaking against their brother Moses: he should not be considered the only intermediary for Israel, since they also have received communications from the Lord (see Ex 4.14–16; 15.20–21; Mic 6.4). At question here is Moses' unique position as the leader of the people; this passage probably reflects issues of a later day when groups who traced their authority to Moses were involved in a power struggle with groups who traced their authority to Miriam or Aaron. **12.3** This verse, because of its laudatory third-person reference to Moses, was a stumbling block to earlier readers who understood the entire Pentateuch to have been written by Moses himself. **12.4** *Come out . . . to the tent.* See 11.16, 26, 30. **12.5** See 9.15–16. **12.6** *Visions* and *dreams* are a valid form of communication from the Lord in Israel (see Joel 2.28; also Gen 15.1; 40–41), but dreams are often distinguished from communications through prophets (Deut 13.1, 3, 5; 1 Sam 28.6, 15; Jer 27.9; 29.8), and sometimes dreams are ranked below a prophet's communications (Jer 23.28). The verbs in this verse are habitual or customary: this is how it is usually done. **12.7** Moses is distinguished from all other prophets,

from what is customary (v. 6). The Lord's *house* is Israel (Jer 12.7; Hos 8.1); see also Gen 24.2; 39.4–6; 41.40 and the frequent reference to Israel as "the house of Israel" (as in Ex 16.31; 40.38). The verse is alluded to in Heb 3.5. **12.8** *Face to face* is not meant to be taken literally here; in fact, the literal translation in this verse is "mouth to mouth." That the Lord spoke to Moses "face to face" perhaps simply means that they spoke directly, without an intermediary or a medium such as a dream (Ex 33.11; Deut 34.10 [both lit. "face to face"]; Num 14.14; Isa 52.8 [both lit. "eye to eye"]). Moses *beholds the form of the LORD*, however (see Ex 33.17–23; cf. Deut 4.12, 15, where the people behold no form; Ps 17.15). **12.10** *Leprous.* See text note *b* and vv. 13–15. We do not know why Miriam is punished, but not Aaron. Aaron, in v. 11, asks that Moses not punish the two of them, as if he too is suffering or about to suffer. **12.11** Aaron addresses Moses as *my lord*, ironically acknowledging Moses' superiority in his plea for help. *Do not punish us.* See note on 12.10. **12.13** Moses' intercession on behalf of Miriam is typical. See 11.10–15. **12.14** *Spit in her face.* On spitting as a sign of humiliation, see Deut 25.9; Job 30.10; Isa 50.6. **12.15** See Lev 13.1–17, esp. v. 4; 14.1–32, esp. v. 8.

13.1–3 Like those who helped with the census, 1.4, the men sent to spy out the land for the people at the Lord's command (cf. Deut 1.22–25) are chosen be-

ing men among the Israelites. 4These were their names: From the tribe of Reuben, Shammua son of Zaccur; 5from the tribe of Simeon, Shaphat son of Hori; 6from the tribe of Judah, Caleb son of Jephunneh; 7from the tribe of Issachar, Igal son of Joseph; 8from the tribe of Ephraim, Hoshea son of Nun; 9from the tribe of Benjamin, Palti son of Raphu; 10from the tribe of Zebulun, Gaddiel son of Sodi; 11from the tribe of Joseph (that is, from the tribe of Manasseh), Gaddi son of Susi; 12from the tribe of Dan, Ammiel son of Gemalli; 13from the tribe of Asher, Sethur son of Michael; 14from the tribe of Naphtali, Nahbi son of Vophsi; 15from the tribe of Gad, Geuel son of Machi. 16These were the names of the men whom Moses sent to spy out the land. And Moses changed the name of Hoshea son of Nun to Joshua.

17 Moses sent them to spy out the land of Canaan, and said to them, "Go up there into the Negeb, and go up into the hill country, 18and see what the land is like, and whether the people who live in it are strong or weak, whether they are few or many, 19and whether the land they live in is good or bad, and whether the towns that they live in are unwalled or fortified, 20and whether the land is

rich or poor, and whether there are trees in it or not. Be bold, and bring some of the fruit of the land." Now it was the season of the first ripe grapes.

21 So they went up and spied out the land from the wilderness of Zin to Rehob, near Lebo-hamath. 22They went up into the Negeb, and came to Hebron; and Ahiman, Sheshai, and Talmai, the Anakites, were there. (Hebron was built seven years before Zoan in Egypt.) 23And they came to the Wadi Eshcol, and cut down from there a branch with a single cluster of grapes, and they carried it on a pole between two of them. They also brought some pomegranates and figs. 24That place was called the Wadi Eshcol,*a* because of the cluster that the Israelites cut down from there.

The Report of the Spies

25 At the end of forty days they returned from spying out the land. 26And they came to Moses and Aaron and to all the congregation of the Israelites in the wilderness of Paran, at Kadesh; they brought back word to them and to all the congregation, and showed them the fruit of the land. 27And they told him, "We

a That is *Cluster*

cause each is a leader in one of the twelve tribes. The setting is the wilderness of Paran; see 12.16. **13.4–16** The order in which the tribes are listed is similar to that in 1.5–15, but the leaders are not the same. This list of names is not duplicated. **13.6** Elsewhere (32.12; Josh 14.6, 14) Caleb is called a Kenizzite; see Num 14.24. **13.17** *Negeb* (pronounced "negev"), the generally dry waste country just north of the Sinai Peninsula, south of what is later Judah, and to the west and south of the Dead Sea. The *hill country* referred to here is either the highlands of the Negeb itself (see 14.40; Deut 1.20) or the highlands of Judah (Judg 1.19), part of the central spine of hills that runs north and south through Canaan. **13.20** *Season of . . . grapes,* July/August. **13.21–24** Cf. Deut 1.24–25a. **13.21** Another note from the Priestly traditions (see Introduction). The following old epic story (vv. 22–24) locates the reconnoitering entirely in the area of the Negeb and Judah, but the Priestly traditions state that the spies went from the far southern end of the promised land in the *wilderness of Zin* (see 34.1–4; Josh 15.1–3) to the far northern end at *Rehob* or Beth-rehob, described as near *Lebo-hamath* (lit. "the entrance to Hamath" in southern Syria), often mentioned as part of Israel's northern border (see 34.7–8; Judg 18.27–28; 2 Sam 10.6, 8). **13.22** *Negeb.* See 13.17. *Hebron,* an important city in Judah, especially in the family narratives in Genesis, is about twenty miles south of Jerusalem. The

Anakites are one of several groups described as the indigenous peoples of Canaan, many of whom are remembered as giants; see vv. 32–33 (see also Gen 6.1–4); Deut 2.9–11, 19–21; 9.1–2; Josh 11.21–22; 14.12–15; 15.13–14; Judg 1.10, 20; see also Gen 14.5; 15.20; Deut 3.11, 13; Josh 12.4–5; 13.12; 17.15; 1 Chr 20.4. *Ahiman, Sheshai, and Talmai.* See Josh 15.14; Judg 1.10. *Zoan in Egypt,* in the eastern Delta (Ex 1.11). **13.23–24** *Wadi Eshcol,* site unknown, is etymologized by being tied to the spies' acquisition of oversized fruit there. In Hebrew an *eshcol* is a cluster of grapes; see text note *a. Grapes, pomegranates,* and *figs* do grow in the Hebron area, as well as many other areas of Palestine. **13.25–33** See Deut 1.25b. **13.25** *Forty days* is a stereotypical expression of time in biblical literature; see, e.g., Gen 7.4; Ex 24.18; 1 Sam 17.16; 1 Kings 19.8; Ezek 4.6. **13.26** This is the first mention of the oasis *Kadesh* (Kadesh-barnea; see, e.g., 32.8), where much of the forty years in the wilderness will be spent (including the events in chs. 13–20). Kadesh is also described in the Priestly tradition (see Introduction) as being in the wilderness of Zin (e.g., 20.1); the relationship between Paran and Zin is not known. Kadesh-barnea was probably one of a group of oases located about fifty miles south of Beer-sheba, one of which is still called "the spring Kadesh." (See Ex 17.7.) **13.27** The spies say the land *flows with milk and honey* in the first

came to the land to which you sent us; it flows with milk and honey, and this is its fruit. 28Yet the people who live in the land are strong, and the towns are fortified and very large; and besides, we saw the descendants of Anak there. 29The Amalekites live in the land of the Negeb; the Hittites, the Jebusites, and the Amorites live in the hill country; and the Canaanites live by the sea, and along the Jordan."

30 But Caleb quieted the people before Moses, and said, "Let us go up at once and occupy it, for we are well able to overcome it." 31Then the men who had gone up with him said, "We are not able to go up against this people, for they are stronger than we." 32So they brought to the Israelites an unfavorable report of the land that they had spied out, saying, "The land that we have gone through as spies is a land that devours its inhabitants; and all the people that we saw in it are of great size. 33There we saw the Nephilim (the Anakites come from the Nephilim); and to ourselves we seemed like grasshoppers, and so we seemed to them."

The People Rebel

14 Then all the congregation raised a loud cry, and the people wept that night. 2And all the Israelites complained against Moses and Aaron; the whole congregation said to them, "Would that we had died in the land of Egypt! Or would that we had died in this wilderness! 3Why is the LORD bringing us into this land to fall by the sword? Our wives and our little ones will become booty; would it not be better for us to go back to Egypt?" 4So they said to one another, "Let us choose a captain, and go back to Egypt."

5 Then Moses and Aaron fell on their faces before all the assembly of the congregation of the Israelites. 6And Joshua son of Nun and Caleb son of Jephunneh, who were among those who had spied out the land, tore their clothes 7and said to all the congregation of the Israelites, "The land that we went through as spies is an exceedingly good land. 8If the LORD is pleased with us, he will bring us into this land and give it to us, a land that flows with milk and honey. 9Only, do not rebel against the

---

use in the book of Numbers of the well-known phrase. See also 14.8; 16.13 (used of Egypt!), 14; Ex 3.8. **13.28** The *descendants of Anak* are the Anakites of v. 22. A common Semitic way of designating the members of a group is to call them "the descendants/children" of an eponymous ancestor or of a typical member of the group: "the children of Israel" are the Israelites; "the sons of the prophets" in 1 Kings 20.34 (see text note *a*) are themselves prophets. **13.29** The *Amalekites* are a perennial enemy of the Israelites (e.g., Gen 14.7; Ex 17.8–16; Judg 3.12–13; 1 Sam 15.1–9) who apparently inhabited the Negeb area where the people are to spend the next forty years. On the *Hittites, Jebusites, Amorites,* and *Canaanites,* see Ex 3.8. The spies' listing of these indigenous peoples divides the land into its constituent parts: the Negeb, the central hill country, the seacoast, and the Jordan Valley. Cf. 14.25, 45, for a slightly different arrangement of peoples. **13.30–31** In this old epic passage (see Introduction) Caleb is the only spy who dissents from the majority opinion voiced in vv. 28–29. Joshua is included only in verses that stem from the Priestly tradition (vv. 8, 16; 14.6, 38; see Introduction). **13.32–33** That the land *devours its inhabitants* can be taken either as a sign of infertility and therefore a contradiction of v. 27 (two verses from different traditions) or as a metaphor for the inevitability of warfare in a place with so many peoples, many of whom are bigger and stronger than the Israelites. Ezek 36.13–15 has been used to support both interpretations. See also Num 14.3, 9. *Nephilim.* See 13.22; Gen 6.4.

14.1–4 The people respond to the spies' negative report (13.27–33) with their complaints; see also Deut 1.26–28; Ps 106.24–25. On the complaint stories, see note on 11.1–3. **14.1** *Raised a loud cry.* See 13.30. **14.3a** *Fall by the sword.* See 13.32–33. On Israelite and foreign women and children as booty, see 31.13–18; Deut 20.10–15; 21.10–14; 1 Sam 30.1–6, 16–20. **14.3b–4** The longing for Egypt is typical of the complaint stories (Ex 14.10–12; 16.3; 17.3; Num 11.5; 14.2; 16.13; 20.5; 21.5; cf. Josh 7.7), but here the people actually plot to return, and with a leader other than Moses; cf. ch. 12; 16.12–14. **14.5–12** Responses to the complaints; cf. Deut 1.29–33. **14.5** Moses and Aaron *fell on their faces* as an act of contrition and entreaty, in hopes of avoiding terrible consequences; see, e.g., 16.4, 22. **14.6** Note *Joshua*'s presence along with Caleb's; cf. 13.30–31. They *tore their clothes* as a sign of grief (e.g., Gen 37.29, 34; Judg 11.35; 2 Sam 1.11). The act is similar to Moses' and Aaron's falling on their faces, because mourning practices in Israel, like tearing clothes and putting dirt on the head, are also obviously acts of contrition and humility before the deity. **14.7–9** See 13.27, 30; cf. 13.32–33. **14.8–9** *If the LORD is pleased with us . . . do not rebel against the LORD* foreshadows the Lord's rejection of this generation, vv. 20–24, 28–35. **14.8** *Land . . . milk and honey.* See 13.27. **14.9** The people of the land are *bread for us,* i.e., the Israelites will conquer them; see 13.32–33; 24.8; Pss 14.4; 53.4; 79.7; Jer 2.3; 10.25. *Protection,* lit. "shadow" (Judg 9.15; Isa 32.2). For a shadow as a god's protection, see Pss 91.1; 121.5; Isa 25.4; and the name Bezalel, "in the shadow of God," Ex 31.2. *Their protection is removed from them* implies that the gods of the people of the

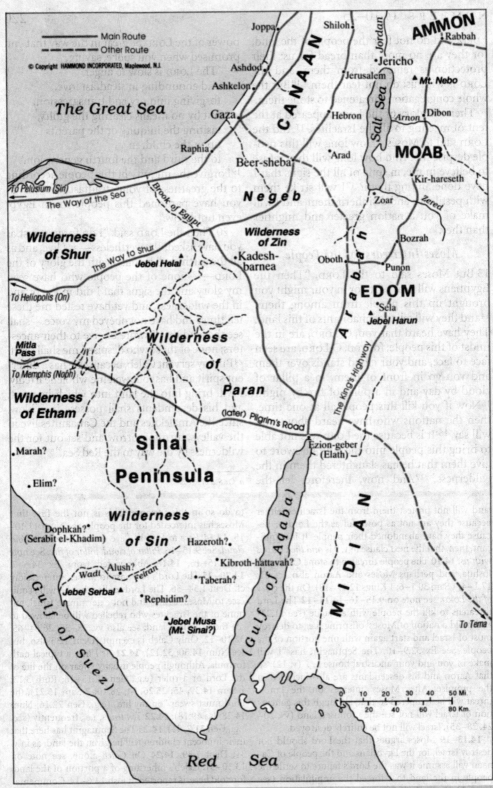

The "Land of Canaan" at the end of the second millennium BCE, showing possible routes into Canaan from Sinai.

LORD; and do not fear the people of the land, for they are no more than bread for us; their protection is removed from them, and the LORD is with us; do not fear them." 10But the whole congregation threatened to stone them.

Then the glory of the LORD appeared at the tent of meeting to all the Israelites. 11And the LORD said to Moses, "How long will this people despise me? And how long will they refuse to believe in me, in spite of all the signs that I have done among them? 12I will strike them with pestilence and disinherit them, and I will make of you a nation greater and mightier than they."

Moses Intercedes for the People

13 But Moses said to the LORD, "Then the Egyptians will hear of it, for in your might you brought up this people from among them, 14and they will tell the inhabitants of this land. They have heard that you, O LORD, are in the midst of this people; for you, O LORD, are seen face to face, and your cloud stands over them and you go in front of them, in a pillar of cloud by day and in a pillar of fire by night. 15Now if you kill this people all at one time, then the nations who have heard about you will say, 16'It is because the LORD was not able to bring this people into the land he swore to give them that he has slaughtered them in the wilderness.' 17And now, therefore, let the

power of the LORD be great in the way that you promised when you spoke, saying,
18 'The LORD is slow to anger,
    and abounding in steadfast love,
    forgiving iniquity and transgression,
    but by no means clearing the guilty,
    visiting the iniquity of the parents
    upon the children
    to the third and the fourth generation.'
19Forgive the iniquity of this people according to the greatness of your steadfast love, just as you have pardoned this people, from Egypt even until now."

20 Then the LORD said, "I do forgive, just as you have asked; 21nevertheless—as I live, and as all the earth shall be filled with the glory of the LORD— 22none of the people who have seen my glory and the signs that I did in Egypt and in the wilderness, and yet have tested me these ten times and have not obeyed my voice, 23shall see the land that I swore to give to their ancestors; none of those who despised me shall see it. 24But my servant Caleb, because he has a different spirit and has followed me wholeheartedly, I will bring into the land into which he went, and his descendants shall possess it. 25Now, since the Amalekites and the Canaanites live in the valleys, turn tomorrow and set out for the wilderness by the way to the Red Sea."[a]

––––––––––
a Or Sea of Reeds

land will not protect them from the Israelites, either because they are not as powerful as the Lord or because they have abandoned their people. It is significant, then, that the next clause in v. 9 is and the LORD is with us. **14.10** The people threaten to stone Caleb and Joshua, and perhaps Moses and Aaron also (cf. Ex 17.1–4; 1 Sam 30.1–6; 1 Kings 12.17–18). On the glory of the LORD, see note on 9.15–16. **14.11–12** The Lord threatens to kill the people with a plague (see 11.33) and build a nation of Moses' offspring, i.e., to destroy most of Israel and start again with one portion of the people. See Ex 32.9–10. The Septuagint has "I will make of you and your ancestral house . . ." (v. 12), so that Aaron and his descendants are also included in the promise. After Moses' intercession the Lord's threat will be tempered so that, although this generation of Israel will not see the promised land (vv. 20–24, 28–35), Israel will not be entirely destroyed. **14.13–19** Moses argues that the Lord should not destroy Israel, for the Egyptians and the people of Canaan will assume it was the Lord's failure to settle the people in the land that forced the annihilation (see Deut 32.26–27; Josh 7.6–9; Ezek 20.8–9; 36.18–32; 39.21–29); furthermore, the Lord has promised (Ex 34.6–7) to "forgive iniquity" and Moses urges the Lord

to do so in this instance. This is not the first time Moses has interceded for the people; see Num 11.10–15. **14.14** Face to face, lit. "eye to eye"; see 12.8. Your cloud. See 9.15–16. Pillar of cloud, pillar of fire. See note on 9.15–16. **14.18** Abbreviated from Ex 34.6–7. **14.20–25** The Lord's response to Moses' intercession; cf. Deut 1.34–36. The Lord replies that he will acquiesce to Moses' wishes and not exterminate Israel, but none of the Israelites who rebelled will be allowed to see the promised land; see also vv. 28–35; 26.64–65; 32.10–12. Only Caleb is exempt (Deut 1.35 also, but see Num 14.30; 32.12). **14.21** As I live, a typical oath formula. Although people usually swear on the life of the Lord or a ruler (e.g., Gen 42.15–16; Ruth 3.13; 1 Sam 14.39, 45; 25.26, 34; 28.10; 2 Sam 15.21), the Lord must swear "on my life" (e.g., Gen 22.16; Num 14.28; Isa 49.18). **14.22** Ten times, i.e., frequently (see, e.g., Gen 31.7, 41). **14.23** The Septuagint has here that their innocent children will be given the land, as in v. 31; Deut 1.39. **14.24** On Caleb alone, see note on 13.30–31. Caleb's inheriting of a portion of the land, foretold here, is reported in Josh 14.6–14. Commentators have long suggested that Caleb represents a family group rather than an individual (perhaps the "dog clan" since the name Caleb means "dog" in Hebrew),

An Attempted Invasion is Repulsed

26 And the LORD spoke to Moses and to Aaron, saying: 27How long shall this wicked congregation complain against me? I have heard the complaints of the Israelites, which they complain against me. 28Say to them, "As I live," says the LORD, "I will do to you the very things I heard you say: 29your dead bodies shall fall in this very wilderness; and of all your number, included in the census, from twenty years old and upward, who have complained against me, 30not one of you shall come into the land in which I swore to settle you, except Caleb son of Jephunneh and Joshua son of Nun. 31But your little ones, who you said would become booty, I will bring in, and they shall know the land that you have despised. 32But as for you, your dead bodies shall fall in this wilderness. 33And your children shall be shepherds in the wilderness for forty years, and shall suffer for your faithlessness, until the last of your dead bodies lies in the wilderness. 34According to the number of the days in which you spied out the land, forty days, for every day a year, you shall bear your iniquity, forty years, and you shall know my displeasure." 35I the LORD have spoken; surely I will do thus to all this wicked congregation gathered together against me: in this wilderness they shall come to a full end, and there they shall die.

36 And the men whom Moses sent to spy out the land, who returned and made all the congregation complain against him by bringing a bad report about the land— 37the men who brought an unfavorable report about the land died by a plague before the LORD. 38But Joshua son of Nun and Caleb son of Jephunneh alone remained alive, of those men who went to spy out the land.

39 When Moses told these words to all the Israelites, the people mourned greatly. 40They rose early in the morning and went up to the heights of the hill country, saying, "Here we are. We will go up to the place that the LORD has promised, for we have sinned." 41But Moses said, "Why do you continue to transgress the command of the LORD? That will not succeed. 42Do not go up, for the LORD is not with you; do not let yourselves be struck down before your enemies. 43For the Amalekites and the Canaanites will confront you there, and you shall fall by the sword; because you have turned back from following the LORD, the LORD will not be with you." 44But they presumed to go up to the heights of the hill country, even though the ark of the covenant of the LORD, and Moses, had not left the camp. 45Then the Amalekites and the Canaanites

---

one that eventually joined with the tribe of Judah. **14.25** *In the valleys.* Cf. 13.29; 14.45. *Turn*, i.e., turn back, because this generation is not to move forward but to remain in the wilderness. *By the way to the Red Sea*, see text note *a*. The Hebrew is "Sea of Reeds"; see Ex 10.19.

14.26–35 Continuation of the Lord's response. Cf. Deut 1.37–40 (although nothing in Num 14.26–35 corresponds to Deut 1.37); Ps 106.26–27. **14.27** *They complain against me.* See 11.20. **14.28–35** Their punishment corresponds to the Israelites' fears. **14.28** *As I live.* See 14.21. **14.29** *Your dead bodies . . . wilderness.* The immediate referent is v. 2. *Included in the census*, lit. "your enrolled ones," in the census in ch. 1. Note that this leaves ambiguous the fate of the Levites, who were not counted in the census in ch. 1; see 1.49; 3.15. There were also no Levites represented among the spies. Moreover, Aaron's son Eleazar, surely twenty years old by now (see 3.32; 4.16), does enter the land (e.g., Josh 14.1; 17.4; 24.33). **14.30** *I swore*, lit. "I raised my hand"; see also Gen 14.22; Ex 6.8; Ps 106.26. On the inclusion of Joshua, see note on 13.30–31. **14.31a** On children as booty, see 14.3. **14.33** *Forty years* is a typical biblical expression for one generation (see Gen 25.20; 26.34). **14.34** *Forty . . . a year.* See 13.25. See the similar phrase in Ezek 4.6. The tradition that Israel spent forty years in the wilderness is reported also in the early prophets (Am 2.10; 5.25; see also Hos 2.14–15), although there is no sense in these passages that the wilderness sojourn is a punishment; cf. Ps 95.10. **14.36–38** The spies, except for Joshua and Caleb, are killed by the Lord. **14.36** See 13.32; 14.1–4. **14.37** *Plague.* See 11.33. The Hebrew word used here simply means some form of death, lit. "a smiting." **14.38** On *Joshua* and *Caleb*, see note on 13.30–31. **14.39–45** An abortive attempt to enter the land from the south; cf. Deut 1.41–45. **14.39–40** The people change their minds when they hear their punishment. **14.40** *They rose early in the morning.* Cf. *tomorrow* in v. 25. **14.41** Moses explains that it is no better to go when the Lord has commanded them to turn back (v. 25) than it was to refuse to go when the Lord commanded them to go. **14.42–43** Moses says that the Lord will not be with them in this venture. Cf. v. 9; see also v. 44; in Deut 1.42 it is the Lord who says this. **14.43, 45** *Amalekites, Canaanites.* See 14.25. On the enmity between Israelites and Amalekites, see 13.29 (cf. Deut 1.44: "Amorites"). *Fall by the sword.* See 14.3, 28–35. **14.44** This verse makes clear what it means that the Lord will not be with the people: the ark will not go up with them; see 7.89; 10.35–36. **14.45** *Hormah*, in the extreme south of Israel's possessions; see 21.1–3

who lived in that hill country came down and defeated them, pursuing them as far as Hormah.

Various Offerings

15 The LORD spoke to Moses, saying: ²Speak to the Israelites and say to them: When you come into the land you are to inhabit, which I am giving you, ³and you make an offering by fire to the LORD from the herd or from the flock—whether a burnt offering or a sacrifice, to fulfill a vow or as a freewill offering or at your appointed festivals—to make a pleasing odor for the LORD, ⁴then whoever presents such an offering to the LORD shall present also a grain offering, one-tenth of an ephah of choice flour, mixed with one-fourth of a hin of oil. ⁵Moreover, you shall offer one-fourth of a hin of wine as a drink offering with the burnt offering or the sacrifice, for each lamb. ⁶For a ram, you shall offer a grain offering, two-tenths of an ephah of choice flour mixed with one-third of a hin of oil; ⁷and as a drink offering you shall offer one-third of a hin of wine, a pleasing odor to the LORD. ⁸When you offer a bull as a burnt offering or a sacrifice, to fulfill a vow or as an offering of well-being to the LORD, ⁹then you shall present with the bull a grain offering, three-tenths of an ephah of choice flour, mixed with half a hin of oil, ¹⁰and you shall present as a drink offering half a hin of wine, as an offering by fire, a pleasing odor to the LORD.

11 Thus it shall be done for each ox or ram, or for each of the male lambs or the kids. ¹²According to the number that you offer, so you shall do with each and every one. ¹³Every native Israelite shall do these things in this way, in presenting an offering by fire, a pleasing odor to the LORD. ¹⁴An alien who lives with you, or who takes up permanent residence among you, and wishes to offer an offering by fire, a pleasing odor to the LORD, shall do as you do. ¹⁵As for the assembly, there shall be for both you and the resident alien a single statute, a perpetual statute throughout your generations; you and the alien shall be alike before the LORD. ¹⁶You and the alien who resides with you shall have the same law and the same ordinance.

17 The LORD spoke to Moses, saying: ¹⁸Speak to the Israelites and say to them: After you come into the land to which I am bringing you, ¹⁹whenever you eat of the bread of the land, you shall present a donation to the LORD. ²⁰From your first batch of dough you shall present a loaf as a donation; you shall present it just as you present a donation from the threshing floor. ²¹Throughout your generations you shall give to the LORD a donation from the first of your batch of dough.

22 But if you unintentionally fail to observe all these commandments that the LORD has spoken to Moses— ²³everything that the LORD has commanded you by Moses, from the day the LORD gave commandment and thereafter, throughout your generations— ²⁴then if it was done unintentionally without the knowledge of the congregation, the whole congregation shall offer one young bull for a burnt offering, a pleasing odor to the LORD, together with its grain offering and its drink

---

(where the name is etymologized as "destruction"); Judg 1.16–17 (with the same etymology); 1 Sam 30.26–31. In Deut 1.44 it is associated with Seir, i.e., Edom. **15.1–16** These verses prescribe grain and drink offerings to go along with burnt offerings and offerings of well-being. Cf. Ezek 46.4–15; see also Num 28–29; Ex 29.38–42. **15.2** *When you come into the land.* The prescribed offerings reflect a settled agricultural life. There is irony in this verse: this generation will not, in fact, "come into the land"; see 14.20–24, 28–35. **15.3** *An offering by fire* perhaps is not specifically a fire offering, but simply any offering, cognate to a word for "gift" in the language of the ancient city of Ugarit. *From the herd . . . flock,* i.e., domestic animals, not wild, are used for sacrifice. On various offerings, see 6.14–17. *Sacrifice,* here the equivalent of an offering of well-being, i.e., an offering in which the worshiper participates. Lev 7.11–18 describes the three kinds of offer-

ings of well-being: thanksgiving, votive, and freewill, two of which are named in Num 15.3 as well. *A pleasing odor for the LORD* describes an acceptable offering; see Gen 8.20–22. **15.4** *Ephah.* See 5.15 (note the grain offering mixed with oil). A *hin* was approximately 12 pints. **15.5** *For each lamb.* See v. 11 where both lambs and goats are included. **15.6–10** The amounts of the accompanying grain and drink offerings increase with the size of the animal offered. **15.11–16** The same rules apply to resident *aliens* as to Israelites; see 9.14; also 15.26, 29. **15.16** See also Ex 12.43–49; cf. Deut 14.21. **15.19** A *donation* is simply an offering dedicated to the Lord, in this case for the priests. **15.20** An offering from the *first batch of dough* is like a first-fruits offering; see Neh 10.36–37; Ezek 44.30; see also Ex 22.29a; 23.19a; 34.26a; Lev 23.9–14; Num 18.13–18; Deut 26.1–11. *A donation from the threshing floor.* See 18.27. **15.22–29** Atonement for unintentional sins; see also Lev 4–5. **15.22** *You* here is plural in Hebrew.

offering, according to the ordinance, and one male goat for a sin offering. 25The priest shall make atonement for all the congregation of the Israelites, and they shall be forgiven; it was unintentional, and they have brought their offering, an offering by fire to the LORD, and their sin offering before the LORD, for their error. 26All the congregation of the Israelites shall be forgiven, as well as the aliens residing among them, because the whole people was involved in the error.

27 An individual who sins unintentionally shall present a female goat a year old for a sin offering. 28And the priest shall make atonement before the LORD for the one who commits an error, when it is unintentional, to make atonement for the person, who then shall be forgiven. 29For both the native among the Israelites and the alien residing among them—you shall have the same law for anyone who acts in error. 30But whoever acts high-handedly, whether a native or an alien, affronts the LORD, and shall be cut off from among the people. 31Because of having despised the word of the LORD and broken his commandment, such a person shall be utterly cut off and bear the guilt.

Penalty for Violating the Sabbath

32 When the Israelites were in the wilderness, they found a man gathering sticks on the sabbath day. 33Those who found him gathering sticks brought him to Moses, Aaron, and to the whole congregation. 34They put him in custody, because it was not clear what should be done to him. 35Then the LORD said to Moses, "The man shall be put to death; all the congregation shall stone him outside the camp." 36The whole congregation brought him outside the camp and stoned him to death, just as the LORD had commanded Moses.

Fringes on Garments

37 The LORD said to Moses: 38Speak to the Israelites, and tell them to make fringes on the corners of their garments throughout their generations and to put a blue cord on the fringe at each corner. 39You have the fringe so that, when you see it, you will remember all the commandments of the LORD and do them, and not follow the lust of your own heart and your own eyes. 40So you shall remember and do all my commandments, and you shall be holy to your God. 41I am the LORD your God, who brought you out of the land of Egypt, to be your God: I am the LORD your God.

Revolt of Korah, Dathan, and Abiram

16 Now Korah son of Izhar son of Kohath son of Levi, along with Dathan and Abiram sons of Eliab, and On son of Peleth— descendants of Reuben—took 2two hundred fifty Israelite men, leaders of the congregation, chosen from the assembly, well-known men,*a*

---

a Cn: Heb *and they confronted Moses, and two hundred fifty men . . . well-known men*

15.24 *According to the ordinance*, i.e., vv. 1–16. 15.25 It is the priest who makes *atonement* for the ones who are in error; see Ex 29.10–37; Lev 1.4; Num 8.10–11. *An offering by fire.* See 15.3. 15.28 See 15.25. 15.30– 31 Intentional sins. One who *acts high-handedly* sins boldly; see the translation *boldly* for *high-handedly* in 33.3; Ex 14.8. *Cut off.* See 9.13. Here execution is plainly meant; see 15.35–36, esp. *just as* in v. 36. 15.32–36 See the similar story in Lev 24.10–23. Intentional violation of the sabbath carries the death penalty (Ex 31.14–15; 35.2). 15.34 *They put him in custody* until a decision was made; see also Lev 24.12. 15.35–36 The man was stoned outside the camp so as not to disturb the sanctity of the camp; see also Lev 24.14, 23; 1 Kings 21.10, 23–24. 15.37–41 *Fringes on . . . garments.* Cf. Deut 22.12. 15.38 The fringes apparently resembled locks of hair; the term rendered *fringe* here is translated "lock (of hair)" in Ezek 8.3. Fringe on garments is known elsewhere in the ancient Near East from pictorial representations. Fringes are still worn on the prayer shawl, or *tallit*, of Orthodox Jewish men.

Blue, or violet, the same color as some of the hangings of the tabernacle enclosure; see 4.5–12. 15.41 For variations on the formulaic sayings in this verse, see, e.g., Ex 6.6–7; 20.2; Lev 26.13; Deut 5.6; cf. Gen 15.7.

16.1–40 In this section on the revolt of Korah, Dathan, and Abiram, there is some mixing of traditions: the complaints are against Moses or Aaron or both; the complaints are about secular or sacred leadership; either Levites or Reubenites or even the whole community are the rebels; the rebels are swallowed whole or are burned by fire from the Lord. Commentators have divided these stories into two major strands (with subplots within them): a Priestly strand with the story of Korah's rebellion and an old epic strand with a secular rebellion led by Reubenites (see Introduction). The two strands are combined by vv. 1, 24, 27a, 32b. Cf. Deut 11.6; Ps 106.16–18. 16.1 For *Korah's* genealogy, see Ex 6.16–21. See also the titles to Pss 42; 44–49; 84– 85; 87–88. Korah is apparently the eponymous ancestor of a group of temple singers (1 Chr 6.16–38). 16.2 *Well-known men,* lit. "men of name." A similar

and they confronted Moses. ³They assembled against Moses and against Aaron, and said to them, "You have gone too far! All the congregation are holy, every one of them, and the LORD is among them. So why then do you exalt yourselves above the assembly of the LORD?" ⁴When Moses heard it, he fell on his face. ⁵Then he said to Korah and all his company, "In the morning the LORD will make known who is his, and who is holy, and who will be allowed to approach him; the one whom he will choose he will allow to approach him. ⁶Do this: take censers, Korah and all your*a* company, ⁷and tomorrow put fire in them, and lay incense on them before the LORD; and the man whom the LORD chooses shall be the holy one. You Levites have gone too far!" ⁸Then Moses said to Korah, "Hear now, you Levites! ⁹Is it too little for you that the God of Israel has separated you from the congregation of Israel, to allow you to approach him in order to perform the duties of the LORD's tabernacle, and to stand before the congregation and serve them? ¹⁰He has allowed you to approach him, and all your brother Levites with you; yet you seek the priesthood as well! ¹¹Therefore you and all your company have gathered together against the LORD. What is Aaron that you rail against him?"

12 Moses sent for Dathan and Abiram sons of Eliab; but they said, "We will not come! ¹³Is

it too little that you have brought us up out of a land flowing with milk and honey to kill us in the wilderness, that you must also lord it over us? ¹⁴It is clear you have not brought us into a land flowing with milk and honey, or given us an inheritance of fields and vineyards. Would you put out the eyes of these men? We will not come!"

15 Moses was very angry and said to the LORD, "Pay no attention to their offering. I have not taken one donkey from them, and I have not harmed any one of them." ¹⁶And Moses said to Korah, "As for you and all your company, be present tomorrow before the LORD, you and they and Aaron; ¹⁷and let each one of you take his censer, and put incense on it, and each one of you present his censer before the LORD, two hundred fifty censers; you also, and Aaron, each his censer." ¹⁸So each man took his censer, and they put fire in the censers and laid incense on them, and they stood at the entrance of the tent of meeting with Moses and Aaron. ¹⁹Then Korah assembled the whole congregation against them at the entrance of the tent of meeting. And the glory of the LORD appeared to the whole congregation.

20 Then the LORD spoke to Moses and to Aaron, saying: ²¹Separate yourselves from this

---

a Heb *his*

phrase is used in Gen 6.4, there translated "warriors of renown"; 1 Chr 5.24; 12.30. In Job 30.8, the "disreputable brood" are "those without name" in Hebrew. **16.3** There are actually two levels of priestly conflict in this Korah narrative: on one level, Korah argues that *all the congregation are holy, every one of them, and the LORD is among them,* thus denying any prerogatives the descendants of Levi might have, whether Aaronite priests or Levites. (See 5.3; 15.40; Ex 19.5–6; Deut 7.6; 14.2, 21a; 28.9; Isa 61.6). On this level, we assume Korah and his followers are not Levites (see 27.1–3, where a Manassite's family feel they must defend their father against any suspicion that he was part of Korah's group) and that the censer test is a matter of nonlevitical people using censers, something that had been a prerogative of the Levites. On a second level, however, Korah's group is addressed as Levites attempting to usurp the prerogatives of the Aaronite priesthood (vv. 1, 7b, 8–11), and the test is one of lesser-ranked Levites using the censers of the Aaronite priesthood (see v. 40; 1 Chr 6.49; 2 Chr 26.16–21). With Korah's complaint here, cf. 12.1–2. *Exalt yourselves.* See 16.13; cf. Ex 2.14. **16.4** *Fell on his face.* See 14.5; 16.22, 45; 20.6. **16.5** *Approach him,* i.e., approach the altar. **16.6–7** The *censers* were apparently trays holding coals onto which in-

cense could be placed (see Ex 25.38; 27.3; 37.23; 38.3; Lev 10.1–2; 16.12). *Before the LORD,* at the entrance to the tent of meeting; see vv. 18–19. **16.9** On the Levites' prescribed *duties,* see 1.47–54; 3; 4; 8. **16.10** *You seek the priesthood as well!* See 3.5–10; 8.5–22, esp. vv. 19, 22. **16.11** *What is Aaron . . . him?* Cf. Ex 16.8. **16.12– 14** The Reubenites' complaint. It is logical that Reubenites should lead a civil revolt since they had once been the preeminent tribe; see Gen 35.22–26; 49.3–4. **16.13–14** This is a typical complaint narrative; see note on 11.1–3. Here it is Moses' leadership on the march that is in question. **16.13** *Land . . . milk and honey,* here used anomalously of Egypt instead of Canaan; see 13.27. *Lord it over us.* See 16.3; 22.14. **16.14** *Put out the eyes,* i.e., deceive them. Cf. the modern phrase "pull the wool over the eyes." **16.15** *Pay no attention to their offering,* a metaphor for withholding favor; see the rejection of Cain in Gen 4. *I have not . . . them.* Cf. 1 Sam 12.1–5. **16.16–17** These verses repeat the information in vv. 6–7, but the addition of Aaron moves the story from the level of congregation vs. Levites to Levites vs. Aaronite priests; see note on 16.3. **16.16** *Before the LORD,* i.e., at the entrance to the tent of meeting; see vv. 18–19. **16.19** *The glory of the LORD.* See note on 9.15–16. **16.21** The Lord threatens to *con-*

congregation, so that I may consume them in a moment. 22 They fell on their faces, and said, "O God, the God of the spirits of all flesh, shall one person sin and you become angry with the whole congregation?"

23 And the LORD spoke to Moses, saying: 24 Say to the congregation: Get away from the dwellings of Korah, Dathan, and Abiram. 25 So Moses got up and went to Dathan and Abiram; the elders of Israel followed him. 26 He said to the congregation, "Turn away from the tents of these wicked men, and touch nothing of theirs, or you will be swept away for all their sins." 27 So they got away from the dwellings of Korah, Dathan, and Abiram; and Dathan and Abiram came out and stood at the entrance of their tents, together with their wives, their children, and their little ones. 28 And Moses said, "This is how you shall know that the LORD has sent me to do all these works; it has not been of my own accord: 29 If these people die a natural death, or if a natural fate comes on them, then the LORD has not sent me. 30 But if the LORD creates something new, and the ground opens its mouth and swallows them up, with all that belongs to them, and they go down alive into Sheol, then you shall know that these men have despised the LORD."

31 As soon as he finished speaking all these words, the ground under them was split apart. 32 The earth opened its mouth and swallowed them up, along with their households—everyone who belonged to Korah and all their goods. 33 So they with all that belonged to them went down alive into Sheol; the earth closed over them, and they perished from the midst of the assembly. 34 All Israel around them fled at their outcry, for they said, "The earth will swallow us too!" 35 And fire came out from the LORD and consumed the two hundred fifty men offering the incense.

36 a Then the LORD spoke to Moses, saying: 37 Tell Eleazar son of Aaron the priest to take the censers out of the blaze; then scatter the fire far and wide. 38 For the censers of these sinners have become holy at the cost of their lives. Make them into hammered plates as a covering for the altar, for they presented them before the LORD and they became holy. Thus they shall be a sign to the Israelites. 39 So Eleazar the priest took the bronze censers that had been presented by those who were burned; and they were hammered out as a covering for the altar— 40 a reminder to the Israelites that

_a_ Ch 17.1 in Heb

---

sume the congregation; see also 16.45; 14.11–12. _In a moment._ This generation will die in the desert, 14.28–30, but here the Lord threatens to kill them immediately. **16.22** _Fell on their faces,_ see 16.4; 14.5. _The God of the spirits of all flesh_ is used elsewhere only in 27.16. But the Hebrew word for "spirit" also means "breath," and the Lord is frequently described as the giver and taker of human breath. See Gen 2.7 (with a different Hebrew word for "breath"); Isa 42.5. _Shall one person sin._ Dathan and Abiram are not at issue here in this strand of the narrative. Cf. Abraham's intercession in Gen 18.23–33. On prophetic intercession, see 11.10–15. **16.24** The number of the punished is reduced to the rebels and their families, in response to Moses and Aaron's intercession (v. 22). The word for _dwellings_ (singular in Hebrew) here and in v. 27 is the same as the word commonly used for the Lord's tabernacle and is elsewhere never used in the singular to mean a secular dwelling. Commentators have suggested that this part of the text has been disturbed by the attempt to connect Korah and his followers to the story of the punishment of Dathan and Abiram. **16.25** On the _elders_ who accompany Moses, see 11.16–30. **16.26** The people are told to _touch nothing_ that belongs to the rebels because their sins are polluting. Elsewhere, similar commands convey the belief that holiness itself is dangerous, that improper contact with it is polluting and life-threatening; see Ex 19.12–13; Num 4.15;

2 Sam 6.6–7; 1 Chr 13.9–10. Even seeing holy things can be dangerous: Num 4.20; cf. the Hebrew of 1 Sam 6.19. **16.27–33** These verses express the belief in corporate guilt and in the family as the extension of the (usually male) head of the family; see Josh 7.24–26. **16.30, 33** _Sheol_ is the underworld home of the dead (see Gen 37.35; 1 Sam 28.11–14; Isa 14.9–11). In Isa 5.14 Sheol opens its mouth to eat the doomed. **16.32** Dathan and Abiram are not mentioned here; instead we have only _everyone who belonged to Korah._ Commentators have assumed this phrase displaced the mention of Dathan and Abiram in an editor's attempt to combine the two strands; cf. Deut 11.6; Ps 106.17. This verse does not say that Korah himself was killed, but cf. 16.40; 26.10–11. **16.35** The _two hundred fifty,_ who are elsewhere "the company of Korah," are killed separately by fire from the Lord; see 11.1. Cf. Lev 10.1–2. In Num 16.17, it is assumed that the two hundred and fifty are Levites; each has his own censer. V. 2, however, implies they came from all the tribes; see 27.1–3. **16.37–39** It is _Eleazar_ instead of Aaron who has contact with the censers, perhaps because of a rule like the one in Lev 21.10–11. See also Num 19.3. _Become holy . . . lives._ The censers are holy because they were presented before the Lord, but since they were offered by those who were not qualified to offer incense, the offering was at the cost of those men's lives. These verses present an etiology of the bronze covering of the

no outsider, who is not of the descendants of Aaron, shall approach to offer incense before the Lord, so as not to become like Korah and his company—just as the Lord had said to him through Moses.

41 On the next day, however, the whole congregation of the Israelites rebelled against Moses and against Aaron, saying, "You have killed the people of the Lord." 42And when the congregation had assembled against them, Moses and Aaron turned toward the tent of meeting; the cloud had covered it and the glory of the Lord appeared. 43Then Moses and Aaron came to the front of the tent of meeting, 44and the Lord spoke to Moses, saying, 45"Get away from this congregation, so that I may consume them in a moment." And they fell on their faces. 46Moses said to Aaron, "Take your censer, put fire on it from the altar and lay incense on it, and carry it quickly to the congregation and make atonement for them. For wrath has gone out from the Lord; the plague has begun." 47So Aaron took it as Moses had ordered, and ran into the middle of the assembly, where the plague had already begun among the people. He put on the incense, and made atonement for the people. 48He stood between the dead and the living; and the plague was stopped. 49Those who died

by the plague were fourteen thousand seven hundred, besides those who died in the affair of Korah. 50When the plague was stopped, Aaron returned to Moses at the entrance of the tent of meeting.

The Budding of Aaron's Rod

17 *The Lord spoke to Moses, saying: 2Speak to the Israelites, and get twelve staffs from them, one for each ancestral house, from all the leaders of their ancestral houses. Write each man's name on his staff, 3and write Aaron's name on the staff of Levi. For there shall be one staff for the head of each ancestral house. 4Place them in the tent of meeting before the covenant,*b* where I meet with you. 5And the staff of the man whom I choose shall sprout; thus I will put a stop to the complaints of the Israelites that they continually make against you. 6Moses spoke to the Israelites; and all their leaders gave him staffs, one for each leader, according to their ancestral houses, twelve staffs; and the staff of Aaron was among theirs. 7So Moses placed the staffs before the Lord in the tent of the covenant.*b*

8 When Moses went into the tent of the covenant*b* on the next day, the staff of Aaron

___
a Ch 17.16 in Heb   *b* Or *treaty,* or *testimony;* Heb *eduth*

___

altar that is different from that in Ex 27.1–2; 38.1–2. **16.40** This event has served to reinforce the prerogatives of Aaron and his descendants; thus, commentators have assumed that the Korah narrative reflects conflicts in later rival priestly groups, with Aaronite priests claiming supremacy based on this story and others like it (see notes on 16.3; 12.2).

16.41–50 Revolt of the whole congregation; see note on 11.1–3. Since it is *the whole congregation* that is at fault, the intercession in 16.22 is no longer valid. The complaint this time concerns the deaths of Korah, Dathan, Abiram, and their families and followers. **16.41** *You have killed the people of the Lord.* Due to an extra pronoun "you" for emphasis in the Hebrew, one might translate "It is you who have killed the people of the Lord," i.e., Moses and Aaron, not God. **16.42** On *tent, cloud,* and *glory,* see 7.89; 12.5; note on 9.15–16. **16.45** On the Lord's *consuming* the congregation, see 16.21. *Fell on their faces.* See 16.4; 14.5. **16.46** The priest makes *atonement;* see 15.25. Incense is not the usual medium of atonement, but it is fitting in this story; cf. 5.21; 21.6–9. On the Lord's *wrath* and *plague,* see 11.33. **16.48** See Lev 21.10–11; such an instruction underlines the seriousness of Aaron's act here. **16.49** *Those who died . . . Korah,* i.e., the two hundred and fifty (v. 35).

17.1–13 Another proof that the tribe of Levi and

Aaron as their leader are chosen above the rest of the community in ritual affairs, necessary because of the renewed rebellion in 16.41–50. **17.2** The *staff* referred to here is a symbol of a leader's authority (see Jer 48.17) and as the symbol of a tribal leader had come itself to mean "tribe," as in 1.16 and elsewhere. The double meaning of the word is appropriate here since the staff/tribe that buds is the one chosen by the Lord. *Leaders.* See 16.2, where they were part of the rebellion. **17.2–3** The command to Moses to *write each man's name on his staff* assumes Moses was literate (see also Ex 17.14; 24.4; 34.27; Num 33.2; Deut 31.9). **17.3** For Aaron's descent from *Levi,* see Ex 6.16–20. There is no hint here of the rivalry between Aaronite priests and other Levites; see notes on 16.3; 16.40. **17.4** *In the tent . . . covenant,* i.e., in front of the ark. See Ex 31.18; 34.29; also Ex 25.16, 21; 40.20; on the name "ark of the covenant," see, e.g., Ex 30.26; 40.3; Num 4.5; 7.89. *Where I meet with you.* See 7.89. **17.5** *The man whom I choose,* i.e., to approach the Lord in ritual; see 16.5, 7. The immediate referent for the *complaints* is 16.41–50, but see note on 11.1–3 for the complaint stories in general. **17.6–7** Moses carries out the Lord's commands, although the narrative does not report the writing of the names. **17.7** *Before the Lord* must mean "before the ark" here; see 17.4. **17.7–8** For *tent of the covenant,* see also 9.15; 18.2. For the tent in general, see

for the house of Levi had sprouted. It put forth buds, produced blossoms, and bore ripe almonds. ⁹Then Moses brought out all the staffs from before the LORD to all the Israelites; and they looked, and each man took his staff. ¹⁰And the LORD said to Moses, "Put back the staff of Aaron before the covenant,ᵃ to be kept as a warning to rebels, so that you may make an end of their complaints against me, or else they will die." ¹¹Moses did so; just as the LORD commanded him, so he did.

12 The Israelites said to Moses, "We are perishing; we are lost, all of us are lost! ¹³Everyone who approaches the tabernacle of the LORD will die. Are we all to perish?"

Responsibility of Priests and Levites

18 The LORD said to Aaron: You and your sons and your ancestral house with you shall bear responsibility for offenses connected with the sanctuary, while you and your sons alone shall bear responsibility for offenses connected with the priesthood. ²So bring with you also your brothers of the tribe of Levi, your ancestral tribe, in order that they may be joined to you, and serve you while you and your sons with you are in front of the tent of the covenant.ᵃ ³They shall perform duties for you and

for the whole tent. But they must not approach either the utensils of the sanctuary or the altar, otherwise both they and you will die. ⁴They are attached to you in order to perform the duties of the tent of meeting, for all the service of the tent; no outsider shall approach you. ⁵You yourselves shall perform the duties of the sanctuary and the duties of the altar, so that wrath may never again come upon the Israelites. ⁶It is I who now take your brother Levites from among the Israelites; they are now yours as a gift, dedicated to the LORD, to perform the service of the tent of meeting. ⁷But you and your sons with you shall diligently perform your priestly duties in all that concerns the altar and the area behind the curtain. I give your priesthood as a gift;ᵇ any outsider who approaches shall be put to death.

The Priests' Portion

8 The LORD spoke to Aaron: I have given you charge of the offerings made to me, all the holy gifts of the Israelites; I have given them to you and your sons as a priestly portion due you in perpetuity. ⁹This shall be yours from the most holy things, reserved from the fire:

a Or *treaty,* or *testimony;* Heb *eduth*   *b* Heb *as a service of gift*

---

notes on 1.1; 2.1–34. **17.8** For other stories of Aaron's miraculous staff, see Ex 7.8–8.19. Narratives of blossoming staffs, clubs, or spears are found in many cultures. **17.10** The Hebrew word for *warning* is the same as the word translated *sign* in 16.38. *Against me.* Cf. v. 5 ("you," plural in Hebrew); Ex 16.8. **17.12–13** The Israelites are convinced that only the tribe of Levi should approach the most holy parts of the tabernacle, but they take the warning in v. 10 so seriously that they become afraid that they will always be in danger of trespassing and dying. These verses serve as an introduction to ch. 18, where the Levites are said to guard the tent from trespass by unqualified persons (18.21–22). **18.1–7** See also 1.50–53; 3.5–10, 14–38; 16. **18.1** A distinction is made in this chapter between Aaron and his descendants, on the one hand, and the rest of the tribe of Levi, on the other. See notes on 3.5–10; 16.3; 16.40; cf. Ezek 44.10–16. *Bear responsibility for offenses,* i.e., suffer the consequences for any offense. This charge is meant to allay the fears expressed in 17.12–13. For offenses connected with the priesthood, see, e.g., v. 3; Ex 28.38, 42–43; 30.20–21; Lev 10.8–9; 16.2; 21.16–23. **18.2** The Levites are *joined to* Aaron and his descendants, a pun in Hebrew on the name Levi (see Gen 29.34), and they *serve* them; see 3.5–10; 8.14–22. *Tent of the covenant.* See 17.7–8. **18.3** The *altar* is the bronze altar; see notes on 3.29, 31; 4.13–14; 16.38–39. *Both they and you will die,* i.e., the priests

will die along with the trespassers, because the priests did not guard the sanctuary properly. See also 4.5–15. **18.4** It is the duty of the Levites to keep nonlevitical people from the most sacred areas; see 1.51. **18.5** For ritual as a means of avoiding the Lord's *wrath,* see 16.46. **18.6** For the Levites as a *gift* to the Aaronites, see 3.9; 8.19. **18.7** The *area behind the curtain* is where the holy of holies is, with the ark and the gold altar; see note on 3.29, 31.

18.8–20 The Aaronite priests' portion. This section stipulates that the priests are to receive, except for those portions that are burned on the altar, all of the grain offerings, sin offerings, and guilt offerings, which may be eaten by any Aaronite males (vv. 9–10). Further, the contributed part of the offerings of well-being, the best of the oil, wine, and grain, the first-fruit offerings, "devoted" things, and the firstborn of clean animals can be eaten by any ritually clean member of an Aaronite household, male or female. Finally, the redemption price for firstborn human beings and unclean animals also is to go to the priests (vv. 15–16). See 1 Sam 2.12–17 for a narrative involving the misuse of this provision. **18.8** The Lord has ordained that part of the Israelites' offerings is to be a means of support for the priesthood and the sanctuary. The word translated *charge* here might also be translated "that which is kept back" from the fire, i.e., held back for the priests. **18.9–10** The *most holy things* include the offer-

every offering of theirs that they render to me as a most holy thing, whether grain offering, sin offering, or guilt offering, shall belong to you and your sons. ¹⁰As a most holy thing you shall eat it; every male may eat it; it shall be holy to you. ¹¹This also is yours: I have given to you, together with your sons and daughters, as a perpetual due, whatever is set aside from the gifts of all the elevation offerings of the Israelites; everyone who is clean in your house may eat them. ¹²All the best of the oil and all the best of the wine and of the grain, the choice produce that they give to the LORD, I have given to you. ¹³The first fruits of all that is in their land, which they bring to the LORD, shall be yours; everyone who is clean in your house may eat of it. ¹⁴Every devoted thing in Israel shall be yours. ¹⁵The first issue of the womb of all creatures, human and animal, which is offered to the LORD, shall be yours; but the firstborn of human beings you shall redeem, and the firstborn of unclean animals you shall redeem. ¹⁶Their redemption price, reckoned from one month of age, you shall fix at five shekels of silver, according to the shekel of the sanctuary (that is, twenty gerahs). ¹⁷But the firstborn of a cow, or the firstborn of a sheep, or the firstborn of a goat, you shall not redeem; they are holy. You shall dash their blood on the altar, and shall turn their fat into smoke as an offering by fire for a pleasing odor to the LORD; ¹⁸but their flesh shall be yours, just as the breast that is elevated and as the

right thigh are yours. ¹⁹All the holy offerings that the Israelites present to the LORD I have given to you, together with your sons and daughters, as a perpetual due; it is a covenant of salt forever before the LORD for you and your descendants as well. ²⁰Then the LORD said to Aaron: You shall have no allotment in their land, nor shall you have any share among them; I am your share and your possession among the Israelites.

21 To the Levites I have given every tithe in Israel for a possession in return for the service that they perform, the service in the tent of meeting. ²²From now on the Israelites shall no longer approach the tent of meeting, or else they will incur guilt and die. ²³But the Levites shall perform the service of the tent of meeting, and they shall bear responsibility for their own offenses; it shall be a perpetual statute throughout your generations. But among the Israelites they shall have no allotment, ²⁴because I have given to the Levites as their portion the tithe of the Israelites, which they set apart as an offering to the LORD. Therefore I have said of them that they shall have no allotment among the Israelites.

25 Then the LORD spoke to Moses, saying: ²⁶You shall speak to the Levites, saying: When you receive from the Israelites the tithe that I have given you from them for your portion, you shall set apart an offering from it to the LORD, a tithe of the tithe. ²⁷It shall be reckoned to you as your gift, the same as the grain

ings listed in v. 9; see Lev 6.14–17. Note the absence of the burnt offering, of which only the skin goes to the priest (Lev 7.8). For that which is not *reserved from the fire*, see, e.g., Lev 2.2, 9, 16; 3.3–5; 5.12; 6.15–16; 7.3–5. **18.11** *Whatever is set aside*, i.e., contributed to the priests. *Elevation offerings*. See 8.13. For the parts set aside from elevation offerings, see, e.g., 18.18; Lev 7.28–36; Num 6.19–20; and the offerings of well-being listed in 6.17–18. *Everyone who is clean*. See Lev 22.3–7; 1 Sam 21.1–6. *In your house*. See Lev 22.10–16. **18.12–13** See also Deut 18.4; Ex 23.19a; Num 15.17–21. **18.14** *Devoted thing*. See Lev 27.21, 28. Here it is devoted to the service of the Lord, but something "devoted" is often "devoted to destruction" or "put to the ban," including in other circumstances human beings (see, e.g., Lev 27.29; Deut 13.12–18; Josh 6.15–21). **18.15–16** On the *firstborn* and redemption of firstborn males, see 3.12, 15, 40–51. Here in Num 18 there is no specification of the sex of the firstborn human being who is to be redeemed. *Their redemption price* refers to the redemption of human beings. The redemption price of unclean animals depended on the valuation by the priest (see Lev 27.11–13, 27). *Shekel of*

the sanctuary. See note on 3.46–48. **18.17–18.** Cf. the description of offerings of well-being in Ex 29.26–28; Lev 7.28–36; 10.14–15. The firstborn of all clean animals belong to the Lord (Lev 27.26) and they are here assigned to the priests as part of their portion. *A pleasing odor to the LORD*. See 15.3. **18.19** The phrase *covenant of salt* apparently refers to an ancient custom of sharing food as part of a covenant ceremony (see Gen 31.54; Ex 24.9–11; cf. Ezra 4.14). Salt was to be added to all sacrifices according to Lev 2.13; see also Ezek 43.18–24. A covenant of salt was perhaps one that could not be broken (see 2 Chr 13.5). **18.20** The Aaronite priests are supposed to have no tribal inheritance; see 26.62; Josh 14.3. Their only support is cultic donations. Cities are provided for all those of the tribe of Levi, however, so that they will have homes and pasture land (but no agricultural land); see 35.1–8; Josh 21.1–42; 1 Chr 6.54–81. Cf. 1 Kings 2.26. **18.21–32** Those Levites other than the Aaronite priests have as their portion the Israelites' tithes, here of agricultural products only; see also Neh 10.37; 13.5, 12. Cf. Lev 27.30–33; 2 Chr 31.6; Deut 14.22–29; 26.12–15. **18.22** *Approach*. See 17.12–13; also 1.51. **18.23–24** See

of the threshing floor and the fullness of the wine press. 28Thus you also shall set apart an offering to the LORD from all the tithes that you receive from the Israelites; and from them you shall give the LORD's offering to the priest Aaron. 29Out of all the gifts to you, you shall set apart every offering due to the LORD; the best of all of them is the part to be consecrated. 30Say also to them: When you have set apart the best of it, then the rest shall be reckoned to the Levites as produce of the threshing floor, and as produce of the wine press. 31You may eat it in any place, you and your households; for it is your payment for your service in the tent of meeting. 32You shall incur no guilt by reason of it, when you have offered the best of it. But you shall not profane the holy gifts of the Israelites, on pain of death.

Ceremony of the Red Heifer

19 The LORD spoke to Moses and Aaron, saying: 2This is a statute of the law that the LORD has commanded: Tell the Israelites to bring you a red heifer without defect, in which there is no blemish and on which no

yoke has been laid. 3You shall give it to the priest Eleazar, and it shall be taken outside the camp and slaughtered in his presence. 4The priest Eleazar shall take some of its blood with his finger and sprinkle it seven times towards the front of the tent of meeting. 5Then the heifer shall be burned in his sight; its skin, its flesh, and its blood, with its dung, shall be burned. 6The priest shall take cedarwood, hyssop, and crimson material, and throw them into the fire in which the heifer is burning. 7Then the priest shall wash his clothes and bathe his body in water, and afterwards he may come into the camp; but the priest shall remain unclean until evening. 8The one who burns the heifer[a] shall wash his clothes in water and bathe his body in water; he shall remain unclean until evening. 9Then someone who is clean shall gather up the ashes of the heifer, and deposit them outside the camp in a clean place; and they shall be kept for the congregation of the Israelites for the water for cleansing. It is a purification offering. 10The

---

a Heb it

18.20. **18.25–29** The Levites themselves must tithe and pay their offering to the Aaronite priests. **18.30–32** Once the Levites have tithed, their "income" is like any other Israelite's. Even though the tithes are technically offered to the Lord and are therefore sacred, the Levites may eat their portion without incurring guilt as long as they have first offered their tithe to the priests. If, however, they have not been faithful in their treatment of their "income," its essentially sacred nature will ensure their deaths.

19.1–22 31.19–24 assumes this chapter; see also Lev 5.3–6; 21.1–4, 10–11; 22.3–7; Num 5.1–3; 6.6–12; 9.6–7, 10–11. The need for ritual after contact with a corpse is felt in many cultures, including other ancient Near Eastern ones. **19.2** The *heifer* here is simply a cow and not necessarily a young one that has not yet calved, as is generally implied by the English term "heifer." Cf. the use of the same Hebrew word in 1 Sam 6.7, 10; Job 21.10. It is not clear why the animal should be red (or brownish-red, cf. Gen 25.29–34) unless it is the color of blood and so, like the *crimson material* in v. 6, symbolically increases the purifying blood in the ritual. Red is a common color choice for sacrificial animals in the ancient world. *Without defect . . . no blemish* (see also, e.g., Lev 4.28; 14.10; 22.20; 21.17–23 for the priests themselves). The cow to be used is one *on which no yoke has been laid;* certain special animals in biblical rituals were to be those that had never been used for profane work; see Deut 15.19; 21.3–4 (a different word for "heifer," meaning a young cow); 1 Sam 6.7. **19.3** *Eleazar,* Aaron's son. See, e.g., Ex 6.23; Num 3.1–4; 16.37–40. That the entire ceremony of this cow

is to take place *outside the camp* makes it something other than ordinary sacrifice, which was performed at the altar. The uniqueness of this ritual must lie in its connection with the pollution associated with corpses. *In his presence,* i.e., the priest must officiate. **19.4** *Seven times.* Seven is often a sacred number in the Bible (e.g., Gen 2.3; 7.2; Lev 4.6; 8.11; Num 23.1–2). *Towards the front of the tent of meeting* (the eastern side), i.e., towards the Lord. **19.5** The dung and skin of a sacrificial animal are sometimes burned (Ex 29.14; Lev 4.11–12; 8.17; 16.27), but never its blood. See 19.2. **19.6** On *cedarwood, hyssop, and crimson material,* see Lev 14.4–6, 49–53; cf. Num 19.18. Cedarwood is perhaps a symbol for endurance since it preserves. *Hyssop* may not be a correct translation for the next term since hyssop is not native to Palestine, but some aromatic, climbing plant is meant (1 Kings 4.33; see also Ex 12.22; Ps 51.7). The crimson material may simply be another symbol of purifying blood; see note on 19.2. Similar materials (aromatic woods, crimson yarn) were used in rituals elsewhere in the ancient world. **19.7–10a** The priest who burns the cow and the person who gathers its ashes must cleanse themselves and remain ritually unclean until evening; see, e.g., Lev 11.24–25, 28, 40; 15; 16.26, 28; 22.3–7. **19.9** The cow's ashes have been made sacred because the cow was an offering (a *purification offering;* see 8.6–7); no one unclean may deal with the ashes and the ashes should be kept ritually clean. *Water for cleansing,* sometimes translated "water of impurity," but here correctly identified as water to *cleanse* from impurity (see 8.6–7; also 31.23; Zech 13.1). On special mixtures of water used for rit-

one who gathers the ashes of the heifer shall wash his clothes and be unclean until evening.

This shall be a perpetual statute for the Israelites and for the alien residing among them. 11Those who touch the dead body of any human being shall be unclean seven days. 12They shall purify themselves with the water on the third day and on the seventh day, and so be clean; but if they do not purify themselves on the third day and on the seventh day, they will not become clean. 13All who touch a corpse, the body of a human being who has died, and do not purify themselves, defile the tabernacle of the LORD; such persons shall be cut off from Israel. Since water for cleansing was not dashed on them, they remain unclean; their uncleanness is still on them.

14 This is the law when someone dies in a tent: everyone who comes into the tent, and everyone who is in the tent, shall be unclean seven days. 15And every open vessel with no cover fastened on it is unclean. 16Whoever in the open field touches one who has been killed by a sword, or who has died naturally,ᵃ or a human bone, or a grave, shall be unclean seven days. 17For the unclean they shall take some ashes of the burnt purification offering, and running water shall be added in a vessel; 18then a clean person shall take hyssop, dip it in the water, and sprinkle it on the tent, on all the furnishings, on the persons who were there, and on whoever touched the bone, the slain, the corpse, or the grave. 19The clean person shall sprinkle the unclean ones on the third day and on the seventh day, thus purifying them on the seventh day. Then they shall wash their clothes and bathe themselves in water, and at evening they shall be clean. 20Any who are unclean but do not purify themselves, those persons shall be cut off from the assembly, for they have defiled the sanctuary of the LORD. Since the water for cleansing has not been dashed on them, they are unclean.

21 It shall be a perpetual statute for them. The one who sprinkles the water for cleansing shall wash his clothes, and whoever touches the water for cleansing shall be unclean until evening. 22Whatever the unclean person touches shall be unclean, and anyone who touches it shall be unclean until evening.

The Waters of Meribah

20 The Israelites, the whole congregation, came into the wilderness of Zin in the first month, and the people stayed in Kadesh. Miriam died there, and was buried there.

---

a Heb lacks *naturally*

---

ual purposes, cf. also Ex 32.20; Num 5.16–28. **19.10** Contact with the sacred can make one "unclean." See 16.26. Both pollution and holiness are outside everyday life and so both require ritual attention before the people in question are once more "clean," i.e., before they can reenter their usual, mundane life for which they must be untouched by the unusual. Holiness can be dangerous (see Ex 19.10–15; 21–24; Num 16.26) and, like pollution, can even be considered contagious, though this is rare (Lev 6.25–29; Ezek 44.19; 46.20; cf. Hag 2.12–13). See 16.37–39, where only Eleazar the priest is to touch the censers made holy by the fire. A *perpetual statute.* See also 19.21; 10.8; 15.15; 18.23. **19.11–22** Uses of the water for cleansing, for people defiled by contact with a corpse or other vestige of human death. See also 31.19–24. **19.11** For people unclean through contact with a corpse, see note on 19.1–22. For a seven-day period of "uncleanness," see also the birth of a male child, Lev 12.2; skin disease, Lev 14.9; menstruation and bodily discharges, Lev 15. **19.12** *With the water,* Hebrew "with it," either the water or the collection of ashes (vv. 9–10). **19.13** Such people would *defile the tabernacle* (see Lev 15.31) because, since the camp is holy (see 5.1–4), any possible contact with uncleanness could endanger the holiness of the tabernacle at the center. *Cut off.* See 9.13. **19.14–22** A repetition of information in vv. 11–13, but with more detail. **19.14–15** The uncleanness of a *tent* (or, probably, any dwelling; the Septuagint translates "house, dwelling") where someone has died is like that from contact with a corpse (see v. 11). The uncleanness is envisioned as contagion that can spread even to open containers. **19.16** This verse treats contact with human death in an environment opposite from the dwelling of vv. 14–15, an *open field.* **19.17–20** Instructions for making and using the water for cleansing (v. 9). **19.17** The *burnt purification offering* is that of the red cow, vv. 2–10, and the *ashes* are mentioned in vv. 9–10. *Running water,* Hebrew "living water," is water that flows continuously, as from a spring, and cannot become stagnant. See also the various translations in Gen 26.19; Lev 14.5, 50; 15.13; Song 4.15; Jer 2.13; 17.13; Zech 14.8. **19.18–19** For *hyssop,* see 19.6. Here the purification process is a matter of being sprinkled with the water for cleansing, of washing clothes, and of bathing. The instruction in v. 12 is less explicit. **19.20** See 19.13. **19.21–22** See 19.10.

20.1–13 This narrative takes place after the forty years of wandering. **20.1** V. 1 presents many chronological and geographical problems. *Wilderness of Zin.* See 13.21. *In the first month,* but the year is not specified. Most commentators propose the fortieth year because of the date of Aaron's death given in 33.38. *The people stayed in Kadesh,* but the length of time is not

2 Now there was no water for the congregation; so they gathered together against Moses and against Aaron. ³The people quarreled with Moses and said, "Would that we had died when our kindred died before the LORD! ⁴Why have you brought the assembly of the LORD into this wilderness for us and our livestock to die here? ⁵Why have you brought us up out of Egypt, to bring us to this wretched place? It is no place for grain, or figs, or vines, or pomegranates; and there is no water to drink." ⁶Then Moses and Aaron went away from the assembly to the entrance of the tent of meeting; they fell on their faces, and the glory of the LORD appeared to them. ⁷The LORD spoke to Moses, saying: ⁸Take the staff, and assemble the congregation, you and your brother Aaron, and command the rock before their eyes to yield its water. Thus you shall bring water out of the rock for them; thus you shall provide drink for the congregation and their livestock.

9 So Moses took the staff from before the LORD, as he had commanded him. ¹⁰Moses and Aaron gathered the assembly together before the rock, and he said to them, "Listen, you rebels, shall we bring water for you out of this rock?" ¹¹Then Moses lifted up his hand and struck the rock twice with his staff; water came out abundantly, and the congregation and their livestock drank. ¹²But the LORD said to Moses and Aaron, "Because you did not trust in me, to show my holiness before the eyes of the Israelites, therefore you shall not bring this assembly into the land that I have given them." ¹³These are the waters of Meribah,ᵃ where the people of Israel quarreled with the LORD, and by which he showed his holiness.

Passage through Edom Refused

14 Moses sent messengers from Kadesh to the king of Edom, "Thus says your brother Israel: You know all the adversity that has befallen us: ¹⁵how our ancestors went down to Egypt, and we lived in Egypt a long time; and the Egyptians oppressed us and our ancestors; ¹⁶and when we cried to the LORD, he heard our voice, and sent an angel and brought us out of

a That is Quarrel

given. V. 12 indicates that forty years have passed: the Israelites in this narrative are to be allowed into the promised land; hence the conclusion that the old generation had died (see 14.21–24, 28–35); note the resumption of the march in v. 22. On *Miriam,* see ch. 12. **20.2–13** The complaint and the waters of Meribah. On complaint stories in general, see note on 11.1–3. Compare this story to its doublet in Ex 17.1–7. This narrative is also referred to in Deut 33.8; Pss 78.15–16, 20; 81.7; 95.8–11; 106.32–33. **20.3** *Quarreled,* from the same root as Meribah, hence the etymology in v. 13. *When . . . LORD,* i.e., in the Korah, Dathan, and Abiram affair, ch. 16 (esp. vv. 32–33, 35, 49). **20.4** *Livestock.* See note on 11.4. **20.5** *No . . . figs, or vines, or pomegranates.* Cf. 13.23. **20.6** *Fell on their faces.* See 14.5; 16.4. *Glory.* See note on 9.15–16. **20.8–9** The mention of *the staff* is phrased in such a way that a particular staff seems to be meant. Since it is taken *from before the LORD,* it must be Aaron's staff of 17.10–11; but see v. 11. See also Ex 7.8–8.19. The reference to *the rock* also implies a known entity, perhaps a well-known feature at Kadesh. The Hebrew word for rock here, *selaʿ,* is also the name of a city in Edom (see Judg 1.36; 2 Kings 14.7) and may be a literary link to the Edom narrative in vv. 14–21. **20.10** For Israel as *rebels,* see 17.10, also concerned with the staff. **20.12** No satisfying explanation has ever been given for the punishment of Moses and Aaron for this incident. Their "sin" is described here as unbelief; in v. 24 and 27.14 it is rebellion; in Deut 32.50–52 they are said to have "broken faith" with the Lord. Ps 106.32–33 blames Moses' "rash words" (perhaps v. 10), and yet other explanations, not always re-

ferring to this narrative at all, are given in Deut 1.37; 3.25–26; 4.21. Commentators have made many suggestions about the nature of the "sin," but none of these explanations is widely accepted. Aaron's death is reported in v. 28, Moses' in Deut 34.5. That *this assembly* will be taken into the promised land implies that this must be the new generation, grown up after the old has died during forty years in the wilderness. *To show my holiness* might also be translated "to treat me as holy." **20.13** *Quarreled.* See 20.3. For the etymologies of place-names, see, e.g., 11.1–3; 13.24; 21.3. *With the LORD.* See Ex 16.8; 17.7.

20.14–21 The relationship between Edom and Israel in the Bible is complicated: sometimes friendly, sometimes hostile (e.g., the stories of Jacob/Israel and Esau/Edom, Gen 25.27–34; 27.1–28.9; 32.3–33.17; and elsewhere, Num 24.18; 1 Sam 14.47; 2 Sam 8.13–14; 1 Kings 11.14–17; 2 Kings 3.4–27; Isa 34.5–7; Obadiah). **20.14** *King.* There is no archaeological evidence that Edom was organized as a kingdom in the early Iron Age; probably the passages that report "chieftains" of Edom are more accurate (see text notes to Gen 36.15–19, 40–43; Ex 15.15). The message in vv. 14–17 is worded in the same way as a typical ancient Near Eastern letter: addressee, sender, message. Moses calls Israel Edom's *brother* in typical diplomatic language. Use of the term *brother* indicates that the message sender believes the two parties to be equals and allies. In this case, of course, there is a double meaning since Israel (Jacob) and Edom (Esau) are recorded as biological brothers in the stories in Genesis (e.g., 25.21–26). **20.16** *Angel.* See Ex 14.19; 23.20–33; 32.34.

Egypt; and here we are in Kadesh, a town on the edge of your territory. 17Now let us pass through your land. We will not pass through field or vineyard, or drink water from any well; we will go along the King's Highway, not turning aside to the right hand or to the left until we have passed through your territory."

18 But Edom said to him, "You shall not pass through, or we will come out with the sword against you." 19The Israelites said to him, "We will stay on the highway; and if we drink of your water, we and our livestock, then we will pay for it. It is only a small matter; just let us pass through on foot." 20But he said, "You shall not pass through." And Edom came out against them with a large force, heavily armed. 21Thus Edom refused to give Israel passage through their territory; so Israel turned away from them.

The Death of Aaron

22 They set out from Kadesh, and the Israelites, the whole congregation, came to Mount Hor. 23Then the LORD said to Moses and Aaron at Mount Hor, on the border of the land of Edom, 24"Let Aaron be gathered to his people. For he shall not enter the land that I have given to the Israelites, because you rebelled against my command at the waters of Meribah. 25Take Aaron and his son Eleazar,

and bring them up Mount Hor; 26strip Aaron of his vestments, and put them on his son Eleazar. But Aaron shall be gathered to his people,[a] and shall die there." 27Moses did as the LORD had commanded; they went up Mount Hor in the sight of the whole congregation. 28Moses stripped Aaron of his vestments, and put them on his son Eleazar; and Aaron died there on the top of the mountain. Moses and Eleazar came down from the mountain. 29When all the congregation saw that Aaron had died, all the house of Israel mourned for Aaron thirty days.

The Bronze Serpent

21 When the Canaanite, the king of Arad, who lived in the Negeb, heard that Israel was coming by the way of Atharim, he fought against Israel and took some of them captive. 2Then Israel made a vow to the LORD and said, "If you will indeed give this people into our hands, then we will utterly destroy their towns." 3The LORD listened to the voice of Israel, and handed over the Canaanites; and they utterly destroyed them and their towns; so the place was called Hormah.[b]

4 From Mount Hor they set out by the way to the Red Sea,[c] to go around the land of Edom;

a Heb lacks *to his people*　b Heb *Destruction*　c Or *Sea of Reeds*

As in many biblical stories, the "angel" is probably meant to be in fact some aspect of the Lord (see, e.g., Gen 16.7–13; Num 22.22–35). **20.17** Because their attack from the south had failed many years earlier (14.39–45), the Israelites are now planning to invade Canaan from the east. To do so they must either pass directly through Edom or make a long detour around. The *King's Highway* was the north-south Transjordanian route connecting the Gulf of Aqaba with Syria. Such a route is still in use today. **20.18** The Edomites refuse, although without explanation. See Judg 11.17–18, but cf. Deut 2.2–8, 26–29. **20.21** See 21.4: the Israelites go south of Edom when they continue their march.

20.22–29 Aaron's successor installed; Aaron dies. **20.22** *They set out*. See 10.11–12. *Mount Hor*. Site unknown, but see v. 23; 33.37; cf. Deut 10.6; Num 33.30–31, 37. **20.24** That an Israelite is *gathered to his people* probably usually refers to burial in a family tomb; see Gen 25.8–10. *Because you rebelled.* "You" is plural; see v. 12; Deut 32.50–52. **20.26** Aaron's son *Eleazar* (see 19.3) will take Aaron's place as chief priest; see also Deut 10.6. On his *vestments,* see Ex 28; Lev 8.7–9. **20.28** Moses will also die on top of a *mountain;* see Deut 32.50; 34.1–6. Num 33.38 places Aaron's death on the first day of the fifth month, year forty.

20.29 The Israelites mourn for Aaron *thirty days,* as they do for Moses (Deut 34.8). The usual period of mourning was seven days (Gen 50.10; 1 Sam 31.13).

21.1–3 The defeat of the king of Arad. This appears to be another story of an attack on the promised land from the south (see v. 4). For other battles of Hormah, see 14.39–45; Judg 1.16–17. **21.1** For *Canaanites* in this region, see also 14.25, 45. *Arad* is approximately fifty miles north of the oases of which Kadesh was a part. For the *king of Arad,* see Josh 12.14. *Negeb.* See 13.17; Judg 1.16. The *way of Atharim.* Site unknown. **21.2–3** See Judg 11.30–31. *We will utterly destroy their towns* is a vow to wage "holy war." See Ex 17.14; Num 18.14; Deut 20.16–18. Such a practice is known also from ancient Moab. *Hormah* is from the same Hebrew root as "utterly destroy"; hence this narrative provides an etymology of the place-name Hormah, as does Judg 1.17. It is odd that, having achieved a victory in the Negeb, the Israelites still turn to the southeast to go through Transjordan and attack Canaan from the east (v. 4), rather than continuing northward into Canaan. Commentators have suggested, therefore, that vv. 1–3 are out of place in their current position.

21.4–9 The bronze serpent. This is the last of the complaint stories (see note on 11.1–3) and the most serious since the people complain directly against God

but the people became impatient on the way. 5The people spoke against God and against Moses, "Why have you brought us up out of Egypt to die in the wilderness? For there is no food and no water, and we detest this miserable food." 6Then the Lord sent poisonous*a* serpents among the people, and they bit the people, so that many Israelites died. 7The people came to Moses and said, "We have sinned by speaking against the Lord and against you; pray to the Lord to take away the serpents from us." So Moses prayed for the people. 8And the Lord said to Moses, "Make a poisonous*b* serpent, and set it on a pole; and everyone who is bitten shall look at it and live." 9So Moses made a serpent of bronze, and put it upon a pole; and whenever a serpent bit someone, that person would look at the serpent of bronze and live.

The Journey to Moab

10 The Israelites set out, and camped in Oboth. 11They set out from Oboth, and camped at Iye-abarim, in the wilderness bordering Moab toward the sunrise. 12From there they set out, and camped in the Wadi Zered. 13From there they set out, and camped on the other side of the Arnon, in*c* the wilderness that extends from the boundary of the Amorites; for the Arnon is the boundary of Moab, between Moab and the Amorites. 14Wherefore it is said in the Book of the Wars of the Lord,

"Waheb in Suphah and the wadis.
The Arnon 15and the slopes of the wadis
    that extend to the seat of Ar,
    and lie along the border of Moab."*d*

16 From there they continued to Beer;*e* that is the well of which the Lord said to Moses, "Gather the people together, and I will give them water." 17Then Israel sang this song:
    "Spring up, O well!—Sing to it!—
18   the well that the leaders sank,

---

a Or *fiery;* Heb *seraphim*   *b* Or *fiery;* Heb *seraph*   *c* Gk: Heb *which is in*   *d* Meaning of Heb uncertain   *e* That is *Well*

---

as well as Moses (v. 5, although cf. Ex 16.8; Num 14.3). **21.4** *They set out.* This is part of the itinerary reported in 33.41. *By the way to the Red Sea.* The Hebrew actually says "Reed Sea," as in 14.25. In this passage, however, Red Sea makes sense, regardless of where the miracle at the sea was thought to have taken place. The Israelites have turned to the Gulf of Aqaba in order *to go around the land of Edom,* because they have been denied passage; see 20.14–21. **21.5** *Against God and against Moses.* See note on 21.4–9. This phrasing is unique. **21.6–7** *Poisonous serpents,* lit. "fiery snakes," so called perhaps because of the burning of their bites. Poisonous snakes do exist in the Sinai and the Negeb. **21.8–9** *Make a poisonous serpent,* lit. "make a fiery one," presumably a "fiery snake." In Isa 30.6 the same word (a flying "fiery one," translated as a flying "serpent") describes an animal of the Negeb. *Set it on a pole,* so that it could be held up for victims to see. Looking at the serpent cures the victims, a process here described as a sort of sympathetic magic (although see Wis 16.5–7). The phrase *serpent of bronze* is a pun in Hebrew, as both words are derived from the same root. Also from that root is Nehushtan, the bronze serpent King Hezekiah destroys because it has become an object of worship; see 2 Kings 18.4. This story in Numbers serves as an etiology for the serpent of Hezekiah's time. Serpent worship is attested elsewhere in the ancient world, as is the belief in a relationship between snakes and healing. In the NT Jn 3.14–15 evokes the image of the serpent as a way of interpreting the death of Jesus.

21.10–11 Cf. 33.41–44, with stops at Zalmonah and Punon not listed in ch. 21 (see v. 4). The location of *Oboth* is unknown. *Iye-abarim,* possibly "the ruins of the Abarim." Abarim, from the root that means "across," i.e., across the Jordan (from the point of view

of an Israelite writer), is a word that describes an area or mountain range in Moab (see 27.12; 33.47). Here the text seems to place the Israelites to the east of Moab, below the Arnon (v. 13); cf. v. 12, where they appear to be south of Moab. **21.12** The style of the itinerary changes in this verse, and the stopping places no longer correspond to the list of "stages" in Num 33 (see 33.45), so commentators generally see a shift here to a different source from the Priestly tradition, possibly simply the old epic sources (see Introduction; 10.29–36). In Deut 2.8–25, the *Wadi Zered* appears to be the southern boundary of Moab, between Moab and Edom, probably modern Wadi el-Hesa. **21.13** The *Arnon,* modern Wadi el-Mujib, was at some periods the northern boundary of Moab. A ninth-century BCE Moabite inscription attributed to King Mesha (2 Kings 3.4–27) describes his regaining the territory north of the Arnon from Israel, in whose control it had been since the time of the Israelite king Omri (1 Kings 16.21–30). The inscription was indeed found north of the Arnon. The *other side* of the Arnon must refer to the north side, since the Israelites were marching from the south. **21.14–15** *The Book of the Wars of the Lord* is otherwise unknown. Cf. the Book of Jashar (Josh 10.13; 2 Sam 1.18). These fragments suggest the existence of collections of poems about Israel's early wars of conquest. Such wars were called "the wars of the Lord" because of the Israelites' belief that the Lord led them in battle (i.e., "holy wars," see, e.g., Josh 6; Judg 4.14–16; 11.30–33; 1 Sam 14.6–10, 23; 18.17; 25.28). The translation of the poem is problematical. For *Ar* as a town in Moab, see 21.28; Deut 2.18. The name probably means "town," in fact. The *seat* of Ar could refer to its location or to some dwelling in the town. **21.16–18** An otherwise unknown miraculous provision of

that the nobles of the people dug,
 with the scepter, with the staff."
From the wilderness to Mattanah, [19]from
Mattanah to Nahaliel, from Nahaliel to Ba-
moth, [20]and from Bamoth to the valley lying
in the region of Moab by the top of Pisgah that
overlooks the wasteland. [a]

King Sihon Defeated

21 Then Israel sent messengers to King Sihon of
the Amorites, saying, [22]"Let me pass through
your land; we will not turn aside into field or
vineyard; we will not drink the water of any
well; we will go by the King's Highway until we
have passed through your territory." [23]But
Sihon would not allow Israel to pass through his
territory. Sihon gathered all his people together,
and went out against Israel to the wilderness; he
came to Jahaz, and fought against Israel. [24]Israel
put him to the sword, and took possession of his
land from the Arnon to the Jabbok, as far as to
the Ammonites; for the boundary of the Ammonites was strong. [25]Israel took all these
towns, and Israel settled in all the towns of the
Amorites, in Heshbon, and in all its villages.
[26]For Heshbon was the city of King Sihon of the
Amorites, who had fought against the former
king of Moab and captured all his land as far as
the Arnon. [27]Therefore the ballad singers say,

"Come to Heshbon, let it be built;
 let the city of Sihon be established.
[28] For fire came out from Heshbon,
 flame from the city of Sihon.
It devoured Ar of Moab,
 and swallowed up [b] the heights of the
 Arnon.
[29] Woe to you, O Moab!
 You are undone, O people of
 Chemosh!
He has made his sons fugitives,
 and his daughters captives,
 to an Amorite king, Sihon.
[30] So their posterity perished
 from Heshbon [c] to Dibon,
 and we laid waste until fire spread to
 Medeba." [d]

31 Thus Israel settled in the land of the Amorites. [32]Moses sent to spy out Jazer; and they
captured its villages, and dispossessed the Amorites who were there.

King Og Defeated

33 Then they turned and went up the road to
Bashan; and King Og of Bashan came out
against them, he and all his people, to battle at

---

a Or *Jeshimon* *b* Gk: Heb *and the lords of* *c* Gk: Heb *we have shot at them; Heshbon has perished* *d* Compare Sam Gk: Meaning of MT uncertain

---

water; cf. Ex 17.1–7; Num 20.2–11, although the "Song of the Well" could obviously be sung about any well. **21.19** *Mattanah* and *Nahaliel* are unknown. *Ba-moth*, "high places," could refer to a number of sites, e.g., Bamoth-baal, 22.41; Josh 13.17; Beth-bamoth in the Mesha Inscription (see note on 21.13). **21.20** *Valley* here could refer to a valley within a series of hills and need not clash with *the top of Pisgah*. For Pisgah as hills, see, e.g., 23.14; Deut 3.17, 27; 34.1. Pisgah is on the Moabite plateau above the Jordan Valley (Deut 34.1), and so the march has come northwest to this point. The *wasteland* referred to in this verse must be the area north of the Dead Sea and east of the Jordan River. The same word is used of that area on the west side of the river as well.
  21.21–35 The defeat of kings Sihon and Og. See the similar narratives in Deut 2.24–3.7; Judg 11.19–22; and many other mentions such as Josh 12.1–5; 13.10–12; Jer 48.45. **21.21** *Amorites*. See 13.29; Gen 10.16. **21.22** Cf. 20.17, 19. The Israelites still need to move farther north in order to press their attack on Canaan from the east, and this brings them to the border of Amorite territory. *The King's Highway*. See 20.17. **21.23** Cf. 20.18, 20–21. *Jahaz* (also mentioned in the Mesha Inscription, see note on 21.13) seems to be the limit of Moab's land (Isa 15.4; Jer 48.34) and was prob-ably near Dibon (see 21.30). **21.24** Earlier in ch. 21 Is-

rael bypassed Edom, but here the Israelites fight with the Amorites. The *Jabbok* is modern Wadi Zerqa. On the *Ammonites*, see Gen 19.38. The area of Ammon in the highlands east of the Jordan Valley was already widely settled in the middle of the second millennium BCE. **21.25–26** *All these towns* has no obvious referent. The site of *Heshbon* in this early period has not been certainly identified but was probably in the highlands east of the Jordan Valley, opposite Jericho. *Villages*, lit. "daughters," i.e., dependent towns. According to these verses, the territory in question (north of the Arnon) had once been Moabite, just as in King Mesha's in-scription (see note on 21.13). **21.27–30** The Song of Heshbon is a song in praise of an Amorite victory over Moab. **21.29** *Chemosh* is the national god of Moab, known also from the Mesha Inscription (see 21.13); see also 1 Kings 11.7, 33; 2 Kings 23.13; Jer 48.7, 13, 46; cf. Judg 11.12–24. Cf. the *people of Chemosh* here and in Jer 48.46 with Israel as "the people of the LORD" in Num 11.29; 2 Kings 9.6; Ezek 36.20; Zeph 2.10. **21.30** *Dibon*, about thirty miles southwest of Amman, and *Medeba*, about twenty miles southwest of Amman. See 33.45; Josh 13.8–9. The Hebrew of v. 30 is not at all clear. **21.32** *Jazer*. Site unknown; see 32.1–4; Josh 13.24–25. **21.33–35** The defeat of King Og, an-other Amorite king. *Bashan* is northern Transjordan, a plateau of volcanic origin and famous in biblical pas-

Edrei. 34But the LORD said to Moses, "Do not be afraid of him; for I have given him into your hand, with all his people, and all his land. You shall do to him as you did to King Sihon of the Amorites, who ruled in Heshbon." 35So they killed him, his sons, and all his people, until there was no survivor left; and they took possession of his land.

Balak Summons Balaam to Curse Israel

22 The Israelites set out, and camped in the plains of Moab across the Jordan from Jericho. 2Now Balak son of Zippor saw all that Israel had done to the Amorites. 3Moab was in great dread of the people, because they were so numerous; Moab was overcome with fear of the people of Israel. 4And Moab said to the elders of Midian, "This horde will now lick up all that is around us, as an ox licks up the grass of the field." Now Balak son of Zippor was king of Moab at that time. 5He sent messengers to Balaam son of Beor at Pethor, which is on the Euphrates, in the land of

Amaw,*a* to summon him, saying, "A people has come out of Egypt; they have spread over the face of the earth, and they have settled next to me. 6Come now, curse this people for me, since they are stronger than I; perhaps I shall be able to defeat them and drive them from the land; for I know that whomever you bless is blessed, and whomever you curse is cursed."

7 So the elders of Moab and the elders of Midian departed with the fees for divination in their hand; and they came to Balaam, and gave him Balak's message. 8He said to them, "Stay here tonight, and I will bring back word to you, just as the LORD speaks to me"; so the officials of Moab stayed with Balaam. 9God came to Balaam and said, "Who are these men with you?" 10Balaam said to God, "King Balak son of Zippor of Moab, has sent me this message: 11'A people has come out of Egypt and has spread over the face of the earth; now come, curse them for me; perhaps I shall be

---

a Or *land of his kinsfolk*

---

sages as a fertile land; see Ps 22.12; Isa 2.13; 33.9; Jer 50.19; Ezek 27.6; 39.18; Mic 7.14; Nah 1.4; Zech 11.2. *Edrei,* about sixty miles south of Damascus; see Deut 3.8–10. **21.34** *Do not be afraid . . . your hand.* Cf. Josh 10.8. **22.1** The last stage in the journey from the wilderness of Sinai, before the crossing of the Jordan River; see Num 33.48–49; 36.13; Deut 1.1–5; Josh 3.1.

22.2–24.25 The story of Balaam, son of Beor. The biblical stories of Balaam have been supplemented by the discovery at Tell Deir 'Alla in Jordan of a plaster inscription dating to the eighth century BCE. The text, which is probably non-Israelite, relates that Balaam, son of Beor, a "seer of the gods," receives an upsetting night visit from the gods and then reports to his people that he has seen a divine council meeting (see Gen 1.26) where impending disaster is apparently planned for the earth. The Balaam story in Num 22–24 combines epic and poetic sources, resulting in a few apparent contradictions: on the one hand, Balaam's journey to Balak seems rather short, with a donkey and two servants (22.21–35), while, on the other, he is said to come from upper Syria (22.5); he is outspokenly loyal to the God of Israel, but his failure to curse Israel continues to surprise Balak; he is portrayed as both prophet and diviner. The connection, if any, between Balaam and Bela son of Beor (an Edomite king, Gen 36.32–33; 1 Chr 1.43–44) is obscure. Some of the mentions of Balaam in the Bible refer to the narrative in chs. 22–24; some refer to the negative Balaam tradition in 31.8, 16; and others have slightly different traditions from either of these (see Deut 23.3–6; Josh 13.22; 24.9–10; Judg 11.25; Neh 13.1–2; Mic 6.5; Rev 2.14). **22.2** *Balak* is mentioned only in these chapters and in references to them (Josh 24.9; Judg 11.25;

Mic 6.5). *All that Israel . . . Amorites.* See 21.21–35. **22.3** *Moab . . . people of Israel.* Cf. Josh 2.8–11. **22.4** On the connection between Balaam and *Midian,* see 31.8, 16. **22.5** *Pethor,* possibly Pitru on the upper Euphrates, where Syrian and Mesopotamian cultures came together; see also 23.7; Deut 23.4. This identification for Pethor, however, accords badly with vv. 21–35, where a short journey seems envisioned (see note on 22.2–24.25). *Amaw,* or "his people"; see text note *a* and cf. 24.14. There is a place-name in northern Syria that might correspond to Hebrew Amaw. Amaw might also be a scribal error for Ammon. *Spread over the face of the earth;* cf. the same expression used of locusts in Ex 10.5, 15. **22.6** Balaam's role here is one who blesses and curses; cf. vv. 7, 40; 23.1–3. **22.7** *Fees for divination.* See the negative interpretation of Balaam's role as diviner in Josh 13.22; see also Deut 18.10–14. Divination was a common ancient cultic practice designed to discover information by interpretation of some object or event, such as the configuration of the entrails of a sacrificed animal or the pattern of oil drops on water. Diviners learned traditional interpretations preserved in long lists of many possible configurations of the various media. **22.8** Balaam, a non-Israelite, maintains unexpectedly that he must confer with the Lord, i.e., with Yahweh, the God of Israel; see also vv. 12–13, 18; Gen 26.28. Not unexpectedly, the God of Israel does not give Balaam permission to curse Israel for Balak king of Moab (v. 6). Equally unusual, the Moabites and Midianites in the story seem to accept that Balaam is dependent on the Lord for his blessings and curses, as if the Lord were the only god Balaam could possibly call on. Cf. 21.29. Balaam here reflects a tradition in which a prophet is the mouthpiece for a deity. See

able to fight against them and drive them out.' " [12]God said to Balaam, "You shall not go with them; you shall not curse the people, for they are blessed." [13]So Balaam rose in the morning, and said to the officials of Balak, "Go to your own land, for the LORD has refused to let me go with you." [14]So the officials of Moab rose and went to Balak, and said, "Balaam refuses to come with us."

15 Once again Balak sent officials, more numerous and more distinguished than these. [16]They came to Balaam and said to him, "Thus says Balak son of Zippor: 'Do not let anything hinder you from coming to me; [17]for I will surely do you great honor, and whatever you say to me I will do; come, curse this people for me.' " [18]But Balaam replied to the servants of Balak, "Although Balak were to give me his house full of silver and gold, I could not go beyond the command of the LORD my God, to do less or more. [19]You remain here, as the others did, so that I may learn what more the LORD may say to me." [20]That night God came to Balaam and said to him, "If the men have come to summon you, get up and go with them; but do only what I tell you to do." [21]So Balaam got up in the morning, saddled his donkey, and went with the officials of Moab.

Balaam, the Donkey, and the Angel

22 God's anger was kindled because he was going, and the angel of the LORD took his stand in the road as his adversary. Now he was riding on the donkey, and his two servants were with him. [23]The donkey saw the angel of the LORD standing in the road, with a drawn sword in his hand; so the donkey turned off the road, and went into the field; and Balaam struck the donkey, to turn it back onto the road. [24]Then the angel of the LORD stood in a narrow path between the vineyards, with a wall on either side. [25]When the donkey saw the angel of the LORD, it scraped against the wall, and scraped Balaam's foot against the wall; so he struck it again. [26]Then the angel of

the LORD went ahead, and stood in a narrow place, where there was no way to turn either to the right or to the left. [27]When the donkey saw the angel of the LORD, it lay down under Balaam; and Balaam's anger was kindled, and he struck the donkey with his staff. [28]Then the LORD opened the mouth of the donkey, and it said to Balaam, "What have I done to you, that you have struck me these three times?" [29]Balaam said to the donkey, "Because you have made a fool of me! I wish I had a sword in my hand! I would kill you right now!" [30]But the donkey said to Balaam, "Am I not your donkey, which you have ridden all your life to this day? Have I been in the habit of treating you this way?" And he said, "No."

31 Then the LORD opened the eyes of Balaam, and he saw the angel of the LORD standing in the road, with his drawn sword in his hand; and he bowed down, falling on his face. [32]The angel of the LORD said to him, "Why have you struck your donkey these three times? I have come out as an adversary, because your way is perverse[a] before me. [33]The donkey saw me, and turned away from me these three times. If it had not turned away from me, surely just now I would have killed you and let it live." [34]Then Balaam said to the angel of the LORD, "I have sinned, for I did not know that you were standing in the road to oppose me. Now therefore, if it is displeasing to you, I will return home." [35]The angel of the LORD said to Balaam, "Go with the men; but speak only what I tell you to speak." So Balaam went on with the officials of Balak.

36 When Balak heard that Balaam had come, he went out to meet him at Ir-moab, on the boundary formed by the Arnon, at the farthest point of the boundary. [37]Balak said to Balaam, "Did I not send to summon you? Why did you not come to me? Am I not able to honor you?" [38]Balaam said to Balak, "I have come to you now, but do I have power to say

---

a Meaning of Heb uncertain

Deut 18.18; also Num 22.18–20, 35, 38; 23.3, 15, 17, 26; 24.13. **22.18** *My God.* Balaam here refers to the Lord as his own god. Cf. v. 8. **22.20** Balaam is given permission to go with the men but not to curse Israel. **22.22–35** The story of Balaam's talking donkey is a fable that perhaps pokes fun at Balaam–the seer whose donkey can see more than he can. Cf. the story of trees talking in Judg 9.7–15. **22.22** God's *anger* is unexplained in the text as we have it; cf. v. 20. **22.23a** Cf.

Josh 5.13–15. **22.28** *Opened the mouth of the donkey.* Cf. v. 31 (although a different Hebrew word is used for "open"). **22.31** *The LORD opened the eyes of Balaam,* so that he could see something supernatural; cf. 2 Kings 6.15–17. **22.32** The *angel* seems to be, in some sense, the Lord; see also 20.16. **22.35** *Angel.* Cf. 22.20, 32. **22.36–39** Balak comes to meet Balaam when he gets to Moab's border. **22.36** *Ir-moab,* or "the city of Moab," perhaps the same as Ar in Moab; see 21.15, 28; Deut

just anything? The word God puts in my mouth, that is what I must say." [39]Then Balaam went with Balak, and they came to Kiriath-huzoth. [40]Balak sacrificed oxen and sheep, and sent them to Balaam and to the officials who were with him.

Balaam's First Oracle

41 On the next day Balak took Balaam and brought him up to Bamoth-baal; and from there he could see part of the people of Israel.[a]

23 [1]Then Balaam said to Balak, "Build me seven altars here, and prepare seven bulls and seven rams for me." [2]Balak did as Balaam had said; and Balak and Balaam offered a bull and a ram on each altar. [3]Then Balaam said to Balak, "Stay here beside your burnt offerings while I go aside. Perhaps the LORD will come to meet me. Whatever he shows me I will tell you." And he went to a bare height.

4 Then God met Balaam; and Balaam said to him, "I have arranged the seven altars, and have offered a bull and a ram on each altar." [5]The LORD put a word in Balaam's mouth, and said, "Return to Balak, and this is what you must say." [6]So he returned to Balak,[b] who was standing beside his burnt offerings with all the officials of Moab. [7]Then Balaam[c] uttered his oracle, saying:

"Balak has brought me from Aram,
the king of Moab from the eastern mountains:
'Come, curse Jacob for me;
Come, denounce Israel!'
[8] How can I curse whom God has not cursed?
How can I denounce those whom the LORD has not denounced?

[9] For from the top of the crags I see him,
from the hills I behold him.
Here is a people living alone,
and not reckoning itself among the nations!
[10] Who can count the dust of Jacob,
or number the dust-cloud[c] of Israel?
Let me die the death of the upright,
and let my end be like his!"

11 Then Balak said to Balaam, "What have you done to me? I brought you to curse my enemies, but now you have done nothing but bless them." [12]He answered, "Must I not take care to say what the LORD puts into my mouth?"

Balaam's Second Oracle

13 So Balak said to him, "Come with me to another place from which you may see them; you shall see only part of them, and shall not see them all; then curse them for me from there." [14]So he took him to the field of Zophim, to the top of Pisgah. He built seven altars, and offered a bull and a ram on each altar. [15]Balaam said to Balak, "Stand here beside your burnt offerings, while I meet the LORD over there." [16]The LORD met Balaam, put a word into his mouth, and said, "Return to Balak, and this is what you shall say." [17]When he came to him, he was standing beside his burnt offerings with the officials of Moab. Balak said to him, "What has the LORD said?" [18]Then Balaam uttered his oracle, saying:

"Rise, Balak, and hear;
listen to me, O son of Zippor:
[19] God is not a human being, that he should lie,

---

a Heb lacks *of Israel*   b Heb *him*   c Heb *he*   d Or *fourth part*

2.9, 18, 29; Isa 15.1. On the *Arnon* as the northern boundary of Moab, see 21.13. **22.39** *Kiriath-huzoth,* "the town of streets." Site unknown. **22.40** The sacrifices could be part of Balaam's divining; see v. 7; 23.2, 14; cf. 24.1. **22.41** *Bamoth-baal, Pisgah* (23.14), and *Peor* (23.28) are in the hills above the eastern Jordan Valley; see 21.19–20; Deut 3.27; 34.1; Josh 13.17–20. **23.1–2** See 22.40. **23.3** See 22.8. **23.5** See 22.8; the *word* is the following oracle, vv. 7–10. **23.7–10** The first of Balaam's oracles. Commentators generally consider oracles one and two separately from oracles three and four. The first and second oracles would make little sense without the prose that surrounds them, while the third and fourth have little necessary connection with the prose narrative. Many would date oracles three and four earlier than one and two, and see some deliberate literary dependence of two on three; see vv.

22, 24. See notes on 24.3–4; 24.8–9; 24.15–16; 24.17–18. **23.7** *Aram* (Syria). See 22.5. *Jacob* and *Israel* are equivalent terms used in parallel in this typical poetic construction; see Gen 32.27–28; 35.9–10. **23.8** See 22.8. **23.9** *Him,* Jacob/Israel. *A people living alone,* a phrase that connotes security; see Jer 49.31; Deut 33.28. **23.10** *Who can . . . Jacob.* See Gen 13.16; 28.14. **23.11–12** See 22.8.

23.13 *You shall see only part of them.* This phrase (see also 22.41) implies a vast number of people camped beyond them (see 22.3–6). **23.14** *The field of Zophim,* "Sentinels' Field." Site unknown. *Pisgah* (see 22.41) was not a particular mountaintop, but a highland range, so "the field of Zophim" could be a part of the Pisgah highlands. On the sacrifices, see 22.40; 23.1–2. **23.16** See v. 5. **23.18–24** The second oracle; see note on 23.7–10. **23.18** See 23.7. **23.19** Balaam and

or a mortal, that he should change his
  mind.
Has he promised, and will he not do it?
Has he spoken, and will he not fulfill
  it?
20 See, I received a command to bless;
  he has blessed, and I cannot revoke it.
21 He has not beheld misfortune in Jacob;
  nor has he seen trouble in Israel.
The LORD their God is with them,
  acclaimed as a king among them.
22 God, who brings them out of Egypt,
  is like the horns of a wild ox for them.
23 Surely there is no enchantment against
  Jacob,
  no divination against Israel;
now it shall be said of Jacob and Israel,
  'See what God has done!'
24 Look, a people rising up like a lioness,
  and rousing itself like a lion!
It does not lie down until it has eaten the
  prey
  and drunk the blood of the slain.'

25 Then Balak said to Balaam, "Do not
curse them at all, and do not bless them at all."
26 But Balaam answered Balak, "Did I not tell
you, 'Whatever the LORD says, that is what I
must do'?"

27 So Balak said to Balaam, "Come now, I
will take you to another place; perhaps it will
please God that you may curse them for me
from there." 28 So Balak took Balaam to the top
of Peor, which overlooks the wasteland.ᵃ 29 Balaam
said to Balak, "Build me seven altars

here, and prepare seven bulls and seven rams
for me." 30 So Balak did as Balaam had said,
and offered a bull and a ram on each altar.

Balaam's Third Oracle

24 Now Balaam saw that it pleased the
  LORD to bless Israel, so he did not go, as
at other times, to look for omens, but set his
face toward the wilderness. 2 Balaam looked
up and saw Israel camping tribe by tribe. Then
the spirit of God came upon him, 3 and he uttered
his oracle, saying:
"The oracle of Balaam son of Beor,
  the oracle of the man whose eye is
  clear,ᵇ
4 the oracle of one who hears the words of
  God,
  who sees the vision of the Almighty,ᶜ
  who falls down, but with eyes
  uncovered:
5 how fair are your tents, O Jacob,
  your encampments, O Israel!
6 Like palm groves that stretch far away,
  like gardens beside a river,
like aloes that the LORD has planted,
  like cedar trees beside the waters.
7 Water shall flow from his buckets,
  and his seed shall have abundant water,
his king shall be higher than Agag,
  and his kingdom shall be exalted.
8 God who brings him out of Egypt,

---

a Or *overlooks Jeshimon* *b* Or *closed* or *open* *c* Traditional
rendering of Heb *Shaddai*

Balak's petitions (and, by implication, all such petitions)
are not effective with God, who, not being a
human being, is not swayed from a course already chosen.
See also vv. 20, 23; but cf., e.g., Gen 18.22–33 and
Moses' many acts of intercession (see 11.10–15).
23.21 Here the Lord is referred to specifically as the
God of Israel; see 22.8, 18. **23.22** *Horns of a wild ox.* The
Hebrew word translated "horns" here and in 24.8 is
not entirely clear. **23.23** Israel's success as a nation reflects
well on the Lord. Cf. Moses' suggestion that the
opposite is also true (14.13–19). **23.24** For a fierce
people portrayed as a *lion,* see 24.9; Gen 49.9; Deut
33.20, 22; Isa 5.29; Ezek 19.1–9; Joel 1.6; Nah 2.11–12.
23.25–26 See 22.8. **23.28** *Peor.* See 22.41. *Which overlooks
the wasteland.* Cf. 21.20. **23.29–30** See 23.1–2.

24.1–14 Balaam's third oracle. The third and fourth
oracles are generally considered older than the first
two (see note on 23.7–10), with very little connection
to the narrative context, although see v. 9. **24.1–2** The
preparation for the third oracle is different from that
for the first two. *As at other times . . . omens.* See 22.40.

The spirit of God . . . him. See 11.17. **24.3–9** The third
oracle itself is a general blessing of Israel and, along
with the fourth oracle, has literary connections to
other poetry thought by many to be quite early—not
from the time of Balaam and Moses, but perhaps from
the early monarchy (see 24.7, 17–18). **24.3–4** That Balaam
seems to be introduced here and in vv. 15–16 is
one reason commentators have suggested this Balak
narrative is not the original context for oracles three
and four. *Oracle . . . eye is clear.* See text note *b*. The
translation is uncertain. See also 2 Sam 23.1; Prov 30.1
(similar in Hebrew). *The Almighty.* See text note *c*. One
group of gods in the Deir 'Alla inscription (see note on
22.2–24.25), to whose council meeting Balaam was
privy, is called the "Shaddai gods." *Who falls down,* perhaps
a reference to ecstatic behavior; see also 11.24–
29; 1 Sam 10.5–13; 19.20–24. **24.7** *Agag.* Those who
would like to date oracles three and four during the
early monarchy compare this verse to the story of
Saul's victory over the Amalekites and their king Agag
in 1 Sam 15. Amalek is also mentioned in Num 24.20.

is like the horns of a wild ox for him;
he shall devour the nations that are his foes
    and break their bones.
He shall strike with his arrows.[a]
9 He crouched, he lay down like a lion,
    and like a lioness; who will rouse him
        up?
Blessed is everyone who blesses you,
    and cursed is everyone who curses you."

10 Then Balak's anger was kindled against Balaam, and he struck his hands together. Balak said to Balaam, "I summoned you to curse my enemies, but instead you have blessed them these three times. 11Now be off with you! Go home! I said, 'I will reward you richly,' but the LORD has denied you any reward." 12And Balaam said to Balak, "Did I not tell your messengers whom you sent to me, 13'If Balak should give me his house full of silver and gold, I would not be able to go beyond the word of the LORD, to do either good or bad of my own will; what the LORD says, that is what I will say'? 14So now, I am going to my people; let me advise you what this people will do to your people in days to come."

Balaam's Fourth Oracle

15 So he uttered his oracle, saying:
"The oracle of Balaam son of Beor,
    the oracle of the man whose eye is clear,[b]
16   the oracle of one who hears the words of
        God,
    and knows the knowledge of the Most
        High,[c]

who sees the vision of the Almighty,[d]
    who falls down, but with his eyes
        uncovered:
17 I see him, but not now;
    I behold him, but not near—
a star shall come out of Jacob,
    and a scepter shall rise out of Israel;
it shall crush the borderlands[e] of Moab,
    and the territory[f] of all the Shethites.
18 Edom will become a possession,
    Seir a possession of its enemies,[g]
        while Israel does valiantly.
19 One out of Jacob shall rule,
    and destroy the survivors of Ir."

20 Then he looked on Amalek, and uttered his oracle, saying:
"First among the nations was Amalek,
    but its end is to perish forever."

21 Then he looked on the Kenite, and uttered his oracle, saying:
"Enduring is your dwelling place,
    and your nest is set in the rock;
22 yet Kain is destined for burning.
    How long shall Asshur take you away
        captive?"

23 Again he uttered his oracle, saying:
"Alas, who shall live when God does this?
24   But ships shall come from Kittim
    and shall afflict Asshur and Eber;
    and he also shall perish forever."

---

a Meaning of Heb uncertain   *b* Or *closed* or *open*   *c* Or *of Elyon*   *d* Traditional rendering of Heb *Shaddai*   *e* Or *forehead*   *f* Some Mss read *skull*   *g* Heb *Seir, its enemies, a possession*

24.8–9 Some verses in oracles three and four are often compared to other early poetry, particularly the tribal lists in Gen 49 and Deut 33. *Horns of a wild ox.* See 23.22; Deut 33.17. For lion imagery, see 23.24; note esp. Gen 49.9; Deut 33.20, 22. The theme of blessing and cursing (see the blessing of Jacob in Gen 27.29) is the suggested literary link that ties oracles three and four to an otherwise unrelated narrative context; see note on 24.1–14. **24.10** Balak *struck his hands together* in contempt. See Job 27.23; Lam 2.15. **24.11** *I said, "I will reward you richly."* See 22.17–18, 37. **24.12–13** See 22.8, 18; 23.3, 5, 8, 11–12, 21, 25–26. **24.14** *My people.* See 22.5.
   24.15–24 The fourth oracle is a prediction that Israel will rule over the Transjordanian kingdoms (see 2 Sam 8–12). Many commentators believe that vv. 21–24 are later additions, some that v. 20 is not original to this oracle. **24.15–16** Slightly expanded over vv. 3–4. *The Most High.* See Gen 14.18–24; Deut 32.8. **24.17–18** These verses have been read as referring to King David's victories over Moab and Edom (2 Sam 8.2,

11–14), again pointing to the early monarchy as a setting for these two oracles. *I see . . . not near.* See 23.9. *Scepter.* See Gen 49.10. *Shethites,* perhaps a reference to the nomadic Sutu, a people known from second-millennium BCE documents. On *Seir* for Edom, see Gen 32.3; Judg 5.4. **24.19** *Ir.* See 22.36. **24.20** On *Amalek,* see 13.29; see also 24.7, 15–24. **24.21–22** *Kenite.* See 10.29–32. *Kain,* the eponymous ancestor of the Kenites, is the same in Hebrew as Cain in Gen 4.1–17 and Tubal-cain in Gen 4.22. *Your nest is set in the rock* contains a pun in Hebrew: the Hebrew word for "nest" is very similar to "Kain." *Asshur* is Assyria, and the Neo-Assyrian Empire was especially famous for deporting conquered populations (see 2 Kings 17.5–41). **24.24** The term *Kittim* refers to Cyprus in Jer 2.10; Ezek 27.6 and is used elsewhere to represent the Greeks (Gen 10.4; 1 Macc 1.1; 8.5) and even the Romans (Dan 11.30 and in the Dead Sea Scrolls). *Asshur.* See v. 22. *Eber,* perhaps the eponymous ancestor of the Hebrews (Gen 10.21–25; 11.10–16), more likely a land "beyond" the river (as in Josh 24.3; Isa 7.20), i.e., Mesopo-

25 Then Balaam got up and went back to his place, and Balak also went his way.

Worship of Baal of Peor

25 While Israel was staying at Shittim, the people began to have sexual relations with the women of Moab. ²These invited the people to the sacrifices of their gods, and the people ate and bowed down to their gods. ³Thus Israel yoked itself to the Baal of Peor, and the LORD's anger was kindled against Israel. ⁴The LORD said to Moses, "Take all the chiefs of the people, and impale them in the sun before the LORD, in order that the fierce anger of the LORD may turn away from Israel." ⁵And Moses said to the judges of Israel, "Each of you shall kill any of your people who have yoked themselves to the Baal of Peor."

6 Just then one of the Israelites came and brought a Midianite woman into his family, in the sight of Moses and in the sight of the whole congregation of the Israelites, while they were weeping at the entrance of the tent of meeting. ⁷When Phinehas son of Eleazar, son of Aaron the priest, saw it, he got up and left the congregation. Taking a spear in his hand, ⁸he went after the Israelite man into the tent, and pierced the two of them, the Israelite and the woman, through the belly. So the plague was stopped among the people of Israel. ⁹Nevertheless those that died by the plague were twenty-four thousand.

10 The LORD spoke to Moses, saying: ¹¹"Phinehas son of Eleazar, son of Aaron the priest, has turned back my wrath from the Israelites by manifesting such zeal among them

---

tamia or specifically Babylonia, used here along with Assyria. *He also shall perish forever.* See v. 20.

25.1–18 This chapter is a combination of two different stories about Israelite men and foreign women: one in vv. 1–5 involving Moabite women, sacrifices, and the Baal of Peor and another in vv. 6–15 involving an apparent marriage between a Midianite woman and a Simeonite man. The two are combined by vv. 16–18, and the combined narrative is known to 31.8, 15–16; Josh 22.17; Ps 106.28–31. **25.1–5** See also Deut 4.3–4; Hos 9.10. **25.1–2** *Shittim,* "the acacias." Site unknown. See the full name Abel-shittim in 33.49, there located in the plains of Moab where the Israelites have camped since 22.1. See also Josh 2.1; 3.1; Mic 6.5 (for Gilgal, see Josh 4.19–24). Shittim is the place where the conquest of the land west of the Jordan begins. *Began.* By a change in the vowels this word could read "defiled themselves." *To have sexual relations with,* lit. "to prostitute themselves with," which phrase can be used of sexual relations or of religious apostasy. *The women of Moab.* Cf. vv. 17–18; 31.15–16. *Sacrifices of their gods,* or "god" (the same Hebrew word can be used for both singular and plural) since only one god is mentioned in v. 3; see Ps 106.28–31, where these sacrifices are said to be part of a cult of the dead. *The people ate,* i.e., they participated in the sacrifices; see, e.g., Ex 32.6; Lev 7.11–18; 1 Sam 1.4, 9. Cf. vv. 1–2; Ex 34.15–16. **25.3** *Baal,* lit. "lord," originally an epithet that came to be used as the equivalent of a personal name for the Syrian storm god Hadad (cf. the Aramean king's name Hadadezer, "Hadad is help," 2 Sam 8.3–12). *Peor* is a place-name; see 23.28. **25.4** *Impale,* sometimes translated "crucify" or "expose." The narrative nowhere states that the execution of the *chiefs of the people* takes place, unless v. 8 is the equivalent. **25.5** Moses' command to the *judges of Israel* (some ancient translations have "tribes of Israel"; the Hebrew words for "tribes" and "judges" differ by only one consonant) is not the same as the Lord's command in v. 4. Here Moses asks only that the guilty parties be executed. Again, there is

no indication in the narrative that this was done. **25.6–15** See also Josh 22.17–18; Ps 106.28–31. **25.6** *Into his family,* lit. "to his brothers." For "brother" as kin in general, see, e.g., 16.10; Gen 13.8; 29.12. What was the offense involved in this story? Perhaps simply bringing home, i.e., marrying, a Midianite woman. That it was done *in the sight of Moses* takes on a special significance then. Even though Moses was aware of the offense, he did nothing about it. Vv. 6–18 are an anti-Midianite story used also to elevate Aaron's family over Moses'; see notes on 12.2; 16.3; 16.40. Moses could hardly punish an Israelite man for marrying a Midianite woman when he had done so himself (see 10.29–32); there is more than one attitude toward intermarriage in the Hebrew Bible; cf. Ex 34.15–16; Deut 7.2–4; Josh 23.12–13. Although the reason is not given until v. 8, the people were apparently *weeping at the entrance of the tent of meeting* because of a plague. Once the two stories in this chapter are combined, the plague becomes a punishment for the worship of the Baal of Peor (see v. 18 [a third punishment, the ones in vv. 4–5 apparently not having been carried out]), and the people are weeping before the tent in supplication to the Lord (see 7.89; 16.16–18). **25.7** *Phinehas son of Eleazar.* See Ex 6.23–25; Num 20.22–29. **25.8** The Hebrew word for *tent* here is not the usual one. In fact, this word is used in the Hebrew Bible only here. The meaning is uncertain, but it was probably a domed tent; it has been suggested that this term is an alternate word for the tabernacle. *Pierced the two of them,* i.e., at once, implying sexual intercourse or some positioning in which the two bodies could be pierced with one thrust of the spear. *Through the belly.* The Hebrew is difficult but seems to mean "through her belly." The Hebrew word for "belly" here, though, is very similar to the word for a special tent earlier in this verse, and one ancient translation has "in the tent" at this point. **25.8–9** *Plague.* See v. 6. **25.10–13** The event becomes the grounds for praise of the Aaronite priestly family (see 1 Chr 6.3–15, 49–53) and an indirect criticism of Moses, who apparently failed to

on my behalf that in my jealousy I did not consume the Israelites. 12Therefore say, 'I hereby grant him my covenant of peace. 13It shall be for him and for his descendants after him a covenant of perpetual priesthood, because he was zealous for his God, and made atonement for the Israelites.' "

14 The name of the slain Israelite man, who was killed with the Midianite woman, was Zimri son of Salu, head of an ancestral house belonging to the Simeonites. 15The name of the Midianite woman who was killed was Cozbi daughter of Zur, who was the head of a clan, an ancestral house in Midian.

16 The LORD said to Moses, 17"Harass the Midianites, and defeat them; 18for they have harassed you by the trickery with which they deceived you in the affair of Peor, and in the affair of Cozbi, the daughter of a leader of Midian, their sister; she was killed on the day of the plague that resulted from Peor."

A Census of the New Generation

26 After the plague the LORD said to Moses and to Eleazar son of Aaron the priest, 2"Take a census of the whole congregation of the Israelites, from twenty years old and upward, by their ancestral houses, everyone in Israel able to go to war." 3Moses and Eleazar the priest spoke with them in the plains of Moab by the Jordan opposite Jericho, saying, 4"Take a census of the people,ᵃ from twenty years old and upward," as the LORD commanded Moses.

The Israelites, who came out of the land of Egypt, were:

5 Reuben, the firstborn of Israel. The descendants of Reuben: of Hanoch, the clan of the Hanochites; of Pallu, the clan of the Palluites; 6of Hezron, the clan of the Hezronites; of Carmi, the clan of the Carmites. 7These are the clans of the Reubenites; the number of those enrolled was forty-three thousand seven hundred thirty. 8And the descendants of Pallu: Eliab. 9The descendants of Eliab: Nemuel, Dathan, and Abiram. These are the same Dathan and Abiram, chosen from the congregation, who rebelled against Moses and Aaron in the company of Korah, when they rebelled against the LORD, 10and the earth opened its mouth and swallowed them up along with Korah, when that company died, when the fire devoured two hundred fifty men; and they became a warning. 11Notwithstanding, the sons of Korah did not die.

12 The descendants of Simeon by their clans: of Nemuel, the clan of the Nemuelites; of Jamin, the clan of the Jaminites; of Jachin, the clan of the Jachinites; 13of Zerah, the clan of the Zerahites; of Shaul, the clan of the Shaulites.ᵇ 14These are the clans of the Simeonites, twenty-two thousand two hundred.

15 The children of Gad by their clans: of Zephon, the clan of the Zephonites; of Haggi, the clan of the Haggites; of Shuni, the clan of

---

a Heb lacks *take a census of the people*: Compare verse 2
b Or *Saul . . . Saulites*

---

carry out either form of punishment in vv. 4–5 and did nothing about the trespass in v. 6. **25.12** *My covenant of peace.* See Isa 54.10; Ezek 34.25; 37.26; Mal 2.4–5. **25.13** *Perpetual priesthood.* See also Ex 29.9; 40.15. **25.14–15** Both the Israelite man and the Midianite woman were important people in their own groups; see also v. 18 and *Zur* in 31.8. **25.16–18** See ch. 31. **25.18** This verse ties together the two stories in this chapter by pairing the Midianites with the Moabites in the *affair of Peor* and by asserting that the plague mentioned in vv. 8–9 was the result of the same Peor incident. *Trickery,* presumably the women's use of sexual contact to draw the Israelite men to sacrifices to a god other than the Lord; see 31.16.

26.1–65 The last obstacle to the conquest is overcome when the plague of ch. 25 apparently kills the remaining Israelites of the wilderness generation (see 26.64), those who were condemned to die because of the incident of the spies in chs. 13–14 (see 14.20–25, 28–35). At this point a new military census is taken, parallel to the census in ch. 1, and from this point the people of Israel are not the condemned generation of the forty years' wandering but rather a new generation that will live to conquer the promised land. **26.1** *After the plague* is v. 19 of ch. 25 in Hebrew. The plague is the one in 25.8–9, 18. *To Moses . . . Aaron.* Cf. 1.3; 20.22–29. **26.2** Cf. 1.2–3. **26.4** *Who came out of the land of Egypt* is an odd introduction to the following list, since these are precisely not those people (vv. 64–65). The phrase may simply mean those who were on the way from Egypt to Canaan. **26.5–50** Cf. 1.20–43. The ordering of the tribes here is different from that in ch. 1, but similar to that in ch. 2; the eastern and southern threesomes have traded places, so that Reuben, the traditional firstborn, is first and Manasseh and Ephraim are switched within the western threesome (cf. Gen 41.50–52; 48.8–20). In this second military census in Numbers, furthermore, the clans of each tribe are listed along with the tribe's totals (cf. Gen 46.8–27). The totals in this list differ from the totals in ch. 1, clan by clan and for Israel as a whole. **26.9–10** *Dathan and Abiram.* See ch. 16. **26.11** On the Korahites, see note on

the Shunites; 16 of Ozni, the clan of the Oznites; of Eri, the clan of the Erites; 17 of Arod, the clan of the Arodites; of Areli, the clan of the Arelites. 18 These are the clans of the Gadites: the number of those enrolled was forty thousand five hundred.

19 The sons of Judah: Er and Onan; Er and Onan died in the land of Canaan. 20 The descendants of Judah by their clans were: of Shelah, the clan of the Shelanites; of Perez, the clan of the Perezites; of Zerah, the clan of the Zerahites. 21 The descendants of Perez were: of Hezron, the clan of the Hezronites; of Hamul, the clan of the Hamulites. 22 These are the clans of Judah: the number of those enrolled was seventy-six thousand five hundred.

23 The descendants of Issachar by their clans: of Tola, the clan of the Tolaites; of Puvah, the clan of the Punites; 24 of Jashub, the clan of the Jashubites; of Shimron, the clan of the Shimronites. 25 These are the clans of Issachar: sixty-four thousand three hundred enrolled.

26 The descendants of Zebulun by their clans: of Sered, the clan of the Seredites; of Elon, the clan of the Elonites; of Jahleel, the clan of the Jahleelites. 27 These are the clans of the Zebulunites; the number of those enrolled was sixty thousand five hundred.

28 The sons of Joseph by their clans: Manasseh and Ephraim. 29 The descendants of Manasseh: of Machir, the clan of the Machirites; and Machir was the father of Gilead; of Gilead, the clan of the Gileadites. 30 These are the descendants of Gilead: of Iezer, the clan of the Iezerites; of Helek, the clan of the Helekites; 31 and of Asriel, the clan of the Asrielites; and of Shechem, the clan of the Shechemites; 32 and of Shemida, the clan of the Shemidaites; and of Hepher, the clan of the Hepherites. 33 Now Zelophehad son of Hepher had no sons, but daughters: and the names of the daughters of Zelophehad were Mahlah, Noah, Hoglah, Milcah, and Tirzah. 34 These are the clans of Manasseh; the number of those enrolled was fifty-two thousand seven hundred.

35 These are the descendants of Ephraim according to their clans: of Shuthelah, the clan of the Shuthelahites; of Becher, the clan of the Becherites; of Tahan, the clan of the Tahanites. 36 And these are the descendants of Shuthelah: of Eran, the clan of the Eranites. 37 These are the clans of the Ephraimites: the number of those enrolled was thirty-two thousand five hundred. These are the descendants of Joseph by their clans.

38 The descendants of Benjamin by their clans: of Bela, the clan of the Belaites; of Ashbel, the clan of the Ashbelites; of Ahiram, the clan of the Ahiramites; 39 of Shephupham, the clan of the Shuphamites; of Hupham, the clan of the Huphamites. 40 And the sons of Bela were Ard and Naaman: of Ard, the clan of the Ardites; of Naaman, the clan of the Naamites. 41 These are the descendants of Benjamin by their clans; the number of those enrolled was forty-five thousand six hundred.

42 These are the descendants of Dan by their clans: of Shuham, the clan of the Shuhamites. These are the clans of Dan by their clans. 43 All the clans of the Shuhamites: sixty-four thousand four hundred enrolled.

44 The descendants of Asher by their families: of Imnah, the clan of the Imnites; of Ishvi, the clan of the Ishvites; of Beriah, the clan of the Beriites. 45 Of the descendants of Beriah: of Heber, the clan of the Heberites; of Malchiel, the clan of the Malchielites. 46 And the name of the daughter of Asher was Serah. 47 These are the clans of the Asherites: the number of those enrolled was fifty-three thousand four hundred.

48 The descendants of Naphtali by their clans: of Jahzeel, the clan of the Jahzeelites; of Guni, the clan of the Gunites; 49 of Jezer, the clan of the Jezerites; of Shillem, the clan of the Shillemites. 50 These are the Naphtalites[a] by their clans: the number of those enrolled was forty-five thousand four hundred.

51 This was the number of the Israelites enrolled: six hundred and one thousand seven hundred thirty.

52 The LORD spoke to Moses, saying: 53 To these the land shall be apportioned for inheritance according to the number of names. 54 To a large tribe you shall give a large inheritance, and to a small tribe you shall give a small inheritance; every tribe shall be given its inheritance according to its enrollment. 55 But the land shall be apportioned by lot; according to the names of their ancestral tribes they shall inherit. 56 Their inheritance shall be apportioned according to lot between the larger and the smaller.

57 This is the enrollment of the Levites by

_____
a Heb clans of Naphtali

their clans: of Gershon, the clan of the Gershonites; of Kohath, the clan of the Kohathites; of Merari, the clan of the Merarites. 58These are the clans of Levi: the clan of the Libnites, the clan of the Hebronites, the clan of the Mahlites, the clan of the Mushites, the clan of the Korahites. Now Kohath was the father of Amram. 59The name of Amram's wife was Jochebed daughter of Levi, who was born to Levi in Egypt; and she bore to Amram: Aaron, Moses, and their sister Miriam. 60To Aaron were born Nadab, Abihu, Eleazar, and Ithamar. 61But Nadab and Abihu died when they offered unholy fire before the LORD. 62The number of those enrolled was twenty-three thousand, every male one month old and upward; for they were not enrolled among the Israelites because there was no allotment given to them among the Israelites.

63 These were those enrolled by Moses and Eleazar the priest, who enrolled the Israelites in the plains of Moab by the Jordan opposite Jericho. 64Among these there was not one of those enrolled by Moses and Aaron the priest, who had enrolled the Israelites in the wilderness of Sinai. 65For the LORD had said of them, "They shall die in the wilderness." Not one of them was left, except Caleb son of Jephunneh and Joshua son of Nun.

The Daughters of Zelophehad

27 Then the daughters of Zelophehad came forward. Zelophehad was son of Hepher son of Gilead son of Machir son of Manasseh son of Joseph, a member of the Manassite clans. The names of his daughters were: Mahlah, Noah, Hoglah, Milcah, and Tirzah. 2They stood before Moses, Eleazar the priest, the leaders, and all the congregation, at the entrance of the tent of meeting, and they said, 3"Our father died in the wilderness; he was not among the company of those who gathered themselves together against the LORD in the company of Korah, but died for his own sin; and he had no sons. 4Why should the name of our father be taken away from his clan because he had no son? Give to us a possession among our father's brothers."

5 Moses brought their case before the LORD. 6And the LORD spoke to Moses, saying: 7The daughters of Zelophehad are right in what they are saying; you shall indeed let them possess an inheritance among their father's brothers and pass the inheritance of their father on to them. 8You shall also say to the Israelites, "If a man dies, and has no son, then you shall pass his inheritance on to his daughter. 9If he has no daughter, then you shall give his inheritance to his brothers. 10If he has no brothers, then you shall give his inheritance to his father's brothers. 11And if his father has no brothers, then you shall give his inheritance to the nearest kinsman of his clan, and he shall possess it. It shall be for the Israelites a statute and ordinance, as the LORD commanded Moses."

Joshua Appointed Moses' Successor

12 The LORD said to Moses, "Go up this mountain of the Abarim range, and see the

16.1. **26.19** See Gen 38. **26.33** See 27.1–11; 36.1–12. **26.51** See 1.46. **26.52–56** A new reason for taking a census is given here, in addition to the need for knowing military power (v. 2), i.e., that after the conquest of Canaan land will be apportioned based on the size of the tribes. **26.57–62** Cf. 3.14–39. **26.61** See Lev 10.1–2. **26.62** Every male . . . up. See 3.15, 40–41. Not enrolled . . . Israelites. See 1.48–49. No allotment. See, e.g., 18.23–24. **26.64–65** See 14.20–25, 28–35.

27.1–11 In Israel, property was passed from father to son, but any patrilineal system must have alternative inheritance arrangements for a man who has no sons (ancestral land is not to be sold; see 1 Kings 21.1–19; Mic 2.1–5). One such arrangement, known also from other ancient Near Eastern documents, is that daughters may inherit, and that solution is here given Mosaic sanction. A restriction is added in 36.1–12, and the decision is carried out in Josh 17.3–6. For alternative solutions, see Deut 25.5–10 (cf. Gen 38.6–11; Ruth); Jer 32.6–15; Lev 25.8–31. **27.1** See 26.33.

27.3 See ch. 16. That Zelophehad, a Manassite, might have been part of Korah's rebellion marks this mention as dependent on the strand of tradition in which Korah and his group are not Levites (see note on 16.3). For his own sin, perhaps simply a reference to chs. 13–14. **27.4** On the name, cf. Deut 25.5–7. The son perpetuates the father's name in his genealogy. Presumably in the case of Zelophehad's daughters, the daughters' sons would carry on as Zelophehad's descendants and would inherit his property, an arrangement also known from other ancient Near Eastern documents; see also 1 Chr 2.34–36; Ezra 2.61; Neh 7.63. The complication that the sons will be part of their fathers' lineages as well is resolved in ch. 36, again in typical fashion. Father's brothers, i.e., male members of his clan. **27.5** Before the LORD, i.e., at the tent of meeting; see v. 2. **27.8–11** The line of inheritance approved here favors direct descendants, male or female, over other relatives, then moves from near to more distant male relatives.

land that I have given to the Israelites. [13]When you have seen it, you also shall be gathered to your people, as your brother Aaron was, [14]because you rebelled against my word in the wilderness of Zin when the congregation quarreled with me." You did not show my holiness before their eyes at the waters." (These are the waters of Meribath-kadesh in the wilderness of Zin.) [15]Moses spoke to the Lord, saying, [16]"Let the Lord, the God of the spirits of all flesh, appoint someone over the congregation [17]who shall go out before them and come in before them, who shall lead them out and bring them in, so that the congregation of the Lord may not be like sheep without a shepherd." [18]So the Lord said to Moses, "Take Joshua son of Nun, a man in whom is the spirit, and lay your hand upon him; [19]have him stand before Eleazar the priest and all the congregation, and commission him in their sight. [20]You shall give him some of your authority, so that all the congregation of the Israelites may obey. [21]But he shall stand before Eleazar the priest, who shall inquire for him by the decision of the Urim before the Lord; at his word they shall go out, and at his word they shall come in, both he and all the Israelites with him, the whole congregation." [22]So Moses did as the Lord commanded him. He took Joshua and had him stand before Eleazar the priest and the whole congregation; [23]he laid his hands on him and commissioned him—as the Lord had directed through Moses.

Daily Offerings

28 The Lord spoke to Moses, saying: [2]Command the Israelites, and say to them: My offering, the food for my offerings by fire, my pleasing odor, you shall take care to offer to me at its appointed time. [3]And you shall say to them, This is the offering by fire that you shall offer to the Lord: two male lambs a year old without blemish, daily, as a regular offering. [4]One lamb you shall offer in the morning, and the other lamb you shall offer at twilight;[b] [5]also one-tenth of an ephah of choice flour for a grain offering, mixed with one-fourth of a hin of beaten oil. [6]It is a regular burnt offering, ordained at Mount Sinai for a pleasing odor, an offering by fire to the Lord. [7]Its drink offering shall be one-fourth of a hin for each lamb; in the sanctuary you shall pour out a drink offering of strong drink to the Lord. [8]The other lamb you shall offer at twilight[b] with a grain offering and a drink offering like the one in the morning; you shall offer it as an offering by fire, a pleasing odor to the Lord.

Sabbath Offerings

9 On the sabbath day: two male lambs a year old without blemish, and two-tenths of an ephah of choice flour for a grain offering, mixed with oil, and its drink offering— [10]this is the burnt offering for every sabbath, in addition to the regular burnt offering and its drink offering.

Monthly Offerings

11 At the beginnings of your months you shall offer a burnt offering to the Lord: two young bulls, one ram, seven male lambs a year old without blemish; [12]also three-tenths of an ephah of choice flour for a grain offering, mixed with oil, for each bull; and two-tenths of choice flour for a grain offering, mixed with oil, for the one ram; [13]and one-tenth of choice flour mixed with oil as a grain offering for every lamb—a burnt offering of pleasing odor, an offering by fire to the Lord. [14]Their drink offerings shall be half a hin of wine for a bull, one-third of a hin for a ram, and one-fourth of a hin for a lamb. This is the burnt of-

a Heb lacks *with me* *b* Heb *between the two evenings*

27.12 See 21.11. **27.13** See 20.22–29. **27.14** See 20.12. **27.16** *The God of the spirits of all flesh.* See 16.22. **27.17** *Go out before them and come in before them* is a phrase often used as a technical military term for the battle march; see v. 21; Josh 14.11; 1 Sam 18.13, 16; 29.6. *Sheep without a shepherd.* See 1 Kings 22.17; Ezek 34.1–10; Zech 11; Mk 6.34. **27.18** On *Joshua,* beside the book of Joshua, see esp. Ex 17.8–14; 24.13; 33.11; Num 11.28; 13.8, 16; 14.6, 30, 38. *A man in whom is the spirit.* See 11.16–30. *Lay your hand upon him,* a form of transfer, in this case, of Moses' authority (v. 20). See

also 8.10–11; Deut 34.9. **27.21** *Eleazar,* not Joshua, is to perform the role of intermediary, using the Urim to determine the Lord's will; see Ex 28.29–30; 1 Sam 14.41; 28.6; Ezra 2.63. *Go out . . . come in.* See v. 17. **27.23** See v. 18.

28.1–29.40 Offerings are described for a number of occasions. Lev 23 has a similar cultic calendar; cf. also Ex 23.14–17; 34.18–24; Deut 16.1–17; Ezek 45.17–46.15. **28.2** *Offerings by fire, my pleasing odor.* See 15.3. **28.3–8** Cf. Ex 29.38–42. **28.11** *Beginnings of your months.* See 10.10; 1 Sam 20.5, 24; 2 Kings 4.23; Isa

fering of every month throughout the months of the year. [15]And there shall be one male goat for a sin offering to the LORD; it shall be offered in addition to the regular burnt offering and its drink offering.

Offerings at Passover

[16] On the fourteenth day of the first month there shall be a passover offering to the LORD. [17]And on the fifteenth day of this month is a festival; seven days shall unleavened bread be eaten. [18]On the first day there shall be a holy convocation. You shall not work at your occupations. [19]You shall offer an offering by fire, a burnt offering to the LORD: two young bulls, one ram, and seven male lambs a year old; see that they are without blemish. [20]Their grain offering shall be of choice flour mixed with oil: three-tenths of an ephah shall you offer for a bull, and two-tenths for a ram; [21]one-tenth shall you offer for each of the seven lambs; [22]also one male goat for a sin offering, to make atonement for you. [23]You shall offer these in addition to the burnt offering of the morning, which belongs to the regular burnt offering. [24]In the same way you shall offer daily, for seven days, the food of an offering by fire, a pleasing odor to the LORD; it shall be offered in addition to the regular burnt offering and its drink offering. [25]And on the seventh day you shall have a holy convocation; you shall not work at your occupations.

Offerings at the Festival of Weeks

[26] On the day of the first fruits, when you offer a grain offering of new grain to the LORD at your festival of weeks, you shall have a holy convocation; you shall not work at your occupations. [27]You shall offer a burnt offering, a pleasing odor to the LORD: two young bulls, one ram, seven male lambs a year old. [28]Their grain offering shall be of choice flour mixed with oil, three-tenths of an ephah for each bull, two-tenths for one ram, [29]one-tenth for each of the seven lambs; [30]with one male goat,

to make atonement for you. [31]In addition to the regular burnt offering with its grain offering, you shall offer them and their drink offering. They shall be without blemish.

Offerings at the Festival of Trumpets

29 On the first day of the seventh month you shall have a holy convocation; you shall not work at your occupations. It is a day for you to blow the trumpets, [2]and you shall offer a burnt offering, a pleasing odor to the LORD: one young bull, one ram, seven male lambs a year old without blemish. [3]Their grain offering shall be of choice flour mixed with oil, three-tenths of one ephah for the bull, two-tenths for the ram, [4]and one-tenth for each of the seven lambs; [5]with one male goat for a sin offering, to make atonement for you. [6]These are in addition to the burnt offering of the new moon and its grain offering, and the regular burnt offering and its grain offering, and their drink offerings, according to the ordinance for them, a pleasing odor, an offering by fire to the LORD.

Offerings on the Day of Atonement

[7] On the tenth day of this seventh month you shall have a holy convocation, and deny yourselves;[a] you shall do no work. [8]You shall offer a burnt offering to the LORD, a pleasing odor: one young bull, one ram, seven male lambs a year old. They shall be without blemish. [9]Their grain offering shall be of choice flour mixed with oil, three-tenths of an ephah for the bull, two-tenths for the one ram, [10]one-tenth for each of the seven lambs; [11]with one male goat for a sin offering, in addition to the sin offering of atonement, and the regular burnt offering and its grain offering, and their drink offerings.

Offerings at the Festival of Booths

[12] On the fifteenth day of the seventh month you shall have a holy convocation; you shall

a Or *and fast*

1.14; Hos 2.11; Am 8.5. **28.16** On the *passover,* see 9.1–14; Ex 12.1–27. No offerings are described here; the celebration is described elsewhere and assumed here. **28.17–25** The festival of *unleavened bread* (Ex 13.3–10), originally a separate festival, is combined with the Passover. **28.26** Fifty days after the Festival of Unleavened Bread, at the beginning of the wheat harvest (June), is the *festival of weeks,* Shavuoth (Lev 23.15–21), or the "festival of harvest" (Ex 23.16). **29.1** The

first day of the seventh month is traditionally New Year's Day (Rosh Hashanah; see Ex 23.16; 34.22 for the end of the year); many commentators have argued that Israel once had an "agricultural year" calendar in which the first month came in the autumn, following the harvest thanksgiving festival (see v. 12). *To blow the trumpets.* See 10.1–10. **29.6** See 28.2. **29.7–11** The Day of Atonement, Yom Kippur; see Lev 16.29–34; 23.26–32. **29.12–34** The Festival of Booths, Sukkoth (Lev

not work at your occupations. You shall celebrate a festival to the LORD seven days. 13You shall offer a burnt offering, an offering by fire, a pleasing odor to the LORD: thirteen young bulls, two rams, fourteen male lambs a year old. They shall be without blemish. 14Their grain offering shall be of choice flour mixed with oil, three-tenths of an ephah for each of the thirteen bulls, two-tenths for each of the two rams, 15and one-tenth for each of the fourteen lambs; 16also one male goat for a sin offering, in addition to the regular burnt offering, its grain offering and its drink offering.

17 On the second day: twelve young bulls, two rams, fourteen male lambs a year old without blemish, 18with the grain offering and the drink offerings for the bulls, for the rams, and for the lambs, as prescribed in accordance with their number; 19also one male goat for a sin offering, in addition to the regular burnt offering and its grain offering, and their drink offerings.

20 On the third day: eleven bulls, two rams, fourteen male lambs a year old without blemish, 21with the grain offering and the drink offerings for the bulls, for the rams, and for the lambs, as prescribed in accordance with their number; 22also one male goat for a sin offering, in addition to the regular burnt offering and its grain offering and its drink offering.

23 On the fourth day: ten bulls, two rams, fourteen male lambs a year old without blemish, 24with the grain offering and the drink offerings for the bulls, for the rams, and for the lambs, as prescribed in accordance with their number; 25also one male goat for a sin offering, in addition to the regular burnt offering, its grain offering and its drink offering.

26 On the fifth day: nine bulls, two rams, fourteen male lambs a year old without blemish, 27with the grain offering and the drink offerings for the bulls, for the rams, and for the lambs, as prescribed in accordance with their number; 28also one male goat for a sin offering, in addition to the regular burnt offering and its grain offering and its drink offering.

29 On the sixth day: eight bulls, two rams, fourteen male lambs a year old without blem-

ish, 30with the grain offering and the drink offerings for the bulls, for the rams, and for the lambs, as prescribed in accordance with their number; 31also one male goat for a sin offering, in addition to the regular burnt offering, its grain offering, and its drink offerings.

32 On the seventh day: seven bulls, two rams, fourteen male lambs a year old without blemish, 33with the grain offering and the drink offerings for the bulls, for the rams, and for the lambs, as prescribed in accordance with their number; 34also one male goat for a sin offering, besides the regular burnt offering, its grain offering, and its drink offering.

35 On the eighth day you shall have a solemn assembly; you shall not work at your occupations. 36You shall offer a burnt offering, an offering by fire, a pleasing odor to the LORD: one bull, one ram, seven male lambs a year old without blemish, 37and the grain offering and the drink offerings for the bull, for the ram, and for the lambs, as prescribed in accordance with their number; 38also one male goat for a sin offering, in addition to the regular burnt offering and its grain offering and its drink offering.

39 These you shall offer to the LORD at your appointed festivals, in addition to your votive offerings and your freewill offerings, as your burnt offerings, your grain offerings, your drink offerings, and your offerings of well-being.

40*a* So Moses told the Israelites everything just as the LORD had commanded Moses.

Vows Made by Women

30 Then Moses said to the heads of the tribes of the Israelites: This is what the LORD has commanded. 2When a man makes a vow to the LORD, or swears an oath to bind himself by a pledge, he shall not break his word; he shall do according to all that proceeds out of his mouth.

3 When a woman makes a vow to the LORD, or binds herself by a pledge, while within her father's house, in her youth, 4and her father

---

a Ch 30.1 in Heb

23.33–36; Deut 16.13–15), or Festival of Ingathering (Ex 23.16; 34.22), is the harvest thanksgiving festival. **29.35–38** Although the Feast of Booths is a grand seven-day festival (see v. 12), these regulations add an eighth day, with far fewer offerings.

30.1–16 Ch. 30 focuses on vows made by women and the limits that husbands and fathers may place on those vows (note the mention of vows in 29.39). **30.3–5** Vows made while a woman is under her father's authority. **30.4–5** The father must speak up as

hears of her vow or her pledge by which she has bound herself, and says nothing to her; then all her vows shall stand, and any pledge by which she has bound herself shall stand. 5But if her father expresses disapproval to her at the time that he hears of it, no vow of hers, and no pledge by which she has bound herself, shall stand; and the LORD will forgive her, because her father had expressed to her his disapproval.

6 If she marries, while obligated by her vows or any thoughtless utterance of her lips by which she has bound herself, 7and her husband hears of it and says nothing to her at the time that he hears, then her vows shall stand, and her pledges by which she has bound herself shall stand. 8But if, at the time that her husband hears of it, he expresses disapproval to her, then he shall nullify the vow by which she was obligated, or the thoughtless utterance of her lips, by which she bound herself; and the LORD will forgive her. 9(But every vow of a widow or of a divorced woman, by which she has bound herself, shall be binding upon her.) 10And if she made a vow in her husband's house, or bound herself by a pledge with an oath, 11and her husband heard it and said nothing to her, and did not express disapproval to her, then all her vows shall stand, and any pledge by which she bound herself shall stand. 12But if her husband nullifies them at the time that he hears them, then whatever proceeds out of her lips concerning her vows, or concerning her pledge of herself, shall not stand. Her husband has nullified them, and the LORD will forgive her. 13Any vow or any binding oath to deny herself,*a* her husband may allow to stand, or her husband may nullify. 14But if her husband says nothing to her from day to day,*b* then he validates all her

vows, or all her pledges, by which she is obligated; he has validated them, because he said nothing to her at the time that he heard of them. 15But if he nullifies them some time after he has heard of them, then he shall bear her guilt.

16 These are the statutes that the LORD commanded Moses concerning a husband and his wife, and a father and his daughter while she is still young and in her father's house.

War against Midian

31 The LORD spoke to Moses, saying, 2"Avenge the Israelites on the Midianites; afterward you shall be gathered to your people." 3So Moses said to the people, "Arm some of your number for the war, so that they may go against Midian, to execute the LORD's vengeance on Midian. 4You shall send a thousand from each of the tribes of Israel to the war." 5So out of the thousands of Israel, a thousand from each tribe were conscripted, twelve thousand armed for battle. 6Moses sent them to the war, a thousand from each tribe, along with Phinehas son of Eleazar the priest,*c* with the vessels of the sanctuary and the trumpets for sounding the alarm in his hand. 7They did battle against Midian, as the LORD had commanded Moses, and killed every male. 8They killed the kings of Midian: Evi, Rekem, Zur, Hur, and Reba, the five kings of Midian, in addition to others who were slain by them; and they also killed Balaam son of Beor with the sword. 9The Israelites took the women of Midian and their little ones captive; and they took all their cattle, their flocks, and all their goods

---

a Or *to fast*   *b* Or *from that day to the next*   *c* Gk: Heb adds *to the war*

---

soon as he hears of his daughter's vow, if he disapproves. *The LORD will forgive her,* i.e., will not punish her or require atonement from her for breaking her vow. **30.6–8** A woman under a vow at the time of her marriage, one that, presumably, her father did not annul. *Thoughtless,* better "impulsive" or "rash"; cf. the same root in Lev 5.4; Ps 106.33. **30.7–8** See 30.4–5. **30.9** A *widow* or *divorced woman* is presumably not under any man's authority. **30.10–15** Vows made while under a husband's authority. **30.11–12** See 30.4–5. **30.13** A specific instance, in which a woman vows to *deny herself,* or to fast (see text note *a;* cf. the same phrase in 29.7). **30.14–15** *He shall bear her guilt.* See 30.4–5. The husband may change his mind at a later date and keep her from carrying out her vow, but

the Lord will hold him responsible, not her (see Deut 23.21–23).

31.2 *Avenge the Israelites,* because of the incident at Peor (25.6–18). Moses' death is predicted (see also 27.13). **31.3–12** The war against Midian is described in holy-war terms (see, e.g., Deut 20; 21.10–14; 23.9–14; 24.5; Josh 6.1–21). **31.5** Compared to 26.2, 51, *twelve thousand* is a very small number. Cf. Deut 20.5–8; Judg 7.2–8; 1 Sam 14.6–15; 2 Sam 17.1; 1 Kings 10.26. **31.6** *Phinehas* instead of Eleazar. See 16.37–39; 25.7. *Trumpets.* See 10.9. The presence of the priest and items from the sanctuary indicates holy war; see Deut 20.2–4. **31.7** *Killed every male.* See Deut 20.12–13. **31.8** The five kings. See also Josh 13.21. *Zur.* See 25.15. *Balaam.* See 31.16; chs. 22–25. **31.9–12** See

as booty. 10All their towns where they had settled, and all their encampments, they burned, 11but they took all the spoil and all the booty, both people and animals. 12Then they brought the captives and the booty and the spoil to Moses, to Eleazar the priest, and to the congregation of the Israelites, at the camp on the plains of Moab by the Jordan at Jericho.

Return from the War

13 Moses, Eleazar the priest, and all the leaders of the congregation went to meet them outside the camp. 14Moses became angry with the officers of the army, the commanders of thousands and the commanders of hundreds, who had come from service in the war. 15Moses said to them, "Have you allowed all the women to live? 16These women here, on Balaam's advice, made the Israelites act treacherously against the LORD in the affair of Peor, so that the plague came among the congregation of the LORD. 17Now therefore, kill every male among the little ones, and kill every woman who has known a man by sleeping with him. 18But all the young girls who have not known a man by sleeping with him, keep alive for yourselves. 19Camp outside the camp seven days; whoever of you has killed any person or touched a corpse, purify yourselves and your captives on the third and on the seventh day. 20You shall purify every garment, every article of skin, everything made of goats' hair, and every article of wood."

21 Eleazar the priest said to the troops who had gone to battle: "This is the statute of the law that the LORD has commanded Moses: 22gold, silver, bronze, iron, tin, and lead— 23everything that can withstand fire, shall be passed through fire, and it shall be clean. Nevertheless it shall also be purified with the water for purification; and whatever cannot withstand fire, shall be passed through the water. 24You must wash your clothes on the seventh day, and you shall be clean; afterward you may come into the camp."

Disposition of Captives and Booty

25 The LORD spoke to Moses, saying, 26"You and Eleazar the priest and the heads of the ancestral houses of the congregation make an inventory of the booty captured, both human and animal. 27Divide the booty into two parts, between the warriors who went out to battle and all the congregation. 28From the share of the warriors who went out to battle, set aside as tribute for the LORD, one item out of every five hundred, whether persons, oxen, donkeys, sheep, or goats. 29Take it from their half and give it to Eleazar the priest as an offering to the LORD. 30But from the Israelites' half you shall take one out of every fifty, whether persons, oxen, donkeys, sheep, or goats—all the animals—and give them to the Levites who have charge of the tabernacle of the LORD."

31 Then Moses and Eleazar the priest did as the LORD had commanded Moses:

32 The booty remaining from the spoil that the troops had taken totaled six hundred seventy-five thousand sheep, 33seventy-two thousand oxen, 34sixty-one thousand donkeys, 35and thirty-two thousand persons in all, women who had not known a man by sleeping with him.

36 The half-share, the portion of those who had gone out to war, was in number three hundred thirty-seven thousand five hundred sheep and goats, 37and the LORD's tribute of sheep and goats was six hundred seventy-five. 38The oxen were thirty-six thousand, of which the LORD's tribute was seventy-two. 39The donkeys were thirty thousand five hundred, of which the LORD's tribute was sixty-one. 40The persons were sixteen thousand, of which the LORD's tribute was thirty-two persons. 41Moses gave the tribute, the offering for the LORD, to Eleazar the priest, as the LORD had commanded Moses.

42 As for the Israelites' half, which Moses separated from that of the troops, 43the congregation's half was three hundred thirty-

31.14 See also 1 Sam 15.10–19. **31.15** See 31.9. **31.16** Cf. ch. 25. Although Balaam is not mentioned there, ch. 25 is juxtaposed to the Balaam narrative, and Balaam is said to be at Peor in 23.28. See also Josh 13.21–22. Midianite women, plural, seem here to be merged with Moabite women (25.1–5, 16–18). **31.17– 18** Even male children are killed, presumably to ensure the extermination of Midian, but cf. Judg 6–8. The women who are to be killed are all those who might have been involved in sexual relations with Israelite men; see 31.16; 25.1. **31.19–24** See 19.1–22. **31.19** On the third . . . seventh day. See 19.12, 19. **31.20** See Lev 11.29–32. **31.23** Water for purification. See 19.9, 11– 22. **31.27–30** Provision for the sanctuary from the living booty (see also 18.8–32), a smaller amount taken from the warriors' share for the priests and a larger amount taken from the rest for the Levites; see also

seven thousand five hundred sheep and goats, [44]thirty-six thousand oxen, [45]thirty thousand five hundred donkeys, [46]and sixteen thousand persons. [47]From the Israelites' half Moses took one of every fifty, both of persons and of animals, and gave them to the Levites who had charge of the tabernacle of the LORD; as the LORD had commanded Moses.

[48] Then the officers who were over the thousands of the army, the commanders of thousands and the commanders of hundreds, approached Moses, [49]and said to Moses, "Your servants have counted the warriors who are under our command, and not one of us is missing. [50]And we have brought the LORD's offering, what each of us found, articles of gold, armlets and bracelets, signet rings, earrings, and pendants, to make atonement for ourselves before the LORD." [51]Moses and Eleazar the priest received the gold from them, all in the form of crafted articles. [52]And all the gold of the offering that they offered to the LORD, from the commanders of thousands and the commanders of hundreds, was sixteen thousand seven hundred fifty shekels. [53](The troops had all taken plunder for themselves.) [54]So Moses and Eleazar the priest received the gold from the commanders of thousands and of hundreds, and brought it into the tent of meeting as a memorial for the Israelites before the LORD.

Conquest and Division of Transjordan

32 Now the Reubenites and the Gadites owned a very great number of cattle. When they saw that the land of Jazer and the land of Gilead was a good place for cattle, [2]the Gadites and the Reubenites came and spoke to Moses, to Eleazar the priest, and to the leaders of the congregation, saying, [3]"Ataroth, Dibon, Jazer, Nimrah, Heshbon, Elealeh, Sebam, Nebo, and Beon— [4]the land that the LORD subdued before the congregation of Israel—is a land for cattle; and your servants have cattle." [5]They continued, "If we have found favor in your sight, let this land be given to your servants for a possession; do not make us cross the Jordan."

[6] But Moses said to the Gadites and to the Reubenites, "Shall your brothers go to war while you sit here? [7]Why will you discourage the hearts of the Israelites from going over into the land that the LORD has given them? [8]Your fathers did this, when I sent them from Kadesh-barnea to see the land. [9]When they went up to the Wadi Eshcol and saw the land, they discouraged the hearts of the Israelites from going into the land that the LORD had given them. [10]The LORD's anger was kindled on that day and he swore, saying, [11]'Surely none of the people who came up out of Egypt, from twenty years old and upward, shall see the land that I swore to give to Abraham, to Isaac, and to Jacob, because they have not unreservedly followed me— [12]none except Caleb son of Jephunneh the Kenizzite and Joshua son of Nun, for they have unreservedly followed the LORD.' [13]And the LORD's anger was kindled against Israel, and he made them wander in the wilderness for forty years, until all the generation that had done evil in the sight of the LORD had disappeared. [14]And now you, a brood of sinners, have risen in place of your fathers, to increase the LORD's fierce anger against Israel! [15]If you turn away from following him, he will again abandon them in the wilderness; and you will destroy all this people."

[16] Then they came up to him and said, "We will build sheepfolds here for our flocks, and towns for our little ones, [17]but we will take up arms as a vanguard[a] before the Israelites, until

_____
a Cn: Heb *hurrying*

1 Sam 30.21–25. **31.35** See 31.14–18. **31.49** The Israelite officers inform Moses that they lost no one in the battle. **31.50** For a possible explanation for the officers' need for *atonement,* see Ex 30.11–16. On the Midianites' *gold,* see Judg 8.24–26. **31.53** The *troops,* i.e., as opposed to the officers. **31.54** *As a memorial* in the tent of meeting; see also 16.39–40; Ex 30.11–16.
32.1–42 See also Deut 3.12–20; Josh 13.8–32; 22. **32.1–5** The Reubenites and the Gadites have cattle, and they point out that Israel has already won good cattle land. **32.1** *Jazer.* See 21.32. *Gilead,* the fertile highland east of the Jordan River; see Gen 31.21, 47–

48. **32.2** *Eleazar.* See 19.3; 20.22–29. **32.6** See Judg 5.16–17, 23. **32.8–15** Moses interprets the request of the Reubenites and Gadites as a fear of failure in war, as in the disastrous earlier incident of the spies, chs. 13–14. This passage is one of several that are negative toward the tribes east of the Jordan. See also 16.1; Gen 35.22a; 49.3–4; Josh 22.10–34; Judg 11.29–40; 1 Chr 5.1, 23–26. **32.16–27** The parties reach a compromise: the Reubenites and Gadites will both inherit the land they want and fight in the remaining battles of conquest on the west side of the Jordan. **32.17** *Before the Israelites,* as if these people are not part of Israel (see v. 22).

we have brought them to their place. Meanwhile our little ones will stay in the fortified towns because of the inhabitants of the land. ¹⁸We will not return to our homes until all the Israelites have obtained their inheritance. ¹⁹We will not inherit with them on the other side of the Jordan and beyond, because our inheritance has come to us on this side of the Jordan to the east."

20 So Moses said to them, "If you do this— if you take up arms to go before the LORD for the war, ²¹and all those of you who bear arms cross the Jordan before the LORD, until he has driven out his enemies from before him ²²and the land is subdued before the LORD—then after that you may return and be free of obligation to the LORD and to Israel, and this land shall be your possession before the LORD. ²³But if you do not do this, you have sinned against the LORD; and be sure your sin will find you out. ²⁴Build towns for your little ones, and folds for your flocks; but do what you have promised."

25 Then the Gadites and the Reubenites said to Moses, "Your servants will do as my lord commands. ²⁶Our little ones, our wives, our flocks, and all our livestock shall remain there in the towns of Gilead; ²⁷but your servants will cross over, everyone armed for war, to do battle for the LORD, just as my lord orders."

28 So Moses gave command concerning them to Eleazar the priest, to Joshua son of Nun, and to the heads of the ancestral houses of the Israelite tribes. ²⁹And Moses said to them, "If the Gadites and the Reubenites, everyone armed for battle before the LORD, will cross over the Jordan with you and the land shall be subdued before you, then you shall give them the land of Gilead for a possession; ³⁰but if they will not cross over with you armed, they shall have possessions among you in the land of Canaan." ³¹The Gadites and the Reubenites answered, "As the LORD has spoken to your servants, so we will do. ³²We will cross over armed before the LORD into the land of Canaan, but the possession of our inheritance shall remain with us on this side of*a* the Jordan."

33 Moses gave to them—to the Gadites and to the Reubenites and to the half-tribe of Manasseh son of Joseph—the kingdom of King Sihon of the Amorites and the kingdom of King Og of Bashan, the land and its towns, with the territories of the surrounding towns. ³⁴And the Gadites rebuilt Dibon, Ataroth, Aroer, ³⁵Atroth-shophan, Jazer, Jogbehah, ³⁶Beth-nimrah, and Beth-haran, fortified cities, and folds for sheep. ³⁷And the Reubenites rebuilt Heshbon, Elealeh, Kiriathaim, ³⁸Nebo, and Baal-meon (some names being changed), and Sibmah; and they gave names to the towns that they rebuilt. ³⁹The descendants of Machir son of Manasseh went to Gilead, captured it, and dispossessed the Amorites who were there; ⁴⁰so Moses gave Gilead to Machir son of Manasseh, and he settled there. ⁴¹Jair son of Manasseh went and captured their villages, and renamed them Havvoth-jair.*b* ⁴²And Nobah went and captured Kenath and its villages, and renamed it Nobah after himself.

The Stages of Israel's Journey from Egypt

33 These are the stages by which the Israelites went out of the land of Egypt in military formation under the leadership of Moses and Aaron. ²Moses wrote down their starting points, stage by stage, by command of the LORD; and these are their stages according to their starting places. ³They set out from Rameses in the first month, on the fifteenth day of the first month; on the day after the passover the Israelites went out boldly in the sight of all the Egyptians, ⁴while the Egyptians were burying all their firstborn, whom the LORD had struck down among them. The LORD executed judgments even against their gods.

5 So the Israelites set out from Rameses, and camped at Succoth. ⁶They set out from Succoth, and camped at Etham, which is on the edge of the wilderness. ⁷They set out from Etham, and turned back to Pi-hahiroth, which faces Baal-zephon; and they camped before Migdol. ⁸They set out from Pi-hahiroth, passed through the sea into the wilderness, went a three days' journey in the wilderness of Etham, and camped at Marah. ⁹They set out from Marah and came to Elim; at Elim there were twelve springs of water and seventy palm trees, and they camped there. ¹⁰They set out from Elim and camped by the Red Sea.*c* ¹¹They set out from the Red Sea*c* and camped in the wilderness of Sin. ¹²They set out from the wilderness of Sin and camped at Dophkah. ¹³They set out from Dophkah and camped at

---

a Heb *beyond*   *b* That is *the villages of Jair*   *c* Or *Sea of Reeds*

Alush. 14They set out from Alush and camped at Rephidim, where there was no water for the people to drink. 15They set out from Rephidim and camped in the wilderness of Sinai. 16They set out from the wilderness of Sinai and camped at Kibroth-hattaavah. 17They set out from Kibroth-hattaavah and camped at Hazeroth. 18They set out from Hazeroth and camped at Rithmah. 19They set out from Rithmah and camped at Rimmon-pcrcz. 20They set out from Rimmon-perez and camped at Libnah. 21They set out from Libnah and camped at Rissah. 22They set out from Rissah and camped at Kehelathah. 23They set out from Kehelathah and camped at Mount Shepher. 24They set out from Mount Shepher and camped at Haradah. 25They set out from Haradah and camped at Makheloth. 26They set out from Makheloth and camped at Tahath. 27They set out from Tahath and camped at Terah. 28They set out from Terah and camped at Mithkah. 29They set out from Mithkah and camped at Hashmonah. 30They set out from Hashmonah and camped at Moseroth. 31They set out from Moseroth and camped at Bene-jaakan. 32They set out from Bene-jaakan and camped at Hor-haggidgad. 33They set out from Hor-haggidgad and camped at Jotbathah. 34They set out from Jotbathah and camped at Abronah. 35They set out from Abronah and camped at Ezion-geber. 36They set out from Ezion-geber and camped in the wilderness of Zin (that is, Kadesh). 37They set out from Kadesh and camped at Mount Hor, on the edge of the land of Edom.

38 Aaron the priest went up Mount Hor at the command of the LORD and died there in the fortieth year after the Israelites had come out of the land of Egypt, on the first day of thc fifth month. 39Aaron was one hundred twenty-three years old when he died on Mount Hor.

40 The Canaanite, the king of Arad, who lived in the Negeb in the land of Canaan, heard of the coming of the Israelites.

41 They set out from Mount Hor and camped at Zalmonah. 42They set out from Zalmonah and camped at Punon. 43They set out from Punon and camped at Oboth. 44They set out from Oboth and camped at Iye-abarim, in the territory of Moab. 45They set out from Iyim and camped at Dibon-gad. 46They set out from Dibon-gad and camped at Almon-diblathaim. 47They set out from Almon-diblathaim and camped in the mountains of Abarim, before Nebo. 48They set out from the mountains of Abarim and camped in the plains of Moab by the Jordan at Jericho; 49they camped by the Jordan from Beth-jeshimoth as far as Abel-shittim in the plains of Moab.

Directions for the Conquest of Canaan

50 In the plains of Moab by the Jordan at Jericho, the LORD spoke to Moses, saying: 51Speak to the Israelites, and say to them: When you cross over the Jordan into the land of Canaan, 52you shall drive out all the inhabitants of the land from before you, destroy all their figured stones, destroy all their cast images, and demolish all their high places. 53You shall take possession of the land and settle in it, for I have given you the land to possess. 54You shall apportion the land by lot according to your clans; to a large one you shall give a large inheritance, and to a small one you shall give a small inheritance; the inheritance shall belong to the person on whom the lot falls; according to your ancestral tribes you shall inherit. 55But if you do not drive out the inhabitants of the land from before you, then those whom you let remain shall be as barbs in your eyes and thorns in your sides; they shall trouble you in

---

32.22 *Free of obligation to the LORD and to Israel* reads almost as if they will no longer be part of the tribal federation. See also 34.1–2, 10–12; Josh 22.9, 21–29. It is also possible that *free of obligation* simply means that they will have participated fully in the holy war of conquest. **32.28** See 32.2. Moses must *give a command* because he will not be with the Israelites (see 20.12; 27.13–14). *Joshua.* See 27.12–23. **32.30** *They shall . . . Canaan,* i.e., they will not be given the choice land they desire east of the Jordan. **32.33** Note the addition of half of *Manasseh. Sihon.* See 21.21–32. *Og.* See 21.33–35. **32.34–38** Cf. Josh 13.15–28. As described here in Numbers, the boundary between Reuben and Gad is not clear-cut. **32.39–42** Not only Reuben and

Gad but also half the tribe of *Manasseh* lived east of the Jordan (see v. 33; Josh 13.29–32, and cf. Josh 17.1–13). On Manasseh's descendants, see 26.29–34; 1 Chr 7.14–19; Gen 50.23. These verses are similar to the descriptions of tribal conquests in Judg 1. **32.39** *Gilead.* Cf. 32.1–4. **32.41** *Havvoth-jair.* See Deut 3.14; Judg 10.3–4; 1 Chr 2.21–23. **32.42** On *Nobah* and *Kenath,* see Judg 8.11; 1 Chr 2.23. **33.3–5** See Ex 12.37. **33.6–15** From Succoth to the wilderness of Sinai. See Ex 13.17–19.1. **33.16–49** From the wilderness of Sinai to the plains of Moab. See 10.11–22.1. **33.38–39** See 20.22–29. **33.50–56** See also, e.g., Ex 23.23–33; 34.11–16; Deut 7.1–6; 12.2–4; cf. Josh 23.4–8; Judg 1.1–2.5; 2.11–3.6.

the land where you are settling. 56And I will do to you as I thought to do to them.

The Boundaries of the Land

34 The LORD spoke to Moses, saying: 2Command the Israelites, and say to them: When you enter the land of Canaan (this is the land that shall fall to you for an inheritance, the land of Canaan, defined by its boundaries), 3your south sector shall extend from the wilderness of Zin along the side of Edom. Your southern boundary shall begin from the end of the Dead Sea^a on the east; 4your boundary shall turn south of the ascent of Akrabbim, and cross to Zin, and its outer limit shall be south of Kadesh-barnea; then it shall go on to Hazar-addar, and cross to Azmon; 5the boundary shall turn from Azmon to the Wadi of Egypt, and its termination shall be at the Sea.

6 For the western boundary, you shall have the Great Sea and its^b coast; this shall be your western boundary.

7 This shall be your northern boundary: from the Great Sea you shall mark out your line to Mount Hor; 8from Mount Hor you shall mark it out to Lebo-hamath, and the outer limit of the boundary shall be at Zedad; 9then the boundary shall extend to Ziphron, and its end shall be at Hazar-enan; this shall be your northern boundary.

10 You shall mark out your eastern boundary from Hazar-enan to Shepham; 11and the boundary shall continue down from Shepham to Riblah on the east side of Ain; and the boundary shall go down, and reach the eastern slope of the sea of Chinnereth; 12and the boundary shall go down to the Jordan, and its end shall be at the Dead Sea.^a This shall be your land with its boundaries all around.

13 Moses commanded the Israelites, saying:

This is the land that you shall inherit by lot, which the LORD has commanded to give to the nine tribes and to the half-tribe; 14for the tribe of the Reubenites by their ancestral houses and the tribe of the Gadites by their ancestral houses have taken their inheritance, and also the half-tribe of Manasseh; 15the two tribes and the half-tribe have taken their inheritance beyond the Jordan at Jericho eastward, toward the sunrise.

Tribal Leaders

16 The LORD spoke to Moses, saying: 17These are the names of the men who shall apportion the land to you for inheritance: the priest Eleazar and Joshua son of Nun. 18You shall take one leader of every tribe to apportion the land for inheritance. 19These are the names of the men: Of the tribe of Judah, Caleb son of Jephunneh. 20Of the tribe of the Simeonites, Shemuel son of Ammihud. 21Of the tribe of Benjamin, Elidad son of Chislon. 22Of the tribe of the Danites a leader, Bukki son of Jogli. 23Of the Josephites: of the tribe of the Manassites a leader, Hanniel son of Ephod, 24and of the tribe of the Ephraimites a leader, Kemuel son of Shiphtan. 25Of the tribe of the Zebulunites a leader, Eli-zaphan son of Parnach. 26Of the tribe of the Issacharites a leader, Paltiel son of Azzan. 27And of the tribe of the Asherites a leader, Ahihud son of Shelomi. 28Of the tribe of the Naphtalites a leader, Pedahel son of Ammihud. 29These were the ones whom the LORD commanded to apportion the inheritance for the Israelites in the land of Canaan.

Cities for the Levites

35 In the plains of Moab by the Jordan at Jericho, the LORD spoke to Moses, say-

a Heb *Salt Sea*   b Syr: Heb lacks *its*

34.1–15 The boundaries of the promised land given here are ideal and do not correspond to Israel's actual boundaries at any time, especially in the case of the western border. They do, however, correspond to the territory "Canaan" as ruled by Egypt in the second half of the second millennium BCE. Cf. Josh 13–19; Ezek 47.13–20; 48.1–7, 23–29. **34.1–2** The "promised land" here is the land west of the Jordan only; see vv. 10–12; 32.22. **34.3** *Wilderness of Zin.* See 13.21, 26; 20.1. **34.4** *Ascent of Akrabbim,* "ascent of scorpions." Site unknown. *Kadesh-barnea.* See 13.26. *Hazar-addar.* Cf. Hezron and Addar in Josh 15.3. **34.4–5** *Azmon.* Site unknown. The *Wadi of Egypt* is modern Wadi el-Arish, south of Gaza. **34.6–7** The *Great Sea* is the Mediterranean. **34.7–8** *Mount Hor* here cannot be

the southern mountain where Aaron died (20.22–29). *Lebo-hamath.* See 13.21. *Zedad,* probably a site northeast of Damascus and east of Byblos. **34.9** *Ziphron, Hazar-enan.* Sites unknown. **34.10–11** *Shepham, Riblah, Ain.* Sites unknown. The *sea of Chinnereth* is the Sea of Galilee. **34.11–12** These verses exclude the Transjordanian holdings (see also vv. 13–15; 32.17, 22; 35.14). **34.13–15** See 32.33–42. **34.16–29** Other than Caleb and Joshua, these leaders have not been mentioned before. The tribes are listed south to north, except for Manasseh, which is listed before the more southern Ephraim because Manasseh was the firstborn (Gen 41.50–52). **34.17** *Eleazar* has replaced Aaron (20.22–29), and *Joshua* will replace Moses when the people cross over into Canaan (27.12–23).

ing: 2Command the Israelites to give, from the inheritance that they possess, towns for the Levites to live in; you shall also give to the Levites pasture lands surrounding the towns. 3The towns shall be theirs to live in, and their pasture lands shall be for their cattle, for their livestock, and for all their animals. 4The pasture lands of the towns, which you shall give to the Levites, shall reach from the wall of the town outward a thousand cubits all around. 5You shall measure, outside the town, for the east side two thousand cubits, for the south side two thousand cubits, for the west side two thousand cubits, and for the north side two thousand cubits, with the town in the middle; this shall belong to them as pasture land for their towns.

6 The towns that you give to the Levites shall include the six cities of refuge, where you shall permit a slayer to flee, and in addition to them you shall give forty-two towns. 7The towns that you give to the Levites shall total forty-eight, with their pasture lands. 8And as for the towns that you shall give from the possession of the Israelites, from the larger tribes you shall take many, and from the smaller tribes you shall take few; each, in proportion to the inheritance that it obtains, shall give of its towns to the Levites.

Cities of Refuge

9 The LORD spoke to Moses, saying: 10Speak to the Israelites, and say to them: When you cross the Jordan into the land of Canaan, 11then you shall select cities to be cities of refuge for you, so that a slayer who kills a person without intent may flee there. 12The cities shall be for you a refuge from the avenger, so that the slayer may not die until there is a trial before the congregation.

13 The cities that you designate shall be six cities of refuge for you: 14you shall designate three cities beyond the Jordan, and three cities in the land of Canaan, to be cities of refuge. 15These six cities shall serve as refuge for the Israelites, for the resident or transient alien among them, so that anyone who kills a person without intent may flee there.

Concerning Murder and Blood Revenge

16 But anyone who strikes another with an iron object, and death ensues, is a murderer; the murderer shall be put to death. 17Or anyone who strikes another with a stone in hand that could cause death, and death ensues, is a murderer; the murderer shall be put to death. 18Or anyone who strikes another with a weapon of wood in hand that could cause death, and death ensues, is a murderer; the murderer shall be put to death. 19The avenger of blood is the one who shall put the murderer to death; when they meet, the avenger of blood shall execute the sentence. 20Likewise, if someone pushes another from hatred, or hurls something at another, lying in wait, and death ensues, 21or in enmity strikes another with the hand, and death ensues, then the one who struck the blow shall be put to death; that person is a murderer; the avenger of blood shall put the murderer to death, when they meet.

22 But if someone pushes another suddenly without enmity, or hurls any object without lying in wait, 23or, while handling any stone that could cause death, unintentionally[a] drops it on another and death ensues, though they were not enemies, and no harm was intended, 24then the congregation shall judge between the slayer and the avenger of blood, in accordance with these ordinances; 25and the congregation shall rescue the slayer from the avenger of blood. Then the congregation shall send the slayer back to the original city of refuge. The slayer shall live in it until the death of the high priest who was anointed with the

---

a Heb without seeing

35.1–8 See also Josh 21; 1 Chr 6.54–81. The Levites were not allotted land as the other tribes were (see 18.20–24). 35.4–5 A thousand cubits, two thousand cubits, about 500 yards, 1,000 yards. 35.6 Cities of refuge. See 35.9–15. 35.8 See 26.52–56. 35.9–15 Cities of refuge were necessary to protect a killer from blood vengeance before a trial could be held; see Ex 21.12–14; Deut 4.41–43; 19.1–13; Josh 20. 35.12 On the avenger, see the order of those who "redeem" (the same Hebrew verb) in Lev 25.25, 47–49 ("uncle" here is father's brother); see also Num 5.8. 35.14 The area beyond the Jordan is Transjordan, the term beyond be-traying the point of view of a narrator from the west. 35.16–34 The distinction is made between murder (including negligence resulting in death) and unintentional killing; see also Ex 21.13–14, but cf. Ex 21.20–21; Deut 4.42; 19.4–6. 35.19, 21 The execution of the murderer is by the avenger; see v. 12. 35.20–23 The concern with whether there was hatred or enmity between the killer and victim helps to establish intention; see also Deut 4.42; 19.4; Josh 20.3–5. 35.25–28 The blood of the victim pollutes the land (v. 33), and that pollution, in the case of unintentional killing, is only masked by the exile of the killer to a city of refuge

holy oil. 26But if the slayer shall at any time go outside the bounds of the original city of refuge, 27and is found by the avenger of blood outside the bounds of the city of refuge, and is killed by the avenger, no bloodguilt shall be incurred. 28For the slayer must remain in the city of refuge until the death of the high priest; but after the death of the high priest the slayer may return home.

29 These things shall be a statute and ordinance for you throughout your generations wherever you live.

30 If anyone kills another, the murderer shall be put to death on the evidence of witnesses; but no one shall be put to death on the testimony of a single witness. 31Moreover you shall accept no ransom for the life of a murderer who is subject to the death penalty; a murderer must be put to death. 32Nor shall you accept ransom for one who has fled to a city of refuge, enabling the fugitive to return to live in the land before the death of the high priest. 33You shall not pollute the land in which you live; for blood pollutes the land, and no expiation can be made for the land, for the blood that is shed in it, except by the blood of the one who shed it. 34You shall not defile the land in which you live, in which I also dwell; for I the LORD dwell among the Israelites.

Marriage of Female Heirs

36 The heads of the ancestral houses of the clans of the descendants of Gilead son of Machir son of Manasseh, of the Josephite clans, came forward and spoke in the presence of Moses and the leaders, the heads of the ancestral houses of the Israelites; 2they said, "The LORD commanded my lord to give the land for inheritance by lot to the Israelites; and my lord was commanded by the LORD to give the inheritance of our brother Zelophehad to his daughters. 3But if they are married into another Israelite tribe, then their inheritance will be taken from the inheritance of our ancestors and added to the inheritance of the tribe into which they marry; so it will be taken away from the allotted portion of our inheritance. 4And when the jubilee of the Israelites comes, then their inheritance will be added to the inheritance of the tribe into which they have married; and their inheritance will be taken from the inheritance of our ancestral tribe."

5 Then Moses commanded the Israelites according to the word of the LORD, saying, "The descendants of the tribe of Joseph are right in what they are saying. 6This is what the LORD commands concerning the daughters of Zelophehad, 'Let them marry whom they think best; only it must be into a clan of their father's tribe that they are married, 7so that no inheritance of the Israelites shall be transferred from one tribe to another; for all Israelites shall retain the inheritance of their ancestral tribes. 8Every daughter who possesses an inheritance in any tribe of the Israelites shall marry one from the clan of her father's tribe, so that all Israelites may continue to possess their ancestral inheritance. 9No inheritance shall be transferred from one tribe to another; for each of the tribes of the Israelites shall retain its own inheritance.' "

10 The daughters of Zelophehad did as the LORD had commanded Moses. 11Mahlah, Tirzah, Hoglah, Milcah, and Noah, the daughters of Zelophehad, married sons of their father's brothers. 12They were married into the clans of the descendants of Manasseh son of Joseph, and their inheritance remained in the tribe of their father's clan.

13 These are the commandments and the ordinances that the LORD commanded through Moses to the Israelites in the plains of Moab by the Jordan at Jericho.

---

until the high priest's death atones for the victim's blood; see also Josh 20.6. If the killer steps outside the city of refuge, the pollution is released again and the avenger is justified in destroying the cause of pollution; cf. 2 Sam 19.18–23; 1 Kings 2.36–46. **35.33** *Pollutes the land.* See 35.25–28; Gen 4.10–11. **35.34** The land is holy because the Lord dwells there. See 5.1–4.

36.1–12 See 27.1–11. **36.1** See 27.1. **36.2** *Brother.* See 25.6; 27.4. **36.3** The complaint in this verse assumes that a wife's property became her husband's upon marriage. In such a case, the solution in 27.7–8 that daughters could inherit might mean that ances-tral land would be moved from one tribe to another, a possibility not considered in framing that earlier solution and one to be avoided (see 27.1–11). **36.4** On the *jubilee of the Israelites,* see Lev 25.8–55; 27.16–25. Since the land was not sold, even the jubilee regulations would not bring it back to its original owners; cf. Lev 25.13–17, 28, 31, 33. **36.6–9** A regulation that women who inherit must marry within a specific family group (or else forfeit their property) is common among societies with patrilineal inheritance laws, including other ancient Near Eastern societies. **36.13** See 22.1; 26.3, 63; 33.48–50; 35.1; Deut 34.1, 8.

DEUTERONOMY

Name and Canonical Significance

DEUTERONOMY IS THE FIFTH BOOK of the Bible and the last of those traditionally ascribed to Moses comprising the canonical division Torah, or Pentateuch. The name, which reflects the Greek designation *deuteronomion* (meaning "second law–giving"), understands the book to be an account of Moses' work as legislator, supplementing and completing the revelation of covenantal law that began at Mount Horeb a generation before (see 1.3; 4.13–14; 5:22–6.3). A similar understanding of the book as an authoritative reprise and amplification of divine legislation is represented by the Hebrew name *Mishneh Torah*. In Jewish tradition the book is also and more generally known by its opening phrase, *'elleh haddevarim* ("These are the words"), frequently shortened to *devarim* ("[Book of] Words").

Deuteronomy is the only part of the Pentateuch to identify itself explicitly and repeatedly as a record of Mosaic *torah* (usually translated "law" in the NRSV): 1.5; 4.8, 44; 17.18–19; 27.3, 8, 26; 28.58, 61; 29.21; 30.10; 31.9, 11, 12, 24, 26; 32.46. *Torah* in these contexts may be characterized as the inspired, comprehensive "polity" (or "constitution") that Moses, unable himself to lead Israel across the Jordan, enacts for the people as a normative guide to their corporate existence in the national homeland they are about to occupy. In short, this authoritative *torah* is a virtual surrogate for Moses himself as the preeminent mediator of the divine word to Israel (see 5.4–5, 23–31; 34.10; cf. Num 12.6–8). From this perspective Deuteronomy is not merely a homiletical appendix to the pentateuchal narrative of Israel's prehistory and political formation under the leadership of Moses. Rather, as Moses' legacy par excellence Deuteronomy is the interpretive key to the Pentateuch understood as a whole to preserve the abiding revelation of God's will for the ongoing life of the covenant people.

In similar fashion Deuteronomy provides the crucial point of reference for an understanding of the canonical unity of the following collection of the Prophets (Hebrew *Nevi'im*) in Jewish scripture. Significantly, affirmations of the Mosaic *torah* in its characteristically Deuteronomic form bracket the collection as a whole (see Josh 1.7–8; Mal 3.22). Deuteronomic influence and perspectives are especially evident in the Former Prophets, consisting of the books of Joshua, Judges, 1 and 2 Samuel, 1 and 2 Kings (see, e.g., Josh 1.1–9; 23–24; Judg 2.11–23; 1 Sam 7.3–14; 12.1–25; 2 Sam 7.1–29; 1 Kings 9.1–9; 11.1–13, 29–39; 14.1–16; 2 Kings

17.7–23; 21.1–23.27). For this reason these books are also known as the Deuteronomistic History in contemporary biblical scholarship. Many believe that Deuteronomy at one stage during its literary formation was an integral part of this national history, before it was detached and incorporated into the Pentateuch. In its dual character, both remembering Israel's past and preparing for its future, the book occupies a pivotal position, both literarily and theologically, in the canons of Jewish and Christian scriptures (see, e.g., "the law of Moses and the prophets," Acts 28.23).

Literary Character, Structure, and Principal Contents

DEUTERONOMY IS CAST in the form of a series of testamentary speeches and acts of Moses. Four editorial prefaces or superscriptions (1.1–5; 4.44–49; 29.1; 33.1) announce the coordinated segments of the work and describe the particular character and content of each major part. The first part (1.1–4.43) consists chiefly of Mosaic memoirs on Israel's prolonged journey from Horeb/Sinai to the plains of Moab in Transjordan (1.6–3.29), followed by a hortatory discourse on Israel's destiny as God's people (4.1–40) and a brief narrative appendix (4.41–43). The second and central part of the book (4.44–28.68) publishes the covenantal *torah*, introducing and systematically articulating the divinely authorized "polity" that Israel must implement in order to secure its collective political existence as the people of God. This central section has three major subdivisions: a review and exposition of the basic terms of the Horeb covenant (5.1–11.30); promulgation of the complementary statutory rulings (11.31–26.15); and a collection of rites of covenantal ratification and sanction (26.16–28.68). The third part of the book (29.1–32.52) describes another, supplementary covenant that the Lord charged Moses to make with the Israelites in Moab. This covenant stresses the social and multigenerational inclusiveness of Israel as well as responsibilities of its individual citizens. It includes reports of the commissioning of Joshua as Moses' successor and of the written consignment of the *torah*, and it ends with the recitation of Moses' eloquent "song" of witness to Israel's future generations. The fourth and final part of the book (33.1–34.12) contains Moses' testamentary blessings of the Israelite tribes and an account of his death and burial, with a concluding epitaph. Maintenance of the covenant relationship between Israel and its divine sovereign through the rule of faith and law within the community is thus the principal concern of Deuteronomy.

Sources and History of Composition

ALTHOUGH DEUTERONOMY EXHIBITS a remarkable coherence in comparison with the preceding books of the Pentateuch, it cannot be considered a unitary literary product. The internal evidence of the book indicates several stages of growth and editing. Among the sources used in composition are earlier pentateuchal narrative traditions, the Decalogue (which appears in a form different from that of Ex 20), legislation in the "Book of the Covenant" (Ex 20–23) together with the supplement in Ex 33–34, collections of blessings and curses, and the poems in chs. 32–33. Although some of the antecedent traditions may be older, the major stages in the compositional history of the book can with some confidence be dated to the two centuries between the fall of Samaria (721 BCE) and the beginning of the Judean restoration (ca. 535 BCE) after the exile to Babylonia. Since the early nineteenth century, critical scholarship has built a convincing case for relating at least the central portion of the book to the document recovered from the Jerusalem temple archives during the reign of King Josiah (621 BCE). Some of the characteristic provisions of the polity bear a close correspondence to reforms attributed to that king (see 2 Kings 22–23), who seems to have renewed the efforts of King Hezekiah a century earlier (see 2 Kings 18.1–7; 2 Chr 29–31). Yet the received form of book points to an exilic setting—when the older Mosaic polity may have been set within an expanded frame of Moses' valedictory addresses to Israel. Authors must be sought among those who bore particular responsibility for the transmission, interpretation, and implementation of the Mosaic legacy of covenantal *torah*. Although reasonable arguments have been set forth on behalf of royal scribes, prophets, and tribal elders, most likely are those identified in the book itself as "levitical priests," whose functions included judicial decision making and instruction as well as officiating in worship (see esp. 7.8–13; 27.9–10; 31.9–13; 33.8–11). [S. DEAN MCBRIDE JR.]

Events at Horeb Recalled

1 These are the words that Moses spoke to all Israel beyond the Jordan—in the wilderness, on the plain opposite Suph, between Paran and Tophel, Laban, Hazeroth, and Dizahab. 2(By the way of Mount Seir it takes eleven days to reach Kadesh-barnea from Horeb.) 3In the fortieth year, on the first day of the eleventh month, Moses spoke to the Israelites just as the LORD had commanded him to speak to them. 4This was after he had defeated King Sihon of the Amorites, who reigned in Heshbon, and King Og of Bashan, who reigned in Ashtaroth and*a* in Edrei. 5Beyond the Jordan in the land of Moab, Moses undertook to expound this law as follows:

6 The LORD our God spoke to us at Horeb, saying, "You have stayed long enough at this mountain. 7Resume your journey, and go into the hill country of the Amorites as well as into the neighboring regions—the Arabah, the hill country, the Shephelah, the Negeb, and the seacoast—the land of the Canaanites and the Lebanon, as far as the great river, the river Euphrates. 8See, I have set the land before you; go in and take possession of the land that I*b* swore to your ancestors, to Abraham, to Isaac, and to Jacob, to give to them and to their descendants after them."

Appointment of Tribal Leaders

9 At that time I said to you, "I am unable by myself to bear you. 10The LORD your God has multiplied you, so that today you are as nu-

---

a Gk Syr Vg Compare Josh 12.4: Heb lacks *and*   *b* Sam Gk: MT *the* LORD

1.1–5 The preface understands Moses' opening address in 1.6–4.40 to be an expository foreword to *this law* (v. 5), which is the Deuteronomic *torah* directly introduced in 4.44. **1.1** *These are the words* and the abbreviation *Words* (Hebrew *devarim*) are often used as the book's title in Jewish tradition (see Introduction). *The plain opposite Suph* and following toponyms may define a natural amphitheater in the valley near Beth-peor; see 3.29. **1.2** Perhaps a comment on 1.19. *Mount Seir*, the Edomite highlands flanking the rift valley from the Dead Sea southward. Once thought to be the mountain refuge of Petra, *Kadesh-barnea* is now usually identified with the oases of 'Ain al-Qudeirat in northern Sinai. In Deuteronomy and some other sources (cf. Ex 3.1) *Horeb* is preferred over "Sinai" as the name for the wilderness mount of revelation. Cf. 33.2; Ex 19.1, 11. **1.3** The date, counting from the first Passover (Ex 12.2), when Moses completed his work as God's spokesman. **1.4** As prelude to the campaign west of the Jordan, these victories vindicate Israel's trust in divine providence; see 2.26–3.22; 4.46–48; cf. Ps 135.10–12.

1.6–3.29 Moses' memoirs review what happened to Israel and why during the post-Horeb epoch of his ca-

reer. The chief lesson is that Israel's national well-being requires strict observance of all that God commands. **1.6–8** The order to depart from Horeb (see v. 2) was an oracular summons to invade and occupy the promised homeland west of the Jordan. Cf. Ex 33.1–3. **1.7** *The hill country of the Amorites* (also 1.19–20) and *the land of the Canaanites* (cf. Ex 13.11; Ezek 16.3), comprehensive terms for western Palestine, using general designations for the land's pre-Israelite occupants. Component regions are the *Arabah* (the Jordan rift valley), the central highland ridge, the western hills of the *Shephelah*, the *Negeb* slope of southern Judah, and the Mediterranean coastal plain. Territory to the northeast, called *the Lebanon* range, which extends into Syria toward the upper reach of the *Euphrates*, was controlled by Aramean states during most of the earlier Iron Age; Israel claimed hegemony over the region in the era of the Davidic-Solomonic empire (2 Sam 8.3–12; 1 Kings 4.21, 24) and briefly again in the heyday of Jeroboam II's reign (2 Kings 14.25). **1.8** Divine promise of *the land* to Israel's *ancestors*. See Gen 13.14–17; 15.12–21; 17.8; 26.4–5; 28.13–14. **1.9–18** Before setting out, a plan of military command and tribal judiciary was implemented to lighten Moses'

merous as the stars of heaven. [11]May the LORD, the God of your ancestors, increase you a thousand times more and bless you, as he has promised you! [12]But how can I bear the heavy burden of your disputes all by myself? [13]Choose for each of your tribes individuals who are wise, discerning, and reputable to be your leaders." [14]You answered me, "The plan you have proposed is a good one." [15]So I took the leaders of your tribes, wise and reputable individuals, and installed them as leaders over you, commanders of thousands, commanders of hundreds, commanders of fifties, commanders of tens, and officials, throughout your tribes. [16]I charged your judges at that time: "Give the members of your community a fair hearing, and judge rightly between one person and another, whether citizen or resident alien. [17]You must not be partial in judging: hear out the small and the great alike; you shall not be intimidated by anyone, for the judgment is God's. Any case that is too hard for you, bring to me, and I will hear it." [18]So I charged you at that time with all the things that you should do.

Israel's Refusal to Enter the Land

19 Then, just as the LORD our God had ordered us, we set out from Horeb and went through all that great and terrible wilderness that you saw, on the way to the hill country of the Amorites, until we reached Kadesh-barnea. [20]I said to you, "You have reached the hill country of the Amorites, which the LORD our God is giving us. [21]See, the LORD your God has given the land to you; go up, take possession, as the LORD, the God of your ancestors, has promised you; do not fear or be dismayed."
22 All of you came to me and said, "Let us send men ahead of us to explore the land for us and bring back a report to us regarding the route by which we should go up and the cities

we will come to." [23]The plan seemed good to me, and I selected twelve of you, one from each tribe. [24]They set out and went up into the hill country, and when they reached the Valley of Eshcol they spied it out [25]and gathered some of the land's produce, which they brought down to us. They brought back a report to us, and said, "It is a good land that the LORD our God is giving us."

26 But you were unwilling to go up. You rebelled against the command of the LORD your God; [27]you grumbled in your tents and said, "It is because the LORD hates us that he has brought us out of the land of Egypt, to hand us over to the Amorites to destroy us. [28]Where are we headed? Our kindred have made our hearts melt by reporting, 'The people are stronger and taller than we; the cities are large and fortified up to heaven! We actually saw there the offspring of the Anakim!' " [29]I said to you, "Have no dread or fear of them. [30]The LORD your God, who goes before you, is the one who will fight for you, just as he did for you in Egypt before your very eyes, [31]and in the wilderness, where you saw how the LORD your God carried you, just as one carries a child, all the way that you traveled until you reached this place. [32]But in spite of this, you have no trust in the LORD your God, [33]who goes before you on the way to seek out a place for you to camp, in fire by night, and in the cloud by day, to show you the route you should take."

The Penalty for Israel's Rebellion

34 When the LORD heard your words, he was wrathful and swore: [35]"Not one of these—not one of this evil generation—shall see the good land that I swore to give to your ancestors, [36]except Caleb son of Jephunneh. He shall see it, and to him and to his descendants I will give the land on which he set foot, because of his

---

burden of governance (cf. Ex 18.13–26; Num 11.10–30). **1.10–11** Divine promise of Israel's *increase*. See Gen 13.16; 15.5; 22.17; 26.4; Ex 32.13. **1.16–17** Because the judges act on God's behalf, all who participate in the life of the community, including alien sojourners, must be given equal access to justice (cf. 10.17–19; 16.18–20). On Moses' role as arbiter in cases *too hard* for tribal courts to resolve, see 17.8–11; cf. Ex 18.13–26. **1.18** Perhaps an allusion to Ex 24.3–8.
1.19–45 This review (see Num 13–14) highlights how Israel's countermanding of divine orders (vv. 26, 43) reversed the expected outcome of the initial march

of conquest. **1.21** A war oracle reiterating the earlier command (vv. 7–8) and urging bold compliance (cf. 20.2–4; Ex 14.13–14). **1.22–33** Neither the communal decision to reconnoiter the route of attack nor the spies' report is faulted here (cf. Num 13.32). The fertile *Valley of Eshcol* (v. 24) lies in the Judean hill country near Hebron, a region whose aborigines were the formidable *Anakim* (v. 28; cf. 2.10–11, 21; 9.2; Num 13.22–33; Josh 14.15). Dread of this foe fueled a grassroots revolt that imputed malice to the Lord, whose salvific presence had been amply shown to the generation that experienced the exodus from Egypt and swift

complete fidelity to the LORD." 37 Even with me the LORD was angry on your account, saying, "You also shall not enter there. 38 Joshua son of Nun, your assistant, shall enter there; encourage him, for he is the one who will secure Israel's possession of it. 39 And as for your little ones, who you thought would become booty, your children, who today do not yet know right from wrong, they shall enter there; to them I will give it, and they shall take possession of it. 40 But as for you, journey back into the wilderness, in the direction of the Red Sea." [a]

41 You answered me, "We have sinned against the LORD! We are ready to go up and fight, just as the LORD our God commanded us." So all of you strapped on your battle gear, and thought it easy to go up into the hill country. 42 The LORD said to me, "Say to them, 'Do not go up and do not fight, for I am not in the midst of you; otherwise you will be defeated by your enemies.'" 43 Although I told you, you would not listen. You rebelled against the command of the LORD and presumptuously went up into the hill country. 44 The Amorites who lived in that hill country then came out against you and chased you as bees do. They beat you down in Seir as far as Hormah. 45 When you returned and wept before the LORD, the LORD would neither heed your voice nor pay you any attention.

The Desert Years

46 After you had stayed at Kadesh as many days as you did, 1 we journeyed back into the wilderness, in the direction of the Red Sea, [a] as the LORD had told me and skirted Mount Seir for many days. 2 Then the LORD said to me: 3 "You have been skirting this hill country long enough. Head north, 4 and charge the people as follows: You are about to pass through the territory of your kindred, the descendants of Esau, who live in Seir. They will be afraid of you, so, be very careful 5 not to engage in battle with them, for I will not give you even so much as a foot's length of their land, since I have given Mount Seir to Esau as a possession. 6 You shall purchase food from them for money, so that you may eat; and you shall also buy water from them for money, so that you may drink. 7 Surely the LORD your God has blessed you in all your undertakings; he knows your going through this great wilderness. These forty years the LORD your God has been with you; you have lacked nothing." 8 So we passed by our kin, the descendants of Esau who live in Seir, leaving behind the route of the Arabah, and leaving behind Elath and Ezion-geber.

When we had headed out along the route of the wilderness of Moab, 9 the LORD said to me: "Do not harass Moab or engage them in battle, for I will not give you any of its land as a possession, since I have given Ar as a possession to the descendants of Lot." 10 (The Emim—a large and numerous people, as tall as the Anakim—had formerly inhabited it. 11 Like the Anakim, they are usually reckoned as Rephaim, though the Moabites call them Emim. 12 Moreover, the Horim had formerly inhabited Seir, but the descendants of Esau dispossessed them, destroying them and settling in their place, as Israel has done in the land that the LORD gave them as a possession.)

---

a Or Sea of Reeds

---

passage through the wilderness (vv. 19, 30–33; cf. Ex 13.21–22). **1.36** Among seniors, *Caleb* alone modeled the zeal demanded of the Lord's warriors; see Josh 14.6–14; 15.13–14. **1.37** *Even with me.* See 3.23–27; cf. Num 20.9–12. **1.39** *Know right from wrong.* The age of accountable discretion (cf. Isa 7.15) was twenty years according to Num 14.29–30. **1.40** *Red Sea,* here the Gulf of Aqaba (cf. 2.8). **1.41–44** Attack on Canaan from the south was not only a foolhardy initiative, resulting in the militia's rout, but another act of brazen rebellion against divine orders. **1.44** *Hormah,* a site in the southeastern Negeb near Arad (cf. Num 21.1–3; Judg 1.16–17).

1.46–2.25 Full renewal of the mandate for conquest accompanied the demise of the rebellious generation. **2.1** Reversing direction away from Canaan and toward Egypt was at least a return to obedience (1.40).

2.3 *Head north,* apparently along the desert route east of the Arabah (see 2.8). **2.4–8** *Esau,* elder brother of Jacob (Israel) and forefather of the Edomites (Gen 25.21–26; 36.1–19), had title to the *Seir* hill country by grant from the Lord; hence Israel had neither right (vv. 5–6) nor reason (v. 7) to challenge Edom's sovereignty. (Num 20.14–21 gives a different account of the passage.) **2.8** *Elath and Ezion-geber,* ports on the Gulf of Aqaba (cf. 1 Kings 9.26). **2.9** *Ar,* the portion of greater Moab between the Zered (2.13) and the Arnon (2.24) which the Lord granted to Lot's Moabite lineage (also 2.18, 29; cf. Gen 19.36–38; Num 21.13–15, 28). **2.10–12** An editorial comment on aboriginal folk dispossessed by Moab and Edom (cf. 2.20–23; 3.11). Both *Emim* (Hebrew, "Frighteners") and Anakim (cf. 1.28) are identified as *Rephaim,* giant warriors of yore who are variously implicated in Israelite and Ugaritic folk-

13"Now then, proceed to cross over the Wadi Zered."

So we crossed over the Wadi Zered. 14And the length of time we had traveled from Kadesh-barnea until we crossed the Wadi Zered was thirty-eight years, until the entire generation of warriors had perished from the camp, as the LORD had sworn concerning them. 15Indeed, the LORD's own hand was against them, to root them out from the camp, until all had perished.

16 Just as soon as all the warriors had died off from among the people, 17the LORD spoke to me, saying, 18"Today you are going to cross the boundary of Moab at Ar. 19When you approach the frontier of the Ammonites, do not harass them or engage them in battle, for I will not give the land of the Ammonites to you as a possession, because I have given it to the descendants of Lot." 20(It also is usually reckoned as a land of Rephaim. Rephaim formerly inhabited it, though the Ammonites call them Zamzummim, 21a strong and numerous people, as tall as the Anakim. But the LORD destroyed them from before the Ammonites so that they could dispossess them and settle in their place. 22He did the same for the descendants of Esau, who live in Seir, by destroying the Horim before them so that they could dispossess them and settle in their place even to this day. 23As for the Avvim, who had lived in settlements in the vicinity of Gaza, the Caphtorim, who came from Caphtor, destroyed them and settled in their place.) 24"Proceed

on your journey and cross the Wadi Arnon. See, I have handed over to you King Sihon the Amorite of Heshbon, and his land. Begin to take possession by engaging him in battle. 25This day I will begin to put the dread and fear of you upon the peoples everywhere under heaven; when they hear report of you, they will tremble and be in anguish because of you."

Defeat of King Sihon

26 So I sent messengers from the wilderness of Kedemoth to King Sihon of Heshbon with the following terms of peace: 27"If you let me pass through your land, I will travel only along the road; I will turn aside neither to the right nor to the left. 28You shall sell me food for money, so that I may eat, and supply me water for money, so that I may drink. Only allow me to pass through on foot— 29just as the descendants of Esau who live in Seir have done for me and likewise the Moabites who live in Ar— until I cross the Jordan into the land that the LORD our God is giving us." 30But King Sihon of Heshbon was not willing to let us pass through, for the LORD your God had hardened his spirit and made his heart defiant in order to hand him over to you, as he has now done.

31 The LORD said to me, "See, I have begun to give Sihon and his land over to you. Begin now to take possession of his land." 32So when Sihon came out against us, he and all his people for battle at Jahaz, 33the LORD our God gave him over to us; and we struck him down,

---

lore with the antediluvian Nephilim and other defunct heroes (cf. Gen 6.4; 14.5; Num 13.33). On the *Horim* of Seir (perhaps "Troglodytes" rather than ethnic "Hurrians"), see Gen 14.6; 36.20–30. **2.13–15** The *Zered* (Wadi el-Hesa), which flows westward into the southern end of the Dead Sea, is the boundary between Edom and Moab; the crossing marked Israel's communal passage, hastened by divine agency, to a new generation of warriors. **2.19** Lot's Ammonite descendants also (cf. 2.9) received by divine grant their homeland on the plateau northeast of Moabite Ar (cf. 2.37). **2.20–23** Folklore with theological commentary continuing vv. 10–12. *Zamzummim* (Hebrew, "Mumblers"?), another subset of Rephaim; cf. "Zuzim" in Gen 14.5. *Avvim* (Hebrew, "Ruiners"?). Cf. Josh 13.3. *Caphtorim . . . from Caphtor,* Philistines or a related people from Crete (cf. Gen 10.14; Jer 47.4; Am 9.7). **2.24** Consignment of *Sihon's* realm to Israel renewed the Lord's war against the Amorites (cf. Gen 15.16; Am 2.9–10). Other ancient claimants to the rich tableland north of the *Arnon* gorge (Wadi el-Mujib) included

Ammon (Judg 11.4–33; cf. 1 Sam 11.1–11) and Moab (Num 21.13–15; Jer 48; cf. the Mesha Inscription). **2.25** Conquest begins with *dread and fear of you.* See also 11.25; Ex 15.14–16; cf. Josh 2.9–11. **2.26–3.7** The era of Israel's conquests began under Moses' command (as promised, Ex 34.10–11), with model holy-war campaigns against the forces of Sihon and Og in Transjordan (cf. Num 21.21–35). **2.26** *Kedemoth,* at the desert's edge east of Ar, near the Arnon's upper reach (cf. Josh 13.18). *Heshbon,* Sihon's capital, near the midpoint on the plateau stretching north from the Arnon to Gilead (cf. Josh 12.2; Jer 48.45; Song 7.4). **2.27–29** The request for peaceful passage may be understood in context (vv. 24–25, 30–31) as the means to draw Sihon into battle (cf. 2.6; 23.3–4). **2.30** Divine action to promote Sihon's bellicose obstinacy and downfall recalls the "hardening of Pharaoh's heart" theme of the exodus drama (e.g., Ex 4.21; 7.3; 14.4; cf. Josh 11.19–20; 1 Sam 16.14; 1 Kings 22.20–23; Isa 6.10). **2.32** *Jahaz,* a fortified town on the plateau south of Heshbon (cf. Josh 13.17–18; Isa 15.4). **2.33–**

along with his offspring and all his people. ³⁴At that time we captured all his towns, and in each town we utterly destroyed men, women, and children. We left not a single survivor. ³⁵Only the livestock we kept as spoil for ourselves, as well as the plunder of the towns that we had captured. ³⁶From Aroer on the edge of the Wadi Arnon (including the town that is in the wadi itself) as far as Gilead, there was no citadel too high for us. The LORD our God gave everything to us. ³⁷You did not encroach, however, on the land of the Ammonites, avoiding the whole upper region of the Wadi Jabbok as well as the towns of the hill country, just as*ᵃ* the LORD our God had charged.

Defeat of King Og

3 When we headed up the road to Bashan, King Og of Bashan came out against us, he and all his people, for battle at Edrei. ²The LORD said to me, "Do not fear him, for I have handed him over to you, along with his people and his land. Do to him as you did to King Sihon of the Amorites, who reigned in Heshbon." ³So the LORD our God also handed over to us King Og of Bashan and all his people. We struck him down until not a single survivor was left. ⁴At that time we captured all his towns; there was no citadel that we did not take from them—sixty towns, the whole region of Argob, the kingdom of Og in Bashan. ⁵All these were fortress towns with high walls, double gates, and bars, besides a great many

villages. ⁶And we utterly destroyed them, as we had done to King Sihon of Heshbon, in each city utterly destroying men, women, and children. ⁷But all the livestock and the plunder of the towns we kept as spoil for ourselves.

8 So at that time we took from the two kings of the Amorites the land beyond the Jordan, from the Wadi Arnon to Mount Hermon ⁹(the Sidonians call Hermon Sirion, while the Amorites call it Senir), ¹⁰all the towns of the tableland, the whole of Gilead, and all of Bashan, as far as Salecah and Edrei, towns of Og's kingdom in Bashan. ¹¹(Now only King Og of Bashan was left of the remnant of the Rephaim. In fact his bed, an iron bed, can still be seen in Rabbah of the Ammonites. By the common cubit it is nine cubits long and four cubits wide.) ¹²As for the land that we took possession of at that time, I gave to the Reubenites and Gadites the territory north of Aroer,ᵇ that is on the edge of the Wadi Arnon, as well as half the hill country of Gilead with its towns, ¹³and I gave to the half-tribe of Manasseh the rest of Gilead and all of Bashan, Og's kingdom. (The whole region of Argob: all that portion of Bashan used to be called a land of Rephaim; ¹⁴Jair the Manassite acquired the whole region of Argob as far as the border of the Geshurites and the Maacathites, and he named them—that is, Bashan—after himself, Havvoth-jair,ᶜ as it is to this day.) ¹⁵To Machir

---

a Gk Tg: Heb *and all*   *b* Heb *territory from Aroer*   *c* That is *Settlement of Jair*

---

35 The "ban" (Hebrew *cherem*) enforced here and against Bashan (3.6–7) straddles the rules of holy war given in 20.10–17: the human populations are totally annihilated (20.16–17), but livestock as well as goods are exempted (20.13–15). Cf. Josh 6.17–19; 7.1; 8.2, 26–27; 11.10–15; 1 Sam 15.3–9. **2.36–37** *Aroer,* a fortress commanding the Arnon's north rim (cf. Josh 13.9). *Gilead,* the fertile hill country of central Transjordan; it is bisected by the *Jabbok* River (Nahr ez-Zerqa), a major eastern tributary of the Jordan, which descends from the heights of Ammon (cf. Gen 32.22; Josh 12.2). **3.1** *Bashan,* a region of rich highland forests, pastures, and fields in northern Transjordan, reaching beyond Gilead across the Yarmuk River into Syria (cf. 32.13–14; Ezek 27.6; 39.18). The battle site, *Edrei* (modern Dar'a), near the upper reach of the Yarmuk's southern tributary, was apparently one of Og's two royal cities (cf. 1.4; Josh 9.10; 12.4). **3.4** *Argob* seems here to designate the broad expanse of south-central Bashan, from the Golan Heights eastward to the Hauran massif (modern Jebel Druze); cf. 3.13–14.

3.8–22 A brief report on the apportionment of conquered regions among the tribes of Reuben, Gad, and Manasseh (cf. Num 32; Josh 13.8–32) plus instructions concerning participation of their militias in the invasion of the land west of the Jordan. **3.8–9** *Mount Hermon* (Jebel esh-Sheikh), the towering southern spur of the Anti-Lebanon range, known also as *Sirion* and *Senir,* marks the northern limit of Israel's primary territorial claims (cf. 4.48; Josh 11.16–17; Ps 29.6; Song 4.8). **3.10** *Salecah,* a town at the eastern boundary of Bashan (cf. Josh 12.5; 13.11). **3.11** The note offers an intriguing glimpse into lore about Og, here not an "Amorite" (cf. v. 8) but last of the giant Rephaim (cf. Josh 12.4; 13.12). His massive *iron bed* (ca. 13 by 6 feet) may have been a megalith or sarcophagus of black basalt. *Rabbah* (modern Amman), the Ammonite royal citadel. **3.13–15** Major clans of eastern *Manasseh* (i.e., *half* [of the] *tribe*) include *Jair,* here allotted most of Bashan (cf. Num 32.41; Judg 10.3–5; 1 Kings 4.13), and *Machir,* receiving Gilead (cf. Num 26.29; 32.39–40; Josh 17.1). *Geshurites and the Maacathites,* Ara-

I gave Gilead. 16And to the Reubenites and the Gadites I gave the territory from Gilead as far as the Wadi Arnon, with the middle of the wadi as a boundary, and up to the Jabbok, the wadi being boundary of the Ammonites; 17the Arabah also, with the Jordan and its banks, from Chinnereth down to the sea of the Arabah, the Dead Sea,*a* with the lower slopes of Pisgah on the east.

18 At that time, I charged you as follows: "Although the LORD your God has given you this land to occupy, all your troops shall cross over armed as the vanguard of your Israelite kin. 19Only your wives, your children, and your livestock—I know that you have much livestock—shall stay behind in the towns that I have given to you. 20When the LORD gives rest to your kindred, as to you, and they too have occupied the land that the LORD your God is giving them beyond the Jordan, then each of you may return to the property that I have given to you." 21And I charged Joshua as well at that time, saying: "Your own eyes have seen everything that the LORD your God has done to these two kings; so the LORD will do to all the kingdoms into which you are about to cross. 22Do not fear them, for it is the LORD your God who fights for you."

Moses Views Canaan from Pisgah

23 At that time, too, I entreated the LORD, saying: 24"O Lord GOD, you have only begun to show your servant your greatness and your might; what god in heaven or on earth can perform deeds and mighty acts like yours! 25Let me cross over to see the good land beyond the Jordan, that good hill country and the Lebanon." 26But the LORD was angry with me on your account and would not heed me. The LORD said to me, "Enough from you! Never speak to me of this matter again! 27Go up to the top of Pisgah and look around you to the west, to the north, to the south, and to the east. Look well, for you shall not cross over this Jordan. 28But charge Joshua, and encourage and strengthen him, because it is he who shall cross over at the head of this people and who shall secure their possession of the land that you will see." 29So we remained in the valley opposite Beth-peor.

Moses Commands Obedience

4 So now, Israel, give heed to the statutes and ordinances that I am teaching you to observe, so that you may live to enter and occupy the land that the LORD, the God of your ancestors, is giving you. 2You must neither add anything to what I command you nor take away anything from it, but keep the commandments of the LORD your God with which I am charging you. 3You have seen for yourselves what the LORD did with regard to the Baal of Peor—how the LORD your God destroyed from among you everyone who followed the Baal of Peor, 4while those of you who held fast to the LORD your God are all alive today.

---

a Heb *Salt Sea*

---

mean clans occupying the Golan Heights (cf. Gen 22.24; Josh 13.13; 2 Sam 3.3; 15.8). **3.17** *Chinnereth,* the Sea of Galilee or Gennesaret. *Pisgah,* the northwestern flank of Mount Nebo (cf. 3.27; 32.49; 34.1). **3.18–20** For the outcome of the commission, see Josh 1.12–18; 4.12; 22.1–6. The promised *rest* means not only relief from the urgency of war but also the Lord's gift to Israel of a stable life in a secure homeland, thus bringing to completion the plan that began to unfold with the exodus (cf. 12.8–9; Ex 3.7–8; 15.17; 33.14; Josh 21.43–45; 1 Kings 8.56). **3.21–22** Anticipation of Joshua's succession. See 31.3–8, 23; Josh 1.3–6. **3.23–29** Moses, who so often had interceded successfully on behalf of others (e.g., 9.20, 25–29; Ex 32.11–14; Num 11.2; 21.7), could not secure divine permission to cross with the new generation of Israel into the land beyond the Jordan. **3.24** Moses' plea begins with hymnic praise extolling the Lord's incomparability (cf. Ex 15.11, 16; 2 Sam 7.22–24; Pss 89.5–8; 113.5–6). **3.26–27** The Lord's rebuke is softened by allowing Moses to survey visually the full expanse of Is-

rael's national homeland. See 32.48–52; 34.1–4. **3.28** See note on 3.21–22. **3.29** The *valley* (Wadi 'Ayun Musa) lies beneath the northwest slope of Pisgah, where Moses is addressing the people (see 1.1, 5; cf. Num 21.20). *Beth-peor,* the "house," or sanctuary, of the Baal of Peor; see 4.3–4.

4.1–40 This grand peroration advances the claim that diligent observance of God's law, as mediated through Moses' instruction, is the wellspring of Israel's life and hence also the discipline that shapes its unique theological witness among the world's nations. **4.1–8** The thesis stated. **4.1** *So now* is a rhetorical device (cf. 10.12; 26.10), here marking a shift in Moses' address from the foregoing memoirs to climactic exhortation and admonition. **4.2–4** *Neither add . . . nor take away.* Because Moses' instruction in what the Lord demands is both authoritative and complete, it is the only guide to life that Israel ever needs or should follow (cf. 12.32; 30.11–14; Prov 30.5–6; Eccl 3.14). The consequences of conflicting claims on Israel's loyalty were demonstrated by the Lord's discriminating judgment in *the*

5 See, just as the LORD my God has charged me, I now teach you statutes and ordinances for you to observe in the land that you are about to enter and occupy. 6 You must observe them diligently, for this will show your wisdom and discernment to the peoples, who, when they hear all these statutes, will say, "Surely this great nation is a wise and discerning people!" 7 For what other great nation has a god so near to it as the LORD our God is whenever we call to him? 8 And what other great nation has statutes and ordinances as just as this entire law that I am setting before you today?

9 But take care and watch yourselves closely, so as neither to forget the things that your eyes have seen nor to let them slip from your mind all the days of your life; make them known to your children and your children's children— 10 how you once stood before the LORD your God at Horeb, when the LORD said to me, "Assemble the people for me, and I will let them hear my words, so that they may learn to fear me as long as they live on the earth, and may teach their children so"; 11 you approached and stood at the foot of the mountain while the mountain was blazing up to the very heavens, shrouded in dark clouds. 12 Then the LORD spoke to you out of the fire. You heard the sound of words but saw no form; there was only a voice. 13 He declared to you his covenant, which he charged you to observe, that is, the ten commandments;[a] and he wrote them on two stone tablets. 14 And the LORD charged me at that time to teach you statutes and ordinances for you to observe in the land that you are about to cross into and occupy.

15 Since you saw no form when the LORD spoke to you at Horeb out of the fire, take care and watch yourselves closely, 16 so that you do not act corruptly by making an idol for yourselves, in the form of any figure—the likeness of male or female, 17 the likeness of any animal that is on the earth, the likeness of any winged bird that flies in the air, 18 the likeness of anything that creeps on the ground, the likeness of any fish that is in the water under the earth. 19 And when you look up to the heavens and see the sun, the moon, and the stars, all the host of heaven, do not be led astray and bow down to them and serve them, things that the LORD your God has allotted to all the peoples everywhere under heaven. 20 But the LORD has taken you and brought you out of the iron-smelter, out of Egypt, to become a people of his very own possession, as you are now.

21 The LORD was angry with me because of you, and he vowed that I should not cross the Jordan and that I should not enter the good land that the LORD your God is giving for your possession. 22 For I am going to die in this land without crossing over the Jordan, but you are going to cross over to take possession of that good land. 23 So be careful not to forget the covenant that the LORD your God made with you, and not to make for yourselves an idol in the form of anything that the LORD your God has forbidden you. 24 For the LORD your God is a devouring fire, a jealous God.

25 When you have had children and children's children, and become complacent in

---

a Heb *the ten words*

Baal of Peor affair (cf. Num 25.1–13; Ps 106.28; Hos 9.10). **4.5–8** Israel will be renowned as a *great nation* (cf. 26.5; Gen 12.2; 18.18; 46.3; Ex 32.10) by virtue of its ethical character and the responsive nearness of its divine sovereign (cf. Ex 3.7; Judg 3.9, 15; 4.3; Ps 145.18; Isa 55.6–7). *This entire law,* whose just provisions and prudent observance by Israel will gain acclaim from other nations (cf. Ezra 7.25; Pss 19.7–10; 147.19–20), is the Mosaic *torah* proclaimed and published in Deuteronomy. See 4.44–45; 31.9–13. **4.9–31** The case against idolatry. **4.9** Transmission through the generations of Israel's normative experience and polity is a major Deuteronomic concern (e.g., 6.7, 20–25; 11.19–21; 29.29; 31.12–13). **4.10–11** The assembly at Horeb: see 5.2–5; 9.10; 10.4. Cf. Ex 19.7–25; 20.18–21. **4.12** Key motifs in the expository argument are *fire . . . no form . . . voice;* see vv. 15–16, 23–25, 33, 36. **4.13–14** The Horeb *covenant* (Hebrew *berit*) was essentially defined by the stipulations of the Decalogue; teaching Israel how to implement them in its national life was Moses' charge. See 5.2–31; 10.4; Ex 34.27–28. **4.15–19** An exposition of 5.8 (Ex 20.4) argues that Israel's imageless worship (cf. Ex 20.23; 34.17; Lev 19.4; 26.1) is a consequence of the visual formlessness of the Lord's presence at Horeb. **4.20** By *iron-smelter* is meant the harshness of servitude in Egypt (cf. 1 Kings 8.51; Isa 48.10; Jer 11.4). In the exodus, Israel became the Lord's *very own possession,* or "heritage" (cf. 32.8–9; 9.26, 29; 1 Sam 10.1; 1 Kings 8.53; Ps 33.12). **4.21–23** The fact of Moses' absence ought never again give rise to idolatry, as happened in the golden calf episode (cf. 9.12–14; Ex 32.1–10). **4.24** Especially in combination, the epithets *devouring fire* (9.3; Ex 24.17; cf. Pss 18.8; 50.3) and *jealous God* (5.9; 6.15; Ex 34.14; Josh 24.19) express the vehement passion of the Lord's self-defense against idolatry and other acts of profanation. See also 32.19–22; Lev 10.1–3; Num 16.35; 25.11. **4.25–27** In view here is the exilic Dispersion as an ac-

the land, if you act corruptly by making an idol in the form of anything, thus doing what is evil in the sight of the LORD your God, and provoking him to anger, 26I call heaven and earth to witness against you today that you will soon utterly perish from the land that you are crossing the Jordan to occupy; you will not live long on it, but will be utterly destroyed. 27The LORD will scatter you among the peoples; only a few of you will be left among the nations where the LORD will lead you. 28There you will serve other gods made by human hands, objects of wood and stone that neither see, nor hear, nor eat, nor smell. 29From there you will seek the LORD your God, and you will find him if you search after him with all your heart and soul. 30In your distress, when all these things have happened to you in time to come, you will return to the LORD your God and heed him. 31Because the LORD your God is a merciful God, he will neither abandon you nor destroy you; he will not forget the covenant with your ancestors that he swore to them.

32 For ask now about former ages, long before your own, ever since the day that God created human beings on the earth; ask from one end of heaven to the other: has anything so great as this ever happened or has its like ever been heard of? 33Has any people ever heard the voice of a god speaking out of a fire, as you have heard, and lived? 34Or has any god ever attempted to go and take a nation for himself from the midst of another nation, by trials, by signs and wonders, by war, by a mighty hand and an outstretched arm, and by terrifying displays of power, as the LORD your God did for you in Egypt before your very eyes? 35To

you it was shown so that you would acknowledge that the LORD is God; there is no other besides him. 36From heaven he made you hear his voice to discipline you. On earth he showed you his great fire, while you heard his words coming out of the fire. 37And because he loved your ancestors, he chose their descendants after them. He brought you out of Egypt with his own presence, by his great power, 38driving out before you nations greater and mightier than yourselves, to bring you in, giving you their land for a possession, as it is still today. 39So acknowledge today and take to heart that the LORD is God in heaven above and on the earth beneath; there is no other. 40Keep his statutes and his commandments, which I am commanding you today for your own well-being and that of your descendants after you, so that you may long remain in the land that the LORD your God is giving you for all time.

Cities of Refuge East of the Jordan

41 Then Moses set apart on the east side of the Jordan three cities 42to which a homicide could flee, someone who unintentionally kills another person, the two not having been at enmity before; the homicide could flee to one of these cities and live: 43Bezer in the wilderness on the tableland belonging to the Reubenites, Ramoth in Gilead belonging to the Gadites, and Golan in Bashan belonging to the Manassites.

Transition to the Second Address

44 This is the law that Moses set before the Israelites. 45These are the decrees and the statutes and ordinances that Moses spoke to the

---

tualization of curses owing to Israel's breach of covenant (cf. 28.64–67; Lev 26.30–39). *Heaven and earth* are invoked as enduring witnesses that Moses had foreseen this fate (cf. 30.19; 31.28). **4.28** *Other gods . . . wood and stone.* See also 28.36, 64; 29.17; 2 Kings 19.18; cf. Pss 115.4–8; 135.15–18; Isa 44.9–20; Jer 10.2–5. **4.29–31** In view too is a renewal of covenant, predicated on Israel's genuinely remorseful seeking of the Lord (see 6.5 on *all your heart and soul*) and the Lord's perennial graciousness (cf. 5.10; 30.1–5; Lev 26.40–45; 1 Kings 8.46–51; Jer 29.10–14; Hos 14.1–7). The latter attribute is invoked by the epithet *merciful God* (Ex 34.6–7; cf. Neh 9.17, 31; Pss 103.8–14; 145.8–9; Jon 4.2). **4.32–40** The Lord's incomparability (see note on 3.24) has its counterpart in Israel's unique experiences of divine providence. The unprecedented events of the exodus and conquest (vv. 34,

37–38) and the revelation at Horeb (vv. 33, 36) give empirical support to Israel's monotheistic creed: *the LORD* (Yahweh) *is God* (lit. "the Deity") and there is *no other* (vv. 35, 39). Cf. 32.39; 1 Kings 8.60; Isa 43.10–13; 44.6; Joel 2.27.

4.41–43 An appended note reports that Moses himself designated three cities in the Transjordan to serve as places of refuge for persons who commit unintentional homicide (19.1–13; cf. Num 35.10–28; Josh 20). **4.44–48** A second preface (cf. 1.1–5) introduces the covenantal legislation promulgated through Moses. **4.44–45** The comprehensive Hebrew term for this corpus is *torah* (translated as *law* in NRSV; see Introduction). Primary components of the legislation are the *decrees* (also 6.17, 20; cf. Ps 25.10), the basic "terms" of the covenant, i.e., the Ten Commandments, and the *statutes and ordinances* (e.g., 5.1; 11.32–12.1;

Israelites when they had come out of Egypt, [46]beyond the Jordan in the valley opposite Beth-peor, in the land of King Sihon of the Amorites, who reigned at Heshbon, whom Moses and the Israelites defeated when they came out of Egypt. [47]They occupied his land and the land of King Og of Bashan, the two kings of the Amorites on the eastern side of the Jordan: [48]from Aroer, which is on the edge of the Wadi Arnon, as far as Mount Sirion[a] (that is, Hermon), [49]together with all the Arabah on the east side of the Jordan as far as the Sea of the Arabah, under the slopes of Pisgah.

The Ten Commandments

5 Moses convened all Israel, and said to them:

Hear, O Israel, the statutes and ordinances that I am addressing to you today; you shall learn them and observe them diligently. [2]The LORD our God made a covenant with us at Horeb. [3]Not with our ancestors did the LORD make this covenant, but with us, who are all of us here alive today. [4]The LORD spoke with you face to face at the mountain, out of the fire. [5](At that time I was standing between the LORD and you to declare to you the words[b] of the LORD; for you were afraid because of the fire and did not go up the mountain.) And he said:

[6]I am the LORD your God, who brought you out of the land of Egypt, out of the house of slavery; [7]you shall have no other gods before[c] me.

[8]You shall not make for yourself an idol, whether in the form of anything that is in heaven above, or that is on the earth beneath, or that is in the water under the earth. [9]You shall not bow down to them or worship them; for I the LORD your God am a jealous God, punishing children for the iniquity of parents, to the third and fourth generation of those who reject me, [10]but showing steadfast love to the thousandth generation[d] of those who love me and keep my commandments.

[11]You shall not make wrongful use of the name of the LORD your God, for the LORD will not acquit anyone who misuses his name.

a Syr: Heb *Sion*   *b* Q Mss Sam Gk Syr Vg Tg: MT *word*   *c* Or *besides*   *d* Or *to thousands*

26.16), a compound designation for the constitutional rules, procedures, and precedents set forth in 12.2–26.15. **4.46–48** A brief reprise of 2.26–3.29.

5.1–12.1 This first major section of Mosaic *torah* consists of a series of hortatory keynotes (5.1–6.3; 6.4–8.20; 9.1–10.11; 10.12–12.1) treating fundamental aspects of the covenant relationship, especially the demand that Israel give willing and undivided allegiance to the Lord. **5.1–6.3** The Israelites at Horeb heard only the Decalogue communicated to them directly by the Lord; they authorized Moses to receive and transmit to them the rest of the Lord's covenantal legislation. See, in brief, 4.13–14. **5.1–3** Moses' audience *today* and their *ancestors* who had originally assembled at Horeb are generational manifestations of the corporate "Israel" with whom the Lord enacts this covenant (cf. 26.16–19; 29.10–15). **5.4** *Face to face.* The Lord's presence was immediate and unmistakable (cf. 34.10; Num 12.8). **5.5** *At that time . . . mountain,* a parenthesis anticipating Moses' role as the intermediary who articulated and amplified the divine speaking (see 5.22–31; cf. Ex 19.3–25). **5.6–21** There are some substantive as well as minor differences between this version of the Decalogue ("the ten words") and the one in Ex 20.2–17. **5.6–10** These verses define the irreducible crux of the covenant relationship (see, e.g., 31.20; Josh 23.16; 2 Kings 17.35–39; Jer 11.9–13). Voiced in the divine first person, the verses form a coherent "word" and comprise a single paragraph in the Hebrew Masoretic Text (which NRSV divides into two segments to lend support to another enumeration of the commandments). The Lord's declaration of sovereignty (v. 6) introduces a series of three injunctions that prohibit association of other deities and any form of idolatry with worship of the Lord (vv. 7–9a). The final clauses proclaim the chief dimensions of the Lord's steadfastness, which should motivate Israel's reciprocal fidelity to the bond of covenant (vv. 9b–10; cf. 4.24, 31; 7.9–10). **5.7** *Other gods* are elsewhere understood to include celestial bodies (e.g., 17.3; cf. 4.19; 2 Kings 23.4–5) as well as various national deities (e.g., 6.14; 13.6–7; 1 Kings 11.4–8), all of which are typically associated with the veneration of their iconographic representations (e.g., 28.36, 64; 2 Kings 17.29–31; Jer 1.16). *Before me,* lit. "upon my face," i.e., masking, eclipsing, or otherwise compromising the Lord's unique identity and presence. **5.8** *An idol* (Hebrew *pesel*) means any cast, carved, or sculpted image, whether ostensibly representing the Lord or some other divine entity or deified power. See, e.g., 4.16–18; 27.15; Judg 17.3–4; 18.30–31; 2 Kings 21.7; Isa 42.17; cf. also Ex 34.17; Lev 19.4; 1 Kings 14.9. **5.9** *Jealous God.* See note on 4.24. *Punishing children . . . parents.* See notes on 7.10; 24.16. **5.10** *Steadfast love* (Hebrew *chesed*) is the ardent faithfulness modeled by the Lord and appropriate to both familial and covenantal relationships. See esp. Ex 15.13; 34.6–7; Hos 2.19–20; 11.1–4; Mic 6.8. **5.11–21** These nine articulated "words" or stipulations include third-person references to the Lord (vv. 11, 12, 14, 15, 16); they are apparently voiced by Moses on the Lord's behalf (see v. 5). **5.11** *Wrongful use,* invocation of the divine name in false oaths or for any magical, malicious, or blasphemous purpose (cf. Lev 19.12; 24.10–23; Ps 24.4; Jer

12 Observe the sabbath day and keep it holy, as the LORD your God commanded you. 13Six days you shall labor and do all your work. 14But the seventh day is a sabbath to the LORD your God; you shall not do any work—you, or your son or your daughter, or your male or female slave, or your ox or your donkey, or any of your livestock, or the resident alien in your towns, so that your male and female slave may rest as well as you. 15Remember that you were a slave in the land of Egypt, and the LORD your God brought you out from there with a mighty hand and an outstretched arm; therefore the LORD your God commanded you to keep the sabbath day.

16 Honor your father and your mother, as the LORD your God commanded you, so that your days may be long and that it may go well with you in the land that the LORD your God is giving you.

17 You shall not murder. *a*

18 Neither shall you commit adultery.

19 Neither shall you steal.

20 Neither shall you bear false witness against your neighbor.

21 Neither shall you covet your neighbor's wife.

Neither shall you desire your neighbor's house, or field, or male or female slave, or ox, or donkey, or anything that belongs to your neighbor.

Moses the Mediator of God's Will

22 These words the LORD spoke with a loud voice to your whole assembly at the mountain, out of the fire, the cloud, and the thick darkness, and he added no more. He wrote them on two stone tablets, and gave them to me. 23When you heard the voice out of the darkness, while the mountain was burning with fire, you approached me, all the heads of your tribes and your elders; 24and you said, "Look, the LORD our God has shown us his glory and greatness, and we have heard his voice out of the fire. Today we have seen that God may speak to someone and the person may still live. 25So now why should we die? For this great fire will consume us; if we hear the voice of the LORD our God any longer, we shall die. 26For who is there of all flesh that has heard the voice of the living God speaking out of fire, as we have, and remained alive? 27Go near, you yourself, and hear all that the LORD our God will say. Then tell us everything that the LORD our God tells you, and we will listen and do it."

28 The LORD heard your words when you spoke to me, and the LORD said to me: "I have heard the words of this people, which they have spoken to you; they are right in all that they have spoken. 29If only they had such a mind as this, to fear me and to keep all my commandments always, so that it might go well with them and with their children forever! 30Go say to them, 'Return to your tents.' 31But you, stand here by me, and I will tell you all the commandments, the statutes and the

---

a Or kill

29.23; Hos 4.2). **5.12–15** The command to hallow the *sabbath day* through observance of broadly inclusive communal rest is connected here with remembrance of the Lord's intervention to release Israel from slavery in Egypt (cf. Ex 20.8–11; 23.12; 31.12–17; 34.21; Isa 58.13–14; Jer 17.21–27). **5.16** *Honor,* respect for parental authority and dignity (cf. 21.18–21; 27.16; Ex 21.15, 17) and faithful performance of filial duties, such as care for aging parents (cf. Sir 3.1–16). **5.17** *Murder* includes both negligent and premeditated homicide (cf. Ex 21.12–14, 29; Num 35.16–34). **5.18–21** *Neither,* lit. "and not"; i.e., the final terse prohibitions are linked in series. **5.18** *Adultery.* Cf. Lev 18.20; 20.10; Prov 6.23–29; Jer 7.9. **5.19** *Steal,* whether persons or property (cf. 24.7; Ex 21.16; 22.1). **5.20** *False witness.* See 19.15–19; Ex 23.1–3; 1 Kings 21.5–14; Prov 25.18. **5.21** Both the ninth and tenth "words" prohibit covetousness, but they distinguish lust to possess a neighbor's *wife* (cf. Prov 6.25) from compulsive desire to alienate a neighbor's *house* or other properties (cf. Isa 5.8; Mic 2.2).

5.22–6.3 Moses' authority to legislate and instruct in matters of the covenant was established through formal agreement at Horeb. **5.22** *These words.* Only the preceding Decalogue. Like *all Israel* in developed Deuteronomic usage (cf. 5.1; 12.7, 12, 18; 29.2, 10–13), *whole assembly* seems to mean the full constituency of the covenant people, inclusive of women and children (cf. 16.16; 23.1–8; 31.12–13, 30; Ex 19.15; cf. Josh 8.35; 2 Kings 23.1–3). The *tablets* document Israel's receipt of the Decalogue as the basic terms of the covenant (see 4.13; 9.9–11, 17; 10.1–5; cf. 31.9, 26). **5.24** *Glory and greatness,* the awesome visual display of the Lord's presence, which served as accompaniment to the divine speaking (cf. 4.10–12; Ex 19.9, 16–18; 24.9, 15–18; Num 16.19; cf. also Ex 33.18–23; 1 Kings 19.11–13). **5.26** *Living God,* the God whose rule is manifest through word and deed (e.g., Josh 3.10; 1 Sam 17.26; 2 Kings 19.4, 16; Jer 10.10; 23.36). **5.27** *Listen and do it.* Israel agreed to heed Moses' voice as the Lord's own. **5.28–31** The Lord ratified Israel's choice of Moses as intermediary, empowering him not

ordinances, that you shall teach them, so that they may do them in the land that I am giving them to possess." 32You must therefore be careful to do as the LORD your God has commanded you; you shall not turn to the right or to the left. 33You must follow exactly the path that the LORD your God has commanded you, so that you may live, and that it may go well with you, and that you may live long in the land that you are to possess.

The Great Commandment

6 Now this is the commandment—the statutes and the ordinances—that the LORD your God charged me to teach you to observe in the land that you are about to cross into and occupy, 2so that you and your children and your children's children may fear the LORD your God all the days of your life, and keep all his decrees and his commandments that I am commanding you, so that your days may be long. 3Hear therefore, O Israel, and observe them diligently, so that it may go well with you, and so that you may multiply greatly in a land flowing with milk and honey, as the LORD, the God of your ancestors, has promised you.

4 Hear, O Israel: The LORD is our God, the LORD alone.*a* 5You shall love the LORD your God with all your heart, and with all your soul, and with all your might. 6Keep these words that I am commanding you today in your heart. 7Recite them to your children and talk about them when you are at home and when you are away, when you lie down and when you rise. 8Bind them as a sign on your hand, fix them as an emblem*b* on your forehead, 9and write them on the doorposts of your house and on your gates.

Caution against Disobedience

10 When the LORD your God has brought you into the land that he swore to your ancestors, to Abraham, to Isaac, and to Jacob, to give you—a land with fine, large cities that you did not build, 11houses filled with all sorts of goods that you did not fill, hewn cisterns that you did not hew, vineyards and olive groves that you did not plant—and when you have eaten your fill, 12take care that you do not forget the LORD, who brought you out of the land of Egypt, out of the house of slavery. 13The LORD your God you shall fear; him you shall serve, and by his name alone you shall swear. 14Do not follow other gods, any of the gods of the peoples who are all around you, 15because the LORD your God, who is present with you, is a jealous God. The anger of the LORD your God would be kindled against you and he would destroy you from the face of the earth.

16 Do not put the LORD your God to the test, as you tested him at Massah. 17You must diligently keep the commandments of the LORD your God, and his decrees, and his statutes that he has commanded you. 18Do what is

---

a Or *The LORD our God is one LORD,* or *The LORD our God, the LORD is one,* or *The LORD is our God, the LORD is one*   *b* Or *as a frontlet*

---

only to transmit divine commandments but also to teach their application. **5.32–6.1** *Now,* a generation later, Moses is about to fulfill his commission by providing Israel with the divinely sanctioned charter for its life in the land. **6.2** *Fear* means to revere and obey the Lord as trustworthy sovereign (e.g., 4.10; 5.29; 6.13, 24; 10.12). **6.3** *Land flowing with milk and honey.* Cf. Ex 3.8; 13.5; 33.3. For the divine promises, see notes on 1.8; 1.10–11.

6.4–8.20 This section offers Moses' instruction on how Israel, when it comes into possession of a national homeland, must conduct its life by disciplined devotion to the Lord. **6.4–9** In Jewish liturgy, this is the lead paragraph of the Shemaʿ (which means *Hear,* the unit's initial word, in Hebrew), which the faithful are instructed to recite twice daily (cf. *Mishnah Berakot* 1.1–3.6). In the synoptic Gospels the creedal injunction of vv. 4–5 is affirmed as the "Great Commandment," which, together with the requirement to love one's neighbor (Lev 19.18), epitomizes the Mosaic law (Mt 22.36–40; Mk 12.28–34; cf. Lk 10.25–28). **6.4–5** *Love* is commanded as the fullest measure of the loy-

alty that Israel owes the Lord (Yahweh), its only divine sovereign (cf. 5.6–10). *Heart,* connoting the human intellect and will, and *soul,* meaning the vitality of selfhood, are often so conjoined in Deuteronomic rhetoric (e.g., 4.29; 10.12; 26.16; Josh 23.14; 2 Kings 23.3); the final item, *might,* or "capacity," appears only here and in a tribute to King Josiah (2 Kings 23.25). **6.6–9** Moses' instruction is to be internalized by the faithful (cf. Ps 37.31; Prov 3.3; Isa 51.7; Jer 31.33) and outwardly displayed in witness to personal and communal identity among the Lord's people. **6.10–19** A concise exposition of 5.6–9, framed as a warning that Israel must never compromise its reliance on the Lord's providence. **6.10–11** The Lord's largess. Cf. 8.7–14; 32.11–15; Josh 24.13; Neh 9.25. **6.13** A summary of positive duties; see also 10.20. *Swear.* Cf. Josh 23.6–8; Isa 48.1; Jer 4.2; 5.7; 12.16. **6.14–15** The perennial injunction and threat; see, e.g., 4.23–26; 8.19–20; 11.16–17; 13.12–18; 29.24–28; 30.17–18; Josh 24.14; Judg 2.11–15; 2 Kings 17.7–18. **6.16** *Test,* by questioning God's presence with or benevolent intentions toward Israel, as exemplified by the incident

right and good in the sight of the LORD, so that it may go well with you, and so that you may go in and occupy the good land that the LORD swore to your ancestors to give you, ¹⁹thrusting out all your enemies from before you, as the LORD has promised.

20 When your children ask you in time to come, "What is the meaning of the decrees and the statutes and the ordinances that the LORD our God has commanded you?" ²¹then you shall say to your children, "We were Pharaoh's slaves in Egypt, but the LORD brought us out of Egypt with a mighty hand. ²²The LORD displayed before our eyes great and awesome signs and wonders against Egypt, against Pharaoh and all his household. ²³He brought us out from there in order to bring us in, to give us the land that he promised on oath to our ancestors. ²⁴Then the LORD commanded us to observe all these statutes, to fear the LORD our God, for our lasting good, so as to keep us alive, as is now the case. ²⁵If we diligently observe this entire commandment before the LORD our God, as he has commanded us, we will be in the right."

A Chosen People

7 When the LORD your God brings you into the land that you are about to enter and occupy, and he clears away many nations before you—the Hittites, the Girgashites, the Amorites, the Canaanites, the Perizzites, the Hivites, and the Jebusites, seven nations mightier and more numerous than you—²and when the LORD your God gives them over to you and you defeat them, then you must utterly destroy them. Make no covenant with them and show them no mercy. ³Do not intermarry with them, giving your daughters to their sons or taking their daughters for your sons, ⁴for that would turn away your children from following me, to serve other gods. Then the anger of the LORD would be kindled against you, and he would destroy you quickly. ⁵But this is how you must deal with them: break down their altars, smash their pillars, hew down their sacred poles,ᵃ and burn their idols with fire. ⁶For you are a people holy to the LORD your God; the LORD your God has chosen you out of all the peoples on earth to be his people, his treasured possession.

7 It was not because you were more numerous than any other people that the LORD set his heart on you and chose you—for you were the fewest of all peoples. ⁸It was because the LORD loved you and kept the oath that he

a Heb Asherim

at *Massah;* see Ex 17.1–7; cf. 1.26–33; Num 14.22; Ps 95.8–9; Mt 4.7. **6.19** For the divine promise, see Ex 23.27; 34.11–12 (cf. Josh 2.22–24). **6.20–25** This catechesis illustrates observance of the instruction in 6.6–9, i.e., how a new generation should be led to acknowledge the Mosaic statutes and ordinances as central to God's gracious design for Israel's well-being (cf. Ex 12.26; 13.14–15; Josh 4.6–7, 21–22). **6.21–23** *We.* The response is succinct, confessional, and experiential; see also 26.5–10 (cf. 5.3; 6.4). **6.24–25** The chief aim of God's law is to secure life (cf. 4.1–4; 30.15–20). *Be in the right,* a verdict of acquittal, anticipated here because of meritorious discharge of covenantal obligations (cf. 24.13; Gen 15.6; Ezek 18.5–9).

7.1–26 In order to safeguard its allegiance to the Lord, Israel must extirpate the nations of Canaan along with their idolatrous cults (cf. 12.2–3; 20.16–18; Ex 23.23–33; 34.11–16; Num 33.51–56). **7.1–6** Prescription. **7.1** Like *Canaanites* and *Amorites* (see 1.7), *Hittites* may be a generic label for Israel's predecessors (cf. Gen 10.15; 23.3–20; 49.29–30; Num 13.29; Josh 1.4; Ezek 16.3, 45). Anatolian antecedents are possible for the *Girgashites* (cf. Gen 10.16), the *Perizzites* (cf. Gen 13.7; 34.30; Josh 17.15; Judg 1.4–5), and Jerusalem's *Jebusites* (cf. Josh 15.63; 2 Sam 5.6–8). *Hivites,* perhaps from north Syria, are associated with Shechem and the Gibeonite cities (cf. Gen 34.2; Josh 9.1–7; Judg 3.3;

2 Sam 21.2). *Seven nations* appear also in Josh 3.10; 24.11; such lists most often have six of the names (e.g., Ex 3.8; Josh 9.1; Judg 3.5; cf. Gen 15.19–21; 1 Kings 9.20). **7.2** *Utterly destroy.* The ban is a radical solution (cf. 20.16–18; Josh 10.40; 11.11–12) that, if enforced, would make the commands of vv. 2b–5 superfluous. *No covenant.* See Ex 23.32–33; 34.12, 15; Josh 9.3–27; 11.19; Judg 2.2–3. **7.3** Prohibition of intermarriage. See Ex 34.16; Josh 23.12–13; Judg 3.5–6 (cf. Gen 34.9–10; 1 Kings 11.1–6). **7.4** *Me,* apparently Moses, speaking as the Lord's surrogate; see 5.27 (cf. 11.13–15; 17.3; 28.20; 29.5). **7.5** Eradication of Canaanizing cult places and practices is a Deuteronomic priority (12.2–4, 29–31; 16.21–22; 18.9–14) which resonates with the measures attributed to kings Hezekiah and Josiah in 2 Kings 18.4; 23.4–24). *Pillars,* commemorative steles (cf. Gen 28.18; 35.14; Ex 24.4; Lev 26.1; 2 Kings 10.26–27). *Asherim* (see text note *a*) were probably cultic *poles* or trees, associated at least indirectly with the goddess Asherah (cf. Ex 34.13; Judg 6.25–30; 1 Kings 14.22–24; 2 Kings 17.16; Isa 27.9; Jer 17.2; Mic 5.14). **7.6** *Holy to the LORD* and *treasured possession* define the character of Israel's election. See 14.2, 21; 26.18–19; cf. Ex 19.5–6; Ps 135.4; Mal 3.17. **7.7–16** God's devotion to Israel is motivated solely by divine love and faithfulness and not by the nation's intrinsic value (variations on 5.6–10). **7.7** *Set his heart,* "was smitten with love" (10.14–15; cf. 21.11; Gen

swore to your ancestors, that the LORD has brought you out with a mighty hand, and redeemed you from the house of slavery, from the hand of Pharaoh king of Egypt. 9Know therefore that the LORD your God is God, the faithful God who maintains covenant loyalty with those who love him and keep his commandments, to a thousand generations, 10and who repays in their own person those who reject him. He does not delay but repays in their own person those who reject him. 11Therefore, observe diligently the commandment—the statutes and the ordinances—that I am commanding you today.

Blessings for Obedience

12 If you heed these ordinances, by diligently observing them, the LORD your God will maintain with you the covenant loyalty that he swore to your ancestors; 13he will love you, bless you, and multiply you; he will bless the fruit of your womb and the fruit of your ground, your grain and your wine and your oil, the increase of your cattle and the issue of your flock, in the land that he swore to your ancestors to give you. 14You shall be the most blessed of peoples, with neither sterility nor barrenness among you or your livestock. 15The LORD will turn away from you every illness; all the dread diseases of Egypt that you experienced, he will not inflict on you, but he will lay them on all who hate you. 16You shall devour all the peoples that the LORD your God is giving over to you, showing them no pity; you shall not serve their gods, for that would be a snare to you.

17 If you say to yourself, "These nations are more numerous than I; how can I dispossess them?" 18do not be afraid of them. Just remember what the LORD your God did to Pharaoh and to all Egypt, 19the great trials that your eyes saw, the signs and wonders, the mighty hand and the outstretched arm by which the LORD your God brought you out. The LORD your God will do the same to all the peoples of whom you are afraid. 20Moreover, the LORD your God will send the pestilence[a] against them, until even the survivors and the fugitives are destroyed. 21Have no dread of them, for the LORD your God, who is present with you, is a great and awesome God. 22The LORD your God will clear away these nations before you little by little; you will not be able to make a quick end of them, otherwise the wild animals would become too numerous for you. 23But the LORD your God will give them over to you, and throw them into great panic, until they are destroyed. 24He will hand their kings over to you and you shall blot out their name from under heaven; no one will be able to stand against you, until you have destroyed them. 25The images of their gods you shall burn with fire. Do not covet the silver or the gold that is on them and take it for yourself, because you could be ensnared by it; for it is abhorrent to the LORD your God. 26Do not bring an abhorrent thing into your house, or you will be set apart for destruction like it. You must utterly detest and abhor it, for it is set apart for destruction.

---

a Or hornets; Meaning of Heb uncertain

34.8; Hos 11.1). **7.8** See 5.6. Redeemed, emancipated or ransomed (also 9.26; 13.5; 15.15; 21.8; 24.18; cf. Num 18.15–17; Ps 78.42; Hos 13.14). **7.9** Echoing 5.10 (cf. Neh 1.5; 9.32; Dan 9.4; Jon 4.2). Faithful, trustworthy, consistent, diligent (cf. 32.4; Pss 89.1–2; 98.3; Isa 49.7). Covenant loyalty, lit. "the covenant [Hebrew berit] and the steadfast love [Hebrew chesed]" (also v. 12). Cf. 1 Kings 8.23–24; Ps 89.24, 28, 33–34; Isa 54.10; 55.3; Mic 7.20). **7.10** An emphatic revision of 5.9b (cf. Ex 34.6–7; Num 14.18). Instead of corporate punishment, which might affect several generations, retribution for breach of covenant is now targeted against individual offenders (cf. 24.16; Jer 31.29–30; 32.18–19; Ezek 18.1–24). **7.13–14** Cf. 15.6; 28.4–14; Ex 23.25–26. Grain, wine, oil, the chief agricultural products of Canaan (11.14; 12.17; 14.23; 18.4; 28.51; cf. Hos 2.8, 22). **7.15** Diseases of Egypt, presumably exemplified by the plagues of Ex 9.3, 9 (cf. Deut 28.27, 60; Ex 15.26; Am 4.10). **7.16** Snare to you. See 12.29–32; cf. 7.25; Ex 23.32–33; 34.12–16; Judg 2.3. **7.17–26** Implementation (the conquest theme). **7.17–19** Divine warfare. Cf. 1.28–30; 3.22; 4.34, 37–38; 9.1–3; 20.1; 29.2–3; Josh 23.3, 9–10. **7.20** Pestilence, perhaps a metaphor for terror as a weapon of divine warfare (cf. 2.25; 32.23–24; Ex 15.14–16; 23.27–28; Josh 24.12; Hab 3.5). **7.22** Little by little. Cf. Ex 23.29–30; Judg 2.3, 20–23; 3.1–6. **7.23** Panic. Cf. 28.20; 1 Sam 5.9–11; 14.18–20. **7.24** See 11.25; 12.3; cf. Josh 13. **7.25–26** Images . . . you shall burn. See 9.21; 1 Kings 15.13; 2 Kings 10.26–27; 23.4, 11, 15. Do not covet. This and the following provisions foreshadow Josh 6.18–19 and the aftermath in Josh 7; cf. Judg 8.24–27; 17.2–4. Abhorrent to the LORD is a label used to proscribe things, practices, and persons deemed fraudulent, idolatrous, or otherwise morally repugnant (e.g., 12.31; 17.1; 18.12; 22.5; 23.18; 24.4; 25.16; Prov 3.32; 6.16; 15.8–9, 26; cf. Gen 43.32; Ex 8.26). Destruction, or "ban" (Hebrew cherem). See note on 2.33–35.

A Warning Not to Forget God in Prosperity

8 This entire commandment that I command you today you must diligently observe, so that you may live and increase, and go in and occupy the land that the LORD promised on oath to your ancestors. 2Remember the long way that the LORD your God has led you these forty years in the wilderness, in order to humble you, testing you to know what was in your heart, whether or not you would keep his commandments. 3He humbled you by letting you hunger, then by feeding you with manna, with which neither you nor your ancestors were acquainted, in order to make you understand that one does not live by bread alone, but by every word that comes from the mouth of the LORD.a 4The clothes on your back did not wear out and your feet did not swell these forty years. 5Know then in your heart that as a parent disciplines a child so the LORD your God disciplines you. 6Therefore keep the commandments of the LORD your God, by walking in his ways and by fearing him. 7For the LORD your God is bringing you into a good land, a land with flowing streams, with springs and underground waters welling up in valleys and hills, 8a land of wheat and barley, of vines and fig trees and pomegranates, a land of olive trees and honey, 9a land where you may eat bread without scarcity, where you will lack nothing, a land whose stones are iron and from whose hills you may mine copper. 10You shall eat your fill and bless the LORD your God for the good land that he has given you.

11 Take care that you do not forget the LORD your God, by failing to keep his commandments, his ordinances, and his statutes, which I am commanding you today. 12When you have eaten your fill and have built fine houses and live in them, 13and when your herds and flocks have multiplied, and your silver and gold is multiplied, and all that you have is multiplied, 14then do not exalt yourself, forgetting the LORD your God, who brought you out of the land of Egypt, out of the house of slavery, 15who led you through the great and terrible wilderness, an arid wasteland with poisonousb snakes and scorpions. He made water flow for you from flint rock, 16and fed you in the wilderness with manna that your ancestors did not know, to humble you and to test you, and in the end to do you good. 17Do not say to yourself, "My power and the might of my own hand have gotten me this wealth." 18But remember the LORD your God, for it is he who gives you power to get wealth, so that he may confirm his covenant that he swore to your ancestors, as he is doing today. 19If you do forget the LORD your God and follow other gods to serve and worship them, I solemnly warn you today that you shall surely perish. 20Like the nations that the LORD is destroying before you, so shall you perish, because you would not obey the voice of the LORD your God.

The Consequences of Rebelling against God

9 Hear, O Israel! You are about to cross the Jordan today, to go in and dispossess na-

---

a Or by anything that the LORD decrees   b Or fiery; Heb seraph

---

8.1–20 The theme that affluent life in Canaan encourages haughtiness and apostasy is a familiar one in prophetic as well as Deuteronomic sources (cf. 4.25; 31.20; 32.13–18; Isa 5.1–7; Jer 2.1–13; Hos 13.4–6; Am 6.1–8). Here the issue is addressed in light of Israel's experience of divine providence during the wilderness era. 8.1–10 Exhortation (remember, v. 2; know, v. 5; keep, v. 6). 8.2 Forty years. Cf. 1.3; 29.5; Ps 95.10; Am 2.10. The Israelites were humbled in the wilderness, treated in a humiliating manner (e.g., 21.14; 22.24; 26.6; Ex 22.22–23; Ps 90.15), to test their willingness to obey. 8.3 Israel survived on manna (cf. Ex 16; Num 11.5–9; Josh 5.12), which was "miserable food" (Num 21.5), because that is what the Lord had provided. The lesson: life is ordered and sustained not by human preferences but by anything and everything that the Lord alone decrees (cf. Ps 104; Prov 30.8). 8.4 Cf. 29.5; Neh 9.21. 8.5 On divine and parental dis-

cipline, see, e.g., 4.36; 11.2; 21.18; Jer 31.18; Ps 94.12; Prov 3.11–12; 19.18; 29.17; Hos 11.1–4. 8.7–9 An encomium on Canaan's bounties (cf. 1.25; 11.9–12; 32.13–14; 33.28; Num 20.5; also the Egyptian "Tale of Sinuhe" 81–84). 8.10 Eat . . . bless, return praise to the Lord for the blessings received (cf. Gen 24.48; Neh 9.5; Pss 34.1; 145.1–2; also Mishnah Berakot 6). 8.11–20 Admonition (Do not forget, v. 11; Do not say, v. 17). 8.11–14 A reprise of 6.10–12. 8.15 Snakes. Cf. Num 21.6–9. Flint rock. See 32.13; cf. Ex 17.6; Num 20.8–11; Ps 114.8. 8.17–18 Because the Lord provides the means to acquire wealth (cf. Gen 34.29; Job 5.5; Prov 13.22; Ezek 28.4–5), prosperity must always be acknowledged as a divine gift and never claimed as a personal right (see also 9.4–5; 12.5–7; 14.28–29; 15.4–18; 26.1–15). 8.19 Solemnly warn, testify against or threaten (cf. 4.26; 30.19; 32.46; 1 Sam 8.9; 2 Kings 17.13).

tions larger and mightier than you, great cities, fortified to the heavens, 2a strong and tall people, the offspring of the Anakim, whom you know. You have heard it said of them, "Who can stand up to the Anakim?" 3Know then today that the LORD your God is the one who crosses over before you as a devouring fire; he will defeat them and subdue them before you, so that you may dispossess and destroy them quickly, as the LORD has promised you.

4 When the LORD your God thrusts them out before you, do not say to yourself, "It is because of my righteousness that the LORD has brought me in to occupy this land"; it is rather because of the wickedness of these nations that the LORD is dispossessing them before you. 5It is not because of your righteousness or the uprightness of your heart that you are going in to occupy their land; but because of the wickedness of these nations the LORD your God is dispossessing them before you, in order to fulfill the promise that the LORD made on oath to your ancestors, to Abraham, to Isaac, and to Jacob.

6 Know, then, that the LORD your God is not giving you this good land to occupy because of your righteousness; for you are a stubborn people. 7Remember and do not forget how you provoked the LORD your God to wrath in the wilderness; you have been rebellious against the LORD from the day you came out of the land of Egypt until you came to this place.

8 Even at Horeb you provoked the LORD to wrath, and the LORD was so angry with you that he was ready to destroy you. 9When I went up the mountain to receive the stone tablets, the tablets of the covenant that the LORD made with you, I remained on the mountain forty days and forty nights; I neither ate bread nor drank water. 10And the LORD gave me the two stone tablets written with the finger of God; on them were all the words that the LORD had spoken to you at the mountain out of the fire on the day of the assembly. 11At the end of forty days and forty nights the LORD gave me the two stone tablets, the tablets of the covenant. 12Then the LORD said to me, "Get up, go down quickly from here, for your people whom you have brought from Egypt have acted corruptly. They have been quick to turn from the way that I commanded them; they have cast an image for themselves." 13Furthermore the LORD said to me, "I have seen that this people is indeed a stubborn people. 14Let me alone that I may destroy them and blot out their name from under heaven; and I will make of you a nation mightier and more numerous than they."

15 So I turned and went down from the mountain, while the mountain was ablaze; the two tablets of the covenant were in my two hands. 16Then I saw that you had indeed sinned against the LORD your God, by casting for yourselves an image of a calf; you had been quick to turn from the way that the LORD had commanded you. 17So I took hold of the two tablets and flung them from my two hands, smashing them before your eyes. 18Then I lay

---

9.1–10.11 This section offers a preemptive challenge to national self-righteousness and triumphalism by reviewing Israel's history of rebelliousness during the wilderness era. **9.1–7** Introduction (resuming the conquest theme of 7.17–26). **9.1–2** A new generation of Israelites must face the threats that undid its predecessor. See 1.28, 41–45; 2.10–11; Num 13.28. **9.3** A reply to the preceding adage: the Lord, leading as a *devouring fire* (see 4.24), will defeat the formidable enemy on Israel's behalf (cf. 31.3–6). *Quickly.* See notes on 6.19; 7.22. **9.4–5** Were the issue to be litigated (cf. 25.1), Israel could not gain title to its homeland on grounds of its own "innocence," *righteousness,* or "integrity," *uprightness of . . . heart* (cf. Pss 32.11; 97.11). The Lord is evicting the nations because of their "guilt," *wickedness* (see 20.18; Gen 15.16; Lev 18.24; 2 Kings 17.8; 21.2); the land only passes to Israel in fulfillment of the divine promise to the patriarchs (see note on 1.8). **9.6** *Stubborn,* or "stiff-necked," indicates an obstinate refusal to heed orders (cf. also 9.13; 10.16;

31.27; Ex 32.9; 33.3; 34.9; Isa 48.4; Jer 17.23; 19.15). **9.7** *From . . . Egypt.* Cf. Ex 14.10–14; 15.22–26; Jer 7.25–26; 2 Kings 21.15. **9.8–24** Rebellions of the wilderness era. **9.8–9** The apostasy at *Horeb,* passed over in Moses' earlier reviews (chs. 1, 4–5), is now introduced as the paradigm case of Israel's unfaithfulness. **9.9** *Tablets of the covenant.* See notes on 4.13–14; 5.22; cf. Ex 24.12. *Forty days . . . nights* is a leitmotif; see also 9.11, 18, 25; 10.10; 1 Kings 19.8; Jon 3.4. **9.10** Cf. Ex 31.18. *The day of the assembly,* when the full convocation heard the Lord speak (also 10.4; 18.16); see note on 5.22. **9.12–14** *Your people whom you have brought.* Israel, already in violation of the chief commandment (5.6–10), was disclaimed by the Lord, who proposed to start over with Moses; see Ex 32.7–10 (cf. Num 14.12). **9.15–17** The metallic *calf,* whether meant to represent the Lord or some other deity, made the case prima facie against Israel for breach of covenant (cf. Ex 32.1–8; 1 Kings 12.28–30; Ps 106.19–22; Hos 8.4–6; 10.5–6; 13.1–2). Moses signaled annulment of the

prostrate before the LORD as before, forty days and forty nights; I neither ate bread nor drank water, because of all the sin you had committed, provoking the LORD by doing what was evil in his sight. ¹⁹For I was afraid that the anger that the LORD bore against you was so fierce that he would destroy you. But the LORD listened to me that time also. ²⁰The LORD was so angry with Aaron that he was ready to destroy him, but I interceded also on behalf of Aaron at that same time. ²¹Then I took the sinful thing you had made, the calf, and burned it with fire and crushed it, grinding it thoroughly, until it was reduced to dust; and I threw the dust of it into the stream that runs down the mountain.

22 At Taberah also, and at Massah, and at Kibroth-hattaavah, you provoked the LORD to wrath. ²³And when the LORD sent you from Kadesh-barnea, saying, "Go up and occupy the land that I have given you," you rebelled against the command of the LORD your God, neither trusting him nor obeying him. ²⁴You have been rebellious against the LORD as long as he has[a] known you.

25 Throughout the forty days and forty nights that I lay prostrate before the LORD when the LORD intended to destroy you, ²⁶I prayed to the LORD and said, "Lord GOD, do not destroy the people who are your very own possession, whom you redeemed in your greatness, whom you brought out of Egypt with a mighty hand. ²⁷Remember your servants, Abraham, Isaac, and Jacob; pay no attention to the stubbornness of this people, their wickedness and their sin, ²⁸otherwise the land from which you have brought us might

say, 'Because the LORD was not able to bring them into the land that he promised them, and because he hated them, he has brought them out to let them die in the wilderness.' ²⁹For they are the people of your very own possession, whom you brought out by your great power and by your outstretched arm."

The Second Pair of Tablets

10 At that time the LORD said to me, "Carve out two tablets of stone like the former ones, and come up to me on the mountain, and make an ark of wood. ²I will write on the tablets the words that were on the former tablets, which you smashed, and you shall put them in the ark." ³So I made an ark of acacia wood, cut two tablets of stone like the former ones, and went up the mountain with the two tablets in my hand. ⁴Then he wrote on the tablets the same words as before, the ten commandments[b] that the LORD had spoken to you on the mountain out of the fire on the day of the assembly; and the LORD gave them to me. ⁵So I turned and came down from the mountain, and put the tablets in the ark that I had made; and there they are, as the LORD commanded me.

6 (The Israelites journeyed from Beeroth-bene-jaakan[c] to Moserah. There Aaron died, and there he was buried; his son Eleazar succeeded him as priest. ⁷From there they journeyed to Gudgodah, and from Gudgodah to Jotbathah, a land with flowing streams. ⁸At that time the LORD set apart the tribe of Levi

---

a Sam Gk: MT *I have*   *b* Heb *the ten words*   *c* Or *the wells of the Bene-jaakan*

---

treaty by *smashing* the tablets. **9.18–19** *Prostrate,* the posture of supplication (cf. Num 16.22). *As before* and *that time also* suppose this to be Moses' second successful intercession in the affair (cf. vv. 25–29; Ex 32.11–14, 30–34). **9.20** The account in Ex 32.1–6, 21–25, 35 recognizes *Aaron's* guilt but says nothing about special pleading on his behalf. **9.21** Cf. Ex 32.20; see note on 7.25–26. **9.22–24** Other incidents are tersely noted by toponyms to establish a pattern of rebelliousness (cf. 31.27): *Taberah* (Num 11.1–3); *Massah* (see Deut 6.16); *Kibroth-hattaavah* (Num 11.31–34); and *Kadesh-barnea* (see 1.19–33). **9.25–10.11** Restoration of the covenant. **9.25–29** Moses' intercessory prayer boldly responded to the Lord's disowning of and threats against Israel in vv. 12–14 (cf. Ex 32.11–14). **9.26** *Your very own possession;* lit. "your people and your possession" (also v. 29; cf. 4.20); i.e., the people belong not to Moses (9.12), but to the Lord,

who *redeemed* them from slavery in Egypt (see 7.8). **9.27–28** Despite Israel's obstinacy (9.13–14) there are reasons for divine restraint: the merit of the ancestors (cf. 7.8) and the Lord's own reputation (cf. 32.26–27; Num 14.13–16; Josh 7.7–9; Ps 115.1–2). **10.1–5** The covenant was reconstituted on its original terms (the Decalogue, vv. 2, 4) when a duplicate set of *tablets* was inscribed by the Lord and transmitted to Israel through Moses (cf. 4.13; 5.22; Ex 34.1–4, 27–29). **10.1** In the tradition represented here, the *ark* was a wooden "chest" (cf. Gen 50.26, "coffin"; 2 Kings 12.9–10) built by Moses for the specific purpose of transporting the stone tablets of the covenant (cf. 10.8; 31.9, 24–26; 1 Kings 8.9 with various views in, e.g., Ex 25.10–22; 37.1–9; Num 10.35–36; 1 Sam 4.3–11; Ps 132.8). **10.6–7** Segments of a wilderness itinerary (with another version in Num 33.31–33) frame a notice on Aaron's death (cf. Deut 32.50) and the succes-

to carry the ark of the covenant of the LORD, to stand before the LORD to minister to him, and to bless in his name, to this day. 9Therefore Levi has no allotment or inheritance with his kindred; the LORD is his inheritance, as the LORD your God promised him.)

10 I stayed on the mountain forty days and forty nights, as I had done the first time. And once again the LORD listened to me. The LORD was unwilling to destroy you. 11The LORD said to me, "Get up, go on your journey at the head of the people, that they may go in and occupy the land that I swore to their ancestors to give them."

The Essence of the Law

12 So now, O Israel, what does the LORD your God require of you? Only to fear the LORD your God, to walk in all his ways, to love him, to serve the LORD your God with all your heart and with all your soul, 13and to keep the commandments of the LORD your God[a] and his decrees that I am commanding you today, for your own well-being. 14Although heaven and the heaven of heavens belong to the LORD your God, the earth with all that is in it, 15yet the LORD set his heart in love on your ancestors alone and chose you, their descendants after them, out of all the peoples, as it is today. 16Circumcise, then, the foreskin of your heart, and do not be stubborn any longer. 17For the LORD your God is God of gods and Lord of lords, the great God, mighty and awesome,

who is not partial and takes no bribe, 18who executes justice for the orphan and the widow, and who loves the strangers, providing them food and clothing. 19You shall also love the stranger, for you were strangers in the land of Egypt. 20You shall fear the LORD your God; him alone you shall worship; to him you shall hold fast, and by his name you shall swear. 21He is your praise; he is your God, who has done for you these great and awesome things that your own eyes have seen. 22Your ancestors went down to Egypt seventy persons; and now the LORD your God has made you as numerous as the stars in heaven.

Rewards for Obedience

11 You shall love the LORD your God, therefore, and keep his charge, his decrees, his ordinances, and his commandments always. 2Remember today that it was not your children (who have not known or seen the discipline of the LORD your God), but it is you who must acknowledge his greatness, his mighty hand and his outstretched arm, 3his signs and his deeds that he did in Egypt to Pharaoh, the king of Egypt, and to all his land; 4what he did to the Egyptian army, to their horses and chariots, how he made the water of the Red Sea[b] flow over them as they pursued you, so that the LORD has destroyed them to this day; 5what he did to you in the wilderness,

---

a Q Ms Gk Syr: MT lacks *your God*   b Or *Sea of Reeds*

---

sion of his son *Eleazar* to priestly leadership (cf. Num 3.1–4, 32; 20.22–29; 26.63–64; 24.33). **10.8–9** Another supplement reports the commissioning of the *tribe of Levi* to perform ritual service. For their duties and prebends, see notes on 18.1–8; 21.5; 33.8–11 (cf. Ex 32.25–29; Num 6.23–27; 8.5–26). **10.10–11** The review ends at the point where Moses' memoirs begin in 1.6 (cf. Ex 33.1).

10.12–12.1 In this finale to Moses' preliminary instruction, primary themes of the preceding sections (5.1–6.3; 6.4–8.20; 9.1–10.11) are rhetorically highlighted, with particular emphasis on love of the Lord as the measure of covenantal obedience (cf. 5.10; 6.5; 7.9; 10.12; 11.1, 13, 22). **10.12–22** The Lord's requirements epitomized. **10.12–13** *So now.* See note on 4.1. The question and answer scheme suggests liturgical usage (cf. Pss 15; 24.3–5, 8, 10; Mic 6.8); here the terms of response are thoroughly Deuteronomic (e.g., 5.29–33; 6.2, 13, 24; 8.6; 11.13, 22). **10.14–15** *Heaven of heavens,* or "the highest heaven" (cf. 1 Kings 8.27; Neh 9.6; Ps 148.4). *Set his heart . . . chose.* See 7.6–8; 14.2; cf. Ex 19.5–6. **10.16** *Circumcise . . . the foreskin of your heart,* a call to conversion that identifies recalcitrant

human minds or individual wills as the barrier to knowing and doing what the Lord requires (cf. 30.6; Lev 26.41; Jer 4.4; 6.10; 9.26; Ezek 44.7, 9). **10.17–18** Both the hymnic titles (cf. Ex 15.3, 11; Ps 47.2; Dan 2.47) and the social agenda of resolute justice (cf. 1.16–17; 16.19; Pss 68.5–6; 99.1–5; 146.5–9) are prerogatives of the Lord's universal suzerainty. **10.19** *You shall also love.* Israel is to imitate the Lord's zeal for egalitarian justice (cf. 24.17–22; Ex 22.21–24; 23.6–9; Lev 19.33–34; also Isa 61.1–9). **10.21** *Your praise,* the one to whom you give praise (cf. Ps 109.1; Jer 17.14). **10.22** *Seventy persons.* See Gen 46.8–27; Ex 1.5; cf. Deut 1.10.

11.1–17 The Lord's providential care. **11.1** *Keep his charge,* perform loyal service as prescribed (cf. Gen 26.5; Lev 8.35; Josh 22.3; 1 Kings 2.3). **11.2** By *discipline* is meant here lessons learned through normative experience of the Lord's sovereign presence (cf. 4.9, 33–39; 5.29; 8.5), i.e., the creedal lore that each generation must assimilate and faithfully transmit to the next (cf. 6.20–25). **11.3–4** The emphasis here on the Lord's victory at the *Red Sea* is singular among the book's witnesses to the exodus (cf. 6.21–22; 7.18–19;

until you came to this place; 6and what he did to Dathan and Abiram, sons of Eliab son of Reuben, how in the midst of all Israel the earth opened its mouth and swallowed them up, along with their households, their tents, and every living being in their company; 7for it is your own eyes that have seen every great deed that the LORD did.

8 Keep, then, this entire commandment that I am commanding you today, so that you may have strength to go in and occupy the land that you are crossing over to occupy, 9and so that you may live long in the land that the LORD swore to your ancestors to give them and to their descendants, a land flowing with milk and honey. 10For the land that you are about to enter to occupy is not like the land of Egypt, from which you have come, where you sow your seed and irrigate by foot like a vegetable garden. 11But the land that you are crossing over to occupy is a land of hills and valleys, watered by rain from the sky, 12a land that the LORD your God looks after. The eyes of the LORD your God are always on it, from the beginning of the year to the end of the year.

13 If you will only heed his every commandment*a* that I am commanding you today—loving the LORD your God, and serving him with all your heart and with all your soul— 14then he*b* will give the rain for your land in its season, the early rain and the later rain, and you will gather in your grain, your wine, and your oil; 15and he*b* will give grass in your fields for your livestock, and you will eat your fill. 16Take care, or you will be seduced into turning away, serving other gods and worshiping them, 17for then the anger of the

LORD will be kindled against you and he will shut up the heavens, so that there will be no rain and the land will yield no fruit; then you will perish quickly off the good land that the LORD is giving you.

18 You shall put these words of mine in your heart and soul, and you shall bind them as a sign on your hand, and fix them as an emblem*c* on your forehead. 19Teach them to your children, talking about them when you are at home and when you are away, when you lie down and when you rise. 20Write them on the doorposts of your house and on your gates, 21so that your days and the days of your children may be multiplied in the land that the LORD swore to your ancestors to give them, as long as the heavens are above the earth.

22 If you will diligently observe this entire commandment that I am commanding you, loving the LORD your God, walking in all his ways, and holding fast to him, 23then the LORD will drive out all these nations before you, and you will dispossess nations larger and mightier than yourselves. 24Every place on which you set foot shall be yours; your territory shall extend from the wilderness to the Lebanon and from the River, the river Euphrates, to the Western Sea. 25No one will be able to stand against you; the LORD your God will put the fear and dread of you on all the land on which you set foot, as he promised you.

26 See, I am setting before you today a blessing and a curse: 27the blessing, if you obey the commandments of the LORD your

---

a Compare Gk: Heb *my commandments*   *b* Sam Gk Vg: MT *I*
c Or *as a frontlet*

26.8; 29.2–3; 34.11; Josh 24.5–7; Ps 106.7–12). **11.6** In the expansive version of Num 16 (usually ascribed to the Priestly tradition; see Introduction to Genesis), the insurrectionist party of the Reubenites *Dathan and Abiram* is subordinated to the ecclesial revolt led by the Levite Korah, who is unmentioned here (cf. Ps 106.16–18). **11.8–9** Echoes 5.32–6.3. **11.10–12** While Egypt's agricultural productivity (cf. Gen 13.10; 41.53–57; Num 11.5) is based on irrigation, exploiting the regularity of the Nile, Canaan's prosperity requires seasonal rains that attest the Lord's special care. **11.13–15** Rainfall in autumn and spring (*the early rain and the later rain;* see Jer 3.3; 5.24; Job 29.23) and the fertility it creates are divine blessings, granted to reward performance of covenantal duties (cf. 7.12–14; 28.12; Lev 26.4–5; Isa 30.23–24; Jer 14.21–22). **11.16** On the danger of entrapment in idolatry (*seduced*), see 7.1–6; 13.1–15. **11.17** *Shut up the heavens,*

to withhold rain (cf. 28.23–24; Gen 7.11; Lev 26.19; 1 Kings 8.35–36; Job 38.25–27). **11.18–12.1** Transition to the Mosaic legislation. **11.18–21** Rhetorical echoes of 6.6–9; 6.1–3 recall attention to the chief aim of the address. **11.21** *As long ... earth,* i.e., forever (cf. Ps 89.29; Jer 31.36–37; 33.25–26). **11.22–23** Cf. 10.12–13, 20; 9.1. **11.24** *Every place ... yours.* Josh 1.3 cites this promise. *Your territory.* The boundaries encompass the broad expanse of Syro-Palestine and correspond approximately to the scope of Davidic hegemony in the early tenth century BCE (see note on 1.7; cf. Ex 23.31). *Western Sea,* the Mediterranean. **11.25** For the promise, see 2.25. **11.26–28** *A blessing and a curse* are the alternatives of weal and woe posed by the constant choice that Israel must make between fidelity to the Lord and apostasy (cf. 30.15–20; Josh 24.14–28). These fundamental options are sanctioned by the specific lists of conditional

God that I am commanding you today; 28 and the curse, if you do not obey the commandments of the LORD your God, but turn from the way that I am commanding you today, to follow other gods that you have not known.

29 When the LORD your God has brought you into the land that you are entering to occupy, you shall set the blessing on Mount Gerizim and the curse on Mount Ebal. 30 As you know, they are beyond the Jordan, some distance to the west, in the land of the Canaanites who live in the Arabah, opposite Gilgal, beside the oak*a* of Moreh.

31 When you cross the Jordan to go in to occupy the land that the LORD your God is giving you, and when you occupy it and live in it, 32 you must diligently observe all the statutes and ordinances that I am setting before you today.

Pagan Shrines to Be Destroyed

12 These are the statutes and ordinances that you must diligently observe in the land that the LORD, the God of your ancestors, has given you to occupy all the days that you live on the earth.

2 You must demolish completely all the places where the nations whom you are about to dispossess served their gods, on the mountain heights, on the hills, and under every leafy tree. 3 Break down their altars, smash their pillars, burn their sacred poles*b* with fire, and hew down the idols of their gods, and thus blot out their name from their places. 4 You shall not worship the LORD your God in such ways. 5 But you shall seek the place that the LORD your God will choose out of all your tribes as his habitation to put his name there. You shall go there, 6 bringing there your burnt offerings and your sacrifices, your tithes and your donations, your votive gifts, your freewill offerings, and the firstlings of your herds and flocks. 7 And

---

a Gk Syr: Compare Gen 12.6; Heb *oaks* or *terebinths*
b Heb *Asherim*

"blessings" and "curses" in ch. 28 (see also Lev 26). **11.28** *Gods . . . not known,* gods whose effective presence you have not experienced (cf. 4.32–39; 32.16–17; Judg 2.11–13; 5.8). **11.29** This anticipates the rites prescribed in ch. 27 (cf. Josh 8.30–35). Ancient Shechem was situated in the valley between *Mount Gerizim* on the south and *Mount Ebal* on the north. **11.30** Geographical sense is not evident in the association of Canaanite inhabitants of the *Arabah* (cf. Num 13.29) with the site of *Gilgal* near Jericho (see Josh 4–5) and the distant *oak of Moreh* at Shechem (Gen 12.6; 35.4; cf. Josh 24.26). **11.31–12.1** These verses form a rhetorical seam between the general instructions, now completed, and the following promulgation of *the statutes and ordinances;* see note on 4.44–45.

12.2–26.15 Articles of the covenantal polity are arranged in five broad topical divisions: the single sanctuary (12.2–28); communal service of the Lord (12.29–17.13); constitutional offices (17.14–18.22); major juridical principles and precedents (19.1–25.19); and liturgical reaffirmations of fidelity (26.1–15). **12.2–28** In this initial division, four complementary articles (vv. 2–7, 8–12, 13–19, 20–28) develop a radical reinterpretation of the sanctuary law in Ex 20.24–26. The revision's chief concern correlates closely with reforms attributed to the Judean kings Hezekiah at the end of the eighth century BCE (2 Kings 18.3–6, 22) and Josiah in the later seventh (2 Kings 23.4–19): suppression of apostasy and cultic pluralism by restricting Israel's performance of sacrificial rites and related ceremonies to the temple in Jerusalem. **12.2–7** A categorical distinction is drawn between the manifold cultic installations that Israel must destroy while conquering its homeland and the single, divinely designated place where Israel's own national worship

center will be established. **12.2–3** Antecedent injunctions are Ex 23.23–24; 34.11–14 (cf. also Deut 7.5; Num 33.51–52). *Heights . . . leafy tree.* See, e.g., 2 Kings 16.4; Jer 2.20. *Their name,* the sovereignty claimed by the defunct nations but also the immanence of putative gods associated with the installations (cf. 7.24–25; 25.19; Gen 35.14–15; Ex 20.24; Josh 23.7). **12.4** According to many witnesses, this is just what happened. See, e.g., Judg 17.3–5; 1 Kings 12.28–30; 14.22–24; 2 Kings 17.8–12; Jer 3.6–10; 17.1–3; Ezek 6.2–7; 18.6; Hos 4.12–13; 10.8. **12.5** Israel should seek the Lord in worship not at "every place" commemorating the divine name (Ex 20.24) but only at the one *place* chosen *out of all your tribes,* i.e., Jerusalem's acropolis, where David's tent shrine for the ark was soon replaced by the Solomonic temple (cf. 2 Sam 6.17; 7.6–7, 13; 24.18–25; 1 Kings 8.16–21; 11.32; 14.21; 2 Kings 21.7; Ps 132). Although in Deuteronomic theology the transcendent God does not "reside" in any earthly abode, the Lord's *name* (Hebrew *shem*) is localized at the one sanctuary as a manifestation of divine presence and cosmic attentiveness (26.15; 1 Kings 8.27–30, 43, 48–49; cf. Ex 23.20; Ps 74.7; Isa 18.7; Jer 3.17; 7.12–14; Tob 13.11). Hence *as his habitation* is a dubious rendering; the Hebrew may be translated instead "to establish it (the divine name)," similarly in 12.11; 14.23; 16.2, 6, 11; 26.2. **12.6** *Burnt offerings,* "holocausts" in which flayed animal carcasses were wholly consumed by fire on the altar, sustained the system of expiatory sacrifices (cf. Lev 1.3–17; 6.9–13; Num 28.2–8, 23–24; Am 5.22). Other *sacrifices* were usually consumed in part by the worshipers who presented them and also by priestly officiants (cf. 18.1–3; Lev 3; 7.29–36). *Tithes . . . firstlings,* i.e., all types of sacred dues (14.22–27; 15.19–23; 23.21–23; 26.12–15; cf. Lev 27.1–8; Num

you shall eat there in the presence of the LORD your God, you and your households together, rejoicing in all the undertakings in which the LORD your God has blessed you.

8 You shall not act as we are acting here today, all of us according to our own desires, ⁹for you have not yet come into the rest and the possession that the LORD your God is giving you. ¹⁰When you cross over the Jordan and live in the land that the LORD your God is allotting to you, and when he gives you rest from your enemies all around so that you live in safety, ¹¹then you shall bring everything that I command you to the place that the LORD your God will choose as a dwelling for his name: your burnt offerings and your sacrifices, your tithes and your donations, and all your choice votive gifts that you vow to the LORD. ¹²And you shall rejoice before the LORD your God, you together with your sons and your daughters, your male and female slaves, and the Levites who reside in your towns (since they have no allotment or inheritance with you).

A Prescribed Place of Worship

13 Take care that you do not offer your burnt offerings at any place you happen to see. ¹⁴But only at the place that the LORD will choose in one of your tribes—there you shall offer your burnt offerings and there you shall do everything I command you.

15 Yet whenever you desire you may slaughter and eat meat within any of your towns, according to the blessing that the LORD your God has given you; the unclean and the clean may eat of it, as they would of gazelle or deer. ¹⁶The blood, however, you must not eat; you shall pour it out on the ground like water. ¹⁷Nor may you eat within your towns the tithe of your grain, your wine, and your oil, the firstlings of your herds and your flocks, any of your votive gifts that you vow, your freewill offerings, or your donations; ¹⁸these you shall eat in the presence of the LORD your God at the place that the LORD your God will choose, you together with your son and your daughter, your male and female slaves, and the Levites resident in your towns, rejoicing in the presence of the LORD your God in all your undertakings. ¹⁹Take care that you do not neglect the Levite as long as you live in your land.

20 When the LORD your God enlarges your territory, as he has promised you, and you say, "I am going to eat some meat," because you wish to eat meat, you may eat meat whenever you have the desire. ²¹If the place where the LORD your God will choose to put his name is too far from you, and you slaughter as I have commanded you any of your herd or flock that the LORD has given you, then you may eat within your towns whenever you desire. ²²Indeed, just as gazelle or deer is eaten, so you may eat it; the unclean and the clean alike may eat it. ²³Only be sure that you do not eat the blood; for the blood is the life, and you shall not eat the life with the meat. ²⁴Do not eat it; you shall pour it out on the ground like water.

15.18–21; 30.2–15; Am 4.4–5). **12.7** Emphasis on inclusive religious celebrations is characteristic of the Deuteronomic polity (cf. 12.12, 18–19; 14.26–27; 15.20; 16.11, 14; 26.11). **12.8–12** A temporal distinction is made between divergent practices *today* and the unification of worship that will become normative for settled Israel. **12.8** *We are acting . . . all of us according to our own desires,* lit. "each person (doing) what is right in his own sight": individual willfulness reigns (cf. Judg 17.6; 21.25) rather than divine authority (*what is right and good in the sight of the LORD;* cf. 6.18; 12.25, 28). **12.9–10** *Rest and . . . possession,* secure territorial dominion (see notes on 3.18–20; 11.24; cf. 33.28–29). According to developed Deuteronomic tradition, the conditions were only met with the creation of David's empire (cf. Josh 23.1–5; 2 Sam 7.1–16; 1 Kings 5.3–5; 8.56). **12.11** *As a dwelling for his name,* better "to establish his name"; see note on 12.5. **12.12** *Levites.* See notes on 10.8–9; 18.1–8. **12.13–19** Two key functional distinctions are made here, one between extant cultic "places" (cf. Ex 20.24; 1 Sam 7.16; Josh 22.10–34), which are not or no longer to be used for sacrificial worship, and the chosen *place,* and the other between animals sacrificed at the altar and animals slaughtered for food. **12.15** *Whenever you desire,* as your appetite dictates (cf. 18.6; Prov 23.2) and the Lord's *blessing* permits (cf. 7.13). *The unclean and the clean may eat of it.* Since domestic slaughter of livestock is no different from the killing of game (*gazelle or deer*) for edible meat, rules of purity that pertain to the consumption of sacrificial offerings and other sacral dues are not applicable (cf. also 12.20–22; 15.22; Lev 7.19–21; 17.3–9). **12.16** *Blood* is the essence of animal "life" and must not be consumed (cf. 12.23; 15.23; Gen 9.4–5; Lev 17.10–14; 19.26; 1 Sam 14.31–35). **12.20–28** A summary paragraph emphasizes orthopraxy and its motives: though nonsacrificial slaughter is permitted as a geographical necessity (*When the LORD . . . enlarges your territory;* cf. 14.24; 19.8–9; Ex 34.24), sacrificial slaughter remains preferable whenever the altar of the single sanctuary is near enough for use (vv. 20–22, 27; cf. Lev 17.3–9). **12.23** The restriction on eating *blood* must never be relaxed (vv. 23–25; cf. 12.16; Lev 17.10–14); requisite offerings and sacral dues must be

25 Do not eat it, so that all may go well with you and your children after you, because you do what is right in the sight of the LORD. 26 But the sacred donations that are due from you, and your votive gifts, you shall bring to the place that the LORD will choose. 27 You shall present your burnt offerings, both the meat and the blood, on the altar of the LORD your God; the blood of your other sacrifices shall be poured out beside*a* the altar of the LORD your God, but the meat you may eat.

28 Be careful to obey all these words that I command you today,*b* so that it may go well with you and with your children after you forever, because you will be doing what is good and right in the sight of the LORD your God.

Warning against Idolatry

29 When the LORD your God has cut off before you the nations whom you are about to enter to dispossess them, when you have dispossessed them and live in their land, 30 take care that you are not snared into imitating them, after they have been destroyed before you: do not inquire concerning their gods, saying, "How did these nations worship their gods? I also want to do the same." 31 You must not do the same for the LORD your God, because every abhorrent thing that the LORD hates they have done for their gods. They would even burn their sons and their daughters in the fire to their gods. 32*c* You must diligently observe everything that I command you; do not add to it or take anything from it.

13 *d* If prophets or those who divine by dreams appear among you and promise you omens or portents, 2 and the omens or the portents declared by them take place, and they say, "Let us follow other gods" (whom you have not known) "and let us serve them," 3 you must not heed the words of those prophets or those who divine by dreams; for the LORD your God is testing you, to know whether you indeed love the LORD your God with all your heart and soul. 4 The LORD your God you shall follow, him alone you shall fear, his commandments you shall keep, his voice you shall obey, him you shall serve, and to him you shall hold fast. 5 But those prophets or those who divine by dreams shall be put to death for having spoken treason against the LORD your God—who brought you out of the land of Egypt and redeemed you from the house of slavery—to turn you from the way in which the LORD your God commanded you to walk. So you shall purge the evil from your midst.

6 If anyone secretly entices you—even if it is your brother, your father's son or*e* your mother's son, or your own son or daughter, or the wife you embrace, or your most intimate friend—saying, "Let us go worship other gods," whom neither you nor your ancestors have known, 7 any of the gods of the peoples that are around you, whether near you or far

a Or *on*   *b* Gk Sam Syr: MT lacks *today*   *c* Ch 13.1 in Heb
d Ch 13.2 in Heb   *e* Sam Gk Compare Tg: MT lacks *your father's son or*

presented regularly at the sanctuary (vv. 26–27; cf. 14.22–27; 15.19–20; 16.16–17; 26.1–15). **12.28** A concluding exhortation composed of familiar phrases (e.g., 4.40; 5.29; 6.3, 17–18; 12.25).
　12.29–17.13 This division treats corporate obligations and institutional structures designed to maintain Israel's national identity as the covenant people of God. **12.29–32** Specific provisions are introduced by another warning against any compromise of Israel's distinctiveness as defined by the Mosaic legislation (cf. 4.1–2; 5.32–6.3; 11.31–12.1). **12.30** *Snared,* here through attraction to aboriginal religious culture rather than by political or nuptial alliance with the condemned nations (cf. 7.1–5, 25; Ex 23.33; 34.12; Judg 2.3). **12.31** *Abhorrent.* See note on 7.25–26. Immolation of children by *fire* is particularly associated with the cult of Molech, practiced during the monarchical era in the Hinnom Valley, southwest of Jerusalem (Lev 18.21; 20.2–5; 2 Kings 23.10; Jer 7.31; 19.5; cf. also 18.10; 2 Kings 3.27; 16.3; 21.6). **12.32** *Everything,* neither less nor more, because worship of the Lord augmented with pagan practices be-

comes paganism (cf. 2 Kings 17.7–41).
　13.1–18 Three cases are summarized to prescribe severe retribution against instigators of sedition. **13.1–5** Mantic incitement to apostasy is a criminal offense, never credible even when supported by accurate prognostication. **13.1–3** *Divine by dreams.* See, e.g., Gen 37.5–10; Num 12.6; Judg 7.13–14; Jer 23.25; 27.9; Joel 2.28. *Omens or portents,* any forecasts or signs offered to authenticate claims of divine empowerment (see 34.11; Ex 4.1–9, 21; 7.9; Judg 6.17–21, 36–40). *Testing.* See 8.2, 16. **13.4** An emphatic restatement of allegiance to the Lord alone (cf. 6.13; 10.20; 11.22). **13.5** *Spoken treason* also describes prophetic duplicity in Jer 28.16; 29.32. *So . . . midst.* The formula emphasizes communal responsibility to eradicate perpetrators of virulent evil from Israel's midst (also 17.7, 12; 19.19; 21.21; 22.21, 22, 24; 24.7). **13.6–11** Clandestine enticement to apostasy must be confronted with equal resolve and harsh punishment. **13.6–8** Loyalty to Israel's divine sovereign takes precedence over even the closest human bonds of kinship, marriage, and collegiality. **13.6** *Intimate friend,* one as beloved as one's

away from you, from one end of the earth to the other, [8]you must not yield to or heed any such persons. Show them no pity or compassion and do not shield them. [9]But you shall surely kill them; your own hand shall be first against them to execute them, and afterwards the hand of all the people. [10]Stone them to death for trying to turn you away from the LORD your God, who brought you out of the land of Egypt, out of the house of slavery. [11]Then all Israel shall hear and be afraid, and never again do any such wickedness.

12 If you hear it said about one of the towns that the LORD your God is giving you to live in, [13]that scoundrels from among you have gone out and led the inhabitants of the town astray, saying, "Let us go and worship other gods," whom you have not known, [14]then you shall inquire and make a thorough investigation. If the charge is established that such an abhorrent thing has been done among you, [15]you shall put the inhabitants of that town to the sword, utterly destroying it and everything in it—even putting its livestock to the sword. [16]All of its spoil you shall gather into its public square; then burn the town and all its spoil with fire, as a whole burnt offering to the LORD your God. It shall remain a perpetual ruin, never to be rebuilt. [17]Do not let anything devoted to destruction stick to your hand, so that the LORD may turn from his fierce anger

and show you compassion, and in his compassion multiply you, as he swore to your ancestors, [18]if you obey the voice of the LORD your God by keeping all his commandments that I am commanding you today, doing what is right in the sight of the LORD your God.

Pagan Practices Forbidden

14 You are children of the LORD your God. You must not lacerate yourselves or shave your forelocks for the dead. [2]For you are a people holy to the LORD your God; it is you the LORD has chosen out of all the peoples on earth to be his people, his treasured possession.

Clean and Unclean Foods

3 You shall not eat any abhorrent thing. [4]These are the animals you may eat: the ox, the sheep, the goat, [5]the deer, the gazelle, the roebuck, the wild goat, the ibex, the antelope, and the mountain-sheep. [6]Any animal that divides the hoof and has the hoof cleft in two, and chews the cud, among the animals, you may eat. [7]Yet of those that chew the cud or have the hoof cleft you shall not eat these: the camel, the hare, and the rock badger, because they chew the cud but do not divide the hoof; they are unclean for you. [8]And the pig, because it divides the hoof but does not chew the cud, is unclean for you. You shall not eat their meat, and you shall not touch their carcasses.

---

own self (cf. 1 Sam 18.3). **13.8** *No pity.* Cf. 7.16; 19.13, 21; 25.12. **13.9–10** To *kill* offenders by stoning on presumption of guilt legitimates communal lynching (cf. 1 Sam 30.6; 1 Kings 12.18). But the Septuagint may preserve the preferable reading, that an accuser must first "decry" or "publicly charge" a culprit, thereby initiating judicial proceedings that may result in capital punishment carried out by accuser and communal court (cf. 17.4–7; 21.18–21; 22.20–24; Josh 7.10–26; 1 Kings 21.8–14). **13.11** Publicized execution in such circumstances is meant as a deterrent (cf. 17.12–13; 21.21). **13.12–18** This case outlines judicial procedure and martial retribution in the event that an entire town in Israel becomes contaminated by apostasy. **13.13** *Scoundrels,* lit. "sons without worth," "outlaws" who defy legitimate authority (cf. Judg 19.22; 20.13; 1 Sam 2.12). **13.14** *Inquire* could connote oracular consultation (cf. Judg 20.18, 23; Josh 7.13–21) but the clear purport of this Deuteronomic usage is judicial initiative to gather empirical evidence (see 17.4, 9; 19.18; cf. Josh 22.10–34). **13.15–17** The apostate town becomes anathema, like the former nations whose practices it assimilated (12.29–30); thus a comprehensive ban must be implemented against it, lest Israel as a whole incur the wrath of God (20.16–18; cf. 7.25–26).

13.16 *Whole burnt offering,* a sacrificial conflagration (33.10; Lev 6.22–23; 1 Sam 7.9; cf. Isa 34.6–7). *Perpetual ruin,* like Ai (Josh 8.28; cf. Jer 49.2).

14.1–21 Select rules pertaining to Israel's comportment as the Lord's holy people. **14.1** *Children of the LORD* is language elsewhere attested especially in prophetic contexts treating Israel's filial waywardness (32.5–6, 19–20; Ps 103.13; Isa 1.2, 4; 30.1; Jer 3.14, 19, 22; cf. Jer 31.9, 20; Hos 1.10; 11.1–4). *Lacerate, shave . . . forelocks.* Self-laceration and tonsure are perhaps prohibited because they were associated with pagan rites (cf. Lev 19.27–28; 21.5; 1 Kings 18.28; Jer 16.6–7; 41.4–5; 47.5; Am 8.10). **14.2** A restatement of covenantal integrity or "holiness" based on Ex 19.5–6 (cf. 7.6) introduces a series of dietary rules. **14.3** *Abhorrent* in the general prohibition makes foods excluded from Israel's diet a matter of the Lord's discretion (see note on 7.25–26; cf. Ex 8.26). **14.4–20** The basic categories of land animals (vv. 4–8), fish (vv. 9–10), and flying creatures (vv. 11–20) reflect the familiar taxonomy of the created order (Gen 1.20–25; 9.2–3). A common antecedent tradition as well as some mutual influence at a late stage of textual formation best account for the detailed similarities and differences between this classification and its counterpart in

9 Of all that live in water you may eat these: whatever has fins and scales you may eat. 10And whatever does not have fins and scales you shall not eat; it is unclean for you.

11 You may eat any clean birds. 12But these are the ones that you shall not eat: the eagle, the vulture, the osprey, 13the buzzard, the kite of any kind; 14every raven of any kind; 15the ostrich, the nighthawk, the sea gull, the hawk of any kind; 16the little owl and the great owl, the water hen 17and the desert owl,*a* the carrion vulture and the cormorant, 18the stork, the heron of any kind; the hoopoe and the bat.*b* 19And all winged insects are unclean for you; they shall not be eaten. 20You may eat any clean winged creature.

21 You shall not eat anything that dies of itself; you may give it to aliens residing in your towns for them to eat, or you may sell it to a foreigner. For you are a people holy to the LORD your God.

You shall not boil a kid in its mother's milk.

Regulations concerning Tithes

22 Set apart a tithe of all the yield of your seed that is brought in yearly from the field. 23In the presence of the LORD your God, in the place that he will choose as a dwelling for his name, you shall eat the tithe of your grain, your wine, and your oil, as well as the firstlings of your herd and flock, so that you may learn to fear the LORD your God always. 24But if, when the LORD your God has blessed you, the distance is so great that you are unable to transport it, because the place where the LORD your God will choose to set his name is too far away from you, 25then you may turn it into money. With the money secure in hand, go to the place that the LORD your God will choose; 26spend the money for whatever you wish— oxen, sheep, wine, strong drink, or whatever you desire. And you shall eat there in the presence of the LORD your God, you and your household rejoicing together. 27As for the Levites resident in your towns, do not neglect them, because they have no allotment or inheritance with you.

28 Every third year you shall bring out the full tithe of your produce for that year, and store it within your towns; 29the Levites, because they have no allotment or inheritance with you, as well as the resident aliens, the orphans, and the widows in your towns, may come and eat their fill so that the LORD your God may bless you in all the work that you undertake.

Laws concerning the Sabbatical Year

15 Every seventh year you shall grant a remission of debts. 2And this is the manner of the remission: every creditor shall remit the claim that is held against a neighbor, not exacting it of a neighbor who is a member of the

---

a Or *pelican*   *b* Identification of several of the birds in verses 12-18 is uncertain

---

Lev 11.2–23. Some of the species identifications, especially of the birds, remain uncertain. **14.21** *Anything that dies of itself,* i.e., carrion or the carcass of an otherwise edible animal from which the blood was not drained (cf. 12.16, 22–27; with Ex 22.31; Lev 17.15; 22.8; Ezek 44.31). The issue is ritual purity, not health per se; hence the affected meat could be eaten by those who did not belong to the sacral community (resident *aliens* or a *foreigner*). The old prohibition against cooking *a kid in its mother's milk* (Ex 23.19; 34.26) concludes the series of rules. The original significance of this prohibition is a matter of some dispute. Some see it as proscribing Canaanite religious practices, others as being directed against the unnatural and callous treatment of animals. The later Jewish dietary practice of not mixing meat and dairy products is based on this law. **14.22–29** The *tithe* probably originated as a 10 percent tax on agricultural produce (*all the yield of your seed*), usually paid in kind to the land's sovereign or to designated government officials (cf. Gen 14.20; 28.22; Lev 27.30–33; Num 18.21–32; 1 Sam 8.15, 17; Am 4.4). Here the ancient practice is roughly adapted to the circumstances of unification of worship. **14.23** *As a dwelling for his name.* See notes on 12.5; 12.11. The three annual pilgrimage festivals (see 16.16–17) are presumably meant as primary occasions for presentation of both agricultural tithes and *firstlings* of livestock (see also 12.17; 15.19–23). **14.24–27** Emphasis again falls on promoting inclusive celebrations (cf. note on 12.7); important social, economic, and administrative implications are ignored (cf. 2 Chr 31.2–19; Neh 12.44; Mk 11.15; Jn 2.13–14). **14.28–29** Provision, however, is added for local storage and distribution of tithes from produce harvested *every third year,* to sustain dispersed levitical clans as well as to provide for others in need of charity (cf. 26.12–15; Ex 22.21–24).

15.1–18 This remarkable revision of older laws (Ex 21.2–11; 22.25; 23.10–11) seeks to strengthen procedures for redressing economic imbalances within Israelite society resulting from usury and debt slavery. (For such abusive practices, see Neh 5.1–13; Job 24.9; Ezek 18.16–18; Am 2.6–8.) **15.1–3** Sabbatical *remission of debts* (Hebrew *shemitta,* only in 15.1, 2, 9; 31.10) regularizes proclamation on the Lord's behalf

community, because the LORD's remission has been proclaimed. 3Of a foreigner you may exact it, but you must remit your claim on whatever any member of your community owes you. 4There will, however, be no one in need among you, because the LORD is sure to bless you in the land that the LORD your God is giving you as a possession to occupy, 5if only you will obey the LORD your God by diligently observing this entire commandment that I command you today. 6When the LORD your God has blessed you, as he promised you, you will lend to many nations, but you will not borrow; you will rule over many nations, but they will not rule over you.

7 If there is among you anyone in need, a member of your community in any of your towns within the land that the LORD your God is giving you, do not be hard-hearted or tight-fisted toward your needy neighbor. 8You should rather open your hand, willingly lending enough to meet the need, whatever it may be. 9Be careful that you do not entertain a mean thought, thinking, "The seventh year, the year of remission, is near," and therefore view your needy neighbor with hostility and give nothing; your neighbor might cry to the LORD against you, and you would incur guilt. 10Give liberally and be ungrudging when you do so, for on this account the LORD your God will bless you in all your work and in all that you undertake. 11Since there will never cease to be some in need on the earth, I therefore command you, "Open your hand to the poor and needy neighbor in your land."

12 If a member of your community, whether a Hebrew man or a Hebrew woman, is sold[a] to you and works for you six years, in the seventh year you shall set that person free. 13And when you send a male slave[b] out from you a free person, you shall not send him out empty-handed. 14Provide liberally out of your flock, your threshing floor, and your wine press, thus giving to him some of the bounty with which the LORD your God has blessed you. 15Remember that you were a slave in the land of Egypt, and the LORD your God redeemed you; for this reason I lay this command upon you today. 16But if he says to you, "I will not go out from you," because he loves you and your household, since he is well off with you, 17then you shall take an awl and thrust it through his earlobe into the door, and he shall be your slave[c] forever.

You shall do the same with regard to your female slave.[d]

18 Do not consider it a hardship when you send them out from you free persons, because for six years they have given you services worth the wages of hired laborers; and the LORD your God will bless you in all that you do.

The Firstborn of Livestock

19 Every firstling male born of your herd and flock you shall consecrate to the LORD your God; you shall not do work with your firstling

---

a Or sells himself or herself   b Heb him   c Or bondman
d Or bondwoman

---

of "liberty" for Israel's oppressed from burdens of indebtedness (cf. 10.17–18; Lev 25; Isa 61.1–2; Jer 34.8–22). **15.2** *Claim*, the debt itself, but also the surety pledged for a loan or taken as distraint after default (cf. 2 Kings 4.1; Prov 6.1–5; 17.18; 22.26–27). **15.3** Debts of a *foreigner* are unaffected (cf. Prov 20.16; 27.13). **15.4–6** Homiletical motivation: fidelity to the covenant will assure ample blessings for all citizens to share, making Israel preeminent among nations (cf. 7.12–14; 26.15; 28.1–14). **15.7–11** These exhortations anticipate that periodic cancellation of debts could seriously curtail lending, thus aggravating the plight of those in need (cf. *Mishnah Shebi'it* 10). Enforcement must be left to the Lord's devices of reward and punishment (cf. 24.19; Ps 37.21–22; Prov 19.17). **15.9** *Cry.* An appeal to the divine judge for redress (24.15; cf. Ex 2.23–24; 22.23–24, 27). **15.12–18** In context, this reworking of older laws of manumission (Ex 21.2–11) apparently favors a collective release of both male and female bond slaves in the fixed sabbatical year of remission (cf. 31.10–13; Jer 34.8–14). **15.12** *Hebrew,*

which seems to mean client status in Ex 21.2, here simply denotes a fellow Israelite; *member of your community,* lit. "your brother," rendered inclusively as sense requires. *Sold,* e.g., as a debtor or distrainee, or indentured by judicial authority to make restitution for a theft (cf. Ex 22.3). **15.13–15** Generous provision for those released is urged as appropriate imitation of the Lord's liberality in redeeming Israel from Egyptian slavery (cf. 5.14–15; 10.17–22; 16.12; 24.18, 22; 26.6–10). *Empty-handed.* Cf. 16.16; also Ex 3.21–22. **15.16–18** A noteworthy revision of Ex 21.2–11 includes the general presumption against permanent enslavement of Israelites as well as the equal treatment now accorded a bondwoman.

15.19–23 Provision is made for disposal of firstlings in accord with the requirements of the single sanctuary. (For antecedent and alternate rulings, see Ex 13.2, 11–16; 22.29–30; 34.19–20; Lev 22.26–27; 27.26–27; Num 18.15–18.) **15.19–20** Though male *firstlings* of livestock must not be used productively, a flexible schedule (*year by year*) is allowed for sacrificial presen-

ox nor shear the firstling of your flock. ²⁰You shall eat it, you together with your household, in the presence of the LORD your God year by year at the place that the LORD will choose. ²¹But if it has any defect—any serious defect, such as lameness or blindness—you shall not sacrifice it to the LORD your God; ²²within your towns you may eat it, the unclean and the clean alike, as you would a gazelle or deer. ²³Its blood, however, you must not eat; you shall pour it out on the ground like water.

The Passover Reviewed

16 Observe the month^a of Abib by keeping the passover to the LORD your God, for in the month of Abib the LORD your God brought you out of Egypt by night. ²You shall offer the passover sacrifice to the LORD your God, from the flock and the herd, at the place that the LORD will choose as a dwelling for his name. ³You must not eat with it anything leavened. For seven days you shall eat unleavened bread with it—the bread of affliction—because you came out of the land of Egypt in great haste, so that all the days of your life you may remember the day of your departure from the land of Egypt. ⁴No leaven shall be seen with you in all your territory for seven days; and none of the meat of what you slaughter on the evening of the first day shall remain until morning. ⁵You are not permitted to offer the passover sacrifice within any of your towns that the LORD your God is giving you. ⁶But at the place that the LORD your God will choose as a dwelling for his name, only there shall you offer the passover sacrifice, in

the evening at sunset, the time of day when you departed from Egypt. ⁷You shall cook it and eat it at the place that the LORD your God will choose; the next morning you may go back to your tents. ⁸For six days you shall continue to eat unleavened bread, and on the seventh day there shall be a solemn assembly for the LORD your God, when you shall do no work.

The Festival of Weeks Reviewed

9 You shall count seven weeks; begin to count the seven weeks from the time the sickle is first put to the standing grain. ¹⁰Then you shall keep the festival of weeks to the LORD your God, contributing a freewill offering in proportion to the blessing that you have received from the LORD your God. ¹¹Rejoice before the LORD your God—you and your sons and your daughters, your male and female slaves, the Levites resident in your towns, as well as the strangers, the orphans, and the widows who are among you—at the place that the LORD your God will choose as a dwelling for his name. ¹²Remember that you were a slave in Egypt, and diligently observe these statutes.

The Festival of Booths Reviewed

13 You shall keep the festival of booths^b for seven days, when you have gathered in the produce from your threshing floor and your wine press. ¹⁴Rejoice during your festival, you and your sons and your daughters, your male and female slaves, as well as the Levites, the

---

a Or new moon b Or tabernacles; Heb succoth

---

tation (cf. 12.6–7, 17–18; 14.23; 16.16; Ex 22.30). **15.21–22** Rules of local slaughter (12.15–16, 22–24) apply to any firstling unacceptable for sacrifice because of *serious defect* (cf. 17.1; Lev 22.17–25; Mal 1.8).

   16.1–17 Deuteronomic restriction of Israel's ritual sacrifices and related ceremonies to a single sanctuary (12.5) culminates in this sketch of a revised liturgical calendar (see Ex 23.14–18; 34.18–24; cf. Lev 23.4–44; Num 28.11–29.39; Ezek 45.18–25). **16.1–8** Communal celebration of the Passover sacrifice (vv. 1–2, 4b–7) is closely correlated with the weeklong consumption of unleavened bread (vv. 3–4a, 8) to commemorate the exodus from Egypt (see Ex 12–13; 23.15; 34.18; cf. Josh 5.10–12; 2 Kings 23.21–23; 2 Chr 30; 35.1–19). **16.1** According to the oldest traditions, the nocturnal escape from Egypt occurred on the "new moon" (preferable to *month*) of *Abib*, the season in early spring when ears of barley began to ripen (cf. Ex 12.29–32, 41–42; 13.3–4; Num 29.6; 1 Sam 20.5, 18;

Isa 1.13; Am 8.5). **16.2** Presumably firstlings of livestock (*flock* and *herd*) were to provide the sacrificial meals during the full term of festivities (cf. Ex 12.5; 2 Chr 30.17–24; 35.7–13). **16.2, 6** *As a dwelling for his name.* See notes on 12.5; 12.11. **16.7** *Cook,* or "boil" (1 Sam 2.13, 15); cf. Ex 12.9; 2 Chr 35.13. **16.8** *Solemn assembly.* A sacral convocation concludes the festivities (cf. Ex 13.6; Lev 23.36; Num 29.35; Isa 1.13; Am 5.21). **16.9–12** *Weeks,* later known as Pentecost (e.g., Acts 2.1), is the harvest festival of early summer, when first fruits of grain were to be presented at the sanctuary (cf. Ex 23.16; 34.22; Lev 23.15–21; Num 28.26). **16.10** *Freewill offering,* apparently in addition to the mandatory tithe of agricultural produce (cf. 12.6, 17). **16.11** *As a dwelling for his name.* See notes on 12.5; 12.11. **16.13–15** *Booths* (cf. Lev 23.34, 42–43; Ezra 3.4; Neh 8.14) is the old autumn festival of "ingathering" at the end of the agricultural year (Ex 23.16; 34.22). It seems to have been the occasion for King Josiah's re-

strangers, the orphans, and the widows resident in your towns. ¹⁵Seven days you shall keep the festival to the LORD your God at the place that the LORD will choose; for the LORD your God will bless you in all your produce and in all your undertakings, and you shall surely celebrate.

16 Three times a year all your males shall appear before the LORD your God at the place that he will choose: at the festival of unleavened bread, at the festival of weeks, and at the festival of booths.ᵃ They shall not appear before the LORD empty-handed; ¹⁷all shall give as they are able, according to the blessing of the LORD your God that he has given you.

Municipal Judges and Officers

18 You shall appoint judges and officials throughout your tribes, in all your towns that the LORD your God is giving you, and they shall render just decisions for the people. ¹⁹You must not distort justice; you must not show partiality; and you must not accept bribes, for a bribe blinds the eyes of the wise and subverts the cause of those who are in the right. ²⁰Justice, and only justice, you shall pursue, so that you may live and occupy the land that the LORD your God is giving you.

Forbidden Forms of Worship

21 You shall not plant any tree as a sacred poleᵇ beside the altar that you make for the LORD your God; ²²nor shall you set up a stone pillar—things that the LORD your God hates.

17 You must not sacrifice to the LORD your God an ox or a sheep that has a defect, anything seriously wrong; for that is abhorrent to the LORD your God.

2 If there is found among you, in one of your towns that the LORD your God is giving you, a man or woman who does what is evil in the sight of the LORD your God, and transgresses his covenant ³by going to serve other gods and worshiping them—whether the sun or the moon or any of the host of heaven, which I have forbidden— ⁴and if it is reported to you or you hear of it, and you make a thorough inquiry, and the charge is proved true that such an abhorrent thing has occurred in Israel, ⁵then you shall bring out to your gates that man or that woman who has committed this crime and you shall stone the man or woman to death. ⁶On the evidence of two or three witnesses the death sentence shall be executed; a person must not be put to death on the evidence of only one witness. ⁷The hands of the witnesses shall be the first raised against the person to execute the death penalty, and afterward the hands of all the people. So you shall purge the evil from your midst.

Legal Decisions by Priests and Judges

8 If a judicial decision is too difficult for you to make between one kind of bloodshed and another, one kind of legal right and another, or one kind of assault and another—any such matters of dispute in your towns—then you

---

a Or *tabernacles*; Heb *succoth*   *b* Heb *Asherah*

newal of the covenant (cf. 31.10–13; 2 Kings 23.1–3) as well as Solomon's dedication of the temple two centuries earlier (1 Kings 8.2, 62–66). **16.16–17** In this summary, the spring pilgrimage is designated only as *unleavened bread*; specification of *males* as participants reflects older practice (Ex 23.17; 34.23) rather than the Deuteronomic emphasis on inclusivity (vv. 11, 14; see note on 12.7).

16.18–17.13 The burden of theocratic governance within Israel is to be born by a two-tiered judiciary comprised of city courts in tribal jurisdictions and a consultative council associated with the single sanctuary. **16.18–20** The whole community (singular *you*) authorizes judicial administration by a corps of professional *judges and officials,* probably consisting in large part of dispersed levitical personnel (cf. 1.13–17; 19.17; 21.5; Ex 32.26–29; Josh 21.1–42; 1 Chr 23.2–6; 26.29; 2 Chr 17.7–9; 19.5–11). **16.19** On the injunctions against *partiality* and taking *bribes,* see 1.16–17; 10.17–18 (cf. Ex 23.2–3, 6–8; Lev 19.15; Prov 17.23;

18.5; Isa 1.23; Mic 7.3). **16.21–17.1** In context, these prohibitions suggest that maintenance of ritual purity is to be a primary judicial concern. For the themes, see 7.5; 15.21 (cf. 2 Kings 23.6, 15). **17.2–7** Due process in adjudicating capital offenses is illustrated by reviewing prosecution of a case of apostasy (cf. 13.1–11). **17.2–3** *Transgresses his covenant.* Cf. Josh 7.11, 15; 23.16; Judg 2.20; 2 Kings 18.12; Jer 34.18; Hos 6.7; 8.1. *Sun... moon... host of heaven.* Cf. 4.19; 2 Kings 17.16; 21.3; 23.5; Jer 8.2; Ezek 8.16. *I have forbidden.* See note on 7.4. **17.4–5** See 13.10. **17.6** *Witnesses.* See 19.15–21; cf. Num 35.30. **17.7** See notes on 13.5; 13.9–10. **17.8–13** Moses' authority to arbitrate in cases *too difficult* for resolution by local courts (cf. 1.17; Ex 18.22, 26) is institutionalized in a judicial council consisting mainly of levitical priests. (This tribunal resembles the one attributed to King Jehoshaphat in 2 Chr 19.8–11.) **17.8** *One kind of bloodshed and another,* e.g., between first-degree murder and accidental homicide (cf. 19.4–13). See note on 5.17. **17.9–12** Levitical compe-

shall immediately go up to the place that the LORD your God will choose, 9where you shall consult with the levitical priests and the judge who is in office in those days; they shall announce to you the decision in the case. 10Carry out exactly the decision that they announce to you from the place that the LORD will choose, diligently observing everything they instruct you. 11You must carry out fully the law that they interpret for you or the ruling that they announce to you; do not turn aside from the decision that they announce to you, either to the right or to the left. 12As for anyone who presumes to disobey the priest appointed to minister there to the LORD your God, or the judge, that person shall die. So you shall purge the evil from Israel. 13All the people will hear and be afraid, and will not act presumptuously again.

Limitations of Royal Authority

14 When you have come into the land that the LORD your God is giving you, and have taken possession of it and settled in it, and you say, "I will set a king over me, like all the nations that are around me," 15you may indeed set over you a king whom the LORD your God will choose. One of your own community you may set as king over you; you are not permitted to put a foreigner over you, who is not of your own community. 16Even so, he must not acquire many horses for himself, or return the people to Egypt in order to acquire more horses, since the LORD has said to you, "You must never return that way again." 17And he must not acquire many wives for himself, or else his heart will turn away; also silver and gold he must not acquire in great quantity for himself. 18When he has taken the throne of his kingdom, he shall have a copy of this law written for him in the presence of the levitical priests. 19It shall remain with him and he shall read in it all the days of his life, so that he may learn to fear the LORD his God, diligently observing all the words of this law and these statutes, 20neither exalting himself above other members of the community nor turning aside from the commandment, either to the right or to the left, so that he and his descendants may reign long over his kingdom in Israel.

Privileges of Priests and Levites

18 The levitical priests, the whole tribe of Levi, shall have no allotment or inheritance within Israel. They may eat the sacrifices that are the LORD's portion*a* 2but they shall have no inheritance among the other members of the community; the LORD is their inheritance, as he promised them.

3 This shall be the priests' due from the people, from those offering a sacrifice, whether an ox or a sheep: they shall give to the priest the shoulder, the two jowls, and the stomach. 4The first fruits of your grain, your wine, and your oil, as well as the first of the fleece of your sheep, you shall give him. 5For

---

a Meaning of Heb uncertain

---

tence in judicial affairs seems here to be associated with transmission and authoritative application of Mosaic law (*the law that they interpret*); cf. 17.18; 31.9; 33.10; 2 Kings 17.27–28; Ezra 7.25–26. *Judge,* perhaps the king or civil governor (cf. 2 Sam 14.3–20; 1 Kings 3.9; Prov 16.10). **17.13** See 13.11. **17.14–18.22** Offices held by virtue of divine election rather than communal empowerment are treated in this central section of the polity.

    17.14–20 Although monarchy is a permissible instrument of theocratic governance, major restrictions are placed on the exercise of royal authority (cf. 1 Sam 10.25). **17.14** *When . . . and settled in it,* a formulaic introduction; cf. 26.1. *Like all the nations.* Cf. 1 Sam 8.5, 20. **17.15** On divine designation of kings, usually through prophetic agency, see, e.g., 1 Sam 10.24; 16.1–13; 1 Kings 19.15–16; 2 Kings 9.1–13 (cf. Hos 8.4). *One of your own community,* lit. "from among your brothers," i.e., a fellow Israelite (cf. 18.15, 18). **17.16–17** These injunctions against abuse of royal power seem to have Solomon's excesses in specific view (1 Kings 10.6–11.8; cf. 1 Sam 8.10–18; Isa 2.7).

17.18 *A copy of this law* (see 4.44–45). The interpretive rendering in the Septuagint, Greek *to deuteronomion touto* ("this second law–giving"; cf. Josh 8.32 [LXX 9.5]), underlies the familiar name "Deuteronomy." **17.19–20** The king's only stated task is to model obedience to the covenantal *torah* incumbent on Israel as a whole; so too dynastic succession and national tenure in the land are parallel rewards for fidelity (cf. 5.32–6.2; 2 Sam 7.10–16; 1 Kings 2.4; Ps 132.11–18).

    18.1–8 Other texts sketch the broader scope of work performed by the levitical bureaucracy (cf. 10.8–9; 17.8–12, 18; 20.2–9; 21.5; 31.9; 33.8–11). Here the concern is to establish the perquisites of Levites who serve at the single sanctuary. **18.1–2** The sacerdotal profession, supported chiefly by sacral prebends, is a prerogative distinguishing the clans or guilds that comprise *the whole tribe of Levi* from Israelite tribes granted territorial dominion (cf. Josh 13.14, 33; 18.7; 21.1–42; 2 Chr 31.2–19). **18.3** *The priests' due.* Cf. Lev 7.28–36; Num 18.8–20. **18.4** *First fruits,* "choice" portions representing the tithes of agricultural produce (cf. 14.22–29; 26.1–15; Num 18.21–32; Neh 13.10–

the LORD your God has chosen Levi[a] out of all your tribes, to stand and minister in the name of the LORD, him and his sons for all time.

6 If a Levite leaves any of your towns, from wherever he has been residing in Israel, and comes to the place that the LORD will choose (and he may come whenever he wishes), 7then he may minister in the name of the LORD his God, like all his fellow-Levites who stand to minister there before the LORD. 8They shall have equal portions to eat, even though they have income from the sale of family possessions.[b]

Child-Sacrifice, Divination, and Magic Prohibited

9 When you come into the land that the LORD your God is giving you, you must not learn to imitate the abhorrent practices of those nations. 10No one shall be found among you who makes a son or daughter pass through fire, or who practices divination, or is a soothsayer, or an augur, or a sorcerer, 11or one who casts spells, or who consults ghosts or spirits, or who seeks oracles from the dead. 12For whoever does these things is abhorrent to the LORD; it is because of such abhorrent practices that the LORD your God is driving them out before you. 13You must remain completely loyal to the LORD your God. 14Although these nations that you are about to dispossess do give heed to soothsayers and diviners, as for you, the LORD your God does not permit you to do so.

A New Prophet Like Moses

15 The LORD your God will raise up for you a prophet[c] like me from among your own people; you shall heed such a prophet.[d] 16This is what you requested of the LORD your God at Horeb on the day of the assembly when you said: "If I hear the voice of the LORD my God any more, or ever again see this great fire, I will die." 17Then the LORD replied to me: "They are right in what they have said. 18I will raise up for them a prophet[c] like you from among their own people; I will put my words in the mouth of the prophet,[e] who shall speak to them everything that I command. 19Anyone who does not heed the words that the prophet[f] shall speak in my name, I myself will hold accountable. 20But any prophet who speaks in the name of other gods, or who presumes to speak in my name a word that I have not commanded the prophet to speak—that prophet shall die." 21You may say to yourself, "How can we recognize a word that the LORD has not spoken?" 22If a prophet speaks in the name of the LORD but the thing does not take place or prove true, it is a word that the LORD has not spoken. The prophet has spoken it presumptuously; do not be frightened by it.

Laws concerning the Cities of Refuge

19 When the LORD your God has cut off the nations whose land the LORD your

---

a Heb *him* b Meaning of Heb uncertain c Or *prophets*
d Or *such prophets* e Or *mouths of the prophets* f Heb *he*

---

13). **18.5** See 10.8; cf. Ex 32.25–29; 1 Sam 2.27–28; Jer 33.17–22; Mal 2.2–7. **18.6–7** *Residing.* Lacking their own tribal territory, Levites "sojourn" among the land-holding tribes (cf. Judg 17.7; 19.1). Eligible Levites retain the right to officiate at the single sanctuary (cf. 2 Kings 23.8–9; 2 Chr 11.13–15). **18.8** *Income,* apparently, e.g., from the sale or lease of family fields and homes (cf. Lev 25.32–34; Num 35.1–8; Jer 32.6–15).

18.9–22 Although prophecy, in contrast to pagan divinatory practices, is a legitimate medium of revelation, individual prophetic claims to speak on the Lord's behalf must be rigorously assessed. **18.9–12** Polemic against *abhorrent practices of those nations* (see 12.29–31; 20.17–18; also notes on 7.1; 7.25–26) frames proscription of various types of occultism (cf. Ex 22.18; Lev 19.31; 20.6, 27; 1 Sam 28.3–19; Isa 8.19–20; Ezek 21.21). **18.10** Child sacrifice (*pass through fire;* see note on 12.31) is also associated with mantic practices in Deuteronomic indictments of both the Northern Kingdom, Israel, and King Manasseh of

Judah (2 Kings 17.17; 21.6), while Josiah is credited with implementing the prohibitions (2 Kings 23.10, 24). **18.13** *Completely loyal* connotes personal "integrity" or "blamelessness" (e.g., Gen 6.9; 17.1; Job 12.4; Ps 18.23; Prov 11.5). **18.15–18** Prophecy, manifest as an authoritative role rather than in a fixed office, is legitimated on the model of Moses' mediation between God and Israel at Horeb (5.23–33; Ex 20.18–21; cf. 2 Kings 17.13; Jer 7.25–26). **18.15** *Like me,* i.e., a fellow Israelite (cf. 17.15); 34.10 is different. **18.18** *I will put . . . prophet.* Cf. Ex 4.12–16; Jer 1.9; 15.19; Ezek 3.1–4. **18.19** Cf. Jer 11.21–23; Am 7.10–17. **18.20** Unauthorized prophesying, whether in *the name of other gods* or the Lord, is a capital offense; see 13.1–5 (cf. Jer 14.13–16; 23.9–40; 28.12–17; Ezek 13). **18.21–22** On the criterion's utility, see 1 Kings 22.5–28; Jer 18.5–12; 28; Ezek 12.21–28; 33.30–33; Jon 3.10–4.5; Hab 2.1–3.

19.1–25.19 The diverse articles in this division of the polity exemplify principles of social justice and

God is giving you, and you have dispossessed them and settled in their towns and in their houses, [2]you shall set apart three cities in the land that the LORD your God is giving you to possess. [3]You shall calculate the distances[a] and divide into three regions the land that the LORD your God gives you as a possession, so that any homicide can flee to one of them.

4 Now this is the case of a homicide who might flee there and live, that is, someone who has killed another person unintentionally when the two had not been at enmity before: [5]Suppose someone goes into the forest with another to cut wood, and when one of them swings the ax to cut down a tree, the head slips from the handle and strikes the other person who then dies; the killer may flee to one of these cities and live. [6]But if the distance is too great, the avenger of blood in hot anger might pursue and overtake and put the killer to death, although a death sentence was not deserved, since the two had not been at enmity before. [7]Therefore I command you: You shall set apart three cities.

8 If the LORD your God enlarges your territory, as he swore to your ancestors—and he will give you all the land that he promised your ancestors to give you, [9]provided you diligently observe this entire commandment that I command you today, by loving the LORD your God and walking always in his ways—then you shall add three more cities to these three, [10]so that the blood of an innocent person may not be shed in the land that the LORD your God is giving you as an inheritance, thereby bringing bloodguilt upon you.

11 But if someone at enmity with another lies in wait and attacks and takes the life of that person, and flees into one of these cities, [12]then the elders of the killer's city shall send to have the culprit taken from there and handed over to the avenger of blood to be put to death. [13]Show no pity; you shall purge the guilt of innocent blood from Israel, so that it may go well with you.

Property Boundaries

14 You must not move your neighbor's boundary marker, set up by former generations, on the property that will be allotted to you in the land that the LORD your God is giving you to possess.

Law concerning Witnesses

15 A single witness shall not suffice to convict a person of any crime or wrongdoing in connection with any offense that may be committed. Only on the evidence of two or three witnesses shall a charge be sustained. [16]If a malicious witness comes forward to accuse someone of wrongdoing, [17]then both parties to the dispute shall appear before the LORD, before the priests and the judges who are in office in those days, [18]and the judges shall make a thorough inquiry. If the witness is a false witness, having testified falsely against another, [19]then you shall do to the false witness just as

---

a Or *prepare roads to them*

---

practices meant to protect individual life and livelihood within the covenant community. **19.1–13** This adaptation of Ex 21.12–14 emphasizes communal responsibility to facilitate legitimate asylum in cases of accidental homicide without compromising either prosecution of those guilty of premeditated murder or, implicitly, the ban on local altars (cf. 4.41–43; Num 35.9–28; Josh 20). **19.1–3** A formulaic introduction (cf. 12.29 is followed by prescriptions for establishment of *three cities* that provide regionally accessible places of refuge. **19.4–7** Rationale for the institution is given in the form of an illustrative case. **19.4** *Unintentionally,* not premeditated (lit. "without knowledge"); cf. Job 35.16; 36.12; 38.2. **19.6** *Avenger of blood,* the agent designated (by the family of the deceased or a city court?) to inflict retaliatory punishment on the murderer (cf. 2 Sam 14.11). *In hot anger,* impetuously (lit. "because his heart is hot"; cf. Ps 39.3). **19.8–9** Provision for an additional three cities when *the LORD . . . enlarges your territory;* cf. 12.20; also 11.22–25. **19.10** *Bloodguilt,* the onus or pollution of illegitimate "bloodshed"; cf. 21.8–9; Ex 22.2; 1 Sam 25.26, 33;

2 Sam 21.1; Ps 51.14; Hos 4.2. **19.11–12** More detail is given in Josh 20.4–6. **19.12** On the jurisdiction of city *elders,* see 21.1–9, 19–20; 22.15–19; 25.7–9. **19.13** *No pity.* See 13.5, 8. **19.14** Concern for the integrity of cairns and the like delimiting familial plots of arable land is widely attested in biblical and other ancient sources (see 27.17; Job 24.2; Prov 22.28; Hos 5.10; cf. Instruction of Amenemope 7.11–19).

19.15–21 In view here is protection of individuals from pernicious accusation and perjured witness (cf. 5.20; Ex 20.16; 23.1). **19.15** The requirement of corroborative testimony to sustain a guilty verdict in capital cases (17.6; Num 35.30) is restated as a general rule of judicial evidence. **19.16** *Malicious witness,* one intent on doing injury or "violence" to another (cf. Gen 6.13; Job 19.7; Ps 35.11). *Wrongdoing* is the capital offense of incitement to "treason" in 13.5 (cf. Isa 59.13). **19.17** *Both parties,* accuser and accused. *Before the LORD* refers to divine presence at the (single) sanctuary (e.g., 12.18; 14.23), here represented by the judicial council (17.8–12; cf. 1.17). **19.18** *Thorough inquiry.* See 13.14; 17.4. **19.19–21** Just retribution as well as ef-

the false witness had meant to do to the other. So you shall purge the evil from your midst. 20The rest shall hear and be afraid, and a crime such as this shall never again be committed among you. 21Show no pity: life for life, eye for eye, tooth for tooth, hand for hand, foot for foot.

Rules of Warfare

20 When you go out to war against your enemies, and see horses and chariots, an army larger than your own, you shall not be afraid of them; for the LORD your God is with you, who brought you up from the land of Egypt. 2Before you engage in battle, the priest shall come forward and speak to the troops, 3and shall say to them: "Hear, O Israel! Today you are drawing near to do battle against your enemies. Do not lose heart, or be afraid, or panic, or be in dread of them; 4for it is the LORD your God who goes with you, to fight for you against your enemies, to give you victory." 5Then the officials shall address the troops, saying, "Has anyone built a new house but not dedicated it? He should go back to his house, or he might die in the battle and another dedicate it. 6Has anyone planted a vineyard but not yet enjoyed its fruit? He should go back to his house, or he might die in the battle and another be first to enjoy its fruit. 7Has anyone become engaged to a woman but not yet married her? He should go back to his house, or he might die in the battle and another marry her." 8The officials shall continue to address the troops, saying, "Is anyone

afraid or disheartened? He should go back to his house, or he might cause the heart of his comrades to melt like his own." 9When the officials have finished addressing the troops, then the commanders shall take charge of them.

10 When you draw near to a town to fight against it, offer it terms of peace. 11If it accepts your terms of peace and surrenders to you, then all the people in it shall serve you at forced labor. 12If it does not submit to you peacefully, but makes war against you, then you shall besiege it; 13and when the LORD your God gives it into your hand, you shall put all its males to the sword. 14You may, however, take as your booty the women, the children, livestock, and everything else in the town, all its spoil. You may enjoy the spoil of your enemies, which the LORD your God has given you. 15Thus you shall treat all the towns that are very far from you, which are not towns of the nations here. 16But as for the towns of these peoples that the LORD your God is giving you as an inheritance, you must not let anything that breathes remain alive. 17You shall annihilate them—the Hittites and the Amorites, the Canaanites and the Perizzites, the Hivites and the Jebusites—just as the LORD your God has commanded, 18so that they may not teach you to do all the abhorrent things that they do for their gods, and you thus sin against the LORD your God.

19 If you besiege a town for a long time, making war against it in order to take it, you must not destroy its trees by wielding an ax

---

fective deterrence (cf. 13.11) commend punishment corresponding to the harm that the culprit intended to do to the victim. The talion formula *life for life . . . foot for foot* (cf. Ex 21.23–25) is invoked to underscore the principle of reciprocity.

20.1–20 Protocols of holy war, sketched in this and subsequent units (21.10–14; 23.9–14; 24.5), are one of the features distinguishing the Deuteronomic polity from other bodies of biblical law. The martial program of the later Judean monarchy (cf. 2 Kings 18.7–19.35; 23.29) as well as the ideology of the conquest era (e.g., 7.1–2, 17–26; 9.1–3; 31.3–8) seems to be reflected in these texts. **20.1** Because the Lord is present as warrior with Israel to give victory (cf. 1.30; 3.22; Ex 14.14; 15.1–4; Judg 4.14), the militia should not be intimidated by a foe's superior numbers and weaponry. *Horses and chariots.* See Josh 11.4; 1 Kings 20.25; Isa 31.1. **20.2–9** The levy. **20.2–4** The only stated task of the *priest* is to deliver a vestigial war oracle (cf. 1.20–21, 29–31; 9.1–3); cf., e.g., Num 31.6; Judg 20.25–28; 1 Sam 7.7–11;

14.36–42. **20.5–8** On the administrative role of the *officials,* see 16.18 (cf. 1.15; Josh 1.10). Implementation of these provisions for exemption is specifically noted in 1 Macc 3.56 (cf. Deut 24.5; Judg 7.3). *Dedicated,* or "inaugurated"; cf. 1 Kings 8.63 (of the temple); also Deut 28.30 (*live in*). **20.6** *Enjoyed its fruit,* made "profane" or ordinary use of the harvest (Jer 31.5; cf. Lev 19.23–25). **20.7** *Engaged,* formally betrothed; cf. 2 Sam 3.14. **20.9** *Commanders,* lit. "officers of hosts" (cf. 1.15; 1 Kings 2.5). **20.10–20** Rules of engagement. **20.10–11** *Terms of peace,* surrender followed by vassalage (cf. 2.26; Josh 9.3–27; 11.19; Judg 1.27–35; 21.13; 2 Sam 10.19). **20.12–15** A mitigated ban is applicable against distant or external foes (cf. 2.33–35; 3.6–7; Num 31.7–54). **20.16–18** A total ban must be inflicted upon the proscribed nations of Canaan (see 7.1–2; cf. 12.29–31). *Anything that breathes,* livestock as well as the human populations (cf. Gen 7.22; Josh 10.40; 11.11, 14; 1 Kings 15.29). **20.19–20** For the tactics called into question, see 2 Kings 3.19, 25; cf. Josephus, *Jewish War* 5.523; 6.5–6.

against them. Although you may take food from them, you must not cut them down. Are trees in the field human beings that they should come under siege from you? 20You may destroy only the trees that you know do not produce food; you may cut them down for use in building siegeworks against the town that makes war with you, until it falls.

Law concerning Murder by Persons Unknown

21 If, in the land that the LORD your God is giving you to possess, a body is found lying in open country, and it is not known who struck the person down, 2then your elders and your judges shall come out to measure the distances to the towns that are near the body. 3The elders of the town nearest the body shall take a heifer that has never been worked, one that has not pulled in the yoke; 4the elders of that town shall bring the heifer down to a wadi with running water, which is neither plowed nor sown, and shall break the heifer's neck there in the wadi. 5Then the priests, the sons of Levi, shall come forward, for the LORD your God has chosen them to minister to him and to pronounce blessings in the name of the LORD, and by their decision all cases of dispute and assault shall be settled. 6All the elders of that town nearest the body shall wash their hands over the heifer whose neck was broken in the wadi, 7and they shall declare: "Our hands did not shed this blood, nor were we witnesses to it. 8Absolve, O LORD, your people Israel, whom you redeemed; do not let the guilt of innocent blood remain in the midst of your people Is-

rael." Then they will be absolved of bloodguilt. 9So you shall purge the guilt of innocent blood from your midst, because you must do what is right in the sight of the LORD.

Female Captives

10 When you go out to war against your enemies, and the LORD your God hands them over to you and you take them captive, 11suppose you see among the captives a beautiful woman whom you desire and want to marry, 12and so you bring her home to your house: she shall shave her head, pare her nails, 13discard her captive's garb, and shall remain in your house a full month, mourning for her father and mother; after that you may go in to her and be her husband, and she shall be your wife. 14But if you are not satisfied with her, you shall let her go free and not sell her for money. You must not treat her as a slave, since you have dishonored her.

The Right of the Firstborn

15 If a man has two wives, one of them loved and the other disliked, and if both the loved and the disliked have borne him sons, the firstborn being the son of the one who is disliked, 16then on the day when he wills his possessions to his sons, he is not permitted to treat the son of the loved as the firstborn in preference to the son of the disliked, who is the firstborn. 17He must acknowledge as firstborn the son of the one who is disliked, giving him a double portion*a* of all that he has; since

a Heb *two-thirds*

21.1–9 This case sketches procedures for restricting communal liability and exculpating bloodguilt in event of a rural homicide in which the culprit cannot be found and prosecuted (cf. 19.4–13; Num 35.30–34). **21.2** Appointed *judges* (see 16.18) exercise concurrent jurisdiction with local *elders* (see note on 19.12) in determining the town nearest the scene of the crime. **21.3–4** Transfer or expurgation of liability is enacted by nonsacrificial slaughter (*break the . . . neck;* cf. Ex 13.13; 34.20) of an unworked *heifer* (cf. Num 19.2; 1 Sam 6.7) in a pristine locale. *Running water.* The "constant flow" (cf. Ps 74.15; Am 5.24) presumably effects the removal of bloodguilt. **21.5** For the jurisdiction of *the priests, the sons of Levi* (also 31.9; cf. 18.1), see 17.8–13. **21.6–8** An exculpatory act (hand washing) and declaration of innocence accompany petitionary prayer for removal of bloodguilt. **21.8** *Absolve,* "cleanse," "forgive," or "expiate" (e.g., 32.43; Ex 32.30; 2 Sam 21.3). **21.9** Cf. 13.5, 18; 19.13.

21.10–21 These three articles (vv. 10–14, 15–17, 18–21) impose restraints on the exercise of authority by male heads of household. **21.10–14** Here a foreign woman acquired as a spoil of war (cf. 20.14) who then becomes a man's slave wife or concubine may not later be sold for profit by the husband (cf. Ex 21.7–11). **21.12–13** The rites mark a transition separating the woman from her former identity and captive status in preparation for her role as bride. **21.14** *Go free* may denote manumission rather than divorce (cf. 15.12–13; Jer 34.16; cf. 22.19, 29; 24.1–3). *As a slave;* i.e., as chattel. *Dishonored,* or "violated," often refers to coerced sexual intercourse (e.g., 22.24, 29; Gen 34.2; Judg 19.24; 2 Sam 13.12). **21.15–17** The legal status of the *firstborn* son, with an attendant share of inheritance, is fixed by priority of birth rather than paternal decision. See, e.g., Gen 21.9–13; 27.1–40; 48.13–49.4; 1 Kings 1.15–21; 1 Chr 5.1–2; cf. Code of Hammurabi 165–170. **21.15** *Disliked.* Cf. Gen 29.31–33. **21.17** *Double portion,* "two-thirds" of

he is the first issue of his virility, the right of the firstborn is his.

Rebellious Children

18 If someone has a stubborn and rebellious son who will not obey his father and mother, who does not heed them when they discipline him, 19then his father and his mother shall take hold of him and bring him out to the elders of his town at the gate of that place. 20They shall say to the elders of his town, "This son of ours is stubborn and rebellious. He will not obey us. He is a glutton and a drunkard." 21Then all the men of the town shall stone him to death. So you shall purge the evil from your midst; and all Israel will hear, and be afraid.

Miscellaneous Laws

22 When someone is convicted of a crime punishable by death and is executed, and you hang him on a tree, 23his corpse must not remain all night upon the tree; you shall bury him that same day, for anyone hung on a tree is under God's curse. You must not defile the land that the LORD your God is giving you for possession.

22 You shall not watch your neighbor's ox or sheep straying away and ignore them; you shall take them back to their owner. 2If the owner does not reside near you or you do not know who the owner is, you shall bring it to your own house, and it shall remain with you until the owner claims it; then you shall return it. 3You shall do the same with a neigh-

bor's donkey; you shall do the same with a neighbor's garment; and you shall do the same with anything else that your neighbor loses and you find. You may not withhold your help.

4 You shall not see your neighbor's donkey or ox fallen on the road and ignore it; you shall help to lift it up.

5 A woman shall not wear a man's apparel, nor shall a man put on a woman's garment; for whoever does such things is abhorrent to the LORD your God.

6 If you come on a bird's nest, in any tree or on the ground, with fledglings or eggs, with the mother sitting on the fledglings or on the eggs, you shall not take the mother with the young. 7Let the mother go, taking only the young for yourself, in order that it may go well with you and you may live long.

8 When you build a new house, you shall make a parapet for your roof; otherwise you might have bloodguilt on your house, if anyone should fall from it.

9 You shall not sow your vineyard with a second kind of seed, or the whole yield will have to be forfeited, both the crop that you have sown and the yield of the vineyard itself.

10 You shall not plow with an ox and a donkey yoked together.

11 You shall not wear clothes made of wool and linen woven together.

12 You shall make tassels on the four corners of the cloak with which you cover yourself.

---

the total estate (cf. 2 Kings 2.9; Zech 13.8). *Virility.* Cf. Gen 49.3; Ps 105.36. **21.18–21** The local community, represented by its elders, has jurisdiction in the capital case of a son charged with chronically dishonorable conduct in defiance of parental authority (cf. 5.16; 27.16; Ex 21.15, 17; Lev 20.9). **21.19** Both parents must appear as plaintiffs before the court at the *town . . . gate* (cf. Isa 29.21; Am 5.10, 12, 15). **21.20** *Stubborn and rebellious,* obstinately unruly (cf. Jer 5.23; Ps 78.8). *A glutton and a drunkard,* dissolute (cf. Prov 23.20–21; 28.7; see also Mt 11.19; Lk 7.34). **21.21** Public execution by stoning treats the offense as comparable to treason; cf. 13.5, 10–11; 22.21, 24; Lev 20.2; 24.14–16. **21.22–23** Limitation on public display of the corpse of an executed criminal; cf. Josh 8.29; 10.26–27; 1 Sam 31.10; 2 Sam 4.12. Exposure of the body (*hang . . . on a tree*) was presumably meant to revile the crime by degrading its perpetrator, supposed to be *under God's curse.* Same-day burial prevented the corpse from becoming carrion (cf. 2 Sam 21.10; Ezek 39.17–20).
    22.1–3 This redraft of Ex 23.4 prescribes initiatives

to aid fellow Israelites in the recovery of straying livestock (cf. 1 Sam 9.3) and, by extension, any other lost property. **22.4** A reformulation of Ex 23.5. **22.5** Classification of cross-dressing as *abhorrent to the LORD* (see note on 7.25–26) suggests that the prohibition has in view pagan cultic practices, perhaps associated with worship of the Mesopotamian goddess Ishtar. **22.6–7** The article urges self-interest (well-being, longevity) as ample motive for ecological sensitivity (cf. 20.19–20; Lev 22.28). **22.8** Flat *roofs* of houses functioned as domestic space (e.g., Josh 2.6). *Bloodguilt* (cf. 19.10). The homeowner was liable for injury or death resulting from negligent construction. **22.9–11** Traditional interpretation understood these and related provisions (Lev 19.19) to exemplify distinctions in the created order that were not to be blurred by human agency; e.g., "nature does not delight in the combination of dissimilar things" (Josephus, *Antiquities* 4.228–29; cf. Philo, *Special Laws* 4.203–12; *Mishnah Kilayim*). **22.9** *Forfeited,* or "hallowed"; i.e., treated like tithed produce (cf. 26.13; Lev 27.10, 21; Josh 6.19).

Laws concerning Sexual Relations

13 Suppose a man marries a woman, but after going in to her, he dislikes her [14]and makes up charges against her, slandering her by saying, "I married this woman; but when I lay with her, I did not find evidence of her virginity." [15]The father of the young woman and her mother shall then submit the evidence of the young woman's virginity to the elders of the city at the gate. [16]The father of the young woman shall say to the elders: "I gave my daughter in marriage to this man but he dislikes her; [17]now he has made up charges against her, saying, 'I did not find evidence of your daughter's virginity.' But here is the evidence of my daughter's virginity." Then they shall spread out the cloth before the elders of the town. [18]The elders of that town shall take the man and punish him; [19]they shall fine him one hundred shekels of silver (which they shall give to the young woman's father) because he has slandered a virgin of Israel. She shall remain his wife; he shall not be permitted to divorce her as long as he lives.

20 If, however, this charge is true, that evidence of the young woman's virginity was not found, [21]then they shall bring the young woman out to the entrance of her father's house and the men of her town shall stone her to death, because she committed a disgraceful act in Israel by prostituting herself in her father's house. So you shall purge the evil from your midst.

22 If a man is caught lying with the wife of another man, both of them shall die, the man who lay with the woman as well as the woman. So you shall purge the evil from Israel.

23 If there is a young woman, a virgin already engaged to be married, and a man meets her in the town and lies with her, [24]you shall bring both of them to the gate of that town and stone them to death, the young woman because she did not cry for help in the town and the man because he violated his neighbor's wife. So you shall purge the evil from your midst.

25 But if the man meets the engaged woman in the open country, and the man seizes her and lies with her, then only the man who lay with her shall die. [26]You shall do nothing to the young woman; the young woman has not committed an offense punishable by death, because this case is like that of someone who attacks and murders a neighbor. [27]Since he found her in the open country, the engaged woman may have cried for help, but there was no one to rescue her.

28 If a man meets a virgin who is not engaged, and seizes her and lies with her, and they are caught in the act, [29]the man who lay with her shall give fifty shekels of silver to the young woman's father, and she shall become his wife. Because he violated her he shall not be permitted to divorce her as long as he lives.

30[a] A man shall not marry his father's wife, thereby violating his father's rights.[b]

---

a Ch 23.1 in Heb   b Heb uncovering his father's skirt

22.12 See Num 15.38–41 (which develops a theological rationale for the practice).

22.13–21 Emphasis in this case as drafted falls on constraining a husband who falsely accuses his bride of losing her virginity prior to marital consummation; a codicil sketches punitive response should the accusation be unrefuted (vv. 20–21). The litigants in contention before the town elders (cf. 21.19–20) are the bride's parents and the husband, whose charges of breach of contract have implicitly defamed them as well as their daughter. **22.13–14** Motive for the slander is not stated; that the husband *dislikes,* or "hates," his wife would suffice as grounds for formal divorce (cf. 21.15; 24.1). *Evidence of her virginity,* a sign of blood from a rupture of the hymen (see v. 17). **22.18–19** Although *punishment* could include flogging (cf. 21.18; 25.1–3), it most clearly refers to monetary damages awarded the bride's father, which are double the amount specified for rape (22.29; cf. Ex 22.7). Since the husband accused his wife of a capital offense comparable to adultery (cf. vv. 21–24), the preclusion of divorce falls well short of talion in severity (see note on 19.19–

21); the woman's wishes are not considered. **22.21** *Disgraceful act,* an "outrage," usually of sexual nature (e.g., Gen 34.7; Judg 19.23–24; 2 Sam 13.12), threatening to the integrity of the social order. *Purge.* See note on 13.5.

22.22–30 The series on sexual offenses continues, first by prescribing the death penalty in the case of a man caught in adultery with another's wife (cf. 5.18; Ex 20.14; Lev 20.10) and then by reviewing related cases complicated by circumstances or rules of evidence. **22.22** *Both . . . shall die,* execution of the pair, presumably by stoning (cf. vv. 21, 24; Lev 20.10; Ezek 16.38–40; Jn 8.5). **22.23–27** Intercourse with an *engaged,* or formally betrothed, woman is equated with the crime of adultery. The question of the woman's culpability distinguishes the two outcomes: she is punished when there is reason, because of locale, to charge her with complicity. **22.26** *This case is like,* reasoning by analogy to accidental homicide (see 19.4–10). **22.28–29** *Seizes, violated* (cf. 21.14). The wording indicates coercion, but biblical law does not sharply distinguish between rape and seduction of an unbetrothed woman (cf. Ex 22.16–17). Preclusion of *divorce.* See 22.19. **22.30** *Vio-*

Those Excluded from the Assembly

23 No one whose testicles are crushed or whose penis is cut off shall be admitted to the assembly of the LORD.

2 Those born of an illicit union shall not be admitted to the assembly of the LORD. Even to the tenth generation, none of their descendants shall be admitted to the assembly of the LORD.

3 No Ammonite or Moabite shall be admitted to the assembly of the LORD. Even to the tenth generation, none of their descendants shall be admitted to the assembly of the LORD, 4because they did not meet you with food and water on your journey out of Egypt, and because they hired against you Balaam son of Beor, from Pethor of Mesopotamia, to curse you. 5(Yet the LORD your God refused to heed Balaam; the LORD your God turned the curse into a blessing for you, because the LORD your God loved you.) 6You shall never promote their welfare or their prosperity as long as you live.

7 You shall not abhor any of the Edomites, for they are your kin. You shall not abhor any of the Egyptians, because you were an alien residing in their land. 8The children of the third generation that are born to them may be admitted to the assembly of the LORD.

Sanitary, Ritual, and Humanitarian Precepts

9 When you are encamped against your enemies you shall guard against any impropriety.

10 If one of you becomes unclean because of a nocturnal emission, then he shall go outside the camp; he must not come within the camp. 11When evening comes, he shall wash himself with water, and when the sun has set, he may come back into the camp.

12 You shall have a designated area outside the camp to which you shall go. 13With your utensils you shall have a trowel; when you relieve yourself outside, you shall dig a hole with it and then cover up your excrement. 14Because the LORD your God travels along with your camp, to save you and to hand over your enemies to you, therefore your camp must be holy, so that he may not see anything indecent among you and turn away from you.

15 Slaves who have escaped to you from their owners shall not be given back to them. 16They shall reside with you, in your midst, in any place they choose in any one of your towns, wherever they please; you shall not oppress them.

17 None of the daughters of Israel shall be a temple prostitute; none of the sons of Israel shall be a temple prostitute. 18You shall not bring the fee of a prostitute or the wages of a male prostitute[a] into the house of the LORD your God in payment for any vow, for both of these are abhorrent to the LORD your God.

19 You shall not charge interest on loans to another Israelite, interest on money, interest on provisions, interest on anything that is lent.

---

a Heb a dog

---

lating his father's rights. The categorical prohibition of a son marrying his widowed or divorced step-mother (*father's wife*) is a matter of decency and respect for paternal privilege (cf. 27.20; Gen 49.4; Lev 18.8; 20.11; Ezek 22.10). **23.1–8** These rules understand the Lord's *assembly* to be a cohort of adult male Israelites, i.e., the covenant community functioning as a restricted religious, military, and political association. (Cf. 16.16; 20.1–9; 33.5 with, e.g., 5.22; 31.30; Isa 56.3–8. Cf. also Judg 20.2; 1 Kings 12.3, 20.) **23.1** Exclusion by reason of genital impairment; cf. Lev 21.17–23. **23.2** *Illicit union* was traditionally understood to mean incest (*Mishnah Yebamot* 4.13; cf. Gen 19.30–38; Lev 18.6–18). **23.3–6** Ethnic disqualifications. Cf. Ezra 10.10–44; Neh 13.1–3, 23–27. **23.4** *Balaam.* See Num 22–24. **23.6** *Welfare* ("peace," Hebrew *shalom*) and *prosperity* may connote political alliance or treaty (cf. Ezra 9.12; Jer 29.7; 38.4); cf. this injunction with 2.9, 19; Isa 16.4. **23.7–8** *Abhor.* Cf. 7.26. *Edomites.* Cf. 2.4–8; Gen 36; Am 1.11. Benevolence toward *Egyptians* is remarkable

in view of 24.22; 26.5, 6; 28.60, 68 (but see Gen 12.10–20). *Children,* apparently the descendants of intermarriage. **23.9–14** Specific rules together with theological rationale for maintenance of personal hygiene during holy-war campaigns (cf. 20.1–20; 2 Sam 11.11). **23.10–11** Cf. Lev 15.16–17; also the Dead Sea Scrolls *Temple Scroll* (11QTª) 45.7–12; 46.18. **23.12** *Designated area,* privy (lit. "hand"); cf. *Temple Scroll* (11QTª) 46.13–16. **23.14** *Travels along.* See, e.g., 1.30; 20.4; 31.6, 8; 2 Sam 7.6–7. *Indecent,* repugnant or "objectionable" (cf. 24.1). **23.15–16** Extradition of *slaves* who seek asylum in Israel is prohibited (contrast 1 Kings 2.39–40; Code of Hammurabi 15–20). **23.17–18** Proscriptions in defense of Israel's sacral integrity. *Temple prostitute.* The term refers to "consecrated" persons, associated in biblical usage with Canaanite or otherwise pagan rites (cf. Gen 38.21–22; 1 Kings 14.24; 15.12; 22.46; 2 Kings 23.7; Hos 4.14). On a harlot's "wages" or *fee,* cf. Isa 23.17–18; Ezek 16.31, 34, 41; Hos 9.1; Mic 1.7. *Abhorrent to the LORD.* See note on 7.25–26. **23.19–20** In accord with 15.1–

²⁰On loans to a foreigner you may charge interest, but on loans to another Israelite you may not charge interest, so that the LORD your God may bless you in all your undertakings in the land that you are about to enter and possess.

21 If you make a vow to the LORD your God, do not postpone fulfilling it; for the LORD your God will surely require it of you, and you would incur guilt. ²²But if you refrain from vowing, you will not incur guilt. ²³Whatever your lips utter you must diligently perform, just as you have freely vowed to the LORD your God with your own mouth.

24 If you go into your neighbor's vineyard, you may eat your fill of grapes, as many as you wish, but you shall not put any in a container.

25 If you go into your neighbor's standing grain, you may pluck the ears with your hand, but you shall not put a sickle to your neighbor's standing grain.

Laws concerning Marriage and Divorce

24 Suppose a man enters into marriage with a woman, but she does not please him because he finds something objectionable about her, and so he writes her a certificate of divorce, puts it in her hand, and sends her out of his house; she then leaves his house ²and goes off to become another man's wife. ³Then suppose the second man dislikes her, writes her a bill of divorce, puts it in her hand, and sends her out of his house (or the second man who married her dies); ⁴her first husband, who sent her away, is not permitted to take her again to be his wife after she has been defiled; for that would be abhorrent to the LORD, and you shall not bring guilt on the land that the LORD your God is giving you as a possession.

Miscellaneous Laws

5 When a man is newly married, he shall not go out with the army or be charged with any related duty. He shall be free at home one year, to be happy with the wife whom he has married.

6 No one shall take a mill or an upper millstone in pledge, for that would be taking a life in pledge.

7 If someone is caught kidnaping another Israelite, enslaving or selling the Israelite, then that kidnaper shall die. So you shall purge the evil from your midst.

8 Guard against an outbreak of a leprous*a* skin disease by being very careful; you shall carefully observe whatever the levitical priests instruct you, just as I have commanded them. ⁹Remember what the LORD your God did to Miriam on your journey out of Egypt.

10 When you make your neighbor a loan of any kind, you shall not go into the house to take the pledge. ¹¹You shall wait outside, while

---

a A term for several skin diseases; precise meaning uncertain

11, distinction is made between interest-free welfare loans to fellow Israelites (cf. 24.10–13; Ex 22.25; Lev 25.35–38) and profit-making commercial loans to foreigners (cf. 15.6; 28.12). *Interest,* increment, lit. "bite," usually taken by the creditor when making the loan (cf. Ezek 18.8, 13, 17; 22.12). **23.21–23** The closely comparable admonitions in Eccl 5.4–6 are derivative. *Vow,* a form of promissory oath, sworn in anticipation of divine favor (e.g., Gen 28.20–22; Num 21.2–3; 1 Sam 1.11; Ps 132.1–5). **23.23** *Whatever,* usually a sacrifice or equivalent monetary payment (cf. Lev 27.2–29; Num 30.2–15; Pss 56.12–13; 66.13–15). **23.24–25** These rulings cogently define the limits of traditional hospitality extended to hungry wayfarers as well as to field hands (cf. 25.4; Mt 12.1; Josephus, *Antiquities* 4.234–37).
24.1–4 Unlike the exceptional cases of 22.19, 29, divorce is here left to a husband's discretion (*does not please,* v. 1; *dislikes,* v. 3). But he is prohibited from remarrying a former spouse after she has become another man's wife, thus preventing interpretation of her second marriage as harlotry or wife swapping (so Nachmanides, a medieval Jewish commentator). **24.1** *Something objectionable* (*indecent,* 23.14) appar-

ently means for any cause, though the sense was already disputed in antiquity (cf. Sir 7.26; 25.25–26; Mt 19.3–9; Josephus, *Antiquities* 4.253). *Certificate of divorce,* a writ proving the husband had relinquished claim on the woman, freeing her to remarry (cf. Isa 50.1; Jer 3.8; Mt 5.31; *Mishnah Gitin*). **24.4** *Been defiled,* by the husband, who had enabled or caused her to seek another marriage. *Abhorrent.* See note on 7.25–26. *Guilt on the land,* pollution comparable to that caused by homicide (19.13; 21.9; cf. Jer 3.1–3; Hos 4.2–3). **24.5** A supplement to 20.7. *Related duty,* e.g., conscripted labor or government service (cf. 1 Sam 8.11–13; 1 Kings 5.13–18; 9.15–21).
24.6–25.4 Most of these otherwise diverse provisions exemplify concern for humane, charitable treatment of persons, especially the economically disadvantaged; together with parallels in other bodies of biblical law, they form the bedrock of biblical social ethics. **24.6** Legitimate surety for creditors must not compromise the means of debtors to subsist. *Pledge,* as collateral for a loan; cf. 24.17; Ex 22.25–27; Job 24.3. **24.7** A redraft of Ex 21.16. *Enslaving or selling,* e.g., abuse of distrainees (cf. 2 Kings 4.1; Job 24.9; Am 2.6). *Purge.* See note on 13.5. **24.8–9** On priestly dermatol-

the person to whom you are making the loan brings the pledge out to you. [12]If the person is poor, you shall not sleep in the garment given you as[a] the pledge. [13]You shall give the pledge back by sunset, so that your neighbor may sleep in the cloak and bless you; and it will be to your credit before the LORD your God.

14 You shall not withhold the wages of poor and needy laborers, whether other Israelites or aliens who reside in your land in one of your towns. [15]You shall pay them their wages daily before sunset, because they are poor and their livelihood depends on them; otherwise they might cry to the LORD against you, and you would incur guilt.

16 Parents shall not be put to death for their children, nor shall children be put to death for their parents; only for their own crimes may persons be put to death.

17 You shall not deprive a resident alien or an orphan of justice; you shall not take a widow's garment in pledge. [18]Remember that you were a slave in Egypt and the LORD your God redeemed you from there; therefore I command you to do this.

19 When you reap your harvest in your field and forget a sheaf in the field, you shall not go back to get it; it shall be left for the alien, the orphan, and the widow, so that the LORD your God may bless you in all your undertakings. [20]When you beat your olive trees, do not strip what is left; it shall be for the alien, the orphan, and the widow.

21 When you gather the grapes of your vineyard, do not glean what is left; it shall be for the alien, the orphan, and the widow. [22]Remember that you were a slave in the land of Egypt; therefore I am commanding you to do this.

25 Suppose two persons have a dispute and enter into litigation, and the judges decide between them, declaring one to be in the right and the other to be in the wrong. [2]If the one in the wrong deserves to be flogged, the judge shall make that person lie down and be beaten in his presence with the number of lashes proportionate to the offense. [3]Forty lashes may be given but not more; if more lashes than these are given, your neighbor will be degraded in your sight.

4 You shall not muzzle an ox while it is treading out the grain.

Levirate Marriage

5 When brothers reside together, and one of them dies and has no son, the wife of the deceased shall not be married outside the family to a stranger. Her husband's brother shall go in to her, taking her in marriage, and performing the duty of a husband's brother to her, [6]and the firstborn whom she bears shall succeed to the name of the deceased brother, so that his name may not be blotted out of Israel. [7]But if the man has no desire to marry his brother's widow, then his brother's widow shall go up to the elders at the gate and say, "My husband's brother refuses to perpetuate his brother's

a Heb lacks the garment given you as

ogy, see Lev 13–14. For the judgment on Miriam, see Num 12.10–15. **24.10–13** Additional restrictions on distraint (see vv. 6, 17), including a redraft of Ex 22.25–27 (cf. Job 22.6; Prov 20.16; 27.13; Am 2.8). **24.13** Be to your credit, counted as "merit" (cf. 6.25), the converse of 15.9; 24.15. **24.14–15** Daily receipt of wages is a laborer's right (cf. Lev 19.13; Jer 22.13; Mt 20.2–15). On equal treatment for aliens ("sojourners"), cf. vv. 17–22; 1.16; 10.17–19; Lev 19.33–34; Ezek 47.22–23. **24.15** Cry to the LORD. See note on 15.9. **24.16** This juridical principle limiting liability for capital offenses to the actual perpetrators of crimes is cited in 2 Kings 14.6. (For theological reverberations, see Deut 7.10; Jer 31.29, 30; Ezek 18.) **24.17–18** For the theological rationale, see 10.17–19; 15.15; 24.22 (cf. also 27.19; Ex 22.21–24; 23.6, 9). **24.19–22** Provisions on gleaning. Cf. Ex 23.10–11; Lev 19.9–10; 23.22; Isa 17.5–6; Ruth 2; Mishnah Pe'a. **25.1–3** Flogging, administered as punishment by a court, should be proportionate to the offense (cf. the rule of talion, note on 19.19–21), with forty stripes fixed as a maxi-

mum in order to protect the culprit from cruel humiliation (cf. 2 Cor 11.24; Josephus, Antiquities 4.238; Mishnah Makkot 3). **25.4** Social equity is exemplified by humane treatment of a working ox (cf. 5.14; Prov 12.10; also 1 Cor 9.9; 1 Tim 5.18).

25.5–10 As drafted, this legislation is concerned with resolving the anomalous relationship between a childless but still youthful widow and her deceased husband's family. Custom preferred an endogamous remarriage of the woman to her husband's brother, levir in Latin, whence the practice is commonly called "levirate marriage." (Cf. the related practices in Gen 38.6–26; Ruth 3–4; also cf. Lev 18.16; 20.21.) **25.5** Though context supports the literal rendering son, the sense was later understood to include female offspring (e.g., Septuagint; Josephus, Antiquities 4.254; Lk 20.28; cf. Num 27.8–11). **25.6** Lineage succession of the male firstborn to the name of the deceased brother implicitly includes claim to patrimony (cf. 21.15–17; Num 27.4; Ruth 4.5, 10; also 2 Sam 14.7). **25.7–8** Jurisdiction of elders in familial disputes; see 19.12; 21.19–20; 22.17–19. **25.9–**

name in Israel; he will not perform the duty of a husband's brother to me." ⁸Then the elders of his town shall summon him and speak to him. If he persists, saying, "I have no desire to marry her," ⁹then his brother's wife shall go up to him in the presence of the elders, pull his sandal off his foot, spit in his face, and declare, "This is what is done to the man who does not build up his brother's house." ¹⁰Throughout Israel his family shall be known as "the house of him whose sandal was pulled off."

Various Commands

11 If men get into a fight with one another, and the wife of one intervenes to rescue her husband from the grip of his opponent by reaching out and seizing his genitals, ¹²you shall cut off her hand; show no pity.

13 You shall not have in your bag two kinds of weights, large and small. ¹⁴You shall not have in your house two kinds of measures, large and small. ¹⁵You shall have only a full and honest weight; you shall have only a full and honest measure, so that your days may be long in the land that the LORD your God is giving you. ¹⁶For all who do such things, all who act dishonestly, are abhorrent to the LORD your God.

17 Remember what Amalek did to you on your journey out of Egypt, ¹⁸how he attacked you on the way, when you were faint and weary, and struck down all who lagged behind you; he did not fear God. ¹⁹Therefore when the LORD your God has given you rest from all your enemies on every hand, in the land that the LORD your God is giving you as an inheritance to possess, you shall blot out the remembrance of Amalek from under heaven; do not forget.

First Fruits and Tithes

26 When you have come into the land that the LORD your God is giving you as an inheritance to possess, and you possess it, and settle in it, ²you shall take some of the first of all the fruit of the ground, which you harvest from the land that the LORD your God is giving you, and you shall put it in a basket and go to the place that the LORD your God will choose as a dwelling for his name. ³You shall go to the priest who is in office at that time, and say to him, "Today I declare to the LORD your God that I have come into the land that the LORD swore to our ancestors to give us." ⁴When the priest takes the basket from your hand and sets it down before the altar of the LORD your God, ⁵you shall make this response before the LORD your God: "A wandering Aramean was my ancestor; he went down into Egypt and lived there as an alien, few in number, and there he became a great nation, mighty and populous. ⁶When the Egyptians treated us harshly and afflicted us, by imposing hard labor on us, ⁷we cried to the LORD, the God of our ancestors; the LORD heard our voice and saw our affliction, our toil, and our oppression. ⁸The LORD brought us out of Egypt with a mighty hand and an outstretched

---

10 Public degradation of the unwilling *levir* (husband's brother; see note on 25.5–10). *Spitting* is an act of contempt (cf. Num 12.14; Job 17.6; 30.10; Isa 50.6); removal of his *sandal* is a rite of quittance, freeing the widow from further obligation to the husband's family (*house*). 25.11–12 The severe penalty, comparable to talion (see note on 19.19–21), presumes the woman has recklessly endangered the man's procreative capacity (cf. 19.21; Ex 21.22–25; *Mishnah Bava Kamma* 8.1). 25.13–16 Such injunctions and the commercial abuses they address are well attested; e.g., Lev 19.35–36; Prov 16.11; 20.23; Ezek 45.10–12; Hos 12.7; Mic 6.10–11; Instruction of Amenemope 17.17–19; 18.14–19.2. 25.16 *Abhorrent.* See note on 7.25–26. 25.17–19 A codicil to 23.3–6 reflecting Ex 17.14–15. On the tradition of enmity between Israel and the Amalekites of northern Sinai, see Num 24.20; Judg 6.3; 10.12; 1 Sam 15.2–33. 25.18 This perfidy goes unreported in Ex 17.8–13. 25.19 *Rest.* Cf. 3.20; 12.9. *Blot out the remembrance.* Cf. 9.14; 25.6; 29.20; 1 Sam 24.21; Pss 9.5–6; 109.13.
26.1–15 This brief concluding section of the polity, which is a counterpart of 12.2–28, prescribes affirma-

tions of covenantal identity that worshipers are to make on particular occasions of pilgrimage to the single sanctuary. 26.1–11 Creedal declarations associated with presentations of first fruits (cf. Lev 23.9–21; Num 28.26–31; *Mishnah Bikkurim*). 26.2 *First* (or "choicest"; cf. Ex 23.19; 34.26) *of all the fruit,* token presentation of each agricultural crop at the sanctuary (*the place;* see 12.5), apparently in conjunction with the annual pilgrimage feasts and as pledge on full payment of tithes (cf. 14.22–23; 16.1–17; 18.4; Ex 22.29; Tob 1.6–7; Philo, *Special Laws* 2.216–20). *As a dwelling for his name.* See notes on 12.5; 12.11. 26.3 *Priest.* Cf. 17.9, 12; 18.3–5; 19.17; 20.2. *Swore to our ancestors.* See 1.8, 20–21. 26.5 *Wandering Aramean* refers to Israel's north Syrian ancestry, traced through Abram (Abraham) (cf. Gen 11.31; 12.1–9; 20.13) as well as Jacob (Israel), who is probably meant here (cf. Gen 29–32). *Few in number.* See 28.62; Ps 105.12 (cf. Gen 34.30; 46.8–27). *Great nation.* See 4.6–8 (cf. Ex 1.7, 9). 26.6 *Hard labor.* See Ex 1.13–14; 6.9 (cf. 1 Kings 12.4). 26.7 *Cried to the LORD.* See Ex 14.10, 15; Num 20.16; Josh 24.7. *God of our ancestors.* See, e.g., 1.11; 6.3; 12.1 (cf. Ex 3.15–16). 26.8 Cf.

arm, with a terrifying display of power, and with signs and wonders; 9and he brought us into this place and gave us this land, a land flowing with milk and honey. 10So now I bring the first of the fruit of the ground that you, O LORD, have given me." You shall set it down before the LORD your God and bow down before the LORD your God. 11Then you, together with the Levites and the aliens who reside among you, shall celebrate with all the bounty that the LORD your God has given to you and to your house.

12 When you have finished paying all the tithe of your produce in the third year (which is the year of the tithe), giving it to the Levites, the aliens, the orphans, and the widows, so that they may eat their fill within your towns, 13then you shall say before the LORD your God: "I have removed the sacred portion from the house, and I have given it to the Levites, the resident aliens, the orphans, and the widows, in accordance with your entire commandment that you commanded me; I have neither transgressed nor forgotten any of your commandments: 14I have not eaten of it while in mourning; I have not removed any of it while I was unclean; and I have not offered any of it to the dead. I have obeyed the LORD my God, doing just as you commanded me. 15Look down from your holy habitation, from heaven, and bless your people Israel and the ground that you have given us, as you swore to our ancestors—a land flowing with milk and honey."

Concluding Exhortation

16 This very day the LORD your God is commanding you to observe these statutes and ordinances; so observe them diligently with all your heart and with all your soul. 17Today you have obtained the LORD's agreement: to be your God; and for you to walk in his ways, to keep his statutes, his commandments, and his ordinances, and to obey him. 18Today the LORD has obtained your agreement: to be his treasured people, as he promised you, and to keep his commandments; 19for him to set you high above all nations that he has made, in praise and in fame and in honor; and for you to be a people holy to the LORD your God, as he promised.

The Inscribed Stones and Altar on Mount Ebal

27 Then Moses and the elders of Israel charged all the people as follows: Keep the entire commandment that I am commanding you today. 2On the day that you cross over the Jordan into the land that the LORD your God is giving you, you shall set up large stones and cover them with plaster. 3You shall write on them all the words of this law when you have crossed over, to enter the land that the LORD your God is giving you, a land flowing with milk and honey, as the LORD, the God of your ancestors, promised you. 4So when you have crossed over the Jordan, you shall set up these stones, about which I am

4.34; 6.21. **26.9** *This place.* Cf. Ex 15.17. **26.11** Cf. 12.7; 16.11, 14. **26.12–15** The worshiper's positive and negative declarations of compliance with the rules of triennial tithing (see 14.28–29; cf. *Mishnah Ma'aser Sheni* 5.10–13) are followed by a prayer for continuance of divine blessing on Israel. **26.13** *Before the LORD,* at the single sanctuary (see, e.g., 14.23; 16.16). **26.14** Protestations of innocence (cf. Job 31.5–40; Ps 26.4–7) regarding misuse of tithed produce in mortuary rites. *Mourning.* Cf. Jer 16.7; Ezek 24.17, 22. *Unclean.* Cf. Lev 11.24–25; 22.3; Num 19.11–22; Hos 9.4; Hag 2.13. *To the dead* may refer to a cult of ancestors (cf. 14.1; Tob 4.17; Sir 30.18–20). **26.15** *Holy habitation . . . heaven.* See, e.g., 1 Kings 8.39, 43, 49; Jer 25.30; Ps 102.19.

26.16–28.68 An archival collection of covenant rites and sanctions concludes the primary corpus of Deuteronomic *torah* (see 4.44–45) and also seals the relationship between God and people previewed in Ex 19.3–8. **26.16–19** The alliance between the Lord and Israel is formally joined or reaffirmed when each party declares its acceptance of reciprocal roles and obligations. See the succinct formulation of covenantal identities in, e.g., 29.13; Ex 6.7; Lev 26.12; 2 Sam 7.24; Jer 7.23; 31.33; Ezek 11.20; Hos 2.23. **26.16** *This very day,* the liturgical present, or anytime the Israel of subsequent generations is gathered in solemn assembly to hear and recommit itself to the covenant (cf. 4.4; 5.1–3; 11.32; 27.9). **26.17** Cf. 8.6; 10.12; 11.22. **26.18–19** Cf. 7.6; 14.2; 28.9; Ex 19.5–6; Jer 13.11; 33.9.

27.1–26 The narrative transition to the blessings and curses in ch. 28 is augmented with ceremonial lore, apparently gleaned from various sources and loosely conflated to encourage observance of covenant obligations. **27.1** The consortium of *Moses and the elders of Israel* (cf. 31.9) may attest a tradition stratum also evident in Ex 3.16–18; 17.5–6; 19.7; 24.1, 9–14; Num 11.16–30. **27.2–3, 8** Memorial *stones,* erected after crossing the Jordan, suggest the shrine at Gilgal (cf. 11.30; Josh 4). *Cover them with plaster,* i.e., to produce a stuccoed writing surface. *All the words of this law* (vv. 3, 8): the articles of Deuteronomic polity (cf. 17.19; 27.26; 28.58; 29.29; 31.12). **27.4** The location at

commanding you today, on Mount Ebal, and you shall cover them with plaster. ⁵And you shall build an altar there to the LORD your God, an altar of stones on which you have not used an iron tool. ⁶You must build the altar of the LORD your God of unhewn*ᵃ* stones. Then offer up burnt offerings on it to the LORD your God, ⁷make sacrifices of well-being, and eat them there, rejoicing before the LORD your God. ⁸You shall write on the stones all the words of this law very clearly.

9 Then Moses and the levitical priests spoke to all Israel, saying: Keep silence and hear, O Israel! This very day you have become the people of the LORD your God. ¹⁰Therefore obey the LORD your God, observing his commandments and his statutes that I am commanding you today.

Twelve Curses

11 The same day Moses charged the people as follows: ¹²When you have crossed over the Jordan, these shall stand on Mount Gerizim for the blessing of the people: Simeon, Levi, Judah, Issachar, Joseph, and Benjamin. ¹³And these shall stand on Mount Ebal for the curse: Reuben, Gad, Asher, Zebulun, Dan, and Naphtali. ¹⁴Then the Levites shall declare in a loud voice to all the Israelites:

15 "Cursed be anyone who makes an idol or casts an image, anything abhorrent to the LORD, the work of an artisan, and sets it up in secret." All the people shall respond, saying, "Amen!"

16 "Cursed be anyone who dishonors father or mother." All the people shall say, "Amen!"

17 "Cursed be anyone who moves a neighbor's boundary marker." All the people shall say, "Amen!"

18 "Cursed be anyone who misleads a blind person on the road." All the people shall say, "Amen!"

19 "Cursed be anyone who deprives the alien, the orphan, and the widow of justice." All the people shall say, "Amen!"

20 "Cursed be anyone who lies with his father's wife, because he has violated his father's rights."ᵇ All the people shall say, "Amen!"

21 "Cursed be anyone who lies with any animal." All the people shall say, "Amen!"

22 "Cursed be anyone who lies with his sister, whether the daughter of his father or the daughter of his mother." All the people shall say, "Amen!"

23 "Cursed be anyone who lies with his mother-in-law." All the people shall say, "Amen!"

24 "Cursed be anyone who strikes down a neighbor in secret." All the people shall say, "Amen!"

25 "Cursed be anyone who takes a bribe to shed innocent blood." All the people shall say, "Amen!"

26 "Cursed be anyone who does not uphold the words of this law by observing them." All the people shall say, "Amen!"

Blessings for Obedience

28 If you will only obey the LORD your God, by diligently observing all his

_____
a Heb *whole*   *b* Heb *uncovered his father's skirt*

Mount Ebal (see 11.29) promotes linkage of vv. 2–3 with vv. 5–7, 12–13 (cf. Josh 8.30–32). **27.5–7** Cf. the covenant-making rites depicted in Ex 24.3–8. **27.5** *Altar of* [unhewn] *stones.* Cf. Ex 20.24–26; *Mishnah Middot* 3.4. **27.7** The term rendered *sacrifices of well-being* (e.g., Ex 20.24; 24.5; 32.6; Lev 3.1–5) is otherwise unattested in the book of Deuteronomy (cf. 12.6, 11, 26–27). **27.9–10** Rhetorical connection is made between 26.16–19 and 28.1. (Cf. 5.32–6.1; 11.31–12.1.) **27.11–13** Further instruction on promulgation of covenant sanctions in the region of Shechem (see 11.26–30; cf. Josephus, *Antiquities* 4.305–308; *Mishnah Sota* 7.5). Implementation, as reported in Josh 8.33–35, relates *the blessing* and *the curse* to the contents of ch. 28. **27.14–26** This liturgy of imprecations and antiphonal responses comprises a loyalty oath, apparently administered by officiating *Levites* to the membership of Israel's tribal "assembly" (cf. 10.8; 23.1–8; 33.4–5, 8–10). By anathematizing any mem-

ber who commits one of these clandestine offenses (*in secret,* vv. 15, 24; cf. 13.6; 29.17–21), the list reinforces the basic communal ethos. Specific items are paralleled in the Decalogue and other biblical codes of law; the whole Deuteronomic polity is encompassed by the final curse (cf. vv. 3, 8). **27.15** See, e.g., 4.15–20; 5.8–9; Ex 20.23; 34.17; Lev 19.4; 26.1; Hos 13.2. On private cults and secretive idolatry, see Judg 17.1–5; Ezek 8.7–13; cf. Job 31.26–27; Ps 64.5–6. *Amen,* or "so be it" (cf. Num 5.22; Jer 11.5; Neh 5.13). **27.16** Cf. 5.16; 21.18–20; Ex 21.17; Lev 20.9. **27.17** See note on 19.14. **27.18** Cf. Lev 19.14. **27.19** See 24.17 (cf. Ex 22.21–22; 23.9; Lev 19.33–34). **27.20–23** Proscribed sexual relations; cf. 22.30; Ex 22.19; Lev 18.7–9, 17, 23; 20.11, 14–17. **27.24** Surreptitious homicide; cf. 21.1; Ex 21.12. **27.25** Abuse of judicial power; cf. 1.16–17; 16.19; Ex 23.6–8. **27.26** Cf. Jer 11.3–5; also Gal 3.10.

28.1–46 Blessings and curses of the covenant. **28.1–14** The blessings affirm that national security, prosper-

commandments that I am commanding you today, the LORD your God will set you high above all the nations of the earth; ²all these blessings shall come upon you and overtake you, if you obey the LORD your God:

3 Blessed shall you be in the city, and blessed shall you be in the field.

4 Blessed shall be the fruit of your womb, the fruit of your ground, and the fruit of your livestock, both the increase of your cattle and the issue of your flock.

5 Blessed shall be your basket and your kneading bowl.

6 Blessed shall you be when you come in, and blessed shall you be when you go out.

7 The LORD will cause your enemies who rise against you to be defeated before you; they shall come out against you one way, and flee before you seven ways. ⁸The LORD will command the blessing upon you in your barns, and in all that you undertake; he will bless you in the land that the LORD your God is giving you. ⁹The LORD will establish you as his holy people, as he has sworn to you, if you keep the commandments of the LORD your God and walk in his ways. ¹⁰All the peoples of the earth shall see that you are called by the name of the LORD, and they shall be afraid of you. ¹¹The LORD will make you abound in prosperity, in the fruit of your womb, in the fruit of your livestock, and in the fruit of your ground in the land that the LORD swore to your ancestors to give you. ¹²The LORD will open for you his rich storehouse, the heavens, to give the rain of your land in its season and to bless all your undertakings. You will lend to many nations, but you will not borrow. ¹³The LORD will make

you the head, and not the tail; you shall be only at the top, and not at the bottom—if you obey the commandments of the LORD your God, which I am commanding you today, by diligently observing them, ¹⁴and if you do not turn aside from any of the words that I am commanding you today, either to the right or to the left, following other gods to serve them.

Warnings against Disobedience

15 But if you will not obey the LORD your God by diligently observing all his commandments and decrees, which I am commanding you today, then all these curses shall come upon you and overtake you:

16 Cursed shall you be in the city, and cursed shall you be in the field.

17 Cursed shall be your basket and your kneading bowl.

18 Cursed shall be the fruit of your womb, the fruit of your ground, the increase of your cattle and the issue of your flock.

19 Cursed shall you be when you come in, and cursed shall you be when you go out.

20 The LORD will send upon you disaster, panic, and frustration in everything you attempt to do, until you are destroyed and perish quickly, on account of the evil of your deeds, because you have forsaken me. ²¹The LORD will make the pestilence cling to you until it has consumed you off the land that you are entering to possess. ²²The LORD will afflict you with consumption, fever, inflammation, with fiery heat and drought, and with blight and mildew; they shall pursue you until you perish. ²³The sky over your head shall be bronze, and the earth under you iron. ²⁴The

---

ity, and preeminence are intrinsic consequences of Israel's fidelity to the covenant relationship (see 26.18–19; cf. also 7.12–16; 11.13–15; Lev 26.1–13). **28.1–2** The preface emphasizes conditionality (*If . . . if*); see also vv. 9, 14. *Set you high.* The language of royal apotheosis (cf. 2 Sam 7.22–29; Ps 89.27–37; Isa 55.3–5) directly echoes 26.19. **28.3–6** This sixfold benediction, together with its imprecatory counterpart in vv. 16–19, may represent an ancient liturgy (cf. 27.12–13). The paired antonyms in vv. 3, 6 (cf. 6.7) express the fullness of productive labors: *city* and *field,* i.e., wherever you work (e.g., Gen 34.28; 1 Kings 14.11; Jer 14.18); *come in* and *go out,* whatever you do (e.g., 31.2; Ps 121.8). Similarly, the central blessings (vv. 4–5) invoke comprehensive fertility for livestock, fields, and their human caretakers (cf. 7.13–14; 32.13–14; Ex 23.26; Lev 26.4–5, 9). **28.7–14** Emphasized here is divine agency in providing the benefactions that will en-

sure well-being and exaltation for Israel, contingent upon its continuing observance of the Lord's commands. **28.7** Defeat of *enemies.* Cf. 9.1–3; Ex 23.27–28; Lev 26.6–8. **28.8** Fertile *land.* Cf. 8.7–10; 11.10–12; Lev 26.10. **28.9** *His holy people.* See 7.6; 14.2; 26.18–19. **28.10** *Called by the name of the LORD* denotes the Lord's active conservatorship of Israel (cf. 2 Chr 7.14; Isa 61.9; 63.19; Jer 14.9; Am 9.12). **28.11** See v. 4. **28.12** Heavenly *storehouse* of seasonal rains. Cf. Job 38.22; Ps 135.7; Jer 10.13. *Lend, not borrow.* Cf. 15.6. **28.14** See 5.32; 6.14–15. **28.15–19** Introductory threat (v. 15) plus the initial series of curses forms a close antithesis to 28.1–6. **28.20–46** An expansive counterpart to the blessing of 28.7–14. **28.20** The terms *disaster, panic,* and *frustration* broadly categorize effects of the following curses (vv. 21–44). *Me.* See note on 7.4. **28.21–22** Debilitation. Cf., e.g., Lev 26.16, 25; 1 Kings 8.37; Jer 14.12; Am 4.9–10; Hag 2.17. **28.23–24** Strik-

LORD will change the rain of your land into powder, and only dust shall come down upon you from the sky until you are destroyed.

25 The LORD will cause you to be defeated before your enemies; you shall go out against them one way and flee before them seven ways. You shall become an object of horror to all the kingdoms of the earth. 26Your corpses shall be food for every bird of the air and animal of the earth, and there shall be no one to frighten them away. 27The LORD will afflict you with the boils of Egypt, with ulcers, scurvy, and itch, of which you cannot be healed. 28The LORD will afflict you with madness, blindness, and confusion of mind; 29you shall grope about at noon as blind people grope in darkness, but you shall be unable to find your way; and you shall be continually abused and robbed, without anyone to help. 30You shall become engaged to a woman, but another man shall lie with her. You shall build a house, but not live in it. You shall plant a vineyard, but not enjoy its fruit. 31Your ox shall be butchered before your eyes, but you shall not eat of it. Your donkey shall be stolen in front of you, and shall not be restored to you. Your sheep shall be given to your enemies, without anyone to help you. 32Your sons and daughters shall be given to another people, while you look on; you will strain your eyes looking for them all day but be powerless to do anything. 33A people whom you do not know shall eat up the fruit of your ground and of all your labors; you shall be continually abused and crushed, 34and driven mad by the sight that your eyes shall see. 35The LORD will strike you on the knees and on the legs with grievous boils of which you cannot be healed, from the sole of your foot to the crown of your head. 36The LORD will bring you, and the king

whom you set over you, to a nation that neither you nor your ancestors have known, where you shall serve other gods, of wood and stone. 37You shall become an object of horror, a proverb, and a byword among all the peoples where the LORD will lead you.

38 You shall carry much seed into the field but shall gather little in, for the locust shall consume it. 39You shall plant vineyards and dress them, but you shall neither drink the wine nor gather the grapes, for the worm shall eat them. 40You shall have olive trees throughout all your territory, but you shall not anoint yourself with the oil, for your olives shall drop off. 41You shall have sons and daughters, but they shall not remain yours, for they shall go into captivity. 42All your trees and the fruit of your ground the cicada shall take over. 43Aliens residing among you shall ascend above you higher and higher, while you shall descend lower and lower. 44They shall lend to you but you shall not lend to them; they shall be the head and you shall be the tail.

45 All these curses shall come upon you, pursuing and overtaking you until you are destroyed, because you did not obey the LORD your God, by observing the commandments and the decrees that he commanded you. 46They shall be among you and your descendants as a sign and a portent forever.

47 Because you did not serve the LORD your God joyfully and with gladness of heart for the abundance of everything, 48therefore you shall serve your enemies whom the LORD will send against you, in hunger and thirst, in nakedness and lack of everything. He will put an iron yoke on your neck until he has destroyed you. 49The LORD will bring a nation from far away, from the end of the earth, to swoop down on you like an eagle, a nation

ingly parallel curses appear in Vassal Treaties of Esarhaddon 526–33. For the imagery, see also Lev 26.19; Job 37.18; 38.38. **28.25** Military rout. Cf. 1.44; 28.7; Lev 26.17–18. *Object of horror*, or "revulsion." Cf. 2 Chr 29.8; Jer 15.4; 34.17; Ezek 23.46. **28.26** *Corpses* as carrion. See note on 21.22–23; cf. also Jer 7.33; 34.20; cf. 2 Sam 21.10; Ps 79.2; Ezek 39.17–20. **28.27** *Boils of Egypt.* Cf. 7.15; 28.60; Ex 9.9–11. **28.28–29** Derangement. Cf. Job 5.14; 12.25; Isa 19.14; 59.10; Zech 12.4. **28.30** Cf. 20.5–7; Am 5.11. **28.31–34** Spoliation. Cf., e.g., Jer 5.17; 38.21–23; Lam 5.2–18; Am 7.17. **28.35** Cf. v. 27; Job 2.7. **28.36–37** Captivity. Cf., e.g., 4.27–28; 2 Kings 25.7, 11; Jer 16.13; 24.8–9; 25.9–10; Ezek 17.12. **28.38–42** Futility of labors. Cf. v. 18; Lev 26.20; Hos 2.8–13; Mic 6.15. **28.43–44** Reversal of

roles. Cf. 15.6; 28.12–13. **28.45** *Inclusio* (a repetition signaling the beginning and end of a unit), echoing 28.15. **28.46** Perduring effects of curse as *sign* and *portent.* Cf. v. 37; also 29.22–28.

28.47–68 Divine retaliation against Israel for breach of covenant is portrayed in scenes (vv. 47–57, 58–68) that threaten reversal of the conquest and even the exodus from Egypt (cf. 6.21–23; 8.11–20; 26.5–9). **28.47–48** Rejection of the Lord's benevolent sovereignty will result in Israel's subjugation to its enemies (cf. Judg 2.11–15). *Joyfully and with gladness of heart* connotes cheerful alacrity (cf. 1 Kings 1.40; 8.66; Esth 5.9). **28.48** *Iron yoke,* heavy, infrangible vassalage (cf. Jer 28.13–14; Mt 11.28–30; *Mishnah Avot* 3.5). **28.49–50** Portrait of the merciless foe wielded by the Lord as

whose language you do not understand, [50]a grim-faced nation showing no respect to the old or favor to the young. [51]It shall consume the fruit of your livestock and the fruit of your ground until you are destroyed, leaving you neither grain, wine, and oil, nor the increase of your cattle and the issue of your flock, until it has made you perish. [52]It shall besiege you in all your towns until your high and fortified walls, in which you trusted, come down throughout your land; it shall besiege you in all your towns throughout the land that the LORD your God has given you. [53]In the desperate straits to which the enemy siege reduces you, you will eat the fruit of your womb, the flesh of your own sons and daughters whom the LORD your God has given you. [54]Even the most refined and gentle of men among you will begrudge food to his own brother, to the wife whom he embraces, and to the last of his remaining children, [55]giving to none of them any of the flesh of his children whom he is eating, because nothing else remains to him, in the desperate straits to which the enemy siege will reduce you in all your towns. [56]She who is the most refined and gentle among you, so gentle and refined that she does not venture to set the sole of her foot on the ground, will begrudge food to the husband whom she embraces, to her own son, and to her own daughter, [57]begrudging even the afterbirth that comes out from between her thighs, and the children that she bears, because she is eating them in secret for lack of anything else, in the desperate straits to which the enemy siege will reduce you in your towns.

[58] If you do not diligently observe all the words of this law that are written in this book, fearing this glorious and awesome name, the LORD your God, [59]then the LORD will overwhelm both you and your offspring with severe and lasting afflictions and grievous and lasting maladies. [60]He will bring back upon you all the diseases of Egypt, of which you were in dread, and they shall cling to you. [61]Every other malady and affliction, even though not recorded in the book of this law, the LORD will inflict on you until you are destroyed. [62]Although once you were as numerous as the stars in heaven, you shall be left few in number, because you did not obey the LORD your God. [63]And just as the LORD took delight in making you prosperous and numerous, so the LORD will take delight in bringing you to ruin and destruction; you shall be plucked off the land that you are entering to possess. [64]The LORD will scatter you among all peoples, from one end of the earth to the other; and there you shall serve other gods, of wood and stone, which neither you nor your ancestors have known. [65]Among those nations you shall find no ease, no resting place for the sole of your foot. There the LORD will give you a trembling heart, failing eyes, and a languishing spirit. [66]Your life shall hang in doubt before you; night and day you shall be in dread, with no assurance of your life. [67]In the morning you shall say, "If only it were evening!" and at evening you shall say, "If only it were morning!"—because of the dread that your heart shall feel and the sights that your eyes shall see. [68]The LORD will bring you back in ships to Egypt, by a route that I promised you would never see again; and there you shall offer yourselves for sale to your enemies as male and female slaves, but there will be no buyer.

29 [a] These are the words of the covenant that the LORD commanded Moses to make with the Israelites in the land of Moab, in addition to the covenant that he had made with them at Horeb.

---

a Ch 28.69 in Heb

---

a weapon against Israel is conventional (cf. Jer 5.14–17; 6.22–26; Joel 1.6; 2.3–11; Hab 1.6–11). *Grim-faced*, imperious, brazen (cf. Prov 7.13; 21.29; Eccl 8.1; Dan 8.23). **28.51** Cf. 7.13; 28.4, 18, 33. **28.52** Broad assault, as practiced by Assyrian and Babylonian armies. See 2 Kings 18.13; Jer 34.7. **28.53–57** Cannibalistic themes epitomize *the desperate straits* of people under prolonged *siege* in Assyrian sources (e.g., Vassal Treaties of Esarhaddon 448–50) as well as biblical texts (e.g., Lev 26.29; 2 Kings 6.28–29; Jer 19.9; Lam 2.20; 4.10). **28.58** *All the words . . . this book,* the whole Deuteronomic polity, recorded and textually transmitted (cf. 17.18–19; 29.20–21, 27; 30.10; 31.9, 24–26). *Fearing this . . . name* means fidelity to the covenantal oath, sworn in acknowledgment of *the* LORD (Yahweh) as Israel's sole divine sovereign (see 5.6; 6.4, 13; 29.12–13; cf. Ex 6.2–3, 7; Josh 24.14–24). **28.59–61** Cf. 7.15; 28.21–22, 27. **28.62** Reversal of proliferation. Cf. 1.10; 10.22; 26.5. **28.63–67** Dispersion. Cf. 4.26–28; 29.28; Lev 26.33–39. **28.68** Displacement to *Egypt.* Cf. Jer 42–44; also Isa 30.1–5; Hos 8.13; 9.3, 6; 11.5. The sense of *in ships . . . never see again* is obscure (cf. 17.16).

29.1 The book's third editorial heading (cf. 1.1–5; 4.44–49) introduces the concluding portion of Moses' valedictory address and apparently also the supple-

The Covenant Renewed in Moab

2[a] Moses summoned all Israel and said to them: You have seen all that the LORD did before your eyes in the land of Egypt, to Pharaoh and to all his servants and to all his land, [3]the great trials that your eyes saw, the signs, and those great wonders. [4]But to this day the LORD has not given you a mind to understand, or eyes to see, or ears to hear. [5]I have led you forty years in the wilderness. The clothes on your back have not worn out, and the sandals on your feet have not worn out; [6]you have not eaten bread, and you have not drunk wine or strong drink—so that you may know that I am the LORD your God. [7]When you came to this place, King Sihon of Heshbon and King Og of Bashan came out against us for battle, but we defeated them. [8]We took their land and gave it as an inheritance to the Reubenites, the Gadites, and the half-tribe of Manasseh. [9]Therefore diligently observe the words of this covenant, in order that you may succeed[b] in everything that you do.

10 You stand assembled today, all of you, before the LORD your God—the leaders of your tribes,[c] your elders, and your officials, all the men of Israel, [11]your children, your women, and the aliens who are in your camp, both those who cut your wood and those who draw your water— [12]to enter into the covenant of the LORD your God, sworn by an oath, which the LORD your God is making with you today; [13]in order that he may establish you today as his people, and that he may be your God, as he promised you and as he swore to your ancestors, to Abraham, to Isaac, and to Jacob. [14]I am making this covenant, sworn by an oath, not only with you who stand here with us today before the LORD our God, [15]but also with those who are not here with us today. [16]You know how we lived in the land of Egypt, and how we came through the midst of the nations through which you passed. [17]You have seen their detestable things, the filthy idols of wood and stone, of silver and gold, that were among them. [18]It may be that there is among you a man or woman, or a family or tribe, whose heart is already turning away from the LORD our God to serve the gods of those nations. It may be that there is among you a root sprouting poisonous and bitter growth. [19]All who hear the words of this oath and bless themselves, thinking in their hearts, "We are safe even though we go our own stubborn ways" (thus bringing disaster on moist and dry alike)[d]— [20]the LORD will be unwilling to pardon them, for the LORD's anger and passion will smoke against them. All the curses written in this book will descend on them, and the LORD will blot out their names from under heaven. [21]The LORD will single them out from all the tribes of Israel for calamity, in accordance with all the curses of the covenant written in this book of the law. [22]The next generation, your children who rise up after you, as well as the foreigner who comes from a distant country, will see the devastation of that land and

a Ch 29.1 in Heb   b Or deal wisely   c Gk Syr: Heb your leaders, your tribes   d Meaning of Heb uncertain

mental depositions that follow in chs. 31–32. These varied contents, designated covenantal words or "provisions," respond to the crisis of continuity posed by Moses' imminent demise. For the setting in Moab, see 3.29; 4.46. For the covenant initiated at Horeb, see 4.10–13; 5.1–3 (cf. 1.2). **29.2–30.20** Principal features of a covenant rite are profiled in this hortatory epilogue to Moses' promulgation of the law. **29.2–9** The retrospect encompasses the era from the exodus through the conquests in the Transjordan (cf. 4.37–38; 6.21–23; 26.5–10). **29.3** Great trials, the plagues (cf. 4.34; 7.19). **29.4** Mind to understand (lit. "heart to know"), the personal capacity to discern providence (cf. Isa 6.9–10; Jer 5.21; 24.7; Ezek 12.2–3). **29.5–6** Cf. 8.2–5. On the apparent shift from Mosaic to divine speech, see note on 7.4. **29.7–8** Sihon and Og. See 1.4; 2.26–3.22. **29.9** Succeed, or "prosper," contingent upon obedience; cf. Josh 1.7–8; 1 Kings 2.3. **29.10–29** Emphasized here is individual accountability as well as the social and multigenerational inclusiveness of Israel's covenant community. **29.10–11** See note on 5.22. Cf. 31.12; Josh 8.33, 35; 9.27; 23.2; 2 Kings 23.2–3. **29.12–15** Covenant . . . sworn by an oath (or "imprecation"). See Gen 26.28–29; cf. Ezek 17.13–21. Here with us and not here with us mean the current and the future generations of Israel; cf. 5.3. **29.16–17** Detestable things (or "abominations"), filthy idols. See, e.g., Lev 26.30; 1 Kings 11.5–7; 21.26; 2 Kings 23.13, 24; Ezek 6.4–6; 20.7–8. **29.18–21** On the threat of secret apostasy, see 13.6–11; 27.15. **29.18** Poisonous and bitter growth. See, e.g., Jer 9.15; 23.15; Hos 10.4; Am 6.12. **29.19** Our own stubborn ways, individual willfulness (cf. 12.8), lit. "the stubbornness of my own heart" (see Ps 81.11–13; Jer 3.17; 7.24). Obstinate idiosyncrasy may threaten the survival of the whole community. Moist and dry alike, apparently an agricultural metaphor (cf. Ps 107.4–9, 33–37; Isa 58.11). **29.20** Divine anger and passion. See v. 27; 4.24; 32.19–22. Blot out their names. See 9.14;

the afflictions with which the LORD has afflicted it— 23 all its soil burned out by sulfur and salt, nothing planted, nothing sprouting, unable to support any vegetation, like the destruction of Sodom and Gomorrah, Admah and Zeboiim, which the LORD destroyed in his fierce anger— 24 they and indeed all the nations will wonder, "Why has the LORD done thus to this land? What caused this great display of anger?" 25 They will conclude, "It is because they abandoned the covenant of the LORD, the God of their ancestors, which he made with them when he brought them out of the land of Egypt. 26 They turned and served other gods, worshiping them, gods whom they had not known and whom he had not allotted to them; 27 so the anger of the LORD was kindled against that land, bringing on it every curse written in this book. 28 The LORD uprooted them from their land in anger, fury, and great wrath, and cast them into another land, as is now the case." 29 The secret things belong to the LORD our God, but the revealed things belong to us and to our children forever, to observe all the words of this law.

God's Fidelity Assured

30 When all these things have happened to you, the blessings and the curses that I have set before you, if you call them to mind among all the nations where the LORD your God has driven you, 2 and return to the LORD your God, and you and your children obey him with all your heart and with all your soul, just as I am commanding you today,

3 then the LORD your God will restore your fortunes and have compassion on you, gathering you again from all the peoples among whom the LORD your God has scattered you. 4 Even if you are exiled to the ends of the world,*a* from there the LORD your God will gather you, and from there he will bring you back. 5 The LORD your God will bring you into the land that your ancestors possessed, and you will possess it; he will make you more prosperous and numerous than your ancestors.

6 Moreover, the LORD your God will circumcise your heart and the heart of your descendants, so that you will love the LORD your God with all your heart and with all your soul, in order that you may live. 7 The LORD your God will put all these curses on your enemies and on the adversaries who took advantage of you. 8 Then you shall again obey the LORD, observing all his commandments that I am commanding you today, 9 and the LORD your God will make you abundantly prosperous in all your undertakings, in the fruit of your body, in the fruit of your livestock, and in the fruit of your soil. For the LORD will again take delight in prospering you, just as he delighted in prospering your ancestors, 10 when you obey the LORD your God by observing his commandments and decrees that are written in this book of the law, because you turn to the LORD your God with all your heart and with all your soul.

a Heb *of heaven*

25.19. **29.22–28** Purview shifts to the aftermath of national disaster (cf. 4.25–28). **29.23** *Sodom and Gomorrah, Admah and Zeboiim,* infamous cities of the Jordan plain. See, e.g., Gen 10.19; 19.24–25; Isa 1.9–10; Jer 49.18; Hos 11.8. **29.24–28** See the interrogation schema in 1 Kings 9.8–9; Jer 5.19; 9.12–16; 16.10–13; 22.8–9. **29.26** *Other gods . . . not allotted to them.* See 4.19; 32.8–9. **29.27–28** See vv. 20–21; Jer 21.5; 32.37. **29.29** The maxim apparently affirms that faithful observance of the law received through Moses (*revealed things*) is sufficient to assure Israel's continuance in covenant relationship with God. See 4.2; cf. 6.25; 30.11–14.

30.1–10 The witness of 4.29–31 to the future of the covenant beyond the devastation of a curse is now developed as a promise of restoration for those in exile who penitently renew their commitment to the Lord (cf. Lev 26.40–45). **30.1** *Call them to mind,* lit. "return [them] to your heart." Continuing reflection on experience yields theological insight; see 4.39 (cf. 1 Kings

8.47; Isa 46.8; Lam 3.21). **30.2** *Return . . . with all your heart and . . . soul.* See v. 10; also 4.29–30; 1 Kings 8.48; 2 Kings 23.25; Jer 3.10; 24.7. **30.3** *Restore your fortunes.* See, e.g., Jer 29.14; 33.26; Ezek 39.25; Am 9.14; Zeph 3.20. **30.4** Neh 1.8–9 cites this promise of ingathering, together with the threat of 28.64. For the theme in prophetic sources, see, e.g., Isa 43.5–7; Jer 31.10; 32.37; Ezek 36.24; 37.21. **30.5** Repatriation. See 28.62–63; Jer 23.3; 30.3. **30.6** Divine initiative to overcome human recalcitrance and spiritual fatuity (*circumcise your heart;* cf. 10.16) accords with the "new covenant" emphases of Jer 31.31–34; 32.37–41; Ezek 11.19–20; 36.26–28 (cf. Ps 51.10). *Love the LORD.* See note on 6.4–5. **30.7** Retribution against arrogant *enemies.* See 7.15; 32.34–35; Ps 137.7–9; Lam 4.21–22. Cf. also Isa 10.5–19; 33.1; Ezek 35; Ob 8–16. **30.9** Cf. 28.4, 11–12, 18. **30.10** *This book of the law,* the scroll of Mosaic *torah* (cf. 29.20–21; 31.9, 24–26). *Turn . . . heart and . . . soul* echoes v. 2. **30.11–14** What the Lord requires of Israel is both perspicuous and practicable (cf. 4.5–8;

Exhortation to Choose Life

11 Surely, this commandment that I am commanding you today is not too hard for you, nor is it too far away. [12]It is not in heaven, that you should say, "Who will go up to heaven for us, and get it for us so that we may hear it and observe it?" [13]Neither is it beyond the sea, that you should say, "Who will cross to the other side of the sea for us, and get it for us so that we may hear it and observe it?" [14]No, the word is very near to you; it is in your mouth and in your heart for you to observe.

15 See, I have set before you today life and prosperity, death and adversity. [16]If you obey the commandments of the LORD your God[a] that I am commanding you today, by loving the LORD your God, walking in his ways, and observing his commandments, decrees, and ordinances, then you shall live and become numerous, and the LORD your God will bless you in the land that you are entering to possess. [17]But if your heart turns away and you do not hear, but are led astray to bow down to other gods and serve them, [18]I declare to you today that you shall perish; you shall not live long in the land that you are crossing the Jordan to enter and possess. [19]I call heaven and earth to witness against you today that I have set before you life and death, blessings and curses. Choose life so that you and your descendants may live, [20]loving the LORD your God, obeying him, and holding fast to him; for that means life to you and length of days, so that you may live in the land that the LORD swore to give to your ancestors, to Abraham, to Isaac, and to Jacob.

Joshua Becomes Moses' Successor

31 When Moses had finished speaking all[b] these words to all Israel, [2]he said to them: "I am now one hundred twenty years old. I am no longer able to get about, and the LORD has told me, 'You shall not cross over this Jordan.' [3]The LORD your God himself will cross over before you. He will destroy these nations before you, and you shall dispossess them. Joshua also will cross over before you, as the LORD promised. [4]The LORD will do to them as he did to Sihon and Og, the kings of the Amorites, and to their land, when he destroyed them. [5]The LORD will give them over to you and you shall deal with them in full accord with the command that I have given to you. [6]Be strong and bold; have no fear or dread of them, because it is the LORD your God who goes with you; he will not fail you or forsake you."

7 Then Moses summoned Joshua and said to him in the sight of all Israel: "Be strong and bold, for you are the one who will go with this people into the land that the LORD has sworn to their ancestors to give them; and you will put them in possession of it. [8]It is the LORD who goes before you. He will be with you; he will not fail you or forsake you. Do not fear or be dismayed."

The Law to Be Read Every Seventh Year

9 Then Moses wrote down this law, and gave it to the priests, the sons of Levi, who carried the

---

a Gk: Heb lacks *If you obey the commandments of the LORD your God* b Q Ms Gk: MT *Moses went and spoke*

10.12–13). **30.11** *This commandment,* the basic protocol of covenantal fidelity, elaborated by Moses (cf. 5.31–6.2; 11.22; 19.9). *Not too hard,* neither infeasible nor esoteric (cf. Ps 139.6). **30.12–13** See the quest after cosmic "wisdom" portrayed in Bar 3.29–31 (cf. Job 28.12–28; Prov 30.4). **30.14** Internalization of the *word.* See 6.6–7; 11.18–19; cf. Jer 1.9. **30.15–20** A climactic appeal for allegiance resounds with familiar expressions. **30.15** The options posed for Israel's decision are "blessing" (*life and prosperity*) and "curse" (*death and adversity*); see 11.26–28 (cf. Jer 21.8; Prov 11.19; 14.27). **30.16** See 4.1; 8.1; 11.22; cf. Lev 18.4–5. **30.17–18** See 4.19, 25–26; 8.19–20. **30.19** *Heaven and earth* as witnesses. See 4.26; 31.28; cf. 32.1; Ps 50.4; Isa 1.2. **30.20** See 1.8; 4.1, 40; 10.20; 11.22.

31.1–32.52 With Moses' death again in immediate view (cf. 3.23–28; 4.21–22), the narrative conjoins the provisions for transition in leadership and preservation of the Mosaic legacy of covenantal lore. **31.1–**

8 Parallel charges reassure the Israelite militia and Joshua of the Lord's own presence as vanguard in the impending conquest west of the Jordan. **31.1** In context, *all these words* should mean the several preceding portions of Moses' valedictory address (see 1.1). **31.2** Moses' age of *one hundred twenty years* spans three normal forty-year generations (cf. 34.7; Ex 7.7; Acts 7.23, 30); according to Gen 6.3 this is the maximum lifetime allowed to any human being (cf. Job 42.16). *To get about,* lit. "to go out and to come in," refers to active leadership, especially exercise of military command (cf. 28.6, 19; Num 27.17, 21; Josh 14.11; 1 Sam 18.16). *You shall not cross.* See 3.27; cf. 1.37; 4.21–22. **31.3–5** On the vanguard and conquest themes, see 1.29–33; 3.21–22, 28; 7.1–5; 9.1–3; 20.16–18. **31.6–8** For the formulaic exhortations to steadfastness and valor, see, e.g., 1.21, 29; Josh 1.6–9; 10.25 (cf. Pss 27.14; 31.24; Isa 7.4). **31.8** *He will be with you.* Reassurance invokes the Lord's accompanying pres-

ark of the covenant of the LORD, and to all the elders of Israel. [10]Moses commanded them: "Every seventh year, in the scheduled year of remission, during the festival of booths,[a] [11]when all Israel comes to appear before the LORD your God at the place that he will choose, you shall read this law before all Israel in their hearing. [12]Assemble the people—men, women, and children, as well as the aliens residing in your towns—so that they may hear and learn to fear the LORD your God and to observe diligently all the words of this law, [13]and so that their children, who have not known it, may hear and learn to fear the LORD your God, as long as you live in the land that you are crossing over the Jordan to possess."

Moses and Joshua Receive God's Charge

14 The LORD said to Moses, "Your time to die is near; call Joshua and present yourselves in the tent of meeting, so that I may commission him." So Moses and Joshua went and presented themselves in the tent of meeting, [15]and the LORD appeared at the tent in a pillar of cloud; the pillar of cloud stood at the entrance to the tent.

16 The LORD said to Moses, "Soon you will lie down with your ancestors. Then this people will begin to prostitute themselves to the foreign gods in their midst, the gods of the land into which they are going; they will forsake me, breaking my covenant that I have made with them. [17]My anger will be kindled against them in that day. I will forsake them and hide my face

from them; they will become easy prey, and many terrible troubles will come upon them. In that day they will say, 'Have not these troubles come upon us because our God is not in our midst?' [18]On that day I will surely hide my face on account of all the evil they have done by turning to other gods. [19]Now therefore write this song, and teach it to the Israelites; put it in their mouths, in order that this song may be a witness for me against the Israelites. [20]For when I have brought them into the land flowing with milk and honey, which I promised on oath to their ancestors, and they have eaten their fill and grown fat, they will turn to other gods and serve them, despising me and breaking my covenant. [21]And when many terrible troubles come upon them, this song will confront them as a witness, because it will not be lost from the mouths of their descendants. For I know what they are inclined to do even now, before I have brought them into the land that I promised them on oath." [22]That very day Moses wrote this song and taught it to the Israelites.

23 Then the LORD commissioned Joshua son of Nun and said, "Be strong and bold, for you shall bring the Israelites into the land that I promised them; I will be with you."

24 When Moses had finished writing down in a book the words of this law to the very end, [25]Moses commanded the Levites who carried the ark of the covenant of the LORD, saying, [26]"Take this book of the law and put it beside

---

a Or *tabernacles*; Heb *succoth*

---

ence (cf. v. 23; Ex 3.12; Josh 1.5, 17; 3.7; 2 Sam 7.9; cf. Ex 33.12–16). **31.9–13** Disposition and periodic proclamation of the written Mosaic *torah;* see also vv. 24–27. **31.9** *This law,* the Deuteronomic polity (see 4.44). *Priests, the sons of Levi.* See 21.5 (cf. 10.8–9; 17.18). *Ark of the covenant.* Cf. 10.1–5, 8; Josh 8.33. *All the elders of Israel.* Cf. note on 27.1. **31.10–11** *Year of remission.* See 15.1–11. *Festival of booths.* See 16.13–15. *The place that he will choose.* See 12.5. On public reading of the polity in the liturgical setting of covenant renewal, see 2 Kings 23.2; Neh 8; cf. *Mishnah Sota* 7.8. **31.12–13** Inclusive assembly. See 29.10–15; cf. also 4.9–14; 5.29–6.2. **31.14–23** A brief account of Joshua's installation to succeed Moses as war leader (vv. 14–15, 23) frames a divine charge introducing the Song of Moses as an oracular witness against Israel (vv. 16–22; see also 31.28–32.44). **31.14** *Your time to die is near.* See Gen 47.29; 1 Kings 2.1. *Tent of meeting.* See Ex 25.22; 29.42–45; 33.7–11; Num 11.16–25. **31.15** On *the pillar of cloud* manifesting divine presence at the tent, see Ex 33.9–10; Num 12.5. **31.16** *Lie*

down with your ancestors. See, e.g., Gen 47.30; 2 Sam 7.12; 1 Kings 2.10; 11.43. Prostitution is frequently used as a metaphor for apostasy, e.g., Ex 34.15–16; Judg 8.27, 33; Hos 4.12; 9.1. Though identified here with *the gods of the land* (Canaan), *foreign gods* most often refers to cultic imports or innovations that compromise Israel's allegiance to the Lord alone (cf. 32.12, 16–17; Gen 35.2–4; Josh 24.2, 14, 20–23; Judg 5.8; 10.6 –16; 1 Kings 11.1–10; 2 Kings 17.29–41). *Breaking my covenant* (also v. 20). See Jer 11.9–10. **31.17–18** Anticipation of 32.19–22. *God is not in our midst.* See 1.42; cf. Ex 17.7; Num 14.14, 42; Jer 14.9. **31.19–22** The written text of the *song* has a mnemonic function (cf. 6.6–9; Ex 17.14) while also documenting divine prescience of Israel's dire fate (cf. Jer 36). **31.20** *Despising me,* neglect or renunciation of the Lord's sovereignty (see Num 14.11, 23; 2 Sam 12.14; Ps 10.3, 13; Isa 1.4). **31.23** See vv. 7–8; cf. Num 27.15–23 (in the Priestly tradition; see Introduction to Genesis). **31.24–29** Preceding themes of the written law (vv. 9–13) and of the Song of Moses as witness (vv. 16–22)

the ark of the covenant of the LORD your God; let it remain there as a witness against you. ²⁷For I know well how rebellious and stubborn you are. If you already have been so rebellious toward the LORD while I am still alive among you, how much more after my death! ²⁸Assemble to me all the elders of your tribes and your officials, so that I may recite these words in their hearing and call heaven and earth to witness against them. ²⁹For I know that after my death you will surely act corruptly, turning aside from the way that I have commanded you. In time to come trouble will befall you, because you will do what is evil in the sight of the LORD, provoking him to anger through the work of your hands."

The Song of Moses

30 Then Moses recited the words of this song, to the very end, in the hearing of the whole assembly of Israel:

32 Give ear, O heavens, and I will speak;
     let the earth hear the words of my
        mouth.
2   May my teaching drop like the rain,
     my speech condense like the dew;
     like gentle rain on grass,
     like showers on new growth.
3   For I will proclaim the name of the LORD;
     ascribe greatness to our God!

4   The Rock, his work is perfect,
     and all his ways are just.
   A faithful God, without deceit,
     just and upright is he;
5   yet his degenerate children have dealt
        falsely with him,ᵃ
     a perverse and crooked generation.
6   Do you thus repay the LORD,
     O foolish and senseless people?
   Is not he your father, who created you,
     who made you and established you?
7   Remember the days of old,
     consider the years long past;
   ask your father, and he will inform you;
     your elders, and they will tell you.
8   When the Most Highᵇ apportioned the
        nations,
     when he divided humankind,
   he fixed the boundaries of the peoples
     according to the number of the gods;ᶜ
9   the LORD's own portion was his people,
     Jacob his allotted share.

10   He sustainedᵈ him in a desert land,
     in a howling wilderness waste;
   he shielded him, cared for him,
     guarded him as the apple of his eye.

a Meaning of Heb uncertain   *b* Traditional rendering of Heb *Elyon*   *c* Q Ms Compare Gk Tg: MT *the Israelites*   *d* Sam Gk Compare Tg: MT *found*

---

are here resumed and conflated; see also 32.44–47. **31.26** The scroll (*this book of the law;* cf. 29.20–21; 30.10) is to be preserved *beside the ark,* i.e., as an authoritative and accessible complement to the tablets of the Decalogue deposited within (cf. 4.13–14; 10.1–5; Ex 40.20; 1 Kings 8.9). **31.27** *Rebellious and stubborn.* See 9.6–7, 23–24; cf. 1.26, 43; Ex 33.3–5; 34.9. **31.28** Tribal *elders* and *officials.* Cf. 1.15; 16.18; Num 11.16. *Heaven and earth* as witnesses. See note on 30.19. **31.29** Future idolatry. See 4.25–28; cf. 11.28; 30.17–18. *Work of your hands.* See, e.g., 2 Kings 22.17; Ps 115.4; Isa 2.8; Jer 44.8; Hos 14.3.
     31.30–32.47 The valedictory *song* ascribed to Moses is an eloquent poetic homily on the vicissitudes of the filial relationship between the Lord and Jacob (Israel). Although origin and date of composition are disputed, forensic themes and the vivid imagery of divine pathos associate the work closely with traditions of classical Israelite prophecy. See esp. Isa 30.1–18; Jer 2–3; Ezek 20.1–44; Hos 13–14; Mic 6.1–5; cf. also Pss 50; 78. **31.30** On Israel's plenary *assembly,* see note on 5.22. **32.1–3** The introductory idiom is both didactic and hymnic. **32.1** On the appeal for *heavens* and *earth* to attend the poet's discourse, see Isa 1.2. Cf. also 4.26; 30.19; 31.28. **32.2** *Teaching,* or "lore." See, e.g., Isa 29.24; Job 11.4; Prov 1.5; 4.2. **32.3** Proclamation of the

name of the LORD here means public defense of divine providence and honor (cf., e.g., Josh 7.7–9; Ps 96.8; Jer 14.21; 32.20). **32.4–18** Poignant contrast between God's superlative character and the waywardness of God's people (vv. 4–5) is developed through narrative retrospect into an indictment of the poet's audience (*you,* vv. 6–7, 15, 18). **32.4** The Lord's stalwart integrity and trustworthiness are underscored by the epithets *Rock* (also vv. 15, 18, 30–31; elsewhere, e.g., 2 Sam 22.3; Ps 18.2, 31, 46; Isa 17.10; 44.8; Hab 1.12) and *faithful God* (see 7.9; Pss 33.4; 89.1–2; Isa 25.1; Hos 2.20). *Just and upright.* See Ps 119.137. **32.5** *Children.* See 14.1. *Dealt falsely* (acted corruptly in 9.12). Cf. Isa 1.2–4; Hos 9.9; Mal 2.8. **32.6** Accusation stresses the Lord's paternal claim on Israel. *Your father, who created you.* Cf. Ex 4.21–23; Jer 31.8–9; Hos 11.1–3. See note on Ex 15.16. **32.7** On the appeal for remembrance of primal events (*days of old,* Isa 51.9–10; 63.11; Mic 7.14–15), see 4.32–34; Job 8.8–10; Isa 46.8–11; 63.11. **32.8** *Most High* (Hebrew *'Elyon*) is an appellation generally expressing the Lord's universal sovereignty (e.g., Gen 14.18–22; Num 24.16; Pss 47.2; 78.35; 83.18); here and occasionally elsewhere (Isa 14.14; Ps 82.6) it denotes the executive of the divine assembly, comprising subordinate *gods* (lit., "sons of God," as in Job 1.6; 2.1; Pss 29.1; 89.5–7). **32.9** *Own*

11 As an eagle stirs up its nest,
     and hovers over its young;
   as it spreads its wings, takes them up,
     and bears them aloft on its pinions,
12 the LORD alone guided him;
     no foreign god was with him.
13 He set him atop the heights of the land,
     and fed him with*a* produce of the field;
   he nursed him with honey from the
        crags,
     with oil from flinty rock;
14 curds from the herd, and milk from the
        flock,
     with fat of lambs and rams;
   Bashan bulls and goats,
     together with the choicest wheat—
   you drank fine wine from the blood of
        grapes.
15 Jacob ate his fill;*b*
   Jeshurun grew fat, and kicked.
   You grew fat, bloated, and gorged!
   He abandoned God who made him,
     and scoffed at the Rock of his
        salvation.
16 They made him jealous with strange gods,
     with abhorrent things they provoked
        him.
17 They sacrificed to demons, not God,
     to deities they had never known,
   to new ones recently arrived,
     whom your ancestors had not feared.
18 You were unmindful of the Rock that
        bore you;*c*

you forgot the God who gave you
     birth.
19 The LORD saw it, and was jealous;*d*
     he spurned*e* his sons and daughters.
20 He said: I will hide my face from them,
     I will see what their end will be;
   for they are a perverse generation,
     children in whom there is no
        faithfulness.
21 They made me jealous with what is no
        god,
     provoked me with their idols.
   So I will make them jealous with what is
        no people,
     provoke them with a foolish nation.
22 For a fire is kindled by my anger,
     and burns to the depths of Sheol;
   it devours the earth and its increase,
     and sets on fire the foundations of the
        mountains.
23 I will heap disasters upon them,
     spend my arrows against them:
24 wasting hunger,
     burning consumption,
     bitter pestilence.
   The teeth of beasts I will send against
        them,
     with venom of things crawling in the
        dust.

---

a Sam Gk Syr Tg: MT *he ate*   *b* Q Mss Sam Gk: MT lacks *Jacob ate his fill*   *c* Or *that begot you*   *d* Q Mss Gk: MT lacks *was jealous*   *e* Cn: Heb *he spurned because of provocation*

---

portion. Cf. 7.6; Jer 10.16; Zech 2.12; Sir 17.17. **32.10–12** For the themes in this portrait of divine providence during the exodus-wilderness era, see esp. Jer 2.2–3, 6; Hos 2.14–15; 9.10; 13.4–6 (cf. also Deut 1.31; 2.7; Ex 15.13; 19.4; Isa 43.10–21). **32.10** *Apple of his eye*. Cf. Ps 17.8; Prov 7.2. **32.11** See Ex 19.4. **32.12** *Foreign god*. See note on 31.16. **32.13** *Heights of the land* (cf. Isa 58.14; Am 4.13; Mic 1.3) refers here to the highlands of Canaan (see 1.7; cf. Ex 15.17). *Honey from the crags*. See Ps 81.16. **32.14** *Bashan*. See note on 3.1. **32.15** Cf. 8.12–17; 31.20; Neh 9.25. The appellations *Jacob* and *Jeshurun* are also paralleled in Isa 44.2; the latter designation (rendered "beloved one, darling" in the Septuagint) is otherwise attested only in Deut 33.5, 26. **32.16** *Strange gods*. See Pss 44.20; 81.9; Isa 43.12; see also note on 31.16. **32.17** *Demons* are associated with abhorrent Canaanite rites in Ps 106.34–39. *New ones*. Cf. Judg 5.8. **32.18** For the imagery of divine maternity, complementing vv. 6–7, see Isa 49.15. **32.19–42** A divine soliloquy contemplating appropriate punishment of Israel's apostasy (vv. 20–27, 34–35), alternates with the narrator's voice (vv. 19, 28–33,

36). **32.19–21** The judgment announced is retaliatory, corresponding to the form of the crime (see note on 19.19–21 on talion). On jealousy as a divine attribute, see 4.24. **32.20** *Hide my face*, withdrawal of divine favor and protective presence, i.e., the converse of Num 6.25–26; see 31.17–18 (cf., e.g., Ps 13.1; Isa 8.17; Jer 33.5; Ezek 39.23–24). **32.21** *No god* is a categorical negation of the anonymous deities referred to in vv. 16–17. So too the anonymous adversary selected as the Lord's instrument of revenge (*no people, foolish nation*) may be intentionally generic; cf. 28.49–50 (cf. Judg 2.14–15; Ps 79.1–7; Isa 9.11–12). **32.22–25** The onslaught of the Lord's wrath is graphically plotted. **32.22** On *fire* as a weapon of divine warfare, see, e.g., Job 31.12; Ps 50.3; Am 1.4; cf. Deut 4.24. For portrayal of the catastrophic cosmic effects (consuming the *depths of Sheol*, i.e., the netherworld as well as the earth's surface and *foundations of the mountains*), see esp. Ps 18.7–8; Am 7.4. **32.23–24** Pestilential *arrows* in the Lord's arsenal (cf. also v. 42; Job 6.4; Pss 7.12–13; 18.14; Lam 3.12–13; Ezek 5.16; Hab 3.9) approximate covenantal curses (cf. Deut 28.21–22; Ps 78.49).

25 In the street the sword shall bereave,
    and in the chambers terror,
  for young man and woman alike,
    nursing child and old gray head.
26 I thought to scatter them[a]
    and blot out the memory of them from
      humankind;
27 but I feared provocation by the enemy,
    for their adversaries might
      misunderstand
  and say, "Our hand is triumphant;
    it was not the LORD who did all this."

28 They are a nation void of sense;
    there is no understanding in them.
29 If they were wise, they would understand
      this;
    they would discern what the end
      would be.
30 How could one have routed a
      thousand,
    and two put a myriad to flight,
  unless their Rock had sold them,
    the LORD had given them up?
31 Indeed their rock is not like our Rock;
    our enemies are fools.[a]
32 Their vine comes from the vinestock of
      Sodom,
    from the vineyards of Gomorrah;
  their grapes are grapes of poison,
    their clusters are bitter;
33 their wine is the poison of serpents,
    the cruel venom of asps.

34 Is not this laid up in store with me,
    sealed up in my treasuries?
35 Vengeance is mine, and recompense,
    for the time when their foot shall slip;
  because the day of their calamity is at
      hand,
    their doom comes swiftly.

36 Indeed the LORD will vindicate his
      people,
    have compassion on his servants,
  when he sees that their power is gone,
    neither bond nor free remaining.
37 Then he will say: Where are their gods,
    the rock in which they took refuge,
38 who ate the fat of their sacrifices,
    and drank the wine of their libations?
  Let them rise up and help you,
    let them be your protection!

39 See now that I, even I, am he;
    there is no god besides me.
  I kill and I make alive;
    I wound and I heal;
    and no one can deliver from my hand.
40 For I lift up my hand to heaven,
    and swear: As I live forever,
41 when I whet my flashing sword,
    and my hand takes hold on judgment;
  I will take vengeance on my adversaries,
    and will repay those who hate me.

---

a Gk: Meaning of Heb uncertain

32.25 Cf. Jer 6.11; 9.20–22; Lam 1.20; 2.21; Ezek 7.15. **32.26–27** Divine wrath is restrained, short of Israel's extinction, to thwart the foe's triumphalism. **32.26** *Blot out the memory.* Cf. 25.19. *Provocation,* vainglory (cf. Isa 10.5–15). On the implied threat to the Lord's reputation, cf., e.g., 9.26–29; Ex 32.11–14; Ps 74.18; Isa 48.9–11. **32.28–33** Descanting on the Lord's deliberations, the poet or prophetic narrator here reproaches the arrogance and brutish character of the enemy. **32.28** *Void of sense,* or "lacking counsel"; cf. Isa 10.13 (boast of Assyria's king) and the ironical interrogation of Edom in Jer 49.7. **32.32** *Sodom* and *Gomorrah.* See note on 29.23. **32.34–35** The agent of chastisement will not itself escape judgment; cf. Isa 10.15–16 (Assyria); Jer 49.12–22 (Edom). See note on 30.7. **32.34** *This,* the foe's transgression, which awaits divine requital (cf. Job 14.17; Hos 13.12). **32.35** *Vengeance,* retribution, vindication (cf., e.g., Judg 16.28; Ps 94.1–3; Isa 61.2). *Recompense,* equitable redress (Isa 59.18; cf. Hos 9.7). *Day of their calamity.* See, e.g., Job 21.30; Ps 18.18; Jer 18.17; Ob 12–13. **32.36–42** Promise of the Lord's intervention as judge and warrior to exact retributive justice. **32.36** Prophetic proclamation of divine intent. *Vindicate,* or "judge," refers to judicial review, here divine prosecution on Israel's behalf (cf., e.g., Gen 15.14; Pss 7.8; 9.8; Isa 3.13); note the parallel in Ps 135.14. The sense of *neither bond nor free* seems to be "(almost) no one" (cf. 1 Kings 14.10; 21.21; 2 Kings 9.8; 14.26). **32.37–38** Interrogation of Israel (cf. Isa 40.25–31) or its adversaries (cf. Isa 41.1–4) or both (cf. Isa 43.8–13; 44.6–8). On mockery of impotent *gods* and those who foolishly worship them, see Judg 10.10–14; 1 Kings 18.27; Isa 46.1–2; Jer 2.26–28. **32.39** The unanswered queries support the Lord's assertion of exclusive sovereignty, as often in the trial scenes of Second Isaiah (Isa 40.28–31; 41.4; 43.10–13; 44.6); cf. 4.32–40. *Kill and . . . make alive.* Cf. 1 Sam 2.6–8; Tob 13.2; Wis 16.13. *I wound and I heal.* See Job 5.18; Isa 30.26; Hos 6.1–2; cf. Ex 15.26. **32.40–42** Promissory oath of the Divine Warrior. *As I live forever.* Cf. Isa 49.18; Jer 22.24; Ezek 5.11; Zeph 2.9. For the themes and carnage depicted, see Isa 1.24; Jer 46.10; Nah 1.2. Portraits of the Lord's retribution against Edom are noteworthy: Isa 34.5–7; 63.1–6; Ezek 25.12–14.

42 I will make my arrows drunk with blood,
        and my sword shall devour flesh—
    with the blood of the slain and the
        captives,
    from the long-haired enemy.

43 Praise, O heavens,*a* his people,
        worship him, all you gods!*b*
    For he will avenge the blood of his
        children,*c*
        and take vengeance on his adversaries;
    he will repay those who hate him,*b*
        and cleanse the land for his people.*d*

44 Moses came and recited all the words of this song in the hearing of the people, he and Joshua*e* son of Nun. 45When Moses had finished reciting all these words to all Israel, 46he said to them: "Take to heart all the words that I am giving in witness against you today; give them as a command to your children, so that they may diligently observe all the words of this law. 47This is no trifling matter for you, but rather your very life; through it you may live long in the land that you are crossing over the Jordan to possess."

Moses' Death Foretold

48 On that very day the LORD addressed Moses as follows: 49"Ascend this mountain of the Abarim, Mount Nebo, which is in the land of Moab, across from Jericho, and view the land of Canaan, which I am giving to the Isra-

elites for a possession; 50you shall die there on the mountain that you ascend and shall be gathered to your kin, as your brother Aaron died on Mount Hor and was gathered to his kin; 51because both of you broke faith with me among the Israelites at the waters of Meribath-kadesh in the wilderness of Zin, by failing to maintain my holiness among the Israelites. 52Although you may view the land from a distance, you shall not enter it—the land that I am giving to the Israelites."

Moses' Final Blessing on Israel

33 This is the blessing with which Moses, the man of God, blessed the Israelites before his death. 2He said:

    The LORD came from Sinai,
        and dawned from Seir upon us;*f*
    he shone forth from Mount Paran.
    With him were myriads of holy ones;*g*
        at his right, a host of his own.*h*
3   Indeed, O favorite among*i* peoples,
        all his holy ones were in your charge;
    they marched at your heels,
        accepted direction from you.
4   Moses charged us with the law,

---

a Q Ms Gk: MT *nations*   *b* Q Ms Gk: MT lacks this line
c Q Ms Gk: MT *his servants*   *d* Q Ms Sam Gk Vg: MT *his land his people*   *e* Sam Gk Syr Vg: MT *Hoshea*   *f* Gk Syr Vg Compare Tg: Heb *upon them*   *g* Cn Compare Gk Sam Syr Vg: MT *He came from Ribeboth-kodesh,*   *h* Cn Compare Gk: meaning of Heb uncertain   *i* Or *O lover of the*

32.43 Concluding summons of the *heavens* to celebrate redemption of the Lord's people (cf. Isa 49.13) forms an *inclusio* (a repetition signaling the beginning and end of a unit) with the appeal of v. 1. Subordination of the *gods* echoes vv. 8, 37. *Cleanse,* or "purify," "expiate"; see 21.8.
    32.44–47 Principal strands of chs. 30–31 especially are woven together in this conclusion to the song and the Moab covenant. For the multiple, overlapping connotations of the leitmotif *word(s)*, cf. 29.1, 9, 19, 29; 30.1 (*things*), 14; 31.1, 12, 24, 28, 30. **32.44** *Joshua* (or *Hoshea;* see text note *e;* cf. Num 13.8, 16) is now in place as Moses' successor; see 31.14–15, 23. **32.47** A final admonition recalls the exhortations of 30.11–20 (cf. 4.26, 40; 6.1–2; Lev 18.5). *No trifling matter,* lit. "no empty word." *Through it,* lit. "by this word." **32.48–52** Transition to the pentateuchal account of Moses' death in ch. 34. With this resumptive paraphrase of Num 27.12–14 (Priestly tradition; see Introduction to Genesis), cf. 3.23–27. **32.49** *Nebo* is a northern promontory of the *Abarim* range, which flanks the eastern shore of the Dead Sea (cf. 3.17, 27; 34.1; Num 33.47–48). **32.50** *Gathered to your kin* (or "people"). See, e.g., Gen 25.8; 35.29; 49.29, 33. For Aaron's death

on Mount Hor, see the Priestly account in Num 20.22–29; 33.38–39; cf. 10.6. **32.51** *Broke faith.* Cf. Ex 17.1–7; Ps 106.32; Num 20.1–13 (Priestly tradition; see Introduction to Genesis). *Meribath-kadesh in the wilderness of Zin* is apparently identical with the oasis of Kadesh-barnea in northern Sinai (see note on 1.2; cf. Josh 15.1–3; Ezek 47.19; 48.28).
    33.1 The last of the book's four editorial headings (cf. 1.1–5; 4.44–49; 29.1) anticipates ch. 34 while specifically introducing Moses' oracular benedictions on the assembled tribes. (For the genre of patriarchal testamentary blessings, see Gen 27.27–29; 48.15–16; 49.1–28.) The prophetic appellation *the man of God* is also used of Moses in Josh 14.6; Ps 90 (heading). Cf., e.g., Judg 13.6, 8; 1 Sam 2.27; 9.6–9; 1 Kings 12.22; 13.1; 17.8. **33.2–29** The composition, which may ultimately derive from a liturgical celebration of the Israelite confederacy, perhaps during the era of Saulide rule (ca. 1000 BCE), is a collocation of tribal epigrams (vv. 6–25) set within the frame of a victory hymn (vv. 2–5, 26–29). **33.2–5** Hymnic poem. **33.2–3** The introit rehearses the Lord's epiphany, advancing into Canaan from *Sinai* (see note on 1.2) across the southeastern highlands of Edom (*Seir, Mount Paran*), ac-

as a possession for the assembly of
Jacob.

5 There arose a king in Jeshurun,
    when the leaders of the people
        assembled—
    the united tribes of Israel.

6 May Reuben live, and not die out,
    even though his numbers are few.

7 And this he said of Judah:
    O Lord, give heed to Judah,
        and bring him to his people;
    strengthen his hands for him,*a*
        and be a help against his adversaries.

8 And of Levi he said:
    Give to Levi*b* your Thummim,
        and your Urim to your loyal one,
    whom you tested at Massah,
        with whom you contended at the
           waters of Meribah;
9 who said of his father and mother,
    "I regard them not";
    he ignored his kin,
        and did not acknowledge his children.
    For they observed your word,
        and kept your covenant.
10 They teach Jacob your ordinances,

and Israel your law;
    they place incense before you,
        and whole burnt offerings on your altar.
11 Bless, O Lord, his substance,
        and accept the work of his hands;
    crush the loins of his adversaries,
        of those that hate him, so that they do
           not rise again.

12 Of Benjamin he said:
    The beloved of the Lord rests in safety—
    the High God*c* surrounds him all day
        long—
    the beloved*d* rests between his
        shoulders.

13 And of Joseph he said:
    Blessed by the Lord be his land,
        with the choice gifts of heaven above,
        and of the deep that lies beneath;
14 with the choice fruits of the sun,
        and the rich yield of the months;
15 with the finest produce of the ancient
        mountains,
        and the abundance of the everlasting
        hills;

a Cn: Heb *with his hands he contended*   *b* Q Ms Gk: MT lacks *Give to Levi*   *c* Heb *above him*   *d* Heb *he*

companied by a vast heavenly cohort and its mundane counterpart, Israel's tribal militia. Variations on this epic theme are attested also in Judg 5.4–5; Ps 68.7–8, 17; Hab 3.3–7; cf. Ex 15.13–18. *Dawned, shown forth* suggest a solar epiphany: cf. Pss 50.1–2; 80.1–2; 94.1; Job 37.15 (lightning). *Myriads of holy ones, host.* Cf. Num 10.36; 1 Kings 22.19; Pss 68.17; 89.7; Zech 14.5; cf. also Mt 26.53; Rev 5.11. **33.4–5** Though formed in response to divine initiative, the confederation of Israel (*assembly of Jacob* [cf. Neh 5.7]; *united tribes*) was formally constituted through Moses' promulgation of *law* (Hebrew *torah*; see 4.44). **33.5** *There arose a king* is perhaps a reference to the inauguration of monarchical governance under Saul (cf. 1 Sam 10.20–25; 11.14–15). The phrase could also be rendered "let there be a king" or "he became king"; the latter has traditionally been understood as a reference either to the Lord's (so, e.g., rsv; cf. Ex 15.18; Num 23.21; Judg 8.23; 1 Sam 8.7; Ps 29.10; Isa 33.17, 22) or to Moses' royal exaltation over tribal Israel (cf. Ex 14.31; 34.10; Num 12.7). *Jeshurun.* See note on 32.15. **33.6–25** Benedictory pronouncements about and petitions on behalf of the individual tribes. Among the traditional twelve tribes only Simeon is missing here. See, e.g., Gen 35.23–26; 49.5; Ex 1.2; cf. Josh 19.1–9. **33.6** Attrition of *Reuben* may be the outcome of warfare with its Transjordanian neighbors during the eleventh century BCE (cf. 3.12, 16; Judg 10.7–11.33; 1 Sam 10.27–11.11). **33.7** The petition on behalf of *Judah* perhaps alludes to Philistine hegemony in the central highlands of Canaan after the defeat of Saul (cf. 1 Sam 31). **33.8–11** This expansive encomium on *Levi* suggests the charter of a clerical guild; see 10.8–9; 18.1–8. *Thummim* and *Urim* are sacred lots (cf. Ex 28.30; Lev 8.8; 1 Sam 14.41–42). The *loyal one* is presumably Moses himself, *tested at Massah* and *Meribah*. See 6.16; 9.22; 32.51; Ex 17.1–7; Num 20.1–13 (cf. also 1 Sam 2.27–28; Pss 77.20; 99.6; Sir 45.1–5). **33.9** On the declaration *I regard them not,* undoing kinship bonds, see Ex 32.25–29; cf. also Lk 14.26. **33.10** *Teach,* or "interpret for" (cognate of the Hebrew noun *torah*). See 17.10–11; cf. Lev 10.10–11; 2 Kings 17.27–28; Jer 18.18; Ezek 7.26; Hos 4.6; Mic 3.11; Mal 2.4–9. **33.12** This cryptic saying may refer to the location of *Benjamin*'s tribal allotment in the central highlands between the major sanctuaries of Bethel and Jerusalem (cf. Josh 18.11–28). *Beloved of the Lord.* Cf. 2 Sam 12.25 (Solomon); Jer 11.15 (Israel). *Rests* (or "tents") *in safety.* See v. 28; 12.10; cf. Prov 1.33; 2.21. *The High God,* Hebrew *'Alu* (also in 1 Sam 2.10), a variant form of the divine appellation *'Elyon*; see 32.8. **33.13–17** This expansive encomium indicates the prominence of *Joseph* among the tribes. *Heaven, deep.* See Gen 7.11; 8.2; 49.25; cf. Ps 107.26; Prov 8.27. **33.15** *Mountains, hills.* Cf. Gen

16 with the choice gifts of the earth and its
        fullness,
      and the favor of the one who dwells on
        Sinai.*
    Let these come on the head of Joseph,
        on the brow of the prince among his
        brothers.
17 A firstborn* bull—majesty is his!
      His horns are the horns of a wild ox;
    with them he gores the peoples,
        driving them to* the ends of the
        earth;
    such are the myriads of Ephraim,
        such the thousands of Manasseh.

18 And of Zebulun he said:
    Rejoice, Zebulun, in your going out;
        and Issachar, in your tents.
19 They call peoples to the mountain;
        there they offer the right sacrifices;
    for they suck the affluence of the seas
        and the hidden treasures of the
        sand.

20 And of Gad he said:
    Blessed be the enlargement of Gad!
      Gad lives like a lion;
        he tears at arm and scalp.
21 He chose the best for himself,
        for there a commander's allotment was
        reserved;
    he came at the head of the people,
        he executed the justice of the Lord,
        and his ordinances for Israel.

22 And of Dan he said:
    Dan is a lion's whelp
        that leaps forth from Bashan.

23 And of Naphtali he said:
    O Naphtali, sated with favor,
        full of the blessing of the Lord,
        possess the west and the south.

24 And of Asher he said:
    Most blessed of sons be Asher;
        may he be the favorite of his brothers,
        and may he dip his foot in oil.
25 Your bars are iron and bronze;
        and as your days, so is your strength.

26 There is none like God, O Jeshurun,
        who rides through the heavens to your
        help,
        majestic through the skies.
27 He subdues the ancient gods,*
        shatters* the forces of old;*
    he drove out the enemy before you,
        and said, "Destroy!"
28 So Israel lives in safety,
        untroubled is Jacob's abode*
    in a land of grain and wine,
        where the heavens drop down dew.
29 Happy are you, O Israel! Who is like you,
        a people saved by the Lord,

---

a Cn: Heb *in the bush*   *b* Q Ms Gk Syr Vg: MT *His firstborn*
c Cn: Heb *the peoples, together*   *d* Or *The eternal God is a*
dwelling place   *e* Cn: Heb *from underneath*   *f* Or *the*
everlasting arms   *g* Or *fountain*

49.26; Hab 3.6. **33.16** *Who dwells* (or "tabernacles") *on*
Sinai. Cf. Ex 24.16. **33.17** *Horns of a wild ox.* Cf. Num
23.22; 24.8. *Ephraim, Manasseh.* See 3.13–14. **33.18–**
19 *Zebulun* and *Issachar* are linked as neighboring
tribes occupying the hills of southern Galilee and the
fertile Esdraelon plain; cf. Josh 19.10–23. **33.19** The
mountain is probably Tabor, in the central Esdraelon
plain (cf. Judg 4.6, 12–14), though Mount Carmel on
the coast is also possible. *Seas* should mean the
Mediterranean and the Sea of Galilee (Chinnereth); cf.
Gen 49.13. **33.20–21** Territorial expansion of *Gad* in
the Transjordan contrasts sharply with Reuben's diminished condition (v. 6). **33.21** *Chose the best.* See
Num 32.1–5. *Commander's allotment* was understood
in early rabbinic tradition to refer to Moses' burial
place; Mahanaim, which served as royal refuge for Ishbaal after the death of his father, Saul, may be a more
likely possibility (cf. 2 Sam 2.8–10). On Gad's military
prowess (*like a lion,* v. 20; *head of the people*), see 3.18–
20; Josh 1.12–14; 1 Chr 12.8–15. *Executed . . . justice* is
another royal theme. Cf. 2 Sam 8.15 (David); Ps 72.1–

4; Jer 22.15–16; 23.5–6. **33.22** Judah receives the epithet *lion's whelp* in Gen 49.9. *Bashan.* See note on 3.1.
On *Dan's* northern provenance, see 34.1; cf. Josh
19.47; Judg 18. **33.23** *Naphtali,* situated in the Galilean
highlands, is encouraged to expand its holdings.
33.24–25 The territory of *Asher* on the slopes of western Galilee was renowned for its orchards that yielded
fine-quality olive *oil.* **33.25** Metallic *bars* perhaps alludes to well-fortified settlements. **33.26–29** The
hymnic postlude resumes the epic themes of the
Lord's advent and incomparability as a warrior, empowering Israel to achieve victories against its enemies. Cf. 3.24; 4.32–40. **33.26** *Jeshurun.* See v. 5 and
note on 32.15. *Who rides,* on the cloud-chariot of the
Divine Warrior; cf. Isa 19.1; Pss 18.10; 68.4, 33; 104.3.
33.27 On the theme of the Lord's triumph over the
otiose gods of Canaan (*ancient gods, forces of old*), see,
e.g., 7.4, 25; Ex 23.23–24; 1 Sam 5.1–7; 2 Sam 7.22–24;
Isa 51.9–10. **33.28–29** Cf. 7.12–24; Gen 27.28.
33.29 *Shield of your help.* Cf. Gen 15.1; 2 Sam 22.3; Pss
28.7; 119.114. *Tread.* Cf. Josh 10.24.

the shield of your help,
    and the sword of your triumph!
Your enemies shall come fawning to you,
    and you shall tread on their backs.

Moses Dies and Is Buried in the Land of Moab

34 Then Moses went up from the plains of Moab to Mount Nebo, to the top of Pisgah, which is opposite Jericho, and the LORD showed him the whole land: Gilead as far as Dan, ²all Naphtali, the land of Ephraim and Manasseh, all the land of Judah as far as the Western Sea, ³the Negeb, and the Plain—that is, the valley of Jericho, the city of palm trees—as far as Zoar. ⁴The LORD said to him, "This is the land of which I swore to Abraham, to Isaac, and to Jacob, saying, 'I will give it to your descendants'; I have let you see it with your eyes, but you shall not cross over there." ⁵Then Moses, the servant of the LORD, died there in the land of Moab, at the LORD's command. ⁶He was buried in a valley in the land of Moab, opposite Beth-peor, but no one knows his burial place to this day. ⁷Moses was one hundred twenty years old when he died; his sight was unimpaired and his vigor had not abated. ⁸The Israelites wept for Moses in the plains of Moab thirty days; then the period of mourning for Moses was ended.

9 Joshua son of Nun was full of the spirit of wisdom, because Moses had laid his hands on him; and the Israelites obeyed him, doing as the LORD had commanded Moses.

10 Never since has there arisen a prophet in Israel like Moses, whom the LORD knew face to face. ¹¹He was unequaled for all the signs and wonders that the LORD sent him to perform in the land of Egypt, against Pharaoh and all his servants and his entire land, ¹²and for all the mighty deeds and all the terrifying displays of power that Moses performed in the sight of all Israel.

34.1–12 This final act of Moses' career, concluding the long pentateuchal story of Israel's formation, seems perfunctory and impassive in this recital. That may be the result of editorial design, abridging the extant traditions, some of which may resurface in later Jewish folklore (cf. *Midrash Rabbah*). What took precedence in Israel's memory was not the grave site of the great leader (whether this was secret or simply forgotten) but his incomparable legacy of *torah* (29.29; 31.9–13; 33.4, 10) and the superlative character of his leadership, handed on through Joshua to subsequent generations, even if only in diminished form (vv. 9–12; cf. Josh 1.1–9; 23; Judg 2.6–10; also *Mishnah Avot*). **34.1–3** A panoramic view of the promised land. *Plains of Moab to Mount Nebo.* See 32.49; Num 22.1. *Pisgah.* See 3.17. The view northward extends beyond *Gilead* (see 2.36) to Danite territory on the lower slopes of Mount Hermon (see 3.8; 33.22). **34.2** *Western Sea.* See 11.24. **34.3** *Negeb.* See 1.7. *Plain,* the basin of the Dead Sea, extending from *Jericho* in the northwest to *Zoar* in the southeast (cf. Gen 13.10–11; 14.2, 8). **34.4** See note on 1.8; cf. 3.27. **34.5–8** Death, burial, and mourning for Moses. *Servant of the LORD,* Moses' principal title. See Ex 14.31; Num 12.7–8; Josh 1.1–2, 7, 13, 15; 1 Kings 8.53, 56; Mal 4.4. *Valley . . . opposite Beth-peor.* See note on 3.29; cf. 4.46. **34.7** On Moses' ripe old age, see 31.2. This notice, together with the date supplied in 1.31, forms a counterpart to Aaron's obituary in Num 33.38–39. **34.8** *Thirty days* of mourning for a deceased leader was apparently traditional; cf. Num 20.29. **34.9** Joshua's initial exaltation. *Full of the spirit of wisdom.* Cf. Gen 41.38–39; Ex 31.3; 35.31; Job 32.8. *Laid his hands on him.* See Num 27.18–23. **34.10–12** *Never since.* The epitaph affirms, from an apparent distance in time, the incomparability of Moses' work as Israel's divinely chosen and empowered deliverer; it serves as a colophon to the completed Pentateuch, which is his enduring memorial (cf. 18.15–18; Mal 4.4–5). **34.10** *A prophet in Israel like Moses.* The point here is Moses' uniqueness (see Num 12.6–8) rather than his role as mediator establishing a model for later prophets (as in 18.15–22). *Face to face* indicates God's intimate knowledge of Moses. See 5.4; Ex 33.11; Num 12.8 (here lit. "mouth to mouth"); Sir 45.5. **34.11** *Signs and wonders.* See, e.g., Ex 7.8–12. **34.12** *Mighty deeds, terrifying displays of power.* Moses performed God's own work. See 4.34, 37; 26.8; Ps 77.11–15; cf. Ex 4.16, 21; 7.1; 34.10.

JOSHUA

THE BOOK OF JOSHUA tells the story of the Israelites who, under Joshua's guidance and with the benefit of divine intervention, crossed the Jordan River to take control of the land of Canaan. Israel takes its orders from Joshua, who gets his orders directly from the Lord. The land was God's gift, promised to the ancestors in the stories of Gen 12–50 and secured by conquest under God's military leadership. In generations to come, Israel's possession of its land would often be endangered by outside attack or foreign domination, but the book of Joshua sustained its claim on the land given to it by God.

Structure

THE BOOK SHOWS FOUR MAIN DIVISIONS: preparations for the attack (chs. 1–5), conquest of the land (chs. 6–12), apportionment of the land to the tribes by lot (chs. 13–21), and two national assemblies called by Joshua (chs. 23–24). There are three decisive demonstrations of divine power: at Jericho (ch. 6), at Ai (chs. 7–8), and at Gibeon (chs. 9–10). Each of these three stories embodies the idea of a miraculous sign and victory won by the Lord in the role of Divine Warrior. The tradition of sacral war confesses, "The LORD fought for Israel" (10.14, 42; cf. 23.3, 10). The geography of conquest falls into three campaigns, central (chs. 6–8), southern (ch. 10), and northern (ch. 11), with a summary in ch. 12. The apportionment of land begins in the south with Judah (chs. 14–15) and then turns to the central territories of Ephraim and Manasseh (chs. 16–17). The remaining tribes west of the Jordan receive their land based on the work of a survey commission (chs. 18–19).

Content and Message

AT THE OUTSET ISRAEL IS DEPICTED as a mighty twelve-tribe army. The people are encamped east of the Jordan River near the northern end of the Dead Sea. The Lord encourages Joshua as their leader (1.1–2, 5–9) and promises Israel a sweeping land (1.3–4). This is the land toward which Moses had led the people in their wanderings for forty years since their departure from Mount Sinai/Horeb. In the concluding chapter, Joshua assembles all the tribes of Israel at the city of Shechem in the heart of the land of promise. There Joshua presides at a covenant ceremony in which rival gods are repudiated and Israel affirms its allegiance to the Lord alone.

Preparations for entrance into the land (ch. 1) are followed by a reconnaissance of Jericho (ch. 2), crossing the Jordan River and setting up memorial stones at Gilgal (chs. 3–4), and finally circumcision of all the males (5.2–9) because circumcision had not been practiced during the wilderness wanderings. With a celebration of the first Passover west of the Jordan (5.10–12), all was at last in readiness for the warfare, as signaled by Joshua's encounter with a mysterious heavenly commander (5.13–15). Stories of warfare (6.1–11.15) stress that the conquest was the result of the Lord's gracious action, for which Israel could claim no credit. Israel's proper role was loyalty and obedience (8.30–35). Sweeping claims are made for military conquest of "all" the land (11.16, 23) and its complete distribution to the tribes (13.8–19.51). This optimistic viewpoint, however, stands in sharp tension with contrary statements that describe the conquest as less than total (13.1–7; 15.63; 16.10; 17.12–13; 23.5–13).

Concluding chapters continue to advocate for loyalty and obedience. To facilitate justice in cases of homicide while at the same time curbing the practice of blood vengeance, asylum towns ("cities of refuge") are designated, three on each side of the Jordan (ch. 20). These and other towns are designated in each of the tribes to provide residential and grazing rights for the priestly tribe of Levi (ch. 21). Deep rifts in national unity are vividly displayed when the building of an altar "near the Jordan" (ch. 22) nearly results in intertribal warfare. Joshua's concluding address spirals downward to a stern warning (ch. 23), followed by a great covenanting ceremony at Shechem (ch. 24). The stage is set for the story of Israel's life in the land from start (Judges) to finish (2 Kings).

Canonical Context, Sources, and Redaction

JOSHUA INCORPORATES THREE TYPES of material. Conquest narratives describing the victories of the Lord, who fights for Israel as the Divine Warrior, make up much of chs. 2–11. Geographical lists and descriptions are found in chs. 12–21. Theological discourses introduce the book in ch. 1 and conclude it in chs. 23–24. All three types of material work together to claim the land of promise for Israel. The individual narratives in Joshua began as folktales about merely local victories, but were eventually gathered into a connected narrative as the triumphs of a unified Israel (chs. 2–11). Later this collection was reedited, growing to chs. 1–12, 23, as part of a historical work that also included the books of Judges, 1 and 2 Samuel, and 1 and 2 Kings. Because the book of Deuteronomy served as its preface and theological foundation, scholars refer to this larger work as the Deuteronomistic History. The main edition of this history probably originated in the reign of the reforming king Josiah, triggered by the discovery of an early form of Deuteronomy during repairs at the Jerusalem temple (ca. 622 BCE; see 2 Kings 22–23). After the defeat of Judah, the geographical material of chs.13–21 and the story of ch. 22 were added, and ch. 24 was appended to form a second conclusion.

The stories and other materials taken up in Joshua cannot be used directly as historical evidence for a violent conquest. The stories were told and the lists preserved to serve theological and nationalistic interests, not historical purposes. Archaeological data frequently provide illustrative light, but rarely decisive corroboration. However, when studied with the aid of social-science perspectives, the texts and excavation data combine to yield a clearer picture of the emergence of Israel in the premonarchical period. [ROBERT G. BOLING, revised by RICHARD D. NELSON]

God's Commission to Joshua

1 After the death of Moses the servant of the LORD, the LORD spoke to Joshua son of Nun, Moses' assistant, saying, 2"My servant Moses is dead. Now proceed to cross the Jordan, you and all this people, into the land that I am giving to them, to the Israelites. 3Every place that the sole of your foot will tread upon I have given to you, as I promised to Moses. 4From the wilderness and the Lebanon as far as the great river, the river Euphrates, all the land of the Hittites, to the Great Sea in the west shall be your territory. 5No one shall be able to stand against you all the days of your life. As I was with Moses, so I will be with you; I will not fail you or forsake you. 6Be strong and courageous; for you shall put this people in possession of the land that I swore to their ancestors to give them. 7Only be strong and very courageous, being careful to act in accordance with all the law that my servant Moses commanded you; do not turn from it to the right hand or to the left, so that you may be successful wherever you go. 8This book of the law shall not depart out of your mouth; you shall meditate on it day and night, so that you may be careful to act in accordance with all that is written in it. For then you shall make your way prosperous, and then you shall be successful. 9I hereby command you: Be strong and courageous; do not be frightened or dismayed, for the LORD your God is with you wherever you go."

Preparations for the Invasion

10 Then Joshua commanded the officers of the people, 11"Pass through the camp, and command the people: 'Prepare your provisions; for in three days you are to cross over the Jordan, to go in to take possession of the land that the LORD your God gives you to possess.' "

12 To the Reubenites, the Gadites, and the half-tribe of Manasseh Joshua said, 13"Remember the word that Moses the servant of the LORD commanded you, saying, 'The LORD your God is providing you a place of rest, and will give you this land.' 14Your wives, your little ones, and your livestock shall remain in the land that Moses gave you beyond the Jordan. But all the warriors among you shall cross over armed before your kindred and shall help them, 15until the LORD gives rest to your kindred as well as to you, and they too take possession of the land that the LORD your God is giving them. Then you shall return to your own land and take possession of it, the land that Moses the servant of the LORD gave you beyond the Jordan to the east."

16 They answered Joshua: "All that you have commanded us we will do, and wherever you send us we will go. 17Just as we obeyed Moses in all things, so we will obey you. Only may the LORD your God be with you, as he was with Moses! 18Whoever rebels against your orders and disobeys your words, whatever you command, shall be put to death. Only be strong and courageous."

1.1–11 God commissions Joshua. Vv. 1–9 emphasize qualities required of Joshua and the leadership he must provide in taking over the land. **1.1** Action begins *after the death of Moses,* who had been denied entrance into the land (Num 20.12; Deut 34.4). **1.3** Walking over land was a way of legally claiming it. **1.4** Canaan lay west of the Jordan, stretching from the Negeb *wilderness* in the south through the mountains of *Lebanon.* The description of the land of promise extending as far north as the *Euphrates* reflects the promise of Gen 15.18; Deut 11.24 as well as royal ideology (Ps 72.8). These expansive, ideal borders were never actually achieved. **1.5** The Lord, speaking as the Divine Warrior who leads heavenly armies into battle and fights for Israel, promises Joshua military success (see v. 3) and effective presence (see v. 9). **1.6** *Strong and courageous* (repeated in vv. 7, 9, 18). Cf. Deut 31.7, 23. The rhetoric of speeches in Joshua frequently echoes Deuteronomy. **1.7–8** This is the theology of Deuteronomy. Obedience to *the law . . . Moses commanded* leads to prosperity and success. Joshua is to resemble the ideal king described

in Deut 17.18–20. In the context of the Deuteronomistic History (see Introduction), *this book of the law* (cf. 2 Kings 22.8) refers to some form of Deuteronomy. **1.11** These *three days* are concluded by 3.2.

1.12–18 Involvement of tribes in Transjordan. In territory east of the Jordan, settled by Reuben, Gad, and half of the tribe of Manasseh, the followers of Moses achieved their first successes. These tribes had already occupied their land, but were now commanded to take part in the seizure of Canaan, where the other half of Manasseh will settle. Deut 3.18–20 reports their agreement with Moses. **1.13** Rest (also v. 15) is security in the land established by the Lord's defeat of the enemy (21.44; 23.1). **1.16–18** The eastern tribes here respond eagerly and echo Joshua's own words from vv. 7, 9. A double use of *only* (vv. 17–18) introduces some tension into the plot, however. Readers may wonder whether the Lord will be *with* Joshua, and whether Joshua will prove to be *strong and courageous.* Cooperative eagerness will turn to suspicion in ch. 22 in a dispute over an altar near the Jordan.

Spies Sent to Jericho

2 Then Joshua son of Nun sent two men secretly from Shittim as spies, saying, "Go, view the land, especially Jericho." So they went, and entered the house of a prostitute whose name was Rahab, and spent the night there. 2 The king of Jericho was told, "Some Israelites have come here tonight to search out the land." 3 Then the king of Jericho sent orders to Rahab, "Bring out the men who have come to you, who entered your house, for they have come only to search out the whole land." 4 But the woman took the two men and hid them. Then she said, "True, the men came to me, but I did not know where they came from. 5 And when it was time to close the gate at dark, the men went out. Where the men went I do not know. Pursue them quickly, for you can overtake them." 6 She had, however, brought them up to the roof and hidden them with the stalks of flax that she had laid out on the roof. 7 So the men pursued them on the way to the Jordan as far as the fords. As soon as the pursuers had gone out, the gate was shut.

8 Before they went to sleep, she came up to them on the roof 9 and said to the men: "I know that the LORD has given you the land, and that dread of you has fallen on us, and that all the inhabitants of the land melt in fear before you. 10 For we have heard how the LORD dried up the water of the Red Sea[a] before you when you came out of Egypt, and what you did to the two kings of the Amorites that were beyond the Jordan, to Sihon and Og, whom you utterly destroyed. 11 As soon as we heard it, our hearts melted, and there was no courage left in any of us because of you. The LORD your God is indeed God in heaven above and on earth below. 12 Now then, since I have dealt kindly with you, swear to me by the LORD that you in turn will deal kindly with my family. Give me a sign of good faith 13 that you will spare my father and mother, my brothers and sisters, and all who belong to them, and deliver our lives from death." 14 The men said to her, "Our life for yours! If you do not tell this business of ours, then we will deal kindly and faithfully with you when the LORD gives us the land."

15 Then she let them down by a rope through the window, for her house was on the outer side of the city wall and she resided within the wall itself. 16 She said to them, "Go toward the hill country, so that the pursuers may not come upon you. Hide yourselves

a Or Sea of Reeds

2.1–24 Rahab outsmarts the spies. Jericho controlled several fords and routes of access into the hill country. Archaeology has shown that by the late thirteenth and early twelfth centuries BCE Jericho had been reduced to at most a small, unfortified village sitting atop the ruins of the previously walled city. **2.1** *Shittim,* the final desert encampment (Num 25.1), lay in the eastern Jordan Valley. Similar stories about *spies* are found in Num 13; Josh 7.2–5; Judg 18.2–10. *Rahab* is a legally independent woman with her own *house.* The nature of her business means that the presence of strangers would not be questioned. Rahab would later be reckoned among the ancestors of Jesus (Mt 1.5), lauded as an example of living faith (Heb 11.31), and justified by her works (Jas 2.25) **2.3– 4** *Come to you* and *came to me* have a double meaning. Understood as "come into you/me," the phrase can imply sexual intercourse as well as arrival at Rahab's house. **2.6–7** Rahab is not just a harlot. She is processing *flax* by spreading it out on her flat roof to dry. Although Rahab has saved them from the king, the spies find themselves trapped in a rather public location on her *roof* (cf. 2 Sam 16.22) and the city *gate was shut.* *Pursuers* block their route back, further deepening their predicament. This puts Rahab in a position to negotiate a favorable agreement. **2.9–11** Rahab provides the content of the spies' eventual report (v. 24).

She confesses the Lord as universal God using language that echoes Deut 4.37–38. The kingdoms of *Sihon and Og* (v. 10), east of the Jordan, had been conquered under Moses' leadership (Num 21; Deut 1–2). They had been *utterly destroyed,* i.e., devoted to destruction in a sacral war in which the Lord fought for Israel in the role of Divine Warrior (cf. 6.17, 21). Rahab seeks to avoid this fate for her family. **2.12– 14** Rahab proposes a covenant of reciprocal protection to protect her extended family. She has *dealt kindly* (using covenant language, "shown *chesed*") with the spies by showing faithfulness to the relationship between host and guest. They are to *deal kindly* in return by honoring a covenant to protect her family. *Our life for yours* indicates that the spies assent to this arrangement. Their agreement violates the prohibition of Deut 20.10–20. **2.15** The location of Rahab's house described here does not fit well with the collapse of Jericho's wall in ch. 6, given that she gathers her family into her house to save them (2.18; 6.22–23). That *she resided within the wall* suggests defensive fortifications of the casemate type, i.e., parallel walls divided by cross walls creating chambers that might be used for storage or residence. **2.16** *Toward the hill country.* Rahab remains in charge of the situation. Having sent the searchers eastward toward the Jordan (v. 7), she directs the spies westward into the hills to hide for a few

there three days, until the pursuers have returned; then afterward you may go your way." [17]The men said to her, "We will be released from this oath that you have made us swear to you [18]if we invade the land and you do not tie this crimson cord in the window through which you let us down, and you do not gather into your house your father and mother, your brothers, and all your family. [19]If any of you go out of the doors of your house into the street, they shall be responsible for their own death, and we shall be innocent; but if a hand is laid upon any who are with you in the house, we shall bear the responsibility for their death. [20]But if you tell this business of ours, then we shall be released from this oath that you made us swear to you." [21]She said, "According to your words, so be it." She sent them away and they departed. Then she tied the crimson cord in the window.

22 They departed and went into the hill country and stayed there three days, until the pursuers returned. The pursuers had searched all along the way and found nothing. [23]Then the two men came down again from the hill country. They crossed over, came to Joshua son of Nun, and told him all that had happened to them. [24]They said to Joshua, "Truly the LORD has given all the land into our hands; moreover all the inhabitants of the land melt in fear before us."

Israel Crosses the Jordan

3 Early in the morning Joshua rose and set out from Shittim with all the Israelites, and they came to the Jordan. They camped there before crossing over. [2]At the end of three days the officers went through the camp [3]and commanded the people, "When you see the ark of the covenant of the LORD your God being carried by the levitical priests, then you shall set out from your place. Follow it, [4]so that you may know the way you should go, for you have not passed this way before. Yet there shall be a space between you and it, a distance of about two thousand cubits; do not come any nearer to it." [5]Then Joshua said to the people, "Sanctify yourselves; for tomorrow the LORD will do wonders among you." [6]To the priests Joshua said, "Take up the ark of the covenant, and pass on in front of the people." So they took up the ark of the covenant and went in front of the people.

7 The LORD said to Joshua, "This day I will begin to exalt you in the sight of all Israel, so that they may know that I will be with you as I was with Moses. [8]You are the one who shall command the priests who bear the ark of the covenant, 'When you come to the edge of the waters of the Jordan, you shall stand still in the Jordan.' " [9]Joshua then said to the Israelites, "Draw near and hear the words of the LORD your God." [10]Joshua said, "By this you shall know that among you is the living God who without fail will drive out from before you the Canaanites, Hittites, Hivites, Perizzites, Girgashites, Amorites, and Jebusites: [11]the ark of the covenant of the Lord of all the earth is going to pass before you into the Jordan. [12]So now select twelve men from the tribes of Israel, one from each tribe. [13]When the soles of the feet of the priests who bear the ark of the LORD, the Lord of all the earth, rest in the waters of the Jordan, the waters of the Jordan flowing from above shall be cut off; they shall stand in a single heap."

14 When the people set out from their tents to cross over the Jordan, the priests bearing the ark of the covenant were in front of the people. [15]Now the Jordan overflows all its

---

days. These *three days* (cf. v. 22) represent a timetable different from the three days of 1.11; 3.2. **2.17–20** Once they are safely out of Rahab's control, the spies seek to clarify their covenant obligations. They insist that she display a conspicuous identification sign, assemble her family at a single location, and keep their secret. **2.24** The spies' report does not go beyond what Rahab has told them (vv. 9, 11). Rahab's story abruptly resumes after the capture of Jericho (6.22–25).

3.1–17 Crossing the Jordan. Israelites in a later time would be exhorted to "remember . . . what happened from Shittim to Gilgal" (Mic 6.5). **3.1** *Early in the morning* signals eager readiness in beginning a commanded task (cf. 6.12; 7.16; 8.10). **3.2** These are the *three days* referred to in 1.11. **3.3** The *levitical priests*

are responsible for the transport of the *ark of the covenant,* which embodies the Lord's presence in sacral warfare. The crossing is described in terms suggestive of a religious procession. **3.4** *Two thousand cubits,* roughly 3,000 feet (1,000 meters). The people must stay at a distance because the ark is dangerously holy (cf. 2 Sam 6.6–7). **3.5** *Sanctify yourselves.* To prepare for a miraculous event, the people are to make themselves holy by means of a ritual. **3.7** Any concern raised in 1.17 is resolved, for the Lord is undeniably *with* Joshua (cf. 6.27). **3.10** Formulaic lists of Canaan's inhabitants also occur in 9.1; 11.3; 12.8; 24.11 and are characteristic of Deuteronomy. **3.15** The detail that the Jordan *overflows all its banks* makes it possible for the priests' feet to touch *the edge of the water.* It also

banks throughout the time of harvest. So when those who bore the ark had come to the Jordan, and the feet of the priests bearing the ark were dipped in the edge of the water, [16]the waters flowing from above stood still, rising up in a single heap far off at Adam, the city that is beside Zarethan, while those flowing toward the sea of the Arabah, the Dead Sea,[a] were wholly cut off. Then the people crossed over opposite Jericho. [17]While all Israel were crossing over on dry ground, the priests who bore the ark of the covenant of the LORD stood on dry ground in the middle of the Jordan, until the entire nation finished crossing over the Jordan.

Twelve Stones Set Up at Gilgal

4 When the entire nation had finished crossing over the Jordan, the LORD said to Joshua: [2]"Select twelve men from the people, one from each tribe, [3]and command them, 'Take twelve stones from here out of the middle of the Jordan, from the place where the priests' feet stood, carry them over with you, and lay them down in the place where you camp tonight.'" [4]Then Joshua summoned the twelve men from the Israelites, whom he had appointed, one from each tribe. [5]Joshua said to them, "Pass on before the ark of the LORD your God into the middle of the Jordan, and each of you take up a stone on his shoulder, one for each of the tribes of the Israelites, [6]so that this may be a sign among you. When your children ask in time to come, 'What do those stones mean to you?' [7]then you shall tell them that the waters of the Jordan were cut off in front of the ark of the covenant of the LORD. When it crossed over the Jordan, the waters of

the Jordan were cut off. So these stones shall be to the Israelites a memorial forever."

[8] The Israelites did as Joshua commanded. They took up twelve stones out of the middle of the Jordan, according to the number of the tribes of the Israelites, as the LORD told Joshua, carried them over with them to the place where they camped, and laid them down there. [9](Joshua set up twelve stones in the middle of the Jordan, in the place where the feet of the priests bearing the ark of the covenant had stood; and they are there to this day.)

[10] The priests who bore the ark remained standing in the middle of the Jordan, until everything was finished that the LORD commanded Joshua to tell the people, according to all that Moses had commanded Joshua. The people crossed over in haste. [11]As soon as all the people had finished crossing over, the ark of the LORD, and the priests, crossed over in front of the people. [12]The Reubenites, the Gadites, and the half-tribe of Manasseh crossed over armed before the Israelites, as Moses had ordered them. [13]About forty thousand armed for war crossed over before the LORD to the plains of Jericho for battle.

[14] On that day the LORD exalted Joshua in the sight of all Israel; and they stood in awe of him, as they had stood in awe of Moses, all the days of his life.

[15] The LORD said to Joshua, [16]"Command the priests who bear the ark of the covenant,[b] to come up out of the Jordan." [17]Joshua therefore commanded the priests, "Come up out of the Jordan." [18]When the priests bearing the ark of the covenant of the LORD came up from

---

a Heb *Salt Sea*   *b* Or *treaty*, or *testimony*; Heb *eduth*

---

makes the miracle more impressive. **3.16** The water that would have flowed downstream was *cut off* because it *stood still* sixteen miles (twenty-six kilometers) upstream at *Adam* (Tell ed-Damiyeh).

4.1–5.1 Israel at Gilgal. These verses appear to describe two sets of twelve stones. One set is installed midstream (v. 9). Another set is erected on shore (vv. 3, 5, 8, 20) and would become a memorial to the crossing: this is the shrine at *Gilgal* (v. 19), which means "Circle." Gilgal was a major political and religious center in the premonarchical period. There Saul was made king (1 Sam 11.15) and David's relations with Judah were later repaired (2 Sam 19.15, 40). Gilgal flourished as a sanctuary in the eighth century BCE, when it was roundly denounced by prophets (Hos 4.15; 9.15; 12.11; Am 4.4; 5.5). **4.1** A comparison of this verse with 3.17; 4.11 shows that readers are to understand

that the actions of vv. 2–10 took place while the crossing was still under way. **4.3** The stones will be temporarily placed in the camp, then set up permanently at Gilgal (v. 20). **4.6–7** The stones will teach future generations about the crossing (cf. Deut 6.20–25). Repetition highlights the marvel that the water was *cut off*. In contrast, vv. 22–24 emphasize that Israel crossed on dry ground. **4.9** *To this day* is a formula that signals an etiology, a story that explains the origin of a name, place, circumstance, or custom known to readers. Cf. 5.9; 6.25; 7.26; 8.28–29; 9.27; 10.27; 13.13; 14.14; 15.63; 16.10. **4.11** The narrative sets aside the topic of the stones and picks up the description of the crossing from v. 1. **4.12–13** The presence of the eastern tribes emphasizes that all Israel engaged in the conquest as a cooperative venture. *As Moses had ordered.* See Deut 3.18–20. **4.14** This fulfills the Lord's

the middle of the Jordan, and the soles of the priests' feet touched dry ground, the waters of the Jordan returned to their place and overflowed all its banks, as before.

19 The people came up out of the Jordan on the tenth day of the first month, and they camped in Gilgal on the east border of Jericho. ²⁰Those twelve stones, which they had taken out of the Jordan, Joshua set up in Gilgal, ²¹saying to the Israelites, "When your children ask their parents in time to come, 'What do these stones mean?' ²²then you shall let your children know, 'Israel crossed over the Jordan here on dry ground.' ²³For the LORD your God dried up the waters of the Jordan for you until you crossed over, as the LORD your God did to the Red Sea,ᵃ which he dried up for us until we crossed over, ²⁴so that all the peoples of the earth may know that the hand of the LORD is mighty, and so that you may fear the LORD your God forever."

The New Generation Circumcised

5 When all the kings of the Amorites beyond the Jordan to the west, and all the kings of the Canaanites by the sea, heard that the LORD had dried up the waters of the Jordan for the Israelites until they had crossed over, their hearts melted, and there was no longer any spirit in them, because of the Israelites.

2 At that time the LORD said to Joshua, "Make flint knives and circumcise the Israelites a second time." ³So Joshua made flint knives, and circumcised the Israelites at Gibeath-haaraloth.ᵇ ⁴This is the reason why Joshua circumcised them: all the males of the people who came out of Egypt, all the warriors, had died during the journey through the wilderness after they had come out of Egypt. ⁵Al-

though all the people who came out had been circumcised, yet all the people born on the journey through the wilderness after they had come out of Egypt had not been circumcised. ⁶For the Israelites traveled forty years in the wilderness, until all the nation, the warriors who came out of Egypt, perished, not having listened to the voice of the LORD. To them the LORD swore that he would not let them see the land that he had sworn to their ancestors to give us, a land flowing with milk and honey. ⁷So it was their children, whom he raised up in their place, that Joshua circumcised; for they were uncircumcised, because they had not been circumcised on the way.

8 When the circumcising of all the nation was done, they remained in their places in the camp until they were healed. ⁹The LORD said to Joshua, "Today I have rolled away from you the disgrace of Egypt." And so that place is called Gilgalᶜ to this day.

The Passover at Gilgal

10 While the Israelites were camped in Gilgal they kept the passover in the evening on the fourteenth day of the month in the plains of Jericho. ¹¹On the day after the passover, on that very day, they ate the produce of the land, unleavened cakes and parched grain. ¹²The manna ceased on the day they ate the produce of the land, and the Israelites no longer had manna; they ate the crops of the land of Canaan that year.

Joshua's Vision

13 Once when Joshua was by Jericho, he looked up and saw a man standing before him

---

ᵃ Or *Sea of Reeds* ᵇ That is *the Hill of the Foreskins* ᶜ Related to Heb *galal* to roll

---

promise made in 3.7. **4.18** These incidents undo each event described in 3.15–16. **4.19** *The first month*, Abib, i.e., March–April, later called Nisan. This note points forward to the date of Passover (5.10). **4.22–23** This response focuses on similarities to the Red Sea crossing on dry ground (in contrast to vv. 6–7). **4.24** The Jordan crossing has two ongoing purposes: that *all the peoples of the earth* will acknowledge the power (*hand*) of the Lord, and that Israel's descendants (the *children* of vv. 21–22) will hold the Lord in reverent awe (*fear*). **5.1** Neighboring *kings* react in fear, confirming Rahab's observations (2.9–11). Their loss of courage will motivate their strategy (9.1–2; 10.1–5; 11.1–5) and make it possible for Israel to win the victories described in chs. 6–11. **5.2–12** Circumcision and Passover. All males par-

ticipating in the Passover must be circumcised (Ex 12.48), but the practice had not been followed during the wilderness period. **5.2** *A second time.* The men previously circumcised had died in the wilderness, so circumcision had to be repeated for the post-exodus generation. **5.3** This narrative explains a place-name near Gilgal, *Gibeath-haaraloth*, "Foreskin Hill." **5.9** *The disgrace of Egypt* signifies Israel's low status as Egyptian slaves and perhaps insults directed at them by their captors. **5.11** *Unleavened cakes and parched grain* are appropriate foods for the first day after the celebration of the Passover because they could be prepared quickly. **5.12** *Manna* is replaced by *the crops of the land of Canaan*, signifying that Israel has moved from wilderness scarcity to agricultural productive land. **5.13–15** The commander of the Lord's celestial army.

with a drawn sword in his hand. Joshua went to him and said to him, "Are you one of us, or one of our adversaries?" [14]He replied, "Neither; but as commander of the army of the LORD I have now come." And Joshua fell on his face to the earth and worshiped, and he said to him, "What do you command your servant, my lord?" [15]The commander of the army of the LORD said to Joshua, "Remove the sandals from your feet, for the place where you stand is holy." And Joshua did so.

Jericho Taken and Destroyed

6 Now Jericho was shut up inside and out because of the Israelites; no one came out and no one went in. [2]The LORD said to Joshua, "See, I have handed Jericho over to you, along with its king and soldiers. [3]You shall march around the city, all the warriors circling the city once. Thus you shall do for six days, [4]with seven priests bearing seven trumpets of rams' horns before the ark. On the seventh day you shall march around the city seven times, the priests blowing the trumpets. [5]When they make a long blast with the ram's horn, as soon as you hear the sound of the trumpet, then all the people shall shout with a great shout; and the wall of the city will fall down flat, and all the people shall charge straight ahead." [6]So Joshua son of Nun summoned the priests and said to them, "Take up the ark of the covenant, and have seven priests carry seven trumpets of rams' horns in front of the ark of the LORD." [7]To the people he said, "Go forward and march around the city; have the armed men pass on before the ark of the LORD."

[8]As Joshua had commanded the people, the seven priests carrying the seven trumpets of rams' horns before the LORD went forward, blowing the trumpets, with the ark of the covenant of the LORD following them. [9]And the armed men went before the priests who blew the trumpets; the rear guard came after the ark, while the trumpets blew continually. [10]To the people Joshua gave this command: "You shall not shout or let your voice be heard, nor shall you utter a word, until the day I tell you to shout. Then you shall shout." [11]So the ark of the LORD went around the city, circling it once; and they came into the camp, and spent the night in the camp.

[12]Then Joshua rose early in the morning, and the priests took up the ark of the LORD. [13]The seven priests carrying the seven trumpets of rams' horns before the ark of the LORD passed on, blowing the trumpets continually. The armed men went before them, and the rear guard came after the ark of the LORD, while the trumpets blew continually. [14]On the second day they marched around the city once and then returned to the camp. They did this for six days.

[15]On the seventh day they rose early, at dawn, and marched around the city in the same manner seven times. It was only on that day that they marched around the city seven times. [16]And at the seventh time, when the priests had blown the trumpets, Joshua said to the people, "Shout! For the LORD has given you the city. [17]The city and all that is in it shall be devoted to the LORD for destruction. Only Rahab the prostitute and all who are with her

---

Somewhere near Jericho, Joshua is granted a theophany—the appearance of a heavenly being—much in the manner of Gideon (Judg 6.11–12). **5.13** Joshua evidently assumes that this *man* is merely a human soldier. His *drawn sword* signals impending battle. **5.14** The presence of this supernatural *commander* signifies sacral war. The Lord's heavenly forces will be fighting on Israel's side. **5.15** A direct quotation of Ex 3.5 recognizes Joshua as the direct successor of Moses.

6.1–27 Jericho is captured first in a classic sacral war and placed off-limits for Israelites. The account is framed by verses that connect with the Rahab story: vv. 1–2, mentioning the king and soldiers, and vv. 22–25, describing the deliverance of Rahab and her household in accordance with Joshua's instructions in v. 17. **6.1** That *Jericho was shut up inside and out* describes Israel's dilemma. Jericho's wall was an impregnable defense. **6.2** A divine promise of victory was a central element of sacral-war tradition (cf. 8.1; 10.8). **6.3–4** The

siege is to reflect ceremonial features of sacral war, with a procession and priests blowing trumpets. **6.5** A *long blast* on a trumpet gives the signal, and the people's *great shout* launches a human assault made possible by a divine miracle (see vv. 16, 20). Archaeology shows that Jericho's last defensive *wall* no longer existed at the time of Israel's emergence. We are in the realm of confessional folklore rather than history. **6.8–9** The order of march: *armed men* followed by *seven priests* blowing trumpets, then the *ark,* and finally a *rear guard.* **6.17** *Devoted to the LORD for destruction.* The Hebrew word *cherem* describes things and people that fall into the distinctive category of being the Lord's exclusive property (cf. Lev 27.20–21, 28–29). Because the Lord achieved Israel's victories, booty and captives won in sacral war were classified as *cherem.* As the Lord's irrevocable possession, such *cherem* had to be kept from human use; because they would be valuable as slaves, the entire enemy population was to be

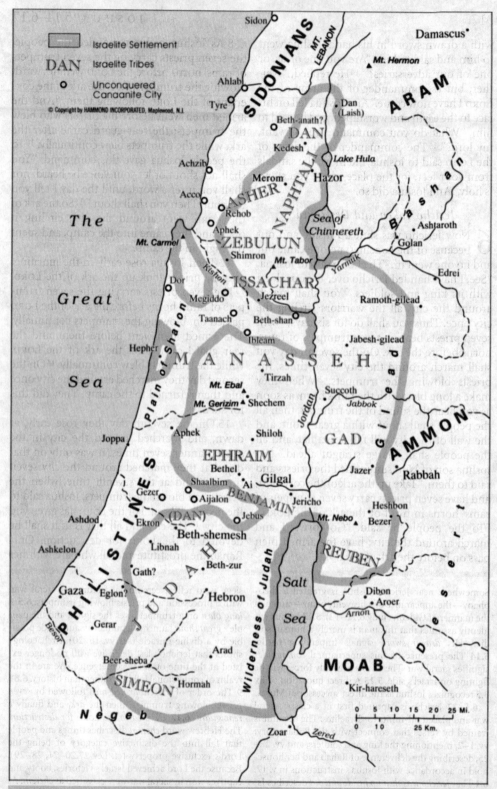

The conquest of Canaan according to the narratives in Joshua. Other sources and archaeological evidence show different patterns of early Israelite settlement.

in her house shall live because she hid the messengers we sent. [18]As for you, keep away from the things devoted to destruction, so as not to covet[a] and take any of the devoted things and make the camp of Israel an object for destruction, bringing trouble upon it. [19]But all silver and gold, and vessels of bronze and iron, are sacred to the LORD; they shall go into the treasury of the LORD." [20]So the people shouted, and the trumpets were blown. As soon as the people heard the sound of the trumpets, they raised a great shout, and the wall fell down flat; so the people charged straight ahead into the city and captured it. [21]Then they devoted to destruction by the edge of the sword all in the city, both men and women, young and old, oxen, sheep, and donkeys.

[22]Joshua said to the two men who had spied out the land, "Go into the prostitute's house, and bring the woman out of it and all who belong to her, as you swore to her." [23]So the young men who had been spies went in and brought Rahab out, along with her father, her mother, her brothers, and all who belonged to her—they brought all her kindred out—and set them outside the camp of Israel. [24]They burned down the city, and everything in it; only the silver and gold, and the vessels of bronze and iron, they put into the treasury of the house of the LORD. [25]But Rahab the prostitute, with her family and all who belonged to her, Joshua spared. Her family[b] has lived in Israel ever since. For she hid the messengers whom Joshua sent to spy out Jericho.

[26]Joshua then pronounced this oath, saying,

"Cursed before the LORD be anyone who tries
     to build this city—this Jericho!
At the cost of his firstborn he shall lay its foundation,
     and at the cost of his youngest he shall set up its gates!"

[27]So the LORD was with Joshua; and his fame was in all the land.

The Sin of Achan and Its Punishment

7 But the Israelites broke faith in regard to the devoted things: Achan son of Carmi son of Zabdi son of Zerah, of the tribe of Judah, took some of the devoted things; and the anger of the LORD burned against the Israelites.

[2]Joshua sent men from Jericho to Ai, which is near Beth-aven, east of Bethel, and said to them, "Go up and spy out the land." And the men went up and spied out Ai. [3]Then they returned to Joshua and said to him, "Not all the people need go up; about two or three thousand men should go up and attack Ai. Since they are so few, do not make the whole people toil up there." [4]So about three thousand of the people went up there; and they fled before the men of Ai. [5]The men of Ai killed about thirty-six of them, chasing them from outside the gate as far as Shebarim and killing them on the

---

a Gk: Heb *devote to destruction* Compare 7.21   *b* Heb *She*

---

killed (Deut 20.16–17). Although material booty and cattle did not usually fall into the *cherem* category (8.2; 11.14), Jericho is an especially rigorous case (vv. 19, 21, 24). **6.18** According to the principle of contagion, to *take any of the devoted things* (i.e., *cherem*) would place Israel itself in the deadly category of *cherem* (*an object for destruction*). This verse foreshadows Achan's crime (7.21).

6.20 *Straight ahead.* Because Israel encircles the city, it can make a frontal assault from all sides simultaneously. **6.23** Israel's sacral-war encampment has to remain ritually clean (Deut 23.9–14), so Rahab and her family must remain *outside the camp.* **6.25** This note shifts focus away from the fall of the city and onto the story of covenant keeping by and with Rahab, explaining how a foreign group *has lived in Israel ever since.* **6.26** *Cursed before the LORD.* Joshua blocks any reconstruction and resettlement of Jericho (cf. Deut 13.16). 1 Kings 16.34 reports the fulfillment of this curse. A story concerning Elisha gives evidence that Jericho's spring was thought to be unhealthy until he miraculously put it right (2 Kings 2.19–22).

7.1–26 The first of two attacks at Ai is repulsed. The embarrassing defeat is traced to Achan's violation of the decree against taking devoted things (6.17–18). The narrative units in ch. 7 are spliced in such a way that the story of Achan (vv. 1, 6–26) is interrupted by the defeat at Ai (vv. 2–5). *Ai,* lit. "The Ruin," is identified as et-Tell (Arabic for "The Ruin"), two miles (three kilometers) east of Bethel. During the period described in Joshua, et-Tell was at most a small unwalled village nestled amid the remains of a long-ruined walled city from the third millennium BCE. As in the case of Jericho, this narrative is folklore, not history. **7.1** Details about Achan's family background portend the procedure by which his crime will be uncovered (vv. 16–18). Even though Achan acted alone in ignoring Joshua's warning (6.18), the principle of corporate responsibility means that all *the Israelites broke faith* (cf. v. 11), so that *the anger of the LORD* is directed against the entire nation. **7.2** Gathering intelligence was sometimes the first step in a sacral war (2.1; Judg 1.23). **7.3** *Not all . . . go up.* As in the first reconnaissance (2.24), these spies bring an optimistic re-

slope. The hearts of the people melted and turned to water.

6 Then Joshua tore his clothes, and fell to the ground on his face before the ark of the LORD until the evening, he and the elders of Israel; and they put dust on their heads. 7 Joshua said, "Ah, Lord GOD! Why have you brought this people across the Jordan at all, to hand us over to the Amorites so as to destroy us? Would that we had been content to settle beyond the Jordan! 8 O Lord, what can I say, now that Israel has turned their backs to their enemies! 9 The Canaanites and all the inhabitants of the land will hear of it, and surround us, and cut off our name from the earth. Then what will you do for your great name?"

10 The LORD said to Joshua, "Stand up! Why have you fallen upon your face? 11 Israel has sinned; they have transgressed my covenant that I imposed on them. They have taken some of the devoted things; they have stolen, they have acted deceitfully, and they have put them among their own belongings. 12 Therefore the Israelites are unable to stand before their enemies; they turn their backs to their enemies, because they have become a thing devoted for destruction themselves. I will be with you no more, unless you destroy the devoted things from among you. 13 Proceed to sanctify the people, and say, 'Sanctify yourselves for tomorrow; for thus says the LORD, the God of Israel, "There are devoted things among you, O Israel; you will be unable to stand before your enemies until you take away the devoted things from among you." 14 In the morning therefore you shall come forward tribe by tribe. The tribe that the LORD takes shall come near by clans, the clan that the LORD takes shall come near by households, and the household that the LORD takes shall come near one by one. 15 And the one who is taken as having the devoted things shall be burned with fire, together with all that he has, for having transgressed the covenant of the LORD, and for having done an outrageous thing in Israel.' "

16 So Joshua rose early in the morning, and brought Israel near tribe by tribe, and the tribe of Judah was taken. 17 He brought near the clans of Judah, and the clan of the Zerahites was taken; and he brought near the clan of the Zerahites, family by family,ᵃ and Zabdi was taken. 18 And he brought near his household one by one, and Achan son of Carmi son of Zabdi son of Zerah, of the tribe of Judah, was taken. 19 Then Joshua said to Achan, "My son, give glory to the LORD God of Israel and make confession to him. Tell me now what you have done; do not hide it from me." 20 And Achan answered Joshua, "It is true; I am the one who sinned against the LORD God of Israel. This is what I did: 21 when I saw among the spoil a beautiful mantle from Shinar, and two hundred shekels of silver, and a bar of gold weighing fifty shekels, then I coveted them and took them. They now lie hidden in the ground inside my tent, with the silver underneath."

22 So Joshua sent messengers, and they ran to the tent; and there it was, hidden in his tent

---

a Mss Syr: MT *man by man*

---

port. **7.5** Israel experiences the panic that the enemy is supposed to feel in sacral war: *the hearts of the people melted* (contrast 2.11; 5.1). Though their losses were only *about thirty-six,* Israel had been expecting an easy victory. **7.6** Exposure of the guilty one begins with rituals of mourning and penitence (cf. 2 Sam 12.15–16; Job 1.20; Jer 16.6–7; Joel 1.8–14) *before the ark of the LORD.* The ark focuses the presence of the Lord (3.4, 10–11) and is a medium for human inquiry and divine response (see Judg 20.27–28). **7.7–9** Joshua seeks to prompt divine action by questioning the Lord's motives and citing possible danger to the Lord's reputation (*your great name,* v. 9). **7.11** Achan's crime violates the *covenant* (also v. 15) and so fundamentally jeopardizes Israel's relationship with the Lord. **7.12** The defeat at Ai is explained. Items under the *cherem* ban have a contagious effect, causing the entire nation to pass into the state of being *devoted for destruction* (see notes on 6.17; 6.18). Thus the Lord's promise to *be with* them is in abeyance (cf. 3.7; 6.27). **7.13** *Proceed to sanctify, sanctify yourselves.* Here the "holiness" root (Hebrew *qdsh*) is used twice to emphasize that the people must prepare themselves for the Lord's intervention (cf. 3.5). **7.14–18** The elimination proceeds, most likely by sacred lot, which is explicitly mentioned in the determination of tribal territories (14.2; 18.6). Three concentric circles within which individual identity was established—house, clan, tribe—are the basis of the proceedings. Apparently the lot gave only yes and no answers. Cf. 1 Sam 10.17–24; 14.37–42. **7.15** An *outrageous thing in Israel* denotes scandalous wrongdoing that puts the whole nation in danger. The purge must be radical, burning up not just the guilty party himself, but also whatever (and whomever; cf. v. 24) the forbidden booty has contaminated. **7.16** *Joshua rose early in the morning,* indicating his eager obedience (3.1; 6.12). **7.19** Confession is the equivalent of giving *glory to the LORD* in that it is a recognition of divine justice. **7.21** *Mantle from Shinar* describes a luxury item imported from Babylon.

with the silver underneath. 23They took them out of the tent and brought them to Joshua and all the Israelites; and they spread them out before the LORD. 24Then Joshua and all Israel with him took Achan son of Zerah, with the silver, the mantle, and the bar of gold, with his sons and daughters, with his oxen, donkeys, and sheep, and his tent and all that he had; and they brought them up to the Valley of Achor. 25Joshua said, "Why did you bring trouble on us? The LORD is bringing trouble on you today." And all Israel stoned him to death; they burned them with fire, cast stones on them, 26and raised over him a great heap of stones that remains to this day. Then the LORD turned from his burning anger. Therefore that place to this day is called the Valley of Achor.*a*

Ai Captured by a Stratagem and Destroyed

8 Then the LORD said to Joshua, "Do not fear or be dismayed; take all the fighting men with you, and go up now to Ai. See, I have handed over to you the king of Ai with his people, his city, and his land. 2You shall do to Ai and its king as you did to Jericho and its king; only its spoil and its livestock you may take as booty for yourselves. Set an ambush against the city, behind it."

3 So Joshua and all the fighting men set out to go up against Ai. Joshua chose thirty thousand warriors and sent them out by night 4with the command, "You shall lie in ambush against the city, behind it; do not go very far from the city, but all of you stay alert. 5I and all the people who are with me will approach the city. When they come out against us, as before, we shall flee from them. 6They will come out after us until we have drawn them away from the city; for they will say, 'They are fleeing from us, as before.' While we flee from them, 7you shall rise up from the ambush and seize the city; for the LORD your God will give it into your hand. 8And when you have taken the city, you shall set the city on fire, doing as the LORD has ordered; see, I have commanded you." 9So Joshua sent them out; and they went to the place of ambush, and lay between Bethel and Ai, to the west of Ai; but Joshua spent that night in the camp.*b*

10 In the morning Joshua rose early and mustered the people, and went up, with the elders of Israel, before the people to Ai. 11All the fighting men who were with him went up, and drew near before the city, and camped on the north side of Ai, with a ravine between them and Ai. 12Taking about five thousand men, he set them in ambush between Bethel and Ai, to the west of the city. 13So they stationed the forces, the main encampment that was north of the city and its rear guard west of the city. But Joshua spent that night in the valley. 14When the king of Ai saw this, he and all his people, the inhabitants of the city, hurried out early in the morning to the meeting place facing the Arabah to meet Israel in battle; but he did not know that there was an ambush against him behind the city. 15And Joshua and all Israel made a pretense of being beaten before them, and fled in the direction of the wilderness. 16So all the people who were in the city were called together to pursue them, and as they pursued Joshua they were drawn away from the city. 17There was not a man left in Ai or Bethel who did not go out after Israel; they left the city open, and pursued Israel.

18 Then the LORD said to Joshua, "Stretch

---

a That is *Trouble*   *b* Heb *among the people*

7.22 The detail regarding the discovery of the *silver underneath* confirms Achan's confession in v. 21. **7.24– 26** A stone cairn in the *Valley of Achor* (Hebrew, "Trouble") marks the place of Achan's execution and reminds readers of the *trouble* (v. 25; cf. 6.18) he caused. **8.1–29** Ambush and victory at Ai. Now the Lord takes charge, Joshua and Israel strictly obey orders, and victory is secured. **8.1** Divine encouragement (*do not fear or be dismayed*) was a traditional element in sacral-war stories (Ex 14.13; Deut 1.21; 3.2; 7.18; 20.1; 31.8). **8.2** Now Israel is to follow a less sweeping pattern of *cherem* (see notes on 6.17; 6.18). All human inhabitants of Ai are to be killed, but the other booty may be kept as the spoils of war (cf. v. 26–27). The

Lord wins this victory (vv. 1, 7, 18) through the strategy of *an ambush* (cf. Judg 20.29–44). **8.3** Different versions of this story have been blended together. Here the ambush numbers *thirty thousand;* in v. 12 it totals five thousand. **8.8** The reason for setting *the city on fire* will only become clear in v. 20. **8.10** *The elders* share Joshua's leadership role in 7.6; 20.4; 23.2; 24.1, 31. **8.12–17** Victory depends on luring the fighters of Ai away from the safety of their city wall. Seeing Israel's main army towards the *north* (vv. 11, 13), the forces of Ai are lured out of the city. Israel's feigned retreat draws them even farther away from the safety of the city defenses *in the direction of the wilderness* (v. 15), i.e., eastward, and thus away from the ambush con-

out the sword that is in your hand toward Ai; for I will give it into your hand." And Joshua stretched out the sword that was in his hand toward the city. 19As soon as he stretched out his hand, the troops in ambush rose quickly out of their place and rushed forward. They entered the city, took it, and at once set the city on fire. 20So when the men of Ai looked back, the smoke of the city was rising to the sky. They had no power to flee this way or that, for the people who fled to the wilderness turned back against the pursuers. 21When Joshua and all Israel saw that the ambush had taken the city and that the smoke of the city was rising, then they turned back and struck down the men of Ai. 22And the others came out from the city against them; so they were surrounded by Israelites, some on one side, and some on the other; and Israel struck them down until no one was left who survived or escaped. 23But the king of Ai was taken alive and brought to Joshua.

24 When Israel had finished slaughtering all the inhabitants of Ai in the open wilderness where they pursued them, and when all of them to the very last had fallen by the edge of the sword, all Israel returned to Ai, and attacked it with the edge of the sword. 25The total of those who fell that day, both men and women, was twelve thousand—all the people of Ai. 26For Joshua did not draw back his hand, with which he stretched out the sword, until he had utterly destroyed all the inhabitants of Ai. 27Only the livestock and the spoil of that city Israel took as their booty, according to the word of the LORD that he had issued to Joshua. 28So Joshua burned Ai, and made it forever a heap of ruins, as it is to this day. 29And he hanged the king of Ai on a tree until evening; and at sunset Joshua commanded, and they took his body down from the tree, threw it down at the entrance of the gate of the city, and raised over it a great heap of stones, which stands there to this day.

Joshua Renews the Covenant

30 Then Joshua built on Mount Ebal an altar to the LORD, the God of Israel, 31just as Moses the servant of the LORD had commanded the Israelites, as it is written in the book of the law of Moses, "an altar of unhewn[a] stones, on which no iron tool has been used"; and they offered on it burnt offerings to the LORD, and sacrificed offerings of well-being. 32And there, in the presence of the Israelites, Joshua[b] wrote on the stones a copy of the law of Moses, which he had written. 33All Israel, alien as well as citizen, with their elders and officers and their judges, stood on opposite

a Heb whole b Heb he

cealed to the west (vv. 12–13). Ai is completely emptied of its defenders. **8.18–19** The Hebrew uses a special word for the *sword* that Joshua holds high at the Lord's command. This is the sickle-shaped sword depicted in Mesopotamian and Egyptian art as symbol of sovereignty. Cf. the outstretched arms of Moses at the battle with Amalek (Ex 17.11). Joshua's brandished sword calls out the ambush party to attack the undefended city. **8.20–21** *The smoke of the city* has two effects. It robs the warriors of Ai of their courage and signals the retreating Israelites to turn around and attack. **8.22** Victory is complete when the ambush party comes out of Ai to attack the enemy from behind, so the enemy was *surrounded by Israelites*. **8.25–27** Following the guidelines given in v. 2, the human inhabitants of Ai are treated as *cherem* and *utterly destroyed,* while the animals and material objects are taken as plunder (see notes on 6.17; 6.18). **8.28** Joshua's action accounts for the name *Ai,* "The Ruin." **8.29** Although Joshua is careful not to violate Deut 21.22–23, public exposure of a corpse was a grave affront (1 Sam 31.10). This *great heap of stones* is one of several well-known landmarks highlighted in Joshua (4.20; 5.3; 7.26; 10.27).

8.30–35 Covenant renewal at Mount Ebal. *Mount Ebal* on the north and Mount Gerizim on the south flank the pass controlled by Shechem, located about twenty miles (thirty kilometers) north of Ai. Whoever commanded the pass below Ebal could control all the hill country from a point not far north of Jerusalem almost to the plain of Esdraelon (or Jezreel). Most of that extensive territory centering in the neighborhood of Shechem, however, lacks a conquest tradition. Joshua carries out the Lord's command given to Moses (Deut 11.29–30; 27.2–13) by building an altar and sacrificing, inscribing the law on stones (v. 32), and dividing the people into two groups for blessing and cursing (v. 33). *Moses* is mentioned five times in this brief unit. **8.30–31** *The book of the law of Moses* almost certainly refers to the form of Deuteronomy rediscovered during King Josiah's reign (2 Kings 22; see Introduction). *Burnt offerings* were consumed entirely by the altar fire, while *offerings of well-being* were partially consumed by the worshipers as sacrifices establishing or maintaining a relationship with God. V. 31 quotes Deut 27.5. **8.32** He, presumably Joshua, *wrote on the stones.* These are not the stones of the altar, but standing stone pillars set up in accordance with Deut 27.4. Treaty inscriptions might characteristically be written on plastered stone surfaces (cf. 24.26–27). **8.33** *Alien as well as citizen.* The inclusive assembly (see also v. 35; Deut 31.12) reflects Deuteronomy's concern for an

sides of the ark in front of the levitical priests who carried the ark of the covenant of the LORD, half of them in front of Mount Gerizim and half of them in front of Mount Ebal, as Moses the servant of the LORD had commanded at the first, that they should bless the people of Israel. 34 And afterward he read all the words of the law, blessings and curses, according to all that is written in the book of the law. 35 There was not a word of all that Moses commanded that Joshua did not read before all the assembly of Israel, and the women, and the little ones, and the aliens who resided among them.

The Gibeonites Save Themselves by Trickery

9 Now when all the kings who were beyond the Jordan in the hill country and in the lowland all along the coast of the Great Sea toward Lebanon—the Hittites, the Amorites, the Canaanites, the Perizzites, the Hivites, and the Jebusites—heard of this, 2 they gathered together with one accord to fight Joshua and Israel.

3 But when the inhabitants of Gibeon heard what Joshua had done to Jericho and to Ai, 4 they on their part acted with cunning: they went and prepared provisions,*a* and took worn-out sacks for their donkeys, and wineskins, worn-out and torn and mended, 5 with worn-out, patched sandals on their feet, and worn-out clothes; and all their provisions were dry and moldy. 6 They went to Joshua in the camp at Gilgal, and said to him and to the Israelites, "We have come from a far country; so now make a treaty with us." 7 But the Israelites said to the Hivites, "Perhaps you live among us; then how can we make a treaty with you?" 8 They said to Joshua, "We are your servants." And Joshua said to them, "Who are you? And where do you come from?" 9 They said to him, "Your servants have come from a very far country, because of the name of the LORD your God; for we have heard a report of him, of all that he did in Egypt, 10 and of all that he did to the two kings of the Amorites who were beyond the Jordan, King Sihon of Heshbon, and King Og of Bashan who lived in Ashtaroth. 11 So our elders and all the inhabitants of our country said to us, 'Take provisions in your hand for the journey; go to meet them, and say to them, "We are your servants; come now, make a treaty with us." ' 12 Here is our bread; it was still warm when we took it from our houses as our food for the journey, on the day we set out to come to you, but now, see, it is dry and moldy; 13 these wineskins were new when we filled them, and see, they are burst; and these garments and sandals of ours are worn out from the very long journey." 14 So the leaders*b* partook of their provisions, and did not ask direction from the LORD. 15 And Joshua made peace with them, guaran-

a Cn: Meaning of Heb uncertain   *b* Gk: Heb *men*

egalitarian public policy. **8.34–35** In conformity to Deut 31.10–12, Joshua reads what was *written in the book of the law. All* is repeated four times in these two verses, emphasizing total obedience. *Blessings and curses* were standard elements in the Assyrian treaty form appropriated in the theology of Deuteronomy to motivate compliance (see esp. Deut 27–28).

9.1–27 An enemy alliance and special status for Gibeonites. News about Israel's victories leads to contrasting reactions. The kings of various peoples *gathered . . . to fight* (v. 2), but the inhabitants of Gibeon *acted with cunning* (v. 4). **9.1** *Hittites . . . Jebusites.* There is no direct correlation between this traditional list (cf. 3.10) and the account of six cities (and seven kings) defeated in 10.28–39. **9.2** *With one accord,* under one command.

9.3–27 The treaty with Gibeon. Vv. 3–15 deal with the protection of Gibeon and vv. 16–27 with the exploitation of Gibeon and its allied towns. This treaty was highly problematical from Israel's side in view of the prohibitions set forth in Deut 20.10–18. The Gibeonites' special status as a foreign enclave within Israel is presumed in the account of a famine during David's reign that was traced to Saul's bloodguilt "because he put the Gibeonites to death" (2 Sam 21.1–6). **9.3** Deliberations are initiated by the *inhabitants* of Gibeon, perhaps indicating that it had no king. *Gibeon* (el-Jib, six miles [nine kilometers] north of Jerusalem) lies on an important east-west road from Jericho that descends to the coastal plain through the Valley of Aijalon. It was at most a small village in the twelfth century BCE, like Jericho, Ai, and the other three towns in this story (v. 17). **9.6–7** This abrupt mention of *Gilgal* is jarring. The Gibeonites claim that they are *from a far country* (also v. 9), which, if true, would exempt them from the annihilation demanded by Deut 20.16–18, but in reality they are *Hivites*, one of the nations to be destroyed (9.1; Deut 20.17). A *treaty* with those who *live among* the Israelites would violate Deut 7.2. **9.8** In calling themselves *servants* the Gibeonites are practicing respectful good manners, but their words foreshadow how things will turn out in vv. 21, 23, 27. **9.9–10** The Gibeonites' hypocritical argument echoes Rahab's speech (2.10–11), based on Deut 2.26–3.17 (cf. Josh 12.1–6) and traditions reflected in Num 21.21–35. **9.14–15** *Did not ask*

teeing their lives by a treaty; and the leaders of the congregation swore an oath to them.

16 But when three days had passed after they had made a treaty with them, they heard that they were their neighbors and were living among them. 17So the Israelites set out and reached their cities on the third day. Now their cities were Gibeon, Chephirah, Beeroth, and Kiriath-jearim. 18But the Israelites did not attack them, because the leaders of the congregation had sworn to them by the LORD, the God of Israel. Then all the congregation murmured against the leaders. 19But all the leaders said to all the congregation, "We have sworn to them by the LORD, the God of Israel, and now we must not touch them. 20This is what we will do to them: We will let them live, so that wrath may not come upon us, because of the oath that we swore to them." 21The leaders said to them, "Let them live." So they became hewers of wood and drawers of water for all the congregation, as the leaders had decided concerning them.

22 Joshua summoned them, and said to them, "Why did you deceive us, saying, 'We are very far from you,' while in fact you are living among us? 23Now therefore you are cursed, and some of you shall always be slaves, hewers of wood and drawers of water for the house of my God." 24They answered Joshua, "Because it

was told to your servants for a certainty that the LORD your God had commanded his servant Moses to give you all the land, and to destroy all the inhabitants of the land before you; so we were in great fear for our lives because of you, and did this thing. 25And now we are in your hand: do as it seems good and right in your sight to do to us." 26This is what he did for them: he saved them from the Israelites; and they did not kill them. 27But on that day Joshua made them hewers of wood and drawers of water for the congregation and for the altar of the LORD, to continue to this day, in the place that he should choose.

The Sun Stands Still

10 When King Adoni-zedek of Jerusalem heard how Joshua had taken Ai, and had utterly destroyed it, doing to Ai and its king as he had done to Jericho and its king, and how the inhabitants of Gibeon had made peace with Israel and were among them, 2he[a] became greatly frightened, because Gibeon was a large city, like one of the royal cities, and was larger than Ai, and all its men were warriors. 3So King Adoni-zedek of Jerusalem sent a message to King Hoham of Hebron, to King

a Heb they

... LORD, perhaps a reference to the sacred lot used in 7.16–18. Joshua finds himself having to ratify an agreement undertaken by others for which he was not originally responsible. **9.16** The fears of v. 7 are realized. The Gibeonites are indeed *living among them*. **9.17** Mention of *their cities* is the first hint that more than one settlement might be involved. The four towns named controlled the entire northwest quadrant of approaches to Jerusalem. **9.18–20** The phrase *sworn to them by the LORD / swore to them* is stated three times in quick succession, emphatically locating responsibility. **9.20–21** Even though the Gibeonites' deception has endangered the community and must be punished, the inviolability of the leaders' oath must be protected. *Hewers of wood and drawers of water* refers to a subordinate class of servants who were part of Israel's covenant assembly nonetheless (Deut 29.11). **9.22** The Gibeonite deception is emphasized by a sharp contrast between *very far* (see vv. 6, 9) and *living among us* (see vv. 7, 16). **9.23** Some Gibeonites are to be support staff for temple ritual as servants of the *house of my God*. **9.27** The etiological formula *to continue to this day* legitimates the ongoing subjugation of the Gibeonites. *The place that he should choose* is how Deuteronomy designates the single, central sanctuary where Israel will offer sacrifice (e.g., Deut 12.5, 11, 14, 18, 21, 26).

10.1–39 Defense of Gibeon and a southern campaign. Gibeon is faced with the threat of a coalition headed by the king of Jerusalem (vv. 1–5). Joshua and Israel fulfill their treaty obligation and repel the attackers thanks to another intervention by the Lord as Divine Warrior (vv. 6–11). The Lord's miraculous intervention is emphasized by inclusion of an ancient, but misunderstood, poetic couplet (vv. 12–14). The story line then resumes, with the capture of the allied enemy kings (vv. 16–27). Then the focus shifts to towns destroyed in the south (vv. 28–39). The units have been strung together in sequence, without any attempt to harmonize differences. **10.1–2** Reports of Israel's victories provoke enemy response (cf. 5.1; 9.1–2; 11.1–3). *Jerusalem* is the only member of the enemy alliance to escape a raid, although its king is eliminated in the defeat of the coalition. Jerusalem remained a Canaanite town until its takeover by David. **10.3** These four cities lay to the south and west of Jerusalem. Judg 1.10 credits the capture of *Hebron* to Judah. Hebron, twenty miles (thirty kilometers) south of Jerusalem, figures prominently in the stories of Israel's ancestors, especially Abraham and Sarah (see Gen 13.18; 18.1; 23.19). After its capture it became the hub of the powerful tribe of Judah, the place where David was first anointed king (2 Sam 2.1–5). *Jarmuth* (Khirbet el-Yarmuk) is the first of three towns situated in a north-

Piram of Jarmuth, to King Japhia of Lachish, and to King Debir of Eglon, saying, 4"Come up and help me, and let us attack Gibeon; for it has made peace with Joshua and with the Israelites." 5Then the five kings of the Amorites—the king of Jerusalem, the king of Hebron, the king of Jarmuth, the king of Lachish, and the king of Eglon—gathered their forces, and went up with all their armies and camped against Gibeon, and made war against it.

6 And the Gibeonites sent to Joshua at the camp in Gilgal, saying, "Do not abandon your servants; come up to us quickly, and save us, and help us; for all the kings of the Amorites who live in the hill country are gathered against us." 7So Joshua went up from Gilgal, he and all the fighting force with him, all the mighty warriors. 8The LORD said to Joshua, "Do not fear them, for I have handed them over to you; not one of them shall stand before you." 9So Joshua came upon them suddenly, having marched up all night from Gilgal. 10And the LORD threw them into a panic before Israel, who inflicted a great slaughter on them at Gibeon, chased them by the way of the ascent of Beth-horon, and struck them down as far as Azekah and Makkedah. 11As they fled before Israel, while they were going down the slope of Beth-horon, the LORD threw down huge stones from heaven on them as far as Azekah, and they died; there were more who died because of the hailstones than the Israelites killed with the sword.

12 On the day when the LORD gave the Amorites over to the Israelites, Joshua spoke to the LORD; and he said in the sight of Israel,

"Sun, stand still at Gibeon,
    and Moon, in the valley of Aijalon."
13 And the sun stood still, and the moon
        stopped,
    until the nation took vengeance on
        their enemies.

Is this not written in the Book of Jashar? The sun stopped in midheaven, and did not hurry to set for about a whole day. 14There has been no day like it before or since, when the LORD heeded a human voice; for the LORD fought for Israel.

15 Then Joshua returned, and all Israel with him, to the camp at Gilgal.

Five Kings Defeated

16 Meanwhile, these five kings fled and hid themselves in the cave at Makkedah. 17And it was told Joshua, "The five kings have been found, hidden in the cave at Makkedah." 18Joshua said, "Roll large stones against the mouth of the cave, and set men by it to guard

---

south line in the foothills separating the central mountain range from the coastal road. *Lachish* (Tell ed-Duweir) was a fortified town already half a millennium old when it was destroyed in the mid-twelfth century BCE. The notice regarding King Debir of Eglon may represent a garbled tradition. *Debir* is a place name in vv. 38–39; 15.7; 21.15. The location of *Eglon* is unknown, possibly Tell Aitun. **10.5** *Amorites,* often a synonym for "Canaanites," may here retain its etymological sense, "westerners." **10.6** *All the kings of the Amorites* is a rhetorical exaggeration on the part of the Gibeonites. **10.8** *The LORD said* presupposes oracular consultation, presumably by some such means as the sacred dice, Urim and Thummim. The Israelites do not repeat the mistake for which they were faulted earlier (9.14). **10.9** A forced march *all night* is plausible (as in the siege of Ai); the straight-line distance of about twenty miles (thirty kilometers) is a strenuous, twisting climb, mostly uphill, out of the Jordan Valley. **10.10** *The LORD threw . . . chased . . . and struck.* This is the victory of the Divine Warrior, not of Joshua or Israel. *Panic* is the classic weapon of the Divine Warrior (Ex 14.24; Judg 7.21–22). The course of pursuit runs westward from Gibeon, through the pass at *the ascent of Beth-horon*, then southward. The *ascent of Beth-horon*, also known as Valley of Aijalon, was a major access route from the northern Shephelah to the hill country. *Azekah* is identified with Tell-Zakariyeh. *Makkedah* is probably Khirbet el-Qom. **10.11** *Stones from heaven* are described in terms of a hailstorm. The Divine Warrior was thought to use weather as a weapon (Isa 30.30). **10.12–14** A prose framework (vv. 12a, 13b–14) reinterprets an older poetic text (vv. 12b–13a) from the *Book of Jashar* (cf. 2 Sam 1.17). The poem addresses the moon and sun (not the Lord), calling upon these heavenly powers to freeze in amazement at Israel's stunning victory (cf. Ex 15.16; Hab 3.11). The prose framework shifts the meaning so that Joshua's request is directed *to the LORD* (v. 12) as an appeal for extended daylight. The sun stops at its noon position (*in midheaven,* v. 13) and postpones setting *for about a whole day*, while the moon is ignored. The conclusion of v. 14 is a perfect summary of the Divine Warrior tradition: *the LORD fought for Israel.*

10.16–27 The sequel to the prose account of the rout of the southern confederacy. Emphasis shifts away from the Lord's action and onto Israel's own military achievement. **10.16** *Makkedah.* The enemy escape route ended here (v. 10). This will also be the starting point for the campaign against southern towns (v. 28). **10.17–21** With *the five kings . . . hidden in . . . Makkedah,* the opposing forces are in leaderless rout. In spite of relentless pursuit (v. 19), *survivors* escape to *the fortified towns* (v. 20), creating a literary

them; [19]but do not stay there yourselves; pursue your enemies, and attack them from the rear. Do not let them enter their towns, for the LORD your God has given them into your hand." [20]When Joshua and the Israelites had finished inflicting a very great slaughter on them, until they were wiped out, and when the survivors had entered into the fortified towns, [21]all the people returned safe to Joshua in the camp at Makkedah; no one dared to speak[a] against any of the Israelites.

[22] Then Joshua said, "Open the mouth of the cave, and bring those five kings out to me from the cave." [23]They did so, and brought the five kings out to him from the cave, the king of Jerusalem, the king of Hebron, the king of Jarmuth, the king of Lachish, and the king of Eglon. [24]When they brought the kings out to Joshua, Joshua summoned all the Israelites, and said to the chiefs of the warriors who had gone with him, "Come near, put your feet on the necks of these kings." Then they came near and put their feet on their necks. [25]And Joshua said to them, "Do not be afraid or dismayed; be strong and courageous; for thus the LORD will do to all the enemies against whom you fight." [26]Afterward Joshua struck them down and put them to death, and he hung them on five trees. And they hung on the trees until evening. [27]At sunset Joshua commanded, and they took them down from the trees and threw them into the cave where they had hidden themselves; they set large stones against the mouth of the cave, which remain to this very day.

[28] Joshua took Makkedah on that day, and struck it and its king with the edge of the sword; he utterly destroyed every person in it; he left no one remaining. And he did to the king of Makkedah as he had done to the king of Jericho.

[29] Then Joshua passed on from Makkedah, and all Israel with him, to Libnah, and fought against Libnah. [30]The LORD gave it also and its king into the hand of Israel; and he struck it with the edge of the sword, and every person in it; he left no one remaining in it; and he did to its king as he had done to the king of Jericho.

[31] Next Joshua passed on from Libnah, and all Israel with him, to Lachish, and laid siege to it, and assaulted it. [32]The LORD gave Lachish into the hand of Israel, and he took it on the second day, and struck it with the edge of the sword, and every person in it, as he had done to Libnah.

[33] Then King Horam of Gezer came up to help Lachish; and Joshua struck him and his people, leaving him no survivors.

[34] From Lachish Joshua passed on with all Israel to Eglon; and they laid siege to it, and assaulted it; [35]and they took it that day, and struck it with the edge of the sword; and every person in it he utterly destroyed that day, as he had done to Lachish.

[36] Then Joshua went up with all Israel from Eglon to Hebron; they assaulted it, [37]and took it, and struck it with the edge of the sword, and its king and its towns, and every person in it; he left no one remaining, just as he had done to Eglon, and utterly destroyed it with every person in it.

[38] Then Joshua, with all Israel, turned back to Debir and assaulted it, [39]and he took it with its king and all its towns; they struck them with the edge of the sword, and utterly destroyed every person in it; he left no one remaining; just as he had done to Hebron, and, as he had done to Libnah and its king, so he did to Debir and its king.

---

a Heb *moved his tongue*

---

bridge to the next series of attacks. **10.24** Putting *feet on their necks* signifies a complete subjugation of the enemy (cf. Ps 110.1). **10.26** This is not death by hanging, but public exposure of corpses after execution so as to inspire fear. Exposing enemy bodies was a way of humiliating them (8.29; 1 Sam 31.10; 2 Sam 4.12). **10.27** Joshua obeys Deut 21.22–23. The *large stones* must have been a familiar landmark (cf. 7.26; 8.29). **10.28–39** It is difficult to harmonize this campaign in the south with the description of the coalition in vv. 1–5, because the editorial process put together preformed literary units. Lachish, Eglon, and Hebron were part of the earlier coalition, yet its other two members, Jerusalem and Jarmuth, are not attacked. No kings are mentioned for Lachish or Eglon because they have already been dealt with (vv. 23, 26), but the presence of a king at Hebron seems to contradict v. 23. **10.28** *Destroyed*, i.e., "devoted to destruction" (Hebrew *cherem*); see note on 6.17. The populations of *Libnah* (probably Tell Bornat) and *Lachish* are also wiped out, although there is no explicit mention of *cherem* (vv. 29–32). **10.33** *King Horam of Gezer* only now joins the action and is the only king mentioned by name in this final southern campaign. This text stands in tension with 16.10; Judg 1.29, which fault the tribe of Ephraim for failure to oust the Canaanites from Gezer (Tell Jezer), a city that only became Israelite in Solomon's reign (1 Kings 9.16–17). **10.36–39** In 14.6–15 Caleb is credited with victory at *Hebron* (see also 15.13–14), but the whole tribe of Judah gets the credit in Judg 1.10. The specification *its towns* (satellite villages) is made only for Hebron and Debir. Debir is

40 So Joshua defeated the whole land, the hill country and the Negeb and the lowland and the slopes, and all their kings; he left no one remaining, but utterly destroyed all that breathed, as the LORD God of Israel commanded. 41 And Joshua defeated them from Kadesh-barnea to Gaza, and all the country of Goshen, as far as Gibeon. 42 Joshua took all these kings and their land at one time, because the LORD God of Israel fought for Israel. 43 Then Joshua returned, and all Israel with him, to the camp at Gilgal.

The United Kings of Northern Canaan Defeated

11 When King Jabin of Hazor heard of this, he sent to King Jobab of Madon, to the king of Shimron, to the king of Achshaph, 2 and to the kings who were in the northern hill country, and in the Arabah south of Chinneroth, and in the lowland, and in Naphoth-dor on the west, 3 to the Canaanites in the east and the west, the Amorites, the Hittites, the Perizzites, and the Jebusites in the hill country, and the Hivites under Hermon in the land of Mizpah. 4 They came out, with all their troops, a great army, in number like the sand on the seashore, with very many horses and chariots. 5 All these kings joined their forces, and came and camped together at the waters of Merom, to fight with Israel.

6 And the LORD said to Joshua, "Do not be afraid of them, for tomorrow at this time I will hand over all of them, slain, to Israel; you shall hamstring their horses, and burn their chariots with fire." 7 So Joshua came suddenly upon them with all his fighting force, by the waters of Merom, and fell upon them. 8 And the LORD handed them over to Israel, who attacked them and chased them as far as Great Sidon and Misrephoth-maim, and eastward as far as the valley of Mizpeh. They struck them down, until they had left no one remaining. 9 And Joshua did to them as the LORD commanded him; he hamstrung their horses, and burned their chariots with fire.

10 Joshua turned back at that time, and took Hazor, and struck its king down with the sword. Before that time Hazor was the head of all those kingdoms. 11 And they put to the sword all who were in it, utterly destroying them; there was no one left who breathed, and he burned Hazor with fire. 12 And all the towns of those kings, and all their kings, Joshua took, and struck them with the edge of the sword, utterly destroying them, as Moses the servant of the LORD had commanded. 13 But Israel burned none of the towns that stood on mounds except Hazor, which Joshua did burn. 14 All the spoil of these towns, and the livestock, the Israelites took for their booty; but all the people they struck down with the edge of the sword, until they had destroyed them, and they did not leave any who breathed. 15 As

probably Khirbet Rabud. **10.40–43** This editorial summary, along with 9.1–2, frames the southern campaign. It covers both more and less than what is reported in the enclosed narrative. **10.40** The *Negeb* is the southern desert stretching from the foot of the Judean hill country into the northern Sinai Peninsula. That he *utterly destroyed all that breathed* (cf. 11.11, 14) shows obedience to Deut 20.16, from which this phrase is taken. The phrase means that the human population was exterminated. **10.41** The southern limit of the land conquered so far runs from *Kadesh-barnea to Gaza* and its northernmost extent is *as far as Gibeon*. The *country of Goshen* (11.16; 15.51) cannot be identified. It should not be confused with Goshen in Egypt (Gen 45.10).

11.1–15 Victory in the far north. Defeat of the Galilean coalition headed by Hazor. Hazor (Tell el-Qedah) was the dominant city in Upper Galilee in the period prior to Israel's emergence (v. 10). **11.1** In Judg 4.2, 23–24 Deborah and Barak also encounter a *King Jabin of Hazor*. Perhaps this was a dynastic name, but more likely separate folk traditions about Hazor used the same well-known name. The king of Hazor *heard* of Israel's victories in the southern hill country, re-

peating the theme of 2.10–11; 5.1; 9.1; 10.1. *Shimron* is Khirbet Sammuniyeh, and *Achshaph* probably Tell Kisan. **11.3** *Mizpah,* Hebrew "Watchtower" or "Lookout." *Land of Mizpah* may be a general term for the area overlooked by Mount Hermon. **11.6** *Do not be afraid of them,* standard Deuteronomic sacral-war encouragement (8.1; 10.8, 25). As at Jericho (6.3–5) and the second battle for Ai (8.18), the Lord takes direct command. The order to *hamstring their horses* (beginning of the action) *and burn their chariots* (conclusion of the action) signifies that Israel is not yet sophisticated enough to use such weaponry; this would have to wait until the monarchy (2 Sam 8.4; 1 Chr 18.4; 2 Sam 15.1; 1 Kings 1.5; 9.19–22). *Hamstring* means to cut a horse's rear leg tendons to make it unfit for war (v. 9; 2 Sam 8.4). **11.8** The panicked rout typical of a victory by the Divine Warrior. The enemy forces seem to have split, some fleeing northwest toward the coastal cities *Sidon* and *Misrephoth-maim.* **11.13** The treatment of Hazor was remembered as an exception to the general rule. Israel did not destroy most captured cities, but took them over in line with Deut 6.10–11. **11.15** *As the LORD . . . Moses.* This verse echoes v. 12 and takes readers back to the rhetoric of the

the LORD had commanded his servant Moses, so Moses commanded Joshua, and so Joshua did; he left nothing undone of all that the LORD had commanded Moses.

Summary of Joshua's Conquests

16 So Joshua took all that land: the hill country and all the Negeb and all the land of Goshen and the lowland and the Arabah and the hill country of Israel and its lowland, 17from Mount Halak, which rises toward Seir, as far as Baal-gad in the valley of Lebanon below Mount Hermon. He took all their kings, struck them down, and put them to death. 18Joshua made war a long time with all those kings. 19There was not a town that made peace with the Israelites, except the Hivites, the inhabitants of Gibeon; all were taken in battle. 20For it was the LORD's doing to harden their hearts so that they would come against Israel in battle, in order that they might be utterly destroyed, and might receive no mercy, but be exterminated, just as the LORD had commanded Moses.

21 At that time Joshua came and wiped out the Anakim from the hill country, from Hebron, from Debir, from Anab, and from all the hill country of Judah, and from all the hill country of Israel; Joshua utterly destroyed them with their towns. 22None of the Anakim was left in the land of the Israelites; some remained only in Gaza, in Gath, and in Ashdod. 23So Joshua took the whole land, according to all that the LORD had spoken to Moses; and Joshua gave it for an inheritance to Israel according to their tribal allotments. And the land had rest from war.

The Kings Conquered by Moses

12 Now these are the kings of the land, whom the Israelites defeated, whose land they occupied beyond the Jordan toward the east, from the Wadi Arnon to Mount Hermon, with all the Arabah eastward: 2King Sihon of the Amorites who lived at Heshbon, and ruled from Aroer, which is on the edge of the Wadi Arnon, and from the middle of the valley as far as the river Jabbok, the boundary of the Ammonites, that is, half of Gilead, 3and the Arabah to the Sea of Chinneroth eastward, and in the direction of Beth-jeshimoth, to the sea of the Arabah, the Dead Sea,*a* southward to the foot of the slopes of Pisgah; 4and King Og*b* of Bashan, one of the last of the Rephaim, who

_____

a Heb *Salt Sea*　*b* Gk: Heb *the boundary of King Og*

Lord's initial command to Joshua (1.7). The intervening stories serve as examples of how Moses' teaching was followed.

11.16–23 Summary of Israel's victories. This is the second such summary. The first one covers the south (10.40–42). The result is a two-phase presentation of the conquest, which will be followed by a two-phase portrayal of the process of settlement, described in 13.1–17.18 and 18.1–19.53, respectively. **11.16** A reiteration of 10.40. **11.17** Israel's territory is envisioned as reaching from *Mount Halak* ("Mount Baldy") far to the southeast on the border with Edom up to *Mount Baal-gad* near *Mount Hermon* on Israel's far north (12.7; 13.5–6). *Seir* refers to the mountains of Edom. **11.19** That *all were taken in battle* presents a picture of total conquest, consistent with the exhortations of Deuteronomy. **11.20** *The* LORD's *doing . . . be exterminated.* The enemy's obstinacy and attacks are interpreted as a divine plan to obliterate them. **11.21** Israel's folklore thought of the *Anakim* as a primordial race of giants (Num 13.28; Deut 2.21; 9.2), descended from a union of divine and human beings (Gen 6.4; Num 13.33). Opponents from the days of Moses, they are found in company with Gaza and Ashkelon in Jer 47.5. This report overlaps with the conquest of Hebron and Debir in 10.36–39, indicating that the actual process of conquest was more complex than previously indicated. **11.22** *Gaza, Gath,* and *Ashdod* are

Philistine cities. The continuing presence of Anakim undermines the sweeping claim that Israel conquered the whole land (v. 16, 20). **11.23** The summary concludes by emphasizing the obedient chain of command—*Joshua* obeys what the LORD commanded through Moses. *Joshua gave . . . tribal allotments* anticipates chs. 14–19. A *land at rest from war* means that the conquest has come to a close.

12.1–24 A summary of the former kingdoms includes towns and kings not otherwise mentioned in the book. **12.1–6** Summary of Transjordanian victories under Moses' leadership, describing land seized from Sihon in vv. 2–3 and that taken from Og in vv. 4–5. **12.1** *Wadi Arnon,* the immense canyon forming a natural and acknowledged northern border of the kingdom of Moab and the southern limit of Israel's territorial claim in Transjordan prior to the reign of King David. **12.2** The story of *King Sihon* is told in Num 21.21–31. *Gilead,* the wooded hill country of Transjordan, was divided by the deep and winding gorge of the *Jabbok,* the northern limit of Sihon's realm. Thus Israel's claim to the southern *half of Gilead* is based on its defeat of Sihon. **12.4** Og ruled *Bashan,* productive land centering on the Golan Heights. *Rephaim* referred originally to an aristocracy of professional chariot warriors, from whose ranks came many of the Canaanite kings. It acquired a secondary sense of "giants" (cf. Og's huge bedstead, Deut 3.11)

lived at Ashtaroth and at Edrei [5] and ruled over Mount Hermon and Salecah and all Bashan to the boundary of the Geshurites and the Maacathites, and over half of Gilead to the boundary of King Sihon of Heshbon. [6] Moses, the servant of the LORD, and the Israelites defeated them; and Moses the servant of the LORD gave their land for a possession to the Reubenites and the Gadites and the half-tribe of Manasseh.

The Kings Conquered by Joshua

7 The following are the kings of the land whom Joshua and the Israelites defeated on the west side of the Jordan, from Baal-gad in the valley of Lebanon to Mount Halak, that rises toward Seir (and Joshua gave their land to the tribes of Israel as a possession according to their allotments, [8] in the hill country, in the lowland, in the Arabah, in the slopes, in the wilderness, and in the Negeb, the land of the Hittites, Amorites, Canaanites, Perizzites, Hivites, and Jebusites):

[9] the king of Jericho	one
the king of Ai, which is next to Bethel	one
[10] the king of Jerusalem	one
the king of Hebron	one
[11] the king of Jarmuth	one
the king of Lachish	one
[12] the king of Eglon	one
the king of Gezer	one
[13] the king of Debir	one
the king of Geder	one
[14] the king of Hormah	one
the king of Arad	one
[15] the king of Libnah	one
the king of Adullam	one
[16] the king of Makkedah	one
the king of Bethel	one
[17] the king of Tappuah	one
the king of Hepher	one
[18] the king of Aphek	one
the king of Lasharon	one
[19] the king of Madon	one
the king of Hazor	one
[20] the king of Shimron-meron	one
the king of Achshaph	one
[21] the king of Taanach	one
the king of Megiddo	one
[22] the king of Kedesh	one
the king of Jokneam in Carmel	one
[23] the king of Dor in Naphath-dor	one
the king of Goiim in Galilee, [a]	one
[24] the king of Tirzah	one

thirty-one kings in all.

The Parts of Canaan Still Unconquered

13 Now Joshua was old and advanced in years; and the LORD said to him, "You are old and advanced in years, and very much of the land still remains to be possessed. [2] This is the land that still remains: all the regions of

a Gk: Heb Gilgal

---

and yet another sense referring to "shades of the dead." **12.5** *Geshurites* and *Maacathites,* two Aramean (Syrian) groups who were sources of continuing resistance to Israel (13.13) until the time of David, one of whose wives was a Geshurite princess (2 Sam 3.3). Israel's claim to the northern *half of Gilead* (12.2) is based on its defeat of Og.

12.7–24 A list of kings dethroned in the era of Joshua making no specific claim to occupation or destruction of towns. **12.7–8** A parallel to 11.16–17. **12.9–13a** These verses are closely related to the sequence of stories in 6.1–10.43; every one of these kings has been previously mentioned in those chapters. Jericho and Ai naturally come first (v. 9). The five cities of 10.3 are listed in vv. 10–12a. **12.13b–16a** A passage related in part to ch. 10, but supplying several names in the south not previously mentioned—*Geder, Hormah, Arad.* **12.16b–24** Kings from the central and northern regions. **12.16b** A tradition about the conquest of *Bethel* is related in Judg 1.22–26. **12.17** *Tappuah* (probably Sheikh Abu Zarad) was an important town on the border between Ephraim and Manasseh. *Hepher,* a clan of Manasseh situated north of Shechem. **12.18** *Aphek* (Ras el-'Ain) was never included in

any of the tribal claims. *Lasharon,* lit. "to (or for) the Sharon(-plain)," perhaps is intended to cover the entire region, which was sparsely settled due to swampy and malarial conditions. **12.19–20** Catalogue of the four cities of 11.1. **12.21** *Megiddo* controlled the southern flank of the Esdraelon plain and the most heavily traveled route through the Mount Carmel range to the Sharon plain. **12.22** *Kedesh,* probably not the great sanctuary town in the far north (19.37) but a smaller site between Megiddo and Taanach. *Jokneam* (Tell Qeimun), at the tip of Zebulun's southwestern wedge, may have become Israelite at a very early period since there is no mention of it among the unconquered towns in 17.11; Judg 1.27. **12.23** *Goiim in Galilee* suggests the name of Sisera's hometown, "Harosheth-ha-goyim" (Judg 4.2). **12.24** *Tirzah,* probably Tell el-Far'ah (ca. six miles [ten kilometers] northeast of Shechem), was first favored as capital of the Northern throne (1 Kings 14–16) when it moved the seat of government away from Shechem.

13.1–19.51 The territorial allotments, with bits of narrative interspersed. Generally the geographical data in chs. 13–19 comes in three forms: "lines of extent" that run out from a stated location, boundary de-

the Philistines, and all those of the Geshurites 3(from the Shihor, which is east of Egypt, northward to the boundary of Ekron, it is reckoned as Canaanite; there are five rulers of the Philistines, those of Gaza, Ashdod, Ashkelon, Gath, and Ekron), and those of the Avvim 4in the south; all the land of the Canaanites, and Mearah that belongs to the Sidonians, to Aphek, to the boundary of the Amorites, 5and the land of the Gebalites, and all Lebanon, toward the east, from Baal-gad below Mount Hermon to Lebo-hamath, 6all the inhabitants of the hill country from Lebanon to Misrephoth-maim, even all the Sidonians. I will myself drive them out from before the Israelites; only allot the land to Israel for an inheritance, as I have commanded you. 7Now therefore divide this land for an inheritance to the nine tribes and the half-tribe of Manasseh."

The Territory East of the Jordan

8 With the other half-tribe of Manasseh*a* the Reubenites and the Gadites received their inheritance, which Moses gave them, beyond the Jordan eastward, as Moses the servant of the LORD gave them: 9from Aroer, which is on the edge of the Wadi Arnon, and the town that is in the middle of the valley, and all the tableland from*b* Medeba as far as Dibon; 10and all the cities of King Sihon of the Amorites, who reigned in Heshbon, as far as the boundary of the Ammonites; 11and Gilead, and the region of the Geshurites and Maacathites, and all Mount Hermon, and all Bashan to Salecah;

12all the kingdom of Og in Bashan, who reigned in Ashtaroth and in Edrei (he alone was left of the survivors of the Rephaim); these Moses had defeated and driven out. 13Yet the Israelites did not drive out the Geshurites or the Maacathites; but Geshur and Maacath live within Israel to this day.

14 To the tribe of Levi alone Moses gave no inheritance; the offerings by fire to the LORD God of Israel are their inheritance, as he said to them.

The Territory of Reuben

15 Moses gave an inheritance to the tribe of the Reubenites according to their clans. 16Their territory was from Aroer, which is on the edge of the Wadi Arnon, and the town that is in the middle of the valley, and all the tableland by Medeba; 17with Heshbon, and all its towns that are in the tableland; Dibon, and Bamoth-baal, and Beth-baal-meon, 18and Jahaz, and Kedemoth, and Mephaath, 19and Kiriathaim, and Sibmah, and Zereth-shahar on the hill of the valley, 20and Beth-peor, and the slopes of Pisgah, and Beth-jeshimoth, 21that is, all the towns of the tableland, and all the kingdom of King Sihon of the Amorites, who reigned in Heshbon, whom Moses defeated with the leaders of Midian, Evi and Rekem and Zur and Hur and Reba, as princes of Sihon, who lived in the land. 22Along with the rest of those they put to death, the Israelites

---

a Cn: Heb *With it*   *b* Compare Gk: Heb lacks *from*

---

scriptions, and town lists. The town lists seem to be derived from older administrative sources. This is particularly clear for 15.20–62 (Judah) and 18.21–28 (Benjamin). **13.1–7** Land in western Palestine remaining to be conquered consisted of Philistine territory and areas to the north in Phoenicia and Lebanon. The Philistines (v. 2) only came under Israelite control, briefly, during the reigns of David and Solomon. Control of Phoenicia (vv. 4–6) was never realized. **13.1** *Now Joshua . . . in years,* in Hebrew a distinctive idiom, occurring again in 23.1. Joshua's age motivates distribution of the land west of the Jordan (vv. 6–7). **13.8–14** This flashback describes the extent of the conquest east of the Jordan and tribal allotments made by Moses and is clearly related to 12.1–5 (and Deut 3.8, 10a). The description moves from south to north. **13.9** *Aroer* ('Ara'ir) forms the boundary with Moab on the south. *The town . . . in the middle of the valley* perhaps refers to the general habitable area between two main courses of the *Wadi Arnon,* which flow together on the west and also meet twice in the east. **13.11–**

12 *Mount Hermon* and the former *kingdom of Og in Bashan* are the northern frontier. **13.13** *Geshur and Maacath* remain as alien enclaves. This is the first of a series of explanatory statements faulting various tribes for failure to achieve total conquest (15.63; 16.10; 17.12–13), contrary to the claim of complete victory found in 11.23; 21.43–45. **13.14** References to Levi here and in v. 33 frame the description of allotments east of the Jordan. *The tribe of Levi* formed the one exception to all tribes sharing in the apportionment of the land. Levites were dispersed with residential and grazing rights in designated towns throughout the land allotted to other tribes (ch. 21). **13.15–31** Reuben receives territory in the south, Gad farther north, and elements of Manasseh occupy land north and east of Gad. **13.15–23** The *Reubenites* receive the larger southern segment of Sihon's realm, described by a line drawn north *from Aroer,* the southern limit of early Israel's claim (v. 16), and a list of towns (vv. 17–20). **13.22** The story of *Balaam son of Beor* is recounted in Num 22–24. Texts referring to Ba-

also put to the sword Balaam son of Beor, who practiced divination. 23 And the border of the Reubenites was the Jordan and its banks. This was the inheritance of the Reubenites according to their families with their towns and villages.

The Territory of Gad

24 Moses gave an inheritance also to the tribe of the Gadites, according to their families. 25 Their territory was Jazer, and all the towns of Gilead, and half the land of the Ammonites, to Aroer, which is east of Rabbah, 26 and from Heshbon to Ramath-mizpeh and Betonim, and from Mahanaim to the territory of Debir,*a* 27 and in the valley Beth-haram, Beth-nimrah, Succoth, and Zaphon, the rest of the kingdom of King Sihon of Heshbon, the Jordan and its banks, as far as the lower end of the Sea of Chinnereth, eastward beyond the Jordan. 28 This is the inheritance of the Gadites according to their clans, with their towns and villages.

The Territory of the Half-Tribe of Manasseh (East)

29 Moses gave an inheritance to the half-tribe of Manasseh; it was allotted to the half-tribe of the Manassites according to their families. 30 Their territory extended from Mahanaim, through all Bashan, the whole kingdom of King Og of Bashan, and all the settlements of Jair, which are in Bashan, sixty towns, 31 and half of Gilead, and Ashtaroth, and Edrei, the towns of the kingdom of Og in Bashan; these were allotted to the people of Machir son of Manasseh according to their clans—for half the Machirites.

32 These are the inheritances that Moses distributed in the plains of Moab, beyond the Jordan east of Jericho. 33 But to the tribe of Levi Moses gave no inheritance; the LORD God of Israel is their inheritance, as he said to them.

The Distribution of Territory West of the Jordan

14 These are the inheritances that the Israelites received in the land of Canaan, which the priest Eleazar, and Joshua son of Nun, and the heads of the families of the tribes of the Israelites distributed to them. 2 Their inheritance was by lot, as the LORD had commanded Moses for the nine and one-half tribes. 3 For Moses had given an inheritance to the two and one-half tribes beyond the Jordan; but to the Levites he gave no inheritance among them. 4 For the people of Joseph were two tribes, Manasseh and Ephraim; and no portion was given to the Levites in the land, but only towns to live in, with their pasture lands for their flocks and herds. 5 The Israelites did as the LORD commanded Moses; they allotted the land.

Hebron Allotted to Caleb

6 Then the people of Judah came to Joshua at Gilgal; and Caleb son of Jephunneh the Kenizzite said to him, "You know what the LORD said to Moses the man of God in Kadesh-barnea concerning you and me. 7 I was forty years old when Moses the servant of the LORD sent me from Kadesh-barnea to spy out the land; and I brought him an honest report. 8 But my companions who went up with me made the heart of the people melt; yet I wholeheartedly followed the LORD my God. 9 And Moses swore on that day, saying, 'Surely the land on which your foot has trodden shall be an inheritance for you and your children forever, be-

---

a Gk Syr Vg: Heb *Lidebir*

---

laam were found in 1967 at Tell Deir 'Alla in Transjordan. **13.24–28** Gad settled north of Reuben in the southern half of Gilead, which represented the northern stretch of Sihon's former kingdom. Two descriptive lines extend northward: *from Heshbon* (Hesban) and *from Mahanaim* (Tell edh-Dhahab el-Garbi, v. 26). The first part of v. 27 catalogs four towns. **13.29–31** Some clans of Manasseh receive territory north and east of Gad. **13.30** *Bashan*, the Golan Heights, lies north of the Yarmuk River. *Jair.* See Num 32.41 (Deut 3.14). **13.31** Manasseh's *half of Gilead* is territory north of the Jabbok (cf. 12.2, 5).
14.1–5 Introduction to the western allotments.

14.1 *Canaan* was the ancient name of the territory west of Jordan. *Eleazar*'s role as keeper of the sacred lot (Urim and Thummim) is stipulated at the commissioning of Joshua (Num 27.21). Casting the lot was a priestly prerogative (Deut 33.8). **14.2** Distribution *by lot* guarantees that it corresponds to God's will. **14.4** The *Levites* receive no territory, and so *the people of Joseph were two tribes, Manasseh and Ephraim*, to make up the total of twelve. **14.6–15** Allotment to Caleb in the south is a special case structurally balanced by the example of Zelophehad's daughters in the north (17.1–6). **14.7–9** Caleb claims an exceptional award of territory to reward his conduct as a spy

cause you have wholeheartedly followed the LORD my God.' 10And now, as you see, the LORD has kept me alive, as he said, these forty-five years since the time that the LORD spoke this word to Moses, while Israel was journeying through the wilderness; and here I am today, eighty-five years old. 11I am still as strong today as I was on the day that Moses sent me; my strength now is as my strength was then, for war, and for going and coming. 12So now give me this hill country of which the LORD spoke on that day; for you heard on that day how the Anakim were there, with great fortified cities; it may be that the LORD will be with me, and I shall drive them out, as the LORD said."

13 Then Joshua blessed him, and gave Hebron to Caleb son of Jephunneh for an inheritance. 14So Hebron became the inheritance of Caleb son of Jephunneh the Kenizzite to this day, because he wholeheartedly followed the LORD, the God of Israel. 15Now the name of Hebron formerly was Kiriath-arba;*a* this Arba was*b* the greatest man among the Anakim. And the land had rest from war.

The Territory of Judah

15 The lot for the tribe of the people of Judah according to their families reached southward to the boundary of Edom, to the wilderness of Zin at the farthest south. 2And their south boundary ran from the end of the Dead Sea,*c* from the bay that faces southward; 3it goes out southward of the ascent of Akrabbim, passes along to Zin, and goes up south of Kadesh-barnea, along by Hezron, up to Addar, makes a turn to Karka, 4passes along to Azmon, goes out by the Wadi of Egypt, and comes to its end at the sea. This shall be your south boundary. 5And the east boundary is the Dead Sea,*c* to the mouth of the Jordan. And the boundary on the north side runs from the bay of the sea at the mouth

of the Jordan; 6and the boundary goes up to Beth-hoglah, and passes along north of Beth-arabah; and the boundary goes up to the Stone of Bohan, Reuben's son; 7and the boundary goes up to Debir from the Valley of Achor, and so northward, turning toward Gilgal, which is opposite the ascent of Adummim, which is on the south side of the valley; and the boundary passes along to the waters of En-shemesh, and ends at En-rogel; 8then the boundary goes up by the valley of the son of Hinnom at the southern slope of the Jebusites (that is, Jerusalem); and the boundary goes up to the top of the mountain that lies over against the valley of Hinnom, on the west, at the northern end of the valley of Rephaim; 9then the boundary extends from the top of the mountain to the spring of the Waters of Nephtoah, and from there to the towns of Mount Ephron; then the boundary bends around to Baalah (that is, Kiriath-jearim); 10and the boundary circles west of Baalah to Mount Seir, passes along to the northern slope of Mount Jearim (that is, Chesalon), and goes down to Beth-shemesh, and passes along by Timnah; 11the boundary goes out to the slope of the hill north of Ekron, then the boundary bends around to Shikkeron, and passes along to Mount Baalah, and goes out to Jabneel; then the boundary comes to an end at the sea. 12And the west boundary was the Mediterranean with its coast. This is the boundary surrounding the people of Judah according to their families.

Caleb Occupies His Portion

13 According to the commandment of the LORD to Joshua, he gave to Caleb son of Jephunneh a portion among the people of Judah, Kiriath-arba,*a* that is, Hebron (Arba was the father of Anak). 14And Caleb drove

---

a That is *the city of Arba* *b* Heb lacks *this Arba was*
c Heb *Salt Sea*

(vv. 7–8; Num 13) and to fulfill an oath sworn by Moses (v. 9). **14.10–11** Caleb supports his case by noting his great age and his undiminished capacity as a fighter. **14.12** That Joshua has already settled accounts with the *Anakim* (11.21–22; see note on 11.21) suggests that this narrative should be read as a flashback. **14.13** *Hebron.* See note on 10.3. The story of Caleb resumes in 15.13–19. **14.15** *And the land . . . war* echoes the identical statement at the end of ch. 11, framing the lengthy explanatory additions, chs. 12–14.

15.1–63 Judah gets pride of place in the description

of the territories in Canaan. Its borders are delineated in vv. 1–12, and its towns are cataloged into districts in vv. 20–63. **15.1–4** Judah's southern border coincides with 13.4–5; Num 34.3–6. **15.5–11** Judah's detailed northern border with Benjamin coincides with 18.15–19. The line carefully excludes Jerusalem by skirting it on the south (vv. 8–9). **15.13–19** A land grant for Caleb interrupts the cartographic description. The story of Othniel and Achsah, repeated nearly verbatim in Judg 1.11–15, explains why descendants of Othniel controlled not only Debir, but two springs near He-

out from there the three sons of Anak: She-shai, Ahiman, and Talmai, the descendants of Anak. 15From there he went up against the in-habitants of Debir; now the name of Debir formerly was Kiriath-sepher. 16And Caleb said, "Whoever attacks Kiriath-sepher and takes it, to him I will give my daughter Achsah as wife." 17Othniel son of Kenaz, the brother of Caleb, took it; and he gave him his daughter Achsah as wife. 18When she came to him, she urged him to ask her father for a field. As she dismounted from her donkey, Caleb said to her, "What do you wish?" 19She said to him, "Give me a present; since you have set me in the land of the Negeb, give me springs of water as well." So Caleb gave her the upper springs and the lower springs.

The Towns of Judah

20 This is the inheritance of the tribe of the people of Judah according to their families. 21The towns belonging to the tribe of the people of Judah in the extreme south, toward the boundary of Edom, were Kabzeel, Eder, Jagur, 22Kinah, Dimonah, Adadah, 23Kedesh, Hazor, Ithnan, 24Ziph, Telem, Bealoth, 25Hazor-hadat-tah, Kerioth-hezron (that is, Hazor), 26Amam, Shema, Moladah, 27Hazar-gaddah, Heshmon, Beth-pelet, 28Hazar-shual, Beer-sheba, Bizioth-iah, 29Baalah, Iim, Ezem, 30Eltolad, Chesil, Hormah, 31Ziklag, Madmannah, Sansannah, 32Lebaoth, Shilhim, Ain, and Rimmon: in all, twenty-nine towns, with their villages.

33 And in the lowland, Eshtaol, Zorah, Ash-nah, 34Zanoah, En-gannim, Tappuah, Enam, 35Jarmuth, Adullam, Socoh, Azekah, 36Shaa-raim, Adithaim, Gederah, Gederothaim: four-teen towns with their villages.

37 Zenan, Hadashah, Migdal-gad, 38Dilan, Mizpeh, Jokthe-el, 39Lachish, Bozkath, Eglon, 40Cabbon, Lahmam, Chitlish, 41Gederoth, Beth-dagon, Naamah, and Makkedah: sixteen towns with their villages.

42 Libnah, Ether, Ashan, 43Iphtah, Ashnah, Nezib, 44Keilah, Achzib, and Mareshah: nine towns with their villages.

45 Ekron, with its dependencies and its vil-lages; 46from Ekron to the sea, all that were near Ashdod, with their villages.

47 Ashdod, its towns and its villages; Gaza, its towns and its villages; to the Wadi of Egypt, and the Great Sea with its coast.

48 And in the hill country, Shamir, Jattir, Socoh, 49Dannah, Kiriath-sannah (that is, Debir), 50Anab, Eshtemoh, Anim, 51Goshen, Holon, and Giloh: eleven towns with their vil-lages.

52 Arab, Dumah, Eshan, 53Janim, Beth-tap-puah, Aphekah, 54Humtah, Kiriath-arba (that is, Hebron), and Zior: nine towns with their villages.

55 Maon, Carmel, Ziph, Juttah, 56Jezreel, Jokdeam, Zanoah, 57Kain, Gibeah, and Tim-nah: ten towns with their villages.

58 Halhul, Beth-zur, Gedor, 59Maarath, Beth-anoth, and Eltekon: six towns with their villages.

60 Kiriath-baal (that is, Kiriath-jearim) and Rabbah: two towns with their villages.

61 In the wilderness, Beth-arabah, Middin, Secacah, 62Nibshan, the City of Salt, and En-gedi: six towns with their villages.

63 But the people of Judah could not drive out the Jebusites, the inhabitants of Jerusalem; so the Jebusites live with the people of Judah in Jerusalem to this day.

The Territory of Ephraim

16 The allotment of the Josephites went from the Jordan by Jericho, east of the

---

bron. **15.18** Achsah urges Othniel to ask *for a field* but immediately takes matters into her own hand. **15.19** Achsah terms her territory *land of the Negeb* to emphasize its aridity. **15.20–63** This list of towns or-ganized into districts, arranged and identified geo-graphically, is probably based on the later administra-tive organization of the kingdom of Judah. The remainder of this district system is used for Benjamin in 18.21–28. Each district description concludes with an enumeration of *towns with their villages.* Eleven districts in the tribe of Judah and the southwestern district of Benjamin preserved in 18.25–28 constitute the kingdom of Judah. **15.21–32** Judah's first district is in the far *south* towards the Negeb desert. **15.33–44** Three districts are in the *lowland,* the Shephelah to the west of the central hill country. **15.45–47** This dis-trict of Philistine towns falls outside the pattern and was probably not part of the original administrative list. **15.48–60** Six districts are in Judah's central *hill country.* The Septuagint (Greek Old Testament) wit-nesses to a district between vv. 59 and 60 that dropped out of the Hebrew text: "Tekoa, Ephrathah (that is, Bethlehem), Peor, Etam, Koulon, Tatam, Sores, Karem, Gallim, Bether, and Manahath: eleven towns with their villages." **15.61–62** One district is in the *wilderness,* the eastern desert leading down to the Dead Sea. **15.63** *Jerusalem* became part of Israel only under David (2 Sam 5.6–9). See also the note on 13.13.
16.1–10 Ephraim comes next as the most impor-tant northern tribe. **16.1–3** Ephraim and Manasseh

waters of Jericho, into the wilderness, going up from Jericho into the hill country to Bethel; 2then going from Bethel to Luz, it passes along to Ataroth, the territory of the Archites; 3then it goes down westward to the territory of the Japhletites, as far as the territory of Lower Beth-horon, then to Gezer, and it ends at the sea.

4 The Josephites—Manasseh and Ephraim—received their inheritance.

5 The territory of the Ephraimites by their families was as follows: the boundary of their inheritance on the east was Ataroth-addar as far as Upper Beth-horon, 6and the boundary goes from there to the sea; on the north is Michmethath; then on the east the boundary makes a turn toward Taanath-shiloh, and passes along beyond it on the east to Janoah, 7then it goes down from Janoah to Ataroth and to Naarah, and touches Jericho, ending at the Jordan. 8From Tappuah the boundary goes westward to the Wadi Kanah, and ends at the sea. Such is the inheritance of the tribe of the Ephraimites by their families, 9together with the towns that were set apart for the Ephraimites within the inheritance of the Manassites, all those towns with their villages. 10They did not, however, drive out the Canaanites who lived in Gezer: so the Canaanites have lived within Ephraim to this day but have been made to do forced labor.

The Other Half-Tribe of Manasseh (West)

17 Then allotment was made to the tribe of Manasseh, for he was the firstborn of Joseph. To Machir the firstborn of Manasseh, the father of Gilead, were allotted Gilead and Bashan, because he was a warrior. 2And allotments were made to the rest of the tribe of Manasseh, by their families, Abiezer, Helek, Asriel, Shechem, Hepher, and Shemida; these were the male descendants of Manasseh son of Joseph, by their families.

3 Now Zelophehad son of Hepher son of Gilead son of Machir son of Manasseh had no sons, but only daughters; and these are the names of his daughters: Mahlah, Noah, Hoglah, Milcah, and Tirzah. 4They came before the priest Eleazar and Joshua son of Nun and the leaders, and said, "The LORD commanded Moses to give us an inheritance along with our male kin." So according to the commandment of the LORD he gave them an inheritance among the kinsmen of their father. 5Thus there fell to Manasseh ten portions, besides the land of Gilead and Bashan, which is on the other side of the Jordan, 6because the daughters of Manasseh received an inheritance along with his sons. The land of Gilead was allotted to the rest of the Manassites.

7 The territory of Manasseh reached from Asher to Michmethath, which is east of Shechem; then the boundary goes along south-

---

together make up *the Josephites*. Ephraim's southern boundary corresponds to the northern border of Benjamin (18.12–13). *Bethel* and *Luz* (v. 2) are the same place in Judg 1.22–26. *Archites* refers to a clan or village population that became part of Benjamin. One of David's most loyal advisers, Hushai, was recruited from them (2 Sam 15.32; 16.16; 17.5). *Gezer*. See note on 10.33. **16.5–9** Ephraim's northern border is mapped first eastward and then westward from a central point: east and south from *Michmethath* (vv. 6–7), then west from neighboring *Tappuah* (v. 8). **16.10** *Canaanites . . . forced labor*. The chapter concludes on a note of partial failure, which appears sporadically throughout the description of the northern tribes (cf. note on 13.13). *Gezer*. See note on 10.33.

17.1–13 Description of Manasseh west of the Jordan, unlike the preceding tribal descriptions, falls into two parts, one concerned with subgroups (vv. 1–6), one with borders (vv. 7–13). **17.1** *Firstborn of Joseph*. See Gen 41.51; 46.20. *Machir*, as "eldest son" of Manasseh, appears to have been a constituency that was originally at home in the west (Judg 5.14) and then in part shifted to Transjordan. *Father of Gilead*. Genealogy adjusts to reflect changing sociopolitical realities (cf.

Num 26.28–34; 1 Chr 7.14–19). Gilead was originally a geographical term (12.2, 5; 13.11, 25, 31). **17.2** *The rest of the tribe of Manasseh* were those who had not already settled in Transjordan. Six clans traced descent through Manasseh's male heirs. *Abiezer* was Gideon's hometown (Judg 6.11, 24, 34). *Helek* is the area to the northwest of Shechem. *Asriel* (1 Chr 7.14) is located northwest of Helek. *Shechem* figures merely as one of the clans of Manasseh. *Hepher* is the area north of Shechem. Shechem is given as a son of *Shemida* in 1 Chr 7.19. **17.3–6** Five clans of Manasseh descended from the daughters of *Zelophehad*. Special provision for them in the north balances the special treatment of Caleb in the south (14.6–15; 15.13–14). Both are based on appeal to a prior ruling from Moses (Num 27.1–11; 36.1–12). Location of the areas identified by the names *Mahlah, Noah, Hoglah*, and *Milcah* are unknown. *Tirzah*. See note on 12.24. **17.4** *Eleazar* is always mentioned before Joshua when they are found together (14.1; 21.1). *The LORD commanded Moses*. See Num 27.1–11. **17.5** Six clans, one of which is "grandfather" of the five daughters, account for *ten portions* for Manasseh west of the river. **17.7–13** The boundaries of western Manasseh were sketchy and presented

ward to the inhabitants of En-tappuah. ⁸The land of Tappuah belonged to Manasseh, but the town of Tappuah on the boundary of Manasseh belonged to the Ephraimites. ⁹Then the boundary went down to the Wadi Kanah. The towns here, to the south of the wadi, among the towns of Manasseh, belong to Ephraim. Then the boundary of Manasseh goes along the north side of the wadi and ends at the sea. ¹⁰The land to the south is Ephraim's and that to the north is Manasseh's, with the sea forming its boundary; on the north Asher is reached, and on the east Issachar. ¹¹Within Issachar and Asher, Manasseh had Beth-shean and its villages, Ibleam and its villages, the inhabitants of Dor and its villages, the inhabitants of En-dor and its villages, the inhabitants of Taanach and its villages, and the inhabitants of Megiddo and its villages (the third is Naphath).ᵃ ¹²Yet the Manassites could not take possession of those towns; but the Canaanites continued to live in that land. ¹³But when the Israelites grew strong, they put the Canaanites to forced labor, but did not utterly drive them out.

The Tribe of Joseph Protests

14 The tribe of Joseph spoke to Joshua, saying, "Why have you given me but one lot and one portion as an inheritance, since we are a numerous people, whom all along the LORD has blessed?" ¹⁵And Joshua said to them, "If you are a numerous people, go up to the forest, and clear ground there for yourselves in the land of the Perizzites and the Rephaim, since

the hill country of Ephraim is too narrow for you." ¹⁶The tribe of Joseph said, "The hill country is not enough for us; yet all the Canaanites who live in the plain have chariots of iron, both those in Beth-shean and its villages and those in the Valley of Jezreel." ¹⁷Then Joshua said to the house of Joseph, to Ephraim and Manasseh, "You are indeed a numerous people, and have great power; you shall not have one lot only, ¹⁸but the hill country shall be yours, for though it is a forest, you shall clear it and possess it to its farthest borders; for you shall drive out the Canaanites, though they have chariots of iron, and though they are strong."

The Territories of the Remaining Tribes

18 Then the whole congregation of the Israelites assembled at Shiloh, and set up the tent of meeting there. The land lay subdued before them.

2 There remained among the Israelites seven tribes whose inheritance had not yet been apportioned. ³So Joshua said to the Israelites, "How long will you be slack about going in and taking possession of the land that the LORD, the God of your ancestors, has given you? ⁴Provide three men from each tribe, and I will send them out that they may begin to go throughout the land, writing a description of it with a view to their inheritances. Then come back to me. ⁵They shall divide it into seven portions, Judah continuing in its territory on

---

ᵃ Meaning of Heb uncertain

---

questions about the tribal "ownership" of certain towns (v. 9). For the allotments to the northern tribes there was apparently no archival source comparable to that for Judah and Benjamin in the south. **17.7–9** Manasseh's southern border corresponds to Ephraim's northern boundary (16.6, 8). **17.11–13** The plain of Esdraelon (or Jezreel), supporting a number of well-fortified city-states, separated Manasseh from the Galilean tribes. *Beth-shean* (Tell el-Husn) was a strongly fortified city controlling the southeast corner of the Jezreel Valley. *Taanach* (Tell Ti'innik) and *Megiddo* (Tell el-Mutesellim) controlled access from the Plain of Sharon to the Jezreel Valley. With the exception of *Dor* (Khirbet el-Burj) and *En-dor* (probably Khirbet Safsafeh), the same towns mentioned here are listed as Manasseh's responsibility, unfulfilled, in Judg 1.27.
17.14–18 A petition of Ephraim and Manasseh together as *the tribe of Joseph* (lit. "the sons of Joseph," v. 14) protests that they have too little land. **17.15** *Perizzites*. See 3.10; 9.1; 11.3; 12.8; 24.11. *Rephaim*. See

note on 12.4. *The hill country of Ephraim* encompassed territory belonging to both Ephraim and Manasseh. *Go up to the forest.* Originally, forests covered much of the watershed ridge and western slopes of the hill country, and clearing them required enormous amounts of cooperative labor. **17.16** *Not enough.* Not only did the heavily forested condition of the hill country pose a problem, but the military strength of the Canaanites also kept them from settling the plains. **17.17–18** Joshua points out that the large population of Ephraim and Manasseh is not a problem, but actually an opportunity. It gives them the resources to clear the highland forests and to *drive out the Canaanites.*

18.1–10 A survey commission prepares for the remaining allotments in western Palestine. **18.1** *Congregation.* See 9.15–21. For this portion of the narrative *Shiloh* has succeeded Gilgal as the rallying point for Israel. Shiloh is Khirbet Seilun, nineteen miles (thirty kilometers) north of Jerusalem. The *tent of meeting* was the portable sanctuary of the wilderness period (Ex

the south, and the house of Joseph in their territory on the north. 6You shall describe the land in seven divisions and bring the description here to me; and I will cast lots for you here before the LORD our God. 7The Levites have no portion among you, for the priesthood of the LORD is their heritage; and Gad and Reuben and the half-tribe of Manasseh have received their inheritance beyond the Jordan eastward, which Moses the servant of the LORD gave them."

8 So the men started on their way; and Joshua charged those who went to write the description of the land, saying, "Go throughout the land and write a description of it, and come back to me; and I will cast lots for you here before the LORD in Shiloh." 9So the men went and traversed the land and set down in a book a description of it by towns in seven divisions; then they came back to Joshua in the camp at Shiloh, 10and Joshua cast lots for them in Shiloh before the LORD; and there Joshua apportioned the land to the Israelites, to each a portion.

The Territory of Benjamin

11 The lot of the tribe of Benjamin according to its families came up, and the territory allotted to it fell between the tribe of Judah and the tribe of Joseph. 12On the north side their boundary began at the Jordan; then the boundary goes up to the slope of Jericho on the north, then up through the hill country westward; and it ends at the wilderness of Beth-aven. 13From there the boundary passes along southward in the direction of Luz, to the slope of Luz (that is, Bethel), then the boundary goes down to Ataroth-addar, on the mountain that lies south of Lower Beth-horon. 14Then the boundary goes in another

direction, turning on the western side southward from the mountain that lies to the south, opposite Beth-horon, and it ends at Kiriath-baal (that is, Kiriath-jearim), a town belonging to the tribe of Judah. This forms the western side. 15The southern side begins at the outskirts of Kiriath-jearim; and the boundary goes from there to Ephron,a to the spring of the Waters of Nephtoah; 16then the boundary goes down to the border of the mountain that overlooks the valley of the son of Hinnom, which is at the north end of the valley of Rephaim; and it then goes down the valley of Hinnom, south of the slope of the Jebusites, and downward to En-rogel; 17then it bends in a northerly direction going on to En-shemesh, and from there goes to Geliloth, which is opposite the ascent of Adummim; then it goes down to the Stone of Bohan, Reuben's son; 18and passing on to the north of the slope of Beth-arabahb it goes down to the Arabah; 19then the boundary passes on to the north of the slope of Beth-hoglah; and the boundary ends at the northern bay of the Dead Sea,c at the south end of the Jordan: this is the southern border. 20The Jordan forms its boundary on the eastern side. This is the inheritance of the tribe of Benjamin, according to its families, boundary by boundary all around.

21 Now the towns of the tribe of Benjamin according to their families were Jericho, Beth-hoglah, Emek-keziz, 22Beth-arabah, Zemaraim, Bethel, 23Avvim, Parah, Ophrah, 24Chephar-ammoni, Ophni, and Geba—twelve towns with their villages: 25Gibeon, Ramah, Beeroth, 26Mizpeh, Chephirah, Mozah, 27Rekem, Irpeel, Taralah, 28Zela, Haeleph,

---

a Cn See 15.9. Heb westward   b Gk: Heb to the slope over against the Arabah   c Heb Salt Sea

---

33.7; Num 11.16; 12.4; Deut 31.14). In ch. 24 the focus will shift to Shechem. **18.6** *I will cast lots.* Readers are unprepared to find Joshua and not Eleazar doing this (cf. 19.51). **18.7** *Levites.* See 13.14, 33; note on 13.14. *Gad and Reuben and the half-tribe of Manasseh.* See 13.8–32. **18.11–28** Benjamin, immediately to the north of Judah, is the first of seven tribes whose land apportionment is determined at Shiloh. This section returns to the pattern displayed in describing Judah (15.1–63): borders (18.11–20; described in a counterclockwise direction) followed by a town list (18.21–28). It may be derived from the same source document. Towns are numerous and close together, concentrated in the area that was the center of action in the warfare recounted in chs.

2–9. The towns are listed in two districts, one crowded onto the watershed ridge north and west of Jerusalem (vv. 25–28), the other on the less desirable eastern ridge and falling away to Jericho and the Jordan. **18.12–13** Benjamin's northern border corresponds to that of Ephraim (16.1–3). **18.15–19** Benjamin's southern border parallels Judah's northern border (15.5–9) traced from west to east. **18.21–24** After Solomon's death, Benjamin was split between Judah and Israel. This district apparently describes that part of Benjamin originally located in the Northern Kingdom and incorporated into the kingdom of Judah during the reign of Josiah. **18.25–28** This district comprises towns located in the kingdom of Judah; see note on 15.20–63.

Jebus[a] (that is, Jerusalem), Gibeah[b] and Kiriath-jearim[c]—fourteen towns with their villages. This is the inheritance of the tribe of Benjamin according to its families.

The Territory of Simeon

19 The second lot came out for Simeon, for the tribe of Simeon, according to its families; its inheritance lay within the inheritance of the tribe of Judah. [2]It had for its inheritance Beer-sheba, Sheba, Moladah, [3]Hazar-shual, Balah, Ezem, [4]Eltolad, Bethul, Hormah, [5]Ziklag, Beth-marcaboth, Hazar-susah, [6]Beth-lebaoth, and Sharuhen—thirteen towns with their villages; [7]Ain, Rimmon, Ether, and Ashan—four towns with their villages; [8]together with all the villages all around these towns as far as Baalath-beer, Ramah of the Negeb. This was the inheritance of the tribe of Simeon according to its families. [9]The inheritance of the tribe of Simeon formed part of the territory of Judah; because the portion of the tribe of Judah was too large for them, the tribe of Simeon obtained an inheritance within their inheritance.

The Territory of Zebulun

10 The third lot came up for the tribe of Zebulun, according to its families. The boundary of its inheritance reached as far as Sarid; [11]then its boundary goes up westward, and on to Maralah, and touches Dabbesheth, then the wadi that is east of Jokneam; [12]from Sarid it goes in the other direction eastward toward the sunrise to the boundary of Chisloth-tabor; from there it goes to Daberath, then up to Ja-

phia; [13]from there it passes along on the east toward the sunrise to Gath-hepher, to Eth-kazin, and going on to Rimmon it bends toward Neah; [14]then on the north the boundary makes a turn to Hannathon, and it ends at the valley of Iphtah-el; [15]and Kattath, Nahalal, Shimron, Idalah, and Bethlehem—twelve towns with their villages. [16]This is the inheritance of the tribe of Zebulun, according to its families—these towns with their villages.

The Territory of Issachar

17 The fourth lot came out for Issachar, for the tribe of Issachar, according to its families. [18]Its territory included Jezreel, Chesulloth, Shunem, [19]Hapharaim, Shion, Anaharath, [20]Rabbith, Kishion, Ebez, [21]Remeth, En-gannim, En-haddah, Beth-pazzez; [22]the boundary also touches Tabor, Shahazumah, and Beth-shemesh, and its boundary ends at the Jordan—sixteen towns with their villages. [23]This is the inheritance of the tribe of Issachar, according to its families—the towns with their villages.

The Territory of Asher

24 The fifth lot came out for the tribe of Asher according to its families. [25]Its boundary included Helkath, Hali, Beten, Achshaph, [26]Allammelech, Amad, and Mishal; on the west it touches Carmel and Shihor-libnath, [27]then it turns eastward, goes to Beth-dagon, and touches Zebulun and the valley of Iphtah-el

---

a Gk Syr Vg: Heb *the Jebusite*   *b* Heb *Gibeath*   *c* Gk: Heb *Kiriath*

19.1–9 In the case of Simeon, situated at the brink of the Negeb desert and entirely surrounded by Judah, there is no trace of boundary descriptions, only a list of towns. The situation is explained in terms of Judah's magnanimity (v. 9). Simeon's towns are listed in two districts (vv. 2–6, 7), which are closely related to the second part of Judah's first district, the northern Negeb around Beer-sheba (15.26–32), and even more closely related to the Simeonite towns in 1 Chr 4.28–32. **19.10–16** Zebulun's territory was the poorer southern flank of the Galilean mountains together with a contiguous wedge out of the Jezreel plain. The boundary descriptions in this chapter look like fragments that vary greatly in their state of preservation. The southern border runs west from Sarid (vv. 10–11) and then east of the same town (v. 12). V. 13 gives the eastern border and v. 14 the northern border. A town list follows (v. 15).

19.17–23 Issachar's territory was the center of a continuing struggle to control the fertile fields and strategic crossroads of the Jezreel Valley. Issachar is de-

scribed by a town list (vv. 18–21) followed by a fragmentary portion of the northern boundary (v. 22). **19.17** *Issachar*, lit. "hired man," which may refer to forced labor at one time supplied by this tribe in the fields and caravans of Jezreel. **19.22** The isolated round dome of Mount *Tabor*, at the southern limit of the Galilean mountains and five miles (eight kilometers) east of Nazareth, is the most conspicuous landmark in the entire region. **19.24–31** The tribe of Asher claimed one of the most prosperous areas, the lush plain of Acco and its narrowing northern extension as far as Rosh ha-Niqra (the ancient "Ladder of Tyre"). The description of Asher's boundary is intermingled with items from a town list. *Sidon* (v. 28) and *Tyre* (v. 29) were not counted as part of Israelite territory; the boundary is described as coming close to their territories. **19.26** The Mount *Carmel* spur juts to the coast just south of Haifa Bay, presenting steep and precipitous slopes, a decisive natural boundary. **19.27** *Cabul* (Kabul), about nine miles (fourteen kilometers) east-

northward to Beth-emek and Neiel; then it continues in the north to Cabul, 28Ebron, Rehob, Hammon, Kanah, as far as Great Sidon; 29then the boundary turns to Ramah, reaching to the fortified city of Tyre; then the boundary turns to Hosah, and it ends at the sea; Maha-lab,*a* Achzib, 30Ummah, Aphek, and Rehob— twenty-two towns with their villages. 31This is the inheritance of the tribe of Asher according to its families—these towns with their villages.

The Territory of Naphtali

32 The sixth lot came out for the tribe of Naphtali, for the tribe of Naphtali, according to its families. 33And its boundary ran from Heleph, from the oak in Zaanannim, and Adami-nekeb, and Jabneel, as far as Lakkum; and it ended at the Jordan; 34then the bound- ary turns westward to Aznoth-tabor, and goes from there to Hukkok, touching Zebulun at the south, and Asher on the west, and Judah on the east at the Jordan. 35The fortified towns are Ziddim, Zer, Hammath, Rakkath, Chin- nereth, 36Adamah, Ramah, Hazor, 37Kedesh, Edrei, En-hazor, 38Iron, Migdal-el, Horem, Beth-anath, and Beth-shemesh—nineteen towns with their villages. 39This is the inheri- tance of the tribe of Naphtali according to its families—the towns with their villages.

The Territory of Dan

40 The seventh lot came out for the tribe of Dan, according to its families. 41The territory

of its inheritance included Zorah, Eshtaol, Ir-shemesh, 42Shaalabbin, Aijalon, Ithlah, 43Elon, Timnah, Ekron, 44Eltekeh, Gibbethon, Baalath, 45Jehud, Bene-berak, Gath-rimmon, 46Me-jarkon, and Rakkon at the border oppo- site Joppa. 47When the territory of the Danites was lost to them, the Danites went up and fought against Leshem, and after capturing it and putting it to the sword, they took posses- sion of it and settled in it, calling Leshem, Dan, after their ancestor Dan. 48This is the in- heritance of the tribe of Dan, according to their families—these towns with their villages.

Joshua's Inheritance

49 When they had finished distributing the several territories of the land as inheritances, the Israelites gave an inheritance among them to Joshua son of Nun. 50By command of the LORD they gave him the town that he asked for, Timnath-serah in the hill country of Ephraim; he rebuilt the town, and settled in it.

51 These are the inheritances that the priest Eleazar and Joshua son of Nun and the heads of the families of the tribes of the Israelites distributed by lot at Shiloh before the LORD, at the entrance of the tent of meeting. So they finished dividing the land.

a Cn Compare Gk: Heb *Mehebel*

---

southeast of Acco, was the center of a district of twenty towns that Solomon traded to Hiram of Tyre in ex- change for building supplies (1 Kings 9.13). **19.32–39** The territory described for Naphtali is the heartland of Galilee. Major trade routes connecting the port of Acco and the coastal plains with all points north and northeast passed through this corridor. A bound- ary description (vv. 33–34) is followed by a town list (vv. 35–38). **19.33** For the *boundary* this verse projects a line running for the most part along the eastern crests of Galilee (but including the plain of Chinnereth). The *oak in Zaananim* figures in the story of Deborah (Judg 4.11). **19.37** *Kedesh.* Tell Qades, in the hills approxi- mately seven miles (eleven kilometers) northwest of Hazor, is perhaps the most impressive archaeological site in the entire land. Despite the presence of walled towns controlling the valleys, the highlands of Galilee in the twelfth century BCE saw a rapid multiplication of unwalled villages whose inhabitants practiced a satis- factory subsistence farming, thanks to the construction of agricultural terraces. These villages can be plausibly recognized as part of a withdrawal from Canaanite so- ciety and expansion of the Israelite movement.

19.40–48 Although tradition located Dan origi- nally in the south, as described here, Dan's relocation to the far north is reported in Judg 18. *Leshem* (v. 47) is "Laish" in Judg 18.27. Dan's territory is described by a town list (vv. 41–46). It is a wedge of coastal region bordering Judah on the south, Ephraim on the north, and Benjamin to the east. **19.49–51** Conclusion to the redistribution of the land. Joshua receives a personal inheritance. **19.50** *Timnath-serah* is properly Tim- nath-heres, in Hebrew "Portion of the Sun." A trans- position of letters has resulted in Timnath-serah ("Leftover Portion"; also Josh 24.30). This is Khirbet Tibnah, fifteen miles (twenty-five kilometers) south- west of Shechem. **19.51** That *the priest Eleazar* cast the *lot* at the *tent of meeting* emphasizes that the distribu- tion accords with God's will. This verse and 14.1, espe- cially the references to the leaders Eleazar and Joshua, form a strong *inclusio* (a repetition signaling the be- ginning and end of a unit). At the same time, this verse echoes 18.1 at the beginning of the Shiloh phase. From this point on, *Eleazar* will be mentioned frequently (21.1; 22.13, 31, 32; 24.33). *The heads of the families* re- calls 14.1. They will appear again in 21.1.

The Cities of Refuge

20 Then the LORD spoke to Joshua, saying, 2 "Say to the Israelites, 'Appoint the cities of refuge, of which I spoke to you through Moses, 3 so that anyone who kills a person without intent or by mistake may flee there; they shall be for you a refuge from the avenger of blood. 4 The slayer shall flee to one of these cities and shall stand at the entrance of the gate of the city, and explain the case to the elders of that city; then the fugitive shall be taken into the city, and given a place, and shall remain with them. 5 And if the avenger of blood is in pursuit, they shall not give up the slayer, because the neighbor was killed by mistake, there having been no enmity between them before. 6 The slayer shall remain in that city until there is a trial before the congregation, until the death of the one who is high priest at the time: then the slayer may return home, to the town in which the deed was done.' "

7 So they set apart Kedesh in Galilee in the hill country of Naphtali, and Shechem in the hill country of Ephraim, and Kiriath-arba (that is, Hebron) in the hill country of Judah. 8 And beyond the Jordan east of Jericho, they appointed Bezer in the wilderness on the tableland, from the tribe of Reuben, and Ramoth in Gilead, from the tribe of Gad, and Golan in Bashan, from the tribe of Manasseh. 9 These were the cities designated for all the Israelites, and for the aliens residing among them, that anyone who killed a person without intent could flee there, so as not to die by the hand of the avenger of blood, until there was a trial before the congregation.

Cities Allotted to the Levites

21 Then the heads of the families of the Levites came to the priest Eleazar and to Joshua son of Nun and to the heads of the families of the tribes of the Israelites; 2 they said to them at Shiloh in the land of Canaan, "The LORD commanded through Moses that we be given towns to live in, along with their pasture lands for our livestock." 3 So by command of the LORD the Israelites gave to the Levites the following towns and pasture lands out of their inheritance.

4 The lot came out for the families of the Kohathites. So those Levites who were descendants of Aaron the priest received by lot thirteen towns from the tribes of Judah, Simeon, and Benjamin.

5 The rest of the Kohathites received by lot ten towns from the families of the tribe of Ephraim, from the tribe of Dan, and the half-tribe of Manasseh.

6 The Gershonites received by lot thirteen towns from the families of the tribe of Issachar, from the tribe of Asher, from the tribe of Naphtali, and from the half-tribe of Manasseh in Bashan.

7 The Merarites according to their families received twelve towns from the tribe of Reuben, the tribe of Gad, and the tribe of Zebulun.

20.1–9 Six towns are designated as *cities of refuge* (v. 2), three on each side of the Jordan. This institution was intended to curb blood feuds. Murders were to be avenged by a near relative of the victim, the *avenger of blood* (vv. 3, 5). Cities of refuge provided asylum for the accused until the case could be classified as murder or unintentional manslaughter (Num 35.13–28; Deut 19.1–13). **20.2** Setting up of cities of refuge completed what God had commanded *Moses* (Num 35.9–34), who so designated three towns east of the Jordan (Deut 4.41–43) and commanded Joshua to do the same west of the river (Deut 19.1–13). **20.4** The *gate of the city* was an elaborate structure, often two stories high, with guardrooms and bench-lined courts and towers; there *the elders* met to hear cases and to conduct other public business. **20.6** The *death of the . . . high priest* was apparently the occasion for a general amnesty (Num 35.25, 28). **20.7** The three towns designated by Joshua were *Kedesh* (Tell Qades in upper Galilee), *Shechem,* in the north-central hill country, and *Kiriath-arba (that is, Hebron),* in the south. **20.8** The three east of the Jordan were *Bezer* (probably Umm el-'Amad) on the southern plateau opposite Hebron, *Ramoth in Gilead* (probably Tell Ramith) opposite Shechem, and *Golan in Bashan* (probably Sahm el-Jolan) opposite Kedesh. Each of these is also included in the list of levitical cities (ch. 21). **20.9** There is no trace of the cities of refuge system functioning during the monarchical period, when it was probably displaced by a system of law courts.

21.1–42 In Num 35.1–8, Moses is commanded to establish a system of levitical cities, designated to provide residential and grazing rights for families of this tribe, which had no territorial inheritance. This roster of towns is mostly paralleled in 1 Chr 6.54–81. Vv. 13–19 derive from an archival list, but the rest of the chapter is a scribal construct based on town names taken from elsewhere in Joshua. **21.4–7** The levitical cities are assigned to four groups. Levi was divided into three clans: Kohathites, Gershonites, and Merarites. The fourth group was composed of the *descendants of Aaron,* the priest, who were also Kohathites (v. 4).

8 These towns and their pasture lands the Israelites gave by lot to the Levites, as the LORD had commanded through Moses.

9 Out of the tribe of Judah and the tribe of Simeon they gave the following towns mentioned by name, 10which went to the descendants of Aaron, one of the families of the Kohathites who belonged to the Levites, since the lot fell to them first. 11They gave them Kiriath-arba (Arba being the father of Anak), that is Hebron, in the hill country of Judah, along with the pasture lands around it. 12But the fields of the town and its villages had been given to Caleb son of Jephunneh as his holding.

13 To the descendants of Aaron the priest they gave Hebron, the city of refuge for the slayer, with its pasture lands, Libnah with its pasture lands, 14Jattir with its pasture lands, Eshtemoa with its pasture lands, 15Holon with its pasture lands, Debir with its pasture lands, 16Ain with its pasture lands, Juttah with its pasture lands, and Beth-shemesh with its pasture lands—nine towns out of these two tribes. 17Out of the tribe of Benjamin: Gibeon with its pasture lands, Geba with its pasture lands, 18Anathoth with its pasture lands, and Almon with its pasture lands—four towns. 19The towns of the descendants of Aaron—the priests—were thirteen in all, with their pasture lands.

20 As to the rest of the Kohathites belonging to the Kohathite families of the Levites, the towns allotted to them were out of the tribe of Ephraim. 21To them were given Shechem, the city of refuge for the slayer, with its pasture lands in the hill country of Ephraim, Gezer with its pasture lands, 22Kibzaim with its pasture lands, and Beth-horon with its pasture lands—four towns. 23Out of the tribe of Dan: Elteke with its pasture lands, Gibbethon with its pasture lands, 24Aijalon with its pasture lands, Gath-rimmon with its pasture lands—four towns. 25Out of the half-tribe of Manasseh: Taanach with its pasture lands, and Gath-rimmon with its pasture lands—two towns. 26The towns of the families of the rest of the Kohathites were ten in all, with their pasture lands.

27 To the Gershonites, one of the families of the Levites, were given out of the half-tribe of Manasseh, Golan in Bashan with its pasture lands, the city of refuge for the slayer, and Beeshterah with its pasture lands—two towns. 28Out of the tribe of Issachar: Kishion with its pasture lands, Daberath with its pasture lands, 29Jarmuth with its pasture lands, En-gannim with its pasture lands—four towns. 30Out of the tribe of Asher: Mishal with its pasture lands, Abdon with its pasture lands, 31Helkath with its pasture lands, and Rehob with its pasture lands—four towns. 32Out of the tribe of Naphtali: Kedesh in Galilee with its pasture lands, the city of refuge for the slayer, Hammoth-dor with its pasture lands, and Kartan with its pasture lands—three towns. 33The towns of the several families of the Gershonites were in all thirteen, with their pasture lands.

34 To the rest of the Levites—the Merarite families—were given out of the tribe of Zebulun: Jokneam with its pasture lands, Kartah with its pasture lands, 35Dimnah with its pasture lands, Nahalal with its pasture lands—four towns. 36Out of the tribe of Reuben: Bezer with its pasture lands, Jahzah with its pasture lands, 37Kedemoth with its pasture lands, and Mephaath with its pasture lands—four towns. 38Out of the tribe of Gad: Ramoth in Gilead with its pasture lands, the city of refuge for the slayer, Mahanaim with its pasture lands, 39Heshbon with its pasture lands, Jazer with its pasture lands—four towns in all. 40As for the towns of the several Merarite families, that is, the remainder of the families of the Levites, those allotted to them were twelve in all.

41 The towns of the Levites within the holdings of the Israelites were in all forty-eight towns with their pasture lands. 42Each of these towns had its pasture lands around it; so it was with all these towns.

43 Thus the LORD gave to Israel all the land that he swore to their ancestors that he would give them; and having taken possession of it, they settled there. 44And the LORD gave them rest on every side just as he had sworn to their ancestors; not one of all their enemies had withstood them, for the LORD had given all their enemies into their hands. 45Not one of all the good promises that the LORD had made to the house of Israel had failed; all came to pass.

The Eastern Tribes Return to Their Territory

22 Then Joshua summoned the Reubenites, the Gadites, and the half-tribe of Manasseh, 2and said to them, "You have observed all that Moses the servant of the LORD

commanded you, and have obeyed me in all that I have commanded you; ³you have not forsaken your kindred these many days, down to this day, but have been careful to keep the charge of the LORD your God. ⁴And now the LORD your God has given rest to your kindred, as he promised them; therefore turn and go to your tents in the land where your possession lies, which Moses the servant of the LORD gave you on the other side of the Jordan. ⁵Take good care to observe the commandment and instruction that Moses the servant of the LORD commanded you, to love the LORD your God, to walk in all his ways, to keep his commandments, and to hold fast to him, and to serve him with all your heart and with all your soul." ⁶So Joshua blessed them and sent them away, and they went to their tents.

7 Now to the one half of the tribe of Manasseh Moses had given a possession in Bashan; but to the other half Joshua had given a possession beside their fellow Israelites in the land west of the Jordan. And when Joshua sent them away to their tents and blessed them, ⁸he said to them, "Go back to your tents with much wealth, and with very much livestock, with silver, gold, bronze, and iron, and with a great quantity of clothing; divide the spoil of your enemies with your kindred." ⁹So the Reubenites and the Gadites and the half-tribe of Manasseh returned home, parting from the Israelites at Shiloh, which is in the land of Canaan, to go to the land of Gilead, their own land of which they had taken possession by command of the LORD through Moses.

A Memorial Altar East of the Jordan

10 When they came to the region*a* near the Jordan that lies in the land of Canaan, the Reubenites and the Gadites and the half-tribe of Manasseh built there an altar by the Jordan, an altar of great size. ¹¹The Israelites heard that the Reubenites and the Gadites and the half-tribe of Manasseh had built an altar at the frontier of the land of Canaan, in the region*a* near the Jordan, on the side that belongs to the Israelites. ¹²And when the people of Israel heard of it, the whole assembly of the Israelites gathered at Shiloh, to make war against them.

13 Then the Israelites sent the priest Phinehas son of Eleazar to the Reubenites and the Gadites and the half-tribe of Manasseh, in the land of Gilead, ¹⁴and with him ten chiefs, one from each of the tribal families of Israel, every one of them the head of a family among the clans of Israel. ¹⁵They came to the Reubenites, the Gadites, and the half-tribe of Manasseh, in the land of Gilead, and they said to them, ¹⁶"Thus says the whole congregation of the LORD, 'What is this treachery that you have committed against the God of Israel in turning away today from following the LORD, by building yourselves an altar today in rebellion against the LORD? ¹⁷Have we not had

a Or to Geliloth

21.13–19 The list of thirteen towns for the *descendants of Aaron* was derived from an older source, but the other three lists were created by assembling place names from chs. 13, 16–17, 19, 20. **21.32** *Naphtali* furnishes only *three towns* instead of four. Because the core list from the older source contained thirteen towns (vv. 13–19), an adjustment had to be made in order to achieve the ideal number forty-eight (v. 41). **21.43–45** This optimistic summary makes no reference, direct or indirect, to the cities of refuge and levitical cities, which suggests that chs. 20–21 were added at a later stage. It is thoroughly Deuteronomic in theology and rhetoric. The goals of the conquest have all been achieved (v. 43), and the Lord has fulfilled all *promises* (v. 45). There is *rest on every side* (v. 44; cf. 1.13, 15; 22.4).
22.1–8 Joshua's farewell exhortation to the two and a half tribes located east of Jordan. This balances their appearance in 1.12–18. **22.4** Promises made in 1.13, 15 (cf. Deut 3.18–21) can now be honored because *rest* has been achieved (cf. 21.44). *Go to your tents* is the traditional call to disperse the national assembly (1 Kings 12.16). **22.5** The call to *love the* LORD (again in an address to all the tribes, 23.11) and to serve *with all your heart and . . . soul* evokes the prime stipulation of Deuteronomy's *commandment and instruction* (in the Shema' in Deut 6.4 9, and repeatedly). **22.7** Manasseh occupies territory both east and west of the Jordan. **22.8** Sharing the *spoil* reflects Israel's traditional custom in warfare (1 Sam 30.21–25). **22.9–34** Controversy over the altar of witness near the Jordan. Only one altar for sacrifice is permissible according to the law of Deut 12. The issue is whether this altar by the Jordan (v. 10) is proof of apostasy (vv. 16–20) or intended as a symbol of national unity and loyalty (vv. 22–29). **22.10** *Great size* seems to point to the altar's intended function as a visible *witness* (vv. 27–28, 34). **22.11** *On the side that belongs to the Israelites* indicates the area west of the Jordan, the side belonging to the group referred to as "Israelites" in vv. 11–13. The story is told from the perspective of the western tribes, described as Israelites to the exclusion of the eastern tribes (see vv. 32, 33). **22.12** *The whole assembly . . . gathered* is wording almost identical to 18.1 (peaceful

enough of the sin at Peor from which even yet we have not cleansed ourselves, and for which a plague came upon the congregation of the LORD, 18that you must turn away today from following the LORD! If you rebel against the LORD today, he will be angry with the whole congregation of Israel tomorrow. 19But now, if your land is unclean, cross over into the LORD's land where the LORD's tabernacle now stands, and take for yourselves a possession among us; only do not rebel against the LORD, or rebel against us*a* by building yourselves an altar other than the altar of the LORD our God. 20Did not Achan son of Zerah break faith in the matter of the devoted things, and wrath fell upon all the congregation of Israel? And he did not perish alone for his iniquity!' "

21 Then the Reubenites, the Gadites, and the half-tribe of Manasseh said in answer to the heads of the families of Israel, 22"The LORD, God of gods! The LORD, God of gods! He knows; and let Israel itself know! If it was in rebellion or in breach of faith toward the LORD, do not spare us today 23for building an altar to turn away from following the LORD; or if we did so to offer burnt offerings or grain offerings or offerings of well-being on it, may the LORD himself take vengeance. 24No! We did it from fear that in time to come your children might say to our children, 'What have you to do with the LORD, the God of Israel? 25For the LORD has made the Jordan a boundary between us and you, you Reubenites and Gadites; you have no portion in the LORD.' So your children might make our children cease to worship the LORD. 26Therefore we said, 'Let us now build an altar, not for burnt offering, nor for sacrifice, 27but to be a witness between us and you, and between the generations after us, that we do perform the service of the LORD

in his presence with our burnt offerings and sacrifices and offerings of well-being; so that your children may never say to our children in time to come, "You have no portion in the LORD." ' 28And we thought, If this should be said to us or to our descendants in time to come, we could say, 'Look at this copy of the altar of the LORD, which our ancestors made, not for burnt offerings, nor for sacrifice, but to be a witness between us and you.' 29Far be it from us that we should rebel against the LORD, and turn away this day from following the LORD by building an altar for burnt offering, grain offering, or sacrifice, other than the altar of the LORD our God that stands before his tabernacle!"

30 When the priest Phinehas and the chiefs of the congregation, the heads of the families of Israel who were with him, heard the words that the Reubenites and the Gadites and the Manassites spoke, they were satisfied. 31The priest Phinehas son of Eleazar said to the Reubenites and the Gadites and the Manassites, "Today we know that the LORD is among us, because you have not committed this treachery against the LORD; now you have saved the Israelites from the hand of the LORD."

32 Then the priest Phinehas son of Eleazar and the chiefs returned from the Reubenites and the Gadites in the land of Gilead to the land of Canaan, to the Israelites, and brought back word to them. 33The report pleased the Israelites; and the Israelites blessed God and spoke no more of making war against them, to destroy the land where the Reubenites and the Gadites were settled. 34The Reubenites and the Gadites called the altar Witness;*b* "For," said they, "it is a witness between us that the LORD is God."

---

a Or make rebels of us   *b* Cn Compare Syr: Heb lacks Witness

partitioning of the land), but the situation is inverted. **22.17** *The sin at Peor.* See Num 25. **22.18** The accepted notion of collective responsibility means that apostasy by one element of Israel endangers the entire nation (cf. the reference to Achan in v. 20; cf. ch. 7). **22.19** Perhaps the erection by the eastern tribes of an altar just to the west of the Jordan (v. 11) means that they think that territory east of Jordan is ritually *unclean;* if so it should be abandoned in favor of easy access to *the LORD's tabernacle.* **22.22** The eastern tribes begin with a liturgical exclamation that confesses their loyalty to the Lord (cf. 1 Kings 18.39). **22.27** That the altar will *be a witness* anticipates 24.27. The eastern tribes use a

rhetoric of repetition, cataloging sacrifices three times in order to deny that they intend to offer them at their altar of witness (vv. 23, 26, 29) and here using a comparable list to affirm their intention to sacrifice properly at the legitimate altar. **22.28** No apostasy was ever intended. The altar is only a *copy,* a replica pointing to loyal worship at the true altar. **22.34** The altar's name, *"Witness,"* does not actually appear in the Hebrew text. The altar's function is to be a *witness between us* to the reality that the tribes all agree *the LORD is God.* This situation is similar to the struggle and truce between Jacob and Laban, also marked by a stone "witness" (Gen 31.43–54).

Joshua Exhorts the People

23 A long time afterward, when the LORD had given rest to Israel from all their enemies all around, and Joshua was old and well advanced in years, ²Joshua summoned all Israel, their elders and heads, their judges and officers, and said to them, "I am now old and well advanced in years; ³and you have seen all that the LORD your God has done to all these nations for your sake, for it is the LORD your God who has fought for you. ⁴I have allotted to you as an inheritance for your tribes those nations that remain, along with all the nations that I have already cut off, from the Jordan to the Great Sea in the west. ⁵The LORD your God will push them back before you, and drive them out of your sight; and you shall possess their land, as the LORD your God promised you. ⁶Therefore be very steadfast to observe and do all that is written in the book of the law of Moses, turning aside from it neither to the right nor to the left, ⁷so that you may not be mixed with these nations left here among you, or make mention of the names of their gods, or swear by them, or serve them, or bow yourselves down to them, ⁸but hold fast to the LORD your God, as you have done to this day. ⁹For the LORD has driven out before you great and strong nations; and as for you, no one has been able to withstand you to this day. ¹⁰One of you puts to flight a thousand, since it is the LORD your God who fights for you, as he promised you. ¹¹Be very careful, therefore, to love the LORD your God. ¹²For if you turn back, and join the survivors of these nations left here among you, and intermarry with them, so that you marry their women and they yours, ¹³know assuredly that the LORD your God will not continue to drive out these nations before you; but they shall be a snare and a trap for you, a scourge on your sides, and thorns in your eyes, until you perish from this good land that the LORD your God has given you.

14 "And now I am about to go the way of all the earth, and you know in your hearts and souls, all of you, that not one thing has failed of all the good things that the LORD your God promised concerning you; all have come to pass for you, not one of them has failed. ¹⁵But just as all the good things that the LORD your God promised concerning you have been fulfilled for you, so the LORD will bring upon you all the bad things, until he has destroyed you from this good land that the LORD your God has given you. ¹⁶If you transgress the covenant of the LORD your God, which he enjoined on you, and go and serve other gods and bow down to them, then the anger of the LORD will be kindled against you, and you shall perish quickly from the good land that he has given to you."

The Tribes Renew the Covenant

24 Then Joshua gathered all the tribes of Israel to Shechem, and summoned the elders, the heads, the judges, and the officers of

---

23.1–16 Joshua's farewell address is another of the edifying discourses that give structure to the Deuteronomistic History (see Introduction). See speeches by Moses (Deut 29–31), God (Josh 1), Samuel (1 Sam 12), Nathan (2 Sam 7), and Solomon (1 Kings 8). Joshua uses the same Deuteronomic rhetoric employed in ch. 1. Joshua's speech falls into two parts (vv. 2b–10, 11–16), each displaying a form of envelope construction. **23.1** *A long time afterward.* Joshua's great age (cf. 13.1) prompts a call for faithfulness and a word of warning. *The LORD had given rest,* the final occurrence of this declaration that the conquest is completed and total (1.13, 15; 21.44; 22.4). **23.2** *Joshua summoned.* The location is unclear. *All Israel.* This inclusive definition of Israel, the tribes on both sides of the river interacting and interdependent, is a special concern of the Deuteronomistic historian (see Introduction). **23.3–10** The first part of Joshua's speech is framed by a description of the Divine Warrior (vv. 3, 9–10) focusing on the recent past and emphasizing that the Lord has indeed kept his promises (vv. 4–5). **23.4** In spite of what has been said in v. 1, some enemy nations *remain.* These will provide opportunities for additional divine victories (v. 5), but also temptations to religious infidelity (vv. 7, 12–13). **23.5** *The LORD your God* will complete the conquest unassisted. **23.6** *Be very steadfast.* Joshua echoes the exhortation the Lord addressed to him in 1.6–9. Future survival requires that Israel as a whole imitate Joshua in undeviating obedience. **23.11–16** The second half of the speech turns the envelope inside out, thunderous warnings (vv. 11–13, 15–16) framing a compact echo of the first part (v. 14). **23.12** Intermarriage with alien peoples would necessarily form social relationships that would lead to religious infidelity (cf. Deut 7.3–4). **23.13** *A snare and a trap* imply limitations on national independence, while a *scourge* is an image of political oppression (1 Kings 12.11). The threat of exile *from this good land* is repeated three times (vv. 13, 15, 16). **23.14–15** The good news is that the Lord has been trustworthy in keeping past promises (21.45); the bad news is that the Lord's consistency means that future threats will certainly take place as well. **23.16** *You shall perish quickly.* The concluding emphasis is on the threat of national destruction and expulsion from the land as just punishment (cf. vv. 13, 15).

Israel; and they presented themselves before God. 2And Joshua said to all the people, "Thus says the LORD, the God of Israel: Long ago your ancestors—Terah and his sons Abraham and Nahor—lived beyond the Euphrates and served other gods. 3Then I took your father Abraham from beyond the River and led him through all the land of Canaan and made his offspring many. I gave him Isaac; 4and to Isaac I gave Jacob and Esau. I gave Esau the hill country of Seir to possess, but Jacob and his children went down to Egypt. 5Then I sent Moses and Aaron, and I plagued Egypt with what I did in its midst; and afterwards I brought you out. 6When I brought your ancestors out of Egypt, you came to the sea; and the Egyptians pursued your ancestors with chariots and horsemen to the Red Sea.*a* 7When they cried out to the LORD, he put darkness between you and the Egyptians, and made the sea come upon them and cover them; and your eyes saw what I did to Egypt. Afterwards you lived in the wilderness a long time. 8Then I brought you to the land of the Amorites, who lived on the other side of the Jordan; they fought with you, and I handed them over to you, and you took possession of their land, and I destroyed them before you. 9Then King Balak son of Zippor of Moab, set out to fight against Israel. He sent and invited Balaam son of Beor to curse you, 10but I would not listen to Balaam; therefore he blessed you; so I rescued you out of his hand. 11When you went over the Jordan and came to Jericho, the citizens of Jericho fought against you, and also the Amorites, the Perizzites, the Canaanites, the Hittites, the Girgashites, the Hivites, and the Jebusites; and I handed them over to you. 12I sent the hornet*b* ahead of you, which drove out before you the two kings of the Amorites; it was not by your sword or by your bow. 13I gave you a land on which you had not labored, and towns that you had not built, and you live in them; you eat the fruit of vineyards and oliveyards that you did not plant.

14 "Now therefore revere the LORD, and serve him in sincerity and in faithfulness; put away the gods that your ancestors served beyond the River and in Egypt, and serve the LORD. 15Now if you are unwilling to serve the LORD, choose this day whom you will serve, whether the gods your ancestors served in the region beyond the River or the gods of the Amorites in whose land you are living; but as for me and my household, we will serve the LORD."

16 Then the people answered, "Far be it from us that we should forsake the LORD to serve other gods; 17for it is the LORD our God who brought us and our ancestors up from the land of Egypt, out of the house of slavery, and who did those great signs in our sight. He protected us along all the way that we went, and among all the peoples through whom we passed; 18and the LORD drove out before us all the peoples, the Amorites who lived in the land. Therefore we also will serve the LORD, for he is our God."

19 But Joshua said to the people, "You cannot serve the LORD, for he is a holy God. He is a jealous God; he will not forgive your trans-

---

a Or *Sea of Reeds* *b* Meaning of Heb uncertain

24.1–28 The major section of ch. 24 describes a covenant made at Shechem at the end of the conquest era. Joshua has already built an altar and engaged in a covenant ceremony there (8.30–35). **24.2–13** A number of parallel recitals of God's saving acts are also clearly related to covenant ceremonies (Ex 19.3b–6; Deut 6.20–25; 26.5–9). **24.1** A detailed list of participants stresses that *all the tribes of Israel* appeared *before God* at the sanctuary of *Shechem*. **24.2** The use of the special messenger formula *thus says the LORD* signals that Joshua speaks as a prophet. **24.3** The *River* signifies the Euphrates. What the Lord did for Abraham foreshadows Israel's potential future: *all the land of Canaan . . . made his offspring many*. **24.6–7** A compact paraphrase of Ex 14, including the shielding *darkness* mentioned in Ex 14.20. **24.9** *Balak . . . set out to fight*. The story of Balaam is reported in Num 22–24. See also 13.22. **24.11** The Israelite takeover west of the Jor-

dan is here represented entirely by the capture of *Jericho*. That the *citizens of Jericho fought* suggests reliance on a tradition different from that in chs. 2 and 6. **24.12** The referent of the *hornet* (see also Ex 23.28; Deut 7.20) is unclear. It may be a metaphor for panic (cf. 10.10). *Two kings of the Amorites*. Sihon (12.2; 13.10, 27) and Og (12.4; 13.12, 30–31). **24.13** An echo of Deut 6.10–11. **24.14–15** All three possible choices for alternative gods have proven to be ineffectual. The Lord took Abraham from the territory of the gods *beyond the River* (v. 2), and neither the gods of *Egypt* nor the gods of *the Amorites* could protect their peoples (vv. 5–7, 8–13). **24.15** *Choose*. The issue is not monotheism in the abstract but allegiance in concrete particularity. **24.17–18** The bulk of the people's response is a polished rhetorical piece, the irreducible minimum of Joshua's recital in vv. 2b–13. **24.19** *You cannot serve the LORD*. Joshua unexpectedly warns of

gressions or your sins. 20If you forsake the LORD and serve foreign gods, then he will turn and do you harm, and consume you, after having done you good." 21And the people said to Joshua, "No, we will serve the LORD!" 22Then Joshua said to the people, "You are witnesses against yourselves that you have chosen the LORD, to serve him." And they said, "We are witnesses." 23He said, "Then put away the foreign gods that are among you, and incline your hearts to the LORD, the God of Israel." 24The people said to Joshua, "The LORD our God we will serve, and him we will obey." 25So Joshua made a covenant with the people that day, and made statutes and ordinances for them at Shechem. 26Joshua wrote these words in the book of the law of God; and he took a large stone, and set it up there under the oak in the sanctuary of the LORD. 27Joshua said to all the people, "See, this stone shall be a witness against us; for it has heard all the words of the LORD that he spoke to us; therefore it shall be a witness against you, if you deal falsely with your God." 28So Joshua sent the people away to their inheritances.

Death of Joshua and Eleazar

29 After these things Joshua son of Nun, the servant of the LORD, died, being one hundred ten years old. 30They buried him in his own inheritance at Timnath-serah, which is in the hill country of Ephraim, north of Mount Gaash.

31 Israel served the LORD all the days of Joshua, and all the days of the elders who outlived Joshua and had known all the work that the LORD did for Israel.

32 The bones of Joseph, which the Israelites had brought up from Egypt, were buried at Shechem, in the portion of ground that Jacob had bought from the children of Hamor, the father of Shechem, for one hundred pieces of money;[a] it became an inheritance of the descendants of Joseph.

33 Eleazar son of Aaron died; and they buried him at Gibeah, the town of his son Phinehas, which had been given him in the hill country of Ephraim.

_____

a Heb one hundred qesitah

the difficulties and dangers implicit in the commitment the people have just made. Israel's danger stems from the Lord's character as a *jealous God,* one who is zealous about remaining Israel's only God. **24.22** *To serve him.* Joshua rules out any other possible motive for choosing the Lord. *We are witnesses.* Cf. Ruth 4.9–11. **24.23** *Incline your hearts.* The heart was understood as the place of the mind and will, the center of decision making. Joshua calls for personal conviction, not just outward conformity (1 Kings 8.58). The ultimatum to *put away the foreign gods* may reflect a practice of burying idols at Shechem (Gen 35.2–4). **24.26** *The oak in the sanctuary.* Cf. "the oak of the pillar at Shechem" (Judg 9.6). **24.27** The inscribed stone is a *witness* in two senses. It will be a reminder to those who come to worship (cf. 22.27, 34), but it is also a witness because it was present when *all the words of the LORD* (i.e., vv. 2–13) were proclaimed. Perhaps the stone was coated with plaster into which words were incised.

24.29–33 The book concludes with a variety of notices. **24.29** The title *servant of the LORD* has been regularly used of Moses (1.1, 2, 13; 8.31, 33; 11.12, 15; 12.6; 13.8; 14.7; 18.7; 22.2, 4, 5); now finally it is applied to Joshua. *One hundred ten years* was considered an ideal lifetime. Joseph also lived one hundred and ten years and Moses one hundred and twenty (Gen 50.26; Deut 34.7). **24.30** *Timnath-serah* was granted to Joshua in 19.49–50. **24.31** This looks forward to the book of Judges (cf. Judg 2.7). **24.32** Reference to *the bones of Joseph* (cf. Gen 50.24–25; Ex 13.19) ties the book of Joshua to the Pentateuch. *Jacob had bought.* See Gen 33.18–20. *Hamor, the father of Shechem.* See Gen 34. *One hundred pieces of money.* The value (weight) of the unit is unknown. **24.33** *Eleazar* and his son *Phinehas* are important figures in the second half of Joshua (14.1; 17.4; 19.51; 21.1; 22.13, 30–32). Along with mention of the tent of meeting (18.1; 19.51) and the tabernacle (22.19, 29), they connect the final form of Joshua to the Pentateuch (see note on 24.32).

JUDGES

Historical Context

THE BOOK OF JUDGES recounts traditional stories that span a critical period in Israelite history, from the death of Joshua to a tragic and costly civil war. After an incomplete conquest that leaves much land in the hands of Israel's foes (ch. 1), Israel follows a recurring pattern of disloyalty to God followed by oppression by its enemies. Israel then cries out in repentance and the Lord sends deliverers, the so-called judges. These judges are national military leaders (chs. 2–12) or, in the case of Samson, a solitary champion (chs. 13–16). In the end, Israel descends into idolatry, bloodshed, and civil war (chs. 17–21). The period that is the book's background extends from the closing decades of the Late Bronze Age through the Iron I period (ca. 1200–1020 BCE). The 410-year span that results from adding up the periods of oppression, the tenures of the judges, and the periods of "rest" mentioned in the book assumes that the judges governed "all Israel" sequentially. In fact, their leadership was more likely local and overlapping.

Despite sweeping claims in the book of Joshua of conquest of all the land, Judges describes continued warfare with Canaanites, plus challenges to Israel's hegemony posed by various tribal groups (Midianites and Amalekites), by emerging territorial states (Moab and Ammon), and by the arrival of the Philistines on the coast. Equally serious was the threat posed by aspirants to kingship within Israel (e.g., Abimelech, ch. 9) and internal anarchy resulting from the absence of kingship (chs. 17–21). The situation described by Judges continues into the narrative of 1 Samuel, named after the prophet who is also remembered as a "judge" and who facilitated the establishment of the monarchy, anointing first Saul, then David.

Protagonists and Terminology

THE BOOK PRESENTS TWELVE LEADERS: Othniel, Ehud, Shamgar, Deborah, Gideon, Tola, Jair, Jephthah, Ibzan, Elon, Abdon, and Samson. The title, Judges, reflects the fact that a majority of the book's protagonists are said to have "judged" (Hebrew *shafat*) Israel. The verb is not limited to strictly judicial function, however, but connotes a general exercise of legitimate "rule." Though scholars often describe the judges' leadership sociologically as "charismatic," "the spirit of the LORD" activates the various leaders with very mixed results. Scholars distinguish between "major judges," military chiefs and heroes whose exploits are recounted in stories, and "minor

346

judges," about whom very little is known apart from their being listed in 10.1–5; 12.7–15. Jephthah is a "major judge" (11.1–12.6), but is also listed in the group of "minor judges" (12.7).

Apart from the introduction (2.16–19), the noun "judge" (Hebrew *shofet*) occurs only once in this book, as a title of the Lord (11.27). As universal Judge, the Lord retains a prerogative that had been attributed to various deities in other ancient Near Eastern societies.

As striking as the absence of the noun "judge" from this book is the presence of the noun "deliverer," or "savior," or its related verb "deliver" in reference to four characters (Othniel, Ehud, Tola, and Samson). It is puzzling, therefore, that this language of deliverance is uniformly absent in regard to those leaders about whom popular lore was most prolific, Deborah, Gideon, and Jephthah. In the case of Gideon, neither "judge" nor "deliverer" language is used. What, then, did Gideon do? Perhaps that is precisely the question. Discerning readers will be alert to a sense of irony throughout the depiction of the judges.

Judges reflects Israel's tradition of sacral war, the conviction that the Lord fought against its enemies as the Divine Warrior. The Lord guided tactics and gave assurance of victory (4.6–7), led supernatural forces into battle (5.20–21), and used panic as an effective weapon (4.15; 7.21–22). Sacral war also could imply the complete slaughter of an enemy population as spoil devoted to the Lord for destruction (1.17; 21.11).

Sources and Development

JUDGES IS PART OF ONE LONG HISTORICAL WORK extending from Joshua through 2 Kings and prefaced by Deuteronomy, which serves as a theological introduction. It continues the Deuteronomistic History (see Introduction to Joshua) from the death of Joshua (Judg 2.8) to just before the birth of Samuel (1 Sam 1). Four stages of development can be discerned in the book. First were various stories of local crises and leaders, classic examples of narrative artistry. These stories, rarely involving more than a few tribes, originated in highland villages that comprised immediate and extended families, the so-called fathers' houses and clans. Israel had begun as a lineage system and developed over time to become an agrarian territorial state. Stories of the judges preserve memories of that tumultuous epoch. Scholars generally think that in the second stage these independent stories were collected for didactic purposes, perhaps by the mid-eighth century BCE. The stories are arranged so that good examples of leadership (Othniel, Deborah, Jephthah) alternate with not so good examples (Ehud, Gideon, Samson), with the whole book centering on Abimelech's abortive reign at Shechem. In the third stage these stories were incorporated into the Deuteronomistic History, composed during the reign of the reforming king Josiah (640–609 BCE) to tell the story of Israel's life in the land. Finally, after the destruction of the nation, this historical work was updated for those living in exile. The era of the judges was enclosed within a grim framework of disobedience and its consequences (1.1–2.5; chs. 17–21).

Israel's possession of the land was often at risk. The stories in Judges provided generations of readers inspiring (though sometimes imperfect) models for resistance and national solidarity. Eventually the kingdoms of Israel and Judah failed, and large numbers were deported from the land. In its final form, Judges gives one answer to what went wrong: disloyalty to God repeatedly resulted in catastrophe. The cyclical pattern of Judges also offered hope in times of national distress. Repentance and obedience might once again lead to deliverance. [ROBERT G. BOLING, revised by RICHARD D. NELSON]

Israel's Failure to Complete the Conquest of Canaan

1 After the death of Joshua, the Israelites inquired of the LORD, "Who shall go up first for us against the Canaanites, to fight against them?" [2]The LORD said, "Judah shall go up. I hereby give the land into his hand." [3]Judah said to his brother Simeon, "Come up with me into the territory allotted to me, that we may fight against the Canaanites; then I too will go with you into the territory allotted to you." So Simeon went with him. [4]Then Judah went up and the LORD gave the Canaanites and the Perizzites into their hand; and they defeated ten thousand of them at Bezek. [5]They came upon Adoni-bezek at Bezek, and fought against him, and defeated the Canaanites and the Perizzites. [6]Adoni-bezek fled; but they pursued him, and caught him, and cut off his thumbs and big toes. [7]Adoni-bezek said, "Seventy kings with their thumbs and big toes cut off used to pick up scraps under my table; as I have done, so God has paid me back." They brought him to Jerusalem, and he died there.

8 Then the people of Judah fought against Jerusalem and took it. They put it to the sword and set the city on fire. [9]Afterward the people of Judah went down to fight against the Canaanites who lived in the hill country, in the Negeb, and in the lowland. [10]Judah went against the Canaanites who lived in Hebron (the name of Hebron was formerly Kiriath-arba); and they defeated Sheshai and Ahiman and Talmai.

11 From there they went against the inhabitants of Debir (the name of Debir was formerly Kiriath-sepher). [12]Then Caleb said, "Whoever attacks Kiriath-sepher and takes it, I will give him my daughter Achsah as wife." [13]And Othniel son of Kenaz, Caleb's younger brother, took it; and he gave him his daughter Achsah as wife. [14]When she came to him, she urged him to ask her father for a field. As she dismounted from her donkey, Caleb said to her, "What do you wish?" [15]She said to him, "Give me a present; since you have set me in the land of the Negeb, give me also Gulloth-mayim."[a] So Caleb gave her Upper Gulloth and Lower Gulloth.

16 The descendants of Hobab[b] the Kenite, Moses' father-in-law, went up with the people of Judah from the city of palms into the wilderness of Judah, which lies in the Negeb near Arad. Then they went and settled with the Amalekites.[c] [17]Judah went with his brother

---

a That is Basins of Water   b Gk: Heb lacks Hobab   c See 1 Sam 15.6: Heb people

---

1.1–36 This introduction reviews the performance of the generation that outlived Joshua and offers a different perspective on the conquest than that given by the book of Joshua. Tribal activities are reported roughly from south to north, beginning with Judah, eager for the offensive, and ending with Dan at a stalemate. Vv. 1–21 describe successful conquests by Judah and Simeon, and vv. 22–36 report the failures of the northern tribes. **1.1** In contrast to what the book of Joshua portrays—a unified, successful conquest under Joshua's leadership (Josh 11.23; 21.43–45)—Judg 1 describes a mixture of successes and failures attributed to the generation *after the death of Joshua*. Tactical guidance from God and an assurance of victory (v. 2) were elements in the tradition of sacral war. In sacral war, the Lord in the role of Divine Warrior fought for Israel. **1.1–2** *Who shall go up first?* This same question and its answer, *Judah*, are repeated in 20.18 with reference to intertribal warfare. Chs. 1 and 20–21 thus frame the book of Judges. **1.3** The tribe of *Simeon* may once have ranged into the north-central highlands (Gen 34.25, 30–31) but finally settled in the south, entirely surrounded by *Judah* (Josh 19.9). The two tribes are personified as individuals. **1.4** The precise meaning of *Perizzites* is uncertain. Perhaps it denotes the rural inhabitants of the land in contrast to the urban *Canaanites*. **1.5** *Adoni-bezek*, or "Lord of Bezek" in He-brew. *Bezek*, Khirbet Bezka, near Gezer, is on the outskirts of Judah. **1.8** This claim is difficult to harmonize with v. 21. *Jerusalem* came under Israelite control only in the time of King David (2 Sam 5.6–9). **1.10** *Hebron* lies twenty miles (thirty kilometers) south of Jerusalem. *Kiriath-arba,* in Hebrew "Town of Arba." Arba was the legendary father of Anak, who gave rise to a lineage of giants (Josh 15.13–14). According to v. 20 and Josh 15.14, Caleb defeated *Sheshai and Ahiman and Talmai,* sons of Anak. **1.11–15** Nearly identical to Josh 15.13–19. **1.11** *Debir* is probably Khirbet Rabud, nine miles (fifteen kilometers) southwest of Hebron. **1.12** *Caleb,* Hebrew, "Dog," perhaps indicating loyalty. **1.13** *Othniel* will reappear in 3.7–11 as the first and model "savior-judge" (see Introduction). **1.14** Although Achsah urges Othniel to ask *for a field,* she immediately takes matters into her own hands. **1.15** *Achsah* contends that she should receive an additional land grant of pools (*Gulloth-mayim,* Hebrew, "Bowls of Water") because she has been assigned dry land (figuratively *land of the Negeb*). **1.16** *Hobab,* probably not *Moses' father-in-law* (Hebrew *choten*), but his son-in-law (*chatan*). The Kenites were a foreign group associated with Israel (5.24; 1 Sam 15.6), perhaps employed as metalworkers. They *settled* with the "people" Israel (a better reading than "Amalekites"). *City of palms,* probably Jericho. **1.17** The name *Hormah* is re-

Simeon, and they defeated the Canaanites who inhabited Zephath, and devoted it to destruction. So the city was called Hormah. 18Judah took Gaza with its territory, Ashkelon with its territory, and Ekron with its territory. 19The LORD was with Judah, and he took possession of the hill country, but could not drive out the inhabitants of the plain, because they had chariots of iron. 20Hebron was given to Caleb, as Moses had said; and he drove out from it the three sons of Anak. 21But the Benjaminites did not drive out the Jebusites who lived in Jerusalem; so the Jebusites have lived in Jerusalem among the Benjaminites to this day.

22 The house of Joseph also went up against Bethel; and the LORD was with them. 23The house of Joseph sent out spies to Bethel (the name of the city was formerly Luz). 24When the spies saw a man coming out of the city, they said to him, "Show us the way into the city, and we will deal kindly with you." 25So he showed them the way into the city; and they put the city to the sword, but they let the man and all his family go. 26So the man went to the land of the Hittites and built a city, and named it Luz; that is its name to this day.

27 Manasseh did not drive out the inhabitants of Beth-shean and its villages, or Taanach and its villages, or the inhabitants of Dor and its villages, or the inhabitants of Ibleam and its villages, or the inhabitants of Megiddo and its villages; but the Canaanites continued to live in that land. 28When Israel grew strong, they put the Canaanites to forced labor, but did not in fact drive them out.

29 And Ephraim did not drive out the Canaanites who lived in Gezer; but the Canaanites lived among them in Gezer.

30 Zebulun did not drive out the inhabitants of Kitron, or the inhabitants of Nahalol; but the Canaanites lived among them, and became subject to forced labor.

31 Asher did not drive out the inhabitants of Acco, or the inhabitants of Sidon, or of Ahlab, or of Achzib, or of Helbah, or of Aphik, or of Rehob; 32but the Asherites lived among the Canaanites, the inhabitants of the land; for they did not drive them out.

33 Naphtali did not drive out the inhabitants of Beth-shemesh, or the inhabitants of Beth-anath, but lived among the Canaanites, the inhabitants of the land; nevertheless the inhabitants of Beth-shemesh and of Beth-anath became subject to forced labor for them.

34 The Amorites pressed the Danites back into the hill country; they did not allow them to come down to the plain. 35The Amorites continued to live in Har-heres, in Aijalon, and in Shaalbim, but the hand of the house of Joseph rested heavily on them, and they became subject to forced labor. 36The border of the Amorites ran from the ascent of Akrabbim, from Sela and upward.

Israel's Disobedience

2 Now the angel of the LORD went up from Gilgal to Bochim, and said, "I brought you up from Egypt, and brought you into the land that I had promised to your ancestors. I said, 'I will never break my covenant with you. 2For your part, do not make a covenant with the in-

---

lated to its status as *cherem* (Hebrew), the spoils of sacral war, in that Judah and Simeon *devoted it to destruction.* See notes on Josh 6.17; 6.18. **1.18** *Gaza, Ashkelon, Ekron,* three cities of the Philistine Pentapolis. **1.19** That *the LORD was with Judah* sounds ironic in light of the following disclaimer. *Chariots of iron.* Chariots were made of wood and leather; iron was used for assemblage and fittings. **1.21** *Jebusites* remained a distinct people even after *Jerusalem* was taken by Israel (2 Sam 24.18). **1.22–26** The capture of *Bethel,* formerly *Luz* and later a royal sanctuary of the Northern Kingdom, is reminiscent of the story of Rahab at Jericho (Josh 2.1–24; 6.22–25). The capture of Bethel is the only success reported for a northern tribe. **1.27–33** The failure of five northern tribes (*Manasseh, Ephraim, Zebulun, Asher,* and *Naphtali*) to drive out the Canaanites results in a situation of mixed ethnicity and Canaanite subordination. **1.27–29** This information is duplicated in Josh 16.10; 17.11–13.

These cities did not become part of Israel until the reigns of David and Solomon. **1.34–35** The *Danites* were the least successful of the tribes, failing in their attempt to control the foothills between the coastal plain and the Judean highlands. This failure led ultimately to their resettlement in the north (chs. 17–18). **2.1–5** Israel's failure to obey leads to revision of the Lord's policy. There will be no more expansionist warfare. **2.1** *The angel of the LORD* is a diplomatic envoy from the heavenly court (cf. 6.11; 13.3), often preparing the way for God's direct appearance and here speaking in unmistakably Deuteronomistic style and theology (see Introduction). This same rhetoric is also present in the speeches of an anonymous prophet (6.8–10) and of the Lord (10.11–14). *Gilgal,* Israel's base camp in Josh 4.19–20; 5.9–10; 9.6, reappears abruptly. **2.2–3** Because Israel has failed to keep separate from *the inhabitants of this land* (Ex 34.12–13; Deut 7.2, 5), they must suffer the consequences threat-

habitants of this land; tear down their altars.' But you have not obeyed my command. See what you have done! ³So now I say, I will not drive them out before you; but they shall become adversaries[a] to you, and their gods shall be a snare to you." ⁴When the angel of the LORD spoke these words to all the Israelites, the people lifted up their voices and wept. ⁵So they named that place Bochim,[b] and there they sacrificed to the LORD.

Death of Joshua

6 When Joshua dismissed the people, the Israelites all went to their own inheritances to take possession of the land. ⁷The people worshiped the LORD all the days of Joshua, and all the days of the elders who outlived Joshua, who had seen all the great work that the LORD had done for Israel. ⁸Joshua son of Nun, the servant of the LORD, died at the age of one hundred ten years. ⁹So they buried him within the bounds of his inheritance in Timnath-heres, in the hill country of Ephraim, north of Mount Gaash. ¹⁰Moreover, that whole generation was gathered to their ancestors, and another generation grew up after them, who did not know the LORD or the work that he had done for Israel.

Israel's Unfaithfulness

11 Then the Israelites did what was evil in the sight of the LORD and worshiped the Baals; ¹²and they abandoned the LORD, the God of their ancestors, who had brought them out of the land of Egypt; they followed other gods,

from among the gods of the peoples who were all around them, and bowed down to them; and they provoked the LORD to anger. ¹³They abandoned the LORD, and worshiped Baal and the Astartes. ¹⁴So the anger of the LORD was kindled against Israel, and he gave them over to plunderers who plundered them, and he sold them into the power of their enemies all around, so that they could no longer withstand their enemies. ¹⁵Whenever they marched out, the hand of the LORD was against them to bring misfortune, as the LORD had warned them and sworn to them; and they were in great distress.

16 Then the LORD raised up judges, who delivered them out of the power of those who plundered them. ¹⁷Yet they did not listen even to their judges; for they lusted after other gods and bowed down to them. They soon turned aside from the way in which their ancestors had walked, who had obeyed the commandments of the LORD; they did not follow their example. ¹⁸Whenever the LORD raised up judges for them, the LORD was with the judge, and he delivered them from the hand of their enemies all the days of the judge; for the LORD would be moved to pity by their groaning because of those who persecuted and oppressed them. ¹⁹But whenever the judge died, they would relapse and behave worse than their ancestors, following other gods, worshiping them and bowing down to them. They would not drop any of their practices or their stub-

a OL Vg Compare Gk: Heb *sides* b That is *Weepers*

---

ened in Josh 23.13. **2.4–5** The Israelites *wept*, as they would again at Bethel on the eve of the solution to the problem of finding wives for Benjamin (21.2). The name of *Bochim* (Hebrew, "Weepers"), an otherwise unknown place of sacrifice, is explained. **2.6–10** A generation gap triggers the state of affairs described in Judges. These verses seem to conclude the assembly of Josh. 24.1–27 and repeat Josh 24.28–31, thus passing over Judg 1.1–2.5 and connecting directly to the end of Joshua. This indicates that Judg 1.1–2.5 was added as a supplement to the Deuteronomistic History (see Introduction). **2.8** The title *servant of the LORD* was first borne by Moses (Josh 1.1), then by Joshua, who left no designated successor. Samson applies the title to himself in 15.18. **2.9** *Timnath-heres*, "Portion of the Sun" in Hebrew, lies some fifteen miles (twenty-five kilometers) southwest of Shechem. A transposition of letters converted the name to "Timnath-serah" ("Leftover Portion") in Josh 19.50; 24.30. **2.10** The observation that, in contrast to the elders of v. 7, the generation

after Joshua *did not know the LORD* marks the turn of an era, a basic change in situation and relationships. **2.11–23** These verses set forth a cyclical pattern—apostasy, hardship, crying out to the Lord, and rescue—that provides a framework for the stories of the "major" judges. **2.13** *Baal* was the Canaanite storm god and divine warrior; *Astarte* was the popular fertility goddess. These names are used in the plural to represent Canaanite religion overall (cf. 3.7; 10.6). **2.14** *Enemies all around*. The first judges deal with threats posed by neighbors in the immediate vicinity: southern highlanders (3.7–11); Moabite invaders from east of the Jordan (3.12–30); Philistines along the coastal plain (3.31); and a Canaanite coalition (4.1–5.31). Thereafter the enemy comes from farther away (Midianites in chs. 6–8, Ammonites in ch. 11) or arises within Israel itself (Abimelech in ch. 9). **2.16–19** The *judges* are local heroes whose military victories (presented generally as results of the Lord's gracious intervention) earn them widespread renown.

born ways. 20So the anger of the LORD was kindled against Israel; and he said, "Because this people have transgressed my covenant that I commanded their ancestors, and have not obeyed my voice, 21I will no longer drive out before them any of the nations that Joshua left when he died." 22In order to test Israel, whether or not they would take care to walk in the way of the LORD as their ancestors did, 23the LORD had left those nations, not driving them out at once, and had not handed them over to Joshua.

Nations Remaining in the Land

3 Now these are the nations that the LORD left to test all those in Israel who had no experience of any war in Canaan 2(it was only that successive generations of Israelites might know war, to teach those who had no experience of it before): 3the five lords of the Philistines, and all the Canaanites, and the Sidonians, and the Hivites who lived on Mount Lebanon, from Mount Baal-hermon as far as Lebo-hamath. 4They were for the testing of Israel, to know whether Israel would obey the commandments of the LORD, which he commanded their ancestors by Moses. 5So the Israelites lived among the Canaanites, the Hit-

tites, the Amorites, the Perizzites, the Hivites, and the Jebusites; 6and they took their daughters as wives for themselves, and their own daughters they gave to their sons; and they worshiped their gods.

Othniel

7 The Israelites did what was evil in the sight of the LORD, forgetting the LORD their God, and worshiping the Baals and the Asherahs. 8Therefore the anger of the LORD was kindled against Israel, and he sold them into the hand of King Cushan-rishathaim of Aram-naharaim; and the Israelites served Cushan-rishathaim eight years. 9But when the Israelites cried out to the LORD, the LORD raised up a deliverer for the Israelites, who delivered them, Othniel son of Kenaz, Caleb's younger brother. 10The spirit of the LORD came upon him, and he judged Israel; he went out to war, and the LORD gave King Cushan-rishathaim of Aram into his hand; and his hand prevailed over Cushan-rishathaim. 11So the land had rest forty years. Then Othniel son of Kenaz died.

Ehud

12 The Israelites again did what was evil in the sight of the LORD; and the LORD strengthened

---

2.20–23 These verses, from a Deuteronomistic editor (see Introduction), underscore the theme of 2.1–5 (v. 20: *have not obeyed my voice;* cf. 2.2; 6.10). Disobedience on Israel's part brings a change in approach from the Lord. Three reasons are given for the survival of remnants of the nations formerly occupying Canaan: as a punishment (vv. 20–21), as a test of obedience (vv. 22–23; 3.1, 4), and to train Israel in the art of war (3.2).

3.1–6 Two lists of peoples (vv. 3, 5) in the midst of whom Israel will be tested are introduced by the explanation that Israel has had inadequate experience of warfare. **3.3** *Lords,* better "tyrants," a reference to the political organization newly introduced to the southern coastal cities by the Philistines. *Hivites,* also relative newcomers, probably from southeastern Asia Minor. **3.4** This verse echoes the note on which the preceding section ends (2.23) and gives the issue of continued resistance by "the nations" a covenantal setting in terms of the commandments. The presence of these communities makes possible the cyclical alternation of times of crisis and peace, depending upon Israel's behavior. **3.5** The list of peoples living among the Israelites includes not only near neighbors (from the geographical perspective of the later nation of Israel), but those living in enclaves in the heart of contested territory. The list is related to Deut 7.1, which mentions seven "nations." *Hittites,* descendants of small kingdoms left behind by the once mighty Anatolian

empire. *Amorites,* originally "Westerners" (from the Mesopotamian perspective), appear often in scripture as synonymous with *Canaanites. Perizzites.* See note on 1.4. *Hivites.* See note on 3.3. *Jebusites,* the pre-Israelite inhabitants of Jerusalem. **3.6** Intermarriage was censured not because it threatened genealogical purity, but because it entangled Israel in idolatry (Deut 7.3–4). **3.7–11** The brief notice for Othniel, conqueror of Debir (1.13), illustrates the cyclical pattern laid out in (see note on) 2.11–23. **3.7** *The Baals and the Asherahs.* The plural implies the worship of these deities at multiple shrines and is used to represent Canaanite religion as a whole. Asherah, represented by a wooden pole (6.25), was viewed as the consort of Baal or Yahweh. **3.8** *Cushan-rishathaim,* in Hebrew "Cushan Double-Wickedness," looks like a distorted name. *Aram-naharaim* is presumably far-off northwestern Mesopotamia. The judges are unified by a chronological structure (*eight years;* see v. 11, *forty years*) that reaches to 1 Kings 6.1. **3.10** *The spirit of the LORD* in Judges stands for a power or force sent by the Lord in which a person might be so absorbed or enveloped as to become capable of extraordinary strength and compelling leadership. In the context of this book, *judged* means mobilizing Israel for successful defensive warfare. **3.11** The round number *forty years* may mean a generation and sounds like an editorial construct. **3.12–30** The swashbuckling story of Ehud, a Benja-

King Eglon of Moab against Israel, because they had done what was evil in the sight of the LORD. [13]In alliance with the Ammonites and the Amalekites, he went and defeated Israel; and they took possession of the city of palms. [14]So the Israelites served King Eglon of Moab eighteen years.

15 But when the Israelites cried out to the LORD, the LORD raised up for them a deliverer, Ehud son of Gera, the Benjaminite, a left-handed man. The Israelites sent tribute by him to King Eglon of Moab. [16]Ehud made for himself a sword with two edges, a cubit in length; and he fastened it on his right thigh under his clothes. [17]Then he presented the tribute to King Eglon of Moab. Now Eglon was a very fat man. [18]When Ehud had finished presenting the tribute, he sent the people who carried the tribute on their way. [19]But he himself turned back at the sculptured stones near Gilgal, and said, "I have a secret message for you, O king." So the king said,[a] "Silence!" and all his attendants went out from his presence. [20]Ehud came to him, while he was sitting alone in his cool roof chamber, and said, "I have a message from God for you." So he rose from his seat. [21]Then Ehud reached with his left hand, took the sword from his right thigh, and thrust it into Eglon's[b] belly; [22]the hilt also went in after the blade, and the fat closed over the blade, for he did not draw the sword out of his belly; and the dirt came out.[c] [23]Then Ehud went out into the vestibule,[d] and closed the doors of the roof chamber on him, and locked them.

24 After he had gone, the servants came. When they saw that the doors of the roof chamber were locked, they thought, "He must be relieving himself[e] in the cool chamber." [25]So they waited until they were embarrassed. When he still did not open the doors of the roof chamber, they took the key and opened them. There was their lord lying dead on the floor.

26 Ehud escaped while they delayed, and passed beyond the sculptured stones, and escaped to Seirah. [27]When he arrived, he sounded the trumpet in the hill country of Ephraim; and the Israelites went down with him from the hill country, having him at their head. [28]He said to them, "Follow after me; for the LORD has given your enemies the Moabites into your hand." So they went down after him, and seized the fords of the Jordan against the Moabites, and allowed no one to cross over. [29]At that time they killed about ten thousand of the Moabites, all strong, able-bodied men; no one escaped. [30]So Moab was subdued that day under the hand of Israel. And the land had rest eighty years.

Shamgar

31 After him came Shamgar son of Anath, who killed six hundred of the Philistines with an oxgoad. He too delivered Israel.

Deborah and Barak

4 The Israelites again did what was evil in the sight of the LORD, after Ehud died. [2]So the LORD sold them into the hand of King

---

a Heb *he said*   *b* Heb *his*   *c* With Tg Vg: Meaning of Heb uncertain   *d* Meaning of Heb uncertain   *e* Heb *covering his feet*

---

minite, unfolds within the cyclical editorial framework (vv. 12–15, 30; see note on 2.11–23). Regarding Ehud, there is no mention of the spirit of the Lord (cf. 3.10). **3.12–13** The agent of the Lord's discipline is *Eglon* ("Young Bull" or "Fat Calf" in Hebrew), king of *Moab*, with support from his northern neighbors, the *Ammonites,* and from Israel's traditional enemies of the wilderness era, the *Amalekites* (Ex 17.8–16). *City of palms,* Jericho, as in 1.16. **3.15–16** Ehud, the *deliverer,* is remembered as a *left-handed man,* allowing him to hide his weapon on his *right thigh,* where it would not be expected. His short sword has *two edges* for stabbing. Left-handedness was supposedly common in the tribe of Benjamin (see 20.16). **3.19** *Stones near Gilgal* (also v. 26). The referent is unclear, but cf. Josh 4.20. **3.20** *Rose from his seat,* a sign of respect in anticipation of hearing *a message from God.* **3.22** Israelite readers would enjoy this scatological humor at the expense of their enemies and their overweight king. **3.24–25** Delay gives Ehud a chance to escape and gather troops. **3.27–28** Ehud rallies forces from the *hill country of Ephraim* to take control of the *fords of the Jordan,* preventing the enemy from escaping back to Moab. **3.30** *Eighty years.* The chronology of round numbers is an editorial construct. **3.31** *Shamgar* is a non-Semitic name. This mysterious figure (cf. 5.6) is not part of the book's chronological system and interrupts the story of Ehud (cf. 4.1). At the same time, his inclusion rounds out the number of judges to twelve. *Son of Anath* may indicate that he was a mercenary, part of a military class dedicated to the war goddess Anath.

4.1–5.31 Deborah outshines Barak as the Israelites oppose a superior Canaanite force in the north. The tradition is told first in prose (ch. 4) and then celebrated in poetry, the "Song of Deborah" (ch. 5). Editorial notices (4.1–3; 5.31b) frame the two chapters. **4.1–24** The exploits of Deborah and Barak. **4.2** *King Jabin of Canaan,* an unusual title in an area of many

Jabin of Canaan, who reigned in Hazor; the commander of his army was Sisera, who lived in Harosheth-ha-goiim. ³Then the Israelites cried out to the LORD for help; for he had nine hundred chariots of iron, and had oppressed the Israelites cruelly twenty years.

4 At that time Deborah, a prophetess, wife of Lappidoth, was judging Israel. ⁵She used to sit under the palm of Deborah between Ramah and Bethel in the hill country of Ephraim; and the Israelites came up to her for judgment. ⁶She sent and summoned Barak son of Abinoam from Kedesh in Naphtali, and said to him, "The LORD, the God of Israel, commands you, 'Go, take position at Mount Tabor, bringing ten thousand from the tribe of Naphtali and the tribe of Zebulun. ⁷I will draw out Sisera, the general of Jabin's army, to meet you by the Wadi Kishon with his chariots and his troops; and I will give him into your hand.' " ⁸Barak said to her, "If you will go with me, I will go; but if you will not go with me, I will not go." ⁹And she said, "I will surely go with you; nevertheless, the road on which you are going will not lead to your glory, for the LORD will sell Sisera into the hand of a woman." Then Deborah got up and went with Barak to Kedesh. ¹⁰Barak summoned Zebulun and Naphtali to Kedesh; and ten thousand warriors went up behind him; and Deborah went up with him.

11 Now Heber the Kenite had separated from the other Kenites,ᵃ that is, the descendants of Hobab the father-in-law of Moses,

and had encamped as far away as Elon-beza-anannim, which is near Kedesh.

12 When Sisera was told that Barak son of Abinoam had gone up to Mount Tabor, ¹³Sisera called out all his chariots, nine hundred chariots of iron, and all the troops who were with him, from Harosheth-ha-goiim to the Wadi Kishon. ¹⁴Then Deborah said to Barak, "Up! For this is the day on which the LORD has given Sisera into your hand. The LORD is indeed going out before you." So Barak went down from Mount Tabor with ten thousand warriors following him. ¹⁵And the LORD threw Sisera and all his chariots and all his army into a panicᵇ before Barak; Sisera got down from his chariot and fled away on foot, ¹⁶while Barak pursued the chariots and the army to Harosheth-ha-goiim. All the army of Sisera fell by the sword; no one was left.

17 Now Sisera had fled away on foot to the tent of Jael wife of Heber the Kenite; for there was peace between King Jabin of Hazor and the clan of Heber the Kenite. ¹⁸Jael came out to meet Sisera, and said to him, "Turn aside, my lord, turn aside to me; have no fear." So he turned aside to her into the tent, and she covered him with a rug. ¹⁹Then he said to her, "Please give me a little water to drink; for I am thirsty." So she opened a skin of milk and gave him a drink and covered him. ²⁰He said to her, "Stand at the entrance of the tent, and if anybody comes and asks you, 'Is anyone here?' say,

---

a Heb *from the Kain*   *b* Heb adds *to the sword*; compare verse 16

city-states. Jabin is king of Hazor in Josh 11. *Sisera* is a non-Semitic name. **4.3** These are *chariots* with *iron* fittings. See note on 1.19. **4.4** As a *prophetess* Deborah ("Bee" in Hebrew) speaks for the Lord (vv. 6–7, 14). *Lappidoth* can mean *torches*, as in 15.4. *Was judging* seems initially to refer to Deborah's role in settling disputes, but the verb can also mean to serve as military leader (3.10). **4.6** The ancient distinction of gender roles means that reluctant *Barak* ("Lightning" in Hebrew), not Deborah, serves as military commander. The territories of *Naphtali* and *Zebulun* touched at *Mount Tabor* at the northern edge of the Esdraelon plain. This location was ideally suited for a muster of troops from Galilee. These are the only tribes mentioned in the prose account. **4.7** The battleground lies where the pass between Megiddo and Taanach opens into Esdraelon, near the confluence of streams that flow together to form the *Kishon* River. The battle is for control of the rich Esdraelon, Acco, and northern Sharon plains. Israelites from the highlands are able successfully to challenge the occupants of the plains. In the tradition of sacral war, the Lord determines tac-

tics and promises victory. **4.8–9** Deborah reproaches Barak for his fainthearted response. *Into the hand of a woman* sets readers up for a surprise fulfillment—the woman will not be Deborah. **4.11** This verse explains why some *Kenites* descended from *Hobab* in the south (see note on 1.16) are encamped in the far north, on the line of Sisera's flight after the battle. The landmark *Elon-bezaanannim* means "Oak in Zaanannim" in Hebrew. **4.13** The waters of *Wadi Kishon* play a role in the poetic account at 5.21. **4.14** Although *Barak* leads the warriors, *Deborah* proclaims the *day* of the Lord's victory. **4.15** The account is strikingly similar to that of the victory at the Red Sea (Ex 14.24). *Panic* is a customary tactic of the Divine Warrior (cf. Josh 10.10). The prose account gives no details of how the LORD created *panic*, but 5.20–21 suggest a natural catastrophe. **4.16** Although *Barak pursued the chariots,* Sisera has abandoned his and escaped (vv. 15, 17). **4.17** *Peace* between Jabin and Heber explains why Sisera feels comfortable seeking sanctuary in the tent of Jael. **4.18–19** Jael makes the first move by inviting Sisera in. At first she seems hospitable (she *covered him* and gave

'No.'" 21 But Jael wife of Heber took a tent peg, and took a hammer in her hand, and went softly to him and drove the peg into his temple, until it went down into the ground—he was lying fast asleep from weariness—and he died. 22 Then, as Barak came in pursuit of Sisera, Jael went out to meet him, and said to him, "Come, and I will show you the man whom you are seeking." So he went into her tent; and there was Sisera lying dead, with the tent peg in his temple.

23 So on that day God subdued King Jabin of Canaan before the Israelites. 24 Then the hand of the Israelites bore harder and harder on King Jabin of Canaan, until they destroyed King Jabin of Canaan.

The Song of Deborah

5 Then Deborah and Barak son of Abinoam sang on that day, saying:
2 "When locks are long in Israel,
    when the people offer themselves
        willingly—
    bless*a* the LORD!

3 "Hear, O kings; give ear, O princes;
    to the LORD I will sing,
    I will make melody to the LORD, the
        God of Israel.

4 "LORD, when you went out from Seir,
    when you marched from the region of
        Edom,
the earth trembled,
    and the heavens poured,
    the clouds indeed poured water.

5 The mountains quaked before the LORD,
    the One of Sinai,
    before the LORD, the God of Israel.

6 "In the days of Shamgar son of Anath,
    in the days of Jael, caravans ceased
    and travelers kept to the byways.
7 The peasantry prospered in Israel,
    they grew fat on plunder,
    because you arose, Deborah,
    arose as a mother in Israel.
8 When new gods were chosen,
    then war was in the gates.
Was shield or spear to be seen
    among forty thousand in Israel?
9 My heart goes out to the commanders of
        Israel
    who offered themselves willingly
        among the people.
    Bless the LORD.

10 "Tell of it, you who ride on white
        donkeys,
    you who sit on rich carpets*b*
    and you who walk by the way.
11 To the sound of musicians*b* at the
        watering places,
    there they repeat the triumphs of the
        LORD,
    the triumphs of his peasantry in Israel.

"Then down to the gates marched the
        people of the LORD.

---

a Or *You who offer yourselves willingly among the people, bless*
b Meaning of Heb uncertain

---

him *milk*), but her actions lull him into a vulnerable sleep. **4.20** Sisera's request reveals his confidence in Jael, but also his unmanly fear. In Hebrew the question can be understood as "Is there a man here?" **4.21** For a nomadic woman, hammering a *tent peg* would be routine. **4.23–24** These verses are an editorial wrap-up.

5.1–31 The Song of Deborah (and Barak, but the verb in v. 1 is singular) is datable to the twelfth century BCE, not far removed from the events being celebrated. The song exhibits repetitive parallelism familiar from fourteenth-century BCE Ugaritic texts, but there are a number of obscurities in the text. Its depiction of events differs from that of ch. 4 in mentioning six participating tribes rather than two, remaining silent about any role for Jabin, and describing Sisera's death in a different way (see note on 5.27). **5.2** This poem's archaic language makes it difficult to interpret at several points. *Locks are long* may describe vows of mili-

tary commitment; Samson's long hair was indicative of his vowed status as a Nazirite (13.5). **5.3** *Hear, O kings* announces the general theme: praising the *God of Israel* as testimony to kings such as those recently defeated by the forces of Deborah and Barak. **5.4–5** The singer describes a theophany of the Lord as Divine Warrior, *the One of Sinai*, arriving in Canaan via *Seir* and the *region of Edom*, in southern Transjordan (cf. Deut 33.2–3). **5.6–7** The crisis is framed by the exploits of *Shamgar* and *Jael*. The insecure situation before Israel's victory (v. 6) is contrasted with the good fortune that it brought about (v. 7). The title *mother in Israel* recognizes Deborah's authority and leadership. **5.8** *Shield* and *spear* were aristocratic weapons belonging to professional military men, not the *forty thousand* Israelite peasants. **5.10** Celebration is appropriate for the entire citizenry: for the elite, *who ride* and possess *rich carpets*, and the general populace, *who walk*.

12 "Awake, awake, Deborah!
  Awake, awake, utter a song!
  Arise, Barak, lead away your captives,
  O son of Abinoam.
13 Then down marched the remnant of the
    noble;
  the people of the LORD marched down
    for him*a* against the mighty.
14 From Ephraim they set out*b* into the
    valley,*c*
  following you, Benjamin, with your
    kin;
  from Machir marched down the
    commanders,
  and from Zebulun those who bear the
    marshal's staff;
15 the chiefs of Issachar came with Deborah,
  and Issachar faithful to Barak;
  into the valley they rushed out at his
    heels.
  Among the clans of Reuben
    there were great searchings of heart.
16 Why did you tarry among the sheepfolds,
    to hear the piping for the flocks?
  Among the clans of Reuben
    there were great searchings of heart.
17 Gilead stayed beyond the Jordan;
  and Dan, why did he abide with the
    ships?
  Asher sat still at the coast of the sea,
    settling down by his landings.
18 Zebulun is a people that scorned death;
  Naphtali too, on the heights of the
    field.

19 "The kings came, they fought;
    then fought the kings of Canaan,
  at Taanach, by the waters of Megiddo;
    they got no spoils of silver.
20 The stars fought from heaven,

from their courses they fought against
    Sisera.
21 The torrent Kishon swept them away,
    the onrushing torrent, the torrent
    Kishon.
  March on, my soul, with might!

22 "Then loud beat the horses' hoofs
    with the galloping, galloping of his
    steeds.

23 "Curse Meroz, says the angel of the LORD,
    curse bitterly its inhabitants,
  because they did not come to the help of
    the LORD,
  to the help of the LORD against the
    mighty.

24 "Most blessed of women be Jael,
    the wife of Heber the Kenite,
  of tent-dwelling women most blessed.
25 He asked water and she gave him milk,
    she brought him curds in a lordly bowl.
26 She put her hand to the tent peg
    and her right hand to the workmen's
    mallet;
  she struck Sisera a blow,
    she crushed his head,
    she shattered and pierced his temple.
27 He sank, he fell,
    he lay still at her feet;
  at her feet he sank, he fell;
    where he sank, there he fell dead.

28 "Out of the window she peered,
    the mother of Sisera gazed*d* through
    the lattice:

---

a Gk: Heb *me*   *b* Cn: Heb *From Ephraim their root*   *c* Gk: Heb
in Amalek   *d* Gk Compare Tg: Heb *exclaimed*

5.11 *Watering places* were the usual spots to gather for social interaction. **5.14–18** In the setting of the victory celebration, the poet reviews the performance of tribal contingents. Six tribes had responded: *Ephraim, Benjamin, Machir* (western Manasseh)*, Zebulun, Issachar,* and *Naphtali.* Four are censured for not responding: *Reuben, Gilead* (possibly Gad)*, Dan, Asher.* These ten groups may reflect a stage of organization earlier than the standard twelve-tribe system. Significantly, Judah, Simeon, and Levi are not mentioned. **5.15** *At his heels,* idiomatic for "under his command" (translated *behind him* in 4.10). **5.19–22** It is possible to read these verses as describing a victory won by a timely maneuver by the Lord—a cloudburst and flash flood—that gave an

advantage to Israel's foot soldiers over enemy chariots. *Stars* fight as the heavenly army of the Divine Warrior (v. 20), and the *Kishon* River engulfs the enemy (v. 21). The hoofbeats of escaping chariot horses are portrayed vividly. **5.23** *Meroz* (a town or clan?) and the incident cited are otherwise unknown. **5.24–27** This description of the demise of Sisera heaps praise upon Jael. **5.26** A *tent peg* and *mallet* were handy because pitching the tent was women's work. **5.27** In this poetic version, Sisera seems to be standing when attacked in contrast to the situation in 4.21. There are probably sexual implications to the penetrating tent peg and his fall *at her feet* ("between her feet"), intended as a bitterly ironic reversal of the common practice of battle-

'Why is his chariot so long in coming?
  Why tarry the hoofbeats of his
    chariots?'
29 Her wisest ladies make answer,
  indeed, she answers the question
    herself:
30 'Are they not finding and dividing the
    spoil?—
  A girl or two for every man;
spoil of dyed stuffs for Sisera,
  spoil of dyed stuffs embroidered,
  two pieces of dyed work embroidered
    for my neck as spoil?'

31 "So perish all your enemies, O LORD!
  But may your friends be like the sun as
    it rises in its might."

And the land had rest forty years.

The Midianite Oppression

6 The Israelites did what was evil in the sight of the LORD, and the LORD gave them into the hand of Midian seven years. ²The hand of Midian prevailed over Israel; and because of Midian the Israelites provided for themselves hiding places in the mountains, caves and strongholds. ³For whenever the Israelites put in seed, the Midianites and the Amalekites and the people of the east would come up against them. ⁴They would encamp against them and destroy the produce of the land, as far as the neighborhood of Gaza, and leave no sustenance in Israel, and no sheep or ox or donkey. ⁵For they and their livestock would come up, and they would even bring their tents, as thick as locusts; neither they nor their camels could be counted; so they wasted the land as they came in. ⁶Thus Israel was greatly impoverished because of Midian; and the Israelites cried out to the LORD for help.

7 When the Israelites cried to the LORD on account of the Midianites, ⁸the LORD sent a prophet to the Israelites; and he said to them, "Thus says the LORD, the God of Israel: I led you up from Egypt, and brought you out of the house of slavery; ⁹and I delivered you from the hand of the Egyptians, and from the hand of all who oppressed you, and drove them out before you, and gave you their land; ¹⁰and I said to you, 'I am the LORD your God; you shall not pay reverence to the gods of the Amorites, in whose land you live.' But you have not given heed to my voice."

The Call of Gideon

11 Now the angel of the LORD came and sat under the oak at Ophrah, which belonged to Joash the Abiezrite, as his son Gideon was beating out wheat in the wine press, to hide it from the Midianites. ¹²The angel of the LORD appeared to him and said to him, "The LORD is with you, you mighty warrior." ¹³Gideon answered him, "But sir, if the LORD is with us,

---

field rape described in v. 30. **5.28** The final scene begins with another woman, the *mother of Sisera* (cf. Deborah as a *mother in Israel*, v. 7), waiting in vain for Sisera's triumphant return. The scene of a woman looking out of a window was common in ancient Near Eastern art and biblical narrative (2 Sam 6.16; 2 Kings 9.30; Prov 7.6). Her reference to *hoofbeats* sounds ironic when read in context with v. 22. **5.30** Contrary to what his mother assumes, Sisera is not capturing girls for his sexual pleasure, but has been ravished himself by a woman. **5.31** *Your friends*, "those who love you." *Forty years* is twice as long as the oppression (4.3) and half as long as the *rest* following Ehud (3.30).

6.1–8.35 Gideon (also identified in ch. 7 as Jerubbaal) mobilizes several central hill-country and Galilean tribes against annual raiding parties from east of the Jordan (Midianites, Amalekites, and other easterners). **6.1–10** This introduction uses the now familiar framework (apostasy, oppression, appeal for help; see note on 2.11–23) in vv. 1–6. Exploitation originating from distant oases was made possible by the recent domestication of the camel. **6.2** *Midian* was a desert confederation sometimes in alliance (Ex 2.15–4.31; 18.1–27) and sometimes at war (Num 25–31) with Israel. **6.3** *Amalekites* were traditional enemies during the wilderness era (Ex 17.8–16). **6.5** *Locusts*, a common image to describe catastrophic destruction (7.12; Isa 33.4; Jer 51.14; Joel 1.6–7; Nah 3.15). **6.7–10** The warning in 2.3 that other gods would be a *snare* is coming true. This time, when *Israelites cried*, instead of the expected deliverer the Lord sends a *prophet* who delivers an indictment, as the angel of the Lord did in 2.1–5. **6.11–32** The Lord receives a new altar (vv. 11–24), and an altar of Baal is destroyed (vv. 25–32). Gideon is slow to recognize the voice of the Lord, foreshadowing Israel's problem in ch. 10. **6.11** Gideon (in contrast to Othniel, Ehud, and Deborah) is first approached by *the angel of the LORD*, a visible manifestation of the Lord's presence in human form, who at points becomes transparent to the Lord himself. *Ophrah*, a village of Manasseh not far from Shechem. *Joash* presides over a pagan shrine. *Abiezrite*. See Josh 17.2. *Gideon* means "Hewer" or "Hacker" in Hebrew, probably a nickname based on his reforming activities. Under normal circumstances, wheat would be threshed on a windy hilltop, not in a *wine press*. **6.12** The designation *mighty warrior* sounds ironic; it does not describe Gideon in chs. 6–7 very well.

why then has all this happened to us? And where are all his wonderful deeds that our ancestors recounted to us, saying, 'Did not the LORD bring us up from Egypt?' But now the LORD has cast us off, and given us into the hand of Midian." 14Then the LORD turned to him and said, "Go in this might of yours and deliver Israel from the hand of Midian; I hereby commission you." 15He responded, "But sir, how can I deliver Israel? My clan is the weakest in Manasseh, and I am the least in my family." 16The LORD said to him, "But I will be with you, and you shall strike down the Midianites, every one of them." 17Then he said to him, "If now I have found favor with you, then show me a sign that it is you who speak with me. 18Do not depart from here until I come to you, and bring out my present, and set it before you." And he said, "I will stay until you return."

19 So Gideon went into his house and prepared a kid, and unleavened cakes from an ephah of flour; the meat he put in a basket, and the broth he put in a pot, and brought them to him under the oak and presented them. 20The angel of God said to him, "Take the meat and the unleavened cakes, and put them on this rock, and pour out the broth." And he did so. 21Then the angel of the LORD reached out the tip of the staff that was in his hand, and touched the meat and the unleavened cakes; and fire sprang up from the rock and consumed the meat and the unleavened cakes; and the angel of the LORD vanished from his sight. 22Then Gideon perceived that it was the angel of the LORD; and Gideon said, "Help me, Lord GOD! For I have seen the angel of the LORD face to face." 23But the LORD said to him, "Peace be to you; do not fear, you shall not die." 24Then Gideon built an altar there to the LORD, and called it, The LORD is peace. To

this day it still stands at Ophrah, which belongs to the Abiezrites.

25 That night the LORD said to him, "Take your father's bull, the second bull seven years old, and pull down the altar of Baal that belongs to your father, and cut down the sacred pole*a* that is beside it; 26and build an altar to the LORD your God on the top of the stronghold here, in proper order; then take the second bull, and offer it as a burnt offering with the wood of the sacred pole*a* that you shall cut down." 27So Gideon took ten of his servants, and did as the LORD had told him; but because he was too afraid of his family and the townspeople to do it by day, he did it by night.

Gideon Destroys the Altar of Baal

28 When the townspeople rose early in the morning, the altar of Baal was broken down, and the sacred pole*a* beside it was cut down, and the second bull was offered on the altar that had been built. 29So they said to one another, "Who has done this?" After searching and inquiring, they were told, "Gideon son of Joash did it." 30Then the townspeople said to Joash, "Bring out your son, so that he may die, for he has pulled down the altar of Baal and cut down the sacred pole*a* beside it." 31But Joash said to all who were arrayed against him, "Will you contend for Baal? Or will you defend his cause? Whoever contends for him shall be put to death by morning. If he is a god, let him contend for himself, because his altar has been pulled down." 32Therefore on that day Gideon*b* was called Jerubbaal, that is to say, "Let Baal contend against him," because he pulled down his altar.

33 Then all the Midianites and the Amalekites and the people of the east came to-

_____
a Heb *Asherah*   b Heb *he*

6.13 The pronoun *you* in v. 12 is singular. Gideon misses the point and replies about the plight of *us*. 6.14 The figure of the angel of the Lord becomes transparent to the LORD himself. 6.15 Objections are a customary feature of call stories (cf. Moses, Ex 3.11; Saul, 1 Sam 9.21). 6.16–17 *I will be with you* is directly reminiscent of Ex 3, as is the request for *a sign* to certify the Lord's call. 6.19 An *ephah of flour*, more than a bushel, signals Gideon's commendably generous hospitality. 6.22 Gideon's response is typical (Gen 32.30). 6.24 One reason the tradition preserved this story was to validate a local altar of sacrifice and explain its name. *Peace* (Hebrew *shalom*) implies comprehensive well-being, individual and communal. 6.25 The dis-

mantling of Joash's *altar* and the hacking down of the *sacred pole* associated with the goddess Asherah will provide legitimacy for Gideon's alternate name, *Jerubbaal* (v. 32). 6.26 Using the sacred pole of Asherah as firewood was a disrespectful and deliberate desecration. 6.27 Gideon remains an ambivalent figure (cf. vv. 15, 17). He is prosperous enough to command the assistance of *ten . . . servants* but is only brave enough to act *by night*. 6.30–31 Joash, facing the zeal of his son, is no longer an avid supporter of Baal. The case against Baal is self-evident. A god unable to defend its own altar deserves no defense from others. 6.32 Reflecting his father's challenge in v. 31, Gideon's assertive action vindicates his name *Jerubbaal*, Hebrew, "Let Baal Con-

gether, and crossing the Jordan they encamped in the Valley of Jezreel. ³⁴But the spirit of the LORD took possession of Gideon; and he sounded the trumpet, and the Abiezrites were called out to follow him. ³⁵He sent messengers throughout all Manasseh, and they too were called out to follow him. He also sent messengers to Asher, Zebulun, and Naphtali, and they went up to meet them.

The Sign of the Fleece

36 Then Gideon said to God, "In order to see whether you will deliver Israel by my hand, as you have said, ³⁷I am going to lay a fleece of wool on the threshing floor; if there is dew on the fleece alone, and it is dry on all the ground, then I shall know that you will deliver Israel by my hand, as you have said." ³⁸And it was so. When he rose early next morning and squeezed the fleece, he wrung enough dew from the fleece to fill a bowl with water. ³⁹Then Gideon said to God, "Do not let your anger burn against me, let me speak one more time; let me, please, make trial with the fleece just once more; let it be dry only on the fleece, and on all the ground let there be dew." ⁴⁰And God did so that night. It was dry on the fleece only, and on all the ground there was dew.

Gideon Surprises and Routs the Midianites

7 Then Jerubbaal (that is, Gideon) and all the troops that were with him rose early and encamped beside the spring of Harod; and the camp of Midian was north of them, below*ᵃ* the hill of Moreh, in the valley.

2 The LORD said to Gideon, "The troops with you are too many for me to give the Midianites into their hand. Israel would only take the credit away from me, saying, 'My own hand has delivered me.' ³Now therefore proclaim this in the hearing of the troops, 'Whoever is fearful and trembling, let him return home.'" Thus Gideon sifted them out;*ᵇ* twenty-two thousand returned, and ten thousand remained.

4 Then the LORD said to Gideon, "The troops are still too many; take them down to the water and I will sift them out for you there. When I say, 'This one shall go with you,' he shall go with you; and when I say, 'This one shall not go with you,' he shall not go." ⁵So he brought the troops down to the water; and the LORD said to Gideon, "All those who lap the water with their tongues, as a dog laps, you shall put to one side; all those who kneel down to drink, putting their hands to their mouths,*ᶜ* you shall put to the other side." ⁶The number of those that lapped was three hundred; but all the rest of the troops knelt down to drink water. ⁷Then the LORD said to Gideon, "With the three hundred that lapped I will deliver you, and give the Midianites into your hand. Let all the others go to their homes." ⁸So he took the jars of the troops from their hands,*ᵈ* and their trumpets; and he sent all the rest of Israel back to their own tents, but retained the three hundred. The camp of Midian was below him in the valley.

9 That same night the LORD said to him, "Get up, attack the camp; for I have given it

a Heb *from*   *b* Cn: Heb *home, and depart from Mount Gilead'"*
c Heb places the words *putting their hands to their mouths* after the word *lapped* in verse 6   *d* Cn: Heb *So the people took provisions in their hands*

---

tend." **6.33–40** Gideon remains an ambivalent hero. He assumes military leadership, but repeatedly seeks confirmation by a sign. **6.34–35** The *spirit of the LORD* finally prods Gideon to action. Beginning with the *Abiezrites*, his home clan, Gideon rallies warriors from his own tribe, *Manasseh*, and from the three Galilean tribes, *Asher, Zebulun, and Naphtali.* **6.36–40** Gideon demands further proof that *God* (not "the LORD" in these verses) really meant what was said in the recruitment scene (vv. 11–24). That a fleece should absorb dew overnight is no surprise. The true miracle is the reverse, and that is what Gideon requires in his second request. Gideon's repeated quest for certainty seems to reflect his ambivalent character (6.15, 17, 27); however, a divine assurance of victory was also fundamental to the tradition of sacral war.

7.1–23 The Lord's rout of the Midianites comprises three scenes: the reduction of the Israelite force (vv. 1–8), an enemy sentry's dream (vv. 9–15), and the rout of the Midianites (vv. 16–23). **7.1** The *spring of Harod* is near the foot of Mount Gilboa in the southeastern Jezreel Valley. **7.2** The Lord alone as Divine Warrior wins the victory in sacral war. **7.3** *Whoever . . . trembling.* See list of exemptions in Deut 20.5–8. **7.5–7** The Hebrew text of the test is perplexing, and the reason for preferring *those who lap* over *those who kneel* (v. 5) is unclear. Is the Lord choosing the more alert or the less cautious? The latter would serve to make it plain that victory is due to divine action, not to human initiative or prowess. The important thing is that lapping is the minority choice, so that only a small portion of the original ten thousand remains. **7.8** Those who remain acquire the provisions of those who go home (following the Hebrew text). The abrupt mention of *trumpets* anticipates vv. 16–17. **7.9–14** The story continues to emphasize Gideon's fearful hesitancy and the

into your hand. 10But if you fear to attack, go down to the camp with your servant Purah; 11and you shall hear what they say, and afterward your hands shall be strengthened to attack the camp." Then he went down with his servant Purah to the outposts of the armed men that were in the camp. 12The Midianites and the Amalekites and all the people of the east lay along the valley as thick as locusts; and their camels were without number, countless as the sand on the seashore. 13When Gideon arrived, there was a man telling a dream to his comrade; and he said, "I had a dream, and in it a cake of barley bread tumbled into the camp of Midian, and came to the tent, and struck it so that it fell; it turned upside down, and the tent collapsed." 14And his comrade answered, "This is no other than the sword of Gideon son of Joash, a man of Israel; into his hand God has given Midian and all the army."

15 When Gideon heard the telling of the dream and its interpretation, he worshiped; and he returned to the camp of Israel, and said, "Get up; for the LORD has given the army of Midian into your hand." 16After he divided the three hundred men into three companies, and put trumpets into the hands of all of them, and empty jars, with torches inside the jars, 17he said to them, "Look at me, and do the same; when I come to the outskirts of the camp, do as I do. 18When I blow the trumpet, I and all who are with me, then you also blow the trumpets around the whole camp, and shout, 'For the LORD and for Gideon!' "

19 So Gideon and the hundred who were with him came to the outskirts of the camp at the beginning of the middle watch, when they had just set the watch; and they blew the trumpets and smashed the jars that were in their

hands. 20So the three companies blew the trumpets and broke the jars, holding in their left hands the torches, and in their right hands the trumpets to blow; and they cried, "A sword for the LORD and for Gideon!" 21Every man stood in his place all around the camp, and all the men in camp ran; they cried out and fled. 22When they blew the three hundred trumpets, the LORD set every man's sword against his fellow and against all the army; and the army fled as far as Beth-shittah toward Zererah,ª as far as the border of Abel-meholah, by Tabbath. 23And the men of Israel were called out from Naphtali and from Asher and from all Manasseh, and they pursued after the Midianites.

24 Then Gideon sent messengers throughout all the hill country of Ephraim, saying, "Come down against the Midianites and seize the waters against them, as far as Beth-barah, and also the Jordan." So all the men of Ephraim were called out, and they seized the waters as far as Beth-barah, and also the Jordan. 25They captured the two captains of Midian, Oreb and Zeeb; they killed Oreb at the rock of Oreb, and Zeeb they killed at the wine press of Zeeb, as they pursued the Midianites. They brought the heads of Oreb and Zeeb to Gideon beyond the Jordan.

Gideon's Triumph and Vengeance

8 Then the Ephraimites said to him, "What have you done to us, not to call us when you went to fight against the Midianites?" And they upbraided him violently. 2So he said to them, "What have I done now in comparison with you? Is not the gleaning of the grapes of Ephraim better than the vintage of Abiezer?

---

a Another reading is Zeredah

Lord's providential response, this time via a pagan sentry's dream. **7.10** Gideon's ambiguous character is reflected by the likelihood that he would still *fear to attack* even after the divine promise in v. 9. The *servant* (Hebrew *na'ar*, generally translated "young man") is Gideon's personal attendant and armor bearer (see 9.54; 1 Sam 14.1, 6). **7.13** The dream's symbolism fits: *barley bread* for Israelite farmers and a *tent* (presumably the leader's command center) for Midianite nomads. **7.15** *Worshiped*, i.e., fell prostrate. **7.16** Dividing the troops *into three companies* allows them to surround the enemy. With *trumpets, empty jars,* and *torches,* the Israelites are prepared to create a spectacular commotion, but there is no mention of weapons. Torches remain *inside the jars* to maintain the element of surprise. **7.19** Attacking at the *beginning of the mid-*

dle watch would have a great psychological impact. **7.21–22** The classic weapon of the Divine Warrior is panic (4.15). The "day of Midian" was a proverbial example of sacral-war victory (Ps 83.9–11; Isa 9.4). The splintered enemy forces retreat southeastward to escape across the Jordan. **7.23** The Israelite militia from *Naphtali, Asher,* and *Manasseh* are mobilized to hunt down the panicked enemy.

7.24–8.3 These verses are transitional. Gideon advocates further mobilization against the Midianites and leads the militia across the Jordan. **7.24** Gideon calls out troops from *Ephraim* to block enemy escape eastward across the Jordan. **7.25** *Oreb and Zeeb,* Hebrew, "Raven" and "Wolf." See Ps 83.9–12; Isa 10.26. Gideon has already crossed over and is *beyond the Jordan* (but contrast 8.4). **8.1** *Ephraimites* complain about not hav-

3God has given into your hands the captains of Midian, Oreb and Zeeb; what have I been able to do in comparison with you?" When he said this, their anger against him subsided.

4 Then Gideon came to the Jordan and crossed over, he and the three hundred who were with him, exhausted and famished.*ª 5So he said to the people of Succoth, "Please give some loaves of bread to my followers, for they are exhausted, and I am pursuing Zebah and Zalmunna, the kings of Midian." 6But the officials of Succoth said, "Do you already have in your possession the hands of Zebah and Zalmunna, that we should give bread to your army?" 7Gideon replied, "Well then, when the LORD has given Zebah and Zalmunna into my hand, I will trample your flesh on the thorns of the wilderness and on briers." 8From there he went up to Penuel, and made the same request of them; and the people of Penuel answered him as the people of Succoth had answered. 9So he said to the people of Penuel, "When I come back victorious, I will break down this tower."

10 Now Zebah and Zalmunna were in Karkor with their army, about fifteen thousand men, all who were left of all the army of the people of the east; for one hundred twenty thousand men bearing arms had fallen. 11So Gideon went up by the caravan route east of Nobah and Jogbehah, and attacked the army; for the army was off its guard. 12Zebah and Zalmunna fled; and he pursued them and took the two kings of Midian, Zebah and Zalmunna, and threw all the army into a panic.

13 When Gideon son of Joash returned from the battle by the ascent of Heres, 14he caught a young man, one of the people of Suc-coth, and questioned him; and he listed for him the officials and elders of Succoth, seventy-seven people. 15Then he came to the people of Succoth, and said, "Here are Zebah and Zalmunna, about whom you taunted me, saying, 'Do you already have in your possession the hands of Zebah and Zalmunna, that we should give bread to your troops who are exhausted?' " 16So he took the elders of the city and he took thorns of the wilderness and briers and with them he trampled*ᵇ the people of Succoth. 17He also broke down the tower of Penuel, and killed the men of the city.

18 Then he said to Zebah and Zalmunna, "What about the men whom you killed at Tabor?" They answered, "As you are, so were they, every one of them; they resembled the sons of a king." 19And he replied, "They were my brothers, the sons of my mother; as the LORD lives, if you had saved them alive, I would not kill you." 20So he said to Jether his firstborn, "Go kill them!" But the boy did not draw his sword, for he was afraid, because he was still a boy. 21Then Zebah and Zalmunna said, "You come and kill us; for as the man is, so is his strength." So Gideon proceeded to kill Zebah and Zalmunna; and he took the crescents that were on the necks of their camels.

Gideon's Idolatry

22 Then the Israelites said to Gideon, "Rule over us, you and your son and your grandson also; for you have delivered us out of the hand of Midian." 23Gideon said to them, "I will not

---

a Gk: Heb *pursuing*   *b* With verse 7, Compare Gk: Heb *he taught*

ing been included in the original summons (6.35; 7.23). **8.2–3** Gideon talks the Ephraimites out of their resentment by complimenting them: the least worthy (*gleaning*) of Ephraim are better than the very best (*vintage*) the clan Abiezer can offer. Gideon is either coining a proverb or adapting one. **8.4–21** The focus shifts from the somewhat miraculous recruitment of Gideon to scenes of Gideon in action. The Lord does not participate apart from being referred to by Gideon (vv. 7, 19). The purpose of this section is to show what becomes of the young reformer who has become a commander. **8.5** *Succoth* ("Huts") is Tell Deir 'Alla in the Jordan Valley. The kings *Zebah and Zalmunna* seem to represent a parallel but different tradition from the story of the captains Oreb and Zeeb (7.25; 8.3). **8.6** The commandeering of provisions is frustrated by distrust of Gideon's capability, despite his threats. The *hands* of the enemy were sometimes cut off as evidence of their capture or death. **8.8** Pursuit continues eastward to *Penuel*, Hebrew, "Face of God" (Gen 32.24–32; Hos 12.4), which was a town and sanctuary at a ford of the Jabbok River. **8.10–11** Pursuit continues far to the southeast into territory east of the Dead Sea. **8.12** The Midianite army is stampeded in the desert terrain by the loss of two kings. **8.16** Gideon makes good on the threat he made in v. 7. **8.18** *Tabor*. Nothing has been said earlier about this event. **8.19** Readers belatedly discover that Gideon is pursuing a private blood feud. *Sons of my mother* specifies that these victims were his full brothers, a matter of great importance in a polygamous society. **8.20–21** Death at the hand of a mere *boy* would mean great disgrace and perhaps greater suffering. **8.22–28** Declining an offer to rule the Israelites, Gideon requests contributions of booty to make an elaborate divinatory device. **8.22** *Rule over us*, Hebrew *mashal* (not *malak*, "be king"). This rule, however, was to

rule over you, and my son will not rule over you; the LORD will rule over you." 24Then Gideon said to them, "Let me make a request of you; each of you give me an earring he has taken as booty." (For the enemy[a] had golden earrings, because they were Ishmaelites.) 25"We will willingly give them," they answered. So they spread a garment, and each threw into it an earring he had taken as booty. 26The weight of the golden earrings that he requested was one thousand seven hundred shekels of gold (apart from the crescents and the pendants and the purple garments worn by the kings of Midian, and the collars that were on the necks of their camels). 27Gideon made an ephod of it and put it in his town, in Ophrah; and all Israel prostituted themselves to it there, and it became a snare to Gideon and to his family. 28So Midian was subdued before the Israelites, and they lifted up their heads no more. So the land had rest forty years in the days of Gideon.

Death of Gideon

29 Jerubbaal son of Joash went to live in his own house. 30Now Gideon had seventy sons, his own offspring, for he had many wives. 31His concubine who was in Shechem also bore him a son, and he named him Abimelech. 32Then Gideon son of Joash died at a good old age, and was buried in the tomb of his father Joash at Ophrah of the Abiezrites.

33 As soon as Gideon died, the Israelites relapsed and prostituted themselves with the Baals, making Baal-berith their god. 34The Is-

raelites did not remember the LORD their God, who had rescued them from the hand of all their enemies on every side; 35and they did not exhibit loyalty to the house of Jerubbaal (that is, Gideon) in return for all the good that he had done to Israel.

Abimelech Attempts to Establish a Monarchy

9 Now Abimelech son of Jerubbaal went to Shechem to his mother's kinsfolk and said to them and to the whole clan of his mother's family, 2"Say in the hearing of all the lords of Shechem, 'Which is better for you, that all seventy of the sons of Jerubbaal rule over you, or that one rule over you?' Remember also that I am your bone and your flesh." 3So his mother's kinsfolk spoke all these words on his behalf in the hearing of all the lords of Shechem; and their hearts inclined to follow Abimelech, for they said, "He is our brother." 4They gave him seventy pieces of silver out of the temple of Baal-berith with which Abimelech hired worthless and reckless fellows, who followed him. 5He went to his father's house at Ophrah, and killed his brothers the sons of Jerubbaal, seventy men, on one stone; but Jotham, the youngest son of Jerubbaal, survived, for he hid himself. 6Then all the lords of Shechem and all Beth-millo came together, and they went and made Abimelech king, by the oak of the pillar[b] at Shechem.

_____

a Heb they   b Cn: Meaning of Heb uncertain

be dynastic: *you and your son and your grandson.* **8.23** *The LORD will rule over you.* The choice of a human king would impinge on the Lord's kingship (1 Sam 8.7). **8.24** *Ishmaelites* were "related" to Israel through Abraham's son by Hagar (Gen 16). Midianites were related to Israel through Abraham's second wife, Keturah (Gen 25.1–4). These two nomadic groups were similar in culture. **8.27** In contrast with preceding judges, Gideon is still alive when apostasy resumes and is faulted for it. In later tradition an *ephod* was an elaborate vestment worn by the high priest, with a "breastpiece of judgment" to hold the sacred lots, Urim and Thummim (Ex 28; 39). Gideon's ephod may have cloaked an idol (cf. 17.4–5) used in oracle seeking (1 Sam 23.9–12; 30.7–8). *Israel prostituted themselves* echoes 2.17; *snare* echoes 2.3. **8.28** The *rest* formula (3.11, 30; 5.31) occurs here for the last time. **8.29–32** Transition describing the political "family" of Gideon, *seventy sons* and *many wives.* **8.31** *Concubine,* a legitimate wife of secondary rank. **8.33–35** Apostasy introduces the story of Abimelech's reign at Shechem,

which interrupts the rest of the familiar framework pattern (punishment, crying out, deliverance; see note on 2.11–23). **8.33** *Baal-berith,* (Hebrew, "Lord of the Covenant"; cf. 9.4) was worshiped in Shechem and is probably the same god as *El-berith* (9.46).

9.1–57 Abimelech becomes commander in Israel, king of the Shechem city-state, and agent of Shechem's destruction. **9.1** Abimelech's entrée into Shechem's politics is based on his mother's belonging to one of the city's clans (8.31). **9.2** *Lords of Shechem* are the local ruling elite. *Seventy* is a politically significant number; cf. Abdon's seventy sons and grandsons (12.14); 2 Kings 10.1, 7. Many of Gideon's *sons* would be half brothers. The appeal to *bone and . . . flesh* is a claim based on close kinship (Gen 2.23). **9.4** The massive *temple* at Shechem would double as a fortress. **9.5** *On one stone* sounds like a parody of sacrifice (1 Sam 14.33–34), but in any case indicates that the mass slaughter was calculated and brutal. **9.6** *Beth-millo,* Hebrew, possibly "House of the Fill," may be named for a huge earthen platform supporting She-

The Parable of the Trees

7 When it was told to Jotham, he went and stood on the top of Mount Gerizim, and cried aloud and said to them, "Listen to me, you lords of Shechem, so that God may listen to you.

8   The trees once went out
        to anoint a king over themselves.
    So they said to the olive tree,
        'Reign over us.'
9   The olive tree answered them,
        'Shall I stop producing my rich oil
            by which gods and mortals are
                honored,
        and go to sway over the trees?'
10 Then the trees said to the fig tree,
        'You come and reign over us.'
11 But the fig tree answered them,
        'Shall I stop producing my sweetness
            and my delicious fruit,
        and go to sway over the trees?'
12 Then the trees said to the vine,
        'You come and reign over us.'
13 But the vine said to them,
        'Shall I stop producing my wine
            that cheers gods and mortals,
        and go to sway over the trees?'
14 So all the trees said to the bramble,
        'You come and reign over us.'
15 And the bramble said to the trees,
        'If in good faith you are anointing me
            king over you,
        then come and take refuge in my
            shade;
        but if not, let fire come out of the
            bramble
        and devour the cedars of Lebanon.'

16 "Now therefore, if you acted in good faith and honor when you made Abimelech king, and if you have dealt well with Jerubbaal and his house, and have done to him as his actions deserved— 17for my father fought for you, and risked his life, and rescued you from the hand of Midian; 18but you have risen up against my father's house this day, and have killed his sons, seventy men on one stone, and have made Abimelech, the son of his slave woman, king over the lords of Shechem, because he is your kinsman— 19if, I say, you have acted in good faith and honor with Jerubbaal and with his house this day, then rejoice in Abimelech, and let him also rejoice in you; 20but if not, let fire come out from Abimelech, and devour the lords of Shechem, and Beth-millo; and let fire come out from the lords of Shechem, and from Beth-millo, and devour Abimelech." 21Then Jotham ran away and fled, going to Beer, where he remained for fear of his brother Abimelech.

The Downfall of Abimelech

22 Abimelech ruled over Israel three years. 23But God sent an evil spirit between Abimelech and the lords of Shechem; and the lords of Shechem dealt treacherously with Abimelech. 24This happened so that the violence done to the seventy sons of Jerubbaal might be avenged[b] and their blood be laid on their brother Abimelech, who killed them, and on the lords of Shechem, who strengthened his hands to kill his brothers. 25So, out of hostility to him, the lords of Shechem set ambushes on the mountain tops. They robbed all who

---

b Heb *might come*

---

chem's fortress-temple. The building denotes an element of Shechem's government (v. 20; cf. White House). *The oak of the pillar.* Cf. Gen 35.4; Josh 24.26. **9.7–21** From a promontory on Mount Gerizim, Jotham denounces the deal with a scathing antimonarchical fable (vv. 8–15) and a curse (vv. 16–20). **9.8–13** A fable is an illustrative story in which animals or plants have speaking parts. Cf. the imagery and literary form of 2 Kings 14.9. The useful plants (*olive, fig,* and *vine*) refuse kingship as a waste of their valuable aptitudes. **9.14–15** Only the worthless *bramble* (Abimelech) aspires to power, but its *shade* would be meager and its potential for *fire* threatens disaster. **9.16–20** The rest of Jotham's speech is an extended curse that denounces monarchy founded on theft and murder and reaches fulfillment in vv. 56–57. **9.17–18** Jotham interrupts his curse to establish that the rulers of

Shechem have acted unfairly. **9.20** *Fire* (cf. v. 15) symbolizes the conflict that is soon to develop.

9.22–33 Abimelech's downfall begins with dissension in the city, described as God's way of bringing Abimelech and his collaborators to justice (vv. 22–25), followed by the return of Gaal, a native Shechemite, who stirs up the citizenry to rebellion (vv. 26–33). **9.22** Mention of *Israel* forms a frame around the story along with the reference to Israelites in 9.55. In the story proper, Abimelech's rule is a purely local affair. **9.23** Split loyalty is Abimelech's undoing. *Evil spirits* from God describe a psychology of mutual distrust (1 Sam 16.14). **9.24** Israel believed that evil deeds automatically brought on a fitting penalty, so that *violence* and *blood* (bloodshed) would rebound on those who perpetrated them. **9.25** With lookouts posted, the Shechem elite take to plundering the caravans (cf.

passed by them along that way; and it was reported to Abimelech.

26 When Gaal son of Ebed moved into Shechem with his kinsfolk, the lords of Shechem put confidence in him. 27 They went out into the field and gathered the grapes from their vineyards, trod them, and celebrated. Then they went into the temple of their god, ate and drank, and ridiculed Abimelech. 28 Gaal son of Ebed said, "Who is Abimelech, and who are we of Shechem, that we should serve him? Did not the son of Jerubbaal and Zebul his officer serve the men of Hamor father of Shechem? Why then should we serve him? 29 If only this people were under my command! Then I would remove Abimelech; I would say*a* to him, 'Increase your army, and come out.' "

30 When Zebul the ruler of the city heard the words of Gaal son of Ebed, his anger was kindled. 31 He sent messengers to Abimelech at Arumah,*b* saying, "Look, Gaal son of Ebed and his kinsfolk have come to Shechem, and they are stirring up*c* the city against you. 32 Now therefore, go by night, you and the troops that are with you, and lie in wait in the fields. 33 Then early in the morning, as soon as the sun rises, get up and rush on the city; and when he and the troops that are with him come out against you, you may deal with them as best you can."

34 So Abimelech and all the troops with him got up by night and lay in wait against Shechem in four companies. 35 When Gaal son of Ebed went out and stood in the entrance of the gate of the city, Abimelech and the troops with him rose from the ambush. 36 And when Gaal saw them, he said to Zebul, "Look, people are coming down from the mountain tops!" And Zebul said to him, "The shadows on the mountains look like people to you." 37 Gaal spoke again and said, "Look, people are coming down from Tabbur-erez, and one company is coming from the direction of Elon-meonenim."*d* 38 Then Zebul said to him, "Where is your boast*e* now, you who said, 'Who is Abimelech, that we should serve him?' Are not these the troops you made light of? Go out now and fight with them." 39 So Gaal went out at the head of the lords of Shechem, and fought with Abimelech. 40 Abimelech chased him, and he fled before him. Many fell wounded, up to the entrance of the gate. 41 So Abimelech resided at Arumah; and Zebul drove out Gaal and his kinsfolk, so that they could not live on at Shechem.

42 On the following day the people went out into the fields. When Abimelech was told, 43 he took his troops and divided them into three companies, and lay in wait in the fields. When he looked and saw the people coming out of the city, he rose against them and killed them. 44 Abimelech and the company that was*f* with him rushed forward and stood at the entrance of the gate of the city, while the two companies rushed on all who were in the fields and killed them. 45 Abimelech fought against the city all that day; he took the city, and killed the people that were in it; and he razed the city and sowed it with salt.

46 When all the lords of the Tower of Shechem heard of it, they entered the stronghold

---

a Gk: Heb *and he said*   *b* Cn See 9.41. Heb *Tormah*
c Cn: Heb *are besieging*   *d* That is *Diviners' Oak*
e Heb *mouth*   *f* Vg and some Gk Mss: Heb *companies that were*

5.6–8). This undercuts Abimelech's authority and weakens his ability to collect tolls. **9.26** *Gaal son of Ebed,* in Hebrew possibly "loathsome son of a slave," an obviously distorted name. **9.27** Celebration of the wine harvest would mean loose talk and volatile emotions. **9.28** Gaal's speech objects to Abimelech's limited family status in Shechem and appears to base its appeal on genealogical purity and ethnic pride. The Shechemites are urged to serve the authentic native leadership, *the men of Hamor father of Shechem* (see Gen 33.19; 34.6), rather than Abimelech, the upstart outsider. **9.33** Zebul (Abimelech's deputy, v. 30) arranges things to ensure that Gaal and his troops *come out against* Abimelech (see also v. 38). **9.34** Dividing his troops into *four companies* lets Abimelech approach unobserved and set up his surprise attack. **9.37** *Tabbur-erez,* Hebrew, "The Navel of the Land," is a mythic designation for the Shechem temple location, a narrow east west pass between Mounts Gerizim and Ebal emptying into the broader north-south plain. *Elon-meonenim,* Hebrew, "Diviner's Oak," possibly the *oak of the pillar* in v. 6. **9.39–40** Shechem's aristocrats venture out from the city under Gaal's leadership but are driven back with heavy casualties. **9.41** Abimelech remains at Arumah (v. 31) and does not take over Shechem at this point; nevertheless, Zebul is able to expel Gaal and his followers. **9.42–43** Abimelech now turns his attention to the common folk who work in the fields. **9.44** The troops directly under Abimelech's command block off the safety of the city while the other two detachments massacre Shechem's ordinary citizens. **9.45** Abimelech wages total war, pulling down buildings and sowing Shechem with *salt* as a curse to prevent resettlement. **9.46–49** This account emphasizes the destruction of the temple and the conspirators. **9.46** *The lords of the Tower of Shechem* are an aris-

of the temple of El-berith. [47] Abimelech was told that all the lords of the Tower of Shechem were gathered together. [48] So Abimelech went up to Mount Zalmon, he and all the troops that were with him. Abimelech took an ax in his hand, cut down a bundle of brushwood, and took it up and laid it on his shoulder. Then he said to the troops with him, "What you have seen me do, do quickly, as I have done." [49] So every one of the troops cut down a bundle and following Abimelech put it against the stronghold, and they set the stronghold on fire over them, so that all the people of the Tower of Shechem also died, about a thousand men and women.

50 Then Abimelech went to Thebez, and encamped against Thebez, and took it. [51] But there was a strong tower within the city, and all the men and women and all the lords of the city fled to it and shut themselves in; and they went to the roof of the tower. [52] Abimelech came to the tower, and fought against it, and came near to the entrance of the tower to burn it with fire. [53] But a certain woman threw an upper millstone on Abimelech's head, and crushed his skull. [54] Immediately he called to the young man who carried his armor and said to him, "Draw your sword and kill me, so people will not say about me, 'A woman killed him.' " So the young man thrust him through, and he died. [55] When the Israelites saw that Abimelech was dead, they all went home. [56] Thus God repaid Abimelech for the crime

he committed against his father in killing his seventy brothers; [57] and God also made all the wickedness of the people of Shechem fall back on their heads, and on them came the curse of Jotham son of Jerubbaal.

Tola and Jair

10 After Abimelech, Tola son of Puah son of Dodo, a man of Issachar, who lived at Shamir in the hill country of Ephraim, rose to deliver Israel. [2] He judged Israel twenty-three years. Then he died, and was buried at Shamir.

3 After him came Jair the Gileadite, who judged Israel twenty-two years. [4] He had thirty sons who rode on thirty donkeys; and they had thirty towns, which are in the land of Gilead, and are called Havvoth-jair to this day. [5] Jair died, and was buried in Kamon.

Oppression by the Ammonites

6 The Israelites again did what was evil in the sight of the LORD, worshiping the Baals and the Astartes, the gods of Aram, the gods of Sidon, the gods of Moab, the gods of the Ammonites, and the gods of the Philistines. Thus they abandoned the LORD, and did not worship him. [7] So the anger of the LORD was kindled against Israel, and he sold them into the hand of the Philistines and into the hand of the Ammonites, [8] and they crushed and oppressed the Israelites that year. For eighteen years they oppressed all the Israelites that were

---

tocratic group who seek safety in the city's last strongholds. The *Tower of Shechem* is probably an alternative designation for *Beth-millo* (v. 6) and *temple of El-berith*. **9.48** *Zalmon,* Hebrew, "Dark One," is probably Mount Ebal, mountain of the covenantal curses (Deut 27.11–26; Josh 8.30–35). **9.49** *Stronghold,* some part of the temple, perhaps a tower. **9.50–57** Abimelech's dishonorable death. **9.53** The tactic that worked at Shechem is foiled at Thebez by an anonymous woman, whose achievement is ironic in light of v. 54, the one thing elsewhere remembered about Abimelech (see 2 Sam 11.21). *An upper millstone* could be easily picked up in two hands and thrown; a woman would find one conveniently at hand. **9.54** *Draw your sword . . . killed him.* Abimelech seeks to avoid the dishonor of being killed by a woman (cf. 4.9), but he was remembered for this nevertheless (2 Sam 11.21). **9.56–57** Jotham's curse (v. 20) and retributive justice (v. 24) have worked together to achieve an appropriate end result.

10.1–5 In addition to the major judges, Judges preserves a list of others who "judged Israel" (10.1–5; 12.7–15). Family details (10.4; 12.9, 14) glorify their

wealth and eminence, but (with the exception of Jephthah) no narratives survive about them. The years of service of the "minor judges" are stated precisely, not in round numbers as in the preceding chronological notices. **10.1–2** *Tola,* possibly "Worm" in Hebrew. *Shamir* seems to be a reference to Samaria. In what sense Tola acted to *deliver Israel* is unclear. Perhaps *after Abimelech* what was needed was *twenty-three years* of effective leadership! Tola and *Puah* (as Puvah) elsewhere represent clans of Issachar (Gen 46.13). **10.3–5** *Jair* was a powerful chief in *Gilead* (north-central Transjordan), elsewhere celebrated as a pioneer in the occupation of Gilead (Josh 13.30; 1 Kings 4.13). *Havvoth-jair* means "tent villages of Jair." **10.6–18** These verses resume the framework cycle (see note on 2.11–23). Oppression by the Ammonites in Transjordan is the setting for Jephthah's career, here given an elaborate and ironic introduction by a Deuteronomistic narrator (see Introduction). **10.6** A list of seven categories of alien gods emphasizes the enormity of Israel's apostasy. *The Baals and the Astartes.* See note on 2.13. **10.7–8** *Ammonites* lived beyond the Jordan, to the east and south of Israel's terri-

beyond the Jordan in the land of the Amorites, which is in Gilead. ⁹The Ammonites also crossed the Jordan to fight against Judah and against Benjamin and against the house of Ephraim; so that Israel was greatly distressed.

10 So the Israelites cried to the LORD, saying, "We have sinned against you, because we have abandoned our God and have worshiped the Baals." ¹¹And the LORD said to the Israelites, "Did I not deliver you* from the Egyptians and from the Amorites, from the Ammonites and from the Philistines? ¹²The Sidonians also, and the Amalekites, and the Maonites, oppressed you; and you cried to me, and I delivered you out of their hand. ¹³Yet you have abandoned me and worshiped other gods; therefore I will deliver you no more. ¹⁴Go and cry to the gods whom you have chosen; let them deliver you in the time of your distress." ¹⁵And the Israelites said to the LORD, "We have sinned; do to us whatever seems good to you; but deliver us this day!" ¹⁶So they put away the foreign gods from among them and worshiped the LORD; and he could no longer bear to see Israel suffer.

17 Then the Ammonites were called to arms, and they encamped in Gilead; and the Israelites came together, and they encamped at Mizpah. ¹⁸The commanders of the people of Gilead said to one another, "Who will begin the fight against the Ammonites? He shall be head over all the inhabitants of Gilead."

Jephthah

11 Now Jephthah the Gileadite, the son of a prostitute, was a mighty warrior. Gilead was the father of Jephthah. ²Gilead's wife

also bore him sons; and when his wife's sons grew up, they drove Jephthah away, saying to him, "You shall not inherit anything in our father's house; for you are the son of another woman." ³Then Jephthah fled from his brothers and lived in the land of Tob. Outlaws collected around Jephthah and went raiding with him.

4 After a time the Ammonites made war against Israel. ⁵And when the Ammonites made war against Israel, the elders of Gilead went to bring Jephthah from the land of Tob. ⁶They said to Jephthah, "Come and be our commander, so that we may fight with the Ammonites." ⁷But Jephthah said to the elders of Gilead, "Are you not the very ones who rejected me and drove me out of my father's house? So why do you come to me now when you are in trouble?" ⁸The elders of Gilead said to Jephthah, "Nevertheless, we have now turned back to you, so that you may go with us and fight with the Ammonites, and become head over us, over all the inhabitants of Gilead." ⁹Jephthah said to the elders of Gilead, "If you bring me home again to fight with the Ammonites, and the LORD gives them over to me, I will be your head." ¹⁰And the elders of Gilead said to Jephthah, "The LORD will be witness between us; we will surely do as you say." ¹¹So Jephthah went with the elders of Gilead, and the people made him head and commander over them; and Jephthah spoke all his words before the LORD at Mizpah.

12 Then Jephthah sent messengers to the king of the Ammonites and said, "What is

---

a Heb lacks *Did I not deliver you*

---

tory *Gilead.* **10.10–14** The cyclical pattern described by (see note on) 2.11–23 is interrupted for a third confrontation between Israel and the Lord (see 2.1–5; 6.7–10). Now the LORD responds directly to Israel's appeal with a sarcastic *let them deliver you.* **10.15** Genuine repentance, nowhere else explicit in Judges, evokes the Lord's compassion for Israel's suffering. **10.16** *No longer bear.* The Lord's affection for Israel is described in strikingly emotional terms. To *put away the foreign gods* may reflect a time-honored ritual in which idols were ceremonially buried (Gen 35.2–4; Josh 24.14). **10.17** *Ammonites were called to arms,* technical language, as in Barak's muster (4.10) and Gideon's muster (6.35; 7.23–24). In contrast, the leaderless *Israelites* merely *came together.* **10.18** The commanders offer a new title, *head over all,* to anyone who will assume leadership.

11.1–11 Jephthah is introduced to readers by the

circumstances of his birth, his expulsion by his half brothers, and his mercenary associates. **11.1** Like Gideon, Jephthah is *a mighty warrior* (6.11–12). **11.3** Jephthah's career as an outlaw is similar to David's early rise to power (1 Sam 22.2). **11.6** In contrast to the proposal made in 10.18, the elders first offer a lower-ranking position of military *commander,* here not Hebrew *sar* (10.18), but *qatsin,* merely a ranking officer (Josh 10.24). **11.7–10** Jephthah negotiates for a better offer. The elders increase the ante by using the term *head* (v. 8; Hebrew *ro'sh*). Perhaps *qatsin* (see note on 11.6) refers to a temporary role as field commander, while *ro'sh* refers to a permanent post, chief *over all the inhabitants of Gilead* (v. 8). **11.11** To conclude the negotiations, Jephthah validates the agreement by reciting it *before the LORD at Mizpah* (Hebrew, "Lookout" or "Watchtower"), a shrine somewhere east of the Jordan. **11.12–28** This is the only narrative of Israelite

there between you and me, that you have come to me to fight against my land?" 13The king of the Ammonites answered the messengers of Jephthah, "Because Israel, on coming from Egypt, took away my land from the Arnon to the Jabbok and to the Jordan; now therefore restore it peaceably." 14Once again Jephthah sent messengers to the king of the Ammonites 15and said to him: "Thus says Jephthah: Israel did not take away the land of Moab or the land of the Ammonites, 16but when they came up from Egypt, Israel went through the wilderness to the Red Sea*a* and came to Kadesh. 17Israel then sent messengers to the king of Edom, saying, 'Let us pass through your land'; but the king of Edom would not listen. They also sent to the king of Moab, but he would not consent. So Israel remained at Kadesh. 18Then they journeyed through the wilderness, went around the land of Edom and the land of Moab, arrived on the east side of the land of Moab, and camped on the other side of the Arnon. They did not enter the territory of Moab, for the Arnon was the boundary of Moab. 19Israel then sent messengers to King Sihon of the Amorites, king of Heshbon; and Israel said to him, 'Let us pass through your land to our country.' 20But Sihon did not trust Israel to pass through his territory; so Sihon gathered all his people together, and encamped at Jahaz, and fought with Israel. 21Then the LORD, the God of Israel, gave Sihon and all his people into the hand of Israel, and they defeated them; so Israel occupied all the land of the Amorites, who inhabited that country. 22They occupied all the territory of the Amorites from the Arnon to the Jabbok and from the wilderness to the Jordan. 23So now the LORD, the God of Israel, has conquered the Amorites for the benefit of his people Israel. Do you intend to take their place? 24Should you not possess what your god Chemosh gives you to possess? And should we not be the ones to possess everything that the LORD our God has conquered for our benefit? 25Now are you any better than King Balak son of Zippor of Moab? Did he ever enter into conflict with Israel, or did he ever go to war with them? 26While Israel lived in Heshbon and its villages, and in Aroer and its villages, and in all the towns that are along the Arnon, three hundred years, why did you not recover them within that time? 27It is not I who have sinned against you, but you are the one who does me wrong by making war on me. Let the LORD, who is judge, decide today for the Israelites or for the Ammonites." 28But the king of the Ammonites did not heed the message that Jephthah sent him.

Jephthah's Vow

29 Then the spirit of the LORD came upon Jephthah, and he passed through Gilead and Manasseh. He passed on to Mizpah of Gilead, and from Mizpah of Gilead he passed on to the Ammonites. 30And Jephthah made a vow

---

a Or *Sea of Reeds*

---

diplomacy in Judges and one of the clearest examples of the genre of the indictment (Hebrew *riv*, "to conduct a lawsuit"). Two delegations are sent. The first (vv. 12–13) addresses a brief, direct question, receives an equally brief, direct answer, and goes home. The second (vv. 14–27) makes an elaborate appeal to historical precedent (cf. Num chs. 21–22) in response to the answer given to the first delegation and receives no reply. **11.13** The Ammonite king charges that Israel has illegitimately occupied land directly west of the Ammonite homeland, north of the *Arnon* River and south of the *Jabbok*. Statements by the second Israelite delegation (vv. 15, 18b) indicate that Ammon is claiming this territory based on the fact that it formerly belonged to Moab. **11.15–27** Jephthah asserts that Israel did not take any *land of Moab* or *land of the Ammonites* (v. 15). Rather, Israel acquired it by wresting it from the Amorite king Sihon (vv. 21–22) three hundred years earlier (v. 26). For the tradition of Israel's progress through Transjordan, see Num 21; Deut 2. **11.18** Jephthah emphasizes that Israel never encroached into Moab proper. Texts referring to the premonarchical period agree that *the Arnon was the boundary of Moab;* it is the territory north of the Arnon that is in dispute. **11.19–21** See Num 21.21–24. **11.20** Jephthah cites how, in connection with Sihon's territory, Israel fought only when negotiations failed. **11.24** *Chemosh* was properly god of Moab, not Ammon, but the region under dispute was associated with him. Early Israel supposed that the gods of other peoples really existed and were active within the limits of their own territories. **11.25** In Num 22–24 a major theme is the great labor exerted to communicate with *King Balak son of Zippor of Moab. Enter into conflict,* i.e., "contend" through diplomacy (Hebrew *riv*; cf. note on 11.12–28). **11.26** *Three hundred years* approximates the book's chronology. The years of oppression and successive judges thus far total 319. **11.27** The noun *judge* (used of the Lord only here in Judges) and the verb *decide* share the Hebrew root *shpt.* Cf. 1 Sam 24.15. **11.29** *The spirit of the* LORD empowers Jephthah, but only after a long delay (contrast 3.10; 6.34),

to the LORD, and said, "If you will give the Ammonites into my hand, ³¹then whoever comes out of the doors of my house to meet me, when I return victorious from the Ammonites, shall be the LORD's, to be offered up by me as a burnt offering." ³²So Jephthah crossed over to the Ammonites to fight against them; and the LORD gave them into his hand. ³³He inflicted a massive defeat on them from Aroer to the neighborhood of Minnith, twenty towns, and as far as Abel-keramim. So the Ammonites were subdued before the people of Israel.

Jephthah's Daughter

34 Then Jephthah came to his home at Mizpah; and there was his daughter coming out to meet him with timbrels and with dancing. She was his only child; he had no son or daughter except her. ³⁵When he saw her, he tore his clothes, and said, "Alas, my daughter! You have brought me very low; you have become the cause of great trouble to me. For I have opened my mouth to the LORD, and I cannot take back my vow." ³⁶She said to him, "My father, if you have opened your mouth to the LORD, do to me according to what has gone out of your mouth, now that the LORD has given you vengeance against your enemies, the Ammonites." ³⁷And she said to her father, "Let this thing be done for me: Grant me two months, so that I may go and wander*ᵃ* on the mountains, and bewail my virginity, my companions and I." ³⁸"Go," he said and sent her

away for two months. So she departed, she and her companions, and bewailed her virginity on the mountains. ³⁹At the end of two months, she returned to her father, who did with her according to the vow he had made. She had never slept with a man. So there arose an Israelite custom that ⁴⁰for four days every year the daughters of Israel would go out to lament the daughter of Jephthah the Gileadite.

Intertribal Dissension

12 The men of Ephraim were called to arms, and they crossed to Zaphon and said to Jephthah, "Why did you cross over to fight against the Ammonites, and did not call us to go with you? We will burn your house down over you!" ²Jephthah said to them, "My people and I were engaged in conflict with the Ammonites who oppressed us*ᵇ* severely. But when I called you, you did not deliver me from their hand. ³When I saw that you would not deliver me, I took my life in my hand, and crossed over against the Ammonites, and the LORD gave them into my hand. Why then have you come up to me this day, to fight against me?" ⁴Then Jephthah gathered all the men of Gilead and fought with Ephraim; and the men of Gilead defeated Ephraim, because they said, "You are fugitives from Ephraim, you Gileadites—in the heart of Ephraim and Manasseh."*ᶜ* ⁵Then the Gileadites took the fords of

---

a Cn: Heb *go down*   *b* Gk OL, Syr H: Heb lacks *who oppressed us*   *c* Meaning of Heb uncertain: Gk omits *because . . . Manasseh*

---

perhaps an echo of the Lord's earlier unwillingness to deliver Israel (10.13–16). **11.30–31** Jephthah's reckless, egocentric vow reveals a tragic flaw in his character. Instead of *whoever*, though, Jephthah may have intended "whatever." Early Israelites often shared their houses with livestock. *Burnt offering* implies a farm animal, although human sacrifice was sometimes practiced in Israel (2 Kings 16.3; Ezek 20.25–26.31; cf. Gen 22). **11.33** *Aroer, Minnith,* and *Abel-keramim* were all located in the district west of the Ammonite capital, Rabbah Ammon. **11.34** A traditional role of women was singing *with timbrels and . . . dancing* after victory (Ex 15.20–21) to welcome the victors home (1 Sam 18.6–7). Cf. the Song of Deborah, esp. 5.28–30. **11.35** *Tore his clothes.* Jephthah is distraught, but also sounds as though he is blaming his daughter for what happened. **11.36** Ancient readers would agree with Jephthah's daughter that a vow once made is irrevocable (cf. Deut 23.22–23; Prov 20.25). **11.37** *Bewail my virginity.* For a woman to die without becoming a mother was seen as a terrible misfortune (reempha-

sized in v. 39). The daughter is courageous, devout, and takes control of how she will spend the last months of her life. Jephthah too experiences tragedy; he is now childless (cf. v. 34). **11.39–40** Jephthah's daughter establishes the precedent for an annual ritual of remembrance, otherwise unknown.
   12.1–6 The final episodes of the career of Jephthah were added as a sequel, loosely joined to the preceding sections. **12.1–4** The powerful tribe of *Ephraim* initiates hostilities with Gilead. Jephthah reacts vigorously. **12.1–2** The Ephraimites claim to have been excluded from the muster of forces against the Ammonites, essentially the same complaint they made to Gideon in the Midianite crisis (8.1). Jephthah replies that he called them. Which side are readers to believe? The book reports no appeal to Ephraim made by Jephthah. **12.3** The argument ends with a question, *Why . . . fight against me?* as did the unsuccessful negotiations with the Ammonite king (11.26). **12.4** The cause of war is an obscure taunt. The Ephraimites apparently mean that *Gileadites* are nothing but *fugitives* or refugees

the Jordan against the Ephraimites. Whenever one of the fugitives of Ephraim said, "Let me go over," the men of Gilead would say to him, "Are you an Ephraimite?" When he said, "No," ⁶they said to him, "Then say Shibboleth," and he said, "Sibboleth," for he could not pronounce it right. Then they seized him and killed him at the fords of the Jordan. Forty-two thousand of the Ephraimites fell at that time.

7 Jephthah judged Israel six years. Then Jephthah the Gileadite died, and was buried in his town in Gilead.*

Ibzan, Elon, and Abdon

8 After him Ibzan of Bethlehem judged Israel. ⁹He had thirty sons. He gave his thirty daughters in marriage outside his clan and brought in thirty young women from outside for his sons. He judged Israel seven years. ¹⁰Then Ibzan died, and was buried at Bethlehem.

11 After him Elon the Zebulunite judged Israel; and he judged Israel ten years. ¹²Then Elon the Zebulunite died, and was buried at Aijalon in the land of Zebulun.

13 After him Abdon son of Hillel the Pirathonite judged Israel. ¹⁴He had forty sons and thirty grandsons, who rode on seventy donkeys; he judged Israel eight years. ¹⁵Then Abdon son of Hillel the Pirathonite died, and was buried at Pirathon in the land of Ephraim, in the hill country of the Amalekites.

The Birth of Samson

13 The Israelites again did what was evil in the sight of the LORD, and the LORD gave them into the hand of the Philistines forty years.

2 There was a certain man of Zorah, of the tribe of the Danites, whose name was Manoah. His wife was barren, having borne no children. ³And the angel of the LORD appeared to the woman and said to her, "Although you are barren, having borne no children, you shall conceive and bear a son. ⁴Now be careful not to drink wine or strong drink, or to eat anything unclean, ⁵for you shall conceive and bear a son. No razor is to come on his head, for the boy shall be a nazirite*ᵇ* to God from birth. It is he who shall begin to deliver Israel from the hand of the Philistines." ⁶Then the woman came and told her husband, "A man of God

---

a Gk: Heb *in the towns of Gilead*   *b* That is *one separated* or *one consecrated*

---

from Ephraim and so are not a real tribe, just a part *of Ephraim and Manasseh.* **12.5–6** Jephthah is not mentioned in this concluding story. **12.5** Gilead blocks the way back across the Jordan and uses a password to detect Ephraimites. These are presumably escapees from the battle in v. 4, and the phrase *fugitives from Ephraim* grimly echoes their earlier insult (v. 4). **12.6** The test turns on regional differences in pronunciation of the word *Shibboleth.* **12.7–15** Jephthah is not only a "major judge"; he was also cataloged in a list of "minor judges" (10.1–5; 12.7–15) into which the stories of the Ammonite crisis were inserted. **12.8** The "minor judges" are all northern and eastern figures, so this *Bethlehem* is the one located in Lower Galilee near Zebulun's border with Asher (Josh 19.15). **12.9** Numerous progeny stand for effective, wide-ranging control as a political ruler (10.4). Ibzan's *outside* marriages represent a quest for wide-ranging familial alliances, similar to royal practice. **12.11–12** *Elon* is mentioned elsewhere as a clan ancestor of Zebulun (Gen 46.14; Num 26.26). Elon's town *Aijalon* is essentially identical to his name. **12.13** *Abdon* is otherwise unknown. **12.14** The decline from *forty sons* to only *thirty grandsons* is a surprising regression, unless the numbers stand for waning political effectiveness, thus anticipating the need for another deliverer-judge. *Pirathon* is probably modern Farʿata, about five miles (eight kilometers) west-southwest of Shechem, in Manasseh near the border with Ephraim.

13.1–16.31 The Samson stories have no close parallel in Judges. They are rowdy tales from the old frontier with Philistia, reflecting Dan's inability to take control of the coastal plain (see 1.34; ch. 18). Samson's primary pursuits, however, are amorous. For injuries to his vanity he kills many Philistines, but he is not an effective deliverer of Israel or any Israelite tribe. Samson's story begins the familiar cycle of apostasy and oppression anew (v. 1), but he will only *begin to deliver Israel* (v. 5). Deliverance from the Philistines must wait until Samuel (1 Sam 7.5–14). **13.1–25** The birth story focuses on Samson's unnamed mother's perceptiveness and her collaboration with the Lord. **13.1** *Philistines* were Sea Peoples from the Aegean and Asia Minor who settled the southern coast of Canaan in the twelfth century BCE, not long after the emergence of Israel in the highlands. **13.2** *Zorah* is in the Shephelah, the foothills near Dan's border with Judah. **13.3** *The angel of the LORD,* representing the deity's visible presence, last appeared in 6.11–24, engaged in another recruitment mission. There are echoes of the Gideon and Jephthah materials in the Samson stories. **13.4–5** *Nazirite,* an Israelite man or woman taking temporary vows of consecration to God according to rules such as those in Num 6.1–21. Here the vow is permanent, *from birth,* and the rule of the Nazirite (no *wine or strong drink*) is urged as prenatal care for Samson, who would begin the liberation of Israel from the Philistines. Cf. 1 Sam 1.11, where Hannah promises that her son will be a Nazirite. **13.6** *Man of God . . . angel of God.* Samson's mother supposes the messen-

came to me, and his appearance was like that of an angel[a] of God, most awe-inspiring; I did not ask him where he came from, and he did not tell me his name; 7but he said to me, 'You shall conceive and bear a son. So then drink no wine or strong drink, and eat nothing unclean, for the boy shall be a nazirite[b] to God from birth to the day of his death.' "

8 Then Manoah entreated the LORD, and said, "O LORD, I pray, let the man of God whom you sent come to us again and teach us what we are to do concerning the boy who will be born." 9God listened to Manoah, and the angel of God came again to the woman as she sat in the field; but her husband Manoah was not with her. 10So the woman ran quickly and told her husband, "The man who came to me the other day has appeared to me." 11Manoah got up and followed his wife, and came to the man and said to him, "Are you the man who spoke to this woman?" And he said, "I am." 12Then Manoah said, "Now when your words come true, what is to be the boy's rule of life; what is he to do?" 13The angel of the LORD said to Manoah, "Let the woman give heed to all that I said to her. 14She may not eat of anything that comes from the vine. She is not to drink wine or strong drink, or eat any unclean thing. She is to observe everything that I commanded her."

15 Manoah said to the angel of the LORD, "Allow us to detain you, and prepare a kid for you." 16The angel of the LORD said to Manoah, "If you detain me, I will not eat your food; but if you want to prepare a burnt offering, then offer it to the LORD." (For Manoah did not know that he was the angel of the LORD.) 17Then Manoah said to the angel of the LORD, "What is your name, so that we may honor you when your words come true?" 18But the

angel of the LORD said to him, "Why do you ask my name? It is too wonderful."

19 So Manoah took the kid with the grain offering, and offered it on the rock to the LORD, to him who works[c] wonders.[d] 20When the flame went up toward heaven from the altar, the angel of the LORD ascended in the flame of the altar while Manoah and his wife looked on; and they fell on their faces to the ground. 21The angel of the LORD did not appear again to Manoah and his wife. Then Manoah realized that it was the angel of the LORD. 22And Manoah said to his wife, "We shall surely die, for we have seen God." 23But his wife said to him, "If the LORD had meant to kill us, he would not have accepted a burnt offering and a grain offering at our hands, or shown us all these things, or now announced to us such things as these."

24 The woman bore a son, and named him Samson. The boy grew, and the LORD blessed him. 25The spirit of the LORD began to stir him in Mahaneh-dan, between Zorah and Eshtaol.

Samson's Marriage

14 Once Samson went down to Timnah, and at Timnah he saw a Philistine woman. 2Then he came up, and told his father and mother, "I saw a Philistine woman at Timnah; now get her for me as my wife." 3But his father and mother said to him, "Is there not a woman among your kin, or among all our[e] people, that you must go to take a wife from the uncircumcised Philistines?" But Samson said to his father, "Get her for me, because she pleases me." 4His father and mother did not

---

a Or the angel   b That is one separated or one consecrated
c Gk Vg: Heb and working   d Heb wonders, while Manoah and his wife looked on   e Cn: Heb my

---

ger is a prophet, but from his striking appearance she nearly guesses the truth. **13.7** The mother's breathless recounting of the interview makes no mention of the prohibition of haircuts. A Nazirite's hair was cut when the period of consecration was complete and the Nazirite returned to secular life. **13.8–14** Manoah prays for a second visit from God's envoy but learns nothing more. **13.15–16** Manoah offers the hospitality appropriate for important visitors (6.19; Gen 18.3–5). **13.18** Too wonderful, i.e., beyond human comprehension. **13.22** We shall surely die is the typical reaction after a divine appearance (cf. Gideon, 6.22). **13.23** Again, it is not the panicky Manoah but the wife who speaks common sense and is more perceptive.

13.24 Samson's name is related to the Hebrew shemesh ("sun"). The boy grew . . . him. Cf. 1 Sam 2.26; Lk 2.52. **13.25** Mention of the spirit of the LORD is anticipatory at this point, only a latent stirring in contrast to 14.6. Mahaneh-dan, Hebrew, "Camp of Dan." **14.1–20** The story of Samson's first love. **14.1** Timnah, Hebrew, "Allotted Portion," is probably Tell el-Batashi, four miles (six kilometers) north of Beth-shemesh. **14.3** The parents' hesitation is proper, for the coming together of families through marriage could bring about apostasy (Deut 7.3–4). Philistines, as far as we know, were the only uncircumcised people in Israel's near vicinity. She pleases me, lit. "she is pleasing in my eyes" (similarly v. 7). The concept of acting

know that this was from the LORD; for he was seeking a pretext to act against the Philistines. At that time the Philistines had dominion over Israel.

5 Then Samson went down with his father and mother to Timnah. When he came to the vineyards of Timnah, suddenly a young lion roared at him. 6 The spirit of the LORD rushed on him, and he tore the lion apart barehanded as one might tear apart a kid. But he did not tell his father or his mother what he had done. 7 Then he went down and talked with the woman, and she pleased Samson. 8 After a while he returned to marry her, and he turned aside to see the carcass of the lion, and there was a swarm of bees in the body of the lion, and honey. 9 He scraped it out into his hands, and went on, eating as he went. When he came to his father and mother, he gave some to them, and they ate it. But he did not tell them that he had taken the honey from the carcass of the lion.

10 His father went down to the woman, and Samson made a feast there as the young men were accustomed to do. 11 When the people saw him, they brought thirty companions to be with him. 12 Samson said to them, "Let me now put a riddle to you. If you can explain it to me within the seven days of the feast, and find it out, then I will give you thirty linen garments and thirty festal garments. 13 But if you cannot explain it to me, then you shall give me thirty linen garments and thirty festal garments." So they said to him, "Ask your riddle; let us hear it." 14 He said to them,

"Out of the eater came something to eat.
Out of the strong came something sweet."

But for three days they could not explain the riddle.

15 On the fourth[a] day they said to Samson's wife, "Coax your husband to explain the riddle to us, or we will burn you and your father's house with fire. Have you invited us here to impoverish us?" 16 So Samson's wife wept before him, saying, "You hate me; you do not really love me. You have asked a riddle of my people, but you have not explained it to me." He said to her, "Look, I have not told my father or my mother. Why should I tell you?" 17 She wept before him the seven days that their feast lasted; and because she nagged him, on the seventh day he told her. Then she explained the riddle to her people. 18 The men of the town said to him on the seventh day before the sun went down,

"What is sweeter than honey?
What is stronger than a lion?"

And he said to them,

"If you had not plowed with my heifer,
you would not have found out my
riddle."

19 Then the spirit of the LORD rushed on him, and he went down to Ashkelon. He killed thirty men of the town, took their spoil, and gave the festal garments to those who had explained the riddle. In hot anger he went back to his father's house. 20 And Samson's wife was given to his companion, who had been his best man.

---

a Gk Syr: Heb *seventh*

rightly in one's own eyes is reiterated in 17.6; 21.25 as the book draws to a close. **14.4** The narrator reveals that an action contrary to basic Israelite standards is actually part of a divine plan (cf. 9.24). **14.5–10a** These verses are framed by an inclusio (a repetition signaling the beginning and end of a unit): first Samson and later his father *went down*. **14.5** The purpose of this initial visit to *Timnah* is a meeting of the couple (v. 7) and presumably negotiations between the parents. **14.6** *The spirit of the LORD* gave other judges a gift for military leadership (3.10; 6.34; 11.29), but equips Samson to face any physical threat (v. 19). **14.8** Samson's second trip was *to marry* the Philistine woman, although she continues to live at home. Ancient Near Eastern evidence describes a type of marriage in which the bride continued to live with her parents rather than join her husband at his family or clan location. Perhaps the tale of Samson suggests such a marital arrangement. *Honey* was regarded as having the po-tential to enlighten and give courage (1 Sam 14.24–30). **14.10–20** How the marriage is providentially annulled. **14.11** *Companions* were a standard feature of marriage celebrations (Ps 45.14), but perhaps Samson's impressive physical presence (*when the people saw him*) suggested to the Philistines the need for thirty of them to provide extra security. **14.14** In the ancient world, proposing and solving riddles was a popular pastime. **14.16–17** *You do not really love me.* Samson's wife is similar to Delilah in her dogged determination (16.15). **14.18** The men's solution contains its own riddle (*What is . . . ?*). Another answer to their question about sweetness and strength could be "love"! Samson's response also operates as a riddle. By taking advantage of his wife, they have *plowed* with his *heifer*. **14.19** Because the people of *Ashkelon* were also Philistines, Samson pays off his bet and still comes out ahead. **14.20** The *best man*, Samson's *companion*, was presumably another Timnite.

Samson Defeats the Philistines

15 After a while, at the time of the wheat harvest, Samson went to visit his wife, bringing along a kid. He said, "I want to go into my wife's room." But her father would not allow him to go in. ²Her father said, "I was sure that you had rejected her; so I gave her to your companion. Is not her younger sister prettier than she? Why not take her instead?" ³Samson said to them, "This time, when I do mischief to the Philistines, I will be without blame." ⁴So Samson went and caught three hundred foxes, and took some torches; and he turned the foxes*ᵃ* tail to tail, and put a torch between each pair of tails. ⁵When he had set fire to the torches, he let the foxes go into the standing grain of the Philistines, and burned up the shocks and the standing grain, as well as the vineyards and*ᵇ* olive groves. ⁶Then the Philistines asked, "Who has done this?" And they said, "Samson, the son-in-law of the Timnite, because he has taken Samson's wife and given her to his companion." So the Philistines came up, and burned her and her father. ⁷Samson said to them, "If this is what you do, I swear I will not stop until I have taken revenge on you." ⁸He struck them down hip and thigh with great slaughter; and he went down and stayed in the cleft of the rock of Etam.

9 Then the Philistines came up and encamped in Judah, and made a raid on Lehi. ¹⁰The men of Judah said, "Why have you come up against us?" They said, "We have come up to bind Samson, to do to him as he did to us." ¹¹Then three thousand men of Judah went down to the cleft of the rock of Etam, and they said to Samson, "Do you not know that the Philistines are rulers over us? What then have you done to us?" He replied, "As they did to me, so I have done to them." ¹²They said to him, "We have come down to bind you, so that we may give you into the hands of the Philistines." Samson answered them, "Swear to me that you yourselves will not attack me." ¹³They said to him, "No, we will only bind you and give you into their hands; we will not kill you." So they bound him with two new ropes, and brought him up from the rock.

14 When he came to Lehi, the Philistines came shouting to meet him; and the spirit of the LORD rushed on him, and the ropes that were on his arms became like flax that has caught fire, and his bonds melted off his hands. ¹⁵Then he found a fresh jawbone of a donkey, reached down and took it, and with it he killed a thousand men. ¹⁶And Samson said,

"With the jawbone of a donkey,
    heaps upon heaps,
with the jawbone of a donkey
    I have slain a thousand men."

¹⁷When he had finished speaking, he threw away the jawbone; and that place was called Ramath-lehi.*ᶜ*

18 By then he was very thirsty, and he called

a Heb *them*   *b* Gk Tg Vg: Heb lacks *and*   *c* That is *The Hill of the Jawbone*

15.1–8 Sometime later, Samson is in Timnah once again. The outraged father of the young woman explains that it had looked like divorce to him, but he tries to make the best of a bad situation by suggesting that the younger sister is better anyway. **15.1** Again, this marriage sounds like one in which the woman continued to live with her parents (see note on 14.8). **15.2** The father's conclusion that Samson had *rejected her* (divorced her) was understandable in light of 14.19. Ancient readers would have seen the offer of *her younger sister* as a reasonable arrangement. **15.4** *Foxes* could spread the fire rapidly and extensively and would be difficult to catch. **15.6** *Burned.* Ironically, the very outcome that Samson's wife had hoped to prevent (14.15). **15.8** *Hip and thigh* implies violent physical combat. The idiom, lit. "calf to thigh," indicates that Samson beat their legs out from under them. **15.9–20** Samson's single-handed victory against an entire Philistine military unit and his extreme thirst afterwards precipitate a direct confrontation with the Lord. **15.10** *Men of Judah.* This is the first hint given in the exploits of Samson that more is at stake than the situation of one man's family. Samson has left home, plundered Philistines, and found a hideout in territory controlled by the tribe of Judah, which must handle the extradition. **15.11–13** Samson is the man in the middle, contending with Philistine belligerence and Judahite servility. He is willing to take his chances with the Philistines rather than exercise his great strength against his Israelite brothers. **15.11** Samson's fearsome reputation is acknowledged by the sending out of *three thousand men* to capture him. **15.13** The details that they use *two ropes* and that the ropes are also *new* increase readers' amazement at Samson's escape. **15.14** The Philistines are *shouting* (Hebrew, "yelling a war cry") in triumph and jubilation, but Samson suddenly manifests *the spirit of the LORD* (cf. 14.6). **15.15** A farmer's sickle, made of an animal *jawbone* fitted with flint teeth, might double as a formidable weapon. **15.16** This Song of Samson, an archaic poetic fragment with repetitive parallelism, is certainly older than the prose story. *Donkey* and *heap* are homonyms in Hebrew. **15.17** *Ramath-lehi*, Hebrew, "Jawbone's Height." Samson's story explains the name of the area

on the LORD, saying, "You have granted this great victory by the hand of your servant. Am I now to die of thirst, and fall into the hands of the uncircumcised?" [19]So God split open the hollow place that is at Lehi, and water came from it. When he drank, his spirit returned, and he revived. Therefore it was named En-hakkore,[a] which is at Lehi to this day. [20]And he judged Israel in the days of the Philistines twenty years.

Samson and Delilah

16 Once Samson went to Gaza, where he saw a prostitute and went in to her. [2]The Gazites were told,[b] "Samson has come here." So they circled around and lay in wait for him all night at the city gate. They kept quiet all night, thinking, "Let us wait until the light of the morning; then we will kill him." [3]But Samson lay only until midnight. Then at midnight he rose up, took hold of the doors of the city gate and the two posts, pulled them up, bar and all, put them on his shoulders, and carried them to the top of the hill that is in front of Hebron.

[4]After this he fell in love with a woman in the valley of Sorek, whose name was Delilah. [5]The lords of the Philistines came to her and said to her, "Coax him, and find out what makes his strength so great, and how we may overpower him, so that we may bind him in order to subdue him; and we will each give you eleven hundred pieces of silver." [6]So Delilah said to Samson, "Please tell me what makes your strength so great, and how you could be bound, so that one could subdue you." [7]Samson said to her, "If they bind me with seven fresh bowstrings that are not dried out, then I shall become weak, and be like anyone else." [8]Then the lords of the Philistines brought her seven fresh bowstrings that had not dried out, and she bound him with them. [9]While men were lying in wait in an inner chamber, she said to him, "The Philistines are upon you, Samson!" But he snapped the bowstrings, as a strand of fiber snaps when it touches the fire. So the secret of his strength was not known.

10 Then Delilah said to Samson, "You have mocked me and told me lies; please tell me how you could be bound." [11]He said to her, "If they bind me with new ropes that have not been used, then I shall become weak, and be like anyone else." [12]So Delilah took new ropes and bound him with them, and said to him, "The Philistines are upon you, Samson!" (The men lying in wait were in an inner chamber.) But he snapped the ropes off his arms like a thread.

13 Then Delilah said to Samson, "Until now you have mocked me and told me lies; tell me how you could be bound." He said to her, "If you weave the seven locks of my head with the web and make it tight with the pin, then I shall become weak, and be like anyone else." [14]So while he slept, Delilah took the seven locks of his head and wove them into the web,[c] and made them tight with the pin. Then she said to him, "The Philistines are upon you, Samson!" But he awoke from his sleep, and pulled away the pin, the loom, and the web.

15 Then she said to him, "How can you say, 'I love you,' when your heart is not with me?

---

a That is *The Spring of the One who Called* *b* Gk: Heb lacks *were told* *c* Compare Gk: in verses 13-14, Heb lacks *and make it tight . . . into the web*

---

where the fight occurred. **15.19** *The hollow place,* apparently a rocky spring. *His spirit returned* indicates that his vigor and positive attitude were restored. The landmark *En-hakkore,* lit. "Spring of the Caller," memorializes the tradition. **15.20** A later repetition of the formula *judged Israel . . . twenty years* in 16.31 suggests that an earlier rendition of the Samson cycle probably ended here.

16.1–31 Three stories answer the question: What became of Samson? **16.1–3** Another tale of lusty Samson's enormous strength. **16.1** *Gaza,* one of five major Philistine cities on the southern coastal plain. **16.3** What a feat! It is thirty-five miles (sixty kilometers) uphill from Gaza to *Hebron.* **16.4–22** This narrative shows similarities with the story of Samson's first love (ch. 14). **16.4** Although we are not told this, *Delilah* is probably a Philistine because she lives in the

valley of Sorek, which begins about thirteen miles (twenty-one kilometers) southwest of Jerusalem. **16.5** *The lords* (better "tyrants") *of the Philistines,* a title imported from their Aegean homeland. A total of 5,500 shekels (each of the five *lords* of the Philistine Pentapolis paying 1,100 shekels) is a fantastically huge payoff. The Levite who serves as priest in 17.10 will make 10 shekels a year. **16.6–17** While Samson teases, Delilah pouts and pesters. Samson is trapped into squandering his great strength. **16.7** These *bowstrings* are explicitly prepared from *fresh* animal tendons; brand-new articles were assumed to have magic powers. **16.11** *New ropes* (cf. 15.13) again point to magical notions (see note on 16.7). **16.13–14** By mentioning his hair, Samson reveals part of his secret. Delilah weaves his hair into the *web* and the *pin* of her loom. The idea may be that entangling Samson in the do-

You have mocked me three times now and have not told me what makes your strength so great." [16]Finally, after she had nagged him with her words day after day, and pestered him, he was tired to death. [17]So he told her his whole secret, and said to her, "A razor has never come upon my head; for I have been a nazirite[a] to God from my mother's womb. If my head were shaved, then my strength would leave me; I would become weak, and be like anyone else."

18 When Delilah realized that he had told her his whole secret, she sent and called the lords of the Philistines, saying, "This time come up, for he has told his whole secret to me." Then the lords of the Philistines came up to her, and brought the money in their hands. [19]She let him fall asleep on her lap; and she called a man, and had him shave off the seven locks of his head. He began to weaken,[b] and his strength left him. [20]Then she said, "The Philistines are upon you, Samson!" When he awoke from his sleep, he thought, "I will go out as at other times, and shake myself free." But he did not know that the LORD had left him. [21]So the Philistines seized him and gouged out his eyes. They brought him down to Gaza and bound him with bronze shackles; and he ground at the mill in the prison. [22]But the hair of his head began to grow again after it had been shaved.

Samson's Death

23 Now the lords of the Philistines gathered to offer a great sacrifice to their god Dagon, and to rejoice; for they said, "Our god has given Samson our enemy into our hand." [24]When the people saw him, they praised their god; for they said, "Our god has given our enemy into our hand, the ravager of our country, who has killed many of us." [25]And when their hearts were merry, they said, "Call Samson, and let him entertain us." So they called Samson out of the prison, and he performed for them. They made him stand between the pillars; [26]and Samson said to the attendant who held him by the hand, "Let me feel the pillars on which the house rests, so that I may lean against them." [27]Now the house was full of men and women; all the lords of the Philistines were there, and on the roof there were about three thousand men and women, who looked on while Samson performed.

28 Then Samson called to the LORD and said, "Lord GOD, remember me and strengthen me only this once, O God, so that with this one act of revenge I may pay back the Philistines for my two eyes."[c] [29]And Samson grasped the two middle pillars on which the house rested, and he leaned his weight against them, his right hand on the one and his left hand on the other. [30]Then Samson said, "Let me die with the Philistines." He strained with all his might; and the house fell on the lords and all the people who were in it. So those he killed at his death were more than those he had killed during his life. [31]Then his brothers and all his family came down and took him and brought him up and buried him between Zorah and Eshtaol in the tomb of his father Manoah. He had judged Israel twenty years.

Micah and the Levite

17 There was a man in the hill country of Ephraim whose name was Micah. [2]He

---

a That is *one separated* or *one consecrated*   b Gk: Heb *She began to torment him*   c Or *so that I may be avenged upon the Philistines for one of my two eyes*

---

mestic task of weaving would charm away his strength as a warrior. **16.15** The *heart*, very important for emotional matters, was also the seat of mind and will. Delilah accuses Samson of not trusting her. **16.16** *He was tired to death.* The prophets Elijah (1 Kings 19.4) and Jonah (Jon 4.8) were so exasperated with God that each requested death, using the same idiom. **16.20** Cutting a Nazirite's hair (v. 17; cf. 13.5, 7) effected discharge from the vow (Num 6.13–20). This means *the LORD had left him* in the sense that the divine spirit would no longer empower impressive exploits (14.6, 19; 15.14). **16.21** Samson the disgraced warrior is forced to engage in a menial task usually carried out by women and slaves (Lam 5.13). **16.23–31** The last Samson story centers on his final settling of accounts during festival time at a Philistine temple.

16.23 *Dagon* was a Canaanite god of grain adopted by the Philistines (1 Sam 5.1–5). **16.26** *Attendant* (Hebrew na'ar, "young man") poignantly evokes an image of the elite warrior's squire who appeared in the stories of Gideon (7.10) and Abimelech (9.54) and who, upon the latter's request, assisted him to an honorable death. The *house* may be Dagon's temple or a public hall. **16.27** The *roof* may refer to some neighboring structure from which spectators watched the proceedings. **16.28** *Lord GOD.* See 6.22. Samson seeks retribution, which he will achieve in his death. In *one act* he will avenge two wrongs. **16.31** *He had judged* repeats the information in 15.20. This repetition probably signals that ch. 16 is a later supplement to ch. 15. **17.1–18.31** The migration of the tribe of Dan and the origin of the sanctuary of Dan and its priesthood.

said to his mother, "The eleven hundred pieces of silver that were taken from you, about which you uttered a curse, and even spoke it in my hearing,—that silver is in my possession; I took it; but now I will return it to you." *a* And his mother said, "May my son be blessed by the LORD!" 3 Then he returned the eleven hundred pieces of silver to his mother; and his mother said, "I consecrate the silver to the LORD from my hand for my son, to make an idol of cast metal." 4 So when he returned the money to his mother, his mother took two hundred pieces of silver, and gave it to the silversmith, who made it into an idol of cast metal; and it was in the house of Micah. 5 This man Micah had a shrine, and he made an ephod and teraphim, and installed one of his sons, who became his priest. 6 In those days there was no king in Israel; all the people did what was right in their own eyes.

7 Now there was a young man of Bethlehem in Judah, of the clan of Judah. He was a Levite residing there. 8 This man left the town of Bethlehem in Judah, to live wherever he could find a place. He came to the house of Micah in the hill country of Ephraim to carry on his work. *b* 9 Micah said to him, "From where do you come?" He replied, "I am a Levite of Bethlehem in Judah, and I am going to live wherever I can find a place." 10 Then Micah said to him, "Stay with me, and be to me a father and a priest, and I will give you ten pieces of silver a year, a set of clothes, and your living." *c* 11 The Levite agreed to stay with the man; and the young man became to him like one of his sons. 12 So Micah installed the Levite, and the young man became his priest, and was in the house of Micah. 13 Then Micah said, "Now I know that the LORD will prosper me, because the Levite has become my priest."

The Migration of Dan

18 In those days there was no king in Israel. And in those days the tribe of the Danites was seeking for itself a territory to live in; for until then no territory among the tribes of Israel had been allotted to them. 2 So the Danites sent five valiant men from the whole number of their clan, from Zorah and from Eshtaol, to spy out the land and to explore it; and they said to them, "Go, explore the land." When they came to the hill country of Ephraim, to the house of Micah, they stayed there. 3 While they were at Micah's house, they recognized the voice of the young Levite; so they went over and asked him, "Who brought you here? What are you doing in this place? What is your business here?" 4 He said to them, "Micah did such and such for me, and he hired me, and I have become his priest." 5 Then they said to him, "Inquire of God that we may know whether the mission we are undertaking will succeed." 6 The priest replied, "Go in peace. The mission you are on is under the eye of the LORD."

7 The five men went on, and when they came to Laish, they observed the people who

---

a The words *but now I will return it to you* are transposed from the end of verse 3 in Heb　*b* Or *Ephraim, continuing his journey*　*c* Heb *living, and the Levite went*

17.1 The *hill country of Ephraim*, the north-central highlands. 17.2–3 The narrative style here is complex, because the narrator begins well past the midpoint in the action. *Eleven hundred pieces of silver*, the same amount that each individual gave Delilah to betray Samson (16.5). Micah's mother seeks to counteract her *curse* with a blessing (v. 2) and a vow (v. 3). 17.4 There is a discrepancy between the mother's pledge (v. 3) and her payment. Israelite readers would view this image negatively (Ex 20.4–6; Deut 5.8–10). 17.5 Micah's household *shrine* (Hebrew, "house of God") has all the appropriate equipment. *Ephod*, a priestly vestment. See 8.27. *Teraphim* were used in divination. *One of his sons* looks ahead to the next unit, where a Levite becomes *like one of his sons* (v. 11) by contractual arrangement. 17.6 This editorial observation is repeated twice in part (18.1; 19.1) and once in its entirety, as the last word on the era (21.25). Here the refrain approves of kingship and communicates displeasure over an ominous situation involving a cultic opportunist and an exploitable careerist. 17.7–13 Dissatisfied with prospects at Bethlehem in Judah, a young Levite finds employment in the north as Micah's priest. 17.7 Although a Levite, he is of the *clan of Judah* in that he is a resident alien living in Judah. 17.10 The honorific title *father* implies his priestly role (cf. Deborah, 5.7). 17.13 *Now I know.* Micah clinches the deal, believing that he has improved the effectiveness of his shrine by hiring the *Levite,* a more proper priest than Micah's son by virtue of his lineage (v. 5). 18.1–31 This polemical story of Dan's migration and rival temple resumes the subject of the final introductory note (1.34). 18.2 Conquest stories often begin with a spy mission (1.24; Josh 2). 18.3 The young Levite's *voice* has a recognizable southern accent. 18.5 To *inquire of God* is to seek an oracle, in this case from a priest, whose job description included supernatural insight into God's will. 18.6 The answer assures a successful mission. 18.7 The people of *Laish* are *living securely,* without defensive fortifications. Far from the

were there living securely, after the manner of the Sidonians, quiet and unsuspecting, lacking[a] nothing on earth, and possessing wealth.[b] Furthermore, they were far from the Sidonians and had no dealings with Aram.[c] 8When they came to their kinsfolk at Zorah and Eshtaol, they said to them, "What do you report?" 9They said, "Come, let us go up against them; for we have seen the land, and it is very good. Will you do nothing? Do not be slow to go, but enter in and possess the land. 10When you go, you will come to an unsuspecting people. The land is broad—God has indeed given it into your hands—a place where there is no lack of anything on earth."

11 Six hundred men of the Danite clan, armed with weapons of war, set out from Zorah and Eshtaol, 12and went up and encamped at Kiriath-jearim in Judah. On this account that place is called Mahaneh-dan[d] to this day; it is west of Kiriath-jearim. 13From there they passed on to the hill country of Ephraim, and came to the house of Micah.

14 Then the five men who had gone to spy out the land (that is, Laish) said to their comrades, "Do you know that in these buildings there are an ephod, teraphim, and an idol of cast metal? Now therefore consider what you will do." 15So they turned in that direction and came to the house of the young Levite, at the home of Micah, and greeted him. 16While the six hundred men of the Danites, armed with their weapons of war, stood by the entrance of the gate, 17the five men who had gone to spy out the land proceeded to enter and take the idol of cast metal, the ephod, and the teraphim.[e] The priest was standing by the entrance of the gate with the six hundred men armed with weapons of war. 18When the men went into Micah's house and took the idol of cast metal, the ephod, and the teraphim, the priest said to them, "What are you doing?" 19They said to him, "Keep quiet! Put your hand over your mouth, and come with us, and be to us a father and a priest. Is it better for you to be priest to the house of one person, or to be priest to a tribe and clan in Israel?" 20Then the priest accepted the offer. He took the ephod, the teraphim, and the idol, and went along with the people.

21 So they resumed their journey, putting the little ones, the livestock, and the goods in front of them. 22When they were some distance from the home of Micah, the men who were in the houses near Micah's house were called out, and they overtook the Danites. 23They shouted to the Danites, who turned around and said to Micah, "What is the matter that you come with such a company?" 24He replied, "You take my gods that I made, and the priest, and go away, and what have I left? How then can you ask me, 'What is the matter?' " 25And the Danites said to him, "You had better not let your voice be heard among us or else hot-tempered fellows will attack you, and you will lose your life and the lives of your household." 26Then the Danites went their way. When Micah saw that they were too strong for him, he turned and went back to his home.

The Danites Settle in Laish

27 The Danites, having taken what Micah had made, and the priest who belonged to him, came to Laish, to a people quiet and unsuspecting, put them to the sword, and burned down the city. 28There was no deliverer, because it was far from Sidon and they had no dealings with Aram.[f] It was in the valley that belongs to Beth-rehob. They rebuilt the city, and lived in it. 29They named the city Dan, after their ancestor Dan, who was born to Israel; but the name of the city was formerly Laish. 30Then the Danites set up the idol for

a Cn Compare 18.10: Meaning of Heb uncertain   b Meaning of Heb uncertain   c Symmachus: Heb with anyone   d That is Camp of Dan   e Compare 17.4, 5; 18.14: Heb teraphim and the cast metal   f Cn Compare verse 7: Heb with anyone

Sidonians on the Phoenician coast, nonaligned with Aram on the north, Laish minds its own business (v. 10). Ironically, Laish sounds like the ideal community Israel was meant to be! 18.12 Kiriath-jearim was a border town of the tribes of Judah, Benjamin, and Dan, lying northeast of Zorah and Eshtaol, about eight miles (thirteen kilometers) northwest of Jerusalem. Presumably this is not the Mahaneh-dan mentioned in 13.25. 18.15 They greeted him, i.e., "asked about his well-being" (Hebrew shalom). 18.19 A father and a priest. See note on 17.10. In Num 26.42 the tribe of Dan consists of a single clan, which might consist of a town and its satellite villages. 18.21 The order of march protects the vulnerable members of the migrating community from pursuit and at the same time provides the expedition with a peaceful facade. 18.25 Danites had a reputation for belligerence (Gen 49.17; Deut 33.22). They are hot-tempered (lit. "bitter of soul") like a bear robbed of her cubs (2 Sam 17.8). 18.28 Far from Sidon . . . no dealings with Aram echoes

themselves. Jonathan son of Gershom, son of Moses,[a] and his sons were priests to the tribe of the Danites until the time the land went into captivity. [31]So they maintained as their own Micah's idol that he had made, as long as the house of God was at Shiloh.

The Levite's Concubine

19 In those days, when there was no king in Israel, a certain Levite, residing in the remote parts of the hill country of Ephraim, took to himself a concubine from Bethlehem in Judah. [2]But his concubine became angry with[b] him, and she went away from him to her father's house at Bethlehem in Judah, and was there some four months. [3]Then her husband set out after her, to speak tenderly to her and bring her back. He had with him his servant and a couple of donkeys. When he reached[c] her father's house, the girl's father saw him and came with joy to meet him. [4]His father-in-law, the girl's father, made him stay, and he remained with him three days; so they ate and drank, and he[d] stayed there. [5]On the fourth day they got up early in the morning, and he prepared to go; but the girl's father said to his son-in-law, "Fortify yourself with a bit of food, and after that you may go." [6]So the two men sat and ate and drank together; and the girl's father said to the man, "Why not spend the night and enjoy yourself." [7]When the man got up to go, his father-in-law kept urging him until he spent the night there again. [8]On the fifth day he got up early in the morning to leave; and the girl's father said, "Fortify yourself." So they lingered[e] until the day declined, and the two of them ate and drank.[f] [9]When the man with his concubine and his servant got up to leave, his father-in-law, the girl's father, said to him, "Look, the day has worn on until it is almost evening. Spend the night. See, the day has drawn to a close. Spend the night here and enjoy yourself. Tomorrow you can get up early in the morning for your journey, and go home."

10 But the man would not spend the night; he got up and departed, and arrived opposite Jebus (that is, Jerusalem). He had with him a couple of saddled donkeys, and his concubine was with him. [11]When they were near Jebus, the day was far spent, and the servant said to his master, "Come now, let us turn aside to this city of the Jebusites, and spend the night in it." [12]But his master said to him, "We will not turn aside into a city of foreigners, who do not belong to the people of Israel; but we will con-

---

a Another reading is *son of Manasseh*   *b* Gk OL: Heb *prostituted herself against*   *c* Gk: Heb *she brought him to*   *d* Compare verse 7 and Gk: Heb *they*   *e* Cn: Heb *Linger*   *f* Gk: Heb lacks *and drank*

---

v. 7 for emphasis. **18.30** *Jonathan* is presumably the Levite who has remained unnamed till now. Dan's priestly family claims descent from *Moses* (*Gershom* is Moses' son according to Ex 2.22). In the Hebrew text a letter has been inserted to turn "Moses" into "Manasseh" (see text note *a*) to avoid associating Moses with idol worship. Along with Bethel, the temple at Dan became a royal shrine of the Northern Kingdom (1 Kings 12.29–30). *Captivity* refers to the destruction of the Northern Kingdom by the Assyrians and the exile of the Danites in 722/1 BCE. **18.31** The Danite sanctuary is devalued by reference to *Shiloh*, regarded by the editors as the one legitimate sanctuary in the premonarchical period (1 Sam 1–4). The narrative consistently emphasizes the illegitimacy of the shrine of Dan. Its silver was dedicated because of a theft (17.2–3), its image was hijacked (17.5–6; 18.16–18, 24), and its priesthood originated in disloyal opportunism (17.9; 18.19–20).

19.1–21.25 Israel reacts to the outrage of gang rape and murder (ch. 19) in such a way as to compound the tragedy. Civil war nearly obliterates the tribe of Benjamin (ch. 20). In the final scenes, Israel maneuvers to recover from these disastrous consequences. Editors in exile (see Introduction) reworked these painful memories, when, once again, it was time for Israel to make a new start. **19.1** Once again, the phrase *no king in Israel* laments the lack of a king who would make such horrifying lawlessness unlikely (17.6; 18.1; 21.25). The story of a *Levite* from the *hill country of Ephraim* who travels to Bethlehem is a narrative inversion of the preceding story of a Levite from Bethlehem (17.7) who migrates to the hill country of Ephraim (17.8). This northern Levite appears to be well established. He has a *concubine,* or wife of secondary rank, from Bethlehem. **19.2** Israelite law did not allow for divorce by the wife. She returns to her family of origin (*father's house*), but the circumstances are unclear. Did she become angry with him or prostitute herself (see text note *b*)? Does she become the equivalent of an adulteress by walking out on him? **19.3** The husband seeks reconciliation, suggesting that she is the offended party. A *servant and a couple of donkeys* give the appearance of prosperous self-sufficiency, in contrast to the circumstances of the young Levite in ch. 17. **19.4–9** The father-in-law will be pleased to see his daughter return with her husband, but his hospitality will create a new crisis. They left much later in the afternoon than was wise. **19.10** The narrator insinuates that the party might have been safe and avoided atrocity at Canaanite *Jebus* (supposedly the pre-Israelite name for Jerusalem; see 1.21). **19.12** Jerusalem as *a city*

tinue on to Gibeah." ¹³Then he said to his servant, "Come, let us try to reach one of these
places, and spend the night at Gibeah or at
Ramah." ¹⁴So they passed on and went their
way; and the sun went down on them near
Gibeah, which belongs to Benjamin. ¹⁵They
turned aside there, to go in and spend the
night at Gibeah. He went in and sat down in
the open square of the city, but no one took
them in to spend the night.

16 Then at evening there was an old man
coming from his work in the field. The man was
from the hill country of Ephraim, and he was
residing in Gibeah. (The people of the place
were Benjaminites.) ¹⁷When the old man
looked up and saw the wayfarer in the open
square of the city, he said, "Where are you going
and where do you come from?" ¹⁸He answered
him, "We are passing from Bethlehem in Judah
to the remote parts of the hill country of
Ephraim, from which I come. I went to Bethlehem in Judah; and I am going to my home.ª Nobody has offered to take me in. ¹⁹We your servants have straw and fodder for our donkeys,
with bread and wine for me and the woman and
the young man along with us. We need nothing
more." ²⁰The old man said, "Peace be to you. I
will care for all your wants; only do not spend
the night in the square." ²¹So he brought him
into his house, and fed the donkeys; they
washed their feet, and ate and drank.

Gibeah's Crime

22 While they were enjoying themselves, the
men of the city, a perverse lot, surrounded the
house, and started pounding on the door.
They said to the old man, the master of the
house, "Bring out the man who came into
your house, so that we may have intercourse
with him." ²³And the man, the master of the
house, went out to them and said to them,
"No, my brothers, do not act so wickedly.
Since this man is my guest, do not do this vile
thing. ²⁴Here are my virgin daughter and his
concubine; let me bring them out now. Ravish
them and do whatever you want to them; but
against this man do not do such a vile thing."
²⁵But the men would not listen to him. So the
man seized his concubine, and put her out to
them. They wantonly raped her, and abused
her all through the night until the morning.
And as the dawn began to break, they let her
go. ²⁶As morning appeared, the woman came
and fell down at the door of the man's house
where her master was, until it was light.

27 In the morning her master got up,
opened the doors of the house, and when he
went out to go on his way, there was his concubine lying at the door of the house, with her
hands on the threshold. ²⁸"Get up," he said to
her, "we are going." But there was no answer.
Then he put her on the donkey; and the man
set out for his home. ²⁹When he had entered
his house, he took a knife, and grasping his
concubine he cut her into twelve pieces, limb
by limb, and sent her throughout all the territory of Israel. ³⁰Then he commanded the men
whom he sent, saying, "Thus shall you say to

---

a Gk Compare 19.29. Heb *to the house of the Lord*

---

of foreigners is ironically rejected in favor of fellow Israelites. *Gibeah,* King Saul's hometown, was a few
miles north of Jerusalem. **19.15** Hospitality was a fundamental virtue, and ancient readers would be outraged that *no one took them in.* **19.16** The only inhabitant of Gibeah to take up the obligation of hospitality
is, like the Levite, a resident alien from the *hill country
of Ephraim* (cf. v. 1). **19.19** The Levite has feed for his
donkeys and food and wine for his entire party. All he
needs is a roof. **19.21** The traveler lets the old man act
as host by feeding the animals. **19.22–30** This story has
striking similarities to that of Sodom and Gomorrah
(Gen 19.4–11). Both stories hinge on a breakdown or
misuse of the obligation of hospitality and the threat
of homosexual rape. **19.22** *They were enjoying themselves* verbally echoes 16.25, where the Philistine crowd
demands that Samson entertain them. *Perverse lot,* lit.
"sons of Belial," a malicious character of the mythic
underworld ("perdition" in Ps 18.4; 2 Sam 22.5–6).
Have intercourse. The Hebrew verb is *yadaʻ,* "to know."

If there is any ambiguity about what this means it disappears with the offer of the young women (v. 24).
19.23–24 *Vile thing,* a loathsome and outrageous act,
usually a sexual crime (20.6, 10; Gen 34.7; Deut 22.21;
2 Sam 13.12). The *master of the house* gives greater
weight to the obligation of hospitality to his male
guest than to any duty he owes to his guest's concubine
or even his own family (cf. Gen 19.8). **19.25** Although
it is not completely clear which man *seized his concubine, and put her out,* the most natural reading is that
the Levite acts to save himself. **19.26** The concubine's
husband (cf. v. 3) is now called *her master,* perhaps a
commentary on how he has treated her. The powerful
description of rape creates outrage against Gibeah on
the part of readers. The poignant final scene at the
door sets the stage for her master's indifference in
the following verses. **19.27–28** The moving image of
the woman's *hands on the threshold* contrasts with the
man's brusque command. *No answer.* We are not actually told that she is dead. **19.29** The man utilizes the

all the Israelites, 'Has such a thing ever happened[a] since the day that the Israelites came up from the land of Egypt until this day? Consider it, take counsel, and speak out.' "

The Other Tribes Attack Benjamin

20 Then all the Israelites came out, from Dan to Beer-sheba, including the land of Gilead, and the congregation assembled in one body before the LORD at Mizpah. 2The chiefs of all the people, of all the tribes of Israel, presented themselves in the assembly of the people of God, four hundred thousand foot-soldiers bearing arms. 3(Now the Benjaminites heard that the people of Israel had gone up to Mizpah.) And the Israelites said, "Tell us, how did this criminal act come about?" 4The Levite, the husband of the woman who was murdered, answered, "I came to Gibeah that belongs to Benjamin, I and my concubine, to spend the night. 5The lords of Gibeah rose up against me, and surrounded the house at night. They intended to kill me, and they raped my concubine until she died. 6Then I took my concubine and cut her into pieces, and sent her throughout the whole extent of Israel's territory; for they have committed a vile outrage in Israel. 7So now, you Israelites, all of you, give your advice and counsel here."

8 All the people got up as one, saying, "We will not any of us go to our tents, nor will any of us return to our houses. 9But now this is what we will do to Gibeah: we will go up[b] against it by lot. 10We will take ten men of a hundred throughout all the tribes of Israel, and a hundred of a thousand, and a thousand of ten thousand, to bring provisions for the troops, who are going to repay[c] Gibeah of

Benjamin for all the disgrace that they have done in Israel." 11So all the men of Israel gathered against the city, united as one.

12 The tribes of Israel sent men through all the tribe of Benjamin, saying, "What crime is this that has been committed among you? 13Now then, hand over those scoundrels in Gibeah, so that we may put them to death, and purge the evil from Israel." But the Benjaminites would not listen to their kinsfolk, the Israelites. 14The Benjaminites came together out of the towns to Gibeah, to go out to battle against the Israelites. 15On that day the Benjaminites mustered twenty-six thousand armed men from their towns, besides the inhabitants of Gibeah. 16Of all this force, there were seven hundred picked men who were left-handed; every one could sling a stone at a hair, and not miss. 17And the Israelites, apart from Benjamin, mustered four hundred thousand armed men, all of them warriors.

18 The Israelites proceeded to go up to Bethel, where they inquired of God, "Which of us shall go up first to battle against the Benjaminites?" And the LORD answered, "Judah shall go up first."

19 Then the Israelites got up in the morning, and encamped against Gibeah. 20The Israelites went out to battle against Benjamin; and the Israelites drew up the battle line against them at Gibeah. 21The Benjaminites came out of Gibeah, and struck down on that day twenty-two thousand of the Israelites. 23[d] The Israelites went up and wept before the

---

a Compare Gk: Heb 30And all who saw it said, "Such a thing has not happened or been seen   b Gk: Heb lacks we will go up
c Compare Gk: Meaning of Heb uncertain   d Verses 22 and 23 are transposed

---

woman's (dead?) body as an object to gain publicity for what has taken place. His actions caricature a practice for raising an emergency force that appears elsewhere in the OT and other texts of the ancient Near East. Cf. Saul summoning the militia with twelve parts of an ox (1 Sam 11.7).
20.1–48 The national assembly is stampeded into wrathful indignation by one man telling half of the truth. **20.1** *From Dan to Beer-sheba*, from the northern to the southern limits of Israel. *Mizpah*, Hebrew, "Lookout" or "Watchtower," probably Tell en-Nasbeh, eight miles (thirteen kilometers) north of Jerusalem, not to be confused with the Mizpah east of the Jordan in 11.11. **20.3** Gibeah is a Benjaminite town (19.16), so the Levite's personal quarrel grows into an intertribal conflict. **20.5** The Levite's testimony passes over his own culpability in surrendering his concubine. *They*

intended to kill me magnifies the threat to himself. **20.6** As a *vile outrage* (see note on 19.23–24), the rape and murder of the concubine was an affront to Israel's foundational principles. **20.9** *By lot* is a reference to how the 10 percent of the next verse will be chosen. **20.11** *All the men of Israel* are *united* as never before in the book, except at Gideon's ephod (8.27). **20.16** The grim odds against Benjamin (400,000, v. 17, against 26,000, v. 15) are offset by a contingent of elite troops who are superb marksmen. Benjamin was proverbially associated with *left-handed* or ambidextrous warriors (3.15; 1 Chr 12.2). **20.18** *Bethel* was the chief sanctuary of central Israel. *Which of us . . . first* is the same question as in 1.1. *Judah* is chosen, as in 1.2, but here it is chosen for civil war. The Lord answers either by the sacred lots or through a priestly oracle. **20.23** V. 26 suggests that this weeping *before the LORD* took place at

LORD until the evening; and they inquired of the LORD, "Shall we again draw near to battle against our kinsfolk the Benjaminites?" And the LORD said, "Go up against them." 22 The Israelites took courage, and again formed the battle line in the same place where they had formed it on the first day.

24 So the Israelites advanced against the Benjaminites the second day. 25 Benjamin moved out against them from Gibeah the second day, and struck down eighteen thousand of the Israelites, all of them armed men. 26 Then all the Israelites, the whole army, went back to Bethel and wept, sitting there before the LORD; they fasted that day until evening. Then they offered burnt offerings and sacrifices of well-being before the LORD. 27 And the Israelites inquired of the LORD (for the ark of the covenant of God was there in those days, 28 and Phinehas son of Eleazar, son of Aaron, ministered before it in those days), saying, "Shall we go out once more to battle against our kinsfolk the Benjaminites, or shall we desist?" The LORD answered, "Go up, for tomorrow I will give them into your hand."

29 So Israel stationed men in ambush around Gibeah. 30 Then the Israelites went up against the Benjaminites on the third day, and set themselves in array against Gibeah, as before. 31 When the Benjaminites went out against the army, they were drawn away from the city. As before they began to inflict casualties on the troops, along the main roads, one of which goes up to Bethel and the other to Gibeah, as well as in the open country, killing about thirty men of Israel. 32 The Benjaminites thought, "They are being routed before us, as previously." But the Israelites said, "Let us retreat and draw them away from the city toward the roads." 33 The main body of the Israelites drew back its battle line to Baal-tamar, while those Israelites who were in ambush rushed out of their place west[a] of Geba. 34 There came against Gibeah ten thousand picked men out of all Israel, and the battle was

fierce. But the Benjaminites did not realize that disaster was close upon them.

35 The LORD defeated Benjamin before Israel; and the Israelites destroyed twenty-five thousand one hundred men of Benjamin that day, all of them armed.

36 Then the Benjaminites saw that they were defeated.[b]

The Israelites gave ground to Benjamin, because they trusted to the troops in ambush that they had stationed against Gibeah. 37 The troops in ambush rushed quickly upon Gibeah. Then they put the whole city to the sword. 38 Now the agreement between the main body of Israel and the men in ambush was that when they sent up a cloud of smoke out of the city 39 the main body of Israel should turn in battle. But Benjamin had begun to inflict casualties on the Israelites, killing about thirty of them; so they thought, "Surely they are defeated before us, as in the first battle." 40 But when the cloud, a column of smoke, began to rise out of the city, the Benjaminites looked behind them—and there was the whole city going up in smoke toward the sky! 41 Then the main body of Israel turned, and the Benjaminites were dismayed, for they saw that disaster was close upon them. 42 Therefore they turned away from the Israelites in the direction of the wilderness; but the battle overtook them, and those who came out of the city[c] were slaughtering them in between.[d] 43 Cutting down[e] the Benjaminites, they pursued them from Nohah[f] and trod them down as far as a place east of Gibeah. 44 Eighteen thousand Benjaminites fell, all of them courageous fighters. 45 When they turned and fled toward the wilderness to the rock of Rimmon, five thousand of them were cut down on the main roads, and they were pursued as far as Gidom, and two thousand of them were slain. 46 So all

---

a Gk Vg: Heb in the plain   b This sentence is continued by verse 45.   c Compare Vg and some Gk Mss: Heb cities
d Compare Syr: Meaning of Heb uncertain   e Gk: Heb Surrounding   f Gk: Heb pursued them at their resting place

---

Bethel. **20.25** The Israelite army is reduced to a decimated level, so that victory can only be attributed to the Lord. **20.26–28** *Bethel* is a fitting place for inquiry because the *ark of the covenant of God was there* (v. 27) in the keeping of a priest properly descended from *Aaron* (v. 28). Only now do the Israelites ask the appropriate prior question, *Shall we go,* and only here is the response reliable: *tomorrow I will give them into your hand.* **20.29–43** Two accounts of the victory are

given (vv. 29–36a, 36b–43). There are strong resemblances to the takeover of Ai (Josh 8.3–23), where simulated retreat and ambush was also the strategy. **20.35** *The LORD* was not explicitly credited with Benjamin's earlier victories. The scale of Benjamin's defeat is clear when the number killed (25,000, v. 46) is compared with Benjamin's starting total (26,000, v. 15). **20.42** Benjamin is trapped *in between* the main army of the *Israelites* and *those who came out of the city.*

who fell that day of Benjamin were twenty-five thousand arms-bearing men, all of them courageous fighters. 47But six hundred turned and fled toward the wilderness to the rock of Rimmon, and remained at the rock of Rimmon for four months. 48Meanwhile, the Israelites turned back against the Benjaminites, and put them to the sword—the city, the people, the animals, and all that remained. Also the remaining towns they set on fire.

The Benjaminites Saved from Extinction

21 Now the Israelites had sworn at Mizpah, "No one of us shall give his daughter in marriage to Benjamin." 2And the people came to Bethel, and sat there until evening before God, and they lifted up their voices and wept bitterly. 3They said, "O LORD, the God of Israel, why has it come to pass that today there should be one tribe lacking in Israel?" 4On the next day, the people got up early, and built an altar there, and offered burnt offerings and sacrifices of well-being. 5Then the Israelites said, "Which of all the tribes of Israel did not come up in the assembly to the LORD?" For a solemn oath had been taken concerning whoever did not come up to the LORD to Mizpah, saying, "That one shall be put to death." 6But the Israelites had compassion for Benjamin their kin, and said, "One tribe is cut off from Israel this day. 7What shall we do for wives for those who are left, since we have sworn by the LORD that we will not give them any of our daughters as wives?"

8 Then they said, "Is there anyone from the tribes of Israel who did not come up to the LORD to Mizpah?" It turned out that no one from Jabesh-gilead had come to the camp, to the assembly. 9For when the roll was called among the people, not one of the inhabitants of Jabesh-gilead was there. 10So the congregation sent twelve thousand soldiers there and commanded them, "Go, put the inhabitants of Jabesh-gilead to the sword, including the women and the little ones. 11This is what you shall do; every male and every woman that has lain with a male you shall devote to destruction." 12And they found among the inhabitants of Jabesh-gilead four hundred young virgins who had never slept with a man and brought them to the camp at Shiloh, which is in the land of Canaan.

13 Then the whole congregation sent word to the Benjaminites who were at the rock of Rimmon, and proclaimed peace to them. 14Benjamin returned at that time; and they gave them the women whom they had saved alive of the women of Jabesh-gilead; but they did not suffice for them.

15 The people had compassion on Benjamin because the LORD had made a breach in the tribes of Israel. 16So the elders of the congregation said, "What shall we do for wives for those who are left, since there are no women left in Benjamin?" 17And they said, "There must be heirs for the survivors of Benjamin, in order that a tribe may not be blotted out from Israel. 18Yet we cannot give any of our daughters to them as wives." For the Israelites had sworn, "Cursed be anyone who gives a wife to Benjamin." 19So they said, "Look, the yearly festival of the LORD is taking

---

20.47–48 A mere *six hundred* fled and went into hiding, to become the only Benjaminite survivors in the story and to set up the situation for the next chapter.
21.1–25 This concluding chapter brings together two stories: one concerning a punitive expedition against Jabesh-gilead, the other a custom involving young women during a vintage festival at Shiloh. 21.1–5 The problem of finding wives for the Benjaminites is emphasized by framing it with repeated mention of the oath at Mizpah in vv. 1, 5. 21.1 The prohibition of marriage with Benjaminites is previously unmentioned. 21.3 *Lacking*, lit. "counted out." The Hebrew verb *paqad* has to do with setting quotas for military service. 21.5 One more small-scale civil war will be necessary. 21.6–12 These verses restate the problem and describe the proposal and implementation of a solution. 21.8 *Jabesh-gilead* lay east of the Jordan. This city would later be friendly and faithful to Saul, who was a Benjaminite from Gibeah (1 Sam 10.27–11.15; 31.11–13). 21.11 *Devote to destruction*, or put under the ban (Hebrew *cherem*). As a result of their vow (v. 5), the Israelites decide to treat this as a sacral war. 21.14–15 Four hundred captive women are not enough for the six hundred surviving men, reinforcing the reality that *the LORD had made a breach in the tribes of Israel.* 21.19 This *yearly festival* at Shiloh (cf. 1 Sam 1.3) seems to have celebrated the grape harvest. 21.21 These instructions may reflect an ongoing custom of obtaining wives by simulated "capture" at Shiloh. 21.22 *Fathers* would lose both honor and money if marriage bypassed the usual negotiations. *Brothers* would be the natural protectors of their unmarried sisters (Song 8.8–9). 21.25 Looking back at chs. 17–21, this verse sees the idolatrous shrine, rape and murder, civil war, and genocide all as a consequence of having no king. In this way, the conclusion of Judges looks forward to Samuel, who will establish the monarchy.

place at Shiloh, which is north of Bethel, on the east of the highway that goes up from Bethel to Shechem, and south of Lebonah." 20And they instructed the Benjaminites, saying, "Go and lie in wait in the vineyards, 21and watch; when the young women of Shiloh come out to dance in the dances, then come out of the vineyards and each of you carry off a wife for himself from the young women of Shiloh, and go to the land of Benjamin. 22Then if their fathers or their brothers come to complain to us, we will say to them, 'Be generous and allow us to have them; because we did not capture in battle a wife for each man. But neither did you incur guilt by giving your daughters to them.' " 23The Benjaminites did so; they took wives for each of them from the dancers whom they abducted. Then they went and returned to their territory, and rebuilt the towns, and lived in them. 24So the Israelites departed from there at that time by tribes and families, and they went out from there to their own territories.

25 In those days there was no king in Israel; all the people did what was right in their own eyes.

R U T H

THE BOOK OF RUTH, a short narrative with a pastoral tone, is one of the most beautiful pieces of literature in the Bible. The few characters in the story, with the exception of Boaz (1 Chr 2.11–12), are unmentioned elsewhere in the Hebrew Bible, and, in contrast to most other biblical narratives, the concern seems to be with a private family rather than national or international affairs. The plot revolves around family relationships—between husbands, wives, children, in-laws, and kinsmen—and the role each member plays in fulfilling the needs of other members and hence the family as a whole. The characters' names seem highly symbolic of their roles. Elimelech, "My God is King," suggests the period before human kings ruled Israel—the time of the judges in which the story is set. The epilogue ends with the human king *par excellence*, King David. Mahlon and Chilion mean "Sickness" and "Spent"; Orpah, "Back of the Neck," turns her back to Naomi. Naomi, whose name means "Pleasant," calls herself Mara, "Bitter," when she returns bereaved and impoverished to Bethlehem. Ruth has been interpreted as deriving from the word meaning "Friend, Companion," and Boaz from two words meaning "In Him is Strength." But the apparent simplicity of the plot and characters belie the seriousness of the book's themes.

Major Themes

ACCORDING TO RABBINIC TRADITION, the main theme is *chesed* (Hebrew), loyalty or faithfulness arising from commitment. *Chesed* may pertain between God and a human community and between members of a family or community. The main characters, Naomi, Ruth, and Boaz, all manifest acts of *chesed*. Naomi shows concern for the welfare of her widowed daughters-in-law, especially Ruth, although technically she has no obligation toward them. Ruth's *chesed* in cleaving to Naomi goes beyond all expectation, and her seeking marriage with Boaz, the family protector, underlines her loyalty to the family. Boaz too acts with *chesed* when he accepts the double responsibility of land purchase and marriage, thereby preserving the lineage and inheritance of a family that were almost lost.

The idea of family continuity, which motivates all the characters and is present in all the acts of *chesed*, is clearly central to the story. Moreover, the continuity is achieved largely by women. In this Ruth echoes the stories of the matriarchs and the story of Judah and Tamar (Gen 38); it is no accident that Boaz is blessed with the words, "May the LORD make the woman who is coming into your house like Rachel and Leah, who together built up the house of Israel. . . . May your house be like the house of Perez, whom Tamar bore to Judah" (4.11–12). But the book of Ruth goes even further, for here the family is preserved not by the wives of patriarchs, but by an elderly widow and her non-Israelite daughter-in-law.

The preservation and continuity of the family is closely related to the preservation and continuity of the nation (cf. Ex 1–2, where the fertility and quick action of women ensure the survival and growth of Israel). Although the plot does not operate on the national level, the ending of the epilogue with the name of David suggests that a royal or national interest may lie below the surface. The Judean elements of the story are strong: a Judean family from Bethlehem; the mention of Judah, Perez, and Tamar; and the genealogy of David. To some readers this suggests that the book may have been intended as a glorification of David through a glorification of his ancestors or perhaps as a kind of "prologue" to the royal dynasty that began with David and remained so crucial in the history of the kingdom of Judah. Others see the main theme as the continuity of the nation, an extension of the idea of family continuity. The Judeans, like the family of Naomi, returned from exile and rebuilt their community.

Literary scholars have observed the theme of emptiness and fullness as it plays out on both the agricultural level, from famine to harvest (both are important settings motivating the action), and the personal level, from Naomi's loss of family to her acquiring a new family through Ruth and Boaz and the birth of their son.

Date and Placement in the Bible

THE DETERMINATION OF THE MAIN THEME or message cannot be separated from the dating of the book, but its date is difficult to ascertain. Basing their assertions on linguistic criteria, some modern scholars place it between 950 and 700 BCE, that is, between the time of David (it could not be earlier) and the end of the Northern Kingdom, Israel (722 BCE). It would then be the product of the cultural flourishing of the United Monarchy or a glorification of the Judean dynasty during the Divided Monarchy. More recent opinions, taking account of certain late linguistic features, especially Aramaisms, date the book to the exilic or postexilic period. Concern with national continuity and the preservation of the Davidic dynasty would naturally have been high when Judah lost its political autonomy and the existence of its community was in danger. The postexilic period saw the rise of short fictional works, like the books of Jonah and Esther, and it seems appropriate to place Ruth among these books. Earlier generations of scholars, who also placed the writing of the book after the exile, thought it was a polemic against the prohibition on taking foreign wives that was a keystone of Ezra's policy. This explanation does not appear so compelling today.

In Christian Bibles, which derive their order from the Septuagint and Vulgate, the book of Ruth is found after Judges, for the story is set in the period of the judges. The placement is thus a chronological one, according to the time of the events of the story. The placement in Jewish Bibles is liturgical; Ruth is located in the Writings, among the Five Scrolls, each of which is read publicly on a specific festival or day of commemoration. Ruth is associated with the festival of Shavuoth, "Weeks," or Pentecost, which marks the end of the barley harvest and the beginning of the wheat harvest. [ADELE BERLIN]

Elimelech's Family Goes to Moab

1 In the days when the judges ruled, there was a famine in the land, and a certain man of Bethlehem in Judah went to live in the country of Moab, he and his wife and two sons. [2]The name of the man was Elimelech and the name of his wife Naomi, and the names of his two sons were Mahlon and Chilion; they were Ephrathites from Bethlehem in Judah. They went into the country of Moab and remained there. [3]But Elimelech, the husband of Naomi, died, and she was left with her two sons. [4]These took Moabite wives; the name of the one was Orpah and the name of the other Ruth. When they had lived there about ten years, [5]both Mahlon and Chilion also died, so that the woman was left without her two sons and her husband.

Naomi and Her Moabite Daughters-in-Law

6 Then she started to return with her daughters-in-law from the country of Moab, for she had heard in the country of Moab that the LORD had considered his people and given them food. [7]So she set out from the place where she had been living, she and her two daughters-in-law, and they went on their way to go back to the land of Judah. [8]But Naomi said to her two daughters-in-law, "Go back each of you to your mother's house. May the LORD deal kindly with you, as you have dealt with the dead and with me. [9]The LORD grant that you may find security, each of you in the house of your husband." Then she kissed them, and they wept aloud. [10]They said to her, "No, we will return with you to your people." [11]But Naomi said, "Turn back, my daughters, why will you go with me? Do I still have sons in my womb that they may become your husbands? [12]Turn back, my daughters, go your way, for I am too old to have a husband. Even if I thought there was hope for me, even if I should have a husband tonight and bear sons, [13]would you then wait until they were grown? Would you then refrain from marrying? No, my daughters, it has been far more bitter for me than for you, because the hand of the LORD has turned against me." [14]Then they wept aloud again. Orpah kissed her mother-in-law, but Ruth clung to her.

15 So she said, "See, your sister-in-law has gone back to her people and to her gods; return after your sister-in-law." [16]But Ruth said,

"Do not press me to leave you
 or to turn back from following you!
Where you go, I will go;
 where you lodge, I will lodge;
your people shall be my people,
 and your God my God.

1.1–5 Naomi gradually emerges as the focus of the story. She is left without male relatives; all that remains of her family are her two Moabite daughters-in-law. Famine, dislocation, and death mark the beginning of the story. These will all be reversed with the return to Bethlehem, the harvest seasons, marriage, and birth. **1.1** *The judges ruled.* The narrative is set in the period of the judges, after the settlement in Canaan and before the monarchy. The judges are portrayed as local or tribal leaders who arose in times of crisis. The tone of the book, however, with its pastoral calmness, is quite different from the tenor of the violent and insecure times portrayed in the book of Judges. *Moab* is the country east of the Dead Sea, between Ammon and Edom, on approximately the same latitude as Judah. There was apparently no famine there. The motif of migration to a foreign land in time of famine occurs in reference to Abraham (Gen 12.10) and Jacob (Gen 42.1). Elsewhere in the Bible (Num 21.29–30; Deut 23.3–4), the name Moab has negative connotations, but they are absent here. **1.2** *Elimelech.* On the characters' names, see Introduction. *Ephrathites,* residents of a geographical area or a subgroup of the Judean populace. Ephrath or Ephrathah is associated with Bethlehem and Judah in several biblical passages (e.g., Gen 35.16, 19; 1 Sam 17.12; 1 Chr 2.18–24, 42–50; Mic

5.2). Mention of the term here presumably underlines the family's long-standing connection with Bethlehem. **1.6–22** Both Orpah and Ruth initially show concern for Naomi, even as she, out of her own concern for them, attempts to persuade them to return to their own families. Ruth's loyalty to Naomi proves unshakable, and she returns to Bethlehem along with her mother-in-law. The key words in this section are *return* (vv. 6, 10, 15, 22) and *turn back* (vv. 11, 12, 16); see also *go/gone back* (vv. 7, 8, 15); all from the same Hebrew root. They are used in the sense of parting and in the sense of rejoining. The issue is how these widows can find security, i.e., a husband and family. **1.11** *Sons in my womb.* Naomi despairs of being able to provide her daughters-in-law with new husbands. This passage is often seen as exemplifying the levirate law in Deut 25.5–10, but it is not a true levirate because these husbands, if they could be born, would not have the same father as Mahlon and Chilion. They would not be brothers of the deceased. **1.16** *Your people . . . my God,* a stirring declaration of loyalty. There was as yet no formal procedure for religious conversion, nor was it even conceived of. One's ethnic identity determined for all time one's religious persuasion. Therefore, Ruth mentions "people" and "God" together. Each people had its own god; or, as it was viewed in the ancient

17 Where you die, I will die—
　　there will I be buried.
　May the LORD do thus and so to me,
　　and more as well,
　if even death parts me from you!"
18 When Naomi saw that she was determined
to go with her, she said no more to her.

19 So the two of them went on until they
came to Bethlehem. When they came to Bethlehem, the whole town was stirred because of
them; and the women said, "Is this Naomi?"
20 She said to them,

　"Call me no longer Naomi,[a]
　　call me Mara,[b]
　for the Almighty[c] has dealt bitterly
　　with me.
21　I went away full,
　　but the LORD has brought me back
　　　empty;
　why call me Naomi
　　when the LORD has dealt harshly with[d]
　　　me,
　　and the Almighty[c] has brought
　　　calamity upon me?"

22 So Naomi returned together with Ruth
the Moabite, her daughter-in-law, who came
back with her from the country of Moab. They
came to Bethlehem at the beginning of the
barley harvest.

Ruth Meets Boaz

2 Now Naomi had a kinsman on her husband's side, a prominent rich man, of the
family of Elimelech, whose name was Boaz.

2 And Ruth the Moabite said to Naomi, "Let
me go to the field and glean among the ears of
grain, behind someone in whose sight I may
find favor." She said to her, "Go, my daughter."
3 So she went. She came and gleaned in the
field behind the reapers. As it happened, she
came to the part of the field belonging to
Boaz, who was of the family of Elimelech.
4 Just then Boaz came from Bethlehem. He
said to the reapers, "The LORD be with you."
They answered, "The LORD bless you." 5 Then
Boaz said to his servant who was in charge of
the reapers, "To whom does this young
woman belong?" 6 The servant who was in
charge of the reapers answered, "She is the
Moabite who came back with Naomi from the
country of Moab. 7 She said, 'Please, let me
glean and gather among the sheaves behind
the reapers.' So she came, and she has been on
her feet from early this morning until now,
without resting even for a moment."[e]

8 Then Boaz said to Ruth, "Now listen, my
daughter, do not go to glean in another field or
leave this one, but keep close to my young
women. 9 Keep your eyes on the field that is
being reaped, and follow behind them. I have
ordered the young men not to bother you. If
you get thirsty, go to the vessels and drink
from what the young men have drawn."
10 Then she fell prostrate, with her face to the
ground, and said to him, "Why have I found

---

a That is Pleasant b That is Bitter c Traditional rendering of
Heb Shaddai d Or has testified against e Compare Gk Vg:
Meaning of Heb uncertain

Near East, each god had its own people. Ruth is adopting a new people, a new ethnic identity, along with a
new faith. 1.20–21 Naomi, whose name means "Pleasant," feels that this name no longer reflects her situation. The name "Bitter," Mara, is now more apt. The
theme of emptiness and fullness is evident.
2.1–23 The fortuitous coming of Ruth to glean in
Boaz's field has the ring of divine guidance. Boaz
shows her special favors—providing food and drink
for her, guaranteeing protection from the workers'
taunts, and inviting her to glean on his estate throughout the harvest. Although readers learn in the first
verse that Boaz is a relative of Naomi's deceased husband, Ruth does not learn this fact until the end of the
chapter when she returns in the evening to Naomi. But
even readers are unaware until Naomi's speech that
Boaz is a near kinsman, a go'el (Hebrew), a family protector. The appearance of this male kinsman and the
plentiful food that he makes available bode well for the
two impoverished, husbandless women. 2.2 Glean.
Gleaning is a form of charity in which the poor are
permitted to gather the grain left by the harvesters (cf.

Lev 19.9; 23.22; Deut 24.19). Naomi and Ruth, having
no other source of income, must resort to this. Notice
that Ruth takes the initiative here in providing for
Naomi. 2.5 Boaz, noticing Ruth, whom he presumably
had not seen before, inquires into her family background. It was family connection, rather than an individual's name, that served as identification. The foreman's answer stresses Ruth's Moabite ancestry and her
attachment to Naomi. 2.8 My daughter, the same term
used by Naomi for Ruth (v. 2). It suggests a familial relationship and a protective stance. Boaz deemphasizes
Ruth's foreignness, although the foreman and Ruth
herself emphasize it (cf. v. 10), and he begins to assume
the role of provider and protector. 2.8–9 The invitation to Ruth to remain in Boaz's field throughout the
harvest signals that he will provide all she needs.
Moreover, he accords her special protection and privileges, keeping the male harvesters from bothering her
and providing her with food and drink, the leftovers of
which she takes home to Naomi (2.18). 2.10 Ruth is
taken aback by these unexpected privileges, especially
given that she is a foreigner. The Hebrew take notice

favor in your sight, that you should take notice of me, when I am a foreigner?" 11But Boaz answered her, "All that you have done for your mother-in-law since the death of your husband has been fully told me, and how you left your father and mother and your native land and came to a people that you did not know before. 12May the LORD reward you for your deeds, and may you have a full reward from the LORD, the God of Israel, under whose wings you have come for refuge!" 13Then she said, "May I continue to find favor in your sight, my lord, for you have comforted me and spoken kindly to your servant, even though I am not one of your servants."

14 At mealtime Boaz said to her, "Come here, and eat some of this bread, and dip your morsel in the sour wine." So she sat beside the reapers, and he heaped up for her some parched grain. She ate until she was satisfied, and she had some left over. 15When she got up to glean, Boaz instructed his young men, "Let her glean even among the standing sheaves, and do not reproach her. 16You must also pull out some handfuls for her from the bundles, and leave them for her to glean, and do not rebuke her."

17 So she gleaned in the field until evening. Then she beat out what she had gleaned, and it was about an ephah of barley. 18She picked it up and came into the town, and her mother-in-law saw how much she had gleaned. Then she took out and gave her what was left over after she herself had been satisfied. 19Her

mother-in-law said to her, "Where did you glean today? And where have you worked? Blessed be the man who took notice of you." So she told her mother-in-law with whom she had worked, and said, "The name of the man with whom I worked today is Boaz." 20Then Naomi said to her daughter-in-law, "Blessed be he by the LORD, whose kindness has not forsaken the living or the dead!" Naomi also said to her, "The man is a relative of ours, one of our nearest kin."ᵃ 21Then Ruth the Moabite said, "He even said to me, 'Stay close by my servants, until they have finished all my harvest.'" 22Naomi said to Ruth, her daughter-in-law, "It is better, my daughter, that you go out with his young women, otherwise you might be bothered in another field." 23So she stayed close to the young women of Boaz, gleaning until the end of the barley and wheat harvests; and she lived with her mother-in-law.

Ruth and Boaz at the Threshing Floor

3 Naomi her mother-in-law said to her, "My daughter, I need to seek some security for you, so that it may be well with you. 2Now here is our kinsman Boaz, with whose young women you have been working. See, he is winnowing barley tonight at the threshing floor. 3Now wash and anoint yourself, and put on your best clothes and go down to the threshing floor; but do not make yourself known to the man until he has finished eating and drinking.

a Or *one with the right to redeem*

---

and *foreigner* are from the same root, thereby forming a wordplay. **2.14** *Sour wine,* a vinegar-based substance into which bread was dipped. **2.15** *Standing sheaves.* Normally the gleaners worked in areas where the grain had been cut, picking up what the harvesters left behind. Ruth is permitted to glean where the cut grain was tied into the sheaves, thereby gaining access to additional grain that fell out of the bundles. Moreover, in the next verse the workers are bidden to actually pull out grain from the bound sheaves for her. This goes beyond the privileges she was initially granted. **2.17** *Ephah,* approximately two-thirds of a bushel, a substantial amount for one day's gleaning. **2.20** *Nearest kin,* Hebrew *go'el,* "one with the right to redeem," a close relative who takes responsibility for protecting the rights of a family in the absence of the head of the household. This usually involves the buying back of property, the redeeming of slaves, or the avenging of murder. Ruth later turns to Boaz as the *go'el* (3.9) but he informs her that there is a *go'el* with prior rights (3.12).

3.1–18 Ruth's initiative in providing for her mother-in-law in ch. 2 is reciprocated by Naomi's initiative in seeking a husband for Ruth. This has been Naomi's concern since ch. 1. Readers have long speculated on what actually transpired between Ruth and Boaz at the threshing floor that night. One senses a romantic attraction, but more important in the eyes of the Bible is the loyalty to family manifested by both Ruth and Boaz. As in ch. 2, there are three scenes here: Ruth and Naomi, Ruth and Boaz, and Ruth and Naomi. As in ch.2, Boaz sends Ruth home with ample provisions of grain. **3.1** As in 1.9, *security* implies finding a husband, as a woman on her own in ancient times had little standing and no protection. **3.2** *Threshing floor,* an elevated open space where the kernels of grain would be separated from the chaff (winnowing). This was done in the evening, when the wind picked up, by beating the grain and tossing it up in the air so that the wind would carry the chaff a distance away. The harvesters or the owner of the field would sleep at or near the threshing floor to protect the harvest at night. **3.3** *Anoint,* put on

4When he lies down, observe the place where he lies; then, go and uncover his feet and lie down; and he will tell you what to do." 5She said to her, "All that you tell me I will do."

6 So she went down to the threshing floor and did just as her mother-in-law had instructed her. 7When Boaz had eaten and drunk, and he was in a contented mood, he went to lie down at the end of the heap of grain. Then she came stealthily and uncovered his feet, and lay down. 8At midnight the man was startled, and turned over, and there, lying at his feet, was a woman! 9He said, "Who are you?" And she answered, "I am Ruth, your servant; spread your cloak over your servant, for you are next-of-kin."[a] 10He said, "May you be blessed by the LORD, my daughter; this last instance of your loyalty is better than the first; you have not gone after young men, whether poor or rich. 11And now, my daughter, do not be afraid, I will do for you all that you ask, for all the assembly of my people know that you are a worthy woman. 12But now, though it is true that I am a near kinsman, there is another kinsman more closely related than I. 13Remain this night, and in the morning, if he will act as next-of-kin[a] for you, good; let him do it. If he is not willing to act as next-of-kin[a] for you, then, as the LORD lives, I will act as next-of-kin[a] for you. Lie down until the morning."

14 So she lay at his feet until morning, but got up before one person could recognize another; for he said, "It must not be known that the woman came to the threshing floor." 15Then he said, "Bring the cloak you are wearing and hold it out." So she held it, and he measured out six measures of barley, and put it on her back; then he went into the city. 16She came to her mother-in-law, who said, "How did things go with you,[b] my daughter?" Then she told her all that the man had done for her, 17saying, "He gave me these six measures of barley, for he said, 'Do not go back to your mother-in-law empty-handed.' " 18She replied, "Wait, my daughter, until you learn how the matter turns out, for the man will not rest, but will settle the matter today."

The Marriage of Boaz and Ruth

4 No sooner had Boaz gone up to the gate and sat down there than the next-of-kin,[a] of whom Boaz had spoken, came passing by. So Boaz said, "Come over, friend; sit down here." And he went over and sat down. 2Then Boaz took ten men of the elders of the city, and said, "Sit down here"; so they sat down. 3He then said to the next-of-kin,[a] "Naomi, who has come back from the country of Moab, is selling the parcel of land that belonged to our kinsman Elimelech. 4So I thought I would tell you of it, and say: Buy it in the presence of those sitting here, and in the presence of the elders of my people. If you will redeem it, redeem it; but if you will not, tell me, so that I may know; for there is no one prior to you to redeem it, and I come after you." So he said, "I will redeem it." 5Then Boaz said, "The day you acquire the field from the

---

a Or one with the right to redeem　b Or "Who are you,

---

perfumed oil, equivalent to putting on cosmetics. **3.7–8** Although Naomi instructed Ruth to lie down near Boaz after he had eaten and drunk, Ruth apparently waited even longer, till after Boaz had fallen asleep. Boaz is startled to sense the presence of someone at midnight. **3.9** *Spread your cloak.* Ruth is asking for marriage; spreading a garment over a woman signifies acquiring her (cf. Ezek 16.8). This phrase echoes 2.12, in which Boaz speaks of Ruth's finding refuge under God's wings (the Hebrew uses the same word for *wings* and *cloak*). **3.10** *Last instance of your loyalty.* Boaz recognizes that Ruth is motivated by *chesed* (Hebrew), "loyalty," i.e., loyalty to the family of Naomi. She did not seek a husband far and wide but chose Boaz because he was the *go'el* (3.9). This is her second act of loyalty; her first was her steadfast cleaving to Naomi (cf. 2.11). **3.11** *Worthy woman,* Hebrew *'eshet chayil* (cf. Prov 31.10). By using this term Boaz equates Ruth's status with his own. He is an *'ish gibbor chayil,* "a prominent rich man" (2.1). Ruth is no longer to be perceived

as a servant or a foreigner (cf. 2.10, 13), but as an appropriate wife for Boaz. **3.12** Just as the agreement of marriage between Boaz and Ruth seems assured, we learn that there is a man who has a prior claim to marry Ruth.

4.1–17 Tension mounts as we wait to see whether the closer kinsman will accept the responsibility of purchasing the land and marrying Ruth. He declines, leaving the way open for Boaz. Boaz and Ruth are married and receive the blessing of the community for progeny. The blessing is realized; a son is born. He is a comfort to Naomi and a fulfillment of the hope for family continuity. He is to become an ancestor of David. **4.1** The city *gate* was the commercial center. Various business and legal transactions took place there. *Friend.* The closer kinsman is not named. In Hebrew he is called *peloni 'almoni,* "So-and-so." **4.3** *Parcel of land.* This is the first we hear that Naomi owned real estate. It is not clear whether it has already been sold or whether it is now up for sale for the first time. The re-

hand of Naomi, you are also acquiring Ruth[a] the Moabite, the widow of the dead man, to maintain the dead man's name on his inheritance." 6At this, the next-of-kin[b] said, "I cannot redeem it for myself without damaging my own inheritance. Take my right of redemption yourself, for I cannot redeem it."

7 Now this was the custom in former times in Israel concerning redeeming and exchanging: to confirm a transaction, the one took off a sandal and gave it to the other; this was the manner of attesting in Israel. 8So when the next-of-kin[b] said to Boaz, "Acquire it for yourself," he took off his sandal. 9Then Boaz said to the elders and all the people, "Today you are witnesses that I have acquired from the hand of Naomi all that belonged to Elimelech and all that belonged to Chilion and Mahlon. 10I have also acquired Ruth the Moabite, the wife of Mahlon, to be my wife, to maintain the dead man's name on his inheritance, in order that the name of the dead may not be cut off from his kindred and from the gate of his native place; today you are witnesses." 11Then all the people who were at the gate, along with the elders, said, "We are witnesses. May the LORD make the woman who is coming into your house like Rachel and Leah, who together built up the house of Israel. May you produce children in Ephrathah and bestow a name in Bethlehem; 12and, through the children that the LORD will give you by this young woman, may your house be like the house of Perez, whom Tamar bore to Judah."

The Genealogy of David

13 So Boaz took Ruth and she became his wife. When they came together, the LORD made her conceive, and she bore a son. 14Then the women said to Naomi, "Blessed be the LORD, who has not left you this day without next-of-kin;[b] and may his name be renowned in Israel! 15He shall be to you a restorer of life and a nourisher of your old age; for your daughter-in-law who loves you, who is more to you than seven sons, has borne him." 16Then Naomi took the child and laid him in her bosom, and became his nurse. 17The women of the neighborhood gave him a name, saying, "A son has been born to Naomi." They named him Obed; he became the father of Jesse, the father of David.

18 Now these are the descendants of Perez: Perez became the father of Hezron, 19Hezron of Ram, Ram of Amminadab, 20Amminadab of Nahshon, Nahshon of Salmon, 21Salmon of Boaz, Boaz of Obed, 22Obed of Jesse, and Jesse of David.

---

a OL Vg: Heb *from the hand of Naomi and from Ruth*   b Or *one with the right to redeem*

---

deeming of land would fall within the duties of the *go'el* to keep the land in the family. **4.5** *Acquiring Ruth.* It is less clear that a *go'el* would be obligated to marry the widow of the deceased landowner. This may be an early form of levirate marriage, which in Deut 25.5–10 is limited to the brother of the deceased (cf. also Gen 38). Or it may be a ploy by Boaz to protect the interests of Naomi and Ruth by ensuring that Ruth and her children would not be separated from this landholding, as would happen if the kinsman redeemed the land but did not marry Ruth. Boaz accepts the double obligation of acquiring the land and Ruth, in order *to maintain the dead man's name on his inheritance* (4.9–10). This echoes the language of the levirate in Deuteronomy. Regardless of the exact legal obligation (which is disputed), Boaz's loyalty to family emerges strongly. In this his loyalty mirrors that of Ruth. **4.7** *Took off a sandal.* This ancient practice, which needed to be explained even to biblical readers, is not to be confused with the pulling off of the sandal in the case of a brother who declines to marry the widow (Deut 25.9). The sandal is a physical representation of the conveying of goods or rights from one party to another. **4.12** *Tamar . . . Judah.* See Gen 38. **4.16** *His nurse.* The child's guardian, like a godmother; not a wet nurse. **4.17** *A son has been born to Naomi,* not a biological son or even a biological grandson, but a son in that he replaces the family that Naomi has lost. The son represents the continuation of the family. Naomi is the central focus at the end of the story, even as she was at the beginning. **4.18–22** The genealogy begins with Perez, the first of the twins born to Judah by Tamar (Gen 38.29). The places of honor in the list, seventh and tenth, are occupied by Boaz, the hero of our story, and David, the preeminent king of Israel and founder of the dynasty of Judah. The genealogy turns the story into a chapter in the ancestry of David and raises the theme of family continuity to a theme of national continuity. The story of a family becomes the story of the royal family and hence the nation.

1 SAMUEL

THE BOOKS OF SAMUEL describe the origins of kingship in Israel and recount the reigns of the first two kings, Saul and David. The two books fall roughly into five narrative sections followed by a miscellany of assorted materials. The first section is the story of Samuel (1 Sam 1.1–7.17), which provides a transition between the period of the judges and the monarchy. The account is dominated by a view of the prophet as a divinely appointed leader capable of functioning as priest, seer, war leader, and judge. It contains as a strong background theme the condemnation of the priestly house of Eli and rejection of the priesthood of Shiloh.

The second section describes the inauguration of kingship in Israel (1 Sam 8.1–15.34). The central figure is Saul, Israel's first king, who is introduced in auspicious terms as a tall, earnest young man capable of leading Israel on the battlefield. He continues to share the stage with Samuel, however, and the predominant atmosphere is suspicious of monarchy in general and of Saul's kingship in particular. Not long after Saul has proven himself in battle, his fortunes change and his life begins to unravel. Soon he is condemned for failing to obey the prophetically mediated divine word.

The third narrative section is the story of David's rise to power (1 Sam 15.35–2 Sam 5.10). It is animated by the conflict between the young David, to whom the Lord has promised Saul's throne, and the increasingly jealous and often irrational old king. David is depicted in the most favorable terms as handsome and charismatic, endowed with extraordinary skills as a musician and soldier, and consistently successful in everything he undertakes because, as the narrator repeatedly reminds us, "The LORD is with him."

The fourth section records a number of events from the reign of David (2 Sam 5.11–12.31). It centers upon the oracle of Nathan in ch. 7, in which David is promised that his descendants will rule after him in Jerusalem in an unending dynasty and that his son will build a temple for the Lord. The fifth section describes the unsuccessful revolt of David's son Absalom (2 Sam 13.1–20.22). David is now a mature and tragic figure who is obliged to flee Jerusalem in fear for his life and very nearly loses his throne while witnessing the death of two of his sons. At the end of 2 Samuel is a miscellany (2 Sam 20.23–24.25) containing poetry attributed to David, lists of his various officers and warriors, and a variety of narrative materials loosely related to other parts of Samuel and Kings.

Literary History

THE LITERARY FOUNDATION of 1 and 2 Samuel is a group of early narrative sources upon which later editors and compilers drew. At least four of these can be specifically identified. The first is the ark narrative, which is found in 1 Sam 4.1–7.1 and parts of 1 Sam 2 (some scholars would also include parts of 2 Sam 6). This narrative explains the capture of the ark by the Philistines as a consequence of the Lord's anger over the corruption of the priesthood of Shiloh (see 2.12–17, 22–25) and shows how the Lord used the occasion to afflict the Philistines with plague. The second early source, which is much less well defined, is a cycle of stories about Saul. These stories underlie various passages in 1 Samuel, including the tale of Saul's anointing in chs. 9–10, the account of his liberation of Jabesh-gilead in ch. 11, and the description of his Philistine wars in chs. 13–14. The third early source is the story of David's rise to power (1 Sam 16.14–2 Sam 5.10), which is designed to demonstrate David's innocence of wrongdoing in his conflict with the house of Saul and to explain his dramatic ascent to the throne as a consequence of divine favor. The fourth early source is the account of Absalom's revolt in 2 Sam 13–20. Its purpose is to disclose the private circumstances leading to the civil war that forced David temporarily into exile. The account explains the death of both Absalom and Amnon, David's firstborn, and it seems to have been combined with the story of David's death and the accession of Solomon in 1 Kings 1–2 to constitute a succession narrative, explaining how Solomon came to the throne instead of one of his several older brothers.

In their present form 1 and 2 Samuel are part of the Deuteronomistic History, which extends from Deuteronomy through 2 Kings (see also the Introduction to Joshua). It recounts the history of the Israelites from the time of their arrival on the plains of Moab and entry into the promised land until the time of their deportation to exile in Babylon after the destruction of Jerusalem by Nebuchadnezzar. The intervening events are reported and evaluated according to principles derived from the Deuteronomic law code (Deut 12–26). Deuteronomistic editing is light in 1 and 2 Samuel, especially in contrast to Judges or Kings. The only major passages that can be attributed to the historian are the oracle against the house of Eli in 1 Sam 2.27–36 establishing the ascendancy of the Zadokite priesthood; the historical retrospective in Samuel's farewell address in 1 Sam 12.6–15, which belongs to a series of such speeches by major figures in the history; and the oracle of Nathan in 2 Sam 7 proclaiming the Davidic dynasty and the erection of the temple in Jerusalem.

Many of the stories in 1 Samuel and to a lesser extent 2 Samuel have been influenced editorially by a point of view that regards the institution of kingship with suspicion while looking to the prophet as the one who can provide a check on royal abuses of power and serve as an avenue through which the divine will can be expressed. In certain parts of Samuel this prophetic viewpoint has given the narrative its primary shape. These include the story of Samuel's childhood and rise to power in 1 Sam 1–8, Samuel's farewell address and the two accounts of the rejection of Saul in 1 Sam 12–15, the story of the anointing of David in 1 Sam 16.1–13, and the account of the Bathsheba affair and Nathan's condemnation of the house of David in 2 Sam 11–12. Though some scholars date this prophetic material to the exile and associate it with the Deuteronomistic revision of the story, others argue that it derives from the time of the monarchy and underlies the final Deuteronomistic edition. In any case, it is necessary to recognize within it a group of passages that present the monarchy in a wholly negative way that makes no room for the Deuteronomistic affirmation of Davidic kingship or even the concept of a prophetically constrained monarchy. These passages include the accounts of Samuel acting as judge in 1 Sam 7.2–17, the people's demand for a king in 8.1–22, the election of Saul as king in 10.17–27a, and Samuel's farewell address in 12.1–25. This material is united not only by its retrospective view of the institution of kingship as a failure, but also by its common representation of the city of Mizpah as the meeting place of all Israel (cf. 1 Sam 7.5; 10.17), a historical situation that existed only after the destruction of Jerusalem, when Mizpah served as the Babylonian provincial capital and headquarters of the government of Gedaliah (2 Kings 25.23). The Mizpah material is best understood as an exilic redaction of the story of the origin of the monarchy told from a uniformly hostile point of view.

The story of the history of Israel recorded in the books of Samuel and Kings is largely retold in the books of Chronicles, which use the books of Samuel and Kings as major sources. That retelling has its own emphases and interests, reflecting the concerns of a later period in the history of Israel.

The Text

FOR A VARIETY OF REASONS, not all of them clear, the Hebrew text of 1 and 2 Samuel has come down to us in defective form. For this reason, translators must rely heavily on the Septuagint and other ancient versions as well as three fragmentary Samuel manuscripts from Qumran (4QSam[a, b, c]). [P. KYLE MCCARTER JR.]

Samuel's Birth and Dedication

1 There was a certain man of Ramathaim, a Zuphite[a] from the hill country of Ephraim, whose name was Elkanah son of Jeroham son of Elihu son of Tohu son of Zuph, an Ephraimite. 2He had two wives; the name of the one was Hannah, and the name of the other Peninnah. Peninnah had children, but Hannah had no children.

3 Now this man used to go up year by year from his town to worship and to sacrifice to the LORD of hosts at Shiloh, where the two sons of Eli, Hophni and Phinehas, were priests of the LORD. 4On the day when Elkanah sacrificed, he would give portions to his wife Peninnah and to all her sons and daughters; 5but to Hannah he gave a double portion,[b] because

he loved her, though the LORD had closed her womb. 6Her rival used to provoke her severely, to irritate her, because the LORD had closed her womb. 7So it went on year by year; as often as she went up to the house of the LORD, she used to provoke her. Therefore Hannah wept and would not eat. 8Her husband Elkanah said to her, "Hannah, why do you weep? Why do you not eat? Why is your heart sad? Am I not more to you than ten sons?"

9 After they had eaten and drunk at Shiloh, Hannah rose and presented herself before the LORD.[c] Now Eli the priest was sitting on the seat beside the doorpost of the temple of the LORD. 10She was deeply distressed and prayed

a Compare Gk and 1 Chr 6.35-36: Heb Ramathaim-zophim
b Syr: Meaning of Heb uncertain c Gk: Heb lacks and presented herself before the LORD

1.1–28 The auspicious story of the birth of Samuel, who dominates the first half of 1 Samuel, and of his dedication as a Nazirite (see vv. 11, 22). **1.1** Ramathaim, NT Arimathea, may have been in the northern Shephelah near Timnah and Lod. Elkanah, though called an Ephraimite here, is given a levitical genealogy in 1 Chr 6.26, where he was listed as a member of the clan of Kohath, which had special responsibility for the ark (see Num 3.29–31); this qualifies his son Samuel for the priestly duties he carries out in chs. 2–3. On Elkanah's designation as a Zuphite, see note on 9.5. **1.3** Shiloh, in the Ephraimite hills about twenty miles north-northeast of Jerusalem, was the central sanctuary of the Israelites at the time of Samuel's birth. **1.6** Her rival, i.e., Peninnah. The Hebrew word became a technical term for a second wife or co-wife in the rabbinic period. **1.7** The references to the house of the LORD in this story are surprising in view of the biblical tradition that no temple existed before the one in Jerusalem (see 2 Sam 7.6; 1 Kings 8.16), but the Shilonite

to the LORD, and wept bitterly. [11] She made this vow: "O LORD of hosts, if only you will look on the misery of your servant, and remember me, and not forget your servant, but will give to your servant a male child, then I will set him before you as a nazirite[a] until the day of his death. He shall drink neither wine nor intoxicants,[b] and no razor shall touch his head."

12 As she continued praying before the LORD, Eli observed her mouth. [13] Hannah was praying silently; only her lips moved, but her voice was not heard; therefore Eli thought she was drunk. [14] So Eli said to her, "How long will you make a drunken spectacle of yourself? Put away your wine." [15] But Hannah answered, "No, my lord, I am a woman deeply troubled; I have drunk neither wine nor strong drink, but I have been pouring out my soul before the LORD. [16] Do not regard your servant as a worthless woman, for I have been speaking out of my great anxiety and vexation all this time." [17] Then Eli answered, "Go in peace; the God of Israel grant the petition you have made to him." [18] And she said, "Let your servant find favor in your sight." Then the woman went to her quarters,[c] ate and drank with her husband,[d] and her countenance was sad no longer.[e]

19 They rose early in the morning and worshiped before the LORD; then they went back to their house at Ramah. Elkanah knew his wife Hannah, and the LORD remembered her. [20] In due time Hannah conceived and bore a son. She named him Samuel, for she said, "I have asked him of the LORD."

21 The man Elkanah and all his household went up to offer to the LORD the yearly sacrifice, and to pay his vow. [22] But Hannah did not go up, for she said to her husband, "As soon as the child is weaned, I will bring him, that he may appear in the presence of the LORD, and remain there forever; I will offer him as a nazirite[a] for all time."[f] [23] Her husband Elkanah said to her, "Do what seems best to you, wait until you have weaned him; only—may the LORD establish his word."[g] So the woman remained and nursed her son, until she weaned him. [24] When she had weaned him, she took him up with her, along with a three-year-old bull,[h] an ephah of flour, and a skin of wine. She brought him to the house of the LORD at Shiloh; and the child was young. [25] Then they slaughtered the bull, and they brought the child to Eli. [26] And she said, "Oh, my lord! As you live, my lord, I am the woman who was standing here in your presence, praying to the LORD. [27] For this child I prayed; and the LORD has granted me the petition that I made to him. [28] Therefore I have lent him to the LORD; as long as he lives, he is given to the LORD."

She left him there for[i] the LORD.

Hannah's Prayer

2 Hannah prayed and said,
   "My heart exults in the LORD;
      my strength is exalted in my God.[j]
   My mouth derides my enemies,
      because I rejoice in my[k] victory.

2   "There is no Holy One like the LORD,
      no one besides you;
         there is no Rock like our God.
3   Talk no more so very proudly,

---

a That is *one separated* or *one consecrated*   b Cn Compare Gk Q Ms 1.22: MT *then I will give him to the LORD all the days of his life*   c Gk: Heb *went her way*   d Gk: Heb lacks *and drank with her husband*   e Gk: Meaning of Heb uncertain   f Cn Compare Q Ms: MT lacks *I will offer him as a nazirite for all time*   g MT: Q Ms Gk Compare Syr *that which goes out of your mouth*   h Q Ms Gk Syr: MT *three bulls*   i Gk (Compare Q Ms) and Gk at 2.11: MT *And he* (that is, Elkanah) *worshiped there before*   j Gk: Heb *the LORD*   k Q Ms: MT *your*

---

temple was known to Jeremiah (Jer 7.12–14). **1.11** According to the regulations in Num 6.1–21, a *nazirite* was a person designated to the service of the Lord by vows of separation and abstention from wine and cutting the hair. Samson is the chief example (see Judg 13.5, 7). **1.19** *Ramah*, a short form of Ramathaim (v. 1), becomes confused in the story of Samuel and Saul with the better-known Ramah of Benjamin, about five miles north of Jerusalem. **1.20** *I have asked him of the LORD.* Hannah is explaining the name Samuel (Hebrew *shemu'el*) as if it meant "He who is from God" (*sheme'el*). **1.28** *He is given to the LORD* continues the wordplay on Samuel's name begun in v. 20; but the Hebrew word translated *given* is *sha'ul*, and some scholars think this statement originally referred to the birth of Saul (*sha'ul*).

2.1–10 Though it is not likely to have had anything to do with the story of Hannah and Samuel originally, this ancient poem of thanksgiving is appropriate to the context because of its theme of a divinely initiated change of fortune, something that the barren Hannah experienced, and its closing reference to the king, the anointed of the Lord. The poem finds strong echoes in the Magnificat (Lk 1.46–55). **2.2** *Holy One, Rock,* terms for a deity; the latter could also be translated "Mountain." **2.3b** The Lord pays attention to human

let not arrogance come from your
mouth;
for the LORD is a God of knowledge,
and by him actions are weighed.
4 The bows of the mighty are broken,
but the feeble gird on strength.
5 Those who were full have hired
themselves out for bread,
but those who were hungry are fat with
spoil.
The barren has borne seven,
but she who has many children is
forlorn.
6 The LORD kills and brings to life;
he brings down to Sheol and raises up.
7 The LORD makes poor and makes rich;
he brings low, he also exalts.
8 He raises up the poor from the dust;
he lifts the needy from the ash heap,
to make them sit with princes
and inherit a seat of honor.*a*
For the pillars of the earth are the LORD's,
and on them he has set the world.

9 "He will guard the feet of his faithful ones,
but the wicked shall be cut off in
darkness;
for not by might does one prevail.
10 The LORD! His adversaries shall be
shattered;
the Most High*b* will thunder in heaven.
The LORD will judge the ends of the
earth;
he will give strength to his king,
and exalt the power of his anointed."

Eli's Wicked Sons

11 Then Elkanah went home to Ramah, while
the boy remained to minister to the LORD, in
the presence of the priest Eli.

12 Now the sons of Eli were scoundrels;
they had no regard for the LORD 13or for the
duties of the priests to the people. When anyone offered sacrifice, the priest's servant
would come, while the meat was boiling, with
a three-pronged fork in his hand, 14and he
would thrust it into the pan, or kettle, or caldron, or pot; all that the fork brought up the
priest would take for himself.*c* This is what
they did at Shiloh to all the Israelites who
came there. 15Moreover, before the fat was
burned, the priest's servant would come and
say to the one who was sacrificing, "Give meat
for the priest to roast; for he will not accept
boiled meat from you, but only raw." 16And if
the man said to him, "Let them burn the fat
first, and then take whatever you wish," he
would say, "No, you must give it now; if not, I
will take it by force." 17Thus the sin of the
young men was very great in the sight of the
LORD; for they treated the offerings of the
LORD with contempt.

The Child Samuel at Shiloh

18 Samuel was ministering before the LORD, a
boy wearing a linen ephod. 19His mother used
to make for him a little robe and take it to him
each year, when she went up with her husband
to offer the yearly sacrifice. 20Then Eli would
bless Elkanah and his wife, and say, "May the
LORD repay*d* you with children by this woman
for the gift that she made to*e* the LORD"; and
then they would return to their home.

21 And*f* the LORD took note of Hannah; she
conceived and bore three sons and two daughters. And the boy Samuel grew up in the presence of the LORD.

---

a Gk (Compare Q Ms) adds *He grants the vow of the one who
vows, and blesses the years of the just* *b* Cn Heb *against him he*
c Gk Syr Vg: Heb *with it* *d* Q Ms Gk: MT *give* *e* Q Ms Gk:
MT *for the petition that she asked of* *f* Q Ms Gk: MT *When*

---

circumstances, weighs them, and, when necessary, sets
them in balance. Vv. 4–8 contain a series of examples
of divinely contrived reversals of human fortune.
2.6 *Sheol,* the dark, dank residence of the dead in the
OT. **2.8–10** This passage is much longer in the Septuagint and in a Samuel scroll from Qumran (4QSama),
both of which append a long passage equivalent to the
Greek version of Jer 9.23–24. **2.10** *The Most High* (Hebrew *'eli*), a rare divine epithet meaning "the exalted
one." It is similar in form, but not necessarily in meaning, to the personal name Eli (see v. 11), borne by the
priest of Shiloh. The references to the *king* and the
Lord's *anointed* (see 9.16) suggest that the original occasion for the composition of this song may have been
the celebration of a royal birth. **2.11–17** The sons of
Eli, the chief priest of Shiloh, are shown to have corrupted the sacrificial cult there and, therefore, to have
proved themselves unfit to succeed their father.
2.16 By asking that they *burn the fat first,* the man is
appealing to the rules that forbid the priests to take the
fat for themselves (see Lev 3.16–17; Num 18.17).
2.18–21 In sharp contrast to the sons of Eli, the young
Samuel earns both divine and human favor (see v. 26)
in carrying out his duties at Shiloh. **2.18** *Linen ephod,* a
simple loincloth that signifies priestly status (cf. 22.18)
but is not as elaborate as the garment worn by Ahijah

Prophecy against Eli's Household

22 Now Eli was very old. He heard all that his sons were doing to all Israel, and how they lay with the women who served at the entrance to the tent of meeting. 23 He said to them, "Why do you do such things? For I hear of your evil dealings from all these people. 24 No, my sons; it is not a good report that I hear the people of the LORD spreading abroad. 25 If one person sins against another, someone can intercede for the sinner with the LORD;[a] but if someone sins against the LORD, who can make intercession?" But they would not listen to the voice of their father; for it was the will of the LORD to kill them.

26 Now the boy Samuel continued to grow both in stature and in favor with the LORD and with the people.

27 A man of God came to Eli and said to him, "Thus the LORD has said, 'I revealed[b] myself to the family of your ancestor in Egypt when they were slaves[c] to the house of Pharaoh. 28 I chose him out of all the tribes of Israel to be my priest, to go up to my altar, to offer incense, to wear an ephod before me; and I gave to the family of your ancestor all my offerings by fire from the people of Israel. 29 Why then look with greedy eye[d] at my sacrifices and my offerings that I commanded, and honor your sons more than me by fattening yourselves on the choicest parts of every offering of my people Israel?' 30 Therefore the LORD the God of Israel declares: 'I promised that your family and the family of your ancestor should go in and out before me forever'; but now the LORD declares: 'Far be it from me; for those who honor me I will honor, and those who de-spise me shall be treated with contempt. 31 See, a time is coming when I will cut off your strength and the strength of your ancestor's family, so that no one in your family will live to old age. 32 Then in distress you will look with greedy eye[e] on all the prosperity that shall be bestowed upon Israel; and no one in your family shall ever live to old age. 33 The only one of you whom I shall not cut off from my altar shall be spared to weep out his[f] eyes and grieve his[g] heart; all the members of your household shall die by the sword.[h] 34 The fate of your two sons, Hophni and Phinehas, shall be the sign to you—both of them shall die on the same day. 35 I will raise up for myself a faithful priest, who shall do according to what is in my heart and in my mind. I will build him a sure house, and he shall go in and out before my anointed one forever. 36 Everyone who is left in your family shall come to implore him for a piece of silver or a loaf of bread, and shall say, Please put me in one of the priest's places, that I may eat a morsel of bread.' "

Samuel's Calling and Prophetic Activity

3 Now the boy Samuel was ministering to the LORD under Eli. The word of the LORD was rare in those days; visions were not widespread.

2 At that time Eli, whose eyesight had begun to grow dim so that he could not see, was lying down in his room; 3 the lamp of God had not yet gone out, and Samuel was lying

---

a Gk Compare Q Ms: MT another, God will mediate for him b Gk Tg Syr: Heb Did I reveal c Q Ms Gk: MT lacks slaves d Q Ms Gk: MT then kick e Q Ms Gk: MT will kick f Q Ms Gk: MT your g Q Ms Gk: Heb your h Q Ms See Gk: MT die like mortals

---

in 14.3, much less the ornate ephod of the high priest described in Ex 28; 39. **2.22–36** An anonymous holy man appears at Shiloh and denounces the house of Eli because of the corruption of his sons. The passage comes from the hand of the Deuteronomistic Historian (see Introduction) and is chiefly concerned with establishing the ascendancy of the Zadokite priesthood (see vv. 35–36). **2.25** Someone can intercede . . . with the LORD was probably originally "gods can intercede for him," a reference to the traditional adjudicatory function of household gods or idols. **2.27** Man of God, a holy man, most often a soothsayer, as in this case. The family of your ancestor, the Levites and perhaps Moses in particular, from whom Eli seems to have been descended. **2.31–33** The prophecy refers to Saul's massacre of the Shilonite priesthood, described in 22.16–19. **2.33** The only one to survive will be Abia-thar (see 22.20–23; 1 Kings 2.26). **2.35** Though in the present context the faithful priest might seem to be Samuel himself, it will turn out to be Zadok, who shared the high-priesthood with Abiathar during David's reign and succeeded him during Solomon's. Subsequently, membership in the sure house of Zadok was required for priestly service in the Jerusalem temple. **2.36** Non-Zadokite priests were relegated to menial roles (see 2 Kings 23.9; Ezek 44.10–16).

3.1–4.1a Samuel's vocation as a prophet formally begins as he becomes, for the first time, a channel for a message from the Lord, in this case a confirmation of the oracle in 2.27–36. **3.3** The lamp of God burned in the sanctuary from evening to morning (see Ex 27.20–21). Samuel must have slept in the nave of the temple near the inner sanctuary where the ark of God, the most sacred object in Israelite worship, marked the

down in the temple of the LORD, where the ark of God was. 4Then the LORD called, "Samuel! Samuel!"*a* and he said, "Here I am!" 5and ran to Eli, and said, "Here I am, for you called me." But he said, "I did not call; lie down again." So he went and lay down. 6The LORD called again, "Samuel!" Samuel got up and went to Eli, and said, "Here I am, for you called me." But he said, "I did not call, my son; lie down again." 7Now Samuel did not yet know the LORD, and the word of the LORD had not yet been revealed to him. 8The LORD called Samuel again, a third time. And he got up and went to Eli, and said, "Here I am, for you called me." Then Eli perceived that the LORD was calling the boy. 9Therefore Eli said to Samuel, "Go, lie down; and if he calls you, you shall say, 'Speak, LORD, for your servant is listening.' " So Samuel went and lay down in his place.

10 Now the LORD came and stood there, calling as before, "Samuel! Samuel!" And Samuel said, "Speak, for your servant is listening." 11Then the LORD said to Samuel, "See, I am about to do something in Israel that will make both ears of anyone who hears of it tingle. 12On that day I will fulfill against Eli all that I have spoken concerning his house, from beginning to end. 13For I have told him that I am about to punish his house forever, for the iniquity that he knew, because his sons were blaspheming God,*b* and he did not restrain them. 14Therefore I swear to the house of Eli that the iniquity of Eli's house shall not be expiated by sacrifice or offering forever."

15 Samuel lay there until morning; then he opened the doors of the house of the LORD. Samuel was afraid to tell the vision to Eli. 16But Eli called Samuel and said, "Samuel, my son." He said, "Here I am." 17Eli said, "What was it that he told you? Do not hide it from

me. May God do so to you and more also, if you hide anything from me of all that he told you." 18So Samuel told him everything and hid nothing from him. Then he said, "It is the LORD; let him do what seems good to him."

19 As Samuel grew up, the LORD was with him and let none of his words fall to the ground. 20And all Israel from Dan to Beer-sheba knew that Samuel was a trustworthy prophet of the LORD. 21The LORD continued to appear at Shiloh, for the LORD revealed himself to Samuel at Shiloh by the word of the LORD. 1And the word of Samuel came to all Israel.

The Ark of God Captured

In those days the Philistines mustered for war against Israel,*c* and Israel went out to battle against them;*d* they encamped at Ebenezer, and the Philistines encamped at Aphek. 2The Philistines drew up in line against Israel, and when the battle was joined,*e* Israel was defeated by the Philistines, who killed about four thousand men on the field of battle. 3When the troops came to the camp, the elders of Israel said, "Why has the LORD put us to rout today before the Philistines? Let us bring the ark of the covenant of the LORD here from Shiloh, so that he may come among us and save us from the power of our enemies." 4So the people sent to Shiloh, and brought from there the ark of the covenant of the LORD of hosts, who is enthroned on the cherubim. The two sons of Eli, Hophni and Phinehas, were there with the ark of the covenant of God.

5 When the ark of the covenant of the LORD

---

a Q Ms Gk See 3.10: MT *the LORD called Samuel*   *b* Another reading is *for themselves*   *c* Gk: Heb lacks *In those days the Philistines mustered for war against Israel*   *d* Gk: Heb *against the Philistines*   *e* Meaning of Heb uncertain

---

presence of the Lord. **3.11–14** Samuel's first vision is a confirmation of the oracle of the anonymous man of God in 2.27–36. **3.14** *Shall not be expiated by sacrifice or offering.* The possibility of ritual expiation (see Lev 4.3–12) is set aside. **3.19–4.1a** Now that he has received his first oracle, Samuel is established as a prophet, the vehicle through which the Lord communicates with Israel.

4.1b–11 In a major battle on the Philistine frontier the ark of the Lord is brought from Shiloh to rally the faltering Israelite troops, but the Philistines prove too strong, Israel is routed, and the ark is captured. When the account is read in conjunction with the materials that precede it, it becomes clear that the Lord's purpose in permitting the capture of the ark is to remove

it from Shiloh, whose priesthood he has just condemned. **4.1b** The *Philistines* had arrived on the coast of Canaan at about the same time the Israelites settled in the hills, and the Israelite monarchy arose amid a struggle between the two peoples for supremacy in the country. *Ebenezer.* Location uncertain. *Aphek,* just east of modern Tel Aviv, guarding a strategically important route from the coastal plain into the hill country. **4.3** The *elders of Israel,* tribal elders with responsibility for important decisions, attribute the rout to the absence of the ark, which marked the presence of the Divine Warrior in the midst of the army. **4.4** *The LORD of hosts . . . enthroned on the cherubim,* an epithet signifying the presence of the Lord above the cherubim, carvings of winged sphinxlike creatures. The ark is

came into the camp, all Israel gave a mighty shout, so that the earth resounded. 6When the Philistines heard the noise of the shouting, they said, "What does this great shouting in the camp of the Hebrews mean?" When they learned that the ark of the LORD had come to the camp, 7the Philistines were afraid; for they said, "Gods have* come into the camp." They also said, "Woe to us! For nothing like this has happened before. 8Woe to us! Who can deliver us from the power of these mighty gods? These are the gods who struck the Egyptians with every sort of plague in the wilderness. 9Take courage, and be men, O Philistines, in order not to become slaves to the Hebrews as they have been to you; be men and fight."

10 So the Philistines fought; Israel was defeated, and they fled, everyone to his home. There was a very great slaughter, for there fell of Israel thirty thousand foot soldiers. 11The ark of God was captured; and the two sons of Eli, Hophni and Phinehas, died.

Death of Eli

12 A man of Benjamin ran from the battle line, and came to Shiloh the same day, with his clothes torn and with earth upon his head. 13When he arrived, Eli was sitting upon his seat by the road watching, for his heart trembled for the ark of God. When the man came into the city and told the news, all the city cried out. 14When Eli heard the sound of the outcry, he said, "What is this uproar?" Then the man came quickly and told Eli. 15Now Eli was ninety-eight years old and his eyes were set, so that he could not see. 16The man said to

Eli, "I have just come from the battle; I fled from the battle today." He said, "How did it go, my son?" 17The messenger replied, "Israel has fled before the Philistines, and there has also been a great slaughter among the troops; your two sons also, Hophni and Phinehas, are dead, and the ark of God has been captured." 18When he mentioned the ark of God, Eli*b* fell over backward from his seat by the side of the gate; and his neck was broken and he died, for he was an old man, and heavy. He had judged Israel forty years.

19 Now his daughter-in-law, the wife of Phinehas, was pregnant, about to give birth. When she heard the news that the ark of God was captured, and that her father-in-law and her husband were dead, she bowed and gave birth; for her labor pains overwhelmed her. 20As she was about to die, the women attending her said to her, "Do not be afraid, for you have borne a son." But she did not answer or give heed. 21She named the child Ichabod, meaning, "The glory has departed from Israel," because the ark of God had been captured and because of her father-in-law and her husband. 22She said, "The glory has departed from Israel, for the ark of God has been captured."

The Philistines and the Ark

5 When the Philistines captured the ark of God, they brought it from Ebenezer to Ashdod; 2then the Philistines took the ark of God and brought it into the house of Dagon

a Or A god has   b Heb he

here envisioned as a portable cherub-throne, an important element in the royal iconography of Canaan. **4.5** The Israelite battle cry, here called *a mighty shout,* was a continuous threatening roar that made the earth seem to shake. **4.8** The Philistines seem to think that Israel has more than one god. They fear *these mighty gods* because they *struck the Egyptians with every sort of plague* (see Ex 7–12), and in fact plague will be the weapon with which the Lord strikes them in ch. 5. The plagues of Exodus were not *in the wilderness,* and the original reading here is likely to have been "and pestilence." **4.11** The death of *Hophni and Phinehas* fulfills the prediction of 2.34. **4.12–22** When word of the capture of the ark is brought to Eli, the old priest collapses and breaks his neck. **4.12** The messenger is a native of *Benjamin,* the small tribal territory immediately north of Jerusalem. **4.18** *Judged Israel forty years.* Eli is incorporated into the succession of "judges" who ruled Israel between Joshua and Saul (see Judg 10.2, 3; 12.7, 9,

11, 14; 16.31; 1 Sam 7.6). **4.19** Shocked by the death of Phinehas, his wife *bowed and gave birth,* assuming the usual crouched position of Israelite women in childbirth. **4.21** The interpretation of the name *Ichabod* given here is close to its literal meaning, "Alas for the glory!" or "Where is the glory?" Such names were probably taken from liturgical laments over the departure of the discernible cultic presence—the "glory"—of a deity.

5.1–12 As the ark is moved around Philistia, pestilence breaks out in one city after another. The story shows that the Lord permitted the capture of the ark to provide an occasion for slaying enemies. **5.1** *Ashdod,* one of the five principal Philistine cities (see note on 5.8), located on the coastal highway a few miles from the sea and almost due west of Jerusalem. **5.2** *House of Dagon,* Ashdod's temple of the god Dagon, a Syrian deity of great antiquity who was adopted as the god of the Philistines after their arrival.

and placed it beside Dagon. [3]When the people of Ashdod rose early the next day, there was Dagon, fallen on his face to the ground before the ark of the LORD. So they took Dagon and put him back in his place. [4]But when they rose early on the next morning, Dagon had fallen on his face to the ground before the ark of the LORD, and the head of Dagon and both his hands were lying cut off upon the threshold; only the trunk of[a] Dagon was left to him. [5]This is why the priests of Dagon and all who enter the house of Dagon do not step on the threshold of Dagon in Ashdod to this day.

6 The hand of the LORD was heavy upon the people of Ashdod, and he terrified and struck them with tumors, both in Ashdod and in its territory. [7]And when the inhabitants of Ashdod saw how things were, they said, "The ark of the God of Israel must not remain with us; for his hand is heavy on us and on our god Dagon." [8]So they sent and gathered together all the lords of the Philistines, and said, "What shall we do with the ark of the God of Israel?" The inhabitants of Gath replied, "Let the ark of God be moved on to us."[b] So they moved the ark of the God of Israel to Gath.[c] [9]But after they had brought it to Gath,[d] the hand of the LORD was against the city, causing a very great panic; he struck the inhabitants of the city, both young and old, so that tumors broke out on them. [10]So they sent the ark of the God of Israel[e] to Ekron. But when the ark of God came to Ekron, the people of Ekron cried out, "Why[f] have they brought around to us[g] the ark of the God of Israel to kill us[g] and our[h] people?" [11]They sent therefore and gathered together all the lords of the Philistines, and said, "Send away the ark of the God of Israel, and let it return to its own place, that it may not kill us

and our people." For there was a deathly panic[i] throughout the whole city. The hand of God was very heavy there; [12]those who did not die were stricken with tumors, and the cry of the city went up to heaven.

The Ark Returned to Israel

6 The ark of the LORD was in the country of the Philistines seven months. [2]Then the Philistines called for the priests and the diviners and said, "What shall we do with the ark of the LORD? Tell us what we should send with it to its place." [3]They said, "If you send away the ark of the God of Israel, do not send it empty, but by all means return him a guilt offering. Then you will be healed and will be ransomed;[j] will not his hand then turn from you?" [4]And they said, "What is the guilt offering that we shall return to him?" They answered, "Five gold tumors and five gold mice, according to the number of the lords of the Philistines; for the same plague was upon all of you and upon your lords. [5]So you must make images of your tumors and images of your mice that ravage the land, and give glory to the God of Israel; perhaps he will lighten his hand on you and your gods and your land. [6]Why should you harden your hearts as the Egyptians and Pharaoh hardened their hearts? After he had made fools of them, did they not let the people go, and they departed? [7]Now then, get ready a new cart and two milch cows that have never borne a yoke, and yoke the cows to the cart, but take their calves home, away from them. [8]Take the

---

a Heb lacks the trunk of   b Gk Compare Q Ms: MT They answered, "Let the ark of the God of Israel be brought around to Gath."   c Gk: Heb lacks to Gath   d Q Ms: MT lacks to Gath   e Q Ms Gk: MT lacks of Israel   f Q Ms Gk: MT lacks Why   g Heb me   h Heb my   i Q Ms reads a panic from the LORD   j Q Ms Gk: MT and it will be known to you

---

5.5 The writer uses the events of the story to explain a contemporary taboo against treading on the *threshold* of Dagon's temple in Ashdod. **5.6** *The hand of the LORD,* plague, a weapon commonly used by the God of Israel against enemies. The specific disease that ravages the Philistines is probably bubonic plague, an epidemic common in coastal cities; it was characterized by *tumors,* nodal swellings or "buboes," and transmitted by fleas borne on rats or mice (see 6.4). **5.8** The *lords of the Philistines* were five in number, one from each of the principal cities, Ashdod, Ekron, Gath, Ashkelon, and Gaza. *Gath,* possibly Tell es-Safi southeast of Tel Miqneh/Ekron (see note on 5.10), but the site is disputed. **5.10** *Ekron,* modern Tel Miqneh, about twenty miles inland at the northern frontier of Philistine territory. **5.11** *Its own place,* the particular

pedestal or alcove where the sacred object used to reside in its native shrine.
6.1–7.1 The Philistines send the ark back to Israelite territory, and it comes to rest in Kiriath-jearim. **6.3** *Guilt offering,* compensation paid to the God of Israel to atone for defiling the ark and to prevent further suffering. **6.4** *Five gold tumors and five gold mice,* a strange but appropriate offering. *Five* corresponds to the number of the Philistine lords or cities (see vv. 17–18), and the Hebrew word for *tumor* also means "acropolis." *Gold* suggests that the offerings can also be thought of as spoils of war. Tumors and mice are characteristic of the plague (see note on 5.6). **6.6** *Egyptians . . . hearts,* an allusion to Pharaoh's repeated resistance to releasing the Israelites during the plagues preceding the exodus (e.g., Ex 10.1–2). **6.7** *New cart, cows that*

ark of the LORD and place it on the cart, and put in a box at its side the figures of gold, which you are returning to him as a guilt offering. Then send it off, and let it go its way. 9And watch; if it goes up on the way to its own land, to Beth-shemesh, then it is he who has done us this great harm; but if not, then we shall know that it is not his hand that struck us; it happened to us by chance."

10 The men did so; they took two milch cows and yoked them to the cart, and shut up their calves at home. 11They put the ark of the LORD on the cart, and the box with the gold mice and the images of their tumors. 12The cows went straight in the direction of Beth-shemesh along one highway, lowing as they went; they turned neither to the right nor to the left, and the lords of the Philistines went after them as far as the border of Beth-she-mesh.

13 Now the people of Beth-shemesh were reaping their wheat harvest in the valley. When they looked up and saw the ark, they went with rejoicing to meet it.*a* 14The cart came into the field of Joshua of Beth-she-mesh, and stopped there. A large stone was there; so they split up the wood of the cart and offered the cows as a burnt offering to the LORD. 15The Levites took down the ark of the LORD and the box that was beside it, in which were the gold objects, and set them upon the large stone. Then the people of Beth-shemesh offered burnt offerings and presented sacrifices on that day to the LORD. 16When the five lords of the Philistines saw it, they returned that day to Ekron.

17 These are the gold tumors, which the Philistines returned as a guilt offering to the LORD: one for Ashdod, one for Gaza, one for Ashkelon, one for Gath, one for Ekron; 18also the gold mice, according to the number of all the cities of the Philistines belonging to the five lords, both fortified cities and unwalled villages. The great stone, beside which they set down the ark of the LORD, is a witness to this day in the field of Joshua of Beth-shemesh.

The Ark at Kiriath-jearim

19 The descendants of Jeconiah did not rejoice with the people of Beth-shemesh when they greeted*b* the ark of the LORD; and he killed seventy men of them.*c* The people mourned because the LORD had made a great slaughter among the people. 20Then the people of Beth-shemesh said, "Who is able to stand before the LORD, this holy God? To whom shall he go so that we may be rid of him?" 21So they sent messengers to the inhabitants of Kiriath-jearim, saying, "The Philistines have returned the ark of the LORD. Come 7 down and take it up to you." 1And the people of Kiriath-jearim came and took up the ark of the LORD, and brought it to the house of Abinadab on the hill. They consecrated his son, Eleazar, to have charge of the ark of the LORD.

2 From the day that the ark was lodged at Kiriath-jearim, a long time passed, some

---

a Gk: Heb *rejoiced to see it* *b* Gk: Heb *And he killed some of the people of Beth-shemesh, because they looked into* *c* Heb *killed seventy men, fifty thousand men*

---

have never borne a yoke. A previously used cart and previously yoked cows would not be ritually pure (see Num 19.2; Deut 21.3), and both are to be used for sacrifice (see v. 15). **6.9** *Beth-shemesh,* in the northeastern Shephelah about twenty miles west of Jerusalem, was at the southwestern end of the Valley of Sorek, the most direct route back from Philistia to Israelite territory. **6.12** The unswerving route of the untrained cows shows the Philistines that the progress of the ark is being divinely guided (see v. 9). **6.14** *Joshua of Beth-shemesh,* not mentioned elsewhere in the Bible, but the field where the sacrifice was made was identified as his in the time of the writer (see v. 18). Both the *wood of the cart* and the *cows* are sacrificed as a *burnt offering,* the highest form of sacrifice, in which the entire victim was consumed on the altar. **6.15** *Levites,* possibly added by a scribe to avoid the implication in v. 14 that the sacrifice was made without the participation of the official priestly tribe. **6.19** Very uncertain textually.

The Septuagint gives us *the descendants of Jeconiah,* but we do not know who they were or why their failure to celebrate would have provoked the Lord to punish Beth-shemesh. The Masoretic Text says that the people angered the Lord by looking into the ark (see Num 4.15, 20). **6.20** *Stand before* often connotes "attend upon (as a priest)" (see Deut 10.8; Judg 20.27–28), and it may be that the people of Beth-shemesh sent the ark to Kiriath-jearim in the hope that a priest might be found there who could safely and properly manage the service of this powerful and dangerous sacred object. In any case, this is apparently what happened (see 7.1–2). **6.21** *Kiriath-jearim,* about fifteen miles east-north-east of Beth-shemesh and eight miles northwest of Jerusalem. It was situated on the border of Benjamin and Judah, and the *hill* (see 7.1) may have been the Benjaminite district. **7.1** *Abinadab* and *Eleazar,* known only from this passage and 2 Sam 6, but both names are prominent in the levitical genealogies.

twenty years, and all the house of Israel lamented[a] after the LORD.

Samuel as Judge

3 Then Samuel said to all the house of Israel, "If you are returning to the LORD with all your heart, then put away the foreign gods and the Astartes from among you. Direct your heart to the LORD, and serve him only, and he will deliver you out of the hand of the Philistines." [4]So Israel put away the Baals and the Astartes, and they served the LORD only.

5 Then Samuel said, "Gather all Israel at Mizpah, and I will pray to the LORD for you." [6]So they gathered at Mizpah, and drew water and poured it out before the LORD. They fasted that day, and said, "We have sinned against the LORD." And Samuel judged the people of Israel at Mizpah.

7 When the Philistines heard that the people of Israel had gathered at Mizpah, the lords of the Philistines went up against Israel. And when the people of Israel heard of it they were afraid of the Philistines. [8]The people of Israel said to Samuel, "Do not cease to cry out to the LORD our God for us, and pray that he may save us from the hand of the Philistines." [9]So Samuel took a sucking lamb and offered it as a whole burnt offering to the LORD; Samuel cried out to the LORD for Israel, and the LORD answered him. [10]As Samuel was offering up the burnt offering, the Philistines drew near to attack Israel; but the LORD thundered with a mighty voice that day against the Philistines and threw them into confusion; and they were routed before Israel. [11]And the men of Israel went out of Mizpah and pursued the Philistines, and struck them down as far as beyond Beth-car.

12 Then Samuel took a stone and set it up between Mizpah and Jeshanah,[b] and named it Ebenezer;[c] for he said, "Thus far the LORD has helped us." [13]So the Philistines were subdued and did not again enter the territory of Israel; the hand of the LORD was against the Philistines all the days of Samuel. [14]The towns that the Philistines had taken from Israel were restored to Israel, from Ekron to Gath; and Israel recovered their territory from the hand of the Philistines. There was peace also between Israel and the Amorites.

15 Samuel judged Israel all the days of his life. [16]He went on a circuit year by year to Bethel, Gilgal, and Mizpah; and he judged Israel in all these places. [17]Then he would come back to Ramah, for his home was there; he administered justice there to Israel, and built there an altar to the LORD.

Israel Demands a King

8 When Samuel became old, he made his sons judges over Israel. [2]The name of his firstborn son was Joel, and the name of

---

a Meaning of Heb uncertain *b* Gk Syr: Heb *Shen* *c* That is *Stone of Help*

7.2–17 Samuel, who has already been presented as both priest and prophet, now becomes a military commander and a judge. The events show that divinely chosen, charismatic leadership is fully sufficient for Israel and, by implication, that kingship is unnecessary. This is one of those passages associated with the city of Mizpah (see v. 5) that were added to the larger Samuel narrative during the Babylonian exile by a writer who viewed Israel's experience with monarchy as an unmitigated disaster (see Introduction). **7.4** *Baals, Astartes,* foreign deities, male and female. **7.5** *Mizpah,* a hilltop town probably located about five miles north of Jerusalem; during the Babylonian exile, when Jerusalem lay in ruins, it served as the provincial capital of Judah (see 2 Kings 25.23). **7.6** We know of no ritual in the biblical period in which people *drew water, poured it out before the LORD,* and *fasted,* but in some respects the ritual anticipates the later observance of the Day of Atonement (Yom Kippur). *Samuel judged the people of Israel* (see also v. 15) incorporates his career into the chronological framework of Judges (see note on 4.18). **7.10** *Thundered with a mighty voice.* The intervention of the Divine Warrior is often expressed in the language of the thunderstorm, especially in early poetry (1 Sam 2.10; 2 Sam 22.14; Pss 18.13; 29; 68.7–8). **7.11** *Beth-car,* mentioned nowhere else; location unknown. **7.12** *Jeshanah,* about seventeen miles north of Jerusalem, was later a border town disputed by the kingdoms of Israel and Judah (2 Chr 13.9). The Israelites were encamped at *Ebenezer* (see 4.1) when the Philistines attacked them earlier, so that Samuel's victory restores the boundaries that existed at the beginning of ch. 4. **7.14** Israel recovers *Ekron* and *Gath* (see 5.8, 10), the Philistines are driven out, and Israel's internal enemies, here called the *Amorites,* are also pacified. **7.16–17** *Bethel,* about ten miles north of Jerusalem, was an important religious center throughout the history of Israel. Along with *Gilgal* (see 11.14), *Mizpah* (see 7.5), and *Ramah* (see 1.19), it was one of the chief cities of the central hill country where Samuel dispensed justice.

8.1–22 A long time has passed, and Samuel is an old man. Despite the security the Israelites enjoyed under his leadership, they approach him and request a king. The people's demand is presented as arbitrary and offensive to Samuel and to the Lord himself. This is an-

his second, Abijah; they were judges in Beer-sheba. ³Yet his sons did not follow in his ways, but turned aside after gain; they took bribes and perverted justice.

4 Then all the elders of Israel gathered together and came to Samuel at Ramah, ⁵and said to him, "You are old and your sons do not follow in your ways; appoint for us, then, a king to govern us, like other nations." ⁶But the thing displeased Samuel when they said, "Give us a king to govern us." Samuel prayed to the LORD, ⁷and the LORD said to Samuel, "Listen to the voice of the people in all that they say to you; for they have not rejected you, but they have rejected me from being king over them. ⁸Just as they have done to me,ᵃ from the day I brought them up out of Egypt to this day, forsaking me and serving other gods, so also they are doing to you. ⁹Now then, listen to their voice; only—you shall solemnly warn them, and show them the ways of the king who shall reign over them."

10 So Samuel reported all the words of the LORD to the people who were asking him for a king. ¹¹He said, "These will be the ways of the king who will reign over you: he will take your sons and appoint them to his chariots and to be his horsemen, and to run before his chariots; ¹²and he will appoint for himself commanders of thousands and commanders of fifties, and some to plow his ground and to reap his harvest, and to make his implements of war and the equipment of his chariots. ¹³He will take your daughters to be perfumers and cooks and bakers. ¹⁴He will take the best of your fields and vineyards and olive orchards and give them to his courtiers. ¹⁵He will take one-tenth of your grain and of your vineyards and give it to his officers and his courtiers. ¹⁶He will take your male and female slaves, and the best of your cattleᵇ and donkeys, and put them to his work. ¹⁷He will take one-tenth of your flocks, and you shall be his slaves. ¹⁸And in that day you will cry out because of your king, whom you have chosen for yourselves; but the LORD will not answer you in that day."

Israel's Request for a King Granted

19 But the people refused to listen to the voice of Samuel; they said, "No! but we are determined to have a king over us, ²⁰so that we also may be like other nations, and that our king may govern us and go out before us and fight our battles." ²¹When Samuel had heard all the words of the people, he repeated them in the ears of the LORD. ²²The LORD said to Samuel, "Listen to their voice and set a king over them." Samuel then said to the people of Israel, "Each of you return home."

Saul Chosen to Be King

9 There was a man of Benjamin whose name was Kish son of Abiel son of Zeror son of Becorath son of Aphiah, a Benjaminite, a man of wealth. ²He had a son whose name was Saul, a handsome young man. There was not a man among the people of Israel more handsome than he; he stood head and shoulders above everyone else.

---

a Gk: Heb lacks to me   b Gk: Heb young men

---

other Mizpah passage (see note on 7.2–17; Introduction). **8.2** Samuel's sons, like Eli's, are unqualified to succeed their father, a detail that carries an implicit warning about dynastic succession in a narrative in which Israel is about to get its first king. According to 1 Chr 6.33, *Joel* was the father of Heman, the chief temple musician appointed by David. Up to this point events have been confined to the central hills, but the sons of Samuel have their headquarters in *Beer-sheba*, at the traditional southern boundary of the country. **8.5** Cf. Moses' anticipation of this request in Deut 17.14. **8.6–7** Samuel feels personally insulted, but the Lord reminds him that the people's demand is a rejection not of Samuel, but of the Lord himself, Israel's true king. The judges were divinely chosen and appointed, but a human king will expect his son to succeed him, taking the choice of leadership away from the Lord. **8.8** This verse interprets the demand for a king in terms of the Deuteronomistic understanding (see Introduction) of Israel's past as a history of repeated apostasy. **8.11–18** *He will take,* used by Samuel six times in warning the people about what to expect from a king. **8.12** *Commanders of thousands, commanders of fifties,* the ranking officers of military units of various size. **8.15** In addition to the religious tithes that supported the temple and priesthood (see Deut 14.22–29; 26.12–15), there apparently were also tithes on agricultural products and livestock (v. 17) that supported the royal estates. **8.19–22** Undeterred by Samuel's warning, the people renew their demand and the Lord acquiesces.

9.1–26 In a story with a folkloric atmosphere, the young Saul goes on a search for some strayed donkeys and finds a kingdom. **9.1** Saul's home in *Benjamin* (see 4.12) was Gibeah (10.26), also known as Gibeah of Saul (11.4) or Gibeah of Benjamin (13.2), a city atop an imposing hill about four miles north of Jerusalem in the direction of Ramah (see notes on 1.1; 1.19).

3 Now the donkeys of Kish, Saul's father, had strayed. So Kish said to his son Saul, "Take one of the boys with you; go and look for the donkeys." 4He passed through the hill country of Ephraim and passed through the land of Shalishah, but they did not find them. And they passed through the land of Shaalim, but they were not there. Then he passed through the land of Benjamin, but they did not find them.

5 When they came to the land of Zuph, Saul said to the boy who was with him, "Let us turn back, or my father will stop worrying about the donkeys and worry about us." 6But he said to him, "There is a man of God in this town; he is a man held in honor. Whatever he says always comes true. Let us go there now; perhaps he will tell us about the journey on which we have set out." 7Then Saul replied to the boy, "But if we go, what can we bring the man? For the bread in our sacks is gone, and there is no present to bring to the man of God. What have we?" 8The boy answered Saul again, "Here, I have with me a quarter shekel of silver; I will give it to the man of God, to tell us our way." 9(Formerly in Israel, anyone who went to inquire of God would say, "Come, let us go to the seer"; for the one who is now called a prophet was formerly called a seer.) 10Saul said to the boy, "Good; come, let us go." So they went to the town where the man of God was.

11 As they went up the hill to the town, they met some girls coming out to draw water, and said to them, "Is the seer here?" 12They answered, "Yes, there he is just ahead of you.

Hurry; he has come just now to the town, because the people have a sacrifice today at the shrine. 13As soon as you enter the town, you will find him, before he goes up to the shrine to eat. For the people will not eat until he comes, since he must bless the sacrifice; afterward those eat who are invited. Now go up, for you will meet him immediately." 14So they went up to the town. As they were entering the town, they saw Samuel coming out toward them on his way up to the shrine.

15 Now the day before Saul came, the LORD had revealed to Samuel: 16"Tomorrow about this time I will send to you a man from the land of Benjamin, and you shall anoint him to be ruler over my people Israel. He shall save my people from the hand of the Philistines; for I have seen the suffering of[a] my people, because their outcry has come to me." 17When Samuel saw Saul, the LORD told him, "Here is the man of whom I spoke to you. He it is who shall rule over my people." 18Then Saul approached Samuel inside the gate, and said, "Tell me, please, where is the house of the seer?" 19Samuel answered Saul, "I am the seer; go up before me to the shrine, for today you shall eat with me, and in the morning I will let you go and will tell you all that is on your mind. 20As for your donkeys that were lost three days ago, give no further thought to them, for they have been found. And on whom is all Israel's desire fixed, if not on you and on all your ancestral house?" 21Saul an-

---

a Gk: Heb lacks the suffering of

9.3 The donkeys, better "some of the donkeys." The ostensible purpose of Saul's mission is not of vital importance (he does not face the economic ruin of the loss of all the animals), a fact that heightens the dramatic irony of the narrative when the higher, divinely intended purpose of the mission is revealed. 9.4 The hill country of Ephraim, a general designation for the highlands north of Benjamin. Land of Shalishah. Location uncertain, but there was a Baal-shalishah (see 2 Kings 4.42) not far from Gilgal (see note on 10.8) in the southeast corner of Ephraim. Land of Shaalim, probably the same as the land of Shual (see 13.17), a designation of the hill country north of Bethel. Land of Benjamin can hardly be correct, since Saul is traveling north and will soon reach Ramathaim (see note on 1.1). 9.5 Samuel's father is called a Zuphite in 1.1; the land of Zuph is his home district. 9.9 This antiquarian notice, which explains the word seer in v. 11, seems to have become misplaced in the text. 9.12 The shrine at Ramathaim was the sort of local place of sacrifice later

condemned (see 2 Kings 23.8–9, 19–20). It is acceptable here because the temple has not yet been built in Jerusalem. 9.13 People . . . eat. In this type of sacrifice portions not set aside for the deity were given to the worshipers to "eat in the presence of the LORD" (Deut 12.18). 9.14 Samuel is mentioned by name for the first time in the story of the anointing of Saul in 9.1–10.16. The seer may have been anonymous in an older version. 9.16 To anoint someone was to smear the head with fat or oil (10.1). The rite sanctified a person for some sacral office (see also 10.6). Ruler (Hebrew nagid), an individual who has been selected to become king either by the reigning king (1 Kings 1.35; 2 Chr 11.22) or, as in this case, by the Lord. From the perspective of ch. 7 the Philistines have been driven to a safe distance, but the author of the present, older story knows nothing of that tradition (see 10.5). 9.20b Better, "And to whom does all of Israel's wealth belong, if not to you and to all your ancestral house?" The point Samuel is making is that Saul need not worry about a

swered, "I am only a Benjaminite, from the least of the tribes of Israel, and my family is the humblest of all the families of the tribe of Benjamin. Why then have you spoken to me in this way?"

22 Then Samuel took Saul and his servant-boy and brought them into the hall, and gave them a place at the head of those who had been invited, of whom there were about thirty. 23And Samuel said to the cook, "Bring the portion I gave you, the one I asked you to put aside." 24The cook took up the thigh and what went with it*a* and set them before Saul. Samuel said, "See, what was kept is set before you. Eat; for it is set*b* before you at the appointed time, so that you might eat with the guests."*c*

So Saul ate with Samuel that day. 25When they came down from the shrine into the town, a bed was spread for Saul*d* on the roof, and he lay down to sleep.*e* 26Then at the break of dawn*f* Samuel called to Saul upon the roof, "Get up, so that I may send you on your way." Saul got up, and both he and Samuel went out into the street.

Samuel Anoints Saul

27 As they were going down to the outskirts of the town, Samuel said to Saul, "Tell the boy to go on before us, and when he has passed on, stop here yourself for a while, that I may make

10 known to you the word of God." 1Samuel took a vial of oil and poured it on

his head, and kissed him; he said, "The LORD has anointed you ruler over his people Israel. You shall reign over the people of the LORD and you will save them from the hand of their enemies all around. Now this shall be the sign to you that the LORD has anointed you ruler*g* over his heritage: 2When you depart from me today you will meet two men by Rachel's tomb in the territory of Benjamin at Zelzah; they will say to you, 'The donkeys that you went to seek are found, and now your father has stopped worrying about them and is worrying about you, saying: What shall I do about my son?' 3Then you shall go on from there further and come to the oak of Tabor; three men going up to God at Bethel will meet you there, one carrying three kids, another carrying three loaves of bread, and another carrying a skin of wine. 4They will greet you and give you two loaves of bread, which you shall accept from them. 5After that you shall come to Gibeath-elohim,*h* at the place where the Philistine garrison is; there, as you come to the town, you will meet a band of prophets coming down from the shrine with harp, tambourine, flute, and lyre playing in front of them; they

---

a Meaning of Heb uncertain   *b* Q Ms Gk: MT *it was kept*
c Cn: Heb *it was kept for you, saying, I have invited the people*
d Gk: Heb *and he spoke with Saul*   *e* Gk: Heb lacks *and he lay down to sleep*   *f* Gk: Heb *and they arose early and at break of dawn*   *g* Gk: Heb lacks *over his people Israel. You shall . . . anointed you ruler*   *h* Or *the Hill of God*

---

few lost donkeys, since all the riches of Israel will soon be his. **9.21** Saul is mystified by Samuel's remarks. As *a Benjaminite*, he belongs to the small tribe descended from the youngest son of Jacob. We learn in 10.21 that Saul's family or clan, which he says is the humblest in Benjamin, is called Matri. **9.24** *Took up* indicates not that the cook physically lifted the *thigh* but that he set it apart or reserved it for a special use. This is the "thigh that is raised" of Lev 10.14, 15 (cf. Ex 29.27; Num 6.20), which was ordinarily reserved for the priests. As when he receives consecrated loaves of bread in 10.4, Saul is being treated as if he were a priest, an indication of the sacral character of kingship. **9.25** As an honored guest, Saul sleeps on the *roof*, where the air is fresh and cool.

9.27–10.8 Samuel anoints Saul king and sends him home with special instructions. **10.1** Samuel anoints Saul (see 9.16) with a *vial of oil*, probably a small ceramic flask containing olive oil impregnated with spices (cf. Ex 30.22–25). Someone's *heritage* was landed property, inalienably held and acquired as a gift, as a result of a military victory, or by inheritance. The Lord's heritage was Israel. **10.2** *Rachel's tomb* was near Ephrathah, where she was going when she died in

childbirth with Benjamin (Gen 35.16–20; 48.7). There were two towns with that name, one near Bethlehem (cf. 17.12) and one near Kiriath-jearim (see 6.21). Though erroneous glosses in Genesis connect the site with Bethlehem, scholars agree that the northern Ephrathah is correct. *Zelzah*, unknown; the text may have sustained errors in transmission. **10.3** *Oak of Tabor*, evidently near Bethel, otherwise unknown. The *three men going up to God at Bethel* are carrying goods for sacrifice at the shrine. **10.4** By being given *two loaves of bread* from the sacrificial goods, Saul is again being treated like a priest (see 9.24). *Loaves* actually appears in no version of the text. The Masoretic Text is defective, reading "two of bread," but both the Septuagint and a scroll from Qumran (4QSam^a) supply the missing term, "elevation offerings," bread ceremonially reserved for priestly use (Num 18.11). **10.5** *Gibeath-elohim*, evidently another name for Gibeah of Saul (see note on 9.1), since people *who knew him before* (v. 11) are there; for the *Philistine garrison*, see 13.3. Prophetic behavior sometimes expressed itself in *a prophetic frenzy*, involving music, dancing, group trances, and even more extreme forms of ecstatic behavior such as self-flagellation or self-mutilation. This

will be in a prophetic frenzy. 6Then the spirit of the LORD will possess you, and you will be in a prophetic frenzy along with them and be turned into a different person. 7Now when these signs meet you, do whatever you see fit to do, for God is with you. 8And you shall go down to Gilgal ahead of me; then I will come down to you to present burnt offerings and offer sacrifices of well-being. Seven days you shall wait, until I come to you and show you what you shall do."

Saul Prophesies

9 As he turned away to leave Samuel, God gave him another heart; and all these signs were fulfilled that day. 10When they were going from there*a* to Gibeah,*b* a band of prophets met him; and the spirit of God possessed him, and he fell into a prophetic frenzy along with them. 11When all who knew him before saw how he prophesied with the prophets, the people said to one another, "What has come over the son of Kish? Is Saul also among the prophets?" 12A man of the place answered, "And who is their father?" Therefore it became a proverb, "Is Saul also among the prophets?" 13When his prophetic frenzy had ended, he went home.*c*

14 Saul's uncle said to him and to the boy, "Where did you go?" And he replied, "To seek the donkeys; and when we saw they were not to be found, we went to Samuel." 15Saul's uncle said, "Tell me what Samuel said to you." 16Saul said to his uncle, "He told us that the donkeys had been found." But about the matter of the kingship, of which Samuel had spoken, he did not tell him anything.

Saul Proclaimed King

17 Samuel summoned the people to the LORD at Mizpah 18and said to them,*d* "Thus says the LORD, the God of Israel, 'I brought up Israel out of Egypt, and I rescued you from the hand of the Egyptians and from the hand of all the kingdoms that were oppressing you.' 19But today you have rejected your God, who saves you from all your calamities and your distresses; and you have said, 'No! but set a king over us.' Now therefore present yourselves before the LORD by your tribes and by your clans."

20 Then Samuel brought all the tribes of Israel near, and the tribe of Benjamin was taken by lot. 21He brought the tribe of Benjamin near by its families, and the family of the Matrites was taken by lot. Finally he brought the family of the Matrites near man by man,*e* and Saul the son of Kish was taken by lot. But when they sought him, he could not be found. 22So they inquired again of the LORD, "Did the man come here?"*f* and the LORD said, "See, he has hidden himself among the baggage." 23Then they ran and brought him from there. When he took his stand among the people, he was head and shoulders taller than any of them. 24Samuel said to all the people, "Do you see the one whom the LORD has chosen? There is no one like him among all the people." And all the people shouted, "Long live the king!"

25 Samuel told the people the rights and

---

a Gk: Heb *they came there* *b* Or *the hill* *c* Cn: Heb *he came to the shrine* *d* Heb *to the people of Israel* *e* Gk: Heb lacks *Finally . . . man by man* *f* Gk: Heb *Is there yet a man to come here?*

---

kind of activity was often regarded as madness by the unaffected (see, e.g., 2 Kings 9.11). **10.6** The chief characteristic of prophetic frenzy was possession by *the spirit of the LORD*, the inspirational power of the God of Israel. The experience involved a loss of self, or rather transformation into *a different person*. **10.8** Samuel's instructions look ahead to 11.14–15. *Gilgal* (see 7.16; 11.14; 13.4) was an important Benjaminite town and place of sacrifice near Jericho; its location is unknown. **10.9–16** On his way home Saul meets a band of prophets and is possessed by the spirit of the Lord. **10.11** The proverb *Is Saul also among the prophets?* is explained differently in 19.19–24. Because of the tradition of prophetic antagonism to Saul, the saying may have originated as a way of remarking on a group that has absorbed or accepted the least likely candidate for membership. **10.12** *And who is their father?* obscure. Does it mean "Saul is not only among

the prophets; he is their leader (father)!"? **10.14** Surprisingly, on his arrival home Saul meets not his father, Kish, but his *uncle*. Is this Ner (14.50)? **10.17–27** Saul's secret anointing becomes public knowledge when a lottery identifies him as the chosen king. The divine selection of Saul as king, mediated through the mechanism of the lottery, is depicted as in no way auspicious but, on the contrary, as a concession to the people's wanton demand for a king (8.1–22). This is another Mizpah passage (see v. 17; note on 7.2–17; Introduction). **10.17** *Mizpah.* See note on 7.5. **10.18** *Kingdoms*, better "kings." **10.19** *You have rejected your God* echoes 8.7 and refers to the people's demand for a king. *Today*, now; it is not intended to suggest that the assembly at Mizpah being described here took place on the same day that the demand for a king was brought to Samuel. **10.21** *Family of the Matrites*, Saul's clan or family, identified nowhere else (see note on

duties of the kingship; and he wrote them in a book and laid it up before the LORD. Then Samuel sent all the people back to their homes. 26Saul also went to his home at Gibeah, and with him went warriors whose hearts God had touched. 27But some worthless fellows said, "How can this man save us?" They despised him and brought him no present. But he held his peace.

Now Nahash, king of the Ammonites, had been grievously oppressing the Gadites and the Reubenites. He would gouge out the right eye of each of them and would not grant Israel a deliverer. No one was left of the Israelites across the Jordan whose right eye Nahash, king of the Ammonites, had not gouged out. But there were seven thousand men who had escaped from the Ammonites and had entered Jabesh-gilead.*a*

Saul Defeats the Ammonites

11 About a month later,*b* Nahash the Ammonite went up and besieged Jabesh-gilead; and all the men of Jabesh said to Nahash, "Make a treaty with us, and we will serve you." 2But Nahash the Ammonite said to them, "On this condition I will make a treaty with you, namely that I gouge out everyone's right eye, and thus put disgrace upon all Israel." 3The elders of Jabesh said to him, "Give us seven days' respite that we may send messengers through all the territory of Israel. Then, if there is no one to save us, we will give ourselves up to you." 4When the messengers came to Gibeah of Saul, they reported the matter in the hearing of the people; and all the people wept aloud.

5 Now Saul was coming from the field behind the oxen; and Saul said, "What is the matter with the people, that they are weeping?" So they told him the message from the inhabitants of Jabesh. 6And the spirit of God came upon Saul in power when he heard these words, and his anger was greatly kindled. 7He took a yoke of oxen, and cut them in pieces and sent them throughout all the territory of Israel by messengers, saying, "Whoever does not come out after Saul and Samuel, so shall it be done to his oxen!" Then the dread of the LORD fell upon the people, and they came out as one. 8When he mustered them at Bezek, those from Israel were three hundred thousand, and those from Judah seventy*c* thousand. 9They said to the messengers who had come, "Thus shall you say to the inhabitants of Jabesh-gilead: 'Tomorrow, by the time the sun is hot, you shall have deliverance.' " When the messengers came and told the inhabitants of Jabesh, they rejoiced. 10So the inhabitants of Jabesh said, "Tomorrow we will give ourselves up to you, and you may do to us whatever seems good to you." 11The next day Saul put the people in three companies. At the morning watch they came into the camp and cut down the Ammonites until the heat of the day; and those who survived were scattered, so that no two of them were left together.

12 The people said to Samuel, "Who is it that said, 'Shall Saul reign over us?' Give them to us so that we may put them to death." 13But Saul said, "No one shall be put to death this

---

a Q Ms Compare Josephus, *Antiquities* VI.v.1 (68-71): MT lacks *Now Nahash . . . entered Jabesh-gilead.* *b* Q Ms Gk: MT lacks *About a month later* *c* Q Ms Gk: MT *thirty*

9.21). **10.25** *Rights and duties of the kingship.* Cf. 8.11–18; Deut 17.18. **10.27a** *Present,* tribute ordinarily paid to a king by his subjects as a gesture of fealty (see, e.g., Judg 3.15).

10.27b–11.15 Saul demonstrates his ability to lead Israel in battle by liberating a Gileadite city from a siege by an Ammonite army. **10.27b** *Now Nahash . . . Jabesh-gilead* has been lost in all the existing witnesses to the text except a manuscript from Qumran (4QSam*a*) and the account of the Jewish historian Josephus. Along with the half-tribe of Manasseh, the *Gadites* and the *Reubenites* were the Israelite tribes that lived east of the Jordan River (see Josh 13.8–13, 15–32). *Jabesh-gilead,* a stronghold in Gilead (Transjordanian Israel; cf. note on 13.7); it was probably situated on the banks of the Wadi Yabis, which preserves the ancient name of Jabesh and empties into the Jordan about twenty miles south of the Sea of Galilee.

Would not grant Israel a deliverer, better "would put the dread of him on Israel" (cf. Josh 2.9). **11.1** *About a month later* may have been removed from the Masoretic Text because it is inconsistent with the chronology of the larger narrative, which permits only seven days to elapse between Saul's departure from Samuel in 10.8 and Samuel's arrival at Gilgal in 14.8–10. **11.4** *Gibeah of Saul* (see note on 9.1) lay across the Jordan slightly more than forty miles away. **11.7** Israelites were bound in covenant by an oath, sanctioned by the slaughter of an animal, to join in any military action needed for the defense of fellow Israelites. Saul's summons of the tribes appeals to this oath and threatens them with the fate of the slaughtered oxen for noncompliance. **11.8** *Bezek,* mentioned nowhere else in the OT, was probably a town west of Jordan facing Jabesh; it has been identified with the modern village of Khirbet Ibzik about fifteen miles northeast of She-

day, for today the LORD has brought deliverance to Israel."

14 Samuel said to the people, "Come, let us go to Gilgal and there renew the kingship." 15So all the people went to Gilgal, and there they made Saul king before the LORD in Gilgal. There they sacrificed offerings of well-being before the LORD, and there Saul and all the Israelites rejoiced greatly.

Samuel's Farewell Address

12 Samuel said to all Israel, "I have listened to you in all that you have said to me, and have set a king over you. 2See, it is the king who leads you now; I am old and gray, but my sons are with you. I have led you from my youth until this day. 3Here I am; testify against me before the LORD and before his anointed. Whose ox have I taken? Or whose donkey have I taken? Or whom have I defrauded? Whom have I oppressed? Or from whose hand have I taken a bribe to blind my eyes with it? Testify against me[a] and I will restore it to you." 4They said, "You have not defrauded us or oppressed us or taken anything from the hand of anyone." 5He said to them, "The LORD is witness against you, and his anointed is witness this day, that you have not found anything in my hand." And they said, "He is witness."

6 Samuel said to the people, "The LORD is witness, who[b] appointed Moses and Aaron and brought your ancestors up out of the land of Egypt. 7Now therefore take your stand, so that I may enter into judgment with you before the LORD, and I will declare to you[c] all the saving deeds of the LORD that he performed for you and for your ancestors. 8When Jacob went into Egypt and the Egyptians oppressed them,[d] then your ancestors cried to the LORD and the LORD sent Moses and Aaron, who brought forth your ancestors out of Egypt, and settled them in this place. 9But they forgot the LORD their God; and he sold them into the hand of Sisera, commander of the army of King Jabin of[e] Hazor, and into the hand of the Philistines, and into the hand of the king of Moab; and they fought against them. 10Then they cried to the LORD, and said, 'We have sinned, because we have forsaken the LORD, and have served the Baals and the Astartes; but now rescue us out of the hand of our enemies, and we will serve you.' 11And the LORD sent Jerubbaal and Barak,[f] and Jephthah, and Samson,[g] and rescued you out of the hand of your enemies on every side; and you lived in safety. 12But when you saw that King Nahash of the Ammonites came against you, you said to me, 'No, but a king shall reign over us,' though the LORD your God was your king. 13See, here is the king whom you have chosen, for whom you have asked; see, the LORD has set a king over you. 14If you will fear the LORD and serve him and heed his voice and not rebel against the commandment of the LORD, and if both you and the king who reigns over you will fol-

a Gk: Heb lacks Testify against me   b Gk: Heb lacks is witness, who   c Gk: Heb lacks and I will declare to you   d Gk: Heb lacks and the Egyptians oppressed them   e Gk: Heb lacks King Jabin of   f Gk Syr: Heb Bedan   g Gk: Heb Samuel

chem. **11.11** On Saul's strategy of *three companies,* cf. Judg 7; 9, where Gideon and Abimelech employ similar battle plans. **11.14** *Gilgal.* See note on 10.8.

12.1–25 Samuel formally turns responsibility for leading Israel over to Saul. His farewell address is punctuated with a fresh demonstration of his prophetic power (see note on 12.17) and a pledge to continue to perform certain indispensable duties in the future (see note on 12.23). Kingship has now been divinely granted to Israel (v. 13), and Samuel sets forth strict terms by which it might succeed (v. 14). But little reason is given for the people to look forward happily to life under the monarchy. On the contrary, the emphasis is clearly on the benefits they are losing with the departure of the great prophet. Though this account embraces a long Deuteronomistic retrospective on the history of Israel (see note on 12.6–15), in its final form, to which a thematic introduction has been provided (vv. 1–15), it is one of the Mizpah passages (see note on 7.2–17; Introduction). **12.1** See 8.22. Samuel is saying that he has been obedient to his instructions. **12.3–5** Samuel reminds the people that he dispensed justice without corruption. **12.6–15** One of a series of long retrospective speeches inserted in the biblical narrative at crucial junctures to express the views of the Deuteronomistic Historian (cf. Josh 23–24; 1 Kings 8.12–61; see Introduction). **12.6** The appointment of *Moses and Aaron* is described in Ex 2–4. **12.9–11** A review of the events recorded in Judges. **12.9** *Sisera.* See Judg 4–5. The *Philistines* are prominent enemies in Judges (see Judg 3.31; 13–16). Eglon, *the king of Moab,* is the oppressor of Israel in Judg 3.12–30. **12.10** *Baals, Astartes,* illicit or foreign gods and goddesses in general. **12.11** *Jerubbaal,* another name for Gideon (see Judg 6–8). The reference to *Barak,* Deborah's colleague in Judg 4–5, is textually doubtful. *Jephthah,* the Gileadite hero of Judg 11. *Samson.* See Judg 13–16. **12.12** This verse relates the people's demand for a king in 8.1–22 to the threat posed by *King Nahash of the Ammonites* (see 11.1–15), a connection not

low the LORD your God, it will be well; 15but if you will not heed the voice of the LORD, but rebel against the commandment of the LORD, then the hand of the LORD will be against you and your king.*a* 16Now therefore take your stand and see this great thing that the LORD will do before your eyes. 17Is it not the wheat harvest today? I will call upon the LORD, that he may send thunder and rain; and you shall know and see that the wickedness that you have done in the sight of the LORD is great in demanding a king for yourselves." 18So Samuel called upon the LORD, and the LORD sent thunder and rain that day; and all the people greatly feared the LORD and Samuel.

19 All the people said to Samuel, "Pray to the LORD your God for your servants, so that we may not die; for we have added to all our sins the evil of demanding a king for ourselves." 20And Samuel said to the people, "Do not be afraid; you have done all this evil, yet do not turn aside from following the LORD, but serve the LORD with all your heart; 21and do not turn aside after useless things that cannot profit or save, for they are useless. 22For the LORD will not cast away his people, for his great name's sake, because it has pleased the LORD to make you a people for himself. 23Moreover as for me, far be it from me that I should sin against the LORD by ceasing to pray for you; and I will instruct you in the good and the right way. 24Only fear the LORD, and serve him faithfully with all your heart; for consider what great things he has done for you. 25But if you still do wickedly, you shall be swept away, both you and your king."

Saul's Unlawful Sacrifice

13 Saul was . . .*b* years old when he began to reign; and he reigned . . . and two*c* years over Israel.

2 Saul chose three thousand out of Israel; two thousand were with Saul in Michmash and the hill country of Bethel, and a thousand were with Jonathan in Gibeah of Benjamin; the rest of the people he sent home to their tents. 3Jonathan defeated the garrison of the Philistines that was at Geba; and the Philistines heard of it. And Saul blew the trumpet throughout all the land, saying, "Let the Hebrews hear!" 4When all Israel heard that Saul had defeated the garrison of the Philistines, and also that Israel had become odious to the Philistines, the people were called out to join Saul at Gilgal.

5 The Philistines mustered to fight with Israel, thirty thousand chariots, and six thousand horsemen, and troops like the sand on the seashore in multitude; they came up and encamped at Michmash, to the east of Beth-aven. 6When the Israelites saw that they were in distress (for the troops were hard pressed), the people hid themselves in caves and in holes and in rocks and in tombs and in cisterns. 7Some Hebrews crossed the Jordan to the land of Gad and Gilead. Saul was still at Gilgal, and all the people followed him trembling.

8 He waited seven days, the time appointed by Samuel; but Samuel did not come to Gilgal,

---

a Gk: Heb *and your ancestors*   *b* The number is lacking in the Heb text (the verse is lacking in the Septuagint).   *c* *Two* is not the entire number; something has dropped out.

---

made in the larger narrative. **12.17** The *wheat harvest* took place in early summer when *thunder and rain* were unnatural (Prov 26.1) and unexpected, a fact that underscores Samuel's special ability to invoke the Lord. **12.18–19** Shocked out of their refusal to see reality by the miracle of the thunderstorm, the people finally acknowledge their mistake and call on Samuel for help. **12.21** *Useless things,* idols, rendered "empty wind" in Isa 41.29 and "nothing" in Isa 44.9. **12.23** Samuel promises to continue to do two things: *pray for* (better, "intercede on behalf of") the people and instruct them *in the good and the right way.* With the advent of kingship, the prophet's role is twofold: he will be an intercessor between Israel and the Lord and an advocate of morality and justice.

13.1–15a Anxious about the onset of a battle with the Philistines, Saul offers a sacrifice without waiting for Samuel to arrive. For this act of disobedience his kingship is repudiated. **13.1** The same formula intro-

duces the reigns of other kings in the Deuteronomistic History (see, e.g., 2 Sam 2.10; 5.4; 1 Kings 14.21; 22.42), but the historian does not seem to have had the necessary chronological data for Saul's reign. Contemporary biblical scholars tend to place Saul's kingship late in the eleventh century BCE. **13.2** *Michmash,* a town about seven miles northeast of Jerusalem, a few miles southeast of *Bethel* (see 7.16–17). *Gibeah of Benjamin.* See note on 9.1. **13.3** *Geba,* a Benjaminite fortress about six miles north-northeast of Jerusalem. By blowing the trumpet, Saul is trying to rally support from other *Hebrews,* who, though kin to the Israelites, have not yet allied themselves politically (see note on 14.21). **13.4** Saul is now in *Gilgal,* where Samuel told him to wait for him (10.8). **13.5** In his oracles against Bethel (Hebrew, "House of God") Hosea uses the name *Beth-aven* ("House of Wickedness") as a pejorative substitute (Hos 4.15; 5.8; 10.5), and Bethel is probably also intended here. **13.7** The tribal claim of

and the people began to slip away from Saul.[a] 9So Saul said, "Bring the burnt offering here to me, and the offerings of well-being." And he offered the burnt offering. 10As soon as he had finished offering the burnt offering, Samuel arrived; and Saul went out to meet him and salute him. 11Samuel said, "What have you done?" Saul replied, "When I saw that the people were slipping away from me, and that you did not come within the days appointed, and that the Philistines were mustering at Michmash, 12I said, 'Now the Philistines will come down upon me at Gilgal, and I have not entreated the favor of the LORD'; so I forced myself, and offered the burnt offering." 13Samuel said to Saul, "You have done foolishly; you have not kept the commandment of the LORD your God, which he commanded you. The LORD would have established your kingdom over Israel forever, 14but now your kingdom will not continue; the LORD has sought out a man after his own heart; and the LORD has appointed him to be ruler over his people, because you have not kept what the LORD commanded you." 15And Samuel left and went on his way from Gilgal.[b] The rest of the people followed Saul to join the army; they went up from Gilgal toward Gibeah of Benjamin.[c]

Preparations for Battle

Saul counted the people who were present with him, about six hundred men. 16Saul, his son Jonathan, and the people who were present with them stayed in Geba of Benjamin; but the Philistines encamped at Michmash. 17And raiders came out of the camp of the Philistines in three companies; one company turned toward Ophrah, to the land of Shual, 18another company turned toward Beth-horon, and another company turned toward the mountain[d] that looks down upon the valley of Zeboim toward the wilderness.

19 Now there was no smith to be found throughout all the land of Israel; for the Philistines said, "The Hebrews must not make swords or spears for themselves"; 20so all the Israelites went down to the Philistines to sharpen their plowshares, mattocks, axes, or sickles;[e] 21The charge was two-thirds of a shekel[f] for the plowshares and for the mattocks, and one-third of a shekel for sharpening the axes and for setting the goads.[g] 22So on the day of the battle neither sword nor spear was to be found in the possession of any of the people with Saul and Jonathan; but Saul and his son Jonathan had them.

Jonathan Surprises and Routs the Philistines

23 Now a garrison of the Philistines had gone out to the pass of Michmash. 14 1One day Jonathan son of Saul said to the young man who carried his armor, "Come, let us go over to the Philistine garrison on the other side." But he did not tell his father. 2Saul was staying in the outskirts of Gibeah under the pomegranate tree that is at Migron; the troops that were with him were about six hundred

---

a Heb *him*   b Gk: Heb *went up from Gilgal to Gibeah of Benjamin*   c Gk: Heb lacks *The rest . . . of Benjamin*   d Cn Compare Gk: Heb *toward the border*   e Gk: Heb *plowshare*   f Heb *was a pim*   g Cn: Meaning of Heb uncertain

---

Gad included most of modern Jordan north of the Dead Sea (see Josh 13.24–28). All but the southern portion of this was *Gilead*, a common designation for Transjordanian Israel (cf. note on 10.27b). **13.8** Saul waits *seven days, the time appointed by Samuel* in 10.8 (but see 11.1). **13.9** Samuel told Saul that he would make the offerings himself (10.8); but Saul, seeing his army begin to desert (v. 8) and fearful of joining battle without sacrificing first (v. 12), goes ahead without him. **13.13** If not for this act of disobedience, the Lord would have established Saul's *kingdom over Israel forever,* i.e., he would have given Saul an enduring dynasty ("kingdom") like David's (see 2 Sam 7.15–16). **13.14** *A man after his own heart,* i.e., a man of his own choosing, rather than one of Saul's sons. For *ruler,* or "king-designate," see note on 9.16. **13.15b–22** Saul and his army prepare to engage the enemy, despite a shortage of weapons caused by Philistine control of metalworking. **13.16** *Geba* and *Michmash* were only a couple of miles apart (see note on 13.2), separated by a steep ravine, part of a strategically important wadi system that drains the Ephraimite hills into the Jordan. **13.17** *Ophrah* (Josh 18.23) was north of Michmash. *Land of Shual.* See note on 9.4. **13.18** There were two towns named *Beth-horon,* Upper and Lower. Upper Beth-horon was about ten miles west of Michmash. The *valley of Zeboim* (Hebrew, "Valley of Hyenas") was southeast of Michmash. **13.19–22** The Philistines strictly controlled access to metalworking so that the Israelites could not arm themselves. **13.21** *Pim* (see text note *f*) occurs nowhere else in the Hebrew Bible, but it has been found inscribed on ancient stone weights averaging about *two-thirds of a shekel.* **13.23–14.23** With only a single companion Jonathan makes his way into the Philistine camp and starts a panic that leads to a rout of the enemy and a major Israelite victory. **14.2** Geba and *Gibeah* are often confused in the text, and the former is likely to be correct

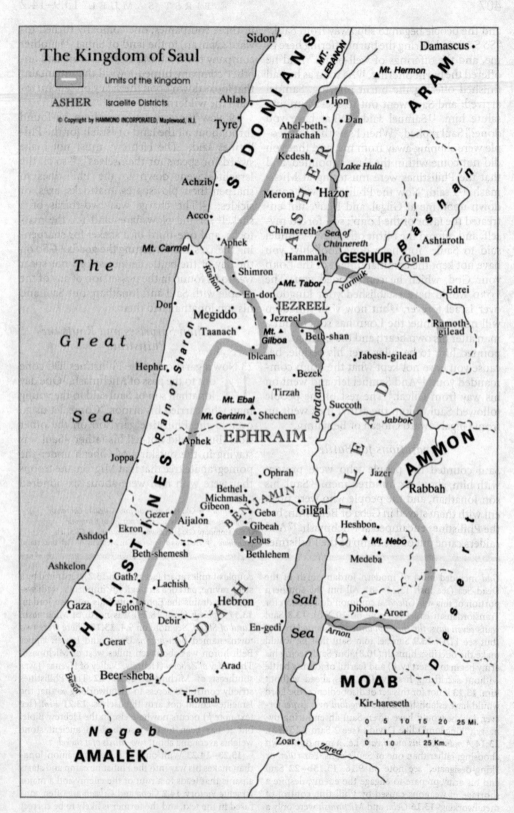

The Kingdom of Saul

— Limits of the Kingdom

ASHER Israelite Districts

© Copyright by HAMMOND INCORPORATED, Maplewood, N.J.

Sidon
Damascus
MT. LEBANON
Mt. Hermon
ARAM
Ahlab
Ijon
SIDONIANS
Dan
Tyre
Abel-beth-maachah
Kedesh
Lake Hula
Achzib
Merom
Hazor
ASHER
Bashan
Acco
Chinnereth
Sea of Chinnereth
Ashtaroth
GESHUR
Golan
Mt. Carmel
Aphek
Hammath
The
Shimron
Kishon
Mt. Tabor
Yarmuk
Edrei
En-dor
JEZREEL
Dor
Megiddo
Jezreel
Ramoth-gilead
Great
Taanach
Mt. Gilboa
Beth-shan
Hepher
Ibleam
Jabesh-gilead
Bezek
Sea
Plain of Sharon
Mt. Ebal
Tirzah
Jordan
Succoth
Mt. Gerizim
Shechem
Jabbok
EPHRAIM
GILEAD
Aphek
AMMON
Joppa
Ophrah
Jazer
Rabbah
Bethel
Michmash
BENJAMIN
Gibeon
Heshbon
Gezer
Geba
Gilgal
Ekron
Aijalon
Gibeah
Mt. Nebo
Ashdod
Jebus
Medeba
Beth-shemesh
Bethlehem
Ashkelon
Gath?
Lachish
Salt
Gaza
Eglon?
Hebron
Sea
Dibon
Aroer
Debir
JUDAH
En-gedi
Arnon
Gerar
Desert
Arad
MOAB
Beer-sheba
Besor
Hormah
Kir-hareseth
Negeb
0 5 10 15 20 25 Mi.
0   10   25 Km.
AMALEK
Zoar
Zered

men, [3]along with Ahijah son of Ahitub, Ichabod's brother, son of Phinehas son of Eli, the priest of the Lord in Shiloh, carrying an ephod. Now the people did not know that Jonathan had gone. [4]In the pass,[a] by which Jonathan tried to go over to the Philistine garrison, there was a rocky crag on one side and a rocky crag on the other; the name of the one was Bozez, and the name of the other Seneh. [5]One crag rose on the north in front of Michmash, and the other on the south in front of Geba.

[6]Jonathan said to the young man who carried his armor, "Come, let us go over to the garrison of these uncircumcised; it may be that the Lord will act for us; for nothing can hinder the Lord from saving by many or by few." [7]His armor-bearer said to him, "Do all that your mind inclines to.[b] I am with you; as your mind is, so is mine."[c] [8]Then Jonathan said, "Now we will cross over to those men and will show ourselves to them. [9]If they say to us, 'Wait until we come to you,' then we will stand still in our place, and we will not go up to them. [10]But if they say, 'Come up to us,' then we will go up; for the Lord has given them into our hand. That will be the sign for us." [11]So both of them showed themselves to the garrison of the Philistines; and the Philistines said, "Look, Hebrews are coming out of the holes where they have hidden themselves." [12]The men of the garrison hailed Jonathan and his armor-bearer, saying, "Come up to us, and we will show you something." Jonathan said to his armor-bearer, "Come up after me; for the Lord has given them into the hand of Israel." [13]Then Jonathan climbed up on his hands and feet, with his armor-bearer following after him. The Philistines[d] fell before Jonathan, and his armor-bearer, coming after him, killed them. [14]In that first slaughter Jonathan and his armor-bearer killed about twenty men

within an area about half a furrow long in an acre[e] of land. [15]There was a panic in the camp, in the field, and among all the people; the garrison and even the raiders trembled; the earth quaked; and it became a very great panic.

[16]Saul's lookouts in Gibeah of Benjamin were watching as the multitude was surging back and forth.[f] [17]Then Saul said to the troops that were with him, "Call the roll and see who has gone from us." When they had called the roll, Jonathan and his armor-bearer were not there. [18]Saul said to Ahijah, "Bring the ark[g] of God here." For at that time the ark[g] of God went with the Israelites. [19]While Saul was talking to the priest, the tumult in the camp of the Philistines increased more and more; and Saul said to the priest, "Withdraw your hand." [20]Then Saul and all the people who were with him rallied and went into the battle; and every sword was against the other, so that there was very great confusion. [21]Now the Hebrews who previously had been with the Philistines and had gone up with them into the camp turned and joined the Israelites who were with Saul and Jonathan. [22]Likewise, when all the Israelites who had gone into hiding in the hill country of Ephraim heard that the Philistines were fleeing, they too followed closely after them in the battle. [23]So the Lord gave Israel the victory that day.

The battle passed beyond Beth-aven, and the troops with Saul numbered altogether about ten thousand men. The battle spread out over the hill country of Ephraim.

Saul's Rash Oath

24 Now Saul committed a very rash act on that day.[h] He had laid an oath on the troops,

---

a Heb *Between the passes*   b Gk: Heb *Do all that is in your mind. Turn*   c Gk: Heb lacks *so is mine*   d Heb *They* e Heb *yoke*   f Gk: Heb *they went and there*   g Gk *the ephod* h Gk: Heb *The Israelites were distressed that day*

---

here. *Migron,* a town associated with Michmash and Geba in Isa 10.28. **14.3** *Ahijah son of Ahitub,* Saul's priest, is one of the Shilonite priests, who are condemned in 2.27–36 and slaughtered in 22.6–23; Ahijah's nephew, Abiathar, is the only survivor. The *ephod,* or priestly garment, that Ahijah is wearing (rather than carrying) is probably more elaborate than Samuel's linen loincloth (see note on 2.18; cf. 22.18). It probably contains a pouch containing the Urim and Thummim used by Saul in v. 41. **14.4** The pass by which Jonathan and his companion cross the deep ravine that separates the two battle camps (see v. 16) is flanked by two outcroppings of rock with names that

suggest that the passage is treacherous, *Bozez* (Hebrew, "Swampy" or "Gleaming") and *Seneh* ("Thorny"). **14.16** *Gibeah,* probably Geba, as in v. 2. **14.18** Better (with the Septuagint), "Saul said to Ahijah, 'Bring the ephod here.' For at that time he wore the ephod before Israel." Saul wants to consult the Urim and Thummim (see note on 14.3) to discover the source of the turmoil in the Philistine camp. **14.21** *Hebrews,* an ethnic, not a political, designation. These Hebrews are people with a recognized kinship to the Israelites who have not yet joined Israel politically (see 13.3). Jonathan's heroism has inspired them to side with their kin. **14.23** *Bethaven,* probably Bethel; see note on 13.5. **14.24–35** Saul

saying, "Cursed be anyone who eats food before it is evening and I have been avenged on my enemies." So none of the troops tasted food. 25All the troops*a* came upon a honeycomb; and there was honey on the ground. 26When the troops came upon the honeycomb, the honey was dripping out; but they did not put their hands to their mouths, for they feared the oath. 27But Jonathan had not heard his father charge the troops with the oath; so he extended the staff that was in his hand, and dipped the tip of it in the honeycomb, and put his hand to his mouth; and his eyes brightened. 28Then one of the soldiers said, "Your father strictly charged the troops with an oath, saying, 'Cursed be anyone who eats food this day.' And so the troops are faint." 29Then Jonathan said, "My father has troubled the land; see how my eyes have brightened because I tasted a little of this honey. 30How much better if today the troops had eaten freely of the spoil taken from their enemies; for now the slaughter among the Philistines has not been great."

31 After they had struck down the Philistines that day from Michmash to Aijalon, the troops were very faint; 32so the troops flew upon the spoil, and took sheep and oxen and calves, and slaughtered them on the ground; and the troops ate them with the blood. 33Then it was reported to Saul, "Look, the troops are sinning against the LORD by eating with the blood." And he said, "You have dealt treacherously; roll a large stone before me here."*b* 34Saul said, "Disperse yourselves among the troops, and say to them, 'Let all bring their oxen or their sheep, and slaughter them here, and eat; and do not sin against the LORD by eating with the blood.' " So all of the troops brought their oxen with them that night, and slaughtered them there. 35And Saul built an altar to the LORD; it was the first altar that he built to the LORD.

Jonathan in Danger of Death

36 Then Saul said, "Let us go down after the Philistines by night and despoil them until the morning light; let us not leave one of them." They said, "Do whatever seems good to you." But the priest said, "Let us draw near to God here." 37So Saul inquired of God, "Shall I go down after the Philistines? Will you give them into the hand of Israel?" But he did not answer him that day. 38Saul said, "Come here, all you leaders of the people; and let us find out how this sin has arisen today. 39For as the LORD lives who saves Israel, even if it is in my son Jonathan, he shall surely die!" But there was no one among all the people who answered him. 40He said to all Israel, "You shall be on one side, and I and my son Jonathan will be on the other side." The people said to Saul, "Do what seems good to you." 41Then Saul said, "O LORD God of Israel, why have you not answered your servant today? If this guilt is in me or in my son Jonathan, O LORD God of Israel, give Urim; but if this guilt is in your people Israel,*c* give Thummim." And Jonathan and Saul were indicated by the lot, but the people were cleared. 42Then Saul said, "Cast the lot between me and my son Jonathan." And Jonathan was taken.

43 Then Saul said to Jonathan, "Tell me what you have done." Jonathan told him, "I tasted a little honey with the tip of the staff

---

a Heb *land*   *b* Gk: Heb *me this day*   *c* Vg Compare Gk: Heb 41*Saul said to the* LORD, *the God of Israel*

---

impetuously makes an oath condemning anyone who eats before sundown, and Jonathan, who knows nothing of the oath, eats honey and finds himself in mortal danger. **14.27** *His eyes brightened.* Jonathan was refreshed or invigorated (see, e.g., Ezra 9.8). **14.31–35** This episode, which blurs the main story's focus on Jonathan, may have originated as an independent tradition about Saul's *first altar* (v. 35). **14.31** *Aijalon* was a few miles southwest of Beth-horon, so that the direction of the rout was to the west (see 13.18) toward Philistine territory. **14.32** When victory is assured, Saul's oath is no longer in effect, and the famished troops slaughter captured livestock for food; but they sin by eating the meat *with the blood,* which was reserved for the deity, thereby violating the prohibition recorded in Lev 19.26; Deut 12.23–27. **14.33–** **34** Slaughtering the livestock on the *large stone,* rather than the ground (v. 32), will permit the blood to drain. **14.36–46** Jonathan's violation of Saul's oath is discovered by casting lots. Saul condemns his son to death, but the people intervene and ransom Jonathan. **14.38** Saul assumes, correctly, that the failure of the divination attempted in v. 37 was a result of some *sin,* but he does not yet know that Jonathan has violated his oath. **14.40–42** As in the lottery that selected Saul king (10.20–21), the lots are cast repeatedly until a particular individual is identified. **14.41** *Urim* and *Thummim,* the names of the objects cast in the lottery, probably dice or something similar inscribed with the first letter of each name, *'aleph* and *taw,* the first and last letters of the Hebrew alphabet. The meanings of the names, "cursed" (i.e., condemned) and "accounted

that was in my hand; here I am, I will die."
⁴⁴Saul said, "God do so to me and more also;
you shall surely die, Jonathan!" ⁴⁵Then the
people said to Saul, "Shall Jonathan die, who
has accomplished this great victory in Israel?
Far from it! As the LORD lives, not one hair of
his head shall fall to the ground; for he has
worked with God today." So the people ransomed Jonathan, and he did not die. ⁴⁶Then
Saul withdrew from pursuing the Philistines;
and the Philistines went to their own place.

Saul's Continuing Wars

47 When Saul had taken the kingship over Israel, he fought against all his enemies on every
side—against Moab, against the Ammonites,
against Edom, against the kings of Zobah, and
against the Philistines; wherever he turned he
routed them. ⁴⁸He did valiantly, and struck
down the Amalekites, and rescued Israel out
of the hands of those who plundered them.

49 Now the sons of Saul were Jonathan,
Ishvi, and Malchishua; and the names of his
two daughters were these: the name of the
firstborn was Merab, and the name of the
younger, Michal. ⁵⁰The name of Saul's wife
was Ahinoam daughter of Ahimaaz. And the
name of the commander of his army was
Abner son of Ner, Saul's uncle; ⁵¹Kish was the
father of Saul, and Ner the father of Abner was
the son of Abiel.

52 There was hard fighting against the Phi-

listines all the days of Saul; and when Saul saw
any strong or valiant warrior, he took him into
his service.

Saul Defeats the Amalekites but Spares Their King

15 Samuel said to Saul, "The LORD sent
me to anoint you king over his people
Israel; now therefore listen to the words of the
LORD. ²Thus says the LORD of hosts, 'I will
punish the Amalekites for what they did in opposing the Israelites when they came up out of
Egypt. ³Now go and attack Amalek, and utterly destroy all that they have; do not spare
them, but kill both man and woman, child and
infant, ox and sheep, camel and donkey.' "

4 So Saul summoned the people, and numbered them in Telaim, two hundred thousand
foot soldiers, and ten thousand soldiers of
Judah. ⁵Saul came to the city of the Amalekites
and lay in wait in the valley. ⁶Saul said to the
Kenites, "Go! Leave! Withdraw from among
the Amalekites, or I will destroy you with
them; for you showed kindness to all the people of Israel when they came up out of Egypt."
So the Kenites withdrew from the Amalekites.
⁷Saul defeated the Amalekites, from Havilah
as far as Shur, which is east of Egypt. ⁸He took
King Agag of the Amalekites alive, but utterly
destroyed all the people with the edge of the
sword. ⁹Saul and the people spared Agag, and
the best of the sheep and of the cattle and of

---

whole" (i.e., acquitted), refer to the possible outcomes
of each cast. **14.47–52** A miscellany of notes regarding
Saul's reign. **14.47** Moab, the Ammonites, Edom, Israel's neighbors east of the Jordan and the Dead Sea.
Zobah, an Aramean kingdom on the western slope of
the Anti-Lebanon mountain range north of Israel,
against which David fights a war in 2 Sam 8.3–12;
10.6–8. **14.48** Did valiantly implies that Saul acquired
territorial gains, restoring lands lost in previous wars
and extending Israel's borders. His victory over the
Amalekites is described in the next chapter in less com-
plimentary terms. **14.49** Of the sons of Saul listed here
only Jonathan has a role in the biblical narrative. Ishvi,
however, may be the same as Ishbaal, Saul's successor
(see 2 Sam 2.8); the list of Saul's sons who died with
him on Mount Gilboa does not mention Ishvi and
adds another name, Abinadab (1 Sam 31.2). For Merab
and Michal, see 18.17–30. **14.50** Ahinoam daughter of
Ahimaaz, mentioned nowhere else. Abner remained
Saul's chief military officer throughout his reign and
set Ishbaal on the throne after Saul's death (2 Sam 2.8).
14.51 Abiel, Kish's father (9.1). Cf. 1 Chr 8.33; 9.39.
15.1–9 Saul is called upon to avenge an ancient
grievance against the Amalekites. **15.2** Amalekites, a

nomadic tribe who lived in the desert south of Judah.
Saul is told to avenge their attack on the Israelites at
the oasis of Rephidim during the journey from Egypt
to Canaan (Ex 17.8–13). At the time the Lord swore to
blot out their memory completely and Moses vowed
continual war with them (Ex 17.14–16). **15.3** The
rules of Israel's holy war required that everything captured in battle be consecrated to the Lord. This meant
that the soldiers could not take spoils and that any person or animal captured alive had to be put to death
(see Deut 20.10–18). Though this fate was normally
reserved for enemies living within the promised land,
the Amalekites are subject to a special directive (see
Deut 25.17–19). **15.4** Telaim, probably another name
for Telem, a town in the extreme southern portion of
Judah (see Josh 15.24). **15.5** It is surprising that there
should be a city of the Amalekites, who were camel-rid-
ing nomads. **15.6** Kenites, desert-dwelling, nomadic
metalworkers or smiths who had settled among the
Amalekites (see Judg 1.16). **15.7** From Havilah . . .
Egypt, perhaps influenced by Gen 25.18. Havilah,
which was somewhere on the western edge of the Arabian Peninsula, seems out of place. The wilderness of
Shur lay northeast of Egypt. **15.9** Agag, known only

the fatlings, and the lambs, and all that was valuable, and would not utterly destroy them; all that was despised and worthless they utterly destroyed.

Saul Rejected as King

10 The word of the LORD came to Samuel: 11"I regret that I made Saul king, for he has turned back from following me, and has not carried out my commands." Samuel was angry; and he cried out to the LORD all night. 12Samuel rose early in the morning to meet Saul, and Samuel was told, "Saul went to Carmel, where he set up a monument for himself, and on returning he passed on down to Gilgal." 13When Samuel came to Saul, Saul said to him, "May you be blessed by the LORD; I have carried out the command of the LORD." 14But Samuel said, "What then is this bleating of sheep in my ears, and the lowing of cattle that I hear?" 15Saul said, "They have brought them from the Amalekites; for the people spared the best of the sheep and the cattle, to sacrifice to the LORD your God; but the rest we have utterly destroyed." 16Then Samuel said to Saul, "Stop! I will tell you what the LORD said to me last night." He replied, "Speak."

17 Samuel said, "Though you are little in your own eyes, are you not the head of the tribes of Israel? The LORD anointed you king over Israel. 18And the LORD sent you on a mission, and said, 'Go, utterly destroy the sinners, the Amalekites, and fight against them until they are consumed.' 19Why then did you not obey the voice of the LORD? Why did you swoop down on the spoil, and do what was evil in the sight of the LORD?" 20Saul said to Samuel, "I have obeyed the voice of the LORD, I have gone on the mission on which the LORD sent me, I have brought Agag the king of Ama-lek, and I have utterly destroyed the Amalek-ites. 21But from the spoil the people took sheep and cattle, the best of the things devoted to destruction, to sacrifice to the LORD your God in Gilgal." 22And Samuel said,

"Has the LORD as great delight in burnt
offerings and sacrifices,
as in obedience to the voice of the
LORD?
Surely, to obey is better than sacrifice,
and to heed than the fat of rams.
23 For rebellion is no less a sin than
divination,
and stubbornness is like iniquity and
idolatry.
Because you have rejected the word of the
LORD,
he has also rejected you from being
king."

24 Saul said to Samuel, "I have sinned; for I have transgressed the commandment of the LORD and your words, because I feared the people and obeyed their voice. 25Now therefore, I pray, pardon my sin, and return with me, so that I may worship the LORD." 26Samuel said to Saul, "I will not return with you; for you have rejected the word of the LORD, and the LORD has rejected you from being king over Israel." 27As Samuel turned to go away, Saul caught hold of the hem of his robe, and it tore. 28And Samuel said to him, "The LORD has torn the kingdom of Israel from you this very day, and has given it to a neighbor of yours, who is better than you. 29Moreover the Glory of Israel will not recant[a] or change his mind; for he is not a mortal, that he should change his mind." 30Then Saul[b] said, "I have sinned; yet honor me now before the elders of

---

a Q Ms Gk: MT *deceive*   *b* Heb *he*

---

from this episode, but Num 24.7 suggests that he was a famous enough king to be a standard of comparison. **15.10–34** By violating the ban on leaving any of the Amalekites alive (see note on 15.3), Saul incurs the anger of the Lord, who rejects him as king. **15.12** *Carmel*, about seven miles south of Hebron (Josh 15.55), is the village where David meets his wife Abigail (see 1 Sam 25.2–42). **15.15** Saul defends himself by claiming that the animals were spared so that they could be sacrificed to the Lord. **15.22–23** Samuel's poetic censure of Saul is reminiscent of the oracles against empty religious practice that abound in the prophetic writings (see, e.g., Isa 66.2b–4; Hos 6.6; Am 5.21–24; Mic 6.6–8). **15.23** *Divination*, here foreign practices (Num 22.7) and false prophecy (Jer 14.14), not the permitted form utilizing the Urim and Thummim (see note on 14.41). *Idolatry,* Hebrew *terapim* (English *teraphim* in 19.13, 16, text notes *b, d*), here idol worship in general. **15.27** Grasping the *hem* of a *robe* is a traditional gesture of supplication widespread in the ancient Near East. **15.28** Samuel turns the accidental tear into a symbolic prophetic act. The prophet Ahijah denounces Jeroboam with a similar gesture in 1 Kings 11.29–32. **15.29** Cf. Num 23.19, but also cf. 1 Sam 15.35; Jon 3.9–10. **15.30–31** These verses seem to represent an alternative ending to the episode. Samuel is now willing to return with Saul without question or comment after angrily refusing to do so in vv. 24–29.

my people and before Israel, and return with me, so that I may worship the LORD your God." [31] So Samuel turned back after Saul; and Saul worshiped the LORD.

32 Then Samuel said, "Bring Agag king of the Amalekites here to me." And Agag came to him haltingly.[a] Agag said, "Surely this is the bitterness of death."[b] [33] But Samuel said,

"As your sword has made women
    childless,
  so your mother shall be childless
    among women."

And Samuel hewed Agag in pieces before the LORD in Gilgal.

34 Then Samuel went to Ramah; and Saul went up to his house in Gibeah of Saul. [35] Samuel did not see Saul again until the day of his death, but Samuel grieved over Saul. And the LORD was sorry that he had made Saul king over Israel.

David Anointed as King

16 The LORD said to Samuel, "How long will you grieve over Saul? I have rejected him from being king over Israel. Fill your horn with oil and set out; I will send you to Jesse the Bethlehemite, for I have provided for myself a king among his sons." [2] Samuel said, "How can I go? If Saul hears of it, he will kill me." And the LORD said, "Take a heifer with you, and say, 'I have come to sacrifice to the LORD.' [3] Invite Jesse to the sacrifice, and I will show you what you shall do; and you shall anoint for me the one whom I name to you." [4] Samuel did what the LORD commanded, and came to Bethlehem. The elders of the city came to meet him trembling, and said, "Do you come peaceably?" [5] He said, "Peaceably; I have come to sacrifice to the LORD; sanctify yourselves and come with me to the sacrifice." And he sanctified Jesse and his sons and invited them to the sacrifice.

6 When they came, he looked on Eliab and thought, "Surely the LORD's anointed is now before the LORD."[c] [7] But the LORD said to Samuel, "Do not look on his appearance or on the height of his stature, because I have rejected him; for the LORD does not see as mortals see; they look on the outward appearance, but the LORD looks on the heart." [8] Then Jesse called Abinadab, and made him pass before Samuel. He said, "Neither has the LORD chosen this one." [9] Then Jesse made Shammah pass by. And he said, "Neither has the LORD chosen this one." [10] Jesse made seven of his sons pass before Samuel, and Samuel said to Jesse, "The LORD has not chosen any of these." [11] Samuel said to Jesse, "Are all your sons here?" And he said, "There remains yet the youngest, but he is keeping the sheep." And Samuel said to Jesse, "Send and bring him; for we will not sit down until he comes here." [12] He sent and brought him in. Now he was ruddy, and had beautiful eyes, and was handsome. The LORD said, "Rise and anoint him; for this is the one." [13] Then Samuel took the horn of oil, and anointed him in the presence of his brothers; and the spirit of the LORD came mightily upon David from that day forward. Samuel then set out and went to Ramah.

David Plays the Lyre for Saul

14 Now the spirit of the LORD departed from Saul, and an evil spirit from the LORD tormented him. [15] And Saul's servants said to

---

a Cn Compare Gk: Meaning of Heb uncertain *b* Q Ms Gk: MT *Surely the bitterness of death is past* *c* Heb *him*

15.32 *Haltingly,* obscure, more likely "in chains" (see Job 38.31). *Samuel hewed Agag in pieces before the LORD.* The execution is a ritual dismemberment of the kind associated with covenant violations (see 11.7).

15.35–16.13 Samuel is sent to Bethlehem to anoint a new king. **16.1** *Fill your horn with oil,* in preparation for anointing a new king (v. 13); see 9.16; 10.1; for the horn, see 1 Kings 1.39. *Jesse,* a member of the tribe of Judah and the clan of Perez (Ruth 4.12, 17–22; 1 Chr 2.3–12), was the grandson of Ruth and Boaz. As a *Bethlehemite,* he lived in Judah about six miles south of Jerusalem. **16.6** Samuel mistakenly assumes that *Eliab,* Jesse's firstborn (1 Chr 2.13), is the LORD's *anointed,* i.e., the *mashiach* (Hebrew, "anointed one" or "messiah") of the Lord. **16.8** *Abinadab,* Jesse's second son (1 Chr 2.13). **16.9** *Shammah* (also 17.13),

elsewhere called Shimeah (2 Sam 13.3, 32), Shimei (2 Sam 21.21), and Shimea (1 Chr 2.13; 20.7). **16.10** Jesse shows Samuel *seven of his sons* before mentioning David, and 17.12 indicates that he had eight sons. According to 1 Chr 2.13–15, however, David was the seventh of seven sons, and the motif of the seventh son who surpasses his brothers is widespread in world folklore. **16.11** *Sit down,* probably to eat the part of the sacrifice (v. 5; cf. 9.13) not reserved for the Lord (see Sir 32.1). **16.13** *The spirit of the LORD* possesses David as it did Saul (see 10.6; 11.6). **16.14–23** David is summoned to court as a musician. **16.14** *The spirit of the LORD* that empowered Saul to prophesy and rule (see 10.6; 11.6) is now replaced by *an evil spirit from the LORD* that will torment him. **16.15** *Saul's servants,* the ranking members of his

him, "See now, an evil spirit from God is tormenting you. 16Let our lord now command the servants who attend you to look for someone who is skillful in playing the lyre; and when the evil spirit from God is upon you, he will play it, and you will feel better." 17So Saul said to his servants, "Provide for me someone who can play well, and bring him to me." 18One of the young men answered, "I have seen a son of Jesse the Bethlehemite who is skillful in playing, a man of valor, a warrior, prudent in speech, and a man of good presence; and the LORD is with him." 19So Saul sent messengers to Jesse, and said, "Send me your son David who is with the sheep." 20Jesse took a donkey loaded with bread, a skin of wine, and a kid, and sent them by his son David to Saul. 21And David came to Saul, and entered his service. Saul loved him greatly, and he became his armor-bearer. 22Saul sent to Jesse, saying, "Let David remain in my service, for he has found favor in my sight." 23And whenever the evil spirit from God came upon Saul, David took the lyre and played it with his hand, and Saul would be relieved and feel better, and the evil spirit would depart from him.

David and Goliath

17 Now the Philistines gathered their armies for battle; they were gathered at

Socoh, which belongs to Judah, and encamped between Socoh and Azekah, in Ephes-dammim. 2Saul and the Israelites gathered and encamped in the valley of Elah, and formed ranks against the Philistines. 3The Philistines stood on the mountain on the one side, and Israel stood on the mountain on the other side, with a valley between them. 4And there came out from the camp of the Philistines a champion named Goliath, of Gath, whose height was six*a* cubits and a span. 5He had a helmet of bronze on his head, and he was armed with a coat of mail; the weight of the coat was five thousand shekels of bronze. 6He had greaves of bronze on his legs and a javelin of bronze slung between his shoulders. 7The shaft of his spear was like a weaver's beam, and his spear's head weighed six hundred shekels of iron; and his shield-bearer went before him. 8He stood and shouted to the ranks of Israel, "Why have you come out to draw up for battle? Am I not a Philistine, and are you not servants of Saul? Choose a man for yourselves, and let him come down to me. 9If he is able to fight with me and kill me, then we will be your servants; but if I prevail against him and kill him, then you shall be our servants and serve us." 10And the Philistine said, "Today I defy the

_a_ MT: Q Ms Gk _four_

---

court. **16.16** The notion that music can tame or banish evil spirits is widespread in world folklore. **16.18** In the tradition underlying the old story of David's rise to power (see Introduction), David was a _warrior_ when he came to Saul's court, not an inexperienced shepherd boy as in the later account that follows (see 17.33, 39). Whatever personal assets David has, however, none is as important as the fact that _the_ LORD _is with him,_ a theme echoed throughout the older narrative (see note on 18.14). **16.21–22** Though subsequent events will poison their relationship, David at first inspires affection and patronage in Saul.

17.1–58 The familiar story of David and Goliath is actually a composite of two accounts of David's victory over a Philistine champion. The first account roughly corresponds to vv. 1–11, 32–54, while the second, which was added late enough to be completely missing from the oldest Greek manuscripts, is contained within vv. 12–31, 55–58 and portions of ch. 18. **17.1** _Socoh,_ a small town in the hills about fourteen miles west of Bethlehem; Israel regarded it as a part of Judah (Josh 15.35), but because of its border location it was disputed with Philistia (see 2 Chr 11.7; 28.18). _Azekah,_ a fortress a few miles northwest of Socoh that guarded the main road across the valley of Elah (v. 2). _Ephes-dammim,_ called Pas-dammim in 1 Chr 11.13,

was probably about four miles northeast of Socoh. **17.2** _Valley of Elah,_ one of the principal wadis, the next south of Sorek (see note on 6.9), in the western watershed of the Judean hills. **17.4** _Champion,_ rendered "infantryman" in the Qumran _War Scroll_ (1QM). The name _Goliath_ is at home in Anatolia, one of the places from which the Philistines and other Sea Peoples came; it occurs only here in the older version of David's fight with the Philistine champion, and it may have been borrowed from 2 Sam 21.19, where the slayer of Goliath the Gittite is not David, but Elhanan, one of his heroes. The Masoretic Text's _six cubits and a span_ make the Philistine champion almost 10 feet tall! According to the Septuagint and a scroll from Qumran (4QSam^a), which probably preserve a superior reading here, he was "four cubits and a span," or about 6 feet, 9 inches tall—a true giant but not a fairy-tale monster. **17.5–6** The description of the Philistine's armor prepares readers for v. 49 by showing that he had no vulnerable spot except his forehead. **17.6** _Javelin_ (Hebrew _kidon_), more likely a curved and flat-bladed sword or scimitar (see v. 51). **17.7** _Like a weaver's beam_ derives from 2 Sam 21.19; it probably means that the spear had a thong attached to a ring, similar to the rod and ring of a weaver's heddle, by which the spear could be slung in battle. The spearhead is _iron,_ a metal harder

ranks of Israel! Give me a man, that we may fight together." [11]When Saul and all Israel heard these words of the Philistine, they were dismayed and greatly afraid.

12 Now David was the son of an Ephrathite of Bethlehem in Judah, named Jesse, who had eight sons. In the days of Saul the man was already old and advanced in years.[a] [13]The three eldest sons of Jesse had followed Saul to the battle; the names of his three sons who went to the battle were Eliab the firstborn, and next to him Abinadab, and the third Shammah. [14]David was the youngest; the three eldest followed Saul, [15]but David went back and forth from Saul to feed his father's sheep at Bethlehem. [16]For forty days the Philistine came forward and took his stand, morning and evening.

17 Jesse said to his son David, "Take for your brothers an ephah of this parched grain and these ten loaves, and carry them quickly to the camp to your brothers; [18]also take these ten cheeses to the commander of their thousand. See how your brothers fare, and bring some token from them."

19 Now Saul, and they, and all the men of Israel, were in the valley of Elah, fighting with the Philistines. [20]David rose early in the morning, left the sheep with a keeper, took the provisions, and went as Jesse had commanded him. He came to the encampment as the army was going forth to the battle line, shouting the war cry. [21]Israel and the Philistines drew up for battle, army against army. [22]David left the things in charge of the keeper of the baggage, ran to the ranks, and went and greeted his brothers. [23]As he talked with them, the champion, the Philistine of Gath, Goliath by name, came up out of the ranks of the Philistines, and spoke the same words as before. And David heard him.

24 All the Israelites, when they saw the man, fled from him and were very much afraid. [25]The Israelites said, "Have you seen this man who has come up? Surely he has come up to defy Israel. The king will greatly enrich the man who kills him, and will give him his daughter and make his family free in Israel." [26]David said to the men who stood by him, "What shall be done for the man who kills this Philistine, and takes away the reproach from Israel? For who is this uncircumcised Philistine that he should defy the armies of the living God?" [27]The people answered him in the same way, "So shall it be done for the man who kills him."

28 His eldest brother Eliab heard him talking to the men; and Eliab's anger was kindled against David. He said, "Why have you come down? With whom have you left those few sheep in the wilderness? I know your presumption and the evil of your heart; for you have come down just to see the battle." [29]David said, "What have I done now? It was only a question." [30]He turned away from him toward another and spoke in the same way; and the people answered him again as before.

31 When the words that David spoke were heard, they repeated them before Saul; and he sent for him. [32]David said to Saul, "Let no one's heart fail because of him; your servant will go and fight with this Philistine." [33]Saul said to David, "You are not able to go against this Philistine to fight with him; for you are just a boy, and he has been a warrior from his youth." [34]But David said to Saul, "Your servant used to keep sheep for his father; and whenever a lion or a bear came, and took a lamb from the flock, [35]I went after it and struck it down, rescuing the lamb from its mouth; and

a Gk Syr: Heb among men

than bronze that was available because of new metalworking techniques being introduced in the region at the time; according to biblical tradition, the Philistines carefully controlled the new technology (see 13.19–22). **17.12** The beginning of the second version of the story, which has been combined with the first by an editor (see note on 17.1–58). Jesse and his sons are introduced as if for the first time (see 16.1–13). Jesse was an *Ephrathite*, a member of a clan that settled in Benjamin near Kiriath-jearim (see 10.2) and in Judah near Bethlehem. **17.25** On the promise of marriage to Saul's *daughter*, see 18.17–30. *Free in Israel*, probably exempt from taxation and the obligations of palace service because of a brave deed at arms. **17.26** David's remarks in this verse, still part of the secondarily added alternate version of the story, seem influenced by the language of v. 36, which belongs to the primary version (see note on 17.1–58). In both verses David refers to the Lord as *the living God,* an epithet that stresses the reality and power of the God of Israel (see Jer 10.10) while implying that anyone who would challenge the authority of the Lord will fail (see 2 Kings 19.4, 16; Isa 37.4, 17; Jer 23.36). **17.33–37** Saul argues that David is unfit to take on the Philistine champion because he is *just a boy.* David's rejoinder is that his experience as a shepherd with lions and bears

if it turned against me, I would catch it by the jaw, strike it down, and kill it. 36 Your servant has killed both lions and bears; and this uncircumcised Philistine shall be like one of them, since he has defied the armies of the living God." 37 David said, "The LORD, who saved me from the paw of the lion and from the paw of the bear, will save me from the hand of this Philistine." So Saul said to David, "Go, and may the LORD be with you!"

38 Saul clothed David with his armor; he put a bronze helmet on his head and clothed him with a coat of mail. 39 David strapped Saul's sword over the armor, and he tried in vain to walk, for he was not used to them. Then David said to Saul, "I cannot walk with these; for I am not used to them." So David removed them. 40 Then he took his staff in his hand, and chose five smooth stones from the wadi, and put them in his shepherd's bag, in the pouch; his sling was in his hand, and he drew near to the Philistine.

41 The Philistine came on and drew near to David, with his shield-bearer in front of him. 42 When the Philistine looked and saw David, he disdained him, for he was only a youth, ruddy and handsome in appearance. 43 The Philistine said to David, "Am I a dog, that you come to me with sticks?" And the Philistine cursed David by his gods. 44 The Philistine said to David, "Come to me, and I will give your flesh to the birds of the air and to the wild animals of the field." 45 But David said to the Philistine, "You come to me with sword and spear and javelin; but I come to you in the name of the LORD of hosts, the God of the armies of Israel, whom you have defied. 46 This very day the LORD will deliver you into my hand, and I will strike you down and cut off your head; and I will give the dead bodies of the Philistine army this very day to the birds of the air and to the wild animals of the earth, so that all the earth may know that there is a God in Israel, 47 and that all this assembly may know that the LORD does not save by sword and spear; for the battle is the LORD's and he will give you into our hand."

48 When the Philistine drew nearer to meet David, David ran quickly toward the battle line to meet the Philistine. 49 David put his hand in his bag, took out a stone, slung it, and struck the Philistine on his forehead; the stone sank into his forehead, and he fell face down on the ground.

50 So David prevailed over the Philistine with a sling and a stone, striking down the Philistine and killing him; there was no sword in David's hand. 51 Then David ran and stood over the Philistine; he grasped his sword, drew it out of its sheath, and killed him; then he cut off his head with it.

When the Philistines saw that their champion was dead, they fled. 52 The troops of Israel and Judah rose up with a shout and pursued the Philistines as far as Gath *a* and the gates of Ekron, so that the wounded Philistines fell on the way from Shaaraim as far as Gath and Ekron. 53 The Israelites came back from chasing the Philistines, and they plundered their camp. 54 David took the head of the Philistine and brought it to Jerusalem; but he put his armor in his tent.

55 When Saul saw David go out against the Philistine, he said to Abner, the commander of the army, "Abner, whose son is this young man?" Abner said, "As your soul lives, O king, I do not know." 56 The king said, "Inquire whose son the stripling is." 57 On David's return from killing the Philistine, Abner took him and brought him before Saul, with the head of the Philistine in his hand. 58 Saul said to him, "Whose son are you, young man?" And David

a Gk Syr: Heb *Gai*

---

has prepared him to deal with the Philistine. **17.38–39** Saul lends David his own armor, but when fully dressed, David, who is depicted in this episode as a shepherd without military training, is unable to walk. **17.40** David chooses *his staff* and *his sling*, the weapons he is comfortable with. The *wadi* that provides the sling stones is the valley (i.e., wadi) of Elah of v. 2. **17.42** *Ruddy and handsome in appearance*, out of place here, was probably added by a scribe who was remembering 16.12. **17.44–45** The Philistine expresses contempt for David's rude weapons, but David's retort expresses the true contrast between the two champions (see v. 47). The Philistine relies on *sword and spear and javelin*, ordinary weapons, but David is armed with the *name of the LORD*, drawing upon the spiritual power of the God of Israel. **17.52** *Shaaraim*, a town in Judah (Josh 15.36) near Socoh and Azekah (see note on 17.1); it apparently lay to the west in the direction of *Gath and Ekron* (see 5.8, 10). **17.54** The mention of *Jerusalem* is surprising, since it did not become an Israelite city until after David became king (see 2 Sam 5.6–9). Although David puts Goliath's *armor in his tent*, he acquires his sword at the shrine of Nob in 21.9. **17.55** *Abner*. See note on 14.50.

answered, "I am the son of your servant Jesse the Bethlehemite."

Jonathan's Covenant with David

18 When David[a] had finished speaking to Saul, the soul of Jonathan was bound to the soul of David, and Jonathan loved him as his own soul. 2Saul took him that day and would not let him return to his father's house. 3Then Jonathan made a covenant with David, because he loved him as his own soul. 4Jonathan stripped himself of the robe that he was wearing, and gave it to David, and his armor, and even his sword and his bow and his belt. 5David went out and was successful wherever Saul sent him; as a result, Saul set him over the army. And all the people, even the servants of Saul, approved.

6 As they were coming home, when David returned from killing the Philistine, the women came out of all the towns of Israel, singing and dancing, to meet King Saul, with tambourines, with songs of joy, and with musical instruments.[b] 7And the women sang to one another as they made merry,

"Saul has killed his thousands,
    and David his ten thousands."

8Saul was very angry, for this saying displeased him. He said, "They have ascribed to David ten thousands, and to me they have ascribed thousands; what more can he have but the kingdom?" 9So Saul eyed David from that day on.

Saul Tries to Kill David

10 The next day an evil spirit from God rushed upon Saul, and he raved within his house, while David was playing the lyre, as he did day by day. Saul had his spear in his hand;

11and Saul threw the spear, for he thought, "I will pin David to the wall." But David eluded him twice.

12 Saul was afraid of David, because the LORD was with him but had departed from Saul. 13So Saul removed him from his presence, and made him a commander of a thousand; and David marched out and came in, leading the army. 14David had success in all his undertakings; for the LORD was with him. 15When Saul saw that he had great success, he stood in awe of him. 16But all Israel and Judah loved David; for it was he who marched out and came in leading them.

David Marries Michal

17 Then Saul said to David, "Here is my elder daughter Merab; I will give her to you as a wife; only be valiant for me and fight the LORD's battles." For Saul thought, "I will not raise a hand against him; let the Philistines deal with him." 18David said to Saul, "Who am I and who are my kinsfolk, my father's family in Israel, that I should be son-in-law to the king?" 19But at the time when Saul's daughter Merab should have been given to David, she was given to Adriel the Meholathite as a wife.

20 Now Saul's daughter Michal loved David. Saul was told, and the thing pleased him. 21Saul thought, "Let me give her to him that she may be a snare for him and that the hand of the Philistines may be against him." Therefore Saul said to David a second time,[c] "You shall now be my son-in-law." 22Saul commanded his servants, "Speak to David in private and say, 'See, the king is delighted with

---

a Heb *he*   b Or *triangles,* or *three-stringed instruments*
c Heb *by two*

18.1–9 David receives Jonathan's loyalty, and as David's success on the battlefield grows, Saul begins to look on him with suspicion. **18.1** *Soul . . . bound to . . . soul,* inseparable devotion, like that of Jacob for his son Benjamin (see Gen 44.30–31). For the political overtones of Jonathan's loving David *as his own soul* (also v. 3), see note on 20.17. **18.3** Jonathan and David enter into a *covenant,* a formal agreement of friendship and mutual loyalty. **18.4** It has been suggested that by giving David his *robe* and other apparel Jonathan is formally transferring his claim on Saul's throne to David. **18.6–9** Saul's jealousy of David begins when David's military exploits become the subject of public celebration. **18.10–16** Saul takes measures to rid himself of David. **18.10–11** This episode is not in the Septuagint; it may have been added in anticipation of 19.9–10. For

the *evil spirit from God,* see 16.14–15. **18.14** Here and throughout the old story of his rise to power (see Introduction) David's extraordinary success is attributed to the fact that *the* LORD *was with him* (see v. 13; 16.18; 17.37; 18.28–29a; 2 Sam 5.10). See also note on 16.18. **18.16** Saul's attempt to protect himself against David's growing popularity by sending him to war (v. 13) proves counterproductive; as a military leader David earns the loyalty of *all Israel and Judah.* **18.17–30** In 17.25 Saul's daughter was promised to the man who slew the Philistine champion. In this section, however, each of Saul's daughters is offered to David as a ruse to get him slain by the Philistines. **18.17** *Merab,* introduced in 14.49. **18.19** *Adriel the Meholathite* was from the town of Abel-meholah, which was east of the Jordan not far from Jabesh-gilead (see 10.27).

you, and all his servants love you; now then, become the king's son-in-law.' " 23 So Saul's servants reported these words to David in private. And David said, "Does it seem to you a little thing to become the king's son-in-law, seeing that I am a poor man and of no repute?" 24 The servants of Saul told him, "This is what David said." 25 Then Saul said, "Thus shall you say to David, 'The king desires no marriage present except a hundred foreskins of the Philistines, that he may be avenged on the king's enemies.' " Now Saul planned to make David fall by the hand of the Philistines. 26 When his servants told David these words, David was well pleased to be the king's son-in-law. Before the time had expired, 27 David rose and went, along with his men, and killed one hundred[a] of the Philistines; and David brought their foreskins, which were given in full number to the king, that he might become the king's son-in-law. Saul gave him his daughter Michal as a wife. 28 But when Saul realized that the LORD was with David, and that Saul's daughter Michal loved him, 29 Saul was still more afraid of David. So Saul was David's enemy from that time forward.

30 Then the commanders of the Philistines came out to battle; and as often as they came out, David had more success than all the servants of Saul, so that his fame became very great.

Jonathan Intercedes for David

19 Saul spoke with his son Jonathan and with all his servants about killing David. But Saul's son Jonathan took great delight in David. 2 Jonathan told David, "My father Saul is trying to kill you; therefore be on guard tomorrow morning; stay in a secret place and hide yourself. 3 I will go out and stand beside my father in the field where you are, and I will speak to my father about you; if I learn anything I will tell you." 4 Jonathan spoke well of David to his father Saul, saying to him, "The king should not sin against his

servant David, because he has not sinned against you, and because his deeds have been of good service to you; 5 for he took his life in his hand when he attacked the Philistine, and the LORD brought about a great victory for all Israel. You saw it, and rejoiced; why then will you sin against an innocent person by killing David without cause?" 6 Saul heeded the voice of Jonathan; Saul swore, "As the LORD lives, he shall not be put to death." 7 So Jonathan called David and related all these things to him. Jonathan then brought David to Saul, and he was in his presence as before.

Michal Helps David Escape from Saul

8 Again there was war, and David went out to fight the Philistines. He launched a heavy attack on them, so that they fled before him. 9 Then an evil spirit from the LORD came upon Saul, as he sat in his house with his spear in his hand, while David was playing music. 10 Saul sought to pin David to the wall with the spear; but he eluded Saul, so that he struck the spear into the wall. David fled and escaped that night.

11 Saul sent messengers to David's house to keep watch over him, planning to kill him in the morning. David's wife Michal told him, "If you do not save your life tonight, tomorrow you will be killed." 12 So Michal let David down through the window; he fled away and escaped. 13 Michal took an idol[b] and laid it on the bed; she put a net[c] of goats' hair on its head, and covered it with the clothes. 14 When Saul sent messengers to take David, she said, "He is sick." 15 Then Saul sent the messengers to see David for themselves. He said, "Bring him up to me in the bed, that I may kill him." 16 When the messengers came in, the idol[d] was in the bed, with the covering[c] of goats' hair on its head. 17 Saul said to Michal, "Why have you deceived me like this, and let my enemy go, so

---

a Gk Compare 2 Sam 3.14: Heb *two hundred*   b Heb *took the teraphim*   c Meaning of Heb uncertain   d Heb *the teraphim*

18.25 The unusual *marriage present*, or bride-price, is calculated both to tempt David, who would otherwise be too poor (v. 23) to marry a king's daughter, and to put him in harm's way.

19.1–7 After learning that Saul is plotting to kill David, Jonathan intervenes and persuades his father to spare David's life. 19.8–17 Despite his oath in v. 6, Saul resumes his plans to kill David, but with Michal's help David is able to escape. 19.9–10 See 18.10–11, where a

duplicate of this incident has been added, probably secondarily, to the story. 19.12 Perhaps Michal's house, like Rahab's (Josh 2.15), was built into the city wall, so that by letting David *down through the window* she made it possible for him to escape the city without risking the gate. 19.13 The *idol*, or *teraphim*, Michal uses to simulate her sleeping husband is a household god like those Rachel steals from Laban in Gen 31.19. The same word is rendered *idolatry* in 15.23. 19.17 Michal lies to

that he has escaped?" Michal answered Saul, "He said to me, 'Let me go; why should I kill you?' "

David Joins Samuel in Ramah

18 Now David fled and escaped; he came to Samuel at Ramah, and told him all that Saul had done to him. He and Samuel went and settled at Naioth. 19Saul was told, "David is at Naioth in Ramah." 20Then Saul sent messengers to take David. When they saw the company of the prophets in a frenzy, with Samuel standing in charge of[a] them, the spirit of God came upon the messengers of Saul, and they also fell into a prophetic frenzy. 21When Saul was told, he sent other messengers, and they also fell into a frenzy. Saul sent messengers again the third time, and they also fell into a frenzy. 22Then he himself went to Ramah. He came to the great well that is in Secu;[b] he asked, "Where are Samuel and David?" And someone said, "They are at Naioth in Ramah." 23He went there, toward Naioth in Ramah; and the spirit of God came upon him. As he was going, he fell into a prophetic frenzy, until he came to Naioth in Ramah. 24He too stripped off his clothes, and he too fell into a frenzy before Samuel. He lay naked all that day and all that night. Therefore it is said, "Is Saul also among the prophets?"

The Friendship of David and Jonathan

20 David fled from Naioth in Ramah. He came before Jonathan and said, "What have I done? What is my guilt? And what is my sin against your father that he is trying to take my life?" 2He said to him, "Far from it! You shall not die. My father does nothing either great or small without disclosing it to me; and why should my father hide this from me?

Never!" 3But David also swore, "Your father knows well that you like me; and he thinks, 'Do not let Jonathan know this, or he will be grieved.' But truly, as the LORD lives and as you yourself live, there is but a step between me and death." 4Then Jonathan said to David, "Whatever you say, I will do for you." 5David said to Jonathan, "Tomorrow is the new moon, and I should not fail to sit with the king at the meal; but let me go, so that I may hide in the field until the third evening. 6If your father misses me at all, then say, 'David earnestly asked leave of me to run to Bethlehem his city; for there is a yearly sacrifice there for all the family.' 7If he says, 'Good!' it will be well with your servant; but if he is angry, then know that evil has been determined by him. 8Therefore deal kindly with your servant, for you have brought your servant into a sacred covenant[c] with you. But if there is guilt in me, kill me yourself; why should you bring me to your father?" 9Jonathan said, "Far be it from you! If I knew that it was decided by my father that evil should come upon you, would I not tell you?" 10Then David said to Jonathan, "Who will tell me if your father answers you harshly?" 11Jonathan replied to David, "Come, let us go out into the field." So they both went out into the field.

12 Jonathan said to David, "By the LORD, the God of Israel! When I have sounded out my father, about this time tomorrow, or on the third day, if he is well disposed toward David, shall I not then send and disclose it to you? 13But if my father intends to do you harm, the LORD do so to Jonathan, and more also, if I do not disclose it to you, and send you away, so

---

a Meaning of Heb uncertain   b Gk reads to the well of the threshing floor on the bare height   c Heb a covenant of the LORD

---

her father, claiming that David threatened her life. **19.18–24** This episode is almost certainly a secondary addition to the story. It was obviously unknown to the author of the statement in 15.35 that Samuel would not see Saul again alive, and it offers an alternate explanation of the saying *Is Saul also among the prophets?* (see note on 10.11). **19.18** *Ramah* of Benjamin, here apparently confused with Samuel's hometown of Ramathaim (see 1.1, 19), was only a few miles north of Gibeah. *Naioth*, "encampments," possibly camps where groups of prophets lived communally. **19.20–21** Each group of Saul's messengers is caught up in the contagious *prophetic frenzy* (see 10.5) as soon as it arrives. **19.22** *Secu,* unknown. The Septuagint reading (see text

note *b*) may be correct, especially since both threshing floors (Hos 9.1) and bare heights (Jer 3.2) were customary places of religious ritual. **19.24** By stripping off *his clothes* and lying *naked* Saul is indulging in another form of ecstatic behavior (see 10.5).

20.1–42 David goes to Jonathan to ask his help again. Jonathan finds it hard to believe that Saul is really plotting to take David's life, but after an elaborate investigation he finds that it is true and passes the word to David. **20.5** The *new moon* was celebrated with special offerings (see Num 28.11–15) and a festival lasting at least three days. **20.8** The *sacred covenant* that binds Jonathan to David is mentioned in 18.3. **20.10** Jonathan's answer to David's question is found

that you may go in safety. May the LORD be with you, as he has been with my father. 14If I am still alive, show me the faithful love of the LORD; but if I die,*a* 15never cut off your faithful love from my house, even if the LORD were to cut off every one of the enemies of David from the face of the earth." 16Thus Jonathan made a covenant with the house of David, saying, "May the LORD seek out the enemies of David." 17Jonathan made David swear again by his love for him; for he loved him as he loved his own life.

18 Jonathan said to him, "Tomorrow is the new moon; you will be missed, because your place will be empty. 19On the day after tomorrow, you shall go a long way down; go to the place where you hid yourself earlier, and remain beside the stone there.*a* 20I will shoot three arrows to the side of it, as though I shot at a mark. 21Then I will send the boy, saying, 'Go, find the arrows.' If I say to the boy, 'Look, the arrows are on this side of you, collect them,' then you are to come, for, as the LORD lives, it is safe for you and there is no danger. 22But if I say to the young man, 'Look, the arrows are beyond you,' then go; for the LORD has sent you away. 23As for the matter about which you and I have spoken, the LORD is witness*b* between you and me forever."

24 So David hid himself in the field. When the new moon came, the king sat at the feast to eat. 25The king sat upon his seat, as at other times, upon the seat by the wall. Jonathan stood, while Abner sat by Saul's side; but David's place was empty.

26 Saul did not say anything that day; for he thought, "Something has befallen him; he is not clean, surely he is not clean." 27But on the second day, the day after the new moon, David's place was empty. And Saul said to his son Jonathan, "Why has the son of Jesse not come to the feast, either yesterday or today?" 28Jonathan answered Saul, "David earnestly asked leave of me to go to Bethlehem; 29he said, 'Let me go; for our family is holding a sacrifice in the city, and my brother has commanded me to be there. So now, if I have found favor in your sight, let me get away, and see my brothers.' For this reason he has not come to the king's table."

30 Then Saul's anger was kindled against Jonathan. He said to him, "You son of a perverse, rebellious woman! Do I not know that you have chosen the son of Jesse to your own shame, and to the shame of your mother's nakedness? 31For as long as the son of Jesse lives upon the earth, neither you nor your kingdom shall be established. Now send and bring him to me, for he shall surely die." 32Then Jonathan answered his father Saul, "Why should he be put to death? What has he done?" 33But Saul threw his spear at him to strike him; so Jonathan knew that it was the decision of his father to put David to death. 34Jonathan rose from the table in fierce anger and ate no food on the second day of the month, for he was grieved for David, and because his father had disgraced him.

35 In the morning Jonathan went out into the field to the appointment with David, and with him was a little boy. 36He said to the boy, "Run and find the arrows that I shoot." As the boy ran, he shot an arrow beyond him. 37When the boy came to the place where Jonathan's arrow had fallen, Jonathan called after the boy and said, "Is the arrow not beyond you?" 38Jonathan called after the boy, "Hurry, be quick, do not linger." So Jonathan's boy gathered up the arrows and came to his master. 39But the boy knew nothing; only Jonathan and David knew the arrangement. 40Jonathan gave his weapons to the boy and said to him, "Go and carry them to the city." 41As soon as the boy had gone, David rose from be-

---

a Meaning of Heb uncertain   *b* Gk: Heb lacks *witness*

---

in vv. 18–23. **20.16** *Thus Jonathan made a covenant with the house of David*, probably originally, "And if the name of Jonathan is cut off from the house of David." *The enemies of David*, probably a scribal euphemism; in the original version Jonathan invoked the Lord's punishment on David himself, but in view of Jonathan's fate a scribe inserted "the enemies of" to protect David from the curse. **20.17** That Jonathan loved David *as he loved his own life* is an indication not only of personal affection but also of political loyalty; it evokes the traditional language of ancient Near-

ern fealty oaths (see also 18.1, 3). **20.26** David's absence on the first day does not arouse Saul's suspicion, because he assumes that David *is not clean*, i.e., that some minor accident has rendered David ritually ineligible to participate in the festival of the new moon (v. 5). **20.30** By calling Jonathan the *son of a perverse, rebellious woman* Saul means to brand Jonathan as genetically disloyal, but the choice of words points the insult at Jonathan's mother. His *mother's nakedness* refers euphemistically to her genitals, which are shamed by her having given birth to Jonathan.

side the stone heap[a] and prostrated himself with his face to the ground. He bowed three times, and they kissed each other, and wept with each other; David wept the more.[b] [42]Then Jonathan said to David, "Go in peace, since both of us have sworn in the name of the LORD, saying, 'The LORD shall be between me and you, and between my descendants and your descendants, forever.'" He got up and left; and Jonathan went into the city.[c]

David and the Holy Bread

21[d] David came to Nob to the priest Ahimelech. Ahimelech came trembling to meet David, and said to him, "Why are you alone, and no one with you?" [2]David said to the priest Ahimelech, "The king has charged me with a matter, and said to me, 'No one must know anything of the matter about which I send you, and with which I have charged you.' I have made an appointment[e] with the young men for such and such a place. [3]Now then, what have you at hand? Give me five loaves of bread, or whatever is here." [4]The priest answered David, "I have no ordinary bread at hand, only holy bread—provided that the young men have kept themselves from women." [5]David answered the priest, "Indeed women have been kept from us as always when I go on an expedition; the vessels of the young men are holy even when it is a common

journey; how much more today will their vessels be holy?" [6]So the priest gave him the holy bread; for there was no bread there except the bread of the Presence, which is removed from before the LORD, to be replaced by hot bread on the day it is taken away.

[7] Now a certain man of the servants of Saul was there that day, detained before the LORD; his name was Doeg the Edomite, the chief of Saul's shepherds.

[8] David said to Ahimelech, "Is there no spear or sword here with you? I did not bring my sword or my weapons with me, because the king's business required haste." [9]The priest said, "The sword of Goliath the Philistine, whom you killed in the valley of Elah, is here wrapped in a cloth behind the ephod; if you will take that, take it, for there is none here except that one." David said, "There is none like it; give it to me."

David Flees to Gath

10 David rose and fled that day from Saul; he went to King Achish of Gath. [11]The servants of Achish said to him, "Is this not David the king of the land? Did they not sing to one another of him in dances,

---

a Gk: Heb *from beside the south* *b* Vg: Meaning of Heb uncertain *c* This sentence is 21.1 in Heb *d* Ch 21.2 in Heb *e* Q Ms Vg Compare Gk: Meaning of MT uncertain

---

20.31 Saul reminds Jonathan that David stands between him and the throne. **20.42** Jonathan again reminds David of the covenantal oath that binds them together (see 18.3; 20.5).

21.1–9 David requests provisions from Ahimelech, the chief priest of Nob. Although he is suspicious, Ahimelech is persuaded by David's dissembling assurances to give him bread and a sword. **21.1** *Nob,* called *the city of the priests* in 22.19, was near Gibeah in Benjamin (see Neh 11.31–32; Isa 10.32); it seems to have been the seat of the house of Eli after the fall of Shiloh (see 1.3; 2.31–33; 4.4, 17). *Ahimelech,* the great-grandson of Eli and chief priest at Nob, is the son of Ahitub (22.9) and the brother of Ahijah (14.3); his anxiety at seeing David alone is probably caused by a suspicion that he is harboring a refugee. **21.2** David's facile lie is intended to allay the priest's concern; the *young men* are David's usual retinue of soldiers. **21.3–6** David solicits food and receives the ceremonial bread used in the rites of the shrine of Nob; this incident is cited in the NT as an instance of an excusable violation of ritual rules (see Mt 12.3–4; Mk 2.25–26; Lk 6.3–4). **21.4** Although Ahimelech has no *ordinary bread,* he does have *holy bread* (see v. 6); but he will make this available to David's men only if they meet the ritual qualification

of abstinence from sexual activity (cf. Ex 19.15). **21.5** David insists that his troops routinely maintain ritual purity when on active duty; *vessels,* if the text is sound, is probably a euphemism. **21.6** For the *bread of the Presence,* see Ex 25.30; Lev 24.5–9. **21.7** *Doeg,* probably a mercenary from Edom (see 14.47), will inform on David and Ahimelech (22.9–10) and serve as the executioner of the priests of Nob (22.18–19); his title, *chief of Saul's shepherds,* is doubtful; many scholars prefer "chief of Saul's guard" on the basis of 22.17. *Detained before the LORD,* found nowhere else in the Hebrew Bible, suggests some kind of ritual confinement at the shrine. **21.9** For the *sword of Goliath,* see 17.54; here it is kept behind an *ephod,* a term that usually designates a priestly garment (see 2.18; 14.3) but sometimes seems to denote an idol or some similar cultic object (see Ex 32.2–4; Judg 8.27). **21.10–15** This episode, probably a late addition to the story, anticipates David's subsequent decision to expatriate and live among the Philistines (see 27.1). **21.10** David later serves as a mercenary of *King Achish* (see chs. 28–30), whose west Anatolian name is probably the same as that of Anchises of Troy, the father of Aeneas. *Gath.* See note on 5.8. **21.11** Why David is called *king of the land* is not known; perhaps it simply means that he is a

'Saul has killed his thousands,
and David his ten thousands'?"
12 David took these words to heart and was
very much afraid of King Achish of Gath.
13 So he changed his behavior before them; he
pretended to be mad when in their presence.*a*
He scratched marks on the doors of the gate,
and let his spittle run down his beard.
14 Achish said to his servants, "Look, you see
the man is mad; why then have you brought
him to me? 15 Do I lack madmen, that you
have brought this fellow to play the madman
in my presence? Shall this fellow come into
my house?"

David and His Followers at Adullam

22 David left there and escaped to the
cave of Adullam; when his brothers
and all his father's house heard of it, they went
down there to him. 2 Everyone who was in distress, and everyone who was in debt, and
everyone who was discontented gathered to
him; and he became captain over them. Those
who were with him numbered about four
hundred.

3 David went from there to Mizpeh of
Moab. He said to the king of Moab, "Please let
my father and mother come*b* to you, until I
know what God will do for me." 4 He left them
with the king of Moab, and they stayed with
him all the time that David was in the stronghold. 5 Then the prophet Gad said to David,
"Do not remain in the stronghold; leave, and
go into the land of Judah." So David left, and
went into the forest of Hereth.

Saul Slaughters the Priests at Nob

6 Saul heard that David and those who were
with him had been located. Saul was sitting at
Gibeah, under the tamarisk tree on the height,
with his spear in his hand, and all his servants
were standing around him. 7 Saul said to his
servants who stood around him, "Hear now,
you Benjaminites; will the son of Jesse give
every one of you fields and vineyards, will he
make you all commanders of thousands and
commanders of hundreds? 8 Is that why all of
you have conspired against me? No one discloses to me when my son makes a league with
the son of Jesse, none of you is sorry for me or
discloses to me that my son has stirred up my
servant against me, to lie in wait, as he is doing
today." 9 Doeg the Edomite, who was in charge
of Saul's servants, answered, "I saw the son of
Jesse coming to Nob, to Ahimelech son of Ahitub; 10 he inquired of the LORD for him, gave
him provisions, and gave him the sword of
Goliath the Philistine."

11 The king sent for the priest Ahimelech
son of Ahitub and for all his father's house, the
priests who were at Nob; and all of them came
to the king. 12 Saul said, "Listen now, son of
Ahitub." He answered, "Here I am, my lord."
13 Saul said to him, "Why have you conspired
against me, you and the son of Jesse, by giving
him bread and a sword, and by inquiring of
God for him, so that he has risen against me,
to lie in wait, as he is doing today?"

---

a Heb *in their hands*   *b* Syr Vg: Heb *come out*

---

powerful and successful military leader. What is clear
is that the Philistines recognize him. This puts him in
danger, and he feigns madness to protect himself.
22.1–5 David becomes a leader of a band of outlaws
recruited from those who, like David himself, have
been discredited or disenfranchised by Saul's regime.
Here in the old story of David's rise to power (see Introduction) the circumstances under which David was
forced to become an outlaw are presented to exonerate
him from possible charges of disloyalty to Saul.
22.1 *Cave* should perhaps be emended to "stronghold"; cf. vv. 4–5. *Adullam,* a fortress of Judah about
sixteen miles southwest of Jerusalem (see 2 Sam
23.13–14). **22.2** David, now a fugitive from Saul's justice, becomes the champion and leader of everyone in
the region who is disfranchised, disenchanted, and
embittered. **22.3** *Mizpeh,* mentioned nowhere else but
assumed to be an important city in *Moab,* which lay
east of the Dead Sea (see 14.47); David traced his connections with Moab to his great-grandmother Ruth

(see Ruth 4.13–22). **22.5** For the *prophet Gad,* whose
appearance at this point is a surprise, see 2 Sam 24.11–
19; 1 Chr 21.9–19; 29.29; 2 Chr 29.25. The *forest of Hereth,* mentioned nowhere else, was probably in the
vicinity of Keilah (see 23.1). **22.6–23** Enraged by his
discovery that Ahimelech gave David provisions and
unimpressed by the priest's explanation that he believed David a loyal servant of Saul, the desperate king
orders the massacre of the priests of Nob. **22.6** This description of Saul corresponds to the classic depiction
of a ruler sitting under a sacred tree (here a *tamarisk*)
judging the people. In this case, Saul's seat of judgment
is located at *the height,* or "high place," i.e., the local
place of sacrifice, at *Gibeah,* Saul's hometown and capital (see note on 9.1). **22.7–8** Saul's angry words to *his
servants* (the ranking members of his court) accuse
them of hoping for favors from David, while implicitly
reminding them that as *Benjaminites* they cannot expect such favors from a Judahite. **22.9** *Doeg.* See note
on 21.7. **22.10** Our account of David's visit to Nob

14 Then Ahimelech answered the king, "Who among all your servants is so faithful as David? He is the king's son-in-law, and is quick[a] to do your bidding, and is honored in your house. 15Is today the first time that I have inquired of God for him? By no means! Do not let the king impute anything to his servant or to any member of my father's house; for your servant has known nothing of all this, much or little." 16The king said, "You shall surely die, Ahimelech, you and all your father's house." 17The king said to the guard who stood around him, "Turn and kill the priests of the LORD, because their hand also is with David; they knew that he fled, and did not disclose it to me." But the servants of the king would not raise their hand to attack the priests of the LORD. 18Then the king said to Doeg, "You, Doeg, turn and attack the priests." Doeg the Edomite turned and attacked the priests; on that day he killed eighty-five who wore the linen ephod. 19Nob, the city of the priests, he put to the sword; men and women, children and infants, oxen, donkeys, and sheep, he put to the sword.

20 But one of the sons of Ahimelech son of Ahitub, named Abiathar, escaped and fled after David. 21Abiathar told David that Saul had killed the priests of the LORD. 22David said to Abiathar, "I knew on that day, when Doeg the Edomite was there, that he would surely tell Saul. I am responsible[b] for the lives of all your father's house. 23Stay with me, and do not be afraid; for the one who seeks my life seeks your life; you will be safe with me."

David Saves the City of Keilah

23 Now they told David, "The Philistines are fighting against Keilah, and are robbing the threshing floors." 2David inquired of the LORD, "Shall I go and attack these Philistines?" The LORD said to David, "Go and attack the Philistines and save Keilah." 3But David's men said to him, "Look, we are afraid here in Judah; how much more then if we go to Keilah against the armies of the Philistines?" 4Then David inquired of the LORD again. The LORD answered him, "Yes, go down to Keilah; for I will give the Philistines into your hand." 5So David and his men went to Keilah, fought with the Philistines, brought away their livestock, and dealt them a heavy defeat. Thus David rescued the inhabitants of Keilah.

6 When Abiathar son of Ahimelech fled to David at Keilah, he came down with an ephod in his hand. 7Now it was told Saul that David had come to Keilah. And Saul said, "God has given[c] him into my hand; for he has shut himself in by entering a town that has gates and bars." 8Saul summoned all the people to war, to go down to Keilah, to besiege David and his men. 9When David learned that Saul was plotting evil against him, he said to the priest Abiathar, "Bring the ephod here." 10David said, "O LORD, the God of Israel, your servant has heard that Saul seeks to come to Keilah, to destroy the city on my account. 11And now, will[d] Saul come down as your servant has heard? O LORD, the God of Israel, I beseech you, tell your servant." The LORD said, "He will come down." 12Then David said, "Will the men of Keilah surrender me and my men into the hand of Saul?" The LORD said, "They will sur-

(21.1–9) does not mention the fact that Ahimelech *inquired of the LORD for him.* **22.14–15** Ahimelech's excuse is true and honest: he believed David to be a fully trusted servant of Saul and knew nothing of the animosity that had developed between the two men. *Quick to do your bidding,* better "commander of your bodyguard," the position that Benaiah son of Jehoiada held in David's own administration (see 2 Sam 23.20–23). **22.17** *Their hand also is with David,* i.e., they too are in collusion with David (cf. 2 Sam 14.19; Jer 26.24). **22.18** As an *Edomite* (and as a scoundrel) Doeg is not as scrupulous as Saul's Israelite servants about doing violence to the priests of the God of Israel. *Linen ephod,* the livery of priesthood (see 2.18; 14.3, 18). **22.20** The only survivor of the massacre at Nob and, therefore, of the Shilonite priesthood (see note on 21.1) is *Abiathar,* a son of Ahimelech (see notes on

2.31–33; 2.33). **22.22–23** Admitting that by deceiving Ahimelech (see 21.1–8) he put the priesthood of Nob in mortal danger, David offers its only survivor his patronage. Abiathar will share the high-priesthood with Zadok during David's reign (see, e.g., 2 Sam 20.25), only to be banished by Solomon (1 Kings 2.26–27) for having supported the succession of Adonijah (1 Kings 1.7).

23.1–14 This episode illustrates the value of David's newly acquired priest. Guided by oracles obtained by Abiathar, David liberates a besieged town and successfully eludes Saul again. **23.1** *Keilah* was just south of Adullam (see 22.1) on the border of Philistine territory. Though it was formally claimed by Judah (Josh 15.44), it seems to have been an independent city at the time of the events described here. **23.6** *Ephod,* here perhaps an instrument of divination or a container for

render you." 13Then David and his men, who were about six hundred, set out and left Keilah; they wandered wherever they could go. When Saul was told that David had escaped from Keilah, he gave up the expedition. 14David remained in the strongholds in the wilderness, in the hill country of the Wilderness of Ziph. Saul sought him every day, but the Lord[a] did not give him into his hand.

David Eludes Saul in the Wilderness

15 David was in the Wilderness of Ziph at Horesh when he learned that[b] Saul had come out to seek his life. 16Saul's son Jonathan set out and came to David at Horesh; there he strengthened his hand through the Lord.[c] 17He said to him, "Do not be afraid; for the hand of my father Saul shall not find you; you shall be king over Israel, and I shall be second to you; my father Saul also knows that this is so." 18Then the two of them made a covenant before the Lord; David remained at Horesh, and Jonathan went home.

19 Then some Ziphites went up to Saul at Gibeah and said, "David is hiding among us in the strongholds of Horesh, on the hill of Hachilah, which is south of Jeshimon. 20Now, O king, whenever you wish to come down, do so; and our part will be to surrender him into the king's hand." 21Saul said, "May you be blessed by the Lord for showing me compassion! 22Go and make sure once more; find out exactly where he is, and who has seen him there; for I am told that he is very cunning.

23Look around and learn all the hiding places where he lurks, and come back to me with sure information. Then I will go with you; and if he is in the land, I will search him out among all the thousands of Judah." 24So they set out and went to Ziph ahead of Saul.

David and his men were in the wilderness of Maon, in the Arabah to the south of Jeshimon. 25Saul and his men went to search for him. When David was told, he went down to the rock and stayed in the wilderness of Maon. When Saul heard that, he pursued David into the wilderness of Maon. 26Saul went on one side of the mountain, and David and his men on the other side of the mountain. David was hurrying to get away from Saul, while Saul and his men were closing in on David and his men to capture them. 27Then a messenger came to Saul, saying, "Hurry and come; for the Philistines have made a raid on the land." 28So Saul stopped pursuing David, and went against the Philistines; therefore that place was called the Rock of Escape.[d] 29[e]David then went up from there, and lived in the strongholds of En-gedi.

David Spares Saul's Life

24 When Saul returned from following the Philistines, he was told, "David is in the wilderness of En-gedi." 2Then Saul took three thousand chosen men out of all Israel, and went to look for David and his men in the

---

a Q Ms Gk: MT *God*   b Or *saw that*   c Compare Q Ms Gk: MT *God*   d Or *Rock of Division*; meaning of Heb uncertain   e Ch 24.1 in Heb

---

such instruments, maybe the Urim and Thummim (see 14.3; 21.9). **23.14** *The hill country of the Wilderness of Ziph,* a part of the Judean hills that lay several miles southeast of Keilah. The town of Ziph was on a hilltop about five miles south-south-east of Hebron. **23.15–29** Another narrow escape for David. **23.15** *Horesh,* "Forest" in Hebrew; there is a ruin with a similar name near the site of ancient Ziph. **23.16** *Strengthened his hand through the Lord.* Jonathan not only offered David encouragement and reassurance (cf. Neh 6.9) but also gave him tangible support (cf. Judg 9.24). **23.17** Jonathan's pledge of loyalty to David echoes the language of 20.12–17, where he sought David's protection for his family. Here he acknowledges that David will become king. *I shall be second to you* may simply mean that Jonathan will be subordinate to David, but there is some evidence to suggest that "second to the king" or "next in authority to the king" was the name of an office Jonathan hoped to fill in David's administration (see 2 Chr 28.7). **23.18** In the present form of the narrative Jonathan and David have *made a covenant* before (see 18.3; 20.8), but this may have

been the first time in an earlier version of the story. **23.19** A group of *Ziphites,* residents of the Wilderness of Ziph, seek to curry favor with Saul by betraying David. *Hill of Hachilah, Jeshimon.* Locations unknown, except that they must be near *Horesh* (see v. 15) and *Maon* (v. 24). **23.24** *Maon* was on a hilltop about eight miles south of Hebron; David's camp is in *the Arabah,* or rift valley east of the town. **23.26** Saul's troops have David trapped on the other side of the mountain; they are *closing in* on him, i.e., circling around the mountain from both directions. **23.27** Saul's army is called away by other duties, affording David a last-minute escape. **23.28** If the name *Rock of Escape* is understood as *Rock of Division* (see text note *d*), the point of the wordplay may be that two hostile parties were divided here and went their separate ways. **23.29** David retreats farther into the Judean wilderness, finding shelter near the oasis of *En-gedi,* about thirty-five miles southeast of Jerusalem, roughly at the midpoint of the western shore of the Dead Sea (see Josh 15.62).

24.1–22 In the first of two very similar episodes (see

direction of the Rocks of the Wild Goats. [3]He came to the sheepfolds beside the road, where there was a cave; and Saul went in to relieve himself.[a] Now David and his men were sitting in the innermost parts of the cave. [4]The men of David said to him, "Here is the day of which the LORD said to you, 'I will give your enemy into your hand, and you shall do to him as it seems good to you.'" Then David went and stealthily cut off a corner of Saul's cloak. [5]Afterward David was stricken to the heart because he had cut off a corner of Saul's cloak. [6]He said to his men, "The LORD forbid that I should do this thing to my lord, the LORD's anointed, to raise my hand against him; for he is the LORD's anointed." [7]So David scolded his men severely and did not permit them to attack Saul. Then Saul got up and left the cave, and went on his way.

[8] Afterwards David also rose up and went out of the cave and called after Saul, "My lord the king!" When Saul looked behind him, David bowed with his face to the ground, and did obeisance. [9]David said to Saul, "Why do you listen to the words of those who say, 'David seeks to do you harm'? [10]This very day your eyes have seen how the LORD gave you into my hand in the cave; and some urged me to kill you, but I spared[b] you. I said, 'I will not raise my hand against my lord; for he is the LORD's anointed.' [11]See, my father, see the corner of your cloak in my hand; for by the fact that I cut off the corner of your cloak, and did not kill you, you may know for certain that there is no wrong or treason in my hands. I have not sinned against you, though you are hunting me to take my life. [12]May the LORD judge between me and you! May the LORD avenge me on you; but my hand shall not be against you. [13]As the ancient proverb says, 'Out of the wicked comes forth wickedness'; but my hand shall not be against you. [14]Against whom has the king of Israel come out? Whom do you pursue? A dead dog? A single flea? [15]May the LORD therefore be judge, and give sentence between me and you. May he see to it, and plead my cause, and vindicate me against you."

[16] When David had finished speaking these words to Saul, Saul said, "Is this your voice, my son David?" Saul lifted up his voice and wept. [17]He said to David, "You are more righteous than I; for you have repaid me good, whereas I have repaid you evil. [18]Today you have explained how you have dealt well with me, in that you did not kill me when the LORD put me into your hands. [19]For who has ever found an enemy, and sent the enemy safely away? So may the LORD reward you with good for what you have done to me this day. [20]Now I know that you shall surely be king, and that the kingdom of Israel shall be established in your hand. [21]Swear to me therefore by the LORD that you will not cut off my descendants after me, and that you will not wipe out my name from my father's house." [22]So David swore this to Saul. Then Saul went home; but David and his men went up to the stronghold.

Death of Samuel

25 Now Samuel died; and all Israel assembled and mourned for him. They buried him at his home in Ramah.

Then David got up and went down to the wilderness of Paran.

---

a Heb *to cover his feet*   *b* Gk Syr Tg Vg: Heb *it* (my eye) spared

---

ch. 26), David passes up an opportunity to kill his pursuer, and Saul is moved to a sincere but fleeting change of heart. The motif of David's unswerving loyalty to Saul despite outward appearances to the contrary is an important element of the old story of David's rise to power (see Introduction). **24.2** *Rocks of the Wild Goats.* Location unknown, but ibexes remain plentiful in the vicinity of En-gedi today. **24.4** We were not told previously that the Lord has promised to deliver David's *enemy* to him; the words of David's men should probably be understood as a traditional saying. David's reason for cutting off *a corner of Saul's cloak* is to use it later (v. 11) as visible evidence that he had an opportunity to harm Saul and declined to do so; in the parallel episode (see 26.12, 16) he will use a spear and a water jar for the same purpose. **24.6–7** David refuses to permit his men to harm Saul, who, as *the LORD's anointed* (see 9.16), is a sacrosanct individual whose slaying or even physical injury (see note on 26.9) would be a sacrilege (see also 26.9, 11, 16, 23; 2 Sam 1.14, 16). **24.14** In this highly rhetorical self-abasement David compares himself to a *dead dog* (see 2 Sam 9.8; 2 Kings 8.13, Septuagint) and even a *single flea* on a dead dog. **24.16–19** Confronted with irrefutable evidence of David's loyalty, Saul admits that David's case is just, but this change of heart will be only temporary. **24.20** Saul acknowledges what Jonathan has already said (23.17), that David will be king. **24.21** Saul's plea for the safety of his family echoes that of Jonathan in 20.15. **24.22** *Stronghold,* probably Adullam (see note on 22.1).

25.1 Samuel's obituary prepares readers for the

David and the Wife of Nabal

2 There was a man in Maon, whose property was in Carmel. The man was very rich; he had three thousand sheep and a thousand goats. He was shearing his sheep in Carmel. ³Now the name of the man was Nabal, and the name of his wife Abigail. The woman was clever and beautiful, but the man was surly and mean; he was a Calebite. ⁴David heard in the wilderness that Nabal was shearing his sheep. ⁵So David sent ten young men; and David said to the young men, "Go up to Carmel, and go to Nabal, and greet him in my name. ⁶Thus you shall salute him: 'Peace be to you, and peace be to your house, and peace be to all that you have. ⁷I hear that you have shearers; now your shepherds have been with us, and we did them no harm, and they missed nothing, all the time they were in Carmel. ⁸Ask your young men, and they will tell you. Therefore let my young men find favor in your sight; for we have come on a feast day. Please give whatever you have at hand to your servants and to your son David.' "

9 When David's young men came, they said all this to Nabal in the name of David; and then they waited. ¹⁰But Nabal answered David's servants, "Who is David? Who is the son of Jesse? There are many servants today who are breaking away from their masters. ¹¹Shall I take my bread and my water and the meat that I have butchered for my shearers, and give it to men who come from I do not know where?" ¹²So David's young men turned away, and came back and told him all this. ¹³David said to his men, "Every man strap on his sword!" And every one of them strapped on his sword; David also strapped on his sword; and about four hundred men went up after David, while two hundred remained with the baggage.

14 But one of the young men told Abigail, Nabal's wife, "David sent messengers out of the wilderness to salute our master; and he shouted insults at them. ¹⁵Yet the men were very good to us, and we suffered no harm, and we never missed anything when we were in the fields, as long as we were with them; ¹⁶they were a wall to us both by night and by day, all the while we were with them keeping the sheep. ¹⁷Now therefore know this and consider what you should do; for evil has been decided against our master and against all his house; he is so ill-natured that no one can speak to him."

18 Then Abigail hurried and took two hundred loaves, two skins of wine, five sheep ready dressed, five measures of parched grain, one hundred clusters of raisins, and two hundred cakes of figs. She loaded them on donkeys ¹⁹and said to her young men, "Go on ahead of me; I am coming after you." But she did not tell her husband Nabal. ²⁰As she rode on the donkey and came down under cover of the mountain, David and his men came down toward her; and she met them. ²¹Now David had said, "Surely it was in vain that I protected all that this fellow has in the wilderness, so that nothing was missed of all that belonged to him; but he has returned me evil for good. ²²God do so to David[a] and more also, if by

---

a Gk Compare Syr: Heb *the enemies of David*

---

story of the evocation of his ghost in 28.3–25. *Ramah.* See notes on 1.1; 1.19. The *wilderness of Paran* was south of Canaan in the northeastern part of the Sinai Peninsula, too far away to fit here, and most scholars prefer to follow the Septuagint and read "wilderness of Maon" (see notes on 23.24; 25.2). **25.2–44** When David seeks help from a prosperous Judahite and is rudely rejected, he angrily marches out to seek revenge but is prevented from incurring bloodguilt by the timely intervention of Abigail, the wife of his offender. **25.2** The towns of *Maon* (see note on 23.24) and *Carmel* (see note on 15.12) were not far apart. **25.3** *Nabal,* a Hebrew word traditionally rendered "fool" in most English Bibles. It refers to someone whose behavior violates the social norms of etiquette or law; it is a very apt name for Abigail's churlish husband. As a *Calebite* he traced his ancestry to Caleb, one of the heroes of the conquest tradition (see Num

13–14). Calebite territory was the region around the city of Hebron (see Josh 14.13–15), a district that included the town where the present story takes place. **25.7** The time of *shearers,* or sheepshearing, was a time of work, but also merrymaking (cf. 2 Sam 13.23–29). **25.8** *A feast day* (lit. "a good day"), a general designation for a legal holiday in postbiblical times; here, however, simply an occasion of celebration, eating, and drinking—in this case, shearing time. In addressing Nabal, who is probably much older and certainly much wealthier, David refers to himself as *your son,* a gesture of courtesy. **25.13** Enraged by the report of Nabal's stingy and discourteous response to his request, David precipitately orders his men to arm themselves and march off to avenge the insult. **25.18** Abigail, determined to prevent a confrontation that would be disastrous for both David and Nabal, assembles the provisions her husband refused to provide. **25.22** *God*

morning I leave so much as one male of all who belong to him."

23 When Abigail saw David, she hurried and alighted from the donkey, and fell before David on her face, bowing to the ground. 24She fell at his feet and said, "Upon me alone, my lord, be the guilt; please let your servant speak in your ears, and hear the words of your servant. 25My lord, do not take seriously this ill-natured fellow, Nabal; for as his name is, so is he; Nabal*a* is his name, and folly is with him; but I, your servant, did not see the young men of my lord, whom you sent.

26 "Now then, my lord, as the LORD lives, and as you yourself live, since the LORD has restrained you from bloodguilt and from taking vengeance with your own hand, now let your enemies and those who seek to do evil to my lord be like Nabal. 27And now let this present that your servant has brought to my lord be given to the young men who follow my lord. 28Please forgive the trespass of your servant; for the LORD will certainly make my lord a sure house, because my lord is fighting the battles of the LORD; and evil shall not be found in you so long as you live. 29If anyone should rise up to pursue you and to seek your life, the life of my lord shall be bound in the bundle of the living under the care of the LORD your God; but the lives of your enemies he shall sling out as from the hollow of a sling. 30When the LORD has done to my lord according to all the good that he has spoken concerning you, and has appointed you prince over Israel, 31my lord shall have no cause of grief, or pangs of conscience, for having shed blood without

cause or for having saved himself. And when the LORD has dealt well with my lord, then remember your servant."

32 David said to Abigail, "Blessed be the LORD, the God of Israel, who sent you to meet me today! 33Blessed be your good sense, and blessed be you, who have kept me today from bloodguilt and from avenging myself by my own hand! 34For as surely as the LORD the God of Israel lives, who has restrained me from hurting you, unless you had hurried and come to meet me, truly by morning there would not have been left to Nabal so much as one male." 35Then David received from her hand what she had brought him; he said to her, "Go up to your house in peace; see, I have heeded your voice, and I have granted your petition."

36 Abigail came to Nabal; he was holding a feast in his house, like the feast of a king. Nabal's heart was merry within him, for he was very drunk; so she told him nothing at all until the morning light. 37In the morning, when the wine had gone out of Nabal, his wife told him these things, and his heart died within him; he became like a stone. 38About ten days later the LORD struck Nabal, and he died.

39 When David heard that Nabal was dead, he said, "Blessed be the LORD who has judged the case of Nabal's insult to me, and has kept back his servant from evil; the LORD has returned the evildoing of Nabal upon his own head." Then David sent and wooed Abigail, to make her his wife. 40When David's servants

a That is Fool

---

do so to David and more also, David's angry oath accompanying his threat to massacre the males of Nabal's family. The threat is never carried out, and a scribe who was concerned about the consequences of the oath changed *David* to *the enemies of David* (see text note *a* on p. 426). *One male,* rendered more literally and less euphemistically in the KJV as "any that pisseth against the wall." **25.24** *Upon me alone, my lord, be the guilt,* a formulaic courtesy meaning, "Please hear me out, and if anything harmful should arise from our conversation, I shall accept responsibility for it." Cf. the words of the woman of Tekoa in 2 Sam 14.9. **25.25** *Nabal.* See note on 25.3. Abigail is saying, "Fool *is his name, and folly is with him.*" Cf. Isa 32.6. **25.28–30** This part of Abigail's speech seems to have been inserted secondarily as an expression of the Deuteronomistic Historian's theme (see Introduction) of David's *sure house* (see 2 Sam 7.16; 1 Kings 11.38); cf. the forecast of the *sure house* of the priest

Zadok in 2.35. **25.29** *Bundle* here is a tied document (cf. Isa 8.16), so that *bundle of the living* is "book of the living" (Ps 69.28), a heavenly book in which the name of every living person is recorded and exclusion from which means death (see Ex 32.32–33). In later Judeo-Christian thought the "book of life" was a record of all those people throughout history who were destined for salvation and eternal life (see Dan 12.1; Rev 3.5; 13.8; 17.8; 20.12; 21.27). **25.30** *Prince* (Hebrew *nagid,* rendered *ruler* in 9.16; 10.1; 13.14). See note on 9.16. **25.33** David acknowledges that Abigail's intervention has prevented his incurring *bloodguilt* by avenging himself rather than leaving vengeance to the Lord, whose justice can be relied upon (see v. 38). **25.35** *I have granted your petition,* lit. "I have lifted up your face," also occurs in Gen 19.21 ("I grant you this favor"); Job 42.8 ("I will accept his prayer"); 42.9 ("and the LORD accepted Job's prayer"). **25.39** *The LORD has returned . . . own head.* Cf. 1 Kings 2.44.

came to Abigail at Carmel, they said to her, "David has sent us to you to take you to him as his wife." [41]She rose and bowed down, with her face to the ground, and said, "Your servant is a slave to wash the feet of the servants of my lord." [42]Abigail got up hurriedly and rode away on a donkey; her five maids attended her. She went after the messengers of David and became his wife.

43 David also married Ahinoam of Jezreel; both of them became his wives. [44]Saul had given his daughter Michal, David's wife, to Palti son of Laish, who was from Gallim.

David Spares Saul's Life a Second Time

26 Then the Ziphites came to Saul at Gibeah, saying, "David is in hiding on the hill of Hachilah, which is opposite Jeshimon."[a] [2]So Saul rose and went down to the Wilderness of Ziph, with three thousand chosen men of Israel, to seek David in the Wilderness of Ziph. [3]Saul encamped on the hill of Hachilah, which is opposite Jeshimon[a] beside the road. But David remained in the wilderness. When he learned that Saul had come after him into the wilderness, [4]David sent out spies, and learned that Saul had indeed arrived. [5]Then David set out and came to the place where Saul had encamped; and David saw the place where Saul lay, with Abner son of Ner, the commander of his army. Saul was lying within the encampment, while the army was encamped around him.

6 Then David said to Ahimelech the Hittite, and to Joab's brother Abishai son of Zeruiah, "Who will go down with me into the camp to Saul?" Abishai said, "I will go down with you."

[7]So David and Abishai went to the army by night; there Saul lay sleeping within the encampment, with his spear stuck in the ground at his head; and Abner and the army lay around him. [8]Abishai said to David, "God has given your enemy into your hand today; now therefore let me pin him to the ground with one stroke of the spear; I will not strike him twice." [9]But David said to Abishai, "Do not destroy him; for who can raise his hand against the LORD's anointed, and be guiltless?" [10]David said, "As the LORD lives, the LORD will strike him down; or his day will come to die; or he will go down into battle and perish. [11]The LORD forbid that I should raise my hand against the LORD's anointed; but now take the spear that is at his head, and the water jar, and let us go." [12]So David took the spear that was at Saul's head and the water jar, and they went away. No one saw it, or knew it, nor did anyone awake; for they were all asleep, because a deep sleep from the LORD had fallen upon them.

13 Then David went over to the other side, and stood on top of a hill far away, with a great distance between them. [14]David called to the army and to Abner son of Ner, saying, "Abner! Will you not answer?" Then Abner replied, "Who are you that calls to the king?" [15]David said to Abner, "Are you not a man? Who is like you in Israel? Why then have you not kept watch over your lord the king? For one of the people came in to destroy your lord the king. [16]This thing that you have done is not good. As the LORD lives, you deserve to die, because you have not kept watch over your lord, the

a Or opposite the wasteland

25.43–44 A catalog of miscellaneous information like 14.47–52. **25.43** *Ahinoam of Jezreel* became the mother of Amnon, David's firstborn (see 2 Sam 3.2; 1 Chr 3.1); her home was not the well-known town of Jezreel situated at the eastern end of the great valley that shares its name (see notes on 29.1; 2 Sam 2.9) but a small Judahite town of the same name near Maon, Ziph, and Carmel (see Josh 15.55–56). Because Ahinoam's name is the same as that of Saul's wife (see 14.50), some scholars have speculated that David married not only Saul's daughters but also his wife (cf. 2 Sam 12.8). **25.44** Saul's annulment of David's marriage to Michal was intended to thwart any claim to the throne David might make on the basis of the marriage; she will be returned to David just before he becomes king of Israel (see 2 Sam 3.13–16). *Palti son of Laish,* called by a longer form of his name, Paltiel, in 2 Sam 3.15; for *Gallim,* his hometown, see Isa 10.30.

26.1–25 As in ch. 24, David, while fleeing from Saul, is given an opportunity to take his pursuer's life. Once again, he spares the king and asks for reconciliation. **26.1** Cf. the details here to those of 23.19. **26.5** *Abner son of Ner,* Saul's uncle (see 14.50–51). **26.6** *Ahimelech the Hittite,* mentioned only here. *Abishai,* one of the three sons of David's sister *Zeruiah* (see 1 Chr 2.16); the others are *Joab* (see 2 Sam 2.13) and Asahel (see 2 Sam 2.18–23); all three are fiercely loyal partisans of David. **26.9** David's command to Abishai is more specific than an admonition not to strike or kill Saul. The verb rendered *destroy* implies mutilation or disfigurement; as in 24.6, David's concern is with violence done to the sacrosanct body of *the LORD's anointed.* **26.12** The *spear* and *the water jar* are taken as proof that David was there; cf. the corner of Saul's cloak in 24.4. *Deep sleep from the LORD* (cf. Gen 2.21; 15.12; Isa 29.10) shows that David is receiving divine help.

LORD's anointed. See now, where is the king's spear, or the water jar that was at his head?"

17 Saul recognized David's voice, and said, "Is this your voice, my son David?" David said, "It is my voice, my lord, O king." ¹⁸And he added, "Why does my lord pursue his servant? For what have I done? What guilt is on my hands? ¹⁹Now therefore let my lord the king hear the words of his servant. If it is the LORD who has stirred you up against me, may he accept an offering; but if it is mortals, may they be cursed before the LORD, for they have driven me out today from my share in the heritage of the LORD, saying, 'Go, serve other gods.' ²⁰Now therefore, do not let my blood fall to the ground, away from the presence of the LORD; for the king of Israel has come out to seek a single flea, like one who hunts a partridge in the mountains."

21 Then Saul said, "I have done wrong; come back, my son David, for I will never harm you again, because my life was precious in your sight today; I have been a fool, and have made a great mistake." ²²David replied, "Here is the spear, O king! Let one of the young men come over and get it. ²³The LORD rewards everyone for his righteousness and his faithfulness; for the LORD gave you into my hand today, but I would not raise my hand against the LORD's anointed. ²⁴As your life was precious today in my sight, so may my life be precious in the sight of the LORD, and may he rescue me from all tribulation." ²⁵Then Saul said to David, "Blessed be you, my son David! You will do many things and will succeed in them." So David went his way, and Saul returned to his place.

David Serves King Achish of Gath

27 David said in his heart, "I shall now perish one day by the hand of Saul; there is nothing better for me than to escape to the land of the Philistines; then Saul will despair of seeking me any longer within the borders of Israel, and I shall escape out of his hand." ²So David set out and went over, he and the six hundred men who were with him, to King Achish son of Maoch of Gath. ³David stayed with Achish at Gath, he and his troops, every man with his household, and David with his two wives, Ahinoam of Jezreel, and Abigail of Carmel, Nabal's widow. ⁴When Saul was told that David had fled to Gath, he no longer sought for him.

5 Then David said to Achish, "If I have found favor in your sight, let a place be given me in one of the country towns, so that I may live there; for why should your servant live in the royal city with you?" ⁶So that day Achish gave him Ziklag; therefore Ziklag has belonged to the kings of Judah to this day. ⁷The length of time that David lived in the country of the Philistines was one year and four months.

8 Now David and his men went up and made raids on the Geshurites, the Girzites, and the Amalekites; for these were the landed settlements from Telam[a] on the way to Shur

_a_ Compare Gk 15.4: Heb _from of old_

26.19 _May he accept an offering,_ lit. "may he smell an offering," as in Gen 8.21. By excluding him from the _heritage of the LORD,_ i.e., from Israel, David's enemies would prevent him from worshiping the God of Israel. 26.20 _A single flea._ See 24.14. David's simile comparing Saul to _one who hunts partridge in the mountains_ is particularly fitting for two reasons; first, the partridge was hunted by relentless pursuit, and second, its Hebrew name meant "the caller" and David is in fact calling in the mountains (see v. 14). 26.21 Once again (see 24.16–19) Saul acknowledges the justice of David's cause.

27.1–28.2 Despite Saul's apparent change of heart in 26.21–25, David despairs any hope of reconciliation and decides that if he is to stay alive he must flee Israel. He enters the service of the king of the Philistine city of Gath. In keeping with the central ideas of the old story of David's rise to power (see Introduction) the narrator shows that David took this step only because he was forced to and that he guilefully used his position in the Philistine army to enrich the people of Israel and Judah and attack their enemies (see 27.8–12; 30.1–31). 27.2 For _King Achish_ and his city, _Gath,_ see note on 21.10. We now learn that his father's name was _Maoch;_ he is called Maacah in 1 Kings 2.39. 27.3 For David's _two wives,_ see 25.42–43. 27.5–6 David requests and receives a military fiefdom, a grant of landed property in return for service at arms. _Ziklag,_ a stronghold in the southwestern Judean hills controlled at this time by Gath, was claimed by the tribe of Simeon (Josh 19.5) and listed among the Judahite cities (Josh 15.31). 27.8–12 David deludes Achish by pretending to raid and plunder Israel and its allies while really fighting against Israel's enemies (see note on 27.1–28.2). 27.8 _Geshurites,_ obscure neighbors of the Philistines (see Josh 13.2–3) with no apparent connection to the land of Geshur in the southern Golan (see 2 Sam 3.3). _Girzites,_ otherwise unknown. The Hebrew text is vocalized as "Gezerites," i.e., people of Gezer, the Israelite-Philistine border city west-northwest of

and on to the land of Egypt. ⁹David struck the land, leaving neither man nor woman alive, but took away the sheep, the oxen, the donkeys, the camels, and the clothing, and came back to Achish. ¹⁰When Achish asked, "Against whom ᵃ have you made a raid today?" David would say, "Against the Negeb of Judah," or "Against the Negeb of the Jerahmeelites," or, "Against the Negeb of the Kenites." ¹¹David left neither man nor woman alive to be brought back to Gath, thinking, "They might tell about us, and say, 'David has done so and so.'" Such was his practice all the time he lived in the country of the Philistines. ¹²Achish trusted David, thinking, "He has made himself utterly abhorrent to his people Israel; therefore he shall always be my servant."

28 In those days the Philistines gathered their forces for war, to fight against Israel. Achish said to David, "You know, of course, that you and your men are to go out with me in the army." ²David said to Achish, "Very well, then you shall know what your servant can do." Achish said to David, "Very well, I will make you my bodyguard for life."

Saul Consults a Medium

3 Now Samuel had died, and all Israel had mourned for him and buried him in Ramah, his own city. Saul had expelled the mediums and the wizards from the land. ⁴The Philistines assembled, and came and encamped at Shunem. Saul gathered all Israel, and they encamped at Gilboa. ⁵When Saul saw the army of the Philistines, he was afraid, and his heart trembled greatly. ⁶When Saul inquired of the LORD, the LORD did not answer him, not by dreams, or by Urim, or by prophets. ⁷Then Saul said to his servants, "Seek out for me a woman who is a medium, so that I may go to her and inquire of her." His servants said to him, "There is a medium at Endor."

8 So Saul disguised himself and put on other clothes and went there, he and two men with him. They came to the woman by night. And he said, "Consult a spirit for me, and bring up for me the one whom I name to you." ⁹The woman said to him, "Surely you know what Saul has done, how he has cut off the mediums and the wizards from the land. Why then are you laying a snare for my life to bring about my death?" ¹⁰But Saul swore to her by the LORD, "As the LORD lives, no punishment shall come upon you for this thing." ¹¹Then the woman said, "Whom shall I bring up for you?" He answered, "Bring up Samuel for me." ¹²When the woman saw Samuel, she cried out with a loud voice; and the woman said to Saul, "Why have you deceived me? You are Saul!" ¹³The king said to her, "Have no fear; what do you see?" The woman said to Saul, "I see a divine being ᵇ coming up out of the ground." ¹⁴He said to her, "What is his appearance?" She said, "An old man is coming up; he is wrapped in a robe." So Saul knew that it was Samuel, and he bowed with his face to the ground, and did obeisance.

15 Then Samuel said to Saul, "Why have you disturbed me by bringing me up?" Saul answered, "I am in great distress, for the Philistines are warring against me, and God has turned away from me and answers me no

---

a Q Ms Gk Vg: MT lacks *whom*   *b* Or *a god*; or *gods*

Jerusalem, but Gezer is much too far away. *Amalekites.* See note on 15.2. *Telam,* probably another name for the town called Telaim in 15.4 and Telem in Josh 15.24. The *way to Shur* (cf. 15.7) was the central east-west route through the Sinai Peninsula. **27.10** *Negeb,* lit. "Southland," the southern desert of Judah. Specifically, the *Negeb of Judah* was the region around Beer-sheba (see 2 Sam 24.7; 2 Chr 28.18), and the *Negeb of the Jerahmeelites* (cf. 30.29) probably lay farther south. *Negeb of the Kenites,* probably "Negeb of the Kenizzites," as in the Septuagint; the territory of the Kenizzites, parent tribe of the Calebites (see 25.3), was in the region around and south of Hebron.

28.3–25 Anxious about the impending battle with the Philistines, Saul engages a medium to bring Samuel up from the dead and seek his advice. **28.3** *Samuel had died,* reported in 25.1. *Mediums* and *wizards,* practitioners of black magic through whom the dead speak

to the living (2 Kings 23.24); their craft was prohibited by priestly law (Lev 19.31; 20.6, 27). **28.4** *Shunem,* a town on the southern slope of the Hill of Moreh, which stood opposite Mount *Gilboa* in the Valley of Jezreel (see 29.1). **28.6** Saul is now estranged from the Lord, and the standard methods of divination are unavailable to him; for *Urim,* divinatory lots, see notes on 14.3; 14.41. **28.7** In his frustration Saul seeks out *a medium,* whose activities he has personally prohibited (v. 3). *Endor,* a town of the tribe of Manasseh (Josh 17.11) located a few miles northeast of the Philistine camp at Shunem on the northern slope of the Hill of Moreh (see v. 4). **28.14** The woman's description of *an old man . . . wrapped in a robe,* Samuel's characteristic garment (see 15.27), is enough for Saul to recognize the ghost of the great prophet. **28.15** *Disturbed,* here specifically the interruption of the rest of the dead (cf. "Sheol beneath is stirred up," Isa 14.9); it occurs in an-

more, either by prophets or by dreams; so I have summoned you to tell me what I should do." 16Samuel said, "Why then do you ask me, since the LORD has turned from you and become your enemy? 17The LORD has done to you just as he spoke by me; for the LORD has torn the kingdom out of your hand, and given it to your neighbor, David. 18Because you did not obey the voice of the LORD, and did not carry out his fierce wrath against Amalek, therefore the LORD has done this thing to you today. 19Moreover the LORD will give Israel along with you into the hands of the Philistines; and tomorrow you and your sons shall be with me; the LORD will also give the army of Israel into the hands of the Philistines."

20 Immediately Saul fell full length on the ground, filled with fear because of the words of Samuel; and there was no strength in him, for he had eaten nothing all day and all night. 21The woman came to Saul, and when she saw that he was terrified, she said to him, "Your servant has listened to you; I have taken my life in my hand, and have listened to what you have said to me. 22Now therefore, you also listen to your servant; let me set a morsel of bread before you. Eat, that you may have strength when you go on your way." 23He refused, and said, "I will not eat." But his servants, together with the woman, urged him; and he listened to their words. So he got up from the ground and sat on the bed. 24Now the woman had a fatted calf in the house. She quickly slaughtered it, and she took flour, kneaded it, and baked unleavened cakes. 25She put them before Saul and his servants, and they ate. Then they rose and went away that night.

The Philistines Reject David

29 Now the Philistines gathered all their forces at Aphek, while the Israelites were encamped by the fountain that is in Jezreel. 2As the lords of the Philistines were passing on by hundreds and by thousands, and David and his men were passing on in the rear with Achish, 3the commanders of the Philistines said, "What are these Hebrews doing here?" Achish said to the commanders of the Philistines, "Is this not David, the servant of King Saul of Israel, who has been with me now for days and years? Since he deserted to me I have found no fault in him to this day." 4But the commanders of the Philistines were angry with him; and the commanders of the Philistines said to him, "Send the man back, so that he may return to the place that you have assigned to him; he shall not go down with us to battle, or else he may become an adversary to us in the battle. For how could this fellow reconcile himself to his lord? Would it not be with the heads of the men here? 5Is this not David, of whom they sing to one another in dances,

'Saul has killed his thousands,
　　and David his ten thousands'?"

6 Then Achish called David and said to him, "As the LORD lives, you have been honest, and to me it seems right that you should march out and in with me in the campaign; for I have found nothing wrong in you from the day of your coming to me until today. Nevertheless the lords do not approve of you. 7So go back now; and go peaceably; do nothing to displease the lords of the Philistines." 8David said to Achish, "But what have I done?

---

cient tomb inscriptions as a description of the activity of grave robbers. **28.17–18** Samuel is alluding to the story of the rejection of Saul's kingship in 15.10–35. *The LORD has torn . . . neighbor,* a direct reference to 15.28. For the Lord's *fierce wrath against Amalek,* see ch. 15 in general. **28.20** *Eaten nothing all day and all night.* Saul probably fasted to purify himself ritually in preparation for the evocation of the ghost of Samuel. **28.24** The familiar NT image of the *fatted calf* (see Lk 15.23) appears elsewhere in the OT only as a metaphor, in Jer. 46.21; Mal 4.2 ("calves from the stall").

29.1–11 Although Achish is convinced of his loyalty, the other Philistine lords are suspicious of David and send him home before the impending battle. In keeping with the viewpoint of the story of David's rise to power (see Introduction) it is made clear that David

will not be a belligerent on the side of the Philistines in the coming battle in which Saul and Jonathan lose their lives (see ch. 31). **29.1** This episode occurs at *Aphek* (see note on 4.1b), far to the south of Shunem, where the Philistines are currently mustering (see 28.4). *Jezreel,* a town on the northwestern slope of Mount Gilboa (see 28.4) thirty-five to forty miles northeast of Aphek. **29.3** The Philistine leaders refer to David and his companions not by the political designation Israelites but by the ethnic term *Hebrews* (see 13.3; 14.21). *Achish,* who has been completely duped by David (see note on 27.8–12), tries to defend his vassal. **29.4** *The place . . . assigned to him,* Ziklag. **29.5** Cf. 18.7; 21.11. **29.6** Achish swears *as the LORD lives* as if he were a worshiper of the God of Israel; perhaps this is a courteous gesture to David. **29.8** Although Achish

What have you found in your servant from the day I entered your service until now, that I should not go and fight against the enemies of my lord the king?" 9 Achish replied to David, "I know that you are as blameless in my sight as an angel of God; nevertheless, the commanders of the Philistines have said, 'He shall not go up with us to the battle.' 10 Now then rise early in the morning, you and the servants of your lord who came with you, and go to the place that I appointed for you. As for the evil report, do not take it to heart, for you have done well before me.*a* Start early in the morning, and leave as soon as you have light." 11 So David set out with his men early in the morning, to return to the land of the Philistines. But the Philistines went up to Jezreel.

David Avenges the Destruction of Ziklag

30 Now when David and his men came to Ziklag on the third day, the Amalekites had made a raid on the Negeb and on Ziklag. They had attacked Ziklag, burned it down, 2 and taken captive the women and all*b* who were in it, both small and great; they killed none of them, but carried them off, and went their way. 3 When David and his men came to the city, they found it burned down, and their wives and sons and daughters taken captive. 4 Then David and the people who were with him raised their voices and wept, until they had no more strength to weep. 5 David's two wives also had been taken captive, Ahinoam of Jezreel, and Abigail the widow of Nabal of Carmel. 6 David was in great danger; for the people spoke of stoning him, because all the people were bitter in spirit for their sons and daughters. But David strengthened himself in the LORD his God.

7 David said to the priest Abiathar son of Ahimelech, "Bring me the ephod." So Abiathar brought the ephod to David. 8 David inquired of the LORD, "Shall I pursue this band? Shall I overtake them?" He answered him, "Pursue; for you shall surely overtake and shall surely rescue." 9 So David set out, he and the six hundred men who were with him. They came to the Wadi Besor, where those stayed who were left behind. 10 But David went on with the pursuit, he and four hundred men; two hundred stayed behind, too exhausted to cross the Wadi Besor.

11 In the open country they found an Egyptian, and brought him to David. They gave him bread and he ate; they gave him water to drink; 12 they also gave him a piece of fig cake and two clusters of raisins. When he had eaten, his spirit revived; for he had not eaten bread or drunk water for three days and three nights. 13 Then David said to him, "To whom do you belong? Where are you from?" He said, "I am a young man of Egypt, servant to an Amalekite. My master left me behind because I fell sick three days ago. 14 We had made a raid on the Negeb of the Cherethites and on that which belongs to Judah and on the Negeb of Caleb; and we burned Ziklag down." 15 David said to him, "Will you take me down to this raiding party?" He said, "Swear to me by God that you will not kill me, or hand me over to my master, and I will take you down to them."

16 When he had taken him down, they were spread out all over the ground, eating and drinking and dancing, because of the great amount of spoil they had taken from the land

---

a Gk: Heb lacks *and go to the place . . . done well before me*
b Gk: Heb lacks *and all*

---

hears only the surface meaning of David's wish to *fight against the enemies of my lord the king*, i.e., the enemies of Achish, the audience of the old story of David's rise to power (see Introduction), who know David's true loyalties, understand that what he really wants is to fight against the enemies of Saul. **29.9** Elsewhere David is given credit for having the juridical insight of *an angel of God* (see 2 Sam 14.17; 19.27), but the Septuagint is probably correct in omitting the phrase in this passage.

30.1–31 David defeats a band of brigands who have plundered his stronghold in his absence and distributes the booty he takes from them to the towns of Judah (see note on 27.1–28.2). **30.1** The *Amalekites*, ancient enemies of Israel (see note on 15.2) against whom David has recently gone raiding (see 27.8), have

used the opportunity of David's absence to attack *Ziklag*. **30.5** For *David's two wives*, see 25.42–43; 27.3. **30.7** As he did after the liberation of Keilah (see 23.6–12) David calls upon *Abiathar* (see 22.20–23) to seek an oracle using the *ephod*, which here, as in 23.6, is an instrument of divination. **30.9** Although the *Wadi Besor* is not mentioned outside of this episode, it must have been one of the prominent wadi systems that drain the Negeb into the Mediterranean. **30.14** On the *Negeb* and its districts, see note on 27.10. The *Cherethites* probably traced their ancestry to Crete or Caphtor, also the place of origin of the Philistines (see Jer 47.4; Am 9.7), and the two peoples are closely associated in the Bible (see Ezek 25.16; Zeph 2.5); when he is king, David's bodyguard will include staunchly loyal Cherethites (see 2 Sam 8.18). *Negeb of Caleb*, probably

of the Philistines and from the land of Judah. ¹⁷David attacked them from twilight until the evening of the next day. Not one of them escaped, except four hundred young men, who mounted camels and fled. ¹⁸David recovered all that the Amalekites had taken; and David rescued his two wives. ¹⁹Nothing was missing, whether small or great, sons or daughters, spoil or anything that had been taken; David brought back everything. ²⁰David also captured all the flocks and herds, which were driven ahead of the other cattle; people said, "This is David's spoil."

21 Then David came to the two hundred men who had been too exhausted to follow David, and who had been left at the Wadi Besor. They went out to meet David and to meet the people who were with him. When David drew near to the people he saluted them. ²²Then all the corrupt and worthless fellows among the men who had gone with David said, "Because they did not go with us, we will not give them any of the spoil that we have recovered, except that each man may take his wife and children, and leave." ²³But David said, "You shall not do so, my brothers, with what the LORD has given us; he has preserved us and handed over to us the raiding party that attacked us. ²⁴Who would listen to you in this matter? For the share of the one who goes down into the battle shall be the same as the share of the one who stays by the baggage; they shall share alike." ²⁵From that day forward he made it a statute and an ordinance for Israel; it continues to the present day.

26 When David came to Ziklag, he sent part of the spoil to his friends, the elders of Judah, saying, "Here is a present for you from the spoil of the enemies of the LORD"; ²⁷it was for those in Bethel, in Ramoth of the Negeb, in Jattir, ²⁸in Aroer, in Siphmoth, in Eshtemoa, ²⁹in Racal, in the towns of the Jerahmeelites, in the towns of the Kenites, ³⁰in Hormah, in Bor-ashan, in Athach, ³¹in Hebron, all the places where David and his men had roamed.

The Death of Saul and His Sons

31 Now the Philistines fought against Israel; and the men of Israel fled before the Philistines, and many fell[a] on Mount Gilboa. ²The Philistines overtook Saul and his sons; and the Philistines killed Jonathan and Abinadab and Malchishua, the sons of Saul. ³The battle pressed hard upon Saul; the archers found him, and he was badly wounded by them. ⁴Then Saul said to his armor-bearer, "Draw your sword and thrust me through with it, so that these uncircumcised may not

---

a Heb *and they fell slain*

---

a subdistrict of the Negeb of the Kenizzites (see note on 27.10). **30.17** *Twilight,* here probably "dawn," as in Job 7.4; Ps 119.147; and postbiblical Hebrew. **30.21–25** The policy David establishes here for the distribution of booty is reminiscent of that in Deut 20.14. **30.26–31** David parcels out the *spoil of the enemies of the LORD* among the towns of Judah. The redistribution of booty is a common way in which a military chieftain earns the loyalty of his followers; David is preparing the way for his assumption of the kingship of Judah (see 2 Sam 2.4). **30.27** *Bethel* was not in Judah; the Septuagint has "Beth-zur," a Calebite town in the Judean hills a few miles north of Hebron (see Josh 15.58). *Ramoth of the Negeb,* called Baalath-beer in Josh 19.8. Location unknown. *Jattir,* a levitical city in the Judean hills about twelve miles south-southwest of Hebron (see Josh 15.48; 21.14). **30.28** *Aroer* (see Num 32.34), a Transjordanian city less likely to have been intended here than Ararah, a town in the Negeb of Judah about twelve miles southeast of Beer-sheba (see Josh 15.22, where Ararah should be read for Adadah). *Siphmoth,* otherwise unknown. *Eshtemoa,* a levitical city in the Judean hills about eight miles south of Hebron (see Josh 15.50; 21.14). **30.29** *Racal,* probably a corruption of Carmel, which the Septuagint preserves (see note on 15.12). Though the *Jerahmeelites* may have once been an independent tribe, they were eventually incorporated into Judah (see 1 Chr 2.9, 25–27); the location of their territory is unknown, but it may have been south of Beer-sheba (see 27.10). *Kenites,* better "Kenizzites," as found in the Septuagint and a manuscript from Qumran (4QSamª); see also note on 27.10. **30.30** *Hormah* must have been close to Ziklag (see note on 27.5–6); it too was formally claimed by Simeon (Josh 19.4) but included in the list of the cities of Judah (Josh 15.30). *Bor-ashan,* or Ashan, a levitical city in the Judean hills a few miles northwest of Beer-sheba (see Josh 15.42; 19.7; 21.16, where Ain should probably be corrected to Ashan). *Athach,* better "Ether," which is paired with Ashan in Josh 15.42; 19.7; it was about fifteen miles northwest of Hebron. **30.31** *Hebron,* the principal city of the region, the traditional capital of Judah, where David was first proclaimed king (see 2 Sam 2.4). It was about nineteen miles south-southwest of Jerusalem in the Judean hills.

31.1–13 Saul, Jonathan, and his brothers lose their lives in a battle with the Philistines on Mount Gilboa. **31.1** *Mount Gilboa.* See note on 28.4. **31.2** *Sons of Saul.* See note on 14.49. **31.4** The armor-bearer's fear of delivering the coup de grace is probably based on his awareness of Saul's status as the sacrosanct

come and thrust me through, and make sport of me." But his armor-bearer was unwilling; for he was terrified. So Saul took his own sword and fell upon it. 5When his armor-bearer saw that Saul was dead, he also fell upon his sword and died with him. 6So Saul and his three sons and his armor-bearer and all his men died together on the same day. 7When the men of Israel who were on the other side of the valley and those beyond the Jordan saw that the men of Israel had fled and that Saul and his sons were dead, they forsook their towns and fled; and the Philistines came and occupied them.

8 The next day, when the Philistines came to strip the dead, they found Saul and his three sons fallen on Mount Gilboa. 9They cut off his

head, stripped off his armor, and sent messengers throughout the land of the Philistines to carry the good news to the houses of their idols and to the people. 10They put his armor in the temple of Astarte;*a* and they fastened his body to the wall of Beth-shan. 11But when the inhabitants of Jabesh-gilead heard what the Philistines had done to Saul, 12all the valiant men set out, traveled all night long, and took the body of Saul and the bodies of his sons from the wall of Beth-shan. They came to Jabesh and burned them there. 13Then they took their bones and buried them under the tamarisk tree in Jabesh, and fasted seven days.

---

a Heb plural

anointed of the Lord (see 24.6; 26.9). **31.7** The Israelites *who were on the other side of the valley* are probably those who lived north of the Valley of Jezreel, where the battle occurred, but *those beyond the Jordan* may be a secondary expansion; the parallel account in 1 Chr 10.7 mentions only the Israelites "who were in the valley." **31.10** Saul's armor, like Goliath's (see 21.9–10), is deposited in a temple. *Astarte,* the name of a prominent Canaanite goddess used by the biblical writers as a generic designation for a goddess (see 7.4); here it probably refers to the goddess of Beth-

shan, whose name was Antit. *Beth-shan,* a major Egyptian and Canaanite fortress that guarded the eastern end of the Valley of Jezreel (see note on 2 Sam 2.9); at this point in the story it seems to be under Philistine control. **31.11–13** *Jabesh-gilead* was not far south of Beth-shan on the other side of the Jordan (see 10.27). The people of Jabesh have a long-standing debt to Saul for rescuing them from Nahash the Ammonite (see 10.27–11.15). David will eventually return the bones of Saul and Jonathan to their family tomb in Benjamin (see 2 Sam 21.12–14).

2 SAMUEL

David Mourns for Saul and Jonathan

1 After the death of Saul, when David had returned from defeating the Amalekites, David remained two days in Ziklag. ²On the third day, a man came from Saul's camp, with his clothes torn and dirt on his head. When he came to David, he fell to the ground and did obeisance. ³David said to him, "Where have you come from?" He said to him, "I have escaped from the camp of Israel." ⁴David said to him, "How did things go? Tell me!" He answered, "The army fled from the battle, but also many of the army fell and died; and Saul and his son Jonathan also died." ⁵Then David asked the young man who was reporting to him, "How do you know that Saul and his son Jonathan died?" ⁶The young man reporting to him said, "I happened to be on Mount Gilboa; and there was Saul leaning on his spear, while the chariots and the horsemen drew close to him. ⁷When he looked behind him, he saw me, and called to me. I answered, 'Here sir.' ⁸And he said to me, 'Who are you?' I answered him, 'I am an Amalekite.' ⁹He said to me, 'Come, stand over me and kill me; for convulsions have seized me, and yet my life still lingers.' ¹⁰So I stood over him, and killed him, for I knew that he could not live after he had fallen. I took the crown that was on his head and the armlet that was on his arm, and I have brought them here to my lord."

11 Then David took hold of his clothes and tore them; and all the men who were with him

---

[For introductory material to 2 Samuel, see the Introduction to 1 Samuel.]

1.1–16 David responds to the news of the death of Saul and Jonathan with genuine sorrow. One of the principal goals of the old story of David's rise to power (see Introduction) is to show that although David was ultimately the beneficiary of Saul's death, he did not seek or desire it, remaining loyal to Saul to the last. **1.1** 2 Samuel begins *After the death of Saul* just as Joshua begins "After the death of Moses" and Judges "After the death of Joshua." For the *Amalekites* in general, see note on 1 Sam 15.2; the present reference is to David's punitive raid, described in 1 Sam 30, against a band of Amalekites who had attacked his personal fortress of *Ziklag* (see 1 Sam 27.6). **1.2** An Amalekite (see v. 8) arrives in David's camp *with his clothes torn and dirt on his head,* conventional gestures of grief (see 1 Sam 4.12; 2 Sam 15.32), but he may be dissembling (cf. Josh 9.3–15). **1.6–10** The Amalekite's account of the death of Saul is quite different from that given in 1 Sam 31.3–5. The simplest explanation of the contradiction is that the Amalekite is lying, on the very erroneous assumption that David would reward him for having taken Saul's life. Readers are probably to understand that the Amalekite came upon the body of Saul, stripped off his crown and armlet, and then conceived of the idea that they might be most valuable to him if he brought them to David. **1.6** *Mount Gilboa,* the scene of the fatal battle (see 1 Sam 31.1), stood at the northern limit of the Samarian hills overlooking the Valley of Jezreel. It has been suggested that Saul was *leaning on his spear* in an attempt to commit suicide (cf. 1 Sam 31.4), but it is more likely that he was supporting himself with the shaft of his weapon after receiving mortal wounds. **1.9** *Convulsions,* obscure, perhaps giddiness or dizziness. **1.10** The *crown* and *armlet* are royal insignia. The former is more likely to have been a diadem worn on the forehead than a crown; the king received it at the time of his investiture (see 2 Kings 11.12). The armlet is mentioned nowhere else in the Bible (though some would restore it in 2 Kings 11.12).

did the same. [12]They mourned and wept, and fasted until evening for Saul and for his son Jonathan, and for the army of the LORD and for the house of Israel, because they had fallen by the sword. [13]David said to the young man who had reported to him, "Where do you come from?" He answered, "I am the son of a resident alien, an Amalekite." [14]David said to him, "Were you not afraid to lift your hand to destroy the LORD's anointed?" [15]Then David called one of the young men and said, "Come here and strike him down." So he struck him down and he died. [16]David said to him, "Your blood be on your head; for your own mouth has testified against you, saying, 'I have killed the LORD's anointed.' "

[17] David intoned this lamentation over Saul and his son Jonathan. [18](He ordered that The Song of the Bow[a] be taught to the people of Judah; it is written in the Book of Jashar.) He said:

[19] Your glory, O Israel, lies slain upon your
     high places!
   How the mighty have fallen!

[20] Tell it not in Gath,
     proclaim it not in the streets of
        Ashkelon;
   or the daughters of the Philistines will
        rejoice,
   the daughters of the uncircumcised
        will exult.

[21] You mountains of Gilboa,
     let there be no dew or rain upon you,
     nor bounteous fields![b]
   For there the shield of the mighty was
        defiled,
     the shield of Saul, anointed with oil no
        more.

[22] From the blood of the slain,
     from the fat of the mighty,
   the bow of Jonathan did not turn back,
     nor the sword of Saul return empty.

[23] Saul and Jonathan, beloved and lovely!
     In life and in death they were not
        divided;
   they were swifter than eagles,
     they were stronger than lions.

[24] O daughters of Israel, weep over Saul,
     who clothed you with crimson, in
        luxury,
     who put ornaments of gold on your
        apparel.

[25] How the mighty have fallen
     in the midst of the battle!

   Jonathan lies slain upon your high places.

---

a Heb *that The Bow*   *b* Meaning of Heb uncertain

1.13–16 *Resident alien,* a foreigner living legally and permanently in Israel, entitled to protection and most of the same privileges as native-born Israelites, but he was also subject to most of the same rules of behavior, including respect for the sanctity of *the LORD's anointed.* David, who has always been scrupulous with regard to this last point where Saul was concerned (see 1 Sam 24.6; 26.9), decides that the Amalekite's own testimony warrants a sentence of death. **1.17–27** One of the Bible's earliest poems; given its antiquity and personal character, its attribution to David might well be authentic. **1.18** *The Song of the Bow* may be the ancient name of David's lament, but it seems unlikely and appears as such in no ancient manuscripts of the text of Samuel. The Masoretic Text has simply "a bow," and some have interpreted this to mean that David commanded that the people should be trained in archery. The Septuagint has nothing at all, understanding *lamentation* of v. 17 to be what David wanted taught to the people. We know of at least two and possibly three poems that were included in the lost *Book of Jashar,* or "Book of the Upright": David's lament, the command to sun and moon to stand still in Josh 10.12–13, and possibly Solomon's verses about the temple of the Lord in 1 Kings 8.12–13, which are assigned to "the Book of

Hashir (the Song)" in the Septuagint. **1.19** If this rendering of this difficult passage is correct, Israel's *glory* is Saul; another interpretation is to understand the word translated *glory* as "gazelle," an example of the common practice of using the names of strong male animals to refer to military commanders. *High places,* presumably the heights of Gilboa, but the expression translated *slain upon . . . high places* is used in the Qumran *War Scroll* (1QM 12.10) to mean "backs of the slain." *How the mighty have fallen!* (also in vv. 25, 27), a refrain unifying this elegant poem. **1.20** *Gath, Ashkelon,* two of the principal cities of the Philistines (see note on 1 Sam 5.8). **1.21** *Bounteous fields,* problematic, possibly "fields of offerings" or "upwellings of the deeps." *Anointed with oil no more,* ambiguous (in translation and in the Hebrew) as to whether this refers to Saul or his shield. Although Saul was the anointed of the Lord (see 1 Sam 9.16; 24.6–7; 26.9), it is probably the shield that is meant; a leather shield was rubbed with oil to keep it supple and ready for battle (see Isa 21.5). **1.24** The dried bodies of "kermes" insects produced the brilliant red dye called *crimson,* which was a sign of luxury (see Prov 31.21). **1.25–26** David's lament is most personal when he expresses his grief over his friend Jonathan; on Jonathan's love for David, see 1 Sam 18.1; 20.17.

26   I am distressed for you, my brother
        Jonathan;
    greatly beloved were you to me;
    your love to me was wonderful,
    passing the love of women.

27 How the mighty have fallen,
    and the weapons of war perished!

David Anointed King of Judah

2 After this David inquired of the LORD, "Shall I go up into any of the cities of Judah?" The LORD said to him, "Go up." David said, "To which shall I go up?" He said, "To Hebron." 2So David went up there, along with his two wives, Ahinoam of Jezreel, and Abigail the widow of Nabal of Carmel. 3David brought up the men who were with him, every one with his household; and they settled in the towns of Hebron. 4Then the people of Judah came, and there they anointed David king over the house of Judah.

When they told David, "It was the people of Jabesh-gilead who buried Saul," 5David sent messengers to the people of Jabesh-gilead, and said to them, "May you be blessed by the LORD, because you showed this loyalty to Saul

your lord, and buried him! 6Now may the LORD show steadfast love and faithfulness to you! And I too will reward you because you have done this thing. 7Therefore let your hands be strong, and be valiant; for Saul your lord is dead, and the house of Judah has anointed me king over them."

Ishbaal King of Israel

8 But Abner son of Ner, commander of Saul's army, had taken Ishbaal*a* son of Saul, and brought him over to Mahanaim. 9He made him king over Gilead, the Ashurites, Jezreel, Ephraim, Benjamin, and over all Israel. 10Ishbaal,*a* Saul's son, was forty years old when he began to reign over Israel, and he reigned two years. But the house of Judah followed David. 11The time that David was king in Hebron over the house of Judah was seven years and six months.

The Battle of Gibeon

12 Abner son of Ner, and the servants of Ishbaal*a* son of Saul, went out from Mahanaim to

---

a Gk Compare 1 Chr 8.33; 9.39: Heb *Ish-bosheth,* "man of shame"

2.1–7 David's kin, the people of Judah, are the first to embrace him as king. **2.1** *Hebron.* See note on 1 Sam 30.31. **2.2** For David's *two wives,* see 1 Sam 25.42–43; 27.3; 30.5. *Jezreel, Carmel,* both towns in the vicinity of Hebron (see notes on 1 Sam 15.12; 25.43). **2.4** *People of Judah,* probably the same as the elders of Judah in 1 Sam 30.26–31, to whom David distributed the booty from his raid against the Amalekites (cf. 2 Sam 19.11, 14). In the present form of the larger story, which has been shaped by a prophetic view of kingship (see Introduction), David has already been anointed in private by Samuel. Here, in an early part of the narrative, he is *anointed* by the leading citizens of Judah in a public ceremony. Saul's burial by *the people of Jabesh-gilead* is reported in 1 Sam 31.11–13. **2.5–7** David's message to the people of Jabesh-gilead is an overture to an alliance with one of Saul's principal constituencies; it will lead to conflict with Saul's heir, as the rest of the chapter shows. **2.8–11** Abner sets up a rump government in Transjordan with Saul's son Ishbaal as king. **2.8** *Abner,* Saul's uncle and chief military officer (see 1 Sam 14.50–51), installs Saul's only surviving son on the throne of Israel. *Ishbaal* in Hebrew means "Man of Baal," but this does not mean that the family of Saul worshiped the god Baal (Jonathan's name contains the name of the God of Israel). *Baal* meant "lord" or "master" and was probably an acceptable way of referring to the God of Israel in Saul's day. In later times the strong association of the word with the Canaanite god Baal caused it to be avoided. Scribes who found *baal* offen-

sive often replaced it with *bosheth,* "shame," so that Saul's heir seems to be called "Man of Shame" (Ish-bosheth; see text note a). *Mahanaim,* a town in the Transjordanian tribal territory of Gad (Josh 13.26, 30; cf. notes on 1 Sam 10.27b; 13.7); its exact location is uncertain. Abner probably moved the government of Israel to Transjordan because of Philistine domination of the central hills in the aftermath of the battle of Mount Gilboa; it was too dangerous to place a son of Saul on the throne in Saul's capital of Gibeah (cf. notes on 1 Sam 9.1; 11.4). **2.9** *Gilead,* a common designation for Transjordanian Israel in general (see notes on 1 Sam 10.27b; 13.7), is here used in its stricter sense as the territory of the tribes of Gad and Reuben, which Saul ruled as a result of his victory over Nahash the Ammonite (see 1 Sam 10.27–11.15). *Ashurites* (Masoretic Text), perhaps "Assyrians," who are wholly out of place here, or "Asherites," i.e., people of the north Galilean tribe of Asher, but they also are too far away. The Peshitta and Vulgate reflect "Geshurites," who lived north of Gilead and east of Jezreel, which fits perfectly into the present list. *Jezreel,* the eastern section of the fertile valley that separated the Galilee from the Ephraimite hills. *Ephraim,* here probably the Samarian hill country in general, including the hills of both Ephraim and Manasseh. *Benjamin,* located to the south, was the home base of the house of Saul (see notes on 1 Sam 4.12; 9.1). *All Israel* (cf. 3.12, 21), probably intended as a summary reference to the territories just listed. **2.10–11** These concluding chronological

Gibeon. [13]Joab son of Zeruiah, and the servants of David, went out and met them at the pool of Gibeon. One group sat on one side of the pool, while the other sat on the other side of the pool. [14]Abner said to Joab, "Let the young men come forward and have a contest before us." Joab said, "Let them come forward." [15]So they came forward and were counted as they passed by, twelve for Benjamin and Ishbaal[a] son of Saul, and twelve of the servants of David. [16]Each grasped his opponent by the head, and thrust his sword in his opponent's side; so they fell down together. Therefore that place was called Helkath-hazzurim,[b] which is at Gibeon. [17]The battle was very fierce that day; and Abner and the men of Israel were beaten by the servants of David.

18 The three sons of Zeruiah were there, Joab, Abishai, and Asahel. Now Asahel was as swift of foot as a wild gazelle. [19]Asahel pursued Abner, turning neither to the right nor to the left as he followed him. [20]Then Abner looked back and said, "Is it you, Asahel?" He answered, "Yes, it is." [21]Abner said to him, "Turn to your right or to your left, and seize one of the young men, and take his spoil." But Asahel would not turn away from following him. [22]Abner said again to Asahel, "Turn away from following me; why should I strike you to the ground? How then could I show my face to your brother Joab?" [23]But he refused to turn away. So Abner struck him in the stomach with the butt of his spear, so that the spear came out at his back. He fell there, and died where he lay. And all those who came to the place where Asahel had fallen and died, stood still.

24 But Joab and Abishai pursued Abner. As the sun was going down they came to the hill of Ammah, which lies before Giah on the way to the wilderness of Gibeon. [25]The Benjaminites rallied around Abner and formed a single band; they took their stand on the top of a hill. [26]Then Abner called to Joab, "Is the sword to keep devouring forever? Do you not know that the end will be bitter? How long will it be before you order your people to turn from the pursuit of their kinsmen?" [27]Joab said, "As God lives, if you had not spoken, the people would have continued to pursue their kinsmen, not stopping until morning." [28]Joab sounded the trumpet and all the people stopped; they no longer pursued Israel or engaged in battle any further.

29 Abner and his men traveled all that night through the Arabah; they crossed the Jordan, and, marching the whole forenoon,[c] they came to Mahanaim. [30]Joab returned from the pursuit of Abner; and when he had gathered all the people together, there were missing of David's servants nineteen men besides Asahel. [31]But the servants of David had killed of Benjamin three hundred sixty of Abner's men. [32]They took up Asahel and buried him in the tomb of his father, which was at Bethlehem. Joab and his men marched all night, and the day broke upon them at Hebron.

Abner Defects to David

3 There was a long war between the house of Saul and the house of David; David grew stronger and stronger, while the house of Saul became weaker and weaker.

---

a Gk Compare 1 Chr 8.33; 9.39: Heb Ish-bosheth, "man of shame"
b That is Field of Sword-edges   c Meaning of Heb uncertain

---

notices derive from the hand of the Deuteronomistic Historian (see Introduction; note on 1 Sam 13.1). **2.12–32** The conflict between David's army and that of Ishbaal erupts in open hostility. **2.12** Abner's expedition should probably be interpreted as a show of force in response to David's overture to the people of Jabesh-gilead. *Gibeon,* about six miles north-north-west of Jerusalem. **2.13** *Joab,* the most prominent of the three sons of David's sister Zeruiah (see 1 Sam 26.6), was the commander of David's army (see 8.16; 20.23). *Pool of Gibeon,* a well-known landmark (see Jer 41.12); it has been identified with the Iron Age water system of the city, a deep, wide circular cavity carved out of the rock on the northern part of the site. **2.14–16** This event is sometimes interpreted as a sporting contest that went out of control, but the term translated *young men* can be used to refer to seasoned sol-diers, and the engagement is more likely to be a battle by representatives similar to the famous contest between the Roman Horatii and Curiatii. Apparently, however, everyone on both sides was slain, so that the contest was inconclusive and a general battle ensued. **2.18** *Abishai.* See 1 Sam 26.6. *Asahel,* the youngest of the sons of Zeruiah and a member of David's elite corps of the Thirty (see 2 Sam 23.24), shares the fierce impetuosity of his older brothers. *Wild gazelle.* Cf. note on 1.19; 1 Chr 12.8. **2.24** *Ammah,* probably "water channel"; *Giah,* probably "spring." The pursuit that began at one water system (v. 13) seems to end at another; the general direction is to the east toward *the wilderness of Gibeon.* **2.29** Abner's troops return by marching northwest through the *Arabah,* or rift valley south of the Sea of Galilee.

3.1–5 The story is interrupted by the insertion of a

2 Sons were born to David at Hebron: his firstborn was Amnon, of Ahinoam of Jezreel; [3]his second, Chileab, of Abigail the widow of Nabal of Carmel; the third, Absalom son of Maacah, daughter of King Talmai of Geshur; [4]the fourth, Adonijah son of Haggith; the fifth, Shephatiah son of Abital; [5]and the sixth, Ithream, of David's wife Eglah. These were born to David in Hebron.

6 While there was war between the house of Saul and the house of David, Abner was making himself strong in the house of Saul. [7]Now Saul had a concubine whose name was Rizpah daughter of Aiah. And Ishbaal[a] said to Abner, "Why have you gone in to my father's concubine?" [8]The words of Ishbaal[b] made Abner very angry; he said, "Am I a dog's head for Judah? Today I keep showing loyalty to the house of your father Saul, to his brothers, and to his friends, and have not given you into the hand of David; and yet you charge me now with a crime concerning this woman. [9]So may God do to Abner and so may he add to it! For just what the LORD has sworn to David, that will I accomplish for him, [10]to transfer the kingdom from the house of Saul, and set up the throne of David over Israel and over Judah, from Dan to Beer-sheba." [11]And Ishbaal[a] could not answer Abner another word, because he feared him.

12 Abner sent messengers to David at Hebron,[c] saying, "To whom does the land belong? Make your covenant with me, and I will give you my support to bring all Israel over to you." [13]He said, "Good; I will make a covenant with you. But one thing I require of you: you shall never appear in my presence unless you bring Saul's daughter Michal when you come to see me." [14]Then David sent messengers to Saul's son Ishbaal,[d] saying, "Give me my wife Michal, to whom I became engaged at the price of one hundred foreskins of the Philistines." [15]Ishbaal[e] sent and took her from her husband Paltiel the son of Laish. [16]But her husband went with her, weeping as he walked

a Heb And he   b Gk Compare 1 Chr 8.33; 9.39: Heb Ish-bosheth, "man of shame"   c Gk: Heb where he was   d Heb Ish-bosheth

list of the sons of David born in Hebron. **3.2** For the story of *Amnon,* David's ill-fated firstborn, see ch. 13; for Amnon's mother, Ahinoam, see 1 Sam 25.43. **3.3** *Chileab* (Masoretic Text), should probably be corrected to "Daluiah" with the Septuagint and a scroll from Qumran (4QSam[a]; cf. Daniel in 1 Chr 3.1). Whatever his name was, he does not figure in the story elsewhere. For his mother, *Abigail,* and her first husband, *Nabal,* see 1 Sam 25.2–43. For the story of *Absalom,* see chs. 13–19; in 13.37 he will seek refuge in the Transjordanian kingdom of *Geshur* (see 2.9) with his grandfather *Talmai.* **3.4–5** For the story of *Adonijah,* see 1 Kings 1–2; nothing else is known of his mother, *Haggith. Shephatiah* and *Ithream,* mentioned only here and in a similar list in 1 Chr 3.3. **3.6–39** After attempting to reach an agreement with David, Abner is slain by Joab for personal reasons. The author of the old story of David's rise to power (see Introduction), aware of the sensibilities of the Benjaminites and others in his audience, places special stress on David's innocence of the death of the popular Benjaminite Abner, who, says the author, initiated private negotiations with David (cf. note on 3.12), came to Jerusalem voluntarily, left his audience with David *in peace* (a point made three times in vv. 21–23!), and was killed without David's knowledge (v. 26) by Joab, who was motivated not by politics but by a family matter of bloodguilt (v. 27). **3.6** A repetition of the essence of v. 1 after the interruption of the list of David's sons, adding now the news of *Abner's* increasing power. **3.7** *Rizpah daughter of Aiah* plays an important role in the grim story in 21.1–14, where we are told that she had borne two sons to Saul. This gave her considerable

status, despite the fact that she was only a *concubine,* a slave woman attached to the house of Saul, so that Ishbaal's sensitivity about her relationship with Abner is understandable. If Abner has made a claim on Saul's harem, as Ishbaal charges, he is only a step away from seizing the throne (see 16.20–22; 1 Kings 2.13–25). **3.8** *A dog's head.* Abner may be euphemistically suggesting that he is being treated like a dog's rear end. Dogs are often mentioned in expressions of self-abasement (see 1 Sam 24.14; 2 Sam 9.8). It has also been suggested that the expression refers to the dog-faced baboon, so that Abner may be claiming that he is being treated like an ape. **3.9–10** These two verses, in which Abner justifies his actions in terms that reflect the editorial viewpoint of the Deuteronomistic historian (see Introduction), are probably a secondary addition to the older story. *From Dan to Beer-sheba,* a convention describing the totality of ancient Israel, from its northernmost city, Dan, on the southern slope of Mount Hermon, to its southernmost, Beer-sheba, the principal town of the northern Negeb. **3.12** Having fallen out with Ishbaal, Abner now offers to swing his support to David. **3.13** David agrees to join forces with Abner, on the condition that Abner return *Saul's daughter Michal* to David; their marriage (see 1 Sam 18.20–28), which Saul annulled (1 Sam 25.44) after Michal helped David escape from Saul (1 Sam 19.8–17), provides David with a claim on the throne of Israel. **3.14** By citing his payment of the bride-*price of one hundred foreskins of the Philistines* (see 1 Sam 18.25, 27) David is stating a legal claim to Michal. **3.15** *Paltiel.* See note on 1 Sam 25.44. **3.16** *Bahurim,* a Benjaminite town just north of Jerusalem on the main

behind her all the way to Bahurim. Then Abner said to him, "Go back home!" So he went back.

17 Abner sent word to the elders of Israel, saying, "For some time past you have been seeking David as king over you. 18 Now then bring it about; for the LORD has promised David: Through my servant David I will save my people Israel from the hand of the Philistines, and from all their enemies." 19 Abner also spoke directly to the Benjaminites; then Abner went to tell David at Hebron all that Israel and the whole house of Benjamin were ready to do.

20 When Abner came with twenty men to David at Hebron, David made a feast for Abner and the men who were with him. 21 Abner said to David, "Let me go and rally all Israel to my lord the king, in order that they may make a covenant with you, and that you may reign over all that your heart desires." So David dismissed Abner, and he went away in peace.

Abner Is Killed by Joab

22 Just then the servants of David arrived with Joab from a raid, bringing much spoil with them. But Abner was not with David at Hebron, for David*a* had dismissed him, and he had gone away in peace. 23 When Joab and all the army that was with him came, it was told Joab, "Abner son of Ner came to the king, and he has dismissed him, and he has gone away in peace." 24 Then Joab went to the king and said, "What have you done? Abner came to you;

why did you dismiss him, so that he got away? 25 You know that Abner son of Ner came to deceive you, and to learn your comings and goings and to learn all that you are doing."

26 When Joab came out from David's presence, he sent messengers after Abner, and they brought him back from the cistern of Sirah; but David did not know about it. 27 When Abner returned to Hebron, Joab took him aside in the gateway to speak with him privately, and there he stabbed him in the stomach. So he died for shedding*b* the blood of Asahel, Joab's*c* brother. 28 Afterward, when David heard of it, he said, "I and my kingdom are forever guiltless before the LORD for the blood of Abner son of Ner. 29 May the guilt*d* fall on the head of Joab, and on all his father's house; and may the house of Joab never be without one who has a discharge, or who is leprous,*e* or who holds a spindle, or who falls by the sword, or who lacks food!" 30 So Joab and his brother Abishai murdered Abner because he had killed their brother Asahel in the battle at Gibeon.

31 Then David said to Joab and to all the people who were with him, "Tear your clothes, and put on sackcloth, and mourn over Abner." And King David followed the bier. 32 They buried Abner at Hebron. The king lifted up his voice and wept at the grave of Abner, and all the people wept. 33 The king lamented for Abner, saying,

a Heb he   b Heb lacks shedding   c Heb his   d Heb May it
e A term for several skin diseases; precise meaning uncertain

road connecting Israel and Judah; it was the home of Shimei, David's nemesis at the time of Absalom's revolt (see 16.5; 19.16; 1 Kings 2.8), and Azmaveth, a member of David's elite corps of the Thirty (23.31). **3.17** We have not been told explicitly that the Israelite leaders wanted David as their king, but it has been implicit in the references to their loyalty to him and his military leadership (see 1 Sam 18.16). **3.18b** A statement probably stemming from the hand of the Deuteronomistic Historian (see Introduction); it looks forward to the Lord's dynastic promise to David in ch. 7, in which the new king is also referred to as *my servant David* (vv. 5, 8; cf. v. 26), and to the synopsis in ch. 8 of his victories over the Philistines (8.1; cf. 5.17–25; 21.15–22; 23.8–17) and Israel's other enemies. **3.19** The narrator reminds the *Benjaminites* and others in his audience who may have been suspicious of David's complicity in Abner's assassination that Abner was negotiating on David's behalf just before his death. **3.21–23** The narrator stresses (three times) that Abner left David *in peace*. **3.25** Joab tries to convince David that Abner came to Jerusalem as a spy to dis-

cover his military plans, or *comings and goings* (see, e.g., 1 Sam 18.13, 16; 29.6). **3.26** Abner traveled two or three miles north from Hebron, where *the cistern of Sirah* was located, before being summoned back by Joab. Again, the narrator insists that *David did not know about it.* **3.27** Joab kills Abner to avenge *the blood of Asahel* (see 2.17–28). **3.28–29** These verses show expansion by a Deuteronomistic editor (see Introduction), who was concerned not only about David's guilt but also that of his *kingdom* or dynasty (cf. 7.12, 16). The oath against Joab anticipates the language of Solomon when he condemns Joab to death in 1 Kings 2.31–33. *Holds a spindle*, if correct, must mean "a man who holds the distaff," i.e., an effeminate male; but another possible rendering is "clings to a crutch." **3.30** For *Abishai*, see 2.18; 1 Sam 26.6. The statement that he too *murdered Abner* contradicts v. 27, which indicates that Joab did it *privately*, but the original text, preserved by the Septuagint and a scroll from Qumran (4QSam*a*), read, "Joab and his brother Abishai had been setting an ambush for Abner" (cf. Prov 1.11, 18). **3.32** Though a Benjaminite, Abner, like Ishbaal (4.12),

"Should Abner die as a fool dies?
34 Your hands were not bound,
    your feet were not fettered;
as one falls before the wicked
    you have fallen."
And all the people wept over him again.
35Then all the people came to persuade David
to eat something while it was still day; but
David swore, saying, "So may God do to me,
and more, if I taste bread or anything else before the sun goes down!" 36All the people took
notice of it, and it pleased them; just as everything the king did pleased all the people. 37So
all the people and all Israel understood that
day that the king had no part in the killing of
Abner son of Ner. 38And the king said to his
servants, "Do you not know that a prince and
a great man has fallen this day in Israel?
39Today I am powerless, even though anointed
king; these men, the sons of Zeruiah, are too
violent for me. The LORD pay back the one
who does wickedly in accordance with his
wickedness!"

Ishbaal Assassinated

4 When Saul's son Ishbaal[a] heard that
Abner had died at Hebron, his courage
failed, and all Israel was dismayed. 2Saul's son
had two captains of raiding bands; the name
of the one was Baanah, and the name of the
other Rechab. They were sons of Rimmon a
Benjaminite from Beeroth—for Beeroth is
considered to belong to Benjamin. 3(Now the

people of Beeroth had fled to Gittaim and are
there as resident aliens to this day).
4 Saul's son Jonathan had a son who was
crippled in his feet. He was five years old when
the news about Saul and Jonathan came from
Jezreel. His nurse picked him up and fled; and,
in her haste to flee, it happened that he fell and
became lame. His name was Mephibosheth.[b]
5 Now the sons of Rimmon the Beerothite,
Rechab and Baanah, set out, and about the
heat of the day they came to the house of Ishbaal,[c] while he was taking his noonday rest.
6They came inside the house as though to take
wheat, and they struck him in the stomach;
then Rechab and his brother Baanah escaped.[d]
7Now they had come into the house while he
was lying on his couch in his bedchamber;
they attacked him, killed him, and beheaded
him. Then they took his head and traveled by
way of the Arabah all night long. 8They
brought the head of Ishbaal[c] to David at Hebron and said to the king, "Here is the head of
Ishbaal,[c] son of Saul, your enemy, who sought
your life; the LORD has avenged my lord the
king this day on Saul and on his offspring."
9 David answered Rechab and his brother
Baanah, the sons of Rimmon the Beerothite,
"As the LORD lives, who has redeemed my life
out of every adversity, 10when the one who
told me, 'See, Saul is dead,' thought he was

---

a Heb lacks *Ishbaal*   b In 1 Chr 8.34 and 9.40, *Merib-baal*
c Heb *Ish-bosheth*   d Meaning of Heb of verse 6 uncertain

---

is buried at *Hebron*. **3.33** The Hebrew term rendered
fool in English Bibles refers to someone who commits
a serious breach of society's norms (see 13.13; note on
1 Sam 25.3); David's point is that Abner, *a prince and a
great man* (v. 38), should not have suffered the igno-
minious death of an outcast lacking the protection of
society. **3.36–37** The narrator of the old story of
David's rise to power (see Introduction) stresses the
popular approval of David's behavior, adding that
David's innocence of complicity in the murder was acknowledged by everyone, including not only Judah but
all Israel, Abner's own kin. **3.39** David says that he cannot control his nephews, *the sons of Zeruiah*, who,
though fiercely loyal to him, are consistently ruthless
and impetuous, as we have already seen (1 Sam 26.8;
2 Sam 2.18–23). *The LORD pay back . . . wickedness,*
lacking in a scroll from Qumran (4QSam[a]); it probably arose as the comment of a pious scribe.
4.1–12 Seeking to gain favor with David, two Benjaminites murder Ishbaal. The author of the old story
of David's rise to power (see Introduction) stresses
that David neither authorized nor approved of the assassination, though it cleared the way for him to be-

come king of Israel. **4.2** *Beeroth,* four to five miles
northwest of Jerusalem, was one of the four Gibeonite
cities that survived destruction during the conquest by
tricking Joshua into making a treaty with them (see
Josh 9, esp. v. 17); it was subsequently assigned to Benjamin by lot (Josh 18.25). **4.3** *Gittaim,* Hebrew, "the
Double Gath (Winepress)." Location unknown; it is
mentioned elsewhere only in Neh 11.33. We are not
told why *the people of Beeroth had fled to Gittaim,* but it
probably had something to do with Saul's hostility toward the Gibeonites (see 21.2). *Resident aliens.* See
note on 1.13–16. **4.4** The flow of the narrative is interrupted for the introduction of *Mephibosheth.* The
name was originally Mephibaal ("Out of the Mouth of
the Lord") before the substitution of *bosheth,* "shame,"
for *baal,* "lord, Baal" (see note on 2.8). The name is
confused in the biblical text with another similar
name, Merib-baal ("The Lord is Advocate"); Mephibaal was probably the name of a son of Saul by his concubine Rizpah (see 21.8); Merib-baal was the name of
Jonathan's crippled son (see 1 Chr 8.34; 9.40). **4.7** As in
2.29, the journey to Mahanaim, Ishbaal's capital (see
2.8), passes through the *Arabah,* or rift valley south of

bringing good news, I seized him and killed him at Ziklag—this was the reward I gave him for his news. 11 How much more then, when wicked men have killed a righteous man on his bed in his own house! And now shall I not require his blood at your hand, and destroy you from the earth?" 12 So David commanded the young men, and they killed them; they cut off their hands and feet, and hung their bodies beside the pool at Hebron. But the head of Ishbaal[a] they took and buried in the tomb of Abner at Hebron.

David Anointed King of All Israel

5 Then all the tribes of Israel came to David at Hebron, and said, "Look, we are your bone and flesh. 2 For some time, while Saul was king over us, it was you who led out Israel and brought it in. The LORD said to you: It is you who shall be shepherd of my people Israel, you who shall be ruler over Israel." 3 So all the elders of Israel came to the king at Hebron; and King David made a covenant with them at Hebron before the LORD, and they anointed David king over Israel. 4 David was thirty years old when he began to reign, and he reigned forty years. 5 At Hebron he reigned over Judah seven years and six months; and at Jerusalem he reigned over all Israel and Judah thirty-three years.

Jerusalem Made Capital of the United Kingdom

6 The king and his men marched to Jerusalem against the Jebusites, the inhabitants of the land, who said to David, "You will not come in here, even the blind and the lame will turn you back"—thinking, "David cannot come in here." 7 Nevertheless David took the stronghold of Zion, which is now the city of David. 8 David had said on that day, "Whoever would strike down the Jebusites, let him get up the water shaft to attack the lame and the blind, those whom David hates."[b] Therefore it is said, "The blind and the lame shall not come into the house." 9 David occupied the stronghold, and named it the city of David. David built the city all around from the Millo inward. 10 And David became greater and greater, for the LORD, the God of hosts, was with him.

11 King Hiram of Tyre sent messengers to

a Heb Ish-bosheth b Another reading is those who hate David

the Sea of Galilee. **4.10** David recalls events of 1.2–16. **4.12** *Tomb of Abner.* See 3.32.

5.1–5 David becomes king a second time, now of the northern tribes. **5.1–2** These two verses, which have a number of verbal parallels with the oracle of Nathan in ch. 7, were inserted by a Deuteronomistic editor in whose time it was natural for the Israelites to describe themselves in relation to David, a Judahite, as *your bone and flesh;* in the older narrative (19.13) David uses the same expression to signify his kinship to the people of Judah in contrast to the people of Israel. David *led out Israel and brought it in,* i.e., he led the army (see Num 27.17; 1 Chr 2.11; cf. 1 Sam 18.13, 16; 29.6). For David as Israel's *shepherd,* see 2 Sam 7.7; *ruler* (Hebrew *nagid*) translates the same word as *prince* in 7.8 (cf. note on 1 Sam 9.16). **5.3** A second, older account of David's appointment as king. By making a *covenant* with the Israelite elders David is binding himself to certain obligations in return for fealty. **5.4–5** These chronological notices belong to the Deuteronomistic framework of the narrative (see Introduction; 2.10–11; note on 1 Sam 13.1). Biblical scholars generally date David's reign to the first half of the tenth century, ca. 1000–960 BCE. **5.6–16** David's private army successfully besieges the city of the Jebusites. **5.6** *Jebusites,* the indigenous inhabitants of Jerusalem whom Joshua failed to drive away (Josh 15.63; Judg 1.21). There have been many attempts to explain the role of the *blind* and the *lame* in this ac-count. The present translation reflects the interpretation that the Jebusites are taunting David: "We are so much stronger than you that even our blind and lame can keep you out." **5.7** *Stronghold of Zion,* a fortified hilltop on the southeast corner of the later city. In the strict sense, then, *Zion* and *the city of David* refer only to this hill (see 1 Kings 8.1), but both terms were extended to mean the city as a whole. **5.8** At this point in the Chronicler's version of the capture of Jerusalem (1 Chr 11.6) Joab wins the position as commander in chief of David's army by leading the attack on the city. *Water shaft,* a vertical passage used by the Jebusites to have access to the Gihon, Jerusalem's primary water source, from within the city walls. Another possible translation of the Hebrew word rendered *water shaft* is "windpipe"; David might be telling his troops to strike at the windpipe, dealing only fatal blows so as not to leave the city full of maimed people (*the lame and the blind*). The narrator uses the story to explain a rule excluding the lame and blind from the *house,* i.e., the temple (cf. Lev 21.16–23; Deut 23.1). **5.9** *Named.* Ancient Near Eastern conquerors often renamed cities in their own honor. *Millo,* Hebrew, "the Fill," an earthwork of some kind, perhaps a building platform created by filling a ravine; Solomon amplified or rebuilt it (1 Kings 9.15, 24; 11.27). **5.10** The old story of David's rise to power (see Introduction) probably ended here, with a final recapitulation of its central motif (see 1 Sam 16.18; 18.14, 28). **5.11** *King Hiram* will later

David, along with cedar trees, and carpenters and masons who built David a house. 12David then perceived that the LORD had established him king over Israel, and that he had exalted his kingdom for the sake of his people Israel.

13 In Jerusalem, after he came from Hebron, David took more concubines and wives; and more sons and daughters were born to David. 14These are the names of those who were born to him in Jerusalem: Shammua, Shobab, Nathan, Solomon, 15Ibhar, Elishua, Nepheg, Japhia, 16Elishama, Eliada, and Eliphelet.

Philistine Attack Repulsed

17 When the Philistines heard that David had been anointed king over Israel, all the Philistines went up in search of David; but David heard about it and went down to the stronghold. 18Now the Philistines had come and spread out in the valley of Rephaim. 19David inquired of the LORD, "Shall I go up against the Philistines? Will you give them into my hand?" The LORD said to David, "Go up; for I will certainly give the Philistines into your hand." 20So David came to Baal-perazim, and David defeated them there. He said, "The LORD has burst forth against[a] my enemies before me, like a bursting flood." Therefore that place is called Baal-perazim.[b] 21The Philis-

tines abandoned their idols there, and David and his men carried them away.

22 Once again the Philistines came up, and were spread out in the valley of Rephaim. 23When David inquired of the LORD, he said, "You shall not go up; go around to their rear, and come upon them opposite the balsam trees. 24When you hear the sound of marching in the tops of the balsam trees, then be on the alert; for then the LORD has gone out before you to strike down the army of the Philistines." 25David did just as the LORD had commanded him; and he struck down the Philistines from Geba all the way to Gezer.

David Brings the Ark to Jerusalem

6 David again gathered all the chosen men of Israel, thirty thousand. 2David and all the people with him set out and went from Baale-judah, to bring up from there the ark of God, which is called by the name of the LORD of hosts who is enthroned on the cherubim. 3They carried the ark of God on a new cart, and brought it out of the house of Abinadab, which was on the hill. Uzzah and Ahio,[c] the sons of Abinadab, were driving the new cart

a Heb *paraz* *b* That is *Lord of Bursting Forth* *c* Or *and his brother*

---

supply Solomon with the skilled workers and materials necessary for the construction of the temple (see 1 Kings 5.1–10); extrabiblical sources indicate that his reign was long and productive. *Tyre,* port and chief city of Phoenicia, ancient Lebanon; it was about fifty miles south of Beirut. For millennia, the cedars of Lebanon were prized for use in the building of temples and royal residences; for David's house of *cedar,* see also 7.2. **5.12** Language anticipating that of the dynastic promise in ch. 7 (see esp. 7.12). **5.13–15** Sons born to David in Jerusalem (see also 1 Chr 14.3–4). For David's sons born in Hebron, cf. 3.2–5. For a composite listing, see 1 Chr 3.1–9. Of the sons mentioned here, only *Solomon* will play a significant role in the story. **5.17–25** A miscellany detailing David's success in the Philistine wars. **5.17** *Stronghold,* probably not Zion (vv. 7, 9), but Adullam, a Judahite fortress about sixteen miles to the southwest where David sought refuge in the past (see 1 Sam 22.1, 4; 24.22) and where he will be in another encounter with Philistines in the valley of Rephaim (see 2 Sam 23.13, 14). **5.18** *Valley of Rephaim,* usually identified with a plain southwest of Jerusalem; it formed part of the boundary of the tribal territories of Benjamin and Judah (see Josh 15.8; 18.16). **5.20** *Baal-perazim* ("the lord of Perazim") must have been a sanctuary on or near Mount Perazim (see Isa 28.21); here its name is playfully traced to

David's victory. **5.21** Just as the Philistines carried off the ark after their victory in 1 Sam 4.1–11, David and his men now carry away *their idols* (lit. "gods"). **5.23** *Balsam trees,* obscure; perhaps some kind of tree or bush or a place-name, "Bachaim." **5.24** The *sound of marching* will indicate that *the LORD has gone out* as the Divine Warrior to fight on David's behalf. **5.25** *Geba,* which was northeast of Jerusalem (see 1 Sam 13.3), should be emended to "Gibeon," which was northwest of the city (see 2.12) and therefore more suited to the geography of the present passage. *Gezer* was about fifteen miles west of Gibeon in the direction of the Philistine plain.

6.1–23 David installs the chief symbol of the religion of Israel in his new capital city. **6.2** *Baale-judah,* another name for Kiriath-jearim (cf. Josh 15.9), where the ark has been since its return from Philistia (see 1 Sam 7.2). **6.2** The *ark of God,* the most sacred object in Israelite worship, marks the presence of the Lord. *The LORD . . . cherubim.* See note on 1 Sam 4.4. **6.3** The cart in which the ark returned from Philistia was burned in a sacrifice (1 Sam 6.14), and in any case *a new cart* is necessary for ritual purposes; see note at 1 Sam 6.7. *The house of Abinadab, which was on the hill.* See 1 Sam 6.21; 7.1. *Uzzah and Ahio* were not mentioned in 1 Sam 7.1, where we were told that Abinadab's son Eleazar was consecrated for service with the

4with the ark of God;*a* and Ahio*b* went in front of the ark. 5David and all the house of Israel were dancing before the LORD with all their might, with songs*c* and lyres and harps and tambourines and castanets and cymbals.

6 When they came to the threshing floor of Nacon, Uzzah reached out his hand to the ark of God and took hold of it, for the oxen shook it. 7The anger of the LORD was kindled against Uzzah; and God struck him there because he reached out his hand to the ark;*d* and he died there beside the ark of God. 8David was angry because the LORD had burst forth with an outburst upon Uzzah; so that place is called Perez-uzzah,*e* to this day. 9David was afraid of the LORD that day; he said, "How can the ark of the LORD come into my care?" 10So David was unwilling to take the ark of the LORD into his care in the city of David; instead David took it to the house of Obed-edom the Gittite. 11The ark of the LORD remained in the house of Obed-edom the Gittite three months; and the LORD blessed Obed-edom and all his household.

12 It was told King David, "The LORD has blessed the household of Obed-edom and all that belongs to him, because of the ark of God." So David went and brought up the ark of God from the house of Obed-edom to the city of David with rejoicing; 13and when those who bore the ark of the LORD had gone six paces, he sacrificed an ox and a fatling. 14David danced before the LORD with all his might; David was girded with a linen ephod. 15So David and all the house of Israel brought up the ark of the LORD with shouting, and with the sound of the trumpet.

16 As the ark of the LORD came into the city of David, Michal daughter of Saul looked out of the window, and saw King David leaping and dancing before the LORD; and she despised him in her heart.

17 They brought in the ark of the LORD, and set it in its place, inside the tent that David had pitched for it; and David offered burnt offerings and offerings of well-being before the LORD. 18When David had finished offering the burnt offerings and the offerings of well-being, he blessed the people in the name of the LORD of hosts, 19and distributed food among all the people, the whole multitude of Israel, both men and women, to each a cake of bread, a portion of meat,*f* and a cake of raisins. Then all the people went back to their homes.

20 David returned to bless his household. But Michal the daughter of Saul came out to meet David, and said, "How the king of Israel honored himself today, uncovering himself today before the eyes of his servants' maids, as any vulgar fellow might shamelessly uncover himself!" 21David said to Michal, "It was before the LORD, who chose me in place of your father and all his household, to appoint me as prince over Israel, the people of the LORD, that I have danced before the LORD. 22I will make myself yet more contemptible than this, and I will be abased in my own eyes; but by the maids of whom you have spoken, by them I

---

a Compare Gk: Heb *and brought it out of the house of Abinadab, which was on the hill with the ark of God*   *b* Or *and his brother*   *c* Q Ms Gk 1 Chr 13.8: Heb *fir trees*   *d* 1 Chr 13.10 Compare Q Ms: Meaning of Heb uncertain   *e* That is *Bursting Out Against Uzzah*   *f* Vg: Meaning of Heb uncertain

---

ark; it is possible that Eleazar and Uzzah are the same person. **6.6–7** Because of its great sacredness the ark is potentially very dangerous (cf. 1 Sam 6.19) and must be treated with great care. Although Uzzah's purpose in reaching for the ark is probably only to steady it, he has not been ritually prepared to touch it, and his lapse proves fatal. **6.8** The meaning of *Perez-uzzah*, as the threshing floor of Nacon was known in the time of the author of this verse, is explained by a reference to the events just described. **6.9–10** David becomes fearful of the holy object and temporarily abandons his plan to bring it into the city. *Obed-edom the Gittite*, perhaps one of the soldiers whose loyalty David won when he served in the army of the king of Gath (see 1 Sam 27) and who followed him when he returned to Israel (see 15.18); because of his association with the ark he had been given a levitical genealogy by the time of the Chronicler (1 Chr 15.18, 21, 24; 16.5, 38). **6.12–19** A ceremony typical of ancient Near Eastern rituals in

which the statue of the national god (to which the ark corresponds in Israel's aniconic religion) is introduced to a newly built or newly captured royal city. In a ceremonial march the god is borne into the city, with numerous sacrifices along the way (v. 13), and installed in the sanctuary (v. 17), followed by the distribution of food and drink to the populace (v. 19). **6.13** For every six paces the ark bearers advance David sacrifices *an ox and a fatling* (i.e., "a fatted ox"), progressively sanctifying the City of David so that it will be ritually suitable to house the ark. **6.14** David's ritual dance has a sacerdotal aspect, as indicated by his garment, *a linen ephod* (see notes on 1 Sam 2.18; 22.18). **6.16** For *Michal daughter of Saul*, see 3.13–16; her displeasure is apparently a reaction to David's scant clothing (see v. 20; cf. note on 6.22). **6.17** The ark customarily resides in a *tent* (see 7.6), and David has prepared one for it here. **6.21** This verse, part of which looks ahead to 7.8, may have been expanded by a Deuteronomistic editor (see

shall be held in honor." 23And Michal the daughter of Saul had no child to the day of her death.

God's Covenant with David

7 Now when the king was settled in his house, and the LORD had given him rest from all his enemies around him, 2the king said to the prophet Nathan, "See now, I am living in a house of cedar, but the ark of God stays in a tent." 3Nathan said to the king, "Go, do all that you have in mind; for the LORD is with you."

4 But that same night the word of the LORD came to Nathan: 5Go and tell my servant David: Thus says the LORD: Are you the one to build me a house to live in? 6I have not lived in a house since the day I brought up the people of Israel from Egypt to this day, but I have been moving about in a tent and a tabernacle. 7Wherever I have moved about among all the people of Israel, did I ever speak a word with any of the tribal leaders*a* of Israel, whom I commanded to shepherd my people Israel,

saying, "Why have you not built me a house of cedar?" 8Now therefore thus you shall say to my servant David: Thus says the LORD of hosts: I took you from the pasture, from following the sheep to be prince over my people Israel; 9and I have been with you wherever you went, and have cut off all your enemies from before you; and I will make for you a great name, like the name of the great ones of the earth. 10And I will appoint a place for my people Israel and will plant them, so that they may live in their own place, and be disturbed no more; and evildoers shall afflict them no more, as formerly, 11from the time that I appointed judges over my people Israel; and I will give you rest from all your enemies. Moreover the LORD declares to you that the LORD will make you a house. 12When your days are fulfilled and you lie down with your ancestors, I will raise up your offspring after you, who shall come forth from your body, and I will establish his kingdom. 13He shall build a house

a Or any of the tribes

Introduction). **6.22** David's retort to Michal's accusation is that what seems vulgar behavior to her is actually pious self-humiliation in the presence of the Lord. **6.23** *No child.* The principal purpose of vv. 20–23 is to explain Michal's childlessness and to show that the blood of the house of Saul was never mixed with that of the house of David.

7.1–17 The royal theology of the Davidic dynasty in oracular form. Because of the thematic centrality of Davidic kingship to ancient Israelite religion, the oracle uttered by Nathan is a watershed event in the biblical narrative as a whole. Accordingly, the passage attracted the attention of biblical writers and editors of every period and point of view (see Introduction). It reflects the royal theology of Jerusalem in its emphasis on the dynastic promise to David and the commissioning of the erection of a temple in Jerusalem. At the same time it expresses prophetic suspicion of dynastic rule, possibly retaining echoes of an early oracle forbidding the building of a temple (see note on 7.6–7). In its final form, though, it is an editorial composition of the Deuteronomistic Historian, affirming the establishment of the Davidic dynasty and the Jerusalem temple as conditions necessary for the realization of the Lord's promise of *rest* for Israel (v. 11; cf. Deut 12.9–10). **7.2** The *prophet Nathan*, previously unmentioned, figures prominently here, in the story of David and Bathsheba (ch. 12), and in the account of the accession of Solomon (1 Kings 1). The contrast David draws between his own *house of cedar* and the *tent* in which the ark is lodged points to 5.11; 6.17; though he does not say so explicitly, David's words clearly imply a wish to build a temple for the Lord. **7.5** *Are you the*

one? The Lord's rhetorical question implies that it is not David but someone else who will build the temple; we soon learn that it will be David's son (v. 13). **7.6– 7** In its present, Deuteronomistically edited form (see Introduction), Nathan's oracle merely defers the erection of a temple to the next generation. These two verses, however, reflect the idea that the ark should be housed in a tent, a portable shrine, and seem hostile to a temple under any circumstances; they may represent the core of an older oracle prohibiting rather than postponing the construction of a temple (see note on 7.1–17). *I brought up . . . from Egypt* refers to the exodus, as in, e.g., 1 Sam 8.8; 2 Kings 21.15. *I have been moving about, Wherever I have moved about,* language that stresses the freedom of the Lord to go where he pleases. For *a house of cedar,* i.e., a temple, see notes on 5.11; 7.2. **7.8** *I took you from the pasture* alludes to 1 Sam 16.11. For *prince,* elsewhere translated *ruler,* see note on 1 Sam 9.16. **7.10** *A place,* not the promised land, in which Israel is already living, but the place where the Lord chooses to be worshiped (see Deut 12.5, 11, 14, 18, 21, 26), i.e., the temple in Jerusalem. *Evildoers,* here probably Hophni and Phinehas (see 1 Sam 2.12–26). **7.11** *I will give you rest* connects the present events with the Deuteronomistic theme of the promise of rest from enemies that the Israelites were given by Moses in Deut 12.9–10; the promise was fulfilled in preliminary form by the conquest of Canaan (see Josh 21.44), but its final realization awaits the erection of the temple (see 1 Kings 8.56). The Lord promises David *a house,* i.e., a dynasty. **7.12** *Offspring,* Solomon, as v. 13 makes clear, but also the Davidic dynasty in general, which Solomon's kingship inaugu-

for my name, and I will establish the throne of his kingdom forever. [14]I will be a father to him, and he shall be a son to me. When he commits iniquity, I will punish him with a rod such as mortals use, with blows inflicted by human beings. [15]But I will not take[a] my steadfast love from him, as I took it from Saul, whom I put away from before you. [16]Your house and your kingdom shall be made sure forever before me;[b] your throne shall be established forever. [17]In accordance with all these words and with all this vision, Nathan spoke to David.

David's Prayer

18 Then King David went in and sat before the LORD, and said, "Who am I, O Lord GOD, and what is my house, that you have brought me thus far? [19]And yet this was a small thing in your eyes, O Lord GOD; you have spoken also of your servant's house for a great while to come. May this be instruction for the people,[c] O Lord GOD! [20]And what more can David say to you? For you know your servant, O Lord GOD! [21]Because of your promise, and according to your own heart, you have wrought all this greatness, so that your servant may know it. [22]Therefore you are great, O LORD God; for there is no one like you, and there is no God besides you, according to all that we have heard with our ears. [23]Who is like your people, like Israel? Is there another[d] nation on earth whose God went to redeem it as a people, and to make a name for himself, doing great and awesome

things for them,[e] by driving out[f] before his people nations and their gods?[g] [24]And you established your people Israel for yourself to be your people forever; and you, O LORD, became their God. [25]And now, O LORD God, as for the word that you have spoken concerning your servant and concerning his house, confirm it forever; do as you have promised. [26]Thus your name will be magnified forever in the saying, 'The LORD of hosts is God over Israel'; and the house of your servant David will be established before you. [27]For you, O LORD of hosts, the God of Israel, have made this revelation to your servant, saying, 'I will build you a house'; therefore your servant has found courage to pray this prayer to you. [28]And now, O Lord GOD, you are God, and your words are true, and you have promised this good thing to your servant; [29]now therefore may it please you to bless the house of your servant, so that it may continue forever before you; for you, O Lord GOD, have spoken, and with your blessing shall the house of your servant be blessed forever."

David's Wars

8 Some time afterward, David attacked the Philistines and subdued them; David took Metheg-ammah out of the hand of the Philistines.

a Gk Syr Vg 1 Chr 17.13: Heb *shall not depart* *b* Gk Heb Mss: MT *before you*; Compare 2 Sam 7.26, 29 *c* Meaning of Heb uncertain *d* Gk: Heb *one* *e* Heb *you* *f* Gk 1 Chr 17.21: Heb *for your land* *g* Cn: Heb *before your people, whom you redeemed for yourself from Egypt, nations and its gods*

rates. **7.13** The *house* that David's offspring will build is the house, or temple, of v. 5; the author is playing on two meanings of *house* in Hebrew—David's *house*, or dynasty, and the Lord's *house*, or temple. *Name,* the Lord's presence in the temple in a way that avoids the theological objection that no earthly dwelling could house such a great deity (see esp. 1 Kings 8.27–30). **7.14** In ancient Israel and contemporary societies, the relationship between *father* and *son* was used to express the special relationship between the dynastic deity and the king, who was regarded the adoptive son of the national god; for David as the adoptive son of the Lord, see also Pss 2.7; 89.26–27. For an early Christian appropriation of the verse, see Heb 1.5. **7.15** As the son of the Lord, the Davidic king will be subject to punishment (v. 14) but not rejection; the pledge of adoption is irrevocable. This means that neither David nor any of his successors will become another *Saul* (see 1 Sam 13.13–14; 15.26–28). **7.18–29** David's response to Nathan's oracle. **7.18** *David went in* (i.e., into the tent, 6.17; 7.2) *and sat before the LORD* (i.e., in front of the ark). But it was not custom-

ary to sit during prayer, so the meaning may be that David remained "before the LORD" after others departed. **7.19** *May this be instruction for the people,* perhaps originally "and you have shown me the generation to come," on the basis of the Hebrew and Greek texts of 1 Chr 17.17. **7.21** *According to your own heart.* See 1 Sam 13.14. The point is that the Lord has acted at his own initiative and not in response to some gesture by David, such as his offer to build a temple (see v. 2). **7.22–26** An expansion of David's prayer, replete with stereotypical language, by the Deuteronomistic Historian (see Introduction), whose purpose was to incorporate the Lord's benefaction toward the house of David into the larger context of his graciousness toward Israel as a whole. **7.23** *Is there another nation . . . their gods?* Cf. Deut 4.7, 8, 32–40. **7.24** The covenant between Israel and the Lord (cf. Deut 29.10–13), which in Deuteronomistic thought was linked to the special relationship between the Davidic king and the Lord (see v. 14).

8.1–14 A summary of David's military achievements. **8.1** *Metheg-ammah,* in Hebrew something like

2 He also defeated the Moabites and, making them lie down on the ground, measured them off with a cord; he measured two lengths of cord for those who were to be put to death, and one length[a] for those who were to be spared. And the Moabites became servants to David and brought tribute.

3 David also struck down King Hadadezer son of Rehob of Zobah, as he went to restore his monument[b] at the river Euphrates. 4David took from him one thousand seven hundred horsemen, and twenty thousand foot soldiers. David hamstrung all the chariot horses, but left enough for a hundred chariots. 5When the Arameans of Damascus came to help King Hadadezer of Zobah, David killed twenty-two thousand men of the Arameans. 6Then David put garrisons among the Arameans of Damascus; and the Arameans became servants to David and brought tribute. The LORD gave victory to David wherever he went. 7David took the gold shields that were carried by the servants of Hadadezer, and brought them to Jerusalem. 8From Betah and from Berothai, towns of Hadadezer, King David took a great amount of bronze.

9 When King Toi of Hamath heard that David had defeated the whole army of Had-adezer, 10Toi sent his son Joram to King David, to greet him and to congratulate him because he had fought against Hadadezer and defeated him. Now Hadadezer had often been at war with Toi. Joram brought with him articles of silver, gold, and bronze; 11these also King David dedicated to the LORD, together with the silver and gold that he dedicated from all the nations he subdued, 12from Edom, Moab, the Ammonites, the Philistines, Amalek, and from the spoil of King Hadadezer son of Rehob of Zobah.

13 David won a name for himself. When he returned, he killed eighteen thousand Edomites[c] in the Valley of Salt. 14He put garrisons in Edom; throughout all Edom he put garrisons, and all the Edomites became David's servants. And the LORD gave victory to David wherever he went.

David's Officers

15 So David reigned over all Israel; and David administered justice and equity to all his people. 16Joab son of Zeruiah was over the army; Jehoshaphat son of Ahilud was recorder;

a Heb one full length   b Compare 1 Sam 15.12 and 2 Sam 18.18
c Gk: Heb returned from striking down eighteen thousand Arameans

"the Bridle of the Aqueduct," occurs nowhere else; the Septuagint has "'the common land." 8.2 David seems to have had an amicable relationship with the Moabites before he became king (see 1 Sam 22.3–4). Measuring lines of prisoners for execution is unique to this passage. 8.3–12 This passage can be read as a sequel to David's Ammonite and Aramean war in ch. 10. 8.3 Hadadezer. The patronymic son of Rehob suggests that he may have been a native of Beth-rehob, an Aramean state that fought against David (see 10.6); he may have united Beth-rehob and Zobah under his rule, just as David did with Judah and Israel. Zobah (cf. 1 Sam 14.47), located on the western slope of Mount Hermon, was the leading Aramean state before the rise of Damascus. If Hadadezer had been marching north to restore his monument at the Euphrates, he would not have been likely to encounter David, who lived far to the south. It seems more likely that it was David who marched north "to leave his monument" at the Euphrates after his victory at Helam (see 10.15–18). 8.4 Apparently David had use for only a hundred chariot horses and hamstrung the rest so that they could not be used against him; but Josh 11.6–9 suggests that David might have been following some kind of ritual requirement. 8.5 Damascus, at this point an ally and probably a vassal of Zobah, will rise to preeminence late in the reign of Solomon under the leadership of a survivor of the present conflict (see 1 Kings 11.23–25).

8.7 Gold shields, ceremonial gold bow cases that were carried by royal officials on formal occasions. 8.8 Betah, probably "Tebah," as in certain Greek and Syriac manuscripts (cf. Tibhath in 1 Chr 18.8); it was in the Bekaa Valley south of modern Homs. Berothai (cf. Berothah in Ezek 47.16) was also in the Bekaa a few miles south of Baalbek. 8.9 Hamath, modern Hama on the middle Orontes, a Neo-Hittite city-state that bordered on Zobah to the north. 8.10 Surprisingly, Toi's son Joram has a name that means "Yahweh [the LORD] is exalted" in Hebrew. His name in 1 Chr 18.10 is Hadoram, which means "(the Aramean god) Hadad is exalted," and many scholars would replace Joram with Hadoram here; but it has also been suggested that Hadoram's name was changed to Joram as a gesture of fealty to David. 8.13 The Valley of Salt probably ran from somewhere in Edom into the Dead Sea; in the Septuagint David's victory there is credited to Abishai son of Zeruiah (see 2.18, 30; 1 Sam 26.6). 8.15–18 The first of two lists (also 20.23–26) of the members of David's administration. 8.16 Joab (see 2.13) may have received the command of the army as a result of his role in the siege of Jerusalem (see note on 5.8). Jehoshaphat will remain in office under Solomon (see 1 Kings 4.3); as recorder he was probably responsible for keeping public records, but the title has been compared to that of an Egyptian officer whose chief responsibility was communication between the king and

17Zadok son of Ahitub and Ahimelech son of Abiathar were priests; Seraiah was secretary; 18Benaiah son of Jehoiada was over*a* the Cherethites and the Pelethites; and David's sons were priests.

David's Kindness to Mephibosheth

9 David asked, "Is there still anyone left of the house of Saul to whom I may show kindness for Jonathan's sake?" 2Now there was a servant of the house of Saul whose name was Ziba, and he was summoned to David. The king said to him, "Are you Ziba?" And he said, "At your service!" 3The king said, "Is there anyone remaining of the house of Saul to whom I may show the kindness of God?" Ziba said to the king, "There remains a son of Jonathan; he is crippled in his feet." 4The king said to him, "Where is he?" Ziba said to the king, "He is in the house of Machir son of Ammiel, at Lo-debar." 5Then King David sent and brought him from the house of Machir son of Ammiel, at Lo-debar. 6Mephibosheth*b* son of Jonathan son of Saul came to David, and fell on his face and did obeisance. David said, "Mephibosheth!"*b* He answered, "I am your servant." 7David said to him, "Do not be afraid, for I will show you kindness for the sake of your father Jonathan; I will restore to you all the land of your grandfather Saul, and you yourself shall eat at my table always." 8He did obeisance and said, "What is your servant, that you should look upon a dead dog such as I?"

9 Then the king summoned Saul's servant Ziba, and said to him, "All that belonged to Saul and to all his house I have given to your master's grandson. 10You and your sons and your servants shall till the land for him, and shall bring in the produce, so that your master's grandson may have food to eat; but your master's grandson Mephibosheth*b* shall always eat at my table." Now Ziba had fifteen sons and twenty servants. 11Then Ziba said to the king, "According to all that my lord the king commands his servant, so your servant will do." Mephibosheth*b* ate at David's*c* table, like one of the king's sons. 12Mephibosheth*b* had a young son whose name was Mica. And all who lived in Ziba's house became Mephibosheth's*d* servants. 13Mephibosheth*b* lived in

---

a Syr Tg Vg 20.23; 1 Chr 18.17: Heb lacks *was over*
b Or *Merib-baal*: See 4.4 note   *c* Gk: Heb *my*   *d* Or *Merib-baal's*: See 4.4 note

---

the public. **8.17** Two high priests served simultaneously during David's reign. One was *Zadok*, who survived Solomon's purge and became the ancestor of the dominant priestly family in Jerusalem, as forecast in the oracle in 1 Sam 2.27–36. The other was not *Ahimelech son of Abiathar* but Abiathar son of Ahimelech, as shown clearly by 15.24, 29, 35; 17.15; 19.11; the mistake in the present passage is replicated in 1 Chr 18.16 but not in 2 Sam 20.25. Abiathar, the only survivor of Saul's massacre of the Shilonite priesthood (see 1 Sam 22.6–23), became David's personal priest (1 Sam 22.20–23) and remained at court until he was banished by Solomon for having sided against his succession (see 1 Kings 1.7; 2.26–27). *Seraiah*, the name is doubtful; the Septuagint points to Shausha, and 20.25 has Sheva. Like recorder, the title of *secretary* has been compared to that of an Egyptian officer who served as the personal secretary of the king. **8.18** For *Benaiah*, see 23.20–23. The *Cherethites* and the *Pelethites* were David's personal bodyguard (cf. 23.23; note on 1 Sam 30.14); like the Philistines, near whose territory they settled, they were probably Aegean in origin (cf. note on 1 Sam 30.14). David probably earned their loyalty while he was in the service of the king of Gath (1 Sam 27–30). *David's sons were priests.* If correct (the textual evidence is unclear), we would have to suppose that membership in the priesthood was not limited to Levites in the time of David.
9.1–13 David finds the surviving heir to the house of Saul and invites him to live at court. If there was any suspicion that David's hospitality was actually a form of house arrest, intended to keep an eye on Mephibosheth, the narrator refutes this by insisting David's only motive was loyalty to the memory of Jonathan (vv. 1, 3, 7). **9.1** Note the connection with 21.7; the account of the execution of the family of Saul in 21.1–14 probably once stood as an introduction to ch. 9. **9.2** *Ziba*, though a *servant of the house of Saul* (i.e., a ranking officer at Saul's court), becomes a valuable supporter of David (see 16.1–4; cf. 19.24–30). **9.4** Like Ziba, *Machir* will prove helpful to David during the crisis provoked by Absalom's revolt (see 17.27). *Lo-debar*, a town in northern Transjordan (see "the territory of Debir," Josh 13.26), not far from Mahanaim (see 2.8) and Jabesh-gilead (see 2.4b–7) in the territory settled by a clan of Manasseh, also known as Machir (see Num 32.39–40; Deut 3.15); the house of Saul always had staunch support in this region because of the memory of Saul's liberation of Jabesh (see 1 Sam 10.27–11.11). **9.6** *Mephibosheth*. See note on 4.4. **9.7** To eat at the king's *table* was a special privilege (see 1 Kings 2.7; 18.19; 2 Kings 25.27–29; Jer 52.31–33; cf. Ps 23.5). **9.8** For the self-abasing expression *dead dog*, see 16.9; cf. note on 1 Sam 24.14. **9.10** The original point of David's remarks in this verse, better preserved in the Greek, was that Ziba and his household would be supported by the income from Mephibosheth's estate and that Mephibosheth himself would be supported at David's expense. **9.12** According to 1 Chr 8.34–35; 9.40–41, *Mica* had four sons, thus en-

Jerusalem, for he always ate at the king's table. Now he was lame in both his feet.

The Ammonites and Arameans Are Defeated

10 Some time afterward, the king of the Ammonites died, and his son Hanun succeeded him. ²David said, "I will deal loyally with Hanun son of Nahash, just as his father dealt loyally with me." So David sent envoys to console him concerning his father. When David's envoys came into the land of the Ammonites, ³the princes of the Ammonites said to their lord Hanun, "Do you really think that David is honoring your father just because he has sent messengers with condolences to you? Has not David sent his envoys to you to search the city, to spy it out, and to overthrow it?" ⁴So Hanun seized David's envoys, shaved off half the beard of each, cut off their garments in the middle at their hips, and sent them away. ⁵When David was told, he sent to meet them, for the men were greatly ashamed. The king said, "Remain at Jericho until your beards have grown, and then return."

6 When the Ammonites saw that they had become odious to David, the Ammonites sent and hired the Arameans of Beth-rehob and the Arameans of Zobah, twenty thousand foot soldiers, as well as the king of Maacah, one thousand men, and the men of Tob, twelve thousand men. ⁷When David heard of it, he sent Joab and all the army with the warriors. ⁸The Ammonites came out and drew up in battle array at the entrance of the gate; but the Arameans of Zobah and of Rehob, and the men of Tob and Maacah, were by themselves in the open country.

9 When Joab saw that the battle was set against him both in front and in the rear, he chose some of the picked men of Israel, and arrayed them against the Arameans; ¹⁰the rest of his men he put in the charge of his brother Abishai, and he arrayed them against the Ammonites. ¹¹He said, "If the Arameans are too strong for me, then you shall help me; but if the Ammonites are too strong for you, then I will come and help you. ¹²Be strong, and let us be courageous for the sake of our people, and for the cities of our God; and may the LORD do what seems good to him." ¹³So Joab and the people who were with him moved forward into battle against the Arameans; and they fled before him. ¹⁴When the Ammonites saw that the Arameans fled, they likewise fled before Abishai, and entered the city. Then Joab returned from fighting against the Ammonites, and came to Jerusalem.

15 But when the Arameans saw that they had been defeated by Israel, they gathered themselves together. ¹⁶Hadadezer sent and brought out the Arameans who were beyond the Euphrates; and they came to Helam, with Shobach the commander of the army of Hadadezer at their head. ¹⁷When it was told David, he gathered all Israel together, and crossed the Jordan, and came to Helam. The Arameans arrayed themselves against David and fought with him. ¹⁸The Arameans fled before Israel; and David killed of the Arameans seven hundred chariot teams, and forty thousand horsemen,ᵃ and wounded Shobach the commander of their army, so that he died there. ¹⁹When all the kings who were servants

---

a 1 Chr 19.18 and some Gk Mss read *foot soldiers*

---

suring the posterity of the house of Saul (cf. 1 Sam 20.14–16; 24.21–22). **9.13** The fact that Mephibosheth, the heir to the house of Saul, is *lame in both his feet* is important; as a cripple he is unlikely to be able to make a successful attempt to revive his line's claim to the throne.

10.1–19 Chronologically, this section seems to be prior to 8.3–14. **10.2** *Nahash* was an enemy of Saul (1 Sam 10.27–11.11) and may have regarded David, after his split with Saul, as an ally. The only occasion on which he is reported to have *dealt loyally* with David was when his son Shobi supplied provisions to him after he fled Jerusalem during Absalom's revolt (17.27). If this is what David is referring to, the revolt must have preceded the events described here. **10.5** *Jericho* was on the west bank of the Jordan at a point intermediate between Jerusalem and the Am-

monite capital. **10.6** *Arameans of Beth-rehob, Zobah.* See note on 8.3. *Maacah,* north of Geshur (see 2.9) in the Golan Heights. *Tob,* a small state southeast of the Sea of Galilee. **10.8** The Ammonites confront Joab's army at *the entrance of the gate,* i.e., of Rabbah, their capital city (see 11.1). **10.10** *Abishai.* See 2.18; 1 Sam 26.6. **10.12** *Cities of our God,* possibly old Israelite centers and sanctuaries of Yahweh in southern Transjordan, a region with strong associations in early Israelite tradition. **10.16** *Hadadezer,* king of Zobah and leader of the Aramean coalition; see note on 8.3. *Arameans who were beyond the Euphrates,* people living in northwestern Mesopotamia in the central and upper Euphrates region. *Helam,* probably the same town or region called Alema in 1 Macc 5.26; it lay east of the Sea of Galilee on the Transjordanian plateau. *Shobach,* called Shopach in 1 Chr 19.16, 18.

of Hadadezer saw that they had been defeated by Israel, they made peace with Israel, and became subject to them. So the Arameans were afraid to help the Ammonites any more.

David Commits Adultery with Bathsheba

11 In the spring of the year, the time when kings go out to battle, David sent Joab with his officers and all Israel with him; they ravaged the Ammonites, and besieged Rabbah. But David remained at Jerusalem.

2 It happened, late one afternoon, when David rose from his couch and was walking about on the roof of the king's house, that he saw from the roof a woman bathing; the woman was very beautiful. 3 David sent someone to inquire about the woman. It was reported, "This is Bathsheba daughter of Eliam, the wife of Uriah the Hittite." 4 So David sent messengers to get her, and she came to him, and he lay with her. (Now she was purifying herself after her period.) Then she returned to her house. 5 The woman conceived; and she sent and told David, "I am pregnant."

6 So David sent word to Joab, "Send me Uriah the Hittite." And Joab sent Uriah to David. 7 When Uriah came to him, David asked how Joab and the people fared, and how the war was going. 8 Then David said to Uriah, "Go down to your house, and wash your feet." Uriah went out of the king's house, and there followed him a present from the king. 9 But Uriah slept at the entrance of the king's house with all the servants of his lord, and did not go down to his house. 10 When they told David, "Uriah did not go down to his house," David said to Uriah, "You have just come from a journey. Why did you not go down to your house?" 11 Uriah said to David, "The ark and Israel and Judah remain in booths;[a] and my lord Joab and the servants of my lord are camping in the open field; shall I then go to my house, to eat and to drink, and to lie with my wife? As you live, and as your soul lives, I will not do such a thing." 12 Then David said to Uriah, "Remain here today also, and tomorrow I will send you back." So Uriah remained in Jerusalem that day. On the next day, 13 David invited him to eat and drink in his presence and made him drunk; and in the evening he went out to lie on his couch with the servants of his lord, but he did not go down to his house.

David Has Uriah Killed

14 In the morning David wrote a letter to Joab, and sent it by the hand of Uriah. 15 In the letter he wrote, "Set Uriah in the forefront of the hardest fighting, and then draw back from him, so that he may be struck down and die." 16 As Joab was besieging the city, he assigned Uriah to the place where he knew there were valiant warriors. 17 The men of the city came out and fought with Joab; and some of the servants of David among the people fell. Uriah the Hittite was killed as well. 18 Then Joab sent

a Or at Succoth

11.1–13 This incident took place during David's Ammonite wars and portrays Israel's greatest king as a sinful human being. This passage (and the materials in chs. 11–12 generally) exhibits the thematic concerns, evident elsewhere in 1 and 2 Samuel, of the writer or editor who views kingship with suspicion and places emphasis on the role of the divinely appointed office of prophet (see Introduction). 11.1 Rabbah, modern Amman, the Ammonite capital. 11.2 David awakens from an afternoon nap on the roof of his palace, the best place to sleep (see note on 1 Sam 9.25). 11.3 Eliam, Bathsheba's father, sometimes identified with Eliam son of Ahithophel, a member of David's elite corps of the Thirty (23.34). Uriah the Hittite was also a member (23.39); although his name (Hebrew, "Yahweh is my light") shows that he was probably a native-born Israelite, his title suggests that he was descended from the Hittites, an Anatolian people of the second millennium BCE whose descendants populated a number of Syrian cities in the time of David. 11.4 Purifying herself after her period indicates both that Bathsheba's intercourse with David occurred at a time that was propitious for conception and that Uriah cannot have been the father of the child she conceives. 11.6–12 David brings Uriah home on furlough in the hope that he will have intercourse with Bathsheba and the child she is carrying will be thought to be his; ironically, though, it is Uriah's loyalty to David as well as his sense of duty as a soldier (see note on 11.11) that prevents this scheme from succeeding. 11.8 Wash your feet, probably a euphemism for sexual intercourse. And there followed ... king, based on a very doubtful Hebrew text. 11.11 Uriah rejects David's suggestion that he go home and sleep with his wife; he is a pious soldier, careful to observe the ritual regulations of the battle camp (Deut 23.9–14), which forbade intimate relations with women (cf. note on 1 Sam 21.5). When in the field, the army lived in tents, not in booths; better is at Succoth (see text note a), a town east of the Jordan and roughly midway between Jerusalem and Rabbah. 11.14–27a Having failed to induce the pious Uriah to violate the ritual regulations of the battle camp, David now plots to have him killed. 11.14–15 Uriah carries his own death sentence to Joab.

and told David all the news about the fighting; [19]and he instructed the messenger, "When you have finished telling the king all the news about the fighting, [20]then, if the king's anger rises, and if he says to you, 'Why did you go so near the city to fight? Did you not know that they would shoot from the wall? [21]Who killed Abimelech son of Jerubbaal?[a] Did not a woman throw an upper millstone on him from the wall, so that he died at Thebez? Why did you go so near the wall?' then you shall say, 'Your servant Uriah the Hittite is dead too.' "

22 So the messenger went, and came and told David all that Joab had sent him to tell. [23]The messenger said to David, "The men gained an advantage over us, and came out against us in the field; but we drove them back to the entrance of the gate. [24]Then the archers shot at your servants from the wall; some of the king's servants are dead; and your servant Uriah the Hittite is dead also." [25]David said to the messenger, "Thus you shall say to Joab, 'Do not let this matter trouble you, for the sword devours now one and now another; press your attack on the city, and overthrow it.' And encourage him."

26 When the wife of Uriah heard that her husband was dead, she made lamentation for him. [27]When the mourning was over, David sent and brought her to his house, and she became his wife, and bore him a son.

Nathan Condemns David

But the thing that David had done displeased **12** the LORD, [1]and the LORD sent Nathan to David. He came to him, and said to him, "There were two men in a certain city, the one rich and the other poor. [2]The rich man had very many flocks and herds; [3]but the poor man had nothing but one little ewe lamb, which he had bought. He brought it up, and it grew up with him and with his children; it used to eat of his meager fare, and drink from his cup, and lie in his bosom, and it was like a daughter to him. [4]Now there came a traveler to the rich man, and he was loath to take one of his own flock or herd to prepare for the wayfarer who had come to him, but he took the poor man's lamb, and prepared that for the guest who had come to him." [5]Then David's anger was greatly kindled against the man. He said to Nathan, "As the LORD lives, the man who has done this deserves to die; [6]he shall restore the lamb fourfold, because he did this thing, and because he had no pity."

7 Nathan said to David, "You are the man! Thus says the LORD, the God of Israel: I anointed you king over Israel, and I rescued you from the hand of Saul; [8]I gave you your master's house, and your master's wives into your bosom, and gave you the house of Israel and of Judah; and if that had been too little, I would have added as much more. [9]Why have you despised the word of the LORD, to do what is evil in his sight? You have struck down Uriah the Hittite with the sword, and have taken his wife to be your wife, and have killed him with the sword of the Ammonites. [10]Now therefore the sword shall never depart from your house,

a Gk Syr Judg 7.1: Heb *Jerubbesheth*

11.21 The death of *Abimelech son of Jerubbaal* is reported in Judg 9.50–55; he was killed by *an upper millstone* thrown by a woman as a result of venturing too close to the city wall during his siege of *Thebez*. **11.27** According to custom, the period of *mourning* was seven days (see Gen 50.10; Jdt 16.24).

11.27b–12.15a Nathan tells David a story as if it were a current court case; but in fact it is a parable. The basis of the parable is tribal law, which permitted someone to slaughter an animal from a neighbor's livestock when the rules of hospitality made it absolutely necessary to do so; but this privilege was forbidden to anyone whose own property included available livestock, and it was strictly forbidden when the neighbor's animal was a personal pet. **12.4** *Took the poor man's lamb* invokes the theme of royal abuse of power as expressed in another prophetically oriented passage, 1 Sam 8.11–18, where the verb *take* is used repeatedly with the king as subject. **12.6** *Fourfold* restitution comes from Ex 22.1, but in the original text of the present passage, preserved in most Greek manuscripts, David demands that the lamb be restored sevenfold (cf. Prov 6.31). **12.7** *I anointed you king over Israel.* See 1 Sam 16.1–13. **12.8** Errors in the transmission of this verse have obscured its main point. *Your master's house* should be "your master's daughter," i.e., Michal (see 3.13–16). *Your master's wives* must refer to Saul's wives, and entry into a king's harem was a way of claiming his throne (see 16.21–22). We have no direct report that David took any of Saul's wives, but the Talmud (*Sanhedrin* 18a) and a number of modern scholars have speculated that David's wife Ahinoam, the mother of Amnon (see 3.2; 1 Sam 25.43), was the same as Saul's wife, Ahinoam daughter of Ahimaaz (1 Sam 14.50). *The house of Israel and of Judah* should be "the daughters of Israel and Judah"; the point is that David was given as many women as he could possibly want, but, like the rich man in the parable, he wantonly took something that belonged to someone who had been less generously treated. **12.10** *Sword . . . never depart*

for you have despised me, and have taken the wife of Uriah the Hittite to be your wife. [11]Thus says the LORD: I will raise up trouble against you from within your own house; and I will take your wives before your eyes, and give them to your neighbor, and he shall lie with your wives in the sight of this very sun. [12]For you did it secretly; but I will do this thing before all Israel, and before the sun." [13]David said to Nathan, "I have sinned against the LORD." Nathan said to David, "Now the LORD has put away your sin; you shall not die. [14]Nevertheless, because by this deed you have utterly scorned the LORD,[a] the child that is born to you shall die." [15]Then Nathan went to his house.

Bathsheba's Child Dies

The LORD struck the child that Uriah's wife bore to David, and it became very ill. [16]David therefore pleaded with God for the child; David fasted, and went in and lay all night on the ground. [17]The elders of his house stood beside him, urging him to rise from the ground; but he would not, nor did he eat food with them. [18]On the seventh day the child died. And the servants of David were afraid to tell him that the child was dead; for they said, "While the child was still alive, we spoke to him, and he did not listen to us; how then can we tell him the child is dead? He may do himself some harm." [19]But when David saw that his servants were whispering together, he perceived that the child was dead; and David said to his servants, "Is the child dead?" They said, "He is dead."

[20] Then David rose from the ground, washed, anointed himself, and changed his clothes. He went into the house of the LORD, and worshiped; he then went to his own house; and when he asked, they set food before him and he ate. [21]Then his servants said to him, "What is this thing that you have done? You fasted and wept for the child while it was alive; but when the child died, you rose and ate food." [22]He said, "While the child was still alive, I fasted and wept; for I said, 'Who knows? The LORD may be gracious to me, and the child may live.' [23]But now he is dead; why should I fast? Can I bring him back again? I shall go to him, but he will not return to me."

Solomon Is Born

[24] Then David consoled his wife Bathsheba, and went to her, and lay with her; and she bore a son, and he named him Solomon. The LORD loved him, [25]and sent a message by the prophet Nathan; so he named him Jedidiah,[b] because of the LORD.

The Ammonites Crushed

[26] Now Joab fought against Rabbah of the Ammonites, and took the royal city. [27]Joab sent messengers to David, and said, "I have fought against Rabbah; moreover, I have taken the water city. [28]Now, then, gather the rest of the people together, and encamp against the city, and take it; or I myself will take the city, and it will be called by my name." [29]So David gathered all the people together and went to Rabbah, and fought against it and took it. [30]He took the crown of Milcom[c] from his head; the weight of it was a talent of gold, and in it was a precious stone; and it was placed on David's head. He also brought forth the spoil

---

a Ancient scribal tradition: Compare 1 Sam 25.22 note: Heb *scorned the enemies of the LORD*   b That is *Beloved of the LORD*   c Gk See 1 Kings 11.5, 33: Heb *their kings*

---

from your house. The prophetic author of chs. 11–12 (see note on 11.1–13) interprets events to come—specifically the violent deaths of David's sons Amnon (13.23–29), Absalom (18.15), and Adonijah (1 Kings 2.25)—as a result of David's contrivance of the death of Uriah. **12.11** *Trouble ... from within your own house.* The grievous events of Absalom's revolt are also interpreted as a consequence of David's sin against Uriah. Specifically, someone (Absalom) will enter David's harem *in the sight of this very sun* (see 16.21–22). **12.13–14** *Put away your sin,* rather "transferred your sin"; David will not die, but someone must, and it will be *the child that is born* to him. **12.15b–23** David fasts, lies in the dirt, and implores the Lord to spare the condemned infant. When the child dies, David bathes and eats. His astonished servants see all this as a reversal of normal behavior, since fasting and self-abasement usually followed a death as gestures of mourning. **12.20** *House of the LORD,* anachronistic; the temple will be built in the time of Solomon (see 7.13). **12.24–25** Though explained differently in 1 Chr 22.9, the name *Solomon,* Hebrew *shelomoh,* means "his replacement," referring to the child who died in v. 18. *Jedidiah,* mentioned nowhere else in the Bible, may have been an official throne name used alongside the personal name Solomon. **12.26–31** The continuation and completion of the siege begun in 11.1. **12.26–27** *Royal city, water city,* designations for the same place; it may have been a royal fortress that stood on the high citadel and guarded the spring that provided the city's water supply. **12.30** *Milcom,* the national god of the Ammonites. His crown with its single jewel (cf. Zech 9.16) would

of the city, a very great amount. ³¹He brought out the people who were in it, and set them to work with saws and iron picks and iron axes, or sent them to the brickworks. Thus he did to all the cities of the Ammonites. Then David and all the people returned to Jerusalem.

Amnon and Tamar

13 Some time passed. David's son Absalom had a beautiful sister whose name was Tamar; and David's son Amnon fell in love with her. ²Amnon was so tormented that he made himself ill because of his sister Tamar, for she was a virgin and it seemed impossible to Amnon to do anything to her. ³But Amnon had a friend whose name was Jonadab, the son of David's brother Shimeah; and Jonadab was a very crafty man. ⁴He said to him, "O son of the king, why are you so haggard morning after morning? Will you not tell me?" Amnon said to him, "I love Tamar, my brother Absalom's sister." ⁵Jonadab said to him, "Lie down on your bed, and pretend to be ill; and when your father comes to see you, say to him, 'Let my sister Tamar come and give me something to eat, and prepare the food in my sight, so that I may see it and eat it from her hand.'" ⁶So Amnon lay down, and pretended to be ill; and when the king came to see him, Amnon said to the king, "Please let my sister Tamar come and make a couple of cakes in my sight, so that I may eat from her hand."

7 Then David sent home to Tamar, saying, "Go to your brother Amnon's house, and prepare food for him." ⁸So Tamar went to her brother Amnon's house, where he was lying down. She took dough, kneaded it, made cakes in his sight, and baked the cakes. ⁹Then she took the pan and set them^a out before him, but he refused to eat. Amnon said, "Send out everyone from me." So everyone went out from him. ¹⁰Then Amnon said to Tamar, "Bring the food into the chamber, so that I may eat from your hand." So Tamar took the cakes she had made, and brought them into the chamber to Amnon her brother. ¹¹But when she brought them near him to eat, he took hold of her, and said to her, "Come, lie with me, my sister." ¹²She answered him, "No, my brother, do not force me; for such a thing is not done in Israel; do not do anything so vile! ¹³As for me, where could I carry my shame? And as for you, you would be as one of the scoundrels in Israel. Now therefore, I beg you, speak to the king; for he will not withhold me from you." ¹⁴But he would not listen to her; and being stronger than she, he forced her and lay with her.

15 Then Amnon was seized with a very great loathing for her; indeed, his loathing was even greater than the lust he had felt for her. Amnon said to her, "Get out!" ¹⁶But she said to him, "No, my brother;^b for this wrong in sending me away is greater than the other that you did to me." But he would not listen to her.

^a Heb and poured   ^b Cn Compare Gk Vg: Meaning of Heb uncertain

have been worn by his cult statue, which to judge by the size of the crown (*a talent of gold,* about 75 pounds) was larger than the size of a man. **12.31** The work assigned to Ammonites *with saws and iron picks and iron axes* is probably the dismantling of the city's fortifications.

13.1–22 This story may be viewed as a prologue to the account of Absalom's rebellion in chs. 15–20. The source for most of the material in chs. 13–20 seems to have been an early account of Absalom's revolt, which, like the story of David's rise to power, is told in such a way that it exonerates David of possible charges of serious wrongdoing in the violent events being reported (see Introduction). The contrast with the prophetic orientation of chs. 11–12 and their unfavorable portrayal of David is striking. In the old story that begins in 13.1 David, the adulterer and murderer of the preceding chapters, is guilty of nothing worse than excessive love and leniency toward his sons (see 13.21, 37–39; 18.5). **13.1** *Tamar,* Absalom's full sister, the daughter of David and Maacah (see 3.3), and Amnon's half

sister. **13.2** For Amnon's lovesickness, cf. Song 2.5; 5.8. Amnon knows that as a *virgin* and a member of the royal family Tamar would be closely guarded. **13.3** *Shimeah.* See note on 1 Sam 16.9. **13.6** The dish Tamar prepares, which is made from dough that is kneaded and boiled (v. 8), seems to be a pudding or dumplings of some kind rather than *cakes.* **13.8** *Baked,* rather "boiled" (cf. v. 6). **13.12** *Anything so vile,* behavior that seriously violates the norms of etiquette or law, rendered *folly* in 1 Sam 25.25; see also note on 13.13. **13.13** *Scoundrels,* in Hebrew the plural of *nabal* (see note on 1 Sam 25.3); by flouting the norms of Israelite society Amnon will, says Tamar, become an outcast. Intercourse with a man's sister or half sister is prohibited by biblical law (Lev 18.9, 11; 20.17; Deut 27.22), so that Tamar's statement that David *will not withhold* her from Amnon, unless she is lying to buy time, must mean that these laws were not in effect at the time, or that the royal family was exempt from them, or that David would be willing to disregard them. **13.16** *This wrong in sending me away.* Tamar is

17 He called the young man who served him and said, "Put this woman out of my presence, and bolt the door after her." 18 (Now she was wearing a long robe with sleeves; for this is how the virgin daughters of the king were clothed in earlier times.*a*) So his servant put her out, and bolted the door after her. 19 But Tamar put ashes on her head, and tore the long robe that she was wearing; she put her hand on her head, and went away, crying aloud as she went.

20 Her brother Absalom said to her, "Has Amnon your brother been with you? Be quiet for now, my sister; he is your brother; do not take this to heart." So Tamar remained, a desolate woman, in her brother Absalom's house. 21 When King David heard of all these things, he became very angry, but he would not punish his son Amnon, because he loved him, for he was his firstborn.*b* 22 But Absalom spoke to Amnon neither good nor bad; for Absalom hated Amnon, because he had raped his sister Tamar.

Absalom Avenges the Violation of His Sister

23 After two full years Absalom had sheepshearers at Baal-hazor, which is near Ephraim, and Absalom invited all the king's sons. 24 Absalom came to the king, and said, "Your servant has sheepshearers; will the king and his servants please go with your servant?" 25 But the king said to Absalom, "No, my son, let us not all go, or else we will be burdensome to you." He pressed him, but he would not go but gave him his blessing. 26 Then Absalom said, "If not, please let my brother Amnon go with us." The king said to him, "Why should he go

with you?" 27 But Absalom pressed him until he let Amnon and all the king's sons go with him. Absalom made a feast like a king's feast.*c* 28 Then Absalom commanded his servants, "Watch when Amnon's heart is merry with wine, and when I say to you, 'Strike Amnon,' then kill him. Do not be afraid; have I not myself commanded you? Be courageous and valiant." 29 So the servants of Absalom did to Amnon as Absalom had commanded. Then all the king's sons rose, and each mounted his mule and fled.

30 While they were on the way, the report came to David that Absalom had killed all the king's sons, and not one of them was left. 31 The king rose, tore his garments, and lay on the ground; and all his servants who were standing by tore their garments. 32 But Jonadab, the son of David's brother Shimeah, said, "Let not my lord suppose that they have killed all the young men the king's sons; Amnon alone is dead. This has been determined by Absalom from the day Amnon*d* raped his sister Tamar. 33 Now therefore, do not let my lord the king take it to heart, as if all the king's sons were dead; for Amnon alone is dead."

34 But Absalom fled. When the young man who kept watch looked up, he saw many people coming from the Horonaim road*e* by the side of the mountain. 35 Jonadab said to the king, "See, the king's sons have come; as your servant said, so it has come about." 36 As soon as he had finished speaking, the king's sons arrived, and raised their voices and wept; and

---

a Cn: Heb *were clothed in robes*   *b* Q Ms Gk: MT lacks *but he would not punish . . . firstborn*   *c* Gk Compare Q Ms: MT lacks *Absalom made a feast like a king's feast*   *d* Heb *he*   *e* Cn Compare Gk: Heb *the road behind him*

---

appealing to a regulation like that in Deut 22.28–29 (cf. Ex 22.16), which says that a man who rapes a virgin is required to marry her and is forbidden to send her away. **13.18** The exact appearance or significance of *a long robe with sleeves* (see also Gen 37.3) is unknown; it may have been a robe that reached the extremities (the wrists and ankles). **13.19** All the actions here are customary gestures of grief. **13.20** Rejected by Amnon and having lost her virginity, Tamar has become *a desolate woman*, i.e., childless and without hope of marriage (see, ironically, Isa 54.1). **13.21** David is depicted as acting too leniently out of love for his son; the same weakness will affect his dealings with Absalom at the time of his revolt (see vv. 37–39; 18.5). **13.23–39** Absalom avenges the violence done to his sister by killing his brother. **13.23** For the festival of *sheepshearers*, see 1 Sam 25.7. *Baal-hazor*, a town in the

central hills about twenty miles north of Jerusalem; about two miles to the southeast was *Ephraim* (see Jn 11.54), also known as Ophrah (see Josh 18.23) and Ephron (2 Chr 13.19). **13.27** As in 1 Sam 25.36, *a king's feast* would be expected to include a lot of drinking, which is, as the next verse shows, an important part of Absalom's plot. **13.29** It seems to have been customary at this time for a king or prince to ride a *mule* rather than a donkey or a horse (see 18.9; 1 Kings 1.33, 38, 44); if Israelites were forbidden to hybridize horses in this period (cf. Lev 19.19), the royal mules must have been imported. **13.32** It is *Jonadab*, Amnon's friend (v. 3), who reports the true state of affairs to the king. **13.34** The royal party approaches the city along the *Horonaim road*, which ran northwest in the direction of "the two Horons" (Hebrew *horonaim*), i.e., Upper and Lower Beth-horon (see Josh 16.3, 5; note on 1 Sam

the king and all his servants also wept very bitterly.

37 But Absalom fled, and went to Talmai son of Ammihud, king of Geshur. David mourned for his son day after day. [38]Absalom, having fled to Geshur, stayed there three years. [39]And the heart of[a] the king went out, yearning for Absalom; for he was now consoled over the death of Amnon.

Absalom Returns to Jerusalem

14 Now Joab son of Zeruiah perceived that the king's mind was on Absalom. [2]Joab sent to Tekoa and brought from there a wise woman. He said to her, "Pretend to be a mourner; put on mourning garments, do not anoint yourself with oil, but behave like a woman who has been mourning many days for the dead. [3]Go to the king and speak to him as follows." And Joab put the words into her mouth.

4 When the woman of Tekoa came to the king, she fell on her face to the ground and did obeisance, and said, "Help, O king!" [5]The king asked her, "What is your trouble?" She answered, "Alas, I am a widow; my husband is dead. [6]Your servant had two sons, and they fought with one another in the field; there was no one to part them, and one struck the other and killed him. [7]Now the whole family has risen against your servant. They say, 'Give up the man who struck his brother, so that we may kill him for the life of his brother whom he murdered, even if we destroy the heir as well.' Thus they would quench my one remaining ember, and leave to my husband neither name nor remnant on the face of the earth."

8 Then the king said to the woman, "Go to your house, and I will give orders concerning you." [9]The woman of Tekoa said to the king, "On me be the guilt, my lord the king, and on my father's house; let the king and his throne be guiltless." [10]The king said, "If anyone says anything to you, bring him to me, and he shall never touch you again." [11]Then she said, "Please, may the king keep the LORD your God in mind, so that the avenger of blood may kill no more, and my son not be destroyed." He said, "As the LORD lives, not one hair of your son shall fall to the ground."

12 Then the woman said, "Please let your servant speak a word to my lord the king." He said, "Speak." [13]The woman said, "Why then have you planned such a thing against the people of God? For in giving this decision the king convicts himself, inasmuch as the king does not bring his banished one home again. [14]We must all die; we are like water spilled on the ground, which cannot be gathered up. But God will not take away a life; he will devise plans so as not to keep an outcast banished forever from his presence.[b] [15]Now I have come to say this to my lord the king because the people have made me afraid; your servant thought, 'I will speak to the king; it may be that the king will perform the request of his servant. [16]For the king will hear, and deliver his servant from the hand of the man who would cut both me and my son off from the heritage of God.' [17]Your servant thought, 'The word of my lord the king will set me at rest'; for my lord the king is like the angel of God, discerning good and evil. The LORD your God be with you!"

18 Then the king answered the woman, "Do not withhold from me anything I ask you." The woman said, "Let my lord the king speak."

---

a Q Ms Gk: MT *And David*   *b* Meaning of Heb uncertain

13.18). **13.37** Absalom finds sanctuary with *Talmai son of Ammihud,* his maternal grandfather (see 3.3). *Geshur.* See notes on 2.9; 3.3.

14.1–24 Joab persuades David to allow Absalom to return to Jerusalem. **14.2** *Tekoa,* the home of the prophet Amos (Am 1.1), was a village in the Judean hills about ten miles south of Jerusalem. Joab arranges for the services of *a wise woman,* a woman skilled in rhetoric (as also in 20.16). **14.5–7** Normal judicial procedures would require that the woman's son, who is guilty of manslaughter, be turned over to the family so that blood vengeance could be exacted; but the king has the power to free the slayer (see v. 16), and she petitions him to do so on the grounds that she is a widow and her son is her late husband's only heir. **14.11** *Keep*

the LORD *your God in mind,* i.e., mention or utter the name of the Lord; the woman is asking David to swear a binding oath, and he does (*as the* LORD *lives*). The *avenger of blood,* the man mentioned in v. 16, is the kinsman who has the responsibility of avenging the death of the woman's son according to the customs of family blood vengeance (see Num 35.16–28; Deut 19.4–13). **14.16** *Heritage of God,* a common way of referring to the promised land, here designates the people of Israel. **14.17** *The word of . . . the king will set me at rest.* The woman is not expressing confidence in a favorable judgment; instead, she is flattering the king by expressing the conviction that whatever he decides will be just. Her comparison of the king's wisdom to that of an *angel of God* is also rhetorical adulation, as in v. 20;

¹⁹The king said, "Is the hand of Joab with you in all this?" The woman answered and said, "As surely as you live, my lord the king, one cannot turn right or left from anything that my lord the king has said. For it was your servant Joab who commanded me; it was he who put all these words into the mouth of your servant. ²⁰In order to change the course of affairs your servant Joab did this. But my lord has wisdom like the wisdom of the angel of God to know all things that are on the earth."

21 Then the king said to Joab, "Very well, I grant this; go, bring back the young man Absalom." ²²Joab prostrated himself with his face to the ground and did obeisance, and blessed the king; and Joab said, "Today your servant knows that I have found favor in your sight, my lord the king, in that the king has granted the request of his servant." ²³So Joab set off, went to Geshur, and brought Absalom to Jerusalem. ²⁴The king said, "Let him go to his own house; he is not to come into my presence." So Absalom went to his own house, and did not come into the king's presence.

David Forgives Absalom

25 Now in all Israel there was no one to be praised so much for his beauty as Absalom; from the sole of his foot to the crown of his head there was no blemish in him. ²⁶When he cut the hair of his head (for at the end of every year he used to cut it; when it was heavy on him, he cut it), he weighed the hair of his head, two hundred shekels by the king's weight. ²⁷There were born to Absalom three sons, and one daughter whose name was Tamar; she was a beautiful woman.

28 So Absalom lived two full years in Jerusalem, without coming into the king's presence. ²⁹Then Absalom sent for Joab to send him to the king; but Joab would not come to him. He sent a second time, but Joab would not come. ³⁰Then he said to his servants,

"Look, Joab's field is next to mine, and he has barley there; go and set it on fire." So Absalom's servants set the field on fire. ³¹Then Joab rose and went to Absalom at his house, and said to him, "Why have your servants set my field on fire?" ³²Absalom answered Joab, "Look, I sent word to you: Come here, that I may send you to the king with the question, 'Why have I come from Geshur? It would be better for me to be there still.' Now let me go into the king's presence; if there is guilt in me, let him kill me!" ³³Then Joab went to the king and told him; and he summoned Absalom. So he came to the king and prostrated himself with his face to the ground before the king; and the king kissed Absalom.

Absalom Usurps the Throne

15 After this Absalom got himself a chariot and horses, and fifty men to run ahead of him. ²Absalom used to rise early and stand beside the road into the gate; and when anyone brought a suit before the king for judgment, Absalom would call out and say, "From what city are you?" When the person said, "Your servant is of such and such a tribe in Israel," ³Absalom would say, "See, your claims are good and right; but there is no one deputed by the king to hear you." ⁴Absalom said moreover, "If only I were judge in the land! Then all who had a suit or cause might come to me, and I would give them justice." ⁵Whenever people came near to do obeisance to him, he would put out his hand and take hold of them, and kiss them. ⁶Thus Absalom did to every Israelite who came to the king for judgment; so Absalom stole the hearts of the people of Israel.

7 At the end of four*a* years Absalom said to the king, "Please let me go to Hebron and pay the vow that I have made to the LORD. ⁸For

---

a Gk Syr: Heb *forty*

19.27. **14.25–33** Through Joab's mediation, David and Absalom are reconciled. **14.25** Absalom's *beauty* partially explains how he *stole the hearts of the people of Israel* (15.6) and why David loved him so deeply that he was unable to discipline him. **14.26** The reference to Absalom's *hair* prepares readers for the bizarre calamity that occurs later in 18.9. *Two hundred shekels,* about 6 pounds. **14.27** That Absalom had *three sons* seems to be contradicted by 18.18; his *one daughter* is evidently named for her aunt (13.1). **14.28–33** Although he has to set a field on fire to get his attention,

Absalom persuades Joab to intervene with his father, and a reconciliation of David and Absalom takes place.

15.1–12 Now that he is back at court, Absalom uses his position to ingratiate himself with the people of Israel. Eventually he claims the throne at Hebron. **15.1** Absalom's *chariot and horses, and fifty men to run ahead of him* are a flamboyant way of claiming the kingship, as 1 Kings 1.5 shows. **15.6** *Stole the hearts of the people.* It is not so much that Absalom won their affection as that he beguiled them; cf. Gen 31.20, where the same expression is translated "deceived."

your servant made a vow while I lived at Geshur in Aram: If the LORD will indeed bring
me back to Jerusalem, then I will worship the
LORD in Hebron."*a* 9The king said to him,
"Go in peace." So he got up, and went to Hebron. 10But Absalom sent secret messengers
throughout all the tribes of Israel, saying, "As
soon as you hear the sound of the trumpet,
then shout: Absalom has become king at Hebron!" 11Two hundred men from Jerusalem
went with Absalom; they were invited guests,
and they went in their innocence, knowing
nothing of the matter. 12While Absalom was
offering the sacrifices, he sent for*b* Ahithophel
the Gilonite, David's counselor, from his city
Giloh. The conspiracy grew in strength, and
the people with Absalom kept increasing.

David Flees from Jerusalem

13 A messenger came to David, saying, "The
hearts of the Israelites have gone after Absalom." 14Then David said to all his officials who
were with him at Jerusalem, "Get up! Let us flee,
or there will be no escape for us from Absalom.
Hurry, or he will soon overtake us, and bring
disaster down upon us, and attack the city with
the edge of the sword." 15The king's officials
said to the king, "Your servants are ready to do
whatever our lord the king decides." 16So the
king left, followed by all his household, except
ten concubines whom he left behind to look
after the house. 17The king left, followed by all
the people; and they stopped at the last house.
18All his officials passed by him; and all the
Cherethites, and all the Pelethites, and all the six
hundred Gittites who had followed him from
Gath, passed on before the king.

19 Then the king said to Ittai the Gittite,
"Why are you also coming with us? Go back,
and stay with the king; for you are a foreigner,
and also an exile from your home. 20You came
only yesterday, and shall I today make you
wander about with us, while I go wherever I
can? Go back, and take your kinsfolk with you;
and may the LORD show*c* steadfast love and
faithfulness to you." 21But Ittai answered the
king, "As the LORD lives, and as my lord the
king lives, wherever my lord the king may be,
whether for death or for life, there also your
servant will be." 22David said to Ittai, "Go
then, march on." So Ittai the Gittite marched
on, with all his men and all the little ones who
were with him. 23The whole country wept
aloud as all the people passed by; the king
crossed the Wadi Kidron, and all the people
moved on toward the wilderness.

24 Abiathar came up, and Zadok also, with
all the Levites, carrying the ark of the covenant
of God. They set down the ark of God, until
the people had all passed out of the city.
25Then the king said to Zadok, "Carry the ark
of God back into the city. If I find favor in the
eyes of the LORD, he will bring me back and let
me see both it and the place where it stays.
26But if he says, 'I take no pleasure in you,' here
I am, let him do to me what seems good to
him." 27The king also said to the priest Zadok,
"Look,*d* go back to the city in peace, you and
Abiathar,*e* with your two sons, Ahimaaz your
son, and Jonathan son of Abiathar. 28See, I will
wait at the fords of the wilderness until word

---

a Gk Mss: Heb lacks *in Hebron*   *b* Or *he sent*   *c* Gk Compare
2.6: Heb lacks *may the LORD show*   *d* Gk: Heb *Are you a seer*
or *Do you see?*   *e* Cn: Heb lacks *and Abiathar*

15.7–8 Absalom must go to Hebron, he says, because
he promised to worship *the LORD in Hebron,* i.e., the
God of Israel in his local Hebronite manifestation, so
that the vow cannot be fulfilled by worshiping the
Lord in Jerusalem. For Absalom's term in exile *at Geshur in Aram,* see 13.38. **15.10** Absalom chooses *Hebron* as the site from which to launch his rebellion; it
was his birthplace (see 3.3) and the traditional capital
of Judah. **15.12** *Ahithophel* was a Judahite; his hometown of *Giloh* was in the hill country of Judah (see
Josh 15.51), but the modern location is unknown.
15.13–31 The news of Absalom's successful rebellion
forces David to abandon the city. **15.16** *Ten concubines* looks ahead to 16.21–22. **15.18** The soldiers
who remain loyal to David are those in his personal
retinue who have been with him since his days as a
fugitive from Saul's justice and a mercenary in the
Philistine army. *Cherethites, Pelethites.* See notes on

1 Sam 30.14; 2 Sam 8.18. David won their loyalty and
that of *the six hundred Gittites* when he lived in Ziklag
and served the king of the Philistine city of *Gath* (see
1 Sam 27; 29–30). **15.19–21** Cf. the language of Ruth
1.8–17. *Ittai,* who is probably the commander of
David's Gittite forces, will command a third of
David's troops in the battle against Absalom's army
(see 18.2). **15.23** David leaves Jerusalem by crossing
the *Wadi Kidron,* the valley separating the City of
David from the Mount of Olives to the east; the Kidron was regarded as the boundary of the city in the
time of David (cf. 1 Kings 2.37). **15.24** For *Abiathar*
and *Zadok,* David's two chief priests, see note on 8.17.
Mention of *the Levites,* the official priestly tribe, may
be a secondary addition (cf. 1 Sam 6.15). **15.25** *The
place where it stays.* The underlying Hebrew suggests a
tent shrine (see 6.17; 7.6) in contrast to the anachronistic *house of the LORD* in 12.20. **15.28** David's plan is

comes from you to inform me." 29So Zadok and Abiathar carried the ark of God back to Jerusalem, and they remained there.

30 But David went up the ascent of the Mount of Olives, weeping as he went, with his head covered and walking barefoot; and all the people who were with him covered their heads and went up, weeping as they went. 31David was told that Ahithophel was among the conspirators with Absalom. And David said, "O Lord, I pray you, turn the counsel of Ahithophel into foolishness."

Hushai Becomes David's Spy

32 When David came to the summit, where God was worshiped, Hushai the Archite came to meet him with his coat torn and earth on his head. 33David said to him, "If you go on with me, you will be a burden to me. 34But if you return to the city and say to Absalom, 'I will be your servant, O king; as I have been your father's servant in time past, so now I will be your servant,' then you will defeat for me the counsel of Ahithophel. 35The priests Zadok and Abiathar will be with you there. So whatever you hear from the king's house, tell it to the priests Zadok and Abiathar. 36Their two sons are with them there, Zadok's son Ahimaaz and Abiathar's son Jonathan; and by them you shall report to me everything you hear." 37So Hushai, David's friend, came into the city, just as Absalom was entering Jerusalem.

David's Adversaries

16 When David had passed a little beyond the summit, Ziba the servant of Mephibosheth[a] met him, with a couple of donkeys saddled, carrying two hundred loaves of bread, one hundred bunches of raisins, one hundred of summer fruits, and one skin of wine. 2The king said to Ziba, "Why have you brought these?" Ziba answered, "The donkeys are for the king's household to ride, the bread and summer fruit for the young men to eat, and the wine is for those to drink who faint in the wilderness." 3The king said, "And where is your master's son?" Ziba said to the king, "He remains in Jerusalem; for he said, 'Today the house of Israel will give me back my grandfather's kingdom.' " 4Then the king said to Ziba, "All that belonged to Mephibosheth[a] is now yours." Ziba said, "I do obeisance; let me find favor in your sight, my lord the king."

Shimei Curses David

5 When King David came to Bahurim, a man of the family of the house of Saul came out whose name was Shimei son of Gera; he came out cursing. 6He threw stones at David and at all the servants of King David; now all the people and all the warriors were on his right and on his left. 7Shimei shouted while he cursed, "Out! Out! Murderer! Scoundrel! 8The Lord has avenged on all of you the blood of the house of Saul, in whose place you have reigned; and the Lord has given the kingdom into the hand of your son Absalom. See, disaster has overtaken you; for you are a man of blood."

9 Then Abishai son of Zeruiah said to the

a Or Merib-baal: See 4.4 note

---

to camp *at the fords of the wilderness,* i.e., on the west bank of the Jordan, until he receives information from Zadok (see 15.27–29; 17.16). **15.31** David's wish for a way to subvert the *counsel of Ahithophel* (see v. 12) will be fulfilled in 17.5–14 through the efforts of the man David will meet at the top of the mountain. **15.32–37** David meets Hushai and asks him to counteract Ahithophel's counsel at Absalom's court. **15.32** We know of no place *where God was worshiped* atop the Mount of Olives except the so-called Mount of Destruction (see 2 Kings 23.13), which was probably farther south than the place where David meets Hushai. *Hushai,* perhaps the same man identified in 1 Kings 4.16 as the father of Baana, one of Solomon's twelve supply officers; but Baana has responsibility for Asher, whereas the *Archite* clan was Benjaminite and inhabited the region southwest of Bethel (Josh 16.2). **15.37** *David's friend.* In a list of civic officials in 1 Chr 27.33 Hushai is called "the king's friend," prob-ably an official title that meant something like "privy counselor," as parallels in Egyptian administrative language suggest.

16.1–4 David receives the support of Ziba, Mephibosheth's steward. **16.1** *Ziba.* See 9.2. *Mephibosheth.* See 4.4. **16.3** When he and David meet after the revolt has been quelled, Mephibosheth will deny Ziba's accusation and accuse him of slander (see 19.24–30). **16.5–14** David endures Shimei's curses with penitential submission to the Lord. **16.5** *Bahurim.* See note on 3.16. The *family of the house of Saul* was Matri (see 1 Sam 10.21). **16.7–8** Shimei's words show that he holds David responsible for the *blood of the house of Saul,* i.e., for the death of many of his kin, including at least the seven sons and grandsons of Saul whom David executed at Gibeon (see ch. 21), but probably also Abner (see ch. 3) and Ishbaal (see ch. 4), and maybe Saul and Jonathan too (see 1 Sam 31; 2 Sam 2). **16.9** It is characteristic of *Abishai* (see 2.18) to think of

king, "Why should this dead dog curse my lord
the king? Let me go over and take off his
head." 10But the king said, "What have I to do
with you, you sons of Zeruiah? If he is cursing
because the LORD has said to him, 'Curse
David,' who then shall say, 'Why have you
done so?' " 11David said to Abishai and to all
his servants, "My own son seeks my life; how
much more now may this Benjaminite! Let
him alone, and let him curse; for the LORD has
bidden him. 12It may be that the LORD will
look on my distress,ᵃ and the LORD will repay
me with good for this cursing of me today."
13So David and his men went on the road,
while Shimei went along on the hillside opposite him and cursed as he went, throwing
stones and flinging dust at him. 14The king
and all the people who were with him arrived
weary at the Jordan;ᵇ and there he refreshed
himself.

The Counsel of Ahithophel

15 Now Absalom and all the Israelitesᶜ came
to Jerusalem; Ahithophel was with him.
16When Hushai the Archite, David's friend,
came to Absalom, Hushai said to Absalom,
"Long live the king! Long live the king!" 17Ab-
salom said to Hushai, "Is this your loyalty to
your friend? Why did you not go with your
friend?" 18Hushai said to Absalom, "No; but
the one whom the LORD and this people and
all the Israelites have chosen, his I will be, and
with him I will remain. 19Moreover, whom
should I serve? Should it not be his son? Just as
I have served your father, so I will serve you."

20 Then Absalom said to Ahithophel, "Give
us your counsel; what shall we do?" 21Ahitho-
phel said to Absalom, "Go in to your father's
concubines, the ones he has left to look after
the house; and all Israel will hear that you have

made yourself odious to your father, and the
hands of all who are with you will be strengthened." 22So they pitched a tent for Absalom
upon the roof; and Absalom went in to his father's concubines in the sight of all Israel.
23Now in those days the counsel that Ahithophel gave was as if one consulted the oracleᵈ of
God; so all the counsel of Ahithophel was esteemed, both by David and by Absalom.

17 Moreover Ahithophel said to Absalom,
"Let me choose twelve thousand men,
and I will set out and pursue David tonight. 2I
will come upon him while he is weary and discouraged, and throw him into a panic; and all
the people who are with him will flee. I will
strike down only the king, 3and I will bring all
the people back to you as a bride comes home
to her husband. You seek the life of only one
man,ᵉ and all the people will be at peace." 4The
advice pleased Absalom and all the elders of
Israel.

The Counsel of Hushai

5 Then Absalom said, "Call Hushai the Archite
also, and let us hear too what he has to say."
6When Hushai came to Absalom, Absalom
said to him, "This is what Ahithophel has said;
shall we do as he advises? If not, you tell us."
7Then Hushai said to Absalom, "This time the
counsel that Ahithophel has given is not
good." 8Hushai continued, "You know that
your father and his men are warriors, and that
they are enraged, like a bear robbed of her
cubs in the field. Besides, your father is expert
in war; he will not spend the night with the
troops. 9Even now he has hidden himself in
one of the pits, or in some other place. And

ᵃ Gk Vg: Heb *iniquity*   ᵇ Gk: Heb lacks *at the Jordan*
ᶜ Gk: Heb *all the people, the men of Israel*   ᵈ Heb *word*
ᵉ Gk: Heb *like the return of the whole (is) the man whom you seek*

---

a quick and violent solution to one of David's problems; cf. 1 Sam 26.8. *Dead dog.* See 9.8; note on 1 Sam
24.14. **16.10–12** David's attitude toward Abishai and
the other ruthless *sons of Zeruiah* is expressed more
fully in 3.29. Here as elsewhere, David is depicted as restrained and lenient in dealing with the kin and partisans of Saul—a depiction that protects him against
charges like those made by Shimei in vv. 7–8; but according to 1 Kings 2.8–9, where the narrator's concern
is to defend Solomon's actions rather than David's, it
was David's deathbed wish that Shimei be executed for
this "terrible curse." **16.15–17.4** Meanwhile, back in
Jerusalem Hushai undermines the counsel of
Ahithophel. **16.16–19** Hushai's dissembling pledge of

allegiance to Absalom is filled with irony and double
entendre; e.g., his acclamation *Long live the king!* is sincere, but he is not thinking of Absalom. *David's friend.*
See note on 15.37. **16.21–22** Absalom's public arroga-
tion of his *father's concubines,* anticipated in Nathan's
warning (see 12.11), constitutes a claim to the throne
(see 3.7; 12.8). **17.1–3** Although Hushai will mislead
Absalom into believing otherwise, Ahithophel's plan is
sound; the best chance of defeating David is to attack
while he is weary and discouraged, but if he is given
time he will be able to draw on his extensive experience as a guerrilla warrior and organize a formidable
resistance.

17.5–14 Using specious arguments Hushai per-

when some of our troops*a* fall at the first attack, whoever hears it will say, 'There has been a slaughter among the troops who follow Absalom.' 10 Then even the valiant warrior, whose heart is like the heart of a lion, will utterly melt with fear; for all Israel knows that your father is a warrior, and that those who are with him are valiant warriors. 11 But my counsel is that all Israel be gathered to you, from Dan to Beer-sheba, like the sand by the sea for multitude, and that you go to battle in person. 12 So we shall come upon him in whatever place he may be found, and we shall light on him as the dew falls on the ground; and he will not survive, nor will any of those with him. 13 If he withdraws into a city, then all Israel will bring ropes to that city, and we shall drag it into the valley, until not even a pebble is to be found there." 14 Absalom and all the men of Israel said, "The counsel of Hushai the Archite is better than the counsel of Ahithophel." For the LORD had ordained to defeat the good counsel of Ahithophel, so that the LORD might bring ruin on Absalom.

Hushai Warns David to Escape

15 Then Hushai said to the priests Zadok and Abiathar, "Thus and so did Ahithophel counsel Absalom and the elders of Israel; and thus and so I have counseled. 16 Therefore send quickly and tell David, 'Do not lodge tonight at the fords of the wilderness, but by all means cross over; otherwise the king and all the people who are with him will be swallowed up.' " 17 Jonathan and Ahimaaz were waiting at En-rogel; a servant-girl used to go and tell them, and they would go and tell King David; for they could not risk being seen entering the city. 18 But a boy saw them, and told Absalom; so both of them went away quickly, and came to the house of a man at Bahurim, who had a well in his courtyard; and they went down into it. 19 The man's wife took a covering, stretched it over the well's mouth, and spread out grain on it; and nothing was known of it. 20 When Absalom's servants came to the woman at the house, they said, "Where are Ahimaaz and Jonathan?" The woman said to them, "They have crossed over the brook*b* of water." And when they had searched and could not find them, they returned to Jerusalem.

21 After they had gone, the men came up out of the well, and went and told King David. They said to David, "Go and cross the water quickly; for thus and so has Ahithophel counseled against you." 22 So David and all the people who were with him set out and crossed the Jordan; by daybreak not one was left who had not crossed the Jordan.

23 When Ahithophel saw that his counsel was not followed, he saddled his donkey and went off home to his own city. He set his house in order, and hanged himself; he died and was buried in the tomb of his father.

24 Then David came to Mahanaim, while Absalom crossed the Jordan with all the men of Israel. 25 Now Absalom had set Amasa over the army in the place of Joab. Amasa was the son of a man named Ithra the Ishmaelite,*c* who had married Abigal daughter of Nahash, sister of Zeruiah, Joab's mother. 26 The Israelites and Absalom encamped in the land of Gilead.

a Gk Mss: Heb *some of them*   *b* Meaning of Heb uncertain
c 1 Chr 2.17: Heb *Israelite*

---

suades Absalom and his supporters to reject the plan of Ahithophel. **17.11** The key to Hushai's strategy is to buy time for David; the size of Absalom's army will not matter if David is able to deploy his expert warriors in rugged terrain. *From Dan to Beer-sheba*. See note on 3.9–10. **17.14** It was the narrator's conviction that the shaping force in these events was the Lord's determination to *bring ruin on Absalom*. **17.15–29** Absalom prefers Hushai's counsel over that of Ahithophel, thus allowing David to escape and regroup. **17.15** David left *Zadok* and *Abiathar* behind in Jerusalem for the specific purpose of sending messages like this one (see 15.27–29). **17.16** *Fords of the wilderness*. See 15.28. **17.17** *Jonathan and Ahimaaz*, the sons of Zadok and Abiathar (see 15.27), carry the actual messages. *En-rogel*, the spring at the confluence of the Wadi Hinnom and the Wadi Kidron (see note on 15.23), not far south of the Gihon, the main spring that served Jerusalem. **17.18** *Bahurim*. See note on 3.16; 16.5. **17.20** *Brook of water*, obscure. The woman is perhaps saying that Ahimaaz and Jonathan have crossed the Jordan. **17.23** Ahithophel's *own city* was Giloh (see 15.12); this report of his death may have had a shaping effect on Matthew's account of the suicide of Judas, who also *hanged himself* (see Mt 27.5). **17.24** *Mahanaim*, once the capital of his enemy, Ishbaal (see 2.8), is now a place of refuge for David. **17.25** *Amasa*, a kinsman of David by marriage and therefore a Judahite; after the revolt David will attempt to placate Absalom's Judahite supporters by putting Amasa in charge of the army (see 19.13). The information about Amasa's parentage is textually uncertain; evidently he was the child of an *Ishmaelite*, i.e., a nomad, and a niece of David's sister *Zeruiah* (see 1 Sam 26.6). **17.26** *Land of*

27 When David came to Mahanaim, Shobi son of Nahash from Rabbah of the Ammonites, and Machir son of Ammiel from Lodebar, and Barzillai the Gileadite from Rogelim, 28brought beds, basins, and earthen vessels, wheat, barley, meal, parched grain, beans and lentils,*a* 29honey and curds, sheep, and cheese from the herd, for David and the people with him to eat; for they said, "The troops are hungry and weary and thirsty in the wilderness."

The Defeat and Death of Absalom

18 Then David mustered the men who were with him, and set over them commanders of thousands and commanders of hundreds. 2And David divided the army into three groups:*b* one third under the command of Joab, one third under the command of Abishai son of Zeruiah, Joab's brother, and one third under the command of Ittai the Gittite. The king said to the men, "I myself will also go out with you." 3But the men said, "You shall not go out. For if we flee, they will not care about us. If half of us die, they will not care about us. But you are worth ten thousand of us;*c* therefore it is better that you send us help from the city." 4The king said to them, "Whatever seems best to you I will do." So the king stood at the side of the gate, while all the army marched out by hundreds and by thousands. 5The king ordered Joab and Abishai and Ittai, saying, "Deal gently for my sake with the young man Absalom." And all the people heard when the king gave orders to all the commanders concerning Absalom.

6 So the army went out into the field against Israel; and the battle was fought in the forest of Ephraim. 7The men of Israel were defeated there by the servants of David, and the slaughter there was great on that day, twenty thousand men. 8The battle spread over the face of all the country; and the forest claimed more victims that day than the sword.

9 Absalom happened to meet the servants of David. Absalom was riding on his mule, and the mule went under the thick branches of a great oak. His head caught fast in the oak, and he was left hanging*d* between heaven and earth, while the mule that was under him went on. 10A man saw it, and told Joab, "I saw Absalom hanging in an oak." 11Joab said to the man who told him, "What, you saw him! Why then did you not strike him there to the ground? I would have been glad to give you ten pieces of silver and a belt." 12But the man said to Joab, "Even if I felt in my hand the weight of a thousand pieces of silver, I would not raise my hand against the king's son; for in our hearing the king commanded you and Abishai and Ittai, saying: For my sake protect the young man Absalom! 13On the other hand, if I had dealt treacherously against his life*e* (and there is nothing hidden from the king), then you yourself would have stood aloof." 14Joab said, "I will not waste time like this with you." He took three spears in his hand, and thrust them into the heart of Absalom, while he was still alive in the oak. 15And ten young men, Joab's

---

a Heb *and lentils and parched grain* *b* Gk: Heb *sent forth the army* *c* Gk Vg Symmachus: Heb *for now there are ten thousand such as we* *d* Gk Syr Tg: Heb *was put* *e* Another reading is *at the risk of my life*

Gilead, here simply the east bank of the Jordan; see notes on 1 Sam 10.27b; 13.7; 2 Sam 2.9. **17.27** *Shobi son of Nahash*, the Ammonite king introduced in 1 Sam 10.27, is mentioned nowhere else; it is possible that the help he gives David here is the act of loyalty David refers to at the time of Nahash's death, which may have occurred after Absalom's revolt (see note on 10.2). *Machir, Lo-debar.* See note on 9.4. In return for his help here, *Barzillai* will receive an invitation to live at court in Jerusalem (see 19.33); although he will decline, his sons will become houseguests of Solomon (see 1 Kings 2.7). *Rogelim.* Location unknown.

18.1–18 In the ensuing battle, troops loyal to David defeat the followers of Absalom, who is killed by Joab. **18.2** *Abishai.* See 2.18. *Ittai the Gittite.* See 15.19–21. **18.3** David receives similar advice in 21.17. **18.5** This narrative seems to be addressed to citizens of Israel and especially Judah who were outraged by the battle-field execution of Absalom; in order to shield David from blame, the author gives special stress not only to his absence from the battle (vv. 3–5) but also to his insistence on the lenient treatment of Absalom. Cf. note on 13.1–22. **18.6** *Forest of Ephraim,* perhaps a wooded region in Transjordan; it may have been settled by Ephraimites moving east from their home in the central hills. **18.8** A battle in which *the forest claimed more victims . . . than the sword* would be greatly to the advantage of David's army, which in contrast to Absalom's conscript militia was a professional fighting force with extensive experience of guerrilla warfare; this situation shows the cleverness of Hushai's disingenuous advice to Absalom (see 17.5–14). **18.9** The *mule* was evidently the customary mount of royalty at this time (see 13.29). The traditional interpretation of Absalom's accident, maintained by many modern scholars, is that he is caught in the tree by his remark-

armor-bearers, surrounded Absalom and struck him, and killed him.

16 Then Joab sounded the trumpet, and the troops came back from pursuing Israel, for Joab restrained the troops. 17They took Absalom, threw him into a great pit in the forest, and raised over him a very great heap of stones. Meanwhile all the Israelites fled to their homes. 18Now Absalom in his lifetime had taken and set up for himself a pillar that is in the King's Valley, for he said, "I have no son to keep my name in remembrance"; he called the pillar by his own name. It is called Absalom's Monument to this day.

David Hears of Absalom's Death

19 Then Ahimaaz son of Zadok said, "Let me run, and carry tidings to the king that the Lord has delivered him from the power of his enemies." 20Joab said to him, "You are not to carry tidings today; you may carry tidings another day, but today you shall not do so, because the king's son is dead." 21Then Joab said to a Cushite, "Go, tell the king what you have seen." The Cushite bowed before Joab, and ran. 22Then Ahimaaz son of Zadok said again to Joab, "Come what may, let me also run after the Cushite." And Joab said, "Why will you run, my son, seeing that you have no reward*a* for the tidings?" 23"Come what may," he said, "I will run." So he said to him, "Run." Then Ahimaaz ran by the way of the Plain, and outran the Cushite.

24 Now David was sitting between the two gates. The sentinel went up to the roof of the gate by the wall, and when he looked up, he saw a man running alone. 25The sentinel shouted and told the king. The king said, "If he is alone, there are tidings in his mouth." He kept coming, and drew near. 26Then the sentinel saw another man running; and the sentinel called to the gatekeeper and said, "See, another man running alone!" The king said,

"He also is bringing tidings." 27The sentinel said, "I think the running of the first one is like the running of Ahimaaz son of Zadok." The king said, "He is a good man, and comes with good tidings."

28 Then Ahimaaz cried out to the king, "All is well!" He prostrated himself before the king with his face to the ground, and said, "Blessed be the Lord your God, who has delivered up the men who raised their hand against my lord the king." 29The king said, "Is it well with the young man Absalom?" Ahimaaz answered, "When Joab sent your servant,*b* I saw a great tumult, but I do not know what it was." 30The king said, "Turn aside, and stand here." So he turned aside, and stood still.

31 Then the Cushite came; and the Cushite said, "Good tidings for my lord the king! For the Lord has vindicated you this day, delivering you from the power of all who rose up against you." 32The king said to the Cushite, "Is it well with the young man Absalom?" The Cushite answered, "May the enemies of my lord the king, and all who rise up to do you harm, be like that young man."

David Mourns for Absalom

33*c* The king was deeply moved, and went up to the chamber over the gate, and wept; and as he went, he said, "O my son Absalom, my son, my son Absalom! Would I had died instead of you, O Absalom, my son, my son!"

19 It was told Joab, "The king is weeping and mourning for Absalom." 2So the victory that day was turned into mourning for all the troops; for the troops heard that day, "The king is grieving for his son." 3The troops stole into the city that day as soldiers steal in who are ashamed when they flee in battle. 4The king covered his face, and the king cried

---

a Meaning of Heb uncertain   *b* Heb *the king's servant, your servant*   *c* Ch 19.1 in Heb

---

able hair (see 14.26), the cause of his pride now becoming the cause of his ruin. **18.18** Added by an editor to identify a monument known in his time (*to this day*). *The King's Valley*, elsewhere called "the Valley of Shaveh" (Gen 14.17); it may have been the name of a broad section of the Wadi Kidron (see note on 15.23) or the place of its confluence with the Valley of Hinnom. *No son* conflicts with 14.27. The reference to *Absalom's Monument* here has led to the designation of a spectacular tomb from the Hellenistic or Roman period in the Wadi Kidron as "Absalom's Tomb." **18.19–**

32 Two messengers inform David of the outcome of the battle. **18.19** *Ahimaaz son of Zadok* (see 15.27; 17.17) is unaware of the death of Absalom (see v. 29). **18.20–21** Joab knows that if he tells Ahimaaz, who has always been loyal to David's wishes, that Absalom has been slain despite David's request to the contrary (see v. 5), Ahimaaz will make an unfavorable report to the king. So Joab declines Ahimaaz's offer to report the news to David and gives the assignment to a *Cushite*, probably an Ethiopian or Nubian. **18.23** *The way of the Plain*, the lower Jordan Valley—the rougher but

with a loud voice, "O my son Absalom, O Absalom, my son, my son!" 5Then Joab came into the house to the king, and said, "Today you have covered with shame the faces of all your officers who have saved your life today, and the lives of your sons and your daughters, and the lives of your wives and your concubines, 6for love of those who hate you and for hatred of those who love you. You have made it clear today that commanders and officers are nothing to you; for I perceive that if Absalom were alive and all of us were dead today, then you would be pleased. 7So go out at once and speak kindly to your servants; for I swear by the Lord, if you do not go, not a man will stay with you this night; and this will be worse for you than any disaster that has come upon you from your youth until now." 8Then the king got up and took his seat in the gate. The troops were all told, "See, the king is sitting in the gate"; and all the troops came before the king.

David Recalled to Jerusalem

Meanwhile, all the Israelites had fled to their homes. 9All the people were disputing throughout all the tribes of Israel, saying, "The king delivered us from the hand of our enemies, and saved us from the hand of the Philistines; and now he has fled out of the land because of Absalom. 10But Absalom, whom we anointed over us, is dead in battle. Now therefore why do you say nothing about bringing the king back?"

11 King David sent this message to the priests Zadok and Abiathar, "Say to the elders of Judah, 'Why should you be the last to bring the king back to his house? The talk of all Israel has come to the king.*a 12You are my kin, you are my bone and my flesh; why then should you be the last to bring back the king?' 13And say to Amasa, 'Are you not my bone and my flesh? So may God do to me, and more, if you are not the commander of my army from now on, in place of Joab.'" 14Amasa*b swayed the hearts of all the people of Judah as one, and they sent word to the king, "Return, both you and all your servants." 15So the king came back to the Jordan; and Judah came to Gilgal to meet the king and to bring him over the Jordan.

16 Shimei son of Gera, the Benjaminite, from Bahurim, hurried to come down with the people of Judah to meet King David; 17with him were a thousand people from Benjamin. And Ziba, the servant of the house of Saul, with his fifteen sons and his twenty servants, rushed down to the Jordan ahead of the king, 18while the crossing was taking place,*c to bring over the king's household, and to do his pleasure.

David's Mercy to Shimei

Shimei son of Gera fell down before the king, as he was about to cross the Jordan, 19and said to the king, "May my lord not hold me guilty or remember how your servant did wrong on the day my lord the king left Jerusalem; may the king not bear it in mind. 20For your servant knows that I have sinned; therefore, see, I have come this day, the first of all the house of Joseph to come down to meet my lord the king." 21Abishai son of Zeruiah answered, "Shall not Shimei be put to death for this, because he cursed the Lord's anointed?" 22But David said, "What have I to do with you, you sons of Zeruiah, that you should today become an adversary to me? Shall anyone be put to death in Israel this day? For do I not know

---

a Gk: Heb to the king, to his house   b Heb He   c Cn: Heb the ford crossed

---

shorter route to Jerusalem. **18.33–19.8a** Joab chides David for his excessive grief over Absalom. **19.6** *Love, hatred,* here political loyalties; cf. 1 Sam 18.1, 3 and note on 1 Sam 20.17. **19.8** David, by *sitting in the gate,* is assuming the traditional role of judge in Israel (cf. 1 Sam 4.12–18), thus symbolically reclaiming his sovereignty.

19.8b–15 David and the people of Judah are reconciled. **19.12** *My bone and my flesh.* See note on 5.1. David's point is that the people of Judah, his kin, should be the first to restore his rule. **19.13** To conciliate the people of Judah, who must have represented Absalom's chief support, David appoints his kinsman Amasa (see 17.25) as commander of the army *in place*

of Joab, who executed Absalom. **19.15** The ancient shrine of *Gilgal* had special associations with kingship; see note on 1 Sam 10.8. **19.16–23** Shimei asks for David's forgiveness. **19.16** The account of David's hostile encounter with *Shimei* is found in 16.5–14. **19.17** *Ziba,* the servant of Mephibosheth. See 9.2; 16.1–4. **19.20** Knowing that his life is in jeopardy, Shimei pleads that he is *the first of all the house of Joseph,* i.e., the first non-Judahite, to welcome the king on his return. **19.21** True to his character (see 2.18; 1 Sam 26.8) and consistent with his role in the earlier Shimei incident (see 16.9), *Abishai* proposes a violent reaction to Shimei's reappearance; he believes that Shimei has committed a capital crime *because he cursed the Lord's*

that I am this day king over Israel?" ²³The king said to Shimei, "You shall not die." And the king gave him his oath.

David and Mephibosheth Meet

24 Mephibosheth*ᵃ* grandson of Saul came down to meet the king; he had not taken care of his feet, or trimmed his beard, or washed his clothes, from the day the king left until the day he came back in safety. ²⁵When he came from Jerusalem to meet the king, the king said to him, "Why did you not go with me, Mephibosheth?"*ᵃ* ²⁶He answered, "My lord, O king, my servant deceived me; for your servant said to him, 'Saddle a donkey for me,*ᵇ* so that I may ride on it and go with the king.' For your servant is lame. ²⁷He has slandered your servant to my lord the king. But my lord the king is like the angel of God; do therefore what seems good to you. ²⁸For all my father's house were doomed to death before my lord the king; but you set your servant among those who eat at your table. What further right have I, then, to appeal to the king?" ²⁹The king said to him, "Why speak any more of your affairs? I have decided: you and Ziba shall divide the land." ³⁰Mephibosheth*ᵃ* said to the king, "Let him take it all, since my lord the king has arrived home safely."

David's Kindness to Barzillai

31 Now Barzillai the Gileadite had come down from Rogelim; he went on with the king to the Jordan, to escort him over the Jordan. ³²Barzillai was a very aged man, eighty years old. He had provided the king with food while he stayed at Mahanaim, for he was a very wealthy man. ³³The king said to Barzillai, "Come over with me, and I will provide for you in Jerusalem at my side." ³⁴But Barzillai said to the king, "How many years have I still to live, that I should go up with the king to Jerusalem? ³⁵Today I am eighty years old; can I discern what is pleasant and what is not? Can your servant taste what he eats or what he drinks? Can I still listen to the voice of singing men and singing women? Why then should your servant be an added burden to my lord the king? ³⁶Your servant will go a little way over the Jordan with the king. Why should the king recompense me with such a reward? ³⁷Please let your servant return, so that I may die in my own town, near the graves of my father and my mother. But here is your servant Chimham; let him go over with my lord the king; and do for him whatever seems good to you." ³⁸The king answered, "Chimham shall go over with me, and I will do for him whatever seems good to you; and all that you desire of me I will do for you." ³⁹Then all the people crossed over the Jordan, and the king crossed over; the king kissed Barzillai and blessed him, and he returned to his own home. ⁴⁰The king went on to Gilgal, and Chimham went on with him; all the people of Judah, and also half the people of Israel, brought the king on his way.

41 Then all the people of Israel came to the king, and said to him, "Why have our kindred the people of Judah stolen you away, and brought the king and his household over the Jordan, and all David's men with him?" ⁴²All the people of Judah answered the people of Israel, "Because the king is near of kin to us. Why then are you angry over this matter? Have we eaten at all at the king's expense? Or has he given us any gift?" ⁴³But the people of Israel answered the people of Judah, "We have ten shares in the king, and in David also we have more than you. Why then did you despise us? Were we not the first to speak of bringing back our king?" But the words of the people of Judah were fiercer than the words of the people of Israel.

---

a Or *Merib-baal*: See 4.4 note   *b* Gk Syr Vg: Heb *said, 'I will saddle a donkey for myself*

---

anointed, who is sacrosanct (see 1 Sam 24.6–7). **19.23** David grants Shimei a royal pardon now, but at the end of his own life he will consign the Benjaminite to death (see 1 Kings 2.8–9, 36–46). **19.24–30** The background to this section is the dispute between Mephibosheth and Ziba, described in 9.1–13; 16.1–4. **19.24** *Not taken care of his feet,* obscure, perhaps related to his crippled condition (see 9.13). **19.27** For the comparison of the king's wisdom to that of *the angel of God,* see 14.17. **19.28** *My father's house,* the house of Saul. *Those who eat at your table.* See note on 9.7. **19.31**–

43 Barzillai was one of those who befriended David when he arrived in Mahanaim after his flight from Jerusalem (see 17.27–29). **19.35** Barzillai declines David's invitation on the grounds that he is too old to be able to enjoy life at court. **19.37** *Chimham,* perhaps one of the sons of Barzillai commended by David on his deathbed in 1 Kings 2.6. **19.41–43** *The people,* here the tribal militia of Judah or Israel; the issue is sectional hostility between the Judahites, to whom David is *near of kin,* and the Israelites, who claim *ten shares in the king* because of the ten northern tribes.

The Rebellion of Sheba

20 Now a scoundrel named Sheba son of Bichri, a Benjaminite, happened to be there. He sounded the trumpet and cried out,

"We have no portion in David,
no share in the son of Jesse!
Everyone to your tents, O Israel!"

2 So all the people of Israel withdrew from David and followed Sheba son of Bichri; but the people of Judah followed their king steadfastly from the Jordan to Jerusalem.

3 David came to his house at Jerusalem; and the king took the ten concubines whom he had left to look after the house, and put them in a house under guard, and provided for them, but did not go in to them. So they were shut up until the day of their death, living as if in widowhood.

4 Then the king said to Amasa, "Call the men of Judah together to me within three days, and be here yourself." 5 So Amasa went to summon Judah; but he delayed beyond the set time that had been appointed him. 6 David said to Abishai, "Now Sheba son of Bichri will do us more harm than Absalom; take your lord's servants and pursue him, or he will find fortified cities for himself, and escape from us." 7 Joab's men went out after him, along with the Cherethites, the Pelethites, and all the warriors; they went out from Jerusalem to pursue Sheba son of Bichri. 8 When they were at the large stone that is in Gibeon, Amasa came to meet them. Now Joab was wearing a soldier's garment and over it was a belt with a sword in its sheath fastened at his waist; as he went forward it fell out. 9 Joab said to Amasa, "Is it well with you, my brother?" And Joab took Amasa by the beard with his right hand to kiss him. 10 But Amasa did not notice the sword in Joab's hand; Joab struck him in the belly so that his entrails poured out on the ground, and he died. He did not strike a second blow.

Then Joab and his brother Abishai pursued Sheba son of Bichri. 11 And one of Joab's men took his stand by Amasa, and said, "Whoever favors Joab, and whoever is for David, let him follow Joab." 12 Amasa lay wallowing in his blood on the highway, and the man saw that all the people were stopping. Since he saw that all who came by him were stopping, he carried Amasa from the highway into a field, and threw a garment over him. 13 Once he was removed from the highway, all the people went on after Joab to pursue Sheba son of Bichri.

14 Sheba[a] passed through all the tribes of Israel to Abel of Beth-maacah;[b] and all the Bichrites[c] assembled, and followed him inside. 15 Joab's forces[d] came and besieged him in Abel of Beth-maacah; they threw up a siege ramp against the city, and it stood against the rampart. Joab's forces were battering the wall to break it down. 16 Then a wise woman called from the city, "Listen! Listen! Tell Joab, 'Come here, I want to speak to you.' " 17 He came near her; and the woman said, "Are you Joab?" He answered, "I am." Then she said to him, "Listen to the words of your servant." He answered, "I am listening." 18 Then she said, "They used to say in the old days, 'Let them inquire at Abel'; and so they would settle a matter. 19 I am one of those who are peaceable and faithful in Israel; you seek to destroy a city that is a mother in Israel; why will you swallow up the heritage of the LORD?" 20 Joab answered, "Far be it from me, far be it, that I should swallow up or destroy! 21 That is not the case! But a man of the hill country of Ephraim, called Sheba son of Bichri, has lifted up his hand against King David; give him up alone, and I will withdraw from the city." The woman said to Joab, "His head shall be thrown over the wall to you." 22 Then the woman went to all the people with her wise plan. And they cut off the

---

a Heb He   b Compare 20.15: Heb and Beth-maacah
c Compare Gk Vg: Heb Berites   d Heb They

20.1–22 The slogan (v. 1) of this revolt contains an anticipation of the revolt that ends the union of Judah and Israel after the death of Solomon (see 1 Kings 12.16). 20.3 David arrests the ten concubines claimed by Absalom during his revolt (see 15.16). 20.7 Cherethites, Pelethites. See notes on 1 Sam 30.14; 2 Sam 8.18. 20.8 The important town of Gibeon (see 2.12) will figure prominently in ch. 21, but the location and significance of the large stone is not known. 20.14 Abel of Beth-maacah. a town about twelve miles north of Lake Huleh near the city of Dan. Bichrites, members of the same clan as Sheba son of Bichri. 20.16 The people of Abel choose a wise woman to negotiate for them; her skills are the same as those of the wise woman of Tekoa employed by Joab (see 14.2). 20.18 Citing an old adage, Let them inquire at Abel, the woman tells Joab that he has come to a town known for its wisdom and good judgment. 20.19 With a bit of rhetorical exaggeration, the woman describes Abel as a mother in Israel, i.e., a principal city or metropolis.

head of Sheba son of Bichri, and threw it out to Joab. So he blew the trumpet, and they dispersed from the city, and all went to their homes, while Joab returned to Jerusalem to the king.

23 Now Joab was in command of all the army of Israel;[a] Benaiah son of Jehoiada was in command of the Cherethites and the Pelethites; 24Adoram was in charge of the forced labor; Jehoshaphat son of Ahilud was the recorder; 25Sheva was secretary; Zadok and Abiathar were priests; 26and Ira the Jairite was also David's priest.

David Avenges the Gibeonites

21 Now there was a famine in the days of David for three years, year after year; and David inquired of the LORD. The LORD said, "There is bloodguilt on Saul and on his house, because he put the Gibeonites to death." 2So the king called the Gibeonites and spoke to them. (Now the Gibeonites were not of the people of Israel, but of the remnant of the Amorites; although the people of Israel had sworn to spare them, Saul had tried to wipe them out in his zeal for the people of Israel and Judah.) 3David said to the Gibeonites, "What shall I do for you? How shall I make expiation, that you may bless the heritage of the LORD?" 4The Gibeonites said to him, "It is not a matter of silver or gold between us and Saul or his house; neither is it for us to put anyone to death in Israel." He said, "What do you say that I should do for you?" 5They said to the king, "The man who consumed us and planned to destroy us, so that we should have no place in all the territory of Israel— 6let seven of his sons be handed over to us, and we will impale them before the LORD at Gibeon

on the mountain of the LORD."[b] The king said, "I will hand them over."

7 But the king spared Mephibosheth,[c] the son of Saul's son Jonathan, because of the oath of the LORD that was between them, between David and Jonathan son of Saul. 8The king took the two sons of Rizpah daughter of Aiah, whom she bore to Saul, Armoni and Mephibosheth;[c] and the five sons of Merab[d] daughter of Saul, whom she bore to Adriel son of Barzillai the Meholathite; 9he gave them into the hands of the Gibeonites, and they impaled them on the mountain before the LORD. The seven of them perished together. They were put to death in the first days of harvest, at the beginning of barley harvest.

10 Then Rizpah the daughter of Aiah took sackcloth, and spread it on a rock for herself, from the beginning of harvest until rain fell on them from the heavens; she did not allow the birds of the air to come on the bodies[e] by day, or the wild animals by night. 11When David was told what Rizpah daughter of Aiah, the concubine of Saul, had done, 12David went and took the bones of Saul and the bones of his son Jonathan from the people of Jabesh-gilead, who had stolen them from the public square of Beth-shan, where the Philistines had hung them up, on the day the Philistines killed Saul on Gilboa. 13He brought up from there the bones of Saul and the bones of his son Jonathan; and they gathered the bones of those who had been impaled. 14They buried the bones of Saul and of his son Jonathan in the land of Benjamin in Zela, in the tomb of his

---

a Cn: Heb Joab to all the army, Israel b Cn Compare Gk and 21.9: Heb at Gibeah of Saul, the chosen of the LORD c Or Meribbaal: See 4.4 note d Two Heb Mss Syr Compare Gk: MT Michal e Heb them

---

20.23–26 Another list of David's officers appears in 8.15–18. **20.24** *Adoram* should be "Adoniram"; he continued in office under Solomon (see 1 Kings 4.6; 5.14) and Rehoboam (1 Kings 12.18; cf. 2 Chr 10.18, Hadoram). He was *in charge of the forced labor,* i.e., the impressing of Israelites into work on state projects, a practice that seems to have generated strong opposition during Solomon's reign (see 1 Kings 9.21; 2 Chr 8.8). **20.26** *Ira the Jairite* was a native of Havvoth-jair in Gilead (see, e.g., Num 32.41; Deut 3.14); in contrast to later periods it seems to have been acceptable during David's reign for the king to have a private priest who was not a Levite.
21.1–14 David puts seven sons and grandsons of Saul to death to avert a famine caused by bloodguilt resulting from Saul's slaughter of the Gibeonites.

21.1 There is no account in the Bible of the crime against the Gibeonites for which Saul incurred *bloodguilt,* but there may have been a connection to his slaughter of the priesthood of Nob (see 1 Sam 22.6–23). **21.2** The story of Israel's unusual alliance with the *Gibeonites* is told in Josh 9. **21.6** *Impale,* obscure, probably some form of crucifixion. **21.7** For *the oath of the LORD* between David and Jonathan, see 1 Sam 20.12–17. **21.8** *Rizpah,* the concubine of Saul over whom Abner and Ishbaal quarreled in 3.7–11. *Merab.* See 1 Sam 18.17–19. *Barzillai,* the father of *Adriel* (see 1 Sam 18.19), may be the same man who appears in 17.27; 19.31–40. **21.9** *In the first days of harvest,* better "in the days of Ziv," the old Canaanite month name also mentioned in 1 Kings 6.1, 37. **21.12** *The bones of Saul and . . . Jonathan.* See 1 Sam 31.12–13. **21.14** *In*

father Kish; they did all that the king commanded. After that, God heeded supplications for the land.

Exploits of David's Men

15 The Philistines went to war again with Israel, and David went down together with his servants. They fought against the Philistines, and David grew weary. 16Ishbi-benob, one of the descendants of the giants, whose spear weighed three hundred shekels of bronze, and who was fitted out with new weapons,*a* said he would kill David. 17But Abishai son of Zeruiah came to his aid, and attacked the Philistine and killed him. Then David's men swore to him, "You shall not go out with us to battle any longer, so that you do not quench the lamp of Israel."

18 After this a battle took place with the Philistines, at Gob; then Sibbecai the Hushathite killed Saph, who was one of the descendants of the giants. 19Then there was another battle with the Philistines at Gob; and Elhanan son of Jaare-oregim, the Bethlehemite, killed Goliath the Gittite, the shaft of whose spear was like a weaver's beam. 20There was again war at Gath, where there was a man of great size, who had six fingers on each hand, and six toes on each foot, twenty-four in number; he too was descended from the giants. 21When he taunted Israel, Jonathan son of David's brother Shimei, killed him. 22These four were descended from the giants in Gath; they fell by the hands of David and his servants.

David's Song of Thanksgiving

22 David spoke to the Lord the words of this song on the day when the Lord delivered him from the hand of all his enemies, and from the hand of Saul. 2He said:

The Lord is my rock, my fortress, and my
   deliverer,
3   my God, my rock, in whom I take
      refuge,
my shield and the horn of my salvation,
   my stronghold and my refuge,
   my savior; you save me from violence.
4   I call upon the Lord, who is worthy to be
      praised,
   and I am saved from my enemies.

5   For the waves of death encompassed me,
      the torrents of perdition assailed me;
6   the cords of Sheol entangled me,
      the snares of death confronted me.

7   In my distress I called upon the Lord;
      to my God I called.
From his temple he heard my voice,
   and my cry came to his ears.

8   Then the earth reeled and rocked;
      the foundations of the heavens
         trembled
      and quaked, because he was angry.
9   Smoke went up from his nostrils,

---

a Heb *was belted anew*

Zela, in the tomb of his father Kish, probably "in a chamber in the tomb of his father Kish"; for Kish, see 1 Sam 9.1. **21.15–22** A series of victories by David's men over Philistines descended from *the giants* (v. 16), possibly an ancient guild of warriors. **21.17** *Abishai.* See 2.18; 1 Sam 26.6. *Quench the lamp of Israel* has no clear linguistic parallel, but for the sentiment, cf. 18.3. **21.18** *Gob,* a town mentioned only here and in the next verse. *Sibbecai,* a native of the town of Hushah, southwest of Bethlehem (cf. 1 Chr 4.4); see also 2 Sam 23.27. **21.19** In the story as we know it (see 1 Sam 17) the *Bethlehemite* warrior who slew *Goliath the Gittite* was David. This has led scholars to suggest that *Elhanan,* who is called *son of Dodo* in 23.24, was another name for David or, as seems more likely, that the Elhanan story caused the name Goliath to become attached secondarily to an anonymous Philistine slain by David. The description of Goliath's spear as being *like a weaver's beam* is also in 1 Sam 17.7. **21.20** At Jericho and an archaeological site in Amman, Neolithic statues have been found with six fingers and toes; the Israelites may have made similar discoveries, leading

them to tell the story in this verse. **21.21** *Shimei.* See note on 1 Sam 16.9.

22.1–51 This magnificent poem is preserved in two very similar versions, here and Ps 18. It has two clearly discernible sections: the first (vv. 2–20) praises the Lord, as revealed in the storm, for the rescue of the psalmist from his enemies; the second section (vv. 29–51) describes the psalmist as a mighty conqueror; an intervening section (vv. 21–28) connects the two major units. The theme of conquest in the second section may have led to the poem's association with David, but features of the language show that it was composed centuries after his lifetime. **22.1** The opening verse, which is not a part of the poem itself, serves to identify the psalm with the events of David's life (cf. Pss 3; 7; 34; 51; 52; 54; 56; 57; 59; 60; 63; 142). **22.2–3** The Lord is praised under the image of a mountain refuge. **22.5–6** For the watery imagery of *Sheol,* the dark abode of the dead, cf. Jon 2.5–6a; Ps 116.3. **22.7** *His temple,* here the Lord's celestial abode (cf. Ps 11.4). **22.8** The image of the cosmic thunderstorm in which the deity is present is introduced at this point.

and devouring fire from his mouth;
 glowing coals flamed forth from him.
10 He bowed the heavens, and came down;
 thick darkness was under his feet.
11 He rode on a cherub, and flew;
 he was seen upon the wings of the
  wind.
12 He made darkness around him a canopy,
 thick clouds, a gathering of water.
13 Out of the brightness before him
 coals of fire flamed forth.
14 The LORD thundered from heaven;
 the Most High uttered his voice.
15 He sent out arrows, and scattered them
 —lightning, and routed them.
16 Then the channels of the sea were seen,
 the foundations of the world were laid
  bare
 at the rebuke of the LORD,
 at the blast of the breath of his
  nostrils.

17 He reached from on high, he took me,
 he drew me out of mighty waters.
18 He delivered me from my strong enemy,
 from those who hated me;
 for they were too mighty for me.
19 They came upon me in the day of my
  calamity,
 but the LORD was my stay.
20 He brought me out into a broad place;
 he delivered me, because he delighted
  in me.

21 The LORD rewarded me according to my
  righteousness;
 according to the cleanness of my hands
  he recompensed me.
22 For I have kept the ways of the LORD,
 and have not wickedly departed from
  my God.
23 For all his ordinances were before me,
 and from his statutes I did not turn
  aside.
24 I was blameless before him,
 and I kept myself from guilt.

25 Therefore the LORD has recompensed me
  according to my righteousness,
 according to my cleanness in his sight.
26 With the loyal you show yourself loyal;
 with the blameless you show yourself
  blameless;
27 with the pure you show yourself pure,
 and with the crooked you show
  yourself perverse.
28 You deliver a humble people,
 but your eyes are upon the haughty to
  bring them down.
29 Indeed, you are my lamp, O LORD,
 the LORD lightens my darkness.
30 By you I can crush a troop,
 and by my God I can leap over a wall.
31 This God—his way is perfect;
 the promise of the LORD proves true;
 he is a shield for all who take refuge in
  him.

32 For who is God, but the LORD?
 And who is a rock, except our God?
33 The God who has girded me with
  strength[a]
 has opened wide my path.[b]
34 He made my[c] feet like the feet of deer,
 and set me secure on the heights.
35 He trains my hands for war,
 so that my arms can bend a bow of
  bronze.
36 You have given me the shield of your
  salvation,
 and your help[d] has made me great.
37 You have made me stride freely,
 and my feet do not slip;
38 I pursued my enemies and destroyed
  them,
 and did not turn back until they were
  consumed.
39 I consumed them; I struck them down, so
  that they did not rise;

a Q Ms Gk Syr Vg Compare Ps 18.32: MT *God is my strong
refuge*   b Meaning of Heb uncertain   c Another reading is *his*
d Q Ms: MT *your answering*

22.9 In his anger the Lord breathes fire and smoke, as
in, e.g., Deut 29.20; Isa 66.15; Ezek 21.31. **22.11** *Cherub*,
a mythological creature, in this case an image of the
storm cloud and the celestial mount of the God of Israel. **22.12** Cf. Job 36.29, where *canopy* is rendered
"pavilion." **22.14** *The Most High* (Hebrew *'elyon*) is an
ancient divine epithet for the most senior of the gods;
Israel appropriated the epithet for its own god. Cf.
note on 1 Sam 2.10. **22.15** *Arrows, lightning.* Cf., e.g.,
Pss 77.18; 97.4; 144.6; Hab 3.11. **22.16** Cf. vv. 5–6.
22.21–28 The language here is reminiscent of that of
Deuteronomy; the section may be an editorial connection between originally distinct poems. **22.31** *His way,*
the rule or dominion of God. **22.38–46** The Lord is

they fell under my feet.
40 For you girded me with strength for the
battle;
you made my assailants sink under me.
41 You made my enemies turn their backs to
me,
those who hated me, and I destroyed
them.
42 They looked, but there was no one to save
them;
they cried to the LORD, but he did not
answer them.
43 I beat them fine like the dust of the
earth,
I crushed them and stamped them
down like the mire of the streets.

44 You delivered me from strife with the
peoples;[a]
you kept me as the head of the nations;
people whom I had not known served
me.
45 Foreigners came cringing to me;
as soon as they heard of me, they
obeyed me.
46 Foreigners lost heart,
and came trembling out of their
strongholds.

47 The LORD lives! Blessed be my rock,
and exalted be my God, the rock of my
salvation,
48 the God who gave me vengeance
and brought down peoples under me,
49 who brought me out from my enemies;
you exalted me above my adversaries,
you delivered me from the violent.

50 For this I will extol you, O LORD, among
the nations,
and sing praises to your name.
51 He is a tower of salvation for his king,
and shows steadfast love to his
anointed,
to David and his descendants forever.

The Last Words of David

23 Now these are the last words of David:
The oracle of David, son of Jesse,
the oracle of the man whom God
exalted,[b]
the anointed of the God of Jacob,
the favorite of the Strong One of Israel:

2 The spirit of the LORD speaks through me,
his word is upon my tongue.
3 The God of Israel has spoken,
the Rock of Israel has said to me:
One who rules over people justly,
ruling in the fear of God,
4 is like the light of morning,
like the sun rising on a cloudless
morning,
gleaming from the rain on the grassy
land.

5 Is not my house like this with God?
For he has made with me an
everlasting covenant,
ordered in all things and secure.
Will he not cause to prosper
all my help and my desire?

---

a Gk: Heb *from strife with my people* *b* Q Ms: MT *who was raised on high*

---

praised for granting the psalmist victory over his foes. **22.47** *The LORD lives!* an oath formula, establishing what follows as a solemn declaration. **22.51** Cf. the language of the promise of dynasty to David in ch. 7.15–16.

23.1–7 A poem centered on the comparison in vv. 3b–4 of a just ruler to a bright morning sun. Though it touches on timeless themes and contains late elements, such as v. 2, there are some indications that it is quite archaic, possibly dating to the early monarchical period (tenth century BCE). **23.1** Cf. the opening of the oracles of Balaam (Num 24.3, 15), which are generally regarded as very ancient. *Whom God exalted.* The expression can be used to stress the elevation of someone without royal ancestry to the throne; cf. "the LORD will raise up for himself a king," a reference to Baasha, in 1 Kings 14.14 (cf. 1 Kings 15.27–30). *Strong One,* a divine epithet probably more concrete in its meaning—

thus, "Stronghold," to which cf. the use of *fortress* and *stronghold* in 22.2–3. **23.2** Possibly a late insertion introducing the notion that the word of God uttered in vv. 3b–4 is a message intended not just for David but for all Israel. **23.3** *Rock of Israel,* a divine epithet likening the Lord to a mountain refuge; cf. *my rock* in 22.2–3. A king who rules *in the fear of God* rules not only in religious awe but also in the knowledge of divine commandments. **23.4** The just ruler is compared to a bright sun that causes vegetation to sprout after rainfall. **23.5** *My house like this,* i.e., members of David's family are like the just rulers just described. *With God,* in the opinion of God (cf. 1 Sam 2.26). God's *everlasting covenant* with David refers to the dynastic promise made in ch. 7; see also 2 Chr 13.5; 21.7; Pss 89.19–37; 132.12; Isa 55.3; Jer 33.17, 20–22. *Ordered in all things and secure,* formal legal terminology indicating that the covenant is clearly articulated on all points and ir-

6 But the godless are*a* all like thorns that
   are thrown away;
 for they cannot be picked up with the
   hand;
7 to touch them one uses an iron bar
   or the shaft of a spear.
 And they are entirely consumed in fire
   on the spot.*b*

David's Mighty Men

8 These are the names of the warriors whom
David had: Josheb-basshebeth a Tahchemonite; he was chief of the Three;*c* he wielded his
spear*d* against eight hundred whom he killed
at one time.

9 Next to him among the three warriors was
Eleazar son of Dodo son of Ahohi. He was
with David when they defied the Philistines
who were gathered there for battle. The Israelites withdrew, 10but he stood his ground. He
struck down the Philistines until his arm grew
weary, though his hand clung to the sword.
The LORD brought about a great victory that
day. Then the people came back to him—but
only to strip the dead.

11 Next to him was Shammah son of Agee,
the Hararite. The Philistines gathered together
at Lehi, where there was a plot of ground full
of lentils; and the army fled from the Philistines. 12But he took his stand in the middle of
the plot, defended it, and killed the Philistines;
and the LORD brought about a great victory.

13 Towards the beginning of harvest three
of the thirty*e* chiefs went down to join David
at the cave of Adullam, while a band of Philis-

tines was encamped in the valley of Rephaim.
14David was then in the stronghold; and the
garrison of the Philistines was then at Bethlehem. 15David said longingly, "O that someone
would give me water to drink from the well of
Bethlehem that is by the gate!" 16Then the
three warriors broke through the camp of the
Philistines, drew water from the well of Bethlehem that was by the gate, and brought it to
David. But he would not drink of it; he poured
it out to the LORD, 17for he said, "The LORD
forbid that I should do this. Can I drink the
blood of the men who went at the risk of their
lives?" Therefore he would not drink it. The
three warriors did these things.

18 Now Abishai son of Zeruiah, the brother
of Joab, was chief of the Thirty.*f* With his spear
he fought against three hundred men and
killed them, and won a name beside the Three.
19He was the most renowned of the Thirty,*g*
and became their commander; but he did not
attain to the Three.

20 Benaiah son of Jehoiada was a valiant
warrior*h* from Kabzeel, a doer of great deeds;
he struck down two sons of Ariel*i* of Moab. He
also went down and killed a lion in a pit on a
day when snow had fallen. 21And he killed an
Egyptian, a handsome man. The Egyptian had
a spear in his hand; but Benaiah went against
him with a staff, snatched the spear out of the

---

a Heb *But worthlessness*   *b* Heb *in sitting*   *c* Gk Vg Compare
1 Chr 11.11: Meaning of Heb uncertain   *d* 1 Chr 11.11:
Meaning of Heb uncertain   *e* Heb adds *head*   *f* Two Heb Mss
Syr: MT *Three*   *g* Syr Compare 1 Chr 11.25: Heb *Was he the
most renowned of the Three?*   *h* Another reading is *the son of
Ish-hai*   *i* Gk: Heb lacks *sons of*

---

revocable. **23.6–7** The text of these two verses is obscure, but they seem to draw on the metaphor of vv.
3b–4: when the bright light of the just ruler shines on
those who are disloyal, they are *consumed in fire* like
uprooted thorns. **23.8–39** An archival relic with three
sections: a report on the Three, who were distinguished warriors in David's army (vv. 8–12); an account of the exploits of Abishai and Benaiah (vv. 18–
23); and a roster of the Thirty, David's elite corps (vv.
24–39). **23.8** *Josheb-basshebeth,* a euphemism for
"Jeshbaal," which was altered by a scribe who believed
it meant "Baal exists," though it might have meant
"The LORD [i.e., Yahweh] exists" (see note on 2.8);
more information about him is given in 1 Chr 11.11,
where he is called Jashobeam. *Tahchemonite,* a mistake
for "Hachmonite" or "son of Hachmoni" (see 1 Chr
11.11). **23.9** *When they defied the Philistines who,* defective; it should be "when the Philistines defied them
at Pas-dammim, and the Philistines" (cf. 1 Chr 11.13;
1 Sam 17.1). **23.11** *Lehi,* the place in Judah where Sam-

son slew a thousand Philistines with the jawbone (Hebrew *lechi*) of an ass (see Judg 15.9–19). **23.13** *Cave of
Adullam,* David's private stronghold during his days as
a leader of outlaws and a refugee from Saul's justice
(see 1 Sam 22.1), and the episode reported here in vv.
13–17 probably belongs to that period. *Valley of Rephaim.* See note on 5.18. **23.15** David's remark is probably motivated more by nostalgia for his hometown of
Bethlehem than by thirst; hence his angry reaction in
vv. 16b–17 when he learns that his men have risked
their lives unnecessarily. **23.16b–17** Because David regards the water as *the blood of the men who went,*
he pours it out on the ground in accordance with
religious law (cf. Lev 17.10–13; Deut 12.23–24).
23.18 *Abishai.* See 2.18. **23.20** *Benaiah.* See 8.18; 20.23.
Kabzeel, a town in southern Judah near Beer-sheba
(Josh 15.21). *Ariel.* Meaning unknown; if not a personal name (cf. Ezra 8.16) or a place-name (cf. Isa
29.1–2), perhaps "altar hearth" (cf. Ezek 43.15–16).
23.21 *A handsome man,* probably "a man of great

Egyptian's hand, and killed him with his own spear. 22Such were the things Benaiah son of Jehoiada did, and won a name beside the three warriors. 23He was renowned among the Thirty, but he did not attain to the Three. And David put him in charge of his bodyguard.

24 Among the Thirty were Asahel brother of Joab; Elhanan son of Dodo of Bethlehem; 25Shammah of Harod; Elika of Harod; 26Helez the Paltite; Ira son of Ikkesh of Tekoa; 27Abiezer of Anathoth; Mebunnai the Hushathite; 28Zalmon the Ahohite; Maharai of Netophah; 29Heleb son of Baanah of Netophah; Ittai son of Ribai of Gibeah of the Benjaminites; 30Benaiah of Pirathon; Hiddai of the torrents of Gaash; 31Abi-albon the Arbathite; Azmaveth of Bahurim; 32Eliahba of Shaalbon; the sons of Jashen: Jonathan 33son of*a* Shammah the Hararite; Ahiam son of Sharar the Hararite; 34Eliphelet son of Ahasbai of Maacah; Eliam son of Ahithophel the Gilonite; 35Hezro*b* of Carmel; Paarai the Arbite; 36Igal son of Na-

than of Zobah; Bani the Gadite; 37Zelek the Ammonite; Naharai of Beeroth, the armor-bearer of Joab son of Zeruiah; 38Ira the Ithrite; Gareb the Ithrite; 39Uriah the Hittite—thirty-seven in all.

David's Census of Israel and Judah

24 Again the anger of the LORD was kindled against Israel, and he incited David against them, saying, "Go, count the people of Israel and Judah." 2So the king said to Joab and the commanders of the army,*c* who were with him, "Go through all the tribes of Israel, from Dan to Beer-sheba, and take a census of the people, so that I may know how many there are." 3But Joab said to the king, "May the LORD your God increase the number of the people a hundredfold, while the eyes of my lord the king can still see it! But why does

a Gk: Heb lacks *son of* *b* Another reading is *Hezrai* *c* 1 Chr 21.2 Gk: Heb *to Joab the commander of the army*

stature," as in 1 Chr 11.23. **23.24** This list must predate the battle of Gibeon, in which *Asahel* was slain by Abner (see 2.18–23). *Elhanan,* the slayer of Goliath (see 21.19). **23.25** The home of these two warriors is less likely to have been the Spring of Herod near Jezreel (see Judg 7.1) than a less well known town southeast of Jerusalem. **23.26** *Helez the Paltite,* a member of the Calebite clan of Pelet (1 Chr 2.47) or a native of the town of Beth-pelet in southern Judah (Josh 15.27) or perhaps both. *Tekoa.* See 14.2. **23.27** *Anathoth,* also the home of the prophet Jeremiah (see Jer 1.1), was the priestly town in Benjamin to which Abiathar was banished (1 Kings 2.26). *Mebunnai,* probably a mistake for Sibbecai (see 21.18; 1 Chr 11.29). **23.28** *Netophah,* a town southeast of Bethlehem. **23.29** *Heleb,* probably Hildai of 1 Chr 27.15, where we learn that he was descended from the judge Othniel (cf. Judg 3.7–11). *Gibeah of the Benjaminites,* Saul's home (see note on 1 Sam 9.1). **23.30** *Pirathon,* home of the minor judge Abdon (Judg 12.13–15), may have been southwest of Shechem in Ephraim in the direction of Mount *Gaash* (Josh 24.30; Judg 2.9). **23.31** *Abi-albon the Arbathite,* probably a corruption of Abial the Beth-arabathite; the town of Beth-arabah was on the border between Judah and Benjamin (Josh 15.6; 18.18). For *Bahurim,* the home of *Azmaveth,* whose name means "The (god) Death is strong," see note on 3.16. **23.32** *Eliahba's* hometown is called Shaalabbin in Josh 19.42 and Shaalbim in Judg 1.35; 1 Kings 4.9; it was northwest of Jerusalem in the territory of Dan. The best Greek manuscript lacks *the sons of* and calls Jashen "the Gunite" (cf. "the Gizonite" in 1 Chr 11.34); perhaps his home was Gimzo, which was not far from Shaalbim (cf. 2 Chr 28.18). **23.33** *Shammah the Hararite.* See v. 11. **23.34** *Eliphelet's* home is less likely to be the Aramean

kingdom of *Maacah* (see 10.6) or Beth-maacah near Dan (see 20.14–15) than the territory of the Judahite clan of Maacah near Eshtemoa south of Hebron (1 Chr 4.19). *Ahithophel the Gilonite.* See 15.12. *Eliam,* perhaps the same as the Eliam who was Bathsheba's father (see 11.3). **23.35** *Carmel.* See note on 1 Sam 25.2. If *Paarai* was really an *Arbite,* he might have come from the town of Arab near Hebron (Josh 15.52), though we would have expected "Arabite"; but some manuscripts call him an Archite (cf. 15.32). **23.36** Better "Igal son of Nathan, the commander of the army of the Hagrites," partially preserved in the Septuagint and 1 Chr 11.37. The Hagrites were a group of nomadic tribes living east of Gilead on the Transjordanian plateau (see 1 Chr 5.10, 19–22). **23.37** David must have won the loyalty of *Zelek the Ammonite* in the days before the incident described in 10.1–5 brought his friendly relations with the Ammonites to an end. *Beeroth.* See 4.2–3. **23.38** Ithrites, one of the leading families of Kiriath-jearim (1 Chr 2.53; cf. 1 Sam 7.1; 2 Sam 6.1). **23.39** *Uriah the Hittite,* the first husband of Bathsheba (see chs. 11–12). We can only guess how the number *thirty-seven* was arrived at; in our list there are only thirty or thirty-one.

24.1–9 David takes a census of Israel and Judah, and the Lord is displeased. **24.1** The *anger of the LORD* seems to function independently of the Lord himself in this passage, inciting David to do something that the Lord condemns; note that the Chronicler, in his version of the story, replaces *the anger of the LORD* with "Satan" (see 1 Chr 21.1). **24.2** *From Dan to Beer-sheba.* See note on 3.9–10. **24.3** Joab's counsel (cf. 19.5–8) about the prospect of a census is rooted in the notion that its primary purpose is to determine the number of men eligible for military service, and soldiers on active

my lord the king want to do this?" 4But the king's word prevailed against Joab and the commanders of the army. So Joab and the commanders of the army went out from the presence of the king to take a census of the people of Israel. 5They crossed the Jordan, and began from*a* Aroer and from the city that is in the middle of the valley, toward Gad and on to Jazer. 6Then they came to Gilead, and to Kadesh in the land of the Hittites;*b* and they came to Dan, and from Dan*c* they went around to Sidon, 7and came to the fortress of Tyre and to all the cities of the Hivites and Canaanites; and they went out to the Negeb of Judah at Beer-sheba. 8So when they had gone through all the land, they came back to Jerusalem at the end of nine months and twenty days. 9Joab reported to the king the number of those who had been recorded: in Israel there were eight hundred thousand soldiers able to draw the sword, and those of Judah were five hundred thousand.

Judgment on David's Sin

10 But afterward, David was stricken to the heart because he had numbered the people. David said to the LORD, "I have sinned greatly in what I have done. But now, O LORD, I pray you, take away the guilt of your servant; for I have done very foolishly." 11When David rose in the morning, the word of the LORD came to the prophet Gad, David's seer, saying, 12"Go and say to David: Thus says the LORD: Three things I offer*d* you; choose one of them, and I

will do it to you." 13So Gad came to David and told him; he asked him, "Shall three*e* years of famine come to you on your land? Or will you flee three months before your foes while they pursue you? Or shall there be three days' pestilence in your land? Now consider, and decide what answer I shall return to the one who sent me." 14Then David said to Gad, "I am in great distress; let us fall into the hand of the LORD, for his mercy is great; but let me not fall into human hands."

15 So the LORD sent a pestilence on Israel from that morning until the appointed time; and seventy thousand of the people died, from Dan to Beer-sheba. 16But when the angel stretched out his hand toward Jerusalem to destroy it, the LORD relented concerning the evil, and said to the angel who was bringing destruction among the people, "It is enough; now stay your hand." The angel of the LORD was then by the threshing floor of Araunah the Jebusite. 17When David saw the angel who was destroying the people, he said to the LORD, "I alone have sinned, and I alone have done wickedly; but these sheep, what have they done? Let your hand, I pray, be against me and against my father's house."

David's Altar on the Threshing Floor

18 That day Gad came to David and said to him, "Go up and erect an altar to the LORD on the

---

a Gk Mss: Heb *encamped in Aroer south of*   *b* Gk: Heb *to the land of Tahtim-hodshi*   *c* Cn Compare Gk: Heb *they came to Dan-jaan and*   *d* Or *hold over*   *e* 1 Chr 21.12 Gk: Heb *seven*

---

duty are subject to a strict regimen of ritual procedures and are especially vulnerable, therefore, to cultic dangers (see Ex 30.11); thus the plague that results is no surprise. **24.5–7** The census itinerary seems to surround the kingdom, but perhaps we are to understand that it includes the interior areas as well. *Aroer* was in southern Transjordan at the southeast corner of David's kingdom (see Deut 4.48; Josh 12.2); *Gad* was the Israelite tribe that inhabited this region (see Josh 13.8–13, 24–28; notes on 1 Sam 10.27b; 13.7). *Jazer* was situated on the Israelite-Ammonite boundary. **24.6** *Gilead.* See note on 2.9. *Kadesh in the land of the Hittites* ought to be Kadesh on the Orontes in Syria, but this is much too far north and Kadesh of Naphtali, near Lake Huleh, seems more likely; in any case, the text is suspicious. *Dan* was the traditional northern border of the promised land (cf. v. 2); *Sidon* was an important Phoenician city, but in this case it probably designates Phoenicia as a whole, modern Lebanon. **24.7** The *fortress of Tyre* was the northwest turning point in the census; it seems to refer to the Phoenician capital, but it is more likely to be an Israelite-Phoeni-

cian border fortification. *Cities of the Hivites and Canaanites,* probably the towns along the coastal plain west of Israel and Judah; the census is now proceeding southward. *Negeb of Judah,* the southern desert. *Beer-sheba,* the traditional southern border corresponding to Dan in the north in v. 6. **24.9** Modern scholarship has still not learned how to interpret population statistics of the kind expressed here; they are much too high to correspond to historical reality. **24.10–17** David's census provokes divine punishment in the form of a pestilence sent against Israel. **24.10** David's change of heart is probably a result of his realization of the ritual danger in which he has placed his subjects, something Joab understood from the beginning. **24.11** The *prophet Gad,* about whom we know very little, made his first appearance in 1 Sam 22.5; he may have been David's personal seer. **24.14** *Hand of the LORD,* plague, as in, e.g., 1 Sam 5.6. **24.15** The cause of the *pestilence* is probably the ritual jeopardy brought on by a census (see note on 24.3); the cause is explained differently in 1 Chr 21.6–7. **24.16** The direct agent of the plague, *the angel,* is re-

threshing floor of Araunah the Jebusite." [19]Following Gad's instructions, David went up, as the LORD had commanded. [20]When Araunah looked down, he saw the king and his servants coming toward him; and Araunah went out and prostrated himself before the king with his face to the ground. [21]Araunah said, "Why has my lord the king come to his servant?" David said, "To buy the threshing floor from you in order to build an altar to the LORD, so that the plague may be averted from the people." [22]Then Araunah said to David, "Let my lord the king take and offer up what seems good to him; here are the oxen for the burnt offering, and the thresh-ing sledges and the yokes of the oxen for the wood. [23]All this, O king, Araunah gives to the king." And Araunah said to the king, "May the LORD your God respond favorably to you."

24 But the king said to Araunah, "No, but I will buy them from you for a price; I will not offer burnt offerings to the LORD my God that cost me nothing." So David bought the thresh-ing floor and the oxen for fifty shekels of silver. [25]David built there an altar to the LORD, and offered burnt offerings and offerings of well-being. So the LORD answered his supplication for the land, and the plague was averted from Israel.

---

strained by the Lord in order to protect Jerusalem; for *Araunah the Jebusite,* see vv. 18–25. **24.18–25** David purchases a piece of land that will become the site of the altar of the Jerusalem temple; cf. the more detailed account in 1 Chr 21–22. **24.18** In the ancient world the *threshing floor* was thought of as a place where divine power might manifest itself; cf. 6.6; Judg 6.37;

1 Kings 22.10. *Araunah,* not a Semitic name, and scholars have proposed that his ancestry was Hurrian or Hittite; the pertinent fact for this account, however, is that he is a *Jebusite,* a member of the pre-Israelite population of Jerusalem (see note on 5.6). **24.21–24** Cf. Abraham's negotiations with the people of Hebron in Gen 23.3–16.

1 KINGS

THE BOOKS OF 1 AND 2 KINGS were originally a single literary work that provided a continuous account of Israel's history from the death of David and the accession of Solomon (ca. 970 BCE) to the release of the exiled King Jehoiachin from prison in Babylon (561/60 BCE). Within this larger work, 1 Kings covers the end of David's reign and the reign of Solomon (1 Kings 1–11), the division of Israel into the two separate kingdoms of Israel and Judah (1 Kings 12), and the history of the two kingdoms to the death of the Israelite king Ahab and the succession of his son Ahaziah (1 Kings 13–22).

Name and Canonical Position

THE DIVISION OF KINGS into two separate books took place in Hebrew texts in the Middle Ages under the influence of much earlier Greek and Latin translations, which saw Kings as the continuation of a history of Israelite kingship beginning in 1 Samuel with an account of Saul's accession. Within this larger history, 1 and 2 Kings constituted the third and fourth books of Reigns or Kingdoms. In Jewish tradition 1 and 2 Kings are part of the division of the Bible known as the Former Prophets, which consists of the books of Joshua, Judges, 1 and 2 Samuel, and 1 and 2 Kings. Together these books recount Israel's history from the conquest of Canaan to the end of the monarchy and the beginning of the exile. Modern scholars usually refer to them as the Deuteronomistic History because they share similar literary styles and theological outlooks and appear to be heavily influenced by the book of Deuteronomy. Scholars also recognize, however, that each of these books also has distinctive literary and theological interests.

Literary Character

THE BOOKS OF KINGS trace a continuous history of the period they cover, but they make no claim to be completely original or comprehensive. At a number of points in the narrative readers are referred to external sources, such as the Book of the Acts of Solomon (1 Kings 11.41), the Book of the Annals of the Kings of Judah (e.g., 1 Kings 14.29; 15.7, 23; 22.45), and the Book of the Annals of the Kings of Israel (e.g., 1 Kings 14.19; 15.31; 16.5, 14). These works, none of which has survived, presumably contained additional information on the reigns of the kings being discussed and may have provided some of the information incorporated in Kings. Scholars also suspect that other sources, both written and oral, may have been used during the process of composition. Additional records from temple or palace archives may lie behind the account of Solomon's court and building activities (1 Kings 4–7), while traditional collections of prophetic stories may form the basis of the history of the Northern Kingdom (Israel) from Ahab to Jehu (1 Kings 17–2 Kings 10).

Although Kings presents readers with a coherent history of Israel, the work contains enough shifts in literary style and point of view to make scholars suspect that it has had a complex literary history. Some specialists maintain that Kings is basically the work of a single author and attribute the shifts to the various sources that were employed in the composition; others have suggested that a preliminary version of Kings was produced and later revised one or more times. There is still much disagreement about the details of the book's editorial history. Some scholars advocate an original edition in the time of Hezekiah (ca. 715–687/6 BCE) or Josiah (ca. 640–609), with final editing taking place sometime early in the exile (586–539), but others argue that the book was created in exilic or postexilic times and revised even later.

In addition to creating an impression of literary unity by presenting events in rough chronological sequence, Kings also uses other devices to give a coherent structure to the whole work. The most obvious of these devices are the formulaic introductions and conclusions used to frame the stories of individual rulers. The reign of each king is introduced with a note on the date of his accession, calculated according to the regnal year of the king in the neighboring kingdom (e.g., 1 Kings 15.1, 25). This system of correlative dating creates insoluble chronological problems within the whole work, but it has the effect of stressing the fundamental unity of Israel and Judah, even though the two kingdoms were technically separate political entities throughout much of their history. (On the problems of chronology in 1 and 2 Kings, see the table, "Chronology of the Kings of the Divided Monarchy," on p. 500.) The note of the king's accession is followed by an indication of the length of his reign (1 Kings 15.2, 25) and, in the case of Judean kings, by a record of his age at accession and the name of his mother (1 Kings 15.2; 22.42). The king's reign is then evaluated by the historian, and sometimes additional information is provided (1 Kings 15.3–5, 26). At the end of the account, readers are referred to other literary works for additional data. The king's death, burial, and successor are then recorded (1 Kings 15.8, 27–28). Another feature of the literary structure of Kings is the use of the motif of prophecy and fulfillment, particularly in the history of the Northern Kingdom (1 Kings 13–2 Kings 17). Whenever the narrative records a prophet's words concerning the fate of a king or dynasty, the fulfillment of that prophecy is usually noted (e.g., 1 Kings 14.7–11; 15.29–30).

Message

ALTHOUGH THE BOOKS OF KINGS in fact contain much historical information, their overall interest is religious rather than historiographic in the modern sense. Kings clearly reflects the theological concerns of Deuteronomy, although there is no unambiguous literary relationship between the two. The theology of Kings is most obvious in the evaluations made of each king and in the occasional comments on crucial historical events, such as the fall of the Northern Kingdom (2 Kings 17.1–23). Underlying this theology is the Deuteronomic principle that the Lord is Israel's only God (Deut 6.4). The worship of other gods is forbidden, and all of the Lord's covenant laws must be obeyed, including the requirement that the Lord may legitimately be worshiped in only one place (Deut 12). According to Kings, all of the Northern kings followed the evil example of their ancestor Jeroboam, who violated divine law by setting up rival sanctuaries outside of Jerusalem and by encouraging the people to worship the bull images he had set up in them (1 Kings 12.25–33). Later Northern kings, with the exception of Jehu, continued to worship other gods, particularly the Canaanite god Baal, and refused prophetic demands for reform. For these crimes the Northern Kingdom was eventually destroyed (2 Kings 17.1–23). In Judah Solomon's willingness to allow the worship of other gods was punished by the loss of the Northern tribes (1 Kings 11). Yet God's promise that David would have an eternal dynasty remained firm (2 Sam 7.1–17), in spite of the fact that Judean kings allowed irregular worship at sanctuaries outside of Jerusalem until the time of Hezekiah. Eventually, however, Judah too followed the evil ways of the Northern Kingdom and was punished. Jerusalem was destroyed, its inhabitants were exiled, and the monarchy came to an end. [ROBERT R. WILSON]

The Struggle for the Succession

1 King David was old and advanced in years; and although they covered him with clothes, he could not get warm. ²So his servants said to him, "Let a young virgin be sought for my lord the king, and let her wait on the king, and be his attendant; let her lie in your bosom, so that my lord the king may be warm." ³So they searched for a beautiful girl throughout all the territory of Israel, and found Abishag the Shunammite, and brought her to the king. ⁴The girl was very beautiful. She became the king's attendant and served him, but the king did not know her sexually.

5 Now Adonijah son of Haggith exalted himself, saying, "I will be king"; he prepared for himself chariots and horsemen, and fifty men to run before him. ⁶His father had never

at any time displeased him by asking, "Why have you done thus and so?" He was also a very handsome man, and he was born next after Absalom. ⁷He conferred with Joab son of Zeruiah and with the priest Abiathar, and they supported Adonijah. ⁸But the priest Zadok, and Benaiah son of Jehoiada, and the prophet Nathan, and Shimei, and Rei, and David's own warriors did not side with Adonijah.

9 Adonijah sacrificed sheep, oxen, and fatted cattle by the stone Zoheleth, which is beside En-rogel, and he invited all his brothers, the king's sons, and all the royal officials of Judah, ¹⁰but he did not invite the prophet Nathan or Benaiah or the warriors or his brother Solomon.

11 Then Nathan said to Bathsheba, Solomon's mother, "Have you not heard that Adonijah son of Haggith has become king and our

---

1.1–53 1 Kings opens with an account of the political intrigue that finally led to the accession of Solomon, whose reign claims a large share of the narrator's attention (chs. 1–11). The first two chapters of the book are actually the conclusion of the "throne succession narrative" (2 Sam 9–20), perhaps an originally independent literary work that some scholars ascribe to an eyewitness to the events being described. As a whole, the narrative shows that in spite of David's character flaws and the self-destructive tendencies within the royal family itself, God was nevertheless willing to honor the promise that David's dynasty would be eternal (2 Sam 7.1–17). For the narrator the accession of Solomon is a definitive sign of the promise's fulfillment. 1.1 A considerable number of years seems to have elapsed between the events recounted in 2 Sam 20 and those recorded here, for David's health has deteriorated drastically enough to trigger various plots to ensure the continued operation of the government. 1.3 The zeal of David's servants to find a beautiful maiden leads them as far as Shunem (modern Solem), a site slightly to the north of the town of Jez-

reel, at the western end of the Jezreel Valley. 1.5–6 With the death of Amnon (2 Sam 13.28–29) and Absalom (2 Sam 18.14–15) and the apparent death of Chileab (2 Sam 3.2–5), Adonijah is David's oldest son and therefore a logical choice to be the ailing king's successor. However, the principle of primogeniture was not yet established in Israel, and the pro-Solomonic narrative hints that Adonijah's actions are treasonous, describing them in the same language used earlier to describe Absalom's failed attempt to seize the throne from his father (2 Sam 14.25; 15.1). 1.7–8 Joab, the veteran commander of David's regular army, and Abiathar, one of David's high priests, support Adonijah, but Zadok, the other high priest, Benaiah, the commander of David's private mercenary forces, and Nathan, the prophet, along with two otherwise unknown officials, are excluded from Adonijah's plans and ultimately support the accession of Solomon. 1.9 En-rogel, a spring a short distance south of Jerusalem, where the stone Zoheleth ("Serpent's Stone") marked a sacred spot. 1.11–27 Nathan's plan to obtain the throne for Solomon involves reminding

lord David does not know it? 12Now therefore come, let me give you advice, so that you may save your own life and the life of your son Solomon. 13Go in at once to King David, and say to him, 'Did you not, my lord the king, swear to your servant, saying: Your son Solomon shall succeed me as king, and he shall sit on my throne? Why then is Adonijah king?' 14Then while you are still there speaking with the king, I will come in after you and confirm your words."

15 So Bathsheba went to the king in his room. The king was very old; Abishag the Shunammite was attending the king. 16Bathsheba bowed and did obeisance to the king, and the king said, "What do you wish?" 17She said to him, "My lord, you swore to your servant by the LORD your God, saying: Your son Solomon shall succeed me as king, and he shall sit on my throne. 18But now suddenly Adonijah has become king, though you, my lord the king, do not know it. 19He has sacrificed oxen, fatted cattle, and sheep in abundance, and has invited all the children of the king, the priest Abiathar, and Joab the commander of the army; but your servant Solomon he has not invited. 20But you, my lord the king—the eyes of all Israel are on you to tell them who shall sit on the throne of my lord the king after him. 21Otherwise it will come to pass, when my lord the king sleeps with his ancestors, that my son Solomon and I will be counted offenders."

22 While she was still speaking with the king, the prophet Nathan came in. 23The king was told, "Here is the prophet Nathan." When he came in before the king, he did obeisance to the king, with his face to the ground. 24Nathan said, "My lord the king, have you said, 'Adonijah shall succeed me as king, and he shall sit on my throne'? 25For today he has gone down and has sacrificed oxen, fatted cattle, and sheep in abundance, and has invited all the king's children, Joab the commander[a] of the army, and the priest Abiathar, who are now

eating and drinking before him, and saying, 'Long live King Adonijah!' 26But he did not invite me, your servant, and the priest Zadok, and Benaiah son of Jehoiada, and your servant Solomon. 27Has this thing been brought about by my lord the king and you have not let your servants know who should sit on the throne of my lord the king after him?"

The Accession of Solomon

28 King David answered, "Summon Bathsheba to me." So she came into the king's presence, and stood before the king. 29The king swore, saying, "As the LORD lives, who has saved my life from every adversity, 30as I swore to you by the LORD, the God of Israel, 'Your son Solomon shall succeed me as king, and he shall sit on my throne in my place,' so will I do this day." 31Then Bathsheba bowed with her face to the ground, and did obeisance to the king, and said, "May my lord King David live forever!"

32 King David said, "Summon to me the priest Zadok, the prophet Nathan, and Benaiah son of Jehoiada." When they came before the king, 33the king said to them, "Take with you the servants of your lord, and have my son Solomon ride on my own mule, and bring him down to Gihon. 34There let the priest Zadok and the prophet Nathan anoint him king over Israel; then blow the trumpet, and say, 'Long live King Solomon!' 35You shall go up following him. Let him enter and sit on my throne; he shall be king in my place; for I have appointed him to be ruler over Israel and over Judah." 36Benaiah son of Jehoiada answered the king, "Amen! May the LORD, the God of my lord the king, so ordain. 37As the LORD has been with my lord the king, so may he be with Solomon, and make his throne greater than the throne of my lord King David."

38 So the priest Zadok, the prophet Nathan,

---

a Gk: Heb *the commanders*

David of an oath not otherwise mentioned in Samuel or Kings. The prophet's reasons for pressing Solomon's case are never stated, but the narrative is careful to exclude Solomon himself from the plots that lead to his enthronement. **1.28** In the dialogues with David the narrator assumes that only one person at a time has an audience with the king. **1.33** In Davidic Israel horses were not yet used for riding, and the *mule* was a mode of transportation reserved for royalty (2 Sam 13.29; 18.9; Zech 9.9). *Gihon,* a spring located south of

Jerusalem on the western side of the Kidron Valley and slightly to the north of En-rogel, well within the hearing of Adonijah and his party. **1.34–35** Solomon is appointed both David's successor and his coregent. The practice of having a king anointed by a prophet recalls the earlier consecration of Saul (1 Sam 10.1) and David (1 Sam 16.1–13) and probably represents God's direct choice of the king (cf. 1 Kings 19.15–16; 2 Kings 9.1–10). Solomon is called both *king* and *ruler,* the latter title being one also given to Saul (1 Sam 9.16; 10.1)

and Benaiah son of Jehoiada, and the Cherethites and the Pelethites, went down and had Solomon ride on King David's mule, and led him to Gihon. 39There the priest Zadok took the horn of oil from the tent and anointed Solomon. Then they blew the trumpet, and all the people said, "Long live King Solomon!" 40And all the people went up following him, playing on pipes and rejoicing with great joy, so that the earth quaked at their noise.

41 Adonijah and all the guests who were with him heard it as they finished feasting. When Joab heard the sound of the trumpet, he said, "Why is the city in an uproar?" 42While he was still speaking, Jonathan son of the priest Abiathar arrived. Adonijah said, "Come in, for you are a worthy man and surely you bring good news." 43Jonathan answered Adonijah, "No, for our lord King David has made Solomon king; 44the king has sent with him the priest Zadok, the prophet Nathan, and Benaiah son of Jehoiada, and the Cherethites and the Pelethites; and they had him ride on the king's mule; 45the priest Zadok and the prophet Nathan have anointed him king at Gihon; and they have gone up from there rejoicing, so that the city is in an uproar. This is the noise that you heard. 46Solomon now sits on the royal throne. 47Moreover the king's servants came to congratulate our lord King David, saying, 'May God make the name of Solomon more famous than yours, and make his throne greater than your throne.' The king bowed in worship on the bed 48and went on to pray thus, 'Blessed be the LORD, the God of Israel, who today has granted one of my offspring[a] to sit on my throne and permitted me to witness it.' "

49 Then all the guests of Adonijah got up trembling and went their own ways. 50Adonijah, fearing Solomon, got up and went to grasp the horns of the altar. 51Solomon was informed, "Adonijah is afraid of King Solomon; see, he has laid hold of the horns of the altar, saying, 'Let King Solomon swear to me first that he will not kill his servant with the sword.' " 52So Solomon responded, "If he proves to be a worthy man, not one of his hairs shall fall to the ground; but if wickedness is found in him, he shall die." 53Then King Solomon sent to have him brought down from the altar. He came to do obeisance to King Solomon; and Solomon said to him, "Go home."

David's Instruction to Solomon

2 When David's time to die drew near, he charged his son Solomon, saying: 2"I am about to go the way of all the earth. Be strong, be courageous, 3and keep the charge of the LORD your God, walking in his ways and keeping his statutes, his commandments, his ordinances, and his testimonies, as it is written in the law of Moses, so that you may prosper in all that you do and wherever you turn. 4Then the LORD will establish his word that he spoke concerning me: 'If your heirs take heed to their way, to walk before me in faithfulness with all their heart and with all their soul, there shall not fail you a successor on the throne of Israel.'

5 "Moreover you know also what Joab son of Zeruiah did to me, how he dealt with the two commanders of the armies of Israel, Abner son of Ner, and Amasa son of Jether,

a Gk: Heb one

and David (1 Sam 25.30). **1.38** *Cherethites, Pelethites,* units in David's private mercenary army (2 Sam 8.18; 20.23). **1.48** David here recalls Nathan's earlier oracle promising the king an eternal dynasty (2 Sam 7.12). **1.49–53** *Horns of the altar,* projections attached to each of the altar's four corners (Ex 29.12; 30.10; Lev 4.7). Because of the sanctity of the altar, a person who had inadvertently committed a crime could touch the altar and claim sanctuary, but this right was not given to willful criminals (Ex 21.14; 1 Kings 2.28–35).

2.1–9 The dying David's advice to Solomon is an example of a common literary genre, the farewell speech. In the OT such speeches often serve to mark important turning points in Israel's history and to provide a theological interpretive framework for subsequent events (Gen 47.29–50.14; Josh 23–24; Deut 33–34; 1 Macc 2.49–70). **2.2–4** David's opening ex-

hortation contains strong echoes of Deuteronomy (Deut 4.29, 40; 6.5; 8.6; 10.12; 11.1, 22; cf. Josh 23.14). Solomon is urged to emulate the ideal Deuteronomic king by keeping the Mosaic law (Deut 17.14–20). Only if he is obedient will God fulfill the promise made to David that his dynasty will be eternal (2 Sam 7.12–16). This stress on the conditional character of God's promise is a hallmark of Deuteronomistic theology. **2.5–6** *Abner,* the former commander of Saul's army, killed *Joab's* brother Asahel during the turbulent years of fighting between Israel and Judah that followed Saul's death and was subsequently slain by Joab (2 Sam 3.22–30). *Amasa* replaced Joab as commander of the army during Absalom's revolt against David and then remained in that position after the king returned to power. Amasa's delay in quelling a later rebellion provoked Joab to kill him (2 Sam 17.25; 19.11–15; 20.4–

whom he murdered, retaliating in time of peace for blood that had been shed in war, and putting the blood of war on the belt around his waist, and on the sandals on his feet. 6 Act therefore according to your wisdom, but do not let his gray head go down to Sheol in peace. 7 Deal loyally, however, with the sons of Barzillai the Gileadite, and let them be among those who eat at your table; for with such loyalty they met me when I fled from your brother Absalom. 8 There is also with you Shimei son of Gera, the Benjaminite from Bahurim, who cursed me with a terrible curse on the day when I went to Mahanaim; but when he came down to meet me at the Jordan, I swore to him by the LORD, 'I will not put you to death with the sword.' 9 Therefore do not hold him guiltless, for you are a wise man; you will know what you ought to do to him, and you must bring his gray head down with blood to Sheol."

Death of David

10 Then David slept with his ancestors, and was buried in the city of David. 11 The time that David reigned over Israel was forty years; he reigned seven years in Hebron, and thirty-three years in Jerusalem. 12 So Solomon sat on the throne of his father David; and his kingdom was firmly established.

Solomon Consolidates His Reign

13 Then Adonijah son of Haggith came to Bathsheba, Solomon's mother. She asked, "Do you come peaceably?" He said, "Peaceably." 14 Then he said, "May I have a word with you?" She said, "Go on." 15 He said, "You know that the kingdom was mine, and that all Israel ex-

pected me to reign; however, the kingdom has turned about and become my brother's, for it was his from the LORD. 16 And now I have one request to make of you; do not refuse me." She said to him, "Go on." 17 He said, "Please ask King Solomon—he will not refuse you—to give me Abishag the Shunammite as my wife." 18 Bathsheba said, "Very well; I will speak to the king on your behalf."

19 So Bathsheba went to King Solomon, to speak to him on behalf of Adonijah. The king rose to meet her, and bowed down to her; then he sat on his throne, and had a throne brought for the king's mother, and she sat on his right. 20 Then she said, "I have one small request to make of you; do not refuse me." And the king said to her, "Make your request, my mother; for I will not refuse you." 21 She said, "Let Abishag the Shunammite be given to your brother Adonijah as his wife." 22 King Solomon answered his mother, "And why do you ask Abishag the Shunammite for Adonijah? Ask for him the kingdom as well! For he is my elder brother; ask not only for him but also for the priest Abiathar and for Joab son of Zeruiah!" 23 Then King Solomon swore by the LORD, "So may God do to me, and more also, for Adonijah has devised this scheme at the risk of his life! 24 Now therefore as the LORD lives, who has established me and placed me on the throne of my father David, and who has made me a house as he promised, today Adonijah shall be put to death." 25 So King Solomon sent Benaiah son of Jehoiada; he struck him down, and he died.

26 The king said to the priest Abiathar, "Go to Anathoth, to your estate; for you deserve death. But I will not at this time put you to

---

10). Both killings could have been considered justifiable under the circumstances. **2.7** *Barzillai* provided food for David and his supporters during Absalom's revolt (2 Sam 17.27–29; 19.31–40). Being invited to eat at the king's table was considered a mark of royal favor (2 Sam 9.7; 19.28; 1 Kings 18.19; 2 Kings 25.29; Neh 5.17). **2.8** When David fled from Jerusalem in the wake of Absalom's revolt, *Shimei* cursed the king for killing members of Saul's family in order to remove rivals to the throne (2 Sam 16.5–13). Although David later swore not to kill Shimei (2 Sam 19.16–23), Solomon would not have been bound by that oath. **2.10–12** In David's time Jerusalem was considered the king's personal property (2 Sam 5.9). David in fact ruled over all Israel, Judah and Israel together, for thirty-three years. In Hebron he ruled Judah alone for seven years and six months (2 Sam 5.4–5). **2.13–**

46 The narrator may feel that Solomon's throne was firmly established immediately after David's death (v. 12), but Solomon himself feels it necessary to secure his kingdom by eliminating anyone who might be a threat to his power. **2.13–25** *Abishag's* status in the court was ambiguous because of her unusual relationship with David (cf. 1.1–4), but Solomon clearly considers her to be a concubine. In this period royal concubines normally became the property of the new king (2 Sam 3.6–7; 12.8; 16.21–22), so Solomon interprets Adonijah's request as a threat and uses it as a pretext to have him killed (vv. 22–25). The text is silent on the question of whether or not Bathsheba anticipated this result. The extraordinary deference shown to her by Solomon (vv. 19–20) is, however, an indication of the power and status the queen mother enjoyed in the Judean royal court. **2.26–27** Abiathar supported Adoni-

death, because you carried the ark of the Lord
GOD before my father David, and because you
shared in all the hardships my father endured." 27 So Solomon banished Abiathar from
being priest to the LORD, thus fulfilling the
word of the LORD that he had spoken concerning the house of Eli in Shiloh.

28 When the news came to Joab—for Joab
had supported Adonijah though he had not
supported Absalom—Joab fled to the tent of
the LORD and grasped the horns of the altar.
29 When it was told King Solomon, "Joab has
fled to the tent of the LORD and now is beside
the altar," Solomon sent Benaiah son of Jehoiada, saying, "Go, strike him down." 30 So Benaiah came to the tent of the LORD and said to
him, "The king commands, 'Come out.'" But
he said, "No, I will die here." Then Benaiah
brought the king word again, saying, "Thus
said Joab, and thus he answered me." 31 The
king replied to him, "Do as he has said, strike
him down and bury him; and thus take away
from me and from my father's house the guilt
for the blood that Joab shed without cause.
32 The LORD will bring back his bloody deeds
on his own head, because, without the knowledge of my father David, he attacked and
killed with the sword two men more righteous and better than himself, Abner son of
Ner, commander of the army of Israel, and
Amasa son of Jether, commander of the army
of Judah. 33 So shall their blood come back on
the head of Joab and on the head of his descendants forever; but to David, and to his descendants, and to his house, and to his
throne, there shall be peace from the LORD
forevermore." 34 Then Benaiah son of Jehoiada went up and struck him down and killed
him; and he was buried at his own house near
the wilderness. 35 The king put Benaiah son of
Jehoiada over the army in his place, and the

king put the priest Zadok in the place of Abiathar.

36 Then the king sent and summoned
Shimei, and said to him, "Build yourself a
house in Jerusalem, and live there, and do not
go out from there to any place whatever. 37 For
on the day you go out, and cross the Wadi Kidron, know for certain that you shall die; your
blood shall be on your own head." 38 And
Shimei said to the king, "The sentence is fair;
as my lord the king has said, so will your servant do." So Shimei lived in Jerusalem many
days.

39 But it happened at the end of three years
that two of Shimei's slaves ran away to King
Achish son of Maacah of Gath. When it was
told Shimei, "Your slaves are in Gath,"
40 Shimei arose and saddled a donkey, and
went to Achish in Gath, to search for his slaves;
Shimei went and brought his slaves from
Gath. 41 When Solomon was told that Shimei
had gone from Jerusalem to Gath and returned, 42 the king sent and summoned
Shimei, and said to him, "Did I not make you
swear by the LORD, and solemnly adjure you,
saying, 'Know for certain that on the day you
go out and go to any place whatever, you shall
die'? And you said to me, 'The sentence is fair;
I accept.' 43 Why then have you not kept your
oath to the LORD and the commandment with
which I charged you?" 44 The king also said to
Shimei, "You know in your own heart all the
evil that you did to my father David; so the
LORD will bring back your evil on your own
head. 45 But King Solomon shall be blessed,
and the throne of David shall be established
before the LORD forever." 46 Then the king
commanded Benaiah son of Jehoiada; and he
went out and struck him down, and he died.

So the kingdom was established in the hand
of Solomon.

---

jah in the struggle over the succession (see 1.7). *Anathoth,* about three miles northeast of Jerusalem. Abiathar's descendants, some of whom were still in Anathoth at the beginning of the exile (Jer 1.1; 32.7–8),
saw his loss of priestly status in Jerusalem as the fulfillment of God's oracle of judgment against the priestly
house of Eli for their corrupt management of the old
shrine at Shiloh (1 Sam 2.27–36). **2.28–35** Joab
rightly suspects that Solomon is conducting a purge of
Adonijah's supporters and therefore seeks sanctuary at
the altar associated with the tent shrine that David had
set up to house the ark of God (2 Sam 6.17). Yet
Solomon chooses not to consider Joab eligible to claim

the protection of the altar (see note on 1 Kings 1.49–
53). After Joab's death, Benaiah, who had been commander of David's private army and an early supporter of Solomon (1.8), becomes commander of the
regular army as well. **2.36–46** Even though David
counseled Solomon to kill Shimei (see vv. 8–9), the
king instead places him under house arrest in
Jerusalem. **2.37** *Wadi Kidron,* the valley to the east of
Jerusalem between the Temple Mount and the Mount
of Olives; Shimei was in effect confined to the city.
2.39 Shimei's ill-considered trip to *Gath* on the coastal
plain is a blatant violation of his agreement with
Solomon.

Solomon's Prayer for Wisdom

3 Solomon made a marriage alliance with Pharaoh king of Egypt; he took Pharaoh's daughter and brought her into the city of David, until he had finished building his own house and the house of the LORD and the wall around Jerusalem. ²The people were sacrificing at the high places, however, because no house had yet been built for the name of the LORD.

3 Solomon loved the LORD, walking in the statutes of his father David; only, he sacrificed and offered incense at the high places. ⁴The king went to Gibeon to sacrifice there, for that was the principal high place; Solomon used to offer a thousand burnt offerings on that altar. ⁵At Gibeon the LORD appeared to Solomon in a dream by night; and God said, "Ask what I should give you." ⁶And Solomon said, "You have shown great and steadfast love to your servant my father David, because he walked before you in faithfulness, in righteousness, and in uprightness of heart toward you; and you have kept for him this great and steadfast love, and have given him a son to sit on his throne today. ⁷And now, O LORD my God, you have made your servant king in place of my father David, although I am only a little child; I do not know how to go out or come in. ⁸And your servant is in the midst of the people whom you have chosen, a great people, so numerous they cannot be numbered or counted. ⁹Give your servant therefore an understanding mind to govern your people, able to discern between good and evil; for who can govern this your great people?"

10 It pleased the Lord that Solomon had asked this. ¹¹God said to him, "Because you have asked this, and have not asked for yourself long life or riches, or for the life of your enemies, but have asked for yourself understanding to discern what is right, ¹²I now do according to your word. Indeed I give you a wise and discerning mind; no one like you has been before you and no one like you shall arise after you. ¹³I give you also what you have not asked, both riches and honor all your life; no other king shall compare with you. ¹⁴If you will walk in my ways, keeping my statutes and my commandments, as your father David walked, then I will lengthen your life."

15 Then Solomon awoke; it had been a dream. He came to Jerusalem where he stood

---

3.1–15 Solomon's dream at Gibeon not only provides divine legitimation for his reign but also indicates the degree to which his kingship at its best will conform to Deuteronomic theological ideals (Deut 17.14–20). **3.1–2** At the beginning of the account the narrator makes two introductory remarks that indicate both Solomon's growing power and the seeds of his eventual downfall. His political alliance with an unnamed king of Egypt indicates that Solomon is now powerful enough to be part of the world of international politics. He is also to become one of Israel's most famous builders, expanding David's original city, fortifying the walls, and building an elaborate royal palace and a splendid temple so that worship could take place appropriately at one site. Solomon, however, also follows the common imperial practice of cementing political alliances with marriages (2 Sam 3.2–5; 5.13), and he participates in or at least tolerates the worship of his wives' native gods in Jerusalem, a situation that ultimately leads to his downfall (ch. 11). **3.2** High places, open-air platforms or shrines where sacrifices and other religious activities took place before the building of the temple. The Lord was sometimes worshiped at the high places, but other deities were worshiped there as well. The Deuteronomistic narrator considered them illegitimate after the building of the temple and often notes their continued use in Judah until Hezekiah's reign (15.14; 22.43; 2 Kings 12.3; 14.4; 15.4, 35; 16.4; 18.4). **3.3** Statutes of . . .

David, Mosaic law, which David himself followed, rather than laws David promulgated (see 3.14; 9.4–5). **3.4** Gibeon (modern el-Jib), about five and a half miles northwest of Jerusalem, was a Hivite enclave well into monarchical times (Josh 9.3–10.15; 2 Sam 21.1–9). The city was an important worship center by Solomon's day, but its early connections with Israelite worship are uncertain (1 Chr 16.39; 21.29; 2 Chr 1.3, 13). **3.5** Many Israelites considered the dream to be a normal means of divine revelation (but see Jer 23.23–32). Revelatory dreams took various forms and sometimes contained dialogues of the sort described here (Gen 20.3–7; 26.24; 28.12–16; 1 Sam 3.1–15; 28.6). **3.6** Steadfast love, God's faithfulness to the demands of the covenant between God and Israel (as expressed in the Mosaic law) and between God and David (as expressed in 2 Sam 7). By invoking the covenant in this context, Solomon indicates his desire to enter into the same relationship with God that his father, David, had accepted. **3.7** A little child . . . not know how to go out or come in, not to be taken literally (see 11.42; 14.21), an expression of humility designed to indicate the king's willingness to be God's servant (vv. 6–9) and to accept divine instruction concerning the duties of kingship. **3.9** Understanding mind, lit. "listening heart." The heart was considered both the seat of the intellect and an organ of perception, so a listening heart is one open to divine direction. Only such a heart is capable of governing God's people and distinguishing good from

before the ark of the covenant of the LORD. He offered up burnt offerings and offerings of well-being, and provided a feast for all his servants.

Solomon's Wisdom in Judgment

16 Later, two women who were prostitutes came to the king and stood before him. 17 The one woman said, "Please, my lord, this woman and I live in the same house; and I gave birth while she was in the house. 18 Then on the third day after I gave birth, this woman also gave birth. We were together; there was no one else with us in the house, only the two of us were in the house. 19 Then this woman's son died in the night, because she lay on him. 20 She got up in the middle of the night and took my son from beside me while your servant slept. She laid him at her breast, and laid her dead son at my breast. 21 When I rose in the morning to nurse my son, I saw that he was dead; but when I looked at him closely in the morning, clearly it was not the son I had borne." 22 But the other woman said, "No, the living son is mine, and the dead son is yours." The first said, "No, the dead son is yours, and the living son is mine." So they argued before the king.

23 Then the king said, "The one says, 'This is my son that is alive, and your son is dead'; while the other says, 'Not so! Your son is dead, and my son is the living one.'" 24 So the king said, "Bring me a sword," and they brought a sword before the king. 25 The king said, "Divide the living boy in two; then give half to the one, and half to the other." 26 But the woman whose son was alive said to the king—because compassion for her son burned within her— "Please, my lord, give her the living boy; certainly do not kill him!" The other said, "It shall be neither mine nor yours; divide it." 27 Then the king responded: "Give the first woman the living boy; do not kill him. She is his mother." 28 All Israel heard of the judgment that the king had rendered; and they stood in awe of the king, because they perceived that the wisdom of God was in him, to execute justice.

Solomon's Administrative Officers

4 King Solomon was king over all Israel, 2 and these were his high officials: Azariah son of Zadok was the priest; 3 Elihoreph and Ahijah sons of Shisha were secretaries; Jehoshaphat son of Ahilud was recorder; 4 Benaiah son of Jehoiada was in command of the army; Zadok and Abiathar were priests; 5 Azariah son of Nathan was over the officials; Zabud son of Nathan was priest and king's friend; 6 Ahishar was in charge of the palace; and Adoniram son of Abda was in charge of the forced labor.

7 Solomon had twelve officials over all Israel, who provided food for the king and his household; each one had to make provision for one month in the year. 8 These were their names: Ben-hur, in the hill country of Ephraim; 9 Ben-deker, in Makaz, Shaalbim,

evil. **3.16–28** The fruit of divine wisdom is immediately apparent in this story meant to illustrate Solomon's success as a judge. Stories of a similar sort are found in other cultures, and it is likely that this tale was part of an oral collection of Solomonic stories before it was incorporated into Kings.
4.1–19 These two lists of Solomon's administrative officers were probably taken from old archives or perhaps from the *Book of the Acts of Solomon* (11.41). Both lists show signs of being slightly garbled during the process of transmission. They are intended to illustrate the effectiveness of Solomon's administrative skills, but they also illustrate the degree to which his kingdom has expanded and become a typical imperial state. His tendencies in this direction run counter to Deuteronomic norms concerning kingship (Deut 17.14–20) and illustrate the dangers of which Samuel warned the Israelites when they asked for a king (1 Sam 8.11–18). **4.2–6** Some of Solomon's officials (*Zadok, Benaiah, Adoniram,* and *Jehoshaphat*) are holdovers from David's regime (2 Sam 8.16–18; 20.23–26; 1 Chr 18.15–17); others (*Azariah son of Zadok, Azariah son of Nathan,* and *Zabud son of Na-*

than) represent the beginning of a hereditary bureaucracy. The inclusion of *Abiathar* in the list suggests that it comes from the beginning of Solomon's reign, before the priest's banishment (2.26–27). **4.3** *Secretaries,* scribes who kept official records but who also had major administrative responsibilities. *Recorder,* perhaps the keeper of the royal archives or the royal herald, but in either case one who functioned at the highest levels of the government. **4.5** The one who *was over the officials* supervised the district administrators listed in vv. 7–19. *King's friend,* the king's chief counselor. **4.6** The official *in charge of the palace* was probably the overseer of all royal estates and buildings. The officer *in charge of the forced labor* was the chief tax collector, who supervised the money, goods, and labor that were owed yearly to the crown (see also 12.18). **4.7–19** The list of Solomon's administrative districts does not seem to conform to Israel's traditional tribal divisions and is probably an indication that the king deliberately tried to break up the older governmental system. If vv. 13, 19 do not refer to the same district, then Judah lies outside the list of twelve administrative units and may not have been taxed in the same way

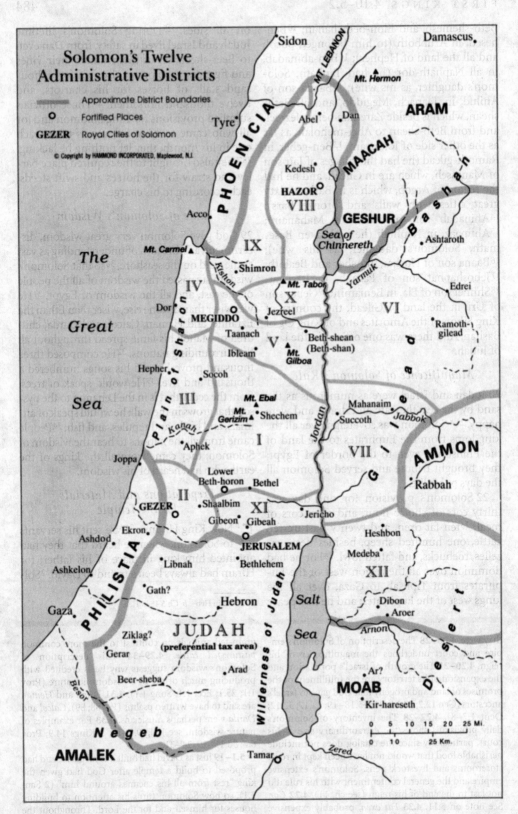

Solomon's Twelve
Administrative Districts

━━━━ Approximate District Boundaries
○ Fortified Places
GEZER Royal Cities of Solomon

© Copyright by HAMMOND INCORPORATED, Maplewood, N.J.

Sidon

Damascus

ARAM

Mt. Hermon ▲

MT. LEBANON

PHOENICIA

Tyre

Abel

Dan

MAACAH

Kedesh

HAZOR ○
VIII

Sea of
Chinnereth

GESHUR

Ashtaroth

Bashan

Acco

IX

Mahanaim

Mt. Carmel ▲

Kishon

Shimron

Mt. Tabor ▲

X

Jezreel

Yarmuk

Edrei

VI

The

IV

Dor

Jezreel

Ramoth-
gilead

Great

MEGIDDO ○

Taanach

V

Beth-shean
(Beth-shan)

Ibleam

Mt.
Gilboa ▲

Hepher

Socoh

Sea

III

Plain of Sharon

Mt. Ebal ▲

Mt.
Gerizim ▲ Shechem

Mahanaim

Succoth

Jabbok

Kanah

Aphek

Gilead

VII

AMMON

Joppa

Lower
Beth-horon Bethel

Rabbah

II

GEZER ○

Shaalbim

Gibeon

XI

Gibeah

Jericho

Ekron

Ashdod

Heshbon

Ashkelon

Libnah

Bethlehem

Medeba

XII

Gath?

JERUSALEM ○

Gaza

PHILISTIA

Hebron

Salt

Dibon

Ziklag?

JUDAH
(preferential tax area)

Aroer

Arnon

Gerar

Arad

Sea

Ar?

MOAB

Beer-sheba

Wilderness of Judah

Kir-haresheth

Besor

Negeb

0 5 10 15 20 25 Mi.

0   10   25 Km.

AMALEK

Tamar

Zered

Desert

483

Beth-shemesh, and Elon-beth-hanan; [10]Ben-hesed, in Arubboth (to him belonged Socoh and all the land of Hepher); [11]Ben-abinadab, in all Naphath-dor (he had Taphath, Solomon's daughter, as his wife); [12]Baana son of Ahilud, in Taanach, Megiddo, and all Beth-shean, which is beside Zarethan below Jezreel, and from Beth-shean to Abel-meholah, as far as the other side of Jokmeam; [13]Ben-geber, in Ramoth-gilead (he had the villages of Jair son of Manasseh, which are in Gilead, and he had the region of Argob, which is in Bashan, sixty great cities with walls and bronze bars); [14]Ahinadab son of Iddo, in Mahanaim; [15]Ahimaaz, in Naphtali (he had taken Basemath, Solomon's daughter, as his wife); [16]Baana son of Hushai, in Asher and Bealoth; [17]Jehoshaphat son of Paruah, in Issachar; [18]Shimei son of Ela, in Benjamin; [19]Geber son of Uri, in the land of Gilead, the country of King Sihon of the Amorites and of King Og of Bashan. And there was one official in the land of Judah.

Magnificence of Solomon's Rule

20 Judah and Israel were as numerous as the sand by the sea; they ate and drank and were happy. [21] [a] Solomon was sovereign over all the kingdoms from the Euphrates to the land of the Philistines, even to the border of Egypt; they brought tribute and served Solomon all the days of his life.

22 Solomon's provision for one day was thirty cors of choice flour, and sixty cors of meal, [23]ten fat oxen, and twenty pasture-fed cattle, one hundred sheep, besides deer, gazelles, roebucks, and fatted fowl. [24]For he had dominion over all the region west of the Euphrates from Tiphsah to Gaza, over all the kings west of the Euphrates; and he had peace

on all sides. [25]During Solomon's lifetime Judah and Israel lived in safety, from Dan even to Beer-sheba, all of them under their vines and fig trees. [26]Solomon also had forty thousand stalls of horses for his chariots, and twelve thousand horsemen. [27]Those officials supplied provisions for King Solomon and for all who came to King Solomon's table, each one in his month; they let nothing be lacking. [28]They also brought to the required place barley and straw for the horses and swift steeds, each according to his charge.

Fame of Solomon's Wisdom

29 God gave Solomon very great wisdom, discernment, and breadth of understanding as vast as the sand on the seashore, [30]so that Solomon's wisdom surpassed the wisdom of all the people of the east, and all the wisdom of Egypt. [31]He was wiser than anyone else, wiser than Ethan the Ezrahite, and Heman, Calcol, and Darda, children of Mahol; his fame spread throughout all the surrounding nations. [32]He composed three thousand proverbs, and his songs numbered a thousand and five. [33]He would speak of trees, from the cedar that is in the Lebanon to the hyssop that grows in the wall; he would speak of animals, and birds, and reptiles, and fish. [34]People came from all the nations to hear the wisdom of Solomon; they came from all the kings of the earth who had heard of his wisdom.

Preparations and Materials for the Temple

5 [b] Now King Hiram of Tyre sent his servants to Solomon, when he heard that they had anointed him king in place of his father; for Hiram had always been a friend to David. [2]Sol-

a Ch 5.1 in Heb   b Ch 5.15 in Heb

they were. **4.20–28** The description of Solomon's empire and court underlines the magnificence of his reign. **4.20–21** The growth of Israel's population and the expansion of its territory are the fulfillment of the promises of land and progeny that God gave to Israel's ancestors (Gen 12.2; 13.14–17; 15.18–19; 22.17; 32.12; Deut 1.7–8). **4.22–28** The inventory of Solomon's daily provisions shows the extraordinary size of his court, particularly since the catalog does not include perishable food that would not have been kept in royal storerooms and livestock pens. Solomon's extensive empire and the general contentment with his rule did not last to the end of his reign (see ch. 11). **4.22** *Cor.* See note on 5.11. **4.23** *Fat oxen*, probably expensive

grain-fed animals, in contrast to the more common *pasture-fed cattle.* **4.29–34** This description of Solomon's wisdom suggests why he is credited with producing much of the OT's wisdom literature (Prov 1.1; 25.1; Eccl 1.1; Song 1.1). **4.31** *Ethan* and *Heman* are said to have written psalms (Pss 88; 89). *Calcol* and *Darda* were perhaps musicians. **4.33** For examples of nature wisdom, see Judg 9.8–15; 2 Kings 14.9; Prov 6.6; 30.15–19, 24–31.

5.1–19 Just as David had built a royal palace and had proposed to build a temple after God had given the king "rest from all his enemies around him" (2 Sam 7.1), so now Solomon turns his attention to building houses for himself and for the Lord. Throughout the

omon sent word to Hiram, saying, ³"You know that my father David could not build a house for the name of the LORD his God because of the warfare with which his enemies surrounded him, until the LORD put them under the soles of his feet.ᵃ ⁴But now the LORD my God has given me rest on every side; there is neither adversary nor misfortune. ⁵So I intend to build a house for the name of the LORD my God, as the LORD said to my father David, 'Your son, whom I will set on your throne in your place, shall build the house for my name.' ⁶Therefore command that cedars from the Lebanon be cut for me. My servants will join your servants, and I will give you whatever wages you set for your servants; for you know that there is no one among us who knows how to cut timber like the Sidonians."

7 When Hiram heard the words of Solomon, he rejoiced greatly, and said, "Blessed be the LORD today, who has given to David a wise son to be over this great people." ⁸Hiram sent word to Solomon, "I have heard the message that you have sent to me; I will fulfill all your needs in the matter of cedar and cypress timber. ⁹My servants shall bring it down to the sea from the Lebanon; I will make it into rafts to go by sea to the place you indicate. I will have them broken up there for you to take away. And you shall meet my needs by providing

food for my household." ¹⁰So Hiram supplied Solomon's every need for timber of cedar and cypress. ¹¹Solomon in turn gave Hiram twenty thousand cors of wheat as food for his household, and twenty cors of fine oil. Solomon gave this to Hiram year by year. ¹²So the LORD gave Solomon wisdom, as he promised him. There was peace between Hiram and Solomon; and the two of them made a treaty.

13 King Solomon conscripted forced labor out of all Israel; the levy numbered thirty thousand men. ¹⁴He sent them to the Lebanon, ten thousand a month in shifts; they would be a month in the Lebanon and two months at home; Adoniram was in charge of the forced labor. ¹⁵Solomon also had seventy thousand laborers and eighty thousand stonecutters in the hill country, ¹⁶besides Solomon's three thousand three hundred supervisors who were over the work, having charge of the people who did the work. ¹⁷At the king's command, they quarried out great, costly stones in order to lay the foundation of the house with dressed stones. ¹⁸So Solomon's builders and Hiram's builders and the Gebalites did the stonecutting and prepared the timber and the stone to build the house.

ᵃ Gk Tg Vg: Heb *my feet* or *his feet*

---

ancient Near East the establishment of a new king was typically followed by palace and temple construction so that the new ruler and his god could be properly enthroned. **5.1** *Tyre,* a Phoenician city just off the coast of southern Lebanon that, along with Sidon, another Phoenician city twenty-two miles to the north, dominated coastal trade around the Mediterranean throughout much of the first millennium BCE. *Hiram is more than a friend to David;* the Hebrew text suggests that the two were treaty partners (see also 2 Sam 5.11). Hiram's interest in continuing this treaty relationship may have prompted him to send goodwill ambassadors to Solomon (see v. 12). **5.3–5** In spite of the fact that 2 Sam 7 gives no explanation for God's forbidding David to build a temple, Solomon here suggests that David could not build a divine house because his kingdom had not been firmly established. He was still engaged in warfare with his enemies. This retrospective explanation defends David's failure to build a temple, but it contradicts 2 Sam 7.1. *Until the LORD put them under the soles of his feet* may be based on 2 Sam 7.11, which seems to imply that God will give David rest from his enemies sometime in the future. The alternate reading *my feet* would suggest that only in Solomon's day was the kingdom established firmly enough to permit temple building, and this reading would provide a better transition to v. 4. Solomon clearly sees the build-

ing of the temple as a fulfillment of Nathan's prophecy (2 Sam 7.13). **5.6** *Lebanon* was famous in the ancient world as a source for *cedar,* a wood whose durability made it highly desirable as a building material. Cedar trees in Lebanon grew particularly tall and straight, characteristics that made them useful in the construction of monumental buildings. Solomon proposes to send workers to aid the Phoenicians (here called simply *Sidonians*) in cutting the timber and offers to pay the wages of the men involved. **5.9** Hiram's counteroffer leaves all of the timber cutting and logging in the hands of the Phoenicians. In return, Solomon will provide food not just for the Phoenician loggers but for Hiram's entire royal court. **5.11** *Cor,* as a dry measure about 14 bushels; as a wet measure 35–60 gallons. *Fine oil,* lit. "beaten oil," olive oil produced by allowing the oil to drip naturally out of a basket of crushed olives. **5.13–17** Work on the temple added to the tax burden already imposed to support Solomon's court. **5.14** *Adoniram.* See 2 Sam 20.24; notes on 1 Kings 4.2–6; 4.6. The remark that Solomon *sent* conscripted workers *to the Lebanon* seems to be at odds with v. 9, which assigns only Phoenicians to the work there. **5.17** *Dressed stones,* ashlars, huge squared, finished blocks whose size made them very difficult to quarry and transport. **5.18** *Gebalites,* inhabitants of the Phoenician coastal city Gebal, later called Byblos by the Greeks.

Solomon Builds the Temple

6 In the four hundred eightieth year after the Israelites came out of the land of Egypt, in the fourth year of Solomon's reign over Israel, in the month of Ziv, which is the second month, he began to build the house of the LORD. ²The house that King Solomon built for the LORD was sixty cubits long, twenty cubits wide, and thirty cubits high. ³The vestibule in front of the nave of the house was twenty cubits wide, across the width of the house. Its depth was ten cubits in front of the house. ⁴For the house he made windows with recessed frames.ᵃ ⁵He also built a structure against the wall of the house, running around the walls of the house, both the nave and the inner sanctuary; and he made side chambers all around. ⁶The lowest storyᵇ was five cubits wide, the middle one was six cubits wide, and the third was seven cubits wide; for around the outside of the house he made offsets on the wall in order that the supporting beams should not be inserted into the walls of the house.

7 The house was built with stone finished at the quarry, so that neither hammer nor ax nor any tool of iron was heard in the temple while it was being built.

8 The entrance for the middle story was on the south side of the house: one went up by winding stairs to the middle story, and from the middle story to the third. ⁹So he built the house, and finished it; he roofed the house with beams and planks of cedar. ¹⁰He built the structure against the whole house, each storyᶜ five cubits high, and it was joined to the house with timbers of cedar.

11 Now the word of the LORD came to Solomon, ¹²"Concerning this house that you are building, if you will walk in my statutes, obey my ordinances, and keep all my commandments by walking in them, then I will establish my promise with you, which I made to your father David. ¹³I will dwell among the children of Israel, and will not forsake my people Israel."

14 So Solomon built the house, and finished it. ¹⁵He lined the walls of the house on the inside with boards of cedar; from the floor of the house to the rafters of the ceiling, he covered them on the inside with wood; and he covered the floor of the house with boards of cypress. ¹⁶He built twenty cubits of the rear of the house with boards of cedar from the floor to the rafters, and he built this within as an inner sanctuary, as the most holy place. ¹⁷The house, that is, the nave in front of the inner sanctuary, was forty cubits long. ¹⁸The cedar within the house had carvings of gourds and open flowers; all was cedar, no stone was seen. ¹⁹The inner sanctuary he prepared in the innermost part of the house, to set there the ark of the covenant of the LORD. ²⁰The interior of the inner sanctuary was twenty cubits long,

---

a Gk: Meaning of Heb uncertain   *b* Gk: Heb *structure*
c Heb lacks *each story*

6.1–22 This detailed description of the building of the temple is designed to impress readers with the building's magnificence and the splendor of Solomon's reign. The account is sometimes confusing because it uses a large number of rare and probably archaic architectural terms, which even the ancient Greek translators no longer understood. Most of the information in ch. 6 is taken from archival sources or from the *Book of the Acts of Solomon* (11.41). **6.1** *Fourth year of Solomon's reign,* between 966 and 956 BCE. This chronology would place the exodus about the middle of the fifteenth century BCE, a date that most modern scholars would consider too early. *Ziv,* the second month in the Canaanite calendar (April–May). The temple was built to the north of David's city on a threshing floor David acquired from Araunah the Jebusite (2 Sam 24.18–25). **6.2** A cubit is about 18 inches. Solomon's temple, a rectangular building 90 feet long, 30 feet wide, and 45 feet high, seems to have been built on Phoenician-Syrian models. **6.3** To the central structure was added an unroofed *vestibule,* or entrance area, 15 feet long and 30 feet wide. A worshiper entering the temple passed through the vestibule and then came to the 60-foot-long *nave* (v. 17). **6.5** The nave in turn led to an *inner sanctuary,* or holy of holies, which was a perfect 30-foot cube (v. 20). Around the outside of the nave and the inner sanctuary was a three-story *structure,* which helped to support the walls and also provided storage space. Latticed windows high in the walls let light in and sacrificial smoke out. **6.11–13** Just as Kings understands God's dynastic promise to David to be conditional on obedience (2.4) and sees the divine promise of longevity to Solomon in a similar way (3.14), so here Kings reminds Solomon that God's willingness to dwell in the temple is also conditional. This typically Deuteronomistic perspective runs counter to the widely held belief that God had promised to dwell eternally in Jerusalem (Pss 68.16; 135.21; Jer 7.1–15). **6.18** The elaborate decorations in the temple probably had religious significance. **6.19** *Ark of the covenant,* an old religious object associated with the Lord, which David had moved to Jerusalem and installed in a tent shrine (2 Sam 6). Solomon later installed the ark in the

twenty cubits wide, and twenty cubits high; he overlaid it with pure gold. He also overlaid the altar with cedar.ᵃ 21 Solomon overlaid the inside of the house with pure gold, then he drew chains of gold across, in front of the inner sanctuary, and overlaid it with gold. 22 Next he overlaid the whole house with gold, in order that the whole house might be perfect; even the whole altar that belonged to the inner sanctuary he overlaid with gold.

The Furnishings of the Temple

23 In the inner sanctuary he made two cherubim of olivewood, each ten cubits high. 24 Five cubits was the length of one wing of the cherub, and five cubits the length of the other wing of the cherub; it was ten cubits from the tip of one wing to the tip of the other. 25 The other cherub also measured ten cubits; both cherubim had the same measure and the same form. 26 The height of one cherub was ten cubits, and so was that of the other cherub. 27 He put the cherubim in the innermost part of the house; the wings of the cherubim were spread out so that a wing of one was touching the one wall, and a wing of the other cherub was touching the other wall; their other wings toward the center of the house were touching wing to wing. 28 He also overlaid the cherubim with gold.

29 He carved the walls of the house all around about with carved engravings of cherubim, palm trees, and open flowers, in the inner and outer rooms. 30 The floor of the house he overlaid with gold, in the inner and outer rooms.

31 For the entrance to the inner sanctuary he made doors of olivewood; the lintel and the doorposts were five-sided.ᵃ 32 He covered the two doors of olivewood with carvings of cherubim, palm trees, and open flowers; he overlaid them with gold, and spread gold on the cherubim and on the palm trees.

33 So also he made for the entrance to the nave doorposts of olivewood, four-sided each, 34 and two doors of cypress wood; the two leaves of the one door were folding, and the two leaves of the other door were folding. 35 He carved cherubim, palm trees, and open flowers, overlaying them with gold evenly applied upon the carved work. 36 He built the inner court with three courses of dressed stone to one course of cedar beams.

37 In the fourth year the foundation of the house of the LORD was laid, in the month of Ziv. 38 In the eleventh year, in the month of Bul, which is the eighth month, the house was finished in all its parts, and according to all its specifications. He was seven years in building it.

Solomon's Palace and Other Buildings

7 Solomon was building his own house thirteen years, and he finished his entire house.

2 He built the House of the Forest of the Lebanon one hundred cubits long, fifty cubits wide, and thirty cubits high, built on four rows of cedar pillars, with cedar beams on the pillars. 3 It was roofed with cedar on the forty-five rafters, fifteen in each row, which were on the pillars. 4 There were window frames in the three rows, facing each other in the three rows. 5 All the doorways and doorposts had four-sided frames, opposite, facing each other in the three rows.

6 He made the Hall of Pillars fifty cubits long and thirty cubits wide. There was a porch in front with pillars, and a canopy in front of them.

---

a Meaning of Heb uncertain

inner sanctuary of the temple, where it was considered the throne of God (2 Kings 19.15; Pss. 80.1; 99.1; Isa 37.16). Other Israelite traditions saw it simply as the container for the Mosaic law (Ex 25.16; 1 Kings 8.9). **6.23–38** The furnishings of the temple were as elaborate and impressive as the building itself. **6.23–28** Cherubim (singular, *cherub*), fantastic composite creatures on which God was sometimes thought to ride (2 Sam 22.11; Ps 18.10; Ezek 1; 10). In the temple they served as guardians of the divine presence. **6.38** *Bul*, the eighth month in the Canaanite calendar (October–November).

7.1–12 Like the description of the temple and its furnishings (6.1–38; 7.13–51), the account of Solomon's other building activities is probably drawn from old archives or from the *Book of the Acts of Solomon* (11.41). The king required considerably more time to build the palace than he did the temple (see 6.38). As in ch. 6, the descriptions of the buildings are sometimes unclear because of the archaic technical terms employed. **7.2–6** The *house* (v. 1) Solomon built was in fact a complex of interrelated buildings just to the south of the new temple. *House of the Forest of Lebanon,* a name deriving from either the cedar from which the building was constructed or its distinctive rows of cedar pillars, which may have given it the look of a forest. Of the five buildings in the complex, three were for public use, while two (the king's house and the house of his Egyptian queen) were Solomon's private domain.

7 He made the Hall of the Throne where he was to pronounce judgment, the Hall of Justice, covered with cedar from floor to floor.

8 His own house where he would reside, in the other court back of the hall, was of the same construction. Solomon also made a house like this hall for Pharaoh's daughter, whom he had taken in marriage.

9 All these were made of costly stones, cut according to measure, sawed with saws, back and front, from the foundation to the coping, and from outside to the great court. 10 The foundation was of costly stones, huge stones, stones of eight and ten cubits. 11 There were costly stones above, cut to measure, and cedarwood. 12 The great court had three courses of dressed stone to one layer of cedar beams all around; so had the inner court of the house of the LORD, and the vestibule of the house.

Products of Hiram the Bronzeworker

13 Now King Solomon invited and received Hiram from Tyre. 14 He was the son of a widow of the tribe of Naphtali, whose father, a man of Tyre, had been an artisan in bronze; he was full of skill, intelligence, and knowledge in working bronze. He came to King Solomon, and did all his work.

15 He cast two pillars of bronze. Eighteen cubits was the height of the one, and a cord of twelve cubits would encircle it; the second pillar was the same.[a] 16 He also made two capitals of molten bronze, to set on the tops of the pillars; the height of the one capital was five cubits, and the height of the other capital was five cubits. 17 There were nets of checker work with wreaths of chain work for the capitals on the tops of the pillars; seven[b] for the one capital, and seven[b] for the other capital. 18 He made the columns with two rows around each latticework to cover the capitals that were above the pomegranates; he did the same with the other capital. 19 Now the capitals that were

---

a Cn: Heb *and a cord of twelve cubits encircled the second pillar;* Compare Jer 52.21 *b* Heb: Gk *a net*

7.9 *Saws,* probably some sort of smoothing tool that gave the stone a more polished surface than was possible with a hammer and chisel. **7.13–51** This archival account of the furnishings of the temple underscores the high quality of craftsmanship involved in Solomon's building projects. Like the temple itself, the furnishings were likely to have been inspired by Phoenician religious practices. **7.13–14** *Hiram from Tyre,* not the king who supplied Solomon with building materials (ch. 5) but an artisan skilled in working bronze. Reference to his Israelite mother is designed to combat the notion that work on the temple was done by a for-

---

1 Kings 5–8 describes the building and dedication of the temple during Solomon's reign and under his direction, a rectangular structure with an overall interior length of 90 feet, a width of 30 feet, and a height of 45 feet, fronted by an unroofed vestibule ("porch") 15 feet long and 30 feet wide.

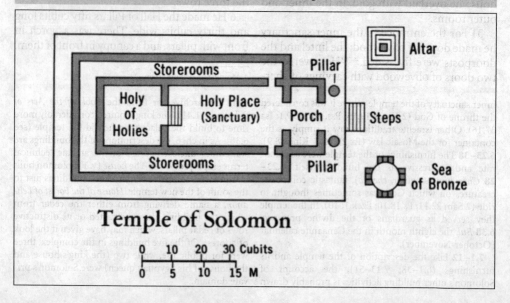

Temple of Solomon

0   10   20   30 Cubits

0   5   10   15 M

on the tops of the pillars in the vestibule were of lily-work, four cubits high. ²⁰The capitals were on the two pillars and also above the rounded projection that was beside the lattice-work; there were two hundred pomegranates in rows all around; and so with the other capital. ²¹He set up the pillars at the vestibule of the temple; he set up the pillar on the south and called it Jachin; and he set up the pillar on the north and called it Boaz. ²²On the tops of the pillars was lily-work. Thus the work of the pillars was finished.

23 Then he made the molten sea; it was round, ten cubits from brim to brim, and five cubits high. A line of thirty cubits would encircle it completely. ²⁴Under its brim were panels all around it, each of ten cubits, surrounding the sea; there were two rows of panels, cast when it was cast. ²⁵It stood on twelve oxen, three facing north, three facing west, three facing south, and three facing east; the sea was set on them. The hindquarters of each

were toward the inside. ²⁶Its thickness was a handbreadth; its brim was made like the brim of a cup, like the flower of a lily; it held two thousand baths. *ᵃ*

27 He also made the ten stands of bronze; each stand was four cubits long, four cubits wide, and three cubits high. ²⁸This was the construction of the stands: they had borders; the borders were within the frames; ²⁹on the borders that were set in the frames were lions, oxen, and cherubim. On the frames, both above and below the lions and oxen, there were wreaths of beveled work. ³⁰Each stand had four bronze wheels and axles of bronze; at the four corners were supports for a basin. The supports were cast with wreaths at the side of each. ³¹Its opening was within the crown whose height was one cubit; its opening was round, as a pedestal is made; it was a cubit and a half wide. At its opening there were

---

a A Heb measure of volume

eigner. **7.15–22** The *two pillars of bronze* flanked the entrance to the temple, where they do not seem to have had any obvious structural function. **7.21** *Jachin* (Hebrew, "he establishes"), *Boaz* (possibly "in strength"), probably catchwords of sentences inscribed on the columns. As an architectural feature, these impressive objects may have served as symbolic markers of the sacredness of the temple enclosure. **7.23–26** *Molten sea*, a

cast bronze vessel of enormous size (a *bath* is about 5.5 gallons), supported by a pedestal of twelve oxen or bulls, traditional Canaanite symbols of fertility. The precise function of this object is uncertain. 2 Chr 4.6 suggests that it was for the priests to wash in, but this seems questionable given the object's height off the ground. The sea may have represented the cosmic sea or had some other religious association. **7.27–39** *Stands,*

A depiction of the temple by T. A. Busnick, an authority on ancient architecture. Although the temple's interior decorations are described in detail in 1 Kings 6, little information is given about its external appearance, which may have been stark and formidable.

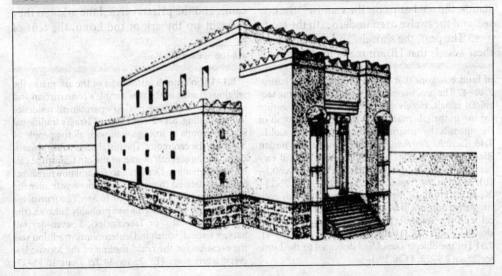

carvings; its borders were four-sided, not round. ³²The four wheels were underneath the borders; the axles of the wheels were in the stands; and the height of a wheel was a cubit and a half. ³³The wheels were made like a chariot wheel; their axles, their rims, their spokes, and their hubs were all cast. ³⁴There were four supports at the four corners of each stand; the supports were of one piece with the stands. ³⁵On the top of the stand there was a round band half a cubit high; on the top of the stand, its stays and its borders were of one piece with it. ³⁶On the surfaces of its stays and on its borders he carved cherubim, lions, and palm trees, where each had space, with wreaths all around. ³⁷In this way he made the ten stands; all of them were cast alike, with the same size and the same form.

38 He made ten basins of bronze; each basin held forty baths,ᵃ each basin measured four cubits; there was a basin for each of the ten stands. ³⁹He set five of the stands on the south side of the house, and five on the north side of the house; he set the sea on the south-east corner of the house.

40 Hiram also made the pots, the shovels, and the basins. So Hiram finished all the work that he did for King Solomon on the house of the LORD: ⁴¹the two pillars, the two bowls of the capitals that were on the tops of the pillars, the two latticeworks to cover the two bowls of the capitals that were on the tops of the pillars; ⁴²the four hundred pomegranates for the two latticeworks, two rows of pomegranates for each latticework, to cover the two bowls of the capitals that were on the pillars; ⁴³the ten stands, the ten basins on the stands; ⁴⁴the one sea, and the twelve oxen underneath the sea.

45 The pots, the shovels, and the basins, all these vessels that Hiram made for King Solo-

mon for the house of the LORD were of burnished bronze. ⁴⁶In the plain of the Jordan the king cast them, in the clay ground between Succoth and Zarethan. ⁴⁷Solomon left all the vessels unweighed, because there were so many of them; the weight of the bronze was not determined.

48 So Solomon made all the vessels that were in the house of the LORD: the golden altar, the golden table for the bread of the Presence, ⁴⁹the lampstands of pure gold, five on the south side and five on the north, in front of the inner sanctuary; the flowers, the lamps, and the tongs, of gold; ⁵⁰the cups, snuffers, basins, dishes for incense, and firepans, of pure gold; the sockets for the doors of the innermost part of the house, the most holy place, and for the doors of the nave of the temple, of gold.

51 Thus all the work that King Solomon did on the house of the LORD was finished. Solomon brought in the things that his father David had dedicated, the silver, the gold, and the vessels, and stored them in the treasuries of the house of the LORD.

Dedication of the Temple

8 Then Solomon assembled the elders of Israel and all the heads of the tribes, the leaders of the ancestral houses of the Israelites, before King Solomon in Jerusalem, to bring up the ark of the covenant of the LORD out of the city of David, which is Zion. ²All the people of Israel assembled to King Solomon at the festival in the month Ethanim, which is the seventh month. ³And all the elders of Israel came, and the priests carried the ark. ⁴So they brought up the ark of the LORD, the tent of

---

ᵃ A Heb measure of volume

---

of bronze wagons that served as supports for basins. **7.40–47** The *pots, shovels,* and *basins,* used during sacrificial rituals, closely resemble those created earlier for use in the tabernacle (Ex 27.3). Hiram cast all of the utensils by pouring bronze into clay molds. **7.46** *Succoth, Zarethan,* on the plain of the Jordan River near the Jabbok. **7.48–50** Another echo of earlier descriptions of the tabernacle (Ex 25.23–40; 30.1–10). *Bread of the Presence.* See Lev 24.5–9; Ex 25.23–30; 40.23; Num 4.7. Apparently the *lampstands* each supported only one lamp and are therefore not identical with the seven-branched lampstands mentioned elsewhere (Ex 25.31–40; 37.17–24; Lev 24.1–4). **7.51** For the objects *David had dedicated* to the Lord, see 2 Sam 8.9–12; 1 Chr 29.1–5.

8.1–13 Solomon's installation of the ark marks the religious climax of the new temple's construction and signifies the beginning of God's permanent residence in the building. **8.1–2** The heads of Israel's traditional kinship groups or lineages join with all the people of Israel for the ceremony. The installation takes place in *Ethanim,* the seventh month of the old Canaanite calendar (September-October), so for unknown reasons Solomon delayed the event for almost a year after the completion of the temple itself (6.38). The *festival* associated with the gathering was probably Sukkoth (the Festival of Booths, or Tabernacles), a seven-day fall harvest festival, which in Deuteronomic tradition was the occasion for the ritual reading of the Mosaic law every seven years (Ex 23.16; 34.22; Deut 16.13–17;

meeting, and all the holy vessels that were in the tent; the priests and the Levites brought them up. 5 King Solomon and all the congregation of Israel, who had assembled before him, were with him before the ark, sacrificing so many sheep and oxen that they could not be counted or numbered. 6 Then the priests brought the ark of the covenant of the LORD to its place, in the inner sanctuary of the house, in the most holy place, underneath the wings of the cherubim. 7 For the cherubim spread out their wings over the place of the ark, so that the cherubim made a covering above the ark and its poles. 8 The poles were so long that the ends of the poles were seen from the holy place in front of the inner sanctuary; but they could not be seen from outside; they are there to this day. 9 There was nothing in the ark except the two tablets of stone that Moses had placed there at Horeb, where the LORD made a covenant with the Israelites, when they came out of the land of Egypt. 10 And when the priests came out of the holy place, a cloud filled the house of the LORD, 11 so that the priests could not stand to minister because of the cloud; for the glory of the LORD filled the house of the LORD.

12 Then Solomon said,

"The LORD has said that he would dwell
    in thick darkness.
13 I have built you an exalted house,
    a place for you to dwell in forever."

Solomon's Speech

14 Then the king turned around and blessed all the assembly of Israel, while all the assembly of Israel stood. 15 He said, "Blessed be the LORD, the God of Israel, who with his hand has fulfilled what he promised with his mouth to my father David, saying, 16 'Since the day that I brought my people Israel out of Egypt, I have not chosen a city from any of the tribes of Israel in which to build a house, that my name might be there; but I chose David to be over my people Israel.' 17 My father David had it in mind to build a house for the name of the LORD, the God of Israel. 18 But the LORD said to my father David, 'You did well to consider building a house for my name; 19 nevertheless you shall not build the house, but your son who shall be born to you shall build the house for my name.' 20 Now the LORD has upheld the promise that he made; for I have risen in the place of my father David; I sit on the throne of Israel, as the LORD promised, and have built the house for the name of the LORD, the God of Israel. 21 There I have provided a place for the ark, in which is the covenant of the LORD that he made with our ancestors when he brought them out of the land of Egypt."

Solomon's Prayer of Dedication

22 Then Solomon stood before the altar of the LORD in the presence of all the assembly of Israel, and spread out his hands to heaven. 23 He said, "O LORD, God of Israel, there is no God like you in heaven above or on earth beneath, keeping covenant and steadfast love for your servants who walk before you with all their heart, 24 the covenant that you kept for your servant my father David as you declared to him; you promised with your mouth and have this day fulfilled with your hand. 25 Therefore, O LORD, God of Israel, keep for your servant my father David that which you promised him, saying, 'There shall never fail you a successor before me to sit on the throne of Israel, if only your children look to their way, to walk before me as you have walked before me.' 26 Therefore, O God of Israel, let your word be

31.9–13; cf. 1 Kings 8.65–66). **8.3–4** The *priests* and the *Levites,* the traditional custodians of the ark (Deut 31.9; 2 Sam 15.24), carried it from the tent in Zion, the older part of Jerusalem that David had occupied (2 Sam 6.1–23), and moved it north to the new temple. **8.6** *Ark.* See note on 6.19. *Cherubim.* See note on 6.23–28. **8.8** The ark's carrying *poles* extended through the veil that blocked the inner sanctuary from public view (2 Chr 3.14) and reminded visitors to the nave of the ark's presence. That the poles *are there to this day* indicates that the account was written sometime after the events being narrated but before the destruction of the temple. **8.10–11** Once the ark was in its proper place, the temple was filled with a *cloud,* a traditional symbol of God's presence (Ex 13.21; 19.16), and with the *glory*

of the LORD, the visible aura or radiance surrounding the deity (Ex 40.34–35; Ezek 1.1–28; 10.18–19; 11.22–23; 43.1–5). **8.12–13** *Thick darkness,* the dark cloud that conceals the deity. **8.14–21** Solomon's speech to the assembled people refers to the fulfillment of God's promise to David (2 Sam 7.1–17). **8.22–53** Solomon's prayer of petition to the Lord is an archetypical statement of Deuteronomistic theology directed to the people and to readers as much as it is to the deity. After introductory references to God's faithfulness to the covenant with David (vv. 22–30; 2 Sam 7.1–17), the king makes seven petitions (vv. 31–32, 33–34, 35–36, 37–40, 41–43, 44–45, 46–51), each of which asks God to hear the prayers of those who are righteous and truly repent of their sins. The last case deals with exile

confirmed, which you promised to your servant my father David.

27 "But will God indeed dwell on the earth? Even heaven and the highest heaven cannot contain you, much less this house that I have built! 28Regard your servant's prayer and his plea, O LORD my God, heeding the cry and the prayer that your servant prays to you today; 29that your eyes may be open night and day toward this house, the place of which you said, 'My name shall be there,' that you may heed the prayer that your servant prays toward this place. 30Hear the plea of your servant and of your people Israel when they pray toward this place; O hear in heaven your dwelling place; heed and forgive.

31 "If someone sins against a neighbor and is given an oath to swear, and comes and swears before your altar in this house, 32then hear in heaven, and act, and judge your servants, condemning the guilty by bringing their conduct on their own head, and vindicating the righteous by rewarding them according to their righteousness.

33 "When your people Israel, having sinned against you, are defeated before an enemy but turn again to you, confess your name, pray and plead with you in this house, 34then hear in heaven, forgive the sin of your people Israel, and bring them again to the land that you gave to their ancestors.

35 "When heaven is shut up and there is no rain because they have sinned against you, and then they pray toward this place, confess your name, and turn from their sin, because you punish*a* them, 36then hear in heaven, and forgive the sin of your servants, your people Israel, when you teach them the good way in which they should walk; and grant rain on your land, which you have given to your people as an inheritance.

37 "If there is famine in the land, if there is plague, blight, mildew, locust, or caterpillar; if their enemy besieges them in any*b* of their cities; whatever plague, whatever sickness there is; 38whatever prayer, whatever plea there is from any individual or from all your people Israel, all knowing the afflictions of their own hearts so that they stretch out their hands toward this house; 39then hear in heaven your dwelling place, forgive, act, and render to all whose hearts you know—according to all their ways, for only you know what is in every human heart— 40so that they may fear you all

the days that they live in the land that you gave to our ancestors.

41 "Likewise when a foreigner, who is not of your people Israel, comes from a distant land because of your name 42—for they shall hear of your great name, your mighty hand, and your outstretched arm—when a foreigner comes and prays toward this house, 43then hear in heaven your dwelling place, and do according to all that the foreigner calls to you, so that all the peoples of the earth may know your name and fear you, as do your people Israel, and so that they may know that your name has been invoked on this house that I have built.

44 "If your people go out to battle against their enemy, by whatever way you shall send them, and they pray to the LORD toward the city that you have chosen and the house that I have built for your name, 45then hear in heaven their prayer and their plea, and maintain their cause.

46 "If they sin against you—for there is no one who does not sin—and you are angry with them and give them to an enemy, so that they are carried away captive to the land of the enemy, far off or near; 47yet if they come to their senses in the land to which they have been taken captive, and repent, and plead with you in the land of their captors, saying, 'We have sinned, and have done wrong; we have acted wickedly'; 48if they repent with all their heart and soul in the land of their enemies, who took them captive, and pray to you toward their land, which you gave to their ancestors, the city that you have chosen, and the house that I have built for your name; 49then hear in heaven your dwelling place their prayer and their plea, maintain their cause 50and forgive your people who have sinned against you, and all their transgressions that they have committed against you; and grant them compassion in the sight of their captors, so that they may have compassion on them 51(for they are your people and heritage, which you brought out of Egypt, from the midst of the iron-smelter). 52Let your eyes be open to the plea of your servant, and to the plea of your people Israel, listening to them whenever they call to you. 53For you have separated them from among all the peoples of the earth, to be your heritage, just as you promised through Moses, your servant, when you brought our ancestors out of Egypt, O Lord GOD."

a Or *when you answer*   *b* Gk Syr: Heb *in the land*

Solomon Blesses the Assembly

54 Now when Solomon finished offering all this prayer and this plea to the LORD, he arose from facing the altar of the LORD, where he had knelt with hands outstretched toward heaven; 55he stood and blessed all the assembly of Israel with a loud voice:

56 "Blessed be the LORD, who has given rest to his people Israel according to all that he promised; not one word has failed of all his good promise, which he spoke through his servant Moses. 57The LORD our God be with us, as he was with our ancestors; may he not leave us or abandon us, 58but incline our hearts to him, to walk in all his ways, and to keep his commandments, his statutes, and his ordinances, which he commanded our ancestors. 59Let these words of mine, with which I pleaded before the LORD, be near to the LORD our God day and night, and may he maintain the cause of his servant and the cause of his people Israel, as each day requires; 60so that all the peoples of the earth may know that the LORD is God; there is no other. 61Therefore devote yourselves completely to the LORD our God, walking in his statutes and keeping his commandments, as at this day."

Solomon Offers Sacrifices

62 Then the king, and all Israel with him, offered sacrifice before the LORD. 63Solomon offered as sacrifices of well-being to the LORD twenty-two thousand oxen and one hundred twenty thousand sheep. So the king and all the people of Israel dedicated the house of the LORD. 64The same day the king consecrated the middle of the court that was in front of the house of the LORD; for there he offered the burnt offerings and the grain offerings and the fat pieces of the sacrifices of well-being, because the bronze altar that was before the LORD was too small to receive the burnt offerings and the grain offerings and the fat pieces of the sacrifices of well-being.

65 So Solomon held the festival at that time, and all Israel with him—a great assembly, people from Lebo-hamath to the Wadi of Egypt—before the LORD our God, seven days.[a] 66On the eighth day he sent the people away; and they blessed the king, and went to their tents, joyful and in good spirits because of all the goodness that the LORD had shown to his servant David and to his people Israel.

God Appears Again to Solomon

9 When Solomon had finished building the house of the LORD and the king's house and all that Solomon desired to build, 2the LORD appeared to Solomon a second time, as he had appeared to him at Gibeon. 3The LORD said to him, "I have heard your prayer and your plea, which you made before me; I have consecrated this house that you have built, and put my name there forever; my eyes and my heart will be there for all time. 4As for you, if you will walk before me, as David your father walked, with integrity of heart and up-

---

a Compare Gk: Heb seven days and seven days, fourteen days

---

and captivity and holds out hope for the exilic audience reading the book. **8.54–61** A resumption of the narrative that frames Solomon's lengthy prayer (cf. vv. 14–22). It consists chiefly of Deuteronomistic exhortation to covenant faithfulness. **8.54** Arose . . . where he had knelt contrasts with v. 22, where Solomon is said to have been praying while standing. **8.55** Blessed all the assembly of Israel. This normally priestly function (cf. Num 6.22–27) is here done by the king (as in v. 14). **8.56** Who has given rest, a fulfillment of the promise given in Deut 12.10–11. **8.62–66** Following common ancient Near Eastern practice, Israel's kings sometimes carried out priestly duties, as Solomon does here (2 Sam 6; 1 Kings 13; 2 Kings 19.14–19), even though such priestly behavior is left out of Deuteronomy's list of royal responsibilities (Deut 17.14–20). **8.65** Lebo-hamath ("Entrance of Hamath"), the traditional northern boundary of the land promised to Israel (Num 34.7–9; Josh 13.5; Ezek 47.15). Its exact location is uncertain, but it has been identified with modern Lebweh, to the south of the city of Hamath (modern Hama) on the Orontes River in Syria. Wadi of Egypt, or Wadi of the Arabah (Am 6.14), the traditional southern boundary, usually identified with the Wadi el-Arish in Egypt's Sinai Peninsula.

9.1–9 The location of Solomon's second vision is not specified, but the divine revelation presumably comes in a dream, as it did at Gibeon (see notes on 3.1–15; 3.5). God's address to Solomon is in good Deuteronomistic style and articulates the theological views that underlie the rest of Kings. The address thus provides a necessary framework for understanding both the narrative of the rest of Solomon's reign (9.10–11.43) and the account of the history of Israel and Judah to the exile. **9.3** God's initial statement concerning the sanctification of the temple verbalizes what readers have already seen in 8.10–11. The temple is now holy because God has caused the divine name to dwell there forever. The promise to keep the temple always in view is a positive answer to Solomon's prayer

rightness, doing according to all that I have commanded you, and keeping my statutes and my ordinances, ⁵then I will establish your royal throne over Israel forever, as I promised your father David, saying, 'There shall not fail you a successor on the throne of Israel.'

6 "If you turn aside from following me, you or your children, and do not keep my commandments and my statutes that I have set before you, but go and serve other gods and worship them, ⁷then I will cut Israel off from the land that I have given them; and the house that I have consecrated for my name I will cast out of my sight; and Israel will become a proverb and a taunt among all peoples. ⁸This house will become a heap of ruins;ᵃ everyone passing by it will be astonished, and will hiss; and they will say, 'Why has the LORD done such a thing to this land and to this house?' ⁹Then they will say, 'Because they have forsaken the LORD their God, who brought their ancestors out of the land of Egypt, and embraced other gods, worshiping them and serving them; therefore the LORD has brought this disaster upon them.' "

10 At the end of twenty years, in which Solomon had built the two houses, the house of the LORD and the king's house, ¹¹King Hiram of Tyre having supplied Solomon with cedar and cypress timber and gold, as much as he desired, King Solomon gave to Hiram twenty cities in the land of Galilee. ¹²But when Hiram came from Tyre to see the cities that Solomon had given him, they did not please him. ¹³Therefore he said, "What kind of cities are these that you have given me, my brother?" So they are called the land of Cabulᵇ to this day.

¹⁴But Hiram had sent to the king one hundred twenty talents of gold.

Other Acts of Solomon

15 This is the account of the forced labor that King Solomon conscripted to build the house of the LORD and his own house, the Millo and the wall of Jerusalem, Hazor, Megiddo, Gezer ¹⁶(Pharaoh king of Egypt had gone up and captured Gezer and burned it down, had killed the Canaanites who lived in the city, and had given it as dowry to his daughter, Solomon's wife; ¹⁷so Solomon rebuilt Gezer), Lower Beth-horon, ¹⁸Baalath, Tamar in the wilderness, within the land, ¹⁹as well as all of Solomon's storage cities, the cities for his chariots, the cities for his cavalry, and whatever Solomon desired to build, in Jerusalem, in Lebanon, and in all the land of his dominion. ²⁰All the people who were left of the Amorites, the Hittites, the Perizzites, the Hivites, and the Jebusites, who were not of the people of Israel— ²¹their descendants who were still left in the land, whom the Israelites were unable to destroy completely—these Solomon conscripted for slave labor, and so they are to this day. ²²But of the Israelites Solomon made no slaves; they were the soldiers, they were his officials, his commanders, his captains, and the commanders of his chariotry and cavalry.

23 These were the chief officers who were over Solomon's work: five hundred fifty, who had charge of the people who carried on the work.

---

a Syr Old Latin: Heb will become high   b Perhaps meaning a land good for nothing

---

(8.29, 52). **9.4–5** Addressing Solomon directly, God again makes the continuation of Davidic rule contingent on Solomon's obedience to the commandments associated with the covenant (cf. 2.4). **9.6–9** In these verses the *you* of the address switches from singular to plural, and God warns Solomon's descendants that they too must obey if the divine presence is to remain in the temple. If they do not obey the law, here summarized by the command to worship only the Lord (Deut 6.4), then king and people together will be punished (cf. 6.11–13). This threat is later recalled in the Deuteronomistic explanation for the destruction of the Northern Kingdom (2 Kings 17.7–8) and ultimately becomes the explanation for the fall of Jerusalem and the exile (2 Kings 21.11–15). **9.10–14** Hiram had already been paid for the building materials (see 5.9–11), so Solomon probably sells the cities in order to replenish his depleted treasury. **9.11** *Galilee* is in

northern Israel between the Jezreel Valley and the Leontes River. The upper part of the region lies just to the east of Tyre. **9.13** *Cabul.* Meaning uncertain. **9.14** Even though Hiram was displeased with the cities when he saw them, he had apparently already paid for them and was unable to cancel the sale. *One hundred twenty talents of gold.* A talent weighs about 75 pounds. **9.15–25** This account of Solomon's other activities probably comes from official archives. **9.15** *Millo,* an artificial platform or terrace of earth constructed to provide a suitable building surface. Its exact location in Jerusalem is unknown. **9.20–22** In addition to the Israelites who were forced to provide labor for Solomon's building activities (5.13–18), he also employed slave labor drawn from the pre-Israelite inhabitants of Canaan, the same people marked for extermination by Deuteronomy (Deut 7.1–6; 20.16–18). The claim that Solomon used Israelites only as

24 But Pharaoh's daughter went up from the city of David to her own house that Solomon had built for her; then he built the Millo.

25 Three times a year Solomon used to offer up burnt offerings and sacrifices of well-being on the altar that he built for the LORD, offering incense*a* before the LORD. So he completed the house.

Solomon's Commercial Activity

26 King Solomon built a fleet of ships at Ezion-geber, which is near Eloth on the shore of the Red Sea,*b* in the land of Edom. 27 Hiram sent his servants with the fleet, sailors who were familiar with the sea, together with the servants of Solomon. 28 They went to Ophir, and imported from there four hundred twenty talents of gold, which they delivered to King Solomon.

Visit of the Queen of Sheba

10 When the queen of Sheba heard of the fame of Solomon (fame due to*c* the name of the LORD), she came to test him with hard questions. 2 She came to Jerusalem with a very great retinue, with camels bearing spices, and very much gold, and precious stones; and when she came to Solomon, she told him all that was on her mind. 3 Solomon answered all her questions; there was nothing hidden from the king that he could not explain to her. 4 When the queen of Sheba had observed all

the wisdom of Solomon, the house that he had built, 5 the food of his table, the seating of his officials, and the attendance of his servants, their clothing, his valets, and his burnt offerings that he offered at the house of the LORD, there was no more spirit in her.

6 So she said to the king, "The report was true that I heard in my own land of your accomplishments and of your wisdom, 7 but I did not believe the reports until I came and my own eyes had seen it. Not even half had been told me; your wisdom and prosperity far surpass the report that I had heard. 8 Happy are your wives!*d* Happy are these your servants, who continually attend you and hear your wisdom! 9 Blessed be the LORD your God, who has delighted in you and set you on the throne of Israel! Because the LORD loved Israel forever, he has made you king to execute justice and righteousness." 10 Then she gave the king one hundred twenty talents of gold, a great quantity of spices, and precious stones; never again did spices come in such quantity as that which the queen of Sheba gave to King Solomon.

11 Moreover, the fleet of Hiram, which carried gold from Ophir, brought from Ophir a great quantity of almug wood and precious stones. 12 From the almug wood the king made

a Gk: Heb *offering incense with it that was*   *b* Or *Sea of Reeds*
c Meaning of Heb uncertain   *d* Gk Syr: Heb *men*

---

overseers does not agree with 5.13–18 or 12.4. **9.26–28** Because Israel was not known for trading by sea, the fleet represents an attempt to expand Solomon's economic base. **9.26** *Ezion-geber* is on the Gulf of Aqaba, so Solomon intends to use the Red Sea for access to ports in eastern Africa and southern Arabia. **9.28** *Ophir,* a renowned source for gold (Job 22.24; 28.16; Ps 45.9; Isa 13.12). Its exact location is uncertain. *Talents.* See note on 9.14.

10.1–29 The building and dedication of the temple mark the religious high point of Solomon's reign; the story of the queen of Sheba's visit shows him at the height of his secular power. The narrator has taken an old legend of the foreign ruler's visit and used it as an occasion to dramatize Solomon's enormous wisdom and the material rewards that wisdom can bring. References to gold and precious objects abound, and the sheer richness of the description is designed to leave readers as awestruck as the queen herself. In the context of the overall narrative, the chapter sharpens the contrast between the brilliance of the Solomonic court (chs. 3–10) and the dark side of his reign, the sins that ultimately bring judgment on the Davidic dynasty and on the nation as a whole (ch. 11). **10.1** *Sheba.* Location

unknown, but possibly to be identified with Saba, the home of the Sabeans, who occupied the southwestern part of the Arabian Peninsula (modern Yemen). This is precisely the area with which Solomon was anxious to establish trading relationships (9.26–28). Ancient Israelite geographers recognized their own kinship with the inhabitants of Sheba (Gen 10.28) but also associated them with Africa (Gen 10.7). This perception of the Sabeans probably reflects their crucial role in transporting spices, gold, and precious stones from Africa, India, and Arabia (Ps 72.10; Isa 60.6; Jer 6.20; Ezek 27.22–23). The queen's *hard questions* are not described in detail, but they might have been riddles of the sort that were the basis of Samson's contest with the Philistines (Judg 14.12–18). The ability to solve riddles was the mark of a wise person (Ps 49.4; Prov 1.6). **10.6–9** The foreigner's praise of Solomon's court serves as the ultimate validation of his status in the international arena and demonstrates the superiority of Israel's God. **10.10** *Talents.* See note on 9.14. An exchange of gifts was customary at meetings between monarchs (cf. v. 13). **10.11** On Solomon's trading ventures with Hiram, see 9.26–28. Here Israelite participation in the voyages is not mentioned. *Ophir.* See

supports for the house of the LORD, and for the king's house, lyres also and harps for the singers; no such almug wood has come or been seen to this day.

13 Meanwhile King Solomon gave to the queen of Sheba every desire that she expressed, as well as what he gave her out of Solomon's royal bounty. Then she returned to her own land, with her servants.

14 The weight of gold that came to Solomon in one year was six hundred sixty-six talents of gold, [15]besides that which came from the traders and from the business of the merchants, and from all the kings of Arabia and the governors of the land. [16]King Solomon made two hundred large shields of beaten gold; six hundred shekels of gold went into each large shield. [17]He made three hundred shields of beaten gold; three minas of gold went into each shield; and the king put them in the House of the Forest of Lebanon. [18]The king also made a great ivory throne, and overlaid it with the finest gold. [19]The throne had six steps. The top of the throne was rounded in the back, and on each side of the seat were arm rests and two lions standing beside the arm rests, [20]while twelve lions were standing, one on each end of a step on the six steps. Nothing like it was ever made in any kingdom. [21]All King Solomon's drinking vessels were of gold, and all the vessels of the House of the Forest of Lebanon were of pure gold; none were of silver—it was not considered as anything in the days of Solomon. [22]For the king had a fleet of ships of Tarshish at sea with the fleet of Hiram. Once every three years the fleet of ships of Tarshish used to come bringing gold, silver, ivory, apes, and peacocks.[a]

23 Thus King Solomon excelled all the kings of the earth in riches and in wisdom. [24]The whole earth sought the presence of Solomon to hear his wisdom, which God had put into his mind. [25]Every one of them brought a present, objects of silver and gold, garments, weaponry, spices, horses, and mules, so much year by year.

26 Solomon gathered together chariots and horses; he had fourteen hundred chariots and twelve thousand horses, which he stationed in the chariot cities and with the king in Jerusalem. [27]The king made silver as common in Jerusalem as stones, and he made cedars as numerous as the sycamores of the Shephelah. [28]Solomon's import of horses was from Egypt and Kue, and the king's traders received them from Kue at a price. [29]A chariot could be imported from Egypt for six hundred shekels of silver, and a horse for one hundred fifty; so through the king's traders they were exported to all the kings of the Hittites and the kings of Aram.

Solomon's Errors

11 King Solomon loved many foreign women along with the daughter of Pharaoh: Moabite, Ammonite, Edomite, Sidonian, and Hittite women, [2]from the nations concerning which the LORD had said to the Israelites, "You shall not enter into marriage with them, neither shall they with you; for they will surely incline your heart to follow their gods"; Solomon clung to these in love. [3]Among his wives were seven hundred princesses and three hundred concubines; and his wives turned away his heart. [4]For when Solomon was old, his wives turned away his

a Or baboons

note on 9.28. Almug wood, perhaps red sandalwood. **10.16** Large shields, probably rectangular and designed to protect the entire body. The ones mentioned here and in v. 17 are decorative rather than functional. Six hundred shekels of gold. The weight of a shekel varied greatly in ancient Israel but averaged about .4 ounce. **10.17** Shields, here likely small circular shields. Three minas of gold. A mina equals 50 shekels. **10.22** Tarshish. Location uncertain, possibly in the Mediterranean (see Gen 10.4) or in India, Africa, or Arabia. The context suggests that the ships were capable of making long voyages. **10.28** Kue, located in southeastern Turkey. **10.29** The kings of the Hittites ruled over parts of northern Syria. Solomon's importation of war horses and chariots from Egypt is a direct violation of the prohibition in Deut 17.16.

11.1–13 A sharp contrast with the rosy picture of Solomon's achievements in chs. 3–10. In characteristic Deuteronomistic style, the narrator provides a theological evaluation of the king's reign and concludes that in the end Solomon violated the conditions attached to God's promise of an eternal Davidic dynasty (2.4; 9.4–5). **11.1–2** Deuteronomy's prohibition against intermarriage with the original inhabitants of Canaan (Deut 7.1–6) is here expanded to include Phoenician trading partners such as Sidon and vassals such as Moab, Ammon, and Edom. The latter three nations, Israel's immediate neighbors to the east and south, had been subjugated by David and were vassals during much of Solomon's reign (2 Sam 8.2, 9–14; 12.26–31). **11.4** Solomon was old, perhaps an oblique attempt to blame his sins on senility. In reality the dif-

heart after other gods; and his heart was not true to the LORD his God, as was the heart of his father David. 5For Solomon followed Astarte the goddess of the Sidonians, and Milcom the abomination of the Ammonites. 6So Solomon did what was evil in the sight of the LORD, and did not completely follow the LORD, as his father David had done. 7Then Solomon built a high place for Chemosh the abomination of Moab, and for Molech the abomination of the Ammonites, on the mountain east of Jerusalem. 8He did the same for all his foreign wives, who offered incense and sacrificed to their gods.

9 Then the LORD was angry with Solomon, because his heart had turned away from the LORD, the God of Israel, who had appeared to him twice, 10and had commanded him concerning this matter, that he should not follow other gods; but he did not observe what the LORD commanded. 11Therefore the LORD said to Solomon, "Since this has been your mind and you have not kept my covenant and my statutes that I have commanded you, I will surely tear the kingdom from you and give it to your servant. 12Yet for the sake of your father David I will not do it in your lifetime; I will tear it out of the hand of your son. 13I will not, however, tear away the entire kingdom; I will give one tribe to your son, for the sake of my servant David and for the sake of Jerusalem, which I have chosen."

Adversaries of Solomon

14 Then the LORD raised up an adversary against Solomon, Hadad the Edomite; he was of the royal house in Edom. 15For when David was in Edom, and Joab the commander of the army went up to bury the dead, he killed every male in Edom 16(for Joab and all Israel remained there six months, until he had eliminated every male in Edom); 17but Hadad fled to Egypt with some Edomites who were servants of his father. He was a young boy at that time. 18They set out from Midian and came to Paran; they took people with them from Paran and came to Egypt, to Pharaoh king of Egypt, who gave him a house, assigned him an allowance of food, and gave him land. 19Hadad found great favor in the sight of Pharaoh, so that he gave him his sister-in-law for a wife, the sister of Queen Tahpenes. 20The sister of Tahpenes gave birth by him to his son Genubath, whom Tahpenes weaned in Pharaoh's house; Genubath was in Pharaoh's house among the children of Pharaoh. 21When Hadad heard in Egypt that David slept with his ancestors and that Joab the commander of the army was dead, Hadad said to Pharaoh, "Let me depart, that I may go to my own country." 22But Pharaoh said to him, "What do you lack with me that you now seek to go to your own country?" And he said, "No, do let me go."

23 God raised up another adversary against Solomon,[a] Rezon son of Eliada, who had fled from his master, King Hadadezer of Zobah. 24He gathered followers around him and became leader of a marauding band, after the slaughter by David; they went to Damascus, settled there, and made him king in Damascus. 25He was an adversary of Israel all the days of Solomon, making trouble as Hadad did; he despised Israel and reigned over Aram.

_a_ Heb _him_

---

ficulties started early in his reign with his marriage to an Egyptian princess (3.1). **11.5** _Followed_ seems to imply that Solomon actually worshiped these deities rather than simply tolerating their worship. _Astarte_ (or Ashtoreth), a Canaanite goddess corresponding to the Mesopotamian goddess Ishtar and later identified with Aphrodite and Venus. In extrabiblical texts as well as in the OT, she is usually portrayed as the consort of Baal, the Canaanite storm god representing fertility. She was particularly popular among the Phoenicians and was the leading female deity in both Tyre and Sidon. _Milcom_, an Ammonite deity whose name is derived from a Semitic root meaning "king" or "ruler"; he is usually identified with Baal. **11.7** _High place._ See note on 3.2. _Chemosh_, the chief deity of Moab, but little is known about his characteristics. _Molech_, usually known only as a deity worshiped outside of Jerusalem

in the Valley of Hinnom (Lev 18.21; 20.2–5; 2 Kings 23.10; Jer 32.35), is not otherwise associated with Ammon, and it is likely that Milcom is intended here (see v. 5). **11.9** For God's appearances to Solomon, see 3.5–14; 9.1–9. **11.13** Because of God's fidelity to the covenant with David, the Davidic line will not be terminated, even though such termination would have been justified. This gracious divine action fulfills one of the promises in Nathan's oracle to David (2 Sam 7.14–15). **11.14–25** Although Solomon is allowed to die before witnessing the judgment against his house, he does see the beginning of the loss of his empire. **11.15–16** For David's campaigns against Edom, see 2 Sam 8.11–14. _Killed every male in Edom,_ undoubtedly an exaggeration. **11.19** _Queen Tahpenes,_ otherwise unknown; _Tahpenes_ may be an Egyptian royal title. **11.23** On David's battles with _Hadadezer of_

Jeroboam's Rebellion

26 Jeroboam son of Nebat, an Ephraimite of Zeredah, a servant of Solomon, whose mother's name was Zeruah, a widow, rebelled against the king. 27 The following was the reason he rebelled against the king. Solomon built the Millo, and closed up the gap in the wall*a* of the city of his father David. 28 The man Jeroboam was very able, and when Solomon saw that the young man was industrious he gave him charge over all the forced labor of the house of Joseph. 29 About that time, when Jeroboam was leaving Jerusalem, the prophet Ahijah the Shilonite found him on the road. Ahijah had clothed himself with a new garment. The two of them were alone in the open country 30 when Ahijah laid hold of the new garment he was wearing and tore it into twelve pieces. 31 He then said to Jeroboam: Take for yourself ten pieces; for thus says the Lord, the God of Israel, "See, I am about to tear the kingdom from the hand of Solomon, and will give you ten tribes. 32 One tribe will remain his, for the sake of my servant David and for the sake of Jerusalem, the city that I have chosen out of all the tribes of Israel. 33 This is because he has*b* forsaken me, worshiped Astarte the goddess of the Sidonians, Chemosh the god of Moab, and Milcom the god of the Ammonites, and has*b* not walked in my ways, doing what is right in my sight and keeping my statutes and my ordinances, as his father David did. 34 Nevertheless I will not take the whole kingdom away from him but will make him ruler all the days of his life, for the sake of my servant David whom I chose and who did keep my commandments and my statutes;

35 but I will take the kingdom away from his son and give it to you—that is, the ten tribes. 36 Yet to his son I will give one tribe, so that my servant David may always have a lamp before me in Jerusalem, the city where I have chosen to put my name. 37 I will take you, and you shall reign over all that your soul desires; you shall be king over Israel. 38 If you will listen to all that I command you, walk in my ways, and do what is right in my sight by keeping my statutes and my commandments, as David my servant did, I will be with you, and will build you an enduring house, as I built for David, and I will give Israel to you. 39 For this reason I will punish the descendants of David, but not forever." 40 Solomon sought therefore to kill Jeroboam; but Jeroboam promptly fled to Egypt, to King Shishak of Egypt, and remained in Egypt until the death of Solomon.

Death of Solomon

41 Now the rest of the acts of Solomon, all that he did as well as his wisdom, are they not written in the Book of the Acts of Solomon? 42 The time that Solomon reigned in Jerusalem over all Israel was forty years. 43 Solomon slept with his ancestors and was buried in the city of his father David; and his son Rehoboam succeeded him.

The Northern Tribes Secede

12 Rehoboam went to Shechem, for all Israel had come to Shechem to make him king. 2 When Jeroboam son of Nebat heard of it (for he was still in Egypt, where he had fled from King Solomon), then Jeroboam returned

a Heb lacks *in the wall*   *b* Gk Syr Vg: Heb *they have*

Zobah, see 2 Sam 8.3–8; 10.15–19. **11.26–40** The story of Jeroboam's rise to power is basically favorable toward the future king, although some early Greek translations give a more negative picture. **11.29** *Ahijah* is identified with the old Israelite shrine at Shiloh and represents a theological viewpoint similar to that of the Deuteronomistic author. For similar prophetic involvement in a change of dynasty, see 1 Sam 15.27–28. **11.31** In contrast to v. 13, this verse seems to imply that two tribes are left to the house of David. The two are presumably Judah and Benjamin (see 12.21). The early absorption of Benjamin into the much larger Judah may have led the author of v. 13 to consider them a single tribe. **11.36** *Lamp.* Meaning uncertain. As translated, the statement seems to mean that David will always have a presence or representative before God in Jerusalem. Some scholars suggest "fief" or "dominion." **11.40** *Shishak,* the Hebrew rendering of Pharaoh Shoshenq I (ca. 931–910 BCE). He later invaded Palestine during the reign of Rehoboam (14.25–26). **11.41–43** This summary marks the end of Solomon's reign. **11.41** *The Book of the Acts of Solomon* is otherwise unknown but is probably the source of much of the archival data in this part of Kings.

12.1–19 As in the case of David's elevation to kingship (1 Sam 16.1–13; 2 Sam 5.1–5), divine legitimation through a prophet here precedes popular election. **12.1** *Shechem,* located about forty-one miles north of Jerusalem, between Mount Gerizim and Mount Ebal. It had been an important religious center for the northern tribes (Josh 24; Deut 27), and Rehoboam's journey may have been intended to placate northern religious and political interests. **12.2–3** The Hebrew text of v. 2 (see text note *a* on p. 499) seems to imply that

from[a] Egypt. 3And they sent and called him; and Jeroboam and all the assembly of Israel came and said to Rehoboam, 4"Your father made our yoke heavy. Now therefore lighten the hard service of your father and his heavy yoke that he placed on us, and we will serve you." 5He said to them, "Go away for three days, then come again to me." So the people went away.

6 Then King Rehoboam took counsel with the older men who had attended his father Solomon while he was still alive, saying, "How do you advise me to answer this people?" 7They answered him, "If you will be a servant to this people today and serve them, and speak good words to them when you answer them, then they will be your servants forever." 8But he disregarded the advice that the older men gave him, and consulted with the young men who had grown up with him and now attended him. 9He said to them, "What do you advise that we answer this people who have said to me, 'Lighten the yoke that your father put on us'?" 10The young men who had grown up with him said to him, "Thus you should say to this people who spoke to you, 'Your father made our yoke heavy, but you must lighten it for us'; thus you should say to them, 'My little finger is thicker than my father's loins. 11Now, whereas my father laid on you a heavy yoke, I will add to your yoke. My father disciplined you with whips, but I will discipline you with scorpions.' "

12 So Jeroboam and all the people came to Rehoboam the third day, as the king had said, "Come to me again the third day." 13The king answered the people harshly. He disregarded the advice that the older men had given him 14and spoke to them according to the advice of the young men, "My father made your yoke heavy, but I will add to your yoke; my father disciplined you with whips, but I will discipline you with scorpions." 15So the king did not listen to the people, because it was a turn of affairs brought about by the Lord that he might fulfill his word, which the Lord had spoken by Ahijah the Shilonite to Jeroboam son of Nebat.

16 When all Israel saw that the king would not listen to them, the people answered the king,

"What share do we have in David?
    We have no inheritance in the son of Jesse.
To your tents, O Israel!
    Look now to your own house, O David."

So Israel went away to their tents. 17But Rehoboam reigned over the Israelites who were living in the towns of Judah. 18When King Rehoboam sent Adoram, who was taskmaster over the forced labor, all Israel stoned him to death. King Rehoboam then hurriedly mounted his chariot to flee to Jerusalem. 19So Israel has been in rebellion against the house of David to this day.

First Dynasty: Jeroboam Reigns over Israel

20 When all Israel heard that Jeroboam had returned, they sent and called him to the assembly and made him king over all Israel. There was no one who followed the house of David, except the tribe of Judah alone.

21 When Rehoboam came to Jerusalem, he assembled all the house of Judah and the tribe of Benjamin, one hundred eighty thousand chosen troops to fight against the house of Israel, to restore the kingdom to Rehoboam son of Solomon. 22But the word of God came to Shemaiah the man of God: 23Say to King Rehoboam of Judah, son of Solomon, and to all the house of Judah and Benjamin, and to the rest of the people, 24"Thus says the Lord, You shall not go up or fight against your kindred the people of Israel. Let everyone go home, for this thing is from me." So they heeded the word of the Lord and went home again, according to the word of the Lord.

_____

a Gk Vg Compare 2 Chr 10.2: Heb *lived in*

Jeroboam remained in political exile in Egypt until the Northern tribes summon him to lead their negotiations with Rehoboam (v. 3). In the Greek text Jeroboam returns before he is summoned. **12.4** *Heavy yoke*, the taxes and forced labor required by Solomon's large court and numerous building projects (see 4.6–19; 5.13–18). **12.6–7** Throughout the ancient Near East it was customary for new monarchs to grant concessions at the beginning of their reigns. **12.11** *Scorpions*, if not simply metaphorical, perhaps a particularly painful kind of whip. **12.15** For Ahijah's oracle, see 11.29–39. **12.16** Israel's call to revolt is reminiscent of the words used by Northerners during the revolts of the Davidic period (2 Sam 20.1). *Tents* evokes Israel's premonarchical past as well as the possibility of military activity. **12.18** In spite of the threats of revolt, Rehoboam apparently tries to enforce his harsher policies in the North. **12.20–24** Shemaiah's oracle underscores the divine legitimation of Jeroboam's rise to power. **12.20–21** On the problem of the number of tribes that

Chronology of the Kings of the Divided Monarchy

JUDAH	ISRAEL
Rehoboam (922–915 BCE)	Jeroboam I (922–901 BCE)
Abijam (915–913)	
Asa (913–873)	Nadab (901–900)
	Baasha (900–877)
	Elah (877–876)
	Zimri (876)
Jehoshaphat (873–849)	Omri (876–869)
	Ahab (869–850)
	Ahaziah (850–849)
Jehoram (849–843/2)	Jehoram (849–843/2)
Ahaziah (843/2)	
Athaliah (843/2–837)	
Jehoash (837–800)	Jehu (843/2–815)
	Jehoahaz (815–802)
Amaziah (800–783)	Joash (802–786)
Azariah/Uzziah (783–742)	Jeroboam II (786–746)
	Zechariah (746–745)
	Shallum (745)
Jotham (742–735)	Menahem (745–737)
	Pekahiah (737–736)
	Pekah (736–732)
Ahaz (735–715)	Hoshea (732–724)
	Fall of Samaria (722/1 BCE)
Hezekiah (715–687/6)	
Mannasseh (687/6–642)	
Amon (642–640)	
Josiah (640–609)	
Jehoahaz (609)	
Jehoiakim (609–598)	
Jehoiachin (598/7)	
Babylonian conquest of Jerusalem	
and first deportation (597 BCE)	
Zedekiah (597–587/6)	
Destruction of Jerusalem and	
second deportation (587/6 BCE)	

Dates following the kings' names are approximate years of their rule. The chronological data given in the books of 1 and 2 Kings pose insurmountable problems, however, for the construction of a firm chronology of the Divided Monarchy. The system adopted here is one of several approximations used by scholars.

Jeroboam's Golden Calves

25 Then Jeroboam built Shechem in the hill country of Ephraim, and resided there; he went out from there and built Penuel. 26 Then Jeroboam said to himself, "Now the kingdom may well revert to the house of David. 27 If this people continues to go up to offer sacrifices in the house of the LORD at Jerusalem, the heart of this people will turn again to their master, King Rehoboam of Judah; they will kill me and return to King Rehoboam of Judah." 28 So the king took counsel, and made two calves of gold. He said to the people, *a* "You have gone up to Jerusalem long enough. Here are your gods, O Israel, who brought you up out of the land of Egypt." 29 He set one in Bethel, and the other he put in Dan. 30 And this thing became a sin, for the people went to worship before the one at Bethel and before the other as far as Dan. *b* 31 He also made houses *c* on high places, and appointed priests from among all the people, who were not Levites. 32 Jeroboam appointed a festival on the fifteenth day of the eighth month like the festival that was in Judah, and he offered sacrifices on the altar; so he did in Bethel, sacrificing to the calves that he had made. And he placed in Bethel the priests of the high places that he had made. 33 He went up to the altar that he had made in Bethel on the fifteenth day in the eighth month, in the month that he alone had devised; he appointed a festival for the people of Israel, and he went up to the altar to offer incense.

A Man of God from Judah

13 While Jeroboam was standing by the altar to offer incense, a man of God came out of Judah by the word of the LORD to Bethel 2 and proclaimed against the altar by the word of the LORD, and said, "O altar, altar, thus says the LORD: 'A son shall be born to the house of David, Josiah by name; and he shall sacrifice on you the priests of the high places who offer incense on you, and human bones shall be burned on you.' " 3 He gave a sign the

a Gk: Heb *to them*   *b* Compare Gk: Heb *went to the one as far as Dan*   *c* Gk Vg Compare 13.32: Heb *a house*

remained faithful to the Davidic house, see note on 11.31. **12.25–33** From the standpoint of the narrator, the new king's reign is problematic from the beginning, for his first royal acts violate most of the Deuteronomistic guidelines for proper worship. **12.25** On the significance of Jeroboam's choice of *Shechem* as the first capital, see note on 12.1. *Penuel* was east of the Jordan at a ford of the Jabbok River, where Jacob wrestled with God (cf. Gen 32.30–31). **12.28** The two *calves* may have been bull images, traditional ancient Near Eastern symbols of power and fertility. In Canaan they were associated with both the god El, the head of the pantheon, and the storm god Baal. The worship of the bull or calf in Israel had ancient roots (see, e.g., Ex 32), and Jeroboam may have thought that he was reinstituting an older and more authentic form of the worship of the Lord. In any case, his actions violate Israel's traditional prohibition against making images of the deity (Ex 20.4–6; Deut 4.15–19; 5.8–10), and the manufacture of two of these objects violates the Deuteronomic ban against worshiping more than one God (Deut 5.7; 6.4). **12.29** *Bethel,* just north of Jerusalem and therefore on the southern boundary of the newly created Northern Kingdom. It had old associations with the worship of the Lord (Gen 28.10–22; Judg 20.18–28). *Dan,* the traditional marker of Israel's northern border. **12.31** *High places.* See note on 3.2. The *houses* were for the cultic activities that took place at the high places. Deuteronomy requires that all priests be *Levites* (Deut 18.1–8). **12.32** *Festival,* the Festival of Tabernacles, a harvest festival usually held on the fifteenth day of the seventh month (Num 29.12–39). **12.33** Jeroboam's priestly activities are not part of a king's proper duties according to Deuteronomy (Deut 17.14–20).

13.1–34 This chapter continues the narrative begun in 12.33 and makes explicit the condemnation of Jeroboam's religious policies implied in the descriptions of 12.26–32. The bulk of ch. 13 is composed of two interrelated legends that focus on prophets and their activities. Both stories may have once circulated orally in prophetic circles. The first story (vv. 1–10) continues the theme of the prophetic condemnation of sinful rulers, a theme that will dominate the remainder of 1 Kings and extend as far as 2 Kings 13. The second story (vv. 11–32) deals with the problem of true and false prophecy and may have originally been intended as a warning to prophets about the conduct of their office. Both stories illustrate an important theological motif of this portion of Kings, the inevitable fulfillment of the word of a genuine prophet (cf. Deut 18.15–22). **13.1** The unnamed Judean is given the title *man of God,* a designation used particularly in the Elijah-Elisha stories (1 Kings 17–2 Kings 10). The title may have originally been used to identify individuals able to use divine power in miraculous ways. On the significance of Jeroboam's cultic installation at *Bethel,* see notes on 12.28; 12.29. **13.2** The judgment oracle is directed against the *altar* itself and not against the king or the dynasty. *Josiah* finally desecrated the altar at Bethel about 620 BCE, roughly three hundred years after the prophecy was originally delivered (2 Kings 23.15–18). Sacrificing the priests and burning their bones on the altar would

same day, saying, "This is the sign that the LORD has spoken: 'The altar shall be torn down, and the ashes that are on it shall be poured out.'" 4When the king heard what the man of God cried out against the altar at Bethel, Jeroboam stretched out his hand from the altar, saying, "Seize him!" But the hand that he stretched out against him withered so that he could not draw it back to himself. 5The altar also was torn down, and the ashes poured out from the altar, according to the sign that the man of God had given by the word of the LORD. 6The king said to the man of God, "Entreat now the favor of the LORD your God, and pray for me, so that my hand may be restored to me." So the man of God entreated the LORD; and the king's hand was restored to him, and became as it was before. 7Then the king said to the man of God, "Come home with me and dine, and I will give you a gift." 8But the man of God said to the king, "If you give me half your kingdom, I will not go in with you; nor will I eat food or drink water in this place. 9For thus I was commanded by the word of the LORD: You shall not eat food, or drink water, or return by the way that you came." 10So he went another way, and did not return by the way that he had come to Bethel.

11 Now there lived an old prophet in Bethel. One of his sons came and told him all that the man of God had done that day in Bethel; the words also that he had spoken to the king, they told to their father. 12Their father said to them, "Which way did he go?" And his sons showed him the way that the man of God who came from Judah had gone. 13Then he said to his sons, "Saddle a donkey for me." So they saddled a donkey for him, and he mounted it. 14He went after the man of God, and found him sitting under an oak tree. He

said to him, "Are you the man of God who came from Judah?" He answered, "I am." 15Then he said to him, "Come home with me and eat some food." 16But he said, "I cannot return with you, or go in with you; nor will I eat food or drink water with you in this place; 17for it was said to me by the word of the LORD: You shall not eat food or drink water there, or return by the way that you came." 18Then the other*a* said to him, "I also am a prophet as you are, and an angel spoke to me by the word of the LORD: Bring him back with you into your house so that he may eat food and drink water." But he was deceiving him. 19Then the man of God*a* went back with him, and ate food and drank water in his house.

20 As they were sitting at the table, the word of the LORD came to the prophet who had brought him back; 21and he proclaimed to the man of God who came from Judah, "Thus says the LORD: Because you have disobeyed the word of the LORD, and have not kept the commandment that the LORD your God commanded you, 22but have come back and have eaten food and drunk water in the place of which he said to you, 'Eat no food, and drink no water,' your body shall not come to your ancestral tomb." 23After the man of God*a* had eaten food and had drunk, they saddled for him a donkey belonging to the prophet who had brought him back. 24Then as he went away, a lion met him on the road and killed him. His body was thrown in the road, and the donkey stood beside it; the lion also stood beside the body. 25People passed by and saw the body thrown in the road, with the lion standing by the body. And they came and told it in the town where the old prophet lived.

---

a Heb *he*

have defiled it, making it unfit for religious purposes. **13.3** Because the fulfillment of a prophecy might be delayed for many years, prophets sometimes gave a *sign* to guarantee the truth of their oracles (Isa 7.11–17). The sign became a visible proof that the prophecy was true. Here the sign, the destruction of the altar, occurs immediately (v. 5). **13.4** The withering of the king's hand demonstrates the power of the prophet and the divine protection given to him. **13.6** Prophets were often thought to be particularly effective in interceding with God (see, e.g., Gen 20.7; 1 Sam 7.5; 12.19). In this case the healing becomes another sign to demonstrate the truth of the prophet's words. **13.9** To eat or drink at Bethel would have suggested

the prophet's willingness to participate in the illegitimate cultic activities taking place there. **13.11** *Son*, perhaps an indication of membership in a prophetic guild rather than actual kinship. The *father* would then have been the head of the guild. **13.18** *An angel spoke* may be an implication that the old prophet did not receive the oracle directly from God, a situation that should have warned the man of God of the possibility that the oracle was false. Subtlety aside, readers are simply told that the old prophet lied. **13.19** Even a genuine prophet cannot determine whether another prophet's oracle is true or false. **13.24** The lion's peculiar behavior, killing the prophet but not the donkey and standing beside the body rather than eating it (cf.

26 When the prophet who had brought him back from the way heard of it, he said, "It is the man of God who disobeyed the word of the LORD; therefore the LORD has given him to the lion, which has torn him and killed him according to the word that the LORD spoke to him." 27Then he said to his sons, "Saddle a donkey for me." So they saddled one, 28and he went and found the body thrown in the road, with the donkey and the lion standing beside the body. The lion had not eaten the body or attacked the donkey. 29The prophet took up the body of the man of God, laid it on the donkey, and brought it back to the city,ᵃ to mourn and to bury him. 30He laid the body in his own grave; and they mourned over him, saying, "Alas, my brother!" 31After he had buried him, he said to his sons, "When I die, bury me in the grave in which the man of God is buried; lay my bones beside his bones. 32For the saying that he proclaimed by the word of the LORD against the altar in Bethel, and against all the houses of the high places that are in the cities of Samaria, shall surely come to pass."

33 Even after this event Jeroboam did not turn from his evil way, but made priests for the high places again from among all the people; any who wanted to be priests he consecrated for the high places. 34This matter became sin to the house of Jeroboam, so as to cut it off and to destroy it from the face of the earth.

Judgment on the House of Jeroboam

14 At that time Abijah son of Jeroboam fell sick. 2Jeroboam said to his wife, "Go, disguise yourself, so that it will not be known that you are the wife of Jeroboam, and go to Shiloh; for the prophet Ahijah is there, who said of me that I should be king over this people. 3Take with you ten loaves, some cakes, and a jar of honey, and go to him; he will tell you what shall happen to the child."

4 Jeroboam's wife did so; she set out and went to Shiloh, and came to the house of Ahijah. Now Ahijah could not see, for his eyes were dim because of his age. 5But the LORD said to Ahijah, "The wife of Jeroboam is coming to inquire of you concerning her son; for he is sick. Thus and thus you shall say to her."

When she came, she pretended to be another woman. 6But when Ahijah heard the sound of her feet, as she came in at the door, he said, "Come in, wife of Jeroboam; why do you pretend to be another? For I am charged with heavy tidings for you. 7Go, tell Jeroboam, 'Thus says the LORD, the God of Israel: Because I exalted you from among the people, made you leader over my people Israel, 8and tore the kingdom away from the house of David to give it to you; yet you have not been like my servant David, who kept my commandments and followed me with all his heart, doing only that which was right in my sight, 9but you have done evil above all those who were before you and have gone and made for yourself other gods, and cast images, provoking me to anger, and have thrust me behind your back; 10therefore, I will bring evil upon the house of Jeroboam. I will cut off from Jeroboam every male, both bond and free in Israel, and will consume the house of Jeroboam, just as one burns up dung until it is all gone. 11Anyone belonging to Jeroboam who dies in the city, the dogs shall eat; and anyone who dies in the open country, the birds of the air shall eat; for the LORD has spoken.' 12Therefore set out, go to your house. When your feet enter the city, the child shall

---

ᵃ Gk: Heb he came to the town of the old prophet

v. 28), is intended to dramatize the supernatural nature of the event. **13.30** The burial of the man of God in the old prophet's grave fulfills the judgment oracle in v. 22. **13.31–32** The incident demonstrates to the old prophet the truth of the words of the man of God, and the old prophet symbolically identifies himself with his colleague's message by requesting burial in the same grave. **13.33** On Jeroboam's nonlevitical priests, see note on 12.31.

14.1–18 This old legend, originally told to demonstrate the prophet's extraordinary powers, is used by the narrator as the occasion for a judgment oracle against the house of Jeroboam. **14.2** The use of a disguise may indicate that Jeroboam wanted to avoid a confrontation with Ahijah over the question of the king's religious ac-

tivities. On Ahijah's earlier contacts with Jeroboam, see 11.29–39. **14.3** The food was probably intended as a fee for the prophet's services. See also 1 Sam 9.1–21; 2 Kings 8.7–15. **14.4** The prophet's weak eyes are mentioned to demonstrate that his knowledge of his visitor's identity could only have come through divine revelation. **14.7–8** The beginning of the oracle implies that Jeroboam's kingship had been divinely instituted and that his dynasty could have been eternal if he had been obedient as David had been (see 11.29–39). **14.9** The comparison must be with Solomon, who also did what was evil in the sight of the Lord (11.6). For a description of Jeroboam's religious practices, see 12.26–32. **14.10–11** Parts of this graphic and somewhat crude judgment oracle are later reapplied to some of Jeroboam's successors (16.2–4;

die. 13All Israel shall mourn for him and bury him; for he alone of Jeroboam's family shall come to the grave, because in him there is found something pleasing to the LORD, the God of Israel, in the house of Jeroboam. 14Moreover the LORD will raise up for himself a king over Israel, who shall cut off the house of Jeroboam today, even right now!ᵃ

15 "The LORD will strike Israel, as a reed is shaken in the water; he will root up Israel out of this good land that he gave to their ancestors, and scatter them beyond the Euphrates, because they have made their sacred poles,ᵇ provoking the LORD to anger. 16He will give Israel up because of the sins of Jeroboam, which he sinned and which he caused Israel to commit."

17 Then Jeroboam's wife got up and went away, and she came to Tirzah. As she came to the threshold of the house, the child died. 18All Israel buried him and mourned for him, according to the word of the LORD, which he spoke by his servant the prophet Ahijah.

Death of Jeroboam

19 Now the rest of the acts of Jeroboam, how he warred and how he reigned, are written in the Book of the Annals of the Kings of Israel. 20The time that Jeroboam reigned was twenty-two years; then he slept with his ancestors, and his son Nadab succeeded him.

Rehoboam Reigns over Judah

21 Now Rehoboam son of Solomon reigned in Judah. Rehoboam was forty-one years old when he began to reign, and he reigned seventeen years in Jerusalem, the city that the LORD had chosen out of all the tribes of Israel, to put his name there. His mother's name was Naamah the Ammonite. 22Judah did what was evil in the sight of the LORD; they provoked him to jealousy with their sins that they committed, more than all that their ancestors had done. 23For they also built for themselves high places, pillars, and sacred polesᵇ on every high hill and under every green tree; 24there were also male temple prostitutes in the land. They committed all the abominations of the nations that the LORD drove out before the people of Israel.

25 In the fifth year of King Rehoboam, King Shishak of Egypt came up against Jerusalem; 26he took away the treasures of the house of the LORD and the treasures of the king's house; he took everything. He also took away all the shields of gold that Solomon had made; 27so King Rehoboam made shields of bronze instead, and committed them to the hands of the officers of the guard, who kept the door of the king's house. 28As often as the king went into the house of the LORD, the guard carried them and brought them back to the guardroom.

29 Now the rest of the acts of Rehoboam, and all that he did, are they not written in the Book of the Annals of the Kings of Judah? 30There was war between Rehoboam and Jeroboam continually. 31Rehoboam slept with his ancestors and was buried with his ancestors in the city of David. His mother's name was Naamah the Ammonite. His son Abijam succeeded him.

---

a Meaning of Heb uncertain b Heb *Asherim*

21.21–24). **14.15** This part of the oracle already envisions the exile and destruction of the whole Northern Kingdom (2 Kings 17.1–23), not just the end of Jeroboam's dynasty. *Sacred poles,* or *Asherim,* wooden cult objects associated with the worship of the Canaanite goddess Asherah, thought to be poles or perhaps representations of trees (cf. Deut 16.21). In second-millennium Syro-Palestine the goddess was portrayed as the consort of the god El, the head of the pantheon. By the OT period, however, she was considered the consort of the storm god Baal. In some circles in Israel she may have been part of the worship of the Lord. **14.16** By setting up illegitimate places of worship, Jeroboam provided an opportunity for Israel to sin. **14.17** Jeroboam had apparently moved his capital to *Tirzah* (cf. 12.25), located about seven miles northeast of Shechem. **14.19–20** The *Book of the Annals of the Kings of Israel* has not survived, but it was probably the source of some of the chronological data included in Kings. *Jeroboam* reigned ca. 922–901 BCE. **14.21–31** Although Rehoboam has already appeared in the narrative (ch. 12), this is a more systematic account of his reign. **14.21** *Rehoboam's* dates are uncertain, but he probably ruled ca. 922–915 BCE. **14.23** *High places.* See note on 3.2. *Pillars,* stones used to mark sacred spots. They were often associated with the worship of Baal. *Sacred poles.* See note on 14.15. **14.24** The word translated *prostitutes* simply means consecrated or sacred individuals (see also 15.12; 22.46; 2 Kings 23.7). Both men and women served in this capacity. They are usually thought to have engaged in some sort of sexual or licentious behavior in cultic contexts, but the exact nature of their activities is uncertain. **14.25** *Shishak.* See note on 11.40. **14.26** *Shields.* See notes on 10.16; 10.17. **14.29** *The Book of the Annals of the Kings of Judah* no longer exists, but it probably provided chronological information on the Judean kings (see Introduction).

Abijam Reigns over Judah: Idolatry and War

15 Now in the eighteenth year of King Jeroboam son of Nebat, Abijam began to reign over Judah. ²He reigned for three years in Jerusalem. His mother's name was Maacah daughter of Abishalom. ³He committed all the sins that his father did before him; his heart was not true to the LORD his God, like the heart of his father David. ⁴Nevertheless for David's sake the LORD his God gave him a lamp in Jerusalem, setting up his son after him, and establishing Jerusalem; ⁵because David did what was right in the sight of the LORD, and did not turn aside from anything that he commanded him all the days of his life, except in the matter of Uriah the Hittite. ⁶The war begun between Rehoboam and Jeroboam continued all the days of his life. ⁷The rest of the acts of Abijam, and all that he did, are they not written in the Book of the Annals of the Kings of Judah? There was war between Abijam and Jeroboam. ⁸Abijam slept with his ancestors, and they buried him in the city of David. Then his son Asa succeeded him.

Asa Reigns over Judah

9 In the twentieth year of King Jeroboam of Israel, Asa began to reign over Judah; ¹⁰he reigned forty-one years in Jerusalem. His mother's name was Maacah daughter of Abishalom. ¹¹Asa did what was right in the sight of the LORD, as his father David had done. ¹²He put away the male temple prostitutes out of the land, and removed all the idols that his ancestors had made. ¹³He also removed his mother Maacah from being queen mother, because she had made an abominable image for Asherah; Asa cut down her image and burned it at the Wadi Kidron. ¹⁴But the high places were not taken away. Nevertheless the heart of Asa was true to the LORD all his days. ¹⁵He brought into the house of the LORD the votive gifts of his father and his own votive gifts—silver, gold, and utensils.

Alliance with Aram against Israel

16 There was war between Asa and King Baasha of Israel all their days. ¹⁷King Baasha of Israel went up against Judah, and built Ramah, to prevent anyone from going out or coming in to King Asa of Judah. ¹⁸Then Asa took all the silver and the gold that were left in the treasures of the house of the LORD and the treasures of the king's house, and gave them into the hands of his servants. King Asa sent them to King Ben-hadad son of Tabrimmon son of Hezion of Aram, who resided in Damascus, saying, ¹⁹"Let there be an alliance between me and you, like that between my father and your father: I am sending you a present of silver and gold; go, break your alliance with King Baasha of Israel, so that he may withdraw from me." ²⁰Ben-hadad listened to King Asa, and sent the commanders of his armies

---

15.1–8 Abijam's brief reign receives a negative evaluation from the Deuteronomistic narrator, although no details of the king's crimes are mentioned. **15.1** *Abijam* reigned ca. 915–913 BCE. **15.4** *Lamp.* See note on 11.36. Because of God's fidelity to the promise to David (2 Sam 7.1–17), the Davidic dynasty is allowed to survive even though individual kings do evil. **15.5** The story of David and *Uriah the Hittite* is told in 2 Sam 11–12. **15.9–15** In contrast to his predecessor's, Asa's relatively long reign receives a positive evaluation from the Deuteronomistic narrator because of the king's religious reforms. **15.9** *Asa* reigned ca. 913–873 BCE. **15.10** According to this verse Asa and Abijam both had the same mother (cf. v. 2). This would make them brothers rather than father and son (v. 8). Alternatively, it may be that Maacah held the important post of queen mother but was not necessarily Asa's biological mother. 2 Chr 13.2 gives a different name for Abijam's mother, thus resolving the problem, but it is not clear which version of the genealogy is correct. **15.12** *Temple prostitutes.* See note on 14.24. **15.13** The nature of the *abominable image* is not indicated. *Asherah.* See note on 14.15. *Wadi Kidron.* See note on 2.37.

15.14 *High places.* See note on 3.2. **15.16–24** The war over the secession of the Northern tribes and the subsequent struggles over borders began in the days of Jeroboam and Rehoboam (14.30) and continued during the reigns of their successors (15.6). **15.16** Because of his interactions with Asa, *Baasha* of Israel is introduced into the narrative at this point, even though the official account of his reign does not appear until 15.33–16.7. **15.17** Baasha was able to extend his southern border to *Ramah* in the tribe of Benjamin. Ramah lay about five miles north of Jerusalem and was an ideal site for a fortress. **15.18** *Aram,* a state or confederation of states to the northeast of the Northern Kingdom in what is now Syria. Throughout much of the monarchical period Aram was engaged in a power struggle with Israel and Judah. Several Aramean kings bore the name *Ben-hadad.* This individual had a treaty relationship with Baasha of Israel (v. 19). **15.19** Asa is probably referring to relations between David and Solomon and the Arameans, which were certainly not peaceful (2 Sam 8.5–12; 1 Kings 11.23–25; 2 Chr 8.3–4). **15.20** These towns and the territories around them all lie on Israel's eastern border, and the Aramean en-

against the cities of Israel. He conquered Ijon, Dan, Abel-beth-maacah, and all Chinneroth, with all the land of Naphtali. 21When Baasha heard of it, he stopped building Ramah and lived in Tirzah. 22Then King Asa made a proclamation to all Judah, none was exempt: they carried away the stones of Ramah and its timber, with which Baasha had been building; with them King Asa built Geba of Benjamin and Mizpah. 23Now the rest of all the acts of Asa, all his power, all that he did, and the cities that he built, are they not written in the Book of the Annals of the Kings of Judah? But in his old age he was diseased in his feet. 24Then Asa slept with his ancestors, and was buried with his ancestors in the city of his father David; his son Jehoshaphat succeeded him.

Nadab Reigns over Israel

25 Nadab son of Jeroboam began to reign over Israel in the second year of King Asa of Judah; he reigned over Israel two years. 26He did what was evil in the sight of the LORD, walking in the way of his ancestor and in the sin that he caused Israel to commit.

27 Baasha son of Ahijah, of the house of Issachar, conspired against him; and Baasha struck him down at Gibbethon, which belonged to the Philistines; for Nadab and all Israel were laying siege to Gibbethon. 28So Baasha killed Nadab*a* in the third year of King Asa of Judah, and succeeded him. 29As soon as he was king, he killed all the house of Jeroboam; he left to the house of Jeroboam not one that breathed, until he had destroyed it, according to the word of the LORD that he spoke by his servant Ahijah the Shilonite— 30because of the sins of Jeroboam that he committed and

that he caused Israel to commit, and because of the anger to which he provoked the LORD, the God of Israel.

31 Now the rest of the acts of Nadab, and all that he did, are they not written in the Book of the Annals of the Kings of Israel? 32There was war between Asa and King Baasha of Israel all their days.

Second Dynasty: Baasha Reigns over Israel

33 In the third year of King Asa of Judah, Baasha son of Ahijah began to reign over all Israel at Tirzah; he reigned twenty-four years. 34He did what was evil in the sight of the LORD, walking in the way of Jeroboam and in the sin that he caused Israel to commit.

16 The word of the LORD came to Jehu son of Hanani against Baasha, saying, 2"Since I exalted you out of the dust and made you leader over my people Israel, and you have walked in the way of Jeroboam, and have caused my people Israel to sin, provoking me to anger with their sins, 3therefore, I will consume Baasha and his house, and I will make your house like the house of Jeroboam son of Nebat. 4Anyone belonging to Baasha who dies in the city the dogs shall eat; and anyone of his who dies in the field the birds of the air shall eat."

5 Now the rest of the acts of Baasha, what he did, and his power, are they not written in the Book of the Annals of the Kings of Israel? 6Baasha slept with his ancestors, and was buried at Tirzah; and his son Elah succeeded him. 7Moreover the word of the LORD came by the prophet Jehu son of Hanani against Baa-

---

a Heb *him*

---

croachment represents a significant loss of territory for the Northern Kingdom. **15.21** The combined pressure from Judah and Aram forces Baasha to abandon his border outpost and withdraw to the capital (see note on 14.17). **15.25–32** The narrator has little to say about Nadab's reign except to repeat the formulaic remark that he *did what was evil in the sight of the LORD, walking in the way* of Jeroboam. **15.25** *Nadab* ruled ca. 901–900 BCE. **15.27** *Gibbethon* lay in Philistine territory slightly beyond the southwestern border of Israel, so Nadab was apparently attempting to extend his kingdom in that direction. **15.29–30** The narrator quotes part of Ahijah's judgment oracle against Jeroboam and his descendants (14.10–11) and interprets Nadab's assassination as the fulfillment of the prophetic word. **15.33–16.7** The formal account of Baasha's twenty-four-year reign contains no further

information on his achievements. From the theological standpoint of the narrator, Baasha is simply another example of a Northern king who did evil by walking in the ways of Jeroboam. **15.33** *Baasha* reigned ca. 900–877 BCE. **16.1** *Jehu son of Hanani*, identified by Chronicles as a prophet active in Jerusalem during this period. He is also said to have delivered an oracle to king Jehoshaphat (2 Chr 19.2–3) and is credited with having written a history of Jehoshaphat's reign (2 Chr 20.34). Jehu's father, Hanani, was also a prophet and may have been the same individual who prophesied against Baasha's Southern contemporary, Asa (2 Chr 16.7–10). **16.4** Jehu's oracle is in part virtually identical with Ahijah's prophecy against Jeroboam (14.11). **16.7** This verse, which repeats the substance of vv. 2–4, seems out of place, coming as it does after Baasha's death has already been

sha and his house, both because of all the evil that he did in the sight of the LORD, provoking him to anger with the work of his hands, in being like the house of Jeroboam, and also because he destroyed it.

Elah Reigns over Israel

8 In the twenty-sixth year of King Asa of Judah, Elah son of Baasha began to reign over Israel in Tirzah; he reigned two years. 9But his servant Zimri, commander of half his chariots, conspired against him. When he was at Tirzah, drinking himself drunk in the house of Arza, who was in charge of the palace at Tirzah, 10Zimri came in and struck him down and killed him, in the twenty-seventh year of King Asa of Judah, and succeeded him.

11 When he began to reign, as soon as he had seated himself on his throne, he killed all the house of Baasha; he did not leave him a single male of his kindred or his friends. 12Thus Zimri destroyed all the house of Baasha, according to the word of the LORD, which he spoke against Baasha by the prophet Jehu— 13because of all the sins of Baasha and the sins of his son Elah that they committed, and that they caused Israel to commit, provoking the LORD God of Israel to anger with their idols. 14Now the rest of the acts of Elah, and all that he did, are they not written in the Book of the Annals of the Kings of Israel?

Third Dynasty: Zimri Reigns over Israel

15 In the twenty-seventh year of King Asa of Judah, Zimri reigned seven days in Tirzah. Now the troops were encamped against Gibbethon, which belonged to the Philistines, 16and the troops who were encamped heard it said, "Zimri has conspired, and he has killed the king"; therefore all Israel made Omri, the commander of the army, king over Israel that day in the camp. 17So Omri went up from Gibbethon, and all Israel with him, and they besieged Tirzah. 18When Zimri saw that the city was taken, he went into the citadel of the king's house; he burned down the king's house over himself with fire, and died— 19because of the sins that he committed, doing evil in the sight of the LORD, walking in the way of Jeroboam, and for the sin that he committed, causing Israel to sin. 20Now the rest of the acts of Zimri, and the conspiracy that he made, are they not written in the Book of the Annals of the Kings of Israel?

Fourth Dynasty: Omri Reigns over Israel

21 Then the people of Israel were divided into two parts; half of the people followed Tibni son of Ginath, to make him king, and half followed Omri. 22But the people who followed Omri overcame the people who followed Tibni son of Ginath; so Tibni died, and Omri became king. 23In the thirty-first year of King Asa of Judah, Omri began to reign over Israel; he reigned for twelve years, six of them in Tirzah.

Samaria the New Capital

24 He bought the hill of Samaria from Shemer for two talents of silver; he fortified the hill, and called the city that he built, Samaria, after the name of Shemer, the owner of the hill.

25 Omri did what was evil in the sight of the LORD; he did more evil than all who were before him. 26For he walked in all the way of Jeroboam son of Nebat, and in the sins that he caused Israel to commit, provoking the LORD, the God of Israel, to anger by their idols. 27Now the rest of the acts of Omri that he did, and the power that he showed, are they not written in the Book of the Annals of the Kings of Israel? 28Omri slept with his ancestors, and was buried in Samaria; his son Ahab succeeded him.

---

reported (v. 6). The narrator here condemns Baasha for destroying the house of Jeroboam, even though Baasha's action carried out God's decree of judgment.

16.8–14 The introduction to Elah's reign omits the customary negative evaluation, although an oblique reference is later made to his sins, along with those of his father (v. 13). The bulk of the account concentrates on the circumstances of Elah's death, which is characteristically interpreted as a judgment on the house of Baasha. As in the case of Jeroboam (14.10–11; 15.27–30), the prophetic judgment oracle is not fulfilled against the king to whom it is delivered but against his son. **16.8** Elah reigned ca. 877–876 BCE. **16.12** Another example of the narrator's interest in noting the fulfill-

ment of prophecies (see vv. 2–4). **16.15–20** The narrative of Zimri's brief reign is in fact simply an account of the aftermath of his coup against Elah. **16.15** On the significance of military activity at *Gibbethon*, see note on 15.27. **16.19** The Deuteronomistic narrator formulaically attributes Zimri's death to his sins, although it is difficult to know what he could have done in seven days. **16.21–23** Omri was one of Israel's most powerful rulers and one of the few whose name has been preserved in extrabiblical sources. The Moabite Stone credits him with capturing Moabite territory, and Assyrian sources continued to call Israel "the Land of Omri" long after his death. **16.23** Omri reigned ca. 876–869 BCE. **16.24–28** The only one of Omri's

Ahab Reigns over Israel

29 In the thirty-eighth year of King Asa of Judah, Ahab son of Omri began to reign over Israel; Ahab son of Omri reigned over Israel in Samaria twenty-two years. 30 Ahab son of Omri did evil in the sight of the LORD more than all who were before him.

Ahab Marries Jezebel and Worships Baal

31 And as if it had been a light thing for him to walk in the sins of Jeroboam son of Nebat, he took as his wife Jezebel daughter of King Ethbaal of the Sidonians, and went and served Baal, and worshiped him. 32 He erected an altar for Baal in the house of Baal, which he built in Samaria. 33 Ahab also made a sacred pole.[a] Ahab did more to provoke the anger of the LORD, the God of Israel, than had all the kings of Israel who were before him. 34 In his days Hiel of Bethel built Jericho; he laid its foundation at the cost of Abiram his firstborn, and set up its gates at the cost of his youngest son Segub, according to the word of the LORD, which he spoke by Joshua son of Nun.

Elijah Predicts a Drought

17 Now Elijah the Tishbite, of Tishbe[b] in Gilead, said to Ahab, "As the LORD the God of Israel lives, before whom I stand, there shall be neither dew nor rain these years, except by my word." 2 The word of the LORD came to him, saying, 3 "Go from here and turn eastward, and hide yourself by the Wadi Cherith, which is east of the Jordan. 4 You shall drink from the wadi, and I have commanded the ravens to feed you there." 5 So he went and did according to the word of the LORD; he went and lived by the Wadi Cherith, which is east of the Jordan. 6 The ravens brought him bread and meat in the morning, and bread and meat in the evening; and he drank from the wadi. 7 But after a while the wadi dried up, because there was no rain in the land.

The Widow of Zarephath

8 Then the word of the LORD came to him, saying, 9 "Go now to Zarephath, which belongs

a Heb Asherah   b Gk: Heb of the settlers

achievements mentioned by the narrator is the king's construction of a new capital at Samaria. **16.29–30** The narrator considers Ahab to be even more sinful than his predecessors, probably because of his introduction of the worship of Baal into Israel. **16.29** Ahab reigned ca. 869–850 BCE. **16.31–34** Just as Solomon was led to sin because of his foreign marriages (ch. 11), so also Ahab's marriage to a Phoenician princess increases the already fatal sins of the Northern Kingdom. **16.31** *Baal,* the Canaanite storm god who provided the rain necessary for the fertility of the land. His worship was widespread in Canaan and had probably infiltrated Israel long before the time of Ahab. Ahab, however, gave the Baal cult official status in the capital. **16.33** *Sacred pole.* See note on 14.15. **16.34** This verse notes the working out of Joshua's curse when the Israelites destroyed Jericho (Josh 6.26). The narrator apparently sees in the event an analogy to the fulfillment of prophecy.

17.1–7 The first of a series of stories concerning prophetic opposition to the Omride dynasty and to the worship of the Phoenician Baal, which King Ahab had introduced into Israel (1 Kings 17–2 Kings 10). Before being incorporated into the book of Kings, many of the stories probably circulated orally in Northern prophetic circles, and the Elijah and Elisha stories may have already been gathered into collections before being written down. Many of the stories focus on the miraculous deeds of the prophets and glorify both the prophets themselves and the God they represent. The writer of Kings has modified some of the stories in order to make them conform to Deuteronomic theology, but many non-Deuteronomic ele-

ments still remain. In general the stories dramatize a central theme of the book: the inevitable destruction of the evil Northern kings and the victory of the Lord over Baal. **17.1** The opening of the first Elijah story seems abrupt, but it must be seen against the background of Ahab's introduction of Baal worship (16.31–33). According to the mythology of the Baal cult, the storm god was responsible for bringing life-giving rains at certain times of the year and thus restoring fertility to the land. After the yearly rainy season, the ground got progressively dryer, and eventually all vegetation died. During this period Baal was thought to be in the power of the god of death and sterility. In this verse Elijah announces that the yearly alternation between life and death is an illusion and that Baal has nothing to do with bringing rain and fertility. In reality the Lord controls both rain and drought, fertility and sterility, and life and death. To illustrate the point, the prophet announces that God has decreed a three-year drought. *Tishbe.* Meaning uncertain. The Greek translators understood it as the name of the otherwise unknown town from which Elijah came. The Hebrew seems to require the translation "of the settlers." *Gilead,* a mountainous region of Transjordan (modern Jordan) between Bashan and Moab (see note on 2 Kings 15.25) near the eastern boundary of the Northern Kingdom. **17.3** *Wadi Cherith.* Location unknown. The journey *east of the Jordan* probably removes Elijah from Ahab's jurisdiction. **17.4** Although God denies rain to apostate Israel, the faithful prophet is provided with both water and food. **17.7** *Wadi,* a stream bed that contains water only

to Sidon, and live there; for I have commanded a widow there to feed you." ¹⁰So he set out and went to Zarephath. When he came to the gate of the town, a widow was there gathering sticks; he called to her and said, "Bring me a little water in a vessel, so that I may drink." ¹¹As she was going to bring it, he called to her and said, "Bring me a morsel of bread in your hand." ¹²But she said, "As the LORD your God lives, I have nothing baked, only a handful of meal in a jar, and a little oil in a jug; I am now gathering a couple of sticks, so that I may go home and prepare it for myself and my son, that we may eat it, and die." ¹³Elijah said to her, "Do not be afraid; go and do as you have said; but first make me a little cake of it and bring it to me, and afterwards make something for yourself and your son. ¹⁴For thus says the LORD the God of Israel: The jar of meal will not be emptied and the jug of oil will not fail until the day that the LORD sends rain on the earth." ¹⁵She went and did as Elijah said, so that she as well as he and her household ate for many days. ¹⁶The jar of meal was not emptied, neither did the jug of oil fail, according to the word of the LORD that he spoke by Elijah.

Elijah Revives the Widow's Son

17 After this the son of the woman, the mistress of the house, became ill; his illness was so severe that there was no breath left in him. ¹⁸She then said to Elijah, "What have you against me, O man of God? You have come to me to bring my sin to remembrance, and to cause the death of my son!" ¹⁹But he said to her, "Give me your son." He took him from her bosom, carried him up into the upper chamber where he was lodging, and laid him on his own bed. ²⁰He cried out to the LORD, "O LORD my God, have you brought calamity even upon the widow with whom I am staying, by killing her son?" ²¹Then he stretched himself upon the child three times, and cried out to the LORD, "O LORD my God, let this child's life come into him again." ²²The LORD listened to the voice of Elijah; the life of the child came into him again, and he revived. ²³Elijah took the child, brought him down from the upper chamber into the house, and gave him to his mother; then Elijah said, "See, your son is alive." ²⁴So the woman said to Elijah, "Now I know that you are a man of God, and that the word of the LORD in your mouth is truth."

Elijah's Message to Ahab

18 After many days the word of the LORD came to Elijah, in the third year of the drought,ᵃ saying, "Go, present yourself to Ahab; I will send rain on the earth." ²So Elijah went to present himself to Ahab. The famine was severe in Samaria. ³Ahab summoned Obadiah, who was in charge of the palace. (Now Obadiah revered the LORD greatly; ⁴when Jezebel was killing off the prophets of the LORD, Obadiah took a hundred prophets, hid them fifty to a cave, and provided them with bread and water.) ⁵Then Ahab said to Obadiah, "Go through the land to all the springs of water and to all the wadis; perhaps we may find grass to keep the horses and mules alive, and not lose some of the animals." ⁶So they divided the land between them to pass through it; Ahab went in one direction by himself, and Obadiah went in another direction by himself.

7 As Obadiah was on the way, Elijah met him; Obadiah recognized him, fell on his face, and said, "Is it you, my lord Elijah?" ⁸He answered him, "It is I. Go, tell your lord that Elijah

---

a Heb lacks *of the drought*

---

in the rainy season. **17.8–16** This prophetic legend originally focused on the prophet's ability to perform miracles. However, in its present context it provides another example of God's care for Elijah and for all faithful Israelites who support him. Cf. the similar tale involving Elisha in 2 Kings 4.1–7. **17.9** The journey to *Zarephath* on the Phoenician coast south of *Sidon* takes the prophet into the heartland of the Baal cult (cf. 16.31). Even here God's power over sterility and fertility is evident. **17.10** *Widows* often had no means of economic support; if they were not sustained by the king or the religious community (cf. Deut 14.28–29), they were quickly reduced to poverty and forced to become scavengers and beggars. **17.17–24** Although this

story of the resurrection of the widow's son serves to demonstrate Elijah's ability to mediate divine power, the account also provides a third dramatic example of God's control over life and death. A similar story is told about Elisha (2 Kings 4.18–37). **17.21** *Three* often figures prominently in rituals.

18.1–19 This account of Ahab's efforts to cope with the drought provides an introduction to one of the most famous of the Elijah stories, the contest with the prophets of Baal on Mount Carmel (vv. 20–40). **18.1** This verse has its counterpart in 17.1. Just as God, not Baal, controls drought (17.1), so also God, not Baal, provides rain. According to the terms of the oath in 17.1, only Elijah's word can end the drought, and he

is here." 9And he said, "How have I sinned, that you would hand your servant over to Ahab, to kill me? 10As the LORD your God lives, there is no nation or kingdom to which my lord has not sent to seek you; and when they would say, 'He is not here,' he would require an oath of the kingdom or nation, that they had not found you. 11But now you say, 'Go, tell your lord that Elijah is here.' 12As soon as I have gone from you, the spirit of the LORD will carry you I know not where; so, when I come and tell Ahab and he cannot find you, he will kill me, although I your servant have revered the LORD from my youth. 13Has it not been told my lord what I did when Jezebel killed the prophets of the LORD, how I hid a hundred of the LORD's prophets fifty to a cave, and provided them with bread and water? 14Yet now you say, 'Go, tell your lord that Elijah is here'; he will surely kill me." 15Elijah said, "As the LORD of hosts lives, before whom I stand, I will surely show myself to him today." 16So Obadiah went to meet Ahab, and told him; and Ahab went to meet Elijah.

17 When Ahab saw Elijah, Ahab said to him, "Is it you, you troubler of Israel?" 18He answered, "I have not troubled Israel; but you have, and your father's house, because you have forsaken the commandments of the LORD and followed the Baals. 19Now therefore have all Israel assemble for me at Mount Carmel, with the four hundred fifty prophets of Baal and the four hundred prophets of Asherah, who eat at Jezebel's table."

Elijah's Triumph over the Priests of Baal

20 So Ahab sent to all the Israelites, and assembled the prophets at Mount Carmel. 21Elijah then came near to all the people, and said, "How long will you go limping with two different opinions? If the LORD is God, follow him; but if Baal, then follow him." The people did not answer him a word. 22Then Elijah said to the people, "I, even I only, am left a prophet of the LORD; but Baal's prophets number four hundred fifty. 23Let two bulls be given to us; let them choose one bull for themselves, cut it in pieces, and lay it on the wood, but put no fire to it; I will prepare the other bull and lay it on the wood, but put no fire to it. 24Then you call on the name of your god and I will call on the name of the LORD; the god who answers by fire is indeed God." All the people answered, "Well spoken!" 25Then Elijah said to the prophets of Baal, "Choose for yourselves one bull and prepare it first, for you are many; then call on the name of your god, but put no fire to it." 26So they took the bull that was given them, prepared it, and called on the name of Baal from morning until noon, crying, "O Baal, answer us!" But there was no voice, and no answer. They limped about the altar that they had made. 27At noon Elijah mocked them, saying, "Cry aloud! Surely he is a god; either he is meditating, or he has wandered away, or he is on a journey, or perhaps he is asleep and must be awakened." 28Then they cried aloud and, as was their custom, they cut themselves with swords and lances until the blood gushed out over them. 29As midday passed, they raved on until the time of the offering of the oblation, but there was no voice, no answer, and no response.

30 Then Elijah said to all the people, "Come closer to me"; and all the people came

---

must at last confront Ahab. **18.12** For a dramatic example of the Lord carrying Elijah away, see 2 Kings 2.11. **18.17** Ahab greets Elijah as *troubler of Israel* because he decreed the three-year drought (17.1). **18.18** The prophet's rejoinder locates the problem with Ahab's institution of Baal worship in Israel. Elijah's use of the plural, *Baals,* is due to the fact that local manifestations of the Canaanite god were sometimes considered independent deities in their own right. **18.19** *Mount Carmel* lies in western Israel at the entrance of the Jezreel Valley. The *four hundred prophets of Asherah* do not appear again in the story. For Asherah, see note on 14.15. Both groups of prophets were part of the royal court. **18.20–40** The contest with the prophets of Baal demonstrates conclusively that there is only one true God in Israel and that that God, not Baal, is responsible for the fertility of the land. **18.21** *Limping.* Meaning uncertain. There is no doubt, however, about the sense of Elijah's question. **18.22** Elijah's claim to be the only remaining prophet of the Lord is an exaggeration for rhetorical effect (see v. 13). **18.24** As a storm god, Baal should have been able to supply fire in the form of lightning. Fire is also often associated with the Lord (see, e.g., Gen 15.17; Ex 14.24; 19.18; Deut 4.11; 5.22–24; Isa 30.27). **18.26** *Limped,* probably some sort of ritual dance (see also v. 21). **18.27** Elijah's taunts mock various aspects of the Baal cult. *Meditating,* perhaps having other things on his mind. *Wandering away,* perhaps a euphemism for taking care of bodily functions. *Journey.* During the dry season Baal travels to the underworld. *Asleep.* Part of the worship of Baal may have involved rituals to waken the god when he was in the power of death. See also note on 17.1. **18.28** Mourners often *cut* themselves during funeral rites, and Baal worshipers may have done the same in an attempt to release the

closer to him. First he repaired the altar of the LORD that had been thrown down; [31]Elijah took twelve stones, according to the number of the tribes of the sons of Jacob, to whom the word of the LORD came, saying, "Israel shall be your name"; [32]with the stones he built an altar in the name of the LORD. Then he made a trench around the altar, large enough to contain two measures of seed. [33]Next he put the wood in order, cut the bull in pieces, and laid it on the wood. He said, "Fill four jars with water and pour it on the burnt offering and on the wood." [34]Then he said, "Do it a second time"; and they did it a second time. Again he said, "Do it a third time"; and they did it a third time, [35]so that the water ran all around the altar, and filled the trench also with water.

[36] At the time of the offering of the oblation, the prophet Elijah came near and said, "O LORD, God of Abraham, Isaac, and Israel, let it be known this day that you are God in Israel, that I am your servant, and that I have done all these things at your bidding. [37]Answer me, O LORD, answer me, so that this people may know that you, O LORD, are God, and that you have turned their hearts back." [38]Then the fire of the LORD fell and consumed the burnt offering, the wood, the stones, and the dust, and even licked up the water that was in the trench. [39]When all the people saw it, they fell on their faces and said, "The LORD indeed is God; the LORD indeed is God." [40]Elijah said to them, "Seize the prophets of Baal; do not let one of them escape." Then they seized them; and Elijah brought them down to the Wadi Kishon, and killed them there.

The Drought Ends

[41] Elijah said to Ahab, "Go up, eat and drink; for there is a sound of rushing rain." [42]So Ahab went up to eat and to drink. Elijah went up to the top of Carmel; there he bowed himself down upon the earth and put his face between his knees. [43]He said to his servant, "Go up now, look toward the sea." He went up and looked, and said, "There is nothing." Then he said, "Go again seven times." [44]At the seventh time he said, "Look, a little cloud no bigger than a person's hand is rising out of the sea." Then he said, "Go say to Ahab, 'Harness your chariot and go down before the rain stops you.'" [45]In a little while the heavens grew black with clouds and wind; there was a heavy rain. Ahab rode off and went to Jezreel. [46]But the hand of the LORD was on Elijah; he girded up his loins and ran in front of Ahab to the entrance of Jezreel.

Elijah Flees from Jezebel

19 Ahab told Jezebel all that Elijah had done, and how he had killed all the prophets with the sword. [2]Then Jezebel sent a messenger to Elijah, saying, "So may the gods do to me, and more also, if I do not make your life like the life of one of them by this time tomorrow." [3]Then he was afraid; he got up and fled for his life, and came to Beer-sheba, which belongs to Judah; he left his servant there.

[4] But he himself went a day's journey into the wilderness, and came and sat down under a solitary broom tree. He asked that he might die: "It is enough; now, O LORD, take away my life, for I am no better than my ancestors."

god from the power of death (Lev 19.28; Deut 14.1; Jer 16.6; 41.5; 47.5; Hos 7.14). **18.29** *Oblation,* an offering made around sunset (Ex 29.39). **18.32** The significance of the *two measures of seed* is unclear. **18.34** Note again the number three in ritual contexts (cf. 17.21). The water probably serves to both symbolize the rain that is coming and underscore the decisiveness of God's response. **18.40** Elijah executes the prophets in accordance with the Deuteronomic law prescribing death as the penalty for prophets who advocate the worship of other gods (Deut 13.1–5). The *Wadi Kishon* runs between Mount Carmel and the Galilean hills. **18.41–46** Now that the people have acknowledged that there is only one God in Israel (v. 39), Elijah speaks the word to end the drought (cf. 17.1). **18.41** Although there is still no sign of rain, Elijah knows that it is coming (v. 1), and he instructs Ahab to begin celebrating the end of the drought. **18.42–**

44 The purpose of Elijah's ritual is unclear. **18.45** In addition to a palace in the capital (Samaria), Ahab also had a royal residence in the town of *Jezreel* at the foot of Mount Gilboa (21.1). **18.46** Possessed by God's spirit, Elijah runs about seventeen miles to Jezreel in front of Ahab's chariot.

19.1–18 Elijah's efforts to flee from Jezebel's wrath inadvertently lead him to reverse Israel's journey through the wilderness until he arrives at Mount Horeb (Sinai), the sacred spot where Israel's covenant with God was first made (Ex 19–34). Throughout the narrative there are a number of allusions to Moses, and it is clear that for the Deuteronomistic narrator Elijah is to be considered a prophet "like Moses" (Deut 18.9–22). **19.3** *Beer-sheba,* a city in the northern Negeb desert, marks the traditional southern boundary of Judah, so Elijah is well beyond Jezebel's reach. **19.4** Like Moses before him, Elijah felt that he was not

⁵Then he lay down under the broom tree and fell asleep. Suddenly an angel touched him and said to him, "Get up and eat." ⁶He looked, and there at his head was a cake baked on hot stones, and a jar of water. He ate and drank, and lay down again. ⁷The angel of the LORD came a second time, touched him, and said, "Get up and eat, otherwise the journey will be too much for you." ⁸He got up, and ate and drank; then he went in the strength of that food forty days and forty nights to Horeb the mount of God. ⁹At that place he came to a cave, and spent the night there.

Then the word of the LORD came to him, saying, "What are you doing here, Elijah?" ¹⁰He answered, "I have been very zealous for the LORD, the God of hosts; for the Israelites have forsaken your covenant, thrown down your altars, and killed your prophets with the sword. I alone am left, and they are seeking my life, to take it away."

Elijah Meets God at Horeb

11 He said, "Go out and stand on the mountain before the LORD, for the LORD is about to pass by." Now there was a great wind, so strong that it was splitting mountains and breaking rocks in pieces before the LORD, but the LORD was not in the wind; and after the wind an earthquake, but the LORD was not in the earthquake; ¹²and after the earthquake a fire, but the LORD was not in the fire; and after the fire a sound of sheer silence. ¹³When Elijah heard it, he wrapped his face in his mantle and went

out and stood at the entrance of the cave. Then there came a voice to him that said, "What are you doing here, Elijah?" ¹⁴He answered, "I have been very zealous for the LORD, the God of hosts; for the Israelites have forsaken your covenant, thrown down your altars, and killed your prophets with the sword. I alone am left, and they are seeking my life, to take it away." ¹⁵Then the LORD said to him, "Go, return on your way to the wilderness of Damascus; when you arrive, you shall anoint Hazael as king over Aram. ¹⁶Also you shall anoint Jehu son of Nimshi as king over Israel; and you shall anoint Elisha son of Shaphat of Abel-meholah as prophet in your place. ¹⁷Whoever escapes from the sword of Hazael, Jehu shall kill; and whoever escapes from the sword of Jehu, Elisha shall kill. ¹⁸Yet I will leave seven thousand in Israel, all the knees that have not bowed to Baal, and every mouth that has not kissed him."

Elisha Becomes Elijah's Disciple

19 So he set out from there, and found Elisha son of Shaphat, who was plowing. There were twelve yoke of oxen ahead of him, and he was with the twelfth. Elijah passed by him and threw his mantle over him. ²⁰He left the oxen, ran after Elijah, and said, "Let me kiss my father and my mother, and then I will follow you." Then Elijah[a] said to him, "Go back again; for what have I done to you?" ²¹He returned

a Heb he

---

up to the task of providing religious leadership for Israel (cf. Num 11.11–15). **19.8** Elijah's journey of *forty days and forty nights* recalls Israel's forty-year sojourn in the wilderness and also the forty days and nights that Moses spent at Sinai, where he did not eat or drink until he had written down the words of God's covenant (Ex 34.27–28). **19.9** *Cave*, perhaps an allusion to be the cleft in the rock where Moses was shielded from God's glory (Ex 33.17–23). **19.10** Elijah's state of depression causes him to exaggerate the problem. There are certainly faithful worshipers of the Lord left in Israel, and Elijah is not the only remaining prophet (17.24; 18.3–4). **19.11–12** *Wind, earthquake,* and *fire* were traditionally associated with God (Ex 19.16; 20.18; Deut 4.11; 5.22–24; Judg 5.4–5; Isa 30.27; Nah 1.3–5; Ps 18.11–15; 68.7–8), but for the Deuteronomistic narrator, God is not to be identified with these natural phenomena. *Sound of sheer silence,* uncertain. This translation suggests that no new revelation followed the appearance of the wind, earthquake, and fire, for the text does not indicate that God was in the silence either. Other renderings are "a gentle little

breeze," "the sound of a light whisper," and the traditional "still small voice." The latter two translations suggest that some sort of verbal revelation did take place. **19.13a** Elijah does not leave the safety of the cave until after the storm, which he heard but did not see. **19.14** Whatever the import of the storm and the silence, the events apparently made no impression on the prophet, who simply repeats his earlier answer (v. 10). **19.15** This time God's response is to issue a new prophetic commission. *Wilderness of Damascus,* the Syrian desert. Elijah's successor, Elisha, actually legitimizes *Hazael* as ruler of *Aram* (Syria; 2 Kings 8.7–15). The command to anoint a foreign ruler indicates God's control over political affairs outside Israel. **19.16** Elisha also anoints *Jehu,* who finally overthrows the dynasty of Omri and wipes out Baal worship in Israel (2 Kings 9–10). **19.18** Kissing the image or symbol of Baal was apparently a common act of worship (Hos 13.2). **19.19–21** Almost immediately Elijah fulfills the third of God's commands (v. 16). **19.19** Elijah does not actually anoint Elisha, but the meaning of his symbolic act is clear. **19.20** Elisha's request indicates that he does

from following him, took the yoke of oxen, and slaughtered them; using the equipment from the oxen, he boiled their flesh, and gave it to the people, and they ate. Then he set out and followed Elijah, and became his servant.

Ahab's Wars with the Arameans

20 King Ben-hadad of Aram gathered all his army together; thirty-two kings were with him, along with horses and chariots. He marched against Samaria, laid siege to it, and attacked it. 2Then he sent messengers into the city to King Ahab of Israel, and said to him: "Thus says Ben-hadad: 3Your silver and gold are mine; your fairest wives and children also are mine." 4The king of Israel answered, "As you say, my lord, O king, I am yours, and all that I have." 5The messengers came again and said: "Thus says Ben-hadad: I sent to you, saying, 'Deliver to me your silver and gold, your wives and children'; 6nevertheless I will send my servants to you tomorrow about this time, and they shall search your house and the houses of your servants, and lay hands on whatever pleases them,*a* and take it away."

7 Then the king of Israel called all the elders of the land, and said, "Look now! See how this man is seeking trouble; for he sent to me for my wives, my children, my silver, and my gold; and I did not refuse him." 8Then all the elders and all the people said to him, "Do not listen or consent." 9So he said to the messengers of Ben-hadad, "Tell my lord the king: All that you first demanded of your servant I will do; but this thing I cannot do." The messengers left and brought him word again. 10Ben-hadad sent to him and said, "The gods do so to me, and more also, if the dust of Samaria will provide a handful for each of the people who follow me." 11The king of Israel answered, "Tell him: One who puts on armor should not brag like one who takes it off." 12When Ben-hadad heard this message—now he had been drinking with the kings in the booths—he said to his men, "Take your positions!" And they took their positions against the city.

Prophetic Opposition to Ahab

13 Then a certain prophet came up to King Ahab of Israel and said, "Thus says the LORD, Have you seen all this great multitude? Look, I will give it into your hand today; and you shall know that I am the LORD." 14Ahab said, "By whom?" He said, "Thus says the LORD, By the young men who serve the district governors." Then he said, "Who shall begin the battle?" He answered, "You." 15Then he mustered the young men who served the district governors, two hundred thirty-two; after them he mustered all the people of Israel, seven thousand.

16 They went out at noon, while Ben-hadad was drinking himself drunk in the booths, he and the thirty-two kings allied with him. 17The young men who served the district governors went out first. Ben-hadad had sent out scouts,*b* and they reported to him, "Men have come out from Samaria." 18He said, "If they have come out for peace, take them alive; if they have come out for war, take them alive."

19 But these had already come out of the city: the young men who served the district governors, and the army that followed them. 20Each killed his man; the Arameans fled and Israel pursued them, but King Ben-hadad of Aram escaped on a horse with the cavalry. 21The king of Israel went out, attacked the horses and chariots, and defeated the Arameans with a great slaughter.

22 Then the prophet approached the king of Israel and said to him, "Come, strengthen

---

a Gk Syr Vg: Heb *you*   *b* Heb lacks *scouts*

---

not yet have the determination to be Elijah's successor. Elijah's response suggests that he wants nothing to do with disciples who are not completely focused on the task at hand. **19.21** The slaughter of the animals is an irrevocable act indicating that Elisha is willing to make a decisive break with his past life.

20.1–12 The first of several stories set against the background of Israel's wars with Aram (modern Syria). After being subdued by David (2 Sam 8.5–12), the Arameans began to harass Israel during Solomon's reign (11.23–25) and continued to do so intermittently thereafter. **20.1** On *Ben-hadad*'s earlier interactions with Israel, see 15.18–21. **20.6** Ben-hadad's second demand would have allowed the Arameans to take anything they wanted from the royal palace. **20.11** Ahab's reply quotes a proverb warning Ben-hadad not to be too confident about the outcome of the battle. **20.12** *Booths,* temporary shelters in which the army lived in the field. **20.13–22** This part of the narrative is unusual in that it indicates prophetic support for Ahab rather than the opposition that characterizes most of the stories about his reign. **20.16** *Kings,* rulers of individual cities. **20.20–21** Israel's decisive victory against superior forces indicates that God supplied divine aid. **20.22** Spring was the traditional time for beginning a military campaign (2 Sam 11.1).

yourself, and consider well what you have to do; for in the spring the king of Aram will come up against you."

The Arameans Are Defeated

23 The servants of the king of Aram said to him, "Their gods are gods of the hills, and so they were stronger than we; but let us fight against them in the plain, and surely we shall be stronger than they. 24Also do this: remove the kings, each from his post, and put commanders in place of them; 25and muster an army like the army that you have lost, horse for horse, and chariot for chariot; then we will fight against them in the plain, and surely we shall be stronger than they." He heeded their voice, and did so.

26 In the spring Ben-hadad mustered the Arameans and went up to Aphek to fight against Israel. 27After the Israelites had been mustered and provisioned, they went out to engage them; the people of Israel encamped opposite them like two little flocks of goats, while the Arameans filled the country. 28A man of God approached and said to the king of Israel, "Thus says the LORD: Because the Arameans have said, 'The LORD is a god of the hills but he is not a god of the valleys,' therefore I will give all this great multitude into your hand, and you shall know that I am the LORD." 29They encamped opposite one another seven days. Then on the seventh day the battle began; the Israelites killed one hundred thousand Aramean foot soldiers in one day. 30The rest fled into the city of Aphek; and the wall fell on twenty-seven thousand men that were left.

Ben-hadad also fled, and entered the city to hide. 31His servants said to him, "Look, we have heard that the kings of the house of Israel are merciful kings; let us put sackcloth around our waists and ropes on our heads, and go out to the king of Israel; perhaps he will spare your life." 32So they tied sackcloth around their waists, put ropes on their heads, went to the king of Israel, and said, "Your servant Ben-hadad says, 'Please let me live.' " And he said, "Is he still alive? He is my brother." 33Now the men were watching for an omen; they quickly took it up from him and said, "Yes, Ben-hadad is your brother." Then he said, "Go and bring him." So Ben-hadad came out to him; and he had him come up into the chariot. 34Ben-hadad[a] said to him, "I will restore the towns that my father took from your father; and you may establish bazaars for yourself in Damascus, as my father did in Samaria." The king of Israel responded,[b] "I will let you go on those terms." So he made a treaty with him and let him go.

A Prophet Condemns Ahab

35 At the command of the LORD a certain member of a company of prophets[c] said to another, "Strike me!" But the man refused to strike him. 36Then he said to him, "Because you have not obeyed the voice of the LORD, as soon as you have left me, a lion will kill you." And when he had left him, a lion met him and killed him. 37Then he found another man and said, "Strike me!" So the man hit him, striking and wounding him. 38Then the prophet departed, and waited for the king along the road,

---

a Heb *He*   *b* Heb lacks *The king of Israel responded*   *c* Heb *of the sons of the prophets*

20.23–34 The second engagement between Israel and Aram is treated as an example of a religious war, which should have been conducted according to the regulations laid down in Deut 20. From the perspective of the narrator the spoil should have been devoted to the deity, and the enemy should have been killed. **20.23** The Aramean civil servants assume that because Israel's God is often associated with mountains (Sinai), the Lord's power is restricted to mountain areas. Readers already know that God's power extends beyond Israel's national boundaries (19.15). **20.24** *Commanders,* probably Benhadad's own officials, who are thus thought to be more professional and strongly motivated than the *kings,* who as semi-independent rulers are looking out for their own interests. **20.26** Several towns bear the name *Aphek,* but the one mentioned here probably lies about three miles east of the Sea of Galilee. **20.28** *Man of God.*

See note on 13.1. **20.31** *Sackcloth,* a dark-colored cloth of goats' hair or camels' hair originally used to make grain sacks. Made into a garment, it was worn in times of mourning or national distress (Gen 37.34; 2 Sam 3.31; Lam 2.10). It was also worn by captives as a sign of submission. **20.32** *Brother,* a term used in treaties to indicate that the parties involved are of equal status. **20.35–43** Although Ahab may see his victory as an opportunity to regain lost territory and establish peace, the prophet in this story sees the outcome as a violation of the terms of the religious war (Deut 20). For a similar story involving Saul and Samuel, see 1 Sam 15. **20.35** *Company of prophets,* one of the prophetic guilds that were active in Israel during this period. The striking was apparently intended to make the prophet look as if he had been in a battle. **20.38** The *bandage* is sometimes thought to have covered a distinctive mark on the fore-

disguising himself with a bandage over his eyes. 39As the king passed by, he cried to the king and said, "Your servant went out into the thick of the battle; then a soldier turned and brought a man to me, and said, 'Guard this man; if he is missing, your life shall be given for his life, or else you shall pay a talent of silver.' 40While your servant was busy here and there, he was gone." The king of Israel said to him, "So shall your judgment be; you yourself have decided it." 41Then he quickly took the bandage away from his eyes. The king of Israel recognized him as one of the prophets. 42Then he said to him, "Thus says the LORD, 'Because you have let the man go whom I had devoted to destruction, therefore your life shall be for his life, and your people for his people.' " 43The king of Israel set out toward home, resentful and sullen, and came to Samaria.

Naboth's Vineyard

21 Later the following events took place: Naboth the Jezreelite had a vineyard in Jezreel, beside the palace of King Ahab of Samaria. 2And Ahab said to Naboth, "Give me your vineyard, so that I may have it for a vegetable garden, because it is near my house; I will give you a better vineyard for it; or, if it seems good to you, I will give you its value in money." 3But Naboth said to Ahab, "The LORD forbid that I should give you my ancestral inheritance." 4Ahab went home resentful and sullen because of what Naboth the Jezreelite had said to him; for he had said, "I will not give you my ancestral inheritance." He lay down on his bed, turned away his face, and would not eat.

5His wife Jezebel came to him and said, "Why are you so depressed that you will not eat?" 6He said to her, "Because I spoke to Naboth the Jezreelite and said to him, 'Give me your vineyard for money; or else, if you prefer, I will give you another vineyard for it'; but he answered, 'I will not give you my vineyard.' " 7His wife Jezebel said to him, "Do you now govern Israel? Get up, eat some food, and be cheerful; I will give you the vineyard of Naboth the Jezreelite."

8So she wrote letters in Ahab's name and sealed them with his seal; she sent the letters to the elders and the nobles who lived with Naboth in his city. 9She wrote in the letters, "Proclaim a fast, and seat Naboth at the head of the assembly; 10seat two scoundrels opposite him, and have them bring a charge against him, saying, 'You have cursed God and the king.' Then take him out, and stone him to death." 11The men of his city, the elders and the nobles who lived in his city, did as Jezebel had sent word to them. Just as it was written in the letters that she had sent to them, 12they proclaimed a fast and seated Naboth at the head of the assembly. 13The two scoundrels came in and sat opposite him; and the scoundrels brought a charge against Naboth, in the presence of the people, saying, "Naboth cursed God and the king." So they took him outside the city, and stoned him to death. 14Then they sent to Jezebel, saying, "Naboth has been stoned; he is dead."

15 As soon as Jezebel heard that Naboth had been stoned and was dead, Jezebel said to Ahab, "Go, take possession of the vineyard of Naboth the Jezreelite, which he refused to give you for

head of prophetic guild members. **20.39–40** This "juridical parable" is designed to trap the hearer into announcing the punishment for his own crime (see also 2 Sam 12.1–12). *Talent.* See note on 9.14.

21.1–16 Like the story of David, Uriah, and Bathsheba (2 Sam 11.1–12.25), this narrative probes the question of the limits of royal power. Unlike the other stories about Elijah and Ahab, where the underlying issue is religious apostasy, this story focuses on the king's willingness to violate individual rights. Elsewhere in the ancient Near East, monarchs had, or sought to have, absolute control over their subjects. As this story illustrates, however, such control was never an ideal in Israel, where the king was never above the law and was always subject to divine judgment. **21.1** Jeroboam had built a second palace in the town of Jezreel, where he lived when he was not in the capital in Samaria (see 18.45–46). **21.3** Israelites normally tried

to prevent inherited property from passing out of the family, although there were no legal barriers against land sales. According to some legal traditions, however, land could not be sold in perpetuity but had to revert eventually to its original owner (Lev 25.8–17, 23–25; 27.16–25). **21.4** Ahab is *resentful and sullen* not just because he does not get his way but because Naboth's oath (v. 3) precludes the possibility of further negotiations. **21.8** This verse seems to imply that Ahab has returned to Samaria. **21.9** Naboth is to be seated with the leaders of the people, but he is not by himself their head. **21.10** In Deuteronomic law two witnesses were required for conviction (Deut 17.6–7; 19.15; cf. Num 35.30), and there were severe penalties for giving false testimony (Ex 20.16; Deut 5.20; 19.16–21). For the prohibitions against cursing God or the king, see Ex 22.28; Lev 24.14–16. **21.15** The property of executed criminals may have been forfeited to the king, or Na-

money; for Naboth is not alive, but dead." 16 As soon as Ahab heard that Naboth was dead, Ahab set out to go down to the vineyard of Naboth the Jezreelite, to take possession of it.

Elijah Pronounces God's Sentence

17 Then the word of the LORD came to Elijah the Tishbite, saying: 18 Go down to meet King Ahab of Israel, who rules*a* in Samaria; he is now in the vineyard of Naboth, where he has gone to take possession. 19 You shall say to him, "Thus says the LORD: Have you killed, and also taken possession?" You shall say to him, "Thus says the LORD: In the place where dogs licked up the blood of Naboth, dogs will also lick up your blood."

20 Ahab said to Elijah, "Have you found me, O my enemy?" He answered, "I have found you. Because you have sold yourself to do what is evil in the sight of the LORD, 21 I will bring disaster on you; I will consume you, and will cut off from Ahab every male, bond or free, in Israel; 22 and I will make your house like the house of Jeroboam son of Nebat, and like the house of Baasha son of Ahijah, because you have provoked me to anger and have caused Israel to sin. 23 Also concerning Jezebel the LORD said, 'The dogs shall eat Jezebel within the bounds of Jezreel.' 24 Anyone belonging to Ahab who dies in the city the dogs shall eat; and anyone of his who dies in the open country the birds of the air shall eat."

25 (Indeed, there was no one like Ahab, who sold himself to do what was evil in the sight of the LORD, urged on by his wife Jezebel. 26 He acted most abominably in going after idols, as the Amorites had done, whom the LORD drove out before the Israelites.)

27 When Ahab heard those words, he tore his clothes and put sackcloth over his bare flesh; he fasted, lay in the sackcloth, and went about dejectedly. 28 Then the word of the LORD came to Elijah the Tishbite: 29 "Have you seen how Ahab has humbled himself before me? Because he has humbled himself before me, I will not bring the disaster in his days; but in his son's days I will bring the disaster on his house."

Joint Campaign with Judah against Aram

22 For three years Aram and Israel continued without war. 2 But in the third year King Jehoshaphat of Judah came down to the king of Israel. 3 The king of Israel said to his servants, "Do you know that Ramoth-gilead belongs to us, yet we are doing nothing to take it out of the hand of the king of Aram?" 4 He said to Jehoshaphat, "Will you go with me to battle at Ramoth-gilead?" Jehoshaphat replied to the king of Israel, "I am as you are; my people are your people, my horses are your horses."

5 But Jehoshaphat also said to the king of Israel, "Inquire first for the word of the LORD." 6 Then the king of Israel gathered the prophets together, about four hundred of them, and said to them, "Shall I go to battle against Ramoth-

---

a Heb *who is*

---

both may have had no relatives to prevent the king from taking the land. **21.17–29** Jezebel may be able to conceal her crime from Ahab and the people, but she cannot conceal it from God. For his involvement in the murder and for his theft of Naboth's land, both the king and his house are condemned. Ironically it is not his apostasy but his willingness to exceed the limits on royal power that brings an end to his rule. **21.19** The first announcement of judgment applies to Ahab personally and not to his house. **21.21–24** The second announcement of judgment is virtually identical with the one made to Jeroboam (14.10–11) and is also similar to the one made to Baasha (16.3–4). **21.22** Ahab's crime of causing *Israel* to *sin* probably refers to his encouragement of illegitimate worship (16.32–33) rather than to his involvement in the Naboth incident. **21.23** The oracle against Ahab and his house is expanded to include *Jezebel,* who in the eyes of the narrator was responsible for introducing Baal worship into Israel and was directly involved in Naboth's murder. **21.27** *Sackcloth,* here a sign of mourning and penitence (see note on 20.31). **21.29** For the motif of penitence leading to a

postponement or modification of judgment, see 2 Sam 12.13–14; 2 Kings 22.11–20. The oracle against Ahab's house is finally fulfilled in 2 Kings 10.17; Jezebel's death is recorded in 2 Kings 9.30–37. The judgment against Ahab personally occurs more quickly (ch. 22). **22.1–12** After the interlude of Naboth's vineyard, the narrator returns to the subject of Israel's wars with Aram (see ch. 20). **22.1** The treaty Ahab made with Ben-hadad of Aram apparently maintained the peace (20.34). **22.2** During this period the Judean king Jehoshaphat was one of Ahab's vassals (v. 44), a relationship Ahab sealed by marrying his daughter, Athaliah, to Jehoshaphat's son, Jehoram (2 Kings 8.18, 26). **22.3** *Ramoth-gilead,* a levitical city east of the Jordan that had been one of Solomon's administrative centers (4.13). Its precise location is unknown. **22.4** As a vassal of Ahab's, Jehoshaphat is bound to fight against Israel's enemies. **22.5** Throughout the ancient Near East, it was customary before battle to seek a divine oracle or omen to determine whether there would be a favorable outcome (see, e.g., 1 Sam 28.3–19; Ezek 21.21–23). **22.6–7** The four hundred prophets were part of the royal

gilead, or shall I refrain?" They said, "Go up; for the LORD will give it into the hand of the king." [7] But Jehoshaphat said, "Is there no other prophet of the LORD here of whom we may inquire?" [8] The king of Israel said to Jehoshaphat, "There is still one other by whom we may inquire of the LORD, Micaiah son of Imlah; but I hate him, for he never prophesies anything favorable about me, but only disaster." Jehoshaphat said, "Let the king not say such a thing." [9] Then the king of Israel summoned an officer and said, "Bring quickly Micaiah son of Imlah." [10] Now the king of Israel and King Jehoshaphat of Judah were sitting on their thrones, arrayed in their robes, at the threshing floor at the entrance of the gate of Samaria; and all the prophets were prophesying before them. [11] Zedekiah son of Chenaanah made for himself horns of iron, and he said, "Thus says the LORD: With these you shall gore the Arameans until they are destroyed." [12] All the prophets were prophesying the same and saying, "Go up to Ramoth-gilead and triumph; the LORD will give it into the hand of the king."

Micaiah Predicts Failure

13 The messenger who had gone to summon Micaiah said to him, "Look, the words of the prophets with one accord are favorable to the king; let your word be like the word of one of them, and speak favorably." [14] But Micaiah said, "As the LORD lives, whatever the LORD says to me, that I will speak."

15 When he had come to the king, the king said to him, "Micaiah, shall we go to Ramoth-gilead to battle, or shall we refrain?" He answered him, "Go up and triumph; the LORD will give it into the hand of the king." [16] But the king said to him, "How many times must I make you swear to tell me nothing but the truth in the name of the LORD?" [17] Then Micaiah[a] said, "I saw all Israel scattered on the mountains, like sheep that have no shepherd; and the LORD said, 'These have no master; let each one go home in peace.' " [18] The king of Israel said to Jehoshaphat, "Did I not tell you that he would not prophesy anything favorable about me, but only disaster?"

19 Then Micaiah[a] said, "Therefore hear the word of the LORD: I saw the LORD sitting on his throne, with all the host of heaven standing beside him to the right and to the left of him. [20] And the LORD said, 'Who will entice Ahab, so that he may go up and fall at Ramoth-gilead?' Then one said one thing, and another said another, [21] until a spirit came forward and stood before the LORD, saying, 'I will entice him.' [22] 'How?' the LORD asked him. He replied, 'I will go out and be a lying spirit in the mouth of all his prophets.' Then the LORD[a] said, 'You are to entice him, and you shall succeed; go out and do it.' [23] So you see, the LORD has put a lying spirit in the mouth of all these your prophets; the LORD has decreed disaster for you."

24 Then Zedekiah son of Chenaanah came up to Micaiah, slapped him on the cheek, and said, "Which way did the spirit of the LORD pass from me to speak to you?" [25] Micaiah replied, "You will find out on that day when you go in to hide in an inner chamber." [26] The king of Israel then ordered, "Take Micaiah, and return him to Amon the governor of the city and to Joash the king's son, [27] and say, 'Thus says the king: Put this fellow in prison, and feed him on reduced rations of bread and water until I come in peace.' " [28] Micaiah said, "If you return in peace, the LORD has not spoken by me." And he said, "Hear, you peoples, all of you!"

Defeat and Death of Ahab

29 So the king of Israel and King Jehoshaphat of Judah went up to Ramoth-gilead. [30] The

___
a Heb he

___

court, but the Judean king apparently doubted that they were prophets of the Lord. **22.11** Zedekiah's prophetic act with the horns was not an illustration of his prophecy; rather, it was believed to have the power to actualize his words. **22.13–28** Micaiah not only supplies a true oracle for Ahab but also provides a rare glimpse into the inner world of the prophet. The story also furnishes a clear example of the conflicts that could arise when one prophet's words disagreed with those of another. **22.13** The messenger apparently wants to avoid the confusion that would result if Micaiah were to go against the prophetic consensus. **22.15–**

16 Micaiah's decision to follow the majority is not credible because his oracle departs from his customary message. **22.19–23** Micaiah attempts to give more authority to his oracle by describing the circumstances in which he received it. He became an observer of the heavenly court and overheard God discussing events with supernatural advisers (cf. Isa 6.1–13). **22.22** The spirit is not described as a being who is inherently evil or as a tempter or adversary (cf. Job 1–2; Zech 3.1–2). Rather, the spirit plans to become a lying spirit temporarily in order to deceive Ahab. **22.24–25** The confrontation between the two prophets indicates that nei-

king of Israel said to Jehoshaphat, "I will disguise myself and go into battle, but you wear your robes." So the king of Israel disguised himself and went into battle. 31Now the king of Aram had commanded the thirty-two captains of his chariots, "Fight with no one small or great, but only with the king of Israel." 32When the captains of the chariots saw Jehoshaphat, they said, "It is surely the king of Israel." So they turned to fight against him; and Jehoshaphat cried out. 33When the captains of the chariots saw that it was not the king of Israel, they turned back from pursuing him. 34But a certain man drew his bow and unknowingly struck the king of Israel between the scale armor and the breastplate; so he said to the driver of his chariot, "Turn around, and carry me out of the battle, for I am wounded." 35The battle grew hot that day, and the king was propped up in his chariot facing the Arameans, until at evening he died; the blood from the wound had flowed into the bottom of the chariot. 36Then about sunset a shout went through the army, "Every man to his city, and every man to his country!"

37 So the king died, and was brought to Samaria; they buried the king in Samaria. 38They washed the chariot by the pool of Samaria; the dogs licked up his blood, and the prostitutes washed themselves in it,*a* according to the word of the LORD that he had spoken. 39Now the rest of the acts of Ahab, and all that he did, and the ivory house that he built, and all the cities that he built, are they not written in the Book of the Annals of the Kings of Israel? 40So Ahab slept with his ancestors; and his son Ahaziah succeeded him.

Jehoshaphat Reigns over Judah

41 Jehoshaphat son of Asa began to reign over Judah in the fourth year of King Ahab of Israel.

42Jehoshaphat was thirty-five years old when he began to reign, and he reigned twenty-five years in Jerusalem. His mother's name was Azubah daughter of Shilhi. 43He walked in all the way of his father Asa; he did not turn aside from it, doing what was right in the sight of the LORD; yet the high places were not taken away, and the people still sacrificed and offered incense on the high places. 44Jehoshaphat also made peace with the king of Israel.

45 Now the rest of the acts of Jehoshaphat, and his power that he showed, and how he waged war, are they not written in the Book of the Annals of the Kings of Judah? 46The remnant of the male temple prostitutes who were still in the land in the days of his father Asa, he exterminated.

47 There was no king in Edom; a deputy was king. 48Jehoshaphat made ships of the Tarshish type to go to Ophir for gold; but they did not go, for the ships were wrecked at Ezion-geber. 49Then Ahaziah son of Ahab said to Jehoshaphat, "Let my servants go with your servants in the ships," but Jehoshaphat was not willing. 50Jehoshaphat slept with his ancestors and was buried with his ancestors in the city of his father David; his son Jehoram succeeded him.

Ahaziah Reigns over Israel

51 Ahaziah son of Ahab began to reign over Israel in Samaria in the seventeenth year of King Jehoshaphat of Judah; he reigned two years over Israel. 52He did what was evil in the sight of the LORD, and walked in the way of his father and mother, and in the way of Jeroboam son of Nebat, who caused Israel to sin. 53He served Baal and worshiped him; he provoked the LORD, the God of Israel, to anger, just as his father had done.

_____
a Heb lacks *in it*

ther prophet was willing to admit that the other might be right. **22.29–40** In spite of Ahab's efforts to nullify the prophetic oracles, the words of Elijah (21.19) and Micaiah (22.17) are inevitably fulfilled. **22.30** Ahab disguises himself so that the enemy will think that the royally attired Jehoshaphat is the king of Israel. **22.32** Jehoshaphat's cry may have been a distinctive battle cry that allowed the Arameans to identify him. **22.35** The Israelites try to prevent the enemy from discovering that the king has been wounded. **22.36** The end of the battle fulfills Micaiah's vision of a scattered Israel (v. 17). **22.38** This verse partially fulfills Elijah's prophecy (21.19), although his original oracle called for Ahab's blood to be spilled in Jezreel. The reference to the *prostitutes* is a bizarre addition to the prophecy. **22.41–50** The formal account of Jehoshaphat's reign portrays him as a good king, although he too fails to remove the high places. **22.41–42** *Jehoshaphat* reigned ca. 873–849 BCE. **22.43** *High places.* See note on 3.2. **22.46** *Temple prostitutes.* See note on 14.24. **22.48–49** Like Solomon, Jehoshaphat tries to become involved in long-distance maritime trade, but he is not successful (see notes on 9.26; 9.28; 10.22). **22.51–53** The stereotypical introduction to Ahaziah's reign gives him the expected negative evaluation. The account of his activities is continued in 2 Kings. **22.51** *Ahaziah* ruled ca. 850–849 BCE.

2 KINGS

THE TWO BOOKS OF KINGS were once a single work, and 2 Kings simply continues the account of Israel's history begun in 1 Kings. The narratives of 2 Kings cover the history of Israel from the reign of Ahaziah (ca. 850–849 BCE) to the Assyrian destruction of Samaria, the capital of the Northern Kingdom (721 BCE). Interwoven with that history is the story of Judah from the reign of Jehoshaphat to the years immediately following the destruction of the Southern Kingdom, the fall of Jerusalem, and the Babylonian exile (586 BCE). For a full introduction to 2 Kings, see the Introduction to 1 Kings. [ROBERT R. WILSON]

Elijah Denounces Ahaziah

1 After the death of Ahab, Moab rebelled against Israel.

2 Ahaziah had fallen through the lattice in his upper chamber in Samaria, and lay injured; so he sent messengers, telling them, "Go, inquire of Baal-zebub, the god of Ekron, whether I shall recover from this injury." ³But the angel of the LORD said to Elijah the Tishbite, "Get up, go to meet the messengers of the king of Samaria, and say to them, 'Is it because there is no God in Israel that you are going to inquire of Baal-zebub, the god of Ekron?' ⁴Now therefore thus says the LORD, 'You shall not leave the bed to which you have gone, but you shall surely die.' " So Elijah went.

5 The messengers returned to the king, who said to them, "Why have you returned?" ⁶They answered him, "There came a man to meet us, who said to us, 'Go back to the king who sent you, and say to him: Thus says the LORD: Is it

---

1.1–18 The story of Ahaziah's illness is used by the narrator as another illustration of the inevitable fulfillment of a prophetic judgment oracle against a corrupt Northern king. The basic narrative has been elaborated by the incorporation of legendary material illustrating the prophet's ability to wield divine power. **1.1** This note on Moab's revolt seems out of place, since Moab plays no role in the narrative until 3.5. On the other hand, it is possible that the narrator understands the revolt as a judgment on the evil dynasty of Ahab (see 1 Kings 22.51–53; cf. 1 Kings 11.1–26). **1.2** *Lattice* implies a woven structure of some sort (1 Kings 7.17; Job 18.8), which probably covered a window. On the practice of consulting a deity through a prophet in times of sickness, cf. 2 Kings 8.7–15; 1 Kings 14.1–18, which is strikingly similar to the

story being told here. *Baal-zebub*, "Baal of the Flies" or "Lord of the Flies," is probably an intentional Israelite corruption of Baal-zebul, "Baal the Prince." The deity would have been a local manifestation of the Canaanite storm god, Baal, whose worship had been introduced into Israel by Ahaziah's father, Ahab (see notes on 1 Kings 16.31; 17.1). The NT preserves the name in the form Beelzebul (Mt 10.25; 12.24; Mk 3.22; Lk 11.15) and reflects the later development of the figure into the prince of demons. *Ekron*, a Philistine city that lay about twenty-two miles west of Jerusalem. Part of the tribe of Judah in David's time (1 Sam 7.14), Ekron may have been back in Philistine hands by the time this story takes place. **1.3** The message Elijah is to deliver reflects the ongoing struggle between the Lord and Baal over the issue of who is the true God in Israel.

because there is no God in Israel that you are sending to inquire of Baal-zebub, the god of Ekron? Therefore you shall not leave the bed to which you have gone, but shall surely die.'" [7]He said to them, "What sort of man was he who came to meet you and told you these things?" [8]They answered him, "A hairy man, with a leather belt around his waist." He said, "It is Elijah the Tishbite."

9 Then the king sent to him a captain of fifty with his fifty men. He went up to Elijah, who was sitting on the top of a hill, and said to him, "O man of God, the king says, 'Come down.'" [10]But Elijah answered the captain of fifty, "If I am a man of God, let fire come down from heaven and consume you and your fifty." Then fire came down from heaven, and consumed him and his fifty.

11 Again the king sent to him another captain of fifty with his fifty. He went up[a] and said to him, "O man of God, this is the king's order: Come down quickly!" [12]But Elijah answered them, "If I am a man of God, let fire come down from heaven and consume you and your fifty." Then the fire of God came down from heaven and consumed him and his fifty.

13 Again the king sent the captain of a third fifty with his fifty. So the third captain of fifty went up, and came and fell on his knees before Elijah, and entreated him, "O man of God, please let my life, and the life of these fifty servants of yours, be precious in your sight. [14]Look, fire came down from heaven and consumed the two former captains of fifty men with their fifties; but now let my life be precious in your sight." [15]Then the angel of the LORD said to Elijah, "Go down with him; do not be afraid of him." So he set out and went down with him to the king, [16]and said to him, "Thus says the LORD: Because you have sent messengers to inquire of Baal-zebub, the god of Ekron, —is it because there is no God in Israel to inquire of his word?—therefore you shall not leave the bed to which you have gone, but you shall surely die."

Death of Ahaziah

17 So he died according to the word of the LORD that Elijah had spoken. His brother,[b] Jehoram succeeded him as king in the second year of King Jehoram son of Jehoshaphat of Judah, because Ahaziah had no son. [18]Now the rest of the acts of Ahaziah that he did, are they not written in the Book of the Annals of the Kings of Israel?

Elijah Ascends to Heaven

2 Now when the LORD was about to take Elijah up to heaven by a whirlwind, Elijah and Elisha were on their way from Gilgal. [2]Elijah said to Elisha, "Stay here; for the LORD has sent me as far as Bethel." But Elisha said, "As the LORD lives, and as you yourself live, I will not leave you." So they went down to Bethel. [3]The company of prophets[c] who were in Bethel came out to Elisha, and said to him, "Do you know that today the LORD will take your master away from you?" And he said, "Yes, I know; keep silent."

4 Elijah said to him, "Elisha, stay here; for the LORD has sent me to Jericho." But he said,

---

a Gk Compare verses 9, 13: Heb He answered   b Gk Syr: Heb lacks His brother   c Heb sons of the prophets

---

For an earlier stage of the contest, see 1 Kings 18.17–40. **1.9–16** The threefold account of attempts to summon Elijah illustrates the divine protection afforded the prophet and also his ability to control God's power. For a similar story, see 1 Sam 19.18–24. **1.9** *Man of God.* See note on 1 Kings 13.1. **1.10** *Fire*, a traditional symbol of God's active presence. See notes on 1 Kings 18.24; 19.11–12. **1.17** The narrator notes the immediate fulfillment of the prophecy. *Jehoram* of Israel should not be confused with *Jehoram son of Jehoshaphat*, king of Judah. The relative chronology of this verse cannot be made to agree with the synchronisms of 3.1; 1 Kings 22.51. It is possible that in these passages the narrator used sources with conflicting chronologies or different systems of reckoning. **1.18** *The Book of the Annals of the Kings of Israel.* See note on 1 Kings 14.19–20.

2.1–18 The dramatic story of Elijah's ascension to heaven in a storm constitutes the climax of the narratives about this mysterious figure. Of all of the acts of power associated with him, this is the one that has most intrigued readers and fueled speculation about the prophet's character and eventual return. By the end of the OT period he had already been connected with the coming of the "day of the LORD" (Mal 4.5); later Jewish and Christian traditions associated him with the Messiah (Mt 11.13–14; 16.13–14; 17.10–13; Mk 6.14–15; 8.27–28; 9.11–13; Lk 1.17; 9.7–8, 18–19). **2.1** *Whirlwind,* elsewhere connected with God's presence (Job 38.1; 40.6; Ps 83.15; Jer 23.19; Zech 9.14). *Gilgal* may not be the site on the Jordan where the Israelites first entered the land of Canaan (Josh 4.19), but a town located elsewhere, perhaps north of Bethel. **2.2** *Bethel.* See note on 1 Kings 12.29. **2.3** *Company of prophets*, a prophetic guild. **2.4** *Jericho* lies in the Jordan Valley about six miles north of the Dead

"As the LORD lives, and as you yourself live, I will not leave you." So they came to Jericho. ⁵The company of prophets *a* who were at Jericho drew near to Elisha, and said to him, "Do you know that today the LORD will take your master away from you?" And he answered, "Yes, I know; be silent."

6 Then Elijah said to him, "Stay here; for the LORD has sent me to the Jordan." But he said, "As the LORD lives, and as you yourself live, I will not leave you." So the two of them went on. ⁷Fifty men of the company of prophets *a* also went, and stood at some distance from them, as they both were standing by the Jordan. ⁸Then Elijah took his mantle and rolled it up, and struck the water; the water was parted to the one side and to the other, until the two of them crossed on dry ground.

9 When they had crossed, Elijah said to Elisha, "Tell me what I may do for you, before I am taken from you." Elisha said, "Please let me inherit a double share of your spirit." ¹⁰He responded, "You have asked a hard thing; yet, if you see me as I am being taken from you, it will be granted you; if not, it will not." ¹¹As they continued walking and talking, a chariot of fire and horses of fire separated the two of them, and Elijah ascended in a whirlwind into heaven. ¹²Elisha kept watching and crying out, "Father, father! The chariots of Israel and its horsemen!" But when he could no longer see him, he grasped his own clothes and tore them in two pieces.

Elisha Succeeds Elijah

13 He picked up the mantle of Elijah that had fallen from him, and went back and stood on the bank of the Jordan. ¹⁴He took the mantle of Elijah that had fallen from him, and struck the water, saying, "Where is the LORD, the God of Elijah?" When he had struck the water, the water was parted to the one side and to the other, and Elisha went over.

15 When the company of prophets *a* who were at Jericho saw him at a distance, they declared, "The spirit of Elijah rests on Elisha." They came to meet him and bowed to the ground before him. ¹⁶They said to him, "See now, we have fifty strong men among your servants; please let them go and seek your master; it may be that the spirit of the LORD has caught him up and thrown him down on some mountain or into some valley." He responded, "No, do not send them." ¹⁷But when they urged him until he was ashamed, he said, "Send them." So they sent fifty men who searched for three days but did not find him. ¹⁸When they came back to him (he had remained at Jericho), he said to them, "Did I not say to you, Do not go?"

Elisha Performs Miracles

19 Now the people of the city said to Elisha, "The location of this city is good, as my lord sees; but the water is bad, and the land is unfruitful." ²⁰He said, "Bring me a new bowl, and put salt in it." So they brought it to him. ²¹Then he went to the spring of water and threw the salt into it, and said, "Thus says the LORD, I have made this water wholesome; from now on neither death nor miscarriage shall come from it." ²²So the water has been

---

a Heb *sons of the prophets*

Sea. **2.8** The *mantle* is a symbol of the prophet's power (cf. 1 Kings 19.19). Elijah's parting of the Jordan's waters recalls both the entry of Israel into Canaan (Josh 4.7–17) and Moses' parting of the sea during the exodus (Ex 14.21–22). For other attempts to portray Elijah as a prophet like Moses, see notes on 1 Kings 19.1–18; 19.4; 19.8; 19.9. **2.9** *A double share of your spirit.* According to Mosaic law, a firstborn son must receive a double portion of the inheritance (Deut 21.15–17). Elisha thus asks to have the status of Elijah's firstborn and to inherit more of his spirit than any other prophetic heirs. Elisha is not requesting more of the spirit than Elijah had, only a fraction of it. **2.10** Although Elijah already knows that Elisha is to be his successor (1 Kings 19.16), the older prophet leaves the final decision to the Lord. **2.11** *Fire.* See note on 1.10. **2.12** *Father,* a traditional title for the head of a prophetic guild and one often used by a disciple speaking to a master. *The chariots of Israel and its horsemen* may simply describe the heavenly army that Elisha is seeing (v. 11) or apply to Elijah and imply that he is more powerful and valuable to Israel than all of its army. Tearing *clothes* is a sign of mourning or distress (e.g., Gen 37.34; Josh 7.6; 2 Sam 13.31; Esth 4.1–3; Job 1.20). **2.13–14** Elisha's ability to use the *mantle* to repeat the earlier miracle demonstrates that he has indeed become Elijah's successor. **2.16** The company of prophets did not see what happened to Elijah and assume that God's spirit has simply transported him to another location (see 1 Kings 18.7–16). Elisha knows that this is not the case and is reluctant to let them search. **2.19–25** Just as the Elijah narratives begin with stories designed to demonstrate the prophet's power and authority (1 Kings 17), so also the Elisha narratives include a number of prophetic legends dealing with his miraculous deeds. **2.19–22** Cf. Moses' sweet-

wholesome to this day, according to the word that Elisha spoke.

23 He went up from there to Bethel; and while he was going up on the way, some small boys came out of the city and jeered at him, saying, "Go away, baldhead! Go away, baldhead!" 24When he turned around and saw them, he cursed them in the name of the LORD. Then two she-bears came out of the woods and mauled forty-two of the boys. 25From there he went on to Mount Carmel, and then returned to Samaria.

Jehoram Reigns over Israel

3 In the eighteenth year of King Jehoshaphat of Judah, Jehoram son of Ahab became king over Israel in Samaria; he reigned twelve years. 2He did what was evil in the sight of the LORD, though not like his father and mother, for he removed the pillar of Baal that his father had made. 3Nevertheless he clung to the sin of Jeroboam son of Nebat, which he caused Israel to commit; he did not depart from it.

War with Moab

4 Now King Mesha of Moab was a sheep breeder, who used to deliver to the king of Israel one hundred thousand lambs, and the wool of one hundred thousand rams. 5But when Ahab died, the king of Moab rebelled against the king of Israel. 6So King Jehoram marched out of Samaria at that time and mustered all Israel. 7As he went he sent word to King Jehoshaphat of Judah, "The king of Moab has rebelled against me; will you go with me to battle against Moab?" He answered, "I will; I am with you, my people are your people, my horses are your horses." 8Then he asked, "By which way shall we march?" Jehoram answered, "By the way of the wilderness of Edom."

9 So the king of Israel, the king of Judah, and the king of Edom set out; and when they had made a roundabout march of seven days, there was no water for the army or for the animals that were with them. 10Then the king of Israel said, "Alas! The LORD has summoned us, three kings, only to be handed over to Moab." 11But Jehoshaphat said, "Is there no prophet of the LORD here, through whom we may inquire of the LORD?" Then one of the servants of the king of Israel answered, "Elisha son of Shaphat, who used to pour water on the hands of Elijah, is here." 12Jehoshaphat said, "The word of the LORD is with him." So the king of Israel and Jehoshaphat and the king of Edom went down to him.

13 Elisha said to the king of Israel, "What have I to do with you? Go to your father's prophets or to your mother's." But the king of Israel said to him, "No; it is the LORD who has summoned us, three kings, only to be handed over to Moab." 14Elisha said, "As the LORD of hosts lives, whom I serve, were it not that I have regard for King Jehoshaphat of Judah, I would give you neither a look nor a glance. 15But get me a musician." And then, while the

---

ening the waters of Marah (Ex 15.23–25). **2.23** The *small boys* may not want the prophet to visit the illegitimate shrine at Bethel (see 1 Kings 12.28–30; 13.1–10), or they may simply be mocking his appearance.

3.1–3 The formal report on Jehoram's reign indicates that he continued in the tradition of Israel's evil kings, although he did try to discourage the worship of Baal. Because for the narrator the real problem in Israel is heterodox worship generally (see 1 Kings 12.25–32), this minor reform makes little difference in the overall evaluation. **3.1** *Jehoram* ruled ca. 849–843/2 BCE. On the chronological problems involved in his dates, see note on 1.17. **3.2** *Pillar.* See note on 1 Kings 14.23. **3.4–27** This report of Israel's war with Moab is unusual in that it portrays Elisha as actively involved in working toward a victory for Israel and its allies (see also 6.8–23; 6.24–7.2; 1 Kings 20.13–22). In this sense the account is in sharp contrast with the otherwise very similar battle report in 1 Kings 22.1–40. **3.7** *Jehoshaphat of Judah* is a vassal of the Northern king, as was also the case during Ahab's reign. The Judeans are therefore obligated to join Israel in quelling the Moab-

ite rebellion (cf. 1 Kings 22.4). **3.8** Jehoram proposes to march south through Judah and then east across the northern part of Edom and through the northeastern desert, the *wilderness of Edom*. This route would require the cooperation of the Edomites, who at the time were vassals of Judah (8.20). The three armies then plan to march north into Moab, approaching their target from the southeast. **3.9** *King of Edom,* an official probably appointed by Jehoshaphat (1 Kings 22.47). **3.11** As in 1 Kings 22.7, it is Jehoshaphat who proposes to seek divine guidance through a prophet of the Lord. Elisha's reputation as Elijah's successor is already well established. *Pour water on the hands.* Elisha acted as Elijah's servant. **3.13** *Father's prophets . . . mother's,* the prophets of Baal and the prophets of Asherah, who were part of Ahab's court (1 Kings 18.19; cf. 1 Kings 22.6, 10–12). Jehoram's reply suggests that the Lord has directed Israel to fight the Moabites. **3.14** Elisha here reflects the point of view of the narrator, who sees all of the Northern kings as illegitimate and apostate but who believes in the eternal divine election of Jerusalem and the Davidic house. **3.15** Prophets some-

musician was playing, the power of the LORD came on him. 16And he said, "Thus says the LORD, 'I will make this wadi full of pools.' 17For thus says the LORD, 'You shall see neither wind nor rain, but the wadi shall be filled with water, so that you shall drink, you, your cattle, and your animals.' 18This is only a trifle in the sight of the LORD, for he will also hand Moab over to you. 19You shall conquer every fortified city and every choice city; every good tree you shall fell, all springs of water you shall stop up, and every good piece of land you shall ruin with stones." 20The next day, about the time of the morning offering, suddenly water began to flow from the direction of Edom, until the country was filled with water.

21 When all the Moabites heard that the kings had come up to fight against them, all who were able to put on armor, from the youngest to the oldest, were called out and were drawn up at the frontier. 22When they rose early in the morning, and the sun shone upon the water, the Moabites saw the water opposite them as red as blood. 23They said, "This is blood; the kings must have fought together, and killed one another. Now then, Moab, to the spoil!" 24But when they came to the camp of Israel, the Israelites rose up and attacked the Moabites, who fled before them; as they entered Moab they continued the attack.*a* 25The cities they overturned, and on every good piece of land everyone threw a stone, until it was covered; every spring of water they stopped up, and every good tree they felled. Only at Kir-hareseth did the stone walls remain, until the slingers surrounded and attacked it. 26When the king of Moab saw that the battle was going against him, he took

with him seven hundred swordsmen to break through, opposite the king of Edom; but they could not. 27Then he took his firstborn son who was to succeed him, and offered him as a burnt offering on the wall. And great wrath came upon Israel, so they withdrew from him and returned to their own land.

Elisha and the Widow's Oil

4 Now the wife of a member of the company of prophets*b* cried to Elisha, "Your servant my husband is dead; and you know that your servant feared the LORD, but a creditor has come to take my two children as slaves." 2Elisha said to her, "What shall I do for you? Tell me, what do you have in the house?" She answered, "Your servant has nothing in the house, except a jar of oil." 3He said, "Go outside, borrow vessels from all your neighbors, empty vessels and not just a few. 4Then go in, and shut the door behind you and your children, and start pouring into all these vessels; when each is full, set it aside." 5So she left him and shut the door behind her and her children; they kept bringing vessels to her, and she kept pouring. 6When the vessels were full, she said to her son, "Bring me another vessel." But he said to her, "There are no more." Then the oil stopped flowing. 7She came and told the man of God, and he said, "Go sell the oil and pay your debts, and you and your children can live on the rest."

Elisha Raises the Shunammite's Son

8 One day Elisha was passing through Shunem, where a wealthy woman lived, who

---

a Compare Gk Syr: Meaning of Heb uncertain   *b* Heb *the sons of the prophets*

---

times used music to induce trance or possession by God's spirit (1 Sam 10.5–6). **3.16–17** The wadi would normally have contained water only during the rainy season. **3.19** The extreme destruction of Moab is a violation of the laws governing religious war (Deut 20.19–20). **3.20** The OT does not specify the precise time of the *morning offering* (Ex 29.38–42), but later Jewish sources require that it be made at dawn. **3.22** *Water . . . red as blood* is probably intended to be a miraculous occurrence, although some scholars have suggested that the Edomites saw water colored by the rising morning sun or by the country's red sandstone. **3.25** *Kir-hareseth*, located about eleven miles east of the Dead Sea and seventeen miles south of the Arnon River. **3.27** Extrabiblical sources indicate that human sacrifices were sometimes offered in times of siege, although there are no other OT references to the practice

(but cf. 16.3; 21.6). *Wrath*, possibly of a deity; the text may be implying that the anger of Moab's god caused the Israelites to withdraw.

4.1–7 This is the first of four prophetic legends in ch. 4 and is designed to enhance the prophet's authority by demonstrating his miraculous powers. All of the stories probably circulated orally before being incorporated in Kings. For a similar story told about Elijah, see 1 Kings 17.8–16. **4.1** In the remaining Elisha stories he is portrayed as the leader of a *company of prophets,* a prophetic guild. The widow has no means of support and cannot repay the debt. The selling of people into slavery in such circumstances was apparently common (Ex 21.7; Am 2.6; 8.6; Mic 2.9). See note on 1 Kings 17.10. **4.2** Elisha's question implies that he is powerless to intervene with the creditor on her behalf. His actual response will be much more dramatic.

urged him to have a meal. So whenever he passed that way, he would stop there for a meal. 9She said to her husband, "Look, I am sure that this man who regularly passes our way is a holy man of God. 10Let us make a small roof chamber with walls, and put there for him a bed, a table, a chair, and a lamp, so that he can stay there whenever he comes to us."

11 One day when he came there, he went up to the chamber and lay down there. 12He said to his servant Gehazi, "Call the Shunammite woman." When he had called her, she stood before him. 13He said to him, "Say to her, Since you have taken all this trouble for us, what may be done for you? Would you have a word spoken on your behalf to the king or to the commander of the army?" She answered, "I live among my own people." 14He said, "What then may be done for her?" Gehazi answered, "Well, she has no son, and her husband is old." 15He said, "Call her." When he had called her, she stood at the door. 16He said, "At this season, in due time, you shall embrace a son." She replied, "No, my lord, O man of God; do not deceive your servant."

17 The woman conceived and bore a son at that season, in due time, as Elisha had declared to her.

18 When the child was older, he went out one day to his father among the reapers. 19He complained to his father, "Oh, my head, my head!" The father said to his servant, "Carry him to his mother." 20He carried him and brought him to his mother; the child sat on her lap until noon, and he died. 21She went up and laid him on the bed of the man of God, closed the door on him, and left. 22Then she called to her husband, and said, "Send me one of the servants and one of the donkeys, so that

I may quickly go to the man of God and come back again." 23He said, "Why go to him today? It is neither new moon nor sabbath." She said, "It will be all right." 24Then she saddled the donkey and said to her servant, "Urge the animal on; do not hold back for me unless I tell you." 25So she set out, and came to the man of God at Mount Carmel.

When the man of God saw her coming, he said to Gehazi his servant, "Look, there is the Shunammite woman; 26run at once to meet her, and say to her, Are you all right? Is your husband all right? Is the child all right?" She answered, "It is all right." 27When she came to the man of God at the mountain, she caught hold of his feet. Gehazi approached to push her away. But the man of God said, "Let her alone, for she is in bitter distress; the LORD has hidden it from me and has not told me." 28Then she said, "Did I ask my lord for a son? Did I not say, Do not mislead me?" 29He said to Gehazi, "Gird up your loins, and take my staff in your hand, and go. If you meet anyone, give no greeting, and if anyone greets you, do not answer; and lay my staff on the face of the child." 30Then the mother of the child said, "As the LORD lives, and as you yourself live, I will not leave without you." So he rose up and followed her. 31Gehazi went on ahead and laid the staff on the face of the child, but there was no sound or sign of life. He came back to meet him and told him, "The child has not awakened."

32 When Elisha came into the house, he saw the child lying dead on his bed. 33So he went in and closed the door on the two of them, and prayed to the LORD. 34Then he got up on the bed*a* and lay upon the child, putting his

---

a Heb lacks *on the bed*

4.8–37 This story of the miraculous birth, death, and resurrection of a child is a gem of Hebrew narrative art and reflects careful shaping and polishing over a long period of time. For a parallel story about Elijah, see 1 Kings 17.17–24. **4.8** *Shunem.* See note on 1 Kings 1.3. **4.10** Because little is known about the second floor of Israelite houses, the precise nature of the structure she proposes to build is unclear. **4.13** The Shunammite's kindness is rewarded by Elisha, whose offer of aid indicates his ability to influence the highest levels of government. Her reply indicates that all of her physical needs can be met by her own family. **4.16–17** The OT has preserved several stories about the miraculous birth of a child to a barren woman, e.g., Gen 18.1–15;

30.1–24; Judg 13.2–25; 1 Sam 1.1–28. *In due time,* probably "next year" (Gen 18.10, 14). **4.16** *You shall embrace a son,* an unusual phrase ironically reflected in v. 20. **4.19** The child probably suffered sunstroke. **4.22–23** The husband does not know that the child has died, so he is puzzled by his wife's desire to visit Elijah. **4.23** New moons and sabbaths were times for special rituals, so these were apparently appropriate times to visit religious figures (Ex 20.8–11; Num 28.11–15; Isa 1.14; 66.23; Hos 2.11; Am 8.5). **4.26** Because of the importance of her errand, the Shunammite wishes to speak to the prophet directly and offers only a courteous reply to Gehazi. **4.29** Without being told directly, the prophet now knows the nature of the

mouth upon his mouth, his eyes upon his eyes, and his hands upon his hands; and while he lay bent over him, the flesh of the child became warm. 35He got down, walked once to and fro in the room, then got up again and bent over him; the child sneezed seven times, and the child opened his eyes. 36Elisha[a] summoned Gehazi and said, "Call the Shunammite woman." So he called her. When she came to him, he said, "Take your son." 37She came and fell at his feet, bowing to the ground; then she took her son and left.

Elisha Purifies the Pot of Stew

38 When Elisha returned to Gilgal, there was a famine in the land. As the company of prophets was[b] sitting before him, he said to his servant, "Put the large pot on, and make some stew for the company of prophets."[c] 39One of them went out into the field to gather herbs; he found a wild vine and gathered from it a lapful of wild gourds, and came and cut them up into the pot of stew, not knowing what they were. 40They served some for the men to eat. But while they were eating the stew, they cried out, "O man of God, there is death in the pot!" They could not eat it. 41He said, "Then bring some flour." He threw it into the pot, and said, "Serve the people and let them eat." And there was nothing harmful in the pot.

Elisha Feeds One Hundred Men

42 A man came from Baal-shalishah, bringing food from the first fruits to the man of God: twenty loaves of barley and fresh ears of grain

in his sack. Elisha said, "Give it to the people and let them eat." 43But his servant said, "How can I set this before a hundred people?" So he repeated, "Give it to the people and let them eat, for thus says the LORD, 'They shall eat and have some left.' " 44He set it before them, they ate, and had some left, according to the word of the LORD.

The Healing of Naaman

5 Naaman, commander of the army of the king of Aram, was a great man and in high favor with his master, because by him the LORD had given victory to Aram. The man, though a mighty warrior, suffered from leprosy.[d] 2Now the Arameans on one of their raids had taken a young girl captive from the land of Israel, and she served Naaman's wife. 3She said to her mistress, "If only my lord were with the prophet who is in Samaria! He would cure him of his leprosy."[d] 4So Naaman[e] went in and told his lord just what the girl from the land of Israel had said. 5And the king of Aram said, "Go then, and I will send along a letter to the king of Israel."

He went, taking with him ten talents of silver, six thousand shekels of gold, and ten sets of garments. 6He brought the letter to the king of Israel, which read, "When this letter reaches you, know that I have sent to you my servant Naaman, that you may cure him of his leprosy."[d] 7When the king of Israel read the letter,

---

a Heb he   b Heb sons of the prophets were   c Heb sons of the prophets   d A term for several skin diseases; precise meaning uncertain   e Heb he

---

problem. **4.30** The woman's persistence convinces Elisha to accompany her. **4.35** Apparently the effort exhausted the prophet so that he has to rest a bit before making a second attempt. The sneezing indicates that the child's breath has returned. *Seven* often appears in rituals (see also 5.10). **4.38–41** This prophetic legend illustrates the prophet's ability to care for his disciples in times of hardship. **4.38** *Gilgal.* See note on 2.1. The *company of prophets,* the prophetic guild, was probably gathered around Elisha for instruction. **4.39** The identification of the *herbs* and the *wild gourds* is uncertain. **4.42–44** This miraculous feeding of the prophetic guild perhaps influenced the later narratives of Jesus feeding large crowds (Mt 14.13–21; 15.32–38; Mk 8.1–10). **4.42** *Baal-shalishah* is southwest of Shechem.
5.1–19a This account of the healing of Naaman may have once been simply a legend that focused on Elisha's miraculous healing powers. The story in its final form, however, has been shaped to emphasize Naaman's conversion and his acknowledgment of the

power of the one true God. The theme of the conversion of foreign officials was particularly meaningful to Israel during and after the Babylonian exile. See, e.g., Dan 2.46–47; 3.28; 4.34–37; 6.25–27. **5.1** For an account of Israel's earlier battles with *Aram* (Syria), see 1 Kings 20.1–34; 22.1–40 and notes there. The notion that the LORD *had given victory to Aram* reflects 1 Kings 22.19–23. *Leprosy,* one of a number of skin diseases, none of which is identical with modern leprosy (Hansen's disease). **5.3** Elisha already has a reputation as a healer, presumably on the basis of stories like 4.8–37. **5.5** *Talents.* See note on 1 Kings 9.14. *Shekels.* See note on 1 Kings 10.16. **5.6** The Syrian king seems to assume that Elisha is employed in the royal court and that the king of Israel will know how to interpret the request for healing. **5.7** The king of Israel does not make the connection with Elisha at all; he assumes that the Syrian is making an impossible request so that the Israelite king's failure to comply will provide an excuse for another Syrian raid. *Tore his clothes.* See note on

he tore his clothes and said, "Am I God, to give death or life, that this man sends word to me to cure a man of his leprosy?ᵃ Just look and see how he is trying to pick a quarrel with me."

8 But when Elisha the man of God heard that the king of Israel had torn his clothes, he sent a message to the king, "Why have you torn your clothes? Let him come to me, that he may learn that there is a prophet in Israel." 9So Naaman came with his horses and chariots, and halted at the entrance of Elisha's house. 10Elisha sent a messenger to him, saying, "Go, wash in the Jordan seven times, and your flesh shall be restored and you shall be clean." 11But Naaman became angry and went away, saying, "I thought that for me he would surely come out, and stand and call on the name of the LORD his God, and would wave his hand over the spot, and cure the leprosy!ᵃ 12Are not Abanaᵇ and Pharpar, the rivers of Damascus, better than all the waters of Israel? Could I not wash in them, and be clean?" He turned and went away in a rage. 13But his servants approached and said to him, "Father, if the prophet had commanded you to do something difficult, would you not have done it? How much more, when all he said to you was, 'Wash, and be clean'?" 14So he went down and immersed himself seven times in the Jordan, according to the word of the man of God; his flesh was restored like the flesh of a young boy, and he was clean.

15 Then he returned to the man of God, he and all his company; he came and stood before him and said, "Now I know that there is no God in all the earth except in Israel; please accept a present from your servant." 16But he said, "As the LORD lives, whom I serve, I will accept nothing!" He urged him to accept, but he refused. 17Then Naaman said, "If not, please let two mule-loads of earth be given to your servant; for your servant will no longer

offer burnt offering or sacrifice to any god except the LORD. 18But may the LORD pardon your servant on one count: when my master goes into the house of Rimmon to worship there, leaning on my arm, and I bow down in the house of Rimmon, when I do bow down in the house of Rimmon, may the LORD pardon your servant on this one count." 19He said to him, "Go in peace."

Gehazi's Greed

But when Naaman had gone from him a short distance, 20Gehazi, the servant of Elisha the man of God, thought, "My master has let that Aramean Naaman off too lightly by not accepting from him what he offered. As the LORD lives, I will run after him and get something out of him." 21So Gehazi went after Naaman. When Naaman saw someone running after him, he jumped down from the chariot to meet him and said, "Is everything all right?" 22He replied, "Yes, but my master has sent me to say, 'Two members of a company of prophetsᶜ have just come to me from the hill country of Ephraim; please give them a talent of silver and two changes of clothing.' " 23Naaman said, "Please accept two talents." He urged him, and tied up two talents of silver in two bags, with two changes of clothing, and gave them to two of his servants, who carried them in front of Gehazi.ᵈ 24When he came to the citadel, he took the bagsᵉ from them, and stored them inside; he dismissed the men, and they left.

25 He went in and stood before his master; and Elisha said to him, "Where have you been, Gehazi?" He answered, "Your servant has not gone anywhere at all." 26But he said to him, "Did I not go with you in spirit when someone

---

ᵃ A term for several skin diseases; precise meaning uncertain
ᵇ Another reading is *Amana* ᶜ Heb *sons of the prophets*
ᵈ Heb *him* ᵉ Heb lacks *the bags*

2.12. **5.10** *Seven*. See note on 4.35. **5.11** Naaman expects Elisha to perform a ritual similar to the ones used by other healers. The Aramean does not realize that a prophetic ritual is unnecessary and also does not yet understand that healing will come only from God's power, not from the power of the prophet. **5.12** The *Abana* (or Amana) River flows just north of Damascus, the capital of Aram. The *Pharpar* River lies to the south of the city. **5.13** *Father*, a title usually used by disciples addressing a master, not by servants. **5.17** Naaman assumes that Israel's God can only be worshiped in the land of Israel, so the dirt is necessary to create a

"miniature Israel" in Syria. The question of how God could be worshiped in a foreign land became a serious one for Israel during the exile (cf. Ps 137.4). **5.18** *Rimmon* (probably "Thunderer"), an epithet of the Syrian storm god Hadad, a deity usually identified with the Canaanite god Baal (see notes on 1 Kings 16.31; 17.1). **5.19b–27** This epilogue to the story of Naaman's healing serves to contrast Gehazi's greed with the unselfishness of Elisha, who will not accept payment for his services (v. 16). **5.22** *Company of prophets*. See notes on 4.1; 4.38. *Talent*. See note on 1 Kings 9.14. **5.26** Apparently Elisha has extrasensory perception

left his chariot to meet you? Is this a time to accept money and to accept clothing, olive orchards and vineyards, sheep and oxen, and male and female slaves? 27Therefore the leprosy*a* of Naaman shall cling to you, and to your descendants forever." So he left his presence leprous,*a* as white as snow.

The Miracle of the Ax Head

6 Now the company of prophets*b* said to Elisha, "As you see, the place where we live under your charge is too small for us. 2Let us go to the Jordan, and let us collect logs there, one for each of us, and build a place there for us to live." He answered, "Do so." 3Then one of them said, "Please come with your servants." And he answered, "I will." 4So he went with them. When they came to the Jordan, they cut down trees. 5But as one was felling a log, his ax head fell into the water; he cried out, "Alas, master! It was borrowed." 6Then the man of God said, "Where did it fall?" When he showed him the place, he cut off a stick, and threw it in there, and made the iron float. 7He said, "Pick it up." So he reached out his hand and took it.

The Aramean Attack Is Thwarted

8 Once when the king of Aram was at war with Israel, he took counsel with his officers. He said, "At such and such a place shall be my camp." 9But the man of God sent word to the king of Israel, "Take care not to pass this place, because the Arameans are going down there." 10The king of Israel sent word to the place of which the man of God spoke. More than once or twice he warned such a place*c* so that it was on the alert.

11 The mind of the king of Aram was greatly perturbed because of this; he called his officers and said to them, "Now tell me who among us sides with the king of Israel?" 12Then one of his officers said, "No one, my lord king. It is Elisha, the prophet in Israel, who tells the king of Israel the words that you speak in your bedchamber." 13He said, "Go and find where he is; I will send and seize him." He was told, "He is in Dothan." 14So he sent horses and chariots there and a great army; they came by night, and surrounded the city.

15 When an attendant of the man of God rose early in the morning and went out, an army with horses and chariots was all around the city. His servant said, "Alas, master! What shall we do?" 16He replied, "Do not be afraid, for there are more with us than there are with them." 17Then Elisha prayed: "O LORD, please open his eyes that he may see." So the LORD opened the eyes of the servant, and he saw; the mountain was full of horses and chariots of fire all around Elisha. 18When the Arameans*d* came down against him, Elisha prayed to the LORD, and said, "Strike this people, please, with blindness." So he struck them with blindness as Elisha had asked. 19Elisha said to them, "This is not the way, and this is not the city; follow me, and I will bring you to the man whom you seek." And he led them to Samaria.

20 As soon as they entered Samaria, Elisha said, "O LORD, open the eyes of these men so that they may see." The LORD opened their eyes, and they saw that they were inside Samaria. 21When the king of Israel saw them he said to Elisha, "Father, shall I kill them? Shall I kill them?" 22He answered, "No! Did

---

a A term for several skin diseases; precise meaning uncertain *b* Heb sons of the prophets *c* Heb warned it *d* Heb they

---

and is able to travel *in spirit* even though his body does not move. See also 6.8–9. Elisha's question elaborates on Gehazi's greed.
6.1–7 The legend of the floating ax head is another illustration of the prophet's extraordinary powers. **6.1** The company of prophets, or prophetic guild, has probably outgrown its meeting space. The other stories about this group suggest that its members do not all live together but do gather periodically, probably for instruction from Elisha (see, e.g., 4.1–2, 38; 5.22). **6.6** Elisha's use of a new ax handle rather than the old one may imply that the miracle requires the use of new objects. Note, e.g., the new bowl in 2.20, and cf. the use of a new garment in Ahijah's prophetic act (1 Kings 11.29). **6.8–23** This story from the time of the Aramean wars again shows Elisha using his miraculous powers on behalf of Israel against the Syrians. For other stories in which Elisha acts for rather than against Israel, see 3.1–27; 6.24–7.2; cf. the story of the unnamed prophet in 1 Kings 20.13–22. **6.8** For earlier episodes in the war between Israel and Aram, see 1 Kings 20.1–34; 22.1–40 and notes. **6.9** Elijah apparently got the information through extrasensory perception (cf. 5.26). **6.13** Dothan, about ten miles north of Samaria. **6.16** The exhortation not to be afraid often introduces prophecies of salvation and deliverance (Isa 41.10; Jer 1.8). **6.17** Horses and chariots of fire, the heavenly army that fights for Israel in times of need (see also 2.11). On the motif of the supernatural protection of the prophet, cf. 1.9–15. *Fire.* See note on 1 Kings 18.24. **6.21** The use of the title *father* (see note on 5.13) here implies that the king acknowledges the

you capture with your sword and your bow those whom you want to kill? Set food and water before them so that they may eat and drink; and let them go to their master." ²³So he prepared for them a great feast; after they ate and drank, he sent them on their way, and they went to their master. And the Arameans no longer came raiding into the land of Israel.

Ben-hadad's Siege of Samaria

24 Some time later King Ben-hadad of Aram mustered his entire army; he marched against Samaria and laid siege to it. ²⁵As the siege continued, famine in Samaria became so great that a donkey's head was sold for eighty shekels of silver, and one-fourth of a kab of dove's dung for five shekels of silver. ²⁶Now as the king of Israel was walking on the city wall, a woman cried out to him, "Help, my lord king!" ²⁷He said, "No! Let the LORD help you. How can I help you? From the threshing floor or from the wine press?" ²⁸But then the king asked her, "What is your complaint?" She answered, "This woman said to me, 'Give up your son; we will eat him today, and we will eat my son tomorrow.' ²⁹So we cooked my son and ate him. The next day I said to her, 'Give

up your son and we will eat him.' But she has hidden her son." ³⁰When the king heard the words of the woman he tore his clothes—now since he was walking on the city wall, the people could see that he had sackcloth on his body underneath— ³¹and he said, "So may God do to me, and more, if the head of Elisha son of Shaphat stays on his shoulders today." ³²So he dispatched a man from his presence.

Now Elisha was sitting in his house, and the elders were sitting with him. Before the messenger arrived, Elisha said to the elders, "Are you aware that this murderer has sent someone to take off my head? When the messenger comes, see that you shut the door and hold it closed against him. Is not the sound of his master's feet behind him?" ³³While he was still speaking with them, the king*a* came down to him and said, "This trouble is from the LORD! Why should I hope in the LORD any longer?"

7 ¹But Elisha said, "Hear the word of the LORD: thus says the LORD, Tomorrow about this time a measure of choice meal shall be sold for a shekel, and two measures of barley for a shekel, at the gate of Samaria." ²Then the

---

a See 7.2: Heb *messenger*

---

authority of the prophet. **6.22** For a very different response in a similar situation, cf. 1 Kings 20.35–43. **6.23** This comment implies that the Syrians were so overwhelmed by the divine power being exercised by the prophet that they broke off hostilities. **6.24–7.20** The gripping account of the Aramean siege of Samaria is a subtle and polished piece of work. In a radical departure from the usual spareness of Hebrew narrative style, the narrator uses extensive detail to create a vivid picture of life in the besieged city. In contrast to many of the Elisha stories, this one does not credit the prophet with being the agent of the city's salvation but focuses almost entirely on God's mysterious act of deliverance. **6.24** Several Aramean kings bore the name *Ben-hadad*. This individual is probably not to be identified with the Ben-hadad of 1 Kings 15.18; 20.1. The chronological relationship of the *siege* to the incident described in vv. 8–23 cannot be established. The events being described here clearly do not reflect the situation of v. 23. **6.25** The extreme scarcity of food during the siege is indicated by the high price being paid for a *donkey's head. Shekels.* See note on 1 Kings 10.16. *Kab*, a little over a quart. Dried dung was used for fuel in the ancient Near East, although in Israel it may have been considered impure, at least by priests (Ezek 4.12–15). This quantity of *dove's dung* would probably not make much of a fire. Some scholars have suggested that dove's dung was a slang term for some sort of inedible seed pods or husks. **6.27** The

king realizes that there is little that he can do to help the woman, but he does ironically point to the solution to the problem. The Lord will eventually help the city (7.6). **6.28–29** Extrabiblical sources report cases of cannibalism in times of siege, and the OT alludes to such behavior during the Babylonian siege of Jerusalem (Lam 2.20; 4.10; Ezek 5.10). Deuteronomic law includes cannibalism as one of the curses to be visited on Israel if it breaks the covenant (Deut 28.53–57). The matter-of-fact way in which the woman presents her case adds to the horror of it. **6.30** *Tore his clothes, sackcloth on.* See notes on 2.12; 1 Kings 20.31. **6.31** There is nothing specific in the story to explain why the king blamed the situation on Elisha. The king, however, views the siege as the work of the Lord (v. 33), so he may assume that the Lord's representative, the prophet, is involved as well. **6.32** *The elders*, the leaders of Israel's traditional kinship groups, have come to Elisha for instruction, just as the company of prophets regularly did (4.38). Elisha is apparently willing to speak with the king personally but not with the messenger. He therefore orders the door to be closed against the messenger until the king arrives (v. 33). **6.33** The king does not see the siege as divine punishment for past sins, which probably was the perspective of the narrator, but as an arbitrary exercise in divine power that warrants rejecting God. **7.1** Elisha's surprising reply indicates that God will soon reverse the city's fortunes. Cf. the prices listed in 6.25. *Gate,* the

captain on whose hand the king leaned said to the man of God, "Even if the LORD were to make windows in the sky, could such a thing happen?" But he said, "You shall see it with your own eyes, but you shall not eat from it."

The Arameans Flee

3 Now there were four leprous[a] men outside the city gate, who said to one another, "Why should we sit here until we die? 4If we say, 'Let us enter the city,' the famine is in the city, and we shall die there; but if we sit here, we shall also die. Therefore, let us desert to the Aramean camp; if they spare our lives, we shall live; and if they kill us, we shall but die." 5So they arose at twilight to go to the Aramean camp; but when they came to the edge of the Aramean camp, there was no one there at all. 6For the Lord had caused the Aramean army to hear the sound of chariots, and of horses, the sound of a great army, so that they said to one another, "The king of Israel has hired the kings of the Hittites and the kings of Egypt to fight against us." 7So they fled away in the twilight and abandoned their tents, their horses, and their donkeys leaving the camp just as it was, and fled for their lives. 8When these leprous[a] men had come to the edge of the camp, they went into a tent, ate and drank, carried off silver, gold, and clothing, and went and hid them. Then they came back, entered another tent, carried off things from it, and went and hid them.

9 Then they said to one another, "What we are doing is wrong. This is a day of good news; if we are silent and wait until the morning light, we will be found guilty; therefore let us go and tell the king's household." 10So they came and called to the gatekeepers of the city, and told them, "We went to the Aramean camp, but there was no one to be seen or heard there, nothing but the horses tied, the donkeys tied, and the tents as they were." 11Then the gatekeepers called out and pro-

claimed it to the king's household. 12The king got up in the night, and said to his servants, "I will tell you what the Arameans have prepared against us. They know that we are starving; so they have left the camp to hide themselves in the open country, thinking, 'When they come out of the city, we shall take them alive and get into the city.'" 13One of his servants said, "Let some men take five of the remaining horses, since those left here will suffer the fate of the whole multitude of Israel that have perished already;[b] let us send and find out." 14So they took two mounted men, and the king sent them after the Aramean army, saying, "Go and find out." 15So they went after them as far as the Jordan; the whole way was littered with garments and equipment that the Arameans had thrown away in their haste. So the messengers returned, and told the king.

16 Then the people went out, and plundered the camp of the Arameans. So a measure of choice meal was sold for a shekel, and two measures of barley for a shekel, according to the word of the LORD. 17Now the king had appointed the captain on whose hand he leaned to have charge of the gate; the people trampled him to death in the gate, just as the man of God had said when the king came down to him. 18For when the man of God had said to the king, "Two measures of barley shall be sold for a shekel, and a measure of choice meal for a shekel, about this time tomorrow in the gate of Samaria," 19the captain had answered the man of God, "Even if the LORD were to make windows in the sky, could such a thing happen?" And he had answered, "You shall see it with your own eyes, but you shall not eat from it." 20It did indeed happen to him; the people trampled him to death in the gate.

---

a A term for several skin diseases; precise meaning uncertain
b Compare Gk Syr Vg: Meaning of Heb uncertain

---

city's main market area. 7.2 The captain on whose hand the king leaned did not literally support the king but was his chief adviser. Captain. Precise meaning uncertain. Windows in the sky, openings through which rain comes (Gen 7.11; Mal 3.10). The captain assumes that the food to which Elisha is referring could appear only as a result of new growth. 7.3 Leprous. See note on 5.1. People in this condition were forbidden to come within the gates of the city (Lev 13.11, 46; Num 12.14–16). 7.6 In this period the Hittites ruled a few city-

states north of Syria, but they were hardly a major threat. The Egyptians would have represented a greater danger. 7.7 According to the narrator, the Arameans are so frightened that they even abandon their horses and donkeys, which would have hastened their flight. 7.13 The servant suggests risking the loss of the horses to the Arameans because the animals would be likely to starve during the siege anyway. 7.17 To be sure readers do not miss the point, the narrator clarifies it in vv. 18–20 (cf. 7.1–3).

The Shunammite Woman's Land Restored

8 Now Elisha had said to the woman whose son he had restored to life, "Get up and go with your household, and settle wherever you can; for the LORD has called for a famine, and it will come on the land for seven years." ²So the woman got up and did according to the word of the man of God; she went with her household and settled in the land of the Philistines seven years. ³At the end of the seven years, when the woman returned from the land of the Philistines, she set out to appeal to the king for her house and her land. ⁴Now the king was talking with Gehazi the servant of the man of God, saying, "Tell me all the great things that Elisha has done." ⁵While he was telling the king how Elisha had restored a dead person to life, the woman whose son he had restored to life appealed to the king for her house and her land. Gehazi said, "My lord king, here is the woman, and here is her son whom Elisha restored to life." ⁶When the king questioned the woman, she told him. So the king appointed an official for her, saying, "Restore all that was hers, together with all the revenue of the fields from the day that she left the land until now."

Death of Ben-hadad

7 Elisha went to Damascus while King Ben-hadad of Aram was ill. When it was told him, "The man of God has come here," ⁸the king said to Hazael, "Take a present with you and go to meet the man of God. Inquire of the LORD through him, whether I shall recover from this illness." ⁹So Hazael went to meet him, taking a present with him, all kinds of goods of Damascus, forty camel loads. When he entered and stood before him, he said, "Your son King Ben-hadad of Aram has sent me to you, saying, 'Shall I recover from this illness?' " ¹⁰Elisha said to him, "Go, say to him, 'You shall certainly recover'; but the LORD has shown me that he shall certainly die." ¹¹He fixed his gaze and stared at him, until he was ashamed. Then the man of God wept. ¹²Hazael asked, "Why does my lord weep?" He answered, "Because I know the evil that you will do to the people of Israel; you will set their fortresses on fire, you will kill their young men with the sword, dash in pieces their little ones, and rip up their pregnant women." ¹³Hazael said, "What is your servant, who is a mere dog, that he should do this great thing?" Elisha answered, "The LORD has shown me that you are to be king over Aram." ¹⁴Then he left Elisha, and went to his master Ben-hadad,[a] who said to him, "What did Elisha say to you?" And he answered, "He told me that you would certainly recover." ¹⁵But the next day he took the bed-cover and dipped it in water and spread it over the king's face, until he died. And Hazael succeeded him.

---

a Heb lacks *Ben-hadad*

8.1–6 This brief story about the Shunammite woman's land claim is a sequel to the account in 4.8–37. The narrative demonstrates Elisha's willingness to use his powers to aid those who support him. **8.1** The story's connection with the preceding narrative is unclear. The seven-year famine does not seem to be related to the starvation caused by the siege but is a new threat of which the Lord has warned the prophet. Famines were common occurrences in ancient Israel (4.38; 1 Kings 17.1), but sometimes people migrated in order to escape them (Gen 12.10; 26.1). **8.2** The woman's temporary residence with the Philistines, somewhere on the west coast of Palestine, indicates that the famine was not widespread. **8.3** Apparently the Shunammite's house and lands had been taken in her absence, although the circumstances of the loss are unclear. They might have become royal property for some reason, or perhaps her neighbors simply expanded their borders. **8.4** In contrast to the preceding narrative (6.31), the king here idolizes Elisha. **8.6** The Shunammite's involvement in Elisha's powerful deed is enough to persuade the king to act favorably on her case. **8.7–15** The illness of the Aramean king Ben-hadad provides Elisha with an opportunity to carry out one of the divine commands to his predecessor, Elijah. Yet rather than anointing Hazael as king over Aram (1 Kings 19.15), the prophet simply plants the seeds of rebellion in the mind of the future king. **8.7** *Ben-hadad.* See note on 6.24. Elisha is portrayed here as a welcome figure in the Aramean capital. **8.8** It was common practice to seek a prophetic oracle in cases of illness (cf. 1.2–8; 1 Kings 14.1–16). **8.9** The *present* Hazael brings to Elisha is enormous and is intended to indicate the high regard in which the Arameans hold the prophet. *Son,* used to designate a disciple, here a sign of subservience. **8.10** The translation correctly indicates that Elisha counseled Hazael to lie, although the Hebrew text and many later commentators tried to avoid that interpretation of events. In the end what the Lord showed the prophet turned out to be true. **8.11** *Until he was ashamed,* possibly simply "for a long time." **8.12** Hazael's attacks on Israel are de-

Jehoram Reigns over Judah

16 In the fifth year of King Joram son of Ahab of Israel,[a] Jehoram son of King Jehoshaphat of Judah began to reign. 17 He was thirty-two years old when he became king, and he reigned eight years in Jerusalem. 18 He walked in the way of the kings of Israel, as the house of Ahab had done, for the daughter of Ahab was his wife. He did what was evil in the sight of the LORD. 19 Yet the LORD would not destroy Judah, for the sake of his servant David, since he had promised to give a lamp to him and to his descendants forever.

20 In his days Edom revolted against the rule of Judah, and set up a king of their own. 21 Then Joram crossed over to Zair with all his chariots. He set out by night and attacked the Edomites and their chariot commanders who had surrounded him;[b] but his army fled home. 22 So Edom has been in revolt against the rule of Judah to this day. Libnah also revolted at the same time. 23 Now the rest of the acts of Joram, and all that he did, are they not written in the Book of the Annals of the Kings of Judah? 24 So Joram slept with his ancestors, and was buried with them in the city of David; his son Ahaziah succeeded him.

Ahaziah Reigns over Judah

25 In the twelfth year of King Joram son of Ahab of Israel, Ahaziah son of King Jehoram of Judah began to reign. 26 Ahaziah was twenty-two years old when he began to reign; he reigned one year in Jerusalem. His mother's name was Athaliah, a granddaughter of King Omri of Israel. 27 He also walked in the way of the house of Ahab, doing what was evil in the sight of the LORD, as the house of Ahab had done, for he was son-in-law to the house of Ahab.

28 He went with Joram son of Ahab to wage war against King Hazael of Aram at Ramoth-gilead, where the Arameans wounded Joram. 29 King Joram returned to be healed in Jezreel of the wounds that the Arameans had inflicted on him at Ramah, when he fought against King Hazael of Aram. King Ahaziah son of Jehoram of Judah went down to see Joram son of Ahab in Jezreel, because he was wounded.

Anointing of Jehu

9 Then the prophet Elisha called a member of the company of prophets[c] and said to him, "Gird up your loins; take this flask of oil in your hand, and go to Ramoth-gilead. 2 When you arrive, look there for Jehu son of Jehoshaphat, son of Nimshi; go in and get him to leave his companions, and take him into an inner chamber. 3 Then take the flask of oil,

---

a Gk Syr: Heb adds *Jehoshaphat being king of Judah,*
b Meaning of Heb uncertain   c Heb *sons of the prophets*

---

scribed less dramatically in 10.32; 13.7. **8.16–24** The reign of Jehoshaphat's son Jehoram (Joram) receives a strong negative evaluation because of his intermarriage with the family of the Northern king Ahab, who represents for the narrator the epitome of evil and apostasy (1 Kings 16.31–33). **8.16** *Jehoram* and *Joram* are variant forms of the same name and are used interchangeably in this narrative for both the Northern and Southern kings. Jehoram of Judah reigned ca. 849–843/2 BCE. **8.17** A comparison with 3.1 reveals a chronological problem usually solved by positing a four-year coregency with Jehoshaphat. **8.18** The marriage between Jehoram and Ahab's daughter Athaliah had been arranged to cement the treaty that made Jehoshaphat Ahab's vassal (see note on 1 Kings 22.2). In the eyes of the narrator, the Israelite princess introduced evil into the Judean royal house in the same way that the Phoenician princess Jezebel introduced evil into the house of Ahab (1 Kings 16.31). **8.19** *Lamp.* See note on 1 Kings 11.36. **8.20** Edom had been a vassal of Judah's during Jehoshaphat's reign. See notes on 3.8; 3.9. **8.21** *Zair,* an unknown location in or near Edom. **8.22** *Libnah* was in western Judah near Philistine territory. **8.23** *The Book of the Annals of the Kings of Judah.* See note on 1 Kings 14.29. **8.25–29** The brief reign of

Ahaziah of Judah was also tainted by his kinship with the house of Ahab and receives the expected negative evaluation from the narrator. **8.25** Ahaziah reigned in 843/2 BCE. **8.26** *Athaliah* was also the daughter of Ahab (v. 18). **8.27** Ahaziah was in fact a blood relative of the house of Ahab, since Ahab was Ahaziah's grandfather. **8.28** For an earlier dispute between Israel and Aram over *Ramoth-gilead,* see 1 Kings 22.1–40. The precise location of the town is unknown. **8.29** *Ramah,* here not the town in Benjamin (see 1 Kings 15.17) but a shortened form of the name Ramoth-gilead.

9.1–13 The story of the prophetic anointing of Jehu introduces a series of narratives that deal with his successful revolt against the Omride dynasty and with his religious reforms (9.1–10.36). In contrast to the other prophetic narratives about Northern kings, the Jehu stories are extraordinarily favorable toward the king, and it is possible that they were originally the climax of a collection of prophetic legends dealing with the eradication of Baal worship in Israel. **9.1–3** The anointing of Jehu fulfills the last of the commands that God gave to Elijah at Mount Horeb (1 Kings 19.15–16; cf. 1 Kings 19.19–21; 2 Kings 8.7–15). **9.1** The anointing is actually performed by a member of a prophetic guild, of which Elisha is the head. **9.2** *Inner chamber,* a

pour it on his head, and say, 'Thus says the LORD: I anoint you king over Israel.' Then open the door and flee; do not linger."

4 So the young man, the young prophet, went to Ramoth-gilead. [5]He arrived while the commanders of the army were in council, and he announced, "I have a message for you, commander." "For which one of us?" asked Jehu. "For you, commander." [6]So Jehu[a] got up and went inside; the young man poured the oil on his head, saying to him, "Thus says the LORD the God of Israel: I anoint you king over the people of the LORD, over Israel. [7]You shall strike down the house of your master Ahab, so that I may avenge on Jezebel the blood of my servants the prophets, and the blood of all the servants of the LORD. [8]For the whole house of Ahab shall perish; I will cut off from Ahab every male, bond or free, in Israel. [9]I will make the house of Ahab like the house of Jeroboam son of Nebat, and like the house of Baasha son of Ahijah. [10]The dogs shall eat Jezebel in the territory of Jezreel, and no one shall bury her." Then he opened the door and fled.

11 When Jehu came back to his master's officers, they said to him, "Is everything all right? Why did that madman come to you?" He answered them, "You know the sort and how they babble." [12]They said, "Liar! Come on, tell us!" So he said, "This is just what he said to me: 'Thus says the LORD, I anoint you king over Israel.' " [13]Then hurriedly they all took their cloaks and spread them for him on the bare[b] steps; and they blew the trumpet, and proclaimed, "Jehu is king."

Joram of Israel Killed

14 Thus Jehu son of Jehoshaphat son of Nimshi conspired against Joram. Joram with all Israel had been on guard at Ramoth-gilead

against King Hazael of Aram; [15]but King Joram had returned to be healed in Jezreel of the wounds that the Arameans had inflicted on him, when he fought against King Hazael of Aram. So Jehu said, "If this is your wish, then let no one slip out of the city to go and tell the news in Jezreel." [16]Then Jehu mounted his chariot and went to Jezreel, where Joram was lying ill. King Ahaziah of Judah had come down to visit Joram.

17 In Jezreel, the sentinel standing on the tower spied the company of Jehu arriving, and said, "I see a company." Joram said, "Take a horseman; send him to meet them, and let him say, 'Is it peace?' " [18]So the horseman went to meet him; he said, "Thus says the king, 'Is it peace?' " Jehu responded, "What have you to do with peace? Fall in behind me." The sentinel reported, saying, "The messenger reached them, but he is not coming back." [19]Then he sent out a second horseman, who came to them and said, "Thus says the king, 'Is it peace?' " Jehu answered, "What have you to do with peace? Fall in behind me." [20]Again the sentinel reported, "He reached them, but he is not coming back. It looks like the driving of Jehu son of Nimshi; for he drives like a maniac."

21 Joram said, "Get ready." And they got his chariot ready. Then King Joram of Israel and King Ahaziah of Judah set out, each in his chariot, and went to meet Jehu; they met him at the property of Naboth the Jezreelite. [22]When Joram saw Jehu, he said, "Is it peace, Jehu?" He answered, "What peace can there be, so long as the many whoredoms and sorceries of your mother Jezebel continue?" [23]Then Joram reined about and fled, saying to Ahaziah, "Treason, Ahaziah!" [24]Jehu drew his

a Heb *he*   b Meaning of Heb uncertain

private room that could be closed off to the public. **9.3** On the practice of the prophetic anointing of kings, see 1 Sam 10.1; 16.3; 1 Kings 1.34. Prophets seem to have been involved particularly in anointing the first king of a new dynasty. **9.4** *Ramoth-gilead.* See note on 8.28. **9.7** Here the death of Ahab is not only grounded in the Naboth's vineyard incident (1 Kings 21.21–24) but is related to retribution against Jezebel for killing God's prophets (1 Kings 18.4; 19.10, 14). **9.8–10** This portion of the oracle repeats in a slightly altered form the earlier prophecy of Elijah (1 Kings 21.21–24; cf. 1 Kings 14.11; 16.4). **9.11** *Madman,* an epithet often applied to prophets with low credibility (Jer 29.26; Hos 9.7). **9.14–26** After the anointing (vv.

1–13), Elisha and the prophets play no further role in the narrative. Instead, Jehu himself is the center of attention, and the detailed narrative of the coup is intended to glorify him and his reign. **9.14–16** A repetition of the essence of 8.28–29 to explain why the two kings, Joram and Ahaziah, were at the palace in Jezreel rather than at the site of the battle. **9.17** Joram's question is a general one. He probably suspects a reversal in the battle rather than a coup. **9.21** The location of the subsequent action at Naboth's property is influenced by the oracle in 1 Kings 21.19. **9.22** *Whoredoms,* not to be taken literally; the language of adultery and prostitution is often used to characterize the worship of other gods (Ex 34.16; Lev 17.7; Deut 31.16; Judg 2.17;

bow with all his strength, and shot Joram between the shoulders, so that the arrow pierced his heart; and he sank in his chariot. 25 Jehu said to his aide Bidkar, "Lift him out, and throw him on the plot of ground belonging to Naboth the Jezreelite; for remember, when you and I rode side by side behind his father Ahab how the LORD uttered this oracle against him: 26 'For the blood of Naboth and for the blood of his children that I saw yesterday, says the LORD, I swear I will repay you on this very plot of ground.' Now therefore lift him out and throw him on the plot of ground, in accordance with the word of the LORD."

Ahaziah of Judah Killed

27 When King Ahaziah of Judah saw this, he fled in the direction of Beth-haggan. Jehu pursued him, saying, "Shoot him also!" And they shot him*a* in the chariot at the ascent to Gur, which is by Ibleam. Then he fled to Megiddo, and died there. 28 His officers carried him in a chariot to Jerusalem, and buried him in his tomb with his ancestors in the city of David.

29 In the eleventh year of Joram son of Ahab, Ahaziah began to reign over Judah.

Jezebel's Violent Death

30 When Jehu came to Jezreel, Jezebel heard of it; she painted her eyes, and adorned her head, and looked out of the window. 31 As Jehu entered the gate, she said, "Is it peace, Zimri, murderer of your master?" 32 He looked up to the window and said, "Who is on my side? Who?" Two or three eunuchs looked out at him. 33 He said, "Throw her down." So they threw her down; some of her blood spattered on the wall and on the horses, which trampled

on her. 34 Then he went in and ate and drank; he said, "See to that cursed woman and bury her; for she is a king's daughter." 35 But when they went to bury her, they found no more of her than the skull and the feet and the palms of her hands. 36 When they came back and told him, he said, "This is the word of the LORD, which he spoke by his servant Elijah the Tishbite, 'In the territory of Jezreel the dogs shall eat the flesh of Jezebel; 37 the corpse of Jezebel shall be like dung on the field in the territory of Jezreel, so that no one can say, This is Jezebel.' "

Massacre of Ahab's Descendants

10 Now Ahab had seventy sons in Samaria. So Jehu wrote letters and sent them to Samaria, to the rulers of Jezreel,*b* to the elders, and to the guardians of the sons of*c* Ahab, saying, 2 "Since your master's sons are with you and you have at your disposal chariots and horses, a fortified city, and weapons, 3 select the son of your master who is the best qualified, set him on his father's throne, and fight for your master's house." 4 But they were utterly terrified and said, "Look, two kings could not withstand him; how then can we stand?" 5 So the steward of the palace, and the governor of the city, along with the elders and the guardians, sent word to Jehu: "We are your servants; we will do anything you say. We will not make anyone king; do whatever you think right." 6 Then he wrote them a second letter, saying, "If you are on my side, and if you are ready to obey me, take the heads of your mas-

---

a Syr Vg Compare Gk: Heb lacks *and they shot him*   *b* Or *of the city*; Vg Compare Gk   *c* Gk: Heb lacks *of the sons of*

8.33; Jer 2.1–13; Hos 1–3). **9.26** Throwing Joram's body on Naboth's land represents a conflation of Elijah's prophecy against Ahab (1 Kings 21.19) and the prophecy against his dynasty (1 Kings 21.21–22). **9.27–29** The text does not explain why Jehu wanted to kill Ahaziah, although the latter was Joram's vassal and might have felt obligated to support one of Joram's sons as the next king of Israel. **9.27** *Beth-haggan*, probably to be identified with modern Jenin, on the main road southwest of Jezreel. *The ascent to Gur, which is by Ibleam*, located just south of Jenin. *Megiddo* lies west-northwest of Jezreel in the Plain of Esdraelon. **9.29** This verse repeats 8.25, but corrects the chronology to take into account the fact that Joram and Ahaziah died in the same year. **9.30–37** The death of Jezebel brings to an end the influence of the most powerful woman in the history of the Northern Kingdom. **9.30** Jezebel's

formal dress and her appearance at the window give the occasion the air of a royal audience. **9.31** Jezebel's taunting greeting recalls Zimri's assassination of the Northern king Elah and the slaughter of all of Baasha's descendants (1 Kings 16.8–14). The taunt may also be intended to remind Jehu of the earlier usurper's extremely short reign (1 Kings 16.15). **9.36–37** Jehu's quotation elaborates Elijah's original oracle (1 Kings 21.23).

10.1–17 Jehu's slaughter of Ahab's descendants follows the familiar practice of usurpers who destroy all rivals (see 2 Sam 3–4; 1 Kings 15.28–30; 16.8–14). **10.1** *Seventy*, probably not precise; it may represent all of the possible claimants to the throne (see Judg 9.5; 12.14). **10.2–4** Jehu invites the guardians to fight to continue the royal line of Ahab, something they are afraid to do. **10.6** Jehu's letter is ambiguous, since in

ter's sons and come to me at Jezreel tomorrow at this time." Now the king's sons, seventy persons, were with the leaders of the city, who were charged with their upbringing. [7]When the letter reached them, they took the king's sons and killed them, seventy persons; they put their heads in baskets and sent them to him at Jezreel. [8]When the messenger came and told him, "They have brought the heads of the king's sons," he said, "Lay them in two heaps at the entrance of the gate until the morning." [9]Then in the morning when he went out, he stood and said to all the people, "You are innocent. It was I who conspired against my master and killed him; but who struck down all these? [10]Know then that there shall fall to the earth nothing of the word of the LORD, which the LORD spoke concerning the house of Ahab; for the LORD has done what he said through his servant Elijah." [11]So Jehu killed all who were left of the house of Ahab in Jezreel, all his leaders, close friends, and priests, until he left him no survivor.

12 Then he set out and went to Samaria. On the way, when he was at Beth-eked of the Shepherds, [13]Jehu met relatives of King Ahaziah of Judah and said, "Who are you?" They answered, "We are kin of Ahaziah; we have come down to visit the royal princes and the sons of the queen mother." [14]He said, "Take them alive." They took them alive, and slaughtered them at the pit of Beth-eked, forty-two in all; he spared none of them.

15 When he left there, he met Jehonadab son of Rechab coming to meet him; he greeted him, and said to him, "Is your heart as true to mine as mine is to yours?"[a] Jehonadab answered, "It is." Jehu said,[b] "If it is, give me your hand." So he gave him his hand. Jehu took him

up with him into the chariot. [16]He said, "Come with me, and see my zeal for the LORD." So he[c] had him ride in his chariot. [17]When he came to Samaria, he killed all who were left to Ahab in Samaria, until he had wiped them out, according to the word of the LORD that he spoke to Elijah.

Slaughter of Worshipers of Baal

18 Then Jehu assembled all the people and said to them, "Ahab offered Baal small service; but Jehu will offer much more. [19]Now therefore summon to me all the prophets of Baal, all his worshipers, and all his priests; let none be missing, for I have a great sacrifice to offer to Baal; whoever is missing shall not live." But Jehu was acting with cunning in order to destroy the worshipers of Baal. [20]Jehu decreed, "Sanctify a solemn assembly for Baal." So they proclaimed it. [21]Jehu sent word throughout all Israel; all the worshipers of Baal came, so that there was no one left who did not come. They entered the temple of Baal, until the temple of Baal was filled from wall to wall. [22]He said to the keeper of the wardrobe, "Bring out the vestments for all the worshipers of Baal." So he brought out the vestments for them. [23]Then Jehu entered the temple of Baal with Jehonadab son of Rechab; he said to the worshipers of Baal, "Search and see that there is no worshiper of the LORD here among you, but only worshipers of Baal." [24]Then they proceeded to offer sacrifices and burnt offerings.

Now Jehu had stationed eighty men outside, saying, "Whoever allows any of those to escape whom I deliver into your hands shall

---

a Gk: Heb *Is it right with your heart, as my heart is with your heart?*   b Gk: Heb lacks *Jehu said*   c Gk Syr Tg: Heb *they*

Hebrew, as in English, *heads* can refer literally to a part of the anatomy or metaphorically to leaders of a group. The recipients of the letter will choose to understand the word literally. **10.8** This display is intended to discourage opposition to Jehu's plans. **10.9–11** Jehu implies that he did not intend the murder of Ahab's descendants, but he sees this turn of events as the fulfillment of Elijah's prophecy (1 Kings 21.21–22, 24). The narrator, however, is clear about Jehu's intentions. **10.12–14** By slaughtering the relatives of Ahaziah, Jehu may have thought that he was eliminating all of the remaining scions of the house of David, thus paving the way for a successful annexation of Judah. **10.12** *Beth-eked of the Shepherds* is on the road between Jezreel and Samaria, but its precise location is uncertain. **10.15** *Jehonadab son of Rechab* was associ-

ated with a group called the Rechabites, who developed a reputation as fanatical worshipers of the Lord. Like the Nazirites (Num 6.1–21), the Rechabites considered all aspects of Canaanite culture to be corrupting, and they therefore avoided cultivating land, planting vineyards, drinking wine, and building houses (Jer 35). Jehonadab presumably saw Jehu's revolt as an opportunity to restore the worship of the Lord in the Northern Kingdom. **10.17** In Samaria Jehu completes the slaughter of the house of Ahab that he began in Jezreel (see v. 11). The narrator then duly notes the fulfillment of Elijah's prophecy (1 Kings 21.21–22, 24). **10.18–31** After destroying all of the house of Ahab, Jehu removes all traces of the worship of Baal, which Ahab and Jezebel had introduced into Israel (1 Kings 16.31–33). **10.19** Jehu's statement is again ambiguous (cf. v.

forfeit his life." 25As soon as he had finished presenting the burnt offering, Jehu said to the guards and to the officers, "Come in and kill them; let no one escape." So they put them to the sword. The guards and the officers threw them out, and then went into the citadel of the temple of Baal. 26They brought out the pillar*a* that was in the temple of Baal, and burned it. 27Then they demolished the pillar of Baal, and destroyed the temple of Baal, and made it a latrine to this day.

28 Thus Jehu wiped out Baal from Israel. 29But Jehu did not turn aside from the sins of Jeroboam son of Nebat, which he caused Israel to commit—the golden calves that were in Bethel and in Dan. 30The LORD said to Jehu, "Because you have done well in carrying out what I consider right, and in accordance with all that was in my heart have dealt with the house of Ahab, your sons of the fourth generation shall sit on the throne of Israel." 31But Jehu was not careful to follow the law of the LORD the God of Israel with all his heart; he did not turn from the sins of Jeroboam, which he caused Israel to commit.

Death of Jehu

32 In those days the LORD began to trim off parts of Israel. Hazael defeated them throughout the territory of Israel: 33from the Jordan eastward, all the land of Gilead, the Gadites, the Reubenites, and the Manassites, from Aroer, which is by the Wadi Arnon, that is, Gilead and Bashan. 34Now the rest of the acts of Jehu, all that he did, and all his power, are they not written in the Book of the Annals of the Kings of Israel? 35So Jehu slept with his ancestors, and they buried him in Samaria. His son Jehoahaz succeeded him. 36The time that Jehu reigned over Israel in Samaria was twenty-eight years.

Athaliah Reigns over Judah

11 Now when Athaliah, Ahaziah's mother, saw that her son was dead, she set about to destroy all the royal family. 2But Jehosheba, King Joram's daughter, Ahaziah's sister, took Joash son of Ahaziah, and stole him away from among the king's children who were about to be killed; she put*b* him and his nurse in a bedroom. Thus she*c* hid him from Athaliah, so that he was not killed; 3he remained with her six years, hidden in the house of the LORD, while Athaliah reigned over the land.

Jehoiada Anoints the Child Joash

4 But in the seventh year Jehoiada summoned the captains of the Carites and of the guards and had them come to him in the house of the LORD. He made a covenant with them and put them under oath in the house of the LORD;

---

a Gk Vg Syr Tg: Heb *pillars*   *b* With 2 Chr 22.11: Heb lacks *she put*   *c* Gk Syr Vg Compare 2 Chr 22.11: Heb *they*

---

6), since the Hebrew word translated *sacrifice* also means "slaughter." **10.26–27** *Pillars.* See note on 1 Kings 14.23. Because the pillars were stone, the burning was probably part of the process of cracking the stone so that it could be demolished. **10.29** Because the narrator considers the real theological problem in the North to be the illegitimate worship of the Lord, which was introduced by Jeroboam (1 Kings 12.26–32), Jehu still receives the standard negative evaluation in spite of his eradication of the worship of Baal. **10.32–36** The closing summary of Jehu's reign has been expanded to include additional references to Hazael's successful attacks on Israelite territory. This activity was probably thought to be a fulfillment of Elisha's prophetic vision (8.12). **10.33** The *land of Gilead* and the areas occupied by the tribes of Gad, Reuben, and Manasseh all lay east of the Jordan and were traditionally Israelite territory. *Aroer* is on the *Arnon* River, which joins the Dead Sea at the midpoint of its eastern shore. The town marks the southern limit of Aramean expansion; *Bashan,* in southern Syria, marks the northern limit. **10.36** *Jehu* reigned ca. 843/2–815 BCE.

11.1–3 In the wake of the confusion caused by Jehu's murder of Ahaziah and his relatives (9.27–28; 10.12–14), Athaliah seizes the throne of Judah. Although she rules seven years (v. 4), the narrator does not consider her a legitimate ruler, both because as a daughter of Ahab of Israel she was not of Davidic descent and because her connections with Jezebel represent a rejection of the worship of the Lord (see notes on 8.18; 8.26). The narrator therefore omits the normal facts about her rule. **11.1** *Athaliah* reigned ca. 843/2–837 BCE. **11.2** The text does not indicate whether *Jehosheba* was also Athaliah's daughter. *Joash* would have been Athaliah's grandson, but his early isolation from her and his association with the priests in the house of the Lord (v. 3) seem to have left him untainted in the eyes of the narrator. **11.4–21** The account of the restoration of the Davidic line is the only major story thus far in 2 Kings to focus completely on the affairs of Judah. The extraordinary detail in the narrative suggests that it came from temple sources in Jerusalem. **11.4** *Jehoiada,* a priest in the house of the Lord (v. 9). In 2 Chr 22.11 he is also said to have been Jehosheba's husband. *Carites,* mercenaries charged with guarding the palace and the temple. Their origins are unknown. On the basis of the Hebrew text of 2 Sam 20.23, some scholars have equated them with

then he showed them the king's son. 5He commanded them, "This is what you are to do: one-third of you, those who go off duty on the sabbath and guard the king's house 6(another third being at the gate Sur and a third at the gate behind the guards), shall guard the palace; 7and your two divisions that come on duty in force on the sabbath and guard the house of the LORD*a* 8shall surround the king, each with weapons in hand; and whoever approaches the ranks is to be killed. Be with the king in his comings and goings."

9 The captains did according to all that the priest Jehoiada commanded; each brought his men who were to go off duty on the sabbath, with those who were to come on duty on the sabbath, and came to the priest Jehoiada. 10The priest delivered to the captains the spears and shields that had been King David's, which were in the house of the LORD; 11the guards stood, every man with his weapons in his hand, from the south side of the house to the north side of the house, around the altar and the house, to guard the king on every side. 12Then he brought out the king's son, put the crown on him, and gave him the covenant;*b* they proclaimed him king, and anointed him; they clapped their hands and shouted, "Long live the king!"

Death of Athaliah

13 When Athaliah heard the noise of the guard and of the people, she went into the house of the LORD to the people; 14when she looked, there was the king standing by the pillar, according to custom, with the captains and the trumpeters beside the king, and all the people of the land rejoicing and blowing trumpets. Athaliah tore her clothes and cried, "Treason!

Treason!" 15Then the priest Jehoiada commanded the captains who were set over the army, "Bring her out between the ranks, and kill with the sword anyone who follows her." For the priest said, "Let her not be killed in the house of the LORD." 16So they laid hands on her; she went through the horses' entrance to the king's house, and there she was put to death.

17 Jehoiada made a covenant between the LORD and the king and people, that they should be the LORD's people; also between the king and the people. 18Then all the people of the land went to the house of Baal, and tore it down; his altars and his images they broke in pieces, and they killed Mattan, the priest of Baal, before the altars. The priest posted guards over the house of the LORD. 19He took the captains, the Carites, the guards, and all the people of the land; then they brought the king down from the house of the LORD, marching through the gate of the guards to the king's house. He took his seat on the throne of the kings. 20So all the people of the land rejoiced; and the city was quiet after Athaliah had been killed with the sword at the king's house.

21*c* Jehoash*d* was seven years old when he began to reign.

The Temple Repaired

12 In the seventh year of Jehu, Jehoash began to reign; he reigned forty years in Jerusalem. His mother's name was Zibiah of Beer-sheba. 2Jehoash did what was right in the sight of the LORD all his days, because the priest Jehoiada instructed him. 3Nevertheless the high places were not taken away; the peo-

---

a Heb *the* LORD *to the king*   *b* Or *treaty* or *testimony;* Heb *eduth*
c Ch 12.1 in Heb   *d* Another spelling is *Joash;* see verse 19

---

the Cherethites, a foreign mercenary unit in David's private army. **11.5–8** The translation here follows closely a rather confusing Hebrew text. Apparently the troops who *guarded the king's house* were divided into three groups, each serving a week ending on the sabbath. Jehoiada took the group about to go off duty (one-third of the total guard), divided it into three subgroups, and assigned one subgroup to each of three stations. The remaining two-thirds of the total guard were brought to the house of the Lord to guard the king (Joash). **11.6** *Gate Sur.* Location unknown. V. 19 implies that the *gate behind the guards* connected the temple with the palace. **11.10** The weapons may have been those that David captured from the Arameans (see 2 Sam 8.7). **11.12** *Covenant,* disputed. If so translated, the reference may be to the book of the law

that the king is supposed to copy and study (Deut 17.18–19). Some scholars argue that the word refers to some sort of royal insignia, perhaps jewelry. **11.14** *Pillar,* probably one of the pair at the entrance to the temple (see note on 1 Kings 7.15–22; cf. 2 Kings 23.3). *People of the land,* probably wealthy landowners. They seem to have been an important social group in Judah and enjoyed a great deal of political influence (21.23–24; 23.30; Jer 1.18; 34.19–20; 37.2). *Tore her clothes.* See note on 2.12. **11.17** The renewal of the *covenant* between the people and the Lord and between the Davidic house and the people is appropriate in the light of the disruption. Unlike the similar ceremony in 23.1–3, the terms of this covenant are not specified. **11.18** There are no earlier references to a temple of Baal in Jerusalem. It may have been introduced by

ple continued to sacrifice and make offerings on the high places.

4 Jehoash said to the priests, "All the money offered as sacred donations that is brought into the house of the LORD, the money for which each person is assessed—the money from the assessment of persons—and the money from the voluntary offerings brought into the house of the LORD, ⁵let the priests receive from each of the donors; and let them repair the house wherever any need of repairs is discovered." ⁶But by the twenty-third year of King Jehoash the priests had made no repairs on the house. ⁷Therefore King Jehoash summoned the priest Jehoiada with the other priests and said to them, "Why are you not repairing the house? Now therefore do not accept any more money from your donors but hand it over for the repair of the house." ⁸So the priests agreed that they would neither accept more money from the people nor repair the house.

9 Then the priest Jehoiada took a chest, made a hole in its lid, and set it beside the altar on the right side as one entered the house of the LORD; the priests who guarded the threshold put in it all the money that was brought into the house of the LORD. ¹⁰Whenever they saw that there was a great deal of money in the chest, the king's secretary and the high priest went up, counted the money that was found in the house of the LORD, and tied it up in bags. ¹¹They would give the money that was weighed out into the hands of the workers who had the oversight of the house of the LORD; then they paid it out to the carpenters and the builders who worked on the house of the LORD, ¹²to the masons and the stonecutters, as well as to buy timber and quarried stone for making repairs on the house of the LORD, as well as for any outlay for repairs of the house. ¹³But for the house of the LORD no basins of silver, snuffers, bowls, trumpets, or any vessels of gold, or of silver, were made from the money that was brought into the house of the LORD, ¹⁴for that was given to the workers who were repairing the house of the LORD with it. ¹⁵They did not ask an accounting from those into whose hand they delivered the money to pay out to the workers, for they dealt honestly. ¹⁶The money from the guilt offerings and the money from the sin offerings was not brought into the house of the LORD; it belonged to the priests.

Hazael Threatens Jerusalem

17 At that time King Hazael of Aram went up, fought against Gath, and took it. But when Hazael set his face to go up against Jerusalem, ¹⁸King Jehoash of Judah took all the votive gifts that Jehoshaphat, Jehoram, and Ahaziah, his ancestors, the kings of Judah, had dedicated, as well as his own votive gifts, all the gold that was found in the treasuries of the house of the LORD and of the king's house, and sent these to King Hazael of Aram. Then Hazael withdrew from Jerusalem.

Athaliah. **11.21** In a formal statement of a Judean king's accession, this information would normally come immediately before the statement of the length of his reign (12.1b; cf. 14.1–2).

12.1–16 The account of Jehoash's reign concentrates primarily on his provisions for the maintenance of the temple and thus illustrates his fidelity to the worship of the Lord. A similar concern for the temple will be exhibited later by Josiah, one of Judah's great kings in the opinion of the narrator (22.3–10). **12.1** *Jehoash* and Joash are variants of the same name and are used interchangeably throughout the narrative. Jehoash ruled ca. 837–800 BCE (cf. 13.1, 10), so the forty-year reign assigned to him here is an approximation. **12.3** *High places.* See note on 1 Kings 3.2. **12.4** The money being referred to here came from the census tax (*the money for which each person is assessed* [Ex 30.11–16]), from the valuation of an individual for the purpose of paying a vow (*the assessment of persons* [Lev 27.1–8]), and from *voluntary offerings.* **12.5** Under this arrangement, the priests were to receive all of the money but were also responsible for temple repairs when they were needed. **12.6** The priests were appar-

ently reluctant to take money out of their own funds, so they did not repair the temple. **12.7–8** Under the new arrangement, the priests would no longer accept the money, but they would also no longer be responsible for paying for repairs. **12.10** Representatives of the king and the temple would jointly take the money from the "bank" and turn it over to the workers. **12.13** The money had to be used to pay for repairs and could not be melted down to make ritual vessels. **12.16** The money from *guilt offerings* and *sin offerings* was distinct from the money mentioned in v. 4 and so was not subject to being banked but remained the property of the priests. On these two offerings, see Lev 4.1–6.7; Num 15.22–31. **12.17–18** Aramean raiding extends into Judah during Jehoash's reign, but the king is able to avoid the loss of territory. **12.17** On *Hazael*'s earlier raids in Israel, see 8.28–29; 10.32–33. *Gath,* a Philistine city on the coastal plain in southern Palestine. It may have briefly been part of the old Davidic empire (2 Chr 26.6). **12.18** *Votive gifts,* gifts donated to the temple as an act of royal piety (1 Kings 7.51; 15.15). This was not the first time they were reclaimed in order to bribe a would-be attacker (see 1 Kings

Death of Joash

19 Now the rest of the acts of Joash, and all that he did, are they not written in the Book of the Annals of the Kings of Judah? 20 His servants arose, devised a conspiracy, and killed Joash in the house of Millo, on the way that goes down to Silla. 21 It was Jozacar son of Shimeath and Jehozabad son of Shomer, his servants, who struck him down, so that he died. He was buried with his ancestors in the city of David; then his son Amaziah succeeded him.

Jehoahaz Reigns over Israel

13 In the twenty-third year of King Joash son of Ahaziah of Judah, Jehoahaz son of Jehu began to reign over Israel in Samaria; he reigned seventeen years. 2 He did what was evil in the sight of the LORD, and followed the sins of Jeroboam son of Nebat, which he caused Israel to sin; he did not depart from them. 3 The anger of the LORD was kindled against Israel, so that he gave them repeatedly into the hand of King Hazael of Aram, then into the hand of Ben-hadad son of Hazael. 4 But Jehoahaz entreated the LORD, and the LORD heeded him; for he saw the oppression of Israel, how the king of Aram oppressed them. 5 Therefore the LORD gave Israel a savior, so that they escaped from the hand of the Arameans; and the people of Israel lived in their homes as formerly. 6 Nevertheless they did not depart from the sins of the house of Jeroboam, which he caused Israel to sin, but walked[a] in them; the sacred pole[b] also remained in Samaria. 7 So Jehoahaz was left with an army of not more than fifty horsemen, ten chariots and ten thousand footmen; for the king of Aram had destroyed them and made them like the dust at threshing. 8 Now the rest of the acts of Jehoahaz and all that he did, including his might, are they not written in the Book of the Annals of the Kings of Israel? 9 So Jehoahaz slept with his ancestors, and they buried him in Samaria; then his son Joash succeeded him.

Jehoash Reigns over Israel

10 In the thirty-seventh year of King Joash of Judah, Jehoash son of Jehoahaz began to reign over Israel in Samaria; he reigned sixteen years. 11 He also did what was evil in the sight of the LORD; he did not depart from all the sins of Jeroboam son of Nebat, which he caused Israel to sin, but he walked in them. 12 Now the rest of the acts of Joash, and all that he did, as well as the might with which he fought against King Amaziah of Judah, are they not written in the Book of the Annals of the Kings of Israel? 13 So Joash slept with his ancestors, and Jeroboam sat upon his throne; Joash was buried in Samaria with the kings of Israel.

Death of Elisha

14 Now when Elisha had fallen sick with the illness of which he was to die, King Joash of Israel went down to him, and wept before him, crying,

a Gk Syr Tg Vg: Heb he walked   b Heb Asherah

15.18), nor would it be the last (see 2 Kings 18.15). **12.19–21** Kings does not give any hint about the reason for Joash's murder, although 2 Chr 24.23–27 claims that the killing was in retribution for the king's murder of the son of the priest Jehoiada. **12.20** *Millo.* See note on 1 Kings 9.15.

13.1–9 In typical Deuteronomistic style, the narrator interprets Aramean military activity during Jehoahaz's reign as a divine judgment on the king's sins. **13.1** *Jehoahaz* reigned ca. 815–802 BCE. **13.2** *On the sins of Jeroboam,* see 1 Kings 12.26–32. **13.3–5** The motif of God using foreign rulers to punish Israel and then sending a deliverer when Israel complains is a common one in Deuteronomistic literature, particularly in the accounts of Israel's early history (Judg 2.11–23 and the formulaic introductions to the stories of most of the judges; see also 1 Kings 11.14–26). **13.3** Ben-hadad continues the military activity against Israel that was begun by his father, Hazael (see 8.28–29; 10.32–33). For earlier episodes in Israel's ongoing war with the Arameans, see 1 Kings 20.1–34; 22.1–40; 2 Kings 6.8–7.20. **13.5** The *savior* is not identified. The

stories in Judges usually mention a specific individual at this point in the narrative. **13.6** After the excursus on foreign oppressors (vv. 3–5), the beginning of this verse alludes to v. 2 in order to return to the subject of Jehoahaz's sins. *Sacred pole.* See note on 1 Kings 14.15. **13.10–13** The formal account of Jehoash's reign offers only the standard remarks about his sin, in spite of the fact that the king is treated sympathetically in the following story dealing with Elisha's death (vv. 14–21). **13.10** *Jehoash* and *Joash* are variants of the same name and are used interchangeably throughout the narrative. Jehoash/Joash of Israel should not be confused with his contemporary Jehoash/Joash of Judah. Jehoash of Israel reigned ca. 802–786 BCE. **13.12–13** Repeated in 14.15–16. Here they seem out of place, since other stories about Jehoash's reign follow in vv. 14–25. **13.12** Jehoash's war with Amaziah is described in 14.8–14. **13.14–21** Elisha first appeared in the narrative in 1 Kings 19.19–21, during the reign of Ahab, so his death marks the end of almost fifty years of prophetic activity. Even on his deathbed the prophet remains a supporter of the Jehu dynasty. **13.14** The king's words

"My father, my father! The chariots of Israel and its horsemen!" 15Elisha said to him, "Take a bow and arrows"; so he took a bow and arrows. 16Then he said to the king of Israel, "Draw the bow"; and he drew it. Elisha laid his hands on the king's hands. 17Then he said, "Open the window eastward"; and he opened it. Elisha said, "Shoot"; and he shot. Then he said, "The LORD's arrow of victory, the arrow of victory over Aram! For you shall fight the Arameans in Aphek until you have made an end of them." 18He continued, "Take the arrows"; and he took them. He said to the king of Israel, "Strike the ground with them"; he struck three times, and stopped. 19Then the man of God was angry with him, and said, "You should have struck five or six times; then you would have struck down Aram until you had made an end of it, but now you will strike down Aram only three times."

20 So Elisha died, and they buried him. Now bands of Moabites used to invade the land in the spring of the year. 21As a man was being buried, a marauding band was seen and the man was thrown into the grave of Elisha; as soon as the man touched the bones of Elisha, he came to life and stood on his feet.

Israel Recaptures Cities from Aram

22 Now King Hazael of Aram oppressed Israel all the days of Jehoahaz. 23But the LORD was gracious to them and had compassion on them; he turned toward them, because of his covenant with Abraham, Isaac, and Jacob, and would not destroy them; nor has he banished them from his presence until now.

24 When King Hazael of Aram died, his son Ben-hadad succeeded him. 25Then Jehoash son of Jehoahaz took again from Ben-hadad son of Hazael the towns that he had taken from his father Jehoahaz in war. Three times Joash defeated him and recovered the towns of Israel.

Amaziah Reigns over Judah

14 In the second year of King Joash son of Joahaz of Israel, King Amaziah son of Joash of Judah, began to reign. 2He was twenty-five years old when he began to reign, and he reigned twenty-nine years in Jerusalem. His mother's name was Jehoaddin of Jerusalem. 3He did what was right in the sight of the LORD, yet not like his ancestor David; in all things he did as his father Joash had done. 4But the high places were not removed; the people still sacrificed and made offerings on the high places. 5As soon as the royal power was firmly in his hand he killed his servants who had murdered his father the king. 6But he did not put to death the children of the murderers; according to what is written in the book of the law of Moses, where the LORD commanded, "The parents shall not be put to death for the children, or the children be put to death for the parents; but all shall be put to death for their own sins."

7 He killed ten thousand Edomites in the Valley of Salt and took Sela by storm; he called it Jokthe-el, which is its name to this day.

8 Then Amaziah sent messengers to King Jehoash son of Jehoahaz, son of Jehu, of Israel, saying, "Come, let us look one another in the

---

had earlier been used by Elisha himself when he witnessed Elijah's disappearance in a whirlwind (see note on 2.12). **13.17** Aram (Syria) lay to the northeast of Israel. *Aphek.* See note on 1 Kings 20.26. **13.18–19** *Three* often plays an important role in rituals, spells, and symbolic actions, but here it does not represent completeness. **13.21** For a similar resurrection brought about by the prophet's touch, see 4.32–35. Stories of this sort are often told about saints and wonder-workers. **13.22–25** The narrator clearly understands Jehoash's victories over Aram as a fulfillment of the blessings of Elisha. **13.22** On *Hazael*'s military activities during Jehoahaz's reign, see vv. 3–5. **13.23** Here for the only time in Kings God's compassion for Israel is grounded in the covenant with Israel's ancestors (Gen 15.1–21; 26.23–25; 28.10–22). As a motive for compassion, this covenant functions in the same way that God's covenant with David serves to preserve Judah and the Davidic dynasty (2 Sam 7.1–17). **14.1–22** The narrator gives Amaziah's reign a rela-

tively positive evaluation, but the main focus of the account is the king's military exploits. Although he was successful in fighting the Edomites, he was not able to free Judah from vassalage to Israel, a relationship that began at least as early as the reign of Ahab (1 Kings 22.4). **14.1–2** According to the synchronisms in v. 23 and 15.8, *Amaziah* could not have reigned as long as the twenty-nine years assigned to him here. Most scholars assume that he shared a coregency with his son Azariah, who was perhaps put on the throne after the disastrous Israelite invasion of Jerusalem. Amaziah's dates therefore remain uncertain; he may have reigned ca. 800–783 BCE. **14.4** *High places.* See note on 1 Kings 3.2. **14.5** On the murder of Joash, see 12.19–21 and note. **14.6** The citation of the law is from Deut 24.16; cf. Jer 31.29–30; Ezek 18.2–4, 20. **14.7** The exact location of the *Valley of Salt* is unknown, although many scholars would locate it in Edom near the southern end of the Dead Sea. David had earlier defeated Edomites there (2 Sam 8.13). The location of *Sela* is also disputed.

face." 9King Jehoash of Israel sent word to King Amaziah of Judah, "A thornbush on Lebanon sent to a cedar on Lebanon, saying, 'Give your daughter to my son for a wife'; but a wild animal of Lebanon passed by and trampled down the thornbush. 10You have indeed defeated Edom, and your heart has lifted you up. Be content with your glory, and stay at home; for why should you provoke trouble so that you fall, you and Judah with you?"

11 But Amaziah would not listen. So King Jehoash of Israel went up; he and King Amaziah of Judah faced one another in battle at Beth-shemesh, which belongs to Judah. 12Judah was defeated by Israel; everyone fled home. 13King Jehoash of Israel captured King Amaziah of Judah son of Jehoash, son of Ahaziah, at Beth-shemesh; he came to Jerusalem, and broke down the wall of Jerusalem from the Ephraim Gate to the Corner Gate, a distance of four hundred cubits. 14He seized all the gold and silver, and all the vessels that were found in the house of the LORD and in the treasuries of the king's house, as well as hostages; then he returned to Samaria.

15 Now the rest of the acts that Jehoash did, his might, and how he fought with King Amaziah of Judah, are they not written in the Book of the Annals of the Kings of Israel? 16Jehoash slept with his ancestors, and was buried in Samaria with the kings of Israel; then his son Jeroboam succeeded him.

17 King Amaziah son of Joash of Judah lived fifteen years after the death of King Jehoash son of Jehoahaz of Israel. 18Now the rest of the deeds of Amaziah, are they not written in the Book of the Annals of the Kings of Judah? 19They made a conspiracy against him in Jerusalem, and he fled to Lachish. But they sent after him to Lachish, and killed him there. 20They brought him on horses; he was buried in Jerusalem with his ancestors in the city of David. 21All the people of Judah took Azariah, who was sixteen years old, and made him king to succeed his father Amaziah. 22He rebuilt Elath and restored it to Judah, after King Amaziah*a* slept with his ancestors.

Jeroboam II Reigns over Israel

23 In the fifteenth year of King Amaziah son of Joash of Judah, King Jeroboam son of Joash of Israel began to reign in Samaria; he reigned forty-one years. 24He did what was evil in the sight of the LORD; he did not depart from all the sins of Jeroboam son of Nebat, which he caused Israel to sin. 25He restored the border of Israel from Lebo-hamath as far as the Sea of the Arabah, according to the word of the LORD, the God of Israel, which he spoke by his servant Jonah son of Amittai, the prophet, who was from Gath-hepher. 26For the LORD saw that the distress of Israel was very bitter; there was no one left, bond or free, and no one to help Israel. 27But the LORD had not said that he would blot out the name of Israel from under heaven, so he saved them by the hand of Jeroboam son of Joash.

_a_ Heb _the king_

14.8 Amaziah's intentions toward Jehoash are ambiguous, but the initiative of the Judean king, who was a vassal of Jehoash's, probably led the Northerner to interpret the message as a hostile act. 14.9–10 Fables of this sort were used in Israel in political and prophetic circles (Judg 9.7–15; Ezek 17.1–10). 14.9 The _thornbush_ (Amaziah), an irritating and worthless plant, is seeking to become the equal of the majestic _cedar_ (Jehoash), but the _wild animal_ (also Jehoash) is capable of destroying the thornbush. 14.11 _Beth-shemesh_, about sixteen miles southwest of Jerusalem. 14.13 The _Ephraim Gate_ was in Jerusalem's northern wall facing Ephraim. The _Corner Gate_ was in the northwest corner of the city. A _cubit_ is about 18 inches, so Jehoash tore down about 600 feet of the wall. 14.14 The _hostages_ may have been taken in exchange for the captured Judean king, who was allowed to remain on the throne. 14.15–16 A duplicate of 13.12–13. 14.19 _Lachish,_ about thirty miles southwest of Jerusalem. 14.22 _Elath_ lies on the northern coast of the Gulf of Aqaba and is closely associated with Ezion-geber, one of Solomon's seaports (1 Kings 9.26). The reference to rebuilding Elath implies that Azariah had regained control of Edom. 14.23–29 Although Jeroboam II was in fact one of Israel's most powerful and successful kings, the narrator says little about the significance of his achievements and concentrates instead on the familiar theme of the king's sins. 14.23 _Jeroboam_ reigned ca. 786–746 BCE. 14.24 On the _sins of Jeroboam_, the first king of Israel, see 1 Kings 12.26–32. 14.25 _Lebo-hamath_ marked the northern border of Solomon's empire; see note on 1 Kings 8.65. _Sea of the Arabah,_ identical with the Salt Sea or the Dead Sea (Josh 3.16; 12.3). Jeroboam thus reconstituted the northern part of the old Solomonic empire. The text implies that this expansion occurred to fulfill an oracle from _Jonah the son of Amittai_, who is otherwise known as the subject of the book of Jonah. Jonah's oracle, however, has not been preserved. _Gath-hepher,_ about two miles east of Sepphoris. 14.26–27 On the motif of God sending deliverers to Israel in time of distress, see 13.3–5. This is an uncharacteristically positive view of God's relationship to the North-

28 Now the rest of the acts of Jeroboam, and all that he did, and his might, how he fought, and how he recovered for Israel Damascus and Hamath, which had belonged to Judah, are they not written in the Book of the Annals of the Kings of Israel? 29Jeroboam slept with his ancestors, the kings of Israel; his son Zechariah succeeded him.

Azariah Reigns over Judah

15 In the twenty-seventh year of King Jeroboam of Israel King Azariah son of Amaziah of Judah began to reign. 2He was sixteen years old when he began to reign, and he reigned fifty-two years in Jerusalem. His mother's name was Jecoliah of Jerusalem. 3He did what was right in the sight of the LORD, just as his father Amaziah had done. 4Nevertheless the high places were not taken away; the people still sacrificed and made offerings on the high places. 5The LORD struck the king, so that he was leprous*a* to the day of his death, and lived in a separate house. Jotham the king's son was in charge of the palace, governing the people of the land. 6Now the rest of the acts of Azariah, and all that he did, are they not written in the Book of the Annals of the Kings of Judah? 7Azariah slept with his ancestors; they buried him with his ancestors in the city of David; his son Jotham succeeded him.

Zechariah Reigns over Israel

8 In the thirty-eighth year of King Azariah of Judah, Zechariah son of Jeroboam reigned over Israel in Samaria six months. 9He did what was evil in the sight of the LORD, as his ancestors had done. He did not depart from the sins of Jeroboam son of Nebat, which he caused Israel to sin. 10Shallum son of Jabesh conspired against him, and struck him down in public and killed him, and reigned in place of him. 11Now the rest of the deeds of Zechariah are written in the Book of the Annals of the Kings of Israel. 12This was the promise of the LORD that he gave to Jehu, "Your sons shall sit on the throne of Israel to the fourth generation." And so it happened.

Shallum Reigns over Israel

13 Shallum son of Jabesh began to reign in the thirty-ninth year of King Uzziah of Judah; he reigned one month in Samaria. 14Then Menahem son of Gadi came up from Tirzah and came to Samaria; he struck down Shallum son of Jabesh in Samaria and killed him; he reigned in place of him. 15Now the rest of the deeds of Shallum, including the conspiracy that he made, are written in the Book of the Annals of the Kings of Israel. 16At that time Menahem sacked Tiphsah, all who were in it and its territory from Tirzah on; because they did not open it to him, he sacked it. He ripped open all the pregnant women in it.

Menahem Reigns over Israel

17 In the thirty-ninth year of King Azariah of Judah, Menahem son of Gadi began to reign over Israel; he reigned ten years in Samaria. 18He did what was evil in the sight of the LORD; he did not depart all his days from any of the sins of Jeroboam son of Nebat, which he caused Israel to sin. 19King Pul of Assyria came

---

a A term for several skin diseases; precise meaning uncertain

ern Kingdom. **14.28** *Damascus,* the capital of Aram (Syria). *Hamath* lies on the Orontes River in Syria between Damascus and Aleppo. This recovery of Aramean territory was possible largely because the Assyrians, the newly dominant power in Mesopotamia, had broken the power of Aram.
15.1–7 In spite of Azariah's long reign, the narrator gives no details of his activities and records only the fact of his leprosy. No explanation is given here for his disease, although 2 Chr 26.16–20 interprets the affliction as punishment for violating ritual regulations. **15.1** *Azariah* is also called Uzziah (vv. 13, 30, 32, 34; 2 Chr 26–27; Isa 1.1; 6.1). He reigned ca. 783–742 BCE. **15.4** *High places.* See note on 1 Kings 3.2. **15.5** *Leprous.* See note on 5.1. Azariah's son *Jotham* served as overseer of all royal estates and buildings and was probably coregent during the latter part of his father's reign. **15.8–12** Zechariah's brief reign receives a typically negative evaluation from the narrator. The king's assassination marks the end of the Jehu dynasty and the beginning of a period of internal political upheaval, complicated by Assyria's increasing involvement in Israel's political affairs. **15.8** *Zechariah* ruled Israel ca. 746–745 BCE. **15.12** For God's dynastic promise to Jehu, see 10.30. **15.13–16** Shallum's reign is so brief that the narrator does not even mention his sins. **15.13** *Shallum* ruled in 745 BCE. **15.14** *Tirzah.* See note on 1 Kings 14.17. **15.16** *Tiphsah.* Location uncertain. *Ripping open pregnant women* was considered a barbarous practice and is elsewhere associated only with foreign armies (8.12; Hos 13.16; Am 1.13). **15.17–22** Menahem's reign is marked by a resurgence in Assyrian military activity that eventually leads to the fall of the Northern Kingdom. **15.17** *Menahem* reigned ca. 745–737 BCE. **15.19** *King Pul,* Tiglath-pileser III, who was king of Assyria 745–727 BCE. Menahem in effect

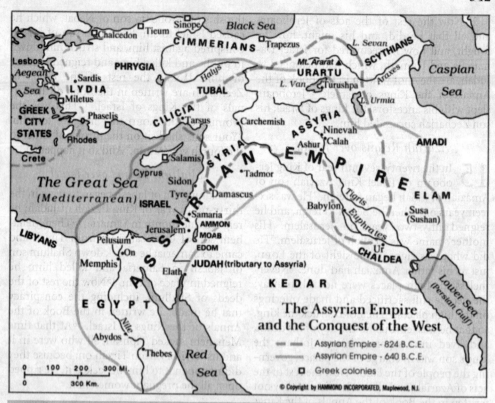

Behind the events narrated in 2 Kings 15–23 are Assyria's expansion in the eighth century BCE and its collision with Egypt's sphere of influence.

against the land; Menahem gave Pul a thousand talents of silver, so that he might help him confirm his hold on the royal power. 20 Menahem exacted the money from Israel, that is, from all the wealthy, fifty shekels of silver from each one, to give to the king of Assyria. So the king of Assyria turned back, and did not stay there in the land. 21 Now the rest of the deeds of Menahem, and all that he did, are they not written in the Book of the Annals of the Kings of Israel? 22 Menahem slept with his ancestors, and his son Pekahiah succeeded him.

Pekahiah Reigns over Israel

23 In the fiftieth year of King Azariah of Judah, Pekahiah son of Menahem began to reign over Israel in Samaria; he reigned two

years. 24 He did what was evil in the sight of the LORD; he did not turn away from the sins of Jeroboam son of Nebat, which he caused Israel to sin. 25 Pekah son of Remaliah, his captain, conspired against him with fifty of the Gileadites, and attacked him in Samaria, in the citadel of the palace along with Argob and Arieh; he killed him, and reigned in place of him. 26 Now the rest of the deeds of Pekahiah, and all that he did, are written in the Book of the Annals of the Kings of Israel.

Pekah Reigns over Israel

27 In the fifty-second year of King Azariah of Judah, Pekah son of Remaliah began to reign over Israel in Samaria; he reigned twenty years. 28 He did what was evil in the sight of the

becomes an Assyrian vassal. **15.19–20** *Talents, shekels.* See notes on 1 Kings 9.14; 10.16. **15.23–26** The reign of Pekahiah receives the usual negative evaluation from the narrator, who mentions only the assassination that ended the king's rule. **15.23** *Pekahiah* ruled ca. 737–736 BCE. **15.25** *Gileadites.* For Gilead, see note on 1 Kings 17.1. The interpretation of *Argob and Arieh*

is disputed. The names are variously interpreted as warriors, cities, and even features of palace architecture.

15.27–31 The official account of Pekah's reign notes only the loss of Israelite territory to Assyria. His extensive involvement in Judean affairs is covered in ch. 16. **15.27** Scholars agree that *Pekah* could not have

LORD; he did not depart from the sins of Jeroboam son of Nebat, which he caused Israel to sin.

29 In the days of King Pekah of Israel, King Tiglath-pileser of Assyria came and captured Ijon, Abel-beth-maacah, Janoah, Kedesh, Hazor, Gilead, and Galilee, all the land of Naphtali; and he carried the people captive to Assyria. 30 Then Hoshea son of Elah made a conspiracy against Pekah son of Remaliah, attacked him, and killed him; he reigned in place of him, in the twentieth year of Jotham son of Uzziah. 31 Now the rest of the acts of Pekah, and all that he did, are written in the Book of the Annals of the Kings of Israel.

Jotham Reigns over Judah

32 In the second year of King Pekah son of Remaliah of Israel, King Jotham son of Uzziah of Judah began to reign. 33 He was twenty-five years old when he began to reign and reigned sixteen years in Jerusalem. His mother's name was Jerusha daughter of Zadok. 34 He did what was right in the sight of the LORD, just as his father Uzziah had done. 35 Nevertheless the high places were not removed; the people still sacrificed and made offerings on the high places. He built the upper gate of the house of the LORD. 36 Now the rest of the acts of Jotham, and all that he did, are they not written in the Book of the Annals of the Kings of Judah? 37 In those days the LORD began to send King Rezin of Aram and Pekah son of Remaliah against Judah. 38 Jotham slept with his ancestors, and was buried with his ancestors in the city of David, his ancestor; his son Ahaz succeeded him.

Ahaz Reigns over Judah

16 In the seventeenth year of Pekah son of Remaliah, King Ahaz son of Jotham of Judah began to reign. 2 Ahaz was twenty years old when he began to reign; he reigned sixteen years in Jerusalem. He did not do what was right in the sight of the LORD his God, as his ancestor David had done, 3 but he walked in the way of the kings of Israel. He even made his son pass through fire, according to the abominable practices of the nations whom the LORD drove out before the people of Israel. 4 He sacrificed and made offerings on the high places, on the hills, and under every green tree.

5 Then King Rezin of Aram and King Pekah son of Remaliah of Israel came up to wage war on Jerusalem; they besieged Ahaz but could not conquer him. 6 At that time the king of Edom[a] recovered Elath for Edom,[b] and drove the Judeans from Elath; and the Edomites came to Elath, where they live to this day. 7 Ahaz sent messengers to King Tiglath-pileser of Assyria, saying, "I am your servant and your son. Come up, and rescue me from the hand of the king of Aram and from the hand of the king of Israel, who are attacking me." 8 Ahaz

---

a Cn: Heb *King Rezin of Aram*   *b* Cn: Heb *Aram*

---

ruled for the twenty years assigned to him here. He may have ruled ca. 736–732 BCE. **15.29** These overlapping references to the towns of *Ijon, Abel-beth-maacah, Janoah, Kedesh,* and *Hazor* and to the regions of *Gilead, Galilee,* and *Naphtali* indicate that Tiglath-pileser took significant portions of north-central Israel and parts of Transjordan. **15.30** Hoshea's coup may have had support from the Assyrians. **15.32–38** The narrator gives no details about Jotham's reign except to note the beginning of attempts to force Judah into an anti-Assyrian coalition. **15.32** *Jotham* ruled ca. 742–735 BCE. **15.35** *High places.* See note on 1 Kings 3.2. *Upper gate* of the temple. Location unknown. **15.37** The kings of Aram (Syria) and Israel were trying to force Judah into a coalition against Assyria (cf. ch. 16; Isa 7.1–8.10). **16.1–20** Ahaz is one of the few Judean kings to receive a negative evaluation from the historian. Part of the reason for this assessment may lie in the king's heterodox religious practices, but the narrator may have also been upset by Ahaz's willingness to make an alliance with Assyria, thus becoming an Assyrian vassal.

16.1 *Ahaz* ruled ca. 735–715 BCE. **16.3** *Made his son pass through fire,* probably a rite carried out as part of the worship of the god Molech, whose cult was practiced just outside of Jerusalem in the Valley of Hinnom. Many scholars, although not all, think that as part of the ritual, children were sacrificed by fire to the god, who was probably an underworld deity. The cult, which may have involved parents sacrificing firstborn children in order to ensure future births, must have had royal patronage. The worship of Molech was banned by Deuteronomy, which associated it with the abominations of the Canaanites (Deut 18.9–14), and later biblical writers condemned it as well (Lev 18.21; 20.2–5; Jer 7.31; 19.5; 32.35). **16.4** *Ahaz* is the first Judean king since Solomon who is said to have personally worshiped at the *high places.* On the significance of these cultic installations, see note on 1 Kings 3.2. **16.5** The kings of Aram and Israel apparently wanted to overthrow Ahaz in order to force Judah into an anti-Assyrian coalition. For a different perspective on the same incident, see Isa 7.1–8.10. **16.6** On Judah's rebuilding of Elath, see 14.22 and note. **16.7** Ignoring

also took the silver and gold found in the house of the LORD and in the treasures of the king's house, and sent a present to the king of Assyria. 9 The king of Assyria listened to him; the king of Assyria marched up against Damascus, and took it, carrying its people captive to Kir; then he killed Rezin.

10 When King Ahaz went to Damascus to meet King Tiglath-pileser of Assyria, he saw the altar that was at Damascus. King Ahaz sent to the priest Uriah a model of the altar, and its pattern, exact in all its details. 11 The priest Uriah built the altar; in accordance with all that King Ahaz had sent from Damascus, just so did the priest Uriah build it, before King Ahaz arrived from Damascus. 12 When the king came from Damascus, the king viewed the altar. Then the king drew near to the altar, went up on it, 13 and offered his burnt offering and his grain offering, poured his drink offering, and dashed the blood of his offerings of well-being against the altar. 14 The bronze altar that was before the LORD he removed from the front of the house, from the place between his altar and the house of the LORD, and put it on the north side of his altar. 15 King Ahaz commanded the priest Uriah, saying, "Upon the great altar offer the morning burnt offering, and the evening grain offering, and the king's burnt offering, and his grain offering, with the burnt offering of all the people of the land, their grain offering, and their drink offering; then dash against it all the blood of the burnt offering, and all the blood of the sacrifice; but the bronze altar shall be for me to inquire by." 16 The priest Uriah did everything that King Ahaz commanded.

17 Then King Ahaz cut off the frames of the stands, and removed the laver from them; he removed the sea from the bronze oxen that were under it, and put it on a pediment of stone. 18 The covered portal for use on the sabbath that had been built inside the palace, and the outer entrance for the king he removed from[a] the house of the LORD. He did this because of the king of Assyria. 19 Now the rest of the acts of Ahaz that he did, are they not written in the Book of the Annals of the Kings of Judah? 20 Ahaz slept with his ancestors, and was buried with his ancestors in the city of David; his son Hezekiah succeeded him.

Hoshea Reigns over Israel

17 In the twelfth year of King Ahaz of Judah, Hoshea son of Elah began to reign in Samaria over Israel; he reigned nine years. 2 He did what was evil in the sight of the LORD, yet not like the kings of Israel who were before him. 3 King Shalmaneser of Assyria came up against him; Hoshea became his vassal, and paid him tribute. 4 But the king of Assyria found treachery in Hoshea; for he had sent messengers to King So of Egypt, and offered no tribute to the king of Assyria, as he had done year by year; therefore the king of Assyria confined him and imprisoned him.

Israel Carried Captive to Assyria

5 Then the king of Assyria invaded all the land and came to Samaria; for three years he besieged it. 6 In the ninth year of Hoshea the king

---

a Cn: Heb lacks from

Isaiah's counsel to trust in the Lord and to avoid foreign entanglements (Isa 7.1–9), Ahaz buys protection from Assyria. **16.9** *Kir,* said to have been the original home of the Arameans (Am 9.7), so it is appropriate that Tiglath-pileser relocates them there. The precise location of Kir is unknown. **16.10** The text does not indicate why Ahaz was attracted to the *altar* he saw in Damascus. There is nothing to indicate that it was anything other than an Aramean cult object, although it might have been a particularly large or grand one (v. 15). *Uriah* the priest appears in Isa 8.2 as one of the prophet's supporters. **16.12–13** As did his predecessors Solomon and Jeroboam (1 Kings 8.63; 12.32), Ahaz dedicates the altar by offering his own sacrifices. **16.17–18** Ahaz apparently takes some of the temple furnishings and uses them as part of his bribe to the king of Assyria. **16.17** *Stands.* See 1 Kings 7.27–37. *Sea, bronze oxen.* See 1 Kings 7.23–26. **16.18** The meaning of *the covered portal for use on the sabbath* continues to be the subject of scholarly debate.

17.1–6 Hoshea was the Israelite king upon whom the punishment for the sins of the Northern Kingdom finally fell. It is therefore odd that the narrator does not judge Hoshea as harshly as some of the other Northern kings and even omits the standard reference to walking in the ways of Jeroboam. **17.1** Here *Hoshea*'s accession is synchronized with the reign of Ahaz of Judah, while in 15.30 the synchronization is with Jotham, a fact that may indicate a coregency in Judah. Hoshea ruled in Samaria ca. 732–724 BCE. **17.3** *King Shalmaneser,* Shalmaneser V, who ruled Assyria 727–722 BCE. **17.4** *King So of Egypt,* controversial; no Egyptian ruler by that name can be identified. Some scholars interpret the phrase as the place at which the messengers met the king of Egypt; others interpret *So* as a misunderstanding of an Egyptian royal title. **17.6** After

of Assyria captured Samaria; he carried the Israelites away to Assyria. He placed them in Halah, on the Habor, the river of Gozan, and in the cities of the Medes.

7 This occurred because the people of Israel had sinned against the LORD their God, who had brought them up out of the land of Egypt from under the hand of Pharaoh king of Egypt. They had worshiped other gods [8]and walked in the customs of the nations whom the LORD drove out before the people of Israel, and in the customs that the kings of Israel had introduced.[a] [9]The people of Israel secretly did things that were not right against the LORD their God. They built for themselves high places at all their towns, from watchtower to fortified city; [10]they set up for themselves pillars and sacred poles[b] on every high hill and under every green tree; [11]there they made offerings on all the high places, as the nations did whom the LORD carried away before them. They did wicked things, provoking the LORD to anger; [12]they served idols, of which the LORD had said to them, "You shall not do this." [13]Yet the LORD warned Israel and Judah by every prophet and every seer, saying, "Turn from your evil ways and keep my commandments and my statutes, in accordance with all the law that I commanded your ancestors and that I sent to you by my servants the prophets." [14]They would not listen but were stubborn, as their ancestors had been, who did not believe in the LORD their God. [15]They despised his statutes, and his covenant that he made with their ancestors, and the warnings that he gave them. They went after false idols and became false; they followed the nations that were around them, concerning whom the LORD had commanded them that they should not do as they did. [16]They rejected all the commandments of the LORD their God and made for themselves cast images of two calves; they made a sacred pole,[c] worshiped all the host of heaven, and served Baal. [17]They made their sons and their daughters pass through fire; they used divination and augury; and they sold themselves to do evil in the sight of the LORD, provoking him to anger. [18]Therefore the LORD was very angry with Israel and removed them out of his sight; none was left but the tribe of Judah alone.

19 Judah also did not keep the commandments of the LORD their God but walked in the customs that Israel had introduced. [20]The LORD rejected all the descendants of Israel; he punished them and gave them into the hand of plunderers, until he had banished them from his presence.

21 When he had torn Israel from the house of David, they made Jeroboam son of Nebat

---

a Meaning of Heb uncertain   *b* Heb *Asherim*   *c* Heb *Asherah*

a siege lasting more than two years, Samaria finally fell in 722/1 BCE to the new Assyrian king, Sargon II. The relocation of populations was a characteristic of Assyrian foreign policy during this period. *Halah,* a city northeast of Nineveh. *Habor* River, the modern Habur, a tributary of the Euphrates. *River of Gozan,* possibly also the Habur. The *cities of the Medes* lay to the east of Assyria. **17.7–23** These verses occupy a crucial position in the book of Kings. Coming as they do immediately after the account of the fall of the Northern Kingdom, they provide a theological framework for understanding Israel's history from the narrator's Deuteronomistic point of view. At the same time, they set up the history of the North as an object lesson for the kingdom of Judah and define the theological terms that will govern the continued existence of the Southern Kingdom and the Davidic dynasty. Although the narrative of Kings up to this point focuses almost entirely on the actions of Israel's kings, here the narrator's theological assessment concentrates instead on the sins of the people and the kings play only an incidental role in the Deuteronomistic explanation of the disaster. **17.7–8** The primary cause of the exile of Israel is the people's worship of other gods, an act that violates Deuteronomy's directive to worship only the Lord and to avoid the gods of Canaan (see Deut 6.4–15; 7.1–6). **17.9** *The people . . . did things that were not right* may indicate the narrator's recognition that there have been relatively few illustrations of the people's sins up to this point. *High places.* See note on 1 Kings 3.2. Their continued use violates the commands in Deut 12.2–4, which requires that the people worship only at the sanctuary of God's choosing. **17.10** *Pillars, sacred poles.* See notes on 1 Kings 14.15; 14.23. These objects too should have been removed (Deut 7.5; 12.2–4). **17.13** Although a number of prophets are mentioned earlier in Kings, none of them are described as calling the people to repent. For later examples, see Jer 7.3, 5; 18.11; Ezek 33.11. **17.16** *Two calves.* See note on 1 Kings 12.28. *Host of heaven,* the sun, moon, and stars. Their worship is prohibited in Deut 4.19; 17.2–5. **17.17** Making sons and daughters *pass through fire* is banned, along with *divination and augury,* in Deut 18.9–14. On the sacrificing of children, see note on 16.3. **17.19–20** Probably the work of an exilic writer who knew Judah's ultimate fate and sought to explain it the same way that the fall of Samaria was earlier explained. **17.21–23** Here the narrator finally returns to the theme of Jeroboam's sin, which has provided the literary and theological struc-

king. Jeroboam drove Israel from following the LORD and made them commit great sin. 22The people of Israel continued in all the sins that Jeroboam committed; they did not depart from them 23until the LORD removed Israel out of his sight, as he had foretold through all his servants the prophets. So Israel was exiled from their own land to Assyria until this day.

Assyria Resettles Samaria

24 The king of Assyria brought people from Babylon, Cuthah, Avva, Hamath, and Sepharvaim, and placed them in the cities of Samaria in place of the people of Israel; they took possession of Samaria, and settled in its cities. 25When they first settled there, they did not worship the LORD; therefore the LORD sent lions among them, which killed some of them. 26So the king of Assyria was told, "The nations that you have carried away and placed in the cities of Samaria do not know the law of the god of the land; therefore he has sent lions among them; they are killing them, because they do not know the law of the god of the land." 27Then the king of Assyria commanded, "Send there one of the priests whom you carried away from there; let him*a* go and live there, and teach them the law of the god of the land." 28So one of the priests whom they had carried away from Samaria came and lived in Bethel; he taught them how they should worship the LORD.

29 But every nation still made gods of its own and put them in the shrines of the high places that the people of Samaria had made, every nation in the cities in which they lived; 30the people of Babylon made Succoth-benoth, the people of Cuth made Nergal, the people of Hamath made Ashima; 31the Avvites made Nibhaz and Tartak; the Sepharvites burned their children in the fire to Adrammelech and Anammelech, the gods of Sepharvaim. 32They also worshiped the LORD and ap-

pointed from among themselves all sorts of people as priests of the high places, who sacrificed for them in the shrines of the high places. 33So they worshiped the LORD but also served their own gods, after the manner of the nations from among whom they had been carried away. 34To this day they continue to practice their former customs.

They do not worship the LORD and they do not follow the statutes or the ordinances or the law or the commandment that the LORD commanded the children of Jacob, whom he named Israel. 35The LORD had made a covenant with them and commanded them, "You shall not worship other gods or bow yourselves to them or serve them or sacrifice to them, 36but you shall worship the LORD, who brought you out of the land of Egypt with great power and with an outstretched arm; you shall bow yourselves to him, and to him you shall sacrifice. 37The statutes and the ordinances and the law and the commandment that he wrote for you, you shall always be careful to observe. You shall not worship other gods; 38you shall not forget the covenant that I have made with you. You shall not worship other gods, 39but you shall worship the LORD your God; he will deliver you out of the hand of all your enemies." 40They would not listen, however, but they continued to practice their former custom.

41 So these nations worshiped the LORD, but also served their carved images; to this day their children and their children's children continue to do as their ancestors did.

Hezekiah's Reign over Judah

18 In the third year of King Hoshea son of Elah of Israel, Hezekiah son of King Ahaz of Judah began to reign. 2He was twenty-

a Syr Vg: Heb *them*

---

ture for Israel's history since the revolt of the Northern Kingdom (1 Kings 12.16–20). **17.24–41** An attempt to explain why the worship of the Lord existed along side of the worship of other gods in the territory that was once the home of the Israelites. **17.24** All of these cities were part of the Assyrian Empire, except for *Babylon,* on the Euphrates River, and *Cuthah,* in central Babylonia; their precise location is uncertain. In keeping with Assyrian practice, *Samaria* is now used to refer to the entire region and not just to the old capital city. **17.25** The *lions* are agents of divine judgment (see 1 Kings 13.24; 20.36). Apparently the Lord still lays

claim to the land, even though the Israelites have been removed. **17.30–31** *Nergal,* a Babylonian underworld god associated with plague. *Nibhaz* and *Tartak,* Elamite gods. The remaining deities cannot be identified with any certainty.

18.1–12 From the standpoint of the narrator, the reign of Hezekiah marks a high point in Judah's history. He is the first king to walk completely in the ways of his ancestor David, and Hezekiah's religious reforms win high praise from the historian. In fact, the stories about his deeds are so favorable that some modern scholars have concluded that 2 Kings once

five years old when he began to reign; he reigned twenty-nine years in Jerusalem. His mother's name was Abi daughter of Zechariah. ³He did what was right in the sight of the LORD just as his ancestor David had done. ⁴He removed the high places, broke down the pillars, and cut down the sacred pole.ᵃ He broke in pieces the bronze serpent that Moses had made, for until those days the people of Israel had made offerings to it; it was called Nehushtan. ⁵He trusted in the LORD the God of Israel; so that there was no one like him among all the kings of Judah after him, or among those who were before him. ⁶For he held fast to the LORD; he did not depart from following him but kept the commandments that the LORD commanded Moses. ⁷The LORD was with him; wherever he went, he prospered. He rebelled against the king of Assyria and would not serve him. ⁸He attacked the Philistines as far as Gaza and its territory, from watchtower to fortified city.

9 In the fourth year of King Hezekiah, which was the seventh year of King Hoshea son of Elah of Israel, King Shalmaneser of Assyria came up against Samaria, besieged it, ¹⁰and at the end of three years, took it. In the sixth year of Hezekiah, which was the ninth year of King Hoshea of Israel, Samaria was taken. ¹¹The king of Assyria carried the Israelites away to Assyria, settled them in Halah, on the Habor, the river of Gozan, and in the cities of the Medes, ¹²because they did not obey the voice of the LORD their God but transgressed his covenant—all that Moses the servant of the LORD had commanded; they neither listened nor obeyed.

Sennacherib Invades Judah

13 In the fourteenth year of King Hezekiah, King Sennacherib of Assyria came up against all the fortified cities of Judah and captured them. ¹⁴King Hezekiah of Judah sent to the king of Assyria at Lachish, saying, "I have done wrong; withdraw from me; whatever you impose on me I will bear." The king of Assyria demanded of King Hezekiah of Judah three hundred talents of silver and thirty talents of gold. ¹⁵Hezekiah gave him all the silver that was found in the house of the LORD and in the treasuries of the king's house. ¹⁶At that time Hezekiah stripped the gold from the doors of the temple of the LORD, and from the doorposts that King Hezekiah of Judah had overlaid and gave it to the king of Assyria. ¹⁷The king of Assyria sent the Tartan, the Rabsaris, and the Rabshakeh with a great army from Lachish to King Hezekiah at Jerusalem. They went up and came to Jerusalem. When they arrived, they came and stood by the conduit of the upper pool, which is on the highway to the Fuller's Field. ¹⁸When they called for the king, there came out to them Eliakim son of Hilkiah, who was in charge of the palace, and Shebnah the secretary, and Joah son of Asaph, the recorder.

19 The Rabshakeh said to them, "Say to Hezekiah: Thus says the great king, the king of Assyria: On what do you base this confidence of yours? ²⁰Do you think that mere words are strategy and power for war? On whom do you now rely, that you have rebelled against me? ²¹See, you are relying now on Egypt, that bro-

---

a Heb *Asherah*

---

ended with an account of his rule. **18.1** *Hezekiah* reigned ca. 715–687/6 BCE. **18.4** Hezekiah was the first Judean king to remove the *high places* (see note on 1 Kings 3.2). *Pillars, sacred pole.* See notes on 1 Kings 14.15; 14.23. The *bronze serpent* attributed to Moses was a cultic object used in rituals to prevent or treat snakebite (Num 21.4–9). Serpents also played a wide variety of roles in the religions of the ancient Near East. **18.8** *Gaza,* a Philistine city near the Mediterranean coast that marked the traditional southern border of Canaan. Hezekiah seems to have tried to push his borders westward to recapture parts of the old Davidic empire. **18.9–12** Much of this material summarizes 17.5–8. See notes on 17.6; 17.7–8. **18.13–37** The beginning of an extended account of Sennacherib's invasion of Palestine in 701 BCE. The account continues through 19.37 and is at least partially paralleled in 2 Chr 32; Isa 36–37. The narrative

includes much traditional material and shows signs of having gone through a long editorial history. **18.13** *Sennacherib* ruled Assyria 705–681 BCE. His invasion was in retaliation for Hezekiah's rebellion (v. 7). **18.14** *Lachish.* See note on 14.19. *Talents.* See note on 1 Kings 9.14. **18.17** *Tartan,* the second-ranking Assyrian officer after the king. The *Rabsaris* was often involved in leading the Assyrian army. The *Rabshakeh* was usually involved in running the royal court and the personal business of the king. *Conduit . . . Fuller's Field.* The site where the two delegations met is mentioned again in Isa 7.3 and seems to have been an important part of Jerusalem's water supply. The precise location is uncertain. **18.18** *Eliakim,* the overseer of royal estates and buildings. *Shebnah* kept the royal records but also had high administrative responsibilities. *Joah,* perhaps the royal herald. **18.21** Hezekiah had sought help from Egypt in his attempt to resist As-

ken reed of a staff, which will pierce the hand of anyone who leans on it. Such is Pharaoh king of Egypt to all who rely on him. 22But if you say to me, 'We rely on the LORD our God,' is it not he whose high places and altars Hezekiah has removed, saying to Judah and to Jerusalem, 'You shall worship before this altar in Jerusalem'? 23Come now, make a wager with my master the king of Assyria: I will give you two thousand horses, if you are able on your part to set riders on them. 24How then can you repulse a single captain among the least of my master's servants, when you rely on Egypt for chariots and for horsemen? 25Moreover, is it without the LORD that I have come up against this place to destroy it? The LORD said to me, Go up against this land, and destroy it."

26 Then Eliakim son of Hilkiah, and Shebnah, and Joah said to the Rabshakeh, "Please speak to your servants in the Aramaic language, for we understand it; do not speak to us in the language of Judah within the hearing of the people who are on the wall." 27But the Rabshakeh said to them, "Has my master sent me to speak these words to your master and to you, and not to the people sitting on the wall, who are doomed with you to eat their own dung and to drink their own urine?"

28 Then the Rabshakeh stood and called out in a loud voice in the language of Judah, "Hear the word of the great king, the king of Assyria! 29Thus says the king: 'Do not let Hezekiah deceive you, for he will not be able to deliver you out of my hand. 30Do not let Hezekiah make you rely on the LORD by saying, The LORD will surely deliver us, and this city will not be given into the hand of the king of Assyria.' 31Do not listen to Hezekiah; for thus says the king of Assyria: 'Make your peace with me and come out to me; then every one of you

will eat from your own vine and your own fig tree, and drink water from your own cistern, 32until I come and take you away to a land like your own land, a land of grain and wine, a land of bread and vineyards, a land of olive oil and honey, that you may live and not die. Do not listen to Hezekiah when he misleads you by saying, The LORD will deliver us. 33Has any of the gods of the nations ever delivered its land out of the hand of the king of Assyria? 34Where are the gods of Hamath and Arpad? Where are the gods of Sepharvaim, Hena, and Ivvah? Have they delivered Samaria out of my hand? 35Who among all the gods of the countries have delivered their countries out of my hand, that the LORD should deliver Jerusalem out of my hand?' "

36 But the people were silent and answered him not a word, for the king's command was, "Do not answer him." 37Then Eliakim son of Hilkiah, who was in charge of the palace, and Shebna the secretary, and Joah son of Asaph, the recorder, came to Hezekiah with their clothes torn and told him the words of the Rabshakeh.

Hezekiah Consults Isaiah

19 When King Hezekiah heard it, he tore his clothes, covered himself with sackcloth, and went into the house of the LORD. 2And he sent Eliakim, who was in charge of the palace, and Shebna the secretary, and the senior priests, covered with sackcloth, to the prophet Isaiah son of Amoz. 3They said to him, "Thus says Hezekiah, This day is a day of distress, of rebuke, and of disgrace; children have come to the birth, and there is no strength to bring them forth. 4It may be that the LORD your God heard all the words of the Rabshakeh, whom his master the king of As-

syria. This policy was firmly opposed by the prophet Isaiah (Isa 30.1–5). **18.22** In contrast to the view of the narrator, the Rabshakeh assumes that the altars and high places removed during Hezekiah's religious reforms were legitimate places for the worship of the Lord (v. 4). In fact, Hezekiah's centralization of worship in Jerusalem is in accordance with the demands of Deut 12. **18.25** The Rabshakeh here appeals to Deuteronomistic theology, which tends to explain disaster as the result of sin. **18.26** The Judeans request that the negotiations be carried out in Aramaic, a West Semitic dialect related to Hebrew. By this time Aramaic had become the language of international diplomacy and trade, but was not well understood by the inhabitants of Jerusalem, who spoke only the local dialect of He-

brew. **18.34** All of these cities had earlier been captured by the Assyrians. **18.37** On tearing clothing, see note on 2.12.

19.1–7 Hezekiah's consultation of Isaiah during the crisis reflects the common practice of seeking divine guidance before or during military activities. See, e.g., 3.9–12; 1 Kings 22.1–12. Here the consultation is intended to be interpreted as a sign of the king's piety. **19.1** On tearing clothing and wearing sackcloth, see notes on 2.12; 1 Kings 20.31. **19.2** *Eliakim, Shebna.* See note on 18.18. **19.3** The *distress* Hezekiah feels is due to the Assyrian threat, and the *rebuke* and *disgrace* are the result of the Rabshakeh's taunts (18.19–35). *Children . . . bring them forth.* The proverb means that the critical moment for deliverance has arrived but that the

syria has sent to mock the living God, and will rebuke the words that the LORD your God has heard; therefore lift up your prayer for the remnant that is left." [5]When the servants of King Hezekiah came to Isaiah, [6]Isaiah said to them, "Say to your master, 'Thus says the LORD: Do not be afraid because of the words that you have heard, with which the servants of the king of Assyria have reviled me. [7]I myself will put a spirit in him, so that he shall hear a rumor and return to his own land; I will cause him to fall by the sword in his own land.' "

Sennacherib's Threat

8 The Rabshakeh returned, and found the king of Assyria fighting against Libnah; for he had heard that the king had left Lachish. [9]When the king[a] heard concerning King Tirhakah of Ethiopia,[b] "See, he has set out to fight against you," he sent messengers again to Hezekiah, saying, [10]"Thus shall you speak to King Hezekiah of Judah: Do not let your God on whom you rely deceive you by promising that Jerusalem will not be given into the hand of the king of Assyria. [11]See, you have heard what the kings of Assyria have done to all lands, destroying them utterly. Shall you be delivered? [12]Have the gods of the nations delivered them, the nations that my predecessors destroyed, Gozan, Haran, Rezeph, and the people of Eden who were in Telassar? [13]Where is the king of Hamath, the king of Arpad, the king of the city of Sepharvaim, the king of Hena, or the king of Ivvah?"

Hezekiah's Prayer

14 Hezekiah received the letter from the hand of the messengers and read it; then Hezekiah

went up to the house of the LORD and spread it before the LORD. [15]And Hezekiah prayed before the LORD, and said: "O LORD the God of Israel, who are enthroned above the cherubim, you are God, you alone, of all the kingdoms of the earth; you have made heaven and earth. [16]Incline your ear, O LORD, and hear; open your eyes, O LORD, and see; hear the words of Sennacherib, which he has sent to mock the living God. [17]Truly, O LORD, the kings of Assyria have laid waste the nations and their lands, [18]and have hurled their gods into the fire, though they were no gods but the work of human hands—wood and stone—and so they were destroyed. [19]So now, O LORD our God, save us, I pray you, from his hand, so that all the kingdoms of the earth may know that you, O LORD, are God alone."

20 Then Isaiah son of Amoz sent to Hezekiah, saying, "Thus says the LORD, the God of Israel: I have heard your prayer to me about King Sennacherib of Assyria. [21]This is the word that the LORD has spoken concerning him:

> She despises you, she scorns you—
>   virgin daughter Zion;
> she tosses her head—behind your back,
>   daughter Jerusalem.

[22] "Whom have you mocked and reviled?
>   Against whom have you raised your
>   voice
> and haughtily lifted your eyes?
>   Against the Holy One of Israel!
[23] By your messengers you have mocked the
>   Lord,
>   and you have said, 'With my many
>   chariots

a Heb *he* *b* Or *Nubia*; Heb *Cush*

---

participants themselves are not able to bring it into existence. **19.6** Isaiah's oracle of salvation opens in typical style with an exhortation not to fear (see, e.g., Isa 7.4). **19.7** The spirit will deceive Sennacherib, although the oracle does not specify the nature of the rumor he will hear (cf. 1 Kings 22.20–23). **19.8–13** This report of Sennacherib's second message to Hezekiah is taken by some scholars to be simply a variant of the report in 18.19–35. Other scholars see here evidence of a second Assyrian campaign, while still others take these verses as the second phase of the negotiations. The narrator clearly intends the last interpretation. **19.8** *Libnah.* See note on 8.22. **19.9** *Tirhakah* ruled Egypt (here called *Ethiopia*) ca. 690–664 BCE, so he must have been commander of the army rather than king when this incident occurred. This

word of an imminent Egyptian attack may have been the rumor mentioned in v. 7. **19.10–13** The arguments advanced here summarize those in 18.19–35. **19.12–13** The cities mentioned were all places where populations had recently been displaced. Several of the cities were connected with the exile of the Northern Kingdom (cf. 17.6, 24). **19.14–34** In contrast to Hezekiah's response to the first Assyrian visit (vv. 1–7), this time Hezekiah himself goes to the temple and prays to the Lord. The answer to the prayer then comes in the form of a second oracle from Isaiah. **19.15** *Before the LORD* implies that the king was before the ark within the holy of holies, an area where normally only priests were allowed to enter. *Cherubim.* See note on 1 Kings 6.23–28. **19.18** *Gods,* statues, usually made of wood, that represented the gods in many temples.

I have gone up the heights of the
 mountains,
 to the far recesses of Lebanon;
I felled its tallest cedars,
 its choicest cypresses;
I entered its farthest retreat,
 its densest forest.
24 I dug wells
 and drank foreign waters,
I dried up with the sole of my foot
 all the streams of Egypt.'

25 "Have you not heard
 that I determined it long ago?
I planned from days of old
 what now I bring to pass,
that you should make fortified cities
 crash into heaps of ruins,
26 while their inhabitants, shorn of strength,
 are dismayed and confounded;
they have become like plants of the field
 and like tender grass,
like grass on the housetops,
 blighted before it is grown.

27 "But I know your rising*a* and your sitting,
 your going out and coming in,
 and your raging against me.
28 Because you have raged against me
 and your arrogance has come to my
    ears,
I will put my hook in your nose
 and my bit in your mouth;
I will turn you back on the way
 by which you came.

29 "And this shall be the sign for you: This
year you shall eat what grows of itself, and in
the second year what springs from that; then
in the third year sow, reap, plant vineyards,
and eat their fruit. 30 The surviving remnant of
the house of Judah shall again take root downward, and bear fruit upward; 31 for from Jerusalem a remnant shall go out, and from Mount
Zion a band of survivors. The zeal of the LORD
of hosts will do this.

32 "Therefore thus says the LORD concerning the king of Assyria: He shall not come into
this city, shoot an arrow there, come before it
with a shield, or cast up a siege ramp against it.
33 By the way that he came, by the same he
shall return; he shall not come into this city,
says the LORD. 34 For I will defend this city to
save it, for my own sake and for the sake of my
servant David."

Sennacherib's Defeat and Death

35 That very night the angel of the LORD set
out and struck down one hundred eighty-five
thousand in the camp of the Assyrians; when
morning dawned, they were all dead bodies.
36 Then King Sennacherib of Assyria left, went
home, and lived at Nineveh. 37 As he was worshiping in the house of his god Nisroch, his
sons Adrammelech and Sharezer killed him
with the sword, and they escaped into the land
of Ararat. His son Esar-haddon succeeded
him.

Hezekiah's Illness

20 In those days Hezekiah became sick
and was at the point of death. The
prophet Isaiah son of Amoz came to him, and
said to him, "Thus says the LORD: Set your

---

a Gk Compare Isa 37.27 Q Ms: MT lacks *rising*

19.25–28 God here implies that the Assyrian victories are all part of a divine plan that has been in existence since the beginning of the world. Sennacherib
is simply the tool God is using to punish the nations.
However, because of the Assyrian king's arrogant assumption that he is in control of the situation, God
will thwart his efforts and make him return to his
land. These themes are also found elsewhere in Isaiah's prophecies (see, e.g., Isa 10.12–19; 14.24–27).
19.28 *Hook in your nose . . . bit in your mouth.* The king
is compared to an animal that can be led wherever its
owner wants it to go. 19.29 Isaiah's sign does not indicate a rapid return to normal living conditions. It will
take the land two years to recover from the ravages of
the Assyrian invasion, and during that time the people
will have to gather grain that grows naturally. Only in
the third year will they be able to plant and reap a nor-

mal harvest. 19.35–37 In spite of many ingenious attempts from antiquity to the present day, there is no
good way to rationalize the miraculous salvation of
Jerusalem. The event is simply a dramatic fulfillment
of Isaiah's oracle of deliverance. 19.37 *Nisroch,* otherwise unknown. The name is probably a corruption of
the name of one of the Mesopotamian deities. *Land of
Ararat,* Urartu, modern Armenia. After a struggle over
the succession, *Esar-haddon* came to the Assyrian
throne in 681 and ruled until 669 BCE.
20.1–11 The story of Hezekiah's illness also exists in
an expanded version in Isa 38.1–22. The incident is
not assigned a specific date, but v. 6 seems to point forward to the miraculous deliverance of Jerusalem in
701 BCE. It is likely, then, that the story is out of place
chronologically and should have preceded the narratives of chs. 18–19. The story is probably in its present

house in order, for you shall die; you shall not recover." ²Then Hezekiah turned his face to the wall and prayed to the LORD: ³"Remember now, O LORD, I implore you, how I have walked before you in faithfulness with a whole heart, and have done what is good in your sight." Hezekiah wept bitterly. ⁴Before Isaiah had gone out of the middle court, the word of the LORD came to him: ⁵"Turn back, and say to Hezekiah prince of my people, Thus says the LORD, the God of your ancestor David: I have heard your prayer, I have seen your tears; indeed, I will heal you; on the third day you shall go up to the house of the LORD. ⁶I will add fifteen years to your life. I will deliver you and this city out of the hand of the king of Assyria; I will defend this city for my own sake and for my servant David's sake." ⁷Then Isaiah said, "Bring a lump of figs. Let them take it and apply it to the boil, so that he may recover."

8 Hezekiah said to Isaiah, "What shall be the sign that the LORD will heal me, and that I shall go up to the house of the LORD on the third day?" ⁹Isaiah said, "This is the sign to you from the LORD, that the LORD will do the thing that he has promised: the shadow has now advanced ten intervals; shall it retreat ten intervals?" ¹⁰Hezekiah answered, "It is normal for the shadow to lengthen ten intervals; rather let the shadow retreat ten intervals." ¹¹The prophet Isaiah cried to the LORD; and he brought the shadow back the ten intervals, by which the sun*ᵃ* had declined on the dial of Ahaz.

Envoys from Babylon

12 At that time King Merodach-baladan son of Baladan of Babylon sent envoys with letters and a present to Hezekiah, for he had heard that Hezekiah had been sick. ¹³Hezekiah welcomed them;*ᵇ* he showed them all his treasure house, the silver, the gold, the spices, the precious oil, his armory, all that was found in his storehouses; there was nothing in his house or in all his realm that Hezekiah did not show them. ¹⁴Then the prophet Isaiah came to King Hezekiah, and said to him, "What did these men say? From where did they come to you?" Hezekiah answered, "They have come from a far country, from Babylon." ¹⁵He said, "What have they seen in your house?" Hezekiah answered, "They have seen all that is in my house; there is nothing in my storehouses that I did not show them."

16 Then Isaiah said to Hezekiah, "Hear the word of the LORD: ¹⁷Days are coming when all that is in your house, and that which your ancestors have stored up until this day, shall be carried to Babylon; nothing shall be left, says the LORD. ¹⁸Some of your own sons who are born to you shall be taken away; they shall be eunuchs in the palace of the king of Babylon." ¹⁹Then Hezekiah said to Isaiah, "The word of the LORD that you have spoken is good." For he

a Syr See Isa 38.8 and Tg: Heb *it*   *b* Gk Vg Syr: Heb *When Hezekiah heard about them*

---

position because of its link in v. 12 with the story of the visit from the messengers of Merodach-baladan. Whatever the reasons for the displacement of 20.1–11, its present position causes the healing to appear as a special favor for the king whose piety and fidelity to the Lord had saved Jerusalem during the Assyrian invasion. **20.4** *Middle court,* part of the royal palace. **20.5** *On the third day* indicates the end of a brief period of time (cf. Hos 6.1–2). **20.6** Here the king's recovery and the salvation of Jerusalem from the Assyrians are linked together in the same prophecy. **20.7** The translation follows the Greek text, which suggests that Isaiah's action set the healing process in motion but that the completion of the process still lay in the future. The Hebrew text reports that the healing took place immediately, thus rendering the following sign superfluous. In antiquity *figs* were thought to have healing properties. **20.8** The *sign* is intended to authenticate the prophecy and guarantee its fulfillment (cf. 1 Kings 13.3 and note). **20.9** For a similar sign involving the sun, see Josh 10.12–13. **20.11** *Dial of Ahaz,* a series of steps on which the movement of a

shadow cast by the sun marked the hours. **20.12–19** The story of Hezekiah's encounter with the messengers of Merodach-baladan also appears to be out of place in the history of Hezekiah's reign. Merodach-baladan ruled Babylon between 722 and 710 BCE and then again briefly from 704 to 703, before Sennacherib deposed him. The visit to Hezekiah must have taken place well before the Assyrian invasion of 701 BCE and probably occurred during Merodach-baladan's first term on the throne. The purpose of the visit was perhaps to encourage trade between Babylon and the west and to secure allies who might be useful in the future. The prophet Isaiah, who was generally opposed to all foreign alliances, opposed any sort of contact with the Babylonians. The compiler of Kings may have placed this negative story about Hezekiah in its present position in order to detract somewhat from the king's reputation for piety. In this way Hezekiah would not overshadow the future achievements of Josiah, whom the narrator regarded as Judah's greatest king. **20.17** In Isaiah's oracle this interchange with the Babylonians becomes an explanation for the destruction of

thought, "Why not, if there will be peace and security in my days?"

Death of Hezekiah

20 The rest of the deeds of Hezekiah, all his power, how he made the pool and the conduit and brought water into the city, are they not written in the Book of the Annals of the Kings of Judah? 21 Hezekiah slept with his ancestors; and his son Manasseh succeeded him.

Manasseh Reigns over Judah

21 Manasseh was twelve years old when he began to reign; he reigned fifty-five years in Jerusalem. His mother's name was Hephzibah. 2 He did what was evil in the sight of the LORD, following the abominable practices of the nations that the LORD drove out before the people of Israel. 3 For he rebuilt the high places that his father Hezekiah had destroyed; he erected altars for Baal, made a sacred pole,*a* as King Ahab of Israel had done, worshiped all the host of heaven, and served them. 4 He built altars in the house of the LORD, of which the LORD had said, "In Jerusalem I will put my name." 5 He built altars for all the host of heaven in the two courts of the house of the LORD. 6 He made his son pass through fire; he practiced soothsaying and augury, and dealt with mediums and with wiz-

ards. He did much evil in the sight of the LORD, provoking him to anger. 7 The carved image of Asherah that he had made he set in the house of which the LORD said to David and to his son Solomon, "In this house, and in Jerusalem, which I have chosen out of all the tribes of Israel, I will put my name forever; 8 I will not cause the feet of Israel to wander any more out of the land that I gave to their ancestors, if only they will be careful to do according to all that I have commanded them, and according to all the law that my servant Moses commanded them." 9 But they did not listen; Manasseh misled them to do more evil than the nations had done that the LORD destroyed before the people of Israel.

10 The LORD said by his servants the prophets, 11 "Because King Manasseh of Judah has committed these abominations, has done things more wicked than all that the Amorites did, who were before him, and has caused Judah also to sin with his idols; 12 therefore thus says the LORD, the God of Israel, I am bringing upon Jerusalem and Judah such evil that the ears of everyone who hears of it will tingle. 13 I will stretch over Jerusalem the measuring line for Samaria, and the plummet for the house of Ahab; I will wipe Jerusalem as

---

a Heb *Asherah*

Jerusalem and the exile in 587/6 BCE. **20.20–21** The concluding summary of Hezekiah's reign finally mentions one of his most impressive achievements, the construction of the Siloam tunnel. To provide Jerusalem with a secure water supply during a siege, the king cut a passage through 1,749 feet of solid rock to lead water from the Gihon spring outside the city to the pool of Siloam safely inside the walls. A wall inscription originally carved in the tunnel still exists to testify to his achievement.

21.1–18 In the eyes of the Deuteronomistic narrator, the long reign of Manasseh was the epitome of evil. Perhaps reacting against the religious reforms of his father, Hezekiah (18.4–6), Manasseh restored the cultic practices of Ahaz (16.2–4) and elaborated on them, in the process violating many of the provisions for worship laid down in Deuteronomy. More to the point, he committed many of the same sins that led to the devastation of the Northern Kingdom and to the exile of its inhabitants (17.7–18). It is not surprising, then, that the narrator blames Manasseh for the Babylonian destruction of Jerusalem and the exile. Chronicles, however, has a more positive view of this king (2 Chr 33.1–20). **21.1** *Manasseh ruled ca.* 687/6–642 BCE. **21.2** Following the *abominable practices of the nations* is forbidden in Deut 12.29–31 (cf. 2 Kings 17.7).

21.3 *High places.* See note on 1 Kings 3.2. *Sacred pole.* See note on 1 Kings 14.15. The destruction of these installations is commanded in Deut 12.2–4 (cf. 2 Kings 17.9–10, 16). In the narrator's view, *Ahab* was the most sinful of all of the Northern kings because of his official encouragement of the worship of Baal and Asherah (see the assessment in 1 Kings 16.31–33). *Host of heaven.* See note on 17.16. **21.5** It is not clear exactly where these altars were placed in the temple courts. **21.6** *Made his son pass through fire.* See note on 16.3. This practice and the various types of divination mentioned here are forbidden in Deut 18.9–14 (cf. 2 Kings 17.17). **21.7** *Asherah.* See note on 1 Kings 14.15. **21.7–8** For the Deuteronomistic narrator, the promise of an eternal Davidic line and the promise of the permanent dwelling of Israel in the land were both always contingent on obedience to the divine law; see, e.g., 1 Kings 9.3–9. **21.10** The *prophets* who delivered this judgment oracle are not identified. **21.11** The *Amorites* were among the original inhabitants of Canaan and therefore one of the peoples whose practices were to be avoided. **21.13** The same standards that were applied to Israel will also be applied to Judah. The parallels between the two are already evident. For the narrator's opinions on the *house of Ahab,* see note on 21.3. One *wipes a dish* and turns it *upside down* to be sure that all

one wipes a dish, wiping it and turning it up-side down. [14]I will cast off the remnant of my heritage, and give them into the hand of their enemies; they shall become a prey and a spoil to all their enemies, [15]because they have done what is evil in my sight and have provoked me to anger, since the day their ancestors came out of Egypt, even to this day."

16 Moreover Manasseh shed very much in-nocent blood, until he had filled Jerusalem from one end to another, besides the sin that he caused Judah to sin so that they did what was evil in the sight of the LORD.

17 Now the rest of the acts of Manasseh, all that he did, and the sin that he committed, are they not written in the Book of the Annals of the Kings of Judah? [18]Manasseh slept with his ancestors, and was buried in the garden of his house, in the garden of Uzza. His son Amon succeeded him.

Amon Reigns over Judah

19 Amon was twenty-two years old when he began to reign; he reigned two years in Jerusa-lem. His mother's name was Meshullemeth daughter of Haruz of Jotbah. [20]He did what was evil in the sight of the LORD, as his father Manasseh had done. [21]He walked in all the way in which his father walked, served the idols that his father served, and worshiped them; [22]he abandoned the LORD, the God of his ancestors, and did not walk in the way of the LORD. [23]The servants of Amon conspired against him, and killed the king in his house.

[24]But the people of the land killed all those who had conspired against King Amon, and the people of the land made his son Josiah king in place of him. [25]Now the rest of the acts of Amon that he did, are they not written in the Book of the Annals of the Kings of Judah? [26]He was buried in his tomb in the garden of Uzza; then his son Josiah succeeded him.

Josiah Reigns over Judah

22 Josiah was eight years old when he began to reign; he reigned thirty-one years in Jerusalem. His mother's name was Je-didah daughter of Adaiah of Bozkath. [2]He did what was right in the sight of the LORD, and walked in all the way of his father David; he did not turn aside to the right or to the left.

Hilkiah Finds the Book of the Law

3 In the eighteenth year of King Josiah, the king sent Shaphan son of Azaliah, son of Me-shullam, the secretary, to the house of the LORD, saying, [4]"Go up to the high priest Hil-kiah, and have him count the entire sum of the money that has been brought into the house of the LORD, which the keepers of the thresh-old have collected from the people; [5]let it be given into the hand of the workers who have the oversight of the house of the LORD; let them give it to the workers who are at the house of the LORD, repairing the house, [6]that is, to the carpenters, to the builders, to the ma-sons; and let them use it to buy timber and quarried stone to repair the house. [7]But no ac-

---

of its contents have been removed. **21.14** After the de-struction of the Northern Kingdom, only Judah re-mained as the *remnant* of God's heritage. **21.18** *Gar-den of Uzza*. Location unknown. **21.19–26** The reign of Amon saw the continuation of all of the evil policies of his father, Manasseh. **21.19** *Amon* ruled ca. 642–640 BCE. **21.24** *People of the land*. See note on 11.14.

22.1–2 The narrator of Kings views Josiah as the Ju-dean king who most closely conformed to the Davidic model. Even more than the highly praised Hezekiah, Josiah was obedient to God's law, a fact the historian il-lustrates by describing in detail the king's religious re-forms. **22.1** *Josiah* reigned ca. 640–609 BCE. **22.3–20** Josiah's pious concern for repairing the temple leads to the discovery of a lawbook, which motivates the king to make a new covenant between the people and the Lord and to carry out a religious reform throughout the land. Most scholars identify this book as an early version of the present book of Deuteron-omy. Like Deuteronomy, the lawbook contains dire threats against people who reject the Lord and wor-

ship other gods (vv. 16–17; cf. Deut 27–28). Similarly, the book leads to the making of a covenant (23.2–3), a concept that plays an important role throughout Deuteronomy (see, e.g., Deut 29). Finally, the reforms carried out by Josiah generally conform to the sort of worship that Deuteronomy demands. In the eyes of the narrator, then, Josiah was the ideal king precisely because his rule was guided by Deuteronomic law (cf. Deut 17.18–20). **22.3** Josiah's *eighteenth year*, 622 BCE. According to 2 Chr 34.3–18, Josiah began his religious reforms in his twelfth year, even though the lawbook was not discovered in the temple until Josiah's eigh-teenth year. Many scholars believe the chronology of Chronicles to be correct, and if it is, then it is likely that the writer of Kings reordered events to emphasize the crucial role of the lawbook. *Shaphan* and his descen-dants seem to have been supporters of the Deuterono-mistic theology advocated by the narrator of Kings, and they later aided the prophet Jeremiah in the final days before the capture of Jerusalem (Jer 26.24; 29.3; 36.10–12). **22.4–7** On the arrangements for making

counting shall be asked from them for the money that is delivered into their hand, for they deal honestly."

8 The high priest Hilkiah said to Shaphan the secretary, "I have found the book of the law in the house of the LORD." When Hilkiah gave the book to Shaphan, he read it. 9Then Shaphan the secretary came to the king, and reported to the king, "Your servants have emptied out the money that was found in the house, and have delivered it into the hand of the workers who have oversight of the house of the LORD." 10Shaphan the secretary informed the king, "The priest Hilkiah has given me a book." Shaphan then read it aloud to the king.

11 When the king heard the words of the book of the law, he tore his clothes. 12Then the king commanded the priest Hilkiah, Ahikam son of Shaphan, Achbor son of Micaiah, Shaphan the secretary, and the king's servant Asaiah, saying, 13"Go, inquire of the LORD for me, for the people, and for all Judah, concerning the words of this book that has been found; for great is the wrath of the LORD that is kindled against us, because our ancestors did not obey the words of this book, to do according to all that is written concerning us."

14 So the priest Hilkiah, Ahikam, Achbor, Shaphan, and Asaiah went to the prophetess Huldah the wife of Shallum son of Tikvah, son of Harhas, keeper of the wardrobe; she resided in Jerusalem in the Second Quarter, where they consulted her. 15She declared to them, "Thus says the LORD, the God of Israel: Tell the man who sent you to me, 16Thus says the LORD, I will indeed bring disaster on this place and on its inhabitants—all the words of the book that the king of Judah has read. 17Because they have abandoned me and have made offerings to other gods, so that they have provoked me to anger with all the work of their hands, therefore my wrath will be kindled against this place, and it will not be quenched. 18But as to the king of Judah, who sent you to inquire of the LORD, thus shall you say to him, Thus says the LORD, the God of Israel: Regarding the words that you have heard, 19because your heart was penitent, and you humbled yourself before the LORD, when you heard how I spoke against this place, and against its inhabitants, that they should become a desolation and a curse, and because you have torn your clothes and wept before me, I also have heard you, says the LORD. 20Therefore, I will gather you to your ancestors, and you shall be gathered to your grave in peace; your eyes shall not see all the disaster that I will bring on this place." They took the message back to the king.

Josiah's Reformation

23 Then the king directed that all the elders of Judah and Jerusalem should be gathered to him. 2The king went up to the

repairs on the temple, see 12.4–16 and notes. **22.8** *Book of the law,* probably a scroll. The precise circumstances of its discovery are not related. Some scholars have speculated that the scroll had been stored in the temple or hidden away during the anti-Deuteronomic reforms of Manasseh (21.2–9). Others have suggested that the book was in fact written by Hilkiah and then conveniently "found." **22.11** *Tore his clothes.* See note on 2.12. **22.13** People inquired of a deity through a prophet in times of personal or national distress (1.2; 8.7–15; 1 Kings 14.1–18; 22.5–12). **22.14** *Huldah* is not mentioned elsewhere, but she was clearly an important figure in Jerusalemite society. The *Second Quarter* was on the western hill of Jerusalem, an area enclosed by a city wall during the reign of Hezekiah. The expansion of the city at that time was perhaps to accommodate refugees from the Assyrian invasion of the Northern Kingdom. **22.16–17** Huldah's judgment oracle is reminiscent of 21.12; Deut 27–28. **22.20** Huldah's prophecy to Josiah implies that the king will have a nonviolent death. In this case, the prophecy was not fulfilled (23.29–30). **23.1–27** Although Josiah's religious reforms were clearly inspired by Deuteronomic regulations con-

cerning worship, some scholars have suggested that the cultic practices he curtailed were of Assyrian origin and that the reforms therefore constituted a revolt against Assyria. However, most of the practices involved seem to have been Canaanite rather than Assyrian, and many of them appear elsewhere in Kings associated with one or another of the native rulers. Yet the lack of connection with Assyrian religion does not necessarily mean that Josiah's reforms did not have political as well as religious motives. In addition to purifying worship of the Lord in Judah and Jerusalem, he also went into the North and destroyed shrines throughout Ephraim, concentrating particularly on Bethel, one of the royal sanctuaries of the old Northern Kingdom (vv. 15–20). At this time Ephraim was technically an Assyrian province, Samaria, and Josiah's activities there could certainly have been understood as hostile acts. Josiah's reforms in the North symbolically made the country fit for the worship of the Lord and may have been intended as a prelude to a political claim that would have reconstituted the old Davidic empire. **23.1–3** Strictly speaking, both the making of the covenant and the reformation of Israelite religion are an exercise in futility, since irrevocable judgment

house of the Lord, and with him went all the people of Judah, all the inhabitants of Jerusalem, the priests, the prophets, and all the people, both small and great; he read in their hearing all the words of the book of the covenant that had been found in the house of the Lord. 3 The king stood by the pillar and made a covenant before the Lord, to follow the Lord, keeping his commandments, his decrees, and his statutes, with all his heart and all his soul, to perform the words of this covenant that were written in this book. All the people joined in the covenant.

4 The king commanded the high priest Hilkiah, the priests of the second order, and the guardians of the threshold, to bring out of the temple of the Lord all the vessels made for Baal, for Asherah, and for all the host of heaven; he burned them outside Jerusalem in the fields of the Kidron, and carried their ashes to Bethel. 5 He deposed the idolatrous priests whom the kings of Judah had ordained to make offerings in the high places at the cities of Judah and around Jerusalem; those also who made offerings to Baal, to the sun, the moon, the constellations, and all the host of the heavens. 6 He brought out the image of[a] Asherah from the house of the Lord, outside Jerusalem, to the Wadi Kidron, burned it at the Wadi Kidron, beat it to dust and threw the dust of it upon the graves of the common people. 7 He broke down the houses of the male temple prostitutes that were in the house of the Lord, where the women did weaving for Asherah. 8 He brought all the priests out of the towns of Judah, and defiled the high places where the priests had made offerings, from Geba to Beersheba; he broke down the high places of the gates that were at the entrance of the gate of Joshua the governor of the city, which were on the left at the gate of the city. 9 The priests of the high places, however, did not come up to the altar of the Lord in Jerusalem, but ate unleavened bread among their kindred. 10 He defiled Topheth, which is in the valley of Ben-hinnom, so that no one would make a son or a daughter pass through fire as an offering to Molech. 11 He removed the horses that the kings of Judah had dedicated to the sun, at the entrance to the house of the Lord, by the chamber of the eunuch Nathan-melech, which was in the precincts;[b] then he burned the chariots of the sun with fire. 12 The altars on the roof of the upper chamber of Ahaz, which the kings of Judah had made, and the altars that Manasseh had made in the two courts of the house of the Lord, he pulled down from there and broke in pieces, and threw the rubble into the Wadi Kidron. 13 The king defiled the high places that were east of Jerusalem, to the south of the Mount of Destruction, which King Solomon of Israel had built for Astarte the abomination of the Sidonians, for Chemosh the abomination of Moab, and for Milcom the abomination of the Ammonites. 14 He broke the pillars in pieces, cut down the sacred poles,[c] and covered the sites with human bones.

15 Moreover, the altar at Bethel, the high place erected by Jeroboam son of Nebat, who caused Israel to sin—he pulled down that altar along with the high place. He burned the high place, crushing it to dust; he also burned the sacred pole.[d] 16 As Josiah turned, he saw the

---

a Heb lacks *image of*   *b* Meaning of Heb uncertain
c Heb *Asherim*   *d* Heb *Asherah*

---

has already been decreed against the city and the people (22.16–17). In the context of the present narrative, Josiah's actions therefore can only be interpreted as a sign of his willingness to obey God's law even though obedience will not bring future benefit. **23.3** *Covenant*, an important Deuteronomic concept constituting an oath of loyalty to the Lord. **23.4** On the worship of *Baal, Asherah*, and *the host of heaven*, which had been introduced (or reintroduced) into Judah by Manasseh, see notes on 1 Kings 14.15; 2 Kings 17.16. *Kidron*. See note on 1 Kings 2.37. Cf. 1 Kings 15.13. Carrying the ashes to *Bethel* shows Josiah's zeal to defile the old royal sanctuary of the Northern Kingdom. **23.7** On the cultic role of prostitutes, see note on 1 Kings 14.24. The women were probably weaving clothes for the statue of the goddess. **23.8** *Priests*, here priests of the Lord, in contrast to the idolatrous priests of v. 5. *High places*. See note on 1 Kings 3.2. The removal of the high places effectively centralizes worship in Jerusalem in accordance with Deut 12. *Geba* lies to the north of the Dead Sea and marks Judah's northern boundary. *Beer-sheba* is the traditional marker of the southern boundary. *Gate of Joshua*. Location unknown. **23.9** The treatment of the *priests of the high places* contradicts Deut 18.6–8, which allows outlying priests to sacrifice at the temple in Jerusalem. **23.10** *Topheth*, an installation for the worship of Molech. See note on 16.3. **23.11** The *horses* and *chariots of the sun* were probably thought to convey the sun across the sky and must have been part of a solar cult. **23.12** On Manasseh's altars, see 21.5. **23.13** *Mount of Destruction*, the Mount of Olives. On Solomon's altars to foreign gods, see 1 Kings 11.5–7 and notes. **23.14** *Pillars, sacred poles*. See notes on 1 Kings 14.15; 14.23. **23.15–18** Jo-

tombs there on the mount; and he sent and took the bones out of the tombs, and burned them on the altar, and defiled it, according to the word of the LORD that the man of God proclaimed,[a] when Jeroboam stood by the altar at the festival; he turned and looked up at the tomb of the man of God who had predicted these things. [17]Then he said, "What is that monument that I see?" The people of the city told him, "It is the tomb of the man of God who came from Judah and predicted these things that you have done against the altar at Bethel." [18]He said, "Let him rest; let no one move his bones." So they let his bones alone, with the bones of the prophet who came out of Samaria. [19]Moreover, Josiah removed all the shrines of the high places that were in the towns of Samaria, which kings of Israel had made, provoking the LORD to anger; he did to them just as he had done at Bethel. [20]He slaughtered on the altars all the priests of the high places who were there, and burned human bones on them. Then he returned to Jerusalem.

The Passover Celebrated

21 The king commanded all the people, "Keep the passover to the LORD your God as prescribed in this book of the covenant." [22]No such passover had been kept since the days of the judges who judged Israel, even during all the days of the kings of Israel and of the kings of Judah; [23]but in the eighteenth year of King Josiah this passover was kept to the LORD in Jerusalem.

24 Moreover Josiah put away the mediums, wizards, teraphim,[b] idols, and all the abominations that were seen in the land of Judah and in Jerusalem, so that he established the words of the law that were written in the book that the priest Hilkiah had found in the house of the LORD. [25]Before him there was no king like him, who turned to the LORD with all his heart, with all his soul, and with all his might, according to all the law of Moses; nor did any like him arise after him.

26 Still the LORD did not turn from the fierceness of his great wrath, by which his anger was kindled against Judah, because of all the provocations with which Manasseh had provoked him. [27]The LORD said, "I will remove Judah also out of my sight, as I have removed Israel; and I will reject this city that I have chosen, Jerusalem, and the house of which I said, My name shall be there."

Josiah Dies in Battle

28 Now the rest of the acts of Josiah, and all that he did, are they not written in the Book of the Annals of the Kings of Judah? [29]In his days Pharaoh Neco king of Egypt went up to the king of Assyria to the river Euphrates. King Josiah went to meet him; but when Pharaoh Neco met him at Megiddo, he killed him. [30]His servants carried him dead in a chariot from Megiddo, brought him to Jerusalem, and buried him in his own tomb. The people of the land took Jehoahaz son of Josiah, anointed him, and made him king in place of his father.

Reign and Captivity of Jehoahaz

31 Jehoahaz was twenty-three years old when he began to reign; he reigned three months in Jerusalem. His mother's name was Hamutal

---

a Gk: Heb proclaimed, who had predicted these things
b Or household gods

---

siah's reforms at Bethel fulfill the prophecy against the altar in 1 Kings 13. **23.18** The old prophet referred to here came from Bethel rather than Samaria (1 Kings 13.11, 31). **23.19–20** The reforms outside of Bethel may have also been considered a fulfillment of prophecy (see 1 Kings 13.32). **23.21–23** Josiah's command resumes the narrative of vv. 1–3. According to Deuteronomic law (Deut 16.5–6), the Passover must be celebrated at the central sanctuary rather than in individual homes. The text claims that the last Passover celebrated in this way took place just after Israel entered Canaan (Josh 5.10–11). **23.24** Diviners are prohibited by Deut 18.9–14. *Teraphim,* images of household deities possibly also used in divination. **23.25** The narrator makes the same statement about Hezekiah in 18.5. **23.26–27** An allusion to the substance of the prophetic oracle against Manasseh in 21.10–15. **23.28–30** Josiah's sudden death comes as a shock and seems to be an anticlimax after the praise the narrator lavishes on the king's reign. **23.29** *Pharaoh Neco,* who had just come to the throne in 610 BCE, was apparently on his way to join the Assyrians in an attempt to curb the growing power of the Babylonians. He met Josiah in 609 BCE at *Megiddo,* which was strategically located in the Plain of Esdraelon in northwestern Palestine on the standard trade route between Egypt and Mesopotamia. It is usually assumed that Josiah attempted to block the Egyptian advance, but the text does not actually mention a battle. It may be that Neco simply murdered Josiah. **23.30** *People of the land.* See note on 11.14. **23.31–35** Jehoahaz's brief reign ends when Neco interferes directly in Judean affairs and places a puppet king on the throne. The text gives no details about the evil Jehoahaz is said to have done.

daughter of Jeremiah of Libnah. [32]He did what was evil in the sight of the LORD, just as his ancestors had done. [33]Pharaoh Neco confined him at Riblah in the land of Hamath, so that he might not reign in Jerusalem, and imposed tribute on the land of one hundred talents of silver and a talent of gold. [34]Pharaoh Neco made Eliakim son of Josiah king in place of his father Josiah, and changed his name to Jehoiakim. But he took Jehoahaz away; he came to Egypt, and died there. [35]Jehoiakim gave the silver and the gold to Pharaoh, but he taxed the land in order to meet Pharaoh's demand for money. He exacted the silver and the gold from the people of the land, from all according to their assessment, to give it to Pharaoh Neco.

Jehoiakim Reigns over Judah

36 Jehoiakim was twenty-five years old when he began to reign; he reigned eleven years in Jerusalem. His mother's name was Zebidah daughter of Pedaiah of Rumah. [37]He did what was evil in the sight of the LORD, just as all his ancestors had done.

Judah Overrun by Enemies

24 In his days King Nebuchadnezzar of Babylon came up; Jehoiakim became his servant for three years; then he turned and rebelled against him. [2]The LORD sent against him bands of the Chaldeans, bands of the Arameans, bands of the Moabites, and bands of the Ammonites; he sent them against Judah to destroy it, according to the word of the LORD

that he spoke by his servants the prophets. [3]Surely this came upon Judah at the command of the LORD, to remove them out of his sight, for the sins of Manasseh, for all that he had committed, [4]and also for the innocent blood that he had shed; for he filled Jerusalem with innocent blood, and the LORD was not willing to pardon. [5]Now the rest of the deeds of Jehoiakim, and all that he did, are they not written in the Book of the Annals of the Kings of Judah? [6]So Jehoiakim slept with his ancestors; then his son Jehoiachin succeeded him. [7]The king of Egypt did not come again out of his land, for the king of Babylon had taken over all that belonged to the king of Egypt from the Wadi of Egypt to the River Euphrates.

Reign and Captivity of Jehoiachin

8 Jehoiachin was eighteen years old when he began to reign; he reigned three months in Jerusalem. His mother's name was Nehushta daughter of Elnathan of Jerusalem. [9]He did what was evil in the sight of the LORD, just as his father had done.

10 At that time the servants of King Nebuchadnezzar of Babylon came up to Jerusalem, and the city was besieged. [11]King Nebuchadnezzar of Babylon came to the city, while his servants were besieging it; [12]King Jehoiachin of Judah gave himself up to the king of Babylon, himself, his mother, his servants, his officers, and his palace officials. The king of Babylon took him prisoner in the eighth year of his reign.

23.31 *Jehoahaz* ruled in 609 BCE. **23.33** *Riblah* lay about seven miles south of Kadesh on the Orontes River on the trade route connecting Egypt, northern Syria, and Mesopotamia. *Talents.* See note on 1 Kings 9.14. **23.36–37** Jehoiakim was the king upon whom God's judgment finally fell. Like all of the other Judean kings after Josiah, he is evaluated negatively by the narrator. **23.36** Jehoiakim ruled ca. 609–598 BCE.

24.1–7 Because in the mind of the narrator the fate of Judah has already been sealed, little time is spent in describing the achievements of Jehoiakim; the text concentrates completely on his relationship with the Babylonians. **24.1** At the battle of Carchemish (605 BCE), Nebuchadnezzar had won a decisive victory over the Egyptians, and he followed this triumph with a campaign in Syria and Palestine. It was during this time that Jehoiakim thought it prudent to conclude a treaty with Nebuchadnezzar, and Judah was a Babylonian vassal from 604 to 602 BCE. In 601/600 BCE, however, the Babylonians were driven back to their homeland by the Egyptians. Jehoiakim concluded that the political tide had turned, and so he rebelled.

24.2 The rebellion was badly timed, for after resupplying his army Nebuchadnezzar again moved west and began to punish the rebels. This invasion is interpreted by the narrator as the promised punishment against Judah and Jerusalem. The OT frequently uses the name *Chaldeans* to refer to the inhabitants of Babylonia during this period. The *Arameans* (Syrians), *Moabites*, and *Ammonites* were Judah's neighbors to the east and had periodically been at war with Israel and Judah during the monarchical period. **24.3–4** On the *sins of Manasseh*, see 21.1–16. **24.7** The battle of Carchemish put an end to Egyptian power, at least temporarily (see v. 1). **24.8–17** Jehoiakim apparently died during Nebuchadnezzar's invasion of Judah, so the brunt of the Babylonian attack fell on the new king, Jehoiachin. The narrator naturally focuses the account on the Babylonian sack of Jerusalem and on the exile of the king and the royal court. **24.8** *Jehoiachin* ruled briefly in 598/7 BCE, before the Babylonians deported him. **24.12** *The eighth year*, the year of Nebuchadnezzar's reign in which the deportations actually began. The city was captured in March, 597 BCE, the seventh year

Capture of Jerusalem

13 He carried off all the treasures of the house of the LORD, and the treasures of the king's house; he cut in pieces all the vessels of gold in the temple of the LORD, which King Solomon of Israel had made, all this as the LORD had foretold. 14 He carried away all Jerusalem, all the officials, all the warriors, ten thousand captives, all the artisans and the smiths; no one remained, except the poorest people of the land. 15 He carried away Jehoiachin to Babylon; the king's mother, the king's wives, his officials, and the elite of the land, he took into captivity from Jerusalem to Babylon. 16 The king of Babylon brought captive to Babylon all the men of valor, seven thousand, the artisans and the smiths, one thousand, all of them strong and fit for war. 17 The king of Babylon made Mattaniah, Jehoiachin's uncle, king in his place, and changed his name to Zedekiah.

Zedekiah Reigns over Judah

18 Zedekiah was twenty-one years old when he began to reign; he reigned eleven years in Jerusalem. His mother's name was Hamutal daughter of Jeremiah of Libnah. 19 He did what was evil in the sight of the LORD, just as Jehoiakim had done. 20 Indeed, Jerusalem and Judah so angered the LORD that he expelled them from his presence.

The Fall and Captivity of Judah

Zedekiah rebelled against the king of Babylon.
25 1 And in the ninth year of his reign, in the tenth month, on the tenth day of the month, King Nebuchadnezzar of Babylon came with all his army against Jerusalem, and laid siege to it; they built siegeworks against it all around. 2 So the city was besieged until the eleventh year of King Zedekiah. 3 On the ninth day of the fourth month the famine became so severe in the city that there was no food for the people of the land. 4 Then a breach was made in the city wall;[a] the king with all the soldiers fled[b] by night by the way of the gate between the two walls, by the king's garden, though the Chaldeans were all around the city. They went in the direction of the Arabah. 5 But the army of the Chaldeans pursued the king, and overtook him in the plains of Jericho; all his army was scattered, deserting him. 6 Then they captured the king and brought him up to the king of Babylon at Riblah, who passed sentence on him. 7 They slaughtered the sons of Zedekiah before his eyes, then put out the eyes of Zedekiah; they bound him in fetters and took him to Babylon.

8 In the fifth month, on the seventh day of the month—which was the nineteenth year of King Nebuchadnezzar, king of Babylon—Nebuzaradan, the captain of the bodyguard, a servant of the king of Babylon, came to Jerusalem. 9 He burned the house of the LORD, the king's house, and all the houses of Jerusalem; every great house he burned down. 10 All the army of the Chaldeans who were with the captain of the guard broke down the walls around Jerusalem. 11 Nebuzaradan the captain of the guard carried into exile the rest of the people who were left in the city and the de-

a Heb lacks wall   b Gk Compare Jer 39.4; 52.7: Heb lacks the king and lacks fled

---

of Nebuchadnezzar's kingship. **24.13** The prediction of the deportation was made by the prophet Isaiah during the reign of Hezekiah (20.12–21). **24.14** Here the number of exiles is set at *ten thousand*, while in v. 16 the figure is eight thousand. **24.18–25.21** Although Zedekiah ruled for eleven years, the narrator concentrates on the last significant events of the king's reign: the fall of Jerusalem and the exile. A condensed version of this account is found in 2 Chr 36.11–21, and the whole account, with small variations, has been appended to the book of Jeremiah (Jer 52). A shortened version of 25.1–21 is also found in Jer 39.1–14. The unusually large number of accounts of the fall indicates the extraordinary political and religious significance of this traumatic event. **24.18** *Zedekiah* reigned 597–587/6 BCE. **24.20** Zedekiah's reign was marked by political indecision as the king struggled unsuccessfully to chart a safe course through troubled Near

Eastern waters. Although Egyptian power had been broken in 605 BCE (see note on 24.1), Pharaoh Psammetichus II began to extend his influence into Palestine in 592 BCE, and thereafter Zedekiah was torn between maintaining his status as a Babylonian vassal and seeking a new alliance with Egypt. He finally decided on the latter course, with disastrous results. **25.1–2** The siege of Jerusalem finally began in January of 587 BCE and lasted for eighteen months. **25.4** The city wall was finally breached in July of 586 BCE. In their unsuccessful attempt to escape, the king and his court fled through a gate in the southeast wall of Jerusalem, where Hezekiah had built a second wall to protect the pool of Siloam (see note on 20.20–21). *Arabah*, land in the Jordan Valley rift between the Sea of Galilee and the Dead Sea. **25.5** *Jericho.* See note on 2.4. **25.6** *Riblah.* See note on 23.33. **25.9** The temple was destroyed in August of 586 BCE. **25.11** This is the sec-

serters who had defected to the king of Babylon—all the rest of the population. 12But the captain of the guard left some of the poorest people of the land to be vinedressers and tillers of the soil.

13 The bronze pillars that were in the house of the LORD, as well as the stands and the bronze sea that were in the house of the LORD, the Chaldeans broke in pieces, and carried the bronze to Babylon. 14They took away the pots, the shovels, the snuffers, the dishes for incense, and all the bronze vessels used in the temple service, 15as well as the firepans and the basins. What was made of gold the captain of the guard took away for the gold, and what was made of silver, for the silver. 16As for the two pillars, the one sea, and the stands, which Solomon had made for the house of the LORD, the bronze of all these vessels was beyond weighing. 17The height of the one pillar was eighteen cubits, and on it was a bronze capital; the height of the capital was three cubits; latticework and pomegranates, all of bronze, were on the capital all around. The second pillar had the same, with the latticework.

18 The captain of the guard took the chief priest Seraiah, the second priest Zephaniah, and the three guardians of the threshold; 19from the city he took an officer who had been in command of the soldiers, and five men of the king's council who were found in the city; the secretary who was the commander of the army who mustered the people of the land; and sixty men of the people of the land who were found in the city. 20Nebuzaradan the captain of the guard took them, and brought them to the king of Babylon at Riblah. 21The king of Babylon struck them down and put them to death at Riblah in the land of Hamath. So Judah went into exile out of its land.

Gedaliah Made Governor of Judah

22 He appointed Gedaliah son of Ahikam son of Shaphan as governor over the people who remained in the land of Judah, whom King Nebuchadnezzar of Babylon had left. 23Now when all the captains of the forces and their men heard that the king of Babylon had appointed Gedaliah as governor, they came with their men to Gedaliah at Mizpah, namely, Ishmael son of Nethaniah, Johanan son of Kareah, Seraiah son of Tanhumeth the Netophathite, and Jaazaniah son of the Maacathite. 24Gedaliah swore to them and their men, saying, "Do not be afraid because of the Chaldean officials; live in the land, serve the king of Babylon, and it shall be well with you." 25But in the seventh month, Ishmael son of Nethaniah son of Elishama, of the royal family, came with ten men; they struck down Gedaliah so that he died, along with the Judeans and Chaldeans who were with him at Mizpah. 26Then all the people, high and low,[a] and the captains of the forces set out and went to Egypt; for they were afraid of the Chaldeans.

Jehoiachin Released from Prison

27 In the thirty-seventh year of the exile of King Jehoiachin of Judah, in the twelfth month, on the twenty-seventh day of the month, King Evil-merodach of Babylon, in the year that he began to reign, released King Jehoiachin of Judah from prison; 28he spoke kindly to him, and gave him a seat above the other seats of the kings who were with him in Babylon. 29So Jehoiachin put aside his prison clothes. Every day of his life he dined regularly in the king's presence. 30For his allowance, a regular allowance was given him by the king, a portion every day, as long as he lived.

---

a Or young and old

---

ond deportation of Jerusalem's inhabitants. **25.13–17** On the origin of these temple furnishings, see 1 Kings 7.15–50 and notes. **25.17** A *cubit* is 18 inches.

25.22–26 In an attempt to maintain political stability, Nebuchadnezzar appoints an administrator from an important Judean family. A more detailed account of Gedaliah's activities is found in Jer 40.7–41.18. **25.22** Gedaliah's grandfather, *Shaphan,* had been the scribe during the reign of Josiah (22.3). Gedaliah's father, *Ahikam,* was part of the delegation sent to Huldah (22.12) and was later a supporter of Jeremiah (Jer 26.24). **25.23** Several Israelite towns bore the name *Mizpah*. The one mentioned here probably lay on the border between Israel and Judah, about eight miles north of Jerusalem. Mizpah may have been one of the few sites left standing after the Babylonian invasion. **25.24** Gedaliah's pro-Babylonian stance was also shared by Jeremiah, who received special treatment from the Babylonians after the fall of Jerusalem (Jer 27.1–22; 39.13–14; 40.1–6). **25.26** This verse seems to imply that the remaining inhabitants fled to Egypt (cf. v. 21). **25.27–30** This brief epilogue recounting Jehoiachin's release from prison introduces a note of hope that the Davidic monarchy might not be finally destroyed. A parallel account is found in Jer 52.31–34. **25.27** *Evil-merodach* ruled Babylon ca. 562–560 BCE.

1 CHRONICLES

IN THE HEBREW BIBLE 1 and 2 Chronicles are called "The Events of the Days." The title Chronicles can be traced back to Jerome in the fifth century CE. 1 and 2 Chronicles were written after the exile and in Jerusalem, probably in the fourth century BCE. The author is conventionally called the Chronicler. Although these books share many themes with the nearly contemporaneous books of Ezra and Nehemiah, a growing number of scholars believe they are separate compositions. Note, however, that the first verses of Ezra (1.1–3a) are identical to the last verses of Chronicles (2 Chr 36.22–23).

Structure and Sources

THE BOOKS OF CHRONICLES consist of four sections: genealogies and lists that trace a historical story from Adam to the community after the exile (1 Chr 1–9); the reign of David (1 Chr 10–29); the reign of Solomon (2 Chr 1–9); and the history of the Davidic monarchy until the Babylonian captivity (2 Chr 10–36).

The books are largely parallel to the books of Samuel and Kings, which are part of the Deuteronomistic History, a portion of the Hebrew Bible running from Deuteronomy to 2 Kings and edited in its final form in the mid-sixth century BCE (2 Sam 9–20 is passed over, and the material on the Northern Kingdom is largely omitted). In fact, Samuel and Kings served as the major source for the Chronicler, though his copy of these books differed in significant ways from the text as we now have it in the Hebrew Bible. Especially useful in establishing the earlier text of Samuel and Kings are the Greek translation of the Bible (the Septuagint, including the recensions known as proto-Lucianic and *kaige*) and the Dead Sea Scrolls. The genealogical notices of 1 Chr 1–8 show strong ties to Genesis, Exodus, Numbers, Joshua, Samuel, and Ruth, although they also contain much unique genealogical material. Pss 96; 105; and 106 are cited in 1 Chr 16. The Chronicler also used the books of Isaiah, Jeremiah, and Zechariah. The Chronicler refers readers to additional sources at the end of every king's history, though most of these references are taken over or revised from the Deuteronomistic History. The genealogies in 1 Chr 1–9 came to the Chronicler from a variety of sources, as did a number of other lists of names (1 Chr 12; 23–27). Material that appears to come from other nonbiblical sources includes the description of the fortifications of Rehoboam (2 Chr 11.5–10), the descriptions of armies (2 Chr 14.8; 17.14–19; 25.5; 26.11–15), and the reference to

Hezekiah's tunnel (2 Chr 32.30). Because of their importance, parallels in Samuel and Kings are cited at the beginning of notes wherever appropriate.

Theology

WHEREAS PAST SCHOLARSHIP OFTEN DEBATED the historical value of the Chronicler's additional material, there is a greater interest today in the theological point the author was making. At the same time archaeological and form-critical judgments are reaching new levels of sophistication. Occasionally no hard data justify a historical judgment. The Chronicler's magnification of an account, often for theological reasons, can be seen in his use of large numbers: Abijah, for example, accompanied by an army of 400,000, attacked the army of Jeroboam, which was 800,000 strong, and inflicted 500,000 casualties (2 Chr 13).

The author frequently expresses his own views in royal speeches and prayers that appeal to an authoritative scriptural text. These compositions play a significant role in the structuring of Chronicles. The speeches (1 Chr 22; 28; 29) and a prayer of David (1 Chr 29.10–19) link David closely with Solomon and place great emphasis on the temple. The period of the Divided Monarchy is framed with speeches calling for repentance by Abijah (2 Chr 13.4–12) and by Hezekiah (2 Chr 30.6–9). Both speeches indicate the Chronicler's openness to the Northern Kingdom's participation in the ritual life of the Jerusalem temple. References to prophets are frequently found in material taken from the parallel accounts in Samuel and Kings, in material added by the Chronicler, and in sources that mention prophets in connection with certain kings (2 Chr 9.29).

Other Matters of Worldview

THE CHRONICLER SHOWS SPECIAL LOYALTY to the Levites and includes in their number singers, gatekeepers, and even bakers (1 Chr 9.31–32). Among the many tasks of the Levites was teaching (2 Chr 17.7–9). They were also in charge of holy objects, prepared the rows of "show" bread (1 Chr 9.28–32; 23.29–31; 2 Chr 29.18), and served as judges and scribes. In addition, they led in singing and praise (1 Chr 15.16–24; 16.4–42).

The author devotes extraordinary attention to David and Solomon and treats them as equals, often omitting negative information contained in his sources. In his presentation, the work of David and Solomon centered on the building of the temple and the installation of its personnel. The Chronicler calls on all Israel of his day, especially people in the area of the former Northern Kingdom, to join in recognizing the Second Temple and its ritual life in Jerusalem.

The Chronicler interprets divine punishments or blessings as retribution for a king's behavior. Such retribution is immediate, with the consequences befalling the evil or righteous king during his own lifetime. Faithful royal behavior is accompanied by many children, building projects, a well-equipped army, victory in war, cultic reforms, or tribute from the nations. A wicked king experiences God's wrath, war, defeat in battle, disease, or conspiracy.

Interpreters of Chronicles now find a far more open attitude to people from the North than was previously recognized. Those willing to return to the Lord and come to his sanctuary were to be welcomed (2 Chr 30.7–8). Hezekiah's Passover celebration was unique in its inclusion of the North, and both he and Josiah conducted reforming activities in the North. The Chronicler seems to be inviting Northerners to acknowledge the claims of the temple in Jerusalem and to participate in its ritual life. [RALPH W. KLEIN]

From Adam to Abraham

1 Adam, Seth, Enosh; [2]Kenan, Mahalalel, Jared; [3]Enoch, Methuselah, Lamech; [4]Noah, Shem, Ham, and Japheth.

5 The descendants of Japheth: Gomer, Magog, Madai, Javan, Tubal, Meshech, and Tiras. [6]The descendants of Gomer: Ashkenaz, Diphath,[a] and Togarmah. [7]The descendants of Javan: Elishah, Tarshish, Kittim, and Rodanim.[b]

8 The descendants of Ham: Cush, Egypt, Put, and Canaan. [9]The descendants of Cush: Seba, Havilah, Sabta, Raama, and Sabteca. The descendants of Raamah: Sheba and Dedan. [10]Cush became the father of Nimrod; he was the first to be a mighty one on the earth.

11 Egypt became the father of Ludim, Anamim, Lehabim, Naphtuhim, [12]Pathrusim, Casluhim, and Caphtorim, from whom the Philistines come.[c]

13 Canaan became the father of Sidon his firstborn, and Heth, [14]and the Jebusites, the Amorites, the Girgashites, [15]the Hivites, the Arkites, the Sinites, [16]the Arvadites, the Zemarites, and the Hamathites.

17 The descendants of Shem: Elam, Asshur, Arpachshad, Lud, Aram, Uz, Hul, Gether, and Meshech.[d] [18]Arpachshad became the father of Shelah; and Shelah became the father of Eber. [19]To Eber were born two sons: the name of the one was Peleg (for in his days the earth was divided), and the name of his brother Joktan. [20]Joktan became the father of Almodad, Sheleph, Hazarmaveth, Jerah, [21]Hadoram, Uzal, Diklah, [22]Ebal, Abimael, Sheba, [23]Ophir, Havilah, and Jobab; all these were the descendants of Joktan.

24 Shem, Arpachshad, Shelah; [25]Eber, Peleg, Reu; [26]Serug, Nahor, Terah; [27]Abram, that is, Abraham.

From Abraham to Jacob

28 The sons of Abraham: Isaac and Ishmael. [29]These are their genealogies: the firstborn of Ishmael, Nebaioth; and Kedar, Adbeel, Mibsam, [30]Mishma, Dumah, Massa, Hadad, Tema, [31]Jetur, Naphish, and Kedemah. These are the sons of Ishmael. [32]The sons of Keturah, Abraham's concubine: she bore Zimran, Jokshan, Medan, Midian, Ishbak, and Shuah. The sons of Jokshan: Sheba and Dedan. [33]The sons of Midian: Ephah, Epher, Hanoch, Abida, and Eldaah. All these were the descendants of Keturah.

34 Abraham became the father of Isaac. The sons of Isaac: Esau and Israel. [35]The sons of Esau: Eliphaz, Reuel, Jeush, Jalam, and Korah. [36]The sons of Eliphaz: Teman, Omar,

---

a Gen 10.3 *Ripath*; See Gk Vg   b Gen 10.4 *Dodanim*; See Syr Vg   c Heb *Casluhim, from which the Philistines come, Caphtorim*; See Am 9.7, Jer 47.4   d *Mash* in Gen 10.23

1.1–2.2 The real goal of the genealogy in ch. 1 is reached with Israel (2.1–2). God's purpose for Israel began at creation. The genealogical materials in 1.1–2.2 relate Israel to the panoply of the nations of the world. Israel understood its role within the family of nations and as a witness to all humanity. One may detect here testimony to Israel's God, who governs the whole world, but focuses attention on Israel—even though there is no mention of God at all in this opening unit. **1.1–27** Cf. Gen 5.1–32; 10.1–29; 11.10–26. The author traces human history from Adam, the first ancestor of humankind, to Abraham, the ancestor of the faithful. Nearly all the genealogies of Genesis are included except Gen 4.17–22 (the genealogy of Cain) and 19.30–38 (the births of Moab and Ben-ammi [Ammonites]). **1.1–4** The list of names is derived from Gen 5, but other details of that genealogy are omitted. **1.5–23** The Table of Nations in Gen 10 divides the then known world into geographical/cultural groups roughly as follows: the children of Shem are in Mesopotamia and Arabia; the children of Ham are in northeast Africa and Syro-Palestine; the children of Japheth are in Europe and Asia. Nations are assigned to eponymous ancestors who fit into a genealogical tree (e.g., Egypt in vv. 8, 11). **1.7** *Rodanim*, the inhabitants of Rhodes. **1.8** *Canaan*, considered a son of Ham, as in Gen 9.22. In modern discussions, Canaan and the Amorites (v. 14) are considered Semites. **1.10** *Nimrod.* Much additional information about this hunter is provided in Gen 10.8–12. **1.12** *Caphtorim*, the people of Crete (cf. Jer 47.4; Am 9.7). **1.24–27** This genealogical list is derived from Gen 11.10–26, with the omission of the details, as in vv. 1–4. There is some overlap with the materials in vv. 17–23. **1.25** *Eber.* Cf. Gen 10.24–25; 11.14–17. The root of this name is a wordplay on the name "Hebrew" and thus portrays Eber as the eponymous ancestor, the namesake, of the Hebrew people. **1.27** *Abram*, changed to *Abraham* in Gen 17.5. **1.28–54** Cf. Gen 25.1–4, 13–16, 19–26; 36.1–5, 10–13, 20–28, 31–43. Abraham's descendants through three separate women (only Keturah is mentioned by name, v. 32), with the subsidiary, nonelect lines reported first. **1.29–31** *Ishmael,* the son of Abraham and his Egyptian slave-girl Hagar (Gen 16; 21). **1.32–33** Perhaps a later addition to the Chronicler's account; note the summary in v. 28. *Keturah,* a concubine Abraham took after the death of Sarah. **1.34** *Israel,* the standard name for Jacob in Chronicles (except for 1 Chr 16.13, 17, where both occurrences are in quotations from Ps 105). **1.35–**

Zephi, Gatam, Kenaz, Timna, and Amalek. 37The sons of Reuel: Nahath, Zerah, Shammah, and Mizzah.

38 The sons of Seir: Lotan, Shobal, Zibeon, Anah, Dishon, Ezer, and Dishan. 39The sons of Lotan: Hori and Homam; and Lotan's sister was Timna. 40The sons of Shobal: Alian, Manahath, Ebal, Shephi, and Onam. The sons of Zibeon: Aiah and Anah. 41The sons of Anah: Dishon. The sons of Dishon: Hamran, Eshban, Ithran, and Cheran. 42The sons of Ezer: Bilhan, Zaavan, and Jaakan.*a* The sons of Dishan:*b* Uz and Aran.

43 These are the kings who reigned in the land of Edom before any king reigned over the Israelites: Bela son of Beor, whose city was called Dinhabah. 44When Bela died, Jobab son of Zerah of Bozrah succeeded him. 45When Jobab died, Husham of the land of the Temanites succeeded him. 46When Husham died, Hadad son of Bedad, who defeated Midian in the country of Moab, succeeded him; and the name of his city was Avith. 47When Hadad died, Samlah of Masrekah succeeded him. 48When Samlah died, Shaul*c* of Rehoboth on the Euphrates succeeded him. 49When Shaul*c* died, Baal-hanan son of Achbor succeeded him. 50When Baal-hanan died, Hadad succeeded him; the name of his city was Pai, and his wife's name Mehetabel daughter of Matred, daughter of Me-zahab. 51And Hadad died.

The clans*d* of Edom were: clans*d* Timna, Aliah,*e* Jetheth, 52Oholibamah, Elah, Pinon, 53Kenaz, Teman, Mibzar, 54Magdiel, and Iram; these are the clans*d* of Edom.

The Sons of Israel and the Descendants of Judah

2 These are the sons of Israel: Reuben, Simeon, Levi, Judah, Issachar, Zebulun, 2Dan, Joseph, Benjamin, Naphtali, Gad, and Asher. 3The sons of Judah: Er, Onan, and Shelah; these three the Canaanite woman Bath-shua bore to him. Now Er, Judah's firstborn, was wicked in the sight of the LORD, and he put him to death. 4His daughter-in-law Tamar also bore him Perez and Zerah. Judah had five sons in all.

5 The sons of Perez: Hezron and Hamul. 6The sons of Zerah: Zimri, Ethan, Heman, Calcol, and Dara,*f* five in all. 7The sons of Carmi: Achar, the troubler of Israel, who transgressed in the matter of the devoted thing; 8and Ethan's son was Azariah.

9 The sons of Hezron, who were born to him: Jerahmeel, Ram, and Chelubai. 10Ram became the father of Amminadab, and Amminadab became the father of Nahshon, prince of the sons of Judah. 11Nahshon became the father of Salma, Salma of Boaz, 12Boaz of Obed, Obed of Jesse. 13Jesse became the father of Eliab his firstborn, Abinadab the second, Shimea the third, 14Nethanel the fourth, Raddai the fifth, 15Ozem the sixth, David the seventh; 16and their sisters were Zeruiah and Abigail. The sons of Zeruiah: Abishai, Joab, and Asahel, three.

---

a Or *and Akan;* See Gen 36.27   *b* See 1.38: Heb *Dishon*
c Or *Saul*   *d* Or *chiefs*   *e* Or *Alvah;* See Gen 36.40
f Or *Darda;* Compare Syr Tg some Gk Mss; See 1 Kings 4.31

---

54 *Esau*/Edom, the brother of Israel, is given lengthy attention. **1.36** *Timna,* in Gen 36.12 a concubine of Eliphaz and mother of Amalek. **1.38–42** The *sons of Seir* inhabited the same territory as Edom (cf. Gen 36.8). **1.43–51a** List of Edomite kings. **1.43** This verse presupposes the existence of the monarchy in Israel. The corresponding verse in Gen 36.31 is used to show that the Pentateuch comes from a time considerably later than Moses. **1.51** *Hadad*'s death is not recorded in Genesis. This addition makes the chiefs clearly subsequent to the list of Edomite kings. *Clans,* preferably *chiefs* (see text note *d*). **2.1–2** Chronicles has an inclusive view of Israel and so lists all twelve tribes. For the order of the tribes in these verses, with the exception of Dan, see Gen 35.23–26. The rest of chs. 2–8 provides details of the Israelite genealogy, though no details are provided for Zebulun and perhaps Dan (but see 7.12). **2.3–4.23** The genealogy of Judah, the most important tribe in the postexilic community, begins the genealogies of individual tribes. The genealogies con-

clude in ch. 8 with Benjamin, another important postexilic tribe. **2.3–4** Based on Gen 38. *Judah* sires twins by his daughter-in-law *Tamar.* **2.3** *Bath-shua,* the daughter of Shua (Gen 38.2). **2.4** *Perez,* a twin, who makes a "breach" and comes out of the womb before his brother *Zerah* (Gen 38.27–30). **2.5** *Hezron and Hamul,* grandsons of Judah (Gen 46.12; Num 26.21). **2.6–8** Descendants of *Zerah,* the younger brother of Perez. **2.7** *Achar* (cf. Achan in Josh 7.1, 18; Achor in Josh 7.24, 26) violated the provisions of holy war by taking booty from Jericho. **2.9** *Chelubai,* Caleb. The descendants of Hezron, grandson of Judah, are divided into the descendants of Ram (2.10–17; 3.1–24 [descendants of David]), Caleb (2.18–24, 42–55), and Jerahmeel (2.25–33; 2.34–41). **2.10–17** *Ram,* Hezron's second son, was the ancestor of David. **2.15** According to 1 Sam 16.10–11; 17.12–14, David is the eighth son. Josephus (*Ant.* 6.161–63) follows the number of sons given by the Chronicler. **2.16–17** *Abishai, Joab, Asahel,* and *Amasa,* nephews of David and his

17 Abigail bore Amasa, and the father of Amasa was Jether the Ishmaelite.

18 Caleb son of Hezron had children by his wife Azubah, and by Jerioth; these were her sons: Jesher, Shobab, and Ardon. 19 When Azubah died, Caleb married Ephrath, who bore him Hur. 20 Hur became the father of Uri, and Uri became the father of Bezalel.

21 Afterward Hezron went in to the daughter of Machir father of Gilead, whom he married when he was sixty years old; and she bore him Segub; 22 and Segub became the father of Jair, who had twenty-three towns in the land of Gilead. 23 But Geshur and Aram took from them Havvoth-jair, Kenath and its villages, sixty towns. All these were descendants of Machir, father of Gilead. 24 After the death of Hezron, in Caleb-ephrathah, Abijah wife of Hezron bore him Ashhur, father of Tekoa.

25 The sons of Jerahmeel, the firstborn of Hezron: Ram his firstborn, Bunah, Oren, Ozem, and Ahijah. 26 Jerahmeel also had another wife, whose name was Atarah; she was the mother of Onam. 27 The sons of Ram, the firstborn of Jerahmeel: Maaz, Jamin, and Eker. 28 The sons of Onam: Shammai and Jada. The sons of Shammai: Nadab and Abishur. 29 The name of Abishur's wife was Abihail, and she bore him Ahban and Molid. 30 The sons of Nadab: Seled and Appaim; and Seled died childless. 31 The son[a] of Appaim: Ishi. The son[a] of Ishi: Sheshan. The son[a] of Sheshan: Ahlai. 32 The sons of Jada, Shammai's brother: Jether and Jonathan; and Jether died childless. 33 The sons of Jonathan: Peleth and Zaza. These were the descendants of Jerahmeel. 34 Now Sheshan had no sons, only daughters; but Sheshan had an Egyptian slave, whose name was Jarha. 35 So Sheshan gave his daughter in marriage to his slave Jarha; and she bore him Attai. 36 Attai became the father of Nathan, and Nathan of Zabad. 37 Zabad became the father of Ephlal, and Ephlal of Obed. 38 Obed became the father of Jehu, and Jehu of Azariah. 39 Azariah became the father of Helez, and Helez of Eleasah. 40 Eleasah became the father of Sismai, and Sismai of Shallum. 41 Shallum became the father of Jekamiah, and Jekamiah of Elishama.

42 The sons of Caleb brother of Jerahmeel: Mesha[b] his firstborn, who was father of Ziph. The sons of Mareshah father of Hebron. 43 The sons of Hebron: Korah, Tappuah, Rekem, and Shema. 44 Shema became father of Raham, father of Jorkeam; and Rekem became the father of Shammai. 45 The son of Shammai: Maon; and Maon was the father of Beth-zur. 46 Ephah also, Caleb's concubine, bore Haran, Moza, and Gazez; and Haran became the father of Gazez. 47 The sons of Jahdai: Regem, Jotham, Geshan, Pelet, Ephah, and Shaaph. 48 Maacah, Caleb's concubine, bore Sheber and Tirhanah. 49 She also bore Shaaph father of Madmannah, Sheva father of Machbenah and father of Gibea; and the daughter of Caleb was Achsah. 50 These were the descendants of Caleb.

The sons[c] of Hur the firstborn of Ephrathah: Shobal father of Kiriath-jearim, 51 Salma father of Bethlehem, and Hareph father of Beth-gader. 52 Shobal father of Kiriath-jearim had other sons: Haroeh, half of the Menuhoth. 53 And the families of Kiriath-jearim: the Ithrites, the Puthites, the Shumathites, and the Mishraites; from these came the Zorathites and the Eshtaolites. 54 The sons of Salma: Bethlehem, the Netophathites, Atroth-beth-joab, and half of the Manahathites, the Zorites. 55 The families also of the scribes that lived at Jabez: the Tirathites, the Shimeathites, and the Sucathites. These are the Kenites who came from Hammath, father of the house of Rechab.

---

a Heb *sons*   *b* Gk reads *Mareshah*   *c* Gk Vg: Heb *son*

---

trusted military leaders. **2.17** *Ishmaelite.* The Hebrew of 2 Sam 17.25 reads "Israelite." **2.18–24** Descendants of *Caleb*/Chelubai, the third son of Hezron. **2.18** The verse should begin, "Caleb . . . had Jerioth by his wife Azubah." Here Jerioth is the mother of the following three men. **2.20** *Bezalel,* a craftsman who worked on the tabernacle (Ex 31.2; 35.30, 38:22). **2.24** *In Caleb-ephrathah . . . Ashhur,* better "Caleb went in to Ephrathah (and Hezron's wife was Abijah) and she bore him Ashhur." The parenthesis supplies the name of the anonymous daughter of Machir in v. 21. **2.25–33, 34–41** Two lists of descendants of *Jerahmeel,* the oldest son of Hezron. At the time of David the Jerahmeelites lived in the Negeb of Judah (1 Sam 27.10; 30.29). According to v. 31 Ahlai is the son of Sheshan, but according to v. 34 *Sheshan* had no sons. **2.35** *His slave Jarha.* The children of a foreign slave who has an Israelite master continue the master's line of descent. **2.41** *Elishama*'s pedigree is certified by a linear genealogy of fourteen generations (vv. 34–41), but his identity is otherwise unknown. **2.42–50a** The additional descendants of Caleb are actually cities in the southern part of Judah. Hebron seems to be the main center around which the other cities cluster. **2.50b–55** A continuation of the genealogy of the Calebite *Hur,* begun in vv. 18–19.

Descendants of David and Solomon

3 These are the sons of David who were born to him in Hebron: the firstborn Amnon, by Ahinoam the Jezreelite; the second Daniel, by Abigail the Carmelite; [2]the third Absalom, son of Maacah, daughter of King Talmai of Geshur; the fourth Adonijah, son of Haggith; [3]the fifth Shephatiah, by Abital; the sixth Ithream, by his wife Eglah; [4]six were born to him in Hebron, where he reigned for seven years and six months. And he reigned thirty-three years in Jerusalem. [5]These were born to him in Jerusalem: Shimea, Shobab, Nathan, and Solomon, four by Bath-shua, daughter of Ammiel; [6]then Ibhar, Elishama, Eliphelet, [7]Nogah, Nepheg, Japhia, [8]Elishama, Eliada, and Eliphelet, nine. [9]All these were David's sons, besides the sons of the concubines; and Tamar was their sister.

10 The descendants of Solomon: Rehoboam, Abijah his son, Asa his son, Jehoshaphat his son, [11]Joram his son, Ahaziah his son, Joash his son, [12]Amaziah his son, Azariah his son, Jotham his son, [13]Ahaz his son, Hezekiah his son, Manasseh his son, [14]Amon his son, Josiah his son. [15]The sons of Josiah: Johanan the firstborn, the second Jehoiakim, the third Zedekiah, the fourth Shallum. [16]The descendants of Jehoiakim: Jeconiah his son, Zedekiah his son; [17]and the sons of Jeconiah, the captive: Shealtiel his son, [18]Malchiram, Pedaiah, Shenazzar, Jekamiah, Hoshama, and Nedabiah; [19]The sons of Pedaiah: Zerubbabel and Shimei; and the sons of Zerubbabel: Meshullam and Hananiah, and Shelomith was their sister; [20]and Hashubah, Ohel, Berechiah, Hasadiah, and Jushab-hesed, five. [21]The sons of Hananiah: Pelatiah and Jeshaiah, his son[a] Rephaiah, his son[a] Arnan, his son[a] Obadiah, his son[a] Shecaniah. [22]The son[b] of Shecaniah: Shemaiah. And the sons of Shemaiah: Hattush, Igal, Bariah, Neariah, and Shaphat, six. [23]The sons of Neariah: Elioenai, Hizkiah, and Azrikam, three. [24]The sons of Elioenai: Hodaviah, Eliashib, Pelaiah, Akkub, Johanan, Delaiah, and Anani, seven.

Descendants of Judah

4 The sons of Judah: Perez, Hezron, Carmi, Hur, and Shobal. [2]Reaiah son of Shobal became the father of Jahath, and Jahath be-

a Gk Compare Syr Vg: Heb sons of b Heb sons

3.1–24 The descendants of David. Cf. 2 Sam 3.2–5; 5.5, 13–16 and the Davidic kings in the book of Kings. The final section of the genealogy, vv. 17–24, is without a biblical parallel. **3.1–4** Sons born to David in Hebron. *Daniel*. The second son of David is called Chileab in 2 Sam 3.3. *Abigail*, widow of Nabal (1 Sam 25). **3.4** 2 Sam 5.5 specifies that David's reign in Hebron was "over Judah," while his reign in Jerusalem was "over all Israel and Judah." **3.5–9** Sons born to David in Jerusalem. Cf. 14.3–7. **3.5** Only *Solomon* is identified as a son of *Bath-shua* (Bathsheba) elsewhere. **3.6–7** *Eliphelet, Nogah*. Cf. 14.5–6; lacking in 2 Sam 5.15. **3.9** This verse is an addition by the Chronicler. *Tamar*. See 2 Sam 13.1. **3.10–16** Kings in Jerusalem. **3.11** Athaliah is not included in the list of monarchs because she was not a descendant of David. **3.12** *Azariah* (cf. 2 Kings 15.1), called Uzziah in 2 Chr 26. **3.15** *Johanan*, otherwise unknown. *Shallum*, Jehoahaz (2 Chr 36.1; Jer 22.11). **3.16** *Jeconiah*, Jehoiachin (2 Chr 36.9), Coniah (Jer 22.24). *Zedekiah his son*. Zedekiah was the successor (son) to Jeconiah, and Jeconiah the successor (son) to Jehoiakim; Zedekiah's father was Josiah, as v. 15 attests. 2 Chr 36.10 makes Zedekiah the brother of Jehoiachin. **3.17–24** The descendants of Jeconiah, who was taken captive in 597 BCE and released from Babylonian prison some thirty-seven years later (2 Kings 25.27–30). The following approximate birth dates have been proposed: Jeconiah, 616 (cf. 2 Kings 24.8; 2 Chr 36.9 [608]); Pedaiah, 595; Zerubbabel, 570; Hananiah, 545; Shecaniah, 520; Shemaiah, 495; Neariah, 470; Elioenai, 445; Hodaviah, 420. If these proposals are correct, the present form of this list would date to about 400 BCE. If this list is part of the original edition of Chronicles, a date for the book prior to 400 BCE would be impossible. **3.17–18** The Babylonian Chronicle, a cuneiform historiographical source dated to 592 BCE, mentions five sons of the king of Judah instead of the seven named here. **3.18** *Shenazzar*, to be distinguished from Sheshbazzar (Ezra 1.8). **3.19** *Zerubbabel* and Joshua were leaders of the postexilic community at the time of Haggai. Elsewhere Zerubbabel is called the son of Shealtiel (Ezra 3.2). Perhaps Shealtiel died childless and Pedaiah engendered Zerubbabel in a levirate marriage (Deut 25.5–10). **3.20** The last five children of Zerubbabel may have been born after their parents' return to Palestine. The etymologies of these names express Israel's hope; e.g., *Hashubah* in Hebrew means "Yahweh has considered," *Berechiah*, "Yahweh has blessed." **3.21** *Rephaiah . . . Shecaniah*, brothers of Pelatiah and Jeshaiah. On the basis of the Septuagint the NRSV understands these names as four additional generations. **3.22** *Six*. Only five names are given. **3.24** *Anani*, mentioned in an Aramaic letter of 407 BCE.

4.1–23 A miscellaneous collection of genealogies related to Judah. **4.1** *Sons*, descendants. *Hezron* was a grandson of Judah (2.5), *Hur* a great-great-grandson (2.19), etc. **4.2** *Zorathites*. Zorah (cf. 2.53) was a city

came the father of Ahumai and Lahad. These were the families of the Zorathites. [3]These were the sons[a] of Etam: Jezreel, Ishma, and Idbash; and the name of their sister was Hazzelelponi, [4]and Penuel was the father of Gedor, and Ezer the father of Hushah. These were the sons of Hur, the firstborn of Ephrathah, the father of Bethlehem. [5]Ashhur father of Tekoa had two wives, Helah and Naarah; [6]Naarah bore him Ahuzzam, Hepher, Temeni, and Haahashtari.[b] These were the sons of Naarah. [7]The sons of Helah: Zereth, Izhar,[c] and Ethnan. [8]Koz became the father of Anub, Zobebah, and the families of Aharhel son of Harum. [9]Jabez was honored more than his brothers; and his mother named him Jabez, saying, "Because I bore him in pain." [10]Jabez called on the God of Israel, saying, "Oh that you would bless me and enlarge my border, and that your hand might be with me, and that you would keep me from hurt and harm!" And God granted what he asked. [11]Chelub the brother of Shuhah became the father of Mehir, who was the father of Eshton. [12]Eshton became the father of Beth-rapha, Paseah, and Tehinnah the father of Ir-nahash. These are the men of Recah. [13]The sons of Kenaz: Othniel and Seraiah; and the sons of Othniel: Hathath and Meonothai.[d] [14]Meonothai became the father of Ophrah; and Seraiah became the father of Joab father of Ge-harashim,[e] so-called because they were artisans. [15]The sons of Caleb son of Jephunneh: Iru, Elah, and Naam; and the son[f] of Elah: Kenaz. [16]The sons of Jehallelel: Ziph, Ziphah, Tiria, and Asarel. [17]The sons of Ezrah: Jether, Mered, Epher, and Jalon. These are the sons of Bithiah, daughter of Pharaoh, whom Mered married;[g] and she conceived and bore[h] Miriam, Shammai, and Ishbah father of Eshtemoa. [18]And his Judean wife bore Jered father of Gedor, Heber father of Soco, and Jekuthiel father of Zanoah. [19]The sons of the wife of Hodiah, the sister of Naham, were the fathers of Keilah the Garmite and Eshtemoa the Maacathite. [20]The sons of Shimon: Amnon, Rinnah, Ben-hanan, and Tilon. The sons of Ishi: Zoheth and Ben-zoheth. [21]The sons of Shelah son of Judah: Er father of Lecah, Laadah father of Mareshah, and the families of the guild of linen workers at Beth-ashbea; [22]and Jokim, and the men of Cozeba, and Joash, and Saraph, who married into Moab but returned to Lehem[i] (now the records[j] are ancient). [23]These were the potters and inhabitants of Netaim and Gederah; they lived there with the king in his service.

Descendants of Simeon

[24] The sons of Simeon: Nemuel, Jamin, Jarib, Zerah, Shaul;[k] [25]Shallum was his son, Mibsam his son, Mishma his son. [26]The sons of Mishma: Hammuel his son, Zaccur his son, Shimei his son. [27]Shimei had sixteen sons and six daughters; but his brothers did not have many children, nor did all their family multiply like the Judeans. [28]They lived in Beersheba, Moladah, Hazar-shual, [29]Bilhah, Ezem, Tolad, [30]Bethuel, Hormah, Ziklag, [31]Bethmarcaboth, Hazar-susim, Beth-biri, and Shaaraim. These were their towns until David became king. [32]And their villages were Etam, Ain, Rimmon, Tochen, and Ashan, five towns, [33]along with all their villages that were around these towns as far as Baal. These were their settlements. And they kept a genealogical record.

[34] Meshobab, Jamlech, Joshah son of Amaziah, [35]Joel, Jehu son of Joshibiah son of Seraiah son of Asiel, [36]Elioenai, Jaakobah, Jeshohaiah, Asaiah, Adiel, Jesimiel, Benaiah, [37]Ziza

a Gk Compare Vg: Heb the father   b Or Ahashtari   c Another reading is Zohar   d Gk Vg: Heb lacks and Meonothai   e That is Valley of artisans   f Heb sons   g The clause: These are . . . married is transposed from verse 18   h Heb lacks and bore   i Vg Compare Gk: Heb and Jashubi-lahem   j Or matters   k Or Saul

fortified by Rehoboam, as were Etam (v. 3) and Tekoa (v. 5; cf. 2 Chr 11.6–10). **4.4** Bethlehem, a town five miles south of Jerusalem. Ephrathah is listed as its "grandmother" and either Hur or Salma (2.51, 54) as its "father." Cf. "Bethlehem of Ephrathah" (Mic 5.2). **4.5** Tekoa, home of Amos; six miles south of Bethlehem. **4.9–10** Jabez, linked etymologically to the Hebrew words for pain and harm. His prayer was meant to counteract the threatening character of his name. **4.13** Sons of Kenaz. The Kenizzites were a southern tribe that joined with Judah, although the genealogical links between Judah and Kenaz are not given. Caleb is a Kenizzite in Num 32.12; Josh 14.6, 14. **4.14** Ge-harashim, the Valley of Craftsmen, northwest of Jerusalem, in which were located Lod and Ono; cf. Neh 11.35. **4.16** Ziph, a town south of Hebron. **4.21** Shelah, the oldest surviving son of Judah. Er, named after his uncle, the oldest son of Judah. Note the mention of guilds: linen workers (v. 21) and potters (v. 23). **4.23** King. The list dates to preexilic times. **4.24–43** This genealogy is made up of descendants of Simeon, especially through Shaul (vv. 24–27; cf. Gen 46.10; Ex 6.15; Num 26.12–14), settlements of the Simeonites near Beer-sheba (vv. 28–33; cf. Josh 15.21–

son of Shiphi son of Allon son of Jedaiah son of Shimri son of Shemaiah— 38these mentioned by name were leaders in their families, and their clans increased greatly. 39They journeyed to the entrance of Gedor, to the east side of the valley, to seek pasture for their flocks, 40where they found rich, good pasture, and the land was very broad, quiet, and peaceful; for the former inhabitants there belonged to Ham. 41These, registered by name, came in the days of King Hezekiah of Judah, and attacked their tents and the Meunim who were found there, and exterminated them to this day, and settled in their place, because there was pasture there for their flocks. 42And some of them, five hundred men of the Simeonites, went to Mount Seir, having as their leaders Pelatiah, Neariah, Rephaiah, and Uzziel, sons of Ishi; 43they destroyed the remnant of the Amalekites that had escaped, and they have lived there to this day.

Descendants of Reuben

5 The sons of Reuben the firstborn of Israel. (He was the firstborn, but because he defiled his father's bed his birthright was given to the sons of Joseph son of Israel, so that he is not enrolled in the genealogy according to the birthright; 2though Judah became prominent among his brothers and a ruler came from him, yet the birthright belonged to Joseph.) 3The sons of Reuben, the firstborn of Israel: Hanoch, Pallu, Hezron, and Carmi. 4The sons of Joel: Shemaiah his son, Gog his son, Shimei his son, 5Micah his son, Reaiah his son, Baal his son, 6Beerah his son, whom King Tilgath-pilneser of Assyria carried away into exile; he was a chieftain of the Reubenites. 7And his kindred by their families, when the genealogy

of their generations was reckoned: the chief, Jeiel, and Zechariah, 8and Bela son of Azaz, son of Shema, son of Joel, who lived in Aroer, as far as Nebo and Baal-meon. 9He also lived to the east as far as the beginning of the desert this side of the Euphrates, because their cattle had multiplied in the land of Gilead. 10And in the days of Saul they made war on the Hagrites, who fell by their hand; and they lived in their tents throughout all the region east of Gilead.

Descendants of Gad

11 The sons of Gad lived beside them in the land of Bashan as far as Salecah: 12Joel the chief, Shapham the second, Janai, and Shaphat in Bashan. 13And their kindred according to their clans: Michael, Meshullam, Sheba, Jorai, Jacan, Zia, and Eber, seven. 14These were the sons of Abihail son of Huri, son of Jaroah, son of Gilead, son of Michael, son of Jeshishai, son of Jahdo, son of Buz; 15Ahi son of Abdiel, son of Guni, was chief in their clan; 16and they lived in Gilead, in Bashan and in its towns, and in all the pasture lands of Sharon to their limits. 17All of these were enrolled by genealogies in the days of King Jotham of Judah, and in the days of King Jeroboam of Israel.

18 The Reubenites, the Gadites, and the half-tribe of Manasseh had valiant warriors, who carried shield and sword, and drew the bow, expert in war, forty-four thousand seven hundred sixty, ready for service. 19They made war on the Hagrites, Jetur, Naphish, and Nodab; 20and when they received help against them, the Hagrites and all who were with them were given into their hands, for they cried to God in the battle, and he granted their entreaty because they trusted in him. 21They

---

32; 19.2–8), and leaders of Simeon and places to which they migrated (vv. 34–43). **4.39** *Gedor.* The Septuagint reads "Gerar," a town in the Negeb, within Simeonite territory. Attacks at the time of Hezekiah were against the Philistines in the southwest and against Edom in the southeast (vv. 39–43).
5.1–10 Ch. 5 deals with the two and a half tribes living east of the Jordan (Reuben, Gad, and the half-tribe of Manasseh). **5.1** Reuben had sexual relations with Bilhah, his father's concubine (Gen 35.22; 49.4). The Chronicler uses this incident to explain why Judah, the fourth oldest son, is listed first in the genealogies. **5.2** *Ruler*, David and his dynasty. The transfer of the birthright to *Joseph* is unknown elsewhere. Both the Northern tribes (Joseph) and the Southern (Judah) have prominence in this verse. **5.3** Cf. Gen 46.9; Ex

6.14; Num 26.5–6. **5.4** *Joel's* connection to the Reubenite genealogy is not stated (cf. v. 8). **5.6** *Tilgath-pilneser.* The Assyrian king Tiglath-pileser III conquered Gilead in 733 BCE. **5.8** *Aroer, Nebo, Baal-meon.* Since these cities were lost to Moab in the late ninth century BCE, according to the Mesha Inscription, the materials in these verses must antedate this time. **5.10** Saul fought with the *Hagrites* (cf. vv. 19–20), an enemy from Transjordan (cf. 11.38; 27.30; Ps 83.6), at the end of the eleventh century BCE. The relationship of the Hagrites to Hagar, the concubine of Abraham, is unclear. **5.11–22** Gad was north of Reuben in Transjordan. **5.16** The Mesha Inscription mentions a people of *Sharon.* **5.17** This enrollment, from about 750 BCE, presupposes that Jotham and Jeroboam II were contemporaries. **5.18–22** The war against the Hagrites

captured their livestock: fifty thousand of their camels, two hundred fifty thousand sheep, two thousand donkeys, and one hundred thousand captives. 22Many fell slain, because the war was of God. And they lived in their territory until the exile.

The Half-Tribe of Manasseh

23 The members of the half-tribe of Manasseh lived in the land; they were very numerous from Bashan to Baal-hermon, Senir, and Mount Hermon. 24These were the heads of their clans: Epher,*a* Ishi, Eliel, Azriel, Jeremiah, Hodaviah, and Jahdiel, mighty warriors, famous men, heads of their clans. 25But they transgressed against the God of their ancestors, and prostituted themselves to the gods of the peoples of the land, whom God had destroyed before them. 26So the God of Israel stirred up the spirit of King Pul of Assyria, the spirit of King Tilgath-pilneser of Assyria, and he carried them away, namely, the Reubenites, the Gadites, and the half-tribe of Manasseh, and brought them to Halah, Habor, Hara, and the river Gozan, to this day.

Descendants of Levi

6 *b* The sons of Levi: Gershom,*c* Kohath, and Merari. 2The sons of Kohath: Amram, Izhar, Hebron, and Uzziel. 3The children of Amram: Aaron, Moses, and Miriam. The sons of Aaron: Nadab, Abihu, Eleazar, and Ithamar. 4Eleazar became the father of Phinehas, Phinehas of Abishua, 5Abishua of Bukki, Bukki of Uzzi, 6Uzzi of Zerahiah, Zerahiah of Meraioth, 7Meraioth of Amariah, Amariah of Ahi-

tub, 8Ahitub of Zadok, Zadok of Ahimaaz, 9Ahimaaz of Azariah, Azariah of Johanan, 10and Johanan of Azariah (it was he who served as priest in the house that Solomon built in Jerusalem). 11Azariah became the father of Amariah, Amariah of Ahitub, 12Ahitub of Zadok, Zadok of Shallum, 13Shallum of Hilkiah, Hilkiah of Azariah, 14Azariah of Seraiah, Seraiah of Jehozadak; 15and Jehozadak went into exile when the LORD sent Judah and Jerusalem into exile by the hand of Nebuchadnezzar.

16*d* The sons of Levi: Gershom, Kohath, and Merari. 17These are the names of the sons of Gershom: Libni and Shimei. 18The sons of Kohath: Amram, Izhar, Hebron, and Uzziel. 19The sons of Merari: Mahli and Mushi. These are the clans of the Levites according to their ancestry. 20Of Gershom: Libni his son, Jahath his son, Zimmah his son, 21Joah his son, Iddo his son, Zerah his son, Jeatherai his son. 22The sons of Kohath: Amminadab his son, Korah his son, Assir his son, 23Elkanah his son, Ebiasaph his son, Assir his son, 24Tahath his son, Uriel his son, Uzziah his son, and Shaul his son. 25The sons of Elkanah: Amasai and Ahimoth, 26Elkanah his son, Zophai his son, Nahath his son, 27Eliab his son, Jeroham his son, Elkanah his son. 28The sons of Samuel: Joel*e* his firstborn, the second Abijah.*f* 29The sons of Merari: Mahli, Libni his son, Shimei his son,

---

a Gk Vg: Heb *and Epher*   *b* Ch 5.27 in Heb   *c* Heb *Gershon,* variant of *Gershom*; See 6.16   *d* Ch 6.1 in Heb   *e* Gk Syr Compare verse 33 and 1 Sam 8.2: Heb lacks *Joel*   *f* Heb reads *Vashni, and Abijah* for *the second Abijah,* taking *the second* as a proper name

---

and others is described in terms of holy war (cf. esp. vv. 20, 22). **5.21** The enormous number of animals and captives demonstrates the size of the God-given victory. **5.23–26** The half-tribe of Manasseh lived in the northernmost part of Transjordan. **5.23** *Senir.* Cf. Deut 3.8–9. *Mount Hermon* (9,230 feet) marked the northernmost limit of Joshua's conquest (Josh 11.3). **5.25–26** A summary of the fate of the two and a half tribes, based in part on 2 Kings 17. **5.26** *Pul,* the Babylonian throne name of Tiglath-pileser III. The Assyrian locales at the end of the verse are derived from 2 Kings 17.6; 18.11.

6.1–30 For other genealogies of Levites, see Gen 46.11; Ex 6.16–25; Num 3.1–4, 17; 26.57–58. **6.2–15** The descendants of Aaron comprise the high priests. Cf. 6.50–53; 9.11; Ezra 7.1–5; Neh 11.10–11. **6.8** *Zadok* is made a descendant of Aaron through his father Ahitub (2 Sam 8.17). Another Ahitub is the grandfather of Abiathar, a high priest at the time of

David (1 Sam 14.3; 22.9, 20). *Ahimaaz.* Cf. 2 Sam 15.27. **6.9–10** *Azariah.* Cf. 1 Kings 4.2. **6.10** The parenthesis, dating this priest to Solomon, should probably be transferred to Azariah in v. 9. **6.11–12** The sequence *Amariah . . . Ahitub . . . Zadok* is duplicated from vv. 7–8. **6.13** *Hilkiah.* Cf. 2 Chr 34–35. **6.14** *Azariah . . . Seraiah.* Seraiah is missing in 9.11, and Azariah in Neh 11.10–11. Seraiah was killed at the beginning of the Babylonian exile (2 Kings 25.18–21). **6.16–30** The genealogy of three sons of Levi. **6.17, 20–21** The genealogy of *Gershom* through Libni, his oldest son. **6.18, 22–28** This genealogy of *Kohath* proceeds to Shaul (v. 24), but then adds a second line (vv. 25–28), beginning with *Elkanah* (v. 23), that makes Samuel a Levite. 1 Sam 1.1 classifies him as an Ephraimite whose father was named Elkanah. **6.19, 29–30** The genealogy of *Merari* through Mahli, his oldest son. **6.28** *Joel, Abijah.* The corruption of Samuel's sons leads the elders to request a king to rule Israel like all the nations

Uzzah his son, [30]Shimea his son, Haggiah his son, and Asaiah his son.

Musicians Appointed by David

31 These are the men whom David put in charge of the service of song in the house of the LORD, after the ark came to rest there. [32]They ministered with song before the tabernacle of the tent of meeting, until Solomon had built the house of the LORD in Jerusalem; and they performed their service in due order. [33]These are the men who served; and their sons were: Of the Kohathites: Heman, the singer, son of Joel, son of Samuel, [34]son of Elkanah, son of Jeroham, son of Eliel, son of Toah, [35]son of Zuph, son of Elkanah, son of Mahath, son of Amasai, [36]son of Elkanah, son of Joel, son of Azariah, son of Zephaniah, [37]son of Tahath, son of Assir, son of Ebiasaph, son of Korah, [38]son of Izhar, son of Kohath, son of Levi, son of Israel; [39]and his brother Asaph, who stood on his right, namely, Asaph son of Berechiah, son of Shimea, [40]son of Michael, son of Baaseiah, son of Malchijah, [41]son of Ethni, son of Zerah, son of Adaiah, [42]son of Ethan, son of Zimmah, son of Shimei, [43]son of Jahath, son of Gershom, son of Levi. [44]On the left were their kindred the sons of Merari: Ethan son of Kishi, son of Abdi, son of Malluch, [45]son of Hashabiah, son of Amaziah, son of Hilkiah, [46]son of Amzi, son of Bani, son of Shemer, [47]son of Mahli, son of Mushi, son of Merari, son of Levi; [48]and their kindred the Levites were appointed for all the service of the tabernacle of the house of God.

49 But Aaron and his sons made offerings on the altar of burnt offering and on the altar of incense, doing all the work of the most holy place, to make atonement for Israel, according to all that Moses the servant of God had commanded. [50]These are the sons of Aaron: Eleazar his son, Phinehas his son, Abishua his son, [51]Bukki his son, Uzzi his son, Zerahiah his son, [52]Meraioth his son, Amariah his son, Ahitub his son, [53]Zadok his son, Ahimaaz his son.

Settlements of the Levites

54 These are their dwelling places according to their settlements within their borders: to the sons of Aaron of the families of Kohathites— for the lot fell to them first— [55]to them they gave Hebron in the land of Judah and its surrounding pasture lands, [56]but the fields of the city and its villages they gave to Caleb son of Jephunneh. [57]To the sons of Aaron they gave the cities of refuge: Hebron, Libnah with its pasture lands, Jattir, Eshtemoa with its pasture lands, [58]Hilen[a] with its pasture lands, Debir with its pasture lands, [59]Ashan with its pasture lands, and Beth-shemesh with its pasture lands. [60]From the tribe of Benjamin, Geba with its pasture lands, Alemeth with its pasture lands, and Anathoth with its pasture lands. All their towns throughout their families were thirteen.

61 To the rest of the Kohathites were given by lot out of the family of the tribe, out of the half-tribe, the half of Manasseh, ten towns. [62]To the Gershomites according to their families were allotted thirteen towns out of the tribes of Issachar, Asher, Naphtali, and Manasseh in Bashan. [63]To the Merarites according to their families were allotted twelve towns out of the tribes of Reuben, Gad, and Zebulun. [64]So the people of Israel gave the Levites the towns with their pasture lands. [65]They also gave them by lot out of the tribes of Judah, Simeon, and Benjamin these towns that are mentioned by name.

66 And some of the families of the sons of Kohath had towns of their territory out of the

---

a Other readings *Hilez, Holon;* See Josh 21.15

(1 Sam 8.1–6). **6.31–53** These genealogies connect the singers Heman, Asaph, and Ethan to Kohath, Gershom, and Merari, respectively, and so make the singers Levites. These genealogies begin with the sons and move "backward" to the fathers. **6.31–32** David appoints the levitical singers; the duties of the priests go back to Moses. **6.33** *Heman,* a grandson of Samuel. **6.44** *Ethan.* See 15.17. In 25.1, 3 Jeduthun is the head of the third family of singers. **6.48** The duties of the singers are distinguished from those of more generic Levites. **6.49–53** The duties of the Aaronite priests (sacrifices and service within the holy of holies) and a list of the high priests up until the time of Solomon

(cf. 6.2–8). **6.54–81** Cf. Josh 21.1–42. Attempts to date this list to a specific century have not been successful. The list may have arisen by selecting four cities per tribe from the cities named in Josh 13–19 in order to create a list that shows levitical and priestly presence throughout the land. The other tribes have their territories and their land possessions; the priests and Levites have only their cities and their pasture lands. It is doubtful whether the levitical cities were ever connected with the administration of Israel. **6.55–59** Cities from the territories of Simeon and Judah. **6.60** Cities from Benjamin. **6.66–81** Cities from Ephraim, Manasseh, Issachar, Asher, Naphtali, Zebu-

tribe of Ephraim. 67They were given the cities of refuge: Shechem with its pasture lands in the hill country of Ephraim, Gezer with its pasture lands, 68Jokmeam with its pasture lands, Beth-horon with its pasture lands, 69Aijalon with its pasture lands, Gath-rimmon with its pasture lands; 70and out of the half-tribe of Manasseh, Aner with its pasture lands, and Bileam with its pasture lands, for the rest of the families of the Kohathites.

71 To the Gershomites: out of the half-tribe of Manasseh: Golan in Bashan with its pasture lands and Ashtaroth with its pasture lands; 72and out of the tribe of Issachar: Kedesh with its pasture lands, Daberath*a* with its pasture lands, 73Ramoth with its pasture lands, and Anem with its pasture lands; 74out of the tribe of Asher: Mashal with its pasture lands, Abdon with its pasture lands, 75Hukok with its pasture lands, and Rehob with its pasture lands; 76and out of the tribe of Naphtali: Kedesh in Galilee with its pasture lands, Hammon with its pasture lands, and Kiriathaim with its pasture lands. 77To the rest of the Merarites out of the tribe of Zebulun: Rimmono with its pasture lands, Tabor with its pasture lands, 78and across the Jordan from Jericho, on the east side of the Jordan, out of the tribe of Reuben: Bezer in the steppe with its pasture lands, Jahzah with its pasture lands, 79Kedemoth with its pasture lands, and Mephaath with its pasture lands; 80and out of the tribe of Gad: Ramoth in Gilead with its pasture lands, Mahanaim with its pasture lands, 81Heshbon with its pasture lands, and Jazer with its pasture lands.

Descendants of Issachar

7 The sons*b* of Issachar: Tola, Puah, Jashub, and Shimron, four. 2The sons of Tola: Uzzi, Rephaiah, Jeriel, Jahmai, Ibsam, and Shemuel, heads of their ancestral houses, namely of Tola, mighty warriors of their generations, their number in the days of David being twenty-two thousand six hundred.

3The son*c* of Uzzi: Izrahiah. And the sons of Izrahiah: Michael, Obadiah, Joel, and Isshiah, five, all of them chiefs; 4and along with them, by their generations, according to their ancestral houses, were units of the fighting force, thirty-six thousand, for they had many wives and sons. 5Their kindred belonging to all the families of Issachar were in all eighty-seven thousand mighty warriors, enrolled by genealogy.

Descendants of Benjamin

6 The sons of Benjamin: Bela, Becher, and Jediael, three. 7The sons of Bela: Ezbon, Uzzi, Uzziel, Jerimoth, and Iri, five, heads of ancestral houses, mighty warriors; and their enrollment by genealogies was twenty-two thousand thirty-four. 8The sons of Becher: Zemirah, Joash, Eliezer, Elioenai, Omri, Jeremoth, Abijah, Anathoth, and Alemeth. All these were the sons of Becher; 9and their enrollment by genealogies, according to their generations, as heads of their ancestral houses, mighty warriors, was twenty thousand two hundred. 10The sons of Jediael: Bilhan. And the sons of Bilhan: Jeush, Benjamin, Ehud, Chenaanah, Zethan, Tarshish, and Ahishahar. 11All these were the sons of Jediael according to the heads of their ancestral houses, mighty warriors, seventeen thousand two hundred, ready for service in war. 12And Shuppim and Huppim were the sons of Ir, Hushim the son*c* of Aher.

Descendants of Naphtali

13 The descendants of Naphtali: Jahziel, Guni, Jezer, and Shallum, the descendants of Bilhah.

Descendants of Manasseh

14 The sons of Manasseh: Asriel, whom his Aramean concubine bore; she bore Machir the father of Gilead. 15And Machir took a wife for

---

a Or Dobrath   *b* Syr Compare Vg: Heb And to the sons
c Heb sons

---

lun, Reuben, and Gad. **6.69** The beginning of the verse should read: "And out of the tribe of Dan: Elteke with its pasture lands, Gibbethon with its pasture lands." Cf. Josh 21.23.

7.1–5 The genealogy of Issachar through his oldest son, Tola (cf. Gen 46.13; Num 26.23–25). The numbers in these verses (vv. 2, 4, 5) suggest that a military census list has been put in genealogical form (cf. 5.23–26). **7.2** Cf. the census of David in ch. 21. **7.6–12** This

genealogy of the Benjaminites also appears to be from the military census list used in 7.1–5 (note the numbers in vv. 7, 9, 11). The Chronicler returns to the genealogy of Benjamin in ch. 8. Cf. Gen 46.21; Num 26.38–41. **7.12** *The sons of Ir.* Some scholars read "the sons of Dan." Hence this verse may contain a fragment of the genealogy of Dan. Cf. Gen 46.23; Num 26.42. **7.13** Cf. Gen 46.24–25; Num 26.48–49. As Gen 46.25 indicates, *Bilhah* is the mother of Dan and Naphtali.

Huppim and for Shuppim. The name of his sister was Maacah. And the name of the second was Zelophehad; and Zelophehad had daughters. [16]Maacah the wife of Machir bore a son, and she named him Peresh; the name of his brother was Sheresh; and his sons were Ulam and Rekem. [17]The son[a] of Ulam: Bedan. These were the sons of Gilead son of Machir, son of Manasseh. [18]And his sister Hammolecheth bore Ishhod, Abiezer, and Mahlah. [19]The sons of Shemida were Ahian, Shechem, Likhi, and Aniam.

Descendants of Ephraim

20 The sons of Ephraim: Shuthelah, and Bered his son, Tahath his son, Eleadah his son, Tahath his son, [21]Zabad his son, Shuthelah his son, and Ezer and Elead. Now the people of Gath, who were born in the land, killed them, because they came down to raid their cattle. [22]And their father Ephraim mourned many days, and his brothers came to comfort him. [23]Ephraim[b] went in to his wife, and she conceived and bore a son; and he named him Beriah, because disaster[c] had befallen his house. [24]His daughter was Sheerah, who built both Lower and Upper Beth-horon, and Uzzen-sheerah. [25]Rephah was his son, Resheph his son, Telah his son, Tahan his son, [26]Ladan his son, Ammihud his son, Elishama his son, [27]Nun[d] his son, Joshua his son. [28]Their possessions and settlements were Bethel and its towns, and eastward Naaran, and westward Gezer and its towns, Shechem and its towns, as far as Ayyah and its towns; [29]also along the borders of the Manassites, Beth-shean and its towns, Taanach and its towns, Megiddo and its towns, Dor and its towns. In these lived the sons of Joseph son of Israel.

Descendants of Asher

30 The sons of Asher: Imnah, Ishvah, Ishvi, Beriah, and their sister Serah. [31]The sons of Beriah: Heber and Malchiel, who was the father of Birzaith. [32]Heber became the father of Japhlet, Shomer, Hotham, and their sister Shua. [33]The sons of Japhlet: Pasach, Bimhal, and Ashvath. These are the sons of Japhlet. [34]The sons of Shemer: Ahi, Rohgah, Hubbah, and Aram. [35]The sons of Helem[e] his brother: Zophah, Imna, Shelesh, and Amal. [36]The sons of Zophah: Suah, Harnepher, Shual, Beri, Imrah, [37]Bezer, Hod, Shamma, Shilshah, Ithran, and Beera. [38]The sons of Jether: Jephunneh, Pispa, and Ara. [39]The sons of Ulla: Arah, Hanniel, and Rizia. [40]All of these were men of Asher, heads of ancestral houses, select mighty warriors, chief of the princes. Their number enrolled by genealogies, for service in war, was twenty-six thousand men.

Descendants of Benjamin

8 Benjamin became the father of Bela his firstborn, Ashbel the second, Aharah the third, [2]Nohah the fourth, and Rapha the fifth. [3]And Bela had sons: Addar, Gera, Abihud,[f] [4]Abishua, Naaman, Ahoah, [5]Gera, Shephuphan, and Huram. [6]These are the sons of Ehud (they were heads of ancestral houses of the inhabitants of Geba, and they were carried into exile to Manahath): [7]Naaman,[g] Ahijah, and Gera, that is, Heglam,[h] who became the father of Uzza and Ahihud. [8]And Shaharaim had sons in the country of Moab after he had sent away his wives Hushim and Baara. [9]He had sons by

a Heb *sons* b Heb *He* c Heb *beraah* d Here spelled *Non*; see Ex 33.11 e Or *Hotham*; see 7.32 f Or *father of Ehud*; see 8.6 g Heb *and Naaman* h Or *he carried them into exile*

7.15 *Maacah,* identified in v. 16 as the wife of Machir, but Machir should probably be emended to Gilead. Inheritance rights in the family of *Zelophehad,* in which there were only daughters, is discussed in Num 27.1–11; 36.1–12; Josh 17.3–6. 7.20–21a, 25–27 A linear genealogy from Ephraim to Joshua, the leader of the conquest, in whom the Chronicler shows little interest elsewhere. 7.21b–24 This anecdote from the life of the ancestor Ephraim interrupts the genealogy. After defeat in an attack upon Gath, Ephraim sires a child, *Beriah,* the etymology of whose name points to the "disaster" that had befallen his house. The family settles farther east near *Lower and Upper Beth-horon,* twin cities in Ephraim near Benjamin that guarded a pass from the coast to Jerusalem. 7.22 *Brothers,* or relatives.

The only true brother of Ephraim known in the Bible is Manasseh. 7.28–29 A list of towns representing the southern and northern boundaries of the territory settled by the sons of Joseph. Cf. Josh 16–18. 7.30–40 The genealogy of Asher (cf. Gen 46.17; Num 26.44–47) based on a military census list (v. 40; cf. vv. 1–12).

8.1–40 An extensive and obscure genealogy of Benjamin concludes the Chronicler's depiction of all Israel and demonstrates the great interest he had in this tribe. 8.1–7 Descendants of Benjamin through his firstborn, Bela, to the fifth generation. 8.3 *Abihud.* Read "the father of Ehud" (Judg 3.15). In v. 6 Ehud's descendants are said to dwell in *Geba,* a town northeast of Jerusalem. 8.8–12 *Moab.* David met with the king of Moab (1 Sam 22.3–4; cf. Ruth 1); perhaps

his wife Hodesh: Jobab, Zibia, Mesha, Malcam, [10]Jeuz, Sachia, and Mirmah. These were his sons, heads of ancestral houses. [11]He also had sons by Hushim: Abitub and Elpaal. [12]The sons of Elpaal: Eber, Misham, and Shemed, who built Ono and Lod with its towns, [13]and Beriah and Shema (they were heads of ancestral houses of the inhabitants of Aijalon, who put to flight the inhabitants of Gath); [14]and Ahio, Shashak, and Jeremoth. [15]Zebadiah, Arad, Eder, [16]Michael, Ishpah, and Joha were sons of Beriah. [17]Zebadiah, Meshullam, Hizki, Heber, [18]Ishmerai, Izliah, and Jobab were the sons of Elpaal. [19]Jakim, Zichri, Zabdi, [20]Elienai, Zillethai, Eliel, [21]Adaiah, Beraiah, and Shimrath were the sons of Shimei. [22]Ishpan, Eber, Eliel, [23]Abdon, Zichri, Hanan, [24]Hananiah, Elam, Anthothijah, [25]Iphdeiah, and Penuel were the sons of Shashak. [26]Shamsherai, Shehariah, Athaliah, [27]Jaareshiah, Elijah, and Zichri were the sons of Jeroham. [28]These were the heads of ancestral houses, according to their generations, chiefs. These lived in Jerusalem.

[29]Jeiel[a] the father of Gibeon lived in Gibeon, and the name of his wife was Maacah. [30]His firstborn son: Abdon, then Zur, Kish, Baal,[b] Nadab, [31]Gedor, Ahio, Zecher, [32]and Mikloth, who became the father of Shimeah. Now these also lived opposite their kindred in Jerusalem, with their kindred. [33]Ner became the father of Kish, Kish of Saul,[c] Saul[c] of Jonathan, Mal-

chishua, Abinadab, and Esh-baal; [34]and the son of Jonathan was Merib-baal; and Merib-baal became the father of Micah. [35]The sons of Micah: Pithon, Melech, Tarea, and Ahaz. [36]Ahaz became the father of Jehoaddah; and Jehoaddah became the father of Alemeth, Azmaveth, and Zimri; Zimri became the father of Moza. [37]Moza became the father of Binea; Raphah was his son, Eleasah his son, Azel his son. [38]Azel had six sons, and these are their names: Azrikam, Bocheru, Ishmael, Sheariah, Obadiah, and Hanan; all these were the sons of Azel. [39]The sons of his brother Eshek: Ulam his firstborn, Jeush the second, and Eliphelet the third. [40]The sons of Ulam were mighty warriors, archers, having many children and grandchildren, one hundred fifty. All these were Benjaminites.

9 So all Israel was enrolled by genealogies; and these are written in the Book of the Kings of Israel. And Judah was taken into exile in Babylon because of their unfaithfulness. [2]Now the first to live again in their possessions in their towns were Israelites, priests, Levites, and temple servants.

Inhabitants of Jerusalem after the Exile

3 And some of the people of Judah, Benjamin, Ephraim, and Manasseh lived in Jerusalem:

a Compare 9.35: Heb lacks *Jeiel* *b* Gk Ms adds *Ner*; Compare 8.33 and 9.36 *c* Or *Shaul*

other Israelites lived in Moab in early times. **8.12** *Ono and Lod,* towns located southeast of Joppa, which were resettled in postexilic times (Ezra 2.33). **8.13** *Aijalon,* a town originally assigned to Dan and later fortified by Rehoboam (2 Chr 11.10); it apparently became part of Benjamin after the division of the kingdom. **8.29–40** The genealogy of Saul is repeated from 9.35–44, where it provides for a transition from the genealogies in chs. 1–9 to the account of Saul's death in ch. 10. The genealogy has its geographical focus at *Gibeon,* a Benjaminite city five and a half miles northwest of Jerusalem. *Jeiel's* relationship to the Benjaminite genealogy is not specified. **8.30** *Ner* should be inserted before *Nadab,* as in Greek manuscript tradition (cf. v. 33). **8.32** Part of the family of the Benjaminites migrated to Jerusalem. **8.33** *Esh-baal.* The form of this name (with the Northwest Semitic divine name "Baal," familiar from the Canaanite deity of this name; cf. vv. 30, 34) indicates the antiquity of this genealogy. The same person elsewhere is called Ishvi (1 Sam 14.49), Ish-bosheth (2 Sam 2.8), and Esh-baal (2 Sam 2.8, Septuagint). **8.34** *Merib-baal,* Mephibosheth (2 Sam 4.4). *Micah,* the last of the descendants of Saul is also known elsewhere in the OT (2 Sam 9.12). **8.35–38** The genealogy of Saul is traced to a point in late preexilic or

exilic times. **8.39–40** These verses do not appear in the parallel genealogy of Saul in 9.35–44 and make the genealogy in ch. 8 typologically later. The military forces associated with Ulam in this genealogical notice claim prestige by identifying themselves as descendants of Israel's first king.

9.1–34 Cf. Neh 11.3–24. The author uses Neh 11, a list of those living in Jerusalem when Nehemiah rebuilt the walls. The nature of the Chronicler's genealogical sources is not clarified by the reference to the *Book of the Kings of Israel* (v. 1). This verse forms a conclusion to the preexilic genealogies in chs. 1–8. Vv. 2–3 anticipate the repopulation of the land and are followed by lists of Judahites (vv. 4–6), Benjaminites (vv. 7–9), priests (vv. 10–13), Levites (vv. 14–16), and gatekeepers (vv. 17–27). Israel and Judah once more live in Jerusalem, the city of the temple, where the clergy functions in accord with the Lord's ordinances. The Chronicler links the community of his day with the Israel described in chs. 1–9. **9.2** *In their towns.* Cf. Neh 11.1. Ch. 9, however, deals only with those living in Jerusalem. *Temple servants,* mentioned only here in Chronicles, but frequent in Ezra and Nehemiah. **9.3** *Ephraim and Manasseh,* not mentioned in Neh 11.4 and probably symbolizing the whole Northern

4Uthai son of Ammihud, son of Omri, son of Imri, son of Bani, from the sons of Perez son of Judah. 5And of the Shilonites: Asaiah the firstborn, and his sons. 6Of the sons of Zerah: Jeuel and their kin, six hundred ninety. 7Of the Benjaminites: Sallu son of Meshullam, son of Hodaviah, son of Hassenuah, 8Ibneiah son of Jeroham, Elah son of Uzzi, son of Michri, and Meshullam son of Shephatiah, son of Reuel, son of Ibnijah; 9and their kindred according to their generations, nine hundred fifty-six. All these were heads of families according to their ancestral houses.

Priestly Families

10 Of the priests: Jedaiah, Jehoiarib, Jachin, 11and Azariah son of Hilkiah, son of Meshullam, son of Zadok, son of Meraioth, son of Ahitub, the chief officer of the house of God; 12and Adaiah son of Jeroham, son of Pashhur, son of Malchijah, and Maasai son of Adiel, son of Jahzerah, son of Meshullam, son of Meshillemith, son of Immer; 13besides their kindred, heads of their ancestral houses, one thousand seven hundred sixty, qualified for the work of the service of the house of God.

Levitical Families

14 Of the Levites: Shemaiah son of Hasshub, son of Azrikam, son of Hashabiah, of the sons of Merari; 15and Bakbakkar, Heresh, Galal, and Mattaniah son of Mica, son of Zichri, son of Asaph; 16and Obadiah son of Shemaiah, son of Galal, son of Jeduthun, and Berechiah son of Asa, son of Elkanah, who lived in the villages of the Netophathites.

17 The gatekeepers were: Shallum, Akkub, Talmon, Ahiman; and their kindred Shallum was the chief, 18stationed previously in the king's gate on the east side. These were the gatekeepers of the camp of the Levites. 19Shallum son of Kore, son of Ebiasaph, son of Korah, and his kindred of his ancestral house, the Korahites, were in charge of the work of the service, guardians of the thresholds of the tent, as their ancestors had been in charge of the camp of the LORD, guardians of the entrance. 20And Phinehas son of Eleazar was chief over them in former times; the LORD was with him. 21Zechariah son of Meshelemiah was gatekeeper at the entrance of the tent of meeting. 22All these, who were chosen as gatekeepers at the thresholds, were two hundred twelve. They were enrolled by genealogies in their villages. David and the seer Samuel established them in their office of trust. 23So they and their descendants were in charge of the gates of the house of the LORD, that is, the house of the tent, as guards. 24The gatekeepers were on the four sides, east, west, north, and south; 25and their kindred who were in their villages were obliged to come in every seven days, in turn, to be with them; 26for the four chief gatekeepers, who were Levites, were in charge of the chambers and the treasures of the house of God. 27And they would spend the night near the house of God; for on them lay the duty of watching, and they had charge of opening it every morning.

28 Some of them had charge of the utensils of service, for they were required to count them when they were brought in and taken out. 29Others of them were appointed over the furniture, and over all the holy utensils, also over the choice flour, the wine, the oil, the incense, and the spices. 30Others, of the sons of the priests, prepared the mixing of the spices, 31and Mattithiah, one of the Levites, the firstborn of Shallum the Korahite, was in charge of making the flat cakes. 32Also some of their kindred of the Kohathites had charge of the rows of bread, to prepare them for each sabbath.

33 Now these are the singers, the heads of ancestral houses of the Levites, living in the chambers of the temple free from other ser-

Kingdom. 9.5–6 Among the Judahites, Chronicles adds references to the descendants of Shelah (cf. Num 26.20 for an alternate vocalization of Shilonites) and Zerah. 9.11 Chief officer of the house of God. Azariah gains this title because of his connection to the list of high priests. 9.17–34 This paragraph identifies the gatekeepers as Levites (v. 26). In Neh 11 the singers are among the Levites, but the gatekeepers and temple servants are not. 9.19 The duties of the gatekeepers continue those of their ancestors in the desert who were in control of the camp of the Lord and guardians of the

entrance. 9.20, 22 The prestige of Phinehas (Num 25.11–13) stands behind the gatekeepers at the time of Moses, and the prestige of David and . . . Samuel lends them authority during the United Monarchy. The reference to Samuel is an anachronism, since Samuel died long before David became king. For the Chronicler Samuel was not only a seer, but a Levite as well. 9.21 Zechariah, a gatekeeper at the time of David (26.2, 14). 9.26 The gatekeepers are identified as Levites. 9.33 The singers are considered important enough to be freed from other levitical duties.

vice, for they were on duty day and night. [34]These were heads of ancestral houses of the Levites, according to their generations; these leaders lived in Jerusalem.

The Family of King Saul

35 In Gibeon lived the father of Gibeon, Jeiel, and the name of his wife was Maacah. [36]His firstborn son was Abdon, then Zur, Kish, Baal, Ner, Nadab, [37]Gedor, Ahio, Zechariah, and Mikloth; [38]and Mikloth became the father of Shimeam; and these also lived opposite their kindred in Jerusalem, with their kindred. [39]Ner became the father of Kish, Kish of Saul, Saul of Jonathan, Malchishua, Abinadab, and Esh-baal; [40]and the son of Jonathan was Merib-baal; and Merib-baal became the father of Micah. [41]The sons of Micah: Pithon, Melech, Tahrea, and Ahaz;[a] [42]and Ahaz became the father of Jarah, and Jarah of Alemeth, Azmaveth, and Zimri; and Zimri became the father of Moza. [43]Moza became the father of Binea; and Rephaiah was his son, Eleasah his son, Azel his son. [44]Azel had six sons, and these are their names: Azrikam, Bocheru, Ishmael, Sheariah, Obadiah, and Hanan; these were the sons of Azel.

Death of Saul and His Sons

10 Now the Philistines fought against Israel; and the men of Israel fled before the Philistines, and fell slain on Mount Gilboa. [2]The Philistines overtook Saul and his sons; and the Philistines killed Jonathan and Abinadab and Malchishua, sons of Saul. [3]The battle pressed hard on Saul; and the archers found him, and he was wounded by the archers. [4]Then Saul said to his armor-bearer, "Draw your sword, and thrust me through with it, so that these uncircumcised may not come and make sport of me." But his armor-bearer was unwilling, for he was terrified. So Saul took his own sword and fell on it. [5]When his armor-bearer saw that Saul was dead, he also fell on his sword and died. [6]Thus Saul died; he and his three sons and all his house died together. [7]When all the men of Israel who were in the valley saw that the army[b] had fled and that Saul and his sons were dead, they abandoned their towns and fled; and the Philistines came and occupied them.

8 The next day when the Philistines came to strip the dead, they found Saul and his sons fallen on Mount Gilboa. [9]They stripped him and took his head and his armor, and sent messengers throughout the land of the Philistines to carry the good news to their idols and to the people. [10]They put his armor in the temple of their gods, and fastened his head in the temple of Dagon. [11]But when all Jabesh-gilead heard everything that the Philistines had done to Saul, [12]all the valiant warriors got up and took away the body of Saul and the bodies of his sons, and brought them to Jabesh. Then they buried their bones under the oak in Jabesh, and fasted seven days.

13 So Saul died for his unfaithfulness; he was unfaithful to the LORD in that he did not keep the command of the LORD; moreover, he had consulted a medium, seeking guidance, [14]and did not seek guidance from the LORD. Therefore the LORD[c] put him to death and turned the kingdom over to David son of Jesse.

---

a Compare 8.35: Heb lacks *and Ahaz*   b Heb *they*   c Heb *he*

9.34 With v. 3 this sentence emphasizes that the list identifies those who had returned from exile and were dwelling in Jerusalem. The Chronicler brought this verse from ch. 8, together with its sequels in 8.29–32 and 8.33–38. The assertion that all the preceding people lived in Jerusalem conflicts with vv. 16, 22, 25. **9.35–44** See note on 8.29–40.
10.1–29.30 The reign of David. **10.1–14** Cf. 1 Sam 31.1–13. Chronicles omits the story of Saul's kingship except for his defeat by the Philistines and his death. **10.1** *Mount Gilboa* is six miles west of Beth-shan. **10.2** Chronicles does not mention another son, Ishbosheth, who succeeded to a portion of his father's kingdom (2 Sam 2.8–10). **10.4** *Uncircumcised*, a term of derision for Israel's non-Semitic neighbors (cf. 1 Sam 17.36; 18.25–27). **10.6** *All his house* (dynasty) indicates the severity of the defeat; the battle of Gilboa marks a decisive change in Israel's history. **10.9** The *head* and *armor*, trophies signaling victory, are carried throughout Philistine territory, giving joy to both idols and people. **10.10** *Dagon*, a fertility deity. The temple of Dagon recalls the Israelite loss of the ark at the battle of Ebenezer (1 Sam 5.1–4). **10.12** *Jabesh*, a city thirteen miles southeast of Beth-shan; it was rescued by Saul from Nahash the Ammonite early in his reign (1 Sam 11). Now its army provides the king and his sons with proper burial. **10.13–14** The king, wounded by archers, actually commits suicide (v. 4). Saul did not observe the Lord's command in general; he sought (the verb is a pun on the name Saul) a medium in order to consult with the spirit world (cf. 1 Sam 28.8–25), thus not seeking the Lord in the wider sense of the word. *Seeking the Lord* in Chronicles means showing loyalty or reverence toward God. In retribution for

David Anointed King of All Israel

11 Then all Israel gathered together to David at Hebron and said, "See, we are your bone and flesh. ²For some time now, even while Saul was king, it was you who commanded the army of Israel. The LORD your God said to you: It is you who shall be shepherd of my people Israel, you who shall be ruler over my people Israel." ³So all the elders of Israel came to the king at Hebron, and David made a covenant with them at Hebron before the LORD. And they anointed David king over Israel, according to the word of the LORD by Samuel.

Jerusalem Captured

4 David and all Israel marched to Jerusalem, that is Jebus, where the Jebusites were, the inhabitants of the land. ⁵The inhabitants of Jebus said to David, "You will not come in here." Nevertheless David took the stronghold of Zion, now the city of David. ⁶David had said, "Whoever attacks the Jebusites first shall be chief and commander." And Joab son of Zeruiah went up first, so he became chief. ⁷David resided in the stronghold; therefore it was called the city of David. ⁸He built the city all around, from the Millo in complete circuit; and Joab repaired the rest of the city. ⁹And David became greater and greater, for the LORD of hosts was with him.

David's Mighty Men and Their Exploits

10 Now these are the chiefs of David's warriors, who gave him strong support in his kingdom, together with all Israel, to make him king, according to the word of the LORD concerning Israel. ¹¹This is an account of David's mighty warriors: Jashobeam, son of Hachmoni,ᵃ was chief of the Three;ᵇ he wielded his spear against three hundred whom he killed at one time.

12 And next to him among the three warriors was Eleazar son of Dodo, the Ahohite. ¹³He was with David at Pas-dammim when the Philistines were gathered there for battle. There was a plot of ground full of barley. Now the people had fled from the Philistines, ¹⁴but he and David took their stand in the middle of the plot, defended it, and killed the Philistines; and the LORD saved them by a great victory.

15 Three of the thirty chiefs went down to the rock to David at the cave of Adullam, while the army of Philistines was encamped in the valley of Rephaim. ¹⁶David was then in the stronghold; and the garrison of the Philistines was then at Bethlehem. ¹⁷David said longingly, "O that someone would give me water to drink from the well of Bethlehem that is by the gate!" ¹⁸Then the Three broke through the camp of the Philistines, and drew water from the well of Bethlehem that was by the gate, and they brought it to David. But David would not drink of it; he poured it out to the LORD, ¹⁹and said, "My God forbid that I should do this. Can I drink the blood of these men? For at the risk of their lives they brought it." Therefore he would not drink it. The three warriors did these things.

20 Now Abishai,ᶜ the brother of Joab, was chief of the Thirty.ᵈ With his spear he fought against three hundred and killed them, and won

---

ᵃ Or *a Hachmonite*   ᵇ Compare 2 Sam 23.8: Heb *Thirty* or *captains*   ᶜ Gk Vg Tg Compare 2 Sam 23.18: Heb *Abishai*   ᵈ Syr: Heb *Three*

Saul's sins, the Lord turns the kingdom over to David, just as he would later divide the kingdom between Rehoboam and Jeroboam (2 Chr 10.15).
11.1–9 Cf. 2 Sam 5.1–10. Chronicles omits the events of 2 Sam 1–4, many of which might be interpreted as negative events following the death of Saul. **11.3** *Hebron,* a city south of Jerusalem. Chronicles does not mention the separate anointings of David by Judah (2 Sam 2.4) and by Israel (2 Sam 5.3); instead, all Israel anoints him at once. David's covenant with the people is echoed by the great feast in 12.38–40. **11.4** *Jebus,* an alternate name for Jerusalem, apparently derived from the name of its inhabitants, the Jebusites. In 2 Sam 5.6–7 David's personal army conquers the future capital; in Chronicles the campaign is waged by David and a united Israel. **11.6** *Joab,* David's nephew, becomes chief officer because of his heroic

actions. **11.8** In Chronicles, blessed kings undertake building projects. The *Millo* was a series of terraces built on the eastern side of the city. **11.9** The Lord is with David as surely as he had departed from Saul.
11.10–47 Cf. 2 Sam 23.8–39. The individual exploits told here are not as important as the unanimous support of these chiefs for David's kingship. The Chronicler puts the list at the beginning of David's reign; in Samuel it comes near the king's death. The first twelve names are repeated in 27.2–15. **11.10** David has the support of all the tribes (ch. 12) in addition to the heroes. David's kingship also results from the divine word of promise. **11.11** *Three.* Jashobeam, Eleazar, and Shammah (2 Sam 23.11–12) make up this elite group of warriors. **11.15–19** David refuses to drink water gained by a daring raid on the Philistines. **11.20–25** *Abishai* and *Benaiah,* though outstanding leaders,

a name beside the Three. 21He was the most renowned[a] of the Thirty,[b] and became their commander; but he did not attain to the Three.

22 Benaiah son of Jehoiada was a valiant man[c] of Kabzeel, a doer of great deeds; he struck down two sons of[d] Ariel of Moab. He also went down and killed a lion in a pit on a day when snow had fallen. 23And he killed an Egyptian, a man of great stature, five cubits tall. The Egyptian had in his hand a spear like a weaver's beam; but Benaiah went against him with a staff, snatched the spear out of the Egyptian's hand, and killed him with his own spear. 24Such were the things Benaiah son of Jehoiada did, and he won a name beside the three warriors. 25He was renowned among the Thirty, but he did not attain to the Three. And David put him in charge of his bodyguard.

26 The warriors of the armies were Asahel brother of Joab, Elhanan son of Dodo of Bethlehem, 27Shammoth of Harod,[e] Helez the Pelonite, 28Ira son of Ikkesh of Tekoa, Abiezer of Anathoth, 29Sibbecai the Hushathite, Ilai the Ahohite, 30Maharai of Netophah, Heled son of Baanah of Netophah, 31Ithai son of Ribai of Gibeah of the Benjaminites, Benaiah of Pirathon, 32Hurai of the wadis of Gaash, Abiel the Arbathite, 33Azmaveth of Baharum, Eliahba of Shaalbon, 34Hashem[f] the Gizonite, Jonathan son of Shagee the Hararite, 35Ahiam son of Sachar the Hararite, Eliphal son of Ur, 36Hepher the Mecherathite, Ahijah the Pelonite, 37Hezro of Carmel, Naarai son of Ezbai, 38Joel the brother of Nathan, Mibhar son of Hagri, 39Zelek the Ammonite, Naharai of Beeroth, the armor-bearer of Joab son of Zeruiah, 40Ira the Ithrite, Gareb the Ithrite, 41Uriah the Hittite, Zabad son of Ahlai, 42Adina son of Shiza the Reubenite, a leader of the Reubenites, and thirty with him, 43Hanan son of Maacah, and Joshaphat the Mithnite, 44Uzzia the Ashterathite, Shama and Jeiel sons of Hotham the Aroerite, 45Jediael son of Shimri, and his brother Joha the Tizite, 46Eliel the Mahavite, and Jeribai and Joshaviah sons of Elnaam, and Ithmah the Moabite, 47Eliel, and Obed, and Jaasiel the Mezobaite.

David's Followers in the Wilderness

12 The following are those who came to David at Ziklag, while he could not move about freely because of Saul son of Kish; they were among the mighty warriors who helped him in war. 2They were archers, and could shoot arrows and sling stones with either the right hand or the left; they were Benjaminites, Saul's kindred. 3The chief was Ahiezer, then Joash, both sons of Shemaah of Gibeah; also Jeziel and Pelet sons of Azmaveth; Beracah, Jehu of Anathoth, 4Ishmaiah of Gibeon, a warrior among the Thirty and a leader over the Thirty; Jeremiah,[g] Jahaziel, Johanan, Jozabad of Gederah, 5Eluzai,[h] Jerimoth, Bealiah, Shemariah, Shephatiah the Haruphite; 6Elkanah, Isshiah, Azarel, Joezer, and Jashobeam, the Korahites; 7and Joelah and Zebadiah, sons of Jeroham of Gedor.

8 From the Gadites there went over to David at the stronghold in the wilderness mighty and experienced warriors, expert with shield and spear, whose faces were like the faces of lions, and who were swift as gazelles on the mountains: 9Ezer the chief, Obadiah second, Eliab third, 10Mishmannah fourth, Jeremiah fifth, 11Attai sixth, Eliel seventh, 12Johanan eighth, Elzabad ninth, 13Jeremiah tenth, Machbannai eleventh. 14These Gadites were officers of the army, the least equal to a hundred and the greatest to a thousand. 15These are the men who crossed the Jordan in the first month, when it was overflowing all its banks, and put to flight all those in the valleys, to the east and to the west.

16 Some Benjaminites and Judahites came to the stronghold to David. 17David went out to meet them and said to them, "If you have come to me in friendship, to help me, then my heart will be knit to you; but if you have come to betray me to my adversaries, though my

---

a Compare 2 Sam 23.19: Heb *more renowned among the two*   b Syr: Heb *Three*   c Syr: Heb *the son of a valiant man*   d See 2 Sam 23.20: Heb lacks *sons of*   e Compare 2 Sam 23.25: Heb *the Harorite*   f Compare Gk and 2 Sam 23.32: Heb *the sons of Hashem*   g Heb verse 5   h Heb verse 6

---

are not included among the Three. **11.41** *Uriah*, husband of Bathsheba. **11.41b–47** Names without parallel in 2 Samuel.

12.1–22 A list of tribal groups who rallied to David already at Hebron. **12.1–7** Twenty-three soldiers from Saul's own tribe of Benjamin support David. **12.1** *Zik-*lag, a city in the southern part of Judah, given to David by Achish, king of Gath (1 Sam 27.5–12). **12.8–15** Eleven Gadites come from their tribal home on the other side of the Jordan River. **12.16–18** Benjamin and Judah are often linked in Chronicles. Clothed with the spirit, the soldier *Amasai* delivers a prophetic oracle

hands have done no wrong, then may the God of our ancestors see and give judgment." [18]Then the spirit came upon Amasai, chief of the Thirty, and he said,

"We are yours, O David;
    and with you, O son of Jesse!
Peace, peace to you,
    and peace to the one who helps you!
For your God is the one who helps
    you."

Then David received them, and made them officers of his troops.

19 Some of the Manassites deserted to David when he came with the Philistines for the battle against Saul. (Yet he did not help them, for the rulers of the Philistines took counsel and sent him away, saying, "He will desert to his master Saul at the cost of our heads.") [20]As he went to Ziklag these Manassites deserted to him: Adnah, Jozabad, Jediael, Michael, Jozabad, Elihu, and Zillethai, chiefs of the thousands in Manasseh. [21]They helped David against the band of raiders,[a] for they were all warriors and commanders in the army. [22]Indeed from day to day people kept coming to David to help him, until there was a great army, like an army of God.

David's Army at Hebron

23 These are the numbers of the divisions of the armed troops who came to David in Hebron to turn the kingdom of Saul over to him, according to the word of the LORD. [24]The people of Judah bearing shield and spear numbered six thousand eight hundred armed troops. [25]Of the Simeonites, mighty warriors, seven thousand one hundred. [26]Of the Levites four thousand six hundred. [27]Jehoiada, leader of the house of Aaron, and with him three thousand seven hundred. [28]Zadok, a young warrior, and twenty-two commanders from his own ancestral house. [29]Of the Benjaminites, the kindred of Saul, three thousand, of whom the majority had continued to keep their allegiance to the house of Saul. [30]Of the Ephraimites, twenty thousand eight hundred, mighty warriors, notables in their ancestral houses. [31]Of the half-tribe of Manasseh, eighteen thousand, who were expressly named to come and make David king. [32]Of Issachar, those who had understanding of the times, to know what Israel ought to do, two hundred chiefs, and all their kindred under their command. [33]Of Zebulun, fifty thousand seasoned troops, equipped for battle with all the weapons of war, to help David[b] with singleness of purpose. [34]Of Naphtali, a thousand commanders, with whom there were thirty-seven thousand armed with shield and spear. [35]Of the Danites, twenty-eight thousand six hundred equipped for battle. [36]Of Asher, forty thousand seasoned troops ready for battle. [37]Of the Reubenites and Gadites and the half-tribe of Manasseh from beyond the Jordan, one hundred twenty thousand armed with all the weapons of war.

38 All these, warriors arrayed in battle order, came to Hebron with full intent to make David king over all Israel; likewise all the rest of Israel were of a single mind to make David king. [39]They were there with David for three days, eating and drinking, for their kindred had provided for them. [40]And also their neighbors, from as far away as Issachar and Zebulun and Naphtali, came bringing food on donkeys, camels, mules, and oxen—abundant

a Or as officers of his troops   b Gk: Heb lacks David

supporting David. He wishes peace to both the king and God. **12.19–22** Seven chiefs of Manasseh, a northern tribe, also join David at Ziklag. **12.19** Though David is allied with the Philistines, the enemies of Saul, he is dismissed by them before Saul's death in battle, thus clearing him of any guilt for that death (1 Sam 29). **12.22** God's help (v. 18) is matched by help offered by numerous military volunteers. *Army of God* can mean a numerous army or one that exerts the power of God's army in holy war. **12.23–40** The size of the armies that rally to David at Hebron from the southern tribes (Judah, Simeon, and Benjamin) is relatively small, but the troops from the north (Ephraim, the half-tribe of Manasseh, Issachar, Zebulun, Naphtali, Dan, and Asher) are quite large, as are the volunteers from Transjordan (Reuben, Gad, and the half-tribe of Manasseh). The more distant tribes show their enthusiasm for David's kingship by their extremely high numbers. Judah has a mere 6,800 men; Zebulun 50,000. There are a total of 339,600 soldiers. Through large numbers the author stresses the overwhelming and unified support of all Israel for David. Ephraim and Manasseh are more enthusiastic than Judah; the remotest tribes are the most enthusiastic of all. **12.28** *Zadok,* possibly to be identified with the high priest who served David in Jerusalem. **12.29** Saul's tribe has supported the short-lived kingdom of Ishbosheth (2 Sam 2–4). **12.38** Even those who do not participate in the army are of *a single mind* (28.9; 2 Chr 19.9; 25.2). **12.40** Three tribes from the far north bring

provisions of meal, cakes of figs, clusters of raisins, wine, oil, oxen, and sheep, for there was joy in Israel.

The Ark Brought from Kiriath-jearim

13 David consulted with the commanders of the thousands and of the hundreds, with every leader. 2David said to the whole assembly of Israel, "If it seems good to you, and if it is the will of the Lord our God, let us send abroad to our kindred who remain in all the land of Israel, including the priests and Levites in the cities that have pasture lands, that they may come together to us. 3Then let us bring again the ark of our God to us; for we did not turn to it in the days of Saul." 4The whole assembly agreed to do so, for the thing pleased all the people.

5 So David assembled all Israel from the Shihor of Egypt to Lebo-hamath, to bring the ark of God from Kiriath-jearim. 6And David and all Israel went up to Baalah, that is, to Kiriath-jearim, which belongs to Judah, to bring up from there the ark of God, the Lord, who is enthroned on the cherubim, which is called by his*a* name. 7They carried the ark of God on a new cart, from the house of Abinadab, and Uzzah and Ahio *b* were driving the cart. 8David and all Israel were dancing before God with all their might, with song and lyres and harps and tambourines and cymbals and trumpets.

9 When they came to the threshing floor of Chidon, Uzzah put out his hand to hold the ark, for the oxen shook it. 10The anger of the Lord was kindled against Uzzah; he struck him down because he put out his hand to the ark; and he died there before God. 11David was angry because the Lord had burst out against Uzzah; so that place is called Perez-uzzah*c* to this day. 12David was afraid of God that day; he said, "How can I bring the ark of God into my care?" 13So David did not take the ark into his care into the city of David; he took it instead to the house of Obed-edom the Gittite. 14The ark of God remained with the household of Obed-edom in his house three months, and the Lord blessed the household of Obed-edom and all that he had.

David Established at Jerusalem

14 King Hiram of Tyre sent messengers to David, along with cedar logs, and masons and carpenters to build a house for him. 2David then perceived that the Lord had established him as king over Israel, and that his kingdom was highly exalted for the sake of his people Israel.

3 David took more wives in Jerusalem, and David became the father of more sons and

---

a Heb lacks *his*   *b* Or *and his brother*   *c* That is *Bursting Out Against Uzzah*

---

abundant foodstuffs, as if to celebrate the king's coronation with a great banquet. Twin themes emerge: unanimity and joy.

13.1–14 Cf. 2 Sam 6.1–11. All Israel, at David's invitation, brings the ark of the covenant from its temporary home in Kiriath-jearim to Jerusalem (cf. 1 Sam 4–6, without parallel in Chronicles, which tells only of the Philistine capture and return of the ark). All Israel also participates in the dedication of Solomon's temple (2 Chr 7.8) and in Hezekiah's Passover (2 Chr 30.5). The Lord's sharp punishment of Uzzah for touching the ark irritates and terrifies David, causing him not to take the ark directly to Jerusalem. Another explanation for this detour is given in 15.2, 13. **13.1–5** These verses are added in Chronicles to emphasize the people's total dedication to the ark, including the participation of priests and Levites in the procession. In 2 Sam 6.1 the ark is brought up by thirty thousand men from David's army. **13.5** *Shihor,* either the Wadi el Arish or one of the eastern branches of the Nile. *Lebo-hamath* (Hebrew, "Entrance of Hamath"), the traditional northern border of Israel. *Kiriath-jearim,* a city eight miles northwest of Jerusalem, where the ark was left by the Philistines. **13.6–14** There are numerous minor variations from the text of Samuel. **13.6** The ep-

ithet *enthroned on the cherubim* first appears in 1 Sam 4.4. **13.9** *Chidon,* in 2 Sam 6.6 "Nacon." **13.11** The Hebrew term translated *burst out* is derived from the same root as Perez in *Perez-uzzah.* **13.13** *Did not take.* In 2 Sam 6.10 David is "unwilling" to take the ark to Jerusalem. This may have struck the Chronicler as too critical of David. *Obed-edom,* apparently a Philistine expatriate who was loyal to David. In the remaining parts of the ark narrative Obed-edom appears as a levitical singer, a gatekeeper, and even a son of Jeduthun (15.18, 21, 24; 16.5, 38).

14.1–17 Chronicles places between the first and second attempts to bring the ark to Jerusalem new materials (14.17–15.24) and passages equivalent to 2 Sam 5.11–25. Hiram's provision of materials for David's building projects (vv. 1–2; 2 Sam 5.11–12), the list of David's children born in Jerusalem (vv. 3–7; 2 Sam 5.13–16), and the victories over the Philistines (vv. 8–16; 2 Sam 5.17–25) appear as rewards for the loyal, though flawed and unsuccessful, initial attempt by David and all Israel to bring the ark to Jerusalem. **14.1–2** Cf. 2 Sam 5.11–12. **14.1** *House.* Cf. 15.1. **14.2** *And that his kingdom was. And* is not in the Hebrew text; read "because his kingdom was . . ." David knew that he himself should be king, since his king-

daughters. 4These are the names of the children whom he had in Jerusalem: Shammua, Shobab, and Nathan; Solomon, 5Ibhar, Elishua, and Elpelet; 6Nogah, Nepheg, and Japhia; 7Elishama, Beeliada, and Eliphelet.

Defeat of the Philistines

8 When the Philistines heard that David had been anointed king over all Israel, all the Philistines went up in search of David; and David heard of it and went out against them. 9Now the Philistines had come and made a raid in the valley of Rephaim. 10David inquired of God, "Shall I go up against the Philistines? Will you give them into my hand?" The LORD said to him, "Go up, and I will give them into your hand." 11So he went up to Baal-perazim, and David defeated them there. David said, "God has burst out *a* against my enemies by my hand, like a bursting flood." Therefore that place is called Baal-perazim.*b* 12They abandoned their gods there, and at David's command they were burned.

13 Once again the Philistines made a raid in the valley. 14When David again inquired of God, God said to him, "You shall not go up after them; go around and come on them opposite the balsam trees. 15When you hear the sound of marching in the tops of the balsam trees, then go out to battle; for God has gone out before you to strike down the army of the Philistines." 16David did as God had com-

manded him, and they struck down the Philistine army from Gibeon to Gezer. 17The fame of David went out into all lands, and the LORD brought the fear of him on all nations.

The Ark Brought to Jerusalem

15 David*c* built houses for himself in the city of David, and he prepared a place for the ark of God and pitched a tent for it. 2Then David commanded that no one but the Levites were to carry the ark of God, for the LORD had chosen them to carry the ark of the LORD and to minister to him forever. 3David assembled all Israel in Jerusalem to bring up the ark of the LORD to its place, which he had prepared for it. 4Then David gathered together the descendants of Aaron and the Levites: 5of the sons of Kohath, Uriel the chief, with one hundred twenty of his kindred; 6of the sons of Merari, Asaiah the chief, with two hundred twenty of his kindred; 7of the sons of Gershom, Joel the chief, with one hundred thirty of his kindred; 8of the sons of Elizaphan, Shemaiah the chief, with two hundred of his kindred; 9of the sons of Hebron, Eliel the chief, with eighty of his kindred; 10of the sons of Uzziel, Amminadab the chief, with one hundred twelve of his kindred.

11 David summoned the priests Zadok and Abiathar, and the Levites Uriel, Asaiah, Joel,

---

a Heb *paraz*   *b* That is *Lord of Bursting Out*   *c* Heb *He*

---

dom prospered through God's commitment to Israel. **14.3–7** Cf. 2 Sam 5.13–16. While Saul and all his sons die (10.6), David, the blessed king, has many children. An almost identical list of children is found in 3.1–9. **14.3** *More wives* and *more sons and daughters* presuppose 2 Sam 3.2–5, a list of David's sons born at Hebron to six different wives, though this list is not mentioned in Chronicles. **14.4** *Solomon*, born in Jerusalem, plays a role equal to David's in Chronicles. **14.7** *Beeliada*, given as *Eliada* in 3.8; 2 Sam 5.16. **14.8–17** Cf. 2 Sam 5.17–25. David's victories over the Philistines reflect God's approval of his attempt to bring the ark to Jerusalem. David inquires of God, follows God's directions, and wins a decisive victory. Note the clear contrast to his predecessor, Saul. **14.11** *Burst out*, from the same Hebrew root that appears in *Baal-perazim*, providing an explanation for the naming of that city. Cf. note on 13.11. **14.12** In 2 Sam 5.21 David and his men take the idols as booty. In Chronicles they burn them according to the law (Deut 7.5; 12.3). Judging by one of the ancient Greek recensions of Samuel (the Lucianic recension), this correction in accordance with the Torah may already have been made in the text of Samuel used by Chronicles. **14.16** The Philistines

are defeated throughout Judah, from *Gibeon,* five and a half miles northwest of Jerusalem, to *Gezer,* about sixteen miles farther west (cf. Isa 28.21). **14.17** An addition in Chronicles, which records David's international fame and God's imposition of the fear of David on the nations. Note the contrast with 10.13–14, where the author summarizes his negative views on Saul.

15.1–24 Chronicles adds a series of preparations for the movement of the ark. **15.1** The *tent* David pitched for the ark in Jerusalem is different from the tabernacle, which, according to Chronicles, is still at Gibeon (16.39). **15.2** Chronicles favors the *Levites;* their duty *to carry the ark* is based on Num 4.15; Deut 10.8. **15.3** The participation by *all Israel* is also affirmed by v. 25. **15.4–10** This list of six Levite chiefs from six different families provides details supplementing v. 11. The numbers associated with the leaders are small and suggest the relative antiquity of this list. The families of *Kohath, Merari,* and *Gershom* are standard in lists of Levites. The fourth family is that of *Elizaphan,* who is identified as a grandson of Kohath through Uzziel (see Ex 6.18, 22). The families of *Hebron* and *Uzziel* are considered elsewhere as descendants of Kohath (6.18). **15.11** *Zadok* and *Abiathar* (cf. 2 Sam 15.24–29) serve

Shemaiah, Eliel, and Amminadab. [12]He said to them, "You are the heads of families of the Levites; sanctify yourselves, you and your kindred, so that you may bring up the ark of the LORD, the God of Israel, to the place that I have prepared for it. [13]Because you did not carry it the first time,[a] the LORD our God burst out against us, because we did not give it proper care." [14]So the priests and the Levites sanctified themselves to bring up the ark of the LORD, the God of Israel. [15]And the Levites carried the ark of God on their shoulders with the poles, as Moses had commanded according to the word of the LORD.

16 David also commanded the chiefs of the Levites to appoint their kindred as the singers to play on musical instruments, on harps and lyres and cymbals, to raise loud sounds of joy. [17]So the Levites appointed Heman son of Joel; and of his kindred Asaph son of Berechiah; and of the sons of Merari, their kindred, Ethan son of Kushaiah; [18]and with them their kindred of the second order, Zechariah, Jaaziel, Shemiramoth, Jehiel, Unni, Eliab, Benaiah, Maaseiah, Mattithiah, Eliphelehu, and Mikneiah, and the gatekeepers Obed-edom and Jeiel. [19]The singers Heman, Asaph, and Ethan were to sound bronze cymbals; [20]Zechariah, Aziel, Shemiramoth, Jehiel, Unni, Eliab, Maaseiah, and Benaiah were to play harps according to Alamoth; [21]but Mattithiah, Eliphelehu, Mikneiah, Obed-edom, Jeiel, and Azaziah were to lead with lyres according to the Sheminith. [22]Chenaniah, leader of the Levites in music,

was to direct the music, for he understood it. [23]Berechiah and Elkanah were to be gatekeepers for the ark. [24]Shebaniah, Joshaphat, Nethanel, Amasai, Zechariah, Benaiah, and Eliezer, the priests, were to blow the trumpets before the ark of God. Obed-edom and Jehiah also were to be gatekeepers for the ark.

25 So David and the elders of Israel, and the commanders of the thousands, went to bring up the ark of the covenant of the LORD from the house of Obed-edom with rejoicing. [26]And because God helped the Levites who were carrying the ark of the covenant of the LORD, they sacrificed seven bulls and seven rams. [27]David was clothed with a robe of fine linen, as also were all the Levites who were carrying the ark, and the singers, and Chenaniah the leader of the music of the singers; and David wore a linen ephod. [28]So all Israel brought up the ark of the covenant of the LORD with shouting, to the sound of the horn, trumpets, and cymbals, and made loud music on harps and lyres.

29 As the ark of the covenant of the LORD came to the city of David, Michal daughter of Saul looked out of the window, and saw King David leaping and dancing; and she despised him in her heart.

The Ark Placed in the Tent

16 They brought in the ark of God, and set it inside the tent that David had

---

a Meaning of Heb uncertain

---

as chief priests under David. Abiathar, a descendant of Eli, was exiled by Solomon to Anathoth, the hometown of Jeremiah, after Bathsheba asked the king to give Abishag, a concubine of David, to Solomon's rival Adonijah (1 Kings 2.26–27). 1 Kings notes that Abiathar had carried the ark in the time of David. **15.12** To *sanctify* oneself probably involved at least bathing, washing of clothes, and refraining from sexual intercourse. **15.13a** The Hebrew Bible, though the text is difficult, suggests that the Levites' failure to carry the ark (or their failure to carry it with poles, v. 15; cf. Ex 25.13–14; 37.4–5) was the cause of the earlier aborted procession of the ark to Jerusalem. **15.16–24** The installation of levitical musicians. **15.16** Chronicles supports many of the cultic activities of its own day by reporting that they were originally commissioned by King David. **15.18** *Obed-edom*, a levitical singer, later demoted with his family to the rank of gatekeeper (v. 24; cf. 26.1–11). **15.19–21** The singers are divided into groups according to their playing of bronze cymbals, harps, and lyres, respectively. **15.25–16.3** Cf. 2 Sam 6.12–19. All Israel

now successfully brings the ark to Jerusalem and puts it in David's tent. Chronicles omits an equivalent for 2 Sam 6.12a (the Lord's blessing of the house of Obed-edom) and 2 Sam 6.20b–23 (an argument between David and his wife Michal about his dancing before the ark). Perhaps the latter verses seemed too negative for this happy occasion, or their criticism of David's wild dancing seemed inappropriate. **15.26** God's approval of the procession is shown by his support for the Levites. **15.27** Since only priests wore the linen ephod in the Chronicler's era, the author considered inappropriate the reference in 2 Sam 6.14 to David's wearing such a garment (perhaps a loincloth). He writes instead that David and all the Levites were *clothed with a robe of fine linen*. The final words of the verse (*David wore a linen ephod*) indicate either a garment worn over the robe of fine linen or they are a later, secondary addition from 2 Sam 6.14. **15.29** As a descendant of Saul's house, Michal despises David's efforts on behalf of the ark, just as her father neglected the ark with disastrous consequences for himself and his house (10.13–14).

pitched for it; and they offered burnt offerings and offerings of well-being before God. 2When David had finished offering the burnt offerings and the offerings of well-being, he blessed the people in the name of the LORD; 3and he distributed to every person in Israel—man and woman alike—to each a loaf of bread, a portion of meat,[a] and a cake of raisins.

4 He appointed certain of the Levites as ministers before the ark of the LORD, to invoke, to thank, and to praise the LORD, the God of Israel. 5Asaph was the chief, and second to him Zechariah, Jeiel, Shemiramoth, Jehiel, Mattithiah, Eliab, Benaiah, Obed-edom, and Jeiel, with harps and lyres; Asaph was to sound the cymbals, 6and the priests Benaiah and Jahaziel were to blow trumpets regularly, before the ark of the covenant of God.

David's Psalm of Thanksgiving

7 Then on that day David first appointed the singing of praises to the LORD by Asaph and his kindred.

8   O give thanks to the LORD, call on his
        name,
      make known his deeds among the
        peoples.
9   Sing to him, sing praises to him,
      tell of all his wonderful works.
10 Glory in his holy name;
      let the hearts of those who seek the
        LORD rejoice.
11 Seek the LORD and his strength,
      seek his presence continually.

12 Remember the wonderful works he has
        done,
      his miracles, and the judgments he
        uttered,
13 O offspring of his servant Israel,[b]
      children of Jacob, his chosen ones.

14 He is the LORD our God;
      his judgments are in all the earth.
15 Remember his covenant forever,
      the word that he commanded, for a
        thousand generations,
16 the covenant that he made with
        Abraham,
      his sworn promise to Isaac,
17 which he confirmed to Jacob as a statute,
      to Israel as an everlasting covenant,
18 saying, "To you I will give the land of
        Canaan
      as your portion for an inheritance."

19 When they were few in number,
      of little account, and strangers in the
        land,[c]
20 wandering from nation to nation,
      from one kingdom to another people,
21 he allowed no one to oppress them;
      he rebuked kings on their account,
22 saying, "Do not touch my anointed ones;
      do my prophets no harm."

23 Sing to the LORD, all the earth.
      Tell of his salvation from day to day.

_____
a Compare Gk Syr Vg: Meaning of Heb uncertain   b Another reading is Abraham (compare Ps 105.6)   c Heb in it

---

16.4–7 Levites and priests are given specific duties in connection with the ark. The Levites are to invoke, thank, and praise until the temple is built, at which time they will also participate in the sacrificial rituals. Prior to that time, sacrifices are offered only at Gibeon (vv. 39–40). The names in this list are related to those in 15.17–18, 19–24. Their inclusion here gives a Davidic pedigree to the musical guilds of the Chronicler's day. **16.8–36** Cf. Pss 105; 95; 106. Chronicles includes three psalms illustrating how the Levites led Israel's praises. This passage also shows one way the Psalter was used in the postexilic temple. **16.8–22** Cf. Ps 105.1–15. In this call to musical praise, the Levites praise God for his saving deeds for the people. The patriarchs were protected by God because of his covenant promise that they would inherit the land (vv. 16–18). **16.11** The community is to seek the LORD in a way Saul did not. **16.13** Israel, a replacement for "Abraham" in Ps 105.6. This change focuses the exhortation

on the faithful community, Israel, whereas Ps 105 itself refers to those genealogically descended from two different ancestors. **16.15** The imperative remember is directed at the author's community; in Ps 105.8 God is construed as the subject of the verb in the phrase "He is mindful." **16.19** When they were few in number. They, as in Ps 105.12, refers to the patriarchs themselves. The Hebrew of Chronicles actually reads "When you were few in number." If this reading is correct, the book's addressees are called to identify themselves with the experience of the patriarchs. **16.22** Anointed ones and prophets may refer in this context to Israel as a royal and prophetic people. In Ps 105.15 both terms refer to the patriarchs themselves. **16.23–30** Cf. Ps 96.1–10. A call to international praise. The Levites urge people to tell God's wonders to the nations and to bow before the LORD, who is coming to judge. Chronicles omits Ps 96.11b, 13b, both of which refer to God's judging of the people, but that idea is present in v. 33.

24 Declare his glory among the nations,
　　his marvelous works among all the
　　　peoples.
25 For great is the LORD, and greatly to be
　　praised;
　　he is to be revered above all gods.
26 For all the gods of the peoples are idols,
　　but the LORD made the heavens.
27 Honor and majesty are before him;
　　strength and joy are in his place.

28 Ascribe to the LORD, O families of the
　　peoples,
　　ascribe to the LORD glory and strength.
29 Ascribe to the LORD the glory due his
　　name;
　　bring an offering, and come before
　　　him.
　　Worship the LORD in holy splendor;
30 　tremble before him, all the earth.
　　The world is firmly established; it shall
　　　never be moved.
31 Let the heavens be glad, and let the earth
　　rejoice,
　　and let them say among the nations,
　　　"The LORD is king!"
32 Let the sea roar, and all that fills it;
　　let the field exult, and everything in it.
33 Then shall the trees of the forest sing for
　　joy
　　before the LORD, for he comes to judge
　　　the earth.
34 O give thanks to the LORD, for he is good;
　　for his steadfast love endures forever.

35 Say also:
　　"Save us, O God of our salvation,
　　and gather and rescue us from among
　　　the nations,

that we may give thanks to your holy
　name,
　and glory in your praise.
36 Blessed be the LORD, the God of Israel,
　from everlasting to everlasting."
Then all the people said "Amen!" and praised
the LORD.

Regular Worship Maintained

37 David left Asaph and his kinsfolk there before the ark of the covenant of the LORD to
minister regularly before the ark as each day
required, 38 and also Obed-edom and his[a]
sixty-eight kinsfolk; while Obed-edom son of
Jeduthun and Hosah were to be gatekeepers.
39 And he left the priest Zadok and his kindred
the priests before the tabernacle of the LORD in
the high place that was at Gibeon, 40 to offer
burnt offerings to the LORD on the altar of
burnt offering regularly, morning and evening,
according to all that is written in the law of the
LORD that he commanded Israel. 41 With them
were Heman and Jeduthun, and the rest of
those chosen and expressly named to render
thanks to the LORD, for his steadfast love endures forever. 42 Heman and Jeduthun had
with them trumpets and cymbals for the
music, and instruments for sacred song. The
sons of Jeduthun were appointed to the gate.

43 Then all the people departed to their
homes, and David went home to bless his
household.

God's Covenant with David

17 Now when David settled in his house,
David said to the prophet Nathan, "I
am living in a house of cedar, but the ark of the

---

a Gk Syr Vg: Heb their

16.27, 29 His place (v. 27) replaces "his sanctuary" in
Ps 96.6, just as before him (v. 29) replaces "into his
courts" in Ps 96.8. Without these changes the poem
would refer to a temple that had not yet been built.
There were no sacrifices at Jerusalem, only the ark and
a tent and the service of song. 16.31–33 Cf. Ps 96.11–
13. A call to cosmic praise. 16.34–36 Cf. Ps 106.1, 47–
48. Most of Ps 106, which recites a long history of Israel's sinful nature and God's decision to hand Israel
over to the enemy, is omitted. 16.34 This verse serves
as a refrain in Chronicles (cf. v. 41; note on 2 Chr 5.13).
16.35 Of our salvation and rescue us, added by Chronicles to the text of Ps 106. Deliverance from Persian
domination may have been a bigger issue at the
Chronicler's time than Israel's dispersal, but the author avoided an explicit attack against the Persians.

16.37–42 Appointment of cultic personnel in
Jerusalem and Gibeon. 16.39 Cf. 21.29; 2 Chr 1.3–6.
16.39–40 The morning and evening sacrifices, required by the Torah (Ex 29.38–42; Num 28.3–8), are
practiced in the time of David at Gibeon. The presence
of the tabernacle and altar at Gibeon makes Solomon's
visit there (2 Chr 1.3) appropriate. 16.43 Cf. 2 Sam
6.19b–20a. Everyone's return home brings the ark
story to an end. Chronicles omits David's altercation
with his wife Michal in 2 Sam 6.20b–23.
17.1–15 Cf. 2 Sam 7.1–17. In response to David's
desire to build a temple (house) for the Lord, the Lord
promises to give David an everlasting dynasty (house).
17.1 House in Hebrew means both temple and dynasty.
Chronicles omits "the LORD had given him rest from all
his enemies around him" (2 Sam 7.1). Additional wars

covenant of the LORD is under a tent." 2Nathan said to David, "Do all that you have in mind, for God is with you."

3 But that same night the word of the LORD came to Nathan, saying: 4Go and tell my servant David: Thus says the LORD: You shall not build me a house to live in. 5For I have not lived in a house since the day I brought out Israel to this very day, but I have lived in a tent and a tabernacle.^a 6Wherever I have moved about among all Israel, did I ever speak a word with any of the judges of Israel, whom I commanded to shepherd my people, saying, Why have you not built me a house of cedar? 7Now therefore thus you shall say to my servant David: Thus says the LORD of hosts: I took you from the pasture, from following the sheep, to be ruler over my people Israel; 8and I have been with you wherever you went, and have cut off all your enemies before you; and I will make for you a name, like the name of the great ones of the earth. 9I will appoint a place for my people Israel, and will plant them, so that they may live in their own place, and be disturbed no more; and evildoers shall wear them down no more, as they did formerly, 10from the time that I appointed judges over my people Israel; and I will subdue all your enemies.

Moreover I declare to you that the LORD will build you a house. 11When your days are fulfilled to go to be with your ancestors, I will raise up your offspring after you, one of your own sons, and I will establish his kingdom. 12He shall build a house for me, and I will establish his throne forever. 13I will be a father to him, and he shall be a son to me. I will not take my steadfast love from him, as I took it from him who was before you, 14but I will confirm him in my house and in my kingdom forever, and his throne shall be established forever. 15In accordance with all these words and all this vision, Nathan spoke to David.

David's Prayer

16 Then King David went in and sat before the LORD, and said, "Who am I, O LORD God, and what is my house, that you have brought me thus far? 17And even this was a small thing in your sight, O God; you have also spoken of your servant's house for a great while to come. You regard me as someone of high rank,^b O LORD God! 18And what more can David say to you for honoring your servant? You know your servant. 19For your servant's sake, O LORD, and according to your own heart, you have done all these great deeds, making known all these great things. 20There is no one like you, O LORD, and there is no God besides you, according to all that we have heard with our ears. 21Who is like your people Israel, one nation on the earth whom God went to redeem to be his people, making for yourself a name for great and terrible things, in driving out nations before your people whom you redeemed from Egypt? 22And you made your people Israel to be your people forever; and you, O LORD, became their God.

---

a Gk 2 Sam 7.6: Heb *but I have been from tent to tent and from tabernacle* *b* Meaning of Heb uncertain

---

of David appear in chs. 18–20, and only their successful conclusion creates a time for temple building. David is disqualified as temple builder because of his warfare (22.8), and Solomon is the man of rest (22.9). Note also the substitution of the verb *subdue* in v. 10 for "give you rest" in 2 Sam 7.11. **17.4** *Not,* a change in Chronicles, although the question posed in 2 Sam 7.5 ("Are you the one to build me a house to live in?") has much the same effect. *Not* already appears in the Septuagint of Samuel. **17.6** *Judges.* The Hebrew of 2 Sam 7.7 has "tribes," although the NRSV there reads "tribal leaders," following the Septuagint. **17.9** *Wear them down.* 2 Sam 7.10 reads "afflict them." **17.10** *Subdue.* See note on 17.1. *I declare to you that the LORD will build you a house.* 2 Sam 7.11 reads "the LORD declares to you that the LORD will make you a house." In this case *house* in Chronicles means temple; in Samuel it refers to the dynasty. **17.11** *One of your own sons.* 2 Sam 7.12 reads "who shall come forth from your body." **17.13a** Chronicles leaves out at this point materials from 2 Sam 7.14:

"When he commits iniquity, I will punish him with a rod such as mortals use, with blows inflicted by human beings." This conforms to the Chronicler's omission elsewhere of negative reports about David and Solomon. **17.14** *I will confirm him in my house and in my kingdom forever, and his throne . . . forever.* 2 Sam 7.16 reads "Your house and your kingdom shall be made sure forever before me; your throne . . . forever." The focus in Chronicles is on Solomon, not David. Again, *house* in Chronicles means temple; in Samuel it means dynasty. The *kingdom* in Chronicles refers to God's kingdom, not David's. **17.16–27** Cf. 2 Sam 7.18–29. In David's prayer in response to Nathan's oracle, God's power, shown in the exodus, is hailed as the authority behind David's dynasty. **17.16** *House* in the prayer always refers to the dynasty. Cf. vv. 17, 23, 24, 25, 27. **17.21–23** The exodus from Egypt guarantees the promises made to David. In the accounts of Solomon, the promise to David becomes the basis for the entire relationship between God and Israel.

23 "And now, O LORD, as for the word that you have spoken concerning your servant and concerning his house, let it be established forever, and do as you have promised. 24Thus your name will be established and magnified forever in the saying, 'The LORD of hosts, the God of Israel, is Israel's God'; and the house of your servant David will be established in your presence. 25For you, my God, have revealed to your servant that you will build a house for him; therefore your servant has found it possible to pray before you. 26And now, O LORD, you are God, and you have promised this good thing to your servant; 27therefore may it please you to bless the house of your servant, that it may continue forever before you. For you, O LORD, have blessed and are blessed*a* forever."

David's Kingdom Established and Extended

18 Some time afterward, David attacked the Philistines and subdued them; he took Gath and its villages from the Philistines.

2 He defeated Moab, and the Moabites became subject to David and brought tribute.

3 David also struck down King Hadadezer of Zobah, toward Hamath,*b* as he went to set up a monument at the river Euphrates. 4David took from him one thousand chariots, seven thousand cavalry, and twenty thousand foot soldiers. David hamstrung all the chariot horses, but left one hundred of them. 5When the Arameans of Damascus came to help King Hadadezer of Zobah, David killed twenty-two thousand Arameans. 6Then David put garrisons*c* in Aram of Damascus; and the Arameans became subject to David, and brought tribute. The LORD gave victory to David wherever he went. 7David took the gold shields that were carried by the servants of Hadadezer, and brought them to Jerusalem. 8From Tibhath and from Cun, cities of Hadadezer, David took a vast quantity of bronze; with it Solomon made the bronze sea and the pillars and the vessels of bronze.

9 When King Tou of Hamath heard that David had defeated the whole army of King Hadadezer of Zobah, 10he sent his son Hadoram to King David, to greet him and to congratulate him, because he had fought against Hadadezer and defeated him. Now Hadadezer had often been at war with Tou. He sent all sorts of articles of gold, of silver, and of bronze; 11these also King David dedicated to the LORD, together with the silver and gold that he had carried off from all the nations, from Edom, Moab, the Ammonites, the Philistines, and Amalek.

12 Abishai son of Zeruiah killed eighteen thousand Edomites in the Valley of Salt. 13He put garrisons in Edom; and all the Edomites became subject to David. And the LORD gave victory to David wherever he went.

David's Administration

14 So David reigned over all Israel; and he administered justice and equity to all his people. 15Joab son of Zeruiah was over the army; Jehoshaphat son of Ahilud was recorder; 16Zadok son of Ahitub and Ahimelech son of Abiathar were priests; Shavsha was secretary; 17Benaiah son of Jehoiada was over the Cherethites and the Pelethites; and David's sons were the chief officials in the service of the king.

---

a Or *and it is blessed*   *b* Meaning of Heb uncertain   *c* Gk Vg 2 Sam 8.6 Compare Syr: Heb lacks *garrisons*

18.1–13 Cf. 2 Sam 8.1–14. In the following three chapters the wars demonstrate why David was unfit to build the temple. **18.1** *Gath and its villages* replaces the obscure "Metheg-ammah" of 2 Sam 8.1. **18.2** *Moab,* a country east of the Dead Sea. David's harsh treatment of the Moabites in 2 Sam 8.2 is omitted. **18.3** *Hadadezer,* an Aramean (Syrian) king located in the Lebanese Beqaa Valley. **18.4** Since the cavalry is not yet a major factor in warfare, David destroys the captured horses. **18.6** The victories given to David fulfill the promise of 17.10. Cf. 18.13; 19.13. **18.8** David's war spoils are used by Solomon to prepare various items for the temple. Cf. v. 11. This information is lacking in the parallel Hebrew text of Samuel but is attested in the Septuagint and in Josephus. **18.9–10** Another Aramean king hears of David's victories and voluntarily sends him tribute.

18.11 *Edom.* 2 Sam 8.12 reads "Aram" (Syria), though the Septuagint has "Idumea" (Edom). **18.12–13** *Abishai,* David's nephew and commander of the "Thirty" (11.20–21). He and his brothers Asahel and Joab are courageous and, at times, foolhardy. *Edom* was located south of Judah and Moab. In 2 Sam 8.13 David himself is credited with these victories. **18.14–17** Cf. 2 Sam 8.15–18. This list of royal officials reveals the growing complexity of David's administration. **18.15a** David entrusts command of the army to his nephew Joab. **18.16** *Zadok ... priests.* The text of Chronicles has been damaged. David has two high priests, Zadok and Abiathar, but not Ahimelech. **18.17** *Benaiah,* a local commander who supported Solomon in his battle with Adonijah for the throne; he became the commander of the army after he had exe-

Defeat of the Ammonites and Arameans

19 Some time afterward, King Nahash of the Ammonites died, and his son succeeded him. ²David said, "I will deal loyally with Hanun son of Nahash, for his father dealt loyally with me." So David sent messengers to console him concerning his father. When David's servants came to Hanun in the land of the Ammonites, to console him, ³the officials of the Ammonites said to Hanun, "Do you think, because David has sent consolers to you, that he is honoring your father? Have not his servants come to you to search and to overthrow and to spy out the land?" ⁴So Hanun seized David's servants, shaved them, cut off their garments in the middle at their hips, and sent them away; ⁵and they departed. When David was told about the men, he sent messengers to them, for they felt greatly humiliated. The king said, "Remain at Jericho until your beards have grown, and then return."

6 When the Ammonites saw that they had made themselves odious to David, Hanun and the Ammonites sent a thousand talents of silver to hire chariots and cavalry from Mesopotamia, from Aram-maacah and from Zobah. ⁷They hired thirty-two thousand chariots and the king of Maacah with his army, who came and camped before Medeba. And the Ammonites were mustered from their cities and came to battle. ⁸When David heard of it, he sent Joab and all the army of the warriors. ⁹The Ammonites came out and drew up in battle array at the entrance of the city, and the kings who had come were by themselves in the open country.

10 When Joab saw that the line of battle was set against him both in front and in the rear, he chose some of the picked men of Israel and arrayed them against the Arameans; ¹¹the rest of his troops he put in the charge of his brother Abishai, and they were arrayed against the Ammonites. ¹²He said, "If the Arameans are too strong for me, then you shall help me; but if the Ammonites are too strong for you, then I will help you. ¹³Be strong, and let us be courageous for our people and for the cities of our God; and may the LORD do what seems good to him." ¹⁴So Joab and the troops who were with him advanced toward the Arameans for battle; and they fled before him. ¹⁵When the Ammonites saw that the Arameans fled, they likewise fled before Abishai, Joab's brother, and entered the city. Then Joab came to Jerusalem.

16 But when the Arameans saw that they had been defeated by Israel, they sent messengers and brought out the Arameans who were beyond the Euphrates, with Shophach the commander of the army of Hadadezer at their head. ¹⁷When David was informed, he gathered all Israel together, crossed the Jordan, came to them, and drew up his forces against them. When David set the battle in array against the Arameans, they fought with him. ¹⁸The Arameans fled before Israel; and David killed seven thousand Aramean charioteers

---

cuted Joab (1 Kings 2.34–35). He also leads foreign mercenary groups such as the *Cherethites* and the *Pelethites*.
    19.1–20.3 Cf. 2 Sam 10.1–19; 11.1; 12.26, 30, 31. David's additional victories demonstrate God's blessing of the king, but they also show why he is barred from building the temple. The Chronicler omits David's affair with Bathsheba, which took place in the course of his Ammonite wars, as well as his murder of her husband, Uriah, and its aftermath. The Chronicler also excludes 2 Sam 9, which indicates that Mephibosheth, a member of Saul's family, survived the battle of Gilboa. Similarly, 2 Sam 13.1–21.17 is omitted both because it refers to the "trouble . . . from within your own house" (2 Sam 12.10–11) that befell David because of his transgressions, and because it indicates that all Israel, including the king's own sons, did *not* support him. Thus we hear nothing in Chronicles about the rape of Tamar, Absalom's murder of Amnon, Absalom's revolt and death and the aftermath of that rebellion, David's role in handing over the descendants of Saul to the Gibeonites, and an anecdote in which David is captured and nearly killed. **19.1** *Nahash*, an opponent of Saul (1 Sam 11). The *Ammonites* lived north and east of Moab; their name is echoed in the modern city of Amman. **19.2–5** A group sent by David to express official grief is shamefully treated by the Ammonites. **19.6–9** Hanun hires mercenaries to fight David. **19.7** The *thirty-two thousand chariots* are an escalation of the thirty-three thousand infantry hired according to 2 Sam 10.6. This text already appears in a manuscript of Samuel among the Dead Sea Scrolls. Cf. also David's destruction of seven thousand charioteers (v. 18) with the parallel account in 2 Sam 10.18 and its seven hundred chariot teams. Again the Chronicler seems to have been working with an alternate form of the Hebrew text of 2 Samuel. **19.10–15** When *Joab* takes on the Arameans and his brother *Abishai* opposes the Ammonites, the two brothers pledge themselves to mutual aid. Both enemy armies flee. **19.16–19** The defeated Arameans summon more of their kin living beyond the Euphrates. David leads all Israel against them, killing some forty-seven thousand Arameans. As a result the Arameans sue David

and forty thousand foot soldiers, and also killed Shophach the commander of their army. [19]When the servants of Hadadezer saw that they had been defeated by Israel, they made peace with David, and became subject to him. So the Arameans were not willing to help the Ammonites any more.

Siege and Capture of Rabbah

20 In the spring of the year, the time when kings go out to battle, Joab led out the army, ravaged the country of the Ammonites, and came and besieged Rabbah. But David remained at Jerusalem. Joab attacked Rabbah, and overthrew it. [2]David took the crown of Milcom[a] from his head; he found that it weighed a talent of gold, and in it was a precious stone; and it was placed on David's head. He also brought out the booty of the city, a very great amount. [3]He brought out the people who were in it, and set them to work[b] with saws and iron picks and axes.[c] Thus David did to all the cities of the Ammonites. Then David and all the people returned to Jerusalem.

Exploits against the Philistines

4 After this, war broke out with the Philistines at Gezer; then Sibbecai the Hushathite killed Sippai, who was one of the descendants of the giants; and the Philistines were subdued. [5]Again there was war with the Philistines; and

Elhanan son of Jair killed Lahmi the brother of Goliath the Gittite, the shaft of whose spear was like a weaver's beam. [6]Again there was war at Gath, where there was a man of great size, who had six fingers on each hand, and six toes on each foot, twenty-four in number; he also was descended from the giants. [7]When he taunted Israel, Jonathan son of Shimea, David's brother, killed him. [8]These were descended from the giants in Gath; they fell by the hand of David and his servants.

The Census and Plague

21 Satan stood up against Israel, and incited David to count the people of Israel. [2]So David said to Joab and the commanders of the army, "Go, number Israel, from Beer-sheba to Dan, and bring me a report, so that I may know their number." [3]But Joab said, "May the LORD increase the number of his people a hundredfold! Are they not, my lord the king, all of them my lord's servants? Why then should my lord require this? Why should he bring guilt on Israel?" [4]But the king's word prevailed against Joab. So Joab departed and went throughout all Israel, and came back to Jerusalem. [5]Joab gave the total count of the people to David. In all Israel there

---

a Gk Vg See 1 Kings 11.5, 33: MT *of their king*   *b* Compare 2 Sam 12.31: Heb *and he sawed*   *c* Compare 2 Sam 12.31: Heb *saws*

20.1 *Jerusalem.* At this point 2 Sam 11.2–12.25 tells the story of David, Bathsheba, Uriah, and the prophetic condemnation by Nathan before reporting the conclusion of the battle with the Ammonites. Since Chronicles idealizes David's and Solomon's work for the temple and its ritual life, to rehearse the sins of the United Monarchy would not have served its purposes. We may be sure that the Chronicler and his readers were well aware of these negative incidents. **20.2** *Milcom,* the national god of the Ammonites. *A talent of gold,* about 67 pounds.

20.4–8 Cf. 2 Sam 21.18–22. The wars end, as they had begun (18.1), with the Philistines. **20.4** *Sibbecai,* a hero who hails from a town near Bethlehem. *Subdued.* Cf. 17.10; 2 Chr 13.18; 28.19. **20.5** *Elhanan's* killing of Goliath (2 Sam 21.19) is later ascribed to David in 1 Sam 17. The name of the victim in Chronicles, *Lahmi the brother of Goliath,* arose through miswriting of the letters of Elhanan's hometown, Bethlehem, but the reference to the brother of Goliath is a harmonization. **20.8** *Giants,* or Raphah, a divine patron of four warriors killed by the Israelites (2 Sam 21.22).

21.1–17 Cf. 2 Sam 24.1–17. Chronicles omits the Song of David (2 Sam 22; Ps 18) and the Last Words of

David (2 Sam 23.1–7). The list of mighty men in 2 Sam 23.8–39 is included in 11.11–41. **21.1** *Satan.* Cf. Job 1–2; Zech 3.1–10, where, however, the figure is called "the satan." In 2 Sam 24.1 the Lord incites David. The Chronicler was unwilling to assign temptation to the deity. **21.2** *Beer-sheba to Dan.* Chronicles describes the land from south to north (cf. 2 Chr 30.5). **21.3** Joab's final accusing question is not found in 2 Sam 24.3. David's census shows reliance on numerical might rather than on the Lord's help. **21.5** It is probable that the numbers in Chronicles originally included nothing for Judah. 2 Sam 24.9 has Israel, "eight hundred thousand," Judah, "five hundred thousand." The Chronicler may have calculated that thirteen tribes (Ephraim and Manasseh replaced Joseph) averaged 100,000 apiece. Since Levi and Benjamin were excluded from this census (v. 6), the total for (all) Israel was reduced to one million one hundred thousand. A later hand understood Israel to include only the territory of the Northern Kingdom and not Judah. The figure of *four hundred seventy thousand* for Judah in Chronicles may result from the figure of four hundred thousand for Judah in the proto-Lucianic text of 2 Sam 24.9, to which seventy thousand were added to make up for the lives that would be lost in the divine

were one million one hundred thousand men who drew the sword, and in Judah four hundred seventy thousand who drew the sword. 6But he did not include Levi and Benjamin in the numbering, for the king's command was abhorrent to Joab.

7 But God was displeased with this thing, and he struck Israel. 8David said to God, "I have sinned greatly in that I have done this thing. But now, I pray you, take away the guilt of your servant; for I have done very foolishly." 9The LORD spoke to Gad, David's seer, saying, 10"Go and say to David, 'Thus says the LORD: Three things I offer you; choose one of them, so that I may do it to you.' " 11So Gad came to David and said to him, "Thus says the LORD, 'Take your choice: 12either three years of famine; or three months of devastation by your foes, while the sword of your enemies overtakes you; or three days of the sword of the LORD, pestilence on the land, and the angel of the LORD destroying throughout all the territory of Israel.' Now decide what answer I shall return to the one who sent me." 13Then David said to Gad, "I am in great distress; let me fall into the hand of the LORD, for his mercy is very great; but let me not fall into human hands."

14 So the LORD sent a pestilence on Israel; and seventy thousand persons fell in Israel. 15And God sent an angel to Jerusalem to destroy it; but when he was about to destroy it, the LORD took note and relented concerning the calamity; he said to the destroying angel, "Enough! Stay your hand." The angel of the LORD was then standing by the threshing floor of Ornan the Jebusite. 16David looked up and saw the angel of the LORD standing between earth and heaven, and in his hand a drawn sword stretched out over Jerusalem. Then David and the elders, clothed in sackcloth, fell on their faces. 17And David said to God, "Was

it not I who gave the command to count the people? It is I who have sinned and done very wickedly. But these sheep, what have they done? Let your hand, I pray, O LORD my God, be against me and against my father's house; but do not let your people be plagued!"

David's Altar and Sacrifice

18 Then the angel of the LORD commanded Gad to tell David that he should go up and erect an altar to the LORD on the threshing floor of Ornan the Jebusite. 19So David went up following Gad's instructions, which he had spoken in the name of the LORD. 20Ornan turned and saw the angel; and while his four sons who were with him hid themselves, Ornan continued to thresh wheat. 21As David came to Ornan, Ornan looked and saw David; he went out from the threshing floor, and did obeisance to David with his face to the ground. 22David said to Ornan, "Give me the site of the threshing floor that I may build on it an altar to the LORD—give it to me at its full price—so that the plague may be averted from the people." 23Then Ornan said to David, "Take it; and let my lord the king do what seems good to him; see, I present the oxen for burnt offerings, and the threshing sledges for the wood, and the wheat for a grain offering. I give it all." 24But King David said to Ornan, "No; I will buy them for the full price. I will not take for the LORD what is yours, nor offer burnt offerings that cost me nothing." 25So David paid Ornan six hundred shekels of gold by weight for the site. 26David built there an altar to the LORD and presented burnt offerings and offerings of well-being. He called upon the LORD, and he answered him with fire from heaven on the altar of burnt offering. 27Then the LORD commanded the angel, and he put his sword back into its sheath.

judgment (v. 14). **21.6** Levi's exclusion is based on Num 1.49; 2.33. Benjamin's exclusion may relate to the presence of the tabernacle in Gibeon. **21.9** *Spoke.* The Lord's address is more direct than in 2 Sam 24.11. *Gad,* a court prophet. **21.12** *Angel of the LORD.* This figure is not mentioned in 2 Sam 24.13, but see v. 16. **21.13** David chooses punishment by (the angel of) the Lord, known for his great mercy. God's grace leads to the choice of the temple site in 22.1. **21.15** *Ornan.* 2 Sam 24.16 reads "Araunah," a variant spelling. The punishment does not include Jerusalem. **21.16** This dramatic depiction of the angel of the Lord does not appear in the standard Hebrew text of 2 Sam 24, but it does occur in the Dead Sea Scrolls. **21.18–27** Cf. 2 Sam

24.18–25. **21.20** Ornan's *sons* are not mentioned in 2 Sam 24.20 and may have arisen from a copyist's error. **21.22** David's offer to buy the threshing floor *at its full price* is an addition by the Chronicler, who relates this purchase to Abraham's offer to buy the cave of Machpelah as a burial site. Cf. also v. 24; Gen 23.9. **21.25** *Six hundred shekels of gold.* 2 Sam 24.24 reads "fifty shekels of silver." The medieval Jewish commentator Rashi suggests that David paid fifty shekels for each tribe. **21.26** The second sentence in this verse is not found in 2 Sam 24.25. The Lord's fire confirms the choice of this site, much as the fire at the first sacrifice at Sinai validated the sacrificial system (Lev 9.24). **21.27** The Lord's command to the angel does not ap-

The Place Chosen for the Temple

28 At that time, when David saw that the LORD had answered him at the threshing floor of Ornan the Jebusite, he made his sacrifices there. 29For the tabernacle of the LORD, which Moses had made in the wilderness, and the altar of burnt offering were at that time in the high place at Gibeon; 30but David could not go before it to inquire of God, for he was afraid of the sword of the angel of the LORD. 22 1Then David said, "Here shall be the house of the LORD God and here the altar of burnt offering for Israel."

David Prepares to Build the Temple

2 David gave orders to gather together the aliens who were residing in the land of Israel, and he set stonecutters to prepare dressed stones for building the house of God. 3David also provided great stores of iron for nails for the doors of the gates and for clamps, as well as bronze in quantities beyond weighing, 4and cedar logs without number—for the Sidonians and Tyrians brought great quantities of cedar to David. 5For David said, "My son Solomon is young and inexperienced, and the house that is to be built for the LORD must be exceedingly magnificent, famous and glorified throughout all lands; I will therefore make preparation for it." So David provided materials in great quantity before his death.

David's Charge to Solomon and the Leaders

6 Then he called for his son Solomon and charged him to build a house for the LORD, the God of Israel. 7David said to Solomon, "My son, I had planned to build a house to the name of the LORD my God. 8But the word of the LORD came to me, saying, 'You have shed much blood and have waged great wars; you shall not build a house to my name, because you have shed so much blood in my sight on the earth. 9See, a son shall be born to you; he shall be a man of peace. I will give him peace from all his enemies on every side; for his name shall be Solomon,ᵃ and I will give peaceᵇ and quiet to Israel in his days. 10He shall build a house for my name. He shall be a son to me, and I will be a father to him, and I will establish his royal throne in Israel forever.' 11Now, my son, the LORD be with you, so that you may succeed in building the house of the LORD your God, as he has spoken concerning you. 12Only, may the LORD grant you discretion and understanding, so that when he gives you charge over Israel you may keep the law of the LORD your God. 13Then you will prosper if you are careful to observe the statutes and the ordinances that the LORD commanded Moses for Israel. Be strong and of good courage. Do not be afraid or dismayed. 14With great pains I have

a Heb *Shelomoh*   *b* Heb *shalom*

pear in the standard text of 2 Samuel. *Sheath*, translation of a Persian loanword. **21.28–22.1** This significant addition by the Chronicler identifies Ornan's threshing floor as the site of the future temple. **21.29** Only in Chronicles do we hear that the tabernacle and the altar of burnt offering were located at Gibeon. This information explains in part why Solomon's famous dream could take place at Gibeon (1 Kings 3.5). **21.30** The angel's *sword* (cf. v. 16) prevents David from worshiping at Gibeon (2 Chr 1.6–13). **22.1** The future site of the temple and its altar is validated by the word of David and the actions of the Lord and his angel. This site has continuity with the Mosaic institutions of tabernacle and altar. The story explains why the nation's worship center is transferred from Gibeon to Jerusalem.

22.2–5 David provides materials for the temple. **22.2** *Aliens* were used in forced labor gangs. It is unclear whether native Israelites were subject to such service (cf. 1 Kings 5.13; 9.20–22). **22.3** *Bronze* was obtained, in part, through wars (18.8, 10). Note the emphasis on quantity: *great stores* and *beyond weighing*. **22.4** *Cedar* from Lebanon was supplied by the Phoenicians for the Second Temple (Ezra 3.7).

22.5 According to the Chronicler, Solomon would have been unable to manage the building of the temple if his father had not assembled all the necessary materials. On the other hand, David was unable to build the temple himself (17.4; 22.7–8; 28.2–3; 2 Chr 6.7–9). **22.6–16** A private speech addressed to Solomon based in part on Moses' commissioning of Joshua (Josh 1). **22.7** Throughout the Deuteronomistic History (see Introduction), the temple is the place where God's *name* dwells (e.g., Deut 12.11; 1 Kings 8.16, 19, 20, 29). **22.8** David's shedding of blood bars him from building the temple. The Chronicler has in mind the seventy thousand who died as a consequence of David's sinful census in the previous chapter. **22.9** Solomon fulfills the promises of a royal heir in Nathan's oracle (17.11–14). The third occurrence of the word *peace* in this verse is a pun in Hebrew on the word Solomon. The other two occurrences might better be translated "rest." Deut 12.9–11 indicates that when the Lord gives the people rest from their enemies, they should gather to one central sanctuary. Only in the reign of Solomon does Israel attain rest. **22.12** Solomon's wisdom enables him to keep the Torah (Josh 1.7–8). **22.14** The amounts of

provided for the house of the LORD one hundred thousand talents of gold, one million talents of silver, and bronze and iron beyond weighing, for there is so much of it; timber and stone too I have provided. To these you must add more. 15 You have an abundance of workers: stonecutters, masons, carpenters, and all kinds of artisans without number, skilled in working 16 gold, silver, bronze, and iron. Now begin the work, and the LORD be with you."

17 David also commanded all the leaders of Israel to help his son Solomon, saying, 18 "Is not the LORD your God with you? Has he not given you peace on every side? For he has delivered the inhabitants of the land into my hand; and the land is subdued before the LORD and his people. 19 Now set your mind and heart to seek the LORD your God. Go and build the sanctuary of the LORD God so that the ark of the covenant of the LORD and the holy vessels of God may be brought into a house built for the name of the LORD."

Families of the Levites and Their Functions

23 When David was old and full of days, he made his son Solomon king over Israel.

2 David assembled all the leaders of Israel and the priests and the Levites. 3 The Levites, thirty years old and upward, were counted, and the total was thirty-eight thousand. 4 "Twenty-four thousand of these," David said, "shall have charge of the work in the house of the LORD, six thousand shall be officers and judges, 5 four thousand gatekeepers, and four thousand shall offer praises to the LORD with the instruments that I have made for praise." 6 And David organized them in divisions corresponding to the sons of Levi: Gershon,[a] Kohath, and Merari.

7 The sons of Gershon[b] were Ladan and Shimei. 8 The sons of Ladan: Jehiel the chief, Zetham, and Joel, three. 9 The sons of Shimei: Shelomoth, Haziel, and Haran, three. These were the heads of families of Ladan. 10 And the sons of Shimei: Jahath, Zina, Jeush, and Beriah. These four were the sons of Shimei. 11 Jahath was the chief, and Zizah the second; but Jeush and Beriah did not have many sons, so they were enrolled as a single family.

12 The sons of Kohath: Amram, Izhar, Hebron, and Uzziel, four. 13 The sons of Amram: Aaron and Moses. Aaron was set apart to consecrate the most holy things, so that he and his sons forever should make offerings before the LORD, and minister to him and pronounce blessings in his name forever; 14 but as for Moses the man of God, his sons were to be reckoned among the tribe of Levi. 15 The sons of Moses: Gershom and Eliezer. 16 The sons of Gershom: Shebuel the chief. 17 The sons of Eliezer: Rehabiah the chief; Eliezer had no other sons, but the sons of Rehabiah were very numerous. 18 The sons of Izhar: Shelomith the

---

a Or Gershom; See 1 Chr 6.1, note, and 23.15   b Vg Compare Gk Syr: Heb to the Gershonite

---

the precious metals are exaggerated in order to stress the magnificence of the temple. The gold amounts to 3,365 tons, the silver to more than 33,000! **22.16** *Begin the work*. The encouragement in David's speech is clarified by a literal translation, "Rise and act." **22.17–19** A speech addressed to the leaders of Israel. **22.18** "Rest" is again preferable to *peace* (see note on 22.9). The Chronicler seeks to suggest that God is with the people of his own period and gives them rest, just as he was with Solomon and gave him rest (vv. 9–11). **22.19** The people's *seeking of the LORD* would result in their building the *sanctuary* for the ark.

23.1–6 Introduction to the levitical organization. It is likely that some of the materials in chs. 23–27 were a later addition to the Chronicler's work. **23.1** The transition from David to Solomon is orderly and honorable and contrasts with the palace intrigues in the second half of 2 Samuel and 1 Kings 1–2. David's death and Solomon's coronation are narrated in 29.22–30. **23.3** *Thirty years old*. Cf. Num 4.3, but in 23.24, 27; 2 Chr 31.17; Ezra 3.8 the beginning age for Levites is twenty. Num 8.23–26 sets the age at

twenty-five. *Thirty-eight thousand*. Note by comparison the small number of Levites among the returnees in Ezra 2 and how few Levites accompany Ezra on his trip home (Ezra 8.15–20). **23.4–5** The four groups of Levites are listed in decreasing numerical order. David is credited with arranging them into four groups and assigning them their duties: those in charge of work in the temple, officers and judges, gatekeepers, and musicians. **23.6** *Gershon, Kohath, and Merari*. The three sons of Levi provide the names for the levitical divisions. **23.7–24** A list of the fathers' houses of the Levites, who are in charge of the work of the house of the Lord. **23.7–11** Descendants of *Gershon*. The genealogy extends only three generations after Levi and hence would not have reached to David. **23.7** *Ladan*. Elsewhere the first son of Gershon is Libni (cf. Ex 6.17; Num 3.18, 21; 1 Chr 6.17, 20). **23.9** *The sons of Shimei*. Read "The sons of Jehiel." **23.12–20** Descendants of *Kohath*. **23.13** Aaron's priestly duties are defined. **23.14–17** The genealogy of Moses is provided. Although Aaron is genealogically a Levite, he and his descendants are distin-

chief. 19The sons of Hebron: Jeriah the chief, Amariah the second, Jahaziel the third, and Jekameam the fourth. 20The sons of Uzziel: Micah the chief and Isshiah the second.

21 The sons of Merari: Mahli and Mushi. The sons of Mahli: Eleazar and Kish. 22Eleazar died having no sons, but only daughters; their kindred, the sons of Kish, married them. 23The sons of Mushi: Mahli, Eder, and Jeremoth, three.

24 These were the sons of Levi by their ancestral houses, the heads of families as they were enrolled according to the number of the names of the individuals from twenty years old and upward who were to do the work for the service of the house of the LORD. 25For David said, "The LORD, the God of Israel, has given rest to his people; and he resides in Jerusalem forever. 26And so the Levites no longer need to carry the tabernacle or any of the things for its service"— 27for according to the last words of David these were the number of the Levites from twenty years old and upward— 28"but their duty shall be to assist the descendants of Aaron for the service of the house of the LORD, having the care of the courts and the chambers, the cleansing of all that is holy, and any work for the service of the house of God; 29to assist also with the rows of bread, the choice flour for the grain offering, the wafers of unleavened bread, the baked offering, the offering mixed with oil, and all measures of quantity or size. 30And they shall stand every morning, thanking and praising the LORD, and likewise at evening, 31and whenever burnt offerings are offered to the LORD on sabbaths, new

moons, and appointed festivals, according to the number required of them, regularly before the LORD. 32Thus they shall keep charge of the tent of meeting and the sanctuary, and shall attend the descendants of Aaron, their kindred, for the service of the house of the LORD."

Divisions of the Priests

24 The divisions of the descendants of Aaron were these. The sons of Aaron: Nadab, Abihu, Eleazar, and Ithamar. 2But Nadab and Abihu died before their father, and had no sons; so Eleazar and Ithamar became the priests. 3Along with Zadok of the sons of Eleazar, and Ahimelech of the sons of Ithamar, David organized them according to the appointed duties in their service. 4Since more chief men were found among the sons of Eleazar than among the sons of Ithamar, they organized them under sixteen heads of ancestral houses of the sons of Eleazar, and eight of the sons of Ithamar. 5They organized them by lot, all alike, for there were officers of the sanctuary and officers of God among both the sons of Eleazar and the sons of Ithamar. 6The scribe Shemaiah son of Nethanel, a Levite, recorded them in the presence of the king, and the officers, and Zadok the priest, and Ahimelech son of Abiathar, and the heads of ancestral houses of the priests and of the Levites; one ancestral house being chosen for Eleazar and one chosen for Ithamar.

7 The first lot fell to Jehoiarib, the second to Jedaiah, 8the third to Harim, the fourth to Seorim, 9the fifth to Malchijah, the sixth to Mijamin, 10the seventh to Hakkoz, the eighth to

---

guished from the rest of the Levites by their priestly responsibilities in v. 13. **23.21–23** Descendants of *Merari.* **23.24** Conclusion of the list. **23.25–32** The duties of the Levites as compared to those of the priests (cf. 9.28–32). **23.25** The *rest* necessary for building the temple is already present in David's time. Cf. the different point of view in 17.1, 10; 22.9. **23.26–27** The construction of the temple obviates the need for the Levites to carry the tabernacle. Elsewhere the Chronicler speaks of the Levites carrying the ark (1 Chr 15.2, 12, 15, 26, 27; 2 Chr 5.4; 35.3), probably indicating that this reference comes from a secondary hand. **23.30** Note the role of the Levites as musicians.
24.1–19 The twenty-four priestly courses. This final organizational development of the priesthood in the OT may have been completed by the mid-fourth century BCE. **24.1** For the descendants of *Aaron,* see

6.2; Ex 6.2–15; Num 3.2–4. **24.2–3** The author of this section does not mention that *Nadab and Abihu* died because they offered illicit fire (Num 3.4). *Zadok,* a leading priest during David's and Solomon's reigns. *Ahimelech,* Abiathar's father, not his son as in v. 6. Abiathar is the other leading priest at the time of David. Ahimelech's tie to Ithamar in this chapter is in tension with other evidence that would link him to Eleazar (18.16; 1 Sam 22.20). **24.4** The descendants of Eleazar are superior to the descendants of Ithamar in numbers and in ranking, despite the implication of v. 5. **24.5** *By lot.* The roles of David, Zadok, and Ahimelech are mentioned in v. 3. **24.7–18** A list in order of the twenty-four priestly houses. Ten of the twenty-four names in the priestly courses are also attested in the list of postexilic priests in Neh 12.1–7, 12–21. **24.7** The family of the Maccabees descend from *Jehoiarib,* but there is no need to date this list that late (1 Macc 2.1; 14.29). **24.10** *Hak-*

Abijah, [11]the ninth to Jeshua, the tenth to Shecaniah, [12]the eleventh to Eliashib, the twelfth to Jakim, [13]the thirteenth to Huppah, the fourteenth to Jeshebeab, [14]the fifteenth to Bilgah, the sixteenth to Immer, [15]the seventeenth to Hezir, the eighteenth to Happizzez, [16]the nineteenth to Pethahiah, the twentieth to Jehezkel, [17]the twenty-first to Jachin, the twenty-second to Gamul, [18]the twenty-third to Delaiah, the twenty-fourth to Maaziah. [19]These had as their appointed duty in their service to enter the house of the LORD according to the procedure established for them by their ancestor Aaron, as the LORD God of Israel had commanded him.

Other Levites

20 And of the rest of the sons of Levi: of the sons of Amram, Shubael; of the sons of Shubael, Jehdeiah. [21]Of Rehabiah: of the sons of Rehabiah, Isshiah the chief. [22]Of the Izharites, Shelomoth; of the sons of Shelomoth, Jahath. [23]The sons of Hebron:[a] Jeriah the chief,[b] Amariah the second, Jahaziel the third, Jekameam the fourth. [24]The sons of Uzziel, Micah; of the sons of Micah, Shamir. [25]The brother of Micah, Isshiah; of the sons of Isshiah, Zechariah. [26]The sons of Merari: Mahli and Mushi. The sons of Jaaziah: Beno.[c] [27]The sons of Merari: of Jaaziah, Beno,[c] Shoham, Zaccur, and Ibri. [28]Of Mahli: Eleazar, who had no sons. [29]Of Kish, the sons of Kish: Jerahmeel. [30]The sons of Mushi: Mahli, Eder, and Jerimoth. These were the sons of the Levites according to their ancestral houses. [31]These also cast lots corresponding to their

kindred, the descendants of Aaron, in the presence of King David, Zadok, Ahimelech, and the heads of ancestral houses of the priests and of the Levites, the chief as well as the youngest brother.

The Temple Musicians

25 David and the officers of the army also set apart for the service the sons of Asaph, and of Heman, and of Jeduthun, who should prophesy with lyres, harps, and cymbals. The list of those who did the work and of their duties was: [2]Of the sons of Asaph: Zaccur, Joseph, Nethaniah, and Asarelah, sons of Asaph, under the direction of Asaph, who prophesied under the direction of the king. [3]Of Jeduthun, the sons of Jeduthun: Gedaliah, Zeri, Jeshaiah, Shimei,[d] Hashabiah, and Mattithiah, six, under the direction of their father Jeduthun, who prophesied with the lyre in thanksgiving and praise to the LORD. [4]Of Heman, the sons of Heman: Bukkiah, Mattaniah, Uzziel, Shebuel, and Jerimoth, Hananiah, Hanani, Eliathah, Giddalti, and Romamti-ezer, Joshbekashah, Mallothi, Hothir, Mahazioth. [5]All these were the sons of Heman the king's seer, according to the promise of God to exalt him; for God had given Heman fourteen sons and three daughters. [6]They were all under the direction of their father for the music in the house of the LORD with cymbals, harps, and lyres for the service of the

---

a See 23.19: Heb lacks *Hebron*   b See 23.19: Heb lacks *the chief*   c Or *his son*: Meaning of Heb uncertain   d One Ms: Gk: MT lacks *Shimei*

---

koz's descendants are barred from the priesthood after the return because they could not find their record in the genealogies (Ezra 2.61). His inclusion in the present list may indicate that this list is later and that the family had made gains in having its claims acknowledged. *Abijah*, the priestly course to which Zechariah, the father of John the Baptist, belonged (Lk 1.5). **24.19** The duties of the priests were given by God as revealed to Aaron. The duties of the Levites in ch. 23 are assigned by David. **24.20–31** A supplementary list of Levites. This list repeats some of the information of 23.7–24, extends five families of Kohath and one of Merari by another generation, and adds another son, Jaaziah, to Merari. **24.31** The Levites, like the priests, have their positions assigned by lot.
25.1–6 The families of levitical singers. The families are listed in a traditional order of Asaph, Heman, and Jeduthun in v. 1, but in vv. 2–6 the order is Asaph, Jeduthun, and Heman. The fourteen people assigned to Heman indicate his increasing prominence. In even

later lists of singers, Jeduthun is replaced by Ethan. The singers are said to *prophesy* (vv. 1, 2, 3), and Heman is called *the king's seer* (v. 5). Their prophetic activity may carry on the tradition of the preexilic prophets associated with ritual activities at shrines, or it may indicate that the hortatory words of Levites (and priests) are viewed as a way in which God reveals himself to his people (cf. the description of levitical singers in prophetic terms elsewhere, 2 Chr 20.14; 29.25; 35.15). Prophetic and musical activities are combined in v. 1. **25.2** Perhaps the number "four" originally appeared after *Asarelah* but has been dropped out; cf. vv. 3, 5. **25.3** *Shimei* is restored on the basis of v. 17 and the Septuagint. **25.4** Some scholars have reconstructed a poem (or the first lines of five poems) out of the names *Hananiah . . . Mahazioth* ("Be gracious to me, O Yahweh, be gracious to me; You are my God. / I have magnified (you), I have exalted (you). / Oh, my helper, fulfill my request. / Give abundant visions."). The number *fourteen* in v. 5, however,

house of God. Asaph, Jeduthun, and Heman were under the order of the king. ⁷They and their kindred, who were trained in singing to the LORD, all of whom were skillful, numbered two hundred eighty-eight. ⁸And they cast lots for their duties, small and great, teacher and pupil alike.

9 The first lot fell for Asaph to Joseph; the second to Gedaliah, to him and his brothers and his sons, twelve; ¹⁰the third to Zaccur, his sons and his brothers, twelve; ¹¹the fourth to Izri, his sons and his brothers, twelve; ¹²the fifth to Nethaniah, his sons and his brothers, twelve; ¹³the sixth to Bukkiah, his sons and his brothers, twelve; ¹⁴the seventh to Jesarelah,ᵃ his sons and his brothers, twelve; ¹⁵the eighth to Jeshaiah, his sons and his brothers, twelve; ¹⁶the ninth to Mattaniah, his sons and his brothers, twelve; ¹⁷the tenth to Shimei, his sons and his brothers, twelve; ¹⁸the eleventh to Azarel, his sons and his brothers, twelve; ¹⁹the twelfth to Hashabiah, his sons and his brothers, twelve; ²⁰to the thirteenth, Shubael, his sons and his brothers, twelve; ²¹to the fourteenth, Mattithiah, his sons and his brothers, twelve; ²²to the fifteenth, to Jeremoth, his sons and his brothers, twelve; ²³to the sixteenth, to Hananiah, his sons and his brothers, twelve; ²⁴to the seventeenth, to Joshbekashah, his sons and his brothers, twelve; ²⁵to the eighteenth, to Hanani, his sons and his brothers, twelve; ²⁶to the nineteenth, to Mallothi, his sons and his brothers, twelve; ²⁷to the twentieth, to Eliathah, his sons and his brothers, twelve; ²⁸to the twenty-first, to Hothir, his sons and his brothers, twelve; ²⁹to the twenty-second, to Giddalti, his sons and his brothers, twelve; ³⁰to the twenty-third, to Mahazioth, his sons and his

brothers, twelve; ³¹to the twenty-fourth, to Romamti-ezer, his sons and his brothers, twelve.

The Gatekeepers

26 As for the divisions of the gatekeepers: of the Korahites, Meshelemiah son of Kore, of the sons of Asaph. ²Meshelemiah had sons: Zechariah the firstborn, Jediael the second, Zebadiah the third, Jathniel the fourth, ³Elam the fifth, Jehohanan the sixth, Eliehoenai the seventh. ⁴Obed-edom had sons: Shemaiah the firstborn, Jehozabad the second, Joah the third, Sachar the fourth, Nethanel the fifth, ⁵Ammiel the sixth, Issachar the seventh, Peullethai the eighth; for God blessed him. ⁶Also to his son Shemaiah sons were born who exercised authority in their ancestral houses, for they were men of great ability. ⁷The sons of Shemaiah: Othni, Rephael, Obed, and Elzabad, whose brothers were able men, Elihu and Semachiah. ⁸All these, sons of Obed-edom with their sons and brothers, were able men qualified for the service; sixty-two of Obed-edom. ⁹Meshelemiah had sons and brothers, able men, eighteen. ¹⁰Hosah, of the sons of Merari, had sons: Shimri the chief (for though he was not the firstborn, his father made him chief), ¹¹Hilkiah the second, Tebaliah the third, Zechariah the fourth: all the sons and brothers of Hosah totaled thirteen.

12 These divisions of the gatekeepers, corresponding to their leaders, had duties, just as their kindred did, ministering in the house of the LORD; ¹³and they cast lots by ancestral houses, small and great alike, for their gates.

ᵃ Or Asarelah; see 25.2

---

presupposes that all these words in v. 4 are to be understood as proper names. **25.7–31** A supplementary list of singers that arranges the singers named in vv. 1–6 into twenty-four courses, like the priests in ch. 24. Small differences in the spelling of names suggest that the supplementary list has developed over a period of time. **25.7** The number *two hundred eighty-eight* is a product of twenty-four courses multiplied by twelve members in each course. **25.8** The assignment to the twenty-four courses was made by *lot*; cf. 24.5; 26.13. David and his officers select the families of levitical singers in the first place without using lots. *Teacher and pupil.* Perhaps there was some kind of instructional program to train the singers. **25.9** After *Joseph* should appear "his sons and his brothers, twelve," as with the other twenty-three names.

26.1–19 A list of the gatekeepers appointed by David (23.5; gatekeepers are also mentioned in 9.17–32; 15.18, 24; 16.38). Since gatekeepers were not originally Levites, this list is relatively late. **26.1** *Korahites.* Korah was from the clan of Kohath (6.22). *Asaph.* Read "Ebiasaph"; cf. the Septuagint. **26.4–8** The materials about *Obed-edom* are intrusive since he is not linked by descent to the Levites and since the total number in his family, sixty-two, is out of proportion with the rest of the chapter. Meshelemiah has eighteen in his family, Hosah thirteen (vv. 9, 11). On Obed-edom, see 15.18, 24; 16.38 (where his number is given as sixty-eight). V. 9 continues the content of v. 3. If vv. 4–8 are a later addition, then vv. 12–18, which presuppose them, are also a later addition. **26.12–18** See note on 26.4–8. **26.13** *Lots.* Cf. 24.5, 31; 25.8. David is not

14The lot for the east fell to Shelemiah. They cast lots also for his son Zechariah, a prudent counselor, and his lot came out for the north. 15Obed-edom's came out for the south, and to his sons was allotted the storehouse. 16For Shuppim and Hosah it came out for the west, at the gate of Shallecheth on the ascending road. Guard corresponded to guard. 17On the east there were six Levites each day,[a] on the north four each day, on the south four each day, as well as two and two at the storehouse; 18and for the colonnade[b] on the west there were four at the road and two at the colonnade.[b] 19These were the divisions of the gatekeepers among the Korahites and the sons of Merari.

The Treasurers, Officers, and Judges

20 And of the Levites, Ahijah had charge of the treasuries of the house of God and the treasuries of the dedicated gifts. 21The sons of Ladan, the sons of the Gershonites belonging to Ladan, the heads of families belonging to Ladan the Gershonite: Jehieli.[c] 22 The sons of Jehieli, Zetham and his brother Joel, were in charge of the treasuries of the house of the LORD. 23Of the Amramites, the Izharites, the Hebronites, and the Uzzielites: 24Shebuel son of Gershom, son of Moses, was chief officer in charge of the treasuries. 25His brothers: from Eliezer were his son Rehabiah, his son Jeshaiah, his son Joram, his son Zichri, and his son Shelomoth. 26This Shelomoth and his brothers were in charge of all the treasuries of the dedicated gifts that King David, and the heads of families, and the officers of the thousands and the hundreds, and the commanders of the army, had dedicated. 27From booty won in battles they dedicated gifts for the maintenance of the house of the LORD. 28Also all that Samuel the seer, and Saul son of Kish, and Abner son of Ner, and Joab son of Zeruiah had dedicated—all dedicated gifts were in the care of Shelomoth[d] and his brothers.

29 Of the Izharites, Chenaniah and his sons were appointed to outside duties for Israel, as officers and judges. 30Of the Hebronites, Hashabiah and his brothers, one thousand seven hundred men of ability, had the oversight of Israel west of the Jordan for all the work of the LORD and for the service of the king. 31Of the Hebronites, Jerijah was chief of the Hebronites. (In the fortieth year of David's reign search was made, of whatever genealogy or family, and men of great ability among them were found at Jazer in Gilead.) 32King David appointed him and his brothers, two thousand seven hundred men of ability, heads of families, to have the oversight of the Reubenites, the Gadites, and the half-tribe of the Manassites for everything pertaining to God and for the affairs of the king.

The Military Divisions

27 This is the list of the people of Israel, the heads of families, the commanders

---

a Gk: Heb lacks *each day*   *b* Heb *parbar*: meaning uncertain   *c* The Hebrew text of verse 21 is confused   *d* Gk Compare 26.28: Heb *Shelomith*

---

mentioned in this chapter since gatekeepers presuppose the existence of the temple, which David did not live to see. **26.14** In order to come up with four names for the four gates, both *Shelemiah* (Meshelemiah of vv. 1–2) and his son *Zechariah* were assigned gates. **26.16** *Shuppim*, a mistaken repetition of the previous Hebrew word. *Gate of Shallecheth*, otherwise unknown. **26.18** *Colonnade*. The *Temple Scroll* from Qumran (11QTemple) describes an area full of pillars in the temple, used for offerings. The total of the number of watches in vv. 17–18 is twenty-four, corresponding to the twenty-four courses of the priests and the singers. **26.20–32** Other Levites. **26.20** *Ahijah*, emended by many to "their brothers," with the Septuagint. These brothers, or Gershonites (absent from vv. 1–19), were in charge of the temple treasuries (vv. 21–22); they (v. 20) or the Kohathites of Amram's line (v. 25) were in charge of the treasuries of dedicated gifts (vv. 25–28). **26.22** The *treasuries of the house of the LORD* contained things like temple vessels. **26.23** These four levitical families are descended from

Kohath. The Uzzielites are not mentioned in the rest of the chapter. **26.24** *Shebuel*. Cf. 23.12–16. A descendant of Moses' son Gershom, he is in charge of both treasuries (but cf. v. 20). **26.25–27** The treasuries of the dedicated gifts contained booty won in battles (v. 27; cf. 18.7–8, 11). **26.25** *Shelomoth*, a descendant of Moses' son Eliezer. **26.28** *Abner*, Saul's general (cf. 27.21); *Joab*, David's general. Samuel too had won military victories (1 Sam 7.3–14). The favorable mention of Saul contrasts with 10.13–14 and may indicate it is a later addition. **26.29** *Izharites* were Kohathites (v. 23). *Officers and judges*. See 23.4; Deut 17.9. **26.30** *Work of the LORD and . . . service of the king*, religious and secular responsibilities, including taxes. Cf. v. 32. *Hashabiah* and seventeen hundred Hebronites have oversight of Cisjordan. **26.31** David's *fortieth* is his last year (29.27; 1 Kings 2.11). **26.31–32** *Jerijah* (cf. 23.19; 24.23) and twenty-seven hundred Hebronites have oversight of the two and a half Transjordanian tribes. **27.1–15** Commanders of the monthly divisions.

of the thousands and the hundreds, and their officers who served the king in all matters concerning the divisions that came and went, month after month throughout the year, each division numbering twenty-four thousand:

2 Jashobeam son of Zabdiel was in charge of the first division in the first month; in his division were twenty-four thousand. 3He was a descendant of Perez, and was chief of all the commanders of the army for the first month. 4Dodai the Ahohite was in charge of the division of the second month; Mikloth was the chief officer of his division. In his division were twenty-four thousand. 5The third commander, for the third month, was Benaiah son of the priest Jehoiada, as chief; in his division were twenty-four thousand. 6This is the Benaiah who was a mighty man of the Thirty and in command of the Thirty; his son Ammizabad was in charge of his division.ᵃ 7Asahel brother of Joab was fourth, for the fourth month, and his son Zebadiah after him; in his division were twenty-four thousand. 8The fifth commander, for the fifth month, was Shamhuth, the Izrahite; in his division were twenty-four thousand. 9Sixth, for the sixth month, was Ira son of Ikkesh the Tekoite; in his division were twenty-four thousand. 10Seventh, for the seventh month, was Helez the Pelonite, of the Ephraimites; in his division were twenty-four thousand. 11Eighth, for the eighth month, was Sibbecai the Hushathite, of the Zerahites; in his division were twenty-four thousand. 12Ninth, for the ninth

month, was Abiezer of Anathoth, a Benjaminite; in his division were twenty-four thousand. 13Tenth, for the tenth month, was Maharai of Netophah, of the Zerahites; in his division were twenty-four thousand. 14Eleventh, for the eleventh month, was Benaiah of Pirathon, of the Ephraimites; in his division were twenty-four thousand. 15Twelfth, for the twelfth month, was Heldai the Netophathite, of Othniel; in his division were twenty-four thousand.

Leaders of Tribes

16 Over the tribes of Israel, for the Reubenites, Eliezer son of Zichri was chief officer; for the Simeonites, Shephatiah son of Maacah; 17for Levi, Hashabiah son of Kemuel; for Aaron, Zadok; 18for Judah, Elihu, one of David's brothers; for Issachar, Omri son of Michael; 19for Zebulun, Ishmaiah son of Obadiah; for Naphtali, Jerimoth son of Azriel; 20for the Ephraimites, Hoshea son of Azaziah; for the half-tribe of Manasseh, Joel son of Pedaiah; 21for the half-tribe of Manasseh in Gilead, Iddo son of Zechariah; for Benjamin, Jaasiel son of Abner; 22for Dan, Azarel son of Jeroham. These were the leaders of the tribes of Israel. 23David did not count those below twenty years of age, for the LORD had promised to make Israel as numerous as the stars of heaven. 24Joab son of Zeruiah began to count them, but did not finish; yet wrath came upon

ᵃ Gk Vg: Heb *Ammizabad was his division*

The twelve commanders in this list are similar to twelve of the first sixteen chiefs recorded in 11.10–47. Two hundred eighty-eight thousand men were at the king's disposal, with twenty-four thousand on duty each month. Since the list does not concern the Levites or the final acts of David, it is a later addition in this context. There is no evidence that civilians at David's time served the king for a month each year. The model for this chapter may lie in the officials who provided food for Solomon's household each month (1 Kings 4.7–19) and the priestly courses and other groups of twelve and twenty-four in the immediate context. The Davidic era is portrayed as a time of perfect order. **27.1** *Commanders of the thousands and the hundreds*, words denoting the military character of the following list. **27.4** *Mikloth was the chief officer of his division*, perhaps a marginal comment about the difference between this verse and 11.12, where Eleazar son of Dodo is called the Ahohite, or a corrupt doublet of v. 6b. **27.7** *Asahel* is killed by Abner early in David's reign (2 Sam 2.18–23), when his kingdom included only

Judah; Asahel could not have commanded troops for a united Israel one month a year. The mention of his son *Zebadiah* is an effort to correct this error. **27.16– 24** The aim of this list of tribal leaders, a later addition to the text, is to lessen the criticism of David for the census described in ch. 21. The number of tribes is kept at twelve by omitting Gad and Asher (the last of the twelve tribes in 2.2), although the tribe of Joseph is represented by three names: the Ephraimites and the two halves of Manasseh. **27.17** *Aaron* is never considered a tribe, and no father's name is provided for *Zadok*. **27.18** *Elihu*. David has a brother Eliab, perhaps here misspelled, or Elihu might be an eighth son of Jesse mentioned, but not named, in 1 Sam 16.10–11; 17.12. **27.23** David's census is compared to the one taken by Moses in the wilderness, which also numbers only those who are over twenty years of age (Num 1.1– 19). This verse is an attempt to remove the guilt of David that permeates the account in ch. 21. *Stars of heaven*. Cf. Gen 15.5; 22.17. **27.24** *Did not finish*. In ch. 21 Joab is the one who objects to the census. The au-

Israel for this, and the number was not entered into the account of the Annals of King David.

Other Civic Officials

25 Over the king's treasuries was Azmaveth son of Adiel. Over the treasuries in the country, in the cities, in the villages and in the towers, was Jonathan son of Uzziah. 26 Over those who did the work of the field, tilling the soil, was Ezri son of Chelub. 27 Over the vineyards was Shimei the Ramathite. Over the produce of the vineyards for the wine cellars was Zabdi the Shiphmite. 28 Over the olive and sycamore trees in the Shephelah was Baal-hanan the Gederite. Over the stores of oil was Joash. 29 Over the herds that pastured in Sharon was Shitrai the Sharonite. Over the herds in the valleys was Shaphat son of Adlai. 30 Over the camels was Obil the Ishmaelite. Over the donkeys was Jehdeiah the Meronothite. Over the flocks was Jaziz the Hagrite. 31 All these were stewards of King David's property.

32 Jonathan, David's uncle, was a counselor, being a man of understanding and a scribe; Jehiel son of Hachmoni attended the king's sons. 33 Ahithophel was the king's counselor, and Hushai the Archite was the king's friend. 34 After Ahithophel came Jehoiada son of Benaiah, and Abiathar. Joab was commander of the king's army.

Solomon Instructed to Build the Temple

28 David assembled at Jerusalem all the officials of Israel, the officials of the tribes, the officers of the divisions that served the king, the commanders of the thousands, the commanders of the hundreds, the stewards of all the property and cattle of the king and his sons, together with the palace officials, the mighty warriors, and all the warriors. 2 Then King David rose to his feet and said: "Hear me, my brothers and my people. I had planned to build a house of rest for the ark of the covenant of the LORD, for the footstool of our God; and I made preparations for building. 3 But God said to me, 'You shall not build a house for my name, for you are a warrior and have shed blood.' 4 Yet the LORD God of Israel chose me from all my ancestral house to be king over Israel forever; for he chose Judah as leader, and in the house of Judah my father's house, and among my father's sons he took delight in making me king over all Israel. 5 And of all my sons, for the LORD has given me many, he has chosen my son Solomon to sit upon the throne of the kingdom of the LORD over Israel. 6 He said to me, 'It is your son Solomon who shall build my house and my courts, for I have chosen him to be a son to me, and I will be a father to him. 7 I will establish his kingdom forever if he continues resolute in keeping my commandments and my ordinances, as he is today.' 8 Now therefore in the sight of all Israel, the assembly of the LORD, and in the hearing of our God, observe and search out all the commandments of the LORD your God; that you may possess this good land, and leave it for an inheritance to your children after you forever.

9 "And you, my son Solomon, know the God of your father, and serve him with single mind and willing heart; for the LORD searches

---

thor explains why the census numbers for individual tribes did not appear in the *Annals of King David*, a source document known to him (but see 21.5, where numbers are given for Israel and Judah). **27.25–31** David's twelve administrators, who manage his treasuries (or storehouses), agricultural endeavors, and livestock. This list indicates the probable sources of the king's income. Cf. also the list of officials in 18.14–17. **27.32–34** David's seven advisers. **27.32** *Jonathan,* not to be confused with Saul's son and David's friend of the same name. **27.33** *Ahithophel.* See 2 Sam 16.23; 17.23. He sides with Absalom and commits suicide. *Hushai.* See 2 Sam 15.32–37. **27.34** *Abiathar,* one of two high priests under David. *Joab.* Cf. 18.15.

28.1–10 David's public charge to Solomon echoes his private admonition (22.6–16). **28.1** The substance of 23.2 repeated. The groups listed include many that were discussed in chs. 23–27. **28.2** *Footstool.* Cf. Ps 132.7. *Rest* in this verse and in Ps 132 refers to the ark's

or to God's rest, not the rest God gives to Israel. Cf. note on 22.9. **28.3** David the *warrior* is contrasted with Solomon, the man of peace. Cf. 22.8–9. **28.4** The choice of David is made through a series of eliminations, much as in earlier lot-casting ceremonies (cf. Josh 7.16–18; 1 Sam 10.20–21). **28.5** The oracle of Nathan (17.1–15) is fulfilled first of all in Solomon. **28.6** Only in Chronicles is Solomon designated as *chosen.* Cf. vv. 5, 10; 29.1. **28.7** The promise to Solomon is made conditionally, but his current obedience indicates that compliance is attainable. **28.8** This verse is addressed to the leaders of Israel and makes presence in the land conditional upon carrying out the commandments (Deut 5.33–6.3). *Possess* and *leave,* a challenge addressed to every generation. **28.9–10** Direct address to Solomon. **28.9** *Plan and thought,* vocabulary drawn from Gen 6.5; 8.21. *Seek* and *abandon,* typical words for obedience and disobedience in Chronicles (10.13–14; 2 Chr 15.2). The Chronicler has David

every mind, and understands every plan and thought. If you seek him, he will be found by you; but if you forsake him, he will abandon you forever. [10]Take heed now, for the LORD has chosen you to build a house as the sanctuary; be strong, and act."

11 Then David gave his son Solomon the plan of the vestibule of the temple, and of its houses, its treasuries, its upper rooms, and its inner chambers, and of the room for the mercy seat;[a] [12]and the plan of all that he had in mind: for the courts of the house of the LORD, all the surrounding chambers, the treasuries of the house of God, and the treasuries for dedicated gifts; [13]for the divisions of the priests and of the Levites, and all the work of the service in the house of the LORD; for all the vessels for the service in the house of the LORD, [14]the weight of gold for all golden vessels for each service, the weight of silver vessels for each service, [15]the weight of the golden lampstands and their lamps, the weight of gold for each lampstand and its lamps, the weight of silver for a lampstand and its lamps, according to the use of each in the service, [16]the weight of gold for each table for the rows of bread, the silver for the silver tables, [17]and pure gold for the forks, the basins, and the cups; for the golden bowls and the weight of each; for the silver bowls and the weight of each; [18]for the altar of incense made of refined gold, and its weight; also his plan for the golden chariot of the cherubim that spread their wings and covered the ark of the covenant of the LORD.

19 "All this, in writing at the LORD's direction, he made clear to me—the plan of all the works."

20 David said further to his son Solomon, "Be strong and of good courage, and act. Do not be afraid or dismayed; for the LORD God, my God, is with you. He will not fail you or forsake you, until all the work for the service of the house of the LORD is finished. [21]Here are the divisions of the priests and the Levites for all the service of the house of God; and with you in all the work will be every volunteer who has skill for any kind of service; also the officers and all the people will be wholly at your command."

Offerings for Building the Temple

29 King David said to the whole assembly, "My son Solomon, whom alone God has chosen, is young and inexperienced, and the work is great; for the temple[b] will not be for mortals but for the LORD God. [2]So I have provided for the house of my God, so far as I was able, the gold for the things of gold, the silver for the things of silver, and the bronze for the things of bronze, the iron for the things of iron, and wood for the things of wood, besides great quantities of onyx and stones for setting, antimony, colored stones, all sorts of precious stones, and marble in abundance. [3]Moreover, in addition to all that I have provided for the holy house, I have a treasure of my own of gold and silver, and because of my devotion to the house of my God I give it to the house of my God: [4]three thousand talents of gold, of the gold of Ophir, and seven thousand talents of refined silver, for overlaying the walls of the house, [5]and for all the work to be done by artisans, gold for the things of gold

---

a Or the cover   b Heb fortress

---

articulate clearly the positive and negative consequences of the doctrine of retribution. **28.11–21** David's provision of the plan for the temple and related items (vv. 11–13, 18b) and his gift of gold and silver for the furnishings of the temple (vv. 14–18a). **28.11** *Plan*, a technical term also used when God gives Moses instructions about the tabernacle (Ex 25.9, 40). David's written plan comes from divine inspiration according to v. 19 (cf. "the hand of the LORD," Ezek 1.3; 3.14). Detailed plans for the Second Temple are also given in Ezek 40–48. *Room for the mercy seat,* a reference to the innermost room, or holy of holies. **28.12** On the treasuries, see 26.22–28. **28.13a** On the *divisions* of the priests and Levites, see chs. 23–24. **28.13b–18** The details about the temple vessels indicate that they serve as a source of continuity between the First and the Second Temples. Cf. 2 Chr 4.1–22;

36.18; Ezra 1.7–11; 7.19; 8.25, 33. The silver vessels are not mentioned elsewhere, but are presupposed in 2 Kings 25.15. **28.18** The ark is given emphasis by a repetition of the word *plan*. The reference to the *golden chariot of the cherubim* evokes the visions of Ezek 1; 10. **28.20–21** A final admonition to Solomon indicates the difficulties he faces. **28.20** *He will not fail you or forsake you.* Cf. Josh 1.5. **28.21** *Skill.* Cf. Ex 35.10. The reference to those who will assist Solomon sets the stage for ch. 29.

29.1–9 Contributions to the temple. Cf. the parallel tabernacle account, Ex 25.1–7; 35.4–9, 20–29. **29.1–5** David's contributions. Cf. 22.2–5, 14. **29.1** The word translated *temple* occurs only in late biblical Hebrew and is a postexilic loanword. Cf. v. 19. **29.4** *Three thousand talents of gold,* 101 tons. *Seven thousand talents of refined silver,* 235 tons. *Ophir,* a source of gold reached

and silver for the things of silver. Who then will offer willingly, consecrating themselves today to the Lord?"

6 Then the leaders of ancestral houses made their freewill offerings, as did also the leaders of the tribes, the commanders of the thousands and of the hundreds, and the officers over the king's work. 7They gave for the service of the house of God five thousand talents and ten thousand darics of gold, ten thousand talents of silver, eighteen thousand talents of bronze, and one hundred thousand talents of iron. 8Whoever had precious stones gave them to the treasury of the house of the Lord, into the care of Jehiel the Gershonite. 9Then the people rejoiced because these had given willingly, for with single mind they had offered freely to the Lord; King David also rejoiced greatly.

David's Praise to God

10 Then David blessed the Lord in the presence of all the assembly; David said: "Blessed are you, O Lord, the God of our ancestor Israel, forever and ever. 11Yours, O Lord, are the greatness, the power, the glory, the victory, and the majesty; for all that is in the heavens and on the earth is yours; yours is the kingdom, O Lord, and you are exalted as head above all. 12Riches and honor come from you, and you rule over all. In your hand are power and might; and it is in your hand to make great and to give strength to all. 13And now, our God, we give thanks to you and praise your glorious name.

14 "But who am I, and what is my people, that we should be able to make this freewill offering? For all things come from you, and of your own have we given you. 15For we are aliens and transients before you, as were all our ancestors; our days on the earth are like a shadow, and there is no hope. 16O Lord our God, all this abundance that we have provided for building you a house for your holy name comes from your hand and is all your own. 17I know, my God, that you search the heart, and take pleasure in uprightness; in the uprightness of my heart I have freely offered all these things, and now I have seen your people, who are present here, offering freely and joyously to you. 18O Lord, the God of Abraham, Isaac, and Israel, our ancestors, keep forever such purposes and thoughts in the hearts of your people, and direct their hearts toward you. 19Grant to my son Solomon that with single mind he may keep your commandments, your decrees, and your statutes, performing all of them, and that he may build the temple*a* for which I have made provision."

20 Then David said to the whole assembly, "Bless the Lord your God." And all the assembly blessed the Lord, the God of their ancestors, and bowed their heads and prostrated themselves before the Lord and the king. 21On the next day they offered sacrifices and burnt offerings to the Lord, a thousand bulls, a thousand rams, and a thousand lambs, with their libations, and sacrifices in abundance for

---

a Heb *fortress*

---

by ship, perhaps in Africa or Arabia. **29.5** David invites the people to contribute and is heeded; cf. the same sequence when Moses invites the people to give to the tabernacle (Ex 35.4–9; 35.20–29). **29.6–9** Contributions by others. In the wilderness period the people make contributions and work on the tabernacle. Since only Levites are permitted in the temple, lay participation in building is impossible. **29.7** *Five thousand talents* (of gold), 168 tons. *Ten thousand darics of gold,* 84,200 grams or 185 pounds. This coin was introduced about 515 BCE by Darius I and is used anachronistically in this passage. *Ten thousand talents of silver,* 336 tons. *Eighteen thousand talents of bronze,* 605 tons. *One hundred thousand talents of iron,* 3,365 tons. All the weights, except perhaps for the darics, are exaggerations. They demonstrate all Israel's dedication to the temple. **29.8** *Jehiel.* Cf. 23.8; 26.21–22. **29.9** The joy of David and the people in contributing echoes the joy of Israel in making David king (12.39–41). **29.10–19** David praises God with joy and humility.

29.11 This verse is the source of the concluding doxology to the Lord's Prayer, which appears in late manuscripts of Mt 6.13: "For the kingdom and the power and the glory are yours forever. Amen." God's kingship is a persistent theme in Chronicles (e.g., 1 Chr 16.23–33; 17.14) and relativizes the upcoming kingship of Solomon. **29.14** The generous gifts of vv. 1–9 are first of all God's gifts to Israel. **29.15** David recalls that the landless *ancestors* were few, but received the promise of the land. Cf. vv. 10, 18. Even in the land the Israelites share their ancestors' vulnerability and dependency. **29.18** David asks that the people maintain their present generous *purposes and thoughts* and that their faith always be directed toward God. The building of the temple is crucial, but it is not the ultimate in religious devotion. **29.19** David prays that Solomon will obey the law, build the temple, and so maintain the dynasty (cf. ch. 17). **29.20–22a** The assembly blesses the Lord. **29.21** *Sacrifices,* peace offerings in which the people eat the sacrificial animal and contribute to the joy

all Israel; 22and they ate and drank before the LORD on that day with great joy.

Solomon Anointed King

They made David's son Solomon king a second time; they anointed him as the LORD's prince, and Zadok as priest. 23Then Solomon sat on the throne of the LORD, succeeding his father David as king; he prospered, and all Israel obeyed him. 24All the leaders and the mighty warriors, and also all the sons of King David, pledged their allegiance to King Solomon. 25The LORD highly exalted Solomon in the sight of all Israel, and bestowed upon him such royal majesty as had not been on any king before him in Israel.

Summary of David's Reign

26 Thus David son of Jesse reigned over all Israel. 27The period that he reigned over Israel was forty years; he reigned seven years in Hebron, and thirty-three years in Jerusalem. 28He died in a good old age, full of days, riches, and honor; and his son Solomon succeeded him. 29Now the acts of King David, from first to last, are written in the records of the seer Samuel, and in the records of the prophet Nathan, and in the records of the seer Gad, 30with accounts of all his rule and his might and of the events that befell him and Israel and all the kingdoms of the earth.

---

mentioned in v. 22. The large number of animals indicates the significance of the event. Cf. 2 Chr 7.4–5; 30.23–27. **29.22b–25** The anointing of Solomon. **29.22b** *A second time*, lacking in Septuagint and added by someone who did not understand that 23.1 was a heading for the whole following section. *Zadok* is already active as priest (16.39) and does not succeed Abiathar as sole priest until later (1 Kings 2.35). The present notice gives the high priest nearly equal standing with the king. **29.23** *Throne of the LORD*. The kingdom is the Lord's (cf. 17.14). **29.24** The claim that all the king's sons and all the leaders obey him is contradicted by 1 Kings 1–2. **29.25** The Lord's exaltation of *Solomon* is also mentioned in 2 Chr 1.1. Cf. Josh 3.7;

4.14. **29.26–30** Cf. 1 Kings 2.10–12. Chronicles puts the notice of David's death after the accession of Solomon and so binds the two reigns closely together. Vv. 28–30 were added by the Chronicler to the summary from 1 Kings. **29.27** David's reign in Hebron is already over all Israel. **29.28** David dies in *riches and honor.* In 1 Kings 1 the frail king has to be warmed by a young virgin and prodded by Bathsheba to prevent Adonijah from taking the throne from Solomon. **29.29** Authorship of the books of Samuel and Kings— and of other records?—is attributed to the prophetic figures of *Samuel* (1 Chr 6.28, 33; 9.22; 11.3; 26.28; 2 Chr 35.18), *Nathan* (1 Chr 17; 2 Chr 9.29; 29.25), and *Gad* (1 Chr 21.9; 2 Chr 29.25).

2 CHRONICLES

Solomon Requests Wisdom

1 Solomon son of David established himself in his kingdom; the LORD his God was with him and made him exceedingly great.

2 Solomon summoned all Israel, the commanders of the thousands and of the hundreds, the judges, and all the leaders of all Israel, the heads of families. ³Then Solomon, and the whole assembly with him, went to the high place that was at Gibeon; for God's tent of meeting, which Moses the servant of the LORD had made in the wilderness, was there. ⁴(But David had brought the ark of God up from Kiriath-jearim to the place that David had prepared for it; for he had pitched a tent for it in Jerusalem.) ⁵Moreover the bronze altar that Bezalel son of Uri, son of Hur, had made, was there in front of the tabernacle of the LORD. And Solomon and the assembly inquired at it. ⁶Solomon went up there to the bronze altar before the LORD, which was at the tent of meeting, and offered a thousand burnt offerings on it.

7 That night God appeared to Solomon, and said to him, "Ask what I should give you." ⁸Solomon said to God, "You have shown great and steadfast love to my father David, and have made me succeed him as king. ⁹O LORD God, let your promise to my father David now be fulfilled, for you have made me king over a people as numerous as the dust of the earth. ¹⁰Give me now wisdom and knowledge to go out and come in before this people, for who can rule this great people of yours?" ¹¹God answered Solomon, "Because this was in your heart, and you have not asked for possessions, wealth, honor, or the life of those who hate you, and have not even asked for long life, but have asked for wisdom and knowledge for yourself that you may rule my people over whom I have made you king, ¹²wisdom and knowledge are granted to you. I will also give you riches, possessions, and honor, such as

---

[For introductory material to 2 Chronicles, see the Introduction to 1 Chronicles.]

1.1–13 Cf. 1 Kings 3.1–15. **1.1** Chronicles omits the reference to Solomon's marriage to Pharaoh's daughter in 1 Kings 3. *Established himself* may include building projects, raising an army, and making reforms. Perhaps there is also an allusion to Solomon's mastering of the troubles that accompany his rise to power in 1 Kings 2.5–46. *Made him exceedingly great.* Cf. Josh 3.7; 4.14; 1 Chr 29.25. **1.2–3** In 1 Kings 3.4 Solomon goes to Gibeon alone; in Chronicles his first act as king is to lead a national pilgrimage to the bronze altar at Gibeon. **1.4** Cf. the Chronicler's version of the ark narrative in 1 Chr 13.1–16.1. **1.5** *Bezalel.* See Ex 31.2–11;

1 Chr 2.20; cf. Ex 38.1–2. *It,* translated by the RSV as "the LORD"; the Hebrew pronoun is ambiguous. For the *tabernacle* at Gibeon, see 1 Chr 16.39 and 21.29. **1.6** The *tent of meeting* makes Gibeon a legitimate place of sacrifice (Lev 17.8–9). **1.7** 1 Kings 3.5 adds "in a dream" after *Solomon,* but see the criticism of dreams in Jer 23.25–28. **1.8** Chronicles omits the notice of Solomon's not knowing "how to go out or come in" from 1 Kings 3.7, but see 1 Chr 22.5; 29.1, where David admits Solomon's youth and inexperience. **1.9** *Fulfilled.* Cf. the promise of numerous offspring made to Jacob in Gen 28.14. **1.10** In Chronicles *wisdom* is the ability to build the temple. In 1 Kings Solomon's wisdom is shown in his judging between two prostitutes (3.16–28), his administrative magnificence (4.1–5.8),

none of the kings had who were before you, and none after you shall have the like." [13]So Solomon came from[a] the high place at Gibeon, from the tent of meeting, to Jerusalem. And he reigned over Israel.

Solomon's Military and Commercial Activity

14 Solomon gathered together chariots and horses; he had fourteen hundred chariots and twelve thousand horses, which he stationed in the chariot cities and with the king in Jerusalem. [15]The king made silver and gold as common in Jerusalem as stone, and he made cedar as plentiful as the sycamore of the Shephelah. [16]Solomon's horses were imported from Egypt and Kue; the king's traders received them from Kue at the prevailing price. [17]They imported from Egypt, and then exported, a chariot for six hundred shekels of silver, and a horse for one hundred fifty; so through them these were exported to all the kings of the Hittites and the kings of Aram.

Preparations for Building the Temple

2[b] Solomon decided to build a temple for the name of the LORD, and a royal palace for himself. [2c] Solomon conscripted seventy thousand laborers and eighty thousand stonecutters in the hill country, with three thousand six hundred to oversee them.

Alliance with Huram of Tyre

3 Solomon sent word to King Huram of Tyre: "Once you dealt with my father David and

sent him cedar to build himself a house to live in. [4]I am now about to build a house for the name of the LORD my God and dedicate it to him for offering fragrant incense before him, and for the regular offering of the rows of bread, and for burnt offerings morning and evening, on the sabbaths and the new moons and the appointed festivals of the LORD our God, as ordained forever for Israel. [5]The house that I am about to build will be great, for our God is greater than other gods. [6]But who is able to build him a house, since heaven, even highest heaven, cannot contain him? Who am I to build a house for him, except as a place to make offerings before him? [7]So now send me an artisan skilled to work in gold, silver, bronze, and iron, and in purple, crimson, and blue fabrics, trained also in engraving, to join the skilled workers who are with me in Judah and Jerusalem, whom my father David provided. [8]Send me also cedar, cypress, and algum timber from Lebanon, for I know that your servants are skilled in cutting Lebanon timber. My servants will work with your servants [9]to prepare timber for me in abundance, for the house I am about to build will be great and wonderful. [10]I will provide for your servants, those who cut the timber, twenty thousand cors of crushed wheat, twenty thousand cors of barley, twenty thousand baths[d] of wine, and twenty thousand baths of oil."

11 Then King Huram of Tyre answered in a

---

a Gk Vg: Heb to   b Ch 1.18 in Heb   c Ch 2.1 in Heb   d A Hebrew measure of volume

---

and his knowledge of nature (5.9–14), all omitted from Chronicles. **1.13** Chronicles omits the sacrifices performed by Solomon on his return to Jerusalem in 1 Kings 3.15, since in its view the only legitimate sacrificial site at this time is Gibeon. **1.14–17** Cf. 1 Kings 10.26–29. Chronicles moves this account of Solomon's riches and commercial activity from the end of Solomon's reign to a point between the revelation at Gibeon and the beginning of temple building. At this position it fulfills v. 12 and implies that these resources were dedicated to constructing the temple. **1.15** Gold, not present in the Hebrew of 1 Kings 10.27. Shephelah, low hills in western Palestine separating the coastal plain from the central mountain ridge. **1.16** Kue, Cilicia, on the southeast coast of Asia Minor. **1.17** Hittites, people living in what is roughly modern Turkey. Solomon is a kind of arms merchant.

2.1–18 Cf. 1 Kings 5.1–8; 7.13–14; 5.9–18. **2.1** Palace. Cf. 2.12; 7.11; 8.1; 9.11. Chronicles omits details about its construction that are reported in

1 Kings 7.1–12. **2.3–10** A letter of Solomon to Huram. According to 1 Kings 5.1 Hiram (note the slight spelling difference) initiates the correspondence with Solomon. **2.4** Chronicles makes the obligation to sacrifice a major reason for building the temple. **2.6a** The inability of any temple to contain God is borrowed from Solomon's speech at the dedication of the temple (6.18). **2.7** The artisan is not mentioned until 1 Kings 7.13–14 in the parallel account, where he is skilled only in bronze work. The wider talents in Chronicles stem from a comparison of Huram-abi (v. 13) with Oholiab, who worked on the tabernacle (cf. Ex 31.1–11; 35.30–35). **2.8** The identity of algum is not certain, but 9.10–11 indicates that it was imported from Ophir. **2.10** A cor was slightly more than 6 bushels. A bath was 6 gallons or 22 liters. The enormous amounts of grain, wine, and oil fit a pattern of Tyrian dependence on Israel for foodstuffs (Ezek 17.17). In 1 Kings 5.11 these are annual payments. **2.11–16** Huram's reply. **2.11–12** Huram expresses piety toward the Lord

letter that he sent to Solomon, "Because the LORD loves his people he has made you king over them." [12] Huram also said, "Blessed be the LORD God of Israel, who made heaven and earth, who has given King David a wise son, endowed with discretion and understanding, who will build a temple for the LORD, and a royal palace for himself.

13 "I have dispatched Huram-abi, a skilled artisan, endowed with understanding, [14] the son of one of the Danite women, his father a Tyrian. He is trained to work in gold, silver, bronze, iron, stone, and wood, and in purple, blue, and crimson fabrics and fine linen, and to do all sorts of engraving and execute any design that may be assigned him, with your artisans, the artisans of my lord, your father David. [15] Now, as for the wheat, barley, oil, and wine, of which my lord has spoken, let him send them to his servants. [16] We will cut whatever timber you need from Lebanon, and bring it to you as rafts by sea to Joppa; you will take it up to Jerusalem."

17 Then Solomon took a census of all the aliens who were residing in the land of Israel, after the census that his father David had taken; and there were found to be one hundred fifty-three thousand six hundred. [18] Seventy thousand of them he assigned as laborers, eighty thousand as stonecutters in the hill country, and three thousand six hundred as overseers to make the people work.

Solomon Builds the Temple

3 Solomon began to build the house of the LORD in Jerusalem on Mount Moriah, where the LORD had appeared to his father David, at the place that David had designated, on the threshing floor of Ornan the Jebusite. [2] He began to build on the second day of the second month of the fourth year of his reign. [3] These are Solomon's measurements[a] for building the house of God: the length, in cubits of the old standard, was sixty cubits, and the width twenty cubits. [4] The vestibule in front of the nave of the house was twenty cubits long, across the width of the house;[b] and its height was one hundred twenty cubits. He overlaid it on the inside with pure gold. [5] The nave he lined with cypress, covered it with fine gold, and made palms and chains on it. [6] He adorned the house with settings of precious stones. The gold was gold from Parvaim. [7] So he lined the house with gold—its beams, its thresholds, its walls, and its doors; and he carved cherubim on the walls.

8 He made the most holy place; its length, corresponding to the width of the house, was twenty cubits, and its width was twenty cubits; he overlaid it with six hundred talents of fine

a Syr: Heb *foundations*   *b* Compare 1 Kings 6.3: Meaning of Heb uncertain

and mentions the Lord's endorsement of Solomon's kingship and his gift of wisdom to him. **2.13** *Huram-abi,* a counterpart to Bezalel and Oholiab from the wilderness period (see note on 2.7). The element *abi* in his name, not attested in 1 Kings 7.13, may be a play on the last part of the name Oholiab. **2.14** *Danite.* According to 1 Kings 7.14, Hiram is the son of a widow from Naphtali. The wilderness artisan Oholiab, however, was from the tribe of Dan (Ex 31.6; 35.34). His skills correspond to those requested by Solomon in v. 7. Both Dan and Naphtali are descendants of Bilhah, Jacob's concubine. *My lord,* a term of respect, used by Huram for both David and Solomon (cf. v. 15). **2.16** *Joppa,* an important harbor city in antiquity, today a suburb of Tel Aviv. The logs could have been carried on ships or towed as rafts. Cf. 1 Kings 5.9; Ezra 3.7. **2.17** *The land of Israel.* Cf. 1 Chr 22.2; 2 Chr 30.25; 34.7. *Census.* Cf. 1 Chr 21; 22.2. Chronicles insists that no Israelite, but only resident *aliens,* had to do forced labor. Cf. 2 Chr 8.7–10. According to 1 Kings 5.13–18, omitted by Chronicles, Solomon sends thirty thousand workers to Lebanon, in three monthly shifts. **2.18** *Three thousand six hundred.* 1 Kings 5.16 has three thousand three hundred, but see the Septuagint of 1 Kings.

3.1–17 Cf. 1 Kings 6.1–7.21. The account of the building of the temple is shorter in Chronicles than in 1 Kings. The Chronicler edits that earlier account to emphasize the parallels between the temple and the tabernacle. **3.1** *Mount Moriah.* The Temple Mount is identified with the place where Abraham attempted to sacrifice Isaac (Gen 22.2, 14). This site is also the place where David saw an angel with a drawn sword at the time of his census and built an altar (1 Chr 21.1–22.1). **3.2** 959 BCE. In 1 Kings 6.1 the temple building begins on the four hundred eightieth anniversary of the exodus. Chronicles generally deemphasizes the exodus. **3.3** The short cubit was 17.4 inches and the long cubit 20.4 inches. It is not clear which of these was considered *the old standard.* By the short cubit, the temple measures 87 by 29 feet; by the long cubit 102 by 34 feet. The height is not given. **3.4** According to 1 Kings 6.3 the vestibule measures 20 by 10 cubits. *One hundred twenty.* Elsewhere the temple is 30 cubits high. The verse has been damaged in transmission. **3.5** *Nave,* the largest room in the temple, where most of the ritual activity takes place. Within it were an incense altar, ten golden lampstands, and the table for the bread of the Presence. **3.6** *Parvaim,* an unknown site. **3.8** *Six hundred talents,* 20 tons. David is said to have contributed

gold. [9]The weight of the nails was fifty shekels of gold. He overlaid the upper chambers with gold.

10 In the most holy place he made two carved cherubim and overlaid[a] them with gold. [11]The wings of the cherubim together extended twenty cubits: one wing of the one, five cubits long, touched the wall of the house, and its other wing, five cubits long, touched the wing of the other cherub; [12]and of this cherub, one wing, five cubits long, touched the wall of the house, and the other wing, also five cubits long, was joined to the wing of the first cherub. [13]The wings of these cherubim extended twenty cubits; the cherubim[b] stood on their feet, facing the nave. [14]And Solomon[c] made the curtain of blue and purple and crimson fabrics and fine linen, and worked cherubim into it.

15 In front of the house he made two pillars thirty-five cubits high, with a capital of five cubits on the top of each. [16]He made encircling[d] chains and put them on the tops of the pillars; and he made one hundred pomegranates, and put them on the chains. [17]He set up the pillars in front of the temple, one on the right, the other on the left; the one on the right he called Jachin, and the one on the left, Boaz.

Furnishings of the Temple

4 He made an altar of bronze, twenty cubits long, twenty cubits wide, and ten cubits high. [2]Then he made the molten sea; it was round, ten cubits from rim to rim, and five cubits high. A line of thirty cubits would encircle it completely. [3]Under it were panels all around, each of ten cubits, surrounding the sea; there were two rows of panels, cast when it was cast. [4]It stood on twelve oxen, three facing north, three facing west, three facing south, and three facing east; the sea was set on them. The hindquarters of each were toward the inside. [5]Its thickness was a handbreadth; its rim was made like the rim of a cup, like the flower of a lily; it held three thousand baths.[e] [6]He also made ten basins in which to wash, and set five on the right side, and five on the left. In these they were to rinse what was used for the burnt offering. The sea was for the priests to wash in.

7 He made ten golden lampstands as prescribed, and set them in the temple, five on the south side and five on the north. [8]He also made ten tables and placed them in the temple, five on the right side and five on the left. And he made one hundred basins of gold. [9]He made the court of the priests, and the great court, and doors for the court; he overlaid their doors with bronze. [10]He set the sea at the southeast corner of the house.

---

a Heb *they overlaid* b Heb *they* c Heb *he* d Cn: Heb *in the inner sanctuary* e A Hebrew measure of volume

---

100,000 talents of gold (1 Chr 22.14). **3.9** *Fifty shekels*, 20 ounces, which is too much for one nail, too little for all the nails. **3.10** *Cherubim*, winged sphinxes, whose backs formed a throne for the invisible Lord. **3.14** Solomon's temple had doors separating the "most holy place" (holy of holies) from the rest of the building (1 Kings 6.31–32). The *curtain* may be a projection onto Solomon's temple from the Second Temple, with influence also from the tabernacle account (Ex 26.31–33; cf. Mt 27.51). At this point Chronicles omits an equivalent to 1 Kings 6.29–7.14. 1 Kings 7.1–12 deals with the king's palace (cf. 2 Chr 2.1). **3.15–17** The *pillars*, lacking in the Second Temple, are symbolic and decorative, not structural. Their height in Chronicles is nearly double that in Kings (18 cubits; 1 Kings 7.15). The Chronicler apparently includes in his calculations the circumference (12 cubits; 1 Kings 7.15) and the height of the capital (5 cubits; 1 Kings 7.16). **3.17** *Jachin*, in Hebrew "he establishes." *Boaz*, meaning unknown (also the name of David's great-grandfather; Ruth 4.17, 21–22). Some scholars interpret these names as the first words in dynastic oracles.

4.1–5.1 Cf. 1 Kings 7.23–51. **4.1** This account of the bronze altar was omitted accidentally in the present text of 1 Kings because this verse and the following verse start the same way: *he made*. For a description of the altar from the exilic period, see Ezek 43.13–17. **4.2–5** According to Chronicles the *molten sea* serves the purposes of purification (cf. Ex 30.18–21). In the temple of Solomon it may have symbolized the cosmic sea dragon. **4.2** The circumference should be 31.4 cubits. Either *thirty* is an approximation, or the measurement was calculated from a different place on the rim (inside versus outside). **4.4** The *twelve* animals supporting the sea face outward and look toward each of the four compass points. The number twelve implies the twelve tribes of Israel (cf. Num 2; Ezek 48.30–35). **4.5** *Three thousand baths.* 1 Kings 7.26 reads "two thousand baths," a calculation based on a hemispherical rather than a cylindrical shape. A *bath* was approximately 6 gallons or 22 liters. **4.6** There are ten basins in Solomon's temple, according to the Chronicler; the tabernacle only had one. Similarly, the tabernacle had but one lampstand and one table, not ten as in Chronicles (vv. 7–8). An elaborate description of the basins and their stands in 1 Kings 7.27–38 is omitted in Chronicles. **4.7** *Golden lampstands*, perhaps symbolizing the presence of God. **4.8** In the tabernacle, a single table was used for the bread of the Presence. The function of the *ten tables* in Chronicles is not clear, though the lampstands may have been placed on them. **4.9** *Court of the priests*, called the inner court in

11 And Huram made the pots, the shovels, and the basins. Thus Huram finished the work that he did for King Solomon on the house of God: 12the two pillars, the bowls, and the two capitals on the top of the pillars; and the two latticeworks to cover the two bowls of the capitals that were on the top of the pillars; 13the four hundred pomegranates for the two latticeworks, two rows of pomegranates for each latticework, to cover the two bowls of the capitals that were on the pillars. 14He made the stands, the basins on the stands, 15the one sea, and the twelve oxen underneath it. 16The pots, the shovels, the forks, and all the equipment for these Huram-abi made of burnished bronze for King Solomon for the house of the LORD. 17In the plain of the Jordan the king cast them, in the clay ground between Succoth and Zeredah. 18Solomon made all these things in great quantities, so that the weight of the bronze was not determined.

19 So Solomon made all the things that were in the house of God: the golden altar, the tables for the bread of the Presence, 20the lampstands and their lamps of pure gold to burn before the inner sanctuary, as prescribed; 21the flowers, the lamps, and the tongs, of purest gold; 22the snuffers, basins, ladles, and firepans, of pure gold. As for the entrance to the temple: the inner doors to the most holy place and the doors of the nave of the temple were of gold.

5 Thus all the work that Solomon did for the house of the LORD was finished. Solomon brought in the things that his father David had dedicated, and stored the silver, the gold, and all the vessels in the treasuries of the house of God.

The Ark Brought into the Temple

2 Then Solomon assembled the elders of Israel and all the heads of the tribes, the leaders of the ancestral houses of the people of Israel, in Jerusalem, to bring up the ark of the covenant of the LORD out of the city of David, which is Zion. 3And all the Israelites assembled before the king at the festival that is in the seventh month. 4And all the elders of Israel came, and the Levites carried the ark. 5So they brought up the ark, the tent of meeting, and all the holy vessels that were in the tent; the priests and the Levites brought them up. 6King Solomon and all the congregation of Israel, who had assembled before him, were before the ark, sacrificing so many sheep and oxen that they could not be numbered or counted. 7Then the priests brought the ark of the covenant of the LORD to its place, in the inner sanctuary of the house, in the most holy place, underneath the wings of the cherubim. 8For the cherubim spread out their wings over the place of the ark, so that the cherubim made a covering above the ark and its poles. 9The poles were so long that the ends of the poles were seen from the holy place in front of the inner sanctuary; but they could not be seen from outside; they are there to this day. 10There was nothing in the ark except the two tablets that Moses put there at Horeb, where

---

1 Kings 6.36; 7.12. **4.10–22** A close parallel to 1 Kings 7.39–50 that is perhaps a later addition. These verses ascribe production of various materials to Huram while the rest of chs. 3–4 gives credit to Solomon. The mention of *inner doors* (v. 22) contradicts the Chronicler's idea that a curtain closed off the holy of holies (3.14). **4.11** Huram-abi from Tyre (2.13) makes other miscellaneous furnishings. **4.16** Chronicles does not tell us where Solomon discovered the great quantities of *bronze*. Recent archaeology demonstrates that the copper from Timna and the valley of Elah was not mined in Solomon's time. **4.17** Solomon makes molds for his bronze castings in the clay of the Jordan River. *Succoth and Zeredah* (better "Zarethan," following 1 Kings 7.46), cities just east of the Jordan River. **5.1** *Dedicated.* Cf. 1 Chr 18.1–13; 26.25–27; 29.1–5. Solomon stores the silver, gold, and temple vessels in the treasuries (1 Chr 28.12). There may be a pun in Hebrew on the name "Solomon" and the verb *was finished.*

5.2–14 Cf. 1 Kings 8.1–11. In Chronicles the whole nation of Israel participates in major cultic events, but in this case the idea is already present in 1 Kings. **5.3** *Festival . . . in the seventh month,* Tabernacles (Booths). **5.4** The Chronicler has the *Levites* carry the ark (cf. 1 Chr 15.2, 11–15) and supports them wherever possible. In 1 Kings 8.3 the priests carry the ark. **5.5** The ark has already been brought to Jerusalem by David (1 Chr 15–16); now the *tent of meeting* (the tabernacle) is brought from Gibeon (1.3) and presumably stored in the temple. *Priests and the Levites,* better "the levitical priests." **5.7** The *priests* alone could enter the most holy place. Cf. Num 4.5–20; Ezek 44.10–14. **5.9** *Holy place.* The NRSV emends, following the Septuagint and 1 Kings 8.8; the Hebrew reads "the ark." *To this day,* taken over from 1 Kings 8.8. The ark no longer existed at the time Chronicles was written. **5.10** *Two tablets.* According to a later tradition attested by Heb 9.4, a jar of manna and Aaron's rod were also in the ark (cf. Ex 16.32–34; Num 17.10–11). *Horeb,* the pre-

the LORD made a covenant*a* with the people of Israel after they came out of Egypt.

11 Now when the priests came out of the holy place (for all the priests who were present had sanctified themselves, without regard to their divisions), 12all the levitical singers, Asaph, Heman, and Jeduthun, their sons and kindred, arrayed in fine linen, with cymbals, harps, and lyres, stood east of the altar with one hundred twenty priests who were trumpeters. 13It was the duty of the trumpeters and singers to make themselves heard in unison in praise and thanksgiving to the LORD, and when the song was raised, with trumpets and cymbals and other musical instruments, in praise to the LORD,

"For he is good,
     for his steadfast love endures forever,"
the house, the house of the LORD, was filled with a cloud, 14so that the priests could not stand to minister because of the cloud; for the glory of the LORD filled the house of God.

Dedication of the Temple

6 Then Solomon said, "The LORD has said that he would reside in thick darkness. 2I have built you an exalted house, a place for you to reside in forever."

3 Then the king turned around and blessed all the assembly of Israel, while all the assembly of Israel stood. 4And he said, "Blessed be the LORD, the God of Israel, who with his hand has fulfilled what he promised with his mouth to my father David, saying, 5'Since the day that I brought my people out of the land of Egypt,

I have not chosen a city from any of the tribes of Israel in which to build a house, so that my name might be there, and I chose no one as ruler over my people Israel; 6but I have chosen Jerusalem in order that my name may be there, and I have chosen David to be over my people Israel.' 7My father David had it in mind to build a house for the name of the LORD, the God of Israel. 8But the LORD said to my father David, 'You did well to consider building a house for my name; 9nevertheless you shall not build the house, but your son who shall be born to you shall build the house for my name.' 10Now the LORD has fulfilled his promise that he made; for I have succeeded my father David, and sit on the throne of Israel, as the LORD promised, and have built the house for the name of the LORD, the God of Israel. 11There I have set the ark, in which is the covenant of the LORD that he made with the people of Israel."

Solomon's Prayer of Dedication

12 Then Solomon*b* stood before the altar of the LORD in the presence of the whole assembly of Israel, and spread out his hands. 13Solomon had made a bronze platform five cubits long, five cubits wide, and three cubits high, and had set it in the court; and he stood on it. Then he knelt on his knees in the presence of the whole assembly of Israel, and spread out his hands toward heaven. 14He said, "O LORD, God of Israel, there is no God like you, in

a Heb lacks *a covenant*   *b* Heb *he*

---

ferred word for Sinai in Deuteronomy–2 Kings (see 1 Kings 8.9). **5.11–13** Most of the text of these verses is an addition by the Chronicler. **5.12** *The levitical singers, Asaph, Heman, and Jeduthun.* Cf. 1 Chr 16.37–41. **5.13** *For he is good . . . forever,* a couplet frequently used in Chronicles (1 Chr 16.34, 41; 2 Chr 7.3, 6; 20.21). **5.13–14** The temple is filled with the *cloud* of the *glory of the LORD,* just as the tabernacle had been at its dedication (Ex 40.34–38). The marks of a theophany are seen by the priests. A second theophany, approving the temple, appears in 7.1–3, where it is visible to all the people.

6.1–11 Cf. 1 Kings 8.12–21. **6.2** Solomon builds a permanent house for the Lord, whose glory had once appeared at Sinai (Ex 20.21) and more frequently at the tabernacle. **6.5–6** Though Chronicles follows 1 Kings very closely in ch. 6, the words *my name might be there . . . and I chose no one* are missing in 1 Kings 8.16 through a copyist's mistake. Solomon is portrayed celebrating the divine choice of Jerusalem and

of his father David. **6.9** Chronicles does not cite here David's bloodshed as the reason for banning him from temple building (cf. 1 Chr 22.8–9; 28.3). **6.10** Solomon is a double fulfillment of the promise: he succeeds his father as king and he builds the temple. **6.11** Instead of *with the people of Israel,* 1 Kings 8.21 reads: "with our ancestors when he brought them out of the land of Egypt." Chronicles stresses the contemporary validity of the covenant more than its antiquity and omits a reference to the exodus. (See also note on 6.41–42; an equivalent for 1 Kings 8.51, 53 is omitted.) The exodus is mentioned in 6.5. **6.12–42** Cf. 1 Kings 8.22–53. Chronicles follows the text of Kings closely in this passage, except that it replaces most of 1 Kings 8.50–53 with its own conclusion in vv. 41–42. **6.13** This verse is missing in 1 Kings because of scribal error. Note how both v. 12 and v. 13 end with *spread out his hands.* **6.14–17** Solomon prays that God would fulfill the dynastic promise, just as he had fulfilled his promise to David about the

heaven or on earth, keeping covenant in steadfast love with your servants who walk before you with all their heart— [15]you who have kept for your servant, my father David, what you promised to him. Indeed, you promised with your mouth and this day have fulfilled with your hand. [16]Therefore, O LORD, God of Israel, keep for your servant, my father David, that which you promised him, saying, 'There shall never fail you a successor before me to sit on the throne of Israel, if only your children keep to their way, to walk in my law as you have walked before me.' [17]Therefore, O LORD, God of Israel, let your word be confirmed, which you promised to your servant David.

18 "But will God indeed reside with mortals on earth? Even heaven and the highest heaven cannot contain you, how much less this house that I have built! [19]Regard your servant's prayer and his plea, O LORD my God, heeding the cry and the prayer that your servant prays to you. [20]May your eyes be open day and night toward this house, the place where you promised to set your name, and may you heed the prayer that your servant prays toward this place. [21]And hear the plea of your servant and of your people Israel, when they pray toward this place; may you hear from heaven your dwelling place; hear and forgive.

22 "If someone sins against another and is required to take an oath and comes and swears before your altar in this house, [23]may you hear from heaven, and act, and judge your servants, repaying the guilty by bringing their conduct on their own head, and vindicating those who are in the right by rewarding them in accordance with their righteousness.

24 "When your people Israel, having sinned against you, are defeated before an enemy but turn again to you, confess your name, pray and plead with you in this house, [25]may you hear from heaven, and forgive the sin of your people Israel, and bring them again to the land that you gave to them and to their ancestors.

26 "When heaven is shut up and there is no rain because they have sinned against you, and then they pray toward this place, confess your name, and turn from their sin, because you punish them, [27]may you hear in heaven, forgive the sin of your servants, your people Israel, when you teach them the good way in which they should walk; and send down rain upon your land, which you have given to your people as an inheritance.

28 "If there is famine in the land, if there is plague, blight, mildew, locust, or caterpillar; if their enemies besiege them in any of the settlements of the lands; whatever suffering, whatever sickness there is; [29]whatever prayer, whatever plea from any individual or from all your people Israel, all knowing their own suffering and their own sorrows so that they stretch out their hands toward this house; [30]may you hear from heaven, your dwelling place, forgive, and render to all whose heart you know, according to all their ways, for only you know the human heart. [31]Thus may they fear you and walk in your ways all the days that they live in the land that you gave to our ancestors.

32 "Likewise when foreigners, who are not of your people Israel, come from a distant land because of your great name, and your mighty hand, and your outstretched arm, when they come and pray toward this house, [33]may you hear from heaven your dwelling place, and do whatever the foreigners ask of you, in order that all the peoples of the earth may know your name and fear you, as do your people Israel, and that they may know that your name has been invoked on this house that I have built.

34 "If your people go out to battle against their enemies, by whatever way you shall send them, and they pray to you toward this city that you have chosen and the house that I have built for your name, [35]then hear from heaven their prayer and their plea, and maintain their cause.

36 "If they sin against you—for there is no one who does not sin—and you are angry with them and give them to an enemy, so that

---

temple. **6.16** *Walk in my law.* 1 Kings 8.25 reads "walk before me." The expression in Chronicles is more concrete and may refer to the Pentateuch. David's obedience in Chronicles contrasts with the record of his many sins in 2 Samuel. **6.18–21** The prayer struggles with ideas about God's presence. Although heaven is God's *dwelling place,* not earth among mortals, his name has been set in the earthly temple. Solomon hopes that his own prayer and that of the people will induce God to hear and forgive. **6.22–23** These verses about oath-taking procedures, even though taken from 1 Kings 8.31–32, express well the Chronicler's theory of divine retribution. **6.24–35** Solomon urges God to respond to calamities like drought, famine,

they are carried away captive to a land far or near; [37] then if they come to their senses in the land to which they have been taken captive, and repent, and plead with you in the land of their captivity, saying, 'We have sinned, and have done wrong; we have acted wickedly'; [38] if they repent with all their heart and soul in the land of their captivity, to which they were taken captive, and pray toward their land, which you gave to their ancestors, the city that you have chosen, and the house that I have built for your name, [39] then hear from heaven your dwelling place their prayer and their pleas, maintain their cause and forgive your people who have sinned against you. [40] Now, O my God, let your eyes be open and your ears attentive to prayer from this place.

[41] "Now rise up, O Lord God, and go to
          your resting place,
       you and the ark of your might.
   Let your priests, O Lord God, be clothed
          with salvation,
       and let your faithful rejoice in your
          goodness.
[42] O Lord God, do not reject your anointed
          one.
       Remember your steadfast love for your
          servant David."

Solomon Dedicates the Temple

7 When Solomon had ended his prayer, fire came down from heaven and consumed the burnt offering and the sacrifices; and the glory of the Lord filled the temple. [2] The

priests could not enter the house of the Lord, because the glory of the Lord filled the Lord's house. [3] When all the people of Israel saw the fire come down and the glory of the Lord on the temple, they bowed down on the pavement with their faces to the ground, and worshiped and gave thanks to the Lord, saying,

"For he is good,
     for his steadfast love endures forever."

[4] Then the king and all the people offered sacrifice before the Lord. [5] King Solomon offered as a sacrifice twenty-two thousand oxen and one hundred twenty thousand sheep. So the king and all the people dedicated the house of God. [6] The priests stood at their posts; the Levites also, with the instruments for music to the Lord that King David had made for giving thanks to the Lord—for his steadfast love endures forever—whenever David offered praises by their ministry. Opposite them the priests sounded trumpets; and all Israel stood.

[7] Solomon consecrated the middle of the court that was in front of the house of the Lord; for there he offered the burnt offerings and the fat of the offerings of well-being because the bronze altar Solomon had made could not hold the burnt offering and the grain offering and the fat parts.

[8] At that time Solomon held the festival for seven days, and all Israel with him, a very great congregation, from Lebo-hamath to the Wadi of Egypt. [9] On the eighth day they held a

---

sickness, and especially military defeat by hearing the people when they repent (or *turn*; vv. 24, 26) and by forgiving them. **6.36–40** The focus is on the plight of Israel in exile; the belief in the effectiveness of prayer from exile reflects the main concern of the prayer in 1 Kings 8. The Chronicler also affirms elsewhere that prayers from exile are effective (33.10–13). **6.40** *To prayer from this place,* an addition to the text of 1 Kings, expressing the theological concern of the Chronicler's own day. **6.41–42** The conclusion of the prayer is made up of a quotation from Ps 132.8–10, 1. Thus, the Chronicler builds his hope on words ascribed to David rather than on those ascribed to Moses in the period of the exodus, as in 1 Kings 8.51, 53. **6.41** *Resting place,* the temple. *Ark of your might.* The ark symbolized the presence of God in military battles. *Salvation,* "righteousness" in Ps 132.9. *In your goodness,* an addition in Chronicles. **6.42** *Steadfast love for your servant David.* Ps 132, by way of contrast, reminds God of David's hardships and the efforts he had expended for God. Chronicles asks God to keep his promises to the anointed king,

indicating that the author expects something from these old promises even after the rebuilding of the temple, perhaps even some form of a messianic hope. Isa 55.3 democratizes the "steadfast, sure love for David" by saying it now applies to all Israel.
   7.1–10 Cf. 1 Kings 8.54–66. **7.1** *Fire* from heaven authenticates the first sacrifices at the new temple, as fire did at the first sacrifices in the wilderness (Lev 9.23–24) and at David's presentation of burnt offerings (1 Chr 21.26). Cf. also Judg 6.20–22; 1 Kings 18. **7.2** A cloud theophany also occurs in 5.13. **7.3** *For he . . . forever.* See note on 5.13. Chronicles omits Solomon's blessing of the people in 1 Kings 8.54–61. **7.5** The large number of sacrifices is probably a hyperbole to emphasize the importance of the occasion. Cf. the similar large figures at ceremonies in the time of Hezekiah (29.32–36) and Josiah (35.7–9). Such sacrifices were to be eaten by the people during the fifteen-day celebration to follow. **7.8** As is fitting for such a momentous event, *all Israel* celebrates the dedication of the temple. The wide geographic area represented

solemn assembly; for they had observed the dedication of the altar seven days and the festival seven days. 10On the twenty-third day of the seventh month he sent the people away to their homes, joyful and in good spirits because of the goodness that the LORD had shown to David and to Solomon and to his people Israel.

11 Thus Solomon finished the house of the LORD and the king's house; all that Solomon had planned to do in the house of the LORD and in his own house he successfully accomplished.

God's Second Appearance to Solomon

12 Then the LORD appeared to Solomon in the night and said to him: "I have heard your prayer, and have chosen this place for myself as a house of sacrifice. 13When I shut up the heavens so that there is no rain, or command the locust to devour the land, or send pestilence among my people, 14if my people who are called by my name humble themselves, pray, seek my face, and turn from their wicked ways, then I will hear from heaven, and will forgive their sin and heal their land. 15Now my eyes will be open and my ears attentive to the prayer that is made in this place. 16For now I have chosen and consecrated this house so that my name may be there forever; my eyes and my heart will be there for all time. 17As for you, if you walk before me, as your father

David walked, doing according to all that I have commanded you and keeping my statutes and my ordinances, 18then I will establish your royal throne, as I made covenant with your father David saying, 'You shall never lack a successor to rule over Israel.'

19 "But if you*a* turn aside and forsake my statutes and my commandments that I have set before you, and go and serve other gods and worship them, 20then I will pluck you*b* up from the land that I have given you;*b* and this house, which I have consecrated for my name, I will cast out of my sight, and will make it a proverb and a byword among all peoples. 21And regarding this house, now exalted, everyone passing by will be astonished, and say, 'Why has the LORD done such a thing to this land and to this house?' 22Then they will say, 'Because they abandoned the LORD the God of their ancestors who brought them out of the land of Egypt, and they adopted other gods, and worshiped them and served them; therefore he has brought all this calamity upon them.' "

Various Activities of Solomon

8 At the end of twenty years, during which Solomon had built the house of the LORD and his own house, 2Solomon rebuilt the cities that Huram had given to him, and settled the people of Israel in them.

a The word *you* in this verse is plural   *b* Heb *them*

by the participants, from *Lebo-hamath,* the traditional northern border of Israel, to the *Wadi of Egypt,* the traditional southern border, recalls the pan-Israelite celebration when David prepared to bring the ark to Jerusalem (1 Chr 13). **7.9–10** The dedication lasts from the eighth to the fourteenth day of the seventh month, followed by the Feast of Tabernacles from the fifteenth to the twenty-second day of the month, with dismissal on the twenty-third day. Hezekiah also is said to have held his great Passover for two weeks (30.23). **7.10** The Chronicler adds a reference to *Solomon* as part of his equal treatment for the two kings of the United Kingdom (cf. 1 Kings 8.66). **7.11–22** Cf. 1 Kings 9.1–9. In this second theophany to Solomon, God gives a positive response to Solomon's prayer at the dedication of the temple (6.14–42). **7.11** Since the building of the king's palace (*the king's house*) took thirteen years, according to 1 Kings 7.1, the second theophany occurs much later than its position in 2 Chronicles would suggest. **7.12** *In the night,* a reference to the theophany at Gibeon (1.7–13). **7.12b–15** This material, not contained in 1 Kings, affirms that God will respond to the petitions of ch. 6. **7.14** Humble repentance will force God to *hear, for-*

give, and *heal.* Throughout the rest of 2 Chronicles this principle of immediate retribution is illustrated through the history of the Southern Kingdom. **7.18** *Made covenant with,* more specific and intense than in 1 Kings 9.5 ("promised"). *Never lack a successor to rule over Israel,* another indication of the low-key messianic hope of the Chronicler. **7.19–22** God's address to the people, announcing the consequences of idolatry. **7.19** *You* includes Solomon, contemporary Israelites, and future generations of Israelites. The Chronicler omits the reference to David's sons in 1 Kings 9.6. The evil behavior of the people would force God to banish all of them from the land. **7.21–22** A similar question-and-answer format dealing with the causes of the desolations of exile appears in Deut 29.24–25.

8.1–18 Cf. 1 Kings 9.10–28. The Chronicler, as here with Solomon, often discloses his approval of a king by recording his many building projects. **8.2** The parallel text in 1 Kings 9.11 reports that Solomon gave Hiram twenty cities, apparently in payment for help with his various building projects or because he needed money for something else. The Chronicler may have been embarrassed that Solomon disposed of some of the land

3 Solomon went to Hamath-zobah, and captured it. 4He built Tadmor in the wilderness and all the storage towns that he built in Hamath. 5He also built Upper Beth-horon and Lower Beth-horon, fortified cities, with walls, gates, and bars, 6and Baalath, as well as all Solomon's storage towns, and all the towns for his chariots, the towns for his cavalry, and whatever Solomon desired to build, in Jerusalem, in Lebanon, and in all the land of his dominion. 7All the people who were left of the Hittites, the Amorites, the Perizzites, the Hivites, and the Jebusites, who were not of Israel, 8from their descendants who were still left in the land, whom the people of Israel had not destroyed—these Solomon conscripted for forced labor, as is still the case today. 9But of the people of Israel Solomon made no slaves for his work; they were soldiers, and his officers, the commanders of his chariotry and cavalry. 10These were the chief officers of King Solomon, two hundred fifty of them, who exercised authority over the people.

11 Solomon brought Pharaoh's daughter from the city of David to the house that he had built for her, for he said, "My wife shall not live in the house of King David of Israel, for the places to which the ark of the LORD has come are holy."

12 Then Solomon offered up burnt offerings to the LORD on the altar of the LORD that he had built in front of the vestibule, 13as the duty of each day required, offering according to the commandment of Moses for the sab-

baths, the new moons, and the three annual festivals—the festival of unleavened bread, the festival of weeks, and the festival of booths. 14According to the ordinance of his father David, he appointed the divisions of the priests for their service, and the Levites for their offices of praise and ministry alongside the priests as the duty of each day required, and the gatekeepers in their divisions for the several gates; for so David the man of God had commanded. 15They did not turn away from what the king had commanded the priests and Levites regarding anything at all, or regarding the treasuries.

16 Thus all the work of Solomon was accomplished from*a* the day the foundation of the house of the LORD was laid until the house of the LORD was finished completely.

17 Then Solomon went to Ezion-geber and Eloth on the shore of the sea, in the land of Edom. 18Huram sent him, in the care of his servants, ships and servants familiar with the sea. They went to Ophir, together with the servants of Solomon, and imported from there four hundred fifty talents of gold and brought it to King Solomon.

Visit of the Queen of Sheba

9 When the queen of Sheba heard of the fame of Solomon, she came to Jerusalem to test him with hard questions, having a very great retinue and camels bearing spices and

---

a Gk Syr Vg: Heb *to*

of Israel or that he was in debt and changed the text to make the cities pass from *Huram* (a variant spelling of Hiram) to Solomon. **8.3–6** Solomon's military successes, otherwise unreported, also show his life under blessing, though elsewhere in Chronicles he is called a man of peace (1 Chr 22.9). **8.3** *Hamath-zobah,* an unknown city, perhaps a scribal error. David strikes down Hadadezer of Zobah, toward Hamath, according to 1 Chr 18.3. **8.4** *Tadmor,* a caravan city (Palmyra) located 140 miles northeast of Damascus. 1 Kings 9.18 reads "Tamar" (a small site in southern Judah; cf. Ezek 47.19; 48.28). *Hamath,* modern Hama, a city located between Damascus and Aleppo on the main overland route to Mesopotamia. **8.5** *Upper Beth-horon and Lower Beth-horon,* twin cities in Ephraim that guarded a major pass on the road from the coast, by way of the valley of Aijalon, to the hill country and Jerusalem. **8.6** *Baalath,* an unidentified city in Judah. **8.7–10** The nations in v. 7 are the traditional inhabitants of the land before the arrival of Israel. Only the descendants of these nations, not the Israelites themselves, are conscripted into forced labor according to the Chronicler.

8.11 Solomon moves his wife, who was Pharaoh's daughter, out of Jerusalem because of the sanctifying presence of the ark in the capital city. Chronicles does not include the other references in Kings to this marriage (1 Kings 3.1; 7.8; 9.16; 11.1). **8.12** Only the priests are allowed to go beyond the vestibule. **8.13– 15** These verses, added by the Chronicler, demonstrate Solomon's conformity to the law of Moses (cf. Num 28–29). His appointment of the Levites follows the precedent of David, his father. Cf. 1 Chr 23–27. **8.17– 18** *Ezion-geber* and *Eloth* were ports on the northeast end of the Gulf of Aqaba. A joint sailing venture with Huram embarks from there and brings back with it *four hundred fifty talents* (more than 15 tons) *of gold. Ophir,* an unknown and presumably distant city; it took three years to get there (9.21).

9.1–12 Cf. 1 Kings 10.1–13. The queen of Sheba admires Solomon's wealth and wisdom. Chronicles begins its account of Solomon with an account of his relationship with the king of Tyre (2.1–16). The queen's trip probably involved commercial interests, since the trade routes to Tyre would pass through Israel.

very much gold and precious stones. When she came to Solomon, she discussed with him all that was on her mind. ²Solomon answered all her questions; there was nothing hidden from Solomon that he could not explain to her. ³When the queen of Sheba had observed the wisdom of Solomon, the house that he had built, ⁴the food of his table, the seating of his officials, and the attendance of his servants, and their clothing, his valets, and their clothing, and his burnt offerings*a* that he offered at the house of the LORD, there was no more spirit left in her.

5 So she said to the king, "The report was true that I heard in my own land of your accomplishments and of your wisdom, ⁶but I did not believe the*b* reports until I came and my own eyes saw it. Not even half of the greatness of your wisdom had been told to me; you far surpass the report that I had heard. ⁷Happy are your people! Happy are these your servants, who continually attend you and hear your wisdom! ⁸Blessed be the LORD your God, who has delighted in you and set you on his throne as king for the LORD your God. Because your God loved Israel and would establish them forever, he has made you king over them, that you may execute justice and righteousness." ⁹Then she gave the king one hundred twenty talents of gold, a very great quantity of spices, and precious stones: there were no spices such as those that the queen of Sheba gave to King Solomon.

10 Moreover the servants of Huram and the servants of Solomon who brought gold from Ophir brought algum wood and precious stones. ¹¹From the algum wood, the king made steps*c* for the house of the LORD and for the king's house, lyres also and harps for the singers; there never was seen the like of them before in the land of Judah.

12 Meanwhile King Solomon granted the queen of Sheba every desire that she expressed, well beyond what she had brought to the king. Then she returned to her own land, with her servants.

Solomon's Great Wealth

13 The weight of gold that came to Solomon in one year was six hundred sixty-six talents of gold, ¹⁴besides that which the traders and merchants brought; and all the kings of Arabia and the governors of the land brought gold and silver to Solomon. ¹⁵King Solomon made two hundred large shields of beaten gold; six hundred shekels of beaten gold went into each large shield. ¹⁶He made three hundred shields of beaten gold; three hundred shekels of gold went into each shield; and the king put them in the House of the Forest of Lebanon. ¹⁷The king also made a great ivory throne, and overlaid it with pure gold. ¹⁸The throne had six steps and a footstool of gold, which were attached to the throne, and on each side of the seat were arm rests and two lions standing beside the arm rests, ¹⁹while twelve lions were standing, one on each end of a step on the six steps. The like of it was never made in any kingdom. ²⁰All King Solomon's drinking vessels were of gold, and all the vessels of the House of the Forest of Lebanon were of pure gold; silver was not considered as anything in the days of Solomon. ²¹For the king's ships went to Tarshish with the servants of Huram; once every three years the ships of Tarshish used to come bringing gold, silver, ivory, apes, and peacocks.*d*

22 Thus King Solomon excelled all the kings of the earth in riches and in wisdom.

---

a Gk Syr Vg 1 Kings 10.5: Heb *ascent* *b* Heb *their* *c* Gk Vg: Meaning of Heb uncertain *d* Or *baboons*

9.1 *Sheba,* modern Yemen, some fourteen hundred miles from Jerusalem. The Sabeans prospered because of trade in myrrh, frankincense, gold, and precious stones. **9.4** The NRSV emendation (see text note *a*) is correct; the difference between *burnt offerings* and *ascent* involves a *yod,* the smallest letter in the Hebrew alphabet. **9.8** *His* (God's) *throne.* 1 Kings 10.9 reads "the throne of Israel." In Chronicles, the throne and kingdom are God's (1 Chr 17.14; 28.5; 29.23; 2 Chr 13.8). God's rule would continue forever, even if there were no human king, as was the case at the time when Chronicles was written. Huram affirms that God's love for Israel led him to place Solomon on the throne (2.11). **9.9** *One hundred twenty talents,* 8,076 pounds.

9.10 Chronicles goes beyond 1 Kings 10.11 by making Solomon an equal partner in Huram's gold trade. *Algum wood.* 1 Kings 10.11 reads "almug wood"; it is perhaps red sandalwood. **9.13–28** Cf. 1 Kings 10.14–29. This idealized picture of the wealth of the United Monarchy may imply that a united Israel in the future might prosper similarly. **9.13** *Six hundred sixty-six talents,* about 44,821 pounds. **9.15** These *shields* will later be taken by King Shishak of Egypt (12.9–11). **9.16** *House of the Forest of Lebanon.* Cf. 1 Kings 7.1–12. **9.18** *A footstool of gold.* 1 Kings 10.19 reads "the top of the throne was rounded in the back." The Chronicler may have found the text of Kings theologically offensive. **9.21** *Tarshish,* probably a site in Spain, or a desig-

23All the kings of the earth sought the presence of Solomon to hear his wisdom, which God had put into his mind. 24Every one of them brought a present, objects of silver and gold, garments, weaponry, spices, horses, and mules, so much year by year. 25Solomon had four thousand stalls for horses and chariots, and twelve thousand horses, which he stationed in the chariot cities and with the king in Jerusalem. 26He ruled over all the kings from the Euphrates to the land of the Philistines, and to the border of Egypt. 27The king made silver as common in Jerusalem as stone, and cedar as plentiful as the sycamore of the Shephelah. 28Horses were imported for Solomon from Egypt and from all lands.

Death of Solomon

29 Now the rest of the acts of Solomon, from first to last, are they not written in the history of the prophet Nathan, and in the prophecy of Ahijah the Shilonite, and in the visions of the seer Iddo concerning Jeroboam son of Nebat? 30Solomon reigned in Jerusalem over all Israel forty years. 31Solomon slept with his ancestors and was buried in the city of his father David; and his son Rehoboam succeeded him.

The Revolt against Rehoboam

10 Rehoboam went to Shechem, for all Israel had come to Shechem to make him king. 2When Jeroboam son of Nebat heard of it (for he was in Egypt, where he had fled from King Solomon), then Jeroboam returned from Egypt. 3They sent and called him; and Jeroboam and all Israel came and said to Rehoboam, 4"Your father made our yoke heavy. Now therefore lighten the hard service of your father and his heavy yoke that he placed on us, and we will serve you." 5He said to them, "Come to me again in three days." So the people went away.

6 Then King Rehoboam took counsel with the older men who had attended his father Solomon while he was still alive, saying, "How do you advise me to answer this people?" 7They answered him, "If you will be kind to this people and please them, and speak good words to them, then they will be your servants forever." 8But he rejected the advice that the older men gave him, and consulted the young men who had grown up with him and now attended him. 9He said to them, "What do you advise that we answer this people who have said to me, 'Lighten the yoke that your father put on us'?" 10The young men who had grown up with him said to him, "Thus should you speak to the people who said to you, 'Your father made our yoke heavy, but you must lighten it for us'; tell them, 'My little finger is thicker than my father's loins. 11Now, whereas my father laid on you a heavy yoke, I will add to your

nation for any distant place. Peacocks. The alternate baboons is preferred by many. 9.25 Solomon's strength in horses is already mentioned at the beginning of his reign (1.14–17; 1 Kings 10.26–29). 9.26 Chronicles adds this description of the wide extent of the kingdom to provide a positive conclusion to the reign of Solomon. The words are taken from 1 Kings 4.21. 9.29–31 Cf. 1 Kings 11.41–43. Chronicles omits 1 Kings 11.1–40, which tells of Solomon's foreign wives, the Lord's decision to give most of the kingdom to one of the king's servants, and rebellions in Edom and Aram and by Jeroboam, the first king of the Northern Kingdom. 9.29 Chronicles ascribes the Book of the Acts of Solomon (1 Kings 11.41) to a series of prophetic authors: Nathan (1 Chr 17), Ahijah (1 Kings 11–15), and Iddo (2 Chr 12.15; 13.22). There is no indication that the Chronicler used any other source than 1 Kings in producing the account of Solomon. Chronicles also cites three prophets in the final summary of David's reign (1 Chr 29.29). 10.1–19 Cf. 1 Kings 12.1–20. The Northern tribes protest against Solomon's oppressive rule, rebel against Rehoboam, and set up the rival Northern Kingdom. They remain part of Israel, according to the Chronicler, but they need to repent of forsaking God.

10.1 Shechem, forty-one miles north of Jerusalem, was important in the patriarchal period (Abraham, Jacob) and was the site of Joshua's farewell address (Josh 24). The choice of the traditional city of Shechem as the site for Rehoboam's coronation may imply resistance to the Davidic dynasty and its capital at Jerusalem. All Israel in Chronicles refers to all of the tribes, in 1 Kings only to the Northern tribes. 10.2 Jeroboam is not mentioned previously in Chronicles, except for 2 Chr 9.29. Chronicles seems to assume knowledge of 1 Kings 11.26–40. Jeroboam rebels against Solomon and flees to Egypt. Solomon seeks to kill Jeroboam after he has been designated king of the ten Northern tribes by Ahijah, a prophet from Shiloh. 10.4 The hard service and heavy yoke probably include taxes and forced labor. Cf. the mention of the taskmaster over forced labor (v. 18) with the denial that Solomon really utilizes the such forced labor within Israel (2.17–18; 8.7–10). The elders counsel moderation and conciliation; Rehoboam's own generation urges a hard-line approach. Rehoboam is already forty-one years old, although v. 8 makes him seem like an impetuous youth. 10.10 My little finger, lit. "my little one," a euphemism for the penis. By using this coarse comparison Rehoboam promises a far harsher rule than his father's.

yoke. My father disciplined you with whips, but I will discipline you with scorpions.' "

12 So Jeroboam and all the people came to Rehoboam the third day, as the king had said, "Come to me again the third day." 13The king answered them harshly. King Rehoboam rejected the advice of the older men; 14he spoke to them in accordance with the advice of the young men, "My father made your yoke heavy, but I will add to it; my father disciplined you with whips, but I will discipline you with scorpions." 15So the king did not listen to the people, because it was a turn of affairs brought about by God so that the LORD might fulfill his word, which he had spoken by Ahijah the Shilonite to Jeroboam son of Nebat.

16 When all Israel saw that the king would not listen to them, the people answered the king,

"What share do we have in David?
We have no inheritance in the son of
Jesse.
Each of you to your tents, O Israel!
Look now to your own house,
O David."

So all Israel departed to their tents. 17But Rehoboam reigned over the people of Israel who were living in the cities of Judah. 18When King Rehoboam sent Hadoram, who was taskmaster over the forced labor, the people of Israel stoned him to death. King Rehoboam hurriedly mounted his chariot to flee to Jerusa-

lem. 19So Israel has been in rebellion against the house of David to this day.

Judah and Benjamin Fortified

11 When Rehoboam came to Jerusalem, he assembled one hundred eighty thousand chosen troops of the house of Judah and Benjamin to fight against Israel, to restore the kingdom to Rehoboam. 2But the word of the LORD came to Shemaiah the man of God: 3Say to King Rehoboam of Judah, son of Solomon, and to all Israel in Judah and Benjamin, 4"Thus says the LORD: You shall not go up or fight against your kindred. Let everyone return home, for this thing is from me." So they heeded the word of the LORD and turned back from the expedition against Jeroboam.

5 Rehoboam resided in Jerusalem, and he built cities for defense in Judah. 6He built up Bethlehem, Etam, Tekoa, 7Beth-zur, Soco, Adullam, 8Gath, Mareshah, Ziph, 9Adoraim, Lachish, Azekah, 10Zorah, Aijalon, and Hebron, fortified cities that are in Judah and in Benjamin. 11He made the fortresses strong, and put commanders in them, and stores of food, oil, and wine. 12He also put large shields and spears in all the cities, and made them very strong. So he held Judah and Benjamin.

Priests and Levites Support Rehoboam

13 The priests and the Levites who were in all Israel presented themselves to him from all

10.11 *Scorpions*, an allusion to the fatal bite of the scorpion or perhaps to a type of scourge. 10.15 *Turn of affairs.* The same Hebrew root used here to refer to God's control of events is also found in 1 Chr 10.14 in speaking of God's handing the kingdom from Saul to David. *Ahijah*'s word about the division of the kingdom (1 Kings 11.29–39) is not contained in 2 Chronicles. 10.16 *Saw.* This verb is lacking in the Hebrew; the NRSV here follows the text of 1 Kings 12.16. *What share ... O David.* The poem rejecting Rehoboam's kingship forms a mirror image to Amasai's cry of support for David (1 Chr 12.18; cf. 1 Sam 25.10; 2 Sam 20.1). 10.18 *Hadoram.* 1 Kings 12.18 reads "Adoram." By sending the leader of the forced labor Rehoboam confirms his hard line and provokes strong opposition. *People of Israel.* The Chronicler includes the citizens of the Northern Kingdom in the concept "Israel." Chronicles omits an equivalent for 1 Kings 12.20, which reports that all Israel anoints Jeroboam to be its king. 11.1–4 Cf. 1 Kings 12.21–24. The prophet Shemaiah successfully warns Rehoboam not to fight against the North, and this results in a temporary truce. 11.1 *One hundred eighty thousand.* The number of troops is much larger than the size of ancient armies,

but Chronicles has even bigger figures elsewhere (580,000 at the time of Asa, 2 Chr 14.8; 307,500 at the time of Uzziah, 2 Chr 26.10). 11.3 *All Israel in Judah and Benjamin.* 1 Kings 12.23 reads "all the house of Judah and Benjamin." In Chronicles both North and South may be called Israel (for the North, see 2 Chr 10.16). 11.4 *Against your kindred.* 1 Kings 12.24 reads "against your kindred the people of Israel." Note that the Northerners in Chronicles are still deemed kindred (brothers). *This thing is from me.* In this verse the Lord takes responsibility for the division of the kingdom. 11.5–12 According to this paragraph, which is unique to Chronicles, Rehoboam erected fortresses at fifteen strategic sites to protect his kingdom from the west, south, and east. A lack of fortresses in the north may imply that he intended to expand his territory in that direction. The western border is pulled back somewhat, perhaps indicating that the territory defended reflects the effects of Shishak's invasion. According to archaeology, Beth-zur (v. 7) was destroyed at the time of Rehoboam, and Lachish (v. 9) was not yet fortified. The list may, therefore, come from a later king. Theologically, Rehoboam's building project shows he was under divine favor. 11.8 *Gath,* possibly

their territories. [14]The Levites had left their common lands and their holdings and had come to Judah and Jerusalem, because Jeroboam and his sons had prevented them from serving as priests of the LORD, [15]and had appointed his own priests for the high places, and for the goat-demons, and for the calves that he had made. [16]Those who had set their hearts to seek the LORD God of Israel came after them from all the tribes of Israel to Jerusalem to sacrifice to the LORD, the God of their ancestors. [17]They strengthened the kingdom of Judah, and for three years they made Rehoboam son of Solomon secure, for they walked for three years in the way of David and Solomon.

Rehoboam's Marriages

18 Rehoboam took as his wife Mahalath daughter of Jerimoth son of David, and of Abihail daughter of Eliab son of Jesse. [19]She bore him sons: Jeush, Shemariah, and Zaham. [20]After her he took Maacah daughter of Absalom, who bore him Abijah, Attai, Ziza, and Shelomith. [21]Rehoboam loved Maacah daughter of Absalom more than all his other wives and concubines (he took eighteen wives and sixty concubines, and became the father of twenty-eight sons and sixty daughters). [22]Rehoboam appointed Abijah son of Maacah as chief prince among his brothers, for he intended to make him king. [23]He dealt wisely, and distributed some of his sons through all the districts of Judah and Benjamin, in all the fortified cities; he gave them abundant provisions, and found many wives for them.

Egypt Attacks Judah

12 When the rule of Rehoboam was established and he grew strong, he abandoned the law of the LORD, he and all Israel with him. [2]In the fifth year of King Rehoboam, because they had been unfaithful to the LORD, King Shishak of Egypt came up against Jerusalem [3]with twelve hundred chariots and sixty thousand cavalry. A countless army came with him from Egypt—Libyans, Sukkiim, and Ethiopians.[a] [4]He took the fortified cities of Judah and came as far as Jerusalem. [5]Then the prophet Shemaiah came to Rehoboam and to the officers of Judah, who had gathered at Jerusalem because of Shishak, and said to them,

_____

a Or Nubians; Heb Cushites

Moresheth-gath (Tell Judeideh). **11.13–17** The priests and Levites, banned from liturgical service by Jeroboam, rally to Rehoboam. Laity join in this movement (cf. v. 16). **11.15** _Goat-demons._ Cf. Lev 17.7. Originally pedestals for Yahweh, the statues of _calves_ are interpreted in the books of Kings and in Chronicles as idolatrous images. **11.16** _Seek the LORD,_ a favorite phrase in Chronicles for faithfulness. Cf. 1 Chr 10.13–14. **11.17** _Three years_ of obedience are followed by apostasy (12.1) and the invasion of Shishak (12.2). Rehoboam's positive behavior in his first years as king is compared to royal conduct during the reigns of David and Solomon (cf. 7.10). The end of Solomon's reign according to 1 Kings had been highly flawed. **11.18–23** Rehoboam establishes a household. **11.18** _Mahalath,_ second cousin to Rehoboam. Her paternal grandfather is David (as is Rehoboam's), and her maternal grandfather is David's brother Eliab. Her parents are first cousins. **11.20** _Maacah,_ granddaughter of David's rebellious son Absalom (2 Sam 13–18). She is descended from Uriel and his wife Tamar, the daughter of Absalom (cf. 13.2). In 1 Kings 15.10 she is the wife of Abijah. _Abijah_ succeeds Rehoboam on the throne even though he is not the eldest son (cf. v. 22). **11.21** Rehoboam's numerous wives and concubines are far fewer than those of his father, Solomon (1 Kings 11.17; but these wives of Solomon are not mentioned in Chronicles). Rehoboam's wives serve as signs of God's blessing. **12.1–14** Cf. 1 Kings 14.25–28. **12.1** _Abandoned,_ one

of the chief terms for disobedience in Chronicles; see v. 5. Specific misdeeds of Judah are listed in 1 Kings 14.22–24. _The law of the LORD._ The Pentateuch probably had canonical status by the time of the Chronicler. **12.2** _Unfaithful,_ another common term (see note on 12.1) for disobedience in Chronicles, without parallel in 1 Kings 14.25. _Shishak_ (Shoshenq I, ca. 945–924 BCE), founder of the twenty-second (Libyan) dynasty in Egypt. His own account of this battle, recorded on the walls of the Amun-Re temple at Karnak, lists more than 150 towns conquered in Palestine. **12.3** _Libyans,_ people from the North African coast, just west of Egypt. _Sukkiim,_ a group of Libyan forces from the western desert. _Ethiopians._ Ethiopia in biblical times was the region between the first and second cataracts of the Nile, south of Aswan, and was not identical with modern Ethiopia. **12.4** _Fortified cities._ Cf. 11.6–10. Aijalon occurs in 11.10 and in Shishak's list. According to Shishak's account, his major attack was on the Negeb region in the south and on Israel in the north. At least part of his forces moved toward Gibeon, where Shishak may have received the submission and tribute of Rehoboam. This would explain why the city was spared, according to the Bible, and account for the lack of any reference to Jerusalem in Shishak's account. Thereafter, Shishak turned north and invaded Israel. **12.5–8** The speech by _Shemaiah_ (cf. 11.2) does not occur in 1 Kings. **12.5** Exact retribution is described in this verse. For the word _abandon,_ see 1 Chr 28.9; 2 Chr 15.2; 24.20 (where the term is translated _forsaken_).

"Thus says the LORD: You abandoned me, so I have abandoned you to the hand of Shishak." 6Then the officers of Israel and the king humbled themselves and said, "The LORD is in the right." 7When the LORD saw that they humbled themselves, the word of the LORD came to Shemaiah, saying: "They have humbled themselves; I will not destroy them, but I will grant them some deliverance, and my wrath shall not be poured out on Jerusalem by the hand of Shishak. 8Nevertheless they shall be his servants, so that they may know the difference between serving me and serving the kingdoms of other lands."

9 So King Shishak of Egypt came up against Jerusalem; he took away the treasures of the house of the LORD and the treasures of the king's house; he took everything. He also took away the shields of gold that Solomon had made; 10but King Rehoboam made in place of them shields of bronze, and committed them to the hands of the officers of the guard, who kept the door of the king's house. 11Whenever the king went into the house of the LORD, the guard would come along bearing them, and would then bring them back to the guardroom. 12Because he humbled himself the wrath of the LORD turned from him, so as not to destroy them completely; moreover, conditions were good in Judah.

Death of Rehoboam

13 So King Rehoboam established himself in Jerusalem and reigned. Rehoboam was forty-one years old when he began to reign; he reigned seventeen years in Jerusalem, the city that the LORD had chosen out of all the tribes of Israel to put his name there. His mother's name was Naamah the Ammonite. 14He did evil, for he did not set his heart to seek the LORD.

15 Now the acts of Rehoboam, from first to last, are they not written in the records of the prophet Shemaiah and of the seer Iddo, recorded by genealogy? There were continual wars between Rehoboam and Jeroboam. 16Rehoboam slept with his ancestors and was buried in the city of David; and his son Abijah succeeded him.

Abijah Reigns over Judah

13 In the eighteenth year of King Jeroboam, Abijah began to reign over Judah. 2He reigned for three years in Jerusalem. His mother's name was Micaiah daughter of Uriel of Gibeah.

Now there was war between Abijah and Jeroboam. 3Abijah engaged in battle, having an army of valiant warriors, four hundred thousand picked men; and Jeroboam drew up his line of battle against him with eight hundred thousand picked mighty warriors. 4Then Abijah stood on the slope of Mount Zemaraim that is in the hill country of Ephraim, and said, "Listen to me, Jeroboam and all Israel! 5Do you not know that the LORD God of Israel gave the kingship over Israel forever to David and his sons by a covenant of salt? 6Yet Jeroboam

---

12.6 The government's repentance takes the form of its leaders *humbling themselves* (cf. 7.14; 12.7, 12) and confessing the righteousness of the Lord. 12.7 The Lord's acceptance of their repentance fulfills the promise in the divine oracle delivered to Solomon in 7.14 and explains why Jerusalem escapes the full brunt of Shishak's attack. 12.8 Service to a foreign king would be more burdensome than service to the Lord. 12.9 *King Shishak . . . Jerusalem.* The first half of this verse repeats the last part of v. 2. 12.10 Judah's diminished circumstances lead Rehoboam to replace the shields of gold with shields of *bronze.* 12.12 *Conditions were good in Judah,* better "in Judah there was some good." Positive retribution explains in part the sparing of Rehoboam from more serious attack. 12.13–16 Cf. 1 Kings 14.21–22, 29–31. 12.13–14 The summary of Rehoboam's reign appears after Shishak's invasion in Chronicles, instead of before it as in Kings. 12.13 *In Jerusalem.* 1 Kings 14.21 reads "in Judah." *Naamah the Ammonite.* Note the foreign origin of Rehoboam's mother, who is mentioned twice in 1 Kings (14.21, 31). 12.14 The effects of Rehoboam's *evil* are illustrated in

this chapter. To *seek* is the opposite of to *abandon* (v. 1). 12.15 Chronicles changes the "Book of the Annals of the Kings of Judah" from 1 Kings 14.29 into prophetic sources written by *Shemaiah* and *Iddo. Genealogy,* unclear, perhaps a reference to another source.

13.1–14.1 Abijah in Chronicles wins a victory against the Northern Kingdom and preaches to his enemy; in 1 Kings 15.3–6 Abijam (note spelling) continues the sins of his ancestors and survives only because of God's loyalty to David. 13.2 *Micaiah, Uriel.* Abijah has a different mother and grandfather in 1 Kings 15.2, Maacah and Abishalom, respectively. The source for the information about constant warfare is 1 Kings 15.7. Cf. 1 Kings 15.6, which reports war between Rehoboam and Jeroboam. 13.3 The size of the armies is enormous (cf. 2 Sam 24.9). God helps Abijah and Judah to victory despite their being outnumbered two to one. 13.4–12 The speech of Abijah was composed by the Chronicler and reflects his theology. 13.4 *Mount Zemaraim.* Cf. Josh 18.22. The territory of Benjamin served as a kind of buffer between the North

son of Nebat, a servant of Solomon son of David, rose up and rebelled against his lord; [7] and certain worthless scoundrels gathered around him and defied Rehoboam son of Solomon, when Rehoboam was young and irresolute and could not withstand them.

8 "And now you think that you can withstand the kingdom of the LORD in the hand of the sons of David, because you are a great multitude and have with you the golden calves that Jeroboam made as gods for you. [9] Have you not driven out the priests of the LORD, the descendants of Aaron, and the Levites, and made priests for yourselves like the peoples of other lands? Whoever comes to be consecrated with a young bull or seven rams becomes a priest of what are no gods. [10] But as for us, the LORD is our God, and we have not abandoned him. We have priests ministering to the LORD who are descendants of Aaron, and Levites for their service. [11] They offer to the LORD every morning and every evening burnt offerings and fragrant incense, set out the rows of bread on the table of pure gold, and care for the golden lampstand so that its lamps may burn every evening; for we keep the charge of the LORD our God, but you have abandoned him. [12] See, God is with us at our head, and his priests have their battle trumpets to sound the call to battle against you. O Israelites, do not fight against the LORD, the God of your ancestors; for you cannot succeed."

13 Jeroboam had sent an ambush around to come on them from behind; thus his troops[a] were in front of Judah, and the ambush was behind them. [14] When Judah turned, the battle was in front of them and behind them. They cried out to the LORD, and the priests blew the trumpets. [15] Then the people of Judah raised the battle shout. And when the people of Judah shouted, God defeated Jeroboam and all Israel before Abijah and Judah. [16] The Israelites fled before Judah, and God gave them into their hands. [17] Abijah and his army defeated them with great slaughter; five hundred thousand picked men of Israel fell slain. [18] Thus the Israelites were subdued at that time, and the people of Judah prevailed, because they relied on the LORD, the God of their ancestors. [19] Abijah pursued Jeroboam, and took cities from him: Bethel with its villages and Jeshanah with its villages and Ephron[b] with its villages. [20] Jeroboam did not recover his power in the days of Abijah; the LORD struck him down, and he died. [21] But Abijah grew strong. He took fourteen wives, and became the father of twenty-two sons and sixteen daughters. [22] The rest of the acts of Abijah, his behavior and his deeds, are written in the story of the prophet Iddo.

Asa Reigns

14 [c] So Abijah slept with his ancestors, and they buried him in the city of David. His son Asa succeeded him. In his days the land had rest for ten years. [2][d] Asa did what was

---

a Heb *they*   b Another reading is *Ephrain*   c Ch 13.23 in Heb
d Ch 14.1 in Heb

---

and the South. **13.5** *Covenant of salt,* an everlasting covenant. Cf. Lev 2.13; Num 18.19. The covenant with David is everlasting. **13.6–7** Jeroboam is criticized for rebellion and for associating with the wrong crowd; Rehoboam's fault is attributed to his youth. With the pious Abijah on the throne, there is no reason for the North to rebel. **13.8–11** The sin of the Northern Kingdom is balanced by the faithfulness of the Southern Kingdom. The North resists God's kingdom as manifested in the Davidic dynasty (1 Chr 17.14), worships the golden calves as gods (2 Chr 11.15), drives out the Aaronite priests and Levites, and makes priests out of all who step forward with a gift in their hand (cf. 11.14–15). Abijah confesses the faith of his people in the Lord (cf. v. 18) and states that the South has not abandoned him (while the North has; 12.1). The legitimate Aaronite priests and the Levites carry out the appropriate sacrifices each day. **13.12** With God on the side of Judah and the priests ready to blow their trumpets to initiate holy war, the situation of the North is hopeless. **13.13–20** A battle report. **13.13** Judah is outnumbered and trapped between two wings of Israel's

army. **13.14–15** Trumpet blasts and battle cries induce God to intervene. **13.16–17** Judah's role is to pursue a fleeing enemy. The casualties are caused by divine intervention; the action of the Judahite army seems incidental to the war itself. *Five hundred thousand.* In all of World War II the United States had about 400,000 fatal casualties. **13.19** *Bethel, Jeshanah,* and *Ephron.* Abijah expands his territory toward the north by taking these cities of Benjamin (Josh 18.21–24). **13.20** The verse implies that Jeroboam outlived Abijah (cf. 1 Kings 15.9). According to 1 Kings 14.20, Jeroboam seems to have died peacefully. **13.21** Abijah's many wives and children indicate divine favor. Cf. 11.22. Note how Abijah also *grew strong.* **13.22** *Story,* lit. "the midrash." See the *visions* of Iddo in 9.29 and his *records* in 12.15. In 1 Kings 15.7 the sources are given as the "Book of the Annals of the Kings of Judah." Chronicles turns this into a prophetic record. **14.1** *Rest,* a characteristic feature of pious reigns (cf. vv. 5–6; 1 Chr 22.9). *Ten years,* proper retribution for the pious king Asa; but 1 Kings 15.16 speaks of continual warfare between Baasha and Asa.

good and right in the sight of the LORD his God. ³He took away the foreign altars and the high places, broke down the pillars, hewed down the sacred poles,ᵃ ⁴and commanded Judah to seek the LORD, the God of their ancestors, and to keep the law and the commandment. ⁵He also removed from all the cities of Judah the high places and the incense altars. And the kingdom had rest under him. ⁶He built fortified cities in Judah while the land had rest. He had no war in those years, for the LORD gave him peace. ⁷He said to Judah, "Let us build these cities, and surround them with walls and towers, gates and bars; the land is still ours because we have sought the LORD our God; we have sought him, and he has given us peace on every side." So they built and prospered. ⁸Asa had an army of three hundred thousand from Judah, armed with large shields and spears, and two hundred eighty thousand troops from Benjamin who carried shields and drew bows; all these were mighty warriors.

Ethiopian Invasion Repulsed

9 Zerah the Ethiopianᵇ came out against them with an army of a million men and three hundred chariots, and came as far as Mareshah. ¹⁰Asa went out to meet him, and they drew up their lines of battle in the valley of Zephathah at Mareshah. ¹¹Asa cried to the LORD his God, "O LORD, there is no difference for you be-

tween helping the mighty and the weak. Help us, O LORD our God, for we rely on you, and in your name we have come against this multitude. O LORD, you are our God; let no mortal prevail against you." ¹²So the LORD defeated the Ethiopiansᶜ before Asa and before Judah, and the Ethiopiansᶜ fled. ¹³Asa and the army with him pursued them as far as Gerar, and the Ethiopiansᶜ fell until no one remained alive; for they were broken before the LORD and his army. The people of Judahᵈ carried away a great quantity of booty. ¹⁴They defeated all the cities around Gerar, for the fear of the LORD was on them. They plundered all the cities; for there was much plunder in them. ¹⁵They also attacked the tents of those who had livestock,ᵉ and carried away sheep and goats in abundance, and camels. Then they returned to Jerusalem.

15 The spirit of God came upon Azariah son of Oded. ²He went out to meet Asa and said to him, "Hear me, Asa, and all Judah and Benjamin: The LORD is with you, while you are with him. If you seek him, he will be found by you, but if you abandon him, he will abandon you. ³For a long time Israel was without the true God, and without a teaching priest, and without law; ⁴but when in their distress they turned to the LORD, the God of

---

a Heb *Asherim*　*b* Or *Nubian*; Heb *Cushite*　*c* Or *Nubians*; Heb *Cushites*　*d* Heb *They*　*e* Meaning of Heb uncertain

---

14.2–8 Cf. 1 Kings 15.11. The Chronicler omits 1 Kings 15.12 and does not return to the Kings text until 15.16 (1 Kings 15.13). **14.3** The *high places* are not removed by the king according to a later summary (15.17; 1 Kings 15.14). Asa's actions in these verses correspond to the directives of Deut 7.5; 12.3; 16.21–22 and make him a reformer somewhat like Hezekiah and Josiah. **14.4** *Seek,* a term for faithfulness that occurs nine times in the three chapters dealing with Asa. **14.5** *Incense altars* or shrines; the meaning of the word in Hebrew is uncertain. **14.6–7** Asa's obedience brings peace and provides the wherewithal to build. Divine protection, however, would seem to obviate the need for additional fortified cities. **14.7** *We have sought him.* Many emend the text correctly to read "He has sought us." **14.8** The army of 580,000 shows the divine favor that rests upon Asa. The army, which lacks horses and chariots, is roughly half the size of Zerah's (v. 9). **14.9–15** Asa shows complete reliance upon the Lord. **14.9** *Zerah,* otherwise unknown. *The Ethiopian,* unclear since it is unlikely that Zerah actually came from Cush/Nubia. *A million men.* The number dramatizes the danger posed by Zerah and the fact that the Lord helps the weak Southern Kingdom (v. 11). *Three hun-*

dred chariots, a more realistic number, or a small number because Zerah and the Ethiopians were seminomadic (note the camels and the tent dwellings in v. 15). *Mareshah,* a city near Lachish, fortified by Rehoboam (11.8). **14.10** *Zephathah,* otherwise unknown. **14.11–12** The Lord answers Asa's prayer just as Solomon had requested in his own prayer (6.34–35). **14.13** *Gerar,* Tell Abu Hureira (cf. Gen 20.1–2; 26.1), a city about thirty miles southwest of Mareshah. The divine army completely destroys the million-person Ethiopian army. All Judah has to do is collect the booty. **14.14** The *fear* instilled by the Lord makes Israel's victory over neighboring cities easy (cf. Ex 23.28; Deut 7.20, 23; Josh 24.12). **14.15** Livestock is taken even from the civilian herdsmen.

15.1–19 Cf. 1 Kings 15.13–15. **15.1** *The spirit of God* connotes prophetic inspiration and authority (cf. 20.14). *Azariah son of Oded,* otherwise unknown. **15.2–7** Azariah's sermon. **15.2** The maxims in this verse seem to be based on the victory over Zerah (cf. 14.4, 7). The Lord has been with Asa because of his early reforms (14.3–5) and because of his faith (14.11). **15.3** This verse seems to describe the period of the judges, when there was no *priest* to give authoritative

Israel, and sought him, he was found by them. [5] In those times it was not safe for anyone to go or come, for great disturbances afflicted all the inhabitants of the lands. [6] They were broken in pieces, nation against nation and city against city, for God troubled them with every sort of distress. [7] But you, take courage! Do not let your hands be weak, for your work shall be rewarded."

8 When Asa heard these words, the prophecy of Azariah son of Oded,[a] he took courage, and put away the abominable idols from all the land of Judah and Benjamin and from the towns that he had taken in the hill country of Ephraim. He repaired the altar of the LORD that was in front of the vestibule of the house of the LORD.[b] [9] He gathered all Judah and Benjamin, and those from Ephraim, Manasseh, and Simeon who were residing as aliens with them, for great numbers had deserted to him from Israel when they saw that the LORD his God was with him. [10] They were gathered at Jerusalem in the third month of the fifteenth year of the reign of Asa. [11] They sacrificed to the LORD on that day, from the booty that they had brought, seven hundred oxen and seven thousand sheep. [12] They entered into a covenant to seek the LORD, the God of their ancestors, with all their heart and with all their

soul. [13] Whoever would not seek the LORD, the God of Israel, should be put to death, whether young or old, man or woman. [14] They took an oath to the LORD with a loud voice, and with shouting, and with trumpets, and with horns. [15] All Judah rejoiced over the oath; for they had sworn with all their heart, and had sought him with their whole desire, and he was found by them, and the LORD gave them rest all around.

16 King Asa even removed his mother Maacah from being queen mother because she had made an abominable image for Asherah. Asa cut down her image, crushed it, and burned it at the Wadi Kidron. [17] But the high places were not taken out of Israel. Nevertheless the heart of Asa was true all his days. [18] He brought into the house of God the votive gifts of his father and his own votive gifts—silver, gold, and utensils. [19] And there was no more war until the thirty-fifth year of the reign of Asa.

Alliance with Aram Condemned

16 In the thirty-sixth year of the reign of Asa, King Baasha of Israel went up against Judah, and built Ramah, to prevent

_a_ Compare Syr Vg: Heb _the prophecy, the prophet Obed_
_b_ Heb _the vestibule of the LORD_

---

direction (_law_). **15.4** Cf. Judg 2.18, where the Lord is moved to pity because of Israel's groaning. **15.7** Azariah urges Asa to complete his work of reform. Readers of Chronicles are to expect the same kind of deliverance that their ancestors experienced in the past (v. 4). The Chronicler cites Jer 31.16 ("There is a reward for your work") and Zeph 3.16 ("Do not let your hands grow weak") in order to make his message compelling for his own generation. **15.8** Since the reform includes portions of _Ephraim_ from the Northern Kingdom, Asa apparently engages in combat against the North before his thirty-sixth year (16.1). _Altar of the LORD_, used for burnt offerings. **15.9** _Ephraim, Manasseh, and Simeon._ The association of the Southern tribe Simeon with the Northern tribes Ephraim and Manasseh is unexplained. Perhaps circumstances have forced elements of Simeon to move north (cf. 1 Chr 4.28–33; 2 Chr 34.6). Asa and other Southern kings (Jehoshaphat, Hezekiah, and Josiah) attempt to include the North within their control and to bring about recognition of the ritual life centered at the Jerusalem temple. The Chronicler cites these examples in support of his own desire to incorporate all Israel into the cult of the Jerusalem temple. **15.10** _Third month,_ at or near the Feast of Weeks, or Pentecost. _Fifteenth year._ The covenant celebration may take place in the same year as the victory over Zerah. **15.11** _Booty,_ from the battle

against Zerah (14.13–15). **15.12** The _covenant_ partners are the king and the people. **15.13** Worship of other gods is a capital crime according to Deut 13.6–10; 17.2–7. **15.15** _Rest._ Cf. 14.1. **15.16–18** Dependent on 1 Kings 15.13–15. **15.16** The authority of the position of _queen mother_ is also seen in the careers of Bathsheba (1 Kings 1.15–21), Jezebel from the Northern Kingdom (1 Kings 17.21; 31–34), and Athaliah (1 Kings 11.1–3). _Asherah,_ a Canaanite goddess, the wife of El, or the consort of Baal. Jezebel was also an advocate for Asherah (1 Kings 18.19). _Wadi Kidron,_ a valley between the Temple Mount and the Mount of Olives. Hezekiah (2 Chr 29.16; 30.14) and Josiah (2 Kings 23.4–6) also destroy cult objects there. **15.17** _High places . . . out of Israel. Out of Israel_ is added by the Chronicler. _Israel_ is here a designation for the Northern Kingdom. **15.19** _No more war until the thirty-fifth year_ is in tension with 1 Kings 15.16, which describes continuous warfare between Asa and Baasha. _More_ is not in the Hebrew text. The Chronicler apparently does not consider the conflicts of 14.9–15; 15.8 to be full warfare. Some scholars believe that the _thirty-fifth year_ should be calculated as dating from the division of the United Monarchy. If so, the thirty-fifth year of v. 19 and the fifteenth year of v. 10 would be the same. **16.1–10** Cf. 1 Kings 15.17–22. **16.1** According to 1 Kings 16.6, 8 Baasha dies in Asa's twenty-sixth year.

anyone from going out or coming into the territory of[a] King Asa of Judah. 2Then Asa took silver and gold from the treasures of the house of the LORD and the king's house, and sent them to King Ben-hadad of Aram, who resided in Damascus, saying, 3"Let there be an alliance between me and you, like that between my father and your father; I am sending to you silver and gold; go, break your alliance with King Baasha of Israel, so that he may withdraw from me." 4Ben-hadad listened to King Asa, and sent the commanders of his armies against the cities of Israel. They conquered Ijon, Dan, Abel-maim, and all the store-cities of Naphtali. 5When Baasha heard of it, he stopped building Ramah, and let his work cease. 6Then King Asa brought all Judah, and they carried away the stones of Ramah and its timber, with which Baasha had been building, and with them he built up Geba and Mizpah.

7 At that time the seer Hanani came to King Asa of Judah, and said to him, "Because you relied on the king of Aram, and did not rely on the LORD your God, the army of the king of Aram has escaped you. 8Were not the Ethiopians[b] and the Libyans a huge army with exceedingly many chariots and cavalry? Yet because you relied on the LORD, he gave them into your hand. 9For the eyes of the LORD range throughout the entire earth, to strengthen those whose heart is true to him. You have done foolishly in

this; for from now on you will have wars." 10Then Asa was angry with the seer, and put him in the stocks, in prison, for he was in a rage with him because of this. And Asa inflicted cruelties on some of the people at the same time.

Asa's Disease and Death

11 The acts of Asa, from first to last, are written in the Book of the Kings of Judah and Israel. 12In the thirty-ninth year of his reign Asa was diseased in his feet, and his disease became severe; yet even in his disease he did not seek the LORD, but sought help from physicians. 13Then Asa slept with his ancestors, dying in the forty-first year of his reign. 14They buried him in the tomb that he had hewn out for himself in the city of David. They laid him on a bier that had been filled with various kinds of spices prepared by the perfumer's art; and they made a very great fire in his honor.

Jehoshaphat's Reign

17 His son Jehoshaphat succeeded him, and strengthened himself against Israel. 2He placed forces in all the fortified cities of Judah, and set garrisons in the land of Judah, and in the cities of Ephraim that his father Asa had taken. 3The LORD was with Je-

---

a Heb lacks *the territory of*   *b* Or *Nubians;* Heb *Cushites*

The date in this verse (the *thirty-sixth year* of Asa) may be calculated historically from the division of the monarchy, making it only the sixteenth year of Asa's reign. The Chronicler dates Baasha's attack to the thirty-sixth year of Asa, making the vast majority of his reign positive. *Baasha,* the third king of the Northern Kingdom. *Ramah,* a town five miles north of Jerusalem. Baasha is trying to prevent people from deserting to the South (cf. v. 9). **16.2** *Ben-hadad,* lit. "son of Hadad" in Hebrew, the name of two or more Aramean kings. *Aram,* the ancient name for Syria. **16.3** Asa bribes Ben-hadad to open a second, northern front against Baasha. **16.4** The three cities lay in the northernmost part of Naphtali. **16.6** When Baasha retreats from Ramah, Asa uses the materials left behind to fortify two neighboring cities. **16.7–10** This prophetic account is added by the Chronicler to express his own theological view of the faithless alliance with Ben-hadad. **16.7** *Hanani* later rebukes Jehoshaphat (19.2). Asa would have defeated Aram if he had remained faithful, and he is indicted for lack of faith as evidenced in his foreign alliance (cf. 14.11). **16.8** Asa's reliance on the Lord in the past led to the defeat of Zerah, the Ethiopians, and the Libyans (14.9–15). **16.9** A quotation from Zech 4.10. God will protect those who are loyal.

16.10 *Stocks.* Asa's treatment of Hanani resembles Pashhur's treatment of the prophet Jeremiah (Jer 20.2–3). *In prison,* not in the Hebrew text. Asa's anger over the prophetic oracle leads to violence against other people as well. **16.11–14** Cf. 1 Kings 15.23–24. **16.11** The Chronicler adds *and Israel* to his source reference, perhaps to indicate that Judah is part of the larger people of Israel. **16.12** A year after his treaty with Ben-hadad, Asa becomes sick with a foot disease, demonstrating the immediate effect of negative retribution (cf. 12.2; 24.23). Even then he does not demonstrate faith but seeks the help of (has faith in) doctors. **16.14** Chronicles adds additional details to the death and burial account of Asa (*spices, a very great fire in his honor*) that underscore the positive evaluation of his life. Through his first thirty-five years he won great victories and led the nation in reform; in his last six years he showed lack of faith and practiced cruelty.

17.1–19 The Chronicler's assessment of Jehoshaphat is positive in chs. 17 and 20, but the chapters in between criticize him for two foreign alliances. Only the first half verse in ch. 17 is dependent on 1 Kings (15.24b); the rest is from the Chronicler. **17.2** The king's military strength indicates divine favor. **17.3–4** *Earlier ways of his father,* the ways of Asa, who is de-

hoshaphat, because he walked in the earlier ways of his father;[a] he did not seek the Baals, [4]but sought the God of his father and walked in his commandments, and not according to the ways of Israel. [5]Therefore the LORD established the kingdom in his hand. All Judah brought tribute to Jehoshaphat, and he had great riches and honor. [6]His heart was courageous in the ways of the LORD; and furthermore he removed the high places and the sacred poles[b] from Judah.

7 In the third year of his reign he sent his officials, Ben-hail, Obadiah, Zechariah, Nethanel, and Micaiah, to teach in the cities of Judah. [8]With them were the Levites, Shemaiah, Nethaniah, Zebadiah, Asahel, Shemiramoth, Jehonathan, Adonijah, Tobijah, and Tob-adonijah; and with these Levites, the priests Elishama and Jehoram. [9]They taught in Judah, having the book of the law of the LORD with them; they went around through all the cities of Judah and taught among the people.

10 The fear of the LORD fell on all the kingdoms of the lands around Judah, and they did not make war against Jehoshaphat. [11]Some of the Philistines brought Jehoshaphat presents, and silver for tribute; and the Arabs also brought him seven thousand seven hundred rams and seven thousand seven hundred male goats. [12]Jehoshaphat grew steadily greater. He built fortresses and storage cities in Judah. [13]He carried out great works in the cities of Judah. He had soldiers, mighty warriors, in Jerusalem. [14]This was the muster of them by ancestral houses: Of Judah, the commanders of the thousands: Adnah the commander, with three hundred thousand mighty warriors, [15]and next to him Jehohanan the commander, with two hundred eighty thousand, [16]and next to him Amasiah son of Zichri, a volunteer for the service of the LORD, with two hundred thousand mighty warriors. [17]Of Benjamin: Eliada, a mighty warrior, with two hundred thousand armed with bow and shield, [18]and next to him Jehozabad with one hundred eighty thousand armed for war. [19]These were in the service of the king, besides those whom the king had placed in the fortified cities throughout all Judah.

Micaiah Predicts Failure

18 Now Jehoshaphat had great riches and honor; and he made a marriage alliance with Ahab. [2]After some years he went down to Ahab in Samaria. Ahab slaughtered an abundance of sheep and oxen for him and for the people who were with him, and in-

---

a Another reading is *his father David*   *b* Heb *Asherim*

---

scribed as faithful for his first thirty-five years. (The Hebrew text mistakenly identifies this ancestor with David.) Jehoshaphat did not *seek the Baals, but sought the God of his father.* Fidelity to God and his commandments is contrasted generically with the conduct of the Northern Kingdom (*the ways of Israel*). **17.5** Because of his faith and pious works, *tribute* and *honor* are paid to Jehoshaphat by the whole kingdom of Judah. **17.6** *High places.* Cf. 20.33. *Sacred poles,* dedicated to the goddess Asherah. Jehoshaphat is a reforming king as evidenced by his removal of the offensive items. **17.7** *Third year.* The Chronicler may have believed that Jehoshaphat was a coregent with Asa during his final two years of illness. Within a year after assuming sole power he sends out a sixteen-person teaching commission. **17.8** *Tob-adonijah,* possibly a mistaken duplication of the two previous names. The list of Levites probably antedates the Chronicler. Note the prominence of the laity and the listing of Levites before priests. It is not clear whether the mission of this group is related to the judicial reform in 19.4–11. **17.9** For the Chronicler, the *book of the law* is the Pentateuch. In Jehoshaphat's time, when the Pentateuch had not yet been completed, this book may have been some kind of royal law code. **17.10–11** *Fear* induced by God prevents surrounding nations from attacking Judah and causes *Philistines* and *Arabs* to pay lavish tribute. **17.13–19** While Jehoshaphat has troops throughout Judah (vv. 2, 19), he also has an extraordinarily large army in Jerusalem: 1,160,000. The size of this army serves to indicate Jehoshaphat's high standing before God. None of the five leaders is known from other sources. *A volunteer for the service of the LORD* (v. 16), an epithet of Amasiah that gives an air of verisimilitude to the whole list.

18.1–19.3 Cf. 1 Kings 22.1–40. This is the only time in Chronicles that a lengthy text from 1 or 2 Kings dealing with a Northern king is included. Chronicles omits the bloody details of Ahab's death (1 Kings 22.35–38) and Ahab's final regnal formula (1 Kings 22.39–40). The Chronicler makes significant changes at the beginning and end of this pericope; the rest is largely unchanged from 1 Kings 22. **18.1** *Now,* better "although." The information about Jehoshaphat's riches in 17.5 should have removed the need for an *alliance.* Jehoshaphat's son Jehoram marries Athaliah, the daughter of Ahab. **18.2** The context in Chronicles makes Jehoshaphat's trip to Samaria part of the marriage agreement, with Ahab preparing a banquet of sheep and cattle. Ahab plays the role of tempter: he *induced,* or "seduced," Jehoshaphat into going with him.

duced him to go up against Ramoth-gilead. 3 King Ahab of Israel said to King Jehoshaphat of Judah, "Will you go with me to Ramoth-gilead?" He answered him, "I am with you, my people are your people. We will be with you in the war."

4 But Jehoshaphat also said to the king of Israel, "Inquire first for the word of the LORD." 5 Then the king of Israel gathered the prophets together, four hundred of them, and said to them, "Shall we go to battle against Ramoth-gilead, or shall I refrain?" They said, "Go up; for God will give it into the hand of the king." 6 But Jehoshaphat said, "Is there no other prophet of the LORD here of whom we may inquire?" 7 The king of Israel said to Jehoshaphat, "There is still one other by whom we may inquire of the LORD, Micaiah son of Imlah; but I hate him, for he never prophesies anything favorable about me, but only disaster." Jehoshaphat said, "Let the king not say such a thing." 8 Then the king of Israel summoned an officer and said, "Bring quickly Micaiah son of Imlah." 9 Now the king of Israel and King Jehoshaphat of Judah were sitting on their thrones, arrayed in their robes; and they were sitting at the threshing floor at the entrance of the gate of Samaria; and all the prophets were prophesying before them. 10 Zedekiah son of Chenaanah made for himself horns of iron, and he said, "Thus says the LORD: With these you shall gore the Arameans until they are destroyed." 11 All the prophets were prophesying the same and saying, "Go up to Ramoth-gilead and triumph; the LORD will give it into the hand of the king."

12 The messenger who had gone to summon Micaiah said to him, "Look, the words of the prophets with one accord are favorable to the king; let your word be like the word of one of them, and speak favorably." 13 But Micaiah said, "As the LORD lives, whatever my God says, that I will speak."

14 When he had come to the king, the king said to him, "Micaiah, shall we go to Ramoth-gilead to battle, or shall I refrain?" He answered, "Go up and triumph; they will be given into your hand." 15 But the king said to him, "How many times must I make you swear to tell me nothing but the truth in the name of the LORD?" 16 Then Micaiah[a] said, "I saw all Israel scattered on the mountains, like sheep without a shepherd; and the LORD said, 'These have no master; let each one go home in peace.' " 17 The king of Israel said to Jehoshaphat, "Did I not tell you that he would not prophesy anything favorable about me, but only disaster?"

18 Then Micaiah[a] said, "Therefore hear the word of the LORD: I saw the LORD sitting on his throne, with all the host of heaven standing to the right and to the left of him. 19 And the LORD said, 'Who will entice King Ahab of Israel, so that he may go up and fall at Ramoth-gilead?' Then one said one thing, and another said another, 20 until a spirit came forward and stood before the LORD, saying, 'I will entice him.' The LORD asked him, 'How?' 21 He replied, 'I will go out and be a lying spirit in the mouth of all his prophets.' Then the LORD[a] said, 'You are to entice him, and you shall succeed; go out and do it.' 22 So you see, the LORD has put a lying spirit in the mouth of these your prophets; the LORD has decreed disaster for you."

23 Then Zedekiah son of Chenaanah came up to Micaiah, slapped him on the cheek, and said, "Which way did the spirit of the LORD pass from me to speak to you?" 24 Micaiah replied, "You will find out on that day when you go in to hide in an inner chamber." 25 The king of Israel then ordered, "Take Micaiah, and return him to Amon the governor of the city and to Joash the king's son; 26 and say, 'Thus says the king: Put this fellow in prison,

------

a Heb he

Ramoth-gilead, a city in the territory of Gad, some twenty-five miles east of the Jordan River. **18.4–11** The four hundred court prophets assure the two kings that God supports the upcoming battle. At Jehoshaphat's request, Ahab agrees to send for Micaiah son of Imlah, a prophet known for his unfavorable messages. A prophet named Zedekiah performs a symbolic act, in which he compares the army to a goring bull, to encourage the kings to attack the Arameans. **18.12–22** After an initial and presumably in-

sincere positive oracle, Micaiah says that Israel will in fact be scattered like sheep without a shepherd (v. 16). Micaiah reports his attendance at a meeting of the divine council, where a spirit offered to be a lying spirit in the mouth of all the prophets so that Ahab would go out and fall at Ramoth-gilead. With God's encouragement, this lying spirit induces all the court prophets to urge Ahab toward disaster. **18.23–27** After a confrontation with Zedekiah, Micaiah is imprisoned by Ahab until he returns safely from battle. Micaiah

and feed him on reduced rations of bread and water until I return in peace.' " 27Micaiah said, "If you return in peace, the LORD has not spoken by me." And he said, "Hear, you peoples, all of you!"

Defeat and Death of Ahab

28 So the king of Israel and King Jehoshaphat of Judah went up to Ramoth-gilead. 29The king of Israel said to Jehoshaphat, "I will disguise myself and go into battle, but you wear your robes." So the king of Israel disguised himself, and they went into battle. 30Now the king of Aram had commanded the captains of his chariots, "Fight with no one small or great, but only with the king of Israel." 31When the captains of the chariots saw Jehoshaphat, they said, "It is the king of Israel." So they turned to fight against him; and Jehoshaphat cried out, and the LORD helped him. God drew them away from him, 32for when the captains of the chariots saw that it was not the king of Israel, they turned back from pursuing him. 33But a certain man drew his bow and unknowingly struck the king of Israel between the scale armor and the breastplate; so he said to the driver of his chariot, "Turn around, and carry me out of the battle, for I am wounded." 34The battle grew hot that day, and the king of Israel propped himself up in his chariot facing the Arameans until evening; then at sunset he died.

19 King Jehoshaphat of Judah returned in safety to his house in Jerusalem. 2Jehu son of Hanani the seer went out to meet him and said to King Jehoshaphat, "Should you help the wicked and love those who hate the LORD? Because of this, wrath has gone out against you from the LORD. 3Nevertheless, some good is found in you, for you destroyed the sacred poles*a* out of the land, and have set your heart to seek God."

The Reforms of Jehoshaphat

4 Jehoshaphat resided at Jerusalem; then he went out again among the people, from Beer-sheba to the hill country of Ephraim, and brought them back to the LORD, the God of their ancestors. 5He appointed judges in the land in all the fortified cities of Judah, city by city, 6and said to the judges, "Consider what you are doing, for you judge not on behalf of human beings but on the LORD's behalf; he is with you in giving judgment. 7Now, let the fear of the LORD be upon you; take care what you do, for there is no perversion of justice with the LORD our God, or partiality, or taking of bribes."

8 Moreover in Jerusalem Jehoshaphat appointed certain Levites and priests and heads of families of Israel, to give judgment for the LORD and to decide disputed cases. They had

---

a Heb *Asheroth*

---

charges that Ahab's safe return would prove that the Lord has not sent Micaiah. **18.28–34** The Arameans at first mistake Jehoshaphat for Ahab, but the Lord deflects the pursuers; a chance shot later wounds the real king of Israel. At the end of the day he dies. **18.31** Although *and the LORD helped him* is not in the Hebrew text of Kings, these words are attested in one of the ancient Greek recensions of the Bible, the Lucianic recension, and were probably in the Hebrew text known by the Chronicler. They are not a theological addition by the Chronicler. *God drew them away from him.* In this addition by the Chronicler, *drew them away* uses the same Hebrew verb as *induce* (seduce) in v. 2. **19.1–3** An addition by the Chronicler. Having ignored the warning of the prophet Micaiah (18.27), Jehoshaphat is met by a prophet of his own kingdom, *Jehu, the son of Hanani* (who prophesies against Baasha in 1 Kings 16.1, 7). **19.2** *The wicked,* namely, Ahab. *Love,* a reference to Jehoshaphat's marriage alliance. The campaign of Jehoshaphat against Ramoth-gilead represents the kind of unholy alliance with the North that the Chronicler bitterly opposes. **19.3** Jehoshaphat's destruction of the sacred poles dedicated to the goddess Asherah

(17.6) and his seeking God mitigate the judgment against him. **19.4–11** This reform and the exemplary behavior of Jehoshaphat in a subsequent military crisis (ch, 20), both without parallel in Kings, illustrate the *good* found in Jehoshaphat (v. 3) that helps him escape divine wrath. **19.4** *Again* presupposes the earlier teaching mission in 17.7–9. **19.5** By *appointing judges,* delegating judicial authority to officials appointed by himself throughout the kingdom, Jehoshaphat extends his own jurisdiction and restricts the influence of the local courts. *Fortified cities.* In some respects the account in Chronicles seems to be typologically older than the laws in Deuteronomy. In Deut 16.18–20, the lawgiver says that judges are to be set up in all towns and not just in the fortified cities. **19.6–7** The Lord's own sense of integrity and justice is to give form to the behavior of the local judges (Deut 10.17–18; 16.19). **19.8** Jehoshaphat establishes a central court in Jerusalem to deal with cases referred to it from local courts. These cases could be resolved by the establishment of precedents or the formulation of new law. *They had their seat at Jerusalem.* This translation results from a changed vocalization of the Hebrew text:

their seat at Jerusalem. [9]He charged them: "This is how you shall act: in the fear of the LORD, in faithfulness, and with your whole heart; [10]whenever a case comes to you from your kindred who live in their cities, concerning bloodshed, law or commandment, statutes or ordinances, then you shall instruct them, so that they may not incur guilt before the LORD and wrath may not come on you and your kindred. Do so, and you will not incur guilt. [11]See, Amariah the chief priest is over you in all matters of the LORD; and Zebadiah son of Ishmael, the governor of the house of Judah, in all the king's matters; and the Levites will serve you as officers. Deal courageously, and may the LORD be with the good!"

Invasion from the East

20 After this the Moabites and Ammonites, and with them some of the Meunites,[a] came against Jehoshaphat for battle. [2]Messengers[b] came and told Jehoshaphat, "A great multitude is coming against you from Edom,[c] from beyond the sea; already they are at Hazazon-tamar" (that is, En-gedi). [3]Jehoshaphat was afraid; he set himself to seek the LORD, and proclaimed a fast throughout all Judah. [4]Judah assembled to seek help from the LORD; from all the towns of Judah they came to seek the LORD.

Jehoshaphat's Prayer and Victory

5 Jehoshaphat stood in the assembly of Judah and Jerusalem, in the house of the LORD, before the new court, [6]and said, "O LORD, God of our ancestors, are you not God in heaven? Do you not rule over all the kingdoms of the nations? In your hand are power and might, so that no one is able to withstand you. [7]Did you not, O our God, drive out the inhabitants of this land before your people Israel, and give it forever to the descendants of your friend Abraham? [8]They have lived in it, and in it have built you a sanctuary for your name, saying, [9]'If disaster comes upon us, the sword, judgment,[d] or pestilence, or famine, we will stand before this house, and before you, for your name is in this house, and cry to you in our distress, and you will hear and save.' [10]See now, the people of Ammon, Moab, and Mount Seir, whom you would not let Israel invade when they came from the land of Egypt, and whom they avoided and did not destroy— [11]they reward us by coming to drive us out of your possession that you have given us to inherit. [12]O our God, will you not execute judgment upon them? For we are powerless against this great multitude that is coming against us. We do not know what to do, but our eyes are on you."

13 Meanwhile all Judah stood before the LORD, with their little ones, their wives, and their children. [14]Then the spirit of the LORD came upon Jahaziel son of Zechariah, son of Benaiah, son of Jeiel, son of Mattaniah, a Levite of the sons of Asaph, in the middle of the assembly. [15]He said, "Listen, all Judah and inhabitants of Jerusalem, and King Jehoshaphat: Thus says the LORD to you: 'Do not fear or be dismayed at this great multitude; for the battle is not yours but God's. [16]Tomorrow go down against them; they will come up by the ascent

---

a Compare 26.7: Heb *Ammonites*   *b* Heb *They*   *c* One Ms: MT *Aram*   *d* Or *the sword of judgment*

"[To decide the disputed cases] of the inhabitants of Jerusalem" (Septuagint, Vulgate); "They returned to Jerusalem" (Hebrew). The NRSV's alternative seems the least likely of the three. **19.11** *Amariah,* probably the third high priest after Solomon built the temple (1 Chr 6.11). *Matters of the LORD,* sacral law; *the king's matters,* civil law. This differentiation of duties may not have arisen until the Persian period (beginning in 539 BCE).

20.1–30 The conduct of this war is mostly liturgical, and little can be established about the historical circumstances. **20.1** *Meunites,* a people named after the town of Maon, eight and a half miles south of Hebron. Later in the chapter the enemies are identified as Ammonites, Moabites, and the people of Mount Seir or Edom. **20.2** *Hazazon-tamar,* a town between En-gedi and Bethlehem. *En-gedi,* a site on the west shore of the Dead Sea. **20.3** Though terrified, Jehoshaphat does the right thing: he *seeks the LORD* and *proclaims a fast.* **20.6–12** A prayer of national lament by Jehoshaphat. **20.9** Jehoshaphat appeals to Solomon's prayer (6.28, 34) at the dedication of the temple and to the Lord's promise to answer it (7.12–14). **20.10** *Mount Seir,* not mentioned in v. 2, but see vv. 22–23. **20.11** Ammon, Moab, and Edom should be grateful for having been spared when Israel entered the land (Deut 2.1–22), but instead they now try to take the land away from Israel. **20.12** Perplexed by the invading horde, Jehoshaphat indicates his strong trust in God. **20.14** *Jahaziel,* a levitical singer (descendant of Asaph) who functions as a prophet and promises Israel a victory in holy war (cf. 1 Chr 25.1–8; 2 Chr 29.25; 35.15). **20.15–17** The speech of Jahaziel answers Jehoshaphat's lament and resembles the speech of a priest before a battle (Deut 20.2–4). **20.16** *Ascent of Ziz,* be-

of Ziz; you will find them at the end of the valley, before the wilderness of Jeruel. 17This battle is not for you to fight; take your position, stand still, and see the victory of the LORD on your behalf, O Judah and Jerusalem.' Do not fear or be dismayed; tomorrow go out against them, and the LORD will be with you."

18 Then Jehoshaphat bowed down with his face to the ground, and all Judah and the inhabitants of Jerusalem fell down before the LORD, worshiping the LORD. 19And the Levites, of the Kohathites and the Korahites, stood up to praise the LORD, the God of Israel, with a very loud voice.

20 They rose early in the morning and went out into the wilderness of Tekoa; and as they went out, Jehoshaphat stood and said, "Listen to me, O Judah and inhabitants of Jerusalem! Believe in the LORD your God and you will be established; believe his prophets." 21When he had taken counsel with the people, he appointed those who were to sing to the LORD and praise him in holy splendor, as they went before the army, saying,

"Give thanks to the LORD,
     for his steadfast love endures forever."
22As they began to sing and praise, the LORD set an ambush against the Ammonites, Moab, and Mount Seir, who had come against Judah, so that they were routed. 23For the Ammonites and Moab attacked the inhabitants of Mount Seir, destroying them utterly; and when they had made an end of the inhabitants of Seir, they all helped to destroy one another.

24 When Judah came to the watchtower of the wilderness, they looked toward the multitude; they were corpses lying on the ground; no one had escaped. 25When Jehoshaphat and his people came to take the booty from them,

they found livestock[a] in great numbers, goods, clothing, and precious things, which they took for themselves until they could carry no more. They spent three days taking the booty, because of its abundance. 26On the fourth day they assembled in the Valley of Beracah, for there they blessed the LORD; therefore that place has been called the Valley of Beracah[b] to this day. 27Then all the people of Judah and Jerusalem, with Jehoshaphat at their head, returned to Jerusalem with joy, for the LORD had enabled them to rejoice over their enemies. 28They came to Jerusalem, with harps and lyres and trumpets, to the house of the LORD. 29The fear of God came on all the kingdoms of the countries when they heard that the LORD had fought against the enemies of Israel. 30And the realm of Jehoshaphat was quiet, for his God gave him rest all around.

The End of Jehoshaphat's Reign

31 So Jehoshaphat reigned over Judah. He was thirty-five years old when he began to reign; he reigned twenty-five years in Jerusalem. His mother's name was Azubah daughter of Shilhi. 32He walked in the way of his father Asa and did not turn aside from it, doing what was right in the sight of the LORD. 33Yet the high places were not removed; the people had not yet set their hearts upon the God of their ancestors.

34 Now the rest of the acts of Jehoshaphat, from first to last, are written in the Annals of Jehu son of Hanani, which are recorded in the Book of the Kings of Israel.

35 After this King Jehoshaphat of Judah joined with King Ahaziah of Israel, who did wickedly. 36He joined him in building ships to

---

a Gk: Heb among them   b That is Blessing

---

tween Tekoa, a town in the highlands of Judah, and En-gedi (see note on 20.2). *Wilderness of Jeruel,* unidentified. **20.17** Despite the fact that Jehoshaphat has more than a million troops in Jerusalem alone (17.14–18), the people are reminded that they are not to fight, but to watch the victory of the Lord. **20.20** In his exhortation, Jehoshaphat seems to refer to Isaiah ("If you do not stand firm in faith, you shall not stand at all," Isa 7.9), to Jahaziel, who had just assured them of victory, and to Jahaziel's fellow Levites who are Kohathites, more specifically Korahites. It is probable that the temple singers of the Chronicler's day claimed prophetic authority. **20.21** The appointment of (prophetic) singers is the trigger that causes the Lord to set the invading nations against one another, leading to their total destruction. **20.25** The magnitude of the victory is

reflected in the overwhelming amount of booty taken. **20.26** The Hebrew for *blessed* has the same consonants as *Beracah.* This verse is an etymological etiology. **20.30** Jehoshaphat is rewarded with *rest.* **20.31–34** Cf. 1 Kings 22.41–45. **20.33** The Chronicler repeats the notice from 1 Kings 22.43 that the *high places* are not removed, but he omits a sentence from 1 Kings that says the people keep worshiping at those high places. In 17.6 the Chronicler states that Jehoshaphat has in fact removed the high places. **20.34** The source reference from 1 Kings is ascribed the prophetic authority of *Jehu son of Hanani.* **20.35–37** Cf. 1 Kings 22.48–49. According to 1 Kings, Jehoshaphat makes ships to go to Ophir, but they never sail since they are destroyed at Ezion-geber. When King Ahaziah subsequently requests Jehoshaphat to allow the servants of the Northern King-

go to Tarshish; they built the ships in Ezion-geber. 37Then Eliezer son of Dodavahu of Ma-reshah prophesied against Jehoshaphat, say-ing, "Because you have joined with Ahaziah, the LORD will destroy what you have made." And the ships were wrecked and were not able to go to Tarshish.

Jehoram's Reign

21 Jehoshaphat slept with his ancestors and was buried with his ancestors in the city of David; his son Jehoram succeeded him. 2He had brothers, the sons of Jehosha-phat: Azariah, Jehiel, Zechariah, Azariah, Mi-chael, and Shephatiah; all these were the sons of King Jehoshaphat of Judah.*a* 3Their father gave them many gifts, of silver, gold, and valu-able possessions, together with fortified cities in Judah; but he gave the kingdom to Jehoram, because he was the firstborn. 4When Jehoram had ascended the throne of his father and was established, he put all his brothers to the sword, and also some of the officials of Israel. 5Jehoram was thirty-two years old when he began to reign; he reigned eight years in Jeru-salem. 6He walked in the way of the kings of Israel, as the house of Ahab had done; for the daughter of Ahab was his wife. He did what was evil in the sight of the LORD. 7Yet the LORD would not destroy the house of David because of the covenant that he had made with David, and since he had promised to give a lamp to him and to his descendants forever.

Revolt of Edom

8 In his days Edom revolted against the rule of Judah and set up a king of their own. 9Then Jehoram crossed over with his commanders and all his chariots. He set out by night and at-tacked the Edomites, who had surrounded him and his chariot commanders. 10So Edom has been in revolt against the rule of Judah to this day. At that time Libnah also revolted against his rule, because he had forsaken the LORD, the God of his ancestors.

Elijah's Letter

11 Moreover he made high places in the hill country of Judah, and led the inhabitants of Jerusalem into unfaithfulness, and made Judah go astray. 12A letter came to him from the prophet Elijah, saying: "Thus says the LORD, the God of your father David: Because you have not walked in the ways of your father Jehoshaphat or in the ways of King Asa of Judah, 13but have walked in the way of the kings of Israel, and have led Judah and the in-habitants of Jerusalem into unfaithfulness, as the house of Ahab led Israel into unfaithful-ness, and because you also have killed your brothers, members of your father's house, who were better than yourself, 14see, the LORD will bring a great plague on your people, your children, your wives, and all your possessions,

---

a Gk Syr: Heb *Israel*

---

dom to go with him, Jehoshaphat refuses. In Chroni-cles, Jehoshaphat first makes a pact with the wicked Ahaziah, with the result that they join in building ships at Ezion-geber. The prophet Eliezer then intervenes and condemns Jehoshaphat for this alliance. As a result the Lord destroys the ships. **21.1–7** Cf. 1 Kings 22.50; 2 Kings 8.16–19. **21.2–4** These verses, which are not in Kings, indicate that the new king has six brothers. All the sons receive rich gifts from Jehoshaphat, but *Jehoram*, as the firstborn, becomes king after his father. By assigning them *forti-fied cities* the king scatters them throughout his realm. **21.2** *Judah.* The Hebrew reads *Israel.* The latter, as the more difficult reading, is preferred. **21.4** Solomon too eliminated rivals at the beginning of his reign (1 Kings 2). In view of the confusion in v. 2, *Israel* here may refer to the Southern Kingdom. **21.6** Jehoram's conduct is like that of the kings of the Northern Kingdom, particu-larly the dynasty of Ahab. Both Kings and Chronicles note that the reason for this misbehavior was that *the daughter of Ahab was his wife.* Later, she will be identi-fied as Athaliah. **21.7** Two things keep Jehoram and the

dynasty from destruction in spite of the negative qual-ities of the king: the *covenant* the Lord made with David and the *lamp* (better "dominion") the Lord promised him forever. The term *covenant* is added by Chronicles, and *the house of David* replaces "Judah" from 2 Kings 8.19. **21.8–10** Cf. 2 Kings 8.20–22. **21.8** *Edom*'s successful revolt continues with only mo-mentary exceptions until the end of the Southern Kingdom. David had conquered Edom, but it had re-belled already under Solomon (1 Kings 11.14–22). Per-haps Asa or Jehoshaphat regained control, but under Jehoram the breach becomes decisive. **21.10** *Libnah,* a city on the western, or Philistine, border of Judah. Since Edom was south to southeast from Judah, Jehoram is faced with conflict on two fronts. This revolt is God's retribution for the king's unfaithfulness. **21.11–20** The lengthy Elijah narrative from 1 Kings 17–19; 2 Kings 1–2 is omitted in Chronicles. **21.11** Jehoram restores the *high places* that Asa and Jehoshaphat had torn down. **21.12–15** Chronicles supplies a letter from the Northern prophet Elijah, Ahab's constant critic, in which Jehoram, Ahab's son-in-law and king in

[15]and you yourself will have a severe sickness with a disease of your bowels, until your bowels come out, day after day, because of the disease."

16 The LORD aroused against Jehoram the anger of the Philistines and of the Arabs who are near the Ethiopians.[a] [17]They came up against Judah, invaded it, and carried away all the possessions they found that belonged to the king's house, along with his sons and his wives, so that no son was left to him except Jehoahaz, his youngest son.

Disease and Death of Jehoram

18 After all this the LORD struck him in his bowels with an incurable disease. [19]In course of time, at the end of two years, his bowels came out because of the disease, and he died in great agony. His people made no fire in his honor, like the fires made for his ancestors. [20]He was thirty-two years old when he began to reign; he reigned eight years in Jerusalem. He departed with no one's regret. They buried him in the city of David, but not in the tombs of the kings.

Ahaziah's Reign

22 The inhabitants of Jerusalem made his youngest son Ahaziah king as his successor; for the troops who came with the Arabs to the camp had killed all the older sons. So Ahaziah son of Jehoram reigned as king of Judah. [2]Ahaziah was forty-two years old when he began to reign; he reigned one year in Jerusalem. His mother's name was Athaliah, a granddaughter of Omri. [3]He also walked in the ways of the house of Ahab, for his mother was his counselor in doing wickedly. [4]He did what was evil in the sight of the LORD, as the house of Ahab had done; for after the death of his father they were his counselors, to his ruin. [5]He even followed their advice, and went with Jehoram son of King Ahab of Israel to make war against King Hazael of Aram at Ramoth-gilead. The Arameans wounded Joram, [6]and he returned to be healed in Jezreel of the wounds that he had received at Ramah, when he fought King Hazael of Aram. And Ahaziah son of King Jehoram of Judah went down to see Joram son of Ahab in Jezreel, because he was sick.

7 But it was ordained by God that the downfall of Ahaziah should come about through his going to visit Joram. For when he came there he went out with Jehoram to meet Jehu son of Nimshi, whom the LORD had anointed to destroy the house of Ahab. [8]When Jehu was executing judgment on the house of Ahab, he met the officials of Judah and the sons of Ahaziah's brothers, who attended Ahaziah, and he killed them. [9]He searched for Ahaziah, who was captured while hiding in

a Or Nubians; Heb Cushites

Jerusalem, is charged with following the kings of the North (v. 11) and with killing his own brothers (v. 4). Elijah announces a plague for the people and a dreadful illness for the king himself. Illness also brings immediate retribution for Asa (16.12–14) and Uzziah (26.16–21). **21.16–17** God's agents of retribution are the Philistines and the Arabs, who deprive the king of wives and children, the normal signs of blessing. **21.18–19** The identity of the *disease* cannot be determined; colitis and dysentery have been suggested. *At the end of two years,* better "two days" (before his death). *Came out,* perhaps prolapsed. In contrast with Asa (16.14), there are no great ceremonial fires at his funeral. Jehoram is the first Davidic king whom the Chronicler judges in a totally negative way. **21.20** Cf. 2 Kings 8.23–24. Chronicles repeats chronological data from v. 5, but omits the source reference listed in 2 Kings 8.23. *Not in the tombs of the kings.* According to 2 Kings 8.24, Jehoram is buried in the tombs of his ancestors. Cf. 2 Chr. 24.25; 26.23.

22.1–9 Cf. 2 Kings 8.24b–10.14. Chronicles abbreviates the account from Kings and focuses on the Southern Kingdom. **22.1** Jehoram, who has killed all his brothers, loses his own *sons* to foreign troops because of divine retribution (cf. 21.16–17). Ahaziah cannot be *forty-two years old,* since his father is said to have died at forty (21.20). 2 Kings 8.26 sets his age at twenty-two. *Granddaughter,* in the Hebrew "daughter" (cf. 21.6). **22.3–4** *Athaliah* and other members of the Northern royal family mislead Ahaziah (cf. 21.6). **22.5** Ahab's son *Jehoram* (the brother of Athaliah) is wounded at Ramoth-gilead, a city of the tribe of Gad, on the border between Aram (Syria) and the Northern Kingdom, Israel. *Hazael* had murdered Ben-hadad and then succeeded him (2 Kings 8.15). **22.6** *Jezreel,* summer palace of the kings of Israel. **22.7a** The first half of v. 7, not taken from 2 Kings, articulates the Chronicler's doctrine of retribution. The Chronicler criticizes each of the Judean kings contemporary with Ahab and his successors for making alliances with their Northern counterparts. **22.7b** After a bloody coup, *Jehu son of Nimshi* rules Israel for twenty-eight years. The Chronicler omits the introduction to his reign from 2 Kings 9.1–20. *Anointed.* See 2 Kings 9.6, where a prophet sent by Elisha anoints Jehu. **22.8** According to 2 Kings 10.12–14, the princes of Judah are killed after the death of King Ahaziah. **22.9** In 2 Kings 9.27–28 Ahaziah is wounded near Ibleam, dies after

Samaria and was brought to Jehu, and put to death. They buried him, for they said, "He is the grandson of Jehoshaphat, who sought the LORD with all his heart." And the house of Ahaziah had no one able to rule the kingdom.

Athaliah Seizes the Throne

10 Now when Athaliah, Ahaziah's mother, saw that her son was dead, she set about to destroy all the royal family of the house of Judah. 11 But Jehoshabeath, the king's daughter, took Joash son of Ahaziah, and stole him away from among the king's children who were about to be killed; she put him and his nurse in a bedroom. Thus Jehoshabeath, daughter of King Jehoram and wife of the priest Jehoiada—because she was a sister of Ahaziah—hid him from Athaliah, so that she did not kill him; 12 he remained with them six years, hidden in the house of God, while Athaliah reigned over the land.

23 But in the seventh year Jehoiada took courage, and entered into a compact with the commanders of the hundreds, Azariah son of Jeroham, Ishmael son of Jehohanan, Azariah son of Obed, Maaseiah son of Adaiah, and Elishaphat son of Zichri. 2 They went around through Judah and gathered the Levites from all the towns of Judah, and the heads of families of Israel, and they came to Jerusalem. 3 Then the whole assembly made a covenant with the king in the house of God. Jehoiada[a] said to them, "Here is the king's son! Let him reign, as the LORD promised concerning the sons of David. 4 This is what you are to do: one-third of you, priests and Levites, who come on duty on the sabbath, shall be gatekeepers, 5 one-third shall be at the king's house, and one-third at the Gate of the Foundation; and all the people shall be in the courts of the house of the LORD. 6 Do not let anyone enter the house of the LORD except the priests and ministering Levites; they may enter, for they are holy, but all the other[b] people shall observe the instructions of the LORD. 7 The Levites shall surround the king, each with his weapons in his hand; and whoever enters the house shall be killed. Stay with the king in his comings and goings."

Joash Crowned King

8 The Levites and all Judah did according to all that the priest Jehoiada commanded; each brought his men, who were to come on duty on the sabbath, with those who were to go off duty on the sabbath; for the priest Jehoiada did not dismiss the divisions. 9 The priest Jehoiada delivered to the captains the spears and the large and small shields that had been King David's, which were in the house of God; 10 and he set all the people as a guard for the king, everyone with weapon in hand, from the south side of the house to the north side of the house, around the altar and the house. 11 Then he brought out the king's son, put the crown on him, and gave him the covenant;[c] they pro-

a Heb He b Heb lacks other c Or treaty, or testimony; Heb eduth

---

fleeing to Megiddo, and is buried in Jerusalem. Ahaziah's burial away from Jerusalem here may express the Chronicler's negative evaluation of him. *He is the grandson . . . kingdom* is not in 2 Kings. Because Ahaziah is the grandson of Jehoshaphat, it is not appropriate to leave him unburied. **22.10–12** Cf. 2 Kings 11.1–3. *Athaliah's* seizure of power here differs little from the account in 2 Kings. Note that *Jehoshabeath* (in Kings "Jehosheba") is the wife of the priest Jehoiada, who plays a prominent role in the revolution against Athaliah (v. 11). Jehoshabeath is the half sister of Ahaziah. Neither Kings nor Chronicles regards Athaliah as legitimate, so both omit the standard royal introductory and concluding notices.
23.1–7 Cf. 2 Kings 11.4–8. **23.1** *Compact,* in the Hebrew "covenant." Cf. vv. 3, 16. Chronicles adds the names of the commanders of the hundreds to materials inherited from 2 Kings. **23.2** Chronicles gives a role in the revolution to the Levites and the family heads of Israel instead of restricting the revolutionaries, with 2 Kings, to the captains of the hundreds, the Carites,

and the royal household. The clergy may have been unhappy with Athaliah's fostering of Baalism (v. 17). The participation of the family heads of Israel indicates that all Israel backs the revolution. **23.3** *The whole assembly* makes a covenant according to Chronicles; in 2 Kings the covenant was only with the military commanders. *King,* an addition, referring to Joash. Jehoiada, according to Chronicles, based the installation of Joash on the promise to David. **23.4–5** It is difficult to identify precisely which people are stationed where. Staging the revolution at the change of shifts is a brilliant strategy. **23.5** *Gate of the Foundation.* 2 Kings 11.6 reads "gate Sur." **23.6** The addition of the first half of this verse by the Chronicler makes it clear that laypeople do not intrude on forbidden areas of the temple. **23.7** *Levites.* The identity of the king's guards is not given in 2 Kings. **23.8–11** Cf. 2 Kings 11.9–12. **23.8** *The Levites and all Judah.* 2 Kings 11.9 reads "The captains." *Jehoiada did not dismiss the divisions.* Thus they stayed in the temple area to help with the revolution. **23.10** *All the people.* 2 Kings 11.11 reads

claimed him king, and Jehoiada and his sons anointed him; and they shouted, "Long live the king!"

Athaliah Murdered

12 When Athaliah heard the noise of the people running and praising the king, she went into the house of the LORD to the people; [13]and when she looked, there was the king standing by his pillar at the entrance, and the captains and the trumpeters beside the king, and all the people of the land rejoicing and blowing trumpets, and the singers with their musical instruments leading in the celebration. Athaliah tore her clothes, and cried, "Treason! Treason!" [14]Then the priest Jehoiada brought out the captains who were set over the army, saying to them, "Bring her out between the ranks; anyone who follows her is to be put to the sword." For the priest said, "Do not put her to death in the house of the LORD." [15]So they laid hands on her; she went into the entrance of the Horse Gate of the king's house, and there they put her to death.

16 Jehoiada made a covenant between himself and all the people and the king that they should be the LORD's people. [17]Then all the people went to the house of Baal, and tore it down; his altars and his images they broke in pieces, and they killed Mattan, the priest of Baal, in front of the altars. [18]Jehoiada assigned the care of the house of the LORD to the levitical priests whom David had organized to be in charge of the house of the LORD, to offer burnt offerings to the LORD, as it is written in the law of Moses, with rejoicing and with singing, according to the order of David. [19]He stationed the gatekeepers at the gates of the house of the LORD so that no one should enter who was in any way unclean. [20]And he took the captains, the nobles, the governors of the people, and all the people of the land, and they brought the king down from the house of the LORD, marching through the upper gate to the king's house. They set the king on the royal throne. [21]So all the people of the land rejoiced, and the city was quiet after Athaliah had been killed with the sword.

Joash Repairs the Temple

24 Joash was seven years old when he began to reign; he reigned forty years in Jerusalem; his mother's name was Zibiah of Beer-sheba. [2]Joash did what was right in the sight of the LORD all the days of the priest Jehoiada. [3]Jehoiada got two wives for him, and he became the father of sons and daughters.

4 Some time afterward Joash decided to restore the house of the LORD. [5]He assembled the priests and the Levites and said to them, "Go out to the cities of Judah and gather money from all Israel to repair the house of your God, year by year; and see that you act quickly." But the Levites did not act quickly. [6]So the king summoned Jehoiada the chief, and said to him, "Why have you not required the Levites to bring in from Judah and Jerusalem the tax levied by Moses, the servant of the LORD, on[a] the congregation of Israel for the tent of the covenant?"[b] [7]For the children of Athaliah, that

---

a Compare Vg: Heb and   b Or treaty, or testimony; Heb eduth

"the guards." **23.12–21** Cf. 2 Kings 11.13–20. **23.12** And praising the king, an addition in Chronicles. **23.13** And the singers . . . celebration, an addition in Chronicles, underlining the writer's interest in music. **23.14** Jehoiada's own son will later die in the temple (24.21). **23.15** Horse Gate. Ironically, Athaliah's mother, Jezebel, was trampled by horses (2 Kings 9.33). **23.16** Jehoiada, the people, and the king are the covenant partners; in 2 Kings 11.17 the covenant partners are the Lord, the king, and the people. **23.18** Chronicles specifies that the guards mentioned in 2 Kings were levitical priests organized by David. Cf. 1 Chr 15–16, 23–27; 2 Chr 29.25–30. The levitical priests offer the sacrifices required in the Pentateuch. **23.19** The Chronicler adds a reference to gatekeepers, who were to keep out all who were unclean. **23.20** Captains, nobles, governors, all the people, a list demonstrating the wide support for Joash. Upper gate. 2 Kings 11.19 reads "the gate of the guards." They set the king. In 2 Kings the king himself takes his

seat. **23.21** Quiet. Cf. 1 Chr 4.40; 22.9; 2 Chr 14.1, 6; 20.30. 2 Kings 11.20 notes that Athaliah was killed at the king's house.

24.1–14 Cf. 2 Kings 12.1–17. Although both Kings and Chronicles record the restoration of the temple, their accounts diverge from one another more widely than usual. **24.2** According to 2 Kings 12.2 Joash did what was right all his days, but Chronicles records a change in Joash's life after the death of Jehoiada. The notice in 2 Kings 12.3 that Joash did not remove the high places is omitted, since it would not conform to the Chronicler's depiction of the first part of Joash's reign. **24.3** Wives and children are signs of God's blessing for the pious Joash. **24.5** Joash requests that the priests and Levites raise a special collection, but the Levites react slowly, possibly because this collection would divert funds from their own income. The Levites play no role in 2 Kings 12. **24.6** Joash prods Jehoiada to get the Levites to collect the tax said to have been inau-

wicked woman, had broken into the house of God, and had even used all the dedicated things of the house of the LORD for the Baals.

8 So the king gave command, and they made a chest, and set it outside the gate of the house of the LORD. 9A proclamation was made throughout Judah and Jerusalem to bring in for the LORD the tax that Moses the servant of God laid on Israel in the wilderness. 10All the leaders and all the people rejoiced and brought their tax and dropped it into the chest until it was full. 11Whenever the chest was brought to the king's officers by the Levites, when they saw that there was a large amount of money in it, the king's secretary and the officer of the chief priest would come and empty the chest and take it and return it to its place. So they did day after day, and collected money in abundance. 12The king and Jehoiada gave it to those who had charge of the work of the house of the LORD, and they hired masons and carpenters to restore the house of the LORD, and also workers in iron and bronze to repair the house of the LORD. 13So those who were engaged in the work labored, and the repairing went forward at their hands, and they restored the house of God to its proper condition and strengthened it. 14When they had finished, they brought the rest of the money to the king and Jehoiada, and with it were made utensils for the house of the LORD, utensils for the service and for the burnt offerings, and ladles, and vessels of gold and silver. They offered burnt offerings in the house of the LORD regularly all the days of Jehoiada.

Apostasy of Joash

15 But Jehoiada grew old and full of days, and died; he was one hundred thirty years old at his death. 16And they buried him in the city of David among the kings, because he had done good in Israel, and for God and his house.

17 Now after the death of Jehoiada the officials of Judah came and did obeisance to the king; then the king listened to them. 18They abandoned the house of the LORD, the God of their ancestors, and served the sacred poles[a] and the idols. And wrath came upon Judah and Jerusalem for this guilt of theirs. 19Yet he sent prophets among them to bring them back to the LORD; they testified against them, but they would not listen.

20 Then the spirit of God took possession of[b] Zechariah son of the priest Jehoiada; he stood above the people and said to them, "Thus says God: Why do you transgress the commandments of the LORD, so that you cannot prosper? Because you have forsaken the LORD, he has also forsaken you." 21But they conspired against him, and by command of the king they stoned him to death in the court of the house of the LORD. 22King Joash did not remember the kindness that Jehoiada, Zechariah's father, had shown him, but killed his son. As he was dying, he said, "May the LORD see and avenge!"

Death of Joash

23 At the end of the year the army of Aram came up against Joash. They came to Judah and Jerusalem, and destroyed all the officials of the people from among them, and sent all the booty they took to the king of Damascus. 24Although the army of Aram had come with few men, the LORD delivered into their hand a very great army, because they had abandoned

---

a Heb Asherim   b Heb clothed itself with

---

gurated by Moses for the building of the tabernacle (Ex 30.12–16; 38.25–26). **24.7** Chronicles provides specifics on what was wrong with the temple; 2 Kings 12.6 speaks vaguely of the need for repairs. **24.8** Chest. A collection box was a common feature in ancient Near Eastern temples. Outside the gate reflects Second Temple practice, when laity had no access to the inner court. In 2 Kings 12.9 the chest is placed beside the altar. **24.10** The joyous generosity of the people repeats the joy of the wilderness community over the tabernacle (Ex 36.4–7) and provides an example for the Chronicler's audience (cf. 1 Chr 29.9). **24.14** Funds are used for various types of temple paraphernalia, as in the construction of the tabernacle (Ex 25; 31.1–10); in 2 Kings 12.13–14 this is explicitly prohibited. **24.15–22** The Chronicler adds a description of Joash's apostasy after the death of Jehoiada. **24.15** Jehoiada's extremely long

life testifies symbolically to his fidelity. **24.16** Jehoiada the priest is given a grave among the kings while Joash himself is not (v. 25). **24.17–19** Joash heeds the bad advice of officials who worship poles and idols dedicated to the goddess Asherah and refuses the admonition of prophets. Note the immediate retribution for their abandoning of the temple. **24.20** Jehoiada's son Zechariah threatens retribution in words reminiscent of Moses' (Num 14.41). **24.21** The officials and the king agree to the murder of Zechariah (cf. Mt 23.35; Lk 11.50–51) and kill him in the temple, where Jehoiada made Joash king and where efforts have been made by Jehoiada to avoid violence (cf. 23.14). **24.22** Zechariah calls for divine retribution. **24.23–27** Cf. 2 Kings 12.19–21. **24.23** An invasion by Aram (Syria) brings the divine retribution earned by the officials. According to 2 Kings 12.7–18 Joash bought off Hazael. **24.24** The small Ara-

the LORD, the God of their ancestors. Thus they executed judgment on Joash.

25 When they had withdrawn, leaving him severely wounded, his servants conspired against him because of the blood of the son[a] of the priest Jehoiada, and they killed him on his bed. So he died; and they buried him in the city of David, but they did not bury him in the tombs of the kings. 26 Those who conspired against him were Zabad son of Shimeath the Ammonite, and Jehozabad son of Shimrith the Moabite. 27 Accounts of his sons, and of the many oracles against him, and of the rebuilding[b] of the house of God are written in the Commentary on the Book of the Kings. And his son Amaziah succeeded him.

Reign of Amaziah

25 Amaziah was twenty-five years old when he began to reign, and he reigned twenty-nine years in Jerusalem. His mother's name was Jehoaddan of Jerusalem. 2 He did what was right in the sight of the LORD, yet not with a true heart. 3 As soon as the royal power was firmly in his hand he killed his servants who had murdered his father the king. 4 But he did not put their children to death, according to what is written in the law, in the book of Moses, where the LORD commanded, "The parents shall not be put to death for the children, or the children be put to death for the parents; but all shall be put to death for their own sins."

Slaughter of the Edomites

5 Amaziah assembled the people of Judah, and set them by ancestral houses under command-

ers of the thousands and of the hundreds for all Judah and Benjamin. He mustered those twenty years old and upward, and found that they were three hundred thousand picked troops fit for war, able to handle spear and shield. 6 He also hired one hundred thousand mighty warriors from Israel for one hundred talents of silver. 7 But a man of God came to him and said, "O king, do not let the army of Israel go with you, for the LORD is not with Israel—all these Ephraimites. 8 Rather, go by yourself and act; be strong in battle, or God will fling you down before the enemy; for God has power to help or to overthrow." 9 Amaziah said to the man of God, "But what shall we do about the hundred talents that I have given to the army of Israel?" The man of God answered, "The LORD is able to give you much more than this." 10 Then Amaziah discharged the army that had come to him from Ephraim, letting them go home again. But they became very angry with Judah, and returned home in fierce anger.

11 Amaziah took courage, and led out his people; he went to the Valley of Salt, and struck down ten thousand men of Seir. 12 The people of Judah captured another ten thousand alive, took them to the top of Sela, and threw them down from the top of Sela, so that all of them were dashed to pieces. 13 But the men of the army whom Amaziah sent back, not letting them go with him to battle, fell on the cities of Judah from Samaria to Beth-horon; they killed three thousand people in them, and took much booty.

---

a Gk Vg: Heb *sons*   *b* Heb *founding*

---

mean army was empowered by the Lord to defeat a far more numerous Judean army that had committed the fatal sin of abandoning God. Chronicles stresses elsewhere that a small Judean army could defeat a larger enemy army (2 Chr 13.3, 13–18; 14.9–13; 20.2, 20–23). **24.25** Joash's servants murder him because he has participated in the murder of Zechariah. 2 Kings provides no rationale for this murder. Joash is denied royal burial by the Chronicler in spite of evidence to the contrary in 2 Kings 12.21. **24.26** The chief conspirators are children of an *Ammonite* woman and a *Moabite* woman. Although the names of the conspirators come from 2 Kings 12.21, the ethnic designations come from the Chronicler. **24.27** *Commentary on the Book of the Kings.* Cf. 13.22.

25.1–4 Cf. 2 Kings 14.1–6. **25.2** As with Joash, the first half of Amaziah's reign is judged favorably. *With a true heart.* 2 Kings 14.3 reads "like his ancestor David." 2 Kings also indicates that Amaziah behaves like Joash

and that the high places are not removed (cf. 2 Chr 24.2; 26.4; 27.2). Amaziah's performance is half-hearted from the beginning. **25.4** Amaziah's reason for not killing the children of his father's murderers is based on Deut 24.16.

25.5–16 Cf. 2 Kings 14.7. **25.5** *Three hundred thousand.* Asa mustered 580,000 and Jehoshaphat 1,160,000. **25.6** *One hundred talents of silver,* roughly one ounce of silver for every man. **25.7–8** The oracle of the anonymous *man of God* is supplied by the Chronicler and shows his usual opposition to an alliance with the North (cf. 13.4–12; 19.1–13). **25.9** God's help would more than make up for the loss of one-fourth of Amaziah's army. **25.11** Based on 2 Kings 14.7. *Valley of Salt,* near the southern end of the Dead Sea (cf. 2 Sam 8.13; 1 Chr 18.12). *Seir,* a mountainous region southeast of Judah. **25.12** *Sela,* Hebrew, "rock, precipice." The exact location is contested. **25.13** *Samaria,* the capital of the Northern Kingdom. Another city may have originally been men-

14 Now after Amaziah came from the slaughter of the Edomites, he brought the gods of the people of Seir, set them up as his gods, and worshiped them, making offerings to them. 15 The LORD was angry with Amaziah and sent to him a prophet, who said to him, "Why have you resorted to a people's gods who could not deliver their own people from your hand?" 16 But as he was speaking the king*a* said to him, "Have we made you a royal counselor? Stop! Why should you be put to death?" So the prophet stopped, but said, "I know that God has determined to destroy you, because you have done this and have not listened to my advice."

Israel Defeats Judah

17 Then King Amaziah of Judah took counsel and sent to King Joash son of Jehoahaz son of Jehu of Israel, saying, "Come, let us look one another in the face." 18 King Joash of Israel sent word to King Amaziah of Judah, "A thornbush on Lebanon sent to a cedar on Lebanon, saying, 'Give your daughter to my son for a wife'; but a wild animal of Lebanon passed by and trampled down the thornbush. 19 You say, 'See, I have defeated Edom,' and your heart has lifted you up in boastfulness. Now stay at home; why should you provoke trouble so that you fall, you and Judah with you?"

20 But Amaziah would not listen—it was God's doing, in order to hand them over, because they had sought the gods of Edom. 21 So King Joash of Israel went up; he and King Amaziah of Judah faced one another in battle at Beth-shemesh, which belongs to Judah. 22 Judah was defeated by Israel; everyone fled home. 23 King Joash of Israel captured King Amaziah of Judah, son of Joash, son of Ahaziah, at Beth-shemesh; he brought him to Jerusalem, and broke down the wall of Jerusalem from the Ephraim Gate to the Corner Gate, a distance of four hundred cubits. 24 He seized all the gold and silver, and all the vessels that were found in the house of God, and Obed-edom with them; he seized also the treasuries of the king's house, also hostages; then he returned to Samaria.

Death of Amaziah

25 King Amaziah son of Joash of Judah, lived fifteen years after the death of King Joash son of Jehoahaz of Israel. 26 Now the rest of the deeds of Amaziah, from first to last, are they not written in the Book of the Kings of Judah and Israel? 27 From the time that Amaziah turned away from the LORD they made a conspiracy against him in Jerusalem, and he fled to Lachish. But they sent after him to Lachish, and killed him there. 28 They brought him back on horses; he was buried with his ancestors in the city of David.

Reign of Uzziah

26 Then all the people of Judah took Uzziah, who was sixteen years old, and made him king to succeed his father Amaziah. 2 He rebuilt Eloth and restored it to Judah,

---

a Heb *he*

---

tioned here. *Beth-horon,* a city in Ephraim near Benjamin. **25.14** In antiquity the gods of defeated nations were sometimes said to abandon their own nation and side with the victor. **25.15–16** Amaziah opposes a second, anonymous prophet, who repeats the inevitability of divine retribution. The king does not listen to divine counsel and follows human counsel (v. 17), to his own harm. **25.17–24** Cf. 2 Kings 14.8–16. **25.18** In this fable, the arrogance of the thistle in proposing a marriage alliance with a cedar is punished by a wild animal. **25.19** Joash castigates Amaziah for his arrogance after the defeat of Edom and warns him to avoid a military confrontation. **25.20** The Chronicler adds his theological interpretation. Amaziah's stubbornness is really God's doing (cf. 10.15; 22.7) to punish him for the idolatry of v. 14. **25.21** *Faced one another.* Note the pun with v. 17 (*look one another in the face*). *Beth-shemesh,* a town sixteen miles southwest of Jerusalem. **25.23** *Ephraim Gate,* in the northern wall of Jerusalem. *Corner Gate,* in the northwestern corner of the city.

25.24 *And Obed-edom with them,* better "in the care of Obed-edom"; this is only in Chronicles. David had put this levitical family in charge of the temple treasuries (1 Chr 13.13–14; 26.4–8, 15). **25.25–28** Cf. 2 Kings 14.17–20. **25.25** Despite his defeat by Joash, Amaziah outlives him by fifteen years. **25.27** *Turned away.* Cf. vv. 14, 20. *In Jerusalem.* The conspirators against Amaziah may be responding to the plundering of Jerusalem by Joash in vv. 23–24. *Lachish,* a city thirty miles southwest of Jerusalem fortified by Rehoboam (11.9). **25.28** *David,* following the Septuagint and 2 Kings 14.20; in the Hebrew "Judah." Jerusalem is called the "city of Judah" in the Babylonian Chronicle, a cuneiform historiographic source of the eighth century BCE.

26.1–15 Cf. 2 Kings 14.21–15.4. Vv. 5–15, which identify the signs of blessings in *Uzziah's* reign, are unique to Chronicles. In 2 Kings, which gives a brief account of his very long reign, he is usually called Azariah. **26.2** *Eloth,* alternate spelling for Elath, a port city

after the king slept with his ancestors. [3]Uzziah was sixteen years old when he began to reign, and he reigned fifty-two years in Jerusalem. His mother's name was Jecoliah of Jerusalem. [4]He did what was right in the sight of the LORD, just as his father Amaziah had done. [5]He set himself to seek God in the days of Zechariah, who instructed him in the fear of God; and as long as he sought the LORD, God made him prosper.

6 He went out and made war against the Philistines, and broke down the wall of Gath and the wall of Jabneh and the wall of Ashdod; he built cities in the territory of Ashdod and elsewhere among the Philistines. [7]God helped him against the Philistines, against the Arabs who lived in Gur-baal, and against the Meunites. [8]The Ammonites paid tribute to Uzziah, and his fame spread even to the border of Egypt, for he became very strong. [9]Moreover Uzziah built towers in Jerusalem at the Corner Gate, at the Valley Gate, and at the Angle, and fortified them. [10]He built towers in the wilderness and hewed out many cisterns, for he had large herds, both in the Shephelah and in the plain, and he had farmers and vinedressers in the hills and in the fertile lands, for he loved the soil. [11]Moreover Uzziah had an army of soldiers, fit for war, in divisions according to the numbers in the muster made by the secretary Jeiel and the officer Maaseiah, under the direction of Hananiah, one of the king's commanders. [12]The whole number of the heads of ancestral houses of mighty warriors was two thousand six hundred. [13]Under their command was an army of three hundred seven thousand five hundred, who could make war with mighty power, to help the king against the enemy. [14]Uzziah provided for all the army the shields, spears, helmets, coats of mail, bows, and stones for slinging. [15]In Jerusalem he set up machines, invented by skilled workers, on the towers and the corners for shooting arrows and large stones. And his fame spread far, for he was marvelously helped until he became strong.

Pride and Apostasy

16 But when he had become strong he grew proud, to his destruction. For he was false to the LORD his God, and entered the temple of the LORD to make offering on the altar of incense. [17]But the priest Azariah went in after him, with eighty priests of the LORD who were men of valor; [18]they withstood King Uzziah, and said to him, "It is not for you, Uzziah, to make offering to the LORD, but for the priests the descendants of Aaron, who are consecrated to make offering. Go out of the sanctuary; for you have done wrong, and it will bring you no honor from the LORD God." [19]Then Uzziah was angry. Now he had a censer in his hand to make offering, and when he became angry with the priests a leprous[a] disease broke out on his forehead, in the presence of the priests in the house of the LORD, by the altar of incense. [20]When the chief priest Azariah, and all the priests, looked at him, he was leprous[a] in his forehead. They hurried him out, and he himself hurried to get out, because the LORD had struck him. [21]King Uzziah was leprous[a] to the day of his death, and being leprous[a] lived in a separate house, for he was excluded from the house of the LORD. His son Jotham was in charge of the palace of the king, governing the people of the land.

22 Now the rest of the acts of Uzziah, from

a A term for several skin diseases; precise meaning uncertain

on the northeastern arm of the Red Sea that revolted during the reign of Jehoram (21.8–10). **26.4** The Chronicler qualifies his positive assessment of Uzziah in vv. 16–21. An early good period is followed by infidelity, just as with the reign of Amaziah. **26.5** *Zechariah,* an unknown adviser, during whose days the king's piety leads to success. Cf. Joash and Zechariah in ch. 24. *God made him prosper* refers to foreign relationships. **26.6** *Gath,* a Philistine city on the coastal plain. *Jabneh,* a city in northwest Judah identical to Jabneel and Jamnia; *Ashdod,* another Philistine city near the coast. **26.7** *Gur-baal.* Emend to "Gur and against." Gur is east of Beer-sheba. *Meunites,* see note on 20.1. Uzziah's expansion is all in a southerly direction; Jeroboam II is too strong in the North. **26.9–10** Royal building activities are a sign of blessing; numerous archaeological remains have been related to Uzziah. *Shephelah,* low hills in western Palestine. *Plain,* perhaps the plain of Sharon. *The hills,* the hill country of Judah. **26.11–13** Large armies are another sign of God's blessing (cf. 1 Chr 12.23–40; 2 Chr 12.3; 13.3, 17; 14.9; 17.12–19; 25.5–6). **26.15** *Machines,* not catapults, but defensive structures that protected the soldiers. **26.16–23** Cf. 2 Kings 15.5–7. Vv. 16–21 are found only in Chronicles. **26.16** *Grew proud.* Uzziah's sinful pride (cf. 12.1) leads to negative consequences in the second half of his reign. *Incense* offerings are to be conducted only by priests (Ex 30.1–10; Num 16.40; 18.1–7). **26.17** *Azariah,* an otherwise unknown priest. **26.20** Because of his illness, Uzziah serves in a coregency with his son Jotham. God effects immediate retribution. **26.22** *Isa-*

first to last, the prophet Isaiah son of Amoz wrote. 23Uzziah slept with his ancestors; they buried him near his ancestors in the burial field that belonged to the kings, for they said, "He is leprous."[a] His son Jotham succeeded him.

Reign of Jotham

27 Jotham was twenty-five years old when he began to reign; he reigned sixteen years in Jerusalem. His mother's name was Jerushah daughter of Zadok. 2He did what was right in the sight of the LORD just as his father Uzziah had done—only he did not invade the temple of the LORD. But the people still followed corrupt practices. 3He built the upper gate of the house of the LORD, and did extensive building on the wall of Ophel. 4Moreover he built cities in the hill country of Judah, and forts and towers on the wooded hills. 5He fought with the king of the Ammonites and prevailed against them. The Ammonites gave him that year one hundred talents of silver, ten thousand cors of wheat and ten thousand of barley. The Ammonites paid him the same amount in the second and the third years. 6So Jotham became strong because he ordered his ways before the LORD his God. 7Now the rest of the acts of Jotham, and all his wars and his ways, are written in the Book of the Kings of Israel and Judah. 8He was twenty-five years old when he began to reign; he reigned sixteen years in Jerusalem. 9Jotham

slept with his ancestors, and they buried him in the city of David; and his son Ahaz succeeded him.

Reign of Ahaz

28 Ahaz was twenty years old when he began to reign; he reigned sixteen years in Jerusalem. He did not do what was right in the sight of the LORD, as his ancestor David had done, 2but he walked in the ways of the kings of Israel. He even made cast images for the Baals; 3and he made offerings in the valley of the son of Hinnom, and made his sons pass through fire, according to the abominable practices of the nations whom the LORD drove out before the people of Israel. 4He sacrificed and made offerings on the high places, on the hills, and under every green tree.

Aram and Israel Defeat Judah

5 Therefore the LORD his God gave him into the hand of the king of Aram, who defeated him and took captive a great number of his people and brought them to Damascus. He was also given into the hand of the king of Israel, who defeated him with great slaughter. 6Pekah son of Remaliah killed one hundred twenty thousand in Judah in one day, all of them valiant warriors, because they had abandoned the LORD, the God of their ancestors. 7And Zichri, a mighty warrior of Ephraim, killed the king's son Maaseiah, Azrikam the

a A term for several skin diseases; precise meaning uncertain

---

iah. The account of Uzziah is traced to prophetic authorship (cf. 1 Chr 29.29; 2 Chr 9.29; 12.15; 32.32). The book of Isaiah refers to Uzziah in 1.1; 6.1; 7.1. 2 Kings 15.6 reads "Are they not written in the Book of the Annals of the Kings of Judah?" **26.23** His grave is near, but not in, the royal cemetery. A later, Hasmonean ossuary text reads: "Herein are the bones of Uzziah, king of Judah. Do not open." The separate burial of the king may have led to the discovery and reburial of his bones in the first century BCE.

27.1–9 Cf. 2 Kings 15.32–38. Unlike his three predecessors, Jotham is given a totally positive judgment. **27.2** Chronicles adds a note that Jotham *did not invade the temple* because of the tradition included in 26.16–20 concerning Uzziah's improper use of incense. *Corrupt practices*, a paraphrase of information in 2 Kings about making sacrifices and burning incense at the high places. **27.3** In Chronicles pious kings usually carry out building projects. *Ophel*, a ridge extending south of Jerusalem that was fortified by David. Jotham's work on the temple gate and on towers echoes the activities of Uzziah. **27.5** The tribute from the Ammonites demonstrates that divine favor rests with Jo-

tham. *One hundred talents*, 6,700 pounds. *Ten thousand cors*, somewhere between 65,000 and 140,000 bushels. **27.6** A clear statement of the doctrine of retribution. **27.7** Chronicles omits the reference to Rezin and Pekah during the reign of Jotham from 2 Kings 15.37 and associates their attack with the next king, Ahaz (28.5–8).

28.1–4 Cf. 2 Kings 16.1–4. Chronicles follows Kings closely in this sharply negative summary of Ahaz. **28.2** *Cast images for the Baals.* Ahaz commits the same sin as Jeroboam, first king of the Northern Kingdom (13.8). **28.3** *Valley of the son of Hinnom*, a wadi south of Jerusalem where child sacrifice was practiced (33.6; Jer 7.31–32). **28.5–7** Cf. 2 Kings 16.5. **28.5** The king of Aram (Syria) is identified in 2 Kings as Rezin. He was allied with Pekah of the Northern Kingdom against Judah in what is known as the Syro-Ephraimite war. Here the two enemies of Judah attack independently. According to Chronicles, the wicked king Ahaz suffers retribution through both opposing countries. **28.6** *One hundred twenty thousand.* The exaggerated number of casualties—and in one day!—shows the penalty for abandoning the Lord (cf. 13.9–12).

commander of the palace, and Elkanah the next in authority to the king.

Intervention of Oded

8 The people of Israel took captive two hundred thousand of their kin, women, sons, and daughters; they also took much booty from them and brought the booty to Samaria. 9But a prophet of the LORD was there, whose name was Oded; he went out to meet the army that came to Samaria, and said to them, "Because the LORD, the God of your ancestors, was angry with Judah, he gave them into your hand, but you have killed them in a rage that has reached up to heaven. 10Now you intend to subjugate the people of Judah and Jerusalem, male and female, as your slaves. But what have you except sins against the LORD your God? 11Now hear me, and send back the captives whom you have taken from your kindred, for the fierce wrath of the LORD is upon you." 12Moreover, certain chiefs of the Ephraimites, Azariah son of Johanan, Berechiah son of Meshillemoth, Jehizkiah son of Shallum, and Amasa son of Hadlai, stood up against those who were coming from the war, 13and said to them, "You shall not bring the captives in here, for you propose to bring on us guilt against the LORD in addition to our present sins and guilt. For our guilt is already great, and there is fierce wrath against Israel." 14So the warriors left the captives and the booty before the officials and all the assembly. 15Then those who were mentioned by name got up and took the captives, and with the booty they clothed all that were naked among them; they clothed them, gave them sandals, provided them with food and drink, and anointed them; and carrying all the feeble among them on donkeys, they brought them to their kindred at Jericho, the city of palm trees. Then they returned to Samaria.

Assyria Refuses to Help Judah

16 At that time King Ahaz sent to the king*a* of Assyria for help. 17For the Edomites had again invaded and defeated Judah, and carried away captives. 18And the Philistines had made raids on the cities in the Shephelah and the Negeb of Judah, and had taken Beth-shemesh, Aijalon, Gederoth, Soco with its villages, Timnah with its villages, and Gimzo with its villages; and they settled there. 19For the LORD brought Judah low because of King Ahaz of Israel, for he had behaved without restraint in Judah and had been faithless to the LORD. 20So King Tilgath-pilneser of Assyria came against him, and oppressed him instead of strengthening him. 21For Ahaz plundered the house of the LORD and the houses of the king and of the officials, and gave tribute to the king of Assyria; but it did not help him.

Apostasy and Death of Ahaz

22 In the time of his distress he became yet more faithless to the LORD—this same King

---

a Gk Syr Vg Compare 2 Kings 16.7: Heb *kings*

28.7 *Next in authority.* Cf. Esth 10.3. **28.8–15** The Chronicler inserts a sermon by a prophet and an admonition by Ephraimite chiefs that lead the Northern troops to change their mind. Certain details of this narrative may have influenced the account of the good Samaritan in the NT. **28.8** *Two hundred thousand* captives plus the fatalities in v. 6 would have depopulated Judah. **28.9–10** *Oded,* otherwise unknown. This prophet concedes the wickedness of Judah but accuses the Northern army of excesses (cf. Isa 10.5–19), the killing of some in anger and the enslaving of the rest (Lev 25.39–55). Note that *the LORD* (Yahweh) is still considered as the God of the North. **28.11** Citizens of the two kingdoms are *kindred* (lit. "brothers"). **28.12** The decisive action by *certain chiefs* may mean that the Northern monarchy is already a thing of the past. **28.13** The four chiefs also admonish the army not to add guilt from the present incident to their existing guilt (cf. 13.4–12). **28.14** Remarkably, the army repents. **28.15** Those *mentioned by name* in v. 12 (or "men nominated for this duty" as translated by the New English Bible) outfit the captives from the booty that had been taken and return them to Judean authorities at Jericho. **28.16–21** Cf. 2 Kings 16.6–9. In 2 Kings Ahaz appeals to the Assyrian king for relief from the Northern invaders. Since the Chronicler had already reported that the North had repented and restored its captives, he identifies the cause of Ahaz's plea as pressure from other neighboring countries, the Edomites and Philistines. This additional material is historically plausible. **28.16** Ahaz should have asked God rather than a foreign king for help (cf. 26.7, 15). **28.18** The *Philistines* capture a number of cities between themselves and Judah. *Gimzo,* a town north of Gezer. **28.19** The Philistine attack metes out appropriate retribution to Ahaz. **28.20** *Tilgath-pilneser,* spelled Tiglath-pileser [III] in 2 Kings 16.7 (but see 1 Chr 5.6). The Assyrian king attacks the South instead of coming to its aid. According to 2 Kings 16.9 the Assyrian king listens to Ahaz and provides him relief by attacking Damascus and killing Rezin. In 733 BCE Tiglath-pileser reorganized the Northern Kingdom into three Assyrian provinces. **28.21** In this added verse, Chronicles attributes Judah's defeat to the fact that Ahaz wrongly

Ahaz. 23For he sacrificed to the gods of Damascus, which had defeated him, and said, "Because the gods of the kings of Aram helped them, I will sacrifice to them so that they may help me." But they were the ruin of him, and of all Israel. 24Ahaz gathered together the utensils of the house of God, and cut in pieces the utensils of the house of God. He shut up the doors of the house of the LORD and made himself altars in every corner of Jerusalem. 25In every city of Judah he made high places to make offerings to other gods, provoking to anger the LORD, the God of his ancestors. 26Now the rest of his acts and all his ways, from first to last, are written in the Book of the Kings of Judah and Israel. 27Ahaz slept with his ancestors, and they buried him in the city, in Jerusalem; but they did not bring him into the tombs of the kings of Israel. His son Hezekiah succeeded him.

Reign of Hezekiah

29 Hezekiah began to reign when he was twenty-five years old; he reigned twenty-nine years in Jerusalem. His mother's name was Abijah daughter of Zechariah. 2He did what was right in the sight of the LORD, just as his ancestor David had done.

The Temple Cleansed

3 In the first year of his reign, in the first month, he opened the doors of the house of the LORD and repaired them. 4He brought in the priests and the Levites and assembled them in the square on the east. 5He said to them, "Listen to me, Levites! Sanctify yourselves, and sanctify the house of the LORD, the God of your ancestors, and carry out the filth from the holy place. 6For our ancestors have been unfaithful and have done what was evil in the sight of the LORD our God; they have forsaken him, and have turned away their faces from the dwelling of the LORD, and turned their backs. 7They also shut the doors of the vestibule and put out the lamps, and have not offered incense or made burnt offerings in the holy place to the God of Israel. 8Therefore the wrath of the LORD came upon Judah and Jerusalem, and he has made them an object of horror, of astonishment, and of hissing, as you see with your own eyes. 9Our fathers have fallen by the sword and our sons and our daughters and our wives are in captivity for this. 10Now it is in my heart to make a covenant with the LORD, the God of Israel, so that his fierce anger may turn away from us. 11My sons, do not now be negligent, for the LORD has chosen you to stand in his presence to minister to him, and to be his ministers and make offerings to him."

12 Then the Levites arose, Mahath son of Amasai, and Joel son of Azariah, of the sons of the Kohathites; and of the sons of Merari, Kish son of Abdi, and Azariah son of Jehallelel; and of the Gershonites, Joah son of Zimmah, and Eden son of Joah; 13and of the sons of Elizaphan, Shimri and Jeuel; and of the sons of Asaph, Zechariah and Mattaniah; 14and of the sons of Heman, Jehuel and Shimei; and of the sons of Jeduthun, Shemaiah and Uzziel. 15They gathered their brothers, sanctified themselves, and went in as the king had commanded, by the

---

paid tribute to the Assyrians. **28.22–27** Cf. 2 Kings 16.10–20. **28.23** Ahaz compounds his guilt by worshiping the Aramean gods. According to 2 Kings 16.10–13 Ahaz copied an Aramean altar and worshiped the Lord with it. **28.24** By closing the Jerusalem temple and thus distancing himself from it, Ahaz acts in a way similar to Jeroboam. In 2 Kings 16.12–14 Ahaz makes special offerings to the temple, but in 2 Kings 16.17–18 the king plunders the temple in order to pay tribute. **28.27** Like Uzziah, Ahaz is buried in Jerusalem, but not with the other kings (cf. 2 Kings 16.20; 2 Chr 21.20; 24.25; 26.23).

29.1–2 Cf. 2 Kings 18.1–3. The opening paragraph for *Hezekiah* is virtually identical to the material in 2 Kings, except that the Chronicler, as usual, omits the synchronism with the Northern king. The Chronicler gives great attention to Hezekiah's reform (chs. 29–31), but less attention than does 2 Kings to the Assyrian invasion (ch. 32), the delegation from Babylon

(32.31), and the king's illness (32.24–26). Unity returns to all Israel under Hezekiah, who is a second David (see 29.2) and especially a second Solomon. **29.3–19** Like Solomon, Hezekiah is concerned with the temple right from the start of his reign—*in the first year . . . in the first month* (cf. chs. 1–2). The actions urged by Hezekiah would reverse those of his father, Ahaz (28.24–25; 29.19). **29.5** *Levites,* used in a broad sense that includes both priests and Levites. **29.8** This description of circumstances at the time of Hezekiah quotes Jer 29.18, which announces the exile that took place more than a century after Hezekiah. **29.10** The temple cleansing renews the *covenant* and sets an example for the postexilic audience. **29.12–14** There are two Levites from each of the families of Kohath, Merari, and Gershon, two from the family of Elizaphan (descended from Kohath), and two from each division of the singers: Asaph, Heman, and Jeduthun. **29.15** *By the words of the LORD.* Hezekiah's reform is given di-

words of the LORD, to cleanse the house of the LORD. 16The priests went into the inner part of the house of the LORD to cleanse it, and they brought out all the unclean things that they found in the temple of the LORD into the court of the house of the LORD; and the Levites took them and carried them out to the Wadi Kidron. 17They began to sanctify on the first day of the first month, and on the eighth day of the month they came to the vestibule of the LORD; then for eight days they sanctified the house of the LORD, and on the sixteenth day of the first month they finished. 18Then they went inside to King Hezekiah and said, "We have cleansed all the house of the LORD, the altar of burnt offering and all its utensils, and the table for the rows of bread and all its utensils. 19All the utensils that King Ahaz repudiated during his reign when he was faithless, we have made ready and sanctified; see, they are in front of the altar of the LORD."

Temple Worship Restored

20 Then King Hezekiah rose early, assembled the officials of the city, and went up to the house of the LORD. 21They brought seven bulls, seven rams, seven lambs, and seven male goats for a sin offering for the kingdom and for the sanctuary and for Judah. He commanded the priests the descendants of Aaron to offer them on the altar of the LORD. 22So they slaughtered the bulls, and the priests received the blood and dashed it against the altar; they slaughtered the rams and their blood was dashed against the altar; they also slaughtered the lambs and their blood was dashed against the altar. 23Then the male goats for the sin offering were brought to the king and the assembly; they laid their hands on them, 24and the priests slaughtered them

and made a sin offering with their blood at the altar, to make atonement for all Israel. For the king commanded that the burnt offering and the sin offering should be made for all Israel.

25 He stationed the Levites in the house of the LORD with cymbals, harps, and lyres, according to the commandment of David and of Gad the king's seer and of the prophet Nathan, for the commandment was from the LORD through his prophets. 26The Levites stood with the instruments of David, and the priests with the trumpets. 27Then Hezekiah commanded that the burnt offering be offered on the altar. When the burnt offering began, the song to the LORD began also, and the trumpets, accompanied by the instruments of King David of Israel. 28The whole assembly worshiped, the singers sang, and the trumpeters sounded; all this continued until the burnt offering was finished. 29When the offering was finished, the king and all who were present with him bowed down and worshiped. 30King Hezekiah and the officials commanded the Levites to sing praises to the LORD with the words of David and of the seer Asaph. They sang praises with gladness, and they bowed down and worshiped.

31 Then Hezekiah said, "You have now consecrated yourselves to the LORD; come near, bring sacrifices and thank offerings to the house of the LORD." The assembly brought sacrifices and thank offerings; and all who were of a willing heart brought burnt offerings. 32The number of the burnt offerings that the assembly brought was seventy bulls, one hundred rams, and two hundred lambs; all these were for a burnt offering to the LORD. 33The consecrated offerings were six hundred bulls and three thousand sheep. 34But the priests were

---

vine sanction. **29.16–17** As prohibited items are removed from the temple, priests and Levites are active in places appropriate to them (cf. 5.4–11). *Kidron*, just east of the city, is also the place for destroying polluted vessels under Asa (15.16) and Josiah (2 Kings 23.4, 6, 12). The purification rites end two days after the normal beginning of Passover. **29.20–36** Temple worship is restored. **29.21** The *bulls, rams,* and *lambs* are for the burnt offering and the *goats* for the sin offering. The sin offering benefited the royal house (*kingdom*), the temple and its personnel (*sanctuary*), and the whole nation (*Judah*). **29.22** *They,* the king and his officials (cf. v. 20). **29.23** Through laying on of hands, the one making the offering identifies with the victim in the sin offering. **29.24** *All Israel.* The king's offering is ex-

plicitly inclusive (cf. v. 21). **29.25–30** The Levites accompany the sacrifices with music. Their role may reflect worship practices from the Chronicler's own time, but their musical performance also echoes their activity at the dedication of the temple (7.6). The restoration of the temple makes Hezekiah a second Solomon. **29.25** David and the prophets are credited with authorizing the levitical activity. **29.31–36** The people join their leaders in bringing sacrifices and so reinaugurate regular worship practices (v. 35; cf. 8.16). Their enthusiasm harks back to popular enthusiasm for the sanctuary at the time of Moses and during the reigns of David and Solomon. **29.32** *Burnt offerings,* expressions of self-giving. **29.33** *Consecrated offerings.* Only parts of these offerings are burned; the rest is

too few and could not skin all the burnt offerings, so, until other priests had sanctified themselves, their kindred, the Levites, helped them until the work was finished—for the Levites were more conscientious[a] than the priests in sanctifying themselves. 35Besides the great number of burnt offerings there was the fat of the offerings of well-being, and there were the drink offerings for the burnt offerings. Thus the service of the house of the LORD was restored. 36And Hezekiah and all the people rejoiced because of what God had done for the people; for the thing had come about suddenly.

The Great Passover

30 Hezekiah sent word to all Israel and Judah, and wrote letters also to Ephraim and Manasseh, that they should come to the house of the LORD at Jerusalem, to keep the passover to the LORD the God of Israel. 2For the king and his officials and all the assembly in Jerusalem had taken counsel to keep the passover in the second month 3(for they could not keep it at its proper time because the priests had not sanctified themselves in sufficient number, nor had the people assembled in Jerusalem). 4The plan seemed right to the king and all the assembly. 5So they decreed to make a proclamation throughout all Israel, from Beer-sheba to Dan, that the people should come and keep the passover to the LORD the God of Israel, at Jerusalem; for they had not kept it in great numbers as prescribed. 6So couriers went throughout all Israel and Judah with letters from the king and his officials, as the king had commanded, saying, "O people of Israel, return to the LORD, the God of Abraham, Isaac, and Israel, so that he may turn again to the remnant of you who have escaped from the hand of the kings of Assyria. 7Do not be like your ancestors and your kindred, who were faithless to the LORD God of their ancestors, so that he made them a desolation, as you see. 8Do not now be stiff-necked as your ancestors were, but yield yourselves to the LORD and come to his sanctuary, which he has sanctified forever, and serve the LORD your God, so that his fierce anger may turn away from you. 9For as you return to the LORD, your kindred and your children will find compassion with their captors, and return to this land. For the LORD your God is gracious and merciful, and will not turn away his face from you, if you return to him."

10 So the couriers went from city to city through the country of Ephraim and Manasseh, and as far as Zebulun; but they laughed them to scorn, and mocked them. 11Only a few from Asher, Manasseh, and Zebulun humbled themselves and came to Jerusalem. 12The hand of God was also on Judah to give them one heart to do what the king and the officials commanded by the word of the LORD.

13 Many people came together in Jerusalem to keep the festival of unleavened bread in the second month, a very large assembly. 14They set to work and removed the altars that were in Jerusalem, and all the altars for offering in-

_____
a Heb upright in heart

consumed by the ones making the offering. **29.34** Although the priests are not required by the law to skin the animals (Lev 1), this verse criticizes them for their delay and offers praise for the Levites who helped them until they had sanctified themselves. **29.36** _Suddenly._ The purification of the temple happens within three weeks during Hezekiah's first year.

30.1–27 In the Chronicler's reckoning, the North is already in exile when Hezekiah begins to rule. One of Hezekiah's first acts is to attempt to unite all Israel around the temple in Jerusalem. Such unification is the main agenda for the author of Chronicles in his postexilic setting. This Passover takes place at the central sanctuary (Deut 16; 2 Kings 23.21–23) and not in the Israelite homes (Ex 12.1–20). **30.2** _Second month._ Individuals who became unclean through contact with a corpse or who had been on a trip could delay the celebration of Passover one month (Num 9.9–11). Hezekiah extends this exception to the priests who had not sanctified themselves and the people who had not assembled (v. 3). **30.5** _Beer-sheba to Dan,_ the south-to-north description of the land characteristic of Chronicles (cf. 1 Chr 21.2). The author uses a wide variety of terms to identify the North. See vv. 11, 12, 18. **30.6** _Israel,_ Jacob (cf. 1 Chr 16.13, 17). The Chronicler demands repentance as the prerequisite for restoration. **30.9** An excellent statement of the doctrine of retribution. **30.10** The Northerners show reluctance (cf. 36.16), perhaps reflecting their attitude toward the Jerusalem temple in the Chronicler's time, but Hezekiah, nevertheless, works for their incorporation in the celebration (vv. 18–20). **30.13** The agricultural _festival of unleavened bread_ was originally celebrated separately from Passover (Ex 23.14–17; 34.18–23). The large attendance at the Passover is frequently mentioned in this account. **30.14** Eating of the Passover meal is preceded by reform of inappropriate installations in Jerusalem. Ahaz had built altars to alien deities

cense they took away and threw into the Wadi Kidron. [15]They slaughtered the passover lamb on the fourteenth day of the second month. The priests and the Levites were ashamed, and they sanctified themselves and brought burnt offerings into the house of the LORD. [16]They took their accustomed posts according to the law of Moses the man of God; the priests dashed the blood that they received[a] from the hands of the Levites. [17]For there were many in the assembly who had not sanctified themselves; therefore the Levites had to slaughter the passover lamb for everyone who was not clean, to make it holy to the LORD. [18]For a multitude of the people, many of them from Ephraim, Manasseh, Issachar, and Zebulun, had not cleansed themselves, yet they ate the passover otherwise than as prescribed. But Hezekiah prayed for them, saying, "The good LORD pardon all [19]who set their hearts to seek God, the LORD the God of their ancestors, even though not in accordance with the sanctuary's rules of cleanness." [20]The LORD heard Hezekiah, and healed the people. [21]The people of Israel who were present at Jerusalem kept the festival of unleavened bread seven days with great gladness; and the Levites and the priests praised the LORD day by day, accompanied by loud instruments for the LORD. [22]Hezekiah spoke encouragingly to all the Levites who showed good skill in the service of the LORD. So the people ate the food of the festival for seven days, sacrificing offerings of well-being and giving thanks to the LORD the God of their ancestors.

23 Then the whole assembly agreed together to keep the festival for another seven days; so they kept it for another seven days with gladness. [24]For King Hezekiah of Judah gave the assembly a thousand bulls and seven thousand sheep for offerings, and the officials gave the assembly a thousand bulls and ten thousand sheep. The priests sanctified themselves in great numbers. [25]The whole assembly of Judah, the priests and the Levites, and the whole assembly that came out of Israel, and the resident aliens who came out of the land of Israel, and the resident aliens who lived in Judah, rejoiced. [26]There was great joy in Jerusalem, for since the time of Solomon son of King David of Israel there had been nothing like this in Jerusalem. [27]Then the priests and the Levites stood up and blessed the people, and their voice was heard; their prayer came to his holy dwelling in heaven.

Pagan Shrines Destroyed

31 Now when all this was finished, all Israel who were present went out to the cities of Judah and broke down the pillars, hewed down the sacred poles,[b] and pulled down the high places and the altars throughout all Judah and Benjamin, and in Ephraim and Manasseh, until they had destroyed them all. Then all the people of Israel returned to their cities, all to their individual properties.

2 Hezekiah appointed the divisions of the priests and of the Levites, division by division, everyone according to his service, the priests and the Levites, for burnt offerings and offerings of well-being, to minister in the gates of the camp of the LORD and to give thanks and praise. [3]The contribution of the king from his own possessions was for the burnt offerings: the burnt offerings of morning and evening, and the burnt offerings for the sabbaths, the new

---

a Heb lacks *that they received* b Heb *Asherim*

(28.24). **30.16** Regulation of the cultic roles of priests and Levites is based on the Pentateuch in general. **30.17** The Levites make great efforts to make the Northerners feel welcome. **30.18–20** Hezekiah prays for the people who *set their hearts to seek God,* even if they have violated ritual regulations in the process. Their intentions and Hezekiah's prayer bring healing. The steps in this incident follow the procedures laid out in the Lord's response to Solomon's prayer at the dedication of the temple (7.14). **30.23** The people decide to celebrate for a second week, just as the celebration at the temple dedication lasted a fortnight (7.9). **30.24** The king and his officials generously provide animals for sacrifice, and the priests are finally ready in sufficient numbers to sacrifice them (cf. 29.34; 30.3). **30.25** Note the all-inclusive makeup of those who celebrate Passover. **30.26** Hezekiah is a kind of second *Solomon,* who unites the people in sacrificial worship. **30.27** Solomon too prayed that his prayer and that of the people would be heard in heaven (6.21).

31.1–10 Cf. 2 Kings 18.4–8. **31.1** The Passover results in wholesale reform, including areas of the Northern Kingdom. *Sacred poles,* named after or dedicated to the goddess Asherah. The destruction of the high places, pillars, and sacred poles is taken from Kings, but Chronicles omits the account of Nehushtan (2 Kings 18.4). **31.2** Hezekiah organizes the cultic personnel, as did Solomon (8.14). The priests sacrifice, and the Levites are gatekeepers and singers. *Camp of the LORD,* the temple (cf. 1 Chr 9.18). **31.3** Hezekiah provides animals for sacrifices, as had many kings before him. Persian kings do the same for postexilic

moons, and the appointed festivals, as it is written in the law of the LORD. [4]He commanded the people who lived in Jerusalem to give the portion due to the priests and the Levites, so that they might devote themselves to the law of the LORD. [5]As soon as the word spread, the people of Israel gave in abundance the first fruits of grain, wine, oil, honey, and of all the produce of the field; and they brought in abundantly the tithe of everything. [6]The people of Israel and Judah who lived in the cities of Judah also brought in the tithe of cattle and sheep, and the tithe of the dedicated things that had been consecrated to the LORD their God, and laid them in heaps. [7]In the third month they began to pile up the heaps, and finished them in the seventh month. [8]When Hezekiah and the officials came and saw the heaps, they blessed the LORD and his people Israel. [9]Hezekiah questioned the priests and the Levites about the heaps. [10]The chief priest Azariah, who was of the house of Zadok, answered him, "Since they began to bring the contributions into the house of the LORD, we have had enough to eat and have plenty to spare; for the LORD has blessed his people, so that we have this great supply left over."

Reorganization of Priests and Levites

11 Then Hezekiah commanded them to prepare store-chambers in the house of the LORD; and they prepared them. [12]Faithfully they brought in the contributions, the tithes and the dedicated things. The chief officer in charge of them was Conaniah the Levite, with his brother Shimei as second; [13]while Jehiel, Azaziah, Nahath, Asahel, Jerimoth, Jozabad, Eliel, Ismachiah, Mahath, and Benaiah were overseers assisting Conaniah and his brother Shimei, by the appointment of King Hezekiah

and of Azariah the chief officer of the house of God. [14]Kore son of Imnah the Levite, keeper of the east gate, was in charge of the freewill offerings to God, to apportion the contribution reserved for the LORD and the most holy offerings. [15]Eden, Miniamin, Jeshua, Shemaiah, Amariah, and Shecaniah were faithfully assisting him in the cities of the priests, to distribute the portions to their kindred, old and young alike, by divisions, [16]except those enrolled by genealogy, males from three years old and upwards, all who entered the house of the LORD as the duty of each day required, for their service according to their offices, by their divisions. [17]The enrollment of the priests was according to their ancestral houses; that of the Levites from twenty years old and upwards was according to their offices, by their divisions. [18]The priests were enrolled with all their little children, their wives, their sons, and their daughters, the whole multitude; for they were faithful in keeping themselves holy. [19]And for the descendants of Aaron, the priests, who were in the fields of common land belonging to their towns, town by town, the people designated by name were to distribute portions to every male among the priests and to everyone among the Levites who was enrolled.

20 Hezekiah did this throughout all Judah; he did what was good and right and faithful before the LORD his God. [21]And every work that he undertook in the service of the house of God, and in accordance with the law and the commandments, to seek his God, he did with all his heart; and he prospered.

Sennacherib's Invasion

32 After these things and these acts of faithfulness, King Sennacherib of As-

---

Judah (Ezra 6.9; 7.21–23). **31.4** The king restores the financial support system for the priests and Levites, which may have been disrupted by Ahaz. The dedication to the study of the law reflects the Chronicler's own time. Since Malachi complains that people are avoiding payments (Mal 3.8–10), the Chronicler may be dealing with a contemporary issue. **31.5** The people's generosity reflects that of the king. **31.7** The people contribute from the *third month* (Pentecost) through the *seventh month* (Tabernacles). **31.10** The chief priest affirms the doctrine of retribution: the people's generosity has led to general prosperity. The people had also contributed generously to the tabernacle (Ex 36.2–7) and to the temple (1 Chr 29.6–9). *Azariah,* perhaps the grandson of the priest mentioned in 26.17. **31.11–13** Two leading Levites and ten

assistants, appointed by Hezekiah, are in charge of the temple storage chambers, where contributions to the clergy are kept. **31.14** *Kore,* keeper of the east gate (1 Chr 9.11), and six assistants are in charge of distributing the contributions to the Levites' kindred living in outlying areas (1 Chr 6.54–60). **31.16** *Three years old and upwards,* after weaning (cf. v. 18). **31.17** The priests are enrolled by their families, the Levites according to their duties. *Twenty years old,* thirty in 1 Chr 23.3, twenty-five in Num 8.24. **31.19** *Fields of common land,* farmland belonging to the priestly cities. **31.20–21** After this summary paragraph, the Chronicler follows the text of 2 Kings more closely. *Prospered.* Cf. Solomon in 7.11.
32.1–19 Cf. 2 Kings 18.13–37. The material in Kings is often divided into three sources: 18.13–16

syria came and invaded Judah and encamped against the fortified cities, thinking to win them for himself. 2When Hezekiah saw that Sennacherib had come and intended to fight against Jerusalem, 3he planned with his officers and his warriors to stop the flow of the springs that were outside the city; and they helped him. 4A great many people were gathered, and they stopped all the springs and the wadi that flowed through the land, saying, "Why should the Assyrian kings come and find water in abundance?" 5Hezekiah*a* set to work resolutely and built up the entire wall that was broken down, and raised towers on it,*b* and outside it he built another wall; he also strengthened the Millo in the city of David, and made weapons and shields in abundance. 6He appointed combat commanders over the people, and gathered them together to him in the square at the gate of the city and spoke encouragingly to them, saying, 7"Be strong and of good courage. Do not be afraid or dismayed before the king of Assyria and all the horde that is with him; for there is one greater with us than with him. 8With him is an arm of flesh; but with us is the LORD our God, to help us and to fight our battles." The people were encouraged by the words of King Hezekiah of Judah.

9 After this, while King Sennacherib of Assyria was at Lachish with all his forces, he sent his servants to Jerusalem to King Hezekiah of Judah and to all the people of Judah that were in Jerusalem, saying, 10"Thus says King Sennacherib of Assyria: On what are you relying, that you undergo the siege of Jerusalem? 11Is not Hezekiah misleading you, handing you over to die by famine and by thirst, when he tells you, 'The LORD our God will save us from the hand of the king of Assyria'? 12Was it not this same Hezekiah who took away his high places and his altars and commanded Judah and Jerusalem, saying, 'Before one altar you shall worship, and upon it you shall make your offerings'? 13Do you not know what I and my ancestors have done to all the peoples of other lands? Were the gods of the nations of those lands at all able to save their lands out of my hand? 14Who among all the gods of those nations that my ancestors utterly destroyed was able to save his people from my hand, that your God should be able to save you from my hand? 15Now therefore do not let Hezekiah deceive you or mislead you in this fashion, and do not believe him, for no god of any nation or kingdom has been able to save his people from my hand or from the hand of my ancestors. How much less will your God save you out of my hand!"

16 His servants said still more against the Lord GOD and against his servant Hezekiah. 17He also wrote letters to throw contempt on the LORD the God of Israel and to speak against him, saying, "Just as the gods of the nations in other lands did not rescue their people from my hands, so the God of Hezekiah will not rescue his people from my hand." 18They shouted it with a loud voice in the language of Judah to the people of Jerusalem who were on the wall, to frighten and terrify them, in order that they might take the city. 19They spoke of the God of Jerusalem as if he were like the gods of the peoples of the earth, which are the work of human hands.

Sennacherib's Defeat and Death

20 Then King Hezekiah and the prophet Isaiah son of Amoz prayed because of this and cried

---

a Heb He   *b* Vg: Heb *and raised on the towers*

(A); 18.17–19.9a, 36–37 (B1); 19.9b–35 (B2), with B1 being parallel to B2. Chronicles omits references to the stripping of the temple, Hezekiah's trust in foreign alliances, and references to Isaiah as recipient of an oracle. In Chronicles Hezekiah is unafraid and directly receives divine messages. **32.1** *Acts of faithfulness,* Hezekiah's reform and Passover. *Sennacherib,* king of Assyria, whose third campaign took him to Judah in 701 BCE. **32.3–4** Hezekiah concealed the water supply and dug a famous tunnel, which can be visited in Jerusalem today. **32.5** *Built up . . . another wall.* Rebuilding the wall was a sign of rebellion against Sennacherib; in Chronicles building projects show that a king is divinely favored. *Millo.* See note on 1 Chr 11.8. **32.6–8** Hezekiah's speech urges trust in God and reflects standard holy-war theology. In 2 Kings 18.19–

25, Sennacherib's officer accuses Hezekiah of trusting in Egypt. **32.9** *Lachish.* See note on 25.27. **32.10–15** The message of Sennacherib is meant to terrify the people and to alienate them from Hezekiah. **32.12** The Assyrian misinterprets the reform of Hezekiah; he sees the destruction of high places and altars as a destruction of the Lord's own sanctuaries. **32.13–15** Since no god of any other nation has been able to stop Sennacherib, the Assyrian suggests that the Lord also could not provide help. **32.16** Cf. Ps 2.2: "[The nations speak] against the LORD and his anointed." **32.18** *The language of Judah,* Hebrew. The standard language of diplomacy was Aramaic. **32.19** In the Chronicler's view, all other gods but Yahweh are impotent idols. **32.20–23** Cf. 2 Kings 19.15, 35–37. **32.20** In 2 Kings 19.1–4; Isa 37.1–4, Hezekiah asks Isaiah to pray; in

to heaven. [21]And the LORD sent an angel who cut off all the mighty warriors and commanders and officers in the camp of the king of Assyria. So he returned in disgrace to his own land. When he came into the house of his god, some of his own sons struck him down there with the sword. [22]So the LORD saved Hezekiah and the inhabitants of Jerusalem from the hand of King Sennacherib of Assyria and from the hand of all his enemies; he gave them rest[a] on every side. [23]Many brought gifts to the LORD in Jerusalem and precious things to King Hezekiah of Judah, so that he was exalted in the sight of all nations from that time onward.

Hezekiah's Sickness

24 In those days Hezekiah became sick and was at the point of death. He prayed to the LORD, and he answered him and gave him a sign. [25]But Hezekiah did not respond according to the benefit done to him, for his heart was proud. Therefore wrath came upon him and upon Judah and Jerusalem. [26]Then Hezekiah humbled himself for the pride of his heart, both he and the inhabitants of Jerusalem, so that the wrath of the LORD did not come upon them in the days of Hezekiah.

Hezekiah's Prosperity and Achievements

27 Hezekiah had very great riches and honor; and he made for himself treasuries for silver, for gold, for precious stones, for spices, for shields, and for all kinds of costly objects; [28]storehouses also for the yield of grain, wine, and oil; and stalls for all kinds of cattle, and sheepfolds.[b] [29]He likewise provided cities for himself, and flocks and herds in abundance; for God had given him very great possessions. [30]This same Hezekiah closed the upper outlet of the waters of Gihon and directed them down to the west side of the city of David. Hezekiah prospered in all his works. [31]So also in the matter of the envoys of the officials of Babylon, who had been sent to him to inquire about the sign that had been done in the land, God left him to himself, in order to test him and to know all that was in his heart.

32 Now the rest of the acts of Hezekiah, and his good deeds, are written in the vision of the prophet Isaiah son of Amoz in the Book of the Kings of Judah and Israel. [33]Hezekiah slept with his ancestors, and they buried him on the ascent to the tombs of the descendants of David; and all Judah and the inhabitants of Jerusalem did him honor at his death. His son Manasseh succeeded him.

Reign of Manasseh

33 Manasseh was twelve years old when he began to reign; he reigned fifty-five years in Jerusalem. [2]He did what was evil in the sight of the LORD, according to the abominable practices of the nations whom the LORD drove out before the people of Israel. [3]For he rebuilt the high places that his father Hezekiah had pulled down, and erected altars to the Baals, made sacred poles,[c] worshiped all the host of

---

a Gk Vg: Heb *guided them*   b Gk Vg: Heb *flocks for folds*
c Heb *Asheroth*

Chronicles they pray together. **32.21** The Lord answers Hezekiah's prayer (cf. 7.13–15) by completely destroying Sennacherib's army. Sennacherib was in fact killed by his son some twenty years later. **32.22** *Rest.* Cf. 14.1. **32.23** The acclaim of the nations demonstrates how favored Hezekiah is in God's eyes. **32.24–26** Cf. 2 Kings 20.1–11 (Isa 38.1–22). In this abbreviated account, Hezekiah is healed in answer to prayer (cf. 7.14). His subsequent pride leads to divine wrath. When he and the citizens of Jerusalem humble themselves (cf. 7.14; 12.1–12; 30.11), the effects of the divine anger are delayed to a later reign. **32.24** *Sign.* Cf. 2 Kings 20.8–11, where the shadow retreats ten intervals. **32.27–33** Cf. 2 Kings 20.12, 20–21. **32.27–30** These verses are added by the Chronicler. Hezekiah's wealth and building projects demonstrate that divine favor is upon him. **32.31** The incident with the Babylonian envoys is interpreted merely as a divine test. In 2 Kings 20.12–19 Hezekiah proudly shows the envoys all his treasures and receives from Isaiah a stern rebuke. *Sign . . . in the land.* Cf. v. 24. **32.32** The source from which Chronicles draws is given prophetic authority (cf. 1 Chr 29.29; 2 Chr 9.29). **32.33a** The location of Hezekiah's grave, added by the Chronicler, gives him special honor.

33.1–9 Cf. 2 Kings 21.1–9. Although *Manasseh* is as wicked in Chronicles as in Kings, Chronicles reports that toward the end of his life Manasseh repents and becomes a religious reformer. **33.1** Beginning with Manasseh and continuing until the end of the monarchy, Chronicles omits the name of the queen mother. *Fifty-five.* In view of his extensive wickedness, Manasseh's long reign seems to contradict the doctrine of retribution. **33.2** In Kings this verse suggests that exile for the nation is inevitable; in Chronicles it leads to the exile of the king himself. **33.3** *Sacred poles,* dedicated to the goddess Asherah. Chronicles omits the comparison with Ahab found in 2 Kings 21.3. In Chronicles Ahaz, not Manasseh, is the most wicked of the Judean kings. *Host of heaven,* probably an old Canaanite cult

heaven, and served them. [4] He built altars in the house of the LORD, of which the LORD had said, "In Jerusalem shall my name be forever." [5] He built altars for all the host of heaven in the two courts of the house of the LORD. [6] He made his son pass through fire in the valley of the son of Hinnom, practiced soothsaying and augury and sorcery, and dealt with mediums and with wizards. He did much evil in the sight of the LORD, provoking him to anger. [7] The carved image of the idol that he had made he set in the house of God, of which God said to David and to his son Solomon, "In this house, and in Jerusalem, which I have chosen out of all the tribes of Israel, I will put my name forever; [8] I will never again remove the feet of Israel from the land that I appointed for your ancestors, if only they will be careful to do all that I have commanded them, all the law, the statutes, and the ordinances given through Moses." [9] Manasseh misled Judah and the inhabitants of Jerusalem, so that they did more evil than the nations whom the LORD had destroyed before the people of Israel.

Manasseh Restored after Repentance

[10] The LORD spoke to Manasseh and to his people, but they gave no heed. [11] Therefore the LORD brought against them the commanders of the army of the king of Assyria, who took Manasseh captive in manacles, bound him with fetters, and brought him to Babylon. [12] While he was in distress he entreated the favor of the LORD his God and humbled himself greatly before the God of his ancestors. [13] He prayed to him, and God received his entreaty, heard his plea, and restored him again to Jerusalem and to his king-

dom. Then Manasseh knew that the LORD indeed was God.

14 Afterward he built an outer wall for the city of David west of Gihon, in the valley, reaching the entrance at the Fish Gate; he carried it around Ophel, and raised it to a very great height. He also put commanders of the army in all the fortified cities in Judah. [15] He took away the foreign gods and the idol from the house of the LORD, and all the altars that he had built on the mountain of the house of the LORD and in Jerusalem, and he threw them out of the city. [16] He also restored the altar of the LORD and offered on it sacrifices of well-being and of thanksgiving; and he commanded Judah to serve the LORD the God of Israel. [17] The people, however, still sacrificed at the high places, but only to the LORD their God.

Death of Manasseh

18 Now the rest of the acts of Manasseh, his prayer to his God, and the words of the seers who spoke to him in the name of the LORD God of Israel, these are in the Annals of the Kings of Israel. [19] His prayer, and how God received his entreaty, all his sin and his faithlessness, the sites on which he built high places and set up the sacred poles [a] and the images, before he humbled himself, these are written in the records of the seers. [b] [20] So Manasseh slept with his ancestors, and they buried him in his house. His son Amon succeeded him.

Amon's Reign and Death

21 Amon was twenty-two years old when he began to reign; he reigned two years in Jerusa-

---

a Heb *Asherim*   *b* One Ms Gk: MT *of Hozai*

and not Assyrian astral worship. **33.6** Manasseh practices child sacrifice in a valley south of Jerusalem (*the valley of the son of Hinnom*) that later became known as Gehenna, a name for hell or everlasting damnation (Mt 5.22, 29–30). On *soothsaying* and similar activities, see Deut 18.9–13. **33.10–17** Cf. 2 Kings 21.10. Kings and Chronicles diverge after v. 10. In Kings, Manasseh's wickedness is the culmination of Southern apostasy and necessitates the nation's exile despite the goodness of Josiah (2 Kings 21.11–16). In Chronicles, retribution happens in one's own generation. **33.11** The exile of Manasseh to Babylon requites him for his misdeeds but is not reported in Kings. Assyrian documents refer to Manasseh as a loyal vassal. It is not clear why the exile took place in Babylon rather than in Assyria. **33.12–14** In captivity Manasseh repents and prays, and the Lord hears his prayer (cf. 7.14) and re-

stores him to Jerusalem, thus confirming the doctrine of retribution. A prayer attributed to Manasseh is contained in the Apocrypha. **33.14** Building projects and powerful armies are signs of Manasseh's forgiven and favored status. *Ophel*. See note on 27.3. **33.15** According to 2 Kings 23.14 Josiah still has to remove *altars* erected by Manasseh from the temple. **33.17** The Chronicler concedes that the reform is not completely successful. **33.18–20** Cf. 2 Kings 21.17–18. **33.18** *Seers*. Cf. v. 10. **33.19** *Records of the seers*. Again the Chronicler's sources are ascribed prophetic authority. **33.20a** Chronicles omits from 2 Kings 21.18 a reference to "the garden of Uzza" (cf. 2 Kings 21.26, according to which Amon is also buried in this garden). Since Uzza was an Arabian astral god, this notice would not conform to the Chronicler's idea of a repentant Manasseh. **33.21–25** Cf. 2 Kings 21.19–26. **33.23** This

lem. 22He did what was evil in the sight of the LORD, as his father Manasseh had done. Amon sacrificed to all the images that his father Manasseh had made, and served them. 23He did not humble himself before the LORD, as his father Manasseh had humbled himself, but this Amon incurred more and more guilt. 24His servants conspired against him and killed him in his house. 25But the people of the land killed all those who had conspired against King Amon; and the people of the land made his son Josiah king to succeed him.

Reign of Josiah

34 Josiah was eight years old when he began to reign; he reigned thirty-one years in Jerusalem. 2He did what was right in the sight of the LORD, and walked in the ways of his ancestor David; he did not turn aside to the right or to the left. 3For in the eighth year of his reign, while he was still a boy, he began to seek the God of his ancestor David, and in the twelfth year he began to purge Judah and Jerusalem of the high places, the sacred poles,[a] and the carved and the cast images. 4In his presence they pulled down the altars of the Baals; he demolished the incense altars that stood above them. He broke down the sacred poles[a] and the carved and the cast images; he made dust of them and scattered it over the graves of those who had sacrificed to them. 5He also burned the bones of the priests on their altars, and purged Judah and Jerusalem. 6In the towns of Manasseh, Ephraim, and Simeon, and as far as Naphtali, in their ruins[b] all around, 7he broke down the altars, beat the sacred poles[a] and the images into powder, and demolished all the incense altars throughout all the land of Israel. Then he returned to Jerusalem.

Discovery of the Book of the Law

8 In the eighteenth year of his reign, when he had purged the land and the house, he sent Shaphan son of Azaliah, Maaseiah the governor of the city, and Joah son of Joahaz, the recorder, to repair the house of the LORD his God. 9They came to the high priest Hilkiah and delivered the money that had been brought into the house of God, which the Levites, the keepers of the threshold, had collected from Manasseh and Ephraim and from all the remnant of Israel and from all Judah and Benjamin and from the inhabitants of Jerusalem. 10They delivered it to the workers who had the oversight of the house of the LORD, and the workers who were working in the house of the LORD gave it for repairing and restoring the house. 11They gave it to the carpenters and the builders to buy quarried stone, and timber for binders, and beams for the buildings that the kings of Judah had let go to ruin. 12The people did the work faithfully. Over them were appointed the Levites Jahath and Obadiah, of the sons of Merari, along with Zechariah and Meshullam, of the sons of the Kohathites, to have oversight. Other Levites, all skillful with instruments of music, 13were over the burden bearers and directed all who did work in every kind of service; and some of the Levites were scribes, and officials, and gatekeepers.

14 While they were bringing out the money that had been brought into the house of the

---

a Heb Asherim b Meaning of Heb uncertain

---

verse adjusts the summary of Amon's reign to fit the Chronicler's version of Manasseh's reign. **33.25** *The people of the land*, variously identified as free landowners, citizens, the population of provincial towns, a proletariat of common people, or a national council of elders. **34.1–7** Cf. 2 Kings 22.1–2; 23.4–20. **34.2** Josiah is the best of all Judean kings in following the example of David, although in Chronicles many of his activities merely repeat those of Hezekiah, who is identified as the real innovator. **34.3** According to Chronicles Josiah begins seeking God at the age of sixteen and his reforming activities at twenty. Note the similar early activities of Hezekiah (29.3). Kings places his main reform in his eighteenth year, after the discovery of the law book, when he was twenty-six. A careful reading of Kings, however, shows that reforming activities (e.g., the temple repair) begin earlier. The few parallels with 2 Kings in vv. 3–7 deal with Josiah's reforms in his eighteenth year. Chronicles antedates the purification of the temple to the reign of Manasseh (33.15–16). **34.4–5** The text implies that Josiah kills the priests of Baal (cf. 2 Kings 10; 23.17). **34.6** Because Assyria's power is rapidly deteriorating, Josiah's reform, as in Kings, extends into the Northern Kingdom. Josiah's territory in Chronicles nearly equals that of David and Solomon—from *Simeon* to *Naphtali*. **34.8–21** Cf. 2 Kings 22.3–13. **34.8** *Maaseiah, Joah*, names added by the Chronicler, or accidentally lost from 2 Kings. **34.9** The Chronicler identifies the *Levites* as the collectors of the temple contribution and includes both Northern and Southern tribes among the contributors. **34.11** *Kings of Judah*, perhaps Ahaz, Manasseh, and Amon. **34.12–13** The Chronicler places *Levites*, including the levitical

LORD, the priest Hilkiah found the book of the law of the LORD given through Moses. 15Hilkiah said to the secretary Shaphan, "I have found the book of the law in the house of the LORD"; and Hilkiah gave the book to Shaphan. 16Shaphan brought the book to the king, and further reported to the king, "All that was committed to your servants they are doing. 17They have emptied out the money that was found in the house of the LORD and have delivered it into the hand of the overseers and the workers." 18The secretary Shaphan informed the king, "The priest Hilkiah has given me a book." Shaphan then read it aloud to the king.

19 When the king heard the words of the law he tore his clothes. 20Then the king commanded Hilkiah, Ahikam son of Shaphan, Abdon son of Micah, the secretary Shaphan, and the king's servant Asaiah: 21"Go, inquire of the LORD for me and for those who are left in Israel and in Judah, concerning the words of the book that has been found; for the wrath of the LORD that is poured out on us is great, because our ancestors did not keep the word of the LORD, to act in accordance with all that is written in this book."

The Prophet Huldah Consulted

22 So Hilkiah and those whom the king had sent went to the prophet Huldah, the wife of Shallum son of Tokhath son of Hasrah, keeper of the wardrobe (who lived in Jerusalem in the Second Quarter) and spoke to her to that effect. 23She declared to them, "Thus says the LORD, the God of Israel: Tell the man who sent you to me, 24Thus says the LORD: I will indeed bring disaster upon this place and upon its inhabitants, all the curses that are written in the book that was read before the king of Judah. 25Because they have forsaken me and have made offerings to other gods, so that they have provoked me to anger with all the works of their hands, my wrath will be poured out on this place and will not be quenched. 26But as to the king of Judah, who sent you to inquire of the LORD, thus shall you say to him: Thus says the LORD, the God of Israel: Regarding the words that you have heard, 27because your heart was penitent and you humbled yourself before God when you heard his words against this place and its inhabitants, and you have humbled yourself before me, and have torn your clothes and wept before me, I also have heard you, says the LORD. 28I will gather you to your ancestors and you shall be gathered to your grave in peace; your eyes shall not see all the disaster that I will bring on this place and its inhabitants." They took the message back to the king.

The Covenant Renewed

29 Then the king sent word and gathered together all the elders of Judah and Jerusalem. 30The king went up to the house of the LORD, with all the people of Judah, the inhabitants of Jerusalem, the priests and the Levites, all the people both great and small; he read in their hearing all the words of the book of the covenant that had been found in the house of the LORD. 31The king stood in his place and made a covenant before the LORD, to follow the LORD, keeping his commandments, his decrees, and his statutes, with all his heart and all his soul, to perform the words of the covenant that were written in this book. 32Then he made all who were present in Jerusalem and in Benjamin pledge themselves to it. And the inhabitants of Jerusalem acted according to the covenant of God, the God of their ancestors. 33Josiah took away all the abominations from all the territory that belonged to the people of Israel, and made all who were in Israel worship the LORD their God. All his days they did not turn away from following the LORD the God of their ancestors.

---

singers, as supervisors and in other offices during the reform. **34.14** *Hilkiah's* discovery of the *book of the law* is a reward for Josiah's generosity and faithfulness to the temple. Modern scholars identify the law book as some form of Deuteronomy; the Chronicler may take it to be the whole Pentateuch. **34.15** 2 Kings 22.8 notes that *Shaphan* reads the book. The Chronicler may think it unlikely that the Pentateuch was read twice by Shaphan in one day (cf. v. 18). **34.21** *Those who are left in Israel.* The Chronicler's interest in all Israel leads him to add a reference to the remnant of the Northern Kingdom. **34.22–28** Cf. 2 Kings 22.14–20. **34.22** *Huldah,* a Jerusalemite prophetess. *Second Quarter,* a part of the city added by Hezekiah. **34.24** *Curses.* Cf. Deut 27.9–26; 28.15–68. **34.27** Josiah's repentance leads to his deliverance. **34.28** *In peace* implies a natural death, even though Josiah died of wounds suffered in battle (35.23–24). Huldah predicts that Josiah will not himself experience the destruction of Jerusalem. **34.29–33** Cf. 2 Kings 23.1–3. **34.30** *Levites.* 2 Kings 23.2 reads "prophets." **34.31** In 2 Kings the *covenant* is followed by the destruction of inappropriate worship sites. In Chronicles these sites were destroyed before the finding of the law book. The covenant leads in Chronicles to the celebration of Passover after a summary of Hezekiah's reforms throughout the land of Israel (v. 33).

Celebration of the Passover

35 Josiah kept a passover to the LORD in Jerusalem; they slaughtered the passover lamb on the fourteenth day of the first month. ²He appointed the priests to their offices and encouraged them in the service of the house of the LORD. ³He said to the Levites who taught all Israel and who were holy to the LORD, "Put the holy ark in the house that Solomon son of David, king of Israel, built; you need no longer carry it on your shoulders. Now serve the LORD your God and his people Israel. ⁴Make preparations by your ancestral houses by your divisions, following the written directions of King David of Israel and the written directions of his son Solomon. ⁵Take position in the holy place according to the groupings of the ancestral houses of your kindred the people, and let there be Levites for each division of an ancestral house.ᵃ ⁶Slaughter the passover lamb, sanctify yourselves, and on behalf of your kindred make preparations, acting according to the word of the LORD by Moses."

7 Then Josiah contributed to the people, as passover offerings for all that were present, lambs and kids from the flock to the number of thirty thousand, and three thousand bulls; these were from the king's possessions. ⁸His officials contributed willingly to the people, to the priests, and to the Levites. Hilkiah, Zechariah, and Jehiel, the chief officers of the house of God, gave to the priests for the passover offerings two thousand six hundred lambs and kids and three hundred bulls. ⁹Conaniah also, and his brothers Shemaiah and Nethanel, and Hashabiah and Jeiel and Jozabad, the chiefs of the Levites, gave to the Levites for the passover offerings five thousand lambs and kids and five hundred bulls.

10 When the service had been prepared for, the priests stood in their place, and the Levites in their divisions according to the king's command. ¹¹They slaughtered the passover lamb, and the priests dashed the blood that they receivedᵇ from them, while the Levites did the skinning. ¹²They set aside the burnt offerings so that they might distribute them according to the groupings of the ancestral houses of the people, to offer to the LORD, as it is written in the book of Moses. And they did the same with the bulls. ¹³They roasted the passover lamb with fire according to the ordinance; and they boiled the holy offerings in pots, in caldrons, and in pans, and carried them quickly to all the people. ¹⁴Afterward they made preparations for themselves and for the priests, because the priests the descendants of Aaron were occupied in offering the burnt offerings and the fat parts until night; so the Levites made preparations for themselves and for the priests, the descendants of Aaron. ¹⁵The singers, the descendants of Asaph, were in their place according to the command of David, and Asaph, and Heman, and the king's seer Jeduthun. The gatekeepers were at each gate; they did not need to interrupt their service, for their kindred the Levites made preparations for them.

16 So all the service of the LORD was prepared that day, to keep the passover and to offer burnt offerings on the altar of the LORD, according to the command of King Josiah. ¹⁷The people of Israel who were present kept the passover at that time, and the festival of unleavened bread seven days. ¹⁸No passover like it had been kept in Israel since the days of the prophet Samuel; none of the kings of Israel

---

a Meaning of Heb uncertain   *b* Heb lacks *that they received*

35.1–19 Cf. 2 Kings 23.21–23. Chronicles greatly expands the report of Josiah's Passover and gives prominence to the Levites. **35.1** *In Jerusalem,* following the precedent of Hezekiah. **35.1** *Fourteenth day of the first month.* Josiah's Passover is held at the normal time (Ex 12.6; Lev 23.5; Num 9.3; cf. 2 Chr 30.2–3). **35.3** *Taught all Israel.* Cf. 17.7–9. According to the Chronicler, the ark had actually been deposited in the temple at the time of Solomon (ch. 5) and the Levites had been given alternate duties since the time of David (1 Chr 16.4). **35.4** The Chronicler links David and Solomon as kings who established the duties of the Levites. See 1 Chr 23–27. Other parallels between David and Solomon are given in 2 Chr 7.10; 11.17. **35.7–9** The generosity of the king and his officials could

serve as an example to the Chronicler's audience. The *bulls* are not part of the Passover ritual but may be associated with the Feast of Unleavened Bread. The number of animals contributed is 41,400 (cf. 30.24, where 19,000 animals were given at Hezekiah's Passover). The population of Judah is about 300,000, not counting participants from the North. **35.11** Because of the large numbers at the centralized Passover, the Levites kill and skin the lambs, while the priests manipulate the blood. **35.13** *They roasted . . . fire,* lit. "They boiled the Passover lamb with fire." According to Ex 12.8–9 the Passover lamb is to be roasted; according to Deut 16.7 it is to be boiled. **35.17** *The people of Israel . . . present.* Josiah's Passover includes people from the North and the South. **35.18** A Passover like

had kept such a passover as was kept by Josiah, by the priests and the Levites, by all Judah and Israel who were present, and by the inhabitants of Jerusalem. 19In the eighteenth year of the reign of Josiah this passover was kept.

Defeat by Pharaoh Neco and Death of Josiah

20 After all this, when Josiah had set the temple in order, King Neco of Egypt went up to fight at Carchemish on the Euphrates, and Josiah went out against him. 21But Neco*a* sent envoys to him, saying, "What have I to do with you, king of Judah? I am not coming against you today, but against the house with which I am at war; and God has commanded me to hurry. Cease opposing God, who is with me, so that he will not destroy you." 22But Josiah would not turn away from him, but disguised himself in order to fight with him. He did not listen to the words of Neco from the mouth of God, but joined battle in the plain of Megiddo. 23The archers shot King Josiah; and the king said to his servants, "Take me away, for I am badly wounded." 24So his servants took him out of the chariot and carried him in his second chariot*b* and brought him to Jerusalem. There he died, and was buried in the tombs of his ancestors. All Judah and Jerusalem mourned for Josiah. 25Jeremiah also uttered a lament for Josiah, and all the singing men and singing women have spoken of Josiah in their laments to this day. They made these a custom in Israel; they are recorded in the Laments. 26Now the rest of the acts of Josiah and his faithful deeds in accordance with what is written in the law of the LORD, 27and his acts, first and last, are written in the Book of the Kings of Israel and Judah.

Reign of Jehoahaz

36 The people of the land took Jehoahaz son of Josiah and made him king to succeed his father in Jerusalem. 2Jehoahaz was twenty-three years old when he began to reign; he reigned three months in Jerusalem. 3Then the king of Egypt deposed him in Jerusalem and laid on the land a tribute of one hundred talents of silver and one talent of gold. 4The king of Egypt made his brother Eliakim king over Judah and Jerusalem, and changed his name to Jehoiakim; but Neco took his brother Jehoahaz and carried him to Egypt.

Reign and Captivity of Jehoiakim

5 Jehoiakim was twenty-five years old when he began to reign; he reigned eleven years in Jerusalem. He did what was evil in the sight of the LORD his God. 6Against him King Nebuchadnezzar of Babylon came up, and bound him

a Heb he   *b* Or the chariot of his deputy

this has not been held since *Samuel.* 2 Kings 23.22 compares Josiah's celebration to the Passover held by the judges, with the issue being centralization of worship by Josiah. Since centralization has already occurred under Hezekiah according to Chronicles, the innovation with Josiah may be the prominent role of the Levites (cf. vv. 3–6). This verse also stresses the significance of an all-Israel celebration. **35.20–27** Cf. 2 Kings 23.28–30a. Josiah's death comes thirteen years after the Passover celebration. Neco was on his way to prop up Assyria as a buffer against Babylon (2 Kings 23.29 indicates that Neco was fighting against Assyria, though this point is not clear in the NRSV). Josiah opposes him because he is anti-Assyrian, because of a league with Babylon, or because he wants independence. **35.20** *Neco,* king of Egypt 610–595 BCE. *Carchemish,* a city sixty miles northeast of Aleppo. **35.21** Since Neco claims he has been sent by God, anyone opposing him would be opposing God. He desires safe passage through Judah. **35.22** Josiah persists in his battle plans and disobeys the word of God as revealed through Neco. Hence the death of this otherwise exemplary king corresponds with the doctrine of retribution. According to 1 Esd 1.26, Jeremiah had authenticated the message from Neco. *Disguised himself,* a detail not mentioned in 2 Kings (cf. Ahab in 1 Kings 22.30). *Megiddo,* a town located on an important pass in the Carmel range. **35.23** The Chronicler observes that the archers wounded the king, who begs his attendants to take him from the battle. **35.24** Transported in a second chariot, Josiah dies in Jerusalem. In 2 Kings 23.29–30 Josiah dies at Megiddo. **35.25** *Jeremiah* expresses public sorrow, and he is joined by other singers. *The Laments,* a work otherwise unknown; not the biblical book of Lamentations. **35.26** The Chronicler notes that the deeds of Josiah were in accord with what is written in the *law of the LORD,* i.e., the Pentateuch. Chronicles places the summary of Josiah's reign after the account of his death, not before it as in Kings.

36.1–4 Cf. 2 Kings 23.30b–34. **36.1** *The people of the land.* Cf. 33.25. **36.3** The tribute is 6,700 pounds of silver and 67 pounds of gold. **36.4** Josiah is succeeded by three sons (Jehoahaz, Eliakim, and Zedekiah) and one grandson (Jehoiachin). Eliakim/Jehoiakim is actually older than Jehoahaz, but we do not know why he is not the first to succeed his father (cf. 1 Chr 3.15). Each of the last four kings winds up in exile and each pays tribute.

36.5–8 Cf. 2 Kings 23.36–24.7. **36.6** *Nebuchadnezzar* ruled Babylon from 605 to 562 BCE. Jehoiakim's death is reported in 2 Kings 24.6; 2 Chronicles reports his (tem-

with fetters to take him to Babylon. 7Nebuchadnezzar also carried some of the vessels of the house of the LORD to Babylon and put them in his palace in Babylon. 8Now the rest of the acts of Jehoiakim, and the abominations that he did, and what was found against him, are written in the Book of the Kings of Israel and Judah; and his son Jehoiachin succeeded him.

Reign and Captivity of Jehoiachin

9 Jehoiachin was eight years old when he began to reign; he reigned three months and ten days in Jerusalem. He did what was evil in the sight of the LORD. 10In the spring of the year King Nebuchadnezzar sent and brought him to Babylon, along with the precious vessels of the house of the LORD, and made his brother Zedekiah king over Judah and Jerusalem.

Reign of Zedekiah

11 Zedekiah was twenty-one years old when he began to reign; he reigned eleven years in Jerusalem. 12He did what was evil in the sight of the LORD his God. He did not humble himself before the prophet Jeremiah who spoke from the mouth of the LORD. 13He also rebelled against King Nebuchadnezzar, who had made him swear by God; he stiffened his neck and hardened his heart against turning to the LORD, the God of Israel. 14All the leading priests and the people also were exceedingly unfaithful, following all the abominations of the nations; and they polluted the house of the LORD that he had consecrated in Jerusalem.

The Fall of Jerusalem

15 The LORD, the God of their ancestors, sent persistently to them by his messengers, because he had compassion on his people and on his dwelling place; 16but they kept mocking the messengers of God, despising his words, and scoffing at his prophets, until the wrath of the LORD against his people became so great that there was no remedy.

17 Therefore he brought up against them the king of the Chaldeans, who killed their youths with the sword in the house of their sanctuary, and had no compassion on young man or young woman, the aged or the feeble; he gave them all into his hand. 18All the vessels of the house of God, large and small, and the treasures of the house of the LORD, and the treasures of the king and of his officials, all these he brought to Babylon. 19They burned the house of God, broke down the wall of Jerusalem, burned all its palaces with fire, and destroyed all its precious vessels. 20He took into exile in Babylon those who had escaped from the sword, and they became servants to him and to his sons until the establishment of the kingdom of Persia, 21to fulfill the word of the LORD by the mouth of Jeremiah, until the land had made up for its sabbaths. All the days that it lay desolate it kept sabbath, to fulfill seventy years.

Cyrus Proclaims Liberty for the Exiles

22 In the first year of King Cyrus of Persia, in fulfillment of the word of the LORD spoken by Jeremiah, the LORD stirred up the spirit of King Cyrus of Persia so that he sent a herald throughout all his kingdom and also declared in a written edict: 23"Thus says King Cyrus of Persia: The LORD, the God of heaven, has given me all the kingdoms of the earth, and he has charged me to build him a house at Jerusalem, which is in Judah. Whoever is among you of all his people, may the LORD his God be with him! Let him go up."

---

porary or possibly his threatened) exile. **36.7** On the temple *vessels*, see 1 Chr 28.14–17; 2 Chr 4.19–22; 36.18; Ezra 1.7–11. **36.9–10** Cf. 2 Kings 24.8–17; 25.27–30. **36.9** A child king for three months, *Jehoiachin* spends thirty-seven years in a Babylonian prison (2 Kings 25.27–30). According to 2 Kings 24.8, he is eighteen when he becomes king. **36.10** *Brother,* perhaps a relative. 2 Kings 24.17 reads "uncle." Cf. also 1 Chr 3.15–16. **36.11–14** Cf. 2 Kings 24.18–25.7. **36.12** Chronicles condemns *Zedekiah* by citing his disobedience toward the prophet Jeremiah (cf. Jer 37.2). **36.13** Zedekiah breaks an oath by rebelling against Nebuchadnezzar. **36.14** The author charges the leading priests and the people with being *unfaithful,* a favorite word for sin in Chronicles. **36.15–16** Exile results from persistent despising of the prophets (cf. Jer 26.5; 29.19). *No remedy.* Cf. 7.14, where

God promises to heal the people. **36.17** *Chaldeans,* the peoples who ruled Mesopotamia during the Neo-Babylonian period. **36.21** *Jeremiah.* Cf. Jer 25.11–12; 29.10. The Chronicler views Palestine as empty during the exilic period, but free to enjoy the sabbaths it had missed (perhaps since the beginning of the monarchy) and to get ready for the exiles who would return (Lev 26.34–35). *Seventy years.* The actual length of the exile was about fifty years. **36.22–23** Cf. Ezra 1.1–3a. The last verses of Chronicles are virtually identical with the first verses of Ezra. This passage views Cyrus as the fulfillment of Jeremiah's prophecy and implicitly accepts Persian rule in the postexilic period. The Persian king authorizes the rebuilding of the temple (cf. Ezra 6.3–5) and gives his blessing to all exiles who desire to return to Palestine. **36.22** *Cyrus* ruled Babylonia from about 539 to 530 BCE.

EZRA

THE BOOKS OF EZRA AND NEHEMIAH are our most important source of evidence for the history of the early postexilic period, from 539 to ca. 430 BCE. They bear the names of the two best-known leaders of the Jewish community of those years, Ezra the priest and Nehemiah the governor, both of whom were active in the middle of the fifth century BCE, though their activity in Jerusalem perhaps never overlapped.

Connections with Other Books

THE NARRATIVE OF EZRA-NEHEMIAH continues directly from the end of 2 Chronicles, and the style and interests of the author are so like those of the Chronicler that it has been customarily thought that the whole sequence of 1 Chronicles through Nehemiah was once a single work by one author. Even if the differences between 1 and 2 Chronicles, on the one hand, and Ezra-Nehemiah, on the other, point to different authorship, as is now the prevailing scholarly view, it seems that Ezra-Nehemiah was composed as a sequel to 1 and 2 Chronicles and that the authors of both works were Jerusalem clergy, perhaps Levites, of the fourth century BCE.

1 Esdras, in the Protestant Apocrypha but not among the Catholic deuterocanonical books, is another work bearing the name of Ezra (Esdras is the Greek form of Ezra). Its narrative parallels the story from 2 Chr 35 to Neh 8, with only its last two chapters being concerned with Ezra. (See the table "The Relation of 1 Esdras to Other Biblical Books" in the Introduction to 1 Esdras.) 2 Esdras is found in the Apocrypha of Anglo-Saxon churches but is usually assigned to the Pseudepigrapha by the Lutheran tradition, and in Catholic Bibles it is either included among the NT Apocrypha or omitted altogether. It has nothing to do with the historical Ezra, though it purports to be his book; it is a collection of visions, and includes Christian material.

Structure

THE BOOKS OF EZRA AND NEHEMIAH are a narrative of the restoration of the Jewish people to their homeland after the exile. What drives that story are the decrees of two Persian kings, Cyrus and Artaxerxes, and what counts as restoration is the fulfillment of their demands. In Ezra 1 Cyrus commands the Jews to return to their land and resume temple worship; in accord with that, Ezra 1–6 narrates the return and the rebuilding of the temple. In Ezra 7 Artaxerxes commands obedience to the law of Moses on the part of all the Jews; and in Neh 2 he authorizes the reestablishment of Jerusalem, which will be the focus of national identity. In accord with these initiatives, Ezra 7 through Neh 13 narrates the imposition of the Mosaic law and its effects; Ezra insists on obedience to the law's demands for separation from non-Jews, and Nehemiah likewise creates a distinctive Jewish identity when he encloses Jerusalem with a wall and purges the community of all things foreign.

Sources

THE AUTHOR HAS DRAWN ON VARIOUS SOURCES for the narrative, at times editing them quite heavily and at other times simply copying them. Extensive sources were an Ezra "memoir," which provided the material for Ezra 7–10 and Neh 8–9, and a Nehemiah memoir, lightly edited to form Neh 1–7; 11.1–2; 12.31–43; 13.4–31 (though it is disputed whether Neh 3 was ever part of such a memoir). Use of first-person language in some of the Ezra material and all of the Nehemiah narrative does not, of course, prove that the documents are authentic, but it is very probable that in the Nehemiah memoir at least we are reading the record of a leading statesman about events in which he was personally involved.

The author has also perhaps drawn on an "Aramaic chronicle," a collection of Persian documents in Aramaic purporting to be official correspondence about Jerusalem. That would explain why Ezra 4.7–6.18 is entirely in Aramaic, while the rest of Ezra-Nehemiah is mostly in Hebrew. The typical bureaucratic language of these documents suggests they are authentic, though there are evidences of editing by a Jewish author. Other purportedly Persian documents are quoted in Ezra 1.2–4 (the edict of Cyrus) and 7.12–28 (Artaxerxes' authorization to Ezra in Aramaic).

Other sources include various Jewish lists, e.g., of inhabitants of Judea (Ezra 2.3–58; Neh 7.8–60; 11.3–9) and of priests and Levites (Neh 11.10–23; 12.1–26), and the document recording the people's pledge to keep the details of the law and the names of those who signed it (Neh 10).

Historical Background

THESE BOOKS HAVE THEIR HISTORICAL SETTING in two distinct periods, in the sixth and in the fifth centuries BCE.

539–515 BCE

THE PERSIAN EMPEROR CYRUS, having gained the Babylonian Empire in 539, gave permission to the Jewish exiles in Babylonia to return to the land of Israel and to rebuild the temple. Sacrifice is said to have been resumed immediately upon their return, but repairs on the temple apparently did not progress. Only in 520, when Zerubbabel was governor of the province of Judea, did temple building start in earnest, and it was finished in 515 (Ezra 6.15).

458–430 BCE

IT IS DEBATED WHETHER Ezra's work is to be dated to 458 or 398, but on the assumption of the earlier date, the second period begins with the commissioning of the Jewish priest Ezra by Artaxerxes I to establish pentateuchal law as state law in the province of Judea and to regulate the temple worship (Ezra 7). Ezra read the law to the people at the Festival of Booths in September 458 (Neh 8), and his commission of enquiry into marriages of Jews with non-Jews sat from December of that year until the spring of 457 (Ezra 9–10).

A decade later, in 445, Nehemiah, a Jewish official in the service of Artaxerxes, was appointed governor of Judea (Neh 2; 5.14) with responsibility to rebuild the wall of Jerusalem and thus presumably to enhance the status of the city. Nehemiah, having completed that task (Neh 6.15), remained governor for twelve years and enlarged the city's population by resettling villagers in the capital. At some time after 433, he returned for a second term of duty and carried out reforms of the religious life of the community (Neh 13.4–31). [DAVID J. A. CLINES]

End of the Babylonian Captivity

1 In the first year of King Cyrus of Persia, in order that the word of the Lord by the mouth of Jeremiah might be accomplished, the Lord stirred up the spirit of King Cyrus of Persia so that he sent a herald throughout all his kingdom, and also in a written edict declared:

2 "Thus says King Cyrus of Persia: The Lord, the God of heaven, has given me all the kingdoms of the earth, and he has charged me to build him a house at Jerusalem in Judah. 3 Any of those among you who are of his people— may their God be with them!—are now permitted to go up to Jerusalem in Judah, and rebuild the house of the Lord, the God of Israel—he is the God who is in Jerusalem; 4 and let all survivors, in whatever place they reside, be assisted by the people of their place with silver and gold, with goods and with animals, besides freewill offerings for the house of God in Jerusalem."

5 The heads of the families of Judah and Benjamin, and the priests and the Levites— everyone whose spirit God had stirred—got ready to go up and rebuild the house of the Lord in Jerusalem. 6 All their neighbors aided them with silver vessels, with gold, with goods, with animals, and with valuable gifts, besides all that was freely offered. 7 King Cyrus himself brought out the vessels of the house of the Lord that Nebuchadnezzar had carried away from Jerusalem and placed in the house of his gods. 8 King Cyrus of Persia had them released into the charge of Mithredath the treasurer, who counted them out to Sheshbazzar the prince of Judah. 9 And this was the inventory: gold basins, thirty; silver basins, one thousand; knives,[a] twenty-nine; 10 gold bowls, thirty; other silver bowls, four hundred ten; other vessels, one thousand; 11 the total of the gold and silver vessels was five thousand four

a Vg: Meaning of Heb uncertain

1.1–11 The Persian king Cyrus authorizes the Jews in exile in Babylonia to return to the land to rebuild the temple; the returning exiles carry with them treasures earlier plundered from the temple. 1.1–2 Mostly the same wording as 2 Chr 36.22, perhaps copied into 2 Chronicles as a link to Ezra. 1.1 *The first year of King Cyrus of Persia.* The first year of the reign of Cyrus II (the Great) over the Babylonian Empire, 539–537 BCE. Cyrus had been king over Anshan (Elam) since 559 BCE; he then conquered Persia, Media, Lydia, Assyria, and finally Babylonia. *The word of the Lord by . . . Jeremiah.* Jer 25.11 predicts subjection to Babylon for seventy years, and Jer 29.10 tells Jewish exiles in Babylon that after seventy years God will bring them back to Jerusalem. The first deportation was in 597 BCE (2 Kings 24.12–16), only sixty years previously. Perhaps seventy is understood as a round number, or perhaps the reference in Dan 1.1 to a deportation in 606 BCE is a genuine historical reminiscence. *Herald . . . written edict.* After the public announcement of the royal edict, the herald would post a copy of it on an official notice board. 1.2–4 Another edict of Cyrus concerning the rebuilding of the temple is in 6.3–5. 1.2 A temple is often called the *house* of the deity who dwells in it. *Judah,* the Persian province of Judea, *Yehud* in Aramaic, the official language of the Persian Empire.

1.3 *Permitted* may mean "commanded," since this is the edict of an autocrat. *Rebuild* implies knowledge of the destruction of the Jerusalem temple (587/6 BCE). 1.4 *Survivors,* from the destruction of Jerusalem, i.e., those exiled to Babylon. *People of their place,* apparently gentile neighbors. 1.5 *Families,* lit. "fathers' houses"; a "father's house" was the extended family consisting of all descendants of a living patriarch (except women married into other families) and the family's slaves or servants. *Judah and Benjamin,* the tribes (contrast Judah the province in 1.2). *Priests* traced their ancestry to Aaron, son of Levi; *Levites* were other members of the tribe of Levi who undertook more menial duties in temple worship (Num 3.5–9). 1.7 *Nebuchadnezzar had carried away,* a reference either to pillaging during the capture of Jerusalem in 597 BCE (2 Kings 24.13) or to the final plundering of the temple in 587 BCE (25.13–15; see also 2 Chr 36.10, 18; Jer 52.17–19). *The house of his gods,* or rather "the house of his god," the temple, called Esagila, of Nebuchadnezzar's preferred deity, Marduk of Babylon. 1.8 *Sheshbazzar,* perhaps Shenazzar, a son of Jehoiachin, the exiled king of Judah (1 Chr 3.18). See also note on 5.14. 1.9–11 The number of items in the inventory comes to 2,499, which differs from the total given as 5,400. The RSV translation emended the 30

hundred. All these Sheshbazzar brought up, when the exiles were brought up from Babylonia to Jerusalem.

List of the Returned Exiles

2 Now these were the people of the province who came from those captive exiles whom King Nebuchadnezzar of Babylon had carried captive to Babylonia; they returned to Jerusalem and Judah, all to their own towns. ²They came with Zerubbabel, Jeshua, Nehemiah, Seraiah, Reelaiah, Mordecai, Bilshan, Mispar, Bigvai, Rehum, and Baanah.

The number of the Israelite people: ³the descendants of Parosh, two thousand one hundred seventy-two. ⁴Of Shephatiah, three hundred seventy-two. ⁵Of Arah, seven hundred seventy-five. ⁶Of Pahath-moab, namely the descendants of Jeshua and Joab, two thousand eight hundred twelve. ⁷Of Elam, one thousand two hundred fifty-four. ⁸Of Zattu, nine hundred forty-five. ⁹Of Zaccai, seven hundred sixty. ¹⁰Of Bani, six hundred forty-two. ¹¹Of Bebai, six hundred twenty-three. ¹²Of Azgad, one thousand two hundred twenty-two. ¹³Of Adonikam, six hundred sixty-six. ¹⁴Of Bigvai, two thousand fifty-six. ¹⁵Of Adin, four hundred fifty-four. ¹⁶Of Ater, namely of Hezekiah, ninety-eight. ¹⁷Of Bezai, three hundred twenty-three. ¹⁸Of Jorah, one hundred twelve. ¹⁹Of Hashum, two hundred twenty-three. ²⁰Of Gibbar, ninety-five. ²¹Of Bethlehem, one hundred twenty-three. ²²The people of Netophah, fifty-six. ²³Of Anathoth, one hundred twenty-eight. ²⁴The descendants of Azmaveth, forty-two. ²⁵Of Kiriatharim, Chephirah, and Beeroth, seven hundred forty-three. ²⁶Of Ramah and Geba, six hundred twenty-one. ²⁷The people of Michmas, one hundred twenty-two. ²⁸Of Bethel and Ai, two hundred

twenty-three. ²⁹The descendants of Nebo, fifty-two. ³⁰Of Magbish, one hundred fifty-six. ³¹Of the other Elam, one thousand two hundred fifty-four. ³²Of Harim, three hundred twenty. ³³Of Lod, Hadid, and Ono, seven hundred twenty-five. ³⁴Of Jericho, three hundred forty-five. ³⁵Of Senaah, three thousand six hundred thirty.

36 The priests: the descendants of Jedaiah, of the house of Jeshua, nine hundred seventy-three. ³⁷Of Immer, one thousand fifty-two. ³⁸Of Pashhur, one thousand two hundred forty-seven. ³⁹Of Harim, one thousand seventeen.

40 The Levites: the descendants of Jeshua and Kadmiel, of the descendants of Hodaviah, seventy-four. ⁴¹The singers: the descendants of Asaph, one hundred twenty-eight. ⁴²The descendants of the gatekeepers: of Shallum, of Ater, of Talmon, of Akkub, of Hatita, and of Shobai, in all one hundred thirty-nine.

43 The temple servants: the descendants of Ziha, Hasupha, Tabbaoth, ⁴⁴Keros, Siaha, Padon, ⁴⁵Lebanah, Hagabah, Akkub, ⁴⁶Hagab, Shamlai, Hanan, ⁴⁷Giddel, Gahar, Reaiah, ⁴⁸Rezin, Nekoda, Gazzam, ⁴⁹Uzza, Paseah, Besai, ⁵⁰Asnah, Meunim, Nephisim, ⁵¹Bakbuk, Hakupha, Harhur, ⁵²Bazluth, Mehida, Harsha, ⁵³Barkos, Sisera, Temah, ⁵⁴Neziah, and Hatipha.

55 The descendants of Solomon's servants: Sotai, Hassophereth, Peruda, ⁵⁶Jaalah, Darkon, Giddel, ⁵⁷Shephatiah, Hattil, Pochereth-hazzebaim, and Ami.

58 All the temple servants and the descendants of Solomon's servants were three hundred ninety-two.

59 The following were those who came up from Tel-melah, Tel-harsha, Cherub, Addan, and Immer, though they could not prove their

---

gold basins to 1,000 (as in the parallel 1 Esd 2.13), the 410 silver bowls to 2,410 (as in 1 Esd 2.13), and the total to 5,469 (as in 1 Esd 2.14).

2.1–2a Apparently a list of leaders from various periods after the return. *Zerubbabel* and *Jeshua* are the governor and the priest of 3.2; perhaps *Nehemiah* is the governor Nehemiah (Neh 1.1), *Seraiah* the father of the priest Ezra (Ezra 7.1), and *Bigvai* the governor of Judea (Aramaic *Yehud*) after Nehemiah known from the Elephantine papyri. **2.2b–58** A census of inhabitants of Judea (the province *Yehud*), at some unknown time after the return from exile. The list is paralleled in Neh 7 and 1 Esd 5, with many variations, especially in the numbers. **2.2b** *The Israelite people*, i.e., laypersons, as distinct from priests, Levites, and other religious

professionals (vv. 36–58). **2.3–35** These are not the names of individuals, but of clans or phratries (vv. 3–20) and of towns (vv. 21–35). **2.36–39** Other lists of postexilic *priests* are in Neh 10.2–8; 12.1–7. **2.40–42** *Levites* are also listed in Neh 10.9–13; 12.8–9. The temple *singers* (cf. 1 Chr 9.33–44) and *gatekeepers* (cf. 1 Chr 9.17–27) seem also to be regarded as Levites (as in Neh 12.9, 24–25). **2.43–54** *Temple servants*, a hereditary caste of temple servitors (Hebrew *netinim*), mostly with non-Israelite names. **2.55–57** *Solomon's servants*, ostensibly the descendants of Solomon's Canaanite slaves (1 Kings 9.20–21; 2 Chr 8.7–8), now temple officials. **2.59–69** Unlike the census of inhabitants of the province in vv. 2b–58, this appears to be a report of

families or their descent, whether they belonged to Israel: 60the descendants of Delaiah, Tobiah, and Nekoda, six hundred fifty-two. 61Also, of the descendants of the priests: the descendants of Habaiah, Hakkoz, and Barzillai (who had married one of the daughters of Barzillai the Gileadite, and was called by their name). 62These looked for their entries in the genealogical records, but they were not found there, and so they were excluded from the priesthood as unclean; 63the governor told them that they were not to partake of the most holy food, until there should be a priest to consult Urim and Thummim.

64 The whole assembly together was forty-two thousand three hundred sixty, 65besides their male and female servants, of whom there were seven thousand three hundred thirty-seven; and they had two hundred male and female singers. 66They had seven hundred thirty-six horses, two hundred forty-five mules, 67four hundred thirty-five camels, and six thousand seven hundred twenty donkeys.

68 As soon as they came to the house of the LORD in Jerusalem, some of the heads of families made freewill offerings for the house of God, to erect it on its site. 69According to their resources they gave to the building fund sixty-one thousand darics of gold, five thousand minas of silver, and one hundred priestly robes.

70 The priests, the Levites, and some of the people lived in Jerusalem and its vicinity;[a] and the singers, the gatekeepers, and the temple servants lived in their towns, and all Israel in their towns.

Worship Restored at Jerusalem

3 When the seventh month came, and the Israelites were in the towns, the people gathered together in Jerusalem. 2Then Jeshua son of Jozadak, with his fellow priests, and Zerubbabel son of Shealtiel with his kin set out to build the altar of the God of Israel, to offer burnt offer-

---

a 1 Esdras 5.46: Heb lacks *lived in Jerusalem and its vicinity*

---

the returned exiles from five towns in Babylonia. **2.61** *Barzillai*, a contemporary of David (2 Sam 17.27–29; 19.31–39). For a male to take the name of his wife's family is unparalleled in the OT. **2.62–63** *Unclean*, in the ritual sense, and so unable to officiate as priests or be fed from the temple revenues (*not to partake of the most holy food*). **2.63** We cannot tell which *governor* (Hebrew *tirshata*, a Persian title signifying "His Excellency") of the Persian province of Judea is intended here. *Urim and Thummim*, sacred lots enabling the answers to difficult questions to be divined, were apparently two small objects kept in a pouch of the high priest's ephod (Ex 28.30; Lev 8.8); they could yield the responses "yes," "no," or "no answer" (cf. 1 Sam 14.36–37; 23.9–12; 30.7–8). **2.64** The figure of 42,360 members of the *assembly* differs from the total of the individual sums (29,818) in vv. 2b–58. Such figures often suffer from scribal errors. But perhaps the 42,360 are returnees, including women, and the 29,818 are inhabitants of the province at a later date including those who had not been exiled, but excluding women. **2.65** Both *male and female servants* and *male and female singers* are counted, so probably women members of the community are also included in the total of v. 64. The *singers* are secular entertainers; the temple singers have been mentioned in v. 41, and there were no female singers in the temple, as far as we know. **2.66–67** *Horses, mules, camels,* and *donkeys* are all pack animals, for carrying loads (horses were not used for riding at this time); the list seems to be something like a caravan inventory. **2.68** The building and furnishing of the Second Temple is here regarded as the responsibility of the community at large rather than of a king, as it was with Solomon's temple (1 Kings 6–7).

The giving of freewill offerings is reminiscent of the accounts of the construction of the tabernacle (Ex 25.2–7; 35.21–29); 1 Chr 29.6–9 also ascribes the funding of the First Temple to the donations of the people. **2.69** *Sixty-one thousand darics.* A daric was a gold coin of 8.4 grams, apparently named for Darius I (522–486 BCE), represented on his coins half-length or kneeling with a bow and arrow. This reference to darics at a time earlier than Darius is anachronistic and suggests a composition or revision of this text later than the time it purports to describe. The total weight of gold in 61,000 darics (41,000 in Neh 7.70–72) is 1,133 pounds. *Minas* are not coins, but weights of about 570 grams (20 ounces), fifty times the weight of a shekel. 5,000 minas of silver would weigh 6,250 pounds. *Priestly robes,* i.e., tunics, of intricately embroidered linen (Ex 28.4–5; cf. 28.39; 39.27–29).

3.1–7 Sacrifices are resumed. **3.1** *The seventh month,* Tishri (September/October) 538 BCE. *The Israelites were in the towns.* The people had settled in their ancestral homes in the country towns and villages, as well, of course, as in Jerusalem. *The people gathered . . . in Jerusalem.* The seventh month, the most important in the liturgical year (Num 29), required in principle the presence in Jerusalem at least of all males in order to celebrate the Festival of Booths (see note on 3.4). **3.2** *Jeshua,* the high priest (cf. Neh 12.10; Hag 1.1, 14; 2.2), called Joshua in Haggai, is here named before Zerubbabel because the context concerns worship. Usually their names are given in the reverse order (e.g., Ezra 2.2; 3.8; 4.3; 5.2). Jeshua's father, *Jozadak* (Jehozadak), was high priest at the time of the exile in 587 BCE (1 Chr 6.15). *Zerubbabel,* grandson of the exiled king of Judah, Jehoiachin (Jeconiah; 1 Chr 3.17–19), is

ings on it, as prescribed in the law of Moses the man of God. ³They set up the altar on its foundation, because they were in dread of the neighboring peoples, and they offered burnt offerings upon it to the LORD, morning and evening. ⁴And they kept the festival of booths,ᵃ as prescribed, and offered the daily burnt offerings by number according to the ordinance, as required for each day, ⁵and after that the regular burnt offerings, the offerings at the new moon and at all the sacred festivals of the LORD, and the offerings of everyone who made a freewill offering to the LORD. ⁶From the first day of the seventh month they began to offer burnt offerings to the LORD. But the foundation of the temple of the LORD was not yet laid. ⁷So they gave money to the masons and the carpenters, and food, drink, and oil to the Sidonians and the Tyrians to bring cedar trees from Lebanon to the sea, to Joppa, according to the grant that they had from King Cyrus of Persia.

Foundation Laid for the Temple

8 In the second year after their arrival at the house of God at Jerusalem, in the second month, Zerubbabel son of Shealtiel and Jeshua son of Jozadak made a beginning, together with the rest of their people, the priests and the Levites and all who had come to Jerusalem from the captivity. They appointed the Levites, from twenty years old and upward, to have the oversight of the work on the house of the LORD. ⁹And Jeshua with his sons and his kin, and Kadmiel and his sons, Binnui and Hodaviah ᵇ along with the sons of Henadad,

---

a Or *tabernacles*; Heb *succoth*   *b* Compare 2.40; Neh 7.43; 1 Esdras 5.58: Heb *sons of Judah*

---

the Jewish governor appointed by the Persians. *To build the altar.* The assumption is that the altar of the First Temple had been destroyed (on destroying altars, cf. 2 Kings 23.15). *As prescribed in the law of Moses,* i.e., built of unhewn stones (Ex 20.25; cf. Deut 27.6; 1 Macc 4.42–47). **3.3** *On its foundation,* i.e., on the foundation of the old altar still remaining. Continuity of tradition is deemed important for the legitimacy of the worship. *Because they were in dread.* The reestablishment of worship is the priority in the restoration of the state as a means of warding off danger from *the neighboring peoples,* lit. "the peoples of the lands," such as Edomites and Ammonites. Cf. the term *people of the land* for the inhabitants of Palestine proper (note on 4.4). *Burnt offerings . . . morning and evening,* the prescribed "perpetual offering" (Hebrew *tamid*), a lamb together with flour, oil, and wine, the staple produce of the land (Ex 29.38–42; Num 28.3–8). **3.4** The *festival of booths* (Tabernacles) was held from the fifteenth to the twenty-second of the seventh month (Lev 23.33–36). The *daily burnt offerings* are detailed in Num 29.12–38, totaling in the week 71 bulls, 15 rams, 105 lambs, and 7 goats. **3.5** Throughout the year sacrifices would be offered: the public *regular burnt offerings* daily, the *new moon* offerings monthly, the offerings at *sacred festivals* seasonally, and the private *freewill* offerings irregularly. The sacred festivals are enumerated in Lev 23. **3.6** The *first day of the seventh month.* According to the narrator's report, the date is September 17, 538 BCE. *The foundation of the temple . . . was not yet laid,* better "work had not yet started on the temple rebuilding." Many of the foundations must have survived from the ruins of the First Temple. The point is that sacrificial worship was resumed long before the temple building itself was repaired. **3.7** The account of the building of the Second Temple is intended to remind readers of the building of Solomon's temple (2 Chr 3; cf. 1 Chr 22.2–4), for the narrator sees the Second Temple as essentially a rebuilding and continuation of the First Temple. *Money,* prob-

ably an anachronistic translation, for coins were not yet in common use. The Hebrew is lit. "silver," which would have been weighed out as wages. *Masons,* i.e., stonecutters (as in 1 Chr 22.2). *Carpenters.* The English word is too specific; the Hebrew is lit. "cutters," i.e., workers in wood, metal, and stone (cf. 1 Chr 22.15). *Food, drink, and oil to the Sidonians and the Tyrians.* Solomon too paid his artisans from Sidon and Tyre in kind (wheat and oil, 1 Kings 5.11). *Cedar trees from Lebanon.* These tall and robust trees, highly prized throughout the ancient Near East, were ideal for roof beams. Isa 60.13 speaks of the "glory of Lebanon" coming to Jerusalem to "beautify" the temple. *To the sea, to Joppa,* better "to the port at Joppa." For Solomon's temple too (according to 2 Chr 2.16) logs bound together as rafts had been towed from Lebanon to Joppa, Tell Qasile, just north of modern Tel Aviv. *The grant . . . from King Cyrus,* probably not the money grant (6.4), but his permission for timber to be taken free from the Lebanon mountains, which had become a royal Persian forest.

3.8–13 Preparations for the rebuilding are made. **3.8** *In the second year,* 537 BCE. Not much is said to have been done at this time (cf. *laid the foundation,* v. 10), for work ceases until the reign of Darius (522–486 BCE; 4.5) and then is resumed and completed in his sixth year (6.15). *In the second month,* Ziv, or Iyyar (April-May). In the same month Solomon too began work on his temple (1 Kings 6.1; 2 Chr 3.2); it was a suitable season for building work, after the spring rains and the early harvest of flax and barley. *Zerubbabel, Jeshua.* See note on 3.2. *All who had come . . . from the captivity.* Those who had not been in exile in Babylonia but had remained in the land seem to be studiously ignored by the author. *Twenty years old,* the minimum age for levitical duties according to the Chronicler (1 Chr 23.24, 27; 2 Chr 31.17). **3.9** In accordance with his custom, the author lingers over the names and functions of the Levites, creating the impression that he himself was a Levite. This *Jeshua* is a Levite,

the Levites, their sons and kin, together took charge of the workers in the house of God.

10 When the builders laid the foundation of the temple of the LORD, the priests in their vestments were stationed to praise the LORD with trumpets, and the Levites, the sons of Asaph, with cymbals, according to the directions of King David of Israel; 11and they sang responsively, praising and giving thanks to the LORD,

"For he is good,
    for his steadfast love endures forever
        toward Israel."

And all the people responded with a great shout when they praised the LORD, because the foundation of the house of the LORD was laid. 12But many of the priests and Levites and heads of families, old people who had seen the first house on its foundations, wept with a loud voice when they saw this house, though many shouted aloud for joy, 13so that the people could not distinguish the sound of the joyful shout from the sound of the people's weeping, for the people shouted so loudly that the sound was heard far away.

Resistance to Rebuilding the Temple

4 When the adversaries of Judah and Benjamin heard that the returned exiles were building a temple to the LORD, the God of Israel, 2they approached Zerubbabel and the heads of families and said to them, "Let us build with you, for we worship your God as you do, and we have been sacrificing to him ever since the days of King Esar-haddon of Assyria who brought us here." 3But Zerubbabel, Jeshua, and the rest of the heads of families in Israel said to them, "You shall have no part with us in building a house to our God; but we alone will build to the LORD, the God of Israel, as King Cyrus of Persia has commanded us."

4 Then the people of the land discouraged the people of Judah, and made them afraid to build, 5and they bribed officials to frustrate their plan throughout the reign of King Cyrus of Persia and until the reign of King Darius of Persia.

Rebuilding of Jerusalem Opposed

6 In the reign of Ahasuerus, in his accession year, they wrote an accusation against the inhabitants of Judah and Jerusalem.

7 And in the days of Artaxerxes, Bishlam and Mithredath and Tabeel and the rest of their associates wrote to King Artaxerxes of Persia; the letter was written in Aramaic and

---

not the high priest (v. 2). **3.10** *Laid the foundation.* Whether there was any foundation laying we do not know (cf. note on 3.6), for the Hebrew says only that they "restored, repaired," which must mean in the context that they began to repair. 2 Kings 25.9 speaks only of the burning of the temple by the Babylonians, and the large dressed foundation stones, up to 12 or 15 feet in length (1 Kings 5.17; 7.10), would not have been much damaged by the collapse of the temple. *In their vestments.* The Hebrew has simply "clothed"; presumably a word like "in linen" has been accidentally omitted. *Trumpets* of silver (Num 10.2) blown by priests and *cymbals* of bronze (1 Chr 15.19) sounded by *the sons of Asaph,* the musicians' guild among the Levites (see Ezra 2.41; 2 Chr 29.25–26), were a rhythmical backing for the vocal music. *According to . . . King David.* See 1 Chr 16.4–6; 25.1, 6. **3.11** *For he is good . . . toward Israel,* a quotation from a psalm such as 106 (v. 1) or 136 intended for responsive singing. The theme of the praise is God's fidelity (*steadfast love*) to the nation; true to his promise, he has enabled them to return to the land. The *shout* is often associated with military victory and the return of the ark of the covenant, seat of the divine king (e.g., 1 Sam 4.5–6; Pss 47.5; 132.16), to the center of the people. *Because the foundation . . . was laid,* rather "because of the rebuilding" (cf. notes on 3.6; 3.10). **3.12** *The first house,* Solomon's temple, destroyed in 587 BCE, fifty years previously. *When they saw this house,* rather, with the Hebrew, "this (or that) was the temple in their eyes

(i.e., as far as they were concerned)," a parenthetical phrase that follows *the first house on its foundations.*

4.1–5 The building of the temple ceases, ostensibly because of opposition from northern neighbors. **4.1** *The adversaries,* presumably the *people of the land* (v. 4). *The returned exiles.* Again, there is no word of those who had stayed in the land (see note on 3.8). **4.2** *Esar-haddon,* king of Assyria (681–669 BCE), who imported colonists from other parts of his empire to settle in northern Israel after the deportation of many inhabitants in 721 BCE (see also v. 10). **4.3** *No part with us.* Perhaps it is implied that those in the land continued worship of their national gods along with Yahweh, as former colonists are said to have done (2 Kings 17.41). **4.4** *People of the land,* non-Jewish settlers in the land of Israel (see note on 4.2). *Discouraged,* lit. "relaxed the hands of," i.e., "weakened the morale of." **4.5** *Until the reign of King Darius* (522–486 BCE). The opposition of the non-Jewish settlers is offered as the explanation of the cessation of temple building from 537 to 520 BCE. **4.6–23** This section has nothing to do with the building of the temple, but with opposition to the building of the city of Jerusalem, many years later. Apparently it has been included here to illustrate the kinds of methods that enemies of the Jews would have employed to *discourage* them (v. 4). **4.6** *Ahasuerus,* the Persian king Xerxes I (486–465 BCE). *In his accession year,* December 486 to April 6, 485 BCE. **4.7** *Artaxerxes* I, 465–424 BCE. *Bishlam,* perhaps Belshunu, the governor of the province Beyond the River. *Translated,* at

translated.[a] [8]Rehum the royal deputy and Shimshai the scribe wrote a letter against Jerusalem to King Artaxerxes as follows [9](then Rehum the royal deputy, Shimshai the scribe, and the rest of their associates, the judges, the envoys, the officials, the Persians, the people of Erech, the Babylonians, the people of Susa, that is, the Elamites, [10]and the rest of the nations whom the great and noble Osnappar deported and settled in the cities of Samaria and in the rest of the province Beyond the River wrote—and now [11]this is a copy of the letter that they sent):

"To King Artaxerxes: Your servants, the people of the province Beyond the River, send greeting. And now [12]may it be known to the king that the Jews who came up from you to us have gone to Jerusalem. They are rebuilding that rebellious and wicked city; they are finishing the walls and repairing the foundations. [13]Now may it be known to the king that, if this city is rebuilt and the walls finished, they will not pay tribute, custom, or toll, and the royal revenue will be reduced. [14]Now because we share the salt of the palace and it is not fitting for us to witness the king's dishonor, therefore we send and inform the king, [15]so that a search may be made in the annals of your ancestors. You will discover in the annals that this is a rebellious city, hurtful to kings and provinces, and that sedition was stirred up in it from long ago. On that account this city was laid waste. [16]We make known to the king that, if this city is rebuilt and its walls finished, you will then have no possession in the province Beyond the River."

[17]The king sent an answer: "To Rehum the royal deputy and Shimshai the scribe and the rest of their associates who live in Samaria and in the rest of the province Beyond the River,

greeting. And now [18]the letter that you sent to us has been read in translation before me. [19]So I made a decree, and someone searched and discovered that this city has risen against kings from long ago, and that rebellion and sedition have been made in it. [20]Jerusalem has had mighty kings who ruled over the whole province Beyond the River, to whom tribute, custom, and toll were paid. [21]Therefore issue an order that these people be made to cease, and that this city not be rebuilt, until I make a decree. [22]Moreover, take care not to be slack in this matter; why should damage grow to the hurt of the king?"

[23] Then when the copy of King Artaxerxes' letter was read before Rehum and the scribe Shimshai and their associates, they hurried to the Jews in Jerusalem and by force and power made them cease. [24]At that time the work on the house of God in Jerusalem stopped and was discontinued until the second year of the reign of King Darius of Persia.

Restoration of the Temple Resumed

5 Now the prophets, Haggai[b] and Zechariah son of Iddo, prophesied to the Jews who were in Judah and Jerusalem, in the name of the God of Israel who was over them. [2]Then Zerubbabel son of Shealtiel and Jeshua son of Jozadak set out to rebuild the house of God in Jerusalem; and with them were the prophets of God, helping them.

[3] At the same time Tattenai the governor of the province Beyond the River and Shethar-bozenai and their associates came to them and spoke to them thus, "Who gave you a decree to

---

a Heb adds *in Aramaic,* indicating that 4.8-6.18 is in Aramaic. Another interpretation is *The letter was written in the Aramaic script and set forth in the Aramaic language*   *b* Aram adds *the prophet*

---

the court, into Persian (cf. v. 18). **4.8–6.18** The text is in Aramaic (as the last word of 4.8 says; see text note *a*), not Hebrew; several Aramaic documents seem to be cited here. **4.8–16** An accusation, no doubt false, by officials of the province of Samaria that the Jews intend to revolt against the Persians. It is in the name of various Persian officials (e.g., *judges, envoys*) and ethnic groups settled there (e.g., *people of Erech*). **4.8–9** The repetitions can best be explained if v. 8 was the summary that typically appeared on the outside of a papyrus letter. **4.10** *Osnappar,* Ashurbanipal (669–ca. 627 BCE), the last of the great Assyrian kings. *The province Beyond the River,* the satrapy Abar-Nahara, of which Samaria and Judea (Aramaic *Yehud*) were provinces. **4.14** *Share the salt.* Partners in a covenant

agreement ratified it by a meal seasoned with salt (cf. Lev 2.13; Num 18.19). **4.15** *The annals.* Cf. 6.1–2; Esth 6.1. **4.21** *Until I make a decree.* A Persian decree for rebuilding the city is mentioned in Neh 2.5–6. **4.23** *Force and power,* military strength. **4.24** This verse resumes from v. 5 the narrative about the temple, after the digression about the city. *The second year of . . . Darius,* 520 BCE.

5.1–17 Restoration of the temple building is resumed. Two prophets provide a new stimulus for the rebuilding (vv. 1–2); the provincial government investigates the work (vv. 3–5) and reports to the central government (vv. 6–17). **5.1** *Haggai and Zechariah.* See Hag 1.1; Zech 1.1. **5.2** *Zerubbabel, Jeshua.* See note on 3.2. **5.3** *The province Beyond the River.* See note on

build this house and to finish this structure?" [4]They[a] also asked them this, "What are the names of the men who are building this building?" [5]But the eye of their God was upon the elders of the Jews, and they did not stop them until a report reached Darius and then answer was returned by letter in reply to it.

[6] The copy of the letter that Tattenai the governor of the province Beyond the River and Shethar-bozenai and his associates the envoys who were in the province Beyond the River sent to King Darius; [7]they sent him a report, in which was written as follows: "To Darius the king, all peace! [8]May it be known to the king that we went to the province of Judah, to the house of the great God. It is being built of hewn stone, and timber is laid in the walls; this work is being done diligently and prospers in their hands. [9]Then we spoke to those elders and asked them, 'Who gave you a decree to build this house and to finish this structure?' [10]We also asked them their names, for your information, so that we might write down the names of the men at their head. [11]This was their reply to us: 'We are the servants of the God of heaven and earth, and we are rebuilding the house that was built many years ago, which a great king of Israel built and finished. [12]But because our ancestors had angered the God of heaven, he gave them into the hand of King Nebuchadnezzar of Babylon, the Chaldean, who destroyed this house and carried away the people to Babylonia. [13]How-

ever, King Cyrus of Babylon, in the first year of his reign, made a decree that this house of God should be rebuilt. [14]Moreover, the gold and silver vessels of the house of God, which Nebuchadnezzar had taken out of the temple in Jerusalem and had brought into the temple of Babylon, these King Cyrus took out of the temple of Babylon, and they were delivered to a man named Sheshbazzar, whom he had made governor. [15]He said to him, "Take these vessels; go and put them in the temple in Jerusalem, and let the house of God be rebuilt on its site." [16]Then this Sheshbazzar came and laid the foundations of the house of God in Jerusalem; and from that time until now it has been under construction, and it is not yet finished.' [17]And now, if it seems good to the king, have a search made in the royal archives there in Babylon, to see whether a decree was issued by King Cyrus for the rebuilding of this house of God in Jerusalem. Let the king send us his pleasure in this matter."

The Decree of Darius

6 Then King Darius made a decree, and they searched the archives where the documents were stored in Babylon. [2]But it was in Ecbatana, the capital in the province of Media, that a scroll was found on which this was written: "A record. [3]In the first year of his reign, King Cyrus issued a decree: Concerning the

---

a Gk Syr: Aram *We*

4.10. **5.5** Strangely, Zerubbabel is not mentioned here or at the completion of the temple (6.14–18), despite Zechariah's assurance that "his hands shall also complete it" (Zech 4.9). Had Zerubbabel died or fallen out of favor with the Persians? *A report*, given in 5.7–17. *Answer*, given in 6.2–12. **5.8** *Timber is laid in the walls.* Timber was layered between stone courses, as in the building edict of Cyrus (6.4), and also in the account of Solomon's temple (1 Kings 6.36; 7.12), possibly to limit damage in case of an earthquake. **5.11** *A great king of Israel*, Solomon. **5.12** *King Nebuchadnezzar of Babylon, the Chaldean.* Nebuchadnezzar II ruled the Neo-Babylonian Empire from 605 to 562 BCE and captured Jerusalem in 597 and again in 587 or 586, taking many inhabitants into captivity (2 Kings 24–25). He was by tribal affiliation a Chaldean from southern Babylonia. **5.13** *Made a decree.* The reference is to 6.3–5; cf. also 1.1. **5.14** *Vessels . . . which Nebuchadnezzar had taken.* See note on 1.7. *Sheshbazzar.* See note on 1.8. *A man named Sheshbazzar* seems deliberately disrespectful; the idiom is often found in Aramaic papyri in reference to slaves. The term translated *governor* may not mean "provincial ruler" (as in v. 6; Neh 5.14),

but simply "commissioner" for this project. **5.16** *Foundations*, or rather the platform on which the temple was built; the term is different from that in 3.10. In all the other evidence it is Zerubbabel, not *Sheshbazzar*, who is said to have begun the rebuilding (3.2; 4.3; 5.2; Hag 1.14; Zech 4.9). Perhaps it was the commissioner Sheshbazzar who was named in the official Persian correspondence and not the governor Zerubbabel. *From that time . . . under construction.* But both 4.4, 24 and Hag 1.2, 4, 9 report that work ceased for about seventeen years. The leaders obviously do not want to admit this; and it is true enough that since work has not yet been completed, it could be said to be still "in progress."

6.1–12 The decree of Darius authorizing the rebuilding of the temple quotes the earlier decree of Cyrus (vv. 2–5). **6.2** *Ecbatana*, modern Hamadan, the former capital of Media and the summer residence of the Persian kings. *Scroll*, or "roll," a rolled piece of leather or papyrus written on in Aramaic and kept in a clay sealing shaped like a napkin ring. **6.3** *Sacrifices.* The Persians themselves did not sacrifice. *Its height . . . and its width.* The length dimension is missing.

house of God at Jerusalem, let the house be rebuilt, the place where sacrifices are offered and burnt offerings are brought;*a* its height shall be sixty cubits and its width sixty cubits, 4with three courses of hewn stones and one course of timber; let the cost be paid from the royal treasury. 5Moreover, let the gold and silver vessels of the house of God, which Nebuchadnezzar took out of the temple in Jerusalem and brought to Babylon, be restored and brought back to the temple in Jerusalem, each to its place; you shall put them in the house of God."

6 "Now you, Tattenai, governor of the province Beyond the River, Shethar-bozenai, and you, their associates, the envoys in the province Beyond the River, keep away; 7let the work on this house of God alone; let the governor of the Jews and the elders of the Jews rebuild this house of God on its site. 8Moreover I make a decree regarding what you shall do for these elders of the Jews for the rebuilding of this house of God: the cost is to be paid to these people, in full and without delay, from the royal revenue, the tribute of the province Beyond the River. 9Whatever is needed— young bulls, rams, or sheep for burnt offerings to the God of heaven, wheat, salt, wine, or oil, as the priests in Jerusalem require—let that be given to them day by day without fail, 10so that they may offer pleasing sacrifices to the God of heaven, and pray for the life of the king and his children. 11Furthermore I decree that if any-

one alters this edict, a beam shall be pulled out of the house of the perpetrator, who then shall be impaled on it. The house shall be made a dunghill. 12May the God who has established his name there overthrow any king or people that shall put forth a hand to alter this, or to destroy this house of God in Jerusalem. I, Darius, make a decree; let it be done with all diligence."

Completion and Dedication of the Temple

13 Then, according to the word sent by King Darius, Tattenai, the governor of the province Beyond the River, Shethar-bozenai, and their associates did with all diligence what King Darius had ordered. 14So the elders of the Jews built and prospered, through the prophesying of the prophet Haggai and Zechariah son of Iddo. They finished their building by command of the God of Israel and by decree of Cyrus, Darius, and King Artaxerxes of Persia; 15and this house was finished on the third day of the month of Adar, in the sixth year of the reign of King Darius.

16 The people of Israel, the priests and the Levites, and the rest of the returned exiles, celebrated the dedication of this house of God with joy. 17They offered at the dedication of this house of God one hundred bulls, two hundred rams, four hundred lambs, and as a sin offering for all Israel, twelve male goats, ac-

---

a Meaning of Aram uncertain

Solomon's temple was 60 cubits long, 20 wide, 30 high (1 Kings 6.2). If the Second Temple was 60 cubits long, it would have been a perfect cube, 60 by 60 by 60 cubits; but it would also have been six times the volume of Solomon's temple! To fit on the same foundations (see note on 3.10), the Second Temple would most likely have had the same dimensions. A *cubit* was about 17.5 inches or, if the "royal" or "long" cubit was used (Ezek 41.8), about 20.4 inches. On the basis of the standard cubit, the temple would have been 90 by 30 by 45 feet. **6.4** *Three courses . . . timber.* See note on 5.8. *Paid from the royal treasury,* hence the necessity for details of size and building materials in the edict. It is said that this is the first time in recorded history that a ruler not only approved the practice of a foreign religion in his empire but also devoted state resources to its maintenance. **6.5** *Vessels . . . Nebuchadnezzar took out of the temple.* See note on 1.7. **6.8** *From . . . the tribute of the province Beyond the River,* i.e., from Tattenai's own revenues, not from central Persian funds. **6.9** *Wheat* was offered as flour, alone or mixed with olive *oil* (cf. Lev 2.1–7; 5.11). *Salt* accompanied cereal offerings (Lev 2.13), and *wine* was a libation with

daily and festival burnt offerings (Ex 29.38–41; Lev 23.13, 18, 37). **6.12** *Established his name there,* a very Jewish, and not at all a Persian, phrase (cf., e.g., Deut 12.11). **6.13–18** The temple is finally completed and dedicated. **6.14** *By command . . . by decree.* The twin impulses, from divine and human sources, are artlessly conjoined. The reference to *King Artaxerxes* (465–424 BCE) is out of place here, since he did not come to the throne until decades after the temple was completed. **6.15** *On the third day . . . in the sixth year,* March 12, 515 BCE. Apparently that was a sabbath, in which case it was the day after the completion of the work (cf. Gen 2.2). But perhaps we should follow 1 Esd 7.5 and read "the twenty-third day," namely, April 1, a Friday. **6.16** *The returned exiles.* See notes on 3.8; 4.1. **6.17** The ceremony of dedication is modeled on that of Solomon (1 Kings 8; 2 Chr 7.4–7), though the number of animals said to have been sacrificed is very much smaller (cf. 1 Kings 8.63). *A sin offering* decontaminates the temple from impurity (cf. Ezek 43.18–27). *The number of the tribes.* Although only members of Judah, Benjamin, and Levi are said to have constituted the postexilic community, they re-

cording to the number of the tribes of Israel. [18]Then they set the priests in their divisions and the Levites in their courses for the service of God at Jerusalem, as it is written in the book of Moses.

The Passover Celebrated

19 On the fourteenth day of the first month the returned exiles kept the passover. [20]For both the priests and the Levites had purified themselves; all of them were clean. So they killed the passover lamb for all the returned exiles, for their fellow priests, and for themselves. [21]It was eaten by the people of Israel who had returned from exile, and also by all who had joined them and separated themselves from the pollutions of the nations of the land to worship the LORD, the God of Israel. [22]With joy they celebrated the festival of unleavened bread seven days; for the LORD had made them joyful, and had turned the heart of the king of Assyria to them, so that he aided them in the work on the house of God, the God of Israel.

The Coming and Work of Ezra

7 After this, in the reign of King Artaxerxes of Persia, Ezra son of Seraiah, son of Azariah, son of Hilkiah, [2]son of Shallum, son of Zadok, son of Ahitub, [3]son of Amariah, son of Azariah, son of Meraioth, [4]son of Zerahiah,

son of Uzzi, son of Bukki, [5]son of Abishua, son of Phinehas, son of Eleazar, son of the chief priest Aaron— [6]this Ezra went up from Babylonia. He was a scribe skilled in the law of Moses that the LORD the God of Israel had given; and the king granted him all that he asked, for the hand of the LORD his God was upon him.

7 Some of the people of Israel, and some of the priests and Levites, the singers and gatekeepers, and the temple servants also went up to Jerusalem, in the seventh year of King Artaxerxes. [8]They came to Jerusalem in the fifth month, which was in the seventh year of the king. [9]On the first day of the first month the journey up from Babylon was begun, and on the first day of the fifth month he came to Jerusalem, for the gracious hand of his God was upon him. [10]For Ezra had set his heart to study the law of the LORD, and to do it, and to teach the statutes and ordinances in Israel.

The Letter of Artaxerxes to Ezra

11 This is a copy of the letter that King Artaxerxes gave to the priest Ezra, the scribe, a scholar of the text of the commandments of the LORD and his statutes for Israel: [12]"Artaxerxes, king of kings, to the priest Ezra, the scribe of the law of the God of heaven: Peace.[a]

_____

a Syr Vg 1 Esdras 8.9: Aram Perfect

---

gard themselves as the authentic Israel and as worshiping on behalf of all the tribes. **6.18** *As it is written in the book of Moses.* In the biblical tradition, however, it was not Moses but David who arranged the divisions and courses of these clergy (1 Chr 23–26); Moses simply established the two classes (Ex 29; Lev 8; Num 3; 4; 8). **6.19–22** Now that the temple is finished, it can serve its purpose as the center for the celebration of the festivals. The first festival that falls due is Passover (cf. Ex 12), some six weeks after the dedication, on April 21, 515 BCE. **6.21** *All who had joined them.* For the first time (see notes on 3.8; 4.1) the presence of a wider circle of Jews than those who had returned from exile is acknowledged. *Pollutions of the nations of the land,* the worship of foreign gods practiced by non-Jews in Judea. **6.22** *The festival of unleavened bread,* an extension of Passover and celebrated from the fifteenth to the twenty-first of the first month (Ex 12.15–20; Lev 23.6–8; Deut 16.1–8). Unleavened bread was a reminder of the food the Israelites ate before they made their hasty escape from Egypt (Deut 16.3). *The king of Assyria.* The Assyrian Empire was of course long since defunct when Cyrus and Darius reigned, but they were its heirs and they reversed the evil against Israel initiated by the Assyrian kings.

7.1–10 Ezra's lineage and office (vv. 1–6) and a brief notice of his coming to Jerusalem (vv. 7–10; more detail in 8.15–36). **7.1** *After this.* The narrative moves suddenly from the end of the sixth century to the middle of the fifth (or beginning of the fourth, if the king is Artaxerxes II; see note on 7.7). *Artaxerxes.* See note on 7.7. Ezra's genealogy shows him to be a member of the high-priestly family, though not high priest himself. **7.6** *Scribe,* doctor of the Jewish law (see also Sir 38.34b–39.11). *All that he asked,* to be inferred from the king's letter of vv. 12–26. **7.7** *In the seventh year of King Artaxerxes,* 458 BCE if the king is Artaxerxes I (465–424), 398 BCE if it is Artaxerxes II (404–358). **7.9** On the assumption that Ezra's journey took place in 458 BCE, he left Babylonia on April 8 and arrived in Jerusalem on August 4. **7.10** To *study,* i.e., to learn and to interpret, and to *do* are the twin ideals of postexilic Judaism. **7.11–26** After an introductory verse in Hebrew (v. 11), there follows a long official document in Aramaic (vv. 12–26), the language in which most documents of this kind are found in Ezra. This is Artaxerxes' firman, or letter of authorization, to Ezra. **7.12** *Peace.* The Aramaic means "perfect," which may be an abbreviation of a greeting formula or else a scribal mark to show that the matter has been dealt

And now ¹³I decree that any of the people of Israel or their priests or Levites in my kingdom who freely offers to go to Jerusalem may go with you. ¹⁴For you are sent by the king and his seven counselors to make inquiries about Judah and Jerusalem according to the law of your God, which is in your hand, ¹⁵and also to convey the silver and gold that the king and his counselors have freely offered to the God of Israel, whose dwelling is in Jerusalem, ¹⁶with all the silver and gold that you shall find in the whole province of Babylonia, and with the freewill offerings of the people and the priests, given willingly for the house of their God in Jerusalem. ¹⁷With this money, then, you shall with all diligence buy bulls, rams, and lambs, and their grain offerings and their drink offerings, and you shall offer them on the altar of the house of your God in Jerusalem. ¹⁸Whatever seems good to you and your colleagues to do with the rest of the silver and gold, you may do, according to the will of your God. ¹⁹The vessels that have been given you for the service of the house of your God, you shall deliver before the God of Jerusalem. ²⁰And whatever else is required for the house of your God, which you are responsible for providing, you may provide out of the king's treasury.

21 "I, King Artaxerxes, decree to all the treasurers in the province Beyond the River: Whatever the priest Ezra, the scribe of the law of the God of heaven, requires of you, let it be done with all diligence, ²²up to one hundred talents of silver, one hundred cors of wheat, one hundred baths*ᵃ* of wine, one hundred baths*ᵃ* of oil, and unlimited salt. ²³Whatever is commanded by the God of heaven, let it be done with zeal for the house of the God of heaven, or wrath will come upon the realm of the king and his heirs. ²⁴We also notify you that it shall not be

lawful to impose tribute, custom, or toll on any of the priests, the Levites, the singers, the doorkeepers, the temple servants, or other servants of this house of God.

25 "And you, Ezra, according to the God-given wisdom you possess, appoint magistrates and judges who may judge all the people in the province Beyond the River who know the laws of your God; and you shall teach those who do not know them. ²⁶All who will not obey the law of your God and the law of the king, let judgment be strictly executed on them, whether for death or for banishment or for confiscation of their goods or for imprisonment."

27 Blessed be the LORD, the God of our ancestors, who put such a thing as this into the heart of the king to glorify the house of the LORD in Jerusalem, ²⁸and who extended to me steadfast love before the king and his counselors, and before all the king's mighty officers. I took courage, for the hand of the LORD my God was upon me, and I gathered leaders from Israel to go up with me.

Heads of Families Who Returned with Ezra

8 These are their family heads, and this is the genealogy of those who went up with me from Babylonia, in the reign of King Artaxerxes: ²Of the descendants of Phinehas, Gershom. Of Ithamar, Daniel. Of David, Hattush, ³of the descendants of Shecaniah. Of Parosh, Zechariah, with whom were registered one hundred fifty males. ⁴Of the descendants of Pahath-moab, Eliehoenai son of Zerahiah, and with him two hundred males. ⁵Of the descendants of Zattu,*ᵇ* Shecaniah son of Jahaziel,

---

a A Heb measure of volume   *b* Gk 1 Esdras 8.32: Heb lacks *of Zattu*

---

with. **7.13** *People . . . priests . . . Levites,* the familiar threefold division of Israel into laity and two types of religious personnel (see also 2.70; 6.16). *Freely offers,* another typically Jewish term (cf. also 1.6; 2.68; 3.5; 8.28), suggesting a Jewish drafting or reworking of this letter. **7.14** *Seven counselors,* known in Greek sources as the king's advisers from the leading aristocratic families (cf. also Esth 1.14). *To make inquiries . . . according to the law,* to discover how far Jewish law is being observed in Judea. *Which is in your hand,* i.e., of which you have the mastery. The law was almost certainly the Pentateuch in more or less its present form. **7.16** *Find,* as donations from fellow Jews and others (cf. 1.4). **7.21–24** Ezra's authorization includes an

edict addressed to the treasurers of the province for support of the temple worship in Jerusalem. The grant seems to be an annual one, except that the amount of silver, *one hundred talents,* more than 3 tons, is hugely disproportionate. Perhaps *talents* is a scribal error for "minas," one-sixtieth of the weight. **7.25** Ezra's authority extends only to Jews in the province, whether they already know pentateuchal law or need to be taught it. **7.27–28** The text changes back to Hebrew at this point, and the narrator quotes a first-person account of Ezra's work.

8.1–14 Ezra's company numbered about fifteen hundred males, all from families of which some members had already returned. The twelve phratry names

and with him three hundred males. 6Of the descendants of Adin, Ebed son of Jonathan, and with him fifty males. 7Of the descendants of Elam, Jeshaiah son of Athaliah, and with him seventy males. 8Of the descendants of Shephatiah, Zebadiah son of Michael, and with him eighty males. 9Of the descendants of Joab, Obadiah son of Jehiel, and with him two hundred eighteen males. 10Of the descendants of Bani,*a* Shelomith son of Josiphiah, and with him one hundred sixty males. 11Of the descendants of Bebai, Zechariah son of Bebai, and with him twenty-eight males. 12Of the descendants of Azgad, Johanan son of Hakkatan, and with him one hundred ten males. 13Of the descendants of Adonikam, those who came later, their names being Eliphelet, Jeuel, and Shemaiah, and with them sixty males. 14Of the descendants of Bigvai, Uthai and Zaccur, and with them seventy males.

Servants for the Temple

15 I gathered them by the river that runs to Ahava, and there we camped three days. As I reviewed the people and the priests, I found there none of the descendants of Levi. 16Then I sent for Eliezer, Ariel, Shemaiah, Elnathan, Jarib, Elnathan, Nathan, Zechariah, and Meshullam, who were leaders, and for Joiarib and Elnathan, who were wise, 17and sent them to Iddo, the leader at the place called Casiphia, telling them what to say to Iddo and his colleagues the temple servants at Casiphia, namely, to send us ministers for the house of our God. 18Since the gracious hand of our God was upon us, they brought us a man of discretion, of the descendants of Mahli son of Levi son of Israel, namely Sherebiah, with his sons and kin, eighteen; 19also Hashabiah and with him Jeshaiah of the descendants of Merari, with his kin and their sons, twenty; 20besides two hundred twenty of the temple ser-

vants, whom David and his officials had set apart to attend the Levites. These were all mentioned by name.

Fasting and Prayer for Protection

21 Then I proclaimed a fast there, at the river Ahava, that we might deny ourselves*b* before our God, to seek from him a safe journey for ourselves, our children, and all our possessions. 22For I was ashamed to ask the king for a band of soldiers and cavalry to protect us against the enemy on our way, since we had told the king that the hand of our God is gracious to all who seek him, but his power and his wrath are against all who forsake him. 23So we fasted and petitioned our God for this, and he listened to our entreaty.

Gifts for the Temple

24 Then I set apart twelve of the leading priests: Sherebiah, Hashabiah, and ten of their kin with them. 25And I weighed out to them the silver and the gold and the vessels, the offering for the house of our God that the king, his counselors, his lords, and all Israel there present had offered; 26I weighed out into their hand six hundred fifty talents of silver, and one hundred silver vessels worth . . . talents,*c* and one hundred talents of gold, 27twenty gold bowls worth a thousand darics, and two vessels of fine polished bronze as precious as gold. 28And I said to them, "You are holy to the LORD, and the vessels are holy; and the silver and the gold are a freewill offering to the LORD, the God of your ancestors. 29Guard them and keep them until you weigh them before the chief priests and the Levites and the heads of families in Israel at Jerusalem, within the chambers of the house of the LORD." 30So

---

a Gk 1 Esdras 8.36: Heb lacks *Bani*   *b* Or *might fast*
c The number of talents is lacking

---

are to be found also in 2.3–15. Unlike in ch. 2, here the priests are mentioned first (v. 2). **8.15–20** The presence of Levites seems to have been needed for the symbolism, so that Ezra's caravan would include representatives of all Israel. The place-names are unknown. **8.20** *Mentioned by name,* perhaps in the first-person Ezra memoir (see Introduction), but omitted by the editor of the present book of Ezra. **8.21** *A fast . . . deny ourselves.* Fasting was apparently a symbolic entering of a near-death state; in such a state one was endangered and therefore in need of divine care. *A safe journey,* lit. "a straight (or level) way," perhaps re-

calling Isa 40.3. **8.24** *The leading priests: Sherebiah, Hashabiah . . . ,* better "the leading priests, and Sherebiah, Hashabiah . . . ," for the named are Levites (vv. 18–19); twelve priests and twelve Levites would be a symbol of all Israel. **8.26** *Six hundred fifty talents,* about 22 tons. *Worth . . . talents.* The numeral is missing; or perhaps the word for *talents* could be read as "two talents." *One hundred talents of gold,* about 3 tons. The figures are either exaggerated or copying errors. **8.27** *Darics.* See note on 2.69. **8.28** *Holy,* i.e. belonging to God, whether objects or persons. Any seizure of the gifts or their guardians would be an as-

the priests and the Levites took over the silver, the gold, and the vessels as they were weighed out, to bring them to Jerusalem, to the house of our God.

The Return to Jerusalem

31 Then we left the river Ahava on the twelfth day of the first month, to go to Jerusalem; the hand of our God was upon us, and he delivered us from the hand of the enemy and from ambushes along the way. 32 We came to Jerusalem and remained there three days. 33 On the fourth day, within the house of our God, the silver, the gold, and the vessels were weighed into the hands of the priest Meremoth son of Uriah, and with him was Eleazar son of Phinehas, and with them were the Levites, Jozabad son of Jeshua and Noadiah son of Binnui. 34 The total was counted and weighed, and the weight of everything was recorded.

35 At that time those who had come from captivity, the returned exiles, offered burnt offerings to the God of Israel, twelve bulls for all Israel, ninety-six rams, seventy-seven lambs, and as a sin offering twelve male goats; all this was a burnt offering to the LORD. 36 They also

delivered the king's commissions to the king's satraps and to the governors of the province Beyond the River; and they supported the people and the house of God.

Denunciation of Mixed Marriages

9 After these things had been done, the officials approached me and said, "The people of Israel, the priests, and the Levites have not separated themselves from the peoples of the lands with their abominations, from the Canaanites, the Hittites, the Perizzites, the Jebusites, the Ammonites, the Moabites, the Egyptians, and the Amorites. 2 For they have taken some of their daughters as wives for themselves and for their sons. Thus the holy seed has mixed itself with the peoples of the lands, and in this faithlessness the officials and leaders have led the way." 3 When I heard this, I tore my garment and my mantle, and pulled hair from my head and beard, and sat appalled. 4 Then all who trembled at the words of the God of Israel, because of the faithlessness of the returned exiles, gathered around me while I sat appalled until the evening sacrifice.

sault on God. **8.35–36** These summary verses, which probably were originally followed by the account of the law-reading ceremony of Neh 7.73b–8.18, are in third-person narrative and so apparently not from the Ezra memoir (see Introduction). **8.36** *Satraps,* used loosely, for there was only one satrap of the province Beyond the River, though Ezra would have encountered various "governors."

9.1–10.44 Ezra is now informed that certain Jews have broken the law by marrying non-Jews (9.1–2); he responds with mourning (9.3–5) and a prayer of repentance (9.5–15), since he feels the people as a whole have been implicated in this breach of the law. A group of rigorists then propose to Ezra the action they think he should take (10.1–5), and Ezra accedes, calling a public assembly that determines that foreign wives should be divorced (10.6–17). A list follows of the 113 men who had married non-Jews. The first-person form in ch. 9 suggests that an Ezra memoir (see Introduction) is being drawn on; in ch. 10 the third-person form resumes. It is hard to fault the desire of the beleaguered postexilic community to maintain its own distinctive way of life, religion, and language (cf. note on Neh 13.23–29), but harder still for modern readers to sympathize with the drastic solution proposed in this narrative. Hints of opposition, in the presence of non-Jewish persons even in noble families in subsequent generations (Neh 6.17–18) and in Nehemiah's less rigorous response to a similar situation (Neh 13.23–27), suggest that Ezra's decision was regarded as extreme even within the postexilic community itself. **9.1** *After*

these things had been done. Most probably the account of the reading of the law in Neh 8, and perhaps also that of the penitential service of Neh 9, earlier came between the moment of Ezra's arrival in Jerusalem and the events of Ezra 9–10. *Peoples of the lands,* non-Jewish or part-Jewish inhabitants. There were no surviving *Canaanites, Hittites, Perizzites, Jebusites,* or *Amorites* still in Palestine in Ezra's time. The names come from an old stereotyped list of foreign nations with whom intermarriage was forbidden (esp. in Deut 7.1–4), and they are mentioned here to invoke the ancient law as relevant to the current situation. Marriage with *Ammonites* and *Moabites,* though they were recognized as members of the Semitic family of nations, had also been strongly prohibited (Deut 23.3–6), but with *Egyptians* it was not forbidden (Deut 23.7). **9.2** *The holy seed,* a phrase from Isa 6.13, with overtones of the language of the blessings to Abraham (e.g., Gen 12.7; 13.14–16; 17.1–8). The exclusivist language expresses a concern with religious rather than simply ethnic identity, but whether that makes it better or worse is a matter of opinion. **9.3** *I tore my garment* (tunic or undergarment) *and my mantle* (cloak or outer garment), an act of mourning, a stylized stripping oneself naked as a symbol of death. *Pulled hair from my head and beard,* a customary modification of the forbidden practice of shaving the head in mourning (Lev 19.27; 21.5). **9.4** *All who trembled . . . Israel,* the strict adherents of the law (cf. 10.9; Isa 66.2, 5). *Appalled,* i.e., dumbfounded, the conventional shocked silence at a time of lamentation (cf. Job 2.12–13; Ezek 26.16). *Until the evening sacrifice,*

Ezra's Prayer

5 At the evening sacrifice I got up from my fasting, with my garments and my mantle torn, and fell on my knees, spread out my hands to the LORD my God, 6and said,

"O my God, I am too ashamed and embarrassed to lift my face to you, my God, for our iniquities have risen higher than our heads, and our guilt has mounted up to the heavens. 7From the days of our ancestors to this day we have been deep in guilt, and for our iniquities we, our kings, and our priests have been handed over to the kings of the lands, to the sword, to captivity, to plundering, and to utter shame, as is now the case. 8But now for a brief moment favor has been shown by the LORD our God, who has left us a remnant, and given us a stake in his holy place, in order that he*a* may brighten our eyes and grant us a little sustenance in our slavery. 9For we are slaves; yet our God has not forsaken us in our slavery, but has extended to us his steadfast love before the kings of Persia, to give us new life to set up the house of our God, to repair its ruins, and to give us a wall in Judea and Jerusalem.

10 "And now, our God, what shall we say after this? For we have forsaken your commandments, 11which you commanded by your servants the prophets, saying, 'The land that you are entering to possess is a land unclean with the pollutions of the peoples of the lands, with their abominations. They have filled it from end to end with their uncleanness. 12Therefore do not give your daughters to their sons, neither take their daughters for your sons, and never seek their peace or prosperity, so that you may be strong and eat the good of the land and leave it for an inheritance to your children forever.' 13After all that has come upon us for our evil deeds and for our great guilt, seeing that you, our God, have punished us less than our iniquities deserved and have given us such a remnant as this, 14shall we break your commandments again and intermarry with the peoples who practice these abominations? Would you not be angry with us until you destroy us without remnant or survivor? 15O LORD, God of Israel, you are just, but we have escaped as a remnant, as is now the case. Here we are before you in our guilt, though no one can face you because of this."

The People's Response

10 While Ezra prayed and made confession, weeping and throwing himself down before the house of God, a very great assembly of men, women, and children gathered to him out of Israel; the people also wept bitterly. 2Shecaniah son of Jehiel, of the descendants of Elam, addressed Ezra, saying, "We have broken faith with our God and have married foreign women from the peoples of the land, but even now there is hope for Israel in spite of this. 3So now let us make a covenant with our God to send away all these wives and their children, according to the counsel of my lord and of those who tremble at the commandment of our God; and let it be done according to the law. 4Take action, for it is your duty, and we are with you; be strong, and do it." 5Then Ezra stood up and made the leading priests, the Levites, and all Israel swear that they would do as had been said. So they swore.

Foreign Wives and Their Children Rejected

6 Then Ezra withdrew from before the house of God, and went to the chamber of Jeho-

---

a Heb *our God*

---

until the ninth hour, about 3 PM, an appropriate time for prayer (1 Kings 18.36; Acts 3.1). **9.5** *Spread out my hands,* palms upward, a gesture of supplication in prayer. **9.7** *Utter shame, as is now the case,* because as a people the Jews are subject to the Persians. **9.8** *A remnant,* those of the nation who remain. *A stake,* lit. "a tent peg," the rebuilt temple as a guarantee of security and God's presence. *Brighten our eyes,* revive our spirits (cf. 1 Sam 14.27). **9.9** *Slaves,* not literally, but, as Persian subjects, lacking national independence. *A wall in Judea and Jerusalem,* a metaphor (cf. Ps 80.2) for the protection of the Persian government. **9.11–12** The words quoted by Ezra come mostly from the Pentateuch, so he must regard Moses as a prophet (as does Deut 18.15; 34.10); there are allusions to Deut 7.1; Lev 18.24–30; Deut 18.9; 2 Kings 21.16; Deut 7.3; 23.6; 11.8; 6.11; 1.38–39.

10.2 *Shecaniah son of Jehiel, of . . . Elam.* Strangely, a Jehiel of the family of Elam was among those who had married foreign wives (see 10.26); so, if it is the same Jehiel, Shecaniah would have been advocating his own excommunication! **10.3** *To send away,* to divorce. *According to the law.* The law sanctions divorce in the case of a man finding some "uncleanness" in his wife (Deut 24.1–4); apparently the law is here being applied to the case of the (ritual) "uncleanness" of foreign birth. Previously, although the law forbade cer-

hanan son of Eliashib, where he spent the night. [a] He did not eat bread or drink water, for he was mourning over the faithlessness of the exiles. [7]They made a proclamation throughout Judah and Jerusalem to all the returned exiles that they should assemble at Jerusalem, [8]and that if any did not come within three days, by order of the officials and the elders all their property should be forfeited, and they themselves banned from the congregation of the exiles.

9 Then all the people of Judah and Benjamin assembled at Jerusalem within the three days; it was the ninth month, on the twentieth day of the month. All the people sat in the open square before the house of God, trembling because of this matter and because of the heavy rain. [10]Then Ezra the priest stood up and said to them, "You have trespassed and married foreign women, and so increased the guilt of Israel. [11]Now make confession to the LORD the God of your ancestors, and do his will; separate yourselves from the peoples of the land and from the foreign wives." [12]Then all the assembly answered with a loud voice, "It is so; we must do as you have said. [13]But the people are many, and it is a time of heavy rain; we cannot stand in the open. Nor is this a task for one day or for two, for many of us have transgressed in this matter. [14]Let our officials represent the whole assembly, and let all in our towns who have taken foreign wives come at appointed times, and with them the elders and judges of every town, until the fierce wrath of our God on this account is averted from us." [15]Only Jonathan son of Asahel and Jahzeiah son of Tikvah opposed this, and Meshullam and Shabbethai the Levites supported them.

16 Then the returned exiles did so. Ezra the priest selected men, [b] heads of families, according to their families, each of them designated by name. On the first day of the tenth month they sat down to examine the matter. [17]By the first day of the first month they had come to the end of all the men who had married foreign women.

18 There were found of the descendants of the priests who had married foreign women, of the descendants of Jeshua son of Jozadak and his brothers: Maaseiah, Eliezer, Jarib, and Gedaliah. [19]They pledged themselves to send away their wives, and their guilt offering was a ram of the flock for their guilt. [20]Of the descendants of Immer: Hanani and Zebadiah. [21]Of the descendants of Harim: Maaseiah, Elijah, Shemaiah, Jehiel, and Uzziah. [22]Of the descendants of Pashhur: Elioenai, Maaseiah, Ishmael, Nethanel, Jozabad, and Elasah.

23 Of the Levites: Jozabad, Shimei, Kelaiah (that is, Kelita), Pethahiah, Judah, and Eliezer. [24]Of the singers: Eliashib. Of the gatekeepers: Shallum, Telem, and Uri.

25 And of Israel: of the descendants of Parosh: Ramiah, Izziah, Malchijah, Mijamin, Eleazar, Hashabiah, [c] and Benaiah. [26]Of the descendants of Elam: Mattaniah, Zechariah, Jehiel, Abdi, Jeremoth, and Elijah. [27]Of the descendants of Zattu: Elioenai, Eliashib, Mattaniah, Jeremoth, Zabad, and Aziza. [28]Of the descendants of Bebai: Jehohanan, Hananiah, Zabbai, and Athlai. [29]Of the descendants of Bani: Meshullam, Malluch, Adaiah, Jashub, Sheal, and Jeremoth. [30]Of the descendants of

---

a 1 Esdras 9.2: Heb where he went   b 1 Esdras 9.16: Syr: Heb And there were selected Ezra,   c 1 Esdras 9.26 Gk: Heb Malchijah

tain intermarriage, there was no rule about what action should be taken once it had occurred. **10.6** *The chamber.* There were rooms in the temple for accommodating priests and Levites when they were on duty. *Jehohanan* (or Johanan) *son of Eliashib,* perhaps the high priest, if the high-priestly genealogy of Neh 12.10–11 is rightly seen to have some gaps. **10.7** *Assemble at Jerusalem.* An assembly of all Israelite males was required in the law for certain festivals (Ex 23.17; Deut 16.16). **10.8** *Forfeited,* lit. "devoted" to God, and so removed from the owner's use for secular purposes. *Banned,* the earliest attestation of excommunication (cf. Jn 9.22; 12.42). **10.9** *The ninth month,* December, when the heavy winter rains, and sometimes even snow, fall in Jerusalem, which lies 2,000 feet above sea level. *The open square,* the scene of Ezra's prayer (v. 1) and perhaps also of his law reading (Neh 8). **10.14** The

appointment of a commission to examine the individual cases casts a veneer of propriety and legality over the proceedings, which had, however, been decided on by a popular assembly of which the vast majority had nothing to lose by the decision. **10.15** The opposition may be to the proposal to postpone the investigations, and these four men may be more rigorous, not more liberal, than the majority; the Levite *Meshullam* may well be Ezra's companion in 8.16, and *Shabbethai*'s name suggests that he came from a strictly religious family (cf. Isa 58.13). **10.16–17** A full three months (from December 29, 458, to March 27, 457 BCE, if the contemporary Persian king was Artaxerxes I; see note on 7.7) were spent on the identification of 113 offenders; it cannot have always been easy to determine the racial status of a woman who was of partly Jewish and partly non-Jewish descent. The list may of course be

Pahath-moab: Adna, Chelal, Benaiah, Maaseiah, Mattaniah, Bezalel, Binnui, and Manasseh. 31Of the descendants of Harim: Eliezer, Isshijah, Malchijah, Shemaiah, Shimeon, 32Benjamin, Malluch, and Shemariah. 33Of the descendants of Hashum: Mattenai, Mattattah, Zabad, Eliphelet, Jeremai, Manasseh, and Shimei. 34Of the descendants of Bani: Maadai, Amram, Uel, 35Benaiah, Bedeiah, Cheluhi, 36Vaniah, Meremoth, Eliashib, 37Mattaniah, Mattenai, and Jaasu. 38Of the descendants of Binnui:*a* Shimei, 39Shelemiah, Nathan, Adaiah, 40Machnadebai, Shashai, Sharai, 41Azarel, Shelemiah, Shemariah, 42Shallum, Amariah, and Joseph. 43Of the descendants of Nebo: Jeiel, Mattithiah, Zabad, Zebina, Jaddai, Joel, and Benaiah. 44All these had married foreign women, and they sent them away with their children.*b*

a Gk: Heb *Bani, Binnui*   *b* 1 Esdras 9.36; meaning of Heb uncertain

incomplete: it includes none of the temple servants or of the inhabitants of the towns listed in 2.20–35. **10.44** The narrative can be reasonably expected to have concluded with some such note, but the Hebrew is not intelligible, and the NRSV adopts the parallel in 1 Esd 9.36.

NEHEMIAH

Nehemiah Prays for His People

1 The words of Nehemiah son of Hacaliah.
In the month of Chislev, in the twentieth year, while I was in Susa the capital, ²one of my brothers, Hanani, came with certain men from Judah; and I asked them about the Jews that survived, those who had escaped the captivity, and about Jerusalem. ³They replied, "The survivors there in the province who escaped captivity are in great trouble and shame; the wall of Jerusalem is broken down, and its gates have been destroyed by fire."

4 When I heard these words I sat down and wept, and mourned for days, fasting and praying before the God of heaven. ⁵I said, "O LORD God of heaven, the great and awesome God who keeps covenant and steadfast love with those who love him and keep his commandments; ⁶let your ear be attentive and your eyes open to hear the prayer of your servant that I now pray before you day and night for your servants, the people of Israel, confessing the sins of the people of Israel, which we have sinned against you. Both I and my family have sinned. ⁷We have offended you deeply, failing to keep the commandments, the statutes, and the ordinances that you commanded your servant Moses. ⁸Remember the word that you commanded your servant Moses, 'If you are unfaithful, I will scatter you among the peoples; ⁹but if you return to me and keep my commandments and do them, though your outcasts are under the farthest skies, I will gather them from there and bring them to the place at which I have chosen to establish my name.' ¹⁰They are your servants and your people, whom you redeemed by your great power and your strong hand. ¹¹O Lord, let your ear be attentive to the prayer of your servant, and

---

[For introductory material to Nehemiah, see the Introduction to Ezra.]

1.1–11 Nehemiah, hearing of a recent attack upon Jerusalem, prays for the success of his planned request to the Persian king to be allowed to rebuild the city walls. The narrative is told in the first person and apparently has been only lightly edited from a memoir composed by Nehemiah himself. **1.1** *Nehemiah,* a Jew who had risen to high office in the Persian administration; see notes on 1.11; 5.14. *Chislev,* the ninth month, November/December. *The twentieth year,* apparently of Artaxerxes I (465–424 BCE), 445. But ch. 2 is dated in the month Nisan (the first month) of the twentieth year; since the month Nisan does not follow Chislev, the year here in v. 1 is apparently an error for "nineteenth," i.e., 446. *Susa,* the winter residence of the Per-sian kings. **1.2** *The Jews that survived,* apparently those who had never been exiled. *Those who had escaped the captivity,* those who had returned from exile. **1.3** This cannot refer to the destruction of the city in 587 BCE, since it is presented as fresh news. Perhaps this assault on the city is the result of the military force deployed against Jerusalem, according to Ezra 4.23, in the reign of Artaxerxes. **1.4** *Sat down,* a customary posture in mourning and fasting (cf. Job 2.8, 13). **1.5–11** Nehemiah's prayer uses much conventional language, taken especially from Deuteronomy. See esp. Deut 5.31; 7.8, 9, 21; 9.29; 12.11; 30.1–5. **1.6** *Confessing.* This is a general confession, without reference to any specific sins (in contrast to Ezra's prayer of Ezra 9). **1.8–9** *The word that you commanded.* A free summary of Deut 30.1–5. **1.11** *This man.* Nehemiah has not yet mentioned the name of his sovereign, but God is expected to know,

to the prayer of your servants who delight in revering your name. Give success to your servant today, and grant him mercy in the sight of this man!"

At the time, I was cupbearer to the king.

Nehemiah Sent to Judah

2 In the month of Nisan, in the twentieth year of King Artaxerxes, when wine was served him, I carried the wine and gave it to the king. Now, I had never been sad in his presence before. ²So the king said to me, "Why is your face sad, since you are not sick? This can only be sadness of the heart." Then I was very much afraid. ³I said to the king, "May the king live forever! Why should my face not be sad, when the city, the place of my ancestors' graves, lies waste, and its gates have been destroyed by fire?" ⁴Then the king said to me, "What do you request?" So I prayed to the God of heaven. ⁵Then I said to the king, "If it pleases the king, and if your servant has found favor with you, I ask that you send me to Judah, to the city of my ancestors' graves, so that I may rebuild it." ⁶The king said to me (the queen also was sitting beside him), "How long will you be gone, and when will you return?" So it pleased the king to send me, and I set him a date. ⁷Then I said to the king, "If it pleases the king, let letters be given me to the governors of the province Beyond the River, that they may grant me passage until I arrive in Judah; ⁸and a letter to Asaph, the keeper of the king's forest, directing him to give me timber to make beams for the gates of the temple fortress, and for the wall of the city, and for the house that I shall occupy." And the king granted me what I asked, for the gracious hand of my God was upon me.

9 Then I came to the governors of the province Beyond the River, and gave them the king's letters. Now the king had sent officers of the army and cavalry with me. ¹⁰When Sanballat the Horonite and Tobiah the Ammonite official heard this, it displeased them greatly that someone had come to seek the welfare of the people of Israel.

Nehemiah's Inspection of the Walls

11 So I came to Jerusalem and was there for three days. ¹²Then I got up during the night, I and a few men with me; I told no one what my God had put into my heart to do for Jerusalem. The only animal I took was the animal I rode. ¹³I went out by night by the Valley Gate past the Dragon's Spring and to the Dung Gate, and I inspected the walls of Jerusalem that had been broken down and its gates that had been destroyed by fire. ¹⁴Then I went on to the Fountain Gate and to the King's Pool;

---

and readers will soon be enlightened. Perhaps Nehemiah's language gives a hint of how he regards him: he is a mere man. *Cupbearer*, an important office in the Persian court. As taster of the king's wine and guard of the royal apartment, he would no doubt have great personal influence on the king's decisions.

2.1–20 Nehemiah gains appointment from the king as (implicit) governor of Judea (vv. 1–8). He meets with hostility from the governors of neighboring provinces (vv. 9–10), arrives in Jerusalem, inspects the state of the walls (vv. 11–16), and determines to rebuild them regardless of the opposition (vv. 17–20). **2.3** *The city.* Nehemiah wisely never mentions the name of Jerusalem, since it was notorious as a rebellious city (cf. Ezra 4.12, 15). **2.4** *What do you request?* The king realizes that Nehemiah's response is no resigned sigh, but demands a reply. **2.5** Nehemiah's rebuilding of Jerusalem would not simply be a pious act in memory of his fathers; it would, by ancient custom, imply rulership of the rebuilt city and, since it was a capital, governorship of the province as well. **2.6** *The queen*, known as Damaspia from Greek sources. **2.7–8** Perhaps it is etiquette that prevents Nehemiah from asking explicitly for the governorship, but 5.14 implies that he was appointed governor of Judea at this time. Nehemiah asks only for a passport for safe conduct through the other Persian provinces and a requisition order for timber from the royal forest. **2.8** This is the first we hear of the *temple fortress;* cf. also 7.2. It may be the Tower of Hananel (3.1), and it may have been the predecessor of the Antonia tower built by Herod. *For the wall of the city*, i.e., for its gates. The city wall itself would have been entirely of stone. **2.9** *The province Beyond the River.* See note on Ezra 4.10. **2.10** *Sanballat*, the governor of the province of Samaria, adjoining Judea on the north. *The Horonite* seems to be a contemptuous reference to Sanballat's humble origins (Horon may be an obscure village); Nehemiah never accords him his official title. *Tobiah*, probably the governor of the province of Ammon, Nehemiah's eastern neighbor. *It displeased them greatly.* Nehemiah's appointment directly by the king perhaps was felt by Sanballat and Tobiah to be a threat to their own political and economic status. They were probably more hostile to Nehemiah personally than to the Jews. **2.13–15** Nehemiah's night ride took him in a counterclockwise direction around Jerusalem, beginning at the north or west of the city. **2.13** *Valley Gate*, in the western wall, 500 yards north of the Dung Gate (3.13). *Dragon's Spring.* No longer known. *Dung Gate*, or Potsherd Gate (Jer 19.2), at the southern tip of the city. **2.14** *Fountain Gate*, in the Kidron Valley on the east of

but there was no place for the animal I was riding to continue. 15So I went up by way of the valley by night and inspected the wall. Then I turned back and entered by the Valley Gate, and so returned. 16The officials did not know where I had gone or what I was doing; I had not yet told the Jews, the priests, the nobles, the officials, and the rest that were to do the work.

Decision to Restore the Walls

17 Then I said to them, "You see the trouble we are in, how Jerusalem lies in ruins with its gates burned. Come, let us rebuild the wall of Jerusalem, so that we may no longer suffer disgrace." 18I told them that the hand of my God had been gracious upon me, and also the words that the king had spoken to me. Then they said, "Let us start building!" So they committed themselves to the common good. 19But when Sanballat the Horonite and Tobiah the Ammonite official, and Geshem the Arab heard of it, they mocked and ridiculed us, saying, "What is this that you are doing? Are you rebelling against the king?" 20Then I replied to them, "The God of heaven is the one who will give us success, and we his servants are going to start building; but you have no share or claim or historic right in Jerusalem."

Organization of the Work

3 Then the high priest Eliashib set to work with his fellow priests and rebuilt the Sheep Gate. They consecrated it and set up its

doors; they consecrated it as far as the Tower of the Hundred and as far as the Tower of Hananel. 2And the men of Jericho built next to him. And next to them*a* Zaccur son of Imri built.

3 The sons of Hassenaah built the Fish Gate; they laid its beams and set up its doors, its bolts, and its bars. 4Next to them Meremoth son of Uriah son of Hakkoz made repairs. Next to them Meshullam son of Berechiah son of Meshezabel made repairs. Next to them Zadok son of Baana made repairs. 5Next to them the Tekoites made repairs; but their nobles would not put their shoulders to the work of their Lord.*b*

6 Joiada son of Paseah and Meshullam son of Besodeiah repaired the Old Gate; they laid its beams and set up its doors, its bolts, and its bars. 7Next to them repairs were made by Melatiah the Gibeonite and Jadon the Meronothite—the men of Gibeon and of Mizpah—who were under the jurisdiction of*c* the governor of the province Beyond the River. 8Next to them Uzziel son of Harhaiah, one of the goldsmiths, made repairs. Next to him Hananiah, one of the perfumers, made repairs; and they restored Jerusalem as far as the Broad Wall. 9Next to them Rephaiah son of Hur, ruler of half the district of*d* Jerusalem, made repairs. 10Next to them Jedaiah son of Harumaph made repairs opposite his house;

---

a Heb *him*   *b* Or *lords*   *c* Meaning of Heb uncertain
d Or *supervisor of half the portion assigned to*

---

the city. *King's Pool,* the Pool of Shelah (Shiloah), fed from the spring Gihon farther up the valley (cf. 3.15; Isa 8.6). *No place for the animal . . . to continue.* The elaborate system of terraces on the eastern slope had collapsed after the Babylonian destruction, and the valley floor was now a vast tumble of stones. The archaeological evidence is that Nehemiah abandoned the old line of wall on the eastern slope and built a new wall on the crest. **2.16** Perhaps Nehemiah is stressing that the rebuilding of the city walls was entirely his initiative. **2.19** *Geshem the Arab,* king of Qedar, the ruler, under nominal Persian control, of a large territory in northern Arabia, Edom, and the Negev of Judah. See also 6.1–6. *Rebelling.* The fortification of the city could be seen as a preparation for revolt.

3.1–32 This list did not perhaps form part of Nehemiah's memoir (see Introduction); it views the wall building as completed (e.g., vv. 1, 3, 6) but it comes between the decision to build (2.18) and the events that occurred during the building (4.1–23). **3.1–5** Gates and wall in the northern sector are mainly said to be *built* (e.g., v. 2), suggesting that they were more dam-

aged than those that were only *repaired* (e.g., v. 6). The north wall fronts the main access road to Jerusalem and would have borne the brunt of military attacks. The "builders" mentioned by name are no doubt those who financed the work rather than those who actually worked with their hands. **3.1** *Sheep Gate,* probably so named because of the market there. It is probably the northeast gate, the Benjamin Gate. *They consecrated it,* perhaps a special ceremony for a section of wall adjoining the temple, for the consecration of the wall as a whole occurs much later (12.27–30). **3.3** *Fish Gate,* naturally enough on the west of the city, nearest the sea. **3.5** The noncooperation of the nobles of Tekoa, in the south, may have been due to the influence of Geshem (see note on 2.19). **3.6–14** The line of wall on the west of the city cannot easily be associated with any archaeological remains. **3.6** *Old Gate,* probably should be emended to Mishneh Gate, the gate of the extended Second Quarter of the city (cf. 2 Kings 22.14). **3.8** *Restored Jerusalem as far as the Broad Wall.* Some translate "abandoned Jerusalem as far as the Broad Wall" (part of the western, or Mishneh, quarter of the preex-

and next to him Hattush son of Hashabneiah made repairs. [11]Malchijah son of Harim and Hasshub son of Pahath-moab repaired another section and the Tower of the Ovens. [12]Next to him Shallum son of Hallohesh, ruler of half the district of[a] Jerusalem, made repairs, he and his daughters.

13 Hanun and the inhabitants of Zanoah repaired the Valley Gate; they rebuilt it and set up its doors, its bolts, and its bars, and repaired a thousand cubits of the wall, as far as the Dung Gate.

14 Malchijah son of Rechab, ruler of the district of[b] Beth-haccherem, repaired the Dung Gate; he rebuilt it and set up its doors, its bolts, and its bars.

15 And Shallum son of Col-hozeh, ruler of the district of[b] Mizpah, repaired the Fountain Gate; he rebuilt it and covered it and set up its doors, its bolts, and its bars; and he built the wall of the Pool of Shelah of the king's garden, as far as the stairs that go down from the City of David. [16]After him Nehemiah son of Azbuk, ruler of half the district of[a] Beth-zur, repaired from a point opposite the graves of David, as far as the artificial pool and the house of the warriors. [17]After him the Levites made repairs: Rehum son of Bani; next to him Hashabiah, ruler of half the district of[a] Keilah, made repairs for his district. [18]After him their kin made repairs: Binnui,[c] son of Henadad, ruler of half the district of[a] Keilah; [19]next to him Ezer son of Jeshua, ruler[d] of Mizpah, repaired another section opposite the ascent to the armory at the Angle. [20]After him Baruch son of Zabbai repaired another section from the Angle to the door of the house of the high priest Eliashib. [21]After him Meremoth son of Uriah son of Hakkoz repaired another section from the door of the house of Eliashib to the end of the house of Eliashib. [22]After him the priests, the men of the surrounding area,

made repairs. [23]After them Benjamin and Hasshub made repairs opposite their house. After them Azariah son of Maaseiah son of Ananiah made repairs beside his own house. [24]After him Binnui son of Henadad repaired another section, from the house of Azariah to the Angle and to the corner. [25]Palal son of Uzai repaired opposite the Angle and the tower projecting from the upper house of the king at the court of the guard. After him Pedaiah son of Parosh [26]and the temple servants living[e] on Ophel made repairs up to a point opposite the Water Gate on the east and the projecting tower. [27]After him the Tekoites repaired another section opposite the great projecting tower as far as the wall of Ophel.

28 Above the Horse Gate the priests made repairs, each one opposite his own house. [29]After them Zadok son of Immer made repairs opposite his own house. After him Shemaiah son of Shecaniah, the keeper of the East Gate, made repairs. [30]After him Hananiah son of Shelemiah and Hanun sixth son of Zalaph repaired another section. After him Meshullam son of Berechiah made repairs opposite his living quarters. [31]After him Malchijah, one of the goldsmiths, made repairs as far as the house of the temple servants and of the merchants, opposite the Muster Gate,[f] and to the upper room of the corner. [32]And between the upper room of the corner and the Sheep Gate the goldsmiths and the merchants made repairs.

Hostile Plots Thwarted

4 [g]Now when Sanballat heard that we were building the wall, he was angry and greatly enraged, and he mocked the Jews. [2]He said in

a Or supervisor of half the portion assigned to   b Or supervisor of the portion assigned to   c Gk Syr Compare verse 24, 10.9: Heb Bavvai   d Or supervisor   e Cn: Heb were living   f Or Hammiphkad Gate   g Ch 3.33 in Heb

---

ilic city). **3.12** *He and his daughters,* the only reference to the participation of women in the building, but we need not assume that these were the only females involved. **3.15–32** The east wall. Especially in its southern half, the builders seem to have been working on an entirely new wall (see note on 2.14). This will explain the large number of gangs that worked on this stretch of wall. **3.15** *Pool of Shelah.* See note on 2.14. **3.16** *Graves of David,* i.e., the graves of the Davidic kings. *House of the warriors,* presumably an army barracks. **3.25** *Upper house of the king,* perhaps Solomon's palace, higher up the hill than David's. **3.26** *Ophel,*

part or all of the southeastern hill overlooking the Kidron Valley. **3.29** *East Gate,* a gate of the temple, not of the city wall. **3.31** *Muster Gate,* probably a gate of the temple court.

4.1–23 This narrative of progress on the wall is interlaced with reports of hostility toward the Jews on the part of the Persian authorities in Samaria. **4.1** *Sanballat.* See note on 2.10. **4.2** *The army of Samaria,* governor Sanballat's troops. *Will they restore things?* Sanballat pokes fun at what he supposes to be the incompetence of the Jews; the sentence might mean "Will they repair for themselves?" suggesting they

the presence of his associates and of the army of Samaria, "What are these feeble Jews doing? Will they restore things? Will they sacrifice? Will they finish it in a day? Will they revive the stones out of the heaps of rubbish—and burned ones at that?" [3]Tobiah the Ammonite was beside him, and he said, "That stone wall they are building—any fox going up on it would break it down!" [4]Hear, O our God, for we are despised; turn their taunt back on their own heads, and give them over as plunder in a land of captivity. [5]Do not cover their guilt, and do not let their sin be blotted out from your sight; for they have hurled insults in the face of the builders.

6 So we rebuilt the wall, and all the wall was joined together to half its height; for the people had a mind to work.

7[a] But when Sanballat and Tobiah and the Arabs and the Ammonites and the Ashdodites heard that the repairing of the walls of Jerusalem was going forward and the gaps were beginning to be closed, they were very angry, [8]and all plotted together to come and fight against Jerusalem and to cause confusion in it. [9]So we prayed to our God, and set a guard as a protection against them day and night.

10 But Judah said, "The strength of the burden bearers is failing, and there is too much rubbish so that we are unable to work on the wall." [11]And our enemies said, "They will not know or see anything before we come upon them and kill them and stop the work." [12]When the Jews who lived near them came, they said to us ten times, "From all the places where they live[b] they will come up against us."[c] [13]So in the lowest parts of the space behind the wall, in open places, I stationed the people according to their families,[d] with their swords, their spears, and their bows. [14]After I looked these things over, I stood up and said to the nobles and the officials

and the rest of the people, "Do not be afraid of them. Remember the LORD, who is great and awesome, and fight for your kin, your sons, your daughters, your wives, and your homes."

15 When our enemies heard that their plot was known to us, and that God had frustrated it, we all returned to the wall, each to his work. [16]From that day on, half of my servants worked on construction, and half held the spears, shields, bows, and body-armor; and the leaders posted themselves behind the whole house of Judah, [17]who were building the wall. The burden bearers carried their loads in such a way that each labored on the work with one hand and with the other held a weapon. [18]And each of the builders had his sword strapped at his side while he built. The man who sounded the trumpet was beside me. [19]And I said to the nobles, the officials, and the rest of the people, "The work is great and widely spread out, and we are separated far from one another on the wall. [20]Rally to us wherever you hear the sound of the trumpet. Our God will fight for us."

21 So we labored at the work, and half of them held the spears from break of dawn until the stars came out. [22]I also said to the people at that time, "Let every man and his servant pass the night inside Jerusalem, so that they may be a guard for us by night and may labor by day." [23]So neither I nor my brothers nor my servants nor the men of the guard who followed me ever took off our clothes; each kept his weapon in his right hand.[e]

Nehemiah Deals with Oppression

5 Now there was a great outcry of the people and of their wives against their Jewish

a Ch 4.1 in Heb   b Cn: Heb *you return*   c Compare Gk Syr: Meaning of Heb uncertain   d Meaning of Heb uncertain   e Cn: Heb *each his weapon the water*

---

would build a makeshift wall unlike the elegant city wall of Samaria. *Sacrifice,* perhaps a foundation or dedication sacrifice. **4.3** *Tobiah.* See note on 2.10; also 2.19. **4.4–5** Nehemiah's plea to God, though doubtless part of his written report of past events, is presented as a prayer composed at the time of Sanballat's mockery. The imprecation on enemies is a feature of several similar psalms of appeal (e.g., Pss 35; 58.6–9). **4.7** *The Arabs,* under their king, Geshem (see note on 2.19). *Ammonites* are on the east, *Ashdodites* on the west of Judah; on all sides Nehemiah is surrounded by enemies. **4.8** *Plotted . . . to come.* But did they come? There is no evidence that they did. **4.10** *Judah,* the Judeans.

Their speech seems to have poetic form and may be a work song. **4.12** *Near them,* near the enemies. **4.13** Nehemiah's tactic seems to have been to mass armed citizens in those places where the wall could be overlooked from outside the city, so as to give to enemy spies the impression of massive defense forces. **4.16–23** There are various public relations and morale-boosting activities here: forming an armed guard for the builders, arming the workers themselves, appointing a trumpeter to sound an alarm in case of attack, and keeping the workers overnight in the city for security and to prevent their intimidation by the enemy. **5.1–13** The threat from without is followed by a

kin. 2For there were those who said, "With our sons and our daughters, we are many; we must get grain, so that we may eat and stay alive." 3There were also those who said, "We are having to pledge our fields, our vineyards, and our houses in order to get grain during the famine." 4And there were those who said, "We are having to borrow money on our fields and vineyards to pay the king's tax. 5Now our flesh is the same as that of our kindred; our children are the same as their children; and yet we are forcing our sons and daughters to be slaves, and some of our daughters have been ravished; we are powerless, and our fields and vineyards now belong to others."

6 I was very angry when I heard their outcry and these complaints. 7After thinking it over, I brought charges against the nobles and the officials; I said to them, "You are all taking interest from your own people." And I called a great assembly to deal with them, 8and said to them, "As far as we were able, we have bought back our Jewish kindred who had been sold to other nations; but now you are selling your own kin, who must then be bought back by us!" They were silent, and could not find a word to say. 9So I said, "The thing that you are doing is not good. Should you not walk in the fear of our God, to prevent the taunts of the nations our enemies? 10Moreover I and my brothers and my servants are lending them money and grain. Let us stop this taking of interest. 11Restore to them, this very day, their fields, their vineyards, their olive orchards, and their houses, and the interest on money, grain, wine, and oil that you have been exacting from them." 12Then they said, "We will restore everything and demand nothing more from them. We will do as you say." And I called the priests, and made them take an oath to do as they had promised. 13I also shook out the fold of my garment and said, "So may God shake out everyone from house and from property who does not perform this promise. Thus may they be shaken out and emptied." And all the assembly said, "Amen," and praised the LORD. And the people did as they had promised.

The Generosity of Nehemiah

14 Moreover from the time that I was appointed to be their governor in the land of Judah, from the twentieth year to the thirty-second year of King Artaxerxes, twelve years, neither I nor my brothers ate the food allowance of the governor. 15The former governors who were before me laid heavy burdens on the people, and took food and wine from them, besides forty shekels of silver. Even their servants lorded it over the people. But I did not do so, because of the fear of God. 16Indeed, I devoted myself to the work on this wall, and acquired no land; and all my servants were gathered there for the work. 17Moreover there were at my table one hundred fifty people, Jews and officials, besides those who came to us from the nations around us. 18Now that which was prepared for one day was one ox and six choice sheep; also fowls were prepared for me, and every ten days skins of wine in abundance; yet with all this I did not demand the food allowance of the governor, because of the heavy burden of labor on the people. 19Remember for my good, O my God, all that I have done for this people.

Intrigues of Enemies Foiled

6 Now when it was reported to Sanballat and Tobiah and to Geshem the Arab and

---

threat to the community's stability from within. A shortage of food has led to large-scale debt slavery, and Nehemiah takes measures in response to an outcry from the people. **5.2** *With our sons and our daughters, we are many,* preferably "we are giving our sons and our daughters as pledges" for borrowings. **5.4** *The king's tax,* the levy from the provinces for the central Persian government. **5.7** *The nobles and the officials,* the lenders of money. *Taking interest.* The Hebrew means rather "seizing (persons, land, and goods) given in pledge against debts." Interest on loans was illegal (Lev 25.36–37; Deut 23.19–20) but taking pledges was sanctioned by the law (Deut 24.10). Nehemiah, himself one of the moneylenders (v. 10), is not confessing to any illegal act, but accepts that pledge-taking from kinspeople is *not good* (v. 9). **5.10** *Stop this taking of interest,* rather "stop this taking in pledge," and perhaps implying also the return of pledges already taken. **5.11** *Interest on,* rather "pledge on." **5.13** *The fold of my garment,* the ancient equivalent of pockets. *The people,* the nobles and moneylenders. **5.14–19** The account of Nehemiah's generosity as governor now continues the theme of the benefits of his rule for the Judeans. **5.14** Nehemiah's appointment as governor was only implicit in 2.5–8. It ran from 445 to 433/2 BCE. As governor, he was entitled to deduct his own expenses from the taxes he collected for the central government, but he refrained from doing so. **5.15** *Forty shekels of silver* a day (about 1 pound). **5.17** *Those . . . from the nations,* imperial and provincial officials.

to the rest of our enemies that I had built the wall and that there was no gap left in it (though up to that time I had not set up the doors in the gates), ²Sanballat and Geshem sent to me, saying, "Come and let us meet together in one of the villages in the plain of Ono." But they intended to do me harm. ³So I sent messengers to them, saying, "I am doing a great work and I cannot come down. Why should the work stop while I leave it to come down to you?" ⁴They sent to me four times in this way, and I answered them in the same manner. ⁵In the same way Sanballat for the fifth time sent his servant to me with an open letter in his hand. ⁶In it was written, "It is reported among the nations—and Geshem*ᵃ also says it—that you and the Jews intend to rebel; that is why you are building the wall; and according to this report you wish to become their king. ⁷You have also set up prophets to proclaim in Jerusalem concerning you, 'There is a king in Judah!' And now it will be reported to the king according to these words. So come, therefore, and let us confer together." ⁸Then I sent to him, saying, "No such things as you say have been done; you are inventing them out of your own mind" ⁹—for they all wanted to frighten us, thinking, "Their hands will drop from the work, and it will not be done." But now, O God, strengthen my hands.

10 One day when I went into the house of Shemaiah son of Delaiah son of Mehetabel, who was confined to his house, he said, "Let us meet together in the house of God, within the temple, and let us close the doors of the temple, for they are coming to kill you; indeed, tonight they are coming to kill you." ¹¹But I said,

"Should a man like me run away? Would a man like me go into the temple to save his life? I will not go in!" ¹²Then I perceived and saw that God had not sent him at all, but he had pronounced the prophecy against me because Tobiah and Sanballat had hired him. ¹³He was hired for this purpose, to intimidate me and make me sin by acting in this way, and so they could give me a bad name, in order to taunt me. ¹⁴Remember Tobiah and Sanballat, O my God, according to these things that they did, and also the prophetess Noadiah and the rest of the prophets who wanted to make me afraid.

The Wall Completed

15 So the wall was finished on the twenty-fifth day of the month Elul, in fifty-two days. ¹⁶And when all our enemies heard of it, all the nations around us were afraid*ᵇ and fell greatly in their own esteem; for they perceived that this work had been accomplished with the help of our God. ¹⁷Moreover in those days the nobles of Judah sent many letters to Tobiah, and Tobiah's letters came to them. ¹⁸For many in Judah were bound by oath to him, because he was the son-in-law of Shecaniah son of Arah: and his son Jehohanan had married the daughter of Meshullam son of Berechiah. ¹⁹Also they spoke of his good deeds in my presence, and reported my words to him. And Tobiah sent letters to intimidate me.

7 Now when the wall had been built and I had set up the doors, and the gatekeepers, the singers, and the Levites had been appointed, ²I gave my brother Hanani charge

---

a Heb *Gashmu*   *b* Another reading is *saw*

6.1–7.4 In spite of traps for Nehemiah, the wall is finished and security arrangements made. **6.1** *Sanballat, Tobiah.* See note on 2.10. *Geshem the Arab.* See notes on 2.19; 4.7. **6.2** *The plain of Ono,* ca. twenty miles northwest of Jerusalem. *To do me harm.* Nehemiah does not know what kind of harm exactly. **6.3** It is a witty reply to make the work his excuse for refusing the invitation when the purpose of the invitation is to make him cease the work. **6.5** An *open letter,* an unsealed sheet of papyrus or an ostracon (a piece of pottery) containing a charge of treason could be fatal for Nehemiah. **6.7** *There is a king in Judah.* It is not impossible that Nehemiah was being hailed by some as a messiah, as Haggai (2.21–23) and Zechariah (3.8; 4.6–10; 6.10–14) had hailed a former governor, Zerubbabel. **6.9** *But now ... hands,* a prayer that suits the time of the events rather than of the writing (cf. note on 4.4–5). **6.10–13** Sanballat engineers another attempt

to discredit Nehemiah and make him stop the wall building. **6.10–11** Shemaiah seems to have been inveigling Nehemiah to enter the temple, which was forbidden to him as a layman, in order to destroy his reputation. How this is connected to what Nehemiah perceived as a threat to his life is hard to tell. **6.10** *Shemaiah,* an otherwise unknown prophet apparently in league with Sanballat. *Confined to his house,* for some religious reason. **6.14** A prayer like that of v. 9 except that it belongs rather to the time of writing. *Noadiah and the rest of the prophets,* allusions to otherwise unknown events. **6.15** The wall, begun on August 11, was finished on October 2, 445 BCE. **6.17–19** Instead of an account of the dedication of the wall, which will come in 12.27–43, we have a further note of hostility toward Nehemiah. It is hard to see what Tobiah hoped to achieve by both threatening Nehemiah and having his friends praise him to Nehemiah. **7.1** *The singers, and*

over Jerusalem, along with Hananiah the commander of the citadel—for he was a faithful man and feared God more than many. [3]And I said to them, "The gates of Jerusalem are not to be opened until the sun is hot; while the gatekeepers[a] are still standing guard, let them shut and bar the doors. Appoint guards from among the inhabitants of Jerusalem, some at their watch posts, and others before their own houses." [4]The city was wide and large, but the people within it were few and no houses had been built.

Lists of the Returned Exiles

5 Then my God put it into my mind to assemble the nobles and the officials and the people to be enrolled by genealogy. And I found the book of the genealogy of those who were the first to come back, and I found the following written in it:

6 These are the people of the province who came up out of the captivity of those exiles whom King Nebuchadnezzar of Babylon had carried into exile; they returned to Jerusalem and Judah, each to his town. [7]They came with Zerubbabel, Jeshua, Nehemiah, Azariah, Raamiah, Nahamani, Mordecai, Bilshan, Mispereth, Bigvai, Nehum, Baanah.

The number of the Israelite people: [8]the descendants of Parosh, two thousand one hundred seventy-two. [9]Of Shephatiah, three hundred seventy-two. [10]Of Arah, six hundred fifty-two. [11]Of Pahath-moab, namely the descendants of Jeshua and Joab, two thousand eight hundred eighteen. [12]Of Elam, one thousand two hundred fifty-four. [13]Of Zattu, eight hundred forty-five. [14]Of Zaccai, seven hundred sixty. [15]Of Binnui, six hundred forty-eight. [16]Of Bebai, six hundred twenty-eight. [17]Of Azgad, two thousand three hundred twenty-two. [18]Of Adonikam, six hundred sixty-seven. [19]Of Bigvai, two thousand sixty-seven. [20]Of Adin, six hundred fifty-five. [21]Of Ater, namely of Hezekiah, ninety-eight. [22]Of Hashum, three hundred twenty-eight. [23]Of Bezai, three hundred twenty-four. [24]Of Hariph, one hundred twelve. [25]Of Gibeon,

ninety-five. [26]The people of Bethlehem and Netophah, one hundred eighty-eight. [27]Of Anathoth, one hundred twenty-eight. [28]Of Beth-azmaveth, forty-two. [29]Of Kiriath-jearim, Chephirah, and Beeroth, seven hundred forty-three. [30]Of Ramah and Geba, six hundred twenty-one. [31]Of Michmas, one hundred twenty-two. [32]Of Bethel and Ai, one hundred twenty-three. [33]Of the other Nebo, fifty-two. [34]The descendants of the other Elam, one thousand two hundred fifty-four. [35]Of Harim, three hundred twenty. [36]Of Jericho, three hundred forty-five. [37]Of Lod, Hadid, and Ono, seven hundred twenty-one. [38]Of Senaah, three thousand nine hundred thirty.

39 The priests: the descendants of Jedaiah, namely the house of Jeshua, nine hundred seventy-three. [40]Of Immer, one thousand fifty-two. [41]Of Pashhur, one thousand two hundred forty-seven. [42]Of Harim, one thousand seventeen.

43 The Levites: the descendants of Jeshua, namely of Kadmiel of the descendants of Hodevah, seventy-four. [44]The singers: the descendants of Asaph, one hundred forty-eight. [45]The gatekeepers: the descendants of Shallum, of Ater, of Talmon, of Akkub, of Hatita, of Shobai, one hundred thirty-eight.

46 The temple servants: the descendants of Ziha, of Hasupha, of Tabbaoth, [47]of Keros, of Sia, of Padon, [48]of Lebana, of Hagaba, of Shalmai, [49]of Hanan, of Giddel, of Gahar, [50]of Reaiah, of Rezin, of Nekoda, [51]of Gazzam, of Uzza, of Paseah, [52]of Besai, of Meunim, of Nephushesim, [53]of Bakbuk, of Hakupha, of Harhur, [54]of Bazlith, of Mehida, of Harsha, [55]of Barkos, of Sisera, of Temah, [56]of Neziah, of Hatipha.

57 The descendants of Solomon's servants: of Sotai, of Sophereth, of Perida, [58]of Jaala, of Darkon, of Giddel, [59]of Shephatiah, of Hattil, of Pochereth-hazzebaim, of Amon.

60 All the temple servants and the descendants of Solomon's servants were three hundred ninety-two.

---

a Heb *while they*

---

the Levites, probably to be omitted as a scribal addition. **7.2** It is likely that the text refers to only one city governor, Hanani, Nehemiah's brother; Hananiah is an alternative writing of the name. **7.3** The strict security precautions are not hard to understand, but obviously not opening the gates *until the sun is hot* was unusual. **7.4** *Wide and large,* 30 or 40 acres. *No houses,* i.e.,

no new houses, for there were already inhabitants of the city (cf., e.g., 3.20; 7.3).

7.5–73a Nehemiah takes a census of the people to prepare for the repopulating of the city (11.1–2). The list that follows is largely identical with Ezra 2. This old list, which Nehemiah says he found, may have been useful in establishing which families were of pure Jew-

61 The following were those who came up from Tel-melah, Tel-harsha, Cherub, Addon, and Immer, but they could not prove their ancestral houses or their descent, whether they belonged to Israel: 62the descendants of Delaiah, of Tobiah, of Nekoda, six hundred forty-two. 63Also, of the priests: the descendants of Hobaiah, of Hakkoz, of Barzillai (who had married one of the daughters of Barzillai the Gileadite and was called by their name). 64These sought their registration among those enrolled in the genealogies, but it was not found there, so they were excluded from the priesthood as unclean; 65the governor told them that they were not to partake of the most holy food, until a priest with Urim and Thummim should come.

66 The whole assembly together was forty-two thousand three hundred sixty, 67besides their male and female slaves, of whom there were seven thousand three hundred thirty-seven; and they had two hundred forty-five singers, male and female. 68They had seven hundred thirty-six horses, two hundred forty-five mules,[a] 69four hundred thirty-five camels, and six thousand seven hundred twenty donkeys.

70 Now some of the heads of ancestral houses contributed to the work. The governor gave to the treasury one thousand darics of gold, fifty basins, and five hundred thirty priestly robes. 71And some of the heads of ancestral houses gave into the building fund twenty thousand darics of gold and two thousand two hundred minas of silver. 72And what the rest of the people gave was twenty thousand darics of gold, two thousand minas of silver, and sixty-seven priestly robes.

73 So the priests, the Levites, the gatekeepers, the singers, some of the people, the temple servants, and all Israel settled in their towns.

Ezra Summons the People to Obey the Law

8 When the seventh month came—the people of Israel being settled in their towns— 1all the people gathered together into the square before the Water Gate. They told the scribe Ezra to bring the book of the law of Moses, which the LORD had given to Israel. 2Accordingly, the priest Ezra brought the law before the assembly, both men and women and all who could hear with understanding. This was on the first day of the seventh month. 3He read from it facing the square before the Water Gate from early morning until midday, in the presence of the men and the women and those who could understand; and the ears of all the people were attentive to the book of the law. 4The scribe Ezra stood on a wooden platform that had been made for the purpose; and beside him stood Mattithiah, Shema, Anaiah, Uriah, Hilkiah, and Maaseiah on his right hand; and Pedaiah, Mishael, Malchijah, Hashum, Hash-baddanah, Zechariah, and Meshullam on his left hand. 5And Ezra opened the book in the sight of all the people, for he was standing above all the people; and when he opened it, all the people stood up. 6Then Ezra blessed the LORD, the great God, and all the people answered, "Amen, Amen," lifting up their hands. Then they bowed their heads and worshiped the LORD with their faces to the ground. 7Also Jeshua, Bani, Sherebiah, Jamin, Akkub, Shabbethai, Hodiah, Maaseiah, Kelita, Azariah, Jozabad, Hanan, Pelaiah, the Levites,[b] helped the people to understand the law, while the people remained in

---

a Ezra 2.66 and the margins of some Hebrew Mss: MT lacks *They had . . . forty-five mules*   b 1 Esdras 9.48 Vg: Heb *and the Levites*

---

ish descent, for only those would have been eligible for transfer to Jerusalem. **7.73b–9.37** In these chapters Ezra is the principal figure, and it seems that they were originally integrated with the Ezra memoir of Ezra 7–10. **7.73b–8.12** Ezra summons the people to a ceremony for the reading of the law. In the present context, it occurs about a week after the finishing of the wall (cf. 6.15), but on the view that Neh 8–9 reports events of 458 BCE and that that was the year of Ezra's arrival, the reading of the law took place two months after Ezra came to Jerusalem (cf. 8.2 with Ezra 7.9). **8.1** *The square before the Water Gate,* on the east of the city, outside the temple area, where even ritually defiled citizens could be present. *They told the scribe Ezra.* Though Ezra is plainly the initiator of the teaching of

the law (cf. Ezra 7.25), he wants to represent it as a response to the people's request. **8.2** *First day of the seventh month,* the new moon day introducing the most important festival month in Israel. This day (Tishri 1) later became New Year's Day (Rosh Hashanah). *All who . . . understanding,* older children. **8.4–8** A narrative parallel to the reading of the "book of the law" in the time of Josiah (2 Chr 34.14–32). **8.4** *Mattithiah . . . Meshullam,* a representative group of thirteen laymen lending their authority; cf. the thirteen Levites in v. 7. **8.5** *Opened the book,* i.e., "unrolled the scroll." **8.6** *Amen,* Hebrew for "It is firm, established," signifying the assent of the listeners. **8.7–8** The Levites apparently moved among the people, ensuring they understood what was read by Ezra. *With interpretation,* in

their places. [8]So they read from the book, from the law of God, with interpretation. They gave the sense, so that the people understood the reading.

9 And Nehemiah, who was the governor, and Ezra the priest and scribe, and the Levites who taught the people said to all the people, "This day is holy to the LORD your God; do not mourn or weep." For all the people wept when they heard the words of the law. [10]Then he said to them, "Go your way, eat the fat and drink sweet wine and send portions of them to those for whom nothing is prepared, for this day is holy to our LORD; and do not be grieved, for the joy of the LORD is your strength." [11]So the Levites stilled all the people, saying, "Be quiet, for this day is holy; do not be grieved." [12]And all the people went their way to eat and drink and to send portions and to make great rejoicing, because they had understood the words that were declared to them.

The Festival of Booths Celebrated

13 On the second day the heads of ancestral houses of all the people, with the priests and the Levites, came together to the scribe Ezra in order to study the words of the law. [14]And they found it written in the law, which the LORD had commanded by Moses, that the people of Israel should live in booths[a] during the festival of the seventh month, [15]and that they should publish and proclaim in all their towns and in Jerusalem as follows, "Go out to the hills and bring branches of olive, wild

olive, myrtle, palm, and other leafy trees to make booths,[a] as it is written." [16]So the people went out and brought them, and made booths[a] for themselves, each on the roofs of their houses, and in their courts and in the courts of the house of God, and in the square at the Water Gate and in the square at the Gate of Ephraim. [17]And all the assembly of those who had returned from the captivity made booths[a] and lived in them; for from the days of Jeshua son of Nun to that day the people of Israel had not done so. And there was very great rejoicing. [18]And day by day, from the first day to the last day, he read from the book of the law of God. They kept the festival seven days; and on the eighth day there was a solemn assembly, according to the ordinance.

National Confession

9 Now on the twenty-fourth day of this month the people of Israel were assembled with fasting and in sackcloth, and with earth on their heads.[b] [2]Then those of Israelite descent separated themselves from all foreigners, and stood and confessed their sins and the iniquities of their ancestors. [3]They stood up in their place and read from the book of the law of the LORD their God for a fourth part of the day, and for another fourth they made confession and worshiped the LORD their God. [4]Then Jeshua, Bani, Kadmiel, Shebaniah, Bunni, Sherebiah, Bani, and Chenani stood on the stairs of the Levites and cried out with a

---

a Or *tabernacles*; Heb *succoth*   *b* Heb *on them*

Hebrew "distinctly" or "with pauses," perhaps implies translation from Hebrew to Aramaic. **8.9** *Nehemiah.* This is the only evidence that Ezra and Nehemiah were contemporaries; and since the verb *said* is singular it seems likely that *Nehemiah, who was the governor* should be deleted as a mistaken scribal addition. *Mourn or weep,* in repentance for having disobeyed the law. **8.10** The people should celebrate the new moon festival as they were planning to and *send portions* to the poor and foreigners (as prescribed in Deut 26.12–13). **8.13–18** The following day a smaller group, the family heads and temple officials in Jerusalem, studied with Ezra the details for exact observance of the next festival, Booths (see note on Ezra 3.4), to begin on the fifteenth of the month. Living for a week in huts commemorated the journeying in the wilderness (Lev 23.42). **8.17** *Jeshua,* Joshua, Moses' successor. The Festival of Booths had always been celebrated, as far as we know (Judg 21.19; 1 Sam 1.3; Ezra 3.4); the novelty now was apparently that all Israel could celebrate it to-

gether in one place, last possible when they were camped by Gilgal with Joshua (though Josh 5.10 speaks of Passover and not specifically of Booths). **9.1–37** Two days later, a day of penitence is held (vv. 1–4), and the prayer of the Levites is reported (vv. 5–37). Strangely, the Day of Atonement (Yom Kippur) on the tenth has not been mentioned; perhaps the ceremony of the twenty-fourth replaces it, or perhaps the narrative deliberately downgrades cultic activities in favor of an increased annual role for scripture. **9.1** Rituals of mourning are often used to express penitence. Mourners and penitents alike want to depict themselves as being like the dead, so they perform a ritual of *fasting* from food, wear *sackcloth,* from which shrouds are made, and put *earth on their heads* as if they were buried. **9.2** *Separated... from all foreigners.* This is not the divorcing of foreign wives as in Ezra 9–10, but it reflects the same concern for religious distinctiveness. Though foreigners living in Judea could participate in the festival (Deut 16.14) and were obliged to keep the

loud voice to the LORD their God. [5]Then the Levites, Jeshua, Kadmiel, Bani, Hashabneiah, Sherebiah, Hodiah, Shebaniah, and Pethahiah, said, "Stand up and bless the LORD your God from everlasting to everlasting. Blessed be your glorious name, which is exalted above all blessing and praise."

6 And Ezra said:[a] "You are the LORD, you alone; you have made heaven, the heaven of heavens, with all their host, the earth and all that is on it, the seas and all that is in them. To all of them you give life, and the host of heaven worships you. [7]You are the LORD, the God who chose Abram and brought him out of Ur of the Chaldeans and gave him the name Abraham; [8]and you found his heart faithful before you, and made with him a covenant to give to his descendants the land of the Canaanite, the Hittite, the Amorite, the Perizzite, the Jebusite, and the Girgashite; and you have fulfilled your promise, for you are righteous.

9 "And you saw the distress of our ancestors in Egypt and heard their cry at the Red Sea.[b] [10]You performed signs and wonders against Pharaoh and all his servants and all the people of his land, for you knew that they acted insolently against our ancestors. You made a name for yourself, which remains to this day. [11]And you divided the sea before them, so that they passed through the sea on dry land, but you threw their pursuers into the depths, like a stone into mighty waters. [12]Moreover, you led them by day with a pillar of cloud, and by night with a pillar of fire, to give them light on the way in which they should go. [13]You came down also upon Mount Sinai, and spoke with them from heaven, and gave them right ordinances and true laws, good statutes and commandments, [14]and you made known your holy sabbath to them and gave them commandments and statutes and a law through your servant Moses. [15]For their hunger you gave them bread from heaven, and for their thirst you brought water for them out of the rock, and you told them to go in to possess the land that you swore to give them.

16 "But they and our ancestors acted presumptuously and stiffened their necks and did not obey your commandments; [17]they refused to obey, and were not mindful of the wonders that you performed among them; but they stiffened their necks and determined to return to their slavery in Egypt. But you are a God ready to forgive, gracious and merciful, slow to anger and abounding in steadfast love, and you did not forsake them. [18]Even when they had cast an image of a calf for themselves and said, 'This is your God who brought you up out of Egypt,' and had committed great blasphemies, [19]you in your great mercies did not forsake them in the wilderness; the pillar of cloud that led them in the way did not leave them by day, nor the pillar of fire by night that gave them light on the way by which they should go. [20]You gave your good spirit to instruct them, and did not withhold your manna from their mouths, and gave them water for their thirst. [21]Forty years you sustained them in the wilderness so that they lacked nothing; their clothes did not wear out and their feet did not swell. [22]And you gave them kingdoms and peoples, and allotted to them every corner,[c] so they took possession of the land of King Sihon of Heshbon and the land of King Og of Bashan. [23]You multiplied their descendants like the stars of heaven, and brought them into the land that you had told their ancestors to enter and possess. [24]So the descendants went in and possessed the land, and you subdued before them the inhabitants of the land, the Canaanites, and gave them into their hands, with their kings and the peoples of the land, to do with them as they pleased. [25]And they captured fortress cities and a rich land, and took possession of houses filled with

_____

a Gk: Heb lacks *And Ezra said*   b Or *Sea of Reeds*   c Meaning of Heb uncertain

_____

law (Num 15.15–16), they had no need to confess Israel's sins as their own. **9.5–37** The Levites first summon the people to *Stand up and bless the LORD* (v. 5a). Their prayer must then begin with *Blessed be your glorious name*, addressed to God. The theme of the prayer is Israelite history viewed as a story of apostasy: there has been divine blessing (vv. 6–15), blessing continued despite rebellion (vv. 16–25), and rebellion renewed (vv. 26–31). It concludes with an appeal for deliverance from foreign domination (vv. 32–37, esp. v. 32, *do not treat lightly all the hardship . . .*). **9.6** There is no good reason to add to the text *And Ezra said*, as NRSV does, for the levitical prayer continues from 9.5b. **9.7** See Gen 11.31–12.3. **9.8** See Gen 15. **9.9** See Ex 3.7; 14.10. **9.10** See Deut 4.34; 29.2–3; Ex 18.11. **9.11** See Ex 14.21–23. **9.12** See Ex 13.21; Num 14.14. **9.13** See Ex 19–23. **9.14** See Ex 20.8–11. **9.15** See Ex 16.4; 17.6. **9.17** See Ex 16.2–3; cf. 34.6. **9.18** See Ex 32.4. **9.20** See Num 11.17; 11.6–9; 20.7–11. **9.21** See Deut 2.7; 8.4. **9.22** See Num 21.32–35; Deut 2.24–

all sorts of goods, hewn cisterns, vineyards, olive orchards, and fruit trees in abundance; so they ate, and were filled and became fat, and delighted themselves in your great goodness.

26 "Nevertheless they were disobedient and rebelled against you and cast your law behind their backs and killed your prophets, who had warned them in order to turn them back to you, and they committed great blasphemies. 27Therefore you gave them into the hands of their enemies, who made them suffer. Then in the time of their suffering they cried out to you and you heard them from heaven, and according to your great mercies you gave them saviors who saved them from the hands of their enemies. 28But after they had rest, they again did evil before you, and you abandoned them to the hands of their enemies, so that they had dominion over them; yet when they turned and cried to you, you heard from heaven, and many times you rescued them according to your mercies. 29And you warned them in order to turn them back to your law. Yet they acted presumptuously and did not obey your commandments, but sinned against your ordinances, by the observance of which a person shall live. They turned a stubborn shoulder and stiffened their neck and would not obey. 30Many years you were patient with them, and warned them by your spirit through your prophets; yet they would not listen. Therefore you handed them over to the peoples of the lands. 31Nevertheless, in your great mercies you did not make an end of them or forsake them, for you are a gracious and merciful God.

32 "Now therefore, our God—the great and mighty and awesome God, keeping covenant and steadfast love—do not treat lightly all the hardship that has come upon us, upon our kings, our officials, our priests, our prophets, our ancestors, and all your people, since the time of the kings of Assyria until today. 33You have been just in all that has come upon us, for you have dealt faithfully and we have acted wickedly; 34our kings, our officials, our priests, and our ancestors have not kept your law or heeded the commandments and the

warnings that you gave them. 35Even in their own kingdom, and in the great goodness you bestowed on them, and in the large and rich land that you set before them, they did not serve you and did not turn from their wicked works. 36Here we are, slaves to this day—slaves in the land that you gave to our ancestors to enjoy its fruit and its good gifts. 37Its rich yield goes to the kings whom you have set over us because of our sins; they have power also over our bodies and over our livestock at their pleasure, and we are in great distress."

Those Who Signed the Covenant

38[a] Because of all this we make a firm agreement in writing, and on that sealed document are inscribed the names of our officials, our Levites, and our priests.

10[b] Upon the sealed document are the names of Nehemiah the governor, son of Hacaliah, and Zedekiah; 2Seraiah, Azariah, Jeremiah, 3Pashhur, Amariah, Malchijah, 4Hattush, Shebaniah, Malluch, 5Harim, Meremoth, Obadiah, 6Daniel, Ginnethon, Baruch, 7Meshullam, Abijah, Mijamin, 8Maaziah, Bilgai, Shemaiah; these are the priests. 9And the Levites: Jeshua son of Azaniah, Binnui of the sons of Henadad, Kadmiel; 10and their associates, Shebaniah, Hodiah, Kelita, Pelaiah, Hanan, 11Mica, Rehob, Hashabiah, 12Zaccur, Sherebiah, Shebaniah, 13Hodiah, Bani, Beninu. 14The leaders of the people: Parosh, Pahath-moab, Elam, Zattu, Bani, 15Bunni, Azgad, Bebai, 16Adonijah, Bigvai, Adin, 17Ater, Hezekiah, Azzur, 18Hodiah, Hashum, Bezai, 19Hariph, Anathoth, Nebai, 20Magpiash, Meshullam, Hezir, 21Meshezabel, Zadok, Jaddua, 22Pelatiah, Hanan, Anaiah, 23Hoshea, Hananiah, Hasshub, 24Hallohesh, Pilha, Shobek, 25Rehum, Hashabnah, Maaseiah, 26Ahiah, Hanan, Anan, 27Malluch, Harim, and Baanah.

Summary of the Covenant

28 The rest of the people, the priests, the Levites, the gatekeepers, the singers, the temple

---

a Ch 10.1 in Heb   *b* Ch 10.2 in Heb

3.11. **9.23** See Gen 22.17. **9.27** Cf. Judg 2.11–18. **9.29** Cf. Deut 4.1.

9.38–10.39 The pledge of reform is here firmly attached to the prayer of penitence (*Because of all this*). Historically it seems more likely that it stemmed from the community of Nehemiah (probably following the events of Neh 13) rather than that of Ezra, who is not

named in it. **10.1–27** The priests' names (vv. 2–8) are probably "course" (or duty roster) names rather than the names of individuals. The laymen's names (vv. 14–27) often correspond to Ezra 2 and Neh 7, suggesting that individuals signed on behalf of their families. **10.28–39** The people pledge to keep not just pentateuchal law in general, but particular interpre-

servants, and all who have separated themselves from the peoples of the lands to adhere to the law of God, their wives, their sons, their daughters, all who have knowledge and understanding, 29join with their kin, their nobles, and enter into a curse and an oath to walk in God's law, which was given by Moses the servant of God, and to observe and do all the commandments of the LORD our Lord and his ordinances and his statutes. 30We will not give our daughters to the peoples of the land or take their daughters for our sons; 31and if the peoples of the land bring in merchandise or any grain on the sabbath day to sell, we will not buy it from them on the sabbath or on a holy day; and we will forego the crops of the seventh year and the exaction of every debt.

32 We also lay on ourselves the obligation to charge ourselves yearly one-third of a shekel for the service of the house of our God: 33for the rows of bread, the regular grain offering, the regular burnt offering, the sabbaths, the new moons, the appointed festivals, the sacred donations, and the sin offerings to make atonement for Israel, and for all the work of the house of our God. 34We have also cast lots among the priests, the Levites, and the people, for the wood offering, to bring it into the house of our God, by ancestral houses, at appointed times, year by year, to burn on the altar of the LORD our God, as it is written in the law. 35We obligate ourselves to bring the first fruits of our soil and the first fruits of all fruit of every tree, year by year, to the house of the LORD; 36also to bring to the house of our God, to the priests who minister in the house of our God, the firstborn of our sons and of our livestock, as it is written in the law, and the firstlings of our herds and of our flocks; 37and to bring the first of our dough, and our contri-

butions, the fruit of every tree, the wine and the oil, to the priests, to the chambers of the house of our God; and to bring to the Levites the tithes from our soil, for it is the Levites who collect the tithes in all our rural towns. 38And the priest, the descendant of Aaron, shall be with the Levites when the Levites receive the tithes; and the Levites shall bring up a tithe of the tithes to the house of our God, to the chambers of the storehouse. 39For the people of Israel and the sons of Levi shall bring the contribution of grain, wine, and oil to the storerooms where the vessels of the sanctuary are, and where the priests that minister, and the gatekeepers and the singers are. We will not neglect the house of our God.

Population of the City Increased

11 Now the leaders of the people lived in Jerusalem; and the rest of the people cast lots to bring one out of ten to live in the holy city Jerusalem, while nine-tenths remained in the other towns. 2And the people blessed all those who willingly offered to live in Jerusalem.

3 These are the leaders of the province who lived in Jerusalem; but in the towns of Judah all lived on their property in their towns: Israel, the priests, the Levites, the temple servants, and the descendants of Solomon's servants. 4And in Jerusalem lived some of the Judahites and of the Benjaminites. Of the Judahites: Athaiah son of Uzziah son of Zechariah son of Amariah son of Shephatiah son of Mahalalel, of the descendants of Perez; 5and Maaseiah son of Baruch son of Col-hozeh son of Hazaiah son of Adaiah son of Joiarib son of Zechariah son of the Shilonite. 6All the descendants of Perez who lived in Jerusalem were four hundred sixty-eight valiant warriors.

---

tations of it amounting to new laws. **10.28** *All who have separated themselves.* Cf. Ezra 6.21. **10.30** Cf. Ex 34.11–16; Deut 7.1–4; note on Ezra 9.1–10.44. **10.31** No former *sabbath* law (e.g., Ex 20.8–11) defined buying food as work. And previously the fallow-year law (Ex 23.10–11), which works to the disadvantage of the farmer, had not been combined with the remission-year law (Deut 15.1–8), which works to the disadvantage of the merchant. **10.32** Previously any temple tax had been only occasional (2 Kings 12.4–15), not annual. **10.33** For the temple expenditures, see Num 28–29. **10.34** The law prescribed a continual fire on the altar (Lev 6.8–13), but not how the wood should be collected. **10.35–39** Most of these gifts for the temple personnel are prescribed in

various parts of the law, but this is the first time they are all brought together. For *first fruits,* see Num 18.12–13; for *firstborn,* see Ex 22.29–30; for *the first,* or better "choice produce," manufactured rather than raw, see Num 18.12; for *tithes,* see Num 18.26–32. **10.38** Priests receive a tenth of the Levites' income (Num 18.26–28).

11.1–36 Nehemiah's memoir seems to resume from the point reached in 7.73a, though it is soon interrupted again in v. 3 by various lists, mostly from a time later than Nehemiah. Those who are forcibly removed by lot from the villages in order to repeople Jerusalem are honored by being called those who *willingly offered.* **11.3–19** These Jerusalemite family heads and clergy are contemporary with Nehemiah (another ver-

7 And these are the Benjaminites: Sallu son of Meshullam son of Joed son of Pedaiah son of Kolaiah son of Maaseiah son of Ithiel son of Jeshaiah. [8]And his brothers[a] Gabbai, Sallai: nine hundred twenty-eight. [9]Joel son of Zichri was their overseer; and Judah son of Hassenuah was second in charge of the city.

10 Of the priests: Jedaiah son of Joiarib, Jachin, [11]Seraiah son of Hilkiah son of Meshullam son of Zadok son of Meraioth son of Ahitub, officer of the house of God, [12]and their associates who did the work of the house, eight hundred twenty-two; and Adaiah son of Jeroham son of Pelaliah son of Amzi son of Zechariah son of Pashhur son of Malchijah, [13]and his associates, heads of ancestral houses, two hundred forty-two; and Amashsai son of Azarel son of Ahzai son of Meshillemoth son of Immer, [14]and their associates, valiant warriors, one hundred twenty-eight; their overseer was Zabdiel son of Haggedolim.

15 And of the Levites: Shemaiah son of Hasshub son of Azrikam son of Hashabiah son of Bunni; [16]and Shabbethai and Jozabad, of the leaders of the Levites, who were over the outside work of the house of God; [17]and Mattaniah son of Mica son of Zabdi son of Asaph, who was the leader to begin the thanksgiving in prayer, and Bakbukiah, the second among his associates; and Abda son of Shammua son of Galal son of Jeduthun. [18]All the Levites in the holy city were two hundred eighty-four.

19 The gatekeepers, Akkub, Talmon and their associates, who kept watch at the gates, were one hundred seventy-two. [20]And the rest of Israel, and of the priests and the Levites, were in all the towns of Judah, all of them in their inheritance. [21]But the temple servants lived on Ophel; and Ziha and Gishpa were over the temple servants.

22 The overseer of the Levites in Jerusalem was Uzzi son of Bani son of Hashabiah son of Mattaniah son of Mica, of the descendants of Asaph, the singers, in charge of the work of the house of God. [23]For there was a command from the king concerning them, and a settled provision for the singers, as was required every day. [24]And Pethahiah son of Meshezabel, of the descendants of Zerah son of Judah, was at the king's hand in all matters concerning the people.

Villages outside Jerusalem

25 And as for the villages, with their fields, some of the people of Judah lived in Kirith-arba and its villages, and in Dibon and its villages, and in Jekabzeel and its villages, [26]and in Jeshua and in Moladah and Beth-pelet, [27]in Hazar-shual, in Beer-sheba and its villages, [28]in Ziklag, in Meconah and its villages, [29]in En-rimmon, in Zorah, in Jarmuth, [30]Zanoah, Adullam, and their villages, Lachish and its fields, and Azekah and its villages. So they camped from Beer-sheba to the valley of Hinnom. [31]The people of Benjamin also lived from Geba onward, at Michmash, Aija, Bethel and its villages, [32]Anathoth, Nob, Ananiah, [33]Hazor, Ramah, Gittaim, [34]Hadid, Zeboim, Neballat, [35]Lod, and Ono, the valley of artisans. [36]And certain divisions of the Levites in Judah were joined to Benjamin.

A List of Priests and Levites

12 These are the priests and the Levites who came up with Zerubbabel son of Shealtiel, and Jeshua: Seraiah, Jeremiah, Ezra, [2]Amariah, Malluch, Hattush, [3]Shecaniah, Rehum, Meremoth, [4]Iddo, Ginnethoi, Abijah, [5]Mijamin, Maadiah, Bilgah, [6]Shemaiah, Joiarib, Jedaiah, [7]Sallu, Amok, Hilkiah, Jedaiah. These were the leaders of the priests and of their associates in the days of Jeshua.

8 And the Levites: Jeshua, Binnui, Kadmiel, Sherebiah, Judah, and Mattaniah, who with his associates was in charge of the songs of thanksgiving. [9]And Bakbukiah and Unno their associates stood opposite them in the service. [10]Jeshua was the father of Joiakim, Joiakim the father of Eliashib, Eliashib the father of Joiada, [11]Joiada the father of Jonathan, and Jonathan the father of Jaddua.

12 In the days of Joiakim the priests, heads of ancestral houses, were: of Seraiah, Meraiah; of Jeremiah, Hananiah; [13]of Ezra, Meshullam;

---

a Gk Mss: Heb And after him

---

sion of the list is in 1 Chr 9). **11.20** A heading that rightly applies to vv. 25–36. **11.21–24** Supplements to vv. 10–19. **11.24** *Pethahiah* seems to be a governor two generations after Nehemiah. **11.25–36** This list of towns in Judah and Benjamin almost certainly does not belong to Nehemiah's time.

12.1–26 Lists of priests and Levites purportedly from ca. 520 BCE (vv. 1–9); high priests down to Jaddua, in 323 (vv. 10–11); priests and Levites from the time of Joiakim, sometime between 520 and 445 (vv.

of Amariah, Jehohanan; [14]of Malluchi, Jonathan; of Shebaniah, Joseph; [15]of Harim, Adna; of Meraioth, Helkai; [16]of Iddo, Zechariah; of Ginnethon, Meshullam; [17]of Abijah, Zichri; of Miniamin, of Moadiah, Piltai; [18]of Bilgah, Shammua; of Shemaiah, Jehonathan; [19]of Joiarib, Mattenai; of Jedaiah, Uzzi; [20]of Sallai, Kallai; of Amok, Eber; [21]of Hilkiah, Hashabiah; of Jedaiah, Nethanel.

22 As for the Levites, in the days of Eliashib, Joiada, Johanan, and Jaddua, there were recorded the heads of ancestral houses; also the priests until the reign of Darius the Persian. [23]The Levites, heads of ancestral houses, were recorded in the Book of the Annals until the days of Johanan son of Eliashib. [24]And the leaders of the Levites: Hashabiah, Sherebiah, and Jeshua son of Kadmiel, with their associates over against them, to praise and to give thanks, according to the commandment of David the man of God, section opposite to section. [25]Mattaniah, Bakbukiah, Obadiah, Meshullam, Talmon, and Akkub were gatekeepers standing guard at the storehouses of the gates. [26]These were in the days of Joiakim son of Jeshua son of Jozadak, and in the days of the governor Nehemiah and of the priest Ezra, the scribe.

Dedication of the City Wall

27 Now at the dedication of the wall of Jerusalem they sought out the Levites in all their places, to bring them to Jerusalem to celebrate the dedication with rejoicing, with thanksgivings and with singing, with cymbals, harps, and lyres. [28]The companies of the singers gathered together from the circuit around Jerusalem and from the villages of the Netophathites; [29]also from Beth-gilgal and from the region of Geba and Azmaveth; for the singers had built for themselves villages around Jerusalem. [30]And the priests and the Levites purified themselves; and they purified the people and the gates and the wall.

31 Then I brought the leaders of Judah up onto the wall, and appointed two great companies that gave thanks and went in procession. One went to the right on the wall to the Dung Gate; [32]and after them went Hoshaiah and half the officials of Judah, [33]and Azariah, Ezra, Meshullam, [34]Judah, Benjamin, Shemaiah, and Jeremiah, [35]and some of the young priests with trumpets: Zechariah son of Jonathan son of Shemaiah son of Mattaniah son of Micaiah son of Zaccur son of Asaph; [36]and his kindred, Shemaiah, Azarel, Milalai, Gilalai, Maai, Nethanel, Judah, and Hanani, with the musical instruments of David the man of God; and the scribe Ezra went in front of them. [37]At the Fountain Gate, in front of them, they went straight up by the stairs of the city of David, at the ascent of the wall, above the house of David, to the Water Gate on the east.

38 The other company of those who gave thanks went to the left,[a] and I followed them with half of the people on the wall, above the Tower of the Ovens, to the Broad Wall, [39]and above the Gate of Ephraim, and by the Old Gate, and by the Fish Gate and the Tower of Hananel and the Tower of the Hundred, to the Sheep Gate; and they came to a halt at the Gate of the Guard. [40]So both companies of those who gave thanks stood in the house of God, and I and half of the officials with me; [41]and the priests Eliakim, Maaseiah, Miniamin, Micaiah, Elioenai, Zechariah, and Hananiah, with trumpets; [42]and Maaseiah, Shemaiah, Eleazar, Uzzi, Jehohanan, Malchijah, Elam, and Ezer. And the singers sang with Jezrahiah as their leader. [43]They offered great sacrifices that day and rejoiced, for God had made them rejoice with great joy; the women and children also rejoiced. The joy of Jerusalem was heard far away.

Temple Responsibilities

44 On that day men were appointed over the chambers for the stores, the contributions, the first fruits, and the tithes, to gather into them

---

a Cn: Heb opposite

12–21, 24–26); and also a note about the source of these lists (vv. 22–23). **12.27–43** The story of the dedication of the wall would have been an appropriate topic for Nehemiah's memoir. **12.27–30** The Levite singers, who normally came up to Jerusalem only for their tours of duty, now assemble en masse for this ceremony. **12.31–43** The circumambulation of the walls is carried out by two processions starting at the same place, walking along the top of the wall in opposite directions, and meeting finally in the temple area. Each procession has a choir, a group of lay nobles, seven priests, and eight Levite musicians. With vocal music in front and instrumental music in the rear, they must have been enveloped in stereophonic sound. The ceremony concludes with many sacrifices (v. 43).

12.44–13.3 An idealized summary of the postexilic

the portions required by the law for the priests and for the Levites from the fields belonging to the towns; for Judah rejoiced over the priests and the Levites who ministered. 45They performed the service of their God and the service of purification, as did the singers and the gatekeepers, according to the command of David and his son Solomon. 46For in the days of David and Asaph long ago there was a leader of the singers, and there were songs of praise and thanksgiving to God. 47In the days of Zerubbabel and in the days of Nehemiah all Israel gave the daily portions for the singers and the gatekeepers. They set apart that which was for the Levites; and the Levites set apart that which was for the descendants of Aaron.

Foreigners Separated from Israel

13 On that day they read from the book of Moses in the hearing of the people; and in it was found written that no Ammonite or Moabite should ever enter the assembly of God, 2because they did not meet the Israelites with bread and water, but hired Balaam against them to curse them—yet our God turned the curse into a blessing. 3When the people heard the law, they separated from Israel all those of foreign descent.

The Reforms of Nehemiah

4 Now before this, the priest Eliashib, who was appointed over the chambers of the house of our God, and who was related to Tobiah, 5prepared for Tobiah a large room where they had previously put the grain offering, the frankincense, the vessels, and the tithes of grain, wine, and oil, which were given by commandment

to the Levites, singers, and gatekeepers, and the contributions for the priests. 6While this was taking place I was not in Jerusalem, for in the thirty-second year of King Artaxerxes of Babylon I went to the king. After some time I asked leave of the king 7and returned to Jerusalem. I then discovered the wrong that Eliashib had done on behalf of Tobiah, preparing a room for him in the courts of the house of God. 8And I was very angry, and I threw all the household furniture of Tobiah out of the room. 9Then I gave orders and they cleansed the chambers, and I brought back the vessels of the house of God, with the grain offering and the frankincense.

10 I also found out that the portions of the Levites had not been given to them; so that the Levites and the singers, who had conducted the service, had gone back to their fields. 11So I remonstrated with the officials and said, "Why is the house of God forsaken?" And I gathered them together and set them in their stations. 12Then all Judah brought the tithe of the grain, wine, and oil into the storehouses. 13And I appointed as treasurers over the storehouses the priest Shelemiah, the scribe Zadok, and Pedaiah of the Levites, and as their assistant Hanan son of Zaccur son of Mattaniah, for they were considered faithful; and their duty was to distribute to their associates. 14Remember me, O my God, concerning this, and do not wipe out my good deeds that I have done for the house of my God and for his service.

Sabbath Reforms Begun

15 In those days I saw in Judah people treading wine presses on the sabbath, and bringing

---

community: the clergy are properly maintained by the community, and they perform the worship of God as prescribed in ancient times. The integrity of the worshiping community is secured by the exclusion of all foreigners forbidden in the law (Num 21.21–23; 22–24; Deut 23.3–6). **13.4–31** The editor's glowing picture of the postexilic community (12.44–13.3) is followed immediately by Nehemiah's account of his reforms, suggesting a less rosy reality. Or is reality whatever is the best that can be said, rather than the sad exceptions to a happy norm? Nehemiah had gone back to Persia in 432 BCE and on his return found several matters amiss. **13.4–9** Nehemiah's old enemy *Tobiah* (2.10; 6.17–19) has during Nehemiah's absence installed himself in a temple apartment with the permission of *Eliashib,* the temple dean, to whom he was apparently related by marriage (v. 4; cf. 6.18). Not only is Tobiah not a priest or Levite, he is an Ammonite (see

v. 1; Deut 23.3)! This is an act of sacrilege and a defilement that must be *cleansed* (v. 9). It is probably also an attack on Nehemiah's personal authority—which explains Nehemiah's reaction. **13.10–14** In reorganizing the temple storerooms Nehemiah realizes that the populace has not provided adequately for the Levites. The *portions* (tithes) of the Levites are their regular income; without them they have to leave Jerusalem and earn their living on their farms (for Levite villages with their pasturelands, see Num 35.1–8). So temple worship has virtually come to a standstill. Nehemiah makes the support of the Levites the responsibility of the lay leaders (*officials,* v. 11), and appoints *treasurers* (v. 13, including priests, since their income derives from the Levites'; cf. note on 10.38) to supervise the delivery of the tithes. The community pledge of Neh 10 goes a step further by establishing levitical depots across the country (10.37) to facilitate collection.

in heaps of grain and loading them on donkeys; and also wine, grapes, figs, and all kinds of burdens, which they brought into Jerusalem on the sabbath day; and I warned them at that time against selling food. 16Tyrians also, who lived in the city, brought in fish and all kinds of merchandise and sold them on the sabbath to the people of Judah, and in Jerusalem. 17Then I remonstrated with the nobles of Judah and said to them, "What is this evil thing that you are doing, profaning the sabbath day? 18Did not your ancestors act in this way, and did not our God bring all this disaster on us and on this city? Yet you bring more wrath on Israel by profaning the sabbath."

19 When it began to be dark at the gates of Jerusalem before the sabbath, I commanded that the doors should be shut and gave orders that they should not be opened until after the sabbath. And I set some of my servants over the gates, to prevent any burden from being brought in on the sabbath day. 20Then the merchants and sellers of all kinds of merchandise spent the night outside Jerusalem once or twice. 21But I warned them and said to them, "Why do you spend the night in front of the wall? If you do so again, I will lay hands on you." From that time on they did not come on the sabbath. 22And I commanded the Levites that they should purify themselves and come and guard the gates, to keep the sabbath day holy. Remember this also in my favor, O my God, and spare me according to the greatness of your steadfast love.

Mixed Marriages Condemned

23 In those days also I saw Jews who had married women of Ashdod, Ammon, and Moab; 24and half of their children spoke the language of Ashdod, and they could not speak the language of Judah, but spoke the language of various peoples. 25And I contended with them and cursed them and beat some of them and pulled out their hair; and I made them take an oath in the name of God, saying, "You shall not give your daughters to their sons, or take their daughters for your sons or for yourselves. 26Did not King Solomon of Israel sin on account of such women? Among the many nations there was no king like him, and he was beloved by his God, and God made him king over all Israel; nevertheless, foreign women made even him to sin. 27Shall we then listen to you and do all this great evil and act treacherously against our God by marrying foreign women?"

28 And one of the sons of Jehoiada, son of the high priest Eliashib, was the son-in-law of Sanballat the Horonite; I chased him away from me. 29Remember them, O my God, because they have defiled the priesthood, the covenant of the priests and the Levites.

30 Thus I cleansed them from everything foreign, and I established the duties of the priests and Levites, each in his work; 31and I provided for the wood offering, at appointed times, and for the first fruits. Remember me, O my God, for good.

13.15–22 Nehemiah finds also that the sabbath law is being contravened: there is work (against Ex 20.8–11), harvesting (against Ex 34.21), and using animals (against Ex 23.12). And there is buying from non-Jewish merchants—which was not specifically forbidden in the law. Nehemiah makes the family heads responsible for enforcing sabbath observance (v. 17), and to prevent sabbath trading he takes direct action by posting guards at the city gates (v. 19). The community pledge of 10.31, no doubt responding to the same situation, relies on the people's conscience rather than a show of force to ensure obedience. 13.23–29 Intermarriage with non-Jews had obviously not ceased when Ezra's community insisted on divorces of foreign wives (Ezra 9–10). That had been about thirty years previously, in a former generation (if Ezra's date is indeed 458 BCE); if Ezra did not precede Nehemiah but came to Jerusalem in 398 BCE, it will of course have been Nehemiah's demands that had been ignored. In either case, Nehemiah, though physically more vigorous than Ezra (v. 25), actually takes a more moderate line, for he only forbids intermarriage in the future and takes no action against existing marriages. The fact that the son (or grandson) of the high priest had married into the family of Nehemiah's archenemy Sanballat (v. 28) shows that Nehemiah's views were far from universally accepted. 13.30–31 Nehemiah's summary of his activities shows well how he would like to be remembered: as a religious reformer rather than simply a civil governor and restorer of Jerusalem's walls.

ESTHER

Purim and Esther

THE BOOK OF ESTHER appears in the Hebrew Bible as one of the Five Scrolls read on festivals or commemorative days of the Jewish year. Read at Purim, Esther legitimizes this celebration of the deliverance of Jews from threatened destruction. Yet tension exists between the theme of the festival, as set out in ch. 9, and the story in chs. 1–8. Many suggest that this connection is a later development in a story of court intrigue and conflict, one that ended in a triumphant celebration for the Jews, but not the massive slaughter of the enemy described in 9.1–19 (seventy-five thousand in v. 16!) and the particulars of Purim in 9.20–32.

Some suggest that Purim reflects a form of New Year's festivity current in the ancient Persian Empire. Diaspora Jewish communities were caught up in the celebrations, which were often linked with casting lots to determine the destinies of peoples and nations for the coming year. The story of Esther and Mordecai linked this popular celebration (called "Mordecai's Day" in 2 Macc 15.36) to events specific to Jewish history. Esther's link to Purim explains the presence of this otherwise nonreligious book in the Jewish canon.

Setting, Plot, Characters, Themes, and Worldview

THE STORY IS SET in the Persian capital of Susa, and its main characters are Jews living in close proximity to foreign rulers. It was composed in the eastern Jewish Diaspora of the Persian Empire in the late Persian or very early Hellenistic period (fourth century BCE).

The story represents a type found in Jewish tradition: an account of the trials and triumphs of figures involved in intrigues in foreign courts, e.g., Joseph and Daniel (Gen 39–41; Dan 1–6). Readers were attracted to stories of contests and conflicts where power and wealth rewarded those clever enough to gain royal favor. Moreover, the story is extremely well told, engaging readers through sustained suspense. Human initiative combines with seeming coincidence to bring about a resolution in which good triumphs over evil.

Characters are sketched with broad strokes. Haman is the archetypical villain. The king is the stock figure of ancient court tales. Mordecai and Esther are more complex. Characters like Vashti and Zeresh make brief and telling appearances; others, including ever present eunuchs, are agents who keep the plot moving.

Emphasis is on plot rather than development of character. A plot laced with twists, turns, and sudden reversals joins rather stock characters, leading to rich depths of irony. Readers experience the universe as ultimately just, a satisfaction real life rarely provides. Three among many ironic elements in the story merit attention.

First, the central figure is a woman. Within postexilic Jewish communities women's roles were quite circumscribed; in public arenas they were generally marginal. It is striking that diaspora Jewish communities, themselves marginal within their larger worlds, placed a woman at the center of a story of deliverance from potential destruction (see also Judith). Esther is a role model for the diaspora Jew.

Second, Esther and Mordecai seem remarkably unconstrained by Torah regulations, which defined Jewish identity for many. Esther can conceal her Jewish identity, and nothing about her dress, diet, or behavior reveals her secret. Her marriage to a Gentile also passes without comment.

Third, absence of any direct mention of the deity in a story about Jews delivered from danger in an alien setting has provoked comment by scholars. The "other quarter" mentioned by Mordecai in 4.14 is sometimes understood as an oblique reference to the deity and providential guidance, and readers are free to assume the activity of the divine behind the so-called coincidences of the plot. Nevertheless, failure to mention God in any direct way lends a remarkably secular and contemporary tone to the story. God works through human instruments to achieve God's purpose, in this case the survival of the Jewish people.

The Greek Text

THE SHORTER AND LONGER FORMS of Greek Esther contain what tradition calls "Additions" addressing perceived problems within the story (for the longer form, see Esther, the Greek Version Containing the Additional Chapters, in the Apocrypha). In spite of qualities of the Greek Esther that align it with traditional Jewish piety, including direct reference to God, prayers, and the keeping of the dietary laws, the shorter Hebrew form of the book was in time included in the Writings of the Hebrew Bible. Its inclusion was not accepted without debate and dissent (Esther is not represented among the Dead Sea Scrolls). This form is also preserved in the Protestant OT. Other Christian Bibles preserve fuller Greek forms of Esther and, like the Protestant, place the story among the historical books. [W. LEE HUMPHREYS, revised by SIDNIE WHITE CRAWFORD]

King Ahasuerus Deposes Queen Vashti

1 This happened in the days of Ahasuerus, the same Ahasuerus who ruled over one hundred twenty-seven provinces from India to Ethiopia.[a] 2 In those days when King Ahasuerus sat on his royal throne in the citadel of Susa, 3 in the third year of his reign, he gave a banquet for all his officials and ministers. The army of Persia and Media and the nobles and governors of the provinces were present, 4 while he displayed the great wealth of his kingdom and the splendor and pomp of his majesty for many days, one hundred eighty days in all.

5 When these days were completed, the king gave for all the people present in the citadel of Susa, both great and small, a banquet lasting for seven days, in the court of the garden of the king's palace. 6 There were white cotton curtains and blue hangings tied with cords of fine linen and purple to silver rings[b] and marble pillars. There were couches of gold and silver on a mosaic pavement of porphyry, marble, mother-of-pearl, and colored stones. 7 Drinks were served in golden goblets, goblets of different kinds, and the royal wine was lavished according to the bounty of the king. 8 Drinking was by flagons, without restraint; for the king had given orders to all the officials

_____
a Or Nubia; Heb Cush   b Or rods

of his palace to do as each one desired. 9Furthermore, Queen Vashti gave a banquet for the women in the palace of King Ahasuerus.

10 On the seventh day, when the king was merry with wine, he commanded Mehuman, Biztha, Harbona, Bigtha and Abagtha, Zethar and Carkas, the seven eunuchs who attended him, 11to bring Queen Vashti before the king, wearing the royal crown, in order to show the peoples and the officials her beauty; for she was fair to behold. 12But Queen Vashti refused to come at the king's command conveyed by the eunuchs. At this the king was enraged, and his anger burned within him.

13 Then the king consulted the sages who knew the laws*a* (for this was the king's procedure toward all who were versed in law and custom, 14and those next to him were Carshena, Shethar, Admatha, Tarshish, Meres, Marsena, and Memucan, the seven officials of Persia and Media, who had access to the king, and sat first in the kingdom): 15"According to the law, what is to be done to Queen Vashti because she has not performed the command of King Ahasuerus conveyed by the eunuchs?" 16Then Memucan said in the presence of the king and the officials, "Not only has Queen Vashti done wrong to the king, but also to all the officials and all the peoples who are in all the provinces of King Ahasuerus. 17For this deed of the queen will be made known to all women, causing them to look with contempt on their husbands, since they will say, 'King Ahasuerus commanded Queen Vashti to be brought before him, and she did not come.' 18This very day the noble ladies of Persia and Media who have heard of the queen's behavior will rebel against*b* the king's officials, and there will be no end of contempt and wrath! 19If it pleases the king, let a royal order go out from him, and let it be written among the laws of the Persians and the Medes so that it may not be altered, that Vashti is never again to come before King Ahasuerus; and let the king give her royal position to another who is better than she. 20So when the decree made by the king is proclaimed throughout all his kingdom, vast as it is, all women will give honor to their husbands, high and low alike."

21 This advice pleased the king and the officials, and the king did as Memucan proposed; 22he sent letters to all the royal provinces, to

---

a Cn: Heb *times*   *b* Cn: Heb *will tell*

1.1–9 Descriptions of the king and his banquets, the extent of the Persian Empire, and of the royal court and its festivities set an opulent stage for a story in which power and wealth are at stake for those engaged in court intrigues. The lavish setting, however, cloaks an underlying hollowness, a lack of deeper ethical and moral concerns. 1.1 *Ahasuerus* (Ezra 4.6; Dan 9.1), whose name means "the chief of rulers," is usually identified as Xerxes I (486–465 BCE), sometimes (as in the Greek and Josephus) as Artaxerxes I or II (465–424 BCE, 404–358 BCE). At its fullest extent the Persian Empire comprised thirty-one satrapies. Xerxes had twenty according to Herodotus (*History* 3.89), each composed of several *provinces.* 1.2 As a royal and religious complex, the *citadel of Susa* was a city within the larger city of Susa, the winter residence of Persian rulers, whose capital was Persepolis. 1.3 Most of the terms for *officials, ministers, nobles,* and *governors* are general, hinting at the complex administrative structures that managed the vast Persian Empire. 1.5 The *king's palace* was an open-air colonnade structure. 1.6 Greek authors mention lavish Persian feasts, with an emphasis on drinking. 1.7–8 Banquets and *drinking* mark many of the critical events in this story (see 2.18; 3.15; 5.4–8; 7.1–8; 8.17; 9.17–19). 1.9 *Vashti* is otherwise unknown. Herodotus names Amestris, from a noble Persian family, as Xerxes' queen. Women could dine with men in Persia; Vashti's separate banquet is a necessary literary device. 1.10–22 King Ahasuerus deposes Queen Vashti. 1.10 *Eunuchs,* men who had been castrated, were functionaries in the Persian court; they appear at key points to facilitate the actions of other characters and move the story along. Lists of names (see also v. 14) give the story an air of authenticity. 1.11 Some rabbinic commentators suggest this summons meant she was to wear only the *royal crown.* 1.12 It is ironic that Vashti is rejected for disobeying the king by refusing to appear when summoned, while in 4.16–5.1 Esther, who refused to obey royal law and stay away until called, is rewarded for disobedience. The timing of events along with good fortune and the ability to capitalize on it bring success to an able courtier. 1.13 The *sages* are possibly a privy council (Ezra 7.14; Herodotus, *History* 3.31). 1.14 Only the most trusted *officials* were allowed physical access to the king. 1.15 The rash decision to do something to Vashti without investigating the causes for her refusal as well as his dependence on others for advice characterize this king as cloaked in symbols of power but actually malleable and controlled by others. 1.18 These *noble ladies* included, of course, the wives of those advising the king. 1.19 The unalterable *laws of the Persians and the Medes* (see 3.12–14; 8.8–14; Dan 6.8) is a literary motif, not otherwise known and historically most improbable. Ironically, because Vashti will not come, she is forbidden ever to come before the king. 1.21–22 All official resources and protocol of state are needed to deal with the danger posed to men by one

every province in its own script and to every people in its own language, declaring that every man should be master in his own house.[a]

Esther Becomes Queen

2 After these things, when the anger of King Ahasuerus had abated, he remembered Vashti and what she had done and what had been decreed against her. [2]Then the king's servants who attended him said, "Let beautiful young virgins be sought out for the king. [3]And let the king appoint commissioners in all the provinces of his kingdom to gather all the beautiful young virgins to the harem in the citadel of Susa under custody of Hegai, the king's eunuch, who is in charge of the women; let their cosmetic treatments be given them. [4]And let the girl who pleases the king be queen instead of Vashti." This pleased the king, and he did so.

5 Now there was a Jew in the citadel of Susa whose name was Mordecai son of Jair son of Shimei son of Kish, a Benjaminite. [6]Kish[b] had been carried away from Jerusalem among the captives carried away with King Jeconiah of Judah, whom King Nebuchadnezzar of Babylon had carried away. [7]Mordecai[c] had brought up Hadassah, that is Esther, his cousin, for she had neither father nor mother; the girl was fair and beautiful, and when her father and her mother died, Mordecai adopted her as his own daughter. [8]So when the king's order and his edict were proclaimed, and

when many young women were gathered in the citadel of Susa in custody of Hegai, Esther also was taken into the king's palace and put in custody of Hegai, who had charge of the women. [9]The girl pleased him and won his favor, and he quickly provided her with her cosmetic treatments and her portion of food, and with seven chosen maids from the king's palace, and advanced her and her maids to the best place in the harem. [10]Esther did not reveal her people or kindred, for Mordecai had charged her not to tell. [11]Every day Mordecai would walk around in front of the court of the harem, to learn how Esther was and how she fared.

12 The turn came for each girl to go in to King Ahasuerus, after being twelve months under the regulations for the women, since this was the regular period of their cosmetic treatment, six months with oil of myrrh and six months with perfumes and cosmetics for women. [13]When the girl went in to the king she was given whatever she asked for to take with her from the harem to the king's palace. [14]In the evening she went in; then in the morning she came back to the second harem in custody of Shaashgaz, the king's eunuch, who was in charge of the concubines; she did not go in to the king again, unless the king delighted in her and she was summoned by name.

---

a Heb adds *and speak according to the language of his people*
b Heb *a Benjaminite* [6]*who*　c Heb *He*

---

willful woman! This is the first in a series of letters and decrees sent by means of the famed Persian courier service. Vashti's banishment creates a place for Esther to enter the royal court and the story.
2.1–4 The search for a new queen. **2.1** Just what he *remembered* of Vashti is left vague; readers must determine among the many possibilities. **2.2** *Servants* are here personal pages, adept at reading the king's mind and addressing his concerns without his speaking a word. **2.3** *Harem,* lit. "the house of the women." **2.4** This is an undertaking in which it seems the king can only benefit. The needs or desires of the young women involved are not taken into consideration. **2.5–7** Esther and Mordecai. **2.5** *Mordecai* is introduced as a Benjaminite linked to Saul, Israel's first king. *Shimei.* See 2 Sam 16.5–14; 19.16–23; 1 Kings 2.8, 36–46. *Kish,* Saul's father; see 1 Sam 9.1. Generations are telescoped, as the phrase *son of* can mean "descendant of." **2.6** Others understand Mordecai, not *Kish,* to be the one exiled by Nebuchadnezzar in 597 BCE with *Jeconiah,* who is elsewhere called Jehoiachin

(2 Kings 24.6–17). This poses chronological problems for a story set in the reign of Xerxes; thus the NRSV has v. 6 refer to Kish as Mordecai's great-grandfather and the one exiled. **2.7** Esther, like other Jews in Diaspora, had both Jewish and non-Jewish names (Dan 1.6–7). *Hadassah* means "Myrtle" in Hebrew. Esther is an orphan, a particularly powerless position. *Beautiful.* Esther clearly fits the requirements of v. 3, but has no other defining characteristics. **2.8–18** Esther becomes queen. **2.9** Esther's success with those charged with custody of the king's women anticipates her future success with the king himself. Receiving her *portion of food,* she appears not to observe Jewish dietary laws, a concern to early interpreters. In this she stands in contrast to Daniel (Dan 1.8–20). See also Addition C in the Greek version. **2.10** Secrecy regarding her kindred is necessary for the plot and also hints at an underlying anti-Semitism in the court. **2.12** *Myrrh* was a resin used as an incense and in ointments and perfumes. **2.14** After their first evening with the king, these women became his concubines, were placed under the

15 When the turn came for Esther daughter of Abihail the uncle of Mordecai, who had adopted her as his own daughter, to go in to the king, she asked for nothing except what Hegai the king's eunuch, who had charge of the women, advised. Now Esther was admired by all who saw her. 16 When Esther was taken to King Ahasuerus in his royal palace in the tenth month, which is the month of Tebeth, in the seventh year of his reign, 17 the king loved Esther more than all the other women; of all the virgins she won his favor and devotion, so that he set the royal crown on her head and made her queen instead of Vashti. 18 Then the king gave a great banquet to all his officials and ministers—"Esther's banquet." He also granted a holiday[a] to the provinces, and gave gifts with royal liberality.

Mordecai Discovers a Plot

19 When the virgins were being gathered together,[b] Mordecai was sitting at the king's gate. 20 Now Esther had not revealed her kindred or her people, as Mordecai had charged her; for Esther obeyed Mordecai just as when she was brought up by him. 21 In those days, while Mordecai was sitting at the king's gate, Bigthan and Teresh, two of the king's eunuchs, who guarded the threshold, became angry and conspired to assassinate[c] King Ahasuerus. 22 But the matter came to the knowledge of Mordecai, and he told it to Queen Esther, and Esther told the king in the name of Mordecai. 23 When the affair was investigated and found to be so, both the men were hanged on the gallows. It was recorded in the book of the annals in the presence of the king.

Haman Undertakes to Destroy the Jews

3 After these things King Ahasuerus promoted Haman son of Hammedatha the Agagite, and advanced him and set his seat above all the officials who were with him. 2 And all the king's servants who were at the king's gate bowed down and did obeisance to Haman; for the king had so commanded concerning him. But Mordecai did not bow down or do obeisance. 3 Then the king's servants who were at the king's gate said to Mordecai, "Why do you disobey the king's command?" 4 When they spoke to him day after day and he would not listen to them, they told Haman, in order to see whether Mordecai's words would avail; for he had told them that he was a Jew. 5 When Haman saw that Mordecai did not bow down or do obeisance to him, Haman was infuriated. 6 But he thought it beneath him to lay hands on Mordecai alone. So, having been told who Mordecai's people were, Haman plotted to destroy all the Jews, the people of Mordecai, throughout the whole kingdom of Ahasuerus.

7 In the first month, which is the month of Nisan, in the twelfth year of King Ahasuerus, they cast Pur—which means "the lot"—before

---

a Or an amnesty   b Heb adds a second time   c Heb to lay hands on

---

charge of another eunuch, and resided in a *second harem.* **2.16** *Tebeth,* December-January in the Babylonian calendar. It took four years to find a new queen. **2.17** Although Esther's success is anticipated (see vv. 9, 15), readers must wait through nine verses of information about harem protocol to be assured that she wins the favor of the man who matters most. Her beauty and charm seem enough to please him, for he inquires no further about her background. **2.18** This wedding *banquet* that includes benefits for the king's subjects is next in a series of feasts punctuating this story. **2.19–23** Mordecai discovers a plot. **2.19** Sitting in the *king's gate,* Mordecai is an official of undetermined rank. **2.20** This repetitive stress on Esther's obedience to Mordecai (v. 10) emphasizes Esther's obedience to the men controlling her (see v. 15). **2.21** Xerxes actually fell victim to a plot by his chamber guards. **2.23** *Hanged,* or "impaled on the stake." The *book of the annals,* lit. "the book of the things of the days," was the official record of royal actions. The king's failure to reward Mordecai becomes an important plot device.

3.1–15 Haman undertakes to destroy the Jews. **3.1** As an *Agagite,* Haman is an Amalekite, the natural enemy of the Jews (Ex 17.8–16; Num 24.20; Deut 25.17–19) and especially of the Benjaminite Mordecai (1 Sam 15). Ironically Haman is rewarded for no stated reason, while Mordecai is not rewarded in 2.19–23 for service to the king. **3.4** *That he was a Jew* does not explain Mordecai's refusal, for elsewhere Jews are depicted as bowing before those in authority (Gen 23.7; 42.6; 2 Sam 14.4; 1 Kings 1.16). The real reason may be that Haman is an Agagite, thus a hereditary enemy of the Jews. **3.5–6** Haman's disproportionate response turns the conflict into an ethnic contest. The verb *to destroy* occurs twenty-five times in this short book, stressing an ever present threat of violence. **3.7** *Nisan* (March-April) is the first month in the Babylonian calendar, the time of Passover. The start of a new year was an appropriate time to cast lots to determine the future. *Pur,* an Akkadian word for *lot,* provides the name for the festival Purim (see ch. 9). *Adar* (February-March) is the twelfth month in

Haman for the day and for the month, and the lot fell on the thirteenth day[a] of the twelfth month, which is the month of Adar. [8]Then Haman said to King Ahasuerus, "There is a certain people scattered and separated among the peoples in all the provinces of your kingdom; their laws are different from those of every other people, and they do not keep the king's laws, so that it is not appropriate for the king to tolerate them. [9]If it pleases the king, let a decree be issued for their destruction, and I will pay ten thousand talents of silver into the hands of those who have charge of the king's business, so that they may put it into the king's treasuries." [10]So the king took his signet ring from his hand and gave it to Haman son of Hammedatha the Agagite, the enemy of the Jews. [11]The king said to Haman, "The money is given to you, and the people as well, to do with them as it seems good to you."

12 Then the king's secretaries were summoned on the thirteenth day of the first month, and an edict, according to all that Haman commanded, was written to the king's satraps and to the governors over all the provinces and to the officials of all the peoples, to every province in its own script and every people in its own language; it was written in the name of King Ahasuerus and sealed with the king's ring. [13]Letters were sent by couriers to all the king's provinces, giving orders to destroy, to kill, and to annihilate all Jews, young and old, women and children, in one day, the thirteenth day of the twelfth month, which is the month of Adar, and to plunder their goods. [14]A copy of the docu-

ment was to be issued as a decree in every province by proclamation, calling on all the peoples to be ready for that day. [15]The couriers went quickly by order of the king, and the decree was issued in the citadel of Susa. The king and Haman sat down to drink; but the city of Susa was thrown into confusion.

Esther Agrees to Help the Jews

4 When Mordecai learned all that had been done, Mordecai tore his clothes and put on sackcloth and ashes, and went through the city, wailing with a loud and bitter cry; [2]he went up to the entrance of the king's gate, for no one might enter the king's gate clothed with sackcloth. [3]In every province, wherever the king's command and his decree came, there was great mourning among the Jews, with fasting and weeping and lamenting, and most of them lay in sackcloth and ashes.

4 When Esther's maids and her eunuchs came and told her, the queen was deeply distressed; she sent garments to clothe Mordecai, so that he might take off his sackcloth; but he would not accept them. [5]Then Esther called for Hathach, one of the king's eunuchs, who had been appointed to attend her, and ordered him to go to Mordecai to learn what was happening and why. [6]Hathach went out to Mordecai in the open square of the city in front of the king's gate, [7]and Mordecai told him all that had happened to him, and the exact sum of money that Haman had promised to pay into the king's treasuries for the destruction of

_____
a Cn Compare Gk and verse 13 below: Heb *the twelfth month*

the Babylonian calendar; the date for the pogrom is fixed well in advance. **3.8** Haman's accusation against the Jews, who are never named by him, moves from truth (*scattered and separated*) to lies (*do not keep the king's laws*). It is necessary for the story that Esther's ability to conceal her Jewish identity not be hampered by these laws that are different. **3.9** *Ten thousand talents of silver* is a huge sum. Inflated figures like this one, the height of Haman's gallows (5.14), and numbers slain by the Jews (9.5–16) give the story an air of the fantastic. **3.10** The *signet ring* gives Haman authority to issue the decree (see 8.8, 10; Gen 41.42). **3.11** *The money is given to you* may mean the king returns Haman's bribe, or it may mean the money is Haman's to use as he wishes. The king authorizes the pogrom with no further inquiry about the people to be destroyed. **3.12** Ironically, the *thirteenth day of the first month* is the day before Jews celebrate Passover (Lev 23.5–8), in which they remember how God de-

livered them in Egypt. **3.13** *Couriers* formed the heart of the famed Persian postal service (1.22; 8.9–14; Herodotus, *History* 5.14; 8.98). The piling up of the terms *to destroy, to kill,* and *to annihilate* and the list of victims, emulating legal language, ensures that the pogrom will be thorough. The Greek version provides a copy of the decree (Addition B). **3.14** Proclamation so far in advance also gives notice to the Jews of the danger, allowing Mordecai and Esther time to act. **3.15** A striking contrast between the leaders and populace ends the scene with another drinking feast that contrasts with those in ch. 1; 2.18.

4.1–17 Esther agrees to help the Jews. **4.1–3** Torn clothing, *sackcloth, ashes,* and *wailing* are all traditional signs of distress and grief (Neh 9.1; Jon 3.6) and are often accompanied by fasting (4.16) and prayer, the last markedly absent from this story (cf. Addition C in the Greek version). **4.4–9** Mordecai's carefully staged demonstration and documentary evidence are

the Jews. [8]Mordecai also gave him a copy of the written decree issued in Susa for their destruction, that he might show it to Esther, explain it to her, and charge her to go to the king to make supplication to him and entreat him for her people.

9 Hathach went and told Esther what Mordecai had said. [10]Then Esther spoke to Hathach and gave him a message for Mordecai, saying, [11]"All the king's servants and the people of the king's provinces know that if any man or woman goes to the king inside the inner court without being called, there is but one law—all alike are to be put to death. Only if the king holds out the golden scepter to someone, may that person live. I myself have not been called to come in to the king for thirty days." [12]When they told Mordecai what Esther had said, [13]Mordecai told them to reply to Esther, "Do not think that in the king's palace you will escape any more than all the other Jews. [14]For if you keep silence at such a time as this, relief and deliverance will rise for the Jews from another quarter, but you and your father's family will perish. Who knows? Perhaps you have come to royal dignity for just such a time as this." [15]Then Esther said in reply to Mordecai, [16]"Go, gather all the Jews to be found in Susa, and hold a fast on my behalf, and neither eat nor drink for three days, night or day. I and my maids will also fast as you do. After that I will go to the king, though it is against the law; and if I perish, I perish." [17]Mordecai then went away and did everything as Esther had ordered him.

Esther's Banquet

5 On the third day Esther put on her royal robes and stood in the inner court of the king's palace, opposite the king's hall. The king was sitting on his royal throne inside the palace opposite the entrance to the palace. [2]As soon as the king saw Queen Esther standing in the court, she won his favor and he held out to her the golden scepter that was in his hand. Then Esther approached and touched the top of the scepter. [3]The king said to her, "What is it, Queen Esther? What is your request? It shall be given you, even to the half of my kingdom." [4]Then Esther said, "If it pleases the king, let the king and Haman come today to a banquet that I have prepared for the king." [5]Then the king said, "Bring Haman quickly, so that we may do as Esther desires." So the king and Haman came to the banquet that Esther had prepared. [6]While they were drinking wine, the king said to Esther, "What is your petition? It shall be granted you. And what is your request? Even to the half of my kingdom, it shall be fulfilled." [7]Then Esther said, "This is my petition and request: [8]If I have won the king's favor, and if it pleases the king to grant my petition and fulfill my request, let the king and Haman come tomorrow to the banquet that I will prepare for them, and then I will do as the king has said."

Haman Plans to Have Mordecai Hanged

9 Haman went out that day happy and in good spirits. But when Haman saw Mordecai in the king's gate, and observed that he neither rose nor trembled before him, he was infuriated with Mordecai; [10]nevertheless Haman restrained himself and went home. Then he sent and called for his friends and his wife Zeresh, [11]and Haman recounted to them the splendor of his riches, the number of his sons, all the promotions with which the king had honored him, and how he had advanced him above the offi-

---

designed to inform Esther, isolated within the harem, and urge her to take advantage of her strategic position. **4.11** Whether this ban on unsummoned appearances reflects actual Persian custom or not, it serves to heighten the narrative tension. Esther's influence with the king is at a low point. **4.14** *Another quarter* is interpreted by some as an oblique reference to the deity, who is so strikingly absent from this story. Many understand Mordecai's statement as an assertion of divine providence. The reference is more allusive than direct and does not lessen the strongly secular character of the story. The choice to act remains with Esther. **4.16** From this point Esther is transformed from one who is passive and obedient to one who takes charge and directs actions to save her people. Mordecai, by contrast, now becomes passive and obedient to her.

The Greek version here has prayers by both Mordecai and Esther (Addition C).

5.1–8 Esther's first banquet. **5.2** The Greek makes this scene more suspenseful and overtly refers to divine providential direction of events (Addition D). **5.3** Herod makes just this exaggerated promise to Salome (Mk 6.23), and Herodotus (*History* 9.109–11) tells of a similar one that Xerxes offered his mistress Artaynte, which came to haunt him. **5.4–5** Esther's invitation to the king and his acceptance obligate him to her. Haman's inclusion disarms and neutralizes him. **5.6** See note on 5.3. **5.8** In light of what might have happened to Mordecai between Esther's first and second banquets, her second delay tempts fate; however, the delay heightens the literary suspense. **5.9–14** Haman plans to have Mordecai hanged. **5.9–13** Dining alone with the king and queen

cials and the ministers of the king. 12Haman added, "Even Queen Esther let no one but myself come with the king to the banquet that she prepared. Tomorrow also I am invited by her, together with the king. 13Yet all this does me no good so long as I see the Jew Mordecai sitting at the king's gate." 14Then his wife Zeresh and all his friends said to him, "Let a gallows fifty cubits high be made, and in the morning tell the king to have Mordecai hanged on it; then go with the king to the banquet in good spirits." This advice pleased Haman, and he had the gallows made.

The King Honors Mordecai

6 On that night the king could not sleep, and he gave orders to bring the book of records, the annals, and they were read to the king. 2It was found written how Mordecai had told about Bigthana and Teresh, two of the king's eunuchs, who guarded the threshold, and who had conspired to assassinate*a* King Ahasuerus. 3Then the king said, "What honor or distinction has been bestowed on Mordecai for this?" The king's servants who attended him said, "Nothing has been done for him." 4The king said, "Who is in the court?" Now Haman had just entered the outer court of the king's palace to speak to the king about having Mordecai hanged on the gallows that he had prepared for him. 5So the king's servants told him, "Haman is there, standing in the court." The king said, "Let him come in." 6So Haman came in, and the king said to him, "What shall be done for the man whom the king wishes to honor?" Haman said to himself, "Whom would the king wish to honor more than me?" 7So Haman said to the king, "For the man

whom the king wishes to honor, 8let royal robes be brought, which the king has worn, and a horse that the king has ridden, with a royal crown on its head. 9Let the robes and the horse be handed over to one of the king's most noble officials; let him*b* robe the man whom the king wishes to honor, and let him*b* conduct the man on horseback through the open square of the city, proclaiming before him: 'Thus shall it be done for the man whom the king wishes to honor.' " 10Then the king said to Haman, "Quickly, take the robes and the horse, as you have said, and do so to the Jew Mordecai who sits at the king's gate. Leave out nothing that you have mentioned." 11So Haman took the robes and the horse and robed Mordecai and led him riding through the open square of the city, proclaiming, "Thus shall it be done for the man whom the king wishes to honor."

12 Then Mordecai returned to the king's gate, but Haman hurried to his house, mourning and with his head covered. 13When Haman told his wife Zeresh and all his friends everything that had happened to him, his advisers and his wife Zeresh said to him, "If Mordecai, before whom your downfall has begun, is of the Jewish people, you will not prevail against him, but will surely fall before him."

Haman's Downfall and Mordecai's Advancement

14 While they were still talking with him, the king's eunuchs arrived and hurried Haman off 7 to the banquet that Esther had prepared. 1So the king and Haman went in to feast

a Heb *to lay hands on*   *b* Heb *them*

---

confirms Haman's elevated position in his own eyes; by contrast the sight of unrepentant Mordecai calls his position into question. **5.10–11** Haman has reached the pinnacle of his glory, possessing wealth, position, and many sons. **5.14** *Fifty cubits* is 75 feet! Haman, Zeresh, and his friends can plot to execute Mordecai, but only the king can condemn someone to death. *Hanged.* See 2.23.

6.1–11 The king honors Mordecai. **6.1** That the *king could not sleep* is the first of several coincidences, interpreted by some as providential, that make this an especially fortunate night for Esther and Mordecai. The Greek version attributes the king's insomnia to God. **6.2** See 2.23. **6.4–5** Ironically, Haman's eagerness to be rid of Mordecai immediately brings him early to court, just at the moment the king needs advice on how to reward one who saved his life. **6.6** In his eagerness for recognition Haman fails to note that the king

has not named the one he wishes to honor; his inflated self-assurance leads to a fatal assumption. **6.8** Cf. Gen 41.42–43. Haman is seeking royal honors. Horses with royal crowns are depicted in Persian reliefs. **6.9, 11** Mordecai's honor and Haman's chagrin are witnessed by all in the *open square.* **6.10** If the king really knows that Mordecai is a *Jew,* he seems not to connect him to the edict issued under his seal (3.12–15). **6.11** The substance of any conversation between Haman and Mordecai and Haman's own feelings are left to readers to supply.

6.12–8.2 Haman's downfall and Mordecai's advancement. **6.12–13** Haman's *covered* head signals grief for indignities just suffered. Unintentionally it also signals the fate awaiting him, as is clear to his wife and friends, who prove wise after the fact (cf. 5.9–14). **6.14** This escort is a sign of honor. Esther's second banquet is Haman's last hope to redeem a disastrous day.

with Queen Esther. 2On the second day, as they were drinking wine, the king again said to Esther, "What is your petition, Queen Esther? It shall be granted you. And what is your request? Even to the half of my kingdom, it shall be fulfilled." 3Then Queen Esther answered, "If I have won your favor, O king, and if it pleases the king, let my life be given me—that is my petition—and the lives of my people—that is my request. 4For we have been sold, I and my people, to be destroyed, to be killed, and to be annihilated. If we had been sold merely as slaves, men and women, I would have held my peace; but no enemy can compensate for this damage to the king."*a* 5Then King Ahasuerus said to Queen Esther, "Who is he, and where is he, who has presumed to do this?" 6Esther said, "A foe and enemy, this wicked Haman!" Then Haman was terrified before the king and the queen. 7The king rose from the feast in wrath and went into the palace garden, but Haman stayed to beg his life from Queen Esther, for he saw that the king had determined to destroy him. 8When the king returned from the palace garden to the banquet hall, Haman had thrown himself on the couch where Esther was reclining; and the king said, "Will he even assault the queen in my presence, in my own house?" As the words left the mouth of the king, they covered Haman's face. 9Then Harbona, one of the eunuchs in attendance on the king, said, "Look, the very gallows that Haman has prepared for Mordecai, whose word saved the king, stands at Haman's house, fifty cubits high." And the king said, "Hang him on that." 10So they hanged Haman on the gallows that he had prepared for Mordecai. Then the anger of the king abated.

Esther Saves the Jews

8 On that day King Ahasuerus gave to Queen Esther the house of Haman, the enemy of the Jews; and Mordecai came before the king, for Esther had told what he was to her. 2Then the king took off his signet ring, which he had taken from Haman, and gave it to Mordecai. So Esther set Mordecai over the house of Haman.

3 Then Esther spoke again to the king; she fell at his feet, weeping and pleading with him to avert the evil design of Haman the Agagite and the plot that he had devised against the Jews. 4The king held out the golden scepter to Esther, 5and Esther rose and stood before the king. She said, "If it pleases the king, and if I have won his favor, and if the thing seems right before the king, and I have his approval, let an order be written to revoke the letters devised by Haman son of Hammedatha the Agagite, which he wrote giving orders to destroy the Jews who are in all the provinces of the king. 6For how can I bear to see the calamity that is coming on my people? Or how can I bear to see the destruction of my kindred?" 7Then King Ahasuerus said to Queen Esther and to the Jew Mordecai, "See, I have given Esther the house of Haman, and they have hanged him on the gallows, because he plotted to lay hands on the Jews. 8You may write as you please with regard to the Jews, in the name of the king, and seal it with the king's ring; for an edict written in the name of the king and sealed with the king's ring cannot be revoked."

9 The king's secretaries were summoned at that time, in the third month, which is the

---

a Meaning of Heb uncertain

7.2 See 5.3, 6. Esther is repeatedly given her title "Queen," aligning her with the king and against Haman. **7.4** Their being *sold* refers to Haman's bribe in 3.9. The last clause of Esther's rationale for her request in v. 3 is not clear. Some follow the Greek to suggest that if they were merely sold as slaves the "problem would not have been worth bothering the king." **7.6** Esther's demonstrative *this* in identifying Haman as the enemy is the narrative equivalent of pointing an accusing finger at him. **7.7–8** The king's exit allows Haman one last plea for his life, ironically to the one whom he unknowingly sought to destroy. His attempt seals his fate, as the king mistakes his posture of supplication before the reclining Esther as an assault upon the queen. The shame foreseen in 6.12–13 is complete, as now they *covered Haman's face*. **7.9–10** The eunuch appears at just the right moment; the ironic reversal of intent and result is complete. **8.1–2** Esther indirectly secures Haman's royal office and power for Mordecai, which he receives with the *signet ring* (see 3.10). She directly provides him the wealth commensurate with his new position by transferring to him Haman's estate.

8.3–17 Esther saves the Jews. **8.3–6** It is not clear whether this is a second audience with the king or a continuation of that in 8.1–2. Esther's dramatic obeisance and courtly language allow her to imply that Haman, not the king, is responsible for the edict ordering her people's death. This helps win his encouragement to present her additional request, shown as he extends the golden scepter (see 5.2). **8.8** See 1.19. **8.8–13** closely parallels 3.9–15, since the second decree cannot simply annul the first, but must allow ac-

month of Sivan, on the twenty-third day; and an edict was written, according to all that Mordecai commanded, to the Jews and to the satraps and the governors and the officials of the provinces from India to Ethiopia,[a] one hundred twenty-seven provinces, to every province in its own script and to every people in its own language, and also to the Jews in their script and their language. 10He wrote letters in the name of King Ahasuerus, sealed them with the king's ring, and sent them by mounted couriers riding on fast steeds bred from the royal herd.[b] 11By these letters the king allowed the Jews who were in every city to assemble and defend their lives, to destroy, to kill, and to annihilate any armed force of any people or province that might attack them, with their children and women, and to plunder their goods 12on a single day throughout all the provinces of King Ahasuerus, on the thirteenth day of the twelfth month, which is the month of Adar. 13A copy of the writ was to be issued as a decree in every province and published to all peoples, and the Jews were to be ready on that day to take revenge on their enemies. 14So the couriers, mounted on their swift royal steeds, hurried out, urged by the king's command. The decree was issued in the citadel of Susa.

15 Then Mordecai went out from the presence of the king, wearing royal robes of blue and white, with a great golden crown and a mantle of fine linen and purple, while the city of Susa shouted and rejoiced. 16For the Jews there was light and gladness, joy and honor. 17In every province and in every city, wherever the king's command and his edict came, there was gladness and joy among the Jews, a festival and a holiday. Furthermore, many of the peoples of the country professed to be Jews, because the fear of the Jews had fallen upon them.

Destruction of the Enemies of the Jews

9 Now in the twelfth month, which is the month of Adar, on the thirteenth day, when the king's command and edict were about to be executed, on the very day when the enemies of the Jews hoped to gain power over them, but which had been changed to a day when the Jews would gain power over their foes, 2the Jews gathered in their cities throughout all the provinces of King Ahasuerus to lay hands on those who had sought their ruin; and no one could withstand them, because the fear of them had fallen upon all peoples. 3All the officials of the provinces, the satraps and the governors, and the royal officials were supporting the Jews, because the fear of Mordecai had fallen upon them. 4For Mordecai was powerful in the king's house, and his fame spread throughout all the provinces as the man Mordecai grew more and more powerful. 5So the Jews struck down all their enemies with the sword, slaughtering, and destroying them, and did as they pleased

a Or Nubia; Heb Cush   b Meaning of Heb uncertain

---

tion by the Jews to counter any who would now act on it even after Haman's fall. The king continues his hands-off administrative style and trusts Esther and Mordecai just as he once trusted Haman. **8.9** Recalling 1.1 and 3.12, this verse sets the stage for the final reversal of Haman's designs, counterbalancing his edict commanding the destruction of the Jews. *Sivan* is May-June. **8.10** *Couriers.* See 1.22; 3.15. **8.11–12** The wording recalls what Haman wrote (3.13) in an exact manner. The effect is to reverse in every detail what Haman planned for the Jews. **8.12** The Greek supplies a copy of the letter (Addition E). **8.13** The distribution is like that of the earlier decree (3.14). **8.15** As the scene progresses, attention shifts from Esther to *Mordecai*, who appears in public arrayed in garb appropriate to his new position, a signal of the change in the fortunes of the Jews (cf. 4.1–2). That the city of Susa *shouted and rejoiced* contrasts with its confusion in 3.15. **8.16** A reversal of 4.3, 16. **8.17** Some interpret the professing *to be Jews* by the people of the country to mean they took sides with the Jews. Others suggest

that they pretended to be Jews out of fear, while still others claim they converted to Judaism (the Greek version claims they were circumcised). This is a final reversal of Haman's schemes: those he sought to set against the Jews now actually join them. The festival provides a final feast in this story punctuated with fateful feasting and drinking. The details for this annual celebration as a *holiday*, or "good day," a term later used for religious celebrations, are given in ch. 9. One Greek version ends at this point, indicating that it is an earlier version of the story.

9.1–19 The destruction of the enemies of the Jews. **9.1** The date determined in 3.7 and mentioned in 8.12 is described now as a day of reversed expectations. **9.3** Cf. the attitude of Mordecai's colleagues in 3.3–4. **9.4** Mordecai now commands the respect that officials showed Haman (3.2); they act in unspecified ways to join him. **9.5–6** That the Jews here would treat their enemies as they would have been treated by them is found to be understandable by some in the light of other pogroms Jewish communities have faced. Others,

to those who hated them. 6In the citadel of Susa the Jews killed and destroyed five hundred people. 7They killed Parshandatha, Dalphon, Aspatha, 8Poratha, Adalia, Aridatha, 9Parmashta, Arisai, Aridai, Vaizatha, 10the ten sons of Haman son of Hammedatha, the enemy of the Jews; but they did not touch the plunder.

11 That very day the number of those killed in the citadel of Susa was reported to the king. 12The king said to Queen Esther, "In the citadel of Susa the Jews have killed five hundred people and also the ten sons of Haman. What have they done in the rest of the king's provinces? Now what is your petition? It shall be granted you. And what further is your request? It shall be fulfilled." 13Esther said, "If it pleases the king, let the Jews who are in Susa be allowed tomorrow also to do according to this day's edict, and let the ten sons of Haman be hanged on the gallows." 14So the king commanded this to be done; a decree was issued in Susa, and the ten sons of Haman were hanged. 15The Jews who were in Susa gathered also on the fourteenth day of the month of Adar and they killed three hundred persons in Susa; but they did not touch the plunder.

16 Now the other Jews who were in the king's provinces also gathered to defend their lives, and gained relief from their enemies, and killed seventy-five thousand of those who hated them; but they laid no hands on the plunder. 17This was on the thirteenth day of the month of Adar, and on the fourteenth day they rested and made that a day of feasting and gladness.

The Feast of Purim Inaugurated

18 But the Jews who were in Susa gathered on the thirteenth day and on the fourteenth, and rested on the fifteenth day, making that a day of feasting and gladness. 19Therefore the Jews of the villages, who live in the open towns, hold the fourteenth day of the month of Adar as a day for gladness and feasting, a holiday on which they send gifts of food to one another.

20 Mordecai recorded these things, and sent letters to all the Jews who were in all the provinces of King Ahasuerus, both near and far, 21enjoining them that they should keep the fourteenth day of the month Adar and also the fifteenth day of the same month, year by year, 22as the days on which the Jews gained relief from their enemies, and as the month that had been turned for them from sorrow into gladness and from mourning into a holiday; that they should make them days of feasting and gladness, days for sending gifts of food to one another and presents to the poor. 23So the Jews adopted as a custom what they had begun to do, as Mordecai had written to them.

24 Haman son of Hammedatha the Agagite, the enemy of all the Jews, had plotted against the Jews to destroy them, and had cast Pur—that is "the lot"—to crush and destroy them; 25but when Esther came before the king, he gave orders in writing that the wicked plot that he had devised against the Jews should come upon his own head, and that he and his sons should be hanged on the gallows. 26Therefore these days are called Purim, from the word Pur. Thus because of all that was written in this letter, and of what they had faced in this matter, and of what had happened to them, 27the Jews established and accepted as a custom for themselves and their descendants and all who joined them, that without fail they would continue to observe these two days every year, as it was written and

however, are troubled by this apparent descent to the level of the brutality of the enemy. **9.7–10** This numbering of Haman's many *sons*, an item in his earlier boasting (5.11), is written in Hebrew texts in a tabular form, one name beneath another and the sum totaled (cf. the list of slain kings in Josh 12.9–24). **9.10** That the Jews *did not touch the plunder* (stressed in vv. 15–16 also), although they were allowed to do so (8.11), suggests they were fighting for survival and not increased wealth. This notice recalls difficulties earlier plunder taken from Agag and the Amalekites (3.1) caused Saul (1 Sam 15). Cf. also Abraham's refusal of plunder in Gen 14.22–24. **9.12** Sensing that Esther is not satisfied, the king gives her carte blanche once again. **9.13–14** See 5.14. As Haman's sons are already dead, this command entails exposure of their bodies, perhaps as a deterrent to others who might attack Jews. **9.15** The second day of killing in *Susa* accounts for the difference between celebrations of Purim in city and country. **9.16** The total of those killed is huge—*seventy-five thousand*. **9.17–19** Different patterns in the celebration of Purim are provided a historical basis. **9.20–32** The feast of Purim is inaugurated. **9.20–23** Mordecai, the most powerful official in the Persian government, authorizes the annual celebration on both the fourteenth and fifteenth of Adar (cf. 9.17–19), including exchange of *gifts of food* and *presents to the poor*. **9.24–25** This terse summary stresses the theme of retributive justice. **9.26** The name *Purim* is expressly linked with the word *Pur* (see 3.7). *This letter* is presumably that sent by Mordecai in 9.20. **9.27–28** The emphasis on keeping the feast annually through the years and generations

at the time appointed. [28]These days should be remembered and kept throughout every generation, in every family, province, and city; and these days of Purim should never fall into disuse among the Jews, nor should the commemoration of these days cease among their descendants.

29 Queen Esther daughter of Abihail, along with the Jew Mordecai, gave full written authority, confirming this second letter about Purim. [30]Letters were sent wishing peace and security to all the Jews, to the one hundred twenty-seven provinces of the kingdom of Ahasuerus, [31]and giving orders that these days of Purim should be observed at their appointed seasons, as the Jew Mordecai and Queen Esther enjoined on the Jews, just as

they had laid down for themselves and for their descendants regulations concerning their fasts and their lamentations. [32]The command of Queen Esther fixed these practices of Purim, and it was recorded in writing.

10 King Ahasuerus laid tribute on the land and on the islands of the sea. [2]All the acts of his power and might, and the full account of the high honor of Mordecai, to which the king advanced him, are they not written in the annals of the kings of Media and Persia? [3]For Mordecai the Jew was next in rank to King Ahasuerus, and he was powerful among the Jews and popular with his many kindred, for he sought the good of his people and interceded for the welfare of all his descendants.

---

and the stress on written records and instructions (see 9.20, 23, 29, 32) seem designed to secure a place in the Jewish calendar for a celebration not authorized in the Torah and whose legitimacy might therefore seem in doubt. **9.29** Presumably this *second letter* is Mordecai's in 9.20. Esther gives the royal sanction to the holiday. **9.30** See 1.1. **9.31** The phrase *their fasts and their lamentations* refers to other Jewish observances.

10.1–3 Mordecai and the king. The story ends as it began, with the focus on the greatness of the king. But now the king's fortunes are firmly linked to those of

Mordecai and the Jews. **10.1** The *tribute* may show the extent of the realm (1.1), including now even the *islands of the sea,* or it may be an alternative and peaceable way to enrich the royal coffers, making up the loss of Haman's ten thousand talents (3.9). **10.2** Reference to these *annals of the kings of Media and Persia* gives an air of historical veracity to the story. **10.3** Although the book bears her name, Esther is missing from this final notice of Mordecai's greatness, goodness, and popularity. The Greek version begins and ends quite differently (Additions A and F).

JOB

THE CENTRAL THEME of the book of Job is the possibility of disinterested righteousness. The author asks whether virtue depends on a universe that operates by the principle of reward and punishment. At stake is the survival of religion, service to God without thought of the carrot or the stick. Then innocent suffering cannot quench the fires of spiritual devotion. Job's response to adversity in the prologue affirms such faith. A secondary theme is innocent suffering, for which several explanations are put forth: the retributive, disciplinary, probative, eschatological, redemptive, revelatory, ineffable, and incidental.

Structure

THE BOOK'S STRUCTURE can be viewed from the standpoint of its diction, drama, or individual components in outline form. A frame narrative, in prose, encloses a poetic debate. This combination is found also in some other ancient wisdom texts, such as the Aramaic tale of "Ahikar" and the Egyptian Instruction of Ankhsheshonky. Alternatively, three dramatic episodes take place, each introduced by brief comments in 1.1–5; 2.11–13; 32.1–5. Thus the hero is afflicted (1.1–2.10), complains, and is rebuked by three friends (2.11–31.40), and after a young enthusiast takes up the task of demonstrating Job's folly, God rebukes Job but restores him (32.1–42.17). A more natural division consists of Job's affliction (chs. 1–2), a dispute between him and three friends (chs. 3–31), a monologue by a previously unmentioned person (chs. 32–37), two divine speeches and two submissions on Job's part (38.1–42.6), and a prose "happy ending" (42.7–17).

Tensions exist between prose and poetry and even within each literary form: the story's patient hero and the defiant Job of the dialogue; a divinely commended hero in the prose and a rebuked one in the poetry; the divine name Yahweh in the folktale and El, Eloah, and Shaddai in the poetry (with one exception); a "happy ending" despite the argument of the hero that God does not deal with humans on the basis of merit; vanishing characters—the Satan and Elihu; a hymn (ch. 28) that anticipates the answer provided by the theophany; and two divine speeches with two responses. Although skilled authors can use dissonance effectively, the book is at odds with itself and irony abounds.

Setting

THE EVENTS OF THE BOOK are set in patriarchal (or prepatriarchal) times when heroes such as Noah, Daniel, and Job (cf. Ezek 14.14, 20) are thought to have lived. Job's possessions are appropriate to that age: cattle and servants. The monetary unit in the epilogue (42.11) is mentioned elsewhere only in Gen 33.19 (and Josh 24.32, alluding to this incident). Job's three friends and the enemy marauders, Sabeans and Chaldeans, belong to clans from the patriarchal world. His sacrifice of animals accords with practice prior to the time of official priests. The life span of the restored hero is at home in patriarchal times. The name Job, which could be translated "enemy," corresponds to Akkadian names with such translations as "Where is the divine father?" and "Inveterate Foe/Hated One."

Date

THE DATE OF COMPOSITION cannot be determined, but several things point to the late sixth or fifth century BCE: the linguistic evidence, the possible allusion to the Behistun Rock, the mention of caravans from Tema and Sheba, the "Persian" nomenclature of officials, and the development of the figure of the Satan corresponding to the stage represented by Zechariah but less developed than that presented in Chronicles. The theological ideas in the book may also support this relatively late date when compared with similar literary complexes, Jeremiah's laments, the lyrical hymns in Second Isaiah (Isa 40–55, sixth century BCE), hymnic fragments in the book of Amos, and Pss 37; 49; 73. The book's monotheism and monogamy are consistent with a late date. The choice of an Edomite for the hero is strange after 587/6 BCE, but the patriarchal setting ruled out an Israelite, and the Edomites were celebrated for wisdom. The book's silence about the events of the exile is surprising, for Job's personal misery is in some ways like that of the exiles. The *Targum of Job* and the *Testament of Job,* works from the Second Temple period, prove that the biblical text of Job was in circulation by the end of the second century BCE. The *Testament of Job* exaggerates Job's charity, depicts his wife favorably, emphasizes his fight against idolatry, speculates about Satan, and alludes to cosmological dualism, magic, and mysticism. The Letter of James recalls the folktale about the endurance of Job (5.11).

Related Texts

THE CLOSEST ANALOGY to the book of Job is "The Babylonian Theodicy." Several other ancient texts resemble the biblical book to some degree. From the twelfth dynasty in Egypt (1990–1785 BCE) come "The Admonitions of Ipuwer," "A Dispute Between a Man and His Ba (Soul)," and "The Eloquent Peasant." Second-millennium Mesopotamia furnishes closer parallels: the Sumerian "A Man and His God," "I Will Praise the Lord of Wisdom," and "A Dialogue Between a Master and His Slave." Parallels to the Canaanite Keret legend are more remote. [JAMES L. CRENSHAW]

Job and His Family

1 There was once a man in the land of Uz whose name was Job. That man was blameless and upright, one who feared God and turned away from evil. [2] There were born to him seven sons and three daughters. [3] He had seven thousand sheep, three thousand camels, five hundred yoke of oxen, five hundred donkeys, and very many servants; so that this man was the greatest of all the people of the east. [4] His sons used to go and hold feasts in one another's houses in turn; and they would send and invite their three sisters to eat and drink with them. [5] And when the feast days had run their course, Job would send and sanctify them, and he would rise early in the morning and offer burnt offerings according to the number of them all; for Job said, "It may be that my children have sinned, and cursed God in their hearts." This is what Job always did.

Attack on Job's Character

6 One day the heavenly beings[a] came to present themselves before the LORD, and Satan[b] also came among them. [7] The LORD said to Satan,[b] "Where have you come from?" Satan[b] answered the LORD, "From going to and fro on the earth, and from walking up and down on it." [8] The LORD said to Satan,[b] "Have you considered my servant Job? There is no one like him on the earth, a blameless and upright man who fears God and turns away from evil." [9] Then Satan[b] answered the LORD, "Does Job fear God for nothing? [10] Have you not put a fence around him and his house and all that he has, on every side? You have blessed the work of his hands, and his possessions have increased in the land. [11] But stretch out your hand now, and touch all that he has, and he will curse you to your face." [12] The LORD said to Satan,[b] "Very well, all that he has is in your power; only do not stretch out your hand against him!" So Satan[b] went out from the presence of the LORD.

Job Loses Property and Children

13 One day when his sons and daughters were eating and drinking wine in the eldest brother's house, [14] a messenger came to Job and said, "The oxen were plowing and the donkeys were feeding beside them, [15] and the Sabe-

---

a Heb sons of God   b Or the Accuser; Heb ha-satan

1.1–2.13 The prologue. A folktale in elevated prose, akin to epic narrative, sets the stage on which the drama of Job's extreme suffering unfolds. The story's action alternates between earth and heaven (e.g., 1.1–5 describes a scene on earth, 1.6–12 one in heaven, with 1.13–22 returning to earth, 2.1–6 occurring in heaven, and 2.7–10 concluding the events on earth). Each scene ends decisively. The first has a remark about Job's habitual conduct; the second and fourth scenes comment on the Adversary's (the Satan's) departure from God's court; and the third and fifth represent the narrator's assessment of Job's innocence despite adverse circumstances. An introduction of Job's three friends (2.11–13) links this earlier story to the poetic dialogue in 3.1–31.40. **1.1** *There was once a man.* The unusual form in Hebrew ("A man there was" instead of "There was a man") emphasizes the name *Job,* well attested in ancient Egypt (letters from Tell el-Amarna and execration texts), Mesopotamia (Mari), and northern Palestine (Alalakh, Ugarit). A possible pun in 13.24 may refer to a popular etymology of the word as "enemy." Perhaps the unknown *Uz* plays on the sound of the Hebrew word for "counsel." Competing traditions place Uz in Hauran and in Edom. The prophet Ezekiel associates Job with ancient heroes Noah and Daniel (Ezek 14.14, 20). According to Israel's sages responsible for the final redaction of Proverbs, Job, Ecclesiastes, Sirach, and the Wisdom of Solomon, the fear of God was the first principle and/or chief ingredient of knowledge (cf. Prov 1.7). Similar hyperbole is used about Solomon in 1 Kings 4.29–34. **1.2** The numbers *seven* and *three* were thought to indicate completion. The Canaanite god Baal had seven sons and three daughters. In Hebrew, the verse begins with a conjunction (*waw,* untranslated by the NRSV), which might be translated "and so," implying that the children and property were a direct consequence of his piety. **1.3** Job's wealth consists of animals and slaves rather than silver and gold. The setting is patriarchal. **1.5** The Hebrew has the verb for "bless" in place of *curse* here and in 1.11; 2.5, 9, presumably a euphemism to avoid the blasphemous thought of actually cursing the Lord, although this is conceivably a literary device to stress the heinousness of the act. The word in both senses, of blessing and cursing, becomes thematic in the story, along with the Hebrew word translated *for nothing* (1.9) and *for no reason* (2.3). **1.6** The article "the" with the word *Satan,* which appears in Hebrew and in some other translations, indicates that an office is involved, something like a CIA agent. The Accuser is therefore in the Lord's imperial service. The word occurs elsewhere in the Hebrew Bible only in Zech 3.1–2; 1 Chr 21.1. It seems to represent the Lord's master spy on the road toward becoming a hostile agent. **1.8** Repetition enhances literary effect (e.g., 1.1, 8 and 2.3; 1.22 and 2.10; 1.15, 16, 17, 18, 19; 1.6–8 and 2.1–3). In this verse it suggests ongoing rivalry. **1.9–10** The Satan responds to a rhetorical question in kind. **1.13** An

ans fell on them and carried them off, and killed the servants with the edge of the sword; I alone have escaped to tell you." [16]While he was still speaking, another came and said, "The fire of God fell from heaven and burned up the sheep and the servants, and consumed them; I alone have escaped to tell you." [17]While he was still speaking, another came and said, "The Chaldeans formed three columns, made a raid on the camels and carried them off, and killed the servants with the edge of the sword; I alone have escaped to tell you." [18]While he was still speaking, another came and said, "Your sons and daughters were eating and drinking wine in their eldest brother's house, [19]and suddenly a great wind came across the desert, struck the four corners of the house, and it fell on the young people, and they are dead; I alone have escaped to tell you."

20 Then Job arose, tore his robe, shaved his head, and fell on the ground and worshiped. [21]He said, "Naked I came from my mother's womb, and naked shall I return there; the LORD gave, and the LORD has taken away; blessed be the name of the LORD."

22 In all this Job did not sin or charge God with wrongdoing.

Attack on Job's Health

2 One day the heavenly beings[a] came to present themselves before the LORD, and Satan[b] also came among them to present himself before the LORD. [2]The LORD said to Satan,[b] "Where have you come from?" Satan[c] answered the LORD, "From going to and fro on the earth, and from walking up and down on it." [3]The LORD said to Satan,[b] "Have you considered my servant Job? There is no one like him on the earth, a blameless and upright

man who fears God and turns away from evil. He still persists in his integrity, although you incited me against him, to destroy him for no reason." [4]Then Satan[b] answered the LORD, "Skin for skin! All that people have they will give to save their lives.[d] [5]But stretch out your hand now and touch his bone and his flesh, and he will curse you to your face." [6]The LORD said to Satan,[b] "Very well, he is in your power; only spare his life."

7 So Satan[b] went out from the presence of the LORD, and inflicted loathsome sores on Job from the sole of his foot to the crown of his head. [8]Job[e] took a potsherd with which to scrape himself, and sat among the ashes.

9 Then his wife said to him, "Do you still persist in your integrity? Curse[f] God, and die." [10]But he said to her, "You speak as any foolish woman would speak. Shall we receive the good at the hand of God, and not receive the bad?" In all this Job did not sin with his lips.

Job's Three Friends

11 Now when Job's three friends heard of all these troubles that had come upon him, each of them set out from his home—Eliphaz the Temanite, Bildad the Shuhite, and Zophar the Naamathite. They met together to go and console and comfort him. [12]When they saw him from a distance, they did not recognize him, and they raised their voices and wept aloud; they tore their robes and threw dust in the air upon their heads. [13]They sat with him on the ground seven days and seven nights, and no one spoke a word to him, for they saw that his suffering was very great.

a Heb sons of God   b Or the Accuser; Heb ha-satan   c Or The Accuser; Heb ha-satan   d Or All that the man has he will give for his life   e Heb He   f Heb Bless

effective illusion of well-being, soon shattered. **1.14–19** Four messengers suggest totality. **1.15** *Sabeans*, perhaps northern Arabians, not southern Arabians or those living in Africa as in other biblical texts (e.g. 1 Kings 10). The queen of Sheba, said in 1 Kings 10 to have visited King Solomon, traveled from a distant land. **1.17** *Chaldeans*, probably seminomadic marauders rather than citizens of the Neo-Babylonian Empire that was founded in the seventh century BCE. **1.21** The adverb *there* refers neither to the mother's womb nor to mother earth; rather, the word is a euphemism for the realm of the dead (cf. 3.17–19; Eccl 5.15; Sir 40.1). This powerful expression of fidelity takes poetic form, using both synonymous and antithetic parallelism. **2.4** *Skin for skin*, a difficult expression, probably associated with barter and meaning an item equivalent to

the one being exchanged. **2.8** The *scraping* was either for relief from the itching or for self-mortification, but hardly an answer to social revulsion accompanying disease of the skin. **2.10** The word for *foolish* is strong, which suggests that Job did not understand his wife as sympathetically suggesting a form of euthanasia. The Septuagint (the Greek OT) gives her a longer speech about both their suffering, and the pseudepigraphical *Testament of Job* depicts the wife favorably. Later interpreters emphasize the decisive change in the narrator's summary statement: *Job did not sin with his lips*, but his heart was a different matter. **2.11** Job's *three friends* are placed in the vicinity of Edom and Arabia. The former was famous for wisdom, according to various OT texts. **2.13** The intermezzo of silence has powerful psychological force.

Job Curses the Day He Was Born

3 After this Job opened his mouth and cursed the day of his birth. [2] Job said:
[3] "Let the day perish in which I was born,
and the night that said,
'A man-child is conceived.'
[4] Let that day be darkness!
May God above not seek it,
or light shine on it.
[5] Let gloom and deep darkness claim it.
Let clouds settle upon it;
let the blackness of the day terrify it.
[6] That night—let thick darkness seize it!
let it not rejoice among the days of the year;
let it not come into the number of the months.
[7] Yes, let that night be barren;
let no joyful cry be heard[a] in it.
[8] Let those curse it who curse the Sea,[b]
those who are skilled to rouse up Leviathan.
[9] Let the stars of its dawn be dark;
let it hope for light, but have none;
may it not see the eyelids of the morning—
[10] because it did not shut the doors of my mother's womb,
and hide trouble from my eyes.

[11] "Why did I not die at birth,
come forth from the womb and expire?
[12] Why were there knees to receive me,
or breasts for me to suck?
[13] Now I would be lying down and quiet;
I would be asleep; then I would be at rest
[14] with kings and counselors of the earth
who rebuild ruins for themselves,
[15] or with princes who have gold,
who fill their houses with silver.
[16] Or why was I not buried like a stillborn child,
like an infant that never sees the light?
[17] There the wicked cease from troubling,
and there the weary are at rest.
[18] There the prisoners are at ease together;
they do not hear the voice of the taskmaster.
[19] The small and the great are there,
and the slaves are free from their masters.

[20] "Why is light given to one in misery,
and life to the bitter in soul,
[21] who long for death, but it does not come,
and dig for it more than for hidden treasures;
[22] who rejoice exceedingly,
and are glad when they find the grave?
[23] Why is light given to one who cannot see the way,
whom God has fenced in?
[24] For my sighing comes like[c] my bread,
and my groanings are poured out like water.
[25] Truly the thing that I fear comes upon me,
and what I dread befalls me.
[26] I am not at ease, nor am I quiet;
I have no rest; but trouble comes."

Eliphaz Speaks: Job Has Sinned

4 Then Eliphaz the Temanite answered:
[2] "If one ventures a word with you, will you be offended?
But who can keep from speaking?

---

a Heb *come*   *b* Cn: Heb *day*   *c* Heb *before*

3.1–42.6 The poetic dialogue. A dispute between Job and three friends begins with his lament. Each of the friends addresses Job, and he responds, for three cycles of speeches. The third is abbreviated by Bildad's short speech and complete silence on Zophar's part. Job's nostalgic glance backward and graphic description of his present woes is interrupted by a hymn on wisdom's inaccessibility (ch. 28). Then Job pronounces an oath of innocence, demanding that God respond. Instead, a brash Elihu challenges Job; afterward, God speaks to Job from a whirlwind. **3.1** The verb for *cursed* differs from that used in the prologue. This anticosmic curse in 3.3–10 uses the language of the creation account in Gen 1.1–2.4 (cf. Jer 20.14–18). **3.3** The unusual word for *man-child* often refers to someone much older than an infant, at times even a soldier. The day of birth and night of conception indicate the end and the beginning of gestation. **3.6** *Rejoice*, a rare word with connotations of sexual pleasure. **3.8** The Hebrew words for *day* (see text note *b*) and *sea* are similar, differing only in a vowel. Both *Sea* and *Leviathan* were thought to represent chaos in ancient myth (cf. Yamm and Lotan in Ugaritic myths). Professional diviners practiced magical cursing (cf. Balaam in Num 22–24). **3.12** An allusion to the practice of placing a newborn infant on a parent's *knees* as an expression of acknowledgment (cf. Sir 15.2). **3.23** The verb for *fenced in* differs from that used in 1.10. **3.26** The threefold use of the same grammatical structure resembles the ticktock of a clock.

3 See, you have instructed many;
    you have strengthened the weak hands.
4 Your words have supported those who
        were stumbling,
    and you have made firm the feeble
        knees.
5 But now it has come to you, and you are
        impatient;
    it touches you, and you are dismayed.
6 Is not your fear of God your confidence,
    and the integrity of your ways your
        hope?

7 "Think now, who that was innocent ever
        perished?
    Or where were the upright cut off?
8 As I have seen, those who plow iniquity
    and sow trouble reap the same.
9 By the breath of God they perish,
    and by the blast of his anger they are
        consumed.
10 The roar of the lion, the voice of the
        fierce lion,
    and the teeth of the young lions are
        broken.
11 The strong lion perishes for lack of prey,
    and the whelps of the lioness are
        scattered.

12 "Now a word came stealing to me,
    my ear received the whisper of it.
13 Amid thoughts from visions of the night,
    when deep sleep falls on mortals,
14 dread came upon me, and trembling,
    which made all my bones shake.
15 A spirit glided past my face;
    the hair of my flesh bristled.
16 It stood still,
    but I could not discern its appearance.
    A form was before my eyes;

    there was silence, then I heard a voice:
17 'Can mortals be righteous before[a] God?
    Can human beings be pure before[a]
        their Maker?
18 Even in his servants he puts no trust,
    and his angels he charges with error;
19 how much more those who live in houses
        of clay,
    whose foundation is in the dust,
    who are crushed like a moth.
20 Between morning and evening they are
        destroyed;
    they perish forever without any
        regarding it.
21 Their tent-cord is plucked up within them,
    and they die devoid of wisdom.'

Job Is Corrected by God

5 "Call now; is there anyone who will
        answer you?
    To which of the holy ones will you turn?
2 Surely vexation kills the fool,
    and jealousy slays the simple.
3 I have seen fools taking root,
    but suddenly I cursed their dwelling.
4 Their children are far from safety,
    they are crushed in the gate,
    and there is no one to deliver them.
5 The hungry eat their harvest,
    and they take it even out of the
        thorns;[b]
    and the thirsty[c] pant after their wealth.
6 For misery does not come from the earth,
    nor does trouble sprout from the
        ground;
7 but human beings are born to trouble
    just as sparks[d] fly upward.

a Or more than b Meaning of Heb uncertain c Aquila
Symmachus Syr Vg: Heb snare d Or birds; Heb sons of Resheph

4.6 Two of Job's four attributes from the story (1.1, 8) recur here, although in different form (the Hebrew lacks the word "God" in fear of God, and your ways qualifies integrity). 4.7–8 The logic of Eliphaz's argument condemns Job's children, and the language of destruction recalls the blast of wind that demolished their house. Eliphaz appeals here to the notion of divine retribution (cf. Ps 37.25). 4.9 The breath of God animated the first human couple, according to Gen 2.7, but now that life-giving force seeks destruction. 4.10–11 Five different Hebrew words for lion occur here; a similar richness of vocabulary in Joel 1.4 mentions four types of locusts. 4.12–21 A little theophany (self-revelation by God). Its theme, that mortals cannot be purer than their Maker, contrasts with that of the extended the-

ophany, 38.1–42.6, which emphasizes Job's ignorance and weakness. Eliphaz's language echoes the theophanies to Abraham ("a deep sleep," Gen 15.12) and to Elijah ("a sound of sheer silence," 1 Kings 19.12). The use of the unexpected verb stealing (v. 12) emphasizes Eliphaz's passive role in the terrifying encounter with God (Eloah, v. 17). 4.14 This description of distress resembles an ancient literary convention, the reaction to a messenger's anticipated bad news.

5.4 Eliphaz's insensitivity erupts in this cruel reference to the death of children, unless 5.3–5 is a standard literary trope. 5.6–7 The pun between the Hebrew words for ground and human beings (or "mortal") recalls Gen 3.17. The allusion to sparks employs the name of a Canaanite deity, Resheph, who was responsible for

8 "As for me, I would seek God,
    and to God I would commit my cause.
9 He does great things and unsearchable,
    marvelous things without number.
10 He gives rain on the earth
    and sends waters on the fields;
11 he sets on high those who are lowly,
    and those who mourn are lifted to
      safety.
12 He frustrates the devices of the crafty,
    so that their hands achieve no success.
13 He takes the wise in their own craftiness;
    and the schemes of the wily are
      brought to a quick end.
14 They meet with darkness in the daytime,
    and grope at noonday as in the night.
15 But he saves the needy from the sword of
      their mouth,
    from the hand of the mighty.
16 So the poor have hope,
    and injustice shuts its mouth.

17 "How happy is the one whom God
      reproves;
    therefore do not despise the discipline
      of the Almighty.[a]
18 For he wounds, but he binds up;
    he strikes, but his hands heal.
19 He will deliver you from six troubles;
    in seven no harm shall touch you.
20 In famine he will redeem you from death,
    and in war from the power of the sword.
21 You shall be hidden from the scourge of
      the tongue,
    and shall not fear destruction when it
      comes.
22 At destruction and famine you shall
      laugh,
    and shall not fear the wild animals of
      the earth.
23 For you shall be in league with the stones
      of the field,

and the wild animals shall be at peace
      with you.
24 You shall know that your tent is safe,
    you shall inspect your fold and miss
      nothing.
25 You shall know that your descendants
      will be many,
    and your offspring like the grass of the
      earth.
26 You shall come to your grave in ripe old
      age,
    as a shock of grain comes up to the
      threshing floor in its season.
27 See, we have searched this out; it is true.
    Hear, and know it for yourself."

Job Replies: My Complaint Is Just

6 Then Job answered:
2 "O that my vexation were weighed,
    and all my calamity laid in the
      balances!
3 For then it would be heavier than the
      sand of the sea;
    therefore my words have been rash.
4 For the arrows of the Almighty[a] are in
      me;
    my spirit drinks their poison;
    the terrors of God are arrayed against
      me.
5 Does the wild ass bray over its grass,
    or the ox low over its fodder?
6 Can that which is tasteless be eaten
      without salt,
    or is there any flavor in the juice of
      mallows?[b]
7 My appetite refuses to touch them;
    they are like food that is loathsome to
      me.[b]

---

a Traditional rendering of Heb *Shaddai*   b Meaning of Heb
uncertain

---

plague and pestilence. **5.8** The general names for *God*,
El and Elohim, appear here. The last word in this verse
is the only one that does not begin with the Hebrew letter *aleph*. **5.17–18** These verses resemble Deut 32.39;
Pss 94.12; 107.42; Prov 3.11; Hos 6.1. **5.17** The meaning
of *Almighty*, or *Shaddai*, remains uncertain; it may relate to an Akkadian word for "mountain" or to the verb
"to destroy." **5.18** An ancient tradition refers to Yahweh
as Israel's healer (Ex 15.26). **5.19–20** *Six . . . seven.* Ascending numerals sometimes refer to a totality (all of
them; cf. Am 1.3–2.16), but at other times specify an
actual number, with emphasis falling on the higher of

the two (cf. Prov 6.16–19; 30.15–16, 18–19, 21–31).
5.21–22 Does the allusion to *destruction* conceal a play
on the divine epithet *Shaddai* (v. 17)? **5.23** Peaceful residence with wild animals achieves classic expression in
Isa 11.6–9, but a pact with stones is found only here.
5.25 *Like the grass.* The usual phrase is "like the stars" or
"like the sands of the sea" (cf. Gen 15.5). **5.26** Eliphaz's
view of *old age* and death contrasts with the dismal
portrait in Eccl 11.7–12.7.

6.4 No evidence exists for the use of *poison* arrows
in the ancient Near East. **6.5–6** Just as Eliphaz cited
traditional maxims (4.8; 5.2, 17), Job relies on impos-

8 "O that I might have my request,
   and that God would grant my desire;
9 that it would please God to crush me,
   that he would let loose his hand and
     cut me off!
10 This would be my consolation;
   I would even exult[a] in unrelenting
     pain;
   for I have not denied the words of the
     Holy One.
11 What is my strength, that I should wait?
   And what is my end, that I should be
     patient?
12 Is my strength the strength of stones,
   or is my flesh bronze?
13 In truth I have no help in me,
   and any resource is driven from me.

14 "Those who withhold[b] kindness from a
     friend
   forsake the fear of the Almighty.[c]
15 My companions are treacherous like a
     torrent-bed,
   like freshets that pass away,
16 that run dark with ice,
   turbid with melting snow.
17 In time of heat they disappear;
   when it is hot, they vanish from their
     place.
18 The caravans turn aside from their course;
   they go up into the waste, and perish.
19 The caravans of Tema look,
   the travelers of Sheba hope.
20 They are disappointed because they were
     confident;
   they come there and are confounded.
21 Such you have now become to me;[d]
   you see my calamity, and are afraid.
22 Have I said, 'Make me a gift'?
   Or, 'From your wealth offer a bribe for
     me'?
23 Or, 'Save me from an opponent's hand'?
   Or, 'Ransom me from the hand of
     oppressors'?

24 "Teach me, and I will be silent;
   make me understand how I have gone
     wrong.
25 How forceful are honest words!
   But your reproof, what does it reprove?
26 Do you think that you can reprove words,
   as if the speech of the desperate were
     wind?
27 You would even cast lots over the orphan,
   and bargain over your friend.

28 "But now, be pleased to look at me;
   for I will not lie to your face.
29 Turn, I pray, let no wrong be done.
   Turn now, my vindication is at stake.
30 Is there any wrong on my tongue?
   Cannot my taste discern calamity?

Job: My Suffering Is without End

7 "Do not human beings have a hard
     service on earth,
   and are not their days like the days of a
     laborer?
2 Like a slave who longs for the shadow,
   and like laborers who look for their
     wages,
3 so I am allotted months of emptiness,
   and nights of misery are apportioned
     to me.
4 When I lie down I say, 'When shall I
     rise?'
   But the night is long,
   and I am full of tossing until dawn.
5 My flesh is clothed with worms and dirt;
   my skin hardens, then breaks out
     again.
6 My days are swifter than a weaver's
     shuttle,
   and come to their end without hope.[e]

---

a Meaning of Heb uncertain   b Syr Vg Compare Tg: Meaning
of Heb uncertain   c Traditional rendering of Heb *Shaddai*
d Cn Compare Gk Syr: Meaning of Heb uncertain   e Or *as the
thread runs out*

---

sible questions to command assent. **6.10** In 5.1 Eliphaz
asked if Job could find protection in one of God's holy
ones. Now Job goes beyond them to deny offense before the *Holy One*. **6.19** *Tema* was located in northern
Arabia. **6.21** The similarity between the words for *see*
and be *afraid* constitutes a pun in Hebrew. **6.26** Perhaps the choice of *desperate* plays on the word for humankind in Hebrew (cf. 7.17). **6.29** A bit of dramatic
acting. The friends appear to be walking away and
must be called back (cf. 17.10).

7.1 In the Mesopotamian creation account *Enuma
Elish*, human beings were created for the purpose of
menial *service* to the gods. **7.5** The *Testament of Job* develops this idea, stating that the pious hero picked up a
worm that had fallen off his skin and placed it back
where it belonged. **7.6** Whereas Eliphaz thought Job—
and the poor generally—had hope, Job rejected such
optimism for caravaneers (6.20) and for himself. A
Hebrew wordplay between *hope* and *thread* occurs
here. The medieval Jewish scholar Ibn Ezra noted that

7 "Remember that my life is a breath;
   my eye will never again see good.
8 The eye that beholds me will see me no
   more;
   while your eyes are upon me, I shall be
   gone.
9 As the cloud fades and vanishes,
   so those who go down to Sheol do not
   come up;
10 they return no more to their houses,
   nor do their places know them any
   more.

11 "Therefore I will not restrain my mouth;
   I will speak in the anguish of my spirit;
   I will complain in the bitterness of my
   soul.
12 Am I the Sea, or the Dragon,
   that you set a guard over me?
13 When I say, 'My bed will comfort me,
   my couch will ease my complaint,'
14 then you scare me with dreams
   and terrify me with visions,
15 so that I would choose strangling
   and death rather than this body.
16 I loathe my life; I would not live forever.
   Let me alone, for my days are a breath.
17 What are human beings, that you make
   so much of them,
   that you set your mind on them,
18 visit them every morning,
   test them every moment?
19 Will you not look away from me for a
   while,
   let me alone until I swallow my spittle?
20 If I sin, what do I do to you, you watcher
   of humanity?
   Why have you made me your target?
   Why have I become a burden to you?
21 Why do you not pardon my transgression
   and take away my iniquity?

For now I shall lie in the earth;
   you will seek me, but I shall not be."

Bildad Speaks: Job Should Repent

8 Then Bildad the Shuhite answered:
2 "How long will you say these things,
   and the words of your mouth be a
   great wind?
3 Does God pervert justice?
   Or does the Almighty[a] pervert the
   right?
4 If your children sinned against him,
   he delivered them into the power of
   their transgression.
5 If you will seek God
   and make supplication to the
   Almighty,[a]
6 if you are pure and upright,
   surely then he will rouse himself for
   you
   and restore to you your rightful place.
7 Though your beginning was small,
   your latter days will be very great.

8 "For inquire now of bygone generations,
   and consider what their ancestors have
   found;
9 for we are but of yesterday, and we know
   nothing,
   for our days on earth are but a shadow.
10 Will they not teach you and tell you
   and utter words out of their
   understanding?

11 "Can papyrus grow where there is no
   marsh?
   Can reeds flourish where there is no
   water?
12 While yet in flower and not cut down,

a Traditional rendering of Heb *Shaddai*

humans weave the threads of daily life. **7.12, 15** Both *Sea* and *Dragon* echo Canaanite myths about the sea as a chaotic force. Baal, the weather god, defeated the sea god. The Hebrew word for *death* recalls the Canaanite deity Mot. **7.14** Both Sirach and the Wisdom of Solomon emphasize God's use of psychological torment through nightmares to punish the wicked (e.g., Sir 40.1–10; Wis 18.17–19). **7.16** Ecclesiastes uses the word for *breath* (*hevel*, rendered "vanity" there) thirty-eight times to characterize life as futile, absurd, and empty. This word also was applied to idols. **7.17–18** A parody of Ps 8.4. **7.20** Job accepts Eliphaz's notion that virtue and vice in human beings amount to nothing in God's sight and reverses the usual idea of divine

guardianship. Job thinks the one who watches over him has evil intentions. **7.21** This verse may allude ironically to Enoch, who according to Gen 5.24 walked with God and "was no more" because God took him.

8.3–7 Bildad addresses Job's legal challenge, denying that God bends the rules of *justice* and asserting that Job's children deserved their fate. The promise of prosperity in the end accords with conventional wisdom, but Bildad's understanding of Job's former status (v. 7, *your beginning was small*) does not coincide with the grand picture in the story. **8.8–10** Wisdom is the accumulation of past insights, according to Bildad. **8.11** Two impossible questions (cf. Prov 6.27–28). The words for *papyrus* and *reeds* derive from Egyptian

they wither before any other plant.

13 Such are the paths of all who forget God;
    the hope of the godless shall perish.
14 Their confidence is gossamer,
    a spider's house their trust.
15 If one leans against its house, it will not
        stand;
    if one lays hold of it, it will not endure.
16 The wicked thrive[a] before the sun,
    and their shoots spread over the
        garden.
17 Their roots twine around the stoneheap;
    they live among the rocks.[b]
18 If they are destroyed from their place,
    then it will deny them, saying, 'I have
        never seen you.'
19 See, these are their happy ways,[c]
    and out of the earth still others will
        spring.

20 "See, God will not reject a blameless
        person,
    nor take the hand of evildoers.
21 He will yet fill your mouth with laughter,
    and your lips with shouts of joy.
22 Those who hate you will be clothed with
        shame,
    and the tent of the wicked will be no
        more."

Job Replies: There Is No Mediator

9 Then Job answered:
2 "Indeed I know that this is so;
    but how can a mortal be just before
        God?
3 If one wished to contend with him,
    one could not answer him once in a
        thousand.

4 He is wise in heart, and mighty in
        strength
    —who has resisted him, and
        succeeded?—
5 he who removes mountains, and they do
        not know it,
    when he overturns them in his anger;
6 who shakes the earth out of its place,
    and its pillars tremble;
7 who commands the sun, and it does not
        rise;
    who seals up the stars;
8 who alone stretched out the heavens
    and trampled the waves of the Sea;[d]
9 who made the Bear and Orion,
    the Pleiades and the chambers of the
        south;
10 who does great things beyond
        understanding,
    and marvelous things without number.
11 Look, he passes by me, and I do not see
        him;
    he moves on, but I do not perceive
        him.
12 He snatches away; who can stop him?
    Who will say to him, 'What are you
        doing?'

13 "God will not turn back his anger;
    the helpers of Rahab bowed beneath
        him.
14 How then can I answer him,
    choosing my words with him?
15 Though I am innocent, I cannot answer
        him;

---

a Heb *He thrives*   *b* Gk Vg: Meaning of Heb uncertain
c Meaning of Heb uncertain   *d* Or *trampled the back of the sea
dragon*

---

terms. **8.13** In 6.8 Job had asked that his *hope*, death,
be granted, but here Bildad pronounces a verdict on all
evil persons, one that stretches language itself: their
hope perishes. **8.14–19** The image of misplaced trust,
the fragility of a spider's web, reinforces that of a
wilted flower in v. 12, both of which gain force as a result of the juxtaposition alongside what—at first—appears a more promising image of well-watered roots.
8.20 Bildad cannot know that both God and the narrator attested to Job's integrity. **8.22** Bildad's speech ends
with the same Hebrew word that concludes Job's complaint in 7.21.

9.2 *Just before God.* Job takes up Eliphaz's point
(4.17), using a different expression ("*just with El*"
rather than "more just than Eloah"). **9.3** Morality gives
way to legality here. The concept *once in a thousand*
occurs in Eccl 7.28 to indicate the rarity of virtuous

men (cf. Sir 16.3, where childlessness is said to be
preferable to having ungodly children). **9.5–10** This
hymn, reminiscent of 5.9–16, uses participles expressing chaotic might, whereas Eliphaz stressed power in
its ordering capacity. With Job praise has assumed the
tone of attack. God's self-manifestation was often associated with an earthquake, and the Israelites coined
the epithet "Worker of wonders" to designate this majestic deity. **9.8** An allusion to a combat myth of creation similar to that of the Mesopotamian Tiamat, the
biblical Tehom. The same imagery occurs in 9.13 with
reference to Rahab, a mythic figure that features
prominently in Psalms and Second Isaiah (chs. 40–55,
sixth century BCE). **9.9** Four constellations are mentioned here, two of which are also referred to in the
similar hymnic fragment in Am 5.8 (perhaps two
more in 5.9). **9.15** The universe is perverse when an in-

I must appeal for mercy to my
accuser.[a]

16 If I summoned him and he answered me,
I do not believe that he would listen to
my voice.

17 For he crushes me with a tempest,
and multiplies my wounds without
cause;

18 he will not let me get my breath,
but fills me with bitterness.

19 If it is a contest of strength, he is the
strong one!
If it is a matter of justice, who can
summon him?[b]

20 Though I am innocent, my own mouth
would condemn me;
though I am blameless, he would prove
me perverse.

21 I am blameless; I do not know myself;
I loathe my life.

22 It is all one; therefore I say,
he destroys both the blameless and the
wicked.

23 When disaster brings sudden death,
he mocks at the calamity[c] of the
innocent.

24 The earth is given into the hand of the
wicked;
he covers the eyes of its judges—
if it is not he, who then is it?

25 "My days are swifter than a runner;
they flee away, they see no good.

26 They go by like skiffs of reed,
like an eagle swooping on the prey.

27 If I say, 'I will forget my complaint;
I will put off my sad countenance and
be of good cheer,'

28 I become afraid of all my suffering,
for I know you will not hold me
innocent.

29 I shall be condemned;

why then do I labor in vain?

30 If I wash myself with soap
and cleanse my hands with lye,

31 yet you will plunge me into filth,
and my own clothes will abhor me.

32 For he is not a mortal, as I am, that I
might answer him,
that we should come to trial together.

33 There is no umpire[d] between us,
who might lay his hand on us both.

34 If he would take his rod away from me,
and not let dread of him terrify me,

35 then I would speak without fear of him,
for I know I am not what I am thought
to be.[e]

Job: I Loathe My Life

10 "I loathe my life;
I will give free utterance to my
complaint;
I will speak in the bitterness of my soul.

2 I will say to God, Do not condemn me;
let me know why you contend against
me.

3 Does it seem good to you to oppress,
to despise the work of your hands
and favor the schemes of the wicked?

4 Do you have eyes of flesh?
Do you see as humans see?

5 Are your days like the days of mortals,
or your years like human years,

6 that you seek out my iniquity
and search for my sin,

7 although you know that I am not guilty,
and there is no one to deliver out of
your hand?

8 Your hands fashioned and made me;
and now you turn and destroy me.[f]

---

a Or for my right   b Compare Gk: Heb me   c Meaning of Heb
uncertain   d Another reading is Would that there were an
umpire   e Cn: Heb for I am not so in myself   f Cn Compare Gk
Syr: Heb made me together all around, and you destroy me

---

nocent person must plead for mercy; guilty individuals
are the ones for whom the quality of mercy comes into
play. **9.16** Job has given up on any hope of obtaining
justice in the presence of blind power. **9.17** The addition of the particle translated by *without cause* carries
explosive force in light of its function in the story.
9.19–21 Daring to assert his own integrity against all
odds, Job quickly takes it back and rejects *life*. This
time, unlike 7.16 (where the NRSV adds "my life"), the
object of the verb "reject," or *loathe* (9.21), is expressed. The cumulative testimony of the book supports Job's initial claim, for everyone has attested to his

integrity—the narrator (1.1), God (1.8; 2.3), Job's wife
(2.9), Eliphaz (4.6, implicitly), and Bildad (8.20).
9.22 Here Job abandons belief in any positive connection between virtue and reward. **9.24** Virtual
monotheism permitted Job no alternative to this disturbing conclusion about divine villainy. **9.33** Because
God acts as plaintiff, judge, and prosecuting attorney,
Job longs for an arbiter to judge between him and the
deity, but promptly discards this wishful thinking.
  10.1 Again Job specifies the object of his disgust, although the language differs altogether: *I loathe*, lit.
"my soul feels loathing." **10.7** The phrase about an ab-

9 Remember that you fashioned me like clay;
    and will you turn me to dust again?
10 Did you not pour me out like milk
    and curdle me like cheese?
11 You clothed me with skin and flesh,
    and knit me together with bones and
        sinews.
12 You have granted me life and steadfast love,
    and your care has preserved my spirit.
13 Yet these things you hid in your heart;
    I know that this was your purpose.
14 If I sin, you watch me,
    and do not acquit me of my iniquity.
15 If I am wicked, woe to me!
    If I am righteous, I cannot lift up my
        head,
    for I am filled with disgrace
    and look upon my affliction.
16 Bold as a lion you hunt me;
    you repeat your exploits against me.
17 You renew your witnesses against me,
    and increase your vexation toward me;
    you bring fresh troops against me. *a*

18 "Why did you bring me forth from the
        womb?
    Would that I had died before any eye
        had seen me,
19 and were as though I had not been,
    carried from the womb to the grave.
20 Are not the days of my life few? *b*
    Let me alone, that I may find a little
        comfort *c*
21 before I go, never to return,
    to the land of gloom and deep darkness,
22 the land of gloom *d* and chaos,
    where light is like darkness."

Zophar Speaks: Job's Guilt Deserves Punishment

11 Then Zophar the Naamathite an-
    swered:

2 "Should a multitude of words go
        unanswered,
    and should one full of talk be
        vindicated?
3 Should your babble put others to silence,
    and when you mock, shall no one
        shame you?
4 For you say, 'My conduct *e* is pure,
    and I am clean in God's *f* sight.'
5 But O that God would speak,
    and open his lips to you,
6 and that he would tell you the secrets of
        wisdom!
    For wisdom is many-sided. *g*
Know then that God exacts of you less
        than your guilt deserves.

7 "Can you find out the deep things of
        God?
    Can you find out the limit of the
        Almighty? *h*
8 It is higher than heaven *i*—what can you
        do?
    Deeper than Sheol—what can you
        know?
9 Its measure is longer than the earth,
    and broader than the sea.
10 If he passes through, and imprisons,
    and assembles for judgment, who can
        hinder him?
11 For he knows those who are worthless;
    when he sees iniquity, will he not
        consider it?
12 But a stupid person will get
        understanding,
    when a wild ass is born human. *g*

---

a Cn Compare Gk: Heb *toward me; changes and a troop are with me*   *b* Cn Compare Gk Syr: Heb *Are not my days few? Let him cease!*   *c* Heb *that I may brighten up a little*   *d* Heb *gloom as darkness, deep darkness*   *e* Gk: Heb *teaching*   *f* Heb *your*   *g* Meaning of Heb uncertain   *h* Traditional rendering of Heb *Shaddai*   *i* Heb *The heights of heaven*

---

sence of anyone to *deliver* from the divine power points to Job's hopelessness. **10.9** According to ancient tradition, the human dilemma after the Fall was precisely this, to return to *dust*. Does Job object to this curse, or does he think of premature death? **10.12, 14** The more common expression for divine protection returns here (cf. the irony when set alongside 2.6). In 10.14 the verb *watch* takes on a negative connotation, like *watcher of humanity* in 7.20. **10.18–20** Job's attitude toward death changes (cf. 3.17–18, 21–22; 7.21). **10.22** An oxymoron, "it shines like *darkness*." **11.4** Zophar emphasizes purity (cf. 11.15, *blemish*),

but Job had concentrated on moral integrity. **11.6** This appeal to divine compassion, a forgetting of some evil and letting Job off lightly, clashes with a strict notion of reward and punishment. The struggle to hold together both sides of the equation, justice and mercy, gave rise to the creedal statement in Ex 34.6–7, part of which occurs often in confessional literature of the Bible (cf. Neh 9.17, 31; Ps 86.15; Joel 2.13; Jon 4.2). Wisdom's hiddenness is noted in Sir 6.22: "For wisdom is like her name; she is not readily perceived by many." **11.8** Cf. Sir 1.3. **11.12** A proverbial "impossible task," like Ovid's "then will the stag fly." Gen 16.12 de-

13 "If you direct your heart rightly,
  you will stretch out your hands toward
    him.
14 If iniquity is in your hand, put it far away,
  and do not let wickedness reside in
    your tents.
15 Surely then you will lift up your face
    without blemish;
  you will be secure, and will not fear.
16 You will forget your misery;
  you will remember it as waters that
    have passed away.
17 And your life will be brighter than the
    noonday;
  its darkness will be like the morning.
18 And you will have confidence, because
    there is hope;
  you will be protected[a] and take your
    rest in safety.
19 You will lie down, and no one will make
    you afraid;
  many will entreat your favor.
20 But the eyes of the wicked will fail;
  all way of escape will be lost to them,
  and their hope is to breathe their last."

Job Replies: I Am a Laughingstock

12 Then Job answered:
  2 "No doubt you are the people,
  and wisdom will die with you.
3 But I have understanding as well as you;
  I am not inferior to you.
  Who does not know such things as
    these?
4 I am a laughingstock to my friends;
  I, who called upon God and he
    answered me,
  a just and blameless man, I am a
    laughingstock.
5 Those at ease have contempt for
    misfortune,[b]

but it is ready for those whose feet are
    unstable.
6 The tents of robbers are at peace,
  and those who provoke God are secure,
  who bring their god in their hands.[c]

7 "But ask the animals, and they will teach
    you;
  the birds of the air, and they will tell
    you;
8 ask the plants of the earth,[d] and they will
    teach you;
  and the fish of the sea will declare to
    you.
9 Who among all these does not know
  that the hand of the LORD has done
    this?
10 In his hand is the life of every living thing
  and the breath of every human being.
11 Does not the ear test words
  as the palate tastes food?
12 Is wisdom with the aged,
  and understanding in length of days?

13 "With God[e] are wisdom and strength;
  he has counsel and understanding.
14 If he tears down, no one can rebuild;
  if he shuts someone in, no one can
    open up.
15 If he withholds the waters, they dry up;
  if he sends them out, they overwhelm
    the land.
16 With him are strength and wisdom;
  the deceived and the deceiver are his.
17 He leads counselors away stripped,
  and makes fools of judges.
18 He looses the sash of kings,
  and binds a waistcloth on their loins.

---

a Or *you will look around*   *b* Meaning of Heb uncertain
c Or *whom God brought forth by his hand*; Meaning of Heb
uncertain   *d* Or *speak to the earth*   *e* Heb *him*

---

scribes Ishmael as a *wild ass* of a man. This proverb in
Job views ignorance, not morality, as the thing that
separates mortals from deity. **11.13** Another discussion of divine justice that isolates the *heart* as the decisive organ in need of attention, Ps 73, clarifies the
issue. The problem, according to Zophar and this
psalmist, is one of cognition. **11.20** Against the background of promised *hope* for those who truly purify
themselves, Zophar threatens Job with perishing
refuge and empty hope, precisely what he had asked
for (3.3; 10.18–22).
  12.2 Sarcasm. **12.3** *Not inferior to you.* Twice in this
speech Job insists on equality with the friends, here and

in 13.2. The story goes further; it describes his superiority over all others. **12.4** The reference indicates a vital
relationship (*called upon . . . answered me*) with God.
12.6 *In their hands.* A reference to idolatry? **12.7** *Animals*, Hebrew *Behemoth*. This allusion to Behemoth,
frighteningly described in 40.15–24, seems out of
place, hence the translation *animals* or "cattle" despite
the singular verb in Hebrew (Behemoth is plural in
form). **12.9** The only mention of the LORD (Yahweh) in
the poetic dialogue between Job and the three friends;
cf. the concluding observation in 28.28. **12.12** Because
the next verse challenges the point of this statement, it
seems that Job cites a proverb in order to refute it.

19 He leads priests away stripped,
   and overthrows the mighty.
20 He deprives of speech those who are
      trusted,
   and takes away the discernment of the
      elders.
21 He pours contempt on princes,
   and looses the belt of the strong.
22 He uncovers the deeps out of darkness,
   and brings deep darkness to light.
23 He makes nations great, then destroys
      them;
   he enlarges nations, then leads them
      away.
24 He strips understanding from the
      leaders*a* of the earth,
   and makes them wander in a pathless
      waste.
25 They grope in the dark without light;
   he makes them stagger like a drunkard.

13 "Look, my eye has seen all this,
   my ear has heard and understood it.
2 What you know, I also know;
   I am not inferior to you.
3 But I would speak to the Almighty,*b*
   and I desire to argue my case with
      God.
4 As for you, you whitewash with lies;
   all of you are worthless physicians.
5 If you would only keep silent,
   that would be your wisdom!
6 Hear now my reasoning,
   and listen to the pleadings of my lips.
7 Will you speak falsely for God,
   and speak deceitfully for him?
8 Will you show partiality toward him,
   will you plead the case for God?
9 Will it be well with you when he searches
      you out?
   Or can you deceive him, as one person
      deceives another?
10 He will surely rebuke you

if in secret you show partiality.
11 Will not his majesty terrify you,
   and the dread of him fall upon you?
12 Your maxims are proverbs of ashes,
   your defenses are defenses of clay.

13 "Let me have silence, and I will speak,
   and let come on me what may.
14 I will take my flesh in my teeth,
   and put my life in my hand.*c*
15 See, he will kill me; I have no hope;*d*
   but I will defend my ways to his face.
16 This will be my salvation,
   that the godless shall not come before
      him.
17 Listen carefully to my words,
   and let my declaration be in your ears.
18 I have indeed prepared my case;
   I know that I shall be vindicated.
19 Who is there that will contend with me?
   For then I would be silent and die.

Job's Despondent Prayer

20 Only grant two things to me,
   then I will not hide myself from your
      face:
21 withdraw your hand far from me,
   and do not let dread of you terrify me.
22 Then call, and I will answer;
   or let me speak, and you reply to me.
23 How many are my iniquities and my sins?
   Make me know my transgression and
      my sin.
24 Why do you hide your face,
   and count me as your enemy?
25 Will you frighten a windblown leaf
   and pursue dry chaff?
26 For you write bitter things against me,
   and make me reap*e* the iniquities of my
      youth.

---

a Heb adds *of the people*   *b* Traditional rendering of Heb
Shaddai   *c* Gk: Heb *Why should I take . . . in my hand?*
d Or *Though he kill me, yet I will trust in him*   *e* Heb *inherit*

13.3 Judicial terminology becomes prominent as
Job turns more and more to address God instead of
the friends. 13.5 In Egypt "the *silent* one" indicated a
professional sage, a person who governed the passions.
13.9 Internal irony. 13.15 *I have no hope,* lit. "I will not
wait/hope." The *qere* reading (an ancient alternative to
what is written in the Hebrew text) suggests that a later
reader considered Job's language excessive and substituted "for him" (lit. "to him") for "not," yielding "I will
for him wait/hope" (see the translation in text note *d*).
Even this change hardly justifies a positive under-

standing of Job's defiant last-ditch stand. 13.16 If sinners cannot appear before God and Job does so without harm, he achieves vindication regardless of the
meaning one assigns to his words in 42.6. This verse
therefore focuses the dramatic action of the book.
13.20 Agur in Prov 30.7–9 also asks *two things* of God:
to banish deception from him and to give him neither
poverty nor riches. 13.24 This reference to *enemy* contains a pun on Job's name in Hebrew. 13.26 Job does
not claim to be sinless, but he does assert that he has
integrity, having done nothing to deserve such foul

27 You put my feet in the stocks,
       and watch all my paths;
       you set a bound to the soles of my feet.
28 One wastes away like a rotten thing,
       like a garment that is moth-eaten.

14

"A mortal, born of woman, few of
       days and full of trouble,
2   comes up like a flower and withers,
       flees like a shadow and does not last.
3   Do you fix your eyes on such a one?
       Do you bring me into judgment with
         you?
4   Who can bring a clean thing out of an
         unclean?
       No one can.
5   Since their days are determined,
       and the number of their months is
         known to you,
       and you have appointed the bounds
         that they cannot pass,
6   look away from them, and desist,[a]
       that they may enjoy, like laborers, their
         days.

7   "For there is hope for a tree,
       if it is cut down, that it will sprout
         again,
       and that its shoots will not cease.
8   Though its root grows old in the earth,
       and its stump dies in the ground,
9   yet at the scent of water it will bud
       and put forth branches like a young
         plant.
10 But mortals die, and are laid low;
       humans expire, and where are they?
11 As waters fail from a lake,
       and a river wastes away and dries up,
12 so mortals lie down and do not rise
         again;
       until the heavens are no more, they will
         not awake
       or be roused out of their sleep.
13 O that you would hide me in Sheol,
       that you would conceal me until your
         wrath is past,

       that you would appoint me a set time,
         and remember me!
14 If mortals die, will they live again?
       All the days of my service I would wait
       until my release should come.
15 You would call, and I would answer you;
       you would long for the work of your
         hands.
16 For then you would not[b] number my
         steps,
       you would not keep watch over my sin;
17 my transgression would be sealed up in a
         bag,
       and you would cover over my iniquity.

18 "But the mountain falls and crumbles
         away,
       and the rock is removed from its place;
19 the waters wear away the stones;
       the torrents wash away the soil of the
         earth;
       so you destroy the hope of mortals.
20 You prevail forever against them, and
         they pass away;
       you change their countenance, and
         send them away.
21 Their children come to honor, and they
         do not know it;
       they are brought low, and it goes
         unnoticed.
22 They feel only the pain of their own
         bodies,
       and mourn only for themselves."

Eliphaz Speaks: Job Undermines Religion

15

Then Eliphaz the Temanite answered:
2 "Should the wise answer with windy
         knowledge,
       and fill themselves with the east wind?
3   Should they argue in unprofitable talk,
       or in words with which they can do no
         good?
4   But you are doing away with the fear of
         God,

_____
a Cn: Heb *that they may desist*   b Syr: Heb lacks *not*

---

treatment. **14.4** Does Job succumb to Eliphaz's low estimate of mortals, calling them guilty as a result of birth? This view occurs in the Sumerian parallel to Job "A Man and His God." **14.8–22** From here until chs. 40, 42 Job only talks *about* God, not *to* God. **14.12** Job dismisses the daring thought of life after death, reconciling himself to future oblivion (like the author of Ec-

clesiastes). Other biblical writers ventured along paths rejected by Job, particularly Dan 12.2; Isa 26.19; and possibly Ps 73.23–28.
     15.2 The *wind* from the eastern desert was hot, so Eliphaz accuses Job of uttering hot air. **15.4** Although Job uses some form of this Hebrew word for *meditation* several times, only in this instance does anyone

and hindering meditation before God.

5 For your iniquity teaches your mouth,
      and you choose the tongue of the
          crafty.

6 Your own mouth condemns you, and not I;
      your own lips testify against you.

7 "Are you the firstborn of the human race?
      Were you brought forth before the
          hills?

8 Have you listened in the council of God?
      And do you limit wisdom to yourself?

9 What do you know that we do not know?
      What do you understand that is not
          clear to us?

10 The gray-haired and the aged are on our
          side,
      those older than your father.

11 Are the consolations of God too small for
          you,
      or the word that deals gently with you?

12 Why does your heart carry you away,
      and why do your eyes flash,^{a}

13 so that you turn your spirit against God,
      and let such words go out of your
          mouth?

14 What are mortals, that they can be clean?
      Or those born of woman, that they can
          be righteous?

15 God puts no trust even in his holy ones,
      and the heavens are not clean in his
          sight;

16 how much less one who is abominable
          and corrupt,
      one who drinks iniquity like water!

17 "I will show you; listen to me;
      what I have seen I will declare—

18 what sages have told,
      and their ancestors have not hidden,

19 to whom alone the land was given,

and no stranger passed among them.

20 The wicked writhe in pain all their days,
      through all the years that are laid up
          for the ruthless.

21 Terrifying sounds are in their ears;
      in prosperity the destroyer will come
          upon them.

22 They despair of returning from darkness,
      and they are destined for the sword.

23 They wander abroad for bread, saying,
          'Where is it?'
      They know that a day of darkness is
          ready at hand;

24 distress and anguish terrify them;
      they prevail against them, like a king
          prepared for battle.

25 Because they stretched out their hands
          against God,
      and bid defiance to the Almighty,^{b}

26 running stubbornly against him
      with a thick-bossed shield;

27 because they have covered their faces with
          their fat,
      and gathered fat upon their loins,

28 they will live in desolate cities,
      in houses that no one should inhabit,
      houses destined to become heaps of
          ruins;

29 they will not be rich, and their wealth will
          not endure,
      nor will they strike root in the earth;^{c}

30 they will not escape from darkness;
      the flame will dry up their shoots,
      and their blossom^d will be swept away^e
          by the wind.

31 Let them not trust in emptiness,
          deceiving themselves;
      for emptiness will be their recompense.

---

a Meaning of Heb uncertain   *b* Traditional rendering of Heb
Shaddai   *c* Vg: Meaning of Heb uncertain   *d* Gk: Heb *mouth*
e Cn: Heb *will depart*

---

else do so. **15.7** A sarcastic response to Job's challenge
that the friends consult earth's creatures in search for
answers, this jibe undercuts any claim on Job's part to
decisive knowledge. The paucity of biblical references
outside Genesis to the primal couple is noteworthy.
The situation changes with Ben Sira, about 190 BCE
(cf. Sir 25.24; 49.16). **15.8** Some prophets, e.g., Amos
and Jeremiah, claim to have listened to the divine
council where human destiny was decided (cf. Am 3.7;
Jer 23.21–22). **15.10** Eliphaz's assumption that length
of years brought wisdom was not shared by Job or the
youthful Elihu, but wisdom literature generally vener-
ated old age even when conceding that some *older* people manifested folly. Suspicion about youthful rash-
ness is best shown in 1 Kings 12.1–16. **15.14–16** Here
Eliphaz links the notions of purity and morality, dismissing the human race as tainted. Such a religious
system affords no rationale for Job's relentless pursuit
of vindication. **15.18** Lit. "which the wise have declared and have not concealed from their ancestors."
15.19 Nowhere else does wisdom literature before Sirach allude to the tradition about Israel's inheriting the
land. The remark about an absence of strangers (cf.
Joel 4.17) does not support such an association with
the earlier tradition, for strangers certainly dwelt in
the newly occupied land.

32 It will be paid in full before their time,
   and their branch will not be green.
33 They will shake off their unripe grape,
      like the vine,
   and cast off their blossoms, like the
      olive tree.
34 For the company of the godless is barren,
   and fire consumes the tents of bribery.
35 They conceive mischief and bring forth
      evil
   and their heart prepares deceit."

Job Reaffirms His Innocence

16 Then Job answered:
2 "I have heard many such things;
   miserable comforters are you all.
3 Have windy words no limit?
   Or what provokes you that you keep
      on talking?
4 I also could talk as you do,
   if you were in my place;
   I could join words together against you,
   and shake my head at you.
5 I could encourage you with my mouth,
   and the solace of my lips would
      assuage your pain.

6 "If I speak, my pain is not assuaged,
   and if I forbear, how much of it leaves
      me?
7 Surely now God has worn me out;
   he has[a] made desolate all my company.
8 And he has[a] shriveled me up,
   which is a witness against me;
   my leanness has risen up against me,
   and it testifies to my face.
9 He has torn me in his wrath, and hated
      me;
   he has gnashed his teeth at me;
   my adversary sharpens his eyes against
      me.
10 They have gaped at me with their
      mouths;
   they have struck me insolently on the
      cheek;

they mass themselves together against
      me.
11 God gives me up to the ungodly,
   and casts me into the hands of the
      wicked.
12 I was at ease, and he broke me in two;
   he seized me by the neck and dashed
      me to pieces;
   he set me up as his target;
13 his archers surround me.
He slashes open my kidneys, and shows
      no mercy;
   he pours out my gall on the ground.
14 He bursts upon me again and again;
   he rushes at me like a warrior.
15 I have sewed sackcloth upon my skin,
   and have laid my strength in the dust.
16 My face is red with weeping,
   and deep darkness is on my eyelids,
17 though there is no violence in my hands,
   and my prayer is pure.

18 "O earth, do not cover my blood;
   let my outcry find no resting place.
19 Even now, in fact, my witness is in
      heaven,
   and he that vouches for me is on high.
20 My friends scorn me;
   my eye pours out tears to God,
21 that he would maintain the right of a
      mortal with God,
   as[b] one does for a neighbor.
22 For when a few years have come,
   I shall go the way from which I shall
      not return.

Job Prays for Relief

17 My spirit is broken, my days are
      extinct,
   the grave is ready for me.
2 Surely there are mockers around me,
   and my eye dwells on their
      provocation.

a Heb you have   b Syr Vg Tg: Heb and

16.7–17 Cf. Lam 3. **16.15** *Sackcloth* was worn during mourning and in periods of intense grief connected with repentance or prayer for forgiveness. **16.17** Job insists that his supplication is *pure* despite Eliphaz's charge in 15.14. The prophets railed against people who prayed with blood-stained hands. **16.18** The Israelites believed that unrequited *blood* of innocent victims cried out until a vindicator acted, as in the case of Abel, the first victim of fraternal rivalry (Gen 4.10). A heavenly advocate was known in Mesopotamia. **16.19** Job's *witness*, already in God's presence, is thought to be sufficiently powerful to exact justice from the deity. In 9.33 Job dismissed any such possibility of a mediator between himself and God. **16.22** Here Job anticipates the lapse of time before his demise. Only a god could return from the netherworld (cf. the Sumerian account of Inanna's descent into the netherworld and the Akkadian "Descent of Ishtar to

3 "Lay down a pledge for me with yourself;
  who is there that will give surety for me?
4 Since you have closed their minds to
    understanding,
  therefore you will not let them
    triumph.
5 Those who denounce friends for
    reward—
  the eyes of their children will fail.

6 "He has made me a byword of the peoples,
  and I am one before whom people spit.
7 My eye has grown dim from grief,
  and all my members are like a shadow.
8 The upright are appalled at this,
  and the innocent stir themselves up
    against the godless.
9 Yet the righteous hold to their way,
  and they that have clean hands grow
    stronger and stronger.
10 But you, come back now, all of you,
  and I shall not find a sensible person
    among you.
11 My days are past, my plans are broken off,
  the desires of my heart.
12 They make night into day;
  'The light,' they say, 'is near to the
    darkness.' *a*
13 If I look for Sheol as my house,
  if I spread my couch in darkness,
14 if I say to the Pit, 'You are my father,'
  and to the worm, 'My mother,' or 'My
    sister,'
15 where then is my hope?
  Who will see my hope?
16 Will it go down to the bars of Sheol?
  Shall we descend together into the
    dust?"

Bildad Speaks: God Punishes the Wicked

18 Then Bildad the Shuhite answered:
   2 "How long will you hunt for words?
    Consider, and then we shall speak.
3 Why are we counted as cattle?

Why are we stupid in your sight?
4 You who tear yourself in your anger—
  shall the earth be forsaken because of
    you,
  or the rock be removed out of its place?

5 "Surely the light of the wicked is put out,
  and the flame of their fire does not
    shine.
6 The light is dark in their tent,
  and the lamp above them is put out.
7 Their strong steps are shortened,
  and their own schemes throw them
    down.
8 For they are thrust into a net by their
    own feet,
  and they walk into a pitfall.
9 A trap seizes them by the heel;
  a snare lays hold of them.
10 A rope is hid for them in the ground,
  a trap for them in the path.
11 Terrors frighten them on every side,
  and chase them at their heels.
12 Their strength is consumed by hunger, *b*
  and calamity is ready for their
    stumbling.
13 By disease their skin is consumed, *c*
  the firstborn of Death consumes their
    limbs.
14 They are torn from the tent in which they
    trusted,
  and are brought to the king of terrors.
15 In their tents nothing remains;
  sulfur is scattered upon their
    habitations.
16 Their roots dry up beneath,
  and their branches wither above.
17 Their memory perishes from the earth,
  and they have no name in the street.
18 They are thrust from light into darkness,
  and driven out of the world.

---

a Meaning of Heb uncertain   *b* Or *Disaster is hungry for them*
c Cn: Heb *It consumes the limbs of his skin*

---

the Netherworld"). **17.13** Ossuaries were shaped like
houses.
  18.4 Bildad's system of reward and retribution will
make no exception for Job, who must be guilty. **18.5–
21** Nothing occurs on earth that was not decreed in
heaven. **18.5–6** In the Bible a *lamp* often points
metaphorically to life, as in Othello's speech ("Put out
the light, and then put out the light"). **18.13** *Death*
here is a mythical figure (see 7.15). In Canaanite
mythology no record of Mot's *firstborn* has survived.

Perhaps one should translate "Death, the firstborn."
18.15 In magical practices of the ancient world, according to the *Odyssey* (22.480–81, 492–94), sulphur
was sprinkled over a site to purge it. **18.16–20** Several
examples of merism (a figure of speech in which parts
symbolize the whole) occur here, e.g., *roots* and
branches; farmlands (*earth*) and grazing lands (*street;*
the Hebrew word can carry either sense); kin (*people*)
and residences (*where they used to live*); and *they of the
west* and *those of the east.* **18.17, 19** The two means of

19 They have no offspring or descendant
       among their people,
   and no survivor where they used to
       live.
20 They of the west are appalled at their fate,
   and horror seizes those of the east.
21 Surely such are the dwellings of the
       ungodly,
   such is the place of those who do not
       know God."

Job Replies: I Know That
My Redeemer Lives

19 Then Job answered:
   2 "How long will you torment me,
   and break me in pieces with words?
3 These ten times you have cast reproach
       upon me;
   are you not ashamed to wrong me?
4 And even if it is true that I have erred,
   my error remains with me.
5 If indeed you magnify yourselves against
       me,
   and make my humiliation an argument
       against me,
6 know then that God has put me in the
       wrong,
   and closed his net around me.
7 Even when I cry out, 'Violence!' I am not
       answered;
   I call aloud, but there is no justice.
8 He has walled up my way so that I cannot
       pass,
   and he has set darkness upon my
       paths.
9 He has stripped my glory from me,
   and taken the crown from my head.
10 He breaks me down on every side, and I
       am gone,
   he has uprooted my hope like a tree.
11 He has kindled his wrath against me,

and counts me as his adversary.
12 His troops come on together;
   they have thrown up siegeworks[a]
       against me,
   and encamp around my tent.

13 "He has put my family far from me,
   and my acquaintances are wholly
       estranged from me.
14 My relatives and my close friends have
       failed me;
15 the guests in my house have forgotten
       me;
   my serving girls count me as a stranger;
   I have become an alien in their eyes.
16 I call to my servant, but he gives me no
       answer;
   I must myself plead with him.
17 My breath is repulsive to my wife;
   I am loathsome to my own family.
18 Even young children despise me;
   when I rise, they talk against me.
19 All my intimate friends abhor me,
   and those whom I loved have turned
       against me.
20 My bones cling to my skin and to my
       flesh,
   and I have escaped by the skin of my
       teeth.
21 Have pity on me, have pity on me, O you
       my friends,
   for the hand of God has touched me!
22 Why do you, like God, pursue me,
   never satisfied with my flesh?

23 "O that my words were written down!
   O that they were inscribed in a book!
24 O that with an iron pen and with lead
       they were engraved on a rock forever!

---

a Cn: Heb their way

surviving death at the time of the author, *memory* and *offspring*, are denied Job. **18.20** *West, east,* perhaps former and subsequent generations rather than geographical designations. **19.3** *Ten times,* a round number (cf. Gen 31.7; Num 14.22). **19.6** *Closed his net,* perhaps an image of a fowler, one that occurs in ancient Near Eastern political treaties as a threat against treacherous conduct. **19.8** Job's view of the divine enclosure (*walled up*) differs from that of Satan, the Adversary, who spoke of it as protection from all harm (see 1.10). **19.9** The Hebrew word translated *glory* can also mean "wealth." **19.16** This negative view of slaves does not recur in

31.13–15. **19.17** *My own family,* lit. "children of my womb," may reflect the sexist views of the ancient Near East—a wife as a husband's property—or it may be an oblique reference to a clan. Job appears to have forgotten that his children are dead, unless his speech merely accords with conventional laments familiar from Mesopotamia, e.g., "I Will Praise the Lord of Wisdom" and "The Babylonian Theodicy." **19.20** *Skin of my teeth,* nothing. **19.24** Evidence exists for use of *lead* as a filler in small tablets and in an inscription, the Behistun Rock, that extols the achievements of the Persian king Darius. Job's eloquence notwithstanding, the written word remains highly unclear in this instance, for its

25 For I know that my Redeemer[a] lives,
  and that at the last he[b] will stand upon
    the earth;[c]
26 and after my skin has been thus
    destroyed,
  then in[d] my flesh I shall see God,[e]
27 whom I shall see on my side,[f]
  and my eyes shall behold, and not
    another.
  My heart faints within me!
28 If you say, 'How we will persecute him!'
  and, 'The root of the matter is found in
    him';
29 be afraid of the sword,
  for wrath brings the punishment of the
    sword,
  so that you may know there is a
    judgment.'"

Zophar Speaks: Wickedness Receives Just Retribution

20 Then Zophar the Naamathite an-
    swered:
2 "Pay attention! My thoughts urge me to
    answer,
  because of the agitation within me.
3 I hear censure that insults me,
  and a spirit beyond my understanding
    answers me.
4 Do you not know this from of old,
  ever since mortals were placed on
    earth,
5 that the exulting of the wicked is short,
  and the joy of the godless is but for a
    moment?
6 Even though they mount up high as the
    heavens,
  and their head reaches to the clouds,
7 they will perish forever like their own
    dung;
  those who have seen them will say,
    'Where are they?'
8 They will fly away like a dream, and not
    be found;

9 they will be chased away like a vision of
    the night.
9 The eye that saw them will see them no
    more,
  nor will their place behold them any
    longer.
10 Their children will seek the favor of the
    poor,
  and their hands will give back their
    wealth.
11 Their bodies, once full of youth,
  will lie down in the dust with them.
12 "Though wickedness is sweet in their
    mouth,
  though they hide it under their
    tongues,
13 though they are loath to let it go,
  and hold it in their mouths,
14 yet their food is turned in their stomachs;
  it is the venom of asps within them.
15 They swallow down riches and vomit
    them up again;
  God casts them out of their bellies.
16 They will suck the poison of asps;
  the tongue of a viper will kill them.
17 They will not look on the rivers,
  the streams flowing with honey and
    curds.
18 They will give back the fruit of their toil,
  and will not swallow it down;
  from the profit of their trading
    they will get no enjoyment.
19 For they have crushed and abandoned the
    poor,
  they have seized a house that they did
    not build.
20 "They knew no quiet in their bellies;
  in their greed they let nothing escape.
21 There was nothing left after they had eaten;

---

a Or Vindicator b Or that he the Last c Heb dust
d Or without e Meaning of Heb of this verse uncertain
f Or for myself

---

meaning defies understanding in vv. 25–27. The prophet Isaiah also mentions a permanent writing (30.8). **19.25–27** Redeemer, an avenger of blood, who, according to Num 35.19; Deut 19.6, would vindicate Job's death by punishing the guilty, in this instance, God. The issue here is revenge, for Job has abandoned any notion of justice. Job's cry resembles a Ugaritic text from the Baal cycle: "And I know that Aleyan Baal is alive," presumably a confession of Baal's annual revivification according to the agricultural calendar. Perhaps the Sumerian patron deity who intercedes with the High God furnishes the background for Job's language. **20.6** Possibly an allusion to the Tower of Babel in Gen 11.1–9. **20.12** Woman Folly entices young men with the promise that "Stolen water is sweet, and bread eaten in secret is pleasant" (Prov 9.17). **20.17** According to ancient Yahwistic tradition, the land of promise was thought to have flowed with milk and honey. **20.18** Ancient futility curses spoke of fruitless effort, e.g., planting without reaping, building a house with-

therefore their prosperity will not
  endure.
22 In full sufficiency they will be in distress;
  all the force of misery will come upon
    them.
23 To fill their belly to the full
  God^a will send his fierce anger into
    them,
  and rain it upon them as their food.^b
24 They will flee from an iron weapon;
  a bronze arrow will strike them
    through.
25 It is drawn forth and comes out of their
    body,
  and the glittering point comes out of
    their gall;
  terrors come upon them.
26 Utter darkness is laid up for their
    treasures;
  a fire fanned by no one will devour
    them;
  what is left in their tent will be
    consumed.
27 The heavens will reveal their iniquity,
  and the earth will rise up against them.
28 The possessions of their house will be
    carried away,
  dragged off in the day of God's^c wrath.
29 This is the portion of the wicked from
    God,
  the heritage decreed for them by God."

*Job Replies: The Wicked Often
  Go Unpunished*

21 Then Job answered:
  2 "Listen carefully to my words,
  and let this be your consolation.
3 Bear with me, and I will speak;
  then after I have spoken, mock on.
4 As for me, is my complaint addressed to
    mortals?
  Why should I not be impatient?
5 Look at me, and be appalled,
  and lay your hand upon your mouth.
6 When I think of it I am dismayed,
  and shuddering seizes my flesh.
7 Why do the wicked live on,
  reach old age, and grow mighty in
    power?
8 Their children are established in their
    presence,
  and their offspring before their eyes.
9 Their houses are safe from fear,
  and no rod of God is upon them.

10 Their bull breeds without fail;
  their cow calves and never miscarries.
11 They send out their little ones like a flock,
  and their children dance around.
12 They sing to the tambourine and the lyre,
  and rejoice to the sound of the pipe.
13 They spend their days in prosperity,
  and in peace they go down to Sheol.
14 They say to God, 'Leave us alone!
  We do not desire to know your ways.
15 What is the Almighty,^d that we should
    serve him?
  And what profit do we get if we pray to
    him?'
16 Is not their prosperity indeed their own
    achievement?^e
  The plans of the wicked are repugnant
    to me.

17 "How often is the lamp of the wicked put
    out?
  How often does calamity come upon
    them?
  How often does God^a distribute pains
    in his anger?
18 How often are they like straw before the
    wind,
  and like chaff that the storm carries
    away?
19 You say, 'God stores up their iniquity for
    their children.'
  Let it be paid back to them, so that
    they may know it.
20 Let their own eyes see their destruction,
  and let them drink of the wrath of the
    Almighty.^d
21 For what do they care for their household
    after them,
  when the number of their months is
    cut off?
22 Will any teach God knowledge,
  seeing that he judges those that are on
    high?
23 One dies in full prosperity,
  being wholly at ease and secure,
24 his loins full of milk
  and the marrow of his bones moist.
25 Another dies in bitterness of soul,
  never having tasted of good.
26 They lie down alike in the dust,
  and the worms cover them.

---

a Heb *he*   *b* Cn: Meaning of Heb uncertain   *c* Heb *his*
d Traditional rendering of Heb *Shaddai*   *e* Heb *in their hand*

27 "Oh, I know your thoughts,
   and your schemes to wrong me.
28 For you say, 'Where is the house of the
   prince?
   Where is the tent in which the wicked
   lived?'
29 Have you not asked those who travel the
   roads,
   and do you not accept their testimony,
30 that the wicked are spared in the day of
   calamity,
   and are rescued in the day of wrath?
31 Who declares their way to their face,
   and who repays them for what they
   have done?
32 When they are carried to the grave,
   a watch is kept over their tomb.
33 The clods of the valley are sweet to them;
   everyone will follow after,
   and those who went before are
   innumerable.
34 How then will you comfort me with
   empty nothings?
   There is nothing left of your answers
   but falsehood."

Eliphaz Speaks: Job's Wickedness Is Great

22 Then Eliphaz the Temanite answered:
   2 "Can a mortal be of use to God?
   Can even the wisest be of service to
   him?
3 Is it any pleasure to the Almighty^a if you
   are righteous,
   or is it gain to him if you make your
   ways blameless?
4 Is it for your piety that he reproves you,
   and enters into judgment with you?
5 Is not your wickedness great?
   There is no end to your iniquities.
6 For you have exacted pledges from your
   family for no reason,
   and stripped the naked of their
   clothing.
7 You have given no water to the weary to
   drink,

and you have withheld bread from the
   hungry.
8 The powerful possess the land,
   and the favored live in it.
9 You have sent widows away empty-
   handed,
   and the arms of the orphans you have
   crushed.^{b}
10 Therefore snares are around you,
   and sudden terror overwhelms you,
11 or darkness so that you cannot see;
   a flood of water covers you.
12 "Is not God high in the heavens?
   See the highest stars, how lofty they
   are!
13 Therefore you say, 'What does God know?
   Can he judge through the deep
   darkness?
14 Thick clouds enwrap him, so that he does
   not see,
   and he walks on the dome of heaven.'
15 Will you keep to the old way
   that the wicked have trod?
16 They were snatched away before their
   time;
   their foundation was washed away by a
   flood.
17 They said to God, 'Leave us alone,'
   and 'What can the Almighty^a do to
   us?'^{c}
18 Yet he filled their houses with good
   things—
   but the plans of the wicked are
   repugnant to me.
19 The righteous see it and are glad;
   the innocent laugh them to scorn,
20 saying, 'Surely our adversaries are cut off,
   and what they left, the fire has
   consumed.'
21 "Agree with God,^{d} and be at peace;
   in this way good will come to you.

---

a Traditional rendering of Heb *Shaddai* b Gk Syr Tg Vg: Heb
were crushed c Gk Syr: Heb *them* d Heb *him*

---

out living in it. **20.24** As in Am 5.19, flight from imminent danger only results in death by another means.
Bronze arrow, lit. "bronze bow," which may function
here as synecdoche for bow and arrow. **21.5** The gesture indicates speechlessness or awe. **21.15** The sufferer in "The Babylonian Theodicy" complains that
"Those who do not seek the god go the way of prosperity, while those who pray to the goddess become

destitute and impoverished" and asks, "What has it
profited me that I have bowed down to my god?"
21.19 Both Jeremiah and Ezekiel challenge the sentiment, expressed in a proverb, that *children* suffer because of their parents' misventures (Ezek 18.2; Jer
31.29).
   22.15 Another vocalization of the Hebrew word rendered *old* yields "hidden," which would imply that the

22 Receive instruction from his mouth,
  and lay up his words in your heart.
23 If you return to the Almighty,[a] you will
      be restored,
  if you remove unrighteousness from
      your tents,
24 if you treat gold like dust,
  and gold of Ophir like the stones of the
      torrent-bed,
25 and if the Almighty[a] is your gold
  and your precious silver,
26 then you will delight yourself in the
      Almighty,[a]
  and lift up your face to God.
27 You will pray to him, and he will hear
      you,
  and you will pay your vows.
28 You will decide on a matter, and it will be
      established for you,
  and light will shine on your ways.
29 When others are humiliated, you say it is
      pride;
  for he saves the humble.
30 He will deliver even those who are guilty;
  they will escape because of the
      cleanness of your hands."[b]

Job Replies: My Complaint Is Bitter

23 Then Job answered:
  2 "Today also my complaint is bitter;[c]
  his[d] hand is heavy despite my
      groaning.
3 Oh, that I knew where I might find him,
  that I might come even to his dwelling!
4 I would lay my case before him,
  and fill my mouth with arguments.
5 I would learn what he would answer me,
  and understand what he would say to
      me.
6 Would he contend with me in the
      greatness of his power?
  No; but he would give heed to me.
7 There an upright person could reason
      with him,
  and I should be acquitted forever by
      my judge.

8 "If I go forward, he is not there;
  or backward, I cannot perceive him;
9 on the left he hides, and I cannot behold
      him;
  I turn[e] to the right, but I cannot see
      him.
10 But he knows the way that I take;
  when he has tested me, I shall come
      out like gold.
11 My foot has held fast to his steps;
  I have kept his way and have not
      turned aside.
12 I have not departed from the
      commandment of his lips;
  I have treasured in[f] my bosom the
      words of his mouth.
13 But he stands alone and who can
      dissuade him?
  What he desires, that he does.
14 For he will complete what he appoints for
      me;
  and many such things are in his mind.
15 Therefore I am terrified at his presence;
  when I consider, I am in dread of him.
16 God has made my heart faint;
  the Almighty[a] has terrified me;
17 If only I could vanish in darkness,
  and thick darkness would cover my
      face![g]

Job Complains of Violence on the Earth

24 "Why are times not kept by the
      Almighty,[a]
  and why do those who know him
      never see his days?
2 The wicked[h] remove landmarks;
  they seize flocks and pasture them.
3 They drive away the donkey of the
      orphan;
  they take the widow's ox for a pledge.
4 They thrust the needy off the road;

---

a Traditional rendering of Heb *Shaddai*   b Meaning of Heb
uncertain   c Syr Vg Tg: Heb *rebellious*   d Gk Syr: Heb *my*
e Syr Vg: Heb *he turns*   f Gk Vg: Heb *from*   g Or *But I am not
destroyed by the darkness; he has concealed the thick darkness from
me*   h Gk: Heb *they*

---

conduct is furtive rather than ancient. **22.21** *Agree with
God.* The Mesopotamian parallel "I Will Praise the Lord
of Wisdom" advises correct ritual and repentance as a
means to restoration. **22.24** Puns accentuate the expression here. The Hebrew word for "treasure," here translated *gold*, resembles that for *like* (or *among*) *the stones,*
and *dust* echoes *Ophir*. **22.27** Neglecting to keep one's

vows brought divine wrath, as the Canaanite hero Keret
discovered. Eccl 5.4 strongly encourages the payment of
vows, lest wrath break out with serious consequences.
23.8–12 Indicators for directions derive from a position
facing the rising sun. Forward is east, backward, west;
to the left, north, to the right, south. Ps 139.7–12 is
similarly comprehensive. **24.1** *Times* of judgment.

the poor of the earth all hide
    themselves.
5 Like wild asses in the desert
    they go out to their toil,
  scavenging in the wasteland
    food for their young.
6 They reap in a field not their own
    and they glean in the vineyard of the
    wicked.
7 They lie all night naked, without
    clothing,
  and have no covering in the cold.
8 They are wet with the rain of the
    mountains,
  and cling to the rock for want of
    shelter.

9 "There are those who snatch the orphan
    child from the breast,
  and take as a pledge the infant of the
    poor.
10 They go about naked, without clothing;
    though hungry, they carry the sheaves;
11 between their terraces*a* they press out oil;
    they tread the wine presses, but suffer
    thirst.
12 From the city the dying groan,
    and the throat of the wounded cries for
    help;
  yet God pays no attention to their
    prayer.

13 "There are those who rebel against the
    light,
  who are not acquainted with its ways,
  and do not stay in its paths.
14 The murderer rises at dusk
    to kill the poor and needy,
  and in the night is like a thief.
15 The eye of the adulterer also waits for the
    twilight,
  saying, 'No eye will see me';
  and he disguises his face.
16 In the dark they dig through houses;
    by day they shut themselves up;
  they do not know the light.
17 For deep darkness is morning to all of
    them;

for they are friends with the terrors of
    deep darkness.

18 "Swift are they on the face of the waters;
    their portion in the land is cursed;
  no treader turns toward their
    vineyards.
19 Drought and heat snatch away the snow
    waters;
  so does Sheol those who have sinned.
20 The womb forgets them;
    the worm finds them sweet;
  they are no longer remembered;
  so wickedness is broken like a tree.

21 "They harm*b* the childless woman,
    and do no good to the widow.
22 Yet God*c* prolongs the life of the mighty
    by his power;
  they rise up when they despair of life.
23 He gives them security, and they are
    supported;
  his eyes are upon their ways.
24 They are exalted a little while, and then
    are gone;
  they wither and fade like the mallow;*d*
  they are cut off like the heads of grain.
25 If it is not so, who will prove me a liar,
    and show that there is nothing in what
    I say?"

Bildad Speaks: How Can a Mortal Be Righteous Before God?

25 Then Bildad the Shuhite answered:
  2 "Dominion and fear are with God;*e*
  he makes peace in his high heaven.
3 Is there any number to his armies?
    Upon whom does his light not arise?
4 How then can a mortal be righteous
    before God?
  How can one born of woman be pure?
5 If even the moon is not bright
    and the stars are not pure in his sight,
6 how much less a mortal, who is a maggot,
    and a human being, who is a worm!"

---

a Meaning of Heb uncertain   *b* Gk Tg: Heb *feed on* or *associate with*   *c* Heb *he*   *d* Gk: Heb *like all others*   *e* Heb *him*

24.9 These accusations recall Am 2.6–8, which mentions garments seized in pledge from the *poor*. **24.11** In the presence of so much, the poor suffer want—a poignant image of the hopelessness of victims of greed. They can't even drink the *wine* they are making.

24.15 The futility of clandestine behavior is described in Prov 7.6–23. **25.1** Bildad's third speech is brief, and Zophar's is missing altogether. Have the friends run out of arguments, or has the text fallen into disarray? In favor of the latter alternative, Job's next speech contains

Job Replies: God's Majesty Is Unsearchable

26 Then Job answered:
²"How you have helped one who has
no power!
How you have assisted the arm that has
no strength!
³ How you have counseled one who has no
wisdom,
and given much good advice!
⁴ With whose help have you uttered words,
and whose spirit has come forth from
you?
⁵ The shades below tremble,
the waters and their inhabitants.
⁶ Sheol is naked before God,
and Abaddon has no covering.
⁷ He stretches out Zaphon*a* over the void,
and hangs the earth upon nothing.
⁸ He binds up the waters in his thick
clouds,
and the cloud is not torn open by
them.
⁹ He covers the face of the full moon,
and spreads over it his cloud.
¹⁰ He has described a circle on the face of
the waters,
at the boundary between light and
darkness.
¹¹ The pillars of heaven tremble,
and are astounded at his rebuke.
¹² By his power he stilled the Sea;
by his understanding he struck down
Rahab.
¹³ By his wind the heavens were made fair;
his hand pierced the fleeing serpent.
¹⁴ These are indeed but the outskirts of his
ways;
and how small a whisper do we hear of
him!
But the thunder of his power who can
understand?"

Job Maintains His Integrity

27 Job again took up his discourse and
said:
² "As God lives, who has taken away my
right,
and the Almighty,*b* who has made my
soul bitter,
³ as long as my breath is in me
and the spirit of God is in my nostrils,
⁴ my lips will not speak falsehood,
and my tongue will not utter deceit.
⁵ Far be it from me to say that you are
right;
until I die I will not put away my
integrity from me.
⁶ I hold fast my righteousness, and will not
let it go;
my heart does not reproach me for any
of my days.

⁷ "May my enemy be like the wicked,
and may my opponent be like the
unrighteous.
⁸ For what is the hope of the godless when
God cuts them off,
when God takes away their lives?
⁹ Will God hear their cry
when trouble comes upon them?
¹⁰ Will they take delight in the Almighty?*b*
Will they call upon God at all times?
¹¹ I will teach you concerning the hand of
God;
that which is with the Almighty*b* I will
not conceal.
¹² All of you have seen it yourselves;
why then have you become altogether
vain?

¹³ "This is the portion of the wicked with
God,

---

a Or *the North*   *b* Traditional rendering of Heb *Shaddai*

sentiments not altogether in line with his previous
thoughts. **26.6** This designation of Death as *Abaddon*
probably comes from the Hebrew verb for "perishing."
26.7 In Canaanite mythology *Zaphon* was a mountain
in the north on which the gods (esp. Baal) dwelt, like
Mount Olympus in Greek literature. **26.9** The Hebrew
has "throne" instead of *moon*. **26.13** *The fleeing serpent*
occurs in Isa 27.1 with reference to Leviathan.
27.1 The introductory formula here and in 29.1 differs from the previous ones; the earlier *Then Job* [Eli-
phaz, Bildad, Zophar] *answered* gives way to *Job again*

took up his discourse and said. The Hebrew word translated *discourse* is the usual one for "likeness," "proverb," or "analogy," sometimes translated "parable."
27.2 *As God lives.* Curiously, the oath is in the name of
the deity who has, in Job's view, demonstrated a lack of
justice. Similarly, Job hopes for justice from God, who
does not act justly. Contradictions may result from his
dire circumstances. Hence he thinks that God cannot
be found, yet that God attacks viciously from all quarters. **27.7–23** The speech, if from Job, must be fully
ironic, for he does not trust in divine justice. **27.14–**

and the heritage that oppressors
   receive from the Almighty:ᵃ

14 If their children are multiplied, it is for
   the sword;
   and their offspring have not enough to
   eat.

15 Those who survive them the pestilence
   buries,
   and their widows make no
   lamentation.

16 Though they heap up silver like dust,
   and pile up clothing like clay—

17 they may pile it up, but the just will wear it,
   and the innocent will divide the silver.

18 They build their houses like nests,
   like booths made by sentinels of the
   vineyard.

19 They go to bed with wealth, but will do
   so no more;
   they open their eyes, and it is gone.

20 Terrors overtake them like a flood;
   in the night a whirlwind carries them
   off.

21 The east wind lifts them up and they are
   gone;
   it sweeps them out of their place.

22 Itᵇ hurls at them without pity;
   they flee from itsᶜ power in headlong
   flight.

23 Itᵇ claps itsᶜ hands at them,
   and hisses at them from itsᶜ place.

Interlude: Where Wisdom Is Found

28 "Surely there is a mine for silver,
   and a place for gold to be refined.

2 Iron is taken out of the earth,
   and copper is smelted from ore.

3 Miners putᵈ an end to darkness,
   and search out to the farthest bound
   the ore in gloom and deep darkness.

4 They open shafts in a valley away from
   human habitation;
   they are forgotten by travelers,
   they sway suspended, remote from
   people.

5 As for the earth, out of it comes bread;
   but underneath it is turned up as by
   fire.

6 Its stones are the place of sapphires,ᵉ
   and its dust contains gold.

7 "That path no bird of prey knows,
   and the falcon's eye has not seen it.

8 The proud wild animals have not trodden
   it;
   the lion has not passed over it.

9 "They put their hand to the flinty rock,
   and overturn mountains by the roots.

10 They cut out channels in the rocks,
   and their eyes see every precious thing.

11 The sources of the rivers they probe;ᶠ
   hidden things they bring to light.

12 "But where shall wisdom be found?
   And where is the place of
   understanding?

13 Mortals do not know the way to it,ᵍ
   and it is not found in the land of the
   living.

14 The deep says, 'It is not in me,'
   and the sea says, 'It is not with me.'

15 It cannot be gotten for gold,
   and silver cannot be weighed out as its
   price.

16 It cannot be valued in the gold of Ophir,
   in precious onyx or sapphire.ᵉ

17 Gold and glass cannot equal it,
   nor can it be exchanged for jewels of
   fine gold.

18 No mention shall be made of coral or of
   crystal;
   the price of wisdom is above pearls.

19 The chrysolite of Ethiopiaʰ cannot
   compare with it,
   nor can it be valued in pure gold.

20 "Where then does wisdom come from?
   And where is the place of
   understanding?

21 It is hidden from the eyes of all living,
   and concealed from the birds of the air.

22 Abaddon and Death say,

---

a Traditional rendering of Heb *Shaddai* *b* Or *He* (that is God)
c Or *his* *d* Heb *He puts* *e* Or *lapis lazuli* *f* Gk Vg: Heb *bind*
g Gk: Heb *its price* *h* Or *Nubia*; Heb *Cush*

---

17 Echoes of a curse formula can be heard in these
verses. **27.15** The word *pestilence* is also the name of a
Canaanite deity. Job's reference to *widows* indicates a
society in which polygyny was practiced. **27.16–
17** Silver and gold are usually paired, but cf. Zech 9.3.

28.15–19 Four different words for *gold* occur in these
verses, and the exact classification of gems remains unclear. Translation of flora, fauna, and the like present
special difficulty. The fleeting nature of wealth is noted
in an Egyptian proverb also found in Prov 23.4–5.

'We have heard a rumor of it with our
ears.'

23 "God understands the way to it,
and he knows its place.
24 For he looks to the ends of the earth,
and sees everything under the heavens.
25 When he gave to the wind its weight,
and apportioned out the waters by
measure;
26 when he made a decree for the rain,
and a way for the thunderbolt;
27 then he saw it and declared it;
he established it, and searched it out.
28 And he said to humankind,
'Truly, the fear of the Lord, that is wisdom;
and to depart from evil is
understanding.' "

Job Finishes His Defense

29 Job again took up his discourse and
said:
2 "O that I were as in the months of old,
as in the days when God watched over
me;
3 when his lamp shone over my head,
and by his light I walked through
darkness;
4 when I was in my prime,
when the friendship of God was upon
my tent;
5 when the Almighty[a] was still with me,
when my children were around me;
6 when my steps were washed with milk,
and the rock poured out for me
streams of oil!
7 When I went out to the gate of the city,
when I took my seat in the square,
8 the young men saw me and withdrew,
and the aged rose up and stood;
9 the nobles refrained from talking,
and laid their hands on their mouths;
10 the voices of princes were hushed,
and their tongues stuck to the roof of
their mouths.
11 When the ear heard, it commended me,
and when the eye saw, it approved;
12 because I delivered the poor who cried,
and the orphan who had no helper.
13 The blessing of the wretched came upon
me,
and I caused the widow's heart to sing
for joy.
14 I put on righteousness, and it clothed me;

my justice was like a robe and a turban.
15 I was eyes to the blind,
and feet to the lame.
16 I was a father to the needy,
and I championed the cause of the
stranger.
17 I broke the fangs of the unrighteous,
and made them drop their prey from
their teeth.
18 Then I thought, 'I shall die in my nest,
and I shall multiply my days like the
phoenix;[b]
19 my roots spread out to the waters,
with the dew all night on my branches;
20 my glory was fresh with me,
and my bow ever new in my hand.'
21 "They listened to me, and waited,
and kept silence for my counsel.
22 After I spoke they did not speak again,
and my word dropped upon them like
dew.[c]
23 They waited for me as for the rain;
they opened their mouths as for the
spring rain.
24 I smiled on them when they had no
confidence;
and the light of my countenance they
did not extinguish.[d]
25 I chose their way, and sat as chief,
and I lived like a king among his troops,
like one who comforts mourners.

30 "But now they make sport of me,
those who are younger than I,
whose fathers I would have disdained
to set with the dogs of my flock.
2 What could I gain from the strength of
their hands?
All their vigor is gone.
3 Through want and hard hunger
they gnaw the dry and desolate
ground,
4 they pick mallow and the leaves of
bushes,
and to warm themselves the roots of
broom.
5 They are driven out from society;
people shout after them as after a thief.
6 In the gullies of wadis they must live,
in holes in the ground, and in the rocks.

---

a Traditional rendering of Heb *Shaddai*   b Or *like sand*
c Heb lacks *like dew*   d Meaning of Heb uncertain

7 Among the bushes they bray;
  under the nettles they huddle together.
8 A senseless, disreputable brood,
  they have been whipped out of the land.

9 "And now they mock me in song;
  I am a byword to them.
10 They abhor me, they keep aloof from me;
  they do not hesitate to spit at the sight
    of me.
11 Because God has loosed my bowstring
    and humbled me,
  they have cast off restraint in my
    presence.
12 On my right hand the rabble rise up;
  they send me sprawling,
  and build roads for my ruin.
13 They break up my path,
  they promote my calamity;
  no one restrains*a* them.
14 As through a wide breach they come;
  amid the crash they roll on.
15 Terrors are turned upon me;
  my honor is pursued as by the wind,
  and my prosperity has passed away like
    a cloud.

16 "And now my soul is poured out within
    me;
  days of affliction have taken hold of me.
17 The night racks my bones,
  and the pain that gnaws me takes no
    rest.
18 With violence he seizes my garment;*b*
  he grasps me by*c* the collar of my tunic.
19 He has cast me into the mire,
  and I have become like dust and ashes.
20 I cry to you and you do not answer me;
  I stand, and you merely look at me.

21 You have turned cruel to me;
  with the might of your hand you
    persecute me.
22 You lift me up on the wind, you make me
    ride on it,
  and you toss me about in the roar of
    the storm.
23 I know that you will bring me to death,
  and to the house appointed for all
    living.

24 "Surely one does not turn against the
    needy,*d*
  when in disaster they cry for help.*e*
25 Did I not weep for those whose day was
    hard?
  Was not my soul grieved for the poor?
26 But when I looked for good, evil came;
  and when I waited for light, darkness
    came.
27 My inward parts are in turmoil, and are
    never still;
  days of affliction come to meet me.
28 I go about in sunless gloom;
  I stand up in the assembly and cry for
    help.
29 I am a brother of jackals,
  and a companion of ostriches.
30 My skin turns black and falls from me,
  and my bones burn with heat.
31 My lyre is turned to mourning,
  and my pipe to the voice of those who
    weep.

31 "I have made a covenant with my eyes;
   how then could I look upon a virgin?

a Cn: Heb *helps*   *b* Gk: Heb *my garment is disfigured*
c Heb *like*   *d* Heb *ruin*   *e* Cn: Meaning of Heb uncertain

---

28.23–24 Emphasis falls on *God* and *he.* **28.28** *Lord,* the only use of Adonai in the book. In Jewish tradition one reads Adonai wherever the Tetragrammaton, YHWH (Yahweh), appears. The Hebrew word *'adonay* refers to a human master but also to the Lord.

29.2–4 The Hebrew alludes to autumn *days,* which, contrary to Western notions, refer to vigor. In the Near East, summer's drought gives way to new growth as the rains during autumn and winter descend on a parched earth. The fall is therefore an appropriate season for the New Year. **29.7** Judicial decisions took place at the city *gate;* here Job represents himself as a city dweller rather than the desert sheik of the prose. **29.12–13** Wisdom literature champions the cause of these three groups: *widows, orphans,* and the *poor.* Kings were charged with their welfare, and neglect of these subjects was cause

for abdication of the throne, according to the Canaanite "Tale of Aqhat." **29.18** In Greek mythology the *phoenix* rises from its own ashes. The Hebrew text has "sand," which makes sense in this context, for the Abraham tradition uses this image to indicate a countless host of descendants. The allusion to a *nest* invites, but does not demand, thought of a bird. **29.20** The warrior's *bow* has sexual overtones in the Canaanite Aqhat tale, where the goddess Anat desires a bow in the possession of the mighty warrior. **30.1–15** Job's disdain for the poor in these verses conflicts with 30.25 and his attitude expressed in 31.16–23.

31.1–40 This chapter has ten abbreviated oaths and three full ones. **31.1** This allusion to a *virgin* probably pertains to a specific one, the virgin goddess Anat of Canaanite mythology. Idolatry, not lust, is the offense.

2 What would be my portion from God
   above,
      and my heritage from the Almighty[a]
      on high?
3 Does not calamity befall the unrighteous,
      and disaster the workers of iniquity?
4 Does he not see my ways,
      and number all my steps?

5 "If I have walked with falsehood,
      and my foot has hurried to deceit—
6 let me be weighed in a just balance,
      and let God know my integrity!—
7 if my step has turned aside from the way,
      and my heart has followed my eyes,
      and if any spot has clung to my
      hands;
8 then let me sow, and another eat;
      and let what grows for me be rooted
      out.

9 "If my heart has been enticed by a
   woman,
      and I have lain in wait at my neighbor's
      door;
10 then let my wife grind for another,
      and let other men kneel over her.
11 For that would be a heinous crime;
      that would be a criminal offense;
12 for that would be a fire consuming down
      to Abaddon,
      and it would burn to the root all my
      harvest.

13 "If I have rejected the cause of my male
      or female slaves,
      when they brought a complaint against
      me;
14 what then shall I do when God rises up?
      When he makes inquiry, what shall I
      answer him?
15 Did not he who made me in the womb
      make them?
      And did not one fashion us in the
      womb?

16 "If I have withheld anything that the poor
      desired,
      or have caused the eyes of the widow
      to fail,
17 or have eaten my morsel alone,
      and the orphan has not eaten from it—
18 for from my youth I reared the orphan[b]
      like a father,
      and from my mother's womb I guided
      the widow[c]—
19 if I have seen anyone perish for lack of
      clothing,
      or a poor person without covering,
20 whose loins have not blessed me,
      and who was not warmed with the
      fleece of my sheep;
21 if I have raised my hand against the
      orphan,
      because I saw I had supporters at the
      gate;
22 then let my shoulder blade fall from my
      shoulder,
      and let my arm be broken from its
      socket.
23 For I was in terror of calamity from
      God,
      and I could not have faced his majesty.

24 "If I have made gold my trust,
      or called fine gold my confidence;
25 if I have rejoiced because my wealth was
      great,
      or because my hand had gotten much;
26 if I have looked at the sun[d] when it
      shone,
      or the moon moving in splendor,
27 and my heart has been secretly enticed,
      and my mouth has kissed my hand;
28 this also would be an iniquity to be
      punished by the judges,
      for I should have been false to God
      above.

---

a Traditional rendering of Heb *Shaddai*   b Heb *him*
c Heb *her*   d Heb *the light*

31.5–40 Similar confessions of innocence are found in Egyptian liturgical texts. Unlike customary curse formulas, Job's oath of innocence mentions the consequences of sinful action, thus abandoning the psychological effect of an unstated curse. **31.10** That the *wife* suffers for her husband's crime accords with the ancient proprietary notion of marriage. In the *Testament of Job* (a work of the Second Temple period; see Introduction) his wife, named Sitis, works as a water carrier and even sells her hair to Satan to buy bread for herself and her ailing husband. The verb *grind* has sexual overtones (cf. the Samson narrative in rabbinic interpretation), as the parallel *kneel over* shows. **31.15** Biblical proverbs affirm this belief that rich and poor have a single maker (cf. Prov 22.2; 29.13). **31.27** *My mouth has kissed my hand*, lit. "my hand has kissed my mouth," may allude to the Babylonian expression for a liturgical gesture of obeisance in which the hand

29 "If I have rejoiced at the ruin of those
        who hated me,
    or exulted when evil overtook them—
30 I have not let my mouth sin
        by asking for their lives with a curse—
31 if those of my tent ever said,
    'O that we might be sated with his
        flesh!'*ª—
32 the stranger has not lodged in the street;
    I have opened my doors to the
        traveler—
33 if I have concealed my transgressions as
        others do,*ᵇ
    by hiding my iniquity in my bosom,
34 because I stood in great fear of the
        multitude,
    and the contempt of families terrified
        me,
    so that I kept silence, and did not go
        out of doors—
35 O that I had one to hear me!
    (Here is my signature! Let the
        Almightyᶜ answer me!)
    O that I had the indictment written by
        my adversary!
36 Surely I would carry it on my shoulder;
    I would bind it on me like a crown;
37 I would give him an account of all my
        steps;
    like a prince I would approach him.

38 "If my land has cried out against me,
    and its furrows have wept together;
39 if I have eaten its yield without payment,
    and caused the death of its owners;
40 let thorns grow instead of wheat,
    and foul weeds instead of barley."

The words of Job are ended.

Elihu Rebukes Job's Friends

32 So these three men ceased to answer
    Job, because he was righteous in his
own eyes. 2 Then Elihu son of Barachel the Buzite, of the family of Ram, became angry. He
was angry at Job because he justified himself
rather than God; 3 he was angry also at Job's
three friends because they had found no answer, though they had declared Job to be in the
wrong.*ᵈ 4 Now Elihu had waited to speak to
Job, because they were older than he. 5 But
when Elihu saw that there was no answer in
the mouths of these three men, he became
angry.

6 Elihu son of Barachel the Buzite answered:
    "I am young in years,
        and you are aged;
    therefore I was timid and afraid
        to declare my opinion to you.
7 I said, 'Let days speak,
        and many years teach wisdom.'
8 But truly it is the spirit in a mortal,
        the breath of the Almighty,ᶜ that makes
        for understanding.
9 It is not the oldᵉ that are wise,
        nor the aged that understand what is
        right.
10 Therefore I say, 'Listen to me;
        let me also declare my opinion.'

11 "See, I waited for your words,
        I listened for your wise sayings,
        while you searched out what to say.
12 I gave you my attention,
        but there was in fact no one that
        confuted Job,
        no one among you that answered his
        words.
13 Yet do not say, 'We have found wisdom;
        God may vanquish him, not a human.'
14 He has not directed his words against me,
        and I will not answer him with your
        speeches.

15 "They are dismayed, they answer no more;
        they have not a word to say.

---

a Meaning of Heb uncertain   *b* Or *as Adam did*
c Traditional rendering of Heb *Shaddai*   *d* Another ancient
tradition reads *answer, and had put God in the wrong*   *e* Gk Syr
Vg: Heb *many*

---

touches the nose. **31.31** *Sated with his flesh,* perhaps an
expression for homosexual abuse. **31.32** Hospitality to
the resident alien was an important obligation in the
ancient world. **31.35** *Signature,* lit. *taw,* the final letter
in the Hebrew alphabet, signifying an identifying
mark like our "X." Literacy was not extensive in the ancient world. **31.36** The prophet Habakkuk speaks in
2.2 of displaying the anticipated vision in a way that it
can be read rapidly, and Isa 22.22 refers to a key worn
on Eliakim's shoulder as a sign of authority. **31.40** The
Hebrew word for *ended* is cognate with that for "integrity." Despite this claim that Job will speak no more,
he does so twice, in 40.3–5 and 42.1–6.
    32.2 Elihu has impeccable credentials; according to
Gen 22.21 "Buz" was a son of Abraham's brother Nahor.
Furthermore, in Hebrew the name *Barachel* means "El
blesses" or "bless El," and *Elihu* means "He is my God"
(cf. Isa 41.4, "I am He"). **32.14** Elihu actually quotes

16 And am I to wait, because they do not
      speak,
   because they stand there, and answer
      no more?
17 I also will give my answer;
   I also will declare my opinion.
18 For I am full of words;
   the spirit within me constrains me.
19 My heart is indeed like wine that has no
      vent;
   like new wineskins, it is ready to burst.
20 I must speak, so that I may find relief;
   I must open my lips and answer.
21 I will not show partiality to any person
   or use flattery toward anyone.
22 For I do not know how to flatter—
   or my Maker would soon put an end to
      me!

Elihu Rebukes Job

33 "But now, hear my speech, O Job,
      and listen to all my words.
2 See, I open my mouth;
   the tongue in my mouth speaks.
3 My words declare the uprightness of my
      heart,
   and what my lips know they speak
      sincerely.
4 The spirit of God has made me,
   and the breath of the Almighty^a gives
      me life.
5 Answer me, if you can;
   set your words in order before me; take
      your stand.
6 See, before God I am as you are;
   I too was formed from a piece of clay.
7 No fear of me need terrify you;
   my pressure will not be heavy on you.

8 "Surely, you have spoken in my hearing,
   and I have heard the sound of your
      words.
9 You say, 'I am clean, without
      transgression;
   I am pure, and there is no iniquity in
      me.
10 Look, he finds occasions against me,
   he counts me as his enemy;
11 he puts my feet in the stocks,
   and watches all my paths.'

12 "But in this you are not right. I will
      answer you:
   God is greater than any mortal.

13 Why do you contend against him,
   saying, 'He will answer none of my^b
      words'?
14 For God speaks in one way,
   and in two, though people do not
      perceive it.
15 In a dream, in a vision of the night,
   when deep sleep falls on mortals,
   while they slumber on their beds,
16 then he opens their ears,
   and terrifies them with warnings,
17 that he may turn them aside from their
      deeds,
   and keep them from pride,
18 to spare their souls from the Pit,
   their lives from traversing the River.
19 They are also chastened with pain upon
      their beds,
   and with continual strife in their
      bones,
20 so that their lives loathe bread,
   and their appetites dainty food.
21 Their flesh is so wasted away that it
      cannot be seen;
   and their bones, once invisible, now
      stick out.
22 Their souls draw near the Pit,
   and their lives to those who bring
      death.
23 Then, if there should be for one of them
      an angel,
   a mediator, one of a thousand,
   one who declares a person upright,
24 and he is gracious to that person, and says,
   'Deliver him from going down into the
      Pit;
   I have found a ransom;
25 let his flesh become fresh with youth;
   let him return to the days of his
      youthful vigor';
26 then he prays to God, and is accepted by
      him,
   he comes into his presence with joy,
   and God^c repays him for his
      righteousness.
27   That person sings to others and says,
   'I sinned, and perverted what was right,
   and it was not paid back to me.
28 He has redeemed my soul from going
      down to the Pit,
   and my life shall see the light.'

---

a Traditional rendering of Heb *Shaddai* b Compare Gk: Heb
his c Heb *he*

29 "God indeed does all these things,
    twice, three times, with mortals,
30 to bring back their souls from the Pit,
    so that they may see the light of life.[a]
31 Pay heed, Job, listen to me;
    be silent, and I will speak.
32 If you have anything to say, answer me;
    speak, for I desire to justify you.
33 If not, listen to me;
    be silent, and I will teach you wisdom."

Elihu Proclaims God's Justice

34 Then Elihu continued and said:
   2 "Hear my words, you wise men,
    and give ear to me, you who know;
3 for the ear tests words
    as the palate tastes food.
4 Let us choose what is right;
    let us determine among ourselves what
        is good.
5 For Job has said, 'I am innocent,
    and God has taken away my right;
6 in spite of being right I am counted a liar;
    my wound is incurable, though I am
        without transgression.'
7 Who is there like Job,
    who drinks up scoffing like water,
8 who goes in company with evildoers
    and walks with the wicked?
9 For he has said, 'It profits one nothing
    to take delight in God.'

10 "Therefore, hear me, you who have sense,
    far be it from God that he should do
        wickedness,
    and from the Almighty[b] that he should
        do wrong.
11 For according to their deeds he will repay
        them,
    and according to their ways he will
        make it befall them.
12 Of a truth, God will not do wickedly,
    and the Almighty[b] will not pervert
        justice.
13 Who gave him charge over the earth
    and who laid on him[c] the whole world?
14 If he should take back his spirit[d] to himself,
    and gather to himself his breath,

15 all flesh would perish together,
    and all mortals return to dust.

16 "If you have understanding, hear this;
    listen to what I say.
17 Shall one who hates justice govern?
    Will you condemn one who is
        righteous and mighty,
18 who says to a king, 'You scoundrel!'
    and to princes, 'You wicked men!';
19 who shows no partiality to nobles,
    nor regards the rich more than the
        poor,
    for they are all the work of his hands?
20 In a moment they die;
    at midnight the people are shaken and
        pass away,
    and the mighty are taken away by no
        human hand.

21 "For his eyes are upon the ways of
        mortals,
    and he sees all their steps.
22 There is no gloom or deep darkness
    where evildoers may hide themselves.
23 For he has not appointed a time[e] for
        anyone
    to go before God in judgment.
24 He shatters the mighty without
        investigation,
    and sets others in their place.
25 Thus, knowing their works,
    he overturns them in the night, and
        they are crushed.
26 He strikes them for their wickedness
    while others look on,
27 because they turned aside from following
        him,
    and had no regard for any of his ways,
28 so that they caused the cry of the poor to
        come to him,
    and he heard the cry of the afflicted—
29 When he is quiet, who can condemn?
    When he hides his face, who can
        behold him,

---

a Syr: Heb *to be lighted with the light of life* *b* Traditional rendering of Heb *Shaddai* *c* Heb lacks *on him* *d* Heb *his heart his spirit* *e* Cn: Heb *yet*

---

earlier *speeches.* **33.1** Only Elihu addresses *Job* by name. **33.23** Do these images of a kind intercessor suggest a patron deity who pleaded one's case before the great God? An intercessory angel appears in *1 Enoch* 9.3; 15.2 and the *Testaments of the Twelve Patriarchs,* e.g., *T. Levi* 3.5–

10. **34.1–9** The word *mishpat* (*right*) occurs here three times. **34.2** Elihu uses a teacher's opening summons to get listeners to pay attention. **34.11** Despite Job's effective refutation of the retributive scheme, it persists in Elihu's thought. **34.14–15** An echo of Gen 2.7; 3.19.

whether it be a nation or an
  individual?—

30 so that the godless should not reign,
  or those who ensnare the people.

31 "For has anyone said to God,
  'I have endured punishment; I will not
    offend any more;

32 teach me what I do not see;
  if I have done iniquity, I will do it no
    more'?

33 Will he then pay back to suit you,
  because you reject it?
  For you must choose, and not I;
  therefore declare what you know.ᵃ

34 Those who have sense will say to me,
  and the wise who hear me will say,

35 'Job speaks without knowledge,
  his words are without insight.'

36 Would that Job were tried to the limit,
  because his answers are those of the
    wicked.

37 For he adds rebellion to his sin;
  he claps his hands among us,
  and multiplies his words against
    God."

Elihu Condemns Self-Righteousness

35 Elihu continued and said:
  2 "Do you think this to be just?
  You say, 'I am in the right before God.'

3 If you ask, 'What advantage have I?
  How am I better off than if I had
    sinned?'

4 I will answer you
  and your friends with you.

5 Look at the heavens and see;
  observe the clouds, which are higher
    than you.

6 If you have sinned, what do you
    accomplish against him?
  And if your transgressions are
    multiplied, what do you do to
    him?

7 If you are righteous, what do you give to
    him;
  or what does he receive from your
    hand?

8 Your wickedness affects others like you,
  and your righteousness, other human
    beings.

9 "Because of the multitude of oppressions
    people cry out;

they call for help because of the arm of
  the mighty.

10 But no one says, 'Where is God my
    Maker,
  who gives strength in the night,

11 who teaches us more than the animals of
    the earth,
  and makes us wiser than the birds of
    the air?'

12 There they cry out, but he does not answer,
  because of the pride of evildoers.

13 Surely God does not hear an empty cry,
  nor does the Almightyᵇ regard it.

14 How much less when you say that you do
    not see him,
  that the case is before him, and you are
    waiting for him!

15 And now, because his anger does not
    punish,
  and he does not greatly heed
    transgression,ᶜ

16 Job opens his mouth in empty talk,
  he multiplies words without
    knowledge."

Elihu Exalts God's Goodness

36 Elihu continued and said:
  2 "Bear with me a little, and I will show
    you,
  for I have yet something to say on
    God's behalf.

3 I will bring my knowledge from far away,
  and ascribe righteousness to my
    Maker.

4 For truly my words are not false;
  one who is perfect in knowledge is
    with you.

5 "Surely God is mighty and does not
    despise any;
  he is mighty in strength of
    understanding.

6 He does not keep the wicked alive,
  but gives the afflicted their right.

7 He does not withdraw his eyes from the
    righteous,
  but with kings on the throne
  he sets them forever, and they are
    exalted.

8 And if they are bound in fetters
  and caught in the cords of affliction,

ᵃ Meaning of Heb of verses 29-33 uncertain ᵇ Traditional
rendering of Heb *Shaddai* ᶜ Theodotion Symmachus Compare
Vg: Meaning of Heb uncertain

9 then he declares to them their work
    and their transgressions, that they are
      behaving arrogantly.
10 He opens their ears to instruction,
    and commands that they return from
      iniquity.
11 If they listen, and serve him,
    they complete their days in prosperity,
    and their years in pleasantness.
12 But if they do not listen, they shall perish
      by the sword,
    and die without knowledge.

13 "The godless in heart cherish anger;
    they do not cry for help when he binds
      them.
14 They die in their youth,
    and their life ends in shame.*a*
15 He delivers the afflicted by their
      affliction,
    and opens their ear by adversity.
16 He also allured you out of distress
    into a broad place where there was no
      constraint,
    and what was set on your table was full
      of fatness.

17 "But you are obsessed with the case of the
      wicked;
    judgment and justice seize you.
18 Beware that wrath does not entice you
      into scoffing,
    and do not let the greatness of the
      ransom turn you aside.
19 Will your cry avail to keep you from
      distress,
    or will all the force of your strength?
20 Do not long for the night,
    when peoples are cut off in their place.
21 Beware! Do not turn to iniquity;
    because of that you have been tried by
      affliction.
22 See, God is exalted in his power;
    who is a teacher like him?
23 Who has prescribed for him his way,
    or who can say, 'You have done wrong'?

Elihu Proclaims God's Majesty

24 "Remember to extol his work,
    of which mortals have sung.

25 All people have looked on it;
    everyone watches it from far away.
26 Surely God is great, and we do not know
      him;
    the number of his years is
      unsearchable.
27 For he draws up the drops of water;
    he distills*b* his mist in rain,
28 which the skies pour down
    and drop upon mortals abundantly.
29 Can anyone understand the spreading of
      the clouds,
    the thunderings of his pavilion?
30 See, he scatters his lightning around him
    and covers the roots of the sea.
31 For by these he governs peoples;
    he gives food in abundance.
32 He covers his hands with the lightning,
    and commands it to strike the mark.
33 Its crashing*c* tells about him;
    he is jealous*c* with anger against
      iniquity.

37 "At this also my heart trembles,
    and leaps out of its place.
2 Listen, listen to the thunder of his voice
    and the rumbling that comes from his
      mouth.
3 Under the whole heaven he lets it loose,
    and his lightning to the corners of the
      earth.
4 After it his voice roars;
    he thunders with his majestic voice
    and he does not restrain the
      lightnings*d* when his voice is
      heard.
5 God thunders wondrously with his voice;
    he does great things that we cannot
      comprehend.
6 For to the snow he says, 'Fall on the
      earth';
    and the shower of rain, his heavy
      shower of rain,
7 serves as a sign on everyone's hand,
    so that all whom he has made may
      know it.*e*
8 Then the animals go into their lairs

---

a Heb *ends among the temple prostitutes*   *b* Cn: Heb *they distill*
c Meaning of Heb uncertain   *d* Heb *them*   *e* Meaning of Heb
of verse 7 uncertain

35.7–8 The argument resembles that of the friends, who exalted God at human expense. **35.16** God later accuses Job of obscuring counsel by *words without* *knowledge* (38.2). **36.4** Apparently Elihu does not subscribe to the idea of limited access to wisdom expressed in 28.21, 23–28, for he claims to possess what

and remain in their dens.

9 From its chamber comes the whirlwind,
   and cold from the scattering winds.
10 By the breath of God ice is given,
   and the broad waters are frozen fast.
11 He loads the thick cloud with moisture;
   the clouds scatter his lightning.
12 They turn round and round by his
      guidance,
   to accomplish all that he commands
      them
   on the face of the habitable world.
13 Whether for correction, or for his land,
   or for love, he causes it to happen.

14 "Hear this, O Job;
   stop and consider the wondrous works
      of God.
15 Do you know how God lays his
      command upon them,
   and causes the lightning of his cloud to
      shine?
16 Do you know the balancings of the
      clouds,
   the wondrous works of the one whose
      knowledge is perfect,
17 you whose garments are hot
   when the earth is still because of the
      south wind?
18 Can you, like him, spread out the skies,
   hard as a molten mirror?
19 Teach us what we shall say to him;
   we cannot draw up our case because of
      darkness.
20 Should he be told that I want to speak?
   Did anyone ever wish to be swallowed
      up?
21 Now, no one can look on the light
   when it is bright in the skies,
   when the wind has passed and cleared
      them.
22 Out of the north comes golden splendor;
   around God is awesome majesty.
23 The Almighty[a]—we cannot find him;
   he is great in power and justice,
   and abundant righteousness he will
      not violate.
24 Therefore mortals fear him;
   he does not regard any who are wise in
      their own conceit."

The LORD Answers Job

38 Then the LORD answered Job out of
   the whirlwind:

2 "Who is this that darkens counsel by
      words without knowledge?
3 Gird up your loins like a man,
   I will question you, and you shall
      declare to me.

4 "Where were you when I laid the
      foundation of the earth?
   Tell me, if you have understanding.
5 Who determined its measurements—
      surely you know!
   Or who stretched the line upon it?
6 On what were its bases sunk,
   or who laid its cornerstone
7 when the morning stars sang together
   and all the heavenly beings[b] shouted
      for joy?

8 "Or who shut in the sea with doors
   when it burst out from the womb?—
9 when I made the clouds its garment,
   and thick darkness its swaddling band,
10 and prescribed bounds for it,
   and set bars and doors,
11 and said, 'Thus far shall you come, and
      no farther,
   and here shall your proud waves be
      stopped'?

12 "Have you commanded the morning
      since your days began,
   and caused the dawn to know its place,
13 so that it might take hold of the skirts of
      the earth,
   and the wicked be shaken out of it?
14 It is changed like clay under the seal,
   and it is dyed[c] like a garment.
15 Light is withheld from the wicked,
   and their uplifted arm is broken.

16 "Have you entered into the springs of the
      sea,
   or walked in the recesses of the deep?
17 Have the gates of death been revealed to
      you,
   or have you seen the gates of deep
      darkness?
18 Have you comprehended the expanse of
      the earth?
   Declare, if you know all this.

---

a Traditional rendering of Heb Shaddai   b Heb sons of God
c Cn: Heb and they stand forth

19 "Where is the way to the dwelling of
          light,
      and where is the place of darkness,
20 that you may take it to its territory
      and that you may discern the paths to
          its home?
21 Surely you know, for you were born then,
      and the number of your days is great!

22 "Have you entered the storehouses of the
          snow,
      or have you seen the storehouses of the
          hail,
23 which I have reserved for the time of
          trouble,
      for the day of battle and war?
24 What is the way to the place where the
          light is distributed,
      or where the east wind is scattered
          upon the earth?

25 "Who has cut a channel for the torrents
          of rain,
      and a way for the thunderbolt,
26 to bring rain on a land where no one lives,
      on the desert, which is empty of
          human life,
27 to satisfy the waste and desolate land,
      and to make the ground put forth
          grass?

28 "Has the rain a father,
      or who has begotten the drops of dew?
29 From whose womb did the ice come forth,
      and who has given birth to the
          hoarfrost of heaven?
30 The waters become hard like stone,
      and the face of the deep is frozen.

31 "Can you bind the chains of the Pleiades,
      or loose the cords of Orion?
32 Can you lead forth the Mazzaroth in their
          season,

or can you guide the Bear with its
          children?
33 Do you know the ordinances of the
          heavens?
      Can you establish their rule on the
          earth?

34 "Can you lift up your voice to the clouds,
      so that a flood of waters may cover
          you?
35 Can you send forth lightnings, so that
          they may go
      and say to you, 'Here we are'?
36 Who has put wisdom in the inward
          parts,[a]
      or given understanding to the mind?[a]
37 Who has the wisdom to number the
          clouds?
      Or who can tilt the waterskins of the
          heavens,
38 when the dust runs into a mass
      and the clods cling together?

39 "Can you hunt the prey for the lion,
      or satisfy the appetite of the young lions,
40 when they crouch in their dens,
      or lie in wait in their covert?
41 Who provides for the raven its prey,
      when its young ones cry to God,
      and wander about for lack of food?

39 "Do you know when the mountain
          goats give birth?
      Do you observe the calving of the deer?
2 Can you number the months that they
          fulfill,
      and do you know the time when they
          give birth,
3 when they crouch to give birth to their
          offspring,
      and are delivered of their young?

_____
a Meaning of Heb uncertain

is there restricted to God. **37.18** The Hebrew word for
skies, or "firmament," implied an object that was
beaten out like metal, hence *hard.* Windows allowed
rain to fall. The Baal cycle has a dispute over placing a
window in his temple.
    38.1 The Hebrew words for the "great wind" ac-
companying the theophany to Elijah in 1 Kings 19.11
occur in 1.19 but not here, where *whirlwind,* or "tempest," is used as in 40.6. **38.3** God's choice of the word
man, or "hero," recalls Job's lament in 3.3, which uses
this strange word with reference to an infant (cf.

40.7). **38.5** In a context dealing with creation mythology Agur, a sage, uses this assurance of knowledge,
surely you know (Prov 30.4). **38.7** In Prov 8.30–31
personified Wisdom rejoices over the creative work.
38.8–11 Tiamat of Mesopotamian tradition was
slain in battle, whereas the chaos monster in this text
survives but moves about under severe constraints
imposed by the victorious deity. Tiamat's body, split
in half like a shellfish, formed the newly constructed
universe. **38.21** The irony here and the near sarcasm
in the following questions resemble the style of

4 Their young ones become strong, they
        grow up in the open;
    they go forth, and do not return to
        them.

5 "Who has let the wild ass go free?
    Who has loosed the bonds of the swift
        ass,
6 to which I have given the steppe for its
        home,
    the salt land for its dwelling place?
7 It scorns the tumult of the city;
    it does not hear the shouts of the
        driver.
8 It ranges the mountains as its pasture,
    and it searches after every green thing.

9 "Is the wild ox willing to serve you?
    Will it spend the night at your crib?
10 Can you tie it in the furrow with ropes,
    or will it harrow the valleys after you?
11 Will you depend on it because its
        strength is great,
    and will you hand over your labor to
        it?
12 Do you have faith in it that it will return,
    and bring your grain to your threshing
        floor?[a]

13 "The ostrich's wings flap wildly,
    though its pinions lack plumage.[b]
14 For it leaves its eggs to the earth,
    and lets them be warmed on the
        ground,
15 forgetting that a foot may crush them,
    and that a wild animal may trample
        them.
16 It deals cruelly with its young, as if they
        were not its own;
    though its labor should be in vain, yet
        it has no fear;
17 because God has made it forget wisdom,
    and given it no share in
        understanding.
18 When it spreads its plumes aloft,[b]
    it laughs at the horse and its rider.

19 "Do you give the horse its might?
    Do you clothe its neck with mane?

20 Do you make it leap like the locust?
    Its majestic snorting is terrible.
21 It paws[c] violently, exults mightily;
    it goes out to meet the weapons.
22 It laughs at fear, and is not dismayed;
    it does not turn back from the sword.
23 Upon it rattle the quiver,
    the flashing spear, and the javelin.
24 With fierceness and rage it swallows the
        ground;
    it cannot stand still at the sound of the
        trumpet.
25 When the trumpet sounds, it says 'Aha!'
    From a distance it smells the battle,
    the thunder of the captains, and the
        shouting.

26 "Is it by your wisdom that the hawk
        soars,
    and spreads its wings toward the
        south?
27 Is it at your command that the eagle
        mounts up
    and makes its nest on high?
28 It lives on the rock and makes its home
    in the fastness of the rocky crag.
29 From there it spies the prey;
    its eyes see it from far away.
30 Its young ones suck up blood;
    and where the slain are, there it is."

40 And the LORD said to Job:
    2 "Shall a faultfinder contend with the
        Almighty?[d]
    Anyone who argues with God must
        respond."

Job's Response to God

3 Then Job answered the LORD:
4 "See, I am of small account; what shall I
        answer you?
    I lay my hand on my mouth.
5 I have spoken once, and I will not
        answer;
    twice, but will proceed no further."

---

a Heb your grain and your threshing floor   b Meaning of Heb
uncertain   c Gk Syr Vg: Heb they dig   d Traditional rendering
of Heb Shaddai

---

school questions in Egyptian literature. **39.13** Unlike
the others, this section on the ostrich does not begin
with a rhetorical question. **39.16–17** This folk tradition about ostriches is not factual. **40.4–5** Against
the background of cosmic wonder, Job recognizes divine silence about human beings and perceives the
futility of greatness, even moral excellence. He therefore vows to abandon his challenge of God's conduct.

God's Challenge to Job

6 Then the LORD answered Job out of the
whirlwind:
7   "Gird up your loins like a man;
        I will question you, and you declare to
            me.
8   Will you even put me in the wrong?
        Will you condemn me that you may be
            justified?
9   Have you an arm like God,
        and can you thunder with a voice like
            his?

10 "Deck yourself with majesty and dignity;
        clothe yourself with glory and
            splendor.
11 Pour out the overflowings of your anger,
        and look on all who are proud, and
            abase them.
12 Look on all who are proud, and bring
            them low;
        tread down the wicked where they
            stand.
13 Hide them all in the dust together;
        · bind their faces in the world below.*a*
14 Then I will also acknowledge to you
        that your own right hand can give you
            victory.

15 "Look at Behemoth,
        which I made just as I made you;
        it eats grass like an ox.
16 Its strength is in its loins,
        and its power in the muscles of its
            belly.
17 It makes its tail stiff like a cedar;
        the sinews of its thighs are knit
            together.
18 Its bones are tubes of bronze,
        its limbs like bars of iron.

19 "It is the first of the great acts of God—
        only its Maker can approach it with the
            sword.
20 For the mountains yield food for it

where all the wild animals play.
21 Under the lotus plants it lies,
        in the covert of the reeds and in the
            marsh.
22 The lotus trees cover it for shade;
        the willows of the wadi surround it.
23 Even if the river is turbulent, it is not
            frightened;
        it is confident though Jordan rushes
            against its mouth.
24 Can one take it with hooks*b*
        or pierce its nose with a snare?

41 *c*"Can you draw out Leviathan*d* with a
        fishhook,
        or press down its tongue with a cord?
2   Can you put a rope in its nose,
        or pierce its jaw with a hook?
3   Will it make many supplications to you?
        Will it speak soft words to you?
4   Will it make a covenant with you
        to be taken as your servant forever?
5   Will you play with it as with a bird,
        or will you put it on leash for your
            girls?
6   Will traders bargain over it?
        Will they divide it up among the
            merchants?
7   Can you fill its skin with harpoons,
        or its head with fishing spears?
8   Lay hands on it;
        think of the battle; you will not do it
            again!
9   *e*Any hope of capturing it*f* will be
            disappointed;
        were not even the gods*g* overwhelmed
            at the sight of it?
10 No one is so fierce as to dare to stir it up.
        Who can stand before it?*h*
11 Who can confront it*h* and be safe?*i*
        —under the whole heaven, who?*j*

---

a Heb *the hidden place*   *b* Cn: Heb *in his eyes*   *c* Ch 40.25 in
Heb   *d* Or *the crocodile*   *e* Ch 41.1 in Heb   *f* Heb *of it*
g Cn Compare Symmachus Syr: Heb *one is*   *h* Heb *me*
i Gk: Heb *that I shall repay*   *j* Heb *to me*

40.6 A second divine speech is introduced, although
Job has already conceded defeat. **40.15** *Behemoth* is
often identified as a hippopotamus, Leviathan as a
crocodile. Egyptian iconography of the god Horus
fighting these two creatures, who represent the forces
of chaos, is usually thought to confirm this reading of
the biblical text. Fantasy plays a role, however, and
these animals are largely figments of the imagination.

If *tail* (v. 17) is not a euphemism for the sexual organ,
Behemoth seems in this respect to resemble a crocodile. **40.19** *Acts*, lit. "ways." According to the creation
hymn in Prov 8.22, wisdom was the *first* of God's acts.
A related root in Ugaritic seems to connote "sovereignty" and thus "powerful deeds" (cf. Prov 31.3).
41.1 Considerable speculation about the ultimate fate
of *Leviathan* occupied the minds of later apocalyptic

12 "I will not keep silence concerning its
limbs,
or its mighty strength, or its splendid
frame.
13 Who can strip off its outer garment?
Who can penetrate its double coat of
mail?*a*
14 Who can open the doors of its face?
There is terror all around its teeth.
15 Its back*b* is made of shields in rows,
shut up closely as with a seal.
16 One is so near to another
that no air can come between them.
17 They are joined one to another;
they clasp each other and cannot be
separated.
18 Its sneezes flash forth light,
and its eyes are like the eyelids of the
dawn.
19 From its mouth go flaming torches;
sparks of fire leap out.
20 Out of its nostrils comes smoke,
as from a boiling pot and burning
rushes.
21 Its breath kindles coals,
and a flame comes out of its mouth.
22 In its neck abides strength,
and terror dances before it.
23 The folds of its flesh cling together;
it is firmly cast and immovable.
24 Its heart is as hard as stone,
as hard as the lower millstone.
25 When it raises itself up the gods are
afraid;
at the crashing they are beside
themselves.
26 Though the sword reaches it, it does not
avail,
nor does the spear, the dart, or the
javelin.
27 It counts iron as straw,
and bronze as rotten wood.

28 The arrow cannot make it flee;
slingstones, for it, are turned to chaff.
29 Clubs are counted as chaff;
it laughs at the rattle of javelins.
30 Its underparts are like sharp potsherds;
it spreads itself like a threshing sledge
on the mire.
31 It makes the deep boil like a pot;
it makes the sea like a pot of ointment.
32 It leaves a shining wake behind it;
one would think the deep to be white-
haired.
33 On earth it has no equal,
a creature without fear.
34 It surveys everything that is lofty;
it is king over all that are proud."

Job Is Humbled and Satisfied

42 Then Job answered the LORD:
2 "I know that you can do all things,
and that no purpose of yours can be
thwarted.
3 'Who is this that hides counsel without
knowledge?'
Therefore I have uttered what I did not
understand,
things too wonderful for me, which I
did not know.
4 'Hear, and I will speak;
I will question you, and you declare to
me.'
5 I had heard of you by the hearing of the
ear,
but now my eye sees you;
6 therefore I despise myself,
and repent in dust and ashes."

Job's Friends Are Humiliated

7 After the LORD had spoken these words to
Job, the LORD said to Eliphaz the Temanite:

---

a Gk: Heb *bridle*   *b* Cn Compare Gk Vg: Heb *pride*

---

thinkers, some of whom envisioned this fishlike creature being served as food for the faithful. **41.18–
21** Fantasy and poetic license reign in this description
of a fire-eating dragon. **42.5** *Hearing* was by no means
denigrated in ancient pedagogy, which relied heavily
on oral presentation (cf. Egyptian instructions). Elevating sight over hearing, Job may say, "I had heard
and now I see." An ancient tradition that none could
see God and live (see Ex 33.20) admitted exceptions in
the narratives about Israel's ancestors. **42.6** The translation and meaning of this verse are uncertain. It can
be read that Job repented of *dust and ashes*, i.e., of re-

pentance. Perhaps Job relinquishes his conviction that
guilt and innocence are taken into account by the ruler
of the universe. Some scholars see irony in Job's response, a concealing of his continued defiance in the
face of divine cruelty. **42.7–17** The epilogue. A prose ending affirms Job's
view of God and condemns that of his friends. God re-
stores Job's health and doubles his former wealth.
42.7 When did Job speak correctly? In the defiant
speeches that denied divine justice? Or in the submission resulting from a new vision of God? The *Testament of Job* reads that the friends have not spoken cor-

"My wrath is kindled against you and against your two friends; for you have not spoken of me what is right, as my servant Job has. ⁸Now therefore take seven bulls and seven rams, and go to my servant Job, and offer up for yourselves a burnt offering; and my servant Job shall pray for you, for I will accept his prayer not to deal with you according to your folly; for you have not spoken of me what is right, as my servant Job has done." ⁹So Eliphaz the Temanite and Bildad the Shuhite and Zophar the Naamathite went and did what the LORD had told them; and the LORD accepted Job's prayer.

Job's Fortunes Are Restored Twofold

10 And the LORD restored the fortunes of Job when he had prayed for his friends; and the LORD gave Job twice as much as he had before. ¹¹Then there came to him all his brothers and sisters and all who had known him before, and they ate bread with him in his house; they showed him sympathy and comforted him for all the evil that the LORD had brought upon him; and each of them gave him a piece of moneyᵃ and a gold ring. ¹²The LORD blessed the latter days of Job more than his beginning; and he had fourteen thousand sheep, six thousand camels, a thousand yoke of oxen, and a thousand donkeys. ¹³He also had seven sons and three daughters. ¹⁴He named the first Jemimah, the second Keziah, and the third Keren-happuch. ¹⁵In all the land there were no women so beautiful as Job's daughters; and their father gave them an inheritance along with their brothers. ¹⁶After this Job lived one hundred and forty years, and saw his children, and his children's children, four generations. ¹⁷And Job died, old and full of days.

---

a Heb a qesitah

---

rectly about Job. **42.8–10** *Job shall pray for you.* In rabbinical interpretation Job's condition changed as a direct consequence of his interceding for the friends, a point that v. 10 seems to make (cf. Gen 20.7). The twofold restitution, that of a convicted criminal, is fully ironic. **42.11** *Evil . . . upon him.* The text freely acknowledges God's responsibility for Job's misfortunes. The monetary unit mentioned here is appropriate for the patriarchal setting of the tale (cf. Gen 33.19; Josh 24.32). This gift was no insignificant one. The *Targum of Job,* discovered in the area of the Dead Sea, seems to have concluded with v. 11. **42.13** The Septuagint doubles the number of children. Surprisingly, slaves are missing from the account of Job's restoration. **42.14** Like Baal's three daughters, Job's are named: *Jemimah* ("Dove"), *Keziah* ("Cinnamon"), and *Keren-happuch* ("Horn of Antinomy"). Neither Baal's nor Job's sons are named. Perhaps the emphasis on Job's daughters' beauty and wealth implies that he will easily find husbands for them (cf. Sir 42.9–11). **42.15** Normally daughters did not inherit unless there were no sons. **42.16** *One hundred and forty years.* The customary life span, according to Ps 90.10, is doubled in Job's case, counting from the time that his calamities ended. **42.17** The same language is used of Abraham and Isaac (Gen 25.8; 35.29).

THE PSALMS

PSALMS, OR THE PSALTER, as it is sometimes called, is a collection of prayers and songs composed throughout Israel's history. Its title, Psalms, is derived from a Greek term meaning "song." The Hebrew title of the book, *Tehillim*, means more specifically "hymns" or "songs of praise."

Poetry and Music

THE POETIC CHARACTER OF THE PSALMS is manifest in the balance or symmetry of each line. A line of poetry, which is often identical with a numbered verse, is composed of two or three parts, usually sentences or clauses, called cola (singular, colon). The balance between or among the cola is evident in three ways, often more approximate than precise: sound or rhythm (accented or stressed syllables), length of line (the number of syllables), and especially parallelism of meaning, in which members or words in one colon are seconded or paralleled in some fashion in another. The forms of such parallelism are many and may involve contrasting elements as well as synonymous ones. The highly poetic form of the psalms is evident also in the use of figures of thought and speech, word pairs, rhyme, and other common poetic devices. The musical character of the psalms is reflected in the title to the book, in many of the superscriptions, or headings, which often contain what seem to be technical music terms, and the long tradition of the musical use of Psalms that continues to the present day.

Psalm Types

THE PSALMS FALL GENERALLY INTO CERTAIN TYPES or genres that reflect usage in various contexts, especially in the worship life of ancient Israel. The title of the book characterizes the psalms as *hymns* and thus identifies the praise of God in worship as their purpose. The conclusion to the first half of the Psalter (Pss 1–72), "the prayers of David . . . are ended," indicates, however, that much of this biblical book was understood as *prayer*, often that of an individual in distress and needing help. In a number of cases one can see that prayers and hymns that may have been originally intended for a setting in worship have become more like *instruction* in character. The reverse may have happened as well. A didactic function for the psalms is confirmed by the introduction to the Psalter, Ps 1, with its focus upon the law, or instruction of the Lord, and its study (cf. Ps 119, which, it has been suggested, may have been the conclusion to an

732

earlier form of the Psalter). Thus, prayers for help, songs of praise, and instruction for life were all joined in this book as different and changing intentions shaped its formation.

PRAYERS FOR HELP (LAMENTS)

THE LARGEST CATEGORY OF PSALMS is composed of prayers for help—usually called laments—either on the part of an individual (e.g., Pss 3–7) or the community as a whole (e.g., Pss 83; 85). In some cases individual prayers have been transformed into community prayers, and in some community prayers one can hear individual and representative voices. These psalms were prayed in situations of severe distress, although the particular circumstances out of which they originated are no longer discernible except in the broadest sense. Sickness and adversity, betrayal and abandonment, sin and guilt, and slander and false accusation as well as other acts of persecution and oppression by those called "enemies" and "wicked" are aspects of suffering reflected in the individual prayers. For the community prayers, situations of national disaster and defeat are indicated, and in some instances it appears as if the Babylonian destruction of Judah (587 BCE) and the exile that followed are in view (e.g., Pss 74; 79; 137). In all of these prayers the circumstances and the effects of the distress on the ones who prayed are set forth in generalized, stylized, and metaphorical ways that have served to loosen these prayers from whatever original setting they may have had and made them more broadly applicable in the life of the community over long periods and for different situations.

The focus of the prayers is on petitions or pleas for help that incorporate lamenting descriptions of the psalmist's distress, including references to physical and emotional suffering, divine affliction, or persecution by other persons. Such prayers, however, also express the petitioner's confidence or trust in God's power and willingness to help and often give reasons why the deity should do so. These usually have to do with the character of the deity, the plight of the psalmist, or the sufferer's trust in God. Frequently the one who prays vows to sacrifice and offer praise to God when deliverance comes. One also may discern indications that the prayer has been heard and God has responded.

SONGS OF THANKSGIVING

THE PROMISE OF PRAISE in the prayer for help is what evokes the song of thanksgiving (e.g., Ps 30). Here the psalmist sings praise to God in gratitude for the help that was given, frequently giving some account of the distress and God's deliverance. Sacrifices may have accompanied these songs. They were, at least, sung in the sanctuary and before the congregation. The song of the psalmist is a testimony inviting others to praise the Lord because of the help God has shown. A few psalms may be communal songs of thanksgiving.

HYMNS

ANOTHER FORM OF PRAISE closely related to the song of thanksgiving is the hymn (e.g., Pss 117; 145). Here the congregation is called to praise or declares its intent to praise the Lord. Reasons for that praise are then given either briefly or at length. These usually have to do with the character and power of God demonstrated in the works of creation and in God's acts of faithfulness and love toward Israel.

ROYAL PSALMS

A NUMBER OF PSALMS center on the king and so have been called royal psalms. Some are prayers and songs of thanksgiving for or by the king (e.g., Ps 18); others may have been composed for occasions such as coronations (e.g., Ps 2) or weddings (e.g., Ps 45). Sporadic references to the king occur in other psalms, and it is possible that sometimes when a voice speaks in the psalms as a representative of the people it is the voice of a king.

OTHER TYPES

OTHER TYPES OF PSALMS occur in smaller numbers, for example, liturgies of thanksgiving (e.g., Ps 118) and liturgies for entrance into the sanctuary (e.g., Pss 15; 24). Some of the other types are developments of particular aspects of the prayer or hymn: the psalms of trust (e.g., Pss 23; 62), the songs exalting Zion (e.g., Pss 48; 87), and those hymns celebrating God's universal rule (commonly called "enthronement psalms," e.g., Pss 47; 93; 96–99). Some psalms with prominent didactic and instructional features must have been initially composed with that aim in mind (e.g., Pss 37; 49).

Setting of the Psalms

THE SPECIFIC RELATIONSHIP of all the psalms to corporate and individual acts of worship is much debated. It is likely that a number of them were a part of public worship. Surely some of them were associated with the great annual festivals. The hymns and liturgies, as well as the songs of thanksgiving, had their place in the worship of the congregation. The relation of the individual prayers for help to the sanctuary and the priestly officials is less clear. There are indications that prayers were uttered in the sanctuary, often at night. They sometimes incorporate or allude to oracles of salvation that may have been mediated through a priest. Some interpreters, however, have claimed that the individual prayers were associated more with the family or clan and less with the sanctuary and its priests.

Composition and Authorship

THE DATE OF COMPOSITION varies from psalm to psalm and is in most cases impossible to determine. Some psalms were probably composed fairly early in Israel's history (e.g., Pss 18; 29; 68). Many may have been composed after the exile. Some psalms show indications of having undergone a process of transmission that, in the course of time, changed them from their original form. That process, which is difficult to reconstruct, has involved adapting individual psalms for communal use, royal motifs for a postmonarchical context, and cultic psalms for noncultic uses (and probably the reverse).

In its present form the Psalter is arranged in five collections, or "books," an arrangement thought to be on analogy with the five books of the Torah. Although the rationale for the internal processes of organization is much debated, the book divisions are evident by the closing doxological verses in Pss 41.13; 72.18–19; 89.52; 106.48; 150.1–6.

Although many of the psalms are associated in their headings with David, who may have written some of them, the authorship of the individual psalms is unknown. The superscriptions of the psalms are secondary to their composition and identify persons other than David with whom the psalms are associated either because of content (e.g., Pss 72; 127) or because the individuals named had some role in the music and worship of the temple (e.g., Asaph and the Korahites). Musical notations of various sorts appear in these headings, but their meaning is often uncertain. Indications of the type of psalm (e.g., Ps 90) or of its use in worship (e.g., Ps 92) are given on occasion.

The superscriptions also serve to identify collections or groupings of psalms within—or sometimes overlapping—the five "book" divisions. At the end of Book II (72.20), for example, a note indicates "the prayers of David son of Jesse are ended." Although, in fact, David's name appears in the headings of several more psalms—especially toward the end of the Psalter (Pss 138–145)—the majority of the psalms in Books I and II have some reference to David in their superscriptions, indicating a sense of these as a collection of Davidic prayers. A few have no name in the title, and there is a small collection of Korahite psalms (Pss 44–49) in their midst. Another collection of Korahite psalms appears in Pss 84–88, and one group of psalms is associated with another musician, Asaph (Pss 73–83; cf. Ps 50). The most obvious collection within the Psalter is the "Songs of Ascents" (Pss 120–134), fifteen psalms that share various features and probably were added as a group (see note on 120.1–7). Contemporary interpretation of Psalms has identified a number of groups of psalms that may be read together as subunits on the basis of formal connections as well as resonances of language and content, without necessarily showing explicit signs of collection such as may be reflected in the superscriptions and the doxologies. Furthermore, important proposals have been put forth for reading the whole Psalter as a book that has not only a beginning and an end, but thematic movement as well.

The formation of the Psalter was a long and complex process. Individual songs and prayers were composed, some of which were used repeatedly by the community; these were brought together into smaller collections first and eventually formed into the larger whole that is now the Psalter. Pss 1 and 2 were placed as an introduction to the whole, probably late in the process of formation, and Ps 150 (or possibly Pss 145–150) seems to have been put at the end as a doxological conclusion. Additional psalms appear in some of the ancient versions as well as in the large Psalms manuscript from Qumran. [PATRICK D. MILLER]

BOOK I: PSALMS 1–41

The Two Ways

1 Happy are those
    who do not follow the advice of the
        wicked,
    or take the path that sinners tread,
        or sit in the seat of scoffers;
2 but their delight is in the law of the
        LORD,
    and on his law they meditate day and
        night.
3 They are like trees
    planted by streams of water,
which yield their fruit in its season,
    and their leaves do not wither.
In all that they do, they prosper.

4 The wicked are not so,
    but are like chaff that the wind drives
        away.
5 Therefore the wicked will not stand in the
        judgment,
    nor sinners in the congregation of the
        righteous;
6 for the LORD watches over the way of the
        righteous,
    but the way of the wicked will
        perish.

1.1–6 A psalm exalting God's instruction, or law, and the blessings of attending to it (cf. Pss 19; 40.8; 119). This psalm, together with Ps 2, serves as an introduction to the Psalter (see Introduction). 1.1–3 The way of the righteous. 1.1 *Happy,* i.e., seen and envied by others as blessed. *Scoffers,* arrogant people who mock the righteous one's trust in God. 1.2 The Hebrew term for *law* is *torah,* i.e., "instruction" or "teaching." For a similar joy in God's law, see 119.77, 92, 97, 113. 1.3 Cf. Jer 17.7–8. 1.4–6 The way of the wicked is ephemeral and unproductive; they will not endure.

God's Promise to His Anointed

2 Why do the nations conspire,
  and the peoples plot in vain?

2 The kings of the earth set themselves,
  and the rulers take counsel together,
  against the LORD and his anointed,
    saying,

3 "Let us burst their bonds asunder,
  and cast their cords from us."

4 He who sits in the heavens laughs;
  the LORD has them in derision.

5 Then he will speak to them in his wrath,
  and terrify them in his fury, saying,

6 "I have set my king on Zion, my holy hill."

7 I will tell of the decree of the LORD:
  He said to me, "You are my son;
    today I have begotten you.

8 Ask of me, and I will make the nations
    your heritage,
  and the ends of the earth your
    possession.

9 You shall break them with a rod of iron,
  and dash them in pieces like a potter's
    vessel."

10 Now therefore, O kings, be wise;
  be warned, O rulers of the earth.

11 Serve the LORD with fear,
  with trembling ¹²kiss his feet,ᵃ
  or he will be angry, and you will perish in
    the way;
  for his wrath is quickly kindled.

  Happy are all who take refuge in him.

Trust in God under Adversity

A Psalm of David, when he fled from his son
Absalom.

3 O LORD, how many are my foes!
  Many are rising against me;

2 many are saying to me,
  "There is no help for youᵇ in God."
                                        Selah

3 But you, O LORD, are a shield around me,
  my glory, and the one who lifts up my
    head.

4 I cry aloud to the LORD,
  and he answers me from his holy hill.
                                        Selah

5 I lie down and sleep;
  I wake again, for the LORD sustains me.

6 I am not afraid of ten thousands of
    people
  who have set themselves against me all
    around.

7 Rise up, O LORD!
  Deliver me, O my God!
For you strike all my enemies on the
    cheek;
  you break the teeth of the wicked.

8 Deliverance belongs to the LORD;
  may your blessing be on your people!
                                        Selah

_____
ᵃ Cn: Meaning of Heb of verses 11b and 12a is uncertain
ᵇ Syr: Heb *him*

2.1–12 A royal psalm perhaps used on occasion of the coronation of a king. It now functions with Ps 1 as part of the introduction to the Psalter (see Introduction), indicating that the ways of the king and the nations are matters to be found within the Psalms. **2.1–3** At a time of transition, subject nations may seek to overthrow the ruling nation. Cf. Acts 4.25–26. **2.2** *Anointed*, or "messiah," God's designated king. Applied to Israel's own kings in the time of the monarchy, the term came to be used in reference to an ideal king who would come in the future and inaugurate God's righteous rule. **2.4–9** The Lord's response to the plot against the king is the installation of the new king, who is given power over the nations. **2.7** *Decree*, the royal protocol legitimating the king at the time of enthronement. *You are . . . begotten you* is a formula of adoption of the king, who from that point on is viewed as God's son (cf. 89.26–27; 2 Sam 7.14). For secondary applications to Jesus, see Acts 13.33; Heb 1.5. **2.9** *You shall*, perhaps to

be read as permissive, "you may." **2.10–12** A warning to rebellious rulers to submit to the rule of God's anointed or they will be destroyed. *Happy.* See note on 1.1. *Refuge*, a thematic image in the Psalms for confident reliance on God's deliverance of the righteous.

3.1–8 A prayer of an individual to God for help. The superscription serves to suggest an occasion in David's life when such words as these would have been appropriate (2 Sam 15–18). **3.1–2** The psalmist laments the threat of enemies and implicitly complains against God. **3.2** *Help*, or deliverance (see vv. 7–8). *Selah*, possibly a liturgical or musical direction of unknown meaning. **3.3–6** In contrast to the apparent abandonment by God, the psalmist expresses confidence in God's protecting care and response to the prayer. **3.4** *Holy hill*, Zion or the Temple Mount. **3.7** The prayer for the deliverance that others (v. 2) assume God will not bring. **3.8** A final expression of confidence that it is in fact God who alone can deliver from threats.

Confident Plea for Deliverance from Enemies

To the leader: with stringed instruments.
A Psalm of David.

4 Answer me when I call, O God of my
   right!
   You gave me room when I was in
      distress.
   Be gracious to me, and hear my
      prayer.

2 How long, you people, shall my honor
      suffer shame?
   How long will you love vain words,
      and seek after lies?   *Selah*
3 But know that the LORD has set apart the
      faithful for himself;
   the LORD hears when I call to him.

4 When you are disturbed,*a* do not sin;
   ponder it on your beds, and be silent.
                                     Selah
5 Offer right sacrifices,
   and put your trust in the LORD.

6 There are many who say, "O that we
      might see some good!
   Let the light of your face shine on us,
      O LORD!"
7 You have put gladness in my heart
   more than when their grain and wine
      abound.

8 I will both lie down and sleep in peace;
   for you alone, O LORD, make me lie
      down in safety.

Trust in God for Deliverance from Enemies

To the leader: for the flutes. A Psalm of David.

5 Give ear to my words, O LORD;
   give heed to my sighing.
2 Listen to the sound of my cry,
   my King and my God,
   for to you I pray.
3 O LORD, in the morning you hear my
      voice;
   in the morning I plead my case to you,
      and watch.

4 For you are not a God who delights in
      wickedness;
   evil will not sojourn with you.
5 The boastful will not stand before your
      eyes;
   you hate all evildoers.
6 You destroy those who speak lies;
   the LORD abhors the bloodthirsty and
      deceitful.

7 But I, through the abundance of your
      steadfast love,
   will enter your house,
   I will bow down toward your holy temple
   in awe of you.
8 Lead me, O LORD, in your righteousness
   because of my enemies;
   make your way straight before me.

9 For there is no truth in their mouths;
   their hearts are destruction;

---

a Or *are angry*

4.1–8 A prayer for help in trouble. *To the leader: with stringed instruments,* apparently musical or liturgical directions, perhaps addressed to the director of temple musicians. **4.1** The cry for help. Deliverance is seen in terms of the imagery of having room and not being hemmed in or trapped. **4.2–5** An address to those who have sought to do in the psalmist. **4.2** A claim that some have brought false accusations against or slandered the petitioner. *Selah.* See note on 3.2. **4.3** The opponents are now challenged to acknowledge the Lord's protection of the one who prays. **4.4–5** The opponents are cautioned against sinful acts and urged to come into the sanctuary like those who do right and trust in the Lord. *Right sacrifices,* either those done in the right manner or, more likely, sacrifices acknowledging God's justice and righteousness manifest in the deliverance of the petitioner. **4.6–8** The fruitless

longing for God's blessing by those who do not trust in God (v. 5) is contrasted with the joyous confidence of the one who trusts and is kept in safety by God. **4.6** *Let . . . shine.* See Num 6.25; note on 31.16.

5.1–12 A prayer for help by an individual in trouble. *To the leader.* See note on 4.1–8. *For the flutes,* a liturgical notation of uncertain meaning. **5.1–3** The petition for God to pay attention to the prayer. *In the morning* is often the time when God comes to help (17.15; 90.14; 143.8; 1 Sam 11.9). **5.4–7** The assurance of being heard is grounded in the knowledge that, although God will not let the wicked appear in the divine presence, the righteous petitioner may enter the temple and stand before God (see Pss 15; 24; 73.17). **5.8** The actual petition for God's saving help, i.e., *righteousness,* and some clear direction for the future, i.e., *your way.* **5.9–10** A call for judgment upon the wicked

their throats are open graves;
   they flatter with their tongues.
10 Make them bear their guilt, O God;
   let them fall by their own counsels;
  because of their many transgressions cast
    them out,
   for they have rebelled against you.

11 But let all who take refuge in you
    rejoice;
   let them ever sing for joy.
  Spread your protection over them,
   so that those who love your name may
    exult in you.
12 For you bless the righteous, O LORD;
   you cover them with favor as with a
    shield.

Prayer for Recovery from Grave Illness

To the leader: with stringed instruments;
according to The Sheminith. A Psalm of David.

6 O LORD, do not rebuke me in your anger,
   or discipline me in your wrath.
2 Be gracious to me, O LORD, for I am
    languishing;
  O LORD, heal me, for my bones are
    shaking with terror.
3 My soul also is struck with terror,
   while you, O LORD—how long?

4 Turn, O LORD, save my life;
   deliver me for the sake of your
    steadfast love.
5 For in death there is no remembrance of
    you;
  in Sheol who can give you praise?

6 I am weary with my moaning;
  every night I flood my bed with tears;
  I drench my couch with my weeping.
7 My eyes waste away because of grief;
  they grow weak because of all my foes.

8 Depart from me, all you workers of evil,
   for the LORD has heard the sound of
    my weeping.
9 The LORD has heard my supplication;
  the LORD accepts my prayer.
10 All my enemies shall be ashamed and
    struck with terror;
  they shall turn back, and in a moment
    be put to shame.

Plea for Help against Persecutors

A Shiggaion of David, which he sang to the
LORD concerning Cush, a Benjaminite.

7 O LORD my God, in you I take refuge;
   save me from all my pursuers, and
    deliver me,

---

who oppress the psalmist. *Throats* and *tongues* suggest that the oppression is some kind of slander or false accusation. The graphic image is used by Paul in Rom 3.13. **5.11–12** A final prayer for protection of the innocent and thus righteous, including the one praying. *Refuge*. See note on 2.10–12.

6.1–10 A prayer for help by an individual in trouble. The first of the seven "penitential psalms" (Pss 6; 32; 38; 51; 102; 130; 143), so called because the early Christian church saw in them a special note of contrition or penitence. *To the leader . . . instruments.* See note on 4.1–8. *According to The Sheminith,* lit. "according to the eighth"; meaning uncertain, perhaps referring to a musical instrument. **6.1–5** Petitions for deliverance by the Lord. The language suggesting physical illness may reflect an actual situation in which a sick person prays for healing or it may be metaphorical for trouble in general. **6.1** Illness or whatever has happened to the psalmist is seen as a judgment of God. **6.3** *My soul . . . is struck.* Cf. Jn 12.27. *How long?* is a typical complaint against God in the cries or prayers for help by the individual (e.g., 13.1–2) or the community (e.g., 74.10; 79.5; 80.4). **6.5** *Sheol,* the abode of the dead. Death is seen as a condition in which one is removed from God's presence and the possibility of

worship and praise (cf. Job 10.21–22; Isa 38.18). That fact is given as a motivation to encourage divine assistance. **6.6–7** The psalmist's physical and emotional distress. **6.7** *Grief,* better "vexation" or "provocation." For the suffering caused by the vexation of others, see 1 Sam 1.6–7. **6.8–10** The confidence of the sufferer that God has heard and will deliver. The particular form of evil (v. 8) or enmity (v. 10) is not indicated. It may be the sort of provocation evidenced by Peninnah in the face of Hannah's personal distress of barrenness (see 1 Sam 1.6–7). **6.8** *Depart from me.* Cf. Mt 7.23; Lk 13.27. **6.10** *Terror.* See vv. 2–3. The fate of the sufferer becomes the fate of those who have caused suffering.

7.1–17 A prayer for help of a person who has probably been falsely accused of some wrong. The psalm would have had its setting in the sanctuary, where an innocent person could come before God for protection and vindication when falsely accused. See 1 Kings 8.31–32; Deut 17.8–9. The accused would declare innocence before God and await a divine decision. The superscription assigns this psalm to an incident in David's life that is unknown in the OT. *Shiggaion,* a word of uncertain meaning that has been taken to mean "lament." **7.1–2** The accused invokes God's protection from those who threaten. *Refuge.* See note on

2 or like a lion they will tear me apart;
      they will drag me away, with no one to
            rescue.

3 O Lord my God, if I have done this,
      if there is wrong in my hands,
4 if I have repaid my ally with harm
      or plundered my foe without cause,
5 then let the enemy pursue and overtake
            me,
      trample my life to the ground,
      and lay my soul in the dust.   *Selah*

6 Rise up, O Lord, in your anger;
      lift yourself up against the fury of my
            enemies;
      awake, O my God;[a] you have
            appointed a judgment.
7 Let the assembly of the peoples be
            gathered around you,
      and over it take your seat[b] on high.
8 The Lord judges the peoples;
      judge me, O Lord, according to my
            righteousness
      and according to the integrity that is in
            me.

9 O let the evil of the wicked come to an
            end,
      but establish the righteous,
   you who test the minds and hearts,
      O righteous God.
10 God is my shield,
      who saves the upright in heart.
11 God is a righteous judge,
      and a God who has indignation every
            day.
12 If one does not repent, God[c] will whet his
            sword;
      he has bent and strung his bow;

13 he has prepared his deadly weapons,
      making his arrows fiery shafts.
14 See how they conceive evil,
      and are pregnant with mischief,
      and bring forth lies.
15 They make a pit, digging it out,
      and fall into the hole that they have
            made.
16 Their mischief returns upon their own
            heads,
      and on their own heads their violence
            descends.

17 I will give to the Lord the thanks due to
            his righteousness,
      and sing praise to the name of the
            Lord, the Most High.

Divine Majesty and Human Dignity

To the leader: according to The Gittith.
A Psalm of David.

8 O Lord, our Sovereign,
      how majestic is your name in all the
            earth!

   You have set your glory above the
            heavens.
2   Out of the mouths of babes and
            infants
   you have founded a bulwark because of
            your foes,
      to silence the enemy and the avenger.

3 When I look at your heavens, the work of
            your fingers,
      the moon and the stars that you have
            established;

---

a Or *awake for me*   *b* Cn: Heb *return*   *c* Heb *he*

2.10–12. **7.2** *Like a lion.* Enemies in Psalms are often compared to wild animals attacking (10.9; 17.12; 22.12–13; 35.17; 57.4; 58.3–6). **7.3–5** A protestation of innocence by the sufferer (cf. 17.3–5; Job 31). **7.3** *If I have done this.* The claim is not of general innocence but of the specific *wrong* of which the praying one is accused. **7.4** *If I have . . . harm.* The accusation against the psalmist may have been betrayal of a trust. **7.5** *Selah.* See note on 3.2. **7.6–11** The appeal to the Lord as righteous judge to render judgment in this case. **7.8** *My righteousness . . . integrity,* i.e., "my innocence in this matter." **7.9–11** The justice of God can be counted upon by the psalmist. **7.12–16** The psalmist

now expresses confidence that the wicked who falsely accuse will suffer the fate they have sought to effect against the accused. **7.12–13** It is not clear whether the subject of this sentence is God or the wicked. See text note c. **7.15** *Pit.* See note on 9.15. **7.17** A vow to give thanks to God when deliverance comes.

8.1–9 A hymn of praise for God's exaltation of the human creature. *To the leader.* See note on 4.1–8. *According to The Gittith,* possibly a kind of melody. **8.1–2** The glory of God. *Out of the mouths . . . infants* may refer to the praise that comes even from the babbling of babies (cf. Mt 21.16). *Founded a bulwark* may be better translated as "established strength" in parallel

4 what are human beings that you are
   mindful of them,
   mortals*a* that you care for them?

5 Yet you have made them a little lower
   than God,*b*
   and crowned them with glory and
   honor.

6 You have given them dominion over the
   works of your hands;
   you have put all things under their feet,

7 all sheep and oxen,
   and also the beasts of the field,

8 the birds of the air, and the fish of the sea,
   whatever passes along the paths of the
   seas.

9 O LORD, our Sovereign,
   how majestic is your name in all the
   earth!

God's Power and Justice

To the leader: according to Muth-labben.
A Psalm of David.

9 I will give thanks to the LORD with my
   whole heart;
   I will tell of all your wonderful deeds.

2 I will be glad and exult in you;
   I will sing praise to your name, O Most
   High.

3 When my enemies turned back,
   they stumbled and perished before
   you.

4 For you have maintained my just cause;
   you have sat on the throne giving
   righteous judgment.

5 You have rebuked the nations, you have
   destroyed the wicked;
   you have blotted out their name
   forever and ever.

6 The enemies have vanished in everlasting
   ruins;
   their cities you have rooted out;
   the very memory of them has perished.

7 But the LORD sits enthroned forever,
   he has established his throne for
   judgment.

8 He judges the world with righteousness;
   he judges the peoples with equity.

9 The LORD is a stronghold for the
   oppressed,
   a stronghold in times of trouble.

10 And those who know your name put
   their trust in you,
   for you, O LORD, have not forsaken
   those who seek you.

11 Sing praises to the LORD, who dwells in
   Zion.
   Declare his deeds among the peoples.

12 For he who avenges blood is mindful of
   them;

---

a Heb *ben adam,* lit. *son of man*   *b* Or *than the divine beings* or *angels:* Heb *elohim*

---

with "set your glory." **8.3–9** Human glory as a manifestation of the glory of God. **8.3–4** Awareness of the awesome universe as God's handiwork raises the question of what value human beings could possibly have in that grand cosmos. **8.3** *The moon . . . established.* The heavenly bodies are God's creation and have no independent character as deities. **8.4** For less positive responses to the same question, see 144.3; Job 7.17. For an application to Christ, cf. Heb 2.6–8. **8.5–6** A similar view of humankind is found in Gen 1.26–28. The terminology used to describe the human creature had its origin in the royal ideology of the ancient Near East. **8.5** *God,* better "divine beings" or "angels," as in text note *b* (cf. "our image," Gen 1.26; Heb 2.7; Ps 8.5, Septuagint). **8.6** *All things . . . feet.* For an eschatological reading, see 1 Cor 15.27; Eph 1.22.

9.1–10.18 Pss 9 and 10 are to be read as a unit. The Septuagint combines them. In the Hebrew they generally follow an alphabetic acrostic pattern in which every other verse begins with a letter of the alphabet,

beginning with the first letter in 9.1 and ending with the last in 10.17. Note also the absence in Ps 10 of a superscription, which is present in most psalms in the first book of the Psalter (Pss 1–41). Furthermore, *Selah,* which concludes Ps 9, nowhere else comes at the end of a psalm. Within the unity, however, one may recognize in Ps 9 a song of thanksgiving by an individual into which has been incorporated a prayer for help in Ps 10. It is uncertain if the song of thanksgiving is meant to be anticipatory of deliverance or praise because it has happened. *To the leader.* See note on 4.1–8. *According to Muth-labben,* probably a musical notation, meaning uncertain. **9.1–2** A hymnic expression of personal thanksgiving and praise for God's saving activity. **9.2** *I will sing . . . name* connects the psalm to 8.1, 9. **9.3–10** God as righteous judge has dealt justly with the oppressed one and with the peoples of the earth generally. The imagery and activity of God as ruler and judge come together as the grounds for praise and thanksgiving. **9.11–12** A call to praise (v.

he does not forget the cry of the
    afflicted.

13 Be gracious to me, O LORD.
    See what I suffer from those who hate
        me;
    you are the one who lifts me up from
        the gates of death,
14 so that I may recount all your praises,
    and, in the gates of daughter Zion,
    rejoice in your deliverance.

15 The nations have sunk in the pit that they
        made;
    in the net that they hid has their own
        foot been caught.
16 The LORD has made himself known, he
        has executed judgment;
    the wicked are snared in the work of
        their own hands.
                     Higgaion. Selah

17 The wicked shall depart to Sheol,
    all the nations that forget God.

18 For the needy shall not always be
        forgotten,
    nor the hope of the poor perish
        forever.

19 Rise up, O LORD! Do not let mortals
        prevail;
    let the nations be judged before you.
20 Put them in fear, O LORD;
    let the nations know that they are only
        human.   *Selah*

Prayer for Deliverance from Enemies

10 Why, O LORD, do you stand far off?
    Why do you hide yourself in times of
        trouble?
2 In arrogance the wicked persecute the
        poor—
    let them be caught in the schemes they
        have devised.

3 For the wicked boast of the desires of
        their heart,
    those greedy for gain curse and
        renounce the LORD.
4 In the pride of their countenance the
        wicked say, "God will not seek it
        out";
    all their thoughts are, "There is no
        God."

5 Their ways prosper at all times;
    your judgments are on high, out of
        their sight;
    as for their foes, they scoff at them.
6 They think in their heart, "We shall not
        be moved;
    throughout all generations we shall not
        meet adversity."

7 Their mouths are filled with cursing and
        deceit and oppression;
    under their tongues are mischief and
        iniquity.
8 They sit in ambush in the villages;
    in hiding places they murder the
        innocent.

---

11) echoes the declaration of praise at the beginning, and the reason (v. 12) is a reiteration of the psalmist's experience of God's positive response to the cry of the sufferer. **9.13–14** Anticipating the extended prayer for help in Ps 10 and believing the claim of v. 12, the psalmist seeks God's gracious attention to the suffering now going on. **9.15–18** The psalmist expresses confidence because of the experience of God's delivering judgment in the nation's history. **9.15** The imagery of *pit* and *net* as weapons of enemies and evildoers is frequent in Psalms and is often a way of speaking about the wicked being caught in their own evil schemes (7.15–16; 10.9; 25.15; 31.4; 35.7–8; 57.6; 140.5; cf. Job 18.8). **9.16** *Higgaion*, translated *melody* in 92.3, perhaps here a musical interlude of some sort. *Selah*. See note on 3.2. **9.17** *Sheol*. See note on 6.5. **9.18** The claim here anticipates the fear that is at the heart of Ps 10, that God has forgotten the weak and

helpless (see 10.2–4, 11–13). **9.19–20** A concluding call to God to rise up in judgment against the nations (cf. 7.6–8; 82.8; 96.13; 98.9). These verses also lead into the complaints and petitions for help of Ps 10. **10.1–11** The psalmist complains to God on behalf of the poor (v. 2; cf. 9.18) and helpless (vv. 8, 10). The wicked believe their successful oppression of the helpless and innocent is a reflection of God's absence or indifference to whatever they do. **10.1** *Why . . . far off?* is a frequent complaint to God in cries for help (22.1, 19; 35.22; 38.21; 71.12). *Why . . . hide yourself?* is also a common form of complaint to God (see 55.1; also the related expression *hide your face* in 13.1; 27.9; 30.7; 44.24; 69.17; 88.14; 102.2; 143.7; note on 27.9) as well as an assumption of the wicked (v. 11). **10.2** Cf. 9.15–16. **10.4** Cf. 14.1. **10.7** *Mouths are filled*. Cf. Rom 3.14. **10.8–11** Vivid imagery to describe the scheming, plotting, and treachery by which the wicked and immoral

Their eyes stealthily watch for the
helpless;
9 they lurk in secret like a lion in its
covert;
they lurk that they may seize the poor;
they seize the poor and drag them off
in their net.

10 They stoop, they crouch,
and the helpless fall by their might.
11 They think in their heart, "God has
forgotten,
he has hidden his face, he will never
see it."

12 Rise up, O LORD; O God, lift up your hand;
do not forget the oppressed.
13 Why do the wicked renounce God,
and say in their hearts, "You will not
call us to account"?

14 But you do see! Indeed you note trouble
and grief,
that you may take it into your hands;
the helpless commit themselves to you;
you have been the helper of the
orphan.

15 Break the arm of the wicked and
evildoers;
seek out their wickedness until you
find none.
16 The LORD is king forever and ever;
the nations shall perish from his land.

17 O LORD, you will hear the desire of the
meek;
you will strengthen their heart, you
will incline your ear
18 to do justice for the orphan and the
oppressed,

so that those from earth may strike
terror no more. [a]

Song of Trust in God

To the leader. Of David.

11 In the LORD I take refuge; how can
you say to me,
"Flee like a bird to the mountains; [b]
2 for look, the wicked bend the bow,
they have fitted their arrow to the
string,
to shoot in the dark at the upright in
heart.
3 If the foundations are destroyed,
what can the righteous do?"

4 The LORD is in his holy temple;
the LORD's throne is in heaven.
His eyes behold, his gaze examines
humankind.
5 The LORD tests the righteous and the
wicked,
and his soul hates the lover of violence.
6 On the wicked he will rain coals of fire
and sulfur;
a scorching wind shall be the portion
of their cup.
7 For the LORD is righteous;
he loves righteous deeds;
the upright shall behold his face.

Plea for Help in Evil Times

To the leader: according to The Sheminith.
A Psalm of David.

12 Help, O LORD, for there is no longer
anyone who is godly;

---

a Meaning of Heb uncertain *b* Gk Syr Jerome Tg: Heb *flee to
your mountain, O bird*

---

do in the innocent and helpless. **10.12–19** Petitions
for help and expressions of confidence that God will
aid the helpless. The Lord will *see* (v. 14) and *hear* (v.
17). **10.14** *Grief,* possibly "provocation" or "vexation."
10.15–16 Association of the wicked and the nations
here and elsewhere in Pss 9 and 10 (e.g., 9.5–6, 15–17)
suggests the possibility that the one who speaks in the
psalm is the king. **10.16** Victory over oppressors is a
demonstration of God's sovereign rule (24.8, 10;
29.10; 47.2; Ex 15.18).
 11.1–7 A psalm of confidence and trust in God by
someone who knows God's protection against the
wicked. It is related to the expressions of confidence in

the prayers for help (3.3–6, 8; 4.6–8; 6.8–10; 7.12–16).
To the leader. See note on 4.1–8. *Refuge.* See note on
2.10–12. **11.1–3** Against the advice of friends or counselors who have recommended that the psalmist in
trouble *flee . . . to the mountains,* the psalmist claims a
sufficient protection in trusting in the Lord. **11.3** See
note on 82.5. The advisers recognize the innocence or
righteousness of the one who prays. **11.4–7** Confidence in God's righteous rule. **11.4** The imagery of
God's throne of judgment is found also in 7.6–8; 9.4,
7; cf. 122.5; Prov 20.8. **11.5** The righteous one trusts in
God's determination of who is righteous or innocent
and who is wicked.

the faithful have disappeared from
humankind.
2 They utter lies to each other;
with flattering lips and a double heart
they speak.

3 May the LORD cut off all flattering lips,
the tongue that makes great boasts,
4 those who say, "With our tongues we will
prevail;
our lips are our own—who is our
master?"

5 "Because the poor are despoiled, because
the needy groan,
I will now rise up," says the LORD;
"I will place them in the safety for
which they long."
6 The promises of the LORD are promises
that are pure,
silver refined in a furnace on the
ground,
purified seven times.

7 You, O LORD, will protect us;
you will guard us from this generation
forever.
8 On every side the wicked prowl,
as vileness is exalted among
humankind.

Prayer for Deliverance from Enemies

To the leader. A Psalm of David.

13 How long, O LORD? Will you forget
me forever?

How long will you hide your face from
me?
2 How long must I bear pain*a* in my soul,
and have sorrow in my heart all day
long?
How long shall my enemy be exalted over
me?

3 Consider and answer me, O LORD my
God!
Give light to my eyes, or I will sleep the
sleep of death,
4 and my enemy will say, "I have
prevailed";
my foes will rejoice because I am
shaken.

5 But I trusted in your steadfast love;
my heart shall rejoice in your salvation.
6 I will sing to the LORD,
because he has dealt bountifully with
me.

Denunciation of Godlessness

To the leader. Of David.

14 Fools say in their hearts, "There is no
God."
They are corrupt, they do abominable
deeds;
there is no one who does good.

2 The LORD looks down from heaven on
humankind

a Syr: Heb *hold counsels*

12.1–8 A general prayer for help that incorporates a divine word of deliverance. A representative figure, possibly priest or prophet, seems to speak on behalf of the community as well as on behalf of God. *To the leader.* See note on 4.1–8. *According to The Sheminith.* See note on 6.1–10. 12.1–4 Pleas to God against those who oppress others by what they say—lies, flattery, arrogance, hypocrisy, and slander. 12.1 *Godly,* often translated as "faithful," those who live a life faithful to the covenant and the instruction of the Lord. The sense of widespread wickedness and the absence of goodness is similar to that expressed even more sharply in 14.1–3. 12.4 *"Who is our master?"* has the same force as the quotations in 10.4, 6; 14.1. The wicked assume that God has no effective power over them. 12.5 The response of God, possibly spoken by a representative figure. *Rise up.* Cf. the petitions asking this of God in, e.g., 3.7; 7.6; 9.19; 10.12; 74.22; 82.8; 132.8. *I will place . . . they long,* possibly to be translated, "I will place in

safety the witness on their behalf." 12.6–8 The confidence of the people in God even though wickedness presently prevails. 12.6 *The promises of the LORD,* or "the utterances of the LORD," given in v. 5, have the integrity and truthfulness that are not present on the lips and tongues of the wicked (vv. 2–4).
13.1–6 The prayer of an individual for help in the face of unspecified trouble. *To the leader.* See note on 4.1–8. 13.1–2 The complaint to God. 13.1 *How long?* See note on 6.3. *Will you forget me forever?* For the frequency of this complaint, see 42.9; 44.24; 74.19; 77.9 (cf. 9.12, 18; 10.11–12). *Hide your face.* See notes on 10.1; 27.9. 13.3–4 The plea for God to respond. 13.3 *Give light to my eyes,* i.e., restore the power to live. 13.5 An expression of confidence in God's help. 13.6 A vow of praise (see note on 7.17).
14.1–7 A psalm expressing confidence in God's protecting help for the poor and innocent even in the face of rampant and unrelenting wickedness and evil. The

to see if there are any who are wise,
    who seek after God.

3 They have all gone astray, they are all
    alike perverse;
    there is no one who does good,
    no, not one.

4 Have they no knowledge, all the evildoers
    who eat up my people as they eat
    bread,
    and do not call upon the LORD?

5 There they shall be in great terror,
    for God is with the company of the
    righteous.
6 You would confound the plans of the
    poor,
    but the LORD is their refuge.

7 O that deliverance for Israel would come
    from Zion!
    When the LORD restores the fortunes
    of his people,
    Jacob will rejoice; Israel will be glad.

Who Shall Abide in God's Sanctuary?

A Psalm of David.

15 O LORD, who may abide in your tent?
    Who may dwell on your holy hill?

2 Those who walk blamelessly, and do what
    is right,
    and speak the truth from their heart;
3 who do not slander with their tongue,
    and do no evil to their friends,
    nor take up a reproach against their
    neighbors;
4 in whose eyes the wicked are despised,
    but who honor those who fear the
    LORD;
    who stand by their oath even to their hurt;
5 who do not lend money at interest,
    and do not take a bribe against the
    innocent.

Those who do these things shall never be
    moved.

Song of Trust and Security in God

A Miktam of David.

16 Protect me, O God, for in you I take
    refuge.
2 I say to the LORD, "You are my Lord;
    I have no good apart from you." [a]

3 As for the holy ones in the land, they are
    the noble,
    in whom is all my delight.

_____
a Jerome Tg: Meaning of Heb uncertain

psalm is repeated in almost the same words as Ps 53. *To the leader.* See note on 4.1–8. **14.1–3** The absence of God is experienced in the absence of good. Quoted in Rom 3.10–12. **14.1** *Fools* are the same as the wicked in the wisdom traditions of Israel (cf. *evildoers* in v. 4). The statement of the fools in this psalm is placed on the lips of the wicked in 10.4 (cf. Isa 32.6). *There is no God,* i.e., God is not present in the world in any effective way. Cf. 10.4, 6, 13; 12.4. *There is no one who does good* echoes "there is no God." **14.2** *Who seek after God.* For the moral character of seeking after God, see Am 5.4–6, 7, 10–11, 14–15, where seeking after God is found in hating evil, loving good, and establishing justice. **14.4–6** The refuge of the poor and righteous is the downfall of the evildoers. These verses counter the empirical claim of vv. 1–3 that God is not present because evil is rampant. **14.4** *Who eat . . . eat bread.* The translation is uncertain. For a similar image, see Mic 3.1–3. **14.5** *God is with . . . the righteous* reflects the primary word of assurance from God to those in distress, "I am with you" (e.g., Gen 26.24; 35.3; Ex 3.12; Isa 41.10; cf. Isa 7.14 for Immanuel, a Hebrew term that means "God is with us"). **14.6** *Refuge.* See note on 2.10–12. **14.7** A prayer of hope and anticipation that God will deliver the people. When that happens, there will be great joy.

15.1–5 A liturgy for entrance into the sanctuary. See Ps 24 (cf. Isa 33.14–16; Ezek 18.5–9; Mic 6.6–8). **15.1** The question, perhaps by a priest, asks what the qualifications are for admission into the worshiping congregation and the presence of God. **15.2–5** The requirements for entry are now listed in response to the question. The general qualifications in v. 2 are specified in v. 3. They involve the morality of speech and conduct toward neighbor (vv. 2–3), association (v. 4ab), integrity of oaths sworn (v. 4c), and ill-gotten gains (v. 5). **15.4** *Fear the LORD.* See note on 34.7. **15.5** For the prohibition of *interest,* see Ex 22.25; Lev 25.36; Deut 23.19. Money was lent in order to help those in need, and profit from the distress of a neighbor was wrong. For the prohibition of *bribes,* see Ex 23.8; Deut 16.19; Isa 1.23; Mic 3.11.

16.1–11 A prayer of an individual for divine help in which emphasis is placed on the confident trust in God of the one who prays. The psalm seems to be more a prayer for continual protection rather than a cry of distress arising out of a particular occasion of suffering, though the latter may have elicited the confidence expressed herein. *Miktam.* Meaning uncertain, but possibly indicating that the psalm was inscribed on a stone or wall. **16.2–11** An elaborate expression of the

4 Those who choose another god multiply
      their sorrows;[a]
   their drink offerings of blood I will not
      pour out
   or take their names upon my lips.

5 The LORD is my chosen portion and my
      cup;
   you hold my lot.
6 The boundary lines have fallen for me in
      pleasant places;
   I have a goodly heritage.

7 I bless the LORD who gives me counsel;
   in the night also my heart instructs me.
8 I keep the LORD always before me;
   because he is at my right hand, I shall
      not be moved.

9 Therefore my heart is glad, and my soul
      rejoices;
   my body also rests secure.
10 For you do not give me up to Sheol,
   or let your faithful one see the Pit.

11 You show me the path of life.
   In your presence there is fullness of joy;
   in your right hand are pleasures
      forevermore.

Prayer for Deliverance from Persecutors

A Prayer of David.

17 Hear a just cause, O LORD; attend to
      my cry;
   give ear to my prayer from lips free of
      deceit.

2 From you let my vindication come;
   let your eyes see the right.

3 If you try my heart, if you visit me by
      night,
   if you test me, you will find no
      wickedness in me;
   my mouth does not transgress.
4 As for what others do, by the word of
      your lips
   I have avoided the ways of the violent.
5 My steps have held fast to your paths;
   my feet have not slipped.

6 I call upon you, for you will answer me,
      O God;
   incline your ear to me, hear my words.
7 Wondrously show your steadfast love,
   O savior of those who seek refuge
   from their adversaries at your right hand.

8 Guard me as the apple of the eye;
   hide me in the shadow of your wings,
9 from the wicked who despoil me,
   my deadly enemies who surround me.
10 They close their hearts to pity;
   with their mouths they speak
      arrogantly.
11 They track me down;[b] now they
      surround me;
   they set their eyes to cast me to the
      ground.
12 They are like a lion eager to tear,
   like a young lion lurking in ambush.

---

a Cn: Meaning of Heb uncertain b One Ms Compare Syr: MT
Our steps

psalmist's experience of God's guidance and protection
and the blessings God has bestowed. **16.2–4** The translation is for the most part very uncertain. **16.5–6** The
terms *portion, cup, boundary lines,* and *heritage* express the fact that the one who prays has received much
good from the Lord. All the terms except *cup* have to do
with the distribution of the promised land. They may
be metaphorical for the richness of life received from
God, or they may reflect the actual receipt of a rich and
valuable allotment of land. It has also been suggested
that these words are spoken by a Levite because the
tribe of Levi received no portion of land but lived off
the offerings of the people. Several texts speak of the
Lord as the portion or heritage of the Levites (Num
18.20; Deut 10.9; Josh 13.14). **16.7** *Bless the Lord,* i.e.,
give thanks. **16.8–10** Cited in Peter's speech in Acts
2.25–28. **16.10** Either in present distress or out of a
past rescue, the psalmist expresses confidence in God's

power to deliver from terrible death and keep the
psalmist alive. *Sheol.* See note on 6.5. *Pit,* a synonym for
Sheol and the grave. Cf. Acts 2.31; 13.35.

17.1–15 A cry for help of a person beset by persecutors and seeking God's judgment and deliverance. See
Ps 7 for a similar setting. Vv. 3, 15 suggest the petitioner may have spent the night in prayer in the sanctuary awaiting God's help, i.e., vindication in the
morning. **17.1–2** The basic petition to be heard and
judged. The one praying may have been falsely accused
(vv. 9–12) and seeks vindication, hoping perhaps for a
divine decision through a priest. **17.3–5** The persecuted one protests that he or she is innocent and righteous and offers to be tested in this regard. **17.6–9** The
petition for God's response and protection goes up
again. **17.7** *Refuge.* See note on 2.10–12. **17.8** *Shadow
of your wings.* See notes on 91.1; 91.4. **17.10–12** The
destructive character and actions of the persecutors

13 Rise up, O Lord, confront them,
    overthrow them!
  By your sword deliver my life from the
    wicked,
14 from mortals—by your hand, O Lord—
    from mortals whose portion in life is
      in this world.
  May their bellies be filled with what you
    have stored up for them;
  may their children have more than
    enough;
  may they leave something over to their
    little ones.

15 As for me, I shall behold your face in
    righteousness;
  when I awake I shall be satisfied,
    beholding your likeness.

Royal Thanksgiving for Victory

To the leader. A Psalm of David the servant of
the Lord, who addressed the words of this
song to the Lord on the day when the Lord
delivered him from the hand of all his
enemies, and from the hand of Saul. He said:

18 I love you, O Lord, my strength.
  2 The Lord is my rock, my fortress,
    and my deliverer,
  my God, my rock in whom I take
    refuge,
  my shield, and the horn of my
    salvation, my stronghold.
3 I call upon the Lord, who is worthy to be
    praised,
  so I shall be saved from my enemies.

4 The cords of death encompassed me;
  the torrents of perdition assailed me;

5 the cords of Sheol entangled me;
  the snares of death confronted me.

6 In my distress I called upon the Lord;
  to my God I cried for help.
  From his temple he heard my voice,
  and my cry to him reached his ears.

7 Then the earth reeled and rocked;
  the foundations also of the mountains
    trembled
  and quaked, because he was angry.
8 Smoke went up from his nostrils,
  and devouring fire from his mouth;
  glowing coals flamed forth from him.
9 He bowed the heavens, and came down;
  thick darkness was under his feet.
10 He rode on a cherub, and flew;
  he came swiftly upon the wings of the
    wind.
11 He made darkness his covering around
    him,
  his canopy thick clouds dark with
    water.
12 Out of the brightness before him
  there broke through his clouds
  hailstones and coals of fire.
13 The Lord also thundered in the heavens,
  and the Most High uttered his voice. *a*
14 And he sent out his arrows, and scattered
    them;
  he flashed forth lightnings, and routed
    them.
15 Then the channels of the sea were seen,
  and the foundations of the world were
    laid bare
  at your rebuke, O Lord,

---

a Gk See 2 Sam 22.14: Heb adds *hailstones and coals of fire*

---

are set forth. **17.12** *Lion, young lion.* See note on 7.2.
17.13–14 A final strong plea to God to thwart and
punish the wicked who threaten the innocent petitioner. **17.13** *Rise up, O Lord.* See note on 12.5.
17.15 The psalmist is confident of God's righteous
judgment when the night is over.
  18.1–50 A royal psalm of thanksgiving, presumably fulfilling a vow to give thanks and praise after
God has helped (see 7.17; 13.6). Although the superscription may not be historical, it suggests the circumstances in which such a song by a king would be
appropriate. The psalm is found also in 2 Sam 22. *To
the leader.* See note on 4.1–8. **18.1–3** Hymnic praise
of God by heaping up metaphors to underscore God's
protecting help. **18.2** *Horn of my salvation.* See note
on 75.4–5. *Refuge.* See v. 30; note on 2.10–12. **18.4–**

5 The near-death distress that evoked the cry to God
for help. **18.5** *Sheol.* See note on 6.5. **18.6** *From his
temple . . . voice.* See 1 Kings 8.37–40. *My cry . . . ears.*
See 2 Chr 6.40; Sir 21.5 (cf. Gen 18.21; Ex 2.23–24;
3.7). **18.7–19** The appearance of God to deliver the
king in trouble. The description is in typical storm-
god imagery, depicting the coming of God as a mighty
warrior from the cosmic abode, represented on earth
by the sanctuary. The elements of nature are both disturbed and used by the Divine Warrior (cf. Ex 15;
Deut 33.2–3; Judg 5.4–5; Ps 68.7–8; Hab 3.15).
18.10 *Cherub,* possibly a synonym for "cloud," but
also referring to the cherubim or winged figures that
served as the throne of the invisible God on the ark of
the covenant (1 Sam 4.4). **18.14** *Arrows,* i.e., flashes of
lightning. **18.16** *Mighty waters,* a common image for

at the blast of the breath of your
    nostrils.

16 He reached down from on high, he took
    me;
    he drew me out of mighty waters.
17 He delivered me from my strong enemy,
    and from those who hated me;
    for they were too mighty for me.
18 They confronted me in the day of my
    calamity;
    but the LORD was my support.
19 He brought me out into a broad place;
    he delivered me, because he delighted
    in me.

20 The LORD rewarded me according to my
    righteousness;
    according to the cleanness of my hands
    he recompensed me.
21 For I have kept the ways of the LORD,
    and have not wickedly departed from
    my God.
22 For all his ordinances were before me,
    and his statutes I did not put away
    from me.
23 I was blameless before him,
    and I kept myself from guilt.
24 Therefore the LORD has recompensed me
    according to my righteousness,
    according to the cleanness of my hands
    in his sight.

25 With the loyal you show yourself loyal;
    with the blameless you show yourself
    blameless;
26 with the pure you show yourself pure;
    and with the crooked you show
    yourself perverse.
27 For you deliver a humble people,
    but the haughty eyes you bring down.
28 It is you who light my lamp;
    the LORD, my God, lights up my
    darkness.
29 By you I can crush a troop,
    and by my God I can leap over a wall.
30 This God—his way is perfect;

the promise of the LORD proves true;
    he is a shield for all who take refuge in
    him.

31 For who is God except the LORD?
    And who is a rock besides our God?—
32 the God who girded me with strength,
    and made my way safe.
33 He made my feet like the feet of a deer,
    and set me secure on the heights.
34 He trains my hands for war,
    so that my arms can bend a bow of
    bronze.
35 You have given me the shield of your
    salvation,
    and your right hand has supported me;
    your help[a] has made me great.
36 You gave me a wide place for my steps
    under me,
    and my feet did not slip.
37 I pursued my enemies and overtook
    them;
    and did not turn back until they were
    consumed.
38 I struck them down, so that they were not
    able to rise;
    they fell under my feet.
39 For you girded me with strength for the
    battle;
    you made my assailants sink under me.
40 You made my enemies turn their backs to
    me,
    and those who hated me I destroyed.
41 They cried for help, but there was no one
    to save them;
    they cried to the LORD, but he did not
    answer them.
42 I beat them fine, like dust before the
    wind;
    I cast them out like the mire of the
    streets.

43 You delivered me from strife with the
    peoples;[b]
    you made me head of the nations;

---

a Or *gentleness* *b* Gk Tg: Heb *people*

---

terrible distress that threatens to overwhelm the sufferer (42.7; 69.1–2, 14–15; 144.7). **18.19** *A broad place*
(cf. v. 36) is a characteristic way of describing God's
gift of salvation (31.8; 66.12; 118.5; cf. Gen 26.22).
18.20–24 Because of the moral integrity of the ruler,
the enemies' persecution has not expressed divine
judgment but rather the grounds for God's powerful

help and protection (see Pss 1; 15). **18.25–29** The reason for the assertions of vv. 20–24 is that God responds appropriately to human conduct. **18.28** *Light*
is an image for life. **18.30–45** The king gives thanks
and praises God (vv. 30–31) by recounting how the
Lord prepared him to fight against his enemies (vv.
32–34) and gave him power over them (vv. 35–42).

people whom I had not known served
me.
44 As soon as they heard of me they obeyed
me;
foreigners came cringing to me.
45 Foreigners lost heart,
and came trembling out of their
strongholds.

46 The LORD lives! Blessed be my rock,
and exalted be the God of my
salvation,
47 the God who gave me vengeance
and subdued peoples under me;
48 who delivered me from my enemies;
indeed, you exalted me above my
adversaries;
you delivered me from the violent.

49 For this I will extol you, O LORD, among
the nations,
and sing praises to your name.
50 Great triumphs he gives to his king,
and shows steadfast love to his
anointed,
to David and his descendants forever.

God's Glory in Creation and the Law

To the leader. A Psalm of David.

19 The heavens are telling the glory of
God;
and the firmament^a proclaims his
handiwork.
2 Day to day pours forth speech,
and night to night declares knowledge.
3 There is no speech, nor are there words;
their voice is not heard;
4 yet their voice^b goes out through all the
earth,

and their words to the end of the
world.

In the heavens^c he has set a tent for the
sun,
5 which comes out like a bridegroom from
his wedding canopy,
and like a strong man runs its course
with joy.
6 Its rising is from the end of the heavens,
and its circuit to the end of them;
and nothing is hid from its heat.

7 The law of the LORD is perfect,
reviving the soul;
the decrees of the LORD are sure,
making wise the simple;
8 the precepts of the LORD are right,
rejoicing the heart;
the commandment of the LORD is clear,
enlightening the eyes;
9 the fear of the LORD is pure,
enduring forever;
the ordinances of the LORD are true
and righteous altogether.
10 More to be desired are they than gold,
even much fine gold;
sweeter also than honey,
and drippings of the honeycomb.

11 Moreover by them is your servant
warned;
in keeping them there is great reward.
12 But who can detect their errors?
Clear me from hidden faults.
13 Keep back your servant also from the
insolent;^d

---

a Or *dome* *b* Gk Jerome Compare Syr: Heb *line* *c* Heb *In them* *d* Or *from proud thoughts*

18.30 *Refuge.* See note on 2.10–12. **18.46–50** Concluding praise and thanksgiving. **18.49** *I will extol.* Cf. Rom 15.9. **18.50** The victories over enemies described in the song are here specifically said to be those of the ruler. *Anointed.* See note on 2.2.

19.1–14 A psalm extolling God's glory as revealed in the creation and the law (cf. Pss 1; 119). *To the leader.* See note on 4.1–8. **19.1–6** The glory of God proclaimed by the created order. **19.1–4b** In a paradoxical way the knowledge of God is passed on, transmitted without speech or words that can be heard in the customary way. Cf. Rom 10.18. **19.4b–6** The *sun* is a particular manifestation of the handiwork of God and, implicitly, not itself divine. The focus is upon the

regular movement of the sun across the heavens. **19.6** *Nothing . . . heat* echoes the ancient Near Eastern notion of the sun god as the god of justice, who has insight into all things, and anticipates the warning that God provides in the law. **19.7–10** God's instruction in the *law* is characterized in terms of its perfection (v. 7a), reliability (v. 7b), clarity (v. 8b), righteousness (vv. 8a, 9b), and truthfulness (v. 9b), and its benefits are set forth. The latter include its enlivening (v. 7a) and illumining (vv. 7b, 8b) effects and its capacity to give joy and delight (cf. 1.2). **19.10** The desirability and value of the law are underscored. **19.11–13** Even with the benefits and warning of the law, the psalmist cannot completely avoid hidden sins and mistakes or the con-

do not let them have dominion over me.
  Then I shall be blameless,
      and innocent of great transgression.

14 Let the words of my mouth and the
        meditation of my heart
      be acceptable to you,
    O LORD, my rock and my redeemer.

Prayer for Victory

To the leader. A Psalm of David.

20 The LORD answer you in the day of
        trouble!
    The name of the God of Jacob protect
        you!
2 May he send you help from the sanctuary,
      and give you support from Zion.
3 May he remember all your offerings,
      and regard with favor your burnt
        sacrifices.   *Selah*

4 May he grant you your heart's desire,
      and fulfill all your plans.
5 May we shout for joy over your victory,
      and in the name of our God set up our
        banners.
    May the LORD fulfill all your petitions.

6 Now I know that the LORD will help his
        anointed;
      he will answer him from his holy
        heaven
    with mighty victories by his right
        hand.
7 Some take pride in chariots, and some in
        horses,
      but our pride is in the name of the
        LORD our God.

8 They will collapse and fall,
      but we shall rise and stand upright.

9 Give victory to the king, O LORD;
      answer us when we call. *a*

Thanksgiving for Victory

To the leader. A Psalm of David.

21 In your strength the king rejoices,
        O LORD,
    and in your help how greatly he exults!
2 You have given him his heart's desire,
      and have not withheld the request of
        his lips.   *Selah*
3 For you meet him with rich blessings;
      you set a crown of fine gold on his
        head.
4 He asked you for life; you gave it to
        him—
      length of days forever and ever.
5 His glory is great through your help;
      splendor and majesty you bestow on
        him.
6 You bestow on him blessings forever;
      you make him glad with the joy of
        your presence.
7 For the king trusts in the LORD,
      and through the steadfast love of the
        Most High he shall not be moved.

8 Your hand will find out all your enemies;
      your right hand will find out those
        who hate you.
9 You will make them like a fiery furnace
      when you appear.

---

a Gk: Heb *give victory, O* LORD; *let the King answer us when we call*

---

trol that presumptuous members of the community could exercise and so needs God's forgiveness. **19.14** A concluding prayer of dedication and offering. See 104.34; 119.108.

20.1–9 A royal psalm seeking God's help for the ruler. It may have been offered as a prayer before the king and the army went out to war or at the time of enthronement. Its liturgical character is suggested by the movement from the intercession of the community to the voice of one who declares God's intention to help and then back to the prayer of the people at the end (cf. Ps 12). *To the leader.* See note on 4.1–8. **20.1–5** A series of prayers all of which would be appropriate when faced by an enemy and its army; they may also address more broadly the needs of the king throughout his rule. **20.1** The *name* of God was understood to

be in the sanctuary; this was the way God could be present there while dwelling continually transcendent in the heavens (1 Kings 8.15–30; cf. Pss 44.5; 54.6; 118.10–12). **20.3** *Selah.* See note on 3.2. **20.6–8** A declaration of God's sure help is given by a representative figure, possibly a priest or prophet. It may have been preceded by an oracle of salvation, a word of assurance from God (cf. note on 22.21b). **20.6** *Anointed.* See note on 2.2. **20.9** A final prayer for God's help in battle.

21.1–13 A royal liturgy of praise and thanksgiving for God's protection of the ruler. *To the leader.* See note on 4.1–8. **21.1–6** Praise of God for all the help and blessings that the Lord has given to the king. **21.2** *Selah.* See note on 3.2. **21.7** The confidence of the king in the Lord. **21.8–12** An announcement is made to the ruler, possibly by a representative figure, that the

The LORD will swallow them up in his
        wrath,
    and fire will consume them.
10 You will destroy their offspring from the
        earth,
    and their children from among
        humankind.
11 If they plan evil against you,
    if they devise mischief, they will not
        succeed.
12 For you will put them to flight;
    you will aim at their faces with your
        bows.

13 Be exalted, O LORD, in your strength!
    We will sing and praise your power.

Plea for Deliverance from Suffering and Hostility

To the leader: according to The Deer of the
        Dawn. A Psalm of David.

22 My God, my God, why have you
        forsaken me?
    Why are you so far from helping me,
        from the words of my groaning?
2 O my God, I cry by day, but you do not
        answer;
    and by night, but find no rest.

3 Yet you are holy,
    enthroned on the praises of Israel.
4 In you our ancestors trusted;
    they trusted, and you delivered
        them.
5 To you they cried, and were saved;

    in you they trusted, and were not put
        to shame.

6 But I am a worm, and not human;
    scorned by others, and despised by the
        people.
7 All who see me mock at me;
    they make mouths at me, they shake
        their heads;
8 "Commit your cause to the LORD; let him
        deliver—
    let him rescue the one in whom he
        delights!"

9 Yet it was you who took me from the
        womb;
    you kept me safe on my mother's breast.
10 On you I was cast from my birth,
    and since my mother bore me you have
        been my God.
11 Do not be far from me,
    for trouble is near
    and there is no one to help.

12 Many bulls encircle me,
    strong bulls of Bashan surround me;
13 they open wide their mouths at me,
    like a ravening and roaring lion.

14 I am poured out like water,
    and all my bones are out of joint;
    my heart is like wax;
    it is melted within my breast;
15 my mouth[a] is dried up like a potsherd,

---

a Cn: Heb strength

Lord will enable the king to overcome all enemies (cf.
note on 20.6–8). **21.13** The congregation sings praise
to God. *Be exalted* is possibly a call to God to "rise up"
in might to deliver the king and so evoke the songs of
thanksgiving (cf. note on 12.5).
22.1–31 The prayer for help of an individual in
great distress (vv. 1–21a) and the song of thanksgiving
and praise (vv. 22–30) that follows God's response of
deliverance (v. 21b). *To the leader.* See note on 4.1–8.
The Deer of the Dawn may be a note about the melody.
The Septuagint gives an alternate possibility, "Concerning the help at dawn," because of the similarity of
the word translated "deer" to the word for "help" in v.
19. **22.1–2** An anguished complaint to God because
God is silent and absent in the petitioner's distress.
22.1 The first part of this verse is quoted in Jesus' cry
from the cross (Mt 27.46; Mk 15.34). *Groaning,* better
"roaring." **22.3–5** The psalmist's trust in God's protection is renewed in remembering that the earlier com-

munity of faith trusted and cried out in trouble and
God heard and delivered them. **22.6–8** Remembering
the earlier community's deliverance, their not being
shamed, the psalmist becomes more aware of the present, as those round about mock and scorn because the
one who prayed suffers without release. These verses
are alluded to in the passion story of Jesus (Mt 27.39–
44; Mk 15.29–32; Lk 23.35–37). **22.9–11** The memory of God's care of the psalmist up to now is a claim
of faith in the face of despair and leads to the plea for
God to be present and to help. Cf. 71.6; 139.13. **22.12–
21a** The sufferer plunges back into the depths and recounts at length the persecutions of others and the
sense of being close to death. **22.12–13** *Bulls, strong
bulls.* See note on 7.2. *Bashan* was an area in Transjordan east of the Sea of Galilee noted for producing
good cattle (cf. Ezek 39.18; Am 4.1). *Roaring lion.* Cf.
1 Pet 5.8. **22.14–15** The picture of sickness unto death
may be metaphorical for severe distress or it may re-

and my tongue sticks to my jaws;
   you lay me in the dust of death.

16 For dogs are all around me;
      a company of evildoers encircles me.
   My hands and feet have shriveled;[a]
17 I can count all my bones.
   They stare and gloat over me;
18 they divide my clothes among themselves,
      and for my clothing they cast lots.

19 But you, O Lord, do not be far away!
      O my help, come quickly to my aid!
20 Deliver my soul from the sword,
      my life[b] from the power of the dog!
21 Save me from the mouth of the lion!

From the horns of the wild oxen you have
      rescued[c] me.
22 I will tell of your name to my brothers
      and sisters;[d]
   in the midst of the congregation I will
      praise you:
23 You who fear the Lord, praise him!
   All you offspring of Jacob, glorify him;
   stand in awe of him, all you offspring
      of Israel!
24 For he did not despise or abhor
      the affliction of the afflicted;
   he did not hide his face from me,[e]
      but heard when I[f] cried to him.

25 From you comes my praise in the great
      congregation;
   my vows I will pay before those who
      fear him.

26 The poor[g] shall eat and be satisfied;
   those who seek him shall praise the
      Lord.
   May your hearts live forever!

27 All the ends of the earth shall remember
      and turn to the Lord;
   and all the families of the nations
      shall worship before him.[h]
28 For dominion belongs to the Lord,
      and he rules over the nations.

29 To him,[i] indeed, shall all who sleep in[j] the
      earth bow down;
   before him shall bow all who go down
      to the dust,
   and I shall live for him.[k]
30 Posterity will serve him;
   future generations will be told about
      the Lord,
31 and[l] proclaim his deliverance to a people
      yet unborn,
   saying that he has done it.

The Divine Shepherd

A Psalm of David.

23 The Lord is my shepherd, I shall not
         want.
2 He makes me lie down in green
      pastures;

---

a Meaning of Heb uncertain   b Heb *my only one*
c Heb *answered*   d Or *kindred*   e Heb *him*   f Heb *he*
g Or *afflicted*   h Gk Syr Jerome: Heb *you*   i Cn: Heb *They have
eaten and*   j Cn: Heb *all the fat ones*   k Compare Gk Syr Vg:
Heb *and he who cannot keep himself alive*   l Compare Gk: Heb *it
will be told about the Lord to the generation*, 31*they will come and*

---

flect actual illness. **22.16–18** *Dogs.* See vv. 12–13; note
on 7.2. The picture here is of one wasted away by illness, and the taunters and persecutors already distributing the victim's clothing as death nears (cf. Mt 27.35;
Mk 15.24; Lk 23.34; Jn 19.23–24). **22.19–21a** The
final desperate petition for God to come and save the
life of the sufferer. *Dog, lion.* See vv. 12–13; note on
7.2. **22.21b–31** The psalmist receives a response from
God and renders extravagant praise for God's delivering help. The thanksgiving may be after God's help has
been received or in anticipation of its coming because
the prayer has been answered. Words of praise (vv. 22–
23, 25–27, 29–31a) are followed by reasons for such
praise (vv. 24, 28, 31b) as the psalmist evokes an ever
widening circle of those who should praise and worship the Lord because of such a marvelous deliverance.
22.21b *Rescued,* more accurately "answered." It is likely
that this point in the psalm reflects the giving by some
priestly or representative figure of an oracle of salva-

tion that is God's promise to be with the psalmist and
to help (e.g., Isa 41.8–13; cf. Ps. 35.3). **22.22–26** The
community of faith in which the psalmist lives is called
to praise the Lord because he has answered the prayer
of the sufferer. **22.22** *I will tell your name.* Set on the
lips of Jesus in Heb 2.12. Cf. 35.18. **22.23** *Fear the
Lord.* See note on 34.7. Cf. 22.25. **22.24** *Hide his face.*
See notes on 10.1; 27.9. **22.27–28** The nations of the
earth are called to praise. **22.29–31** Those who have
died and those yet unborn are expected to serve the
Lord, who has done such a marvelous deed in saving
the psalmist from death.
   23.1–6 A song of trust that may have been evoked
by an experience of deliverance such as the one described in Ps 22. **23.1–3** The imagery of the Lord as
shepherd and the people as the flock is developed here
in detail (cf. 95.7; 100.3; Isa 40.11; Ezek 34.11–16; Jn
10.11, 14). **23.1** *I shall not want,* as Israel lacked nothing when wandering in the wilderness (Neh 9.21).

he leads me beside still waters;[a]

3   he restores my soul.[b]
     He leads me in right paths[c]
        for his name's sake.

4   Even though I walk through the darkest
        valley,[d]
     I fear no evil;
        for you are with me;
     your rod and your staff—
        they comfort me.

5   You prepare a table before me
        in the presence of my enemies;
     you anoint my head with oil;
        my cup overflows.

6   Surely[e] goodness and mercy[f] shall follow
        me
     all the days of my life,
     and I shall dwell in the house of the LORD
        my whole life long.[g]

Entrance into the Temple

Of David. A Psalm.

24   The earth is the LORD's and all that is
     in it,
        the world, and those who live in it;

2   for he has founded it on the seas,
        and established it on the rivers.

3   Who shall ascend the hill of the LORD?
        And who shall stand in his holy place?

4   Those who have clean hands and pure
        hearts,

who do not lift up their souls to what
        is false,
     and do not swear deceitfully.

5   They will receive blessing from the LORD,
        and vindication from the God of their
        salvation.

6   Such is the company of those who seek
        him,
     who seek the face of the God of Jacob.[h]
                                        Selah

7   Lift up your heads, O gates!
        and be lifted up, O ancient doors!
        that the King of glory may come in.

8   Who is the King of glory?
        The LORD, strong and mighty,
        the LORD, mighty in battle.

9   Lift up your heads, O gates!
        and be lifted up, O ancient doors!
        that the King of glory may come in.

10   Who is this King of glory?
        The LORD of hosts,
        he is the King of glory.   *Selah*

Prayer for Guidance and for Deliverance

Of David.

25   To you, O LORD, I lift up my soul.
     2 O my God, in you I trust;
        do not let me be put to shame;
        do not let my enemies exult over me.

---

a Heb *waters of rest* *b* Or *life* *c* Or *paths of righteousness*
d Or *the valley of the shadow of death* *e* Or *Only*
f Or *kindness* *g* Heb *for length of days* *h* Gk Syr: Heb *your
face, O Jacob*

23.4 The confidence here reflects the assuring words of the oracle of salvation that came to those in distress who cried out to God: "Do not fear. I am with you" (cf. note on 22.21b). *Darkest valley* is an image for the experience of terrible distress or suffering, the nearness of death. *Rod,* a club used to fend off wild animals. *Staff,* an instrument used to keep sheep from wandering off. **23.5–6** The image of the Lord as host conveys the psalmist's experience of the goodness of God. These verses may reflect a sacrificial meal in thanksgiving for God's deliverance. **23.5** *You prepare . . . me,* as God spread a table of provision for Israel in the wilderness (78.19). *You anoint . . . oil* reflects the custom of pouring oil over the head of an honored guest. **23.6** The psalmist is now pursued by God's goodness and mercy instead of by enemies and persecutors (7.5; 71.11).
24.1–10 A liturgy for entrance into the sanctuary. See Ps 15 (cf. Isa 33.14–16; Ezek 18.5–9; Mic 6.6–8). **24.1–2** A confession that everything belongs to the Lord, who created the world and everything in it. Cf.

1 Cor 10.26. **24.3–6** A question is asked, perhaps by a priest or representative figure, about the qualifications for admission into the sanctuary (v. 3), and those qualifications are then listed (v. 4). Cf. Ps 15. A final affirmation accepts these conditions as the requisites for divine blessing (vv. 5–6). **24.6** *Selah.* See note on 3.2. **24.7–10** The liturgy continues, but now centers on the entrance of the Lord into the city and sanctuary, presumably by means of the ark of the covenant, which, as the throne of the invisible God, accompanied the people into battle against their enemies (Num 10.35–36; 1 Sam 4.4). **24.7** The call of those who bear the ark as they approach the gates or doors. **24.8a** The question posed by those at the doors. **24.8b–9** The response of those with the ark. **24.10** The question and answer repeated once more (cf. 2 Sam 6.12–15).
25.1–22 This acrostic psalm (see note on 9.1–10.18), presents an individual's prayer for help in a situation of unspecified trouble. The prayer is marked by various petitions, undergirded by reasons for God's

3 Do not let those who wait for you be put
     to shame;
     let them be ashamed who are wantonly
       treacherous.

4 Make me to know your ways, O LORD;
     teach me your paths.
5 Lead me in your truth, and teach me,
     for you are the God of my salvation;
     for you I wait all day long.

6 Be mindful of your mercy, O LORD, and
     of your steadfast love,
     for they have been from of old.
7 Do not remember the sins of my youth or
     my transgressions;
     according to your steadfast love
       remember me,
     for your goodness' sake, O LORD!

8 Good and upright is the LORD;
     therefore he instructs sinners in the
       way.
9 He leads the humble in what is right,
     and teaches the humble his way.
10 All the paths of the LORD are steadfast
       love and faithfulness,
     for those who keep his covenant and
       his decrees.

11 For your name's sake, O LORD,
     pardon my guilt, for it is great.
12 Who are they that fear the LORD?
     He will teach them the way that they
       should choose.

13 They will abide in prosperity,
     and their children shall possess the
       land.

14 The friendship of the LORD is for those
     who fear him,
     and he makes his covenant known to
       them.
15 My eyes are ever toward the LORD,
     for he will pluck my feet out of the net.

16 Turn to me and be gracious to me,
     for I am lonely and afflicted.
17 Relieve the troubles of my heart,
     and bring me *a* out of my distress.
18 Consider my affliction and my trouble,
     and forgive all my sins.

19 Consider how many are my foes,
     and with what violent hatred they hate
       me.
20 O guard my life, and deliver me;
     do not let me be put to shame, for I
       take refuge in you.
21 May integrity and uprightness preserve
     me,
     for I wait for you.

22 Redeem Israel, O God,
     out of all its troubles.

Plea for Justice and Declaration of Righteousness

Of David.

26 Vindicate me, O LORD,
     for I have walked in my integrity,
     and I have trusted in the LORD without
       wavering.
2 Prove me, O LORD, and try me;
     test my heart and mind.

_____

a Or *The troubles of my heart are enlarged; bring me*

positive response, and it expresses trust in God's goodness. **25.1–7** The one who trusts prays for help, direction, and forgiveness. **25.2–3** The shame of the psalmist may be in being afflicted and receiving no response from God (cf. 4.2; 22.2–8; 31.1, 17; 69.7, 19), but those *who are wantonly treacherous* have probably accused or persecuted the psalmist in some way. **25.4–5** A prayer for instruction in the Lord's way. **25.6–7** A prayer for forgiveness. **25.8–15** Affirmations of the goodness and faithfulness of the Lord, the ground of the petitioner's hope for help. **25.11** The realization of God's faithfulness to those who keep God's instruction (v. 10) leads the psalmist, who is mindful of failure to do that in the past, to insert a prayer for forgiveness. **25.12** *Fear the LORD.* See note on 34.7. Cf. 25.14. **25.15** *Net.* See note on 9.15. **25.16–21** Renewed and

passionate pleas for deliverance and forgiveness. **25.16** For loneliness as a symptom of the suffering of those who cry for help, see 22.6; 69.8, 20; 102.7; Jer 15.17. **25.20** *Refuge.* See note on 2.10–12. **25.22** The prayer of an individual concludes with a prayer for the whole community in trouble (cf. 14.7; 28.9; 130.7; 131.3).

26.1–12 An individual's prayer seeking God's judgment of the psalmist's righteousness. Such a prayer may be that of one who has come before God in the sanctuary seeking vindication in the face of false accusations (vv. 9–10; cf. Ps 7; 1 Kings 8.31–32) or it may be the prayer of one who seeks entrance into the sanctuary and claims to have fulfilled the requirements of a righteous life (vv. 7–8; cf. Pss 15; 24). **26.1** The initial plea to God. *Vindicate me,* or "judge me." **26.2–8** The

3 For your steadfast love is before my eyes,
   and I walk in faithfulness to you.*ᵃ*

4 I do not sit with the worthless,
   nor do I consort with hypocrites;
5 I hate the company of evildoers,
   and will not sit with the wicked.

6 I wash my hands in innocence,
   and go around your altar, O LORD,
7 singing aloud a song of thanksgiving,
   and telling all your wondrous deeds.

8 O LORD, I love the house in which you
      dwell,
   and the place where your glory abides.
9 Do not sweep me away with sinners,
   nor my life with the bloodthirsty,
10 those in whose hands are evil devices,
   and whose right hands are full of
      bribes.

11 But as for me, I walk in my integrity;
   redeem me, and be gracious to me.
12 My foot stands on level ground;
   in the great congregation I will bless
      the LORD.

Triumphant Song of Confidence

Of David.

27 The LORD is my light and my
      salvation;
   whom shall I fear?
   The LORD is the stronghold*ᵇ* of my life;
   of whom shall I be afraid?

2 When evildoers assail me
   to devour my flesh—
   my adversaries and foes—
   they shall stumble and fall.

3 Though an army encamp against me,
   my heart shall not fear;
   though war rise up against me,
   yet I will be confident.

4 One thing I asked of the LORD,
   that will I seek after:
   to live in the house of the LORD
   all the days of my life,
   to behold the beauty of the LORD,
   and to inquire in his temple.

5 For he will hide me in his shelter
   in the day of trouble;
   he will conceal me under the cover of his
      tent;
   he will set me high on a rock.

6 Now my head is lifted up
   above my enemies all around me,
   and I will offer in his tent
   sacrifices with shouts of joy;
   I will sing and make melody to the LORD.

7 Hear, O LORD, when I cry aloud,
   be gracious to me and answer me!
8 "Come," my heart says, "seek his face!"
   Your face, LORD, do I seek.
9 Do not hide your face from me.

Do not turn your servant away in anger,
   you who have been my help.
Do not cast me off, do not forsake me,
   O God of my salvation!
10 If my father and mother forsake me,
   the LORD will take me up.

11 Teach me your way, O LORD,
   and lead me on a level path

---

a Or *in your faithfulness*   *b* Or *refuge*

petitioner offers to be tested and submits the case for a righteous and faithful life. **26.4–5** See 1.1. **26.6–7** Washing the hands may have been part of a ritual in the sanctuary as a way of testifying to cleanness or innocence. **26.9–12** A concluding sharp contrast is drawn between the ways of sinners and their fate and the way and hope of the righteous one who prays to God. **26.10** *Evil devices,* a term that often refers to sexual immorality (Lev 18.17; 19.29; 20.14; Job 31.11; Jer 13.27).

27.1–14 A song of trust (vv. 1–6) by one of the faithful is the basis for a prayer for help in the face of false accusations (vv. 7–14). **27.1–6** The psalmist expresses trust in the Lord against all enemies (vv. 1–3) and eagerness to be in God's presence (vv. 4–6). Cf. 23.6; 42.1–2; 43.3–4; 84.1–4. **27.1** *Stronghold.* Or *refuge;* see note on 2.10–12. **27.2** *Devour my flesh.* See note on 7.2. **27.4** *The beauty of the LORD,* i.e., the graciousness or favor of the Lord (cf. 90.17; 135.3). *To inquire in his temple* probably means to seek after an oracle of salvation from the Lord, though it may have a more general reference. **27.6** Sacrifices and praise were offered in the sanctuary by the one God delivered from distress. **27.7–13** The prayer of the oppressed. **27.8** *Seek his face,* seek God's favor. **27.9** *Do not hide your face,* i.e., "do not withhold your favor"; see also

because of my enemies.
12 Do not give me up to the will of my
        adversaries,
    for false witnesses have risen against
        me,
    and they are breathing out violence.

13 I believe that I shall see the goodness of
        the LORD
    in the land of the living.
14 Wait for the LORD;
    be strong, and let your heart take
        courage;
    wait for the LORD!

Prayer for Help and Thanksgiving for It

Of David.

28 To you, O LORD, I call;
    my rock, do not refuse to hear me,
    for if you are silent to me,
        I shall be like those who go down to
        the Pit.
2 Hear the voice of my supplication,
    as I cry to you for help,
    as I lift up my hands
        toward your most holy sanctuary.[a]

3 Do not drag me away with the wicked,
    with those who are workers of evil,
    who speak peace with their neighbors,
        while mischief is in their hearts.
4 Repay them according to their work,
    and according to the evil of their
        deeds;
    repay them according to the work of their
        hands;
    render them their due reward.

5 Because they do not regard the works of
        the LORD,
    or the work of his hands,
    he will break them down and build them
        up no more.

6 Blessed be the LORD,
    for he has heard the sound of my
        pleadings.
7 The LORD is my strength and my shield;
    in him my heart trusts;
    so I am helped, and my heart exults,
        and with my song I give thanks to him.

8 The LORD is the strength of his people;
    he is the saving refuge of his anointed.
9 O save your people, and bless your
        heritage;
    be their shepherd, and carry them
        forever.

The Voice of God in a Great Storm

A Psalm of David.

29 Ascribe to the LORD, O heavenly
        beings,[b]
    ascribe to the LORD glory and strength.
2 Ascribe to the LORD the glory of his
        name;
    worship the LORD in holy splendor.

3 The voice of the LORD is over the waters;
    the God of glory thunders,
    the LORD, over mighty waters.
4 The voice of the LORD is powerful;
    the voice of the LORD is full of majesty.

---

a Heb *your innermost sanctuary*   b Heb *sons of gods*

note on 10.1. **27.12** At least one facet of the trouble is false accusation brought against the one praying. *They are . . . violence,* more accurately "violent witnesses." **27.13** An expression of trust that the petitioner will be kept alive and well by the Lord. **27.14** A response of encouragement to the prayer of the preceding verses. *Wait for the LORD* means to expect the Lord's deliverance.

   28.1–9 An individual's prayer for help when beset by members of the community who are carrying out some sort of persecution, or when in fear of being caught up in the judgment that God will bring against them. **28.1–2** The initial plea for God to pay attention to the prayer. **28.1** *Pit.* See note on 16.10. **28.2** For lifting up hands toward the sanctuary, see 1 Kings 8.38–39. **28.3–4** A cry to God to do in the wicked who persecute the praying one. The psalmist fears being drawn

into the punishment that they rightfully deserve. **28.5** A claim that God's just judgment against the wicked will happen. It is either a response to the prayer of the petitioner by a representative figure like a priest or an expression of trust on the part of the one who prays. **28.6–7** A song of thanksgiving by the one who has cried out because God has heeded the prayer. **28.6** *Blessed.* See note on 103.1–2. **28.8–9** A final confession and prayer that transforms the prayer of an individual into one incorporating the community and its ruler. See note on 25.22. **28.8** *Anointed.* See note on 2.2.

   29.1–11 A hymn of praise in honor of God's glory and power as revealed in a thunderstorm. **29.1–2** Opening call to worship God. *Heavenly beings,* the heavenly court of gods or semidivine beings (see 82.1, 6; Ex 15.11; Deut 32.8), who are to acknowledge the supremacy of the Lord as universal ruler. **29.3–9** De-

5 The voice of the Lord breaks the cedars;
  the Lord breaks the cedars of
  Lebanon.
6 He makes Lebanon skip like a calf,
  and Sirion like a young wild ox.

7 The voice of the Lord flashes forth
  flames of fire.
8 The voice of the Lord shakes the
  wilderness;
  the Lord shakes the wilderness of
  Kadesh.

9 The voice of the Lord causes the oaks to
  whirl,ª
  and strips the forest bare;
  and in his temple all say, "Glory!"

10 The Lord sits enthroned over the flood;
  the Lord sits enthroned as king forever.
11 May the Lord give strength to his people!
  May the Lord bless his people with
  peace!

Thanksgiving for Recovery from Grave Illness

A Psalm. A Song at the dedication of the
temple. Of David.

30 I will extol you, O Lord, for you have
  drawn me up,
  and did not let my foes rejoice over me.
2 O Lord my God, I cried to you for help,

and you have healed me.
3 O Lord, you brought up my soul from
  Sheol,
  restored me to life from among those
  gone down to the Pit.ᵇ

4 Sing praises to the Lord, O you his
  faithful ones,
  and give thanks to his holy name.
5 For his anger is but for a moment;
  his favor is for a lifetime.
  Weeping may linger for the night,
  but joy comes with the morning.

6 As for me, I said in my prosperity,
  "I shall never be moved."
7 By your favor, O Lord,
  you had established me as a strong
  mountain;
  you hid your face;
  I was dismayed.

8 To you, O Lord, I cried,
  and to the Lord I made supplication:
9 "What profit is there in my death,
  if I go down to the Pit?
  Will the dust praise you?
  Will it tell of your faithfulness?
10 Hear, O Lord, and be gracious to me!
  O Lord, be my helper!"

---

a Or causes the deer to calve b Or that I should not go down to the Pit

---

scription of the thunderstorm as it rises over the Mediterranean, moves inland with devastating effects across the Lebanon and Anti-Lebanon mountain ranges, and spends itself in the Syrian desert. **29.3** *Waters* and *mighty waters* refer to the Mediterranean Sea, perhaps with mythic overtones relating to the primordial waters of chaos the Lord was said to have vanquished in creating the world (see 74.12–14; 89.9–10; Isa 51.9). **29.6** *Sirion*, Phoenician name for Mount Hermon in the Anti-Lebanon range. **29.8** *Kadesh*, here not the well-known oasis in Sinai (Num 20.1) but the desert east of the Syrian city of Kadesh on the Orontes River. **29.9** The alternate reading *causes the deer to calve* (see text note *a*) is equally plausible in the light of the ancient belief that thunderstorms could induce labor. **29.10–11** Concluding affirmation of confidence, possibly with a polemic thrust. In Canaanite mythology, Baal, the storm god, was enthroned over the conquered flood or primordial waters of chaos. Here is affirmed the universal kingship of the Lord, who dethrones all other powers and thus is the only one able to grant security and peace.

30.1–12 A song of thanksgiving and praise by one who has gone from security and prosperity to near death and has been delivered by God. *A Song . . . temple* is a secondary superscription indicating that the psalm came to be used at the Feast of Dedication (Hanukkah) after the cleansing of the temple by Judas Maccabeus in 164 BCE. **30.1–3** The psalmist praises God for being healed. The references to healing may be metaphorical, but their sustained use in this psalm suggests physical illness and near death as the plight from which the psalmist was delivered. **30.1** *My foes,* here probably those who declare the sufferer's illness to be the proper punishment from God. **30.3** *Sheol.* See note on 6.5. *Pit.* See note on 16.10. **30.4–5** A call to the community to praise God, who is always more inclined toward favor than anger (cf. Isa 54.7–8), and a declaration that the latter is a response to particular sins by the people. **30.6–12** The psalmist recounts what happened and how the Lord helped. **30.6–7** From a position of security the psalmist is thrown into some terrible personal distress. Both situations are seen as God's activity. **30.7** *Hid your face.* See notes

11 You have turned my mourning into
        dancing;
    you have taken off my sackcloth
    and clothed me with joy,
12 so that my soul *a* may praise you and not
        be silent.
    O Lord my God, I will give thanks to
        you forever.

Prayer and Praise for Deliverance from Enemies

To the leader. A Psalm of David.

31 In you, O Lord, I seek refuge;
    do not let me ever be put to shame;
    in your righteousness deliver me.
2 Incline your ear to me;
    rescue me speedily.
    Be a rock of refuge for me,
    a strong fortress to save me.

3 You are indeed my rock and my
        fortress;
    for your name's sake lead me and guide
        me,
4 take me out of the net that is hidden for
        me,
    for you are my refuge.
5 Into your hand I commit my spirit;
    you have redeemed me, O Lord,
        faithful God.

6 You hate *b* those who pay regard to
        worthless idols,
    but I trust in the Lord.
7 I will exult and rejoice in your steadfast
        love,
    because you have seen my affliction;
    you have taken heed of my
        adversities,

8 and have not delivered me into the hand
        of the enemy;
    you have set my feet in a broad place.

9 Be gracious to me, O Lord, for I am in
        distress;
    my eye wastes away from grief,
    my soul and body also.
10 For my life is spent with sorrow,
    and my years with sighing;
    my strength fails because of my misery, *c*
    and my bones waste away.

11 I am the scorn of all my adversaries,
    a horror *d* to my neighbors,
    an object of dread to my acquaintances;
    those who see me in the street flee
        from me.
12 I have passed out of mind like one who is
        dead;
    I have become like a broken vessel.
13 For I hear the whispering of many—
        terror all around!—
    as they scheme together against me,
    as they plot to take my life.

14 But I trust in you, O Lord;
    I say, "You are my God."
15 My times are in your hand;
    deliver me from the hand of my
        enemies and persecutors.
16 Let your face shine upon your servant;
    save me in your steadfast love.
17 Do not let me be put to shame, O Lord,
    for I call on you;
    let the wicked be put to shame;
    let them go dumbfounded to Sheol.

a Heb *that glory* *b* One Heb Ms Gk Syr Jerome: MT *I hate*
c Gk Syr: Heb *my iniquity* *d* Cn: Heb *exceedingly*

---

on 10.1; 27.9. **30.8–10** The cry to God for help. **30.9** See note on 6.5. **30.11–12** The psalmist gives thanks to God for hearing the prayer and giving the desired help. **30.11** *Sackcloth,* clothing representing mourning or penitence.

31.1–24 A prayer for God's help in which petition, lament, and expressions of confidence lead into a final song of thanksgiving for the help that has been received. *To the leader.* See note on 4.1–8. **31.1–5** Prayer for deliverance. **31.1** *Shame.* See note on 25.2–3. **31.4** *Net.* See note on 9.15. **31.5** According to Lk 23.46 these are Jesus' last words on the cross. **31.6–8** Either a song of thanksgiving or a vow to express such thanksgiving in the future. **31.8** *Broad place.* See note on

18.19. **31.9–13** A petition (v. 9a) leading into an extended lament over physical (vv. 9b–10) and social distress (vv. 11–13). The former may be actual sickness unto death or a metaphor of personal dissolution to express suffering. The latter involves both scorn by neighbors and some sort of scheming that threatens the petitioner's life. **31.9** *Grief,* or "provocation." **31.12** *Like a broken vessel.* See Jer 22.28; 48.38. **31.13** Cf. Jer 11.19; 20.10. *Terror all around.* See Jer 6.25; 20.3, 10; 46.5; 49.29. **31.14–18** Additional pleas for God's help (vv. 15b–18) arising out of the trust in God (vv. 14–15a). **31.16** *Let your face shine,* i.e., show favor (4.6; 67.1; 80.3, 7, 19; 119.135). **31.17** *Put to shame.* See note on 25.2–3. *Sheol.* See note on 6.5.

18 Let the lying lips be stilled
   that speak insolently against the
      righteous
   with pride and contempt.

19 O how abundant is your goodness
   that you have laid up for those who
      fear you,
   and accomplished for those who take
      refuge in you,
   in the sight of everyone!
20 In the shelter of your presence you hide
      them
   from human plots;
   you hold them safe under your shelter
   from contentious tongues.

21 Blessed be the Lord,
   for he has wondrously shown his
      steadfast love to me
   when I was beset as a city under siege.
22 I had said in my alarm,
   "I am driven far[a] from your sight."
   But you heard my supplications
   when I cried out to you for help.

23 Love the Lord, all you his saints.
   The Lord preserves the faithful,
   but abundantly repays the one who
      acts haughtily.
24 Be strong, and let your heart take
      courage,
   all you who wait for the Lord.

The Joy of Forgiveness

Of David. A Maskil.

32 Happy are those whose transgression
   is forgiven,
   whose sin is covered.

2 Happy are those to whom the Lord
   imputes no iniquity,
   and in whose spirit there is no deceit.

3 While I kept silence, my body wasted away
   through my groaning all day long.
4 For day and night your hand was heavy
      upon me;
   my strength was dried up[b] as by the
      heat of summer.   Selah

5 Then I acknowledged my sin to you,
   and I did not hide my iniquity;
   I said, "I will confess my transgressions to
      the Lord,"
   and you forgave the guilt of my sin.
                                          Selah

6 Therefore let all who are faithful
   offer prayer to you;
   at a time of distress,[c] the rush of mighty
      waters
   shall not reach them.
7 You are a hiding place for me;
   you preserve me from trouble;
   you surround me with glad cries of
      deliverance.   Selah

8 I will instruct you and teach you the way
   you should go;
   I will counsel you with my eye upon
   you.
9 Do not be like a horse or a mule, without
      understanding,
   whose temper must be curbed with bit
      and bridle,
   else it will not stay near you.

---

a Another reading is *cut off*   b Meaning of Heb uncertain
c Cn: Heb *at a time of finding* only

31.18 Slanderous accusations seem to have been made against the one praying. 31.19 *Fear.* See note on 34.7. 31.19–24 A song of thanksgiving and praise for deliverance. An oracle of salvation may have been given between vv. 18 and 19 that provided the assurance evoking these expressions. See note on 22.21b. 31.21 *Blessed.* See note on 103.1–2. 31.23–24 The salvation of the individual is an impetus for all the community of the faithful to trust in God's help.

32.1–11 A song of thanksgiving by an individual who has been forgiven by God. One of the penitential psalms (see note on 6.1–10). *Maskil,* either an "artful song" or a "didactic song," probably the former, indicating a song that has been composed with artistic

skill, though didactic elements are present also (e.g., vv. 8–9). 32.1–2 The joy of the psalmist in receiving God's forgiveness. Quoted in Rom 4.7–8. *Happy.* See note on 1.1. 32.3–5 The psalmist tells about the experience of personal disintegration and distress until the acknowledgment of sin. 32.3–4 This may be a depiction of illness understood to be the result of God's anger over sin or of the effects of sin and guilt unconfessed. *Selah.* See note on 3.2. 32.6–7 Instruction to others to pray to God in distress as did the psalmist. *Mighty waters.* See note on 18.16. 32.8–9 Probably a divine word of instruction, reflecting the character and concerns of wisdom. 32.9 See Prov 26.3. *Else . . . you,* possibly to be translated as an assurance, "Noth-

10 Many are the torments of the wicked,
   but steadfast love surrounds those who
      trust in the LORD.
11 Be glad in the LORD and rejoice,
      O righteous,
   and shout for joy, all you upright in
      heart.

The Greatness and Goodness of God

33 Rejoice in the LORD, O you righteous.
   Praise befits the upright.
2 Praise the LORD with the lyre;
   make melody to him with the harp of
      ten strings.
3 Sing to him a new song;
   play skillfully on the strings, with loud
      shouts.

4 For the word of the LORD is upright,
   and all his work is done in faithfulness.
5 He loves righteousness and justice;
   the earth is full of the steadfast love of
      the LORD.

6 By the word of the LORD the heavens
      were made,
   and all their host by the breath of his
      mouth.
7 He gathered the waters of the sea as in a
      bottle;
   he put the deeps in storehouses.

8 Let all the earth fear the LORD;
   let all the inhabitants of the world
      stand in awe of him.
9 For he spoke, and it came to be;
   he commanded, and it stood firm.

10 The LORD brings the counsel of the
      nations to nothing;
   he frustrates the plans of the peoples.
11 The counsel of the LORD stands forever,

the thoughts of his heart to all
      generations.
12 Happy is the nation whose God is the
      LORD,
   the people whom he has chosen as his
      heritage.

13 The LORD looks down from heaven;
   he sees all humankind.
14 From where he sits enthroned he watches
      all the inhabitants of the earth—
15 he who fashions the hearts of them all,
   and observes all their deeds.
16 A king is not saved by his great army;
   a warrior is not delivered by his great
      strength.
17 The war horse is a vain hope for victory,
   and by its great might it cannot save.

18 Truly the eye of the LORD is on those who
      fear him,
   on those who hope in his steadfast
      love,
19 to deliver their soul from death,
   and to keep them alive in famine.

20 Our soul waits for the LORD;
   he is our help and shield.
21 Our heart is glad in him,
   because we trust in his holy name.
22 Let your steadfast love, O LORD, be upon
      us,
   even as we hope in you.

Praise for Deliverance from Trouble

Of David, when he feigned madness before
Abimelech, so that he drove him out, and he
went away.

34 I will bless the LORD at all times;
   his praise shall continually be in my
      mouth.
2 My soul makes its boast in the LORD;

---

ing will come near you." The text, however, is very uncertain. **32.10** The lesson learned by the psalmist.
32.11 A call to the faithful to trust also and join in the
psalmist's joy (see 31.23–24).
   33.1–22 A hymn of praise of God as creator of the
world and Lord of history. **33.1–3** A call to praise.
33.4–9 The reason for praise is God's creation of the
world through God's righteous and powerful word.
See Gen 1. **33.6** *Host,* i.e., sun, moon, and stars. *Waters
of the sea,* probably the waters above the dome of
heaven (cf. Gen 1.7; Job 38.37). **33.8** *Fear the LORD.* See

note on 34.7. **33.10–12** The Lord's rule of the nations.
33.12 *Happy.* See note on 1.1. *His heritage.* See Deut
7.6–8; 32.8–9. **33.13–19** The Lord's discerning and
providential watch over all the inhabitants of the
earth. **33.20–22** The community of faith expresses its
hope in God's steadfast love.
   34.1–22 A song of thanksgiving that becomes instructional and didactic in character. The address or
instruction to the community that often concludes
songs of thanksgiving (see 31.2–4; 32.11) is accentu-
ated in this psalm. The historical superscription is sec-

let the humble hear and be glad.
3 O magnify the LORD with me,
    and let us exalt his name together.

4 I sought the LORD, and he answered me,
    and delivered me from all my fears.
5 Look to him, and be radiant;
    so your[a] faces shall never be ashamed.
6 This poor soul cried, and was heard by
        the LORD,
    and was saved from every trouble.
7 The angel of the LORD encamps
        around those who fear him, and
        delivers them.
8 O taste and see that the LORD is good;
    happy are those who take refuge in
        him.
9 O fear the LORD, you his holy ones,
    for those who fear him have no want.
10 The young lions suffer want and hunger,
    but those who seek the LORD lack no
        good thing.

11 Come, O children, listen to me;
    I will teach you the fear of the LORD.
12 Which of you desires life,
    and covets many days to enjoy good?
13 Keep your tongue from evil,
    and your lips from speaking deceit.
14 Depart from evil, and do good;
    seek peace, and pursue it.

15 The eyes of the LORD are on the
        righteous,
    and his ears are open to their cry.
16 The face of the LORD is against evildoers,
    to cut off the remembrance of them
        from the earth.

17 When the righteous cry for help, the
        LORD hears,
    and rescues them from all their
        troubles.
18 The LORD is near to the brokenhearted,
    and saves the crushed in spirit.

19 Many are the afflictions of the righteous,
    but the LORD rescues them from them
        all.
20 He keeps all their bones;
    not one of them will be broken.
21 Evil brings death to the wicked,
    and those who hate the righteous will
        be condemned.
22 The LORD redeems the life of his servants;
    none of those who take refuge in him
        will be condemned.

Prayer for Deliverance from Enemies

Of David.

35 Contend, O LORD, with those who
        contend with me;
    fight against those who fight against
        me!
2 Take hold of shield and buckler,
    and rise up to help me!
3 Draw the spear and javelin
        against my pursuers;
    say to my soul,
        "I am your salvation."

4 Let them be put to shame and dishonor
        who seek after my life.
    Let them be turned back and confounded

_____
a Gk Syr Jerome: Heb their

---

ondarily attached to the psalm (1 Sam 21.10–15; *Abimelech* is an error for Achish). The psalm is an alphabetic acrostic in its Hebrew text (see note on 9.1–10.18). **34.1–3** Introductory praise and thanksgiving. **34.1** *Bless.* See note on 103.1–2. **34.4–10** Testimony to the goodness of God, who delivers the afflicted from their fears. The psalmist reports on God's hearing the prayer and invites others to know the goodness of the Lord through worship and trust. **34.7** *Angel of the LORD,* both a messenger of the Lord and an extension of the Lord's power (see 35.5–6; Josh 5.13–15). *Fear,* an all-encompassing term for worship and obedience, the proper relationship to God (cf. vv. 9, 11). **34.8** Taste. Cf. 1 Pet 2.3. **34.9** *His holy ones,* members of the community of faith. **34.10** Even when the most successful and self-sufficient, i.e., the *young lions,* go hungry, those who trust in the Lord do not want (cf. 23.1).

34.11–14 The psalmist's reported deliverance leads into wise teaching about what is involved in *the fear of the LORD* (v. 11). Cf. 1 Pet 3.10–12. **34.14** Wisdom's teaching is like the prophetic exhortations. See Isa 1.16–17; Am 5.14–15; Mic 6.8; cf. Ps 37.27. **34.15–22** The teaching continues about the Lord's actions toward the innocent and righteous and toward the wicked. The accent is on God's attention to the cries of the righteous in their sufferings. *Righteous* often refers to the innocent victims who suffer at the hands of those who do evil.

35.1–28 A prayer for God's help by a person persecuted and falsely accused. The psalm is primarily a series of petitions against the persecutors and tormentors. **35.1–8** Petitions to God to fight against and undo the power of those who pursue the psalmist. **35.3b** The persecuted one seeks an oracle of salvation, a divine

who devise evil against me.

5 Let them be like chaff before the wind,
    with the angel of the LORD driving
        them on.

6 Let their way be dark and slippery,
    with the angel of the LORD pursuing
        them.

7 For without cause they hid their net[a] for
        me;
    without cause they dug a pit[b] for my
        life.

8 Let ruin come on them unawares.
    And let the net that they hid ensnare
        them;
    let them fall in it—to their ruin.

9 Then my soul shall rejoice in the LORD,
    exulting in his deliverance.

10 All my bones shall say,
    "O LORD, who is like you?
    You deliver the weak
        from those too strong for them,
        the weak and needy from those who
            despoil them."

11 Malicious witnesses rise up;
    they ask me about things I do not
        know.

12 They repay me evil for good;
    my soul is forlorn.

13 But as for me, when they were sick,
    I wore sackcloth;
    I afflicted myself with fasting.
    I prayed with head bowed[c] on my bosom,

14   as though I grieved for a friend or a
        brother;
    I went about as one who laments for a
        mother,
    bowed down and in mourning.

15 But at my stumbling they gathered in glee,
    they gathered together against me;
    ruffians whom I did not know

tore at me without ceasing;

16 they impiously mocked more and more,[d]
    gnashing at me with their teeth.

17 How long, O LORD, will you look on?
    Rescue me from their ravages,
    my life from the lions!

18 Then I will thank you in the great
        congregation;
    in the mighty throng I will praise you.

19 Do not let my treacherous enemies
        rejoice over me,
    or those who hate me without cause
        wink the eye.

20 For they do not speak peace,
    but they conceive deceitful words
    against those who are quiet in the land.

21 They open wide their mouths against me;
    they say, "Aha, Aha,
    our eyes have seen it."

22 You have seen, O LORD; do not be silent!
    O Lord, do not be far from me!

23 Wake up! Bestir yourself for my defense,
    for my cause, my God and my Lord!

24 Vindicate me, O LORD, my God,
    according to your righteousness,
    and do not let them rejoice over me.

25 Do not let them say to themselves,
    "Aha, we have our heart's desire."
    Do not let them say, "We have swallowed
        you[e] up."

26 Let all those who rejoice at my calamity
    be put to shame and confusion;
    let those who exalt themselves against me
    be clothed with shame and dishonor.

27 Let those who desire my vindication
    shout for joy and be glad,

---

a Heb *a pit, their net* b The word *pit* is transposed from the preceding line c Or *My prayer turned back* d Cn Compare Gk: Heb *like the profanest of mockers of a cake* e Heb *him*

---

word giving assurance of God's presence and help. See note on 22.21b. **35.5** *Chaff.* See 1.4. *Angel of the LORD.* See note on 34.7. **35.7–8** See note on 9.15. **35.9–10** The afflicted one vows to praise the Lord when delivered. **35.11–16** The lament of the psalmist over the persecutions rendered by others. A comparison is drawn between the support of the afflicted one for others in their sickness and their glee over the distress of the psalmist. **35.15** In light of v. 13a, the *stumbling* may be an illness, but the primary focus of the prayer is against the tormenting activity of others. **35.17–18** The praying one complains to God (v. 17) and vows to give thanks to God when deliverance comes (v. 18). **35.17** *How long?* See note on 6.3. *Lions.* See note on 7.2. **35.19–25** Petitions once again asking for God's defense against the machinations and torments of the wicked who delight in the undoing of the psalmist. **35.26–27** A call for the downfall or shame of those who rejoice in the misfortune of the psalmist and for the joy and praise to God of those who support the

and say evermore,
"Great is the LORD,
who delights in the welfare of his
servant."
28 Then my tongue shall tell of your
righteousness
and of your praise all day long.

Human Wickedness and Divine Goodness

To the leader. Of David, the servant of
the LORD.

36 Transgression speaks to the wicked
deep in their hearts;
there is no fear of God
before their eyes.
2 For they flatter themselves in their own
eyes
that their iniquity cannot be found out
and hated.
3 The words of their mouths are mischief
and deceit;
they have ceased to act wisely and do
good.
4 They plot mischief while on their beds;
they are set on a way that is not good;
they do not reject evil.

5 Your steadfast love, O LORD, extends to
the heavens,
your faithfulness to the clouds.
6 Your righteousness is like the mighty
mountains,
your judgments are like the great deep;
you save humans and animals alike,
O LORD.

7 How precious is your steadfast love,
O God!

All people may take refuge in the
shadow of your wings.
8 They feast on the abundance of your
house,
and you give them drink from the river
of your delights.
9 For with you is the fountain of life;
in your light we see light.

10 O continue your steadfast love to those
who know you,
and your salvation to the upright of
heart!
11 Do not let the foot of the arrogant tread
on me,
or the hand of the wicked drive me
away.
12 There the evildoers lie prostrate;
they are thrust down, unable to rise.

Exhortation to Patience and Trust

Of David.

37 Do not fret because of the wicked;
do not be envious of wrongdoers,
2 for they will soon fade like the grass,
and wither like the green herb.

3 Trust in the LORD, and do good;
so you will live in the land, and enjoy
security.
4 Take delight in the LORD,
and he will give you the desires of your
heart.

5 Commit your way to the LORD;
trust in him, and he will act.
6 He will make your vindication shine like
the light,

psalmist in trouble. **35.28** The afflicted psalmist vows to praise God for the righteousness that supports the weak and undoes the wicked.

36.1–12 An individual's prayer for help that is highly reflective in the manner of the wisdom traditions, esp. vv. 1–4. *To the leader.* See note on 4.1–8. *Servant of the LORD.* See 78.70; 89.3. **36.1–4** A reflection on the character and attitude of the wicked that here serves as a generalized lament in anticipation of the prayer for help against the wicked in v. 11. **36.1** *Fear of God.* See note on 34.7. Cf. Rom 3.18. **36.4** *They plot . . . beds.* Cf. Mic 2.1. **36.5–9** The psalmist now praises God as an act of trust, describing the character of God and the protecting and life-giving care of God. **36.6b** The life and well-being of humans and animals depends on the Lord. Cf. v. 9; Ps

104. **36.7** *Shadow of your wings.* See notes on 91.1; 91.4. **36.10–12** The attributes of God extolled in the preceding verses, *steadfast love* (vv. 5, 7) and *salvation* (v. 6), here become the grounds for the psalmist's prayer for help in the face of the threats of the wicked described in vv. 1–4.

37.1–40 An instructional psalm in which an older, more experienced person (v. 25) instructs others, particularly about the Lord's protection of the righteous and the inevitable judgment that comes upon the wicked. The psalm is an exhortation to trust in the Lord, who will vindicate the righteous, and not to be disturbed by the wicked, who will soon pass away. An acrostic psalm (see note on 9.1–10.18). **37.1** *Do not fret* is repeated several times (vv. 7–8), suggesting the psalm is addressed to someone who may have come

and the justice of your cause like the
  noonday.

7 Be still before the LORD, and wait
    patiently for him;
  do not fret over those who prosper in
    their way,
  over those who carry out evil devices.

8 Refrain from anger, and forsake wrath.
  Do not fret—it leads only to evil.
9 For the wicked shall be cut off,
  but those who wait for the LORD shall
    inherit the land.

10 Yet a little while, and the wicked will be
    no more;
  though you look diligently for their
    place, they will not be there.
11 But the meek shall inherit the land,
  and delight themselves in abundant
    prosperity.

12 The wicked plot against the righteous,
  and gnash their teeth at them;
13 but the LORD laughs at the wicked,
  for he sees that their day is coming.

14 The wicked draw the sword and bend
    their bows
  to bring down the poor and needy,
  to kill those who walk uprightly;
15 their sword shall enter their own heart,
  and their bows shall be broken.

16 Better is a little that the righteous person
    has
  than the abundance of many wicked.
17 For the arms of the wicked shall be
    broken,
  but the LORD upholds the righteous.

18 The LORD knows the days of the
    blameless,
  and their heritage will abide forever;
19 they are not put to shame in evil times,
  in the days of famine they have
    abundance.

20 But the wicked perish,
  and the enemies of the LORD are like
    the glory of the pastures;
  they vanish—like smoke they vanish
    away.

21 The wicked borrow, and do not pay back,
  but the righteous are generous and
    keep giving;
22 for those blessed by the LORD shall inherit
    the land,
  but those cursed by him shall be cut
    off.

23 Our steps*a* are made firm by the LORD,
  when he delights in our*b* way;
24 though we stumble,*c* we*d* shall not fall
    headlong,
  for the LORD holds us*e* by the hand.

25 I have been young, and now am old,
  yet I have not seen the righteous
    forsaken
  or their children begging bread.
26 They are ever giving liberally and
    lending,
  and their children become a blessing.

27 Depart from evil, and do good;
  so you shall abide forever.
28 For the LORD loves justice;
  he will not forsake his faithful ones.

  The righteous shall be kept safe forever,
  but the children of the wicked shall be
    cut off.
29 The righteous shall inherit the land,
  and live in it forever.

30 The mouths of the righteous utter
    wisdom,
  and their tongues speak justice.
31 The law of their God is in their hearts;
  their steps do not slip.

---

a Heb *A man's steps* *b* Heb *his* *c* Heb *he stumbles*
d Heb *he* *e* Heb *him*

---

under some persecution or thinks that God's rule is
not effective (cf. Prov 24.19–20). **37.9** *Inherit the land,*
i.e., enjoy the rich blessings provided in the land God
has given the people (cf. vv. 3, 11, 22, 29, 34). **37.13** *The
LORD laughs.* Cf. 2.4; 59.8. **37.14–15** The language is a

metaphorical way of saying that the violent acts of
wicked persons shall be their undoing. **37.22** See Deut
28. **37.25** The instruction given is gained from long experience. It is not meant to be absolute, but the
psalmist's presentation of the way things are is borne

32 The wicked watch for the righteous,
    and seek to kill them.
33 The LORD will not abandon them to their
        power,
    or let them be condemned when they
        are brought to trial.

34 Wait for the LORD, and keep to his way,
    and he will exalt you to inherit the land;
    you will look on the destruction of the
        wicked.

35 I have seen the wicked oppressing,
    and towering like a cedar of Lebanon.[a]
36 Again I[b] passed by, and they were no
        more;
    though I sought them, they could not
        be found.

37 Mark the blameless, and behold the
        upright,
    for there is posterity for the peaceable.
38 But transgressors shall be altogether
        destroyed;
    the posterity of the wicked shall be cut
        off.

39 The salvation of the righteous is from the
        LORD;
    he is their refuge in the time of trouble.
40 The LORD helps them and rescues them;
    he rescues them from the wicked, and
        saves them,
    because they take refuge in him.

A Penitent Sufferer's Plea for Healing

A Psalm of David, for the memorial offering.

38 O LORD, do not rebuke me in your
        anger,
    or discipline me in your wrath.
2 For your arrows have sunk into me,
    and your hand has come down on me.

3 There is no soundness in my flesh
    because of your indignation;
    there is no health in my bones

because of my sin.
4 For my iniquities have gone over my head;
    they weigh like a burden too heavy for
        me.

5 My wounds grow foul and fester
    because of my foolishness;
6 I am utterly bowed down and prostrate;
    all day long I go around mourning.
7 For my loins are filled with burning,
    and there is no soundness in my flesh.
8 I am utterly spent and crushed;
    I groan because of the tumult of my
        heart.

9 O Lord, all my longing is known to you;
    my sighing is not hidden from you.
10 My heart throbs, my strength fails me;
    as for the light of my eyes—it also has
        gone from me.
11 My friends and companions stand aloof
        from my affliction,
    and my neighbors stand far off.
12 Those who seek my life lay their snares;
    those who seek to hurt me speak of
        ruin,
    and meditate treachery all day long.

13 But I am like the deaf, I do not hear;
    like the mute, who cannot speak.
14 Truly, I am like one who does not hear,
    and in whose mouth is no retort.

15 But it is for you, O LORD, that I wait;
    it is you, O Lord my God, who will
        answer.
16 For I pray, "Only do not let them rejoice
        over me,
    those who boast against me when my
        foot slips."

17 For I am ready to fall,
    and my pain is ever with me.
18 I confess my iniquity;

a Gk: Meaning of Heb uncertain   b Gk Syr Jerome: Heb he

out in life over the long haul. **37.35** *Cedar of Lebanon.*
See note on 92.12.
    38.1–22 This penitential psalm (see note on 6.1–
10) offers prayer for help by one who feels God's judgment for sin. The language of sickness may be
metaphorical, but it is likely that the psalm envisions

real sickness and the taunts and rejection of others
that sickness may evoke. **38.1** The plea of the psalmist
that God take away the effects of God's anger. Cf. 6.1.
38.2–10 A description of the psalmist's sickness.
38.10 *Light of my eyes,* either actual sight or one's
power of life. Cf. 36.9. **38.11–20** The reaction of others

I am sorry for my sin.
19 Those who are my foes without cause[a]
    are mighty,
and many are those who hate me
    wrongfully.
20 Those who render me evil for good
    are my adversaries because I follow
    after good.

21 Do not forsake me, O LORD;
    O my God, do not be far from me;
22 make haste to help me,
    O Lord, my salvation.

Prayer for Wisdom and Forgiveness

To the leader: to Jeduthun. A Psalm of David.

39 I said, "I will guard my ways
    that I may not sin with my tongue;
I will keep a muzzle on my mouth
    as long as the wicked are in my
    presence."
2 I was silent and still;
    I held my peace to no avail;
my distress grew worse,
3   my heart became hot within me.
While I mused, the fire burned;
    then I spoke with my tongue:

4 "LORD, let me know my end,
    and what is the measure of my days;
    let me know how fleeting my life is.
5 You have made my days a few
    handbreadths,
    and my lifetime is as nothing in your
    sight.
Surely everyone stands as a mere breath.
            Selah
6   Surely everyone goes about like a
    shadow.
Surely for nothing they are in
    turmoil;

they heap up, and do not know who
    will gather.

7 "And now, O Lord, what do I wait for?
    My hope is in you.
8 Deliver me from all my transgressions.
    Do not make me the scorn of the fool.
9 I am silent; I do not open my mouth,
    for it is you who have done it.
10 Remove your stroke from me;
    I am worn down by the blows[b] of your
    hand.

11 "You chastise mortals
    in punishment for sin,
consuming like a moth what is dear to
    them;
    surely everyone is a mere breath.   *Selah*

12 "Hear my prayer, O LORD,
    and give ear to my cry;
    do not hold your peace at my tears.
For I am your passing guest,
    an alien, like all my forebears.
13 Turn your gaze away from me, that I may
    smile again,
    before I depart and am no more."

Thanksgiving for Deliverance and Prayer for Help

To the leader. Of David. A Psalm.

40 I waited patiently for the LORD;
    he inclined to me and heard my cry.
2 He drew me up from the desolate pit,[c]
    out of the miry bog,
and set my feet upon a rock,
    making my steps secure.
3 He put a new song in my mouth,

---

a Q Ms: MT *my living foes*   *b* Heb *hostility*   *c* Cn: Heb *pit of tumult*

to the illness of the one praying. The psalmist is alienated from other human beings in various ways. **38.21–22** A final cry to God for help.

39.1–13 A prayer for help by an individual who complains to God against a divine chastisement (v. 10) and seeks release. *To the leader.* See note on 4.1–8. *To Jeduthun.* See note on 77.1–20. **39.1–3** The psalmist has held back from complaining about the distress in hopes that silence would be rewarded, but that has not happened. So now the complaint to God comes forth. **39.4–6** A strong sense of the transiency of human existence arises out of the distress. Cf. 90.9–12; 103.15–16; Isa 40.6–8. **39.5** *Selah.* See note on 3.2. **39.7–13** The petitions of the psalmist punctuated by reiterated complaint. The sense of the transiency of human life persists (vv. 11c, 12b). **39.13** *Turn . . . me,* i.e., "spare me further punishment."

40.1–17 A song of thanksgiving by an individual leads into and is the ground for a prayer for help (cf. Ps 27). *To the leader.* See note on 4.1–8. **40.1–10** A song of thanksgiving by one who trusted in the Lord and was delivered. **40.1–3a** Report of how the Lord helped. **40.2** *Pit.* See note on 16.10. **40.3b–4** The deliverance of the psalmist is a lesson in trust for others.

a song of praise to our God.
Many will see and fear,
    and put their trust in the LORD.

4 Happy are those who make
        the LORD their trust,
    who do not turn to the proud,
        to those who go astray after false
            gods.
5 You have multiplied, O LORD my God,
        your wondrous deeds and your
            thoughts toward us;
    none can compare with you.
    Were I to proclaim and tell of them,
        they would be more than can be
            counted.

6 Sacrifice and offering you do not desire,
        but you have given me an open ear. *a*
    Burnt offering and sin offering
        you have not required.
7 Then I said, "Here I am;
        in the scroll of the book it is written
            of me. *b*
8 I delight to do your will, O my God;
        your law is within my heart."

9 I have told the glad news of deliverance
        in the great congregation;
    see, I have not restrained my lips,
        as you know, O LORD.
10 I have not hidden your saving help within
            my heart,
    I have spoken of your faithfulness and
            your salvation;
    I have not concealed your steadfast love
        and your faithfulness
        from the great congregation.

11 Do not, O LORD, withhold
        your mercy from me;

let your steadfast love and your faithfulness
        keep me safe forever.
12 For evils have encompassed me
        without number;
    my iniquities have overtaken me,
        until I cannot see;
    they are more than the hairs of my head,
        and my heart fails me.

13 Be pleased, O LORD, to deliver me;
    O LORD, make haste to help me.
14 Let all those be put to shame and
            confusion
        who seek to snatch away my life;
    let those be turned back and brought to
            dishonor
        who desire my hurt.
15 Let those be appalled because of their
            shame
        who say to me, "Aha, Aha!"

16 But may all who seek you
        rejoice and be glad in you;
    may those who love your salvation
        say continually, "Great is the LORD!"
17 As for me, I am poor and needy,
        but the Lord takes thought for me.
    You are my help and my deliverer;
        do not delay, O my God.

Assurance of God's Help and a Plea for Healing

To the leader. A Psalm of David.

41 Happy are those who consider the
        poor; *c*
    the LORD delivers them in the day of
        trouble.

---

a Heb *ears you have dug for me*   *b* Meaning of Heb uncertain
c Or *weak*

Happy. See note on 1.1. **40.5** The recounting of God's marvelous deeds is part of the act of thanksgiving. **40.6–8** Instead of sacrifice, the act of thanksgiving is accompanied by a commitment to do God's will. Quoted in Heb 10.5–7. Cf. 51.16–17. **40.7** *Scroll of the book* is interpreted variously. If the song is by a king, this could refer to the "law of the king" in Deut 17.14–20. More likely, it is the heavenly record of human deeds of good or ill, though some have assumed it refers to the written record of this song of thanksgiving, offered in place of a sacrifice. **40.8** *Your law is within my heart.* See Jer 31.33; Heb 10.16. **40.9–10** The one who has been delivered has borne witness to God's

love and faithfulness before the community (cf. v. 3; 22.22–23). **40.11–17** A cry to God for help in a new situation of distress and trouble. Vv. 13–17 are the same as Ps 70. **40.16–17** The prayer concludes with the psalmist's expression of trust and anticipated praise and joy when God's help comes (cf. 35.27).

41.1–13 An individual prayer for help and deliverance from sickness is set before the congregation as instruction about God's care of the weak and the sick. *To the leader.* See note on 4.1–8. **41.1–3** A didactic introduction expressing the certainty of the Lord's healing of the sick. It is the ground of confidence on which the prayer that follows was uttered and the conclusion

2 The Lord protects them and keeps them
     alive;
   they are called happy in the land.
   You do not give them up to the will of
     their enemies.
3 The Lord sustains them on their sickbed;
   in their illness you heal all their
     infirmities.ᵃ

4 As for me, I said, "O Lord, be gracious to
     me;
   heal me, for I have sinned against you."
5 My enemies wonder in malice
   when I will die, and my name perish.
6 And when they come to see me, they
     utter empty words,
   while their hearts gather mischief;
   when they go out, they tell it abroad.
7 All who hate me whisper together about
     me;
   they imagine the worst for me.

8 They think that a deadly thing has
     fastened on me,
   that I will not rise again from where I lie.
9 Even my bosom friend in whom I
     trusted,
   who ate of my bread, has lifted the heel
     against me.
10 But you, O Lord, be gracious to me,
    and raise me up, that I may repay them.

11 By this I know that you are pleased with
     me;
   because my enemy has not triumphed
     over me.

12 But you have upheld me because of my
     integrity,
    and set me in your presence forever.

13 Blessed be the Lord, the God of Israel,
    from everlasting to everlasting.
       Amen and Amen.

BOOK II: PSALMS 42–72

Longing for God and His Help in Distress

To the leader. A Maskil of the Korahites.

42 As a deer longs for flowing streams,
     so my soul longs for you, O God.
2 My soul thirsts for God,
   for the living God.
   When shall I come and behold
     the face of God?
3 My tears have been my food
     day and night,
   while people say to me continually,
     "Where is your God?"

4 These things I remember,
     as I pour out my soul:
   how I went with the throng,ᵇ
     and led them in procession to the
       house of God,
   with glad shouts and songs of
     thanksgiving,
   a multitude keeping festival.
5 Why are you cast down, O my soul,
     and why are you disquieted within me?

_____
a Heb *you change all his bed*   b Meaning of Heb uncertain

reached by the psalmist in light of the answered
prayer. **41.1** *Happy.* See note on 1.1. **41.4–10** The
prayer is reported, beginning and ending with petitions for the Lord to *be gracious* and *heal* (or *raise up*)
the sick person (vv. 4, 10) and lamenting the malice of
those, including friends, who may say kind words but
really spread slanderous things and anticipate happily
the death of the one who is sick. **41.4** *For I have sinned
against you* reflects the understanding that the illness
has also to do with God's judgment for sin and that
God's healing involves forgiveness. **41.9** *Who ate of my
bread.* Applied to Judas in Jn 13.18. **41.11–12** Having
been healed, the one who was sick acknowledges
God's vindication and providential care and the consequent defeat of the enemies. **41.13** A doxology
marks the end of each of the five sections, or "books,"
of the Psalter (41.13; 72.18–19; 89.52; 106.48; 150.1–
6). This doxology, which concludes the first book of
the Psalter (Pss 1–41), also serves as praise and

thanksgiving for God's deliverance. *Blessed.* See note
on 103.1–2.
   42.1–43.5 An individual prayer for help by one who
is cut off from the presence of God and oppressed by
enemies. The psalmist seeks both to be led again into
the sanctuary and defended against those who have
dealt unjustly. The absence of a superscription at the
beginning of Ps 43, the repetition of the refrain in 42.5,
11; 43.5, the repetition of 42.9b in 43.2b, and the common theme of coming to the sanctuary all suggest that
the two psalms are to be read as a single psalm. *To the
leader.* See note on 4.1–8. *Maskil.* See note on 32.1–11.
Korahites, a group of temple singers (2 Chr 20.19) who
may have collected and transmitted a number of
psalms. **42.1–5** The intense longing to come again into
the presence of God is tempered by remembrance of
previous pilgrimages to the sanctuary (cf. 84.1–2).
42.3 *"Where is your God?"* See v. 10; note on 79.10.
42.4 *Festival,* one of Israel's three great pilgrimage festi-

Hope in God; for I shall again praise him,
  my help ⁶and my God.

My soul is cast down within me;
  therefore I remember you
from the land of Jordan and of Hermon,
  from Mount Mizar.
7 Deep calls to deep
  at the thunder of your cataracts;
all your waves and your billows
  have gone over me.
8 By day the LORD commands his steadfast
    love,
  and at night his song is with me,
  a prayer to the God of my life.

9 I say to God, my rock,
  "Why have you forgotten me?
Why must I walk about mournfully
  because the enemy oppresses me?"
10 As with a deadly wound in my body,
  my adversaries taunt me,
while they say to me continually,
  "Where is your God?"

11 Why are you cast down, O my soul,
  and why are you disquieted within me?
Hope in God; for I shall again praise him,
  my help and my God.

Prayer to God in Time of Trouble

43 Vindicate me, O God, and defend my
    cause
  against an ungodly people;
from those who are deceitful and unjust
  deliver me!
2 For you are the God in whom I take
    refuge;
  why have you cast me off?
Why must I walk about mournfully

because of the oppression of the
  enemy?

3 O send out your light and your truth;
  let them lead me;
let them bring me to your holy hill
  and to your dwelling.
4 Then I will go to the altar of God,
  to God my exceeding joy;
and I will praise you with the harp,
  O God, my God.

5 Why are you cast down, O my soul,
  and why are you disquieted within me?
Hope in God; for I shall again praise him,
  my help and my God.

National Lament and Prayer for Help

To the leader. Of the Korahites. A Maskil.

44 We have heard with our ears, O God,
    our ancestors have told us,
what deeds you performed in their days,
  in the days of old:
2 you with your own hand drove out the
    nations,
  but them you planted;
you afflicted the peoples,
  but them you set free;
3 for not by their own sword did they win
    the land,
  nor did their own arm give them
    victory;
but your right hand, and your arm,
  and the light of your countenance,
  for you delighted in them.

4 You are my King and my God;
  you command *a* victories for Jacob.

---

a Gk Syr: Heb *You are my King, O God; command*

---

vals (Deut 16). **42.6–11** In despair again, the psalmist once more remembers God. But that memory makes all the sharper the present experience of distress and the absence of God's presence and power. **42.6** *My soul is cast down.* Cf. Mt 26.38; Mk 14.34. *From the land . . . Hermon,* the headwaters of the Jordan and the great Mount Hermon in the north of Syro-Palestine, suggesting that the one praying may have been in that locale. *Mount Mizar* is unknown but may have been a peak in the Hermon range. **43.1–5** The sufferer pleads for God's powerful defense against injustice and asks with great confidence to be led into the sanctuary to praise and thank God. Cf. 23.6; 27.4–6; 84.1–4.

43.3 *Your holy hill,* probably the temple on Zion in Jerusalem, though some have speculated that a sanctuary in the north of Palestine may have been meant.
44.1–26 A prayer by the community for help after having been severely defeated by its enemies (cf. Pss 74; 79). *To the leader.* See note on 4.1–8. *Korahites.* See note on 42.1–43.5. *Maskil.* See note on 32.1–11. **44.1–3** Remembrance of the mighty deeds of God in the past on behalf of Israel. Later generations have been told the story of how the Lord gave the Israelites the land and victory over their enemies. **44.3** See Deut 8.17–18. **44.4–8** An acknowledgment of God's help against the nation's enemies together with thanksgiving. The first-

5 Through you we push down our foes;
    through your name we tread down our
        assailants.
6 For not in my bow do I trust,
    nor can my sword save me.
7 But you have saved us from our foes,
    and have put to confusion those who
        hate us.
8 In God we have boasted continually,
    and we will give thanks to your name
        forever.   *Selah*

9 Yet you have rejected us and abased us,
    and have not gone out with our
        armies.
10 You made us turn back from the foe,
    and our enemies have gotten spoil.
11 You have made us like sheep for
        slaughter,
    and have scattered us among the
        nations.
12 You have sold your people for a trifle,
    demanding no high price for them.

13 You have made us the taunt of our
        neighbors,
    the derision and scorn of those around
        us.
14 You have made us a byword among the
        nations,
    a laughingstock*a* among the peoples.
15 All day long my disgrace is before me,
    and shame has covered my face
16 at the words of the taunters and revilers,
    at the sight of the enemy and the
        avenger.

17 All this has come upon us,
    yet we have not forgotten you,
    or been false to your covenant.
18 Our heart has not turned back,

nor have our steps departed from your
        way,
19 yet you have broken us in the haunt of
        jackals,
    and covered us with deep darkness.

20 If we had forgotten the name of our God,
    or spread out our hands to a strange god,
21 would not God discover this?
    For he knows the secrets of the heart.
22 Because of you we are being killed all day
        long,
    and accounted as sheep for the
        slaughter.

23 Rouse yourself! Why do you sleep,
        O Lord?
    Awake, do not cast us off forever!
24 Why do you hide your face?
    Why do you forget our affliction and
        oppression?
25 For we sink down to the dust;
    our bodies cling to the ground.
26 Rise up, come to our help.
    Redeem us for the sake of your
        steadfast love.

Ode for a Royal Wedding

To the leader: according to Lilies. Of the
    Korahites. A Maskil. A love song.

45 My heart overflows with a goodly
        theme;
    I address my verses to the king;
    my tongue is like the pen of a ready
        scribe.

2 You are the most handsome of men;
    grace is poured upon your lips;

_____
a Heb *a shaking of the head*

person voice in these verses could have been a king's,
though any representative voice could speak these
words on behalf of the community. **44.8** *Selah.* See note
on 3.2. **44.9–16** But now God has abandoned the people, and they have been defeated by their enemies.
44.12 *Sold your people,* i.e., made them in effect slaves
to their enemies (cf. Deut 32.30; Judg 2.14; 3.8; 1 Sam
12.9). **44.13** *Taunt* (cf. v. 10). See note on 79.10.
44.14 See 79.4; 80.6; Deut 28.37. *Made us a byword.* The
disaster was so great that it has become proverbial
among other peoples. **44.17–22** The people protest
their innocence and complain that God has abandoned
them unjustly. **44.18** *Haunt of jackals,* either the desert
where jackals roam or a place of devastation where

jackals eat the remains of bodies (cf. Isa 34.13; 35.7; Jer
9.11; 10.22). **44.22** Because of the people's faithfulness
to the Lord they are being defeated, so God's honor is at
stake. Quoted in Rom 8.36. **44.23–26** The prayer of the
people for God to help them rather than to reject them.
44.23 *Sleep,* an image to convey God's inactivity. Cf.
78.65; 121.4. **44.24** *Hide your face.* See notes on 10.1;
27.9. **44.26** *Rise up.* See note on 12.5.

   45.1–17 A royal psalm probably composed for the
wedding of the king. *To the leader.* See note on 4.1–8.
According to Lilies. Meaning uncertain, probably referring to a particular melody. *Korahites.* See note on
42.1–43.5. *Maskil.* See note on 32.1–11. **45.1** A composer or singer addresses these words to the king to

therefore God has blessed you forever.

3 Gird your sword on your thigh, O mighty
   one,
   in your glory and majesty.

4 In your majesty ride on victoriously
   for the cause of truth and to defend[a]
   the right;
   let your right hand teach you dread
   deeds.

5 Your arrows are sharp
   in the heart of the king's enemies;
   the peoples fall under you.

6 Your throne, O God,[b] endures forever
   and ever.
   Your royal scepter is a scepter of
   equity;

7 you love righteousness and hate
   wickedness.
   Therefore God, your God, has anointed
   you
   with the oil of gladness beyond your
   companions;

8 your robes are all fragrant with myrrh
   and aloes and cassia.
   From ivory palaces stringed instruments
   make you glad;

9 daughters of kings are among your
   ladies of honor;
   at your right hand stands the queen in
   gold of Ophir.

10 Hear, O daughter, consider and incline
   your ear;
   forget your people and your father's
   house,

11 and the king will desire your beauty.
   Since he is your lord, bow to him;

12 the people[c] of Tyre will seek your favor
   with gifts,

the richest of the people [13]with all
kinds of wealth.

The princess is decked in her chamber
   with gold-woven robes;[d]

14 in many-colored robes she is led to the
   king;
   behind her the virgins, her
   companions, follow.

15 With joy and gladness they are led along
   as they enter the palace of the king.

16 In the place of ancestors you, O king,[e]
   shall have sons;
   you will make them princes in all the
   earth.

17 I will cause your name to be celebrated in
   all generations;
   therefore the peoples will praise you
   forever and ever.

God's Defense of His City and People

To the leader. Of the Korahites. According to
Alamoth. A Song.

46 God is our refuge and strength,
   a very present[f] help in trouble.

2 Therefore we will not fear, though the
   earth should change,
   though the mountains shake in the
   heart of the sea;

3 though its waters roar and foam,
   though the mountains tremble with its
   tumult.   Selah

4 There is a river whose streams make glad
   the city of God,

---

a Cn: Heb and the meekness of   b Or Your throne is a throne of
God, it   c Heb daughter   d Or people. [13]All glorious is the
princess within, gold embroidery is her clothing   e Heb lacks
O king   f Or well proved

---

praise him. **45.2–9** Praise of the king's appearance and
strength, his love of the right and hatred of wickedness. **45.6a** The meaning of this sentence is unclear. Although the king is called "my son" by God (2.7),
nowhere else in the OT is the king called "God" or regarded as divine. Quoted in Heb 1.8. **45.7** The more
characteristic understanding of kingship in Israel (as
opposed to that in 45.6a) is found here in the notion
that the king is the anointed of God. **45.8** *Ivory palaces,*
the homes of the wealthy that contained furnishings
inlaid with carved ivory. **45.9–15** The princess or
queen is now addressed and praised. **45.9** *Gold of
Ophir* was probably the finest gold then known; the lo-

cation of Ophir is unknown (cf. Job 28.16; Isa 13.12).
45.10–11 These verses may actually reflect aspects of
the marriage ceremony, or they may describe more
generally the appropriate attitude of the bride in this
marital relationship. **45.16–17** A final paean of blessing and praise to the king by the singer or composer.
   46.1–11 A song of Zion expressing confidence in
God's protecting care in the midst of whatever trouble
comes. *To the leader.* See note on 4.1–8. *Korahites.* See
note on 42.1–43.5. *Alamoth,* probably a musical notation; meaning uncertain. **46.1–3** God as secure protection in the midst of cosmic and natural tumult.
46.3 *Selah.* See note on 3.2. **46.4–7** God's secure pro-

the holy habitation of the Most High.
5 God is in the midst of the city;[a] it shall
    not be moved;
  God will help it when the morning
    dawns.
6 The nations are in an uproar, the
    kingdoms totter;
  he utters his voice, the earth melts.
7 The LORD of hosts is with us;
  the God of Jacob is our refuge.[b]   Selah

8 Come, behold the works of the LORD;
  see what desolations he has brought on
    the earth.
9 He makes wars cease to the end of the
    earth;
  he breaks the bow, and shatters the spear;
  he burns the shields with fire.
10 "Be still, and know that I am God!
   I am exalted among the nations,
   I am exalted in the earth."
11 The LORD of hosts is with us;
   the God of Jacob is our refuge.[b]   Selah

God's Rule over the Nations

To the leader. Of the Korahites. A Psalm.

47 Clap your hands, all you peoples;
     shout to God with loud songs of joy.
2 For the LORD, the Most High, is awesome,
    a great king over all the earth.
3 He subdued peoples under us,
    and nations under our feet.
4 He chose our heritage for us,
    the pride of Jacob whom he loves.   Selah

5 God has gone up with a shout,
    the LORD with the sound of a trumpet.

6 Sing praises to God, sing praises;
  sing praises to our King, sing praises.
7 For God is the king of all the earth;
  sing praises with a psalm.[c]

8 God is king over the nations;
  God sits on his holy throne.
9 The princes of the peoples gather
    as the people of the God of Abraham.
  For the shields of the earth belong to
    God;
  he is highly exalted.

The Glory and Strength of Zion

A Song. A Psalm of the Korahites.

48 Great is the LORD and greatly to be
     praised
  in the city of our God.
His holy mountain, 2beautiful in
    elevation,
  is the joy of all the earth,
Mount Zion, in the far north,
  the city of the great King.
3 Within its citadels God
  has shown himself a sure defense.

4 Then the kings assembled,
  they came on together.
5 As soon as they saw it, they were
    astounded;
  they were in panic, they took to flight;
6 trembling took hold of them there,
  pains as of a woman in labor,
7 as when an east wind shatters
  the ships of Tarshish.

---

a Heb of it   b Or fortress   c Heb Maskil

---

tection of the holy city in the face of historical tumult.
46.4 *River,* probably a mythological image for the
source of blessing. *City of God* would have been
Jerusalem when the psalm was composed (cf. 48.1, 8;
87.3). **46.7** A refrain (see v. 11) echoing the opening
verse and identifying the theme of the psalm. **46.8–
11** The Lord's destruction of the implements of war.
46.10 These words may have been like an oracle of salvation giving divine assurance of help against enemies.
  47.1–9 A hymn of praise celebrating God's rule
over the nations and belonging to a group of psalms
called "enthronement psalms." See note on 93.1–5. *To
the leader.* See note on 4.1–8. *Korahites.* See note on
42.1–43.5. **47.1–4** Call to the people of the earth to acclaim the Lord of Israel, who is king over all. **47.3–
4** These verses may refer to the conquest of peoples

when God gave the land (*heritage*) to Israel. *Selah.* See
note on 3.2. **47.5** The announcement that God has
gone up in victory to the sanctuary. The procession of
the ark of the covenant, God's invisible throne, is
probably in view. **47.6–9** A reiterated call to the peoples to praise the Lord of Israel, who is king over all.
47.8 *God is king.* See note on 93.1–2.
  48.1–14 A song of Zion in praise of the Lord, whose
protecting presence is found in the temple in
Jerusalem. *Korahites.* See note on 42.1–43.5. **48.1–
3** Extolling the glory of Zion as the habitation of Israel's God. **48.2** *The far north,* probably a reference to
Mount Zaphon (Hebrew, "north"), a divine dwelling
place in Canaanite mythology; Jerusalem is here identified with it. **48.4–8** Encountering Zion as described
in the preceding verses, the kings of the earth were
frightened and fled. Because God has established it,

8 As we have heard, so have we seen
       in the city of the LORD of hosts,
   in the city of our God,
       which God establishes forever.   *Selah*

9 We ponder your steadfast love,
       O God,
   in the midst of your temple.
10 Your name, O God, like your praise,
       reaches to the ends of the earth.
   Your right hand is filled with victory.
11   Let Mount Zion be glad,
   let the towns[a] of Judah rejoice
       because of your judgments.

12 Walk about Zion, go all around it,
       count its towers,
13 consider well its ramparts;
       go through its citadels,
   that you may tell the next generation
14   that this is God,
   our God forever and ever.
       He will be our guide forever.

The Folly of Trust in Riches

To the leader. Of the Korahites. A Psalm.

49 Hear this, all you peoples;
       give ear, all inhabitants of the world,
2 both low and high,
       rich and poor together.
3 My mouth shall speak wisdom;
       the meditation of my heart shall be
           understanding.
4 I will incline my ear to a proverb;
       I will solve my riddle to the music of
           the harp.

5 Why should I fear in times of trouble,
       when the iniquity of my persecutors
           surrounds me,
6 those who trust in their wealth
       and boast of the abundance of their
           riches?
7 Truly, no ransom avails for one's life,[b]
       there is no price one can give to God
           for it.
8 For the ransom of life is costly,
       and can never suffice,
9 that one should live on forever
       and never see the grave.[c]

10 When we look at the wise, they die;
       fool and dolt perish together
   and leave their wealth to others.
11 Their graves[d] are their homes forever,
       their dwelling places to all
           generations,
   though they named lands their own.
12 Mortals cannot abide in their pomp;
       they are like the animals that perish.

13 Such is the fate of the foolhardy,
       the end of those[e] who are pleased with
           their lot.   *Selah*
14 Like sheep they are appointed for Sheol;
       Death shall be their shepherd;
   straight to the grave they descend,[f]
       and their form shall waste away;
   Sheol shall be their home.[g]

---

a Heb *daughters*   b Another reading is *no one can ransom a brother*   c Heb *the pit*   d Gk Syr Compare Tg: Heb *their inward* (thought)   e Tg: Heb *after them*   f Cn: Heb *the upright shall have dominion over them in the morning*   g Meaning of Heb uncertain

---

the city is invincible. **48.7** The meaning is debated, but *Tarshish* may refer to the Phoenician colony of Tartessus in Spain (1 Kings 10.22). **48.8–11** The congregation responds in praise of God and calls Zion and all its surroundings to the praise of God, who rules and protects them. **48.8** *City of our God.* See 46.4; 87.3; Rev 3.12; 21.2, 10. *Selah.* See note on 3.2. **48.12–14** A representative figure instructs the community to make a solemn procession around Zion to see its greatness as a pointer to God, who dwells there and guides the people through all generations.

49.1–20 A psalm of instruction about life and death and the fact that wealth cannot save one from death or be carried beyond the grave. Lying behind this instruction is the experience of an individual who has been persecuted (v. 5) and expresses confidence in God's deliverance (v, 15). *To the leader.* See note on 4.1–8. *Korahites.* See note on 42.1–43.5. **49.1–4** A didactic

introduction by the psalmist, who here functions as a teacher of wisdom. Cf. 78.1–2; Deut 32.1–2. **49.4** *Proverb, riddle,* in Hebrew the same terms as in 78.2, the former probably referring to an instruction, the latter to a perplexing problem. **49.5–12** Instruction about not fearing the wealthy and their power, for rich and poor alike suffer the same fate in the end. **49.5–6** The personal concern toward which the instruction is directed is indicated here in a rhetorical question. **49.7–11** Assurance is given that wealth is finally of no avail. **49.8** A parenthetic verse that interrupts the direct connection between vv. 7 and 9. **49.12** A refrain (cf. v. 20), in typical fashion stating the point of the instruction (e.g., 46.7, 11). **49.13–20** The destiny of the psalmist, who trusts in God, is contrasted with the *fate of the foolhardy* (v. 13) and the *rich* (v. 16). **49.13** *Selah.* See note on 3.2. **49.14** The text of this verse is very uncertain. *Sheol.* See note on 6.5.

15 But God will ransom my soul from the
　　power of Sheol,
　　for he will receive me. *Selah*

16 Do not be afraid when some become
　　rich,
　　when the wealth of their houses
　　increases.
17 For when they die they will carry nothing
　　away;
　　their wealth will not go down after
　　them.
18 Though in their lifetime they count
　　themselves happy
　　—for you are praised when you do well
　　for yourself—
19 they[a] will go to the company of their
　　ancestors,
　　who will never again see the light.
20 Mortals cannot abide in their pomp;
　　they are like the animals that perish.

The Acceptable Sacrifice

A Psalm of Asaph.

50 The mighty one, God the LORD,
　　speaks and summons the earth
　　from the rising of the sun to its setting.
2 Out of Zion, the perfection of beauty,
　　God shines forth.

3 Our God comes and does not keep
　　silence,
　　before him is a devouring fire,
　　and a mighty tempest all around him.
4 He calls to the heavens above
　　and to the earth, that he may judge his
　　people:
5 "Gather to me my faithful ones,

who made a covenant with me by
　　sacrifice!"
6 The heavens declare his righteousness,
　　for God himself is judge. *Selah*

7 "Hear, O my people, and I will speak,
　　O Israel, I will testify against you.
　　I am God, your God.
8 Not for your sacrifices do I rebuke you;
　　your burnt offerings are continually
　　before me.
9 I will not accept a bull from your house,
　　or goats from your folds.
10 For every wild animal of the forest is
　　mine,
　　the cattle on a thousand hills.
11 I know all the birds of the air,[b]
　　and all that moves in the field is mine.

12 "If I were hungry, I would not tell you,
　　for the world and all that is in it is
　　mine.
13 Do I eat the flesh of bulls,
　　or drink the blood of goats?
14 Offer to God a sacrifice of thanksgiving,[c]
　　and pay your vows to the Most High.
15 Call on me in the day of trouble;
　　I will deliver you, and you shall glorify
　　me."

16 But to the wicked God says:
　　"What right have you to recite my
　　statutes,
　　or take my covenant on your lips?
17 For you hate discipline,
　　and you cast my words behind you.

---

a Cn: Heb *you*　b Gk Syr Tg: Heb *mountains*　c Or *make
thanksgiving your sacrifice to God*

49.15 The assurance of the psalmist over against the
fear of persecutors (v. 5) and in the knowledge that
one cannot ransom one's own life (v. 7). It is debated as
to whether the psalmist envisions a life with God beyond the grave. *Receive.* See Gen 5.24; 2 Kings 2.3, 5.
49.16–20 The instruction and its assurance are reiterated: one need not fear the rich, who lose everything in
death.
　50.1–23 A liturgy with priestly or prophetic ad-
monishment of the people, probably to be sung at a
festival of covenant renewal (cf. Pss 81; 95 for similar
language and character). *Asaph,* one of David's chief
musicians (1 Chr 6.39; 15.17; 16.5–7). The designation may refer to a psalm composed or handed down
by Asaph or the guild of singers associated with him

or under his leadership, as in the case of the Korahites
(e.g., Ps 42). **50.1–6** The coming of God for judgment
and the summons of the congregation of the faithful.
50.2 *Shines forth.* See note on 80.1. Cf. 18.8; Hab 3.3–
5. **50.4** *The heavens above and . . . the earth* are probably being called as witnesses to the covenant. See Deut
31.28; 32.1; Isa 1.2. **50.5** A covenant-renewal occasion
is suggested. **50.6** *Selah.* See note on 3.2. **50.7–
15** God's rebuke of the people for misunderstanding
the meaning of sacrifice. Its purpose is not to sustain
or strengthen the deity, who does not need food, but
to represent and manifest thanksgiving to God for divine help. **50.16–21** God's rebuke of the wicked for
their violation of the covenant laws, the Ten Commandments and other laws. Stealing (v. 18a), adultery

18 You make friends with a thief when you
        see one,
    and you keep company with adulterers.

19 "You give your mouth free rein for evil,
    and your tongue frames deceit.
20 You sit and speak against your kin;
    you slander your own mother's child.
21 These things you have done and I have
        been silent;
    you thought that I was one just like
        yourself.
    But now I rebuke you, and lay the charge
        before you.

22 "Mark this, then, you who forget God,
    or I will tear you apart, and there will
        be no one to deliver.
23 Those who bring thanksgiving as their
        sacrifice honor me;
    to those who go the right way*a*
    I will show the salvation of God."

Prayer for Cleansing and Pardon

To the leader. A Psalm of David, when the
prophet Nathan came to him, after he had
gone in to Bathsheba.

51 Have mercy on me, O God,
    according to your steadfast love;
    according to your abundant mercy
        blot out my transgressions.
2 Wash me thoroughly from my iniquity,
    and cleanse me from my sin.

3 For I know my transgressions,
    and my sin is ever before me.
4 Against you, you alone, have I sinned,
    and done what is evil in your sight,

so that you are justified in your sentence
    and blameless when you pass
        judgment.
5 Indeed, I was born guilty,
    a sinner when my mother conceived
        me.

6 You desire truth in the inward being;*b*
    therefore teach me wisdom in my
        secret heart.
7 Purge me with hyssop, and I shall be
        clean;
    wash me, and I shall be whiter than
        snow.
8 Let me hear joy and gladness;
    let the bones that you have crushed
        rejoice.
9 Hide your face from my sins,
    and blot out all my iniquities.

10 Create in me a clean heart, O God,
    and put a new and right*c* spirit within
        me.
11 Do not cast me away from your
        presence,
    and do not take your holy spirit from
        me.
12 Restore to me the joy of your salvation,
    and sustain in me a willing*d* spirit.

13 Then I will teach transgressors your ways,
    and sinners will return to you.
14 Deliver me from bloodshed, O God,
    O God of my salvation,
    and my tongue will sing aloud of your
        deliverance.

a Heb *who set a way*   b Meaning of Heb uncertain
c Or *steadfast*   d Or *generous*

(v. 18b), and false witness (vv. 19–20) are specifically
in view. **50.22–23** God utters a final warning about
disobedience (v. 22) and a promise to those who bring
thanksgiving as sacrifice (v. 23), reflecting the two
primary concerns of the divine judgment in this
psalm.

51.1–19 A prayer for God's help by an individual
who is deeply aware of sin and guilt and needs God's
forgiveness. One of the penitential psalms (see note on
6.1–10). *To the leader.* See note on 4.1–8. *A Psalm of
David . . . Bathsheba* is a secondary association of the
psalm with that event (2 Sam 12.1–15). Cf. v. 4a; 2 Sam
12.13. **51.1–2** A plea for mercy and God's cleansing of
the guilt of the petitioner. **51.3–6** Confession of sin
and acknowledgment of guilt. **51.4** The conviction of
the sin against God does not mean that there is no sin

against the neighbor involved, as the similar statement
in 2 Sam 12.13 indicates. *So that you . . . judgment.*
Quoted in Rom 3.4. **51.5** An expression of the depth of
the sense of sin, not a statement about original sin.
51.7–12 Prayer for forgiveness and restoration.
51.7 *Purge me with hyssop* probably refers to a cleansing ceremony using the hyssop bush (cf. Lev 14.2–9,
48–53; Num 19.6, 18). The petition here may have a
metaphorical sense. **51.8** *The bones . . . crushed,* actual
sickness or a metaphor for any situation of distress.
51.11 *Your holy spirit,* i.e., God's sustaining, powerful
presence. **51.13–15** A vow to instruct and to praise.
51.13 *Your ways* can refer both to the divine commandments and to God's merciful and forgiving way
of dealing with sinners. **51.14** *Bloodshed* is an enigmatic term that may mean the death that should come

15 O Lord, open my lips,
    and my mouth will declare your praise.
16 For you have no delight in sacrifice;
    if I were to give a burnt offering, you
      would not be pleased.
17 The sacrifice acceptable to God[a] is a
    broken spirit;
    a broken and contrite heart, O God,
      you will not despise.

18 Do good to Zion in your good pleasure;
    rebuild the walls of Jerusalem,
19 then you will delight in right sacrifices,
    in burnt offerings and whole burnt
      offerings;
    then bulls will be offered on your
      altar.

Judgment on the Deceitful

To the leader. A Maskil of David, when Doeg
the Edomite came to Saul and said to him,
"David has come to the house of Ahimelech."

52 Why do you boast, O mighty one,
    of mischief done against the godly?[b]
    All day long 2you are plotting
      destruction.
    Your tongue is like a sharp razor,
    you worker of treachery.
3 You love evil more than good,
    and lying more than speaking the
      truth.   *Selah*
4 You love all words that devour,
    O deceitful tongue.

5 But God will break you down forever;
    he will snatch and tear you from your
      tent;

    he will uproot you from the land of the
      living.   *Selah*
6 The righteous will see, and fear,
    and will laugh at the evildoer,[c] saying,
7 "See the one who would not take
    refuge in God,
    but trusted in abundant riches,
    and sought refuge in wealth!"[d]

8 But I am like a green olive tree
    in the house of God.
    I trust in the steadfast love of God
    forever and ever.
9 I will thank you forever,
    because of what you have done.
    In the presence of the faithful
    I will proclaim[e] your name, for it is
      good.

Denunciation of Godlessness

To the leader: according to Mahalath.
A Maskil of David.

53 Fools say in their hearts, "There is no
    God."
    They are corrupt, they commit
      abominable acts;
    there is no one who does good.

2 God looks down from heaven on
    humankind
    to see if there are any who are wise,
    who seek after God.

---

a Or *My sacrifice, O God,* *b* Cn Compare Syr: Heb *the kindness
of God* *c* Heb *him* *d* Syr Tg: Heb *in his destruction*
e Cn: Heb *wait for*

---

either from the illness, if such is to be assumed, or
from the guilt acknowledged in the psalm. **51.16–17** A
recognition of the need for penitence as the necessary
offering to God by the sinner. Cf. 50.7–15, 23. **51.18–
19** Probably a later addition relating the prayer to the
needs of the larger community and placing sacrifice in
the context of proper worship in the temple and a
proper spirit. **51.19** *Right sacrifices* can mean those
done according to the appropriate prescriptions of the
law or those offered with the right attitude and in the
right relationship to God.

    52.1–9 An announcement of judgment against one
of the wicked and a song of thanksgiving. *To the leader.*
See note on 4.1–8. *Maskil.* See note on 32.1–11. The
occasion alluded to in the superscription (cf. 1 Sam
21.1–8; 22.6–19) fits only very loosely with the details
of the psalm. **52.1–4** The accusation against the wicked

one. For a similar use of questions as an indictment, see
50.16; Isa 22.15–19. The accusation is of scheming to
oppress members of the community (*the godly*), who
are probably among the poor and less powerful. Vv.
1b–4 suggest that the principal manifestation is lying,
i.e., slander or false accusation against others, though
acts of fraud and deception to secure the wealth of others may be meant. **52.1** *Mighty one,* a term of sarcasm
that points to the power and wealth (v. 7) as well as the
self-image of the one accused. **52.3** *Selah.* See note on
3.2. **52.5–7** An announcement of judgment against the
wicked one who believes security is found in riches
rather than God. **52.8–9** A song of thanksgiving by the
psalmist who, in distinction from the *mighty one* (v. 1),
trusts in God and is delivered (v. 9a).

    53.1–6 With slight variations, the psalm is the same
as Ps 14. See notes on that psalm. *Mahalath.* See note

3 They have all fallen away, they are all alike
      perverse;
   there is no one who does good,
      no, not one.

4 Have they no knowledge, those evildoers,
      who eat up my people as they eat
         bread,
   and do not call upon God?

5 There they shall be in great terror,
      in terror such as has not been.
   For God will scatter the bones of the
         ungodly;[a]
   they will be put to shame,[b] for God has
         rejected them.

6 O that deliverance for Israel would come
      from Zion!
   When God restores the fortunes of his
         people,
   Jacob will rejoice; Israel will be glad.

Prayer for Vindication

To the leader: with stringed instruments.
A Maskil of David, when the Ziphites went
and told Saul, "David is in hiding among us."

54 Save me, O God, by your name,
      and vindicate me by your might.
2 Hear my prayer, O God;
      give ear to the words of my mouth.

3 For the insolent have risen against me,
      the ruthless seek my life;
   they do not set God before them. *Selah*

4 But surely, God is my helper;
      the Lord is the upholder of[c] my life.
5 He will repay my enemies for their evil.
      In your faithfulness, put an end to
         them.

6 With a freewill offering I will sacrifice to
      you;
   I will give thanks to your name,
      O LORD, for it is good.
7 For he has delivered me from every
         trouble,
   and my eye has looked in triumph on
         my enemies.

Complaint about a Friend's Treachery

To the leader: with stringed instruments.
A Maskil of David.

55 Give ear to my prayer, O God;
      do not hide yourself from my
         supplication.
2 Attend to me, and answer me;
      I am troubled in my complaint.
   I am distraught 3by the noise of the
         enemy,
   because of the clamor of the wicked.
   For they bring[d] trouble upon me,
      and in anger they cherish enmity
         against me.

4 My heart is in anguish within me,
      the terrors of death have fallen upon me.
5 Fear and trembling come upon me,
      and horror overwhelms me.
6 And I say, "O that I had wings like a dove!
      I would fly away and be at rest;
7 truly, I would flee far away;
      I would lodge in the wilderness; *Selah*
8 I would hurry to find a shelter for myself
      from the raging wind and tempest."

9 Confuse, O Lord, confound their speech;
      for I see violence and strife in the city.

---

a Cn Compare Gk Syr: Heb *him who encamps against you*
b Gk: Heb *you have put (them) to shame*   c Gk Syr Jerome: Heb
is of those who uphold or *is with those who uphold*
d Cn Compare Gk: Heb *they cause to totter*

---

on 88.1–18. *Maskil.* See note on 32.1–11. **53.3** *There is
. . . not one.* Cited in Rom 3.10–12.
   54.1–7 A prayer by an individual for help. *To the
leader . . . instruments.* See note on 4.1–8. *Maskil.* See
note on 32.1–11. For the incident alluded to in the superscription, see 1 Sam 23.19. **54.1–2** Pleas for God to
hear and help. **54.3** Description of the distress of the one
praying. *Selah.* See note on 86.14. *Selah.* See note on 3.2. **54.4–
5** The confidence of the psalmist in God's help and a
final plea for help against the persecutors. **54.6–7** A vow
of thanksgiving because God has heard and responded
to the prayer (cf. 6.9–10; 22.21b–22; 28.6–7; 56.12–13).

55.1–23 The prayer of an individual for God's help.
The psalm speaks of various enemies but twice indicates that the object of the complaint is a friend. *To the
leader . . . instruments.* See note on 4.1–8. *Maskil.* See
note on 32.1–11. **55.1–2a** Plea to God to hear the
prayer. *Do not hide yourself.* See notes on 10.1; 27.9.
55.2b–5 The distress of the psalmist, who is undone
and terrified by the trouble inflicted by an enemy. **55.6–
8** The wish to escape the trouble. **55.7** *Selah.* See note on
3.2. **55.9–11** Further description of the trouble discerned by the petitioner, but this time it is social violence and injustice in the community. For this part and

10 Day and night they go around it
       on its walls,
   and iniquity and trouble are within it;
11   ruin is in its midst;
   oppression and fraud
       do not depart from its marketplace.

12 It is not enemies who taunt me—
       I could bear that;
   it is not adversaries who deal insolently
           with me—
       I could hide from them.
13 But it is you, my equal,
       my companion, my familiar friend,
14 with whom I kept pleasant company;
   we walked in the house of God with
           the throng.
15 Let death come upon them;
       let them go down alive to Sheol;
       for evil is in their homes and in their
           hearts.

16 But I call upon God,
       and the LORD will save me.
17 Evening and morning and at noon
       I utter my complaint and moan,
       and he will hear my voice.
18 He will redeem me unharmed
       from the battle that I wage,
       for many are arrayed against me.
19 God, who is enthroned from of old, *Selah*
       will hear, and will humble them—
   because they do not change,
       and do not fear God.

20 My companion laid hands on a friend
       and violated a covenant with me[a]
21 with speech smoother than butter,
       but with a heart set on war;
   with words that were softer than oil,
       but in fact were drawn swords.

22 Cast your burden[b] on the LORD,
       and he will sustain you;
   he will never permit
       the righteous to be moved.

23 But you, O God, will cast them down
       into the lowest pit;
   the bloodthirsty and treacherous
       shall not live out half their days.
   But I will trust in you.

Trust in God under Persecution

To the leader: according to The Dove on Far-
off Terebinths. Of David. A Miktam, when the
       Philistines seized him in Gath.

56 Be gracious to me, O God, for people
           trample on me;
       all day long foes oppress me;
2 my enemies trample on me all day long,
       for many fight against me.
   O Most High, 3when I am afraid,
       I put my trust in you.
4 In God, whose word I praise,
       in God I trust; I am not afraid;
       what can flesh do to me?

5 All day long they seek to injure my cause;
       all their thoughts are against me for
           evil.
6 They stir up strife, they lurk,
       they watch my steps.
   As they hoped to have my life,
7   so repay[c] them for their crime;
       in wrath cast down the peoples, O God!

8 You have kept count of my tossings;
       put my tears in your bottle.

---

a Heb lacks *with me*   *b* Or *Cast what he has given you*
c Cn: Heb *rescue*

the psalm as a whole, cf. Mic 7.1–8 (cf. Hab 1.2–4).
55.12–15 A lament over being betrayed by a friend.
55.12 *Taunt.* See notes on 79.4; 79.10. **55.15** A strong
petition against all the persecutors tormenting the one
praying and the community. *Let them . . . Sheol.* Cf. Num
16.33. *Sheol.* See note on 6.5. **55.16–19** Expression of
confidence in God's attention to the cries and God's deliverance. **55.19** *Fear God.* See note on 34.7. **55.20–
21** The psalmist returns to the complaint against the
friend who has betrayed the relationship. **55.22–23** A
word of encouragement that may have been addressed
to the petitioner by someone else (v. 22), followed by the
psalmist's own final words of trust in God (v. 23).

56.1–13 An individual's prayer for help when persecuted by enemies. *To the leader.* See note on 4.1–8.
According to . . . Terebinths may be a note about the
melody or tune. *Miktam.* See note on 16.1–11. *When
the Philistines . . . Gath.* See 1 Sam 21.11–15. Gath was
one of the five main cities of the Philistines. **56.1–2** A
plea for help and a description of the distress that is the
basis for the plea. **56.3–4** Expressions of trust and
confidence in God's help. V. 4 is a refrain repeated in
vv. 10–11. **56.5–7** A description of the distress culminating in an additional petition for God's help. **56.8–
11** Further assertion of confidence in God. **56.8** Two
images show that God cares by keeping track of the af-

Are they not in your record?
9 Then my enemies will retreat
    in the day when I call.
  This I know, that[a] God is for me.
10 In God, whose word I praise,
    in the LORD, whose word I praise,
11 in God I trust; I am not afraid.
  What can a mere mortal do to me?

12 My vows to you I must perform, O God;
    I will render thank offerings to you.
13 For you have delivered my soul from
        death,
  and my feet from falling,
  so that I may walk before God
    in the light of life.

Praise and Assurance under Persecution

To the leader: Do Not Destroy. Of David.
A Miktam, when he fled from Saul, in the cave.

57 Be merciful to me, O God, be merciful
        to me,
    for in you my soul takes refuge;
  in the shadow of your wings I will take
        refuge,
    until the destroying storms pass by.
2 I cry to God Most High,
    to God who fulfills his purpose for me.
3 He will send from heaven and save me,
    he will put to shame those who
        trample on me.   *Selah*
  God will send forth his steadfast love and
    his faithfulness.

4 I lie down among lions
    that greedily devour[b] human prey;
  their teeth are spears and arrows,
    their tongues sharp swords.

5 Be exalted, O God, above the heavens.
    Let your glory be over all the earth.

6 They set a net for my steps;
    my soul was bowed down.
  They dug a pit in my path,
    but they have fallen into it themselves.
                                    Selah
7 My heart is steadfast, O God,
    my heart is steadfast.
  I will sing and make melody.
8   Awake, my soul!
  Awake, O harp and lyre!
    I will awake the dawn.
9 I will give thanks to you, O Lord, among
        the peoples;
    I will sing praises to you among the
        nations.
10 For your steadfast love is as high as the
        heavens;
    your faithfulness extends to the clouds.

11 Be exalted, O God, above the heavens.
    Let your glory be over all the earth.

Prayer for Vengeance

To the leader: Do Not Destroy. Of David.
A Miktam.

58 Do you indeed decree what is right,
        you gods?[c]
  Do you judge people fairly?
2 No, in your hearts you devise wrongs;
    your hands deal out violence on earth.

3 The wicked go astray from the womb;
    they err from their birth, speaking lies.

a Or *because*   *b* Cn: Heb *are aflame for*   *c* Or *mighty lords*

flictions of the sufferer: collecting the tears and writing the afflictions in a book. *Record.* See 40.7; 69.28; 139.16. **56.10** *Word.* Probably an oracle of salvation. See note on 22.21b. **56.12–13** A vow of thanksgiving for help received or anticipated. *Light,* a symbol for the power of life; see 13.3; 27.1; 36.9; 38.10.
  57.1–11 A prayer for help by one who has been beset by other people. *To the leader.* See note on 4.1–8. *Do Not Destroy.* Meaning uncertain. *Miktam.* See note on 16.1–11. *When he fled ... cave.* See 1 Sam 22–24. **57.1–3** A plea for help expressed in confidence that God will save. **57.1** *Shadow of your wings.* See notes on 91.1; 91.4. **57.3** *Selah.* See note on 3.2. **57.4** The enemies of the petitioner are portrayed as lions lying in wait and devouring their prey (see note on 7.2). **57.5** A refrain express-

ing praise to God (cf. v. 11). **57.6** The enemies, now pictured as hunters, fall into their own trap. *Net, pit.* See note on 9.15. **57.7–11** Expressions of trust, thanksgiving, and praise in anticipation of God's continued faithfulness to the psalmist. Repeated in 108.1–5.
  58.1–11 A call to God to destroy the power of the wicked. The depiction of the wicked in vv. 3–5 and the plea of v. 6 associate the psalm with the prayers for help that surround this psalm. *To the leader.* See note on 4.1–8. *Do Not Destroy.* Meaning uncertain. *Miktam.* See note on 16.1–11. **58.1–2** An indictment of the gods of the nations, who are responsible for justice on the earth (see Ps 82) but in fact support the wicked, as the next verses suggest. For the conceptual background of these verses, see note on 82.1–8. **58.3–5** A

4 They have venom like the venom of a
      serpent,
   like the deaf adder that stops its ear,
5 so that it does not hear the voice of
      charmers
   or of the cunning enchanter.

6 O God, break the teeth in their mouths;
   tear out the fangs of the young lions,
      O Lord!
7 Let them vanish like water that runs
      away;
   like grass let them be trodden down[a]
      and wither.
8 Let them be like the snail that dissolves
      into slime;
   like the untimely birth that never sees
      the sun.
9 Sooner than your pots can feel the heat of
      thorns,
   whether green or ablaze, may he sweep
      them away!

10 The righteous will rejoice when they see
      vengeance done;
   they will bathe their feet in the blood
      of the wicked.
11 People will say, "Surely there is a reward
      for the righteous;
   surely there is a God who judges on
      earth."

Prayer for Deliverance from Enemies

To the leader: Do Not Destroy. Of David.
A Miktam, when Saul ordered his house to be
      watched in order to kill him.

59 Deliver me from my enemies, O my
      God;
   protect me from those who rise up
      against me.

2 Deliver me from those who work evil;
   from the bloodthirsty save me.

3 Even now they lie in wait for my life;
   the mighty stir up strife against me.
   For no transgression or sin of mine,
      O Lord,
4 for no fault of mine, they run and
      make ready.

   Rouse yourself, come to my help and see!
5   You, Lord God of hosts, are God of
      Israel.
   Awake to punish all the nations;
   spare none of those who treacherously
      plot evil.   Selah

6 Each evening they come back,
   howling like dogs
   and prowling about the city.
7 There they are, bellowing with their
      mouths,
   with sharp words[b] on their lips—
   for "Who," they think,[c] "will hear us?"

8 But you laugh at them, O Lord;
   you hold all the nations in derision.
9 O my strength, I will watch for you;
   for you, O God, are my fortress.
10 My God in his steadfast love will meet me;
   my God will let me look in triumph on
      my enemies.

11 Do not kill them, or my people may
      forget;
   make them totter by your power, and
      bring them down,
      O Lord, our shield.

---

a Cn: Meaning of Heb uncertain   b Heb with swords
c Heb lacks they think

---

description of the wicked with particular emphasis
upon their deceit (v. 3), deadliness (v. 4a), and uncon-
trollability (vv. 4a–5; cf. Jer 8.17). They are the agents
of the violence perpetuated by the cosmic powers or
demonic forces of vv. 1–2. **58.6–9** A series of imprecations, or curses, calling for God to destroy the wicked.
58.6 *Young lions.* See note on 7.2. **58.8** *Untimely birth,*
i.e., miscarriage. **58.9** The text is disturbed and the
meaning uncertain. **58.10–11** The confidence of the
righteous or innocent in God's vindicating judgment.
   59.1–17 An individual prayer for help. *To the leader.*
See note on 4.1–8. *Do Not Destroy.* Meaning uncertain.
Miktam. See note on 16.1–11. *When Saul . . . kill him.*

See 1 Sam 19.11–17. **59.1–2** Plea for deliverance from
the psalmist's enemies. **59.3–4a** Description of the
persecution by the enemies and a protestation of innocence on the part of the psalmist, suggesting the persecution may be a matter of false accusations (cf. vv. 7,
12). **59.4b–5** Additional plea for God's active involvement to help. *Selah.* See note on 3.2. **59.6–7** A reference to the enemies as prowling and scavenging dogs
(cf. vv. 14–15) who believe they will not be called to
account when they persecute (cf. 10.4, 13; 14.1; 73.11;
94.7). **59.8–10** Expressions of confidence in God.
59.8 See 2.4; 37.13. **59.11–13** A final plea for God to
bring down the wicked as a lesson and witness to all

12 For the sin of their mouths, the words of
        their lips,
    let them be trapped in their pride.
    For the cursing and lies that they utter,
13   consume them in wrath;
    consume them until they are no more.
    Then it will be known to the ends of the
        earth
    that God rules over Jacob.   *Selah*

14 Each evening they come back,
        howling like dogs
    and prowling about the city.
15 They roam about for food,
    and growl if they do not get their fill.

16 But I will sing of your might;
    I will sing aloud of your steadfast love
        in the morning.
    For you have been a fortress for me
    and a refuge in the day of my distress.
17 O my strength, I will sing praises to you,
    for you, O God, are my fortress,
    the God who shows me steadfast love.

Prayer for National Victory after Defeat

To the leader: according to the Lily of the
Covenant. A Miktam of David; for
instruction; when he struggled with Aram-
naharaim and with Aram-zobah, and when
Joab on his return killed twelve thousand
Edomites in the Valley of Salt.

60 O God, you have rejected us, broken
        our defenses;
    you have been angry; now restore us!
2   You have caused the land to quake; you
        have torn it open;

repair the cracks in it, for it is tottering.
3   You have made your people suffer hard
        things;
    you have given us wine to drink that
        made us reel.

4   You have set up a banner for those who
        fear you,
    to rally to it out of bowshot.[a]   *Selah*
5   Give victory with your right hand, and
        answer us,[b]
    so that those whom you love may be
        rescued.

6   God has promised in his sanctuary:[c]
    "With exultation I will divide up
        Shechem,
    and portion out the Vale of Succoth.
7   Gilead is mine, and Manasseh is mine;
    Ephraim is my helmet;
    Judah is my scepter.
8   Moab is my washbasin;
    on Edom I hurl my shoe;
    over Philistia I shout in triumph."

9   Who will bring me to the fortified city?
    Who will lead me to Edom?
10 Have you not rejected us, O God?
    You do not go out, O God, with our
        armies.
11 O grant us help against the foe,
    for human help is worthless.
12 With God we shall do valiantly;
    it is he who will tread down our foes.

---

a Gk Syr Jerome: Heb *because of the truth*   *b* Another reading
is *me*   *c* Or *by his holiness*

---

people that God rules in power. **59.16–17** A vow of
thanksgiving and praise for God's help.
60.1–12 A prayer of the community for God's help.
To the leader. See note on 4.1–8. *According to . . . Covenant,* perhaps a melody. *Miktam.* See note on 16.1–
11. *When he struggled . . . Aram-zobah.* See 2 Sam 8.3–
8; 10.6–18. *Twelve thousand . . . Valley of Salt.* See
2 Sam 8.13. *Joab* was David's general. These historical
allusions are probably secondary. A national defeat
may lie behind this psalm, but it is not possible to determine which one with any certainty. **60.1–4** A complaint to God, who is seen as the ultimate source of the
national suffering. **60.4** *You have set up a banner.* Perhaps to be understood as a request rather than a declaration, i.e., "Set up a banner." *Selah.* See note on 3.2.
60.5–12 Repeated in 108.6–13. **60.5** Plea for help (v.
5a) and motivation offered (v. 5b). **60.6–8** Divine re-

sponse asserting God's power and rule over Israel and
Judah and their enemies. It was probably delivered by a
priest or prophet in the temple. **60.6** *I will divide up . . .
and portion out* is God's claim of ownership. *Shechem*
was one of the main towns in the Northern Kingdom,
Israel. **60.6b–7** *Succoth, Gilead,* and *Manasseh* were
areas east of the Jordan. *Ephraim* may be the hill country of the Northern Kingdom or a term for the kingdom as a whole. *Judah* is the Southern Kingdom,
where the Davidic king ruled (i.e., God's *scepter*).
60.8 *Moab, Edom,* and *Philistia* were often in conflict
with Israel. *Hurl my shoe* is an image indicating possession (cf. Ruth 4.7–8). **60.9–12** A plea for help on the
part of the king or some representative figure. The
meaning of v. 9 is unclear. The complaint of v. 10 echoes the complaint of v. 1 and leads into the final petition (v. 11) and the expression of confidence (v. 12).

Assurance of God's Protection

To the leader: with stringed instruments.
Of David.

61 Hear my cry, O God;
     listen to my prayer.

2 From the end of the earth I call to you,
     when my heart is faint.

Lead me to the rock
     that is higher than I;
3 for you are my refuge,
     a strong tower against the enemy.

4 Let me abide in your tent forever,
     find refuge under the shelter of your
          wings.   *Selah*
5 For you, O God, have heard my vows;
     you have given me the heritage of
          those who fear your name.

6 Prolong the life of the king;
     may his years endure to all
          generations!
7 May he be enthroned forever before God;
     appoint steadfast love and faithfulness
          to watch over him!

8 So I will always sing praises to your name,
     as I pay my vows day after day.

Song of Trust in God Alone

To the leader: according to Jeduthun.
A Psalm of David.

62 For God alone my soul waits in
     silence;
     from him comes my salvation.
2 He alone is my rock and my salvation,
     my fortress; I shall never be shaken.

3 How long will you assail a person,
     will you batter your victim, all of
          you,
     as you would a leaning wall, a tottering
          fence?
4 Their only plan is to bring down a person
     of prominence.
     They take pleasure in falsehood;
they bless with their mouths,
     but inwardly they curse.   *Selah*

5 For God alone my soul waits in silence,
     for my hope is from him.
6 He alone is my rock and my salvation,
     my fortress; I shall not be shaken.
7 On God rests my deliverance and my
          honor;
     my mighty rock, my refuge is in God.

8 Trust in him at all times, O people;
     pour out your heart before him;
     God is a refuge for us.   *Selah*

9 Those of low estate are but a breath,
     those of high estate are a delusion;
in the balances they go up;
     they are together lighter than a
          breath.
10 Put no confidence in extortion,
     and set no vain hopes on robbery;
     if riches increase, do not set your heart
          on them.

11 Once God has spoken;
     twice have I heard this:
that power belongs to God,
12   and steadfast love belongs to you,
          O Lord.
For you repay to all
     according to their work.

61.1–8 A prayer by an individual for help. *To the leader . . . instruments.* See note on 4.1–8. **61.1–2a** A cry for help. *From the end of the earth* suggests the psalmist is distant from the sanctuary (cf. 42.6; 84.2). **61.2b–5** The psalmist seeks refuge and expresses confidence in God's protection. **61.4** *Tent,* the sanctuary or temple. *Shelter of your wings.* See notes on 91.1; 91.4. *Selah.* See note on 3.2. **61.5** *Fear.* See note on 34.7. **61.6–7** Intercession for the king (cf. 63.11; 84.9). **61.6** Cf. 72.5, 15. **61.7** For *steadfast love and faithfulness* as personifications, see note on 85.10–13. **61.8** Vow of praise when the psalmist is secure in the safety of God's presence. See note on 65.1–2a.
62.1–12 A prayer of trust in God in the face of perse-

cution. *To the leader.* See note on 4.1–8. *According to Jeduthun.* See note on 77.1–20. **62.1–7** Expression of trust by the psalmist. The theme is set at the beginning (vv. 1–2) and then repeated at the end (vv. 5–7). In between (vv. 3–4) the psalmist laments over the oppression inflicted by others that has evoked this prayer. The psalmist has been battered for some time by the lies, curses (magical incantations), and hypocrisy of the enemies. **62.4** *Selah.* See note on 3.2. **62.8–10** Instruction to the community to trust in God and not in immoral and oppressive acts. **62.11–12** Reference to God's promise of protection, possibly an oracle of salvation, that evokes the confidence expressed in the prayer. **62.12** *You repay . . . work.* Cited in Mt 16.27; Rom 2.6.

Comfort and Assurance in God's Presence

A Psalm of David, when he was in the
Wilderness of Judah.

63 O God, you are my God, I seek you,
my soul thirsts for you;
my flesh faints for you,
as in a dry and weary land where there
is no water.
2 So I have looked upon you in the sanctuary,
beholding your power and glory.
3 Because your steadfast love is better than
life,
my lips will praise you.
4 So I will bless you as long as I live;
I will lift up my hands and call on your
name.

5 My soul is satisfied as with a rich feast,*a*
and my mouth praises you with joyful
lips
6 when I think of you on my bed,
and meditate on you in the watches of
the night;
7 for you have been my help,
and in the shadow of your wings I sing
for joy.
8 My soul clings to you;
your right hand upholds me.

9 But those who seek to destroy my life
shall go down into the depths of the
earth;
10 they shall be given over to the power of
the sword,
they shall be prey for jackals.
11 But the king shall rejoice in God;
all who swear by him shall exult,
for the mouths of liars will be stopped.

Prayer for Protection from Enemies

To the leader. A Psalm of David.

64 Hear my voice, O God, in my
complaint;
preserve my life from the dread enemy.
2 Hide me from the secret plots of the
wicked,
from the scheming of evildoers,
3 who whet their tongues like swords,
who aim bitter words like arrows,
4 shooting from ambush at the blameless;
they shoot suddenly and without fear.
5 They hold fast to their evil purpose;
they talk of laying snares secretly,
thinking, "Who can see us?*b*
6 Who can search out our crimes?*c*
We have thought out a cunningly
conceived plot."
For the human heart and mind are
deep.

7 But God will shoot his arrow at them;
they will be wounded suddenly.
8 Because of their tongue he will bring
them to ruin;*d*
all who see them will shake with
horror.
9 Then everyone will fear;
they will tell what God has brought
about,
and ponder what he has done.

10 Let the righteous rejoice in the LORD
and take refuge in him.
Let all the upright in heart glory.

---

a Heb *with fat and fatness* *b* Syr: Heb *them* *c* Cn: Heb *They
search out crimes* *d* Cn: Heb *They will bring him to ruin, their
tongue being against them*

63.1–11 A prayer for help in the sanctuary, in
which the psalmist is confident of God's overthrow of
those who are persecuting. *When he was . . . Judah* may
refer to 1 Sam 23.14–15 or 24.1. This secondary historical allusion may be suggested by v. 1b. **63.1–2** The
longing of the psalmist for the divine presence.
63.1 Cf. 42.1–2. **63.2** It is unclear if the psalmist is
looking for or has already seen God in some way in
the sanctuary (cf. 5.3; 27.4). **63.3–8** Confident of
God's help, the psalmist gives praise. **63.4** *Bless.* See
note on 103.1–2. **63.6** Cf. 4.4; 16.7; 77.2, 6. *Watches.*
See note on 90.4. There may be an allusion here to
waiting through the night in the sanctuary for God's
help in the morning. **63.7** *Shadow of your wings.* See
notes on 91.1; 91.4. **63.9–10** Confidence of the
psalmist in the downfall of the oppressors. Here, as

elsewhere, they may be false accusers or slanderers
(see v. 11b). **63.11** A form of intercession for the king
as God's representative (cf. 61.6–7; 84.9). *By him,* i.e.,
by the king. For oaths sworn in the name of the king,
see 1 Sam 17.55; 25.26; 2 Sam 11.11; 15.21.

   64.1–10 A prayer by an individual for help. *To the
leader.* See note on 4.1–8. **64.1–2** A cry for help. **64.2–
6** Beginning already in the plea, the psalmist lays out
the distress brought about by wicked enemies. Cf. note
on 10.1–11. **64.7–9** God's destruction of the enemies.
These verses should probably be read as a report of
what God did in the past and the testimony to it by
those who witnessed it. **64.7** *Shoot his arrow,* poetic
justice—the judgment of God corresponds to the sins
of the wicked (vv. 3–4). **64.10** Concluding call to
praise. *Refuge.* See note on 2.10–12.

Thanksgiving for Earth's Bounty

To the leader. A Psalm of David. A Song.

65 Praise is due to you,
     O God, in Zion;
  and to you shall vows be performed,
2   O you who answer prayer!
  To you all flesh shall come.
3 When deeds of iniquity overwhelm us,
     you forgive our transgressions.
4 Happy are those whom you choose and
        bring near
     to live in your courts.
  We shall be satisfied with the goodness of
        your house,
     your holy temple.

5 By awesome deeds you answer us with
        deliverance,
     O God of our salvation;
  you are the hope of all the ends of the
        earth
     and of the farthest seas.
6 By your*a* strength you established the
        mountains;
     you are girded with might.
7 You silence the roaring of the seas,
     the roaring of their waves,
     the tumult of the peoples.
8 Those who live at earth's farthest bounds
     are awed by your signs;
  you make the gateways of the morning
     and the evening shout for joy.

9 You visit the earth and water it,
     you greatly enrich it;
  the river of God is full of water;
     you provide the people with grain,
     for so you have prepared it.
10 You water its furrows abundantly,

  settling its ridges,
  softening it with showers,
     and blessing its growth.
11 You crown the year with your bounty;
     your wagon tracks overflow with
        richness.
12 The pastures of the wilderness overflow,
     the hills gird themselves with joy,
13 the meadows clothe themselves with
        flocks,
     the valleys deck themselves with grain,
     they shout and sing together for joy.

Praise for God's Goodness to Israel

To the leader. A Song. A Psalm.

66 Make a joyful noise to God, all the
     earth;
2   sing the glory of his name;
     give to him glorious praise.
3 Say to God, "How awesome are your
        deeds!
  Because of your great power, your
        enemies cringe before you.
4 All the earth worships you;
     they sing praises to you,
  sing praises to your name."   *Selah*

5 Come and see what God has done:
     he is awesome in his deeds among
        mortals.
6 He turned the sea into dry land;
     they passed through the river on foot.
  There we rejoiced in him,
7   who rules by his might forever,
  whose eyes keep watch on the nations—
     let the rebellious not exalt themselves.
                                          Selah

---

a Gk Jerome: Heb *his*

65.1–13 A hymn of praise to God, who has redeemed the people and sustains their life on the earth. Either particular or repeated occasions in which Israel experienced a good harvest may have given rise to the singing of this hymn. *To the leader.* See note on 4.1–8. **65.1–5** The people give praise to God, who dwells in Zion and has forgiven and saved them. **65.1–2a** The praise arises out of vows made in prayers for help (cf. 22.25; 50.14; 56.12; 61.5, 8; 66.13; 116.14, 18). **65.4** *Happy.* See note on 1.1. **65.6–8** Praise to God as the creator of the world. God's subduing of the waters of chaos may lie behind v. 7 (cf. 74.12–14; 89.9–10; note on 77.16). **65.9–13** Praise to God, who nourishes the earth and so provides bountiful harvest and many

flocks. **65.9** *River of God.* See note on 46.4. **65.11** *Your wagon tracks,* either the imagery of God riding the clouds in a chariot (e.g., 68.4, 33) or a poetic way of speaking about God's providential presence in the land.

66.1–20 A song of thanksgiving (vv. 13–20) by an individual that is prefaced by a general hymn of praise (vv. 1–12). *To the leader.* See note on 4.1–8. **66.1–12** Hymn of praise for God's mighty deeds of salvation for the people. **66.4** *Selah.* See note on 3.2. **66.5a** See 46.8. **66.6** *He turned . . . land,* the crossing of the sea in the exodus (Ex 14–15). *They passed . . . foot,* the crossing of the Jordan into Canaan (Josh 3.14–17). These mighty acts of the Lord may have been re-presented in

8 Bless our God, O peoples,
  let the sound of his praise be heard,
9 who has kept us among the living,
  and has not let our feet slip.
10 For you, O God, have tested us;
  you have tried us as silver is tried.
11 You brought us into the net;
  you laid burdens on our backs;
12 you let people ride over our heads;
  we went through fire and through
    water;
  yet you have brought us out to a spacious
    place.[a]

13 I will come into your house with burnt
    offerings;
  I will pay you my vows,
14 those that my lips uttered
  and my mouth promised when I was in
    trouble.
15 I will offer to you burnt offerings of
    fatlings,
  with the smoke of the sacrifice of rams;
  I will make an offering of bulls and goats.
    Selah

16 Come and hear, all you who fear God,
  and I will tell what he has done
    for me.
17 I cried aloud to him,
  and he was extolled with my tongue.
18 If I had cherished iniquity in my heart,
  the Lord would not have listened.
19 But truly God has listened;
  he has given heed to the words of my
    prayer.

20 Blessed be God,
  because he has not rejected my prayer
  or removed his steadfast love from me.

The Nations Called to Praise God

To the leader: with stringed instruments.
A Psalm. A Song.

67 May God be gracious to us and bless us
  and make his face to shine upon us,
    Selah
2 that your way may be known upon earth,
  your saving power among all nations.
3 Let the peoples praise you, O God;
  let all the peoples praise you.

4 Let the nations be glad and sing for joy,
  for you judge the peoples with equity
  and guide the nations upon earth. *Selah*
5 Let the peoples praise you, O God;
  let all the peoples praise you.

6 The earth has yielded its increase;
  God, our God, has blessed us.
7 May God continue to bless us;
  let all the ends of the earth revere him.

Praise and Thanksgiving

To the leader. Of David. A Psalm. A Song.

68 Let God rise up, let his enemies be
  scattered;
  let those who hate him flee before him.

_____
a Cn Compare Gk Syr Jerome Tg: Heb *to a saturation*

some fashion in worship (cf. 114.1–8). **66.8–12** While
the people experienced God's judgment as a testing
and refinement, God kept them secure and gave them
the land. **66.8** *Bless.* See note on 103.1–2. **66.13–20** A
song of thanksgiving as one who has been helped pays
vows of sacrifice (vv. 13–15; cf. 65.1–2a and note) and
bears witness to God's gracious attention (vv. 17–19,
20a) and deliverance (v. 16, 20b). **66.16** *Fear God.* See
note on 34.7. **66.20** *Blessed.* See note on 103.1–2.
67.1–7 A prayer of benediction or blessing together
with a call to all peoples to praise the Lord, who blesses
Israel. *To the leader . . . instruments.* See note on 4.1–8.
67.1–2 Prayer for God's blessing in the language of the
Aaronite benediction (Num 6.24–26). The reason for
the blessing is that Israel's experience of God's favor
may be a witness to all the nations (cf. Pss 117; 126.2).
67.1 *Make his face to shine.* See note on 31.16. *Selah.*
See note on 3.2. **67.3–5** Call to the nations to praise
the Lord who rules justly over all peoples. **67.6–7** A

final prayer for God's blessing in the provision of produce from the land. V. 6 perhaps should be read like
v. 1, i.e., as a prayer, "May the earth yield its increase;
may God, our God, bless us."
  68.1–35 A hymn of praise for God's awesome appearance to the people in power and victory. The unity
and order of the hymn are difficult to discern and
some have seen it as a collection of fragments. Its interpretation as a whole is problematic. It may have
been associated in its origin with God's appearance at
one of the sanctuaries, but in its present form it has
been adapted for worship in the Jerusalem temple (v.
29). The various references to marching and procession (vv. 7–8, 17–18, 24–27) and to music (vv. 4, 25,
32) suggest use of the psalm in the festivals of Israel's
worship. *To the leader.* See note on 4.1–8. **68.1–3** Call
to God to go forth in victory against the enemy. The
words are a form of the ancient Song of the Ark in
Num 10.35. It was sung as the Lord, enthroned on the

2   As smoke is driven away, so drive them
         away;
      as wax melts before the fire,
      let the wicked perish before God.
3   But let the righteous be joyful;
      let them exult before God;
      let them be jubilant with joy.

4   Sing to God, sing praises to his name;
      lift up a song to him who rides upon
         the clouds*—
      his name is the LORD—
      be exultant before him.

5   Father of orphans and protector of
         widows
      is God in his holy habitation.
6   God gives the desolate a home to live in;
      he leads out the prisoners to
         prosperity,
      but the rebellious live in a parched
         land.

7   O God, when you went out before your
         people,
      when you marched through the
         wilderness,   Selah
8   the earth quaked, the heavens poured
         down rain
      at the presence of God, the God of
         Sinai,
      at the presence of God, the God of
         Israel.
9   Rain in abundance, O God, you showered
         abroad;
      you restored your heritage when it
         languished;
10 your flock found a dwelling in it;
      in your goodness, O God, you
         provided for the needy.

11 The Lord gives the command;
      great is the company of those*b* who
         bore the tidings:
12 "The kings of the armies, they flee,
         they flee!"
   The women at home divide the spoil,
13   though they stay among the
         sheepfolds—
      the wings of a dove covered with silver,
         its pinions with green gold.
14 When the Almighty*c* scattered kings
         there,
      snow fell on Zalmon.

15 O mighty mountain, mountain of
         Bashan;
      O many-peaked mountain, mountain
         of Bashan!
16 Why do you look with envy, O many-
         peaked mountain,
      at the mount that God desired for his
         abode,
      where the LORD will reside forever?

17 With mighty chariotry, twice ten
         thousand,
      thousands upon thousands,
      the Lord came from Sinai into the holy
         place.*d*
18 You ascended the high mount,
      leading captives in your train
      and receiving gifts from people,
      even from those who rebel against the
         LORD God's abiding there.
19 Blessed be the Lord,
      who daily bears us up;

———————
a Or *cast up a highway for him who rides through the deserts*
b Or *company of the women* *c* Traditional rendering of Heb
Shaddai *d* Cn: Heb *The Lord among them Sinai in the holy*
(place)

ark, went forth to war, leading the people (cf. 1 Sam 4).
68.4–6 Hymn of praise exalting God as protector of
the weak. **68.4** *Rides upon the clouds* is an ancient epithet of the Canaanite storm god applied to the Lord of
Israel. The *clouds* are the chariot of God, who goes
forth to lead the armies (cf. 104.3–4). **68.6** *Prisoners,*
or "captives." **68.7–10** The march of God before the
people to lead them into the land and provide for
them. Cf. vv. 7–8; Judg 5.4–5; Deut 33.2–3. The imagery again is of the Lord as a storm god, marching in
battle and making the land fertile through rain.
68.7 *Selah.* See note on 3.2. **68.11–14** The victory of
God over the kings of Canaan. An allusion to Judg 5
may be present in these verses also (see Judg 5.19). Vv.

12b–13 are enigmatic. There may be an allusion to
Judg 5.16 in v. 13a. **68.13** *The wings of a dove,* possibly
some treasure from the spoil (cf. Judg 5.19b).
68.14 *Snow fell on Zalmon.* Meaning uncertain. **68.15–
18** The Lord ascends the holy mountain, which is the
divine abode. Unidentified in the psalm, it came to be
understood as Mount Zion. **68.15** *Bashan,* a mountain
of unknown location here seen as envious of the
mount of God's dwelling (cf. note on 22.12–13).
68.17 A possible reading of this difficult verse is: "The
chariots of God were twice ten thousand, / A thousand
the warriors of the LORD, / When he came from Sinai
with the holy ones." **68.18** *You ascended.* See Eph 4.8–
10. **68.19–20** Praise to God, who has saved the people.

God is our salvation.   *Selah*

20 Our God is a God of salvation,
and to GOD, the Lord, belongs escape
from death.

21 But God will shatter the heads of his
enemies,
the hairy crown of those who walk in
their guilty ways.

22 The Lord said,
"I will bring them back from Bashan,
I will bring them back from the depths of
the sea,

23 so that you may bathe*a* your feet in blood,
so that the tongues of your dogs may
have their share from the foe."

24 Your solemn processions are seen,*b*
O God,
the processions of my God, my King,
into the sanctuary—

25 the singers in front, the musicians last,
between them girls playing
tambourines:

26 "Bless God in the great congregation,
the LORD, O you who are of Israel's
fountain!"

27 There is Benjamin, the least of them, in
the lead,
the princes of Judah in a body,
the princes of Zebulun, the princes of
Naphtali.

28 Summon your might, O God;
show your strength, O God, as you
have done for us before.

29 Because of your temple at Jerusalem
kings bear gifts to you.

30 Rebuke the wild animals that live among
the reeds,
the herd of bulls with the calves of the
peoples.
Trample*c* under foot those who lust after
tribute;

scatter the peoples who delight in war.*d*

31 Let bronze be brought from Egypt;
let Ethiopia*e* hasten to stretch out its
hands to God.

32 Sing to God, O kingdoms of the earth;
sing praises to the Lord,   *Selah*

33 O rider in the heavens, the ancient
heavens;
listen, he sends out his voice, his
mighty voice.

34 Ascribe power to God,
whose majesty is over Israel;
and whose power is in the skies.

35 Awesome is God in his*f* sanctuary,
the God of Israel;
he gives power and strength to his
people.

Blessed be God!

Prayer for Deliverance from Persecution

To the leader: according to Lilies. Of David.

69 Save me, O God,
for the waters have come up to my
neck.

2 I sink in deep mire,
where there is no foothold;
I have come into deep waters,
and the flood sweeps over me.

3 I am weary with my crying;
my throat is parched.
My eyes grow dim
with waiting for my God.

4 More in number than the hairs of my
head
are those who hate me without cause;
many are those who would destroy me,
my enemies who accuse me falsely.

---

a Gk Syr Tg: Heb *shatter* *b* Or *have been seen* *c* Cn: Heb
Trampling *d* Meaning of Heb of verse 30 is uncertain
e Or *Nubia*; Heb *Cush* *f* Gk: Heb *from your*

68.21–23 God's defeat of the enemies. V. 22 is enigmatic but probably also has to do with conquest. **68.24–27** The procession of God, whose rule is secured in victory, into the sanctuary. **68.27** *Benjamin . . . in the lead* has been seen as suggesting an origin of the psalm in the time of Saul, who was from the tribe of Benjamin. **68.28–31** Call to God to show power over the kings and nations of the earth. **68.32–35** Concluding hymn of praise. **68.33** Cf. 18.9–13; Ps 29.
69.1–36 An individual prayer for help. *To the leader.*

See note on 4.1–8. *According to Lilies.* See note on 45.1–17. **69.1–4** Plea for God's deliverance and lament over physical and emotional distress and the persecution of others. The particular situation is not described, but aspects of the psalm (e.g., vv. 26, 29) suggest illness seen as God's judgment and evoking the taunts and insults of others. For the likely character of the insults and reproach, see notes on 79.4; 79.10 (cf. 42.4, 10). **69.1–2** For the imagery of *waters* and drowning to express personal distress, see vv. 14–15;

What I did not steal
  must I now restore?
5 O God, you know my folly;
  the wrongs I have done are not hidden
    from you.

6 Do not let those who hope in you be put
    to shame because of me,
  O Lord GOD of hosts;
  do not let those who seek you be
    dishonored because of me,
  O God of Israel.
7 It is for your sake that I have borne
    reproach,
  that shame has covered my face.
8 I have become a stranger to my kindred,
  an alien to my mother's children.

9 It is zeal for your house that has
    consumed me;
  the insults of those who insult you
    have fallen on me.
10 When I humbled my soul with fasting,[a]
  they insulted me for doing so.
11 When I made sackcloth my clothing,
  I became a byword to them.
12 I am the subject of gossip for those who
    sit in the gate,
  and the drunkards make songs about
    me.

13 But as for me, my prayer is to you,
    O LORD.
  At an acceptable time, O God,
  in the abundance of your steadfast
    love, answer me.
  With your faithful help [14]rescue me
    from sinking in the mire;
  let me be delivered from my enemies
    and from the deep waters.
15 Do not let the flood sweep over me,
    or the deep swallow me up,
    or the Pit close its mouth over me.

16 Answer me, O LORD, for your steadfast
    love is good;
  according to your abundant mercy,
    turn to me.
17 Do not hide your face from your servant,
  for I am in distress—make haste to
    answer me.
18 Draw near to me, redeem me,
  set me free because of my enemies.

19 You know the insults I receive,
  and my shame and dishonor;
  my foes are all known to you.
20 Insults have broken my heart,
  so that I am in despair.
  I looked for pity, but there was none;
  and for comforters, but I found none.
21 They gave me poison for food,
  and for my thirst they gave me vinegar
    to drink.

22 Let their table be a trap for them,
  a snare for their allies.
23 Let their eyes be darkened so that they
    cannot see,
  and make their loins tremble
    continually.
24 Pour out your indignation upon them,
  and let your burning anger overtake
    them.
25 May their camp be a desolation;
  let no one live in their tents.
26 For they persecute those whom you have
    struck down,
  and those whom you have wounded,
    they attack still more.[b]
27 Add guilt to their guilt;
  may they have no acquittal from you.
28 Let them be blotted out of the book of
    the living;

---

a Gk Syr: Heb *I wept, with fasting my soul*, or *I made my soul mourn with fasting* *b* Gk Syr: Heb *recount the pain of*

32.6; 42.7; 88.7, 17; 124.4–5; 144.7; Jon 2.3–5. **69.5** Confession of sin. **69.6–12** Additional plea for help on the basis of the fact that the sufferer has been taunted and abandoned because of enthusiasm for the service of God and the temple. **69.6** God's failure to help the petitioner will be a negative reflection on other faithful servants as well as himself. **69.9** *Zeal for your house* suggests the possibility that the psalmist was an enthusiastic supporter of the efforts to rebuild the temple (cf. vv. 35–36; also Ezra 4.1–5, 23–24; Haggai; Zech 1.16; 8.2–3). Cf. Jn 2.17. *Those who insult you.* It is God who is the ultimate object of the insults by the enemies (cf. v. 7). Cf. Rom 15.3. **69.11** *Sackcloth.* See note on 30.11. **69.12** *Gate*, the place of public assembly. **69.13–18** Additional cries for help rooted in the knowledge of the love and mercy of God. **69.15** *Pit.* See note on 16.10. **69.17** *Hide your face.* See notes on 10.1; 27.9. **69.19–28** Continued recounting of the taunting insults of the oppressors and prayers for their downfall. **69.21** *Vinegar to drink.* See Mt 27.34, 48. **69.22** Quoted at Rom 11.9. **69.25** Quoted at Acts 1.20. **69.28** *Book of the living*, a heavenly record of human

let them not be enrolled among the
righteous.
29 But I am lowly and in pain;
let your salvation, O God, protect me.

30 I will praise the name of God with a song;
I will magnify him with thanksgiving.
31 This will please the LORD more than
an ox
or a bull with horns and hoofs.
32 Let the oppressed see it and be glad;
you who seek God, let your hearts
revive.
33 For the LORD hears the needy,
and does not despise his own that are
in bonds.

34 Let heaven and earth praise him,
the seas and everything that moves in
them.
35 For God will save Zion
and rebuild the cities of Judah;
and his servants shall live*a* there and
possess it;
36 the children of his servants shall
inherit it,
and those who love his name shall live
in it.

Prayer for Deliverance from Enemies

To the leader. Of David, for the memorial
offering.

70 Be pleased, O God, to deliver me.
O LORD, make haste to help me!
2 Let those be put to shame and confusion
who seek my life.
Let those be turned back and brought to
dishonor
who desire to hurt me.
3 Let those who say, "Aha, Aha!"
turn back because of their shame.

4 Let all who seek you
rejoice and be glad in you.
Let those who love your salvation
say evermore, "God is great!"
5 But I am poor and needy;
hasten to me, O God!
You are my help and my deliverer;
O LORD, do not delay!

Prayer for Lifelong Protection and Help

71 In you, O LORD, I take refuge;
let me never be put to shame.
2 In your righteousness deliver me and
rescue me;
incline your ear to me and save me.
3 Be to me a rock of refuge,
a strong fortress,*b* to save me,
for you are my rock and my fortress.

4 Rescue me, O my God, from the hand of
the wicked,
from the grasp of the unjust and cruel.
5 For you, O Lord, are my hope,
my trust, O LORD, from my youth.
6 Upon you I have leaned from my birth;
it was you who took me from my
mother's womb.
My praise is continually of you.

7 I have been like a portent to many,
but you are my strong refuge.
8 My mouth is filled with your praise,
and with your glory all day long.
9 Do not cast me off in the time of old
age;
do not forsake me when my strength is
spent.
10 For my enemies speak concerning me,

---

a Syr: Heb *and they shall live* *b* Gk Compare 31.3: Heb *to come
continually you have commanded*

---

deeds of good or ill, or a record of the righteous (cf.
40.7). **69.29** Final prayer for God's help. **69.30–36** A
vow of praise and thanksgiving because God has heard
the prayer. **69.31** Cf. 40.6; 50.9–14; 51.15–17. **69.35–
36** The individual prayer is placed in the context of a
confident expectation of God's help for a destroyed
Jerusalem and exiled people.

70.1–5 An individual prayer for help in the face of
oppression. This psalm also appears as vv. 13–17 of Ps
40. *To the leader.* See note on 4.1–8. **70.1** Cry for help.
70.2–3 Plea for God to put to shame the persecutors of
the psalmist. **70.4** Anticipated praise by those who

have been saved. **70.5** A final cry for help uttered in
trust and urgency. *Poor and needy* may refer to spiritual need and humility or material poverty.

71.1–24 A prayer for help by an aged person in distress. **71.1–8** Pleas for help interspersed with expressions of trust as a basis for hope in God's action.
71.1 *Refuge.* See note on 2.10–12. **71.6** Cf. 22.9–10.
71.7 *Portent,* a negative sign of God's wrath. This may
refer to some ill health or distress seen by others as an
affliction bestowed by God and so an opportunity (see
v. 11) for the persecution mentioned in vv. 4, 10–13,
24. **71.9–13** Further cries for help in the face of those

and those who watch for my life
  consult together.
11 They say, "Pursue and seize that person
  whom God has forsaken,
  for there is no one to deliver."

12 O God, do not be far from me;
  O my God, make haste to help me!
13 Let my accusers be put to shame and
  consumed;
  let those who seek to hurt me
  be covered with scorn and disgrace.
14 But I will hope continually,
  and will praise you yet more and more.
15 My mouth will tell of your righteous
  acts,
  of your deeds of salvation all day
  long,
  though their number is past my
  knowledge.
16 I will come praising the mighty deeds of
  the Lord GOD,
  I will praise your righteousness, yours
  alone.

17 O God, from my youth you have taught
  me,
  and I still proclaim your wondrous
  deeds.
18 So even to old age and gray hairs,
  O God, do not forsake me,
  until I proclaim your might
  to all the generations to come.[a]
  Your power 19and your righteousness,
  O God,
  reach the high heavens.

  You who have done great things,
  O God, who is like you?
20 You who have made me see many
  troubles and calamities
  will revive me again;
  from the depths of the earth
  you will bring me up again.

21 You will increase my honor,
  and comfort me once again.

22 I will also praise you with the harp
  for your faithfulness, O my God;
  I will sing praises to you with the lyre,
  O Holy One of Israel.
23 My lips will shout for joy
  when I sing praises to you;
  my soul also, which you have rescued.
24 All day long my tongue will talk of your
  righteous help,
  for those who tried to do me harm
  have been put to shame, and disgraced.

Prayer for Guidance and Support for the King

Of Solomon.

72 Give the king your justice, O God,
  and your righteousness to a king's son.
2 May he judge your people with
  righteousness,
  and your poor with justice.
3 May the mountains yield prosperity for
  the people,
  and the hills, in righteousness.
4 May he defend the cause of the poor of
  the people,
  give deliverance to the needy,
  and crush the oppressor.

5 May he live[b] while the sun endures,
  and as long as the moon, throughout
  all generations.
6 May he be like rain that falls on the
  mown grass,
  like showers that water the earth.
7 In his days may righteousness flourish
  and peace abound, until the moon is
  no more.

a Gk Compare Syr: Heb *to a generation, to all that come*
b Gk: Heb *may they fear you*

who have taken advantage of the psalmist's distress to bring accusations of some offense. **71.14–24** Vows of praise and thanksgiving in the confidence that God, who has been a refuge in earlier years, will also protect the aged sufferer.
  72.1–19 A royal psalm possibly on the occasion of the coronation of a king. Cf. the concluding doxology (vv. 17–18) with David's doxology upon hearing of the coronation of Solomon (1 Kings 1.48). The ascription to *Solomon* is suggested by several features of the psalm, including his being *a king's son* and a wise judge (vv. 1–2), the broad extent of his rule (v. 8), and rulers coming to him from afar bearing tribute and gifts (vv. 8–11, 15; cf. 1 Kings 10). **72.1–7** A prayer for the king to live long, ruling justly. *Justice,* or "judgments" in the Hebrew, possibly the specific righteous judgments of the king (cf. 2 Sam 15.1–6; 1 Kings 3.16–28). **72.4** The particular concern of the just king is the *poor* and the *needy,* who could appeal to the king when there was no other way of gaining justice.

8 May he have dominion from sea to sea,
   and from the River to the ends of the
      earth.
9 May his foes[a] bow down before him,
   and his enemies lick the dust.
10 May the kings of Tarshish and of the
      isles
   render him tribute,
may the kings of Sheba and Seba
   bring gifts.
11 May all kings fall down before him,
   all nations give him service.

12 For he delivers the needy when they call,
   the poor and those who have no
      helper.
13 He has pity on the weak and the needy,
   and saves the lives of the needy.
14 From oppression and violence he
      redeems their life;
   and precious is their blood in his sight.

15 Long may he live!
   May gold of Sheba be given to him.
May prayer be made for him continually,
   and blessings invoked for him all day
      long.
16 May there be abundance of grain in the
      land;
   may it wave on the tops of the
      mountains;
   may its fruit be like Lebanon;
and may people blossom in the cities
   like the grass of the field.
17 May his name endure forever,
   his fame continue as long as the sun.
May all nations be blessed in him;[b]
   may they pronounce him happy.

18 Blessed be the LORD, the God of Israel,
   who alone does wondrous things.
19 Blessed be his glorious name forever;
   may his glory fill the whole earth.
      Amen and Amen.

20 The prayers of David son of Jesse are
      ended.

BOOK III: PSALMS 73–89

Plea for Relief from Oppressors

A Psalm of Asaph.

73 Truly God is good to the upright,[c]
   to those who are pure in heart.
2 But as for me, my feet had almost
      stumbled;
   my steps had nearly slipped.
3 For I was envious of the arrogant;
   I saw the prosperity of the wicked.

4 For they have no pain;
   their bodies are sound and sleek.
5 They are not in trouble as others are;
   they are not plagued like other people.
6 Therefore pride is their necklace;
   violence covers them like a garment.
7 Their eyes swell out with fatness;
   their hearts overflow with follies.
8 They scoff and speak with malice;
   loftily they threaten oppression.
9 They set their mouths against heaven,
   and their tongues range over the earth.

---

a Cn: Heb *those who live in the wilderness*   b Or *bless themselves by him*   c Or *good to Israel*

72.8–14 The rule of this righteous king is universal (vv. 8–11) because (v. 12) he is totally committed to delivering the weak and the poor from violence and oppression (vv. 12–14). **72.15–17** A reiteration of the prayer for the long life of the king and blessings upon him and through him. **72.15** *Gold of Sheba*. Sheba, located most likely in the southwest of the Arabian peninsula, was known in the OT for its gold and legendary wealth (see 1 Kings 10.2; Isa 60.6; Ezek 27.22). **72.17** *All nations ... blessed in him* is an allusion to the blessing to the nations through Abraham (Gen 12.3; 18.18; 22.18; 28.14). Through the righteous king that blessing will be effected in a kingdom of righteousness and peace. **72.18–19** A doxology marking the end of the second book of the Psalter (Pss 42–72). See note on 41.13. *Blessed*. See note on 103.1–2. **72.20** An editorial note added to the end of the second book of the

Psalter identifying the first two books as containing the prayers of David. In fact, later psalms in the Psalter are also ascribed to him.

73.1–28 A psalm of trust in God and praise for divine deliverance. Its reflective character in vv. 4–20 connects it with the wisdom and didactic tradition. *Asaph*. See note on 50.1–23. **73.1–3** In a basic affirmation of trust the psalmist agrees with others that God is good to the upright (Pss 1; 37; 49) but tells of almost being led astray from God and the righteous way out of envy of the prosperity of the wicked while the pure in heart are frequently in trouble (vv. 5, 13–14; cf. Job). **73.4–12** The character and prosperity of the wicked are laid out. **73.4–5** They have an easy life despite their unrighteous ways. **73.6–8** Their affluence is gained by violence and oppression against others. **73.9–11** In their arrogance, the wicked do not believe God will see

10 Therefore the people turn and praise
        them,[a]
     and find no fault in them.[b]
11 And they say, "How can God know?
     Is there knowledge in the Most High?"
12 Such are the wicked;
     always at ease, they increase in riches.
13 All in vain I have kept my heart clean
     and washed my hands in innocence.
14 For all day long I have been plagued,
     and am punished every morning.

15 If I had said, "I will talk on in this way,"
     I would have been untrue to the circle
        of your children.
16 But when I thought how to understand
        this,
     it seemed to me a wearisome task,
17 until I went into the sanctuary of God;
     then I perceived their end.
18 Truly you set them in slippery places;
     you make them fall to ruin.
19 How they are destroyed in a moment,
     swept away utterly by terrors!
20 They are[c] like a dream when one awakes;
     on awaking you despise their
        phantoms.

21 When my soul was embittered,
     when I was pricked in heart,
22 I was stupid and ignorant;
     I was like a brute beast toward you.
23 Nevertheless I am continually with you;
     you hold my right hand.
24 You guide me with your counsel,
     and afterward you will receive me with
        honor.[d]
25 Whom have I in heaven but you?
     And there is nothing on earth that I
        desire other than you.
26 My flesh and my heart may fail,
     but God is the strength[e] of my heart
        and my portion forever.

27 Indeed, those who are far from you will
        perish;
     you put an end to those who are false
        to you.
28 But for me it is good to be near God;
     I have made the Lord GOD my refuge,
        to tell of all your works.

Plea for Help in Time of National Humiliation

A Maskil of Asaph.

74 O God, why do you cast us off
        forever?
     Why does your anger smoke against
        the sheep of your pasture?
2 Remember your congregation, which you
        acquired long ago,
     which you redeemed to be the tribe of
        your heritage.
     Remember Mount Zion, where you
        came to dwell.
3 Direct your steps to the perpetual ruins;
     the enemy has destroyed everything in
        the sanctuary.

4 Your foes have roared within your holy
        place;
     they set up their emblems there.
5 At the upper entrance they hacked
     the wooden trellis with axes.[f]
6 And then, with hatchets and hammers,
     they smashed all its carved work.
7 They set your sanctuary on fire;
     they desecrated the dwelling place of
        your name,
     bringing it to the ground.
8 They said to themselves, "We will utterly
        subdue them";

---

a Cn: Heb *his people return here*   b Cn: Heb *abundant waters
are drained by them*   c Cn: Heb *Lord*   d Or *to glory*
e Heb *rock*   f Cn Compare Gk Syr: Meaning of Heb uncertain

---

or punish their wickedness. **73.12** A concluding summary of the seemingly enviable state of the wicked.
73.13–14 The contrasting state of the psalmist, who is
innocent but suffers. **73.15–16** The temptation to
think and act like the wicked is felt and resisted, but
trying to comprehend is troublesome. **73.17–20** In the
turning point of the psalm (v. 17), an encounter with
God (cf. Job 42.1–6) in the sanctuary gives the
psalmist an understanding that in the end God will
deal justly with the wicked (vv. 18–20; cf. Ps 37).
73.21–28 The psalmist now sees the stupidity of fo-

cusing on the prosperity of the wicked (vv. 21–22) and
expresses confidence in God's presence (vv. 23, 27–
28), guidance (v. 24), and protection (vv. 26, 28).
74.1–23 A community prayer for help that seems to
assume the destruction of Jerusalem and so may date
between 587 and 520 BCE. *Maskil.* See note on 32.1–
11. *Asaph.* See note on 50.1–23. **74.1–2** Address and
introductory cry for help. **74.1** *Why . . . forever?* anticipates the later complaint *How long?* (v. 10). **74.3–8** A
description of the destruction of Jerusalem. **74.4** *Emblems,* lit. "signs" (cf. v. 10), perhaps military stan-

they burned all the meeting places of
God in the land.

9 We do not see our emblems;
there is no longer any prophet,
and there is no one among us who
knows how long.

10 How long, O God, is the foe to scoff?
Is the enemy to revile your name
forever?

11 Why do you hold back your hand;
why do you keep your hand in*a* your
bosom?

12 Yet God my King is from of old,
working salvation in the earth.

13 You divided the sea by your might;
you broke the heads of the dragons in
the waters.

14 You crushed the heads of Leviathan;
you gave him as food*b* for the creatures
of the wilderness.

15 You cut openings for springs and
torrents;
you dried up ever-flowing streams.

16 Yours is the day, yours also the night;
you established the luminaries*c* and the
sun.

17 You have fixed all the bounds of the
earth;
you made summer and winter.

18 Remember this, O Lord, how the enemy
scoffs,
and an impious people reviles your
name.

19 Do not deliver the soul of your dove to
the wild animals;

do not forget the life of your poor
forever.

20 Have regard for your*d* covenant,
for the dark places of the land are full
of the haunts of violence.

21 Do not let the downtrodden be put to
shame;
let the poor and needy praise your
name.

22 Rise up, O God, plead your cause;
remember how the impious scoff at
you all day long.

23 Do not forget the clamor of your foes,
the uproar of your adversaries that
goes up continually.

Thanksgiving for God's Wondrous Deeds

To the leader: Do Not Destroy. A Psalm of
Asaph. A Song.

75 We give thanks to you, O God;
we give thanks; your name is near.
People tell of your wondrous deeds.

2 At the set time that I appoint
I will judge with equity.

3 When the earth totters, with all its
inhabitants,
it is I who keep its pillars steady.   *Selah*

4 I say to the boastful, "Do not boast,"
and to the wicked, "Do not lift up your
horn;

5 do not lift up your horn on high,
or speak with insolent neck."

---

a Cn: Heb *do you consume your right hand from*   *b* Heb *food for
the people*   *c* Or *moon;* Heb *light*   *d* Gk Syr: Heb *the*

---

dards. **74.8** *Meeting places of God,* perhaps other places
of worship besides the temple. **74.9–11** A complaint to
God over the absence of divine intervention. **74.9** *Emblems,* probably "signs" here. It may mean that the
prophetic signs that promised a quick end to suffering
have not come true. *There is no . . . prophet* may mean
that the speakers have lost all confidence in those
prophets still around. There is no prophet who *knows
how long* the suffering is to last. For prophetic signs
that tell how long something will last, see 2 Kings
19.29; Isa 7.14–16. Such failure of contemporary
prophecy may be demonstrated in Jer 28.1–4.
74.10 *How long?* See note on 6.3. **74.12–17** Expression
of trust and praise of the creator. **74.13–15** The picture is of the mythological creation battle in which the
watery forces of chaos, portrayed as monsters, are de-

feated by the Lord at the beginning of creation. See
93.3; 104.7–9; Job 38.8–11; cf. Isa 27.1. Israel associated this language with God's "creation" of the people
in the crossing of the sea (cf. Ex 15.1–18; Isa 51.9–11).
Both images may be in view here. **74.18–23** A series of
petitions urging God to help and giving various motivations that suggest that God's cause, name, and covenant are at stake in Israel's distress.

75.1–10 A community prayer of thanksgiving. The
psalm gives thanks to God and announces divine judgment on the arrogant wicked. *To the leader.* See note on
4.1–8. *Do Not Destroy.* Meaning uncertain. *Asaph.* See
note on 50.1–23. **75.1** The community praises God for
marvelous acts of deliverance. **75.2–5** The Lord speaks
through a prophetic or priestly voice to announce righteous judgment. **75.3** *Totters.* See 46.2–3, 6. *Selah.* See

6 For not from the east or from the west
  and not from the wilderness comes
    lifting up;
7 but it is God who executes judgment,
  putting down one and lifting up
    another.
8 For in the hand of the LORD there is a cup
  with foaming wine, well mixed;
  he will pour a draught from it,
  and all the wicked of the earth
  shall drain it down to the dregs.
9 But I will rejoice[a] forever;
  I will sing praises to the God of Jacob.

10 All the horns of the wicked I will cut off,
   but the horns of the righteous shall be
     exalted.

Israel's God–Judge of All the Earth

To the leader: with stringed instruments. A
Psalm of Asaph. A Song.

76 In Judah God is known,
     his name is great in Israel.
2 His abode has been established in Salem,
  his dwelling place in Zion.
3 There he broke the flashing arrows,
  the shield, the sword, and the weapons
    of war.   *Selah*

4 Glorious are you, more majestic
  than the everlasting mountains.[b]
5 The stouthearted were stripped of their
    spoil;
  they sank into sleep;
  none of the troops

was able to lift a hand.
6 At your rebuke, O God of Jacob,
  both rider and horse lay stunned.

7 But you indeed are awesome!
  Who can stand before you
  when once your anger is roused?
8 From the heavens you uttered judgment;
  the earth feared and was still
9 when God rose up to establish judgment,
  to save all the oppressed of the earth.
                                       Selah

10 Human wrath serves only to praise you,
   when you bind the last bit of your[c]
     wrath around you.
11 Make vows to the LORD your God, and
     perform them;
   let all who are around him bring gifts
   to the one who is awesome,
12 who cuts off the spirit of princes,
   who inspires fear in the kings of the
     earth.

God's Mighty Deeds Recalled

To the leader: according to Jeduthun.
Of Asaph. A Psalm.

77 I cry aloud to God,
     aloud to God, that he may hear me.
2 In the day of my trouble I seek the Lord;
  in the night my hand is stretched out
    without wearying;

---

a Gk: Heb *declare*   *b* Gk: Heb *the mountains of prey*
c Heb lacks *your*

---

note on 3.2. **75.4–5** *Horn,* a symbol of might or power
(cf. v. 10). **75.6–8** God's judgment of the wicked.
75.7 *Putting . . . another* is a frequent way of expressing
God's vindication of the innocent and righteous and
judgment of the wicked (see 113.7; 145.8; 146.6).
75.8 *Cup,* a symbol of divine judgment (see 11.6; Isa
51.17; Jer 25.15, 28; Hab 2.16). **75.9–10** The themes of
praise and divine judgment are brought together in the
conclusion. *I,* either the community or its representative in v. 9, but the Lord in v. 10.

76.1–12 A song of Zion. See Pss 46; 48; 137.3. *To the
leader . . . instruments.* See note on 4.1–8. *Asaph.* See
note on 50.1–23. **76.1–2** God's abode and place of
powerful activity is Zion or Jerusalem. **76.2** *Abode,* lit.
"lair" or "covert" (of a fierce animal). *Salem,* an ancient
name for Jerusalem (see Gen 14.18). **76.3–6** The Lord's
battle against the armies. **76.3** God's destruction of all
the weapons of war is associated with the divine activity
from Zion (see 46.9). *Flashing arrows,* lit. "flames of the

bow," perhaps the fiery arrows of besiegers. *Selah.* See
note on 3.2. **76.4–6** The destruction of the weapons is
matched by rendering the warriors powerless, a theme
of Israel's ancient holy wars. **76.6** *Rider and horse.* See
Ex 15.1. **76.7–9** The victory is an act of divine judgment against the oppressive rulers and of salvation for
the weak and afflicted. **76.10** The underlying Hebrew of
this verse is uncertain and ambiguous. *Human wrath*
could also be read as God's "wrath against humans."
The meaning may be that God's crushing those that rise
against him will redound to God's praise. God's wrath
in the OT is a dimension of God's righteousness and justice directed against evildoers. It is tempered by God's
love and compassion (see 103.8; Ex 34.6; Num 14.18;
Isa 54.7–8; Hos 11.8–9; Jon 4.2). **76.11–12** An exhortation to the community to praise the God (v. 11), who
does what the psalm has declared so vividly (v. 12).

77.1–20 A prayer for help that develops into a
hymn as the psalmist recalls God's wondrous acts. *To*

my soul refuses to be comforted.
3 I think of God, and I moan;
   I meditate, and my spirit faints.   *Selah*

4 You keep my eyelids from closing;
   I am so troubled that I cannot speak.
5 I consider the days of old,
   and remember the years of long ago.
6 I commune[a] with my heart in the night;
   I meditate and search my spirit:[b]
7 "Will the Lord spurn forever,
   and never again be favorable?
8 Has his steadfast love ceased forever?
   Are his promises at an end for all time?
9 Has God forgotten to be gracious?
   Has he in anger shut up his
      compassion?"   *Selah*
10 And I say, "It is my grief
   that the right hand of the Most High
     has changed."

11 I will call to mind the deeds of the
   Lord;
   I will remember your wonders of old.
12 I will meditate on all your work,
   and muse on your mighty deeds.
13 Your way, O God, is holy.
   What god is so great as our God?
14 You are the God who works wonders;
   you have displayed your might among
     the peoples.
15 With your strong arm you redeemed your
     people,
   the descendants of Jacob and Joseph.
                   Selah

16 When the waters saw you, O God,
   when the waters saw you, they were
     afraid;
   the very deep trembled.
17 The clouds poured out water;
   the skies thundered;
   your arrows flashed on every side.
18 The crash of your thunder was in the
     whirlwind;
   your lightnings lit up the world;
   the earth trembled and shook.
19 Your way was through the sea,
   your path, through the mighty waters;
   yet your footprints were unseen.
20 You led your people like a flock
   by the hand of Moses and Aaron.

God's Goodness and Israel's Ingratitude

A Maskil of Asaph.

78 Give ear, O my people, to my
     teaching;
   incline your ears to the words of my
     mouth.
2 I will open my mouth in a parable;
   I will utter dark sayings from of old,
3 things that we have heard and known,
   that our ancestors have told us.
4 We will not hide them from their children;
   we will tell to the coming generation
   the glorious deeds of the Lord, and his
     might,
   and the wonders that he has done.

---

a Gk Syr: Heb *My music*   b Syr Jerome: Heb *my spirit searches*

---

the leader. See note on 4.1–8. *According to Jeduthun*, i.e., in the style of one of David's musicians (1 Chr 9.16; 16.38). *Asaph*. See note on 50.1–23. **77.1–10** The prayer for help. **77.1–3** A cry to God. **77.2, 6** *In the night* is often the time of prayer. *My hand is stretched out*, in prayer. **77.3** *Selah*. See note on 3.2. **77.4–10** A complaint against God that centers in questions about God's love and faithfulness. **77.11–20** The song of praise. **77.11–15** As a way of gaining confidence that God has not forgotten to be gracious (v. 9) but will give help in the present distress, the one praying recalls the wonderful redemptive acts of God for the people in the past. **77.16–20** A recollection of the powerful appearance of God at the crossing of the Red Sea by the Israelites in their escape from Egypt. **77.16** *The waters* and *the very deep* may be the primeval waters of chaos at the creation as well as the waters of the Red Sea. **77.17** *Your arrows*, i.e., lightning bolts. **77.19** *Your way . . . through the sea*, in leading the Israelites across the Red Sea. *Your footprints were unseen* refers to the

appearance and work of God that is without visible proof, in the present as well as in the past. **77.20** *Moses and Aaron*, the leaders of Israel during the exodus and the journey through the wilderness. See the book of Exodus.

78.1–72 A historical psalm (cf. Pss 105; 106; 136) recounting the story of God's care of Israel and the people's response of continuing sin and faithlessness. The account goes only down to the time of David (vv. 70–71). It may be compared with Deut 32. The recital is meant to be instructive. *Maskil*. See note on 32.1–11. *Asaph*. See note on 50.1–23. **78.1–8** Passing on God's instruction (vv. 1–5) so that each generation may learn to trust in God and not forget the divine teaching (vv. 6–8). **78.1** The speaker of this verse is probably some priest or teacher of wisdom. **78.2** *Parable*, a poem or song that is didactic in character. *Dark sayings*, lit. "riddles." The story is seen as having mysterious or enigmatic dimensions, possibly the puzzle of why Israel rebelled against God, who cared for them.

5 He established a decree in Jacob,
  and appointed a law in Israel,
which he commanded our ancestors
  to teach to their children;
6 that the next generation might know
    them,
  the children yet unborn,
and rise up and tell them to their
    children,
7 so that they should set their hope in
    God,
and not forget the works of God,
  but keep his commandments;
8 and that they should not be like their
    ancestors,
  a stubborn and rebellious generation,
a generation whose heart was not
    steadfast,
  whose spirit was not faithful to God.

9 The Ephraimites, armed with*a* the bow,
  turned back on the day of battle.
10 They did not keep God's covenant,
  but refused to walk according to his
    law.
11 They forgot what he had done,
  and the miracles that he had shown
    them.
12 In the sight of their ancestors he worked
    marvels
  in the land of Egypt, in the fields of
    Zoan.
13 He divided the sea and let them pass
    through it,
  and made the waters stand like a
    heap.
14 In the daytime he led them with a cloud,
  and all night long with a fiery light.
15 He split rocks open in the wilderness,
  and gave them drink abundantly as
    from the deep.
16 He made streams come out of the rock,
  and caused waters to flow down like
    rivers.

17 Yet they sinned still more against him,
  rebelling against the Most High in the
    desert.
18 They tested God in their heart
  by demanding the food they craved.
19 They spoke against God, saying,
  "Can God spread a table in the
    wilderness?
20 Even though he struck the rock so that
    water gushed out
  and torrents overflowed,
can he also give bread,
  or provide meat for his people?"

21 Therefore, when the LORD heard, he was
    full of rage;
  a fire was kindled against Jacob,
  his anger mounted against Israel,
22 because they had no faith in God,
  and did not trust his saving power.
23 Yet he commanded the skies above,
  and opened the doors of heaven;
24 he rained down on them manna to eat,
  and gave them the grain of heaven.
25 Mortals ate of the bread of angels;
  he sent them food in abundance.
26 He caused the east wind to blow in the
    heavens,
  and by his power he led out the south
    wind;
27 he rained flesh upon them like dust,
  winged birds like the sand of the seas;
28 he let them fall within their camp,
  all around their dwellings.
29 And they ate and were well filled,
  for he gave them what they craved.
30 But before they had satisfied their
    craving,
  while the food was still in their mouths,
31 the anger of God rose against them
  and he killed the strongest of them,
  and laid low the flower of Israel.

---

a Heb *armed with shooting*

78.5 *Decree*, i.e., covenant. See the term *covenant* in parallel with *law* in v. 10 as *decree* is in parallel with it here. **78.8** Cf. the Deuteronomic law for punishing a "stubborn and rebellious" son in Deut 21.18–21. **78.9–16** The people forgot all that the Lord had done for them in the deliverance from Egypt and in guiding them through the wilderness. **78.9** It is unclear what incident is referred to here. **78.12** *Marvels in the land of Egypt*, the plagues. *Zoan*, a city in the Nile Delta, probably the "supply city" called Rameses in Ex 1.11.

78.13 The crossing of the Red Sea. *Heap.* Cf. Ex 15.8. **78.14–16** God's leading and care of the Israelites in the wilderness. Cf. Ex 17.1–6; Num 20.2–13. **78.17–31** The people continued to rebel in the wilderness despite God's provision (Ex 16–17). So God came in wrath against them. **78.18** *Tested God.* See Ex 17.7. **78.19** *Spread a table.* Cf. 23.5. **78.24** Quoted in Jn 6.31. *Manna*, God's provision of food in the wilderness, possibly a natural substance from the tamarisk tree released by the actions of certain insects and hardening

32 In spite of all this they still sinned;
   they did not believe in his wonders.
33 So he made their days vanish like a
      breath,
   and their years in terror.
34 When he killed them, they sought for
      him;
   they repented and sought God
      earnestly.
35 They remembered that God was their
      rock,
   the Most High God their redeemer.
36 But they flattered him with their mouths;
   they lied to him with their tongues.
37 Their heart was not steadfast toward him;
   they were not true to his covenant.
38 Yet he, being compassionate,
      forgave their iniquity,
   and did not destroy them;
   often he restrained his anger,
   and did not stir up all his wrath.
39 He remembered that they were but flesh,
   a wind that passes and does not come
      again.
40 How often they rebelled against him in
      the wilderness
   and grieved him in the desert!
41 They tested God again and again,
   and provoked the Holy One of Israel.
42 They did not keep in mind his power,
   or the day when he redeemed them
      from the foe;
43 when he displayed his signs in Egypt,
   and his miracles in the fields of Zoan.
44 He turned their rivers to blood,
   so that they could not drink of their
      streams.
45 He sent among them swarms of flies,
      which devoured them,
   and frogs, which destroyed them.
46 He gave their crops to the caterpillar,
   and the fruit of their labor to the
      locust.

47 He destroyed their vines with hail,
   and their sycamores with frost.
48 He gave over their cattle to the hail,
   and their flocks to thunderbolts.
49 He let loose on them his fierce anger,
   wrath, indignation, and distress,
   a company of destroying angels.
50 He made a path for his anger;
   he did not spare them from death,
   but gave their lives over to the plague.
51 He struck all the firstborn in Egypt,
   the first issue of their strength in the
      tents of Ham.
52 Then he led out his people like sheep,
   and guided them in the wilderness like
      a flock.
53 He led them in safety, so that they were
      not afraid;
   but the sea overwhelmed their
      enemies.
54 And he brought them to his holy hill,
   to the mountain that his right hand
      had won.
55 He drove out nations before them;
   he apportioned them for a possession
   and settled the tribes of Israel in their
      tents.
56 Yet they tested the Most High God,
   and rebelled against him.
   They did not observe his decrees,
57 but turned away and were faithless like
      their ancestors;
   they twisted like a treacherous bow.
58 For they provoked him to anger with
      their high places;
   they moved him to jealousy with their
      idols.
59 When God heard, he was full of wrath,
   and he utterly rejected Israel.
60 He abandoned his dwelling at Shiloh,
   the tent where he dwelt among
      mortals,

at night (see Num 11.7–9). **78.26–31** See Num 11.31–35. **78.32–55** The continued sin of the people is met by divine anger, but anger tempered with compassion, so that the Lord does not destroy them despite the degree to which they test God. **78.33–34** Probably the death of the wilderness generation (Num 14.22–24; Deut 1.34–36; 2.14–15). **78.42–51** A recounting of the plagues as a powerful manifestation of God's redemptive care of Israel, which the people continually forgot (Ex 7–12). **78.43** *Zoan.* See note on 78.12. **78.51** *Ham,* a son of Noah and traditionally viewed as the ancestor of the Egyptians according to Gen 10.6. **78.52–55** The journey from Egypt into Canaan as a divine leading. **78.54** *Holy hill, mountain,* probably the land of Canaan. **78.56–66** The people's sin and God's consequent anger in the time of settlement in Canaan, the period of the judges. **78.56** *Decrees,* the commandments and statutes that made up the requirements of the covenant. See note on 78.5. **78.58** *High places,* sites of idolatrous worship. **78.60** *Dwelling at Shiloh,* the tent shrine at the central sanctuary of Israel during the period of the judges (Josh 18.1; 1 Sam 1.9). Its destruc-

61 and delivered his power to captivity,
   his glory to the hand of the foe.
62 He gave his people to the sword,
   and vented his wrath on his heritage.
63 Fire devoured their young men,
   and their girls had no marriage song.
64 Their priests fell by the sword,
   and their widows made no
      lamentation.
65 Then the Lord awoke as from sleep,
   like a warrior shouting because of
      wine.
66 He put his adversaries to rout;
   he put them to everlasting disgrace.

67 He rejected the tent of Joseph,
   he did not choose the tribe of
      Ephraim;
68 but he chose the tribe of Judah,
   Mount Zion, which he loves.
69 He built his sanctuary like the high
      heavens,
   like the earth, which he has founded
      forever.
70 He chose his servant David,
   and took him from the sheepfolds;
71 from tending the nursing ewes he
      brought him
   to be the shepherd of his people Jacob,
      of Israel, his inheritance.
72 With upright heart he tended them,
   and guided them with skillful hand.

Plea for Mercy for Jerusalem

A Psalm of Asaph.

79 O God, the nations have come into
      your inheritance;
   they have defiled your holy temple;
      they have laid Jerusalem in ruins.
2 They have given the bodies of your
      servants
   to the birds of the air for food,
   the flesh of your faithful to the wild
      animals of the earth.
3 They have poured out their blood like
      water
   all around Jerusalem,
   and there was no one to bury them.
4 We have become a taunt to our
      neighbors,
   mocked and derided by those around us.

5 How long, O Lord? Will you be angry
      forever?
   Will your jealous wrath burn like fire?
6 Pour out your anger on the nations
   that do not know you,
and on the kingdoms
   that do not call on your name.
7 For they have devoured Jacob
   and laid waste his habitation.

8 Do not remember against us the
      iniquities of our ancestors;
   let your compassion come speedily to
      meet us,
   for we are brought very low.
9 Help us, O God of our salvation,
   for the glory of your name;
deliver us, and forgive our sins,
   for your name's sake.
10 Why should the nations say,
      "Where is their God?"
Let the avenging of the outpoured blood
      of your servants
   be known among the nations before
      our eyes.

---

tion is mentioned by Jeremiah in Jer 7.12–15; 26.6.
78.61 *His power* and *his glory* are references to the ark
of the covenant, taken by the Philistines at the battle of
Ebenezer (1 Sam 4.1–7.1). The Philistine conquest
was an act of judgment upon Israel by the Lord.
78.65–66 The defeat of the Philistines through the
victories of Saul and David. The imagery is of God as a
mighty warrior roused for battle and stimulated by
wine. **78.67–72** God's choice of Zion as the place of
divine dwelling and of David as king. The psalm sees
the culmination of the story of Israel in the Lord's rejection of the northern tribes (Ephraim) in favor of
Judah as the locus of worship and human leadership.
79.1–13 A prayer by the community for help because Jerusalem and the temple have been destroyed,
probably the Babylonian destruction in 587 BCE. The
frequent use of *your* in reference to God indicates that
the community sees the destruction as in some sense
an attack on God and expects a divine response as a
defense of God's own reputation. *Asaph.* See note on
50.1–23. **79.1–5** A complaint to God because of the
destruction of Jerusalem and its people. **79.1** *Your inheritance.* See Deut 32.8–9. Judah's loss is God's loss as
well. **79.2–3** Mass executions are reported after the
Babylonian destruction of Jerusalem, though not in
Jerusalem itself (2 Kings 25.18–21). *No one to bury
them.* See Deut 21.23; 28.26; Jer 7.33; 8.2. **79.4** The
specific character of the *taunt* is seen in the question in
v. 10. **79.5** *How long?* See note on 6.3. **79.6–12** Petitions for deliverance of the people and destruction of
the enemies. **79.10** *"Where is their God?"* is the typical
taunt of the enemy (cf. 42.3, 10; 115.2; Joel 2.17; Mic

11 Let the groans of the prisoners come
before you;
according to your great power preserve
those doomed to die.
12 Return sevenfold into the bosom of our
neighbors
the taunts with which they taunted
you, O Lord!
13 Then we your people, the flock of your
pasture,
will give thanks to you forever;
from generation to generation we will
recount your praise.

Prayer for Israel's Restoration

To the leader: on Lilies, a Covenant. Of Asaph.
A Psalm.

80 Give ear, O Shepherd of Israel,
you who lead Joseph like a flock!
You who are enthroned upon the
cherubim, shine forth
2 before Ephraim and Benjamin and
Manasseh.
Stir up your might,
and come to save us!

3 Restore us, O God;
let your face shine, that we may be saved.

4 O Lord God of hosts,
how long will you be angry with your
people's prayers?
5 You have fed them with the bread of
tears,

and given them tears to drink in full
measure.
6 You make us the scorn[a] of our neighbors;
our enemies laugh among themselves.

7 Restore us, O God of hosts;
let your face shine, that we may be
saved.

8 You brought a vine out of Egypt;
you drove out the nations and planted
it.
9 You cleared the ground for it;
it took deep root and filled the land.
10 The mountains were covered with its
shade,
the mighty cedars with its branches;
11 it sent out its branches to the sea,
and its shoots to the River.
12 Why then have you broken down its walls,
so that all who pass along the way
pluck its fruit?
13 The boar from the forest ravages it,
and all that move in the field feed on it.

14 Turn again, O God of hosts;
look down from heaven, and see;
have regard for this vine,
15 the stock that your right hand
planted.[b]
16 They have burned it with fire, they have
cut it down;[c]

---

a Syr: Heb strife   b Heb adds from verse 17 and upon the one
whom you made strong for yourself   c Cn: Heb it is cut down

7.10). **79.12** Sevenfold designates completeness of retaliation (Gen 4.15, 24; Lev 26.21, 24, 28). Taunted you.
See note on 79.10. **79.13** An expression of confidence
or vow as the community anticipates its praise of and
thanksgiving to the Lord.
80.1–19 A community prayer for the restoration of
the people; one of the people's prayers (v. 4). To the
leader. See note on 4.1–8. On Lilies, a Covenant. See
notes on 45.1–17; 60.1–12. Asaph. See note on 50.1–
23. **80.1–3** Petitions for God as shepherd and warrior
to deliver the people. **80.1** Shepherd. See 23.1; 78.52;
Isa 40.11. The image is associated with kings and rulers
(e.g., Jer 23.1–6; Ezek 34). Enthroned upon the cherubim refers to the Lord's invisible abode upon the cherubim of the ark of the covenant (1 Sam 4.4). Shine
forth is a way of speaking of God's appearing in might
to do battle (cf. 50.2; 94.1). Before Ephraim and Benjamin and Manasseh may refer to all the tribes of the
Northern Kingdom or to those left after other tribal
groups had been exiled by the Assyrians. The tribes

were understood to have marched in this order behind
the ark in the journey through the wilderness (Num
2.32–34). **80.3** A refrain (see vv. 7, 19), as in Pss 42–43;
46. Let your face shine. See Num 6.25; note on 31.16.
80.4–7 The complaint of the people against God.
80.4 How long? See note on 6.3. People's prayers is
probably the term for the community laments or
prayers for help such as are found here and in Pss 44;
74; 79. **80.6** Scorn. See note on 79.10. **80.8–19** The vine
(Israel) that the Lord brought out of Egypt and
planted is now ravaged. For vine and vineyard imagery
in relation to Israel and Judah, see Isa 5.1–7; 27.2–6;
Jer 2.21; 12.10; Ezek 15.1–8; Hos 10.1. **80.8** The redemption of Israel in the exodus and their settlement
in the land. **80.9–11** Israel's gradual spread in and
control of the land. **80.10** Mighty cedars. See 104.16.
80.11 The extent of the Davidic empire. Sea, the
Mediterranean. River, the Euphrates River in Mesopotamia. **80.12–13** A reiteration of the complaint to
God. **80.14–19** A plea to God to restore the vine of Is-

may they perish at the rebuke of your
   countenance.
17 But let your hand be upon the one at
   your right hand,
    the one whom you made strong for
    yourself.
18 Then we will never turn back from you;
   give us life, and we will call on your
    name.

19 Restore us, O LORD God of hosts;
   let your face shine, that we may be
    saved.

God's Appeal to Stubborn Israel

To the leader: according to The Gittith.
Of Asaph.

81 Sing aloud to God our strength;
   shout for joy to the God of Jacob.
2 Raise a song, sound the tambourine,
   the sweet lyre with the harp.
3 Blow the trumpet at the new moon,
   at the full moon, on our festal day.
4 For it is a statute for Israel,
   an ordinance of the God of Jacob.
5 He made it a decree in Joseph,
   when he went out over*a* the land of
    Egypt.

I hear a voice I had not known:
6 "I relieved your*b* shoulder of the burden;
   your*b* hands were freed from the
    basket.
7 In distress you called, and I rescued you;
   I answered you in the secret place of
    thunder;

I tested you at the waters of Meribah.
                Selah
8 Hear, O my people, while I admonish
   you;
    O Israel, if you would but listen to
    me!
9 There shall be no strange god among you;
   you shall not bow down to a foreign
    god.
10 I am the LORD your God,
   who brought you up out of the land of
    Egypt.
   Open your mouth wide and I will fill
    it.

11 "But my people did not listen to my
   voice;
    Israel would not submit to me.
12 So I gave them over to their stubborn
   hearts,
    to follow their own counsels.
13 O that my people would listen to me,
   that Israel would walk in my ways!
14 Then I would quickly subdue their
   enemies,
    and turn my hand against their foes.
15 Those who hate the LORD would cringe
   before him,
    and their doom would last forever.
16 I would feed you*c* with the finest of the
   wheat,
    and with honey from the rock I would
    satisfy you."

---

a Or *against*   *b* Heb *his*   *c* Cn Compare verse 16b: Heb *he
would feed him*

---

rael to life. **80.17** *The one at your right hand,* i.e., the
king.
  81.1–16 A liturgy with priestly or prophetic ad-
monishment of the people, probably to be sung at the
fall Festival of Tabernacles (cf. Pss 50; 95 for similar
language and character). *To the leader.* See note on
4.1–8. *According to The Gittith.* See note on 8.1–9.
Asaph. See note on 50.1–23. **81.1–5a** A summons to
worship with festival shouting and celebration.
81.3 *Our festal day* suggests one of the three major festivals, in this case Tabernacles (or Booths). **81.4–
5a** The festival has been appointed by God as a regulation of the people's life (Lev 23.33–36, 39–43; Deut
16.13–15; cf. Num 29). **81.5a** For the Festival of Tabernacles (or Booths) as a statute from the time of the exodus out of Egypt, see Lev 23.41–43. *Joseph,* a term for
Israel in Egypt. **81.5b–16** A prophetic or priestly voice
speaks for God. **81.5b–10** The Lord's deliverance of

Israel in the exodus is a lesson for the people. The one
who redeemed the Israelites called them to an uncompromising loyalty as God's people. **81.5b** *A voice . . . not
known,* probably the mysterious voice of the Lord,
thus giving authority to the words of God that are
quoted in the following verses. **81.6** *Burden* and *basket*
refer to the labors in Egypt. **81.7** *In distress you called.*
Cf. Ex 2.23; 3.7–8. *Waters of Meribah.* Cf. Ex 17.1–7;
Num 20.1–13. *Selah.* See note on 3.2. **81.9–10** Allusion to the primary commandment (v. 9) and the prologue (v. 10) to the Ten Commandments (Ex 20.2–5;
Deut 5.6–9). *Open . . . fill it* may be dislocated from an
original location after v. 5b. **81.11–12** Divine judgment because of the people's failure to keep the commandment. **81.13–16** God's admonishing hope that
the people will repent and be delivered. **81.15** *Hate the
LORD,* another allusion to the primary commandment
to worship the Lord alone (Ex 20.5b; Deut 5.9b).

A Plea for Justice

A Psalm of Asaph.

82 God has taken his place in the divine council;
in the midst of the gods he holds judgment:

2 "How long will you judge unjustly
and show partiality to the wicked? *Selah*

3 Give justice to the weak and the orphan;
maintain the right of the lowly and the destitute.

4 Rescue the weak and the needy;
deliver them from the hand of the wicked."

5 They have neither knowledge nor understanding,
they walk around in darkness;
all the foundations of the earth are shaken.

6 I say, "You are gods,
children of the Most High, all of you;

7 nevertheless, you shall die like mortals,
and fall like any prince."[a]

8 Rise up, O God, judge the earth;
for all the nations belong to you!

Prayer for Judgment on Israel's Foes

A Song. A Psalm of Asaph.

83 O God, do not keep silence;
do not hold your peace or be still,
O God!

2 Even now your enemies are in tumult;
those who hate you have raised their heads.

3 They lay crafty plans against your people;
they consult together against those you protect.

4 They say, "Come, let us wipe them out as a nation;
let the name of Israel be remembered no more."

5 They conspire with one accord;
against you they make a covenant—

6 the tents of Edom and the Ishmaelites,
Moab and the Hagrites,

7 Gebal and Ammon and Amalek,
Philistia with the inhabitants of Tyre;

8 Assyria also has joined them;
they are the strong arm of the children of Lot.   *Selah*

9 Do to them as you did to Midian,
as to Sisera and Jabin at the Wadi Kishon,

10 who were destroyed at En-dor,
who became dung for the ground.

11 Make their nobles like Oreb and Zeeb,
all their princes like Zebah and Zalmunna,

12 who said, "Let us take the pastures of God
for our own possession."

13 O my God, make them like whirling dust,[b]
like chaff before the wind.

_____

a Or *fall as one man, O princes*   *b* Or *a tumbleweed*

82.1–8 A call for God's rule of the nations to ensure justice for the weak. The psalm is a literary report of the action of the divine council or heavenly assembly similar to the prophetic reports recounted in 1 Kings 22.19–23; Isa 6.1–13; Jer 23.18–22. As commonly conceived in the ancient Near East, the council of the gods was where the governance of the universe was managed. *Asaph.* See note on 50.1–23. **82.1–4** The God of Israel rises in the council of the gods to accuse the gods of the nations of not having maintained the right to justice of the weak and the poor, the primary criterion of a just order in ancient Israel. **82.2** *How long?* is the typical complaint against God of the sufferer in prayer. Here it is taken up by God on behalf of the victims of oppression (cf. 6.3; 13.1–2; 74.10; 94.3). It also becomes a part of prophetic indictment of the wickedness of the people (Jer 4.14; 13.27; 23.26; Hos 8.5; Hab 2.6). *Selah.* See note on 3.2. **82.5** Either blindly or intentionally the gods do not know the way

of justice. As a consequence, the just order of the universe is undermined. **82.6–7** The God of Israel strips the heavenly powers of their divine character and condemns the immortal gods to mortality. V. 6a is quoted in Jn 10.34. **82.8** The psalmist, perhaps a priestly or prophetic voice, calls upon God to take over the rule of the nations from all the other gods.

83.1–18 A prayer of the community for God's help against enemies. *Asaph.* See note on 50.1–23. **83.1–8** A plea to God not to be inactive and quiescent in the face of the conspiracy of the nations against Israel. In their plotting against Israel they conspire also against God (v. 5) and so are God's enemies as well (v. 2). The fate of the Lord of Israel is seen as allied to the fate of the Lord's people. **83.6–8** There is no particular historical moment with which such a grouping of nations against Israel can be associated. **83.8** *Children of Lot,* the Moabites and Ammonites (Gen 19.36–38). *Selah.* See note on 3.2. **83.9–18** Petitions for God's destruc-

14 As fire consumes the forest,
    as the flame sets the mountains ablaze,
15 so pursue them with your tempest
    and terrify them with your hurricane.
16 Fill their faces with shame,
    so that they may seek your name,
      O LORD.
17 Let them be put to shame and dismayed
      forever;
    let them perish in disgrace.
18 Let them know that you alone,
    whose name is the LORD,
    are the Most High over all the earth.

The Joy of Worship in the Temple

To the leader: according to The Gittith. Of the
Korahites. A Psalm.

84 How lovely is your dwelling place,
    O LORD of hosts!
2 My soul longs, indeed it faints
    for the courts of the LORD;
  my heart and my flesh sing for joy
    to the living God.

3 Even the sparrow finds a home,
    and the swallow a nest for herself,
    where she may lay her young,
  at your altars, O LORD of hosts,
    my King and my God.
4 Happy are those who live in your house,
    ever singing your praise.   *Selah*

5 Happy are those whose strength is in you,
    in whose heart are the highways to
      Zion.[a]
6 As they go through the valley of Baca
    they make it a place of springs;
    the early rain also covers it with
      pools.

7 They go from strength to strength;
    the God of gods will be seen in Zion.

8 O LORD God of hosts, hear my prayer;
    give ear, O God of Jacob!   *Selah*
9 Behold our shield, O God;
    look on the face of your anointed.

10 For a day in your courts is better
    than a thousand elsewhere.
  I would rather be a doorkeeper in the
      house of my God
    than live in the tents of wickedness.
11 For the LORD God is a sun and shield;
    he bestows favor and honor.
  No good thing does the LORD withhold
    from those who walk uprightly.
12 O LORD of hosts,
    happy is everyone who trusts in you.

Prayer for the Restoration of God's Favor

To the leader. Of the Korahites. A Psalm.

85 LORD, you were favorable to your
        land;
    you restored the fortunes of Jacob.
2 You forgave the iniquity of your people;
    you pardoned all their sin.   *Selah*
3 You withdrew all your wrath;
    you turned from your hot anger.

4 Restore us again, O God of our salvation,
    and put away your indignation toward
      us.
5 Will you be angry with us forever?
    Will you prolong your anger to all
      generations?
6 Will you not revive us again,

___
a Heb lacks *to Zion*

tion of the enemies. **83.9** *Midian* alludes to Gideon's destruction of the Midianites (Judg 6–8). *Sisera and Jabin* were defeated by the Israelites under the leadership of Deborah and Barak (Judg 4–5). **83.11** *Oreb, Zeeb, Zebah, Zalmunna*, Midianite leaders defeated by Israel (Judg 7.25; 8.4–21).
  84.1–12 A song of Zion for one who makes pilgrimage to the temple, possibly at the autumn Festival of Tabernacles (Booths), and rejoices in being able to be in the presence of God. *To the leader.* See note on 4.1–8. *According to The Gittith.* See note on 8.1–9. *Korahites.* See note on 42.1–43.5. **84.1–4** Longing for the sanctuary (cf. 42.1–2). **84.4** *Selah.* See note on 3.2. **84.5–7** The joy and blessing of journeying to the sanctuary. **84.6** The *valley of Baca* is unknown but seems to

be an arid place on the way to Jerusalem. *Place of springs.* For the notion of God opening up springs of water for people journeying through arid desert on their way to Jerusalem, see 107.33; Isa 35.6–7; 41.18; 43.20; 48.21. **84.7** *From strength to strength.* Cf. Isa 40.31. **84.8–9** A prayer of intercession for the king (*our shield, your anointed*). **84.10–12** The favor and protection of God in the sanctuary.
  85.1–13 A community prayer for deliverance by God. *To the leader.* See note on 4.1–8. *Korahites.* See note on 42.1–43.5. **85.1–3** Recollection of God's forgiveness and favor in the past. The particular occasion referred to is not indicated in the psalm. It may have been the return from exile in Babylon. *Selah.* See note on 3.2. **85.4–7** The prayer itself that God may grant

so that your people may rejoice in you?

7 Show us your steadfast love, O Lᴏʀᴅ,
   and grant us your salvation.

8 Let me hear what God the Lᴏʀᴅ will
      speak,
   for he will speak peace to his people,
   to his faithful, to those who turn to
      him in their hearts.*

9 Surely his salvation is at hand for those
      who fear him,
   that his glory may dwell in our land.

10 Steadfast love and faithfulness will meet;
   righteousness and peace will kiss each
      other.

11 Faithfulness will spring up from the
      ground,
   and righteousness will look down from
      the sky.

12 The Lᴏʀᴅ will give what is good,
   and our land will yield its increase.

13 Righteousness will go before him,
   and will make a path for his steps.

Supplication for Help against Enemies

A Prayer of David.

86 Incline your ear, O Lᴏʀᴅ, and answer
      me,
   for I am poor and needy.

2 Preserve my life, for I am devoted to you;
   save your servant who trusts in you.
   You are my God; ³be gracious to me,
      O Lord,
   for to you do I cry all day long.

4 Gladden the soul of your servant,
   for to you, O Lord, I lift up my soul.

5 For you, O Lord, are good and forgiving,

abounding in steadfast love to all who
   call on you.

6 Give ear, O Lᴏʀᴅ, to my prayer;
   listen to my cry of supplication.

7 In the day of my trouble I call on you,
   for you will answer me.

8 There is none like you among the gods,
      O Lord,
   nor are there any works like yours.

9 All the nations you have made shall
      come
   and bow down before you, O Lord,
   and shall glorify your name.

10 For you are great and do wondrous
      things;
   you alone are God.

11 Teach me your way, O Lᴏʀᴅ,
   that I may walk in your truth;
   give me an undivided heart to revere
      your name.

12 I give thanks to you, O Lord my God,
      with my whole heart,
   and I will glorify your name forever.

13 For great is your steadfast love toward
      me;
   you have delivered my soul from the
      depths of Sheol.

14 O God, the insolent rise up against me;
   a band of ruffians seeks my life,
   and they do not set you before them.

15 But you, O Lord, are a God merciful and
      gracious,
   slow to anger and abounding in
      steadfast love and faithfulness.

16 Turn to me and be gracious to me;

_____
a Gk: Heb but let them not turn back to folly

forgiveness and favor in the present distress. **85.8– 13** The word of the Lord, declared in this situation, is an announcement of salvation by the psalmist or possibly by a priest or prophet. The message is one of peace or well-being (v. 8), which is then elaborated in the following verses. **85.9** *Fear.* See note on 34.7. **85.10–13** *Steadfast love, faithfulness, righteousness,* and *peace* are divine attributes here personified as messengers or servants who meet in concord (v. 10), fill and cover the earth (v. 12), and go before the Lord as heralds before a king (v. 13). Cf. 89.14.

86.1–17 An individual's prayer for help. **86.1–7** A series of petitions for God's attention (vv. 1, 6–7) and help (vv. 2–4) are grounded in a number of reasons justifying the prayer and God's help. The reasons have

to do with the plight of the psalmist (vv. 1b, 7a), the devotion of the psalmist (vv. 2a, 2b, 3b, 4b), and the nature of God (vv. 2b, 5, 7b). **86.8–13** Praise and thanksgiving for God's help. **86.8–10** Hymnic exaltation of the power and glory of God. **86.8** See Ex 15.11; Deut 33.26. **86.11** A prayer for guidance. **86.12–13** A vow of thanksgiving in anticipation of deliverance by God. **86.13** *Sheol.* See note on 6.5. **86.14–17** The prayer for help is renewed; the reasons set forth are rooted in God's gracious character (vv. 15, 17b). **86.14** The enemies of the psalmist are often characterized as arrogant and indifferent toward God. **86.15** The psalmist characterizes God in terms of the ancient confessional and liturgical formula of Ex 33.19; 34.6; Num 14.18; Pss 103.8; 145.8. Cf. 86.5.

give your strength to your servant;
  save the child of your serving girl.
17 Show me a sign of your favor,
  so that those who hate me may see it
      and be put to shame,
  because you, Lord, have helped me
      and comforted me.

The Joy of Living in Zion

Of the Korahites. A Psalm. A Song.

87 On the holy mount stands the city he
          founded;
2   the Lord loves the gates of Zion
      more than all the dwellings of Jacob.
3   Glorious things are spoken of you,
      O city of God.   *Selah*

4   Among those who know me I mention
        Rahab and Babylon;
    Philistia too, and Tyre, with
        Ethiopia*a*—
    "This one was born there," they say.

5   And of Zion it shall be said,
    "This one and that one were born in
        it";
    for the Most High himself will
        establish it.
6   The Lord records, as he registers the
        peoples,
    "This one was born there."   *Selah*

7   Singers and dancers alike say,
    "All my springs are in you."

Prayer for Help in Despondency

A Song. A Psalm of the Korahites. To the
leader: according to Mahalath Leannoth.
A Maskil of Heman the Ezrahite.

88 O Lord, God of my salvation,
          when, at night, I cry out in your
          presence,
2   let my prayer come before you;
      incline your ear to my cry.

3   For my soul is full of troubles,
      and my life draws near to Sheol.
4   I am counted among those who go down
        to the Pit;
    I am like those who have no help,
5   like those forsaken among the dead,
      like the slain that lie in the grave,
    like those whom you remember no more,
      for they are cut off from your hand.
6   You have put me in the depths of the Pit,
      in the regions dark and deep.
7   Your wrath lies heavy upon me,
      and you overwhelm me with all your
          waves.   *Selah*

8   You have caused my companions to shun
        me;
    you have made me a thing of horror to
        them.
    I am shut in so that I cannot escape;
9   my eye grows dim through sorrow.
    Every day I call on you, O Lord;

----

a Or *Nubia*; Heb *Cush*

86.16 *Child of your serving girl,* a synonym for *your servant;* cf. 116.16.
  87.1–7 A song in praise of Zion. *Korahites.* See note
on 42.1–43.5. **87.1–3** Praise of Zion, or Jerusalem, as
God's beloved city. *Holy mount,* lit. "hills of holiness,"
possibly reflecting the fact that Jerusalem is built on several hills, but maybe referring to a more mythological
notion of primeval mountains. *The dwellings of Jacob,*
probably the other towns and cities. *City of God.* See
46.4; 48.1, 8. *Selah.* See note on 3.2. **87.4–6** Zion is the
mother city of all who know the Lord, wherever they are
born. **87.4** The places may represent proselytes to the
worship of the God of Israel, or Israelites who have been
dispersed to those countries and cities, or both. *Rahab,*
the name of an ancient mythological monster defeated
by the Lord, later used as a poetic name for Egypt
(89.10; Job 26.12; Isa 30.7; 51.9). **87.5** *Most High.* See
Deut 32.8, where this epithet is used to designate God as
the one who allotted the nations. **87.6** *The Lord records*
probably refers to the book of life or the book of re-

membrance, in which are recorded the names of the
faithful worshipers of the Lord (Ex 32.32–33; Ps 69.28;
Isa 4.3; Dan 12.1; Mal 3.16; Rev 3.5; 13.8; 20.12, 15;
21.27). **87.7** Although the verse is unclear, the *singers
and dancers* are probably worshipers or those on pilgrimage, and *springs* is an image of blessing. For *springs*
welling up on the pilgrimage to Zion, see 84.6. For water
flowing through Jerusalem as a symbol of life, see 46.4;
Ezek 47.1–12; Zech 14.8; Rev 22.1–2.
  88.1–18 A prayer for help that is relentless in complaint against God and does not see any assurance of deliverance. *Korahites.* See note on 42.1–43.5. *To the
leader.* See note on 4.1–8. *According to Mahalath Leannoth.* Meaning unknown, possibly a melody. *Maskil.* See
note on 32.1–11. *Heman the Ezrahite,* a wise man
(1 Kings 4.31) or leader of a guild of temple musicians
(1 Chr 6.33; 15.19; 25.1–8). **88.1–9a** Near death and deserted by friends, the psalmist attributes that plight to
God's wrath. **88.1–2** A plea for God to hear the persistent prayer. **88.3–6** *Sheol, Pit.* See notes on 6.5; 16.10.

I spread out my hands to you.
10 Do you work wonders for the dead?
   Do the shades rise up to praise you?
                                    Selah
11 Is your steadfast love declared in the
      grave,
   or your faithfulness in Abaddon?
12 Are your wonders known in the darkness,
   or your saving help in the land of
      forgetfulness?

13 But I, O LORD, cry out to you;
   in the morning my prayer comes
      before you.
14 O LORD, why do you cast me off?
   Why do you hide your face from me?
15 Wretched and close to death from my
      youth up,
   I suffer your terrors; I am desperate.*ᵃ*
16 Your wrath has swept over me;
   your dread assaults destroy me.
17 They surround me like a flood all day long;
   from all sides they close in on me.
18 You have caused friend and neighbor to
      shun me;
   my companions are in darkness.

God's Covenant with David

A Maskil of Ethan the Ezrahite.

89 I will sing of your steadfast love,
   O LORD,*ᵇ* forever;
with my mouth I will proclaim your
      faithfulness to all generations.
2 I declare that your steadfast love is
      established forever;
   your faithfulness is as firm as the
      heavens.

3 You said, "I have made a covenant with
      my chosen one,
   I have sworn to my servant David:
4 'I will establish your descendants forever,
   and build your throne for all
      generations.' "
                                    Selah

5 Let the heavens praise your wonders,
      O LORD,
   your faithfulness in the assembly of the
      holy ones.
6 For who in the skies can be compared to
      the LORD?
   Who among the heavenly beings is like
      the LORD,
7 a God feared in the council of the holy
      ones,
   great and awesome*ᶜ* above all that are
      around him?
8 O LORD God of hosts,
   who is as mighty as you, O LORD?
   Your faithfulness surrounds you.
9 You rule the raging of the sea;
   when its waves rise, you still them.
10 You crushed Rahab like a carcass;
   you scattered your enemies with your
      mighty arm.
11 The heavens are yours, the earth also is
      yours;
   the world and all that is in it—you
      have founded them.
12 The north and the south*ᵈ*—you created
      them;
   Tabor and Hermon joyously praise
      your name.

---

a Meaning of Heb uncertain   *b* Gk: Heb *the steadfast love of the* LORD   *c* Gk Syr: Heb *greatly awesome*   *d* Or *Zaphon and Yamin*

88.7 *Selah.* See note on 3.2. **88.9b–12** The plea to be heard is followed again by the fear of death and questions designed to urge God's help by pointing out that in the realm of death and Sheol not only is the psalmist cut off from God, but God cannot be praised and glorified. *Abaddon,* "ruin" in Hebrew, a term for the netherworld. **88.13–18** Questions and assertions complaining of God's abandonment and the effects of God's wrath. If the plight of the psalmist is sickness, it is understood as the result of divine punishment. The psalmist is again depicted as near death and suffering the loss of community and companionship. **88.13** The morning was the time when God was expected to help (cf. 46.5; 90.14; 143.8). **88.14** *Hide your face.* See notes on 10.1; 27.9.

89.1–18 A hymn of praise to God as creator and as the one who chose David and his descendants to be kings forever. *Maskil.* See note on 32.1–11. *Ethan the*

Ezrahite, a sage (1 Kings 4.31) or temple musician (1 Chr 15.17, 19). **89.3–4** For the choice of David and his line as a perpetual dynasty, see vv. 19–37; 2 Sam 7.8–16. *Covenant . . . chosen one.* Cf. 132.11–12. **89.4** This verse gives the content of the covenant or oath referred to in v. 3. *Selah.* See note on 3.2. **89.5–7** *Holy ones,* the host of heavenly beings (cf. v. 6) who are understood to make up the divine assembly surrounding the heavenly throne of God. They serve as a court or council in which the Lord utters the divine decrees. On this conception, see 1 Kings 22.19–23; Job 1–2; Ps 82; Jer 23.18, 21–22. **89.9–10** The creative work of God is seen in terms of a defeat of the powers of chaos. *Rahab.* See note on 87.4. **89.12** *The north and the south* may be either directions, signifying the whole universe, or terms for mountains. The Hebrew term for "north" is *Zaphon,* also the name of a mountain

13 You have a mighty arm;
        strong is your hand, high your right
            hand.
14 Righteousness and justice are the
        foundation of your throne;
        steadfast love and faithfulness go
            before you.
15 Happy are the people who know the
        festal shout,
        who walk, O LORD, in the light of your
            countenance;
16 they exult in your name all day long,
        and extol^a your righteousness.
17 For you are the glory of their strength;
        by your favor our horn is exalted.
18 For our shield belongs to the LORD,
        our king to the Holy One of Israel.

19 Then you spoke in a vision to your
        faithful one, and said:
    "I have set the crown^b on one who is
        mighty,
    I have exalted one chosen from the
        people.
20 I have found my servant David;
        with my holy oil I have anointed him;
21 my hand shall always remain with him;
        my arm also shall strengthen him.
22 The enemy shall not outwit him,
        the wicked shall not humble him.
23 I will crush his foes before him
        and strike down those who hate him.
24 My faithfulness and steadfast love shall be
        with him;
        and in my name his horn shall be
            exalted.
25 I will set his hand on the sea
        and his right hand on the rivers.
26 He shall cry to me, 'You are my Father,

my God, and the Rock of my
        salvation!'
27 I will make him the firstborn,
        the highest of the kings of the earth.
28 Forever I will keep my steadfast love for
        him,
        and my covenant with him will stand
            firm.
29 I will establish his line forever,
        and his throne as long as the heavens
            endure.
30 If his children forsake my law
        and do not walk according to my
            ordinances,
31 if they violate my statutes
        and do not keep my commandments,
32 then I will punish their transgression
        with the rod
        and their iniquity with scourges;
33 but I will not remove from him my
        steadfast love,
        or be false to my faithfulness.
34 I will not violate my covenant,
        or alter the word that went forth from
            my lips.
35 Once and for all I have sworn by my
        holiness;
        I will not lie to David.
36 His line shall continue forever,
        and his throne endure before me like
            the sun.
37 It shall be established forever like the
        moon,
        an enduring witness in the skies." *Selah*

38 But now you have spurned and rejected
        him;

_____

a Cn: Heb *are exalted in*   *b* Cn: Heb *help*

that was the abode of the Canaanite god Baal. It may
represent the abode of God here (cf. note on 48.2). The
Hebrew term for "south" is *yamin.* It is not the name of
a mountain but has been identified by some as referring to the Amanus range in Lebanon. *Tabor,* a mountain in northern Israel, south of the Sea of Galilee. *Hermon,* a mountain in Syria, frequently mentioned in the
Bible because of its great height (cf. 42.6; 133.3).
89.14 *Righteousness and justice* are here divine attributes seen as supports for the divine throne and thus as
characterizing God's rule. *Steadfast love and faithfulness* are other characteristics of God here personified
as companions or servants who lead the way of the
Lord (cf. 85.10–11). **89.15** *Festal shout,* shouts of the
people at the festival celebration of the Lord's rule (cf.

2 Sam 6.15). **89.17** *Horn,* an image for the king. **89.19–
37** An oracle of God in a vision, establishing the
covenant with David and his descendants as the kings
of Israel (cf. 2 Sam 7.4–17; Ps 132). **89.19** *Spoke in a
vision,* probably to a prophet (cf. 2 Sam 7.4, 17).
89.24 *Faithfulness and steadfast love.* Cf. v. 14. *Horn,*
i.e., strength. **89.26** *Father.* For the notion of the king
as adopted by God, cf. 2.7; 2 Sam 7.14. **89.30–37** God
will punish any of the Davidic kings who disobey
God's will as reflected in the laws but will not take
away the kingship bestowed by covenant. **89.38–51** A
lament or prayer for help for a defeated king. **89.38–
46** Words of complaint to and against God, characteristic of prayers for help. Here they presume that the
defeat of the king represents God's abandonment of

you are full of wrath against your
    anointed.
39 You have renounced the covenant with
    your servant;
    you have defiled his crown in the dust.
40 You have broken through all his walls;
    you have laid his strongholds in ruins.
41 All who pass by plunder him;
    he has become the scorn of his
    neighbors.
42 You have exalted the right hand of his
    foes;
    you have made all his enemies rejoice.
43 Moreover, you have turned back the edge
    of his sword,
    and you have not supported him in
    battle.
44 You have removed the scepter from his
    hand,[a]
    and hurled his throne to the ground.
45 You have cut short the days of his youth;
    you have covered him with shame.
                                        Selah

46 How long, O LORD? Will you hide
    yourself forever?
    How long will your wrath burn like fire?
47 Remember how short my time is—[b]
    for what vanity you have created all
    mortals!
48 Who can live and never see death?
    Who can escape the power of Sheol?
                                        Selah

49 Lord, where is your steadfast love of old,
    which by your faithfulness you swore
    to David?
50 Remember, O Lord, how your servant is
    taunted;
    how I bear in my bosom the insults of
    the peoples,[c]

51 with which your enemies taunt, O LORD,
    with which they taunted the footsteps
    of your anointed.

52 Blessed be the LORD forever.
    Amen and Amen.

BOOK IV: PSALMS 90–106

God's Eternity and Human Frailty

A Prayer of Moses, the man of God.

90 Lord, you have been our dwelling
    place[d]
    in all generations.
2 Before the mountains were brought
    forth,
    or ever you had formed the earth and
    the world,
    from everlasting to everlasting you are
    God.

3 You turn us[e] back to dust,
    and say, "Turn back, you mortals."
4 For a thousand years in your sight
    are like yesterday when it is past,
    or like a watch in the night.

5 You sweep them away; they are like a
    dream,
    like grass that is renewed in the
    morning;
6 in the morning it flourishes and is
    renewed;
    in the evening it fades and withers.

7 For we are consumed by your anger;
    by your wrath we are overwhelmed.

---

a Cn: Heb *removed his cleanness*   *b* Meaning of Heb uncertain
c Cn: Heb *bosom all of many peoples*   *d* Another reading is *our
refuge*   *e* Heb *humankind*

---

the covenant and promises to the Davidic line.
89.41 *Neighbors,* perhaps neighboring nations.
89.46 *How long?* See note on 6.3. **89.47–51** The petition of the king for restoration through God's *steadfast
love* (vv. 1, 2, 14, 24, 28, 33) and *faithfulness* (vv. 1, 2, 5,
8, 14, 24, 33) to the covenant or oath to David.
89.48 *Sheol.* See note on 6.5. **89.50–51** The *insults* with
which the king is *taunted* are probably taunts that God
has abandoned him (cf. 42.3, 10; 79.10). *Anointed.* See
note on 2.2. **89.52** A doxology concluding the third
book of the Psalter (Pss 73–89). See note on 41.13.
Blessed. See note on 103.1–2.
90.1–17 A prayer of the community reflecting on

human frailty and seeking wisdom and God's favor. It
is the only psalm attributed to *Moses.* The association
may be because of the tradition that recalls Moses as
the one who asked God to *turn* (so v. 13) from wrath
in Ex 32.12. **90.1–6** The eternal nature of God contrasted with the transient nature of human beings.
90.1 *Dwelling place,* or "refuge" (cf. 71.3; 91.9; Deut
33.27). God has provided a place of belonging and protection for the people from the beginning of time (cf.
Ps 46). **90.2** Cf. Job 38.4. **90.3** Cf. 103.14; Gen 2.7; 3.19;
Job 34.14–15. **90.4** Cf. 2 Pet 3.8. *Watch,* one of the three
periods into which the nighttime hours were divided.
90.5–6 Cf. 103.15–18; Isa 40.6–8. **90.7–12** Human

8 You have set our iniquities before you,
    our secret sins in the light of your
        countenance.

9 For all our days pass away under your
        wrath;
    our years come to an end[a] like a sigh.
10 The days of our life are seventy years,
    or perhaps eighty, if we are strong;
    even then their span[b] is only toil and
        trouble;
    they are soon gone, and we fly away.

11 Who considers the power of your anger?
    Your wrath is as great as the fear that is
        due you.
12 So teach us to count our days
    that we may gain a wise heart.

13 Turn, O LORD! How long?
    Have compassion on your servants!
14 Satisfy us in the morning with your
        steadfast love,
    so that we may rejoice and be glad all
        our days.
15 Make us glad as many days as you have
        afflicted us,
    and as many years as we have seen evil.
16 Let your work be manifest to your servants,
    and your glorious power to their
        children.
17 Let the favor of the Lord our God be
        upon us,
    and prosper for us the work of our
        hands—
    O prosper the work of our hands!

Assurance of God's Protection

91 You who live in the shelter of the
    Most High,

who abide in the shadow of the
        Almighty,[c]
2 will say to the LORD, "My refuge and my
        fortress;
    my God, in whom I trust."
3 For he will deliver you from the snare of
        the fowler
    and from the deadly pestilence;
4 he will cover you with his pinions,
    and under his wings you will find
        refuge;
    his faithfulness is a shield and buckler.
5 You will not fear the terror of the night,
    or the arrow that flies by day,
6 or the pestilence that stalks in darkness,
    or the destruction that wastes at
        noonday.

7 A thousand may fall at your side,
    ten thousand at your right hand,
    but it will not come near you.
8 You will only look with your eyes
    and see the punishment of the wicked.

9 Because you have made the LORD your
        refuge,[d]
    the Most High your dwelling place,
10 no evil shall befall you,
    no scourge come near your tent.

11 For he will command his angels
        concerning you
    to guard you in all your ways.
12 On their hands they will bear you up,
    so that you will not dash your foot
        against a stone.
13 You will tread on the lion and the adder,

---

a Syr: Heb *we bring our years to an end*   *b* Cn Compare Gk Syr
Jerome Tg: Heb *pride*   *c* Traditional rendering of Heb *Shaddai*
d Cn: Heb *Because you, LORD, are my refuge; you have made*

mortality issues from the judgment of God on human
sin (cf. Rom 6.23). **90.8** Cf. 19.12. **90.11** *Fear.* See note
on 34.7. **90.12** Cf. 39.4–6. *Wise heart,* the ability to discern the purposes of God. Acknowledging human
frailty and the certainty of death may lead to the proper
perspective with which to live in the present. **90.13–
17** Prayer for God to redeem the time and deal favorably with the people. **90.13** *How long?* See note on 6.3.
90.14 Cf. 81.16; 91.16; 103.5; 107.8–9. **90.17** *Prosper,*
lit. "establish." A prayer that God may give enduring
value to the work of the community.
    91.1–13 A didactic or wisdom psalm elaborating
with many images that God's protection from harm

and danger is manifest and reliable. **91.1–2** Address to
one who enters the sanctuary. *Refuge.* See vv. 2, 9; 90.1;
note on 2.10–12. **91.1** *Shelter* may allude to the protective area of the sanctuary (cf. 27.5; 31.20; 61.4).
Shadow refers to wings (see v. 4; 17.8; 36.7; 57.1; 63.7).
91.2 The one addressed is invited to make a confession
of personal trust in God. **91.3–13** The justification for
that confidence is laid out in detail. The Lord's protection is against human enemies or persecutors (v. 3) as
well as demonic forces or sickness (vv. 5–6, 10).
91.4 *Pinions* and *wings* suggest the image of God as an
eagle protecting its young (cf. v. 1; Deut 32.10–11; Isa
31.5). **91.5** *Arrow that flies by day,* possibly sunstroke.

the young lion and the serpent you will
trample under foot.

14 Those who love me, I will deliver;
  I will protect those who know my
    name.
15 When they call to me, I will answer them;
  I will be with them in trouble,
  I will rescue them and honor them.
16 With long life I will satisfy them,
  and show them my salvation.

Thanksgiving for Vindication

A Psalm. A Song for the Sabbath Day.

92 It is good to give thanks to the LORD,
  to sing praises to your name, O Most
    High;
2 to declare your steadfast love in the
    morning,
  and your faithfulness by night,
3 to the music of the lute and the harp,
  to the melody of the lyre.
4 For you, O LORD, have made me glad by
    your work;
  at the works of your hands I sing for
    joy.

5 How great are your works, O LORD!
  Your thoughts are very deep!
6 The dullard cannot know,
  the stupid cannot understand this:
7 though the wicked sprout like grass
  and all evildoers flourish,

they are doomed to destruction forever,
8 but you, O LORD, are on high forever.
9 For your enemies, O LORD,
  for your enemies shall perish;
  all evildoers shall be scattered.

10 But you have exalted my horn like that of
    the wild ox;
  you have poured over me*a* fresh oil.
11 My eyes have seen the downfall of my
    enemies;
  my ears have heard the doom of my
    evil assailants.

12 The righteous flourish like the palm tree,
  and grow like a cedar in Lebanon.
13 They are planted in the house of the LORD;
  they flourish in the courts of our God.
14 In old age they still produce fruit;
  they are always green and full of sap,
15 showing that the LORD is upright;
  he is my rock, and there is no
    unrighteousness in him.

The Majesty of God's Rule

93 The LORD is king, he is robed in
    majesty;
  the LORD is robed, he is girded with
    strength.
He has established the world; it shall
    never be moved;

_____
a Syr: Meaning of Heb uncertain

91.11–12 Cf. Mt 4.6; Lk 4.10–11. *Bear you up.* See Ex
19.4. 91.13 *Lion, adder, serpent,* symbolic of dangers
and enemies. See note on 7.2. 91.14–16 A divine oracle of salvation that typically was given, perhaps
through a priest (see 1 Sam 1.17) or a prophet (e.g., Isa
41.8–13), to those who cried to God in trouble. Cf.
22.21b; 35.3.
    92.1–15 A hymn of thanksgiving for God's just
order as demonstrated in the psalmist's deliverance
from enemies. *A Song for the Sabbath Day,* a later designation of the psalm as part of the Sabbath celebration, the only psalm so designated in the Hebrew text
of the Psalter. 92.1–3 Hymnic introduction (cf. 106.1;
107.1; 118.1; 136.1). 92.2 *Morning and . . . night,* i.e.,
continually, though the psalm may also have in mind
morning sacrifices and nightly praise. (134.1–2).
92.4–15 The grounds for praising and giving thanks.
92.4–11 The greatness of God's wonderful work as
demonstrated in the defeat of the enemies of God and
in the exaltation of the one who gives thanks.
92.10 *Horn.* See note on 75.4–5. *Oil,* a symbol of favor

and well-being (23.5; 45.7; 133.2). 92.12–15 In contrast to the temporary success of the wicked (v. 7), the
righteous endure and flourish in God's presence
throughout their life. 92.12 *Palm tree, cedar in Lebanon,* symbols of prosperity and longevity (cf. 1.3; 52.8;
104.16; Jer 17.8).
    93.1–5 A hymn of praise celebrating God's rule over
the world. It belongs to a group of psalms (Pss 47; 93;
95–99) that have been called "enthronement psalms"
because they may have been used on festival occasions
when God was declared to be king (see 93.1; 95.3;
96.10; 97.1; 98.6; 99.1). Similar language and themes
are to be found in the prophecy of Isa 40–55. 93.1–
2 The establishment of God's rule. *The LORD is king,* or
"The LORD has become king," is to be understood as a
declaration of God's enduring kingship or, in the latter
case, as the declaration that at a particular moment in
the festival celebration the Lord's enthronement is formally declared. The psalm assumes that God's rule as
sovereign is from eternity (v. 2; cf. 29.10), but it is possible that at one of the annual festivals, perhaps the Fes-

2   your throne is established from of old;
        you are from everlasting.

3   The floods have lifted up, O LORD,
        the floods have lifted up their voice;
        the floods lift up their roaring.
4   More majestic than the thunders of
            mighty waters,
        more majestic than the waves*a* of the sea,
        majestic on high is the LORD!

5   Your decrees are very sure;
        holiness befits your house,
        O LORD, forevermore.

God the Avenger of the Righteous

94 O LORD, you God of vengeance,
        you God of vengeance, shine forth!
2   Rise up, O judge of the earth;
        give to the proud what they deserve!
3   O LORD, how long shall the wicked,
        how long shall the wicked exult?

4   They pour out their arrogant words;
        all the evildoers boast.
5   They crush your people, O LORD,
        and afflict your heritage.
6   They kill the widow and the stranger,
        they murder the orphan,
7   and they say, "The LORD does not see;
        the God of Jacob does not perceive."

8   Understand, O dullest of the people;
        fools, when will you be wise?

9   He who planted the ear, does he not hear?
        He who formed the eye, does he not see?
10 He who disciplines the nations,
        he who teaches knowledge to
            humankind,
        does he not chastise?
11 The LORD knows our thoughts,*b*
        that they are but an empty breath.

12 Happy are those whom you discipline,
            O LORD,
        and whom you teach out of your law,
13 giving them respite from days of trouble,
        until a pit is dug for the wicked.
14 For the LORD will not forsake his people;
        he will not abandon his heritage;
15 for justice will return to the righteous,
        and all the upright in heart will follow it.

16 Who rises up for me against the wicked?
        Who stands up for me against
            evildoers?
17 If the LORD had not been my help,
        my soul would soon have lived in the
            land of silence.
18 When I thought, "My foot is slipping,"
        your steadfast love, O LORD, held me
            up.
19 When the cares of my heart are many,
        your consolations cheer my soul.
20 Can wicked rulers be allied with you,
        those who contrive mischief by statute?

---

a Cn: Heb *majestic are the waves*   *b* Heb *the thoughts of humankind*

---

tival of Booths, or Tabernacles, in the fall, the Lord's victory over the forces of chaos and disorder (see vv. 3–4) was celebrated by the people in a ritual and hymnic act of enthronement declaring the Lord's rule anew. **93.3–4** The establishment of God's eternal rule is accomplished by the defeat of the powers of chaos as represented in the floods and waters. Lying behind this notion are Mesopotamian and Canaanite conceptions of divine kingship as established by victory over the sea and the deep (cf. 74.13; Job 38.8–11; Isa 27.1; 51.9–10). **93.5** Praise of the Lord is also because of the reliability of God's law and God's holy house, the temple.

94.1–23 A prayer for God's help by an individual whose present suffering at the hands of the powerful is representative of the larger community's distress. **94.1–2** The initial call for God to render judgment. **94.1** *Vengeance,* i.e., vindication and compassion for the righteous or innocent and judgment for the wicked (cf. Deut 32.35–36; Rom 12.19). *Shine forth.* See note on 80.1. **94.2** *Judge of the earth.* See 7.8; 9.8–9; 58.11;

76.8–9; 82.8; Gen 18.25. **94.3–7** The complaint against the wicked. The power of the wicked against the people is a challenge to God's power and care. **94.3** *How long?* See note on 6.3. **94.5** *Heritage,* the property of the Lord; cf. Deut 32.8–9. **94.6** *Widow, stranger, orphan,* the dependent, whose care by the community is the mark of true justice (Ex 22.21–24; Deut 24.17, 21; 26.12; 27.19; Isa 1.17; Jer 7.6; 22.3) and for whom God has special concern (Ex 22.24; Pss 68.5; 82.3–4; 146.9). V. 20 suggests that the oppression is judicial in character, carried out by judges and rulers who use the courts to oppress the weak, possibly even committing legal murder (cf. 1 Kings 21). **94.8–11** The foolishness of the wicked, who think that God does not see and care about their wickedness. Cf. 10.3–4; 14.1; 53.1. **94.12–15** The ultimate confidence and blessing of the righteous is in God, who will not forsake and will ensure that justice is done. *Happy.* See note on 1.1. **94.16–23** The psalmist proclaims God's saving help against the machinations of the wicked. **94.17** *Land of silence,* i.e., death (115.17).

21 They band together against the life of the
   righteous,
   and condemn the innocent to death.
22 But the LORD has become my stronghold,
   and my God the rock of my refuge.
23 He will repay them for their iniquity
   and wipe them out for their
   wickedness;
   the LORD our God will wipe them out.

A Call to Worship and Obedience

95 O come, let us sing to the LORD;
   let us make a joyful noise to the rock
   of our salvation!
2 Let us come into his presence with
   thanksgiving;
   let us make a joyful noise to him with
   songs of praise!
3 For the LORD is a great God,
   and a great King above all gods.
4 In his hand are the depths of the earth;
   the heights of the mountains are his
   also.
5 The sea is his, for he made it,
   and the dry land, which his hands have
   formed.

6 O come, let us worship and bow down,
   let us kneel before the LORD, our Maker!
7 For he is our God,
   and we are the people of his pasture,
   and the sheep of his hand.

   O that today you would listen to his voice!
8   Do not harden your hearts, as at
      Meribah,

   as on the day at Massah in the
   wilderness,
9 when your ancestors tested me,
   and put me to the proof, though they
   had seen my work.
10 For forty years I loathed that generation
   and said, "They are a people whose
   hearts go astray,
   and they do not regard my ways."
11 Therefore in my anger I swore,
   "They shall not enter my rest."

Praise to God Who Comes in Judgment

96 O sing to the LORD a new song;
   sing to the LORD, all the earth.
2 Sing to the LORD, bless his name;
   tell of his salvation from day to day.
3 Declare his glory among the nations,
   his marvelous works among all the
   peoples.
4 For great is the LORD, and greatly to be
   praised;
   he is to be revered above all gods.
5 For all the gods of the peoples are idols,
   but the LORD made the heavens.
6 Honor and majesty are before him;
   strength and beauty are in his
   sanctuary.

7 Ascribe to the LORD, O families of the
   peoples,
   ascribe to the LORD glory and strength.
8 Ascribe to the LORD the glory due his
   name;
   bring an offering, and come into his
   courts.

94.20–21 See note on 94.6. 94.22 Refuge. See note on 2.10–12.

95.1–11 A liturgy of praise and admonition. This psalm may have been a temple liturgy consisting of a procession into the sanctuary (vv. 1–5) and prostration before God's presence (vv. 6–7a), followed by words of admonition (vv. 7b–11), perhaps in preparation for the public reading of the Torah, or law of God, at the Festival of Booths, or Tabernacles (Deut 31.10–11). Cf. Pss 50; 81 for similar language and character. 95.1–7a Praise of God's kingship and rule over all. 95.1–2 A call to praise. Rock of our salvation. See 89.26; cf. 94.22. 95.3–5 The reason for praise is God's greatness and rule (cf. 93.1–2; 96.10); God is above all gods (cf. 82; 96.4–5) and rules the depths and heights, i.e., the whole earth, and the sea and the dry land (Gen 1.9–10; cf. Ps 24.1). 95.6–7a A call to worship God, who is creator and ruler not only of the universe (vv.

3–5) but also of people (Isa 43.1, 15). The shepherd image is a royal one, signifying rule of the people (100.3; cf. 80.1; Isa 40.11). 95.7b–11 A word of admonition to be spoken by a priest or prophet in preparation for hearing God's law (cf. 81.8–9). On Meribah, in Hebrew "place of contention," and Massah, "place of testing," see Ex 17.1–7; Num 20.1–13; also Pss 78.18–20; 81.7; 106.32. Rest, the divine gift of the land. For a homiletic elaboration of vv. 7b–11, see Heb 3–4.

96.1–13 A hymn of praise to God as ruler and judge. The Lord of Israel rules the universe (image of king) and does so in righteousness (image of judge). See note on 93.1–5. 96.1–3 A call to praise God in song. 96.1 A new song. See 33.3; 40.3; 98.1; 144.9; 149.1; Isa 42.10; Rev 5.9; Jdt 16.1, 13. 96.2 Bless. See note on 103.1–2. 96.4–6 The reason for praise is God's greatness and majesty above all other claims for worship, i.e., above all other gods (95.3; 97.7; cf. 115.3–8). 96.7–9 A call to praise the glory

9   Worship the LORD in holy splendor;
       tremble before him, all the earth.

10 Say among the nations, "The LORD is king!
       The world is firmly established; it shall
          never be moved.
    He will judge the peoples with equity."
11 Let the heavens be glad, and let the earth
       rejoice;
    let the sea roar, and all that fills it;
12   let the field exult, and everything in it.
    Then shall all the trees of the forest sing
       for joy
13   before the LORD; for he is coming,
       for he is coming to judge the earth.
    He will judge the world with
       righteousness,
    and the peoples with his truth.

The Glory of God's Reign

97 The LORD is king! Let the earth
          rejoice;
    let the many coastlands be glad!
2   Clouds and thick darkness are all around
       him;
    righteousness and justice are the
       foundation of his throne.
3   Fire goes before him,
    and consumes his adversaries on every
       side.
4   His lightnings light up the world;
       the earth sees and trembles.
5   The mountains melt like wax before the
       LORD,
    before the Lord of all the earth.

6   The heavens proclaim his righteousness;
    and all the peoples behold his glory.
7   All worshipers of images are put to shame,
       those who make their boast in
          worthless idols;
    all gods bow down before him.
8   Zion hears and is glad,
    and the towns[a] of Judah rejoice,
    because of your judgments, O God.
9   For you, O LORD, are most high over all
       the earth;
    you are exalted far above all gods.

10 The LORD loves those who hate[b] evil;
    he guards the lives of his faithful;
    he rescues them from the hand of the
       wicked.
11 Light dawns[c] for the righteous,
    and joy for the upright in heart.
12 Rejoice in the LORD, O you righteous,
    and give thanks to his holy name!

Praise the Judge of the World

A Psalm.

98 O sing to the LORD a new song,
          for he has done marvelous things.
    His right hand and his holy arm
       have gotten him victory.
2   The LORD has made known his victory;
    he has revealed his vindication in the
       sight of the nations.
3   He has remembered his steadfast love and
       faithfulness
    to the house of Israel.
    All the ends of the earth have seen
       the victory of our God.

4   Make a joyful noise to the LORD, all the
       earth;

---

a Heb *daughters*   *b* Cn: Heb *You who love the LORD hate*
c Gk Syr Jerome: Heb *is sown*

---

of God. Cf. 29.1–2. **96.10–13** The Lord is proclaimed king and judge of all the earth. **96.10** *The LORD is king.* See note on 93.1–2. For God as judge, cf. 7.11; 50.6; 82.8; Ezek 18.30; 33.17, 20. **96.11–13** See 98.7–9.

97.1–12 A hymn of praise celebrating the rule of God. See note on 93.1–5. **97.1** The whole earth is called to rejoice in the realization of the Lord's rule. *The LORD is king.* See note on 93.1–2. **97.2–6** The divine king appears in a storm theophany (18.7–15; 50.1–3; 68.7–8; 77.18; cf. Judg 5.4–5). **97.2** On *righteousness* and *justice* as central to kingship, human and divine, see 72; 82; 85.10–13; Isa 9.7; 11.3–5). **97.3** For fire in the descriptions of God's appearing, see Ex 19.18; 24.17; Deut 4.11–12, 15, 33; 5.4; 9.10, 15. **97.7–**

9 The effects of the Lord's appearing. **97.7** Cf. Isa 42.17; 45.16; Jer 10.14. **97.9** Cf. 47.2, 9; 83.18; 95.3; 96.4–6. **97.10–12** The justice of God is security for the righteous. **97.11** For the dawning of the light of the righteous, see 112.4; Isa 58.10; 60.1–3.

98.1–9 A hymn celebrating the salvation given by God as ruler and judge. See note on 93.1–5. **98.1–3** A call to praise the Lord for marvelous things done for Israel. The imagery of these verses is of God as a mighty warrior, victorious on behalf of the divine purposes and the care of the people. Cf. Ex 15. **98.1** *New song.* See note on 96.1. *Right hand . . . holy arm* are images of God's power in battle. Cf. Ex 15.6, 12; Pss 44.2–3; 89.13; Isa 52.10; 59.16. **98.2** *Victory,* or salvation.

break forth into joyous song and sing
   praises.
5 Sing praises to the LORD with the lyre,
   with the lyre and the sound of melody.
6 With trumpets and the sound of the horn
   make a joyful noise before the King,
   the LORD.

7 Let the sea roar, and all that fills it;
   the world and those who live in it.
8 Let the floods clap their hands;
   let the hills sing together for joy
9 at the presence of the LORD, for he is
   coming
   to judge the earth.
He will judge the world with righteousness,
   and the peoples with equity.

Praise to God for His Holiness

99 The LORD is king; let the peoples
   tremble!
He sits enthroned upon the cherubim;
   let the earth quake!
2 The LORD is great in Zion;
   he is exalted over all the peoples.
3 Let them praise your great and awesome
   name.
   Holy is he!
4 Mighty King,[a] lover of justice,
   you have established equity;
you have executed justice
   and righteousness in Jacob.
5 Extol the LORD our God;
   worship at his footstool.
   Holy is he!

6 Moses and Aaron were among his
   priests,

Samuel also was among those who
   called on his name.
They cried to the LORD, and he
   answered them.
7 He spoke to them in the pillar of cloud;
   they kept his decrees,
   and the statutes that he gave them.

8 O LORD our God, you answered them;
   you were a forgiving God to them,
   but an avenger of their wrongdoings.
9 Extol the LORD our God,
   and worship at his holy mountain;
   for the LORD our God is holy.

All Lands Summoned to Praise God

A Psalm of thanksgiving.

100 Make a joyful noise to the LORD,
   all the earth.
2 Worship the LORD with gladness;
   come into his presence with singing.

3 Know that the LORD is God.
   It is he that made us, and we are his;[b]
   we are his people, and the sheep of his
   pasture.

4 Enter his gates with thanksgiving,
   and his courts with praise.
   Give thanks to him, bless his name.

5 For the LORD is good;
   his steadfast love endures forever,
   and his faithfulness to all generations.

---

a Cn: Heb *And a king's strength*   b Another reading is *and not
we ourselves*

Vindication, or righteousness. **98.4–8** Reiterated summons to the praise of God by the whole earth, the created order (cf. Ps 148) and its inhabitants. **98.9** The reason for all this praise is now given. It is in anticipation of the appearance of God to rule righteously over the earth and its peoples. Cf. 96.13; 97.2.
99.1–9 A hymn in praise of God's holy and righteous rule. See note on 93.1–5. Each stanza concludes with a call to praise God, who is holy. **99.1–3** Praise of God the great ruler. **99.1** *The LORD is king.* See note on 93.1–2. *Enthroned upon the cherubim.* See note on 80.1. **99.4–5** Praise for God's justice and righteousness. **99.5** *Footstool*, either the ark on Mount Zion or Mount Zion itself (1 Chr 28.2; Ps 132.7; cf. Isa 66.1). **99.6–9** Praise for God's forgiving response to the intercessors for Israel. For Moses' intercession, see Ex

32.11–14; Deut 9.26–29. Aaron is given the responsibility of praying for God's blessing upon the people (Num 6.22–26). Samuel cried out to the Lord for the people in the face of the Philistines, and the Lord answered him (1 Sam 7.9). Cf. Jer 15.1.
100.1–5 A hymn of praise and thanksgiving for the goodness of the Lord. **100.1–3** A summons to worship and praise (vv. 1–2) because of God's shepherding care of the people (v. 3). **100.4–5** A further summons to thanksgiving and praise because of God's goodness and faithfulness. These verses are a reflection of the prayer of thanksgiving in its essence, quoted in some form when reference is made to the people or the priests praising or giving thanks (106.1; 107.1; 118.1, 29; 136.1; 2 Chr 5.13; 7.3, 6; 20.21; Ezra 3.10–11). **100.4** *Bless.* See note on 103.1–2.

A Sovereign's Pledge of Integrity and Justice

Of David. A Psalm.

101 I will sing of loyalty and of justice;
to you, O LORD, I will sing.
2 I will study the way that is blameless.
When shall I attain it?

I will walk with integrity of heart
within my house;
3 I will not set before my eyes
anything that is base.

I hate the work of those who fall away;
it shall not cling to me.
4 Perverseness of heart shall be far from
me;
I will know nothing of evil.

5 One who secretly slanders a neighbor
I will destroy.
A haughty look and an arrogant
heart
I will not tolerate.

6 I will look with favor on the faithful in
the land,
so that they may live with me;
whoever walks in the way that is
blameless
shall minister to me.

7 No one who practices deceit
shall remain in my house;
no one who utters lies
shall continue in my presence.

8 Morning by morning I will destroy
all the wicked in the land,
cutting off all evildoers
from the city of the LORD.

Prayer to the Eternal King for Help

A prayer of one afflicted, when faint and
pleading before the LORD.

102 Hear my prayer, O LORD;
let my cry come to you.
2 Do not hide your face from me
in the day of my distress.
Incline your ear to me;
answer me speedily in the day when I
call.

3 For my days pass away like smoke,
and my bones burn like a furnace.
4 My heart is stricken and withered like
grass;
I am too wasted to eat my bread.
5 Because of my loud groaning
my bones cling to my skin.
6 I am like an owl of the wilderness,
like a little owl of the waste places.
7 I lie awake;
I am like a lonely bird on the housetop.
8 All day long my enemies taunt me;
those who deride me use my name for
a curse.
9 For I eat ashes like bread,
and mingle tears with my drink,
10 because of your indignation and anger;
for you have lifted me up and thrown
me aside.
11 My days are like an evening shadow;
I wither away like grass.

12 But you, O LORD, are enthroned forever;
your name endures to all generations.
13 You will rise up and have compassion on
Zion,
for it is time to favor it;
the appointed time has come.
14 For your servants hold its stones dear,
and have pity on its dust.

101.1–8 A royal psalm expressing the commitment of the ruler to a just rule. It may have been used at the king's coronation. 101.1 A hymnic introduction by the king. 101.2 The king's vow of integrity and blameless conduct. 101.3–8 The ruler vows to support the righteous and eliminate all such manifestations of wickedness as perversity, evil, slander, arrogance, and deceit. 101.8 *Morning by morning*. The king administered justice in the morning (2 Sam 15.2; Jer 21.12; cf. 1 Kings 3.16–28; Ps 72; Isa 11.4). *The city of the LORD*, Jerusalem.
102.1–28 A prayer for help by one whose situation

is well described in the superscription. One of the penitential psalms (see note on 6.1–10). 102.1–2 A plea for help. 102.2 *Hide your face*. See notes on 10.1; 27.9. 102.3–11 A lament over personal suffering including physical and emotional distress (vv. 3–7, 9, 11), the taunts of enemies (v. 8), and the affliction of God's wrath (v. 10). 102.8 *Taunt*. See note on 79.10. 102.12–22 Hymnic in form, these verses express the confidence of the psalmist, who is anticipating and declaring that God will restore Zion. The individual suffering of the psalmist is joined with the larger suffering of

15 The nations will fear the name of the
        LORD,
    and all the kings of the earth your
        glory.
16 For the LORD will build up Zion;
    he will appear in his glory.
17 He will regard the prayer of the destitute,
    and will not despise their prayer.

18 Let this be recorded for a generation to
        come,
    so that a people yet unborn may praise
        the LORD:
19 that he looked down from his holy
        height,
    from heaven the LORD looked at the
        earth,
20 to hear the groans of the prisoners,
    to set free those who were doomed to
        die;
21 so that the name of the LORD may be
        declared in Zion,
    and his praise in Jerusalem,
22 when peoples gather together,
    and kingdoms, to worship the LORD.

23 He has broken my strength in midcourse;
    he has shortened my days.
24 "O my God," I say, "do not take me away
        at the midpoint of my life,
    you whose years endure
        throughout all generations."

25 Long ago you laid the foundation of the
        earth,
    and the heavens are the work of your
        hands.
26 They will perish, but you endure;
    they will all wear out like a garment.
    You change them like clothing, and they
        pass away;
27   but you are the same, and your years
        have no end.

28 The children of your servants shall live
        secure;
    their offspring shall be established in
        your presence.

Thanksgiving for God's Goodness

Of David.

103 Bless the LORD, O my soul,
        and all that is within me,
    bless his holy name.
2 Bless the LORD, O my soul,
    and do not forget all his benefits—
3 who forgives all your iniquity,
    who heals all your diseases,
4 who redeems your life from the Pit,
    who crowns you with steadfast love
        and mercy,
5 who satisfies you with good as long as
        you live [a]
    so that your youth is renewed like the
        eagle's.

6 The LORD works vindication
    and justice for all who are oppressed.
7 He made known his ways to Moses,
    his acts to the people of Israel.
8 The LORD is merciful and gracious,
    slow to anger and abounding in
        steadfast love.
9 He will not always accuse,
    nor will he keep his anger forever.
10 He does not deal with us according to our
        sins,
    nor repay us according to our
        iniquities.
11 For as the heavens are high above the
        earth,
    so great is his steadfast love toward
        those who fear him;
12 as far as the east is from the west,

_____
a Meaning of Heb uncertain

an exiled people. **102.23–24** Return to lament over
God's affliction of the sufferer. **102.25–28** The confidence of the psalmist is once again expressed in praise,
here of the God who, in the midst of transiency,
change, and insecurity, endures forever and does not
change. **102.25–27** Quoted in Heb 1.10–12.
    103.1–22 A hymn of praise that may have func-
tioned as a song of thanksgiving for one who had been
helped by God. **103.1–2** The psalmist's self-exhortation to give thanks to God. *Bless* is one of the charac-

teristic terms for expressing gratitude to God. See, e.g.,
28.6–7; 31.21; 66.20. **103.3–5** Hymnic description of
the benefits (v. 2) from God. They are generalized and
universalized for the whole congregation but may reflect the particular benefits the psalmist has experienced in answer to prayer. **103.4** *Pit.* See note on 16.10,
but cf. note on 9.15. **103.5b** Cf. Isa 40.31. **103.6–**
18 Praise of God's grace and mercy showered upon the
people throughout their history. **103.8** Quotation of
the ancient confession of Ex 34.6. Cf. Num 14.18; Neh

so far he removes our transgressions
  from us.

13 As a father has compassion for his children,
  so the LORD has compassion for those
  who fear him.

14 For he knows how we were made;
  he remembers that we are dust.

15 As for mortals, their days are like grass;
  they flourish like a flower of the field;

16 for the wind passes over it, and it is gone,
  and its place knows it no more.

17 But the steadfast love of the LORD is from
  everlasting to everlasting
  on those who fear him,
  and his righteousness to children's
  children,

18 to those who keep his covenant
  and remember to do his
  commandments.

19 The LORD has established his throne in
  the heavens,
  and his kingdom rules over all.

20 Bless the LORD, O you his angels,
  you mighty ones who do his bidding,
  obedient to his spoken word.

21 Bless the LORD, all his hosts,
  his ministers that do his will.

22 Bless the LORD, all his works,
  in all places of his dominion.
  Bless the LORD, O my soul.

God the Creator and Provider

104 Bless the LORD, O my soul.
  O LORD my God, you are very
  great.
  You are clothed with honor and majesty,
2   wrapped in light as with a garment.
  You stretch out the heavens like a tent,
3   you set the beams of your[a] chambers
  on the waters,

you make the clouds your[a] chariot,
  you ride on the wings of the wind,
4 you make the winds your[a] messengers,
  fire and flame your[a] ministers.

5 You set the earth on its foundations,
  so that it shall never be shaken.
6 You cover it with the deep as with a
  garment;
  the waters stood above the mountains.
7 At your rebuke they flee;
  at the sound of your thunder they take
  to flight.
8 They rose up to the mountains, ran down
  to the valleys
  to the place that you appointed for
  them.
9 You set a boundary that they may not
  pass,
  so that they might not again cover the
  earth.

10 You make springs gush forth in the
  valleys;
  they flow between the hills,
11 giving drink to every wild animal;
  the wild asses quench their thirst.
12 By the streams[b] the birds of the air have
  their habitation;
  they sing among the branches.
13 From your lofty abode you water the
  mountains;
  the earth is satisfied with the fruit of
  your work.

14 You cause the grass to grow for the cattle,
  and plants for people to use,[c]
  to bring forth food from the earth,
15   and wine to gladden the human heart,
  oil to make the face shine,

---

a Heb his b Heb By them c Or to cultivate

9.17, 31; Jon 4.2. **103.11** *Fear him* (also vv. 13, 17). See note on 34.7. **103.15–17** Cf. 90.5–6; Isa 40.7–8. **103.19–22** The psalmist's concluding call to all creation to give praise and thanks to the gracious ruler of all. **103.20–21** *Angels, mighty ones, hosts, ministers,* the heavenly hosts, the members of the divine assembly who make up the heavenly court of the Lord (see note on 82.1–8).
  104.1–35 A hymn in praise of God the creator (cf. Pss 8; 19; 33). The psalm has similarities with both the Egyptian *Hymn to Aten* ("Hymn to the Sun Disk") and

Gen 1. **104.1–4** God the creator of the heavens. **104.1** Cf. v. 35; 103.1, 22b. **104.3–4** See note on 68.4. **104.4** Quoted in Heb 1.7. **104.5–9** God the creator of the earth. God gives stability to the earth and orders the unruly, chaotic waters. **104.6** The primeval waters covered the earth. **104.7** Echoes of God's victory over the watery chaos are heard here; see notes on 74.12–17; 93.3–4. **104.8** *Rose up to the mountains,* i.e., became mountain streams. **104.10–18** By means of the controlled waters, God refreshes and sustains the earth and its creatures. **104.12** Jesus' parable of the mustard

and bread to strengthen the human
    heart.

16 The trees of the LORD are watered
    abundantly,
    the cedars of Lebanon that he planted.

17 In them the birds build their nests;
    the stork has its home in the fir trees.

18 The high mountains are for the wild goats;
    the rocks are a refuge for the coneys.

19 You have made the moon to mark the
    seasons;
    the sun knows its time for setting.

20 You make darkness, and it is night,
    when all the animals of the forest come
    creeping out.

21 The young lions roar for their prey,
    seeking their food from God.

22 When the sun rises, they withdraw
    and lie down in their dens.

23 People go out to their work
    and to their labor until the evening.

24 O LORD, how manifold are your works!
    In wisdom you have made them all;
    the earth is full of your creatures.

25 Yonder is the sea, great and wide,
    creeping things innumerable are there,
    living things both small and great.

26 There go the ships,
    and Leviathan that you formed to
    sport in it.

27 These all look to you
    to give them their food in due season;

28 when you give to them, they gather it up;
    when you open your hand, they are
    filled with good things.

29 When you hide your face, they are
    dismayed;

when you take away their breath, they
    die
    and return to their dust.

30 When you send forth your spirit,[a] they
    are created;
    and you renew the face of the ground.

31 May the glory of the LORD endure forever;
    may the LORD rejoice in his works—

32 who looks on the earth and it trembles,
    who touches the mountains and they
    smoke.

33 I will sing to the LORD as long as I live;
    I will sing praise to my God while I
    have being.

34 May my meditation be pleasing to him,
    for I rejoice in the LORD.

35 Let sinners be consumed from the earth,
    and let the wicked be no more.
Bless the LORD, O my soul.
Praise the LORD!

God's Faithfulness to Israel

105 O give thanks to the LORD, call on
    his name,
    make known his deeds among the
    peoples.

2 Sing to him, sing praises to him;
    tell of all his wonderful works.

3 Glory in his holy name;
    let the hearts of those who seek the
    LORD rejoice.

4 Seek the LORD and his strength;
    seek his presence continually.

5 Remember the wonderful works he has
    done,

_____
a Or your breath

seed evokes this reference to where the *birds* find *habitation.* Cf. Mt 13.32; Mk 4.32; Lk 13.19. **104.15** *Oil,* used to protect and heal, was also a sign of gladness (45.7). **104.16** *Cedars of Lebanon.* See note on 92.12. **104.17–18** The watered and flourishing trees and mountains are a home for the wild animals. **104.19– 23** God, the provider of times and seasons, orders the lives of all creatures. **104.24** A summary affirmation and praise. **104.25–26** The sea as a place of other creatures and human transportation. **104.26** *Leviathan,* elsewhere one of the monsters of chaos defeated by God (see note on 74.13–15), is here simply one of God's playful creatures. **104.27–30** The dependence upon God of everything created. **104.31–35** Concluding exultation and praise. The joy of God in the cre-

ation (v. 31) is echoed in the joy of the creatures in God (v. 34). **104.34** See 19.14; 119.108. **104.35** In God's marvelous creation there is no place for the perversion of it by the presence of sin and wickedness. The psalm sustains to its end the vision of God's good creation.

    105.1–45 A hymn of praise for God's wonderful deeds in the history of the people Israel (cf. Ps 78). It has its negative counterpart in the history of sin and judgment in Ps 106. Part of this psalm (vv. 1–15) appears in the context of the community's worship in 1 Chr 16.8–22. **105.1–6** Call to the people to give thanks to God for the wonderful works on their behalf. Declaration of what God has done is a standard part of thanksgiving in the psalms (cf. 18.16–19; 22.22–24;

his miracles, and the judgments he has
    uttered,
6 O offspring of his servant Abraham,[a]
    children of Jacob, his chosen ones.

7 He is the LORD our God;
    his judgments are in all the earth.
8 He is mindful of his covenant forever,
    of the word that he commanded, for a
      thousand generations,
9 the covenant that he made with
    Abraham,
    his sworn promise to Isaac,
10 which he confirmed to Jacob as a statute,
    to Israel as an everlasting covenant,
11 saying, "To you I will give the land of
    Canaan
    as your portion for an inheritance."

12 When they were few in number,
    of little account, and strangers in it,
13 wandering from nation to nation,
    from one kingdom to another people,
14 he allowed no one to oppress them;
    he rebuked kings on their account,
15 saying, "Do not touch my anointed ones;
    do my prophets no harm."

16 When he summoned famine against the
    land,
    and broke every staff of bread,
17 he had sent a man ahead of them,
    Joseph, who was sold as a slave.
18 His feet were hurt with fetters,
    his neck was put in a collar of iron;
19 until what he had said came to pass,
    the word of the LORD kept testing him.
20 The king sent and released him;
    the ruler of the peoples set him free.
21 He made him lord of his house,
    and ruler of all his possessions,
22 to instruct[b] his officials at his pleasure,
    and to teach his elders wisdom.

23 Then Israel came to Egypt;
    Jacob lived as an alien in the land of
    Ham.
24 And the LORD made his people very
    fruitful,
    and made them stronger than their
      foes,
25 whose hearts he then turned to hate his
    people,
    to deal craftily with his servants.
26 He sent his servant Moses,
    and Aaron whom he had chosen.
27 They performed his signs among them,
    and miracles in the land of Ham.
28 He sent darkness, and made the land
    dark;
    they rebelled[c] against his words.
29 He turned their waters into blood,
    and caused their fish to die.
30 Their land swarmed with frogs,
    even in the chambers of their kings.
31 He spoke, and there came swarms of flies,
    and gnats throughout their country.
32 He gave them hail for rain,
    and lightning that flashed through
      their land.
33 He struck their vines and fig trees,
    and shattered the trees of their country.
34 He spoke, and the locusts came,
    and young locusts without number;
35 they devoured all the vegetation in their
    land,
    and ate up the fruit of their ground.
36 He struck down all the firstborn in their
    land,
    the first issue of all their strength.

37 Then he brought Israel[d] out with silver
    and gold,

---

a Another reading is *Israel* (compare 1 Chr 16.13) b Gk Syr
Jerome: Heb *to bind* c Cn Compare Gk Syr: Heb *they did not
rebel* d Heb *them*

30.1–3). **105.7–11** Praise for God's faithfulness to
the eternal covenant with Israel. **105.9** See Gen 15.18–
21; 26.3–5. **105.10** See Gen 28.13–15; 35.11–12.
105.11 *Inheritance,* a hereditary allotment to be
handed down through the generations. **105.12–45** A
recounting of God's faithfulness from the time of the
fathers and mothers (vv. 12–15; cf. Gen 12–36)
through the story of Joseph's slavery in Egypt (vv. 16–
19; cf. Gen 37; 39.1–40.36) and his leadership in time
of famine (vv. 20–22; cf. Gen 40.37–50.26), the multiplication of the Hebrews in Egypt (vv. 23–25; cf. Ex

1.1–22), the calling of Moses and Aaron to lead the
people out of slavery (vv. 26–27; cf. Ex 2.1–6.30), the
plagues in Egypt (vv. 28–36; cf. Ex 7.8–12.32), the exodus (vv. 37–38; cf. Ex 12.33–15.21), care during the
wandering in the wilderness (vv. 39–42; cf. Ex 15.22–
Num 36.13), and the entry into Canaan (vv. 43–45; cf.
Josh 1.1–24.33). **105.14** *Rebuked kings.* See Gen 12.17;
20.3. **105.15** *Anointed ones,* here those chosen or
called, specifically Abraham, Isaac, and Jacob, not
kings or messianic leaders. *Prophets.* See Gen 20.7.
105.23 *Ham,* the ancestor of the Egyptians in biblical

and there was no one among their
tribes who stumbled.
38 Egypt was glad when they departed,
for dread of them had fallen upon it.
39 He spread a cloud for a covering,
and fire to give light by night.
40 They asked, and he brought quails,
and gave them food from heaven in
abundance.
41 He opened the rock, and water gushed out;
it flowed through the desert like a river.
42 For he remembered his holy promise,
and Abraham, his servant.

43 So he brought his people out with joy,
his chosen ones with singing.
44 He gave them the lands of the nations,
and they took possession of the wealth
of the peoples,
45 that they might keep his statutes
and observe his laws.
Praise the Lord!

A Confession of Israel's Sins

106 Praise the Lord!
O give thanks to the Lord, for he is
good;
for his steadfast love endures forever.
2 Who can utter the mighty doings of the
Lord,
or declare all his praise?
3 Happy are those who observe justice,
who do righteousness at all times.

4 Remember me, O Lord, when you show
favor to your people;

help me when you deliver them;
5 that I may see the prosperity of your
chosen ones,
that I may rejoice in the gladness of
your nation,
that I may glory in your heritage.

6 Both we and our ancestors have sinned;
we have committed iniquity, have done
wickedly.
7 Our ancestors, when they were in Egypt,
did not consider your wonderful works;
they did not remember the abundance of
your steadfast love,
but rebelled against the Most High[a] at
the Red Sea.[b]
8 Yet he saved them for his name's sake,
so that he might make known his
mighty power.
9 He rebuked the Red Sea,[b] and it became
dry;
he led them through the deep as
through a desert.
10 So he saved them from the hand of the
foe,
and delivered them from the hand of
the enemy.
11 The waters covered their adversaries;
not one of them was left.
12 Then they believed his words;
they sang his praise.

13 But they soon forgot his works;
they did not wait for his counsel.

---

a Cn Compare 78.17, 56: Heb *rebelled at the sea*   b Or *Sea of Reeds*

---

tradition (Gen 10.6). **105.37** *Silver and gold.* See Ex 3.21–22; 11.2; 12.35–36. *No one . . . stumbled,* i.e., all were kept from harm as they left by God's guidance and providence. **105.45** This is what the book of Deuteronomy is about, providing *statutes* and *laws* for life in the land and exhorting the people to follow them.

106.1–48 A hymn of praise to the Lord who has remained faithful to God's people despite a long history of sin and apostasy (vv. 1–3, 6–46) together with petitions for God's continued help in present distress (vv. 4–5, 47). Contrasting with the history of salvation recounted in the preceding psalm, this psalm recounts, penitentially (v. 6), the story of the frequent sins of the people (vv. 6–7, 13–14, 16, 19–22, 28–29, 32–39, 43b) and the consequent judgment by God (vv. 15, 17–18, 26–27, 29, 40–42, 43c), who, nevertheless, dealt compassionately with them, protecting and delivering them

time and again (vv. 8–12, 23, 30–31, 43a, 44–46) because of the covenant and God's own loving nature (vv. 44–45). That history, therefore, is the ground for continued pleas for help as well as praise and thanksgiving (vv. 47–48). Like Ps 105, parts of this psalm (vv. 1, 47–48) also appear in the context of the community's worship in 1 Chr 16.34–36. **106.1–3** The psalm begins, as it ends, in praise and thanks to God. **106.1** The paradigms of praise and thanksgiving are to be found here in the Hallelujah, or "Praise the Lord" (33.2; 104.35; 105.45; 106.48; 111.1; 112.1; and *passim;* Jer 20.13; Rom 15.11), and in the rest of this verse (see 107.1; 118.1, 29; 136.1; 1 Chr 16.34; 2 Chr 5.13; 7.3; 20.21; Ezra 3.11; Jer 33.11; Sir 51 [Hebrew additions]). **106.3** *Happy.* See note on 1.1. **106.4–5** The plea of the psalmist for help is placed in the context of the prayer for deliverance of the community, anticipating the petitions of v. 47. **106.7** *Rebelled . . . Red Sea.* See Ex 14.10–

14 But they had a wanton craving in the
        wilderness,
    and put God to the test in the desert;
15 he gave them what they asked,
    but sent a wasting disease among
        them.

16 They were jealous of Moses in the camp,
    and of Aaron, the holy one of the
        LORD.
17 The earth opened and swallowed up
        Dathan,
    and covered the faction of Abiram.
18 Fire also broke out in their company;
    the flame burned up the wicked.

19 They made a calf at Horeb
    and worshiped a cast image.
20 They exchanged the glory of God[a]
    for the image of an ox that eats grass.
21 They forgot God, their Savior,
    who had done great things in Egypt,
22 wondrous works in the land of Ham,
    and awesome deeds by the Red Sea.[b]
23 Therefore he said he would destroy
        them—
    had not Moses, his chosen one,
    stood in the breach before him,
        to turn away his wrath from destroying
            them.

24 Then they despised the pleasant land,
    having no faith in his promise.
25 They grumbled in their tents,
    and did not obey the voice of the LORD.
26 Therefore he raised his hand and swore to
        them
    that he would make them fall in the
        wilderness,
27 and would disperse[c] their descendants
        among the nations,
    scattering them over the lands.

28 Then they attached themselves to the Baal
        of Peor,
    and ate sacrifices offered to the dead;
29 they provoked the LORD to anger with
        their deeds,

and a plague broke out among them.
30 Then Phinehas stood up and interceded,
    and the plague was stopped.
31 And that has been reckoned to him as
        righteousness
    from generation to generation forever.

32 They angered the LORD[d] at the waters of
        Meribah,
    and it went ill with Moses on their
        account;
33 for they made his spirit bitter,
    and he spoke words that were rash.

34 They did not destroy the peoples,
    as the LORD commanded them,
35 but they mingled with the nations
    and learned to do as they did.
36 They served their idols,
    which became a snare to them.
37 They sacrificed their sons
    and their daughters to the demons;
38 they poured out innocent blood,
    the blood of their sons and daughters,
    whom they sacrificed to the idols of
        Canaan;
    and the land was polluted with blood.
39 Thus they became unclean by their acts,
    and prostituted themselves in their
        doings.

40 Then the anger of the LORD was kindled
        against his people,
    and he abhorred his heritage;
41 he gave them into the hand of the
        nations,
    so that those who hated them ruled
        over them.
42 Their enemies oppressed them,
    and they were brought into subjection
        under their power.
43 Many times he delivered them,
    but they were rebellious in their
        purposes,

---

a Compare Gk Mss: Heb *exchanged their glory*   *b* Or *Sea of
Reeds*   *c* Syr Compare Ezek 20.23: Heb *cause to fall*   *d* Heb *him*

---

12. **106.9** *Rebuked.* See note on 104.7. **106.13–15** See
Num 11.4–6, 31–35. **106.16–18** See Num 16. **106.19–
23** See Ex 32. **106.19** *Horeb* is the alternate name for
Mount Sinai. **106.24–27** See Num 14.1–35. **106.28–
31** See Num 25.1–13. **106.32–33** See Ex 17.1–7; Num

20.2–13. **106.34–39** Israel's sins during the period of
the judges and later. **106.34** *As the LORD commanded
them.* See Deut 7.1–5; 20.16–18. **106.36** *Snare.* See Ex
23.32–33. **106.37–38** See 2 Kings 16.3; 21.6; 23.10.
106.41 *Gave them . . . nations.* See Judg 6.1; 13.1.

and were brought low through their
    iniquity.
44 Nevertheless he regarded their distress
    when he heard their cry.
45 For their sake he remembered his
    covenant,
    and showed compassion according to
        the abundance of his steadfast love.
46 He caused them to be pitied
    by all who held them captive.

47 Save us, O LORD our God,
    and gather us from among the nations,
    that we may give thanks to your holy
        name
    and glory in your praise.

48 Blessed be the LORD, the God of Israel,
    from everlasting to everlasting.
    And let all the people say, "Amen."
    Praise the LORD!

BOOK V: PSALMS 107–150

Thanksgiving for Deliverance from Many Troubles

107 O give thanks to the LORD, for he is good;
    for his steadfast love endures forever.
2 Let the redeemed of the LORD say so,
    those he redeemed from trouble
3 and gathered in from the lands,
    from the east and from the west,
    from the north and from the south.[a]

4 Some wandered in desert wastes,
    finding no way to an inhabited town;
5 hungry and thirsty,
    their soul fainted within them.
6 Then they cried to the LORD in their
        trouble,

and he delivered them from their
    distress;
7 he led them by a straight way,
    until they reached an inhabited town.
8 Let them thank the LORD for his steadfast
    love,
    for his wonderful works to
        humankind.
9 For he satisfies the thirsty,
    and the hungry he fills with good
        things.

10 Some sat in darkness and in gloom,
    prisoners in misery and in irons,
11 for they had rebelled against the words of
        God,
    and spurned the counsel of the Most
        High.
12 Their hearts were bowed down with hard
        labor;
    they fell down, with no one to help.
13 Then they cried to the LORD in their
        trouble,
    and he saved them from their distress;
14 he brought them out of darkness and
        gloom,
    and broke their bonds asunder.
15 Let them thank the LORD for his steadfast
    love,
    for his wonderful works to
        humankind.
16 For he shatters the doors of bronze,
    and cuts in two the bars of iron.

17 Some were sick[b] through their sinful
    ways,
    and because of their iniquities endured
        affliction;
18 they loathed any kind of food,

_____
a Cn: Heb *sea*   *b* Cn: Heb *fools*

106.44 *Heard their cry.* See Judg 3.9, 15; 4.3; 6.7; 10.10–16. **106.47** *Gather us... nations* suggests that the psalm was composed during the time of exile or later, when the people were dispersed among different nations, e.g., Babylon and Egypt. **106.48** A doxology closing the fourth book of the Psalter (Pss 90–106). See note on 41.13. *Blessed.* See note on 103.1–2.
    107.1–32 A liturgy of thanksgiving. Four different distressful situations are described (vv. 4–5, 10–12, 17–18, 23–27). In each case the psalmist recounts how those in peril cried out to the Lord, i.e., prayed (vv. 6a, 13a, 19a, 28a), and God delivered them (vv. 6b–7,

13b–14, 19b–20, 28b–29). Because of this they are now called to give thanks and praise (vv. 8–9, 15–16, 21–22, 31–32). **107.1–3** Introductory general call to give thanks. **107.1** This verse of the general call to give thanks is echoed in the particular calls that follow (vv. 8, 15, 21, 31). See note on 106.1. **107.2–3** These verses may have in mind the exiles who have been freed from Babylonian captivity and returned home. *Redeemed of the LORD.* See Isa 62.12. **107.4–9** Thanksgiving of those delivered from the dangers of thirst and starvation in the desert. **107.10–16** Thanksgiving of freed prisoners. **107.17–22** Thanksgiving of those healed

and they drew near to the gates of
    death.
19 Then they cried to the LORD in their
    trouble,
    and he saved them from their distress;
20 he sent out his word and healed them,
    and delivered them from destruction.
21 Let them thank the LORD for his steadfast
    love,
    for his wonderful works to humankind.
22 And let them offer thanksgiving
    sacrifices,
    and tell of his deeds with songs of joy.

23 Some went down to the sea in ships,
    doing business on the mighty waters;
24 they saw the deeds of the LORD,
    his wondrous works in the deep.
25 For he commanded and raised the stormy
    wind,
    which lifted up the waves of the sea.
26 They mounted up to heaven, they went
    down to the depths;
    their courage melted away in their
    calamity;
27 they reeled and staggered like drunkards,
    and were at their wits' end.
28 Then they cried to the LORD in their
    trouble,
    and he brought them out from their
    distress;
29 he made the storm be still,
    and the waves of the sea were hushed.
30 Then they were glad because they had
    quiet,
    and he brought them to their desired
    haven.
31 Let them thank the LORD for his steadfast
    love,
    for his wonderful works to humankind.
32 Let them extol him in the congregation of
    the people,
    and praise him in the assembly of the
    elders.

33 He turns rivers into a desert,
    springs of water into thirsty ground,

34 a fruitful land into a salty waste,
    because of the wickedness of its
    inhabitants.
35 He turns a desert into pools of water,
    a parched land into springs of water.
36 And there he lets the hungry live,
    and they establish a town to live in;
37 they sow fields, and plant vineyards,
    and get a fruitful yield.
38 By his blessing they multiply greatly,
    and he does not let their cattle
    decrease.

39 When they are diminished and brought
    low
    through oppression, trouble, and
    sorrow,
40 he pours contempt on princes
    and makes them wander in trackless
    wastes;
41 but he raises up the needy out of distress,
    and makes their families like flocks.
42 The upright see it and are glad;
    and all wickedness stops its mouth.
43 Let those who are wise give heed to these
    things,
    and consider the steadfast love of the
    LORD.

Praise and Prayer for Victory

A Song. A Psalm of David.

108 My heart is steadfast, O God, my
heart is steadfast;[a]
I will sing and make melody.
Awake, my soul![b]
2 Awake, O harp and lyre!
    I will awake the dawn.
3 I will give thanks to you, O LORD, among
    the peoples,
    and I will sing praises to you among
    the nations.
4 For your steadfast love is higher than the
    heavens,

---

a Heb Mss Gk Syr: MT lacks *my heart is steadfast* b Compare
57.8: Heb *also my soul*

---

and forgiven. **107.22** Here a specific call is made to
offer sacrifices of thanksgiving (66.13–15; 116.17) and
bear witness to God's salvation (18.49–50; 22.22; 40.9;
66.16–19). **107.23–32** Thanksgiving of those saved
from the dangers of the sea. **107.32** Thanksgiving to
God was rendered in the midst of the gathered congregation (22.22–25; 40.9–10; 116.18). **107.33–43** A
hymn of praise for God's provision for the hungry and
needy, which forms a fitting conclusion to the liturgy
of thanksgiving in vv. 1–32. **107.35** Cf. Isa 41.17–18.
107.39–41 Cf. 1 Sam 2.4–8.
108.1–5 The same as (see note on) 57.7–11.

and your faithfulness reaches to the
  clouds.

5 Be exalted, O God, above the heavens,
  and let your glory be over all the earth.
6 Give victory with your right hand, and
    answer me,
  so that those whom you love may be
    rescued.

7 God has promised in his sanctuary:[a]
  "With exultation I will divide up
    Shechem,
  and portion out the Vale of Succoth.
8 Gilead is mine; Manasseh is mine;
  Ephraim is my helmet;
  Judah is my scepter.
9 Moab is my washbasin;
  on Edom I hurl my shoe;
  over Philistia I shout in triumph."

10 Who will bring me to the fortified city?
  Who will lead me to Edom?
11 Have you not rejected us, O God?
  You do not go out, O God, with our
    armies.
12 O grant us help against the foe,
  for human help is worthless.
13 With God we shall do valiantly;
  it is he who will tread down our foes.

Prayer for Vindication and Vengeance

To the leader. Of David. A Psalm.

109 Do not be silent, O God of my
  praise.
2 For wicked and deceitful mouths are
    opened against me,
  speaking against me with lying
    tongues.
3 They beset me with words of hate,

and attack me without cause.
4 In return for my love they accuse me,
  even while I make prayer for them.[b]
5 So they reward me evil for good,
  and hatred for my love.

6 They say,[c] "Appoint a wicked man against
    him;
  let an accuser stand on his right.
7 When he is tried, let him be found guilty;
  let his prayer be counted as sin.
8 May his days be few;
  may another seize his position.
9 May his children be orphans,
  and his wife a widow.
10 May his children wander about and beg;
  may they be driven out of[d] the ruins
    they inhabit.
11 May the creditor seize all that he has;
  may strangers plunder the fruits of his
    toil.
12 May there be no one to do him a
    kindness,
  nor anyone to pity his orphaned
    children.
13 May his posterity be cut off;
  may his name be blotted out in the
    second generation.
14 May the iniquity of his father[e] be
    remembered before the LORD,
  and do not let the sin of his mother be
    blotted out.
15 Let them be before the LORD continually,
  and may his[f] memory be cut off from
    the earth.
16 For he did not remember to show
    kindness,
  but pursued the poor and needy

---

a Or by his holiness b Syr: Heb I prayer c Heb lacks They say
d Gk: Heb and seek e Cn: Heb fathers f Gk: Heb their

108.6–13 The same as (see notes on) 60.5–12.
108.10 For a possible historical context, see note on
137.7.
  109.1–31 An individual prayer for help against enemies who have uttered false accusations and pronounced curses that endanger the life of the petitioner.
To the leader. See note on 4.1–8. **109.1** Cry for help.
109.2–5 Lament over the false accusations (cf. v. 20) and
hateful curses (cf. v. 28) rendered against the psalmist,
who has acted benevolently toward those who now persecute. The lament urges God's intervention. **109.6–
19** The lament continues as the accusation (v. 16) and
the curses (vv. 8–15, 17–19) that have been uttered

against the petitioner are now quoted. Because the
curses and accusation are directed against an individual
rather than a group, as in vv. 2–5, some, including the
NRSV (see text note c), see these verses as spoken by the
accusers of the psalmist. **109.6–7** The accusers have
called for a judicial process against the psalmist to prove
guilt and bring about a punishment of death (v. 31).
109.8 The phrase *seize his position* is cited at the replacement of Judas in Acts 1.20. **109.15b** Better translated according to text note *f*; the reference is to the family.
109.16 The false accusation is that the psalmist oppressed the poor and needy even to their death, and so
the curse is that the psalmist also shall not be treated

and the brokenhearted to their death.

17 He loved to curse; let curses come on
   him.
   He did not like blessing; may it be far
      from him.
18 He clothed himself with cursing as his
      coat,
   may it soak into his body like water,
   like oil into his bones.
19 May it be like a garment that he wraps
      around himself,
   like a belt that he wears every day."

20 May that be the reward of my accusers
      from the LORD,
   of those who speak evil against my life.
21 But you, O LORD my Lord,
   act on my behalf for your name's sake;
   because your steadfast love is good,
      deliver me.
22 For I am poor and needy,
   and my heart is pierced within me.
23 I am gone like a shadow at evening;
   I am shaken off like a locust.
24 My knees are weak through fasting;
   my body has become gaunt.
25 I am an object of scorn to my accusers;
   when they see me, they shake their
      heads.

26 Help me, O LORD my God!
   Save me according to your steadfast
      love.
27 Let them know that this is your hand;
   you, O LORD, have done it.
28 Let them curse, but you will bless.

Let my assailants be put to shame;[a]
   may your servant be glad.
29 May my accusers be clothed with dishonor;
   may they be wrapped in their own
      shame as in a mantle.
30 With my mouth I will give great thanks to
      the LORD;
   I will praise him in the midst of the
      throng.
31 For he stands at the right hand of the
      needy,
   to save them from those who would
      condemn them to death.

Assurance of Victory for God's Priest-King

Of David. A Psalm.

110 The LORD says to my lord,
   "Sit at my right hand
until I make your enemies your
   footstool."

2 The LORD sends out from Zion
   your mighty scepter.
   Rule in the midst of your foes.
3 Your people will offer themselves willingly
   on the day you lead your forces
   on the holy mountains.[b]
From the womb of the morning,
   like dew, your youth[c] will come to you.
4 The LORD has sworn and will not change
      his mind,

---

a Gk: Heb *They have risen up and have been put to shame*
b Another reading is *in holy splendor*   c Cn: Heb *the dew of your youth*

---

kindly (v. 12) and be pursued to death (v. 31). **109.17–19** Here, as in v. 12 (cf. v. 16a), the curses call for a punishment corresponding to the supposed crime. **109.20–29** The petitions of the psalmist asking God to stop the persecutors are couched in language somewhat similar to their curses and accusations (vv. 22, 28–29, 31). **109.20** This verse has been understood by some interpreters as concluding the preceding part, i.e., "This is the work of my accusers, those who speak evil against my life." **109.22** *For I am poor and needy*. Accused of having oppressed the *poor and needy* (v. 16), the psalmist is in the same state and so can claim God's help (cf. Ex 22.22–26). **109.30–31** Vow of praise and thanksgiving. **109.31** *He stands . . . the needy*, over against the efforts of the persecutors to place an accuser *on his right* (v. 6).
   110.1–7 A royal psalm declaring God's establishment of the ruling and priestly office of the king. The psalm probably originally had to do with rights and traditions given to the king at his enthronement in

Jerusalem. Textual problems prohibit a clear and certain reading of the text. **110.1** An oracle probably delivered by a prophetic or priestly figure. *My lord*, i.e., the king. *At my right hand* is a place of power and honor. The ruler here is the Lord (cf. 1 Kings 2.19). *Your footstool* refers to the practice of victorious kings placing their feet on the backs of captured enemies. The verse is frequently cited in the NT in reference to the exaltation of Christ; see Acts 2.34; 1 Cor 15.25; Heb 1.3, 13. It appears also in a controversy between Jesus and his opponents; see Mt 22.44; Mk 12.36; Lk 20.42. **110.2** The *scepter* of the king is given by God as a symbol of rule over enemies. **110.3** *On the day you lead your forces* probably should be read "On the day of your power," i.e., on the day of the king's enthronement. The second half of the verse may be another oracle referring to the divine adoption of the king: "From the womb of the morning, like dew I have begotten you" (cf. 2.7). *Dew*. Cf. 72.6. **110.4** An addi-

"You are a priest forever according to
the order of Melchizedek." [a]

5   The Lord is at your right hand;
       he will shatter kings on the day of his
          wrath.
6   He will execute judgment among the
          nations,
       filling them with corpses;
    he will shatter heads
       over the wide earth.
7   He will drink from the stream by the
          path;
       therefore he will lift up his head.

Praise for God's Wonderful Works

111 Praise the LORD!
       I will give thanks to the LORD with
          my whole heart,
       in the company of the upright, in the
          congregation.
2   Great are the works of the LORD,
       studied by all who delight in them.
3   Full of honor and majesty is his work,
       and his righteousness endures forever.
4   He has gained renown by his wonderful
          deeds;
       the LORD is gracious and merciful.
5   He provides food for those who fear him;
       he is ever mindful of his covenant.
6   He has shown his people the power of his
          works,
       in giving them the heritage of the
          nations.

7   The works of his hands are faithful and
          just;
       all his precepts are trustworthy.
8   They are established forever and ever,
       to be performed with faithfulness and
          uprightness.
9   He sent redemption to his people;
       he has commanded his covenant
          forever.
       Holy and awesome is his name.
10 The fear of the LORD is the beginning of
          wisdom;
       all those who practice it [b] have a good
          understanding.
       His praise endures forever.

Blessings of the Righteous

112 Praise the LORD!
       Happy are those who fear the LORD,
       who greatly delight in his
          commandments.
2   Their descendants will be mighty in the
          land;
       the generation of the upright will be
          blessed.
3   Wealth and riches are in their houses,
       and their righteousness endures
          forever.
4   They rise in the darkness as a light for the
          upright;
       they are gracious, merciful, and
          righteous.

---

a Or *forever, a rightful king by my edict*   *b* Gk Syr: Heb *them*

---

tional oracle giving the king priestly functions and
prerogatives (cf. 2 Sam 6.13–14, 18; 8.18; 24.25;
1 Kings 3.4; 8.14, 55). *Melchizedek,* a figure who seems
to have been a king of Jerusalem; he was called "priest
of God Most High" in the pre-Israelite era (Gen 14.17–
20). Israel seems to have taken over traditions from the
Jebusites, who inhabited Jerusalem prior to David's
conquest of the city (1 Sam 5.6–10). In the Letter to
the Hebrews, Jesus' priestly role is associated with
Melchizedek through citation of this verse (see Heb
5.6, 10; 6.20–7.10, 15–17). **110.5–6** God's defeat of
the enemies of the king. **110.7** The meaning of the
verse is uncertain, but it may refer to some ritual act of
the king at the enthronement.
    111.1–10 A hymn of praise and thanksgiving. Its
conclusion and its alphabetic acrostic form (see note
on 9.1–10.18) show that it was composed for instruction as well as praise. Although an individual voice
gives thanks, the psalm focuses on the wonderful
deeds of God for the people rather than the particular

way in which God has helped an individual, as is the
case in such psalms as Pss 18; 22; 30; 116. Ps 66 gives an
example of the combination of thanksgiving for the
works of God on behalf of the people and the help rendered to an individual in distress. **111.4** *The LORD . . .
merciful.* See note on 103.8. **111.5** *He is . . . covenant.*
See 105.8–10; 106.45. **111.6** *Heritage of the nations,*
presumably the land of Canaan, which was occupied
by various nations when Israel took the land.
111.10 See Job 28.28; Prov 1.7; 9.10. *Fear of the LORD.*
See note on 34.7.
    112.1–10 Instruction about the characteristics and
benefits of righteous living. Cf. Pss 1; 19; 119. Like Ps
111, with which this psalm shares various expressions
and vocabulary, Ps 112 is an alphabetic acrostic (see
note on 9.1–10.18). **112.1** *Happy.* See note on 1.1. *Fear
the LORD.* See note on 34.7. *Delight in his commandments.* See Ps 1.2. **112.4** *They are gracious, merciful.*
The righteous are seen to imitate the attributes of God
according to the ancient confession of Ex 34.6. Cf.

5 It is well with those who deal generously
        and lend,
    who conduct their affairs with justice.
6 For the righteous will never be moved;
    they will be remembered forever.
7 They are not afraid of evil tidings;
    their hearts are firm, secure in the
        LORD.
8 Their hearts are steady, they will not be
        afraid;
    in the end they will look in triumph on
        their foes.
9 They have distributed freely, they have
        given to the poor;
    their righteousness endures forever;
    their horn is exalted in honor.
10 The wicked see it and are angry;
    they gnash their teeth and melt away;
    the desire of the wicked comes to
        nothing.

God the Helper of the Needy

113 Praise the LORD!
    Praise, O servants of the LORD;
    praise the name of the LORD.

2 Blessed be the name of the LORD
    from this time on and forevermore.
3 From the rising of the sun to its setting
    the name of the LORD is to be praised.
4 The LORD is high above all nations,
    and his glory above the heavens.

5 Who is like the LORD our God,
    who is seated on high,
6 who looks far down
    on the heavens and the earth?
7 He raises the poor from the dust,
    and lifts the needy from the ash heap,

8 to make them sit with princes,
    with the princes of his people.
9 He gives the barren woman a home,
    making her the joyous mother of
        children.
Praise the LORD!

God's Wonders at the Exodus

114 When Israel went out from Egypt,
    the house of Jacob from a people
        of strange language,
2 Judah became God's[a] sanctuary,
    Israel his dominion.

3 The sea looked and fled;
    Jordan turned back.
4 The mountains skipped like rams,
    the hills like lambs.

5 Why is it, O sea, that you flee?
    O Jordan, that you turn back?
6 O mountains, that you skip like rams?
    O hills, like lambs?

7 Tremble, O earth, at the presence of the
        LORD,
    at the presence of the God of Jacob,
8 who turns the rock into a pool of water,
    the flint into a spring of water.

The Impotence of Idols and the Greatness of God

115 Not to us, O LORD, not to us, but
    to your name give glory,
    for the sake of your steadfast love and
        your faithfulness.

---

a Heb his

103.8; 111.4; 116.5. **112.6** See Ps 15, esp. v. 5b.
112.9 *Horn.* See note on 75.4–5. **112.10** As in Ps 1, the
wicked are contrasted with the righteous but are given
less attention. Like the chaff, with which they are compared in Ps 1, they are worthless and disappear.
    113.1–9 A hymn in praise of God, who does won-
derful things on behalf of the weak and needy. In Jewish tradition this is one of the "Egyptian Hallel"
("praise") psalms (Pss 113–118), sung before (Pss
113–114) and after (Pss 115–118) the Passover meal
(cf. Mt 26.30; Mk 14.26). Because of vv. 7–9 particularly, the song stands in a line of tradition with 1 Sam
2.1–10; Lk 1.46–55. **113.2** *Blessed.* See note on 103.1–
2. **113.5** Cf. Ex 15.11. **113.6** Cf. 14.2; 138.6. **113.7–
8** Cf. 1 Sam 2.8. **113.9** Cf. 1 Sam 2.5.

114.1–8 A hymn in praise of God's marvelous
power in bringing Israel out of slavery in Egypt and
across the Jordan into the promised land. One of the
Hallel psalms (see note on 113.1–9). **114.2** *Judah became God's sanctuary* suggests a date of composition
after Jerusalem had become the site of the central
sanctuary. **114.3–6** The miraculous phenomena of
nature during the exodus and the crossing of the Jordan are here given poetic interpretation as manifestations of divine power. *The sea . . . fled* refers to the turning back of the waters during the exodus. *Jordan
turned back.* Cf. Josh 3.14–17. **114.8** See Ex 17.6; Num
20.11.
    115.1–18 A liturgical prayer of the people. The
changing pattern of the personal pronouns suggests

2 Why should the nations say,
   "Where is their God?"

3 Our God is in the heavens;
   he does whatever he pleases.
4 Their idols are silver and gold,
   the work of human hands.
5 They have mouths, but do not speak;
   eyes, but do not see.
6 They have ears, but do not hear;
   noses, but do not smell.
7 They have hands, but do not feel;
   feet, but do not walk;
   they make no sound in their throats.
8 Those who make them are like them;
   so are all who trust in them.

9 O Israel, trust in the LORD!
   He is their help and their shield.
10 O house of Aaron, trust in the LORD!
   He is their help and their shield.
11 You who fear the LORD, trust in the
   LORD!
   He is their help and their shield.

12 The LORD has been mindful of us; he will
   bless us;
   he will bless the house of Israel;
   he will bless the house of Aaron;
13 he will bless those who fear the LORD,
   both small and great.

14 May the LORD give you increase,
   both you and your children.

15 May you be blessed by the LORD,
   who made heaven and earth.
16 The heavens are the LORD's heavens,
   but the earth he has given to human
   beings.
17 The dead do not praise the LORD,
   nor do any that go down into silence.
18 But we will bless the LORD
   from this time on and forevermore.
   Praise the LORD!

Thanksgiving for Recovery from Illness

116 I love the LORD, because he has
    heard
    my voice and my supplications.
2 Because he inclined his ear to me,
   therefore I will call on him as long as I
   live.
3 The snares of death encompassed me;
   the pangs of Sheol laid hold on me;
   I suffered distress and anguish.
4 Then I called on the name of the
   LORD:
   "O LORD, I pray, save my life!"

5 Gracious is the LORD, and righteous;
   our God is merciful.
6 The LORD protects the simple;
   when I was brought low, he saved me.
7 Return, O my soul, to your rest,
   for the LORD has dealt bountifully with
   you.

---

antiphonal or alternating speakers in the course of the prayer. One of the Hallel psalms (see note on 113.1–9). **115.1–2** The first verse ascribes glory to God, but the second is more of a complaint suggesting some experience of distress on the part of the people. Their situation is understood to be a challenge to God's glory and honor. Their words are therefore praise and a call for demonstration of God's glory. **115.2** *"Where is their God?"* See note on 79.10. **115.3–8** As a response to the taunt of the nations, Israel or a representative voice declares the vitality and power of the God of Israel over against the impotent idols worshiped by the nations. **115.9–11** A voice or voices follow up this claim by calling upon people and priests to trust in the Lord, whose power over the gods of the nations has just been described. **115.11** *Fear the LORD.* See note on 34.7 (cf. 115.13). Some interpret this as a reference to proselytes in the postexilic community (cf. 1 Kings 8.41–45; Isa 56.6; Acts 13.16, 26) as distinct from the Israelite laity (*O Israel,* v. 9) and priests (*O house of Aaron,* v. 10). **115.12–13** The people respond, express-

ing their confidence in God's blessing of them. It is possible, however, to understand these verses as the voice of a representative figure announcing that God has heard the prayer and will bless the people. **115.14–15** A priestly voice (cf. Num 6.22–27) prays a blessing prayer for the people. **115.16–18** Concluding hymn of praise by the people. **115.17** See note on 6.5. **115.18** *Bless.* See note on 103.1–2.
   116.1–19 A song of thanksgiving for God's help in time of distress. As in most of the prayers for help, the nature of the distress is not indicated except to say that the psalmist felt close to death (vv. 3, 8, 15). One of the Hallel psalms (see note on 113.1–9). **116.1–2** The basic word of gratitude because God has heard the prayer for help and delivered the sufferer. The testimony of the psalmist before the congregation (v. 18; cf. 22.22–25; 40.9–10; 107.32) begins at this point. **116.3–11** Testimony about the distress and God's deliverance. **116.3–4** The suffering and the prayer it evoked. **116.3** *Sheol.* See note on 6.5. **116.5–9** The graciousness of God manifest in the salvation of the suf-

8 For you have delivered my soul from death,
  my eyes from tears,
  my feet from stumbling.
9 I walk before the LORD
  in the land of the living.
10 I kept my faith, even when I said,
  "I am greatly afflicted";
11 I said in my consternation,
  "Everyone is a liar."

12 What shall I return to the LORD
  for all his bounty to me?
13 I will lift up the cup of salvation
  and call on the name of the LORD,
14 I will pay my vows to the LORD
  in the presence of all his people.
15 Precious in the sight of the LORD
  is the death of his faithful ones.
16 O LORD, I am your servant;
  I am your servant, the child of your
    serving girl.
  You have loosed my bonds.
17 I will offer to you a thanksgiving sacrifice
  and call on the name of the LORD.
18 I will pay my vows to the LORD
  in the presence of all his people,
19 in the courts of the house of the LORD,
  in your midst, O Jerusalem.
Praise the LORD!

Universal Call to Worship

117 Praise the LORD, all you nations!
    Extol him, all you peoples!

2 For great is his steadfast love toward us,
  and the faithfulness of the LORD
  endures forever.
Praise the LORD!

A Song of Victory

118 O give thanks to the LORD, for he is
    good;
  his steadfast love endures forever!

2 Let Israel say,
  "His steadfast love endures forever."
3 Let the house of Aaron say,
  "His steadfast love endures forever."
4 Let those who fear the LORD say,
  "His steadfast love endures forever."

5 Out of my distress I called on the
    LORD;
  the LORD answered me and set me in a
    broad place.
6 With the LORD on my side I do not fear.
  What can mortals do to me?
7 The LORD is on my side to help me;
  I shall look in triumph on those who
    hate me.
8 It is better to take refuge in the LORD
  than to put confidence in mortals.
9 It is better to take refuge in the LORD
  than to put confidence in princes.
10 All nations surrounded me;
  in the name of the LORD I cut them off!

---

ferer. **116.10–11** Looking back, the psalmist reports a continuing trust in God even when complaining and lamenting over affliction and persecution. *Everyone is a liar* may indicate that the distress was due to slander or a false accusation, or it may have been a general reaction of despair in the face of how everyone responded to the afflicted. **116.12–19** Fulfillment of the vow of thanksgiving that was part of the cry for help. **116.13** In worship the grateful psalmist now offers a libation and praises the name of the God who delivered. **116.15** The Lord cares about those who trust in the Lord and will seek to keep them from the defeat of death. **116.16** *Child of your serving girl.* See note on 86.16. **116.17** *Thanksgiving sacrifice.* Cf. 66.13–15; 107.22. **116.18–19** See note on 116.1–2.
117.1–2 A hymn of praise. One of the Hallel psalms (see note on 113.1–9). **117.1** Call to praise. For the praise of the *nations*, see 67.3–5; 68.32. **117.2** The reason for praise is God's overwhelming love manifested toward Israel. Cf. 126.2–3.
118.1–29 A liturgy of thanksgiving in which an individual comes to the temple to give thanks to God in

the context of the festival worship of the community. One of the Hallel psalms (see note on 113.1–9). **118.1–4** Call to praise. The short model of praise in v. 1 (cf. v. 29; note on 106.1) becomes a liturgical response in vv. 2–4 (cf. Ps 136). **118.2–4** See note on 115.11. **118.5–18** A song of thanksgiving of an individual who recounts the cry to the Lord in distress and how the Lord helped. Vv. 10–14, with their references to being surrounded by the nations, have suggested the possibility that the original speaker was a king. Although that is possible, a composition date after the exile would require a nonroyal speaker either using royal motifs or in some sense being beset by people of other nationalities. Nehemiah and the community of his time would be an example of this, though there is nothing to associate the psalm with him. **118.5** A summary report of the cry for help and God's answer. *A broad place.* See note on 18.19. **118.6–9** Expressions of confidence in God. **118.6** Quoted in Heb 13.6. *I do not fear* may reflect the suppliant's receiving an oracle of salvation with the assuring words "Do not fear" (cf. note on 22.21b). **118.8–9** Cf. 60.11; 146.3. **118.9** *Refuge.* See note on 2.10–12.

11 They surrounded me, surrounded me on
      every side;
   in the name of the LORD I cut them off!
12 They surrounded me like bees;
   they blazed[a] like a fire of thorns;
   in the name of the LORD I cut them off!
13 I was pushed hard,[b] so that I was falling,
   but the LORD helped me.
14 The LORD is my strength and my might;
   he has become my salvation.

15 There are glad songs of victory in the
      tents of the righteous:
   "The right hand of the LORD does
      valiantly;
16   the right hand of the LORD is exalted;
   the right hand of the LORD does
      valiantly."
17 I shall not die, but I shall live,
   and recount the deeds of the LORD.
18 The LORD has punished me severely,
   but he did not give me over to death.

19 Open to me the gates of righteousness,
   that I may enter through them
   and give thanks to the LORD.

20 This is the gate of the LORD;
   the righteous shall enter through it.

21 I thank you that you have answered me
   and have become my salvation.
22 The stone that the builders rejected
   has become the chief cornerstone.

23 This is the LORD's doing;
   it is marvelous in our eyes.
24 This is the day that the LORD has made;
   let us rejoice and be glad in it.[c]
25 Save us, we beseech you, O LORD!
   O LORD, we beseech you, give us
      success!

26 Blessed is the one who comes in the name
      of the LORD.[d]
   We bless you from the house of the
      LORD.
27 The LORD is God,
   and he has given us light.
   Bind the festal procession with branches,
   up to the horns of the altar.[e]

28 You are my God, and I will give thanks to
      you;
   you are my God, I will extol you.

29 O give thanks to the LORD, for he is good,
   for his steadfast love endures forever.

The Glories of God's Law

119 Happy are those whose way is
      blameless,
   who walk in the law of the LORD.
2 Happy are those who keep his decrees,
   who seek him with their whole heart,

---

a Gk: Heb *were extinguished*   *b* Gk Syr Jerome: Heb *You pushed
me hard*   *c* Or *in him*   *d* Or *Blessed in the name of the LORD is
the one who comes*   *e* Meaning of Heb uncertain

118.10–13 Account of the situation of distress.
118.14–18 Praise and thanksgiving to God for the
help that was given. **118.14** Cf. Ex 15.2; Isa 12.2.
118.15–16 Perhaps an ancient victory song. **118.19–
21** These verses suggest that the previous verses are
part of a processional to the gates of the temple, where
the suppliant now asks for entry to continue to give
thanks to the Lord before the assembled congregation.
118.19 The request for entry. **118.20** The qualifications for entry into the sanctuary (cf. Pss 15; 24), probably spoken by a priest. **118.21** The thanksgiving of
the individual now in the sanctuary. **118.22–27** The
voices of the congregation or singers are heard praising God for the marvelous deliverance of the one in
distress. **118.22** Either the words of the particular individual or those of the congregation. Quoted in Mt
21.42; Mk 12.10; Lk 20.17; Acts 4.11; 1 Pet 2.7.
118.23 Quoted in Mt 21.42; Mk 12.11. **118.25–
26** Quoted or alluded to in Mt 21.9; Mk 11.9; Lk 19.38.
Save us is the translation of the Hebrew expression
"Hosanna." V. 26 is probably a blessing uttered upon
the one who comes to give thanks. **118.26** *Bless.* See

note on 103.1–2. **118.27** The *horns of the altar* were
four projections at the corners of the altar. **118.28** The
act of thanksgiving by the individual in the sanctuary.
118.29 Concluding praise of the people or singers (cf.
2 Chr 5.13).

119.1–176 A prayer for God's help in time of trouble as well as in the keeping of the law. It may be an anthology of psalm pieces. Elements of prayers for help
and songs of thanksgiving intermix with exaltation of
the law and expressions of commitment to it, giving the
psalm the character of both instruction and prayer. It is
an alphabetic acrostic psalm (see note on 9.1–10.18)
made up of twenty-two stanzas of eight lines each. Following the order of the Hebrew alphabet, each stanza
uses one letter of the alphabet to begin each of its eight
lines. Eight different terms for the law (*commandments,
statutes, ordinances, decrees, words, precepts, promise,*
and *law*) are used, most of them in each stanza, and all
of them in four stanzas. In its delight in the law of the
Lord and commitment to it, the psalm is to be compared with Pss 1; 19. **119.1–8** Praise of the law and the
benefits of keeping God's instruction. **119.1–2** *Happy.*

3 who also do no wrong,
      but walk in his ways.
4 You have commanded your precepts
      to be kept diligently.
5 O that my ways may be steadfast
      in keeping your statutes!
6 Then I shall not be put to shame,
      having my eyes fixed on all your
         commandments.
7 I will praise you with an upright heart,
      when I learn your righteous ordinances.
8 I will observe your statutes;
      do not utterly forsake me.

9 How can young people keep their way
         pure?
      By guarding it according to your word.
10 With my whole heart I seek you;
      do not let me stray from your
         commandments.
11 I treasure your word in my heart,
      so that I may not sin against you.
12 Blessed are you, O LORD;
      teach me your statutes.
13 With my lips I declare
      all the ordinances of your mouth.
14 I delight in the way of your decrees
      as much as in all riches.
15 I will meditate on your precepts,
      and fix my eyes on your ways.
16 I will delight in your statutes;
      I will not forget your word.

17 Deal bountifully with your servant,
      so that I may live and observe your
         word.
18 Open my eyes, so that I may behold
      wondrous things out of your law.
19 I live as an alien in the land;
      do not hide your commandments from
         me.
20 My soul is consumed with longing
      for your ordinances at all times.
21 You rebuke the insolent, accursed ones,
      who wander from your
         commandments;
22 take away from me their scorn and
         contempt,

for I have kept your decrees.
23 Even though princes sit plotting against
         me,
      your servant will meditate on your
         statutes.
24 Your decrees are my delight,
      they are my counselors.

25 My soul clings to the dust;
      revive me according to your word.
26 When I told of my ways, you answered
         me;
      teach me your statutes.
27 Make me understand the way of your
         precepts,
      and I will meditate on your wondrous
         works.
28 My soul melts away for sorrow;
      strengthen me according to your
         word.
29 Put false ways far from me;
      and graciously teach me your law.
30 I have chosen the way of faithfulness;
      I set your ordinances before me.
31 I cling to your decrees, O LORD;
      let me not be put to shame.
32 I run the way of your commandments,
      for you enlarge my understanding.

33 Teach me, O LORD, the way of your
         statutes,
      and I will observe it to the end.
34 Give me understanding, that I may keep
         your law
      and observe it with my whole heart.
35 Lead me in the path of your
         commandments,
      for I delight in it.
36 Turn my heart to your decrees,
      and not to selfish gain.
37 Turn my eyes from looking at vanities;
      give me life in your ways.
38 Confirm to your servant your promise,
      which is for those who fear you.
39 Turn away the disgrace that I dread,
      for your ordinances are good.
40 See, I have longed for your precepts;
      in your righteousness give me life.

See note on 1.1. **119.9–16** Prayer for help in keeping
the law. **119.12** *Blessed*. See note on 103.1–2. **119.17–
24** Prayer for help against enemies, as the one who
prays keeps all the law. **119.25–32** Prayer to be
strengthened and rejuvenated through keeping the way
of God's commandments. **119.33–40** Plea for understanding in order to keep God's law. **119.35** *Delight*
(also v. 47). See 1.2. **119.38** *Fear you* (also vv. 63, 74, 79).
See note on 34.7. **119.41–48** Prayer for God's deliverance so that the taunts of persecutors will be answered

41 Let your steadfast love come to me,
    O Lord,
      your salvation according to your
        promise.
42 Then I shall have an answer for those
      who taunt me,
    for I trust in your word.
43 Do not take the word of truth utterly out
      of my mouth,
    for my hope is in your ordinances.
44 I will keep your law continually,
    forever and ever.
45 I shall walk at liberty,
    for I have sought your precepts.
46 I will also speak of your decrees before
      kings,
    and shall not be put to shame;
47 I find my delight in your commandments,
    because I love them.
48 I revere your commandments, which I
      love,
    and I will meditate on your statutes.

49 Remember your word to your servant,
    in which you have made me hope.
50 This is my comfort in my distress,
    that your promise gives me life.
51 The arrogant utterly deride me,
    but I do not turn away from your law.
52 When I think of your ordinances from of
      old,
    I take comfort, O Lord.
53 Hot indignation seizes me because of the
      wicked,
    those who forsake your law.
54 Your statutes have been my songs
    wherever I make my home.
55 I remember your name in the night,
    O Lord,
    and keep your law.
56 This blessing has fallen to me,
    for I have kept your precepts.

57 The Lord is my portion;
    I promise to keep your words.
58 I implore your favor with all my heart;
    be gracious to me according to your
      promise.
59 When I think of your ways,
    I turn my feet to your decrees;
60 I hurry and do not delay
    to keep your commandments.
61 Though the cords of the wicked ensnare
      me,

    I do not forget your law.
62 At midnight I rise to praise you,
    because of your righteous ordinances.
63 I am a companion of all who fear you,
    of those who keep your precepts.
64 The earth, O Lord, is full of your
      steadfast love;
    teach me your statutes.

65 You have dealt well with your servant,
    O Lord, according to your word.
66 Teach me good judgment and knowledge,
    for I believe in your commandments.
67 Before I was humbled I went astray,
    but now I keep your word.
68 You are good and do good;
    teach me your statutes.
69 The arrogant smear me with lies,
    but with my whole heart I keep your
      precepts.
70 Their hearts are fat and gross,
    but I delight in your law.
71 It is good for me that I was humbled,
    so that I might learn your statutes.
72 The law of your mouth is better to me
    than thousands of gold and silver pieces.

73 Your hands have made and fashioned me;
    give me understanding that I may learn
      your commandments.
74 Those who fear you shall see me and
      rejoice,
    because I have hoped in your word.
75 I know, O Lord, that your judgments are
      right,
    and that in faithfulness you have
      humbled me.
76 Let your steadfast love become my
      comfort
    according to your promise to your
      servant.
77 Let your mercy come to me, that I may
      live;
    for your law is my delight.
78 Let the arrogant be put to shame,
    because they have subverted me with
      guile;
    as for me, I will meditate on your
      precepts.
79 Let those who fear you turn to me,
    so that they may know your decrees.
80 May my heart be blameless in your
      statutes,
    so that I may not be put to shame.

81 My soul languishes for your salvation;
    I hope in your word.
82 My eyes fail with watching for your
        promise;
    I ask, "When will you comfort me?"
83 For I have become like a wineskin in the
        smoke,
    yet I have not forgotten your statutes.
84 How long must your servant endure?
    When will you judge those who
        persecute me?
85 The arrogant have dug pitfalls for me;
    they flout your law.
86 All your commandments are enduring;
    I am persecuted without cause; help me!
87 They have almost made an end of me on
        earth;
    but I have not forsaken your precepts.
88 In your steadfast love spare my life,
    so that I may keep the decrees of your
        mouth.

89 The LORD exists forever;
    your word is firmly fixed in heaven.
90 Your faithfulness endures to all
        generations;
    you have established the earth, and it
        stands fast.
91 By your appointment they stand today,
    for all things are your servants.
92 If your law had not been my delight,
    I would have perished in my misery.
93 I will never forget your precepts,
    for by them you have given me life.
94 I am yours; save me,
    for I have sought your precepts.
95 The wicked lie in wait to destroy me,
    but I consider your decrees.
96 I have seen a limit to all perfection,
    but your commandment is exceedingly
        broad.

97 Oh, how I love your law!
    It is my meditation all day long.
98 Your commandment makes me wiser
        than my enemies,

for it is always with me.
99 I have more understanding than all my
        teachers,
    for your decrees are my meditation.
100 I understand more than the aged,
    for I keep your precepts.
101 I hold back my feet from every evil way,
    in order to keep your word.
102 I do not turn away from your ordinances,
    for you have taught me.
103 How sweet are your words to my taste,
    sweeter than honey to my mouth!
104 Through your precepts I get
        understanding;
    therefore I hate every false way.

105 Your word is a lamp to my feet
    and a light to my path.
106 I have sworn an oath and confirmed it,
    to observe your righteous ordinances.
107 I am severely afflicted;
    give me life, O LORD, according to your
        word.
108 Accept my offerings of praise, O LORD,
    and teach me your ordinances.
109 I hold my life in my hand continually,
    but I do not forget your law.
110 The wicked have laid a snare for me,
    but I do not stray from your precepts.
111 Your decrees are my heritage forever;
    they are the joy of my heart.
112 I incline my heart to perform your
        statutes
    forever, to the end.

113 I hate the double-minded,
    but I love your law.
114 You are my hiding place and my shield;
    I hope in your word.
115 Go away from me, you evildoers,
    that I may keep the commandments of
        my God.
116 Uphold me according to your promise,
    that I may live,
    and let me not be put to shame in my
        hope.

by the one who trusts and keeps God's law. **119.49–56** Prayer for help (v. 49) and expressions of confidence in the face of the arrogant and the wicked because God's *servant* (v. 49) keeps the law. **119.57–64** Prayer, praise, and commitment to God's law. **119.65–72** The psalmist has experienced God's chastening help and has learned from it the value of the law of the Lord. **119.73–80** Prayer for help and understanding of God's commandments. **119.81–88** Cry for help by one who has kept the divine decrees. **119.89–96** Praise of the Lord, whose law gives life. **119.97–104** The constant devotion of the psalmist to God's law. **119.103** See 19.10. **119.105–112** Whatever afflictions come, the psalmist holds to God's decrees. **119.113–120** The psalmist's obedience to the law is contrasted with the ways of evildoers, and a prayer for help is uttered.

117 Hold me up, that I may be safe
        and have regard for your statutes
            continually.
118 You spurn all who go astray from your
            statutes;
        for their cunning is in vain.
119 All the wicked of the earth you count as
            dross;
        therefore I love your decrees.
120 My flesh trembles for fear of you,
        and I am afraid of your judgments.

121 I have done what is just and right;
        do not leave me to my oppressors.
122 Guarantee your servant's well-being;
        do not let the godless oppress me.
123 My eyes fail from watching for your
            salvation,
        and for the fulfillment of your
            righteous promise.
124 Deal with your servant according to your
            steadfast love,
        and teach me your statutes.
125 I am your servant; give me
            understanding,
        so that I may know your decrees.
126 It is time for the LORD to act,
        for your law has been broken.
127 Truly I love your commandments
        more than gold, more than fine gold.
128 Truly I direct my steps by all your
            precepts;*a*
        I hate every false way.

129 Your decrees are wonderful;
        therefore my soul keeps them.
130 The unfolding of your words gives light;
        it imparts understanding to the simple.
131 With open mouth I pant,
        because I long for your
            commandments.
132 Turn to me and be gracious to me,
        as is your custom toward those who
            love your name.
133 Keep my steps steady according to your
            promise,

and never let iniquity have dominion
            over me.
134 Redeem me from human oppression,
        that I may keep your precepts.
135 Make your face shine upon your servant,
        and teach me your statutes.
136 My eyes shed streams of tears
        because your law is not kept.

137 You are righteous, O LORD,
        and your judgments are right.
138 You have appointed your decrees in
            righteousness
        and in all faithfulness.
139 My zeal consumes me
        because my foes forget your words.
140 Your promise is well tried,
        and your servant loves it.
141 I am small and despised,
        yet I do not forget your precepts.
142 Your righteousness is an everlasting
            righteousness,
        and your law is the truth.
143 Trouble and anguish have come upon
            me,
        but your commandments are my
            delight.
144 Your decrees are righteous forever;
        give me understanding that I may live.

145 With my whole heart I cry; answer me,
            O LORD.
        I will keep your statutes.
146 I cry to you; save me,
        that I may observe your decrees.
147 I rise before dawn and cry for help;
        I put my hope in your words.
148 My eyes are awake before each watch of
            the night,
        that I may meditate on your promise.
149 In your steadfast love hear my voice;
        O LORD, in your justice preserve my
            life.

_____
a Gk Jerome: Meaning of Heb uncertain

119.121–128 Claims of righteousness and prayers for help against persecutors join with the prayer that God will instruct the psalmist. 119.127 See 19.10. 119.129–136 Praise of God's law and prayer for help against oppression. 119.135 *Make your face shine.* See note on 31.16. 119.137–144 Praise of the Lord's righteousness as seen in the law. 119.145–152 A cry for help and confidence in God's presence. 119.151 Cf. Deut 4.7–8; 30.14. 119.153–160 A plea for God to preserve the life of the faithful servant. 119.161–168 The devotion of the psalmist to the words of the Lord. 119.169–176 The psalmist asks God to hear the cry for help and to save in order that praise may come forth from God's servant.

150 Those who persecute me with evil
        purpose draw near;
    they are far from your law.
151 Yet you are near, O Lord,
        and all your commandments are true.
152 Long ago I learned from your decrees
        that you have established them forever.

153 Look on my misery and rescue me,
        for I do not forget your law.
154 Plead my cause and redeem me;
        give me life according to your
            promise.
155 Salvation is far from the wicked,
        for they do not seek your statutes.
156 Great is your mercy, O Lord;
        give me life according to your justice.
157 Many are my persecutors and my
            adversaries,
        yet I do not swerve from your decrees.
158 I look at the faithless with disgust,
        because they do not keep your
            commands.
159 Consider how I love your precepts;
        preserve my life according to your
            steadfast love.
160 The sum of your word is truth;
        and every one of your righteous
            ordinances endures forever.

161 Princes persecute me without cause,
        but my heart stands in awe of your
            words.
162 I rejoice at your word
        like one who finds great spoil.
163 I hate and abhor falsehood,
        but I love your law.
164 Seven times a day I praise you
        for your righteous ordinances.
165 Great peace have those who love your
            law;
        nothing can make them stumble.
166 I hope for your salvation, O Lord,
        and I fulfill your commandments.
167 My soul keeps your decrees;
        I love them exceedingly.

168 I keep your precepts and decrees,
        for all my ways are before you.

169 Let my cry come before you, O Lord;
        give me understanding according to
            your word.
170 Let my supplication come before you;
        deliver me according to your promise.
171 My lips will pour forth praise,
        because you teach me your statutes.
172 My tongue will sing of your promise,
        for all your commandments are right.
173 Let your hand be ready to help me,
        for I have chosen your precepts.
174 I long for your salvation, O Lord,
        and your law is my delight.
175 Let me live that I may praise you,
        and let your ordinances help me.
176 I have gone astray like a lost sheep; seek
            out your servant,
        for I do not forget your
            commandments.

Prayer for Deliverance from Slanderers

A Song of Ascents.

120 In my distress I cry to the Lord,
        that he may answer me:
2   "Deliver me, O Lord,
        from lying lips,
        from a deceitful tongue."

3   What shall be given to you?
        And what more shall be done to you,
            you deceitful tongue?
4   A warrior's sharp arrows,
        with glowing coals of the broom tree!

5   Woe is me, that I am an alien in Meshech,
        that I must live among the tents of
            Kedar.
6   Too long have I had my dwelling
        among those who hate peace.
7   I am for peace;
        but when I speak,
        they are for war.

120.1–7 A prayer by an individual for help. *A Song of Ascents,* the superscription to each psalm in the collection Pss 120–134. Most of the psalms are brief, often reflecting concerns of and images from the family and agricultural life of the common people. The meaning of the superscription is debated. It may refer to an ascending style of poetic form, but more likely it has some reference to the ascent of pilgrims on their way to Jerusalem and/or to the sanctuary there. These psalms may have been sung on such pilgrimages. **120.5** *Meshech,* listed in Gen 10.2 as a descendant of Japhet, in the OT usually refers to a distant region and its inhabitants in eastern Asia Minor near the Black Sea. *Kedar,* a descendant of Abraham and Hagar via Ishmael (see Gen 25.12–13; 1 Chr 1.29), is a general designation for certain Arab tribes inhabiting the northern regions of the

Assurance of God's Protection

A Song of Ascents.

121 I lift up my eyes to the hills—
from where will my help come?
2 My help comes from the LORD,
who made heaven and earth.

3 He will not let your foot be moved;
he who keeps you will not slumber.
4 He who keeps Israel
will neither slumber nor sleep.

5 The LORD is your keeper;
the LORD is your shade at your right
hand.
6 The sun shall not strike you by day,
nor the moon by night.

7 The LORD will keep you from all evil;
he will keep your life.
8 The LORD will keep
your going out and your coming in
from this time on and forevermore.

Song of Praise and Prayer for Jerusalem

A Song of Ascents. Of David.

122 I was glad when they said to me,
"Let us go to the house of the
LORD!"
2 Our feet are standing
within your gates, O Jerusalem.

3 Jerusalem—built as a city
that is bound firmly together.

4 To it the tribes go up,
the tribes of the LORD,
as was decreed for Israel,
to give thanks to the name of the
LORD.
5 For there the thrones for judgment were
set up,
the thrones of the house of David.

6 Pray for the peace of Jerusalem:
"May they prosper who love you.
7 Peace be within your walls,
and security within your towers."
8 For the sake of my relatives and friends
I will say, "Peace be within you."
9 For the sake of the house of the LORD our
God,
I will seek your good.

Supplication for Mercy

A Song of Ascents.

123 To you I lift up my eyes,
O you who are enthroned in the
heavens!
2 As the eyes of servants
look to the hand of their master,
as the eyes of a maid
to the hand of her mistress,
so our eyes look to the LORD our God,
until he has mercy upon us.

3 Have mercy upon us, O LORD, have
mercy upon us,
for we have had more than enough of
contempt.

Arabian peninsula (cf. Jer 49.28–33). The psalmist here uses these names symbolically, as representing the war-like people among whom he is forced to live (see v. 6). **121.1–8** A song of confidence in God's providential care. *A Song of Ascents.* See note on 120.1–7. **121.1–2** The psalmist asks a question about the source of help when one is in trouble of any sort and then answers it. **121.1** *Hills*, probably those around Jerusalem. **121.3–8** A representative figure, possibly a priest, elaborates the answer, identifying the constancy of the Lord's care through all of life in every circumstance. **121.4** *Sleep.* Cf. 44.23; 78.65. **121.6** *The moon by night.* Although some have seen here a belief in negative effects of the moon on human life, it is likely that the phrase is simply a poetic parallel to *the sun . . . by day*, indicating that the Lord's care is day and night, i.e., continual. **122.1–9** A song of Zion probably sung on pilgrimage to the holy city. *A Song of Ascents.* See note on 120.1–7. **122.1–2** The joy of the psalmist in anticipat-

ing the pilgrimage to Jerusalem with others and in arriving there. **122.3–5** Jerusalem is praised as a secure city (v. 3), the center of Israel's worship (v. 4), and as a place where just judgment may be found (cf. Deut 17.8–13; Isa 2.2–4; Mic 4.1–4). **122.5** See 1 Kings 7.7. On the responsibility of kings for rendering justice and judgment in Jerusalem, see 2 Sam 15.1–6; 1 Kings 3.16–28; Jer 21.12; 22.15–16. **122.6–9** Prayer for Jerusalem's peace and well-being. The Hebrew of these verses contains several instances of wordplay on the sounds of the last part of the word "Jerusalem," including the word for *peace* (shalom).

123.1–4 A community prayer for help. It may have been uttered by an individual on behalf of the whole community or leading them in prayer. *A Song of Ascents.* See note on 120.1–7. **123.1–2** The petitioner and the people pray in an attitude of dependence. **123.3–4** The cry for help against the taunts and ridicule of others; cf. (notes on) 44.14; 79.4.

4 Our soul has had more than its fill
    of the scorn of those who are at ease,
    of the contempt of the proud.

Thanksgiving for Israel's Deliverance

A Song of Ascents. Of David.

124 If it had not been the LORD who
        was on our side
    —let Israel now say—

2 if it had not been the LORD who was on
    our side,
    when our enemies attacked us,

3 then they would have swallowed us up
    alive,
    when their anger was kindled against us;

4 then the flood would have swept us away,
    the torrent would have gone over us;

5 then over us would have gone
    the raging waters.

6 Blessed be the LORD,
    who has not given us
    as prey to their teeth.

7 We have escaped like a bird
    from the snare of the fowlers;
    the snare is broken,
    and we have escaped.

8 Our help is in the name of the LORD,
    who made heaven and earth.

The Security of God's People

A Song of Ascents.

125 Those who trust in the LORD are
        like Mount Zion,
    which cannot be moved, but abides
        forever.

2 As the mountains surround Jerusalem,
    so the LORD surrounds his people,
    from this time on and forevermore.

3 For the scepter of wickedness shall not
        rest
    on the land allotted to the righteous,
    so that the righteous might not stretch
        out
    their hands to do wrong.

4 Do good, O LORD, to those who are good,
    and to those who are upright in their
        hearts.

5 But those who turn aside to their own
        crooked ways
    the LORD will lead away with evildoers.
    Peace be upon Israel!

A Harvest of Joy

A Song of Ascents.

126 When the LORD restored the
        fortunes of Zion,*a*
    we were like those who dream.

2 Then our mouth was filled with laughter,
    and our tongue with shouts of joy;
    then it was said among the nations,
    "The LORD has done great things for
        them."

3 The LORD has done great things for us,
    and we rejoiced.

4 Restore our fortunes, O LORD,
    like the watercourses in the Negeb.

—————
a Or brought back those who returned to Zion

124.1–8 A song of thanksgiving by the community. *A Song of Ascents.* See note on 120.1–7. **124.1–7** An account of the Lord's deliverance of the people from their enemies. **124.1** *Let Israel now say,* liturgical direction. Cf. 118.2–4; 129.1. **124.4–5** See note on 69.1–2. **124.6** Exclamation of thanksgiving and praise. *Blessed.* See note on 103.1–2. **124.8** A concluding confession of faith in hymnic form.

125.1–5 A community prayer for help against national enemies. *A Song of Ascents.* See note on 120.1–7. **125.1–3** Expression of confidence and trust in the Lord. **125.3** *Scepter of wickedness,* probably a foreign power that oppresses the people of Israel in the land. *The land allotted* refers to the Lord's granting or allotting the land of Canaan to Israel. *So that . . . do wrong* expresses a concern that the dominance of a foreign and ungodly power will lead those in the community to fall into immoral practices and an unfaithful way of

life. **125.4–5** Prayer for help to secure the confidence expressed in v. 3. God is asked to do good to those who keep the covenant and do right and to remove those influenced by wickedness from the righteous way.

126.1–6 A community prayer for help. *A Song of Ascents.* See note on 120.1–7. **126.1–3** The community looks back in memory to the Lord's deliverance of Zion and its joy on that occasion. It is possible that these verses are to be read in a future tense as a dreaming anticipation of restoration. **126.1** *Restored the fortunes of Zion,* if in reference to the past, may have in mind the return of the exiles from captivity in Babylon and the rebuilding of Jerusalem. **126.2** The restoration of Zion evokes the joy of the people and the testimony of other nations to the Lord's marvelous work for Israel. **126.3** Israel echoes the testimony and affirms it to be true. **126.4–6** The present prayer for restoration assumes that the community is in distress again and

5 May those who sow in tears
  reap with shouts of joy.
6 Those who go out weeping,
  bearing the seed for sowing,
shall come home with shouts of joy,
  carrying their sheaves.

God's Blessings in the Home

A Song of Ascents. Of Solomon.

127 Unless the Lord builds the house,
      those who build it labor in vain.
Unless the Lord guards the city,
  the guard keeps watch in vain.
2 It is in vain that you rise up early
  and go late to rest,
eating the bread of anxious toil;
  for he gives sleep to his beloved. *a*

3 Sons are indeed a heritage from the
  Lord,
  the fruit of the womb a reward.
4 Like arrows in the hand of a warrior
  are the sons of one's youth.
5 Happy is the man who has
  his quiver full of them.
He shall not be put to shame
  when he speaks with his enemies in the
  gate.

The Happy Home of the Faithful

A Song of Ascents.

128 Happy is everyone who fears the
      Lord,
  who walks in his ways.

2 You shall eat the fruit of the labor of your
  hands;
  you shall be happy, and it shall go well
  with you.

3 Your wife will be like a fruitful vine
  within your house;
  your children will be like olive shoots
  around your table.
4 Thus shall the man be blessed
  who fears the Lord.

5 The Lord bless you from Zion.
  May you see the prosperity of Jerusalem
  all the days of your life.
6 May you see your children's children.
  Peace be upon Israel!

Prayer for the Downfall of Israel's Enemies

A Song of Ascents.

129 "Often have they attacked me from
      my youth"
  —let Israel now say—
2 "often have they attacked me from my
  youth,
  yet they have not prevailed against me.
3 The plowers plowed on my back;
  they made their furrows long."
4 The Lord is righteous;
  he has cut the cords of the wicked.
5 May all who hate Zion
  be put to shame and turned backward.

------

a Or *for he provides for his beloved during sleep*

------

wishes God's help so that its weeping may once again be turned into joy. **126.4** *Watercourses in the Negeb*, the dry beds in the desert that become torrential streams in times of rain and flood.

127.1–5 Instruction about the Lord as the source of security and of the gift of children. *A Song of Ascents.* See note on 120.1–7. *Solomon* was the master builder in Israel's history, building houses (1 Kings 3.1–2; 7; 8.13; 9.1) and cities (2 Chr 8.1–11). **127.1–2** Human labors to build structures and secure human communities are useless unless God is involved in these enterprises. **127.1** *House* can mean a building, such as the house of the Lord (the temple), or a human household or family line (see v. 4). **127.2** *Sleep.* The text is quite uncertain here. The reference may be to honor or prosperity—rather than sleep—as given by God rather than the fruit of driven, frantic work. *Beloved.* Elsewhere the term refers specifically to Israel or one of the tribes (60.5; 108.6; Deut 33.12; Isa 5.1; Jer

11.15). **127.3–5** Many children are a gift of God to provide security for parents. The text has sons particularly in mind as able to protect against enemies.

128.1–5 Instruction about the rewards of living in obedience to the Lord. The psalm carries forward the themes of fruitful work and the blessing of children from Ps 127. *A Song of Ascents.* See note on 120.1–7. **128.1** *Happy.* See note on 1.1. *Fears the Lord* is a way of speaking of the right relationship to God. See note on 34.7.

129.1–8 A community song of thanksgiving or trust. *A Song of Ascents.* See note on 120.1–7. **129.1–4** The people recount their long history of being oppressed and how God freed them from the wicked oppressors. **129.1** *Let Israel now say.* See note on 124.1. **129.5–8** Expression of confidence that God will put the oppressors to naught. **129.5–6** These verses may be translated as a prayer wish, e.g., "May all . . . be put to shame," or as a declaration, e.g., "All . . . will be put to

6 Let them be like the grass on the
       housetops
    that withers before it grows up,
7 with which reapers do not fill their hands
    or binders of sheaves their arms,
8 while those who pass by do not say,
    "The blessing of the LORD be upon
       you!
    We bless you in the name of the LORD!"

Waiting for Divine Redemption

A Song of Ascents.

130 Out of the depths I cry to you,
        O LORD.
2   Lord, hear my voice!
    Let your ears be attentive
       to the voice of my supplications!

3 If you, O LORD, should mark iniquities,
    Lord, who could stand?
4 But there is forgiveness with you,
    so that you may be revered.

5 I wait for the LORD, my soul waits,
    and in his word I hope;
6 my soul waits for the Lord
    more than those who watch for the
       morning,
    more than those who watch for the
       morning.

7 O Israel, hope in the LORD!
    For with the LORD there is steadfast love,
    and with him is great power to redeem.
8 It is he who will redeem Israel
    from all its iniquities.

Song of Quiet Trust

A Song of Ascents. Of David.

131 O LORD, my heart is not lifted up,
        my eyes are not raised too high;
    I do not occupy myself with things
       too great and too marvelous for me.
2 But I have calmed and quieted my soul,
    like a weaned child with its mother;
    my soul is like the weaned child that is
       with me. [a]

3 O Israel, hope in the LORD
    from this time on and forevermore.

The Eternal Dwelling of God in Zion

A Song of Ascents.

132 O LORD, remember in David's
        favor
    all the hardships he endured;
2 how he swore to the LORD
    and vowed to the Mighty One of Jacob,
3 "I will not enter my house
    or get into my bed;
4 I will not give sleep to my eyes
    or slumber to my eyelids,
5 until I find a place for the LORD,
    a dwelling place for the Mighty One of
       Jacob."

6 We heard of it in Ephrathah;
    we found it in the fields of Jaar.
7 "Let us go to his dwelling place;
    let us worship at his footstool."

---

a Or *my soul within me is like a weaned child*

---

shame." **129.8** For the blessing given to reapers, see Ruth 2.4. No harvesting means no blessings exchanged during the harvest.

130.1–8 A prayer for help by one who seeks God's forgiveness and favor. One of the penitential psalms (see note on 6.1–10). *A Song of Ascents*. See note on 120.1–7. **130.1–2** The plea of the psalmist for God to hear the prayer. **130.3–6** Trust in God's forgiveness and eager expectation that it will be granted. **130.6** There may be allusion here to the fact that confirmation of God's help often came in the early morning after a night of praying and waiting (cf. 5.3; 30.5; 46.5; 88.13; 90.14). **130.7–8** The hope of the individual is now commended to the community as the ground of its own confidence (cf. 131.3).

131.1–3 A prayer of humility and trust in God. *A Song of Ascents.* See note on 120.1–7. **131.1** *Great and . . . marvelous*, usually the great and marvelous deeds

of the Lord. **131.2** *Calmed and quieted* suggests some struggle of the soul. *Weaned child . . . with me* suggests that the one speaking in the prayer is a mother. **131.3** The trust of the psalmist is commended to the larger community (cf. 130.7–8).

132.1–18 A royal psalm celebrating God's election of Zion and the sanctuary there as the divine abode on earth and the election of David and the Davidic line as God's ruling representatives. *A Song of Ascents.* See note on 120.1–7. **132.1–5** A prayer for God to remember David (and so the Davidic dynasty; cf. vv. 11–12) as the one who swore an oath to build a sanctuary for the Lord. This prayer may have been uttered by a priest or prophet or possibly by the king himself. **132.5** *A dwelling place*, the tent David set up as a sanctuary for the ark of the covenant (2 Sam 6.17). **132.6–10** Recollection of the bringing of the ark into the sanctuary on Zion. **132.6–7** Although these verses are customarily

8 Rise up, O Lord, and go to your resting
place,
    you and the ark of your might.
9 Let your priests be clothed with
righteousness,
    and let your faithful shout for joy.
10 For your servant David's sake
    do not turn away the face of your
    anointed one.

11 The Lord swore to David a sure oath
    from which he will not turn back:
"One of the sons of your body
    I will set on your throne.
12 If your sons keep my covenant
    and my decrees that I shall teach
    them,
their sons also, forevermore,
    shall sit on your throne."

13 For the Lord has chosen Zion;
    he has desired it for his habitation:
14 "This is my resting place forever;
    here I will reside, for I have desired it.
15 I will abundantly bless its provisions;
    I will satisfy its poor with bread.
16 Its priests I will clothe with salvation,
    and its faithful will shout for joy.
17 There I will cause a horn to sprout up for
David;
    I have prepared a lamp for my
    anointed one.

18 His enemies I will clothe with disgrace,
    but on him, his crown will gleam."

The Blessedness of Unity

A Song of Ascents.

133 How very good and pleasant it is
    when kindred live together in
    unity!
2 It is like the precious oil on the head,
    running down upon the beard,
on the beard of Aaron,
    running down over the collar of his
    robes.
3 It is like the dew of Hermon,
    which falls on the mountains of Zion.
For there the Lord ordained his blessing,
    life forevermore.

Praise in the Night

A Song of Ascents.

134 Come, bless the Lord, all you
    servants of the Lord,
who stand by night in the house of
    the Lord!
2 Lift up your hands to the holy place,
    and bless the Lord.

3 May the Lord, maker of heaven and
earth,
    bless you from Zion.

---

understood as referring to David's finding the ark in
the old sanctuary in Kiriath-jearim (1 Sam 7.1–2), i.e.,
Jaar (v. 6), and his bringing it to Jerusalem (2 Sam 6),
they may refer to David's finding the ark (v. 6) and
then worshiping before it in the old tent shrine where
it had remained for some time. **132.8–10** The call to
God to go forth in triumph to the new divine abode in
Zion. **132.8** *Go to your resting place,* probably better
"Go from your resting place," i.e., from the old shrine
where the ark had lodged to the new shrine David had
set up in Jerusalem. The verse is reminiscent of the war
song of the ark in Num 10.35 and thus signals that this
section is a call to God to march forth in victory into
the new sanctuary (cf. Ps 24). **132.11–12** God's oath
electing David and his line as rulers over the people in
perpetuity. The covenant with the Davidic dynasty,
however, is made explicitly conditional on the obedience of David's successors (cf. 2 Sam 7.14–15).
132.13–18 God's choice of David as king is now
paired with God's choice of Zion as the divine
dwelling place on earth. It is now the permanent *resting place* (cf. v. 8) of the ark, the visible throne of the
invisible God. **132.17** *Horn.* See note on 89.17. *Lamp* is
an image representing the promise to David that there

would always be a descendant of his on the throne of
Israel/Judah. See 2 Sam 21.17; 1 Kings 11.36; 15.4;
2 Kings 8.19.
    133.1–3 A didactic or wisdom poem transformed
into a song for communal worship that may have been
used in connection with journeys to Jerusalem. *A Song
of Ascents.* See note on 120.1–7. **133.1** *Kindred live together in unity* is to be seen in relation to such texts as
Deut 25.5; Gen 13.6; 36.7 and refers to the custom of
clan and family groups living in proximity to each
other. **133.2** *Precious oil* refers to the custom of anointing the head of an honored guest with the finest oil.
Beard of Aaron. See Ex 29.7; Lev 8.12. **133.3** *Hermon*
was the highest mountain in Syro-Palestine.
    134.1–3 A liturgy of praise and blessing. *A Song of
Ascents.* See note on 120.1–7. **134.1–2** A call to the
people who are gathered in the sanctuary, apparently
during the night and possibly at one of the major festivals, to praise and give thanks, i.e., *bless* the Lord (see
note on 103.1–2). **134.1** *Servants of the Lord* could be
a reference to the priests, but in Psalms it does not ordinarily have that restricted reference. **134.3** A blessing
is prayed over the people, probably by a priest or
priests (cf. Num 6.22–27).

Praise for God's Goodness and Might

135 Praise the LORD!
Praise the name of the LORD;
give praise, O servants of the LORD,

2 you that stand in the house of the LORD,
in the courts of the house of our
God.

3 Praise the LORD, for the LORD is good;
sing to his name, for he is gracious.

4 For the LORD has chosen Jacob for
himself,
Israel as his own possession.

5 For I know that the LORD is great;
our Lord is above all gods.

6 Whatever the LORD pleases he does,
in heaven and on earth,
in the seas and all deeps.

7 He it is who makes the clouds rise at the
end of the earth;
he makes lightnings for the rain
and brings out the wind from his
storehouses.

8 He it was who struck down the firstborn
of Egypt,
both human beings and animals;

9 he sent signs and wonders
into your midst, O Egypt,
against Pharaoh and all his servants.

10 He struck down many nations
and killed mighty kings—

11 Sihon, king of the Amorites,
and Og, king of Bashan,
and all the kingdoms of Canaan—

12 and gave their land as a heritage,
a heritage to his people Israel.

13 Your name, O LORD, endures forever,
your renown, O LORD, throughout all
ages.

14 For the LORD will vindicate his people,
and have compassion on his servants.

15 The idols of the nations are silver and
gold,
the work of human hands.

16 They have mouths, but they do not speak;
they have eyes, but they do not see;

17 they have ears, but they do not hear,
and there is no breath in their mouths.

18 Those who make them
and all who trust them
shall become like them.

19 O house of Israel, bless the LORD!
O house of Aaron, bless the LORD!

20 O house of Levi, bless the LORD!
You that fear the LORD, bless the LORD!

21 Blessed be the LORD from Zion,
he who resides in Jerusalem.
Praise the LORD!

God's Work in Creation and in History

136 O give thanks to the LORD, for
he is good,
for his steadfast love endures forever.

2 O give thanks to the God of gods,
for his steadfast love endures forever.

3 O give thanks to the Lord of lords,
for his steadfast love endures forever;

4 who alone does great wonders,
for his steadfast love endures forever;

5 who by understanding made the heavens,

135.1–21 A hymn of praise to God. Pieces and elements from other biblical texts have been woven together into a new and unified vehicle of praise. 135.1–4 Call to praise (vv. 1–3b) and the reason for praise (vv. 3b–4). 135.1 Cf. 113.1. *Servants of the LORD.* See note on 134.1. 135.2 Cf. 134.1. 135.3 Cf. 100.4–5; 136.1. 135.4 Cf. Ex 19.5; Deut 7.6. 135.5–7 A singer praises the Lord as the creator and ruler of the natural world. 135.5 Cf. 95.3. 135.6 Cf. 115.3. 135.7 Cf. Jer 10.13; 51.16. 135.8–12 Praise continues, now for God's liberating the people from slavery in Egypt and bringing them safely into the land. The focus is upon the plagues in Egypt, the victory over the foreign kings on the way into the land, and the granting of the land to Israel. 135.8 Cf. 136.10. 135.10–12 Cf. 136.17–22. *Sihon, Og.* See Num 21.21–35; Deut 2.26–3.11. 135.13–14 Praise of God's compassionate care of the

people. 135.13 Cf. Ex 3.15. 135.14 Cf. Deut 32.36. 135.15–18 Using 115.4–8, the psalmist contrasts implicitly the impotence of the idols of the nations with the God who has been praised in the preceding verses. 135.19–21 Concluding call to *bless the Lord,* i.e., give thanks and praise. On the enumeration of the groups in vv. 19–20, see note on 115.11; see also 118.2–4. The *house of Levi* has been added to the list. In formal worship after the exile, the Levites were a group who assisted the Aaronite priests.

136.1–26 A hymn of praise for God's marvelous works. The second half of each verse was probably a response by the people (cf. Ps 106). 136.1–3 Call to the community to offer thankful praise of God. 136.1 See note on 106.1. The paradigm of praise and thanksgiving in v. 1 provides the vehicle of congregational response throughout the rest of the psalm. 136.4–9 Praise of God

for his steadfast love endures forever;
6 who spread out the earth on the waters,
    for his steadfast love endures forever;
7 who made the great lights,
    for his steadfast love endures forever;
8 the sun to rule over the day,
    for his steadfast love endures forever;
9 the moon and stars to rule over the night,
    for his steadfast love endures forever;

10 who struck Egypt through their firstborn,
    for his steadfast love endures forever;
11 and brought Israel out from among them,
    for his steadfast love endures forever;
12 with a strong hand and an outstretched
    arm,
    for his steadfast love endures forever;
13 who divided the Red Sea*a* in two,
    for his steadfast love endures forever;
14 and made Israel pass through the midst
    of it,
    for his steadfast love endures forever;
15 but overthrew Pharaoh and his army in
    the Red Sea,*a*
    for his steadfast love endures forever;
16 who led his people through the
    wilderness,
    for his steadfast love endures forever;
17 who struck down great kings,
    for his steadfast love endures forever;
18 and killed famous kings,
    for his steadfast love endures forever;
19 Sihon, king of the Amorites,
    for his steadfast love endures forever;
20 and Og, king of Bashan,
    for his steadfast love endures forever;
21 and gave their land as a heritage,
    for his steadfast love endures forever;
22 a heritage to his servant Israel,
    for his steadfast love endures forever.

23 It is he who remembered us in our low
    estate,
    for his steadfast love endures forever;
24 and rescued us from our foes,
    for his steadfast love endures forever;
25 who gives food to all flesh,
    for his steadfast love endures forever.

26 O give thanks to the God of heaven,
    for his steadfast love endures forever.

Lament over the Destruction of Jerusalem

137 By the rivers of Babylon—
    there we sat down and there we
      wept
    when we remembered Zion.
2 On the willows*b* there
    we hung up our harps.
3 For there our captors
    asked us for songs,
and our tormentors asked for mirth,
    saying,
    "Sing us one of the songs of Zion!"

4 How could we sing the LORD's song
    in a foreign land?
5 If I forget you, O Jerusalem,
    let my right hand wither!
6 Let my tongue cling to the roof of my
    mouth,
    if I do not remember you,
if I do not set Jerusalem
    above my highest joy.

7 Remember, O LORD, against the Edomites
    the day of Jerusalem's fall,
how they said, "Tear it down! Tear it down!

---

a Or *Sea of Reeds* *b* Or *poplars*

---

for the marvelous works of creation. **136.4** The praise begins with a general reference that incorporates all the particular wonderful deeds that follow in the rest of the hymn. **136.10–22** Praise of God for the wonderful deeds on behalf of the people at the beginning of their history. **136.10–15** The deliverance from slavery in Egypt. **136.16** God's guidance and care of the people in the wilderness. **136.17–22** The victory over opposing kings and God's allotment (*heritage*) of the land of Canaan to Israel. **136.19–20** See Num 21.21–35; Deut 2.26–3.11. **136.23–25** Summary praise of God for the mercy and protection shown to the people. **136.26** The initial call to praise and thanksgiving is reiterated at the end.

137.1–9 A prayer of the community for God to destroy its oppressors and enemies. Although it refers to the exile in Babylon, it is probably a later recollection of the event. **137.1–4** Lament over Jerusalem's destruction and the plight of the exiles in Babylonian captivity. **137.3** *Songs of Zion,* such as Pss 46; 48; 76; 84. **137.5–6** Glorification of Zion in the form of a self-imprecation. The psalmist vows always to remember and care about Jerusalem. **137.7–9** An imprecation, or curse prayer, in which the psalmist calls for God's destruction of those who destroyed Jerusalem and sent the people into captivity. **137.7** *Edomites* joined in the sacking and pillaging of Jerusalem and handed over fleeing survivors to the Babylonians (Ob

Down to its foundations!"
8 O daughter Babylon, you devastator![a]
    Happy shall they be who pay you back
      what you have done to us!
9 Happy shall they be who take your little
      ones
    and dash them against the rock!

Thanksgiving and Praise

Of David.

138 I give you thanks, O Lord, with
    my whole heart;
    before the gods I sing your praise;
2 I bow down toward your holy temple
    and give thanks to your name for your
      steadfast love and your
      faithfulness;
    for you have exalted your name and
      your word
    above everything.[b]
3 On the day I called, you answered me,
    you increased my strength of soul.[c]

4 All the kings of the earth shall praise you,
    O Lord,
    for they have heard the words of your
      mouth.
5 They shall sing of the ways of the Lord,
    for great is the glory of the Lord.
6 For though the Lord is high, he regards
    the lowly;
    but the haughty he perceives from far
      away.

7 Though I walk in the midst of trouble,
    you preserve me against the wrath of
      my enemies;
    you stretch out your hand,
    and your right hand delivers me.

8 The Lord will fulfill his purpose for me;
    your steadfast love, O Lord, endures
      forever.
    Do not forsake the work of your
      hands.

The Inescapable God

To the leader. Of David. A Psalm.

139 O Lord, you have searched me and
    known me.
2 You know when I sit down and when I
      rise up;
    you discern my thoughts from far
      away.
3 You search out my path and my lying
      down,
    and are acquainted with all my ways.
4 Even before a word is on my tongue,
    O Lord, you know it completely.
5 You hem me in, behind and before,
    and lay your hand upon me.
6 Such knowledge is too wonderful for me;
    it is so high that I cannot attain it.

7 Where can I go from your spirit?
    Or where can I flee from your
      presence?
8 If I ascend to heaven, you are there;
    if I make my bed in Sheol, you are
      there.
9 If I take the wings of the morning
    and settle at the farthest limits of the
      sea,
10 even there your hand shall lead me,
    and your right hand shall hold me fast.

---

a Or *you who are devastated*   *b* Cn: Heb *you have exalted your word above all your name*   *c* Syr Compare Gk Tg: Heb *you made me arrogant in my soul with strength*

8–14; cf. Ezek 25.12–14; 35.2–9). **137.8–9** *Happy.* See note on 1.1.
    138.1–8 A song of thanksgiving for deliverance by God. **138.1–3** Expression of thanksgiving (vv. 1–2) and testimony to what the Lord did to help (v. 3). *Before the gods* probably means before the heavenly assembly that surrounds the Lord of hosts, but the expression could refer to the gods of the nations, whose power is understood to be nothing in comparison to that of the Lord. **138.4–6** The kings of the nations are called to praise the ways of the Lord. Cf. 67.3–5; 68.32; 126.2. **138.6** Cf. 113.5–8. **138.7–8** An expression of confidence by the psalmist ending in a prayer for God's continued care. **138.8** *Work of your hands,* any of

God's works, from creation to the redemption of an individual.
    139.1–24 A prayer for God's help against certain enemies or persecutors by one who claims to be innocent and offers to be tested by God. *To the leader.* See note on 4.1–8. **139.1–6** Everything about the psalmist, even the innermost thoughts, are known to the Lord. Nothing the psalmist does or thinks has escaped the Lord. Such divine knowledge of the psalmist's thoughts has to do especially with commitment to the ways of the Lord and comes from God's searching and testing to discern the psalmist's inclination of heart and mind (see vv. 23–24). **139.7–12** There is nowhere that one can hide or escape from the presence of God.

11 If I say, "Surely the darkness shall cover
       me,
   and the light around me become
       night,"
12 even the darkness is not dark to you;
   the night is as bright as the day,
   for darkness is as light to you.

13 For it was you who formed my inward
       parts;
   you knit me together in my mother's
       womb.
14 I praise you, for I am fearfully and
       wonderfully made.
   Wonderful are your works;
   that I know very well.
15   My frame was not hidden from you,
   when I was being made in secret,
   intricately woven in the depths of the
       earth.
16 Your eyes beheld my unformed
       substance.
   In your book were written
   all the days that were formed for me,
   when none of them as yet existed.
17 How weighty to me are your thoughts,
       O God!
   How vast is the sum of them!
18 I try to count them—they are more than
       the sand;
   I come to the end[a]—I am still with
       you.

19 O that you would kill the wicked, O God,
   and that the bloodthirsty would depart
       from me—
20 those who speak of you maliciously,
   and lift themselves up against you for
       evil![b]
21 Do I not hate those who hate you,
       O LORD?
   And do I not loathe those who rise up
       against you?

22 I hate them with perfect hatred;
   I count them my enemies.
23 Search me, O God, and know my heart;
   test me and know my thoughts.
24 See if there is any wicked[c] way in me,
   and lead me in the way everlasting.[d]

Prayer for Deliverance from Enemies

To the leader. A Psalm of David.

140 Deliver me, O LORD, from
       evildoers;
   protect me from those who are violent,
2 who plan evil things in their minds
   and stir up wars continually.
3 They make their tongue sharp as a
       snake's,
   and under their lips is the venom of
       vipers.   Selah

4 Guard me, O LORD, from the hands of
       the wicked;
   protect me from the violent
   who have planned my downfall.
5 The arrogant have hidden a trap for me,
   and with cords they have spread a net,[e]
   along the road they have set snares for
       me.   Selah

6 I say to the LORD, "You are my God;
   give ear, O LORD, to the voice of my
       supplications."
7 O LORD, my Lord, my strong deliverer,
   you have covered my head in the day of
       battle.
8 Do not grant, O LORD, the desires of the
       wicked;
   do not further their evil plot.[f]   Selah

---

a Or I awake   b Cn: Meaning of Heb uncertain
c Heb hurtful   d Or the ancient way. Compare Jer 6.16
e Or they have spread cords as a net   f Heb adds they are exalted

---

139.13–19 The beginning (vv. 13–16a) and end (vv. 16b–18) of the psalmist are known and determined by God. **139.19–22** A prayer for the defeat of those who are hostile to the psalmist because they are also opposed to God and God's ways. **139.23–24** The psalmist submits to God's testing, confident of being judged innocent or righteous and committed to following the Lord's way.

140.1–13 An individual prayer for help against those who have slandered and falsely accused the one who prays. *To the leader.* See note on 4.1–8. **140.1–**

3 Cry for help and description of the persecution. **140.3** Together with vv. 9, 11, this verse indicates that the distress of the petitioner is caused by lies and slander on the part of those who would cause violence (vv. 1, 4, 9, 11). *Selah.* See note on 3.2. **140.4–5** Another cry for help and description of the violence directed against the one who cries out. On the imagery of trap and net, cf., e.g., 9.15; 10.9; 25.15; 31.4; 35.7, 8; 57.6; 141.9; 142.3. **140.6–11** Further pleas for help against the wicked intermingled with expressions of trust and confidence (vv. 6–7). **140.9–**

9 Those who surround me lift up their
       heads;[a]
   let the mischief of their lips overwhelm
       them!
10 Let burning coals fall on them!
   Let them be flung into pits, no more to
       rise!
11 Do not let the slanderer be established in
       the land;
   let evil speedily hunt down the violent!

12 I know that the LORD maintains the cause
       of the needy,
   and executes justice for the poor.
13 Surely the righteous shall give thanks to
       your name;
   the upright shall live in your presence.

Prayer for Preservation from Evil

A Psalm of David.

141 I call upon you, O LORD; come
       quickly to me;
   give ear to my voice when I call to you.
2 Let my prayer be counted as incense
       before you,
   and the lifting up of my hands as an
       evening sacrifice.

3 Set a guard over my mouth, O LORD;
   keep watch over the door of my lips.
4 Do not turn my heart to any evil,
   to busy myself with wicked deeds
   in company with those who work iniquity;
   do not let me eat of their delicacies.

5 Let the righteous strike me;
   let the faithful correct me.
   Never let the oil of the wicked anoint my
       head,[b]

for my prayer is continually[c] against
       their wicked deeds.
6 When they are given over to those who
       shall condemn them,
   then they shall learn that my words
       were pleasant.
7 Like a rock that one breaks apart and
       shatters on the land,
   so shall their bones be strewn at the
       mouth of Sheol.[d]

8 But my eyes are turned toward you,
       O GOD, my Lord;
   in you I seek refuge; do not leave me
       defenseless.
9 Keep me from the trap that they have laid
       for me,
   and from the snares of evildoers.
10 Let the wicked fall into their own nets,
   while I alone escape.

Prayer for Deliverance from Persecutors

A Maskil of David. When he was in the cave.
A Prayer.

142 With my voice I cry to the LORD;
   with my voice I make supplication
       to the LORD.
2 I pour out my complaint before him;
   I tell my trouble before him.
3 When my spirit is faint,
   you know my way.

   In the path where I walk
       they have hidden a trap for me.
4 Look on my right hand and see—

---

a Cn Compare Gk: Heb *those who surround me are uplifted in head*; Heb divides verses 8 and 9 differently   *b* Gk: Meaning of Heb uncertain   *c* Cn: Heb *for continually and my prayer*
d Meaning of Heb of verses 5-7 is uncertain

---

11 Explicit calls for God's judgment against the oppressors. **140.12–13** The confidence of the petitioner in God's justice for the weak (v. 12) and a vow of praise (v. 13). **140.12** Cf. Ps 82.

141.1–10 An individual prayer for help against the danger of being drawn into association with the wicked. **141.1–2** Plea to God to hear and respond to the prayer. **141.2** *Incense.* Cf. Ex 30.8. *Evening sacrifice.* Cf. Ex 29.38–42; Num 28.3–8. Accounts are given of prayer offered at the time of the evening sacrifice and with incense in Ezra 9.4–5; Dan 9.20–21; Jdt 9.1. **141.3–7** Specific petitions whose primary content is the prayer for God to keep the psalmist from harmful speech and from association with the wicked (cf. 1.1).

Vv. 5–7 are difficult to interpret because of the condition of the Hebrew text. **141.4** *Eat of their delicacies,* i.e., enjoy their fancy hospitality. **141.7** *Sheol.* See note on 6.5. **141.8–10** Additional pleas for God's help to keep the petitioner from being drawn in and caught up by those who do wrong. *Trap.* See note on 140.4–5. **141.10** The prayer for help against the enticement of the wicked is also a prayer for judgment of them; cf. 7.15–16; 9.15.

142.1–7 An individual prayer for help against persecutors. *Maskil.* See note on 32.1–11. *Cave.* See note on 57.1–11. **142.1–3a** Cry for help. **142.3b–4** Lament over the psalmist's distress. Enemies are plotting and there is no one who will help or pay any attention to the suffer-

there is no one who takes notice of me;
no refuge remains to me;
no one cares for me.

5 I cry to you, O LORD;
I say, "You are my refuge,
my portion in the land of the living."
6 Give heed to my cry,
for I am brought very low.

Save me from my persecutors,
for they are too strong for me.
7 Bring me out of prison,
so that I may give thanks to your
name.
The righteous will surround me,
for you will deal bountifully with me.

Prayer for Deliverance from Enemies

A Psalm of David.

143 Hear my prayer, O LORD;
give ear to my supplications in
your faithfulness;
answer me in your righteousness.
2 Do not enter into judgment with your
servant,
for no one living is righteous before you.

3 For the enemy has pursued me,
crushing my life to the ground,
making me sit in darkness like those
long dead.
4 Therefore my spirit faints within me;
my heart within me is appalled.

5 I remember the days of old,
I think about all your deeds,
I meditate on the works of your hands.
6 I stretch out my hands to you;

my soul thirsts for you like a parched
land.   *Selah*

7 Answer me quickly, O LORD;
my spirit fails.
Do not hide your face from me,
or I shall be like those who go down to
the Pit.
8 Let me hear of your steadfast love in the
morning,
for in you I put my trust.
Teach me the way I should go,
for to you I lift up my soul.

9 Save me, O LORD, from my enemies;
I have fled to you for refuge.[a]
10 Teach me to do your will,
for you are my God.
Let your good spirit lead me
on a level path.

11 For your name's sake, O LORD, preserve
my life.
In your righteousness bring me out of
trouble.
12 In your steadfast love cut off my enemies,
and destroy all my adversaries,
for I am your servant.

Prayer for National Deliverance and Security

Of David.

144 Blessed be the LORD, my rock,
who trains my hands for war, and
my fingers for battle;
2 my rock[b] and my fortress,

---

a One Heb Ms Gk: MT *to you I have hidden*   *b* With 18.2 and
2 Sam 22.2: Heb *my steadfast love*

---

ing of the petitioner. *Trap.* See note on 140.4–5. **142.5–7** Further cries for help (vv. 5a, 6, 7a) intermingled with expressions of trust (vv. 5b, 7b). **142.7** *Bring me out of prison,* a metaphorical reference to the experience of distress, or an actual imprisonment or captivity of the one who cries out in the psalm; cf. 107.10–16. *So that . . . your name* is a vow of praise, which often concludes a prayer for help (cf. 7.17; 13.6; 35.28; 59.16–17; 61.8).

143.1–12 An individual prayer for help. One of the penitential psalms (see note on 6.1–10). **143.1–2** Cry for help. **143.2** The implicit acknowledgment of inadequacy before God's judgment has led to the inclusion of this psalm in the penitential psalms. **143.3–4** Description of the affliction from oppressive elements and the internal distress it has caused. **143.5–6** Recollection of

God's saving works in the past is the ground for the present plea. *Selah.* See note on 3.2. **143.7–12** Urgent pleas for help are followed by laments and expressions of confidence that are submitted as grounds for God's attention. **143.7** *Hide your face.* See notes on 10.1; 27.9. *Pit.* See note on 16.10. **143.8b–10** In addition to the plea for help, these verses seek divine instruction in the proper way to go. **143.11–12** The plea for help is rooted in the character of God as the psalmist pleads for the Lord to act in accordance with God's own nature.

144.1–11 A royal prayer for God's help. The psalm uses themes and traditions found in Ps 18 (2 Sam 22), a royal song of thanksgiving. **144.1–2** The king gives thanks and praise for God's instruction, protection, and victory over other nations (cf. Pss 18.2; 34; 46–47).

my stronghold and my deliverer,
my shield, in whom I take refuge,
who subdues the peoples[a] under me.

3 O LORD, what are human beings that you
regard them,
or mortals that you think of them?
4 They are like a breath;
their days are like a passing shadow.

5 Bow your heavens, O LORD, and come
down;
touch the mountains so that they
smoke.
6 Make the lightning flash and scatter
them;
send out your arrows and rout them.
7 Stretch out your hand from on high;
set me free and rescue me from the
mighty waters,
from the hand of aliens,
8 whose mouths speak lies,
and whose right hands are false.

9 I will sing a new song to you, O God;
upon a ten-stringed harp I will play to
you,
10 the one who gives victory to kings,
who rescues his servant David.
11 Rescue me from the cruel sword,
and deliver me from the hand of aliens,
whose mouths speak lies,
and whose right hands are false.

12 May our sons in their youth
be like plants full grown,
our daughters like corner pillars,
cut for the building of a palace.
13 May our barns be filled,
with produce of every kind;

may our sheep increase by thousands,
by tens of thousands in our fields,
14 and may our cattle be heavy with young.
May there be no breach in the walls,[b] no
exile,
and no cry of distress in our streets.

15 Happy are the people to whom such
blessings fall;
happy are the people whose God is the
LORD.

The Greatness and the Goodness of God

Praise. Of David.

145 I will extol you, my God and King,
and bless your name forever and
ever.
2 Every day I will bless you,
and praise your name forever and ever.
3 Great is the LORD, and greatly to be
praised;
his greatness is unsearchable.

4 One generation shall laud your works to
another,
and shall declare your mighty acts.
5 On the glorious splendor of your majesty,
and on your wondrous works, I will
meditate.
6 The might of your awesome deeds shall
be proclaimed,
and I will declare your greatness.
7 They shall celebrate the fame of your
abundant goodness,
and shall sing aloud of your
righteousness.

---

a Heb Mss Syr Aquila Jerome: MT *my people* b Heb lacks *in the walls*

144.3–4 Reflection on human frailty in anticipation of the prayer that follows (cf. Job 7.17–18; Pss 8.4; 90.5–6; 103.15–16; 146.3–4). 144.5–8 Prayer for God's help couched in the theophanic language of 18.7–19; see notes on 18.7–19; 18.14; 18.16. 144.7–8 *Aliens*, hostile nations or peoples. *Whose right hands are false* refers to violating oaths sworn by raising the right hand; the verse may refer to nations that have broken political alliances or treaties (cf. v. 11b). 144.9–11 Vow of praise and another plea for help (cf. vv. 7–8). 144.9–10 The basis for associating the psalm with a king and particularly with David, who was a musician and also experienced God's deliverance from his enemies, is seen in these verses. *David* could refer to a member of the Davidic line (cf. Ezek 34.23; Hos 3.5). 144.12–15 A com-

munity prayer for God's blessing of the nation in prosperity and security. The relation of these verses to the royal psalm in vv. 1–11 is unclear. They may have been a prayer uttered by the king, or they may have been originally a separate prayer later joined to the royal psalm. 144.15 *Happy*. See note on 1.1.

145.1–21 A hymn of praise. An alphabetic acrostic psalm (so also Pss 9–10; 25; 34; 37; 111; 112; 119; Lam 1–4), in which each verse begins with a successive letter of the Hebrew alphabet (see note on 9.1–10.18). 145.1–2 An individual makes a vow of praise and thanksgiving to the Lord that is carried out in the verses that follow (cf. 7.17; 9.1–2; 13.6; 116.12–19; 138.1–2; 144.9–10). *Bless*. Cf. vv. 10, 21; note on 103.1–2. 145.3–7 The psalmist's praise becomes a part of a chain of praise that

8 The LORD is gracious and merciful,
    slow to anger and abounding in
        steadfast love.
9 The LORD is good to all,
    and his compassion is over all that he
        has made.

10 All your works shall give thanks to you,
    O LORD,
    and all your faithful shall bless you.
11 They shall speak of the glory of your
        kingdom,
    and tell of your power,
12 to make known to all people your[a]
        mighty deeds,
    and the glorious splendor of your[b]
        kingdom.
13 Your kingdom is an everlasting kingdom,
    and your dominion endures
        throughout all generations.

    The LORD is faithful in all his words,
    and gracious in all his deeds.[c]
14 The LORD upholds all who are falling,
    and raises up all who are bowed down.
15 The eyes of all look to you,
    and you give them their food in due
        season.
16 You open your hand,
    satisfying the desire of every living thing.
17 The LORD is just in all his ways,
    and kind in all his doings.
18 The LORD is near to all who call on him,
    to all who call on him in truth.
19 He fulfills the desire of all who fear him;
    he also hears their cry, and saves them.
20 The LORD watches over all who love him,
    but all the wicked he will destroy.

21 My mouth will speak the praise of the
    LORD,
    and all flesh will bless his holy name
        forever and ever.

Praise for God's Help

146 Praise the LORD!
    Praise the LORD, O my soul!
2 I will praise the LORD as long as I live;
    I will sing praises to my God all my life
        long.

3 Do not put your trust in princes,
    in mortals, in whom there is no help.
4 When their breath departs, they return to
        the earth;
    on that very day their plans perish.

5 Happy are those whose help is the God of
        Jacob,
    whose hope is in the LORD their God,
6 who made heaven and earth,
    the sea, and all that is in them;
    who keeps faith forever;
7   who executes justice for the oppressed;
    who gives food to the hungry.

    The LORD sets the prisoners free;
8   the LORD opens the eyes of the blind.
    The LORD lifts up those who are bowed
        down;
    the LORD loves the righteous.
9 The LORD watches over the strangers;
    he upholds the orphan and the widow,

---

a Gk Jerome Syr: Heb *his*   *b* Heb *his*   *c* These two lines supplied by Q Ms Gk Syr

---

stretches out across the generations (cf. 22.30). **145.8–9** The substance of the praise of God is found in these verses, which draw upon the ancient confession of Ex 34.6; cf. note on 103.8 as well as the paradigm song of praise and thanksgiving (see note on 106.1). **145.10–13a** All of God's creatures as well as all the faithful members of the congregation are now called to praise the splendor of the Lord's eternal rule, the kingdom of God. **145.13b–20** An echo of vv. 8–9, praising the faithfulness and compassion of God, especially for the weak and afflicted (vv. 13b–14, 17b), the providence of God (vv. 15–16, 20a), the justice of God (vv. 17a, 20b), and God's presence and responsiveness to those who cry out for help (vv. 18–19). The comprehensiveness and inclusiveness of these divine ways and deeds is seen in the constant repetition of the word *all* in these verses and vv. 10–13. **145.19** *Fear him.* See note on 34.7. **145.21** A

concluding expression of the purpose of the psalm, the praise of the Lord by the psalmist (cf. vv. 1–2, 5–6) joined with the praise by *all flesh* (cf. vv. 10–13).

146.1–10 A hymn of praise. **146.1–2** Introductory call to praise as self-exhortation (cf. note on 145.1–2). **146.3–4** Reflection on the inadequacy of human help addressed as a warning to the congregation (cf. 56.11; 118.6–9). **146.5–9** Over against human inadequacy, the psalmist points out the benefits of trusting in the Lord by enumerating the many ways God cares, particularly for the weak, the suffering, and the oppressed (cf. 1 Sam 2.1–10; Ps 145.14–20). **146.5** *Happy.* See note on 1.1. *The God of Jacob,* a divine title often found in psalms that focus on Zion (v. 10; 20.1; 24.6; 46.7, 11; 76.6; 84.8). **146.6** The power of God is attested first in praise of God as creator of all that is. **146.7** Cf. 82.1–8; 107.10–16; 140.12; 142.7. **146.9** *The way of the wicked.*

but the way of the wicked he brings to
ruin.

10 The LORD will reign forever,
your God, O Zion, for all generations.
Praise the LORD!

Praise for God's Care for Jerusalem

147 Praise the LORD!
How good it is to sing praises to
our God;
for he is gracious, and a song of praise
is fitting.
2 The LORD builds up Jerusalem;
he gathers the outcasts of Israel.
3 He heals the brokenhearted,
and binds up their wounds.
4 He determines the number of the stars;
he gives to all of them their names.
5 Great is our Lord, and abundant in power;
his understanding is beyond measure.
6 The LORD lifts up the downtrodden;
he casts the wicked to the ground.

7 Sing to the LORD with thanksgiving;
make melody to our God on the lyre.
8 He covers the heavens with clouds,
prepares rain for the earth,
makes grass grow on the hills.
9 He gives to the animals their food,
and to the young ravens when they cry.
10 His delight is not in the strength of the
horse,
nor his pleasure in the speed of a
runner;[a]
11 but the LORD takes pleasure in those who
fear him,

in those who hope in his steadfast love.

12 Praise the LORD, O Jerusalem!
Praise your God, O Zion!
13 For he strengthens the bars of your gates;
he blesses your children within you.
14 He grants peace[b] within your borders;
he fills you with the finest of wheat.
15 He sends out his command to the earth;
his word runs swiftly.
16 He gives snow like wool;
he scatters frost like ashes.
17 He hurls down hail like crumbs—
who can stand before his cold?
18 He sends out his word, and melts them;
he makes his wind blow, and the waters
flow.
19 He declares his word to Jacob,
his statutes and ordinances to Israel.
20 He has not dealt thus with any other
nation;
they do not know his ordinances.
Praise the LORD!

Praise for God's Universal Glory

148 Praise the LORD!
Praise the LORD from the heavens;
praise him in the heights!
2 Praise him, all his angels;
praise him, all his host!

3 Praise him, sun and moon;
praise him, all you shining stars!
4 Praise him, you highest heavens,
and you waters above the heavens!

_____

a Heb *legs of a person*   b Or *prosperity*

Cf. 1.6. **146.10** Concluding praise of God's eternal rule
(cf. Ex 15.18; Pss 29.10; 145.13; 93; 95–99).
147.1–20 A hymn of praise. Motifs and themes
from other psalms, Job, and Isa 40–66 appear
throughout the psalm. **147.1–6** Call to praise (v. 1)
and the reason for praise, which is found in the Lord's
power and care. The psalmist joins praise of God's
power and wisdom in creation with God's attention to
the lowliest and weakest creatures. **147.2** *The LORD
builds up Jerusalem.* Cf. 51.18; 102.16; 127.1. *Outcasts
of Israel.* Cf. Neh 1.9; Isa 11.12; 56.8; Zeph 3.19.
147.3 Cf. 6.2; 30.2; 34.18; 41.4; Isa 61.1. **147.4–5** Cf.
145.3; Isa 40.26–28. **147.6** Cf. 113.7; 145.14, 20; 146.8–
9. **147.7–11** Call to praise and thanksgiving (v. 7)
and the reason for praise, found in the Lord's provision of food for the creatures (vv. 8–9) and in God's
joy in those who are faithful (vv. 10–11). **147.8–9** Cf.

104.10–14, 21. *Ravens.* Cf. Job 38.41; Lk 12.24.
147.10–11 Cf. 20.7; 33.16–18. *Fear him.* See note on
34.7. **147.12–20** Call to praise (v. 12) and the reason
for praise, centering especially in the creative and effective *word* (or *command, statutes, ordinances*) of God
(cf. 33.4–7; Gen 1; Isa 55.10–11). **147.13** Cf. v. 2. On
the building up and strengthening of the city together
with the blessing of children, cf. Ps 127. **147.14a** Cf. Isa
60.17–18. **147.14b** Cf. 81.16. **147.15–18** Cf. Job 37.1–
13. **147.18** *Makes his wind blow.* Cf. Isa 40.7. **147.19–
20** Cf. Deut 4.6–8, 12–13.
148.1–14 A hymn of praise consisting primarily of
a long series of calls to the elements of creation and the
inhabitants of the earth to praise the Lord. Its influence is felt in the apocryphal Song of the Three Jews.
148.1–6 The heavens and their natural and angelic inhabitants are called to praise the Lord because God is

5 Let them praise the name of the LORD,
   for he commanded and they were
      created.
6 He established them forever and ever;
   he fixed their bounds, which cannot be
      passed.[a]

7 Praise the LORD from the earth,
   you sea monsters and all deeps,
8 fire and hail, snow and frost,
   stormy wind fulfilling his command!

9 Mountains and all hills,
   fruit trees and all cedars!
10 Wild animals and all cattle,
   creeping things and flying birds!

11 Kings of the earth and all peoples,
   princes and all rulers of the earth!
12 Young men and women alike,
   old and young together!

13 Let them praise the name of the LORD,
   for his name alone is exalted;
   his glory is above earth and heaven.
14 He has raised up a horn for his people,
   praise for all his faithful,
   for the people of Israel who are close to
      him.
   Praise the LORD!

Praise for God's Goodness to Israel

149 Praise the LORD!
   Sing to the LORD a new song,
   his praise in the assembly of the
      faithful.
2 Let Israel be glad in its Maker;
   let the children of Zion rejoice in their
      King.

3 Let them praise his name with dancing,
   making melody to him with
      tambourine and lyre.
4 For the LORD takes pleasure in his people;
   he adorns the humble with victory.
5 Let the faithful exult in glory;
   let them sing for joy on their couches.
6 Let the high praises of God be in their
      throats
   and two-edged swords in their hands,
7 to execute vengeance on the nations
   and punishment on the peoples,
8 to bind their kings with fetters
   and their nobles with chains of iron,
9 to execute on them the judgment
      decreed.
   This is glory for all his faithful ones.
   Praise the LORD!

Praise for God's Surpassing Greatness

150 Praise the LORD!
   Praise God in his sanctuary;
   praise him in his mighty firmament![b]
2 Praise him for his mighty deeds;
   praise him according to his surpassing
      greatness!

3 Praise him with trumpet sound;
   praise him with lute and harp!
4 Praise him with tambourine and dance;
   praise him with strings and pipe!
5 Praise him with clanging cymbals;
   praise him with loud clashing
      cymbals!
6 Let everything that breathes praise the
      LORD!
   Praise the LORD!

---

a Or *he set a law that cannot pass away*   *b* Or *dome*

---

their creator (cf. 19.1; Job 38.7). **148.2** Cf. 29.1; 103.20–22. **148.6** Cf. Job 38.8–11. **148.7–14** The earth and all its natural elements, animals, and human inhabitants are called to praise the Lord because of God's glory. **148.14** *Horn.* See note on 75.4–5.

149.1–9 A hymn of praise for God's salvation. **149.1–4** Call for the congregation to praise the Lord because of God's favor seen in saving the humble, i.e., the lowly and helpless, which is how the community sees itself. **149.1** *Sing . . . new song.* Cf. 33.3; 40.3; 96.1; 98.1; 144.1; Isa 42.10. **149.5–9** Call for the people to praise and go forth in battle. It is debated as to whether these verses describe a ritual occasion of martial singing and dancing during one of the religious festi-

vals or envision an eschatological victory celebration. The opening verses of the psalm tend to suggest a liturgical event of praise and celebration of God's victory and rule over the nations. **149.5–6** Cf. Jdt 15.13. **149.7** Cf. Isa 34.8; 61.2; 62.1–2.

150.1–6 A hymn of praise in which all of creation is called to glorify God. The Psalter is thus given a doxological conclusion. Whereas in other hymns in Psalms the emphasis is often upon the reasons for praise in God's marvelous works, here the emphasis is upon the call to praise and the universality of that praise in all the earth, by every creature, and with every instrument that can make music.

PROVERBS

THE BOOK OF PROVERBS is a series of collections whose authorship was traditionally attributed to Solomon, as were Ecclesiastes and Song of Solomon. The ascription to Solomon, however, is an honorary one, making sense in light of his fabled wisdom (1 Kings 3–4). The sages who first began to write and collect these sayings were court- and temple-based men who served as counselors, bureaucrats, and teachers during the Divided Monarchy. The final stages of composition and editing occurred much later, however, probably in the late Persian or Hellenistic period (fifth–third century BCE) by scribes and teachers associated with the Jerusalem temple. Hence, Proverbs—like the other Hebrew wisdom books Job and Ecclesiastes—reflects the worldview of the intellectual elite. Though aspects of that outlook changed as cultural conditions altered, the final editors had no trouble crafting a book that combined received tradition with new insights.

Leading Ideas

THE FUNDAMENTAL GOAL of the book of Proverbs is to teach the acquisition of wisdom and the avoidance of folly. Both these words are rich in nuance and conveyed by a plethora of overlapping Hebrew terms. Wisdom is seen as insight, understanding, knowledge, advice, prudence, discretion, discipline, intelligence, good sense, and more; folly means ignorance, lacking sense or discipline, knavishness, stupidity, smug obtuseness, prideful scorn, arrogance, insolence, and callow gullibility. Wisdom thus involves good judgment at the practical level, but it is also an ethical virtue: prudence comes engrained with the moral order, and intelligence is an act of will, not an innate attribute. Folly likewise entails moral culpability: the callow youth is trainable but also responsible for accepting discipline, while willful ignorance sets one on the path to death. Proverbial contrasts between the righteous and the wicked as well as the wise and the foolish show the sages' concern for morality as it was lived out on a day-to-day basis.

Concern with retribution marks the thinking of this group. It was believed that a person's character and behavior produced predictable consequences, making it easy to blame fools for their inevitable misfortunes or recommend corporal punishment for children lest their disobedience produce worse consequences later in life. At such points we become aware that we are listening to the discourse of a privileged group, whose members find moral validation of their own status in this same way. The sages also know that appearances can be deceptive, that

849

the poor deserve care rather than blame, and that God's purposes transcend human plans. Indeed, "fear of the LORD" is a key concept, referring to the obedience and proper relationship to God that is the "beginning of wisdom" and that matures into a full moral conscience.

Divine revelation is nonetheless not the source of authority for the wisdom tradition. Covenant, historical redemption, and the legal tradition, although known to the sages, are less important here than elsewhere. This "wisdom of the marketplace" looks to human experience of the social and natural orders, confirmed over the generations, as the basis for theological and moral insight and is cast in the voice of a "father" speaking to a "son." This is in part because the world of wisdom is an international one. Many of the sages' writings have direct parallels from Mesopotamia and Egypt (in fact, Prov 22.17–24.22 derives indirectly but clearly from the earlier Egyptian Instruction of Amenemope), making this a markedly universal rather than national literature.

Woman Wisdom

THE FIGURE OF WISDOM personified as a woman who reaches out to the human world is another intriguing feature. The meaning of this exalted female figure in a strongly male-centered society has been much debated, for female imagery begins (chs. 1–9) and ends (ch. 31) the book, providing both the theological introduction and human postscript to the collections of individual sayings. Some find in this figure—and in her direct opposites, Woman Folly (NRSV, "foolish woman," 9.13–18), Woman Stranger (NRSV, "loose woman," 2.16–19), and the adulteress—the remnant of a goddess once worshiped by Israelites. Others see her as an extension of God's attributes that have subsequently taken on independent life, or as a prophet. To others she is modeled after the real roles of teacher, counselor, and household planner played by Israelite women in their homes and societies. In the paternal rhetoric of Proverbs, Woman Wisdom provides an appealing antidote for young men to the allures of more dangerous women. More than this, though, she embodies for the sages the universal wisdom of which they see their own work as part, as she speaks with divine authority (1.20–33) and plays a role in creation (ch. 8). Resisting categorization as a simple literary device of personification, Woman Wisdom gains additional stature in the apocryphal/deuterocanonical books of Sirach and the Wisdom of Solomon, and even enters the New Testament canon in the masculinized form of the divine Logos (cf. Prov 8.22–36; Jn 1.1–18).

Formal Characteristics

DIVERSE LITERARY FORMS make up the book, though all conform to the canons of parallelism in Hebrew poetry. In parallelism, a poetic verse consists of two (sometimes three) lines, the second of which in some way restates the thought of the first. In synonymous parallelism the second line agrees with the first; in antithetic parallelism the relationship is one of contrast between the two lines; and in formal, or synthetic, parallelism the second line advances the thought of the first in some way. Because the sages are concerned with the inculcation of moral values, they often use antithetic parallelism to heighten the contrast between approved and disapproved behavior.

Proverbs 1–9 consists primarily of lengthy "wisdom poems," which celebrate the virtues of Woman Wisdom, and ten "instructions." The instruction, a form borrowed from the Egyptian wisdom tradition, is an extended poem characterized by positive and negative admonitions to youth, issued in direct address from parent to child or teacher to pupil (1.8–19; 2.1–22; 3.1–12, 21–35; 4.1–9, 10–19, 20–27, 5.1–23; 6.20–35; 7.1–27; 22.17–24.22; 31.1–9). Prov 31.1–9 is extraordinary because it purports to be an instruction by a queen mother. The acrostic poem of the Woman of Worth, or the capable wife, in 31.10–31, in which each line begins with a successive letter of the Hebrew alphabet, is another type of extended composition.

In chs. 10–30, readers encounter the highly crafted, two-line artistic proverbs of the sages, which are simple observations, but most moral mini-lessons. Specialized forms of proverbs are the "better than" sayings (e.g., 3.14; 15.16–17), their "not right" variation (e.g., 17.26a; 18.5a), and riddles (identified in 1.6, but not represented in the collection; but see 23.29–35). Admonitions and prohibitions add a motivation to the proverbial observations (4.21–22; 5.7–10). "Numerical sayings," a favorite among Israel's neighbors, use the pattern of x number in the first line followed by $x + 1$ in the next ("Three things are stately in their stride; four are stately in their gait," 30.29). The arrangement of these forms is not haphazard: the sages used wordplays, key words, alliteration, content, and other devices in their ordering and editing of diverse sayings. Cross-references to repeated vocabulary are given in the notes the first time the term appears. [CLAUDIA V. CAMP and CAROLE R. FONTAINE]

1

The proverbs of Solomon son of David, king of Israel:

Prologue

2 For learning about wisdom and
      instruction,
   for understanding words of insight,
3 for gaining instruction in wise dealing,
      righteousness, justice, and equity;
4 to teach shrewdness to the simple,
      knowledge and prudence to the young—
5 let the wise also hear and gain in learning,

and the discerning acquire skill,
6 to understand a proverb and a figure,
   the words of the wise and their riddles.

7 The fear of the LORD is the beginning of
      knowledge;
   fools despise wisdom and instruction.

Warnings against Evil Companions

8 Hear, my child, your father's instruction,
      and do not reject your mother's
         teaching;

1.1 The book's title. "Proverbs," Hebrew *meshalim*, are sayings expressing commonly held wisdom. Solomon's legendary wisdom is invoked, though the book's themes and perspectives are not at all monarchical. In the royal ideology, the king's wisdom gave him the capacity to administer legal justice and bring righteous order to society (see also 8.14–16; 16.10, 13; 20.26, 28; 25.1–7; 28.2–3, 15–16; 29.2, 12, 14, 16, 26; 30.27–31; 31.1–9; 1 Kings 3.4–28; 4.29–34; 10.1–13), functions here assumed by the wisdom teachers. **1.2–7** The prologue introduces the book as a whole, describing the goals of its sayings. It addresses the wise man who will be studying wisdom from the book; he will teach it orally to his students, but also gain from it himself. **1.2–5** The concatenation of terms related to *wisdom* (*learning, instruction, understanding, insight, righteousness, justice, equity, shrewdness, knowledge, prudence*) shows the broad scope of the wisdom to be instilled in the young (see Introduction; cf. 2.2–11; 3.13, 21; 4.1, 5, 7; 5.1–2; 8.1, 5, 12, 14). **1.3** *Instruction*, more precisely "discipline" must be taken; it cannot be forced. The association of *wise dealing* with *righteousness, justice, and equity* is typical of wisdom thought:

worldly wisdom makes one right with God (see also 2.9; 3.33–35; 8.8, 18–20). *Equity*, from the Hebrew root meaning "straight, (up)right," a concept common in Proverbs in both the concrete and the abstract sense, is often found with *path* or *way* (see, e.g., 2.7, 13, 15, 21; 3.6, 32; 4.11, 25–26; 5.6; 8.8–9; 9.15; 11.3, 5, 6; 28.10; 29.27; 30.20). **1.4** *Shrewdness, prudence,* morally neutral terms indicating cunning and private plans, yet here appropriated by the author as virtues, since all intellectual powers had moral potential. Proverbs knows several degrees of fool. Here the *simple* and *young* can be trained; elsewhere recalcitrant students *without sense* become the doomed *scoffers, scorners,* and *fools* who *hate knowledge* (see, e.g., 1.7, 22, 32; 3.34; 6.32; 7.7; 9.4, 6, 7, 12, 16; 10.1, 8; 14.9; 21.24; 27.22; 29.1, 8). The message is: wisdom leads to life, folly to death. **1.5** The wise as well as the simple can learn from the book (see also 9.7–12). *Hear,* pay attention, in this case to the written book, not an oral teacher. *Learning* connotes verbal eloquence. One can learn from the book to speak persuasively. *Skill,* the sophisticated abilities to direct events that come with experience, again not inherently moral. **1.6** Proper and truthful speech is a cen-

9 for they are a fair garland for your head,
  and pendants for your neck.
10 My child, if sinners entice you,
  do not consent.
11 If they say, "Come with us, let us lie in
    wait for blood;
  let us wantonly ambush the innocent;
12 like Sheol let us swallow them alive
  and whole, like those who go down to
    the Pit.
13 We shall find all kinds of costly things;

  we shall fill our houses with booty.
14 Throw in your lot among us;
  we will all have one purse"—
15 my child, do not walk in their way,
  keep your foot from their paths;
16 for their feet run to evil,
  and they hurry to shed blood.
17 For in vain is the net baited
  while the bird is looking on;
18 yet they lie in wait—to kill themselves!
  and set an ambush—for their own lives!

---

tral concern of the wisdom tradition, both as a practical skill and as a manifestation of an orderly society; listening and speaking well determine worldly success and can be a matter of life and death (see, e.g., 1.23; 2.1, 6, 12, 16; 4.4–5, 10, 20, 24; 5.2–3, 7, 13; 6.2, 17, 19; 7.2, 21, 24; 8.6–8, 13; 10.8, 11, 13–14, 18–21, 31–32; 25.11–15; 26.4–5, 7, 9, 22–25, 28; 29.20). Advanced study in wisdom includes the *proverb* (Hebrew *mashal;* see note on 1.1), the *figure* (an artistic epigram), and *riddles* (none obvious in the book—cf. Samson's riddle in Judg 14.14, 18—itself an enigma!). **1.7** *Fear of the LORD* is the *beginning* (i.e., prerequisite) of knowledge or wisdom (cf. 4.7; see also 1.29; 2.5; 3.7; 8.13; 9.10; 10.27; 14.26–27; 15.33; 16.6; 19.23; 28.14; 29.25; 31.30; Job 28.28). Obedience to the precepts of righteousness may begin from childlike fear of punishment but matures into adult moral conscience.

1.8–9.18 Using antithesis, these instructional and wisdom poems identify and interrelate fundamental values: wisdom vs. folly, good vs. evil, life vs. death, parental instruction vs. the lure of outsiders' speech. These concepts are often presented metaphorically by means of two contrasting female figures, personified Wisdom and the *strange woman* (see 2.16; text note *a*), and of two "ways" (e.g., 2.13).

1.8–19 The first of ten instructional poems cast as paternal lectures, this one against men whose greed breeds violence. Each lecture has three parts: the exordium or introduction (including address, exhortation, and motivation), the lesson itself, and a conclusion. **1.8** *Hear, my child,* a typical formula to introduce an instruction; sometimes it appears without *hear,* sometimes in the plural, *children* (see also 1.10, 15; 2.1; 3.1, 21; 4.1, 10, 20; 5.1, 7; 6.1, 3, 20; 7.1, 24; 8.32; 27.11). Students of the time were usually male; "Hear, my son(s)" in the RSV translation is more accurate. Both *mother* and *father* are regularly named as teachers, though the mother's voice is only heard in 31.1 (see also 4.3; 6.20; 10.1; 15.20; 23.22; 28.7, 24; 29.3, 15, 17; 30.17). The family setting may here be a literary fiction disguising a school, but parental teaching was also an important social reality. *Instruction, teaching* (Hebrew *torah*), along with *discipline, reproof, counsel,* words typical of wisdom discourse (see, e.g., 1.25, 30; 3.1, 11–13; 4.1; 5.12; 6.20, 23; 7.2; 9.7–9; 10.17; 11.14; 29.1). *Torah,* elsewhere a term for covenant law, in Proverbs usually refers to more general parental instruction (cf. *commandment,* 2.1; 10.8; for possible exceptions, see

28.4, 7, 9; 29.18). **1.9** *Fair garland,* also Woman Wisdom's prize (4.9); parental instruction is thus associated with Wisdom's authority. The depiction of virtue visibly worn is common; it is unclear whether it is intended literally (see also 3.3, 22; 4.9; 6.21; 7.3; Job 31.35–36; Song 8.6). *Pendants,* better "necklace," a multistranded adornment. **1.10–19** The motif of the violent men to be avoided appears also in 2.12–15; 3.31–32; 6.11–19; 28.17, 24; 29.10. **1.10** *Sinners,* habitual criminals, not occasional transgressors. **1.11–14** Though the instructor purports to quote the *sinners'* speech, the rhetoric shows it to be his own construction (see also 7.14–20; 8.4–36; 9.4–6, 16–17). **1.11** *Come with us* resembles the invitations of both female Wisdom and the Strange Woman (7.18; 9.5). The latter will also *lie in wait* (7.12; 23.28). **1.12** *Sheol, Pit,* the place of the dead. In Canaanite myth, Death was depicted as having a gaping maw with which to *swallow* victims; the sinners thus equate themselves with personified Death (see also 5.5; 7.27; 9.18; 23.27; 27.20; 30.16). **1.13** *Find.* Seeking and finding is a common motif usually applied to the quest for wisdom (v. 28; 2.4–5; 3.13; 4.22; 8.9, 17, 35), though it is used once of the Strange Woman's seduction of the simple youth (7.15; see also 25.2–3; 28.11–13, 28; 29.10). *Costly things.* Wealth and treasure are among the blessings of seeking Wisdom (8.18, 21; cf. 25.11–12); they are not without value, but only sinners quest for the things in themselves (2.1, 4; 3.14–15; 8.10–11, 19). *Houses.* The choice of which house to enter becomes important in developing the portraits of Woman Wisdom and Woman Stranger/Folly (2.18; 3.33; 5.8, 10; 7.6, 8, 11, 19, 27; 9.1, 14; 14.1; cf. 31.15). *Booty,* or *gain,* is also what the good wife brings her husband (31.11). **1.14** *One purse,* a temptingly egalitarian offer to a young man in a society where the family patriarch controlled the wealth until his death. **1.15–16** *Way, paths,* imagery for life decisions, often concretized with images of *feet* that *run* or *walk* in one moral direction or another (see, e.g., 2.7–20; 3.6, 17, 23; 4.11–19, 26–27; 5.5–8, 21; 6.23; 7.25; 8.13, 20, 32; 9.6; 10.9; 11.5; 28.6; 28.18). A variation of v. 16 appears in Isa 59.7a. **1.17** An originally independent proverb included here for persuasion: greed is its own snare (see also 3.26; 5.22; 6.2, 5; 7.22–23; 12.13; 29.6, 25), though the sinners are too foolish to see it. **1.18** *Lie in wait, ambush.* The sinners' own words are repeated, but with the meaning inverted to reveal their folly.

19 Such is the end[a] of all who are greedy for
      gain;
   it takes away the life of its possessors.

The Call of Wisdom

20 Wisdom cries out in the street;
   in the squares she raises her voice.
21 At the busiest corner she cries out;
   at the entrance of the city gates she
      speaks:
22 "How long, O simple ones, will you love
      being simple?
   How long will scoffers delight in their
      scoffing
   and fools hate knowledge?
23 Give heed to my reproof;
   I will pour out my thoughts to you;
   I will make my words known to you.
24 Because I have called and you refused,
   have stretched out my hand and no
      one heeded,
25 and because you have ignored all my
      counsel
   and would have none of my reproof,
26 I also will laugh at your calamity;
   I will mock when panic strikes you,

27 when panic strikes you like a storm,
   and your calamity comes like a
      whirlwind,
   when distress and anguish come upon
      you.
28 Then they will call upon me, but I will
      not answer;
   they will seek me diligently, but will
      not find me.
29 Because they hated knowledge
   and did not choose the fear of the
      LORD,
30 would have none of my counsel,
   and despised all my reproof,
31 therefore they shall eat the fruit of their
      way
   and be sated with their own devices.
32 For waywardness kills the simple,
   and the complacency of fools destroys
      them;
33 but those who listen to me will be
      secure
   and will live at ease, without dread of
      disaster."

----

a Gk: Heb *are the ways*

1.19 *End,* lit. "ways." See note on 1.15–16. Violent, untimely death meets evildoers, rather than the peaceful
death of old age anticipated by the good.

1.20–33 Female personified *Wisdom,* here Hebrew
chokmot, a plural form construed as a singular, as also
in 9.1; the singular, *chokmah,* appears in 8.1. Perhaps
the plural is one of majesty (cf. Hebrew *Elohim,*
"gods/God"). She appears here as a prophet or street
teacher (see also 3.13–18; 4.5–9; 5.15–19; 7.4–5; 8.1–
36; 9.1–6), and the poem has verbal, structural, and
thematic links to, e.g., Jer 7; Zech 7. Though she forms
the antithesis to the Strange Woman (see 2.16–19; 5.3–
14, 19–20; 6.24–35; 7.1–27), their portrayals contain
many similarities. Shared vocabulary also links her to
the capable wife (31.10–31). **1.20–21** *Cries out, raises
her voice.* Her daring approach is personal and verbal,
as is the Strange Woman's (v. 24; 8.1; 9.3, 15). *Street,
squares, corner, city gates.* Woman Wisdom is found
where the economic and juridical life of society takes
place, as are the Strange Woman and the capable wife
(7.8, 12; 8.2–3; 9.3, 14; 31.23, 31). **1.22** *How long* evokes
prophetic as well as psalmic speech (e.g., Jer 4.14, 21;
12.4; Pss 6.3; 74.10). *Simple ones, scoffers, fools.* See note
on 1.4. Like a prophet, Wisdom addresses both the
teachable and the intractable. One relates to her in the
personal terms of *love* or *hate* (see also v. 29; 4.6; 5.12;
6.16; 8.13, 17–21, 36; 9.8; 29.3). **1.23** *Reproof,* chastisement, an important educational concept (1.23, 25, 30;
3.11; 5.12; 6.23; 10.17 (rebuke); 12.1; 13.18; 15.5 (admonition), 10 (rebuke), 31 (admonition), 32 (admonition); 27.5; 29.1, 15), that may imply corporal or verbal

punishment. *Pour out.* Wisdom is like a fountain or
spring (see also 13.14; 16.22; 25.26). *Thoughts,* lit.
"spirit," but here an attribute of the mind combining
emotion and intellect that Wisdom will convey along
with her *words* to a hypothetical audience of sinners.
1.24–33 *Called, refused, stretched out my hand,* vocabulary that evokes the prophets (see Jer 7.13; Isa 6.9–10;
65.1–2). Woman Wisdom, though, speaks in her own
behalf, rather than God's. The gesture is intimidating,
not welcoming. **1.26–27** *Laugh, mock.* Wisdom's attitude matches the fool's, and the capable wife's (31.25);
God also mocks his enemies (Ps 2.4). *Panic.* The effect
of accepting or rejecting Wisdom is experienced internally as well as externally (see v. 33; 3.25–26; 4.16;
6.22). **1.28** Wisdom now turns to her real audience, the
readers. *Call.* Her approach should be matched by the
student's (see v. 20; 2.3). *Seek, find.* See note on 1.13;
elsewhere the terms describe the worshiper's relationship to God (Hos 5.6; Am 8.12; 2 Chr 15.2). God, when
angry, does not let himself be found (Mic 3.4; Isa 1.15;
Jer 11.11). **1.30** *Counsel, reproof.* The language of the
teacher (see note on 1.8) replaces that of the prophet.
1.31 *Eat the fruit, be sated.* Food is a metaphor for attitude and action, particularly the enjoyment and fruits
of learning or the choice and outcome of refusing to
learn (see also 4.17; 9.2, 5, 17; 18.21; 26.22; 27.7, 18;
28.7; 30.20). **1.32–33** Wisdom does not herself execute
the punishment. **1.32** A proverb suggesting evil brings
its own reward. **1.33** *Be secure* (lit. "dwell secure"); the
same phrase describes faithful Israel's life in the land
(Deut 33.28). *Dread.* See vv. 26–27.

The Value of Wisdom

2 My child, if you accept my words
and treasure up my commandments
within you,

2 making your ear attentive to wisdom
and inclining your heart to
understanding;

3 if you indeed cry out for insight,
and raise your voice for understanding;

4 if you seek it like silver,
and search for it as for hidden
treasures—

5 then you will understand the fear of the
LORD
and find the knowledge of God.

6 For the LORD gives wisdom;
from his mouth come knowledge and
understanding;

7 he stores up sound wisdom for the upright;
he is a shield to those who walk
blamelessly,

8 guarding the paths of justice
and preserving the way of his faithful
ones.

9 Then you will understand righteousness
and justice
and equity, every good path;

10 for wisdom will come into your heart,
and knowledge will be pleasant to your
soul;

11 prudence will watch over you;
and understanding will guard you.

12 It will save you from the way of evil,
from those who speak perversely,

13 who forsake the paths of uprightness
to walk in the ways of darkness,

14 who rejoice in doing evil
and delight in the perverseness of evil;

15 those whose paths are crooked,
and who are devious in their ways.

16 You will be saved from the loose*a* woman,
from the adulteress with her smooth
words,

17 who forsakes the partner of her youth
and forgets her sacred covenant;

18 for her way*b* leads down to death,

_____

a Heb *strange* *b* Cn: Heb *house*

2.1–22 This second instruction repeats several key themes from ch. 1 and introduces *treasure* as a symbol for wisdom (vv. 1, 4; see note on 1.13). It does not itself teach wisdom, but rather prepares and encourages listeners/readers for the ensuing instructions. **2.1** *Commandments,* here the words of a human teacher, elsewhere in the Bible God's commandments (see note on 1.8; also 3.1; 4.4; 6.20, 23; 7.2). **2.2–11** In the extended introduction (exordium), the father presents his own words as the *wisdom* to be sought. **2.2** The *heart,* the seat of the mind, must be connected to the *ear* (cf. the "understanding mind," lit. "listening heart" requested by wise Solomon, 1 Kings 3.9; see, e.g., Prov 3.5; 4.20–21, 23; 5.1, 13; 6.18, 25; 7.3, 25; 15.14; 25.12). *Inclining* the heart thus means desiring and choosing understanding. **2.3** *Cry out, raise your voice.* The same verbs describe Wisdom's call (1.20; cf. 1.28). **2.4–5** *Hidden treasures.* Wisdom must be actively sought, a variation on the theme of her public accessibility. **2.5** Although *fear of the* LORD is the beginning of wisdom (1.7), finding wisdom allows one to *understand* that fear. Thus wisdom leads to *knowledge of God,* to conscience and religious awareness (see also 9.10). **2.6–11** The LORD is the source of *wisdom* and its protective power, yet *wisdom, prudence,* and *understanding* are active agents in vv. 10–12 (see also 3.21–26; 4.6; 6.24). **2.6** *From his mouth.* Not verbal revelation, but the source of God's gift of wisdom. **2.7** *Sound wisdom,* neither an intellectual nor a moral faculty, but practical resourcefulness. **2.12–15** Cf. the portrayal of the violent men in 1.10–19. Perverse speech is as much at issue as evil actions. *Uprightness.* See note on 1.3. *Crookedness* characterizes

the wicked. **2.13** *Darkness* suggests both evil and ignorance; cf. the light of wisdom (see also 4.18–19; 6.23; 7.9). **2.16–19** These verses introduce a key female figure typically described with two closely related Hebrew words. Better than *loose woman, adulteress* are the more literal translations "strange woman," "alien woman" (cf. the masculine form, 5.10; 20.16; 27.2, 13). Extramarital sexuality was regarded as a fundamental evil in its own right, but the doubled, multivalent, and evocative terms for strangeness may intimate a more pervasive male sense of female danger (see also 5.3–14, 19–20; 6.24–35; 7.1–27). The terms can mean "foreign in nationality," but that does not seem to be the issue here; contrast Neh 13. The postexilic period seems nonetheless to have had its problems with women regarded as outsiders to whatever group was in charge (e.g., Ezra 9–10; Mal 2.10–16), and the Proverbs figure may channel some of that anxiety. Woman Stranger is equated with Woman Folly in 9.13–18 (cf. 5.22–23). **2.16** The woman's *smooth words* may at first sound sweeter than the evil men's crooked speech, but they are no less dangerous (see note on 1.6; also 2.12). **2.17** Marital faithlessness is linked with religious deviation (cf. Mal 2.10–16; also cf. Prov 5.15–18; 7.4). *Her sacred covenant* (lit. "the covenant of her God") may refer simply to her marriage contract, but evokes the marital metaphor often used for God and Israel. **2.18–19** *Way* parallels *paths* (see note on 1.15–16), but the images of the "way" and the woman's deadly *house* (see text note *b*) are often connected (see 1.13, 15; 5.8, 10; 7.8, 11, 19, 27; 9.13–15; note on 1.13). *Those who go* [lit. "come"] *to her* has a sexual connotation in Hebrew

and her paths to the shades;
19 those who go to her never come back,
   nor do they regain the paths of life.

20 Therefore walk in the way of the good,
   and keep to the paths of the just.
21 For the upright will abide in the land,
   and the innocent will remain in it;
22 but the wicked will be cut off from the
   land,
   and the treacherous will be rooted out
   of it.

Admonition to Trust and Honor God

3 My child, do not forget my teaching,
   but let your heart keep my
      commandments;
2 for length of days and years of life
   and abundant welfare they will give
      you.

3 Do not let loyalty and faithfulness forsake
      you;
   bind them around your neck,
   write them on the tablet of your heart.
4 So you will find favor and good repute
   in the sight of God and of people.

5 Trust in the LORD with all your heart,
   and do not rely on your own insight.
6 In all your ways acknowledge him,
   and he will make straight your paths.
7 Do not be wise in your own eyes;

fear the LORD, and turn away from evil.
8 It will be a healing for your flesh
   and a refreshment for your body.

9 Honor the LORD with your substance
   and with the first fruits of all your
      produce;
10 then your barns will be filled with plenty,
   and your vats will be bursting with wine.

11 My child, do not despise the LORD's
      discipline
   or be weary of his reproof,
12 for the LORD reproves the one he loves,
   as a father the son in whom he
      delights.

The True Wealth

13 Happy are those who find wisdom,
   and those who get understanding,
14 for her income is better than silver,
   and her revenue better than gold.
15 She is more precious than jewels,
   and nothing you desire can compare
      with her.
16 Long life is in her right hand;
   in her left hand are riches and honor.
17 Her ways are ways of pleasantness,
   and all her paths are peace.
18 She is a tree of life to those who lay hold
      of her;
   those who hold her fast are called
      happy.

---

as in English. **2.20–22** *Cut off from the land* probably means premature death or death without heirs, but may sound undertones of the covenant tradition.
3.1–35 This chapter is stitched together with the motifs of commandments (v. 1; cf. the list in vv. 27–31), long life (vv. 2, 16), honor (vv. 4, 9, 16, 35), virtue imaged as adornments (vv. 3, 22), and material blessings (vv. 2, 8, 10, 16, 33; cf. 4.8, 10, 22; 5.9–11; 6.33; 8.18–20; 9.11). **3.1–12** In the third person, the father's *teaching* and *commandments* (v. 1) are aligned with *the* LORD's *discipline* (vv. 11–12; see notes on 1.8; 2.1). This wisdom, though human, has a status beyond the "merely" human; thus one should not *rely on* one's *own insight* or *be wise in* one's *own eyes* (vv. 5, 7; see also 12.15; 26.5, 12, 16; 28.11; 28.26). **3.3** *Loyalty* (Hebrew *chesed;* see 31.26) is always given by a superior to an inferior; thus, the pupil is admonished to live so as not to be abandoned by God. **3.3** *Bind . . . neck.* See 1.9. *Write . . . heart,* internalize the father's teachings in order to remember them. **3.4** Social approval or disapproval (often termed *honor* and *shame/disgrace*) defined the relationship of the individual to society (see

vv. 16, 35; 4.8; 5.9, 14; 6.33–35; 8.18; 11.16; 15.33; 18.12; 20.3; 25.2–3, 7c–10, 27; 26.1, 8; 27.11; 28.7; 29.15, 23). **3.5, 7** *Not rely on your own insight, not be wise in your own eyes,* a rare but important caution against hubris in wisdom; *fear the LORD* is the corrective. **3.8** On healing vs. destruction of the body, see also 4.22; 5.11; 6.33. *Body,* lit. "bones," is paired, as often, with "flesh." **3.9–10** An admonition to observe ritual law (Lev 2.14; Num 28.6), rare in wisdom literature. **3.11–12** Not all discipline is punishment. **3.13–18** Hymn to personified Wisdom (see 1.20–33) using several conventional motifs: comparison to treasure (see 1.13); *long life, riches, honor* as Wisdom's gifts (see 3.1–12); and calling her a *tree of life* (see also 11.30; 13.12; 15.4). **3.13** *Happy are those,* a typical wisdom formula (macarism) identical to that in the Beatitudes (Mt 5:3–12; Lk 6:20–23; see also Prov 8.34; 20.7; 28.14; 29.18; 31.28). **3.16** The Egyptian goddess Maat, depicted with symbols of life and wealth in her hands, is possibly a source for female Wisdom. **3.18** *Lay hold of, hold . . . fast.* Strong words of physical embrace describe the student's relationship to Woman Wisdom or

God's Wisdom in Creation

19 The LORD by wisdom founded the earth;
  by understanding he established the
    heavens;
20 by his knowledge the deeps broke open,
  and the clouds drop down the dew.

The True Security

21 My child, do not let these escape from
    your sight:
  keep sound wisdom and prudence,
22 and they will be life for your soul
  and adornment for your neck.
23 Then you will walk on your way securely
  and your foot will not stumble.
24 If you sit down,ᵃ you will not be afraid;
  when you lie down, your sleep will be
    sweet.
25 Do not be afraid of sudden panic,
  or of the storm that strikes the
    wicked;
26 for the LORD will be your confidence
  and will keep your foot from being
    caught.

27 Do not withhold good from those to
    whom it is due,ᵇ
  when it is in your power to do it.
28 Do not say to your neighbor, "Go, and
    come again,
  tomorrow I will give it"—when you
    have it with you.
29 Do not plan harm against your neighbor
  who lives trustingly beside you.

30 Do not quarrel with anyone without
    cause,
  when no harm has been done to you.
31 Do not envy the violent
  and do not choose any of their ways;
32 for the perverse are an abomination to
    the LORD,
  but the upright are in his confidence.
33 The LORD's curse is on the house of the
    wicked,
  but he blesses the abode of the
    righteous.
34 Toward the scorners he is scornful,
  but to the humble he shows favor.
35 The wise will inherit honor,
  but stubborn fools, disgrace.

Parental Advice

4 Listen, children, to a father's instruction,
  and be attentive, that you may gain
    ᶜinsight;
2 for I give you good precepts:
  do not forsake my teaching.
3 When I was a son with my father,
  tender, and my mother's favorite,
4 he taught me, and said to me,
  "Let your heart hold fast my words;
  keep my commandments, and live.
5 Get wisdom; get insight: do not forget,
    nor turn away
  from the words of my mouth.
6 Do not forsake her, and she will keep you;
  love her, and she will guard you.

---

a Gk: Heb *lie down*   *b* Heb *from its owners*   *c* Heb *know*

---

the Strange Woman (see also 4.4, 8, 13; 5.2, 20; 7.13).
3.19–20 A short hymn to the creator God that gives wisdom cosmological significance. The connection between God, Wisdom, and creation is elaborated in 8.22–36. Control of the water of *the deeps* under the earth and in the heavens above is crucial to life on earth. **3.21–35** The father's fourth lecture. **3.21–26** On the inner and outer effects of wisdom and wickedness. **3.22** The artistry of the couplet is hard to capture in translation. *Adornment* (Hebrew *hen*) forms an alliteration with *life* (*chayyim*). The first line (*life, soul*) seems to represent an inner state, while the second line (*adornment, neck*) its outer manifestation. But the word for soul (*nephesh*) can also mean "throat," breaking the inner-outer distinction in typical Israelite fashion. On virtue as adornment, see 1.9. **3.24–26** See 1.26–27. **3.26** *Caught.* See 1.17. **3.27–32** Admonitions to treat others fairly. The apodictic *do not* is like that of the Ten Commandments. **3.27–29** *Good.* The context suggests something that is owed.

On the sages' concern for financial obligations, see 6.1–5; 7.19–20. *Neighbor,* not just someone who lives nearby, but anyone one has dealings with. **3.31–32** See 1.8–19. **3.33–35** *Wicked/righteous, wise/fools,* two central word pairs, here equated (cf. 1.3; 5.21–23), elsewhere independent (see, e.g., ch. 10; 25.5). **3.35** A proverb closes the instruction with persuasive force (see 1.17).

4.1–5.23 Woman Wisdom, the Violent Men, and the Strange Woman elaborated. **4.1–9** An instruction poem focused on love of Woman Wisdom (see 1.20–33). Though the speaker's mother is mentioned, the poem presents a father's teaching of his father's instruction to his sons on Wisdom, the woman they should love. **4.4–6** Not *turning away* from the father's words and *not forsaking* Woman Wisdom are poetically identified; here female imagery increases the desirability and authority of male teaching. If the student *keeps* the commandments, Woman Wisdom will *keep, guard* him (see 2.7–8). **4.5, 7** *Get wisdom, get insight.*

7   The beginning of wisdom is this: Get
      wisdom,
    and whatever else you get, get insight.
8   Prize her highly, and she will exalt you;
    she will honor you if you embrace her.
9   She will place on your head a fair garland;
    she will bestow on you a beautiful
      crown."

Admonition to Keep to the Right Path

10 Hear, my child, and accept my words,
    that the years of your life may be many.
11 I have taught you the way of wisdom;
    I have led you in the paths of
      uprightness.
12 When you walk, your step will not be
      hampered;
    and if you run, you will not stumble.
13 Keep hold of instruction; do not let go;
    guard her, for she is your life.
14 Do not enter the path of the wicked,
    and do not walk in the way of
      evildoers.
15 Avoid it; do not go on it;
    turn away from it and pass on.
16 For they cannot sleep unless they have
      done wrong;
    they are robbed of sleep unless they
      have made someone stumble.
17 For they eat the bread of wickedness
    and drink the wine of violence.
18 But the path of the righteous is like the
      light of dawn,
    which shines brighter and brighter
      until full day.
19 The way of the wicked is like deep
      darkness;
    they do not know what they stumble
      over.
20 My child, be attentive to my words;

    incline your ear to my sayings.
21 Do not let them escape from your sight;
    keep them within your heart.
22 For they are life to those who find them,
    and healing to all their flesh.
23 Keep your heart with all vigilance,
    for from it flow the springs of life.
24 Put away from you crooked speech,
    and put devious talk far from you.
25 Let your eyes look directly forward,
    and your gaze be straight before you.
26 Keep straight the path of your feet,
    and all your ways will be sure.
27 Do not swerve to the right or to the left;
    turn your foot away from evil.

Warning against Impurity and Infidelity

5   My child, be attentive to my wisdom;
      incline your ear to my understanding,
2   so that you may hold on to prudence,
    and your lips may guard knowledge.
3   For the lips of a loose*a* woman drip honey,
    and her speech is smoother than oil;
4   but in the end she is bitter as wormwood,
    sharp as a two-edged sword.
5   Her feet go down to death;
    her steps follow the path to Sheol.
6   She does not keep straight to the path of
      life;
    her ways wander, and she does not
      know it.

7   And now, my child,*b* listen to me,
    and do not depart from the words of
      my mouth.
8   Keep your way far from her,
    and do not go near the door of her
      house;

a Heb strange   b Gk Vg: Heb children

The same verb describes the Lord's approach to Wisdom in (see note on) 8.22. **4.7** Note the tautology: the goal and the process are of the same order; cf. 1.7. **4.8–9** A scene of a marriage festival with the groom in kingly array (cf. Song 3.6–11), or of a ceremony in which a high-status woman confers *honor* (see note on 3.4) on her protégé? Imagery of Woman Wisdom as lover and guardian is mixed throughout Prov 1–9 (see 1.20–33; 2.10–12), perhaps merging in the idealization of the wife (5.15–18; 12.4; 31.10–31). *Embrace.* See note on 3.18. *Garland, crown.* See 1.9. **4.10–27** The motif of wisdom's path or way connects the sixth (vv. 10–19) and seventh (vv. 20–27) instructions. **4.13** *Keep hold, do not let go.* To gain Wisdom's guardianship (see 2.7–8), the student must *guard her.*

4.16 On the psychology of the way of evil, see 1.26–27. **4.17** See note on 1.31. **4.18–19** Two aphorisms on *light* and *darkness* (see 2.13) conclude the unit. **4.20–27** Note the theme of body parts: *ear, eyes, heart, flesh,* mouth (here, *speech*), lips (here, *talk*), *feet* (see also 2.2; 3.8). **4.23** *Springs.* On water imagery for life and wisdom, see also 1.23; 5.15–18.

5.1–23 The eighth instruction, polarizing two female figures, the Strange (*loose*) Woman (see 2.16–19) and the wife. **5.3** *Lips, speech.* See note on 1.6; also 2.16. *Honey,* a favorite image for a good that can go bad (see 25.16, 27; 27.7) as well as for a woman's sexual delights. **5.4** *Two-edged sword,* lit., "sword of mouths," an appropriate image for the combined verbal/sexual danger of the Strange Woman. **5.8** *Way, house.* See note on 2.18–

9 or you will give your honor to others,
    and your years to the merciless,
10 and strangers will take their fill of your
    wealth,
    and your labors will go to the house of
    an alien;
11 and at the end of your life you will groan,
    when your flesh and body are
    consumed,
12 and you say, "Oh, how I hated discipline,
    and my heart despised reproof!
13 I did not listen to the voice of my teachers
    or incline my ear to my instructors.
14 Now I am at the point of utter ruin
    in the public assembly."

15 Drink water from your own cistern,
    flowing water from your own well.
16 Should your springs be scattered abroad,
    streams of water in the streets?
17 Let them be for yourself alone,
    and not for sharing with strangers.
18 Let your fountain be blessed,
    and rejoice in the wife of your youth,
19   a lovely deer, a graceful doe.
    May her breasts satisfy you at all times;
    may you be intoxicated always by her
    love.

20 Why should you be intoxicated, my son,
    by another woman
    and embrace the bosom of an adulteress?
21 For human ways are under the eyes of the
    LORD,
    and he examines all their paths.
22 The iniquities of the wicked ensnare them,
    and they are caught in the toils of their
    sin.
23 They die for lack of discipline,
    and because of their great folly they are
    lost.

Practical Admonitions

6 My child, if you have given your pledge
    to your neighbor,
    if you have bound yourself to another,*
2 you are snared by the utterance of your
    lips,*
    caught by the words of your mouth.
3 So do this, my child, and save yourself,
    for you have come into your neighbor's
    power:
    go, hurry,* and plead with your
    neighbor.

---

a Or *a stranger*   *b* Cn Compare Gk Syr: Heb *the words of your
mouth*   *c* Or *humble yourself*

---

19. *Door,* perhaps an allusion to the maw of Sheol (see
note on 1.12; also 8.34; 9.14), but lit. "opening," hence
also a sexual connotation. **5.9–14** The fool will eventually rue his loss of social status, wealth, and health.
5.10 *Strangers, alien,* the same word pair describing the
Strange Woman (see note on 2.16–19), but here in
masculine form. As with the female figure, the terminology denotes outsiders to a man's household, but
they are of a faceless and ruthless sort; the image thus
also hints at the danger of anyone who is "not us."
House of an alien recalls both the violent men (see 1.13)
and the Strange Woman (see notes on 1.13; 2.16–19).
5.14 Public dishonor had more meaning in ancient
times than today, implying a permanent judgment on
one's personhood and social status (see note on 3.4;
also 6.33–35). **5.15–19** A poem in which *water* is a
metaphor for the male student's sexual enjoyment of
his wife. Typically in Prov 1–9, the more abstract female personification of Wisdom (see 1.20–33) is the
Strange Woman's counterpart; here the imagery of female sexuality governs the discourse, and the wife replaces Woman Wisdom (see 2.17; 7.4). As elsewhere in
these poems, the language of proper and improper sexuality blends with that describing wisdom vs. folly and
life vs. death. **5.15–16** The water imagery referring to
the woman in v. 15 balances that referring to the man
in v. 16. **5.17** A difficult verse perhaps referring to v. 10:
a man's sexual pleasure with a strange woman, proba-

bly here an adulteress, will mean sharing his wife with
strange men. **5.18** *Fountain.* Properly contained and
enjoyed waters will yield offspring (see also note on
1.23). **5.19–20** *Deer, doe.* Celebrating the beloved's
beauty by comparison with animals is typical of ancient love poetry, as is delight in anatomical description, here *breasts,* though this word in Hebrew may be
revocalized to yield the alternate translation "lovemaking" (see Song 1.9–10, 15; 2.9; 4.1–5; 5.10–16; 6.5–7;
7.1–9; cf. Prov 7.18). *Be intoxicated.* Repeated vocabulary links the wife and the Strange Woman, even in
their opposition. **5.21–23** The conclusion of the poem
moves abruptly to the larger significance of sexual misbehavior. *Folly* is equated with the *iniquities of the
wicked;* both lead to death (see note on 1.4; also 2.16–
19; 3.33–35; 9.13–18).
   6.1–19 Four epigrams (brief poems with a single
point) on folly and evil. **6.1–5** Control of one's financial resources is urged (cf. 3.27–28). The motif of en-
snarement (6.1, 2, 5), repeated from 5.22, stitches this
unit to the preceding one (see also 1.17). Though material self-interest is strong, one's inheritance was also
a sign of the Lord's blessing. **6.1** *Given your pledge,
bound yourself,* offered oneself or one's resources as
collateral for another's loan. *Neighbor, another* could
be translated "associate," "stranger"; the latter may
have been willing to pay someone to vouch for him
(see 5.10; 11.15; 20.16). **6.2** Verbal agreements were

4   Give your eyes no sleep
       and your eyelids no slumber;
5   save yourself like a gazelle from the
           hunter,[a]
       like a bird from the hand of the fowler.

6   Go to the ant, you lazybones;
       consider its ways, and be wise.
7   Without having any chief
       or officer or ruler,
8   it prepares its food in summer,
       and gathers its sustenance in harvest.
9   How long will you lie there, O lazybones?
       When will you rise from your sleep?
10 A little sleep, a little slumber,
       a little folding of the hands to rest,
11 and poverty will come upon you like a
           robber,
       and want, like an armed warrior.

12 A scoundrel and a villain
       goes around with crooked speech,
13 winking the eyes, shuffling the feet,
       pointing the fingers,
14 with perverted mind devising evil,
       continually sowing discord;
15 on such a one calamity will descend
           suddenly;
       in a moment, damage beyond repair.

16 There are six things that the LORD hates,
       seven that are an abomination to him:
17 haughty eyes, a lying tongue,
       and hands that shed innocent blood,
18 a heart that devises wicked plans,
       feet that hurry to run to evil,
19 a lying witness who testifies falsely,
       and one who sows discord in a family.

20 My child, keep your father's
           commandment,
       and do not forsake your mother's
           teaching.
21 Bind them upon your heart always;
       tie them around your neck.
22 When you walk, they[b] will lead you;
       when you lie down, they[b] will watch
           over you;
       and when you awake, they[b] will talk
           with you.
23 For the commandment is a lamp and the
           teaching a light,
       and the reproofs of discipline are the
           way of life,
24 to preserve you from the wife of another,[c]
       from the smooth tongue of the
           adulteress.
25 Do not desire her beauty in your heart,
       and do not let her capture you with her
           eyelashes;
26 for a prostitute's fee is only a loaf of
           bread,[d]
       but the wife of another stalks a man's
           very life.
27 Can fire be carried in the bosom
       without burning one's clothes?
28 Or can one walk on hot coals
       without scorching the feet?
29 So is he who sleeps with his neighbor's
           wife;
       no one who touches her will go
           unpunished.
30 Thieves are not despised who steal only

---

a Cn: Heb *from the hand*   b Heb *it*   c Gk: MT *the evil woman*
d Cn Compare Gk Syr Vg Tg: Heb *for because of a harlot to a
piece of bread*

---

apparently binding. **6.6–11** Wisdom may be taught through comparison of human life with the natural world (see also 27.8; 28.1, 15; 30.15–19, 24–31). Diligent labor is a virtue (see, e.g., 10.4–5; 22.13; 24.30–34; 26.13–16; 27.23–27; 31.13–27). **6.10** *Sleep* stitches this epigram to the preceding one. **6.11** *Robber, armed warrior.* Cf. 1.10–19. **6.12–15** These verses are connected to preceding unit by the theme of the evil man. **6.13** *Winking, shuffling, pointing,* body language as a clear sign of character. **6.15b** *Suddenly.* Fate is sure, if not immediate (also in 7.22; 29.1b). **6.16–19** A numerical saying, with the typical *x, x* + 1 introductory formula, that develops the motif of the body parts from the preceding epigram. **6.16** More typically the student is advised on what to *hate* or love, but see 8.13 for Woman Wisdom's hating. **6.20–35** The lecture in the ninth instruction returns to the theme of proper

sexual behavior with an explicit focus on adultery. **6.20–21** See 1.9; 3.3. **6.22** *They,* or *it* (text note *b*), but "she" (Woman Wisdom?) is also possible, especially as the subject of *talk with you.* **6.23** *Lamp.* See note on 2.13. **6.24** *Wife of another, adulteress.* Although the poem's topic is adultery, this verse uses the more evocative "evil woman," "strange woman." **6.26** Adultery violates a man's exclusive right to his wife's sexuality and his ability to be sure his sons (inheritors) are his own; hence, it threatens the stability of the social system. As outsiders to the system, *prostitutes* were tolerated for their services, but they are not worth the instructor's consideration (see also 7.10; cf. 6.30). **6.27–28** Two proverbs, whose heat imagery makes them particularly appropriate as rhetoric against sexual promiscuity. **6.30–31** Like the prostitute whose fee is a mere *loaf of bread* (v. 26), the hungry thief is not a

to satisfy their appetite when they are
  hungry.
31 Yet if they are caught, they will pay
    sevenfold;
  they will forfeit all the goods of their
    house.
32 But he who commits adultery has no
    sense;
  he who does it destroys himself.
33 He will get wounds and dishonor,
    and his disgrace will not be wiped
      away.
34 For jealousy arouses a husband's fury,
    and he shows no restraint when he
      takes revenge.
35 He will accept no compensation,
    and refuses a bribe no matter how
      great.

The False Attractions of Adultery

7 My child, keep my words
    and store up my commandments with
      you;
2 keep my commandments and live,
    keep my teachings as the apple of your
      eye;
3 bind them on your fingers,
    write them on the tablet of your heart.
4 Say to wisdom, "You are my sister,"
    and call insight your intimate friend,

5 that they may keep you from the loose[a]
    woman,
  from the adulteress with her smooth
    words.
6 For at the window of my house
    I looked out through my lattice,
7 and I saw among the simple ones,
    I observed among the youths,
    a young man without sense,
8 passing along the street near her corner,
    taking the road to her house
9 in the twilight, in the evening,
    at the time of night and darkness.
10 Then a woman comes toward him,
    decked out like a prostitute, wily of
      heart.[b]
11 She is loud and wayward;
    her feet do not stay at home;
12 now in the street, now in the squares,
    and at every corner she lies in wait.
13 She seizes him and kisses him,
    and with impudent face she says to
      him:
14 "I had to offer sacrifices,
    and today I have paid my vows;
15 so now I have come out to meet you,

---

a Heb *strange*   b Meaning of Heb uncertain

major moral problem; but thieves are still punished severely. **6.32** Senselessness in sexual behavior is especially deadly (see note on 1.4). **6.33–35** The exact nature of the adulterer's punishment is unclear. The law (Lev 20.10) takes it as an offense against God, thus warranting automatic execution. Here, the offended husband seems to have a choice in exacting punishment. *Wounds.* Symbolic or literal (see 3.8)? *Dishonor, disgrace.* See 3.4; 5.14. *Jealousy,* not moral necessity, produces the punishment.

7.1–27 The tenth instruction returns to the more complex portrayal of the Strange Woman with her smooth words as both a social reality and embodiment of death (see note on 2.16–19). The poem's *inclusio* (a symmetrical structure in which the end repeats the beginning) is created by scene changes: it opens (vv. 1–5) and closes (vv. 24–27) with an instructor in a classroom; vv. 6–12 and vv. 21–23 describe an (imaginary?) scene observed at a distance; in the center, vv. 13–20, a conversation is supposedly overheard at close range. **7.2** *Apple,* lit. "pupil." **7.3** See 3.3; Song 8.6. **7.4** *Sister,* a term of endearment for a lover, not biological kin (see Song 4.9), though "intimate friend" does not necessarily have erotic overtones. **7.6** The scene unfolds as a narrative account of the teacher's experience. Could this place of concealment inside a *house*

hint at a mother's instruction? The woman looking from a window was a popular motif on Phoenician ivories (see 2 Kings 9.30; also the place of the waiting lover in Song 2.9). **7.7** See notes on 1.4; 6.32. **7.8** *Street, house.* See notes on 1.13; 1.15–16; 2.18–19. **7.9** See note on 2.13. The scene twists the female lover's nighttime search for her beloved in Song 3.1–4; 5.2–7. **7.10–20** The description of the woman teases with details of her appearance and speech. She is dressed *like a prostitute* and approaches the young man in this fashion; we do not discover until v. 19 that she is the deadly adulteress. Though he has foolishly wandered near her house, she comes out to meet him. **7.11** *Loud.* See 9.13. **7.12** *Street, squares, corner,* Woman Wisdom's haunts as well (see 1.20). *Lies in wait.* See 1.11. **7.13** *Seizes.* See note on 3.18. *Impudent face,* the same Hebrew words translated *bold face* when applied to the evil man in 21.29. **7.14–20** The woman's words are as imagined by the sage; cf. 1.11–14. **7.14–18** The woman's mention of sacrifices is not a reference to foreign worship but to the "offering of well-being" in Lev 7.11–21. She might legitimately serve the meat from the offering to a guest, but it must be eaten in a state of ritual purity. Such a meal in the midst of a sexual encounter will "cut [the transgressor] off from . . . kin" (Lev 7.20–21). Still, the poet does not flinch from the attractiveness of

to seek you eagerly, and I have found
    you!

16 I have decked my couch with coverings,
    colored spreads of Egyptian linen;
17 I have perfumed my bed with myrrh,
    aloes, and cinnamon.
18 Come, let us take our fill of love until
    morning;
    let us delight ourselves with love.
19 For my husband is not at home;
    he has gone on a long journey.
20 He took a bag of money with him;
    he will not come home until full
    moon."

21 With much seductive speech she
    persuades him;
    with her smooth talk she compels
    him.
22 Right away he follows her,
    and goes like an ox to the slaughter,
    or bounds like a stag toward the trap*a*
23   until an arrow pierces its entrails.
He is like a bird rushing into a snare,
    not knowing that it will cost him his
    life.

24 And now, my children, listen to me,
    and be attentive to the words of my
    mouth.
25 Do not let your hearts turn aside to her
    ways;
    do not stray into her paths.
26 For many are those she has laid low,
    and numerous are her victims.
27 Her house is the way to Sheol,
    going down to the chambers of death.

The Gifts of Wisdom

8 Does not wisdom call,
    and does not understanding raise her
    voice?
2 On the heights, beside the way,
    at the crossroads she takes her stand;
3 beside the gates in front of the town,
    at the entrance of the portals she cries
    out:
4 "To you, O people, I call,
    and my cry is to all that live.
5 O simple ones, learn prudence;
    acquire intelligence, you who lack it.
6 Hear, for I will speak noble things,
    and from my lips will come what is
    right;
7 for my mouth will utter truth;
    wickedness is an abomination to my
    lips.
8 All the words of my mouth are righteous;
    there is nothing twisted or crooked in
    them.
9 They are all straight to one who
    understands
    and right to those who find knowledge.
10 Take my instruction instead of silver,
    and knowledge rather than choice
    gold;
11 for wisdom is better than jewels,
    and all that you may desire cannot
    compare with her.
12 I, wisdom, live with prudence,*b*
    and I attain knowledge and discretion.

---

a Cn Compare Gk: Meaning of Heb uncertain *b* Meaning of Heb uncertain

---

her offer, only adding to the danger she represents. **7.15** *Seek you*, lit. "seek out your face"; with v. 13, this image provides a close-up of the woman's face pressed close to the man's. **7.16–17** The visual beauty of the bed *coverings* is enhanced with the aroma of *myrrh, aloes, cinnamon,* the sources of valued extracts and fragrances associated with both love (Song 4.14) and sacrifice (Ex 30.22–33). **7.18** *Fill of love,* with a change of a vowel in the Hebrew, "fill of breasts," as in the instruction on marital satisfaction in 5.19. **7.19–20** The false but seductive promise that the two can sin without being caught. **7.21–23** A resumption of the more distanced perspective of vv. 6–9. **7.22–23** Although translation is difficult, the imagery of *trap* and *snare* is unmistakable (see 1.17). *Slaughter,* also an action of Woman Wisdom in her house (see 9.2). **7.24–27** The scene returns to the classroom as the concatenation of increasingly deadly female attributes in ch. 7 (prosti-

tute, defiler of sacrifice, adulterer) builds to its inevitable conclusion: the woman is death.
    8.1–36 The most fully developed poetic personification of Wisdom, standing in contrast to the Strange Woman's allures. Speaking in the first person, she praises herself to induce her listeners to heed her call (see note on 1.20–33). **8.1–3** On Wisdom's location and her *call,* see note on 1.20–21. **8.4** *People, all that live,* lit. "men," "human beings" (see notes on 1.8; 4.1–9). The call is universal in scope. **8.5** *Simple ones,* a special appeal to the still-educable fools. *Intelligence,* lit. "heart" (see 2.2). **8.6–9** *Speak, mouth, words.* See note on 1.6. *Wickedness, righteous.* See notes on 1.3; 3.33–35. *Crooked, straight.* See note on 1.3; also 2.12–15. *Find.* Also in 8.12, 17; see note on 1.13. **8.10–11** *Silver, gold, jewels.* Also in 8.19; see note on 1.13. **8.12** *Live with prudence,* lit. "inhabit cunning." *Attain discretion,* lit. "find shrewdness."

13 The fear of the LORD is hatred of evil.
   Pride and arrogance and the way of evil
      and perverted speech I hate.
14 I have good advice and sound wisdom;
   I have insight, I have strength.
15 By me kings reign,
   and rulers decree what is just;
16 by me rulers rule,
   and nobles, all who govern rightly.
17 I love those who love me,
   and those who seek me diligently find
      me.
18 Riches and honor are with me,
   enduring wealth and prosperity.
19 My fruit is better than gold, even fine gold,
   and my yield than choice silver.
20 I walk in the way of righteousness,
   along the paths of justice,
21 endowing with wealth those who love me,
   and filling their treasuries.

Wisdom's Part in Creation

22 The LORD created me at the beginning*a* of
      his work,*b*
   the first of his acts of long ago.
23 Ages ago I was set up,
   at the first, before the beginning of the
      earth.
24 When there were no depths I was brought
      forth,

when there were no springs abounding
      with water.
25 Before the mountains had been shaped,
   before the hills, I was brought
      forth—
26 when he had not yet made earth and
      fields,*c*
   or the world's first bits of soil.
27 When he established the heavens, I was
      there,
   when he drew a circle on the face of
      the deep,
28 when he made firm the skies above,
   when he established the fountains of
      the deep,
29 when he assigned to the sea its limit,
   so that the waters might not transgress
      his command,
   when he marked out the foundations of
      the earth,
30 then I was beside him, like a master
      worker;*d*
   and I was daily his*e* delight,
   rejoicing before him always,
31 rejoicing in his inhabited world
   and delighting in the human race.

---

a Or *me as the beginning*   *b* Heb *way*   *c* Meaning of Heb
uncertain   *d* Another reading is *little child*   *e* Gk: Heb lacks *his*

8.13 *Fear of the LORD.* See note on 1.7. The previous verse's pragmatic virtues are embedded in a larger piety. *Hatred, hate.* See notes on 1.22; 6.16. *Way. Perverted speech.* See notes on 1.6; 2.12–15. **8.14–16** On wisdom and just rule, see note on 1.1. **8.14** *Good advice,* a Hebrew word designating the powerful counsel a king expected from his advisers; note *strength* in the next line; cf. qualities of the capable wife (31.17, 25–26). **8.17–21** The love of wisdom and its material blessings (see note on 1.13). *Love* can define the loyal relationship of treaty partners or royal subjects as well as the affections of lovers (see also note on 1.22). **8.18** *Prosperity,* usually translated *righteousness* (v. 20), though the moral state and its material rewards were inseparable (see note on 1.13). Through parallelism, the couplet shows *riches, enduring wealth* to be the concrete signs of *honor,* "righteousness" (see notes on 1.3; 3.4). **8.22–31** A remarkable statement of Woman Wisdom's antiquity and authority. Depending on translation, one of two pictures emerges: Wisdom is a child born of the deity before the creation of the cosmos, or she is a preexistent being who aligns with God; see also 3.19–20; Jn 1.1–4. **8.22** *Created.* The Hebrew verb *qnh* is usually translated "acquire" (thus in 4.5, 7 *get* describes the student's approach to wisdom). Also possible is "conceive,

engender" in the biological sense (Gen 4.1). "Create" is introduced by the Greek translation. **8.23** *Set up,* used elsewhere only to refer to God's installing of the king in Zion (Ps 2.6). The Hebrew verb can also mean "to weave" and a variant form portrays the divine weaving of baby's sinews in the womb (Ps 139.13; Job 10.11). **8.24–29** Cf. the account of creation in Gen 1. **8.24–25** *Depths, springs.* Water was taken to be the original substance (Gen 1.2). *Brought forth* usually refers to the birthing of a child. If one reads "conceived/woven in the womb" for the ambiguous verbs in vv. 22–23 (see notes on 8.22; 8.23), then Wisdom is portrayed as born of God as mother (see Isa 49.14–15; 42.14). *Mountains, hills,* not just features of the natural landscape, but the home of the gods, and the peaks of the pillars that supported the earth; they are lit. "sunk," not *shaped,* and they precede the *earth* (v. 26). **8.27–29** God is portrayed ordering and regulating, rather than creating substance; in particular God commands and limits the primordial waters as an essential part of maintaining the earth's viability in the face of ever threatening chaos (cf. Job 38.8–11). **8.30–31** *Master worker,* or "little child" (see text note *d*); the ambiguous portrait of Wisdom persists. *Delight, rejoicing, rejoicing, delighting.* Repeated verbs in a "mirror pattern" unite Wisdom's playful activity

32 "And now, my children, listen to me:
    happy are those who keep my ways.
33 Hear instruction and be wise,
    and do not neglect it.
34 Happy is the one who listens to me,
    watching daily at my gates,
    waiting beside my doors.
35 For whoever finds me finds life
    and obtains favor from the LORD;
36 but those who miss me injure themselves;
    all who hate me love death."

Wisdom's Feast

9 Wisdom has built her house,
    she has hewn her seven pillars.
2 She has slaughtered her animals, she has
        mixed her wine,
    she has also set her table.
3 She has sent out her servant-girls, she calls
    from the highest places in the town,
4 "You that are simple, turn in here!"
    To those without sense she says,
5 "Come, eat of my bread
    and drink of the wine I have mixed.
6 Lay aside immaturity,^{a} and live,
    and walk in the way of insight."

General Maxims

7 Whoever corrects a scoffer wins abuse;
    whoever rebukes the wicked gets hurt.
8 A scoffer who is rebuked will only hate you;
    the wise, when rebuked, will love you.
9 Give instruction^b to the wise, and they
    will become wiser still;

teach the righteous and they will gain
    in learning.
10 The fear of the LORD is the beginning of
        wisdom,
    and the knowledge of the Holy One is
        insight.
11 For by me your days will be multiplied,
    and years will be added to your life.
12 If you are wise, you are wise for yourself;
    if you scoff, you alone will bear it.

Folly's Invitation and Promise

13 The foolish woman is loud;
    she is ignorant and knows nothing.
14 She sits at the door of her house,
    on a seat at the high places of the town,
15 calling to those who pass by,
    who are going straight on their way,
16 "You who are simple, turn in here!"
    And to those without sense she says,
17 "Stolen water is sweet,
    and bread eaten in secret is pleasant."
18 But they do not know that the dead^c are
        there,
    that her guests are in the depths of
        Sheol.

Wise Sayings of Solomon

10 The proverbs of Solomon.

A wise child makes a glad father,
    but a foolish child is a mother's grief.

---

a Or *simpleness*   *b* Heb lacks *instruction*   *c* Heb *shades*

---

with God to her delight in humans on earth. **8.32–
36** Woman Wisdom's discourse continues. Wisdom's
ways lead from the public arena (8.1–3) to her *gates*
and *doors* (her house; see notes on 1.13; 1.15–16;
2.18–19; 5.8; 9.1). **8.34** *Watching* and *waiting* outside
a house recall the lover in Song 2.9, but also the path
of the foolish youth in 7.8. **8.35–36** Wisdom mediates *life* from the Lord.

9.1–18 Closely matching poetic portrayals of
Woman Wisdom (vv. 1–6) and Woman Folly (9.13–
18) frame a central collection of sayings (vv. 7–12).
The focus on the *houses* of the two women continues
familiar themes (see note on 1.13) and also seems to
expand upon the proverb in 14.1. On food as
metaphor for gaining wisdom and moral perspective,
see note on 1.31. **9.1** *Wisdom* (see note on 1.20–33)
evokes 14.1a (which is lit. "The wisdom of women
builds a house"). Like the house of the capable wife
(31.10–31; cf. 5.7–23), Wisdom's *house* is the center
of the good society, though it may be hard to discern
from the home of Woman Folly (see vv. 13–17).

Seven pillars may recall the mythic foundations of the
earth (cf. 8.22–31), but are also found in ancient
temples. **9.2** *Slaughtered*. See 7.22. Wisdom's meal
may reflect the common Hellenistic institution of
philosophical *symposia*, where the wise gathered to
dine and discourse. **9.3** *Calls*. See 1.20. *Highest places
in the town*. See 1.20; 8.2; 9.14. **9.4–6** *Simple, without
sense, immaturity*. See note on 1.4; also 9.16. *Bread,
wine*. See 9.17. **9.7–12** Reflections on education for
advanced students, *the wise* (see 1.5; note on 1.8).
9.13–18 The Woman of Folly (lit.) is identical to the
Strange Woman (see note on 2.16–19) and the direct
opposite of Wisdom in vv. 1–6. **9.13** *Loud*. See 7.11.
9.14–15 An image perhaps drawn from the alewife,
whose establishment was also often a house of prostitution; but her location and words are also similar to
those of Woman Wisdom (see 1.20; 8.1–5, 34; 9.1–
6). **9.17** See 9.5. **9.18** See 2.18–19; 5.5; 7.27; cf. 6.33–
35.

10.1–22.16 This section departs from the generally
unified compositions of the instructions and wisdom

2 Treasures gained by wickedness do not
profit,
but righteousness delivers from
death.
3 The Lord does not let the righteous go
hungry,
but he thwarts the craving of the
wicked.
4 A slack hand causes poverty,
but the hand of the diligent makes
rich.
5 A child who gathers in summer is
prudent,
but a child who sleeps in harvest brings
shame.
6 Blessings are on the head of the
righteous,
but the mouth of the wicked conceals
violence.
7 The memory of the righteous is a
blessing,
but the name of the wicked will rot.
8 The wise of heart will heed
commandments,
but a babbling fool will come to ruin.
9 Whoever walks in integrity walks
securely,
but whoever follows perverse ways will
be found out.
10 Whoever winks the eye causes trouble,
but the one who rebukes boldly makes
peace.[a]
11 The mouth of the righteous is a fountain
of life,
but the mouth of the wicked conceals
violence.
12 Hatred stirs up strife,
but love covers all offenses.

13 On the lips of one who has
understanding wisdom is found,
but a rod is for the back of one who
lacks sense.
14 The wise lay up knowledge,
but the babbling of a fool brings ruin
near.
15 The wealth of the rich is their fortress;
the poverty of the poor is their ruin.
16 The wage of the righteous leads to life,
the gain of the wicked to sin.
17 Whoever heeds instruction is on the path
to life,
but one who rejects a rebuke goes astray.
18 Lying lips conceal hatred,
and whoever utters slander is a fool.
19 When words are many, transgression is
not lacking,
but the prudent are restrained in
speech.
20 The tongue of the righteous is choice
silver;
the mind of the wicked is of little
worth.
21 The lips of the righteous feed many,
but fools die for lack of sense.
22 The blessing of the Lord makes rich,
and he adds no sorrow with it.[b]
23 Doing wrong is like sport to a fool,
but wise conduct is pleasure to a
person of understanding.
24 What the wicked dread will come upon
them,
but the desire of the righteous will be
granted.

---

a Gk: Heb *but a babbling fool will come to ruin*   *b* Or *and toil
adds nothing to it*

---

poems in chs. 1–9 but continues their teachings in an explicit way in the vehicle of two-lined sayings using parallelism (see Introduction). Although many of the sayings are simply observational, most are shaped to recommend a specific virtue or behavior to the students of the sages. **10.1–15.33** The antithetic collection. This section makes use of antithetic parallelisms (the second line contrasts with the first) to drive home the sages' views. Typical themes already seen in chs. 1–9 are taken up in antithetical word pairs (*father/mother*, e.g., 10.1b; *righteous/wicked*, e.g., 10.2–3, 24–25, 27–32; *wise/fool*, e.g., 10.8, 14, 23). Other common concerns of the sages appear: the power of language (e.g., 10.6, 11, 13–14, 18–21, 31–32), the doctrine of retribution (every act contains its own consequence, e.g., 10.2, 4, 16, 28, 30), and the excellence of wisdom (e.g., 10.1, 17). **10.1** *The proverbs of*

Solomon. This subtitle to the book's second collection (omitted in the Septuagint) reveals its independent origin (cf. 22.17; 24.23; 25.1; 30.1; 31.1). *Mothers* bore the responsibility for teaching the young (see note on 1.8; also 31.1). *Foolish,* the same word used for the woman in 9.13, helping to link this new section to the preceding one. **10.3** *The righteous,* probably equivalent to "the wise." **10.4–5** Diligence brings rewards (also in 12.11, 24). **10.7** Concern for a good reputation was common with the sages (Job 18.17; Eccl 7.1; see note on 3.4). **10.8, 11, 13–14, 18–21, 31–32** See note on 1.6 on the importance of true and effective speech. **10.10** *Winking the eye* may be a reference to malevolent (e.g., "evil eye"?) or sorcerous behavior (see 6.13; Ps 35.19). The Septuagint reading opts for an antithetic statement. **10.15** A purely observational saying. **10.22** See text note *b:* God's blessing is sufficient.

25 When the tempest passes, the wicked are
    no more,
  but the righteous are established
    forever.
26 Like vinegar to the teeth, and smoke to
    the eyes,
  so are the lazy to their employers.
27 The fear of the LORD prolongs life,
  but the years of the wicked will be
    short.
28 The hope of the righteous ends in
    gladness,
  but the expectation of the wicked
    comes to nothing.
29 The way of the LORD is a stronghold for
    the upright,
  but destruction for evildoers.
30 The righteous will never be removed,
  but the wicked will not remain in the
    land.
31 The mouth of the righteous brings forth
    wisdom,
  but the perverse tongue will be cut off.
32 The lips of the righteous know what is
    acceptable,
  but the mouth of the wicked what is
    perverse.

11 A false balance is an abomination to
    the LORD,
  but an accurate weight is his delight.
2 When pride comes, then comes disgrace;
  but wisdom is with the humble.
3 The integrity of the upright guides them,
  but the crookedness of the treacherous
    destroys them.
4 Riches do not profit in the day of wrath,
  but righteousness delivers from death.
5 The righteousness of the blameless keeps
    their ways straight,
  but the wicked fall by their own
    wickedness.
6 The righteousness of the upright saves
    them,
  but the treacherous are taken captive
    by their schemes.
7 When the wicked die, their hope perishes,

and the expectation of the godless
    comes to nothing.
8 The righteous are delivered from trouble,
  and the wicked get into it instead.
9 With their mouths the godless would
    destroy their neighbors,
  but by knowledge the righteous are
    delivered.
10 When it goes well with the righteous, the
    city rejoices;
  and when the wicked perish, there is
    jubilation.
11 By the blessing of the upright a city is
    exalted,
  but it is overthrown by the mouth of
    the wicked.
12 Whoever belittles another lacks sense,
  but an intelligent person remains
    silent.
13 A gossip goes about telling secrets,
  but one who is trustworthy in spirit
    keeps a confidence.
14 Where there is no guidance, a nation[a] falls,
  but in an abundance of counselors
    there is safety.
15 To guarantee loans for a stranger brings
    trouble,
  but there is safety in refusing to do so.
16 A gracious woman gets honor,
  but she who hates virtue is covered
    with shame.[b]
  The timid become destitute,[c]
  but the aggressive gain riches.
17 Those who are kind reward themselves,
  but the cruel do themselves harm.
18 The wicked earn no real gain,
  but those who sow righteousness get a
    true reward.
19 Whoever is steadfast in righteousness will
    live,
  but whoever pursues evil will die.
20 Crooked minds are an abomination to
    the LORD,

_____
a Or an army   b Compare Gk Syr: Heb lacks but she . . . shame
c Gk: Heb lacks The timid . . . destitute

_____
10.25a Unlooked-for death was considered a punishment for sin.
  11.1–31 Contrasts between the righteous, upright,
and gracious and the wicked, crooked, greedy, and
godless bind the proverbs of this section together, as
the theory of retribution is acted out in daily life.
11.1 A false balance is used to cheat the poor (16.11;

20.10, 23; Deut 25.13–16; Am 8.5–6; Hos 12.8; Mic
6.10–11). Abomination here and in v. 20 recalls the
numerical saying of 6.16–19. **11.3** Crookedness is the
physical attribute that consistently characterizes moral
perversity. **11.7** A departure from contrastive statements. **11.18–19, 21** For the sage, faith in retribution
outweighs any temporary discrepancies in the good

but those of blameless ways are his
    delight.
21 Be assured, the wicked will not go
    unpunished,
  but those who are righteous will
    escape.
22 Like a gold ring in a pig's snout
  is a beautiful woman without good
    sense.
23 The desire of the righteous ends only in
    good;
  the expectation of the wicked in wrath.
24 Some give freely, yet grow all the richer;
  others withhold what is due, and only
    suffer want.
25 A generous person will be enriched,
  and one who gives water will get water.
26 The people curse those who hold back
    grain,
  but a blessing is on the head of those
    who sell it.
27 Whoever diligently seeks good seeks
    favor,
  but evil comes to the one who searches
    for it.
28 Those who trust in their riches will
    wither,^{a}
  but the righteous will flourish like
    green leaves.
29 Those who trouble their households will
    inherit wind,
  and the fool will be servant to the wise.
30 The fruit of the righteous is a tree of life,
  but violence^b takes lives away.
31 If the righteous are repaid on earth,
  how much more the wicked and the
    sinner!

12 Whoever loves discipline loves
    knowledge,
  but those who hate to be rebuked are
    stupid.
2 The good obtain favor from the LORD,
  but those who devise evil he
    condemns.
3 No one finds security by wickedness,
  but the root of the righteous will never
    be moved.

4 A good wife is the crown of her husband,
  but she who brings shame is like
    rottenness in his bones.
5 The thoughts of the righteous are just;
  the advice of the wicked is treacherous.
6 The words of the wicked are a deadly
    ambush,
  but the speech of the upright delivers
    them.
7 The wicked are overthrown and are no
    more,
  but the house of the righteous will
    stand.
8 One is commended for good sense,
  but a perverse mind is despised.
9 Better to be despised and have a servant,
  than to be self-important and lack food.
10 The righteous know the needs of their
    animals,
  but the mercy of the wicked is cruel.
11 Those who till their land will have plenty
    of food,
  but those who follow worthless
    pursuits have no sense.
12 The wicked covet the proceeds of
    wickedness,^{c}
  but the root of the righteous bears
    fruit.
13 The evil are ensnared by the transgression
    of their lips,
  but the righteous escape from trouble.
14 From the fruit of the mouth one is filled
    with good things,
  and manual labor has its reward.
15 Fools think their own way is right,
  but the wise listen to advice.
16 Fools show their anger at once,
  but the prudent ignore an insult.
17 Whoever speaks the truth gives honest
    evidence,
  but a false witness speaks deceitfully.
18 Rash words are like sword thrusts,
  but the tongue of the wise brings
    healing.

---

a Cn: Heb *fall*   *b* Cn Compare Gk Syr: Heb *a wise man*
c Or *covet the catch of the wicked*

---

fortune gained by wickedness. **11.22** A vivid comparative statement. See also 31.30. **11.24–25** The mysteries
of generosity. **11.26** *Hold back grain,* waiting for higher
prices. **11.28, 30** *Tree of life* imagery recalls Woman
Wisdom (3.18; Pss 1.3; 52.7–8). **12.1** The wise learn
from correction. **12.3** *Root,* that which holds the tree
of life secure (Ps 1). **12.4** A *wife* either enhances or
threatens a man's life; the negative possibility departs
from the good wives in chs. 1–9 and 31. **12.6a** An echo
of the instruction of 1.8–19. **12.9** "Better than" sayings
are popular with the sages (15.16–17; 16.8; Eccl 9.4b;
Sir 10.27). **12.13–14, 17–19, 22, 25** The sages empha-

19 Truthful lips endure forever,
  but a lying tongue lasts only a
    moment.
20 Deceit is in the mind of those who plan
    evil,
  but those who counsel peace have joy.
21 No harm happens to the righteous,
  but the wicked are filled with trouble.
22 Lying lips are an abomination to the
    LORD,
  but those who act faithfully are his
    delight.
23 One who is clever conceals knowledge,
  but the mind of a fool[a] broadcasts
    folly.
24 The hand of the diligent will rule,
  while the lazy will be put to forced
    labor.
25 Anxiety weighs down the human heart,
  but a good word cheers it up.
26 The righteous gives good advice to
    friends,[b]
  but the way of the wicked leads astray.
27 The lazy do not roast[c] their game,
  but the diligent obtain precious wealth.[c]
28 In the path of righteousness there is life,
  in walking its path there is no death.

13 A wise child loves discipline,[d]
  but a scoffer does not listen to rebuke.
2 From the fruit of their words good
    persons eat good things,
  but the desire of the treacherous is for
    wrongdoing.
3 Those who guard their mouths preserve
    their lives;
  those who open wide their lips come to
    ruin.
4 The appetite of the lazy craves, and gets
    nothing,
  while the appetite of the diligent is
    richly supplied.
5 The righteous hate falsehood,
  but the wicked act shamefully and
    disgracefully.
6 Righteousness guards one whose way is
    upright,

but sin overthrows the wicked.
7 Some pretend to be rich, yet have
    nothing;
  others pretend to be poor, yet have
    great wealth.
8 Wealth is a ransom for a person's life,
  but the poor get no threats.
9 The light of the righteous rejoices,
  but the lamp of the wicked goes out.
10 By insolence the heedless make strife,
  but wisdom is with those who take
    advice.
11 Wealth hastily gotten[e] will dwindle,
  but those who gather little by little will
    increase it.
12 Hope deferred makes the heart sick,
  but a desire fulfilled is a tree of life.
13 Those who despise the word bring
    destruction on themselves,
  but those who respect the
    commandment will be rewarded.
14 The teaching of the wise is a fountain of
    life,
  so that one may avoid the snares of
    death.
15 Good sense wins favor,
  but the way of the faithless is their
    ruin.[f]
16 The clever do all things intelligently,
  but the fool displays folly.
17 A bad messenger brings trouble,
  but a faithful envoy, healing.
18 Poverty and disgrace are for the one who
    ignores instruction,
  but one who heeds reproof is honored.
19 A desire realized is sweet to the soul,
  but to turn away from evil is an
    abomination to fools.
20 Whoever walks with the wise becomes
    wise,
  but the companion of fools suffers
    harm.

---

a Heb *the heart of fools* b Syr: Meaning of Heb uncertain
c Meaning of Heb uncertain d Cn: Heb *A wise child the
discipline of his father* e Gk Vg: Heb *from vanity*
f Cn Compare Gk Syr Vg Tg: Heb *is enduring*

---

size the importance of using language properly (see
also note on 1.6). **12.23a** Discretion is a virtue in civil
servants and others. **12.25** A psychological insight.
12.27 Parallelism is forced due to uncertainties in
translation.
13.1–25 Throughout this chapter the sages stress
the importance of listening to wise counsel and using
language well (vv. 1–3, 13–14, 17–18; see also note on

1.6). **13.2, 4** Eating has both literal and metaphorical
meanings. **13.7** "Don't judge a book by its cover."
13.8 An observational saying. **13.9** *Light, lamp,*
metaphors for life. **13.11** *Hastily gotten.* The Hebrew
text *from vanity* (see text note e) stresses impermanence or worthless pursuits. **13.12** *Tree of life.* See
3.18; 11.30; 15.4. **13.14** Formal (synthetic) parallelism
(see Introduction). **13.17** *Bad,* "lazy" or "dishonest."

21 Misfortune pursues sinners,
    but prosperity rewards the righteous.
22 The good leave an inheritance to their
        children's children,
    but the sinner's wealth is laid up for
        the righteous.
23 The field of the poor may yield much
        food,
    but it is swept away through injustice.
24 Those who spare the rod hate their
        children,
    but those who love them are diligent to
        discipline them.
25 The righteous have enough to satisfy
        their appetite,
    but the belly of the wicked is empty.

14 The wise woman[a] builds her house,
    but the foolish tears it down with her
        own hands.
2 Those who walk uprightly fear the Lord,
    but one who is devious in conduct
        despises him.
3 The talk of fools is a rod for their backs,[b]
    but the lips of the wise preserve them.
4 Where there are no oxen, there is no grain;
    abundant crops come by the strength
        of the ox.
5 A faithful witness does not lie,
    but a false witness breathes out lies.
6 A scoffer seeks wisdom in vain,
    but knowledge is easy for one who
        understands.
7 Leave the presence of a fool,
    for there you do not find words of
        knowledge.
8 It is the wisdom of the clever to
        understand where they go,
    but the folly of fools misleads.
9 Fools mock at the guilt offering,[c]
    but the upright enjoy God's favor.
10 The heart knows its own bitterness,
    and no stranger shares its joy.
11 The house of the wicked is destroyed,
    but the tent of the upright flourishes.
12 There is a way that seems right to a
        person,
    but its end is the way to death.[d]

13 Even in laughter the heart is sad,
    and the end of joy is grief.
14 The perverse get what their ways deserve,
    and the good, what their deeds
        deserve.[e]
15 The simple believe everything,
    but the clever consider their steps.
16 The wise are cautious and turn away
        from evil,
    but the fool throws off restraint and is
        careless.
17 One who is quick-tempered acts
        foolishly,
    and the schemer is hated.
18 The simple are adorned with[f] folly,
    but the clever are crowned with
        knowledge.
19 The evil bow down before the good,
    the wicked at the gates of the
        righteous.
20 The poor are disliked even by their
        neighbors,
    but the rich have many friends.
21 Those who despise their neighbors are
        sinners,
    but happy are those who are kind to
        the poor.
22 Do they not err that plan evil?
    Those who plan good find loyalty and
        faithfulness.
23 In all toil there is profit,
    but mere talk leads only to poverty.
24 The crown of the wise is their wisdom,[g]
    but folly is the garland[h] of fools.
25 A truthful witness saves lives,
    but one who utters lies is a betrayer.
26 In the fear of the Lord one has strong
        confidence,
    and one's children will have a refuge.
27 The fear of the Lord is a fountain of life,
    so that one may avoid the snares of
        death.

---

a Heb *Wisdom of women*   b Cn: Heb *a rod of pride*
c Meaning of Heb uncertain   d Heb *ways of death*   e Cn: Heb
from upon him   f Or *inherit*   g Cn Compare Gk: Heb *riches*
h Cn: Heb *is the folly*

13.23 Poverty is sometimes the result of injustice rather than laziness or wickedness (cf. 13.25; 14.23; 19.15). 13.24 The sages, who condemn violence between people, recommend it to control households (see 19.18, 25; 20.30; 29.15, 17, 19, 21; see also Deut 21.18–22). 14.1a See 9.1; 24.3. *Wise woman.* The Hebrew reading (text note *a*) may refer to the important roles played by women in ancient households (see 31.10–31). 14.10, 13, 30 Astute psychological insights. 14.12 Humans are seldom omniscient (16.1–2, 25). 14.15–16 Caution is an attribute of the wise. 14.17 The sages deplore hot-tempered or hasty behavior. See 15.18; 16.32; 19.19; 21.5b; 29.22. 14.20 A simple observation. 14.21 An ethical response to v. 20.

28 The glory of a king is a multitude of
        people;
   without people a prince is ruined.
29 Whoever is slow to anger has great
        understanding,
   but one who has a hasty temper exalts
        folly.
30 A tranquil mind gives life to the flesh,
   but passion makes the bones rot.
31 Those who oppress the poor insult their
        Maker,
   but those who are kind to the needy
        honor him.
32 The wicked are overthrown by their
        evildoing,
   but the righteous find a refuge in their
        integrity. *a*
33 Wisdom is at home in the mind of one
        who has understanding,
   but it is not *b* known in the heart of
        fools.
34 Righteousness exalts a nation,
   but sin is a reproach to any people.
35 A servant who deals wisely has the king's
        favor,
   but his wrath falls on one who acts
        shamefully.

15 A soft answer turns away wrath,
     but a harsh word stirs up anger.
2 The tongue of the wise dispenses
        knowledge, *c*
   but the mouths of fools pour out folly.
3 The eyes of the LORD are in every place,
   keeping watch on the evil and the
        good.
4 A gentle tongue is a tree of life,
   but perverseness in it breaks the spirit.
5 A fool despises a parent's instruction,
   but the one who heeds admonition is
        prudent.
6 In the house of the righteous there is
        much treasure,
   but trouble befalls the income of the
        wicked.

7 The lips of the wise spread knowledge;
   not so the minds of fools.
8 The sacrifice of the wicked is an
        abomination to the LORD,
   but the prayer of the upright is his
        delight.
9 The way of the wicked is an abomination
        to the LORD,
   but he loves the one who pursues
        righteousness.
10 There is severe discipline for one who
        forsakes the way,
   but one who hates a rebuke will die.
11 Sheol and Abaddon lie open before the
        LORD,
   how much more human hearts!
12 Scoffers do not like to be rebuked;
   they will not go to the wise.
13 A glad heart makes a cheerful
        countenance,
   but by sorrow of heart the spirit is
        broken.
14 The mind of one who has understanding
        seeks knowledge,
   but the mouths of fools feed on folly.
15 All the days of the poor are hard,
   but a cheerful heart has a continual
        feast.
16 Better is a little with the fear of the LORD
   than great treasure and trouble with it.
17 Better is a dinner of vegetables where
        love is
   than a fatted ox and hatred with it.
18 Those who are hot-tempered stir up
        strife,
   but those who are slow to anger calm
        contention.
19 The way of the lazy is overgrown with
        thorns,
   but the path of the upright is a level
        highway.

a Gk Syr: Heb *in their death*   *b* Gk Syr: Heb lacks *not*
c Cn: Heb *makes knowledge good*

Concern for the poor is also expressed in v. 31.
14.28a Population flourishes under wise leadership.
Only the occasional proverb in this section deals with
matters related to royalty (also vv. 34–35), despite the
attribution to Solomon. **15.1, 4, 23** Reflections on the
effects of thoughtful use of language, taught by the
sages (see note on 1.6). Contrast this sensitivity with
other advice to reprove with word or rod. **15.3** Watchfulness is a typical attribute of sky gods (5.21; 15.11;
Ps 139.1; Zech 4.10b). **15.6** Judgment of the righ-

teous and wicked is expected in this life. **15.8** A rare
comment on worship practices, tying them to ethical
behavior (cf. Am 5.21–24). **15.9** See 11.20; 12.22.
15.11 *Sheol, Abaddon,* the underworld, home of the
dead (see also note on 1.12). **15.13, 30** More psychology based on careful observation. **15.16–17** "Better
than" sayings that develop the point of v. 15, stressing
times when, contrary to expected appearances, little
is to be preferred to much. See 16.8; 17.1; Ps 37.16.
15.18 See 14.17. **15.19, 21** Straightness is the physical

20 A wise child makes a glad father,
    but the foolish despise their mothers.
21 Folly is a joy to one who has no sense,
    but a person of understanding walks
        straight ahead.
22 Without counsel, plans go wrong,
    but with many advisers they succeed.
23 To make an apt answer is a joy to anyone,
    and a word in season, how good it is!
24 For the wise the path of life leads upward,
    in order to avoid Sheol below.
25 The LORD tears down the house of the
        proud,
    but maintains the widow's boundaries.
26 Evil plans are an abomination to the
        LORD,
    but gracious words are pure.
27 Those who are greedy for unjust gain
        make trouble for their households,
    but those who hate bribes will live.
28 The mind of the righteous ponders how
        to answer,
    but the mouth of the wicked pours out
        evil.
29 The LORD is far from the wicked,
    but he hears the prayer of the righteous.
30 The light of the eyes rejoices the heart,
    and good news refreshes the body.
31 The ear that heeds wholesome
        admonition
    will lodge among the wise.
32 Those who ignore instruction despise
        themselves,
    but those who heed admonition gain
        understanding.
33 The fear of the LORD is instruction in
        wisdom,
    and humility goes before honor.

16 The plans of the mind belong to
        mortals,
    but the answer of the tongue is from
        the LORD.
2 All one's ways may be pure in one's own
        eyes,
    but the LORD weighs the spirit.
3 Commit your work to the LORD,
    and your plans will be established.
4 The LORD has made everything for its
        purpose,
    even the wicked for the day of
        trouble.
5 All those who are arrogant are an
        abomination to the LORD;
    be assured, they will not go
        unpunished.
6 By loyalty and faithfulness iniquity is
        atoned for,
    and by the fear of the LORD one avoids
        evil.
7 When the ways of people please the
        LORD,
    he causes even their enemies to be at
        peace with them.
8 Better is a little with righteousness
    than large income with injustice.
9 The human mind plans the way,
    but the LORD directs the steps.
10 Inspired decisions are on the lips of a
        king;
    his mouth does not sin in judgment.
11 Honest balances and scales are the
        LORD's;
    all the weights in the bag are his work.
12 It is an abomination to kings to do evil,
    for the throne is established by
        righteousness.

---

attribute associated with wisdom and righteousness.
15.20 See 10.1; 17.25; note on 1.8. **15.22** See 11.14.
This proverb did not hold in the case of Absalom
(2 Sam 15–18). **15.25** Widows and orphans were
under God's special protection (23.10–11; see also
22.28; Deut 19.14; Hos 5.10). **15.30** *The light of the
eyes,* the cheerful look of the messenger; *refreshes the
body,* lit. "makes fat the bones" (see Ps 63.5).
    16.1–22.16 The "royal" collection. In the second
half of the wise sayings of Solomon, the sages depart
from the mostly antithetic style of the earlier section
in favor of synonymous parallelism (second line restates the first). This group of sayings also shows a
greater attempt at thematic arrangement, as well as
strong emphasis on court values and settings. **16.1–7,
9, 11, 20, 33** LORD. A series of Yahweh ("the LORD")
sayings forms a bridge between this collection and

the previous chapters (see 14.2, 26–27; 15.3, 8–9, 11,
16, 25–26, 29, 33). **16.1, 9** Ultimately, God is the
source of all things, even though humans do have a
measure of freedom in their acts. **16.2** *The LORD
weighs the spirit,* an image possibly drawn from the
Egyptian belief that the scribal god weighs the heart
of the deceased in an underworld hall of judgment.
See 21.2. **16.4** The sages here suggest that perhaps
negative things are also part of the divine plan; cf.
Eccl 3.1–8; 7.13; Rom 9.22. **16.8** See 15.16–17. **16.10,
12–15** Placement of sayings about the ideal king after
those stressing the Lord's ways enhances the idea of
the king as God's worthy representative. See also note
on 1.1. **16.11** *Balances and scales.* See note on 11.1.
16.12 In Egypt, wisdom, or "Maat," was the foundation of the pharaoh's throne conceptually and perhaps literally, for one of the Egyptian hieroglyphs for

13 Righteous lips are the delight of a king,
    and he loves those who speak what is
      right.
14 A king's wrath is a messenger of death,
    and whoever is wise will appease it.
15 In the light of a king's face there is life,
    and his favor is like the clouds that
      bring the spring rain.
16 How much better to get wisdom than
      gold!
    To get understanding is to be chosen
      rather than silver.
17 The highway of the upright avoids evil;
    those who guard their way preserve
      their lives.
18 Pride goes before destruction,
    and a haughty spirit before a fall.
19 It is better to be of a lowly spirit among
      the poor
    than to divide the spoil with the proud.
20 Those who are attentive to a matter will
      prosper,
    and happy are those who trust in the
      LORD.
21 The wise of heart is called perceptive,
    and pleasant speech increases
      persuasiveness.
22 Wisdom is a fountain of life to one who
      has it,
    but folly is the punishment of fools.
23 The mind of the wise makes their speech
      judicious,
    and adds persuasiveness to their lips.
24 Pleasant words are like a honeycomb,
    sweetness to the soul and health to the
      body.
25 Sometimes there is a way that seems to be
      right,
    but in the end it is the way to death.
26 The appetite of workers works for them;
    their hunger urges them on.
27 Scoundrels concoct evil,
    and their speech is like a scorching fire.

28 A perverse person spreads strife,
    and a whisperer separates close friends.
29 The violent entice their neighbors,
    and lead them in a way that is not
      good.
30 One who winks the eyes plans*a* perverse
      things;
    one who compresses the lips brings
      evil to pass.
31 Gray hair is a crown of glory;
    it is gained in a righteous life.
32 One who is slow to anger is better than
      the mighty,
    and one whose temper is controlled
      than one who captures a city.
33 The lot is cast into the lap,
    but the decision is the LORD's alone.

17 Better is a dry morsel with quiet
    than a house full of feasting with strife.
2 A slave who deals wisely will rule over a
      child who acts shamefully,
    and will share the inheritance as one of
      the family.
3 The crucible is for silver, and the furnace
      is for gold,
    but the LORD tests the heart.
4 An evildoer listens to wicked lips;
    and a liar gives heed to a mischievous
      tongue.
5 Those who mock the poor insult their
      Maker;
    those who are glad at calamity will not
      go unpunished.
6 Grandchildren are the crown of the aged,
    and the glory of children is their
      parents.
7 Fine speech is not becoming to a fool;
    still less is false speech to a ruler.*b*
8 A bribe is like a magic stone in the eyes of
      those who give it;
    wherever they turn they prosper.

---

a Gk Syr Vg Tg: Heb *to plan*   *b* Or *a noble person*

Maat represents a side view of the dais upon which the pharaoh's throne was placed. **16.14** Cf. Joab's counsel to the messenger he sends to David (2 Sam 11.18–24). **16.15** *Rain,* always a positive image in the arid Near East. **16.16** See 3.14; 4.5. **16.18** See 11.2; 15.33. **16.22** *Fountain of life.* See 10.11; 13.14; 14.27. **16.24** Language can be a sensual pleasure. **16.25** See 14.12. **16.26** Bodily appetites are not always bad. **16.30** *One who winks.* See note on 10.10. **16.31** One of the benefits of wisdom and righteousness is long life (3.16; 20.29). **16.32.**The sages deplore hot-tempered

or hasty behavior. See 15.18; 19.2; 21.5b. **16.33** *Lot.* Urim and Thummim were sacred dice used in oracles. Does the sage challenge the authority of priestly knowledge? **17.1** See 15.16–17. **17.2** See Eccl 4.13–14. Reflections on role reversals of this type are also common in the Egyptian wisdom tradition. **17.3** See 16.2; 27.21; Jer 11.20. *Silver/gold* is a common proverbial word pair (22.1; 25.11; see note on 10.1–15.33). **17.5a** See 14.31. **17.8** An ethically neutral comment on the success of bribery (so too 18.16; 21.14); for condemnations, see v. 23; Ex 23.8; Deut 16.19.

9 One who forgives an affront fosters
      friendship,
    but one who dwells on disputes will
      alienate a friend.

10 A rebuke strikes deeper into a discerning
      person
    than a hundred blows into a fool.

11 Evil people seek only rebellion,
    but a cruel messenger will be sent
      against them.

12 Better to meet a she-bear robbed of its
      cubs
    than to confront a fool immersed in
      folly.

13 Evil will not depart from the house
    of one who returns evil for good.

14 The beginning of strife is like letting out
      water;
    so stop before the quarrel breaks out.

15 One who justifies the wicked and one
      who condemns the righteous
    are both alike an abomination to the
      Lord.

16 Why should fools have a price in hand
    to buy wisdom, when they have no
      mind to learn?

17 A friend loves at all times,
    and kinsfolk are born to share
      adversity.

18 It is senseless to give a pledge,
    to become surety for a neighbor.

19 One who loves transgression loves strife;
    one who builds a high threshold invites
      broken bones.

20 The crooked of mind do not prosper,
    and the perverse of tongue fall into
      calamity.

21 The one who begets a fool gets trouble;
    the parent of a fool has no joy.

22 A cheerful heart is a good medicine,
    but a downcast spirit dries up the
      bones.

23 The wicked accept a concealed bribe
    to pervert the ways of justice.

24 The discerning person looks to wisdom,
    but the eyes of a fool to the ends of the
      earth.

25 Foolish children are a grief to their father
    and bitterness to her who bore them.

26 To impose a fine on the innocent is not
      right,
    or to flog the noble for their integrity.

27 One who spares words is knowledgeable;
    one who is cool in spirit has
      understanding.

28 Even fools who keep silent are considered
      wise;
    when they close their lips, they are
      deemed intelligent.

18 The one who lives alone is
      self-indulgent,
    showing contempt for all who have
      sound judgment.[a]

2 A fool takes no pleasure in
      understanding,
    but only in expressing personal
      opinion.

3 When wickedness comes, contempt
      comes also;
    and with dishonor comes disgrace.

4 The words of the mouth are deep waters;
    the fountain of wisdom is a gushing
      stream.

5 It is not right to be partial to the guilty,
    or to subvert the innocent in judgment.

6 A fool's lips bring strife,
    and a fool's mouth invites a flogging.

7 The mouths of fools are their ruin,
    and their lips a snare to themselves.

8 The words of a whisperer are like
      delicious morsels;
    they go down into the inner parts of
      the body.

9 One who is slack in work
    is close kin to a vandal.

10 The name of the Lord is a strong tower;

_____
a Meaning of Heb uncertain

17.10 See 12.1. An example of formal (synthetic) parallelism (second line advances the thought of the first). Some are harder to teach than others, and some may be impossible (v. 16). **17.11** Perhaps a political reference. On *messengers*, see 13.17; 16.14. **17.12** A common proverbial image (2 Sam 17.8; Hos 13.8). **17.13** Retribution theory in action. **17.14** *Like letting out water*, a poignant image (cf. 2 Sam 14.14a). **17.15** See Deut 16.18–20. **17.18** See 6.1–2; 11.15. Guaranteeing others' loans was apparently a common social problem. **17.22** See 14.30. **17.25** See 10.1. **17.27a** Sound counsel in the world of court intrigue; see also 10.19; 12.23.

18.1 The Hebrew is unclear. **18.4** The relationship between the two lines is unclear (synonymous or antithetic parallelism? See Introduction). **18.5** See 17.15. Here the legal context is in the foreground: the innocent must be protected in court (see also Ex 23.1–3). **18.8** Slander attracts listeners to deadly effect. See 26.22. **18.10–11** Real and deceptive sources of strength.

the righteous run into it and are safe.

11 The wealth of the rich is their strong city;
   in their imagination it is like a high
   wall.
12 Before destruction one's heart is haughty,
   but humility goes before honor.
13 If one gives answer before hearing,
   it is folly and shame.
14 The human spirit will endure sickness;
   but a broken spirit—who can bear?
15 An intelligent mind acquires knowledge,
   and the ear of the wise seeks
   knowledge.
16 A gift opens doors;
   it gives access to the great.
17 The one who first states a case seems right,
   until the other comes and cross-
   examines.
18 Casting the lot puts an end to disputes
   and decides between powerful
   contenders.
19 An ally offended is stronger than a city;[a]
   such quarreling is like the bars of a
   castle.
20 From the fruit of the mouth one's
   stomach is satisfied;
   the yield of the lips brings satisfaction.
21 Death and life are in the power of the
   tongue,
   and those who love it will eat its fruits.
22 He who finds a wife finds a good thing,
   and obtains favor from the LORD.
23 The poor use entreaties,
   but the rich answer roughly.
24 Some[b] friends play at friendship[c]
   but a true friend sticks closer than
   one's nearest kin.

19 Better the poor walking in integrity
   than one perverse of speech who is a
   fool.
2 Desire without knowledge is not good,
   and one who moves too hurriedly
   misses the way.

3 One's own folly leads to ruin,
   yet the heart rages against the LORD.
4 Wealth brings many friends,
   but the poor are left friendless.
5 A false witness will not go unpunished,
   and a liar will not escape.
6 Many seek the favor of the generous,
   and everyone is a friend to a giver of
   gifts.
7 If the poor are hated even by their kin,
   how much more are they shunned by
   their friends!
   When they call after them, they are not
   there.[d]
8 To get wisdom is to love oneself;
   to keep understanding is to prosper.
9 A false witness will not go unpunished,
   and the liar will perish.
10 It is not fitting for a fool to live in
   luxury,
   much less for a slave to rule over
   princes.
11 Those with good sense are slow to anger,
   and it is their glory to overlook an
   offense.
12 A king's anger is like the growling of a
   lion,
   but his favor is like dew on the grass.
13 A stupid child is ruin to a father,
   and a wife's quarreling is a continual
   dripping of rain.
14 House and wealth are inherited from
   parents,
   but a prudent wife is from the LORD.
15 Laziness brings on deep sleep;
   an idle person will suffer hunger.
16 Those who keep the commandment will
   live;
   those who are heedless of their ways
   will die.

---

a Gk Syr Vg Tg: Meaning of Heb uncertain   b Syr Tg: Heb A
man of   c Cn Compare Syr Vg Tg: Meaning of Heb uncertain
d Meaning of Heb uncertain

See 10.15a. **18.12** See 15.33; 16.18. **18.14** See 17.22b.
18.15 *Mind,* lit. "heart," seat of the intellect and the will
(cf. note on 2.2). In oral societies one learns by listening. **18.16** See 17.8; 21.14. **18.17–18** Two more neutral
observations. **18.20** See 12.14a; 13.2a. The sages reflect
on material and intellectual rewards of their vocation.
18.21 *Power of the tongue,* language, used aptly (see
note on 1.6). **18.22** See 19.14. A nice contrast to the implicit misogyny of 19.13b, 14a. **18.23** See Sir 13.3.
18.24 See 27.10b. **19.1** See 28.6. **19.2** See 15.18; 16.32;
21.5b. **19.3** Fools seldom take responsibility for their
own actions; see 22.13; 26.12; Sir 15.11–12. **19.4** See
14.20. No wonder the sages counsel mercy toward the
poor (14.21, 31; 17.5; 21.13; 22.9, 16; 28.8, 27; 29.7, 14;
31.9, 20). **19.5** See v. 9. **19.8** *Wisdom, lit.,* "heart," see
note on 18.15. **19.10** See 30.22. **19.11** See 14.29.
19.12a See 20.2. **19.13–14** Note the juxtaposition of
good and bad examples. **19.13a** See 17.25a. **19.13b** See
27.15. This is one of the few places where water imagery
is negative. **19.14** See 18.22. **19.15** *Laziness* and *sleep* go
together. See 6.9–10. **19.16** *Commandment* here means
precept, not revealed law; in parallel with *ways,* it

17 Whoever is kind to the poor lends to the
LORD,
and will be repaid in full.
18 Discipline your children while there is
hope;
do not set your heart on their
destruction.
19 A violent tempered person will pay the
penalty;
if you effect a rescue, you will only
have to do it again.*
20 Listen to advice and accept instruction,
that you may gain wisdom for the
future.
21 The human mind may devise many
plans,
but it is the purpose of the LORD that
will be established.
22 What is desirable in a person is loyalty,
and it is better to be poor than a liar.
23 The fear of the LORD is life indeed;
filled with it one rests secure
and suffers no harm.
24 The lazy person buries a hand in the dish,
and will not even bring it back to the
mouth.
25 Strike a scoffer, and the simple will learn
prudence;
reprove the intelligent, and they will
gain knowledge.
26 Those who do violence to their father and
chase away their mother
are children who cause shame and
bring reproach.
27 Cease straying, my child, from the words
of knowledge,
in order that you may hear instruction.
28 A worthless witness mocks at justice,
and the mouth of the wicked devours
iniquity.
29 Condemnation is ready for scoffers,
and flogging for the backs of fools.
20 Wine is a mocker, strong drink a
brawler,
and whoever is led astray by it is not
wise.

2 The dread anger of a king is like the
growling of a lion;
anyone who provokes him to anger
forfeits life itself.
3 It is honorable to refrain from strife,
but every fool is quick to quarrel.
4 The lazy person does not plow in season;
harvest comes, and there is nothing to
be found.
5 The purposes in the human mind are like
deep water,
but the intelligent will draw them out.
6 Many proclaim themselves loyal,
but who can find one worthy of trust?
7 The righteous walk in integrity—
happy are the children who follow
them!
8 A king who sits on the throne of
judgment
winnows all evil with his eyes.
9 Who can say, "I have made my heart
clean;
I am pure from my sin"?
10 Diverse weights and diverse measures
are both alike an abomination to the
LORD.
11 Even children make themselves known by
their acts,
by whether what they do is pure and
right.
12 The hearing ear and the seeing eye—
the LORD has made them both.
13 Do not love sleep, or else you will come
to poverty;
open your eyes, and you will have
plenty of bread.
14 "Bad, bad," says the buyer,
then goes away and boasts.
15 There is gold, and abundance of costly
stones;
but the lips informed by knowledge are
a precious jewel.
16 Take the garment of one who has given
surety for a stranger;

_____
a Meaning of Heb uncertain

matches the usage in the paternal instructions in chs.
1–9. **19.17** See 14.31; 28.27. **19.18** *On their destruction,*
lit. "to kill him." Sparing reproof might do much worse
damage than merely spoiling the child. See also 23.13–
14. **19.21** See 16.1, 9. **19.23** See 4.27. **19.24** The epitome
of laziness encapsulated in an amusing visual image.
19.26 See 20.20; 30.17; Ex 20.12; 21.17. **19.27** A return
to the instruction style (see Introduction).

20.1 See 23.29–35; 31.4–5. **20.2a** See 19.12. **20.5** See
18.4. **20.8** *Winnows,* sifts. Solomon's judicial wisdom is
the model (1 Kings 3.16–28). See also 20.26. **20.9** The
form of the rhetorical question implies a negative answer. **20.10** See 11.1. **20.11** "By their fruits, you shall
know them." **20.13** Negative and positive admonitions.
20.14 Another amusing encapsulation of a social type.
20.15 See 3.13–15. **20.16** See note on 6.1; also 27.13; Ex

seize the pledge given as surety for
    foreigners.
17 Bread gained by deceit is sweet,
    but afterward the mouth will be full of
       gravel.
18 Plans are established by taking advice;
    wage war by following wise guidance.
19 A gossip reveals secrets;
    therefore do not associate with a
       babbler.
20 If you curse father or mother,
    your lamp will go out in utter
       darkness.
21 An estate quickly acquired in the
       beginning
    will not be blessed in the end.
22 Do not say, "I will repay evil";
    wait for the LORD, and he will help
       you.
23 Differing weights are an abomination to
       the LORD,
    and false scales are not good.
24 All our steps are ordered by the LORD;
    how then can we understand our own
       ways?
25 It is a snare for one to say rashly, "It is
       holy,"
    and begin to reflect only after making a
       vow.
26 A wise king winnows the wicked,
    and drives the wheel over them.
27 The human spirit is the lamp of the
       LORD,
    searching every inmost part.
28 Loyalty and faithfulness preserve the
       king,
    and his throne is upheld by
       righteousness.[a]
29 The glory of youths is their strength,
    but the beauty of the aged is their gray
       hair.
30 Blows that wound cleanse away evil;
    beatings make clean the innermost
       parts.

21 The king's heart is a stream of water
    in the hand of the LORD;

    he turns it wherever he will.
2 All deeds are right in the sight of the
       doer,
    but the LORD weighs the heart.
3 To do righteousness and justice
    is more acceptable to the LORD than
       sacrifice.
4 Haughty eyes and a proud heart—
    the lamp of the wicked—are sin.
5 The plans of the diligent lead surely to
       abundance,
    but everyone who is hasty comes only
       to want.
6 The getting of treasures by a lying tongue
    is a fleeting vapor and a snare[b] of
       death.
7 The violence of the wicked will sweep
       them away,
    because they refuse to do what is just.
8 The way of the guilty is crooked,
    but the conduct of the pure is right.
9 It is better to live in a corner of the
       housetop
    than in a house shared with a
       contentious wife.
10 The souls of the wicked desire evil;
    their neighbors find no mercy in their
       eyes.
11 When a scoffer is punished, the simple
       become wiser;
    when the wise are instructed, they
       increase in knowledge.
12 The Righteous One observes the house of
       the wicked;
    he casts the wicked down to ruin.
13 If you close your ear to the cry of the
       poor,
    you will cry out and not be heard.
14 A gift in secret averts anger;
    and a concealed bribe in the bosom,
       strong wrath.
15 When justice is done, it is a joy to the
       righteous,
    but dismay to evildoers.

---

a Gk: Heb loyalty   b Gk: Heb seekers

22.26–27. **20.17** See 9.17–18; Job 20.12–14. **20.18** See
24.6. Wise men provided political guidance to kings,
e.g., 2 Sam 16.20, 23; 17.5, 14. **20.24** Such pessimism
about the search for understanding is rare in Proverbs.
20.30 A particularly strong attempt to justify corporal
punishment. **21.1** *Heart*, here translated literally, but
still meaning "mind." Cf. the relationship of king and

God in 25.3. **21.2** Cf. 24.12; see note on 16.2. **21.3** See Ps
50. **21.4** *Lamp of the wicked.* See note on 13.9; also 24.20.
21.6 *Fleeting vapor*, the Hebrew term translated "vanity"
in Ecclesiastes (see Eccl 1.2, 14). **21.9** See 25.24; the Hebrew for *wife* also means "woman." **21.13** The relationship between act and consequence in action: "Do unto
others . . ." **21.14** Another pure observation (see 17.8; cf.

16 Whoever wanders from the way of
        understanding
    will rest in the assembly of the dead.
17 Whoever loves pleasure will suffer want;
    whoever loves wine and oil will not be
        rich.
18 The wicked is a ransom for the righteous,
    and the faithless for the upright.
19 It is better to live in a desert land
    than with a contentious and fretful
        wife.
20 Precious treasure remains *a* in the house
        of the wise,
    but the fool devours it.
21 Whoever pursues righteousness and
        kindness
    will find life *b* and honor.
22 One wise person went up against a city of
        warriors
    and brought down the stronghold in
        which they trusted.
23 To watch over mouth and tongue
    is to keep out of trouble.
24 The proud, haughty person, named
        "Scoffer,"
    acts with arrogant pride.
25 The craving of the lazy person is fatal,
    for lazy hands refuse to labor.
26 All day long the wicked covet, *c*
    but the righteous give and do not hold
        back.
27 The sacrifice of the wicked is an
        abomination;
    how much more when brought with
        evil intent.
28 A false witness will perish,
    but a good listener will testify
        successfully.
29 The wicked put on a bold face,
    but the upright give thought to *d* their
        ways.
30 No wisdom, no understanding, no
        counsel,
    can avail against the LORD.

31 The horse is made ready for the day of
        battle,
    but the victory belongs to the LORD.

22 A good name is to be chosen rather
        than great riches,
    and favor is better than silver or gold.
2 The rich and the poor have this in
        common:
    the LORD is the maker of them all.
3 The clever see danger and hide;
    but the simple go on, and suffer for it.
4 The reward for humility and fear of the
        LORD
    is riches and honor and life.
5 Thorns and snares are in the way of the
        perverse;
    the cautious will keep far from them.
6 Train children in the right way,
    and when old, they will not stray.
7 The rich rule over the poor,
    and the borrower is the slave of the
        lender.
8 Whoever sows injustice will reap calamity,
    and the rod of anger will fail.
9 Those who are generous are blessed,
    for they share their bread with the
        poor.
10 Drive out a scoffer, and strife goes out;
    quarreling and abuse will cease.
11 Those who love a pure heart and are
        gracious in speech
    will have the king as a friend.
12 The eyes of the LORD keep watch over
        knowledge,
    but he overthrows the words of the
        faithless.
13 The lazy person says, "There is a lion
        outside!
    I shall be killed in the streets!"
14 The mouth of a loose *e* woman is a deep
        pit;

---

a Gk: Heb *and oil*   *b* Gk: Heb *life and righteousness*
c Gk: Heb *all day long one covets covetously*   *d* Another reading
is *establish*   *e* Heb *strange*

17.23). **21.19** See v. 9. Abusive husbands are not a topic
for the sages. **21.22** An unusual bit of narrative form
among the sayings. **21.24** Sages describe here the
meaning of *scoffer*. See also note on 1.4. **21.27** An echo
of v. 3. **21.28** A *good listener* is one who hears truth and
acts accordingly. **21.30–31** Though the sages praise
wisdom, no human understanding can fathom God's.
22.1–16 A series of contrasts between the wise way and
the fool's way. **22.1** *Good name,* "reputation." See note
on 10.7. **22.2** See 29.13; Job 31.15. The same grammatical frame appears in 20.12. **22.3** The instruction on the
simpleton who meets the Strange Woman in ch. 7 develops this point. **22.4** *Fear of the LORD,* an ongoing
concern for the sages, praised here, as in 10.27; 14.27;
19.23, for its beneficial consequences. See note on 1.7.
22.7 The simple observation in v. 7a provides an analogy to make a teaching point in v. 7b. **22.8** *Sow, reap,* a
proverbial word pair (Ps 126.5; Jer 12.13; Hos 8.7;
10.12). **22.13** Sluggards make ludicrous excuses for
their behavior (26.13). **22.14** *Loose woman.* The He-

he with whom the Lord is angry falls
into it.

15 Folly is bound up in the heart of a boy,
but the rod of discipline drives it far
away.

16 Oppressing the poor in order to enrich
oneself,
and giving to the rich, will lead only to
loss.

Sayings of the Wise

17 The words of the wise:

Incline your ear and hear my words,[a]
and apply your mind to my teaching;

18 for it will be pleasant if you keep them
within you,
if all of them are ready on your lips.

19 So that your trust may be in the Lord,
I have made them known to you
today—yes, to you.

20 Have I not written for you thirty sayings
of admonition and knowledge,

21 to show you what is right and true,
so that you may give a true answer to
those who sent you?

22 Do not rob the poor because they are poor,
or crush the afflicted at the gate;

23 for the Lord pleads their cause
and despoils of life those who despoil
them.

24 Make no friends with those given to anger,
and do not associate with hotheads,

25 or you may learn their ways
and entangle yourself in a snare.

26 Do not be one of those who give pledges,
who become surety for debts.

27 If you have nothing with which to pay,
why should your bed be taken from
under you?

28 Do not remove the ancient landmark
that your ancestors set up.

29 Do you see those who are skillful in their
work?
They will serve kings;
they will not serve common people.

23 When you sit down to eat with a ruler,
observe carefully what[b] is before you,

2 and put a knife to your throat
if you have a big appetite.

3 Do not desire the ruler's[c] delicacies,
for they are deceptive food.

4 Do not wear yourself out to get rich;
be wise enough to desist.

5 When your eyes light upon it, it is gone;
for suddenly it takes wings to itself,
flying like an eagle toward heaven.

6 Do not eat the bread of the stingy;
do not desire their delicacies;

7 for like a hair in the throat, so are they.[d]
"Eat and drink!" they say to you;
but they do not mean it.

8 You will vomit up the little you have
eaten,
and you will waste your pleasant
words.

9 Do not speak in the hearing of a fool,
who will only despise the wisdom of
your words.

---

a Cn Compare Gk: Heb *Incline your ear, and hear the words of the wise* *b* Or *who* *c* Heb *his* *d* Meaning of Heb uncertain

---

brew reads "strange woman," i.e., the repository of all the dangers the sages contrast with the figure of Woman Wisdom. See note on 2.16–19. *Deep pit,* the land of the dead is evoked here, as this major collection ends with the same imagery that shaped chs. 1–9. **22.17–24.22** The sayings of the wise. This section departs from the proverb collections of 10.1–22.16, as it makes a free adaptation from the popular Egyptian wisdom text Instruction of Amenemope. Many of the topics treated seem especially suited to educating young civil servants for their roles in court life (22.29; 23.1–3, 6–8; 23.20–21, 29–35), although typical wisdom themes (e.g., the poor, family relationships, fools and kings) also appear. Although inspired by the Egyptian work, sentiments have been thoroughly reworked according to the sages' Yahwistic theology and the order of topics has been altered. **22.17** *The words of the wise.* The title of the book's

third collection (see 1.1; 10.1; 24.23; 25.1; 30.1; 31.1) has been restored from the Septuagint. Notice the use of direct address as the text reverts to the instruction style (cf. 23.19, 26). **22.20** *Thirty sayings.* The original Amenemope contained thirty "houses," or chapters. **22.22** *At the gate,* the place where legal matters were decided. **22.28** The moving of boundary markers was also a concern for Amenemope (see note on 22.17–24.22), but see 23.10–11; 25.25; Deut 19.14; 27.17; Isa 5.8–10 for the Hebrew context. Such standing stones established legal ownership of land, the source of life.
   23.1–8 Words of caution for those who associate with their social betters. **23.1** *What is before you.* The Hebrew reading, *who is before you* (see text note b), might well attest to the sages' concern for circumspect behavior in exalted company. **23.4–5** See Eccl 2 for similar reflections on the fleeting nature of ma-

10 Do not remove an ancient landmark
       or encroach on the fields of
           orphans,
11 for their redeemer is strong;
       he will plead their cause against you.
12 Apply your mind to instruction
       and your ear to words of knowledge.
13 Do not withhold discipline from your
           children;
       if you beat them with a rod, they will
           not die.
14 If you beat them with the rod,
       you will save their lives from Sheol.
15 My child, if your heart is wise,
       my heart too will be glad.
16 My soul will rejoice
       when your lips speak what is right.
17 Do not let your heart envy sinners,
       but always continue in the fear of the
           LORD.
18 Surely there is a future,
       and your hope will not be cut off.

19 Hear, my child, and be wise,
       and direct your mind in the way.
20 Do not be among winebibbers,
       or among gluttonous eaters of meat;
21 for the drunkard and the glutton will
           come to poverty,
       and drowsiness will clothe them with
           rags.

22 Listen to your father who begot you,
       and do not despise your mother when
           she is old.
23 Buy truth, and do not sell it;
       buy wisdom, instruction, and
           understanding.

24 The father of the righteous will greatly
           rejoice;
       he who begets a wise son will be glad
           in him.
25 Let your father and mother be glad;
       let her who bore you rejoice.

26 My child, give me your heart,
       and let your eyes observe*a* my ways.
27 For a prostitute is a deep pit;
       an adulteress*b* is a narrow well.
28 She lies in wait like a robber
       and increases the number of the faithless.

29 Who has woe? Who has sorrow?
       Who has strife? Who has complaining?
       Who has wounds without cause?
       Who has redness of eyes?
30 Those who linger late over wine,
       those who keep trying mixed wines.
31 Do not look at wine when it is red,
       when it sparkles in the cup
       and goes down smoothly.
32 At the last it bites like a serpent,
       and stings like an adder.
33 Your eyes will see strange things,
       and your mind utter perverse things.
34 You will be like one who lies down in the
           midst of the sea,
       like one who lies on the top of a mast.*c*
35 "They struck me," you will say,*d* "but I
           was not hurt;
       they beat me, but I did not feel it.
       When shall I awake?
       I will seek another drink."

---

a Another reading is *delight in*   *b* Heb *an alien woman*
c Meaning of Heb uncertain   *d* Gk Syr Vg Tg: Heb lacks *you will say*

terial pleasures. **23.10** See 22.28; Job 24.2–3; Deut 27.19. **23.11** *Redeemer,* a blood relative charged with prosecuting legal wrongs; the sages may be thinking here of God, often pictured as redeemer to orphans and widows (see Ex 22.22–24; Job 19.25). **23.12** *Mind* (lit. "heart"), *ear,* a traditional word pair in 18.15; 22.17; Deut 29.4. *Apply your mind* occurs also in 22.17; Eccl 1.13, 17; 8.9. **23.13–14** See 4.10; 15.10; 19.18; 22.15. Public stoning was provided as a last resort for parents who could not control their children (Deut 21.18–21). **23.17** Similar sentiments are found in two wisdom psalms, Pss 37; 73; see also Prov 3.31; 24.1; 24.19, 21. **23.18** See Ps 1, where long life belongs to those who study (cf. Prov 24.14); in Job 27.8, God cuts off the hope of the godless. **23.21** *Drunkards* (26.9–10) and *gluttons* (28.7) are favorite targets of the sages, but see Lemuel's mother's advice for a

change in a different context (31.4–7). **23.23** *Buy,* lit. "acquire." Like the Lord (8.22), the sages must acquire wisdom. **23.24–25** See 10.1; 13.1; 15.20; 19.13; 28.7; 29.3. **23.27–28** See 22.14, where the *loose* (lit. "strange") woman's mouth is a *deep pit.* In the instructional poems, it is not the prostitute but the adulteress who is the real problem (2.16–19; 6.26; ch.7); v. 27a may be the result of a scribal error, as the Hebrew word for "prostitute" differs from "stranger" by only one consonant. In 1.11–12 male sinners lie in wait and lead the ignorant down to the Pit (Death; see note on 1.12). **23.29–30** Perhaps a disintegrated fragment of a popular old riddle; the answer here, though, is no surprise. **23.32** *Serpent, adder.* See Pss 58.4; 91.13. **23.33–35** A dead-on caricature of the drunkard's behavior. **23.33** *Strange things.* The feminine plural noun could as easily be translated "strange

24 Do not envy the wicked,
     nor desire to be with them;
2 for their minds devise violence,
     and their lips talk of mischief.

3 By wisdom a house is built,
     and by understanding it is established;
4 by knowledge the rooms are filled
     with all precious and pleasant riches.
5 Wise warriors are mightier than strong
     ones,[a]
     and those who have knowledge than
          those who have strength;
6 for by wise guidance you can wage your
          war,
     and in abundance of counselors there
          is victory.
7 Wisdom is too high for fools;
     in the gate they do not open their
          mouths.

8 Whoever plans to do evil
     will be called a mischief-maker.
9 The devising of folly is sin,
     and the scoffer is an abomination to all.

10 If you faint in the day of adversity,
     your strength being small;
11 if you hold back from rescuing those
          taken away to death,
     those who go staggering to the slaughter;
12 if you say, "Look, we did not know
          this"—
     does not he who weighs the heart
          perceive it?
     Does not he who keeps watch over your
          soul know it?
     And will he not repay all according to
          their deeds?

13 My child, eat honey, for it is good,
     and the drippings of the honeycomb
          are sweet to your taste.

14 Know that wisdom is such to your
          soul;
     if you find it, you will find a future,
     and your hope will not be cut off.

15 Do not lie in wait like an outlaw against
          the home of the righteous;
     do no violence to the place where the
          righteous live;
16 for though they fall seven times, they will
          rise again;
     but the wicked are overthrown by
          calamity.

17 Do not rejoice when your enemies fall,
     and do not let your heart be glad when
          they stumble,
18 or else the LORD will see it and be
          displeased,
     and turn away his anger from them.

19 Do not fret because of evildoers.
     Do not envy the wicked;
20 for the evil have no future;
     the lamp of the wicked will go out.

21 My child, fear the LORD and the king,
     and do not disobey either of them;[b]
22 for disaster comes from them suddenly,
     and who knows the ruin that both can
          bring?

Further Sayings of the Wise

23 These also are sayings of the wise:

Partiality in judging is not good.
24 Whoever says to the wicked, "You are
          innocent,"
     will be cursed by peoples, abhorred by
          nations;

---

a Gk Compare Syr Tg: Heb *A wise man is strength*   *b* Gk: Heb
do not associate with those who change

---

women." **24.3a** Woman Wisdom builds her house in
9.1 and the "Woman of Worth" (or the capable wife)
performs similar tasks on the human level in 31.26–
27. See also 1 Kings 10.4 (2 Chr 9.3); Acts 7.10 for
other examples of wisdom building "households."
24.5–6 Intelligence trumps brute strength. **24.10–
12** Pretending ignorance of others' suffering carries
no weight with God. *Weighs the heart.* See 21.2; note
on 16.2. **24.13** *Honey, honeycomb,* traditional word
pair for exemplary sweetness and desirability (Ps
19.10). Too much of a good thing can become bad,

however (25.16, 27; 27.7), or dangerous (5.3).
24.14 See note on 23.18. **24.15** See the instruction of
1.10–19. **24.20** The same view expressed in 13.9 (cf.
21.4), but Job questions it in Job 21.17. **24.21–
22** *Fear the LORD and the king.* Both can be equally
dangerous!
   24.23–34 Further sayings of the wise. **24.23a** *These
also are the sayings of the wise,* lit. "also these (belong)
to the wise ones," a title linking this short collection
with 22.17–22. **24.23b–25** An admonition against
partiality in judging; see 18.5; 28.21; 31.5; Lev 19.15;

25 but those who rebuke the wicked will
    have delight,
    and a good blessing will come upon
    them.
26 One who gives an honest answer
    gives a kiss on the lips.

27 Prepare your work outside,
    get everything ready for you in the
    field;
    and after that build your house.

28 Do not be a witness against your
    neighbor without cause,
    and do not deceive with your lips.
29 Do not say, "I will do to others as they
    have done to me;
    I will pay them back for what they have
    done."

30 I passed by the field of one who was
    lazy,
    by the vineyard of a stupid person;
31 and see, it was all overgrown with thorns;
    the ground was covered with nettles,
    and its stone wall was broken down.
32 Then I saw and considered it;
    I looked and received instruction.
33 A little sleep, a little slumber,
    a little folding of the hands to rest,

34 and poverty will come upon you like a
    robber,
    and want, like an armed warrior.

Further Wise Sayings of Solomon

25 These are other proverbs of Solomon
    that the officials of King Hezekiah of
Judah copied.

2 It is the glory of God to conceal things,
    but the glory of kings is to search
    things out.
3 Like the heavens for height, like the earth
    for depth,
    so the mind of kings is unsearchable.
4 Take away the dross from the silver,
    and the smith has material for a vessel;
5 take away the wicked from the presence
    of the king,
    and his throne will be established in
    righteousness.
6 Do not put yourself forward in the king's
    presence
    or stand in the place of the great;
7 for it is better to be told, "Come up here,"
    than to be put lower in the presence of
    a noble.

What your eyes have seen
8   do not hastily bring into court;

Deut 1.17; 16.19. **24.26** A delightfully pithy saying. **24.29** See Mt 6.12, 14–15. **24.30–34** An example story warning against laziness. The tradition is aware that not all poverty is the victim's fault (see 28.15; 29.7; Pss 10.2; 37.14). **24.33–34** Same as 6.10–11. **25.1–29.27** Further wise sayings of Solomon, an independent collection (see headings at 25.1; 30.1) composed of two discrete units, chs. 25–27 and 28–29 (see notes on 25.1–27.27; 27.23–27; 28.1–29.27). **25.1–27.27** One scholar argues for considerable thematic and structural unity in this section. Some of the evidence for this view will be noted. The artistry of the similes here is unsurpassed. **25.1** *Solomon.* See 1.1; Introduction. The proverbs' artistry and worldview suggest education and wealth, if not the royal court itself. *Officials,* lit. "men," presumably court scribes. *Hezekiah* reigned 715–687 BCE. The numerical equivalent of one spelling of his name is 140, the number of lines in this collection. **25.2–27** A carefully constructed unit marked by a double *inclusio* (repetition of one or more words at the beginning and end of a passage): *glory/honor* (the same Hebrew word) appears twice and *search* (*seek*) once in vv. 2, 27; and the word pair *wicked/righteous* appears in vv. 5, 26. **25.2–7** These verses establish the proper relationships of God, king, and subject, with much less distance between the first two than the second two. **25.2–3** *God* and *kings* (see 1.1) are intimately related; the *glory* of each is tied to the other. Hebrew *kabod* can be translated either "glory," a divine attribute, or "honor" a central social value, the opposite of which is shame (see note on 3.4). *Search, unsearchable.* See note on 1.13. *Heavens, earth.* The *mind of kings* is comparable to the whole of creation, thus, like God, not to be questioned. **25.4–5** The saying in v. 4 provides a metaphor for the main point in v. 5. Moral worth is imaged as refinement (see also 27.21–22). *Throne will be established,* formulaic language from the Davidic promise (see 29.14b; 2 Sam 7.13, 16). On *righteousness* and kingship, see note on 1.1; Ps 72. **25.5** The word pair *righteous, wicked* (see note on 3.33–35) is common in chs. 25–29 (25.26; 28.1, 4–5, 10, 28; 29.6, 7, 16, 27). **25.6–7** Better to recognize one's subordinate status than to lose face, a form of shame (see note on 3.4; also 25.7c–10). On the value of humility, see also 11.2; 27.1–2, 21; 29.23. References to social tensions pervade chs. 25–26. **25.7c–10** These verses are related to what precedes by the motifs of the law *court,* once under the jurisdiction of the monarchy, and of *shame.* The inability to settle one's own disputes brings loss of face, but was apparently common (see also 25.18; 26.17; 28.25; 29.9, 22, 24; 30.33).

for[a] what will you do in the end,
    when your neighbor puts you to
        shame?
9 Argue your case with your neighbor
        directly,
    and do not disclose another's secret;
10 or else someone who hears you will bring
        shame upon you,
    and your ill repute will have no end.

11 A word fitly spoken
    is like apples of gold in a setting of silver.
12 Like a gold ring or an ornament of gold
    is a wise rebuke to a listening ear.
13 Like the cold of snow in the time of
        harvest
    are faithful messengers to those who
        send them;
    they refresh the spirit of their masters.
14 Like clouds and wind without rain
    is one who boasts of a gift never given.
15 With patience a ruler may be persuaded,
    and a soft tongue can break bones.
16 If you have found honey, eat only enough
        for you,
    or else, having too much, you will
        vomit it.
17 Let your foot be seldom in your
        neighbor's house,
    otherwise the neighbor will become
        weary of you and hate you.
18 Like a war club, a sword, or a sharp arrow
    is one who bears false witness against a
        neighbor.
19 Like a bad tooth or a lame foot
    is trust in a faithless person in time of
        trouble.

20 Like vinegar on a wound[b]
    is one who sings songs to a heavy
        heart.
Like a moth in clothing or a worm in
        wood,
    sorrow gnaws at the human heart.[c]
21 If your enemies are hungry, give them
        bread to eat;
    and if they are thirsty, give them water
        to drink;
22 for you will heap coals of fire on their
        heads,
    and the LORD will reward you.
23 The north wind produces rain,
    and a backbiting tongue, angry looks.
24 It is better to live in a corner of the
        housetop
    than in a house shared with a
        contentious wife.
25 Like cold water to a thirsty soul,
    so is good news from a far country.
26 Like a muddied spring or a polluted
        fountain
    are the righteous who give way before
        the wicked.
27 It is not good to eat much honey,
    or to seek honor on top of honor.
28 Like a city breached, without walls,
    is one who lacks self-control.

26 Like snow in summer or rain in
        harvest,
    so honor is not fitting for a fool.
2 Like a sparrow in its flitting, like a
        swallow in its flying,

---

a Cn: Heb *or else* *b* Gk: Heb *Like one who takes off a garment on a cold day, like vinegar on lye* *c* Gk Syr Tg: Heb lacks *Like a moth . . . human heart*

25.11–15 Four elegant metaphors on the power of language culminate in practical advice for the prospective courtier. **25.11–12** *Gold, silver.* See notes on 1.13; 17.3. **25.13** Cf. v. 25. Weather similes also occur in vv. 14, 23; 26.1; 27.15–16. **25.14** What is anticipated does not come forth; see v. 23 for the opposite problem. **25.15** Wise advisers exercise power indirectly, with well-chosen words, not weapons (see note on 1.6; cf. 25.18; 26.6–10, 18–19). **25.16–27** Except for v. 25, a series of visceral images of undesirable relationships. *Honey* (vv. 16, 27; see 4.17; note on 5.3) creates an *inclusio* (see note on 25.2–27) for this subsection. **25.16–17** Two admonitions, the first a metaphor to reinforce the point of the second. **25.16** *Vomit.* See 26.11. **25.17** See 27.10. **25.18** *War club, sword, sharp arrow.* See v. 15. *False witness.* Malicious speech is a cause and a symbol of social disruption (see note on 1.6; also 26.19–28; 29.12), here set in a legal context (see 25.7c–10; Ex 20.16; Deut 5.20).

25.21–22 "Turn the other cheek" or "Vengeance is the Lord's" (Mt 5.39; Rom 12.20). **25.23** The *north wind* brings unanticipated rain (cf. 25.14); however, the Hebrew word for "north" can also mean "hidden." *Backbiting* (lit. "hidden"), a wordplay on "hidden wind"/"hidden tongue." **25.24** *Contentious wife.* See also 21.9; 27.15. **25.25** See v. 13. **25.26–27** *Righteous, wicked, seek, honor.* See note on 25.2–27. **25.26** *Spring, fountain,* symbols of wisdom (see 1.23), which is lacking here. **25.27** The unit concludes with typical advice against overreaching oneself (see vv. 6–7, 16–17). **25.28** An odd verse in the overall composition, perhaps added for the sake of the line count (see note on 25.1). *Self-control,* a virtue of the sages (see also 29.8, 11, 22; 30.33).

26.1–12 A unit on the fool. **26.1–3** Things that "land" where they do not belong (vv. 1–2) and things that land appropriately (v. 3). On animal comparisons, see note on 6.6–11. **26.1** *Snow, rain.* See 25.13–14.

an undeserved curse goes nowhere.

3 A whip for the horse, a bridle for the
      donkey,
   and a rod for the back of fools.
4 Do not answer fools according to their
      folly,
   or you will be a fool yourself.
5 Answer fools according to their folly,
   or they will be wise in their own eyes.
6 It is like cutting off one's foot and
      drinking down violence,
   to send a message by a fool.
7 The legs of a disabled person hang limp;
   so does a proverb in the mouth of a fool.
8 It is like binding a stone in a sling
   to give honor to a fool.
9 Like a thornbush brandished by the hand
      of a drunkard
   is a proverb in the mouth of a fool.
10 Like an archer who wounds everybody
   is one who hires a passing fool or
      drunkard.*a*
11 Like a dog that returns to its vomit
   is a fool who reverts to his folly.
12 Do you see persons wise in their own eyes?
   There is more hope for fools than for
      them.
13 The lazy person says, "There is a lion in
      the road!
   There is a lion in the streets!"
14 As a door turns on its hinges,
   so does a lazy person in bed.
15 The lazy person buries a hand in the dish,
   and is too tired to bring it back to the
      mouth.
16 The lazy person is wiser in self-esteem
   than seven who can answer discreetly.
17 Like somebody who takes a passing dog
      by the ears
   is one who meddles in the quarrel of
      another.

18 Like a maniac who shoots deadly
      firebrands and arrows,
19 so is one who deceives a neighbor
   and says, "I am only joking!"
20 For lack of wood the fire goes out,
   and where there is no whisperer,
      quarreling ceases.
21 As charcoal is to hot embers and wood to
      fire,
   so is a quarrelsome person for kindling
      strife.
22 The words of a whisperer are like
      delicious morsels;
   they go down into the inner parts of
      the body.
23 Like the glaze*b* covering an earthen vessel
   are smooth*c* lips with an evil heart.
24 An enemy dissembles in speaking
   while harboring deceit within;
25 when an enemy speaks graciously, do not
      believe it,
   for there are seven abominations
      concealed within;
26 though hatred is covered with guile,
   the enemy's wickedness will be exposed
      in the assembly.
27 Whoever digs a pit will fall into it,
   and a stone will come back on the one
      who starts it rolling.
28 A lying tongue hates its victims,
   and a flattering mouth works ruin.

27 Do not boast about tomorrow,
   for you do not know what a day may
      bring.
2 Let another praise you, and not your own
      mouth—
   a stranger, and not your own lips.
3 A stone is heavy, and sand is weighty,

---

a Meaning of Heb uncertain   *b* Cn: Heb *silver of dross*
c Gk: Heb *burning*

26.3 The trainable fool. **26.4–5** Proverbs are not timeless absolutes but must be applied in their season (see note on 1.6; cf. 26.6, 7, 9). *Wise in their own eyes.* See 3.5. **26.6–10** These verses are linked by artfully crafted images of violence and weapons (see 25.25). **26.6–7** "Lame" language (see vv. 4–5). **26.6** See 25.13, 15. **26.9** See 26.4–5. **26.10** Only a fool hires a fool (see 26.4–5). **26.11** Fools refuse instruction at the price of their own humanity (see 25.16). **26.12** See note on 3.5. **26.12b** Same as 29.20b. **26.13–16** A humorous unit on the lazy (see 6.6–10; 19.24). **26.16** *Wiser in self-esteem,* lit. "wise in his own eyes." See 3.5; 26.12. **26.17–28** Social tension and wound-

ing speech. **26.17–19** The unit's themes. **26.20–21** On "heat" and *strife,* see 29.8, 22. **26.22–26a** Inner intent must be distinguished from outward appearance; see also 27.6; 31.30. **26.22** Same as 18.8. **26.23** *Smooth,* lit. "burning," the same imagery as in vv. 20–21. **26.26** *Assembly.* See 5.14. **26.27–28** See 1.32. **26.27** Proverbial assurance of retribution (see 1.32). *Pit.* See also 28.10, 17–18.

  27.1–22 A miscellany composed mostly of proverb pairs. **27.1–2** See 25.6–7. *Bring,* lit. "give birth to." *Another, stranger,* the same word pair used for the Strange Woman (see note on 2.16–19), though here without negative connotation. **27.3–6** Problematic relation-

but a fool's provocation is heavier than
both.

4 Wrath is cruel, anger is overwhelming,
but who is able to stand before
jealousy?

5 Better is open rebuke
than hidden love.

6 Well meant are the wounds a friend
inflicts,
but profuse are the kisses of an enemy.

7 The sated appetite spurns honey,
but to a ravenous appetite even the
bitter is sweet.

8 Like a bird that strays from its nest
is one who strays from home.

9 Perfume and incense make the heart glad,
but the soul is torn by trouble. *a*

10 Do not forsake your friend or the friend
of your parent;
do not go to the house of your kindred
in the day of your calamity.
Better is a neighbor who is nearby
than kindred who are far away.

11 Be wise, my child, and make my heart glad,
so that I may answer whoever
reproaches me.

12 The clever see danger and hide;
but the simple go on, and suffer for it.

13 Take the garment of one who has given
surety for a stranger;
seize the pledge given as surety for
foreigners. *b*

14 Whoever blesses a neighbor with a loud
voice,
rising early in the morning,
will be counted as cursing.

15 A continual dripping on a rainy day
and a contentious wife are alike;

16 to restrain her is to restrain the wind
or to grasp oil in the right hand. *c*

17 Iron sharpens iron,
and one person sharpens the wits *d* of
another.

18 Anyone who tends a fig tree will eat its
fruit,
and anyone who takes care of a master
will be honored.

19 Just as water reflects the face,
so one human heart reflects another.

20 Sheol and Abaddon are never satisfied,
and human eyes are never satisfied.

21 The crucible is for silver, and the furnace
is for gold,
so a person is tested *e* by being praised.

22 Crush a fool in a mortar with a pestle
along with crushed grain,
but the folly will not be driven out.

23 Know well the condition of your flocks,
and give attention to your herds;

24 for riches do not last forever,
nor a crown for all generations.

25 When the grass is gone, and new growth
appears,
and the herbage of the mountains is
gathered,

26 the lambs will provide your clothing,
and the goats the price of a field;

27 there will be enough goats' milk for your
food,
for the food of your household
and nourishment for your servant-
girls.

---

a Gk: Heb *the sweetness of a friend is better than one's own
counsel* *b* Vg and 20.16: Heb *for a foreign woman* *c* Meaning
of Heb uncertain *d* Heb *face* *e* Heb lacks *is tested*

---

ships. **27.3–4** *Stone, sand, overwhelming* (the last term
is lit. "a flood"). Natural weights and forces embody
the experiences of folly and jealousy. **27.4** See Song
8.6–7 for a similar description of passionate love.
27.6 Appearances deceive (see 26.22–26a). **27.7–
10** Satiation and appetite provide a metaphor (v. 7) for
the difficulty in maintaining the proper relational distance (vv. 8–10). **27.7** *Appetite, honey.* See notes on
1.31; 5.3. **27.9b** The translation in text note *a* is preferable. When one is too close to a situation, comradely
advice is welcome. *Sweetness* echoes *honey* (v. 7).
27.10 See 25.17. **27.11** Public honor or shame depends
on success in child rearing (see notes on 1.8; 3.4).
27.13 *Garment.* See Ex 22.26–27; Am 2.8. *Given surety.*
See 6.1–5. **27.15–16** The contentious wife seems to
have a mind of her own. See 21.9; 25.24. **27.17–18** The
first line of each verse cites a proverb, and the second

applies it concretely. **27.19** A subtle reflection on relationship. **27.20** *Sheol, Abaddon.* See notes on 1.12;
15.11. **27.21–22** *Crucible, mortar.* Two modes of testing for what is worthy (see 25.4). *Being praised.* See
25.6–7; 27.1–2; in 17.3 it is the Lord who tests.
27.22 The unteachable fool (see note on 1.4). **27.23–
27** An admonitory poem. Though the imagery is
largely bucolic, one scholar suggests that *riches* and
crown (v. 24) make the poem a metaphor of proper
kingly rule (on king as shepherd, people as flock, see,
e.g., Jer 23.1–6; Ezek 34). *Clothing, field, food, household, servant-girls,* vocabulary and concerns identical
to those of the capable wife (31.10–31); this poem
may mark the end of the unit beginning in 25.1, as
31.10–31 closes the book as a whole (see note on 25.1–
29.27). **27.27** *Servant-girls.* Female servants were undoubtedly often adult women (see also 31.15).

28

The wicked flee when no one pursues,
but the righteous are as bold as a lion.

2 When a land rebels
it has many rulers;
but with an intelligent ruler
there is lasting order.[a]

3 A ruler[b] who oppresses the poor
is a beating rain that leaves no food.

4 Those who forsake the law praise the
wicked,
but those who keep the law struggle
against them.

5 The evil do not understand justice,
but those who seek the LORD
understand it completely.

6 Better to be poor and walk in integrity
than to be crooked in one's ways even
though rich.

7 Those who keep the law are wise
children,
but companions of gluttons shame
their parents.

8 One who augments wealth by exorbitant
interest
gathers it for another who is kind to
the poor.

9 When one will not listen to the law,
even one's prayers are an abomination.

10 Those who mislead the upright into evil
ways
will fall into pits of their own making,
but the blameless will have a goodly
inheritance.

11 The rich is wise in self-esteem,
but an intelligent poor person sees
through the pose.

12 When the righteous triumph, there is
great glory,
but when the wicked prevail, people go
into hiding.

13 No one who conceals transgressions will
prosper,
but one who confesses and forsakes
them will obtain mercy.

14 Happy is the one who is never without
fear,
but one who is hard-hearted will fall
into calamity.

15 Like a roaring lion or a charging bear
is a wicked ruler over a poor people.

16 A ruler who lacks understanding is a
cruel oppressor;
but one who hates unjust gain will
enjoy a long life.

17 If someone is burdened with the blood of
another,
let that killer be a fugitive until death;
let no one offer assistance.

18 One who walks in integrity will be safe,
but whoever follows crooked ways will
fall into the Pit.[c]

19 Anyone who tills the land will have plenty
of bread,
but one who follows worthless pursuits
will have plenty of poverty.

20 The faithful will abound with blessings,

---

a Meaning of Heb uncertain   *b* Cn: Heb *A poor person*
c Syr: Heb *fall all at once*

28.1–29.27 The literary style returns to the independent antithetical proverbs favored in chs. 10–15. **28.2–3** Textual difficulties prevent certain translation, but observations about just rule and care for the poor are frequent in chs. 28–29 (28.8, 12, 15, 16, 27, 28; 29.2, 4, 7, 12, 13, 14, 16, 26; see also note on 1.1). *Rulers* translates a variety of Hebrew words for authority figures; here it probably refers to later foreign rulers, not the Davidic monarchs. **28.2** *Intelligent ruler.* Just rule requires wisdom (see note on 1.1). **28.4, 7, 9** See also 29.18. *The law* (Hebrew *torah*). The lack of the definite article in the Hebrew may suggest that this is still a teacher's instruction, not covenantal law; on the other hand, unlike elsewhere in Proverbs no specific instruction is indicated by the term (cf., e.g., 1.8), which seems to have a self-standing weight. The book of Sirach will later equate wisdom and law, and these sayings seem to mark the path to that conclusion. **28.6** Poverty is not always a consequence of evil or laziness (see 15.15–16; 28.2–3, 11; cf. 6.6–10; 28.19). *Walk, ways.* **28.7–8** Both verses seem to reference pentateuchal laws. On *children*

(sons) who are *gluttons,* see Deut 21.20. On not taking *interest* on loans, see Ex 22.25. **28.10** See 1.10–19; 26.27. **28.11–13** These verses are linked by "searching"/"hiding" (see notes on 1.13; 28.11). **28.11** See 28.6. *Wise in self-esteem.* See 3.5; 26.5. *Sees through the pose,* lit. "searches him out." **28.12b** Same as 28.28a. *People go into hiding,* lit. "a man is searched for." Do the people hide or do they search for a just ruler? **28.14** *Happy. Hard-hearted,* stubborn (see 29.1; Ex 7.3); the allusion to Pharaoh suggests that *fear* refers to fear of the Lord (see note on 1.7). **28.15–16** See 28.2–3. **28.17** *Burdened,* lit. "oppressed," a catchword tying this verse to preceding. *Let that killer . . . assistance,* lit. "let him flee to the pit; do not seize him"; bloodguilt brings its own punishment (the pit is the grave); see 1.11–12; 5.22; 26.27; cf. Ex 21.13; Num 35.6–15; Deut 4.41–43; 19.1–10. **28.18** Perhaps explanatory of v. 17. *Walks, ways.* **28.19–22** On wealth and poverty. A clear statement of the work ethic (v. 19; see 6.6–10) gets clouded: the poor thief may deserve mercy (vv. 21; see vv. 2–3; Ex 23.3), and the greedy may (temporarily) achieve their aims

but one who is in a hurry to be rich
  will not go unpunished.

21 To show partiality is not good—
  yet for a piece of bread a person may
    do wrong.

22 The miser is in a hurry to get rich
  and does not know that loss is sure to
    come.

23 Whoever rebukes a person will afterward
    find more favor
  than one who flatters with the tongue.

24 Anyone who robs father or mother
  and says, "That is no crime,"
  is partner to a thug.

25 The greedy person stirs up strife,
  but whoever trusts in the LORD will be
    enriched.

26 Those who trust in their own wits are
    fools;
  but those who walk in wisdom come
    through safely.

27 Whoever gives to the poor will lack
    nothing,
  but one who turns a blind eye will get
    many a curse.

28 When the wicked prevail, people go into
    hiding;
  but when they perish, the righteous
    increase.

29 One who is often reproved, yet
    remains stubborn,
  will suddenly be broken beyond
    healing.

2 When the righteous are in authority, the
    people rejoice;
  but when the wicked rule, the people
    groan.

3 A child who loves wisdom makes a parent
    glad,
  but to keep company with prostitutes
    is to squander one's substance.

4 By justice a king gives stability to the
    land,
  but one who makes heavy exactions
    ruins it.

5 Whoever flatters a neighbor
  is spreading a net for the neighbor's
    feet.

6 In the transgression of the evil there is a
    snare,
  but the righteous sing and rejoice.

7 The righteous know the rights of the
    poor;
  the wicked have no such
    understanding.

8 Scoffers set a city aflame,
  but the wise turn away wrath.

9 If the wise go to law with fools,
  there is ranting and ridicule without
    relief.

10 The bloodthirsty hate the blameless,
  and they seek the life of the upright.

11 A fool gives full vent to anger,
  but the wise quietly holds it back.

12 If a ruler listens to falsehood,
  all his officials will be wicked.

13 The poor and the oppressor have this in
    common:
  the LORD gives light to the eyes of
    both.

14 If a king judges the poor with equity,
  his throne will be established forever.

15 The rod and reproof give wisdom,
  but a mother is disgraced by a
    neglected child.

16 When the wicked are in authority,
    transgression increases,
  but the righteous will look upon their
    downfall.

17 Discipline your children, and they will
    give you rest;
  they will give delight to your heart.

(vv. 20b, 22). **28.23** Rebuke, flatter. See 25.12. **28.24–25** Cf. 29.24–25. **28.24** See Ex 20.12; 21.15–17; Deut 5.16; 27.16. **28.25–26** Trusts in the LORD and walk in wisdom are identified via parallelism (see 1.7). **28.26** Trust in their own wits, lit. "heart," or mind. See 3.5. **28.27** Almsgiving was a matter of honor. **28.28a** Same as 28.12b.

29.1a See note on 1.4. Stubborn, lit. "hard-necked"; cf. 28.14. **29.1b** Suddenly. See note on 6.15b. **29.3** Prostitutes appear more dangerous here than in 6.26. **29.5–6** The images of net and snare link these two sayings (see also 1.17). **29.6** Rejoice. See 29.2. **29.8** This translation misses the wordplay on words involving breath.

Read either lit. "Scoffers set a city panting / but the wise turn aside the nose" or, completing the metaphor, "Scoffers set a city aflame / but the wise turn aside burning anger." A "(burning) nose" is a typical Hebrew euphemism for anger (cf. 25.28; 26.20–21; 30.33). **29.9** See 25.7c–10. **29.10** See 1.10–19. **29.11** See, e.g., 12.16. **29.13** Bitter realism or hope for the poor (see 22.2)? **29.14** This verse perhaps qualifies the preceding saying; the reverse situation appears in 28.3. **29.14b** See note on 25.4–5. **29.15** Rod, reproof. See 13.24; cf. 29.19, 21, where similar harsh discipline is applied to slaves. Mother is disgraced. See notes on 1.8; 3.4. **29.17** See 13.24; 29.3.

18 Where there is no prophecy, the people
    cast off restraint,
       but happy are those who keep the
       law.
19 By mere words servants are not
    disciplined,
       for though they understand, they will
       not give heed.
20 Do you see someone who is hasty in
    speech?
       There is more hope for a fool than for
       anyone like that.
21 A slave pampered from childhood
    will come to a bad end.ᵃ
22 One given to anger stirs up strife,
    and the hothead causes much
    transgression.
23 A person's pride will bring humiliation,
    but one who is lowly in spirit will
    obtain honor.
24 To be a partner of a thief is to hate one's
    own life;
       one hears the victim's curse, but
       discloses nothing.ᵇ
25 The fear of othersᶜ lays a snare,
    but one who trusts in the LORD is
    secure.
26 Many seek the favor of a ruler,
    but it is from the LORD that one gets
    justice.
27 The unjust are an abomination to the
    righteous,
       but the upright are an abomination to
       the wicked.

Sayings of Agur

30 The words of Agur son of Jakeh. An oracle.
    Thus says the man: I am weary, O God,
       I am weary, O God. How can I
       prevail?ᵈ
2 Surely I am too stupid to be human;
    I do not have human understanding.
3 I have not learned wisdom,
    nor have I knowledge of the holy
    ones.ᵉ
4 Who has ascended to heaven and come
    down?
    Who has gathered the wind in the
    hollow of the hand?
    Who has wrapped up the waters in a
    garment?
    Who has established all the ends of the
    earth?
    What is the person's name?
    And what is the name of the person's
    child?
    Surely you know!

5 Every word of God proves true;
    he is a shield to those who take refuge
    in him.
6 Do not add to his words,
    or else he will rebuke you, and you will
    be found a liar.

---

a Vg: Meaning of Heb uncertain   b Meaning of Heb uncertain
c Or human fear   d Or I am spent. Meaning of Heb uncertain
e Or Holy One

29.18 See note on 28.4, 7, 9. *Law* (without the definite article) may refer to written Torah, especially here in parallel with *prophecy;* the latter word refers to the prophetic vision and is not the term used for either the prophets or their books. 29.20b Same as 26.12b. 29.22 See, e.g., 14.17. 29.23 *Pride, humiliation.* See 25.6–7. 29.24–25 Imagery and message similar to those in 1.10–33 (esp. 1.17–18, 26–27, 33); 28.24–25. 29.25 *Snare.* See 1.17. 29.26 *Justice* may establish a throne (see 25.5), but not all thrones are just (see 28.3, 5).

30.1–33 A series of short, independent epigrams (short poems that make a point). 30.1–6 Questions of a skeptic and a pious response. 30.1 *The words of Agur son of Jakeh,* a title, but the extent of the original unit is uncertain, as is Agur's identity, though he may be a foreigner. *Oracle,* prophetic terminology, though some translate as a place-name, Massa; see also 31.1. *Thus says* in the prophets is always followed by "the LORD," but here by *the man,* lit. "strong man, war-

rior." *I am weary, O God.* Some translate "There is no God" or "I am not God"; others read proper names in the beginning clauses of the oracle, "to Ithiel, to Ithiel and Ucal" (RSV). The context supplies a sense of distance from a transcendent God, not doctrinal atheism. 30.2–3 A tone more likely ironic than submissive (see Job 9.2). *Holy ones,* a plural form translated in the singular in 9.10, though the foreign Agur may refer to gods rather than God. 30.4 Perhaps a riddle whose answer is "God" (cf. Job 38.5–11); perhaps a challenge to proponents of a know-it-all piety. *Person's name . . . person's child,* lit. "his name . . . his sons' [plural in Greek] name"; thus the referent could be human (sage and pupil) or divine (God and other member[s] of the heavenly realm who are sometimes called "sons of God" [Job 1.6]; cf. v. 3). *Surely you know.* See Job 38.21. 30.5–6 A pious response to vv. 1–4 in the mode of those of Job's friends or Eccl 12.9–14. *Word of God* may or may not refer to written scripture. 30.5 Cf. Ps 18.30. 30.6a Cf. Deut 4.2.

7 Two things I ask of you;
       do not deny them to me before I die:
8 Remove far from me falsehood and lying;
       give me neither poverty nor riches;
       feed me with the food that I need,
9 or I shall be full, and deny you,
       and say, "Who is the LORD?"
   or I shall be poor, and steal,
       and profane the name of my God.

10 Do not slander a servant to a master,
       or the servant will curse you, and you
           will be held guilty.

11 There are those who curse their fathers
       and do not bless their mothers.
12 There are those who are pure in their
           own eyes
       yet are not cleansed of their filthiness.
13 There are those—how lofty are their eyes,
       how high their eyelids lift!—
14 there are those whose teeth are swords,
       whose teeth are knives,
   to devour the poor from off the earth,
       the needy from among mortals.

15 The leech[a] has two daughters;
       "Give, give," they cry.
   Three things are never satisfied;
       four never say, "Enough":
16 Sheol, the barren womb,
       the earth ever thirsty for water,
       and the fire that never says, "Enough."[a]

17 The eye that mocks a father
       and scorns to obey a mother
   will be pecked out by the ravens of the
           valley
       and eaten by the vultures.

18 Three things are too wonderful for me;
       four I do not understand:
19 the way of an eagle in the sky,
       the way of a snake on a rock,
   the way of a ship on the high seas,
       and the way of a man with a girl.

20 This is the way of an adulteress:
       she eats, and wipes her mouth,
       and says, "I have done no wrong."

21 Under three things the earth trembles;
       under four it cannot bear up:
22 a slave when he becomes king,
       and a fool when glutted with food;
23 an unloved woman when she gets a
           husband,
       and a maid when she succeeds her
           mistress.

24 Four things on earth are small,
       yet they are exceedingly wise:
25 the ants are a people without strength,
       yet they provide their food in the
           summer;

_____
a Meaning of Heb uncertain

30.7–9 A model of pious prayer (cf. Job 13.20–21). The catchword *lying* connects the unit to v. 6. The request for neither too much nor too little assesses human nature realistically (cf. Mt 6.11; Mk 10.25). **30.10** An isolated admonition, but for the catchword *curse* (also in v. 11). Do not interfere in the affairs of other households. **30.11–14** Four reprehensible groups: the unfilial, the hypocritical, the proud, and the avaricious.
   30.15–33 A collection of five numerical sayings (vv. 15b–16, 18–19, 21–23, 24–28, 29–31; see 6.16–19) interspersed with sayings (vv. 15a, 17, 20, 33) and an admonition (v. 32). On the natural world as a source of learning (vv. 15–16, 19, 24–31), see note on 6.6–11. **30.15a** Originally an independent saying connected to the following numerical saying by its use of the number *two* and its image of things that demand ("*Give, give*") a continuous supply of life substance. **30.15b– 16** *Barren womb.* Recall Rachel's cry to Jacob, "Give me children, or I shall die!" (Gen 30.1). **30.17–20** The numerical saying in v. 18–19 is framed by sayings representing two major themes of chs. 1–9: obedience to parents (v. 17; see 1.8) and avoidance of the adulteress (v. 20; see 6.20–35). **30.17–19** These verses are linked by imagery of carnivorous birds. **30.17** See Ex 21.17; horror of lack of proper burial reinforces the message. **30.18–19** Four items lacking visible means of operation and leaving no trace when gone. **30.19** *Girl,* a young woman of marriageable age. **30.20** This verse is linked to vv. 18–19 by the catchword *way* (see note on 1.15–16) and the allusion to sexual relations; to vv. 15–16 by imagery of deadly appetite (see note on 1.31; also 9.17). **30.21–23** Four unbearable things: the first and last are inversions of appropriate order; the middle two do not know how to use their blessings wisely; all may be prone to taunt others. **30.22a** See 29.19. **30.23a** *When she gets a husband,* or "when she is married." The problem is being married and unloved, not unloved and unmarried; see Gen 29.31–35; Deut 20.15–16; 1 Sam 1.2–6. **30.23b** See Gen 16.1–6. **30.24–28** V. 24 breaks the "three things plus a fourth" pattern. There are several messages: wisdom does not depend on size or strength; joint effort succeeds where the individual might fail; neither power nor a king is

26 the badgers are a people without power,
        yet they make their homes in the rocks;
27 the locusts have no king,
        yet all of them march in rank;
28 the lizard*a* can be grasped in the hand,
        yet it is found in kings' palaces.

29 Three things are stately in their stride;
        four are stately in their gait:
30 the lion, which is mightiest among wild
            animals
        and does not turn back before any;
31 the strutting rooster,*b* the he-goat,
        and a king striding before*c* his people.

32 If you have been foolish, exalting
            yourself,
        or if you have been devising evil,
        put your hand on your mouth.
33 For as pressing milk produces curds,
        and pressing the nose produces blood,
        so pressing anger produces strife.

The Teaching of King Lemuel's Mother

31 The words of King Lemuel. An oracle
        that his mother taught him:

2 No, my son! No, son of my womb!
        No, son of my vows!
3 Do not give your strength to women,
        your ways to those who destroy kings.
4 It is not for kings, O Lemuel,
        it is not for kings to drink wine,

or for rulers to desire*d* strong drink;
5 or else they will drink and forget what
            has been decreed,
        and will pervert the rights of all the
            afflicted.
6 Give strong drink to one who is
            perishing,
        and wine to those in bitter distress;
7 let them drink and forget their poverty,
        and remember their misery no more.
8 Speak out for those who cannot speak,
        for the rights of all the destitute.*e*
9 Speak out, judge righteously,
        defend the rights of the poor and
            needy.

Ode to a Capable Wife

10 A capable wife who can find?
        She is far more precious than jewels.
11 The heart of her husband trusts in her,
        and he will have no lack of gain.
12 She does him good, and not harm,
        all the days of her life.
13 She seeks wool and flax,
        and works with willing hands.
14 She is like the ships of the merchant,
        she brings her food from far away.
15 She rises while it is still night
        and provides food for her household
        and tasks for her servant-girls.

---

a Or *spider*   *b* Gk Syr Tg Compare Vg: Meaning of Heb
uncertain   *c* Meaning of Heb uncertain   *d* Cn: Heb *where*
e Heb *all children of passing away*

---

necessary for survival (a message, perhaps, to the community living under Persian and Greek rule after the exile). **30.29–31** If this restoration of a corrupt text is accurate, the message contrasts with vv. 24–28 in its positive image of the mighty. **30.32–33** Seemingly an instruction (v. 32) plus a motivation (v. 33), but the exact relationship is not clear. **30.33** *Pressing anger*, lit. "pressing noses" (anger is usually described as a "hot nose"), a pun on *pressing the nose* in the preceding line. *Strife*, more specifically a lawsuit. The punch line relates two products of physical pressure to an undesirable outcome of social pressure (see 25.7c–10). **31.1–31** Two originally independent poems (vv. 1–9; vv. 10–31), joined here under the heading of a queen mother's instruction, share vocabulary, theme, and structure. **31.1** *King Lemuel* is otherwise unknown, but presumably foreign. *Oracle*. See note on 30.1. *Mother*. See note on 1.8; also 31.26, 28. **31.2** *Son of my vows*. The phrase is unique in the Bible, though the idea of a child granted by God in response to a woman's vow is not (see 1 Sam 1.9–28). **31.3** *Strength*. The same Hebrew word, translated *capable* in v. 10 and

excellently in v. 29, is used to describe the woman in the second poem, mitigating this verse's apparent warning against strong women. **31.4–7** The abuse and use of alcohol (see 23.29–35). Although a king should not *drink* and *forget* his duty to justice (v. 5; see note on 1.1), those in distress do well to *drink and forget* their *poverty* (v. 7). **31.8–9** The capable woman also *speaks out* (v. 26) and cares for the *poor and needy* (v. 20).

   31.10–31 An acrostic poem (see Introduction). The capable wife (lit. "woman of worth") exemplifies wisdom in the world, thus providing a fitting conclusion to a book that begins with Woman Wisdom. Her assumption of kingly duties (see 27.23–27; 31.1–9) may suggest a social context in which the wisdom and order provided the family household replaced that of a vanished monarchy. **31.10** *Capable*. See note on 31.3. *Find, more precious than jewels,* both motifs for Woman Wisdom (see note on 1.13; also 3.15; cf. Job 28). **31.11** *Trusts in her.* Elsewhere, gain comes through trust in the Lord or heeding wisdom (1.29–33; 8.17–21; 28.25b; 29.25b). *Gain*. See note on 1.13. **31.15bc** See 27.27. *Her household,* an unusual attribution in a culture that typically speaks of "the father's

16 She considers a field and buys it;
   with the fruit of her hands she plants a
      vineyard.
17 She girds herself with strength,
   and makes her arms strong.
18 She perceives that her merchandise is
      profitable.
   Her lamp does not go out at night.
19 She puts her hands to the distaff,
   and her hands hold the spindle.
20 She opens her hand to the poor,
   and reaches out her hands to the needy.
21 She is not afraid for her household when
      it snows,
   for all her household are clothed in
      crimson.
22 She makes herself coverings;
   her clothing is fine linen and purple.
23 Her husband is known in the city gates,
   taking his seat among the elders of the
      land.

24 She makes linen garments and sells
      them;
   she supplies the merchant with sashes.
25 Strength and dignity are her clothing,
   and she laughs at the time to come.
26 She opens her mouth with wisdom,
   and the teaching of kindness is on her
      tongue.
27 She looks well to the ways of her
      household,
   and does not eat the bread of idleness.
28 Her children rise up and call her happy;
   her husband too, and he praises her:
29 "Many women have done excellently,
   but you surpass them all."
30 Charm is deceitful, and beauty is vain,
   but a woman who fears the LORD is to
      be praised.
31 Give her a share in the fruit of her hands,
   and let her works praise her in the city
      gates.

house"; see also vv. 21, 27 and the mother's house in Song 8.2. *Servant-girls.* See note on 27.27. **31.16** She engages in public economic enterprise (see v. 18, 24). **31.16b** She has the vineyard planted with profits she has made (cf. v. 31a). **31.17** Both physical and moral *strength* are implied (see 8.14; 31.25). **31.18** See v. 16. **31.19–20** *Puts her hands* (v. 19a), the same Hebrew words as *reaches out her hands* (v. 20b). The woman's ability to provide for her household is linked to her care for the poor. **31.21** See v. 15. **31.23** The woman's work is publicly effaced by her husband's leadership role, though see v. 31. *City gates.* See note on 1.20–21. **31.24** See v. 16. **31.25** See 1.26; 8.14; 31.17. **31.26** See vv. 8–9. *Teaching* (Hebrew *torah*) *of kindness* (*chesed*, often translated "steadfast love"), elsewhere often covenantal terms, but here, as in 1.8, more likely general parental instruction. **31.27** There is possibly a wordplay between the Hebrew *tsophiyyah, she looks well to,* and the Greek *sophia* ("wisdom"); thus the beginning of the verse may be translated "the ways of her house are wisdom" (see 9.1–6). A Greek-Hebrew wordplay would date the poem in or close to the Hellenistic period (late fourth century BCE). **31.28a** See 3.13; 27.11. **31.29** *Excellently.* See note on 31.3. **31.30** A proverb used to clinch the argument. On deceitful appearances, see note on 26.22–26a. *Vain,* meaningless (see Eccl 1.2). **31.31a** See 31.16. **31.31b** See 31.23. Woman Wisdom teaches and *praises* herself in the city gates (1.21; 8.3).

ECCLESIASTES

"ECCLESIASTES" IS THE LATIN TRANSCRIPTION of the Greek translation of the Hebrew *Qoheleth*, often rendered "Preacher" (a tradition from Luther) or "Teacher." Qoheleth's wisdom is attributed to the "son of David," Solomon (a name that never appears in the book), who is Israel's archetypal gatherer of wisdom (1 Kings 4.29–34; Prov 1.1; Song 1.1). Qoheleth urges readers to take joy in what they have and to fear God despite knowing that "for everything there is a season" (3.1).

Dating and Language

THE UNIQUE LANGUAGE, syntax, and grammar of Ecclesiastes suggest that the book can be dated between the fifth and third centuries BCE. At one time some thought that the book was originally written in Aramaic and poorly translated into Hebrew, but that view is entirely rejected today. It is conceded that the Persian loanwords, Aramaisms, and the structure of the Hebrew require a date after Israel's release from exile in 539 BCE. Issues regarding the influence of Phoenician on the language and thought of Ecclesiastes, the possibility of the author's familiarity with Greek, and the relationship between standard biblical Hebrew (preexilic) and late biblical Hebrew are debated.

No internal references to historical dates appear, and the external evidence is indecisive. The social, economic, and political evidence in the book points to a time of change and upheaval, of risk and possibility. As many commentators note, the fifth century BCE was a period of commercialization and the standardization of currency, a time when not everyone benefited equally. Certainly Qoheleth speaks out of such a context. Two fragments of the book dating from the second and first centuries BCE were found among the Dead Sea Scrolls; the larger contains sections of chs. 5–7. This discovery confirms that the book was written prior to the end of the third century BCE.

Canonical Status

THE ATTRIBUTION OF THE BOOK to Solomon was certainly a later development. This attribution probably assisted in the book's gaining canonical status in Judaism and Christianity even though other books associated with Solomon's name were not so acclaimed (e.g., *Odes of Solomon*). A tradition within first-century CE rabbinical debates over which books are worthy resulted in a growing consensus that Ecclesiastes was inspired and deserving of a place in the canon.

The canonical location of Ecclesiastes varies in Judaism and Christianity. In some of the oldest Greek manuscripts it is found in the third division of the canon, the "Writings" or Hagiographa, a kind of miscellaneous collection that was variously arranged in those manuscripts. The Hebrew Bible places Ecclesiastes among the five scrolls, *Megillot* (Song of Solomon, Ruth, Lamentations, Ecclesiastes, Esther), a relatively late grouping based on the order in which the books were read in the succession of Jewish festivals. In other Bibles it comes between Proverbs and the Song of Solomon, two other works attributed to Solomon.

Literary Structure

ATTEMPTS TO FIND A CLEAR STRUCTURE in the book have depended largely on the diverse perspectives readers bring to the book. Few read the book as an entirely haphazard collection, although some see no easily discernable structure. Others see it organized around numerological theories or concentric circles; still others discover different editorial levels and rearrange the text; and finally some see a logical development or the adaptation of some earlier literary form or pattern. The book exhibits a complex consistency of language, perspective, and themes. Themes are introduced, then dropped and picked up, and sometimes advanced within a series of repeated words and phrases in refrainlike fashion.

Content

ECCLESIASTES FOCUSES upon the limits and contradictions of life in order to teach wisdom (see Ps 90). From the pinnacle of human success and power (1.12–2.26) Qoheleth surveys life and finds it "vanity." Even the best life is limited in knowledge, virtue, and power, troubled by evil and injustice, and ultimately ended by death. This focus on human limits and absurdity attacks those, like Job's friends, who selectively misuse traditional wisdom (see Proverbs) to argue neat connections between godly goodness and success or wickedness and failure (7.15; 8.10–17; 9.1–12). Yet Qoheleth maintains that wisdom, in spite of its limits and destruction by death, is better than folly (see 2.11, 12–17; 6.8). In the face of death and "vanity," Qoheleth repeatedly urges humans to embrace life and its goods—food, drink, love, work, and play—as gifts from God (9.7–10).

Interpretation

ECCLESIASTES IS READ in the Jewish community during the feast of Sukkoth (Festival of Booths, Tabernacles, or Ingathering, Lev 23.39–43; Deut 16.13–15; Neh 8.13–18), a joyous pilgrimage festival that normally occurs in September or October. This festival underscores the precariousness of life and yet the joy to be found even in the enigmatic nature of life. The correlation between joy and the ephemeral requires one to follow the inclination of the heart (11.9–10), remembering one's creator (12.1). Those who read the contents of the book as marginal, pessimistic, and not given to answering the perplexing questions of life have not attended carefully to its affirmations.

Interpreters offer conflicting readings of Ecclesiastes. Some see it as a portrait of "life without God," for they do not see how life with God can be described as "vanity." Some have seen it at odds with the dominant expressions of the religion of the Hebrew scriptures. It does not speak of covenants or tell of God acting in history; and it focuses, when speaking of God, on the mysterious, unfathomable nature of the divine.

The tensions and contradictions of Ecclesiastes are precisely its point. The book recognizes that it is impossible to know what will come with death, which is inevitable for both the righteous and unrighteous, yet it never lets go of God. Part of the tension surrounds the key word "vanity" (Hebrew *hevel*). Translated as "meaninglessness," "absurdity," "emptiness," "incongruity," and "uselessness," its literal meaning is "breath," "breeze," "vapor," or "mist." Whether understood more as liquid or as air, *hevel* is fundamental to sustaining life despite the fact that it evaporates and dissipates. If meaning is found only in the permanent and unchanging, then Ecclesiastes will seem incredibly frustrating. On the other hand, the book emphasizes the value of rationality despite the irrationality of life. As one writer has said, it is God's presence that is present and, one might add, precious.

What, then, is good for humans according to Ecclesiastes? First, never give up questing, seeking, and searching. The book begins with that note (1.12–14) and continually provokes readers to reflect on the musings it sets forth. Second, as clearly stated in the epilogue, "Fear God, and keep his commandments; for that is the whole duty of everyone" (12.13; see 3.9–17; 5.1–7; 7.13–14, 18; 8.12–13). Ecclesiastes, while forever discerning and certainly breaking the mold in the quest undertaken, reminds readers of Deuteronomy's traditional call "to fear the LORD your God, to walk in all his ways, to love him" (Deut 10.12). Human beings are not power brokers of the universe, but afflicted by *hevel* in all its forms. The good is simply to enjoy life—both work and play—as God's gift and the "lot" for which all are responsible. [RAYMOND C. VAN LEEUWEN, revised by KENT HAROLD RICHARDS]

Reflections of a Royal Philosopher

1 The words of the Teacher,[a] the son of David, king in Jerusalem.

2 Vanity of vanities, says the Teacher,[a]
  vanity of vanities! All is vanity.

3 What do people gain from all the toil
  at which they toil under the sun?

4 A generation goes, and a generation comes,
  but the earth remains forever.

5 The sun rises and the sun goes down,
  and hurries to the place where it rises.

6 The wind blows to the south,
  and goes around to the north;
  round and round goes the wind,
  and on its circuits the wind returns.

7 All streams run to the sea,
  but the sea is not full;
  to the place where the streams flow,
  there they continue to flow.

8 All things[b] are wearisome;
  more than one can express;
  the eye is not satisfied with seeing,
  or the ear filled with hearing.

9 What has been is what will be,
  and what has been done is what will be done;
  there is nothing new under the sun.

10 Is there a thing of which it is said,
  "See, this is new"?
  It has already been,
  in the ages before us.

11 The people of long ago are not remembered,
  nor will there be any remembrance
of people yet to come
  by those who come after them.

The Futility of Seeking Wisdom

12 I, the Teacher,[a] when king over Israel in Jerusalem, 13applied my mind to seek and to search out by wisdom all that is done under heaven; it is an unhappy business that God has given to human beings to be busy with. 14I saw all the deeds that are done under the sun; and see, all is vanity and a chasing after wind.[c]

15 What is crooked cannot be made straight,
  and what is lacking cannot be counted.

---

a Heb *Qoheleth*, traditionally rendered *Preacher*   b Or *words*
c Or *a feeding on wind*. See Hos 12.1

16 I said to myself, "I have acquired great wisdom, surpassing all who were over Jerusalem before me; and my mind has had great experience of wisdom and knowledge." 17And I applied my mind to know wisdom and to know madness and folly. I perceived that this also is but a chasing after wind.[a]

18 For in much wisdom is much vexation,
   and those who increase knowledge
      increase sorrow.

The Futility of Self-Indulgence

2 I said to myself, "Come now, I will make a test of pleasure; enjoy yourself." But again, this also was vanity. 2I said of laughter, "It is mad," and of pleasure, "What use is it?" 3I searched with my mind how to cheer my body with wine—my mind still guiding me with wisdom—and how to lay hold on folly, until I might see what was good for mortals to do under heaven during the few days of their life.

4I made great works; I built houses and planted vineyards for myself; 5I made myself gardens and parks, and planted in them all kinds of fruit trees. 6I made myself pools from which to water the forest of growing trees. 7I bought male and female slaves, and had slaves who were born in my house; I also had great possessions of herds and flocks, more than any who had been before me in Jerusalem. 8I also gathered for myself silver and gold and the treasure of kings and of the provinces; I got singers, both men and women, and delights of the flesh, and many concubines.[b]

9 So I became great and surpassed all who were before me in Jerusalem; also my wisdom remained with me. 10Whatever my eyes desired I did not keep from them; I kept my heart from no pleasure, for my heart found

---

a Or a feeding on wind. See Hos 12.1   b Meaning of Heb uncertain

---

1.1 Superscription or title. *Words of* is a typical title for a collection usually followed by the individual to whom the collection is attributed. *Qoheleth* is mentioned five times in the book (1.1, 2, 12; 7.27; 12.8). The word *Qoheleth* has to do with the act of gathering something, in this case wisdom (at other times wealth), and suggests someone who addresses the "assembly" (Hebrew *kahal;* Deut 31.30; 1 Kings 8.22). *Son of David* is an important link with the wisdom tradition's supreme gatherer, Solomon. **1.2–11** Preface. **1.2** *Vanity of vanities,* meaning "utterly ephemeral," is the book's theme or motto, placed at its beginning and end (12.8). *Vanity* renders *hevel,* a Hebrew word difficult to translate with any single English word but used extensively in the book (fifty-seven times) referring to the ephemeral, unknowable, mysterious, absurd, and ironic. The Hebrew term literally refers to "breath" (Isa 57.13) and is often parallel to *chasing after wind* (e.g., vv. 14, 17). For human life as "breath," see Job 7.7; Pss 39.4–6; 62.9; 78.33; 144.4. **1.3–11** A poem placing human existence in a cosmological and epistemological frame. Human existence is situated in the east-west journey of the sun (v. 5), the north-south circuit of the wind (v. 6), and the four ancient elements: earth, fire (sun), air (wind), and water (Ps 148.7–8). Some read this passage negatively (both cosmos and life consist of meaningless cycles), and some positively (the cyclical world order *remains forever* [v. 4], thus making life possible; Gen 8.22; Pss 104.1–30; 147.8–9, 16–18). *Gain,* or advantage (v. 3), has to do not with economic benefit per se but rather with having a "surplus" (2.11; 3.9; 5.9, 16; 6.8; 7.12; 10.11). **1.5** *Hurries,* lit. "pants" like a runner (Ps 19.5–6). **1.6** Ironically, the restless *wind* remains while humans, who come and go (v. 4; 5.15–16), are mere "breath" (vanity). **1.8–11** A move from cosmology to epistemology, on the limits of human knowledge. **1.8** *All things are wearisome.* The

Hebrew is ambiguous; some translate positively, "All things are constantly active," and beyond human mastery (v. 18; 3.11; 8.17; 12.12). *The eye is not satisfied.* See Prov 27.20. *The ear* is not *filled* ironically parallels *the sea is not full* (v. 7). **1.9–11** Possibly a commentary explaining in more direct language the meaning of the difficult poetry found in vv. 3–8. See 6.10. **1.9** *Under the sun* appears only in Ecclesiastes in the Hebrew scriptures, although it does appear in other ancient Near Eastern texts. **1.11** *People of long ago . . . people yet to come,* or "things of long ago . . . things yet to come."

   1.12–2.26 *Chasing after wind* (1.14, 17) is the theme of this section. The book turns to a predominantly first-person autobiographical style reminiscent of royal inscriptions, exploring the limits of the human condition and the inscrutability of God. **1.13** *Wisdom* includes knowledge, insight, and technical or artistic skills. *All . . . under heaven,* usually *under the sun* (e.g., vv. 3, 9, 14). This quest to understand all that happens on earth is an *unhappy business* because it cannot be attained; see note on 3.11. **1.14–15** Thus, from a human viewpoint, what happens is vanity. Moreover, humans cannot straighten what God has bent (3.14; 7.13). **1.17** *Madness and folly* may be an interpreter's addition, or, as polar opposite of wisdom, the pair may indicate the universal scope of the quest of v. 13 (2.2–3, 12; 7.25). **1.18** See note on 7.3. **2.2** See 10.19; Prov 14.13. **2.3** *Wisdom* and *folly* anticipate vv. 12–17; see note on 1.17. Given death and human limits, the "king" seeks *what was good . . . to do.* **2.4–11** Accomplishments summarized as in many royal inscriptions. Mastery over nature and culture and over humans as servants and instruments of pleasure. The "king" achieves all his goals, yet this too is *vanity* (v. 11). **2.5–6** In arid Palestine mastery of water is a *great work* (v. 4). **2.10** *Toil* is ambiguous, denoting both the process and result of work (wealth, etc.; v. 18). *Reward,* also

pleasure in all my toil, and this was my reward for all my toil. [11]Then I considered all that my hands had done and the toil I had spent in doing it, and again, all was vanity and a chasing after wind,[a] and there was nothing to be gained under the sun.

Wisdom and Joy Given to One Who Pleases God

12 So I turned to consider wisdom and madness and folly; for what can the one do who comes after the king? Only what has already been done. [13]Then I saw that wisdom excels folly as light excels darkness.

14 The wise have eyes in their head,
    but fools walk in darkness.

Yet I perceived that the same fate befalls all of them. [15]Then I said to myself, "What happens to the fool will happen to me also; why then have I been so very wise?" And I said to myself that this also is vanity. [16]For there is no enduring remembrance of the wise or of fools, seeing that in the days to come all will have been long forgotten. How can the wise die just like fools? [17]So I hated life, because what is done under the sun was grievous to me; for all is vanity and a chasing after wind.[a]

18 I hated all my toil in which I had toiled under the sun, seeing that I must leave it to those who come after me [19]—and who knows whether they will be wise or foolish? Yet they will be master of all for which I toiled and used my wisdom under the sun. This also is vanity. [20]So I turned and gave my heart up to despair concerning all the toil of my labors under the sun, [21]because sometimes one who has toiled with wisdom and knowledge and skill must leave all to be enjoyed by another who did not toil for it. This also is vanity and a great evil. [22]What do mortals get from all the toil and strain with which they toil under the sun? [23]For all their days are full of pain, and their work is a vexation; even at night their minds do not rest. This also is vanity.

24 There is nothing better for mortals than to eat and drink, and find enjoyment in their toil. This also, I saw, is from the hand of God; [25]for apart from him[b] who can eat or who can have enjoyment? [26]For to the one who pleases him God gives wisdom and knowledge and joy; but to the sinner he gives the work of gathering and heaping, only to give to one who pleases God. This also is vanity and a chasing after wind.[a]

Everything Has Its Time

3 For everything there is a season, and a time for every matter under heaven:
2 a time to be born, and a time to die;
   a time to plant, and a time to pluck up
       what is planted;
3 a time to kill, and a time to heal;
   a time to break down, and a time to build
       up;
4 a time to weep, and a time to laugh;
   a time to mourn, and a time to dance;
5 a time to throw away stones, and a time
       to gather stones together;

---

a Or a feeding on wind. See Hos 12.1 b Gk Syr: Heb apart from me

---

translated lot (3.22), share (9.6), or portion (9.9), is generally a positive gift of God (5.17–18; 9.9). This important term can be used of land given to heirs (Gen 31.14; Josh 19.9), who are both responsible for their portion and free to enjoy its benefits. **2.11** Nothing . . . gained, an answer to 1.3, but see 2.13, where lit. "there is more gain in wisdom than in folly." **2.12–17** Wisdom is better than folly (v. 12), yet death destroys both the wise and fools (6.8; Ps 49.10), and the wise are forgotten (v. 16; 1.11; Wis 2.4). **2.12** Madness and folly, a hendiadys, "senseless folly" (7.25; see note on 1.17). **2.14** The fate or "event" is death (3.19–20; 6.6; 9.2–3). **2.17** I hated life, perhaps, "I was disillusioned with life" because of its limits and vanity; "hate" in Hebrew has a range of meanings opposite to "love." Elsewhere life is positive, despite vanity (vv. 24–26; 9.4–6; 11.7–8). **2.18–26** Death and heirs; the royal experiment concludes. **2.18** I hated. See note on 2.17. Toil. See note on 2.10. One can leave a business ("toil" as process) or wealth ("toil" as result) to an heir (v. 21; 6.2). Toil can

bring pleasure (vv. 10, 24; 3.13, 22; 5.18–19; 9.9) or despair (vv. 18, 20). **2.19** Who knows? a rhetorical question expecting the answer "nobody," with the implicit exception of God. **2.21** Evil, because humans cut off by death do not reap the good they sow. **2.22–23** What advantage then for human toil? **2.24–26** A modestly positive but realistic answer to the question of v. 22. Qoheleth constantly associates enjoyment with both work (toil) and play (to eat and drink); see notes on 3.12–15; 3.16–22; 5.18–20; 9.7–10.

3.1–22 Everything has a season. **3.1–8** Life's good and evil conditioned by God's time. The antithetical pairs are a literary device using opposites to represent life's totality and variety, which are also represented by their sum (twice seven). The times, which simply happen to people or which require appropriate human action (8.5–6; Am 5.13), are inscrutably in God's hands (vv. 1, 11, 13; Ps 31.15; Sir 33.7–15; 39.33–34). The opposed items seem good or bad in themselves, but time or circumstance can invert the value of actions (see v.

a time to embrace, and a time to refrain
   from embracing;
6 a time to seek, and a time to lose;
   a time to keep, and a time to throw away;
7 a time to tear, and a time to sew;
   a time to keep silence, and a time to speak;
8 a time to love, and a time to hate;
   a time for war, and a time for peace.

The God-Given Task

9 What gain have the workers from their toil?
10I have seen the business that God has given
to everyone to be busy with. 11He has made
everything suitable for its time; moreover he
has put a sense of past and future into their
minds, yet they cannot find out what God has
done from the beginning to the end. 12I know
that there is nothing better for them than to be
happy and enjoy themselves as long as they
live; 13moreover, it is God's gift that all should
eat and drink and take pleasure in all their toil.
14I know that whatever God does endures forever; nothing can be added to it, nor anything
taken from it; God has done this, so that all
should stand in awe before him. 15That which
is, already has been; that which is to be, already
is; and God seeks out what has gone by.*a*

Judgment and the Future Belong to God

16 Moreover I saw under the sun that in the
place of justice, wickedness was there, and in
the place of righteousness, wickedness was
there as well. 17I said in my heart, God will
judge the righteous and the wicked, for he has
appointed a time for every matter, and for
every work. 18I said in my heart with regard to
human beings that God is testing them to
show that they are but animals. 19For the fate
of humans and the fate of animals is the same;
as one dies, so dies the other. They all have the
same breath, and humans have no advantage
over the animals; for all is vanity. 20All go to
one place; all are from the dust, and all turn to
dust again. 21Who knows whether the human
spirit goes upward and the spirit of animals
goes downward to the earth? 22So I saw that
there is nothing better than that all should
enjoy their work, for that is their lot; who can
bring them to see what will be after them?

4 Again I saw all the oppressions that are
  practiced under the sun. Look, the tears of
the oppressed—with no one to comfort them!
On the side of their oppressors there was
power—with no one to comfort them. 2And I
thought the dead, who have already died,
more fortunate than the living, who are still
alive; 3but better than both is the one who has
not yet been, and has not seen the evil deeds
that are done under the sun.

4 Then I saw that all toil and all skill in work
come from one person's envy of another. This
also is vanity and a chasing after wind.*b*

5 Fools fold their hands
      and consume their own flesh.
6 Better is a handful with quiet
      than two handfuls with toil,
      and a chasing after wind.*b*

7 Again, I saw vanity under the sun: 8the
case of solitary individuals, without sons or
brothers; yet there is no end to all their toil,
and their eyes are never satisfied with riches.
"For whom am I toiling," they ask, "and depriving myself of pleasure?" This also is vanity
and an unhappy business.

a Heb *what is pursued*   *b* Or *a feeding on wind*. See Hos 12.1

11; 7.1–4). **3.11** *Suitable.* Wisdom requires actions
that fit their time (Prov 10.5; 26.1; 27.14; Mt 11.16–
19). *A sense of past and future* (Hebrew *ha'olam*, lit.
"the age" or "the world"), a difficult expression; suggested translations include "the world," "eternity," of
"darkness" ("ignorance"). The quest to know all things
("the world") cannot be attained (1.12–13; 7.25; 8.17;
11.5). **3.12–15** In the face of limits, enjoy the good,
both play and work (2.10, 24; 3.22; 5.17–18; but see
2.18) as God's gift. God's deeds intend to lead humans
to revere him (v. 14; see note on 7.18). **3.15** Not a form
of "the myth of the eternal return," for humans do not
know what will be (6.12; 8.7). *What has gone by,* uncertain but may mean "what is pursued." **3.16–22** Injustice resides even in the law court (see 8.14). God's justice is timely (v. 17; see v. 1; 12.14) but is uncertain
since humans lack knowledge beyond death (vv. 21–

22). It is best to enjoy one's present *work* (v. 17; the Hebrew is plural and includes both activities and their
products) as divine gift or *lot* (v. 22; see 2.24–25; 3.13).
3.17 Some seek to resolve the tension concerning ultimate justice by attributing this verse to a later, more
"orthodox" editor of the book. **3.18** *Is testing them.*
Hebrew uncertain. *Animals,* as explained in v. 19.
3.20 *One place,* Sheol (9.10), the place of the dead (Isa
14.9–20). *Dust.* See 12.7; Gen 3.19. **3.21** *Who knows?*
See note on 2.19. *Spirit.* See 12.7; perhaps Prov 15.24.
   4.1–16 What is better? Oppression and evil can be
so great that nonexistence seems better than life; see
6.1–6. **4.4** Negative and positive aspects of *toil.*
4.4 *All toil . . . envy of another,* perhaps "all toil and all
success in work are [inseparable from] human competition." **4.5–6** Proverbial sayings: neither self-destructive sloth nor frenetic toil are good. **4.7–12** Solitary

The Value of a Friend

9 Two are better than one, because they have a good reward for their toil. [10]For if they fall, one will lift up the other; but woe to one who is alone and falls and does not have another to help. [11]Again, if two lie together, they keep warm; but how can one keep warm alone? [12]And though one might prevail against another, two will withstand one. A threefold cord is not quickly broken.

13 Better is a poor but wise youth than an old but foolish king, who will no longer take advice. [14]One can indeed come out of prison to reign, even though born poor in the kingdom. [15]I saw all the living who, moving about under the sun, follow that[a] youth who replaced the king;[b] [16]there was no end to all those people whom he led. Yet those who come later will not rejoice in him. Surely this also is vanity and a chasing after wind.[c]

Reverence, Humility, and Contentment

5[d] Guard your steps when you go to the house of God; to draw near to listen is better than the sacrifice offered by fools; for they do not know how to keep from doing evil.[e] [2f] Never be rash with your mouth, nor let your heart be quick to utter a word before God, for God is in heaven, and you upon earth; therefore let your words be few.

3 For dreams come with many cares, and a fool's voice with many words.

4 When you make a vow to God, do not delay fulfilling it; for he has no pleasure in fools. Fulfill what you vow. [5]It is better that you should not vow than that you should vow and not fulfill it. [6]Do not let your mouth lead you into sin, and do not say before the messenger that it was a mistake; why should God be angry at your words, and destroy the work of your hands?

7 With many dreams come vanities and a multitude of words;[g] but fear God.

8 If you see in a province the oppression of the poor and the violation of justice and right, do not be amazed at the matter; for the high official is watched by a higher, and there are yet higher ones over them. [9]But all things considered, this is an advantage for a land: a king for a plowed field.[g]

10 The lover of money will not be satisfied with money; nor the lover of wealth, with gain. This also is vanity.

11 When goods increase, those who eat them increase; and what gain has their owner but to see them with his eyes?

12 Sweet is the sleep of laborers, whether they eat little or much; but the surfeit of the rich will not let them sleep.

13 There is a grievous ill that I have seen under the sun: riches were kept by their owners to their hurt, [14]and those riches were lost in a bad venture; though they are parents of children, they have nothing in their hands. [15]As they came from their mother's womb, so they shall go again, naked as they came; they shall take nothing for their toil, which they may carry away with their hands. [16]This also is a grievous ill: just as they came, so shall they go; and what gain do they have from toiling for the wind? [17]Besides, all their days they eat in darkness, in much vexation and sickness and resentment.

---

a Heb the second   b Heb him   c Or a feeding on wind. See Hos 12.1   d Ch 4.17 in Heb   e Cn: Heb they do not know how to do evil   f Ch 5.1 in Heb   g Meaning of Heb uncertain

---

toil (vv. 7–8; see 2.18–23) is pointless compared to toil and life together (vv. 9–12). **4.13–16** An obscure passage portraying paradoxical reversals of traditional expectations concerning roles and qualities (see 9.13–16; 10.5–7, 16–17; Prov 17.2; 20.29 [gray hair means wisdom]; 26.1; 30.21–23). **5.1–7** Fear God (v. 7). Though he wrestles with questions of God's justice and knowability, Qoheleth here affirms traditional practices and views. Right worship (including sacrifice and vows), wisdom, speech (see Jas 1.26), and living all belong together. **5.1** Guard your steps means care for right behavior; to listen means to obey (see 1 Sam 15.22; Ps 15; Isa 1.11–17). **5.4–7** Vows and commitments are to be kept, lest God destroy one's work (v. 6; see Deut 23.21–23; Ps 90.11, 17). **5.6** It is not clear who the messenger is, but it is possibly a priest (see Num 15.22–31).

5.8–6.9 Enjoyment enabled. **5.8** A government hierarchy may or may not be implied here. But watched by means that the high and mighty "look out for" one another, so the poor have no chance for justice. **5.9** There is no satisfactory explanation of this verse given the complications of the Hebrew; it may mean that land should be obtained only for its advantage or yield, not merely to possess. **5.10–20** Wealth in negative (vv. 10–17) and positive (vv. 18–20) perspective. **5.10–12** Three proverbs argue that lust for wealth is insatiable and wealth brings sleepless nights of worry. **5.13–17** The uncertainty of wealth. Carefully guarded (kept, v. 13) riches are lost in a business venture gone bad. The heirs, like all humans, "come and go" (see 1.3–4). Naked, empty-handed (vv. 15–16; see Job 1.21). **5.16** They came . . . shall they go . . . what gain? an echo of 1.3–4. **5.17** Perhaps a description of miserli-

18 This is what I have seen to be good: it is fitting to eat and drink and find enjoyment in all the toil with which one toils under the sun the few days of the life God gives us; for this is our lot. 19Likewise all to whom God gives wealth and possessions and whom he enables to enjoy them, and to accept their lot and find enjoyment in their toil—this is the gift of God. 20For they will scarcely brood over the days of their lives, because God keeps them occupied with the joy of their hearts.

The Frustration of Desires

6 There is an evil that I have seen under the sun, and it lies heavy upon humankind: 2those to whom God gives wealth, possessions, and honor, so that they lack nothing of all that they desire, yet God does not enable them to enjoy these things, but a stranger enjoys them. This is vanity; it is a grievous ill. 3A man may beget a hundred children, and live many years; but however many are the days of his years, if he does not enjoy life's good things, or has no burial, I say that a stillborn child is better off than he. 4For it comes into vanity and goes into darkness, and in darkness its name is covered; 5moreover it has not seen the sun or known anything; yet it finds rest rather than he. 6Even though he should live a thousand years twice over, yet enjoy no good—do not all go to one place?

7 All human toil is for the mouth, yet the appetite is not satisfied. 8For what advantage have the wise over fools? And what do the poor have who know how to conduct themselves before the living? 9Better is the sight of the eyes than the wandering of desire; this also is vanity and a chasing after wind. *a*

10 Whatever has come to be has already been named, and it is known what human beings are, and that they are not able to dispute with those who are stronger. 11The more words, the more vanity, so how is one the better? 12For who knows what is good for mortals while they live the few days of their vain life, which they pass like a shadow? For who can tell them what will be after them under the sun?

A Disillusioned View of Life

7 A good name is better than precious
        ointment,
    and the day of death, than the day of
        birth.
2 It is better to go to the house of
        mourning
    than to go to the house of feasting;
    for this is the end of everyone,
        and the living will lay it to heart.
3 Sorrow is better than laughter,

---

a Or *a feeding on wind.* See Hos 12.1

---

ness, anticipating death, what one scholar has called "the long darkness yet to come." **5.18–20** On the *good*, an echo and elaboration of 2.24–26; 3.12–13, 22. Although wealth is futile as an attempt to gain security (vv. 10–18), the responsible enjoyment (see 11.9) of life, *toil*, and even *wealth* (v. 19) as God's gifts is *fitting*. Cf. Mt 6.25–34. **5.18** *Fitting,* rendered *suitable* in 3.11; Qoheleth's call to responsible enjoyment, made with awareness of death and uncertainty, is not escapist or ill-timed (Isa 22.12–13), but it presupposes the principle of the right time (3.1–15; Prov 6.6–8; 10.5; 2 Kings 5.26) and thus is a balance of play and work (see 8.15; 9.7–10). *Lot.* See note on 2.10. **6.1–6** Examples of wealth possessed but not enjoyed; see 2.18–21; 4.1–3. **6.3** *No burial,* an evil fate in ancient Israel; see 8.10; 2 Kings 9.33–37; Jer 16.5–6; 22.18–19. *A stillborn child is better off,* an inversion of the usual views (Ps 58.8); see Job 3.16–18. **6.6** *One place.* See note on 3.20. **6.7** See Prov 16.26. **6.8** *What advantage?* See the positive answer in 7.11–12, 19; 2.13–14. Wisdom is better than folly, but death destroys its advantage.

6.10–7.14 God knows. A group of sayings echoing a variety of Qoheleth's concerns and vocabulary and leading into the paradoxical proverbs of 7.1–14. **6.10** See 1.9–11. *Named . . . known.* The passives indi-

cate that God is the namer and knower. To name something is to express its "nature," or character. Some place a period after *it is known* (*it* referring to *whatever*) and continue, "*Human beings* are not able to dispute . . ." *Those who are stronger.* The Hebrew is singular and probably refers to God: "the one who is stronger." Hebrew traditions mark this as the midpoint of the book. **6.11** *Words.* Ironic, for Qoheleth himself trades in "words" or proverbs such as those following in 7.1–14. *How is one the better?* lit. "What gain do humans have?" See note on 1.3–11. **6.12** *Who knows?* See note on 2.19. *What is good* does not refer to human activity (see 5.18), but to the divine disposition of events for humans (3.11; 7.14; 8.17). **7.1–14** A series of proverbs mingling traditional wisdom with Qoheleth's critical contradictions (see Prov 26.4–5; 17.27–28), often using the "better . . . than" form. **7.1–6** These sayings encapsulate much of Qoheleth's wisdom: joy in life without awareness of vanity and death is folly. **7.1** *Good name,* a traditional judgment (Prov 22.1), with a pun on the Hebrew terms *shem* ("name") and *shemen* ("ointment"), followed by a paradox; see v. 8; Sir 11.21–28. **7.3** *Sorrow,* the same Hebrew word (*ka'as*) translated as *vexation* in 1.18, *anger* in 7.9, and *anxiety* in 11.10, creating verbal contradictions in He-

for by sadness of countenance the
       heart is made glad.
4   The heart of the wise is in the house of
       mourning;
     but the heart of fools is in the house of
       mirth.
5   It is better to hear the rebuke of the wise
       than to hear the song of fools.
6   For like the crackling of thorns under a
       pot,
     so is the laughter of fools;
     this also is vanity.
7   Surely oppression makes the wise foolish,
       and a bribe corrupts the heart.
8   Better is the end of a thing than its
       beginning;
     the patient in spirit are better than the
       proud in spirit.
9   Do not be quick to anger,
     for anger lodges in the bosom of fools.
10 Do not say, "Why were the former days
       better than these?"
     For it is not from wisdom that you ask
       this.
11 Wisdom is as good as an inheritance,
     an advantage to those who see the sun.
12 For the protection of wisdom is like the
       protection of money,
     and the advantage of knowledge is that
       wisdom gives life to the one who
       possesses it.
13 Consider the work of God;
     who can make straight what he has
       made crooked?

14 In the day of prosperity be joyful, and in
the day of adversity consider; God has made the
one as well as the other, so that mortals may not
find out anything that will come after them.

The Riddles of Life

15 In my vain life I have seen everything; there
are righteous people who perish in their righteousness, and there are wicked people who
prolong their life in their evildoing. 16Do not
be too righteous, and do not act too wise; why
should you destroy yourself? 17Do not be too
wicked, and do not be a fool; why should you
die before your time? 18It is good that you
should take hold of the one, without letting go
of the other; for the one who fears God shall
succeed with both.

19 Wisdom gives strength to the wise more
than ten rulers that are in a city.

20 Surely there is no one on earth so righteous as to do good without ever sinning.

21 Do not give heed to everything that people say, or you may hear your servant cursing
you; 22your heart knows that many times you
have yourself cursed others.

23 All this I have tested by wisdom; I said, "I
will be wise," but it was far from me. 24That
which is, is far off, and deep, very deep; who
can find it out? 25I turned my mind to know
and to search out and to seek wisdom and the
sum of things, and to know that wickedness is
folly and that foolishness is madness. 26I
found more bitter than death the woman who
is a trap, whose heart is snares and nets, whose
hands are fetters; one who pleases God escapes
her, but the sinner is taken by her. 27See, this is
what I found, says the Teacher,[a] adding one
thing to another to find the sum, 28which my
mind has sought repeatedly, but I have not
found. One man among a thousand I found,

---

a *Qoheleth*, traditionally rendered *Preacher*

---

brew concerning contrary aspects of the term. *Counte-*
nance . . . heart, a contrast between inner and outer: a
sad face may conceal a joyful heart or vice versa (Prov
14.13). **7.7** See Deut 16.19. *Oppression,* in the sense of
extortion. **7.8** See 7.1–2; 1 Kings 20.11. **7.9** *Anger* may
be translated *sorrow;* see note on 7.3. **7.10** See 1.11.
7.11–12 An answer to 6.8. Wisdom is as good as or
better than wealth (Prov 16.16), but each has its limits
(9.15–16; Prov 19.21; 21.30–31). **7.13–14** See 1.15;
3.1–15; Sir 11.14; 33.7–15. *After them.* See 3.11; 6.12;
10.14; 11.6; Prov 27.1.

7.15–29 The riddles of life. The normal causal sequence of good actions leading to good consequences
and evil to evil sometimes fails. See 3.16–17; 8.5, 14;
9.1–2. **7.16–17** *Do not be too righteous . . . too wise.*
One should not pretend to be something one is not,
i.e., very righteous and wise; cf. Prov 13.7; 25.6–7. *Do*
not be too wicked . . . a fool. On the other hand, one
should not abandon oneself to wickedness. **7.17** *Your*
time. See note on 3.1–8; Prov 10.27. Qoheleth still
maintains that God is free to judge the wicked with an
early death (3.17; 8.13). **7.18** *The one . . . the other,* the
two precepts in 7.16–17. *Fears God* includes both worship and daily life in relation to God and his will,
sometimes *to stand in awe* of God (3.14; 5.1–7; 8.12–
13; 12.13; Gen 20.11; Deut 8.6; Prov 1.7; Job 28.28).
7.20 See 7.29; 9.3; Gen 6.5; 8.21; Ps 14.1–3; Rom 3.9–
18. **7.26** Some read this (and v. 28) as a polemic against
women. More likely it echoes Proverbs' warning
against the seductiveness of Folly and adultery, in
which males are responsible for sexual restraint toward women other than their wives (Prov 7.5–27;
9.13–18; 22.14; 23.27). Marital love is good (9.9; Prov
5.15–20). **7.28** Like v. 26, this seems misogynist, yet its

but a woman among all these I have not found. 29See, this alone I found, that God made human beings straightforward, but they have devised many schemes.

Obey the King and Enjoy Yourself

8 Who is like the wise man?
    And who knows the interpretation of a
        thing?
  Wisdom makes one's face shine,
    and the hardness of one's countenance
        is changed.

2 Keep*a* the king's command because of your sacred oath. 3Do not be terrified; go from his presence, do not delay when the matter is unpleasant, for he does whatever he pleases. 4For the word of the king is powerful, and who can say to him, "What are you doing?" 5Whoever obeys a command will meet no harm, and the wise mind will know the time and way. 6For every matter has its time and way, although the troubles of mortals lie heavy upon them. 7Indeed, they do not know what is to be, for who can tell them how it will be? 8No one has power over the wind*b* to restrain the wind,*b* or power over the day of death; there is no discharge from the battle, nor does wickedness deliver those who practice it. 9All this I observed, applying my mind to all that is done under the sun, while one person exercises authority over another to the other's hurt.

God's Ways Are Inscrutable

10 Then I saw the wicked buried; they used to go in and out of the holy place, and were praised in the city where they had done such things.*c* This also is vanity. 11Because sentence against an evil deed is not executed speedily, the human heart is fully set to do evil.

12Though sinners do evil a hundred times and prolong their lives, yet I know that it will be well with those who fear God, because they stand in fear before him, 13but it will not be well with the wicked, neither will they prolong their days like a shadow, because they do not stand in fear before God.

14 There is a vanity that takes place on earth, that there are righteous people who are treated according to the conduct of the wicked, and there are wicked people who are treated according to the conduct of the righteous. I said that this also is vanity. 15So I commend enjoyment, for there is nothing better for people under the sun than to eat, and drink, and enjoy themselves, for this will go with them in their toil through the days of life that God gives them under the sun.

16 When I applied my mind to know wisdom, and to see the business that is done on earth, how one's eyes see sleep neither day nor night, 17then I saw all the work of God, that no one can find out what is happening under the sun. However much they may toil in seeking, they will not find it out; even though those who are wise claim to know, they cannot find it out.

Take Life as It Comes

9 All this I laid to heart, examining it all, how the righteous and the wise and their deeds are in the hand of God; whether it is love or hate one does not know. Everything that confronts them 2is vanity,*d* since the same fate comes to all, to the righteous and the wicked, to the good and the evil,*e* to the clean and the unclean, to those who sacrifice and those who

---

a Heb *I keep* *b* Or *breath* *c* Meaning of Heb uncertain
d Syr Compare Gk: Heb *Everything that confronts them* 2*is
everything* *e* Gk Syr Vg: Heb lacks *and the evil*

---

sense in context is unclear. Perhaps it is a hyperbolic idiom using the image of rarity to express the great value of a good man and woman. Cf. Prov 31.10, where "Who can find?" expects the answer "No one" (see Prov 18.22). Cf. the numerical hyperbole in 1 Sam 18.7. **8.1–17** Who is like the wise man? Here the limits of wisdom are made clear. **8.2–5** See 10.4; Prov 24.21–22. **8.2–3** *Sacred oath . . . terrified* may be translated "Concerning an oath before God, do not be hasty." See 5.2, 4; 9.2. **8.5–6** *Time and way,* lit. "time and judgment," probably a hendiadys, "time of judgment"; see 3.1, 16–17; 11.9. **8.7** See 6.12; 7.14. **8.8** *Wind,* perhaps ironic in light of the refrains *vanity* ("breath" or "wind," e.g., 1.2, 14) and *chasing after wind* (e.g., 1.14, 17; see Jn 3.8), but it may refer to death ("wind" as *spirit,* 3.21). *Battle.* See Prov 21.30–31. **8.10–**

17 Human experience of God's justice is mysterious, even inverted (thus *vanity*), leading the wicked to think it does not exist. Even the wise cannot know it (v. 17; 3.11), yet Qoheleth insists on its reality (3.16–17; 11.9) and commends joy (v. 15). **8.17** See note on 3.11.
  9.1–11.6 One fate comes to all. Humans cannot distinguish good and bad people by what happens to them (7.15; 8.10–17; the fallacy of Job's friends). Death, chance, and the evil in every human heart can level the distinctions between just and unjust, wise and foolish, the competent and incompetent (9.11–12). Yet life is better than death (9.4; cf. 4.2–3) and to be enjoyed (9.7–10). **9.1** *Love or hate,* of God or humans is uncertain, perhaps the sort of literary device found in 3.1–8 indicating lack of total knowledge (see 9.6; note on 9.1–11.6). **9.2** For the converse, see Mt

do not sacrifice. As are the good, so are the sinners; those who swear are like those who shun an oath. 3This is an evil in all that happens under the sun, that the same fate comes to everyone. Moreover, the hearts of all are full of evil; madness is in their hearts while they live, and after that they go to the dead. 4But whoever is joined with all the living has hope, for a living dog is better than a dead lion. 5The living know that they will die, but the dead know nothing; they have no more reward, and even the memory of them is lost. 6Their love and their hate and their envy have already perished; never again will they have any share in all that happens under the sun.

7 Go, eat your bread with enjoyment, and drink your wine with a merry heart; for God has long ago approved what you do. 8Let your garments always be white; do not let oil be lacking on your head. 9Enjoy life with the wife whom you love, all the days of your vain life that are given you under the sun, because that is your portion in life and in your toil at which you toil under the sun. 10Whatever your hand finds to do, do with your might; for there is no work or thought or knowledge or wisdom in Sheol, to which you are going.

11 Again I saw that under the sun the race is not to the swift, nor the battle to the strong, nor bread to the wise, nor riches to the intelligent, nor favor to the skillful; but time and chance happen to them all. 12For no one can anticipate the time of disaster. Like fish taken in a cruel net, and like birds caught in a snare, so mortals are snared at a time of calamity, when it suddenly falls upon them.

Wisdom Superior to Folly

13 I have also seen this example of wisdom under the sun, and it seemed great to me.

14There was a little city with few people in it. A great king came against it and besieged it, building great siegeworks against it. 15Now there was found in it a poor wise man, and he by his wisdom delivered the city. Yet no one remembered that poor man. 16So I said, "Wisdom is better than might; yet the poor man's wisdom is despised, and his words are not heeded."

17 The quiet words of the wise are more to
   be heeded
  than the shouting of a ruler among
   fools.
18 Wisdom is better than weapons of war,
  but one bungler destroys much good.

Miscellaneous Observations

10 Dead flies make the perfumer's
   ointment give off a foul odor;
  so a little folly outweighs wisdom and
   honor.
2 The heart of the wise inclines to the right,
  but the heart of a fool to the left.
3 Even when fools walk on the road, they
   lack sense,
  and show to everyone that they are
   fools.
4 If the anger of the ruler rises against you,
   do not leave your post,
  for calmness will undo great offenses.

5 There is an evil that I have seen under the sun, as great an error as if it proceeded from the ruler: 6folly is set in many high places, and the rich sit in a low place. 7I have seen slaves on horseback, and princes walking on foot like slaves.

8 Whoever digs a pit will fall into it;
  and whoever breaks through a wall will
   be bitten by a snake.
9 Whoever quarries stones will be hurt by
   them;

5.45. Qoheleth does not mean that the righteous and the wicked, the good and the evil, etc., are equal, but that death comes to all. **9.3** *Hearts . . . evil.* See note on 7.20. In biblical terms, the heart is the spiritual center of the self, the ultimate source of thought, will, emotion, and action. See Prov 4.23; Jer 7.24 ("will" here translates the Hebrew word usually rendered "heart"); 31.33; Ezek 18.31; 36.26–27; Mk 7.20–21. **9.7–10** The practical sum of Qoheleth's teaching, given imperative force: in the face of death and vanity, embrace the good in life—both work and play—with passion, as God's gift (2.24–26; 3.12–14, 22; 5.18–20; 6.3, 6; 7.14; 8.14–15; 11.6–10; 12.1). **9.11** *Time and chance,* ultimately determined by God (3.1–17; 7.14).

9.13–18 A parable followed by proverbial observations (vv. 17–18; cf. 4.13–16) that *wisdom* provides no assurances. **9.15** Ambiguous in Hebrew. Poverty limits wisdom, for either the poor man delivered the city and was not honored, or he would have been able to deliver it, had he been taken seriously. **10.1–11.6** Traditional sayings of the sort found in Proverbs, mingled with observations characteristic of Qoheleth (10.5–7, 14–15; 11.2b–6). **10.2** Not a political judgment! The *right* hand symbolizes strength and competence (wisdom). **10.4** See 8.2; Prov 19.12; 20.2; 24.21–22; 25.15. **10.5–7** The social world "upside down"; see 10.16; Prov 26.1; 30.21–23; Isa 3.4–5. **10.8–9** See Prov 26.27; Pss 7.14–16; 9.15–16, which

and whoever splits logs will be
endangered by them.
10 If the iron is blunt, and one does not
whet the edge,
then more strength must be exerted;
but wisdom helps one to succeed.
11 If the snake bites before it is charmed,
there is no advantage in a charmer.

12 Words spoken by the wise bring them
favor,
but the lips of fools consume them.
13 The words of their mouths begin in
foolishness,
and their talk ends in wicked madness;
14 yet fools talk on and on.
No one knows what is to happen,
and who can tell anyone what the
future holds?
15 The toil of fools wears them out,
for they do not even know the way to
town.

16 Alas for you, O land, when your king is a
servant,[a]
and your princes feast in the morning!
17 Happy are you, O land, when your king is
a nobleman,
and your princes feast at the proper
time—
for strength, and not for drunkenness!
18 Through sloth the roof sinks in,
and through indolence the house leaks.
19 Feasts are made for laughter;
wine gladdens life,
and money meets every need.
20 Do not curse the king, even in your
thoughts,
or curse the rich, even in your
bedroom;
for a bird of the air may carry your
voice,
or some winged creature tell the
matter.

The Value of Diligence

11 Send out your bread upon the waters,
for after many days you will get it back.
2 Divide your means seven ways, or even
eight,
for you do not know what disaster may
happen on earth.
3 When clouds are full,
they empty rain on the earth;
whether a tree falls to the south or to the
north,
in the place where the tree falls, there it
will lie.
4 Whoever observes the wind will not sow;
and whoever regards the clouds will
not reap.

5 Just as you do not know how the breath
comes to the bones in the mother's womb, so
you do not know the work of God, who makes
everything.

6 In the morning sow your seed, and at
evening do not let your hands be idle; for you
do not know which will prosper, this or that,
or whether both alike will be good.

Youth and Old Age

7 Light is sweet, and it is pleasant for the eyes
to see the sun.

8 Even those who live many years should rejoice in them all; yet let them remember that
the days of darkness will be many. All that
comes is vanity.

9 Rejoice, young man, while you are young,
and let your heart cheer you in the days of
your youth. Follow the inclination of your
heart and the desire of your eyes, but know
that for all these things God will bring you
into judgment.

10 Banish anxiety from your mind, and put
away pain from your body; for youth and the
dawn of life are vanity.

_____
a Or a child

---

focus on judgment. **10.10** Translation uncertain.
10.16–20 Concerning political issues. **10.16–17** See
note on 10.5–7; Prov 31.4–5. **10.19** See Ps 104.15.
11.1–6 Concerning economic issues. **11.1–2** Sometimes taken as metaphorical for almsgiving; probably
literal and metaphorical advice concerning sea trade
in grain (*bread,* v. 1) and other endeavors; see v. 6.
11.5 See Ps 139.13–16. **11.6** *Sow,* both literal and
metaphorical for every sort of human undertaking;

see note on 11.1–2; Job 31.8; Prov 11.18; 22.8; Mic
6.15; Gal 6.7.

11.7–12.8 Conclusions. The possibility of enjoyment is mandatory for youth to understand. Even as
youth, itself *hevel,* gives way to an old age and decay, depicted in graphic, almost apocalyptic, images, death
places everything in perspective. The "breath" infused
into creation will now return to God (12.7). **11.9** *Judgment.* See notes on 3.17; 8.5–6. **11.10** *Anxiety.* See note

12 Remember your creator in the days of your youth, before the days of trouble come, and the years draw near when you will say, "I have no pleasure in them"; ²before the sun and the light and the moon and the stars are darkened and the clouds return with ᵃ the rain; ³in the day when the guards of the house tremble, and the strong men are bent, and the women who grind cease working because they are few, and those who look through the windows see dimly; ⁴when the doors on the street are shut, and the sound of the grinding is low, and one rises up at the sound of a bird, and all the daughters of song are brought low; ⁵when one is afraid of heights, and terrors are in the road; the almond tree blossoms, the grasshopper drags itself along ᵇ and desire fails; because all must go to their eternal home, and the mourners will go about the streets; ⁶before the silver cord is snapped, ᶜ and the golden bowl is broken, and the pitcher is broken at the fountain, and the wheel broken at the cistern, ⁷and the dust returns to the earth as it was, and the breath ᵈ returns to God who gave it. ⁸Vanity of vanities, says the Teacher; ᵉ all is vanity.

Epilogue

9 Besides being wise, the Teacher ᵉ also taught the people knowledge, weighing and studying and arranging many proverbs. ¹⁰The Teacher ᵉ sought to find pleasing words, and he wrote words of truth plainly.

11 The sayings of the wise are like goads, and like nails firmly fixed are the collected sayings that are given by one shepherd. ᶠ ¹²Of anything beyond these, my child, beware. Of making many books there is no end, and much study is a weariness of the flesh.

13 The end of the matter; all has been heard. Fear God, and keep his commandments; for that is the whole duty of everyone. ¹⁴For God will bring every deed into judgment, including ᵍ every secret thing, whether good or evil.

---

a Or *after*; Heb *'ahar*   *b* Or *is a burden*   *c* Syr Vg Compare Gk: Heb *is removed*   *d* Or *the spirit*   *e* *Qoheleth*, traditionally rendered *Preacher*   *f* Meaning of Heb uncertain   *g* Or *into the judgment on*

---

on 7.3. **12.1–8** A prose poem on death variously read as a house falling to pieces, the image of a funeral passing, or an allegory of aging, in which images represent parts of the aging body (e.g., *women who grind* are the teeth and *those who look* the eyes, v. 3). The passage most likely portrays a village funeral (vv. 5–7) to remind readers (v. 1) of their own coming death. **12.1** Continuation of the advice to enjoy life in the face of death (see note on 9.7–10). *Creator.* See v. 7. **12.2** For the dead, the world is no more. For mourners, death seems the un-creation of the entire world (human as microcosm) in which the light-bearers of Gen 1 are undone (11.7–8; see Job 3.4–5, 9; Isa 13.9–10). *Clouds.* See Ezek 32.7–8; Joel 2.2. **12.3** The effects of mourning described; people are wracked with dismay and work ceases. *Are bent,* perhaps "writhe." *See dimly,* because of grief (see Lam 5.17). **12.4** *One rises,* or "the sound of a bird rises," as the mourners grow silent. **12.5** The sense of the first part of this verse is very uncertain. **12.6** Images of death. *Wheel,* or "jar." **12.7** See Gen 2.7; 3.19. The thought of this verse seems to contradict 3.21. *Breath* does not refer to an "immortal soul," a notion foreign to Qoheleth. **12.8** *Vanity of vanities.* The body of the book ends as it began (1.2). **12.9–14** Epilogue. An assurance, probably by someone other than the author, that all has been faithfully and honestly written.

THE SONG OF SOLOMON

THE SONG OF SOLOMON (also known as the "Song of Songs," "Canticles," and "the Song") is a rich and sensual love song.

Purpose

THE SONG OF SOLOMON has been understood in radically different ways. In the traditional Jewish understanding, the Song is a *religious allegory* recounting God's love for Israel and the history of their relationship. For Christians it is an allegory of Christ's love for the church. These allegorical interpretations enabled the Song to become sacred scripture. According to another theory, the Song is, or at least is derived from, a *sacred marriage liturgy*, a Mesopotamian ritual of marriage between two gods, the fertility god Dumuzi-Tammuz (perhaps represented by the king) and his sister, Inanna-Astarte (represented by a priestess). Many Mesopotamian rituals celebrate love between different gods, drawing on a reservoir of ancient Near Eastern love imagery, to which the Song of Songs is heir as well. A *mortuary song* theory identifies the Song's setting as funerary repasts (or orgies) that affirmed life by setting the power of love against the power of death. According to the *wedding song* interpretation, the poem describes an actual wedding. The lovers are regarded as bride and groom celebrating their nuptials. Parallels to songs sung at nineteenth-century Palestinian Arab weddings have been used to support this theory. The Song has also been read as *secular love poetry*. In this view, the poem portrays erotic love between two young people who are not yet betrothed and whose union is not yet recognized by the young woman's family, but who look forward to public acceptance of their union and to its culmination in marriage. The following notes adopt the last interpretation.

The other approaches do not necessarily deny that the Song depicts erotic, premarital love, but they regard this level of meaning as superficial or incomplete. There are, however, no signs that the author intended to depict any sort of experience other than human sexual love. Nevertheless, one may draw meanings from a book beyond the author's intentions, and traditional interpreters, Jewish and Christian, did so with rich results. As a lush and subtle portrayal of adolescent erotic love, the words of the Song can—by a bold reinterpretation—be applied to other types of love, such as the divine benevolence that bestows loving blessings on humanity, the human devotion that transcends death, or the mature sexual communion solemnized in marriage.

903

Setting

JUDGING FROM ITS SKILLFUL control of language, the Song is a product of deliberate artistry, perhaps composed by a professional singer for entertainment at festivities. Similar Egyptian love songs occasionally define themselves as "entertainment" (lit. "diverting the heart") and were sung by professional male and female singers at banquets, which are portrayed in many tombs. Similar festivities are a likely setting for the Song's original use.

Like Proverbs and Ecclesiastes, the Song is attributed to King Solomon (1.1), the archetypal wise man and lover. Nothing in the poem supports that identification, and the title is probably a later addition. The Song's actual author is unknown.

Opinions on the book's structure vary greatly. Some scholars believe it is a unified poem constructed on a tight, intricate pattern, while others consider it a loose anthology of originally independent poems from different sources. One view, popular in the nineteenth century, holds that the poem is a drama whose unity resides in a cohesive plot (such as a story of Solomon taking an unwilling rustic maiden to his palace). Others hold that the Song is a single poem written by a single author but lacking any strict overall pattern. Its cohesiveness comes from the presentation of consistent characters who express the same emotions in similar language throughout.

The dating of the Song is uncertain, since there is nothing to tie it to a specific historical setting. It has been assigned dates ranging from the time of Solomon (mid-tenth century BCE) down to third or second century BCE. The linguistic characteristics of the poem tend to confirm a later (fourth or third century) dating for its present form, but it incorporates themes and usages from much earlier—probably pre-Israelite—times.

The Song belongs to a tradition of love poetry known elsewhere in the ancient Near East. Similar language and motifs appear in Mesopotamian love rituals. Even closer are the Egyptian love songs (early thirteenth to mid-twelfth century BCE), which speak of love between unmarried young people who express their longings, joys, and pains, as well as their fascination with the new experiences of love.

By portraying lovers, the Song represents an idea—and an ideal—of love. It shows a relationship charged with erotic energy and a joyous, sensual world in which the land's rebirth in spring is the counterpart of the maiden's blossoming into womanhood. Sexuality is treated with restraint and indirection and affirmed without coyness or apology. The love portrayed is thoroughly egalitarian and mutual; both lovers desire, behave, feel, and speak in the same way and with the same intensity. The constraints of a patriarchal society do not seem to determine the lovers' behavior toward each other, though they do restrict the young woman's freedom of movement. As the Song portrays the lovers, they are in transition from youth to maturity. She is unmarried, and in the ancient world there was little time between puberty and marriage. She is still living under her brothers' authority, but she believes that she is mature (8.10), and it seems that even her brothers are about to recognize her readiness for marriage (8.8–9).

Love in the Song is seen as a communion of souls, expressed by tightly interlocking dialogue (e.g., 1.9–17; 2.1–3a; 4.1–5.1). It is also a mode of perception, for when the lovers look at each other they see a world of their own. Each describes the other's body, dwelling lovingly on each part as if to caress it with words and capturing its essence in striking (sometimes startling) images. These images come to life on their own and combine to describe a rich and blessed landscape (4.1–7; 5.10–16; 6.4–10; 7.2–10a), the Arcady of love. [MICHAEL V. FOX]

1 The Song of Songs, which is Solomon's.

Colloquy of Bride and Friends

2 Let him kiss me with the kisses of his
      mouth!
  For your love is better than wine,
3   your anointing oils are fragrant,
  your name is perfume poured out;
      therefore the maidens love you.
4 Draw me after you, let us make haste.
      The king has brought me into his
      chambers.
  We will exult and rejoice in you;
      we will extol your love more than
      wine;
  rightly do they love you.

5 I am black and beautiful,
      O daughters of Jerusalem,
  like the tents of Kedar,
      like the curtains of Solomon.
6 Do not gaze at me because I am dark,
      because the sun has gazed on me.
  My mother's sons were angry with me;
      they made me keeper of the vineyards,
      but my own vineyard I have not kept!
7 Tell me, you whom my soul loves,
      where you pasture your flock,
      where you make it lie down at noon;
  for why should I be like one who is veiled
      beside the flocks of your companions?

8 If you do not know,
      O fairest among women,

follow the tracks of the flock,
    and pasture your kids
    beside the shepherds' tents.

Colloquy of Bridegroom, Friends, and Bride

9 I compare you, my love,
      to a mare among Pharaoh's chariots.
10 Your cheeks are comely with
      ornaments,
  your neck with strings of jewels.
11 We will make you ornaments of gold,
      studded with silver.

12 While the king was on his couch,
      my nard gave forth its fragrance.
13 My beloved is to me a bag of myrrh
      that lies between my breasts.
14 My beloved is to me a cluster of henna
      blossoms
  in the vineyards of En-gedi.

15 Ah, you are beautiful, my love;
      ah, you are beautiful;
      your eyes are doves.
16 Ah, you are beautiful, my beloved,
      truly lovely.
  Our couch is green;
17   the beams of our house are cedar,
      our rafters^a are pine.

2 I am a rose^b of Sharon,
    a lily of the valleys.

---

a Meaning of Heb uncertain   *b* Heb *crocus*

1.1 *Song of Songs,* a superlative meaning "the sublime song." **1.2–8** The maiden's complaint. **1.2** *Let him . . . your.* The lovers sometimes address each other in the third person (e.g., 1.12; 2.1–3), which carries a tone of respect. *Let him kiss me,* Hebrew *yishakeni,* suggests a pun on *yashkeyni,* "give to drink" (used in 8.2). *Love* (Hebrew *dodim*), meaning physical expressions of love. **1.4** *King,* probably a term of affection and esteem referring to the youth. **1.5–8** The young woman's brothers grew angry at her (for her new love interests?) and tried to coop her up at home. **1.5** *Black and beautiful,* better "black but beautiful." As v. 6 shows, the maiden does not consider "blackness," i.e., sunburn, to be part of her beauty. The *daughters of Jerusalem* are the Shulammite's girlfriends, who listen to her effusions and tease her a bit (5.9). *Kedar,* an Arabian tribe whose name means "dark." *Curtains,* i.e., tent curtains. *Solomon,* or read "Salmah," also an Arabian tribe. **1.6** *Vineyard,* an allusion to womanhood (cf. 8.12). **1.7–8** *One who is veiled,* a harlot (Gen

38.14–15). The woman is being provocative and gets teased in return in v. 8. To *pasture,* or "graze" (Hebrew *ro'eh*), together with homonyms, often enters into wordplays alluding to lovemaking (his beloved is called *ra' yati, my love* [v. 9], from a homonymous root). As for where this shepherd "grazes," see 2.16; 4.16–5.1.

1.9–2.7 An admiration dialogue in which the lovers speak to each other and praise each other's beauty as a whole; set in a bower in the fields. **1.12–14** The *king* is the youth, reclining royally on a leafy "couch" under the trees (vv. 16–17). *Nard* is an expensive spice that emits scent when rubbed; *myrrh* and *henna* too are fragrant spices. The woman's beloved lies nestled between her breasts like a pouch of spices. *En-gedi,* where henna grows, is an oasis on the Dead Sea. **1.15–16** The man speaks in v. 15; the woman replies in v. 16. **2.1** *I am a rose* (better "crocus") *of Sharon* is not a boast, but a modest self-appraisal; the woman says she is but one of thousands. Her beloved turns this into high praise:

2 As a lily among brambles,
  so is my love among maidens.

3 As an apple tree among the trees of the
    wood,
  so is my beloved among young men.
  With great delight I sat in his shadow,
  and his fruit was sweet to my taste.

4 He brought me to the banqueting house,
  and his intention toward me was love.

5 Sustain me with raisins,
  refresh me with apples;
  for I am faint with love.

6 O that his left hand were under my head,
  and that his right hand embraced me!

7 I adjure you, O daughters of Jerusalem,
  by the gazelles or the wild does:
do not stir up or awaken love
  until it is ready!

Springtime Rhapsody

8 The voice of my beloved!
  Look, he comes,
leaping upon the mountains,
  bounding over the hills.

9 My beloved is like a gazelle
  or a young stag.
Look, there he stands
  behind our wall,
gazing in at the windows,
  looking through the lattice.

10 My beloved speaks and says to me:
"Arise, my love, my fair one,
  and come away;

11 for now the winter is past,
  the rain is over and gone.

12 The flowers appear on the earth;
  the time of singing has come,
and the voice of the turtledove
  is heard in our land.

13 The fig tree puts forth its figs,
  and the vines are in blossom;
  they give forth fragrance.
Arise, my love, my fair one,
  and come away.

14 O my dove, in the clefts of the rock,
  in the covert of the cliff,
let me see your face,
  let me hear your voice;
for your voice is sweet,
  and your face is lovely.

15 Catch us the foxes,
  the little foxes,
that ruin the vineyards—
  for our vineyards are in blossom."

16 My beloved is mine and I am his;
  he pastures his flock among the lilies.

17 Until the day breathes
  and the shadows flee,
turn, my beloved, be like a gazelle
  or a young stag on the cleft
    mountains.[a]

Love's Dream

3 Upon my bed at night
  I sought him whom my soul loves;
I sought him, but found him not;
  I called him, but he gave no answer.[b]

2 "I will rise now and go about the city,
  in the streets and in the squares;
I will seek him whom my soul loves."
  I sought him, but found him not.

3 The sentinels found me,
  as they went about in the city.
"Have you seen him whom my soul
    loves?"

---

a Or *on the mountains of Bether*; meaning of Heb uncertain
b Gk: Heb lacks this line

---

she is unique (v. 2); and she replies in kind (v. 3). **2.4** *Banqueting house* (lit. "house of wine") alludes to a garden booth (cf. 1.17). **2.5** The fruits that the lovesick woman requires are her lover's caresses (cf. v. 3). **2.6** This sentence should probably be translated as a statement. **2.7** This same request recurs in 3.5; 8.4. The maiden does not want her friends to disturb *love*, i.e., the couple's embrace. *Gazelles, does,* words for making "oaths" without mentioning God's name. **2.8–17** The man appears at his beloved's window just before dawn and urges her to come away with him to the countryside, now abloom in the splendor of spring. **2.11** *Winter* in Israel is the rainy season. In April and May the figs and vines begin to ripen and the migrant birds

reappear. **2.12** *Singing.* The Hebrew *zamir* may also mean "pruning season" and so may be a wordplay pointing in two directions. **2.15** *Foxes* is a metaphor for lusty youths, *vineyards* for nubile women. The woman in an Egyptian love song affectionately refers to her lover as a "(little) fox." **2.16** *He pastures his flock* (the Hebrew lacks "his flock"). Her beloved "pastures" or "grazes" among the most delicate and lovely of flowers—the maiden herself (cf. 5.13; 4.16–5.1a). **2.17** The maiden urges her beloved to flee—we may recall her irritable brothers!—before daybreak. *The cleft mountains.* An anatomical allusion? Better might be "mountains of Bether," hills outside Jerusalem.

3.1–5 A nighttime search for the beloved; cf. 5.2–8.

4 Scarcely had I passed them,
  when I found him whom my soul
      loves.
I held him, and would not let him go
  until I brought him into my mother's
      house,
  and into the chamber of her that
      conceived me.
5 I adjure you, O daughters of Jerusalem,
  by the gazelles or the wild does:
do not stir up or awaken love
  until it is ready!

The Groom and His Party Approach

6 What is that coming up from the
      wilderness,
  like a column of smoke,
perfumed with myrrh and frankincense,
  with all the fragrant powders of the
      merchant?
7 Look, it is the litter of Solomon!
  Around it are sixty mighty men
  of the mighty men of Israel,
8 all equipped with swords
  and expert in war,
each with his sword at his thigh
  because of alarms by night.
9 King Solomon made himself a palanquin
  from the wood of Lebanon.
10 He made its posts of silver,
  its back of gold, its seat of purple;
its interior was inlaid with love. *a*
  Daughters of Jerusalem,
11 come out.
Look, O daughters of Zion,
  at King Solomon,
at the crown with which his mother
  crowned him

on the day of his wedding,
  on the day of the gladness of his heart.

The Bride's Beauty Extolled

4 How beautiful you are, my love,
  how very beautiful!
Your eyes are doves
  behind your veil.
Your hair is like a flock of goats,
  moving down the slopes of Gilead.
2 Your teeth are like a flock of shorn ewes
  that have come up from the washing,
all of which bear twins,
  and not one among them is bereaved.
3 Your lips are like a crimson thread,
  and your mouth is lovely.
Your cheeks are like halves of a
      pomegranate
  behind your veil.
4 Your neck is like the tower of David,
  built in courses;
on it hang a thousand bucklers,
  all of them shields of warriors.
5 Your two breasts are like two fawns,
  twins of a gazelle,
  that feed among the lilies.
6 Until the day breathes
  and the shadows flee,
I will hasten to the mountain of myrrh
  and the hill of frankincense.
7 You are altogether beautiful, my love;
  there is no flaw in you.
8 Come with me from Lebanon, my bride;
  come with me from Lebanon.
Depart *b* from the peak of Amana,
  from the peak of Senir and Hermon,

---

a Meaning of Heb uncertain   *b* Or *Look*

This might all be a dream. **3.5** The happy conclusion; cf. 2.7. **3.6–11** "Solomon's wedding." Though usually understood as an actual royal wedding, this may be a fantasy disguise for the beloved in his humble bower, which is extravagantly pictured as a royal pavilion. **3.6** *What* (Hebrew "who") *is that*, probably an exclamation of surprise (as in the identically phrased 8.5), not a real question. *Frankincense* is a fragrant balsamic gum whose Hebrew name, *lebonah*, sometimes plays on "Lebanon." **3.7–8** A *litter* is a portable couch; the Hebrew simply has "couch," and it may be stationary. *Sixty mighty men.* Armed guards surround the royal chamber, here perhaps in imagination. The *alarms by night* may be nocturnal demons. **3.9–11** *Palanquin*, or "pavilion," not necessarily portable. *Inlaid with love.* Emendation yields "inlaid with stones"; cf. Esth 1.6. The *crown* may allude to a floral garland.

4.1–7 A praise song (cf. 5.10–16; 6.4–10; 7.1–9) that describes the beloved part by part with bold and sometimes startling metaphors. The metaphors are often extended by a description pertaining only to the image itself, not to the beloved's appearance. **4.1** *Flock of goats* suggests wavy black tresses cascading over head and shoulders. **4.3** The woman's *veil* casts a shadow that recalls the webbing of membranes in a split pomegranate. **4.4** This image suggests a necklace made up of rows of beads, each of which is like a shield hung on a wall (cf. Ezek 27.11). An actual *tower of David* is otherwise unknown. **4.6** *The day . . . flee*, i.e., at dawn. The hills of myrrh and spices seem to allude to the maiden's breasts. **4.8–5.1** The youth invites his beloved to come away with him, speaking as if she were in far and inaccessible mountains (cf. 2.14) and then lauds her caresses. **4.8** *Lebanon*, a mountain

from the dens of lions,
    from the mountains of leopards.

9 You have ravished my heart, my sister, my
    bride,
    you have ravished my heart with a
        glance of your eyes,
    with one jewel of your necklace.
10 How sweet is your love, my sister, my
    bride!
    how much better is your love than wine,
    and the fragrance of your oils than any
        spice!
11 Your lips distill nectar, my bride;
    honey and milk are under your tongue;
    the scent of your garments is like the
        scent of Lebanon.
12 A garden locked is my sister, my bride,
    a garden locked, a fountain sealed.
13 Your channel^a is an orchard of
        pomegranates
    with all choicest fruits,
    henna with nard,
14 nard and saffron, calamus and cinnamon,
    with all trees of frankincense,
    myrrh and aloes,
    with all chief spices—
15 a garden fountain, a well of living water,
    and flowing streams from Lebanon.

16 Awake, O north wind,
    and come, O south wind!
Blow upon my garden
    that its fragrance may be wafted
        abroad.
Let my beloved come to his garden,
    and eat its choicest fruits.

5 I come to my garden, my sister, my bride;
    I gather my myrrh with my spice,
    I eat my honeycomb with my honey,
    I drink my wine with my milk.

Eat, friends, drink,
    and be drunk with love.

Another Dream

2 I slept, but my heart was awake.
Listen! my beloved is knocking.
"Open to me, my sister, my love,
    my dove, my perfect one;
for my head is wet with dew,
    my locks with the drops of the night."
3 I had put off my garment;
    how could I put it on again?
I had bathed my feet;
    how could I soil them?
4 My beloved thrust his hand into the
        opening,
    and my inmost being yearned for him.
5 I arose to open to my beloved,
    and my hands dripped with myrrh,
my fingers with liquid myrrh,
    upon the handles of the bolt.
6 I opened to my beloved,
    but my beloved had turned and was
        gone.
My soul failed me when he spoke.
I sought him, but did not find him;
    I called him, but he gave no answer.
7 Making their rounds in the city
    the sentinels found me;
    they beat me, they wounded me,

---

a Meaning of Heb uncertain

---

range north of Israel. *Amana, Senir,* and *Hermon* are tall mountains in the Anti-Lebanon range, running along the border of present-day Syria and Lebanon. **4.9** *Sister* is a term of endearment, as in the Egyptian love songs, and in no way implies consanguinity. *Bride* too is a term of affection, but it also expresses hopes for the future. **4.11** *Your lips distill nectar* (or "drip honeycomb"), *my bride,* a striking assonance in Hebrew: *nofet tittofnah siftotayik kallah. The scent of Lebanon.* The fragrant cedars of Lebanon can be smelled from miles away. **4.12** *Garden* and *fountain* are images of feminine sexuality (cf. Prov 5.15–17). The youth extols his beloved's modesty and sexual exclusiveness, while hinting at his wish to be admitted. **4.13–14** *Channel,* rather the area of a garden irrigated by the channel. *Saffron, calamus,* and the others mentioned are all aromatic spices. The profusion of fruits and spices suggests a fullness of sensual delights. **4.16** The

maiden invites the beloved into her *garden*—her own fresh and fragrant body—which is now *his garden* too, to taste the fruits of love. **5.1** *I come to my garden.* The youth accepts the invitation and enters the garden, which he now calls his. Then a chorus—the daughters of Jerusalem?—encourages the couple to drink their fill of love. *Be drunk with love* (Hebrew *dodim,* "lovemaking") means to give oneself over to sexual ecstasy, as in Prov 5.19; 7.18.

5.2–8 Another nighttime visit and search for the beloved (cf. 3.1–4). **5.2** *I slept … awake.* Perhaps the entire passage relates a dream, but the words may also mean that the maiden woke up. **5.4** *Into the opening,* through a window. **5.5** The woman had prepared for the visit by anointing herself with perfumed unguents; cf. Prov 7.17. **5.6** The woman runs about the streets at night seeking her lover—a strange and dangerous deed. **5.7** The *sentinels* who guard *the walls*—perhaps a

they took away my mantle,
    those sentinels of the walls.
8 I adjure you, O daughters of
        Jerusalem,
    if you find my beloved,
    tell him this:
    I am faint with love.

Colloquy of Friends and Bride

9 What is your beloved more than another
        beloved,
    O fairest among women?
    What is your beloved more than another
        beloved,
    that you thus adjure us?

10 My beloved is all radiant and ruddy,
    distinguished among ten thousand.
11 His head is the finest gold;
    his locks are wavy,
        black as a raven.
12 His eyes are like doves
        beside springs of water,
    bathed in milk,
        fitly set.*a*
13 His cheeks are like beds of spices,
        yielding fragrance.
    His lips are lilies,
        distilling liquid myrrh.
14 His arms are rounded gold,
        set with jewels.
    His body is ivory work,*a*
        encrusted with sapphires.*b*
15 His legs are alabaster columns,
        set upon bases of gold.
    His appearance is like Lebanon,
        choice as the cedars.
16 His speech is most sweet,
        and he is altogether desirable.
    This is my beloved and this is my
        friend,
    O daughters of Jerusalem.

6 Where has your beloved gone,
        O fairest among women?
    Which way has your beloved turned,
        that we may seek him with you?

2 My beloved has gone down to his garden,
        to the beds of spices,
    to pasture his flock in the gardens,
        and to gather lilies.
3 I am my beloved's and my beloved is
        mine;
    he pastures his flock among the lilies.

The Bride's Matchless Beauty

4 You are beautiful as Tirzah, my love,
        comely as Jerusalem,
    terrible as an army with banners.
5 Turn away your eyes from me,
        for they overwhelm me!
    Your hair is like a flock of goats,
        moving down the slopes of Gilead.
6 Your teeth are like a flock of ewes,
        that have come up from the washing;
    all of them bear twins,
        and not one among them is bereaved.
7 Your cheeks are like halves of a
        pomegranate
    behind your veil.
8 There are sixty queens and eighty
        concubines,
    and maidens without number.
9 My dove, my perfect one, is the only one,
        the darling of her mother,
    flawless to her that bore her.
    The maidens saw her and called her
        happy;
    the queens and concubines also, and
        they praised her.
10 "Who is this that looks forth like the
        dawn,

---

a Meaning of Heb uncertain   *b* Heb *lapis lazuli*

symbol of social conventions (cf. 8.9)—beat her and
strip off her garment. Perhaps they are treating her as a
prostitute (cf. the behavior of the woman in Prov 7.5–
21). Although the woman is exposed, hurt, and confused, she gives no reason for the sentinels' brutality, as
if shrugging it off as a triviality in the face of her need
for her lover. **5.8** *Tell him this,* better "Do not tell him."
The maiden begs her friends *not* to tell her beloved
about her love-crazed, distraught behavior. **5.9–16** A
praise song using imagery from the plastic arts.
5.10 To be *radiant and ruddy* was considered a sign of
health and vigor (Ps 104.15; 1 Sam 16.12; 17.42).

5.16 *His speech is most sweet,* lit. "his palate is sweet
drink"—the maiden alludes to her beloved's kisses (cf.
1.2) as well as his speech.
    6.1–3 A transition to the next song, returning to the
dialogue form of 5.9. **6.4–10** The youth offers another
praise song, repeating and expanding 4.1–3. **6.4** The
beloved's beauty and majesty equal that of two grand
cities, *Jerusalem* (capital of the Southern Kingdom)
and *Tirzah* (for a brief time capital of the North). The
maiden is not just a pretty girl, but a dignified, even
"awesome," woman (cf. 6.10). **6.8–10** There are a great
many women of rank, but this maiden is unique and

fair as the moon, bright as the sun,
　　terrible as an army with banners?"

11　I went down to the nut orchard,
　　to look at the blossoms of the valley,
　　to see whether the vines had budded,
　　　whether the pomegranates were in
　　　　bloom.

12　Before I was aware, my fancy set me
　　in a chariot beside my prince.[a]

13　[b] Return, return, O Shulammite!
　　Return, return, that we may look upon
　　　you.

Why should you look upon the
　　Shulammite,
　　as upon a dance before two armies?[c]

Expressions of Praise

7　How graceful are your feet in sandals,
　　O queenly maiden!
Your rounded thighs are like jewels,
　　the work of a master hand.

2　Your navel is a rounded bowl
　　that never lacks mixed wine.
Your belly is a heap of wheat,
　　encircled with lilies.

3　Your two breasts are like two fawns,
　　twins of a gazelle.

4　Your neck is like an ivory tower.
Your eyes are pools in Heshbon,
　　by the gate of Bath-rabbim.
Your nose is like a tower of Lebanon,

overlooking Damascus.

5　Your head crowns you like Carmel,
　　and your flowing locks are like purple;
　　a king is held captive in the tresses.[c]

6　How fair and pleasant you are,
　　O loved one, delectable maiden![d]

7　You are stately[e] as a palm tree,
　　and your breasts are like its clusters.

8　I say I will climb the palm tree
　　and lay hold of its branches.
O may your breasts be like clusters of the
　　vine,
　　and the scent of your breath like
　　　apples,

9　and your kisses[f] like the best wine
　　that goes down[g] smoothly,
　　gliding over lips and teeth.[h]

10　I am my beloved's,
　　and his desire is for me.

11　Come, my beloved,
　　let us go forth into the fields,
　　and lodge in the villages;

12　let us go out early to the vineyards,
　　and see whether the vines have
　　　budded,
　　whether the grape blossoms have opened
　　and the pomegranates are in bloom.
　　There I will give you my love.

---

a　Cn: Meaning of Heb uncertain　　b　Ch 7.1 in Heb
c　Or dance of Mahanaim　　d　Meaning of Heb uncertain
e　Syr: Heb in delights　　f　Heb This your stature is　　g　Heb palate
h　Heb down for my lover　　f　Gk Syr Vg: Heb lips of sleepers

---

flawless, as even the (hypothetical) noblewomen declare in v. 10. **6.12** In this obscure verse, the woman seems to be saying that she was overwhelmed by emotion in the presence of her beloved, who is—for her—a nobleman. **6.13a** This verse seems to be spoken by a group (the women of Jerusalem?), while v. 13b (where the *you* is plural) is the youth's response. *Shulammite,* actually *the* Shulammite; the word is not a proper name but an epithet that probably means "the perfect one." *A dance before two armies* with a minor change may be read as "a camp dancer," i.e., a woman who dances in the camps of soldiers or shepherds.

7.1–7 A praise song with metaphors evoking intangible qualities: plenitude, preciousness, nobility, and grandeur. **7.2** *That never . . . wine,* praise of the bowl, not the belly. **7.4** *Ivory tower,* decorated with ivory, an image suggestive of a long and graceful neck adorned with an ivory necklace. *Heshbon,* eighty kilometers east of Jerusalem, retains ruins of a large reservoir dating from the eighth century BCE. *Bath-rabbim,* presumably the name of a gate or location in Hesh-

bon, means "daughter of noblemen" and alludes to the beloved. The *tower of Lebanon* suggests loftiness and pride and plays on the Hebrew *lebonah,* "frankincense." **7.5** The *Carmel* is a verdant mountain range in northwestern Israel. Its name plays on *karmil,* a redpurple cloth. *Purple* cloth was a sign of royalty. A "king"—the youth himself—is trapped by the maiden's long, curled tresses. **7.8–14** An admiration dialogue in which the lovers speak to each other and praise each other's beauty as a whole (cf. 1.9–17; 2.1–3). **7.8** *Breath,* lit. "nose," an allusion to the custom of nose kissing. **7.9** *That goes down smoothly.* The Hebrew reads, "that flows smoothly to my lover." The NRSV's emendation obscures the fact that the maiden speaks here. She breaks into her lover's sentence and completes it with an offer of her kisses, showing that she reciprocates his desire. *Gliding over lips and teeth.* Emendation produces "flowing smoothly to my beloved, dripping on scarlet lips." **7.11** *Villages* (Hebrew *kefarim*), a pun, meaning both villages and henna bushes. **7.12** *My love.* The Hebrew here is

13 The mandrakes give forth fragrance,
   and over our doors are all choice fruits,
new as well as old,
   which I have laid up for you, O my
      beloved.

8 O that you were like a brother to me,
   who nursed at my mother's breast!
If I met you outside, I would kiss you,
   and no one would despise me.
2 I would lead you and bring you
   into the house of my mother,
   and into the chamber of the one who
      bore me.*a*
I would give you spiced wine to drink,
   the juice of my pomegranates.
3 O that his left hand were under my head,
   and that his right hand embraced me!
4 I adjure you, O daughters of Jerusalem,
   do not stir up or awaken love
   until it is ready!

Homecoming

5 Who is that coming up from the
      wilderness,
   leaning upon her beloved?

Under the apple tree I awakened you.
There your mother was in labor with you;
   there she who bore you was in labor.

6 Set me as a seal upon your heart,
   as a seal upon your arm;
for love is strong as death,
   passion fierce as the grave.
Its flashes are flashes of fire,
   a raging flame.
7 Many waters cannot quench love,
   neither can floods drown it.
If one offered for love

all the wealth of one's house,
   it would be utterly scorned.

8 We have a little sister,
   and she has no breasts.
What shall we do for our sister,
   on the day when she is spoken for?
9 If she is a wall,
   we will build upon her a battlement of
      silver;
but if she is a door,
   we will enclose her with boards of
      cedar.
10 I was a wall,
   and my breasts were like towers;
then I was in his eyes
   as one who brings*b* peace.
11 Solomon had a vineyard at Baal-hamon;
   he entrusted the vineyard to keepers;
   each one was to bring for its fruit a
      thousand pieces of silver.
12 My vineyard, my very own, is for
      myself;
you, O Solomon, may have the
      thousand,
and the keepers of the fruit two
      hundred!
13 O you who dwell in the gardens,
   my companions are listening for your
      voice;
   let me hear it.
14 Make haste, my beloved,
   and be like a gazelle
or a young stag
   upon the mountains of spices!

---

a Gk Syr: Heb *my mother; she* (or *you*) *will teach me*   *b* Or *finds*

---

dodim, which means "lovemaking" (1.2). **7.13** *Man-drakes* (Hebrew *duda'im,* suggestive of *dodim,* "love-making") were considered an aphrodisiac (Gen 30.14–24). *New as well as old,* i.e., fruits of all sorts. **8.1–7** Expressions of love. **8.1** The woman wishes she could demonstrate her love publicly as she could to a brother. **8.2** *My pomegranates,* her breasts. **8.5a** As in 3.6 an exclamation of unknown meaning, not a real question. **8.5b** *I awakened you,* perhaps after spending the night in the countryside (7.11). *Was in labor,* or "conceived." The setting of coitus was thought to af-fect the offspring (Gen 30.31–43). Note that the youth is as sweet as apples (2.3). **8.6–7** The maiden declares the fierce power of love and the eternality of its bond. A *seal* was used to stamp documents and functioned like a signature; it would always be kept on one's per-

son. *Flashes,* flaming arrows. *Raging flame* is a better translation for *shalhevetyah* than the traditional "flame of the Lord [Yah]." The name of God does not appear in this book. **8.8–10** Reconciliation with the brothers (cf. 1.6). They promise to lavish wedding or-naments upon their sister when she is mature. They doubt that she is ready, but she insists that she is (v. 10). *I was a wall,* Hebrew, "I am a wall." She is a *wall* (probably implying chastity) with *towers*—mature breasts. **8.11–12** The youth asserts that not even Solomon's rich vineyard could compare to *his* vine-yard, which is the maiden herself. And whereas Solomon gave his vineyards to *keepers,* the youth will tend his alone. *Baal-hamon.* The location is unknown; the name means "possessor of wealth" and alludes to Solomon.

ISAIAH

THE BOOK OF ISAIAH is a composite work, the product of several different prophets who ministered at different periods in the history of Israel. Scholars normally distinguish between three main sections in the book: chs. 1–39, referred to as First Isaiah and attributed in general to the eighth-century BCE Judean prophet whose name the book bears; chs. 40–55, referred to as Second Isaiah, or Deutero-Isaiah, and attributed to an unknown prophet who lived in Babylon during the Babylonian exile of the sixth century; and chs. 56–66, referred to as Third Isaiah, or Trito-Isaiah, and attributed to a prophet or prophets who lived in Judah after the return from Babylonian exile in 539 BCE.

First Isaiah

ACCORDING TO THE SUPERSCRIPTION (1.1), Isaiah son of Amoz prophesied in Jerusalem during the reign of the four Judean kings Uzziah, Jotham, Ahaz, and Hezekiah. If the vision in 6.1 was Isaiah's inaugural vision, he began prophesying in the year of Uzziah's death (ca. 738 BCE), and although the end of his ministry is less certain, it extended at least until 701 and perhaps as late as 688. Isaiah's datable oracles cluster in three main periods: the period of the Syro-Ephraimite war (735–732 BCE), when Syria and Israel attacked Judah (7.1–2); the period of anti-Assyrian agitation in the west against Sargon II (ca. 720–710); and the period of Hezekiah's revolt against Sennacherib (ca. 705–701, possibly again in 689–88). There is evidence that during his long ministry Isaiah adapted and reused early oracles in new historical settings; some oracles originally directed against Syria and Israel at the time of the Syro-Ephraimite war were later given an anti-Assyrian slant.

Though the editorial process cannot be fully recovered, the genuine Isaian oracles seem to have been preserved in several subcollections. Chs. 1–5 primarily contain oracles against God's own people. The core of chs. 6–11 appears to be a collection from the time of the Syro-Ephraimite war. Chs. 13–23 contain oracles against the nations; chs. 28–33 have oracles on the revolt against Sennacherib.

Not all the material in chs. 1–39 can be attributed to Isaiah of Jerusalem, however. In addition to individual oracles whose authenticity is questioned by one scholar or another, three major blocks of material in chs. 1–39 are clearly not the work of Isaiah of Jerusalem. Chs. 36–39 are largely prose narrative taken from 2 Kings 18.13–20.19 and secondarily inserted into the book of Isaiah. Chs. 34–35 are much closer in style and content to Second or Third Isaiah and should probably be dated to the exilic or postexilic period. Chs. 24–27, often referred to as the Isaiah Apocalypse, contain protoapocalyptic oracles that stand in marked contrast to those of Isaiah of Jerusalem. Although Isaiah's oracles are rooted in particular historical contexts and his threats and promises do not dissolve the reality of those contexts, the oracles in chs. 24–27 are very difficult to root in any historical context and are marked by a heavy dependence on mythological motifs. Scholars normally date these chapters to the early sixth century BCE or later.

Isaiah of Jerusalem was rooted in the Zion tradition, which celebrated God as the great king of heaven and earth, Jerusalem (Zion) as the city God chose to be his royal dwelling, and the kings of the Davidic line as God's anointed vice-regents on earth. The influence of all three aspects of this tradition is evident in the prophet's message. Isaiah's inaugural vision (6.1–4) portrays God as the exalted king, from whose terrifying holiness even the most august angels must hide their eyes. That vision colors the prophet's attitude toward anything that humans might lift up as a rival for the fear and allegiance that rightly belong only to the divine suzerain (see 2.12–22; 8.13). Isaiah assumed that God had founded Zion/Jerusalem (14.32), lived in it (8.18), and hence would ultimately save it. Nevertheless, since the holy God would not live in a moral slum, a morally defiled Jerusalem must be purified by judgment before the city could be saved (1.21–28; 29.1–8). Isaiah's adherence to the Davidic royal tradition is clear from his assurance to Ahaz (7.3–17) and his several portrayals of the ideal king (9.1–7; 11.1–10; 32.1–2).

Second Isaiah

CHAPTERS 40–55 PRESUPPOSE an Israelite audience living in Babylon toward the end of the Babylonian exile (597–539 BCE). The prophet announces to his listeners that the end of their exile in Babylon is imminent. Babylon, not Assyria, is Israel's main enemy, and the burden of the prophet's message is the promise of deliverance, not the threat of judgment. Moreover, the prophet twice mentions the Persian ruler Cyrus (44.28; 45.1) as a figure who has come to the attention of his audience. Such notice certainly presupposes Cyrus's dethroning of his Median overlord Astyages (550) and perhaps Cyrus's defeat of the Lydian king Croesus (547/6) as well. Thus this anonymous prophet's work can probably be dated between 545 and 539 BCE.

Though clearly dependent on First Isaiah's message, Second Isaiah is also easily distinguishable. Second Isaiah shares the eighth-century prophet's emphasis on the holiness of God and his vision of God as the great king, and he at least adapts the earlier prophet's ideal of the Davidic king, democratizing it to apply it to the entire nation. Unlike First Isaiah, however, the message of Second Isaiah is primarily that of consolation, and this message is couched in a distinctive style. In relatively long, markedly lyrical oracles, Second Isaiah reassures the exiles that God still controls history. Despite present appearances, the Lord will soon demonstrate his power by bringing the Israelites back to their own country in a second exodus more glorious than the first. Before this God, who has created all things, the Babylonian idols are as nothing; God's judgment on both the Babylonians and their gods is imminent.

Third Isaiah

CHAPTERS 56–66 ARE SO SIMILAR stylistically to Second Isaiah that they must be attributed either to the same author or to some disciple or disciples who used the poetry of Second Isaiah as a model. The historical setting presupposed is, however, different from that of Second Isaiah.

The audience addressed by Third Isaiah is once more living in the land of Judah. Isa 66.1 suggests that work had already begun on rebuilding the temple, work completed in the years 520–515 BCE. The initial return from Babylonian exile has already taken place, but this second exodus has not been as glorious as Second Isaiah predicted, and life for the returnees in Judah remains very harsh. In these difficult circumstances there are both economic oppression and, in an attempt to cope with life's problems, a resurgence in the pagan rituals long indigenous in Israel. In response to this situation Third Isaiah announces God's imminent judgment on the oppressors and syncretists. The prophet promises the righteous that God's glorious deliverance of Israel, long promised by Second Isaiah, is soon to be realized. Soon the wealth of the nations will pour into Jerusalem along with the rest of Israel's exiles, and the shame and sorrow of the recent past will be replaced with eternal joy and prosperity.

An Overarching Unity

DESPITE THE DIFFERENT HISTORICAL SETTINGS to which the various parts of the book may be attributed and the clear evidence of multiple authorship, there is also a certain overarching unity to the book. All parts of the book share a common theological tradition, and the later parts seem to take up, adapt, respond to, or reverse announcements made in earlier parts of the book while staying in that same theological tradition. Like most other prophetic books, the book of Isaiah moves in a general way from oracles predominantly of judgment to those of salvation. In response to these observations, recent scholarship has begun to turn its primary attention away from the traditional historical-critical issues of historical setting and authorship toward an attempt to explain this overarching unity. Some scholars see this unity as the result of a thorough reediting of the book by the latest authors or their disciples in the exilic or postexilic periods. In its most extreme form, this scholarly trend also explores how the prophetic collection as a whole has been edited to shape interconnections within the whole prophetic corpus.

Most scholars, even of the most traditional historical-critical mold, would admit there has been some late editing of the earlier parts of the book, but the evidence for a thorough, intentional, coherent editing of the book as a whole is not very persuasive. Such reconstructions are far more hypothetical than the reconstructions of traditional historical criticism. Historical reconstructions at least have attested external historical events as a control over pure speculation. Battles and political crises are public events that leave records elsewhere than in the prophetic book itself. In contrast, editorial work by its very nature is private and, barring the discovery of earlier manuscripts showing variant text forms, the reconstruction of such work never rises above the level of more or less plausible hypotheses. In this author's opinion, the editorial processes even within the material that may be confidently attributed to the eighth-century BCE Isaiah of Jerusalem are often less than transparent. Thus the opinion reflected in these notes is that the overarching unity of the book owes more to a common theological tradition in which all the authors stood than to any consistent and coherent editing the book has undergone. The common theological tradition and the fact that the later authors were responding to and commenting on the earlier oracles in the book are sufficient explanation for the overarching unity.

[J. J. M. ROBERTS]

1 The vision of Isaiah son of Amoz, which he saw concerning Judah and Jerusalem in the days of Uzziah, Jotham, Ahaz, and Hezekiah, kings of Judah.

The Wickedness of Judah

2 Hear, O heavens, and listen, O earth;
   for the LORD has spoken:
I reared children and brought them up,
   but they have rebelled against me.
3 The ox knows its owner,
   and the donkey its master's crib;
but Israel does not know,
   my people do not understand.

4 Ah, sinful nation,
   people laden with iniquity,
offspring who do evil,
   children who deal corruptly,
who have forsaken the LORD,
   who have despised the Holy One of
      Israel,
who are utterly estranged!

5 Why do you seek further beatings?
   Why do you continue to rebel?
The whole head is sick,
   and the whole heart faint.

6 From the sole of the foot even to the
      head,
   there is no soundness in it,
but bruises and sores
   and bleeding wounds;
they have not been drained, or
      bound up,
   or softened with oil.

7 Your country lies desolate,
   your cities are burned with fire;
in your very presence
   aliens devour your land;
it is desolate, as overthrown by
      foreigners.
8 And daughter Zion is left
   like a booth in a vineyard,
like a shelter in a cucumber field,
   like a besieged city.
9 If the LORD of hosts
   had not left us a few survivors,
we would have been like Sodom,
   and become like Gomorrah.

10 Hear the word of the LORD,
   you rulers of Sodom!
Listen to the teaching of our God,
   you people of Gomorrah!

1.1 Superscription. In contrast to other superscriptions found in Isaiah (2.1; 13.1; 14.28; 15.1; 17.1; 19.1; 21.1, 11, 13; 22.1; 23.1; 30.6), this superscription is intended as a heading for all of chs. 1–39 (cf. Jer 1.1–3; Ezek 1.1–3). It characterizes the book as a prophetic message from God given to Judah by Isaiah, and it puts the message in a limited historical context. **1.2–20** God brings a legal suit against his people because of their breach of the Mosaic covenant. **1.2–3** The accusation. *Heavens* and *earth* are summoned as witnesses (cf. Deut 32.1; Ps 50; Mic 6.1–8) in this lawsuit because they were witnesses when the covenant was originally made (Deut 4.23–26; 30.19; 31.24–30). God, the father of the people of Israel, charges them with being rebellious children (Deut 32.5–6), a crime subject to the death penalty in Israelite law (Deut 21.18–21). **1.3** *Israel* is sometimes used as a specific reference to the Northern Kingdom, but here it is an inclusive designation for God's people, since Zion, the capital city of Judah, the Southern Kingdom, is mentioned (v. 8). The nation's behavior shows less understanding than that normally encountered in dumb animals (cf. Jer 8.7). **1.4–9** Direct address to Israel underscoring the folly of its wicked behavior. **1.4** *Ah,* sometimes translated *Ho* (55.1), a simple exclamation to get the attention of those being addressed (5.8, 11, 18). The following words identify them as God's wicked *children* mentioned in v. 2. *Holy One of Israel,* one of Isaiah's fa-

vorite designations for God (5.19, 24; 10.20; 12.6; 17.7; 29.19; 30.11–12, 15; 31.1; 37.23). It expresses the unapproachable majesty and sanctity of this God (cf. 6.1–5), who nonetheless graciously chose Israel and lives in its midst (12.6; Ex 24.9–11). **1.5–6** To treat such a holy God with contempt is utter folly. Israel has already been disciplined so harshly that it is like a person whose whole body is covered with untreated wounds yet who continues to provoke more punishment. **1.7–8** The historical reality behind Isaiah's metaphor of discipline appears to be the desolation of the land caused by one of the Assyrian invasions, probably that of Sennacherib in 701 BCE. *Zion,* another name for Jerusalem, which Sennacherib isolated and besieged. *Daughter Zion,* personification of the city as a young woman carrying an undertone of affection or sympathy. **1.9** LORD *of hosts,* another of Isaiah's choice designations for God; it occurs fifty-six times in chs. 1–39. The epithet portrays God as the king and leader of the army of heavenly beings (1 Kings 22.19) and thus underscores God's great imperial power (2 Sam 6.2; Ps 24.10; Isa 6.3). *Sodom* and *Gomorrah* were proverbial as cities utterly destroyed by God (13.19; Gen 19.24–29; Deut 29.23; Jer 49.18; 50.40; Am 4.11; Zeph 2.9). **1.10–17** God rejects ritual worship until such rituals are accompanied by a genuine change to moral behavior (cf. 29.13–14; Jer 6.20; 7.1–15; Am 5.21–24). **1.10** *Sodom* and *Gomorrah* were also

11 What to me is the multitude of your
sacrifices?
says the LORD;
I have had enough of burnt offerings of
rams
and the fat of fed beasts;
I do not delight in the blood of bulls,
or of lambs, or of goats.

12 When you come to appear before me,ᵃ
who asked this from your hand?
Trample my courts no more;
13 bringing offerings is futile;
incense is an abomination to me.
New moon and sabbath and calling of
convocation—
I cannot endure solemn assemblies
with iniquity.
14 Your new moons and your appointed
festivals
my soul hates;
they have become a burden to me,
I am weary of bearing them.
15 When you stretch out your hands,
I will hide my eyes from you;
even though you make many prayers,
I will not listen;
your hands are full of blood.
16 Wash yourselves; make yourselves clean;
remove the evil of your doings
from before my eyes;
cease to do evil,
17 learn to do good;
seek justice,
rescue the oppressed,
defend the orphan,
plead for the widow.

18 Come now, let us argue it out,
says the LORD:

though your sins are like scarlet,
they shall be like snow;
though they are red like crimson,
they shall become like wool.
19 If you are willing and obedient,
you shall eat the good of the land;
20 but if you refuse and rebel,
you shall be devoured by the sword;
for the mouth of the LORD has spoken.

The Degenerate City

21 How the faithful city
has become a whore!
She that was full of justice,
righteousness lodged in her—
but now murderers!
22 Your silver has become dross,
your wine is mixed with water.
23 Your princes are rebels
and companions of thieves.
Everyone loves a bribe
and runs after gifts.
They do not defend the orphan,
and the widow's cause does not come
before them.

24 Therefore says the Sovereign, the LORD of
hosts, the Mighty One of Israel:
Ah, I will pour out my wrath on my
enemies,
and avenge myself on my foes!
25 I will turn my hand against you;
I will smelt away your dross as with lye
and remove all your alloy.
26 And I will restore your judges as at the
first,
and your counselors as at the
beginning.

_____
ᵃ Or see my face

proverbial as utterly wicked cities (3.9; Gen 19.1–23; Deut 32.32; Jer 23.14; Lam 4.6). **1.14** _My soul,_ a Hebrew idiom meaning "I." **1.15** _Hands . . . full of blood,_ hands stained by murder and violent oppression. **1.17** Because of their relative powerlessness _orphans_ and _widows_ were two classes of people often subject to oppression in ancient Near Eastern societies. Following the Near Eastern legal tradition, Israelite law extended special concern for their protection (Ex 22.21; Deut 24.17; 27.19), and this concern is also reflected in Israel's other religious literature (Job 31.16; Ps 94.6; Jer 7.6; Zech 7.10). **1.18–20** The covenantal choice of life or death (cf. Deut 30.19–20). **1.18** _Argue,_ as in a lawsuit before a judge (cf. Job 23.7). The use of _scarlet_ and _crimson_ as metaphors for wickedness probably arose from the association of these colors with blood (cf. v. 15); cloth of this color was used in certain sin offerings (Lev 14.4–6, 49–52; Num 19.6). **1.21–28** The once glorious city must be purged to restore it to its former honor. **1.21–23** God laments the city's corruption. _Whore._ Cf. Jer 3.6–10; Ezek 16, 23; Hos 1–3. **1.24–28** God's solution is a purging judgment. **1.24** _Mighty One of Israel,_ a unique Isaian variant of the more common epithet _Mighty One of Jacob_ (49.26; 60.16; Gen 49.24; Ps 132.2, 5) portraying God as a warrior. **1.25** _As with lye,_ better "in a furnace" (cf. 48.10), since lye was not used in the smelting process. **1.26** The _judges_ and _counselors_ can only refer to royal officials of the Da-

Afterward you shall be called the city of
    righteousness,
        the faithful city.

27 Zion shall be redeemed by justice,
        and those in her who repent, by
            righteousness.
28 But rebels and sinners shall be destroyed
            together,
        and those who forsake the LORD shall
            be consumed.
29 For you shall be ashamed of the oaks
        in which you delighted;
    and you shall blush for the gardens
        that you have chosen.
30 For you shall be like an oak
        whose leaf withers,
    and like a garden without water.
31 The strong shall become like tinder,
        and their work[a] like a spark;
    they and their work shall burn together,
        with no one to quench them.

The Future House of God

2 The word that Isaiah son of Amoz saw
    concerning Judah and Jerusalem.

2 In days to come
    the mountain of the LORD's house
shall be established as the highest of the
        mountains,
    and shall be raised above the hills;
all the nations shall stream to it.
3   Many peoples shall come and say,
    "Come, let us go up to the mountain of
        the LORD,
    to the house of the God of Jacob;
        that he may teach us his ways

and that we may walk in his paths."
For out of Zion shall go forth instruction,
    and the word of the LORD from
        Jerusalem.
4 He shall judge between the nations,
    and shall arbitrate for many peoples;
they shall beat their swords into
        plowshares,
    and their spears into pruning hooks;
nation shall not lift up sword against
        nation,
    neither shall they learn war any more.

Judgment Pronounced on Arrogance

5 O house of Jacob,
    come, let us walk
        in the light of the LORD!
6 For you have forsaken the ways of[b] your
        people,
    O house of Jacob.
Indeed they are full of diviners[c] from the
        east
    and of soothsayers like the Philistines,
    and they clasp hands with foreigners.
7 Their land is filled with silver and gold,
    and there is no end to their treasures;
their land is filled with horses,
    and there is no end to their chariots.
8 Their land is filled with idols;
    they bow down to the work of their
        hands,
    to what their own fingers have made.
9 And so people are humbled,
    and everyone is brought low—
        do not forgive them!

---

a Or its makers b Heb lacks the ways of c Cn: Heb lacks of
diviners

---

vidic era, since Jerusalem first became an Israelite city
in his day (2 Sam 5.6–9). **1.27–28** Only the repentant
will survive the judgment (cf. vv. 18–20; 33.14–16).
1.29–31 The prophet condemns sacred groves as
pagan cult symbols (17.10–11); in the religious reform
of his contemporary King Hezekiah they were destroyed (2 Kings 18.4). **1.31** *Strong* here refers to the
oak (cf. Am 2.9). *Their work,* better *its makers* (see text
note *a*); it refers to the human keepers of the grove.
There is a wordplay in Hebrew between *its makers* and
their work in the following line.
    2.1 Second superscription. This can be for ch. 2 or
chs. 2–4. **2.2–4** Elevated above all other sites as the divine abode (for this motif, cf. Pss 48.1–2; 78.68–69;
Ezek 40.2; Zech 14.10), Jerusalem will one day be acknowledged by the nations as the imperial capital. Just
as political suzerains in the ancient Near East arbi-

trated disputes among their vassals, so God as suzerain
over all the nations will settle international disputes by
arbitration at Jerusalem, thus bringing an end to war.
This oracle also occurs in Mic 4.1–3. **2.5–22** Judgment
threatened against the house of Jacob and every rival
to God's majesty. **2.5–6a** These verses form a logical
connection between the preceding and following oracles. *House of Jacob,* presumably the Northern Kingdom, Israel (9.8; 17.4; cf. 8.17; 10.20–21). Since the nations are going to come to God in Jerusalem, Israel,
which has forsaken the ways of its people, is also invited to return and once more walk with God. Mic
4.4–5 ends the oracle differently. **2.6b–22** The sin of
Jacob/Israel is illustrated (vv. 6–9) and God's judgment is announced (vv. 10–22). **2.6b** *Diviners* and
soothsayers were regarded as pagan fortune-tellers and
were not to be consulted in Israel (Deut 18.14). In par-

10 Enter into the rock,
    and hide in the dust
  from the terror of the LORD,
    and from the glory of his majesty.
11 The haughty eyes of people shall be
        brought low,
    and the pride of everyone shall be
        humbled;
  and the LORD alone will be exalted on
        that day.
12 For the LORD of hosts has a day
    against all that is proud and lofty,
    against all that is lifted up and high;[a]
13 against all the cedars of Lebanon,
    lofty and lifted up;
    and against all the oaks of Bashan;
14 against all the high mountains,
    and against all the lofty hills;
15 against every high tower,
    and against every fortified wall;
16 against all the ships of Tarshish,
    and against all the beautiful craft.[b]
17 The haughtiness of people shall be
        humbled,
    and the pride of everyone shall be
        brought low;
  and the LORD alone will be exalted on
        that day.
18 The idols shall utterly pass away.
19 Enter the caves of the rocks
    and the holes of the ground,
  from the terror of the LORD,
    and from the glory of his majesty,
    when he rises to terrify the earth.
20 On that day people will throw away
    to the moles and to the bats
  their idols of silver and their idols of
        gold,
    which they made for themselves to
        worship,

21 to enter the caverns of the rocks
    and the clefts in the crags,
  from the terror of the LORD,
    and from the glory of his majesty,
    when he rises to terrify the earth.
22 Turn away from mortals,
    who have only breath in their nostrils,
    for of what account are they?

3 For now the Sovereign, the LORD of hosts,
    is taking away from Jerusalem and from
        Judah
  support and staff—
    all support of bread,
    and all support of water—
2 warrior and soldier,
    judge and prophet,
    diviner and elder,
3 captain of fifty
    and dignitary,
  counselor and skillful magician
    and expert enchanter.
4 And I will make boys their princes,
    and babes shall rule over them.
5 The people will be oppressed,
    everyone by another
    and everyone by a neighbor;
  the youth will be insolent to the elder,
    and the base to the honorable.

6 Someone will even seize a relative,
    a member of the clan, saying,
  "You have a cloak;
    you shall be our leader,
  and this heap of ruins
    shall be under your rule."
7 But the other will cry out on that day,
        saying,

a Cn Compare Gk: Heb low   b Compare Gk: Meaning of Heb
uncertain

allel to the Philistines on the west, *east* must refer to
the Arameans (9.12). **2.11–12** Just as God's city is exalted above all rivals (v. 2), so God is exalted above all
rivals (cf. 6.1–5). *On that day* and *the LORD . . . has a
day* pick up the common prophetic theme of the "day
of the LORD," that day on which God will judge his enemies and manifest his glory (13.6, 9; Ezek 13.5; Joel
1.15; 2.11, 31; 3.14; Am 5.18–20; Ob 15; Zeph 1.7, 14;
Mal 4.5). **2.13–14** *Lebanon,* the mountainous area just
north of Israel ruled by the Phoenician king of Tyre.
Bashan, the high plateau in northern Transjordan
controlled in this period by the Aramean king of Damascus. The mention of Lebanon, Bashan, and *high
mountains* may suggest the Aramean state and its Tyrian ally as God's political and religious rival (cf. Ps

68.15–16). **2.16** *Ships* can symbolize forces hostile to
God and his city (33.21–23; Ps 48.7). **2.19–20** Palestine's innumerable limestone *caves* have always served
as a refuge, as hiding places for abandoned goods, and
as a home for *bats.*
  3.1–15 Judgment on Jerusalem and Judah. **3.1–
9** The breakdown of Judean society. **3.1** *Support and
staff,* originally the human functionaries deemed necessary for the continuity and stability of the society
(vv. 2–3); *bread* and *water* represent a secondary reinterpretation (Ezek 4.16). **3.4–5** *Boys, babes, youth.* God
will replace the experienced officials with inexperienced and naive rulers, and the result will be social
chaos, including open oppression and violence. **3.6–
7** The breakdown in authority will be so complete that

"I will not be a healer;
    in my house there is neither bread nor
        cloak;
you shall not make me
    leader of the people."
8 For Jerusalem has stumbled
    and Judah has fallen,
because their speech and their deeds are
        against the LORD,
    defying his glorious presence.

9 The look on their faces bears witness
        against them;
    they proclaim their sin like Sodom,
    they do not hide it.
Woe to them!
    For they have brought evil on
        themselves.
10 Tell the innocent how fortunate they are,
    for they shall eat the fruit of their
        labors.
11 Woe to the guilty! How unfortunate they
        are,
    for what their hands have done shall be
        done to them.
12 My people—children are their
        oppressors,
    and women rule over them.
O my people, your leaders mislead you,
    and confuse the course of your paths.

13 The LORD rises to argue his case;
    he stands to judge the peoples.
14 The LORD enters into judgment
    with the elders and princes of his
        people:
It is you who have devoured the vineyard;
    the spoil of the poor is in your houses.
15 What do you mean by crushing my
        people,

by grinding the face of the poor? says
    the Lord GOD of hosts.

16 The LORD said:
Because the daughters of Zion are
        haughty
    and walk with outstretched necks,
    glancing wantonly with their eyes,
mincing along as they go,
    tinkling with their feet;
17 the Lord will afflict with scabs
    the heads of the daughters of Zion,
    and the LORD will lay bare their secret
        parts.

18 In that day the Lord will take away the
finery of the anklets, the headbands, and the
crescents; 19the pendants, the bracelets, and
the scarfs; 20the headdresses, the armlets, the
sashes, the perfume boxes, and the amulets;
21the signet rings and nose rings; 22the festal
robes, the mantles, the cloaks, and the hand-
bags; 23the garments of gauze, the linen garments, the turbans, and the veils.
24 Instead of perfume there will be a stench;
    and instead of a sash, a rope;
    and instead of well-set hair, baldness;
    and instead of a rich robe, a binding of
        sackcloth;
    instead of beauty, shame.ᵃ
25 Your men shall fall by the sword
    and your warriors in battle.
26 And her gates shall lament and mourn;
    ravaged, she shall sit upon the ground.
4 Seven women shall take hold of one man
    in that day, saying,
"We will eat our own bread and wear our
        own clothes;

_____
a Q Ms: MT lacks shame

no one will want the thankless task of being *leader* and
ruling Judah. **3.8–9** *The look on their faces.* Judah's
rulers, by their shameless, brazen sinfulness, have
brought this judgment on themselves. **3.10–11** A wisdom saying distinguishing the fate of the *innocent* and
the *guilty.* **3.12–15** An indictment of Judah's leadership. **3.12** *Children, women.* Judah's childish rulers are
unduly influenced by the selfish desires of their
women (vv. 16–17; 32.9–14; cf. Am 4.1–3). **3.13–
14** The Lord takes the leaders of his people to court. *Elders,* prominent representatives of the people who had
an influential voice in governmental policies and the
administration of justice (Deut 21.19–21; 2 Kings
23.1). *Princes,* government officials not necessarily re-

lated to the royal family. *Vineyard,* a metaphor for
God's people (5.1–7). **3.16–4.1** The humiliation of
Zion's haughty women (32.9–14; Am 4.1–3).
3.17 *Their secret parts,* better "their foreheads"; God
threatens the women with baldness (cf. v. 24). **3.18–
24** All their stylish clothes and accessories will be lost
on the day of judgment. **3.26** *Her gates.* The prophet
shifts from the image of the humiliated women of
Jerusalem to a personification of the city itself as a
woman. *Ground,* an inappropriate resting place for a
noblewoman (47.1). **4.1** Because of the severe reduction of the male population (3.25), women will be
forced to accept humiliating conditions for even a
token respectability.

just let us be called by your name;
    take away our disgrace."

The Future Glory of the Survivors in Zion

2 On that day the branch of the LORD shall be beautiful and glorious, and the fruit of the land shall be the pride and glory of the survivors of Israel. ³Whoever is left in Zion and remains in Jerusalem will be called holy, everyone who has been recorded for life in Jerusalem, ⁴once the Lord has washed away the filth of the daughters of Zion and cleansed the bloodstains of Jerusalem from its midst by a spirit of judgment and by a spirit of burning. ⁵Then the LORD will create over the whole site of Mount Zion and over its places of assembly a cloud by day and smoke and the shining of a flaming fire by night. Indeed over all the glory there will be a canopy. ⁶It will serve as a pavilion, a shade by day from the heat, and a refuge and a shelter from the storm and rain.

The Song of the Unfruitful Vineyard

5 Let me sing for my beloved
    my love-song concerning his vineyard:
My beloved had a vineyard
    on a very fertile hill.
2 He dug it and cleared it of stones,
    and planted it with choice vines;
he built a watchtower in the midst of it,
    and hewed out a wine vat in it;
he expected it to yield grapes,
    but it yielded wild grapes.

3 And now, inhabitants of Jerusalem

and people of Judah,
judge between me
    and my vineyard.
4 What more was there to do for my
        vineyard
    that I have not done in it?
When I expected it to yield grapes,
    why did it yield wild grapes?

5 And now I will tell you
    what I will do to my vineyard.
I will remove its hedge,
    and it shall be devoured;
I will break down its wall,
    and it shall be trampled down.
6 I will make it a waste;
    it shall not be pruned or hoed,
    and it shall be overgrown with briers
        and thorns;
I will also command the clouds
    that they rain no rain upon it.

7 For the vineyard of the LORD of hosts
    is the house of Israel,
and the people of Judah
    are his pleasant planting;
he expected justice,
    but saw bloodshed;
righteousness,
    but heard a cry!

Social Injustice Denounced

8 Ah, you who join house to house,
    who add field to field,
until there is room for no one but you,

4.2–6 The purified Jerusalem. **4.2** *Branch,* either the messiah (11.1, 10; Jer 23.5; 33.15; Zech 3.8; 6.12) or the righteous remnant (60.21; 61.3). *Fruit of the land,* the righteous remnant (27.6; 37.31–32; 44.1–5). **4.3** *Called holy,* an idiom implying a real change in character, not just a forensic designation (cf. 1.26). *Recorded for life,* inscribed in God's book of life (Ex 32.32; Ps 69.28; Dan 12.1; Mal 3.16; Rev 20.12, 15). **4.4** Zion purified by a burning judgment (cf. 1.25–28). **4.5** *Cloud by day, fire by night,* imagery from the exodus tradition (Ex 13.21–22; 40.34–38) symbolizing God's protecting presence in Jerusalem. **4.6** *Shelter . . . rain.* See 25.4.

5.1–7 This unique poem, sung by the prophet on behalf of his friend, operates on several levels—as a love song, judicial parable, and judgment oracle. **5.1** The poem works metaphorically as a *love-song,* since *vineyard* is a standard metaphor for "lover" in Israelite love poetry (Song 1.6, 14; 2.3, 15; 4.12–16; 7.6–13; 8.12). **5.2** The friend's love for the "vineyard" is un-

requited. **5.3–4** The prophet's friend, now quoted directly, calls upon the people of Judah to judge his "vineyard," but in judging the vineyard the people unwittingly pass judgment on themselves. They are entrapped by Isaiah's love song much as David was entrapped by Nathan's parable (2 Sam 12.1–12). **5.7** *Vineyard,* a common metaphor for God's people in Israelite poetry (27.2–6; Ps 80.8–16; Jer 2.21; Ezek 19.10–14; Hos 10.1). The prophet plays on the similarity in sound between the Hebrew words for *justice* (*mishpat*) and *bloodshed* (*mispach*), *righteousness* (*tsedaqah*) and *cry* (*tse'aqah*), the cry of the oppressed. **5.8–24** Series of oracles against social injustice (vv. 8–10, 11–13, 14–17, 18–19, 20, 21, 22–24). Such oracles introduced by *Ah* are often arranged in a series (cf. 28.1; 29.1, 15; 30.1; 31.1; 33.1; Hab 2.6–19). **5.8–10** Against the amassing of property at others' expense (Mic 2.1–6, 8–9). *Bath,* a liquid measure of approximately 5.5 gallons, a grotesquely small yield for 10 acres of vineyard. *Homer,* a dry measure of ap-

and you are left to live alone
in the midst of the land!
9 The LORD of hosts has sworn in my
hearing:
Surely many houses shall be desolate,
large and beautiful houses, without
inhabitant.
10 For ten acres of vineyard shall yield but
one bath,
and a homer of seed shall yield a mere
ephah.*a*

11 Ah, you who rise early in the morning
in pursuit of strong drink,
who linger in the evening
to be inflamed by wine,
12 whose feasts consist of lyre and harp,
tambourine and flute and wine,
but who do not regard the deeds of the
LORD,
or see the work of his hands!
13 Therefore my people go into exile
without knowledge;
their nobles are dying of hunger,
and their multitude is parched with
thirst.

14 Therefore Sheol has enlarged its appetite
and opened its mouth beyond measure;
the nobility of Jerusalem*b* and her
multitude go down,
her throng and all who exult in her.
15 People are bowed down, everyone is
brought low,
and the eyes of the haughty are
humbled.

16 But the LORD of hosts is exalted by
justice,
and the Holy God shows himself holy
by righteousness.
17 Then the lambs shall graze as in their
pasture,
fatlings and kids*c* shall feed among the
ruins.

18 Ah, you who drag iniquity along with
cords of falsehood,
who drag sin along as with cart
ropes,
19 who say, "Let him make haste,
let him speed his work
that we may see it;
let the plan of the Holy One of Israel
hasten to fulfillment,
that we may know it!"
20 Ah, you who call evil good
and good evil,
who put darkness for light
and light for darkness,
who put bitter for sweet
and sweet for bitter!
21 Ah, you who are wise in your own eyes,
and shrewd in your own sight!
22 Ah, you who are heroes in drinking
wine
and valiant at mixing drink,
23 who acquit the guilty for a bribe,
and deprive the innocent of their
rights!

---

a The Heb *bath, homer,* and *ephah* are measures of quantity
b Heb *her nobility*   *c* Cn Compare Gk: Heb *aliens*

proximately 6.5 bushels. *Ephah,* a dry measure equal to only one-tenth of a *homer* (see Ezek 45.11). **5.11–13** Against drink and debauchery (Am 6.4–7). **5.11** *Strong drink,* an ambiguously misleading translation for a word that probably means barley beer. It has that meaning in modern Hebrew, and the Akkadian cognate means "beer" in Mesopotamian sources contemporary with Isaiah. Beer was well known in both Egypt and Mesopotamia, and it would be curious if beer were not brewed in the barley-raising areas between these two cultures. *Strong drink* suggests distilled liquors, which were probably still unknown, though some recent archaeological evidence suggests that an early form of pomace brandy similar to grappa or marc was known. *To be inflamed by wine,* a remarkable wordplay better rendered "until wine chases them." Until the very last syllable readers or hearers expect simple parallelism—"to pursue beer, . . . to chase wine"—but the last syllable subverts expectations, so

that those who pursue alcoholic drinks end up no longer in control, being chased by the very thing they pursued. **5.12** The *deeds, work,* or plan of God is a central motif in Isaiah's message (5.19; 10.12; 14.24–27; 19.12, 17; 23.9; 28.21; 30.1). **5.13** *Without knowledge,* because of a lack of knowledge (1.3; Hos 4.1, 6). **5.14–17** A fragmentary oracle against Jerusalem. The introduction to this oracle with the explicit denunciation of the city has apparently been lost, leaving only the announcement of judgment. **5.14** *Sheol,* the underworld, where the dead go (14.9–18). A similar threat that the city would sink into the underworld is found in 29.4. **5.15** Cf. 2.9, 17. **5.16** *Justice . . . righteousness.* God's judgment is just (cf. 28.23–29). **5.18–19** Against scoffers who urged God to hurry up with the divine work so they could discern it (v. 12; cf. Jer 17.15–16). **5.20** Against moral confusion (32.5; Prov 17.15). **5.21** Against the conceit of the wise (Prov 3.7; 26.5, 12, 16; 28.11). **5.22–23** Against indulgence and bribery

Foreign Invasion Predicted

24 Therefore, as the tongue of fire devours
         the stubble,
    and as dry grass sinks down in the
         flame,
 so their root will become rotten,
    and their blossom go up like dust;
 for they have rejected the instruction of
         the LORD of hosts,
    and have despised the word of the
         Holy One of Israel.

25 Therefore the anger of the LORD was
         kindled against his people,
    and he stretched out his hand against
         them and struck them;
    the mountains quaked,
 and their corpses were like refuse
    in the streets.
 For all this his anger has not turned away,
    and his hand is stretched out still.

26 He will raise a signal for a nation far
         away,
    and whistle for a people at the ends of
         the earth;
 Here they come, swiftly, speedily!
27 None of them is weary, none stumbles,
    none slumbers or sleeps,
 not a loincloth is loose,
    not a sandal-thong broken;
28 their arrows are sharp,
    all their bows bent,
 their horses' hoofs seem like flint,
    and their wheels like the whirlwind.
29 Their roaring is like a lion,
    like young lions they roar;

    they growl and seize their prey,
       they carry it off, and no one can
          rescue.
30 They will roar over it on that day,
       like the roaring of the sea.
    And if one look to the land—
       only darkness and distress;
    and the light grows dark with clouds.

A Vision of God in the Temple

6 In the year that King Uzziah died, I saw the Lord sitting on a throne, high and lofty; and the hem of his robe filled the temple. ²Seraphs were in attendance above him; each had six wings: with two they covered their faces, and with two they covered their feet, and with two they flew. ³And one called to another and said:

    "Holy, holy, holy is the LORD of hosts;
       the whole earth is full of his glory."

⁴The pivots[a] on the thresholds shook at the voices of those who called, and the house filled with smoke. ⁵And I said: "Woe is me! I am lost, for I am a man of unclean lips, and I live among a people of unclean lips; yet my eyes have seen the King, the LORD of hosts!"

6 Then one of the seraphs flew to me, holding a live coal that had been taken from the altar with a pair of tongs. ⁷The seraph[b] touched my mouth with it and said: "Now that this has touched your lips, your guilt has departed and your sin is blotted out." ⁸Then I heard the voice of the Lord saying, "Whom shall I send, and who will go for us?" And I said, "Here am I; send me!" ⁹And he said, "Go and say to this people:

---

a Meaning of Heb uncertain   b Heb He

(cf. Prov 31.4–5). **5.24** Concluding judgment on these perpetrators of social injustice. **5.25–30** These verses should probably follow 9.8–21. **5.25** As in 9.8–21, this past judgment on Israel did not lead to its repentance, so God's anger is still unabated (see 9.12, 17, 21; 10.4). **5.26–30** God will summon the Assyrians as his agent to punish Israel (cf. 7.18–20; 8.7; 10.5–6). The negative use of the lion metaphor to characterize the punishing Assyrians is picked up in 31.4 to characterize God as the punisher of Jerusalem.

6.1–13 Isaiah's prophetic commission is described as a response to an awesome vision of God as divine suzerain (cf. the portrayals of the enthroned deity in 1 Kings 22.19–23; Ezek 1.4–2.1). **6.1** *Year,* probably 738 BCE. *The Lord sitting on a throne, high and lofty,* better "The Lord sitting on a high and lofty throne," the 15-foot-high throne in the inner sanctum of the

temple formed by the outspread wings of the two giant cherubim (1 Kings 6.22–29; 2 Kings 19.15; Ezek 10.1–2; 1 Chr 28.18). *Hem,* the border on the bottom of God's robe or the part hanging down from the knees; the image is that of a God too gigantic to be contained in the temple (66.1; 1 Kings 8.27). **6.2** *Seraphs,* winged cobras (14.29; 30.6) often represented in Egyptian art, in association with Syro-Phoenician thrones, and on late eighth-century Judean seals, with wings outstretched to protect the deity. *Covered their faces.* Here, rather than protect the deity, they must protect themselves from the glory of God. **6.5** *I am lost,* a double entendre that could also be rendered "I am silenced." *Unclean lips.* See 29.13. It was life-threatening for sinful mortals to see God (Ex 33.20; Judg 13.22). **6.6–8** Cleansed by the burning coal from the altar, Isaiah may now speak for God. **6.9–12** The message God

'Keep listening, but do not comprehend;
keep looking, but do not understand.'

10 Make the mind of this people dull,
    and stop their ears,
    and shut their eyes,
so that they may not look with their eyes,
    and listen with their ears,
and comprehend with their minds,
    and turn and be healed."

11 Then I said, "How long, O Lord?" And he
    said:
"Until cities lie waste
    without inhabitant,
and houses without people,
    and the land is utterly desolate;

12 until the LORD sends everyone far away,
    and vast is the emptiness in the midst
      of the land.

13 Even if a tenth part remain in it,
    it will be burned again,
like a terebinth or an oak
    whose stump remains standing
    when it is felled." [a]
The holy seed is its stump.

Isaiah Reassures King Ahaz

7 In the days of Ahaz son of Jotham son of Uzziah, king of Judah, King Rezin of Aram and King Pekah son of Remaliah of Israel went up to attack Jerusalem, but could not mount an attack against it. 2When the house of David heard that Aram had allied itself with Ephraim, the heart of Ahaz [b] and the heart of his people shook as the trees of the forest shake before the wind.

3 Then the LORD said to Isaiah, Go out to meet Ahaz, you and your son Shear-jashub, [c] at the end of the conduit of the upper pool on the highway to the Fuller's Field, 4and say to him, Take heed, be quiet, do not fear, and do not let your heart be faint because of these two smoldering stumps of firebrands, because of the fierce anger of Rezin and Aram and the son of Remaliah. 5Because Aram—with Ephraim and the son of Remaliah—has plotted evil against you, saying, 6Let us go up against Judah and cut off Jerusalem [d] and conquer it for ourselves and make the son of Tabeel king in it; 7therefore thus says the Lord GOD:

It shall not stand,
    and it shall not come to pass.

8 For the head of Aram is Damascus,
    and the head of Damascus is Rezin.
(Within sixty-five years Ephraim will be shattered, no longer a people.)

9 The head of Ephraim is Samaria,
    and the head of Samaria is the son of
      Remaliah.
If you do not stand firm in faith,
    you shall not stand at all.

Isaiah Gives Ahaz the Sign of Immanuel

10 Again the LORD spoke to Ahaz, saying, 11Ask a sign of the LORD your God; let it be deep as Sheol or high as heaven. 12But Ahaz said, I will not ask, and I will not put the LORD to the test. 13Then Isaiah [e] said: "Hear then, O house of David! Is it too little for you to

---

a Meaning of Heb uncertain   *b* Heb *his heart*   *c* That is *A remnant shall return*   *d* Heb *cut it off*   *e* Heb *he*

---

gives Isaiah will not lead to repentance, but to the hardening of the people's heart, thus making them ripe for God's judgment. Cf. 29.9–14; see also the NT citations of vv. 9–10 in Mt 13.10–17; Mk 4.10–12; Lk 8.9–10; Jn 12.40; Acts 28.25–29. **6.13** The last part of the verse is textually uncertain and unclear.

7.1–8.18 Isaiah and the Syro-Ephraimite war (735–732 BCE). The prophet's message is organized around the symbolic names given to his three children (see 8.18; cf. Hos 1.4–9). For the historical background, see 2 Kings 15.29–16.20; 2 Chr 28.1–27. **7.1–9** The symbolic name of Isaiah's first child assures Ahaz that Israel and Aram's plan against Judah will not succeed. **7.1** *Aram,* Syria, with its capital at Damascus. **7.2** *Ephraim,* the Northern Kingdom; this coalition of Aram and Israel planned to remove Ahaz and end the Davidic dynasty's rule over Judah (see v. 6). **7.3** *Shear-jashub,* in Hebrew "A remnant shall return"; only a remnant of the hostile Northern Kingdom will survive

(v. 8; 10.20–22). **7.6** *Tabeel,* perhaps a garbled transcription of (It)tobaal, king of Tyre in 738 BCE; Tyre was allied with the coalition. **7.8–9** God chose both Jerusalem and the Davidic dynasty (Pss 2.6; 132.11–14), so the humanly chosen kings and capital cities of Judah's enemies cannot prevail against them. The repetitive nature of these verses appears to have led to a serious haplography and subsequent corruption. A promise *sixty-five years* in the future would be irrelevant to Ahaz's immediate danger, and no known historical event occurred at that time, so it makes little sense as a later gloss. The original text probably read something like: "For the head of Aram is Damascus, and the head of Damascus is Rezin, and the head of Ephraim is Samaria, and the head of Samaria is the son of Remaliah; within five years Ephraim will be shattered from being a people, and within six Damascus will be removed from being a city" (cf. 17.1). **7.10–17** The symbolic name of the second child gives fur-

weary mortals, that you weary my God also? [14]Therefore the Lord himself will give you a sign. Look, the young woman[a] is with child and shall bear a son, and shall name him Immanuel.[b] [15]He shall eat curds and honey by the time he knows how to refuse the evil and choose the good. [16]For before the child knows how to refuse the evil and choose the good, the land before whose two kings you are in dread will be deserted. [17]The Lord will bring on you and on your people and on your ancestral house such days as have not come since the day that Ephraim departed from Judah—the king of Assyria."

18 On that day the Lord will whistle for the fly that is at the sources of the streams of Egypt, and for the bee that is in the land of Assyria. [19]And they will all come and settle in the steep ravines, and in the clefts of the rocks, and on all the thornbushes, and on all the pastures.

20 On that day the Lord will shave with a razor hired beyond the River—with the king of Assyria—the head and the hair of the feet, and it will take off the beard as well.

21 On that day one will keep alive a young cow and two sheep, [22]and will eat curds because of the abundance of milk that they give; for everyone that is left in the land shall eat curds and honey.

23 On that day every place where there used to be a thousand vines, worth a thousand shekels of silver, will become briers and thorns. [24]With bow and arrows one will go there, for all the land will be briers and thorns; [25]and as for all the hills that used to be hoed with a hoe, you will not go there for fear of briers and thorns; but they will become a place where cattle are let loose and where sheep tread.

Isaiah's Son a Sign of the Assyrian Invasion

8 Then the Lord said to me, Take a large tablet and write on it in common characters, "Belonging to Maher-shalal-hash-baz,"[c] [2]and have it attested[d] for me by reliable witnesses, the priest Uriah and Zechariah son of Jeberechiah. [3]And I went to the prophetess, and she conceived and bore a son. Then the Lord said to me, Name him Maher-shalal-hash-baz; [4]for before the child knows how to call "My father" or "My mother," the wealth of Damascus and the spoil of Samaria will be carried away by the king of Assyria.

5 The Lord spoke to me again: [6]Because this people has refused the waters of Shiloah that flow gently, and melt in fear before[e] Rezin and the son of Remaliah; [7]therefore, the Lord is bringing up against it the mighty flood waters of the River, the king of Assyria and all his glory; it will rise above all its channels and overflow all its banks; [8]it will sweep on into Judah as a flood, and, pouring over, it will

---

a Gk *the virgin*   *b* That is *God is with us*   *c* That is *The spoil speeds, the prey hastens*   *d* Q Ms Gk Syr: MT *and I caused to be attested*   *e* Cn: Meaning of Heb uncertain

---

ther reassurance to Ahaz. **7.13** The prophet treats Ahaz's pious-sounding remark as merely masking a refusal to trust the divine promise. **7.14** *Immanuel*, in Hebrew "God is with us," embodies the divine promise of protection to Jerusalem (Ps 46.4–7, 11; cf. Isa 8.9–10). **7.15** *Curds and honey*, choice foods for a newly weaned child, but hard to obtain in a city under siege. **7.16** *Before the child knows . . . good*, by the time the child is weaned—within two or three years—the besieging enemies will have long since been destroyed (cf. 8.4). **7.17** Whether the verse is a promise or a threat to Judah is ambiguous. **7.18–25** Four sayings that expand on v. 17. **7.18** *Fly*, a metaphor for Egyptian troops. *Bee*, a metaphor for Assyrian troops. **7.20** *Razor hired beyond the River*, a reference to Assyria as the agent God employed to punish Israel (see 10.5–15). *The River*, the Euphrates. *Feet*, a euphemism for the genitals (Ex 4.25). **7.21–25** The small remnant left in the devastated land will have sufficient to eat; with the cultivated land reverted to pasture there will be abundant grazing for the few livestock remaining.

8.1–4 The symbolic name of yet a third child reaffirms God's promise to Ahaz. **8.2** *Uriah*. See 2 Kings 16.10–16. *Zechariah*, possibly Ahaz's father-in-law (2 Kings 18.2). **8.3** *Prophetess*, Isaiah's wife. **8.4** *Before the child knows . . . "My mother*," before the child says his first words—within about a year. Note that with each succeeding child the time limit for the destruction of Ahaz's enemies is reduced—from five to six years (see note on 7.8–9), to two to three (see note on 7.16), to around one here. **8.5–10** Oracle threatening the devastation of Israel but the ultimate deliverance of Judah. **8.6** *Shiloah*, a gentle stream fed by Jerusalem's Gihon spring (cf. Neh 3.15), symbolizing the Davidic dynasty. *Melt in fear before*. The Hebrew may mean "delight in." *Rezin*, Aramean king of Damascus. *Son of Remaliah*, Pekah, king of Israel. **8.7** *The River*, the Euphrates, symbolizing Assyria. **8.8** *And its outspread wings*, better "But his (God's) outspread wings." The antecedent of the pronoun is probably *the Lord* in v. 7; although a standard metaphor for God's protection (Deut 32.11; Pss 17.8; 36.7; 57.1; 61.4; 63.7;

reach up to the neck; and its outspread wings will fill the breadth of your land, O Immanuel.

9 Band together, you peoples, and be
          dismayed;
      listen, all you far countries;
   gird yourselves and be dismayed;
      gird yourselves and be dismayed!
10 Take counsel together, but it shall be
          brought to naught;
      speak a word, but it will not stand,
          for God is with us. [a]

11 For the Lord spoke thus to me while his hand was strong upon me, and warned me not to walk in the way of this people, saying: 12 Do not call conspiracy all that this people calls conspiracy, and do not fear what it fears, or be in dread. 13 But the Lord of hosts, him you shall regard as holy; let him be your fear, and let him be your dread. 14 He will become a sanctuary, a stone one strikes against; for both houses of Israel he will become a rock one stumbles over—a trap and a snare for the inhabitants of Jerusalem. 15 And many among them shall stumble; they shall fall and be broken; they shall be snared and taken.

Disciples of Isaiah

16 Bind up the testimony, seal the teaching among my disciples. 17 I will wait for the Lord, who is hiding his face from the house of Jacob, and I will hope in him. 18 See, I and the children whom the Lord has given me are signs and portents in Israel from the Lord of hosts, who dwells on Mount Zion. 19 Now if people say to you, "Consult the ghosts and the familiar spirits that chirp and mutter; should not a people consult their gods, the dead on behalf of the living, 20 for teaching and for instruction?" surely, those who speak like this will have no dawn! 21 They will pass through the land, [b] greatly distressed and hungry; when they are hungry, they will be enraged and will curse [c] their king and their gods. They will turn their faces upward, 22 or they will look to the earth, but will see only distress and darkness, the gloom of anguish; and they will be thrust into thick darkness. [d]

The Righteous Reign of the Coming King

9 [e] But there will be no gloom for those who were in anguish. In the former time he brought into contempt the land of Zebulun and the land of Naphtali, but in the latter time he will make glorious the way of the sea, the land beyond the Jordan, Galilee of the nations.
2 [f] The people who walked in darkness
          have seen a great light;
      those who lived in a land of deep
          darkness—
          on them light has shined.
3 You have multiplied the nation,
          you have increased its joy;
      they rejoice before you
          as with joy at the harvest,
          as people exult when dividing plunder.
4 For the yoke of their burden,

---

a Heb *immanu el*   b Heb *it*   c Or *curse by*   d Meaning of Heb uncertain   e Ch 8.23 in Heb   f Ch 9.1 in Heb

---

91.1–4), *wings* is never used of rivers, and *Immanuel* suggests a positive word (see v. 10). **8.9–10** A promise of deliverance for Judah ending with a repetition of the symbolic name *God is with us,* "Immanuel" (cf. 7.7–9; 17.12–14). **8.11–15** The people are to sanctify and fear God, not what the crowd fears. **8.11** *His hand was strong upon me,* a technical expression for the onset of prophetic inspiration (Ezek 1.3; 3.14, 22; 33.22). **8.14** *Sanctuary,* a place of refuge. Both *stone* and *rock* were used in Israelite religious language as metaphors for God as a place of refuge (1 Sam 7.12; Ps 31.3); Isaiah adds a shocking modifier to each term to set up a terrifying contrast. God will be either a *sanctuary* or the *stone* or *rock* that destroys (cf. 28.16–17), depending on whether one fears God more than anything else. **8.16–18** The message preserved among Isaiah's circle of supporters while Israel remains disobedient (cf. 30.8–11). **8.16** *Bind, seal,* as one does a scroll (29.11). **8.18** *Signs,* the symbolic names of Isaiah's children. **8.19–22** Condemnation of necromancy (see 1 Sam 28.3–14 for this practice of consulting the dead). **8.19** *Chirp and mutter,* a disparaging comment about the necromancer's customary manner of speaking during the consultation of the dead (29.4).

9.1–7 This passage served originally as an oracle for the coronation of a Judean king, probably Hezekiah. It celebrates the accession of the new king with the traditional ideals of Davidic kingship (see 11.1–9). **9.1** The areas mentioned were turned into three Assyrian provinces by Tiglath-pileser III in 733–32 BCE: *Zebulun* and *Naphtali* represent the Assyrian province of *Galilee; the way of the sea* corresponds to the Assyrian province of Dor, south of Mount Carmel; and *the land beyond the Jordan* is equivalent to the province of Gilead. **9.2** *People,* the Israelite inhabitants of the areas annexed by Assyria (v. 1). *Darkness* is standard imagery for oppression, *light* for royal relief from such oppression. **9.3** *You have multiplied the nation, you have increased its joy,* better "You have multiplied exultation, you have increased rejoicing." **9.4** *Day of Mid-*

and the bar across their shoulders,
the rod of their oppressor,
you have broken as on the day of
Midian.
5 For all the boots of the tramping warriors
and all the garments rolled in blood
shall be burned as fuel for the fire.
6 For a child has been born for us,
a son given to us;
authority rests upon his shoulders;
and he is named
Wonderful Counselor, Mighty God,
Everlasting Father, Prince of Peace.
7 His authority shall grow continually,
and there shall be endless peace
for the throne of David and his kingdom.
He will establish and uphold it
with justice and with righteousness
from this time onward and
forevermore.
The zeal of the LORD of hosts will do this.

Judgment on Arrogance and Oppression

8 The Lord sent a word against Jacob,
and it fell on Israel;
9 and all the people knew it—
Ephraim and the inhabitants of
Samaria—
but in pride and arrogance of heart
they said:
10 "The bricks have fallen,
but we will build with dressed stones;
the sycamores have been cut down,
but we will put cedars in their place."
11 So the LORD raised adversaries^a against
them,
and stirred up their enemies,
12 the Arameans on the east and the
Philistines on the west,
and they devoured Israel with open
mouth.
For all this his anger has not turned away;
his hand is stretched out still.

13 The people did not turn to him who
struck them,
or seek the LORD of hosts.
14 So the LORD cut off from Israel head and
tail,
palm branch and reed in one day—
15 elders and dignitaries are the head,
and prophets who teach lies are the
tail;
16 for those who led this people led them
astray,
and those who were led by them were
left in confusion.
17 That is why the Lord did not have pity
on^b their young people,
or compassion on their orphans and
widows;
for everyone was godless and an evildoer,
and every mouth spoke folly.
For all this his anger has not turned away;
his hand is stretched out still.

18 For wickedness burned like a fire,
consuming briers and thorns;
it kindled the thickets of the forest,
and they swirled upward in a column
of smoke.
19 Through the wrath of the LORD of hosts
the land was burned,
and the people became like fuel for the
fire;
no one spared another.
20 They gorged on the right, but still were
hungry,
and they devoured on the left, but were
not satisfied;
they devoured the flesh of their own
kindred;^c
21 Manasseh devoured Ephraim, and
Ephraim Manasseh,

a Cn: Heb *the adversaries of Rezin* b Q Ms: MT *rejoice over*
c Or *arm*

---

ian. See Judg 7.15–25. **9.6** *Child, son.* The divine birth or adoption of the king was announced on his coronation day (see Ps 2.7). As in the Egyptian coronation ritual, where the birth is announced to the other gods, the *for us* probably refers to the angelic members of God's divine council. *Wonderful Counselor, Mighty God, Everlasting Father, Prince of Peace,* coronation names like those given Egyptian kings at their accession. **9.8–10.4** Israel's failure to learn from past judgments is a warning to Judah. Note the refrain (9.12, 17, 21; 10.4; 5.25). **9.8–12** Judgment on the Northern

Kingdom's unrepentant pride. **9.8** *Word,* prophetic announcement of judgment that sets in motion the judgment it proclaims (55.10–11; Jer 23.18–20). **9.9** *Ephraim,* designation for the Northern Kingdom; *Samaria,* its royal capital. **9.10** *Bricks, sycamores,* common building material. *Dressed stones, cedars,* expensive material used in palaces. **9.13–17** Judgment on Israel's leaders who led the people astray (see 3.12). **9.18–21** Wickedness led to the judgment of civil war. **9.20** *Flesh of their own kindred,* a striking metaphorical description of Israel's self-destruction in the sec-

and together they were against Judah.
For all this his anger has not turned away;
    his hand is stretched out still.

10

Ah, you who make iniquitous decrees,
    who write oppressive statutes,
2 to turn aside the needy from justice
    and to rob the poor of my people of
        their right,
that widows may be your spoil,
    and that you may make the orphans
        your prey!
3 What will you do on the day of
        punishment,
    in the calamity that will come from far
        away?
To whom will you flee for help,
    and where will you leave your wealth,
4 so as not to crouch among the prisoners
    or fall among the slain?
For all this his anger has not turned away;
    his hand is stretched out still.

Arrogant Assyria Also Judged

5 Ah, Assyria, the rod of my anger—
    the club in their hands is my fury!
6 Against a godless nation I send him,
    and against the people of my wrath I
        command him,
to take spoil and seize plunder,
    and to tread them down like the mire
        of the streets.
7 But this is not what he intends,
    nor does he have this in mind;
but it is in his heart to destroy,
    and to cut off nations not a few.
8 For he says:
"Are not my commanders all kings?
9 Is not Calno like Carchemish?
    Is not Hamath like Arpad?

Is not Samaria like Damascus?
10 As my hand has reached to the kingdoms
        of the idols
    whose images were greater than those
        of Jerusalem and Samaria,
11 shall I not do to Jerusalem and her idols
    what I have done to Samaria and her
        images?"

12 When the Lord has finished all his work
on Mount Zion and on Jerusalem, he[a] will
punish the arrogant boasting of the king of
Assyria and his haughty pride. 13 For he says:
"By the strength of my hand I have done
        it,
    and by my wisdom, for I have
        understanding;
I have removed the boundaries of
        peoples,
    and have plundered their treasures;
like a bull I have brought down those
        who sat on thrones.
14 My hand has found, like a nest,
    the wealth of the peoples;
and as one gathers eggs that have been
        forsaken,
    so I have gathered all the earth;
and there was none that moved a wing,
    or opened its mouth, or chirped."

15 Shall the ax vaunt itself over the one who
        wields it,
    or the saw magnify itself against the
        one who handles it?
As if a rod should raise the one who lifts
        it up,
    or as if a staff should lift the one who is
        not wood!

---

a Heb *I*

tional conflicts climaxing in the Syro-Ephraimite war.
9.21 *Manasseh, Ephraim,* tribes that constituted the
two major sectional rivals for dominance in the
Northern Kingdom. *Judah,* the Southern Kingdom.
10.1–4 Judgment on those who pervert justice by oppressive laws (Jer 8.8).
  10.5–19 Isaiah reassures Judah that God, not Assyria, controls history. Despite its arrogant pride, Assyria is just God's temporary instrument for punishing
others; soon it too will experience God's punishment.
10.9 *Calno,* or "Calneh" (Am 6.2), north Syrian city
that twice fell to the Assyrian king Tiglath-pileser (740
and 738 BCE). *Carchemish,* north Syrian city dominated by Tiglath-pileser and recaptured by the Assyr-

ian king Sargon II after a brief revolt against Assyrian
rule (717). *Hamath,* central Syrian territory captured
by Tiglath-pileser (738) and recaptured by Sargon in
720. *Arpad,* north Syrian city captured by Tiglath-pileser (740). *Samaria,* capital of Israel; it fell to Assyria
(722 and 720). *Damascus,* capital of southern Syria; it
fell to Tiglath-pileser in 732. **10.10–11** To the Assyrian
king, the God of Judah was just another idol (cf. 36.7–
10). **10.12** *Work,* God's strange work (28.21) of purging Zion by judgment (1.21–28; 29.1–8). **10.13** *Removed the boundaries.* Assyria absorbed whole nations
into their provincial system and used widespread resettlement of their populations to destroy former national identities. **10.15** Rhetorical questions that un-

16 Therefore the Sovereign, the Lord of
        hosts,
    will send wasting sickness among his
        stout warriors,
    and under his glory a burning will be
        kindled,
    like the burning of fire.
17 The light of Israel will become a fire,
        and his Holy One a flame;
    and it will burn and devour
        his thorns and briers in one day.
18 The glory of his forest and his fruitful
        land
    the Lord will destroy, both soul and
        body,
    and it will be as when an invalid wastes
        away.
19 The remnant of the trees of his forest will
        be so few
    that a child can write them down.

The Repentant Remnant of Israel

20 On that day the remnant of Israel and the
survivors of the house of Jacob will no more
lean on the one who struck them, but will lean
on the Lord, the Holy One of Israel, in truth.
21A remnant will return, the remnant of
Jacob, to the mighty God. 22For though your
people Israel were like the sand of the sea,
only a remnant of them will return. Destruction is decreed, overflowing with righteous-

ness. 23For the Lord God of hosts will make a
full end, as decreed, in all the earth. *a*

24 Therefore thus says the Lord God of
hosts: O my people, who live in Zion, do not
be afraid of the Assyrians when they beat you
with a rod and lift up their staff against you as
the Egyptians did. 25For in a very little while
my indignation will come to an end, and my
anger will be directed to their destruction.
26The Lord of hosts will wield a whip against
them, as when he struck Midian at the rock of
Oreb; his staff will be over the sea, and he will
lift it as he did in Egypt. 27On that day his burden will be removed from your shoulder, and
his yoke will be destroyed from your neck.

    He has gone up from Rimmon, *b*
28   he has come to Aiath;
    he has passed through Migron,
        at Michmash he stores his baggage;
29   they have crossed over the pass,
        at Geba they lodge for the night;
    Ramah trembles,
        Gibeah of Saul has fled.
30   Cry aloud, O daughter Gallim!
        Listen, O Laishah!
        Answer her, O Anathoth!
31   Madmenah is in flight,

---

a Or land   *b* Cn: Heb and his yoke from your neck, and a yoke
will be destroyed because of fatness

derscore Assyria's foolish misconception of its significance. **10.16–19** The original target of this oracle may
have been Damascus and Israel (cf. the imagery in
17.1–6), but it now portrays the destruction of Assyria.
10.17 Light of Israel, an epithet for God that suggests
the image of the deity as a devouring fire (29.6; 30.27–
33; 31.9; 33.14). **10.20–23** Originally a threat to the
Northern Kingdom, but a promise to Judah. In its
present location this oracle conveys the ambiguous
message of Judah's salvation through judgment (see
1.21–28; 29.1–8). **10.20** Israel, Jacob, designations for
the Northern Kingdom. One who struck them, the Aramean ruler of Damascus (9.11–12). **10.21** A remnant
will return, the name of Isaiah's first child, Shear-
jashub (7.3). Israel's return to God implied its acceptance of the Davidic dynasty in Jerusalem (2.5–6; 8.5–
8). Mighty God, a coronation name of the Judean king
in 9.6. **10.22** Your people Israel. Note contrast to my
people, who live in Zion (v. 24). Sand of the sea, only a
small remnant of the North will survive despite the ancient promise (Gen 22.17; 32.12; Hos 1.10). **10.24–
27c** The promise of deliverance from the rod of Assyria
resumes the imagery of vv. 5, 15. **10.26** Oreb. See Judg
7.25. Staff. See Ex 14.16. Over the sea . . . Egypt. God's

deliverance of his people from Assyria is compared to
the first exodus from Egypt. **10.27** Cf. 9.4. **10.27d–
32** This oracle describes the march of an enemy army
along the main north-south route from Israelite territory toward Jerusalem in the south. It is the logical approach for the Syro-Ephraimite army to have taken in
its attack on the city (7.1), but there is no evidence any
Assyrian army ever took this route. **10.27d** Rimmon,
not in the Hebrew text; a better reading is "Samaria,"
the Northern capital. **10.28** Aiath, a variant spelling of
Ai, a village two miles east-southeast of Bethel. Migron,
unidentified site in Benjamin (1 Sam 14.2). Michmash,
a village located about seven miles northeast of
Jerusalem and just north of a strategic pass across the
Wadi es-Suwenit. **10.29** The crossing of the pass at
Michmash through Geba, located just south of the
Wadi es-Suwenit, suggests a wide swing off the main
route, probably to bypass the Judean border fortress of
Mizpeh, before regaining the main road at Ramah, five
miles north of Jerusalem. Gibeah of Saul, modern Tell
el-Ful, about three and a half miles north of Jerusalem.
10.30 Gallim, Laishah, unidentified villages near
Anathoth, a village three miles north of Jerusalem.
10.31 Madmenah, Gebim, unidentified villages north

the inhabitants of Gebim flee for
  safety.
32 This very day he will halt at Nob,
  he will shake his fist
  at the mount of daughter Zion,
  the hill of Jerusalem.

33 Look, the Sovereign, the LORD of hosts,
  will lop the boughs with terrifying
    power;
  the tallest trees will be cut down,
  and the lofty will be brought low.
34 He will hack down the thickets of the
    forest with an ax,
  and Lebanon with its majestic trees[a]
    will fall.

The Peaceful Kingdom

11 A shoot shall come out from the
    stump of Jesse,
  and a branch shall grow out of his
    roots.
2 The spirit of the LORD shall rest on him,
  the spirit of wisdom and
    understanding,
  the spirit of counsel and might,
  the spirit of knowledge and the fear of
    the LORD.
3 His delight shall be in the fear of the LORD.

He shall not judge by what his eyes see,
  or decide by what his ears hear;
4 but with righteousness he shall judge the
    poor,
  and decide with equity for the meek of
    the earth;
he shall strike the earth with the rod of
    his mouth,

and with the breath of his lips he shall
    kill the wicked.
5 Righteousness shall be the belt around his
    waist,
  and faithfulness the belt around his
    loins.

6 The wolf shall live with the lamb,
  the leopard shall lie down with the
    kid,
  the calf and the lion and the fatling
    together,
  and a little child shall lead them.
7 The cow and the bear shall graze,
  their young shall lie down together;
  and the lion shall eat straw like the ox.
8 The nursing child shall play over the hole
    of the asp,
  and the weaned child shall put its hand
    on the adder's den.
9 They will not hurt or destroy
  on all my holy mountain;
for the earth will be full of the knowledge
    of the LORD
  as the waters cover the sea.

Return of the Remnant of Israel and Judah

10 On that day the root of Jesse shall stand as a
signal to the peoples; the nations shall inquire
of him, and his dwelling shall be glorious.

11 On that day the Lord will extend his
hand yet a second time to recover the remnant
that is left of his people, from Assyria, from
Egypt, from Pathros, from Ethiopia,[b] from

---

a Cn Compare Gk Vg: Heb *with a majestic one* b Or *Nubia*;
Heb *Cush*

---

of Jerusalem. **10.32** *Nob,* probably situated on Mount
Scopus, about a mile northeast of Jerusalem. *Shake his
fist,* a derisive gesture. **10.33–34** God, who founded
(14.32) and lives in Zion (8.18), will respond to the
enemy's haughty derision by felling his proud troops
like a forest (see 2.12–13; 9.18–19; 10.16–19).
  11.1–9 This portrayal probably stems from the period of the Syro-Ephraimite war (cf. 9.1–7) when the
Davidic dynasty appeared a mere stump compared to
its enemies (10.33–34). **11.1** *Jesse,* the father of David
(1 Sam 16.1–20). **11.2** Just as the *spirit of the LORD*
once came upon David (1 Sam 16.13), so it will abide
on the new king, equipping him for his royal tasks.
11.3–5 The traditional ideal of royal justice involved
extraordinary judicial insight (1 Kings 3.4–28) and
harsh justice on oppressors (Pss 72; 101). **11.6–9** The
king's reign will be marked by the peace and harmony

of paradise. **11.9** *My holy mountain,* Mount Zion (see
65.25). **11.10–16** During the new king's rule, God will
gather and reunite the remnant of Israel and Judah.
These verses need not presuppose the Babylonian
exile in 587 BCE. During Isaiah's lifetime Israel suffered major deportations in 733–731 and 722–720.
According to Sennacherib's Assyrian annals more
than two hundred thousand people were deported
from Judah in 701, and others undoubtedly sought
refuge in Egypt. **11.10** *Inquire of him,* go to him in
Jerusalem (*his glorious dwelling*) to obtain the word of
the Lord (cf. 2.2–4). **11.11** *Pathros,* Upper or southern
Egypt. *Ethiopia,* Nubia or the northern part of modern Sudan. *Elam,* a kingdom on the north shore of the
Persian Gulf occupying the Zagros Mountains and
modern Luristan and Khuzistan. *Shinar,* Babylonia.
Hamath, an important city on the Orontes River in

Elam, from Shinar, from Hamath, and from
the coastlands of the sea.

12 He will raise a signal for the nations,
    and will assemble the outcasts of Israel,
  and gather the dispersed of Judah
    from the four corners of the earth.
13 The jealousy of Ephraim shall depart,
    the hostility of Judah shall be cut off;
  Ephraim shall not be jealous of Judah,
    and Judah shall not be hostile towards
        Ephraim.
14 But they shall swoop down on the backs
        of the Philistines in the west,
    together they shall plunder the people
        of the east.
  They shall put forth their hand against
        Edom and Moab,
    and the Ammonites shall obey them.
15 And the LORD will utterly destroy
    the tongue of the sea of Egypt;
  and will wave his hand over the River
    with his scorching wind;
  and will split it into seven channels,
    and make a way to cross on foot;
16 so there shall be a highway from Assyria
    for the remnant that is left of his
        people,
  as there was for Israel
    when they came up from the land of
        Egypt.

Thanksgiving and Praise

12 You will say in that day:
    I will give thanks to you, O LORD,
  for though you were angry with me,
  your anger turned away,
    and you comforted me.

2 Surely God is my salvation;
    I will trust, and will not be afraid,
  for the LORD GOD*a* is my strength and my
        might;
    he has become my salvation.

3 With joy you will draw water from the
wells of salvation. 4 And you will say in that day:
  Give thanks to the LORD,
    call on his name;
  make known his deeds among the nations;
    proclaim that his name is exalted.

5 Sing praises to the LORD, for he has done
        gloriously;
    let this be known*b* in all the earth.
6 Shout aloud and sing for joy, O royal*c*
        Zion,
    for great in your midst is the Holy One
        of Israel.

Proclamation against Babylon

13 The oracle concerning Babylon that
    Isaiah son of Amoz saw.

2 On a bare hill raise a signal,
    cry aloud to them;
  wave the hand for them to enter
    the gates of the nobles.
3 I myself have commanded my
        consecrated ones,
  have summoned my warriors, my
        proudly exulting ones,
    to execute my anger.

4 Listen, a tumult on the mountains
    as of a great multitude!
  Listen, an uproar of kingdoms,
    of nations gathering together!
  The LORD of hosts is mustering
    an army for battle.
5 They come from a distant land,
    from the end of the heavens,
  the LORD and the weapons of his
        indignation,
    to destroy the whole earth.

a Heb *for Yah, the* LORD   b Or *this is made known*
c Or *O inhabitant of*

Syria. **11.14** *People of the east,* Arameans of Damascus
(9.12). **11.15** *Sea of Egypt,* the Red Sea. *The River,* the
Euphrates. **11.16** This future deliverance is portrayed
as a new exodus (cf. Jer 23.7–8).
  12.1–6 Brief songs of praise for God's deliverance
end this section of the book. **12.2b** Cf. Ex 15.2; Ps
118.14. **12.6** *Royal Zion.* The city is portrayed as a
princess sitting enthroned (cf. 47.1). *In your midst.* God
lives in Zion (8.18). *Holy One of Israel.* See note on 1.4.
13.1–23.18 Oracles against foreign nations (cf. Jer 46–
51; Ezek 25–32). **13.1–22** In Isaiah's lifetime, Babylon

experienced a resurgence under the Chaldean rule of
Merodach-baladan (39.1) and his successors, and Assyria was forced to recapture it at least four times (708,
703, 700, 689 BCE), the last after a prolonged siege that
led to its total destruction. Such an occasion, rather
than the later uncontested surrender of Babylon to Persia (539), may be the background for this oracle. In the
later period, however, after the fall of Babylon to Persia,
the text would likely have been reread in the light of that
more recent conquest of Babylon. **13.3** *Consecrated
ones,* the enemy soldiers used by God to carry out the

6 Wail, for the day of the LORD is near;
  it will come like destruction from the
    Almighty!*a*

7 Therefore all hands will be feeble,
  and every human heart will melt,
8 and they will be dismayed.
  Pangs and agony will seize them;
  they will be in anguish like a woman in
    labor.
  They will look aghast at one another;
  their faces will be aflame.

9 See, the day of the LORD comes,
  cruel, with wrath and fierce anger,
  to make the earth a desolation,
  and to destroy its sinners from it.

10 For the stars of the heavens and their
    constellations
  will not give their light;
  the sun will be dark at its rising,
  and the moon will not shed its light.

11 I will punish the world for its evil,
  and the wicked for their iniquity;
  I will put an end to the pride of the
    arrogant,
  and lay low the insolence of tyrants.

12 I will make mortals more rare than fine
    gold,
  and humans than the gold of Ophir.

13 Therefore I will make the heavens tremble,
  and the earth will be shaken out of its
    place,
  at the wrath of the LORD of hosts
  in the day of his fierce anger.

14 Like a hunted gazelle,
  or like sheep with no one to gather
    them,
  all will turn to their own people,
  and all will flee to their own lands.

15 Whoever is found will be thrust through,
  and whoever is caught will fall by the
    sword.

16 Their infants will be dashed to pieces
  before their eyes;

their houses will be plundered,
  and their wives ravished.

17 See, I am stirring up the Medes against
    them,
  who have no regard for silver
  and do not delight in gold.

18 Their bows will slaughter the young men;
  they will have no mercy on the fruit of
    the womb;
  their eyes will not pity children.

19 And Babylon, the glory of kingdoms,
  the splendor and pride of the
    Chaldeans,
  will be like Sodom and Gomorrah
  when God overthrew them.

20 It will never be inhabited
  or lived in for all generations;
  Arabs will not pitch their tents there,
  shepherds will not make their flocks lie
    down there.

21 But wild animals will lie down there,
  and its houses will be full of howling
    creatures;
  there ostriches will live,
  and there goat-demons will dance.

22 Hyenas will cry in its towers,
  and jackals in the pleasant palaces;
  its time is close at hand,
  and its days will not be prolonged.

Restoration of Judah

14 But the LORD will have compassion on
  Jacob and will again choose Israel, and
will set them in their own land; and aliens will
join them and attach themselves to the house
of Jacob. 2And the nations will take them and
bring them to their place, and the house of Israel will possess the nations*b* as male and female slaves in the LORD's land; they will take
captive those who were their captors, and rule
over those who oppressed them.

---

a Traditional rendering of Heb *Shaddai*   *b* Heb *them*

divine judgment (5.26; 10.5–6). **13.5** *Distant land.* Cf.
5.26. **13.6–19** The destruction of Babylon is portrayed
with the traditional imagery of the "day of the LORD"
(see 2.11). **13.12** *Ophir,* a country of disputed location
famous for its fine gold (1 Kings 9.26–28; Job 22.24;
28.16; Ps 45.9). **13.17** *Medes,* a people northwest of
Persia who were vassals of Assyria in Isaiah's time.
13.19 *Chaldeans,* an Aramean tribe from southern
Babylonia that dominated Babylon during the Neo-
Babylonian Empire from about 725 until 539 BCE.
13.20–22 The fate portrayed in this traditional descrip-

tion of a destroyed and abandoned city (34.8–17; Jer
50.39–40; Zeph 2.13–15) befell Babylon in 689 BCE; it
remained in ruins until its rebuilding late in the reign of
Esar-haddon (681–669). **13.21** *Goat-demons.* Demons
as well as wild animals were thought to inhabit ruins.
14.1–2 Restored to its land, Israel will be served by
the nations who once oppressed it (cf. 60.4–16; 61.5–
7). Originally the exile referred to here could easily have
been the eighth-century Assyrian exile of the Northern
tribes; only later would it have been reinterpreted to
refer to the Babylonian exile of the sixth century. **14.3–**

Downfall of the King of Babylon

3 When the LORD has given you rest from your pain and turmoil and the hard service with which you were made to serve, ⁴you will take up this taunt against the king of Babylon:

How the oppressor has ceased!
    How his insolence*a* has ceased!
5 The LORD has broken the staff of the
            wicked,
    the scepter of rulers,
6 that struck down the peoples in wrath
            with unceasing blows,
    that ruled the nations in anger
            with unrelenting persecution.
7 The whole earth is at rest and quiet;
    they break forth into singing.
8 The cypresses exult over you,
    the cedars of Lebanon, saying,
"Since you were laid low,
    no one comes to cut us down."
9 Sheol beneath is stirred up
    to meet you when you come;
it rouses the shades to greet you,
    all who were leaders of the earth;
it raises from their thrones
    all who were kings of the nations.
10 All of them will speak
    and say to you:
"You too have become as weak as we!
    You have become like us!"
11 Your pomp is brought down to Sheol,
    and the sound of your harps;
maggots are the bed beneath you,
    and worms are your covering.

12 How you are fallen from heaven,
    O Day Star, son of Dawn!
How you are cut down to the ground,
    you who laid the nations low!
13 You said in your heart,
    "I will ascend to heaven;
I will raise my throne
    above the stars of God;
I will sit on the mount of assembly
    on the heights of Zaphon;*b*
14 I will ascend to the tops of the clouds,
    I will make myself like the Most High."
15 But you are brought down to Sheol,
    to the depths of the Pit.
16 Those who see you will stare at you,
    and ponder over you:
"Is this the man who made the earth
            tremble,
    who shook kingdoms,
17 who made the world like a desert
    and overthrew its cities,
who would not let his prisoners go
            home?"
18 All the kings of the nations lie in glory,
    each in his own tomb;
19 but you are cast out, away from your grave,
    like loathsome carrion,*c*
clothed with the dead, those pierced by
            the sword,
    who go down to the stones of the Pit,
    like a corpse trampled underfoot.
20 You will not be joined with them in burial,
    because you have destroyed your land,
    you have killed your people.

May the descendants of evildoers
    nevermore be named!
21 Prepare slaughter for his sons
    because of the guilt of their father.*d*

---

a Q Ms Compare Gk Syr Vg: Meaning of MT uncertain
b Or *assembly in the far north*   *c* Cn Compare Gk: Heb *like a loathed branch*   *d* Syr Compare Gk: Heb *fathers*

---

23 This mocking dirge may have originally celebrated the violent death of the Assyrian king Sargon II or Sennacherib, both of whom were also kings of Babylon. **14.3–4a** Prose introduction. **14.4b–8** Following the tyrant's death, the earth is at peace. **14.8** Assyrian and Babylonian kings cut *the cedars of Lebanon* for their building projects (see 37.24). **14.9–11** The dead tyrant is greeted in *Sheol* by the *shades*, or spirits, of earlier rulers (see note on 5.14). **14.12–15** Attempting to displace God in heaven, this tyrant, like a figure from Canaanite mythology, fell into Sheol instead. **14.12** *Day star, Dawn,* names of deities. **14.13** *Mount of assembly,* mountain where the assembly of the gods met. *Zaphon,* the name of Baal's mountain in Canaanite mythology, in Israel identified with Mount Zion (see Ps 48.2, where the same expression is translated "in the far north"). **14.14** *Most High,* Hebrew *Elyon,* an archaic name for the head of the pantheon, identified with the Lord in Israel (Deut 32.8–9; Ps 82.6). **14.15** *The Pit,* another name for the underworld. **14.16–20** The tyrant has lost his former glory in death; he does not even receive proper burial. This description best fits Sargon II, whose body was not recovered after he died in battle against mountain tribesmen. It possibly also fits Sennacherib, who was murdered by his own sons and may not have received a state funeral. **14.20** *Killed your people.* Sargon and especially Sennacherib slaughtered many of Babylon's inhabitants in their attempt to gain and maintain control of the city. **14.21** A curse on the descendants of the king of Babylon. **14.22–23** Prose

Let them never rise to possess the earth
  or cover the face of the world with cities.

22 I will rise up against them, says the LORD of hosts, and will cut off from Babylon name and remnant, offspring and posterity, says the LORD. 23 And I will make it a possession of the hedgehog, and pools of water, and I will sweep it with the broom of destruction, says the LORD of hosts.

An Oracle concerning Assyria

24 The LORD of hosts has sworn:
  As I have designed,
    so shall it be;
  and as I have planned,
    so shall it come to pass:
25 I will break the Assyrian in my land,
  and on my mountains trample him
      under foot;
  his yoke shall be removed from them,
    and his burden from their shoulders.
26 This is the plan that is planned
    concerning the whole earth;
  and this is the hand that is stretched out
    over all the nations.
27 For the LORD of hosts has planned,
    and who will annul it?
  His hand is stretched out,
    and who will turn it back?

An Oracle concerning Philistia

28 In the year that King Ahaz died this oracle came:

29 Do not rejoice, all you Philistines,
    that the rod that struck you is broken,

for from the root of the snake will come
      forth an adder,
  and its fruit will be a flying fiery
      serpent.
30 The firstborn of the poor will graze,
    and the needy lie down in safety;
  but I will make your root die of famine,
    and your remnant I*a* will kill.
31 Wail, O gate; cry, O city;
    melt in fear, O Philistia, all of you!
  For smoke comes out of the north,
    and there is no straggler in its ranks.

32 What will one answer the messengers of
      the nation?
  "The LORD has founded Zion,
    and the needy among his people
    will find refuge in her."

An Oracle concerning Moab

15 An oracle concerning Moab.

Because Ar is laid waste in a night,
    Moab is undone;
  because Kir is laid waste in a night,
    Moab is undone.
2 Dibon*b* has gone up to the temple,
    to the high places to weep;
  over Nebo and over Medeba
    Moab wails.
  On every head is baldness,
    every beard is shorn;
3 in the streets they bind on sackcloth;
    on the housetops and in the squares
  everyone wails and melts in tears.

_____

a Q Ms Vg: MT *he*   *b* Cn: Heb *the house and Dibon*

conclusion. **14.24–27** God's plan is to destroy Assyria in the land of Israel (see 29.1–8; 30.27–33; 31.8–9), and no power can thwart the divine will. **14.28–32** In ca. 714 BCE, Philistia, under the leadership of Ashdod and supported by Egypt and Ethiopia, began a revolt against Assyria that was sustained for three years. **14.28** *Year that King Ahaz died.* Ahaz apparently died in 715 BCE (cf. 2 Kings 18.1). In that year Sargon II removed Azuri of Ashdod from the throne for plotting revolt, but after the Assyrian army departed, the revolt was restarted under new leadership (see note on 20.1–6). **14.29** *Do not rejoice.* Philistia's respite will be brief. The referent of *the rod* is ambiguous—is it the Judean king Ahaz or one of the Assyrian kings such as Tiglath-pileser III? **14.31** *Smoke . . . out of the north,* the Assyrian army (see 5.26–30). **14.32** Philistia tried to induce Judah to join the revolt, but Isaiah opposed it (see 18.1–7; 20.1–6), urging Judah to trust instead in God's promises to Zion.

15.1–16.14 Moab, Judah's neighbor east of the Dead Sea (Gen 19.30–37), will be destroyed (Jer 48.1–47; Ezek 25.8–11). **15.1–9** The refugees from the ruined cities of Moab are in mourning. **15.1** *Ar,* Moabite city located near Moab's ancient northern border on the south bank of the Arnon River (Num 21.15, 28). *Kir,* probably *Kir-hareseth* (see 16.7), modern Kerak, eleven miles east of the Dead Sea and seventeen miles south of the Arnon. **15.2** *Dibon,* modern Dhiban, three miles north of the Arnon. *Nebo,* another city of Moab in the vicinity of Heshbon (Num 32.3, 38). *Medeba,* Moabite city fifteen miles southeast of the northern end of the Dead Sea. *Baldness . . . beard is shorn.* One shaved the head and beard as a sign of mourning (Lev 21.5). There is probably a wordplay here, since the Hebrew word for baldness (*qorchah*) has the same consonantal spelling as a Moabite place-name mentioned several times in Mesha's Moabite

4 Heshbon and Elealeh cry out,
   their voices are heard as far as Jahaz;
 therefore the loins of Moab quiver;[a]
   his soul trembles.
5 My heart cries out for Moab;
   his fugitives flee to Zoar,
   to Eglath-shelishiyah.
 For at the ascent of Luhith
   they go up weeping;
 on the road to Horonaim
   they raise a cry of destruction;
6 the waters of Nimrim
   are a desolation;
 the grass is withered, the new growth
      fails,
   the verdure is no more.
7 Therefore the abundance they have
      gained
   and what they have laid up
 they carry away
   over the Wadi of the Willows.
8 For a cry has gone
   around the land of Moab;
 the wailing reaches to Eglaim,
   the wailing reaches to Beer-elim.
9 For the waters of Dibon[b] are full of
      blood;
   yet I will bring upon Dibon[b] even
      more—
 a lion for those of Moab who escape,
   for the remnant of the land.

16 Send lambs
   to the ruler of the land,
 from Sela, by way of the desert,
   to the mount of daughter Zion.
2 Like fluttering birds,
   like scattered nestlings,
 so are the daughters of Moab
   at the fords of the Arnon.
3 "Give counsel,
   grant justice;
 make your shade like night
   at the height of noon;
 hide the outcasts,
   do not betray the fugitive;

4 let the outcasts of Moab
   settle among you;
 be a refuge to them
   from the destroyer."

 When the oppressor is no more,
   and destruction has ceased,
 and marauders have vanished from the
      land,
5 then a throne shall be established in
      steadfast love
   in the tent of David,
   and on it shall sit in faithfulness
 a ruler who seeks justice
   and is swift to do what is right.

6 We have heard of the pride of Moab
   —how proud he is!—
 of his arrogance, his pride, and his
      insolence;
   his boasts are false.
7 Therefore let Moab wail,
   let everyone wail for Moab.
 Mourn, utterly stricken,
   for the raisin cakes of Kir-hareseth.

8 For the fields of Heshbon languish,
   and the vines of Sibmah,
 whose clusters once made drunk
   the lords of the nations,
 reached to Jazer
   and strayed to the desert;
 their shoots once spread abroad
   and crossed over the sea.
9 Therefore I weep with the weeping of
      Jazer
   for the vines of Sibmah;
 I drench you with my tears,
   O Heshbon and Elealeh;
 for the shout over your fruit harvest
   and your grain harvest has ceased.
10 Joy and gladness are taken away

---

a Cn Compare Gk Syr: Heb *the armed men of Moab cry aloud*
b Q Ms Vg Compare Syr: MT *Dimon*

Stone. **15.3** The wearing of *sackcloth* was another sign of mourning. **15.4** *Heshbon*, modern Hesban, in Moab fifty miles due east of Jerusalem. *Elealeh*, another city near Heshbon. *Jahaz*, another Moabite city of disputed location. **15.5–8** *Zoar, Eglath-shelishiyah, Luhith, Horonaim, waters of Nimrim, Wadi of the Willows, Eglaim, Beer-elim*, sites in Moab of uncertain location. **16.1–5** Moabite refugees seek asylum in Judah, and the Judean crown is urged to give them shelter.

16.1 *Lambs*, Moabite tribute to Judah (cf. 2 Kings 3.4). *Sela*, another unidentified site in Moab. **16.2** *Arnon*, the modern Wadi el-Mujib, which flows into the Dead Sea. **16.5** *Tent of David*. A future descendant of David will once again rule over Moab in justice. **16.6–11** Lament over the destruction of the vineyards of Moab. *Kir-hareseth*. See note on 15.1. *Sibmah*, a Moabite city known for its vineyards; its site is still disputed. *Jazer*, a site near the border with Ammon (Num

from the fruitful field;
and in the vineyards no songs are sung,
no shouts are raised;
no treader treads out wine in the presses;
the vintage-shout is hushed.*a*

11 Therefore my heart throbs like a harp for
Moab,
and my very soul for Kir-heres.

12 When Moab presents himself, when he wearies himself upon the high place, when he comes to his sanctuary to pray, he will not prevail.

13 This was the word that the LORD spoke concerning Moab in the past. 14But now the LORD says, In three years, like the years of a hired worker, the glory of Moab will be brought into contempt, in spite of all its great multitude; and those who survive will be very few and feeble.

An Oracle concerning Damascus

17 An oracle concerning Damascus.

See, Damascus will cease to be a city,
and will become a heap of ruins.
2 Her towns will be deserted forever;*b*
they will be places for flocks,
which will lie down, and no one will
make them afraid.
3 The fortress will disappear from
Ephraim,
and the kingdom from Damascus;
and the remnant of Aram will be
like the glory of the children of Israel,
says the LORD of hosts.

4 On that day
the glory of Jacob will be brought low,

and the fat of his flesh will grow lean.
5 And it shall be as when reapers gather
standing grain
and their arms harvest the ears,
and as when one gleans the ears of grain
in the Valley of Rephaim.
6 Gleanings will be left in it,
as when an olive tree is beaten—
two or three berries
in the top of the highest bough,
four or five
on the branches of a fruit tree,
says the LORD God of Israel.

7 On that day people will regard their Maker, and their eyes will look to the Holy One of Israel; 8they will not have regard for the altars, the work of their hands, and they will not look to what their own fingers have made, either the sacred poles*c* or the altars of incense.

9 On that day their strong cities will be like the deserted places of the Hivites and the Amorites,*d* which they deserted because of the children of Israel, and there will be desolation.

10 For you have forgotten the God of your
salvation,
and have not remembered the Rock of
your refuge;
therefore, though you plant pleasant
plants
and set out slips of an alien god,
11 though you make them grow on the day
that you plant them,

---

a Gk: Heb *I have hushed*   *b* Cn Compare Gk: Heb *the cities of Aroer are deserted*   *c* Heb *Asherim*   *d* Cn Compare Gk: Heb *places of the wood and the highest bough*

21.24 in the Septuagint). *Kir-heres,* alternate form of *Kir-hareseth.* **16.12–14** Moab's prayers will be to no avail; within three years it will be almost completely devastated.
17.1–6 The Aramean and Israelite nations allied against Judah in the Syro-Ephraimite war (735–732 BCE) will be totally destroyed (cf. 7.1–8.4). **17.1** *Damascus,* the capital of the Aramean state. **17.3** *Ephraim,* a designation for the Northern Kingdom, Israel. **17.4** Cf. the imagery in 10.16. **17.5** *Rephaim,* a valley just outside of Jerusalem (2 Sam 5.18); its proximity to the heavily populated city meant that it would be thoroughly *gleaned* (see Deut 24.19–22; Ruth 2.2–23) by the landless urban poor. **17.7–11** Judgment on idolatry (cf. 1.29–31; 2.8, 20). **17.7–8** After God's judgment on Israel the people will turn back to him from their idols. *The work of their hands.*

Altars and altars of incense were used in the worship of the Lord; the prophet probably takes exception to these because they were dedicated to either a foreign deity or a Northern form of the Lord, such as the "Yahweh of Samaria" attested from Kuntillet 'Ajrud, which the Judean prophet considered idolatrous. *Sacred pole,* a wooden cult object or actual tree that represented the Canaanite goddess Asherah; in syncretistic popular Israelite religion Asherah was sometimes identified as the spouse of the Lord. **17.9** Israel's cities will be as devastated as those of the *Hivites* and *Amorites,* the original inhabitants of Palestine (Deut 7.1), when Israel displaced them. **17.10–11** This devastation will befall Israel because it had deserted God, who saved it. **17.10** *Rock,* a standard metaphor for God as a source of refuge (30.29). *Plants, slips,* perhaps sacred groves planted in honor of other gods (1.29–31).

and make them blossom in the
   morning that you sow;
yet the harvest will flee away
   in a day of grief and incurable pain.

12 Ah, the thunder of many peoples,
   they thunder like the thundering of the
      sea!
Ah, the roar of nations,
   they roar like the roaring of mighty
      waters!
13 The nations roar like the roaring of many
      waters,
   but he will rebuke them, and they will
      flee far away,
chased like chaff on the mountains before
      the wind
   and whirling dust before the storm.
14 At evening time, lo, terror!
   Before morning, they are no more.
This is the fate of those who despoil us,
   and the lot of those who plunder us.

An Oracle concerning Ethiopia

18 Ah, land of whirring wings
    beyond the rivers of Ethiopia,ᵃ
2 sending ambassadors by the Nile
   in vessels of papyrus on the waters!
Go, you swift messengers,
   to a nation tall and smooth,
to a people feared near and far,
   a nation mighty and conquering,
   whose land the rivers divide.

3 All you inhabitants of the world,
   you who live on the earth,
when a signal is raised on the mountains,
      look!
When a trumpet is blown, listen!
4 For thus the LORD said to me:
I will quietly look from my dwelling
   like clear heat in sunshine,

like a cloud of dew in the heat of
     harvest.
5 For before the harvest, when the blossom
    is over
   and the flower becomes a ripening
     grape,
he will cut off the shoots with pruning
     hooks,
   and the spreading branches he will hew
     away.
6 They shall all be left
   to the birds of prey of the mountains
   and to the animals of the earth.
And the birds of prey will summer on
     them,
   and all the animals of the earth will
     winter on them.

7 At that time gifts will be brought to the
LORD of hosts fromᵇ a people tall and smooth,
from a people feared near and far, a nation
mighty and conquering, whose land the rivers
divide, to Mount Zion, the place of the name
of the LORD of hosts.

An Oracle concerning Egypt

19 An oracle concerning Egypt.

See, the LORD is riding on a swift cloud
   and comes to Egypt;
the idols of Egypt will tremble at his
     presence,
   and the heart of the Egyptians will
     melt within them.
2 I will stir up Egyptians against Egyptians,
   and they will fight, one against the
     other,
neighbor against neighbor,
city against city, kingdom against
     kingdom;

---

a Or *Nubia*; Heb *Cush*   b Q Ms Gk Vg: MT *of*

17.12–14 Though Jerusalem's enemies roar like the chaotic waters of the stormy sea (Pss 46.1–3; 93.3–4), God will drive them away before morning. Perhaps originally directed against the Syro-Ephraimite coalition (cf. 8.9–10), this oracle could easily be reapplied to the later threat from Assyria (5.30; 8.7; 28.17; 29.7). 18.1–7 The background for this oracle may be Ethiopia's support for Ashdod's revolt against Assyria in 714 BCE. In opposition to the Ethiopian messengers encouraging Judah to join this revolt (see 14.32; 20.1–6), Isaiah insists that one must wait for God's appointed time of harvest. **18.2** *A nation tall and smooth.*

The Nubians of ancient Ethiopia were black, tall, and, unlike the soldiers of most armies Israel encountered, clean shaven. *Land the rivers divide,* ancient Ethiopia or Nubia, divided by the branches of the Nile. **18.4** *My dwelling,* Mount Zion (see v. 7). **19.1–15** The Lord will bring judgment on Egypt's gods, its leaders, and its people. **19.1–4** The internal conflict in Egypt may reflect the period before the Ethiopian Piankhi, founder of the twenty-fifth dynasty, united Egypt under his rule beginning ca. 727 BCE or the later imposition of Ethiopian rule over the delta rulers by Shabaqo ca. 715. If the latter, the oracle would come from the pe-

3 the spirit of the Egyptians within them
      will be emptied out,
   and I will confound their plans;
  they will consult the idols and the spirits
         of the dead
   and the ghosts and the familiar spirits;
4 I will deliver the Egyptians
      into the hand of a hard master;
  a fierce king will rule over them,
      says the Sovereign, the LORD of hosts.

5 The waters of the Nile will be dried up,
      and the river will be parched and dry;
6 its canals will become foul,
      and the branches of Egypt's Nile will
         diminish and dry up,
   reeds and rushes will rot away.
7 There will be bare places by the Nile,
      on the brink of the Nile;
   and all that is sown by the Nile will dry
         up,
   be driven away, and be no more.
8 Those who fish will mourn;
      all who cast hooks in the Nile will
         lament,
   and those who spread nets on the
         water will languish.
9 The workers in flax will be in despair,
      and the carders and those at the loom
         will grow pale.
10 Its weavers will be dismayed,
      and all who work for wages will be
         grieved.

11 The princes of Zoan are utterly foolish;
      the wise counselors of Pharaoh give
         stupid counsel.
   How can you say to Pharaoh,
      "I am one of the sages,
      a descendant of ancient kings"?
12 Where now are your sages?
      Let them tell you and make known
   what the LORD of hosts has planned
         against Egypt.
13 The princes of Zoan have become fools,

and the princes of Memphis are
      deluded;
   those who are the cornerstones of its tribes
      have led Egypt astray.
14 The LORD has poured into them[a]
      a spirit of confusion;
   and they have made Egypt stagger in all
         its doings
      as a drunkard staggers around in
         vomit.
15 Neither head nor tail, palm branch or
         reed,
      will be able to do anything for Egypt.

16 On that day the Egyptians will be like
women, and tremble with fear before the hand
that the LORD of hosts raises against them.
17And the land of Judah will become a terror
to the Egyptians; everyone to whom it is mentioned will fear because of the plan that the
LORD of hosts is planning against them.

Egypt, Assyria, and Israel Blessed

18 On that day there will be five cities in the
land of Egypt that speak the language of Canaan and swear allegiance to the LORD of
hosts. One of these will be called the City of
the Sun.
   19 On that day there will be an altar to the
LORD in the center of the land of Egypt, and a
pillar to the LORD at its border. 20It will be a
sign and a witness to the LORD of hosts in the
land of Egypt; when they cry to the LORD because of oppressors, he will send them a savior, and will defend and deliver them. 21The
LORD will make himself known to the Egyptians; and the Egyptians will know the LORD
on that day, and will worship with sacrifice
and burnt offering, and they will make vows to
the LORD and perform them. 22The LORD will
strike Egypt, striking and healing; they will return to the LORD, and he will listen to their
supplications and heal them.

_____
a Gk Compare Tg: Heb it

---

riod of Ashdod's revolt (see ch. 20). **19.4** *Hard master,*
either Piankhi or Shabaqo of Ethiopia (see note on
19.1–4) or possibly Sargon II of Assyria. **19.5–
10** Egypt's collapse is portrayed using the imagery of
the drying up of the Nile, Egypt's source of life and
economic well-being. **19.11–15** Despite their reputation for wisdom, the leaders of Egypt have proven
themselves foolish and incompetent. **19.11** *Zoan,*
Greek Tanis, an important Egyptian city in the Delta

region. **19.13** *Memphis,* ancient capital of Lower
Egypt. **19.14** Cf. 28.7–8. **19.15** *Palm branch, reed,*
metaphors for the ruler and the ruled (9.14–15).
19.16–25 Five prose sayings, each beginning with *on
that day,* expand on the preceding oracle against
Egypt. **19.16–17** Egypt will fear Judah because of
God's plan against Egypt. **19.18** *Language of Canaan,*
Canaanite, of which Hebrew is a dialect. *City of the
Sun,* perhaps Heliopolis (cf. Jer 43.13). **19.19–22** The

23 On that day there will be a highway from Egypt to Assyria, and the Assyrian will come into Egypt, and the Egyptian into Assyria, and the Egyptians will worship with the Assyrians.

24 On that day Israel will be the third with Egypt and Assyria, a blessing in the midst of the earth, 25whom the LORD of hosts has blessed, saying, "Blessed be Egypt my people, and Assyria the work of my hands, and Israel my heritage."

Isaiah Dramatizes the Conquest of Egypt and Ethiopia

20 In the year that the commander-in-chief, who was sent by King Sargon of Assyria, came to Ashdod and fought against it and took it— 2at that time the LORD had spoken to Isaiah son of Amoz, saying, "Go, and loose the sackcloth from your loins and take your sandals off your feet," and he had done so, walking naked and barefoot. 3Then the LORD said, "Just as my servant Isaiah has walked naked and barefoot for three years as a sign and a portent against Egypt and Ethiopia,*a* 4so shall the king of Assyria lead away the Egyptians as captives and the Ethiopians*b* as exiles, both the young and the old, naked and barefoot, with buttocks uncovered, to the shame of Egypt. 5And they shall be dismayed and confounded because of Ethiopia*a* their hope and of Egypt their boast. 6In that day the inhabitants of this coastland will say, 'See, this is what has happened to those in

whom we hoped and to whom we fled for help and deliverance from the king of Assyria! And we, how shall we escape?' "

Oracles concerning Babylon, Edom, and Arabia

21 The oracle concerning the wilderness of the sea.

As whirlwinds in the Negeb sweep on,
　it comes from the desert,
　from a terrible land.
2 A stern vision is told to me;
　the betrayer betrays,
　and the destroyer destroys.
Go up, O Elam,
　lay siege, O Media;
all the sighing she has caused
　I bring to an end.
3 Therefore my loins are filled with
　　anguish;
　pangs have seized me,
　like the pangs of a woman in labor;
I am bowed down so that I cannot hear,
　I am dismayed so that I cannot see.
4 My mind reels, horror has appalled me;
　the twilight I longed for
　has been turned for me into trembling.
5 They prepare the table,
　they spread the rugs,
　they eat, they drink.

---

a Or Nubia; Heb Cush   *b* Or Nubians; Heb Cushites

Egyptians will come to know and worship the Lord even as Israel does. **19.23** Assyria will join Egypt in this worship. **19.24–25** Egypt, Assyria, and Israel will all be blessed by God in that day (cf. Gen 12.3).

20.1–6 In 715 BCE, Sargon II replaced the rebellious Azuri of Ashdod with his brother Ahimeti. Sometime after the Assyrian army withdrew, however, the inhabitants of Ashdod drove Ahimeti out and replaced him with a commoner variously called Yamani or Yadna, perhaps variant nicknames meaning "Greek" or "Cypriot." He promptly wrote letters to the surrounding states inviting them to join a revolt against Assyria, promising the support of Egypt and far-off Ethiopia. Isaiah tried to dissuade Hezekiah from joining the revolt by demonstrating naked in front of the palace, thus symbolizing the shameful captivity that would first befall the expected Egyptian and Ethiopian relief troops, leaving Ashdod and any other allies without hope. Apparently Isaiah was successful. Hezekiah did not join the revolt, the promised help from Egypt and Ethiopia did not materialize, and in 711 Sargon's general captured Ashdod, exiled its population, and resettled it with foreigners. Yamani escaped to the border of

Ethiopia, however, and did not fall into Assyrian hands until four years later when Ethiopia extradited him to Assyria.

21.1–17 These three oracles all seem to presuppose the Assyrian struggle to gain control of southern Mesopotamia against the Chaldean rulers of Babylon and their Elamite, Aramean, and Arab allies in 691–689 BCE. Following the bloody battle at Halule (691), which pitted Sennacherib's Assyrian army against a large coalition led by the king of Elam, Assyria regrouped and continued to campaign against Babylon and its allies, eventually destroying Babylon completely in 689. **21.1–10** Announcement of the fall of Babylon. **21.1** *Wilderness of the sea*, probably a reference to the steppe regions in lower Mesopotamia, which was known as the Sealand. *Negeb*, steppe region in southern Palestine. **21.2** *Betrayer, destroyer*, probably a reference to Assyria (16.4; 33.1). *Elam* led the large anti-Assyrian coalition, which included contingents from Persia and perhaps *Media*. **21.3–4** The vision dismays the prophet because it reveals the fall of Babylon, Israel's ally (39.1–4), rather than the fall of Assyria he longed for. **21.5** *Oil the shield*, to keep the

Rise up, commanders,
 oil the shield!
6 For thus the Lord said to me:
 "Go, post a lookout,
  let him announce what he sees.
7 When he sees riders, horsemen in pairs,
  riders on donkeys, riders on camels,
 let him listen diligently,
  very diligently."
8 Then the watcher[a] called out:
 "Upon a watchtower I stand, O Lord,
  continually by day,
 and at my post I am stationed
  throughout the night.
9 Look, there they come, riders,
  horsemen in pairs!"
 Then he responded,
  "Fallen, fallen is Babylon;
 and all the images of her gods
  lie shattered on the ground."
10 O my threshed and winnowed one,
  what I have heard from the LORD of
   hosts,
  the God of Israel, I announce to you.

11 The oracle concerning Dumah.

 One is calling to me from Seir,
  "Sentinel, what of the night?
  Sentinel, what of the night?"
12 The sentinel says:
  "Morning comes, and also the night.
  If you will inquire, inquire;
  come back again."

13 The oracle concerning the desert plain.

 In the scrub of the desert plain you will
  lodge,
 O caravans of Dedanites.

14 Bring water to the thirsty,
 meet the fugitive with bread,
 O inhabitants of the land of Tema.
15 For they have fled from the swords,
 from the drawn sword,
 from the bent bow,
 and from the stress of battle.

16 For thus the Lord said to me: Within a year, according to the years of a hired worker, all the glory of Kedar will come to an end; [17]and the remaining bows of Kedar's warriors will be few; for the LORD, the God of Israel, has spoken.

A Warning of Destruction of Jerusalem

22 The oracle concerning the valley of vision.

 What do you mean that you have gone
  up,
 all of you, to the housetops,
2 you that are full of shoutings,
  tumultuous city, exultant town?
 Your slain are not slain by the sword,
  nor are they dead in battle.
3 Your rulers have all fled together;
  they were captured without the use of
   a bow.[b]
 All of you who were found were
  captured,
  though they had fled far away.[c]
4 Therefore I said:
 Look away from me,
  let me weep bitter tears;
 do not try to comfort me
  for the destruction of my beloved
   people.

a Q Ms: MT *a lion* b Or *without their bows* c Gk Syr Vg: Heb *fled from far away*

leather supple (cf. 2 Sam 1.21). **21.6–8** *Lookout . . . watcher.* For this image of the prophet as a sentinel, see v. 11; Ezek 3.17; Hab 2.1. **21.9** *The images of her gods lie shattered.* In shocking contrast to their normal practice, the victorious Assyrians destroyed the images of the Babylonian gods when Babylon fell to Sennacherib in 689 BCE. **21.11–12** There is as yet no clear answer on the fate of Dumah. **21.11** *Dumah,* Adummatu in the northern Arabian desert, plundered by Sennacherib in connection with his campaign against Babylon. *Seir.* There is a Seir in Edom, but the present context suggests another site of the same name in the northern Arabian desert. **21.13–17** Other Arab groups are urged to give comfort to those Arabs who must flee Sennacherib's attacks. **21.13** *Dedanites,* a northern

Arabian group (Ezek 25.13). **21.14** *Tema,* an oasis in northwest Arabia (Jer 25.23). **21.16** *Kedar,* a seminomadic tribal group of the northern Arabian desert (42.11; Ezek 27.21).

22.1–14 The occasion for this oracle may have been news of Sennacherib's successful first campaign against Babylon (703 BCE), Judah's ally, that freed the Assyrian king to attack Judah in the west (701). **22.1** *Valley of vision,* possibly a reference to the Babylonian plain seen only in the prophet's vision. **22.2–3** In Sennacherib's first campaign, Merodach-baladan, king of Babylon, fled the battlefield, and his Elamite, Chaldean, and Aramaic allies were routed and many prisoners taken. **22.4** *My beloved people,* Judah, exposed to attack because of the collapse of its

5 For the Lord GOD of hosts has a day
        of tumult and trampling and
            confusion
    in the valley of vision,
    a battering down of walls
        and a cry for help to the mountains.
6 Elam bore the quiver
        with chariots and cavalry,*
        and Kir uncovered the shield.
7 Your choicest valleys were full of chariots,
        and the cavalry took their stand at the
            gates.
8 He has taken away the covering of Judah.

On that day you looked to the weapons of
the House of the Forest, 9and you saw that
there were many breaches in the city of David,
and you collected the waters of the lower pool.
10You counted the houses of Jerusalem, and
you broke down the houses to fortify the wall.
11You made a reservoir between the two walls
for the water of the old pool. But you did not
look to him who did it, or have regard for him
who planned it long ago.

12 In that day the Lord GOD of hosts
        called to weeping and mourning,
        to baldness and putting on sackcloth;
13 but instead there was joy and festivity,
        killing oxen and slaughtering sheep,
        eating meat and drinking wine.
    "Let us eat and drink,
        for tomorrow we die."
14 The LORD of hosts has revealed himself in
        my ears:
    Surely this iniquity will not be forgiven
        you until you die,
    says the Lord GOD of hosts.

Denunciation of Self-Seeking Officials

15 Thus says the Lord GOD of hosts: Come, go
to this steward, to Shebna, who is master of
the household, and say to him: 16What right
do you have here? Who are your relatives here,
that you have cut out a tomb here for yourself,
cutting a tomb on the height, and carving a
habitation for yourself in the rock? 17The
LORD is about to hurl you away violently, my
fellow. He will seize firm hold on you, 18whirl
you round and round, and throw you like a
ball into a wide land; there you shall die, and
there your splendid chariots shall lie, O you
disgrace to your master's house! 19I will thrust
you from your office, and you will be pulled
down from your post.

20 On that day I will call my servant Eliakim son of Hilkiah, 21and will clothe him with
your robe and bind your sash on him. I will
commit your authority to his hand, and he
shall be a father to the inhabitants of Jerusalem and to the house of Judah. 22I will place
on his shoulder the key of the house of David;
he shall open, and no one shall shut; he shall
shut, and no one shall open. 23I will fasten him
like a peg in a secure place, and he will become
a throne of honor to his ancestral house.
24And they will hang on him the whole weight
of his ancestral house, the offspring and issue,
every small vessel, from the cups to all the
flagons. 25On that day, says the LORD of hosts,
the peg that was fastened in a secure place will
give way; it will be cut down and fall, and the
load that was on it will perish, for the LORD
has spoken.

_____

a Meaning of Heb uncertain

allies in the east. **22.5** *Day.* See note on 2.11–12.
22.6 *Elam,* Babylon's major ally against Assyria (see
note on 11.11). *Kir,* the Aramean allies of Babylon
(Am 1.5; 9.7); this Kir is not the one mentioned in
15.1. **22.7** *Choicest valleys, the gates,* perhaps referring to the major engagements at the Babylonian cities of
Kutha and Kish. **22.8a** *The covering of Judah,* the protection provided by its allies on the Babylonian front.
22.8b–11 News of Babylon's fall led to frenzied military preparations in Judah against the threat of Assyrian invasion, but God was ignored in these preparations (cf. 30.1–2, 15–16). **22.8b** *House of the Forest,*
the royal palace with its armory (1 Kings 7.2; 10.17).
22.9 *City of David,* the oldest (southeastern) section of Jerusalem. *Collected the waters,* perhaps a reference to Hezekiah's excavation of the Siloam tunnel

(2 Kings 20.20). **22.12–14** God was angered by the Judean leaders' failure to turn to him, by the cynical fa-
talism with which they faced imminent disaster (see
28.14–15). **22.15–25** Shebna, Hezekiah's major-
domo, has overreached his authority and is threatened with the loss of his office. **22.15–16** Shebna's
tomb has been plausibly identified with the tomb cut
out of rock at Silwan in the Kidron Valley with a late
eighth-century BCE inscription giving the fuller form
of the name: "This is [the grave of Sheban]yahu who
was *master of the household.*" **22.20–23** Shebna's office is promised to *Eliakim,* who apparently replaced
Shebna before the siege of Jerusalem (36.3; 2 Kings
18.18). **22.24–25** Eventually Eliakim, weighed down
by his family's claims, also proved to be a disappointment.

An Oracle concerning Tyre

23 The oracle concerning Tyre.

Wail, O ships of Tarshish,
   for your fortress is destroyed.[a]
When they came in from Cyprus
   they learned of it.
2 Be still, O inhabitants of the coast,
   O merchants of Sidon,
your messengers crossed over the sea[b]
3   and were on the mighty waters;
your revenue was the grain of Shihor,
   the harvest of the Nile;
   you were the merchant of the nations.
4 Be ashamed, O Sidon, for the sea has
      spoken,
   the fortress of the sea, saying:
"I have neither labored nor given birth,
   I have neither reared young men
   nor brought up young women."
5 When the report comes to Egypt,
   they will be in anguish over the report
      about Tyre.
6 Cross over to Tarshish—
   wail, O inhabitants of the coast!
7 Is this your exultant city
   whose origin is from days of old,
whose feet carried her
   to settle far away?
8 Who has planned this
   against Tyre, the bestower of crowns,
whose merchants were princes,
   whose traders were the honored of the
      earth?
9 The LORD of hosts has planned it—
   to defile the pride of all glory,
   to shame all the honored of the
      earth.
10 Cross over to your own land,
   O ships of[c] Tarshish;
   this is a harbor[d] no more.

11 He has stretched out his hand over the
      sea,
   he has shaken the kingdoms;
the LORD has given command concerning
      Canaan
   to destroy its fortresses.
12 He said:
You will exult no longer,
   O oppressed virgin daughter Sidon;
rise, cross over to Cyprus—
   even there you will have no rest.

13 Look at the land of the Chaldeans! This
is the people; it was not Assyria. They destined
Tyre for wild animals. They erected their siege
towers, they tore down her palaces, they made
her a ruin.[e]
14 Wail, O ships of Tarshish,
   for your fortress is destroyed.
15From that day Tyre will be forgotten for seventy years, the lifetime of one king. At the end
of seventy years, it will happen to Tyre as in
the song about the prostitute:
16 Take a harp,
   go about the city,
   you forgotten prostitute!
Make sweet melody,
   sing many songs,
   that you may be remembered.
17At the end of seventy years, the LORD will
visit Tyre, and she will return to her trade, and
will prostitute herself with all the kingdoms of
the world on the face of the earth. 18Her merchandise and her wages will be dedicated to
the LORD; her profits[f] will not be stored or
hoarded, but her merchandise will supply
abundant food and fine clothing for those
who live in the presence of the LORD.

---

a Cn Compare verse 14: Heb *for it is destroyed, without houses*
b Q Ms: MT *crossing over the sea, they replenished you*
c Cn Compare Gk: Heb *like the Nile, daughter*   d Cn: Heb
restraint   e Meaning of Heb uncertain   f Heb *it*

23.1–18 The original oracle against Tyre probably
reflects an Assyrian campaign against Phoenicia, possibly that of Tiglath-pileser III (734 BCE) or Sennacherib (701). **23.1** *Tarshish,* a seaport in the western
Mediterranean, probably Tartessus in southern Spain.
Cyprus traded with Phoenicia. **23.2** *Sidon,* a neighboring city to Tyre. **23.3** *Shihor,* an area in the Egyptian
Delta along the Pelusiac arm of the Nile. **23.4** Sidon is
left barren without inhabitants. **23.5–11** Tyre's trading
partners will lament their loss of trade with devastated
Phoenicia. **23.7** *Settle far away.* Phoenician settlers
founded colonies in Cyprus, North Africa, and other
distant sites in the Mediterranean. **23.13** This verse is a
later gloss (perhaps the time of Nebuchadnezzar, 605–
562 BCE; see Ezek 26–28) that attributes the destruction of Tyre to Babylon, *the land of the Chaldeans,*
rather than Assyria. **23.15–18** These verses are probably also from the Babylonian period. **23.17** *Seventy
years.* See Jer 25.11–12; a seventy year period of judgment is also predicted for Babylon in a text of Esar-
haddon. *Prostitute herself,* make whatever international agreements are necessary for economic gain.
23.18 Tyre's future wealth, however, will be dedicated
to God.

Impending Judgment on the Earth

24 Now the LORD is about to lay waste
     the earth and make it desolate,
and he will twist its surface and scatter
     its inhabitants.
2 And it shall be, as with the people, so
     with the priest;
as with the slave, so with his master;
as with the maid, so with her mistress;
as with the buyer, so with the seller;
as with the lender, so with the
     borrower;
as with the creditor, so with the debtor.
3 The earth shall be utterly laid waste and
     utterly despoiled;
for the LORD has spoken this word.

4 The earth dries up and withers,
     the world languishes and withers;
the heavens languish together with the
     earth.
5 The earth lies polluted
     under its inhabitants;
for they have transgressed laws,
     violated the statutes,
     broken the everlasting covenant.
6 Therefore a curse devours the earth,
     and its inhabitants suffer for their guilt;
therefore the inhabitants of the earth
     dwindled,
and few people are left.
7 The wine dries up,
     the vine languishes,
     all the merry-hearted sigh.
8 The mirth of the timbrels is stilled,
     the noise of the jubilant has ceased,
     the mirth of the lyre is stilled.
9 No longer do they drink wine with
     singing;

strong drink is bitter to those who
     drink it.
10 The city of chaos is broken down,
     every house is shut up so that no one
     can enter.
11 There is an outcry in the streets for lack
     of wine;
all joy has reached its eventide;
     the gladness of the earth is banished.
12 Desolation is left in the city,
     the gates are battered into ruins.
13 For thus it shall be on the earth
     and among the nations,
as when an olive tree is beaten,
     as at the gleaning when the grape
     harvest is ended.

14 They lift up their voices, they sing for joy;
     they shout from the west over the
     majesty of the LORD.
15 Therefore in the east give glory to the
     LORD;
in the coastlands of the sea glorify the
     name of the LORD, the God of
     Israel.
16 From the ends of the earth we hear songs
     of praise,
     of glory to the Righteous One.
But I say, I pine away,
     I pine away. Woe is me!
For the treacherous deal treacherously,
     the treacherous deal very treacherously.

17 Terror, and the pit, and the snare
     are upon you, O inhabitant of the
     earth!
18 Whoever flees at the sound of the terror
     shall fall into the pit;
and whoever climbs out of the pit
     shall be caught in the snare.

24.1–27.13 The Isaiah Apocalypse. The designation is due to the fact that these chapters, usually attributed to a period at least a hundred years later than the eighth-century BCE Isaiah of Jerusalem, contain a number of themes popular in later apocalyptic writings. Older Isaian material has been reworked in developing these themes, however. **24.1–23** The earth is about to be laid waste in a universal judgment. **24.2** Cf. Hos 4.9. **24.4–6** The whole creation suffers because of human transgressions (33.8–9; Hos 4.1–3). **24.7–11** The vineyards dry up, ending the mirth of the drinking parties (1.11–12; 32.9–14). **24.10** City of chaos, a portrait of a society so disrupted by famine that every house is shut up against normal social inter-

course (3.1–8). **24.13** Survivors will be as rare as the gleaning after a fruit harvest (17.6). **24.14–16** While the whole world praises God's glory, the prophet complains that the judgment has not yet ended the treachery of the evil oppressors. **24.17–23** Universal judgment will overtake the whole world as God manifests his rule on Mount Zion in Jerusalem. **24.17–18b** See the identical imagery in Jer 48.43–44; cf. Am 5.18–19. **24.18c** Windows of heaven are opened, imagery taken from the Genesis story of Noah and the flood (see Gen 7.11). There may also be an allusion here to an incident in Canaanite myth in which Baal enters his temple, opens a window, and "utters his voice" (i.e., thunders), whereupon the earth quakes and his enemies

For the windows of heaven are opened,
and the foundations of the earth
tremble.
19 The earth is utterly broken,
the earth is torn asunder,
the earth is violently shaken.
20 The earth staggers like a drunkard,
it sways like a hut;
its transgression lies heavy upon it,
and it falls, and will not rise again.

21 On that day the LORD will punish
the host of heaven in heaven,
and on earth the kings of the earth.
22 They will be gathered together
like prisoners in a pit;
they will be shut up in a prison,
and after many days they will be
punished.
23 Then the moon will be abashed,
and the sun ashamed;
for the LORD of hosts will reign
on Mount Zion and in Jerusalem,
and before his elders he will manifest his
glory.

Praise for Deliverance from Oppression

25 O LORD, you are my God;
I will exalt you, I will praise your name;
for you have done wonderful things,
plans formed of old, faithful and sure.
2 For you have made the city a heap,
the fortified city a ruin;
the palace of aliens is a city no more,
it will never be rebuilt.
3 Therefore strong peoples will glorify you;
cities of ruthless nations will fear you.

4 For you have been a refuge to the poor,
a refuge to the needy in their distress,
a shelter from the rainstorm and a
shade from the heat.
When the blast of the ruthless was like a
winter rainstorm,
5 the noise of aliens like heat in a dry
place,
you subdued the heat with the shade of
clouds;
the song of the ruthless was stilled.

6 On this mountain the LORD of hosts will
make for all peoples
a feast of rich food, a feast of well-aged
wines,
of rich food filled with marrow, of
well-aged wines strained clear.
7 And he will destroy on this mountain
the shroud that is cast over all
peoples,
the sheet that is spread over all nations;
8 he will swallow up death forever.
Then the Lord GOD will wipe away the
tears from all faces,
and the disgrace of his people he will
take away from all the earth,
for the LORD has spoken.
9 It will be said on that day,
Lo, this is our God; we have waited for
him, so that he might save us.
This is the LORD for whom we have
waited;
let us be glad and rejoice in his
salvation.
10 For the hand of the LORD will rest on this
mountain.

---

flee. **24.18d–20** Earthquake imagery. **24.21–23** The judgment embraces the pagan gods as well as their human worshipers. **24.21** *Host of heaven,* astral deities (Jer 19.13; Zeph 1.5). **24.22** *Pit,* the underworld, where God's enemies are imprisoned until the final judgment (14.15; Rev 20.1–3). **24.23** *The moon . . . abashed, the sun ashamed,* two of the astral deities (Deut 17.3) responding to God's rebuke. *Elders.* See Ex 24.9–11.

25.1–5 A psalm praising God for saving the weak by his judgment on the mighty oppressors. **25.1** *Plans formed of old,* an old Isaian theme (14.24–27). **25.2** Whether a specific *city* is in mind is unclear; for the imagery, see 17.1. **25.4** *Poor, needy.* See 14.30, 32. **25.4c–5** For this imagery of protection from storm and heat, see 4.6; 32.2. **25.6–10a** God prepares a joyous banquet for all peoples on his royal mountain. **25.6** *This mountain,* Mount Zion, the site of God's royal rule (24.23). *Feast.* A new king celebrated his ac-

cession by providing a feast for his supporters (1 Kings 1.24–25); cf. the banquet before God on Mount Sinai (Ex 24.9–11). The motif suggests a new level of communion and intimacy between God and human subjects. **25.7** *Destroy, swallow up,* translations of the same Hebrew verb meaning to "swallow up." The notion of God's swallowing up death is a reversal of a Canaanite mythological motif in which death "swallows" everything (see 5.14; cf. 1 Cor 15.54–57). *Shroud* and *sheet* do not designate burial garments. They are usually taken to refer to garments worn by mourners, but they may refer to the curtains in the tabernacle or temple that shielded the inner sanctum from public view (Ex 26.36; 27.16; Num 3.31), since humans could not look upon God and live (Ex 33.20). In either case, they symbolize the alienation between God and humans that is removed by God's destruction of death. **25.8** *Wipe away the tears.* See Rev 7.17; 21.4. **25.10b–12** Moab,

The Moabites shall be trodden down in
  their place
    as straw is trodden down in a dung-pit.
11 Though they spread out their hands in
  the midst of it,
    as swimmers spread out their hands to
      swim,
    their pride will be laid low despite the
      struggle[a] of their hands.
12 The high fortifications of his walls will be
  brought down,
    laid low, cast to the ground, even to the
      dust.

Judah's Song of Victory

26 On that day this song will be sung in
    the land of Judah:
We have a strong city;
  he sets up victory
    like walls and bulwarks.
2 Open the gates,
  so that the righteous nation that keeps
    faith
  may enter in.
3 Those of steadfast mind you keep in
    peace—
  in peace because they trust in you.
4 Trust in the Lord forever,
  for in the Lord God[b]
    you have an everlasting rock.
5 For he has brought low
  the inhabitants of the height;
    the lofty city he lays low.
  He lays it low to the ground,
    casts it to the dust.
6 The foot tramples it,
  the feet of the poor,
    the steps of the needy.

7 The way of the righteous is level;
  O Just One, you make smooth the path
    of the righteous.
8 In the path of your judgments,
  O Lord, we wait for you;

your name and your renown
  are the soul's desire.
9 My soul yearns for you in the night,
  my spirit within me earnestly seeks
    you.
For when your judgments are in the
  earth,
    the inhabitants of the world learn
      righteousness.
10 If favor is shown to the wicked,
  they do not learn righteousness;
in the land of uprightness they deal
  perversely
  and do not see the majesty of the
    Lord.
11 O Lord, your hand is lifted up,
  but they do not see it.
Let them see your zeal for your people,
  and be ashamed.
Let the fire for your adversaries
  consume them.
12 O Lord, you will ordain peace for us,
  for indeed, all that we have done, you
    have done for us.
13 O Lord our God,
  other lords besides you have ruled over
    us,
  but we acknowledge your name alone.
14 The dead do not live;
  shades do not rise—
because you have punished and destroyed
  them,
  and wiped out all memory of them.
15 But you have increased the nation,
    O Lord,
  you have increased the nation; you are
    glorified;
  you have enlarged all the borders of the
    land.
16 O Lord, in distress they sought you,
  they poured out a prayer[a]

a Meaning of Heb uncertain   b Heb in Yah, the Lord

Judah's hostile neighbor, will be cast down to drown in shame as in a dung heap. **26.1–6** A processional song celebrating God's defense of Jerusalem and his defeat of its enemies (cf. Pss 24; 46; 48). **26.2** *Righteous nation,* a reformed Judah. **26.5** Cf. the humiliation of Jerusalem in 29.4. **26.6** *Poor, needy.* See 25.4. **26.7–27.1** The community pleads for God's judgment on the wicked, and a prophetic voice responds with a demand for patience and a promise that God's intervention will soon come.

26.7 *O Just One.* The characterization of God as just provides the basis for the community's complaint that God's justice is currently anything but evident (cf. Jer 12.1; Hab 1.12–13). **26.9–11** Unless they are punished, the wicked neither acknowledge God nor change their behavior, so the community urges God to punish them. **26.12–15** There will be deliverance for Judah, who acknowledges God, but destruction for its enemies. **26.14** Cf. v. 19. **26.16–18** Judah, under God's chastening, was like a pregnant woman unable to give

when your chastening was on them.
17 Like a woman with child,
    who writhes and cries out in her pangs
    when she is near her time,
so were we because of you, O LORD;
18   we were with child, we writhed,
    but we gave birth only to wind.
We have won no victories on earth,
    and no one is born to inhabit the
        world.
19 Your dead shall live, their corpses*a* shall
    rise.
    O dwellers in the dust, awake and sing
        for joy!
For your dew is a radiant dew,
    and the earth will give birth to those
        long dead.*b*

20 Come, my people, enter your chambers,
    and shut your doors behind you;
hide yourselves for a little while
    until the wrath is past.
21 For the LORD comes out from his place
    to punish the inhabitants of the earth
        for their iniquity;
the earth will disclose the blood shed on it,
    and will no longer cover its slain.

Israel's Redemption

27 On that day the LORD with his cruel
and great and strong sword will punish
Leviathan the fleeing serpent, Leviathan the
twisting serpent, and he will kill the dragon
that is in the sea.

2 On that day:
    A pleasant vineyard, sing about it!
3   I, the LORD, am its keeper;
    every moment I water it.
I guard it night and day
    so that no one can harm it;
4   I have no wrath.
If it gives me thorns and briers,
    I will march to battle against it.
    I will burn it up.

5 Or else let it cling to me for protection,
    let it make peace with me,
    let it make peace with me.

6 In days to come*c* Jacob shall take root,
    Israel shall blossom and put forth
        shoots,
    and fill the whole world with fruit.

7 Has he struck them down as he struck
        down those who struck them?
    Or have they been killed as their killers
        were killed?
8 By expulsion,*d* by exile you struggled
        against them;
    with his fierce blast he removed them
        in the day of the east wind.
9 Therefore by this the guilt of Jacob will be
        expiated,
    and this will be the full fruit of the
        removal of his sin:
when he makes all the stones of the altars
    like chalkstones crushed to pieces,
    no sacred poles*e* or incense altars will
        remain standing.
10 For the fortified city is solitary,
    a habitation deserted and forsaken, like
        the wilderness;
the calves graze there,
    there they lie down, and strip its
        branches.
11 When its boughs are dry, they are broken;
    women come and make a fire of them.
For this is a people without
        understanding;
therefore he that made them will not
        have compassion on them,
he that formed them will show them
        no favor.

12 On that day the LORD will thresh from
the channel of the Euphrates to the Wadi of

---

a Cn Compare Syr Tg: Heb *my corpse*   *b* Heb *to the shades*
c Heb *Those to come*   *d* Meaning of Heb uncertain
e Heb *Asherim*

---

birth (2 Kings 19.3). **26.19** *Your dead.* For his people,
in contrast to the wicked (see v. 14), God promises a
resurrection to new life (cf. Ezek 37.1–14). **26.20–
21** The people must be patient a little longer, however,
until God's judgment comes. **27.1** Well known from
Canaanite myth, *Leviathan* and the *dragon* are mythological sea monsters (Ps 74.13–14) that personify the
powers of chaos, evil, and destruction.
27.2–13 This section is composed of several frag-

ments, all of which portray Israel's future salvation
using agricultural imagery. **27.2–6** A reversal of Isaiah's earlier song of the vineyard (5.1–7); under God's
protection Israel will prove very fruitful. **27.7–11** God
has punished Israel, but for disciplinary reasons, not to
destroy it as its enemies have been destroyed. **27.9** Israel's sin will be expiated by the removal of every symbol of its idolatry. **27.11** *People without understanding,*
an earlier characterization of Israel (1.3; 5.13). *Will not*

Egypt, and you will be gathered one by one, O people of Israel. [13] And on that day a great trumpet will be blown, and those who were lost in the land of Assyria and those who were driven out to the land of Egypt will come and worship the Lord on the holy mountain at Jerusalem.

Judgment on Corrupt Rulers, Priests, and Prophets

28 Ah, the proud garland of the
    drunkards of Ephraim,
and the fading flower of its glorious
  beauty,
which is on the head of those bloated
  with rich food, of those overcome
  with wine!

[2] See, the Lord has one who is mighty and
  strong;
like a storm of hail, a destroying
  tempest,
like a storm of mighty, overflowing waters;
  with his hand he will hurl them down
  to the earth.

[3] Trampled under foot will be
  the proud garland of the drunkards of
  Ephraim.

[4] And the fading flower of its glorious
  beauty,
which is on the head of those bloated
  with rich food,
will be like a first-ripe fig before the
  summer;
whoever sees it, eats it up
  as soon as it comes to hand.

[5] In that day the Lord of hosts will be a
  garland of glory,

and a diadem of beauty, to the
  remnant of his people;

[6] and a spirit of justice to the one who sits
  in judgment,
and strength to those who turn back
  the battle at the gate.

[7] These also reel with wine
  and stagger with strong drink;
the priest and the prophet reel with
  strong drink,
  they are confused with wine,
  they stagger with strong drink;
they err in vision,
  they stumble in giving judgment.

[8] All tables are covered with filthy vomit;
  no place is clean.

[9] "Whom will he teach knowledge,
  and to whom will he explain the
  message?
Those who are weaned from milk,
  those taken from the breast?

[10] For it is precept upon precept, precept
  upon precept,
  line upon line, line upon line,
  here a little, there a little." [a]

[11] Truly, with stammering lip
  and with alien tongue
he will speak to this people,

[12] to whom he has said,
"This is rest;
  give rest to the weary;
and this is repose";
  yet they would not hear.

_____
a Meaning of Heb of this verse uncertain

have compassion. Cf. Hos 1.6. **27.12–13** The Lord will gather up the remnant of Israel like the kernels of grain at the grain harvest. **27.12** The *Wadi of Egypt* marks the traditional southwestern boundary of Canaan (Num 34.5) and is usually identified with the Wadi el-Arish, midway between Gaza and Pelusium. **27.13** As the *trumpet* summoned Israel to assemble for worship (Num 10.2–10; Joel 2.15), so in the day of salvation it will summon the exiles back to Judah to worship on Mount Zion (cf. Mt 24.31; 1 Thess 4.16).

28.1–33.24 Oracles concerning Ephraim and Judah. **28.1–29** An early oracle against Ephraim (vv. 1–6) is used to introduce an elaborate oracle against Judah (vv. 7–29). **28.1–6** This oracle against Ephraim was probably originally composed at the time of the Syro-Ephraimite war (7.1–6). **28.1** *Garland,* a metaphor for the walls of Samaria, capital of the

Northern Kingdom. **28.2** *Overflowing waters,* Assyria (see 8.7). **28.4** *Like a first-ripe fig,* a simile that underscores how open to hostile attack Israel will be (cf. 17.6). **28.5–6** Israel's remnant will turn to God as its *garland* of pride (see 10.20–23). **28.7–13** This former judgment on Israel's leaders is now applied to the drunken leaders of Judah (see 5.11–12, 22). **28.7** *Strong drink.* See note on 5.11. *Priest* and *prophet,* presumably those who opposed Isaiah's counsel. **28.9–10** The opponents mocked Isaiah's teaching. The Hebrew behind *precept* and *line* may not represent actual words, but simply nonsense sounds uttered in mockery of the prophet's speech. **28.11–13** Since the leaders rejected as unintelligible nonsense the prophet's simple message that would have given them rest (see 30.15), God will speak to them in the incomprehensible *stammering lip* and *alien tongue* of the Assyrians.

13 Therefore the word of the LORD will be to
        them,
   "Precept upon precept, precept upon
        precept,
   line upon line, line upon line,
   here a little, there a little;"[a]
   in order that they may go, and fall
        backward,
   and be broken, and snared, and taken.

14 Therefore hear the word of the LORD, you
        scoffers
   who rule this people in Jerusalem.
15 Because you have said, "We have made a
        covenant with death,
   and with Sheol we have an agreement;
   when the overwhelming scourge passes
        through
   it will not come to us;
   for we have made lies our refuge,
   and in falsehood we have taken
        shelter";
16 therefore thus says the Lord GOD,
   See, I am laying in Zion a foundation
        stone,
   a tested stone,
   a precious cornerstone, a sure
        foundation:
   "One who trusts will not panic."
17 And I will make justice the line,
   and righteousness the plummet;
   hail will sweep away the refuge of lies,
   and waters will overwhelm the shelter.
18 Then your covenant with death will be
        annulled,
   and your agreement with Sheol will
        not stand;
   when the overwhelming scourge passes
        through
   you will be beaten down by it.
19 As often as it passes through, it will take
        you;

for morning by morning it will pass
        through,
   by day and by night;
   and it will be sheer terror to understand
        the message.
20 For the bed is too short to stretch oneself
        on it,
   and the covering too narrow to wrap
        oneself in it.
21 For the LORD will rise up as on Mount
        Perazim,
   he will rage as in the valley of Gibeon
   to do his deed—strange is his deed!—
   and to work his work—alien is his
        work!
22 Now therefore do not scoff,
   or your bonds will be made stronger;
   for I have heard a decree of destruction
   from the Lord GOD of hosts upon the
        whole land.

23 Listen, and hear my voice;
   Pay attention, and hear my speech.
24 Do those who plow for sowing plow
        continually?
   Do they continually open and harrow
        their ground?
25 When they have leveled its surface,
   do they not scatter dill, sow cummin,
   and plant wheat in rows
   and barley in its proper place,
   and spelt as the border?
26 For they are well instructed;
   their God teaches them.

27 Dill is not threshed with a threshing
        sledge,
   nor is a cart wheel rolled over cummin;
   but dill is beaten out with a stick,
   and cummin with a rod.

_____

a Meaning of Heb of this verse uncertain

28.14–22 The foolish plans of these scoffers who
sought a military alliance with Egypt against Assyria
will be destroyed by God's strange work in Zion.
28.14 *Scoffers . . . in Jerusalem,* the Judean authorities.
28.15 *Covenant with death,* presumably a treaty with
Egypt (30.1–2; cf. 22.13). *Overwhelming scourge,* Assyria (8.7–8; cf. 30.28). **28.16** *Foundation stone.* God's
presence in Jerusalem will constitute either a rock of
sanctuary or a stone of stumbling (see 8.14). **28.17** Just
as *line* and *plummet* are used to check the alignment of
walls, so *justice* and *righteousness* will be the criteria
used to determine whether one has built on God's firm

foundation. *Refuge of lies,* military preparation that
depended on deceitful alliances and oppressive demands on the populace (see 30.12; cf. 22.10).
28.20 Proverbial description of an impossible situation. **28.21** As God once fought on *Mount Perazim*
(2 Sam 5.17–21) and at *Gibeon* (Josh 10.10) against
Judah's enemies, now he will rise up to do his *strange
work,* to fight against his own city Jerusalem (29.1–3).
28.23–29 An agricultural parable showing that just as
a farmer adjusts his actions to fit the crop and the season, so even God's strange work makes sense in terms
of God's larger purpose. **28.27–28** Just as a farmer is

28 Grain is crushed for bread,
    but one does not thresh it forever;
    one drives the cart wheel and horses over it,
    but does not pulverize it.
29 This also comes from the LORD of hosts;
    he is wonderful in counsel,
    and excellent in wisdom.

The Siege of Jerusalem

29 Ah, Ariel, Ariel,
    the city where David encamped!
Add year to year;
    let the festivals run their round.
2 Yet I will distress Ariel,
    and there shall be moaning and
      lamentation,
    and Jerusalem*a* shall be to me like an
      Ariel.*b*
3 And like David*c* I will encamp against you;
    I will besiege you with towers
    and raise siegeworks against you.
4 Then deep from the earth you shall speak,
    from low in the dust your words shall
      come;
    your voice shall come from the ground
      like the voice of a ghost,
    and your speech shall whisper out of
      the dust.
5 But the multitude of your foes*d* shall be
    like small dust,
    and the multitude of tyrants like flying
      chaff.
And in an instant, suddenly,
6   you will be visited by the LORD of hosts
with thunder and earthquake and great
    noise,

with whirlwind and tempest, and the
    flame of a devouring fire.
7 And the multitude of all the nations that
    fight against Ariel,
    all that fight against her and her
      stronghold, and who distress her,
    shall be like a dream, a vision of the
      night.
8 Just as when a hungry person dreams of
    eating
    and wakes up still hungry,
    or a thirsty person dreams of drinking
    and wakes up faint, still thirsty,
    so shall the multitude of all the nations be
    that fight against Mount Zion.

9 Stupefy yourselves and be in a stupor,
    blind yourselves and be blind!
Be drunk, but not from wine;
    stagger, but not from strong drink!
10 For the LORD has poured out upon you
    a spirit of deep sleep;
    he has closed your eyes, you prophets,
    and covered your heads, you seers.
11 The vision of all this has become for you
like the words of a sealed document. If it is given
to those who can read, with the command,
"Read this," they say, "We cannot, for it is sealed."
12And if it is given to those who cannot read,
saying, "Read this," they say, "We cannot read."

13 The Lord said:
    Because these people draw near with
      their mouths

---

a Heb *she* *b* Probable meaning, *altar hearth*; compare Ezek 43.15 *c* Gk: Meaning of Heb uncertain *d* Cn: Heb *strangers*

---

careful not to destroy his crop when harvesting it, so God's work of judgment is measured and is not intended to destroy the harvest (27.12–13).

29.1–8 God first besieges and humiliates Jerusalem before coming to its rescue (cf. 1.21–28). **29.1** *Ariel,* probably an altar hearth (cf. Ezek 43.15), an allusion to Jerusalem. **29.2** *Like an Ariel.* The city will be burned like an altar hearth (1.25; 4.4; 33.14). **29.3** *Like David,* as David once besieged Jerusalem (2 Sam 5.6–9). **29.4** Jerusalem will be brought down to the underworld (5.14–15). *Voice of a ghost,* a reference to the muttering or chirping sound that necromancers made when invoking the spirits of the dead (see 8.19). **29.5–8** Then after he has punished Jerusalem, the Lord will suddenly intervene to drive away all those nations he has used as his agents to fight against the city (see 10.12). **29.5** *Small dust, flying chaff,* quickly blown away (17.13). **29.6** Cf. 30.30. **29.7–8** The enemy van-ishes overnight (17.14; 31.4–9; 2 Kings 19.35). **29.9–16** Judah is incapable of discerning what God is doing, so his work seems shocking and amazing, while the plans of its shrewd political counselors come to naught. **29.9–10** Mere drunkenness cannot explain Judah's lack of vision and judgment (28.7); God must have blinded them (cf. 6.9–10; but see 30.10). **29.10** *Your eyes, you prophets . . . your heads, you seers,* perhaps better "your eyes, the prophets . . . your heads, the seers." The question is whether God has blinded the prophets who opposed Isaiah's message, or whether God blinded the people by withholding a prophetic message from those who did not want to hear what the prophets had to say (cf. 30.9–10). **29.11** *Sealed document,* a scroll that cannot be unrolled and read without breaking the seal that secures it. **29.13** Judah's worship is only pretense, not a genuine response to God from the heart (see 1.10–17).

and honor me with their lips,
while their hearts are far from me,
and their worship of me is a human
commandment learned by rote;
14 so I will again do
amazing things with this people,
shocking and amazing.
The wisdom of their wise shall perish,
and the discernment of the discerning
shall be hidden.

15 Ha! You who hide a plan too deep for the
LORD,
whose deeds are in the dark,
and who say, "Who sees us? Who
knows us?"
16 You turn things upside down!
Shall the potter be regarded as the clay?
Shall the thing made say of its maker,
"He did not make me";
or the thing formed say of the one who
formed it,
"He has no understanding"?

Hope for the Future

17 Shall not Lebanon in a very little while
become a fruitful field,
and the fruitful field be regarded as a
forest?
18 On that day the deaf shall hear
the words of a scroll,
and out of their gloom and darkness
the eyes of the blind shall see.
19 The meek shall obtain fresh joy in the
LORD,
and the neediest people shall exult in
the Holy One of Israel.
20 For the tyrant shall be no more,
and the scoffer shall cease to be;

all those alert to do evil shall be cut
off—
21 those who cause a person to lose a
lawsuit,
who set a trap for the arbiter in the
gate,
and without grounds deny justice to
the one in the right.

22 Therefore thus says the LORD, who redeemed Abraham, concerning the house of
Jacob:
No longer shall Jacob be ashamed,
no longer shall his face grow pale.
23 For when he sees his children,
the work of my hands, in his midst,
they will sanctify my name;
they will sanctify the Holy One of
Jacob,
and will stand in awe of the God of
Israel.
24 And those who err in spirit will come to
understanding,
and those who grumble will accept
instruction.

The Futility of Reliance on Egypt

30 Oh, rebellious children, says the
LORD,
who carry out a plan, but not mine;
who make an alliance, but against my
will,
adding sin to sin;
2 who set out to go down to Egypt
without asking for my counsel,
to take refuge in the protection of
Pharaoh,
and to seek shelter in the shadow of
Egypt;

29.14 Thus even Judah's wise cannot discern God's plan (5.12–13). **29.15** *Hide a plan.* Some try to keep their own political plans secret from God and his prophet (30.1–2), apparently on the premise that international politics are too subtle and complicated for the simple religious mind to grasp (28.9–10). **29.16** But believing plans can be hidden is to forget who is the creature and who the creator. **29.17–24** These verses reverse earlier judgments and are generally dated to the later period of chs. 40–66. **29.17** *Lebanon,* a metaphor for God's people; once decimated (10.18–19, 33–34), they will again become as numerous as a forest (4.2; 60.21–22; 61.3). **29.18** A reversal of vv. 9–12. **29.19** *Holy One of Israel.* See note on 1.4. **29.20–21** The *scoffer* will no longer rule (28.14) and oppress God's people (10.1–3). **29.22** *Abraham.*

Cf. 41.8; 51.2. **29.23** *Sanctify,* count as holy. *Stand in awe of,* be in dread of (see 8.12–13).

30.1–5 Isaiah condemns Judah's negotiations with Egypt (703–701 BCE) as rebellion against God and the resulting defensive alliance against Assyria as ultimately useless. **30.1** *Rebellious children.* See 1.2, 4. **30.2** *Without asking for my counsel.* One normally consulted the deity through prophets or the priestly oracle before making a treaty; the failure to do so implied an impious attitude of human self-sufficiency (29.15; cf. Josh 9.14–21). The royal court, because it was apparently trying to keep its rebellious negotiations with Egypt secret from Assyrian spies, refused to consult such prophets as Isaiah, who had publicly opposed such diplomatic moves in the past (cf. 20.1); public opposition by prophets would alert the Assyrians to

3 Therefore the protection of Pharaoh shall
become your shame,
and the shelter in the shadow of Egypt
your humiliation.
4 For though his officials are at Zoan
and his envoys reach Hanes,
5 everyone comes to shame
through a people that cannot profit
them,
that brings neither help nor profit,
but shame and disgrace.

6 An oracle concerning the animals of the
Negeb.
Through a land of trouble and distress,
of lioness and roaring*a* lion,
of viper and flying serpent,
they carry their riches on the backs of
donkeys,
and their treasures on the humps of
camels,
to a people that cannot profit them.
7 For Egypt's help is worthless and empty,
therefore I have called her,
"Rahab who sits still."*b*

A Rebellious People

8 Go now, write it before them on a tablet,
and inscribe it in a book,
so that it may be for the time to come
as a witness forever.
9 For they are a rebellious people,
faithless children,
children who will not hear
the instruction of the LORD;
10 who say to the seers, "Do not see";
and to the prophets, "Do not prophesy
to us what is right;
speak to us smooth things,
prophesy illusions,

11 leave the way, turn aside from the path,
let us hear no more about the Holy
One of Israel."
12 Therefore thus says the Holy One of
Israel:
Because you reject this word,
and put your trust in oppression and
deceit,
and rely on them;
13 therefore this iniquity shall become for
you
like a break in a high wall, bulging out,
and about to collapse,
whose crash comes suddenly, in an
instant;
14 its breaking is like that of a potter's vessel
that is smashed so ruthlessly
that among its fragments not a sherd is
found
for taking fire from the hearth,
or dipping water out of the cistern.

15 For thus said the Lord GOD, the Holy
One of Israel:
In returning and rest you shall be saved;
in quietness and in trust shall be your
strength.
But you refused 16and said,
"No! We will flee upon horses"—
therefore you shall flee!
and, "We will ride upon swift steeds"—
therefore your pursuers shall be swift!
17 A thousand shall flee at the threat of one,
at the threat of five you shall flee,
until you are left
like a flagstaff on the top of a
mountain,
like a signal on a hill.

---

a Cn: Heb *from them*   *b* Meaning of Heb uncertain

---

the revolt that was brewing. **30.4** *Zoan*. See note
on 19.11. *Hanes*, an Egyptian city fifty miles south
of Memphis. **30.6–7** The military assistance Judah
hoped to acquire by sending a treasure caravan
through the desert to Egypt will prove totally useless.
30.6 *Land of trouble . . . flying serpent*, traditional description of the desert between Palestine and Egypt
(Deut 8.15). **30.7** *Rahab*, a mythological sea dragon
slain by God in the cosmogonic battle that led to creation (51.9–10; 89.9–10; Job 9.13; 26.12–13; Ps 89.9–
10). **30.8–17** Isaiah is told to record his message as a
future witness against Judah, because at the present
time the people are unwilling to listen (8.16–18).
30.9 *Rebellious people*. See 30.1. *Faithless children*. See

1.2–4. **30.10** The people effectively silenced their *seers*
and *prophets* (see 29.10). *Smooth things, illusions*,
pleasant words confirming their own plans and hopes,
even if false. **30.11** *Hear no more about the Holy One of
Israel*, keep silent about God's demands and plans.
30.12 *This word*, the promise recorded in v. 15. Judah's
rival military option involved the *oppression* of heavy
taxation, forced labor, government appropriation of
property (22.8–11) and the *deceit* of secret alliances
(28.15; 29.15). **30.15** Judah's salvation lay in trusting
God (cf. 28.12). **30.16** The *horses* they chose to trust in
instead of God will only speed their cowardly flight
(cf. Ps 20.7). **30.17** *A thousand shall flee*. See Lev
26.36–37; Deut 32.30. *Signal on a hill*, a metaphor for

God's Promise to Zion

18 Therefore the LORD waits to be gracious
          to you;
      therefore he will rise up to show mercy
          to you.
    For the LORD is a God of justice;
      blessed are all those who wait for him.

19 Truly, O people in Zion, inhabitants of Jerusalem, you shall weep no more. He will surely be gracious to you at the sound of your cry; when he hears it, he will answer you. 20 Though the Lord may give you the bread of adversity and the water of affliction, yet your Teacher will not hide himself any more, but your eyes shall see your Teacher. 21 And when you turn to the right or when you turn to the left, your ears shall hear a word behind you, saying, "This is the way; walk in it." 22 Then you will defile your silver-covered idols and your gold-plated images. You will scatter them like filthy rags; you will say to them, "Away with you!"

23 He will give rain for the seed with which you sow the ground, and grain, the produce of the ground, which will be rich and plenteous. On that day your cattle will graze in broad pastures; 24 and the oxen and donkeys that till the ground will eat silage, which has been winnowed with shovel and fork. 25 On every lofty mountain and every high hill there will be brooks running with water—on a day of the great slaughter, when the towers fall. 26 Moreover the light of the moon will be like the light of the sun, and the light of the sun will be sevenfold, like the light of seven days, on the day when the LORD binds up the injuries of his people, and heals the wounds inflicted by his blow.

Judgment on Assyria

27 See, the name of the LORD comes from
          far away,
      burning with his anger, and in thick
          rising smoke;[a]
    his lips are full of indignation,

    and his tongue is like a devouring fire;
28   his breath is like an overflowing stream
      that reaches up to the neck—
    to sift the nations with the sieve of
          destruction,
      and to place on the jaws of the peoples
          a bridle that leads them astray.

29 You shall have a song as in the night when a holy festival is kept; and gladness of heart, as when one sets out to the sound of the flute to go to the mountain of the LORD, to the Rock of Israel. 30 And the LORD will cause his majestic voice to be heard and the descending blow of his arm to be seen, in furious anger and a flame of devouring fire, with a cloudburst and tempest and hailstones. 31 The Assyrian will be terror-stricken at the voice of the LORD, when he strikes with his rod. 32 And every stroke of the staff of punishment that the LORD lays upon him will be to the sound of timbrels and lyres; battling with brandished arm he will fight with him. 33 For his burning place[b] has long been prepared; truly it is made ready for the king,[c] its pyre made deep and wide, with fire and wood in abundance; the breath of the LORD, like a stream of sulfur, kindles it.

Alliance with Egypt Is Futile

31 Alas for those who go down to Egypt
          for help
    and who rely on horses,
    who trust in chariots because they are
          many
      and in horsemen because they are very
          strong,
    but do not look to the Holy One of Israel
      or consult the LORD!
2   Yet he too is wise and brings disaster;
      he does not call back his words,
    but will rise against the house of the
          evildoers,
      and against the helpers of those who
          work iniquity.

_____
a Meaning of Heb uncertain   b Or Topheth   c Or Molech

an isolated and exposed remnant (see 31.9). **30.18–26** An oracle of promise is inserted here, perhaps because of the *signal* metaphor (v. 17), which is often used in promises of Israel's restoration (11.10–11; 13.2; 49.22). **30.18** *Waits.* See 8.17. Because the LORD *is a God of justice,* his desire to save must wait until Jerusalem has been transformed by judgment (1.27). **30.19** See 65.19, 24. **30.20** *Hide himself.* Cf. 8.17.

30.25–26 These blessings presuppose God's judgment. **30.27–33** This oracle probably dates to 701 BCE (see 37.21–29). For the fire imagery, cf. 10.16–17; 33.10–14. **30.28** *Bridle.* See 37.29. **30.29** *Rock of Israel,* an epithet for God as a source of refuge for his people (17.10; 26.4). **30.33** *Burning place,* Topheth, where children were sacrificed in the fire (2 Kings 23.10; Jer 7.31; 19.4–9).

3 The Egyptians are human, and not
        God;
    their horses are flesh, and not spirit.
  When the LORD stretches out his hand,
        the helper will stumble, and the one
        helped will fall,
    and they will all perish together.

4 For thus the LORD said to me,
  As a lion or a young lion growls over its
        prey,
    and—when a band of shepherds is
        called out against it—
  is not terrified by their shouting
    or daunted at their noise,
  so the LORD of hosts will come down
    to fight upon Mount Zion and upon its
        hill.
5 Like birds hovering overhead, so the
        LORD of hosts
  will protect Jerusalem;
  he will protect and deliver it,
    he will spare and rescue it.

6 Turn back to him whom you[a] have deeply
betrayed, O people of Israel. 7 For on that day
all of you shall throw away your idols of silver
and idols of gold, which your hands have sin-
fully made for you.
8 "Then the Assyrian shall fall by a sword,
        not of mortals;
    and a sword, not of humans, shall
        devour him;
  he shall flee from the sword,
    and his young men shall be put to
        forced labor.
9 His rock shall pass away in terror,
    and his officers desert the standard in
        panic,"
  says the LORD, whose fire is in Zion,
    and whose furnace is in Jerusalem.

Government with Justice Predicted

32 See, a king will reign in righteousness,
      and princes will rule with justice.

2 Each will be like a hiding place from the
        wind,
    a covert from the tempest,
  like streams of water in a dry place,
    like the shade of a great rock in a weary
        land.
3 Then the eyes of those who have sight
    will not be closed,
  and the ears of those who have hearing
    will listen.
4 The minds of the rash will have good
        judgment,
  and the tongues of stammerers will
    speak readily and distinctly.
5 A fool will no longer be called noble,
  nor a villain said to be honorable.
6 For fools speak folly,
    and their minds plot iniquity:
  to practice ungodliness,
    to utter error concerning the LORD,
  to leave the craving of the hungry
        unsatisfied,
    and to deprive the thirsty of drink.
7 The villainies of villains are evil;
    they devise wicked devices
  to ruin the poor with lying words,
    even when the plea of the needy is
        right.
8 But those who are noble plan noble things,
    and by noble things they stand.

Complacent Women Warned of Disaster

9 Rise up, you women who are at ease, hear
        my voice;
    you complacent daughters, listen to my
        speech.
10 In little more than a year
    you will shudder, you complacent
        ones;
  for the vintage will fail,
    the fruit harvest will not come.
11 Tremble, you women who are at ease,
    shudder, you complacent ones;

_____
a Heb they

31.1–3 Cf. 30.1–17; Jer. 17.5–8. 31.4–9 The mixed
imagery of an attacking lion (5.29) and protecting
birds (Deut 32.11) suggests God's siege of Jerusalem
followed by his deliverance of the city (see 29.1–8).
31.4 Cf. Jer 25.30, 34–38. 31.6–7 A call to repentance
originally addressed to the Northern Kingdom (cf.
2.20; 17.7–8). 31.8–9 God will destroy Assyria; the
Lord dwells in Jerusalem like a _fire_ or a _furnace,_ ready
to refine his own people or consume his enemies (see

1.25; 30.27–33; 33.14). 32.1–8 In the future the rule of
the ideal king (9.1–7; 11.1–9) and his princes (cf. 1.26)
will be marked by righteousness and justice. 32.2 Unlike the former officials who oppressed the people
(1.23; 3.14–15), these rulers, like God, will offer relief
(cf. 25.4–5; 28.12). 32.3 A reversal of the judgment in
6.9–10. 32.5–8 In those days _fools_ and _villains_ will all
be called by their right names (cf. 5.20). 32.9–14 Cf.
3.16–4.1. 32.10 The failure of the vintage will end the

strip, and make yourselves bare,
  and put sackcloth on your loins.
12 Beat your breasts for the pleasant fields,
  for the fruitful vine,
13 for the soil of my people
  growing up in thorns and briers;
  yes, for all the joyous houses
  in the jubilant city.
14 For the palace will be forsaken,
  the populous city deserted;
  the hill and the watchtower
  will become dens forever,
  the joy of wild asses,
  a pasture for flocks;
15 until a spirit from on high is poured out
  on us,
  and the wilderness becomes a fruitful
  field,
  and the fruitful field is deemed a forest.

The Peace of God's Reign

16 Then justice will dwell in the wilderness,
  and righteousness abide in the fruitful
  field.
17 The effect of righteousness will be peace,
  and the result of righteousness,
  quietness and trust forever.
18 My people will abide in a peaceful
  habitation,
  in secure dwellings, and in quiet
  resting places.
19 The forest will disappear completely,[a]
  and the city will be utterly laid low.
20 Happy will you be who sow beside every
  stream,
  who let the ox and the donkey range
  freely.

A Prophecy of Deliverance from Foes

33 Ah, you destroyer,
  who yourself have not been destroyed;

you treacherous one,
  with whom no one has dealt
  treacherously!
When you have ceased to destroy,
  you will be destroyed;
and when you have stopped dealing
  treacherously,
  you will be dealt with treacherously.

2 O LORD, be gracious to us; we wait for
  you.
  Be our arm every morning,
  our salvation in the time of trouble.
3 At the sound of tumult, peoples fled;
  before your majesty, nations scattered.
4 Spoil was gathered as the caterpillar
  gathers;
  as locusts leap, they leaped[b] upon it.
5 The LORD is exalted, he dwells on high;
  he filled Zion with justice and
  righteousness;
6 he will be the stability of your times,
  abundance of salvation, wisdom, and
  knowledge;
  the fear of the LORD is Zion's treasure.[c]

7 Listen! the valiant[b] cry in the streets;
  the envoys of peace weep bitterly.
8 The highways are deserted,
  travelers have quit the road.
The treaty is broken,
  its oaths[d] are despised,
  its obligation[e] is disregarded.
9 The land mourns and languishes;
  Lebanon is confounded and withers
  away;
  Sharon is like a desert;

---

a Cn: Heb And it will hail when the forest comes down
b Meaning of Heb uncertain   c Heb his treasure; meaning of
Heb uncertain   d Q Ms: MT cities   e Or everyone

---

former leisurely life of feasting (5.10–12). **32.11–12** Typical mourning rites (Jer 4.8). **32.15–20** The desolation of judgment will only be ended when the pouring out of God's spirit brings justice and righteousness to the people so that they live in security (see 11.2–9).

33.1–24 An extended prophetic liturgy that includes a communal prayer (vv. 2–9), oracles promising deliverance from the Assyrian oppressor (vv. 1, 10–12), and a call to righteous living in God's presence (vv. 13–16). **33.1** Warning to the treacherous oppressor that his turn will come (see 10.5–12). **33.2–9** Communal lament praising God as the defender of

Zion and describing the treachery of the oppressor. **33.2** *Arm*, source of strength. *Morning*, the time of God's intervention (Ps 46.5). **33.3–4** Traditional imagery from the Zion tradition (see Introduction) for God's protection of Jerusalem; see Pss 48.4–6; 76.5. **33.5–6** God's presence in Jerusalem is its *treasure*, the source of its security (Pss 46.7, 11; 48.1–3; 76.1–3). **33.7–9** The situation of need is described as one of imminent war caused by the treacherous disregard of peace initiatives and earlier treaty commitments. Sennacherib's continuation of the campaign against Jerusalem despite Hezekiah's offer of submission provides a possible historical setting (2 Kings 18.13–37).

and Bashan and Carmel shake off their
        leaves.

10 "Now I will arise," says the LORD,
        "now I will lift myself up;
        now I will be exalted.
11 You conceive chaff, you bring forth
        stubble;
        your breath is a fire that will consume
        you.
12 And the peoples will be as if burned to
        lime,
        like thorns cut down, that are burned
        in the fire."

13 Hear, you who are far away, what I have
        done;
        and you who are near, acknowledge my
        might.
14 The sinners in Zion are afraid;
        trembling has seized the godless:
    "Who among us can live with the
        devouring fire?
    Who among us can live with
        everlasting flames?"
15 Those who walk righteously and speak
        uprightly,
        who despise the gain of oppression,
    who wave away a bribe instead of
        accepting it,
    who stop their ears from hearing of
        bloodshed
    and shut their eyes from looking on
        evil,
16 they will live on the heights;
        their refuge will be the fortresses of
        rocks;
        their food will be supplied, their water
        assured.

The Land of the Majestic King

17 Your eyes will see the king in his beauty;
        they will behold a land that stretches
        far away.

18 Your mind will muse on the terror:
    "Where is the one who counted?
    Where is the one who weighed the
        tribute?
    Where is the one who counted the
        towers?"
19 No longer will you see the insolent
        people,
        the people of an obscure speech that
        you cannot comprehend,
        stammering in a language that you
        cannot understand.
20 Look on Zion, the city of our appointed
        festivals!
    Your eyes will see Jerusalem,
        a quiet habitation, an immovable tent,
    whose stakes will never be pulled up,
        and none of whose ropes will be
        broken.
21 But there the LORD in majesty will be for
        us
        a place of broad rivers and streams,
        where no galley with oars can go,
        nor stately ship can pass.
22 For the LORD is our judge, the LORD is
        our ruler,
        the LORD is our king; he will save us.

23 Your rigging hangs loose;
        it cannot hold the mast firm in its
        place,
        or keep the sail spread out.

    Then prey and spoil in abundance will be
        divided;
        even the lame will fall to plundering.
24 And no inhabitant will say, "I am sick";
        the people who live there will be
        forgiven their iniquity.

Judgment on the Nations

34 Draw near, O nations, to hear;
        O peoples, give heed!
    Let the earth hear, and all that fills it;

33.10–12 Oracular response in which God threatens
to arise and burn the enemy like *thorns* (see 10.16–17;
30.27–33). 33.13–16 In response to this mighty display of God's power before the nations, the sinners
among his own people are terrified, for only the righteous can live in the presence of such a God (see Pss 15;
24.3–5). 33.17–24 In that golden future the righteous
will rejoice in the glory of their king and in the security
of Jerusalem. 33.18–20 In that day the former terror
will seem but a dream (29.7–8); in place of enemy of-

ficers speaking an incomprehensible language (28.11–
13), it will be Judah itself who counts Jerusalem's towers in thankful admiration (Ps 48.12–14). 33.21–
23 This portrayal of Jerusalem makes use of Canaanite
mythological motifs about the abode of the gods.
Jerusalem will be well watered (Ezek 47.1–12), but not
exposed to attack by sea, for the divine king will smash
all such hostile ships (Ps 48.12).
    34.1–17 This is probably a postexilic oracle from
the same period as chs. 56–66. For the prominence

the world, and all that comes from it.
2 For the LORD is enraged against all the
        nations,
    and furious against all their hordes;
    he has doomed them, has given them
        over for slaughter.
3 Their slain shall be cast out,
    and the stench of their corpses shall
        rise;
    the mountains shall flow with their
        blood.
4 All the host of heaven shall rot away,
    and the skies roll up like a scroll.
    All their host shall wither
    like a leaf withering on a vine,
    or fruit withering on a fig tree.

5 When my sword has drunk its fill in the
        heavens,
    lo, it will descend upon Edom,
    upon the people I have doomed to
        judgment.
6 The LORD has a sword; it is sated with
        blood,
    it is gorged with fat,
    with the blood of lambs and goats,
    with the fat of the kidneys of rams.
    For the LORD has a sacrifice in Bozrah,
    a great slaughter in the land of Edom.
7 Wild oxen shall fall with them,
    and young steers with the mighty bulls.
    Their land shall be soaked with blood,
    and their soil made rich with fat.

8 For the LORD has a day of vengeance,
    a year of vindication by Zion's cause.*ᵃ*
9 And the streams of Edom*ᵇ* shall be
        turned into pitch,
    and her soil into sulfur;
    her land shall become burning pitch.

10 Night and day it shall not be quenched;
    its smoke shall go up forever.
    From generation to generation it shall lie
        waste;
    no one shall pass through it forever
        and ever.
11 But the hawk*ᶜ* and the hedgehog*ᶜ* shall
        possess it;
    the owl*ᶜ* and the raven shall live in it.
    He shall stretch the line of confusion over
        it,
    and the plummet of chaos over*ᵈ* its
        nobles.
12 They shall name it No Kingdom There,
    and all its princes shall be nothing.
13 Thorns shall grow over its strongholds,
    nettles and thistles in its fortresses.
    It shall be the haunt of jackals,
    an abode for ostriches.
14 Wildcats shall meet with hyenas,
    goat-demons shall call to each other;
    there too Lilith shall repose,
    and find a place to rest.
15 There shall the owl nest
    and lay and hatch and brood in its
        shadow;
    there too the buzzards shall gather,
    each one with its mate.
16 Seek and read from the book of the LORD:
    Not one of these shall be missing;
    none shall be without its mate.
    For the mouth of the LORD has
        commanded,
    and his spirit has gathered them.
17 He has cast the lot for them,
    his hand has portioned it out to them
        with the line;

---

a Or *of recompense by Zion's defender*   *b* Heb *her streams*
c Identification uncertain   *d* Heb lacks *over*

---

given to Edom in this judgment, cf. esp. 63.1. **34.4** *Host of heaven,* the moon, stars, and planets worshiped by other nations and symbolizing the spiritual powers that lay behind their human governments (see 24.21). **34.5** *My sword,* the sword of the Lord (see Ezek 21.3–32). The judgment on *Edom* simply illustrates the destruction that will befall all the nations (Ob 15–16). **34.6** *Sacrifice.* Cf. Jer 46.10; Ezek 39.17–20. *Bozrah,* an important Edomite city (63.1). **34.8** *A day of vengeance, a year of vindication,* time for God to save Zion and to punish the nations for their treatment of it (61.2; 63.4). **34.9–10** Edom, like Babylon (13.19–22), will share the fate of Sodom and Gomorrah (Gen 19.24–28). **34.11–15** Edom's ruins will be overgrown and inhabited by wild creatures and demons. **34.11** *Line* and *plummet* were aids used by builders to ensure straight horizontal and vertical lines, but they were also used to decide if a building needed to be torn down (28.16–17; Am 7.7–9). **34.12** *No Kingdom There,* a mocking name given to the Edomite ruins. **34.14** *Goat-demons, Lilith,* two varieties of demons thought to inhabit abandoned ruins. **34.16** *Book of the LORD,* perhaps a reference to an earlier scroll containing the similar judgment against Babylon (13.19–22). **34.17** As the Israelites were assigned their inheritance in the land of Canaan by *lot* (Josh 14.1–2), these wild creatures have been assigned the ruins of Babylon as their allotted inheritance.

they shall possess it forever,
  from generation to generation they
    shall live in it.

The Return of the Redeemed to Zion

35 The wilderness and the dry land shall
    be glad,
  the desert shall rejoice and blossom;
like the crocus 2it shall blossom
    abundantly,
  and rejoice with joy and singing.
The glory of Lebanon shall be given to it,
  the majesty of Carmel and Sharon.
They shall see the glory of the LORD,
  the majesty of our God.

3 Strengthen the weak hands,
  and make firm the feeble knees.
4 Say to those who are of a fearful heart,
  "Be strong, do not fear!
Here is your God.
  He will come with vengeance,
with terrible recompense.
  He will come and save you."

5 Then the eyes of the blind shall be
    opened,
  and the ears of the deaf unstopped;
6 then the lame shall leap like a deer,
  and the tongue of the speechless sing
    for joy.
For waters shall break forth in the
    wilderness,
  and streams in the desert;
7 the burning sand shall become a pool,
  and the thirsty ground springs of water;
the haunt of jackals shall become a
    swamp,*a*
  the grass shall become reeds and rushes.

8 A highway shall be there,
  and it shall be called the Holy Way;
the unclean shall not travel on it,*b*
  but it shall be for God's people;*c*
no traveler, not even fools, shall go
    astray.
9 No lion shall be there,
  nor shall any ravenous beast come up
    on it;
they shall not be found there,
  but the redeemed shall walk there.
10 And the ransomed of the LORD shall
    return,
  and come to Zion with singing;
everlasting joy shall be upon their heads;
  they shall obtain joy and gladness,
  and sorrow and sighing shall flee away.

Sennacherib Threatens Jerusalem

36 In the fourteenth year of King Hezekiah, King Sennacherib of Assyria
came up against all the fortified cities of Judah
and captured them. 2The king of Assyria sent
the Rabshakeh from Lachish to King Hezekiah
at Jerusalem, with a great army. He stood by
the conduit of the upper pool on the highway
to the Fuller's Field. 3And there came out to
him Eliakim son of Hilkiah, who was in charge
of the palace, and Shebna the secretary, and
Joah son of Asaph, the recorder.

4 The Rabshakeh said to them, "Say to Hezekiah: Thus says the great king, the king of Assyria: On what do you base this confidence of
yours? 5Do you think that mere words are
strategy and power for war? On whom do you
now rely, that you have rebelled against me?

---

a Cn: Heb *in the haunt of jackals is her resting place*   *b* Or *pass
it by*   *c* Cn: Heb *for them*

35.1–10 This oracle originally belonged to the exilic
collection in chs. 40–55. **35.1–2** The wilderness will
bloom (41.18–19; 51.3), and all shall see the *glory of
the LORD* (40.5). **35.3–4** An unnamed group, perhaps
the angelic members of God's divine council (cf. 40.1–
2), is commissioned to strengthen the disheartened
with the good news that God is coming to save them
(cf. 40.9–10; 41.10, 13–14; 43.1, 5; 44.2; 51.7; 54.4).
35.5–6a The spiritual disabilities of God's people (see
6.9–10; 29.9–10; 32.3; 42.18–20) will be corrected.
35.6b–7 Cf. 41.18–19. **35.8** There will be a *highway*
through the wilderness that no one can miss (30.20–
21; 40.3–4; 42.16). **35.9** Cf. 11.6–9. **35.10** See 51.11.

36.1–39.8 Historical appendix. Apart from 38.9–
20, this material seems to have been inserted from
2 Kings 18.13; 18.17–20.19. **36.1–22** Sennacherib's

campaign against Jerusalem. **36.1** *Fourteenth year of
King Hezekiah.* According to his annals, Sennacherib
besieged Judah in 701 BCE during the course of his
third campaign; hence Hezekiah began his reign in
715; two other passages date the beginning of Hezekiah's reign to 729 based on a synchronism with the Israelite king Hoshea (2 Kings 18.1, 9), but that synchronism is probably artificial and certainly less reliable
than the synchronism with the Assyrian king. *All the
fortified cities,* forty-six according to the Assyrian account. **36.2** *Rabshakeh,* "chief steward," Assyrian title
for a high official. *Lachish,* a major Judean fortress city
lying southwest of Jerusalem midway between
Jerusalem and Gaza; Sennacherib's siege of Lachish
is graphically portrayed on a bas-relief from Sennacherib's palace in Nineveh. **36.3** *Eliakim, Shebna.*

6See, you are relying on Egypt, that broken reed of a staff, which will pierce the hand of anyone who leans on it. Such is Pharaoh king of Egypt to all who rely on him. 7But if you say to me, 'We rely on the LORD our God,' is it not he whose high places and altars Hezekiah has removed, saying to Judah and to Jerusalem, 'You shall worship before this altar'? 8Come now, make a wager with my master the king of Assyria: I will give you two thousand horses, if you are able on your part to set riders on them. 9How then can you repulse a single captain among the least of my master's servants, when you rely on Egypt for chariots and for horsemen? 10Moreover, is it without the LORD that I have come up against this land to destroy it? The LORD said to me, Go up against this land, and destroy it."

11 Then Eliakim, Shebna, and Joah said to the Rabshakeh, "Please speak to your servants in Aramaic, for we understand it; do not speak to us in the language of Judah within the hearing of the people who are on the wall." 12But the Rabshakeh said, "Has my master sent me to speak these words to your master and to you, and not to the people sitting on the wall, who are doomed with you to eat their own dung and drink their own urine?"

13 Then the Rabshakeh stood and called out in a loud voice in the language of Judah, "Hear the words of the great king, the king of Assyria! 14Thus says the king: 'Do not let Hezekiah deceive you, for he will not be able to deliver you. 15Do not let Hezekiah make you rely on the LORD by saying, The LORD will surely deliver us; this city will not be given into the hand of the king of Assyria.' 16Do not listen to Hezekiah; for thus says the king of Assyria: 'Make your peace with me and come out to me; then every one of you will eat from your own vine and your own fig tree and drink water from your own cistern, 17until I come

and take you away to a land like your own land, a land of grain and wine, a land of bread and vineyards. 18Do not let Hezekiah mislead you by saying, The LORD will save us. Has any of the gods of the nations saved their land out of the hand of the king of Assyria? 19Where are the gods of Hamath and Arpad? Where are the gods of Sepharvaim? Have they delivered Samaria out of my hand? 20Who among all the gods of these countries have saved their countries out of my hand, that the LORD should save Jerusalem out of my hand?' "

21 But they were silent and answered him not a word, for the king's command was, "Do not answer him." 22Then Eliakim son of Hilkiah, who was in charge of the palace, and Shebna the secretary, and Joah son of Asaph, the recorder, came to Hezekiah with their clothes torn, and told him the words of the Rabshakeh.

Hezekiah Consults Isaiah

37 When King Hezekiah heard it, he tore his clothes, covered himself with sackcloth, and went into the house of the LORD. 2And he sent Eliakim, who was in charge of the palace, and Shebna the secretary, and the senior priests, covered with sackcloth, to the prophet Isaiah son of Amoz. 3They said to him, "Thus says Hezekiah, This day is a day of distress, of rebuke, and of disgrace; children have come to the birth, and there is no strength to bring them forth. 4It may be that the LORD your God heard the words of the Rabshakeh, whom his master the king of Assyria has sent to mock the living God, and will rebuke the words that the LORD your God has heard; therefore lift up your prayer for the remnant that is left."

5 When the servants of King Hezekiah came to Isaiah, 6Isaiah said to them, "Say to your master, 'Thus says the LORD: Do not be

---

See 22.15–25. **36.6** Cf. 31.1–3. **36.7** Sennacherib misconstrues the character of Hezekiah's religious reform (2 Kings 18.3–6; 2 Chr 29.3–31.21); for a similar Assyrian misunderstanding of the religious situation in Judah, see 10.10–11. **36.9** Cf. 10.8. **36.10** This is typical Assyrian propaganda. **36.11** *Aramaic* was the diplomatic language of the period; the *language of Judah* was Hebrew. The average Judean did not understand Aramaic. **36.12** Horrible conditions resulting from a prolonged siege. **36.13–20** A propaganda speech aimed at the rank and file of Jerusalem's defenders. **36.19** *Hamath, Arpad, Samaria.* See note on 10.9.

Sepharvaim ("Sibraim," Ezek 47.16), a city located between Damascus and Hamath.

37.1–35 From 2 Kings 19; also cf. 2 Chr 32.16–23. **37.1–7** Hezekiah's first consultation with Isaiah. **37.1** *Tore his clothes, covered himself with sackcloth,* signs of mourning. **37.2** Delegations sent from the king to consult a prophet were normal in such circumstances (2 Kings 22.11–14; Jer 37.3). **37.5–7** Isaiah reassures Hezekiah. *Rumor,* report of problems back in Assyria. *Fall by the sword.* Sennacherib was murdered by his own sons in Assyria, but he was not killed until 681 BCE, twenty years after his third campaign. This

afraid because of the words that you have heard, with which the servants of the king of Assyria have reviled me. [7]I myself will put a spirit in him, so that he shall hear a rumor, and return to his own land; I will cause him to fall by the sword in his own land.' "

8 The Rabshakeh returned, and found the king of Assyria fighting against Libnah; for he had heard that the king had left Lachish. [9]Now the king[a] heard concerning King Tirhakah of Ethiopia,[b] "He has set out to fight against you." When he heard it, he sent messengers to Hezekiah, saying, [10]"Thus shall you speak to King Hezekiah of Judah: Do not let your God on whom you rely deceive you by promising that Jerusalem will not be given into the hand of the king of Assyria. [11]See, you have heard what the kings of Assyria have done to all lands, destroying them utterly. Shall you be delivered? [12]Have the gods of the nations delivered them, the nations that my predecessors destroyed, Gozan, Haran, Rezeph, and the people of Eden who were in Telassar? [13]Where is the king of Hamath, the king of Arpad, the king of the city of Sepharvaim, the king of Hena, or the king of Ivvah?"

Hezekiah's Prayer

14 Hezekiah received the letter from the hand of the messengers and read it; then Hezekiah went up to the house of the LORD and spread it before the LORD. [15]And Hezekiah prayed to the LORD, saying: [16]"O LORD of hosts, God of Israel, who are enthroned above the cherubim, you are God, you alone, of all the kingdoms of the earth; you have made heaven and earth. [17]Incline your ear, O LORD, and hear; open your eyes, O LORD, and see; hear all the words of Sennacherib, which he has sent to mock the living God. [18]Truly, O LORD, the

kings of Assyria have laid waste all the nations and their lands, [19]and have hurled their gods into the fire, though they were no gods, but the work of human hands—wood and stone—and so they were destroyed. [20]So now, O LORD our God, save us from his hand, so that all the kingdoms of the earth may know that you alone are the LORD."

21 Then Isaiah son of Amoz sent to Hezekiah, saying: "Thus says the LORD, the God of Israel: Because you have prayed to me concerning King Sennacherib of Assyria, [22]this is the word that the LORD has spoken concerning him:

> She despises you, she scorns you—
>   virgin daughter Zion;
> she tosses her head—behind your back,
>   daughter Jerusalem.

[23] "Whom have you mocked and reviled?
>   Against whom have you raised your
>   voice
> and haughtily lifted your eyes?
>   Against the Holy One of Israel!
[24] By your servants you have mocked the
>   Lord,
>   and you have said, 'With my many
>   chariots
> I have gone up the heights of the
>   mountains,
>   to the far recesses of Lebanon;
> I felled its tallest cedars,
>   its choicest cypresses;
> I came to its remotest height,
>   its densest forest.
[25] I dug wells
>   and drank waters,
> I dried up with the sole of my foot
>   all the streams of Egypt.'

a Heb he   b Or Nubia; Heb Cush

has led some scholars to posit a second campaign against Judah sometime after his conquest of Babylon in 689. **37.8–13** Sennacherib's second message. **37.8** *Libnah*. The precise identification and location of this Judean fortress is still debated. *Lachish* (see note on 36.2) had apparently been captured in the meantime. **37.9** Sennacherib mentions a battle with an Egyptian army, but it is questionable whether *Tirhakah* was already king in 701 BCE, a fact that has also been cited to support a second campaign of Sennacherib against Jerusalem in 689–88, when Tirhakah was king of Ethiopia. **37.12** Sites in Mesopotamia: *Gozan*, on the Habor (Khabur) River (2 Kings 17.6); *Haran*, on the Balikh River (Gen 11.27–32); *Rezeph*, near the west end of the Jebel Singar; *Eden*, territory of

Bit-adini between the Euphrates and the Balikh (Amos 1.5; Ezek 27.23); *Telassar*, a city of Bit-adini. **37.13** The locations of *Hena* and *Ivvah* are unknown. **37.14–20** Hezekiah shows God the Assyrian's boastful letter, and, after the Lord has read it, Hezekiah prays to God for deliverance. **37.14** *Before the LORD*, before the ark within the "most holy place" (holy of holies) in the temple (1 Kings 8.6–7). **37.16** *Enthroned above the cherubim*. The cherubim that overshadowed the ark in the temple were thought of as God's throne (see 6.1). **37.17–20** The Assyrian reproach is a threat to God's own reputation among the nations (see Ex 32.12; Num 14.13–16). **37.21–35** God's response through Isaiah is to taunt the proud Assyrian king and assure Hezekiah of deliverance. **37.23–25** By mocking God, Sen-

26 "Have you not heard
      that I determined it long ago?
   I planned from days of old
      what now I bring to pass,
   that you should make fortified cities
      crash into heaps of ruins,
27 while their inhabitants, shorn of strength,
      are dismayed and confounded;
   they have become like plants of the field
      and like tender grass,
   like grass on the housetops,
      blighted[a] before it is grown.

28 "I know your rising up[b] and your sitting
         down,
      your going out and coming in,
      and your raging against me.
29 Because you have raged against me
      and your arrogance has come to my
         ears,
   I will put my hook in your nose
      and my bit in your mouth;
   I will turn you back on the way
      by which you came.

30 "And this shall be the sign for you: This
year eat what grows of itself, and in the second
year what springs from that; then in the third
year sow, reap, plant vineyards, and eat their
fruit. 31 The surviving remnant of the house of
Judah shall again take root downward, and
bear fruit upward; 32 for from Jerusalem a
remnant shall go out, and from Mount Zion a
band of survivors. The zeal of the LORD of
hosts will do this.

33 "Therefore thus says the LORD concerning the king of Assyria: He shall not come into

this city, shoot an arrow there, come before it
with a shield, or cast up a siege ramp against it.
34 By the way that he came, by the same he
shall return; he shall not come into this city,
says the LORD. 35 For I will defend this city to
save it, for my own sake and for the sake of my
servant David."

Sennacherib's Defeat and Death

36 Then the angel of the LORD set out and
struck down one hundred eighty-five thousand in the camp of the Assyrians; when
morning dawned, they were all dead bodies.
37 Then King Sennacherib of Assyria left, went
home, and lived at Nineveh. 38 As he was worshiping in the house of his god Nisroch, his
sons Adrammelech and Sharezer killed him
with the sword, and they escaped into the land
of Ararat. His son Esar-haddon succeeded
him.

Hezekiah's Illness

38 In those days Hezekiah became sick
and was at the point of death. The
prophet Isaiah son of Amoz came to him, and
said to him, "Thus says the LORD: Set your
house in order, for you shall die; you shall not
recover." 2 Then Hezekiah turned his face to
the wall, and prayed to the LORD: 3 "Remember now, O LORD, I implore you, how I have
walked before you in faithfulness with a whole
heart, and have done what is good in your
sight." And Hezekiah wept bitterly.

4 Then the word of the LORD came to Isa-

---

a With 2 Kings 19.26: Heb *field*   b Q Ms Gk: MT lacks *your rising up*

---

nacherib overreached himself (see 10.7–15; 14.4–15).
37.26–27 God was simply using Sennacherib for
God's own purposes (10.5–6). **37.28–29** Now God
will silence Sennacherib's arrogance by leading him
back home (see 30.28). **37.30** *The sign* confirming this
oracle of salvation is the time limit: within three years
the siege will be long over and agriculture will be back
to normal. For similar signs, cf. 7.14–16; 8.4. **37.33–
35** God promises that Sennacherib will not capture
Jerusalem. **37.35** *For my own sake and . . . David,* God's
action is to preserve his own reputation and to uphold
his covenant with David. **37.36–38** God takes vengeance on Sennacherib by first destroying his army
and then, after he had returned to Assyria, by having
him assassinated. **37.36** *Angel of the LORD,* a transcen-
dental explanation for plague (2 Sam 24.15–17),
which apparently devastated the besieging Assyrian
army; the historian Herodotus (in *Persian Wars* 2.141)

speaks of a plague of mice that overran the Assyrian
camp. **37.38** Sennacherib died in 681 BCE, apparently
murdered in a quarrel among his sons over the right of
succession. *Nisroch,* the name of the god, seems to be
garbled; no such divine name is attested in Assyrian.
Adrammelech, plausibly identified with Arda-Mulishi,
a son of Sennacherib mentioned in Assyrian sources.
Sharezer would correspond to Akkadian Shar-usur,
"Protect the king," but no son of Sennacherib with that
name is attested in Assyrian sources.
38.1–22 Hezekiah becomes ill and God tells him he
will die, but in response to Hezekiah's prayer God
grants him fifteen more years. **38.1** *In those days,* a
vague temporal phrase found again in 39.1; though
the date of Hezekiah's illness is still disputed, the concerns of 38.6 and the connection with the Babylonian
embassy in 39.1 suggest the period just prior to the revolt against Assyria (ca. 705–703 BCE). **38.3** For the

iah: 5"Go and say to Hezekiah, Thus says the LORD, the God of your ancestor David: I have heard your prayer, I have seen your tears; I will add fifteen years to your life. 6I will deliver you and this city out of the hand of the king of Assyria, and defend this city.

7 "This is the sign to you from the LORD, that the LORD will do this thing that he has promised: 8See, I will make the shadow cast by the declining sun on the dial of Ahaz turn back ten steps." So the sun turned back on the dial the ten steps by which it had declined.*a*

9 A writing of King Hezekiah of Judah, after he had been sick and had recovered from his sickness:

10 I said: In the noontide of my days
  I must depart;
I am consigned to the gates of Sheol
  for the rest of my years.
11 I said, I shall not see the LORD
  in the land of the living;
I shall look upon mortals no more
  among the inhabitants of the world.
12 My dwelling is plucked up and removed
    from me
  like a shepherd's tent;
like a weaver I have rolled up my life;
  he cuts me off from the loom;
from day to night you bring me to an
    end;*a*
13   I cry for help*b* until morning;
like a lion he breaks all my bones;
  from day to night you bring me to an
    end.*a*

14 Like a swallow or a crane*a* I clamor,
  I moan like a dove.
My eyes are weary with looking upward.
  O Lord, I am oppressed; be my
    security!
15 But what can I say? For he has spoken to
    me,

and he himself has done it.
All my sleep has fled*c*
  because of the bitterness of my soul.
16 O Lord, by these things people live,
  and in all these is the life of my spirit.*a*
  Oh, restore me to health and make me
    live!
17 Surely it was for my welfare
  that I had great bitterness;
but you have held back*d* my life
  from the pit of destruction,
for you have cast all my sins
  behind your back.
18 For Sheol cannot thank you,
  death cannot praise you;
those who go down to the Pit cannot
    hope
  for your faithfulness.
19 The living, the living, they thank you,
  as I do this day;
fathers make known to children
  your faithfulness.

20 The LORD will save me,
  and we will sing to stringed
    instruments*e*
all the days of our lives,
  at the house of the LORD.

21 Now Isaiah had said, "Let them take a lump of figs, and apply it to the boil, so that he may recover." 22Hezekiah also had said, "What is the sign that I shall go up to the house of the LORD?"

Envoys from Babylon Welcomed

39 At that time King Merodach-baladan son of Baladan of Babylon sent envoys

a Meaning of Heb uncertain   *b* Meaning of Heb uncertain   *c* Cn Compare Syr: Heb *I will walk slowly all my years*   *d* Cn Compare Gk Vg: Heb *loved*   *e* Heb *my stringed instruments*

content of this petition, cf. Ps 26. **38.8** *Dial,* steps or stairs on which the movement of the shadow of a nearby object was used to mark the passage of time. **38.9–20** This song, attributed to Hezekiah as a written votive offering celebrating his recovery, is a typical thanksgiving song used when presenting a thank offering for personal deliverance in the temple liturgy (see Ps 30). **38.10–16** These verses quote the earlier lament and petition of the psalmist. **38.17–20** Then the psalmist announces the deliverance for which he gives thanks. *Death cannot praise you.* If God had al-

lowed Hezekiah to die, God would have lost a voice to sing God's praises; because God cured him, Hezekiah will continue to sing to others of God's faithfulness (see Pss 6.5; 30.9). **38.21–22** These verses would fit better between vv. 6 and 7 (see 2 Kings 20.7–8).

39.1–8 Isaiah is disturbed by Hezekiah's open reception of a delegation from the king of Babylon. **39.1** *Merodach-baladan,* a Chaldean king of Babylon, subjugated by Tiglath-pileser III of Assyria, who revolted against Sargon II and succeeded in ruling an independent Babylon for twelve years (721–709 BCE)

with letters and a present to Hezekiah, for he heard that he had been sick and had recovered. 2 Hezekiah welcomed them; he showed them his treasure house, the silver, the gold, the spices, the precious oil, his whole armory, all that was found in his storehouses. There was nothing in his house or in all his realm that Hezekiah did not show them. 3 Then the prophet Isaiah came to King Hezekiah and said to him, "What did these men say? From where did they come to you?" Hezekiah answered, "They have come to me from a far country, from Babylon." 4 He said, "What have they seen in your house?" Hezekiah answered, "They have seen all that is in my house; there is nothing in my storehouses that I did not show them."

5 Then Isaiah said to Hezekiah, "Hear the word of the LORD of hosts: 6 Days are coming when all that is in your house, and that which your ancestors have stored up until this day, shall be carried to Babylon; nothing shall be left, says the LORD. 7 Some of your own sons who are born to you shall be taken away; they shall be eunuchs in the palace of the king of Babylon." 8 Then Hezekiah said to Isaiah, "The word of the LORD that you have spoken is good." For he thought, "There will be peace and security in my days."

God's People Are Comforted

40 Comfort, O comfort my people,
says your God.
2 Speak tenderly to Jerusalem,
and cry to her

that she has served her term,
that her penalty is paid,
that she has received from the LORD's
hand
double for all her sins.

3 A voice cries out:
"In the wilderness prepare the way of the
LORD,
make straight in the desert a highway
for our God.
4 Every valley shall be lifted up,
and every mountain and hill be made
low;
the uneven ground shall become level,
and the rough places a plain.
5 Then the glory of the LORD shall be
revealed,
and all people shall see it together,
for the mouth of the LORD has
spoken."

6 A voice says, "Cry out!"
And I said, "What shall I cry?"
All people are grass,
their constancy is like the flower of the
field.
7 The grass withers, the flower fades,
when the breath of the LORD blows
upon it;
surely the people are grass.
8 The grass withers, the flower fades;
but the word of our God will stand
forever.
9 Get you up to a high mountain,

before Sargon recaptured it. After Sargon's death (705), Merodach-baladan again revolted and, though he soon lost Babylon (703), he remained a thorn in Assyria's side for another ten years. **39.2** Hezekiah's display of his *treasure house* and *armory* to these envoys suggests that the real motivation for this visit was an attempt to forge an anti-Assyrian alliance between Babylon and Judah. **39.3–4** Isaiah suspected such intrigue. The fact that Isaiah had to ask about the foreign envoys after their visit with the king suggests that the prophet had been intentionally kept in the dark about the diplomatic plans being hatched in the royal court (see 29.15; 30.1–2; 31.1). **39.5–7** The judgment appears to refer to the later events of 597 BCE (2 Kings 24.10–17).

40.1–55.13 Consolation of Judah. These chapters, which console the people of Judah with the promise of a joyous return to their homeland, presuppose the Babylonian exile and probably date from the period between 545 and 539 BCE. See Introduction. **40.1–** 11 God commissions the divine council to issue a message of consolation to the people of Israel, and the prophet, who overhears the voices of the council, clarifies the message. **40.1–2** *Comfort, speak, cry.* These imperatives are all plural, addressed to the angelic members of God's royal council (see 6.8; 1 Kings 22.19–22). *My people . . . your God,* covenant language (Jer 31.33). *Served her term.* The period of punishment in exile is passed (see Jer 29.10). *Double.* See Ex 22.7. **40.3–5** Quoted in Lk 3.4–6 (cf. Mt 3.3; Mk 1.3; Jn 1.23). *Way of the LORD,* the highway God will use to come to his people; behind this imagery are the roads especially prepared by the Babylonians for the festive processionals of their gods. *Desert.* The road will extend across the desert from Babylon to Judah. *The glory of the LORD* will be seen when he returns to Judah on this road (vv. 9–10). **40.6–8** A *voice* from God's council proclaims the eternal reliability of God's word (55.10–11) in contrast to the transitoriness of human existence (see 1 Pet 1.24–25). **40.7** *Breath,* wind.

O Zion, herald of good tidings;[a]
lift up your voice with strength,
O Jerusalem, herald of good tidings,[b]
lift it up, do not fear;
say to the cities of Judah,
"Here is your God!"

10 See, the Lord GOD comes with might,
and his arm rules for him;
his reward is with him,
and his recompense before him.

11 He will feed his flock like a shepherd;
he will gather the lambs in his arms,
and carry them in his bosom,
and gently lead the mother sheep.

12 Who has measured the waters in the
hollow of his hand
and marked off the heavens with a span,
enclosed the dust of the earth in a
measure,
and weighed the mountains in scales
and the hills in a balance?

13 Who has directed the spirit of the LORD,
or as his counselor has instructed him?

14 Whom did he consult for his
enlightenment,
and who taught him the path of
justice?
Who taught him knowledge,
and showed him the way of
understanding?

15 Even the nations are like a drop from a
bucket,
and are accounted as dust on the
scales;
see, he takes up the isles like fine dust.

16 Lebanon would not provide fuel enough,
nor are its animals enough for a burnt
offering.

17 All the nations are as nothing before him;
they are accounted by him as less than
nothing and emptiness.

18 To whom then will you liken God,
or what likeness compare with him?

19 An idol? —A workman casts it,
and a goldsmith overlays it with gold,
and casts for it silver chains.

20 As a gift one chooses mulberry wood[c]
—wood that will not rot—
then seeks out a skilled artisan
to set up an image that will not topple.

21 Have you not known? Have you not
heard?
Has it not been told you from the
beginning?
Have you not understood from the
foundations of the earth?

22 It is he who sits above the circle of the
earth,
and its inhabitants are like
grasshoppers;
who stretches out the heavens like a
curtain,
and spreads them like a tent to live in;

23 who brings princes to naught,
and makes the rulers of the earth as
nothing.

24 Scarcely are they planted, scarcely sown,
scarcely has their stem taken root in
the earth,
when he blows upon them, and they
wither,
and the tempest carries them off like
stubble.

25 To whom then will you compare me,
or who is my equal? says the Holy One.

26 Lift up your eyes on high and see:
Who created these?

---

a Or O herald of good tidings to Zion   b Or O herald of good
tidings to Jerusalem   c Meaning of Heb uncertain

40.9 Jerusalem is called upon to be the *herald* to announce the good news of God's return to the rest of
the cities of Judah. 40.10–11 God is portrayed in the
typology of a Jacob returning from Mesopotamia with
his flock (the Judean exiles) as his wages (see Gen
31.1–33.14). This portrait reflects traditional royal
imagery; the Babylonian king Hammurabi describes
himself as "the beneficent shepherd" and asserts, "In
my *bosom* I carried the peoples of the land of Sumer
and Akkad" (Code of Hammurabi, Prologue). 40.12–
31 The God who created all things is more than a
match for Judah's oppressors and their idols. 40.12–

14 A series of rhetorical questions intended to show
the incomparable power and wisdom of God. 40.15–
17 Neither nature nor the nations can thwart the will
of such a God; as obstacles to the accomplishment of
God's purpose, they are as insignificant as a few specks
of fine *dust on the scales* are to a merchant when weighing produce. 40.18–20 God cannot be compared to
idols made by human hands (see 42.17; 45.16, 20;
46.1–2; Jer 10.1–16). 40.21–24 God, who created the
world and its peoples, also controls their history
(44.24–28). 40.24 *He blows upon them, and they
wither.* See v. 7. 40.26 Far from being rival gods, the

He who brings out their host and
    numbers them,
  calling them all by name;
because he is great in strength,
  mighty in power,
  not one is missing.

27 Why do you say, O Jacob,
    and speak, O Israel,
  "My way is hidden from the LORD,
  and my right is disregarded by my
      God"?
28 Have you not known? Have you not
    heard?
  The LORD is the everlasting God,
    the Creator of the ends of the earth.
  He does not faint or grow weary;
    his understanding is unsearchable.
29 He gives power to the faint,
    and strengthens the powerless.
30 Even youths will faint and be weary,
    and the young will fall exhausted;
31 but those who wait for the LORD shall
    renew their strength,
  they shall mount up with wings like
    eagles,
  they shall run and not be weary,
  they shall walk and not faint.

Israel Assured of God's Help

41 Listen to me in silence, O coastlands;
    let the peoples renew their strength;
let them approach, then let them speak;
  let us together draw near for judgment.

2 Who has roused a victor from the east,
    summoned him to his service?
He delivers up nations to him,
    and tramples kings under foot;
he makes them like dust with his sword,
  like driven stubble with his bow.

3 He pursues them and passes on safely,
    scarcely touching the path with his
    feet.
4 Who has performed and done this,
    calling the generations from the
    beginning?
I, the LORD, am first,
    and will be with the last.
5 The coastlands have seen and are afraid,
    the ends of the earth tremble;
  they have drawn near and come.
6 Each one helps the other,
    saying to one another, "Take courage!"
7 The artisan encourages the goldsmith,
    and the one who smooths with the
      hammer encourages the one who
      strikes the anvil,
saying of the soldering, "It is good";
  and they fasten it with nails so that it
    cannot be moved.
8 But you, Israel, my servant,
    Jacob, whom I have chosen,
  the offspring of Abraham, my friend;
9 you whom I took from the ends of the
    earth,
  and called from its farthest corners,
saying to you, "You are my servant,
  I have chosen you and not cast you
    off";
10 do not fear, for I am with you,
    do not be afraid, for I am your God;
I will strengthen you, I will help you,
  I will uphold you with my victorious
    right hand.

11 Yes, all who are incensed against you
    shall be ashamed and disgraced;
those who strive against you
    shall be as nothing and shall perish.
12 You shall seek those who contend with
    you,

---

heavenly *host* (24.21) were created by God and are
subject to him, appearing promptly at God's call.
40.27–31 God is aware of his people's situation and by
his creative power the Lord will renew their strength if
they *wait* on him (49.23; see Ps 103.5).
  41.1–10 The nations are called upon to go to court
with God to resolve the question of who actually controls history. The early victories of Cyrus of Persia,
who was becoming a threat to Babylon, form the background to this oracle. **41.2** *Victor from the east,* Cyrus
of Persia (44.28; 45.1). *Summoned him to his service.*
God is the real power behind the rise of Cyrus, who is
simply an agent in God's service (10.5; Jer 27.6).
41.3 *Scarcely touching the path,* a reference to the speed

of the Persian army. **41.4** *First . . . last.* The God of Israel controls history from beginning to end; the Lord
has no rival (43.10; 44.6). **41.5–6** Terrified by the victorious advance of Cyrus, the nations try to encourage
one another against him—a reference perhaps to the
defensive treaties concluded between Babylon, Lydia,
and Egypt. **41.7** Securing their idols is part of the nations' defensive preparations. **41.8–10** Just as God is
summoning Cyrus from the east, so God called Abraham and his descendants from the ends of the earth
(Gen 12.1–3). That summons to be God's special people still stands, so Israel, God's *servant,* need not fear
like the other nations. **41.11–20** God will protect Israel against its enemies and meet its needs in the

but you shall not find them;
those who war against you
shall be as nothing at all.
13 For I, the LORD your God,
hold your right hand;
it is I who say to you, "Do not fear,
I will help you."

14 Do not fear, you worm Jacob,
you insect[a] Israel!
I will help you, says the LORD;
your Redeemer is the Holy One of
Israel.
15 Now, I will make of you a threshing
sledge,
sharp, new, and having teeth;
you shall thresh the mountains and crush
them,
and you shall make the hills like chaff.
16 You shall winnow them and the wind
shall carry them away,
and the tempest shall scatter them.
Then you shall rejoice in the LORD;
in the Holy One of Israel you shall
glory.

17 When the poor and needy seek water,
and there is none,
and their tongue is parched with thirst,
I the LORD will answer them,
I the God of Israel will not forsake them.
18 I will open rivers on the bare heights,[b]
and fountains in the midst of the
valleys;
I will make the wilderness a pool of
water,
and the dry land springs of water.
19 I will put in the wilderness the cedar,
the acacia, the myrtle, and the olive;

I will set in the desert the cypress,
the plane and the pine together,
20 so that all may see and know,
all may consider and understand,
that the hand of the LORD has done this,
the Holy One of Israel has created it.

The Futility of Idols

21 Set forth your case, says the LORD;
bring your proofs, says the King of
Jacob.
22 Let them bring them, and tell us
what is to happen.
Tell us the former things, what they are,
so that we may consider them,
and that we may know their outcome;
or declare to us the things to come.
23 Tell us what is to come hereafter,
that we may know that you are gods;
do good, or do harm,
that we may be afraid and terrified.
24 You, indeed, are nothing
and your work is nothing at all;
whoever chooses you is an
abomination.

25 I stirred up one from the north, and he
has come,
from the rising of the sun he was
summoned by name.[c]
He shall trample[d] on rulers as on mortar,
as the potter treads clay.
26 Who declared it from the beginning, so
that we might know,
and beforehand, so that we might say,
"He is right"?

---

a Syr: Heb *men of*   b Or *trails*   c Cn Compare Q Ms Gk: MT
and he shall call on my name   d Cn: Heb *come*

---

wilderness. **41.11–13** Israel's enemies will vanish, because God is with Israel. **41.14** *Worm Jacob ... insect Israel*. Israel seemed insignificant in comparison to its powerful enemies (cf. Ps 22.6). *Redeemer*, the one who avenges or liberates an oppressed kinsman (cf. Lev 25.47–55). *Holy One of Israel*, an epithet for God (see note on 1.4). **41.15–16** Just as Cyrus treated his enemies as stubble (v. 2), so Israel will thresh its enemies. *Mountains, hills* suggest the strength of Israel's enemies. **41.17–20** God will provide water and shade for Israel when it crosses the desert in its return from exile to its own land. **41.20** *The hand of the LORD has done this.* God's care for Israel in the wilderness will prove that it was God who raised up Cyrus to defeat Babylon and bring about Israel's restoration. **41.21–29** The idols of the nations are called upon to provide some

proof that they are gods and that they, rather than the Lord, the God of Israel, control the destiny of nations. **41.21** *King of Jacob*, God. **41.22–23** The idols are called upon to cite their past prophecies that have now been fulfilled or to predict the outcome of present events in order to prove that they know and control the course of history. *Do good, or do harm*. A god that neither blesses nor harms humans is nothing of which humans need to be *afraid* or *terrified;* such a god can safely be ignored (see Zeph 1.12). **41.24** *Nothing*. An idol is a nonentity incapable of action. *Abomination.* The one who chooses such a god becomes as detestable as the idol chosen (see Hos 9.10). **41.25** God, in contrast, is the one who called Cyrus. *From the north*, here from the Medo-Persian territory north and east of Babylon; earlier used of enemies from Assyria (14.31)

There was no one who declared it, none
    who proclaimed,
  none who heard your words.
27 I first have declared it to Zion,ᵃ
    and I give to Jerusalem a herald of
      good tidings.
28 But when I look there is no one;
    among these there is no counselor
  who, when I ask, gives an answer.
29 No, they are all a delusion;
    their works are nothing;
  their images are empty wind.

The Servant, a Light to the Nations

42 Here is my servant, whom I uphold,
    my chosen, in whom my soul delights;
  I have put my spirit upon him;
    he will bring forth justice to the
      nations.
2 He will not cry or lift up his voice,
    or make it heard in the street;
3 a bruised reed he will not break,
    and a dimly burning wick he will not
      quench;
  he will faithfully bring forth justice.
4 He will not grow faint or be crushed
    until he has established justice in the
      earth;
  and the coastlands wait for his
      teaching.

5 Thus says God, the LORD,
    who created the heavens and stretched
      them out,
  who spread out the earth and what
      comes from it,
  who gives breath to the people upon it
    and spirit to those who walk in it:
6 I am the LORD, I have called you in
      righteousness,
    I have taken you by the hand and kept
      you;
  I have given you as a covenant to the
      people,ᵇ
    a light to the nations,
7   to open the eyes that are blind,
  to bring out the prisoners from the
      dungeon,
    from the prison those who sit in
      darkness.
8 I am the LORD, that is my name;
    my glory I give to no other,
    nor my praise to idols.
9 See, the former things have come to
      pass,
    and new things I now declare;
  before they spring forth,
    I tell you of them.

A Hymn of Praise

10 Sing to the LORD a new song,
    his praise from the end of the earth!
  Let the sea roarᶜ and all that fills it,
    the coastlands and their inhabitants.

---

a Cn: Heb *First to Zion—Behold, behold them*   *b* Meaning of
Heb uncertain   *c* Cn Compare Ps 96.11; 98.7: Heb *Those who
go down to the sea*

and Babylon (Jer 6.22). **41.26–27** No other god announced the rise of Cyrus; God proclaimed it first to
Jerusalem. **41.28–29** The silence of the idols of the nations demonstrates their nonexistence.
  42.1–9 This text, or a part of this text (vv. 1–4), is
one of four texts (49.1–7; 50.4–11; 52.13–53.12) that
some scholars have identified as "servant songs." Both
the isolation of these songs from their larger context
and the identification of the servant in them are disputed. Those who isolate the songs often identify the
servant as an individual. The position taken here is
that the songs should be read in context and that the
servant is the nation Israel (see, e.g., note on 44.1–2).
42.1–4 The passage is cited as messianic prophecy in
Mt 12.18–20. **42.1** *My servant, whom I uphold, my chosen.* The language points to the identification of Israel
as the servant (41.8–10; 44.1–2; 44.21); God only used
Cyrus for the sake of God's servant Israel (45.1–4).
Spirit, bring forth justice. Israel is equipped for (cf.
44.3) and given the task assigned to the ideal king in
11.1–5. **42.2–3** Unlike the ideal king, however, the servant neither strikes the earth nor kills the wicked with

his royal command (11.4); his *voice* is not even *heard*.
He *brings forth justice* in a different way. **42.4** *Be
crushed.* It is the servant's endurance of suffering that
leads to the establishment of justice (see 53.11). *Wait
for his teaching.* Cf. 11.10. **42.5–6a** Despite appearances, Israel will not fail in its mission, for the one who
called and sustains Israel is the creator and sustainer of
the whole world. **42.6b–7** The light imagery used here
is traditional imagery for a king's establishment of justice. God's servant will be a model to make that justice
clear to all the nations. **42.6b** *A covenant to the people*
(49.8), a difficult expression, perhaps better "a cleansing for the people." **42.7** *To open the eyes . . . to bring out
. . . from the dungeon.* The subject of the infinitives is
not the servant, but God, better conveyed by, "that I
might open the eyes that are blind, bring out the prisoners from the dungeon." The same Hebrew construction is found in 51.16, where *stretching out the heavens
and laying the foundations of the earth* clearly refers to
God's actions, not those of Israel. **42.8** *The LORD,* Yahweh, the name of the only true God, a God who will
allow no rival (Deut 4.23–24). **42.10–17** A song of

11 Let the desert and its towns lift up their
     voice,
       the villages that Kedar inhabits;
     let the inhabitants of Sela sing for joy,
       let them shout from the tops of the
         mountains.
12 Let them give glory to the LORD,
     and declare his praise in the coastlands.
13 The LORD goes forth like a soldier,
     like a warrior he stirs up his fury;
   he cries out, he shouts aloud,
     he shows himself mighty against his
       foes.

14 For a long time I have held my peace,
     I have kept still and restrained myself;
   now I will cry out like a woman in labor,
     I will gasp and pant.
15 I will lay waste mountains and hills,
     and dry up all their herbage;
   I will turn the rivers into islands,
     and dry up the pools.
16 I will lead the blind
     by a road they do not know,
   by paths they have not known
     I will guide them.
   I will turn the darkness before them into
     light,
       the rough places into level ground.
   These are the things I will do,
     and I will not forsake them.
17 They shall be turned back and utterly put
     to shame—
       those who trust in carved images,
   who say to cast images,
     "You are our gods."

18 Listen, you that are deaf;
     and you that are blind, look up and
       see!
19 Who is blind but my servant,

or deaf like my messenger whom I send?
Who is blind like my dedicated one,
  or blind like the servant of the LORD?
20 He sees many things, but does[a] not
     observe them;
   his ears are open, but he does not hear.

Israel's Disobedience

21 The LORD was pleased, for the sake of his
     righteousness,
       to magnify his teaching and make it
         glorious.
22 But this is a people robbed and
     plundered,
       all of them are trapped in holes
       and hidden in prisons;
   they have become a prey with no one to
     rescue,
       a spoil with no one to say, "Restore!"
23 Who among you will give heed to this,
     who will attend and listen for the time
       to come?
24 Who gave up Jacob to the spoiler,
     and Israel to the robbers?
   Was it not the LORD, against whom we
       have sinned,
     in whose ways they would not walk,
       and whose law they would not obey?
25 So he poured upon him the heat of his
     anger
     and the fury of war;
   it set him on fire all around, but he did
       not understand;
     it burned him, but he did not take it to
       heart.

Restoration and Protection Promised

43 But now thus says the LORD,
   he who created you, O Jacob,

a Heb *You see many things but do*

victory to be sung by the whole world for God the warrior (Pss 96; 98). **42.11** *Kedar.* See note on 21.16. *Sela,* a
city of Edom. This city is different from the Sela mentioned in 16.1. **42.13** *Soldier, warrior.* See Ex 15.3.
42.14–17 These verses quote God's shout referred to
in v. 13. **42.14** *For a long time,* during the long period
of Israel's punishment and exile. *Held my peace . . . restrained myself.* God's silence is a metaphor for his failure to intervene in history (see Hab 1.13). **42.15–
16** God's work of destruction is to provide a path for
his people to return to their land in a new exodus
(11.15–16; Ex 13.21–22). **42.17** Having seen this intervention of the true God, idolaters will be ashamed

of their misplaced trust in dead images. **42.18–25** Israel has not understood the significance of all that has
befallen it in its history. **42.18–20** Cf. 6.9–10. **42.21–
22** Though God wanted to glorify his teaching among
the nations (2.3), blind and deaf Israel, God's intended
messenger, sits in exile as a pathetically plundered and
helpless people. **42.23–25** Why is Israel languishing in
exile? It has been punished for transgressing God's
teaching, though it did not understand. **42.24** *Law,*
rendered *teaching* in v. 21. **42.25** Israel's failure to learn
from the *fire* of God's judgment is a recurring motif in
First Isaiah (1.5–7; 9.18–21).

43.1–7 Now this period of punishment is ended,

he who formed you, O Israel:
Do not fear, for I have redeemed you;
　　I have called you by name, you are mine.
2　When you pass through the waters, I will
　　　　be with you;
　　and through the rivers, they shall not
　　　　overwhelm you;
　　when you walk through fire you shall not
　　　　be burned,
　　and the flame shall not consume you.
3　For I am the LORD your God,
　　　　the Holy One of Israel, your Savior.
　　I give Egypt as your ransom,
　　　　Ethiopia[a] and Seba in exchange for you.
4　Because you are precious in my sight,
　　　　and honored, and I love you,
　　I give people in return for you,
　　　　nations in exchange for your life.
5　Do not fear, for I am with you;
　　　　I will bring your offspring from the
　　　　　　east,
　　and from the west I will gather you;
6　I will say to the north, "Give them up,"
　　　　and to the south, "Do not withhold;
　　bring my sons from far away
　　　　and my daughters from the end of the
　　　　　　earth—
7　everyone who is called by my name,
　　　　whom I created for my glory,
　　　　whom I formed and made."

8　Bring forth the people who are blind, yet
　　　　have eyes,
　　who are deaf, yet have ears!
9　Let all the nations gather together,
　　　　and let the peoples assemble.
　　Who among them declared this,
　　　　and foretold to us the former things?
　　Let them bring their witnesses to justify
　　　　them,

and let them hear and say, "It is true."
10　You are my witnesses, says the LORD,
　　　　and my servant whom I have chosen,
　　so that you may know and believe me
　　　　and understand that I am he.
　　Before me no god was formed,
　　　　nor shall there be any after me.
11　I, I am the LORD,
　　　　and besides me there is no savior.
12　I declared and saved and proclaimed,
　　　　when there was no strange god among
　　　　　　you;
　　and you are my witnesses, says the
　　　　LORD.
13　I am God, and also henceforth I am He;
　　　　there is no one who can deliver from
　　　　　　my hand;
　　I work and who can hinder it?

14　Thus says the LORD,
　　　　your Redeemer, the Holy One of Israel:
　　For your sake I will send to Babylon
　　　　and break down all the bars,
　　　　and the shouting of the Chaldeans will
　　　　　　be turned to lamentation.[b]
15　I am the LORD, your Holy One,
　　　　the Creator of Israel, your King.
16　Thus says the LORD,
　　　　who makes a way in the sea,
　　　　a path in the mighty waters,
17　who brings out chariot and horse,
　　　　army and warrior;
　　they lie down, they cannot rise,
　　　　they are extinguished, quenched like a
　　　　　　wick:
18　Do not remember the former things,
　　　　or consider the things of old.
19　I am about to do a new thing;

_____

a Or Nubia; Heb Cush   b Meaning of Heb uncertain

and God will redeem Israel. **43.1** Israel need not fear, for God its creator (44.2, 21, 24) and redeemer (41.14; 48.17; 49.7) has claimed Israel as his own (Ex 19.5–6). *By name* indicates the intimate personal relationship to God (45.3–4; Ex 33.17). **43.2** God will protect his people through all the dangers they encounter (Ps 66.12). **43.3–4** God will give *Egypt, Ethiopia,* and the kingdom of *Seba* in Arabia to Cyrus as a ransom for his people. **43.5–7** God will gather the exiles of his people from the four corners of the world (11.11–12). **43.7** *For my glory.* Israel was created to bring glory to God (cf. 43.21). **43.8–13** Though they have been blind and deaf, the people of Israel will be God's witnesses to the nations that the Lord is the only true God. **43.9** The nations are called upon to bring proof that

their gods predicted the course of history (41.21–24). **43.10** *My witnesses.* Israel will testify on behalf of God. *My servant.* Note that the collective Israel is referred to in the plural as God's witnesses and in the singular as God's servant (see note on 42.1–9). **43.11–13** God has no rival or opponent worthy of the name. **43.14–21** God will break Israel out of its Babylonian exile in a new exodus. **43.14** The mention of *Babylon* and the *Chaldeans* shows that this oracle presupposes the Babylonian exile (597–539 BCE). *Bars,* the wooden or metal crosspieces that held gates shut; to *break* them was to open the gates, allowing Israel to leave Babylon. **43.15** God was Israel's *king* (52.7). **43.16–17** An allusion to the exodus from Egypt (Ex 14–15; cf. Isa 51.9–11). **43.18–19** The new exodus from Babylon, when

now it springs forth, do you not
    perceive it?
I will make a way in the wilderness
    and rivers in the desert.
20 The wild animals will honor me,
        the jackals and the ostriches;
    for I give water in the wilderness,
        rivers in the desert,
    to give drink to my chosen people,
21   the people whom I formed for myself
    so that they might declare my praise.

22 Yet you did not call upon me, O Jacob;
        but you have been weary of me,
            O Israel!
23 You have not brought me your sheep for
            burnt offerings,
        or honored me with your sacrifices.
    I have not burdened you with offerings,
        or wearied you with frankincense.
24 You have not bought me sweet cane with
            money,
        or satisfied me with the fat of your
            sacrifices.
    But you have burdened me with your sins;
        you have wearied me with your
            iniquities.

25 I, I am He
        who blots out your transgressions for
            my own sake,
    and I will not remember your sins.
26 Accuse me, let us go to trial;
        set forth your case, so that you may be
            proved right.
27 Your first ancestor sinned,
        and your interpreters transgressed
            against me.
28 Therefore I profaned the princes of the
        sanctuary,

I delivered Jacob to utter destruction,
    and Israel to reviling.

God's Blessing on Israel

44 But now hear, O Jacob my servant,
        Israel whom I have chosen!
2 Thus says the LORD who made you,
        who formed you in the womb and will
            help you:
    Do not fear, O Jacob my servant,
        Jeshurun whom I have chosen.
3 For I will pour water on the thirsty land,
        and streams on the dry ground;
    I will pour my spirit upon your
            descendants,
        and my blessing on your offspring.
4 They shall spring up like a green
            tamarisk,
        like willows by flowing streams.
5 This one will say, "I am the LORD's,"
        another will be called by the name of
            Jacob,
    yet another will write on the hand, "The
            LORD's,"
        and adopt the name of Israel.

6 Thus says the LORD, the King of Israel,
        and his Redeemer, the LORD of hosts:
    I am the first and I am the last;
        besides me there is no god.
7 Who is like me? Let them proclaim it,
        let them declare and set it forth before
            me.
    Who has announced from of old the
            things to come?[a]
        Let them tell us[b] what is yet to be.
8 Do not fear, or be afraid;

---

a Cn: Heb *from my placing an eternal people and things to come*
b Tg: Heb *them*

God will lead Israel home to Palestine through the wilderness, will be even more glorious than the former exodus. **43.20** *Water in the wilderness.* See Ex 15.22–25; 17.1–7; Num 20.2–13. **43.21** See v. 7. **43.22–28** God did not wrong Israel; it was Israel who sinned against God and brought punishment upon itself. **43.22–23** Cf. Mic 6.3. **43.24** *Sweet cane.* See Ex 30.23; Jer 6.20. **43.25** God forgives Israel for God's own sake, not because Israel is worthy of forgiveness. **43.26–28** If Israel wants to challenge this view of Israel's history, Israel should present its evidence that God is the transgressor. For this point of view, see Ps 44.9–26. **43.27** *First ancestor,* Jacob (Gen 27–38; Hos 12.2–4). *Interpreters,* perhaps prophets and priests who were supposed to speak God's word to the people (Hos 4.4–

6; Jer 23.9–15). **43.28** *Princes of the sanctuary,* priests (2 Kings 25.18–21).
    44.1–5 Now, however, God will restore his blessings to his people. **44.1–2** *My servant.* Note the identification of the servant as Jacob/Israel, Jacob/Jeshurun. **44.2** *Jeshurun* (Deut 32.15; 33.5, 26), an old poetic name for Israel, perhaps meaning "upright one" in Hebrew. **44.3–4** God's *spirit* causes the people to flourish like plants in a well-watered land (see 32.15). **44.5** Then the people will exult in their relationship to the Lord (cf. 4.3; Ps 87.5–6). **44.6–8** The Lord alone has demonstrated his control of history by his prophetic word; there is no other god to challenge the Lord (see 41.21–24). **44.8** *Rock,* an epithet for God as Israel's protector (17.10; 26.4; 30.29; Deut 32.4, 18).

have I not told you from of old and
declared it?
You are my witnesses!
Is there any god besides me?
There is no other rock; I know not one.

The Absurdity of Idol Worship

9 All who make idols are nothing, and the
things they delight in do not profit; their witnesses neither see nor know. And so they will
be put to shame. 10Who would fashion a god
or cast an image that can do no good? 11Look,
all its devotees shall be put to shame; the artisans too are merely human. Let them all assemble, let them stand up; they shall be terrified, they shall all be put to shame.

12 The ironsmith fashions it[a] and works it
over the coals, shaping it with hammers, and
forging it with his strong arm; he becomes
hungry and his strength fails, he drinks no
water and is faint. 13The carpenter stretches a
line, marks it out with a stylus, fashions it with
planes, and marks it with a compass; he makes
it in human form, with human beauty, to be
set up in a shrine. 14He cuts down cedars or
chooses a holm tree or an oak and lets it grow
strong among the trees of the forest. He plants
a cedar and the rain nourishes it. 15Then it can
be used as fuel. Part of it he takes and warms
himself; he kindles a fire and bakes bread.
Then he makes a god and worships it, makes it
a carved image and bows down before it.
16Half of it he burns in the fire; over this half
he roasts meat, eats it and is satisfied. He also
warms himself and says, "Ah, I am warm, I can
feel the fire!" 17The rest of it he makes into a
god, his idol, bows down to it and worships it;
he prays to it and says, "Save me, for you are
my god!"

18 They do not know, nor do they comprehend; for their eyes are shut, so that they cannot see, and their minds as well, so that they
cannot understand. 19No one considers, nor is
there knowledge or discernment to say, "Half
of it I burned in the fire; I also baked bread on

its coals, I roasted meat and have eaten. Now
shall I make the rest of it an abomination?
Shall I fall down before a block of wood?"
20He feeds on ashes; a deluded mind has led
him astray, and he cannot save himself or say,
"Is not this thing in my right hand a fraud?"

Israel Is Not Forgotten

21 Remember these things, O Jacob,
and Israel, for you are my servant;
I formed you, you are my servant;
O Israel, you will not be forgotten by
me.
22 I have swept away your transgressions like
a cloud,
and your sins like mist;
return to me, for I have redeemed you.

23 Sing, O heavens, for the LORD has done it;
shout, O depths of the earth;
break forth into singing, O mountains,
O forest, and every tree in it!
For the LORD has redeemed Jacob,
and will be glorified in Israel.

24 Thus says the LORD, your Redeemer,
who formed you in the womb:
I am the LORD, who made all things,
who alone stretched out the heavens,
who by myself spread out the earth;
25 who frustrates the omens of liars,
and makes fools of diviners;
who turns back the wise,
and makes their knowledge foolish;
26 who confirms the word of his servant,
and fulfills the prediction of his
messengers;
who says of Jerusalem, "It shall be
inhabited,"
and of the cities of Judah, "They shall
be rebuilt,
and I will raise up their ruins";
27 who says to the deep, "Be dry—

_____
a Cn: Heb an ax

44.9–20 A prose satire on the absurdity of idolatry
(cf. 40.18–20; 41.6–7). **44.18** Cf. 6.9–10; 42.18–20.
44.21–28 Reassurance to Israel. **44.21–23** These
verses resume the theme of God's redemption of Israel
found in vv. 1–8. **44.21** _My servant._ Because of Israel's
special status as God's uniquely created servant, God
will never forget Israel. **44.22** God has _swept away_ Israel's sins as completely as the morning mists vanish
before the sun. **44.23** All of nature is called upon to

praise God for his redemption of Israel (cf. 42.10–12;
Jer 51.48). **44.24–28** These verses summarize most of
the themes in the preceding material. **44.24** _Who alone
. . . by myself._ The Lord, the God of Israel, created the
whole world without any assistance from any other
deity (40.12–26; 42.5). **44.25–26** God by his guidance
of history _frustrates_ the predictions of the pagan diviners and _confirms_ the predictions of the Israelite prophets who promised the restoration of Judah (cf. 41.21–

I will dry up your rivers";
28 who says of Cyrus, "He is my shepherd,
        and he shall carry out all my purpose";
and who says of Jerusalem, "It shall be
        rebuilt,"
    and of the temple, "Your foundation
        shall be laid."

Cyrus, God's Instrument

45 Thus says the LORD to his anointed, to
        Cyrus,
    whose right hand I have grasped
to subdue nations before him
    and strip kings of their robes,
to open doors before him—
    and the gates shall not be closed:
2 I will go before you
        and level the mountains, [a]
    I will break in pieces the doors of bronze
        and cut through the bars of iron,
3 I will give you the treasures of darkness
        and riches hidden in secret places,
    so that you may know that it is I, the
        LORD,
    the God of Israel, who call you by your
        name.
4 For the sake of my servant Jacob,
        and Israel my chosen,
    I call you by your name,
        I surname you, though you do not
            know me.
5 I am the LORD, and there is no other;
        besides me there is no god.
    I arm you, though you do not know
        me,
6 so that they may know, from the rising of
        the sun
    and from the west, that there is no one
        besides me;

I am the LORD, and there is no other.
7 I form light and create darkness,
        I make weal and create woe;
    I the LORD do all these things.

8 Shower, O heavens, from above,
        and let the skies rain down
            righteousness;
    let the earth open, that salvation may
        spring up, [b]
    and let it cause righteousness to sprout
        up also;
    I the LORD have created it.

9 Woe to you who strive with your Maker,
        earthen vessels with the potter! [c]
    Does the clay say to the one who fashions
        it, "What are you making"?
    or "Your work has no handles"?
10 Woe to anyone who says to a father,
        "What are you begetting?"
    or to a woman, "With what are you in
        labor?"
11 Thus says the LORD,
        the Holy One of Israel, and its Maker:
    Will you question me [d] about my
        children,
    or command me concerning the work
        of my hands?
12 I made the earth,
        and created humankind upon it;
    it was my hands that stretched out the
        heavens,
    and I commanded all their host.
13 I have aroused Cyrus [e] in righteousness,
        and I will make all his paths straight;

---

a Q Ms Gk: MT the swellings   b Q Ms: MT that they may bring
forth salvation   c Cn: Heb with the potsherds, or with the potters
d Cn: Heb Ask me of things to come   e Heb him

29; 42.9; 43.8–13; 44.7–8). **44.27** *Deep,* double allusion to Babylon as the site of the new exodus from
bondage and as the primordial sea of the cosmogonic
myth whose waters must be dried up so that Israel can
return home (see 11.15–16; 51.10; Ps 74.12–17).
44.28 *Cyrus,* the founder of the Persian Empire, identified as God's agent for effecting Israel's salvation. *Shepherd,* a standard metaphor for king (see Jer 23.1–6).

45.1–8 God's commission to Cyrus. **45.1** Cyrus is
the only non-Israelite designated in the OT as God's
anointed (i.e., messiah), a term usually reserved for Israel's kings or high priests. The closest parallel is found
in Jeremiah, where the prophet has God refer to the
Babylonian king Nebuchadnezzar as "my servant" (Jer
25.9; 27.6; 43.10). **45.2–3** God will assist and reward
Cyrus for carrying out God's commission, so that

Cyrus will recognize that God is responsible for his
success. **45.4–5** Though Cyrus does not know the
Lord, the God of Israel, it is the Lord who has summoned and armed Cyrus for the sake of God's servant
Israel. **45.6–7** The Lord is doing this so that the whole
world will recognize that the Lord alone is God, creator of nature and controller of history. **45.7** *Light . . .
darkness, weal . . . woe.* God is in control of all the twists
and turns of history, whether good or bad from a
human standpoint. **45.8** Concluding command to
heaven and earth to bring forth God's salvation. **45.9–
19** As the creator and lord of history, God is free to
save Israel however God pleases. **45.9–12** There is no
logical basis for Israel to challenge God's way of working in the world (see 29.15–16; Rom 9.20), since Israel
was created by God just like heaven and earth and the

he shall build my city
   and set my exiles free,
not for price or reward,
   says the LORD of hosts.

14 Thus says the LORD:
The wealth of Egypt and the merchandise
   of Ethiopia,*
and the Sabeans, tall of stature,
shall come over to you and be yours,
   they shall follow you;
   they shall come over in chains and bow
     down to you.
They will make supplication to you,
   saying,
"God is with you alone, and there is no
   other;
   there is no god besides him."

15 Truly, you are a God who hides himself,
   O God of Israel, the Savior.

16 All of them are put to shame and
   confounded,
   the makers of idols go in confusion
    together.

17 But Israel is saved by the LORD
   with everlasting salvation;
you shall not be put to shame or
   confounded
   to all eternity.

18 For thus says the LORD,
who created the heavens
   (he is God!),
who formed the earth and made it
   (he established it;
he did not create it a chaos,
   he formed it to be inhabited!):
I am the LORD, and there is no other.

19 I did not speak in secret,
   in a land of darkness;
I did not say to the offspring of Jacob,

"Seek me in chaos."
I the LORD speak the truth,
   I declare what is right.

Idols Cannot Save Babylon

20 Assemble yourselves and come together,
   draw near, you survivors of the
    nations!
They have no knowledge—
   those who carry about their wooden
    idols,
and keep on praying to a god
   that cannot save.

21 Declare and present your case;
   let them take counsel together!
Who told this long ago?
   Who declared it of old?
Was it not I, the LORD?
   There is no other god besides me,
a righteous God and a Savior;
   there is no one besides me.

22 Turn to me and be saved,
   all the ends of the earth!
For I am God, and there is no other.

23 By myself I have sworn,
   from my mouth has gone forth in
    righteousness
   a word that shall not return:
"To me every knee shall bow,
   every tongue shall swear."

24 Only in the LORD, it shall be said of me,
   are righteousness and strength;
all who were incensed against him
   shall come to him and be ashamed.

25 In the LORD all the offspring of Israel
   shall triumph and glory.

---

a Or *Nubia*; Heb *Cush*

rest of humanity. **45.13** God is the one who raised up Cyrus, and he will free Israel and rebuild Jerusalem for God. **45.14** The nations will bring their wealth to Israel as tribute, will serve Israel, and will acknowledge that Israel's God alone is God (49.22–23; 60.4–16; 61.5–6). **45.15** *Hides himself,* a reference to God's penchant for temporarily withdrawing from visible involvement in the world (8.17) and working in strange ways (28.21) that suggests that God's use of Cyrus is totally in character. **45.16–17** Those who make idols will be put to shame, but Israel will be saved. **45.18–19** Israel's exile in Babylon is not God's final purpose for Israel. As the creator, God did not intend Israel to live in a disordered and chaotic universe, but in a habitable one of order, truth, and right. *Chaos,* the disor-

dered state prior to creation (Gen 1.2). **45.20–25** The remnant of the nations is summoned to gather and recognize the Lord as the only God in order that it may be saved. **45.20** *Carry about their wooden idols.* Just prior to Cyrus's conquest of Babylon the Babylonian king Nabonidus had the images of the Babylonian gods carried from their local shrines to Babylon for safekeeping. **45.21** Unlike the Lord, the pagan gods did not predict the rise of Cyrus or the fall of Babylon. **45.22–23** The pagans are invited to acknowledge God and be saved. **45.23** *By myself.* God swears by himself since there is no higher power (cf. Heb 6.13). *Every knee shall bow.* Cf. Rom 14.11; Phil 2.10. **45.24** *All who were incensed against him,* all who were hostile to Israel (see 41.11–13; cf. Gen 12.1–3).

46

Bel bows down, Nebo stoops,
their idols are on beasts and cattle;
these things you carry are loaded
as burdens on weary animals.
2 They stoop, they bow down together;
they cannot save the burden,
but themselves go into captivity.

3 Listen to me, O house of Jacob,
all the remnant of the house of Israel,
who have been borne by me from your
birth,
carried from the womb;
4 even to your old age I am he,
even when you turn gray I will carry
you.
I have made, and I will bear;
I will carry and will save.

5 To whom will you liken me and make me
equal,
and compare me, as though we were
alike?
6 Those who lavish gold from the purse,
and weigh out silver in the scales—
they hire a goldsmith, who makes it into a
god;
then they fall down and worship!
7 They lift it to their shoulders, they carry
it,
they set it in its place, and it stands
there;
it cannot move from its place.
If one cries out to it, it does not answer
or save anyone from trouble.

8 Remember this and consider,[a]
recall it to mind, you transgressors,
9 remember the former things of old;
for I am God, and there is no other;

I am God, and there is no one like me,
10 declaring the end from the beginning
and from ancient times things not yet
done,
saying, "My purpose shall stand,
and I will fulfill my intention,"
11 calling a bird of prey from the east,
the man for my purpose from a far
country.
I have spoken, and I will bring it to pass;
I have planned, and I will do it.

12 Listen to me, you stubborn of heart,
you who are far from deliverance:
13 I bring near my deliverance, it is not far
off,
and my salvation will not tarry;
I will put salvation in Zion,
for Israel my glory.

The Humiliation of Babylon

47

Come down and sit in the dust,
virgin daughter Babylon!
Sit on the ground without a throne,
daughter Chaldea!
For you shall no more be called
tender and delicate.
2 Take the millstones and grind meal,
remove your veil,
strip off your robe, uncover your legs,
pass through the rivers.
3 Your nakedness shall be uncovered,
and your shame shall be seen.
I will take vengeance,
and I will spare no one.
4 Our Redeemer—the LORD of hosts is his
name—
is the Holy One of Israel.

_____
a Meaning of Heb uncertain

46.1–13 Idols must be carried by their worshipers, but God has always carried his people, and God will yet carry and save them. 46.1 Bel, "Lord," an epithet that became an alternate name for Marduk, the chief god of Babylon. Nebo, the Babylonian god Nabu, city god of Borsippa and son of Marduk. 46.2 The Babylonian gods cannot even save their own images, which weigh down the pack animals (see note on 45.20). 46.3–4 God has carried and will carry Israel from the womb (cf. Pss 22.9–11; 71.5–6) to old age (Ps 71.18). 46.5–7 Cf. 40.18–20. 46.7 The reference could be to the yearly processions of the divine images in Babylon, or it could refer to Nabonidus's vain attempt to prevent the Persians from capturing the images (45.20). 46.8–11 Cf. 45.9–13. 46.8 This, the prophetic

history of God's dealing with Israel (44.21). 46.9 Cf. 41.22–29; 42.8–9. 46.10 My purpose shall stand. Cf. 14.24–27. 46.11 Bird of prey, a reference to Cyrus and the swiftness of his assault (41.2–3; 44.28). 46.12–13 Stubborn unbelievers are warned that God's salvation of Israel is near.

47.1–15 God will punish Babylon for its treatment of Israel. 47.1–4 Babylon is portrayed as a royal princess stripped of her glory and taken into captivity. 47.1 Virgin daughter, daughter (also v. 5), parallel terms of endearment for a city or country (37.22; Jer 31.4; 46.11). Chaldea, a name for the country of Babylon derived from the Chaldeans (see note on 13.19). 47.2–3 The former princess is stripped of her finery (3.16–24), forced to do common labor, and subjected

5 Sit in silence, and go into darkness,
    daughter Chaldea!
  For you shall no more be called
    the mistress of kingdoms.
6 I was angry with my people,
    I profaned my heritage;
  I gave them into your hand,
    you showed them no mercy;
  on the aged you made your yoke
    exceedingly heavy.
7 You said, "I shall be mistress forever,"
    so that you did not lay these things to
      heart
    or remember their end.

8 Now therefore hear this, you lover of
      pleasures,
    who sit securely,
  who say in your heart,
    "I am, and there is no one besides me;
  I shall not sit as a widow
    or know the loss of children"—
9 both these things shall come upon you
    in a moment, in one day:
  the loss of children and widowhood
    shall come upon you in full measure,
  in spite of your many sorceries
    and the great power of your
      enchantments.

10 You felt secure in your wickedness;
     you said, "No one sees me."
   Your wisdom and your knowledge
     led you astray,
   and you said in your heart,
     "I am, and there is no one besides me."
11 But evil shall come upon you,
     which you cannot charm away;
   disaster shall fall upon you,

which you will not be able to ward off;
  and ruin shall come on you suddenly,
    of which you know nothing.

12 Stand fast in your enchantments
     and your many sorceries,
   with which you have labored from
     your youth;
   perhaps you may be able to succeed,
     perhaps you may inspire terror.
13 You are wearied with your many
       consultations;
     let those who study[a] the heavens
   stand up and save you,
     those who gaze at the stars,
   and at each new moon predict
     what[b] shall befall you.

14 See, they are like stubble,
     the fire consumes them;
   they cannot deliver themselves
     from the power of the flame.
   No coal for warming oneself is this,
     no fire to sit before!
15 Such to you are those with whom you
       have labored,
     who have trafficked with you from
       your youth;
   they all wander about in their own paths;
     there is no one to save you.

God the Creator and Redeemer

48 Hear this, O house of Jacob,
   who are called by the name of Israel,
   and who came forth from the loins[c] of
     Judah;

---

a Meaning of Heb uncertain   *b* Gk Syr Compare Vg: Heb *from what*   *c* Cn: Heb *waters*

---

to sexual humiliation. **47.6–7** God used Babylon to punish his people, but Babylon did not understand her role and in thoughtless self-conceit failed to show mercy (cf. 10.5–15). **47.8–11** Babylon's haughty sense of security will prove false. **47.9** *Sorceries, enchantments,* a reference to the many Babylonian rituals for divining the future and warding off evil omens. **47.11** *Charm away, ward off.* Babylonian religion had rituals for warding off evils predicted by divination. *Know nothing.* Divination will fail to alert Babylon to the destruction that will suddenly overtake her. **47.13** *Many consultations.* There were many different methods in Babylonian divination, but the inspection of the internal organs of sacrificial animals was the dominant one, always requiring a second consultation to confirm the first. If two consultations did not pro-

duce the desired favorable response from the deity, one tried again; since each consultation required another sacrificial animal, one could exhaust oneself and one's economic resources in attempting to get a reliable response. *Study the heavens.* Astrology was an important means of divination in the Neo-Babylonian period. **47.14–15** Her diviners and astrologers may try, but they cannot deliver Babylon from its destruction; they cannot even save themselves.

48.1–22 God warns his obstinate people to pay attention this time, for God the creator is about to redeem them from Babylonian bondage. **48.1** As elsewhere in chs. 40–66, *house of Jacob* and *Israel* are used here inclusively for the whole people of God, though the vast majority of the people addressed would be the exiles from the Southern Kingdom, *Judah. Not in truth*

who swear by the name of the LORD,
  and invoke the God of Israel,
    but not in truth or right.
2 For they call themselves after the holy city,
    and lean on the God of Israel;
  the LORD of hosts is his name.

3 The former things I declared long ago,
    they went out from my mouth and I
      made them known;
  then suddenly I did them and they
    came to pass.
4 Because I know that you are obstinate,
    and your neck is an iron sinew
  and your forehead brass,
5 I declared them to you from long ago,
    before they came to pass I announced
      them to you,
  so that you would not say, "My idol did
    them,
  my carved image and my cast image
    commanded them."

6 You have heard; now see all this;
    and will you not declare it?
  From this time forward I make you hear
    new things,
  hidden things that you have not known.
7 They are created now, not long ago;
    before today you have never heard of
      them,
  so that you could not say, "I already
    knew them."
8 You have never heard, you have never
    known,
  from of old your ear has not been
    opened.
  For I knew that you would deal very
    treacherously,
  and that from birth you were called a
    rebel.

9 For my name's sake I defer my anger,
    for the sake of my praise I restrain it
      for you,

so that I may not cut you off.
10 See, I have refined you, but not like[a]
    silver;
  I have tested you in the furnace of
    adversity.
11 For my own sake, for my own sake, I do
    it,
  for why should my name[b] be profaned?
  My glory I will not give to another.

12 Listen to me, O Jacob,
    and Israel, whom I called:
  I am He; I am the first,
    and I am the last.
13 My hand laid the foundation of the earth,
    and my right hand spread out the
      heavens;
  when I summon them,
    they stand at attention.

14 Assemble, all of you, and hear!
    Who among them has declared these
      things?
  The LORD loves him;
    he shall perform his purpose on
      Babylon,
    and his arm shall be against the
      Chaldeans.
15 I, even I, have spoken and called him,
    I have brought him, and he will
      prosper in his way.
16 Draw near to me, hear this!
    From the beginning I have not spoken
      in secret,
    from the time it came to be I have been
      there.
  And now the Lord GOD has sent me and
    his spirit.

17 Thus says the LORD,
    your Redeemer, the Holy One of Israel:
  I am the LORD your God,
    who teaches you for your own good,

_____
a Cn: Heb *with*   *b* Gk Old Latin: Heb *for why should it*

or right. Despite their outward affirmations, the people have not followed the Lord (29.13; Zeph 1.5–6). **48.2** *Holy city,* Jerusalem. **48.3–5** To prevent the people of Israel from attributing events to their idols, God announced to Israel what would happen to it and the other nations long before it came to pass (30.8–9; Jer 36.27–32). **48.6–8** God calls upon Israel to testify to the previously unexpected new things the Lord was doing for it. **48.6** *New things,* the deliverance from Bab-

ylon and return to Palestine (43.18–21). **48.8** *Rebel.* See 1.2. **48.9–11** God is saving Israel, not because Israel deserves it, but in order to preserve and enhance God's own reputation (Ex 32.11–12; Ezek 20.22). **48.10** See 1.24–25; Jer 6.27–30. **48.12–13** Israel's God is the creator of the whole world. **48.14–15** *You,* Israel. *Them,* the idols. *Him,* Cyrus. **48.16** The first-person references at the beginning of the verse refer to God, but the final phrase refers either to the prophet or to Israel as

who leads you in the way you should
go.

18 O that you had paid attention to my
commandments!
Then your prosperity would have been
like a river,
and your success like the waves of the
sea;

19 your offspring would have been like the
sand,
and your descendants like its grains;
their name would never be cut off
or destroyed from before me.

20 Go out from Babylon, flee from Chaldea,
declare this with a shout of joy,
proclaim it,
send it forth to the end of the earth;
say, "The LORD has redeemed his
servant Jacob!"

21 They did not thirst when he led them
through the deserts;
he made water flow for them from the
rock;
he split open the rock and the water
gushed out.

22 "There is no peace," says the LORD, "for
the wicked."

The Servant's Mission

49 Listen to me, O coastlands,
pay attention, you peoples from far
away!
The LORD called me before I was born,
while I was in my mother's womb he
named me.

2 He made my mouth like a sharp sword,

in the shadow of his hand he hid me;
he made me a polished arrow,
in his quiver he hid me away.

3 And he said to me, "You are my servant,
Israel, in whom I will be glorified."

4 But I said, "I have labored in vain,
I have spent my strength for nothing
and vanity;
yet surely my cause is with the LORD,
and my reward with my God."

5 And now the LORD says,
who formed me in the womb to be his
servant,
to bring Jacob back to him,
and that Israel might be gathered to
him,
for I am honored in the sight of the
LORD,
and my God has become my strength—

6 he says,
"It is too light a thing that you should be
my servant
to raise up the tribes of Jacob
and to restore the survivors of Israel;
I will give you as a light to the nations,
that my salvation may reach to the end
of the earth."

7 Thus says the LORD,
the Redeemer of Israel and his Holy
One,
to one deeply despised, abhorred by the
nations,
the slave of rulers,
"Kings shall see and stand up,
princes, and they shall prostrate
themselves,

God's servant (42.1–4; 61.1) **48.17** *Teaches, leads.* See
30.20–21. **48.18–19** Had Israel followed God, its prosperity would have come (Ps 81.13–16), fulfilling the
ancient promises (Gen 22.17). **48.20–21** Israel's departure from Babylon is seen as a new exodus (Ex
17.1–7). **48.22** This salvation will not benefit those
who persist in their wickedness (57.20–21).
  49.1–7 The second of the so-called servant songs
(see note on 42.1–9). Despite Israel's present reputation among the nations, God has chosen it to be his
servant, and Israel will ultimately manifest God's glory
and salvation to the whole world. **49.1** *Before I was
born . . . mother's womb.* See Jer 1.5; Gal 1.15. **49.2** God
made the servant's mouth *like a sharp sword* through
the words God gave him to speak (51.16; Eph 6.17;
Heb 4.12). *Arrow, quiver.* Cf. Ps 127.4–5. **49.3** The
identification of the servant with Israel is here explicit.

49.4–7 In the despair of exile it seemed to Israel that
its labor had been for naught (cf. Hab 2.13), but God
reassures Israel of its significance. **49.5** *To bring Jacob
back to him* is not a description of the servant's mission, but a statement of God's action; hence a better
rendering would be "that he might bring Israel back to
himself." **49.6** *It is too light . . . Israel.* The subject of *to
raise up* and *to restore* is again God, which suggests the
translation, "It is too light a thing, you being my servant, that I should only raise up the tribes of Jacob and
restore the survivors of Israel." *End of the earth.* God
will not only restore Israel, but this restoration of Israel will be the means by which God's salvation will extend to the whole earth (42.4, 6). **49.7** *One deeply despised.* The nations had no regard for Israel as long as
it was in exile, apparently rejected by God (53.2–3).
Kings shall . . . prostrate themselves, in response to Is-

because of the LORD, who is faithful,
  the Holy One of Israel, who has chosen
    you."

Zion's Children to Be Brought Home

8 Thus says the LORD:
  In a time of favor I have answered you,
    on a day of salvation I have helped you;
  I have kept you and given you
    as a covenant to the people,^{a}
  to establish the land,
    to apportion the desolate heritages;
9 saying to the prisoners, "Come out,"
    to those who are in darkness, "Show
      yourselves."
  They shall feed along the ways,
    on all the bare heights^b shall be their
      pasture;
10 they shall not hunger or thirst,
    neither scorching wind nor sun shall
      strike them down,
  for he who has pity on them will lead
    them,
  and by springs of water will guide them.
11 And I will turn all my mountains into a
      road,
  and my highways shall be raised up.
12 Lo, these shall come from far away,
    and lo, these from the north and from
      the west,
  and these from the land of Syene.^{c}

13 Sing for joy, O heavens, and exult,
      O earth;
  break forth, O mountains, into singing!
  For the LORD has comforted his people,
    and will have compassion on his
      suffering ones.

14 But Zion said, "The LORD has forsaken me,
    my Lord has forgotten me."

15 Can a woman forget her nursing child,
    or show no compassion for the child of
      her womb?
  Even these may forget,
    yet I will not forget you.
16 See, I have inscribed you on the palms of
      my hands;
    your walls are continually before me.
17 Your builders outdo your destroyers,^{d}
    and those who laid you waste go away
      from you.
18 Lift up your eyes all around and see;
    they all gather, they come to you.
  As I live, says the LORD,
    you shall put all of them on like an
      ornament,
    and like a bride you shall bind them
      on.

19 Surely your waste and your desolate
      places
    and your devastated land—
  surely now you will be too crowded for
      your inhabitants,
    and those who swallowed you up will
      be far away.
20 The children born in the time of your
      bereavement
    will yet say in your hearing:
  "The place is too crowded for me;
    make room for me to settle."
21 Then you will say in your heart,
    "Who has borne me these?
  I was bereaved and barren,
    exiled and put away—
    so who has reared these?
  I was left all alone—
    where then have these come from?"

---

a Meaning of Heb uncertain   *b* Or *the trails*   *c* Q Ms: MT
Sinim   *d* Or *Your children come swiftly; your destroyers*

---

rael's unexpected deliverance and exaltation (52.10–15). **49.8–26** A collection of sayings celebrating God's deliverance of his people. **49.8** *To establish . . . to apportion.* The subject of the verbs is God, not the servant; better "establishing the land, apportioning the desolate heritages." See 42.6–7. **49.9** *Prisoners,* the Israelite exiles. *Come out.* See 48.20. **49.9c–12** Israel's restoration to Palestine is described in the imagery of a new exodus (41.17–20; 42.16; 43.19–21; 48.21). **49.11** See 40.3–4. **49.12** The exiles will return from all directions, not just from Babylon (see 43.5–7). *Syene,* modern Assuan, in southern Egypt at its ancient boundary with Ethiopia (Ezek 29.10). **49.13** See 44.23.

49.14–16 God refutes *Zion's* complaint that God has *forgotten* his city. **49.16** *Inscribed.* God cannot forget Zion, because its plan is tattooed on God's palms. **49.17** The very slight distinction in one vowel between the Hebrew words for *your builders* and *your children* (see text note *d*) suggests an intentional double entendre. **49.18** The imagery shifts from builders/children, and the exiles returning to repopulate Jerusalem are portrayed as *ornaments* of jewelry worn by the city (cf. Lam 4.1–2). **49.19–21** Jerusalem will be surprised at the size of its new population because of the large numbers of returnees who were born in exile. **49.22–23** At God's *signal* the nations will bring Jerusalem's

22 Thus says the Lord GOD:
    I will soon lift up my hand to the nations,
        and raise my signal to the peoples;
    and they shall bring your sons in their
            bosom,
    and your daughters shall be carried on
            their shoulders.
23 Kings shall be your foster fathers,
        and their queens your nursing mothers.
    With their faces to the ground they shall
            bow down to you,
        and lick the dust of your feet.
    Then you will know that I am the LORD;
        those who wait for me shall not be put
            to shame.

24 Can the prey be taken from the mighty,
        or the captives of a tyrant *a* be rescued?
25 But thus says the LORD:
    Even the captives of the mighty shall be
            taken,
        and the prey of the tyrant be rescued;
    for I will contend with those who
            contend with you,
        and I will save your children.
26 I will make your oppressors eat their own
            flesh,
        and they shall be drunk with their own
            blood as with wine.
    Then all flesh shall know
        that I am the LORD your Savior,
        and your Redeemer, the Mighty One of
            Jacob.

50 Thus says the LORD:
    Where is your mother's bill of divorce
        with which I put her away?
    Or which of my creditors is it
        to whom I have sold you?
    No, because of your sins you were sold,

and for your transgressions your
        mother was put away.
2 Why was no one there when I came?
        Why did no one answer when I called?
    Is my hand shortened, that it cannot
            redeem?
        Or have I no power to deliver?
    By my rebuke I dry up the sea,
        I make the rivers a desert;
    their fish stink for lack of water,
        and die of thirst. *b*
3 I clothe the heavens with blackness,
        and make sackcloth their covering.

The Servant's Humiliation and Vindication

4 The Lord GOD has given me
        the tongue of a teacher, *c*
    that I may know how to sustain
        the weary with a word.
    Morning by morning he wakens—
        wakens my ear
    to listen as those who are taught.
5 The Lord GOD has opened my ear,
        and I was not rebellious,
        I did not turn backward.
6 I gave my back to those who struck me,
        and my cheeks to those who pulled out
            the beard;
    I did not hide my face
        from insult and spitting.

7 The Lord GOD helps me;
        therefore I have not been disgraced;
    therefore I have set my face like flint,
        and I know that I shall not be put to
            shame;

---

a Q Ms Syr Vg: MT *of a righteous person*   *b* Or *die on the thirsty ground*   *c* Cn: Heb *of those who are taught*

---

children home (11.10–12; 62.10), and the royalty of the nations will serve Israel (60.9–10, 16). *Bow down . . . lick the dust,* obeisance normally given to a great king (Ps 72.9). **49.24–26** Even though Babylon still seems a mighty power, God will destroy it to rescue his people (see Jer 50–51), and all flesh will acknowledge the Lord as God (45.14–17, 22–25; 52.10; 60.16). **50.1–3** Nothing in Israel's past signifies God's inability to save his people. **50.1** There is no *bill of divorce* to mark God's putting away of Israel as irrevocable (Deut 24.1–4; Jer 3.1), nor did God have to sell his people to pay off a *creditor;* Israel's suffering was not due to God's weakness, but to Israel's sin. **50.2–3** Despite Israel's failure to respond, God still has the power

and will to save, just as in the first exodus. **50.4–11** The third of the so-called servant songs (see note on 42.1–9). The speaker, either the prophet or the servant proclaimed by the prophet, portrays himself in imagery borrowed from the experience of prophets like Jeremiah. **50.4** Constantly instructed by God (Jer 1.4–10), the speaker encourages the discouraged exiles (42.3; 49.5–6). **50.5–6** Unlike Israel as a whole (1.4; 30.9–11), the speaker did not turn away from God, though he was persecuted for his faithfulness (53.3–5, 7–8; Jer 20.1–2; 26.7–24). **50.7–9** Despite these persecutions, the speaker is confident that God will vindicate him against these adversaries (53.10–12; Jer 11.20–12.3; 20.7–13). **50.7** *Set my face like flint.* The speaker will be

8   he who vindicates me is near.
    Who will contend with me?
        Let us stand up together.
    Who are my adversaries?
        Let them confront me.
9   It is the Lord GOD who helps me;
        who will declare me guilty?
    All of them will wear out like a garment;
        the moth will eat them up.

10 Who among you fears the LORD
        and obeys the voice of his servant,
    who walks in darkness
        and has no light,
    yet trusts in the name of the LORD
        and relies upon his God?
11 But all of you are kindlers of fire,
        lighters of firebrands. *a*
    Walk in the flame of your fire,
        and among the brands that you have
            kindled!
    This is what you shall have from my
            hand:
        you shall lie down in torment.

Blessings in Store for God's People

51 Listen to me, you that pursue
            righteousness,
        you that seek the LORD.
    Look to the rock from which you were
            hewn,
        and to the quarry from which you were
            dug.
2   Look to Abraham your father
        and to Sarah who bore you;
    for he was but one when I called him,
        but I blessed him and made him many.
3   For the LORD will comfort Zion;
        he will comfort all her waste places,
    and will make her wilderness like Eden,

her desert like the garden of the LORD;
joy and gladness will be found in her,
    thanksgiving and the voice of song.

4   Listen to me, my people,
        and give heed to me, my nation;
    for a teaching will go out from me,
        and my justice for a light to the peoples.
5   I will bring near my deliverance swiftly,
        my salvation has gone out
    and my arms will rule the peoples;
    the coastlands wait for me,
        and for my arm they hope.
6   Lift up your eyes to the heavens,
        and look at the earth beneath;
    for the heavens will vanish like smoke,
        the earth will wear out like a garment,
    and those who live on it will die like
            gnats; *b*
    but my salvation will be forever,
        and my deliverance will never be ended.

7   Listen to me, you who know
            righteousness,
        you people who have my teaching in
            your hearts;
    do not fear the reproach of others,
        and do not be dismayed when they
            revile you.
8   For the moth will eat them up like a
            garment,
        and the worm will eat them like wool;
    but my deliverance will be forever,
        and my salvation to all generations.

9   Awake, awake, put on strength,
        O arm of the LORD!

---

a Syr: Heb *you gird yourselves with firebrands*   *b* Or *in like manner*

---

just as adamant as his persecutors (Ezek 3.8–9). **50.9** His opponents will perish like old moth-eaten clothes (51.7–8). **50.10–11** But who among his listeners will obey the servant remains a question (42.23); the majority (*all of you*) are disobedient and destined to burn in judgment (1.25–28; 31.9; 33.11–14; 42.25; 47.14).

51.1–8 Three sayings (vv. 1–3, 4–6, 7–8), each introduced with a similar command to listen, containing promises to God's people. **51.1–3** The example of Abraham is proof that God can fulfill the divine promises even if the people are few in number. **51.1** *You that pursue righteousness.* At least some of the exiles were trying to follow God's teaching (see v. 7; 50.10). *Rock,*

quarry, Israel's ancestors, Abraham and Sarah (Gen 11.26–25.11). **51.2** *For he was but one.* Cf. Ezek 33.24. **51.3** *Eden . . . garden of the LORD.* The time of salvation is often portrayed in prophetic literature as a return to the conditions of paradise (Ezek 36.35; 47.1–12). **51.4–6** God's salvation will soon go forth to the whole world. **51.4** *Teaching, justice.* See 2.2–5. **51.5** Even the pagan nations hope for the imposition of God's righteous rule (see Ps 82). **51.6** The present order of reality with its old heavens and earth will vanish, but God's salvation will last (24.21–23; 65.17). **51.7–8** Those who follow God should not fear the reproaches of those who revile them, for their persecutors will perish (50.9). **51.9–11** In response to the preceding promises

Awake, as in days of old,
    the generations of long ago!
Was it not you who cut Rahab in pieces,
    who pierced the dragon?
10 Was it not you who dried up the sea,
    the waters of the great deep;
who made the depths of the sea a way
    for the redeemed to cross over?
11 So the ransomed of the Lord shall
        return,
    and come to Zion with singing;
everlasting joy shall be upon their heads;
    they shall obtain joy and gladness,
    and sorrow and sighing shall flee away.

12 I, I am he who comforts you;
    why then are you afraid of a mere
        mortal who must die,
    a human being who fades like grass?
13 You have forgotten the Lord, your Maker,
    who stretched out the heavens
    and laid the foundations of the earth.
You fear continually all day long
    because of the fury of the oppressor,
who is bent on destruction.
    But where is the fury of the oppressor?
14 The oppressed shall speedily be released;
    they shall not die and go down to the
        Pit,
    nor shall they lack bread.
15 For I am the Lord your God,
    who stirs up the sea so that its waves
        roar—
    the Lord of hosts is his name.
16 I have put my words in your mouth,
    and hidden you in the shadow of my
        hand,

stretching out*a* the heavens
    and laying the foundations of the
        earth,
    and saying to Zion, "You are my people."

17 Rouse yourself, rouse yourself!
    Stand up, O Jerusalem,
you who have drunk at the hand of the
        Lord
    the cup of his wrath,
who have drunk to the dregs
    the bowl of staggering.
18 There is no one to guide her
    among all the children she has borne;
there is no one to take her by the hand
    among all the children she has brought
        up.
19 These two things have befallen you
    —who will grieve with you?—
devastation and destruction, famine and
        sword—
    who will comfort you?*b*
20 Your children have fainted,
    they lie at the head of every street
    like an antelope in a net;
they are full of the wrath of the Lord,
    the rebuke of your God.

21 Therefore hear this, you who are
        wounded,*c*
    who are drunk, but not with wine:
22 Thus says your Sovereign, the Lord,
    your God who pleads the cause of his
        people:

a Syr: Heb *planting*   *b* Q Ms Gk Syr Vg: MT *how may I comfort you?*   *c* Or *humbled*

the *arm of the Lord* is called upon to demonstrate anew its ancient victories (Hab 3.2). **51.9–10** *Awake,* a cry sometimes addressed to God in laments when the deity's inaction suggests God is asleep (see Ps 44.23). *Arm,* a traditional metaphor for God's power, particularly as it was displayed in God's mighty signs at the exodus (Ex 6.6; 15.16; Deut 4.34; 2 Kings 17.36; Ps 136.12–13; Jer 32.21; Ezek 20.33–34). The exodus is here identified with God's cosmogonic victory over the primeval chaos-dragon (Ps 74.12–17). *Rahab.* See 30.7; Job 26.12. *Dragon.* See 27.1; Ezek 29.3. *Sea.* See Job 26.12. *Great deep.* See Gen 7.11; Am 7.4. **51.11** *The ransomed of the Lord,* those freed from the Babylonian exile (35.8–10; 43.1–21). **51.12–16** Israel need not fear, for God, who created Israel and the world, is more powerful than Israel's mortal oppressors. **51.12** *Fades like grass.* See 40.6–8. **51.14** *Oppressed.* The Babylonian exiles are portrayed as prisoners bending over in a cramped dungeon (42.7). *Pit,* realm of the dead (14.9–11, 15). **51.15** *Who stirs up the sea so that its waves roar,* better "who stills the sea though its waves roar" (Job 26.12–13); Israel need not fear the fury of the oppressor, for God will still the fury of Babylon just as he once stilled the fury of the cosmogonic sea. **51.16** See 49.2. **51.17–23** Jerusalem is called upon to stand up, because her punishment is ended, and now her oppressors will receive their punishment. **51.17** *Cup of his wrath,* a common symbol of judgment that plays on the disorientation, shame, and vulnerability of intoxicated individuals to point to the same characteristics among the politically oppressed (Jer 25.15–29; Hab 2.15–16). **51.18–20** The depopulation of Jerusalem is portrayed through the image of a woman who has no children left to help or comfort her in her old age. **51.21** *Not with wine.* Jerusalem's disorientation was caused by the oppression of her tormentors

See, I have taken from your hand the cup
    of staggering;
you shall drink no more
    from the bowl of my wrath.
23 And I will put it into the hand of your
    tormentors,
    who have said to you,
    "Bow down, that we may walk on you";
and you have made your back like the
    ground
    and like the street for them to walk on.

Let Zion Rejoice

52 Awake, awake,
    put on your strength, O Zion!
Put on your beautiful garments,
    O Jerusalem, the holy city;
for the uncircumcised and the unclean
    shall enter you no more.
2 Shake yourself from the dust, rise up,
    O captive*a* Jerusalem;
loose the bonds from your neck,
    O captive daughter Zion!

3 For thus says the LORD: You were sold for
nothing, and you shall be redeemed without
money. 4 For thus says the Lord GOD: Long
ago, my people went down into Egypt to reside there as aliens; the Assyrian, too, has oppressed them without cause. 5 Now therefore
what am I doing here, says the LORD, seeing
that my people are taken away without cause?
Their rulers howl, says the LORD, and continually, all day long, my name is despised. 6 Therefore my people shall know my name; therefore
in that day they shall know that it is I who
speak; here am I.

7 How beautiful upon the mountains
    are the feet of the messenger who
        announces peace,
who brings good news,
    who announces salvation,
    who says to Zion, "Your God reigns."
8 Listen! Your sentinels lift up their voices,
    together they sing for joy;
for in plain sight they see
    the return of the LORD to Zion.
9 Break forth together into singing,
    you ruins of Jerusalem;
for the LORD has comforted his people,
    he has redeemed Jerusalem.
10 The LORD has bared his holy arm
    before the eyes of all the nations;
and all the ends of the earth shall see
    the salvation of our God.
11 Depart, depart, go out from there!
    Touch no unclean thing;
go out from the midst of it, purify
    yourselves,
    you who carry the vessels of the
        LORD.
12 For you shall not go out in haste,
    and you shall not go in flight;
for the LORD will go before you,
    and the God of Israel will be your rear
        guard.

The Suffering Servant

13 See, my servant shall prosper;
    he shall be exalted and lifted up,
    and shall be very high.

_____
a Cn: Heb *rise up, sit*

(v. 23). **51.22–23** Jerusalem will no longer drink from
the cup of oppression, because God has now given it to
her tormenters, who will now suffer as the same judgment that they imposed on Jerusalem.
   52.1–12 A series of sayings stressing God's redemption of Jerusalem. **52.1–2** Jerusalem should arise and
dress up because her captivity is ended (cf. 51.17). The
uncircumcised and the *unclean* are the foreigners and
sinful Israelites who will no longer have access to the
holy city (33.10–16). **52.3–6** A prose saying. Just as
God once redeemed Israel from Egyptian and Assyrian
oppression, so now God will redeem it from Babylonian oppression. **52.4–5** *Without cause.* Other nations
have mistreated Israel without sufficient justification,
and because they have done this with impunity God's
name has been *despised* (see 10.10–11). **52.6** *Know my
name.* God will soon act to restore the reputation of
the divine name. **52.7–10** God's salvation is an-

nounced to Jerusalem and displayed before the whole
world. **52.7–8** The imagery is that of a royal city waiting in suspense when a swift messenger arrives with
the good news of their king's victory. This is followed
by the joyous shout of the city watchmen who now see
the royal entourage, with the divine king returning in
triumph from victory over his enemies (Pss 24.7–10;
47.1–9). **52.10** *Arm.* See note on 51.9–10. *Holy arm.*
See Ps 98.1. **52.11–12** The exiles are called upon to
leave Babylon. As in the first exodus, God will guide
and protect Israel (Ex 14.19–20), but unlike the first
exodus (Ex 12.33–39), this one will not be in haste.
   52.13–53.12 The last and most striking of the so-
called servant songs (see note on 42.1–9). The early
church identified the servant in this passage with Jesus
(Acts 8.32–35), and Jesus' own sense of identity and
mission may have been shaped by this figure (Mk 8.31;
9.30–32; 10.33–34). In the original historical context,

14 Just as there were many who were
          astonished at him[a]
      —so marred was his appearance,
          beyond human semblance,
      and his form beyond that of mortals—
15 so he shall startle[b] many nations;
      kings shall shut their mouths because
          of him;
      for that which had not been told them
          they shall see,
      and that which they had not heard
          they shall contemplate.

53 Who has believed what we have heard?
      And to whom has the arm of the LORD
          been revealed?
2   For he grew up before him like a young
          plant,
      and like a root out of dry ground;
      he had no form or majesty that we should
          look at him,
      nothing in his appearance that we
          should desire him.
3   He was despised and rejected by others;
      a man of suffering[c] and acquainted
          with infirmity;
      and as one from whom others hide their
          faces[d]
      he was despised, and we held him of
          no account.

4   Surely he has borne our infirmities
      and carried our diseases;
      yet we accounted him stricken,
      struck down by God, and afflicted.
5   But he was wounded for our
          transgressions,
      crushed for our iniquities;
      upon him was the punishment that made
          us whole,
      and by his bruises we are healed.
6   All we like sheep have gone astray;

      we have all turned to our own way,
      and the LORD has laid on him
          the iniquity of us all.

7   He was oppressed, and he was afflicted,
      yet he did not open his mouth;
      like a lamb that is led to the slaughter,
      and like a sheep that before its shearers
          is silent,
      so he did not open his mouth.
8   By a perversion of justice he was taken
          away.
      Who could have imagined his future?
      For he was cut off from the land of the
          living,
      stricken for the transgression of my
          people.
9   They made his grave with the wicked
      and his tomb[e] with the rich,[f]
      although he had done no violence,
      and there was no deceit in his mouth.

10 Yet it was the will of the LORD to crush
          him with pain.[g]
      When you make his life an offering for
          sin,[b]
      he shall see his offspring, and shall
          prolong his days;
      through him the will of the LORD shall
          prosper.
11 Out of his anguish he shall see light;[h]
      he shall find satisfaction through his
          knowledge.
      The righteous one,[i] my servant, shall
          make many righteous,
      and he shall bear their iniquities.

---

a Syr Tg: Heb *you*   b Meaning of Heb uncertain   c Or *a man
of sorrows*   d Or *as one who hides his face from us*   e Q Ms: MT
and in his death   f Cn: Heb *with a rich person*   g Or *by disease*;
meaning of Heb uncertain   h Q Mss: MT lacks *light*   i Or *and
he shall find satisfaction. Through his knowledge, the righteous one*

---

however, the servant appears to have been exiled Israel. **52.13–15** God's deliverance and exaltation of Israel will astound the nations, who formerly despised
this disfigured slave (49.7). **53.1–6** The nations speak,
expressing their astonishment at the deliverance of Israel, which forces them to revise their assessment of Israel. **53.1–3** The servant's outward appearance suggested nothing special. **53.2** There may be an allusion
in the term *root* to Israel's messianic expectations
(11.1, 10), but the servant had no *majesty* to suggest a
royal status. **53.3** The servant was *despised* by the nations. **53.4–6** Israel's suffering suggested God had rejected it. Now, however, contrary to the nations' origi-

nal impression, they see that the servant's suffering
was vicarious, God's surprising way of restoring all
people to himself (42.2–3; Mt 8.17; 1 Pet 2.22–25).
53.7–12 The servant's willing submission to suffering
leads to his exaltation (cf. Phil 2.6–11). **53.7–9** The
servant suffered silently, though unjustly. **53.8** The
Babylonian exile could be seen as a *perversion of justice*
despite Israel's sins, since it was more righteous than
its Babylonian oppressors (Hab 1.12–17). *Cut off from
. . . the living.* Many Israelites saw the Babylonian exile
as the death and burial of their nation (Ezek 37.11–
14). **53.9** Cf. Mt 27.57–60. **53.10–12** Like a sin offering, the servant's suffering brings forgiveness to many.

12 Therefore I will allot him a portion with
        the great,
   and he shall divide the spoil with the
        strong;
   because he poured out himself to death,
        and was numbered with the
        transgressors;
   yet he bore the sin of many,
        and made intercession for the
        transgressors.

The Eternal Covenant of Peace

54 Sing, O barren one who did not bear;
        burst into song and shout,
   you who have not been in labor!
   For the children of the desolate woman
        will be more
        than the children of her that is
        married, says the LORD.
2 Enlarge the site of your tent,
        and let the curtains of your habitations
        be stretched out;
   do not hold back; lengthen your cords
        and strengthen your stakes.
3 For you will spread out to the right and
        to the left,
        and your descendants will possess the
        nations
        and will settle the desolate towns.

4 Do not fear, for you will not be ashamed;
        do not be discouraged, for you will not
        suffer disgrace;
   for you will forget the shame of your
        youth,
        and the disgrace of your widowhood
        you will remember no more.
5 For your Maker is your husband,
        the LORD of hosts is his name;
   the Holy One of Israel is your Redeemer,
        the God of the whole earth he is called.
6 For the LORD has called you

like a wife forsaken and grieved in
        spirit,
   like the wife of a man's youth when she is
        cast off,
        says your God.
7 For a brief moment I abandoned you,
        but with great compassion I will gather
        you.
8 In overflowing wrath for a moment
        I hid my face from you,
   but with everlasting love I will have
        compassion on you,
        says the LORD, your Redeemer.

9 This is like the days of Noah to me:
        Just as I swore that the waters of Noah
        would never again go over the earth,
   so I have sworn that I will not be angry
        with you
        and will not rebuke you.
10 For the mountains may depart
        and the hills be removed,
   but my steadfast love shall not depart
        from you,
        and my covenant of peace shall not be
        removed,
        says the LORD, who has compassion on
        you.

11 O afflicted one, storm-tossed, and not
        comforted,
        I am about to set your stones in
        antimony,
        and lay your foundations with
        sapphires.ᵃ
12 I will make your pinnacles of rubies,
        your gates of jewels,
        and all your wall of precious stones.
13 All your children shall be taught by the
        LORD,

_____
a Or *lapis lazuli*

53.12 The servant will be exalted among the *great* and *strong* (52.13). *Numbered with the transgressors.* Cf. Lk 22.37.
54.1–17 Jerusalem is comforted by God with the announcement of her restoration. **54.1–3** Israel, personified as the feminine figure of its capital city, Jerusalem, which remained desolate and uninhabited during the exile, will soon overflow with a burgeoning population (49.14–21). **54.1** *Barren one,* Zion, or Jerusalem. *Children,* Zion's inhabitants. **54.4–8** Zion will not remain abandoned. **54.4** *Shame, widowhood,* the destruction caused by the exile, which signified God's abandon-

ment of the city (cf. 4.1 and the similar language used of Babylon's destruction, 47.3, 8–9). **54.5** *Husband,* God. **54.6–8** God has not rejected Zion permanently; there was no divorce (50.1), only a brief estrangement, and God will soon redeem her (Hos 2.14–20). *Hid my face,* a recurring image for God's anger (8.17; 30.20; 45.15; 57.17; 59.2; 64.7). **54.9–10** God's eternal covenant with Jerusalem. **54.9** See Gen 8.21–22; 9.8–17. **54.10** *Mountains may depart . . . hills be removed.* See Ps 46.1–3. *Covenant of peace.* See Ezek 34.25. **54.11–17** Though formerly *afflicted* (51.21), the new Jerusalem will be established in beauty and security. **54.11–**

and great shall be the prosperity of
    your children.
14 In righteousness you shall be established;
    you shall be far from oppression, for
        you shall not fear;
    and from terror, for it shall not come
        near you.
15 If anyone stirs up strife,
    it is not from me;
  whoever stirs up strife with you
    shall fall because of you.
16 See it is I who have created the smith
    who blows the fire of coals,
  and produces a weapon fit for its
    purpose;
  I have also created the ravager to destroy.
17 No weapon that is fashioned against
    you shall prosper,
  and you shall confute every tongue that
    rises against you in judgment.
  This is the heritage of the servants of the
    LORD
  and their vindication from me, says the
    LORD.

An Invitation to Abundant Life

55 Ho, everyone who thirsts,
    come to the waters;
and you that have no money,
    come, buy and eat!
Come, buy wine and milk
    without money and without price.
2 Why do you spend your money for that
    which is not bread,
  and your labor for that which does not
    satisfy?
Listen carefully to me, and eat what is good,

    and delight yourselves in rich food.
3 Incline your ear, and come to me;
    listen, so that you may live.
I will make with you an everlasting
    covenant,
  my steadfast, sure love for David.
4 See, I made him a witness to the peoples,
    a leader and commander for the
        peoples.
5 See, you shall call nations that you do not
    know,
  and nations that do not know you shall
    run to you,
because of the LORD your God, the Holy
    One of Israel,
  for he has glorified you.

6 Seek the LORD while he may be found,
    call upon him while he is near;
7 let the wicked forsake their way,
    and the unrighteous their thoughts;
let them return to the LORD, that he may
    have mercy on them,
  and to our God, for he will abundantly
    pardon.
8 For my thoughts are not your thoughts,
    nor are your ways my ways, says the
        LORD.
9 For as the heavens are higher than the
    earth,
  so are my ways higher than your ways
    and my thoughts than your thoughts.

10 For as the rain and the snow come down
    from heaven,
  and do not return there until they have
    watered the earth,

---

12 Cf. Rev 21.10–21. **54.13** *Taught by the* LORD. See
30.20–21; Jer 31.34; 1 Thess 4.9. **54.14** Cf. 33.18–22.
54.15–17 Since God, the creator of all craftsmen and
thus all weapons, is on Zion's side, no enemy will successfully raise any weapon against her.
  55.1–13 Israel should come to God now, for his salvation is about to be realized. **55.1–3a** This invitation
to a free banquet may be modeled on ritual meals for
the dead in which the dead were summoned to partake
in the food offering. *Ho,* a particle that was sometimes
used to get the attention of the dead in funerary
laments. If this is the background, Israel in exile is
being addressed as though it is dead in exile (cf. Ezek
37.11–14). *That you may live.* The free food and drink
offered by God will give the people life. Note that the
destruction of death is also associated with God's royal
banquet on Mount Zion in 25.6–7. Cf. also the covenant banquet on Mount Sinai, where mere humans

see God and eat in his presence, yet live (Ex 24.9–11).
The metaphor of the free banquet (cf. also Prov 9.1–5;
Jn 7.37) functions as an invitation to Israel to accept
God's coming restoration of the nation. **55.3b–5** If
Israel turns to him, God will turn his former covenant
with David (2 Sam 7.4–17) into a covenant with the
whole nation. **55.3** *Sure love for David.* See Ps 89.24,
28, 33. **55.4–5** The nations will come to Israel, their
leader and commander, as they once came to the Davidic king in Jerusalem (Ps 72.8–11; cf. Isa 2.3–4;
11.10, 12; 49.22–23). **55.6–9** Israel should seek God
now in repentance, because God has positive plans for
those who return to him. **55.6** *While he is near,* now
that God has come out of hiding and is ready to save.
55.7 A change of life and thought is demanded of the
wicked. **55.8–9** God's *ways* and *thoughts,* the divine
plan to redeem Israel, are beyond Israel's comprehension. **55.10–11** As *the rain and the snow,* sent by God to

making it bring forth and sprout,
> giving seed to the sower and bread to
> > the eater,
11 so shall my word be that goes out from
> my mouth;
> it shall not return to me empty,
but it shall accomplish that which I
> purpose,
> and succeed in the thing for which I
> > sent it.

12 For you shall go out in joy,
> and be led back in peace;
the mountains and the hills before you
> shall burst into song,
> and all the trees of the field shall clap
> > their hands.
13 Instead of the thorn shall come up the
> cypress;
> instead of the brier shall come up the
> > myrtle;
and it shall be to the LORD for a memorial,
> for an everlasting sign that shall not be
> > cut off.

The Covenant Extended to All Who Obey

56 Thus says the LORD:
Maintain justice, and do what is right,
for soon my salvation will come,
and my deliverance be revealed.

2 Happy is the mortal who does this,
> the one who holds it fast,
who keeps the sabbath, not profaning it,
> and refrains from doing any evil.

3 Do not let the foreigner joined to the
> LORD say,
> "The LORD will surely separate me
> > from his people";

and do not let the eunuch say,
> "I am just a dry tree."
4 For thus says the LORD:
To the eunuchs who keep my sabbaths,
> who choose the things that please me
> and hold fast my covenant,
5 I will give, in my house and within my
> walls,
> a monument and a name
> better than sons and daughters;
I will give them an everlasting name
> that shall not be cut off.

6 And the foreigners who join themselves
> to the LORD,
> to minister to him, to love the name of
> > the LORD,
> and to be his servants,
all who keep the sabbath, and do not
> profane it,
> and hold fast my covenant—
7 these I will bring to my holy mountain,
> and make them joyful in my house of
> > prayer;
their burnt offerings and their sacrifices
> will be accepted on my altar;
for my house shall be called a house of
> prayer
> for all peoples.
8 Thus says the Lord GOD,
> who gathers the outcasts of Israel,
I will gather others to them
> besides those already gathered.[a]

The Corruption of Israel's Rulers

9 All you wild animals,
> all you wild animals in the forest, come
> > to devour!

---

a Heb *besides his gathered ones*

---

give new life to the earth, succeed, so shall God's promise to save Israel. **55.12–13** Even nature itself will be transformed in a reversal of former judgments (5.6; 7.23–25) and join in the rejoicing at Israel's return to its land (41.18–19; 51.3).

56.1–66.24 Admonitions to Judah. These chapters, often referred to as Third Isaiah, contain a miscellaneous collection of oracles that seem to presuppose a setting in Palestine after the return of the exiles to Judah after 539 BCE. See Introduction. **56.1–8** If they do what is right, even those formerly excluded from the religious community will share in the salvation God is about to reveal. **56.2** *Happy is the mortal.* Cf. Pss 1.1; 106.3; Mt 5.3–12. Observance of the *sabbath* became a

major concern in the exilic and postexilic period (58.13; Neh 13.15–22; Jer 17.21–27; Ezek 20.12–38). **56.3** Some biblical legislation might incline the *foreigner* and *eunuch* to consider themselves excluded from God's blessings (Deut 23.1–3; cf. Lev 21.18–20), but it is not to be so in the coming salvation. **56.5** *Monument,* a stele or plaque set up to preserve one's memory in the absence of children (2 Sam 18.18). **56.6–7** God will accept the offerings of faithful proselytes. *My holy mountain,* the Temple Mount in Jerusalem. *House of prayer for all peoples.* Quoted in Mk 11.17. **56.8** *Others,* proselytes (cf. Jn 10.16). **56.9–12** Israel's leaders are failing to discharge their responsibilities. **56.9** *Wild animals,* foreign nations (5.26–30; Jer 4.7;

10 Israel's[a] sentinels are blind,
        they are all without knowledge;
    they are all silent dogs
        that cannot bark;
    dreaming, lying down,
        loving to slumber.
11 The dogs have a mighty appetite;
        they never have enough.
    The shepherds also have no
        understanding;
        they have all turned to their own way,
        to their own gain, one and all.
12 "Come," they say, "let us[b] get wine;
        let us fill ourselves with strong drink.
    And tomorrow will be like today,
        great beyond measure."

Israel's Futile Idolatry

57 The righteous perish,
        and no one takes it to heart;
    the devout are taken away,
        while no one understands.
    For the righteous are taken away from
        calamity,
2   and they enter into peace;
    those who walk uprightly
        will rest on their couches.
3   But as for you, come here,
        you children of a sorceress,
        you offspring of an adulterer and a
        whore.[c]
4   Whom are you mocking?
        Against whom do you open your
            mouth wide
        and stick out your tongue?
    Are you not children of transgression,
        the offspring of deceit—
5   you that burn with lust among the
        oaks,
        under every green tree;

    you that slaughter your children in the
        valleys,
        under the clefts of the rocks?
6   Among the smooth stones of the valley is
        your portion;
        they, they, are your lot;
    to them you have poured out a drink
        offering,
        you have brought a grain offering.
    Shall I be appeased for these things?
7   Upon a high and lofty mountain
        you have set your bed,
        and there you went up to offer sacrifice.
8   Behind the door and the doorpost
        you have set up your symbol;
    for, in deserting me,[d] you have uncovered
        your bed,
        you have gone up to it,
        you have made it wide;
    and you have made a bargain for yourself
        with them,
        you have loved their bed,
        you have gazed on their nakedness.[e]
9   You journeyed to Molech[f] with oil,
        and multiplied your perfumes;
    you sent your envoys far away,
        and sent down even to Sheol.
10 You grew weary from your many
        wanderings,
        but you did not say, "It is useless."
    You found your desire rekindled,
        and so you did not weaken.

11 Whom did you dread and fear
        so that you lied,
    and did not remember me
        or give me a thought?

---

a Heb *His*   b Q Ms Syr Vg Tg: MT *me*   c Heb *an adulterer
and she plays the whore*   d Meaning of Heb uncertain
e Or *their phallus*; Heb *the hand*   f Or *the king*

5.6). **56.10** *Sentinels,* prophets (Ezek 3.16–21; 33.1–9)
or leaders who mislead for lack of knowledge (5.11–13;
9.14–16). *Silent dogs,* a disparaging reference to the
leaders or prophets as useless (cf. 9.14; Job 30.1).
56.11 *Mighty appetite.* The leaders are only good for
devouring what they are supposed to guard (3.12–15;
cf. Mic 3.5). *Shepherds,* rulers (Ezek 34.1–16; Zech
11.4–17). **56.12** Cf. 5.11–12.
    57.1–13 Pagan religious practices still threaten the
struggling postexilic community in Judah. **57.1–2** The
righteous die without regard, but their evil detractors
are unaware that death brings the righteous *peace* and
rest from the greater evil to come. *Couches,* a reference
to proper burial in a tomb. **57.3–4** *You.* Those who

mock the righteous are addressed as illegitimate offspring of the foreign gods they worship (Hos 2.4–5).
57.5–8 The apostates continue the old fertility cults
and their sexually immoral practices. *Among the oaks,
under every green tree, upon a . . . lofty mountain,* where
these cultic practices take place (Deut 12.2; Jer 2.20;
3.6; Ezek 6.13). Because they practiced child sacrifice
(*slaughter your children*) in the valleys, their *lot* would
be to end up in the same place (cf. Jer 19.4–13).
57.9 *Molech,* the deity to whom child sacrifices were
offered. *Sheol,* the underworld personified as a deity.
57.10 Despite the futility of these practices, Israel persists in them (Jer 2.23–25). **57.11–13** The object of
their *fear* and *dread* was not God (8.13), because he

Have I not kept silent and closed my
    eyes,*a*
  and so you do not fear me?
12 I will concede your righteousness and
    your works,
  but they will not help you.
13 When you cry out, let your collection of
    idols deliver you!
  The wind will carry them off,
    a breath will take them away.
  But whoever takes refuge in me shall
    possess the land
  and inherit my holy mountain.

A Promise of Help and Healing

14 It shall be said,
  "Build up, build up, prepare the way,
    remove every obstruction from my
    people's way."
15 For thus says the high and lofty one
  who inhabits eternity, whose name is
    Holy:
  I dwell in the high and holy place,
    and also with those who are contrite
      and humble in spirit,
  to revive the spirit of the humble,
    and to revive the heart of the contrite.
16 For I will not continually accuse,
    nor will I always be angry;
  for then the spirits would grow faint
    before me,
  even the souls that I have made.
17 Because of their wicked covetousness I
    was angry;
  I struck them, I hid and was angry;
  but they kept turning back to their
    own ways.
18 I have seen their ways, but I will heal
    them;
  I will lead them and repay them with
    comfort,
  creating for their mourners the fruit of
    the lips.*b*

19 Peace, peace, to the far and the near, says
    the LORD;
  and I will heal them.
20 But the wicked are like the tossing sea
    that cannot keep still;
  its waters toss up mire and mud.
21 There is no peace, says my God, for the
    wicked.

False and True Worship

58 Shout out, do not hold back!
  Lift up your voice like a trumpet!
  Announce to my people their rebellion,
    to the house of Jacob their sins.
2 Yet day after day they seek me
    and delight to know my ways,
  as if they were a nation that practiced
    righteousness
  and did not forsake the ordinance of
    their God;
  they ask of me righteous judgments,
    they delight to draw near to God.
3 "Why do we fast, but you do not see?
    Why humble ourselves, but you do not
      notice?"
  Look, you serve your own interest on
    your fast day,
  and oppress all your workers.
4 Look, you fast only to quarrel and to fight
    and to strike with a wicked fist.
  Such fasting as you do today
    will not make your voice heard on
      high.
5 Is such the fast that I choose,
    a day to humble oneself?
  Is it to bow down the head like a
    bulrush,
    and to lie in sackcloth and ashes?
  Will you call this a fast,
    a day acceptable to the LORD?

---

a Gk Vg: Heb *silent even for a long time*   *b* Meaning of Heb uncertain

---

kept silent, but they will learn that idols are useless; only God can save (42.14–17). **57.14–21** The prophet assures the penitent of God's presence and peace. **57.14** Cf. 40.3–4. **57.15** The transcendent God will dwell with the contrite and humble (6.1–7). **57.16–18** God's anger, though justified, will not last forever. **57.17** Though God *struck them*, the Israelites *kept turning back* in rebellion (cf. 1.5–6). **57.18** Despite the people's past, God will heal them. *Mourners*, the repentant. *Fruit of the lips*, perhaps praise for God's deliverance (see Hos 14.2). **57.19** *The far and the near*,

those still in exile and those in Judah. **57.20–21** This consolation is not for the unrepentant wicked.

58.1–14 The prophet here contrasts mere religious ritual with the service God desires. **58.1–2** Israel must be made aware of its sin (Mic 3.8); its delight in ritual does not make it the righteous nation it imagines (1.10–17). *Draw near to God.* Cf. 29.13. **58.3–4** Fasting that serves self-interest and contributes to the oppression of the weak does not move God to respond favorably. **58.5** Wearing *sackcloth* and sitting in *ashes* were rituals of mourning often accompanying a fast (Joel

6 Is not this the fast that I choose:
    to loose the bonds of injustice,
    to undo the thongs of the yoke,
  to let the oppressed go free,
    and to break every yoke?
7 Is it not to share your bread with the
      hungry,
    and bring the homeless poor into your
      house;
  when you see the naked, to cover them,
    and not to hide yourself from your
      own kin?
8 Then your light shall break forth like the
      dawn,
    and your healing shall spring up
      quickly;
  your vindicator *a* shall go before you,
    the glory of the LORD shall be your rear
      guard.
9 Then you shall call, and the LORD will
      answer;
    you shall cry for help, and he will say,
      Here I am.

  If you remove the yoke from among you,
    the pointing of the finger, the speaking
      of evil,
10 if you offer your food to the hungry
    and satisfy the needs of the afflicted,
  then your light shall rise in the darkness
    and your gloom be like the noonday.
11 The LORD will guide you continually,
    and satisfy your needs in parched
      places,
    and make your bones strong;
  and you shall be like a watered garden,
    like a spring of water,
    whose waters never fail.
12 Your ancient ruins shall be rebuilt;
    you shall raise up the foundations of
      many generations;

you shall be called the repairer of the
      breach,
    the restorer of streets to live in.

13 If you refrain from trampling the
      sabbath,
    from pursuing your own interests on
      my holy day;
  if you call the sabbath a delight
    and the holy day of the LORD honorable;
  if you honor it, not going your own ways,
    serving your own interests, or pursuing
      your own affairs; *b*
14 then you shall take delight in the LORD,
    and I will make you ride upon the
      heights of the earth;
  I will feed you with the heritage of your
      ancestor Jacob,
    for the mouth of the LORD has spoken.

Injustice and Oppression to Be Punished

59 See, the LORD's hand is not too short
      to save,
    nor his ear too dull to hear.
2 Rather, your iniquities have been barriers
    between you and your God,
  and your sins have hidden his face from
      you
    so that he does not hear.
3 For your hands are defiled with blood,
    and your fingers with iniquity;
  your lips have spoken lies,
    your tongue mutters wickedness.
4 No one brings suit justly,
    no one goes to law honestly;
  they rely on empty pleas, they speak lies,
    conceiving mischief and begetting
      iniquity.
5 They hatch adders' eggs,

---

a Or *vindication*   *b* Heb *or speaking words*

1.8, 13–14; Jon 3.5–6). **58.6–14** Three parallel formulations (vv. 6–9a, 9b–12, 13–14) stating what God expects of his people, if they want him to hear them. **58.6–9a** The fast that God wants involves saving other people from oppression and satisfying their needs (cf. Mt 25.31–46). **58.7** Cf. Job 31.16–23. **58.8** *Light,* a metaphor for deliverance and for salvation (42.6–7). *Rear guard.* See 52.12. **58.9b–12** Obedience will result in the restoration of Israel's ancient ruins. **58.9b** *Pointing of the finger* probably involves a legal accusation (cf. Prov 6.13). **58.10–11** *Satisfy . . . needs.* God's treatment of his worshipers corresponds to their treatment of fellow humans in need (cf. Mt 7.2). **58.13** Observance of the *sabbath* is a significant part in this true worship of God. **58.14** *Ride upon the heights of the earth,* an idiom for triumph or success (Deut 32.13; cf. Ps 18.33; Hab 3.19).

59.1–21 Although salvation is God's work, it may be hastened or delayed by Israel's response. **59.1–8** It is not God's lack of power, but Israel's wickedness, that prevents its salvation. **59.2–3** *Hidden his face, does not hear, hands . . . defiled with blood.* See 1.15. **59.4** *No one.* Israel's wickedness is so great, a single righteous person cannot be found (Ps 14.1–4; Jer 5.1–5; Rom 3.10–18). **59.5** *Adder, viper,* standard metaphors for the wicked (Pss 58.3–4; 140.1–3; Mt 3.7; 12.34; 23.33). **59.6** *Their*

and weave the spider's web;
whoever eats their eggs dies,
and the crushed egg hatches out a
viper.
6 Their webs cannot serve as clothing;
they cannot cover themselves with
what they make.
Their works are works of iniquity,
and deeds of violence are in their
hands.
7 Their feet run to evil,
and they rush to shed innocent blood;
their thoughts are thoughts of iniquity,
desolation and destruction are in their
highways.
8 The way of peace they do not know,
and there is no justice in their paths.
Their roads they have made crooked;
no one who walks in them knows peace.

9 Therefore justice is far from us,
and righteousness does not reach us;
we wait for light, and lo! there is darkness;
and for brightness, but we walk in
gloom.
10 We grope like the blind along a wall,
groping like those who have no eyes;
we stumble at noon as in the twilight,
among the vigorous*a* as though we
were dead.
11 We all growl like bears;
like doves we moan mournfully.
We wait for justice, but there is none;
for salvation, but it is far from us.
12 For our transgressions before you are
many,
and our sins testify against us.
Our transgressions indeed are with us,
and we know our iniquities:
13 transgressing, and denying the LORD,
and turning away from following our
God,
talking oppression and revolt,
conceiving lying words and uttering
them from the heart.

14 Justice is turned back,
and righteousness stands at a distance;
for truth stumbles in the public square,
and uprightness cannot enter.
15 Truth is lacking,
and whoever turns from evil is
despoiled.

The LORD saw it, and it displeased him
that there was no justice.
16 He saw that there was no one,
and was appalled that there was no one
to intervene;
so his own arm brought him victory,
and his righteousness upheld him.
17 He put on righteousness like a
breastplate,
and a helmet of salvation on his head;
he put on garments of vengeance for
clothing,
and wrapped himself in fury as in a
mantle.
18 According to their deeds, so will he repay;
wrath to his adversaries, requital to his
enemies;
to the coastlands he will render
requital.
19 So those in the west shall fear the name of
the LORD,
and those in the east, his glory;
for he will come like a pent-up stream
that the wind of the LORD drives on.

20 And he will come to Zion as Redeemer,
to those in Jacob who turn from
transgression, says the LORD.
21And as for me, this is my covenant with
them, says the LORD: my spirit that is upon
you, and my words that I have put in your
mouth, shall not depart out of your mouth, or
out of the mouths of your children, or out of
the mouths of your children's children, says
the LORD, from now on and forever.

---

a Meaning of Heb uncertain

webs. The machinations of the wicked will not stand
(Job 8.13–15). **59.7–8** The ways of the wicked will not
lead to peace (cf. Ps 34.11–14). **59.9–15a** Israel's sin is
the reason it stumbles about groaning and oppressed.
59.9 See Job 30.26. **59.10** This was the proverbial fate
of the wicked (Job 5.14). **59.12–15** Israel confesses its
sins. **59.15a** Injustice is so rampant in the postexilic
community that it is an extremely hostile environment
to anyone who *turns from evil* (see Am 5.10). **59.15b–**

21 Finding no human concerned with righteousness to
help deliver Israel, God established his victory on his
own. **59.17** God dressed himself in the armor that
brings victory (cf. Eph 6.14–17). **59.18–20** God, the
Divine Warrior, will punish his enemies, redeem Zion,
and save the Israelites who turn from their sins.
59.18 *According to their deeds.* The judgment is just.
59.19 *Pent-up stream.* Cf. 30.28. **59.21** God's new covenant with Israel (Jer 31.31–34; Ezek 36.26–27).

The Ingathering of the Dispersed

60 Arise, shine; for your light has come,
and the glory of the LORD has risen
upon you.
2 For darkness shall cover the earth,
and thick darkness the peoples;
but the LORD will arise upon you,
and his glory will appear over you.
3 Nations shall come to your light,
and kings to the brightness of your
dawn.

4 Lift up your eyes and look around;
they all gather together, they come to
you;
your sons shall come from far away,
and your daughters shall be carried on
their nurses' arms.
5 Then you shall see and be radiant;
your heart shall thrill and rejoice,*a*
because the abundance of the sea shall be
brought to you,
the wealth of the nations shall come to
you.
6 A multitude of camels shall cover you,
the young camels of Midian and
Ephah;
all those from Sheba shall come.
They shall bring gold and frankincense,
and shall proclaim the praise of the
LORD.
7 All the flocks of Kedar shall be gathered
to you,
the rams of Nebaioth shall minister to
you;
they shall be acceptable on my altar,
and I will glorify my glorious house.

8 Who are these that fly like a cloud,
and like doves to their windows?

9 For the coastlands shall wait for me,
the ships of Tarshish first,
to bring your children from far away,
their silver and gold with them,
for the name of the LORD your God,
and for the Holy One of Israel,
because he has glorified you.
10 Foreigners shall build up your walls,
and their kings shall minister to you;
for in my wrath I struck you down,
but in my favor I have had mercy on
you.
11 Your gates shall always be open;
day and night they shall not be shut,
so that nations shall bring you their
wealth,
with their kings led in procession.
12 For the nation and kingdom
that will not serve you shall perish;
those nations shall be utterly laid
waste.
13 The glory of Lebanon shall come to you,
the cypress, the plane, and the pine,
to beautify the place of my sanctuary;
and I will glorify where my feet rest.
14 The descendants of those who oppressed
you
shall come bending low to you,
and all who despised you
shall bow down at your feet;
they shall call you the City of the LORD,
the Zion of the Holy One of Israel.
15 Whereas you have been forsaken and
hated,
with no one passing through,
I will make you majestic forever,
a joy from age to age.
16 You shall suck the milk of nations,
you shall suck the breasts of kings;

a Heb *be enlarged*

60.1–22 A vision of Jerusalem's coming exaltation.
60.1–3 The *light* of God's glory has dawned for
Jerusalem (4.5; 9.2), and the nations will be drawn to
that light (2.2–5; 11.10; 42.6–7; 49.6). **60.4** The nations will return Jerusalem's children, the Israelite exiles (11.12; 49.18, 22–23). **60.5–7** Jerusalem will be
enriched by the tribute of the nations, including that
of several northern Arabian tribal groups from the
east: *Midian* (Ex 2.15); *Ephah* (Gen 25.4); *Sheba* (Gen
10.7; one might also think of the southern Arabian
kingdom of the same name, 1 Kings 10.1–13); *Kedar*
(21.13–17; Jer 49.28–29); and *Nebaioth* (Gen 25.13).
60.8–9 Other nations from the west will send their

tribute and return the Israelite exiles by ship. *Tarshish.*
See note on 23.1. **60.10** Jerusalem, destroyed by foreigners because of God's anger, will be rebuilt by them
because of God's favor. **60.11** Cf. Rev 21.24–26.
60.12 Cf. Zech 14.16–19. **60.13** *Glory of Lebanon.* The
fine lumber of Lebanon (cf. 1 Kings 5.8–10) will be
used in the rebuilding of the temple. **60.14** Even its
former oppressors will acknowledge and exalt
Jerusalem as the special *City of the LORD*, the Holy
One of Israel. **60.15** God will once again make
Jerusalem *majestic* and a *joy* (Ps 48.2; Lam 2.15), but
this time forever. **60.16** *Suck the milk of nations.*
Jerusalem will be nourished by the wealth of the na-

and you shall know that I, the LORD, am
　　your Savior
and your Redeemer, the Mighty One of
　　Jacob.

17 Instead of bronze I will bring gold,
　　instead of iron I will bring silver;
instead of wood, bronze,
　　instead of stones, iron.
I will appoint Peace as your overseer
　　and Righteousness as your taskmaster.
18 Violence shall no more be heard in your
　　land,
　　devastation or destruction within your
　　　borders;
you shall call your walls Salvation,
　　and your gates Praise.

God the Glory of Zion

19 The sun shall no longer be
　　your light by day,
nor for brightness shall the moon
　　give light to you by night;[a]
but the LORD will be your everlasting
　　light,
　　and your God will be your glory.
20 Your sun shall no more go down,
　　or your moon withdraw itself;
for the LORD will be your everlasting light,
　　and your days of mourning shall be
　　　ended.
21 Your people shall all be righteous;
　　they shall possess the land forever.
They are the shoot that I planted, the
　　work of my hands,
　　so that I might be glorified.
22 The least of them shall become a clan,
　　and the smallest one a mighty nation;
I am the LORD;
　　in its time I will accomplish it quickly.

The Good News of Deliverance

61 The spirit of the Lord GOD is upon
　　me,
　　because the LORD has anointed me;
he has sent me to bring good news to the
　　oppressed,
to bind up the brokenhearted,
to proclaim liberty to the captives,
　　and release to the prisoners;
2 to proclaim the year of the LORD's favor,
　　and the day of vengeance of our God;
to comfort all who mourn;
3 to provide for those who mourn in
　　Zion—
　　to give them a garland instead of
　　　ashes,
the oil of gladness instead of mourning,
　　the mantle of praise instead of a faint
　　　spirit.
They will be called oaks of righteousness,
　　the planting of the LORD, to display his
　　　glory.
4 They shall build up the ancient ruins,
　　they shall raise up the former
　　　devastations;
they shall repair the ruined cities,
　　the devastations of many generations.

5 Strangers shall stand and feed your
　　flocks,
　　foreigners shall till your land and dress
　　　your vines;
6 but you shall be called priests of the LORD,
　　you shall be named ministers of our
　　　God;
you shall enjoy the wealth of the nations,
　　and in their riches you shall glory.

---

a Q Ms Gk Old Latin Tg: MT lacks by night

---

tions. **60.17–18** Wealth (cf. 1 Kings 10.21) and tranquility will characterize the restored city. **60.19–
20** God will be the city's *light* (vv. 1–2; Rev 21.23).
60.21 The inhabitants of the renewed Jerusalem will
all be righteous (1.26–28), God's special *planting* that
brings God glory (see 4.2–4). This is a clear reversal of
the judgment on Israel as the worthless vineyard (5.1–
7). **60.22** *A mighty nation.* Like Abraham (see 51.2),
even the most insignificant member of the restored
postexilic community will have numerous progeny,
and it is God who will accomplish this rebuilding of
the nation.
　　61.1–11 The prophet brings good news to Zion of
its deliverance and glorification. **61.1** The speaker, ei-

ther the prophet or the servant portrayed by the
prophet, announces that God has commissioned him
through an *anointing* with the *spirit* (see 11.2; 42.1–4).
The portrayal of the speaker's task could be described
as either royal or prophetic and is reminiscent of that
of the servant in Second Isaiah (42.1–9). Luke saw this
passage fulfilled in Jesus' ministry (Lk 4.16–21).
61.2 *Year of the LORD's favor.* See 49.8. **61.3** *Oaks of
righteousness, the planting of the LORD.* The agricultural metaphor of Israel as God's planting is common
in the book of Isaiah (4.2; 5.7; 27.2–6; 60.21). **61.4–
5** Israelites will rebuild the ruined cities, and foreigners will serve them (cf. 60.10–12). **61.6** *Priests.* In contrast to the other nations, Israel will have a special

7 Because their[a] shame was double,
    and dishonor was proclaimed as their
        lot,
    therefore they shall possess a double
        portion;
    everlasting joy shall be theirs.

8 For I the LORD love justice,
    I hate robbery and wrongdoing;[b]
    I will faithfully give them their
        recompense,
    and I will make an everlasting
        covenant with them.
9 Their descendants shall be known among
        the nations,
    and their offspring among the peoples;
    all who see them shall acknowledge
        that they are a people whom the LORD
            has blessed.
10 I will greatly rejoice in the LORD,
    my whole being shall exult in my God;
    for he has clothed me with the garments
        of salvation,
    he has covered me with the robe of
        righteousness,
    as a bridegroom decks himself with a
        garland,
    and as a bride adorns herself with her
        jewels.
11 For as the earth brings forth its shoots,
    and as a garden causes what is sown in
        it to spring up,
    so the Lord GOD will cause righteousness
        and praise
    to spring up before all the nations.

The Vindication and Salvation of Zion

62 For Zion's sake I will not keep silent,
    and for Jerusalem's sake I will not rest,
    until her vindication shines out like the
        dawn,
    and her salvation like a burning
        torch.
2 The nations shall see your vindication,
    and all the kings your glory;
    and you shall be called by a new name
        that the mouth of the LORD will give.
3 You shall be a crown of beauty in the
        hand of the LORD,
    and a royal diadem in the hand of your
        God.
4 You shall no more be termed Forsaken,[c]
    and your land shall no more be termed
        Desolate;[d]
    but you shall be called My Delight Is in
        Her,[e]
    and your land Married;[f]
    for the LORD delights in you,
    and your land shall be married.
5 For as a young man marries a young
        woman,
    so shall your builder[g] marry you,
    and as the bridegroom rejoices over the
        bride,
    so shall your God rejoice over you.
6 Upon your walls, O Jerusalem,
    I have posted sentinels;
    all day and all night
        they shall never be silent.
    You who remind the LORD,
        take no rest,
7 and give him no rest
    until he establishes Jerusalem
    and makes it renowned throughout the
        earth.
8 The LORD has sworn by his right hand
        and by his mighty arm:
    I will not again give your grain
        to be food for your enemies,

---

a Heb *your*   b Or *robbery with a burnt offering*   c Heb *Azubah*
d Heb *Shemamah*   e Heb *Hephzibah*   f Heb *Beulah*
g Cn: Heb *your sons*

priestly relationship to God (Ex 19.6). **61.7** *Double portion,* a double reward in place of the double punishment Jerusalem once received (40.2). **61.8–9** When God has redeemed his people, the nations will change their estimate of Israel (52.13–53.12) and acknowledge that God has blessed Israel. *Everlasting covenant.* See 54.9–10. **61.10** While God dresses himself in *salvation* and *righteousness* as armor for battle (59.17), God dresses Israel or Zion in *garments of salvation* and *robes of righteousness* as the festive clothing or ornaments of a bridegroom or bride. **61.11** Zion's *righteousness* (or "salvation") and *praise* before the nations will spring up like the green shoots of a garden in springtime. **62.1–12** Anticipation of the vindication and res-toration of the holy city. **62.1–5** The prophet will not cease reminding God of the Lord's promise to redeem Zion (vv. 6–7) until God has vindicated the city before the whole world. **62.2** *Your glory.* See 60.1–3. A *new name* implies a change in status (1.26). **62.3** *Crown of beauty.* The encircling walls of a city set on the crest of a hill lie behind this image of Jerusalem as a crown (see 28.1–5). **62.4–5** City and land will no longer be like an abandoned wife (54.5–6; 60.14–15). *Your builder,* God. God will *delight in* Zion and *rejoice over* her land with all the attention that a *bridegroom* gives to a new *bride.* **62.6–9** The prophets must remind God of his sworn promise to glorify Jerusalem. **62.8** God swears by symbols of his own power—his *right hand* (48.13) and his

and foreigners shall not drink the
  wine
    for which you have labored;
9 but those who garner it shall eat it
    and praise the LORD,
  and those who gather it shall drink it
    in my holy courts.

10 Go through, go through the gates,
    prepare the way for the people;
  build up, build up the highway,
    clear it of stones,
  lift up an ensign over the peoples.
11 The LORD has proclaimed
    to the end of the earth:
  Say to daughter Zion,
    "See, your salvation comes;
  his reward is with him,
    and his recompense before him."
12 They shall be called, "The Holy People,
    The Redeemed of the LORD";
  and you shall be called, "Sought Out,
    A City Not Forsaken."

Vengeance on Edom

63 "Who is this that comes from Edom,
    from Bozrah in garments stained
    crimson?
Who is this so splendidly robed,
    marching in his great might?"

"It is I, announcing vindication,
    mighty to save."

2 "Why are your robes red,
    and your garments like theirs who
    tread the wine press?"

3 "I have trodden the wine press alone,
    and from the peoples no one was with
    me;

I trod them in my anger
    and trampled them in my wrath;
  their juice spattered on my garments,
    and stained all my robes.
4 For the day of vengeance was in my heart,
    and the year for my redeeming work
    had come.
5 I looked, but there was no helper;
    I stared, but there was no one to
    sustain me;
  so my own arm brought me victory,
    and my wrath sustained me.
6 I trampled down peoples in my anger,
    I crushed them in my wrath,
    and I poured out their lifeblood on the
    earth."

God's Mercy Remembered

7 I will recount the gracious deeds of the
    LORD,
    the praiseworthy acts of the LORD,
  because of all that the LORD has done for
    us,
  and the great favor to the house of Israel
  that he has shown them according to his
    mercy,
    according to the abundance of his
    steadfast love.
8 For he said, "Surely they are my people,
    children who will not deal falsely";
  and he became their savior
9   in all their distress.
  It was no messenger[a] or angel
    but his presence that saved them;[b]
  in his love and in his pity he redeemed
    them;
    he lifted them up and carried them all
    the days of old.

---

a Gk: Heb *anguish* *b* Or *savior.* *9In all their distress he was
distressed; the angel of his presence saved them;*

---

arm (59.16). The threat that enemies would enjoy the
food, drink, or other goods for which one had *labored*
was a traditional curse or punishment for breach of
covenant (Deut 28.30–34). **62.10–11** Zion's vindication is proclaimed in words reminiscent of Second Isaiah (40.3–5, 10; 49.22). **62.12** See v. 4.
  63.1–6 The triumphant return of the Divine Warrior. **63.1** *Who is this?* Challenged by the prophet, the
majestic figure coming from Edom identifies himself
as the mighty Savior (see Ps 24.8–10). *Edom,* a symbol
of wicked, foreign enemies (Jer 49.7–22). *Bozrah,* a
major city of Edom (34.6). **63.2–3** In response to the
question why his robes are *red,* God the warrior ex-

plains that he has been trampling the *wine press,* a
symbol of judgment (Joel 3.13; Rev 14.19–20), and his
clothes have been spattered by its *juice,* a metaphor for
the *lifeblood* of his enemies (v. 6). **63.4** *Day of
vengeance.* See 34.8; 61.2. **63.5** Cf. 59.16. **63.7–
64.12** On the basis of God's gracious activity in the
past, the community appeals to God for mercy and
help in its present miserable circumstances. **63.7–
14** An introductory historical recitation of God's
mighty redemptive acts in the exodus, the wilderness
wandering, and the settlement of the land. This recitation serves both as praise and as the basis for the
laments and petitions that follow. **63.9** *His presence.*

10 But they rebelled
    and grieved his holy spirit;
  therefore he became their enemy;
    he himself fought against them.
11 Then they[a] remembered the days of old,
    of Moses his servant.[b]
  Where is the one who brought them up
      out of the sea
  with the shepherds of his flock?
  Where is the one who put within them
    his holy spirit,
12 who caused his glorious arm
    to march at the right hand of Moses,
  who divided the waters before them
    to make for himself an everlasting
      name,
13 who led them through the depths?
  Like a horse in the desert,
    they did not stumble.
14 Like cattle that go down into the valley,
    the spirit of the LORD gave them rest.
  Thus you led your people,
    to make for yourself a glorious name.

A Prayer of Penitence

15 Look down from heaven and see,
    from your holy and glorious
      habitation.
  Where are your zeal and your might?
    The yearning of your heart and your
      compassion?
  They are withheld from me.
16 For you are our father,
    though Abraham does not know us
    and Israel does not acknowledge us;
  you, O LORD, are our father;
    our Redeemer from of old is your
      name.
17 Why, O LORD, do you make us stray from
      your ways
    and harden our heart, so that we do
      not fear you?
  Turn back for the sake of your servants,
    for the sake of the tribes that are your
      heritage.
18 Your holy people took possession for a
    little while;

  but now our adversaries have trampled
    down your sanctuary.
19 We have long been like those whom you
    do not rule,
  like those not called by your name.

64 O that you would tear open the
    heavens and come down,
  so that the mountains would quake at
    your presence—
2 [c] as when fire kindles brushwood
    and the fire causes water to boil—
  to make your name known to your
    adversaries,
  so that the nations might tremble at
    your presence!
3 When you did awesome deeds that we did
      not expect,
  you came down, the mountains
    quaked at your presence.
4 From ages past no one has heard,
    no ear has perceived,
  no eye has seen any God besides you,
    who works for those who wait for him.
5 You meet those who gladly do right,
    those who remember you in your ways.
  But you were angry, and we sinned;
    because you hid yourself we
      transgressed.[d]
6 We have all become like one who is
      unclean,
  and all our righteous deeds are like a
    filthy cloth.
  We all fade like a leaf,
    and our iniquities, like the wind, take
      us away.
7 There is no one who calls on your name,
    or attempts to take hold of you;
  for you have hidden your face from us,
    and have delivered[e] us into the hand of
      our iniquity.
8 Yet, O LORD, you are our Father;
    we are the clay, and you are our potter;
  we are all the work of your hand.

---

a Heb *he*   b Cn: Heb *his people*   c Ch 64.1 in Heb
d Meaning of Heb uncertain   e Gk Syr Old Latin Tg: Heb
melted

See Ex 33.12–16. *Carried them.* Cf. Ex 19.4. **63.10** Rebellion, punishment, and repentance characterized Israel's relationship with God (Ps 78). **63.11** *Put within
them his holy spirit,* perhaps a reference to the impart-
ing of the spirit to the seventy elders of Israel (Num
11.16–17, 25–29). **63.15–16** God is petitioned to have
compassion on his people again, for God is their true
father, not the mortal patriarchs Abraham and Israel,
who no longer care about their descendants (cf. 51.1–
2). **63.17** Israel's continuing transgression is attributed
to a divine hardening of the heart (6.9–10; Ex 4.21;
7.3; Jn 12.40; Rom 9.18). **63.18–19** Cf. Ps 79. **64.1–
3** God is petitioned to reveal his awesome might in a
theophany as of old (Judg 5.4–5; Ps 68.7–8; Hab 3.2–

9 Do not be exceedingly angry, O LORD,
  and do not remember iniquity
    forever.
  Now consider, we are all your people.
10 Your holy cities have become a
    wilderness,
  Zion has become a wilderness,
  Jerusalem a desolation.
11 Our holy and beautiful house,
  where our ancestors praised you,
  has been burned by fire,
  and all our pleasant places have
    become ruins.
12 After all this, will you restrain yourself,
    O LORD?
  Will you keep silent, and punish us so
    severely?

The Righteousness of God's Judgment

65 I was ready to be sought out by those
    who did not ask,
  to be found by those who did not seek
    me.
  I said, "Here I am, here I am,"
  to a nation that did not call on my
    name.
2 I held out my hands all day long
    to a rebellious people,
  who walk in a way that is not good,
    following their own devices;
3 a people who provoke me
    to my face continually,
  sacrificing in gardens
  and offering incense on bricks;
4 who sit inside tombs,
  and spend the night in secret places;
  who eat swine's flesh,

with broth of abominable things in
    their vessels;
5 who say, "Keep to yourself,
  do not come near me, for I am too
    holy for you."
  These are a smoke in my nostrils,
  a fire that burns all day long.
6 See, it is written before me:
  I will not keep silent, but I will repay;
  I will indeed repay into their laps
7   their[a] iniquities and their[a] ancestors'
    iniquities together,
                              says the LORD;
  because they offered incense on the
    mountains
  and reviled me on the hills,
  I will measure into their laps
  full payment for their actions.
8 Thus says the LORD:
  As the wine is found in the cluster,
  and they say, "Do not destroy it,
  for there is a blessing in it,"
  so I will do for my servants' sake,
  and not destroy them all.
9 I will bring forth descendants[b] from
    Jacob,
  and from Judah inheritors[c] of my
    mountains;
  my chosen shall inherit it,
  and my servants shall settle there.
10 Sharon shall become a pasture for flocks,
  and the Valley of Achor a place for
    herds to lie down,
  for my people who have sought me.
11 But you who forsake the LORD,

_____

a Gk Syr: Heb your   b Or a descendant   c Or an inheritor

_____

15). **64.5–7** Confession of sins. **64.8–12** Prayer that God turn aside from his anger and comfort his people against the enemies who have destroyed God's cities (Ps 79). **64.8–9** Since God fathered and fashioned Israel as his own people, why should he destroy the work of his own hand (see Job 10.8–12)? **64.12** *Restrain yourself,* either from further acts of wrath or from continuing indifference to Israel's plight (see 42.14–17). Either way, the plaintive question constitutes a mild rebuke of God.

65.1–25 As if to answer the rebuke implicit in the questions of 64.12, this chapter provides a defense of God's action. Israel's judgment is deserved; nevertheless God will save a remnant. **65.1–7** Israel will be judged because of its constant rebellion. **65.1–2** God spoke, but Israel did not listen (Rom 10.20–21). *Held out my hands,* a gesture of prayer or entreaty (1.15; 1 Kings 8.22, 38, 54; Ps 143.6; Lam 1.17). **65.3–5** Israel

continues the pagan rituals that anger God: *sacrificing in gardens,* presumably a syncretistic fertility ritual; sitting *inside tombs,* for consulting the dead (Deut 18.11–12); eating *swine's flesh* (Deut 14.8). *Too holy.* The participants in these pagan practices claimed a dangerous holiness that set them apart from others. **65.6–7** God will not *keep silent* (see 64.12), but will punish the Israelites fully for these iniquities. **65.8–16** Nevertheless, God will not destroy all Israel; a remnant will be saved. **65.8** *Servants.* In contrast to Second Isaiah, this writer uses the plural when speaking of Israel as God's servants. **65.9** *Jacob,* descendants of the Northern Kingdom. *Judah,* descendants of the Southern Kingdom. **65.10** *Sharon,* rich pastureland along the Mediterranean between Joppa and Mount Carmel (1 Chr 27.29). *Valley of Achor,* a valley near Jericho (Josh 7.24–26; Hos 2.15). **65.11–12** Those who forsake God for such pagan deities as *Fortune* and *Destiny*

who forget my holy mountain,
who set a table for Fortune
   and fill cups of mixed wine for
      Destiny;
12 I will destine you to the sword,
   and all of you shall bow down to the
      slaughter;
because, when I called, you did not
      answer,
   when I spoke, you did not listen,
but you did what was evil in my sight,
   and chose what I did not delight in.
13 Therefore thus says the Lord GOD:
My servants shall eat,
   but you shall be hungry;
my servants shall drink,
   but you shall be thirsty;
my servants shall rejoice,
   but you shall be put to shame;
14 my servants shall sing for gladness of
      heart,
   but you shall cry out for pain of heart,
   and shall wail for anguish of spirit.
15 You shall leave your name to my chosen
      to use as a curse,
and the Lord GOD will put you to
      death;
but to his servants he will give a
      different name.
16 Then whoever invokes a blessing in the
      land
   shall bless by the God of faithfulness,
and whoever takes an oath in the land
   shall swear by the God of faithfulness;
because the former troubles are forgotten
   and are hidden from my sight.

The Glorious New Creation

17 For I am about to create new heavens
   and a new earth;
the former things shall not be
      remembered
   or come to mind.
18 But be glad and rejoice forever
   in what I am creating;
for I am about to create Jerusalem as a joy,
   and its people as a delight.

19 I will rejoice in Jerusalem,
   and delight in my people;
no more shall the sound of weeping be
      heard in it,
   or the cry of distress.
20 No more shall there be in it
   an infant that lives but a few days,
   or an old person who does not live out
      a lifetime;
for one who dies at a hundred years will
      be considered a youth,
   and one who falls short of a hundred
      will be considered accursed.
21 They shall build houses and inhabit
      them;
   they shall plant vineyards and eat their
      fruit.
22 They shall not build and another inhabit;
   they shall not plant and another eat;
for like the days of a tree shall the days of
      my people be,
   and my chosen shall long enjoy the
      work of their hands.
23 They shall not labor in vain,
   or bear children for calamity;[a]
for they shall be offspring blessed by the
      LORD—
   and their descendants as well.
24 Before they call I will answer,
   while they are yet speaking I will hear.
25 The wolf and the lamb shall feed
      together,
   the lion shall eat straw like the ox;
   but the serpent—its food shall be dust!
They shall not hurt or destroy
   on all my holy mountain,
             says the LORD.

The Worship God Demands

66 Thus says the LORD:
Heaven is my throne
   and the earth is my footstool;
what is the house that you would build
      for me,
   and what is my resting place?

---

a Or *sudden terror*

---

will perish. **65.13–16** God's servants will prosper, while the wicked suffer. **65.16** *God of faithfulness.* Blessings and oaths in this era of salvation will emphasize God's faithfulness, because the former experience of God's anger, punishment, and absence will be a forgotten and hidden thing of the past. **65.17–25** God will create new heavens and a new earth of joy, peace,

and tranquility for his people. **65.17** *Former things.* See 43.18. **65.20–23** God's people will enjoy long life and the fruits of their labor (62.8–9). *Days of a tree.* See Job 14.7–9. **65.24** Cf. 30.19. **65.25** Cf. 11.6–9.

    66.1–5 True worship differentiated from false worship. **66.1** *House that you would build for me* presupposes the work of rebuilding the temple in Jerusalem

2 All these things my hand has made,
    and so all these things are mine,[a]
                        says the LORD.
But this is the one to whom I will look,
    to the humble and contrite in spirit,
    who trembles at my word.

3 Whoever slaughters an ox is like one who
        kills a human being;
    whoever sacrifices a lamb, like one who
        breaks a dog's neck;
    whoever presents a grain offering, like
        one who offers swine's blood;[b]
    whoever makes a memorial offering of
        frankincense, like one who blesses
        an idol.
These have chosen their own ways,
    and in their abominations they take
        delight;
4 I also will choose to mock[c] them,
    and bring upon them what they fear;
because, when I called, no one
        answered,
    when I spoke, they did not listen;
but they did what was evil in my sight,
    and chose what did not please me.

The LORD Vindicates Zion

5 Hear the word of the LORD,
    you who tremble at his word:
Your own people who hate you
    and reject you for my name's sake
have said, "Let the LORD be glorified,
    so that we may see your joy";
    but it is they who shall be put to
        shame.

6 Listen, an uproar from the city!
    A voice from the temple!
The voice of the LORD,
    dealing retribution to his enemies!

7 Before she was in labor
        she gave birth;
before her pain came upon her
        she delivered a son.
8 Who has heard of such a thing?
    Who has seen such things?
Shall a land be born in one day?
    Shall a nation be delivered in one
        moment?
Yet as soon as Zion was in labor
        she delivered her children.
9 Shall I open the womb and not deliver?
    says the LORD;
shall I, the one who delivers, shut the
        womb?
    says your God.

10 Rejoice with Jerusalem, and be glad for her,
    all you who love her;
rejoice with her in joy,
    all you who mourn over her—
11 that you may nurse and be satisfied
    from her consoling breast;
that you may drink deeply with delight
    from her glorious bosom.

12 For thus says the LORD:
    I will extend prosperity to her like a river,

---

a Gk Syr: Heb *these things came to be*   *b* Meaning of Heb uncertain   *c* Or *to punish*

---

after the return from exile (520–515 BCE). In contrast to Haggai and Zechariah, this prophet does not show much enthusiasm for the rebuilding project. **66.2** Since the creator of the whole world cannot be contained in a temple built by humans (1 Kings 8.27), it is not the temple, but the right attitude among God's worshipers, that guarantees God's continuing presence with the people (33.14–16; 57.15). **66.3** *Like one.* Each of the four occurrences of this phrase links an appropriate ritual action with a sinful action. The NRSV translation suggests a blanket condemnation of the sacrificial system, but this is only one possible interpretation. The word *like* is not in the Hebrew, and the verse may be translated in a way that simply condemns normal worship practices when the worshiper is also engaging in pagan rituals or an immoral life (1.10–17; 65.1–7, 11). The latter interpretation fits better with the complaint that the wicked *have chosen their own ways.* **66.4** God will *choose* to mock the wicked, because they refused to listen to God's word and *chose* what displeased God (65.12–16). **66.5** *"Let the LORD ... your joy,"* the mocking words of those Israelites who reject God's promises and hate those who take these promises seriously (cf. 5.19; Jer 17.15). **66.6–16** Contrary to what the skeptics say, God's promises to Jerusalem are about to be fulfilled. **66.6–9** God's vindication of the righteous and punishment of the wicked in Zion is as imminent and certain as birth to a woman in labor. **66.7** *Before ... labor she gave birth.* Zion's delivery will be quick and painless. **66.8** The easy birth is incredible because the prophet is talking about the rebirth of a whole *nation,* which normally does not happen in a *day* or a *moment.* **66.9** God's rhetorical questions may be a response to an Israelite complaint that Israel's distress was as desperate as that of pregnant woman who could not give birth (see 26.18; 37.3). **66.10–13** When Zion gives birth to her children, those who love her will delight in Mother

and the wealth of the nations like an
  overflowing stream;
and you shall nurse and be carried on her
  arm,
and dandled on her knees.
13 As a mother comforts her child,
  so I will comfort you;
  you shall be comforted in Jerusalem.

The Reign and Indignation of God

14 You shall see, and your heart shall rejoice;
  your bodies[a] shall flourish like the
    grass;
and it shall be known that the hand of the
  LORD is with his servants,
  and his indignation is against his
    enemies.
15 For the LORD will come in fire,
  and his chariots like the whirlwind,
to pay back his anger in fury,
  and his rebuke in flames of fire.
16 For by fire will the LORD execute
    judgment,
  and by his sword, on all flesh;
  and those slain by the LORD shall be
    many.

17 Those who sanctify and purify themselves to go into the gardens, following the one
in the center, eating the flesh of pigs, vermin,
and rodents, shall come to an end together,
says the LORD.

18 For I know[b] their works and their
thoughts, and I am[c] coming to gather all nations and tongues; and they shall come and

shall see my glory, 19and I will set a sign
among them. From them I will send survivors
to the nations, to Tarshish, Put,[d] and Lud—
which draw the bow—to Tubal and Javan, to
the coastlands far away that have not heard of
my fame or seen my glory; and they shall declare my glory among the nations. 20They
shall bring all your kindred from all the nations as an offering to the LORD, on horses,
and in chariots, and in litters, and on mules,
and on dromedaries, to my holy mountain Jerusalem, says the LORD, just as the Israelites
bring a grain offering in a clean vessel to the
house of the LORD. 21And I will also take some
of them as priests and as Levites, says the
LORD.

22 For as the new heavens and the new
    earth,
  which I will make,
shall remain before me, says the LORD;
  so shall your descendants and your
    name remain.
23 From new moon to new moon,
  and from sabbath to sabbath,
all flesh shall come to worship before me,
  says the LORD.

24 And they shall go out and look at the
dead bodies of the people who have rebelled
against me; for their worm shall not die, their
fire shall not be quenched, and they shall be an
abhorrence to all flesh.

a Heb *bones*   *b* Gk Syr: Heb lacks *know*   *c* Gk Syr Vg Tg: Heb
it is   *d* Gk: Heb *Pul*

Zion's consolations. **66.12** Cf. 60.4–5. **66.13** The
prophet switches from the image of Zion as comforting mother to that of God who comforts like a mother.
66.14–16 While the righteous rejoice, God will come
in fire to punish the wicked (30.27–33; 33.10–14).
66.17–24 Concluding comments underscoring the
Lord's judgment and the revelation of God's glory before the nations. **66.17** See 65.3–4. **66.18–19** God's
glory will be announced even to the most distant nations. *Tarshish.* See note on 23.1. *Put,* a part of Libya
(Ezek 30.5). *Lud,* Lydia in Asia Minor. *Tubal,* a country
in Asia Minor referred to in the Assyrian sources as
Tabal. *Javan,* Ionia or Greece. **66.20–23** The nations

will bring the exiles from Israel back to Jerusalem as an
offering to God, and all nations will serve the Lord (see
60.4–12). **66.21** *Take some of them as priests and as Levites.* The antecedent of *them* is ambiguous. Does it
refer to Israelites brought back from distant exile by
the nations, or to the foreigners who now acknowledge
the glory of God and enter into his priestly service?
66.23 However one interprets (see note on) 66.21, all
the nations will continually come to worship before
God in Jerusalem (cf. Zech 14.16–19). **66.24** The
worm-eaten, burning corpses of the wicked dead will
remain as an eternal warning against rebellion. Cf. Mk
9.48.

JEREMIAH

THE PROPHET JEREMIAH CAME FROM ANATHOTH, a village in the hill country of Benjamin, a small tribe to the north of Judah. Though often controlled by its powerful neighbor to the south, Benjamin was culturally and religiously more at home with the tribes who comprised the Northern Kingdom.

Jeremiah was a descendant of Abiathar, one of the two chief priests of King David (1 Sam 22–23; 2 Sam 20.25). Abiathar was a levitical priest, belonging to a priesthood that was prominent during the period of the judges (ca. 1200–1000 BCE) and that was connected by tradition to the shrine at Shiloh (1 Kings 2.27). David's other chief priest, Zadok, was the founder of the Zadokite priesthood, which contended with the Levites for priestly control of royal religion in Jerusalem. Solomon banished Abiathar to Anathoth because he supported the efforts of Adonijah, Solomon's rival, to succeed David to the throne (1 Kings 2.26–27). Allied with Solomon, Zadok and his descendants gained control of the temple in Jerusalem and were strong supporters of the Davidic monarchy. Jeremiah's strong criticism of the house of David and the Jerusalem temple is due in part to his levitical and Benjaminite heritage.

Jeremiah's Mosaic theology emphasizes particularly the traditions of the exodus from Egypt, the wilderness wandering, the gift of the land of Canaan, and the covenant of Sinai. Indeed, Jeremiah is presented as the "prophet like Moses" (Deut 18.15–22) whom, like the early lawgiver, people were to hear and obey.

Historical Background

THE PROSE NARRATIVES AND SERMONS (1.2; 25.3) place Jeremiah's call to prophesy in the "thirteenth year of King Josiah" (627 BCE) and note that the prophet was active during this king's reign (cf. 3.6; 36.2). The year 627 was an auspicious time in the history of Judah; it witnessed the death of Ashurbanipal, the last powerful Assyrian king. Judah had become a vassal of the Assyrian Empire in 735 BCE. With Ashurbanipal's death, the Assyrian Empire began to crumble. Asshur, a major Assyrian city, fell to the Medes in 614, and Nineveh, the capital, fell in 612. After Nebuchadrezzar's (also spelled Nebuchadnezzar; see note on 21.2) defeat of the Egyptians at Carchemish in 605, Babylonia conquered much of the ancient Near East.

In 627 the vassal nations in the Assyrian Empire revolted; these included Judah, ruled by King Josiah, whose ambition was to reestablish the empire of David and Solomon. Five years later Josiah launched a religious reform that reaffirmed the covenant of Moses and centralized the worship of Yahweh in Jerusalem. The reform also had political implications. The king pressed the reform not only in Judah but also in the territory of the old Northern Kingdom, which at that time was under the political control of the Assyrians. Josiah was initially successful, but his dreams of independence ended with his death at the hands of the Egyptians at Megiddo (609 BCE).

Within a year or two after the battle of Carchemish Judah became a part of the Babylonian Empire. A later king of Judah, Jehoiakim (609–598 BCE), died during an unsuccessful revolt against Babylon, and the first exiles from Jerusalem were taken to Babylon (597). A second rebellion, led by the last king of Judah, Zedekiah (597–587/6), resulted in the destruction of Jerusalem and the second, more comprehensive exile in 587. After zealots assassinated the Judean governor, Gedaliah, Jeremiah was forced to accompany a group of Jews seeking exile in Egypt. The Babylonian captivity lasted until 539, when the Persian king, Cyrus, conquered Babylon and allowed the exiles to return home (538; see Ezra 1.1–4).

Jeremiah's prophetic career coincided with these critical events in Judah's history. The early period of his life is difficult to reconstruct. It is likely that he opposed the unabashed enthusiasm for the political ambitions of Josiah and spoke of a "foe from the north" who would bring destruction (see chs. 4–10). This foe was not clearly identified as Babylon until the battle of Carchemish. If active at the time, Jeremiah may have initially supported Josiah's reform, though this support probably ended with the king's death in 609 BCE. Some of Jeremiah's oracles addressed to the Northern Kingdom may come from this period of religious reform. Before coming to Jerusalem after Josiah's death, the prophet preached both repentance by returning to the ancestral faith (ch. 3) and acquiescence to the Babylonians as the sole means of avoiding national destruction, thus gaining for himself powerful enemies within Judah. The so-called "laments of Jeremiah" (see 11.18–20.18) reflect his experience of persecution.

Jeremiah's temple sermon (see chs. 7, 26), dating to the beginning of Jehoiakim's reign (609 BCE), assaulted the theological undergirding of royal religion by arguing that obedience to the commandments and the covenant of Moses, not temple worship, was Judah's only hope for survival. Comparable are Jeremiah's oracles of judgment against Jerusalem and the kings of the house of David (21.11–23.8). In Jeremiah's view, temple worship and the eternal covenant of God with the dynasty of David, so central to royal religion in Jerusalem (2 Sam 7), were a "false" (Hebrew *sheqer*) religion, sure to fail.

After the exile of 587 BCE, Jeremiah chose to stay in Jerusalem to help those who remained rebuild their lives. Although he had earlier occasionally delivered oracles of salvation to both Judah and the Northern Kingdom, now he emphasized oracles of hope rather than of judgment. The remnants of both Israel and Judah would enter into a new covenant and faithfully follow God's law, for it would be written upon their hearts (chs. 30–31). After the assassination of Gedaliah by Jewish partisans, Jeremiah was forced to go into Egyptian exile. Sometime later the prophet disappeared from history.

Composition and Literary Character

THE BOOK OF JEREMIAH consists of several kinds of literature that underwent numerous editions before the book achieved its present form. Three major types of literature compose much of the book. Poetic oracles of judgment are found throughout chs. 1–25. These may contain much that originated with the prophet. Narratives about incidents in the life of Jeremiah are found mainly in chs. 26–45. Prose exhortations or "sermons" in the literary style of speeches in Deuteronomy and the books of Samuel and Kings are embedded in the first forty-five chapters. Indeed, both the narratives and the prose exhortations may derive from later scribes, called by scholars Deuteronomic authors or editors because of their affinities in thought and style to the Deuteronomic literature (Deuteronomy–2 Kings). These later writers were responsible for the final form of the book. Their efforts were designed to enable Jeremiah to speak to later exilic and early postexilic Jewish communities.

Several independent collections of literary materials appear to have been compiled and transmitted separately, at least for a time, before being brought together in the present book. These collections include the oracles "concerning the house of David" (21.11–23.8), speeches "concerning the prophets" (23.9–40), speeches "concerning the nations" (chs. 46–51), and possibly two others: the "laments of Jeremiah" (found throughout 11.18–20.18) and the oracles concerning the "foe from the north" (found throughout chs. 4–10).

In addition, several clues to the composition and growth of the book are given in ch. 36. This chapter mentions two "scrolls of Baruch," Jeremiah's scribe, who is presented as writing down in the first scroll the oracles the prophet spoke from the "days of Josiah" until the battle of Carchemish. After the first scroll's destruction Baruch wrote a second scroll that repeated the contents of the first and added "many similar words." The call of Jeremiah (ch. 1), his laments (found in parts of 11.18–20.18), and the oracles concerning the "foe from the north" (chs. 4–10), along with other early oracles in chs. 1–25, may have composed the book's first scroll (or edition). The second scroll made allowances for the addition of other materials, including the biographical narratives and the prose exhortations.

Part of the literary history of the book also may be reconstructed by comparing the Septuagint (Greek) of Jeremiah with its Masoretic (Hebrew) counterpart. The Septuagint is one-eighth shorter than the Masoretic Text and represents a different arrangement of materials (especially the location of the "oracles against the nations," chs. 46–51). The manuscript evidence for Jeremiah contained in the Qumran scrolls, discovered near the Dead Sea in the 1940s, suggests that the Septuagint is based on an older Hebrew edition of Jeremiah. Some later editor or editors supplemented that early edition to produce what became the canonical form of the present book.

The rather complex composition and editing of the book should obscure neither the beauty of its literary character nor the power of its prophetic message. Here indeed was a prophet who combined elegance of form with the ethical and redemptive content of the "word of the LORD." Perhaps more than anyone in his time, Jeremiah provided the means by which a despairing people could hope for a new future. [LEO G. PERDUE, revised by ROBERT R. WILSON]

1 The words of Jeremiah son of Hilkiah, of the priests who were in Anathoth in the land of Benjamin, ²to whom the word of the LORD came in the days of King Josiah son of Amon of Judah, in the thirteenth year of his reign. ³It came also in the days of King Jehoiakim son of Josiah of Judah, and until the end of the eleventh year of King Zedekiah son of Josiah of Judah, until the captivity of Jerusalem in the fifth month.

Jeremiah's Call and Commission

4 Now the word of the LORD came to me saying,
5 "Before I formed you in the womb I knew
      you,
   and before you were born I consecrated
      you;
   I appointed you a prophet to the
      nations."
⁶Then I said, "Ah, Lord GOD! Truly I do not know how to speak, for I am only a boy." ⁷But the LORD said to me,

"Do not say, 'I am only a boy';
   for you shall go to all to whom I send
      you,
   and you shall speak whatever I command
      you.
8 Do not be afraid of them,
   for I am with you to deliver you,
                              says the LORD."
⁹Then the LORD put out his hand and touched my mouth; and the LORD said to me,
   "Now I have put my words in your
      mouth.
10 See, today I appoint you over nations and
      over kingdoms,
   to pluck up and to pull down,
   to destroy and to overthrow,
   to build and to plant."

11 The word of the LORD came to me, saying, "Jeremiah, what do you see?" And I said, "I see a branch of an almond tree." *a* ¹²Then the

---

a Heb *shaqed*

1.1–3 Superscription. Added by later editors, superscriptions to prophetic books contain all or some of the following features: the title (*the words of Jeremiah*), personal background (*son of . . . Benjamin*), reception of the revelation (*to whom the word of the LORD came*), whom the revelation concerned (*the nations*; see vv. 4–10), and the date (vv. 2–3). See Isa 1.1; Am 1.1; Mic 1.1; Zeph 1.1. **1.1** *Jeremiah*, in Hebrew "Yahweh exalts." *Priests . . . in Anathoth.* See Introduction. *Anathoth* (located at modern Ras el Kharuba), a levitical village in Benjamin less than three miles northeast of Jerusalem. **1.2** *Josiah* reigned 640–609 BCE. *Thirteenth year*, 627. **1.3** *Jehoiakim* reigned 609–598 BCE. Zedekiah reigned 597–587/6. *Captivity of Jerusalem*, 587. The superscription dates Jeremiah's prophetic activity from 627 to 587. **1.4–19** Jeremiah's call and commission. The date of Jeremiah's call is a matter of debate. The prose texts (1.2; 25.3) place the call in the *thirteenth year of King Josiah* (627 BCE) and note that Jeremiah was active in this king's reign (see 3.6; 36.2). However, the poetry may imply Jeremiah was born in 627, was called from the *womb*, and then, as a *boy* (vv. 5–6), began to prophesy in 609. Ch. 1 presents an overture to the book. Key themes and words are introduced and later repeated throughout the various collections. The chapter contains the poetic call of Jeremiah (vv. 4–10), two accompanying visions (vv. 11–14), and two editorial expansions (vv. 15–16, 17–19). Of the two forms of prophetic call, the encounter with (the word of) God (Ex 3.1–4.17; Judg 6.11–18; 1 Sam 3) and the vision of God in the heavenly court (1 Kings 22.19–22; Isa 40.1–11; Ezek 1.1–3.11), Jeremiah's followed the first. The first form consists of the divine confrontation (v. 4), introductory word (v. 5ab), commission (v. 5c), objection (v. 6), reassurance (vv. 7–8), and sign

(vv. 9–10). The striking parallels with the call of Moses (Ex 3.1–4.17) present Jeremiah as the "prophet like Moses" (Deut 18.15–22). **1.5** Jeremiah is predestined to be a prophet even before his birth and to be a *prophet to the nations* (see "oracles against the nations," chs. 46–51). The origin of the world and that of the individual (conception, formation in the womb, birth, and nurture) are the two major creation traditions in the Hebrew Bible (world: Gen 1.1–2.4a; Pss 33; 74.12–17; 104; individual: Gen 2.4b–25; Job 3; 10; Ps 139.13–16; both are combined in the birth of Wisdom, Prov 8.22–31). In his final lament Jeremiah curses his birth, thus perhaps attempting to negate his call (20.14–18). The point of the prenatal call, however, may be that the prophet's call is both early and irresistible. **1.6** *Ah, Lord GOD* introduces a complaint against God (see 4.10; 14.13; 32.17; Josh 7.7; Ezek 4.14; 9.8; 11.13; 20.49). *I do not know how to speak* refers to the role of the prophet as one who speaks on behalf of God and may be intended to echo Moses' objection to his own call (Ex 3.11–4.17, esp. 4.10-12). *Boy*, either a child, adolescent, or young man. The term echoes the call of another "prophet like Moses," the lad Samuel (1 Sam 3). **1.8** *I am with you to deliver you* promises divine presence and aid in the face of persecution (see the laments in 11.18–20.18). **1.9** Touching and placing divine words in the mouth reflects the "prophet like Moses" (Deut 15.15, 18; 18.15–22; cf. Jer 15.19). **1.10** God appoints Jeremiah, not kings, over nations to destroy and then to build. *To pluck up . . . overthrow* points to the oracles of judgment in chs. 2–25. *To build and to plant* echoes the oracles of salvation in chs. 30–31. The theme of this verse is a recurring motif aptly summarizing the message of the prophet. See 18.7–9; 24.6; 31.28; 42.10; 45.4 (cf. 31.4, 40; 32.41). **1.11–14** Vision

LORD said to me, "You have seen well, for I am watching*a* over my word to perform it." 13The word of the LORD came to me a second time, saying, "What do you see?" And I said, "I see a boiling pot, tilted away from the north."

14 Then the LORD said to me: Out of the north disaster shall break out on all the inhabitants of the land. 15For now I am calling all the tribes of the kingdoms of the north, says the LORD; and they shall come and all of them shall set their thrones at the entrance of the gates of Jerusalem, against all its surrounding walls and against all the cities of Judah. 16And I will utter my judgments against them, for all their wickedness in forsaking me; they have made offerings to other gods, and worshiped the works of their own hands. 17But you, gird up your loins; stand up and tell them everything that I command you. Do not break down before them, or I will break you before them. 18And I for my part have made you today a fortified city, an iron pillar, and a bronze wall, against the whole land—against the kings of Judah, its princes, its priests, and the people of the land. 19They will fight against you; but they shall not prevail against you, for I am with you, says the LORD, to deliver you.

God Pleads with Israel to Repent

2 The word of the LORD came to me, saying: 2Go and proclaim in the hearing of Jerusalem, Thus says the LORD:

I remember the devotion of your youth,
    your love as a bride,
how you followed me in the wilderness,
    in a land not sown.
3 Israel was holy to the LORD,
    the first fruits of his harvest.
All who ate of it were held guilty;
    disaster came upon them,
                              says the LORD.

4 Hear the word of the LORD, O house of Jacob, and all the families of the house of Israel. 5Thus says the LORD:

_____

a Heb *shoqed*

---

reports consist of several parts: introduction (God shows or the prophet sees something), description of what is seen, dialogue between God and the prophet, and interpretation (God explains the meaning of the vision). See ch. 24; Am 7.1–9.10. In the first vision a wordplay, *branch of an almond tree* (Hebrew *shaqed*) and *watching* (*shoqed*), stresses that God will enact the content of the prophetic word. In the second vision the *boiling pot* points to destruction from the *north* (see "foe from the north" oracles, chs. 4–10). **1.15–16** An exilic or postexilic editorial expansion of the second vision, explaining that the Babylonian conquest resulted from violation of the Mosaic covenant. **1.17–19** A second editorial expansion in which Jeremiah is encouraged to fight against his enemies, the leaders of Judah: *kings of Judah, its princes* (i.e., royal officers), *its priests* (both levitical and Zadokite), and the *people of the land* (landowners in the countryside). Unlike Jerusalem, he is to be invincible, *a fortified city, an iron pillar, a bronze wall* (see 15.20), because the Lord will sustain and deliver him (see 1.8).

2.1–37 Ch. 2 is an oracular poem dealing with the theme of Israel's and Judah's religious and political disloyalty to the Lord and the covenant. With the deterioration of Assyrian power after 627 BCE, Josiah moved into the territory of the former Northern Kingdom to bring it under his control. The oracles in ch. 2, perhaps from the first stage of Jeremiah's activity, assume the form of a "lawsuit" (Hebrew *riv*, v. 9), in which the Lord serves as both plaintiff and judge (see Isa 5.1–7; Hos 9.10–13; 13.4–8; Mic 6.1–8). "Lawsuits" include an appeal to heaven and earth as witnesses, a summons to the defendant to hear the charges, a listing of charges, rhetorical questions, a description of the Lord's gracious acts on behalf of the accused, and an announcement of guilt and punishment. The poem has five parts: vv. 1–3 (Israel and Judah's faithfulness as a young bride), vv. 4–13 (religious apostasy—Baal worship), vv. 14–19 (political disloyalty—alliances with Assyria and Egypt), vv. 20–28 (religious apostasy—Baal worship), and vv. 29–37 (political disloyalty—alliance with Egypt). The pattern is A, B, C, B′, C′. The wilderness and bridal imagery of the first oracle is repeated in the final one, thus forming an *inclusio* (a repetition signaling the beginning and end of a unit). Echoing Hosea, a Northern prophet of the eighth century BCE, Jeremiah contrasts Israel's faithfulness in the Sinai wilderness with its disloyalty after entrance into Canaan. **2.1–2** *The word of the LORD . . . Jerusalem,* a prose introduction inserted by a postexilic editor. **2.2** *Devotion* (Hebrew *chesed*), love or faithfulness within a covenant relationship (marriage, friendship, and the covenant between God and Israel). *Bride,* a common metaphor for Israel in the relationship with God, the husband (Isa 49.18; 61.10; 62.5; see esp. Hos 2). *Wilderness,* the Sinai wilderness, where Israel entered into covenant with the Lord after the exodus from Egypt. **2.3** *Holy,* set apart, consecrated for divine service. *First fruits,* the initial and presumably the best yield of the harvest given as an offering to the Lord (see Ex 23.19; 34.26; Deut 26.2, 10). **2.4–13** The oracle contrasts exodus theology (God's liberation of Israel from Egyptian slavery, guidance through the treacherous Sinai wilderness, and gift of the land of Canaan) with Israel's later disloyalty in following the Canaanite god

What wrong did your ancestors find in
   me
   that they went far from me,
and went after worthless things, and
   became worthless themselves?
6 They did not say, "Where is the LORD
   who brought us up from the land of
      Egypt,
who led us in the wilderness,
   in a land of deserts and pits,
in a land of drought and deep darkness,
   in a land that no one passes through,
   where no one lives?"
7 I brought you into a plentiful land
   to eat its fruits and its good things.
But when you entered you defiled my
      land,
   and made my heritage an
      abomination.
8 The priests did not say, "Where is the
      LORD?"
   Those who handle the law did not
      know me;
the rulers[a] transgressed against me;
   the prophets prophesied by Baal,
   and went after things that do not
      profit.

9 Therefore once more I accuse you,
                        says the LORD,
   and I accuse your children's children.
10 Cross to the coasts of Cyprus and look,
   send to Kedar and examine with care;
   see if there has ever been such a thing.

11 Has a nation changed its gods,
   even though they are no gods?
But my people have changed their glory
   for something that does not profit.
12 Be appalled, O heavens, at this,
   be shocked, be utterly desolate,
                        says the LORD,
13 for my people have committed two evils:
   they have forsaken me,
the fountain of living water,
   and dug out cisterns for themselves,
cracked cisterns
   that can hold no water.

14 Is Israel a slave? Is he a homeborn
      servant?
   Why then has he become plunder?
15 The lions have roared against him,
   they have roared loudly.
They have made his land a waste;
   his cities are in ruins, without
      inhabitant.
16 Moreover, the people of Memphis and
      Tahpanhes
   have broken the crown of your head.
17 Have you not brought this upon yourself
   by forsaking the LORD your God,
   while he led you in the way?
18 What then do you gain by going to Egypt,
   to drink the waters of the Nile?
Or what do you gain by going to Assyria,
   to drink the waters of the Euphrates?

_____
a Heb *shepherds*

Baal (lit. "husband" in Canaanite and Hebrew).
2.5 *Worthless things,* idols, false gods (8.19; Deut 32.21;
1 Kings 16.13, 26; 10.8; 14.22). **2.7** *Plentiful land,* the
land of Canaan. **2.8** *Priests, rulers,* and *prophets* led the
people into religious apostasy. **2.10–11** *Cyprus,* an island in the eastern Mediterranean about sixty miles
west of the coast of Phoenicia. It was a center for maritime trade. *Kedar,* a powerful league of Arab tribes in
the north Arabian desert east of the Transjordan who
raided surrounding countries and controlled the eastern trade route from Arabia to the Fertile Crescent
(49.28–33; Isa 21.16–17; Ezek 27.21). From west to
east (including all areas crisscrossed by trade routes),
Jeremiah contends, no nation changes its gods, even
though they are not real. Yet Israel exchanges its *glory*
(lit. "divine presence," God) for false gods who *do not
profit.* **2.12** The *heavens* are personified as witnesses at
Israel's trial. **2.13** Rock-cut *cisterns* were normally
plastered to protect against leakage. **2.14–19** Israel's
political apostasy, establishing alliances with Egypt
and Assyria, is another example of covenant faithlessness. Unlike a *slave* or a *homeborn servant* (i.e., one
born to a family as a slave), who is property to be
bought and sold, Israel was a nation of slaves liberated
by God for responsible freedom within a covenant relationship. Yet Israel willingly sacrificed this freedom
to become a slave of Assyria (*lions*) and of Egypt.
2.16 *Memphis,* on the west bank of the Nile about fifteen miles south of Cairo. It was the capital of Egypt
during the Old Kingdom (ca. 2700–2200 BCE) and the
cultic center of Ptah, a creator deity and patron of
skilled crafts (44.1; Isa 19.13; Ezek 30.13; Hos 9.6). Although no longer the capital in Jeremiah's day, it was
still a politically and religiously important city. *Tahpanhes,* modern Tell Defenneh, located on Lake Men-
zaleh in the northeast Delta. King Psammetichus I
(664–610 BCE) built a garrison there for Greek mercenaries to defend against the Assyrians. Both cities
would have been places where emissaries from Judah
met with Egyptian officials to discuss alliances against
Babylonia. Jewish refugees fled to these cities in the aftermath of the Babylonian invasion of Judah (43.7–9;

19 Your wickedness will punish you,
  and your apostasies will convict you.
  Know and see that it is evil and bitter
    for you to forsake the LORD your God;
  the fear of me is not in you,
                says the Lord GOD of hosts.

20 For long ago you broke your yoke
    and burst your bonds,
    and you said, "I will not serve!"
  On every high hill
    and under every green tree
    you sprawled and played the whore.

21 Yet I planted you as a choice vine,
    from the purest stock.
  How then did you turn degenerate
    and become a wild vine?

22 Though you wash yourself with lye
    and use much soap,
  the stain of your guilt is still before me,
                says the Lord GOD.

23 How can you say, "I am not defiled,
    I have not gone after the Baals"?
  Look at your way in the valley;
    know what you have done—
  a restive young camel interlacing her
        tracks,

24   a wild ass at home in the wilderness,
  in her heat sniffing the wind!
    Who can restrain her lust?
  None who seek her need weary themselves;
    in her month they will find her.

25 Keep your feet from going unshod
    and your throat from thirst.
  But you said, "It is hopeless,
    for I have loved strangers,
    and after them I will go."

26 As a thief is shamed when caught,
    so the house of Israel shall be shamed—

they, their kings, their officials,
  their priests, and their prophets,
27 who say to a tree, "You are my father,"
  and to a stone, "You gave me birth."
  For they have turned their backs to me,
    and not their faces.
  But in the time of their trouble they say,
    "Come and save us!"

28 But where are your gods
    that you made for yourself?
  Let them come, if they can save you,
    in your time of trouble;
  for you have as many gods
    as you have towns, O Judah.

29 Why do you complain against me?
    You have all rebelled against me,
                says the LORD.

30 In vain I have struck down your children;
    they accepted no correction.
  Your own sword devoured your prophets
    like a ravening lion.

31 And you, O generation, behold the word
        of the LORD! [a]
  Have I been a wilderness to Israel,
    or a land of thick darkness?
  Why then do my people say, "We are free,
    we will come to you no more"?

32 Can a girl forget her ornaments,
    or a bride her attire?
  Yet my people have forgotten me,
    days without number.

33 How well you direct your course
    to seek lovers!
  So that even to wicked women
    you have taught your ways.

34 Also on your skirts is found

----
a Meaning of Heb uncertain

44.1). **2.19** Israel is condemned for abandoning the Lord of the exodus for alliances with human kings. **2.20–28** Judah is charged with religious infidelity in worshiping Baal. Graphic images of apostasy include an insatiable whore, an ox that breaks its yoke, a vine that bears strange fruit, a stain that will not wash off, and the lust of a young camel and a wild ass in heat. **2.23** *Way*, both a road and a lifestyle. **2.26** Once again the leaders of Judah are condemned: *kings, officials, priests,* and *prophets* (see 1.18). **2.27** *Tree* and *stone* are connected with Canaanite worship. Normally, Asherah (a Canaanite goddess portrayed variously as the consort of the Canaanite storm god Baal and as the consort of El, the head of the Canaanite pantheon) is

associated with a tree. Male deities like Baal are represented in cult places by a *matsebah* (a Hebrew term for an upright cultic stone). Jeremiah sarcastically reverses the sexual imagery. Unlike the Lord, who redeems, the Canaanite deities are idols created by their worshipers and incapable of saving them (see the idol satires in 10.1–16; Isa 40.18–20; 41.5–7, 21–29; 44.6–20; 46; Pss 115; 135). **2.29–37** Israel's social injustice will lead to its humiliation at the hands of the very nations with whom it sought alliances. Josiah was killed by Neco II (610–594 BCE) at Megiddo in 609, when the Egyptians were marching north to join with the Assyrians at Carchemish in the futile attempt to stall the Babylonian advance.

the lifeblood of the innocent poor,
  though you did not catch them breaking in.
  Yet in spite of all these things[a]
35 you say, "I am innocent;
  surely his anger has turned from me."
Now I am bringing you to judgment
  for saying, "I have not sinned."
36 How lightly you gad about,
  changing your ways!
You shall be put to shame by Egypt
  as you were put to shame by Assyria.
37 From there also you will come away
  with your hands on your head;
for the LORD has rejected those in whom
    you trust,
  and you will not prosper through
    them.

Unfaithful Israel

3 If[b] a man divorces his wife
  and she goes from him
and becomes another man's wife,
  will he return to her?
Would not such a land be greatly polluted?
You have played the whore with many
    lovers;
  and would you return to me?
              says the LORD.

2 Look up to the bare heights,[c] and see!
  Where have you not been lain with?
By the waysides you have sat waiting for
    lovers,
  like a nomad in the wilderness.
You have polluted the land
  with your whoring and wickedness.
3 Therefore the showers have been
    withheld,
  and the spring rain has not come;
yet you have the forehead of a whore,
  you refuse to be ashamed.
4 Have you not just now called to me,
  "My Father, you are the friend of my
    youth—
5 will he be angry forever,
  will he be indignant to the end?"
This is how you have spoken,
  but you have done all the evil that you
    could.

A Call to Repentance

6 The LORD said to me in the days of King Josiah: Have you seen what she did, that faithless one, Israel, how she went up on every high hill

---

a Meaning of Heb uncertain   b Q Ms Gk Syr: MT *Saying, If*
c Or *the trails*

3.1–4.4 Jeremiah's call to repentance is a collection of primarily poetic oracles directing Israel to *return* to the Lord, i.e., "repent," Hebrew *shub. Shub* occurs sixteen times in this collection and provides the key theme. The "summons to repentance" occurs four times: 3.12b; 3.14a; 3.22a; 4.1a. 3.1–5 is a continuation of the lawsuit in ch. 2, while the other poetic sections form a "call to repentance" (see Am 5.4–7, 14–15; Hos 14.2). The poetic sections include: 3.1–5 (the adulterous wife and the faithless child); 3.12b–13 (the adulterous wife); 3.14, 19–20 (faithless children); 3.21–23 (faithless sons); and 4.1–4 (faithless Israel and Judah exhorted to repent). The poetic call to repentance, addressed to Israel and Judah, was most likely issued during the early stage of Jeremiah's activity. The contingents of Israelites in Assyrian exile, those remaining in the North after the destruction of Samaria in 722 BCE, the Israelite refugees who migrated south to Judah, especially to the western hill in Jerusalem, and Judah are all addressed by Jeremiah. Using two metaphors, an unfaithful wife and rebellious children, Jeremiah urges Israel to repent, i.e., to return to God, who is both husband and father. Jeremiah's use of these two metaphors follows Hosea. Editors, sometime after the destruction of Jerusalem in 587 BCE, inserted three prose speeches: 3.6–12a; 3.15–18; 3.24–25. These additions indict *false sister Judah* (3.7) for being more guilty of religious adultery than

Israel, promise a new future with faithful rulers who dwell in a Jerusalem that is the throne of God and the city to which the nations will come, and express hope for the return of a united Israel and Judah from exile in Mesopotamia. **3.1–5** Israel and Judah are presented as both the Lord's faithless wife, who has become a prostitute, and his disobedient child. The lawsuit draws on the legal case of divorce in Deut 24.1–4 and its application in Hos 2. The case in Deuteronomy forbids a man who divorces his wife to remarry her, even if her second husband has died or divorced her. Jeremiah replaces the law in Deut 24.1–4 with two rhetorical questions: *Will he* (the husband) *return to her? Would not such a land be greatly polluted?* (v. 1). Although the Lord has not divorced his people, they have forsaken the marriage by having many *lovers* (false gods). For Jeremiah divine grace allows a repentant people to return. This sets the stage for the four "summons to repentance" that follow. Immoral actions pollute the land, i.e., desecrate the holiness of the land, which God both gave to Israel and Judah and blesses with divine presence and fertility (see Lev 19.29; Num 35.33–34). Desecration leads to God's withholding the rain. *Forehead of a whore* may allude to a phylactery or crown of cord worn around the head by prostitutes. **3.6–11** A prose commentary on vv. 1–5 set in the reign of Josiah. Israel did not *return* and is divorced by the Lord, i.e., sent into Assyrian exile. *False sister Judah* (v. 8) did

and under every green tree, and played the whore there? 7And I thought, "After she has done all this she will return to me"; but she did not return, and her false sister Judah saw it. 8She*a* saw that for all the adulteries of that faithless one, Israel, I had sent her away with a decree of divorce; yet her false sister Judah did not fear, but she too went and played the whore. 9Because she took her whoredom so lightly, she polluted the land, committing adultery with stone and tree. 10Yet for all this her false sister Judah did not return to me with her whole heart, but only in pretense, says the LORD.

11 Then the LORD said to me: Faithless Israel has shown herself less guilty than false Judah. 12Go, and proclaim these words toward the north, and say:

Return, faithless Israel,
                                    says the LORD.
I will not look on you in anger,
    for I am merciful,
                                    says the LORD;
    I will not be angry forever.
13 Only acknowledge your guilt,
        that you have rebelled against the LORD
            your God,
    and scattered your favors among
            strangers under every green tree,
        and have not obeyed my voice,
                                    says the LORD.
14 Return, O faithless children,
                                    says the LORD,
        for I am your master;
    I will take you, one from a city and two
            from a family,
        and I will bring you to Zion.

15 I will give you shepherds after my own heart, who will feed you with knowledge and understanding. 16And when you have multiplied and increased in the land, in those days, says the LORD, they shall no longer say, "The ark of the covenant of the LORD." It shall not come to mind, or be remembered, or missed; nor shall another one be made. 17At that time Jerusalem shall be called the throne of the LORD, and all nations shall gather to it, to the presence of the LORD in Jerusalem, and they shall no longer stubbornly follow their own evil will. 18In those days the house of Judah shall join the house of Israel, and together they shall come from the land of the north to the land that I gave your ancestors for a heritage.

19 I thought
        how I would set you among my
            children,
    and give you a pleasant land,
        the most beautiful heritage of all the
            nations.
    And I thought you would call me, My
        Father,
    and would not turn from following
        me.
20 Instead, as a faithless wife leaves her
        husband,
    so you have been faithless to me,
        O house of Israel,
                                    says the LORD.

21 A voice on the bare heights*b* is heard,
        the plaintive weeping of Israel's
            children,
    because they have perverted their way,
        they have forgotten the LORD their
            God:

_____
a Q Ms Gk Mss Syr: MT *I*   *b* Or *the trails*

not learn from Israel's experience. She too became a prostitute by following false gods. Judah also did not return. Indeed, Israel was judged less guilty than Judah. This commentary explains the Babylonian exile. **3.8–9** *Decree of divorce.* See Deut 24.1–4. *Adultery with stone and tree.* See note on 2.27. **3.12–13** *Merciful* (Hebrew *chasid*). The loyalty between two covenant partners includes divine grace as the basis for forgiveness and reconciliation. **3.14, 19–21** A second "summons to repentance," addressed to Israel. The faithful refugees from the former Northern Kingdom will return to Zion as a part of the new people of God. **3.15–18** A prose speech by later editors that comments on v. 14. In the restoration, new and faithful rulers will guide a reunited Israel and Judah, Jerusalem will be the center of divine rule, all nations shall come to Jerusalem, and all will follow the will of God. **3.15** *Shepherds,* a figurative expression for kings (see 10.21; 22.22; 23.1–4; 25.34–38; Ps 78.70–72; Isa 44.28; Ezek 34.1–10). God was the true shepherd of Israel (Ps 23; Ezek 34). **3.16** *Ark of the covenant,* a chest that was originally a portable shrine signifying divine presence and considered the throne of God (cf. Ex 25.10–15; Deut 10.8). Originally kept in the tent of meeting (2 Sam 6.17), it contained the two tablets of the law (Deut 10.2, 5) and perhaps the sacred lots (Urim and Thummim, Judg 20.27; 1 Sam 14.17–18). David brought the ark to Jerusalem, signifying the unification of the Northern and Southern Kingdoms (2 Sam 6), and Solomon placed it in the holy of holies of the new temple (1 Kings 8.4–7). Here it was considered a throne, guarded by two cherubim (2 Kings 19.15). The

22 Return, O faithless children,
        I will heal your faithlessness.

    "Here we come to you;
        for you are the LORD our God.
23 Truly the hills are[a] a delusion,
        the orgies on the mountains.
    Truly in the LORD our God
        is the salvation of Israel.
24 "But from our youth the shameful thing
has devoured all for which our ancestors had
labored, their flocks and their herds, their sons
and their daughters. 25Let us lie down in our
shame, and let our dishonor cover us; for we
have sinned against the LORD our God, we and
our ancestors, from our youth even to this
day; and we have not obeyed the voice of the
LORD our God."

4 If you return, O Israel,
                        says the LORD,
    if you return to me,
    if you remove your abominations from
        my presence,
        and do not waver,

2 and if you swear, "As the LORD lives!"
        in truth, in justice, and in uprightness,
    then nations shall be blessed[b] by him,
        and by him they shall boast.
3 For thus says the LORD to the people of
Judah and to the inhabitants of Jerusalem:
    Break up your fallow ground,
        and do not sow among thorns.
4 Circumcise yourselves to the LORD,
        remove the foreskin of your hearts,
    O people of Judah and inhabitants of
        Jerusalem,
    or else my wrath will go forth like fire,
        and burn with no one to quench it,
        because of the evil of your doings.

Invasion and Desolation of Judah Threatened

5 Declare in Judah, and proclaim in Jerusalem, and say:
    Blow the trumpet through the land;
        shout aloud[c] and say,

---

a Gk Syr Vg: Heb *Truly from the hills is*   b Or *shall bless themselves*   c Or *shout, take your weapons*: Heb *shout, fill* (your hand)

---

ark was captured or destroyed by the Babylonians in
587 BCE. **3.22–23** The third "summons to repentance,"
also addressed to Israel. *Hills* and *mountains* were important locations for shrines and temples. These sacred
sites are sometimes identified as "high places" (Hebrew
bamot; see 1 Kings 3.2; 2 Kings 12.4). *Orgies*, lit. "noise,"
the sounds made during illegitimate worship at the
high places. Many scholars think that such worship involved sexual activity. **3.24–25** A third editorial addition that places a liturgical confession of sin in the
mouth of the exilic or postexilic community; it is a ritual response to the prophetic "summons to repentance." **4.1–4** The final poem in the section 3.1–4.4 is
also a "summons to repentance," though shaped as a
conditional clause (*if you return . . .*) to conform to the
opening line of the unit (3.1, *if a man . . .*). This provides
an *inclusio* (a repetition signaling the beginning and
end of a unit) for the entire section. **4.1** *Abominations*,
idols and practices associated with idol worship (7.30;
13.27; 16.18; Deut 29.17). **4.2** *Swear*. In oaths that either
begin with or imply the use of the phrase *as the LORD
lives*, the Lord is the guarantor of the oath, and lies or
broken oaths would receive divine punishment. This
oath is probably the ritual swearing during occasions of
covenant renewal (Gen 26.28). Oaths are sacred words
of promise, and to violate them is to take God's name in
vain (Ex 20.7; Lev 19.12). *Blessed*, also sacred language.
A blessing is a ritual pronouncement, usually by God
through a priest, that effects good fortune or well-being
for the recipient. This may include life, health,
longevity, children, fertility, prosperity, and peace. Both
swearing and blessing are power-laden forms of lan-

guage; they enact the content of the words they contain.
4.3a A prose insertion specifying, at least in the mind of
the editor, the recipient of the last "summons." **4.4** *Circumcise*, to ritually remove the foreskin of the penis,
signifying a male's membership in the covenant community (Gen 17.9–27; Lev 12.1–5). Here circumcision
is used metaphorically to describe repentance and submission of the human will to divine purpose.

4.5–10.25 Most of chs. 4–10 is a collection of oracular poems of Jeremiah with the theme of the "foe from
the north." These oracles consist mainly of prophecies
of judgment containing a commission/appeal for attention (e.g., 5.20–21), an indication of the situation
(often introduced by *Thus says the LORD*, e.g., 5.22–
28), a prediction of disaster (e.g., 5.29), and a concluding characterization (e.g., 5.30–31). These poetic
prophecies of judgment were probably delivered in the
early stage of Jeremiah's prophetic career, prior to his
coming to Jerusalem in 609 BCE. They are addressed to
both Israel and Judah, partially reunited during the
reign of Josiah. The identification of the foe is not clear
from the poetry itself. The prose identifies the foe as
Babylonia (25.8–14). The collection dealing with the
"foe from the north" consists of eleven sections: 4.5–
26+28–31; 5.1–9; 5.10–17; 5.20–31; 6.1–8; 6.9–15;
6.16–30; 8.4–13; 8.14–9.11; 9.17–22; 10.17–25. It was
edited during the exile (after 587 BCE) and following it
(after 539), and the following prose speeches were inserted: 4.27; 5.18–19; 7.1–8.3; 9.12–16; 9.23–26. These
additions indicate that the destruction by the "foe from
the north" will not be total, that the failure to be faithful
to the Mosaic covenant led to the destruction of the

"Gather together, and let us go
　　into the fortified cities!"
6　Raise a standard toward Zion,
　　flee for safety, do not delay,
　for I am bringing evil from the north,
　　and a great destruction.
7　A lion has gone up from its thicket,
　　a destroyer of nations has set out;
　he has gone out from his place
　to make your land a waste;
　　your cities will be ruins
　　without inhabitant.
8　Because of this put on sackcloth,
　　lament and wail:
　"The fierce anger of the LORD
　　has not turned away from us."

9On that day, says the LORD, courage shall fail
the king and the officials; the priests shall be
appalled and the prophets astounded. 10Then
I said, "Ah, Lord GOD, how utterly you have
deceived this people and Jerusalem, saying, 'It
shall be well with you,' even while the sword is
at the throat!"

11 At that time it will be said to this people
and to Jerusalem: A hot wind comes from me
out of the bare heights[a] in the desert toward
my poor people, not to winnow or cleanse—
12a wind too strong for that. Now it is I who
speak in judgment against them.
13　Look! He comes up like clouds,
　　his chariots like the whirlwind;
　his horses are swifter than eagles—
　woe to us, for we are ruined!

14　O Jerusalem, wash your heart clean of
　　wickedness
　　so that you may be saved.
　How long shall your evil schemes
　　lodge within you?
15　For a voice declares from Dan
　　and proclaims disaster from Mount
　　Ephraim.
16　Tell the nations, "Here they are!"
　　Proclaim against Jerusalem,
　"Besiegers come from a distant land;
　　they shout against the cities of Judah.
17　They have closed in around her like
　　watchers of a field,
　because she has rebelled against me,
　　　　　　　　　　　　says the LORD.
18　Your ways and your doings
　　have brought this upon you.
　This is your doom; how bitter it is!
　　It has reached your very heart."

Sorrow for a Doomed Nation

19　My anguish, my anguish! I writhe in pain!
　　Oh, the walls of my heart!
　My heart is beating wildly;
　　I cannot keep silent;
　for I[b] hear the sound of the trumpet,
　　the alarm of war.
20　Disaster overtakes disaster,
　　the whole land is laid waste.
　Suddenly my tents are destroyed,
　　my curtains in a moment.
21　How long must I see the standard,

---

a Or the trails　b Another reading is for you, O my soul,

Jerusalem temple and the Babylonian exile, and that
the uncircumcised foreign nations and Jews uncircumcised in the heart will be punished. 4.5–31 The invasion from the north threatened. This section is addressed to Judah and Jerusalem. God is sending an
unidentified enemy to invade and devastate the Southern Kingdom. There will be mass destruction, likened
to the end of the world. Three oracles of judgment,
plus two interludes, are woven together into a literary
masterpiece: first prophecy of judgment (vv. 5–8),
first interlude (vv. 9–12), second prophecy of judgment (vv. 13–18), second interlude (vv. 19–26), and
third prophecy of judgment (vv. 28–31; v. 27 is a prose
insertion). The inclusio (a repetition signaling the beginning and end of a unit) for the section is Jerusalem/
Zion in vv. 5–6 and Zion in v. 31. 4.5–8 This speech
describes the sounding of the alarm to signal people in
the countryside and unfortified villages to take refuge
in Zion because of an approaching invader. 4.8 Put on
sackcloth, lament and wail, a ritual of lamentation designed to arouse the Lord to defend his city (see Pss 44;
60; 74; 79; 80; 83; 89; 123; 129). 4.9–12 First interlude.
The prophet's anguish over the invasion is expressed
in vv. 9–10 (the leaders are appalled and . . . astounded
over the invasion, and the prophet objects). Ah, Lord
GOD. See note on 1.6. The prophet accuses God of deception by promising peace but then bringing destruction (see 1 Kings 22). 4.13–18 Second prophecy
of judgment. The enemy lays siege to Jerusalem, and
Jeremiah urges its inhabitants to repent and engage in
lamentation (v. 14). 4.19–26 The anguish of God is
experienced by the prophet who sees the holocaust
rendered by the invaders (vv. 19–22). Vv. 23–26 contain a macabre poem depicting the result of the invasion as the return of chaos (i.e., the state of reality
prior to creation). The strong literary allusions to Gen
1.1–2.4a (the first creation account) point to a reversal of creation. Although hyperbolic, the poem indicates that the devastation of war is like the end of
the world and a return to primordial nothingness.

and hear the sound of the trumpet?
22 "For my people are foolish,
    they do not know me;
they are stupid children,
    they have no understanding.
They are skilled in doing evil,
    but do not know how to do good."

23 I looked on the earth, and lo, it was waste
        and void;
    and to the heavens, and they had no
        light.
24 I looked on the mountains, and lo, they
        were quaking,
    and all the hills moved to and fro.
25 I looked, and lo, there was no one at all,
    and all the birds of the air had fled.
26 I looked, and lo, the fruitful land was a
        desert,
    and all its cities were laid in ruins
    before the LORD, before his fierce
        anger.
27 For thus says the LORD: The whole land
shall be a desolation; yet I will not make a full
end.
28 Because of this the earth shall mourn,
    and the heavens above grow black;
for I have spoken, I have purposed;
    I have not relented nor will I turn back.

29 At the noise of horseman and archer
    every town takes to flight;
they enter thickets; they climb among
        rocks;
    all the towns are forsaken,
    and no one lives in them.
30 And you, O desolate one,
    what do you mean that you dress in
        crimson,
    that you deck yourself with ornaments
        of gold,
    that you enlarge your eyes with paint?
In vain you beautify yourself.
    Your lovers despise you;
    they seek your life.

31 For I heard a cry as of a woman in labor,
    anguish as of one bringing forth her
        first child,
    the cry of daughter Zion gasping for
        breath,
    stretching out her hands,
    "Woe is me! I am fainting before killers!"

The Utter Corruption of God's People

5 Run to and fro through the streets of
        Jerusalem,
    look around and take note!
Search its squares and see
    if you can find one person
who acts justly
    and seeks truth—
so that I may pardon Jerusalem.[a]
2 Although they say, "As the LORD lives,"
    yet they swear falsely.
3 O LORD, do your eyes not look for truth?
You have struck them,
    but they felt no anguish;
you have consumed them,
    but they refused to take correction.
They have made their faces harder than
        rock;
    they have refused to turn back.

4 Then I said, "These are only the poor,
    they have no sense;
for they do not know the way of the LORD,
    the law of their God.
5 Let me go to the rich[b]
    and speak to them;
surely they know the way of the LORD,
    the law of their God."
But they all alike had broken the yoke,
    they had burst the bonds.

6 Therefore a lion from the forest shall kill
        them,
    a wolf from the desert shall destroy
        them.

---

a Heb *it*   *b* Or *the great*

4.27 A later prose insertion promising that the devastation will not be total. **4.28–31** The final prophecy of
judgment in the larger poem describes the lamentation
of *earth* and *the heavens*, the two spheres of creation
(see Gen 1.1; 2.1, 4); the destruction of the nation; and
the failure of *Zion*, personified as a woman, to escape
death. Zion (Jerusalem) takes on the appearance of a
prostitute to offer herself to the invaders to avoid death,
but to no avail (see 3.2–3).

5.1–31 A series of judgment oracles. **5.1–9** This
oracle of judgment describes the continued disobedience and sinfulness of the inhabitants of Jerusalem,
in spite of the siege. **5.1** Like Abraham's efforts to save
Sodom and Gomorrah for the sake of ten righteous
people (Gen 18.22–33), Jeremiah is commissioned to
find one righteous person who may save Jerusalem.
5.2 The oath probably involves faithfulness to the
covenant, but it is *sworn falsely* (see note on 4.2).

A leopard is watching against their
    cities;
  everyone who goes out of them shall
    be torn in pieces—
because their transgressions are many,
    their apostasies are great.

7 How can I pardon you?
    Your children have forsaken me,
    and have sworn by those who are no
      gods.
  When I fed them to the full,
    they committed adultery
    and trooped to the houses of
      prostitutes.
8 They were well-fed lusty stallions,
    each neighing for his neighbor's wife.
9 Shall I not punish them for these things?
                        says the LORD;
    and shall I not bring retribution
    on a nation such as this?

10 Go up through her vine-rows and
      destroy,
    but do not make a full end;
  strip away her branches,
    for they are not the LORD's.
11 For the house of Israel and the house of
      Judah
    have been utterly faithless to me,
                        says the LORD.
12 They have spoken falsely of the LORD,
    and have said, "He will do nothing.
  No evil will come upon us,
    and we shall not see sword or famine."
13 The prophets are nothing but wind,
    for the word is not in them.
  Thus shall it be done to them!

14 Therefore thus says the LORD, the God of
      hosts:
  Because they*a* have spoken this word,

I am now making my words in your
    mouth a fire,
  and this people wood, and the fire shall
    devour them.
15 I am going to bring upon you
    a nation from far away, O house of
      Israel,
                        says the LORD.
  It is an enduring nation,
    it is an ancient nation,
  a nation whose language you do not know,
    nor can you understand what they say.
16 Their quiver is like an open tomb;
    all of them are mighty warriors.
17 They shall eat up your harvest and your
      food;
    they shall eat up your sons and your
      daughters;
  they shall eat up your flocks and your
      herds;
    they shall eat up your vines and your
      fig trees;
  they shall destroy with the sword
    your fortified cities in which you trust.

18 But even in those days, says the LORD, I
will not make a full end of you. 19And when
your people say, "Why has the LORD our God
done all these things to us?" you shall say to
them, "As you have forsaken me and served
foreign gods in your land, so you shall serve
strangers in a land that is not yours."

20 Declare this in the house of Jacob,
    proclaim it in Judah:
21 Hear this, O foolish and senseless people,
    who have eyes, but do not see,
    who have ears, but do not hear.
22 Do you not fear me? says the LORD;
    Do you not tremble before me?

----

a Heb *you*

5.10–17 Faithlessness leads to destruction. This oracle
of judgment is directed against the cities and countryside of Israel and Judah for being unfaithful to the covenant. **5.13** *The prophets are nothing but wind,* a play
on Hebrew *ruach* ("spirit," "wind," "breath"). One of
the forms of prophetic inspiration is the "spirit" or
"breath" of God (see Num 27.18; 2 Kings 2.15; Isa
29.10). Jeremiah, in effect, calls the false prophets
"windbags" or "full of hot air." **5.18–19** A prose speech
inserted by a later editor that, while promising that destruction is not to be total, still explains the invasion as
punishment for unfaithfulness to God. **5.20–31** A

prophecy of judgment against Israel (*house of Jacob,* v.
20) and Judah. God's power as creator to still the powers of chaos and to bring fertility to the land does not
inspire fear and covenantal obedience in the people.
5.22 The *sea* (Hebrew *yam*) is often personified as
chaos or its ruler (Prince Yam). In Canaanite mythology Prince Yam, representing saltwater, was the nemesis of Baal, the storm god, who provided freshwater
and therefore fertility. The two deities contended for
rulership of the earth. Chaos is a destructive power
that threatens the order of creation (see Job 38.8–11;
Ps 74.12–14), but one that is limited here by the Lord.

I placed the sand as a boundary for the sea,
  a perpetual barrier that it cannot pass;
though the waves toss, they cannot
    prevail,
  though they roar, they cannot pass
    over it.
23 But this people has a stubborn and
    rebellious heart;
  they have turned aside and gone away.
24 They do not say in their hearts,
  "Let us fear the LORD our God,
who gives the rain in its season,
  the autumn rain and the spring rain,
and keeps for us
  the weeks appointed for the harvest."
25 Your iniquities have turned these away,
  and your sins have deprived you of
    good.
26 For scoundrels are found among my
    people;
  they take over the goods of others.
Like fowlers they set a trap;[a]
  they catch human beings.
27 Like a cage full of birds,
  their houses are full of treachery;
therefore they have become great and
    rich,
28   they have grown fat and sleek.
They know no limits in deeds of
    wickedness;
  they do not judge with justice
the cause of the orphan, to make it prosper,
  and they do not defend the rights of
    the needy.
29 Shall I not punish them for these things?
                              says the LORD,
  and shall I not bring retribution
    on a nation such as this?

30 An appalling and horrible thing
  has happened in the land:
31 the prophets prophesy falsely,
  and the priests rule as the prophets
    direct;[b]
my people love to have it so,
  but what will you do when the end
    comes?

The Imminence and Horror of the Invasion

6 Flee for safety, O children of Benjamin,
    from the midst of Jerusalem!
Blow the trumpet in Tekoa,
    and raise a signal on Beth-haccherem;
for evil looms out of the north,
    and great destruction.
2 I have likened daughter Zion
    to the loveliest pasture.[c]
3 Shepherds with their flocks shall come
        against her.
    They shall pitch their tents around her;
    they shall pasture, all in their places.
4 "Prepare war against her;
    up, and let us attack at noon!"
"Woe to us, for the day declines,
    the shadows of evening lengthen!"
5 "Up, and let us attack by night,
    and destroy her palaces!"
6 For thus says the LORD of hosts:
Cut down her trees;
    cast up a siege ramp against Jerusalem.
This is the city that must be punished;[d]
    there is nothing but oppression within
        her.
7 As a well keeps its water fresh,
    so she keeps fresh her wickedness;
violence and destruction are heard within
        her;
    sickness and wounds are ever before
        me.
8 Take warning, O Jerusalem,
    or I shall turn from you in disgust,
and make you a desolation,
    an uninhabited land.

9 Thus says the LORD of hosts:
Glean[e] thoroughly as a vine
    the remnant of Israel;
like a grape-gatherer, pass your hand
        again
    over its branches.

---

a Meaning of Heb uncertain   b Or rule by their own authority
c Or I will destroy daughter Zion, the loveliest pasture   d Or the
city of license   e Cn: Heb They shall glean

6.1–8 The approach of the invader. In this prophecy of judgment, the enemy's conquest of Jerusalem is launched. 6.1 Jeremiah warns his fellow Benjaminites to flee *Jerusalem*. Warnings for Jerusalem are to be issued from *Tekoa* and *Beth-haccherem* (possibly modern Ramet Rahel), twelve miles and two miles south of Jerusalem, respectively. The invading army is now marching toward the capital. 6.3–8 The assault on the city is launched. 6.3 *Shepherds . . . flocks*, here invading kings and their armies (cf. 3.15). 6.9–15 Jeremiah's warnings go unheeded. As the assault against Jerusalem intensifies, children, married couples, and

10 To whom shall I speak and give warning,
      that they may hear?
   See, their ears are closed,[a]
      they cannot listen.
   The word of the LORD is to them an
         object of scorn;
      they take no pleasure in it.
11 But I am full of the wrath of the LORD;
      I am weary of holding it in.

   Pour it out on the children in the street,
      and on the gatherings of young men as
         well;
   both husband and wife shall be taken,
      the old folk and the very aged.
12 Their houses shall be turned over to
         others,
      their fields and wives together;
   for I will stretch out my hand
      against the inhabitants of the land,
                           says the LORD.

13 For from the least to the greatest of them,
      everyone is greedy for unjust gain;
   and from prophet to priest,
      everyone deals falsely.
14 They have treated the wound of my
         people carelessly,
      saying, "Peace, peace,"
      when there is no peace.
15 They acted shamefully, they committed
         abomination;
      yet they were not ashamed,
      they did not know how to blush.
   Therefore they shall fall among those
         who fall;
      at the time that I punish them, they
         shall be overthrown,
                           says the LORD.
16 Thus says the LORD:

Stand at the crossroads, and look,
   and ask for the ancient paths,
where the good way lies; and walk in it,
   and find rest for your souls.
But they said, "We will not walk in it."
17 Also I raised up sentinels for you:
   "Give heed to the sound of the
      trumpet!"
But they said, "We will not give heed."
18 Therefore hear, O nations,
   and know, O congregation, what will
      happen to them.
19 Hear, O earth; I am going to bring
      disaster on this people,
   the fruit of their schemes,
because they have not given heed to my
      words;
   and as for my teaching, they have
      rejected it.
20 Of what use to me is frankincense that
      comes from Sheba,
   or sweet cane from a distant land?
Your burnt offerings are not acceptable,
   nor are your sacrifices pleasing to me.
21 Therefore thus says the LORD:
See, I am laying before this people
   stumbling blocks against which they
      shall stumble;
parents and children together,
   neighbor and friend shall perish.

22 Thus says the LORD:
See, a people is coming from the land of
      the north,
   a great nation is stirring from the
      farthest parts of the earth.
23 They grasp the bow and the javelin,
   they are cruel and have no mercy,

_____

a Heb *are uncircumcised*

the elderly will experience the *wrath of the LORD* (i.e.,
divine judgment, v. 9) in the form of suffering, death,
and exile. **6.16–30** Forsaking the ancient paths. The
ancient paths (v. 16) are the covenant of Moses and its
laws, which were to guide the religious and moral
lives of the people. In this prophecy of judgment
against Zion (Jerusalem), the people have disobeyed
the covenant and not given heed to the warnings of
the prophets (*sentinels*, v. 17). The fierce enemy from
the north will destroy all (*parents and children . . .
neighbor and friend*, v. 21) without distinction and
without mercy. **6.20** Sacrifices and gifts do not appease God's wrath (see Hos 9.4). *Frankincense*, a fragrant gum resin from the *Boswellia* tree, which grows
in southern Arabia, northeastern Africa, and India. It

was imported into Israel by caravans from *Sheba* (a
country in southwest Arabia; see 1 Kings 10.1–13; Isa
60.6; Ezek 27.22–23) and was used as perfume (Song
3.6; 4.6, 14) and ritual incense (Ex 30.34–38). *Sweet
cane*, also known as calamus, one of several varieties
of cane or grasses yielding sweet-scented and volatile
oils. It was used in holy anointing oil (Ex 30.23).
Burnt offerings and *sacrifices* cover the array of animal
sacrifices connected with the temple. Animals offered
as burnt offerings were totally consumed by fire on
the altar, while the edible parts of sacrifices were to be
eaten by the worshipers. *Acceptable*, an indicator of
the Lord's willingness to receive the offering and the
spirit with which it is given. The sacrificial laws in
Leviticus specify the type and condition of acceptable

their sound is like the roaring sea;
they ride on horses,
  equipped like a warrior for battle,
  against you, O daughter Zion!

24 "We have heard news of them,
  our hands fall helpless;
anguish has taken hold of us,
  pain as of a woman in labor.
25 Do not go out into the field,
  or walk on the road;
for the enemy has a sword,
  terror is on every side."

26 O my poor people, put on sackcloth,
  and roll in ashes;
make mourning as for an only child,
  most bitter lamentation:
for suddenly the destroyer
  will come upon us.

27 I have made you a tester and a refiner[a]
  among my people
so that you may know and test their
  ways.
28 They are all stubbornly rebellious,

going about with slanders;
they are bronze and iron,
  all of them act corruptly.
29 The bellows blow fiercely,
  the lead is consumed by the fire;
in vain the refining goes on,
  for the wicked are not removed.
30 They are called "rejected silver,"
  for the LORD has rejected them.

Jeremiah Proclaims God's Judgment on the Nation

7 The word that came to Jeremiah from the
LORD: 2Stand in the gate of the LORD's
house, and proclaim there this word, and say,
Hear the word of the LORD, all you people of
Judah, you that enter these gates to worship
the LORD. 3Thus says the LORD of hosts, the
God of Israel: Amend your ways and your doings, and let me dwell with you[b] in this place.
4Do not trust in these deceptive words: "This
is[c] the temple of the LORD, the temple of the
LORD, the temple of the LORD."

5 For if you truly amend your ways and

a Or a fortress b Or and I will let you dwell c Heb They are

---

animals (see Lev 1–7). **6.26** Rites of lamentation do
not avail. **6.27–30** Jeremiah is a *tester and a refiner*
who, like a metalsmith, examines the metal or religious character of the people and discards them like
rejected silver, i.e., metal not containing enough silver
to use for jewelry and decorations (see Job 23.10;
Zech 13.9).

7.1–8.3 This section comprises a series of prose
speeches written by editors: the temple sermon (7.1–
15), the forbidding of Jeremiah's intercession by God,
(7.16–20), disobedience and rejection of sacrificial ritual (7.21–28), the fate of Judah and the disinterment
of the faithless dead (7.29–8.3). These speeches were
written during the exilic or postexilic period to explain
that illicit worship and disobedience to the Mosaic
covenant were the reasons for the exile. The theme of
illicit worship continues in 10.1–16, a poetic polemic
against idol worship. **7.1–15** The temple sermon (an
abbreviated version appears in 26.1–6). Although 26.1
places the sermon in the accession year of King Jehoiakim (609 BCE), shortly after the death of Josiah,
the sermon we have was most likely written later, during or after the exile. However, it is probable that Jeremiah delivered an oracle of judgment against the temple and that the content of the prose sermon reflects
his own views. Josiah's death marked both the end of
Judah's political ambitions for self-determination and
the religious reform. Neco II's victory over Judah's
army at Megiddo and the death of Josiah in 609 led to
Egyptian control of Israel, until the defeat of Egypt by
the Babylonians at the battle of Carchemish in 605. Is-

rael and Judah were soon incorporated into the Babylonian Empire. The son who succeeded Josiah to the
throne, Jehoahaz, only ruled for three months. Neco II
took him to Egypt and placed on the throne Jehoiakim, another son of Josiah. Jehoiakim received
neither the endorsement of the elders of the land nor
prophetic anointing. The sermon consists of an introduction (vv. 1–2), a first admonition (vv. 3–4), a second admonition (vv. 5–8), two rhetorical questions
(vv. 9–11), and a threat (vv. 12–15). **7.2** LORD's house,
the Jerusalem temple. With the death of Josiah and the
end of the dreams for national destiny, the people of
Judah make a pilgrimage to Jerusalem to celebrate a
festival, possibly the Festival of Booths (Tabernacles,
September-October), an eight-day festival that gave
thanks for the autumn harvest and recalled God's
guidance of Israel during the wilderness wanderings
(Lev 23.39–43). This festival was also the time when
Solomon's temple was dedicated (1 Kings 8). Every
seven years the Torah was read publicly during this festival (Deut 31.10–11). It has also been suggested that
the sermon was delivered at Jehoiakim's coronation
(see 26.1) during the New Year's festivities, which took
place at roughly the same time as the Festival of
Booths. **7.3** The Hebrew may be read two ways: *let me
dwell with you in this place* (i.e., divine presence in the
temple), or *I will let you dwell in this place* (i.e., not go
into exile). **7.4** *Deceptive words* (Hebrew *sheqer*, "lie,
falsehood"). The notion that the *temple of the LORD*
(repeated three times for emphasis) is the basis of security, grounded in the belief that God will defend

your doings, if you truly act justly one with another, [6] if you do not oppress the alien, the orphan, and the widow, or shed innocent blood in this place, and if you do not go after other gods to your own hurt, [7] then I will dwell with you in this place, in the land that I gave of old to your ancestors forever and ever.

8 Here you are, trusting in deceptive words to no avail. [9] Will you steal, murder, commit adultery, swear falsely, make offerings to Baal, and go after other gods that you have not known, [10] and then come and stand before me in this house, which is called by my name, and say, "We are safe!"—only to go on doing all these abominations? [11] Has this house, which is called by my name, become a den of robbers in your sight? You know, I too am watching, says the LORD. [12] Go now to my place that was in Shiloh, where I made my name dwell at first, and see what I did to it for the wickedness of my people Israel. [13] And now, because you have done all these things, says the LORD, and when I spoke to you persistently, you did not listen, and when I called you, you did not answer, [14] therefore I will do to the house that is called by my name, in which you trust, and to the place that I gave to you and to your ancestors, just what I did to Shiloh. [15] And I will cast you out of my sight, just as I cast out all your kinsfolk, all the offspring of Ephraim.

The People's Disobedience

16 As for you, do not pray for this people, do not raise a cry or prayer on their behalf, and do not intercede with me, for I will not hear you. [17] Do you not see what they are doing in the towns of Judah and in the streets of Jerusalem? [18] The children gather wood, the fathers kindle fire, and the women knead dough, to make cakes for the queen of heaven; and they pour out drink offerings to other gods, to provoke me to anger. [19] Is it I whom they provoke? says the LORD. Is it not themselves, to their own hurt? [20] Therefore thus says the Lord GOD: My anger and my wrath shall be poured out on this place, on human beings and animals, on the trees of the field and the fruit of the ground; it will burn and not be quenched.

21 Thus says the LORD of hosts, the God of Israel: Add your burnt offerings to your sacrifices, and eat the flesh. [22] For in the day that I brought your ancestors out of the land of Egypt, I did not speak to them or command them concerning burnt offerings and sacrifices. [23] But this command I gave them, "Obey my voice, and I will be your God, and you shall be my people; and walk only in the way that I command you, so that it may be well with you." [24] Yet they did not obey or incline their ear, but, in the stubbornness of their evil will, they walked in their own counsels, and looked backward rather than forward. [25] From the day

---

Zion against its enemies (see Pss 46; 48; 76; Isa 31.4–5), is rejected. **7.5** Repentance (returning to the Mosaic covenant), not the temple and its worship, is the one hope for divine presence and the people's continued dwelling in Judah. **7.6** *Alien, orphan, widow.* See Deut 10.18–19; 24.17–22; 27.19. Aliens are resident foreigners who do not enjoy the same economic or legal status as native-born Israelites. Orphans and widows do not have families to sustain them. All three are therefore socially vulnerable and require outside support from the king or the Israelite community as a whole. In Deuteronomy, Israel's responsibility for the destitute is linked with God's merciful deliverance of the people when they were slaves in Egypt at the time of the exodus. **7.9** Five of the Ten Commandments (Ex 20.1–17; Deut 5.6–21) are mentioned. Here they serve as a symbol of all of Israel's covenant obligations. **7.11** *Den of robbers.* See Mt 21.13. **7.12–15** *Shiloh,* eighteen miles north of Jerusalem, is Khirbet Seilun. The seat of the levitical priesthood and the location of an important sanctuary (Josh 21.1–2; 1 Sam 1.3, 9), the town was a major religious center during the period of the judges (twelfth century BCE). It was destroyed, probably by the Philistines, in the eleventh

century BCE (see Jer 26.6–9). This destruction was eventually understood as God's judgment on the priestly house of Eli for the abuses it committed at the shrine. Eli's descendants, including Abiathar and perhaps Jeremiah himself, traced their loss of priestly power to these early events (1 Kings 2.27). Jeremiah's reference to Shiloh therefore carries a particularly powerful message for his priestly relatives at Anathoth (1.1). Jeremiah's threat of destruction and exile parallels that of Micah in the eighth century BCE (see Mic 3.9–12). **7.15** *Offspring of Ephraim,* the Northern Kingdom, which fell to the Assyrians in the eighth century BCE. **7.16–20** Jeremiah is forbidden to intercede to save the nation. Intercession is a primary function of the prophetic office (see 11.14; 15.1; Am 7–9). **7.18** *Queen of heaven* (see 44.15–30), the Assyro-Babylonian goddess Ishtar, an astral deity associated with Venus. She was a goddess of both war and fertility. **7.21–28** Obedience, including moral behavior, not sacrifice, is the basis for the covenantal relationship with God. **7.21** *Eating the flesh* of burnt offerings was forbidden by ritual law, for the flesh was to be burned and thus reserved for God (Lev 1). **7.25** *My servants the prophets* suggests the image of a king sending his

that your ancestors came out of the land of Egypt until this day, I have persistently sent all my servants the prophets to them, day after day; 26yet they did not listen to me, or pay attention, but they stiffened their necks. They did worse than their ancestors did.

27 So you shall speak all these words to them, but they will not listen to you. You shall call to them, but they will not answer you. 28You shall say to them: This is the nation that did not obey the voice of the LORD their God, and did not accept discipline; truth has perished; it is cut off from their lips.

29　Cut off your hair and throw it away;
　　　raise a lamentation on the bare
　　　　heights, *a*
　　for the LORD has rejected and forsaken
　　　the generation that provoked his
　　　　wrath.

30 For the people of Judah have done evil in my sight, says the LORD; they have set their abominations in the house that is called by my name, defiling it. 31And they go on building the high place *b* of Topheth, which is in the valley of the son of Hinnom, to burn their sons and their daughters in the fire—which I did not command, nor did it come into my mind. 32Therefore, the days are surely coming, says the LORD, when it will no more be called Topheth, or the valley of the son of Hinnom, but the valley of Slaughter: for they will bury in Topheth until there is no more room. 33The corpses of this people will be food for the birds of the air, and for the animals of the earth; and no one will frighten them away. 34And I will bring to an end the sound of mirth and glad-

ness, the voice of the bride and bridegroom in the cities of Judah and in the streets of Jerusalem; for the land shall become a waste.

8 At that time, says the LORD, the bones of the kings of Judah, the bones of its officials, the bones of the priests, the bones of the prophets, and the bones of the inhabitants of Jerusalem shall be brought out of their tombs; 2and they shall be spread before the sun and the moon and all the host of heaven, which they have loved and served, which they have followed, and which they have inquired of and worshiped; and they shall not be gathered or buried; they shall be like dung on the surface of the ground. 3Death shall be preferred to life by all the remnant that remains of this evil family in all the places where I have driven them, says the LORD of hosts.

The Blind Perversity of the Whole Nation

4　You shall say to them, Thus says the
　　　LORD:
　　When people fall, do they not get up
　　　again?
　　If they go astray, do they not turn
　　　back?
5　Why then has this people *c* turned away
　　　in perpetual backsliding?
　　They have held fast to deceit,
　　　they have refused to return.
6　I have given heed and listened,
　　　but they do not speak honestly;
　　no one repents of wickedness,

---

a Or *the trails*　*b* Gk Tg: Heb *high places*　*c* One Ms Gk: MT *this people, Jerusalem,*

---

couriers and emissaries to announce royal proclamations (see 23.1; 25.4). God has sought to address the covenant people with a long series of emissaries, but to no avail. **7.29–8.3** A prose sermon on the fate of Judah and the disinterment of its leaders. **7.29** An earlier poetic fragment from Jeremiah, embedded within the prose. *Cut off your hair,* part of the ritual of lamentation (16.6; Mic 1.16). **7.31** *Topheth* (from Aramaic, "fireplace") was pronounced with the vowels of the word "shame" in Hebrew. This cultic place for child sacrifice was located in the *valley of the son of Hinnom* (Gehenna), just west and south of the walls of Jerusalem. The valley received notoriety for being the site of idolatrous practices, including child sacrifice (2 Chr 28.3; 33.6). The law requiring the giving of the firstborn to God (Ex 22.29–30) may have been interpreted to mean child sacrifice, a view Jeremiah counters (see Lev 18.21). **7.32** *Valley of Slaughter,* lit. "valley of murder." **8.1–2** In Assyrian practice, corpses of

leaders were disinterred when a vassal violated a treaty (see 2 Kings 23.16, which tells of Josiah's desecration of tombs at the sanctuary of Bethel). *Sun, moon, host of heaven,* astral deities (Deut 4.19; 17.3; 2 Kings 23.5).

8.4–10.25 These chapters return to the theme of the "foe from the north" (see 4.5–6.30). This section contains the following poetic oracles of judgment: 8.4–13; 8.14–9.11; 9.17–22; 10.17–25. Later prose additions include 9.12–16; 9.23–26. Inserted within these chapters is a diatribe against idol worship (10.1–16) with a prose addition (10.11). See note on 7.1–8.3. **8.4–13** An oracle of judgment consisting of two parts: an indictment of the people for their refusal to repent (vv. 4–7) and a diatribe against the religious leaders (scribes, prophets, and priests, vv. 8–13). **8.4–6** The Hebrew root *shub,* "repent" or "turn," occurs six times in these verses: *go astray, turn back, turned away, backsliding, return, turn. Repents* in v. 6 translates a different Hebrew word (*nicham*). See note on 3.1–4.4.

saying, "What have I done!"
All of them turn to their own course,
  like a horse plunging headlong into
    battle.
7 Even the stork in the heavens
    knows its times;
and the turtledove, swallow, and crane[a]
    observe the time of their coming;
but my people do not know
    the ordinance of the LORD.

8 How can you say, "We are wise,
    and the law of the LORD is with us,"
when, in fact, the false pen of the scribes
    has made it into a lie?
9 The wise shall be put to shame,
    they shall be dismayed and taken;
since they have rejected the word of the
    LORD,
  what wisdom is in them?
10 Therefore I will give their wives to others
    and their fields to conquerors,
because from the least to the greatest
    everyone is greedy for unjust gain;
from prophet to priest
    everyone deals falsely.
11 They have treated the wound of my
    people carelessly,
  saying, "Peace, peace,"
    when there is no peace.
12 They acted shamefully, they committed
    abomination;
  yet they were not at all ashamed,
    they did not know how to blush.
Therefore they shall fall among those
    who fall;
at the time when I punish them, they
    shall be overthrown,
                              says the LORD.

13 When I wanted to gather them, says the
    LORD,
  there are[b] no grapes on the vine,
    nor figs on the fig tree;
even the leaves are withered,
    and what I gave them has passed away
      from them.[a]

14 Why do we sit still?
Gather together, let us go into the
    fortified cities
  and perish there;
for the LORD our God has doomed us to
    perish,
  and has given us poisoned water to
    drink,
because we have sinned against the
    LORD.
15 We look for peace, but find no good,
    for a time of healing, but there is terror
      instead.

16 The snorting of their horses is heard
    from Dan;
  at the sound of the neighing of their
    stallions
  the whole land quakes.
They come and devour the land and all
    that fills it,
  the city and those who live in it.
17 See, I am letting snakes loose among
    you,
  adders that cannot be charmed,
    and they shall bite you,
                              says the LORD.

---

a Meaning of Heb uncertain   b Or I will make an end of them, says the LORD. There are

---

8.7 Birds instinctively know and act in accord with the natural order, but the people do not know God's revealed order of justice. **8.8–13** The prophetic "word" (revealed through the prophet's encounter with God) conflicts with written law if the latter is corrupted and misinterpreted. The *wise* are scribes who served two institutions, the royal court and the temple. Temple scribes wrote religious legislation, interpreted priestly law, and taught the nation God's Torah. Royal sages formulated civil legislation, served in legal settings as judges and lawyers, gave advice to kings and other high officials, and administered the kingdom. The "wise" were often in conflict with prophets over the proper discernment and source of the divine will (see 18.18; Isa 3.1–4; 30.1–5; 31.1–3; Ob 8). *Wisdom* is the ability to discern God's righteous order and to teach people and the king how to act in conformity with that order. Wise behavior was thought to lead to *peace* (Hebrew *shalom*), which also means "well-being" and "harmony." **8.14–9.26** This lengthy poem is fashioned out of several prophetic speeches: the people's resignation and the approach of the "foe" (8.14–17); an interlude describing Jeremiah's and God's anguish over the coming destruction (8.18–9.3); an indictment of the neighbor's deceit (9.4–9); and three admonitions to lament over imminent destruction (9.10–22). Two prose additions are inserted: 9.12–16; 9.23–26. **8.14–17.** The people are resigned to divine destruction and the approach of the "foe." **8.16** *Dan,* either a Northern tribe or more probably a city (Tel Dan) situated on the northern border of Israel. *The whole land quakes* echoes the chaos tradition, in which the order of the cos-

The Prophet Mourns for the People

18 My joy is gone, grief is upon me,
    my heart is sick.
19 Hark, the cry of my poor people
    from far and wide in the land:
    "Is the LORD not in Zion?
    Is her King not in her?"
    ("Why have they provoked me to anger
        with their images,
        with their foreign idols?")
20 "The harvest is past, the summer is
        ended,
    and we are not saved."
21 For the hurt of my poor people I am
        hurt,
    I mourn, and dismay has taken hold of
        me.
22 Is there no balm in Gilead?
    Is there no physician there?
    Why then has the health of my poor
        people
    not been restored?

9ᵃ O that my head were a spring of water,
    and my eyes a fountain of tears,
    so that I might weep day and night
    for the slain of my poor people!
2ᵇ O that I had in the desert
    a traveler's lodging place,
    that I might leave my people
    and go away from them!
    For they are all adulterers,
    a band of traitors.
3 They bend their tongues like bows;
    they have grown strong in the land for
        falsehood, and not for truth;
    for they proceed from evil to evil,
    and they do not know me, says the
        LORD.

4 Beware of your neighbors,
    and put no trust in any of your kin;ᶜ
    for all your kinᵈ are supplanters,
    and every neighbor goes around like a
        slanderer.
5 They all deceive their neighbors,

and no one speaks the truth;
    they have taught their tongues to speak
        lies;
    they commit iniquity and are too
        weary to repent.ᵉ
6 Oppression upon oppression, deceitᶠ
        upon deceit!
    They refuse to know me, says the LORD.

7 Therefore thus says the LORD of hosts:
    I will now refine and test them,
        for what else can I do with my sinful
        people?ᵍ
8 Their tongue is a deadly arrow;
    it speaks deceit through the mouth.
    They all speak friendly words to their
        neighbors,
    but inwardly are planning to lay an
        ambush.
9 Shall I not punish them for these things?
        says the LORD;
    and shall I not bring retribution
    on a nation such as this?

10 Take upʰ weeping and wailing for the
        mountains,
    and a lamentation for the pastures of
        the wilderness,
    because they are laid waste so that no one
        passes through,
    and the lowing of cattle is not heard;
    both the birds of the air and the animals
    have fled and are gone.
11 I will make Jerusalem a heap of ruins,
    a lair of jackals;
    and I will make the towns of Judah a
        desolation,
        without inhabitant.

12 Who is wise enough to understand this?
To whom has the mouth of the LORD spoken,
so that they may declare it? Why is the land ru-

ᵃ Ch 8.23 in Heb   ᵇ Ch 9.1 in Heb   ᶜ Heb *in a brother*
ᵈ Heb *for every brother*   ᵉ Cn Compare Gk: Heb *they weary
themselves with iniquity.* ⁶*Your dwelling*   ᶠ Cn: Heb *Your dwelling
in the midst of deceit*   ᵍ Or *my poor people*   ʰ Gk Syr: Heb *I
will take up*

---

mos is destabilized by the approach of divine judgment (see Hab 3; note on 4.19–26). **8.18–9.3** The
prophet experiences divine suffering over the imminent destruction of the people. **8.19** See note on 7.1–
8.3. **8.22** *Balm,* resin or gum of the balsam tree, used to
heal wounds. *Gilead,* a region in the Transjordan lo-

cated between Bashan and Moab (see Gen 37.25). **9.4–
9** A neighbor's *deceit* ("treachery") resides at the heart
of social discord and corruption. **9.10–22** Three admonitions (vv. 10–11, 17–19, 20–22) to engage in ritual lament over the death of the cosmos and the destruction of Jerusalem. **9.12–16** A prose addition

ined and laid waste like a wilderness, so that no one passes through? 13And the LORD says: Because they have forsaken my law that I set before them, and have not obeyed my voice, or walked in accordance with it, 14but have stubbornly followed their own hearts and have gone after the Baals, as their ancestors taught them. 15Therefore thus says the LORD of hosts, the God of Israel: I am feeding this people with wormwood, and giving them poisonous water to drink. 16I will scatter them among nations that neither they nor their ancestors have known; and I will send the sword after them, until I have consumed them.

The People Mourn in Judgment

17 Thus says the LORD of hosts:
  Consider, and call for the mourning
      women to come;
    send for the skilled women to come;
18 let them quickly raise a dirge over us,
    so that our eyes may run down with
        tears,
    and our eyelids flow with water.
19 For a sound of wailing is heard from Zion:
    "How we are ruined!
    We are utterly shamed,
  because we have left the land,
    because they have cast down our
        dwellings."

20 Hear, O women, the word of the LORD,
    and let your ears receive the word of
        his mouth;
  teach to your daughters a dirge,
    and each to her neighbor a lament.
21 "Death has come up into our windows,
    it has entered our palaces,
  to cut off the children from the streets
    and the young men from the squares."
22 Speak! Thus says the LORD:
  "Human corpses shall fall
    like dung upon the open field,
  like sheaves behind the reaper,
    and no one shall gather them."

23 Thus says the LORD: Do not let the wise boast in their wisdom, do not let the mighty boast in their might, do not let the wealthy boast in their wealth; 24but let those who boast boast in this, that they understand and know me, that I am the LORD; I act with steadfast love, justice, and righteousness in the earth, for in these things I delight, says the LORD.

25 The days are surely coming, says the LORD, when I will attend to all those who are circumcised only in the foreskin: 26Egypt, Judah, Edom, the Ammonites, Moab, and all those with shaven temples who live in the desert. For all these nations are uncircumcised, and all the house of Israel is uncircumcised in heart.

Idolatry Has Brought Ruin on Israel

10 Hear the word that the LORD speaks to you, O house of Israel. 2Thus says the LORD:
  Do not learn the way of the nations,
    or be dismayed at the signs of the
        heavens;
    for the nations are dismayed at them.
3 For the customs of the peoples are false:
  a tree from the forest is cut down,
    and worked with an ax by the hands of
        an artisan;
4 people deck it with silver and gold;
    they fasten it with hammer and nails
    so that it cannot move.
5 Their idols*a* are like scarecrows in a
        cucumber field,
    and they cannot speak;
  they have to be carried,
    for they cannot walk.
  Do not be afraid of them,
    for they cannot do evil,
    nor is it in them to do good.

6 There is none like you, O LORD;
    you are great, and your name is great
        in might.

_____
a Heb They

---

blaming the destruction on disobedience to God's law. **9.17** *Mourning women, skilled women,* professional mourners who are paid to lament during a funeral or over destruction of a city (see 22.18–19; Lamentations). In the ancient Near East, goddesses and their priestesses ritually mourned over the destruction of their sacred cities, at times as a prelude to new life. **9.21–22** Some scholars see here an allusion to the Canaanite god of *death* (Mot). **9.23–26** A prose inser-

tion reassuring the exiles of God's *steadfast love* (Hebrew *chesed,* "covenant love"), *justice,* and *righteousness* and promising future punishment for the *uncircumcised* pagan *nations* as well as those Jews who are *uncircumcised in heart* (i.e., disobedient to God's will). **9.26** *Shaven temples,* a religious rite of hair cutting practiced by Arab tribes (see 25.23; 49.32).

10.1–16 The greatness and power of God as Creator and Lord of history are contrasted with the origins and

7 Who would not fear you, O King of the
          nations?
      For that is your due;
      among all the wise ones of the nations
      and in all their kingdoms
          there is no one like you.
8 They are both stupid and foolish;
      the instruction given by idols
          is no better than wood![a]
9 Beaten silver is brought from Tarshish,
      and gold from Uphaz.
   They are the work of the artisan and of
          the hands of the goldsmith;
      their clothing is blue and purple;
      they are all the product of skilled
          workers.
10 But the LORD is the true God;
      he is the living God and the everlasting
          King.
   At his wrath the earth quakes,
      and the nations cannot endure his
          indignation.

11 Thus shall you say to them: The gods
who did not make the heavens and the earth
shall perish from the earth and from under the
heavens.[b]

12 It is he who made the earth by his power,
      who established the world by his
          wisdom,
      and by his understanding stretched out
          the heavens.
13 When he utters his voice, there is a
          tumult of waters in the heavens,
      and he makes the mist rise from the
          ends of the earth.
   He makes lightnings for the rain,
      and he brings out the wind from his
          storehouses.
14 Everyone is stupid and without knowledge;
      goldsmiths are all put to shame by
          their idols;
   for their images are false,
      and there is no breath in them.

15 They are worthless, a work of delusion;
      at the time of their punishment they
          shall perish.
16 Not like these is the LORD,[c] the portion of
          Jacob,
      for he is the one who formed all things,
   and Israel is the tribe of his inheritance;
      the LORD of hosts is his name.

The Coming Exile

17 Gather up your bundle from the ground,
      O you who live under siege!
18 For thus says the LORD:
   I am going to sling out the inhabitants of
          the land
      at this time,
   and I will bring distress on them,
      so that they shall feel it.

19 Woe is me because of my hurt!
      My wound is severe.
   But I said, "Truly this is my punishment,
      and I must bear it."
20 My tent is destroyed,
      and all my cords are broken;
   my children have gone from me,
      and they are no more;
   there is no one to spread my tent again,
      and to set up my curtains.
21 For the shepherds are stupid,
      and do not inquire of the LORD;
   therefore they have not prospered,
      and all their flock is scattered.

22 Hear, a noise! Listen, it is coming—
      a great commotion from the land of
          the north
   to make the cities of Judah a desolation,
      a lair of jackals.
23 I know, O LORD, that the way of human
          beings is not in their control,

---

a Meaning of Heb uncertain   *b* This verse is in Aramaic
c Heb lacks *the* LORD

---

weakness of idols. See Ps 115.3–8; Isa 40.18–20; 41.6–
7; 44.9–20. **10.9** *Tarshish,* an unidentified seaport famous for commerce (1 Kings 10.22; Isa 23.1, 14; 60.9;
Ezek 27.25). *Uphaz.* Location unknown. Some scholars see the term as a corruption for Ophir, a place well
known for its gold (1 Kings 9.28). **10.10** *At his wrath
the earth quakes.* God's coming in judgment destabi-
lizes creation (see 9.10). **10.11** A prose addition in Aramaic, unique in Jeremiah. **10.12–13** A fragment of a

hymn describing God as Lord of creation (see Pss 29;
33; 104; Am 4.13; 5.8–9; 9.5–6). **10.17–25** The final
siege. In this final oracle about the "foe from the
north," the siege against the cities will not be lifted.
The inhabitants are admonished to prepare for exile.
10.19–21 Mother Zion laments over her wounds and
the loss of her children (see 31.15–22). *Shepherds.* See
note on 3.15. To *inquire of the* LORD, to consult the
Lord through a prophet. **10.23–25** An intercessory

that mortals as they walk cannot direct
  their steps.
24 Correct me, O LORD, but in just
    measure;
  not in your anger, or you will bring me
    to nothing.

25 Pour out your wrath on the nations that
    do not know you,
  and on the peoples that do not call on
    your name;
  for they have devoured Jacob;
  they have devoured him and consumed
    him,
  and have laid waste his habitation.

Israel and Judah Have Broken the Covenant

11 The word that came to Jeremiah from
    the LORD: 2 Hear the words of this cov-
enant, and speak to the people of Judah and
the inhabitants of Jerusalem. 3 You shall say to
them, Thus says the LORD, the God of Israel:
Cursed be anyone who does not heed the
words of this covenant, 4 which I commanded
your ancestors when I brought them out of
the land of Egypt, from the iron-smelter, saying, Listen to my voice, and do all that I command you. So shall you be my people, and I
will be your God, 5 that I may perform the oath
that I swore to your ancestors, to give them a
land flowing with milk and honey, as at this
day. Then I answered, "So be it, LORD."

6 And the LORD said to me: Proclaim all
these words in the cities of Judah, and in the
streets of Jerusalem: Hear the words of this
covenant and do them. 7 For I solemnly
warned your ancestors when I brought them
up out of the land of Egypt, warning them
persistently, even to this day, saying, Obey my
voice. 8 Yet they did not obey or incline their

ear, but everyone walked in the stubbornness
of an evil will. So I brought upon them all the
words of this covenant, which I commanded
them to do, but they did not.

9 And the LORD said to me: Conspiracy exists among the people of Judah and the inhabitants of Jerusalem. 10 They have turned back
to the iniquities of their ancestors of old, who
refused to heed my words; they have gone after
other gods to serve them; the house of Israel
and the house of Judah have broken the
covenant that I made with their ancestors.
11 Therefore, thus says the LORD, assuredly I
am going to bring disaster upon them that
they cannot escape; though they cry out to
me, I will not listen to them. 12 Then the cities
of Judah and the inhabitants of Jerusalem will
go and cry out to the gods to whom they make
offerings, but they will never save them in the
time of their trouble. 13 For your gods have become as many as your towns, O Judah; and as
many as the streets of Jerusalem are the altars
to shame you have set up, altars to make offerings to Baal.

14 As for you, do not pray for this people, or
lift up a cry or prayer on their behalf, for I will
not listen when they call to me in the time of
their trouble. 15 What right has my beloved in
my house, when she has done vile deeds? Can
vows*a* and sacrificial flesh avert your doom?
Can you then exult? 16 The LORD once called
you, "A green olive tree, fair with goodly fruit";
but with the roar of a great tempest he will set
fire to it, and its branches will be consumed.
17 The LORD of hosts, who planted you, has
pronounced evil against you, because of the
evil that the house of Israel and the house of
Judah have done, provoking me to anger by
making offerings to Baal.

---

a Gk: Heb *Can many*

---

prayer in which the prophet asks God for both merciful chastisement for his sins and punishment upon the
enemies who have destroyed God's people.
  11.1–17 The broken covenant. The prose sermon,
built around a partial poetic oracle of judgment, is an
addition in the form of a speech of judgment against
Judah's violation of the covenant. The sermon explains
the destruction of Judah and Jerusalem and the Babylonian exile. Both language and theology reflect the
Mosaic covenant and its ritual renewal found in
Deuteronomy (also see 7.16–28; Josh 24). The formal
character of the covenant consists of a historical prologue describing God's acts of salvation on the people's

behalf (the exodus from Egypt and the gift of the land
of Canaan, vv. 4–5); stipulations necessary for maintaining the covenantal relationship (*heed the words of
this covenant*, v. 3); curses for violating the covenant (vv.
3, 8–13); blessings for keeping trust; and witnesses (Jeremiah serves as witness: "*So be it, LORD*," v. 5). **11.3** See
Deut 27.26. **11.4** See Deut 4.20. **11.5** *That I may perform
. . . ancestors.* See Deut 7.8; 8.18; 9.5. *A land flowing with
milk and honey.* See Deut 6.3; 11.9; 26.9, 15; 27.3. *As at
this day.* Cf. Deut 2.30; 4.20, 38; 6.24; 8.18; 10.15; 29.28.
11.14 Jeremiah is not allowed to intercede for Judah to
avert divine judgment (see 7.16; 14.11; Ex 32.30–32).
11.15 *Sacrificial flesh.* See 6.20; 7.21–22.

Jeremiah's Life Threatened

18 It was the LORD who made it known to
   me, and I knew;
      then you showed me their evil deeds.
19 But I was like a gentle lamb
      led to the slaughter.
   And I did not know it was against me
      that they devised schemes, saying,
   "Let us destroy the tree with its fruit,
      let us cut him off from the land of the
         living,
      so that his name will no longer be
         remembered!"
20 But you, O LORD of hosts, who judge
      righteously,
   who try the heart and the mind,
   let me see your retribution upon them,
      for to you I have committed my cause.

21 Therefore thus says the LORD concerning
the people of Anathoth, who seek your life,
and say, "You shall not prophesy in the name
of the LORD, or you will die by our hand"—
22therefore thus says the LORD of hosts: I am
going to punish them; the young men shall die
by the sword; their sons and their daughters
shall die by famine; 23and not even a remnant
shall be left of them. For I will bring disaster
upon the people of Anathoth, the year of their
punishment.

Jeremiah Complains to God

12 You will be in the right, O LORD,
   when I lay charges against you;
      but let me put my case to you.
   Why does the way of the guilty prosper?
      Why do all who are treacherous thrive?
2 You plant them, and they take root;

11.18–20.18 These chapters consist of various
types of materials in both poetry and prose: laments,
judgment oracles, biographical narratives, and oracles
of salvation. However, dominating chs. 11–20 are the
laments by Jeremiah, the Lord, and the people of Judah
and Jerusalem. Jeremiah utters seven laments: 11.18–
23; 12.1–6; 15.10–21; 17.14–18; 18.18–23; 20.7–12;
20.14–18. The usual structure consists of two parts:
the prophet's complaint and the Lord's response. A
fragment of a lament describes the conversion of
pagan nations (16.19–20). Parts of two thanksgiving
psalms, often found as a response to laments, are inserted (17.12–13; 20.13). Two laments are attributed
to the Lord (12.7–13; 14.17–18) and two others to the
people of Jerusalem (14.1–10; 14.19–22). In two prose
additions, Jeremiah is told to cease intercession, i.e., to
stop offering a lament on behalf of the people in the
effort to divert punishment for their sin (14.11–12;
16.1–13). Another prose addition indicates that even
if Moses and Samuel, two of Israel's greatest prophets,
were to intercede, punishment would not be avoided
(15.1–4). Common in the Psalter (e.g., Pss 3; 4; 5; 6; 7;
9–10) and the book of Job, laments contain all or at
least some of the following elements: invocation (call
to God and initial pleas), complaint (description of
suffering, reproachful questions), plea for help, condemnation of or imprecation against enemies, affirmation of confidence, confession of sins, acknowledgment of divine response, and hymnic elements (praise
of God, blessings). Laments are often followed by
thanksgiving psalms in which the worshiper praises
and gives thanks to God for salvation (e.g., Pss 18; 21;
32; 34). The laments attributed to Jeremiah provide a
unique look at the prophet's inner struggle with faith,
persecution, and human suffering. If they are Jeremiah's own words, the laments could be placed in any
period of his life. These laments interact with various
judgment oracles, in both poetry and prose, which figure prominently in these chapters: 13.1–11, 12–14;

13.15–17, 18–19, 20–27; 14.13–16; 15.5–9; 16.16–18,
21; 17.1–4. The setting presupposed by the judgment
oracles is the siege of Jerusalem and the imminent
exile, either in 597 or in 587 BCE. Biographical narratives also appear for the first time, to illustrate graphically the reasons for the laments and the reality of
judgment and salvation: the potter and the clay (18.1–
12), the broken earthenware jug (19.1–15), and persecution of Jeremiah by Pashhur the priest (20.1–6).
Also present in the form of prose speeches (12.14–17;
16.14–15) is the promise of salvation, similar to the
ones found in the Book of Consolation in chs. 30–31.
Finally, a conditional, "either-or" prose sermon offers
judgment or salvation depending on whether the sabbath is honored (17.19–27). **11.18–23** The plot
against Jeremiah's life. The first lament of Jeremiah
consists of a poetic complaint (vv. 18–20) and a prose
response (vv. 21–23). In the complaint, Jeremiah indicates he is the innocent, unwitting target (*gentle lamb,*
v. 19) of a plot against his life. As is common to
laments in general and Jeremiah's own complaints, the
prophet seeks God's protection and asks for divine retribution against the would-be evildoers. **11.19** To have
one's (good) *name . . . remembered* was greatly desired.
Survival by means of memory was greatly coveted, for
this, along with children, were the two major means of
life beyond death in ancient Israel (see Gen 12.2; Eccl
2.16; 7.1.) A belief in resurrection did not clearly develop in Judaism until the second century BCE (see
Dan 12.2). **11.20** The request for punishment of enemies is common in laments (e.g., Pss 3.7; 7.6). **11.21–
23** The enemies of Jeremiah are identified in a prose
addition as the *people of Anathoth,* i.e., his own family
and neighbors. The reason for their persecution of Jeremiah is unclear.
   12.1–6 Jeremiah's second lament (see note on
11.18–23), the question of divine justice. In his complaint (vv. 1–4), Jeremiah accuses God of injustice: it is
God who supports the wicked. **12.1–2** *Put my case* re-

they grow and bring forth fruit;
you are near in their mouths
   yet far from their hearts.
3 But you, O LORD, know me;
   You see me and test me—my heart is
      with you.
Pull them out like sheep for the slaughter,
   and set them apart for the day of
      slaughter.
4 How long will the land mourn,
   and the grass of every field wither?
For the wickedness of those who live in it
   the animals and the birds are swept
      away,
   and because people said, "He is blind
      to our ways."*a*

God Replies to Jeremiah

5 If you have raced with foot-runners and
      they have wearied you,
   how will you compete with horses?
And if in a safe land you fall down,
   how will you fare in the thickets of the
      Jordan?
6 For even your kinsfolk and your own
      family,
   even they have dealt treacherously with
      you;
   they are in full cry after you;
do not believe them,
   though they speak friendly words to
      you.

7 I have forsaken my house,
   I have abandoned my heritage;
I have given the beloved of my heart
   into the hands of her enemies.
8 My heritage has become to me
   like a lion in the forest;
she has lifted up her voice against me—
   therefore I hate her.
9 Is the hyena greedy*b* for my heritage at
      my command?
   Are the birds of prey all around her?
Go, assemble all the wild animals;

   bring them to devour her.
10 Many shepherds have destroyed my
      vineyard,
   they have trampled down my portion,
they have made my pleasant portion
   a desolate wilderness.
11 They have made it a desolation;
   desolate, it mourns to me.
The whole land is made desolate,
   but no one lays it to heart.
12 Upon all the bare heights*c* in the desert
   spoilers have come;
for the sword of the LORD devours
   from one end of the land to the other;
   no one shall be safe.
13 They have sown wheat and have reaped
      thorns,
   they have tired themselves out but
      profit nothing.
They shall be ashamed of their*d* harvests
   because of the fierce anger of the LORD.

14 Thus says the LORD concerning all my evil neighbors who touch the heritage that I have given my people Israel to inherit: I am about to pluck them up from their land, and I will pluck up the house of Judah from among them. 15 And after I have plucked them up, I will again have compassion on them, and I will bring them again to their heritage and to their land, every one of them. 16 And then, if they will diligently learn the ways of my people, to swear by my name, "As the LORD lives," as they taught my people to swear by Baal, then they shall be built up in the midst of my people. 17 But if any nation will not listen, then I will completely uproot it and destroy it, says the LORD.

The Linen Loincloth

13 Thus said the LORD to me, "Go and buy yourself a linen loincloth, and put it on your loins, but do not dip it in water." 2 So I

---

a Gk: Heb *to our future* *b* Cn: Heb *Is the hyena, the bird of prey*
c Or *the trails* *d* Heb *your*

---

flects the law court in which Jeremiah brings charges against God, who serves as judge. The theory of retribution, in which the righteous are rewarded and the wicked are punished, is questioned by the prophet. **12.5–6** God's response is a warning that the present persecution of the prophet is only going to intensify. **12.7–13** The lament pictures God weeping over the destruction of Judah by invading enemies. The Lord, having abandoned the people, is the one who gives vic-

tory to the invaders. **12.7** *My house,* either the nation of Judah (Hos 9.15) or the temple (Jer 7.10). **12.14–17** Judgment against Judah's neighbors, a prose oracle of salvation added during the exile. Judah's neighbors may escape God's future judgment at the conclusion of the exile only if they are converted to the worship of Yahweh. Common to oracles of salvation is the promise of the punishment of enemies (see 30.10–11). **13.1–11** The linen loincloth. This prose narrative

bought a loincloth according to the word of the LORD, and put it on my loins. ³And the word of the LORD came to me a second time, saying, ⁴"Take the loincloth that you bought and are wearing, and go now to the Euphrates,ᵃ and hide it there in a cleft of the rock." ⁵So I went, and hid it by the Euphrates,ᵇ as the LORD commanded me. ⁶And after many days the LORD said to me, "Go now to the Euphrates,ᵃ and take from there the loincloth that I commanded you to hide there." ⁷Then I went to the Euphrates,ᵃ and dug, and I took the loincloth from the place where I had hidden it. But now the loincloth was ruined; it was good for nothing.

8 Then the word of the LORD came to me: ⁹Thus says the LORD: Just so I will ruin the pride of Judah and the great pride of Jerusalem. ¹⁰This evil people, who refuse to hear my words, who stubbornly follow their own will and have gone after other gods to serve them and worship them, shall be like this loincloth, which is good for nothing. ¹¹For as the loincloth clings to one's loins, so I made the whole house of Israel and the whole house of Judah cling to me, says the LORD, in order that they might be for me a people, a name, a praise, and a glory. But they would not listen.

Symbol of the Wine-Jars

12 You shall speak to them this word: Thus says the LORD, the God of Israel: Every wine-jar should be filled with wine. And they will say to you, "Do you think we do not know that every wine-jar should be filled with wine?" ¹³Then you shall say to them: Thus says the LORD: I am about to fill all the inhabitants of this land—the kings who sit on David's throne, the priests, the prophets, and all the inhabitants of Jerusalem—with drunkenness. ¹⁴And I will dash them one against another, parents and children together, says the LORD. I will not pity or spare or have compassion when I destroy them.

Exile Threatened

15 Hear and give ear; do not be haughty,
        for the LORD has spoken.
16 Give glory to the LORD your God
        before he brings darkness,
    and before your feet stumble
        on the mountains at twilight;
    while you look for light,
        he turns it into gloom

_____

ᵃ Or to Parah; Heb perath   ᵇ Or by Parah; Heb perath

recounts a symbolic action by Jeremiah. A symbolic action graphically illustrates the message of a prophet (see chs. 19, 32). The structure involves three parts: the prophet is commanded by God to perform a symbolic act, the narrative reports that the act was carried out, and an explanation of the act is given. *Loincloth,* an undergarment covering the middle of the body. *Linen* was used for various types of clothing, sheets, curtains, and burial shrouds. All garments worn by priests were made of linen (Lev 16.4). **13.4** The *Euphrates* and the Tigris were the two major rivers that coursed through Babylonia. Carrying out the symbolic act beside the Euphrates may suggest that the ultimate interpretation of the action refers to exiles from Jerusalem deported to Babylon in 597 or 587/6 BCE. However, a broader interpretation that includes the exiles from the Northern Kingdom (722/1 BCE) cannot be ruled out (see v. 11). That Jeremiah actually twice made such a long journey of some four hundred miles is doubtful. The alternative *Parah* (see text note a), modern Khirbet Farah, is about five miles northeast of Jerusalem. A more likely possibility is that the journey, like the larger narrative, is a symbolic action, not to be taken literally. **13.7** That *the loincloth was ruined* points to Israel's and Judah's corruption by their stubborn sinfulness. **13.12–14** The symbol of the wine-jars. A prose speech, this oracle of judgment is issued against the leaders of Judah—kings, priests, and prophets—

and against the citizens of Jerusalem. Quoting a popular proverb, *every wine-jar should be filled with wine* (v. 12), the speech is similar to the preceding narrative. Either the wine-jar filled with wine symbolizes a complacency that is expressed in the belief there will always be plenty, or the saying is a truism: wine-jars are made to hold wine. **13.13** The leaders and the inhabitants of Jerusalem will be filled with wine and become *drunk,* an image that suggests both a condition of stupor that prohibits wise decisions and a "cup of wrath" from which the leaders and people of Jerusalem will be made to drink (see 25.15–29). **13.15–27** Three poetic oracles shaped into a larger poem that describes the tragedy of exile. Two periods are plausible: the time just prior to the exile in 597 BCE or that prior to the exile of 587. The first oracle calls for repentance (vv. 15–17); the second is a judgment speech addressing the king and queen mother, who have lost their positions (vv. 18–19); and the third is a lawsuit that attributes the ravages of exile to religious apostasy (vv. 20–27). **13.16** *Glory to the LORD,* a doxology, i.e., a word of praise to God in which a person found guilty of a crime acknowledges the judgment is fair (see Josh 7.16–21; 2 Chr 30.8). Guilty Judah, threatened with exile unless there is full-scale repentance, is exhorted to utter a doxology. *Darkness, twilight, gloom, deep darkness,* images of primordial chaos used to describe the devastation of impending doom (see Gen 1.2;

and makes it deep darkness.
17 But if you will not listen,
    my soul will weep in secret for your
        pride;
    my eyes will weep bitterly and run down
        with tears,
    because the LORD's flock has been
        taken captive.

18 Say to the king and the queen mother:
    "Take a lowly seat,
    for your beautiful crown
        has come down from your head." *a*
19 The towns of the Negeb are shut up
        with no one to open them;
    all Judah is taken into exile,
        wholly taken into exile.

20 Lift up your eyes and see
        those who come from the north.
    Where is the flock that was given you,
        your beautiful flock?
21 What will you say when they set as head
        over you
    those whom you have trained
        to be your allies?
    Will not pangs take hold of you,
        like those of a woman in labor?
22 And if you say in your heart,
        "Why have these things come upon me?"
    it is for the greatness of your iniquity
        that your skirts are lifted up,
        and you are violated.
23 Can Ethiopians *b* change their skin
        or leopards their spots?
    Then also you can do good
        who are accustomed to do evil.
24 I will scatter you *c* like chaff
        driven by the wind from the desert.
25 This is your lot,
        the portion I have measured out to
            you, says the LORD,

because you have forgotten me
    and trusted in lies.
26 I myself will lift up your skirts over your
        face,
    and your shame will be seen.
27 I have seen your abominations,
    your adulteries and neighings, your
        shameless prostitutions
    on the hills of the countryside.
Woe to you, O Jerusalem!
    How long will it be
    before you are made clean?

The Great Drought

14 The word of the LORD that came to Jeremiah concerning the drought:
2 Judah mourns
    and her gates languish;
    they lie in gloom on the ground,
    and the cry of Jerusalem goes up.
3 Her nobles send their servants for water;
    they come to the cisterns,
    they find no water,
    they return with their vessels empty.
    They are ashamed and dismayed
        and cover their heads,
4 because the ground is cracked.
    Because there has been no rain on the
        land
    the farmers are dismayed;
        they cover their heads.
5 Even the doe in the field forsakes her
        newborn fawn
    because there is no grass.
6 The wild asses stand on the bare
        heights, *d*
    they pant for air like jackals;
    their eyes fail
        because there is no herbage.

---

a Gk Syr Vg: Meaning of Heb uncertain   *b* Or *Nubians*; Heb
Cushites   *c* Heb *them*   *d* Or *the trails*

Job 3). **13.17** The theme of lament returns as Jeremiah anticipates weeping over the captivity of the nation. **13.18** *Queen mother*, the mother of the ruling king; she had significant political power (see 1 Kings 2.19; 15.13; 2 Kings 8.26; 11.1–3). If the exile in 597 BCE is in mind, the king and queen mother would be Jehoiachin and Nehushta (2 Kings 24.8–17). Jehoiachin ruled only three months, prior to his exile. If the exile in 587 BCE is in view, the king and queen mother would be Zedekiah and Hamutal (2 Kings 24.18–20). **13.19** *Negeb*, the southern part of Judah; it is a hot, arid region with under eight inches of annual rainfall. During the

monarchy there were in the Negeb many small villages engaged in agriculture and fortresses to protect Judah to the north and the trade routes that traversed the region. **13.20** *Those who come from the north*. See chs. 4–10. **13.23** Using proverbial language in a rhetorical question, Jeremiah addresses the impossibility of a corrupt people doing good. *Ethiopians*, the inhabitants of Cush, the region south of Egypt.
14.1–10 The people's lament. Occasioned by a drought, the first section (vv. 1–6) describes the devastating effects of a prolonged drought. The second part (vv. 7–9) contains the lament of the people in which

7 Although our iniquities testify against us,
        act, O LORD, for your name's sake;
    our apostasies indeed are many,
        and we have sinned against you.
8 O hope of Israel,
        its savior in time of trouble,
    why should you be like a stranger in the
            land,
        like a traveler turning aside for the
            night?
9 Why should you be like someone
            confused,
        like a mighty warrior who cannot give
            help?
    Yet you, O LORD, are in the midst of us,
        and we are called by your name;
        do not forsake us!

10 Thus says the LORD concerning this
            people:
    Truly they have loved to wander,
        they have not restrained their feet;
    therefore the LORD does not accept them,
        now he will remember their iniquity
        and punish their sins.

11 The LORD said to me: Do not pray for the
welfare of this people. 12Although they fast, I
do not hear their cry, and although they offer
burnt offering and grain offering, I do not accept them; but by the sword, by famine, and by
pestilence I consume them.

Denunciation of Lying Prophets

13 Then I said: "Ah, Lord GOD! Here are the
prophets saying to them, 'You shall not see the
sword, nor shall you have famine, but I will
give you true peace in this place.'" 14And the
LORD said to me: The prophets are prophesying lies in my name; I did not send them, nor
did I command them or speak to them. They

are prophesying to you a lying vision, worthless divination, and the deceit of their own
minds. 15Therefore thus says the LORD concerning the prophets who prophesy in my
name though I did not send them, and who
say, "Sword and famine shall not come on this
land": By sword and famine those prophets
shall be consumed. 16And the people to whom
they prophesy shall be thrown out into the
streets of Jerusalem, victims of famine and
sword. There shall be no one to bury them—
themselves, their wives, their sons, and their
daughters. For I will pour out their wickedness upon them.

17 You shall say to them this word:
    Let my eyes run down with tears night
            and day,
        and let them not cease,
    for the virgin daughter—my people—is
            struck down with a crushing
            blow,
        with a very grievous wound.
18 If I go out into the field,
        look—those killed by the sword!
    And if I enter the city,
        look—those sick with a famine!
    For both prophet and priest ply their
            trade throughout the land,
        and have no knowledge.

The People Plead for Mercy

19 Have you completely rejected Judah?
        Does your heart loathe Zion?
    Why have you struck us down
        so that there is no healing for us?
    We look for peace, but find no good;
        for a time of healing, but there is terror
            instead.

_____
a Heb look—the sicknesses of

they acknowledge their iniquities and call upon the
Lord for deliverance. **14.8–9** The people reproach God
for being one who is neither moved nor able to bring
redemption. **14.10** The conclusion contains God's rejection of the people's petition, because they continue
in their wickedness. **14.11–12** Jeremiah is forbidden
to intercede on behalf of his people and thus to redeem them from destruction (see 7.16; 11.14; 15.1;
16.5–9). The laments and sacrifices of the people will
not avert destruction (6.20; 7.21–29). **14.12** _Burnt of-
ferings._ See note on 6.20. _Grain offerings,_ sacrifices of
grains and vegetables, which could be given raw or
cooked (see Lev 2). **14.13–16** Lying prophets. Jere-

miah protests (_Ah, Lord GOD;_ see note on 1.6) the
words of prophets whose promises of well-being have
deceived the people. **14.13** It may be that Jeremiah objects that God is responsible for deceiving the people
with lying words (see 1 Kings 22). **14.14–15** God denies the charge, indicating that the prophets speak lies
and will be punished (see 23.9–40; 28). **14.16** Those
who are deceived will be killed and will suffer the curse
of not being buried (see 7.29–8.3). **14.17–18** God's
second lament. Once again God laments over the destruction of his _daughter_ (see 12.7–13). **14.19–22** The
people lament once more. God is addressed again by
the people with a lament containing reproach, confes-

20 We acknowledge our wickedness,
        O LORD,
    the iniquity of our ancestors,
        for we have sinned against you.
21 Do not spurn us, for your name's sake;
        do not dishonor your glorious throne;
    remember and do not break your
        covenant with us.
22 Can any idols of the nations bring rain?
        Or can the heavens give showers?
    Is it not you, O LORD our God?
    We set our hope on you,
        for it is you who do all this.

Punishment Is Inevitable

15 Then the LORD said to me: Though Moses and Samuel stood before me, yet my heart would not turn toward this people. Send them out of my sight, and let them go! 2And when they say to you, "Where shall we go?" you shall say to them: Thus says the LORD:

    Those destined for pestilence, to
        pestilence,
    and those destined for the sword, to
        the sword;
    those destined for famine, to famine,
    and those destined for captivity, to
        captivity.

3And I will appoint over them four kinds of destroyers, says the LORD: the sword to kill, the dogs to drag away, and the birds of the air and the wild animals of the earth to devour and destroy. 4I will make them a horror to all the kingdoms of the earth because of what King Manasseh son of Hezekiah of Judah did in Jerusalem.

5 Who will have pity on you, O Jerusalem,
        or who will bemoan you?
    Who will turn aside
        to ask about your welfare?
6 You have rejected me, says the LORD,
        you are going backward;
    so I have stretched out my hand against
        you and destroyed you—
    I am weary of relenting.
7 I have winnowed them with a winnowing
        fork
    in the gates of the land;
    I have bereaved them, I have destroyed
        my people;
    they did not turn from their ways.
8 Their widows became more numerous
        than the sand of the seas;
    I have brought against the mothers of
        youths
    a destroyer at noonday;
    I have made anguish and terror
        fall upon her suddenly.
9 She who bore seven has languished;
        she has swooned away;
    her sun went down while it was yet day;
        she has been shamed and disgraced.
    And the rest of them I will give to the
        sword
    before their enemies,
                                says the LORD.

Jeremiah Complains Again and Is Reassured

10 Woe is me, my mother, that you ever bore me, a man of strife and contention to the whole land! I have not lent, nor have I borrowed, yet all of them curse me. 11The LORD said: Surely I

---

sion of sin, and an implicit appeal for salvation (see vv. 1–10). **14.21** Jerusalem is known as the *throne* of God (see 3.17), as is the temple (see 17.12; Ezek 43.7). **15.1–4** Intercession cannot divert destruction. A prose speech originating during the exile. Even if Moses (Ex 32.11–14, 30–34; Num 14.13–19) and Samuel (1 Sam 12.17–18), two of the greatest prophetic intercessors, were to plead Judah's case, the Lord would not save the nation from destruction (see 7.16; 11.14; 14.11–12; 16.5–9). Jeremiah is understood as the "prophet like Moses" (Deut 18.15–22) and stands in the line of succession from Moses and Samuel. **15.4** *Manasseh,* king over Judah for forty-five years (687/6–642 BCE). A loyal vassal to Assyria, he was condemned for leading Israel into religious infidelity. The editors of 2 Kings blame him for the eventual destruction of Jerusalem and the exile of Judah (2 Kings 21.1–18). Judah's punishment for the sins of Manas-

seh represents the theory of retribution common in Deuteronomy, 1 and 2 Samuel, 1 and 2 Kings, and the prose edition of Jeremiah. **15.5–9** A town without pity. A poetic judgment oracle in which the final destruction of Jerusalem is announced. Even the great losses suffered at the hands of the Egyptians and Babylonians prior to 587 BCE did not result in Jerusalem's turning to the Lord. **15.9** *She who bore seven.* Bearing seven children is a sign of divine blessing (Ruth 4.15; 1 Sam 2.5). **15.10–21** Jeremiah's third lament (see note on 11.18–23). This lament consists of a poetic complaint by the prophet (vv. 15–18) and divine reassurance (vv. 19–21). Added later is an exilic or postexilic prose insertion (vv. 10–14). **15.10** The prose addition begins with a lament (*Woe is me!*) in which the prophet regrets he was born. Note that his call was from the womb and that God decreed from birth that he would be a prophet (see 1.5; 20.14–18). *Strife* (He-

have intervened in your life^a for good, surely I
have imposed enemies on you in a time of trouble and in a time of distress.^b 12Can iron and
bronze break iron from the north?

13 Your wealth and your treasures I will
give as plunder, without price, for all your sins,
throughout all your territory. 14I will make
you serve your enemies in a land that you do
not know, for in my anger a fire is kindled that
shall burn forever.

15 O Lord, you know;
        remember me and visit me,
        and bring down retribution for me on
            my persecutors.
     In your forbearance do not take me away;
        know that on your account I suffer
            insult.
16 Your words were found, and I ate them,
        and your words became to me a joy
        and the delight of my heart;
     for I am called by your name,
        O Lord, God of hosts.
17 I did not sit in the company of
            merrymakers,
        nor did I rejoice;
     under the weight of your hand I sat
            alone,
        for you had filled me with indignation.
18 Why is my pain unceasing,
        my wound incurable,

refusing to be healed?
     Truly, you are to me like a deceitful brook,
        like waters that fail.

19 Therefore thus says the Lord:
     If you turn back, I will take you back,
        and you shall stand before me.
     If you utter what is precious, and not
            what is worthless,
        you shall serve as my mouth.
     It is they who will turn to you,
        not you who will turn to them.
20 And I will make you to this people
        a fortified wall of bronze;
     they will fight against you,
        but they shall not prevail over you,
     for I am with you
        to save you and deliver you,
                            says the Lord.
21 I will deliver you out of the hand of the
            wicked,
        and redeem you from the grasp of the
            ruthless.

Jeremiah's Celibacy and Message

16 The word of the Lord came to me:
2You shall not take a wife, nor shall you
have sons or daughters in this place. 3For thus

a Heb intervened with you   b Meaning of Heb uncertain

---

brew *riv*). Jeremiah is both the object of contention
and the mediator of God's lawsuit against the people
(see 2.1–37). His wish not to have been born is
grounded in both his prophetic call and the subsequent opposition and persecution he has received
from the leaders of Judah for proclaiming divine judgment (see the trial in ch. 26, Jehoiakim's efforts to arrest him in 36.20–26, and his imprisonment by Zedekiah in 37.11–38.13). Even his own priestly family
plotted against him (11.21–23). *Curse* (Hebrew *qalal*),
verbal abuse (Eccl 7.21–22) and even physical harm
(Gen 8.21). **15.11** God assumes responsibility for the
contempt and persecution of the prophet, yet intervenes in the prophet's life *for good*. **15.12** Such persecution hardens the prophet's character, enabling him
to endure the disaster from the north (see 1.17–19).
15.13–14 Jeremiah and his opponents will be plundered and forced into exile. As a prophet of the people, Jeremiah is to experience their disastrous fate.
15.16 *Your words . . . I ate them,* a metaphor for God's
putting in the prophet's mouth the divine words he is
to speak (1.9; see Isa 55.1–11; Ezek 2.8–3.3). *I am
called by your name.* Jeremiah's name in Hebrew
means "Yahweh exalts." **15.17** *Under the weight of your
hand,* a metaphor for prophetic inspiration (see
1 Kings 18.46; 2 Kings 3.15; Isa 8.11; Ezek 1.3; 3.14).

15.18 Jeremiah likens God to a *deceitful brook* and wa-
ters that fail in order to counter God's claim to be a
fountain of living waters (2.13) and denial of being a
wilderness to Israel (2.31). This imagery reflects the experience of one who, traveling through the wilderness,
seeks to find water in a stream bed only to find it dry.
15.19 The Lord's reply indicates Jeremiah has abandoned the prophetic office. *Turn back, turn, turn* (all
Hebrew *shub*). The threefold repetition echoes the call
to repentance in 3.1–4.4. *Stand before* the Lord, as a
messenger stands before the king and awaits the royal
word. **15.20** This verse brings to mind the language of
the call in 1.18–19. Jeremiah is reminded of his call
and is admonished to return to the prophetic office.

16.1–13 Celibacy and judgment. A prose sermon,
added by later editors, combines an announcement of
judgment with a symbolic act: the prophet is commanded by the Lord not to marry and have a family
(cf. symbolic acts in 13.1–11, 12–14). The prohibition
against marriage and family is to underscore the coming death and destruction that will face parents and
children. Even burial will be denied the dead. The
theme of lament is repeated in God's refusal to allow
Jeremiah to intercede on the people's behalf (7.16;
14.11–12; 15.1). He is also forbidden to rejoice with
them, for joy will be taken from the land during the

says the LORD concerning the sons and daughters who are born in this place, and concerning the mothers who bear them and the fathers who beget them in this land: 4They shall die of deadly diseases. They shall not be lamented, nor shall they be buried; they shall become like dung on the surface of the ground. They shall perish by the sword and by famine, and their dead bodies shall become food for the birds of the air and for the wild animals of the earth.

5 For thus says the LORD: Do not enter the house of mourning, or go to lament, or bemoan them; for I have taken away my peace from this people, says the LORD, my steadfast love and mercy. 6Both great and small shall die in this land; they shall not be buried, and no one shall lament for them; there shall be no gashing, no shaving of the head for them. 7No one shall break bread*a* for the mourner, to offer comfort for the dead; nor shall anyone give them the cup of consolation to drink for their fathers or their mothers. 8You shall not go into the house of feasting to sit with them, to eat and drink. 9For thus says the LORD of hosts, the God of Israel: I am going to banish from this place, in your days and before your eyes, the voice of mirth and the voice of gladness, the voice of the bridegroom and the voice of the bride.

10 And when you tell this people all these words, and they say to you, "Why has the LORD pronounced all this great evil against us? What is our iniquity? What is the sin that we have committed against the LORD our God?" 11then you shall say to them: It is because your ancestors have forsaken me, says the LORD, and have gone after other gods and have served and worshiped them, and have forsaken me and have not kept my law; 12and because you have behaved worse than your ancestors, for here you are, every one of you, following your stub-

born evil will, refusing to listen to me. 13Therefore I will hurl you out of this land into a land that neither you nor your ancestors have known, and there you shall serve other gods day and night, for I will show you no favor.

God Will Restore Israel

14 Therefore, the days are surely coming, says the LORD, when it shall no longer be said, "As the LORD lives who brought the people of Israel up out of the land of Egypt," 15but "As the LORD lives who brought the people of Israel up out of the land of the north and out of all the lands where he had driven them." For I will bring them back to their own land that I gave to their ancestors.

16 I am now sending for many fishermen, says the LORD, and they shall catch them; and afterward I will send for many hunters, and they shall hunt them from every mountain and every hill, and out of the clefts of the rocks. 17For my eyes are on all their ways; they are not hidden from my presence, nor is their iniquity concealed from my sight. 18And*b* I will doubly repay their iniquity and their sin, because they have polluted my land with the carcasses of their detestable idols, and have filled my inheritance with their abominations.

19   O LORD, my strength and my stronghold,
        my refuge in the day of trouble,
     to you shall the nations come
        from the ends of the earth and say:
     Our ancestors have inherited nothing but
        lies,
        worthless things in which there is no
        profit.
20   Can mortals make for themselves gods?
        Such are no gods!

---

a Two Mss Gk: MT *break for them*   *b* Gk: Heb *And first*

---

impending destruction and exile. **16.5** *House of mourning,* the room or hall in a house in which a funeral banquet that included feasting and drinking occurred (see Am 6.7, where "the revelry of the loungers" refers to participants at funeral banquets; also see the *bread* and the *cup* in Jer 16.7 and the corresponding expression *house of feasting* in v. 8). **16.6** *Gashing* and *shaving* of the head were funerary practices associated with pagan worship and forbidden by Israelite law (Lev 19.28; 21.5; Deut 14.1). **16.10–13** The question and answer form is common in the prose tradition (5.19; 13.12–14; 15.1–4; 22.8–9). **16.14–15** The re-

turn from exile. A prose sermon of hope predicts the future return of the exiles from Babylonia. This passage duplicates almost exactly 23.7–8. The return from exile will be remembered and celebrated in religious faith and practice, as once was the exodus from Egypt. **16.16–18, 21** Fishers and hunters of Judah. The prose sermon continues v. 13. **16.16** The *fishermen* and *hunters* may represent, respectively, the Egyptians (Isa 19.5–10) and Babylonians (Lam 4.18–19). **16.18** Being repaid double may suggest the defeat by the Egyptians (Neco II) and the Babylonian conquest. **16.19–20** A fragment of a lament and possibly a thanksgiving

21 "Therefore I am surely going to teach them, this time I am going to teach them my power and my might, and they shall know that my name is the LORD."

Judah's Sin and Punishment

17 The sin of Judah is written with an iron pen; with a diamond point it is engraved on the tablet of their hearts, and on the horns of their altars, 2while their children remember their altars and their sacred poles,*a* beside every green tree, and on the high hills, 3on the mountains in the open country. Your wealth and all your treasures I will give for spoil as the price of your sin*b* throughout all your territory. 4By your own act you shall lose the heritage that I gave you, and I will make you serve your enemies in a land that you do not know, for in my anger a fire is kindled*c* that shall burn forever.

5 Thus says the LORD:
Cursed are those who trust in mere
    mortals
and make mere flesh their strength,
    whose hearts turn away from the LORD.

6 They shall be like a shrub in the desert,
    and shall not see when relief comes.
They shall live in the parched places of
    the wilderness,
        in an uninhabited salt land.

7 Blessed are those who trust in the LORD,
    whose trust is the LORD.
8 They shall be like a tree planted by water,
    sending out its roots by the stream.
It shall not fear when heat comes,
    and its leaves shall stay green;
in the year of drought it is not anxious,
    and it does not cease to bear fruit.

9 The heart is devious above all else;
    it is perverse—
        who can understand it?
10 I the LORD test the mind
    and search the heart,
to give to all according to their ways,
    according to the fruit of their doings.

---

a Heb *Asherim*   *b* Cn: Heb *spoil your high places for sin*
c Two Mss Theodotion: *you kindled*

---

psalm that speaks of Jeremiah's faith in God and the conversion of the nations (see Ps 22; Isa 2.3; Mic 4.2), **16.21** A continuation of v. 18.
17.1–4 Judgment against Judah. This prose sermon, deriving from the exile or the postexilic period, indicts Judah for involvement in Canaanite religion. Despoliation and exile are the judgment. **17.1** *Iron pen*, used to incise wood or metal (Job 19.24). *Diamond point*, an engraving instrument; the point was probably not diamond, but rather a very hard stone, perhaps emery. *Engraved on the tablet of their hearts* calls to mind engraving the Ten Commandments on tablets of stone (Ex 31.18; 32.16). *Altars*, places for the offering of oblations, foodstuffs, incense, and animals. Some altars had *horns*, i.e., projections from their four corners (Ex 27.2) on which the blood of sacrificial animals was placed (Lev 4.7). Those who desired asylum could cling to the altar's horns (1 Kings 1.50–51; 2.28–34). Tablets were made of stone, metal, or wood. Engraved writings, especially on stone and metal, were meant to endure permanently, unlike writings on leather and papyrus or notes and records written with ink on broken pottery. Writing or engraving Judah's sins on the tablets of its people's hearts and on the horns of its stone altars suggests a record that will endure for a very long time. This contrasts with the writing of the law on the hearts of the faithful generation in the future (31.33). **17.2** *Sacred poles* (Hebrew *'asherim*), carved wood (Judg 6.25) or living trees (Deut 16.21) representing the goddess Asherah. A Canaanite goddess, Asherah was the consort of El and perhaps of Baal at Ugarit, but certainly of Baal in Israel (see 1 Kings 15.13; 18.19; 2 Kings 21.7; 23.4; Mic 5.13–14). Scholars are still debating her possible role in Israelite worship. **17.5–11** These verses consist of a wisdom poem (vv. 5–8), a rhetorical question (v. 9), a first-person proverb (v. 10), and a comparative proverb (v. 11). These are forms typically found in wisdom literature (Job, Proverbs, and Ecclesiastes). Although it is possible Jeremiah used wisdom texts, it is more probable that these materials were inserted by later editors. **17.5–8** A poem of two strophes (vv. 5–6, vv. 7–8) very similar to Ps 1. Ps 1 emphasizes that avoidance of the wicked and study of the Torah are the key to blessing; the poem in Jeremiah finds the key to well-being in trusting in the Lord. *Tree planted by water*, imagery suggesting the "tree of life," a common motif taken from mythology and associated with wisdom (Prov 3.13–18). For the sages who wrote wisdom literature, wisdom is the ability to perceive the order of God in creation, the intelligence to act in accordance with God's order, and moral behavior that leads to well-being. Wise behavior produces life in all of its fullness. **17.9** Rhetorical questions, common in wisdom texts, are queries that do not expect answers, for the answers are obvious (see "the voice from the whirlwind" in Job 38–41; Am 3.3–8). For the sages, the *heart* is the mind and seat of volition (will; Prov 14.10; 16.9, 23; 25.3). **17.10** In wisdom literature, God is the one who oversees the just order in nature and society. God is able to distribute to all their just deserts because of divine knowledge of the human heart (see 20.12; Pss. 7.10;

11 Like the partridge hatching what it did
        not lay,
     so are all who amass wealth unjustly;
   in mid-life it will leave them,
     and at their end they will prove to be
        fools.

12 O glorious throne, exalted from the
        beginning,
     shrine of our sanctuary!
13 O hope of Israel! O LORD!
     All who forsake you shall be put to
        shame;
   those who turn away from you[a] shall be
        recorded in the underworld,[b]
   for they have forsaken the fountain of
        living water, the LORD.

Jeremiah Prays for Vindication

14 Heal me, O LORD, and I shall be healed;
     save me, and I shall be saved;
   for you are my praise.
15 See how they say to me,
     "Where is the word of the LORD?
     Let it come!"
16 But I have not run away from being a
        shepherd[c] in your service,
     nor have I desired the fatal day.
   You know what came from my lips;
     it was before your face.
17 Do not become a terror to me;
     you are my refuge in the day of
        disaster;
18 Let my persecutors be shamed,
     but do not let me be shamed;

   let them be dismayed,
     but do not let me be dismayed;
   bring on them the day of disaster;
     destroy them with double destruction!

Hallow the Sabbath Day

19 Thus said the LORD to me: Go and stand in the People's Gate, by which the kings of Judah enter and by which they go out, and in all the gates of Jerusalem, 20 and say to them: Hear the word of the LORD, you kings of Judah, and all Judah, and all the inhabitants of Jerusalem, who enter by these gates. 21 Thus says the LORD: For the sake of your lives, take care that you do not bear a burden on the sabbath day or bring it in by the gates of Jerusalem. 22 And do not carry a burden out of your houses on the sabbath or do any work, but keep the sabbath day holy, as I commanded your ancestors. 23 Yet they did not listen or incline their ear; they stiffened their necks and would not hear or receive instruction.

24 But if you listen to me, says the LORD, and bring in no burden by the gates of this city on the sabbath day, but keep the sabbath day holy and do no work on it, 25 then there shall enter by the gates of this city kings[d] who sit on the throne of David, riding in chariots and on horses, they and their officials, the people of Judah and the inhabitants of Jerusalem; and this city shall be inhabited forever. 26 And people shall come from the towns of Judah and

---

a Heb me   b Or in the earth   c Meaning of Heb uncertain
d Cn: Heb kings and officials

17.3; 139.14). **17.11** Comparative proverbs bring together two different things to discover a common feature. This proverb expresses clearly the theory of retribution (the righteous are rewarded and the wicked punished), so common to proverbial wisdom. **17.12–13** A fragment of a hymn that praises both the Lord and the sacred ark; it probably is a later addition to vv. 5–11. Hymns are common in the Psalter (see, e.g., Pss 8; 19; 33; 47). The *throne* is the ark, located in the temple, considered the seat of the invisible deity and guarded by cherubim (see note on 3.16). **17.14–18** Jeremiah's fourth lament (see note on 11.18–23). Unlike the earlier laments, Jeremiah's complaint is not answered. The prophet cries out for healing and redemption (see Pss 41.4; 147.3). **17.16** Jeremiah denies he has desired the *fatal day* (see *day of disaster* in v. 18), i.e., the "day of the LORD" when destruction from the invading enemy will come (see Am 5.18; 8.9–14; Zeph 1.14–18). Jeremiah has seen his role as intercessor, hoping to move Judah to repentance and to avert the

wrath from the northern enemy. **17.19–27** Honor the sabbath. This probably postexilic prose sermon calls upon Judah, in the form of "either-or," to honor the sabbath day. It is a matter of life and death, punishment and blessing. *Sabbath* occurs seven times in this text. The sabbath was the seventh day of the week and was observed as a day of rest and worship (see Ex 16.23; 20.8–11; 23.12; 31.12–17; Lev 23.3; Deut 5.12–15). Its observance was central to the Mosaic covenant. Am 8.5 points to abstaining from business on the sabbath, while Nehemiah in the fifth century BCE locked the gates of Jerusalem on the sabbath to prevent commercial activity (Neh 13.15–22). The passage in Jeremiah promises the possibility of the restoration of kingship and kingdom if the people observe the sabbath and recalls the temple sermon in 7.1–15, where Jeremiah stands at a temple gate, addresses kings and people, and underscores obedience to God's law as necessary for salvation. **17.19** *People's Gate*, probably one of the gates to the temple. **17.26** The geographical

the places around Jerusalem, from the land of Benjamin, from the Shephelah, from the hill country, and from the Negeb, bringing burnt offerings and sacrifices, grain offerings and frankincense, and bringing thank offerings to the house of the LORD. 27But if you do not listen to me, to keep the sabbath day holy, and to carry in no burden through the gates of Jerusalem on the sabbath day, then I will kindle a fire in its gates; it shall devour the palaces of Jerusalem and shall not be quenched.

The Potter and the Clay

18 The word that came to Jeremiah from the LORD: 2"Come, go down to the potter's house, and there I will let you hear my words." 3So I went down to the potter's house, and there he was working at his wheel. 4The vessel he was making of clay was spoiled in the potter's hand, and he reworked it into another vessel, as seemed good to him.

5 Then the word of the LORD came to me: 6Can I not do with you, O house of Israel, just as this potter has done? says the LORD. Just like the clay in the potter's hand, so are you in my hand, O house of Israel. 7At one moment I may declare concerning a nation or a kingdom, that I will pluck up and break down and destroy it, 8but if that nation, concerning

which I have spoken, turns from its evil, I will change my mind about the disaster that I intended to bring on it. 9And at another moment I may declare concerning a nation or a kingdom that I will build and plant it, 10but if it does evil in my sight, not listening to my voice, then I will change my mind about the good that I had intended to do to it. 11Now, therefore, say to the people of Judah and the inhabitants of Jerusalem: Thus says the LORD: Look, I am a potter shaping evil against you and devising a plan against you. Turn now, all of you from your evil way, and amend your ways and your doings.

Israel's Stubborn Idolatry

12 But they say, "It is no use! We will follow our own plans, and each of us will act according to the stubbornness of our evil will."

13 Therefore thus says the LORD:
   Ask among the nations:
      Who has heard the like of this?
   The virgin Israel has done
      a most horrible thing.
14 Does the snow of Lebanon leave
      the crags of Sirion?a

———
a Cn: Heb of the field

areas are those near Jerusalem, making temple worship accessible. The *Shephelah* designates the low hills that separate the coastal plain from the central hill country. See 32.44; 33.13. Most biblical references are to the Shephelah of Judah. The Negeb is the southern region of Judah. For *burnt offerings, sacrifices,* and *frankincense,* see note on 6.20. For *grain offerings,* see note on 14.12. Frankincense was associated with grain offerings (Lev 2). A *thank offering,* consisting of meat and breads that could be eaten by priests and worshipers, is the type of sacrifice offered in thanks for salvation of various types (e.g., recovery from an illness; see Lev 7.11–18; Ps 107). **18.1–12** This prose narrative, originating during the exile or after it, involves another symbolic act coupled with a judgment oracle (see 13.1–11, 12–14). God has devised evil against Judah and Jerusalem, but will alter this fate if they will turn from their evil ways. The conclusion in v. 12 quotes the people as saying they will follow their own evil will. **18.2–4** The craft of the potter was a highly skilled one. Pottery was an important industry and most villages and cities had pottery workshops. Pottery was shaped by hand in several ways: pressing clay to the inside of a basket which was then fired; shaping clay in the palm of one hand with the other hand; piecing clay strips around a base; and connecting lengths of clay with slip (clay mixed with

water); but a potter's wheel was the most common way of producing vessels. The wheel was turned by hand or foot, while the free hand or hands shaped the clay. Some vessels were sun-dried, but most were hardened by firing. Decorations consisted of incision, painting, and especially burnishing (polishing the slip that coated the dried pottery before firing). **18.7–9** *Pluck up, break down, build, plant.* See note on 1.10. **18.11** The image of God as *potter* is common in the Bible. Gen 2.7 presents God as the potter fashioning humanity from clay. In other texts God shapes peoples and nations like a potter (see Isa 29.16; 64.8; Rom 9.20–24). **18.12** The people's rejection of God's will is as absurd as a vessel that argues against the potter, its creator (Isa 45.9). **18.13–17** The foolishness of idolatry. Once again Jeremiah brings charges against Israel for idolatry (see 2.1–3.5). God is both plaintiff and judge, the charges of religious apostasy and idolatry are set forth, the nations are called as witnesses to testify against Israel for abandoning God, rhetorical questions are raised with obvious though unspoken answers, and the judgment is rendered. The passage in form and content is strikingly similar to ch. 2. The oracle was probably uttered during the reign of Josiah as he sought to annex the former Northern Kingdom within his expanding territory. **18.14** *Snow of Lebanon* and *crags of Sirion* refer to the mountain range just to

Do the mountain*a* waters run dry,*b*
　　the cold flowing streams?
15 But my people have forgotten me,
　　they burn offerings to a delusion;
　they have stumbled*c* in their ways,
　　in the ancient roads,
　and have gone into bypaths,
　　not the highway,
16 making their land a horror,
　　a thing to be hissed at forever.
　All who pass by it are horrified
　　and shake their heads.
17 Like the wind from the east,
　　I will scatter them before the enemy.
　I will show them my back, not my face,
　　in the day of their calamity.

A Plot against Jeremiah

18 Then they said, "Come, let us make plots
against Jeremiah—for instruction shall not
perish from the priest, nor counsel from the
wise, nor the word from the prophet. Come,
let us bring charges against him,*d* and let us
not heed any of his words."

19 　Give heed to me, O LORD,
　　and listen to what my adversaries say!
20 　Is evil a recompense for good?
　　Yet they have dug a pit for my life.
　Remember how I stood before you
　　to speak good for them,
　　to turn away your wrath from them.
21 　Therefore give their children over to
　　　famine;

hurl them out to the power of the
　　sword,
　let their wives become childless and
　　widowed.
　May their men meet death by
　　pestilence,
　their youths be slain by the sword in
　　battle.
22 May a cry be heard from their houses,
　　when you bring the marauder
　　　suddenly upon them!
　For they have dug a pit to catch me,
　　and laid snares for my feet.
23 Yet you, O LORD, know
　　all their plotting to kill me.
　Do not forgive their iniquity,
　　do not blot out their sin from your
　　　sight.
　Let them be tripped up before you;
　　deal with them while you are angry.

The Broken Earthenware Jug

19 Thus said the LORD: Go and buy a potter's earthenware jug. Take with you*e*
some of the elders of the people and some of
the senior priests, 2 and go out to the valley of
the son of Hinnom at the entry of the Potsherd Gate, and proclaim there the words that
I tell you. 3 You shall say: Hear the word of the
LORD, O kings of Judah and inhabitants of Jerusalem. Thus says the LORD of hosts, the God

---

a Cn: Heb *foreign*　*b* Cn: Heb *Are . . . plucked up?*　*c* Gk Syr
Vg: Heb *they made them stumble*　*d* Heb *strike him with the
tongue*　*e* Syr Tg Compare Gk: Heb lacks *take with you*

---

the north of Israel, which extends northward for a
hundred miles. Sirion is another name for Mount Hermon, a mountain with three peaks (Deut 3.9; 4.48). It
is some 9,230 feet above sea level and is the highest
point in the region. **18.15** *My people have forgotten me.*
See 2.32; 13.24–25. *Delusion,* a metaphor for idols (Ps
31.6; Jon 2.8). *Ancient roads,* the traditional Mosaic religion (see 6.16), which Israel has abandoned to follow
other paths. **18.17** *Wind from the east,* often a violent
and scorching wind that comes from the desert
("sirocco"). See Ex 10.13; 14.21; Ps 48.7; Jon 4.8.
18.18–23 Jeremiah's fifth lament (see note on 11.18–
23). The initial verse describes a plot against the life of
Jeremiah (see the enemies of Jeremiah in other personal laments: 11.18–23; 12.1–6; 15.10–21; 17.14–18;
20.7–12). The efforts against Jeremiah seek to preserve
the priestly *instruction (torah),* the *counsel* of the wise,
and the prophetic *word* (see Ezek 7.26). The Torah,
counsel, and word were the three forms of divine revelation and teaching. Jeremiah is seen as standing contrary to the legitimate revelation of God announced by

the three offices of religious leadership. Those plotting
intend to kill the prophet (see v. 23). The *wise* were
probably counselors to kings (cf. note on 8.8–13).
18.20 Jeremiah had even interceded for his enemies
(4.10, 19–22). See 14.11–12; 15.1; also 16.5–9, where
Jeremiah was forbidden to intercede. **18.21–23** The
call for vengeance against enemies is common in Jeremiah's laments (see 11.18–23; 12.6; 15.15; see also Pss
3.7; 5.4–10; 7.6). Jeremiah desires that his enemies
perish during the invasion from the north.
　19.1–15 This prose narrative, coming from the
exile, combines a symbolic act with a prophetic word
of judgment (see 13.1–11, 12–14; 16.1–13; 18.1–12).
19.2 *Valley of . . . Hinnom.* See note on 7.31. *Potsherd
Gate,* probably another name for the Dung Gate (Neh
2.13; 3.13–14; 12.31), possibly located in the south
wall of Jerusalem. The gate was probably the exit for
removing the garbage of the city. Among the garbage
would probably have been broken pottery. **19.3–
9** Idolatrous practices, including child sacrifice, are
also condemned in 7.29–8.3. *Topheth.* See 7.30–34;

of Israel: I am going to bring such disaster upon this place that the ears of everyone who hears of it will tingle. [4]Because the people have forsaken me, and have profaned this place by making offerings in it to other gods whom neither they nor their ancestors nor the kings of Judah have known, and because they have filled this place with the blood of the innocent, [5]and gone on building the high places of Baal to burn their children in the fire as burnt offerings to Baal, which I did not command or decree, nor did it enter my mind; [6]therefore the days are surely coming, says the LORD, when this place shall no more be called Topheth, or the valley of the son of Hinnom, but the valley of Slaughter. [7]And in this place I will make void the plans of Judah and Jerusalem, and will make them fall by the sword before their enemies, and by the hand of those who seek their life. I will give their dead bodies for food to the birds of the air and to the wild animals of the earth. [8]And I will make this city a horror, a thing to be hissed at; everyone who passes by it will be horrified and will hiss because of all its disasters. [9]And I will make them eat the flesh of their sons and the flesh of their daughters, and all shall eat the flesh of their neighbors in the siege, and in the distress with which their enemies and those who seek their life afflict them.

10 Then you shall break the jug in the sight of those who go with you, [11]and shall say to them: Thus says the LORD of hosts: So will I break this people and this city, as one breaks a potter's vessel, so that it can never be mended. In Topheth they shall bury until there is no more room to bury. [12]Thus will I do to this place, says the LORD, and to its inhabitants, making this city like Topheth. [13]And the houses of Jerusalem and the houses of the kings of Judah shall be defiled like the place of Topheth—all the houses upon whose roofs offerings have been made to the whole host of heaven, and libations have been poured out to other gods.

14 When Jeremiah came from Topheth, where the LORD had sent him to prophesy, he stood in the court of the LORD's house and said to all the people: [15]Thus says the LORD of hosts, the God of Israel: I am now bringing upon this city and upon all its towns all the disaster that I have pronounced against it, because they have stiffened their necks, refusing to hear my words.

Jeremiah Persecuted by Pashhur

20 Now the priest Pashhur son of Immer, who was chief officer in the house of the LORD, heard Jeremiah prophesying these things. [2]Then Pashhur struck the prophet Jeremiah, and put him in the stocks that were in the upper Benjamin Gate of the house of the LORD. [3]The next morning when Pashhur released Jeremiah from the stocks, Jeremiah said to him, The LORD has named you not Pashhur but "Terror-all-around." [4]For thus says the LORD: I am making you a terror to yourself and to all your friends; and they shall fall by the sword of their enemies while you look on. And I will give all Judah into the hand of the king of Babylon; he shall carry them captive to Babylon, and shall kill them with the sword. [5]I will give all the wealth of this city, all its gains, all its prized belongings, and all the treasures of the kings of Judah into the hand of their enemies, who shall plunder them, and seize

---

note on 7.31. Eating children happened in times of famine and siege when food supplies ran out (2 Kings 6.24–31; Lam 4.10). **19.9** Eating the flesh of one's children was a curse for disobedience to the law and covenant (Lev 26.29; Deut 28.53; Isa 9.20; 49.26; Zech 11.9). **19.10–13** The breaking of a vessel of pottery is a common symbol of destruction (see Ps 2.9). The most common example is Egyptian execration texts. The names of the king's enemies were inscribed on pottery vessels, curses were uttered, and the pottery was smashed. This ritual was designed to break the power of the king's enemies magically and to defeat them.
20.1–6 Pashhur's public persecution of Jeremiah. This prose narrative identifies one of Jeremiah's enemies and is an example of the persecution about which the prophet complains in his laments. **20.1** *Pashhur*, a priest in charge of the temple police, who were to maintain order in the sacred precinct. **20.2** Pashhur took Jeremiah into custody, beat him, and put him in stocks for a day. **20.3–6** Jeremiah's judgment oracle against Judah, Jerusalem, and Pashhur. **20.3** The act of naming and the meaning of names were important. Names at times embodied the character, faith, or fate of a person. Jacob in Hebrew means "supplanter," for he supplanted his older twin brother in obtaining the birthright from Isaac (see Gen 25.24–34). Jacob's name is later changed to Israel when he is blessed by God (see Gen 32.27–29). "Israel" means "he who strives with God" in Hebrew. Jeremiah's changing of Pashhur's name to *Terror-all-around* (see 6.25; 20.10) points to the coming siege of Jerusalem and exile, a fate that Pashhur and his family will share (see the prophecy against Hananiah in ch. 28; and the prophecy of Amos against Amaziah, priest of Bethel, in Am

them, and carry them to Babylon. 6And you, Pashhur, and all who live in your house, shall go into captivity, and to Babylon you shall go; there you shall die, and there you shall be buried, you and all your friends, to whom you have prophesied falsely.

Jeremiah Denounces His Persecutors

7 O LORD, you have enticed me,
     and I was enticed;
   you have overpowered me,
     and you have prevailed.
   I have become a laughingstock all day
       long;
     everyone mocks me.
8 For whenever I speak, I must cry out,
     I must shout, "Violence and
       destruction!"
   For the word of the LORD has become for
       me
     a reproach and derision all day long.
9 If I say, "I will not mention him,
     or speak any more in his name,"
   then within me there is something like a
       burning fire
     shut up in my bones;
   I am weary with holding it in,
     and I cannot.
10 For I hear many whispering:
     "Terror is all around!
   Denounce him! Let us denounce him!"
     All my close friends
     are watching for me to stumble.
   "Perhaps he can be enticed,

and we can prevail against him,
     and take our revenge on him."
11 But the LORD is with me like a dread
       warrior;
     therefore my persecutors will stumble,
     and they will not prevail.
   They will be greatly shamed,
     for they will not succeed.
   Their eternal dishonor
     will never be forgotten.
12 O LORD of hosts, you test the righteous,
     you see the heart and the mind;
   let me see your retribution upon them,
     for to you I have committed my cause.

13 Sing to the LORD;
     praise the LORD!
   For he has delivered the life of the needy
     from the hands of evildoers.

14 Cursed be the day
     on which I was born!
   The day when my mother bore me,
     let it not be blessed!
15 Cursed be the man
     who brought the news to my father,
       saying,
   "A child is born to you, a son,"
     making him very glad.
16 Let that man be like the cities
     that the LORD overthrew without pity;
   let him hear a cry in the morning
     and an alarm at noon,
17 because he did not kill me in the womb;

7.10–17). **20.7–12** Jeremiah's sixth lament (see note on 11.18–23). A thanksgiving, presumably sung by the prophet, follows in v. 13. The complaint is the most blasphemous in the Bible. **20.7–8** *Enticed,* which occurs twice in the first line, has two important meanings: "to deceive" and "to seduce." The first may express God's deception of a prophet (see the case of Micaiah ben Imlah in 1 Kings 22.19–22). The second, used for the seduction of a virgin in Ex 22.16–17, is metaphorically applied to God's "seducing" Israel (Hos 2.14). A wife may "seduce" (i.e., deceive) her husband by her beauty and cunning (Judg 14.15; 16.5). *Overpowered* may suggest rape (see 2 Sam 13.14). In Deut 22.25–27, the law requires that a man who "overpowers" a betrothed virgin in the open countryside be put to death. The woman is spared, for when she "cries out" (see Jer 20.8) there is no one to rescue her. Thus, Jeremiah uses very harsh language, the language of rape, to describe his treatment by God. God has seduced and then raped him. When he cries out "*Violence and destruction,*" there is no one to hear and to save. Jeremiah's enemies, called his *close friends,* use

the same language of seduction and rape in their plans to take revenge against him (v. 10). **20.13** A fragment of a thanksgiving psalm, which, if delivered by Jeremiah, expresses his joy and thanks for God's merciful acts of delivering the *needy* from the *evildoers.* Thanksgiving psalms are uttered either after salvation has come or in sure anticipation of its occurrence. They usually are in response to laments (see note on 11.18–20.18). **20.14–18** Jeremiah's seventh and last lament. Jeremiah curses his own existence, i.e., the day of his birth (see Job 3). For other curses, see 11.1–17; 17.5–8. **20.14–15** Curses, power-filled language designed to bring death and destruction, were opposed to blessings, which were to enhance life and well-being. God is the creator who brings about conception, shapes the fetus in the womb, is the midwife who delivers the baby, and nurtures the newborn throughout life (see note on 1.5). Jeremiah's curse against his birth (15.10) is also a rejection of his call (1.5). *A child . . . glad.* The birth of a son was considered good news and a reason for rejoicing (see Ruth 4.13–17; Prov 4.3; Isa 9.6). **20.16** *Cities,* Sodom and Gomorrah (Gen 19; see Isa

so my mother would have been my
    grave,
and her womb forever great.
18 Why did I come forth from the womb
    to see toil and sorrow,
    and spend my days in shame?

Jerusalem Will Fall to Nebuchadrezzar

21 This is the word that came to Jeremiah from the LORD, when King Zedekiah sent to him Pashhur son of Malchiah and the priest Zephaniah son of Maaseiah, saying, 2 "Please inquire of the LORD on our behalf, for King Nebuchadrezzar of Babylon is making war against us; perhaps the LORD will perform a wonderful deed for us, as he has often done, and will make him withdraw from us."

3 Then Jeremiah said to them: 4 Thus you shall say to Zedekiah: Thus says the LORD, the God of Israel: I am going to turn back the weapons of war that are in your hands and with which you are fighting against the king of Babylon and against the Chaldeans who are besieging you outside the walls; and I will bring them together into the center of this city. 5 I myself will fight against you with outstretched hand and mighty arm, in anger, in fury, and in great wrath. 6 And I will strike down the inhabitants of this city, both human beings and animals; they shall die of a great pestilence. 7 Afterward, says the LORD, I will give King Zedekiah of Judah, and his servants, and the people in this city—those who survive the pestilence, sword, and famine—into the hands of King Nebuchadrezzar of Babylon, into the hands of their enemies, into the hands of those who seek their lives. He shall strike them down with the edge of the sword; he shall not pity them, or spare them, or have compassion.

8 And to this people you shall say: Thus says the LORD: See, I am setting before you the way

---

1.9–10; 3.9; Jer 23.14; Am 4.11; Zeph 2.9). **20.17** The prophet wishes he had been aborted.

21.1–10 Oracle against Zedekiah and Jerusalem. The setting given to the narrative appears to be 588 BCE, after Zedekiah had rebelled against Babylonian rule. The narrative consists of two parts: an oracle against Jerusalem and Zedekiah (vv. 1–7) and a conditional offer of salvation only to those who surrender (vv. 8–10). The narrative is similar to another one that tells of two other emissaries sent to the prophet by Zedekiah, perhaps a short time after this occasion (37.3–10). Also cf. 34.1–7, which contains another warning to Zedekiah. **21.1** *Zedekiah* reigned 597–587/6 BCE. A son of Josiah and a descendant of David, Zedekiah was placed on the throne by Nebuchadrezzar (605/4–562) after his first conquest of Jerusalem in 597. Against Jeremiah's repeated warnings, Zedekiah rebelled against the Babylonians, leading to the destruction of Jerusalem and the second exile in 587. Zedekiah was blinded by Nebuchadrezzar and taken to Babylon (2 Kings 24.18–25.7). *Pashhur*, the son of *Malchiah*, a prince who owned the cistern in which Jeremiah was imprisoned (38.6). *Malchiah* may have been a son of Zedekiah. Not to be confused with the priest of the same name in 20.1–6, this Pashhur was a royal prince under Zedekiah (see 38.1). One of his descendants served as a priest during the time of Nehemiah (1 Chr 9.12; Neh 11.12). *Zephaniah*, a priest, was the overseer of the temple who had been rebuked by Shemaiah, a Jewish prophet in Babylonia, for not opposing Jeremiah's prophecy to the first exiles in 597 BCE that the exile would be a long one. Shemaiah insisted Jeremiah be imprisoned. Refusing to imprison the prophet, Zephaniah simply read the letter to Jeremiah, who in turn issued an oracle of judgment against Shemaiah and his descendants (see ch. 29).

Zephaniah was executed by Nebuchadrezzar at Riblah after the fall of Jerusalem in 587. **21.2** *Inquire of the LORD*, consult the Lord through a prophet (10.21; 37.2). *A wonderful deed*, one of God's mighty acts, especially deeds of judgment and redemption, in the realm of history (Ex 3.20; Pss 9.1; 26.7; 86.10). The "mighty deeds" celebrated in Jewish faith were the exodus from Egypt, victory at the Red Sea, guidance in the Sinai wilderness, and the taking of the land of Canaan. Zedekiah is hoping for a similar act of deliverance in the face of the Babylonian invasion and siege. *Nebuchadrezzar* (Akkadian *Nabu-kudurri-utzur*) means both "May Nabu [a Babylonian deity] protect the boundary" and "May Nabu protect the offspring." A variant spelling, Nebuchadnezzar, occurs elsewhere in the OT. See, e.g., 27.6, 8, 20; 28.11; 29.3; 2 Kings 24.10–11; 25.1, 8; Dan 1.1, 18; 2.1, 28; 3.1; 4.1; 5.1. **21.3–7** The Lord will not protect the city as was expected in traditional Jewish faith (Pss 46; 48; 76; Isa 31.4–5). Instead, God will fight against Jerusalem and bring victory to the Babylonians (here and elsewhere in the OT also called *Chaldeans*). This is a reversal of "holy war" theology, in which God fights on Israel's behalf (see the holy-war campaigns in Josh 1–12). Equally devastating is the news that the Lord will not defend the king who is a son of David. Royal theology is based on a covenant between God and David (2 Sam 7; Ps 89). Because of a divine promise and steadfast love (Hebrew *chesed*), God would support forever the royal line, even though there would be descendants of David evil enough to be punished. The king, who ruled on behalf of God, would receive divine aid against his enemies as long as he was faithful (see the royal psalms: Pss 2; 18; 20; 21; 45; 72; 89; 110). **21.8–10** This speech addresses the people of Jerusalem, not the king. The oracle of conditional salvation follows a

of life and the way of death. ⁹Those who stay in this city shall die by the sword, by famine, and by pestilence; but those who go out and surrender to the Chaldeans who are besieging you shall live and shall have their lives as a prize of war. ¹⁰For I have set my face against this city for evil and not for good, says the LORD: it shall be given into the hands of the king of Babylon, and he shall burn it with fire.

Message to the House of David

11 To the house of the king of Judah say: Hear the word of the LORD, ¹²O house of David! Thus says the LORD:

Execute justice in the morning,
  and deliver from the hand of the
    oppressor
anyone who has been robbed,
or else my wrath will go forth like fire,
  and burn, with no one to quench it,
  because of your evil doings.

13 See, I am against you, O inhabitant of the
    valley,
  O rock of the plain,
                                    says the LORD;
  you who say, "Who can come down
    against us,

---

covenantal formula found elsewhere only in Deut 30.15, 19: *I am setting before you the way of life and the way of death*. This "either-or" formula, which asks the audience to choose life or death by obedience to or rejection of the covenant requirements, occurs in the prose narratives and sermons in Jeremiah 7.1–15; 17.19–27; 22.1–5 (see Deut 28; 30.15–20; Josh 24). Jeremiah believed that the Babylonians were the instrument of God's will. To resist them was to resist God. Thus, the prophet consistently warned both leaders and people to bow the knee to Nebuchadrezzar or face disastrous consequences (27.6; 38.17–18). As a result of his position on the Babylonian question Jeremiah was considered a traitor by some leaders (see 37.13–14).

21.11–23.8 Concerning the house of David. This collection consists of poetic oracles and prose sermons that address the related themes of Davidic kingship ("the house of David") and Jerusalem (the political capital and religious center of the kingdom of Judah). The key expressions are *house* (dynasty and palace) and (*cedars of*) *Lebanon* (representing the city of Jerusalem, palace, and temple). The collection consists of general speeches addressed to the house of David, oracles concerning specific kings, oracles mentioning future rulers and a messiah, and others that speak of Jerusalem. The references to Lebanon recall that cedars of Lebanon were used in the construction of the palace and temple (1 Kings 5–7; 9.10–28). The general oracles addressed to the house of David are 21.11–12 (poetry); 22.1–5 (prose); 22.6–7 (poetry). The poetic oracles concerning individual kings are 22.10 (Jehoahaz, or Shallum); 22.13–19 (Jehoiakim); 22.28–30 (Jehoiachin, or Coniah). The prose sermons about specific kings are 22.11–12 (Jehoahaz); 22.24–27 (Jehoiachin). Curiously, two kings who are not the direct subject of an oracle are Josiah (indirectly mentioned in 22.15–16) and Zedekiah (an allusion to him may occur in wordplays on *righteous Branch* and *The LORD is our righteousness* in 23.5–6). 23.1–8 contains prose sermons about the future, including the promise of *shepherds* (i.e., kings; see note on 3.15) who will rule faithfully in contrast to their evil predecessors, and a messianic oracle about a *righteous Branch*, who will

rule according to wisdom and justice. Finally, several speeches deal with Jerusalem (*this city, Lebanon*): 21.13–14 (poetry); 22.8–9 (prose); 22.20–23 (poetry). The strong criticism of kings and the city of Jerusalem (the location of palace and temple) indicate that Jeremiah blamed the Jerusalem establishment (kings, princes [officers], prophets, and priests) for the violation of the Mosaic covenant, including especially religious and political apostasy. Although Jeremiah may not have been opposed in principle to the existence of the related institutions of palace and temple, they did not have an important place in his theological understanding of the relationship between God, Israel and Judah, and the pagan nations. Later prose sermons attributed to the prophet point to the reestablishment of kingship and temple in Jerusalem and their importance to the future restoration (23.1–8; 30.9; 33.14–26), but whether they accurately reflect Jeremiah's own view is questionable. **21.11–14** General oracles against the house of David and Jerusalem. Two poetic oracles introduce the collection: a warning for kings to rule justly (vv. 11–12) and a judgment against Jerusalem (vv. 13–14). **21.11–12** This warning to the monarchy takes the form of an admonition in apodictic (unconditional) style (see Isa 1.16–17; 56.1; Ezek 45.9; Am 5.4b, 14–15). *Execute* (or "act with") *justice* recurs in 22.3, 15; 23.5. For Jeremiah, destruction is avoided only by the practice of justice, not by an unconditional promise to preserve the monarchy forever (cf. 2 Sam 7.11–16; Ps 89). Although ruling descendants of David would be punished for evil acts and injustice, the Lord's covenant with the house of David, outlined in 2 Sam 7; Ps 89, promises an eternal reign for the dynasty. To *execute justice* involves more than simply a judicial responsibility. To rule justly means that the king maintains the cosmic and social order and produces well-being for the nation (see Ps 72). **21.13–14** This introductory oracle includes a threat in v. 13 (see 23.30–32; 50.31; 51.25) and judgment in v. 14. *Inhabitant of the valley*, better "one enthroned over the valley," Jerusalem. *Inhabitant* in Hebrew is a feminine participle, thus agreeing with the Hebrew word for "city," which is also feminine. *Rock of the plain* is not an appellation for Jerusalem elsewhere in the Bible, but

or who can enter our places of refuge?"
14 I will punish you according to the fruit of
        your doings,
                              says the LORD;
I will kindle a fire in its forest,
and it shall devour all that is around it.

Exhortation to Repent

22 Thus says the LORD: Go down to the
house of the king of Judah, and speak
there this word, 2and say: Hear the word of the
LORD, O King of Judah sitting on the throne of
David—you, and your servants, and your people who enter these gates. 3Thus says the LORD:
Act with justice and righteousness, and deliver
from the hand of the oppressor anyone who has
been robbed. And do no wrong or violence to
the alien, the orphan, and the widow, or shed innocent blood in this place. 4For if you will indeed obey this word, then through the gates of
this house shall enter kings who sit on the
throne of David, riding in chariots and on
horses, they, and their servants, and their people. 5But if you will not heed these words, I
swear by myself, says the LORD, that this house

shall become a desolation. 6For thus says the
LORD concerning the house of the king of Judah:
    You are like Gilead to me,
        like the summit of Lebanon;
    but I swear that I will make you a desert,
        an uninhabited city.*a*
7   I will prepare destroyers against you,
        all with their weapons;
    they shall cut down your choicest cedars
        and cast them into the fire.

8 And many nations will pass by this city,
and all of them will say one to another, "Why
has the LORD dealt in this way with that great
city?" 9And they will answer, "Because they
abandoned the covenant of the LORD their
God, and worshiped other gods and served
them."

10 Do not weep for him who is dead,
        nor bemoan him;
    weep rather for him who goes away,
        for he shall return no more
        to see his native land.

_____
a Cn: Heb *uninhabited cities*

"rock" is a common metaphor for God, occurring
some thirty-three times (see Deut 32; Isa 17.10; Pss
31.3; 62.7; 71.3). The reference may be a parody of
Zion theology, i.e., the belief that God will defend the
city against its enemies (Pss 46; 48; 76; Isa 31.4–5).
Forest (of Lebanon), the palace (see 1 Kings 7.2–12;
10.17, 21; Isa 22.8) and possibly the temple as well
(1 Kings 6.9–36), since both were built from the cedars
of Lebanon. Thus the fire will burn down the city and
its two major buildings, the palace and the temple.
22.1–5 An exhortation to kings. This prose sermon,
deriving from the exile or later, is an elaboration of the
poetic oracle in 21.11–12. It is also in the conditional
"either-or" style: obey the covenant by ruling justly
and the monarchy will continue; disobey and suffer
the end of the dynasty. The sermon seeks to provide
the reason for the destruction of the palace and the
ending of monarchical succession. **22.1** Jeremiah is to
go down to the house of the king of Judah, i.e., descend
from the temple to the palace. **22.3** *Alien, orphan,
widow.* See Deut 16.11, 14; 24.19–21; note on 7.6.
22.5 *I swear by myself.* Oaths in the Hebrew Bible generally invoked the name of God for validation. They
were serious expressions of obligation and were expected to be kept (Lev 5.1–4; Ps 15.4). Oaths were accompanied by symbolic acts, most often the raising of
the hand toward heaven (Dan 12.7; Rev 10.5–6). Even
God raises the hand in oath-taking (Isa 62.8; Ezek
20.5). Curses, expressed or implied, often accompanied oaths (Ruth 1.17; 1 Sam 3.17; 1 Kings 2.23). Here
the curse is replaced with a stern warning: *this house*
(palace) *shall become a desolation. Desolation* often

refers to the ruins of cities ravaged by disaster (25.18;
27.17; 44.2, 6; Lev 26.31; Isa 44.26). **22.6–7** Judgment
against the palace. This poetic oracle of judgment contains language that connects it to 21.13–14 (*cedars* and
fire, 22.7; *fire in its forest,* 21.14). **22.6** The introduction
addresses the oracle to the *house of the king of Judah*
(i.e., the monarchy or the palace). *Gilead,* a region in
the Transjordan located between Bashan and Moab. It
was a mountainous and heavily forested area. *Summit
of Lebanon,* a mountainous area also noted for its
forests. Both are mentioned because of their forests.
The palace of Solomon was designated as a forest, because it was constructed of cedars from Lebanon
(1 Kings 7.1–12; see note on 21.13–14). *Uninhabited
city,* lit. "uninhabited cities," a hyperbole indicating the
terrible destruction that is facing the palace. **22.8–
9** An explanation of Jerusalem's destruction. Originating in the exile, this prose commentary in the form of a
question and answer explains why Jerusalem and the
palace were destroyed. The answer is the violation of
the Mosaic covenant and the worship of other gods
(see 5.19; 9.12–16; 13.12–14; 15.1–4; 16.10–13; Deut
29.22–28; 1 Kings 9.8–9). **22.10–12** Concerning Jehoahaz (Shallum). A fragment of a poetic oracle concerning two unidentified males (one dead and the
other in exile) is followed by a prose sermon naming
the exiled male as Shallum (Jehoahaz). **22.10** An admonition to the citizens of Judah and Jerusalem not to
engage in lamentation over King Josiah, who died at
the hands of the Egyptians at Megiddo in 609 BCE, thus
bringing to an end the nationalistic dream of a Jewish
state free from foreign domination. Rather, the people

Message to the Sons of Josiah

11 For thus says the LORD concerning Shallum son of King Josiah of Judah, who succeeded his father Josiah, and who went away from this place: He shall return here no more, 12but in the place where they have carried him captive he shall die, and he shall never see this land again.

13 Woe to him who builds his house by
        unrighteousness,
    and his upper rooms by injustice;
    who makes his neighbors work for
        nothing,
    and does not give them their wages;
14 who says, "I will build myself a spacious
        house
    with large upper rooms,"
    and who cuts out windows for it,
        paneling it with cedar,
        and painting it with vermilion.
15 Are you a king
    because you compete in cedar?
    Did not your father eat and drink

    and do justice and righteousness?
    Then it was well with him.
16 He judged the cause of the poor and
        needy;
    then it was well.
    Is not this to know me?
    says the LORD.
17 But your eyes and heart
    are only on your dishonest gain,
    for shedding innocent blood,
    and for practicing oppression and
        violence.

18 Therefore thus says the LORD concerning King Jehoiakim son of Josiah of Judah:
    They shall not lament for him, saying,
        "Alas, my brother!" or "Alas, sister!"
    They shall not lament for him, saying,
        "Alas, lord!" or "Alas, his majesty!"
19 With the burial of a donkey he shall be
        buried—
    dragged off and thrown out beyond
        the gates of Jerusalem.

20 Go up to Lebanon, and cry out,
    and lift up your voice in Bashan;

---

should lament the exile of Jehoahaz (609), who was chosen by the "people of the land" (male landowners, 2 Kings 23.30) to succeed his father, Josiah, to the throne. After only three months Neco replaced him with another son of Josiah, Jehoiakim (2 Kings 23.34). **22.11–12** A prose commentary, deriving from the exile or later, explaining that the person in v. 10 who is exiled is *Shallum* (see Ezek 19.2–4). "Shallum" is the personal name (see 1 Chr 3.15) of the king whose royal name, given to him upon ascending the throne, is Jehoahaz. Jehoahaz died in Egyptian exile (2 Kings 23.34). **22.13–19** Against King Jehoiakim. Jehoiakim (throne name; Eliakim, birth name; 2 Kings 23.34; 609–598 BCE), a son of Josiah and descendant of David, was put on the throne by Neco II (see Introduction) to replace his younger brother, Jehoahaz. Thus, Jehoiakim ruled without a contract with the male landowners ("the people of the land") and with no evidence of prophetic or priestly anointing. After Nebuchadrezzar defeated the Egyptians at Carchemish in 605, Jehoiakim became a Babylonian vassal. After three years Jehoiakim rebelled against the Babylonians, resulting in his death during the siege of Jerusalem. The city surrendered to Nebuchadrezzar in 597 (see 2 Kings 23.34–24.7). The speech against Jehoiakim is a poetic judgment oracle. The indictment (vv. 13–17) includes using compulsory, uncompensated labor to build a luxurious palace and practicing injustice. The announcement of judgment (vv. 18–19) speaks of the eventual demise of Jehoiakim, who will neither be lamented nor buried with royal honors. **22.13–14** *Woe,* a cry that derives from funeral lamen-

tation (see the repetition of the word in v. 18, where it is translated "alas"). It announces the "funeral" of the one or ones addressed and was commonly used by prophets in introducing judgment oracles (see Isa 10.5; 17.12; 28.1; Am 5.18; 6.1; Hab 2.6, 9, 12, 15, 19; Zech 11.17). *Unrighteousness* and *injustice.* See 21.12; 22.3–4. *House,* probably the palace, a project of renovation and expansion. Compulsory labor, without remuneration, was used by Solomon in building the temple, palace, and other projects (see 1 Kings 5.13–18; 9.15–22). *Paneling it with cedar* calls to mind Solomon's palace (1 Kings 7.7). *Vermilion,* red ocher (hematite). **22.15–17** The just reign of Josiah contrasted with the oppressive rule of his son Jehoiakim. The language throughout this speech indicates that Jehoiakim attempted to rule in the manner and style of his famous ancestor Solomon instead of imitating the good and just king Josiah. *Shedding innocent blood,* one of the twelve curses associated with violating the Mosaic covenant (Deut 27.25). **22.18** For Jehoiakim there will be no public ritual of lamentation, in which mourners weep over the deceased. *Brother, sister, lord* (father), and *majesty* indicate that the king symbolically fulfilled various family roles on behalf of his people. **22.19** *Burial of a donkey.* Jehoiakim's carcass will be dragged out of the city and dumped in the open to rot and provide food for scavengers (see 36.30). The denial of burial was a horrible curse (see 8.1–3; Deut 28.26). 2 Kings 24.6 simply mentions the death of Jehoiakim, while 2 Chr 36.6 indicates that he was put in fetters by Nebuchadrezzar to be taken to Babylon. Neither mentions his burial. **22.20–23** This poetic judg-

cry out from Abarim,
    for all your lovers are crushed.
21 I spoke to you in your prosperity,
    but you said, "I will not listen."
This has been your way from your youth,
    for you have not obeyed my voice.
22 The wind shall shepherd all your
    shepherds,
    and your lovers shall go into captivity;
then you will be ashamed and dismayed
    because of all your wickedness.
23 O inhabitant of Lebanon,
    nested among the cedars,
how you will groan[a] when pangs come
      upon you,
    pain as of a woman in labor!

Judgment on Coniah (Jehoiachin)

24 As I live, says the LORD, even if King Coniah son of Jehoiakim of Judah were the signet ring on my right hand, even from there I would tear you off 25 and give you into the hands of those who seek your life, into the hands of those of whom you are afraid, even into the hands of King Nebuchadrezzar of Babylon and into the hands of the Chaldeans. 26 I will hurl you and the mother who bore you into another country, where you were not born, and there you shall die. 27 But they shall not return to the land to which they long to return.
28 Is this man Coniah a despised broken
      pot,
    a vessel no one wants?
Why are he and his offspring hurled out
    and cast away in a land that they do
      not know?
29 O land, land, land,
    hear the word of the LORD!
30 Thus says the LORD:
Record this man as childless,
    a man who shall not succeed in his
      days;
for none of his offspring shall succeed
    in sitting on the throne of David,
    and ruling again in Judah.

Restoration after Exile

23 Woe to the shepherds who destroy and scatter the sheep of my pasture! says the LORD. 2 Therefore thus says the LORD, the God of Israel, concerning the shepherds who shepherd my people: It is you who have scattered

***

a Gk Vg Syr: Heb *will be pitied*

***

ment oracle calls upon the city of Jerusalem, personified as an adulterous woman, to lament over her approaching humiliation (see 4.8; 9.17–22; 14.1–10). **22.20** *Lebanon, Bashan, Abarim,* mountainous locations (north, northeast, and southeast of Israel) from which Jerusalem is to wail over her fate (see Jephthah's daughter in Judg 11.37–38; Rachel in Jer 31.15). *Lovers,* either false deities (Hos 2) or allies (Ezek 23.5, 9) who promised Jerusalem protection. See also 30.14. **22.21** *Your youth.* See 2.2; Ezek 16.22, 43, 60; Hos 2.17. **22.22** *Shepherds.* See note on 3.15. **22.23** *Inhabitant of Lebanon,* lit. "one enthroned in Lebanon," here the city of Jerusalem (see note on 21.13–14). **22.24–30** Jehoiachin, the throne name of *Coniah,* the king who succeeded Jehoiakim to the throne in the final days of the Babylonian siege of Jerusalem. Jehoiachin ruled for only three months before the city fell (598/7 BCE). Deported to Babylon along with the people of Jerusalem, including his royal family and important leaders (2 Kings 24.6–17), Jehoiachin died in exile. However, 2 Kings ends with the hopeful report that in the thirty-seventh year of Jehoiachin's exile (560), he was released from prison by the Babylonian king Evil-merodach, given a place of honor above the other exiled kings, and provided with both food from the king's table and a regular allowance. This passage consists of a prose judgment speech that includes a divine oath (vv. 24–27) and a poetic judgment speech (vv. 28–30). The two speeches are directed against the popular hope of the return of Jehoiachin and his children from exile to rule over Judah (28.4). A pro-Jehoiachin political party looked to the exiled king as the legitimate ruler, and not his uncle, Zedekiah, placed on the throne by Nebuchadrezzar. The Babylonian Jewish community calculated their calendar by reference to the exile of Jehoiachin (e.g., Ezek 1.2). Babylonian texts call Jehoiachin "King of Judah" and indicate that he received a pension from Nebuchadrezzar. Inscriptions on jar handles from the period indicate that royal property belonged to Jehoiachin. Contrary to this popular view, Jeremiah's argument was that Jehoiachin's legal right to kingship expired with his exile. Indeed, Jeremiah predicted that the exiled king would never return home. **22.24–27** A prose judgment speech, deriving from the exile, announcing that Jehoiachin and his mother, the queen (see note on 13.18), will not return from exile. *As I live* introduces an oath (see notes on 4.2; 22.5). *Signet ring* points to the authority of the king as God's representative, since the bearer of the king's seal has the authority to stamp documents with the royal signature (see Hag 2.20–23, where Zerubbabel, a Davidic descendant, is likened to the Lord's signet ring). **22.28–30** A judgment speech dispelling any hope that Jehoiachin will rule again in Judah. The same is true of his offspring. It is as though Jehoiachin were childless (actually he had seven sons; 1 Chr 3.17–18). **23.1–8** Three prose sermons about the future: return from exile and faithful rulers (vv. 1–4), the *righteous Branch* (vv. 5–6), and return from the north

my flock, and have driven them away, and you have not attended to them. So I will attend to you for your evil doings, says the LORD. ³Then I myself will gather the remnant of my flock out of all the lands where I have driven them, and I will bring them back to their fold, and they shall be fruitful and multiply. ⁴I will raise up shepherds over them who will shepherd them, and they shall not fear any longer, or be dismayed, nor shall any be missing, says the LORD.

The Righteous Branch of David

5 The days are surely coming, says the LORD, when I will raise up for David a righteous Branch, and he shall reign as king and deal wisely, and shall execute justice and righteousness in the land. ⁶In his days Judah will be saved and Israel will live in safety. And this is the name by which he will be called: "The LORD is our righteousness."

7 Therefore, the days are surely coming, says the LORD, when it shall no longer be said, "As the LORD lives who brought the people of Israel up out of the land of Egypt," ⁸but "As the LORD lives who brought out and led the offspring of the house of Israel out of the land of the north and out of all the lands where he*a* had driven them." Then they shall live in their own land.

False Prophets of Hope Denounced

9 Concerning the prophets:
My heart is crushed within me,
    all my bones shake;
I have become like a drunkard,
    like one overcome by wine,
because of the LORD
    and because of his holy words.
10   For the land is full of adulterers;

------

a Gk: Heb *I*

------

country (vv. 7–8). These three sermons may have originated during the exile or shortly thereafter. **23.1–4** Return from exile and faithful rulers. This prose sermon combines a judgment oracle against faithless rulers with a prophecy of salvation that speaks of faithful rulers after the return from captivity. Vv. 1–2 are modeled on the form of a "woe oracle" (see note on 22.13–14). *Shepherds,* kings (see note on 3.15) who are condemned for their evil rule. **23.3** *Be fruitful and multiply.* See the promises to Abraham and Jacob, the two great ancestors of Israel, in Gen 17.1–8, 20; 28.3; 48.4. **23.5–6** *Righteous Branch.* This prose sermon, repeated with modifications in 33.15–16, predicts the coming of a future king who will rule wisely and establish justice (see Isa 11.1–9). *Branch* is a messianic title in Zech 3.8; 6.12 (Isa 11.1 uses a different Hebrew word for "branch"). One of the leaders of the return from exile was Zerubbabel (whose name in Hebrew means "branch/shoot of Babylon"), a descendant of David. Hag 2.20–23 identifies him as the heir to kingship. Here the future ruler will bear the name *The LORD is our righteousness,* perhaps a wordplay on the name Zedekiah, in Hebrew "Yahweh is righteousness." Nebuchadrezzar gave this name to Mattaniah when he was appointed king (2 Kings 24.17). Zedekiah was the last king of Judah (597–587/6 BCE). Hebrew *tsedeq,* "righteousness," also means "legitimate." Although Jeremiah did not oppose Zedekiah, his legitimacy as ruler was questioned by many, even within Judah. The implication may be that the future king will rule in such a way as to demonstrate that "The LORD is our legitimate (ruler)." **23.7–8** Return from the north country. This passage is a prose prediction of salvation that makes use of the oath formula (*as the LORD lives;* see note on 4.2). The exodus from Egypt was central to Israel's ancient faith (see Deut 26.5–9; Josh 24; Pss 78; 105; 106; 135; 136; Neh 9). In the future the return

from captivity in Babylon will replace the ancient creed's emphasis on the exodus. The "new exodus" is a major theme in Second Isaiah (the anonymous prophet of the exile whose oracles are collected in Isa 40–55; see Isa 43.15–21; 51.9–11). **23.9–40** This collection of various materials about prophets divides into a largely poetic section in vv. 9–22 and a prose sermon in vv. 23–40. The poetic section includes: a description of general wickedness that priest and prophet share (vv. 9–12), a judgment oracle against the prophets of Samaria and of Jerusalem (vv. 13–15), a warning in prose not to pay heed to the false prophets (vv. 16–17), rhetorical questions and a vision report about the failure of the false prophets to see the coming judgment of the Lord (vv. 18–20), and a rejection of the false prophets (vv. 21–22). The prose section consists of a sermon stating God's opposition to false prophets (vv. 23–32) and a midrash, an interpretive commentary, on the meaning of *the burden of the LORD* (vv. 33–40). The problems involved in distinguishing between true and false prophets were considerable (see ch. 28; 1 Kings 13; 22). Deut 18.15–22 provides the most detailed attempt: false prophets spoke in the name of false gods, prophesied good fortune instead of judgment, lied in claiming to speak in the name of God, and predicted things that did not come to pass. Jeremiah adds his own tests: false prophets are immoral, speak at times in the name of Baal, see visions and dreams of their own mind, prophesy weal not woe, tell lies, and have not stood in the *council of the LORD* (v. 18). Even so, Jeremiah had a very difficult time convincing others he was a true prophet and that his prophetic opponents were false prophets. **23.9** A lamentation (see note on 11.18–23) that mentions prophetic ecstasy, i.e., the physical and mental state of one who receives a divine revelation (see 4.19–21; 1 Sam 10.1–13; 19.23–24). **23.10** *The land is full.* See

because of the curse the land mourns,
  and the pastures of the wilderness are
    dried up.
Their course has been evil,
  and their might is not right.
11 Both prophet and priest are ungodly;
    even in my house I have found their
      wickedness,
                              says the LORD.
12 Therefore their way shall be to them
    like slippery paths in the darkness,
    into which they shall be driven and
      fall;
for I will bring disaster upon them
  in the year of their punishment,
                              says the LORD.
13 In the prophets of Samaria
    I saw a disgusting thing:
  they prophesied by Baal
    and led my people Israel astray.
14 But in the prophets of Jerusalem
    I have seen a more shocking thing:
  they commit adultery and walk in lies;
    they strengthen the hands of evildoers,
    so that no one turns from wickedness;
  all of them have become like Sodom to
    me,
    and its inhabitants like Gomorrah.
15 Therefore thus says the LORD of hosts
      concerning the prophets:
  "I am going to make them eat
      wormwood,
    and give them poisoned water to drink;
  for from the prophets of Jerusalem
    ungodliness has spread throughout the
      land."

16 Thus says the LORD of hosts: Do not listen to the words of the prophets who prophesy
to you; they are deluding you. They speak visions of their own minds, not from the mouth
of the LORD. 17They keep saying to those who
despise the word of the LORD, "It shall be well
with you"; and to all who stubbornly follow
their own stubborn hearts, they say, "No
calamity shall come upon you."

18 For who has stood in the council of the
    LORD
  so as to see and to hear his word?
  Who has given heed to his word so as
    to proclaim it?
19 Look, the storm of the LORD!
  Wrath has gone forth,
a whirling tempest;
  it will burst upon the head of the
    wicked.
20 The anger of the LORD will not turn back
  until he has executed and
    accomplished
  the intents of his mind.
In the latter days you will understand it
  clearly.

21 I did not send the prophets,
  yet they ran;
I did not speak to them,
  yet they prophesied.
22 But if they had stood in my council,
  then they would have proclaimed my
    words to my people,
  and they would have turned them from
    their evil way,
  and from the evil of their doings.

23 Am I a God near by, says the LORD, and
not a God far off? 24Who can hide in secret
places so that I cannot see them? says the
LORD. Do I not fill heaven and earth? says the
LORD. 25I have heard what the prophets have
said who prophesy lies in my name, saying, "I
have dreamed, I have dreamed!" 26How long?
Will the hearts of the prophets ever turn
back—those who prophesy lies, and who
prophesy the deceit of their own heart? 27They
plan to make my people forget my name by
their dreams that they tell one another, just as
their ancestors forgot my name for Baal. 28Let
the prophet who has a dream tell the dream,
but let the one who has my word speak my
word faithfully. What has straw in common
with wheat? says the LORD. 29Is not my word
like fire, says the LORD, and like a hammer that

Gen 6.13; Lev 19.29. **23.12** *Slippery paths.* See Ps 35.6.
23.13 For a description of Baal prophecy, see 1 Kings
18.25–29. **23.14** *Sodom, Gomorrah* (Gen 18–19). See
Jer 20.16 and note; Isa 1.10. **23.16–17** For an example
of a prophet of good fortune, see Hananiah in ch. 28.
23.18 *The council of the LORD,* an assembly of divine
beings over which God presides (1 Kings 22.19–23;
Job 1–2; Pss 82; 89.7; Isa 6.1–8). In this assembly God
issues divine edicts for governing the cosmos and history. **23.19–20** These verses are almost duplicated in
30.23–24. *Storm of the LORD,* an image taken from
theophanic judgment scenes in which the Lord as warrior comes to execute judgment against the wicked
(25.32; Job 38.1; 40.6; Hab 3). **23.21** Prophets *ran* in
the sense that they were messengers of God. **23.23–
24** God is both immanent and transcendent (see Ps

breaks a rock in pieces? 30See, therefore, I am against the prophets, says the LORD, who steal my words from one another. 31See, I am against the prophets, says the LORD, who use their own tongues and say, "Says the LORD." 32See, I am against those who prophesy lying dreams, says the LORD, and who tell them, and who lead my people astray by their lies and their recklessness, when I did not send them or appoint them; so they do not profit this people at all, says the LORD.

33 When this people, or a prophet, or a priest asks you, "What is the burden of the LORD?" you shall say to them, "You are the burden,*a* and I will cast you off, says the LORD." 34And as for the prophet, priest, or the people who say, "The burden of the LORD," I will punish them and their households. 35Thus shall you say to one another, among yourselves, "What has the LORD answered?" or "What has the LORD spoken?" 36But "the burden of the LORD" you shall mention no more, for the burden is everyone's own word, and so you pervert the words of the living God, the LORD of hosts, our God. 37Thus you shall ask the prophet, "What has the LORD answered you?" or "What has the LORD spoken?" 38But if you say, "the burden of the LORD," thus says the LORD: Because you have said these words, "the burden of the LORD," when I sent to you, saying, You shall not say, "the burden of the LORD," 39therefore, I will surely lift you up*b* and cast you away from my presence, you and the city that I gave to you and your ancestors. 40And I will bring upon you everlasting disgrace and perpetual shame, which shall not be forgotten.

The Good and the Bad Figs

24 The LORD showed me two baskets of figs placed before the temple of the LORD. This was after King Nebuchadrezzar of Babylon had taken into exile from Jerusalem King Jeconiah son of Jehoiakim of Judah, together with the officials of Judah, the artisans, and the smiths, and had brought them to Babylon. 2One basket had very good figs, like first-ripe figs, but the other basket had very bad figs, so bad that they could not be eaten. 3And the LORD said to me, "What do you see, Jeremiah?" I said, "Figs, the good figs very good, and the bad figs very bad, so bad that they cannot be eaten."

4 Then the word of the LORD came to me: 5Thus says the LORD, the God of Israel: Like these good figs, so I will regard as good the exiles from Judah, whom I have sent away from this place to the land of the Chaldeans. 6I will set my eyes upon them for good, and I will bring them back to this land. I will build them up, and not tear them down; I will plant them, and not pluck them up. 7I will give them a heart to know that I am the LORD; and they shall be my people and I will be their God, for they shall return to me with their whole heart.

---

a Gk Vg: Heb *What burden*   *b* Heb Mss Gk Vg: MT *forget you*

139.7–12; Am 9.1–4). **23.30–32** Note the threefold occurrence of *I am against,* a challenge formula issued to opponents (see 21.13). **23.33** This verse, in a question and answer form (5.19; 9.12–16; 13.12–14; 15.1–4; 16.10–13; 22.8–9), identifies the people, priests, and prophets as the *burden of the LORD.* Hebrew *massa',* "burden," also means "oracle" (see Nah 1.1; Hab 1.1; Mal 1.1). Hence the verse involves a wordplay: when Jeremiah is asked for an oracle from God, he is to respond: "You are the 'burden' of the LORD." **23.34–40** A later pointed commentary, or midrash, that prohibits the use of the term *burden* for a revelation from God.

24.1–10 This prose narrative contains a prophetic vision report (see 1.11–14, 15–16; Am 7.1–9.10). See note on 1.11–14. The formal structure includes an introduction (*The LORD showed me,* v. 1), a description (v. 2), a dialogue (v. 3), and an interpretation (vv. 4–10). Although written during the exile, the narrative is situated in the period after the first exiles were taken to Babylonia in 597 BCE. Its purpose is to stress that the first exiles (the *good figs*) were the chosen remnant whom God would use to build a new future once the return to the Jewish homeland occurred. Chief among

these, of course, was the exiled king, Jehoiachin. By contrast the *bad* (rotten) *figs* were those who remained behind in Jerusalem, including Zedekiah and his officials, and those who were in Egypt (Jehoahaz and his entourage). In view of the earlier speech about Jehoiachin (22.24–30), it seems unlikely the present narrative reflects the view of Jeremiah. Rather, the story appears to be a piece of religious propaganda designed to enhance the importance of the first exiles in 597 BCE, including Jehoiachin and his officials, in rebuilding the future (see 28.3–4; 2 Kings 25.27–30). This view of divine favor for the first exiles rather than for the remnant left behind in Judah is found in the book of Ezekiel and became especially pronounced in the time of Ezra and Nehemiah in the fifth–fourth centuries BCE. **24.1** *Two baskets of figs.* See 29.17; Hos 9.10. *Jeconiah,* an alternate spelling for Jehoiachin. **24.6** *Build, tear down, plant, pluck up.* See note on 1.10. **24.7** *I will give them a heart to know.* See 31.33–34; 32.39; Deut 29.4. *They shall be my people and I will be their God,* a covenant formula for the sealing of the relationship between God and Israel (see 7.23; 11.4; 30.22; 31.1, 33; 32.38). *Return.* See note on 3.1–4.4. This text anticipates the new covenant

8 But thus says the LORD: Like the bad figs that are so bad they cannot be eaten, so will I treat King Zedekiah of Judah, his officials, the remnant of Jerusalem who remain in this land, and those who live in the land of Egypt. 9I will make them a horror, an evil thing, to all the kingdoms of the earth—a disgrace, a byword, a taunt, and a curse in all the places where I shall drive them. 10And I will send sword, famine, and pestilence upon them, until they are utterly destroyed from the land that I gave to them and their ancestors.

The Babylonian Captivity Foretold

25 The word that came to Jeremiah concerning all the people of Judah, in the fourth year of King Jehoiakim son of Josiah of Judah (that was the first year of King Nebuchadrezzar of Babylon), 2which the prophet Jeremiah spoke to all the people of Judah and all the inhabitants of Jerusalem: 3For twenty-three years, from the thirteenth year of King Josiah son of Amon of Judah, to this day, the word of the LORD has come to me, and I have spoken persistently to you, but you have not listened. 4And though the LORD persistently sent you all his servants the prophets, you have neither listened nor inclined your ears to hear 5when they said, "Turn now, every one of you, from your evil way and wicked doings, and you will remain upon the land that the LORD has given to you and your ancestors from of old and forever; 6do not go after other gods to serve and worship them, and do not provoke me to anger with the work of your hands. Then I will do you no harm." 7Yet you did not listen to me, says the

LORD, and so you have provoked me to anger with the work of your hands to your own harm.

8 Therefore thus says the LORD of hosts: Because you have not obeyed my words, 9I am going to send for all the tribes of the north, says the LORD, even for King Nebuchadrezzar of Babylon, my servant, and I will bring them against this land and its inhabitants, and against all these nations around; I will utterly destroy them, and make them an object of horror and of hissing, and an everlasting disgrace.a 10And I will banish from them the sound of mirth and the sound of gladness, the voice of the bridegroom and the voice of the bride, the sound of the millstones and the light of the lamp. 11This whole land shall become a ruin and a waste, and these nations shall serve the king of Babylon seventy years. 12Then after seventy years are completed, I will punish the king of Babylon and that nation, the land of the Chaldeans, for their iniquity, says the LORD, making the land an everlasting waste. 13I will bring upon that land all the words that I have uttered against it, everything written in this book, which Jeremiah prophesied against all the nations. 14For many nations and great kings shall make slaves of them also; and I will repay them according to their deeds and the work of their hands.

The Cup of God's Wrath

15 For thus the LORD, the God of Israel, said to me: Take from my hand this cup of the wine of wrath, and make all the nations to whom I

---

a Gk Compare Syr: Heb and everlasting desolations

---

passage in 31.31–34. **24.9** A disgrace, a byword, a taunt, and a curse. See 19.8; 25.9, 18; 29.18; 42.18; 44.8, 12, 22; Deut 28.37; 1 Kings 9.7; 2 Chr 7.20.

25.1–14 This prose sermon, originating in the exile or later, summarizes the content of Jeremiah's speeches from the beginning of his prophetic activity (627 BCE, the thirteenth year of King Josiah, v. 3) to the battle of Carchemish (605, the fourth year of King Jehoiakim, v. 1); see Introduction. The section divides into a superscription (vv. 1–2) and an appeal for repentance followed by an announcement of judgment (vv. 3–14). In the appeal Judah is called upon to repent or face destruction; in the announcement Judah has not repented and subsequently will be destroyed. **25.1** King Jehoiakim (609–598 BCE). See note on 22.13–19. Nebuchadrezzar (605–562). See Introduction. **25.3** King Josiah (640–609 BCE). Twenty-three years, 627 to 605. Jeremiah's speeches these twenty-three years primarily announce judgment and may

compose the first scroll (ch. 36; see Introduction). **25.4** His servants the prophets. See note on 7.25. The rejection of Jeremiah's message stands in a long tradition of refusing to listen to the Lord's emissaries. **25.5** Turn now. See the summons to repentance in 3.1–4.4; 18.11. **25.9** The first clear indication that the "foe from the north" (tribes of the north) is Babylonia. Nebuchadrezzar . . . my servant (27.6), i.e., the instrument of the divine will (cf. Cyrus in Isa 45.1–7, who is the "anointed" of God). **25.10** See 7.34; 16.9. **25.11** Seventy years is difficult to put into an exact chronology. From 605 to 539 BCE (the conquest of Babylon by Cyrus) is sixty-six years (perhaps rounded to "seventy"). In Zech 1.12 the period of seventy years begins with the destruction of the temple (587) and concludes with its rebuilding (516/5). The number also may represent either the period of a normal life span (Ps 90.10) or the traditional, figurative time for a city to remain in ruins. **25.13** This book, perhaps originally the first or, more likely, the

send you drink it. [16]They shall drink and stagger and go out of their minds because of the sword that I am sending among them.

17 So I took the cup from the LORD's hand, and made all the nations to whom the LORD sent me drink it: [18]Jerusalem and the towns of Judah, its kings and officials, to make them a desolation and a waste, an object of hissing and of cursing, as they are today; [19]Pharaoh king of Egypt, his servants, his officials, and all his people; [20]all the mixed people;[a] all the kings of the land of Uz; all the kings of the land of the Philistines—Ashkelon, Gaza, Ekron, and the remnant of Ashdod; [21]Edom, Moab, and the Ammonites; [22]all the kings of Tyre, all the kings of Sidon, and the kings of the coastland across the sea; [23]Dedan, Tema, Buz, and all who have shaven temples; [24]all the kings of Arabia and all the kings of the mixed peoples[a] that live in the desert; [25]all the kings of Zimri, all the kings of Elam, and all the kings of Media; [26]all the kings of the north, far and near, one after another, and all the kingdoms of the world that are on the face of the earth. And after them the king of Sheshach[b] shall drink.

27 Then you shall say to them, Thus says the LORD of hosts, the God of Israel: Drink, get drunk and vomit, fall and rise no more, because of the sword that I am sending among you.

28 And if they refuse to accept the cup from your hand to drink, then you shall say to them: Thus says the LORD of hosts: You must drink! [29]See, I am beginning to bring disaster on the city that is called by my name, and how can you possibly avoid punishment? You shall not go unpunished, for I am summoning a sword against all the inhabitants of the earth, says the LORD of hosts.

30 You, therefore, shall prophesy against them all these words, and say to them:

The LORD will roar from on high,
    and from his holy habitation utter his
        voice;
he will roar mightily against his fold,
    and shout, like those who tread grapes,
    against all the inhabitants of the earth.
[31]   The clamor will resound to the ends of
        the earth,
    for the LORD has an indictment against
        the nations;
    he is entering into judgment with all
        flesh,
    and the guilty he will put to the sword,
                            says the LORD.

[32]   Thus says the LORD of hosts:
    See, disaster is spreading

a Meaning of Heb uncertain   b Sheshach is a cryptogram for Babel, Babylon

second scroll (see ch. 36; Introduction). **25.15–29** This prose narrative contains a symbolic action in which Jeremiah takes from God's hand the cup of wrath and makes the nations who are listed drink and become drunk (see 13.1–11, 12–14; 18.1–12; 19.1–15). The nations listed are cursed with destruction. This section may have originally introduced the "oracles against the nations" in chs. 46–51. In the Septuagint, the "oracles against the nations" in chs. 46–51 follow 25.13a. 25.15–38 is found as 32.1–24 in the Septuagint. The nations listed in this passage roughly parallel those in chs. 46–51. Judgment oracles against foreign nations are found in Isa 13–23; Ezek 25–32; Am 1.3–2.3. **25.15** Drinking from a cup as punishment is a common image (49.12; 51.7; Pss 11.6; 75.8; Isa 51.17, 22; Lam 4.21; Ezek 23.31–34; Hab 2.15–16; Rev 14.10; 16.19; 17.4; 18.6). Cf. the "cup of blessing" in Pss 16.5; 23.5. **25.18** The judgment that will engulf all the nations begins with Jerusalem. **25.20** *Mixed people*, probably people of various cultural and ethnic identities who are politically connected to a larger cultural and ethnic group. *Uz*, an area in the desert east of Israel, possibly in Edom. *Ashkelon, Gaza, Ekron, Ashdod*, Philistine cities located on the southern coastal plain. Ashdod was destroyed by Psammetichus I (664–

610 BCE) of Egypt after a siege lasting twenty-nine years (Herodotus *History* 2.157). **25.21** *Edom, Moab, and the Ammonites* compose the countries in the Transjordan, east of Israel. **25.22** *Coastland across the sea*, islands and coastal areas in the Mediterranean settled by the Phoenicians. **25.23** *Dedan, Tema*, tribes in northwest Arabia. *Buz*. Location unknown. *Shaven temples*. See note on 9.26. **25.25** *Elam* and *Media* were in what is now western Iran. *Zimri*. Location unknown. **25.26** In an example of the athbash cipher, in which Hebrew letters are substituted in reverse alphabetical order, Babylon is referred to as *Sheshach* (see 51.41). Although all the nations listed are threatened by Babylonia, ultimately it too shall drink from the same cup. **25.30–38** Judgment against the nations. Continuing the theme of the preceding section are two poetic oracles: vv. 30–32 (announcement of judgment) and vv. 34–38 (call to lamentation). V. 33 is a prose insert that speaks of the widespread destruction brought by the Lord and the lack of burial and funeral rites. **25.30** *The LORD will roar* like a lion from heaven. Cf. Am 1.2, where the Lord roars from Zion (Jerusalem). **25.31** *An indictment against the nations*. See Hos 4.1. The Lord enters into a lawsuit against all the nations. **25.32** See note on 23.19. **25.33** A prose addi-

from nation to nation,
and a great tempest is stirring
from the farthest parts of the earth!

33 Those slain by the LORD on that day shall extend from one end of the earth to the other. They shall not be lamented, or gathered, or buried; they shall become dung on the surface of the ground.

34 Wail, you shepherds, and cry out;
roll in ashes, you lords of the flock,
for the days of your slaughter have
come—and your dispersions,[a]
and you shall fall like a choice vessel.
35 Flight shall fail the shepherds,
and there shall be no escape for the
lords of the flock.
36 Hark! the cry of the shepherds,
and the wail of the lords of the flock!
For the LORD is despoiling their pasture,
37 and the peaceful folds are devastated,
because of the fierce anger of the LORD.
38 Like a lion he has left his covert;
for their land has become a waste
because of the cruel sword,
and because of his fierce anger.

Jeremiah's Prophecies in the Temple

26 At the beginning of the reign of King Jehoiakim son of Josiah of Judah, this word came from the LORD: 2Thus says the LORD: Stand in the court of the LORD's house, and speak to all the cities of Judah that come to worship in the house of the LORD; speak to them all the words that I command you; do not hold back a word. 3It may be that they will listen, all of them, and will turn from their evil way, that I may change my mind about the disaster that I intend to bring on them because of their evil doings. 4You shall say to them: Thus says the LORD: If you will not listen to

me, to walk in my law that I have set before you, 5and to heed the words of my servants the prophets whom I send to you urgently— though you have not heeded— 6then I will make this house like Shiloh, and I will make this city a curse for all the nations of the earth.

7 The priests and the prophets and all the people heard Jeremiah speaking these words in the house of the LORD. 8And when Jeremiah had finished speaking all that the LORD had commanded him to speak to all the people, then the priests and the prophets and all the people laid hold of him, saying, "You shall die! 9Why have you prophesied in the name of the LORD, saying, 'This house shall be like Shiloh, and this city shall be desolate, without inhabitant'?" And all the people gathered around Jeremiah in the house of the LORD.

10 When the officials of Judah heard these things, they came up from the king's house to the house of the LORD and took their seat in the entry of the New Gate of the house of the LORD. 11Then the priests and the prophets said to the officials and to all the people, "This man deserves the sentence of death because he has prophesied against this city, as you have heard with your own ears."

12 Then Jeremiah spoke to all the officials and all the people, saying, "It is the LORD who sent me to prophesy against this house and this city all the words you have heard. 13Now therefore amend your ways and your doings, and obey the voice of the LORD your God, and the LORD will change his mind about the disaster that he has pronounced against you. 14But as for me, here I am in your hands. Do with me as seems good and right to you. 15Only know for certain that if you put me to

---

a Meaning of Heb uncertain

---

tion. For the curse of being denied burial and funeral rites, see 8.1–2; 9.22; 16.4. **25.34** For the call for *shepherds* (i.e., kings; see note on 3.15) to lament, see 4.8; Joel 1.13–14. **25.38** The image of the *lion* (see v. 30) provides an *inclusio* (see note on 4.5–31) for this section.

26.1–29.32 Three episodes in the life of Jeremiah, each of which illustrates his conflict with the priests and the prophets. The first episode involves the temple sermon and the trial of the prophet (26.1–24; see note on 7.1–15); the second, the yoke incident and confrontation with Hananiah (27.1–28.17); the third, Jeremiah's letters to the Babylonian exiles and the ensuing confrontation with false prophets among them

(29.1–32). **26.1–24** The prose sermon is abbreviated in vv. 1–6; the rest of the chapter is devoted to narrating Jeremiah's trial for his life. **26.1** *The beginning of the reign of King Jehoiakim,* probably his accession year, which was 609 BCE. See note on 7.2. **26.6** *Shiloh.* See note on 7.12–15. **26.7–9** Although Jeremiah's sermon in vv. 1–6 was in conditional terms (*If you will not listen . . . then I will make this house like Shiloh,* vv. 4–6) the priests, the prophets, and all the people hear the sermon as an absolute threat against the temple and the city. They therefore consider Jeremiah's words to be treasonous. **26.10** The officials of Judah could hear the commotion from their location in the palace, which was nearby (see ch. 36). *New Gate.* Location un-

death, you will be bringing innocent blood upon yourselves and upon this city and its inhabitants, for in truth the LORD sent me to you to speak all these words in your ears."

16 Then the officials and all the people said to the priests and the prophets, "This man does not deserve the sentence of death, for he has spoken to us in the name of the LORD our God." [17] And some of the elders of the land arose and said to all the assembled people, [18] "Micah of Moresheth, who prophesied during the days of King Hezekiah of Judah, said to all the people of Judah: 'Thus says the LORD of hosts,

Zion shall be plowed as a field;
Jerusalem shall become a heap of
    ruins,
and the mountain of the house a
    wooded height.'

[19] Did King Hezekiah of Judah and all Judah actually put him to death? Did he not fear the LORD and entreat the favor of the LORD, and did not the LORD change his mind about the disaster that he had pronounced against them? But we are about to bring great disaster on ourselves!"

20 There was another man prophesying in the name of the LORD, Uriah son of Shemaiah from Kiriath-jearim. He prophesied against this city and against this land in words exactly like those of Jeremiah. [21] And when King Jehoiakim, with all his warriors and all the officials, heard his words, the king sought to put him to death; but when Uriah heard of it, he was afraid and fled and escaped to Egypt. [22] Then King Jehoiakim sent[a] Elnathan son of Achbor and men with him to Egypt, [23] and they took Uriah from Egypt and brought him to King Jehoiakim, who struck him down with the sword and threw his dead body into the burial place of the common people.

24 But the hand of Ahikam son of Shaphan was with Jeremiah so that he was not given over into the hands of the people to be put to death.

The Sign of the Yoke

27 In the beginning of the reign of King Zedekiah[b] son of Josiah of Judah, this word came to Jeremiah from the LORD. [2] Thus the LORD said to me: Make yourself a yoke of straps and bars, and put them on your neck. [3] Send word[c] to the king of Edom, the king of

a Heb adds men to Egypt b Another reading is Jehoiakim
c Cn: Heb send them

---

known. **26.16** Deuteronomy stipulated death for prophets who spoke in the name of a false god or falsely claimed to speak a word in the Lord's name. In the latter case the only test for authenticity was whether the prophecy came to pass (18.15–22). **26.17–19** Micah's prophecy against Jerusalem during Hezekiah's attempt to throw off Assyrian rule (Hezekiah, 715–687/6 BCE) provided a precedent for Jeremiah's temple sermon (Mic 3.12). *Elders of the land,* leaders among the citizen landowners in the countryside. **26.20–24** The story of Uriah's execution illustrates King Jehoiakim's ruthlessness in dealing with prophets who incurred his disfavor. Jehoiakim sought to take Jeremiah captive (36.26). For the execution of a prophet named Zechariah, see 2 Chr 24.20–22. **26.22** *Elnathan son of Achbor.* See 36.12, 25. **26.24** *Ahikam,* an officer who served Josiah (2 Kings 22.12, 14). His father, *Shaphan,* who was Josiah's secretary, was involved in reporting the discovery of the law in the temple to the king. According to the story, this law became the basis for Josiah's reforms. Ahikam also was among the entourage who consulted the prophet Huldah after the discovery of the law (see 2 Kings 22). Ahikam was the father of Gedaliah, the governor of Judah after the fall of Jerusalem; he was later assassinated by a Jewish zealot (ch. 40). The association between Jeremiah and the upright family of Shaphan was an important one.

27.1–28.17 Jeremiah opposes the efforts to persuade King Zedekiah (597–587/6 BCE) to rebel against the Babylonians. The date was probably 594/3 (see 28.1), when emissaries from Edom, Moab, Ammon, Tyre, and Sidon met in Jerusalem to plan revolution. In the Jewish court, pro-Egyptian conspirators probably looked to Egypt for help, especially with the accession of the new king, Psammetichus II (594–589). Jeremiah opposed rebellion, arguing that Judah's only hope was to remain a vassal to the Babylonians (see note on 26.1–29.32). **27.1–22** The yoke of Babylon. This prose text centers on a symbolic act: the making and wearing of a yoke, which means submission to Babylon (see 13.1–11, 12–14; 16.1–13; 18.1–12; 19.1–15; 24.1–10). The chapter divides into three sermons: one to foreign kings (vv. 1–11), one to King Zedekiah (vv. 12–15), and one to priests and people (vv. 16–22). **27.1** *In the beginning of the reign of King Zedekiah* (597 BCE) does not fit the chronology for the events in chs. 27–28. Most Hebrew manuscripts read, "In the beginning of the reign of King Jehoiakim," but this is undoubtedly a scribal error. The events described in chs. 27–28 occurred in the fourth year of Zedekiah (594/3 BCE; see 28.1). Since the verse is absent in the Septuagint (i.e., the short text; see Introduction), it is likely an editorial or scribal error. **27.2** *Yoke,* used by two oxen to pull a heavy load. Normally, yokes consisted of a crossbar with leather or rope nooses or rods of wood placed around the animals' necks. Attached to the crossbar was a wooden shaft for pulling the load (see Deut 21.3; 1 Sam 6.7; 11.5; 1 Kings 19.19). For the yoke as a symbol of servi-

Moab, the king of the Ammonites, the king of Tyre, and the king of Sidon by the hand of the envoys who have come to Jerusalem to King Zedekiah of Judah. 4Give them this charge for their masters: Thus says the LORD of hosts, the God of Israel: This is what you shall say to your masters: 5It is I who by my great power and my outstretched arm have made the earth, with the people and animals that are on the earth, and I give it to whomever I please. 6Now I have given all these lands into the hand of King Nebuchadnezzar of Babylon, my servant, and I have given him even the wild animals of the field to serve him. 7All the nations shall serve him and his son and his grandson, until the time of his own land comes; then many nations and great kings shall make him their slave.

8 But if any nation or kingdom will not serve this king, Nebuchadnezzar of Babylon, and put its neck under the yoke of the king of Babylon, then I will punish that nation with the sword, with famine, and with pestilence, says the LORD, until I have completed its*a* destruction by his hand. 9You, therefore, must not listen to your prophets, your diviners, your dreamers,*b* your soothsayers, or your sorcerers, who are saying to you, "You shall not serve the king of Babylon." 10For they are prophesying a lie to you, with the result that you will be removed far from your land; I will drive you out, and you will perish. 11But any nation that will bring its neck under the yoke of the king of Babylon and serve him, I will leave on its own land, says the LORD, to till it and live there.

12 I spoke to King Zedekiah of Judah in the same way: Bring your necks under the yoke of the king of Babylon, and serve him and his people, and live. 13Why should you and your peo-

ple die by the sword, by famine, and by pestilence, as the LORD has spoken concerning any nation that will not serve the king of Babylon? 14Do not listen to the words of the prophets who are telling you not to serve the king of Babylon, for they are prophesying a lie to you. 15I have not sent them, says the LORD, but they are prophesying falsely in my name, with the result that I will drive you out and you will perish, you and the prophets who are prophesying to you.

16 Then I spoke to the priests and to all this people, saying, Thus says the LORD: Do not listen to the words of your prophets who are prophesying to you, saying, "The vessels of the LORD's house will soon be brought back from Babylon," for they are prophesying a lie to you. 17Do not listen to them; serve the king of Babylon and live. Why should this city become a desolation? 18If indeed they are prophets, and if the word of the LORD is with them, then let them intercede with the LORD of hosts, that the vessels left in the house of the LORD, in the house of the king of Judah, and in Jerusalem may not go to Babylon. 19For thus says the LORD of hosts concerning the pillars, the sea, the stands, and the rest of the vessels that are left in this city, 20which King Nebuchadnezzar of Babylon did not take away when he took into exile from Jerusalem to Babylon King Jeconiah son of Jehoiakim of Judah, and all the nobles of Judah and Jerusalem— 21thus says the LORD of hosts, the God of Israel, concerning the vessels left in the house of the LORD, in the house of the king of Judah, and in Jerusalem: 22They shall be carried to Babylon, and there they shall stay, until the day when I give attention to them, says the LORD. Then I will bring them up and restore them to this place.

---

a Heb *their*   *b* Gk Syr Vg: Heb *dreams*

tude, also see 1 Kings 12.1–11. **27.6** *Nebuchadnezzar* (see note on 21.2) is God's *servant,* i.e., the one who carries out God's will (see 25.9). **27.7** This verse is absent in the Septuagint. The prediction was not fulfilled, at least literally, since the last king of the Babylonian Empire was Nabonidus (556–539 BCE), the fourth king to succeed Nebuchadnezzar. Also, Nabonidus was not a descendant of Nebuchadnezzar. The reference may be to Nebuchadnezzar, Nabonidus, and Belshazzar (Dan 5.2). Belshazzar was the son of Nabonidus. **27.12–15** Zedekiah receives essentially the same warning delivered to the foreign kings: submit to the yoke of Nebuchadnezzar or face destruction. False *prophets.* See note on 23.9–40. **27.16** *Priests,* mentioned because they desire the return of the sacred objects carried away to

Babylon in 597 BCE. **27.18–22** The sacred objects that remained after 597 BCE will be taken away to Babylon. There were two cast bronze, freestanding *pillars* (Jachin and Boaz) at the entrance of the temple (1 Kings 7.15–22). A huge basin or tank standing perhaps some ten feet in height, the *sea* was also cast bronze, perhaps located at the entrance to the temple and before the altar (1 Kings 7.23–26). Its estimated capacity was approximately 12,000 gallons. 2 Chr 4.6 indicates it was used as a basin in which the priests washed. The *stands* were ornamented bronze wagons upon which were mounted the ten lavers or wash basins (see 1 Kings 7.27–39). The pillars, basin, and stands were broken into pieces, and these and other vessels were taken to Babylon in 587 (see 2 Kings 25.13–17).

Hananiah Opposes Jeremiah and Dies

28 In that same year, at the beginning of the reign of King Zedekiah of Judah, in the fifth month of the fourth year, the prophet Hananiah son of Azzur, from Gibeon, spoke to me in the house of the LORD, in the presence of the priests and all the people, saying, 2"Thus says the LORD of hosts, the God of Israel: I have broken the yoke of the king of Babylon. 3Within two years I will bring back to this place all the vessels of the LORD's house, which King Nebuchadnezzar of Babylon took away from this place and carried to Babylon. 4I will also bring back to this place King Jeconiah son of Jehoiakim of Judah, and all the exiles from Judah who went to Babylon, says the LORD, for I will break the yoke of the king of Babylon."

5 Then the prophet Jeremiah spoke to the prophet Hananiah in the presence of the priests and all the people who were standing in the house of the LORD; 6and the prophet Jeremiah said, "Amen! May the LORD do so; may the LORD fulfill the words that you have prophesied, and bring back to this place from Babylon the vessels of the house of the LORD, and all the exiles. 7But listen now to this word that I speak in your hearing and in the hearing of all the people. 8The prophets who preceded you and me from ancient times prophesied war, famine, and pestilence against many countries and great kingdoms. 9As for the prophet who prophesies peace, when the word of that prophet comes true, then it will be known that the LORD has truly sent the prophet."

10 Then the prophet Hananiah took the yoke from the neck of the prophet Jeremiah, and broke it. 11And Hananiah spoke in the presence of all the people, saying, "Thus says the LORD: This is how I will break the yoke of King Nebuchadnezzar of Babylon from the neck of all the nations within two years." At this, the prophet Jeremiah went his way.

12 Sometime after the prophet Hananiah had broken the yoke from the neck of the prophet Jeremiah, the word of the LORD came to Jeremiah: 13Go, tell Hananiah, Thus says the LORD: You have broken wooden bars only to forge iron bars in place of them! 14For thus says the LORD of hosts, the God of Israel: I have put an iron yoke on the neck of all these nations so that they may serve King Nebuchadnezzar of Babylon, and they shall indeed serve him; I have even given him the wild animals. 15And the prophet Jeremiah said to the prophet Hananiah, "Listen, Hananiah, the LORD has not sent you, and you made this people trust in a lie. 16Therefore thus says the LORD: I am going to send you off the face of the earth. Within this year you will be dead, because you have spoken rebellion against the LORD."

17 In that same year, in the seventh month, the prophet Hananiah died.

Jeremiah's Letter to the Exiles in Babylon

29 These are the words of the letter that the prophet Jeremiah sent from Jerusalem to the remaining elders among the exiles, and to the priests, the prophets, and all the people, whom Nebuchadnezzar had taken

---

28.1–17 This prose narrative is the best illustration of conflict between two prophets who claim to be spokespersons for God (see 23.9–40). *Hananiah* (in Hebrew "Yahweh has been gracious") utters an oracle of salvation: the yoke of Babylon has been broken and within two years God will bring back to Jerusalem King Jehoiachin, the exiles of 597 BCE, and the sacred vessels stolen from the temple. Jeremiah, wearing a yoke that symbolizes submission to Babylon (see ch. 27), opposes Hananiah and his hopeful word. Indeed, he announces an oracle of judgment against Hananiah, a prophecy that comes to pass in his death *that same year* (v. 17). 28.1 The Septuagint reads only "in the fourth year of Zedekiah king of Judah, in the fifth month" (v. 1a), which must be correct. The Hebrew, which is translated here, is contradictory, for the *beginning* would be 597 BCE and the *fourth year* 594/3. *Gibeon*, modern el-Jib, five and a half miles northwest of Jerusalem. It contained a great high place where

Solomon prayed for wisdom (1 Kings 3.4–15). 28.8–9 Although there were occasional oracles of salvation from true prophets, the prophetic tradition was dominated by announcements of punishment. By contrast, false prophets generally promised good fortune (see Deut 18.20–22).

29.1–32 This prose narrative describes how the exiles in Babylon were incited to consider rebellion by false prophets who predicted an early return from exile. The time frame is apparently the same as that for chs. 27–28 (594/3 BCE). Jeremiah wrote letters to oppose these false hopes for an early return. Singled out for condemnation in the first letter were two prophets, *Ahab son of Kolaiah* and *Zedekiah son of Maaseiah*. In the second letter, *Shemaiah of Nehelam*, who had attempted without success to silence Jeremiah, received the judgment of the prophet (see note on 26.1–29.32). The chapter consists of a general letter to the exiles (vv. 1–23) and a letter concerning Shemaiah (vv. 24–32).

into exile from Jerusalem to Babylon. ²This was after King Jeconiah, and the queen mother, the court officials, the leaders of Judah and Jerusalem, the artisans, and the smiths had departed from Jerusalem. ³The letter was sent by the hand of Elasah son of Shaphan and Gemariah son of Hilkiah, whom King Zedekiah of Judah sent to Babylon to King Nebuchadnezzar of Babylon. It said: ⁴Thus says the LORD of hosts, the God of Israel, to all the exiles whom I have sent into exile from Jerusalem to Babylon: ⁵Build houses and live in them; plant gardens and eat what they produce. ⁶Take wives and have sons and daughters; take wives for your sons, and give your daughters in marriage, that they may bear sons and daughters; multiply there, and do not decrease. ⁷But seek the welfare of the city where I have sent you into exile, and pray to the LORD on its behalf, for in its welfare you will find your welfare. ⁸For thus says the LORD of hosts, the God of Israel: Do not let the prophets and the diviners who are among you deceive you, and do not listen to the dreams that they dream,ᵃ ⁹for it is a lie that they are prophesying to you in my name; I did not send them, says the LORD.

10 For thus says the LORD: Only when Babylon's seventy years are completed will I visit you, and I will fulfill to you my promise and bring you back to this place. ¹¹For surely I know the plans I have for you, says the LORD, plans for your welfare and not for harm, to give you a future with hope. ¹²Then when you call upon me and come and pray to me, I will hear you. ¹³When you search for me, you will find me; if you seek me with all your heart, ¹⁴I will let you find me, says the LORD, and I will restore your fortunes and gather you from all the nations and all the places where I have driven you, says the LORD, and I will bring you back to the place from which I sent you into exile.

15 Because you have said, "The LORD has raised up prophets for us in Babylon,"—

¹⁶Thus says the LORD concerning the king who sits on the throne of David, and concerning all the people who live in this city, your kinsfolk who did not go out with you into exile: ¹⁷Thus says the LORD of hosts, I am going to let loose on them sword, famine, and pestilence, and I will make them like rotten figs that are so bad they cannot be eaten. ¹⁸I will pursue them with the sword, with famine, and with pestilence, and will make them a horror to all the kingdoms of the earth, to be an object of cursing, and horror, and hissing, and a derision among all the nations where I have driven them, ¹⁹because they did not heed my words, says the LORD, when I persistently sent to you my servants the prophets, but theyᵇ would not listen, says the LORD. ²⁰But now, all you exiles whom I sent away from Jerusalem to Babylon, hear the word of the LORD: ²¹Thus says the LORD of hosts, the God of Israel, concerning Ahab son of Kolaiah and Zedekiah son of Maaseiah, who are prophesying a lie to you in my name: I am going to deliver them into the hand of King Nebuchadrezzar of Babylon, and he shall kill them before your eyes. ²²And on account of them this curse shall be used by all the exiles from Judah in Babylon: "The LORD make you like Zedekiah and Ahab, whom the king of Babylon roasted in the fire," ²³because they have perpetrated outrage in Israel and have committed adultery with their neighbors' wives, and have spoken in my name lying words that I did not command them; I am the one who knows and bears witness, says the LORD.

The Letter of Shemaiah

24 To Shemaiah of Nehelam you shall say: ²⁵Thus says the LORD of hosts, the God of Israel: In your own name you sent a letter to all the people who are in Jerusalem, and to the priest Zephaniah son of Maaseiah, and to all the priests, saying, ²⁶The LORD himself has

---

ᵃ Cn: Heb *your dreams that you cause to dream*   ᵇ Syr: Heb *you*

29.2 *Jeconiah,* another spelling of Jehoiachin (see 22.24–30). **29.3** *Elasah,* probably the brother of Ahikam son of Shaphan (see note on 26.24). *Gemariah,* perhaps the son of Hilkiah the high priest, who was involved in the discovery of the book of the law during the reign of Josiah (see 2 Kings 22–23). If so, Jeremiah was supported by two very powerful families in Judah who had been involved in Josiah's reform. **29.4–7** The exiles are to build their lives in Babylon and not expect immediate restoration. Indeed, they are to seek the welfare of Babylon. **29.10–14** *Seventy years,* see note on 25.11. **29.16–20** See ch. 24. These verses are absent in the Septuagint. **29.24–32** The letter against Shemaiah condemns him for attempting to have Jeremiah imprisoned. Shemaiah is also condemned as a false prophet whose descendants shall not live to experience the restoration. **29.25** *Zephaniah.* See 21.1; 37.3; 52.24–27.

made you priest instead of the priest Jehoiada, so that there may be officers in the house of the LORD to control any madman who plays the prophet, to put him in the stocks and the collar. 27 So now why have you not rebuked Jeremiah of Anathoth who plays the prophet for you? 28 For he has actually sent to us in Babylon, saying, "It will be a long time; build houses and live in them, and plant gardens and eat what they produce."

29 The priest Zephaniah read this letter in the hearing of the prophet Jeremiah. 30 Then the word of the LORD came to Jeremiah: 31 Send to all the exiles, saying, Thus says the LORD concerning Shemaiah of Nehelam: Because Shemaiah has prophesied to you, though I did not send him, and has led you to trust in a lie, 32 therefore thus says the LORD: I am going to punish Shemaiah of Nehelam and his descendants; he shall not have anyone living among this people to see[a] the good that I am going to do to my people, says the LORD, for he has spoken rebellion against the LORD.

Restoration Promised for Israel and Judah

30 The word that came to Jeremiah from the LORD: 2 Thus says the LORD, the God of Israel: Write in a book all the words that I have spoken to you. 3 For the days are surely coming, says the LORD, when I will restore the fortunes of my people, Israel and Judah, says the LORD, and I will bring them back to the land that I gave to their ancestors and they shall take possession of it.

4 These are the words that the LORD spoke concerning Israel and Judah:

5   Thus says the LORD:
    We have heard a cry of panic,
      of terror, and no peace.
6   Ask now, and see,
      can a man bear a child?
    Why then do I see every man
      with his hands on his loins like a
        woman in labor?
    Why has every face turned pale?
7   Alas! that day is so great
      there is none like it;
    it is a time of distress for Jacob;
      yet he shall be rescued from it.

8 On that day, says the LORD of hosts, I will break the yoke from off his[b] neck, and I will burst his[b] bonds, and strangers shall no more make a servant of him. 9 But they shall serve the LORD their God and David their king, whom I will raise up for them.

10   But as for you, have no fear, my servant
      Jacob, says the LORD,
    and do not be dismayed, O Israel;
    for I am going to save you from far away,
      and your offspring from the land of
        their captivity.
    Jacob shall return and have quiet and ease,

---

a Gk: Heb and he shall not see   b Cn: Heb your

30.1–31.40 The Book of Consolation. The poetic and prose oracles in this collection speak of the future restoration of Israel and Judah. There is considerable debate as to which of these oracles may derive from Jeremiah. The best cases may be made for Jeremian authorship of 30.5–7, 12–15; 31.2–6; 31.15–22. Two dates are often assigned to the oracles uttered by Jeremiah: the early part of his ministry and after the fall of Jerusalem in 587 BCE. Some of the salvation oracles directed to the Northern Kingdom may be in the former category and may be the counterpart of judgment oracles directed against the North earlier in the book. Many scholars, however, date the majority of the salvation oracles to a later period, during the governorship of Gedaliah, who was appointed by the Babylonians to administer the provincial district into which Judah was incorporated (40.7–41.18; 2 Kings 25.22–26). The other oracles derive from the exilic and postexilic periods. The form that predominates in this collection is the "prophecy of salvation." It contains the following parts: the appeal for attention and/or the introductory messenger formula (e.g., "Thus says the LORD"), the description of the present situation, the prediction of salvation, a final characterization of either God or the message, and the concluding messenger formula ("says the LORD"). 30.1–4 A general editorial introduction to the oracles of salvation in chs. 30–31. The oracles pertain to both Israel and Judah. 30.5–7 The day of God's judgment upon Israel. Dominated by rhetorical questions, this poem is a lament over the great and terrible day of God's judgment against Jacob. For the "day of the LORD," see Isa 2.12–21; Am 5.18–20; Zeph 1.14–18. Laments dominate Jer 11.18–20.18. The last line of v. 7 is added to form a transition to vv. 8–9. 30.8–9 This prose oracle of salvation by a later hand promises the removal of the yoke (see chs. 27–28) and the restoration of the Davidic monarchy (23.5–6; 33.14–26; Ezek 34.24; Hos 3.5). Jeremiah himself placed little importance on the restoration of the monarchy (see 21.11–23.8). 30.10–11 The salvation of Jacob, i.e., Israel, the Lord's servant. 46.27–28 almost duplicates this oracle of salvation. The language and content resonates with Second Isaiah (an anonymous poet of the exile whose oracles are collected in Isa 40–55; see Isa 41.8–14; 43.1–5). Israel as the servant of the Lord is a common expression in Sec-

and no one shall make him afraid.

11 For I am with you, says the LORD, to save
        you;
  I will make an end of all the nations
        among which I scattered you,
    but of you I will not make an end.
  I will chastise you in just measure,
    and I will by no means leave you
        unpunished.

12 For thus says the LORD:
  Your hurt is incurable,
    your wound is grievous.
13 There is no one to uphold your cause,
    no medicine for your wound,
    no healing for you.
14 All your lovers have forgotten you;
    they care nothing for you;
  for I have dealt you the blow of an enemy,
    the punishment of a merciless foe,
  because your guilt is great,
    because your sins are so numerous.
15 Why do you cry out over your hurt?
    Your pain is incurable.
  Because your guilt is great,
    because your sins are so numerous,
    I have done these things to you.
16 Therefore all who devour you shall be
        devoured,
    and all your foes, every one of them,
        shall go into captivity;
  those who plunder you shall be plundered,
    and all who prey on you I will make a
        prey.
17 For I will restore health to you,
    and your wounds I will heal,
                            says the LORD,
  because they have called you an outcast:
    "It is Zion; no one cares for her!"

18 Thus says the LORD:
  I am going to restore the fortunes of the
        tents of Jacob,
    and have compassion on his dwellings;
  the city shall be rebuilt upon its mound,
    and the citadel set on its rightful site.
19 Out of them shall come thanksgiving,
    and the sound of merrymakers.
  I will make them many, and they shall not
        be few;
  I will make them honored, and they
        shall not be disdained.
20 Their children shall be as of old,
    their congregation shall be established
        before me;
  and I will punish all who oppress
        them.
21 Their prince shall be one of their own,
    their ruler shall come from their midst;
  I will bring him near, and he shall
        approach me,
    for who would otherwise dare to
        approach me?
                            says the LORD.
22 And you shall be my people,
    and I will be your God.

23 Look, the storm of the LORD!
    Wrath has gone forth,
  a whirling*a* tempest;
    it will burst upon the head of the
        wicked.
24 The fierce anger of the LORD will not turn
        back
  until he has executed and
        accomplished
    the intents of his mind.
  In the latter days you will understand this.

The Joyful Return of the Exiles

31 At that time, says the LORD, I will be the
   God of all the families of Israel, and
they shall be my people.
2 Thus says the LORD:

---

a One Ms: Meaning of MT uncertain

ond Isaiah (see Isa 44.1, 2, 21). **30.12–17** Though Jerusalem is incurably wounded (see 15.18), nevertheless the divine healer will restore Zion to health and will make an end of her enemies. For a similar description of Zion's distress and lamentation, see 4.31; 8.18–21; 9.17–19. **30.14** Zion's *lovers* (probably allies) have abandoned her. Jeremiah may be speaking of the Egyptians, who withdrew before the Babylonian advance (37.5). Other states that joined in the rebellion beginning in 589 BCE included at least Tyre and Ammon. **30.18–22** This oracle of salvation speaks of the restoration of Jacob (Israel), the Israelites thanksgiving over their return, their increase in population, and their own prince who shall approach the Lord. The ruler shall be an Israelite, not a foreigner (see Deut 17.15). **30.21** To *approach* God was normally a priestly prerogative (see Ex 29.4, 8; 40.12, 14; Lev 7.35). Cf. Ezekiel's prince in Ezek 46.1–18. **30.22** A repetition of the covenant formula (see note on 24.7). **30.23–24** The storm of the Lord. This poem occurs also in (see note on) 23.19–20. **31.1** A covenant formula. See note on 24.7. **31.2–6** This oracle of salvation grounds

The people who survived the sword
   found grace in the wilderness;
when Israel sought for rest,
3   the LORD appeared to him[a] from far
      away.[b]
I have loved you with an everlasting love;
   therefore I have continued my
     faithfulness to you.
4 Again I will build you, and you shall be
     built,
   O virgin Israel!
Again you shall take[c] your tambourines,
   and go forth in the dance of the
     merrymakers.
5 Again you shall plant vineyards
   on the mountains of Samaria;
the planters shall plant,
   and shall enjoy the fruit.
6 For there shall be a day when sentinels
     will call
   in the hill country of Ephraim:
"Come, let us go up to Zion,
   to the LORD our God."

7 For thus says the LORD:
Sing aloud with gladness for Jacob,
   and raise shouts for the chief of the
     nations;
proclaim, give praise, and say,
   "Save, O LORD, your people,
   the remnant of Israel."
8 See, I am going to bring them from the
     land of the north,
   and gather them from the farthest
     parts of the earth,
among them the blind and the lame,
   those with child and those in labor,
     together;
   a great company, they shall return here.
9 With weeping they shall come,
   and with consolations[d] I will lead them
     back,

I will let them walk by brooks of water,
   in a straight path in which they shall
     not stumble;
for I have become a father to Israel,
   and Ephraim is my firstborn.

10 Hear the word of the LORD, O nations,
   and declare it in the coastlands far
     away;
say, "He who scattered Israel will gather
     him,
   and will keep him as a shepherd a flock."
11 For the LORD has ransomed Jacob,
   and has redeemed him from hands too
     strong for him.
12 They shall come and sing aloud on the
     height of Zion,
   and they shall be radiant over the
     goodness of the LORD,
over the grain, the wine, and the oil,
   and over the young of the flock and the
     herd;
their life shall become like a watered
     garden,
   and they shall never languish again.
13 Then shall the young women rejoice in
     the dance,
   and the young men and the old shall
     be merry.
I will turn their mourning into joy,
   I will comfort them, and give them
     gladness for sorrow.
14 I will give the priests their fill of fatness,
   and my people shall be satisfied with
     my bounty,
                says the LORD.

15 Thus says the LORD:
A voice is heard in Ramah,

---

a Gk: Heb me b Or to him long ago c Or adorn yourself with
d Gk Compare Vg Tg: Heb supplications

Israel's future redemption in the everlasting love of
God. The poem addresses the Northern Kingdom (*Israel, mountains of Samaria,* and *hill country of Ephraim*). **31.2** *Found grace in the wilderness* refers to the period of wandering in the Sinai after the exodus from Egypt and before entrance into Canaan (see Exodus; Numbers). In Hosea and Jeremiah the time in the wilderness was a period of intimacy between the Lord and Israel (Jer 2.2–3; Hos 2). **31.6** In the restoration, North and South will be united and will worship God in Jerusalem. **31.7–9** In this oracle of salvation, Israel's return from the Diaspora is praised in hymnic celebration (see Second Isaiah, i.e., Isa 40–55). **31.9** *Father,* a common metaphor for God in the Hebrew Bible (see esp. Jer 3.19; 31.20; Hos 11.1). Israel is designated as the Lord's *firstborn,* a designation of election (Ex 4.22). In Israel the firstborn was privileged with a double share of the father's estate, received the paternal blessing, and succeeded him in authority. **31.10–14** Exiles rejoice as they return. Another oracle of salvation in which Israel returns from exile and in Jerusalem praises God for many blessings. The lamentation during periods of peril will turn into thanksgiving. **31.15–22** Rachel's weeping and the return of her

lamentation and bitter weeping.
Rachel is weeping for her children;
　she refuses to be comforted for her
　　children,
　because they are no more.
16 Thus says the LORD:
Keep your voice from weeping,
　and your eyes from tears;
for there is a reward for your work,
　　　　　　　　　　　　says the LORD:
　they shall come back from the land of
　　the enemy;
17 there is hope for your future,
　　　　　　　　　　　　says the LORD:
　your children shall come back to their
　　own country.

18 Indeed I heard Ephraim pleading:
"You disciplined me, and I took the
　discipline;
I was like a calf untrained.
Bring me back, let me come back,
　for you are the LORD my God.
19 For after I had turned away I repented;
　and after I was discovered, I struck my
　　thigh;
I was ashamed, and I was dismayed
　because I bore the disgrace of my youth."
20 Is Ephraim my dear son?
　Is he the child I delight in?
As often as I speak against him,
　I still remember him.
Therefore I am deeply moved for him;
　I will surely have mercy on him,
　　　　　　　　　　　says the LORD.

21 Set up road markers for yourself,
　make yourself signposts;

consider well the highway,
　the road by which you went.
Return, O virgin Israel,
　return to these your cities.
22 How long will you waver,
　O faithless daughter?
For the LORD has created a new thing on
　　the earth:
　a woman encompasses*a* man.

23 Thus says the LORD of hosts, the God of
Israel: Once more they shall use these words in
the land of Judah and in its towns when I restore their fortunes:
"The LORD bless you, O abode of
　righteousness,
　O holy hill!"
24And Judah and all its towns shall live there
together, and the farmers and those who wander*b* with their flocks.
25 I will satisfy the weary,
　and all who are faint I will replenish.

26 Thereupon I awoke and looked, and my
sleep was pleasant to me.

Individual Retribution

27 The days are surely coming, says the LORD,
when I will sow the house of Israel and the
house of Judah with the seed of humans and
the seed of animals. 28And just as I have
watched over them to pluck up and break
down, to overthrow, destroy, and bring evil, so
I will watch over them to build and to plant,
says the LORD. 29In those days they shall no
longer say:

---

a Meaning of Heb uncertain　*b* Cn Compare Syr Vg Tg: Heb
and they shall wander

children. **31.15** In biblical tradition, *Rachel*, the more
favored wife of Jacob (Israel, Gen 35.10), was the
mother of Joseph and Benjamin. Joseph had two sons,
Ephraim and Manasseh. Along with her sister Leah
and their handmaidens, Rachel is one of the matriarchs of the nation (see Gen 25–35). *Ramah* (modern
er-Ram), located five miles north of Jerusalem, appears to have been the place where the exiles were
gathered for deportation to Babylon (40.1, 4). According to one tradition (1 Sam 10.2), Rachel's grave was
located in the territory of Benjamin, thus to the north
of Jerusalem. For an alternate location, see Gen 35.16–
20; 48.7; Mt 2.18. The dead Rachel is heard weeping
over her children, who were either killed or deported.
31.22 The verb in the last line of the poem, *a woman
encompasses a man,* is subject to many translations
and interpretations: "a woman protects a man," "the

woman woos the man," "the woman sets out to find
her husband again," "the woman must encompass the
man with devotion," and "a woman is turned into a
man." The NRSV translation suggests two possibilities:
in a reversal of traditional roles, the woman (Israel?)
embraces the man (God?); or, in contrast to Rachel bereaved of children, Virgin Israel will bear a son, a posterity, and thus have a future. **31.23–26** The restoration of Judah. This oracle of salvation anticipates the
restoration of worship in the destroyed temple in
Jerusalem and the resettlement of Judah. **31.26** An editor placed these words in Jeremiah's mouth to indicate he had been dreaming of the future restoration.
31.27–30 The repopulation of Israel and Judah and
individual retribution. **31.27** The land of Israel and
Judah will be repopulated with people and herds (Ezek
36.9–11). **31.28** See note on 1.10. **31.29–30** These

"The parents have eaten sour grapes,
and the children's teeth are set on
edge."
30But all shall die for their own sins; the teeth of everyone who eats sour grapes shall be set on edge.

A New Covenant

31 The days are surely coming, says the LORD, when I will make a new covenant with the house of Israel and the house of Judah. 32It will not be like the covenant that I made with their ancestors when I took them by the hand to bring them out of the land of Egypt—a covenant that they broke, though I was their husband,[a] says the LORD. 33But this is the covenant that I will make with the house of Israel after those days, says the LORD: I will put my law within them, and I will write it on their hearts; and I will be their God, and they shall be my people. 34No longer shall they teach one another, or say to each other, "Know the LORD," for they shall all know me, from the least of them to the greatest, says the LORD; for I will forgive their iniquity, and remember their sin no more.

35 Thus says the LORD,
who gives the sun for light by day
and the fixed order of the moon and
the stars for light by night,
who stirs up the sea so that its waves
roar—
the LORD of hosts is his name:
36 If this fixed order were ever to cease
from my presence, says the LORD,

then also the offspring of Israel would
cease
to be a nation before me forever.

37 Thus says the LORD:
If the heavens above can be measured,
and the foundations of the earth below
can be explored,
then I will reject all the offspring of Israel
because of all they have done,
says the LORD.

Jerusalem to Be Enlarged

38 The days are surely coming, says the LORD, when the city shall be rebuilt for the LORD from the tower of Hananel to the Corner Gate. 39And the measuring line shall go out farther, straight to the hill Gareb, and shall then turn to Goah. 40The whole valley of the dead bodies and the ashes, and all the fields as far as the Wadi Kidron, to the corner of the Horse Gate toward the east, shall be sacred to the LORD. It shall never again be uprooted or overthrown.

Jeremiah Buys a Field During the Siege

32 The word that came to Jeremiah from the LORD in the tenth year of King Zedekiah of Judah, which was the eighteenth year of Nebuchadrezzar. 2At that time the army of the king of Babylon was besieging Jerusalem, and the prophet Jeremiah was confined in the court of the guard that was in the palace of the king of Judah, 3where King Zedekiah of Judah had confined him. Zedekiah

_____
a Or master

words and thoughts are borrowed from Ezekiel (see Ezek 18.1–32). **31.31–34** The new covenant. See Lk 22.20; 1 Cor 11.25; 2 Cor 3.5–14; Heb 8.8–12; 10.16–17. In this prose oracle of salvation, Jeremiah promises a new covenant, not a new law. The old (Mosaic) covenant had been broken, but the new covenant will continue because of an inward transformation of the human heart that will allow the people to know God intimately and to be obedient to the commandments. And God will forgive and forget the people's sins. **31.33** *I will make*, lit. "I will cut." "Cutting a covenant" involved the sacrifice of animals and a ceremony in which the covenant partners walked between the slaughtered animals (see 34.18; Gen 15.7–21). **31.35–37** The continuation of Israel. This oracle of salvation makes use of hymnic language praising the God of creation. The power of God revealed in the endless cycle of days and seasons and the unfathomable character of the heavens and the earth guarantees Israel's continua-

tion (see Isa 40.12, 26; 42.5; 44.24; 45.7, 18; 54.10). **31.38–40** Jerusalem will be rebuilt and enlarged, and the areas desecrated by death will be purified (see Zech 14.10–11). The boundaries of Jerusalem are mentioned: the *tower of Hananel* in the northeast (Neh 3.1), the *Corner Gate* in the northwest (2 Kings 14.13), the southern boundary of Hinnom (7.31–32), the eastern boundary of *Kidron* (2 Kings 23.4, 6), and the *Horse Gate* in the southeast corner (Neh 3.28). *Gareb, Goah,* unknown. *Valley of the dead bodies and the ashes,* most likely the valley of Hinnom, where child sacrifice was practiced (see 7.31–32; 19.2, 6; 32.35; 2 Kings 23.10).

32.1–44 Jeremiah's purchase of a field in Anathoth, another symbolic act, illustrates Jeremiah's preaching (see note on 13.1–11). **32.1** This prose narrative is set in 588 BCE, during the siege of Jerusalem by Nebuchadrezzar. **32.2** Jeremiah was imprisoned for attempting to leave the city to go to Anathoth when the

had said, "Why do you prophesy and say: Thus says the LORD: I am going to give this city into the hand of the king of Babylon, and he shall take it; 4King Zedekiah of Judah shall not escape out of the hands of the Chaldeans, but shall surely be given into the hands of the king of Babylon, and shall speak with him face to face and see him eye to eye; 5and he shall take Zedekiah to Babylon, and there he shall remain until I attend to him, says the LORD; though you fight against the Chaldeans, you shall not succeed?"

6 Jeremiah said, The word of the LORD came to me: 7Hanamel son of your uncle Shallum is going to come to you and say, "Buy my field that is at Anathoth, for the right of redemption by purchase is yours." 8Then my cousin Hanamel came to me in the court of the guard, in accordance with the word of the LORD, and said to me, "Buy my field that is at Anathoth in the land of Benjamin, for the right of possession and redemption is yours; buy it for yourself." Then I knew that this was the word of the LORD.

9 And I bought the field at Anathoth from my cousin Hanamel, and weighed out the money to him, seventeen shekels of silver. 10I signed the deed, sealed it, got witnesses, and weighed the money on scales. 11Then I took the sealed deed of purchase, containing the terms and conditions, and the open copy; 12and I gave the deed of purchase to Baruch son of Neriah son of Mahseiah, in the presence of my cousin Hanamel, in the presence of the witnesses who signed the deed of purchase, and in the presence of all the Judeans who were sitting in the court of the guard. 13In their presence I charged Baruch, saying, 14Thus says the LORD of hosts, the God of Israel: Take these deeds, both this sealed deed of purchase and this open deed, and put them in an earthenware jar, in order that they may last for a long time. 15For thus says the LORD of hosts, the God of Israel: Houses and fields and vineyards shall again be bought in this land.

Jeremiah Prays for Understanding

16 After I had given the deed of purchase to Baruch son of Neriah, I prayed to the LORD, saying: 17Ah Lord GOD! It is you who made the heavens and the earth by your great power and by your outstretched arm! Nothing is too hard for you. 18You show steadfast love to the thousandth generation,[a] but repay the guilt of parents into the laps of their children after them, O great and mighty God whose name is the LORD of hosts, 19great in counsel and mighty in deed; whose eyes are open to all the ways of mortals, rewarding all according to their ways and according to the fruit of their doings. 20You showed signs and wonders in the land of Egypt, and to this day in Israel and among all humankind, and have made yourself a name that continues to this very day. 21You brought your people Israel out of the land of Egypt with signs and wonders, with a strong hand and outstretched arm, and with great terror; 22and you gave them this land, which you swore to their ancestors to give them, a land flowing with milk and honey; 23and they entered and took possession of it. But they did not obey your voice or follow your law; of all you commanded them to do, they did nothing. Therefore you have made all these disasters come upon them. 24See, the siege ramps have been cast up against the city to take it, and the city, faced with sword, famine, and pestilence, has been given into the hands of the Chaldeans who are fighting against it. What you spoke has happened, as you yourself can see. 25Yet you, O Lord GOD, have said to me, "Buy the field for money and get witnesses"—though the city has been given into the hands of the Chaldeans.

God's Assurance of the People's Return

26 The word of the LORD came to Jeremiah: 27See, I am the LORD, the God of all flesh; is

a Or to thousands

---

siege was temporarily lifted. He was accused of deserting to the enemy (see 37.11–21). **32.3–5** Zedekiah accused Jeremiah of treason and insurrection (see Am 7.10–17). **32.6–8** *Right of redemption,* a means to prevent the threatened loss of family property (see Lev 25.25–28). **32.9–15** *Seventeen shekels of silver,* an amount by weight (about 7 ounces), not coins; coins were probably not used until the Persian period (beginning in 539 BCE). The official copy of the scroll was rolled up and sealed, while the *open copy* was unsealed for easy reference. *Baruch,* Jeremiah's secretary (amanuensis) and companion (see chs. 36, 45). The purchase of a field at the time of conquest and threatened exile underscores the prophet's faith in a future restoration. **32.16–25** A prayer of Jeremiah. See Neh 9.6–38. This prose prayer is similar to hymns praising God for great acts of salvation (Pss 78; 105; 106; 135; 136). **32.26–44** This response of God to Jeremiah's

anything too hard for me? 28Therefore, thus says the LORD: I am going to give this city into the hands of the Chaldeans and into the hand of King Nebuchadrezzar of Babylon, and he shall take it. 29The Chaldeans who are fighting against this city shall come, set it on fire, and burn it, with the houses on whose roofs offerings have been made to Baal and libations have been poured out to other gods, to provoke me to anger. 30For the people of Israel and the people of Judah have done nothing but evil in my sight from their youth; the people of Israel have done nothing but provoke me to anger by the work of their hands, says the LORD. 31This city has aroused my anger and wrath, from the day it was built until this day, so that I will remove it from my sight 32because of all the evil of the people of Israel and the people of Judah that they did to provoke me to anger—they, their kings and their officials, their priests and their prophets, the citizens of Judah and the inhabitants of Jerusalem. 33They have turned their backs to me, not their faces; though I have taught them persistently, they would not listen and accept correction. 34They set up their abominations in the house that bears my name, and defiled it. 35They built the high places of Baal in the valley of the son of Hinnom, to offer up their sons and daughters to Molech, though I did not command them, nor did it enter my mind that they should do this abomination, causing Judah to sin.

36 Now therefore thus says the LORD, the God of Israel, concerning this city of which you say, "It is being given into the hand of the king of Babylon by the sword, by famine, and by pestilence": 37See, I am going to gather them from all the lands to which I drove them in my anger and my wrath and in great indignation; I will bring them back to this place, and I will settle them in safety. 38They shall be my people, and I will be their God. 39I will give them one heart and one way, that they may fear me for all time, for their own good and the good of their children after them. 40I will make an everlasting covenant with them,

never to draw back from doing good to them; and I will put the fear of me in their hearts, so that they may not turn from me. 41I will rejoice in doing good to them, and I will plant them in this land in faithfulness, with all my heart and all my soul.

42 For thus says the LORD: Just as I have brought all this great disaster upon this people, so I will bring upon them all the good fortune that I now promise them. 43Fields shall be bought in this land of which you are saying, It is a desolation, without human beings or animals; it has been given into the hands of the Chaldeans. 44Fields shall be bought for money, and deeds shall be signed and sealed and witnessed, in the land of Benjamin, in the places around Jerusalem, and in the cities of Judah, of the hill country, of the Shephelah, and of the Negeb; for I will restore their fortunes, says the LORD.

Healing after Punishment

33 The word of the LORD came to Jeremiah a second time, while he was still confined in the court of the guard: 2Thus says the LORD who made the earth,ᵃ the LORD who formed it to establish it—the LORD is his name: 3Call to me and I will answer you, and will tell you great and hidden things that you have not known. 4For thus says the LORD, the God of Israel, concerning the houses of this city and the houses of the kings of Judah that were torn down to make a defense against the siege ramps and before the sword:ᵇ 5The Chaldeans are coming in to fightᶜ and to fill them with the dead bodies of those whom I shall strike down in my anger and my wrath, for I have hidden my face from this city because of all their wickedness. 6I am going to bring it recovery and healing; I will heal them and reveal to them abundanceᵇ of prosperity and security. 7I will restore the fortunes of Judah and the fortunes of Israel, and rebuild them as they were at first. 8I will cleanse them

---

a Gk: Heb *it* b Meaning of Heb uncertain c Cn: Heb *They are coming in to fight against the Chaldeans*

---

prayer lists the sins of the people as the basis for the fall of Jerusalem. It is a history of disobedience (see Ezek 20.1–32). Yet God also promises a restoration in which the covenant will be renewed (cf. vv. 39–40; 31.31–34). Even as Jeremiah purchased his field, so once again fields will be bought in the land. **33.1–26** Promises of future restoration. Continuing

the theme of salvation in chs. 30–32, this chapter consists of various sections that speak of future restoration. **33.1–9** Destroyed Jerusalem will be rebuilt. **33.1** See ch. 32. **33.2–3** The prose sermon begins with a hymnic acclamation of the Lord as Creator (see 31.35–37). **33.4–5** The imminent destruction of Jerusalem is reaffirmed. **33.6–9** Nevertheless, Israel and

from all the guilt of their sin against me, and I will forgive all the guilt of their sin and rebellion against me. [9]And this city[e] shall be to me a name of joy, a praise and a glory before all the nations of the earth who shall hear of all the good that I do for them; they shall fear and tremble because of all the good and all the prosperity I provide for it.

10 Thus says the LORD: In this place of which you say, "It is a waste without human beings or animals," in the towns of Judah and the streets of Jerusalem that are desolate, without inhabitants, human or animal, there shall once more be heard [11]the voice of mirth and the voice of gladness, the voice of the bridegroom and the voice of the bride, the voices of those who sing, as they bring thank offerings to the house of the LORD:

"Give thanks to the LORD of hosts,
    for the LORD is good,
    for his steadfast love endures forever!"

For I will restore the fortunes of the land as at first, says the LORD.

12 Thus says the LORD of hosts: In this place that is waste, without human beings or animals, and in all its towns there shall again be pasture for shepherds resting their flocks. [13]In the towns of the hill country, of the Shephelah, and of the Negeb, in the land of Benjamin, the places around Jerusalem, and in the towns of Judah, flocks shall again pass under the hands of the one who counts them, says the LORD.

The Righteous Branch and the Covenant with David

14 The days are surely coming, says the LORD, when I will fulfill the promise I made to the house of Israel and the house of Judah. [15]In those days and at that time I will cause a righteous Branch to spring up for David; and he shall execute justice and righteousness in the land. [16]In those days Judah will be saved and Jerusalem will live in safety. And this is the name by which it will be called: "The LORD is our righteousness."

17 For thus says the LORD: David shall never lack a man to sit on the throne of the house of Israel, [18]and the levitical priests shall never lack a man in my presence to offer burnt offerings, to make grain offerings, and to make sacrifices for all time.

19 The word of the LORD came to Jeremiah: [20]Thus says the LORD: If any of you could break my covenant with the day and my covenant with the night, so that day and night would not come at their appointed time, [21]only then could my covenant with my servant David be broken, so that he would not have a son to reign on his throne, and my covenant with my ministers the Levites. [22]Just as the host of heaven cannot be numbered and the sands of the sea cannot be measured, so I will increase the offspring of my servant David, and the Levites who minister to me.

23 The word of the LORD came to Jeremiah: [24]Have you not observed how these people say, "The two families that the LORD chose have been rejected by him," and how they hold my people in such contempt that they no longer regard them as a nation? [25]Thus says the LORD: Only if I had not established my covenant with day and night and the ordinances of heaven and earth, [26]would I reject the offspring of Jacob and of my servant David and not choose any of his descendants as rulers over the offspring of Abraham, Isaac, and Jacob. For I will restore their fortunes, and will have mercy upon them.

Death in Captivity Predicted for Zedekiah

34 The word that came to Jeremiah from the LORD, when King Nebuchadrezzar of Babylon and all his army and all the kingdoms of the earth and all the peoples under his dominion were fighting against Jerusalem

---

a Heb *And it*

Judah will be forgiven and restored, and Jerusalem rebuilt. **33.10–11** This oracle of salvation announces the return of gladness to a desolate land. For thank offerings and thanksgiving psalms, see Lev 7.11–18; Ps 107. The poetic quotation (v. 11b) comes from Ps 136.1, a thanksgiving psalm that praises God for mighty acts of salvation. **33.12–13** A prose oracle of salvation that promises pastures and flocks in the restoration period. **33.14–26** Future leaders. This prose oracle of salvation is an expansion of 23.5–6. Coming from the exile, it promises the restoration of the Davidic monarchy and the levitical priesthood. These verses are not in the Septuagint. God's promises to David and the Levites will be honored (Deut 18.1–8; 2 Sam 7). See Hag 1.1; 2.23; Zech 4.11–14; 6.9–13. **33.15–16** Jerusalem, not the future king, will be called *The LORD is our righteousness* (see 23.5–6).

34.1–7 A prose oracle of judgment against Zedekiah (cf. the oracle against Hananiah in ch. 28). The sermon is set at the onset of the siege of Jerusalem. Jer-

and all its cities: 2Thus says the LORD, the God of Israel: Go and speak to King Zedekiah of Judah and say to him: Thus says the LORD: I am going to give this city into the hand of the king of Babylon, and he shall burn it with fire. 3And you yourself shall not escape from his hand, but shall surely be captured and handed over to him; you shall see the king of Babylon eye to eye and speak with him face to face; and you shall go to Babylon. 4Yet hear the word of the LORD, O King Zedekiah of Judah! Thus says the LORD concerning you: You shall not die by the sword; 5you shall die in peace. And as spices were burned*a* for your ancestors, the earlier kings who preceded you, so they shall burn spices*b* for you and lament for you, saying, "Alas, lord!" For I have spoken the word, says the LORD.

6 Then the prophet Jeremiah spoke all these words to Zedekiah king of Judah, in Jerusalem, 7when the army of the king of Babylon was fighting against Jerusalem and against all the cities of Judah that were left, Lachish and Azekah; for these were the only fortified cities of Judah that remained.

Treacherous Treatment of Slaves

8 The word that came to Jeremiah from the LORD, after King Zedekiah had made a covenant with all the people in Jerusalem to make a proclamation of liberty to them— 9that all should set free their Hebrew slaves, male and female, so that no one should hold another Judean in slavery. 10And they obeyed, all the officials and all the people who had entered into the covenant that all would set free their slaves, male or female, so that they would not be enslaved again; they obeyed and set them free. 11But afterward they turned around and took back the male and female slaves they had

set free, and brought them again into subjection as slaves. 12The word of the LORD came to Jeremiah from the LORD: 13Thus says the LORD, the God of Israel: I myself made a covenant with your ancestors when I brought them out of the land of Egypt, out of the house of slavery, saying, 14"Every seventh year each of you must set free any Hebrews who have been sold to you and have served you six years; you must set them free from your service." But your ancestors did not listen to me or incline their ears to me. 15You yourselves recently repented and did what was right in my sight by proclaiming liberty to one another, and you made a covenant before me in the house that is called by my name; 16but then you turned around and profaned my name when each of you took back your male and female slaves, whom you had set free according to their desire, and you brought them again into subjection to be your slaves. 17Therefore, thus says the LORD: You have not obeyed me by granting a release to your neighbors and friends; I am going to grant a release to you, says the LORD—a release to the sword, to pestilence, and to famine. I will make you a horror to all the kingdoms of the earth. 18And those who transgressed my covenant and did not keep the terms of the covenant that they made before me, I will make like*c* the calf when they cut it in two and passed between its parts: 19the officials of Judah, the officials of Jerusalem, the eunuchs, the priests, and all the people of the land who passed between the parts of the calf 20shall be handed over to their enemies and to those who seek their lives. Their corpses shall become food for the birds

a Heb *as there was burning*   *b* Heb *shall burn*   *c* Cn: Heb lacks *like*

emiah was not yet imprisoned. **34.3–5** Zedekiah was blinded and exiled to Babylon, where he died in prison (39.7; 52.8–11; 2 Kings 25.5–7). In contrast to Jehoiakim (see 22.13–19), Zedekiah will have a funeral and be lamented. To *burn spices* was part of a royal funeral (2 Chr 16.14; 21.19). **34.7** *Lachish*, modern Tell ed-Duweir, located about thirty miles southwest of Jerusalem. It was a major walled fortress city located between Jerusalem and Gaza. *Azekah* (modern Tell ez-Zahariyeh), lying to the northeast of Lachish, was also a fortified city. In the fourth letter of the Lachish ostraca, recovered from a tower in the outer city gate and dated to the period just before the fall of Jerusalem, Hoshaiah, an official in an outpost to the north of Lachish, writes to Yaosh, its military commander: "We

are looking for the signals of Lachish, according to all the indications my Lord has given, because we do not see Azekah." **34.8–22** Slaves and the broken covenant. This prose narrative is set during the siege of Jerusalem (588 BCE). King Zedekiah and the population entered into covenant to release their Hebrew slaves in the hopes of gaining God's help. However, when Nebuchadrezzar temporarily lifted the siege to oppose an advancing Egyptian army (cf. 37.6–11), the people broke their covenantal oath by re-enslaving the slaves they had set free. This act of bad faith leads to an oracle of judgment against Jerusalem. **34.14** The law quoted is Deut 15.1, 12 (see Ex 21.2). **34.18–19** These verses describe the ritual of covenant making, "to cut a covenant" (see note on 31.33; Gen 15.7–21).

of the air and the wild animals of the earth. [21]And as for King Zedekiah of Judah and his officials, I will hand them over to their enemies and to those who seek their lives, to the army of the king of Babylon, which has withdrawn from you. [22]I am going to command, says the LORD, and will bring them back to this city; and they will fight against it, and take it, and burn it with fire. The towns of Judah I will make a desolation without inhabitant.

The Rechabites Commended

35 The word that came to Jeremiah from the LORD in the days of King Jehoiakim son of Josiah of Judah: [2]Go to the house of the Rechabites, and speak with them, and bring them to the house of the LORD, into one of the chambers; then offer them wine to drink. [3]So I took Jaazaniah son of Jeremiah son of Habazziniah, and his brothers, and all his sons, and the whole house of the Rechabites. [4]I brought them to the house of the LORD into the chamber of the sons of Hanan son of Igdaliah, the man of God, which was near the chamber of the officials, above the chamber of Maaseiah son of Shallum, keeper of the threshold. [5]Then I set before the Rechabites pitchers full of wine, and cups; and I said to them, "Have some wine." [6]But they answered, "We will drink no wine, for our ancestor Jonadab son of Rechab commanded us, 'You shall never drink wine, neither you nor your children; [7]nor shall you ever build a house, or sow seed; nor shall you plant a vineyard, or even own one; but you shall live in tents all your days, that you may live many days in the land where you reside.' [8]We have obeyed the charge of our ancestor Jonadab son of Rechab in all that he commanded us, to drink no wine all our days, ourselves, our wives, our sons, or our daughters, [9]and not to build houses to live in. We have no vineyard or field or seed; [10]but we have lived in tents, and have obeyed and done all that our ancestor Jonadab commanded us. [11]But when King Nebuchadrezzar of Babylon

came up against the land, we said, 'Come, and let us go to Jerusalem for fear of the army of the Chaldeans and the army of the Arameans.' That is why we are living in Jerusalem."

[12]Then the word of the LORD came to Jeremiah: [13]Thus says the LORD of hosts, the God of Israel: Go and say to the people of Judah and the inhabitants of Jerusalem, Can you not learn a lesson and obey my words? says the LORD. [14]The command has been carried out that Jonadab son of Rechab gave to his descendants to drink no wine; and they drink none to this day, for they have obeyed their ancestor's command. But I myself have spoken to you persistently, and you have not obeyed me. [15]I have sent to you all my servants the prophets, sending them persistently, saying, "Turn now every one of you from your evil way, and amend your doings, and do not go after other gods to serve them, and then you shall live in the land that I gave to you and your ancestors." But you did not incline your ear or obey me. [16]The descendants of Jonadab son of Rechab have carried out the command that their ancestor gave them, but this people has not obeyed me. [17]Therefore, thus says the LORD, the God of hosts, the God of Israel: I am going to bring on Judah and on all the inhabitants of Jerusalem every disaster that I have pronounced against them; because I have spoken to them and they have not listened, I have called to them and they have not answered.

[18]But to the house of the Rechabites Jeremiah said: Thus says the LORD of hosts, the God of Israel: Because you have obeyed the command of your ancestor Jonadab, and kept all his precepts, and done all that he commanded you, [19]therefore thus says the LORD of hosts, the God of Israel: Jonadab son of Rechab shall not lack a descendant to stand before me for all time.

The Scroll Read in the Temple

36 In the fourth year of King Jehoiakim son of Josiah of Judah, this word came

---

35.1–19 Set in the reign of Jehoiakim (609–598 BCE), this prose narrative describes the faithfulness of the Rechabites, a religious sect named in honor of their founder, Jonadab the son of Rechab, during the reign of Jehu (843/2–815). Presumably the editor who positioned chs. 34 and 35 next to each other wished to contrast the covenant loyalty of the Rechabites with the faithlessness the citizens of Jerusalem exhibited in taking back their slaves. The Rechabites abstained

from wine, lived as nomads in tents, and did not practice agriculture, all in accordance with the principles of Jonadab. **35.19** *To stand before* God is a priestly prerogative. The Rechabites were not priests, but their devotion was a form of divine service.

36.1–32 The two scrolls of Baruch. Clues to the composition of the book of Jeremiah are contained in this chapter. The story begins with the *fourth year of King Jehoiakim* (605 BCE, v. 1), the year of the battle of

to Jeremiah from the LORD: 2Take a scroll and write on it all the words that I have spoken to you against Israel and Judah and all the nations, from the day I spoke to you, from the days of Josiah until today. 3It may be that when the house of Judah hears of all the disasters that I intend to do to them, all of them may turn from their evil ways, so that I may forgive their iniquity and their sin.

4 Then Jeremiah called Baruch son of Neriah, and Baruch wrote on a scroll at Jeremiah's dictation all the words of the LORD that he had spoken to him. 5And Jeremiah ordered Baruch, saying, "I am prevented from entering the house of the LORD; 6so you go yourself, and on a fast day in the hearing of the people in the LORD's house you shall read the words of the LORD from the scroll that you have written at my dictation. You shall read them also in the hearing of all the people of Judah who come up from their towns. 7It may be that their plea will come before the LORD, and that all of them will turn from their evil ways, for great is the anger and wrath that the LORD has pronounced against this people." 8And Baruch son of Neriah did all that the prophet Jeremiah ordered him about reading from the scroll the words of the LORD in the LORD's house.

9 In the fifth year of King Jehoiakim son of Josiah of Judah, in the ninth month, all the people in Jerusalem and all the people who came from the towns of Judah to Jerusalem proclaimed a fast before the LORD. 10Then, in the hearing of all the people, Baruch read the words of Jeremiah from the scroll, in the house of the LORD, in the chamber of Gemariah son of Shaphan the secretary, which was in the upper court, at the entry of the New Gate of the LORD's house.

The Scroll Read in the Palace

11 When Micaiah son of Gemariah son of Shaphan heard all the words of the LORD from the scroll, 12he went down to the king's house, into the secretary's chamber; and all the officials were sitting there: Elishama the secretary, Delaiah son of Shemaiah, Elnathan son of Achbor, Gemariah son of Shaphan, Zedekiah son of Hananiah, and all the officials. 13And Micaiah told them all the words that he had heard, when Baruch read the scroll in the hearing of the people. 14Then all the officials sent Jehudi son of Nethaniah son of Shelemiah son of Cushi to say to Baruch, "Bring the scroll that you read in the hearing of the people, and come." So Baruch son of Neriah took the scroll in his hand and came to them. 15And they said to him, "Sit down and read it to us." So Baruch read it to them. 16When they heard all the words, they turned to one another in alarm, and said to Baruch, "We certainly must report all these words to the king." 17Then they questioned Baruch, "Tell us now, how did you write all these words? Was it at his dictation?" 18Baruch answered them, "He dictated all these words to me, and I wrote them with ink on the scroll." 19Then the officials said to Baruch, "Go and hide, you and Jeremiah, and let no one know where you are."

Jehoiakim Burns the Scroll

20 Leaving the scroll in the chamber of Elishama the secretary, they went to the court of the

---

Carchemish (see Introduction), and describes the formation of two scrolls of Baruch. The first scroll contained the prophecies of Jeremiah from 627 to 605 BCE, described primarily as oracles of judgment. The purpose of this scroll was to present the "house of Judah" an opportunity to repent, be forgiven, and avoid destruction (see 25.1–14). Baruch, Jeremiah's companion and secretary, belonged to an important family in Jerusalem and was a royal scribe (36.32; see chs. 32, 45). His brother, Seraiah, was minister to Zedekiah (51.59). Seals of the two brothers have been excavated. Baruch's reads: "to/from Baruch / son of Neriah / the scribe." Numerous efforts to reconstruct the two scrolls have been undertaken (see Introduction). If ch. 36 is historical, we may have indications of the first two editions of the book of Jeremiah. **36.5** Jeremiah was barred from the temple precinct, possibly because of the temple sermon (see chs. 7, 26). **36.6** Public fasts

were held periodically, especially during times of distress (see 2 Chr 20.3; Ezra 8.21–23; Neh 1.4–11). Since these were periods of penance in which lamenting, wearing sackcloth, offering sacrifices, and fasting made up the ritual, a *fast day* was appropriate for reading Jeremiah's oracles of judgment to the people assembled in the temple. **36.9** *The fifth year of King Jehoiakim* (604 BCE) would coincide with Nebuchadrezzar's advance into the Philistine plain, where he conquered Ashkelon. Shortly thereafter Jehoiakim declared his allegiance to Nebuchadrezzar. **36.11–13** *Elnathan,* the father of Nehushta (the mother of Jehoiachin, 2 Kings 24.8) and the leader of the party that captured Uriah and brought him to Jehoiakim for execution (26.22–23). *Gemariah,* the son of *Shaphan,* the royal secretary to whom Hilkiah, the high priest, revealed the discovery of the "book of the law" in the temple (2 Kings 22). *Micaiah* was his son. Interestingly, Shaphan read the

king; and they reported all the words to the king. 21Then the king sent Jehudi to get the scroll, and he took it from the chamber of Elishama the secretary; and Jehudi read it to the king and all the officials who stood beside the king. 22Now the king was sitting in his winter apartment (it was the ninth month), and there was a fire burning in the brazier before him. 23As Jehudi read three or four columns, the king*a* would cut them off with a penknife and throw them into the fire in the brazier, until the entire scroll was consumed in the fire that was in the brazier. 24Yet neither the king, nor any of his servants who heard all these words, was alarmed, nor did they tear their garments. 25Even when Elnathan and Delaiah and Gemariah urged the king not to burn the scroll, he would not listen to them. 26And the king commanded Jerahmeel the king's son and Seraiah son of Azriel and Shelemiah son of Abdeel to arrest the secretary Baruch and the prophet Jeremiah. But the LORD hid them.

Jeremiah Dictates Another

27 Now, after the king had burned the scroll with the words that Baruch wrote at Jeremiah's dictation, the word of the LORD came to Jeremiah: 28Take another scroll and write on it all the former words that were in the first scroll, which King Jehoiakim of Judah has burned. 29And concerning King Jehoiakim of Judah you shall say: Thus says the LORD, You have dared to burn this scroll, saying, Why have you written in it that the king of Babylon will certainly come and destroy this land, and will cut off from it human beings and animals? 30Therefore thus says the LORD concerning King Jehoiakim of Judah: He shall have no one to sit upon the throne of David, and his dead body shall be cast out to the heat by day and the frost by night. 31And I will punish him and his offspring and his servants for their iniquity; I will bring on them, and on the inhabitants of Jerusalem, and on the people of Judah, all the disasters with which I have threatened them—but they would not listen.

32 Then Jeremiah took another scroll and gave it to the secretary Baruch son of Neriah, who wrote on it at Jeremiah's dictation all the words of the scroll that King Jehoiakim of Judah had burned in the fire; and many similar words were added to them.

Zedekiah's Vain Hope

37 Zedekiah son of Josiah, whom King Nebuchadrezzar of Babylon made king in the land of Judah, succeeded Coniah son of Jehoiakim. 2But neither he nor his servants nor the people of the land listened to the words of the LORD that he spoke through the prophet Jeremiah.

3 King Zedekiah sent Jehucal son of Shelemiah and the priest Zephaniah son of Maaseiah to the prophet Jeremiah saying, "Please pray for us to the LORD our God." 4Now Jeremiah was still going in and out among the people, for he had not yet been put in prison. 5Meanwhile, the army of Pharaoh had come out of Egypt; and when the Chaldeans who were besieging Jerusalem heard news of them, they withdrew from Jerusalem.

6 Then the word of the LORD came to the prophet Jeremiah: 7Thus says the LORD, God of Israel: This is what the two of you shall say to the king of Judah, who sent you to me to inquire of me: Pharaoh's army, which set out to help you, is going to return to its own land, to Egypt. 8And the Chaldeans shall return and fight against this city; they shall take it and burn it with fire. 9Thus says the LORD: Do not deceive yourselves, saying, "The Chaldeans will surely go away from us," for they will not go away. 10Even if you defeated the whole army of Chaldeans who are fighting against you, and there remained of them only wounded men in their tents, they would rise up and burn this city with fire.

Jeremiah Is Imprisoned

11 Now when the Chaldean army had withdrawn from Jerusalem at the approach of

a Heb he

---

newly discovered law to King Josiah and received a positive response. **36.30** See note on 22.13–19. Jehoiakim was succeeded by his son Jehoiachin, who ruled for three months (see note on 22.24–30).

37.1–38.28 Jeremiah and Zedekiah. The prose narratives in these two chapters are sequential accounts of Jeremiah's dealings with Zedekiah during the Babylonian siege of Jerusalem. **37.1–10** News of an ad-

vancing Egyptian army led to Nebuchadrezzar's withdrawal from Jerusalem to meet the threat (see 34.21). When Zedekiah sends emissaries to ask Jeremiah to intercede on the behalf of Jerusalem (see 21.1–10), the prophet responds with an oracle that the Babylonians will return to destroy the city. **37.5** Pharaoh, Hophra (589–570 BCE). See 44.30. Zedekiah's rebellion, which began in 589, was no doubt stimulated in part by an al-

Pharaoh's army, 12Jeremiah set out from Jerusalem to go to the land of Benjamin to receive his share of property*a* among the people there. 13When he reached the Benjamin Gate, a sentinel there named Irijah son of Shelemiah son of Hananiah arrested the prophet Jeremiah saying, "You are deserting to the Chaldeans." 14And Jeremiah said, "That is a lie; I am not deserting to the Chaldeans." But Irijah would not listen to him, and arrested Jeremiah and brought him to the officials. 15The officials were enraged at Jeremiah, and they beat him and imprisoned him in the house of the secretary Jonathan, for it had been made a prison. 16Thus Jeremiah was put in the cistern house, in the cells, and remained there many days.

17 Then King Zedekiah sent for him, and received him. The king questioned him secretly in his house, and said, "Is there any word from the LORD?" Jeremiah said, "There is!" Then he said, "You shall be handed over to the king of Babylon." 18Jeremiah also said to King Zedekiah, "What wrong have I done to you or your servants or this people, that you have put me in prison? 19Where are your prophets who prophesied to you, saying, 'The king of Babylon will not come against you and against this land'? 20Now please hear me, my lord king: be good enough to listen to my plea, and do not send me back to the house of the secretary Jonathan to die there." 21So King Zedekiah gave orders, and they committed Jeremiah to the court of the guard; and a loaf of bread was given him daily from the bakers' street, until all the bread of the city was gone. So Jeremiah remained in the court of the guard.

Jeremiah in the Cistern

38 Now Shephatiah son of Mattan, Gedaliah son of Pashhur, Jucal son of Shelemiah, and Pashhur son of Malchiah heard the words that Jeremiah was saying to all the people, 2Thus says the LORD, Those who stay in this city shall die by the sword, by famine, and by pestilence; but those who go out to the Chaldeans shall live; they shall have their lives as a prize of war, and live. 3Thus says the LORD, This city shall surely be handed over to the army of the king of Babylon and be taken. 4Then the officials said to the king, "This man ought to be put to death, because he is discouraging the soldiers who are left in this city, and all the people, by speaking such words to them. For this man is not seeking the welfare of this people, but their harm." 5King Zedekiah said, "Here he is; he is in your hands; for the king is powerless against you." 6So they took Jeremiah and threw him into the cistern of Malchiah, the king's son, which was in the court of the guard, letting Jeremiah down by ropes. Now there was no water in the cistern, but only mud, and Jeremiah sank in the mud.

Jeremiah Is Rescued by Ebed-melech

7 Ebed-melech the Ethiopian,*b* a eunuch in the king's house, heard that they had put Jeremiah into the cistern. The king happened to be sitting at the Benjamin Gate, 8So Ebed-melech left the king's house and spoke to the king, 9"My lord king, these men have acted wickedly in all they did to the prophet Jeremiah by throwing him into the cistern to die there of hunger, for there is no bread left in the city." 10Then the king commanded Ebed-melech the Ethiopian,*b* "Take three men with you from here, and pull the prophet Jeremiah up from the cistern before he dies." 11So Ebed-melech took the men with him and went to the house of the king, to a wardrobe of*c* the storehouse, and took from there old rags and worn-out clothes, which he let down to Jeremiah in the cistern by ropes. 12Then Ebed-melech the Ethiopian*b* said to Jeremiah, "Just put the rags and clothes between your armpits and the ropes." Jeremiah did so. 13Then they drew Jeremiah up by the ropes and pulled him

a Meaning of Heb uncertain *b* Or Nubian; Heb Cushite
c Cn: Heb to under

liance with Egypt. **37.11–15** At the time of the lifting of the siege, Jeremiah is accused of deserting to the Babylonians when he attempts to travel to the territory of Benjamin to receive his share of the family property. This is probably not connected with the redeeming of the field in Anathoth (ch. 32), which occurred when he was in prison. **37.16–21** Zedekiah's renewed efforts to find a hopeful prophetic word fail. Jeremiah does succeed in being transferred to more comfortable quarters. **38.1–13** Jeremiah's enemies, officials who were pro-Egyptian and supportive of the rebellion, succeed in having the prophet imprisoned and presumably left to die in a muddy but waterless cistern. **38.4** The charge of treason against Jeremiah is similar to a charge in letter six of the Lachish letters against some officials in Jerusalem (see note on 34.7). **38.7** *Ebed-melech*, an Ethiopian and either a eunuch or palace official (Hebrew *saris*). Later he receives an oracle from

out of the cistern. And Jeremiah remained in the court of the guard.

Zedekiah Consults Jeremiah Again

14 King Zedekiah sent for the prophet Jeremiah and received him at the third entrance of the temple of the LORD. The king said to Jeremiah, "I have something to ask you; do not hide anything from me." 15 Jeremiah said to Zedekiah, "If I tell you, you will put me to death, will you not? And if I give you advice, you will not listen to me." 16 So King Zedekiah swore an oath in secret to Jeremiah, "As the LORD lives, who gave us our lives, I will not put you to death or hand you over to these men who seek your life."

17 Then Jeremiah said to Zedekiah, "Thus says the LORD, the God of hosts, the God of Israel, If you will only surrender to the officials of the king of Babylon, then your life shall be spared, and this city shall not be burned with fire, and you and your house shall live. 18 But if you do not surrender to the officials of the king of Babylon, then this city shall be handed over to the Chaldeans, and they shall burn it with fire, and you yourself shall not escape from their hand." 19 King Zedekiah said to Jeremiah, "I am afraid of the Judeans who have deserted to the Chaldeans, for I might be handed over to them and they would abuse me." 20 Jeremiah said, "That will not happen. Just obey the voice of the LORD in what I say to you, and it shall go well with you, and your life shall be spared. 21 But if you are determined not to surrender, this is what the LORD has shown me— 22 a vision of all the women remaining in the house of the king of Judah being led out to the officials of the king of Babylon and saying,

'Your trusted friends have seduced you
    and have overcome you;
Now that your feet are stuck in the mud,
    they desert you.'

23 All your wives and your children shall be led out to the Chaldeans, and you yourself shall not escape from their hand, but shall be seized by the king of Babylon; and this city shall be burned with fire."

24 Then Zedekiah said to Jeremiah, "Do not let anyone else know of this conversation, or you will die. 25 If the officials should hear that I have spoken with you, and they should come and say to you, 'Just tell us what you said to the king; do not conceal it from us, or we will put you to death. What did the king say to you?' 26 then you shall say to them, 'I was presenting my plea to the king not to send me back to the house of Jonathan to die there.' " 27 All the officials did come to Jeremiah and questioned him; and he answered them in the very words the king had commanded. So they stopped questioning him, for the conversation had not been overheard. 28 And Jeremiah remained in the court of the guard until the day that Jerusalem was taken.

The Fall of Jerusalem

39 In the ninth year of King Zedekiah of Judah, in the tenth month, King Nebuchadrezzar of Babylon and all his army came against Jerusalem and besieged it; 2 in the eleventh year of Zedekiah, in the fourth month, on the ninth day of the month, a breach was made in the city. 3 When Jerusalem was taken,[a] all the officials of the king of Babylon came and sat in the middle gate: Nergal-sharezer, Samgar-nebo, Sarsechim the Rabsaris, Nergal-sharezer the Rabmag, with all the rest of the officials of the king of Babylon. 4 When King Zedekiah of Judah and all the soldiers saw them, they fled, going out of the city at night by way of the king's garden through the gate between the two walls; and they went toward the Arabah. 5 But the army of the Chaldeans pursued them, and overtook Zedekiah in the plains of Jericho; and when they

---

a This clause has been transposed from 38.28

Jeremiah promising he would survive the destruction of Jerusalem (39.15–18). **38.14–28** In this final consultation between Jeremiah and Zedekiah, Jeremiah advises the king to surrender in order to save the city and himself. Zedekiah's fear of both the pro-Babylonian and pro-Egyptian factions is obvious. **38.14** *Third entrance.* The various entrances to the temple are not currently known. **38.16** *Oath.* See note on 4.2.
   39.1–40.6 The fall of Jerusalem. **39.1–10** A summary of 52.4–16 (see 2 Kings 25.1–12). **39.3** *Nergal-*

sharezer, Samgar-nebo, Sarsechim the Rabsaris, Nergal-sharezer the Rabmag, possibly combinations of proper names and titles (see v. 13). Some scholars suggest: "Nergal-sharezer the Simmagir, Nebushazban the chief court official, and Nergal-sharezer the Rabmag," in which Simmagir and Rabmag are understood as Babylonian official titles. Some scholars identify Nergal-sharezer (here and in v. 13) as Nergalsharusur (Neriglissar), Nebuchadrezzar's son-in-law, who succeeded to the Babylonian throne in 560 and ruled until

had taken him, they brought him up to King Nebuchadrezzar of Babylon, at Riblah, in the land of Hamath; and he passed sentence on him. 6The king of Babylon slaughtered the sons of Zedekiah at Riblah before his eyes; also the king of Babylon slaughtered all the nobles of Judah. 7He put out the eyes of Zedekiah, and bound him in fetters to take him to Babylon. 8The Chaldeans burned the king's house and the houses of the people, and broke down the walls of Jerusalem. 9Then Nebuzaradan the captain of the guard exiled to Babylon the rest of the people who were left in the city, those who had deserted to him, and the people who remained. 10Nebuzaradan the captain of the guard left in the land of Judah some of the poor people who owned nothing, and gave them vineyards and fields at the same time.

Jeremiah, Set Free, Remembers Ebed-melech

11 King Nebuchadrezzar of Babylon gave command concerning Jeremiah through Nebuzaradan, the captain of the guard, saying, 12"Take him, look after him well and do him no harm, but deal with him as he may ask you." 13So Nebuzaradan the captain of the guard, Nebushazban the Rabsaris, Nergal-sharezer the Rabmag, and all the chief officers of the king of Babylon sent 14and took Jeremiah from the court of the guard. They entrusted him to Gedaliah son of Ahikam son of Shaphan to be brought home. So he stayed with his own people.

15 The word of the LORD came to Jeremiah while he was confined in the court of the guard: 16Go and say to Ebed-melech the Ethiopian:*a* Thus says the LORD of hosts, the God of Israel: I am going to fulfill my words against this city for evil and not for good, and they shall be accomplished in your presence on that day. 17But I will save you on that day, says the LORD, and you shall not be handed over to those whom you dread. 18For I will surely save you, and you shall not fall by the sword; but you shall have your life as a prize of war, because you have trusted in me, says the LORD.

Jeremiah with Gedaliah the Governor

40 The word that came to Jeremiah from the LORD after Nebuzaradan the captain of the guard had let him go from Ramah, when he took him bound in fetters along with all the captives of Jerusalem and Judah who were being exiled to Babylon. 2The captain of the guard took Jeremiah and said to him, "The LORD your God threatened this place with this disaster; 3and now the LORD has brought it about, and has done as he said, because all of you sinned against the LORD and did not obey his voice. Therefore this thing has come upon you. 4Now look, I have just released you today from the fetters on your hands. If you wish to come with me to Babylon, come, and I will take good care of you; but if you do not wish to come with me to Babylon, you need not come. See, the whole land is before you; go wherever you think it good and right to go. 5If you remain,*b* then return to Gedaliah son of Ahikam son of Shaphan, whom the king of Babylon appointed governor of the towns of Judah, and stay with him among the people; or go wherever you think it right to go." So the captain of the guard gave him an allowance of food and a present, and let him go. 6Then Jeremiah went to Gedaliah son of Ahikam at Mizpah, and stayed with him among the people who were left in the land.

7 When all the leaders of the forces in the open country and their troops heard that the king of Babylon had appointed Gedaliah son of Ahikam governor in the land, and had committed to him men, women, and children, those of the poorest of the land who had not been taken into exile to Babylon, 8they went to

a Or Nubian; Heb Cushite   *b* Syr: Meaning of Heb uncertain

---

556 BCE, but this identification is not universally accepted. **39.6** *Riblah,* a city in the Beqaa Valley in Lebanon that guarded the highway between Egypt and Mesopotamia. It was an important military base in the seventh and sixth centuries BCE. **39.11–14** For a slightly different account regarding Jeremiah's release from prison, cf. 40.1–6. **39.15–18** See 38.7–13.

40.7–41.18 The governorship and assassination of Gedaliah. See 2 Kings 25.22–26. **40.7–16** After the fall of Jerusalem Judah was incorporated into the provincial system of the Babylonian Empire. With the destruction of its cities, the decimation of its economy, and the deportation of its leaders, including the best educated and the highly skilled artisans, Judah was left largely with poor peasants. Nebuchadrezzar appointed as governor *Gedaliah,* the son of the same *Ahikam* who set Jeremiah free at the conclusion of the trial in ch. 26, and the grandson of *Shaphan,* Josiah's royal secretary (2 Kings 22). How long Gedaliah's government lasted is unclear, although certainly no longer than 582 BCE. He set up his government in *Mizpah,* probably modern Tell en-Nasbeh, about eight miles north of

Gedaliah at Mizpah—Ishmael son of Nethaniah, Johanan son of Kareah, Seraiah son of Tanhumeth, the sons of Ephai the Netophathite, Jezaniah son of the Maacathite, they and their troops. 9Gedaliah son of Ahikam son of Shaphan swore to them and their troops, saying, "Do not be afraid to serve the Chaldeans. Stay in the land and serve the king of Babylon, and it shall go well with you. 10As for me, I am staying at Mizpah to represent you before the Chaldeans who come to us; but as for you, gather wine and summer fruits and oil, and store them in your vessels, and live in the towns that you have taken over." 11Likewise, when all the Judeans who were in Moab and among the Ammonites and in Edom and in other lands heard that the king of Babylon had left a remnant in Judah and had appointed Gedaliah son of Ahikam son of Shaphan as governor over them, 12then all the Judeans returned from all the places to which they had been scattered and came to the land of Judah, to Gedaliah at Mizpah; and they gathered wine and summer fruits in great abundance.

13 Now Johanan son of Kareah and all the leaders of the forces in the open country came to Gedaliah at Mizpah 14and said to him, "Are you at all aware that Baalis king of the Ammonites has sent Ishmael son of Nethaniah to take your life?" But Gedaliah son of Ahikam would not believe them. 15Then Johanan son of Kareah spoke secretly to Gedaliah at Mizpah, "Please let me go and kill Ishmael son of Nethaniah, and no one else will know. Why should he take your life, so that all the Judeans who are gathered around you would be scattered, and the remnant of Judah would perish?" 16But Gedaliah son of Ahikam said to Johanan son of Kareah, "Do not do such a thing, for you are telling a lie about Ishmael."

Insurrection against Gedaliah

41 In the seventh month, Ishmael son of Nethaniah son of Elishama, of the royal family, one of the chief officers of the king, came with ten men to Gedaliah son of

Ahikam, at Mizpah. As they ate bread together there at Mizpah, 2Ishmael son of Nethaniah and the ten men with him got up and struck down Gedaliah son of Ahikam son of Shaphan with the sword and killed him, because the king of Babylon had appointed him governor in the land. 3Ishmael also killed all the Judeans who were with Gedaliah at Mizpah, and the Chaldean soldiers who happened to be there.

4 On the day after the murder of Gedaliah, before anyone knew of it, 5eighty men arrived from Shechem and Shiloh and Samaria, with their beards shaved and their clothes torn, and their bodies gashed, bringing grain offerings and incense to present at the temple of the LORD. 6And Ishmael son of Nethaniah came out from Mizpah to meet them, weeping as he came. As he met them, he said to them, "Come to Gedaliah son of Ahikam." 7When they reached the middle of the city, Ishmael son of Nethaniah and the men with him slaughtered them, and threw them[a] into a cistern. 8But there were ten men among them who said to Ishmael, "Do not kill us, for we have stores of wheat, barley, oil, and honey hidden in the fields." So he refrained, and did not kill them along with their companions.

9 Now the cistern into which Ishmael had thrown all the bodies of the men whom he had struck down was the large cistern[b] that King Asa had made for defense against King Baasha of Israel; Ishmael son of Nethaniah filled that cistern with those whom he had killed. 10Then Ishmael took captive all the rest of the people who were in Mizpah, the king's daughters and all the people who were left at Mizpah, whom Nebuzaradan, the captain of the guard, had committed to Gedaliah son of Ahikam. Ishmael son of Nethaniah took them captive and set out to cross over to the Ammonites.

11 But when Johanan son of Kareah and all the leaders of the forces with him heard of all

---

a Syr: Heb lacks *and threw them*; compare verse 9   b Gk: Heb *whom he had killed by the hand of Gedaliah*

Jerusalem on the border between Benjamin and Judah. **41.1–3** When Gedaliah attempted to persuade the survivors to settle down and accept Babylonian rule, the government was overthrown and Gedaliah was assassinated by *Ishmael*, a member of the royal family and a superpatriot who collaborated with Baalis, king of the Ammonites (40.14), to continue resistance against the Babylonians. **41.4–10** Ishmael

slaughters pilgrims from cities in the old Northern Kingdom going to Jerusalem to make sacrifices. Perhaps they were engaged in lamentation rituals in their mourning over the destruction of Jerusalem and the temple. **41.11–18** *Johanan*, a Jewish military commander and strong supporter of Gedaliah, intercepted and defeated Ishmael, though he made good his escape to Ammon. Fearful of Babylonian reprisals for the

the crimes that Ishmael son of Nethaniah had done, [12]they took all their men and went to fight against Ishmael son of Nethaniah. They came upon him at the great pool that is in Gibeon. [13]And when all the people who were with Ishmael saw Johanan son of Kareah and all the leaders of the forces with him, they were glad. [14]So all the people whom Ishmael had carried away captive from Mizpah turned around and came back, and went to Johanan son of Kareah. [15]But Ishmael son of Nethaniah escaped from Johanan with eight men, and went to the Ammonites. [16]Then Johanan son of Kareah and all the leaders of the forces with him took all the rest of the people whom Ishmael son of Nethaniah had carried away captive[a] from Mizpah after he had slain Gedaliah son of Ahikam—soldiers, women, children, and eunuchs, whom Johanan brought back from Gibeon.[b] [17]And they set out, and stopped at Geruth Chimham near Bethlehem, intending to go to Egypt [18]because of the Chaldeans; for they were afraid of them, because Ishmael son of Nethaniah had killed Gedaliah son of Ahikam, whom the king of Babylon had made governor over the land.

Jeremiah Advises Survivors Not to Migrate

42 Then all the commanders of the forces, and Johanan son of Kareah and Azariah[c] son of Hoshaiah, and all the people from the least to the greatest, approached [2]the prophet Jeremiah and said, "Be good enough to listen to our plea, and pray to the LORD your God for us—for all this remnant. For there are only a few of us left out of many, as your eyes can see. [3]Let the LORD your God show us where we should go and what we should do." [4]The prophet Jeremiah said to them, "Very well: I am going to pray to the LORD your God as you request, and whatever the LORD answers you I will tell you; I will keep nothing back from you." [5]They in their turn said to Jeremiah, "May the LORD be a true and faithful witness against us if we do not act according to everything that the LORD your God sends us

through you. [6]Whether it is good or bad, we will obey the voice of the LORD our God to whom we are sending you, in order that it may go well with us when we obey the voice of the LORD our God."

7 At the end of ten days the word of the LORD came to Jeremiah. [8]Then he summoned Johanan son of Kareah and all the commanders of the forces who were with him, and all the people from the least to the greatest, [9]and said to them, "Thus says the LORD, the God of Israel, to whom you sent me to present your plea before him: [10]If you will only remain in this land, then I will build you up and not pull you down; I will plant you, and not pluck you up; for I am sorry for the disaster that I have brought upon you. [11]Do not be afraid of the king of Babylon, as you have been; do not be afraid of him, says the LORD, for I am with you, to save you and to rescue you from his hand. [12]I will grant you mercy, and he will have mercy on you and restore you to your native soil. [13]But if you continue to say, 'We will not stay in this land,' thus disobeying the voice of the LORD your God [14]and saying, 'No, we will go to the land of Egypt, where we shall not see war, or hear the sound of the trumpet, or be hungry for bread, and there we will stay,' [15]then hear the word of the LORD, O remnant of Judah. Thus says the LORD of hosts, the God of Israel: If you are determined to enter Egypt and go to settle there, [16]then the sword that you fear shall overtake you there, in the land of Egypt; and the famine that you dread shall follow close after you into Egypt; and there you shall die. [17]All the people who have determined to go to Egypt to settle there shall die by the sword, by famine, and by pestilence; they shall have no remnant or survivor from the disaster that I am bringing upon them.

18 "For thus says the LORD of hosts, the God of Israel: Just as my anger and my wrath were poured out on the inhabitants of Jerusalem, so my wrath will be poured out on you when you

---

a Cn: Heb *whom he recovered from Ishmael son of Nethaniah*
b Meaning of Heb uncertain   *c* Gk: Heb *Jezaniah*

---

slaughter at Mizpah, Johanan and his forces began to seek refuge in Egypt. This fear was not unfounded, as a third exile was carried out in 582 BCE (52.30). **41.12** *Great pool that is in Gibeon.* See 2 Sam 2.13. **41.17** *Geruth Chimham,* unidentified. Geruth may mean "inn," thus Chimham's Inn.

42.1–43.7 The survivors of Mizpah and their res-

cuers decide to flee to Egypt and force Jeremiah to accompany them. **42.1–6** Jeremiah is asked to intercede with God to tell the survivors what to do. **42.7–22** God's reply is the survivors should remain and rebuild the land. If they do so, God will bless them and deliver them from Nebuchadrezzar. However, should they flee to Egypt, even there war, famine, and pesti-

go to Egypt. You shall become an object of execration and horror, of cursing and ridicule. You shall see this place no more. [19]The LORD has said to you, O remnant of Judah, Do not go to Egypt. Be well aware that I have warned you today [20]that you have made a fatal mistake. For you yourselves sent me to the LORD your God, saying, 'Pray for us to the LORD our God, and whatever the LORD our God says, tell us and we will do it.' [21]So I have told you today, but you have not obeyed the voice of the LORD your God in anything that he sent me to tell you. [22]Be well aware, then, that you shall die by the sword, by famine, and by pestilence in the place where you desire to go and settle."

Taken to Egypt, Jeremiah Warns of Judgment

43 When Jeremiah finished speaking to all the people all these words of the LORD their God, with which the LORD their God had sent him to them, [2]Azariah son of Hoshaiah and Johanan son of Kareah and all the other insolent men said to Jeremiah, "You are telling a lie. The LORD our God did not send you to say, 'Do not go to Egypt to settle there'; [3]but Baruch son of Neriah is inciting you against us, to hand us over to the Chaldeans, in order that they may kill us or take us into exile in Babylon." [4]So Johanan son of Kareah and all the commanders of the forces and all the people did not obey the voice of the LORD, to stay in the land of Judah. [5]But Johanan son of Kareah and all the commanders of the forces took all the remnant of Judah who had returned to settle in the land of Judah from all the nations to which they had been driven— [6]the men, the women, the children, the princesses, and everyone whom Nebuzaradan the captain of the guard had left

with Gedaliah son of Ahikam son of Shaphan; also the prophet Jeremiah and Baruch son of Neriah. [7]And they came into the land of Egypt, for they did not obey the voice of the LORD. And they arrived at Tahpanhes.

8 Then the word of the LORD came to Jeremiah in Tahpanhes: [9]Take some large stones in your hands, and bury them in the clay pavement[a] that is at the entrance to Pharaoh's palace in Tahpanhes. Let the Judeans see you do it, [10]and say to them, Thus says the LORD of hosts, the God of Israel: I am going to send and take my servant King Nebuchadrezzar of Babylon, and he[b] will set his throne above these stones that I have buried, and he will spread his royal canopy over them. [11]He shall come and ravage the land of Egypt, giving

> those who are destined for pestilence, to
>   pestilence,
> and those who are destined for
>   captivity, to captivity,
> and those who are destined for the
>   sword, to the sword.

[12]He[c] shall kindle a fire in the temples of the gods of Egypt; and he shall burn them and carry them away captive; and he shall pick clean the land of Egypt, as a shepherd picks his cloak clean of vermin; and he shall depart from there safely. [13]He shall break the obelisks of Heliopolis, which is in the land of Egypt; and the temples of the gods of Egypt he shall burn with fire.

Denunciation of Persistent Idolatry

44 The word that came to Jeremiah for all the Judeans living in the land of Egypt, at Migdol, at Tahpanhes, at Memphis, and in

---

a Meaning of Heb uncertain   *b* Gk Syr: Heb *I*   *c* Gk Syr Vg: Heb *I*

---

lence will overtake them, and no remnant will remain. **43.1–7** Jeremiah is accused of lying and following the counsel of Baruch, who is accused of wishing to turn the survivors over to the Babylonians. The survivors and their rescuers flee to Egypt, and Jeremiah and Baruch are forced to go with them. **43.7** *Tahpanhes.* See note on 2.16.

43.8–44.30 Jeremiah's condemnation of the Jewish refugees who fled to Egypt. The story is set in the years following the assassination of Gedaliah, i.e., ca. 582–570 BCE. **43.8–13** The narrative begins with a symbolic act designed to demonstrate that Nebuchadrezzar will conquer Egypt (see 13.1–11, 12–14; 16.1–13; 18.1–12; 19.1–15; 27.1–22; 32.1–44). **43.9** *Pharaoh's*

palace, probably a royal building, since the capital was in Sais in the western Delta. **43.11** See 15.2. **43.13** *Heliopolis,* also called On (Egyptian, "city of the pillar"; see Gen 41.45), is modern Tell Hisn and Matariyeh, seven miles northeast of downtown Cairo. It was the cultic center for the worship of the sun god Re and well known for its *obelisks:* four-sided, freestanding granite pillars with pyramidal tops. According to the oracle, the Jewish refugees will not escape their dreaded foe. Nebuchadrezzar did invade Egypt in 568/7 BCE and fought Pharaoh Amasis, though the outcome of the battle is not known. However, Babylonia did not conquer Egypt. **44.1–14** The narrative continues with Jeremiah's rather lengthy sermon condemning all Jewish

the land of Pathros, [2]Thus says the LORD of hosts, the God of Israel: You yourselves have seen all the disaster that I have brought on Jerusalem and on all the towns of Judah. Look at them; today they are a desolation, without an inhabitant in them, [3]because of the wickedness that they committed, provoking me to anger, in that they went to make offerings and serve other gods that they had not known, neither they, nor you, nor your ancestors. [4]Yet I persistently sent to you all my servants the prophets, saying, "I beg you not to do this abominable thing that I hate!" [5]But they did not listen or incline their ear, to turn from their wickedness and make no offerings to other gods. [6]So my wrath and my anger were poured out and kindled in the towns of Judah and in the streets of Jerusalem; and they became a waste and a desolation, as they still are today. [7]And now thus says the LORD God of hosts, the God of Israel: Why are you doing such great harm to yourselves, to cut off man and woman, child and infant, from the midst of Judah, leaving yourselves without a remnant? [8]Why do you provoke me to anger with the works of your hands, making offerings to other gods in the land of Egypt where you have come to settle? Will you be cut off and become an object of cursing and ridicule among all the nations of the earth? [9]Have you forgotten the crimes of your ancestors, of the kings of Judah, of their[a] wives, your own crimes and those of your wives, which they committed in the land of Judah and in the streets of Jerusalem? [10]They have shown no contrition or fear to this day, nor have they walked in my law and my statutes that I set before you and before your ancestors.

11 Therefore thus says the LORD of hosts, the God of Israel: I am determined to bring disaster on you, to bring all Judah to an end. [12]I will take the remnant of Judah who are determined to come to the land of Egypt to settle, and they shall perish, everyone; in the land of Egypt they shall fall; by the sword and by famine they shall perish; from the least to the greatest, they shall die by the sword and by famine; and they shall become an object of ex-

ecration and horror, of cursing and ridicule. [13]I will punish those who live in the land of Egypt, as I have punished Jerusalem, with the sword, with famine, and with pestilence, [14]so that none of the remnant of Judah who have come to settle in the land of Egypt shall escape or survive or return to the land of Judah. Although they long to go back to live there, they shall not go back, except some fugitives.

15 Then all the men who were aware that their wives had been making offerings to other gods, and all the women who stood by, a great assembly, all the people who lived in Pathros in the land of Egypt, answered Jeremiah: [16]"As for the word that you have spoken to us in the name of the LORD, we are not going to listen to you. [17]Instead, we will do everything that we have vowed, make offerings to the queen of heaven and pour out libations to her, just as we and our ancestors, our kings and our officials, used to do in the towns of Judah and in the streets of Jerusalem. We used to have plenty of food, and prospered, and saw no misfortune. [18]But from the time we stopped making offerings to the queen of heaven and pouring out libations to her, we have lacked everything and have perished by the sword and by famine." [19]And the women said,[b] "Indeed we will go on making offerings to the queen of heaven and pouring out libations to her; do you think that we made cakes for her, marked with her image, and poured out libations to her without our husbands' being involved?"

20 Then Jeremiah said to all the people, men and women, all the people who were giving him this answer: [21]"As for the offerings that you made in the towns of Judah and in the streets of Jerusalem, you and your ancestors, your kings and your officials, and the people of the land, did not the LORD remember them? Did it not come into his mind? [22]The LORD could no longer bear the sight of your evil doings, the abominations that you committed; therefore your land became a desolation and a waste and a curse, without in-

---

a Heb *his*   *b* Compare Syr: Heb lacks *And the women said*

refugees in Egypt for abandoning their homeland and engaging in idolatry. **44.1** *Migdol,* a city in northern Egypt, possibly identified with modern Tell el-Heir (see 46.14). *Tahpanhes.* See 43.7; note on 2.16. *Memphis.* See note on 2.16. *Pathros,* Upper Egypt, the area south of Memphis and the Delta (see Isa 11.11; Ezek 29.14; 30.14). **44.15–19** The response of the people is defiant: they intend to continue in their idolatry. **44.17** *Queen of heaven.* See note on 7.18. **44.20–28** Jeremiah continues to condemn the refugees, predicting

habitant, as it is to this day. ²³It is because you burned offerings, and because you sinned against the LORD and did not obey the voice of the LORD or walk in his law and in his statutes and in his decrees, that this disaster has befallen you, as is still evident today."

24 Jeremiah said to all the people and all the women, "Hear the word of the LORD, all you Judeans who are in the land of Egypt, ²⁵Thus says the LORD of hosts, the God of Israel: You and your wives have accomplished in deeds what you declared in words, saying, 'We are determined to perform the vows that we have made, to make offerings to the queen of heaven and to pour out libations to her.' By all means, keep your vows and make your libations! ²⁶Therefore hear the word of the LORD, all you Judeans who live in the land of Egypt: Lo, I swear by my great name, says the LORD, that my name shall no longer be pronounced on the lips of any of the people of Judah in all the land of Egypt, saying, 'As the Lord GOD lives.' ²⁷I am going to watch over them for harm and not for good; all the people of Judah who are in the land of Egypt shall perish by the sword and by famine, until not one is left. ²⁸And those who escape the sword shall return from the land of Egypt to the land of Judah, few in number; and all the remnant of Judah, who have come to the land of Egypt to settle, shall know whose words will stand, mine or theirs! ²⁹This shall be the sign to you, says the LORD, that I am going to punish you in this place, in order that you may know that my words against you will surely be carried out: ³⁰Thus says the LORD, I am going to give Phar-

aoh Hophra, king of Egypt, into the hands of his enemies, those who seek his life, just as I gave King Zedekiah of Judah into the hand of King Nebuchadrezzar of Babylon, his enemy who sought his life."

A Word of Comfort to Baruch

45 The word that the prophet Jeremiah spoke to Baruch son of Neriah, when he wrote these words in a scroll at the dictation of Jeremiah, in the fourth year of King Jehoiakim son of Josiah of Judah: ²Thus says the LORD, the God of Israel, to you, O Baruch: ³You said, "Woe is me! The LORD has added sorrow to my pain; I am weary with my groaning, and I find no rest." ⁴Thus you shall say to him, "Thus says the LORD: I am going to break down what I have built, and pluck up what I have planted—that is, the whole land. ⁵And you, do you seek great things for yourself? Do not seek them; for I am going to bring disaster upon all flesh, says the LORD; but I will give you your life as a prize of war in every place to which you may go."

Judgment on Egypt

46 The word of the LORD that came to the prophet Jeremiah concerning the nations.

2 Concerning Egypt, about the army of Pharaoh Neco, king of Egypt, which was by the river Euphrates at Carchemish and which King Nebuchadrezzar of Babylon defeated in the fourth year of King Jehoiakim son of Josiah of Judah:

3   Prepare buckler and shield,

---

that most will die, while a few will escape to return to Judah. **44.30** *Hophra* (Aphries), king of Egypt 589–570 BCE (see 37.5). He was assassinated by Amasis (570–526), a former court official who ruled as co-regent for three years before killing Hophra. **45.1–5** An oracle of salvation addressed to Baruch, Jeremiah's secretary and companion (see note on 36.1–32). Set in 605 BCE, when Baruch wrote down the judgment oracles of Jeremiah (see ch. 36), Jeremiah's words promise the scribe that his own life will be spared when the disasters against Judah and Jerusalem take place. **45.3** The oracle refers to Baruch's lament. Cf. Jeremiah's laments in 11.18–20.18 (see note on 11.18–23). **45.4** See 1.10; 18.7–9; 24.6. **45.5** What Baruch sought for himself is not clear. However, he does seem to have held an important position in government (see note on 36.1–32). For one's *life as a prize of war*, cf. 21.9; 38.2; 39.18. **46.1–51.58** Oracles against the nations. This collec-

tion of oracles, with its own superscription (46.1), had its own history of transmission before being included in the growing corpus that became the book of Jeremiah. The location of this collection in the Septuagint (after 25.13a) is probably original (see the similar positioning of oracles concerning foreign nations in Isa 13–23; Ezek 25–32, where they follow oracles of judgment against Judah and precede oracles of salvation and hope). The question of the authorship of these oracles is greatly debated by scholars. Some of the oracles may have been original to Jeremiah (e.g., the oracle against Egypt in 46.3–12); others are by later prophets and editors. **46.2–26** Two oracles of judgment are against Egypt: the defeat at Carchemish, vv. 2–12, and the approach of Nebuchadrezzar, vv. 13–26. **46.2** The defeat of Neco II by Nebuchadrezzar, first at Carchemish, and then near Hamath, opened the way to Syro-Palestine for the expanding Babylonian Empire. By 604 or 603 BCE, Judah became a vassal to the Babyloni-

and advance for battle!

4 Harness the horses;
   mount the steeds!
Take your stations with your helmets,
   whet your lances,
   put on your coats of mail!

5 Why do I see them terrified?
   They have fallen back;
their warriors are beaten down,
   and have fled in haste.
They do not look back—
   terror is all around!
                         says the LORD.

6 The swift cannot flee away,
   nor can the warrior escape;
in the north by the river Euphrates
   they have stumbled and fallen.

7 Who is this, rising like the Nile,
   like rivers whose waters surge?

8 Egypt rises like the Nile,
   like rivers whose waters surge.
It said, Let me rise, let me cover the earth,
   let me destroy cities and their
      inhabitants.

9 Advance, O horses,
   and dash madly, O chariots!
Let the warriors go forth:
   Ethiopia[a] and Put who carry the shield,
   the Ludim, who draw[b] the bow.

10 That day is the day of the Lord GOD of
      hosts,
   a day of retribution,
   to gain vindication from his foes.
The sword shall devour and be sated,
   and drink its fill of their blood.
For the Lord GOD of hosts holds a
      sacrifice
   in the land of the north by the river
      Euphrates.

11 Go up to Gilead, and take balm,
   O virgin daughter Egypt!
In vain you have used many medicines;
   there is no healing for you.

12 The nations have heard of your shame,
   and the earth is full of your cry;
for warrior has stumbled against warrior;
   both have fallen together.

Babylonia Will Strike Egypt

13 The word that the LORD spoke to the prophet Jeremiah about the coming of King Nebuchadrezzar of Babylon to attack the land of Egypt:

14 Declare in Egypt, and proclaim in
      Migdol;
   proclaim in Memphis and Tahpanhes;
Say, "Take your stations and be ready,
   for the sword shall devour those
      around you."

15 Why has Apis fled?[c]
   Why did your bull not stand?
   —because the LORD thrust him down.

16 Your multitude stumbled[d] and fell,
   and one said to another,[e]
"Come, let us go back to our own people
   and to the land of our birth,
   because of the destroying sword."

17 Give Pharaoh, king of Egypt, the name
   "Braggart who missed his chance."

18 As I live, says the King,
   whose name is the LORD of hosts,
one is coming
   like Tabor among the mountains,
   and like Carmel by the sea.

19 Pack your bags for exile,
   sheltered daughter Egypt!
For Memphis shall become a waste,
   a ruin, without inhabitant.

20 A beautiful heifer is Egypt—
   a gadfly from the north lights upon her.

21 Even her mercenaries in her midst
   are like fatted calves;
they too have turned and fled together,
   they did not stand;
for the day of their calamity has come
      upon them,
   the time of their punishment.

22 She makes a sound like a snake gliding
      away;

---

a Or *Nubia*; Heb *Cush*   b Cn: Heb *who grasp, who draw*
c Gk: Heb *Why was it swept away*   d Gk: Meaning of Heb uncertain   e Gk: Heb *and fell one to another and they said*

---

ans. The oracle either predicts or celebrates the Egyptian defeat. **46.9** *Ethiopia, Put* (probably a region in Libya), and *Ludim* (a group of people in North Africa), three nations fighting with the Egyptians. **46.11** *Gilead.* See note on 8.22. **46.13–26** This oracle supposes

Jeremiah predicted an invasion of Egypt by Nebuchadrezzar. Although Nebuchadrezzar invaded Egypt, he did not conquer the country (see Ezek. 29.19–21; notes on Jer 43.8–13; 48.13). **46.14** *Migdol.* See note on 44.1. *Memphis, Tahpanhes.* See note on

for her enemies march in force,
and come against her with axes,
like those who fell trees.
23 They shall cut down her forest,
            says the LORD,
though it is impenetrable,
because they are more numerous
            than locusts;
they are without number.
24 Daughter Egypt shall be put to shame;
she shall be handed over to a people
from the north.

25 The LORD of hosts, the God of Israel, said: See, I am bringing punishment upon Amon of Thebes, and Pharaoh, and Egypt and her gods and her kings, upon Pharaoh and those who trust in him. 26 I will hand them over to those who seek their life, to King Nebuchadrezzar of Babylon and his officers. Afterward Egypt shall be inhabited as in the days of old, says the LORD.

God Will Save Israel

27 But as for you, have no fear, my servant
            Jacob,
and do not be dismayed, O Israel;
for I am going to save you from far away,
and your offspring from the land of
            their captivity.
Jacob shall return and have quiet and
            ease,
and no one shall make him afraid.
28 As for you, have no fear, my servant
            Jacob,
            says the LORD,
for I am with you.
I will make an end of all the nations
among which I have banished you,
but I will not make an end of you!
I will chastise you in just measure,
and I will by no means leave you
            unpunished.

Judgment on the Philistines

47 The word of the LORD that came to the prophet Jeremiah concerning the Philistines, before Pharaoh attacked Gaza:
2 Thus says the LORD:
See, waters are rising out of the north
and shall become an overflowing
            torrent;
they shall overflow the land and all that
            fills it,
the city and those who live in it.
People shall cry out,
and all the inhabitants of the land shall
            wail.
3 At the noise of the stamping of the hoofs
            of his stallions,
at the clatter of his chariots, at the
            rumbling of their wheels,
parents do not turn back for children,
so feeble are their hands,
4 because of the day that is coming
to destroy all the Philistines,
to cut off from Tyre and Sidon
every helper that remains.
For the LORD is destroying the Philistines,
the remnant of the coastland of
            Caphtor.
5 Baldness has come upon Gaza,
Ashkelon is silenced.
O remnant of their power![a]
How long will you gash yourselves?
6 Ah, sword of the LORD!
How long until you are quiet?
Put yourself into your scabbard,
rest and be still!
7 How can it[b] be quiet,
when the LORD has given it an order?
Against Ashkelon and against the
            seashore—
there he has appointed it.

---

a Gk: Heb their valley   b Gk Vg: Heb you

2.16. **46.15** *Apis,* an Egyptian god of fertility worshiped in Memphis as a sacred bull. **46.25–26** A later commentary on the two oracles. *Amon,* an Egyptian sun god whose cult center was the temple of Karnak in Thebes. **46.27–28** An oracle of salvation for Israel found also in 30.10–11.
47.1–7 The prose introduction points to an imminent attack on Gaza, one of the major Philistine cities, by an unidentified pharaoh as the occasion for this judgment oracle. Herodotus (*History* 2.159) indicates that, after the battle of Megiddo (609 BCE), Neco II conquered Kadytis (Gaza). However, the *waters . . . rising out of the north* and the reference to Ashkelon suggest Nebuchadrezzar's invasion of Philistia in 604 BCE after he defeated the Egyptians at Carchemish. **47.4** *Tyre and Sidon,* Phoenician cities presumably allied with the Philistines. *Caphtor,* the island of Crete (see Am 9.7), one of the places from which the Philistines came. **47.5** *Gaza,* taken by Neco II after 609 BCE, came within the Babylonian orbit along with the other cities of Philistia after the battle of Carchemish. *Ashkelon,* destroyed by Nebuchadrezzar in late 604.

Judgment on Moab

48 Concerning Moab.

Thus says the LORD of hosts, the God of Israel:
Alas for Nebo, it is laid waste!
  Kiriathaim is put to shame, it is taken;
  the fortress is put to shame and broken
    down;
2   the renown of Moab is no more.
In Heshbon they planned evil against her:
  "Come, let us cut her off from being a
    nation!"
You also, O Madmen, shall be brought to
    silence;[a]
  the sword shall pursue you.

3 Hark! a cry from Horonaim,
  "Desolation and great destruction!"
4 "Moab is destroyed!"
  her little ones cry out.
5 For at the ascent of Luhith
    they go[b] up weeping bitterly;
  for at the descent of Horonaim
    they have heard the distressing cry of
      anguish.
6 Flee! Save yourselves!
  Be like a wild ass[c] in the desert!

7 Surely, because you trusted in your
    strongholds[d] and your treasures,
    you also shall be taken;
  Chemosh shall go out into exile,
    with his priests and his attendants.
8 The destroyer shall come upon every
    town,
  and no town shall escape;
  the valley shall perish,
  and the plain shall be destroyed,
    as the LORD has spoken.

9 Set aside salt for Moab,
    for she will surely fall;
  her towns shall become a desolation,
    with no inhabitant in them.

10 Accursed is the one who is slack in doing
the work of the LORD; and accursed is the one
who keeps back the sword from bloodshed.

11 Moab has been at ease from his youth,
    settled like wine[e] on its dregs;
  he has not been emptied from vessel to
    vessel,
    nor has he gone into exile;
  therefore his flavor has remained
    and his aroma is unspoiled.
12 Therefore, the time is surely coming, says
the LORD, when I shall send to him decanters to
decant him, and empty his vessels, and break
his[f] jars in pieces. 13 Then Moab shall be
ashamed of Chemosh, as the house of Israel
was ashamed of Bethel, their confidence.

14 How can you say, "We are heroes
    and mighty warriors"?
15 The destroyer of Moab and his towns has
    come up,
  and the choicest of his young men have
    gone down to slaughter,
    says the King, whose name is the LORD
    of hosts.
16 The calamity of Moab is near at hand
    and his doom approaches swiftly.
17 Mourn over him, all you his neighbors,
    and all who know his name;
  say, "How the mighty scepter is broken,
    the glorious staff!"

---

a The place-name Madmen sounds like the Hebrew verb to be
silent   b Cn: Heb he goes   c Gk Aquila: Heb like Aroer
d Gk: Heb works   e Heb lacks like wine   f Gk Aquila: Heb their

---

48.1–47 A series of oracles of judgment against
Moab: the advance of Nebuchadrezzar (vv. 1–10), destruction is at hand (vv. 11–17), a taunt of destroyed
Moab (vv. 18–28), a lament over fallen Moab (vv. 29–
39), judgment against Moab (vv. 40–42), and a woe
oracle ending with the promise of salvation (vv. 43–
47). The oracles and prose additions (vv. 10, 12, 21–27,
34–39) feature extensive borrowings from Isa 15–16.
Located east of Israel in the Transjordan, Moab was a
historic enemy of Israel, often receiving prophetic
condemnation (Isa 15–16; Zeph 2.8–11). When Jehoiakim rebelled against Nebuchadrezzar, Moabites
joined in raids on Judah (2 Kings 24.2). According to
27.1–11, Moab joined in the conspiracy against the

Babylonians (595 BCE). It is possible that Moab joined
in the later revolt. 48.1 Nebo, a Moabite city (probably
modern Khirbet Mekhayyet) approximately five miles
southwest of Heshbon (see Isa 15.2). Kiriathaim, a city
in Moab, probably located near modern el-Qereiyat,
five and a half miles north-northwest of Dibon (see
Ezek 25.9). 48.2 Heshbon, modern Tell Hesban,
located near the Jordanian village of Hesban, was
an important city in northern Moab (see Isa 15.4;
16.8–9). 48.3 Horonaim, a town in Moab (see Isa.
15.5). 48.5 Luhith, a city of Moab, probably near the
south end of the Dead Sea (see Isa 15.5). 48.7 Chemosh, the national deity of Moab (see 1 Kings 11.7).
48.13 Bethel. See 1 Kings 12.25–33; Am 7.10–17.

18 Come down from glory,
    and sit on the parched ground,
    enthroned daughter Dibon!
For the destroyer of Moab has come up
    against you;
he has destroyed your strongholds.
19 Stand by the road and watch,
    you inhabitant of Aroer!
Ask the man fleeing and the woman
    escaping;
say, "What has happened?"
20 Moab is put to shame, for it is broken
    down;
wail and cry!
Tell it by the Arnon,
    that Moab is laid waste.

21 Judgment has come upon the tableland, upon Holon, and Jahzah, and Mephaath, 22 and Dibon, and Nebo, and Beth-diblathaim, 23 and Kiriathaim, and Beth-gamul, and Beth-meon, 24 and Kerioth, and Bozrah, and all the towns of the land of Moab, far and near. 25 The horn of Moab is cut off, and his arm is broken, says the LORD.

26 Make him drunk, because he magnified himself against the LORD; let Moab wallow in his vomit; he too shall become a laughingstock. 27 Israel was a laughingstock for you, though he was not caught among thieves; but whenever you spoke of him you shook your head!

28 Leave the towns, and live on the rock,
    O inhabitants of Moab!
Be like the dove that nests
    on the sides of the mouth of a gorge.
29 We have heard of the pride of Moab—
    he is very proud—
of his loftiness, his pride, and his
    arrogance,
    and the haughtiness of his heart.
30 I myself know his insolence, says the
    LORD;
his boasts are false,
    his deeds are false.
31 Therefore I wail for Moab;

I cry out for all Moab;
    for the people of Kir-heres I mourn.
32 More than for Jazer I weep for you,
    O vine of Sibmah!
Your branches crossed over the sea,
    reached as far as Jazer;[a]
upon your summer fruits and your
    vintage
    the destroyer has fallen.
33 Gladness and joy have been taken away
    from the fruitful land of Moab;
I have stopped the wine from the wine
    presses;
no one treads them with shouts of joy;
    the shouting is not the shout of joy.

34 Heshbon and Elealeh cry out;[b] as far as Jahaz they utter their voice, from Zoar to Horonaim and Eglath-shelishiyah. For even the waters of Nimrim have become desolate. 35 And I will bring to an end in Moab, says the LORD, those who offer sacrifice at a high place and make offerings to their gods. 36 Therefore my heart moans for Moab like a flute, and my heart moans like a flute for the people of Kir-heres; for the riches they gained have perished.

37 For every head is shaved and every beard cut off; on all the hands there are gashes, and on the loins sackcloth. 38 On all the housetops of Moab and in the squares there is nothing but lamentation; for I have broken Moab like a vessel that no one wants, says the LORD. 39 How it is broken! How they wail! How Moab has turned his back in shame! So Moab has become a derision and a horror to all his neighbors.
40 For thus says the LORD:
    Look, he shall swoop down like an eagle,
    and spread his wings against Moab;
41 the towns[c] shall be taken
    and the strongholds seized.
The hearts of the warriors of Moab, on
    that day,
    shall be like the heart of a woman in
    labor.

---

a Two Mss and Isa 16.8: MT *the sea of Jazer*   b Cn: Heb *From the cry of Heshbon to Elealeh*   c Or *Kerioth*

48.18 *Dibon,* modern Dhiban, was an important city located on the King's Highway, thirteen miles east of the Dead Sea (see Isa 15.2, 9). **48.19** *Aroer,* a fortress on the Arnon River, identified with modern Khirbet Araʿir. **48.20** The *Arnon* River flows through Moab from the east into the Dead Sea. **48.21–24** Various towns and cities in Moab. **48.29–39** See the laments, both of God for the people (14.17–18) and of Judah and Jerusalem for themselves (14.1–10, 19–22). **48.31** *Kir-heres,* identified with modern el-Kerak (see Isa 15.1), was a capital city of Moab; it is about eleven miles east of the Dead Sea. **48.32** *Sibmah,* a Moabite city, may be modern Qurn el-Kibsh, five miles southwest of Hesban. *Jazer,* a Moabite city probably located just to the west of Amman. **48.34** A

42 Moab shall be destroyed as a people,
    because he magnified himself against
        the LORD.
43 Terror, pit, and trap
    are before you, O inhabitants of Moab!
                    says the LORD.
44 Everyone who flees from the terror
    shall fall into the pit,
and everyone who climbs out of the pit
    shall be caught in the trap.
For I will bring these things[a] upon Moab
    in the year of their punishment,
                    says the LORD.

45 In the shadow of Heshbon
    fugitives stop exhausted;
for a fire has gone out from Heshbon,
    a flame from the house of Sihon;
it has destroyed the forehead of Moab,
    the scalp of the people of tumult.[b]
46 Woe to you, O Moab!
    The people of Chemosh have perished,
for your sons have been taken captive,
    and your daughters into captivity.
47 Yet I will restore the fortunes of Moab
    in the latter days, says the LORD.
Thus far is the judgment on Moab.

Judgment on the Ammonites

49 Concerning the Ammonites.

Thus says the LORD:
    Has Israel no sons?
    Has he no heir?
Why then has Milcom dispossessed Gad,
    and his people settled in its towns?
2 Therefore, the time is surely coming,

says the LORD,
    when I will sound the battle alarm
        against Rabbah of the Ammonites;
it shall become a desolate mound,
    and its villages shall be burned with fire;
then Israel shall dispossess those who
        dispossessed him,
    says the LORD.

3 Wail, O Heshbon, for Ai is laid waste!
    Cry out, O daughters[c] of Rabbah!
Put on sackcloth,
    lament, and slash yourselves with
        whips![d]
For Milcom shall go into exile,
    with his priests and his attendants.
4 Why do you boast in your strength?
    Your strength is ebbing,
O faithless daughter.
    You trusted in your treasures, saying,
    "Who will attack me?"
5 I am going to bring terror upon you,
    says the Lord GOD of hosts,
    from all your neighbors,
and you will be scattered, each headlong,
    with no one to gather the fugitives.

6 But afterward I will restore the fortunes of
the Ammonites, says the LORD.

Judgment on Edom

7 Concerning Edom.

Thus says the LORD of hosts:
    Is there no longer wisdom in Teman?

---

a Gk Syr: Heb bring upon it   b Or of Shaon   c Or villages
d Cn: Meaning of Heb uncertain

---

list of various Moabite sites. **48.45–47** These verses are missing in the Septuagint, an indication that they were added later. **48.45** Sihon, an Amorite king whose capital was Heshbon. He was defeated by the Israelites during their migration prior to the settlement in Canaan (see Num 21.21–30; Deut 2.24–37; Judg 11.18–22).

49.1–6 Ammon, a country in the Transjordan, east of Israel, and a perennial enemy. After the fall of Assyria, Ammon soon came under the control of the Babylonians and joined with them in the attack on Judah when Jehoiakim revolted (see 2 Kings 24.2). Later they joined in a conspiracy against Babylonia (Jer 27.3) and eventually revolted (see Ezek 21.18–23). After the fall of Judah in 587 BCE, Ammon continued the rebellion, even supporting a Jewish partisan, Ishmael, who assassinated Gedaliah (see ch. 41). Sometime later, Nebuchadrezzar sent punitive expeditions that led to the end of the Ammonite state. The

oracle of judgment indicates destruction will come upon Ammon. **49.1** Milcom, the national deity of Ammon and, like Baal, a god of war and fertility (see 1 Kings 11.5, 33). Gad, an Israelite tribe that occupied land east of the Jordan between the Jabbok and Arnon rivers. Ammon took over territory formerly claimed by Israel (see Judg 10.6–12.6; 2 Sam 12.26–31). **49.2** Rabbah, the capital of Ammon, modern Amman (see Ezek 25.5; Am 1.14). **49.3** Heshbon (see note on 48.2) may have fallen into Ammonite hands. Ai, possibly an Israelite settlement just south of the ancient city of Ai (located two miles southeast of Bethel) or, since Ai means "ruin" in Hebrew, Rabbah. Cf. the calls for Judah and Jerusalem to lament (6.26; 9.10; 9.17–22). **49.6** This verse, a promise of salvation, is absent in the Septuagint, an indication it was added later (see 48.45–47). **49.7–22** Against Edom, a bitter rival of Israel. Tradition traced Edom's origins back to Esau, the

Has counsel perished from the
    prudent?
Has their wisdom vanished?

8 Flee, turn back, get down low,
    inhabitants of Dedan!
For I will bring the calamity of Esau upon
    him,
    the time when I punish him.

9 If grape-gatherers came to you,
    would they not leave gleanings?
If thieves came by night,
    even they would pillage only what they
    wanted.

10 But as for me, I have stripped Esau bare,
    I have uncovered his hiding places,
    and he is not able to conceal himself.
His offspring are destroyed, his kinsfolk
    and his neighbors; and he is no more.

11 Leave your orphans, I will keep them alive;
    and let your widows trust in me.

12 For thus says the LORD: If those who do
not deserve to drink the cup still have to drink
it, shall you be the one to go unpunished? You
shall not go unpunished; you must drink it.
13 For by myself I have sworn, says the LORD,
that Bozrah shall become an object of horror
and ridicule, a waste, and an object of cursing;
and all her towns shall be perpetual wastes.

14 I have heard tidings from the LORD,
    and a messenger has been sent among
    the nations:
"Gather yourselves together and come
    against her,
    and rise up for battle!"

15 For I will make you least among the
    nations,
    despised by humankind.

16 The terror you inspire
    and the pride of your heart have
    deceived you,

you who live in the clefts of the rock,[a]
    who hold the height of the hill.
Although you make your nest as high as
    the eagle's,
    from there I will bring you down,
        says the LORD.

17 Edom shall become an object of horror;
everyone who passes by it will be horrified
and will hiss because of all its disasters. 18 As
when Sodom and Gomorrah and their neighbors were overthrown, says the LORD, no one
shall live there, nor shall anyone settle in it.
19 Like a lion coming up from the thickets of
the Jordan against a perennial pasture, I will
suddenly chase Edom[b] away from it; and I
will appoint over it whomever I choose.[c] For
who is like me? Who can summon me? Who
is the shepherd who can stand before me?
20 Therefore hear the plan that the LORD has
made against Edom and the purposes that he
has formed against the inhabitants of Teman:
Surely the little ones of the flock shall be
dragged away; surely their fold shall be appalled at their fate. 21 At the sound of their fall
the earth shall tremble; the sound of their cry
shall be heard at the Red Sea.[d] 22 Look, he
shall mount up and swoop down like an
eagle, and spread his wings against Bozrah,
and the heart of the warriors of Edom in that
day shall be like the heart of a woman in
labor.

Judgment on Damascus

23 Concerning Damascus.

Hamath and Arpad are confounded,
    for they have heard bad news;

---

a Or of Sela   b Heb him   c Or and I will single out the choicest
of his rams: Meaning of Heb uncertain   d Or Sea of Reeds

---

twin brother of Jacob (Israel; see Gen 25.19–28). Its
territory was to the east and south of Israel. The
Edomites were often the object of prophetic invective
(see Ps 137; Isa 11.14; 34.5–17; Ezek 35; Am 1.6, 9, 11;
2.1; Obadiah; Mal 1.2–5). A vassal of Nebuchadrezzar's expanding empire as early as 604 BCE, Edom
joined in his conquest of Jerusalem in 587 BCE and exulted over the devastation of the city (Ps 137.7; Lam
4.21–22; Ob 10–16). After the exile in 587 BCE, some
Edomites moved into southern Judah, making Hebron their capital. The present oracle is closely related
to Obadiah (vv. 14–16 are close to Ob 1–4; vv. 9–10a
are similar to Ob 5–6). **49.7** *Teman,* a significant military and commercial city in central Edom. Edom was
famous for its wisdom. **49.8** *Dedan,* a country in

northwest Arabia known for its commerce (see Ezek
25.13). **49.13** *Bozrah* was the chief city of northern
Edom (see Isa 34.6; Am 1.12). **49.18** *Sodom and Gomorrah.* See note on 20.16. **49.23–27** *Damascus,* the
capital of Syria (see 1 Kings 11.24; 15.18; 19.15; 20.34;
2 Kings 8.7, 9; 16.10–12; Isa 7.8). It was conquered by
the Assyrians in 733/2 BCE and became the center of a
province ruled by successive empires. Little is known
of its history for the next several centuries. It is not in
the list of nations doomed to drink the cup of the
Lord's wrath in 25.18–26 and thus was probably a
later addition to this collection. **49.23** *Hamath* (modern Hama), both a Syrian city on the Orontes River
between Damascus and Aleppo and a kingdom in its
own right. *Arpad* (Tell Erfad), a city in northern Syria

they melt in fear, they are troubled like
the sea[a]
that cannot be quiet.
24 Damascus has become feeble, she turned
to flee,
and panic seized her;
anguish and sorrows have taken hold of
her,
as of a woman in labor.
25 How the famous city is forsaken,[b]
the joyful town![c]
26 Therefore her young men shall fall in her
squares,
and all her soldiers shall be destroyed
in that day,
says the LORD of hosts.
27 And I will kindle a fire at the wall of
Damascus,
and it shall devour the strongholds of
Ben-hadad.

Judgment on Kedar and Hazor

28 Concerning Kedar and the kingdoms of
Hazor that King Nebuchadrezzar of Babylon
defeated.

Thus says the LORD:
Rise up, advance against Kedar!
Destroy the people of the east!
29 Take their tents and their flocks,
their curtains and all their goods;
carry off their camels for yourselves,
and a cry shall go up: "Terror is all
around!"
30 Flee, wander far away, hide in deep places,
O inhabitants of Hazor!
says the LORD.
For King Nebuchadrezzar of Babylon
has made a plan against you
and formed a purpose against you.

31 Rise up, advance against a nation at
ease,

that lives secure,
says the LORD,
that has no gates or bars,
that lives alone.
32 Their camels shall become booty,
their herds of cattle a spoil.
I will scatter to every wind
those who have shaven temples,
and I will bring calamity
against them from every side,
says the LORD.
33 Hazor shall become a lair of jackals,
an everlasting waste;
no one shall live there,
nor shall anyone settle in it.

Judgment on Elam

34 The word of the LORD that came to the
prophet Jeremiah concerning Elam, at the beginning of the reign of King Zedekiah of Judah.

35 Thus says the LORD of hosts: I am going
to break the bow of Elam, the mainstay of
their might; 36and I will bring upon Elam the
four winds from the four quarters of heaven;
and I will scatter them to all these winds, and
there shall be no nation to which the exiles
from Elam shall not come. 37I will terrify Elam
before their enemies, and before those who
seek their life; I will bring disaster upon them,
my fierce anger, says the LORD. I will send the
sword after them, until I have consumed
them; 38and I will set my throne in Elam, and
destroy their king and officials, says the LORD.

39 But in the latter days I will restore the
fortunes of Elam, says the LORD.

Judgment on Babylon

50 The word that the LORD spoke concerning Babylon, concerning the land
of the Chaldeans, by the prophet Jeremiah:

---

a Cn: Heb *there is trouble in the sea*   *b* Vg: Heb *is not forsaken*
c Syr Vg Tg: Heb *the town of my joy*

---

located some twenty-five miles north of Aleppo. Hamath and Arpad were destroyed by the Assyrians (see
2 Kings 18.34; 19.13; Isa 10.9; 36.19; 37.13). **49.27** This
verse is taken from Am 1.4. *Ben-hadad,* the name of
several kings of Damascus (1 Kings 15.18, 20; 2 Kings
13.24). **49.28–33** An oracle of judgment against Arabian tribes (see 25.23–24). *Kedar* (see note on 2.10–
11) was apparently conquered by Nebuchadrezzar.
Hazor, an unknown site in the Arabian desert, possibly conquered by Nebuchadrezzar. **49.32** *Shaven
temples.* See note on 9.26. **49.34–39** *Elam,* a country

located east of the Tigris River. Its capital was Susa.
Conquered by the Assyrians, Elam helped in the
Assyrian war against Israel (see Isa 11.11; 21.2; 22.6).
Eventually Elam came under Babylonian and then
Persian control. The oracle is dated at the beginning
of the reign of Zedekiah (597 BCE). **49.39** This verse
is probably a later addition (see 46.25–26; 48.47;
49.6). **50.1–51.58** A collection of poetic and prose judgment oracles that speak of the destruction of Babylon
and the return of the Jews from captivity (see chs. 24,

2 Declare among the nations and proclaim,
　　set up a banner and proclaim,
　　　do not conceal it, say:
　Babylon is taken,
　　Bel is put to shame,
　　Merodach is dismayed.
　Her images are put to shame,
　　her idols are dismayed.

3 For out of the north a nation has come up against her; it shall make her land a desolation, and no one shall live in it; both human beings and animals shall flee away.

4 In those days and in that time, says the LORD, the people of Israel shall come, they and the people of Judah together; they shall come weeping as they seek the LORD their God. 5They shall ask the way to Zion, with faces turned toward it, and they shall come and join*a* themselves to the LORD by an everlasting covenant that will never be forgotten.

6 My people have been lost sheep; their shepherds have led them astray, turning them away on the mountains; from mountain to hill they have gone, they have forgotten their fold. 7All who found them have devoured them, and their enemies have said, "We are not guilty, because they have sinned against the LORD, the true pasture, the LORD, the hope of their ancestors."

8 Flee from Babylon, and go out of the land of the Chaldeans, and be like male goats leading the flock. 9For I am going to stir up and bring against Babylon a company of great nations from the land of the north; and they shall array themselves against her; from there she shall be taken. Their arrows are like the arrows of a skilled warrior who does not return empty-handed. 10Chaldea shall be plundered; all who plunder her shall be sated, says the LORD.

11 Though you rejoice, though you exult,
　　O plunderers of my heritage,
　though you frisk about like a heifer on
　　　the grass,
　　and neigh like stallions,
12 your mother shall be utterly shamed,
　　and she who bore you shall be
　　　disgraced.
　Lo, she shall be the last of the nations,
　　a wilderness, dry land, and a desert.
13 Because of the wrath of the LORD she
　　　shall not be inhabited,
　but shall be an utter desolation;
　everyone who passes by Babylon shall be
　　　appalled
　　and hiss because of all her wounds.
14 Take up your positions around Babylon,
　　all you that bend the bow;
　shoot at her, spare no arrows,
　　for she has sinned against the LORD.
15 Raise a shout against her from all sides,
　　"She has surrendered;
　her bulwarks have fallen,
　　her walls are thrown down."
　For this is the vengeance of the LORD:
　　take vengeance on her,
　　do to her as she has done.
16 Cut off from Babylon the sower,
　　and the wielder of the sickle in time of
　　　harvest;
　because of the destroying sword
　all of them shall return to their own
　　　people,
　and all of them shall flee to their own
　　　land.

17 Israel is a hunted sheep driven away by lions. First the king of Assyria devoured it, and now at the end King Nebuchadrezzar of Babylon has gnawed its bones. 18Therefore, thus says the LORD of hosts, the God of Israel:

―――――――――

a Gk: Heb *toward it. Come! They shall join*

―――――――――

25, 29). Whether or not these two chapters contain a nucleus of material from Jeremiah is debated. Prior to the fall of Jerusalem the prophet speaks favorably of Babylon: Nebuchadrezzar is the servant of God, the Babylonians are the instrument of God's will, the exiles are to pray for Babylon, and Judah should submit to Babylonian rule. After the fall of Jerusalem the prophet may have changed his views. Now the devastator of nations will be destroyed because of its arrogance. It is more likely, however, that most of the collection derives from prophets of the exile and the early postexilic period who announce and celebrate the collapse of the empire and the return home. The Babylonian Empire fell in 539 BCE to the Persians, and shortly thereafter Cyrus, the Persian king, allowed the Jews to return home (Ezra 1.1–4). **50.1** Superscription (see Hag 1.1; Mal 1.1). **50.2** *Bel*, one of the names of Marduk, the leading god of Babylonia. *Merodach,* the biblical name for Marduk. **50.3** The imagery of the "foe from the north" (see chs. 4–10) is transferred to the enemies of Babylonia (the Medes and the Persians). **50.11–16** Babylon surrendered to the armies of

I am going to punish the king of Babylon and his land, as I punished the king of Assyria. ¹⁹I will restore Israel to its pasture, and it shall feed on Carmel and in Bashan, and on the hills of Ephraim and in Gilead its hunger shall be satisfied. ²⁰In those days and at that time, says the LORD, the iniquity of Israel shall be sought, and there shall be none; and the sins of Judah, and none shall be found; for I will pardon the remnant that I have spared.

21 Go up to the land of Merathaim;ᵃ
        go up against her,
    and attack the inhabitants of Pekodᵇ
        and utterly destroy the last of them,ᶜ
                            says the LORD;
        do all that I have commanded you.
22 The noise of battle is in the land,
        and great destruction!
23 How the hammer of the whole earth
        is cut down and broken!
    How Babylon has become
        a horror among the nations!
24 You set a snare for yourself and you were
            caught, O Babylon,
        but you did not know it;
    you were discovered and seized,
        because you challenged the LORD.
25 The LORD has opened his armory,
        and brought out the weapons of his
            wrath,
    for the Lord GOD of hosts has a task
            to do
        in the land of the Chaldeans.
26 Come against her from every quarter;
        open her granaries;
    pile her up like heaps of grain, and
            destroy her utterly;
        let nothing be left of her.
27 Kill all her bulls,
        let them go down to the slaughter.
    Alas for them, their day has come,
        the time of their punishment!

28 Listen! Fugitives and refugees from the land of Babylon are coming to declare in Zion the vengeance of the LORD our God, vengeance for his temple.

29 Summon archers against Babylon, all who bend the bow. Encamp all around her; let no one escape. Repay her according to her deeds; just as she has done, do to her—for she has arrogantly defied the LORD, the Holy One of Israel. ³⁰Therefore her young men shall fall in her squares, and all her soldiers shall be destroyed on that day, says the LORD.

31 I am against you, O arrogant one,
        says the Lord GOD of hosts;
    for your day has come,
        the time when I will punish you.
32 The arrogant one shall stumble and fall,
        with no one to raise him up,
    and I will kindle a fire in his cities,
        and it will devour everything around
            him.

33 Thus says the LORD of hosts: The people of Israel are oppressed, and so too are the people of Judah; all their captors have held them fast and refuse to let them go. ³⁴Their Redeemer is strong; the LORD of hosts is his name. He will surely plead their cause, that he may give rest to the earth, but unrest to the inhabitants of Babylon.

35 A sword against the Chaldeans, says the
            LORD,
        and against the inhabitants of Babylon,
        and against her officials and her
            sages!
36 A sword against the diviners,
        so that they may become fools!
    A sword against her warriors,
        so that they may be destroyed!
37 A sword against herᵈ horses and against
            herᵈ chariots,
        and against all the foreign troops in
            her midst,
        so that they may become women!
    A sword against all her treasures,
        that may be plundered!
38 A droughtᵉ against her waters,
        that they may be dried up!
    For it is a land of images,
        and they go mad over idols.

39 Therefore wild animals shall live with hyenas in Babylon,ᶠ and ostriches shall inhabit her; she shall never again be peopled, or inhabited for all generations. ⁴⁰As when God overthrew Sodom and Gomorrah and their neighbors, says the LORD, so no one shall live there, nor shall anyone settle in her.

---

a Or of Double Rebellion b Or of Punishment c Tg: Heb destroy after them d Cn: Heb his e Another reading is A sword f Heb lacks in Babylon

41 Look, a people is coming from the north;
    a mighty nation and many kings
        are stirring from the farthest parts of
            the earth.
42 They wield bow and spear,
        they are cruel and have no mercy.
    The sound of them is like the roaring sea;
        they ride upon horses,
    set in array as a warrior for battle,
        against you, O daughter Babylon!

43 The king of Babylon heard news of them,
        and his hands fell helpless;
    anguish seized him,
        pain like that of a woman in labor.

44 Like a lion coming up from the thickets of the Jordan against a perennial pasture, I will suddenly chase them away from her; and I will appoint over her whomever I choose.[a] For who is like me? Who can summon me? Who is the shepherd who can stand before me? 45 Therefore hear the plan that the LORD has made against Babylon, and the purposes that he has formed against the land of the Chaldeans: Surely the little ones of the flock shall be dragged away; surely their[b] fold shall be appalled at their fate. 46 At the sound of the capture of Babylon the earth shall tremble, and her cry shall be heard among the nations.

51 Thus says the LORD:
    I am going to stir up a destructive
        wind[c]
    against Babylon
    and against the inhabitants of Leb-
        qamai;[d]
2 and I will send winnowers to Babylon,
        and they shall winnow her.
    They shall empty her land
        when they come against her from every
            side
        on the day of trouble.
3 Let not the archer bend his bow,
        and let him not array himself in his
            coat of mail.

Do not spare her young men;
    utterly destroy her entire army.
4 They shall fall down slain in the land of
        the Chaldeans,
    and wounded in her streets.
5 Israel and Judah have not been forsaken
        by their God, the LORD of hosts,
    though their land is full of guilt
        before the Holy One of Israel.

6 Flee from the midst of Babylon,
        save your lives, each of you!
    Do not perish because of her guilt,
        for this is the time of the LORD's
            vengeance;
        he is repaying her what is due.
7 Babylon was a golden cup in the LORD's
        hand,
        making all the earth drunken;
    the nations drank of her wine,
        and so the nations went mad.
8 Suddenly Babylon has fallen and is
        shattered;
        wail for her!
    Bring balm for her wound;
        perhaps she may be healed.
9 We tried to heal Babylon,
        but she could not be healed.
    Forsake her, and let each of us go
        to our own country;
    for her judgment has reached up to
            heaven
        and has been lifted up even to the
            skies.
10 The LORD has brought forth our
            vindication;
        come, let us declare in Zion
            the work of the LORD our God.

11 Sharpen the arrows!
        Fill the quivers!
    The LORD has stirred up the spirit of the kings

_____
a Or *and I will single out the choicest of her rams*: Meaning of Heb uncertain   b Syr Gk Tg Compare 49.20: Heb lacks *their*   c Or *stir up the spirit of a destroyer*   d *Leb-qamai* is a cryptogram for *Kasdim,* Chaldea

_____
Persia, led by Gobryas. It was not taken by force and destroyed. **50.21** This verse contains two wordplays. *Merathaim* means "double rebellion" and is a word-play on a region in southern Babylonia, *nar marratu*. *Pekod,* "punishment" in Hebrew, refers to an Aramean tribe on the eastern bank of the lower Tigris River (see Ezek 23.23). **50.29–32** The pride of rulers that leads to self-exaltation and the desire to rule in the place of

God is the basis for Babylonia's judgment (see Ezek 28). **50.40** *Sodom and Gomorrah.* See 20.16 and note; 23.14. **51.1** *Leb-qamai,* in Hebrew "the heart of those who rise up against me." It is another example of ath-bash (see note on 25.26) that works out to mean *kas-dim,* the Chaldeans (Babylonians). **51.11** *Medes.* Media, located in northwest Iran, was a separate em-pire that helped in the overthrow of the Assyrians at

of the Medes, because his purpose concerning Babylon is to destroy it, for that is the vengeance of the LORD, vengeance for his temple.

12 Raise a standard against the walls of
        Babylon;
      make the watch strong;
    post sentinels;
      prepare the ambushes;
    for the LORD has both planned and done
        what he spoke concerning the
        inhabitants of Babylon.
13 You who live by mighty waters,
      rich in treasures,
    your end has come,
      the thread of your life is cut.
14 The LORD of hosts has sworn by himself:
    Surely I will fill you with troops like a
        swarm of locusts,
      and they shall raise a shout of victory
        over you.

15 It is he who made the earth by his
        power,
      who established the world by his
        wisdom,
    and by his understanding stretched out
        the heavens.
16 When he utters his voice there is a tumult
        of waters in the heavens,
      and he makes the mist rise from the
        ends of the earth.
    He makes lightnings for the rain,
      and he brings out the wind from his
        storehouses.
17 Everyone is stupid and without
        knowledge;
      goldsmiths are all put to shame by
        their idols;
    for their images are false,
      and there is no breath in them.
18 They are worthless, a work of delusion;
      at the time of their punishment they
        shall perish.
19 Not like these is the LORD,[a] the portion of
        Jacob,
      for he is the one who formed all things,
    and Israel is the tribe of his inheritance;
      the LORD of hosts is his name.

Israel the Creator's Instrument

20 You are my war club, my weapon of
        battle:
    with you I smash nations;
      with you I destroy kingdoms;

21   with you I smash the horse and its rider;
        with you I smash the chariot and the
          charioteer;
22   with you I smash man and woman;
        with you I smash the old man and the
          boy;
      with you I smash the young man and the
          girl;
23   with you I smash shepherds and their
          flocks;
      with you I smash farmers and their
          teams;
      with you I smash governors and
          deputies.

The Doom of Babylon

24 I will repay Babylon and all the inhabitants of Chaldea before your very eyes for all the wrong that they have done in Zion, says the LORD.

25   I am against you, O destroying mountain,
                                        says the LORD,
        that destroys the whole earth;
      I will stretch out my hand against you,
        and roll you down from the crags,
        and make you a burned-out mountain.
26   No stone shall be taken from you for a
          corner
        and no stone for a foundation,
      but you shall be a perpetual waste,
        says the LORD.

27   Raise a standard in the land,
        blow the trumpet among the nations;
      prepare the nations for war against her,
        summon against her the kingdoms,
          Ararat, Minni, and Ashkenaz;
      appoint a marshal against her,
        bring up horses like bristling locusts.
28   Prepare the nations for war against her,
        the kings of the Medes, with their
          governors and deputies,
        and every land under their dominion.
29   The land trembles and writhes,
        for the LORD's purposes against
          Babylon stand,
      to make the land of Babylon a desolation,
        without inhabitant.
30   The warriors of Babylon have given up
          fighting,
        they remain in their strongholds;

---

a Heb lacks the LORD

their strength has failed,
they have become women;
her buildings are set on fire,
her bars are broken.

31 One runner runs to meet another,
and one messenger to meet another,
to tell the king of Babylon
that his city is taken from end to end:

32 the fords have been seized,
the marshes have been burned with
fire,
and the soldiers are in panic.

33 For thus says the LORD of hosts, the God
of Israel:
Daughter Babylon is like a threshing floor
at the time when it is trodden;
yet a little while
and the time of her harvest will come.

34 "King Nebuchadrezzar of Babylon has
devoured me,
he has crushed me;
he has made me an empty vessel,
he has swallowed me like a monster;
he has filled his belly with my delicacies,
he has spewed me out.

35 May my torn flesh be avenged on
Babylon,"
the inhabitants of Zion shall say.
"May my blood be avenged on the
inhabitants of Chaldea,"
Jerusalem shall say.

36 Therefore thus says the LORD:
I am going to defend your cause
and take vengeance for you.
I will dry up her sea
and make her fountain dry;

37 and Babylon shall become a heap of
ruins,
a den of jackals,
an object of horror and of hissing,
without inhabitant.

38 Like lions they shall roar together;
they shall growl like lions' whelps.

39 When they are inflamed, I will set out
their drink

and make them drunk, until they
become merry
and then sleep a perpetual sleep
and never wake, says the LORD.

40 I will bring them down like lambs to the
slaughter,
like rams and goats.

41 How Sheshach[a] is taken,
the pride of the whole earth seized!
How Babylon has become
an object of horror among the nations!

42 The sea has risen over Babylon;
she has been covered by its tumultuous
waves.

43 Her cities have become an object of
horror,
a land of drought and a desert,
a land in which no one lives,
and through which no mortal passes.

44 I will punish Bel in Babylon,
and make him disgorge what he has
swallowed.
The nations shall no longer stream to
him;
the wall of Babylon has fallen.

45 Come out of her, my people!
Save your lives, each of you,
from the fierce anger of the LORD!

46 Do not be fainthearted or fearful
at the rumors heard in the land—
one year one rumor comes,
the next year another,
rumors of violence in the land
and of ruler against ruler.

47 Assuredly, the days are coming
when I will punish the images of
Babylon;
her whole land shall be put to shame,
and all her slain shall fall in her midst.

48 Then the heavens and the earth,
and all that is in them,
shall shout for joy over Babylon;

---

a Sheshach is a cryptogram for Babel, Babylon

the end of the seventh century BCE. It became a Persian
province in 549 BCE and participated in the defeat of
the Babylonians (see Isa 13.17). 51.15–19 These verses
are taken from 10.12–16. 51.20–23 These words appear to be addressed to Cyrus (see Isa 41.2–4).
51.27 Ararat (Urartu), a people inhabiting a region
near Lake Van (southeast Turkey and northwest Iran).
Minni (Mannaya), a people who lived in an area south
of Lake Urmia in modern northern Iraq. Ashkenaz,
probably an Indo-European people who lived near
modern Armenia and were identified by Herodotus as
the Scythians. 51.41 Sheshach. See note on 25.26.

for the destroyers shall come against
them out of the north,
    says the LORD.
49 Babylon must fall for the slain of Israel,
 as the slain of all the earth have fallen
  because of Babylon.

50 You survivors of the sword,
  go, do not linger!
 Remember the LORD in a distant land,
  and let Jerusalem come into your
   mind:
51 We are put to shame, for we have heard
  insults;
 dishonor has covered our face,
for aliens have come
 into the holy places of the LORD's
  house.

52 Therefore the time is surely coming, says
  the LORD,
 when I will punish her idols,
and through all her land
 the wounded shall groan.
53 Though Babylon should mount up to
  heaven,
 and though she should fortify her
  strong height,
from me destroyers would come upon
  her,
 says the LORD.

54 Listen!—a cry from Babylon!
 A great crashing from the land of the
  Chaldeans!
55 For the LORD is laying Babylon waste,
 and stilling her loud clamor.
Their waves roar like mighty waters,
 the sound of their clamor resounds;
56 for a destroyer has come against her,
  against Babylon;
her warriors are taken,
 their bows are broken;
for the LORD is a God of recompense,
 he will repay in full.
57 I will make her officials and her sages
  drunk,

also her governors, her deputies, and
 her warriors;
they shall sleep a perpetual sleep and
 never wake,
 says the King, whose name is the LORD
  of hosts.

58 Thus says the LORD of hosts:
The broad wall of Babylon
 shall be leveled to the ground,
and her high gates
 shall be burned with fire.
The peoples exhaust themselves for
 nothing,
 and the nations weary themselves only
  for fire.[a]

Jeremiah's Command to Seraiah

59 The word that the prophet Jeremiah commanded Seraiah son of Neriah son of Mahseiah, when he went with King Zedekiah of Judah to Babylon, in the fourth year of his reign. Seraiah was the quartermaster. 60 Jeremiah wrote in a[b] scroll all the disasters that would come on Babylon, all these words that are written concerning Babylon. 61 And Jeremiah said to Seraiah: "When you come to Babylon, see that you read all these words, 62 and say, 'O LORD, you yourself threatened to destroy this place so that neither human beings nor animals shall live in it, and it shall be desolate forever.' 63 When you finish reading this scroll, tie a stone to it, and throw it into the middle of the Euphrates, 64 and say, 'Thus shall Babylon sink, to rise no more, because of the disasters that I am bringing on her.' "[c]
Thus far are the words of Jeremiah.

The Destruction of Jerusalem Reviewed

52 Zedekiah was twenty-one years old when he began to reign; he reigned eleven years in Jerusalem. His mother's name was Hamutal daughter of Jeremiah of Libnah. 2 He did what was evil in the sight of the LORD,

---

a Gk Syr Compare Hab 2.13: Heb *and the nations for fire, and they are weary*   *b* Or *one*   *c* Gk: Heb *on her. And they shall weary themselves*

51.59–64 This narrative purports to tell how the oracles against Babylonia were written in a book and carried to Babylon by Seraiah when he accompanied King Zedekiah on his trip to Babylon in the fourth year of his reign (593 BCE). Seraiah was a brother of Baruch (see 32.12). It may be that Zedekiah made such a trip in order to explain his participation in the conspiracy mentioned in ch. 27. The oracles against Babylon do not agree with Jeremiah's pro-Babylonian stance prior to the fall of Jerusalem. It is likely that the editor of the collection of oracles against Babylon composed this narrative in order to attribute them to Jeremiah. **51.63** A symbolic act (see note on 13.1–11). **52.1–34** A historical appendix principally taken

just as Jehoiakim had done. ³Indeed, Jerusalem and Judah so angered the LORD that he expelled them from his presence.

Zedekiah rebelled against the king of Babylon. ⁴And in the ninth year of his reign, in the tenth month, on the tenth day of the month, King Nebuchadrezzar of Babylon came with all his army against Jerusalem, and they laid siege to it; they built siegeworks against it all around. ⁵So the city was besieged until the eleventh year of King Zedekiah. ⁶On the ninth day of the fourth month the famine became so severe in the city that there was no food for the people of the land. ⁷Then a breach was made in the city wall;ᵃ and all the soldiers fled and went out from the city by night by the way of the gate between the two walls, by the king's garden, though the Chaldeans were all around the city. They went in the direction of the Arabah. ⁸But the army of the Chaldeans pursued the king, and overtook Zedekiah in the plains of Jericho; and all his army was scattered, deserting him. ⁹Then they captured the king, and brought him up to the king of Babylon at Riblah in the land of Hamath, and he passed sentence on him. ¹⁰The king of Babylon killed the sons of Zedekiah before his eyes, and also killed all the officers of Judah at Riblah. ¹¹He put out the eyes of Zedekiah, and bound him in fetters, and the king of Babylon took him to Babylon, and put him in prison until the day of his death.

12 In the fifth month, on the tenth day of the month—which was the nineteenth year of King Nebuchadrezzar, king of Babylon—Nebuzaradan the captain of the bodyguard who served the king of Babylon, entered Jerusalem. ¹³He burned the house of the LORD, the king's house, and all the houses of Jerusalem; every great house he burned down. ¹⁴All the army of the Chaldeans, who were with the captain of the guard, broke down all the walls around Jerusalem. ¹⁵Nebuzaradan the captain of the guard carried into exile some of the poorest of the people and the rest of the people who were left in the city and the deserters who had defected to the king of Babylon, together with the rest of the artisans. ¹⁶But Nebuzaradan the captain of the guard left some of the poorest people of the land to be vinedressers and tillers of the soil.

17 The pillars of bronze that were in the house of the LORD, and the stands and the bronze sea that were in the house of the LORD, the Chaldeans broke in pieces, and carried all the bronze to Babylon. ¹⁸They took away the pots, the shovels, the snuffers, the basins, the ladles, and all the vessels of bronze used in the temple service. ¹⁹The captain of the guard took away the small bowls also, the firepans, the basins, the pots, the lampstands, the ladles, and the bowls for libation, both those of gold and those of silver. ²⁰As for the two pillars, the one sea, the twelve bronze bulls that were under the sea, and the stands,ᵇ which King Solomon had made for the house of the LORD, the bronze of all these vessels was beyond weighing. ²¹As for the pillars, the height of the one pillar was eighteen cubits, its circumference was twelve cubits; it was hollow and its thickness was four fingers. ²²Upon it was a capital of bronze; the height of the capital was five cubits; latticework and pomegranates, all of bronze, encircled the top of the capital. And the second pillar had the same, with pomegranates. ²³There were ninety-six pomegranates on the sides; all the pomegranates encircling the latticework numbered one hundred.

24 The captain of the guard took the chief priest Seraiah, the second priest Zephaniah, and the three guardians of the threshold; ²⁵and from the city he took an officer who had been in command of the soldiers, and seven men of the king's council who were found in the city; the secretary of the commander of the army who mustered the people of the land; and sixty men of the people of the land who were found inside the city. ²⁶Then Nebuzaradan the captain of the guard took them, and brought them to the king of Babylon at Riblah. ²⁷And the king of Babylon struck them down, and put them to death at Riblah in the land of Hamath. So Judah went into exile out of its land.

---

a Heb lacks *wall*   *b* Cn: Heb *that were under the stands*

---

from 2 Kings 24.18–25.30 in order to provide additional information about the rebellion of Zedekiah, the fall of Jerusalem, and the exile (see chs. 39–43). **52.1–3** A brief summary of the reign of Zedekiah (see 2 Kings 24.18–20). **52.4–11** The siege, fall of Jerusalem, and capture of Zedekiah. **52.12–16** The commander of the Babylonian army, *Nebuzaradan* (cf. 39.9–14; 40.1–6), ordered the burning of Jerusalem, including the temple and palace, and took into exile all but the country's very poor. **52.17–23** The spoils taken from the temple are

28 This is the number of the people whom Nebuchadrezzar took into exile: in the seventh year, three thousand twenty-three Judeans; 29in the eighteenth year of Nebuchadrezzar he took into exile from Jerusalem eight hundred thirty-two persons; 30in the twenty-third year of Nebuchadrezzar, Nebuzaradan the captain of the guard took into exile of the Judeans seven hundred forty-five persons; all the persons were four thousand six hundred.

Jehoiachin Favored in Captivity

31 In the thirty-seventh year of the exile of King Jehoiachin of Judah, in the twelfth month, on the twenty-fifth day of the month, King Evil-merodach of Babylon, in the year he began to reign, showed favor to King Jehoiachin of Judah and brought him out of prison; 32he spoke kindly to him, and gave him a seat above the seats of the other kings who were with him in Babylon. 33So Jehoiachin put aside his prison clothes, and every day of his life he dined regularly at the king's table. 34For his allowance, a regular daily allowance was given him by the king of Babylon, as long as he lived, up to the day of his death.

---

listed (cf. 28.3). **52.24–27** *Seraiah.* See 36.26. *Zephaniah.* See 21.1; 29.24–32. **52.28–30** The lists of exiles from three deportations (597, 587, 582 BCE). These verses are not in the account in 2 Kings. **52.31–34** The release of *Jehoiachin* from prison in 560 BCE indicates that the book of Jeremiah was edited sometime after this event. *Evil-merodach* (Akkadian *Amel-Marduk*), the son and successor of Nebuchadrezzar. He ruled only two years (562–560 BCE) before being replaced by his brother-in-law, Neriglissar, in a rebellion.

LAMENTATIONS

THE BOOK OF LAMENTATIONS is a work of art produced in response to a historical disaster. Its five poems grieve over the destruction of Jerusalem, military occupation, and the deportation of its leading citizens by King Nebuchadnezzar and the Babylonians in 586 BCE. Historical background appears in 2 Kings 25.8–21. The book's evocative poetry enables it to encompass the sorrows of the world.

Name and Canonical Context

THE BOOK'S NAME in the Hebrew Bible is *'ekah* ("How!"), after the initial word in 1.1, repeated in 2.1; 4.1. The title is a conventional cry of shock at a death, which also implies a question: "How could this happen to God's beloved city?" The English "Lamentations" translates the Latin *threni* (Greek *threnoi*), which reflects another Hebrew title, *qinot*, attested in the Babylonian Talmud (*Bava Batra* 14b). In most English Bibles, which follow the order of the Latin and Greek versions, Lamentations comes after Jeremiah, but in the Hebrew Bible Lamentations appears among the Writings (Hebrew *ketuvim*) as one of the five liturgical scrolls (Hebrew *megillot*). Jewish communities read Lamentations on the "Ninth of Av" to commemorate the destruction of the temple by the Roman emperor Titus in 70 CE as well as subsequent attacks on the Jewish people. Christians read portions of Lamentations during Holy Week. The text of Lamentations has frequently been set to music.

Literary Form and Character

THE FIRST FOUR SECTIONS of this poetic book are acrostic compositions; the strophes or verses begin with the twenty-two letters of the Hebrew alphabet in succession. The significance of acrostic order, which is found in Pss 9–10; 25; 34; 111; 112; 119; 145; Prov 31.10–31, is unclear. Some interpreters believe that such compositions are mnemonic devices. Others detect literary meaning. The movement from *a* to *z* (*aleph* to *taw*) suggests that suffering is complete, total, and allows room for no more. Or the acrostic form may be an effort to put order into the chaotic experience that followed invasion and persisted during military occupation of Judah.

The arrangement of the poems is also puzzling. The first two are of equal length and similar acrostic structure; each verse begins with a different letter. The central poem (ch. 3) intensifies the acrostic, devoting three verses to each letter of the alphabet. Since this is the only place in

1085

the poetry where hope finds strong expression, this alteration in acrostic form has led some commentators to call it the heart of the book. But this is to overlook the next two chapters, which thin out the alphabetic structuring. The fourth poem resumes the acrostic style of chs. 1 and 2, but ch. 5 drops the acrostic form altogether, even though its twenty-two verses mimic the twenty-two-letter alphabet. The movement of the acrostics across the book suggests hope emerging and fading, confidence breaking though grief and anger and then dwindling. Such a breakdown of confidence in God and the world is a common response to the trauma experienced by individuals and communities.

Formally, the poetry of Lamentations exhibits affinities to such other biblical genres as the elegy, or funeral lament, and the individual and communal psalms of lamentation. Laments over the destruction of cities and temples are known also from extrabiblical sources going back to the second millennium BCE; see, e.g., the "Lamentation over the Destruction of Sumer and Ur." Yet in keeping with the specificity of the historical occasion, Lamentations, while incorporating and adapting several traditional elements, is a unique literary composition addressed to the survivors of the destruction of Jerusalem and designed to help them come to terms with the historical reality and the religious implications of that catastrophic experience. It has been suggested, with some degree of plausibility, that these poems were used in public rites of mourning, such as those known to have been carried on at the site of the ruins of the Jerusalem temple (see Jer 41.5; Zech 7.1–7; 8.19).

Lamentations is an eloquent expression of grief that helped survivors come to terms with the historical calamity they had experienced. Appeals for repentance, however, are frequently interspersed with appeals for God's mercy and compassion on the penitent survivors. A cautious note of hope is sounded in the center of the book (see 3.21–33), where the poet gives expression to the belief that, although God's wrath is limited (3.31), divine mercy and compassion are limitless (3.22–24). This message has continued to reverberate through subsequent ages and calamities to the present day.

Authorship and Date of Composition

THE GREEK VERSION OF LAMENTATIONS contains a sentence not present in the older Hebrew text: "These are the words of the prophet Jeremiah as he sat upon the hill weeping over Jerusalem." Although it is unlikely that Jeremiah wrote this book, he symbolically presides over it as one who predicted Jerusalem's fall and whose prophetic book also abounds with lamentation and weeping.

The oldest Hebrew manuscripts of Lamentations make no reference to Jeremiah, and both content and style of the prophetic book differ sharply from Lamentations (contrast 1.10 with Jer 7.14; 4.17 with Jer 2.18 and 37.5–10; and 4.20 with Jer 37.17). Lamentations is probably the work of a survivor (or survivors) of the nation's destruction who poured out sorrow, anger, and dismay after the city's traumatic defeat and occupation by the Babylonians. Because the book of Jeremiah tells of citizens going to worship at the site of the destroyed temple (41.4–5), some interpreters imagine it to be the place where this book took form in worship that continued among the ruins. [WERNER E. LEMKE, revised by KATHLEEN O'CONNOR]

The Deserted City

1 How lonely sits the city
　　that once was full of people!
How like a widow she has become,
　　she that was great among the nations!
She that was a princess among the provinces
　　has become a vassal.

2　She weeps bitterly in the night,
　　　with tears on her cheeks;
among all her lovers
　　she has no one to comfort her;
all her friends have dealt treacherously
　　　with her,
　　they have become her enemies.

3　Judah has gone into exile with suffering
　　　and hard servitude;
she lives now among the nations,
　　and finds no resting place;
her pursuers have all overtaken her
　　in the midst of her distress.

4　The roads to Zion mourn,
　　　for no one comes to the festivals;
all her gates are desolate,
　　her priests groan;
her young girls grieve,*a*
　　and her lot is bitter.

5　Her foes have become the masters,
　　　her enemies prosper,
because the Lord has made her suffer
　　for the multitude of her transgressions;
her children have gone away,
　　captives before the foe.

6　From daughter Zion has departed
　　　all her majesty.
Her princes have become like stags
　　that find no pasture;
they fled without strength
　　before the pursuer.

7　Jerusalem remembers,
　　　in the days of her affliction and
　　　　　wandering,
all the precious things
　　that were hers in days of old.
When her people fell into the hand of the
　　　foe,
　　and there was no one to help her,
the foe looked on mocking
　　over her downfall.

8　Jerusalem sinned grievously,
　　　so she has become a mockery;
all who honored her despise her,
　　for they have seen her nakedness;
she herself groans,
　　and turns her face away.

9　Her uncleanness was in her skirts;
　　　she took no thought of her future;
her downfall was appalling,
　　with none to comfort her.
"O Lord, look at my affliction,
　　for the enemy has triumphed!"

10　Enemies have stretched out their hands
　　　over all her precious things;
she has even seen the nations

_____

a Meaning of Heb uncertain

1.1–22 A moving description of the plight of the city following its destruction. Two voices mark the main sections of the poem. The narrator speaks in vv. 1–11b, and Daughter Zion in vv. 11c–22. The former speaks as an observer, and the latter as the victim of violence and destruction. Together they portray a totality of pain. They both blame the city for the disaster. **1.1–11** The poet contrasts the present miserable condition of the city with its former glory. **1.1** *How* (Hebrew *'ekah*) suggests a sharp intake of breath in astonishment and disbelief about the fall of the city. The term characteristically appears in funeral elegies (see 2 Sam 1.19, 25, 27; Isa 1.21; 14.4; Jer 48.17; Ezek 26.17). **1.2** *Lovers, friends,* nations with whom Judah had entered into political alliances, which were denounced by the prophets (see Isa 31.1–3; Jer 4.30; 27.1–7; 30.14; Ezek 16.33). Some of these former allies made common cause with the Babylonians when they attacked Jerusalem (see 2 Kings 24.2; Ezek 25.12–17). The speaker accuses the city of adulterous infidelity, but notes that she is alone and without a comforter (see 1.9, 16, 19; 2.13). **1.4** *Roads . . . mourn,* or "roads are dried up," perhaps for lack of religious pilgrims. City *gates* were normally bustling with activity (see 5.14). **1.5** *Foes . . . the masters* (*the masters,* lit. "the heads") alludes to the covenant blessing and curse in Deut 28.13, 44. God punished Jerusalem for breach of covenant, a theme more fully developed in ch. 2. **1.6** *Daughter Zion* or the like (see 1.15; 2.1, 4, 8, 10, 13, 15; 4.21, 22; cf. 3.48; 4.3, 6, 10, where the Hebrew reads lit. "daughter of my people") is a poetic expression of endearment personifying a city, land, or people. **1.8** *Nakedness* was considered shameful and humiliating (see Gen 9.22–23; Ex 20.26; Isa 47.3; Ezek 16.37–39). Ancient reliefs show prisoners being marched into captivity stark naked. **1.9** *Uncleanness,* a metaphor drawn from ritual purity laws and barring Zion from

invade her sanctuary,
 those whom you forbade
  to enter your congregation.

11 All her people groan
  as they search for bread;
 they trade their treasures for food
  to revive their strength.
 Look, O LORD, and see
  how worthless I have become.

12 Is it nothing to you,*ᵃ* all you who pass by?
  Look and see
 if there is any sorrow like my sorrow,
  which was brought upon me,
 which the LORD inflicted
  on the day of his fierce anger.

13 From on high he sent fire;
  it went deep into my bones;
 he spread a net for my feet;
  he turned me back;
 he has left me stunned,
  faint all day long.

14 My transgressions were bound*ᵃ* into a
   yoke;
 by his hand they were fastened
   together;
 they weigh on my neck,
  sapping my strength;
 the Lord handed me over
  to those whom I cannot withstand.

15 The LORD has rejected
  all my warriors in the midst of me;
 he proclaimed a time against me
  to crush my young men;
 the Lord has trodden as in a wine press
  the virgin daughter Judah.

16 For these things I weep;
  my eyes flow with tears;
 for a comforter is far from me,
  one to revive my courage;
 my children are desolate,
  for the enemy has prevailed.

17 Zion stretches out her hands,
  but there is no one to comfort her;
 the LORD has commanded against Jacob
  that his neighbors should become his
   foes;
 Jerusalem has become
  a filthy thing among them.

18 The LORD is in the right,
  for I have rebelled against his word;
 but hear, all you peoples,
  and behold my suffering;
 my young women and young men
  have gone into captivity.

19 I called to my lovers
  but they deceived me;
 my priests and elders
  perished in the city
 while seeking food
  to revive their strength.

20 See, O LORD, how distressed I am;
  my stomach churns,
 my heart is wrung within me,
  because I have been very rebellious.
 In the street the sword bereaves;
  in the house it is like death.

21 They heard how I was groaning,
  with no one to comfort me.

---

a Meaning of Heb uncertain

worship (see Lev 15.16–24). **1.10** *Precious things*, the temple treasures plundered by the Babylonians (2 Kings 25.13–17; Jer 28.1–3). Ironically, foreigners barred by law from entering the Lord's *congregation* (Deut 23.3) had invaded God's *sanctuary*. **1.11** *Treasures*, rendered *precious things* in v. 10, here probably refers to humans rather than valuables (cf. Ezek 24.16; Hos 9.16). **1.12–22** Zion is speaking from within a world of pain. **1.12** *On the day of his fierce anger*, a reference to the prophetic concept of "the day of the LORD," on which God comes to judge Israel or the nations (see Isa 10.3; 13.13; 22.5; Ezek 7.7–12; Joel 2.1–2; Am 5.18, 20; Ob 15–18). Here it is identified with the destruction of Jerusalem. **1.13** Traditional metaphors drawn from in-dividual laments (see Job 30.30; Pss 10.9; 35.7–8; 57.6; 102.3; Jer 20.9) and here suggesting physical abuse by a spouse. **1.14** The *yoke*, or heavy burden (see 1 Kings 12.3–14; Isa 9.4; Jer 27–28), has been brought on by Israel's rebellious acts against the Lord (cf. Deut 28.47–48). **1.15** *Virgin daughter Judah*. See note on 1.6. **1.17** *Filthy thing* belongs to the same semantic realm as *uncleanness* in v. 9 (cf. Lev. 12.2; 15.19–32; 2 Chr 29.5; Ezra 9.11; Zech 13.1). **1.18** Zion concedes that God's punishment is just because she had *rebelled against his word* (lit. "mouth"), i.e., disobeyed divine directives given through prophetic mediators (see Num 20.24; Deut 1.26, 43; 1 Sam 12.14–15; 1 Kings 13.21, 26). **1.19** *Lovers*. See note on 1.2. **1.21–22** Peti-

All my enemies heard of my trouble;
    they are glad that you have done it.
Bring on the day you have announced,
    and let them be as I am.

22 Let all their evil doing come before you;
    and deal with them
as you have dealt with me
    because of all my transgressions;
for my groans are many
    and my heart is faint.

God's Warnings Fulfilled

2 How the Lord in his anger
    has humiliated[a] daughter Zion!
He has thrown down from heaven to earth
    the splendor of Israel;
he has not remembered his footstool
    in the day of his anger.

2 The Lord has destroyed without mercy
    all the dwellings of Jacob;
in his wrath he has broken down
    the strongholds of daughter Judah;
he has brought down to the ground in
      dishonor
    the kingdom and its rulers.

3 He has cut down in fierce anger
    all the might of Israel;
he has withdrawn his right hand from
      them
    in the face of the enemy;
he has burned like a flaming fire in
      Jacob,
    consuming all around.

4 He has bent his bow like an enemy,
    with his right hand set like a foe;
he has killed all in whom we took pride
    in the tent of daughter Zion;
he has poured out his fury like fire.

5 The Lord has become like an enemy;
    he has destroyed Israel.
He has destroyed all its palaces,
    laid in ruins its strongholds,
and multiplied in daughter Judah
    mourning and lamentation.

6 He has broken down his booth like a
      garden,
    he has destroyed his tabernacle;
the LORD has abolished in Zion
    festival and sabbath,
and in his fierce indignation has spurned
    king and priest.

7 The Lord has scorned his altar,
    disowned his sanctuary;
he has delivered into the hand of the
      enemy
    the walls of her palaces;
a clamor was raised in the house of the
    LORD
    as on a day of festival.

8 The LORD determined to lay in ruins
    the wall of daughter Zion;
he stretched the line;
    he did not withhold his hand from
      destroying;
he caused rampart and wall to lament;
    they languish together.

9 Her gates have sunk into the ground;
    he has ruined and broken her bars;
her king and princes are among the
      nations;
    guidance is no more,
and her prophets obtain
    no vision from the LORD.

---

a Meaning of Heb uncertain

---

tions for God to see Zion's suffering and to intervene against her enemies.

2.1–22 The narrator describes the enormity of Zion's suffering but now shows sympathy for her pain and accuses God of being merciless and cruel in punishing Zion. This poem suggests the narrator has changed and protests the divine treatment of Zion. **2.1** *Daughter Zion.* See note on 1.6. *The splendor of Israel* is a reference to the capital city (cf. Isa 13.19; Ezek 24.25) or its sanctuary (cf. Ps 78.61; Isa 64.11). God's *footstool,* the ark of the Lord or the temple where it was housed (see 1 Chr 28.2; Pss 99.5; 132.7). *In the day of his anger.* See also vv. 3, 4, 6, 21, 22;

note on 1.12. **2.2** *Without mercy,* i.e., unsparingly, but without exhausting divine capabilities for mercy (cf. 3.22–23, 32–33). **2.3–5** The Divine Warrior who used to fight Israel's enemies (see Ex 15.3–10; Judg 5.10–11; Hab 3.1–16) has now withdrawn his *right hand,* or protective power, and become *like an enemy* to Israel (cf. Jer 30.14). **2.6** *Booth, tabernacle,* the temple (see v. 7). *King and priest,* the two pillars of the Jerusalemite ruling class. Temple and palace were both part of the building complex destroyed by the Babylonians (2 Kings 25.8–12, 18–21), and kings played an important role in the Israelite religion (2 Kings 23.1–25). **2.9** *Guidance,* or priestly "in-

10 The elders of daughter Zion
    sit on the ground in silence;
they have thrown dust on their heads
    and put on sackcloth;
the young girls of Jerusalem
    have bowed their heads to the ground.

11 My eyes are spent with weeping;
    my stomach churns;
my bile is poured out on the ground
    because of the destruction of my people,
because infants and babes faint
    in the streets of the city.

12 They cry to their mothers,
    "Where is bread and wine?"
as they faint like the wounded
    in the streets of the city,
as their life is poured out
    on their mothers' bosom.

13 What can I say for you, to what compare
    you,
    O daughter Jerusalem?
To what can I liken you, that I may
    comfort you,
    O virgin daughter Zion?
For vast as the sea is your ruin;
    who can heal you?

14 Your prophets have seen for you
    false and deceptive visions;
they have not exposed your iniquity
    to restore your fortunes,
but have seen oracles for you
    that are false and misleading.

15 All who pass along the way
    clap their hands at you;
they hiss and wag their heads
    at daughter Jerusalem;
"Is this the city that was called
    the perfection of beauty,
    the joy of all the earth?"

16 All your enemies
    open their mouths against you;
they hiss, they gnash their teeth,
    they cry: "We have devoured her!
Ah, this is the day we longed for;
    at last we have seen it!"

17 The LORD has done what he purposed,
    he has carried out his threat;
as he ordained long ago,
    he has demolished without pity;
he has made the enemy rejoice over you,
    and exalted the might of your foes.

18 Cry aloud[a] to the Lord!
    O wall of daughter Zion!
Let tears stream down like a torrent
    day and night!
Give yourself no rest,
    your eyes no respite!

19 Arise, cry out in the night,
    at the beginning of the watches!
Pour out your heart like water
    before the presence of the Lord!
Lift your hands to him
    for the lives of your children,
who faint for hunger
    at the head of every street.

20 Look, O LORD, and consider!
    To whom have you done this?
Should women eat their offspring,
    the children they have borne?
Should priest and prophet be killed
    in the sanctuary of the Lord?

21 The young and the old are lying
    on the ground in the streets;
my young women and my young men
    have fallen by the sword;

a Cn: Heb *Their heart cried*

struction." **2.10** This verse describes traditional rites of mourning in the face of calamity (see Job 2.12–13; Jer 4.8; 6.26; Jon 3.6). **2.13** *Daughter Jerusalem, virgin daughter Zion.* See note on 1.6. The narrator offers comfort by recognizing the vastness of her suffering. **2.14** *Deceptive visions.* See Jer 14.13–16; 23.9–22; 28.1–17; 29.8–9. **2.15–16** Cf. 1 Kings 9.8–9; Ps 22.7; Jer 19.8; Zeph 2.15. **2.15** *Is this . . . the joy of all the earth*, a derisive question that mocks the exalted praise of the city found in the songs of Zion (Pss 46; 48). **2.17** The claims of her

enemies notwithstanding (v. 16b), Jerusalem's destruction was the Lord's purposive doing (cf. 1.5, 12–15, 18). **2.18–19** Zion is encouraged to engage in weeping, shouting, and entreaty before God. **2.20–22** Zion's plaintive prayer appeals to God's mercy through a heartrending description of her misery. She asks again for God to see her suffering, to recognize her misery. Perhaps God will act. **2.20** *Should women eat their offspring?* The horrors of cannibalism during severe famine are mentioned in traditional treaty curses and prophetic

in the day of your anger you have killed
them,
slaughtering without mercy.

22 You invited my enemies from all around
as if for a day of festival;
and on the day of the anger of the LORD
no one escaped or survived;
those whom I bore and reared
my enemy has destroyed.

God's Steadfast Love Endures

3 I am one who has seen affliction
under the rod of God's[a] wrath;
2 he has driven and brought me
into darkness without any light;
3 against me alone he turns his hand,
again and again, all day long.

4 He has made my flesh and my skin waste
away,
and broken my bones;
5 he has besieged and enveloped me
with bitterness and tribulation;
6 he has made me sit in darkness
like the dead of long ago.

7 He has walled me about so that I cannot
escape;
he has put heavy chains on me;
8 though I call and cry for help,
he shuts out my prayer;
9 he has blocked my ways with hewn
stones,
he has made my paths crooked.

10 He is a bear lying in wait for me,
a lion in hiding;
11 he led me off my way and tore me to
pieces;
he has made me desolate;
12 he bent his bow and set me
as a mark for his arrow.

13 He shot into my vitals
the arrows of his quiver;
14 I have become the laughingstock of all
my people,
the object of their taunt-songs all day
long.
15 He has filled me with bitterness,
he has sated me with wormwood.

16 He has made my teeth grind on gravel,
and made me cower in ashes;
17 my soul is bereft of peace;
I have forgotten what happiness is;
18 so I say, "Gone is my glory,
and all that I had hoped for from the
LORD."

19 The thought of my affliction and my
homelessness
is wormwood and gall!
20 My soul continually thinks of it
and is bowed down within me.
21 But this I call to mind,
and therefore I have hope:

---

a Heb his

threats (see Lev 26.29; Deut 28.53–57; Jer 19.9; Ezek 5.10) and reported on at least some occasions (Lam 4.10; 2 Kings 6.28–29). **2.21** Cf. Jer 9.21–22.

3.1–66 A new speaker, a male charged with the protection of women and children (Hebrew *geber*), laments his own captivity and torture. He vacillates between despair and hope. The community either joins or replaces him in vv. 42–47. **3.1–39** The speaker, in the first person, describes his affliction with personal authority. **3.1** *I am one who.* The Hebrew *geber,* translated *one* here and in v. 27, *human* in v. 35, and (with Hebrew *'adam*) *any* in v. 39, means "man," showing that the speaker here is not Zion but an individual male. **3.2–18** The description of the speaker's suffering is so traditional that attempts to identify him are misplaced. He is a typical sufferer, like the "I" in the individual psalms of lamentation. **3.3** The *hand* of God often produces sickness or calamity (see v. 4; cf. 1 Sam 5.6–12; Job 19.21; Pss 32.4; 38.2). Hebraic monotheism precludes dualistic explanations of evil. All the attacks described in vv. 2–18 are

from God, but the poem withholds explicit identification of this enemy until v. 31, making the discovery all the more shocking. **3.4** *Flesh, bones.* See Pss 38.3; 51.8; cf. Ps 34.20. **3.6–7** *Darkness* is traditionally associated with prison (Ps 107.10–14) and the netherworld (Job 10.21; Ps 88.6, 12, 18). Prison here is viewed as a form of death. **3.6** Cf. Ps 143.3. **3.10–11** The enemies of the sufferer are often pictured as wild animals (see Pss 7.2; 17.12; 22.12–13, 16), but here the enemy is the Lord, as in Job 10.16; Hos 13.7–8; Am 5.18–19. **3.12** *Bow, arrow,* refer to the divine archer who produces disaster and death (see Deut 32.23–24; Job 16.12–13; Pss 7.12–13; 38.2). **3.13** *Vitals,* or "kidneys," internal organs essential for life. **3.14** On the pain of mockery, see also v. 63; Job 30.9; Pss 22.6–7; 44.13–16. **3.15** *Wormwood,* a bitter-tasting plant and a symbol of extreme calamity or sorrow (see v. 19; Jer 9.15; 23.15). **3.20–21** These verses mark an important transition from despair to hope (vv. 22–33) that is not uncommon in psalms of lamentation (see Pss 42.5, 6, 11; 73.15–17). Here hope is restored

22 The steadfast love of the LORD never
      ceases,[a]
   his mercies never come to an end;
23 they are new every morning;
   great is your faithfulness.
24 "The LORD is my portion," says my soul,
   "therefore I will hope in him."

25 The LORD is good to those who wait for
      him,
   to the soul that seeks him.
26 It is good that one should wait quietly
   for the salvation of the LORD.
27 It is good for one to bear
   the yoke in youth,
28 to sit alone in silence
   when the Lord has imposed it,
29 to put one's mouth to the dust
   (there may yet be hope),
30 to give one's cheek to the smiter,
   and be filled with insults.

31 For the Lord will not
   reject forever.
32 Although he causes grief, he will have
      compassion
   according to the abundance of his
      steadfast love;
33 for he does not willingly afflict
   or grieve anyone.

34 When all the prisoners of the land
   are crushed under foot,
35 when human rights are perverted
   in the presence of the Most High,
36 when one's case is subverted
   —does the Lord not see it?

37 Who can command and have it done,
   if the Lord has not ordained it?

38 Is it not from the mouth of the Most High
   that good and bad come?
39 Why should any who draw breath complain
   about the punishment of their sins?

40 Let us test and examine our ways,
   and return to the LORD.
41 Let us lift up our hearts as well as our
      hands
   to God in heaven.
42 We have transgressed and rebelled,
   and you have not forgiven.

43 You have wrapped yourself with anger
      and pursued us,
   killing without pity;
44 you have wrapped yourself with a cloud
   so that no prayer can pass through.
45 You have made us filth and rubbish
   among the peoples.

46 All our enemies
   have opened their mouths against us;
47 panic and pitfall have come upon us,
   devastation and destruction.
48 My eyes flow with rivers of tears
   because of the destruction of my people.

49 My eyes will flow without ceasing,
   without respite,
50 until the LORD from heaven
   looks down and sees.
51 My eyes cause me grief
   at the fate of all the young women in
      my city.

52 Those who were my enemies without cause
   have hunted me like a bird;

---

a Syr Tg: Heb LORD, we are not cut off

through remembrance. **3.22–23** These verses express a biblical belief (see Ex 34.6; Ps 103.8; Jon 4.2). **3.24–26** *Portion,* tribal inheritance of land (see Josh 18.2–10), but here, symbolically, of the Lord, as in Pss 16.5; 73.26; 142.5. *Hope* entails patient waiting and intense longing for God (cf. Pss 40.1; 130.5–7). **3.27–30** Speaking like a sage, the sufferer counsels humble submission to suffering as divine chastisement (cf. Ps 37.7; Prov 23.13–14; Isa 50.6). **3.31–33** Affirmation of the triumph of God's love over God's wrath, as in vv. 22–23; Ps 103.8–14. **3.34–36** God is not indifferent to wrongs. **3.37–39** Since nothing happens apart from God's will, divine chastisement should be accepted willingly. **3.40–41** In the light of the foregoing verses (1–39), a communal appeal is now issued for penitential self-examination,

which must go beyond external ritual (*hands*) to interior renewal (*hearts*); cf. 1 Sam 16.7; Jer 4.4; 12.2 . **3.42–47** A communal lament acknowledging guilt but complaining over the continuing experience of divine wrath as if taking back the acceptance of the previous verses. **3.43–44** On the hiddenness or absence of God, see Isa 45.15. **3.44** The *cloud,* normally a symbol of God's protective presence (see Ex 14.19–25; Num 9.15–23), is here a symbol of God's inaccessibility. **3.45** This verse describes a stark reversal of fortune from Deut 7.6. **3.46** See Ps 22.13. **3.48–51** This section describes the poet's grief over the ruin of his people (cf. 1.16; 2.11, 18–19). **3.50** *Until . . . looks down,* i.e., in answer to the people's prayers (see Ps 102.19–20). **3.52–66** The speaker recalls a past saving experience and returns to a mode of

53 they flung me alive into a pit
　　and hurled stones on me;
54 water closed over my head;
　　I said, "I am lost."

55 I called on your name, O LORD,
　　from the depths of the pit;
56 you heard my plea, "Do not close your
　　　ear
　　to my cry for help, but give me relief!"
57 You came near when I called on you;
　　you said, "Do not fear!"

58 You have taken up my cause, O Lord,
　　you have redeemed my life.
59 You have seen the wrong done to me,
　　　O LORD;
　　judge my cause.
60 You have seen all their malice,
　　all their plots against me.

61 You have heard their taunts, O LORD,
　　all their plots against me.
62 The whispers and murmurs of my
　　　assailants
　　are against me all day long.
63 Whether they sit or rise—see,
　　I am the object of their taunt-songs.

64 Pay them back for their deeds, O LORD,
　　according to the work of their hands!
65 Give them anguish of heart;
　　your curse be on them!

66 Pursue them in anger and destroy them
　　from under the LORD's heavens.

The Punishment of Zion

4 How the gold has grown dim,
　　how the pure gold is changed!
The sacred stones lie scattered
　　at the head of every street.

2 The precious children of Zion,
　　worth their weight in fine gold—
how they are reckoned as earthen pots,
　　the work of a potter's hands!

3 Even the jackals offer the breast
　　and nurse their young,
but my people has become cruel,
　　like the ostriches in the wilderness.

4 The tongue of the infant sticks
　　to the roof of its mouth for thirst;
the children beg for food,
　　but no one gives them anything.

5 Those who feasted on delicacies
　　perish in the streets;
those who were brought up in purple
　　cling to ash heaps.

6 For the chastisement[a] of my people has
　　been greater

---

a Or iniquity

hope in God. If he is the same speaker as in vv. 1–39, his movement toward hope has been unsteady and fragile, as is often the case in situations of extreme suffering. **3.52** *Without cause*, or treacherously. See note on 1.2. *Hunted . . . bird*. See Pss 11.1; 124.7; Prov 6.5. **3.54** *Water closed over my head*, a metaphor for Sheol or death (see Pss 69.1–2, 14–15; 88.16–17; Jon 2.2–3). **3.55–66** The verbs in this section alternate between past tenses and imperatives, thus making the speaker appear to look back and forward at the same time, in remembrance of past events and in hope of future divine intervention. **3.55** *Pit*, a metaphor for Sheol (see Pss 28.1; 30.3; 88.4, 6; 143.7). **3.56** *You heard* (cf. Ps 130.2). The speaker believes God is attending to his predicament. **3.57** *You came . . . you said*, or "Come near when I call on you, and say!" *Do not fear*, a standard divine assurance when God comes near to humans (see Gen 15.1; 21.17; 26.24; Ex 14.13; Isa 41.10, 13–14; 43.1, 5). These are the only words directly attributed to God in the book, and they are set in the past. **3.58–59** *You have taken up, redeemed*, and *seen*, or "Take up," "redeem," "see!" These are appeals for God to have pity on the speaker and to judge the enemy (see Pss 7.6–8; 35.24; 82.8; 94.2). **3.60–63** These verses provide

motivations for the petitions that follow in vv. 64–66. **3.63** *Whether they sit or rise*, i.e., "in whatever they do" (see Deut 6.7; Ps 139.2). **3.64–66** Awareness of their own sin does not preclude the people from petitioning God to requite the excessive cruelties of their tormentors (cf. 1.21–22; Pss 74.18–23; 79.1–13; 94.1–7, 23).

4.1–22 A description of the horrors of the final siege of Jerusalem, focusing on the suffering of her people. Here the acrostic form shortens and the poetic tone looses emotional intensity. A narrator describes the destruction of the society in a seemingly numbed state (vv. 1–16). The community recalls its trauma and wishes punishment on its enemies (vv. 17–22). **4.1** *How*. See note on 1.1. *Sacred stones*, precious stones or jewels, here metaphorically the children of the city (see v. 2; 2.19; cf. Song 5.11–16), now scattered at *every street* corner (cf. Isa 51.20). **4.2** *Earthen pots* were common utensils that, when broken, were thrown away (cf. Jer 22.28). **4.3** For similarly unfavorable comparisons of human and animal behavior, see Isa 1.3; Jer 8.7. *Ostriches* had a reputation for neglecting their young (Job 39.13–18). **4.6** *Sodom*. See Gen 19.24–25; Deut 29.23; Isa 1.9–10; 13.19; Jer 23.14; Ezek 16.44–52. In comparison,

than the punishment[a] of Sodom,
which was overthrown in a moment,
though no hand was laid on it.[b]

7   Her princes were purer than snow,
whiter than milk;
their bodies were more ruddy than coral,
their hair[b] like sapphire.[c]

8   Now their visage is blacker than soot;
they are not recognized in the streets.
Their skin has shriveled on their bones;
it has become as dry as wood.

9   Happier were those pierced by the sword
than those pierced by hunger,
whose life drains away, deprived
of the produce of the field.

10 The hands of compassionate women
have boiled their own children;
they became their food
in the destruction of my people.

11 The LORD gave full vent to his wrath;
he poured out his hot anger,
and kindled a fire in Zion
that consumed its foundations.

12 The kings of the earth did not believe,
nor did any of the inhabitants of the
world,
that foe or enemy could enter
the gates of Jerusalem.

13 It was for the sins of her prophets
and the iniquities of her priests,
who shed the blood of the righteous
in the midst of her.

14 Blindly they wandered through the streets,
so defiled with blood
that no one was able
to touch their garments.

15 "Away! Unclean!" people shouted at them;
"Away! Away! Do not touch!"
So they became fugitives and wanderers;
it was said among the nations,
"They shall stay here no longer."

16 The LORD himself has scattered them,
he will regard them no more;
no honor was shown to the priests,
no favor to the elders.

17 Our eyes failed, ever watching
vainly for help;
we were watching eagerly
for a nation that could not save.

18 They dogged our steps
so that we could not walk in our streets;
our end drew near; our days were
numbered;
for our end had come.

19 Our pursuers were swifter
than the eagles in the heavens;
they chased us on the mountains,
they lay in wait for us in the wilderness.

20 The LORD's anointed, the breath of our life,
was taken in their pits—
the one of whom we said, "Under his
shadow
we shall live among the nations."

21 Rejoice and be glad, O daughter Edom,
you that live in the land of Uz;
but to you also the cup shall pass;
you shall become drunk and strip
yourself bare.

22 The punishment of your iniquity,
O daughter Zion, is accomplished,
he will keep you in exile no longer;

---

a Or *sin*   b Meaning of Heb uncertain   c Or *lapis lazuli*

Jerusalem suffered a worse fate: whereas Sodom was overthrown *in a moment* and without a *hand laid on it*, Jerusalem went through a long siege and famine before it was destroyed. **4.10** See note on 2.20. **4.11** *Fire*, a symbol of divine wrath (see 2.3–4; Deut 32.22; Isa 10.17), here perhaps also meant literally (see 2 Kings 25.8–9). **4.12** An allusion to Zion's alleged inviolability as celebrated in Ps 48.4–5, 12–13. *Inhabitants*, or "rulers." **4.13–14** *Prophets . . . priests.* Cf. Jer 6.13; 23.11; 26.7–8. **4.17** Perhaps an allusion to expected relief from Egypt

during the siege (see Jer 34.21–22; 37.3–10). **4.20** *The LORD's anointed*, the Judean king, here perhaps a reference to Zedekiah (see 2 Kings 25.1–7; Jer 39.1–7). *The breath of our life* (lit. "nostrils") and *under his shadow* are traditional royal epithets reflecting a high view of kingship. **4.21–22** Punishment is announced on Edom (cf. Ps 137.7; Ezek 25.12–14; Ob 10–15). **4.21** *Rejoice . . . daughter Edom* is ironic (cf. note on 1.6). On the *cup* of God's wrath, see Ps 75.8; Jer 25.15–28. **4.22** *Accomplished . . . no longer*, or "complete, he will not exile you

but your iniquity, O daughter Edom, he
will punish,
he will uncover your sins.

A Plea for Mercy

5 Remember, O LORD, what has befallen us;
look, and see our disgrace!
2 Our inheritance has been turned over to
strangers,
our homes to aliens.
3 We have become orphans, fatherless;
our mothers are like widows.
4 We must pay for the water we drink;
the wood we get must be bought.
5 With a yoke*a* on our necks we are hard
driven;
we are weary, we are given no rest.
6 We have made a pact with*b* Egypt and
Assyria,
to get enough bread.
7 Our ancestors sinned; they are no more,
and we bear their iniquities.
8 Slaves rule over us;
there is no one to deliver us from their
hand.
9 We get our bread at the peril of our lives,
because of the sword in the wilderness.
10 Our skin is black as an oven
from the scorching heat of famine.
11 Women are raped in Zion,
virgins in the towns of Judah.
12 Princes are hung up by their hands;
no respect is shown to the elders.
13 Young men are compelled to grind,
and boys stagger under loads of wood.
14 The old men have left the city gate,
the young men their music.
15 The joy of our hearts has ceased;
our dancing has been turned to
mourning.
16 The crown has fallen from our head;
woe to us, for we have sinned!
17 Because of this our hearts are sick,
because of these things our eyes have
grown dim:
18 because of Mount Zion, which lies desolate;
jackals prowl over it.

19 But you, O LORD, reign forever;
your throne endures to all generations.
20 Why have you forgotten us completely?
Why have you forsaken us these many
days?
21 Restore us to yourself, O LORD, that we
may be restored;
renew our days as of old—
22 unless you have utterly rejected us,
and are angry with us beyond measure.

a Symmachus: Heb lacks *With a yoke* *b* Heb *have given the hand to*

again," sounds a note of hope for Zion, but this poem does not end with a petition (cf. 3.64–66).
5.1–22 A communal lament that describes life in the occupied land; it is entirely in petition form as if completing the previous chapter. The community begs God to see their unspeakable pain and sorrow. **5.1** The *disgrace*, or "derision" (cf. Pss 44.13; 79.4, 12), that God is asked to *remember* (cf. Pss 74.2, 18, 22; 137.7) is spelled out in greater detail in vv. 2–18. **5.2** *Our inheritance*, the land God gave Israel (see Deut 4.38; 25.19; 26.1). Israel in turn was called God's inheritance (see Deut 4.20; 9.26, 29; 32.9). **5.3** *Orphans . . . widows*, marginalized groups vulnerable to abuse and in need of special protection (see Ex 22.21–14; Deut 24.17–18, 21–22; 27.19). Here the terms are used metaphorically. **5.5** *Yoke.* See note on 1.14. **5.7** Like Jer 31.29; Ezek 18.2, this verse could be read as a complaint about unmerited suffering caused by the ancestors, i.e., as a denial of present responsibility—but see v. 16 (see also 1.14, 18; 3.42)—or it may express identification with the people's sinful ancestors. Cf. also Ex 20.5; 34.7; Deut 5.9; Deut 7.10; 24.16. **5.10** *Our skin is black,* probably from malnutrition. See 4.8. **5.12** *Their hands,* the enemy's hands. **5.14** *Old men . . . city gate.* The elders customarily carried out judicial functions in the city gate (see Deut 22.15; 25.7; Ruth 4.1–2, 11).

5.15 The cessation of joy signifies the vast interruption of daily life (Jer 16.9; Ezek 24.25; Hos 2.11). **5.16** *The crown . . . from our head* figuratively refers to Israel's humiliation (cf. Job 19.9; Isa 62.3). **5.17** *Because of this . . . these things* looks back to vv. 2–16 as well as forward to v. 18. **5.18** An alternate translation of this verse is possible: "On Mount Zion, which is desolate, jackals roam about." The roaming of *jackals* (or "foxes") over ruins is a traditional picture of desolation found in treaty or covenant curses (see Isa 13.22; 34.13; Jer 9.11; 10.22; 49.33; 51.37). **5.19** The hymnic declaration of faith in God's sovereign rule (cf. Pss 93.1–2; 102.12) provides the context for the petition that follows. **5.20** Such impassioned questioning of God is characteristic of biblical prayer (see Pss 10.1; 13.1–2; 22.1; 44.23–24; 74.11; 79.5, 10). **5.21** *Restore us . . . that we may be restored* acknowledges the necessity of divine intervention to effect true penitence, much as in Ps 80.3, 7, 19; Jer 31.18; 23.22; cf. Deut 30.6. **5.22** *Unless you have utterly rejected us.* The possibility of such rejection is left open and the book ends in a state of uncertainty. Its expression of doubt in God's fidelity to the people is appropriate and honest. The book can serve as a step toward healing because it does not whitewash the pain of people who have survived trauma and disaster.

EZEKIEL

EZEKIEL AND THE BOOK ASSOCIATED WITH HIM have perplexed readers for centuries. Ezekiel, of priestly lineage, becomes a prophet. He speaks, falls down, acts out God's word, travels between Mesopotamia and Syro-Palestine in a trance, sees strange things, and proclaims dangerous messages. Perhaps it is not surprising that according to some Jewish traditions the book was to be read only by those over thirty. Nonetheless, discerning readers of Ezekiel have the opportunity to encounter one of ancient Israel's most vigorous religious thinkers, an individual concerned with both classical priestly concerns—purity and holiness—and prophetic issues—righteousness and religious propriety.

Historical Context

THE NUMEROUS CHRONOLOGICAL FORMULAS that occur throughout the book (e.g., 1.1–3; 20.1; 24.1; 32.1; 40.1) attest to the pivotal times during which Ezekiel lived. Such formulas indicate that Ezekiel prophesied from 593 to 571 BCE. These years span the decisive moment—587 BCE —when Jerusalem fell to Nebuchadnezzar (whom Ezekiel deemed an instrument of God, 29.19–20). Before Ezekiel was commissioned as prophet, he had been taken into exile, along with other prominent Judahites, in 597 BCE, the year in which Nebuchadnezzar first defeated Jerusalem. After that date there were prominent Yahwistic communities in both Babylon and Judah. In fact, there were two kings—the exiled Jehoiachin and the puppet Zedekiah—in these two areas, respectively. Ezek 11.14–21 attests to Ezekiel's solidarity with the community in exile, though he also addressed those who remained in the land.

Prophet

EZEKIEL HAD BEEN BORN INTO A PRIESTLY FAMILY (1.3), probably Zadokite, and had followed the ritual requirements that allowed one to work as a priest. He was married, though his wife predeceased him (24.15–27); the book mentions no offspring. Before 597 he lived in Jerusalem; afterward not far from Nippur, on the banks of an irrigation canal. In exile, other Judahites consulted him on a regular basis (8.1; 14.1; 20.1), which suggests that he had significant stature in that expatriate community. Although the book includes vision reports with vivid imagery, such literature, which is stylized, does not readily allow readers to make judgments about the personality of the prophet.

Book

THE BOOK IS MADE up of four primary sections: chs. 1–24, judgment concerning Judah and Jerusalem; chs. 25–32, oracles about foreign nations; chs. 33–39, restoration discourses; and chs. 40–48, a vision of the new temple and polity. These divisions are not absolute, however, since promises of restoration (e.g., 17.22–24) appear in the first section and an oracle of restoration appears in the second section (28.25–26). Unlike Isaiah and more like Jeremiah, much of the book is written in prose—though the NRSV discerns more poetry than did the RSV (e.g., ch. 7). Divine utterance, rather than prophetic utterance, is the predominant rhetorical style.

Ezekiel used diverse literary forms in his prophetic proclamation, including vision reports (1.1–3.15; 8.1–11.25; 37.1–14; 40.1–48.35) and at least twelve symbolic actions (e.g., 4.1–3). The three long vision reports may be understood as the beginning, middle, and end of the book. In both vision and symbolic action reports, the prophet is described as physically involved—he is transported and tours in visions; he acts out oracles. Other important forms include allegory (e.g., chs. 15–17), quotations (e.g., 8.12; 9.9), some of which introduce disputations (e.g. 18.2, 19, 25), and proof sayings, which incorporate the formulaic expression "You shall know that I am the LORD," an expression that appears more than fifty times. Moreover, priestly legal argumentation (e.g., ch. 18) as well as priestly vocabulary and imagery (e.g., of the enthroned "glory of the LORD") characterize the book. The so-called Holiness Code, Lev 17–26, one type of priestly literature, seems particular close to ideas and expressions present in Ezekiel (e.g., one may compare Lev 17 with Ezek 14.1–11 and Lev 26.4–13 with Ezek 34.25–31).

Scholars have explained the composition of the book in diverse ways. Some have discerned a long process of editorial reinterpretation, which may have begun with Ezekiel himself. Others maintain that most of the book may be attributed directly to the prophet. Moreover, while some hold that the prophet originally delivered his discourses orally, others maintain that much in the book was, from the outset, written.

The Septuagint (Greek version) of Ezekiel is roughly 5 percent shorter than the Masoretic (Hebrew) Text and probably derives from an early form of the book. Ezek 12.26–28, 32.25–26; 36.23b–38, not present on one important septuagintal papyrus, are likely later additions to the emerging book. This newer material reflects eschatological concerns.

Message

EZEKIEL RESPONDED DIRECTLY to the circumstances that the Israelites, particularly those in exile, confronted. Before 587 BCE words of judgment predominated; after 587 words of consolation and restoration were prominent. None were immune from judgment, even those already in exile. Those still in Judah were, however, singled out for the brunt of God's attack (9.3–11).

The book presents distinctive theological formulations. The three primary visions offer a creative theology of divine presence. In the first, Ezekiel depicts the deity in both traditional (light imagery, 1.4) and innovative ways (moving wheels, 1.19). This motif of mobility is of fundamental theological importance: the deity can leave the temple (ch. 10), be experienced in exile, and then return to the temple (ch. 43).

Concern for the religious status of the individual works itself out in several ways. The prophet's task is defined as that of a sentinel who may personally succeed or fail (3.16–21; 33.7–16). More generally, God will respond to individual Israelites according to their deeds (18.20).

Consistent with his priestly status, Ezekiel construed the problems of and promise for Israel in priestly theological terms. Instead of injustice, as in Amos, Ezekiel speaks of "abominations," a Hebrew word for ritual impurity. Idolatrous behavior at the temple required punishment (ch. 8). As a result, the "glory of the Lord" had to leave Jerusalem. Then the defiled temple and those who worshiped there could be destroyed. Once the defilement was removed, a new temple with new regulations would provide the focus for a restored Israel.

Though imbued with Israel's theological traditions, Ezekiel thought in creative ways. In his reviews of Israel's history, he deemed Israel fundamentally foreign and recalcitrant from its beginnings (ch. 16). Moreover, Israel's ensuing experiences with God justified radical punishment—obliteration without regard for a remnant. Such finality made it difficult to imagine a viable future. Hence, the well-known vision of dry bones (37.1–14) is truly remarkable—expressing the notion that what is dead, God's people, might live again. The comprehensive vision of new life (chs. 40–48) may properly be termed utopian. The new "torah of the temple" will reorder religious and political life as well as redefine geographic boundaries. Ezekiel's theology is one in which God is other and acts to preserve the sanctity of the deity's name. When God acts, foreign nations (28.23), as well as Israel, will know that the Lord—and no other—is God.

[DAVID L. PETERSEN]

The Vision of the Chariot

1 In the thirtieth year, in the fourth month, on the fifth day of the month, as I was among the exiles by the river Chebar, the heavens were opened, and I saw visions of God. ²On the fifth day of the month (it was the fifth year of the exile of King Jehoiachin), ³the word of the Lord came to the priest Ezekiel son of Buzi, in the land of the Chaldeans by the river Chebar; and the hand of the Lord was on him there.

4 As I looked, a stormy wind came out of the north: a great cloud with brightness around it and fire flashing forth continually, and in the middle of the fire, something like gleaming amber. ⁵In the middle of it was something like four living creatures. This was their appearance: they were of human form. ⁶Each had four faces, and each of them had four wings. ⁷Their legs were straight, and the soles of their feet were like the sole of a calf's foot; and they sparkled like burnished bronze. ⁸Under their wings on their four sides they had human

---

1.1–3.15 Ezekiel's inaugural vision, which may be compared with shorter, though similar, accounts in Isa 6; Jer 1. God calls Ezekiel to act as a prophet and provides him with instructions about fulfilling this task. Other vision reports are in 8.1–11.25; 37.1–14; 40.1–48.35. **1.1–3** The book's introduction places the prophet in Babylonia and dates his activity by reference to a Judahite king, Jehoiachin, now in exile. **1.1** *Thirtieth year,* probably Ezekiel's age when he experienced this vision. *The river Chebar,* a canal, not a natural river, near Nippur. **1.2** Jehoiachin, Ezekiel, and others were exiled to Babylon in 597 BCE. *The fifth year of the exile* would have been 593. This is the first of thirteen such chronological notices (1.2; 8.1; 20.1; 24.1; 26.1; 29.1; 29.17; 30.20; 31.1; 32.1; 32.17; 33.21; 40.1). **1.3** *The priest,* either Ezekiel or Buzi, though most probably Ezekiel. Ezekiel is defined as a priest because of his lineage, whereas he becomes a prophet because of this visionary experience. *The land of the Chaldeans,* the plains of southern Mesopotamia, associated with an Aramean-speaking people who had entered this area earlier in the first millennium BCE. *The*

hand of the Lord, a phrase indicative of spirit possession; cf. 3.14.22; 8.1; 33.22; 37.1; 40.1. This phrase is present at the beginning of each of Ezekiel's four vision reports. **1.4–28** Ezekiel encounters God. The combination of cloud, fire, creatures, the spirit, and wheels makes it impossible to reduce this vision to some readily understandable phenomenon. **1.4–14** Ezekiel perceives strange creatures. **1.4** *Fire* and *cloud* are often associated with an appearance of the deity (e.g., Ps 18). *Something like gleaming amber,* also in 8.2. **1.5** The author uses *like* (see also vv. 22, 26, 27) to emphasize that the vision is proximate. The prophet does not actually see the deity and his accoutrements. The *living creatures* are part animal, part human, with the latter dominant, i.e., they have two legs and stand upright. Such winged creatures with animal features are related to the seraphim in Isa 6, another "prophetic call" narrative. Ancient Near Eastern mythology knows such creatures, often minor deities, some of which support the divine or royal throne. Cf. 10.15, 20, where similar creatures are labeled cherubim. **1.7** *Bronze,* also in the description of a *man* in 40.3.

hands. And the four had their faces and their wings thus: [9]their wings touched one another; each of them moved straight ahead, without turning as they moved. [10]As for the appearance of their faces: the four had the face of a human being, the face of a lion on the right side, the face of an ox on the left side, and the face of an eagle; [11]such were their faces. Their wings were spread out above; each creature had two wings, each of which touched the wing of another, while two covered their bodies. [12]Each moved straight ahead; wherever the spirit would go, they went, without turning as they went. [13]In the middle of[a] the living creatures there was something that looked like burning coals of fire, like torches moving to and fro among the living creatures; the fire was bright, and lightning issued from the fire. [14]The living creatures darted to and fro, like a flash of lightning.

15 As I looked at the living creatures, I saw a wheel on the earth beside the living creatures, one for each of the four of them.[b] [16]As for the appearance of the wheels and their construction: their appearance was like the gleaming of beryl; and the four had the same form, their construction being something like a wheel within a wheel. [17]When they moved, they moved in any of the four directions without veering as they moved. [18]Their rims were tall and awesome, for the rims of all four were full of eyes all around. [19]When the living creatures moved, the wheels moved beside them; and when the living creatures rose from the earth, the wheels rose. [20]Wherever the spirit would go, they went, and the wheels rose along with

them; for the spirit of the living creatures was in the wheels. [21]When they moved, the others moved; when they stopped, the others stopped; and when they rose from the earth, the wheels rose along with them; for the spirit of the living creatures was in the wheels.

22 Over the heads of the living creatures there was something like a dome, shining like crystal,[c] spread out above their heads. [23]Under the dome their wings were stretched out straight, one toward another; and each of the creatures had two wings covering its body. [24]When they moved, I heard the sound of their wings like the sound of mighty waters, like the thunder of the Almighty,[d] a sound of tumult like the sound of an army; when they stopped, they let down their wings. [25]And there came a voice from above the dome over their heads; when they stopped, they let down their wings.

26 And above the dome over their heads there was something like a throne, in appearance like sapphire;[e] and seated above the likeness of a throne was something that seemed like a human form. [27]Upward from what appeared like the loins I saw something like gleaming amber, something that looked like fire enclosed all around; and downward from what looked like the loins I saw something that looked like fire, and there was a splendor all around. [28]Like the bow in a cloud on a rainy day, such was the appearance of the

---

a Gk OL: Heb *And the appearance of*   *b* Heb *of their faces*
c Gk: Heb *like the awesome crystal*   *d* Traditional rendering of Heb *Shaddai*   *e* Or *lapis lazuli*

1.10 Four *faces* (human, lion, ox, eagle) on one head is otherwise unattested. The imagery may emphasize alertness: as the wheels turn, the creature will be able to look in any direction. **1.12** *The spirit*, not the deity, but *the spirit of the living creatures* in v. 21 (see also v. 20; 3.12). **1.13–14** The creatures are associated with fire or lightning; cf. Gen 3.24 for an analogous creature who brandishes a flaming sword; Gen 15.17, where torches symbolize the presence of the deity. **1.15–21** Crystalline wheels associated with the creatures. Although the writer mentions *a wheel* (v. 15), there are apparently four wheels, one for each creature. Either a chariot with four wheels on one axle (two wheels on each side of the carriage) or a ceremonial cart with two axles (and two wheels per axle) may be presumed in this description. The imagery of wheels emphasizes that *the glory of the LORD* (v. 28) was capable of movement. The motif of wheels symbolizes the mobility of the deity, who will later leave the temple (10.18–19). **1.18** *Full of eyes* implies the ability to see everything

(cf. 10.12; Zech 4.10). **1.22–25** Below the dome. **1.22** *Dome*, the heavenly vault (see Gen 1.7–8). **1.24** Auditory imagery (e.g., *like the thunder*) rather than visual imagery, fire and light, prevails. Both sound and visual imagery attend the appearance of the deity (e.g., Ex 19.16–19). *The sound of mighty waters.* Cf. 43.2. In Rev 14.2, the sound is further defined in association with thunder. **1.25** *A voice*, or "a sound," from above the dome indicates that even the deafening roar created by the creatures' wings under the dome is not the ultimate sound. **1.26–28** Above the dome. The *throne* above the heavenly vault signifies the throne or council room of the deity. The deity enthroned in the heavens truly transcends the temple. *Like*, used ten times in three verses to emphasize that Ezekiel does not actually see the deity. *Sapphire.* Cf. Ex 24.10. *Like a human form* begins the description of the deity, above the loins (waist) like amber, below the loins like fire. **1.28** Rather than proceed with a more detailed and hence dangerous description, the author moves to an

splendor all around. This was the appearance of the likeness of the glory of the LORD.

When I saw it, I fell on my face, and I heard the voice of someone speaking.

The Vision of the Scroll

2 He said to me: O mortal,[a] stand up on your feet, and I will speak with you. 2 And when he spoke to me, a spirit entered into me and set me on my feet; and I heard him speaking to me. 3 He said to me, Mortal, I am sending you to the people of Israel, to a nation[b] of rebels who have rebelled against me; they and their ancestors have transgressed against me to this very day. 4 The descendants are impudent and stubborn. I am sending you to them, and you shall say to them, "Thus says the Lord GOD." 5 Whether they hear or refuse to hear (for they are a rebellious house), they shall know that there has been a prophet among them. 6 And you, O mortal, do not be afraid of them, and do not be afraid of their words, though briers and thorns surround you and you live among scorpions; do not be afraid of their words, and do not be dismayed at their looks, for they are a rebellious house. 7 You shall speak my words to them, whether they hear or refuse to hear; for they are a rebellious house.

8 But you, mortal, hear what I say to you; do not be rebellious like that rebellious house; open your mouth and eat what I give you. 9 I

looked, and a hand was stretched out to me, and a written scroll was in it. 10 He spread it before me; it had writing on the front and on the back, and written on it were words of lamentation and mourning and woe.

3 He said to me, O mortal, eat what is offered to you; eat this scroll, and go, speak to the house of Israel. 2 So I opened my mouth, and he gave me the scroll to eat. 3 He said to me, Mortal, eat this scroll that I give you and fill your stomach with it. Then I ate it; and in my mouth it was as sweet as honey.

4 He said to me: Mortal, go to the house of Israel and speak my very words to them. 5 For you are not sent to a people of obscure speech and difficult language, but to the house of Israel— 6 not to many peoples of obscure speech and difficult language, whose words you cannot understand. Surely, if I sent you to them, they would listen to you. 7 But the house of Israel will not listen to you, for they are not willing to listen to me; because all the house of Israel have a hard forehead and a stubborn heart. 8 See, I have made your face hard against their faces, and your forehead hard against their foreheads. 9 Like the hardest stone, harder than flint, I have made your forehead; do not fear them or be dismayed at their looks, for they are a rebellious house. 10 He said to

a Or son of man; Heb ben adam (and so throughout the book when Ezekiel is addressed)   b Syr: Heb to nations

analogy, the splendor of a rainbow, and the summation This was the appearance of the likeness of the glory of the LORD, which again emphasizes that the prophet did not see God directly (see note on 1.5). **1.28b** The author is careful not to impute the voice to God, though the deity is almost certainly speaking.

2.1–3.3 Ezekiel is made to stand up and provided with a commission. **2.1** Mortal, lit. "son of man" (see text note a). The Hebrew phrase "son of x" means a member of a certain class, e.g., "son of Israel" is properly translated "Israelite." Mortal occurs over ninety times in Ezekiel. It is appropriate here since the other characters, whether spirits or living creatures, belong to the divine realm. Stand up signifies that this is a waking as opposed to a sleeping (incubation) vision. Cf. Dan 8.17–18; 10.9–11; Zech 4.1. **2.2** A spirit. See also, e.g., 3.12, 14, 24, where the Hebrew does not have the definite article. Is this a minor deity, the deity's spirit (cf. 11.5, 24; 37.1) or simply human energy? This spirit, and not the prophet's own power, enables him to stand up. **2.3** Israel's rebellion against God has been going on for generations, a standard theme for Ezekiel; see ch. 16. **2.4** Thus says the Lord GOD, a standard phrase with which a prophetic utterance may be intro-

duced. Without an ensuing oracle, however, the phrase alone is ironic; cf. 3.11, 27. **2.6** Do not be afraid. Cf. the call of Jeremiah (Jer 1.8). The descendants (v. 4) are here characterized as plants (briers and thorns) and animals (scorpions). The commission recognizes that Israel may not hear (vv. 5, 7), but emphasizes the importance of having someone who is recognizably a prophet speak (v. 7). **2.8–10** Open your mouth. Oral imagery is prominent in prophetic call narratives. Cf. Isa 6.6–7; Jer 1.9. **2.9–10** The scroll has been fully inscribed and bears bad news; cf. Zech 5.1–4. **2.10** Lamentation and mourning and woe may reflect funeral rites in ancient Israel. **3.1–3** There is no precedent for eating scrolls, which were made of either papyrus or leather. Cf. Jer 15.16, where "words" are eaten, but not scrolls. If Ezekiel's consumption of the scroll is surprising, his palate is shocking, namely, that funeral words could be as sweet as honey. Cf. "joy," "delight" in Jer 15.16.

3.4–11 Words to Israel. **3.4** A reiteration of 2.7, though now presuming the content of the scroll. **3.5** Obscure speech and difficult language, no doubt a reference to Akkadian, the Northeast Semitic cuneiform language of ancient Mesopotamia, which, as a

me: Mortal, all my words that I shall speak to you receive in your heart and hear with your ears; 11 then go to the exiles, to your people, and speak to them. Say to them, "Thus says the Lord GOD"; whether they hear or refuse to hear.

Ezekiel at the River Chebar

12 Then the spirit lifted me up, and as the glory of the LORD rose[a] from its place, I heard behind me the sound of loud rumbling; 13 it was the sound of the wings of the living creatures brushing against one another, and the sound of the wheels beside them, that sounded like a loud rumbling. 14 The spirit lifted me up and bore me away; I went in bitterness in the heat of my spirit, the hand of the LORD being strong upon me. 15 I came to the exiles at Tel-abib, who lived by the river Chebar.[b] And I sat there among them, stunned, for seven days.

16 At the end of seven days, the word of the LORD came to me: 17 Mortal, I have made you a sentinel for the house of Israel; whenever you hear a word from my mouth, you shall give them warning from me. 18 If I say to the wicked, "You shall surely die," and you give them no warning, or speak to warn the wicked from their wicked way, in order to save their life, those wicked persons shall die for their iniquity; but their blood I will require at your hand. 19 But if you warn the wicked, and they do not turn from their wickedness, or from their wicked way, they shall die for their iniquity; but you will have saved your life. 20 Again, if the righteous turn from their righteousness and commit iniquity, and I lay a stumbling block before them, they shall die; because you have not warned them, they shall die for their sin, and their righteous deeds that they have done shall not be remembered; but their blood I will require at your hand. 21 If, however, you warn the righteous not to sin, and they do not sin, they shall surely live, because they took warning; and you will have saved your life.

Ezekiel Isolated and Silenced

22 Then the hand of the LORD was upon me there; and he said to me, Rise up, go out into the valley, and there I will speak with you. 23 So I rose up and went out into the valley; and the glory of the LORD stood there, like the glory that I had seen by the river Chebar; and I fell on my face. 24 The spirit entered into me, and set me on my feet; and he spoke with me and said to me: Go, shut yourself inside your house. 25 As for you, mortal, cords shall be placed on you, and you shall be bound with them, so that you cannot go out among the people; 26 and I will make your tongue cling to

a Cn: Heb and blessed be the glory of the LORD   b Two Mss Syr: Heb Chebar, and to where they lived. Another reading is Chebar, and I sat where they sat

more fully inflected language than Hebrew, would have been viewed as difficult; cf. Isa 33.19. **3.12–15** Conclusion of the vision. **3.12** The spirit, lit. "a spirit," here probably a wind. Cf. other instances of wind impelling the prophet in a vision (8.3; 11.1, 24; 43.5). The glory of the LORD also moves, though of its own accord. **3.12–13** The sound of loud rumbling ("a great earthquake," RSV) suggests (so 1.22–25), and v. 13 makes explicit, that the creatures' wings, along with the wheels, assist in this movement. **3.14** The spirit (cf. "The Spirit," RSV, an interpretive rendering), again lit. "a spirit," best understood as the wind. The Septuagint omits in bitterness. Heat of my spirit, probably anger. **3.15** Tel-abib reflects the Akkadian til-abubi, "mound of the flood." In Hebrew 'abib means "ears of grain." **3.16–21** Ezekiel as sentinel. This conception of the prophet's role is used elsewhere in the OT (Jer 6.17; Hos 9.8; cf. Isa 21.6) and is more fully developed in 33.1–9. The logic is informed by that used in chs. 18 and 33, chapters that insist that each individual is responsible for his or her fate. In this instance, the prophet as sentinel is accountable to the Lord. That accountability is expressed in the sentinel's providing a warning. There are four cases, one per verse, in vv. 18,

19, 20, 21; concerns of the latter two are not part of the discourse in ch. 33, but 33.8 parallels the case in 3.18 and 33.9 parallels the one in 3.19. **3.16** The word of the LORD came to me, a phrase characteristic of Ezekiel (occurring almost fifty times) emphasizing the "private" character of these revelations. **3.17** I have made you suggests that vv. 16–21 present a way of understanding the earlier commissioning, not a new call.

3.22–5.17 Ezekiel communicates God's message through bodily action. The Lord requires Ezekiel to act out his prophetic message in a series of discrete performances. Numerous prophets prior to Ezekiel had used nonverbal behavior to convey a message from the deity, e.g., Elisha (2 Kings 13.14–19); Hosea (Hos 1); Jeremiah (Jer 16.1–9; 19). Yet reports of symbolic actions occur more frequently in Ezekiel (twelve times) than in any other prophetic book. **3.22–27** The prophet experiences again the glory of the LORD (v. 23), which results in directions to perform certain actions. **3.22** There and the valley (better "the plain," RSV, a broad alluvial river basin typical of Mesopotamia) emphasize that Ezekiel is in Babylon when he perceives the Lord and when the spirit speaks with him. **3.24a** Cf. 2.2. **3.26** I will make . . . so that you shall be

the roof of your mouth, so that you shall be speechless and unable to reprove them; for they are a rebellious house. 27 But when I speak with you, I will open your mouth, and you shall say to them, "Thus says the Lord GOD"; let those who will hear, hear; and let those who refuse to hear, refuse; for they are a rebellious house.

The Siege of Jerusalem Portrayed

4 And you, O mortal, take a brick and set it before you. On it portray a city, Jerusalem; 2 and put siegeworks against it, and build a siege wall against it, and cast up a ramp against it; set camps also against it, and plant battering rams against it all around. 3 Then take an iron plate and place it as an iron wall between you and the city; set your face toward it, and let it be in a state of siege, and press the siege against it. This is a sign for the house of Israel.

4 Then lie on your left side, and place the punishment of the house of Israel upon it; you shall bear their punishment for the number of the days that you lie there. 5 For I assign to you a number of days, three hundred ninety days, equal to the number of the years of their punishment; and so you shall bear the punishment of the house of Israel. 6 When you have completed these, you shall lie down a second time, but on your right side, and bear the punishment of the house of Judah; forty days I assign you, one day for each year. 7 You shall set your face toward the siege of Jerusalem, and with your arm bared you shall prophesy against it. 8 See, I am putting cords on you so that you cannot turn from one side to the other until you have completed the days of your siege.

9 And you, take wheat and barley, beans and lentils, millet and spelt; put them into one vessel, and make bread for yourself. During the number of days that you lie on your side, three hundred ninety days, you shall eat it. 10 The food that you eat shall be twenty shekels a day by weight; at fixed times you shall eat it. 11 And you shall drink water by measure, one-sixth of a hin; at fixed times you shall drink. 12 You shall eat it as a barley-cake, baking it in their sight on human dung. 13 The LORD said, "Thus shall the people of Israel eat their bread, unclean, among the nations to which I will drive them." 14 Then I said, "Ah Lord GOD! I have never defiled myself; from my youth up until now I have never eaten what died of itself or was torn by animals, nor has carrion flesh come into my mouth." 15 Then he said to me, "See, I will let you have cow's dung instead of human dung, on which you may prepare your bread."

---

speechless. Here the absence of prophetic speech is attributed to the Lord's prohibition, not malfeasance by the prophet. **3.26–27** Cf. 24.27; 34.22, a text that links news about the destruction of Jerusalem to the removal of Ezekiel's speechlessness. Only when the Lord permits will Ezekiel be able to perform his prophetic task, namely, by saying *Thus says the Lord GOD* (cf. 2.4; 3.11). **4.1–3** Siege and separation. This symbolic act uses imagery attested in an earlier prophetic text, Jer 1.18. **4.1** *Brick,* i.e., brick made out of mud and dried in the sun. Ezekiel is probably being commanded to etch the city and siege works into a still damp brick, though the verbs seem to call for sculpting, which would have been possible with damp clay. Such bricks could vary widely in size and general configuration (square or rectangular), though one 40 by 20 by 12 centimeters would not be unusual. **4.3** *Iron plate,* probably an iron cooking griddle. This vignette is to be an uninterpreted sign for Israel. **4.4–8** Ezekiel is commanded to lie first on his left and then on his right side to communicate the length of punishment for Israel and Judah, respectively. The numbers of days—390 and 40—do not conform to the chronology of either nation's exile. The Septuagint offers different figures, 150 and 40 years, respectively. **4.4** *Punishment,* sin or guilt. The prophet may serve as a "scapegoat" (Lev 16.20–22), evoking a priestly role in ancient Israel (Lev 16.17); Ezekiel was both priest and prophet. **4.9–17** Ezekiel is commanded to bake bread and eat it and then to drink water according to a specific rationing. **4.9** *Wheat . . . spelt.* This mixture of six foodstuffs, known in both Israel and Babylon, probably symbolizes that no one grain or legume is found in sufficient quantity to allow the preparation of something to eat. **4.10** *Twenty shekels.* One shekel weighed almost half an ounce; hence twenty shekels would weigh almost half a pound. **4.11** *One-sixth of a hin,* about two-thirds of a quart. One hin (the word belongs to an Egyptian system) equals slightly less than a gallon. **4.12–13** The Hebrew syntax and term *barley-cake* make it unclear whether the barley bread is the one Ezekiel baked (v. 9). V. 12 may begin a new symbolic action that emphasizes impurity rather than scarcity, which appears to be the point in vv. 9–11. *Human dung* as fuel is otherwise unattested in ancient Israel. According to Deut 23.12–14 human fecal material violates holiness. **4.14** For Ezekiel to have cooked over a fire fueled with human offal would have introduced impurity; it would have *defiled* him, which would have been especially pernicious since Ezekiel was a priest. The cases that Ezekiel attests, eating something that was not properly slaughtered (Lev 22.8) and meat that has not been eaten within a specific time limit (*carrion flesh;* Lev 7.18), are forbidden in Israel's ritual legislation.

16 Then he said to me, Mortal, I am going to break the staff of bread in Jerusalem; they shall eat bread by weight and with fearfulness; and they shall drink water by measure and in dismay. 17Lacking bread and water, they will look at one another in dismay, and waste away under their punishment.

A Sword against Jerusalem

5 And you, O mortal, take a sharp sword; use it as a barber's razor and run it over your head and your beard; then take balances for weighing, and divide the hair. 2One third of the hair you shall burn in the fire inside the city, when the days of the siege are completed; one third you shall take and strike with the sword all around the city;*a* and one third you shall scatter to the wind, and I will unsheathe the sword after them. 3Then you shall take from these a small number, and bind them in the skirts of your robe. 4From these, again, you shall take some, throw them into the fire and burn them up; from there a fire will come out against all the house of Israel.

5 Thus says the Lord GOD: This is Jerusalem; I have set her in the center of the nations, with countries all around her. 6But she has rebelled against my ordinances and my statutes, becoming more wicked than the nations and the countries all around her, rejecting my ordinances and not following my statutes. 7Therefore thus says the Lord GOD: Because you are more turbulent than the nations that are all around you, and have not followed my statutes or kept my ordinances, but have acted according to the ordinances of the nations that are all around you; 8therefore thus says

the Lord GOD: I, I myself, am coming against you; I will execute judgments among you in the sight of the nations. 9And because of all your abominations, I will do to you what I have never yet done, and the like of which I will never do again. 10Surely, parents shall eat their children in your midst, and children shall eat their parents; I will execute judgments on you, and any of you who survive I will scatter to every wind. 11Therefore, as I live, says the Lord GOD, surely, because you have defiled my sanctuary with all your detestable things and with all your abominations—therefore I will cut you down;*b* my eye will not spare, and I will have no pity. 12One third of you shall die of pestilence or be consumed by famine among you; one third shall fall by the sword around you; and one third I will scatter to every wind and will unsheathe the sword after them.

13 My anger shall spend itself, and I will vent my fury on them and satisfy myself; and they shall know that I, the LORD, have spoken in my jealousy, when I spend my fury on them. 14Moreover I will make you a desolation and an object of mocking among the nations around you, in the sight of all that pass by. 15You shall be*c* a mockery and a taunt, a warning and a horror, to the nations around you, when I execute judgments on you in anger and fury, and with furious punishments—I, the LORD, have spoken— 16when I loose against you*d* my deadly arrows of famine, arrows for destruction, which I will let loose to destroy

---

a Heb *it*   *b* Another reading is *I will withdraw*   *c* Gk Syr Vg Tg: Heb *It shall be*   *d* Heb *them*

4.16–17 The prophet returns to the imagery of vv. 9–11, that of scarcity; cf. Lev 26.26 for similar language. 5.1–4 Ezekiel and the blade of a barber. In the final symbolic action of this series, Ezekiel is to take a sharp instrument (*sword*, or "sharp blade") and use it to cut his hair and beard (cf. Isa 7.20 for the imagery of a foreign enemy as a razor). The manipulation of the hair in three parts and then *a small number* (vv. 2–4) suggests that no part of Israel will be immune from destruction. What Ezekiel does to the hair—weighing, dividing, burning, striking, scattering, binding—may symbolize God's punishment. Fire is a destructive element at both beginning and end. 5.5–17 God vows that he will destroy Jerusalem using various weapons. This long speech is replete with the prophetic speech formulas *thus says the Lord GOD* in vv. 5, 7, 8, 11 and *I, the LORD, have spoken* in vv. 13, 15, 17. 5.5 *This is Jerusalem* signifies that the divine oracle interprets the

purport of the foregoing symbolic actions, especially the last one, as referring to Jerusalem. *In the center of the nations* resonates with traditions of a holy site or city being located at the earth's central point (cf. 38.12). Here, however, that tradition involves no divine protection for the city and, instead, allows for judgment in the next verse. 5.6 *My ordinances and my statutes*, i.e., specific requirements created by God's covenant with Israel. Jerusalem's becoming *more wicked than the nations* is a theme also present in ch. 16. 5.8 *I . . . against you*. Cf. Nah 2.13; 3.5. 5.10 Ezekiel takes the case of parents consuming children (cf. Lev 26.29; 2 Kings 6.29; Jer 19.9) and adds its converse, otherwise unattested, children consuming parents. Here and in v. 12 Ezekiel uses imagery drawn from covenant curses. 5.11 *Defiled my sanctuary*. See chs. 8, 11 for specific desecrations. 5.12 This verse builds on the fractional symbolism of 5.1–2. 5.16–17 On God's

you, and when I bring more and more famine upon you, and break your staff of bread. 17I will send famine and wild animals against you, and they will rob you of your children; pestilence and bloodshed shall pass through you; and I will bring the sword upon you. I, the LORD, have spoken.

Judgment on Idolatrous Israel

6 The word of the LORD came to me: 2O mortal, set your face toward the mountains of Israel, and prophesy against them, 3and say, You mountains of Israel, hear the word of the Lord GOD! Thus says the Lord GOD to the mountains and the hills, to the ravines and the valleys: I, I myself will bring a sword upon you, and I will destroy your high places. 4Your altars shall become desolate, and your incense stands shall be broken; and I will throw down your slain in front of your idols. 5I will lay the corpses of the people of Israel in front of their idols; and I will scatter your bones around your altars. 6Wherever you live, your towns shall be waste and your high places ruined, so that your altars will be waste and ruined,ᵃ your idols broken and destroyed, your incense stands cut down, and your works wiped out. 7The slain shall fall in your midst; then you shall know that I am the LORD.

8 But I will spare some. Some of you shall escape the sword among the nations and be scattered through the countries. 9Those of you who escape shall remember me among the nations where they are carried captive, how I was crushed by their wanton heart that turned away from me, and their wanton eyes that turned after their idols. Then they will be loathsome in their own sight for the evils that they have committed, for all their abominations. 10And they shall know that I am the LORD; I did not threaten in vain to bring this disaster upon them.

11 Thus says the Lord GOD: Clap your hands and stamp your foot, and say, Alas for all the vile abominations of the house of Israel! For they shall fall by the sword, by famine, and by pestilence. 12Those far off shall die of pestilence; those nearby shall fall by the sword; and any who are left and are spared shall die of famine. Thus I will spend my fury upon them. 13And you shall know that I am the LORD, when their slain lie among their idols around their altars, on every high hill, on all the mountain tops, under every green tree, and under every leafy oak, wherever they offered pleasing odor to all their idols. 14I will stretch out my hand against them, and make the land desolate and waste, throughout all their settlements, from the wilderness to Riblah.ᵇ Then they shall know that I am the LORD.

Impending Disaster

7 The word of the LORD came to me: 2You, O mortal, thus says the Lord GOD to the land of Israel:

a Syr Vg Tg: Heb *and be made guilty*   *b* Another reading is *Diblah*

arsenal, cf. Deut 32.23–24, which suggests Ezekiel is using standard notions of ways in which God can inflict punishment.

6.1–14 Destruction with survivors. **6.1–7** Ezekiel addresses first the mountains of Israel and then all Israel. Cf. ch. 36 for similar imagery, employed after the destruction foretold in ch. 6; see also 3.22, where Ezekiel is speaking in a valley. Geographic imagery is prominent throughout the book. **6.2–4** The mountains themselves are personified and addressed, as are valleys. Mountains are important because Israel had built improper religious sites on them. *High place,* anything from a small ritual platform to a temple complex. High places are frequently related to Canaanite religious practices. For OT polemic against such places, see, e.g., 2 Kings 23.8; Jer 19.5 (high places could also be located in valleys; so Jer 7.31). Even Yahwistic high places were to have been destroyed after the reforms of Josiah. *Altars, incense stands,* and *idols* indicate that Ezekiel understands these shrines to have been major installations. *Idols* (Hebrew *gillulim*), used thirty-nine times in Ezekiel, is characteristic of this book. **6.5–6** Instead of the sacrifices normally expected at the high places, God will provide corpses (cf. Jer 7.31–33). **6.6** *Your works,* a reference to religious implements made by human hands (see Isa 17.7–8). **6.7** *You shall know that I am the LORD,* a sentence, common in Ezekiel (over sixty times), that regularly marks the boundary of a speech, e.g., 7.27. Here remembering and self-loathing lead to knowledge. **6.8–10** Those who survive will be exiled. **6.9** *I was crushed.* God has been affected personally and does not simply enforce covenant curses. **6.11–14** An oracle that begins with a new device, ritual use of hands, foot, and voice. On *alas,* cf. the related Hebrew word translated *aha* in 25.3; 26.2; 36.2. **6.12** The possibility for survivors seems remote. *Far off, nearby* may refer to proximity to Jerusalem. **6.13** An allusion to the imagery of vv. 1–7. **6.14** *From the wilderness to Riblah,* a general description of Israel's boundaries at their greatest extent. *Wilderness,* southern Judah (Ex 23.31); *Riblah* (*Diblah* in Hebrew; the letters *r* and *d* may be easily confused) lies in Syria (2 Kings 23.33).

7.1–27 Sayings concerning the end for Israel. *Thus*

An end! The end has come
    upon the four corners of the land.
3 Now the end is upon you,
    I will let loose my anger upon you;
I will judge you according to your ways,
    I will punish you for all your
      abominations.
4 My eye will not spare you, I will have no
      pity.
I will punish you for your ways,
    while your abominations are among
      you.
Then you shall know that I am the Lord.
  5 Thus says the Lord God:
Disaster after disaster! See, it comes.
6   An end has come, the end has come.
It has awakened against you; see, it comes!
7 Your doom[a] has come to you,
    O inhabitant of the land.
The time has come, the day is near—
    of tumult, not of reveling on the
      mountains.
8   Soon now I will pour out my wrath upon
      you;
I will spend my anger against you.
I will judge you according to your ways,
    and punish you for all your
      abominations.
9 My eye will not spare; I will have no pity.
    I will punish you according to your
      ways,
    while your abominations are among
      you.
Then you shall know that it is I the Lord who
strike.
10 See, the day! See, it comes!
    Your doom[a] has gone out.
The rod has blossomed, pride has
      budded.

11 Violence has grown into a rod of
      wickedness.
None of them shall remain,
    not their abundance, not their wealth;
    no pre-eminence among them.[a]
12 The time has come, the day draws near;
    let not the buyer rejoice, nor the seller
      mourn,
    for wrath is upon all their multitude.
13 For the sellers shall not return to what has
been sold as long as they remain alive. For the
vision concerns all their multitude; it shall not
be revoked. Because of their iniquity, they
cannot maintain their lives.[a]
14 They have blown the horn and made
      everything ready;
    but no one goes to battle,
    for my wrath is upon all their
      multitude.
15 The sword is outside, pestilence and
      famine are inside;
    those in the field die by the sword;
    those in the city—famine and
      pestilence devour them.
16 If any survivors escape,
    they shall be found on the mountains
    like doves of the valleys,
all of them moaning over their iniquity.
17 All hands shall grow feeble,
    all knees turn to water.
18 They shall put on sackcloth,
    horror shall cover them.
Shame shall be on all faces,
    baldness on all their heads.
19 They shall fling their silver into the
      streets,
    their gold shall be treated as unclean.

---

a Meaning of Heb uncertain

---

says the Lord God introduces two of the three oracles that make up this chapter, vv. 1–4, 5–9, 10–27. The formula *Then you shall know that I am the Lord* occurs at the end of each oracle. These oracles share much imagery and phraseology with other OT texts, e.g., Isa 13–14. **7.1–4** *End* occurs three times and provides the basic theme of the first oracle. Am 8.2 also understands God's judgment to be "the end." *Four corners of the land,* possibly "four corners of the earth," emphasizing the destruction's cosmic scope, but Hebrew *'adamah,* "land," is regularly used by Ezekiel to refer to Israelite territory, e.g., 11.17. Cf. Isa 11.12. **7.3** *Let loose my anger.* See Ex 15.7; Ps 78.49. **7.4** *Eye.* Cf. Pss 33.18; 34.15. **7.5–9** The end is defined as *the day,* which is imminent. The "day of the Lord" as a time for destruction and disorder is a prominent motif in other

prophetic texts, e.g., Joel 1.15; Zeph 1.14; Zech 14.1; Mal 4.1. The general terms *doom, end, disaster,* and *tumult* are presented as God's personal *wrath,* which will be meted out in proportion to the people's *ways;* cf. ch. 18. **7.10–27** What will happen to humans on *the day* is spelled out. **7.10–11** *Rod.* Another word with the same consonants in Hebrew could mean "injustice" (RSV). *Pride, wickedness,* symbolized by twigs that grow larger. **7.12–13** Normal life, as exemplified in market transactions, is inappropriate since many will die. **7.14–17** *They have blown the horn.* Those on guard and responsible for mustering defensive forces have issued the call, but the onslaught of sword, pestilence, and famine has prevented a military response. Some may flee, but they will only be able to *moan.* **7.18** Wearing *sackcloth* and shaving the head (*baldness*) are lamenta-

Their silver and gold cannot save them on the day of the wrath of the LORD. They shall not satisfy their hunger or fill their stomachs with it. For it was the stumbling block of their iniquity. 20From their[a] beautiful ornament, in which they took pride, they made their abominable images, their detestable things; therefore I will make of it an unclean thing to them.

21 I will hand it over to strangers as booty,
   to the wicked of the earth as plunder;
   they shall profane it.
22 I will avert my face from them,
   so that they may profane my treasured[b] place;
   the violent shall enter it,
   they shall profane it.
23 Make a chain![c]
   For the land is full of bloody crimes;
   the city is full of violence.
24 I will bring the worst of the nations
   to take possession of their houses.
   I will put an end to the arrogance of the strong,
   and their holy places shall be profaned.
25 When anguish comes, they will seek peace,
   but there shall be none.
26 Disaster comes upon disaster,
   rumor follows rumor;
   they shall keep seeking a vision from the prophet;
   instruction shall perish from the priest,
   and counsel from the elders.
27 The king shall mourn,
   the prince shall be wrapped in despair,

and the hands of the people of the land shall tremble.
   According to their way I will deal with them;
   according to their own judgments I will judge them.
And they shall know that I am the LORD.

Abominations in the Temple

8 In the sixth year, in the sixth month, on the fifth day of the month, as I sat in my house, with the elders of Judah sitting before me, the hand of the Lord GOD fell upon me there. 2I looked, and there was a figure that looked like a human being;[d] below what appeared to be its loins it was fire, and above the loins it was like the appearance of brightness, like gleaming amber. 3It stretched out the form of a hand, and took me by a lock of my head; and the spirit lifted me up between earth and heaven, and brought me in visions of God to Jerusalem, to the entrance of the gateway of the inner court that faces north, to the seat of the image of jealousy, which provokes to jealousy. 4And the glory of the God of Israel was there, like the vision that I had seen in the valley.

5 Then God[e] said to me, "O mortal, lift up your eyes now in the direction of the north." So I lifted up my eyes toward the north, and there, north of the altar gate, in the entrance, was this image of jealousy. 6He said to me, "Mortal, do you see what they are doing, the

---

a Syr Symmachus: Heb *its* b Or *secret* c Meaning of Heb uncertain d Gk: Heb *like fire* e Heb *he*

---

tion practices. **7.19–20** *Silver* and *gold*. Wealth generally, as well as specific objects made out of precious metal, including idols, provide no protection from disaster. **7.21–22** *It* (v. 21), riches (as in v. 20), which God can give over to the foreign army in order to fulfill the promise of desecration, which also includes profanation of the temple. **7.23** *Make a chain* may refer to the fetters worn by the people as they were led away to exile (Nah 3.10). **7.24–27** Though the *people of the land* (v. 27) will suffer, special attention is devoted to prominent functionaries (priest, prophet, elders, king, prince), who are characterized by the *arrogance of the strong* (v. 24). Cf. Isa 3.2–3; Jer 4.9 for similar lists of prominent officials in a city.

8.1–11.25 Second vision report: visions at the temple and God's response. **8.1–18** Acts of religious impropriety in and around the temple. **8.1–4** Vision introduction. **8.1** *The sixth year*, 592 BCE; see note on 1.2. Leaders of the community consult with Ezekiel (cf. also 14.1; 20.1; 33.31), an important glimpse into ex-

ilic life. *The hand of the Lord GOD.* See note on 1.3. **8.2** The *figure* is described using vocabulary from the first vision, 1.4, 26–27. **8.3** *Visions of God,* visions enabled by God by means of which Ezekiel is about to see and experience Jerusalem via visionary transport. **8.4** *In the valley* alludes to 3.22–23, where Ezekiel also perceived the *glory.* **8.5–6** The first scene of religious impropriety. Ezekiel is told to look north. From where he was located, the gate of the inner temple courtyard (v. 3; 10.5 refers to an outer court), his gaze is directed toward the *image of jealousy,* probably an image of a god or goddess that made the Lord "jealous." This object was doubly inappropriate since it violated the command against making images (Deut 4.15–18). The scene concludes with formulaic question and response, which are repeated with slight variations in vv. 13, 15, 17. **8.5** Either the *figure* (v. 2) or God speaking to Ezekiel. **8.6** *Drive me far from my sanctuary.* The prophet alludes to the ultimate effect of these indictments—God will leave the temple (described in ch.

great abominations that the house of Israel are committing here, to drive me far from my sanctuary? Yet you will see still greater abominations."

7 And he brought me to the entrance of the court; I looked, and there was a hole in the wall. 8Then he said to me, "Mortal, dig through the wall"; and when I dug through the wall, there was an entrance. 9He said to me, "Go in, and see the vile abominations that they are committing here." 10So I went in and looked; there, portrayed on the wall all around, were all kinds of creeping things, and loathsome animals, and all the idols of the house of Israel. 11Before them stood seventy of the elders of the house of Israel, with Jaazaniah son of Shaphan standing among them. Each had his censer in his hand, and the fragrant cloud of incense was ascending. 12Then he said to me, "Mortal, have you seen what the elders of the house of Israel are doing in the dark, each in his room of images? For they say, 'The LORD does not see us, the LORD has forsaken the land.' " 13He said also to me, "You will see still greater abominations that they are committing."

14 Then he brought me to the entrance of the north gate of the house of the LORD; women were sitting there weeping for Tammuz. 15Then he said to me, "Have you seen this, O mortal? You will see still greater abominations than these."

16 And he brought me into the inner court of the house of the LORD; there, at the entrance of the temple of the LORD, between the porch and the altar, were about twenty-five men, with their backs to the temple of the LORD, and their faces toward the east, prostrating themselves to the sun toward the east. 17Then he said to me, "Have you seen this, O mortal? Is it not bad enough that the house of Judah commits the abominations done here? Must they fill the land with violence, and provoke my anger still further? See, they are putting the branch to their nose! 18Therefore I will act in wrath; my eye will not spare, nor will I have pity; and though they cry in my hearing with a loud voice, I will not listen to them."

The Slaughter of the Idolaters

9 Then he cried in my hearing with a loud voice, saying, "Draw near, you executioners of the city, each with his destroying weapon in his hand." 2And six men came from the direction of the upper gate, which faces north, each with his weapon for slaughter in his hand; among them was a man clothed in linen, with a writing case at his side. They went in and stood beside the bronze altar.

---

10). *Abominations,* a favorite term of Ezekiel for describing ritual sin. **8.7–13** A second scene of religious impropriety. The prophet is commanded to dig and discover a secret area. The prophet sees wall art (engravings or paintings) of various animals and more *idols* termed as *of the house of Israel.* Moreover, representatives of the Judahite community, including *Jaazaniah* (who belonged to a prominent family; Shaphan, his father, is mentioned in 2 Kings 22), perform an incense ritual. This second scene is "worse" than the first since it depicts people actively disregarding Israelite traditions. Here the people attempt to justify their behavior by asserting that *the LORD has forsaken the land* (v. 12). **8.14–15** Ezekiel is now apparently closer to the temple itself. This third and briefest scene of impropriety is even worse than the second since the name of another deity appears. *Tammuz* (also known as Dumuzi) was worshiped in Mesopotamia as early as the third millennium BCE. Since he was thought to die and be held captive in the underworld, lamentation rites belonged to his worship. Ritual *weeping* by women (cf. 32.16) would be natural, especially as a part of the annual cycle of vegetation. Plant growth and fertility were associated with the life power of Tammuz, harvest and drought with his death. Veneration of Tammuz was probably incorporated in the worship of

Canaanite gods, especially Baal, who was also associated with vegetation and time in the underworld. **8.16–17** The fourth and most heinous scene of impropriety, probably because it occurs at the temple's doorway. Judahites were bowing down to worship the sun. Veneration of the sun god Shamash (associated with wisdom and law) was prominent in Mesopotamia. Worship of Yahweh, however, had also been associated with the sun (e.g., Ps 84.11; 2 Kings 23.11). **8.17** The focus shifts from abominations at the temple complex to *violence* throughout the land. *Putting the branch to their nose* is obscure, since there is no obvious connection between this image and the veneration of the sun. **8.18** If vv. 5–17 provide indictment, v. 18 constitutes the sentence. God promises radical justice with no possibility for intercession by the prophet or for mercy by God.

9.1–11 Execution in Jerusalem. **9.1–2** *Executioners of the city,* individuals who have been given the task of executing those in the city. Although the text defines these persons as *men,* Israelite tradition normally attributed this punitive role to minor deities or angels, e.g., Ex 12.23 ("the destroyer"); 2 Sam 24.16; 2 Kings 19.35. Ezekiel presents the first instance in which multiple individuals carry out this task; cf. Rev 15.6. *Among them,* lit. "in their midst." *A man clothed in linen,* probably a priest, since priests normally wore

3 Now the glory of the God of Israel had gone up from the cherub on which it rested to the threshold of the house. The LORD called to the man clothed in linen, who had the writing case at his side; 4and said to him, "Go through the city, through Jerusalem, and put a mark on the foreheads of those who sigh and groan over all the abominations that are committed in it." 5To the others he said in my hearing, "Pass through the city after him, and kill; your eye shall not spare, and you shall show no pity. 6Cut down old men, young men and young women, little children and women, but touch no one who has the mark. And begin at my sanctuary." So they began with the elders who were in front of the house. 7Then he said to them, "Defile the house, and fill the courts with the slain. Go!" So they went out and killed in the city. 8While they were killing, and I was left alone, I fell prostrate on my face and cried out, "Ah Lord GOD! will you destroy all who remain of Israel as you pour out your wrath upon Jerusalem?" 9He said to me, "The guilt of the house of Israel and Judah is exceedingly great; the land is full of bloodshed and the city full of perversity; for they say, 'The LORD has forsaken the land, and the LORD does not see.' 10As for me, my eye will not spare, nor will I have pity, but I will bring down their deeds upon their heads."

11 Then the man clothed in linen, with the writing case at his side, brought back word, saying, "I have done as you commanded me."

God's Glory Leaves Jerusalem

10 Then I looked, and above the dome that was over the heads of the cherubim there appeared above them something like a sapphire,ᵃ in form resembling a throne. 2He said to the man clothed in linen, "Go within the wheelwork underneath the cherubim; fill your hands with burning coals from among the cherubim, and scatter them over the city." He went in as I looked on. 3Now the cherubim were

ᵃ Or *lapis lazuli*

---

linen garments (Ex 28.39; in Dan 10.5, however, an angel wears a linen garment). *Writing case,* implements of a scribe; Egyptian writing cases included, minimally, brushes and various inks. All seven men positioned themselves near the *bronze altar,* which belonged to the Solomonic temple, but which had been repositioned by Ahaz (2 Kings 16.14), i.e., they were in the northern area of the temple courtyard. **9.3** As alluded to in 8.6, *the glory of the God of Israel* begins to leave the temple. God was understood to be enthroned above the cherubim. At this point, the glory moves to the temple doorway; cf. 10.4. **9.3b–6** God's charge to the seven men. **9.3b–4** God commands the scribe to place a *mark on those who sigh and groan over all the abominations.* The Hebrew word translated *mark* is a vocalization of the last letter of the Hebrew alphabet, *taw,* which would have been written as an X. One might think that the individuals so designated were to be spared (cf. the protective marking of Passover, Ex 12.23), but the remainder of the vision does not explicitly report that any individuals were marked and spared (although cf. v. 11). **9.5–6** Then the six are authorized to *kill* everyone whom they encounter, regardless of gender or age. They begin at the temple (*at my sanctuary*), where they are now located, so that it could not offer sanctuary to those under attack and because abominations at the temple itself had just been identified. The first to be slain, the *elders,* are probably those men indicted in 8.11, 16. **9.7** *Defile the house,* corpse defilement (Num 19) in the temple complex (cf. 6.4–5). Since God is leaving the temple, it is possible for that structure to become impure. **9.8** Ezekiel attempts to intercede on behalf of Israel. Cf. 11.11; Isa 6.11; Am 7.1–6. **9.9–10** To Ezekiel's question, God responds in the negative, affirming again (see 8.18; 9.5) that the destruction will occur without pity. However, unlike earlier language in this vision, God speaks of more than just the city: *the house of Israel and Judah, the land.* The vast geographic scope of wrongdoing appears to justify radical punishment. The quotation of the people in v. 9 revises a similar statement in 8.12. There is a play on the motif of God seeing. The people think *the LORD does not see,* but God responds, *my eye will not spare.* **9.11** The scribe accomplished his work, just as the executioners performed their task (v. 7).

10.1–22 God's glory leaves the temple. **10.1** Ezekiel perceives the divine throne (cf. 1.26), but this time there is nothing seated above the throne. *Cherubim* have replaced the living creatures of ch. 1. (There are important and complex similarities and differences between the imagery in ch. 10 and that in ch. 1.) **10.2–8** *The man clothed in linen* receives a new task. **10.2** This verse continues the narrative of 9.11. *Go within the wheelwork* and 1.16 suggest that the wheels comprise a structure large enough to enter. The location of the wheelwork is unclear; presumably it is outside the temple (v. 3). The man is charged with gathering some *burning coals;* cf. 1.13, which refers to *something that looked like burning coals.* What was a simile now becomes literal. Since priests normally manipulated the coals of the altar fire, there is additional reason for thinking that this man was a priest. Such coals could function in different ways. According to Isa 6.6, coals purify the prophet. Here, however, they are to be scattered *over the city,* presumably to start a fire that would destroy the city. By implication, Jerusalem is as sinful as Sodom and Gomorrah (cf. Gen 19).

standing on the south side of the house when the man went in; and a cloud filled the inner court. 4 Then the glory of the LORD rose up from the cherub to the threshold of the house; the house was filled with the cloud, and the court was full of the brightness of the glory of the LORD. 5 The sound of the wings of the cherubim was heard as far as the outer court, like the voice of God Almighty*a* when he speaks.

6 When he commanded the man clothed in linen, "Take fire from within the wheelwork, from among the cherubim," he went in and stood beside a wheel. 7 And a cherub stretched out his hand from among the cherubim to the fire that was among the cherubim, took some of it and put it into the hands of the man clothed in linen, who took it and went out. 8 The cherubim appeared to have the form of a human hand under their wings.

9 I looked, and there were four wheels beside the cherubim, one beside each cherub; and the appearance of the wheels was like gleaming beryl. 10 And as for their appearance, the four looked alike, something like a wheel within a wheel. 11 When they moved, they moved in any of the four directions without veering as they moved; but in whatever direction the front wheel faced, the others followed without veering as they moved. 12 Their entire body, their rims, their spokes, their wings, and the wheels—the wheels of the four of them— were full of eyes all around. 13 As for the wheels, they were called in my hearing "the wheelwork." 14 Each one had four faces: the first face was that of the cherub, the second face was that of a human being, the third that of a lion, and the fourth that of an eagle.

15 The cherubim rose up. These were the living creatures that I saw by the river Chebar. 16 When the cherubim moved, the wheels moved beside them; and when the cherubim lifted up their wings to rise up from the earth, the wheels at their side did not veer. 17 When they stopped, the others stopped, and when they rose up, the others rose up with them; for the spirit of the living creatures was in them.

18 Then the glory of the LORD went out from the threshold of the house and stopped above the cherubim. 19 The cherubim lifted up their wings and rose up from the earth in my sight as they went out with the wheels beside them. They stopped at the entrance of the east gate of the house of the LORD; and the glory of the God of Israel was above them.

20 These were the living creatures that I saw underneath the God of Israel by the river Chebar; and I knew that they were cherubim. 21 Each had four faces, each four wings, and underneath their wings something like human hands. 22 As for what their faces were like, they were the same faces whose appearance I had seen by the river Chebar. Each one moved straight ahead.

Judgment on Wicked Counselors

11 The spirit lifted me up and brought me to the east gate of the house of the LORD, which faces east. There, at the entrance of the gateway, were twenty-five men; among them I saw Jaazaniah son of Azzur, and Pelatiah son of Benaiah, officials of the people. 2 He said to me, "Mortal, these are the men

a Traditional rendering of Heb *El Shaddai*

10.4–5 *The glory of the LORD* begins to move, as do certain of the cherubim. The biblical writer is careful to note that the glory moves from the *cherub*, since this sole cherub was affixed to the ark. Other cherubim were part of the divine retinue and depart from the temple. The *cloud* could represent God's presence (Ex 19.9; 1 Kings 8.10–11). 10.6–7 The man is given burning coals by one of the cherubim because, for some unknown reason, he does not himself approach the coals. 10.8–14 The author provides a detailed description of the cherubim vis-à-vis the wheelwork similar to that in 1.4–21. 10.15–17 As if to underline the similarity between chs. 1 and 10, the author mentions *the river Chebar* again (see 1.3). Mobility is the hallmark of the cherubim wheelwork. The structure rises up with cherubim wings beating and with wheels turning. 10.18–19 *The glory of the LORD* moves from the threshold of the house (cf. v. 4) and is located *above the*

cherubim, which are themselves moving. The glory is at its accustomed position, namely, enthroned above cherubim, but now they are movable. *East gate*, the main ceremonial entrance into the temple complex, known elsewhere as "the gate of the LORD" (Ps 118.20). 10.20–22 Ezekiel reaffirms the identity of the living creatures as cherubim. Three times in short compass (vv. 15, 20, 22) he states that he perceived them while *by the river Chebar*. This repetition verifies Ezekiel's ability to experience God while he is in exile. 11.1–13 Ezekiel performs as prophet during his visionary transport. 11.1–4 Just as the cherubim and the glory of the Lord paused at the *east gate* as they left the temple complex (10.19), now Ezekiel is taken to this site. *Twenty-five men*, possibly the group in 8.16. *Jaazaniah son of Azzur* and *Pelatiah son of Benaiah* do not appear elsewhere in Ezekiel. Unlike the other twenty-three, they were *officials of the people*, a phrase

who devise iniquity and who give wicked counsel in this city; ³they say, 'The time is not near to build houses; this city is the pot, and we are the meat.' ⁴Therefore prophesy against them; prophesy, O mortal."

5 Then the spirit of the LORD fell upon me, and he said to me, "Say, Thus says the LORD: This is what you think, O house of Israel; I know the things that come into your mind. ⁶You have killed many in this city, and have filled its streets with the slain. ⁷Therefore thus says the Lord GOD: The slain whom you have placed within it are the meat, and this city is the pot; but you shall be taken out of it. ⁸You have feared the sword; and I will bring the sword upon you, says the Lord GOD. ⁹I will take you out of it and give you over to the hands of foreigners, and execute judgments upon you. ¹⁰You shall fall by the sword; I will judge you at the border of Israel. And you shall know that I am the LORD. ¹¹This city shall not be your pot, and you shall not be the meat inside it; I will judge you at the border of Israel. ¹²Then you shall know that I am the LORD, whose statutes you have not followed, and whose ordinances you have not kept, but you have acted according to the ordinances of the nations that are around you."

13 Now, while I was prophesying, Pelatiah son of Benaiah died. Then I fell down on my face, cried with a loud voice, and said, "Ah Lord GOD! will you make a full end of the remnant of Israel?"

God Will Restore Israel

14 Then the word of the LORD came to me: ¹⁵Mortal, your kinsfolk, your own kin, your fellow exiles,ᵃ the whole house of Israel, all of them, are those of whom the inhabitants of Jerusalem have said, "They have gone far from the LORD; to us this land is given for a possession." ¹⁶Therefore say: Thus says the Lord GOD: Though I removed them far away among the nations, and though I scattered them among the countries, yet I have been a sanctuary to them for a little whileᵇ in the countries where they have gone. ¹⁷Therefore say: Thus says the Lord GOD: I will gather you from the peoples, and assemble you out of the countries where you have been scattered, and I will give you the land of Israel. ¹⁸When they come there, they will remove from it all its detestable things and all its abominations. ¹⁹I will give them oneᶜ heart, and put a new spirit within them; I will remove the heart of stone from their flesh and give them a heart of flesh, ²⁰so that they may follow my statutes and keep my ordinances and obey them. Then they shall be my people, and I will be their God. ²¹But as

---

ᵃ Gk Syr: Heb *people of your kindred* ᵇ Or *to some extent*
ᶜ Another reading is *a new*

---

that elsewhere occurs only in postexilic texts (Neh 11.1; 1 Chr 21.2; 2 Chr 24.23; Esth 3.12). Normally the phrase distinguishes lay from priestly leaders or public officials. **11.2** God proffers an indictment that focuses on ethical rather than religious malfeasance, as it did in ch. 8. *Counsel* was the provenance of "elders" (7.26), who could be characterized as officials. **11.3** *The time is not near to build houses,* perhaps because it is a time for investing in defense, or perhaps because those taken into exile in 597 BCE had left houses available for use by others (see v. 15); cf. Jer 32.15. *Pot, meat.* The image of the pot appears in greater detail in 24.1–14. The sense here is apparently one of the pot protecting the meat, i.e., the twenty-five men. In v. 7 God identifies the meat with those whom the men have killed, not the men themselves. **11.5–13** Ezekiel, empowered by the prophetic spirit, prophesies as God has commanded. **11.5–6** Ezekiel's indictment continues the motif begun in v. 2, devising or plotting evil. The effect of such plots has been slaughter in Jerusalem (cf. 19.3; 22.6), though whether in war or not is unclear. **11.7–10** A sentence of doom in which the image of the pot in v. 4 is recast. The men will be removed from the protection of the pot and subjected to attack by foreign swords. *At the border of Israel,* at Riblah, a city in Syria,

many Judahites were executed in 588/7 BCE (Jer 52.10, 24–27). **11.12** Destruction by foreigners is appropriate because Judahites have behaved according to the *ordinances of the nations,* the foreign religious practices described in ch. 8 (cf. 5.7). **11.13** Pelatiah dies before his execution, an event that enhances the power of Ezekiel's sentence (cf. Jer 28). Then Ezekiel again (cf. 9.8) attempts to intercede on behalf of the *remnant of Israel.* **11.14–21** The problem of land ownership. An answer to the question with which v. 13 concludes. **11.15** *Fellow exiles,* Hebrew, "people of your kin." A dispute is placed within the context of the relations between those in exile and those in Judah. The latter claim possession of the land vacated by those taken into exile and do so on theological grounds: *they have gone far from the LORD.* **11.16** The first of two divine oracles introduced by *Thus says the Lord GOD.* In support of those who have been dispossessed by exile, to them God has been *a sanctuary . . . for a little while,* or "a minor sanctuary." This provision would counter the claim of those in the land that the exiles had *gone far from the LORD* (v. 15). **11.17–19** The second divine oracle includes a sequence of promises: return to *the land of Israel,* removal of *abominations,* and a different *heart* and *spirit.* **11.19** *One heart,* or "new heart" (see

for those whose heart goes after their detestable things and their abominations,[a] I will bring their deeds upon their own heads, says the Lord GOD.

22 Then the cherubim lifted up their wings, with the wheels beside them; and the glory of the God of Israel was above them. 23And the glory of the LORD ascended from the middle of the city, and stopped on the mountain east of the city. 24The spirit lifted me up and brought me in a vision by the spirit of God into Chaldea, to the exiles. Then the vision that I had seen left me. 25And I told the exiles all the things that the LORD had shown me.

Judah's Captivity Portrayed

12 The word of the LORD came to me: 2Mortal, you are living in the midst of a rebellious house, who have eyes to see but do not see, who have ears to hear but do not hear; 3for they are a rebellious house. Therefore, mortal, prepare for yourself an exile's baggage, and go into exile by day in their sight; you shall go like an exile from your place to another place in their sight. Perhaps they will understand, though they are a rebellious house. 4You shall bring out your baggage by day in their sight, as baggage for exile; and you shall go out yourself at evening in their sight, as those do who go into exile. 5Dig through the wall in their sight, and carry the baggage through it. 6In their sight you shall lift the baggage on your shoulder, and carry it out in the dark; you shall cover your face, so that you may not see the land; for I have made you a sign for the house of Israel.

7 I did just as I was commanded. I brought out my baggage by day, as baggage for exile, and in the evening I dug through the wall with my own hands; I brought it out in the dark, carrying it on my shoulder in their sight.

8 In the morning the word of the LORD came to me: 9Mortal, has not the house of Israel, the rebellious house, said to you, "What are you doing?" 10Say to them, "Thus says the Lord GOD: This oracle concerns the prince in Jerusalem and all the house of Israel in it." 11Say, "I am a sign for you: as I have done, so shall it be done to them; they shall go into exile, into captivity." 12And the prince who is among them shall lift his baggage on his shoulder in the dark, and shall go out; he[b] shall dig through the wall and carry it through; he shall cover his face, so that he may not see the land with his eyes. 13I will spread my net over him, and he shall be caught in my snare; and I will bring him to Babylon, the land of the Chaldeans, yet he shall not see it; and he shall die there. 14I will scatter to every wind all who are around him, his helpers and all his troops; and I will unsheathe the sword behind them. 15And they shall know that I am the LORD, when I disperse them among the

---

a Cn: Heb And to the heart of their detestable things and their abominations their heart goes   b Gk Syr: Heb they

---

text note c on p. 1110); cf. Jer 32.39; Ezek 18.31; 36.26. **11.20** Cf. Jer 31.33–34; Ezek 16.59–63. **11.22–25** Ezekiel's vision concludes with a return to the primary images: cherubim, wheels, and the glory. *The glory of the LORD* leaves the city and is located on a massif to the east, namely, the Mount of Olives. In visionary transport Ezekiel returns to Babylonia and reports to those in exile what he has seen.

12.1–16 Symbolic action and its interpretation concerning exile. **12.1–7** The symbolic act commanded and performed. **12.1–2** The condition of Judah as *a rebellious house* is characterized as having eyes to see but not seeing. Hence something visible, vv. 3–4, becomes an appropriate mode of prophetic communication. **12.3–6** God commands Ezekiel to perform a series of acts that symbolize someone going into exile. **12.3** *An exile's baggage,* apparently all of one's portable belongings. *In their sight,* which occurs repeatedly in vv. 3–7, emphasizes the visual character of Ezekiel's prophetic task. At first Ezekiel is commanded to act out the exile role in daylight so that *they will understand,* lit. "they will see." **12.4–5** Then the prophet is to act as an exile at night, which approxi-

mates the actual behavior of those escaping from a city. Digging *through the wall* suggests that the wall as a defensive fortification has already been partially destroyed. **12.6** *Cover your face.* See v. 12. *I have made you a sign.* See also v. 11; 24.24; Isa 8.18. The prophet's action, not just words, can become part of God's communication. **12.7** Ezekiel's self-report that the symbolic action has been carried out. **12.8–16** An interpretation of the symbolic action. **12.8** *In the morning* suggests that the act concluded during the previous evening. **12.10–16** The oracle answers the people's question to Ezekiel, *What are you doing?* (v. 9). **12.10** *The prince in Jerusalem,* probably Zedekiah, whose fate is described in Jer 39.1–7; 52.6–11; 2 Kings 25.3–7. He fled at night "through the gate between the two walls" (Jer 39.4), was captured by Babylonian forces, taken into Riblah, and blinded before being taken into exile. A symbolic act that initially addresses the *house of Israel* (v. 6) focuses now on the fate of the prince as well as the people (v. 11). **12.12–14** The plight of the prince foreshadows the flight and exile of Zedekiah. V. 14, however, continues the theme of other people driven into exile. *Sword* (vv. 14, 16) recalls ch. 5.

nations and scatter them through the countries. [16]But I will let a few of them escape from the sword, from famine and pestilence, so that they may tell of all their abominations among the nations where they go; then they shall know that I am the Lord.

Judgment Not Postponed

17 The word of the Lord came to me: [18]Mortal, eat your bread with quaking, and drink your water with trembling and with fearfulness; [19]and say to the people of the land, Thus says the Lord God concerning the inhabitants of Jerusalem in the land of Israel: They shall eat their bread with fearfulness, and drink their water in dismay, because their land shall be stripped of all it contains, on account of the violence of all those who live in it. [20]The inhabited cities shall be laid waste, and the land shall become a desolation; and you shall know that I am the Lord.

21 The word of the Lord came to me: [22]Mortal, what is this proverb of yours about the land of Israel, which says, "The days are prolonged, and every vision comes to nothing"? [23]Tell them therefore, "Thus says the Lord God: I will put an end to this proverb, and they shall use it no more as a proverb in Israel." But say to them, The days are near, and the fulfillment of every vision. [24]For there shall no longer be any false vision or flattering divination within the house of Israel. [25]But I the Lord will speak the word that I speak, and it will be fulfilled. It will no longer be delayed; but in your days, O rebellious house, I will speak the word and fulfill it, says the Lord God.

26 The word of the Lord came to me: [27]Mortal, the house of Israel is saying, "The vision that he sees is for many years ahead; he prophesies for distant times." [28]Therefore say to them, Thus says the Lord God: None of my words will be delayed any longer, but the word that I speak will be fulfilled, says the Lord God.

False Prophets Condemned

13 The word of the Lord came to me: [2]Mortal, prophesy against the prophets of Israel who are prophesying; say to those who prophesy out of their own imagination: "Hear the word of the Lord!" [3]Thus says the Lord God, Alas for the senseless prophets who follow their own spirit, and have seen nothing! [4]Your prophets have been like jackals among ruins, O Israel. [5]You have not gone up into the breaches, or repaired a wall for the house of Israel, so that it might stand in battle on the day of the Lord. [6]They have envisioned falsehood and lying divination; they say, "Says the Lord," when the Lord has not sent them, and yet they wait for the fulfillment of their word! [7]Have you not seen a false vision or uttered a lying divination, when you have said, "Says the Lord," even though I did not speak?

8 Therefore thus says the Lord God: Because you have uttered falsehood and envisioned lies, I am against you, says the Lord God. [9]My hand will be against the prophets who see false visions and utter lying divinations; they shall not

---

12.15–16 A remnant in exile will attest to abominations performed in the land. 12.17–20 God commands Ezekiel to consume *bread* and *water* so as to act out the way in which Jerusalemites will eat and drink after the destruction throughout the land begins. 12.21–28 The people's perceptions of prophetic visions. Two sayings of the people (in vv. 22, 27) require a divine response. 12.22 *Proverb*, a brief saying that expresses popular consensus. *The days are prolonged*, time passes. The point of the saying is that, even though time passes, visions that prefigure the future do not come to pass. 12.23 God provides a contrary saying: the time approaches when prophetic visions will be verified. 12.24–25 God will enact quickly the *word*, so that no ineffectual visions can hold sway. 12.27 In the second saying, people argue that Ezekiel's visions do not affect their own times.

13.1–23 Judgment on false prophets. 13.1–7 Indictment of prophets, whom Ezekiel characterizes as those who prophesy *out of their own imagination* (v. 2) and as those *who follow their own spirit* (v. 3), in contrast to Ezekiel who speaks *the word of the Lord* (v. 2). For similar language about conflict between prophets, see Jer 23.9–32; 1 Kings 22. 13.4 *Like jackals among ruins*, a simile that probably refers to wild animals rooting in a destroyed city (see Lam 5.18). 13.5 *You*, plural in the Hebrew, which means that the prophets are being condemned. 13.6–7 These prophets perceive *falsehood* (which Jeremiah also uses to describe other prophets; Jer 14.14; 23.21), *lying divination*, and *false vision* despite the fact that they use standard prophetic language: *says the Lord*. *Divination*, a human means of securing information from the deity often involving physically observable data, e.g., examining the organs of a sacrificed animal for signs (as in 21.21) or in standard Israelite practice the Urim and Thummim (Ex 28.30). 13.8–16 Punishment of false prophets. 13.9 *Council of my people*. Cf. Gen 49.6. *Council* does not necessarily mean a political assembly. *The register*. Cf. Ezra 2.62. To be excluded from such a written doc-

be in the council of my people, nor be enrolled in the register of the house of Israel, nor shall they enter the land of Israel; and you shall know that I am the Lord God. [10]Because, in truth, because they have misled my people, saying, "Peace," when there is no peace; and because, when the people build a wall, these prophets[a] smear whitewash on it. [11]Say to those who smear whitewash on it that it shall fall. There will be a deluge of rain,[b] great hailstones will fall, and a stormy wind will break out. [12]When the wall falls, will it not be said to you, "Where is the whitewash you smeared on it?" [13]Therefore thus says the Lord God: In my wrath I will make a stormy wind break out, and in my anger there shall be a deluge of rain, and hailstones in wrath to destroy it. [14]I will break down the wall that you have smeared with whitewash, and bring it to the ground, so that its foundation will be laid bare; when it falls, you shall perish within it; and you shall know that I am the Lord. [15]Thus I will spend my wrath upon the wall, and upon those who have smeared it with whitewash; and I will say to you, The wall is no more, nor those who smeared it— [16]the prophets of Israel who prophesied concerning Jerusalem and saw visions of peace for it, when there was no peace, says the Lord God.

17 As for you, mortal, set your face against the daughters of your people, who prophesy out of their own imagination; prophesy against them [18]and say, Thus says the Lord God: Woe to the women who sew bands on all wrists, and make veils for the heads of persons of every height, in the hunt for human lives! Will you hunt down lives among my people, and maintain your own lives? [19]You have profaned me among my people for handfuls of barley and for pieces of bread, putting to death persons who should not die and keeping alive persons who should not live, by your lies to my people, who listen to lies.

20 Therefore thus says the Lord God: I am against your bands with which you hunt lives;[c] I will tear them from your arms, and let the lives go free, the lives that you hunt down like birds. [21]I will tear off your veils, and save my people from your hands; they shall no longer be prey in your hands; and you shall know that I am the Lord. [22]Because you have disheartened the righteous falsely, although I have not disheartened them, and you have encouraged the wicked not to turn from their wicked way and save their lives; [23]therefore you shall no longer see false visions or practice divination; I will save my people from your hand. Then you will know that I am the Lord.

God's Judgments Justified

14 Certain elders of Israel came to me and sat down before me. [2]And the word of the Lord came to me: [3]Mortal, these men have taken their idols into their hearts, and placed their iniquity as a stumbling block before them; shall I let myself be consulted by them? [4]Therefore speak to them, and say to

---

a Heb *they* b Heb *rain and you* c Gk Syr: Heb *lives for birds*

---

ument was tantamount to losing membership among the people of Israel. The register was especially important after the exile; hence its prominence in Ezra and Nehemiah. *Nor shall they enter the land* presumes that one form of punishment will be exile. **13.10** *Peace.* Cf. Jer 23; 27–29 for similar conflict over whether or not a message of peace was appropriate before 587 BCE. **13.10–16** The imagery involves a wall of friable construction, the strength of which might be minimally enhanced with a light coating of plaster (*whitewash*). The people build the wall; the prophets apply the *whitewash.* God intends to destroy the wall using a storm; since it is inherently weak, the wall will fall. Both the people and their prophets will be punished. **13.17–23** Judgment upon prophetesses. **13.17** *The daughters of your people.* Both in Israel (the prophetess Huldah, 2 Kings 22.14) and elsewhere (e.g., the ancient city-state of Mari) women functioned as prophets. **13.18** The *bands* and *veils* have more to do with magic than intermediation. Unfortunately, practices having to do with these textiles remain obscure. Hunting *lives* involves the very life and death of a person; see v. 19.

13.19 *For handfuls of barley and for pieces of bread,* probably payment for services rendered; see 1 Sam 9.7. **13.20–23** Punishment of the prophetesses. **13.20–21** *With which you hunt lives,* or "with which you hunt persons like birds." God punishes the prophetesses by removing the *bands* and *veils* and in so doing liberates those who had been trapped. **13.22** The indictment is further clarified: those trapped were the *righteous,* an action that *encouraged the wicked.* **13.23** *I will save my people,* strikingly positive, when compared to texts such as 9.9–10.

14.1–11 Prophet and people. Similar to formulations in the sacral laws of the Holiness Code (Lev 17–26), e.g., Lev 17.3–4, 8–9; 20.6. **14.1** The scene is similar to 8.1; Ezekiel is consulted by representatives of the exilic community. **14.3** God provides an assessment of the people before they are able to ask a question. *Taken their idols into their hearts,* unclear. Ezekiel used the term *idols* in diverse ways. Typically it refers to representations of non-Yahwistic religious entities. If such objects were destroyed or left in the land, those in exile may not actually possess idols but may still be venerat-

them, Thus says the Lord GOD: Any of those of the house of Israel who take their idols into their hearts and place their iniquity as a stumbling block before them, and yet come to the prophet—I the LORD will answer those who come with the multitude of their idols, [5]in order that I may take hold of the hearts of the house of Israel, all of whom are estranged from me through their idols.

6 Therefore say to the house of Israel, Thus says the Lord GOD: Repent and turn away from your idols; and turn away your faces from all your abominations. [7]For any of those of the house of Israel, or of the aliens who reside in Israel, who separate themselves from me, taking their idols into their hearts and placing their iniquity as a stumbling block before them, and yet come to a prophet to inquire of me by him, I the LORD will answer them myself. [8]I will set my face against them; I will make them a sign and a byword and cut them off from the midst of my people; and you shall know that I am the LORD.

9 If a prophet is deceived and speaks a word, I, the LORD, have deceived that prophet, and I will stretch out my hand against him, and will destroy him from the midst of my people Israel. [10]And they shall bear their punishment—the punishment of the inquirer and the punishment of the prophet shall be the same— [11]so that the house of Israel may no longer go astray from me, nor defile themselves any more with all their transgressions. Then they shall be my people, and I will be their God, says the Lord GOD.

12 The word of the LORD came to me: [13]Mortal, when a land sins against me by acting faithlessly, and I stretch out my hand against it, and break its staff of bread and send famine upon it, and cut off from it human beings and animals, [14]even if Noah, Daniel, [a] and Job, these three, were in it, they would save only their own lives by their righteousness, says the Lord GOD. [15]If I send wild animals through the land to ravage it, so that it is made desolate, and no one may pass through because of the animals; [16]even if these three men were in it, as I live, says the Lord GOD, they would save neither sons nor daughters; they alone would be saved, but the land would be desolate. [17]Or if I bring a sword upon that land and say, "Let a sword pass through the land," and I cut off human beings and animals from it; [18]though these three men were in it, as I live, says the Lord GOD, they would save neither sons nor daughters, but they alone would be saved. [19]Or if I send a pestilence into that land, and pour out my wrath upon it with blood, to cut off humans and animals from it; [20]even if Noah, Daniel, [a] and Job were in it, as I live, says the Lord GOD, they would save neither son nor daughter; they would save only their own lives by their righteousness.

21 For thus says the Lord GOD: How much more when I send upon Jerusalem my four deadly acts of judgment, sword, famine, wild animals, and pestilence, to cut off humans and animals from it! [22]Yet, survivors shall be left in

---

a Or, as otherwise read, *Danel*

---

ing what the idols represented. On the prophet as consultant, see 20.3. **14.6** Instead of a sentence, the prophet offers an admonition, *repent and turn away.* **14.7** *Aliens who reside in Israel* appears unusual when referring to the exilic context. Cf. Isa 56.3, "the foreigner joined to the LORD." Originally, an alien was a non-Israelite who lived in Israelite territory and who had defined rights (e.g., Deut 1.16; 14.29). Ezek 47.22–23 allows for land inheritance by aliens. **14.7–8** Those who do not repent will be accursed. The actual punishment would constitute a *sign,* whereas those who observed the situation would summarize and express it using a saying (a *byword*). *Cut them off . . . people,* a sentiment similar to that in 13.9. **14.9–11** If a prophet provides a word to idolaters, contrary to v. 3, that prophet will be destroyed. **14.9** God claims responsibility for the deceit of such a prophet; cf. 1 Kings 13 for an instance in which a prophet is misled through divine instrumentality. **14.12–23** Sin, destruction, and survival. **14.12–20** A formulaic discourse (signaled by

the repetition of *if, even if, they would save neither sons nor daughters,* and *they would save only their own lives*) concerning the severity of God's punishment, which is a direct response to radical sin. These verses build on four different modes of punishment: *famine* (v. 13), *wild animals* (v. 15), *sword* (v. 17), and *pestilence* (v. 19). Ezekiel identifies three individuals and reports that, although they would escape destruction, they would not be able to save others. *Noah, Daniel,* and *Job,* figures known widely in the ancient Near East as especially righteous. Their righteousness worked itself out on behalf of others, namely, their children. Noah enabled his family to survive the deluge; Job's children exist at the end of the book. Danel, the righteous king described in the Ugaritic Aqhat epic, who is related to the biblical Daniel, is apparently able to engender life for his son. **14.21–23** The four modes of punishment are repeated (cf. 5.16) and focused on Jerusalem. There will, however, be survivors, *sons and daughters,* an implicit literary link with the three heroes men-

it, sons and daughters who will be brought out; they will come out to you. When you see their ways and their deeds, you will be consoled for the evil that I have brought upon Jerusalem, for all that I have brought upon it. 23 They shall console you, when you see their ways and their deeds; and you shall know that it was not without cause that I did all that I have done in it, says the Lord GOD.

The Useless Vine

15 The word of the LORD came to me: 2 O mortal, how does the wood of the vine surpass all other wood—
the vine branch that is among the trees of the forest?
3   Is wood taken from it to make anything?
Does one take a peg from it on which to hang any object?
4   It is put in the fire for fuel;
when the fire has consumed both ends of it
and the middle of it is charred,
is it useful for anything?
5   When it was whole it was used for nothing;
how much less—when the fire has consumed it,
and it is charred—
can it ever be used for anything!

6 Therefore thus says the Lord GOD: Like the wood of the vine among the trees of the forest, which I have given to the fire for fuel, so I will give up the inhabitants of Jerusalem. 7 I

will set my face against them; although they escape from the fire, the fire shall still consume them; and you shall know that I am the LORD, when I set my face against them. 8 And I will make the land desolate, because they have acted faithlessly, says the Lord GOD.

God's Faithless Bride

16 The word of the LORD came to me: 2 Mortal, make known to Jerusalem her abominations, 3 and say, Thus says the Lord GOD to Jerusalem: Your origin and your birth were in the land of the Canaanites; your father was an Amorite, and your mother a Hittite. 4 As for your birth, on the day you were born your navel cord was not cut, nor were you washed with water to cleanse you, nor rubbed with salt, nor wrapped in cloths. 5 No eye pitied you, to do any of these things for you out of compassion for you; but you were thrown out in the open field, for you were abhorred on the day you were born.

6 I passed by you, and saw you flailing about in your blood. As you lay in your blood, I said to you, "Live! 7 and grow up[a] like a plant of the field." You grew up and became tall and arrived at full womanhood;[b] your breasts were formed, and your hair had grown; yet you were naked and bare.

8 I passed by you again and looked on you;

---

a Gk Syr: Heb *Live! I made you a myriad*   *b* Cn: Heb *ornament of ornaments*

---

tioned in vv. 14–20. **14.22–23** These survivors will provide consolation for the earlier generation. **15.1– 8** The useless vine. **15.1** *To me* signals a "private" oracle. **15.2** The first in a series of rhetorical questions. Despite the prominence of vine imagery in OT literature (e.g., Judg 9.8–15; Isa 5.1–5; Hos 10.1), questions about the quality of the wood from a vine are innovative. The initial question elicits an understood response—wood from a vine does not surpass any wood of the forest. **15.3** The second and third questions concerning the utility of vine wood that has been worked imply brief negative answers. **15.4** The poet adduces an obvious case, a fragment of partially burned vine. The ensuing question implies another negative answer. **15.5** An indicative judgment summarizing the cases presented in vv. 3–4. **15.6–8** The foregoing poem is viewed as a simile, the *wood of the vine* being likened to the *inhabitants of Jerusalem*. They are destined for destruction, whether by fire or not.

16.1–63 An extended discourse in which Jerusalem is understood as God's adulterous wife. **16.1–7** Jerusalem the orphan. **16.2** *Make known . . . her abominations* has legal connotations. **16.3** *Land of the Canaan-*

ites, ancient Syro-Palestine, which is roughly equivalent to Lebanon and Israel today. Jerusalem was under Jebusite (or Canaanite) control before David conquered it. *Amorite* culture is generally associated with Syria and the Transjordan; *Hittite* with ancient Anatolia (but some Hittites lived in Syro-Palestine, e.g., Uriah the Hittite, 2 Sam 11.3). In biblical traditions, Amorites and Hittites are generally the pre-Israelite population. These three ethnolinguistic categories— Canaanite, Amorite, and Hittite—define Jerusalem's origin as different from that of Israel, which traced its lineage through Abraham to Nahor (see Gen 11.22– 26). Jerusalem is a "foreigner." **16.4–5** Standard birth rituals were not performed, possibly because the parents intended to commit infanticide by exposure in a field. **16.6–7** God discovers the foundling and admonishes her to remain alive. *And grow up*, in Hebrew "I made you a myriad" or "I made you flourish." In this translation, God assists the child at the very first instance. **16.8–14** On the image of covering with a garment in order to symbolize an intent to marry, cf. Ruth 3.9. *I pledged myself to you . . . and you became mine* echoes standard covenant language (e.g., Ex 6.7).

you were at the age for love. I spread the edge of my cloak over you, and covered your nakedness: I pledged myself to you and entered into a covenant with you, says the Lord God, and you became mine. 9Then I bathed you with water and washed off the blood from you, and anointed you with oil. 10I clothed you with embroidered cloth and with sandals of fine leather; I bound you in fine linen and covered you with rich fabric.*a* 11I adorned you with ornaments: I put bracelets on your arms, a chain on your neck, 12a ring on your nose, earrings in your ears, and a beautiful crown upon your head. 13You were adorned with gold and silver, while your clothing was of fine linen, rich fabric,*a* and embroidered cloth. You had choice flour and honey and oil for food. You grew exceedingly beautiful, fit to be a queen. 14Your fame spread among the nations on account of your beauty, for it was perfect because of my splendor that I had bestowed on you, says the Lord God.

15 But you trusted in your beauty, and played the whore because of your fame, and lavished your whorings on any passer-by.*b* 16You took some of your garments, and made for yourself colorful shrines, and on them played the whore; nothing like this has ever been or ever shall be.*a* 17You also took your beautiful jewels of my gold and my silver that I had given you, and made for yourself male images, and with them played the whore; 18and you took your embroidered garments to cover them, and set my oil and my incense before them. 19Also my bread that I gave you—I fed you with choice flour and oil and honey—you set it before them as a pleasing odor; and so it was, says the Lord God. 20You took your sons and your daughters, whom you had borne to me, and these you sacrificed to them to be devoured. As if your whorings were not enough!

21You slaughtered my children and delivered them up as an offering to them. 22And in all your abominations and your whorings you did not remember the days of your youth, when you were naked and bare, flailing about in your blood.

23 After all your wickedness (woe, woe to you! says the Lord God), 24you built yourself a platform and made yourself a lofty place in every square; 25at the head of every street you built your lofty place and prostituted your beauty, offering yourself to every passer-by, and multiplying your whoring. 26You played the whore with the Egyptians, your lustful neighbors, multiplying your whoring, to provoke me to anger. 27Therefore I stretched out my hand against you, reduced your rations, and gave you up to the will of your enemies, the daughters of the Philistines, who were ashamed of your lewd behavior. 28You played the whore with the Assyrians, because you were insatiable; you played the whore with them, and still you were not satisfied. 29You multiplied your whoring with Chaldea, the land of merchants; and even with this you were not satisfied.

30 How sick is your heart, says the Lord God, that you did all these things, the deeds of a brazen whore; 31building your platform at the head of every street, and making your lofty place in every square! Yet you were not like a whore, because you scorned payment. 32Adulterous wife, who receives strangers instead of her husband! 33Gifts are given to all whores; but you gave your gifts to all your lovers, bribing them to come to you from all around for your whorings. 34So you were different from other women in your whorings: no one solicited you to play the whore; and you gave

---

a Meaning of Heb uncertain   *b* Heb adds *let it be his*

God performs various ministrations on behalf of his new wife. They involve cleansing, clothing and jewelry, and special food. **16.15–34** Jerusalem, understood now as an adulterous wife, commits various sinful acts. Hos 2 and Jer 2–3 also liken Israel to an unfaithful wife. **16.16** Using textiles, the wife makes *colorful shrines*, whether for veneration of other deities or for illicit sexual practice (or both, as in sacral prostitution) is unclear. **16.17–19** Using precious metals and garments the woman makes and clothes *male images* and sets food before them. **16.20–21** Children born to the woman are sacrificed; cf. Jer 19.4–6; 32.35, which attribute child sacrifice to vener-

ation of Baal. **16.23–26** The wife is indicted for having built a structure (*platform*), whether ritual or not is uncertain, where she engaged in prostitution (cf. ch. 23). *Egyptians*, allusion to a treaty made with Egypt. **16.27–29** God's sentence includes punishment by *the daughters of the Philistines*, but mention of *whoring* with Assyria and Babylon (*Chaldea*) continues the tone of indictment. The order of foreign nations parallels a sketch of Israelite history: slavery in Egypt, conflict with Philistia, and confrontation with the Neo-Assyrian and Neo-Babylonian empires. **16.30–34** Jerusalem gave presents to rather than received income from those with whom she had intercourse.

payment, while no payment was given to you; you were different.

35 Therefore, O whore, hear the word of the Lord: [36]Thus says the Lord God, Because your lust was poured out and your nakedness uncovered in your whoring with your lovers, and because of all your abominable idols, and because of the blood of your children that you gave to them, [37]therefore, I will gather all your lovers, with whom you took pleasure, all those you loved and all those you hated; I will gather them against you from all around, and will uncover your nakedness to them, so that they may see all your nakedness. [38]I will judge you as women who commit adultery and shed blood are judged, and bring blood upon you in wrath and jealousy. [39]I will deliver you into their hands, and they shall throw down your platform and break down your lofty places; they shall strip you of your clothes and take your beautiful objects and leave you naked and bare. [40]They shall bring up a mob against you, and they shall stone you and cut you to pieces with their swords. [41]They shall burn your houses and execute judgments on you in the sight of many women; I will stop you from playing the whore, and you shall also make no more payments. [42]So I will satisfy my fury on you, and my jealousy shall turn away from you; I will be calm, and will be angry no longer. [43]Because you have not remembered the days of your youth, but have enraged me with all these things; therefore, I have returned your deeds upon your head, says the Lord God.

Have you not committed lewdness beyond all your abominations? [44]See, everyone who uses proverbs will use this proverb about you, "Like mother, like daughter." [45]You are the daughter of your mother, who loathed her husband and her children; and you are the sister of your sisters, who loathed their husbands and their children. Your mother was a Hittite and your father an Amorite. [46]Your elder sister is Samaria, who lived with her daughters to the north of you; and your younger sister, who lived to the south of you, is Sodom with her daughters. [47]You not only followed their ways, and acted according to their abominations; within a very little time you were more corrupt than they in all your ways. [48]As I live, says the Lord God, your sister Sodom and her daughters have not done as you and your daughters have done. [49]This was the guilt of your sister Sodom: she and her daughters had pride, excess of food, and prosperous ease, but did not aid the poor and needy. [50]They were haughty, and did abominable things before me; therefore I removed them when I saw it. [51]Samaria has not committed half your sins; you have committed more abominations than they, and have made your sisters appear righteous by all the abominations that you have committed. [52]Bear your disgrace, you also, for you have brought about for your sisters a more favorable judgment; because of your sins in which you acted more abominably than they, they are more in the right than you. So be ashamed, you also, and bear your disgrace, for you have made your sisters appear righteous.

53 I will restore their fortunes, the fortunes of Sodom and her daughters and the fortunes of Samaria and her daughters, and I will restore your own fortunes along with theirs, [54]in order that you may bear your disgrace and be ashamed of all that you have done, becoming a consolation to them. [55]As for your sisters, Sodom and her daughters shall return to their former state, Samaria and her daughters shall return to their former state, and you and your daughters shall return to your former state. [56]Was not your sister Sodom a byword in your mouth in the day of your pride, [57]before your wickedness was uncovered? Now you are a mockery to the daughters of Aram[a] and all her neighbors, and to the daughters of the Philistines, those all around who despise you. [58]You must bear the penalty of your lewdness and your abominations, says the Lord.

---

a Another reading is *Edom*

16.35–43 God will punish Jerusalem by using the foreign nations with whom she has committed adultery. **16.40** See Deut 22.22–24 for laws concerning adultery, which involve death by stoning. **16.41** *Burn your houses.* On destruction by fire, see 23.47. **16.44–52** Though *mother-daughter* imagery continues, siblings now appear: Samaria the elder and Sodom the younger. Sodom's sins centered on injustice (v. 49); Samaria's sins remain unnamed. Both cities had already been destroyed, Sodom in the distant past (Gen 19), Samaria in 721 BCE. Jerusalem has, however, *committed more abominations* (v. 51) than either sister. **16.53–58** Restoration for Sodom, Samaria, and Jerusalem. (Cf. Jer 12.14–17 on the concept of restoration of many Syro-Palestinian cities and states.) The goal of the restoration is, however, their suffering *disgrace* and being *ashamed* (v. 54). **16.57** *Aram*, in Hebrew; a variant manuscript tradition reads "Edom"; cf.

An Everlasting Covenant

59 Yes, thus says the Lord GOD: I will deal with you as you have done, you who have despised the oath, breaking the covenant; 60 yet I will remember my covenant with you in the days of your youth, and I will establish with you an everlasting covenant. 61 Then you will remember your ways, and be ashamed when I[a] take your sisters, both your elder and your younger, and give them to you as daughters, but not on account of my[b] covenant with you. 62 I will establish my covenant with you, and you shall know that I am the LORD, 63 in order that you may remember and be confounded, and never open your mouth again because of your shame, when I forgive you all that you have done, says the Lord GOD.

The Two Eagles and the Vine

17 The word of the LORD came to me: 2 O mortal, propound a riddle, and speak an allegory to the house of Israel. 3 Say: Thus says the Lord GOD:

A great eagle, with great wings and long
    pinions,
    rich in plumage of many colors,
    came to the Lebanon.
He took the top of the cedar,
4   broke off its topmost shoot;
he carried it to a land of trade,
    set it in a city of merchants.
5   Then he took a seed from the land,
    placed it in fertile soil;
a plant[c] by abundant waters,
    he set it like a willow twig.
6   It sprouted and became a vine

spreading out, but low;
    its branches turned toward him,
    its roots remained where it stood.
So it became a vine;
    it brought forth branches,
    put forth foliage.

7   There was another great eagle,
    with great wings and much plumage.
And see! This vine stretched out
    its roots toward him;
it shot out its branches toward him,
    so that he might water it.
From the bed where it was planted
8   it was transplanted
to good soil by abundant waters,
    so that it might produce branches
    and bear fruit
    and become a noble vine.

9 Say: Thus says the Lord GOD:
    Will it prosper?
Will he not pull up its roots,
    cause its fruit to rot[c] and wither,
    its fresh sprouting leaves to fade?
No strong arm or mighty army will be
    needed
    to pull it from its roots.
10   When it is transplanted, will it thrive?
When the east wind strikes it,
    will it not utterly wither,
    wither on the bed where it grew?

11 Then the word of the LORD came to me: 12 Say now to the rebellious house: Do you not know what these things mean? Tell them: The king of Babylon came to Jerusalem, took its

---

a Syr: Heb you b Heb lacks my c Meaning of Heb uncertain

25.12. **16.59–63** An everlasting covenant. **16.59** *Oath, covenant,* complementary terms; in taking an oath one makes a covenant (cf. Deut 29.12). Deuteronomic vocabulary and rhetoric make it clear that the prophet alludes to the Sinai covenant. **16.60** References to an earlier covenant and *an everlasting covenant* suggest that the latter refers to a new covenant. Cf. 37.26; Jer 31.31–34. **16.61** God will introduce new kinship relationships. Samaria and Sodom, which had earlier been "sisters," will now become daughters of Jerusalem. **16.62** God will, ultimately, absolve Jerusalem of her sin.

17.1–24 The two eagles, the vine, and the cedar. **17.2** *Riddle* and *allegory* normally refer to different kinds of sayings. On riddle in the OT, cf. Judg 14.12–19. *Allegory,* translated *proverb* in 12.23; 16.44, 18.2. Hence, though there may be allegorical elements in ch. 17, the Hebrew word itself does not define these verses as an allegory. **17.3–10** Most of the important symbols

allude to kings and international politics from 598 to 588 BCE. **17.3–6** The *cedar,* traditionally associated with Lebanon, is a majestic tree; cf. ch. 31; Ps 92.12. *A great eagle,* Nebuchadnezzar, who took *a city of merchants* into exile. *Topmost shoot,* Jehoiachin. *Seed, vine,* Zedekiah, who was placed on the throne by and was initially loyal to Nebuchadnezzar. **17.7–8** *Another great eagle,* the pharaoh Psammetichus II, to whom Zedekiah expressed allegiance, abandoning his oath of loyalty to the Neo-Babylonians. This transfer of loyalty is expressed by the imagery of transplanting. **17.9–10** Various symbols (*pull up its roots, the east wind*) refer to Nebuchadnezzar's attack and siege (January 588–August 587 BCE) of Zedekiah in Jerusalem. Rhetorical questions underline the impossibility of survival. **17.11–15** In prose the prophet recounts the individuals and events to which earlier poetry alludes. As with the poem, the prose version concludes with a

king and its officials, and brought them back with him to Babylon. 13He took one of the royal offspring and made a covenant with him, putting him under oath (he had taken away the chief men of the land), 14so that the kingdom might be humble and not lift itself up, and that by keeping his covenant it might stand. 15But he rebelled against him by sending ambassadors to Egypt, in order that they might give him horses and a large army. Will he succeed? Can one escape who does such things? Can he break the covenant and yet escape? 16As I live, says the Lord GOD, surely in the place where the king resides who made him king, whose oath he despised, and whose covenant with him he broke—in Babylon he shall die. 17Pharaoh with his mighty army and great company will not help him in war, when ramps are cast up and siege walls built to cut off many lives. 18Because he despised the oath and broke the covenant, because he gave his hand and yet did all these things, he shall not escape. 19Therefore thus says the Lord GOD: As I live, I will surely return upon his head my oath that he despised, and my covenant that he broke. 20I will spread my net over him, and he shall be caught in my snare; I will bring him to Babylon and enter into judgment with him there for the treason he has committed against me. 21All the pick*a* of his troops shall fall by the sword, and the survivors shall be scattered to every wind; and you shall know that I, the LORD, have spoken.

Israel Exalted at Last

22 Thus says the Lord GOD:
  I myself will take a sprig
    from the lofty top of a cedar;
  I will set it out.
  I will break off a tender one
    from the topmost of its young twigs;
  I myself will plant it
    on a high and lofty mountain.
23 On the mountain height of Israel
  I will plant it,
    in order that it may produce boughs and
      bear fruit,
    and become a noble cedar.
  Under it every kind of bird will live;
    in the shade of its branches will nest
      winged creatures of every kind.
24 All the trees of the field shall know
    that I am the LORD.
  I bring low the high tree,
    I make high the low tree;
  I dry up the green tree
    and make the dry tree flourish.
  I the LORD have spoken;
    I will accomplish it.

Individual Retribution

18 The word of the LORD came to me: 2What do you mean by repeating this proverb concerning the land of Israel, "The parents have eaten sour grapes, and the children's teeth are set on edge"? 3As I live, says the Lord GOD, this proverb shall no more be used by you in Israel. 4Know that all lives are mine; the life of the parent as well as the life of the child is mine: it is only the person who sins that shall die.

5 If a man is righteous and does what is lawful and right— 6if he does not eat upon the mountains or lift up his eyes to the idols of the

---

a Another reading is *fugitives*

---

series of questions. **17.16–21** Two divine oaths. The first (vv. 16–18) foresees Zedekiah's death in Babylonian exile due to inadequate Egyptian military assistance. Zedekiah is condemned for having violated his treaty obligation to Nebuchadnezzar. The second (vv. 19–21) focuses on the military defeat, capture, and exile of Zedekiah as acts of God. **17.21** *The pick,* or "fugitives" as attested in some Greek manuscript traditions. **17.22** God, instead of *a great eagle* (v. 3), will plant a cedar shoot in Israel. **17.23** *The mountain height,* possibly Zion (Ps 48.1–2), which would be consistent with a replanting or restoration of the Davidic house (cf. Isa 11.1; Jer 23.5–6; 33.15). *Every kind of bird* (cf. Gen 7.14), along with the reference to a high mountain and a singular tree, provides cosmic scale for the deity's action. **17.24** Typical for Ezekiel, God's action redounds to his glory and demonstrates the

deity's ability to enact a word. *Bring low . . . make high,* a rhetorical figure that defines God's power; cf. 1 Sam 2.7; Pss 75.7; 147.6.

18.1–32 Justice for the individual. **18.1–4** A popular saying prompts reflection and rejection by both Ezekiel and Jeremiah (Jer 31.29–30). Quoting such terse Israelite sayings is typical of Ezekiel, e.g., 12.21; 16.44. The saying grows logically out of provisions for the unlimited liability of covenant punishment, which regularly extended well beyond the individual violating a stipulation, e.g., "to the third and fourth generation" (Ex 20.5). By contrast, Ezekiel provides a postulate that focuses on God's concern for *all lives.* Individuals will live or die according to their own deeds. **18.5–9** The first generation, in which an individual is righteous and lives. **18.6–9** A catalogue of virtues—many are described in negative fashion—

house of Israel, does not defile his neighbor's wife or approach a woman during her menstrual period, 7does not oppress anyone, but restores to the debtor his pledge, commits no robbery, gives his bread to the hungry and covers the naked with a garment, 8does not take advance or accrued interest, withholds his hand from iniquity, executes true justice between contending parties, 9follows my statutes, and is careful to observe my ordinances, acting faithfully—such a one is righteous; he shall surely live, says the Lord GOD.

10 If he has a son who is violent, a shedder of blood, 11who does any of these things (though his father*a* does none of them), who eats upon the mountains, defiles his neighbor's wife, 12oppresses the poor and needy, commits robbery, does not restore the pledge, lifts up his eyes to the idols, commits abomination, 13takes advance or accrued interest; shall he then live? He shall not. He has done all these abominable things; he shall surely die; his blood shall be upon himself.

14 But if this man has a son who sees all the sins that his father has done, considers, and does not do likewise, 15who does not eat upon the mountains or lift up his eyes to the idols of the house of Israel, does not defile his neighbor's wife, 16does not wrong anyone, exacts no pledge, commits no robbery, but gives his bread to the hungry and covers the naked with a garment, 17withholds his hand from iniquity,*b* takes no advance or accrued interest, observes my ordinances, and follows my statutes; he shall not die for his father's iniquity; he

shall surely live. 18As for his father, because he practiced extortion, robbed his brother, and did what is not good among his people, he dies for his iniquity.

19 Yet you say, "Why should not the son suffer for the iniquity of the father?" When the son has done what is lawful and right, and has been careful to observe all my statutes, he shall surely live. 20The person who sins shall die. A child shall not suffer for the iniquity of a parent, nor a parent suffer for the iniquity of a child; the righteousness of the righteous shall be his own, and the wickedness of the wicked shall be his own.

21 But if the wicked turn away from all their sins that they have committed and keep all my statutes and do what is lawful and right, they shall surely live; they shall not die. 22None of the transgressions that they have committed shall be remembered against them; for the righteousness that they have done they shall live. 23Have I any pleasure in the death of the wicked, says the Lord GOD, and not rather that they should turn from their ways and live? 24But when the righteous turn away from their righteousness and commit iniquity and do the same abominable things that the wicked do, shall they live? None of the righteous deeds that they have done shall be remembered; for the treachery of which they are guilty and the sin they have committed, they shall die.

25 Yet you say, "The way of the Lord is un-

---

a Heb *he*   *b* Gk: Heb *the poor*

consistent with the Decalogue. Both sacral and secular topics are included. **18.6** *Eat upon the mountains,* i.e., consume food from sacrifices to gods other than Yahweh; cf. 6.13; Hos 4.13. *Idols of the house of Israel.* Cf. 8.10; 18.6, 15. The phrase does not necessarily involve veneration of deities other than Yahweh. **18.7** *Does not oppress.* Cf. Lev 25.17. *Restores . . . pledge.* See Ex 22.26. **18.8** On debt *interest,* see Ex 22.25; Deut 23.20. *Executes true justice,* i.e., comports himself properly in the law court convened in the city gate (Lev 19.15). **18.9** *Such a one is righteous,* the sort of judgment that might normally have occurred at the temple. Ezekiel, however, lived in Babylonia, which made a judgment of this sort almost revolutionary; and it leads to life. **18.10–13** The second generation, in which an individual is sinful and dies. The righteousness of the father does not affect the fate of the son. The individual is characterized as *a shedder of blood* (v. 10), a phrase characteristic of Ezekiel (also in v. 13 as *blood . . . upon himself*) and influenced by priestly rhetoric (Lev 17.4).

18.11–12 The evildoer behaves conversely from the person in the first generation. **18.14–18** The third generation, in which an individual is righteous and lives. **18.14** This individual reviews the life of his father and acts in a different manner. The behavior of the sinful father does not prejudice the fate of his son. **18.15–17** A repetition of the case of the individual in the first generation, vv. 6–9. **18.18** Instead of concluding with the grandson, this case refers to that of the sinful son. **18.19–20** Ezekiel quotes yet another saying, which sounds more like a response to the foregoing analysis than an epigram; see 2 Kings 14.6; cf. Deut 24.16. Such insistence upon the separate fate of discrete generations reflects the concerns of those in exile. Were they to be punished for the sins of their fathers, who had already been subject to attack? **18.21–24** *If the wicked . . . their sins.* Now the case of the wicked is couched in the plural and has meaning for the life of one individual, for one may speak here of repentance that engenders life. **18.24** Conversely, one

fair." Hear now, O house of Israel: Is my way unfair? Is it not your ways that are unfair? ²⁶When the righteous turn away from their righteousness and commit iniquity, they shall die for it; for the iniquity that they have committed they shall die. ²⁷Again, when the wicked turn away from the wickedness they have committed and do what is lawful and right, they shall save their life. ²⁸Because they considered and turned away from all the transgressions that they had committed, they shall surely live; they shall not die. ²⁹Yet the house of Israel says, "The way of the Lord is unfair." O house of Israel, are my ways unfair? Is it not your ways that are unfair?

30 Therefore I will judge you, O house of Israel, all of you according to your ways, says the Lord GOD. Repent and turn from all your transgressions; otherwise iniquity will be your ruin.ᵃ ³¹Cast away from you all the transgressions that you have committed against me, and get yourselves a new heart and a new spirit! Why will you die, O house of Israel? ³²For I have no pleasure in the death of anyone, says the Lord GOD. Turn, then, and live.

Israel Degraded

19 As for you, raise up a lamentation for the princes of Israel, ²and say:
What a lioness was your mother
    among lions!
She lay down among young lions,
    rearing her cubs.
³ She raised up one of her cubs;

he became a young lion,
and he learned to catch prey;
    he devoured humans.
4 The nations sounded an alarm against
        him;
    he was caught in their pit;
and they brought him with hooks
    to the land of Egypt.
5 When she saw that she was thwarted,
    that her hope was lost,
she took another of her cubs
    and made him a young lion.
6 He prowled among the lions;
    he became a young lion,
and he learned to catch prey;
    he devoured people.
7 And he ravaged their strongholds,ᵇ
    and laid waste their towns;
the land was appalled, and all in it,
    at the sound of his roaring.
8 The nations set upon him
    from the provinces all around;
they spread their net over him;
    he was caught in their pit.
9 With hooks they put him in a cage,
    and brought him to the king of Babylon;
    they brought him into custody,
so that his voice should be heard no more
    on the mountains of Israel.
10 Your mother was like a vine in a
        vineyardᶜ

---

a Or *so that they shall not be a stumbling block of iniquity to you*
b Heb *his widows*   *c* Cn: Heb *in your blood*

---

who had led a righteous life but then *commits iniquity* will die. **18.25–29** *The way of the Lord is unfair* (repeated in v. 29; 33.17). It is not clear to which of the numerous foregoing cases this saying might refer. The prophet responds by citing the cases developed in vv. 21–24. If an individual is treated according to what she or he does, then, Ezekiel claims, God is fair. **18.30–32** *Repent . . .get a new heart and a new spirit*, i.e., get what enables a new form of life. What has been implicit becomes explicit in words associated with a new covenant.

19.1–14 Two laments, one using lion imagery and the other vine symbolism, describe the fate of the mother of the princes. **19.1** *Lamentation*, a dirge or funeral song. *The princes*. The Greek manuscript tradition reads "a prince." **19.2–9** The lion may serve as a metaphor for Judah, the territory ruled by the house of David (Gen 49.9–10). *Lioness*, according to some scholars a symbol for Hamutal, a queen mother and wife of Josiah. **19.3–4** *One of her cubs*, probably Jehoahaz, son of Josiah and Hamutal, who was captured by the pharaoh Neco and taken to Egypt, where he died

(2 Kings 23.31–34). **19.5–9** *Another of her cubs,* identity uncertain. Jehoiakim, also a son of Hamutal, was not taken into exile, whereas both Jehoiachin and Zedekiah were exiled to Babylon. Cf. Jer 22 for laments on Jehoahaz and Jehoiachin. The poem may be read as a general lament over the Davidic lineage without identifying either the lioness or the cubs as specific persons. The poem stresses certain features common to both cubs: *he was caught in their pit* (vv. 4, 8), *the nations* responded to both animals (vv. 4, 8), both *devoured humans* (vv. 3, 6), and both were taken with *hooks* (vv. 4, 9). Nonetheless, the fate of the second cub receives greater attention than that of the first. **19.7** *He ravaged their strongholds*, in Hebrew "he knew his widows," possibly with sexual connotations; cf. the Greek manuscript tradition, "he ravaged his widows." **19.8** *Set upon him from the provinces*. Cf. "set against him snares" (RSV). The *net* was used throughout the ancient Near East as a military implement. **19.10–14** A second lament, which uses vine imagery. Cf. chs. 15, 17. **19.10** *Your*, singular in Hebrew. *Like a vine*. In this lament, Ezekiel uses a simile instead of a

transplanted by the water,
fruitful and full of branches
from abundant water.

11 Its strongest stem became
a ruler's scepter;[a]
it towered aloft
among the thick boughs;
it stood out in its height
with its mass of branches.

12 But it was plucked up in fury,
cast down to the ground;
the east wind dried it up;
its fruit was stripped off,
its strong stem was withered;
the fire consumed it.

13 Now it is transplanted into the
wilderness,
into a dry and thirsty land.

14 And fire has gone out from its stem,
has consumed its branches and fruit,
so that there remains in it no strong stem,
no scepter for ruling.

This is a lamentation, and it is used as a
lamentation.

Israel's Continuing Rebellion

20 In the seventh year, in the fifth month,
on the tenth day of the month, certain
elders of Israel came to consult the LORD, and
sat down before me. 2And the word of the
LORD came to me: 3Mortal, speak to the elders
of Israel, and say to them: Thus says the Lord
GOD: Why are you coming? To consult me? As

I live, says the Lord GOD, I will not be consulted by you. 4Will you judge them, mortal,
will you judge them? Then let them know the
abominations of their ancestors, 5and say to
them: Thus says the Lord GOD: On the day
when I chose Israel, I swore to the offspring of
the house of Jacob—making myself known to
them in the land of Egypt—I swore to them,
saying, I am the LORD your God. 6On that day
I swore to them that I would bring them out of
the land of Egypt into a land that I had
searched out for them, a land flowing with
milk and honey, the most glorious of all lands.
7And I said to them, Cast away the detestable
things your eyes feast on, every one of you,
and do not defile yourselves with the idols of
Egypt; I am the LORD your God. 8But they rebelled against me and would not listen to me;
not one of them cast away the detestable
things their eyes feasted on, nor did they forsake the idols of Egypt.

Then I thought I would pour out my wrath
upon them and spend my anger against them
in the midst of the land of Egypt. 9But I acted
for the sake of my name, that it should not be
profaned in the sight of the nations among
whom they lived, in whose sight I made myself
known to them in bringing them out of the
land of Egypt. 10So I led them out of the land
of Egypt and brought them into the wilderness. 11I gave them my statutes and showed
them my ordinances, by whose observance

---

a Heb Its strongest stems became rulers' scepters

---

metaphor. Just as the lioness was grand, so too this
vine flourished in an ideal location. *In a vineyard,* conjectural; cf. the Hebrew, "in your blood." **19.11** *Its
strongest stem became a ruler's scepter,* in Hebrew, "its
strongest stems became rulers' scepters," which accords with the imagery of more than one king in vv. 2–
9. *Scepter,* a ceremonial staff used by the king (Isa
14.5); it could symbolize Judah and the Davidic house
(Ps 60.7). **19.12** The vine is destroyed by various
means: it is pulled out, dried up by an east wind (cf.
17.10), and consumed by fire. As a result, the stem
(and so too the scepter) is also destroyed. **19.13** *Transplanted,* surely an allusion to the Babylonian exile.
19.14 *And fire . . . for ruling.* The emphasis on the entire plant and not just the strongest stem focuses on
the demise of the entire Davidic house as a royal line
and not just the defeat of one or another king. *This is a
lamentation* underlines the ritual use to which dirges
were put as well as the individuals who chanted them;
cf. 32.16.
20.1–32 Israel's rebellious past. **20.1–4** Again Ezekiel meets with the elders (8.1; 14.1), who seek God's

word. **20.1** *Seventh year . . . month,* August 14, 591 BCE
(see note on 1.2), five years before the temple was destroyed. Ezekiel had been acting as a prophet for two
years and had been in exile since 597. Note the prominence of the first-person pronoun *me* in the mouth of
the deity, who is the preeminent actor. **20.2–4** Instead
of acting as an intermediary for the people, Ezekiel is
commanded by God to *judge them;* see also 22.2;
23.36. **20.5–31** Various periods when Israel rebelled
against God. For another version of Israel's history
with God, see Ps 106. **20.5** *Chose Israel,* virtually royal
language since God also "chose" David as king. **20.7–
8** In Egypt, Israel had been venerating *detestable things,
idols of Egypt.* Israel's rebellion involved continuing to
worship such objects. **20.9–26** The wilderness experiences. **20.9** *For the sake of my name.* Ezekiel emphasizes here (and elsewhere, vv. 14, 22; 36.22) that such
action is not undertaken because Israel deserves such
bounty. **20.10** The exodus and the time in the wilderness are concisely conjoined. Throughout this historical reprise, Ezekiel distills longer accounts. **20.11** The
Sinai event is linked immediately to these other

everyone shall live. ¹²Moreover I gave them my sabbaths, as a sign between me and them, so that they might know that I the LORD sanctify them. ¹³But the house of Israel rebelled against me in the wilderness; they did not observe my statutes but rejected my ordinances, by whose observance everyone shall live; and my sabbaths they greatly profaned.

Then I thought I would pour out my wrath upon them in the wilderness, to make an end of them. ¹⁴But I acted for the sake of my name, so that it should not be profaned in the sight of the nations, in whose sight I had brought them out. ¹⁵Moreover I swore to them in the wilderness that I would not bring them into the land that I had given them, a land flowing with milk and honey, the most glorious of all lands, ¹⁶because they rejected my ordinances and did not observe my statutes, and profaned my sabbaths; for their heart went after their idols. ¹⁷Nevertheless my eye spared them, and I did not destroy them or make an end of them in the wilderness.

18 I said to their children in the wilderness, Do not follow the statutes of your parents, nor observe their ordinances, nor defile yourselves with their idols. ¹⁹I the LORD am your God; follow my statutes, and be careful to observe my ordinances, ²⁰and hallow my sabbaths that they may be a sign between me and you, so that you may know that I the LORD am your God. ²¹But the children rebelled against me; they did not follow my statutes, and were not careful to observe my ordinances, by whose observance everyone shall live; they profaned my sabbaths.

Then I thought I would pour out my wrath upon them and spend my anger against them in the wilderness. ²²But I withheld my hand, and acted for the sake of my name, so that it should not be profaned in the sight of the nations, in whose sight I had brought them out. ²³Moreover I swore to them in the wilderness that I would scatter them among the nations and disperse them through the countries, ²⁴because they had not executed my ordinances, but had rejected my statutes and profaned my sabbaths, and their eyes were set on their ancestors' idols. ²⁵Moreover I gave them statutes that were not good and ordinances by which they could not live. ²⁶I defiled them through their very gifts, in their offering up all their firstborn, in order that I might horrify them, so that they might know that I am the LORD.

27 Therefore, mortal, speak to the house of Israel and say to them, Thus says the Lord GOD: In this again your ancestors blasphemed me, by dealing treacherously with me. ²⁸For when I had brought them into the land that I swore to give them, then wherever they saw any high hill or any leafy tree, there they offered their sacrifices and presented the provocation of their offering; there they sent up their pleasing odors, and there they poured out their drink offerings. ²⁹(I said to them, What is the high place to which you go? So it is called Bamah *a* to this day.) ³⁰Therefore say to the house of Israel, Thus says the Lord GOD: Will you defile yourselves after the manner of your ancestors and go astray after their de-

a That is *High Place*

epochal episodes. *Everyone shall live.* Cf. Lev 18.5. **20.12** *Sabbaths,* remarkably important in this chapter; see vv. 13, 16, 20, 21, 24. Observance of the sabbath is associated with the covenant at Sinai; see Ex 31.13 on the sabbath as a *sign.* For a contemporaneous prophetic perspective on the sabbath observances, see Jer 17.19–27. The sabbath is to make the people holy, to *sanctify them.* **20.13–17** After the Sinai event, the people again *rebelled,* whereupon God was tempted to annihilate them. However, concern for the viability of the deity's name among the nations prevented this punitive response. **20.18–21** Introduction of the motif of the next generation, *their children;* cf. ch. 18. These individuals are challenged to obey in a way that their fathers did not obey. And yet they also rebelled, unlike the case in ch. 18. **20.22–26** The generation of children, in the wilderness, is threatened with exile; see also Ps 106.26–27. **20.25** Moreover, God gives the children *statutes that were not good and ordinances by* *which they could not live.* Ezekiel's charge is radical, but it is not outside the pale of other OT assessments, e.g., Isa 63.17. **20.26** This verse defines the sort of laws to which Ezekiel refers in v. 25, namely, offering the *firstborn.* Certain obligations involving the firstborn are ambiguous, e.g., Ex 22.29. Nonetheless, child sacrifice is attested in ancient Israel (Deut 12.31; Jer 7.31; 19.4–6; 32.35). **20.27–29** Another geographic setting, now in *the land that* God *swore to give them.* The promised land provided occasions for ritual malfeasance: *sacrifices, offering, pleasing odors* (incense), *drink offerings,* and the *high place.* **20.30–31** Ezekiel addresses his generation (*the house of Israel*), which can now be compared to those who have gone before. V. 31 suggests that those in exile are guilty of misdeeds like those performed by their forebears. To wit, with the effect of an *inclusio* (a repetition signaling the beginning and end of a unit; see vv. 3–4), God asks, *Shall I be consulted by you?* To this question the deity answers in the negative,

testable things? [31]When you offer your gifts and make your children pass through the fire, you defile yourselves with all your idols to this day. And shall I be consulted by you, O house of Israel? As I live, says the Lord GOD, I will not be consulted by you.

32 What is in your mind shall never happen—the thought, "Let us be like the nations, like the tribes of the countries, and worship wood and stone."

God Will Restore Israel

33 As I live, says the Lord GOD, surely with a mighty hand and an outstretched arm, and with wrath poured out, I will be king over you. [34]I will bring you out from the peoples and gather you out of the countries where you are scattered, with a mighty hand and an outstretched arm, and with wrath poured out; [35]and I will bring you into the wilderness of the peoples, and there I will enter into judgment with you face to face. [36]As I entered into judgment with your ancestors in the wilderness of the land of Egypt, so I will enter into judgment with you, says the Lord GOD. [37]I will make you pass under the staff, and will bring you within the bond of the covenant. [38]I will purge out the rebels among you, and those who transgress against me; I will bring them out of the land where they reside as aliens, but they shall not enter the land of Israel. Then you shall know that I am the LORD.

39 As for you, O house of Israel, thus says the Lord GOD: Go serve your idols, every one of you now and hereafter, if you will not listen to me; but my holy name you shall no more profane with your gifts and your idols.

40 For on my holy mountain, the mountain height of Israel, says the Lord GOD, there all the house of Israel, all of them, shall serve me in the land; there I will accept them, and there I will require your contributions and the choicest of your gifts, with all your sacred things. [41]As a pleasing odor I will accept you, when I bring you out from the peoples, and gather you out of the countries where you have been scattered; and I will manifest my holiness among you in the sight of the nations. [42]You shall know that I am the LORD, when I bring you into the land of Israel, the country that I swore to give to your ancestors. [43]There you shall remember your ways and all the deeds by which you have polluted yourselves; and you shall loathe yourselves for all the evils that you have committed. [44]And you shall know that I am the LORD, when I deal with you for my name's sake, not according to your evil ways, or corrupt deeds, O house of Israel, says the Lord GOD.

A Prophecy against the Negeb

45[a] The word of the LORD came to me: [46]Mortal, set your face toward the south, preach against the south, and prophesy against the forest land in the Negeb; [47]say to the forest of the Negeb, Hear the word of the LORD: Thus says the Lord GOD, I will kindle a fire in you, and it shall devour every green tree in you and every dry tree; the blazing flame shall not be quenched, and all faces from south to north shall be scorched by it. [48]All flesh shall see that I the LORD have kindled it; it shall not be

---

a Ch 21.1 in Heb

---

which is a much milder response than it was to earlier audiences. **20.32** Again Ezekiel quotes those whom he addresses: *Let us be like the nations,* or "we will be like the nations." *Worship wood and stone,* the most overt reference to veneration of objects representing gods other than Yahweh in this chapter; cf. Jer 2.27. **20.33–44** These verses offer hope. **20.33–35** *With wrath poured out* indicates that this new exodus will be accompanied by harsh trials en route. *Wilderness of the peoples,* through which Israel will have to pass on its way from Babylon to Syro-Palestine. *Face to face,* imagery of direct encounter, similar to the prior encounter in the wilderness at Mount Sinai (Deut 5.4). **20.37** *I . . . will bring you within the bond of the covenant.* Cf. the Greek manuscript tradition and RSV, "I will let you go by number." **20.38** Certain Israelites, *rebels,* will be removed from the community before it enters the *land.* Cf. 13.9 for the motif of being re-

moved from among the people. **20.39** The first part of the verse is an ironic admonition to worship religious objects. The final clause demonstrates the purpose of such language, to prevent God's *holy name* from being profaned. **20.40–44** The scene shifts to Jerusalem and Zion, *my holy mountain,* the site of the temple. Ezekiel describes a hopeful future in which the people resume proper religious practices. *Contributions, choicest of . . . gifts, sacred things,* ritual offerings at the temple. **20.41** Israel itself will be like a *pleasing odor,* the incense and smoke from various sacrifices. **20.43** Memory will lead to contrition. **20.45–48** A prophecy against the South. **20.46** *The south, the south,* and *the Negeb,* three different Hebrew terms that should probably all be understood as referring to the Southern Kingdom, or tribal territory of Judah. According to this imagery, Ezekiel is in the north; on the enemy from the north, see ch. 38; Jer 5.14–17. **20.47–48** Fire

quenched. ⁴⁹Then I said, "Ah Lord GOD! they are saying of me, 'Is he not a maker of allegories?' "

The Drawn Sword of God

21 ᵃ The word of the LORD came to me: ²Mortal, set your face toward Jerusalem and preach against the sanctuaries; prophesy against the land of Israel ³and say to the land of Israel, Thus says the LORD: I am coming against you, and will draw my sword out of its sheath, and will cut off from you both righteous and wicked. ⁴Because I will cut off from you both righteous and wicked, therefore my sword shall go out of its sheath against all flesh from south to north; ⁵and all flesh shall know that I the LORD have drawn my sword out of its sheath; it shall not be sheathed again. ⁶Moan therefore, mortal; moan with breaking heart and bitter grief before their eyes. ⁷And when they say to you, "Why do you moan?" you shall say, "Because of the news that has come. Every heart will melt and all hands will be feeble, every spirit will faint and all knees will turn to water. See, it comes and it will be fulfilled," says the Lord GOD.

8 And the word of the LORD came to me: ⁹Mortal, prophesy and say: Thus says the Lord; Say:

A sword, a sword is sharpened,
    it is also polished;
¹⁰ it is sharpened for slaughter,
    honed to flash like lightning!
How can we make merry?
    You have despised the rod,
    and all discipline.ᵇ
¹¹ The swordᶜ is given to be polished,
    to be grasped in the hand;
it is sharpened, the sword is polished,

to be placed in the slayer's hand.
¹² Cry and wail, O mortal,
    for it is against my people;
it is against all Israel's princes;
    they are thrown to the sword,
    together with my people.
Ah! Strike the thigh!
¹³For consider: What! If you despise the rod, will it not happen?ᵇ says the Lord GOD.
¹⁴ And you, mortal, prophesy;
    strike hand to hand.
Let the sword fall twice, thrice;
    it is a sword for killing.
A sword for great slaughter—
    it surrounds them;
¹⁵ therefore hearts melt
    and many stumble.
At all their gates I have set
    the pointᵇ of the sword.
Ah! It is made for flashing,
    it is polishedᵈ for slaughter.
¹⁶ Attack to the right!
    Engage to the left!
    —wherever your edge is directed.
¹⁷ I too will strike hand to hand,
    I will satisfy my fury;
    I the LORD have spoken.

18 The word of the LORD came to me: ¹⁹Mortal, mark out two roads for the sword of the king of Babylon to come; both of them shall issue from the same land. And make a signpost, make it for a fork in the road leading to a city; ²⁰mark out the road for the sword to come to Rabbah of the Ammonites or to Judah and toᵉ Jerusalem the fortified. ²¹For the king of Babylon stands at the parting of the way, at the fork in the two roads, to use

---

a Ch 21.6 in Heb   b Meaning of Heb uncertain   c Heb It
d Tg: Heb wrapped up   e Gk Syr: Heb Judah in

---

imagery is prominent in Ezekiel (e.g., 5.4; 10.2; 15.4–7; 16.41; 19.12, 14; 21.32; 23.25). For such a great fire, cf. Am 7.4–5. **20.49** Ezekiel laments (so the formulaic *Ah*) that the people perceive him as speaking unclearly. **21.1–32** Sayings that have in common sword imagery, which appears elsewhere in Ezekiel (e.g., 14.21). **21.1–7** The audience is diverse: *Jerusalem, the sanctuaries, the land of Israel.* Moreover, God will attack *all flesh,* which includes both *righteous and wicked.* The oracle therefore stresses the totality of the coming destruction; cf. chs. 9, 18. **21.6–7** The prophet laments symbolically, which elicits a question from the people, thereby allowing for a new utterance about the universal scope of God's punitive action: *every heart, all hands, every spirit, all knees.* **21.8–17** The number of

text notes indicates the difficulty of this poem. Descriptions of the sword are interposed with comments from the prophet and God respectively (vv. 10, 12). **21.12** Again Ezekiel is commanded to lament (v. 6). That the sword is against *Israel's princes* (cf. 19.1; 22.60) does not, however, limit the scope of the punishment; see *my people* twice in this verse. *Strike the thigh,* an expression of sorrow; see Jer 31.19. **21.13–17** These verses are built on the foregoing poem; the *rod* in v. 13 alludes to the rod in v. 10. Now imperative language predominates as God addresses the sword and its function, e.g., v. 16. **21.18–24** The sword of Babylon. Ezekiel is admonished to direct Nebuchadnezzar's sword, which is at a crossroads. **21.20** *Rabbah,* the capital of Ammon, modern Amman, Jordan.

divination; he shakes the arrows, he consults the teraphim,[a] he inspects the liver. 22Into his right hand comes the lot for Jerusalem, to set battering rams, to call out for slaughter, for raising the battle cry, to set battering rams against the gates, to cast up ramps, to build siege towers. 23But to them it will seem like a false divination; they have sworn solemn oaths; but he brings their guilt to remembrance, bringing about their capture.

24 Therefore thus says the Lord GOD: Because you have brought your guilt to remembrance, in that your transgressions are uncovered, so that in all your deeds your sins appear—because you have come to remembrance, you shall be taken in hand.[b]

25 As for you, vile, wicked prince of Israel,
   you whose day has come,
   the time of final punishment,
26 thus says the Lord GOD:
   Remove the turban, take off the crown;
      things shall not remain as they are.
   Exalt that which is low,
      abase that which is high.
27 A ruin, a ruin, a ruin—
      I will make it!
   (Such has never occurred.)
   Until he comes whose right it is;
      to him I will give it.

28 As for you, mortal, prophesy, and say, Thus says the Lord GOD concerning the Ammonites, and concerning their reproach; say:
   A sword, a sword! Drawn for slaughter,
      polished to consume,[c] to flash like
         lightning.
29 Offering false visions for you,
      divining lies for you,
   they place you over the necks
      of the vile, wicked ones—
   those whose day has come,

the time of final punishment.
30 Return it to its sheath!
   In the place where you were created,
      in the land of your origin,
         I will judge you.
31 I will pour out my indignation upon you,
      with the fire of my wrath
         I will blow upon you.
   I will deliver you into brutish hands,
      those skillful to destroy.
32 You shall be fuel for the fire,
      your blood shall enter the earth;
   you shall be remembered no more,
      for I the LORD have spoken.

The Bloody City

22 The word of the LORD came to me: 2You, mortal, will you judge, will you judge the bloody city? Then declare to it all its abominable deeds. 3You shall say, Thus says the Lord GOD: A city! Shedding blood within itself; its time has come; making its idols, defiling itself. 4You have become guilty by the blood that you have shed, and defiled by the idols that you have made; you have brought your day near, the appointed time of your years has come. Therefore I have made you a disgrace before the nations, and a mockery to all the countries. 5Those who are near and those who are far from you will mock you, you infamous one, full of tumult.

6 The princes of Israel in you, everyone according to his power, have been bent on shedding blood. 7Father and mother are treated with contempt in you; the alien residing within you suffers extortion; the orphan and the widow are wronged in you. 8You have de-

___

a Or the household gods b Or be taken captive c Cn: Heb to contain

___

21.21 Nebuchadnezzar employs various divinatory techniques to determine which road to take. On *teraphim* as sources of information, see Hos 3.4; Zech 10.2. Hepatoscopy, *liver* divination, was prominent in Mesopotamia. In the ancient Near East kings regularly consulted various omens before entering battle. Ezekiel as an intermediary could affect the king's decision. **21.22** *The lot,* which symbolizes a divinatory decision, designates Jerusalem. The repertoire of siege and destruction ensues. **21.25–27** God addresses a *wicked prince of Israel,* almost certainly Zedekiah. *Exalt . . . low, abase . . . high,* a reversal of social order, which exemplifies dysfunction (cf. Isa 3.4–5). **21.27** *He,* probably Nebuchadnezzar, the one whom God has designated to administer judgment; cf. Gen 49.10. **21.28–**

32 Concerning the *Ammonites,* whose capital had been Nebuchadnezzar's alternate site for attack (v. 20). The sense of v. 29 remains unclear. Ammon appears first in the collection of oracles against the nations, 25.1–7. **21.30** Presumably Nebuchadnezzar is addressed. God's judgment will also fall on Babylon; cf. Isa 13–14; Jer 50–51. The sword is under God's control. **22.1–31** Oracles of judgment on Jerusalem and Judah. **22.2–5** Bloodshed (cf. the indictment of Nineveh as a "city of bloodshed," Nah 3.1) and veneration of idols are the hallmark indictments. **22.5** On Jerusalem as scorned, cf. 16.57. **22.6–12** *Shedding blood* (vv. 6, 9, 12), attributed to *the princes of Israel* (v. 6). Other OT texts attest leaders (Num 4.34; 31.13; 32.2). **22.7** Cases that violate Israelite legal formula-

spised my holy things, and profaned my sabbaths. 9In you are those who slander to shed blood, those in you who eat upon the mountains, who commit lewdness in your midst. 10In you they uncover their fathers' nakedness; in you they violate women in their menstrual periods. 11One commits abomination with his neighbor's wife; another lewdly defiles his daughter-in-law; another in you defiles his sister, his father's daughter. 12In you, they take bribes to shed blood; you take both advance interest and accrued interest, and make gain of your neighbors by extortion; and you have forgotten me, says the Lord God.

13 See, I strike my hands together at the dishonest gain you have made, and at the blood that has been shed within you. 14Can your courage endure, or can your hands remain strong in the days when I shall deal with you? I the Lord have spoken, and I will do it. 15I will scatter you among the nations and disperse you through the countries, and I will purge your filthiness out of you. 16And I*a* shall be profaned through you in the sight of the nations; and you shall know that I am the Lord.

17 The word of the Lord came to me: 18Mortal, the house of Israel has become dross to me; all of them, silver,*b* bronze, tin, iron, and lead. In the smelter they have become dross. 19Therefore thus says the Lord God: Because you have all become dross, I will gather you into the midst of Jerusalem. 20As one gathers silver, bronze, iron, lead, and tin into a smelter, to blow the fire upon them in order to melt them; so I will gather you in my anger and in my wrath, and I will put you in and melt you. 21I will gather you and blow upon you with the fire of my wrath, and you shall be melted within it. 22As silver is melted in a

smelter, so you shall be melted in it; and you shall know that I the Lord have poured out my wrath upon you.

23 The word of the Lord came to me: 24Mortal, say to it: You are a land that is not cleansed, not rained upon in the day of indignation. 25Its princes*c* within it are like a roaring lion tearing the prey; they have devoured human lives; they have taken treasure and precious things; they have made many widows within it. 26Its priests have done violence to my teaching and have profaned my holy things; they have made no distinction between the holy and the common, neither have they taught the difference between the unclean and the clean, and they have disregarded my sabbaths, so that I am profaned among them. 27Its officials within it are like wolves tearing the prey, shedding blood, destroying lives to get dishonest gain. 28Its prophets have smeared whitewash on their behalf, seeing false visions and divining lies for them, saying, "Thus says the Lord God," when the Lord has not spoken. 29The people of the land have practiced extortion and committed robbery; they have oppressed the poor and needy, and have extorted from the alien without redress. 30And I sought for anyone among them who would repair the wall and stand in the breach before me on behalf of the land, so that I would not destroy it; but I found no one. 31Therefore I have poured out my indignation upon them; I have consumed them with the fire of my wrath; I have returned their conduct upon their heads, says the Lord God.

---

a Gk Syr Vg: Heb *you*   *b* Transposed from the end of the verse; compare verse 20   *c* Gk: Heb *indignation.* 25*A conspiracy of its prophets*

---

tions: *father and mother,* Ex 21.17; *the alien,* Ex 22.21; *the orphan and the widow,* Deut 16.11. **22.8–9** Violations of the orders involving holiness. Cf. Lev 18–20. **22.10–11** Concerning illicit sexual practice. Cf. Lev 18. **22.12** Concerning illegal monetary practices. **22.13–16** Judgment for the iniquity just cited. Punishment will occur in the form of exile. **22.13** Strike my hands together. Cf. 21.14. **22.17–22** Judgment on the *house of Israel* based on smelting imagery. Cf. Isa 1.22, 25; Jer 9.7; Zech 13.9; Mal 3.2–3. As with ore in which the desired metal is still present, so Israel will be gathered to one furnace, Jerusalem, for a decisive smelting. Ezekiel emphasizes the diverse elements collected— *silver, bronze, tin, iron, and lead* (v. 17). At the outset, however, God views Israel as dross, not the essential metal sought in the smelting process. **22.22** A focus on

the most precious of these metals, *silver,* as opposed to the earlier dross. Nonetheless, wrath remains the hallmark. **22.23–31** Those in certain social roles—prince, priest, official, and prophet—have acted improperly; cf. Jer 8.8–10; esp. Zeph 3.3–4. The malfeasance may be identified: *princes* who are to foster peace kill (v. 25), *priests* do not distinguish between the sacred and the common (v. 26), *officials* do not administer impartial justice (v. 27), and *prophets* do not speak on behalf of God (v. 28). *The people of the land* (v. 29; cf. 7.27) moves the discourse beyond discrete classes to all Israel. **22.30** For the search for *anyone,* cf. Jer 5.1. There as here, no such person was found. The absence of such an individual results in judgment, which is described in v. 31. **22.31** *Fire* (see vv. 17–22) will destroy those just indicted.

Oholah and Oholibah

23 The word of the LORD came to me: 2Mortal, there were two women, the daughters of one mother; 3they played the whore in Egypt; they played the whore in their youth; their breasts were caressed there, and their virgin bosoms were fondled. 4Oholah was the name of the elder and Oholibah the name of her sister. They became mine, and they bore sons and daughters. As for their names, Oholah is Samaria, and Oholibah is Jerusalem.

5 Oholah played the whore while she was mine; she lusted after her lovers the Assyrians, warriors[a] 6clothed in blue, governors and commanders, all of them handsome young men, mounted horsemen. 7She bestowed her favors upon them, the choicest men of Assyria all of them; and she defiled herself with all the idols of everyone for whom she lusted. 8She did not give up her whorings that she had practiced since Egypt; for in her youth men had lain with her and fondled her virgin bosom and poured out their lust upon her. 9Therefore I delivered her into the hands of her lovers, into the hands of the Assyrians, for whom she lusted. 10These uncovered her nakedness; they seized her sons and her daughters; and they killed her with the sword. Judgment was executed upon her, and she became a byword among women.

11 Her sister Oholibah saw this, yet she was more corrupt than she in her lusting and in her whorings, which were worse than those of her sister. 12She lusted after the Assyrians, governors and commanders, warriors[a] clothed in full armor, mounted horsemen, all of them handsome young men. 13And I saw that she was defiled; they both took the same way. 14But she carried her whorings further; she saw male figures carved on the wall, images of the Chaldeans portrayed in vermilion, 15with belts around their waists, with flowing turbans on their heads, all of them looking like officers—a picture of Babylonians whose native land was Chaldea. 16When she saw them she lusted after them, and sent messengers to them in Chaldea. 17And the Babylonians came to her into the bed of love, and they defiled her with their lust; and after she defiled herself with them, she turned from them in disgust. 18When she carried on her whorings so openly and flaunted her nakedness, I turned in disgust from her, as I had turned from her sister. 19Yet she increased her whorings, remembering the days of her youth, when she played the whore in the land of Egypt 20and lusted after her paramours there, whose members were like those of donkeys, and whose emission was like that of stallions. 21Thus you longed for the lewdness of your youth, when the Egyptians[b] fondled your bosom and caressed[c] your young breasts.

22 Therefore, O Oholibah, thus says the Lord GOD: I will rouse against you your lovers from whom you turned in disgust, and I will bring them against you from every side: 23the Babylonians and all the Chaldeans, Pekod and

___

a Meaning of Heb uncertain   b Two Mss: MT from Egypt
c Cn: Heb for the sake of

___

23.1–49 Oholah and Oholibah, symbols for Samaria and Jerusalem. Cf. ch. 16 for a similar indictment of Jerusalem. **23.2** *Daughters of one mother.* Who is the mother? Perhaps all of Israel in Egypt, where Israel's whoredom begins; see 20.8. **23.4** *Oholah,* lit. "her tent." *Oholibah,* lit. "my tent is in her." If "tent" refers to a tent shrine (cf. the tent of meeting, Ex 33.7–11), then the names allude to the royal shrines at the national capitals: Samaria and Jerusalem. God identifies the latter as having "my tent," which makes Oholibah's whoring worse than that of her sister. **23.5–9** Indictment and sentence of Oholah. *Governors, commanders,* and *horsemen* presume the presence of Neo-Assyrian provincial political and military officials in Syro-Palestine. Her licentious behavior with Assyrians may symbolize treaties with the Neo-Assyrian Empire. Such alliances required oaths of fealty and payment of tribute as early as the late ninth century BCE. **23.9–10** The death of Oholah and her children reflects the destruction of Samaria by the Neo-Assyrians in 721 BCE. *Delivered . . . lovers.* Cf. 16.37–39. **23.11–27** Indictment and sentence of Oholibah. **23.11–21** The indictment. Like her sister, Oholibah lusts after Neo-Assyrian officials. However, *she was more corrupt,* which Ezekiel argues in vv. 14–15. *Male figures carved on the wall* (v. 14), probably Neo-Assyrian wall reliefs, which were sometimes tinted red. Ezekiel may have known a tradition according to which Judahites sent emissaries to Neo-Assyrian (or Neo-Babylonian, *Chaldean*) cities. The greater sin would result from the Judahites' sexual misbehavior in Mesopotamia. After God rejects Oholibah, she continues *her whorings,* as she had done earlier with her sexually vigorous partners (vv. 19–20). **23.22–27** The sentence. As with Oholah, the woman will be turned over to her lovers, who now include both Assyrians and Babylonians. Note the prominence of the *o* vowel in the tribal names (v. 23), which creates assonance with the names Oholah and

Shoa and Koa, and all the Assyrians with them, handsome young men, governors and commanders all of them, officers and warriors,[a] all of them riding on horses. 24They shall come against you from the north[b] with chariots and wagons and a host of peoples; they shall set themselves against you on every side with buckler, shield, and helmet, and I will commit the judgment to them, and they shall judge you according to their ordinances. 25I will direct my indignation against you, in order that they may deal with you in fury. They shall cut off your nose and your ears, and your survivors shall fall by the sword. They shall seize your sons and your daughters, and your survivors shall be devoured by fire. 26They shall also strip you of your clothes and take away your fine jewels. 27So I will put an end to your lewdness and your whoring brought from the land of Egypt; you shall not long for them, or remember Egypt any more. 28For thus says the Lord GOD: I will deliver you into the hands of those whom you hate, into the hands of those from whom you turned in disgust; 29and they shall deal with you in hatred, and take away all the fruit of your labor, and leave you naked and bare, and the nakedness of your whorings shall be exposed. Your lewdness and your whorings 30have brought this upon you, because you played the whore with the nations, and polluted yourself with their idols. 31You have gone the way of your sister; therefore I will give her cup into your hand. 32Thus says the Lord GOD:

You shall drink your sister's cup,
   deep and wide;
you shall be scorned and derided,
   it holds so much.
33 You shall be filled with drunkenness and
   sorrow.
A cup of horror and desolation
   is the cup of your sister Samaria;

34 you shall drink it and drain it out,
   and gnaw its sherds,
   and tear out your breasts;
for I have spoken, says the Lord GOD. 35Therefore thus says the Lord GOD: Because you have forgotten me and cast me behind your back, therefore bear the consequences of your lewdness and whorings.

36 The LORD said to me: Mortal, will you judge Oholah and Oholibah? Then declare to them their abominable deeds. 37For they have committed adultery, and blood is on their hands; with their idols they have committed adultery; and they have even offered up to them for food the children whom they had borne to me. 38Moreover this they have done to me: they have defiled my sanctuary on the same day and profaned my sabbaths. 39For when they had slaughtered their children for their idols, on the same day they came into my sanctuary to profane it. This is what they did in my house.

40 They even sent for men to come from far away, to whom a messenger was sent, and they came. For them you bathed yourself, painted your eyes, and decked yourself with ornaments; 41you sat on a stately couch, with a table spread before it on which you had placed my incense and my oil. 42The sound of a raucous multitude was around her, with many of the rabble brought in drunken from the wilderness; and they put bracelets on the arms[c] of the women, and beautiful crowns upon their heads.

43 Then I said, Ah, she is worn out with adulteries, but they carry on their sexual acts with her. 44For they have gone in to her, as one goes in to a whore. Thus they went in to Oholah and to Oholibah, wanton women. 45But righteous judges shall declare them guilty of

---

a Compare verses 6 and 12: Heb *officers and called ones*
b Gk: Meaning of Heb uncertain   c Heb *hands*

Oholibah. **23.23–24** Horsemen, *chariots and wagons,* and *buckler, shield, and helmet* attest to the power of the Neo-Babylonian army. **23.25–27** As prisoners of war, Oholibah and her children are subject to physical mutilation and death. *Egypt.* Ezekiel continues to emphasize that the whoring dates far back in Israel's existence. **23.28–49** Diverse judgments and reflections based on the Oholah and Oholibah discourse. **23.28–30** A general oracle of judgment, probably directed to Oholibah (Jerusalem); *you* (v. 28) is feminine singular. **23.30** Use of *idols* becomes part of the indictment.

23.31–35 Address to Oholibah and description of her punishment using the imagery of her *sister's cup;* cf. Isa 51.17, 22; Jer 25.15–28; 51.7; Hab 2.16. **23.36–49** Final reflections, which point in a new direction. **23.36–39** More indictments, which recall chs. 16, 20, 38–39. *My sanctuary* focuses on ritual infractions. **23.40–44** One woman, probably Oholibah, undertakes self-adornment, but with some materials belonging to religious ritual (*my incense,* v. 41). **23.40–42** *Men* and *rabble* are imported for Oholibah; cf. 23.17. **23.45–49** The scene shifts to human judgment (*righteous judges*) and

adultery and of bloodshed; because they are adulteresses and blood is on their hands.

46 For thus says the Lord GOD: Bring up an assembly against them, and make them an object of terror and of plunder. 47The assembly shall stone them and with their swords they shall cut them down; they shall kill their sons and their daughters, and burn up their houses. 48Thus will I put an end to lewdness in the land, so that all women may take warning and not commit lewdness as you have done. 49They shall repay you for your lewdness, and you shall bear the penalty for your sinful idolatry; and you shall know that I am the Lord GOD.

The Boiling Pot

24 In the ninth year, in the tenth month, on the tenth day of the month, the word of the LORD came to me: 2Mortal, write down the name of this day, this very day. The king of Babylon has laid siege to Jerusalem this very day. 3And utter an allegory to the rebellious house and say to them, Thus says the Lord GOD:

Set on the pot, set it on,
    pour in water also;
4   put in it the pieces,
    all the good pieces, the thigh and the
        shoulder;
    fill it with choice bones.
5   Take the choicest one of the flock,
    pile the logs[a] under it;
    boil its pieces,[b]
    seethe[c] also its bones in it.

6 Therefore thus says the Lord GOD:
    Woe to the bloody city,
    the pot whose rust is in it,
    whose rust has not gone out of it!
    Empty it piece by piece,

making no choice at all.[d]
7   For the blood she shed is inside it;
    she placed it on a bare rock;
    she did not pour it out on the ground,
    to cover it with earth.
8   To rouse my wrath, to take vengeance,
    I have placed the blood she shed
        on a bare rock,
    so that it may not be covered.
9Therefore thus says the Lord GOD:
    Woe to the bloody city!
    I will even make the pile great.
10 Heap up the logs, kindle the fire;
    boil the meat well, mix in the spices,
    let the bones be burned.
11 Stand it empty upon the coals,
    so that it may become hot, its copper
        glow,
    its filth melt in it, its rust be consumed.
12 In vain I have wearied myself;[e]
    its thick rust does not depart.
    To the fire with its rust![f]
13 Yet, when I cleansed you in your filthy
        lewdness,
    you did not become clean from your
        filth;
    you shall not again be cleansed
    until I have satisfied my fury upon you.
14I the LORD have spoken; the time is coming, I will act. I will not refrain, I will not spare, I will not relent. According to your ways and your doings I will judge you, says the Lord GOD.

Ezekiel's Bereavement

15 The word of the LORD came to me: 16Mortal, with one blow I am about to take away

---

a Compare verse 10: Heb the bones   b Two Mss: Heb its boilings   c Cn: Heb its bones seethe   d Heb piece, no lot has fallen on it   e Cn: Meaning of Heb uncertain   f Meaning of Heb uncertain

---

Israelite laws regarding adultery (Lev 20.10). **23.48** *That all women may take warning*. The conclusion has an admonitory tone, characteristic of wisdom literature, rather than one of annihilation.

24.1–14 The boiling pot. **24.1–2** *Ninth year . . . month*, January 15, 588 BCE (see note on 1.2), a date that the prophet is to inscribe, since Nebuchadnezzar began his siege of Jerusalem on that day. **24.3** *Another allegory*. Cf. 17.2. **24.3–5** One individual is directed to cook an animal in boiling water. Cf. Mic 3.3 for the motif of flesh and bones (though there human) in one pot. Also cf. Ezek 11.3. **24.6–8** The imagery becomes complicated, with attention now devoted to corrosion

in the pot. **24.7–8** Then blood contaminates what is inside the pot. On Jerusalem and blood, see ch. 22. On blood manipulation, see 33.25; Gen 9.4; Lev 7.10–14; Deut 12.16. God will not allow the blood that Jerusalem has shed to be *covered;* cf. Gen 4.10–11; Job 16.18. **24.9–14** Though this oracle of woe commences with reference to blood, the imagery of the pot returns. The fire will be hotter, the rust will contaminate the pot, the pot will be emptied (so also v. 6b), and nothing will be clean. This flurry of prophetic rhetoric—which is consonant with *my fury*—provides images rather than a definitive picture of destruction by fire. **24.15–27** Ezekiel's bereavement. **24.15–18** God commands

from you the delight of your eyes; yet you shall not mourn or weep, nor shall your tears run down. 17 Sigh, but not aloud; make no mourning for the dead. Bind on your turban, and put your sandals on your feet; do not cover your upper lip or eat the bread of mourners. *a* 18 So I spoke to the people in the morning, and at evening my wife died. And on the next morning I did as I was commanded.

19 Then the people said to me, "Will you not tell us what these things mean for us, that you are acting this way?" 20 Then I said to them: The word of the LORD came to me: 21 Say to the house of Israel, Thus says the Lord GOD: I will profane my sanctuary, the pride of your power, the delight of your eyes, and your heart's desire; and your sons and your daughters whom you left behind shall fall by the sword. 22 And you shall do as I have done; you shall not cover your upper lip or eat the bread of mourners. *a* 23 Your turbans shall be on your heads and your sandals on your feet; you shall not mourn or weep, but you shall pine away in your iniquities and groan to one another. 24 Thus Ezekiel shall be a sign to you; you shall do just as he has done. When this comes, then you shall know that I am the Lord GOD.

25 And you, mortal, on the day when I take from them their stronghold, their joy and glory, the delight of their eyes and their heart's affection, and also *b* their sons and their daughters, 26 on that day, one who has escaped will come to you to report to you the news. 27 On that day your mouth shall be opened to the one who has escaped, and you shall speak and no longer be silent. So you shall be a sign to them; and they shall know that I am the LORD.

Proclamation against Ammon

25 The word of the LORD came to me: 2 Mortal, set your face toward the Ammonites and prophesy against them. 3 Say to the Ammonites, Hear the word of the Lord GOD: Thus says the Lord GOD, Because you said, "Aha!" over my sanctuary when it was profaned, and over the land of Israel when it was made desolate, and over the house of Judah when it went into exile; 4 therefore I am handing you over to the people of the east for a possession. They shall set their encampments among you and pitch their tents in your midst; they shall eat your fruit, and they shall drink your milk. 5 I will make Rabbah a pasture for camels and Ammon a fold for flocks. Then you shall know that I am the LORD. 6 For thus says the Lord GOD: Because you have

_____

a Vg Tg: Heb *of men*   *b* Heb lacks *and also*

the prophet to undertake another symbolic act (cf. 4.1–5.17; 12.1–16), which involves the absence of standard mourning rituals for his wife, who is about to die. Cf. Jer 16.5 for another prohibition of mourning. **24.17** Certain of these lamentation practices, i.e., not wearing the normal headdress, not wearing sandals, covering part of the face (*upper lip*), would create a different appearance for the mourner and in so doing protect the individual from the netherworld. *Bread of mourners* (Hebrew, "bread of humans") may refer to the feasting that was part of the funeral rites. **24.19–24** The act explained. God interprets the destruction of the temple to be like the death of Ezekiel's wife. Both shall occur without the expected and appropriate lamentation. Just as Ezekiel's wife was the *delight* of his eyes (v. 16), so the temple was the *delight* of the people's eyes (v. 21). **24.24** Ezekiel, the person, and not simply what he says, becomes a *sign*. **24.25– 27** *On the day* or *on that day*, a formula prominent in late prophetic texts; cf. Zech 14. The sequel to these verses, 33.21–22, reports that Ezekiel will be able to speak again as a prophet and be, again, a *sign* to the people.

25.1–32.32 Oracles against foreign nations. As in other books (Isa 13–23; Jer 46–51; Am 1.3–2.3; Nahum), prophets often directed oracles against nations and rulers other than Israel and Judah. Ezekiel addresses one empire, Egypt, and a number of smaller Syro-Palestinian states, Ammon, Moab, Edom, Philistia, Tyre, which form a geographic arc around Judah. Tyre (chs. 26–28) and Egypt (chs. 29–32)—and their respective kings—receive primary attention. Many of these oracles postdate the demise of Judah in 587 BCE. The punishment of other nations sets the stage for the announcements of well-being for Israel that follow. **25.1–17** Four oracles against nations on the eastern and western flanks of Israel: Ammon, Moab, Edom, and Philistia. **25.1–7** Proclamation against Ammon, a nation east of the Jordan River, north of Moab. Its southern border began approximately halfway up the Dead Sea and continued for almost half the Jordan Valley between the Dead Sea and the Sea of Galilee. In 21.28, Ezekiel had already focused attention on this nation. Ammon had, in league with the Moabites and Arameans, cooperated with the Neo-Babylonians in their first major attack against Jerusalem (2 Kings 24.1–2). Later however, Ammon and Judah together attempted to withstand the Neo-Babylonians (Jer 27). **25.3** Not Ammonite history (see note on 25.1–7), but Ammonite delight in the destruction of the temple and Judah serves as Ezekiel's indictment. **25.4** *People of the east, encampments, tents* suggest that other, though unnamed, foreign peoples—desert nomads— will destroy Ammon. **25.5** *Rabbah*. See note on 21.20.

clapped your hands and stamped your feet and rejoiced with all the malice within you against the land of Israel, [7]therefore I have stretched out my hand against you, and will hand you over as plunder to the nations. I will cut you off from the peoples and will make you perish out of the countries; I will destroy you. Then you shall know that I am the LORD.

Proclamation against Moab

8 Thus says the Lord GOD: Because Moab[a] said, The house of Judah is like all the other nations, [9]therefore I will lay open the flank of Moab from the towns[b] on its frontier, the glory of the country, Beth-jeshimoth, Baal-meon, and Kiriathaim. [10]I will give it along with Ammon to the people of the east as a possession. Thus Ammon shall be remembered no more among the nations, [11]and I will execute judgments upon Moab. Then they shall know that I am the LORD.

Proclamation against Edom

12 Thus says the Lord GOD: Because Edom acted revengefully against the house of Judah and has grievously offended in taking vengeance upon them, [13]therefore thus says the Lord GOD, I will stretch out my hand against Edom, and cut off from it humans and animals, and I will make it desolate; from

Teman even to Dedan they shall fall by the sword. [14]I will lay my vengeance upon Edom by the hand of my people Israel; and they shall act in Edom according to my anger and according to my wrath; and they shall know my vengeance, says the Lord GOD.

Proclamation against Philistia

15 Thus says the Lord GOD: Because with unending hostilities the Philistines acted in vengeance, and with malice of heart took revenge in destruction; [16]therefore thus says the Lord GOD, I will stretch out my hand against the Philistines, cut off the Cherethites, and destroy the rest of the seacoast. [17]I will execute great vengeance on them with wrathful punishments. Then they shall know that I am the LORD, when I lay my vengeance on them.

Proclamation against Tyre

26 In the eleventh year, on the first day of the month, the word of the LORD came to me: [2]Mortal, because Tyre said concerning Jerusalem,

"Aha, broken is the gateway of the
        peoples;
    it has swung open to me;

---

a Gk Old Latin: Heb *Moab and Seir*   *b* Heb *towns from its towns*

25.8–11 Proclamation against Moab, a nation that lay south of Ammon. This and the previous oracle (vv. 1–7) are closely related. The method of punishment for Moab is the same as that of Ammon (destruction by the *people of the east*); Ammon is mentioned explicitly in both oracles; and Israel understood itself to stand in a kinship relation with both Ammon and Moab (Gen 19; 37–38). 25.8 *Like all the other nations.* Cf. 20.32; 1 Sam 8.5. In all three texts the phrase bears a negative connotation. 25.9 *The towns.* Cf. Jer 47, which also emphasizes destruction of cities and villages and not just the capital. *Beth-jeshimoth, Baal-meon, Kiriathaim,* cities near Moab's border with Israel. 25.12–14 Proclamation against Edom, which lies next to Moab just south of the Dead Sea. As with the other nations, there was a kinship relationship to Israel, in this case through Esau (see Gen 25.23–26). Both Edom and Philistia (25.15) are indicted for taking revenge. 25.12 Other biblical texts allude to Edomite action against Israel (Ps 137.7; Isa 34.5–17; Jer 49.7–22; Lam 4.21–22; Ob 1–14; Mal 1.2–5), which results in a particularly spiteful relationship between Judah and Edom; cf. Am 1.9. 25.13 *My hand.* God will act directly with Edom, not through an intermediary as was the case with Ammon and Moab. *Teman, Dedan.* Locations uncertain, though Teman was probably not located on a border. 25.14 *By the hand of my people* seems to stand in contrast to v. 13. On the demise of Edom, cf. 32.29. 25.15–17 Proclamation against Philistia. Cf. Jer 47, though there is less evidence for a Philistine nation as such in the early sixth century BCE than there is for the other three territories.

26.1–28.19 Pronouncements against Tyre and its rulers. Tyre was one city-state, in contrast to the larger geographic units addressed in ch. 25. Its maritime trade and geographic remove just off the Phoenician coast made it a particularly prominent city. After defeating Jerusalem, Nebuchadnezzar laid siege to Tyre for thirteen years, though without obtaining a decisive victory (cf. 29.18). Ezekiel probably devotes so much attention to Tyre (and Egypt) because they, unlike Judah, were able to resist the instrument of God's punishment, Nebuchadnezzar and the Neo-Babylonians. 26.1–21 Four distinct oracles, vv. 2–6, 7–14, 15–18, 19–21, the last three of which are introduced by the same formula. 26.1 *The eleventh year,* probably of King Jehoiachin (see note on 1.2), which was 587 BCE, the year in which Jerusalem fell (cf. 33.21). 26.2–6 Indictment and sentence. 26.2 Ezekiel quotes Tyre's apparent delight at the destruction of Jerusalem as an indictment. *Gateway,* in Hebrew "gateways." Whether singular or plural, the Tyrians refer to Judah as a com-

I shall be replenished,
   now that it is wasted,"
3 therefore, thus says the Lord GOD:
   See, I am against you, O Tyre!
   I will hurl many nations against you,
      as the sea hurls its waves.
4 They shall destroy the walls of Tyre
      and break down its towers.
   I will scrape its soil from it
      and make it a bare rock.
5 It shall become, in the midst of the sea,
      a place for spreading nets.
I have spoken, says the Lord GOD.
   It shall become plunder for the nations,
6   and its daughter-towns in the country
      shall be killed by the sword.
Then they shall know that I am the LORD.

7 For thus says the Lord GOD: I will bring against Tyre from the north King Nebuchadrezzar of Babylon, king of kings, together with horses, chariots, cavalry, and a great and powerful army.
8 Your daughter-towns in the country
      he shall put to the sword.
   He shall set up a siege wall against you,
      cast up a ramp against you,
      and raise a roof of shields against
         you.
9 He shall direct the shock of his battering
         rams against your walls
      and break down your towers with his
         axes.
10 His horses shall be so many
      that their dust shall cover you.
   At the noise of cavalry, wheels, and
         chariots
      your very walls shall shake,
   when he enters your gates
      like those entering a breached city.
11 With the hoofs of his horses
      he shall trample all your streets.
   He shall put your people to the sword,

and your strong pillars shall fall to the
      ground.
12 They will plunder your riches
      and loot your merchandise;
   they shall break down your walls
      and destroy your fine houses.
   Your stones and timber and soil
      they shall cast into the water.
13 I will silence the music of your songs;
      the sound of your lyres shall be heard
         no more.
14 I will make you a bare rock;
      you shall be a place for spreading nets.
   You shall never again be rebuilt,
      for I the LORD have spoken,
      says the Lord GOD.

15 Thus says the Lord GOD to Tyre: Shall not the coastlands shake at the sound of your fall, when the wounded groan, when slaughter goes on within you? 16 Then all the princes of the sea shall step down from their thrones; they shall remove their robes and strip off their embroidered garments. They shall clothe themselves with trembling, and shall sit on the ground; they shall tremble every moment, and be appalled at you. 17 And they shall raise a lamentation over you, and say to you:

   How you have vanished[a] from the seas,
      O city renowned,
   once mighty on the sea,
      you and your inhabitants,[b]
   who imposed your[c] terror
      on all the mainland![d]
18 Now the coastlands tremble
      on the day of your fall;
   the coastlands by the sea
      are dismayed at your passing.

19 For thus says the Lord GOD: When I make you a city laid waste, like cities that are

---

a Gk OL Aquila: Heb have vanished, O inhabited one,   b Heb it and its inhabitants   c Heb their   d Cn: Heb its inhabitants

---

mercial competitor, whose absence will enrich Tyre. **26.3** *Many nations.* Cf. the singular focus on Nebuchadnezzar in vv. 7–10. **26.5** *Spreading nets.* Cf. 47.10. **26.6** *Daughter-towns,* those cities (especially coastal ones) in Syro-Palestine over which Tyre exerted political and economic influence. **26.7–14** Destruction by Nebuchadnezzar. **26.7** *Nebuchadrezzar,* a more correct spelling of the Akkadian name, which may be translated "May Nabu preserve my offspring"; in the Bible more often "Nebuchadnezzar." *King of kings,* a royal title used throughout the ancient Near East as early as the second millennium BCE. **26.8** Unlike Nebuchad-

nezzar, Alexander the Great was able to build a *ramp* and *siege wall* to conquer Tyre. **26.13** Cf. Am 5.23. **26.14a** A repetition of imagery in the first oracle (vv. 4–5). **26.15–18** Lament described and intoned. **26.15** Cf. 27.26–36; 31.16. **26.16** *Princes of the sea,* either a mythological allusion or a reference to rulers of other coastal city-states who begin traditional lament practices. **26.17–18** Composed in the Hebrew *qinah,* or lament rhythm, this short poem emphasizes the prior and present position of Tyre vis-à-vis the *seas.* **26.19–21** God proclaims to Tyre its final fate. The destruction of Tyre is viewed as a direct act of God, who

not inhabited, when I bring up the deep over you, and the great waters cover you, 20then I will thrust you down with those who descend into the Pit, to the people of long ago, and I will make you live in the world below, among primeval ruins, with those who go down to the Pit, so that you will not be inhabited or have a place*a* in the land of the living. 21I will bring you to a dreadful end, and you shall be no more; though sought for, you will never be found again, says the Lord GOD.

Lamentation over Tyre

27 The word of the LORD came to me: 2Now you, mortal, raise a lamentation over Tyre, 3and say to Tyre, which sits at the entrance to the sea, merchant of the peoples on many coastlands, Thus says the Lord GOD:
O Tyre, you have said,
　"I am perfect in beauty."
4　Your borders are in the heart of the seas;
　　your builders made perfect your
　　　beauty.
5　They made all your planks
　　of fir trees from Senir;
　they took a cedar from Lebanon
　　to make a mast for you.
6　From oaks of Bashan
　　they made your oars;
　they made your deck of pines*b*
　　from the coasts of Cyprus,
　　inlaid with ivory.
7　Of fine embroidered linen from Egypt
　　was your sail,

　serving as your ensign;
　blue and purple from the coasts of Elishah
　　was your awning.
8　The inhabitants of Sidon and Arvad
　　were your rowers;
　skilled men of Zemer*c* were within you,
　　they were your pilots.
9　The elders of Gebal and its artisans were
　　　within you,
　　caulking your seams;
　all the ships of the sea with their mariners
　　　were within you,
　　to barter for your wares.
10　Paras*d* and Lud and Put
　　were in your army,
　　your mighty warriors;
　they hung shield and helmet in you;
　　they gave you splendor.
11　Men of Arvad and Helech*e*
　　were on your walls all around;
　　men of Gamad were at your towers.
　They hung their quivers all around your
　　　walls;
　　they made perfect your beauty.

12 Tarshish did business with you out of the abundance of your great wealth; silver, iron, tin, and lead they exchanged for your wares. 13Javan, Tubal, and Meshech traded with you; they exchanged human beings and vessels of bronze for your merchandise. 14Beth-togarmah exchanged for your wares horses, war

a Gk: Heb *I will give beauty*　*b* Or *boxwood*　*c* Cn Compare Gen 10.18: Heb *your skilled men, O Tyre*　*d* Or *Persia*
e Or *and your army*

---

manipulates the *great waters,* i.e., the primeval deep, against Tyre (cf. 31.4). **26.20** *The Pit,* the netherworld, abode of the dead; cf. 32.17–32; Pss 63.9; 139.15; Isa 44.23. Tyrians will live in the netherworld, thus allowing for a city *not inhabited. The world below.* Cf. Deut 32.22; Pss 86.13; 88.6; Lam 3.55. *Land of the living.* Cf. 32.23–27, 32.
　27.1–36 Lamentation over Tyre, which uses the limping Hebrew *qinah,* or lament rhythm, in vv. 3–9, 25–36. A prose description of economic transactions interrupts the poem, which uses the primary metaphor of a large sailing ship. Ezekiel uses metaphors in other laments; see 19.1; 28.12; 32.3. **27.3** *Entrance to the sea,* i.e., a description from the perspective of those who live on land, which is consistent with a description of Tyre as a *merchant of the peoples.* Tyre's self-description of perfection has a negative connotation that stands in contrast with vv. 4–9. **27.4–9** The ship described. **27.4** *Your borders,* the shape of the hull below the surface of the sea. *Beauty.* Cf. 28.12, 17. **27.5–6** Ezekiel stresses the variety of woods used for this masted galley. Such variety comes from diverse locales: Senir—

the Anti-Lebanon, Lebanon, Bashan—east of the sea of Galilee in southern Syria, and Cyprus. *Inlaid with ivory.* The Hebrew is problematic. **27.7** Textiles on board—sails, ensigns, awnings—also come from abroad. *Elishah,* another name for Cyprus. The trade attested to in vv. 5–9 underlines Tyre as *merchant of the peoples* (v. 3). **27.8** The crew came from *Zemer* (Hebrew *Tyre*), *Arvad,* and *Sidon,* Phoenician coastal cities north of Tyre (moving south to north). **27.8–9** Portions of these verses are problematic. **27.10–11** Land-based military mercenaries and their armaments. *Paras,* Persia. *Lud,* Lydia. *Put,* Libya. *Arvad,* Phoenicia. *Helech,* in Hebrew lit. "your army," and *Gamad* are difficult. **27.12–25a** This prose section provides a virtual catalog of ancient Near Eastern international commerce, which begins and ends with Tarshish (vv. 12, 25a), a port (Tartessos) located in southern Spain and important for metal ore. Apart from this literary envelope, the toponyms move generally from the western Mediterranean to the eastern Mesopotamian environs, e.g., from western places like *Javan* (v. 13, Ionia), *Tubal,* and *Meshech* (v. 13, Asia Minor), *Beth-togarmah* (v. 14,

horses, and mules. 15The Rhodians*a* traded with you; many coastlands were your own special markets; they brought you in payment ivory tusks and ebony. 16Edom*b* did business with you because of your abundant goods; they exchanged for your wares turquoise, purple, embroidered work, fine linen, coral, and rubies. 17Judah and the land of Israel traded with you; they exchanged for your merchandise wheat from Minnith, millet,*c* honey, oil, and balm. 18Damascus traded with you for your abundant goods—because of your great wealth of every kind—wine of Helbon, and white wool. 19Vedan and Javan from Uzal*c* entered into trade for your wares; wrought iron, cassia, and sweet cane were bartered for your merchandise. 20Dedan traded with you in saddlecloths for riding. 21Arabia and all the princes of Kedar were your favored dealers in lambs, rams, and goats; in these they did business with you. 22The merchants of Sheba and Raamah traded with you; they exchanged for your wares the best of all kinds of spices, and all precious stones, and gold. 23Haran, Canneh, Eden, the merchants of Sheba, Asshur, and Chilmad traded with you. 24These traded with you in choice garments, in clothes of blue and embroidered work, and in carpets of colored material, bound with cords and made secure; in these they traded with you.*d* 25The ships of Tarshish traveled for you in your trade.

So you were filled and heavily laden
   in the heart of the seas.
26 Your rowers have brought you
      into the high seas.
   The east wind has wrecked you
      in the heart of the seas.
27 Your riches, your wares, your
         merchandise,
      your mariners and your pilots,
   your caulkers, your dealers in
         merchandise,

and all your warriors within you,
   with all the company
      that is with you,
   sink into the heart of the seas
      on the day of your ruin.
28 At the sound of the cry of your pilots
      the countryside shakes,
29 and down from their ships
      come all that handle the oar.
   The mariners and all the pilots of the sea
      stand on the shore
30 and wail aloud over you,
      and cry bitterly.
   They throw dust on their heads
      and wallow in ashes;
31 they make themselves bald for you,
      and put on sackcloth,
   and they weep over you in bitterness of
         soul,
      with bitter mourning.
32 In their wailing they raise a lamentation
         for you,
      and lament over you:
   "Who was ever destroyed*e* like Tyre
      in the midst of the sea?
33 When your wares came from the seas,
      you satisfied many peoples;
   with your abundant wealth and
         merchandise
      you enriched the kings of the earth.
34 Now you are wrecked by the seas,
      in the depths of the waters;
   your merchandise and all your crew
      have sunk with you.
35 All the inhabitants of the coastlands
      are appalled at you;
   and their kings are horribly afraid,
      their faces are convulsed.

---

a Gk: Heb *The Dedanites*   *b* Another reading is *Aram*
c Meaning of Heb uncertain   *d* Cn: Heb *in your market*
e Tg Vg: Heb *like silence*

---

in Armenia), and Rhodes (v. 15, in the Aegean Sea) to eastern ones like *Sheba* (v. 23, the southern Arabian Peninsula), *Asshur* (v. 23, northern Mesopotamia), and *Chilmad* (v. 23, a reference to Media). *You* and *your* emphasize the central role of Tyre as an intermediary in these trade routes. **27.17** *Judah* and *Israel* provided agricultural goods. *Minnith,* if a place-name, lies outside Israelite territory (Judg 11.33). *Wheat, oil,* and *honey* are part of the standard inventory for the promised land; see, e.g., Deut 8.8. Hebrew *pannag,* translated *millet,* is uncertain; it may refer to a fig. *Balm,* resin from a tree; see Gen 37.25; 43.11; Jer 8.22; 46.11; 51.8.

27.25b–36 The poem resumes, in virtual narrative form. **27.25b–27** The ship founders; the entire cargo and crew are lost. **27.26** *The east wind,* a destructive agent attested elsewhere (Ps 48.7). Cf. Ezek 19.12; Jer 18.17. **27.28–36** The lament. Cf. 26.17–18. Poignantly, other mariners mourn the fate of those drowned. **27.32b** The Hebrew is difficult. Alternately, "Who like Tyre like such silence" or, preferably, "Who may be compared to Tyre?" **27.33–35** The prominence of royalty (*kings*) in such international trade as well as the role of the *seas* in the destruction of the ship is emphasized.

36 The merchants among the peoples hiss at
     you;
   you have come to a dreadful end
   and shall be no more forever."

Proclamation against the King of Tyre

28 The word of the LORD came to me:
     2 Mortal, say to the prince of Tyre, Thus
says the Lord GOD:
   Because your heart is proud
     and you have said, "I am a god;
   I sit in the seat of the gods,
     in the heart of the seas,"
   yet you are but a mortal, and no god,
     though you compare your mind
     with the mind of a god.
3 You are indeed wiser than Daniel;[a]
     no secret is hidden from you;
4 by your wisdom and your understanding
     you have amassed wealth for yourself,
   and have gathered gold and silver
     into your treasuries.
5 By your great wisdom in trade
     you have increased your wealth,
   and your heart has become proud in
     your wealth.
6 Therefore thus says the Lord GOD:
   Because you compare your mind
     with the mind of a god,
7 therefore, I will bring strangers against
     you,
     the most terrible of the nations;
   they shall draw their swords against the
     beauty of your wisdom
   and defile your splendor.
8 They shall thrust you down to the Pit,

and you shall die a violent death
   in the heart of the seas.
9 Will you still say, "I am a god,"
     in the presence of those who kill you,
   though you are but a mortal, and no god,
     in the hands of those who wound you?
10 You shall die the death of the
     uncircumcised
   by the hand of foreigners;
     for I have spoken, says the Lord GOD.

Lamentation over the King of Tyre

11 Moreover the word of the LORD came to
me: 12 Mortal, raise a lamentation over the
king of Tyre, and say to him, Thus says the
Lord GOD:
   You were the signet of perfection,[b]
     full of wisdom and perfect in beauty.
13 You were in Eden, the garden of God;
     every precious stone was your
       covering,
   carnelian, chrysolite, and moonstone,
     beryl, onyx, and jasper,
   sapphire,[c] turquoise, and emerald;
     and worked in gold were your settings
     and your engravings.[b]
   On the day that you were created
     they were prepared.
14 With an anointed cherub as guardian I
     placed you;[b]
     you were on the holy mountain of
       God;
   you walked among the stones of fire.

---

a Or, as otherwise read, *Danel*   *b* Meaning of Heb uncertain
c Or *lapis lazuli*

28.1–10 Proclamation of indictment (vv. 2–6) and
sentence (vv. 7–10) against the king of Tyre. The fate
of the city is personified through the figure of its
prince or ruler. **28.2** *Your heart is proud*, elsewhere explicitly an affront to God (Prov 16.5). *The seat of the
gods*, related to Tyre's island setting. El, head of the
Canaanite pantheon, is described in Canaanite epic
texts as dwelling "at the springs of two rivers, amid the
channels of the double watery deep." On such self-deification, cf. Isa 14.13–14. The deity's response echoes
language in Isa 31.3 and introduces the motif of wisdom. **28.3** On *Daniel*, see note on 14.12–20. The legendary king Danel was not only righteous but also
wise, a typical attribute of kings (see 1 Kings 3; Isa
11.2). Ezekiel, however, admits that the prince was
even wiser than Danel. **28.4–5** The working out of
such wisdom results in vast *wealth* (cf. 1 Kings 10.14–
22), which itself has engendered pride. **28.6** A recapitulation of the theme of self-deification (introduced in

v. 2) and the conclusion of the indictment. **28.7** Cf.
26.7–12, which suggests that the *strangers* are the Neo-
Babylonians. **28.8** *The Pit*. See note on 26.20; cf.
32.17–32. **28.10** *The death of the uncircumcised*, i.e.,
the fate of non-Israelites, particularly Mesopotamians,
who did not practice the rite of circumcision, on
which see 32.17–32. **28.11–19** Lamentation over the
king of Tyre. The text is obscure at numerous points,
though it seems clear that Ezekiel attests a variant
form of the Eden story focusing on the expulsion of
the king from the primal garden. **28.12** *Signet*, as in a
royal signet ring. The initial perfection involves wisdom, beauty, and adornment. **28.13** *Eden*, here as in
Gen 2.8, 10, is a place; cf. Gen 2.15. On the precious
stones and metals, cf. Gen 2.11–12 and the description
of the ephod, Ex 28.17–20. **28.14** The *cherub* functions
here as a guardian of, not against, the human; cf. 10.2;
esp. Gen 3.24. *The holy mountain of God*, the divine
dwelling place, upon which in this tradition the divine

15 You were blameless in your ways
 from the day that you were created,
 until iniquity was found in you.
16 In the abundance of your trade
 you were filled with violence, and you
 sinned;
 so I cast you as a profane thing from the
 mountain of God,
 and the guardian cherub drove you out
 from among the stones of fire.
17 Your heart was proud because of your
 beauty;
 you corrupted your wisdom for the
 sake of your splendor.
 I cast you to the ground;
 I exposed you before kings,
 to feast their eyes on you.
18 By the multitude of your iniquities,
 in the unrighteousness of your trade,
 you profaned your sanctuaries.
 So I brought out fire from within you;
 it consumed you,
 and I turned you to ashes on the earth
 in the sight of all who saw you.
19 All who know you among the peoples
 are appalled at you;
 you have come to a dreadful end
 and shall be no more forever.

Proclamation against Sidon

20 The word of the LORD came to me: 21 Mortal, set your face toward Sidon, and prophesy against it, 22 and say, Thus says the Lord GOD:
 I am against you, O Sidon,
 and I will gain glory in your midst.
 They shall know that I am the LORD

when I execute judgments in it,
 and manifest my holiness in it;
23 for I will send pestilence into it,
 and bloodshed into its streets;
 and the dead shall fall in its midst,
 by the sword that is against it on every
 side.
 And they shall know that I am the LORD.

24 The house of Israel shall no longer find a pricking brier or a piercing thorn among all their neighbors who have treated them with contempt. And they shall know that I am the Lord GOD.

Future Blessing for Israel

25 Thus says the Lord GOD: When I gather the house of Israel from the peoples among whom they are scattered, and manifest my holiness in them in the sight of the nations, then they shall settle on their own soil that I gave to my servant Jacob. 26 They shall live in safety in it, and shall build houses and plant vineyards. They shall live in safety, when I execute judgments upon all their neighbors who have treated them with contempt. And they shall know that I am the LORD their God.

Proclamation against Egypt

29 In the tenth year, in the tenth month, on the twelfth day of the month, the word of the LORD came to me: 2 Mortal, set your face against Pharaoh king of Egypt, and prophesy against him and against all Egypt; 3 speak, and say, Thus says the Lord GOD:
 I am against you,
 Pharaoh king of Egypt,

garden was located; cf. Isa 14.13; Ps 48.13. *Stones of fire,* possibly the aforementioned gems (v. 13). **28.15–19** The imagery of expulsion focuses on removal from the mountain. **28.18** Instead of *iniquity* (v. 15) the poet now offers specific indictments: improper trade practices, defilement of sanctuaries. Punishment is multiple: being cast down, exposure, fire. **28.20–23** Pronouncement against Sidon, another Phoenician port, twenty-five miles north of Tyre. The two cities often occur as a formulaic pair, e.g., in Joel 3.4; Zech 9.2. The language is typical of other Ezekiel texts: *I am against you* (5.8), *gain glory* (39.13), *execute judgments* (5.10), *pestilence* (5.12). No specific reason is offered for the punishment of Sidon.
 28.24–26 Conclusion to chs. 25–28. **28.24** The aforementioned Syro-Palestinian states are likened to *briers* and *thorns,* imagery used elsewhere to describe the pre-Israelite population of the land (Num 33.55; Josh 23.13) and as instruments of torture (Judg 8.7).

28.25–26 Oracle of return and renewal. God promises to bring back those who lived in exile, a theme elsewhere important to Ezekiel (11.17; 20.41; 34.13; 39.27). On *living in safety,* see chs. 34, 36. The imagery of restoration is primarily rural and agricultural; cf. Isa 65.21 on the motif of building houses and planting vineyards.
 29.1–32.32 Seven pronouncements against Egypt and its rulers. As with his contemporary Jeremiah, Ezekiel addresses Egypt more than any other foreign state. Like Tyre, Egypt had remained outside the sway of God's punitive force, the Neo-Babylonians; hence they, along with Israel, deserved judgment. All the pronouncements except 30.1–19 are prefaced by a date formula, which refers to Jehoiachin's regnal years. **29.1** *Tenth year ... month,* January 7, 587 BCE (see note on 1.2). This date precedes that in 26.1. **29.2** *Pharaoh king of Egypt,* Hophra (589–570 BCE). **29.3–7** A poem in which Pharaoh is likened to a *great dragon,* probably

the great dragon sprawling
  in the midst of its channels,
saying, "My Nile is my own;
  I made it for myself."
4 I will put hooks in your jaws,
    and make the fish of your channels
      stick to your scales.
  I will draw you up from your channels,
    with all the fish of your channels
      sticking to your scales.
5 I will fling you into the wilderness,
    you and all the fish of your channels;
  you shall fall in the open field,
    and not be gathered and buried.
  To the animals of the earth and to the
      birds of the air
    I have given you as food.
6 Then all the inhabitants of Egypt shall
      know
    that I am the LORD
  because you*a* were a staff of reed
    to the house of Israel;
7 when they grasped you with the hand,
      you broke,
    and tore all their shoulders;
  and when they leaned on you, you broke,
    and made all their legs unsteady.*b*

8 Therefore, thus says the Lord GOD: I will bring a sword upon you, and will cut off from you human being and animal; 9and the land of Egypt shall be a desolation and a waste. Then they shall know that I am the LORD.

Because you*c* said, "The Nile is mine, and I made it," 10therefore, I am against you, and against your channels, and I will make the land of Egypt an utter waste and desolation, from Migdol to Syene, as far as the border of Ethiopia.*d* 11No human foot shall pass

through it, and no animal foot shall pass through it; it shall be uninhabited forty years. 12I will make the land of Egypt a desolation among desolated countries; and her cities shall be a desolation forty years among cities that are laid waste. I will scatter the Egyptians among the nations, and disperse them among the countries.

13 Further, thus says the Lord GOD: At the end of forty years I will gather the Egyptians from the peoples among whom they were scattered; 14and I will restore the fortunes of Egypt, and bring them back to the land of Pathros, the land of their origin; and there they shall be a lowly kingdom. 15It shall be the most lowly of the kingdoms, and never again exalt itself above the nations; and I will make them so small that they will never again rule over the nations. 16The Egyptians*e* shall never again be the reliance of the house of Israel; they will recall their iniquity, when they turned to them for aid. Then they shall know that I am the Lord GOD.

Babylonia Will Plunder Egypt

17 In the twenty-seventh year, in the first month, on the first day of the month, the word of the LORD came to me: 18Mortal, King Nebuchadrezzar of Babylon made his army labor hard against Tyre; every head was made bald and every shoulder was rubbed bare; yet neither he nor his army got anything from Tyre to pay for the labor that he had expended against it. 19Therefore thus says the Lord GOD: I will give the land of Egypt to King Nebuchadrez-

---

a Gk Syr Vg: Heb *they*   *b* Syr: Heb *stand*   *c* Gk Syr Vg: Heb *he*
d Or *Nubia*; Heb *Cush*   *e* Heb *It*

---

an allusion to a Nile crocodile. Because of boasting, Pharaoh will be captured and along with others—the *fish of your channels* (the various channels of the Nile)—will be destroyed. **29.5** *Not . . . buried,* a violation of standard pharaonic funerary practice. **29.6** *A staff of reed,* a new image, that of the bulrush (cf. Isa 36.6), to depict the pharaoh. **29.7** *When they grasped you,* a reference to Judah's unsuccessful alliance with Egypt against the Babylonians (cf. Jer 37). **29.8–9a** Language of judgment typical of Ezekiel (cf. 14.13; 25.13). **29.9b–16** Pharaoh's boast (v. 3) is repeated, thereby allowing another statement of judgment that highlights the extent of destruction. *Migdol,* probably in the Nile Delta region. though the site is unknown; *Syene,* just north of the first cataract on the Nile; *from Migdol to Syene* is therefore a portion of the land signifying its entirety (cf. Hebrew, "from Dan to Beer-

sheba," e.g., Judg 20.1). *Ethiopia* (Hebrew, "Cush"), another reference to the southern border. **29.11** *Forty years,* a traditional number of years for national exile; cf. 4.6; Num 14.33. **29.13–16** Just as with Israel (11.17; 20.34; 28.25), God will return Egypt to its land. **29.14** *Pathros,* a reference to Upper or southern Egypt. Egypt will be limited, as *a lowly kingdom,* to a smaller territory than it possessed under Hophra. Though a nation, Egypt will no longer be an empire; cf. Jer 46.26. **29.17–21** The second pronouncement is prefaced by the latest date in the book, later than the pronouncements that follow it, April 26, 571 BCE (v. 17; see note on 1.2). **29.18** Ezekiel refers to Nebuchadnezzar's thirteen-year siege against Tyre, which ended ca. 573 BCE. This verse makes it clear that Nebuchadnezzar did not despoil Tyre (cf. 26.7–14). **29.19–20** Since Nebuchadnezzar had *worked for* God and without sufficient re-

zar of Babylon; and he shall carry off its wealth and despoil it and plunder it; and it shall be the wages for his army. 20I have given him the land of Egypt as his payment for which he labored, because they worked for me, says the Lord God.

21 On that day I will cause a horn to sprout up for the house of Israel, and I will open your lips among them. Then they shall know that I am the Lord.

Lamentation for Egypt

30 The word of the Lord came to me: 2Mortal, prophesy, and say, Thus says the Lord God:
Wail, "Alas for the day!"
3   For a day is near,
        the day of the Lord is near;
    it will be a day of clouds,
        a time of doom*a* for the nations.
4   A sword shall come upon Egypt,
        and anguish shall be in Ethiopia,*b*
    when the slain fall in Egypt,
        and its wealth is carried away,
        and its foundations are torn down.
5Ethiopia,*b* and Put, and Lud, and all Arabia, and Libya,*c* and the people of the allied land*d* shall fall with them by the sword.

6   Thus says the Lord:
    Those who support Egypt shall fall,
        and its proud might shall come down;
    from Migdol to Syene
        they shall fall within it by the sword,
    says the Lord God.

7   They shall be desolated among other
        desolated countries,
    and their cities shall lie among cities
        laid waste.
8   Then they shall know that I am the Lord,
        when I have set fire to Egypt,
        and all who help it are broken.
9 On that day, messengers shall go out from me in ships to terrify the unsuspecting Ethiopians;*e* and anguish shall come upon them on the day of Egypt's doom;*f* for it is coming!

10 Thus says the Lord God:
    I will put an end to the hordes of Egypt,
        by the hand of King Nebuchadrezzar of
            Babylon.
11 He and his people with him, the most
        terrible of the nations,
        shall be brought in to destroy the land;
    and they shall draw their swords against
            Egypt,
        and fill the land with the slain.
12 I will dry up the channels,
        and will sell the land into the hand of
            evildoers;
    I will bring desolation upon the land and
            everything in it
        by the hand of foreigners;
    I the Lord have spoken.

13 Thus says the Lord God:
    I will destroy the idols

---

a Heb lacks *of doom* *b* Or *Nubia*; Heb *Cush* *c* Compare Gk Syr Vg: Heb *Cub* *d* Meaning of Heb uncertain *e* Or *Nubians*; Heb *Cush* *f* Heb *the day of Egypt*

---

ward, he will be permitted to attack Egypt instead. Such an attack was launched in 568 BCE, again without conclusive results. **29.21** *A horn.* Cf. Ps 132.17, which suggests that the promise involves restoration of Davidic kingship. *Open your lips,* a reference to exercise of the prophetic role; cf. 16.63.

30.1–19 The third, and undated, pronouncement, which is itself made up of several distinct utterances (vv. 2–9, 10–12, 13–19). **30.2–9** By commencing with *Wail,* a plural imperative, the prophet admonishes his audience to begin lamenting the destruction of Egypt. **30.3** *The day of the Lord.* Cf. other prophetic texts in which God's day is one of doom and destruction (Am 5.18; Zeph 1.14–18). *A day of clouds,* one in which the darkness of God's day is envisioned (Joel 2.2; Zeph 1.15). **30.4** *Ethiopia,* here understood to be part of Egypt, as in Isa 20.3, 5. **30.5** With the exception of *all Arabia* and *the people of the allied land,* the other four names rhyme in Hebrew. On *Put, Lud,* see note on 27.10–11. *Them,* i.e., the Egyptians. The destruction

will be so vast that it affects peoples far and near. **30.6** The key word *fall* (vv. 4, 5) is repeated, but now it is Egypt's allies who will fall, perhaps those identified in v. 5. **30.9** As with v. 5, this prose verse appears intrusive; and both verses emphasize that nations other than Egypt will be affected on this terrible day. The Hebrew does not include *doom.* Cf. Isa 18.2, which also refers to divine emissaries arriving via ship. **30.10–12** Again (29.18–20), Ezekiel identifies *Nebuchadrezzar* (see note on 26.7) as the one designated by God, i.e., Nebuchadnezzar is to *be brought in* to destroy Egypt; cf. 26.7–14. **30.12** *I,* God, the ultimate author of Egypt's destruction. The drying up of the Nile and sale of Egyptian land are new motifs. **30.13–19** Ezekiel cites various place-names to make God's judgment geographically specific. The forms of destruction remain general. Moreover, there is no apparent order to the listings. Many of the cities were associated with specific gods, e.g., On (v. 17) with Re-Atum, Pi-beseth (v. 17) with Bastis. Apart from v. 13, there are no overt re-

and put an end to the images in
Memphis;
there shall no longer be a prince in the
land of Egypt;
so I will put fear in the land of Egypt.
14 I will make Pathros a desolation,
and will set fire to Zoan,
and will execute acts of judgment on
Thebes.
15 I will pour my wrath upon Pelusium,
the stronghold of Egypt,
and cut off the hordes of Thebes.
16 I will set fire to Egypt;
Pelusium shall be in great agony;
Thebes shall be breached,
and Memphis face adversaries by day.
17 The young men of On and of Pi-beseth
shall fall by the sword;
and the cities themselves[a] shall go into
captivity.
18 At Tehaphnehes the day shall be dark,
when I break there the dominion of
Egypt,
and its proud might shall come to an end;
the city[b] shall be covered by a cloud,
and its daughter-towns shall go into
captivity.
19 Thus I will execute acts of judgment on
Egypt.
Then they shall know that I am the
LORD.

Proclamation against Pharaoh

20 In the eleventh year, in the first month, on
the seventh day of the month, the word of the
LORD came to me: 21Mortal, I have broken the
arm of Pharaoh king of Egypt; it has not been
bound up for healing or wrapped with a bandage, so that it may become strong to wield
the sword. 22Therefore thus says the Lord
GOD: I am against Pharaoh king of Egypt, and
will break his arms, both the strong arm and
the one that was broken; and I will make the
sword fall from his hand. 23I will scatter the
Egyptians among the nations, and disperse
them throughout the lands. 24I will strengthen
the arms of the king of Babylon, and put my
sword in his hand; but I will break the arms of
Pharaoh, and he will groan before him with
the groans of one mortally wounded. 25I will
strengthen the arms of the king of Babylon,
but the arms of Pharaoh shall fall. And they
shall know that I am the LORD, when I put my
sword into the hand of the king of Babylon.
He shall stretch it out against the land of
Egypt, 26and I will scatter the Egyptians
among the nations and disperse them
throughout the countries. Then they shall
know that I am the LORD.

The Lofty Cedar

31 In the eleventh year, in the third
month, on the first day of the month,
the word of the LORD came to me: 2Mortal, say
to Pharaoh king of Egypt and to his hordes:
Whom are you like in your greatness?
3   Consider Assyria, a cedar of Lebanon,
with fair branches and forest shade,

_a_ Heb and they   _b_ Heb she

---

ligious polemics. **30.13** _Memphis,_ about fifteen miles
south of Cairo, the early capital and largest city in
Egypt during most of its history. Both religious images
(though the words for _idols_ and _images_ are uncertain
and may refer to humans) and leaders (a _prince_) will
be destroyed. **30.14** _Pathros,_ or "land of Pathros" (so
reads the Greek manuscript tradition); see note on
29.14. _Zoan,_ a city (probably Avaris, Greek Tanis) in
the eastern Nile Delta. _Thebes,_ the capital of Egypt
during much of its history, located in Middle Egypt.
30.15 _Pelusium,_ near Zoan in the northeast Delta.
30.17 _On,_ Heliopolis, only six miles northeast of
Cairo. _Pi-beseth,_ Bubastis, in the eastern Delta.
30.18 _Tehaphnehes,_ near the northern shore of the
Suez Gulf. **30.20–26** The fourth pronouncement. The
date in v. 20 is April 29, 587 BCE (see note on 1.2).
30.21 The bodily imagery probably refers to a military
defeat of Hophra by Nebuchadnezzar, when the pharaoh came to Judah's aid during the siege of Jerusalem
by the Babylonians (Jer 37.5). The defeat probably occurred in 588 BCE. **30.23–24** The historical allusion
sets the stage for an announcement that both Hophra's
arms will be broken, an act that symbolizes total defeat
for Egypt (_mortally wounded_). In other "arm" imagery,
God will strengthen Nebuchadnezzar's arms. **30.26** Cf.
29.12.
    31.1–18 The fifth pronouncement. The date in v. 1
is June 21, 587 BCE (see note on 1.2). This pronouncement utilizes the imagery of a cedar from Lebanon in a
poem (vv. 2b–9), and two interpretations (vv. 10–14,
15–18). As with the first pronouncement, the fifth is
directed to Pharaoh (vv. 2, 18), though apart from
these verses there is no explicit reference to Egypt.
31.2 Cf. the analogous question in v. 18. **31.3** _Consider
Assyria._ Cf. "Behold I will liken you" (RSV). However,
the word translated _Assyria_ may result from a scribal
error in a word meaning "cypress." The tree is greater
than life; some have termed it a cosmic or world tree,
with its top in the clouds (cf. Gen 11.4) and its roots in
the primeval deep. Cf. 17.23; Dan 4; Mk 4.32; and the

and of great height,
   its top among the clouds.[a]
4 The waters nourished it,
   the deep made it grow tall,
making its rivers flow[b]
   around the place it was planted,
sending forth its streams
   to all the trees of the field.
5 So it towered high
   above all the trees of the field;
its boughs grew large
   and its branches long,
from abundant water in its shoots.
6 All the birds of the air
   made their nests in its boughs;
under its branches all the animals of the
      field
   gave birth to their young;
and in its shade
   all great nations lived.
7 It was beautiful in its greatness,
   in the length of its branches;
for its roots went down
   to abundant water.
8 The cedars in the garden of God could
      not rival it,
   nor the fir trees equal its boughs;
the plane trees were as nothing
   compared with its branches;
no tree in the garden of God
   was like it in beauty.
9 I made it beautiful
   with its mass of branches,
the envy of all the trees of Eden
   that were in the garden of God.

10 Therefore thus says the Lord GOD: Because it[c] towered high and set its top among

the clouds,[a] and its heart was proud of its height, 11I gave it into the hand of the prince of the nations; he has dealt with it as its wickedness deserves. I have cast it out. 12Foreigners from the most terrible of the nations have cut it down and left it. On the mountains and in all the valleys its branches have fallen, and its boughs lie broken in all the watercourses of the land; and all the peoples of the earth went away from its shade and left it.
13   On its fallen trunk settle
      all the birds of the air,
   and among its boughs lodge
      all the wild animals.
14All this is in order that no trees by the waters may grow to lofty height or set their tops among the clouds,[a] and that no trees that drink water may reach up to them in height.

For all of them are handed over to death,
   to the world below;
along with all mortals,
   with those who go down to the Pit.

15 Thus says the Lord GOD: On the day it went down to Sheol I closed the deep over it and covered it; I restrained its rivers, and its mighty waters were checked. I clothed Lebanon in gloom for it, and all the trees of the field fainted because of it. 16I made the nations quake at the sound of its fall, when I cast it down to Sheol with those who go down to the Pit; and all the trees of Eden, the choice and best of Lebanon, all that were well watered, were consoled in the world below. 17They also went down to Sheol with it, to

a Gk: Heb thick boughs   b Gk: Heb rivers going   c Syr Vg: Heb you

---

tree of life, Gen 2–3. **31.4** The deep. See Gen 1.2; 7.11; 8.2; 49.25; Deut 33.13; Isa 51.9–11. The tree is so important that the poet may speak of its rivers. **31.5** Towered and branches present Aramaic spellings. **31.6** All the birds, all the animals, all great nations. The poet uses hyperbole to reinforce the cosmic scale of this tree. It provides protection for birthing and living; cf. 17.23. **31.7** Beautiful in its greatness. Cf. Gen 3.6 for a tree that was "a delight to the eyes." **31.8–9** A new tone of rivalry and envy between the great tree and the cedars in the garden of God. This element suggests the great tree was not located in the Garden; see v. 18. Moreover, 17.23 speaks of a tree being planted on the mountain of God. Plane trees, perhaps a form of pine; cf. Isa 41.19. **31.9** God is the explicit creator of this tree. **31.10–14** Indictment and sentence passed. **31.10** The tree ("you" in the Hebrew, though other manuscript traditions read it) took inappropriate

pride in its stature. Cf. 28.17 for similar language applied to the king of Tyre. **31.11** The prince of the nations, lit. "a ram," which probably refers to Nebuchadnezzar. **31.12** Foreigners, the Neo-Babylonians, cut down the tree, leaving both timber and detritus. **31.13** Ironically, the tree still appears to provide shelter for birds and animals, though people have left (v. 12). All taint of civilization has disappeared. **31.14** An almost sermonic conclusion for the benefit of other "trees." **31.14b** Related to vv. 15–18. **31.15–18** Fate in the underworld; cf. 26.19–21; 28.8; 32.17–32. **31.15–16** I closed the deep over it and covered it. Cf. "I will make the deep mourn for it" (the Greek manuscript tradition and the RSV). The tree, as would a person, descends into Sheol, the netherworld (see also 32.21, 27), which could be viewed as a watery abyss. God controls the watery powers (cf. Gen 8.2). Whereas the trees of the field fainted, the trees of Eden apparently are also in

those killed by the sword, along with its allies,[a] those who lived in its shade among the nations.

18 Which among the trees of Eden was like you in glory and in greatness? Now you shall be brought down with the trees of Eden to the world below; you shall lie among the uncircumcised, with those who are killed by the sword. This is Pharaoh and all his horde, says the Lord GOD.

Lamentation over Pharaoh and Egypt

32 In the twelfth year, in the twelfth month, on the first day of the month, the word of the LORD came to me: 2Mortal, raise a lamentation over Pharaoh king of Egypt, and say to him:

You consider yourself a lion among the
        nations,
    but you are like a dragon in the seas;
you thrash about in your streams,
    trouble the water with your feet,
    and foul your[b] streams.
3   Thus says the Lord GOD:
    In an assembly of many peoples
    I will throw my net over you;
    and I[c] will haul you up in my dragnet.
4   I will throw you on the ground,
        on the open field I will fling you,
    and will cause all the birds of the air to
        settle on you,
    and I will let the wild animals of the
        whole earth gorge themselves
        with you.
5   I will strew your flesh on the mountains,
        and fill the valleys with your carcass.[d]
6   I will drench the land with your flowing
        blood
        up to the mountains,

and the watercourses will be filled with
    you.
7   When I blot you out, I will cover the
        heavens,
    and make their stars dark;
I will cover the sun with a cloud,
    and the moon shall not give its light.
8   All the shining lights of the heavens
        I will darken above you,
    and put darkness on your land,
                    says the Lord GOD.
9   I will trouble the hearts of many peoples,
        as I carry you captive[e] among the
            nations,
    into countries you have not known.
10 I will make many peoples appalled at you;
        their kings shall shudder because of
            you.
    When I brandish my sword before them,
        they shall tremble every moment
    for their lives, each one of them,
        on the day of your downfall.
11 For thus says the Lord GOD:
    The sword of the king of Babylon shall
        come against you.
12 I will cause your hordes to fall
        by the swords of mighty ones,
    all of them most terrible among the
        nations.
    They shall bring to ruin the pride of
        Egypt,
        and all its hordes shall perish.
13 I will destroy all its livestock
        from beside abundant waters;
    and no human foot shall trouble them
        any more,

---

a Heb its arms   b Heb their   c Gk Vg: Heb they
d Symmachus Syr Vg: Heb your height   e Gk: Heb bring your
destruction

Sheol and are comforted, since they share the same fate as that of the great tree. **31.17** Hebrew text is problematic here. **31.18** The question now asks the pharaoh for a comparison with *the trees of Eden;* cf. 28.10 on the motif of the *uncircumcised.*

32.1–16 The sixth pronouncement, March 3, 586 BCE (see note on 1.2). Vv. 2, 16 suggest that these verses are one lament; cf. ch. 19. Yet only v. 2 contains the language and form of lament. Other sections (vv. 3–8, 9–10, 11–14, 15) are oracular utterances. **32.2** Ezekiel addresses Pharaoh directly and likens him to a sea dragon (not the crocodile as in 29.3) instead of the self-proffered and typical royal heraldic symbol, the lion. The parallel nouns *seas* and *streams* connote mythic waters; cf. 31.4. The lament functions to indict the pharaoh for contaminating all waters. **32.3–**

8 Judgment on the dragon. **32.3** *My net* may allude to the archetypal combat, attested in the Babylonian *Enuma Elish,* when Marduk netted and then killed Tiamat, the sea dragon. **32.4–6** A vivid depiction of the fate of the dragon's carcass; cf. 29.5. The immense scale—*animals of the whole earth, fill the valleys*—demonstrate the mythic proportions of the dragon that has been slain; cf. Isa 51.9. **32.7–8** The motif of darkness suggests that this is the "day of the LORD" (cf. 30.3; Joel 2.1–2; 3.15; Zeph 1.15), though v. 8 here recalls the plague of darkness (Ex 10.21–29). **32.9–10** Pharaoh (or Egypt), now as *captive,* will be paraded among various nations, perhaps a reference to exile; cf. 29.12–13. **32.11** *The king of Babylon,* Nebuchadnezzar; cf. 29.19. **32.12** *Mighty ones,* or "warriors"; cf. 32.21, 27. **32.13–14** On the motif of turbid versus

nor shall the hoofs of cattle trouble
        them.
14 Then I will make their waters clear,
        and cause their streams to run like oil,
            says the Lord GOD.
15 When I make the land of Egypt desolate
        and when the land is stripped of all
            that fills it,
        when I strike down all who live in it,
            then they shall know that I am the LORD.
16 This is a lamentation; it shall be chanted.
        The women of the nations shall chant it.
    Over Egypt and all its hordes they shall
            chant it,
        says the Lord GOD.

Dirge over Egypt

17 In the twelfth year, in the first month,[a] on
the fifteenth day of the month, the word of the
LORD came to me:
18 Mortal, wail over the hordes of Egypt,
        and send them down,
    with Egypt[b] and the daughters of
            majestic nations,
        to the world below,
        with those who go down to the Pit.
19 "Whom do you surpass in beauty?
        Go down! Be laid to rest with the
            uncircumcised!"
20They shall fall among those who are killed
by the sword. Egypt[b] has been handed over to
the sword; carry away both it and its hordes.
21The mighty chiefs shall speak of them, with
their helpers, out of the midst of Sheol: "They
have come down, they lie still, the uncircumcised, killed by the sword."

22 Assyria is there, and all its company,
their graves all around it, all of them killed,
fallen by the sword. 23Their graves are set in
the uttermost parts of the Pit. Its company is
all around its grave, all of them killed, fallen by
the sword, who spread terror in the land of the
living.

24 Elam is there, and all its hordes around
its grave; all of them killed, fallen by the sword,
who went down uncircumcised into the world
below, who spread terror in the land of the living. They bear their shame with those who go
down to the Pit. 25They have made Elam[b] a
bed among the slain with all its hordes, their
graves all around it, all of them uncircumcised, killed by the sword; for terror of them
was spread in the land of the living, and they
bear their shame with those who go down to
the Pit; they are placed among the slain.

26 Meshech and Tubal are there, and all
their multitude, their graves all around them,
all of them uncircumcised, killed by the
sword; for they spread terror in the land of the
living. 27And they do not lie with the fallen
warriors of long ago[c] who went down to Sheol
with their weapons of war, whose swords were
laid under their heads, and whose shields[d] are
upon their bones; for the terror of the warriors was in the land of the living. 28So you
shall be broken and lie among the uncircumcised, with those who are killed by the sword.

29 Edom is there, its kings and all its princes,
who for all their might are laid with those who

---

a Gk: Heb lacks *in the first month*   b Heb *it*   c Gk Old Latin:
Heb *of the uncircumcised*   d Cn: Heb *iniquities*

---

clear water, cf. v. 2. Cf. 29.11 for similar imagery of desolation. **32.15** A final and summary saying, which includes language typical of Ezekiel. **32.16** *The women of
the nations.* Apparently women regularly undertook
the role of public lamentation; see similarly Jer 9.17–
18. **32.17–32** The seventh pronouncement, April 27,
586 BCE (see note on 1.2), depicts the demography of
the Pit or Sheol, to which Pharaoh and his army will
descend (see note on 26.20). **32.18** *Wail,* a word different from "lamentation" (v. 16); cf. Jer 9.10, 17–19.
Ezekiel not only is to wail; the utterance is performative—it will *send them down. With Egypt . . . below.* The
Hebrew is difficult; perhaps "majestic nations have
brought her down to the world below." **32.19–20** V. 19
is the beginning of the song of wailing. If one includes
the first three Hebrew words of v. 20, lit. "in the midst
of those killed by the sword," with v. 19, one discovers
that *the Pit* is populated with the *uncircumcised* and
those who suffer a violent death (in distinction from

those who, as a common biblical formula says, "go
down to peace in Sheol"). Egypt is personified in the
masculine singular in the Hebrew, translated *it* here.
One infers that in the netherworld there is a separate
place (the Pit?) for the unclean, the nations listed here.
32.21 *Mighty chiefs,* or "mighty gods," an ironic reference to minor deities in the underworld. **32.22–
23** The first in a series of nations who are already in the
netherworld, *Assyria* was defeated at Nineveh by the
Babylonians (and Medes) in 612 BCE. *All around it,* or
simply "round its grave." *Uttermost parts.* Cf. Isa 14.15.
32.24–25 *Elam,* an empire just to the east of Babylonia, defeated decisively by the Assyrians in the mid-
seventh century BCE. **32.26–28** *Meshech and Tubal,* lit.
"Meshech-Tubal," the area of Asia Minor, though the
specific nation is uncertain (cf. 27.13). **32.27** The
honorable burials of ancient military heroes; cf. Gen
10.8–9. **32.29–30** Syro-Palestinian groups in the Pit:
Edom (cf. 25.12–14); *princes of the north* (Phoenician

are killed by the sword; they lie with the uncircumcised, with those who go down to the Pit.

30 The princes of the north are there, all of them, and all the Sidonians, who have gone down in shame with the slain, for all the terror that they caused by their might; they lie uncircumcised with those who are killed by the sword, and bear their shame with those who go down to the Pit.

31 When Pharaoh sees them, he will be consoled for all his hordes—Pharaoh and all his army, killed by the sword, says the Lord God. 32For he*a* spread terror in the land of the living; therefore he shall be laid to rest among the uncircumcised, with those who are slain by the sword—Pharaoh and all his multitude, says the Lord God.

Ezekiel Israel's Sentry

33 The word of the Lord came to me: 2O Mortal, speak to your people and say to them, If I bring the sword upon a land, and the people of the land take one of their number as their sentinel; 3and if the sentinel sees the sword coming upon the land and blows the trumpet and warns the people; 4then if any who hear the sound of the trumpet do not take warning, and the sword comes and takes them away, their blood shall be upon their own heads. 5They heard the sound of the trumpet and did not take warning; their blood shall be upon themselves. But if they had taken warning, they would have saved their lives. 6But if the sentinel sees the sword coming and does not blow the trumpet, so that the people are not warned, and the sword comes and takes any of them, they are taken away in their iniquity, but their blood I will require at the sentinel's hand.

7 So you, mortal, I have made a sentinel for the house of Israel; whenever you hear a word from my mouth, you shall give them warning from me. 8If I say to the wicked, "O wicked ones, you shall surely die," and you do not speak to warn the wicked to turn from their ways, the wicked shall die in their iniquity, but their blood I will require at your hand. 9But if you warn the wicked to turn from their ways, and they do not turn from their ways, the wicked shall die in their iniquity, but you will have saved your life.

God's Justice and Mercy

10 Now you, mortal, say to the house of Israel, Thus you have said: "Our transgressions and our sins weigh upon us, and we waste away because of them; how then can we live?" 11Say to them, As I live, says the Lord God, I have no pleasure in the death of the wicked, but that the wicked turn from their ways and live; turn back, turn back from your evil ways; for why will you die, O house of Israel? 12And you, mortal, say to your people, The righteousness of the righteous shall not save them when they transgress; and as for the wickedness of the wicked, it shall not make them stumble when they turn from their wickedness; and the righteous shall not be able to live by their righteousness*b* when they sin. 13Though I say to the righteous that they shall surely live, yet if they trust in their righteousness and commit iniquity, none of their righteous deeds shall be remembered; but in the iniquity that they have committed they shall die. 14Again, though I say to the wicked, "You shall surely die," yet if they turn from their sin and do

a Cn: Heb *I*   *b* Heb *by it*

rulers?); *Sidonians* (28.20–23). **32.31–32** Pharaoh *consoled* by his colleagues in the Pit (31.16).

33.1–39.29 The third major section in Ezekiel, which includes many oracles of restoration along with more oracles against foreign nations. **33.1–33** Ch. 33 comprises diverse material, much of which is paralleled elsewhere in the book. **33.1–9** The prophet as sentinel, a way of understanding the prophetic role addressed earlier in 3.16–21. **33.2–6** Those with Ezekiel in exile are to hear this description of the prophet's task. **33.2–5** The first case, in which the sentinel sounds the alarm, but the people do not respond. *Blood . . . upon their own heads.* Cf. 17.19. **33.6** The case in which the sentinel does not sound the alarm. In both this case and the previous one (vv. 2–5) the people die. *Their blood I will require.* The Hebrew uses a

parallel but different term for "require" in v. 8; cf. 3.18. The implication is that God will avenge the death of the person who had not been warned. **33.7–9** An oracle to Ezekiel in which two more cases are adduced. In v. 8 the wicked are not warned. In v. 9 the wicked are warned, but do not turn. Again, in both cases the wicked die. *You shall surely die,* the pronouncement of a legal death sentence; cf. Gen 2.17; 20.7; 1 Sam 14.44; 22.16. **33.10–20** God responds to the people's plight; see similarly ch. 18. **33.10** As in ch. 18, the section begins with a quotation from the people, which, however, focuses on the *sins* of the present generation, not the past. **33.11** *Turn back from your evil ways,* the key admonition. **33.12** To act righteously is to save oneself; cf. 18.26–27. **33.13–16** Neither the fate of those deemed righteous nor that of those called wicked is

what is lawful and right— [15]if the wicked restore the pledge, give back what they have taken by robbery, and walk in the statutes of life, committing no iniquity—they shall surely live, they shall not die. [16]None of the sins that they have committed shall be remembered against them; they have done what is lawful and right, they shall surely live.

17 Yet your people say, "The way of the Lord is not just," when it is their own way that is not just. [18]When the righteous turn from their righteousness, and commit iniquity, they shall die for it.[a] [19]And when the wicked turn from their wickedness, and do what is lawful and right, they shall live by it.[a] [20]Yet you say, "The way of the Lord is not just." O house of Israel, I will judge all of you according to your ways!

The Fall of Jerusalem

21 In the twelfth year of our exile, in the tenth month, on the fifth day of the month, someone who had escaped from Jerusalem came to me and said, "The city has fallen." [22]Now the hand of the LORD had been upon me the evening before the fugitive came; but he had opened my mouth by the time the fugitive came to me in the morning; so my mouth was opened, and I was no longer unable to speak.

The Survivors in Judah

23 The word of the LORD came to me: [24]Mortal, the inhabitants of these waste places in the land of Israel keep saying, "Abraham was only one man, yet he got possession of the land; but we are many; the land is surely given us to possess." [25]Therefore say to them, Thus says the Lord GOD: You eat flesh with the blood, and lift up your eyes to your idols, and shed blood;

shall you then possess the land? [26]You depend on your swords, you commit abominations, and each of you defiles his neighbor's wife; shall you then possess the land? [27]Say this to them, Thus says the Lord GOD: As I live, surely those who are in the waste places shall fall by the sword; and those who are in the open field I will give to the wild animals to be devoured; and those who are in strongholds and in caves shall die by pestilence. [28]I will make the land a desolation and a waste, and its proud might shall come to an end; and the mountains of Israel shall be so desolate that no one will pass through. [29]Then they shall know that I am the LORD, when I have made the land a desolation and a waste because of all their abominations that they have committed.

30 As for you, mortal, your people who talk together about you by the walls, and at the doors of the houses, say to one another, each to a neighbor, "Come and hear what the word is that comes from the LORD." [31]They come to you as people come, and they sit before you as my people, and they hear your words, but they will not obey them. For flattery is on their lips, but their heart is set on their gain. [32]To them you are like a singer of love songs,[b] one who has a beautiful voice and plays well on an instrument; they hear what you say, but they will not do it. [33]When this comes—and come it will!—then they shall know that a prophet has been among them.

Israel's False Shepherds

34 The word of the LORD came to me: [2]Mortal, prophesy against the shep-

---

a Heb them b Cn: Heb like a love song

---

unchangeable. **33.13** Cf. 18.24. **33.15** Two specific cases in which the *wicked* might act righteously; cf. 18.5–17. **33.17–20** These verses mirror directly 18.25–30. The issue is one of theodicy, or God's justice. **33.21–22** *Twelfth year . . . month,* January 19, 585 BCE (see note on 1.2), the day on which news of Jerusalem's fall came to Ezekiel in exile. *Unable to speak.* Cf. 24.15–27. *The hand of the LORD,* a reference to spirit possession, which may have also involved lack of speech; see also note on 1.3. **33.23–29** Judahites in the land. As with 11.14–16, the issue involves claims to land ownership in Judah. *Waste,* a leitmotif characterizing the land after it had been devastated by the Babylonians. **33.24** A proverbial saying, quite different from the people's rationale in 11.15. **33.25–26** Specific ritual and ethical indictments of those who live in Judah. **33.27** The punishments are typical of Ezekiel

(5.12; 7.15; 14.15–19). **33.28–29** The *land,* which had already been destroyed, might suffer further devastation; cf. 6.14. The people in the land have lost their claim to that territory *because of all their abominations.* **33.30–33** Judahites in exile. **33.30** Now those in Babylon are quoted, providing the rationale for gatherings attested in 8.1; 14.1; 20.1. **33.31** *As people come,* in groups. *As my people,* i.e., as a religious assembly; cf. 37.12. **33.33** Cf. 2.5. Vv. 31–33 are related to 33.1–9, since they portray a prophet functioning as sentinel and the people not heeding his words.

34.1–31 The structure of this chapter devoted to shepherds is complex. Two primary sections (vv. 1–16, 17–31) may be subdivided further. **34.1–16** The first half of the chapter focuses primarily on shepherds, a symbol for kings throughout the ancient Near East, including Israel. **34.1–10** A woe oracle. *Ah,* "Woe." Ne-

herds of Israel: prophesy, and say to them—to the shepherds: Thus says the Lord GOD: Ah, you shepherds of Israel who have been feeding yourselves! Should not shepherds feed the sheep? ³You eat the fat, you clothe yourselves with the wool, you slaughter the fatlings; but you do not feed the sheep. ⁴You have not strengthened the weak, you have not healed the sick, you have not bound up the injured, you have not brought back the strayed, you have not sought the lost, but with force and harshness you have ruled them. ⁵So they were scattered, because there was no shepherd; and scattered, they became food for all the wild animals. ⁶My sheep were scattered, they wandered over all the mountains and on every high hill; my sheep were scattered over all the face of the earth, with no one to search or seek for them.

7 Therefore, you shepherds, hear the word of the LORD: ⁸As I live, says the Lord GOD, because my sheep have become a prey, and my sheep have become food for all the wild animals, since there was no shepherd; and because my shepherds have not searched for my sheep, but the shepherds have fed themselves, and have not fed my sheep; ⁹therefore, you shepherds, hear the word of the LORD: ¹⁰Thus says the Lord GOD, I am against the shepherds; and I will demand my sheep at their hand, and put a stop to their feeding the sheep; no longer shall the shepherds feed themselves. I will rescue my sheep from their mouths, so that they may not be food for them.

God, the True Shepherd

11 For thus says the Lord GOD: I myself will search for my sheep, and will seek them out. ¹²As shepherds seek out their flocks when they are among their scattered sheep, so I will seek out my sheep. I will rescue them from all the places to which they have been scattered on a day of clouds and thick darkness. ¹³I will bring them out from the peoples and gather them from the countries, and will bring them into their own land; and I will feed them on the mountains of Israel, by the watercourses, and in all the inhabited parts of the land. ¹⁴I will feed them with good pasture, and the mountain heights of Israel shall be their pasture; there they shall lie down in good grazing land, and they shall feed on rich pasture on the mountains of Israel. ¹⁵I myself will be the shepherd of my sheep, and I will make them lie down, says the Lord GOD. ¹⁶I will seek the lost, and I will bring back the strayed, and I will bind up the injured, and I will strengthen the weak, but the fat and the strong I will destroy. I will feed them with justice.

17 As for you, my flock, thus says the Lord GOD: I shall judge between sheep and sheep, between rams and goats: ¹⁸Is it not enough for you to feed on the good pasture, but you must tread down with your feet the rest of your pasture? When you drink of clear water, must you foul the rest with your feet? ¹⁹And must my sheep eat what you have trodden with your feet, and drink what you have fouled with your feet?

20 Therefore, thus says the Lord GOD to them: I myself will judge between the fat sheep and the lean sheep. ²¹Because you pushed with flank and shoulder, and butted at all the weak animals with your horns until you scattered them far and wide, ²²I will save my flock, and they shall no longer be ravaged; and I will judge between sheep and sheep.

---

glect of duties is the primary indictment; all are articulated using the metaphoric sphere of the shepherd's life. **34.3** *Fat.* The Greek manuscript tradition reads "milk." Not all the action in this verse appears improper. **34.4** Specific acts of omission are cited. **34.5–6** Because of improper care, the flock was scattered, attacked, and dispersed in dangerous territory. *My sheep.* God owns the flock. *All the face of the earth,* perhaps a hyperbolic description of exile, which included Egypt as well as Babylon. **34.7–8** These verses seem intrusive. V. 7 duplicates v. 9. **34.8** A shift to a third-person address about *my shepherds.* **34.9–10** A judgment upon the shepherds. God will reclaim the flock and rescue them. Concern for the well-being of the sheep appears more prominent than does punishment of the shepherds. **34.11–15** God restores the flock, places them in *their own land* (v. 13), and performs properly the role of shepherd. **34.12** *When they are among,* lit. "when he is among"; the Hebrew is awkward. *Day of clouds and thick darkness,* the "day of the LORD," which has already transpired; cf. 30.3. **34.14** See similarly Ps 23. **34.16** A verse transitional between vv. 1–15 and vv. 17–31. *I will destroy* foreshadows the language of judgment in vv. 17–22. **34.17–30** Various sayings concerning the proper administration of the flock by God. **34.17–19** God addresses the *flock,* which is made up of diverse animals. **34.18–19** God questions the flock over feeding and drinking in ways that make it difficult for them all to eat and drink. **34.19** *My sheep . . . you,* i.e., a distinction within the flock. **34.20–21** Judgment ensues, though in what it consists is unclear. Physical condition (*fat* versus *lean*), which results from the behavior described in vv. 18–19, provides the criterion for judgment. **34.21** *You,* apparently the fat sheep.

23 I will set up over them one shepherd, my servant David, and he shall feed them: he shall feed them and be their shepherd. 24And I, the LORD, will be their God, and my servant David shall be prince among them; I, the LORD, have spoken.

25 I will make with them a covenant of peace and banish wild animals from the land, so that they may live in the wild and sleep in the woods securely. 26I will make them and the region around my hill a blessing; and I will send down the showers in their season; they shall be showers of blessing. 27The trees of the field shall yield their fruit, and the earth shall yield its increase. They shall be secure on their soil; and they shall know that I am the LORD, when I break the bars of their yoke, and save them from the hands of those who enslaved them. 28They shall no more be plunder for the nations, nor shall the animals of the land devour them; they shall live in safety, and no one shall make them afraid. 29I will provide for them a splendid vegetation so that they shall no more be consumed with hunger in the land, and no longer suffer the insults of the nations. 30They shall know that I, the LORD their God, am with them, and that they, the house of Israel, are my people, says the Lord GOD. 31You are my sheep, the sheep of my pasture*a* and I am your God, says the Lord GOD.

Judgment on Mount Seir

35 The word of the LORD came to me: 2Mortal, set your face against Mount Seir, and prophesy against it, 3and say to it, Thus says the Lord GOD:

I am against you, Mount Seir;
  I stretch out my hand against you
    to make you a desolation and a waste.
4 I lay your towns in ruins;
    you shall become a desolation,
    and you shall know that I am the
      LORD.

5Because you cherished an ancient enmity, and gave over the people of Israel to the power of the sword at the time of their calamity, at the time of their final punishment; 6therefore, as I live, says the Lord GOD, I will prepare you for blood, and blood shall pursue you; since you did not hate bloodshed, bloodshed shall pursue you. 7I will make Mount Seir a waste and a desolation; and I will cut off from it all who come and go. 8I will fill its mountains with the slain; on your hills and in your valleys and in all your watercourses those killed with the sword shall fall. 9I will make you a perpetual desolation, and your cities shall never be inhabited. Then you shall know that I am the LORD.

10 Because you said, "These two nations and these two countries shall be mine, and we will take possession of them,"—although the LORD was there— 11therefore, as I live, says the Lord GOD, I will deal with you according to the anger and envy that you showed because of your hatred against them; and I will make myself known among you,*b* when I judge you. 12You shall know that I, the LORD, have heard all the abusive speech that you uttered against

a Gk OL: Heb *pasture, you are people*   *b* Gk: Heb *them*

34.22 *Saving* and *judging* the flock are interdependent; cf. v. 10. **34.23–24** A member of the Davidic line will function as shepherd, though as *prince* (so also 37.25; 44.1–3), not as king (but cf. 37.24). Num 2.3 knows the *prince* (Hebrew *nasi'*) as a tribal leader. *My servant,* a typical designation of David (e.g., 2 Sam 3.18). On a future David, cf. Hos 3.5; Jer 30.9. *One shepherd,* not multiple rulers, as was the case during 597–587 BCE, when Jehoiachin was in exile and Zedekiah on the throne in Judah; cf. 37.19. **34.25–30** *A covenant of peace.* The blessings that conclude the so-called Holiness Code (Lev 26.4–6) provide striking parallels to the weal depicted here; cf. Ezek 16.60; 37.26; Isa 54.10. The covenant obligations devolve on God. **34.26** *My hill,* probably Zion. **34.31** A concluding pronouncement using flock and shepherd imagery to convey the reality of a covenant relationship; cf. 11.20; 14.11.

35.1–36.15 Oracles concerning mountains, both Edomite and Israelite. The structure is complex. Ch. 35 is made up of four "proof sayings" ("Because . . . therefore": vv. 3–4, 5–9, 10–13, 14–15); 36.1–15 may be construed as an elaborated oracle of salvation. **35.1–2** *Mount Seir,* a mountainous area east of the Arabah that extends north–south throughout Edom. *Seir* may be equated with Edom, e.g., Gen 36.8; Num 24.18. Ezekiel had addressed Edom earlier (25.12–14). **35.3–4** The language is typical of Ezekiel. **35.5–6** *Ancient enmity.* Cf. the prior indictment of the Philistines, 25.15. In the case of Edom and Israel, such enmity exists within kinship lines (Gen 25.27–34; 27.41–45; cf. Jer 49.7–22; Obadiah). For reference to Edomite action during the defeat of Judah, see Ob 11–14. *Blood, bloodshed* belong to the concept of bloodguilt (cf. Gen 9.6). **35.8** Imagery used earlier (9.7; 11.6; 30.11; 32.5–6). **35.9** Cf. Mal 1.2–5 for the notion of God's *perpetual* (eternal) anger at Edom. **35.10** *Two nations . . . two countries,* Israel and Judah; cf. 37.22. Israelites and non-Israelites in the land lay claim to it (11.15; 33.24). **35.12–13** *Abusive speech, you uttered, your mouth, your words.* Verbal impropriety receives special attention.

the mountains of Israel, saying, "They are laid desolate, they are given us to devour." [13] And you magnified yourselves against me with your mouth, and multiplied your words against me; I heard it. [14] Thus says the Lord GOD: As the whole earth rejoices, I will make you desolate. [15] As you rejoiced over the inheritance of the house of Israel, because it was desolate, so I will deal with you; you shall be desolate, Mount Seir, and all Edom, all of it. Then they shall know that I am the LORD.

Blessing on Israel

36 And you, mortal, prophesy to the mountains of Israel, and say: O mountains of Israel, hear the word of the LORD. [2] Thus says the Lord GOD: Because the enemy said of you, "Aha!" and, "The ancient heights have become our possession," [3] therefore prophesy, and say: Thus says the Lord GOD: Because they made you desolate indeed, and crushed you from all sides, so that you became the possession of the rest of the nations, and you became an object of gossip and slander among the people; [4] therefore, O mountains of Israel, hear the word of the Lord GOD: Thus says the Lord GOD to the mountains and the hills, the watercourses and the valleys, the desolate wastes and the deserted towns, which have become a source of plunder and an object of derision to the rest of the nations all around; [5] therefore thus says the Lord GOD: I am speaking in my hot jealousy against the rest of the nations, and against all Edom, who, with wholehearted joy and utter contempt,

took my land as their possession, because of its pasture, to plunder it. [6] Therefore prophesy concerning the land of Israel, and say to the mountains and hills, to the watercourses and valleys, Thus says the Lord GOD: I am speaking in my jealous wrath, because you have suffered the insults of the nations; [7] therefore thus says the Lord GOD: I swear that the nations that are all around you shall themselves suffer insults.

8 But you, O mountains of Israel, shall shoot out your branches, and yield your fruit to my people Israel; for they shall soon come home. [9] See now, I am for you; I will turn to you, and you shall be tilled and sown; [10] and I will multiply your population, the whole house of Israel, all of it; the towns shall be inhabited and the waste places rebuilt; [11] and I will multiply human beings and animals upon you. They shall increase and be fruitful; and I will cause you to be inhabited as in your former times, and will do more good to you than ever before. Then you shall know that I am the LORD. [12] I will lead people upon you—my people Israel—and they shall possess you, and you shall be their inheritance. No longer shall you bereave them of children.

13 Thus says the Lord GOD: Because they say to you, "You devour people, and you bereave your nation of children," [14] therefore you shall no longer devour people and no longer bereave your nation of children, says the Lord GOD; [15] and no longer will I let you hear the insults of the nations, no longer shall you bear the disgrace of the peoples; and no longer

---

35.12 The *mountains of Israel* are addressed in 36.1–15. *To devour,* the language of destruction by animals, birds, or fire (15.4, 6; 29.5; 34.5, 8) **35.14–15** Punishment in kind for Edom. Just as Edom gloated at the destruction of Judah, the *whole earth* will gloat at the destruction of Edom; cf. Ob 12–13. **36.1–15** Concerning salvation for Israel's mountains, a discourse with a complex structure consisting of the numerous oracular formulas (vv. 2, 3, 4, 5, 6, 7, 13). **36.1** *Mountains of Israel* (cf. 35.12; Deut 3.25), a way of referring to the entire country. **36.2** *Aha,* quoted earlier in the mouths of the Ammonites (25.3) and the Tyrians (26.2). *Ancient heights,* poetic diction for the mountains. *Heights,* rendered *high place(s)* in 6.3, 6; 20.29; cf. Num 21.28; Deut 32.13; Mic 3.12. *Our possession.* Cf. the claim in v. 10. **36.3** *The rest of the nations,* also in v. 5; cf. 25.16; all probably refer to the nations elsewhere indicted in the book. **36.4** God continues to speak to Israel using geographic vocabulary. **36.5** *Hot jealousy.* Cf. the variant in v. 6 (cf. Ex 20.5; Josh 24.19; 1 Kings 14.22). As befits ch.

35, *Edom* is the only nation singled out. **36.6** Vocabulary found in vv. 4–5. **36.7** *I swear,* lit. "I lift up my hand." **36.8** God continues to speak to the depopulated mountains, whose inhabitants, now in exile, will *soon come home.* Instead of being desolate, the mountains will produce verdure and consumable crops for the benefit of the people (see similarly 17.8). **36.9** *I am for you.* On this terse affirmation of the covenant relationship, cf. Lev 26.9. **36.10–11** God addresses the issue of repopulation, which was a serious problem after 587 BCE. **36.12** *Inheritance.* Cf. 35.15; Deut 26.9. *Bereave them of children,* perhaps an addition in which the mountains are viewed as negative; see 6.1–14; Deut 12.1–3. **36.13** The nations observe that the mountains, i.e., the land, *devour people.* Cf. the similar rhetoric in Num 13.32. An external observer might think that those who lived in Israel were doomed because of all the wars fought in that area. **36.15** *Cause your nation to stumble.* See note on 36.12. The mountains were not simply neutral geographic venues.

shall you cause your nation to stumble, says
the Lord God.

The Renewal of Israel

16 The word of the Lord came to me: [17]Mor-
tal, when the house of Israel lived on their own
soil, they defiled it with their ways and their
deeds; their conduct in my sight was like the
uncleanness of a woman in her menstrual period. [18]So I poured out my wrath upon them
for the blood that they had shed upon the
land, and for the idols with which they had defiled it. [19]I scattered them among the nations,
and they were dispersed through the countries; in accordance with their conduct and
their deeds I judged them. [20]But when they
came to the nations, wherever they came, they
profaned my holy name, in that it was said of
them, "These are the people of the Lord, and
yet they had to go out of his land." [21]But I had
concern for my holy name, which the house of
Israel had profaned among the nations to
which they came.

22 Therefore say to the house of Israel,
Thus says the Lord God: It is not for your sake,
O house of Israel, that I am about to act, but
for the sake of my holy name, which you have
profaned among the nations to which you
came. [23]I will sanctify my great name, which
has been profaned among the nations, and
which you have profaned among them; and
the nations shall know that I am the Lord,
says the Lord God, when through you I display my holiness before their eyes. [24]I will take
you from the nations, and gather you from all
the countries, and bring you into your own
land. [25]I will sprinkle clean water upon you,
and you shall be clean from all your uncleannesses, and from all your idols I will cleanse
you. [26]A new heart I will give you, and a new
spirit I will put within you; and I will remove
from your body the heart of stone and give
you a heart of flesh. [27]I will put my spirit
within you, and make you follow my statutes
and be careful to observe my ordinances.
[28]Then you shall live in the land that I gave to
your ancestors; and you shall be my people,
and I will be your God. [29]I will save you from
all your uncleannesses, and I will summon the
grain and make it abundant and lay no famine
upon you. [30]I will make the fruit of the tree
and the produce of the field abundant, so that
you may never again suffer the disgrace of
famine among the nations. [31]Then you shall
remember your evil ways, and your dealings
that were not good; and you shall loathe yourselves for your iniquities and your abominable
deeds. [32]It is not for your sake that I will act,
says the Lord God; let that be known to you.
Be ashamed and dismayed for your ways,
O house of Israel.

33 Thus says the Lord God: On the day that
I cleanse you from all your iniquities, I will
cause the towns to be inhabited, and the waste
places shall be rebuilt. [34]The land that was
desolate shall be tilled, instead of being the
desolation that it was in the sight of all who
passed by. [35]And they will say, "This land that
was desolate has become like the garden of
Eden; and the waste and desolate and ruined

36.16–38 Discourse on the restoration of Israel,
which is made up of several discrete utterances (vv.
17–21, 22–32, 33–36, 37–38). **36.17–21** A cursory
theological survey of Israelite history that adumbrates
themes and images used elsewhere in the book and
serves as a prologue to the longest section in the discourse. **36.17** *Their own soil,* "their land" (cf. 28.25).
On menstrual *uncleanness,* which is used here in a simile, see Lev 15.19–30. **36.18** *Blood,* here of violence; cf.
22.4. **36.20** By dint of the response of those countries
to which Israel came, God's name was *profaned. My
holy name.* It is holiness that is subject to profanation.
The conception is dialectical: the people of Israel have
profaned God's name, even though it is God who exiled them. **36.21** *I had concern for,* lit. "I grieved for."
36.22–32 The rationale for and design of God's new
plan for Israel. **36.22, 32** Both at beginning and end,
Ezekiel makes clear that God acts on behalf of the *holy
name,* not for the sake of the people; cf. Isa 43.22–28.
36.23 *I will sanctify my great name,* presumably by the
purificatory acts that follow, which will be apparent to
Israelites and non-Israelites alike. Israel must return
and remain in its land in order for God's name to be
holy. **36.24** Purification will occur after the people
have returned to their *own land.* **36.25** On cleansing
lustration rites, which here remove the uncleanness
and idols; cf. Num 19.9–22; Ps 51.7. **36.26** Then God
will give the people a *new heart . . . and a new spirit;* cf.
11.19; 18.31; Jer 31.31–34; Ps 51.10. For Ezekiel the
new heart is to the old heart as flesh is to stone; the old
heart did not enable life. **36.27** The *new spirit* (v. 26) is
construed as *my spirit,* God's spirit (cf. Lev 26.3; Gen
2.7), which will enable Israelites to obey the covenant
statutes. **36.28** The covenant formula (e.g., 11.20;
14.11) reinforces Israel's ability to remain in the land.
36.29–30 Cf. 34.27. **36.33–36** Destroyed towns and
fields, of a sort described in v. 4, will be rebuilt.
36.35 Just as foreigners commented on the ignomin-
ious state of Israel in exile, they will attest verbally to
the restored country—it will be *like the garden of Eden;*

towns are now inhabited and fortified." ³⁶Then the nations that are left all around you shall know that I, the LORD, have rebuilt the ruined places, and replanted that which was desolate; I, the LORD, have spoken, and I will do it.

37 Thus says the Lord GOD: I will also let the house of Israel ask me to do this for them: to increase their population like a flock. ³⁸Like the flock for sacrifices,ᵃ like the flock at Jerusalem during her appointed festivals, so shall the ruined towns be filled with flocks of people. Then they shall know that I am the LORD.

The Valley of Dry Bones

37 The hand of the LORD came upon me, and he brought me out by the spirit of the LORD and set me down in the middle of a valley; it was full of bones. ²He led me all around them; there were very many lying in the valley, and they were very dry. ³He said to me, "Mortal, can these bones live?" I answered, "O Lord GOD, you know." ⁴Then he said to me, "Prophesy to these bones, and say to them: O dry bones, hear the word of the LORD. ⁵Thus says the Lord GOD to these bones: I will cause breathᵇ to enter you, and you shall live. ⁶I will lay sinews on you, and will cause flesh to come upon you, and cover you with skin, and put breathᵇ in you, and you shall live; and you shall know that I am the LORD."

7 So I prophesied as I had been commanded; and as I prophesied, suddenly there was a noise, a rattling, and the bones came to-

gether, bone to its bone. ⁸I looked, and there were sinews on them, and flesh had come upon them, and skin had covered them; but there was no breath in them. ⁹Then he said to me, "Prophesy to the breath, prophesy, mortal, and say to the breath:ᶜ Thus says the Lord GOD: Come from the four winds, O breath,ᶜ and breathe upon these slain, that they may live." ¹⁰I prophesied as he commanded me, and the breath came into them, and they lived, and stood on their feet, a vast multitude.

11 Then he said to me, "Mortal, these bones are the whole house of Israel. They say, 'Our bones are dried up, and our hope is lost; we are cut off completely.' ¹²Therefore prophesy, and say to them, Thus says the Lord GOD: I am going to open your graves, and bring you up from your graves, O my people; and I will bring you back to the land of Israel. ¹³And you shall know that I am the LORD, when I open your graves, and bring you up from your graves, O my people. ¹⁴I will put my spirit within you, and you shall live, and I will place you on your own soil; then you shall know that I, the LORD, have spoken and will act, says the LORD."

The Two Sticks

15 The word of the LORD came to me: ¹⁶Mortal, take a stick and write on it, "For Judah, and the Israelites associated with it"; then take another stick and write on it, "For Joseph (the

ᵃ Heb *flock of holy things*   ᵇ Or *spirit*   ᶜ Or *wind* or *spirit*

---

cf. Jer 31.23–28; Isa 51.3. **36.37–38** The first instance of Israel being allowed to request something (cf. 14.3; 20.3)—repopulation; cf. vv. 10–11. The request recalls the covenant blessings of population (Lev 26.9). The evidence for great numbers, two flocks for sacrifice, allows for a return to the imagery of God's people as a flock (cf. ch. 34).

37.1–14 The third vision report: the valley of dry bones (vv. 1–10) and its meaning (vv. 11–14). **37.1** *The hand of the LORD.* See note on 1.3. *He brought me out by the spirit of the LORD* seems awkward if *he* is the deity; cf. 11.5, 24. *Valley,* or "plain"; see note on 3.22. The venue is Mesopotamia. **37.3** After having shown Ezekiel the bones in the valley, God asks him a question that, if rhetorical, deserves a negative answer. The prophet demurs with a response that affirms the power of the deity. **37.4–5** The prophet is ordered to address the bones with an oracle, which concludes with an echo of the "know" motif (v. 6). **37.6** *Breath,* or "spirit"; cf. 36.26–27. **37.7–10** Ezekiel performs as ordered but must utter a second oracle to the *breath,* or

the "spirit"; cf. Gen 2.7; Eccl 3.20–21; 12.7. *The four winds.* Cf. 42.20; Jer 49.36; Dan 8.8; Zech 2.6; 6.5; but the *breath* comes from and is not identical with the winds of the compass points. *Slain.* One senses the imagery of a battlefield full of long dead warriors; cf. 32.4–5. If so, the valley of dry bones is no straightforward allegory of Israel in exile. **37.11** An interpretation of the bones as the *whole house of Israel,* i.e., those in various diaspora settings as well as those still in the land (cf. vv. 15–22). The quotation reflects the vocabulary and style of lamentation (e.g., Pss 31.10; 35.10) over *bones,* in which various symbolically graphic descriptions of physical malaise may occur. On being *cut off,* cf. Ps 88.5; Isa 53.8; Lam 3.54. **37.12–14** The prophet continues to speak to all Israel as if the people were dead. The imagery, however, is new—not that of unburied bones but of corpses in graves. **37.14** Cf. 36.27–28. **37.15–28** The two sticks become one, a symbolic action with several interpretations. **37.15–19** The symbolic action and its primary interpretation. **37.16** *Stick,* perhaps a wooden staff (cf. Num

stick of Ephraim) and all the house of Israel associated with it"; [17] and join them together into one stick, so that they may become one in your hand. [18] And when your people say to you, "Will you not show us what you mean by these?" [19] say to them, Thus says the Lord GOD: I am about to take the stick of Joseph (which is in the hand of Ephraim) and the tribes of Israel associated with it; and I will put the stick of Judah upon it,[a] and make them one stick, in order that they may be one in my hand. [20] When the sticks on which you write are in your hand before their eyes, [21] then say to them, Thus says the Lord GOD: I will take the people of Israel from the nations among which they have gone, and will gather them from every quarter, and bring them to their own land. [22] I will make them one nation in the land, on the mountains of Israel; and one king shall be king over them all. Never again shall they be two nations, and never again shall they be divided into two kingdoms. [23] They shall never again defile themselves with their idols and their detestable things, or with any of their transgressions. I will save them from all the apostasies into which they have fallen,[b] and will cleanse them. Then they shall be my people, and I will be their God.

24 My servant David shall be king over them; and they shall all have one shepherd. They shall follow my ordinances and be careful to observe my statutes. [25] They shall live in the land that I gave to my servant Jacob, in which your ancestors lived; they and their children and their children's children shall live there forever; and my servant David shall be

their prince forever. [26] I will make a covenant of peace with them; it shall be an everlasting covenant with them; and I will bless[c] them and multiply them, and will set my sanctuary among them forevermore. [27] My dwelling place shall be with them; and I will be their God, and they shall be my people. [28] Then the nations shall know that I the LORD sanctify Israel, when my sanctuary is among them forevermore.

Invasion by Gog

38 The word of the LORD came to me: [2] Mortal, set your face toward Gog, of the land of Magog, the chief prince of Meshech and Tubal. Prophesy against him [3] and say: Thus says the Lord GOD: I am against you, O Gog, chief prince of Meshech and Tubal; [4] I will turn you around and put hooks into your jaws, and I will lead you out with all your army, horses and horsemen, all of them clothed in full armor, a great company, all of them with shield and buckler, wielding swords. [5] Persia, Ethiopia,[d] and Put are with them, all of them with buckler and helmet; [6] Gomer and all its troops; Beth-togarmah from the remotest parts of the north with all its troops—many peoples are with you.

7 Be ready and keep ready, you and all the companies that are assembled around you, and hold yourselves in reserve for them. [8] After many days you shall be mustered; in the latter years you shall go against a land restored from

---

a Heb *I will put them upon it*　*b* Another reading is *from all the settlements in which they have sinned*　*c* Tg: Heb *give*　*d* Or *Nubia*; Heb *Cush*

17.1–13, a narrative in which the names of Israelite ancestral houses were written upon staffs), or a wooden writing board. Less likely is a shepherd's crook or a royal scepter. The Hebrew noun is the generic word for "tree" or "wood." The most probable forms of the original inscriptions were: *for Judah* and *for Joseph*, symbolizing the Southern and Northern Kingdoms, respectively. **37.19** National reunification—*one stick*—is the goal (so also vv. 21–22). **37.22** *One king.* Cf. v. 25; 34.23–24; 46.1–18, though the term *king* is not used in those places. **37.24b–26** The people will be in a covenant relationship; cf. 34.25. **37.27–28** *My sanctuary,* the temple in Jerusalem, which foreshadows chs. 40–48.
38.1–39.29 Discourse against Gog of Magog. Two complex chapters directed against Gog, the ruler and general of Magog's forces. His army will be decimated in a cataclysmic defeat, once it attacks Israel. After the drama has been played out, Israel will dwell securely in

the land. Gog and Magog appear transhistorical, though the name Gog may derive from the name of the Lydian ruler Gyges. The name of the land Magog was probably created to rhyme with Gog; for another toponymic rhyme, cf. 27.10; 30.5. **38.2** *Chief prince* does not imply subordination to someone, but highest status among a plurality of rulers, e.g., a regional group of rulers (26.16; 32.30). *Meshech and Tubal.* Cf. 27.13; note on 32.26–28; Gen 10.2. **38.4** *I will turn you . . . lead you out.* God physically drags Gog and his army out for battle; cf. 19.4. Mention of numerous weapons becomes especially important in light of 39.9–10. **38.5** The force is international, though these names may be later additions to the passage. **38.6** *Gomer* (the Cimmerians) and *Beth-togarmah* (cf. 27.14; Gen 10.3) are both associated with Asia Minor, i.e., *from the remotest parts of the north.* **38.8** *After many days,* often viewed as an eschatological formula pertaining to an end-time or a future time of judg-

war, a land where people were gathered from many nations on the mountains of Israel, which had long lain waste; its people were brought out from the nations and now are living in safety, all of them. [9]You shall advance, coming on like a storm; you shall be like a cloud covering the land, you and all your troops, and many peoples with you.

10 Thus says the Lord God: On that day thoughts will come into your mind, and you will devise an evil scheme. [11]You will say, "I will go up against the land of unwalled villages; I will fall upon the quiet people who live in safety, all of them living without walls, and having no bars or gates"; [12]to seize spoil and carry off plunder; to assail the waste places that are now inhabited, and the people who were gathered from the nations, who are acquiring cattle and goods, who live at the center[a] of the earth. [13]Sheba and Dedan and the merchants of Tarshish and all its young warriors[b] will say to you, "Have you come to seize spoil? Have you assembled your horde to carry off plunder, to carry away silver and gold, to take away cattle and goods, to seize a great amount of booty?"

14 Therefore, mortal, prophesy, and say to Gog: Thus says the Lord God: On that day when my people Israel are living securely, you will rouse yourself[c] [15]and come from your place out of the remotest parts of the north, you and many peoples with you, all of them riding on horses, a great horde, a mighty army; [16]you will come up against my people Israel, like a cloud covering the earth. In the latter days I will bring you against my land, so that the nations may know me, when through you, O Gog, I display my holiness before their eyes.

Judgment on Gog

17 Thus says the Lord God: Are you he of whom I spoke in former days by my servants the prophets of Israel, who in those days prophesied for years that I would bring you against them? [18]On that day, when Gog comes against the land of Israel, says the Lord God, my wrath shall be aroused. [19]For in my jealousy and in my blazing wrath I declare: On that day there shall be a great shaking in the land of Israel; [20]the fish of the sea, and the birds of the air, and the animals of the field, and all creeping things that creep on the ground, and all human beings that are on the face of the earth, shall quake at my presence, and the mountains shall be thrown down, and the cliffs shall fall, and every wall shall tumble to the ground. [21]I will summon the sword against Gog[d] in[e] all my mountains, says the Lord God; the swords of all will be against their comrades. [22]With pestilence and bloodshed I will enter into judgment with him; and I will pour down torrential rains and hailstones, fire and sulfur, upon him and his troops and the many peoples that are with him. [23]So I will display my greatness and my holiness and make myself known in the eyes of many nations. Then they shall know that I am the Lord.

Gog's Armies Destroyed

39 And you, mortal, prophesy against Gog, and say: Thus says the Lord God:

---

a Heb *navel*   *b* Heb *young lions*   *c* Gk: Heb *will you not know?*
d Heb *him*   *e* Heb to or for

---

ment and transformation. *A land restored from war,* presumably a reference to Israel restored after exile, i.e., in the quite distant future from the perspective of Ezekiel and his contemporaries. **38.9** For similar descriptions of military *advance,* see Isa 10.3; Jer 4.13; Joel 2.2. **38.10–13** Gog and his scheme for plunder. For similar language concerning an enemy of Israel, see Jer 4.13. **38.11** *Unwalled villages.* Cf. Esth 9.19; Zech 2.4. **38.12** *Center,* or navel, of the earth (Greek *omphalos*) must refer to Jerusalem, so 5.5. **38.13** *Sheba, Dedan, Tarshish,* all nations cited in the commercial nation listing (27.22, 20, 12). Their interest in plunder is conveyed in prolix questions. **38.14–18** God declaims to Gog. **38.14** *On that day,* another eschatological formula; cf. note on 38.8. For the remainder of the verse, cf. vv. 4–5. **38.16** *Through you,* a foreshadowing of Gog's fate. **38.17** The Hebrew Masoretic tradition preserves a textual error that results in the verse being

construed as a question. It is preferable to read with the Greek (Septuagint) and Latin (Vulgate): "You are he of whom I spoke . . . " For the notion of earlier prophets, cf. Zech 1.4. Such earlier oracles might have been similar to Jer 4.5–6.26. **38.18–23** God's theophanic response. **38.18–19** *On that day,* the "day of the Lord"; cf. 30.3. **38.19–22** A classic description of a theophany in which the deity's appearance wreaks havoc with the natural order and, when it occurs in a military context, with any enemy of the Lord. **38.19** On theophanic *shaking,* cf. Joel 2.10; 2.30. **38.20** *The fish . . . the earth.* Using vocabulary drawn from the Priestly creation account in Gen 1, the objects of such *shaking* are specified. On geographic disorder, cf. Isa 2.14; Zech 14.4–5. **38.22** An eclectic assemblage of destructive natural phenomena directed at Gog. **38.23** Reflexive verbs in the Hebrew highlight God's role in the destruction of Gog. **39.1–5** Destruc-

I am against you, O Gog, chief prince of Meshech and Tubal! 2I will turn you around and drive you forward, and bring you up from the remotest parts of the north, and lead you against the mountains of Israel. 3I will strike your bow from your left hand, and will make your arrows drop out of your right hand. 4You shall fall on the mountains of Israel, you and all your troops and the peoples that are with you; I will give you to birds of prey of every kind and to the wild animals to be devoured. 5You shall fall in the open field; for I have spoken, says the Lord GOD. 6I will send fire on Magog and on those who live securely in the coastlands; and they shall know that I am the LORD.

7 My holy name I will make known among my people Israel; and I will not let my holy name be profaned any more; and the nations shall know that I am the LORD, the Holy One in Israel. 8It has come! It has happened, says the Lord GOD. This is the day of which I have spoken.

9 Then those who live in the towns of Israel will go out and make fires of the weapons and burn them—bucklers and shields, bows and arrows, handpikes and spears—and they will make fires of them for seven years. 10They will not need to take wood out of the field or cut down any trees in the forests, for they will make their fires of the weapons; they will despoil those who despoiled them, and plunder those who plundered them, says the Lord GOD.

The Burial of Gog

11 On that day I will give to Gog a place for burial in Israel, the Valley of the Travelers*a* east of the sea; it shall block the path of the travelers, for there Gog and all his horde will be buried; it shall be called the Valley of Hamon-gog.*b* 12Seven months the house of Israel shall spend burying them, in order to cleanse the land. 13All the people of the land shall bury them; and it will bring them honor on the day that I show my glory, says the Lord GOD. 14They will set apart men to pass through the land regularly and bury any invaders*c* who remain on the face of the land, so as to cleanse it; for seven months they shall make their search. 15As the searchers*c* pass through the land, anyone who sees a human bone shall set up a sign by it, until the buriers have buried it in the Valley of Hamon-gog.*b* 16(A city Hamonah*d* is there also.) Thus they shall cleanse the land.

17 As for you, mortal, thus says the Lord GOD: Speak to the birds of every kind and to all the wild animals: Assemble and come, gather from all around to the sacrificial feast that I am preparing for you, a great sacrificial feast on the mountains of Israel, and you shall eat flesh and drink blood. 18You shall eat the flesh of the mighty, and drink the blood of the princes of the earth—of rams, of lambs, and of goats, of bulls, all of them fatlings of Bashan. 19You shall eat fat until you are filled, and drink blood until you are drunk, at the sacrificial feast that I am preparing for you. 20And you shall be filled at my table with horses and charioteers,*e* with warriors and all kinds of soldiers, says the Lord GOD.

---

a Or *of the Abarim*   *b* That is, *the Horde of Gog*
c Heb *travelers*   *d* That is *The Horde*   *e* Heb *chariots*

---

tion on the mountains of Israel. **39.1–2** Parallel in formulation to 38.1–2, 8. **39.3** Personal combat between God the warrior and Gog, who is depicted as an archer. **39.4** *Birds . . . wild animals.* Cf. 29.5. **39.6** *Send fire on* reflects the mode of punishment in Amos's oracles against the nations (1.4, 7, 10, 12; 2.5). *Coastlands*, perhaps Tyre (26.15, 18; 27.3) or, more generally, the maritime trading regions (38.13). **39.7** *My holy name.* Cf. v. 25; 36.20–23. **39.8** *It has come! It has happened*, better "Behold, it is coming and it will be brought about" (RSV), since the reference is to the "day of the LORD." **39.9–10** Destruction of Gog's weaponry; cf. Ps 46.9. *Those who live in towns.* Cf. v. 13, *all the people of the land.* On the specific *weapons*, cf. 23.24. *Buckler*, a small shield. *Seven years*, an idealized number based on the sabbath and sabbatical cycle; cf. vv. 12, 14. **39.10** Israel apparently uses the *wood* for domestic

purposes. **39.11–16** Burying Gog. **39.11** *Valley of the Travelers*, Hebrew "Valley of the Obarim"; however, perhaps one should read "Abarim," a mountain range east of the Dead Sea in northern Moab. The place of burial would be outside the land, hence avoiding contamination from corpse impurity (see Num 19.11–13) and allowing for purification (Ezek 39.12, 16). **39.14** A group *set apart* from all the people, who search for bones for another *seven months.* **39.15** *Buriers*, another group. **39.17–20** An elaboration of v. 4b. Ezekiel is to summon birds and animals for a *sacrificial feast*, perhaps with allusions to earlier Canaanite myths; cf. Isa 34.5–7; Zeph 1.7. **39.18** The proper sacrificial character is underlined by construing the dead warriors as animals acceptable for sacrifice. *Fatlings of Bashan.* Cf. Ps 22.12; Am 4.1. In standard Israelite practice, humans did not consume the blood and fat (so 44.7, 15;

Israel Restored to the Land

21 I will display my glory among the nations; and all the nations shall see my judgment that I have executed, and my hand that I have laid on them. 22 The house of Israel shall know that I am the LORD their God, from that day forward. 23 And the nations shall know that the house of Israel went into captivity for their iniquity, because they dealt treacherously with me. So I hid my face from them and gave them into the hand of their adversaries, and they all fell by the sword. 24 I dealt with them according to their uncleanness and their transgressions, and hid my face from them.

25 Therefore thus says the Lord GOD: Now I will restore the fortunes of Jacob, and have mercy on the whole house of Israel; and I will be jealous for my holy name. 26 They shall forget[a] their shame, and all the treachery they have practiced against me, when they live securely in their land with no one to make them afraid, 27 when I have brought them back from the peoples and gathered them from their enemies' lands, and through them have displayed my holiness in the sight of many nations. 28 Then they shall know that I am the LORD their God because I sent them into exile among the nations, and then gathered them into their own land. I will leave none of them

behind; 29 and I will never again hide my face from them, when I pour out my spirit upon the house of Israel, says the Lord GOD.

The Vision of the New Temple

40 In the twenty-fifth year of our exile, at the beginning of the year, on the tenth day of the month, in the fourteenth year after the city was struck down, on that very day, the hand of the LORD was upon me, and he brought me there. 2 He brought me, in visions of God, to the land of Israel, and set me down upon a very high mountain, on which was a structure like a city to the south. 3 When he brought me there, a man was there, whose appearance shone like bronze, with a linen cord and a measuring reed in his hand; and he was standing in the gateway. 4 The man said to me, "Mortal, look closely and listen attentively, and set your mind upon all that I shall show you, for you were brought here in order that I might show it to you; declare all that you see to the house of Israel."

5 Now there was a wall all around the outside of the temple area. The length of the measuring reed in the man's hand was six long cubits, each being a cubit and a handbreadth in length; so he measured the thickness of the

a Another reading is *They shall bear*

Lev 3.16–17). **39.21–29** Concluding oracles. **39.21–22** God's actions perceived by both the nations and Israel; cf. 39.6–8. **39.23–24** Defeat and exile are treated as God's just punishment. *Hid my face.* Cf. Pss 13.1; 22.24; 27.9; 104.29; Isa 54.8; 57.17; 59.2; 64.7; Num 6.24–26. **39.25–29** *Restore the fortunes.* Cf. 16.53–58; 29.14; Jer 33.26. *Jealous for my holy name.* Cf. 36.22–23; Joel 2.18. **39.27** *When I have brought them back.* Return is still a future event. **39.29** *Pour out my spirit.* Cf. 36.26–27; Joel 2.28–29.

40.1–48.35 The new temple and polity. Chs. 40–48, the fourth major section of the book, is the fourth vision report. Ezekiel travels to Jerusalem, receives a tour of the new temple complex (chs. 40–42), and perceives the glory of the Lord returning to the rebuilt temple (43.4–5). Then he is instructed in the Torah (43.12–46.24) relevant to the new structure and the community gathered around it. Finally, in chs. 47–48, the land beyond the temple is defined and described. **40.1–42.20** The temple and its courtyards. **40.1–4** Prologue. The date in v. 1 is April 28, 573 BCE (see note on 1.2). A quarter century after Ezekiel and the first deportees were taken into exile and fourteen years after Jerusalem was razed, he returns via visionary experience (*the hand of the LORD* [see note on 1.3], *in visions of God*) to Jerusalem. **40.2** *A very high mountain,*

Mount Zion, upon which the temple stood; cf. 17.22; 20.40; 43.12; Isa 2.2. *A city to the south* places Jerusalem south of the temple; cf. 48.15–19. **40.3** *A man* will guide Ezekiel throughout this final vision; the last mention of the man is in 47.6. *Like bronze.* As with the creatures in 1.7, bronze characterizes the man as something other than a human; cf. the figure described in 8.2. *A linen cord and a measuring reed,* two instruments for linear measurement. The reed (also in v. 5) was a little longer than 10 feet, or 3 meters. The cord does not recur; cf. Zech 2.1. **40.4** The rationale for Ezekiel's experience is the imperative to *declare all that you see;* cf. 43.10. **40.5** *A long cubit* was about 518 millimeters, or 20 inches, long; the ratio of a short to long cubit was 6 to 7, a distinction known throughout the ancient Near East. **40.5–16** The eastern gate (*gateway facing east*) to the temple compound, which has the basic configuration of city gates excavated at Gezer, Hazor, and Megiddo, in this case a passageway with four recessed rooms (three recesses and one vestibule on either side). Such fortified gates make Ezekiel's temple rather like a religious citadel. As with other city gates, this wall met the gate before the first recess, with the rest of the gate structure inside the *temple area.* Apart from v. 5b, which may be a later addition, the measurements provide a ground plan, i.e., with no ele-

wall, one reed; and the height, one reed. ⁶Then he went into the gateway facing east, going up its steps, and measured the threshold of the gate, one reed deep.ᵃ There were ⁷recesses, and each recess was one reed wide and one reed deep; and the space between the recesses, five cubits; and the threshold of the gate by the vestibule of the gate at the inner end was one reed deep. ⁸Then he measured the inner vestibule of the gateway, one cubit. ⁹Then he measured the vestibule of the gateway, eight cubits; and its pilasters, two cubits; and the vestibule of the gate was at the inner end. ¹⁰There were three recesses on either side of the east gate; the three were of the same size; and the pilasters on either side were of the same size. ¹¹Then he measured the width of the opening of the gateway, ten cubits; and the width of the gateway, thirteen cubits. ¹²There was a barrier before the recesses, one cubit on either side; and the recesses were six cubits on either side. ¹³Then he measured the gate from the backᵇ of the one recess to the backᵇ of the other, a width of twenty-five cubits, from wall to wall.ᶜ ¹⁴He measuredᵈ also the vestibule, twenty cubits; and the gate next to the pilaster on every side of the court.ᵉ ¹⁵From the front of the gate at the entrance to the end of the inner vestibule of the gate was fifty cubits. ¹⁶The recesses and their pilasters had windows, with shuttersᵉ on the inside of the gateway all around, and the vestibules also had windows on the inside all around; and on the pilasters were palm trees.

17 Then he brought me into the outer court; there were chambers there, and a pavement, all around the court; thirty chambers fronted on the pavement. ¹⁸The pavement ran along the side of the gates, corresponding to the length of the gates; this was the lower pavement. ¹⁹Then he measured the distance from the inner front ofᶠ the lower gate to the outer front of the inner court, one hundred cubits.ᵍ

20 Then he measured the gate of the outer court that faced north—its depth and width. ²¹Its recesses, three on either side, and its pi-

lasters and its vestibule were of the same size as those of the first gate; its depth was fifty cubits, and its width twenty-five cubits. ²²Its windows, its vestibule, and its palm trees were of the same size as those of the gate that faced toward the east. Seven steps led up to it; and its vestibule was on the inside.ʰ ²³Opposite the gate on the north, as on the east, was a gate to the inner court; he measured from gate to gate, one hundred cubits.

24 Then he led me toward the south, and there was a gate on the south; and he measured its pilasters and its vestibule; they had the same dimensions as the others. ²⁵There were windows all around in it and in its vestibule, like the windows of the others; its depth was fifty cubits, and its width twenty-five cubits. ²⁶There were seven steps leading up to it; its vestibule was on the inside.ʰ It had palm trees on its pilasters, one on either side. ²⁷There was a gate on the south of the inner court; and he measured from gate to gate toward the south, one hundred cubits.

28 Then he brought me to the inner court by the south gate, and he measured the south gate; it was of the same dimensions as the others. ²⁹Its recesses, its pilasters, and its vestibule were of the same size as the others; and there were windows all around in it and in its vestibule; its depth was fifty cubits, and its width twenty-five cubits. ³⁰There were vestibules all around, twenty-five cubits deep and five cubits wide. ³¹Its vestibule faced the outer court, and palm trees were on its pilasters, and its stairway had eight steps.

32 Then he brought me to the inner court on the east side, and he measured the gate; it was of the same size as the others. ³³Its recesses, its pilasters, and its vestibule were of the same dimensions as the others; and there were windows all around in it and in its vestibule; its depth was fifty cubits, and its width twenty-five cubits. ³⁴Its vestibule faced

a Heb *deep, and one threshold, one reed deep*   b Gk: Heb *roof*
c Heb *opening facing opening*   d Heb *made*   e Meaning of Heb uncertain   f Compare Gk: Heb *from before*   g Heb adds *the east and the north*   h Gk: Heb *before them*

---

vations, though there were seven stairs just before the gate (see v. 22). The entire gate complex was almost ninety feet long. Windows provided light in the rooms. **40.16** *Pilasters,* projecting columns, which may have been door jambs, were decorated with *palm trees;* cf. 1 Kings 6.29, 32, 35; 7.36. **40.17–19** The *outer court* was lined with *thirty chambers;* cf. Jer 35.2–4; Neh

13.4–14 for such rooms, which could have been used for meeting or storage. **40.20–27** The north and south gates, which are fundamentally similar to the east gate. The steps reflect multiple elevations. **40.28–37** Three gates (south, east, north) leading from the outer to the inner courtyards, which involved an elevation of eight stairs, were used exclusively by priests. These inner

the outer court, and it had palm trees on its pilasters, on either side; and its stairway had eight steps.

35 Then he brought me to the north gate, and he measured it; it had the same dimensions as the others. 36Its recesses, its pilasters, and its vestibule were of the same size as the others;[a] and it had windows all around. Its depth was fifty cubits, and its width twenty-five cubits. 37Its vestibule[b] faced the outer court, and it had palm trees on its pilasters, on either side; and its stairway had eight steps.

38 There was a chamber with its door in the vestibule of the gate,[c] where the burnt offering was to be washed. 39And in the vestibule of the gate were two tables on either side, on which the burnt offering and the sin offering and the guilt offering were to be slaughtered. 40On the outside of the vestibule[d] at the entrance of the north gate were two tables; and on the other side of the vestibule of the gate were two tables. 41Four tables were on the inside, and four tables on the outside of the side of the gate, eight tables, on which the sacrifices were to be slaughtered. 42There were also four tables of hewn stone for the burnt offering, a cubit and a half long, and one cubit and a half wide, and one cubit high, on which the instruments were to be laid with which the burnt offerings and the sacrifices were slaughtered. 43There were pegs, one handbreadth long, fastened all around the inside. And on the tables the flesh of the offering was to be laid.

44 On the outside of the inner gateway there were chambers for the singers in the inner court, one[e] at the side of the north gate facing south, the other at the side of the east gate facing north. 45He said to me, "This chamber that faces south is for the priests who have charge of the temple, 46and the chamber that faces north is for the priests who have

charge of the altar; these are the descendants of Zadok, who alone among the descendants of Levi may come near to the LORD to minister to him." 47He measured the court, one hundred cubits deep, and one hundred cubits wide, a square; and the altar was in front of the temple.

The Temple

48 Then he brought me to the vestibule of the temple and measured the pilasters of the vestibule, five cubits on either side; and the width of the gate was fourteen cubits; and the sidewalls of the gate were three cubits[f] on either side. 49The depth of the vestibule was twenty cubits, and the width twelve[g] cubits; ten steps led up[h] to it; and there were pillars beside the pilasters on either side.

41 Then he brought me to the nave, and measured the pilasters; on each side six cubits was the width of the pilasters.[i] 2The width of the entrance was ten cubits; and the sidewalls of the entrance were five cubits on either side. He measured the length of the nave, forty cubits, and its width, twenty cubits. 3Then he went into the inner room and measured the pilasters of the entrance, two cubits; and the width of the entrance, six cubits; and the sidewalls[j] of the entrance, seven cubits. 4He measured the depth of the room, twenty cubits, and its width, twenty cubits, beyond the nave. And he said to me, This is the most holy place.

5 Then he measured the wall of the temple, six cubits thick; and the width of the side chambers, four cubits, all around the temple.

---

a One Ms: Compare verses 29 and 33: MT lacks *were of the same size as the others* b Gk Vg Compare verses 26, 31, 34: Heb *pilasters* c Cn: Heb *at the pilasters of the gates* d Cn: Heb *to him who goes up* e Heb lacks *one* f Gk: Heb *and the width of the gate was three cubits* g Gk: Heb *eleven* h Gk: Heb *and by steps that went up* i Compare Gk: Heb *tent* j Gk: Heb *width*

---

gates are similar to the outer gates, though with a reversal in the order of vestibule and recesses. **40.38–43** Chambers, located in one of the inside gates (probably the north one since it has just been described), were to be used for preparation of animals for sacrifices—washing and slaughter. On *burnt, sin,* and *guilt* offerings, see Lev 1; 4–7. **40.44–46** Rooms for the priests: the north chamber for Zadokites, who alone could perform the altar sacrifice (cf. 44.15), the south for priests of lesser status. *Singers,* levitical singers (1 Chr 16). **40.44** *East gate,* better "south gate," based on the north–south orientation of the gates and the Septuagint. **40.47** The inner court was a square, with

the altar (43.13–17) near the temple itself; cf. 1 Kings 8.64; 2 Kings 16.14. **40.48–41.4** Ten steps lead up to the temple's entrance—into the *vestibule.* The three rooms, the *vestibule* (35 feet long by 21 feet wide), the *nave* (71 by 25), and the *inner room* (35 by 35), are arranged on a linear axis. Cf. the dimensions of the Solomonic temple (1 Kings 6), from which Ezekiel's temple differs in important ways. Though the man entered the inner room, Ezekiel did not. Silence throughout their tour is broken when the man announces *the most holy place.* **40.49** *Pillars,* similar to the placement of Solomon's pillars, but without names; cf. 1 Kings 7.15–22. **41.5–11** Three stories of thirty rooms each

6The side chambers were in three stories, one over another, thirty in each story. There were offsets[a] all around the wall of the temple to serve as supports for the side chambers, so that they should not be supported by the wall of the temple. 7The passageway[b] of the side chambers widened from story to story; for the structure was supplied with a stairway all around the temple. For this reason the structure became wider from story to story. One ascended from the bottom story to the uppermost story by way of the middle one. 8I saw also that the temple had a raised platform all around; the foundations of the side chambers measured a full reed of six long cubits. 9The thickness of the outer wall of the side chambers was five cubits; and the free space between the side chambers of the temple 10and the chambers of the court was a width of twenty cubits all around the temple on every side. 11The side chambers opened onto the area left free, one door toward the north, and another door toward the south; and the width of the part that was left free was five cubits all around.

12 The building that was facing the temple yard on the west side was seventy cubits wide; and the wall of the building was five cubits thick all around, and its depth ninety cubits.

13 Then he measured the temple, one hundred cubits deep; and the yard and the building with its walls, one hundred cubits deep; 14also the width of the east front of the temple and the yard, one hundred cubits.

15 Then he measured the depth of the building facing the yard at the west, together with its galleries[c] on either side, one hundred cubits.

The nave of the temple and the inner room and the outer[d] vestibule 16were paneled,[e] and, all around, all three had windows with re-

cessed[f] frames. Facing the threshold the temple was paneled with wood all around, from the floor up to the windows (now the windows were covered), 17to the space above the door, even to the inner room, and on the outside. And on all the walls all around in the inner room and the nave there was a pattern.[g] 18It was formed of cherubim and palm trees, a palm tree between cherub and cherub. Each cherub had two faces: 19a human face turned toward the palm tree on the one side, and the face of a young lion turned toward the palm tree on the other side. They were carved on the whole temple all around; 20from the floor to the area above the door, cherubim and palm trees were carved on the wall.[h]

21 The doorposts of the nave were square. In front of the holy place was something resembling 22an altar of wood, three cubits high, two cubits long, and two cubits wide;[i] its corners, its base,[j] and its walls were of wood. He said to me, "This is the table that stands before the LORD." 23The nave and the holy place had each a double door. 24The doors had two leaves apiece, two swinging leaves for each door. 25On the doors of the nave were carved cherubim and palm trees, such as were carved on the walls; and there was a canopy of wood in front of the vestibule outside. 26And there were recessed windows and palm trees on either side, on the sidewalls of the vestibule.[k]

The Holy Chambers and the Outer Wall

42 Then he led me out into the outer court, toward the north, and he

---

a Gk Compare 1 Kings 6.6: Heb they entered   b Cn: Heb it was surrounded   c Cn: Meaning of Heb uncertain   d Gk: Heb of the court   e Gk: Heb the thresholds   f Cn Compare Gk 1 Kings 6.4: Meaning of Heb uncertain   g Heb measures h Cn Compare verse 25: Heb and the wall   i Gk: Heb lacks two cubits wide   j Gk: Heb length   k Cn: Heb vestibule. And the side chambers of the temple and the canopies

---

abutting the exterior walls; cf. 1 Kings 6.5–10. **41.8** Raised platform, probably an allusion to the final elevation upon which the temple was built. **41.12– 15a.** Concluding exterior measurements of both the temple and the building, which was similar in size to the temple, though the purpose of this latter structure is unknown; cf. 1 Chr 26.18. **41.15b–26** Interior decoration of the temple, expressed in ways different from the language and motifs typical of accounts of Ezekiel's tour through the temple complex. **41.15b– 16** Only the vestibule and nave are explicitly mentioned in the Hebrew text. They are paneled (cf. 1 Kings 6.9; 7.3, 7), but much remains obscure, esp. in

v. 16, though the windows appear similar to those in the gates. **41.17–20** Some repeating patterns of cherubim (with human and lion faces) and palm trees appear on one register of the walls (cf. 1 Kings 6.29), probably as reliefs carved in wood. **41.21–22** Something resembling an altar of wood, a table typologically similar to the table for rows of bread of the Presence (Ex 25.23–30; Lev 24.7–9; 1 Kings 6.20–22). **41.23– 26** There were two swinging doors per aperture; on doors, cf. v. 21a, and windows, v. 16. Canopy of wood, obscure; cf. 1 Kings 7.6. **42.1–14** The Hebrew text is at many places problematic; moreover, the precise physical character and location of the buildings is difficult

brought me to the chambers that were opposite the temple yard and opposite the building
on the north. [2] The length of the building that
was on the north side[a] was[b] one hundred cubits, and the width fifty cubits. [3] Across the
twenty cubits that belonged to the inner court,
and facing the pavement that belonged to the
outer court, the chambers rose[c] gallery[d] by
gallery[d] in three stories. [4] In front of the chambers was a passage on the inner side, ten cubits
wide and one hundred cubits deep,[e] and its[f]
entrances were on the north. [5] Now the upper
chambers were narrower, for the galleries[d]
took more away from them than from the
lower and middle chambers in the building.
[6] For they were in three stories, and they had
no pillars like the pillars of the outer[g] court;
for this reason the upper chambers were set
back from the ground more than the lower
and the middle ones. [7] There was a wall outside parallel to the chambers, toward the outer
court, opposite the chambers, fifty cubits long.
[8] For the chambers on the outer court were
fifty cubits long, while those opposite the temple were one hundred cubits long. [9] At the foot
of these chambers ran a passage that one entered from the east in order to enter them
from the outer court. [10] The width of the passage[h] was fixed by the wall of the court.

On the south[i] also, opposite the vacant area
and opposite the building, there were chambers [11] with a passage in front of them; they
were similar to the chambers on the north, of
the same length and width, with the same
exits[j] and arrangements and doors. [12] So the
entrances of the chambers to the south were
entered through the entrance at the head of
the corresponding passage, from the east,
along the matching wall.[d]

[13] Then he said to me, "The north chambers and the south chambers opposite the vacant area are the holy chambers, where the
priests who approach the LORD shall eat the
most holy offerings; there they shall deposit
the most holy offerings—the grain offering,
the sin offering, and the guilt offering—for
the place is holy. [14] When the priests enter the
holy place, they shall not go out of it into the
outer court without laying there the vestments
in which they minister, for these are holy; they
shall put on other garments before they go
near to the area open to the people."

[15] When he had finished measuring the interior of the temple area, he led me out by the
gate that faces east, and measured the temple
area all around. [16] He measured the east side
with the measuring reed, five hundred cubits
by the measuring reed. [17] Then he turned and
measured[k] the north side, five hundred cubits
by the measuring reed. [18] Then he turned and
measured[k] the south side, five hundred cubits
by the measuring reed. [19] Then he turned to
the west side and measured, five hundred cubits by the measuring reed. [20] He measured it
on the four sides. It had a wall around it, five
hundred cubits long and five hundred cubits
wide, to make a separation between the holy
and the common.

The Divine Glory Returns to the Temple

43 Then he brought me to the gate, the gate
facing east. [2] And there, the glory of the
God of Israel was coming from the east; the

---

a Gk: Heb *door*   *b* Gk: Heb *before the length*   *c* Heb lacks *the
chambers rose*   *d* Meaning of Heb uncertain   *e* Gk Syr: Heb *a
way of one cubit*   *f* Heb *their*   *g* Gk: Heb lacks *outer*
h Heb lacks *of the passage*   *i* Gk: Heb *east*   *j* Heb *and all their
exits*   *k* Gk: Heb *measuring reed all around. He measured*

---

to determine, though they are related to the *outer court*
(v. 1; cf. 40.17). The buildings function as temple sacristies and may be related to the tradition of the two
chambers described in 40.44–46. Each was three stories high. Specific attention is devoted to passages and
doors, which is consistent with the concern to limit access to the holy. **42.1** The *building*, a structure west of
and hence behind the temple; see 41.12. **42.13** The
grain offering, the sin offering, and the guilt offering are
reserved for priestly consumption (see 44.29); cf. 40.39
for a similar list of sacrifices. Such ritually prepared
food is to remain in the sacristies, a holy precinct.
42.14 Requirements for the use of ritual apparel.
Priestly *vestments* that are worn in the temple building
are not to be worn in the temple's outer courtyard (see
similarly 44.19). **42.15–20** The temple complex is a

square with sides of 500 cubits each. The process of
measuring parallels the description in 40.6–37; movement is from the east to the north, south, and then
west. **42.20** The purpose of the wall is defined not as a
defensive structure but as a boundary between *the holy
and the common* (i.e., the sacred and the profane). On
this distinction elsewhere in Ezekiel, cf. 22.26; 44.23.
Given this statement about the function of the wall,
the defensive character of the gates becomes even
more important, since they must guard against the intrusion of the common into the holy.
43.1–12 The glory of God returns to the temple.
43.1–2 *The gate facing east,* i.e., the gate from which
the glory of God departed (10.19) and the gate at
which Ezekiel's visionary tour had begun (40.6). *From
the east.* Cf. 11.23 for the last explicit reference to the

sound was like the sound of mighty waters; and the earth shone with his glory. ³The[a] vision I saw was like the vision that I had seen when he came to destroy the city, and[b] like the vision that I had seen by the river Chebar; and I fell upon my face. ⁴As the glory of the LORD entered the temple by the gate facing east, ⁵the spirit lifted me up, and brought me into the inner court; and the glory of the LORD filled the temple.

6 While the man was standing beside me, I heard someone speaking to me out of the temple. ⁷He said to me: Mortal, this is the place of my throne and the place for the soles of my feet, where I will reside among the people of Israel forever. The house of Israel shall no more defile my holy name, neither they nor their kings, by their whoring, and by the corpses of their kings at their death.[c] ⁸When they placed their threshold by my threshold and their doorposts beside my doorposts, with only a wall between me and them, they were defiling my holy name by their abominations that they committed; therefore I have consumed them in my anger. ⁹Now let them put away their idolatry and the corpses of their kings far from me, and I will reside among them forever.

10 As for you, mortal, describe the temple to the house of Israel, and let them measure the pattern; and let them be ashamed of their iniquities. ¹¹When they are ashamed of all that they have done, make known to them the plan of the temple, its arrangement, its exits and its entrances, and its whole form—all its ordinances and its entire plan and all its laws; and write it down in their sight, so that they may observe and follow the entire plan and all its ordinances. ¹²This is the law of the temple: the whole territory on the top of the mountain all around shall be most holy. This is the law of the temple.

The Altar

13 These are the dimensions of the altar by cubits (the cubit being one cubit and a handbreadth): its base shall be one cubit high,[d] and one cubit wide, with a rim of one span around its edge. This shall be the height of the altar: ¹⁴From the base on the ground to the lower ledge, two cubits, with a width of one cubit; and from the smaller ledge to the larger ledge, four cubits, with a width of one cubit; ¹⁵and the altar hearth, four cubits; and from the altar hearth projecting upward, four horns. ¹⁶The altar hearth shall be square, twelve cubits long by twelve wide. ¹⁷The ledge also shall be square,

---

a Gk: Heb *Like the vision*   *b* Syr: Heb *and the visions*   *c* Or *on their high places*   *d* Gk: Heb lacks *high*

---

eastward movement of the glory of God. *The sound of mighty waters.* See note on 1.24. *The earth shone.* Cf. 1.4, 13 for the symbolism of light. **43.3** Allusions to 8.1–11.25 and 1.1–28a, respectively. And Ezekiel's behavior is similar—*I fell upon my face* (see 1.28b). **43.5** *The spirit lifted me up.* Cf. 3.12, 14; 8.3; 11.1, 24. *The glory of the LORD filled the temple,* an event analogous to the presence of God filling the tabernacle and temple, respectively (Ex 40.34–35; 1 Kings 8.10–13). **43.6** The *man,* the one who has been conducting Ezekiel's visionary tour of the temple compound and who, despite God's presence in the temple, continues to perform this role. **43.7–12** God's new Torah. God promises never again to leave the temple (vv. 7, 9). Cf. 37.28. **43.7** *Place of my throne,* Jerusalem (Jer 3.16–17; 17.12). *Soles of my feet.* The ark of the covenant was understood to be the object upon which the feet of the deity might rest (cf. esp. 1 Chr 28.2; also Ps 132.7; Isa 60.13; Lam 2.1; and, for an entirely different conception, Isa 66.1). *Their kings,* perhaps a reference to royal burials near the temple (cf. 2 Kings 21.18; 21.26), or to royal steles erected in the temple area and commemorating the dead kings (the final Hebrew phrase in the Masoretic Text is ambiguous). **43.8** A specific critique of the earlier proximity of palace to temple as well as more general reference to *their abominations.* **43.9** A challenge and promise to the present generation.

43.10 The first portion corresponds to the charge in 40.4; *let them measure . . . iniquities* involves the people's pragmatic and emotional response. **43.11** In distinction to 40.4, Ezekiel is charged with writing down the plans for the temple. *Its exits and its entrances,* the permeable portions of the boundary between the sacred and the profane. **43.12** *This is the law of the temple.* Law, Hebrew *torah.* The claim is extraordinary, since Israel already knew an authoritative book of Torah (2 Kings 22.8). *The whole territory . . . shall be most holy,* the primary theme of chs. 40–48. **43.13–27** The construction and consecration of the altar. **43.13–17** The dimensions of the *altar,* a stepped structure, with each ascending level smaller in area than the one before (base, 18 square cubits; lower ledge, 16; upper ledge, 14; hearth with four horns, 12). **43.13** *Cubit.* See note on 40.5. **43.14** *From the base on the ground,* lit. "from the lap of the earth." **43.15–16** *Altar hearth,* a difficult term that in the Hebrew looks like "the mountain of God" (v. 15) or "the lion of God" (vv. 15–16). The latter phrase is very similar to "Ariel" in Isa 29.1–2, 7. Some have suggested that the configuration of the altar is similar to the Mesopotamian ziggurat. **43.15** Archaeologists have discovered numerous stone altars with *horns* at the four corners of their tops. Cf. Ex 27.2; 29.12; 1 Kings 1.50–51; Am 3.14. **43.17** The altar was so high (over 20 feet) that it required *steps.*

fourteen cubits long by fourteen wide, with a rim around it half a cubit wide, and its surrounding base, one cubit. Its steps shall face east.

18 Then he said to me: Mortal, thus says the Lord GOD: These are the ordinances for the altar: On the day when it is erected for offering burnt offerings upon it and for dashing blood against it, 19you shall give to the levitical priests of the family of Zadok, who draw near to me to minister to me, says the Lord GOD, a bull for a sin offering. 20And you shall take some of its blood, and put it on the four horns of the altar, and on the four corners of the ledge, and upon the rim all around; thus you shall purify it and make atonement for it. 21You shall also take the bull of the sin offering, and it shall be burnt in the appointed place belonging to the temple, outside the sacred area.

22 On the second day you shall offer a male goat without blemish for a sin offering; and the altar shall be purified, as it was purified with the bull. 23When you have finished purifying it, you shall offer a bull without blemish and a ram from the flock without blemish. 24You shall present them before the LORD, and the priests shall throw salt on them and offer them up as a burnt offering to the LORD. 25For seven days you shall provide daily a goat for a sin offering; also a bull and a ram from the flock, without blemish, shall be provided. 26Seven days shall they make atonement for the altar and cleanse it, and so consecrate it. 27When these days are over, then from the eighth day onward the priests shall offer upon the altar your burnt offerings and your offerings of well-being; and I will accept you, says the Lord GOD.

The Closed Gate

44 Then he brought me back to the outer gate of the sanctuary, which faces east; and it was shut. 2The LORD said to me: This gate shall remain shut; it shall not be opened, and no one shall enter by it; for the LORD, the God of Israel, has entered by it; therefore it shall remain shut. 3Only the prince, because he is a prince, may sit in it to eat food before the LORD; he shall enter by way of the vestibule of the gate, and shall go out by the same way.

Admission to the Temple

4 Then he brought me by way of the north gate to the front of the temple; and I looked, and lo! the glory of the LORD filled the temple of the LORD; and I fell upon my face. 5The LORD said to me: Mortal, mark well, look closely, and listen attentively to all that I shall tell you concerning all the ordinances of the temple of the LORD and all its laws; and mark well those who may be admitted to[a] the temple and all those who are to be excluded from the sanctuary. 6Say to the rebellious house,[b] to the house of Israel, Thus says the Lord GOD: O house of Israel, let there be an end to all your abominations 7in admitting foreigners, uncircumcised in heart and flesh, to be in my sanctuary, profaning my temple when you offer to me my food, the fat and the blood. You[c] have broken my covenant with all your abominations. 8And you have not kept charge of my sacred offerings; but you have ap-

a Cn: Heb *the entrance of*   *b* Gk: Heb lacks *house*   *c* Gk Syr Vg: Heb *They*

43.18–27 Consecration of the altar requires one week. **43.19** *Family of Zadok.* Only Zadokites, not all levitical priests, may offer sacrifices on the altar. On the first day, both anointing rituals with blood (cf. Lev 16.18; Ex 29.16) and burnt offerings will take place. *Sin offering.* See Lev 4.1–5.13. **43.20** *Purify . . . make atonement,* both cleanse and remove any residual impurity; cf. Ex 29.36; Lev 8.15. **43.21** *Outside the sacred area.* See Lev 4.12, 21; 8.17. **43.22–24** The second day's offerings. **43.24** *Salt,* elsewhere used only for vegetarian offerings; see Lev 2.13; Num 18.19; 2 Chr 13.5; Ezek 47.11. **43.25–27** *Seven days* of offerings mirrors other rituals for dedication. (Ex 29.37; Lev 8.33, 35). **43.27** *Offerings of well-being,* which priests and supplicants could eat; see Lev 3.1–17.

44.1–3 The exterior east gate closed. The east gate, described in 40.6–16, is shut because God is now in the temple. Such action makes the gate function as part of the wall, which is a boundary between the holy

and the common (42.20). **44.2** The closed gate apparently symbolizes the final (43.7, 9) reentry of God into the temple. **44.3** *Prince,* the "civil" ruler in Ezekiel's new polity; see 46.1–18; note on 34.23–24. *Eat food before the LORD,* consume food prepared as part of a sacrifice, e.g., a well-being sacrifice. What was a gate becomes a ritual dining area. **44.4–5** Reprise recapitulating much in 40.4; 43.2–3, 12. One key difference is that the gate now used is the north one, presumably due to the closing of the east gate (v. 2). In addition, v. 5b links the language of *ordinances* and *laws* to the ensuing regulations regarding admission to the temple complex. **44.6–16** Admission of priests to the temple. **44.6–8** The prophet inveighs against Israel for allowing *foreigners* to worship at the sanctuary; see similarly Lev 22.25; cf. Ezek 47.22–23; Isa 56.3–8. For specific instances, see 1 Chr 9.2; Neh 13.4–9. **44.7,9** *Uncircumcised in heart and flesh.* Cf. Lev 26.41; Deut 10.16; Jer 4.4; 9.25. Consistent with Deut 23.2–4, no foreigners

pointed foreigners*a* to act for you in keeping my charge in my sanctuary.

9 Thus says the Lord God: No foreigner, uncircumcised in heart and flesh, of all the foreigners who are among the people of Israel, shall enter my sanctuary. 10But the Levites who went far from me, going astray from me after their idols when Israel went astray, shall bear their punishment. 11They shall be ministers in my sanctuary, having oversight at the gates of the temple, and serving in the temple; they shall slaughter the burnt offering and the sacrifice for the people, and they shall attend on them and serve them. 12Because they ministered to them before their idols and made the house of Israel stumble into iniquity, therefore I have sworn concerning them, says the Lord God, that they shall bear their punishment. 13They shall not come near to me, to serve me as priest, nor come near any of my sacred offerings, the things that are most sacred; but they shall bear their shame, and the consequences of the abominations that they have committed. 14Yet I will appoint them to keep charge of the temple, to do all its chores, all that is to be done in it.

The Levitical Priests

15 But the levitical priests, the descendants of Zadok, who kept the charge of my sanctuary when the people of Israel went astray from me, shall come near to me to minister to me; and they shall attend me to offer me the fat and the blood, says the Lord God. 16It is they who shall enter my sanctuary, it is they who shall approach my table, to minister to me, and they shall keep my charge. 17When they enter the gates of the inner court, they shall wear linen vestments; they shall have nothing of wool on them, while they minister at the gates of the inner court, and within. 18They shall have linen turbans on their heads, and linen undergarments on their loins; they shall not bind themselves with anything that causes sweat. 19When they go out into the outer court to the people, they shall remove the vestments in which they have been ministering, and lay them in the holy chambers; and they shall put on other garments, so that they may not communicate holiness to the people with their vestments. 20They shall not shave their heads or let their locks grow long; they shall only trim the hair of their heads. 21No priest shall drink wine when he enters the inner court. 22They shall not marry a widow, or a divorced woman, but only a virgin of the stock of the house of Israel, or a widow who is the widow of a priest. 23They shall teach my people the difference between the holy and the common, and show them how to distinguish between the unclean and the clean. 24In a controversy they shall act as judges, and they shall decide it according to my judgments. They shall keep my laws and my statutes regarding all my appointed festivals, and they shall keep my sabbaths holy. 25They shall not defile themselves by going near to a dead person; for father or mother, however, and for son or daughter, and for brother or unmarried sister they may defile themselves. 26After he has become clean, they shall count seven days for him. 27On the day that he goes into the holy place, into the inner court, to minister in the holy place, he shall offer his sin offering, says the Lord God.

28 This shall be their inheritance: I am their inheritance; and you shall give them no holding in Israel; I am their holding. 29They shall eat the grain offering, the sin offering, and the

---

a Heb lacks *foreigners*

---

who reside in Judahite territory are to be allowed into the temple precinct. **44.10–14** The *Levites,* who were enfranchised to sacrifice in Deut 18.6–8, are demoted because of idolatrous behavior. Though no specific charges are leveled, there may be an allusion to levitical malfeasance as narrated in Num 16. Nonetheless, they are to have a role in the temple compound, i.e., oversight of the gates and preparation of sacrifices, especially since foreigners have been barred from such activity. **44.15–31** Zadokite priests and their duties. **44.15–16** The Zadokites, because of past orthodox behavior, will conduct sacrifices. *Zadok,* a priest in Jerusalem when David ruled (2 Sam 20.25), became prominent during Solomon's reign (1 Kings 1.41–45). Cf. 40.46. **44.16** *My table.* See 41.22. **44.17–18** Priestly *apparel. Linen.* See note on 9.1–2. **44.19** Cf. the description of *holy chambers* (42.1–14). *Communicate holiness.* See note on 46.20. **44.20** Tonsure is forbidden; cf. Lev 21.5. Deut 14.1–2 indicates that shaving one's head as a form of lamentation (cf. Jer 7.29) could be construed as non-Yahwistic. **44.21** *Drink wine.* See Lev 10.9. **44.22** *Marry.* Cf. Lev 21.7, 13–14. **44.23** *Teach my people.* Cf. Deut 33.8–10. **44.24** *Act as judges.* Cf. Ex 22.9 for such a case; Deut 17.8–9; 19.17; 21.1–5. **44.25** Corpse defilement. See Lev 21.1–3; Num 19. **44.26** It takes seven days to remove corpse defilement for the laity, twice that for priests. **44.28** *No holding,* or "no inheritance" (RSV), i.e., the tradition that the levitical priests had no land holdings (Num 18.20–24; Josh 13.14; 18.7); cf. Ezek 45.1–5; 48.8–14.

guilt offering; and every devoted thing in Israel shall be theirs. 30 The first of all the first fruits of all kinds, and every offering of all kinds from all your offerings, shall belong to the priests; you shall also give to the priests the first of your dough, in order that a blessing may rest on your house. 31 The priests shall not eat of anything, whether bird or animal, that died of itself or was torn by animals.

The Holy District

45 When you allot the land as an inheritance, you shall set aside for the LORD a portion of the land as a holy district, twenty-five thousand cubits long and twenty*a* thousand cubits wide; it shall be holy throughout its entire extent. 2 Of this, a square plot of five hundred by five hundred cubits shall be for the sanctuary, with fifty cubits for an open space around it. 3 In the holy district you shall measure off a section twenty-five thousand cubits long and ten thousand wide, in which shall be the sanctuary, the most holy place. 4 It shall be a holy portion of the land; it shall be for the priests, who minister in the sanctuary and approach the LORD to minister to him; and it shall be both a place for their houses and a holy place for the sanctuary. 5 Another section, twenty-five thousand cubits long and ten thousand cubits wide, shall be for the Levites who minister at the temple, as their holding for cities to live in.*b*

6 Alongside the portion set apart as the holy district you shall assign as a holding for the city an area five thousand cubits wide, and twenty-five thousand cubits long; it shall belong to the whole house of Israel.

7 And to the prince shall belong the land on both sides of the holy district and the holding of the city, alongside the holy district and the holding of the city, on the west and on the east, corresponding in length to one of the tribal portions, and extending from the western to the eastern boundary 8 of the land. It is to be his property in Israel. And my princes shall no longer oppress my people; but they shall let the house of Israel have the land according to their tribes.

9 Thus says the Lord GOD: Enough, O princes of Israel! Put away violence and oppression, and do what is just and right. Cease your evictions of my people, says the Lord GOD.

Weights and Measures

10 You shall have honest balances, an honest ephah, and an honest bath.*c* 11 The ephah and the bath shall be of the same measure, the bath containing one-tenth of a homer, and the ephah one-tenth of a homer; the homer shall be the standard measure. 12 The shekel shall be twenty gerahs. Twenty shekels, twenty-five shekels, and fifteen shekels shall make a mina for you.

Offerings

13 This is the offering that you shall make: one-sixth of an ephah from each homer of

---

a Gk: Heb *ten*   *b* Gk: Heb *as their holding, twenty chambers*
c A Heb measure of volume

44.29 On the priestly portion of the *grain offering,* see Lev 2.3; the *sin offering,* Lev 6.24; and the *guilt offering,* Lev 7.6; more generally, see Num 18.9–13. On *every devoted thing,* cf. Num 18.14; Lev 27.28–29. **44.30** On other priestly income, see Num 18.25–30. *Dough,* "coarse meal" (RSV). **44.31** See Ex 22.31; Lev 17.15, where the prohibition applies to all people, but cf. Lev 22.8, where the stipulation devolves specifically on priests.

45.1–8 Instruction about a holy district in the restored land, which treats the matter of priestly inheritance differently from 44.28 and continues the distinction between Levites and priests. **45.1** *Inheritance,* i.e., in perpetuity; see 48.14. The district is a square plot 25,000 cubits on a side. Cf. the longer description of land divisions in 48.8–22. **45.2** Land for the sanctuary, a *plot* 500 cubits square, and *open space;* cf. 42.20; 48.8, 17. **45.3–4** The share of the land *for the priests* in the South. According to 48.10, the temple is located in this priestly allotment. **45.5** The *Levites'* share, which lies in the North. The forty-eight levitical *cities* (Josh 21.1–

42) are all to be located in this section. **45.6** Land *for the city.* Cf. 48.15–20. **45.7** The *prince's* portion, which lies to the east and west of all three other allocations. **45.9** *Princes of Israel,* language reminiscent of Ezekiel before 587 BCE (e.g., 21.12), which in this context may have been secondarily applied to the priests in the new polity. On earlier *evictions,* see 1 Kings 21.1–16; Isa 5.8; Mic 2.2. But land possession was important for Ezekiel as well, e.g., 11.14–16. **45.10–12** Dry volume and weight. Not only are measures standardized, but Israel is admonished to adhere to them. Such admonitions are consistent with earlier stipulations (Lev 19.35–36; Deut 25.13–16). Earlier prophets had inveighed against violation of standard measures, e.g., Am 8.5; Mic 6.10–11. Cf. Prov 11.1; 20.10. *Homer,* the base for dry measurement, 5–6 bushels (the Hebrew word suggests that it was the load one donkey could bear). *Shekel,* the standard for weight, a little less than a half ounce, though both a "heavy" and a "light" shekel are known—thus justifying such a call for standardization. **45.13–17** Offerings. The people's agricultural

wheat, and one-sixth of an ephah from each homer of barley, [14]and as the fixed portion of oil,[a] one-tenth of a bath from each cor (the cor,[b] like the homer, contains ten baths); [15]and one sheep from every flock of two hundred, from the pastures of Israel. This is the offering for grain offerings, burnt offerings, and offerings of well-being, to make atonement for them, says the Lord GOD. [16]All the people of the land shall join with the prince in Israel in making this offering. [17]But this shall be the obligation of the prince regarding the burnt offerings, grain offerings, and drink offerings, at the festivals, the new moons, and the sabbaths, all the appointed festivals of the house of Israel: he shall provide the sin offerings, grain offerings, the burnt offerings, and the offerings of well-being, to make atonement for the house of Israel.

Festivals

18 Thus says the Lord GOD: In the first month, on the first day of the month, you shall take a young bull without blemish, and purify the sanctuary. [19]The priest shall take some of the blood of the sin offering and put it on the doorposts of the temple, the four corners of the ledge of the altar, and the posts of the gate of the inner court. [20]You shall do the same on the seventh day of the month for anyone who has sinned through error or ignorance; so you shall make atonement for the temple.

21 In the first month, on the fourteenth day of the month, you shall celebrate the festival of the passover, and for seven days unleavened bread shall be eaten. [22]On that day the prince shall provide for himself and all the people of the land a young bull for a sin offering. [23]And

during the seven days of the festival he shall provide as a burnt offering to the LORD seven young bulls and seven rams without blemish, on each of the seven days; and a male goat daily for a sin offering. [24]He shall provide as a grain offering an ephah for each bull, an ephah for each ram, and a hin of oil to each ephah. [25]In the seventh month, on the fifteenth day of the month and for the seven days of the festival, he shall make the same provision for sin offerings, burnt offerings, and grain offerings, and for the oil.

Miscellaneous Regulations

46 Thus says the Lord GOD: The gate of the inner court that faces east shall remain closed on the six working days; but on the sabbath day it shall be opened and on the day of the new moon it shall be opened. [2]The prince shall enter by the vestibule of the gate from outside, and shall take his stand by the post of the gate. The priests shall offer his burnt offering and his offerings of well-being, and he shall bow down at the threshold of the gate. Then he shall go out, but the gate shall not be closed until evening. [3]The people of the land shall bow down at the entrance of that gate before the LORD on the sabbaths and on the new moons. [4]The burnt offering that the prince offers to the LORD on the sabbath day shall be six lambs without blemish and a ram without blemish; [5]and the grain offering with the ram shall be an ephah, and the grain offering with the lambs shall be as much as he wishes to give, together with a hin of oil to each ephah. [6]On the day of the new moon he

---

a Cn: Heb oil, the bath the oil   b Vg: Heb homer

---

products are subject to a tax of the following percentages: grain, 1.5 percent; olive oil, 1 percent; livestock, .5 percent. These are payable in the form of offerings in kind (*grain offerings, burnt offerings, and offerings of well-being*). **45.16** Cf. "All the people of the land shall give this offering to the prince of Israel" (RSV). **45.17** The *prince* is subject to a higher tax; cf. 45.22–46.15 on the prince's obligations for the sacrificial system. **45.18–25** Rites of purification and festivals. **45.18–20** An otherwise unattested annual rite of temple purification. For the use of blood in purification rites, cf. 43.18–27; on the Day of Atonement, cf. Lev 16. **45.20** Purification of the individual (*anyone*), though the text is difficult. **45.21–25** *Passover* and Festival of Booths (Tabernacles). Ezekiel has revised significantly the standard festival calendar (cf. Num 28) by highlighting these two primary feasts. **45.21** Calendar for

the Passover celebration. **45.22–24** The prince's responsibilities for Passover sacrifices. **45.25** *The festival*, the fall harvest festival otherwise known as Booths, Ingathering, or Tabernacles. Cf. Lev 23.33–36; Num 29.12–38; Deut 16.13–15, where it continues for eight days.

46.1–18 Stipulations regarding the prince. **46.1–7** The prince and sacrifices. The inner east gate is to be closed except on the sabbath and new moon (cf. the closing of the exterior east gate, 44.1–3). When the *prince* (note on 34.23–24) enters and moves through the gate to stand at the interior door with the appropriate offerings (v. 2), the priests will perform his sacrifices. By contrast, the *people of the land* (v. 3) may only come near the outside opening of the gate. **46.4** On the *sabbath* sacrifices, cf. Num 28.9–10. The sabbath was important for Ezekiel; see 20.12–13.

shall offer a young bull without blemish, and six lambs and a ram, which shall be without blemish; 7 as a grain offering he shall provide an ephah with the bull and an ephah with the ram, and with the lambs as much as he wishes, together with a hin of oil to each ephah. 8 When the prince enters, he shall come in by the vestibule of the gate, and he shall go out by the same way.

9 When the people of the land come before the LORD at the appointed festivals, whoever enters by the north gate to worship shall go out by the south gate; and whoever enters by the south gate shall go out by the north gate: they shall not return by way of the gate by which they entered, but shall go out straight ahead. 10 When they come in, the prince shall come in with them; and when they go out, he shall go out.

11 At the festivals and the appointed seasons the grain offering with a young bull shall be an ephah, and with a ram an ephah, and with the lambs as much as one wishes to give, together with a hin of oil to an ephah. 12 When the prince provides a freewill offering, either a burnt offering or offerings of well-being as a freewill offering to the LORD, the gate facing east shall be opened for him; and he shall offer his burnt offering or his offerings of well-being as he does on the sabbath day. Then he shall go out, and after he has gone out the gate shall be closed.

13 He shall provide a lamb, a yearling, without blemish, for a burnt offering to the LORD daily; morning by morning he shall provide it. 14 And he shall provide a grain offering with it morning by morning regularly, one-sixth of an ephah, and one-third of a hin of oil to moisten the choice flour, as a grain offering to the LORD; this is the ordinance for all time. 15 Thus the lamb and the grain offering and the oil shall be provided, morning by morning, as a regular burnt offering.

16 Thus says the Lord GOD: If the prince makes a gift to any of his sons out of his inheritance,[a] it shall belong to his sons, it is their holding by inheritance. 17 But if he makes a gift out of his inheritance to one of his servants, it shall be his to the year of liberty; then it shall revert to the prince; only his sons may keep a gift from his inheritance. 18 The prince shall not take any of the inheritance of the people, thrusting them out of their holding; he shall give his sons their inheritance out of his own holding, so that none of my people shall be dispossessed of their holding.

19 Then he brought me through the entrance, which was at the side of the gate, to the north row of the holy chambers for the priests; and there I saw a place at the extreme western end of them. 20 He said to me, "This is the place where the priests shall boil the guilt offering and the sin offering, and where they shall bake the grain offering, in order not to bring them out into the outer court and so communicate holiness to the people."

21 Then he brought me out to the outer court, and led me past the four corners of the court; and in each corner of the court there was a court— 22 in the four corners of the court were small[b] courts, forty cubits long and thirty wide; the four were of the same size. 23 On the inside, around each of the four courts[c] was a row of masonry, with hearths made at the bottom of the rows all around.

a Gk: Heb it is his inheritance b Gk Syr Vg: Meaning of Heb uncertain c Heb the four of them

---

46.6 On new moon sacrifices, cf. Num 28.11–15. 46.8–10 Entering and exiting during festivals. As with v. 2, the prince approaches the interior east gate from the outside and proceeds to the inner door. Though he makes his ritual entrance at the same time as the people, they must use different exterior gates from those through which they entered. Moreover, they must move according to either a north–south or south–north axis, apparently a form of traffic control during major festivals. 46.11 See v. 7. 46.12–15 Instructions for the prince when making a freewill (noncalendrical) or daily (calendrical) offering. On the freewill or voluntary offering, which may result from payment of a vow, see Lev 22.18–23; on the daily offering, see Num 28.3–8. 46.16–18 The prince's land (45.7; 48.21–22) may be inherited by his sons, but it is to remain in that family in perpetuity. Such land could be temporarily granted to someone outside, one of his servants, but the land would revert to kin ownership on the year of liberty, i.e., the year of release associated with the jubilee celebration (Lev 25.8–17). 46.18a The prince is not to take others' inheritance; cf. note on 45.9. 46.19–24 Sacrifice preparation areas for priests and laity. Near the inner north gate and in the holy chambers is a room where priests prepare the guilt, sin, and grain offerings; cf. 42.13. 46.20 Not to . . . communicate holiness to the people. The holy is a threat to the people, e.g., when Uzzah touched the ark and died (2 Sam 6.6–7); cf. 44.19. 46.21–24 Sizable cooking areas in the four corners of the exterior court. Those who serve at the temple, i.e., the Levites, prepare foodstuffs on behalf of the people; cf. 2 Chr 35.11–13.

24Then he said to me, "These are the kitchens where those who serve at the temple shall boil the sacrifices of the people."

Water Flowing from the Temple

47 Then he brought me back to the entrance of the temple; there, water was flowing from below the threshold of the temple toward the east (for the temple faced east); and the water was flowing down from below the south end of the threshold of the temple, south of the altar. 2Then he brought me out by way of the north gate, and led me around on the outside to the outer gate that faces toward the east;*a* and the water was coming out on the south side.

3 Going on eastward with a cord in his hand, the man measured one thousand cubits, and then led me through the water; and it was ankle-deep. 4Again he measured one thousand, and led me through the water; and it was knee-deep. Again he measured one thousand, and led me through the water; and it was up to the waist. 5Again he measured one thousand, and it was a river that I could not cross, for the water had risen; it was deep enough to swim in, a river that could not be crossed. 6He said to me, "Mortal, have you seen this?"

Then he led me back along the bank of the river. 7As I came back, I saw on the bank of the river a great many trees on the one side and on the other. 8He said to me, "This water flows to-ward the eastern region and goes down into the Arabah; and when it enters the sea, the sea of stagnant waters, the water will become fresh. 9Wherever the river goes,*b* every living creature that swarms will live, and there will be very many fish, once these waters reach there. It will become fresh; and everything will live where the river goes. 10People will stand fishing beside the sea*c* from En-gedi to En-eglaim; it will be a place for the spreading of nets; its fish will be of a great many kinds, like the fish of the Great Sea. 11But its swamps and marshes will not become fresh; they are to be left for salt. 12On the banks, on both sides of the river, there will grow all kinds of trees for food. Their leaves will not wither nor their fruit fail, but they will bear fresh fruit every month, because the water for them flows from the sanctuary. Their fruit will be for food, and their leaves for healing."

The New Boundaries of the Land

13 Thus says the Lord God: These are the boundaries by which you shall divide the land for inheritance among the twelve tribes of Israel. Joseph shall have two portions. 14You shall divide it equally; I swore to give it to your ancestors, and this land shall fall to you as your inheritance.

---

a Meaning of Heb uncertain   *b* Gk Syr Vg Tg: Heb *the two rivers go*   *c* Heb *it*

47.1–12 The guide returns to show Ezekiel a stream flowing out from beneath the temple, past the altar, and out under the exterior east gate. Water imagery has already been associated with the presence of the deity (1.24; 43.2). The river apparently reflects the motif of the deity's garden or dwelling as a watery and fertile place (e.g., Gen 2.10–14; Ps 46.4), which clearly links the river to Jerusalem; see note on 28.2. The late prophetic writings Joel 3.18; Zech 13.1; 14.8 share Ezekiel's basic expectation. **47.2** The flow is to the southeast. **47.3–5** The man takes four measurements at 1,000 cubit intervals, which reveal that the river is growing progressively larger and deeper—it is *ankle-deep, knee-deep, up to the waist*, and finally *could not be crossed*. **47.6–7** As they retrace their steps, Ezekiel observes the fertile growth on the riverbanks; cf. descriptions of the Jordan banks (Jer 12.5; Zech 11.3). **47.8** The river continues southeast into the *Arabah*, which means here the Jordan rift valley just north of *the sea*, the Dead Sea. The *water will become fresh;* cf. 2 Kings 2.22 for the same Hebrew expression. **47.9–12** The river as a source of fertility. **47.9** *The river goes.* The Masoretic tradition reads "the two rivers go," which reflects an expectation of two rivers attested in Zech 14.8. *Living creature, swarms, fish*, vocabulary from Gen 1. **47.10** Fish will be prolific and the fishing excellent (cf. 26.5, 14 on earlier fishing imagery). *En-gedi*, an oasis with spring, waterfall, and small canyon on the western bank of the Dead Sea. *En-eglaim.* Site unknown, though some scholars think it lies on the eastern bank of the Dead Sea. *Like the fish of the Great Sea* probably refers to a prolific fishery and not specific saltwater species. **47.11** Saline wetlands will be preserved, not for ecological reasons but for salt production, i.e., *they are to be left for salt*, which was used in ritual practice (43.24). **47.12** Cf. v. 7, a picture of preternatural fertility: deciduous trees whose leaves do not fall and that bear fruit *every month*. The fertility provides for food and healing. All this is attributable to the source of the river: *the sanctuary.*

47.13–48.29 New configuration of the land, a continuation of the process begun in 45.1–8. **47.13–22** Boundaries and allocation of the land. This process suggests that Ezekiel envisions a new settlement preceded by a new exodus and wilderness wanderings (20.33–35). **47.13** *Joseph . . . two portions*, i.e., Manasseh and Ephraim, 48.4–5. **47.14** What was promised to the ancestors will be fulfilled for a future generation.

15 This shall be the boundary of the land: On the north side, from the Great Sea by way of Hethlon to Lebo-hamath, and on to Zedad,[a] 16Berothah, Sibraim (which lies between the border of Damascus and the border of Hamath), as far as Hazer-hatticon, which is on the border of Hauran. 17So the boundary shall run from the sea to Hazar-enon, which is north of the border of Damascus, with the border of Hamath to the north.[b] This shall be the north side.

18 On the east side, between Hauran and Damascus; along the Jordan between Gilead and the land of Israel; to the eastern sea and as far as Tamar.[c] This shall be the east side.

19 On the south side, it shall run from Tamar as far as the waters of Meribath-kadesh, from there along the Wadi of Egypt[d] to the Great Sea. This shall be the south side.

20 On the west side, the Great Sea shall be the boundary to a point opposite Lebo-hamath. This shall be the west side.

21 So you shall divide this land among you according to the tribes of Israel. 22You shall allot it as an inheritance for yourselves and for the aliens who reside among you and have begotten children among you. They shall be to you as citizens of Israel; with you they shall be allotted an inheritance among the tribes of Israel. 23In whatever tribe aliens reside, there you shall assign them their inheritance, says the Lord God.

The Tribal Portions

48 These are the names of the tribes: Beginning at the northern border, on the Hethlon road,[e] from Lebo-hamath, as far as Hazar-enon (which is on the border of Damascus, with Hamath to the north), and[f] extending from the east side to the west,[g] Dan, one portion. 2Adjoining the territory of Dan, from the east side to the west, Asher, one portion. 3Adjoining the territory of Asher, from the east side to the west, Naphtali, one portion. 4Adjoining the territory of Naphtali, from the east side to the west, Manasseh, one portion. 5Adjoining the territory of Manasseh, from the east side to the west, Ephraim, one portion. 6Adjoining the territory of Ephraim, from the east side to the west, Reuben, one portion. 7Adjoining the territory of Reuben, from the east side to the west, Judah, one portion.

8 Adjoining the territory of Judah, from the east side to the west, shall be the portion that you shall set apart, twenty-five thousand cubits in width, and in length equal to one of the tribal portions, from the east side to the west, with the sanctuary in the middle of it. 9The portion that you shall set apart for the Lord shall be twenty-five thousand cubits in length, and twenty[h] thousand in width. 10These shall be the allotments of the holy portion: the priests shall have an allotment measuring twenty-five thousand cubits on the northern side, ten thousand cubits in width on the western side, ten thousand in width on the eastern side, and twenty-five thousand in length on the southern side, with the sanctuary of the Lord in the middle of it. 11This shall be for the consecrated priests, the descendants[i] of Zadok, who kept my charge, who did not go astray when the people of Israel went astray, as the Levites did. 12It shall belong to them as a special portion from the holy portion of the land, a most holy place, adjoining the territory of the Levites. 13Alongside the territory of the priests, the Levites shall have an allotment twenty-five thousand cubits in length and ten

---

a Gk: Heb Lebo-zedad, 16Hamath   b Meaning of Heb uncertain
c Compare Syr: Heb you shall measure   d Heb lacks of Egypt
e Compare 47.15: Heb by the side of the way   f Cn: Heb and
they shall be his   g Gk Compare verses 2-8: Heb the east side the
west   h Compare 45.1: Heb ten   i One Ms Gk: Heb of the
descendants

47.15–21 The idealized perimeter *boundary of the land:* on the north, basically Damascus to the coast; on the east, the Jordan; south, a line through Kadesh-barnea on the southern side; and west, the Mediterranean. Cf. earlier boundaries, e.g., in Num 34; Josh 15. Striking is the absence of Transjordanian tribal land (Num 34.13–15). **47.22–23** Quite a liberal allowance concerning *inheritance* and *aliens.* Cf. 44.6–9; Lev 19.34; 24.22; Num 15.29; Deut 23.2–8 on the status of the so-called resident aliens. In order to "inherit" land, the alien family must be of two generations. **48.1–29** Boundaries inside the land. **48.1–7** Tribal alloca-tions to the north of the holy sector (vv. 8–22): Dan, Asher, Naphtali, Manasseh, Ephraim, Reuben, Judah. Each tribe receives an equal portion of land. The grants are strips of land that extend from the eastern to the western borders. The rationale for the ordering of the tribal land is unclear, e.g., Benjamin south of Judah. Cf. the tribal allocations in Josh 13–19. **48.8–22** The holy sector, the description of which dominates this depiction of the land. Cf. 45.1–8, which is an abbreviated form of this description. **48.12** The Zadokites' allocation is *a most holy place,* an expression that presupposes various gradations of holiness in comparison to the bi-

thousand in width. The whole length shall be twenty-five thousand cubits and the width twenty[a] thousand. 14They shall not sell or exchange any of it; they shall not transfer this choice portion of the land, for it is holy to the LORD.

15 The remainder, five thousand cubits in width and twenty-five thousand in length, shall be for ordinary use for the city, for dwellings and for open country. In the middle of it shall be the city; 16and these shall be its dimensions: the north side four thousand five hundred cubits, the south side four thousand five hundred, the east side four thousand five hundred, and the west side four thousand five hundred. 17The city shall have open land: on the north two hundred fifty cubits, on the south two hundred fifty, on the east two hundred fifty, on the west two hundred fifty. 18The remainder of the length alongside the holy portion shall be ten thousand cubits to the east, and ten thousand to the west, and it shall be alongside the holy portion. Its produce shall be food for the workers of the city. 19The workers of the city, from all the tribes of Israel, shall cultivate it. 20The whole portion that you shall set apart shall be twenty-five thousand cubits square, that is, the holy portion together with the property of the city.

21 What remains on both sides of the holy portion and of the property of the city shall belong to the prince. Extending from the twenty-five thousand cubits of the holy portion to the east border, and westward from the twenty-five thousand cubits to the west border, parallel to the tribal portions, it shall belong to the prince. The holy portion with the sanctuary of the temple in the middle of it, 22and the property of the Levites and of the city, shall be in the middle of that which belongs to the prince. The portion of the prince

shall lie between the territory of Judah and the territory of Benjamin.

23 As for the rest of the tribes: from the east side to the west, Benjamin, one portion. 24Adjoining the territory of Benjamin, from the east side to the west, Simeon, one portion. 25Adjoining the territory of Simeon, from the east side to the west, Issachar, one portion. 26Adjoining the territory of Issachar, from the east side to the west, Zebulun, one portion. 27Adjoining the territory of Zebulun, from the east side to the west, Gad, one portion. 28And adjoining the territory of Gad to the south, the boundary shall run from Tamar to the waters of Meribath-kadesh, from there along the Wadi of Egypt[b] to the Great Sea. 29This is the land that you shall allot as an inheritance among the tribes of Israel, and these are their portions, says the Lord GOD.

30 These shall be the exits of the city: On the north side, which is to be four thousand five hundred cubits by measure, 31three gates, the gate of Reuben, the gate of Judah, and the gate of Levi, the gates of the city being named after the tribes of Israel. 32On the east side, which is to be four thousand five hundred cubits, three gates, the gate of Joseph, the gate of Benjamin, and the gate of Dan. 33On the south side, which is to be four thousand five hundred cubits by measure, three gates, the gate of Simeon, the gate of Issachar, and the gate of Zebulun. 34On the west side, which is to be four thousand five hundred cubits, three gates,[c] the gate of Gad, the gate of Asher, and the gate of Naphtali. 35The circumference of the city shall be eighteen thousand cubits. And the name of the city from that time on shall be, The LORD is There.

---

a Gk: Heb ten   b Heb lacks of Egypt   c One Ms Gk Syr: MT their gates three

nary distinction between holy and common; cf. 45.4. **48.14** The priests, like other Israelites, hold the land in perpetuity; cf. 46.16–18; 47.13–14. **48.15–20** *The city,* Jerusalem, though not so explicitly stated. The city is a square a little over one and a half miles per side. **48.15** Land *for ordinary use for the city,* a portion of which is designated for agriculture. **48.21–22** The *prince*'s holdings, a grant that, consistent with 43.8, does not place the prince in direct proximity to the temple. **48.21** *Sanctuary of the temple,* a peculiar phrase, but one that emphasizes the intensely holy character of the Zadokites' sector. **48.23–29** Allocations *for the rest of the tribes* to the south of the holy sector: Benjamin, Simeon, Issachar, Zebulun, Gad. Of

these tribes only Simeon was, according to other tribal allocation traditions, a Southern tribe (Josh 19.1–9). **48.30–35** The perimeter and name of the *city.* Each side of the city wall will have three gates, which are given tribal names. Unlike the list in vv.1–7, 23–27, Levi is present, which means that Joseph replaces Manasseh and Ephraim in order to preserve the number twelve; cf. Jer 31.38–39; Zech 14.10–11; Rev 21.12–14. **48.35** A new name for Jerusalem, the name of which has not been explicitly mentioned in descriptions of the *city* (vv. 15–20; 43.6). *The LORD is There,* a natural expression of sentiments such as those in Isa 60.14. Cf. other new names for Jerusalem (Isa 62.4, "My Delight Is in Her"; Jer 33.16, "The LORD is our righteousness").

DANIEL

THE BOOK APPEARING UNDER THE NAME OF DANIEL is actually by an unknown author. A Daniel is mentioned in Ezek 14.14–20; 28.3 as a righteous sage of antiquity alongside two non-Israelite heroes of the Hebrew Bible, Noah and Job. A non-Israelite Daniel (or Danel) is mentioned as a just judge in the Aqhat legend from Ugarit (fourteenth century BCE). The name of such a wise and righteous legendary figure was probably chosen to enhance the text. The stories about Daniel in chs. 1–6 have a legendary character and are clearly fictitious.

Genre and Structure

THE BOOK AS A WHOLE is usually described as an apocalypse, a genre in which revelation is mediated in a narrative framework to a human recipient through otherworldly beings and that discloses a heavenly world and a coming judgment. Apocalypses often use conventions such as pseudonymity and employ a variety of literary forms. Daniel is the only full-fledged example of the genre in the Hebrew Bible, but other examples include Revelation and the pseudepigraphical books of *1 Enoch, 4 Ezra,* and *2 Baruch.* The book of Daniel has two distinct parts, a collection of stories in chs. 1–6 and four visions in chs. 7–12. The stories, narrated mostly in the third person, are about a Jew named Daniel and his companions, who are among the prisoners from Jerusalem taken into exile in Babylon. The visions, largely in the first person, are received by Daniel. The two parts are unified by the narrative framework and the character, Daniel.

Setting, Date, and Languages

THE PORTRAYAL OF DANIEL as a Jewish exile in Babylon creates a literary setting in the sixth century BCE, and his visions there appear to provide insight into events in Judea in later centuries. The literary setting is not, however, the setting in which the book was actually written. The fact that ch. 11 obviously refers to Antiochus IV Epiphanes, the Seleucid ruler from Syria, makes it clear that the book took its final form during Antiochus's persecution of the Jews, which began with the desecration of the temple in 167 BCE. While one group of Jews led by the Maccabees resisted militarily, others offered passive resistance (1 Macc 1.29–38).

Much of the material in chs. 1–6 probably originated in the fourth and third centuries BCE and circulated independently before being joined to the visions. The inaccurate description of the end of Antiochus's reign and of his death indicates that the book was finished before these events of 164 BCE. The process by which the book was composed is further complicated by the fact that it is written in two languages, Hebrew (1.1–2.4a; 8.1–12.13) and Aramaic (2.4b–7.28). The language divisions do not correspond to the content divisions. The traditional stories about Daniel circulated in Aramaic, and the first vision (ch. 7) was also composed in Aramaic. The use of Hebrew in the later visions may reflect growing nationalism in the time of persecution. Ch. 1 may have been translated from Aramaic into Hebrew to form an *inclusio* (a repetition signaling the beginning and end of a unit) with the Hebrew chapters at the end of the book.

The book was further expanded when it was translated into Greek by the insertion of the Prayer of Azariah and the Song of the Three Jews in ch. 3, and the addition of the stories of Susanna and Bel and the Dragon.

Authorship and Audience

CLUES SCATTERED THROUGH THE BOOK indicate that the author (or authors) belonged to "the wise," those faithful to the covenant in the time of Antiochus's persecution, but not advocates of active resistance. They are sometimes identified with the Hasidim, but the latter were militant supporters of the Maccabees. The tales were probably originally composed for a general audience in the eastern Diaspora, the visions for a more learned audience in Judea.

Intention

AS A WHOLE, THE BOOK OF DANIEL encourages and consoles Jews facing persecution in the reign of Antiochus. In chs. 1–6, it provides them with heroic role models who thrive because they remain faithful to Jewish law while serving a foreign king. Chs. 7–12 hold out the promise of deliverance in the new kingdom of God and individual resurrection and exaltation for those who remain faithful in the face of persecution. Throughout the book insists on the sovereignty of the God of Israel.

Place in the Canon

DANIEL'S PLACE AMONG THE PROPHETIC BOOKS derives from its location in the Greek Septuagint. The Hebrew canon, on the other hand, places it among the Writings, between Esther and Ezra. The placement of the book bears significantly on the history of its interpretation as prophecy or apocalyptic. There are significant differences between the book found in the Hebrew (and Protestant) biblical canon and that found in Greek and Latin (and modern Catholic) Bibles. The two major Greek versions, the Septuagint and that of Theodotion, contain the Prayer of Azariah (3.24–45), the Song of the Three Jews (3.46–90), and the stories of Susanna (13.1–64), Bel (14.1–22), and the Dragon (14.23–42), which are relegated to the Apocrypha in Protestant Bibles. Manuscript fragments of Daniel were found among the Dead Sea Scrolls in three caves at Qumran. Some other Aramaic compositions related to Daniel were also found there: the *Prayer of Nabonidus* (4Q242), which may reflect an earlier form of the story in Daniel 4, two apocalyptic texts that mention the name of Daniel (4Q243–44 and 4Q245), and another apocalyptic text that does not mention him but uses language reminiscent of Daniel 7 (4Q246, the "Son of God" text). [PAMELA J. MILNE, revised by JOHN J. COLLINS]

Four Young Israelites at the Babylonian Court

1 In the third year of the reign of King Jehoiakim of Judah, King Nebuchadnezzar of Babylon came to Jerusalem and besieged it. ²The Lord let King Jehoiakim of Judah fall into his power, as well as some of the vessels of the house of God. These he brought to the land of Shinar,ᵃ and placed the vessels in the treasury of his gods.

3 Then the king commanded his palace master Ashpenaz to bring some of the Israelites of the royal family and of the nobility, ⁴young men without physical defect and handsome, versed in every branch of wisdom, endowed with knowledge and insight, and competent to serve in the king's palace; they were to be taught the literature and language of the Chaldeans. ⁵The king assigned them a daily portion of the royal rations of food and wine. They were to be educated for three years, so that at the end of that time they could be stationed in the king's court. ⁶Among them were Daniel, Hananiah, Mishael, and Azariah, from the tribe of Judah. ⁷The palace master gave them other names: Daniel he called Belteshazzar, Hananiah he called Shadrach, Mishael he called Meshach, and Azariah he called Abednego.

8 But Daniel resolved that he would not defile himself with the royal rations of food and wine; so he asked the palace master to allow him not to defile himself. ⁹Now God allowed Daniel to receive favor and compassion from the palace master. ¹⁰The palace master said to Daniel, "I am afraid of my lord the king; he has appointed your food and your drink. If he should see you in poorer condition than the other young men of your own age, you would endanger my head with the king." ¹¹Then Daniel asked the guard whom the palace master had appointed over Daniel, Hananiah, Mishael, and Azariah: ¹²"Please test your servants for ten days. Let us be given vegetables to eat and water to drink. ¹³You can then compare our appearance with the appearance of the young men who eat the royal rations, and deal with your servants according to what you observe." ¹⁴So he agreed to this proposal and tested them for ten days. ¹⁵At the end of ten days it was observed that they appeared better and fatter than all the young men who had been eating the royal rations. ¹⁶So the guard

---

ᵃ Gk Theodotion: Heb adds *to the house of his own gods*

1.1–6.28 The edifying popular tales in chs. 1–6 are linked to the visions in chs. 7–12 by the central character, Daniel, and a focus on the sovereignty and power of God. They incorporate older, traditional material and exhibit many characteristics of folklore including stereotyped characters, stylized plots, marvelous interventions, and extensive repetition and elaboration. In chs. 2, 4, and 5 wise courtiers compete to interpret dreams and visions, while in chs. 3 and 6 Jewish courtiers are miraculously delivered from mortal danger after coming into conflict with foreign courtiers and their king. There are many parallels with the stories of Joseph (Gen 39–41), Esther, and Ahikar (Aramaic). **1.1–21** This introduction in Hebrew to the Aramaic stories in chs. 2–6 sets the time, place, and general circumstance of exile in Babylon and introduces five of the eight major characters in the remaining stories. The superiority of the Jews' God-given wisdom introduces the theme of the sovereignty of their God. **1.1** *Third year of . . . Jehoiakim*, 606 BCE. See 2 Chr 36.5–7. Jerusalem was actually captured in 597 BCE during the reign of Jehoiachin, Jehoiakim's son; see 2 Kings 24.10–12 and the *Babylonian Chronicle*, a cuneiform source. *Nebuchadnezzar* II (605–562 BCE), alternately spelled "Nebuchadrezzar" (Jer 24.1; 25.1, 9) can be translated "Nabu/Nebo [a Babylonian deity], guard of the frontier"; see Isa 46.1. **1.2** See 2 Kings 24.10–16; 2 Chr 36.7, 18–20; Ezra 5.14. *Shinar*, the ancient name of Babylon, ordinarily with negative connotations; see Gen 10.10; 11.2; 14.1, 9; Isa 11.11; Zech 5.11. *His gods*, Marduk (Bel), the chief god of Babylon, and his son, Nabu/Nebo, the personal god of Nebuchadnezzar. **1.3** *Palace master*, lit. "chief eunuch." Such royal servants were sometimes castrated, but the word does not necessarily have that connotation; see Gen 37.36; 39.1. *The Israelites . . . of the nobility*, the bulk of those taken to Babylon in 597 BCE; see 2 Kings 24.14–16. **1.4** *Without physical defect*, used of priests (Lev 21.17–23) and sacrificial animals (Lev 22.19–21), but also of slaves in papyri from Wadi Daliyeh. *Chaldeans*, usually Aramaic-speaking, Neo-Babylonian peoples (5.30; 9.1; Ezra 5.12), but here and elsewhere in Daniel (2.2–5, 10; 4.7; 5.7, 11) a generic term for wise men who practiced astrology and divination; see 2.2. **1.5** *Portion*, from an Old Persian word meaning "government-supplied food ration"; see vv. 8, 15, 16; 11.26; 2 Kings 25.30; Jer 52.34. **1.6–7** The Hebrew names contain references to the God of Israel. For service in the royal court the young men are given new names incorporating references to Babylonian deities: Bel, Marduk, and Nabu. **1.8** By the second century BCE observance of the dietary laws (Lev 11) was a cornerstone of orthodoxy; see Tob 1.10–11; Jdt 10.5; 12.1–2; 1 Macc 1.62–63; 2 Macc 5.27; 6.8, 18–31; 7.1. **1.14** *Ten days*, a typical period for a spiritual test; see Rev 2.10; *Jubilees* 19.8. In v. 20, the four Jews prove to be *ten times better*.

continued to withdraw their royal rations and the wine they were to drink, and gave them vegetables. [17]To these four young men God gave knowledge and skill in every aspect of literature and wisdom; Daniel also had insight into all visions and dreams.

18 At the end of the time that the king had set for them to be brought in, the palace master brought them into the presence of Nebuchadnezzar, [19]and the king spoke with them. And among them all, no one was found to compare with Daniel, Hananiah, Mishael, and Azariah; therefore they were stationed in the king's court. [20]In every matter of wisdom and understanding concerning which the king inquired of them, he found them ten times better than all the magicians and enchanters in his whole kingdom. [21]And Daniel continued there until the first year of King Cyrus.

Nebuchadnezzar's Dream

2 In the second year of Nebuchadnezzar's reign, Nebuchadnezzar dreamed such dreams that his spirit was troubled and his sleep left him. [2]So the king commanded that the magicians, the enchanters, the sorcerers, and the Chaldeans be summoned to tell the king his dreams. When they came in and stood before the king, [3]he said to them, "I have had such a dream that my spirit is troubled by the desire to understand it." [4]The Chaldeans said to the king (in Aramaic),[a] "O king, live forever! Tell your servants the dream, and we will reveal the interpretation." [5]The king answered the Chaldeans, "This is a

public decree: if you do not tell me both the dream and its interpretation, you shall be torn limb from limb, and your houses shall be laid in ruins. [6]But if you do tell me the dream and its interpretation, you shall receive from me gifts and rewards and great honor. Therefore tell me the dream and its interpretation." [7]They answered a second time, "Let the king first tell his servants the dream, then we can give its interpretation." [8]The king answered, "I know with certainty that you are trying to gain time, because you see I have firmly decreed: [9]if you do not tell me the dream, there is but one verdict for you. You have agreed to speak lying and misleading words to me until things take a turn. Therefore, tell me the dream, and I shall know that you can give me its interpretation." [10]The Chaldeans answered the king, "There is no one on earth who can reveal what the king demands! In fact no king, however great and powerful, has ever asked such a thing of any magician or enchanter or Chaldean. [11]The thing that the king is asking is too difficult, and no one can reveal it to the king except the gods, whose dwelling is not with mortals."

12 Because of this the king flew into a violent rage and commanded that all the wise men of Babylon be destroyed. [13]The decree was issued, and the wise men were about to be executed; and they looked for Daniel and his companions, to execute them. [14]Then Daniel responded with prudence and discretion to

---

a The text from this point to the end of chapter 7 is in Aramaic

---

1.20 The Hebrew term translated *magicians* is derived from Egyptian and found only in the stories of Joseph (Gen 41.8, 24) and Moses and Aaron (Ex 7.11, 22; 8.3, 14, 15; 9.11), both of which are set at the Egyptian royal court. *Enchanters,* a term derived from Akkadian meaning "incantation priest"; see 2.2; 4.7; 5.7. **1.21** *First year of King Cyrus,* 539 BCE, the end of Daniel's service at the royal court but not the end of his career, which continues until 536 BCE (10.1), seventy years after date in 1.1.

2.1–49 God's superiority demonstrated through a contest to interpret a king's dream; in this contest the wisdom skills of Daniel are pitted against those of the Babylonian wise men. The plot is similar to the Joseph story (Gen 41) and the Aramaic story of Ahikar. Duplications (e.g., vv. 16, 25) and inconsistencies (e.g., vv. 34–35, 45) suggest that an older story was expanded. **2.1** *Second year of Nebuchadnezzar's reign,* 603 BCE; this is inconsistent with 1.1, where Nebuchadnezzar is already king during the three years Dan-

iel and his friends are in training. *Dreams,* believed to be important vehicles for divine-human communication; see chs. 4, 7; Gen 15.12; 20.3; 28.10–12; 37.5–10; 41.1–32; 1 Sam 3.3–5; Mt 27.19; kings were regarded as favored recipients of divine oracles. **2.2** *Magicians . . . Chaldeans.* See 1.4, 20. Originally these terms designated different religious specialists, but here they are used synonymously; see 4.7. *To tell . . . his dreams,* a difficult task (repeated in vv. 6, 9). Providing interpretations was a common practice, attested in numerous Mesopotamian divination tablets, but not the telling of the dream itself (v. 11). **2.4** *O king, live forever,* a royal greeting used for Persian kings until the Islamic period (beginning in the mid-seventh century CE); see 3.9; 5.10; 6.6, 21. **2.5** On the threat of punishment, see vv. 9, 12. *Torn . . . laid in ruins.* See 3.29; Ezra 6.11. **2.6** On the promise of reward, see v. 48. **2.9** This verse suggests the king has not forgotten his dreams but is testing the competence of the wise men. **2.11** The task exceeds human ability. **2.13–23** Widely regarded as a

Arioch, the king's chief executioner, who had gone out to execute the wise men of Babylon; [15]he asked Arioch, the royal official, "Why is the decree of the king so urgent?" Arioch then explained the matter to Daniel. [16]So Daniel went in and requested that the king give him time and he would tell the king the interpretation.

God Reveals Nebuchadnezzar's Dream

17 Then Daniel went to his home and informed his companions, Hananiah, Mishael, and Azariah, [18]and told them to seek mercy from the God of heaven concerning this mystery, so that Daniel and his companions with the rest of the wise men of Babylon might not perish. [19]Then the mystery was revealed to Daniel in a vision of the night, and Daniel blessed the God of heaven.

20 Daniel said:

"Blessed be the name of God from age to age,
    for wisdom and power are his.
21 He changes times and seasons,
    deposes kings and sets up kings;
he gives wisdom to the wise
    and knowledge to those who have understanding.
22 He reveals deep and hidden things;
    he knows what is in the darkness,
    and light dwells with him.
23 To you, O God of my ancestors,
    I give thanks and praise,
for you have given me wisdom and power,
    and have now revealed to me what we asked of you,
    for you have revealed to us what the king ordered."

Daniel Interprets the Dream

24 Therefore Daniel went to Arioch, whom the king had appointed to destroy the wise men of Babylon, and said to him, "Do not destroy the wise men of Babylon; bring me in before the king, and I will give the king the interpretation."

25 Then Arioch quickly brought Daniel before the king and said to him: "I have found among the exiles from Judah a man who can tell the king the interpretation." [26]The king said to Daniel, whose name was Belteshazzar, "Are you able to tell me the dream that I have seen and its interpretation?" [27]Daniel answered the king, "No wise men, enchanters, magicians, or diviners can show to the king the mystery that the king is asking, [28]but there is a God in heaven who reveals mysteries, and he has disclosed to King Nebuchadnezzar what will happen at the end of days. Your dream and the visions of your head as you lay in bed were these: [29]To you, O king, as you lay in bed, came thoughts of what would be hereafter, and the revealer of mysteries disclosed to you what is to be. [30]But as for me, this mystery has not been revealed to me because of any wisdom that I have more than any other living being, but in order that the interpretation may be known to the king and that you may understand the thoughts of your mind.

31 "You were looking, O king, and lo! there was a great statue. This statue was huge, its brilliance extraordinary; it was standing before you, and its appearance was frightening. [32]The head of that statue was of fine gold, its chest and arms of silver, its middle and thighs of bronze, [33]its legs of iron, its feet partly of iron and partly of clay. [34]As you looked on, a

---

late addition to harmonize with ch. 1. Daniel has direct access to the king, in contrast to v. 24, where Arioch introduces him to the king as an exile. **2.17** See 1.6–7; 2.49. **2.18** *The God of heaven,* a Persian title for the God of the Jews, occurs frequently in texts from the beginning of the Persian period (539 BCE) onward; see vv. 19, 37, 44; Ezra 1.2; 5.11, 12; 6.9, 10; 7.12, 21, 23; Neh 1.4, 5; 2.4, 20; Jon 1.9; Tob 10.11; Jdt 5.8; 6.19; 11.17. *Mystery,* a loanword from Old Persian meaning something secret, implying knowledge gained through divine revelation, not conventional wisdom. It is found only in Dan 2.19, 27, 28, 29, 30; 4.9 in the Bible but is frequent in the Dead Sea Scrolls from Qumran. **2.19** *Vision of the night.* See 7.2; Gen 46.2; Zech 1.8. **2.20–23** A doxology in the form of a short psalm of praise and thanksgiving; see Neh 9.5;

Job 12.13, 22; Pss 36.9; 41.13; 106.48; 139.11–12; Prov 2.6; Isa 60.19–20; Hab 3.4; Rev 5.12. **2.24–25** See vv. 13–16. **2.28** *End of days* in biblical Hebrew means only "in the indefinite future." In the Dead Sea Scrolls it comes to refer to a period at the end of history. See 10.14; Isa 2.2; Jer 23.20; Ezek 38.16; Hos 3.5. **2.29–30** A repetition of the theme of v. 28; possibly an editorial expansion (see vv. 13–23). **2.31–35** The difficult task successfully completed by Daniel (see note on 2.2). **2.31** *You . . . and lo,* a formulaic introduction. **2.32–33** The five parts of the statue are constructed from materials of decreasing value. The motif of four metals in order of descending value is also found in Greek (Hesiod), Roman (Ovid), and Persian (Bahman Yasht) sources. **2.33** *Clay,* baked clay or terra-cotta. **2.34** *Not by human hands* emphasizes the divine na-

stone was cut out, not by human hands, and it struck the statue on its feet of iron and clay and broke them in pieces. 35Then the iron, the clay, the bronze, the silver, and the gold, were all broken in pieces and became like the chaff of the summer threshing floors; and the wind carried them away, so that not a trace of them could be found. But the stone that struck the statue became a great mountain and filled the whole earth.

36 "This was the dream; now we will tell the king its interpretation. 37You, O king, the king of kings—to whom the God of heaven has given the kingdom, the power, the might, and the glory, 38into whose hand he has given human beings, wherever they live, the wild animals of the field, and the birds of the air, and whom he has established as ruler over them all—you are the head of gold. 39After you shall arise another kingdom inferior to yours, and yet a third kingdom of bronze, which shall rule over the whole earth. 40And there shall be a fourth kingdom, strong as iron; just as iron crushes and smashes everything,a it shall crush and shatter all these. 41As you saw the feet and toes partly of potter's clay and partly of iron, it shall be a divided kingdom; but some of the strength of iron shall be in it, as you saw the iron mixed with the clay. 42As the toes of the feet were part iron and part clay, so the kingdom shall be partly strong and partly brittle. 43As you saw the iron mixed with clay, so will they mix with one an-other in marriage,b but they will not hold to-gether, just as iron does not mix with clay. 44And in the days of those kings the God of heaven will set up a kingdom that shall never be destroyed, nor shall this kingdom be left to another people. It shall crush all these king-doms and bring them to an end, and it shall stand forever; 45just as you saw that a stone was cut from the mountain not by hands, and that it crushed the iron, the bronze, the clay, the silver, and the gold. The great God has in-formed the king what shall be hereafter. The dream is certain, and its interpretation trust-worthy."

Daniel and His Friends Promoted

46 Then King Nebuchadnezzar fell on his face, worshiped Daniel, and commanded that a grain offering and incense be offered to him. 47The king said to Daniel, "Truly, your God is God of gods and Lord of kings and a revealer of mysteries, for you have been able to reveal this mystery!" 48Then the king promoted Daniel, gave him many great gifts, and made him ruler over the whole province of Babylon and chief prefect over all the wise men of Bab-ylon. 49Daniel made a request of the king, and he appointed Shadrach, Meshach, and Abed-nego over the affairs of the province of Bab-ylon. But Daniel remained at the king's court.

a Gk Theodotion Syr Vg: Aram adds *and like iron that crushes*
b Aram *by human seed*

---

ture of the intervention; see 8.25; Ps 118.22; Isa 28.16. The *feet* are the weakest point because of the fragile clay, but a strategic point because they support the statue; see Jer 51.20–23. **2.35** Here the stone *became . . . a mountain*, but in v. 45 it *was cut* from the moun-tain. Stones and mountains are frequently associated with the divine presence; see Gen 28.10–22; Deut 32.4, 15, 18, 30–31; Ps 36.6; Isa 8.14; 11.9–10; Ezek 17.22–24. The mountain brings to mind Mount Zion. **2.36–45** Daniel interprets the dream symbolically or allegorically as a political oracle; many regard the in-terpretation as a later addition because it does not correspond completely to the dream. The four king-doms are not named, but they can be identified as Neo-Babylonian, Median, Persian, and Greek, since these are the kingdoms mentioned elsewhere in Dan-iel; similar four-kingdom schemes are found in sev-eral ancient sources (the *Fourth Sibylline Oracle*, the Babylonian Dynastic Prophecy, the writings of Aemil-ius Sura). **2.37** *King of kings*, a title for Persian mon-archs; see Ezra 7.12; Ezek 26.7. **2.37–38** God's power extends even to foreign rulers; see Gen 1.26; Ps 8.5–8; Jer 27.5–7; 28.14. **2.38** See 4.12. The king is flattered as the head of gold, even though the statue will ulti-mately be destroyed. **2.41** After the death of Alexander the Great, the Greek empire was divided among four of his generals. Judea was controlled by the Ptolemies until 198 BCE, then by the Seleucids; see 8.8; 11.4. *Toes* are not mentioned in the dream itself (vv. 31–35). **2.42** It is *brittle* because it is baked clay. **2.43** The Ptolemies and Seleucids unsuccessfully sought peace and stability between themselves through intermar-riage; see 11.6–7, 17. **2.44** *Those kings*, the kings of the fourth kingdom. **2.45** A *stone* symbolizes the everlast-ing kingdom of God. The destruction of the statue symbolizes not only the fall of the kingdoms but also the destruction of idols. **2.46** See Gen 17.3; Ezek 3.23. *Worshiped.* The RSV translated this "did homage," but more than civic honor is implied; the specifically reli-gious sense of the word is reinforced by the strictly re-ligious terms *grain offering* and *incense*; see 3.5–7, 10, 15; 8.17; Isa 44.15–19; 46.6. **2.47** A very brief doxol-ogy like vv. 20–23, but here it is spoken by the king, not Daniel. **2.48** The hero is rewarded, a favorite folk-tale motif; see Gen 41.37–45; Esth 8.1–2. **2.49** A liter-ary link to 3.12.

The Golden Image

3 King Nebuchadnezzar made a golden statue whose height was sixty cubits and whose width was six cubits; he set it up on the plain of Dura in the province of Babylon. 2Then King Nebuchadnezzar sent for the satraps, the prefects, and the governors, the counselors, the treasurers, the justices, the magistrates, and all the officials of the provinces, to assemble and come to the dedication of the statue that King Nebuchadnezzar had set up. 3So the satraps, the prefects, and the governors, the counselors, the treasurers, the justices, the magistrates, and all the officials of the provinces, assembled for the dedication of the statue that King Nebuchadnezzar had set up. When they were standing before the statue that Nebuchadnezzar had set up, 4the herald proclaimed aloud, "You are commanded, O peoples, nations, and languages, 5that when you hear the sound of the horn, pipe, lyre, trigon, harp, drum, and entire musical ensemble, you are to fall down and worship the golden statue that King Nebuchadnezzar has set up. 6Whoever does not fall down and worship shall immediately be thrown into a furnace of blazing fire." 7Therefore, as soon as all the peoples heard the sound of the horn, pipe, lyre, trigon, harp, drum, and entire musical ensemble, all the peoples, nations, and languages fell down and worshiped the golden statue that King Nebuchadnezzar had set up.

8 Accordingly, at this time certain Chaldeans came forward and denounced the Jews. 9They said to King Nebuchadnezzar, "O king, live forever! 10You, O king, have made a decree, that everyone who hears the sound of the horn, pipe, lyre, trigon, harp, drum, and entire musical ensemble, shall fall down and worship the golden statue, 11and whoever does not fall down and worship shall be thrown into a furnace of blazing fire. 12There are certain Jews whom you have appointed over the affairs of the province of Babylon: Shadrach, Meshach, and Abednego. These pay no heed to you, O king. They do not serve your gods and they do not worship the golden statue that you have set up."

13 Then Nebuchadnezzar in furious rage commanded that Shadrach, Meshach, and Abednego be brought in; so they brought those men before the king. 14Nebuchadnezzar said to them, "Is it true, O Shadrach, Meshach, and Abednego, that you do not serve my gods and you do not worship the golden statue that I have set up? 15Now if you are ready when you hear the sound of the horn, pipe, lyre, trigon, harp, drum, and entire musical ensemble to fall down and worship the statue that I have

3.1–30 A legend of conflict between three Jewish courtiers and rival Babylonian wise men over acknowledging the divine sovereignty of the Babylonian king. The issue is resolved in a wondrous way in favor of God by a mysterious figure who protects the Jews from harm in the fire. Extensive use of repetition and hyperbole adds to the story's folktale quality. The unified structure and Daniel's absence suggest the story originated independently of the others in chs. 1–6, possibly in the late Persian or early Hellenistic period. 3.1 Golden statue, of a Babylonian god or of the king; see Jdt 3.8; 6.2. The motif of the statue provides continuity with Nebuchadnezzar's dream in ch. 2. Colossal statues were widely used free-standing art forms in Egypt and Mesopotamia; Diodorus Siculus (first century BCE) and Herodotus (fifth century BCE) report a gold statue of Zeus (Bel?) in Babylon; see Isa 40.19; Jer 10.3–10. Sixty . . . six cubits, about 30 by 3 meters, obelisk-shaped; the proportions reflect the Babylonian sexagesimal number system. Dura in Aramaic or dûru in Babylonian, meaning "fortress" or "city wall," is usually the first part of a place-name and is not to be identified with any specific place. 3.2 The list of officials is given in order of precedence; the terms for prefects and governors derive from Akkadian, all others from Old Persian; see vv. 3, 27. Dedication. See 1 Kings 8.63; 2 Chr 7.9; Neh 12.27. 3.4–6 The order to worship the statue creates a problem for the Jews, who cannot obey without breaching a basic tenet of their faith. 3.4 Peoples, nations, and languages, a stereotyped phrase used as a rhetorical device to create hyperbole; e.g., vv. 7, 29; 4.1; 5.19; 7.14; Esth 1.22; 3.12; 8.9; Rev 5.9; 7.9. 3.5 The list of instruments, used as hyperbole, is repeated in vv. 7, 10, 15; see 1 Chr 25.1. Lyre, a Greek loanword; an Asiatic variant of an instrument with three to twelve strings. Trigon, a triangular four-stringed instrument. Harp, a Greek loanword; an instrument with ten strings across a sound board. Drum. The Greek loanword symphonia usually means "harmony," but it is attested as an instrument from 200 BCE; the RSV translated "bagpipe." Fall down and worship, repeated in vv. 6, 11, 15; see 2.46. 3.6 A known, but not common, form of execution; see Gen 38.24 (probably in an open fire, not in a furnace); Jer 29.21–22; 2 Macc 6.11; 7.5; 13.4–6. 3.8 Chaldeans. See note on 1.4. Denounced, lit. "ate pieces of," an idiom indicating maliciousness. This is not a false accusation, but one motivated by envy; see v. 12; 2.49; Esth 3. 3.9 O king, live forever! See note on 2.4. 3.12 See 2.49. 3.13–18 The interrogation repeats much of the accusation. 3.13 Furious rage, a stock motif; see Esth 1.12; 7.7; 2 Macc 7.3. 3.15 Who . . . hands. See 2 Kings 18.20–22,

made, well and good.*ᵃ* But if you do not worship, you shall immediately be thrown into a furnace of blazing fire, and who is the god that will deliver you out of my hands?"

16 Shadrach, Meshach, and Abednego answered the king, "O Nebuchadnezzar, we have no need to present a defense to you in this matter. ¹⁷If our God whom we serve is able to deliver us from the furnace of blazing fire and out of your hand, O king, let him deliver us.*ᵇ* ¹⁸But if not, be it known to you, O king, that we will not serve your gods and we will not worship the golden statue that you have set up."

The Fiery Furnace

19 Then Nebuchadnezzar was so filled with rage against Shadrach, Meshach, and Abednego that his face was distorted. He ordered the furnace heated up seven times more than was customary, ²⁰and ordered some of the strongest guards in his army to bind Shadrach, Meshach, and Abednego and to throw them into the furnace of blazing fire. ²¹So the men were bound, still wearing their tunics,*ᶜ* their trousers,*ᶜ* their hats, and their other garments, and they were thrown into the furnace of blazing fire. ²²Because the king's command was urgent and the furnace was so overheated, the raging flames killed the men who lifted Shadrach, Meshach, and Abednego. ²³But the three men, Shadrach, Meshach, and Abednego, fell down, bound, into the furnace of blazing fire.

24 Then King Nebuchadnezzar was astonished and rose up quickly. He said to his counselors, "Was it not three men that we threw bound into the fire?" They answered the king,

"True, O king." ²⁵He replied, "But I see four men unbound, walking in the middle of the fire, and they are not hurt; and the fourth has the appearance of a god."*ᵈ* ²⁶Nebuchadnezzar then approached the door of the furnace of blazing fire and said, "Shadrach, Meshach, and Abednego, servants of the Most High God, come out! Come here!" So Shadrach, Meshach, and Abednego came out from the fire. ²⁷And the satraps, the prefects, the governors, and the king's counselors gathered together and saw that the fire had not had any power over the bodies of those men; the hair of their heads was not singed, their tunics*ᶜ* were not harmed, and not even the smell of fire came from them. ²⁸Nebuchadnezzar said, "Blessed be the God of Shadrach, Meshach, and Abednego, who has sent his angel and delivered his servants who trusted in him. They disobeyed the king's command and yielded up their bodies rather than serve and worship any god except their own God. ²⁹Therefore I make a decree: Any people, nation, or language that utters blasphemy against the God of Shadrach, Meshach, and Abednego shall be torn limb from limb, and their houses laid in ruins; for there is no other god who is able to deliver in this way." ³⁰Then the king promoted Shadrach, Meshach, and Abednego in the province of Babylon.

Nebuchadnezzar's Second Dream

4*ᵉ* King Nebuchadnezzar to all peoples, nations, and languages that live throughout

---

a Aram lacks *well and good*   *b* Or *If our God whom we serve is able to deliver us, he will deliver us from the furnace of blazing fire and out of your hand, O king.*   *c* Meaning of Aram word uncertain   *d* Aram *a son of the gods*   *e* Ch 3.31 in Aram

---

29–35; Isa 36.13–20; 37.8–12. **3.19** *Seven times.* An ordinary fire would have been sufficient; the extreme heat is stressed for hyperbole and to heighten drama. **3.20** *Strongest guards,* hyperbole. **3.21** *Tunics . . . garments.* The listing of clothing, similar to the listing of officials (v. 2) and musical instruments (v. 5), delays the plot and increases tension. Clothing would intensify the burning, thereby heightening the marvelous effect of the deliverance; see v. 27. **3.22** The death of the other men confirms the peril facing the three Jews. **3.23** *Fell down . . . fire.* The furnace has an opening in the top and a door (v. 26) near the bottom, like a kiln. **3.25** A *god,* one of a class of beings associated with the divine council as attendants to the deity; see Gen 6.2; Job 1.6; 2.1; 38.7; Ps 29.1. The fourth figure is described as an *angel* in v. 28. **3.26** *Most High God,* a title used by both Jews and non-Jews; see 4.2; Gen 14.19–

20; Num 24.16; Deut 32.8; Isa 14.14; 1 Esd 6.31; 2 Macc 3.31; Mk 5.7; Acts 16.17. **3.28** A doxology in the form of a short hymn of praise. **3.29** A royal decree granting legitimacy and protection to the Jewish religion. Persians, Greeks, and Romans all issued decrees protecting the right of Jews to practice their religion, but this decree goes further. *Torn . . . laid in ruins.* See 2.5. **3.30** A typical folk motif of reward for heroes; see 2.48. **4.1–47** This text differs markedly from the other stories in chs. 1–6. Although many folk elements are present, including the motif of dream interpretation, the literary form is not the tale but the epistle or public proclamation. It begins (vv. 1–18) and ends (vv. 34–37) in the first person with a third-person tale in between (vv. 19–33). The tightly circular rhetorical structure emphasizes the central theme of God's sovereignty. The king first acknowledges God's sovereignty

the earth: May you have abundant prosperity! [2]The signs and wonders that the Most High God has worked for me I am pleased to recount.

[3] How great are his signs,
 how mighty his wonders!
His kingdom is an everlasting kingdom,
 and his sovereignty is from generation
  to generation.

[4][a] I, Nebuchadnezzar, was living at ease in my home and prospering in my palace. [5]I saw a dream that frightened me; my fantasies in bed and the visions of my head terrified me. [6]So I made a decree that all the wise men of Babylon should be brought before me, in order that they might tell me the interpretation of the dream. [7]Then the magicians, the enchanters, the Chaldeans, and the diviners came in, and I told them the dream, but they could not tell me its interpretation. [8]At last Daniel came in before me—he who was named Belteshazzar after the name of my god, and who is endowed with a spirit of the holy gods[b]—and I told him the dream: [9]"O Belteshazzar, chief of the magicians, I know that you are endowed with a spirit of the holy gods[b] and that no mystery is too difficult for you. Hear[c] the dream that I saw; tell me its interpretation.
[10][d] Upon my bed this is what I saw;

there was a tree at the center of the
  earth,
 and its height was great.
[11] The tree grew great and strong,
 its top reached to heaven,
 and it was visible to the ends of the
  whole earth.
[12] Its foliage was beautiful,
 its fruit abundant,
 and it provided food for all.
The animals of the field found shade
  under it,
 the birds of the air nested in its
  branches,
 and from it all living beings were fed.

[13] "I continued looking, in the visions of my head as I lay in bed, and there was a holy watcher, coming down from heaven. [14]He cried aloud and said:
'Cut down the tree and chop off its
  branches,
 strip off its foliage and scatter its fruit.
Let the animals flee from beneath it
 and the birds from its branches.

---

a Ch 4.1 in Aram *b* Or *a holy, divine spirit* *c* Theodotion: Aram *The visions of* *d* Theodotion Syr Compare Gk: Aram adds *The visions of my head*

---

and greatness (vv. 2–3) and prospers (v. 4), then asserts his own sovereignty and greatness (v. 30) and is brought low (vv. 32–33) as predicted (v. 22), only to accept God's sovereignty again (vv. 34–35) and have his own greatness restored by God. Daniel's role is less prominent than in ch. 2. The Old Greek translation preserves a substantially different form of this story. It is generally believed that the king in this story was originally Nabonidus, not Nebuchadnezzar, and this view is supported by the *Prayer of Nabonidus* (4Q242) from Qumran, which resembles this tale but is by no means identical with it. **4.1–2** Epistolary introduction and greeting; see, e.g., 1 Macc 10.18; 14.20; 15.2, 16; 2 Macc 1.1, 10; 1 Cor 1.1–3; Rom 1.1, 7; Gal 1.1–3; Eph 1.1–2. **4.1** *Peoples, nations, and languages.* See note on 3.4. **4.2** *Signs and wonders,* a typical description of marvelous acts of God, especially in relation to the exodus from Egypt; see v. 3; 6.27; Ex 7.3; Deut 4.34; 6.22; Isa 8.18; Mk 13.22; Jn 4.48. *Most High God.* See note on 3.26. **4.3** A doxology. See 2.20–23. It is paralleled by 4.34–35 and is a typical opening for an epistle; see 2 Cor 1.3–4; Eph 1.3–4; 1 Pet 1.3–5. Here the pagan king is said to acknowledge the God of Daniel as the true God. Nebuchadnezzar had already acknowledged the God of Daniel in 2.47. *His kingdom . . . generation.* See v. 34; Ps 145.13. **4.5** *Dream.* See 2.1. *Frightened, terrified.* See 5.6; 7.15. The effect of the dream is stronger than in 2.1, which creates foreboding about the inter-

pretation. **4.6–7** The task is only to interpret, not tell the dream, but the Chaldeans still fail; no punishment is threatened; see 2.2–11. **4.7** *Magicians . . . Chaldeans.* See notes on 1.4; 2.2. *Diviners* were the most important type of religious intermediary in Babylonia; here the term is used simply as a synonym for "wise men." **4.8** *Name of my god.* See note on 1.6–7. *Holy gods,* either Babylonian deities or the God of the Jews; see 2.11; 4.9, 18; 5.11, 14; Gen 41.38. **4.9** *Mystery.* See note on 2.18. **4.10–17** The dream has two parts: a vision of a great tree (vv. 10–12) and the decree of a watcher (vv. 13–17). **4.10** *Tree at the center of the earth,* a widely used image in ancient Near Eastern mythology. Here it is used allegorically for the king's greatness and might; see Ps 37.35–36; Isa 10.33–11.1; 14.4–20; Ezek 31; Zech 11.2. **4.11** *Great,* a key term used allegorically of the king; see vv. 20, 22, 30; it is used of God in v. 3. *Its top reached to heaven.* See Isa 14.13–14; Ezek 31.3. **4.12** See Ezek 17.23; 31.6. **4.13–17** A cryptic interpretation in the form of a command or decree, which Nebuchadnezzar cannot understand. **4.13** *A holy watcher,* lit. "a watcher, a holy one"; see vv. 17, 20. This is the only biblical occurrence of this term to designate an angelic being, but it is commonly found in pseudepigraphical texts and the Dead Sea Scrolls; see, e.g., *1 Enoch* 1.5; 20.1; *Jubilees* 4.15; *Genesis Apocryphon* (1QapGen) 2.1. It is used especially of angels who come down to earth. "Holy one" typically means an

15 But leave its stump and roots in the
        ground,
    with a band of iron and bronze,
    in the tender grass of the field.
  Let him be bathed with the dew of
        heaven,
    and let his lot be with the animals of
        the field
    in the grass of the earth.
16 Let his mind be changed from that of a
        human,
    and let the mind of an animal be given
        to him.
  And let seven times pass over him.
17 The sentence is rendered by decree of the
        watchers,
    the decision is given by order of the
        holy ones,
  in order that all who live may know
    that the Most High is sovereign over
        the kingdom of mortals;
  he gives it to whom he will
    and sets over it the lowliest of human
        beings.'

18 "This is the dream that I, King Nebuchadnezzar, saw. Now you, Belteshazzar, declare the interpretation, since all the wise men
of my kingdom are unable to tell me the interpretation. You are able, however, for you are
endowed with a spirit of the holy gods." [a]

Daniel Interprets the Second Dream

19 Then Daniel, who was called Belteshazzar,
was severely distressed for a while. His
thoughts terrified him. The king said, "Belteshazzar, do not let the dream or the interpretation terrify you." Belteshazzar answered, "My
lord, may the dream be for those who hate
you, and its interpretation for your enemies!
20 The tree that you saw, which grew great and
strong, so that its top reached to heaven and

was visible to the end of the whole earth,
21 whose foliage was beautiful and its fruit
abundant, and which provided food for all,
under which animals of the field lived, and in
whose branches the birds of the air had
nests— 22 it is you, O king! You have grown
great and strong. Your greatness has increased
and reaches to heaven, and your sovereignty to
the ends of the earth. 23 And whereas the king
saw a holy watcher coming down from heaven
and saying, 'Cut down the tree and destroy it,
but leave its stump and roots in the ground,
with a band of iron and bronze, in the grass of
the field; and let him be bathed with the dew
of heaven, and let his lot be with the animals of
the field, until seven times pass over him'—
24 this is the interpretation, O king, and it is a
decree of the Most High that has come upon
my lord the king: 25 You shall be driven away
from human society, and your dwelling shall
be with the wild animals. You shall be made to
eat grass like oxen, you shall be bathed with
the dew of heaven, and seven times shall pass
over you, until you have learned that the Most
High has sovereignty over the kingdom of
mortals, and gives it to whom he will. 26 As it
was commanded to leave the stump and roots
of the tree, your kingdom shall be re-established for you from the time that you learn
that Heaven is sovereign. 27 Therefore, O king,
may my counsel be acceptable to you: atone
for [b] your sins with righteousness, and your iniquities with mercy to the oppressed, so that
your prosperity may be prolonged."

Nebuchadnezzar's Humiliation

28 All this came upon King Nebuchadnezzar.
29 At the end of twelve months he was walking
on the roof of the royal palace of Babylon,
30 and the king said, "Is this not magnificent

---

a Or *a holy, divine spirit*   *b* Aram *break off*

---

angel or divinity. **4.15** *Stump and roots* implies potential for regeneration; see Isa 6.13; 11.1. *Band of iron and
bronze*. Metal bands were sometimes put on sacred
trees to prevent them from cracking; more likely the
image here foreshadows a fettered king. *Him.* The tree's
stump becomes a man. **4.16** *Let his mind be changed,* a
mental illness. *Seven times,* a conventional number; see
3.19; 4.25, 32. **4.17** *Watchers* and *holy ones* are made
parallel by the verse structure and recall mythological
imagery of the divine council; both terms refer to angelic beings; see notes on 3.25; 4.13; cf. Job 5.1; 15.15;
Ps 89.7; Zech 14.5. **4.19–27** Daniel makes the watcher's

interpretation explicit. The identification of Nebuchadnezzar is intensified by repeating *you/your.*
4.25 Prediction of affliction. **4.26** Promise of restoration. *Heaven* is capitalized here as the equivalent of
"God"; see 1 Macc 3.18–19; 4.10, 55. **4.27** Admonition
to atone and repent; see Ps 34.14–17; Isa 1.16–17; Jer
22.3; Am 5.6–7. **4.28–33** Prediction of affliction fulfilled. This legend may have been inspired by
Nabonidus, the last king of Babylon, who spent years in
Teima in the Arabian desert because of his devotion to
the moon god Sin. See the *Nabonidus Chronicle* and the
Haran inscriptions. The Qumran *Prayer of Nabonidus*

Babylon, which I have built as a royal capital by my mighty power and for my glorious majesty?" 31While the words were still in the king's mouth, a voice came from heaven: "O King Nebuchadnezzar, to you it is declared: The kingdom has departed from you! 32You shall be driven away from human society, and your dwelling shall be with the animals of the field. You shall be made to eat grass like oxen, and seven times shall pass over you, until you have learned that the Most High has sovereignty over the kingdom of mortals and gives it to whom he will." 33Immediately the sentence was fulfilled against Nebuchadnezzar. He was driven away from human society, ate grass like oxen, and his body was bathed with the dew of heaven, until his hair grew as long as eagles' feathers and his nails became like birds' claws.

Nebuchadnezzar Praises God

34 When that period was over, I, Nebuchadnezzar, lifted my eyes to heaven, and my reason returned to me.

I blessed the Most High,
   and praised and honored the one who
      lives forever.
For his sovereignty is an everlasting
      sovereignty,
   and his kingdom endures from
      generation to generation.
35 All the inhabitants of the earth are
      accounted as nothing,

and he does what he wills with the host
   of heaven
   and the inhabitants of the earth.
There is no one who can stay his hand
   or say to him, "What are you doing?"
36At that time my reason returned to me; and my majesty and splendor were restored to me for the glory of my kingdom. My counselors and my lords sought me out, I was re-established over my kingdom, and still more greatness was added to me. 37Now I, Nebuchadnezzar, praise and extol and honor the King of heaven,

for all his works are truth,
   and his ways are justice;
and he is able to bring low
   those who walk in pride.

Belshazzar's Feast

5 King Belshazzar made a great festival for a thousand of his lords, and he was drinking wine in the presence of the thousand.

2 Under the influence of the wine, Belshazzar commanded that they bring in the vessels of gold and silver that his father Nebuchadnezzar had taken out of the temple in Jerusalem, so that the king and his lords, his wives, and his concubines might drink from them. 3So they brought in the vessels of gold and silver*a* that had been taken out of the temple, the

_____
a Theodotion Vg: Aram lacks and silver

(4Q242) says that the king was smitten with disease for seven years. **4.30** Nebuchadnezzar's arrogance in asserting his own greatness (see vv. 11, 20, 22); irony is achieved by having his downfall occur as he reaches his highest self-glorification. *Magnificent Babylon.* Many of Babylon's most beautiful monumental buildings were built by Nebuchadnezzar. Later "Babylon" could symbolize another great and hostile city, as in Rev 14.8; 16.19. **4.34–37** Epistolary conclusion. **4.34–35** A doxology; see v. 3. **4.34** *My reason returned.* The prediction is fulfilled; see v. 36. *Sovereignty . . . generation.* See v. 3. **4.35** *All the inhabitants of the earth.* See v. 1. *Host of heaven* (see 1 Kings 22.19; Isa 24.21), members of the divine council (see v. 17) or stars (see Deut 4.19; 17.3; Isa 34.4; Jer 8.2; 19.13). **4.36** Reward for recognizing God's sovereignty. **4.37** A doxology and final hymn of praise; see Ps 47; Isa 40.17; Ezek 21.26. *King of heaven,* only occurrence of this precise epithet in Daniel or the Hebrew scriptures, but see comparable imagery in Deut 33.26 and terminology in Gen 24.7. Equilibrium has been restored—Nebuchadnezzar is recognized as sovereign king of Babylon and God as sovereign King of heaven; see Pss 93.1–2; 97.1; 99.1; Jer 10.7, 10.

5.1–31 The contest here involves the interpretation

of mysterious writing, not a dream (chs. 2, 4). The sovereignty of God is asserted against a king who is unrepentant in his arrogance and sacrilege. The repetitive style of vv. 1–23 contrasts with the economical style of vv. 24–31. The Old Greek translation of this chapter is much shorter. Direct references to earlier chapters, especially to ch. 4, suggest a late date. As in all of chs. 1–6, historical information is unreliable. **5.1** *King Belshazzar,* a new king whose name in Babylonian means "Bel, protect the king." A person named Belshazzar existed in this period, but he was never king of Babylon, only regent while Nabonidus was at Teima; see note on 4.28–33; see also 7.1; 8.1. *A great festival.* See Esth 1.3–8. **5.2** *Under the influence of wine.* See Esth 1.7–9. *Vessels . . . of the temple in Jerusalem.* See 1.2. *His father Nebuchadnezzar.* See vv. 11–12, 22; Bar 1.11. Belshazzar's father was actually Nabonidus. *The king . . . concubines.* A listing as in, e.g., 3.2, 5, 21; 4.7. Women attend the banquet, in contrast to Esth 1.9. Some biblical texts speak of two classes of women in royal harems (see 1 Kings 11.3; Song 6.8): *wives,* queenly consorts (see Neh 2.6; Ps 45.9), and *concubines,* lower-rank women. **5.3–4** Belshazzar profanes the temple vessels by having his whole retinue, including his concubines,

house of God in Jerusalem, and the king and his lords, his wives, and his concubines drank from them. ⁴They drank the wine and praised the gods of gold and silver, bronze, iron, wood, and stone.

The Writing on the Wall

5 Immediately the fingers of a human hand appeared and began writing on the plaster of the wall of the royal palace, next to the lampstand. The king was watching the hand as it wrote. ⁶Then the king's face turned pale, and his thoughts terrified him. His limbs gave way, and his knees knocked together. ⁷The king cried aloud to bring in the enchanters, the Chaldeans, and the diviners; and the king said to the wise men of Babylon, "Whoever can read this writing and tell me its interpretation shall be clothed in purple, have a chain of gold around his neck, and rank third in the kingdom." ⁸Then all the king's wise men came in, but they could not read the writing or tell the king the interpretation. ⁹Then King Belshazzar became greatly terrified and his face turned pale, and his lords were perplexed.

10 The queen, when she heard the discussion of the king and his lords, came into the banqueting hall. The queen said, "O king, live forever! Do not let your thoughts terrify you or your face grow pale. ¹¹There is a man in your kingdom who is endowed with a spirit of the holy gods.ᵃ In the days of your father he was found to have enlightenment, understanding, and wisdom like the wisdom of the gods. Your father, King Nebuchadnezzar, made him chief of the magicians, enchanters,

Chaldeans, and diviners,ᵇ ¹²because an excellent spirit, knowledge, and understanding to interpret dreams, explain riddles, and solve problems were found in this Daniel, whom the king named Belteshazzar. Now let Daniel be called, and he will give the interpretation."

The Writing on the Wall Interpreted

13 Then Daniel was brought in before the king. The king said to Daniel, "So you are Daniel, one of the exiles of Judah, whom my father the king brought from Judah? ¹⁴I have heard of you that a spirit of the godsᶜ is in you, and that enlightenment, understanding, and excellent wisdom are found in you. ¹⁵Now the wise men, the enchanters, have been brought in before me to read this writing and tell me its interpretation, but they were not able to give the interpretation of the matter. ¹⁶But I have heard that you can give interpretations and solve problems. Now if you are able to read the writing and tell me its interpretation, you shall be clothed in purple, have a chain of gold around your neck, and rank third in the kingdom."

17 Then Daniel answered in the presence of the king, "Let your gifts be for yourself, or give your rewards to someone else! Nevertheless I will read the writing to the king and let him know the interpretation. ¹⁸O king, the Most High God gave your father Nebuchadnezzar kingship, greatness, glory, and majesty. ¹⁹And because of the greatness that he gave him, all

---

a Or *a holy, divine spirit*   *b* Aram adds *the king your father*
c Or *a divine spirit*

---

drink from them and commits a sacrilege by using them in the praise of idols; both acts mock the power and sovereignty of God, as v. 23 makes explicit. **5.4** *The gods of . . . stone,* a list of elements very similar to one in the *Prayer of Nabonidus* (4Q242) from Qumran, in which Nabonidus is indicted for idolatry. It recalls elements of the statue in Dan 2. See 5.23; Deut 4.28; Pss 115.4–8; 135.15–18. **5.5** *Immediately,* swiftness of response similar to the speed of punishment in v. 30. *Fingers of a human hand,* a popular marvelous motif in folktales; see Ex 31.18. **5.6** See v. 9. Here fear is so intense it has physical manifestations; see Ps 69.23; Isa 21.3; Ezek 21.7; Nah 2.10. **5.7–8** The double task of reading and interpreting the writing (see 2.2–9). As usual, the Babylonian wise men fail; see 2.2–11; 4.7, 18. Political reward is promised those who are successful (see vv. 16, 29; 2.6) but there is no threat of punishment for failure (see 2.5, 9, 13). **5.7** *Purple,* a sign of dignity and/or royalty; see Esth 8.15; Song 3.10;

1 Macc 10.20; 14.43–44; 2 Macc 4.38; 1 Esd 3.6; Mt 27.28. *Chain,* lit. "collar," a Persian ornament signifying rank; see Gen 41.42. *Rank third,* be a high official; see 2.48; 5.16, 29; 6.2; Gen 41.40–41; Ezek 23.23. **5.10** *The queen,* usually regarded as queen mother rather than queen consort because of her position of influence and power, her use of *your father, King Nebuchadnezzar* (v. 11), and her knowledge of Daniel's high position in Nebuchadnezzar's court; see 2.48; 4.9; 1 Kings 15.13; 2 Kings 10.13; 24.12. *O king, live forever!* See note on 2.4. **5.11** *Holy gods.* See note on 4.8. *Chief of the . . . diviners.* See 2.48; 4.9. **5.12** *Excellent spirit . . . solve problems.* See 1.17, 20; 4.9, 18; Gen 41.38. *Explain riddles.* See Prov 1.5–6; Sir 39.1–3. *Whom the king named Belteshazzar.* See 1.7. **5.13** The new king does not seem to know Daniel; see vv. 11–12; Ex 1.8. **5.17–21** See 4.22–27, 30–33. **5.18–19** *Gave* emphasizes the king's sovereignty as a gift from the Most High God; see ch. 4. **5.19** *Peoples, nations, and languages.* See note

peoples, nations, and languages trembled and feared before him. He killed those he wanted to kill, kept alive those he wanted to keep alive, honored those he wanted to honor, and degraded those he wanted to degrade. 20 But when his heart was lifted up and his spirit was hardened so that he acted proudly, he was deposed from his kingly throne, and his glory was stripped from him. 21 He was driven from human society, and his mind was made like that of an animal. His dwelling was with the wild asses, he was fed grass like oxen, and his body was bathed with the dew of heaven, until he learned that the Most High God has sovereignty over the kingdom of mortals, and sets over it whomever he will. 22 And you, Belshazzar his son, have not humbled your heart, even though you knew all this! 23 You have exalted yourself against the Lord of heaven! The vessels of his temple have been brought in before you, and you and your lords, your wives and your concubines have been drinking wine from them. You have praised the gods of silver and gold, of bronze, iron, wood, and stone, which do not see or hear or know; but the God in whose power is your very breath, and to whom belong all your ways, you have not honored.

24 "So from his presence the hand was sent and this writing was inscribed. 25 And this is the writing that was inscribed: MENE, MENE, TEKEL, and PARSIN. 26 This is the interpretation of the matter: MENE, God has numbered the days of[a] your kingdom and brought it to an end; 27 TEKEL, you have been weighed on the scales and found wanting; 28 PERES,[b] your kingdom is divided and given to the Medes and Persians."

29 Then Belshazzar gave the command, and Daniel was clothed in purple, a chain of gold was put around his neck, and a proclamation was made concerning him that he should rank third in the kingdom.

30 That very night Belshazzar, the Chaldean king, was killed. 31[c] And Darius the Mede received the kingdom, being about sixty-two years old.

The Plot against Daniel

6 It pleased Darius to set over the kingdom one hundred twenty satraps, stationed throughout the whole kingdom, 2 and over them three presidents, including Daniel; to these the satraps gave account, so that the king might suffer no loss. 3 Soon Daniel distin-

---

a Aram lacks the days of   b The singular of Parsin   c Ch 6.1 in Aram

---

on 3.4. He killed . . . degrade, a surprising description of royal power more usually reserved for God alone; see Deut 32.39; 1 Sam 2.6–7; Job 5.11; Ps 75.7–8; Tob 4.19; Sir 7.11. 5.22–23 Repetition of you/yours focuses the rebuke forcefully on Belshazzar, who is quite unlike Nebuchadnezzar; see 4.37; Jer 22.15–19. 5.23 The gods of . . . stone. See note on 5.4; gold and silver are reversed here. 5.24–28 A succinct interpretation contrasts with lengthy preliminary remarks. 5.25 MENE . . . PARSIN, units of monetary weight or value in Aramaic: the mina, shekel, and half-mina. A mina was worth between 50 and 60 shekels. 5.26–28 The enigmatic words require further interpretation; Daniel's explanation is allegorical, not literal, and creates puns by reading the Aramaic nouns as similar-sounding verbal roots; see Am 8.1–2. 5.26 MENE sounds like mn', "to number"; see Ps 90.12. 5.27 TEKEL sounds like tkl, "to weigh"; see Job 31.6; Prov 16.2; 21.2; 24.12. 5.28 PERES sounds like prs, "to divide"; there is a second pun on the word Persians. Medes, people of Media, an obscure kingdom with its capital at Ecbatana. Media played a role in the Babylonian conquest of the Assyrians at Nineveh in 612 BCE but was incorporated into the Persian Empire by 550/49 BCE; see 7.5; 8.3–4; 9.1. Persians, people in the territory roughly corresponding to modern Iran; they defeated the Medes in 550/49 BCE; in 331 BCE their empire fell to Alexander the Great; see 6.8, 12, 15; 7.6; 8.3–4; 9.1. 5.29 Daniel accepts the re-

ward spurned earlier (v. 17); see 2.48; Gen 41.40–45; Esth 8.15. 5.30 Punishment is swift and severe with no chance for repentance; see Isa 13.17–22; 21.1–10; Jer 51.8–16, 39–46. 5.31 Darius the Mede is not a historical figure; Babylon was conquered by Cyrus the Great of Persia in 539 BCE, not by the Medes, despite the prophecies of Isa 13.17–22; 21.1–10; Jer 50.9, 41; 51.11, 28; see Dan 9.1. There were three kings of Persia named Darius, of whom the first ruled 522–486 BCE.

6.1–28 A legend similar in structure and style to the one in ch. 3. Despite an unusually benevolent king, conflict with jealous rivals puts Daniel in a life-threatening situation from which he is wondrously delivered by an angel. The underlying issue is again God's sovereignty, which is introduced in v. 7 and culminates in vv. 26–27. Extensive use is made of repetition and elaboration (e.g., vv. 3–4, 7–8, 12). A different form of this story is preserved in the Old Greek. 6.1 Darius. See note on 5.31. Satraps, officials who administered large regions called satrapies, which were subdivided into provinces ruled by governors (see 3.2); only twenty to thirty satrapies are known from Persian records, so the number here may include provinces (see Esth 1.1; 8.9; 1 Esd 3.2). Darius I of Persia was noted for organizing the satrapies. 6.2 Three might be an allusion to third in 5.7, 16, 29; see Gen 41.41–42; 1 Esd 3.9. Presidents. No such officials are known from Persian documents. 6.3 An excellent spirit. See 5.12. Appoint . . . kingdom.

guished himself above all the other presidents and satraps because an excellent spirit was in him, and the king planned to appoint him over the whole kingdom. 4So the presidents and the satraps tried to find grounds for complaint against Daniel in connection with the kingdom. But they could find no grounds for complaint or any corruption, because he was faithful, and no negligence or corruption could be found in him. 5The men said, "We shall not find any ground for complaint against this Daniel unless we find it in connection with the law of his God."

6 So the presidents and satraps conspired and came to the king and said to him, "O King Darius, live forever! 7All the presidents of the kingdom, the prefects and the satraps, the counselors and the governors are agreed that the king should establish an ordinance and enforce an interdict, that whoever prays to anyone, divine or human, for thirty days, except to you, O king, shall be thrown into a den of lions. 8Now, O king, establish the interdict and sign the document, so that it cannot be changed, according to the law of the Medes and the Persians, which cannot be revoked." 9Therefore King Darius signed the document and interdict.

Daniel in the Lions' Den

10 Although Daniel knew that the document had been signed, he continued to go to his house, which had windows in its upper room open toward Jerusalem, and to get down on his knees three times a day to pray to his God and praise him, just as he had done previously. 11The conspirators came and found Daniel

praying and seeking mercy before his God. 12Then they approached the king and said concerning the interdict, "O king! Did you not sign an interdict, that anyone who prays to anyone, divine or human, within thirty days except to you, O king, shall be thrown into a den of lions?" The king answered, "The thing stands fast, according to the law of the Medes and Persians, which cannot be revoked." 13Then they responded to the king, "Daniel, one of the exiles from Judah, pays no attention to you, O king, or to the interdict you have signed, but he is saying his prayers three times a day."

14 When the king heard the charge, he was very much distressed. He was determined to save Daniel, and until the sun went down he made every effort to rescue him. 15Then the conspirators came to the king and said to him, "Know, O king, that it is a law of the Medes and Persians that no interdict or ordinance that the king establishes can be changed."

16 Then the king gave the command, and Daniel was brought and thrown into the den of lions. The king said to Daniel, "May your God, whom you faithfully serve, deliver you!" 17A stone was brought and laid on the mouth of the den, and the king sealed it with his own signet and with the signet of his lords, so that nothing might be changed concerning Daniel. 18Then the king went to his palace and spent the night fasting; no food was brought to him, and sleep fled from him.

Daniel Saved from the Lions

19 Then, at break of day, the king got up and hurried to the den of lions. 20When he came

---

See Gen 41.41–44. **6.5** The conspiracy is politically, not religiously, motivated. **6.6** *O King Darius, live forever!* See note on 2.4. **6.7** A typically fanciful plan, but it makes sovereignty the central issue of the conflict. *Prefects . . . governors.* See note on 3.2. *Whoever prays . . . O king.* The king is the only lawfully worshiped deity. When the king agrees to make this law (v. 9), he unwittingly challenges the sovereignty of God. *Den,* a pit or subterranean area with a small opening (see v. 17); there is no evidence of lions being kept this way, though the hunting and caging of *lions* is well documented in Mesopotamian inscriptions and art. The danger posed by the lions' power took on symbolic value. See 1 Kings 13.24; Pss 22.21; 58.6; 91.13; Ezek 19.2–9. **6.8** *Cannot be revoked,* a folkloristic motif, not a Persian custom. The scheme is designed to trap both Daniel and the king; see Esth 1.19; 8.8. *Medes, Persians.* See note on 5.28. **6.10** *Windows.* See Tob 3.11. *Upper*

room. See Judg 3.20; 1 Kings 17.19–20; 2 Kings 1.2; 4.10; Jer 22.14; Acts 1.13. Praying *toward Jerusalem* was especially important in the exilic and postexilic periods; see 1 Kings 8.35–44; Pss 5.7; 138.2; 1 Esd 4.58. *Down on his knees.* Jews ordinarily stood for public prayer but during the postexilic period began the custom of kneeling for private prayer; see 1 Kings 8.54; 2 Chr 6.13; Ezra 9.5; Lk 22.41; Acts 9.40; 20.36. *Three times a day.* See 9.21; Ps 55.17; Jdt 9.1; Acts 3.1. **6.12** *Approached,* in the sense of "bringing a charge" in a legal manner; see Isa 41.1; Mal 3.5. **6.14** The king is remarkably sympathetic to Daniel; see vv. 16, 18–19, 23. He is *distressed* at Daniel's plight and the realization he had been tricked; see 2.1; 3.13; 4.5; 5.6. Despite his royal power, the king cannot *save* Daniel; only the power of God will save him; see vv. 16, 22–23, 27. **6.17** *The king sealed . . . lords,* an assurance that no human help could be given. Seals were made by press-

near the den where Daniel was, he cried out anxiously to Daniel, "O Daniel, servant of the living God, has your God whom you faithfully serve been able to deliver you from the lions?" 21Daniel then said to the king, "O king, live forever! 22My God sent his angel and shut the lions' mouths so that they would not hurt me, because I was found blameless before him; and also before you, O king, I have done no wrong." 23Then the king was exceedingly glad and commanded that Daniel be taken up out of the den. So Daniel was taken up out of the den, and no kind of harm was found on him, because he had trusted in his God. 24The king gave a command, and those who had accused Daniel were brought and thrown into the den of lions—they, their children, and their wives. Before they reached the bottom of the den the lions overpowered them and broke all their bones in pieces.

25 Then King Darius wrote to all peoples and nations of every language throughout the whole world: "May you have abundant prosperity! 26I make a decree, that in all my royal

dominion people should tremble and fear before the God of Daniel:

For he is the living God,
  enduring forever.
His kingdom shall never be destroyed,
  and his dominion has no end.
27   He delivers and rescues,
  he works signs and wonders in heaven
    and on earth;
  for he has saved Daniel
    from the power of the lions."
28So this Daniel prospered during the reign of Darius and the reign of Cyrus the Persian.

Visions of the Four Beasts

7 In the first year of King Belshazzar of Babylon, Daniel had a dream and visions of his head as he lay in bed. Then he wrote down the dream:*a* 2I,*b* Daniel, saw in my vision by night the four winds of heaven stirring up the great sea, 3and four great beasts came up out of the

a Q Ms Theodotion: MT adds *the beginning of the words; he said*
b Theodotion: Aram *Daniel answered and said, I*

ing the signet into clay and were regularly used on official correspondence; see 1 Kings 21.8; Esth 3.12; 8.8, 10. **6.20–22** The king does not observe the angel himself, unlike in ch. 3. **6.20** *The living God.* See Deut 5.26; Ps 42.2; Jer 10.10; 23.36. **6.21** *O king, live forever!* See note on 2.4. **6.22** Daniel insists on his legal innocence; see Ps 91.9–16; 1 Macc 2.60. *Angel.* Postexilic Jewish writers increasingly depicted divine-human encounters as mediated through heavenly beings; see 3.28; 2 Kings 1.3; 1 Chr 21.12; Ps 91.11; Zech 3; Tob 5.4. **6.24** Punishment for false witness. See Deut 19.16–19; Esth 9.25; Ps 140.9–11. As the property of men, *children and . . . wives* could be punished along with them; see Num 16.25–33; Josh 7.24; Judg 20.48; 21.10; 2 Sam 21.5–9; Esth 9.12–14. **6.25** *Peoples and nations of every language.* See note on 3.4. **6.26a** Darius's edict goes even further than that of Nebuchadnezzar (3.29) in ordering all to revere God. **6.26–27** The rationale for the edict is a doxology, as in 4.3, 34–35, 37, recognizing the sovereignty of God. **6.26** The *living God.* See 6.20. *Enduring forever . . . no end.* See 4.3, 34; Ex 15.18; Pss 10.16; 29.10; 66.7; 102.12. **6.27** *Signs and wonders.* See 4.2–3. **6.28** *Cyrus the Persian* allowed Jewish exiles to return home in 539 BCE, exhibiting moderation and religious sensitivity toward conquered peoples; see 5.31; 10.1; Ezra 1.1–4; 6.3–5; Isa 44.28; he is called the Lord's anointed (or messiah) in Isa 45.1.

7.1–12.13 It is generally agreed that these chapters focus on the reign of Antiochus IV Epiphanes (175–164 BCE). The chronological sequence of the visions parallels that of the stories in chs. 1–6. Although ch. 6 was set in the reign of Darius and mentioned Cyrus of Persia, ch. 7 reverts to Belshazzar of Babylon. These visions are similar to the visions in Am 7.7–9; Zech 1.8–17, 18–21; 2.1–5; 4.1–5; 5.1–4, 5–11; 6.1–8, but are more elaborate. Although the visions of chs. 7 and 8 are symbolic, the others are direct revelations to Daniel. The symbolic vision in ch. 7 is received in a dream (as in ch. 2); in both visions a detailed description is given and an interpretation requested and received. In ch. 7 this contact with the divine realm produces a feeling of fear; see 4.5; 5.5, 6; 7.15, 28. All the visions present past events as if they were future. There are indications of editorial activity in these chapters, but the unevenness in the imagery may be due to deliberate contrasts by the author. **7.1–28** Although the translation indicates a mixture of prose and poetical sections, the whole chapter has a rhythmic prose style often very close to poetry. Ch. 7 is connected in its language, Aramaic, to chs. 2–6 and in theme to ch. 2 and chs. 8–12. The theme of four world kingdoms superseded by a fifth more ideal kingdom has a long history in the Near East before and after the time of the composition of Daniel. Here the persecution of Antiochus Epiphanes has negatively colored the portrayal of the entire fourth kingdom, and indeed of all four kingdoms, a view much more negative than in ch. 2. **7.1** *The first year of King Belshazzar of Babylon* (see 5.1, 30), a sixth-century date to present the vision as an ancient prediction. **7.2** *Four winds . . . stirring up.* Ordinary winds would blow from one direction. Daniel's dream and night vision give a setting beyond the mundane. As in other ancient Near Eastern creation traditions, the *sea* is associated with mythological monsters, forces of chaos; see Job 26.12–13; Pss 74.13–17; 89.9–10; Isa 27.1; 51.9–10. Here the sea spawns

sea, different from one another. ⁴The first was like a lion and had eagles' wings. Then, as I watched, its wings were plucked off, and it was lifted up from the ground and made to stand on two feet like a human being; and a human mind was given to it. ⁵Another beast appeared, a second one, that looked like a bear. It was raised up on one side, had three tusks*a* in its mouth among its teeth and was told, "Arise, devour many bodies!" ⁶After this, as I watched, another appeared, like a leopard. The beast had four wings of a bird on its back and four heads; and dominion was given to it. ⁷After this I saw in the visions by night a fourth beast, terrifying and dreadful and exceedingly strong. It had great iron teeth and was devouring, breaking in pieces, and stamping what was left with its feet. It was different from all the beasts that preceded it, and it had ten horns. ⁸I was considering the horns, when another horn appeared, a little one coming up among them; to make room for it, three of the earlier horns were plucked up by the roots. There were eyes like human eyes in this horn, and a mouth speaking arrogantly.

Judgment before the Ancient One

⁹ As I watched,
     thrones were set in place,
         and an Ancient One*b* took his throne,

his clothing was white as snow,
     and the hair of his head like pure wool;
his throne was fiery flames,
     and its wheels were burning fire.
¹⁰ A stream of fire issued
     and flowed out from his presence.
A thousand thousands served him,
     and ten thousand times ten thousand
         stood attending him.
The court sat in judgment,
     and the books were opened.
¹¹I watched then because of the noise of the arrogant words that the horn was speaking. And as I watched, the beast was put to death, and its body destroyed and given over to be burned with fire. ¹²As for the rest of the beasts, their dominion was taken away, but their lives were prolonged for a season and a time. ¹³As I watched in the night visions,

I saw one like a human being*c*
     coming with the clouds of heaven.
And he came to the Ancient One*d*
     and was presented before him.
¹⁴ To him was given dominion
     and glory and kingship,
         that all peoples, nations, and languages

---

a Or ribs *b* Aram *an Ancient of Days* *c* Aram *one like a son of man* *d* Aram *the Ancient of Days*

---

mythological beasts symbolizing kingdoms (v. 17). On the four kingdoms, see note on 2.36–45. **7.4** *First,* the Babylonian Empire, as in 2.36. *Like a lion . . . eagles' wings.* Winged lions are well known from Assyro-Babylonian art. *Wings . . . plucked off* may refer to 4.10–33; *human being* and *human mind* to 4.36. **7.5** *Another beast,* the Median Empire; see 5.28. The savage Median attack on Babylon by divine command had been predicted (Jer 51.11) but did not occur. *Up on one side,* perhaps ready to spring. *Three tusks* may refer to its ravenous appetite for booty (if *three ribs* [see text note a] refers to the booty being devoured). **7.6** *Another beast,* the Persian Empire; see 5.28. *Four wings* may allude to the rapidity of Persia's conquests under Cyrus; see Isa 41.3. *Four heads* may refer to Persia's dominion in all directions or to the four kings of Persia mentioned in Ezra 1.1; 4.6, 7; Neh 12.22. **7.7** *Fourth beast,* the empire of Alexander the Great. *Ten horns,* the line of rulers of the Seleucid dynasty (which ruled Syria after the death of Alexander) culminating in Antiochus IV. The first Seleucid kings had coins decorated with horns, symbols of divine power; see vv. 23–24. **7.8** *Eyes* and *mouth* indicate that the horn represents a human character, the contemporary ruler Antiochus IV Epiphanes, who disposed of other claimants to the throne (see v. 24; 11.21). **7.9–14** The imagery becomes more cryptic and more poetic as the future and the

heavenly realm are described; much of this judgment scene imagery partakes of traditions preserved in Psalms and the prophets; see Pss 82.1; 90.2; Isa 6; Ezek 1; see also 1 Kings 22.19. Some of the motifs suggest aspects of ancient Canaanite mythology. The image of an *Ancient One* and of *one like a human being . . . clouds of heaven* (v. 13) has been compared to myths that refer to the god El as king and father of years and to Baal as a triumphant warrior god. There is, however, no cosmic battle here, only a judgment. **7.11** A violent end to the fourth kingdom. **7.12** Respite for the other kingdoms accentuates the wickedness of the fourth kingdom and anticipates v. 27. **7.13–14** The symbol of the fifth kingdom, a human figure, stands in contrast to the animal symbols from the abyss by being associated with the heavenly realm; the animals were connected with historical events, but in these two verses the scene moves beyond history. *One like a human being,* lit. "one like a son of man," stands in contrast to those ominous kingdoms symbolized by what looked like animals. Some scholars think that this figure is a corporate symbol for Israel. It is more likely, however, that he is an angel who represents Israel on the heavenly level, as the archangel Michael does in 10.21; 12.1. Angels are said to appear in human likeness in, e.g., 8.15; 10.5, 16, 18; 12.6–7. In the Gospels Jesus is identified as the Son of Man who comes on the clouds of heaven

should serve him.
His dominion is an everlasting dominion
    that shall not pass away,
and his kingship is one
    that shall never be destroyed.

Daniel's Visions Interpreted

15 As for me, Daniel, my spirit was troubled within me,[a] and the visions of my head terrified me. 16I approached one of the attendants to ask him the truth concerning all this. So he said that he would disclose to me the interpretation of the matter: 17"As for these four great beasts, four kings shall arise out of the earth. 18But the holy ones of the Most High shall receive the kingdom and possess the kingdom forever—forever and ever."

19 Then I desired to know the truth concerning the fourth beast, which was different from all the rest, exceedingly terrifying, with its teeth of iron and claws of bronze, and which devoured and broke in pieces, and stamped what was left with its feet; 20and concerning the ten horns that were on its head, and concerning the other horn, which came up and to make room for which three of them fell out—the horn that had eyes and a mouth that spoke arrogantly, and that seemed greater than the others. 21As I looked, this horn made war with the holy ones and was prevailing over them, 22until the Ancient One[b] came; then judgment was given for the holy ones of the Most High, and the time arrived when the holy ones gained possession of the kingdom.

23 This is what he said: "As for the fourth beast,
there shall be a fourth kingdom on earth
    that shall be different from all the
        other kingdoms;
it shall devour the whole earth,
    and trample it down, and break it to
        pieces.

24 As for the ten horns,
    out of this kingdom ten kings shall arise,
    and another shall arise after them.
This one shall be different from the
        former ones,
    and shall put down three kings.
25 He shall speak words against the Most
        High,
    shall wear out the holy ones of the
        Most High,
    and shall attempt to change the sacred
        seasons and the law;
and they shall be given into his power
    for a time, two times,[c] and half a time.
26 Then the court shall sit in judgment,
    and his dominion shall be taken away,
    to be consumed and totally destroyed.
27 The kingship and dominion
    and the greatness of the kingdoms
        under the whole heaven
    shall be given to the people of the holy
        ones of the Most High;
their kingdom shall be an everlasting
        kingdom,
    and all dominions shall serve and obey
        them."

28 Here the account ends. As for me, Daniel, my thoughts greatly terrified me, and my face turned pale; but I kept the matter in my mind.

Vision of a Ram and a Goat

8 In the third year of the reign of King Belshazzar a vision appeared to me, Daniel, after the one that had appeared to me at first. 2In the vision I was looking and saw myself in Susa the capital, in the province of Elam,[d] and I was by the river Ulai.[e] 3I looked up and saw a ram standing beside the river.[f] It had two

---

a Aram *troubled in its sheath*   b Aram *the Ancient of Days*
c Aram *a time, times*   d Gk Theodotion: MT Q Ms repeat *in the vision I was looking*   e Or *the Ulai Gate*   f Or *gate*

(e.g., Mk 13.26; 14.62). **7.15** *Troubled*, like Nebuchadnezzar; see 2.1; 4.4. **7.16** In chs. 1–6 Daniel was the interpreter; here he needs an interpreter. **7.18** *Holy ones of the Most High*, the angelic host. Cf. 8.10–13. **7.20–21** The little horn of v. 8 has now become greater than the others; the persecution of Antiochus Epiphanes begins. **7.25** Antiochus Epiphanes banned the observance of the sabbath and feast days (1 Macc 1.41–53). A *time . . . time*. The persecution is for a limited time, three and a half years, half of the perfect number seven. **7.27** *The people . . . Most High*, the Jewish people, who are protected by the angelic host. There is no

description of the kingdom they receive, but evidently they will rule over the other nations.

8.1–27 The language returns to Hebrew and the literary style deteriorates, possibly because the author was more at home in Aramaic. There is also increasing concern with actual contemporary history from the time of the Medes and Persians through to Antiochus IV. The chapter refers to some of the same events as ch. 7. **8.1** *Third year of . . . Belshazzar*, two years later than 7.1. **8.2** The text is obscure, but Daniel, while still in Babylon, seems to be transported in vision to *Susa*, the winter capital of the Medo-Persian Empire in the

horns. Both horns were long, but one was longer than the other, and the longer one came up second. ⁴I saw the ram charging westward and northward and southward. All beasts were powerless to withstand it, and no one could rescue from its power; it did as it pleased and became strong.

5 As I was watching, a male goat appeared from the west, coming across the face of the whole earth without touching the ground. The goat had a horn*a* between its eyes. ⁶It came toward the ram with the two horns that I had seen standing beside the river,*b* and it ran at it with savage force. ⁷I saw it approaching the ram. It was enraged against it and struck the ram, breaking its two horns. The ram did not have power to withstand it; it threw the ram down to the ground and trampled upon it, and there was no one who could rescue the ram from its power. ⁸Then the male goat grew exceedingly great; but at the height of its power, the great horn was broken, and in its place there came up four prominent horns toward the four winds of heaven.

9 Out of one of them came another*c* horn, a little one, which grew exceedingly great toward the south, toward the east, and toward the beautiful land. ¹⁰It grew as high as the host of heaven. It threw down to the earth some of the host and some of the stars, and trampled on

them. ¹¹Even against the prince of the host it acted arrogantly; it took the regular burnt offering away from him and overthrew the place of his sanctuary. ¹²Because of wickedness, the host was given over to it together with the regular burnt offering;*d* it cast truth to the ground, and kept prospering in what it did. ¹³Then I heard a holy one speaking, and another holy one said to the one that spoke, "For how long is this vision concerning the regular burnt offering, the transgression that makes desolate, and the giving over of the sanctuary and host to be trampled?"*d* ¹⁴And he answered him,*e* "For two thousand three hundred evenings and mornings; then the sanctuary shall be restored to its rightful state."

Gabriel Interprets the Vision

15 When I, Daniel, had seen the vision, I tried to understand it. Then someone appeared standing before me, having the appearance of a man, ¹⁶and I heard a human voice by the Ulai, calling, "Gabriel, help this man understand the vision." ¹⁷So he came near where I stood; and when he came, I became frightened and fell prostrate. But he said to me, "Understand, O mortal,*f* that the vision is for the time of the end."

a Theodotion: Gk *one horn*; Heb *a horn of vision*   *b* Or *gate*
c Cn Compare 7.8: Heb *one*   *d* Meaning of Heb uncertain
e Gk Theodotion Syr Vg: Heb *me*   *f* Heb *son of man*

province of *Elam. The river Ulai,* at or near Susa, a setting similar to that of Ezek 1.1 (Ezekiel's vision by the river Chebar). Rivers and gates (see text note *e* on p. 1184) provide equally good "boundary" places where communication with divine beings is possible; see Gen 32.22–32 (a river); Gen 28.10–19 (Bethel, "house of God," "gate of heaven"). **8.3** *Ram* with *two horns,* the Medes and the Persians symbolically merged as in 6.8, 12; cf. chs. 2 and 7, where separate symbols were used. *Longer one,* Persia; see note on 5.28. **8.4** The expansion of the Medo-Persian Empire. **8.5–7** The *goat* advancing so swiftly from the *west* refers to the Macedonian army, which quickly conquered the whole Persian Empire. *Horn between its eyes,* Alexander the Great, as v. 21 indicates; see 2.40; 7.7; 11.3. **8.8** *Height of its power.* Alexander died in 323 BCE, and the kingdom was divided up among four generals, the *four prominent horns;* see 2.41. **8.9** *A little one.* The author is interested only in the Seleucid kingdom in Syria and especially in one of its rulers, represented by the little horn. It is generally agreed that this refers to Antiochus Epiphanes and his campaigns: *south* to Egypt, *east* to Parthia, and finally toward *the beautiful land,* namely, Judea, as indicated by the references to the *sanctuary,* or temple, in vv. 10–13; see 11.16, 41, 45. **8.10** Cf. Isa 14.12–14; Antiochus is pictured as challenging heaven

itself. *Host,* the angelic host; see 4.35. *Stars,* the host of heaven, often represent gods or angels; see Judg 5.20. The motif of a rebellion by lower powers against the heavenly forces is found in Canaanite and other Near Eastern myths. **8.11–12** Antiochus interfered with the offerings in the temple, a direct affront to *the prince of the host* (God). 1 Macc 1.41–59 describes his profanation of the temple and erection, on the altar of burnt offering, of a foreign altar, referred to as the *transgression that makes desolate* in v. 13 and as an *abomination that desolates* in 9.27; 11.31; 12.11; see 1 Macc 4.36–59. Cf. Mk 13.14, where "the desolating sacrilege" is a sign of the end. **8.13–14** Daniel overhears the conversation of *a holy one* and *another holy one* (angels; see Zech 2.3–4) and learns *how long* the desolation of the sanctuary and the interference with the daily burnt offerings will last: *two thousand three hundred . . . mornings,* 1,150 days, almost as long as the length of time in 7.25 and 12.7, namely, three and a half years, about 1,260 days. According to 1 Macc 1.54–4.52, the period of the desecration of the sanctuary lasted exactly three years. **8.13** *Transgression . . . desolate.* See note on 8.11–12. **8.15** *Appearance of a man.* Celestial beings are said to have the appearance of humans; see 7.13; 10.5–6, 16–19; Ezek 1.5, 26–28; 40.3–4. **8.16** *Gabriel,* one of the principal angels; see 6.22; 9.21. **8.17** *Mortal,* a title ac-

18 As he was speaking to me, I fell into a trance, face to the ground; then he touched me and set me on my feet. 19 He said, "Listen, and I will tell you what will take place later in the period of wrath; for it refers to the appointed time of the end. 20 As for the ram that you saw with the two horns, these are the kings of Media and Persia. 21 The male goat[a] is the king of Greece, and the great horn between its eyes is the first king. 22 As for the horn that was broken, in place of which four others arose, four kingdoms shall arise from his[b] nation, but not with his power.

23 At the end of their rule,
  when the transgressions have reached
    their full measure,
  a king of bold countenance shall arise,
    skilled in intrigue.
24 He shall grow strong in power,[c]
  shall cause fearful destruction,
    and shall succeed in what he does.
  He shall destroy the powerful
    and the people of the holy ones.
25 By his cunning
  he shall make deceit prosper under his
    hand,
  and in his own mind he shall be great.
  Without warning he shall destroy many
    and shall even rise up against the
      Prince of princes.

But he shall be broken, and not by
    human hands.
26 The vision of the evenings and the mornings that has been told is true. As for you, seal up the vision, for it refers to many days from now."

27 So I, Daniel, was overcome and lay sick for some days; then I arose and went about the king's business. But I was dismayed by the vision and did not understand it.

Daniel's Prayer for the People

9 In the first year of Darius son of Ahasuerus, by birth a Mede, who became king over the realm of the Chaldeans— 2 in the first year of his reign, I, Daniel, perceived in the books the number of years that, according to the word of the LORD to the prophet Jeremiah, must be fulfilled for the devastation of Jerusalem, namely, seventy years.

3 Then I turned to the Lord God, to seek an answer by prayer and supplication with fasting and sackcloth and ashes. 4 I prayed to the LORD my God and made confession, saying,

"Ah, Lord, great and awesome God, keeping covenant and steadfast love with those who

a Or shaggy male goat   b Gk Theodotion Vg: Heb the
c Theodotion and one Gk Ms: Heb repeats (from 8.22) but not with his power

centuating the distance between the human and the divine; see, e.g., Ezek 1.28–2.1; 3.1; 3.4; 3.16. The time of the end in this context (vv. 14, 25) refers to the end of the persecution; see v. 19; 10.14. There is no explicit mention of an eternal kingdom as in 7.14, 18, 22, 27. **8.18** On Daniel's reaction and the angel touching him, see 10.8–10, 16, 18; Ezek 1.28–2.2. **8.19** The period of wrath, possibly the wrath of Antiochus or the wrath of God; contexts here and in 11.36 may suggest a fixed time during which God is angry with the Jewish people and uses Antiochus as the rod of divine anger; see Isa 5.1–30; 10.1–12; Zech 1.12–17. **8.20–25** Gabriel's explanation spells out the meaning of the vision in vv. 5–12; it reflects what is known of the historical period from the time of the Medes and Persians to the reign of Antiochus IV. **8.22** The four kingdoms (horns) mentioned in v. 8 are here said to lack Alexander's power. **8.23–25** Brief rhythmic phrases spell out the acts of the tyrant Antiochus; both form and content are reminiscent of Isa 14.4–21. See vv. 9–11; 11.21–45. **8.25** Prince of princes, a title for God; see v. 11. Not by human hands, divine intervention in the defeat of Antiochus; see 2.34; 7.26. **8.26** Seal up. Daniel is to keep the vision secret until later, since it is supposedly being given in the middle of the sixth century BCE (v. 1) but in fact is only written down in the second. **8.27** King's, Belshazzar's (8.1). Did not understand. Daniel's lack of

understanding after the explanation of vv. 19–26 may be a literary artifice pointing ahead to the detailed presentation in ch. 11.

9.1–27 A reinterpretation of Jeremiah's prophecy of a seventy-year exile; it now extends to the time of Antiochus Epiphanes but will soon end. **9.1** Darius. See note on 5.31. Ahasuerus, Hebrew for Xerxes. Both Darius and Xerxes were names of later Persian, not Median, kings. Who became king over the . . . Chaldeans, a reminder of the fall of the Babylonian Empire in 539 BCE. **9.2** Seventy years (Jer 25.11, 12; 29.10), a round number indicating a long exile, lasting a lifetime; see Ps 90.10; Isa 23.15. 2 Chr 36.22–23 considers this prophecy fulfilled by Cyrus's decree in 539 BCE, but the persecution by Antiochus and the continued devastation of Jerusalem would have called this fulfillment into question. As a sixth-century BCE character, Daniel would have been disturbed about the Babylonian devastation of Jerusalem, but in the second century BCE, the actual time of composition, the ravages of Antiochus are the underlying and central concern of the book. This double perspective must be kept in mind in reading the prayer in vv. 4–19. **9.3** Supplication. See v. 17, 18, 20, 23. Sackcloth and ashes, traditional signs of mourning; see 10.2–3; Neh 9.1; Esth 4.1–3; Jer 4.8; 6.26; 49.3; Joel 1.13–14. **9.4–19** A communal confession of sin and petition for mercy. The quality of the

love you and keep your commandments, 5we have sinned and done wrong, acted wickedly and rebelled, turning aside from your commandments and ordinances. 6We have not listened to your servants the prophets, who spoke in your name to our kings, our princes, and our ancestors, and to all the people of the land.

7 "Righteousness is on your side, O Lord, but open shame, as at this day, falls on us, the people of Judah, the inhabitants of Jerusalem, and all Israel, those who are near and those who are far away, in all the lands to which you have driven them, because of the treachery that they have committed against you. 8Open shame, O LORD, falls on us, our kings, our officials, and our ancestors, because we have sinned against you. 9To the Lord our God belong mercy and forgiveness, for we have rebelled against him, 10and have not obeyed the voice of the LORD our God by following his laws, which he set before us by his servants the prophets.

11 "All Israel has transgressed your law and turned aside, refusing to obey your voice. So the curse and the oath written in the law of Moses, the servant of God, have been poured out upon us, because we have sinned against you. 12He has confirmed his words, which he spoke against us and against our rulers, by bringing upon us a calamity so great that what has been done against Jerusalem has never before been done under the whole heaven. 13Just as it is written in the law of Moses, all this calamity has come upon us. We did not entreat the favor of the LORD our God, turning from our iniquities and reflecting on his*a* fidelity. 14So the LORD kept watch over this calamity until he brought it upon us. Indeed, the LORD our God is right in all that he has done; for we have disobeyed his voice.

15 "And now, O Lord our God, who brought your people out of the land of Egypt with a mighty hand and made your name renowned even to this day—we have sinned, we have done wickedly. 16O Lord, in view of all your righteous acts, let your anger and wrath, we pray, turn away from your city Jerusalem, your holy mountain; because of our sins and the iniquities of our ancestors, Jerusalem and your people have become a disgrace among all our neighbors. 17Now therefore, O our God, listen to the prayer of your servant and to his supplication, and for your own sake, Lord,*b* let your face shine upon your desolated sanctuary. 18Incline your ear, O my God, and hear. Open your eyes and look at our desolation and the city that bears your name. We do not present our supplication before you on the ground of our righteousness, but on the ground of your great mercies. 19O Lord, hear; O Lord, forgive; O Lord, listen and act and do not delay! For your own sake, O my God, because your city and your people bear your name!"

The Seventy Weeks

20 While I was speaking, and was praying and confessing my sin and the sin of my people Israel, and presenting my supplication before the LORD my God on behalf of the holy mountain of my God— 21while I was speaking in prayer, the man Gabriel, whom I had seen before in a vision, came to me in swift flight at the time of the evening sacrifice. 22He came*c* and said to me, "Daniel, I have now come out to give you wisdom and understanding. 23At the beginning of your supplications a word went out, and I have come to declare it, for you

---

a Heb *your*   *b* Theodotion Vg Compare Syr: Heb *for the Lord's sake*   *c* Gk Syr: Heb *He made to understand*

Hebrew is superior to that in surrounding verses; hence it is sometimes considered a later addition. More likely it is a traditional prayer reminiscent in language and theology of the Deuteronomistic corpus in Deuteronomy through 2 Kings; see 1 Kings 8.23–53; Ezra 9.6–15; Neh 1.5–11; 9.6–37. The prayer assumes that the people's troubles are not the result of a predetermined divine plan, as the visions suggest, but are due to sin. **9.4** *Great and awesome God.* See Deut 7.21; Neh 1.5; 9.32. *Covenant and steadfast love.* See Deut 7.9, 12. *Keep your commandments.* See Ex 20.6; Deut 7.9; 1 Kings 8.23; Neh 1.5. **9.5** See 1 Kings 8.47; Ps 106.6. **9.6** *Not listened to . . . prophets.* See 9.10; Jer 7.25–26; 29.19. *Kings . . . land.* See Jer 44.21. **9.7–8** See Lev 26.40; 1 Kings 8.46–50; Ezra 9.7. **9.9–10** See Neh 9.17; Ps 130.4. **9.11** See Lev 26.14–45; Deut 28.15–68; 29.10–29. **9.12–14** A shift from second to third person; the text now addresses the people instead of God. A *calamity . . . Jerusalem,* the sixth-century BCE destruction and the second-century BCE desecration; the latter would be uppermost in the mind of the author. **9.14** *Kept watch.* Here God keeps watch to punish disobedience; see Jer 1.11–12; 31.28; 44.27. **9.15** See Deut 6.21; Neh 9.10; Jer 32.20–21. **9.16** *Your holy mountain.* See 9.20. *Disgrace,* language typical of exilic and postexilic laments; see Ps 44.13–16. **9.17** See Num 6.25; 1 Kings 8.28–30. *Desolated.* See vv. 18, 27; the language of the prayer resonates in the other verses of ch. 9; see also 8.11–13. **9.21** *Gabriel.* See 8.15–18. *Evening sacrifice.* See Ex 29.38–42. **9.23** *A word went out.* See Isa

are greatly beloved. So consider the word and understand the vision:

24 "Seventy weeks are decreed for your people and your holy city: to finish the transgression, to put an end to sin, and to atone for iniquity, to bring in everlasting righteousness, to seal both vision and prophet, and to anoint a most holy place. [a] 25 Know therefore and understand: from the time that the word went out to restore and rebuild Jerusalem until the time of an anointed prince, there shall be seven weeks; and for sixty-two weeks it shall be built again with streets and moat, but in a troubled time. 26 After the sixty-two weeks, an anointed one shall be cut off and shall have nothing, and the troops of the prince who is to come shall destroy the city and the sanctuary. Its [b] end shall come with a flood, and to the end there shall be war. Desolations are decreed. 27 He shall make a strong covenant with many for one week, and for half of the week he shall make sacrifice and offering cease; and in their place [c] shall be an abomination that desolates, until the decreed end is poured out upon the desolator."

Conflict of Nations and Heavenly Powers

10 In the third year of King Cyrus of Persia a word was revealed to Daniel, who was named Belteshazzar. The word was true, and it concerned a great conflict. He understood the word, having received understanding in the vision.

2 At that time I, Daniel, had been mourning for three weeks. 3 I had eaten no rich food, no meat or wine had entered my mouth, and I had not anointed myself at all, for the full three weeks. 4 On the twenty-fourth day of the first month, as I was standing on the bank of the great river (that is, the Tigris), 5 I looked up and saw a man clothed in linen, with a belt of gold from Uphaz around his waist. 6 His body was like beryl, his face like lightning, his eyes like flaming torches, his arms and legs like the gleam of burnished bronze, and the sound of his words like the roar of a multitude. 7 I, Daniel, alone saw the vision; the people who were with me did not see the vision, though a great trembling fell upon them, and they fled and hid themselves. 8 So I was left alone to see this great vision. My strength left me, and my complexion grew deathly pale, and I retained no strength. 9 Then I heard the sound of his words; and when I heard the sound of his words, I fell into a trance, face to the ground.

10 But then a hand touched me and roused me to my hands and knees. 11 He said to me, "Daniel, greatly beloved, pay attention to the words that I am going to speak to you. Stand on your feet, for I have now been sent to you."

_____

a Or thing or one   b Or His   c Cn: Meaning of Heb uncertain

55.11. _Greatly beloved_ becomes an epithet for the prophet in 10.11, 19. **9.24** _Seventy weeks are decreed._ The seventy years of v. 2 are interpreted as seventy weeks of years, perhaps because Israel merited such a sevenfold punishment (Lev 26.18). 2 Chr 36.21 also connects Jeremiah's prophecy with the sabbatical years of Lev 26.34–35. Contrary to the assumption of Daniel's prayer, the period of punishment is decreed and is not affected by human actions. _To seal both vision and prophet,_ either as their ratification, or their termination as they are no longer necessary. _Most holy place,_ the sanctuary. **9.25** The final week is the author's main focus. The remaining sixty-nine weeks are then divided into _seven_ and _sixty-two weeks. Anointed prince,_ either Zerubbabel or the high priest Joshua; see Ezra 2.2; 3.2; Hag 1.1–14; Zech 6.9–14. _Sixty-two weeks,_ a round number to describe the period down to Antiochus. _Troubled time_ could refer to the struggle for control of the country between the Seleucid and Ptolemaic dynasties; see 2.41, 43; 11.4–20. **9.26** _Anointed one,_ Onias III, the deposed high priest murdered in 171 BCE (2 Macc 4.32–34). _The prince,_ Antiochus IV. **9.27** _With many,_ with hellenizing Jews; see 1 Macc 1.11–15. _Half of the week,_ the second half of the last week; see 7.25; see 8.13–14 for these three and a half years from 167 to 164 BCE. _Abomination that desolates._ See 8.11–13; 1 Macc 1.54. _Decreed end._ See 7.26–27.

10.1–12.4 Chs. 10–12 comprise a single vision: a long preparation in 10.1–11.1 and then in 11.2–12.4 another survey of the future. The survey contains brief references to the Persian Empire and the conquests and demise of Alexander, then lengthy descriptions of the conflict between Ptolemies and Seleucids with its effects on Judea; everything leads up to the rise and fall of Antiochus IV. All this takes place against the backdrop of a heavenly struggle and culminates in the deliverance of the elect, especially the wise, in a resurrection from the dead. **10.1** _Third year of . . . Cyrus,_ 536 BCE, seventy years after the date given in 1.1. _Belteshazzar._ See 1.7. _Conflict,_ the wars of 11.5–45 and the heavenly struggle of 10.13, 20. **10.2** _Mourning._ See 9.3; 10.12. **10.3** See 9.3; 10.12. **10.4** _River._ See 8.2. **10.5–6** See Ezekiel, esp. chs. 1, 9–11, for the imagery. _A man,_ an angel in human form, probably Gabriel; see 8.15–17. _Uphaz,_ an unknown place. **10.7** The cause of the _trembling_ is not stated; see v. 11. The scene enhances Daniel's position. **10.8–9** Both the vision and the sound of the words are overpowering; see 8.17–18; 10.15–17. **10.10–11** See 8.18; Ezek 1.28–2.2. Superhuman support is needed; see also vv. 16, 18. _Greatly_

So while he was speaking this word to me, I stood up trembling. [12]He said to me, "Do not fear, Daniel, for from the first day that you set your mind to gain understanding and to humble yourself before your God, your words have been heard, and I have come because of your words. [13]But the prince of the kingdom of Persia opposed me twenty-one days. So Michael, one of the chief princes, came to help me, and I left him there with the prince of the kingdom of Persia,[a] [14]and have come to help you understand what is to happen to your people at the end of days. For there is a further vision for those days."

15 While he was speaking these words to me, I turned my face toward the ground and was speechless. [16]Then one in human form touched my lips, and I opened my mouth to speak, and said to the one who stood before me, "My lord, because of the vision such pains have come upon me that I retain no strength. [17]How can my lord's servant talk with my lord? For I am shaking,[b] no strength remains in me, and no breath is left in me."

18 Again one in human form touched me and strengthened me. [19]He said, "Do not fear, greatly beloved, you are safe. Be strong and courageous!" When he spoke to me, I was strengthened and said, "Let my lord speak, for you have strengthened me." [20]Then he said, "Do you know why I have come to you? Now I must return to fight against the prince of Persia, and when I am through with him, the prince of Greece will come. [21]But I am to tell you what is inscribed in the book of truth. There is no one with me who contends against

11 these princes except Michael, your prince. [1]As for me, in the first year of Darius the Mede, I stood up to support and strengthen him.

2 "Now I will announce the truth to you. Three more kings shall arise in Persia. The fourth shall be far richer than all of them, and when he has become strong through his riches, he shall stir up all against the kingdom of Greece. [3]Then a warrior king shall arise, who shall rule with great dominion and take action as he pleases. [4]And while still rising in power, his kingdom shall be broken and divided toward the four winds of heaven, but not to his posterity, nor according to the dominion with which he ruled; for his kingdom shall be uprooted and go to others besides these.

5 "Then the king of the south shall grow strong, but one of his officers shall grow stronger than he and shall rule a realm greater than his own realm. [6]After some years they shall make an alliance, and the daughter of the king of the south shall come to the king of the north to ratify the agreement. But she shall not retain her power, and his offspring shall not endure. She shall be given up, she and her attendants and her child and the one who supported her.

"In those times [7]a branch from her roots shall rise up in his place. He shall come against the army and enter the fortress of the king of the north, and he shall take action against

---

a Gk Theodotion: Heb *I was left there with the kings of Persia*
b Gk: Heb *from now*

---

beloved. See 9.23; 10.19. **10.13** *Prince,* the patron angel of a people. The idea of struggles between angelic princes is an adaptation of the common mythology of the ancient Near East. With a god over every nation, if nations battled, the more significant battle was waged between their gods; see Isa 36.18–20. *Twenty-one days,* the duration of the fast in vv. 2–3. *Michael,* protector of the Jewish people; see v. 21; 12.1. **10.14** *End of days.* The events foretold in 11.40–12.4 are construed as the end of history. *A further vision,* supplementing chs. 7– 9. **10.20–21** *Do you know ... to you?* The answer is that Gabriel is to reveal the contents of the *book of truth,* and he begins to do so in 11.2: the future is under divine control. *Return to fight,* in the heavenly struggle; Michael will be the only support for Gabriel in the successive conflicts with the angelic patrons of Persia and Greece. **11.1** *First year of Darius* (see 9.1), possibly an editorial addition, but it may be part of the speech that began in 10.20; the angel would be speaking of

strengthening Darius in the supposed Median conquest of Babylon (5.30–31; note on 5.31; Jer 51.11). **11.2** *Three more kings,* possibly Ahasuerus, Artaxerxes, and Darius II (see 7.6), although no names are mentioned and there is no scholarly consensus about who is meant. The author evidently did not know how many Persian kings there had been. **11.3** *Warrior king,* Alexander the Great. See 7.7; 8.5–8, 21. **11.4** *Broken and divided.* See 2.41; 8.8. **11.5** *King of the south,* Ptolemy I of Egypt. *One of his officers,* Seleucus I, who established a greater kingdom in Syria. **11.6** *They,* the Ptolemies and the Seleucids. *An alliance,* an unsuccessful interdynastic marriage; see 2.43. *Daughter,* Berenice, the daughter of Ptolemy II (now *king of the south*) to Antiochus II of Syria (now *king of the north*) in 252 BCE; Berenice, her child, and her attendants were murdered after Antiochus himself died under suspicious circumstances. **11.7–8** *A branch,* Berenice's brother, Ptolemy III, who took revenge for her death.

them and prevail. 8Even their gods, with their idols and with their precious vessels of silver and gold, he shall carry off to Egypt as spoils of war. For some years he shall refrain from attacking the king of the north; 9then the latter shall invade the realm of the king of the south, but will return to his own land.

10 "His sons shall wage war and assemble a multitude of great forces, which shall advance like a flood and pass through, and again shall carry the war as far as his fortress. 11Moved with rage, the king of the south shall go out and do battle against the king of the north, who shall muster a great multitude, which shall, however, be defeated by his enemy. 12When the multitude has been carried off, his heart shall be exalted, and he shall overthrow tens of thousands, but he shall not prevail. 13For the king of the north shall again raise a multitude, larger than the former, and after some years*a* he shall advance with a great army and abundant supplies.

14 "In those times many shall rise against the king of the south. The lawless among your own people shall lift themselves up in order to fulfill the vision, but they shall fail. 15Then the king of the north shall come and throw up siegeworks, and take a well-fortified city. And the forces of the south shall not stand, not even his picked troops, for there shall be no strength to resist. 16But he who comes against him shall take the actions he pleases, and no one shall withstand him. He shall take a position in the beautiful land, and all of it shall be in his power. 17He shall set his mind to come with the strength of his whole kingdom, and he shall bring terms of peace*b* and perform them. In order to destroy the kingdom,*c* he shall give him a woman in marriage; but it shall not succeed or be to his advantage. 18Afterward he shall turn to the coastlands, and

shall capture many. But a commander shall put an end to his insolence; indeed,*d* he shall turn his insolence back upon him. 19Then he shall turn back toward the fortresses of his own land, but he shall stumble and fall, and shall not be found.

20 "Then shall arise in his place one who shall send an official for the glory of the kingdom; but within a few days he shall be broken, though not in anger or in battle. 21In his place shall arise a contemptible person on whom royal majesty had not been conferred; he shall come in without warning and obtain the kingdom through intrigue. 22Armies shall be utterly swept away and broken before him, and the prince of the covenant as well. 23And after an alliance is made with him, he shall act deceitfully and become strong with a small party. 24Without warning he shall come into the richest parts*e* of the province and do what none of his predecessors had ever done, lavishing plunder, spoil, and wealth on them. He shall devise plans against strongholds, but only for a time. 25He shall stir up his power and determination against the king of the south with a great army, and the king of the south shall wage war with a much greater and stronger army. But he shall not succeed, for plots shall be devised against him 26by those who eat of the royal rations. They shall break him, his army shall be swept away, and many shall fall slain. 27The two kings, their minds bent on evil, shall sit at one table and exchange lies. But it shall not succeed, for there remains an end at the time appointed. 28He shall return to his land with great wealth, but his heart shall be set against the holy covenant. He shall work his will, and return to his own land.

---

a Heb *and at the end of the times years*   *b* Gk: Heb *kingdom, and upright ones with him*   *c* Heb *it*   *d* Meaning of Heb uncertain   *e* Or *among the richest men*

11.9 *The latter,* Seleucus II, who unsuccessfully invaded Egypt. **11.10** *Sons,* Seleucus III and Antiochus III. **11.10–19** Reign of Antiochus III the Great. **11.11–12** Ptolemy IV (*king of the south*) does not capitalize on his victory over Antiochus III (*king of the north*). **11.13–16** Antiochus III defeats Ptolemy V. **11.14** Revolts in Egypt. *The lawless,* very likely Jewish supporters of the Seleucids; see 11.30, 32. **11.15** *Forces of the south,* the Egyptians, defeated at Paneas by Antiochus III in 200 BCE. **11.16** *He,* Antiochus III, in complete control. *Beautiful land,* Judea; see 8.9. **11.17** *Marriage.* Whatever Antiochus intended by giving his daughter in marriage to Ptolemy V, the marriage did not further

the father's ambitions. **11.18** *A commander,* the Roman commander Lucius Cornelius Scipio, who defeated Antiochus III at the battle of Magnesia in Asia Minor. **11.19** *Fall.* Antiochus III was assassinated. **11.20** *One who . . . kingdom,* Antiochus III's successor, Seleucus IV, who sent Heliodorus to rob the temple treasury in Jerusalem (2 Macc 3.1–40); Seleucus was later assassinated. **11.21–45** The reign of Antiochus IV (175–164 BCE). **11.21** *Obtain . . . intrigue.* Antiochus IV usurped the throne, which belonged to his nephew. **11.22** *The prince of the covenant,* Onias III; see note on 9.26. **11.24** See 1 Macc 3.30. **11.25–28** The successful campaign against Egypt. **11.28** *Against the holy cov-*

29 "At the time appointed he shall return and come into the south, but this time it shall not be as it was before. 30For ships of Kittim shall come against him, and he shall lose heart and withdraw. He shall be enraged and take action against the holy covenant. He shall turn back and pay heed to those who forsake the holy covenant. 31Forces sent by him shall occupy and profane the temple and fortress. They shall abolish the regular burnt offering and set up the abomination that makes desolate. 32He shall seduce with intrigue those who violate the covenant; but the people who are loyal to their God shall stand firm and take action. 33The wise among the people shall give understanding to many; for some days, however, they shall fall by sword and flame, and suffer captivity and plunder. 34When they fall victim, they shall receive a little help, and many shall join them insincerely. 35Some of the wise shall fall, so that they may be refined, purified, and cleansed,[a] until the time of the end, for there is still an interval until the time appointed.

36 "The king shall act as he pleases. He shall exalt himself and consider himself greater than any god, and shall speak horrendous things against the God of gods. He shall prosper until the period of wrath is completed, for what is determined shall be done. 37He shall pay no respect to the gods of his ancestors, or to the one beloved by women; he shall pay no respect to any other god, for he shall consider himself greater than all. 38He

shall honor the god of fortresses instead of these; a god whom his ancestors did not know he shall honor with gold and silver, with precious stones and costly gifts. 39He shall deal with the strongest fortresses by the help of a foreign god. Those who acknowledge him he shall make more wealthy, and shall appoint them as rulers over many, and shall distribute the land for a price.

The Time of the End

40 "At the time of the end the king of the south shall attack him. But the king of the north shall rush upon him like a whirlwind, with chariots and horsemen, and with many ships. He shall advance against countries and pass through like a flood. 41He shall come into the beautiful land, and tens of thousands shall fall victim, but Edom and Moab and the main part of the Ammonites shall escape from his power. 42He shall stretch out his hand against the countries, and the land of Egypt shall not escape. 43He shall become ruler of the treasures of gold and of silver, and all the riches of Egypt; and the Libyans and the Ethiopians[b] shall follow in his train. 44But reports from the east and the north shall alarm him, and he shall go out with great fury to bring ruin and complete destruction to many. 45He shall pitch his palatial tents between the sea and the beautiful holy mountain. Yet he shall come to his end, with no one to help him.

_____
a Heb made them white   b Or Nubians; Heb Cushites

enant, the attack on Jerusalem and the Jewish religion; see 11.30. **11.29-35** The unsuccessful campaign in Egypt and attack on Jerusalem. **11.30** Kittim, from Citium in Cyprus, is used as a name for westerners. Alexander "came from the land of Kittim" (1 Macc 1.1). Here and in the Dead Sea Scrolls it means the Romans. Forsake the holy covenant. See 2 Macc 4. **11.31** See 8.11-14; 9.27. **11.33** The wise, those steadfast ones like the author to whom truth has been revealed, give understanding, sharing the messages preserved in the book of Daniel, central of which is that God controls events. Fall. The wise suffer martyrdom, but see 12.3. **11.34** A little help, probably more a reference to the small number who sincerely join "the wise" than to the activities of the Maccabees, Jews who confront the forces of Antiochus militarily and eventually succeed (167-164 BCE). **11.36-39** The character and pretensions of Antiochus; see 7.8; 8.9-12, 23-25. **11.36** As he pleases, a Danielic expression for a ruler's excesses just prior to his demise; see 8.4; 11.3, 16. Exalt . . . any god. Antiochus claims divine honors as

Epiphanes, from the Greek meaning "manifestation" of a god. The imagery may be influenced by the old Canaanite myth of a rebellion in heaven, which is reflected in Isa 14.3-21; Ezek 28.2-19. What is determined, divine control of events; see 7.22, 26-27; 8.19, 25; 9.26-27. **11.37** The one beloved by women, Tammuz, Mesopotamian god of vegetation (Adonis); see Ezek 8.14. **11.38** God of fortresses, probably the Olympian Zeus, the Hellenistic equivalent of Baal Shamem. **11.39** A foreign god. Such a god was unknown to his ancestors. **11.40-45** This passage is not historical; it represents the author's hopes for this climactic moment in history, based perhaps in part on Ezek 38-39. **11.41** Beautiful land. See note on 11.16. But Edom . . . escape. Why the peoples east of the Jordan are spared or even mentioned is not clear, except perhaps to imply their cooperation with Antiochus. **11.45** Between the sea . . . mountain. The idea of Antiochus coming to his end between the Mediterranean and Mount Zion could be influenced by prophetic texts about such a final climactic battle, including

The Resurrection of the Dead

12 "At that time Michael, the great prince, the protector of your people, shall arise. There shall be a time of anguish, such as has never occurred since nations first came into existence. But at that time your people shall be delivered, everyone who is found written in the book. [2]Many of those who sleep in the dust of the earth*a* shall awake, some to everlasting life, and some to shame and everlasting contempt. [3]Those who are wise shall shine like the brightness of the sky,*b* and those who lead many to righteousness, like the stars forever and ever. [4]But you, Daniel, keep the words secret and the book sealed until the time of the end. Many shall be running back and forth, and evil*c* shall increase."

[5] Then I, Daniel, looked, and two others appeared, one standing on this bank of the stream and one on the other. [6]One of them said to the man clothed in linen, who was upstream, "How long shall it be until the end of these wonders?" [7]The man clothed in linen, who was upstream, raised his right hand and his left hand toward heaven. And I heard him swear by the one who lives forever that it would be for a time, two times, and half a time,*d* and that when the shattering of the power of the holy people comes to an end, all these things would be accomplished. [8]I heard but could not understand; so I said, "My lord, what shall be the outcome of these things?" [9]He said, "Go your way, Daniel, for the words are to remain secret and sealed until the time of the end. [10]Many shall be purified, cleansed, and refined, but the wicked shall continue to act wickedly. None of the wicked shall understand, but those who are wise shall understand. [11]From the time that the regular burnt offering is taken away and the abomination that desolates is set up, there shall be one thousand two hundred ninety days. [12]Happy are those who persevere and attain the thousand three hundred thirty-five days. [13]But you, go your way,*e* and rest; you shall rise for your reward at the end of the days."

---

a Or *the land of dust* *b* Or *dome* *c* Cn Compare Gk: Heb *knowledge* *d* Heb *a time, times, and a half* *e* Gk Theodotion: Heb adds *to the end*

Ezek 38.17–23; 39.4–5. Antiochus actually died in Persia during his eastern campaign in 164 BCE. **12.1** *At that time,* after the death of Antiochus. With the reference to *Michael* here and in 10.13–14, 20–21, just as in 7.9–10, 13–14, the scene moves beyond the bounds of earth. *Time of anguish.* See Jer 30.7 and the many references to the anguish associated with the "day of the LORD," e.g., Joel 2–3; Am 5.18–20; Zeph 1.14–18. *Book.* See Ex 32.32–33; Ps 69.28; Isa 4.3. **12.2** *Many,* so not everyone. *Sleep,* death. *In the dust of the earth,* lit. "in the land of dust," probably Sheol rather than the grave. *Shall awake,* rise from the dead. Cf. Isa 26.19. *Some . . . and some . . . ,* contrasting consequences. Implicit is a worldview strongly dividing between "saved" and "damned." **12.3** Probably synonymous parallel structure characteristic of Hebrew poetry: not two groups, but one—the wise who lead many to righteousness. *Like the stars,* like the angelic host. See 8.10, 1 Enoch 104.2–6. **12.4** *Keep . . . book sealed.* See 8.26.

12.5–13 Epilogue attempting to recalculate the date of the end. **12.5–6** *Two others,* beside the one *clothed in linen* (10.5). **12.7** *Swear,* sworn testimony about the time of the end; see 7.25. **12.10** See 11.33. **12.11–12** The contradictory numbers reflect an attempt to recalculate the time of the end when the first calculation failed. Note that even the first of these numbers points to a time after the rededication of the temple by Judas Maccabeus (1 Macc 4.52–58), so the author evidently did not regard that as "the end." **12.13** *Rest . . . rise for your reward.* Daniel's reward at the end is certain; see vv. 2–3. The *end of days* here is expected shortly after the death of Antiochus, after the predicted number of days has elapsed.

HOSEA

THE PROPHECY OF HOSEA revolves around God's unfathomable love for wayward Israel. Nowhere else in scripture do we feel so intensely God's agony over the betrayal of God's people (cf. 3.1; 11.1, 8–9; 14.4). The body of tradition informing Hosea's message is summarized in one declaration of the Lord found in his book: "I have been the LORD your God ever since the land of Egypt; you know no God but me, and besides me there is no savior" (13.4). Hosea's task was to apply that venerable word in an era when its meaning had been virtually lost.

Historical and Social Setting

HOSEA'S CAREER TOOK PLACE in the Northern Kingdom, Israel, which Hosea often calls Ephraim (after the name of its largest tribe), and began during the prosperous and relatively quiet reign of King Jeroboam II (ca. 786–746 BCE). The tranquility of this era was disrupted from 738 on by Assyria's military incursions into the region, and some of Hosea's sayings reflect the war of Israel and Syria against Judah to force the Southern Kingdom into an anti-Assyrian alliance (the Syro-Ephraimite war, 734–732 BCE). Later, Hosea seems to have been active particularly during the time of King Hoshea's fatal rebellion against Assyria that led to the end of the Northern Kingdom in 722. The biblical accounts of Hosea's era are found in 2 Kings 14.23–17.41.

Hosea confronted two doleful developments: a proliferation of sexualized fertility worship and an escalation of reckless political intriguing. The flourishing fertility cult centered on Baal, the storm god in the Canaanite pantheon, believed by many to be the source of rain and agricultural bounty in the land. The tumultuous politics of the era took two main forms. It entailed a series of murderous coups after Jeroboam's reign and an incessant conspiring with various foreign powers by the acting kings to cope with Assyrian pressure.

A key basis for these developments was societal centralization in the Northern Kingdom since ca. 930 BCE, specifically Israel's growth as a hierarchical monarchy (8.4; 10.7; 13.10). New, royally appointed priests perverted worship at Israel's traditional shrines (4.4–10; 5.1; 6.9; 9.8; 10.5). Self-absorption and satiety now issued from a centralized economy that was generating benumbing wealth (10.1; 12.7–8; 13.6). To set things right, Hosea announced that God would return the people to a bygone village-based society where traditional, covenantal lifestyles could flourish (2.14–15; 3.4; 12.9).

Prophet

HOSEA'S LANGUAGE AND THOUGHT fit a bygone era when Israel lacked a monarchy and organized itself based on family ties and kinship (1.11; 12.9, 13). His prophecies reflect confusion and conflict among the Israelite people as their traditional village-based and lineage-based society regrouped and entrenched itself as a centralized state. Alienated from society's new hierarchical arrangement, Hosea confronted apostasy at the royal capital of Samaria and the royal sanctuaries of Bethel and Gilgal as a dissident.

Hosea appears to have operated out of membership in a traditional priestly lineage, the Levites, whose forebears had lost their stations at old Israel's traditional shrines with the rise of the Northern monarchy (10.5; 2 Chr 11.14–15; 13.9). Having experienced disenfranchisement, the Levites subsisted on society's fringe until the great reforms of King Hezekiah and King Josiah in Judah. The psalms of Asaph, associated with the Levites, had an especially marked influence on Hosea's prophecies.

The narratives about Hosea's marriage in chs. 1 and 3—though they are prophetic communications and not biography—allow us an unusual glimpse of an Israelite prophet's personal life. On the Lord's orders Hosea chose a sexually promiscuous wife, Gomer, leading to a tumultuous marriage. His tortured experience presented Israel with a living, symbolic demonstration of God's heartbreak over the people's love affair with foreign deities. As part of this symbolism Hosea gave doomful symbolic names to Gomer's children, such as "Not my people" (1.9). All this surely entailed an emotional trauma for Hosea and his family that is left unspecified and can only be imagined.

Book

IN THE FIRST PART of the book, narrative descriptions of Hosea's marriage (chs. 1 and 3) frame a long divine speech in ch. 2 portraying Israel as both an adulterous wife and a land of whoredom. Prophetic promises of restoration appear in 1.10–11; 2.14–23; 3.5. The second part of Hosea, chs. 4–14, presents a variety of prophetic sayings, including legal indictments, recollections of Israel's past, and heartrending divine monologues. The sayings have been worked up into conflated literary compositions of varying lengths arranged in roughly chronological order. Near the end of ch. 11, a promise of salvation rounds off preceding messages of judgment. Then, additional sayings of judgment in chs. 12–13 lead to the book's finale, another promise of restoration in ch. 14.

Among the NRSV's text notes, twelve call the Hebrew text uncertain and seventeen signal that translators have made conjectural changes. It is obvious that the Hebrew text is unusually difficult. The book's opening verse and some of its internal references (1.7; 3.5; 11.12; 12.2) indicate that it took on new life in Judah after the fall of Israel. Northern refugees settling in Jerusalem, including groups of Levites, must have introduced Hosea's prophecies into the Judean royal court together with other texts such as the psalms of Asaph (2 Chr 29.30).

Prophecy

HOSEA'S PROPHECY IS BASED on covenantal traditions shared with both earlier and later scriptural sources, including the psalms of Asaph, the E strand of the Pentateuch (see Introduction to Genesis), and the book of Micah. These sources understand the Sinai covenant to unite God and Israel in a mutual, binding relationship entailing both grace and obligation (see 4.6; 6.7; 8.1). Having received the Lord's personal fiefdom as its homeland (9.3, 15; cf. Ex 13.5, E), Israel must not credit the bounty of the land to Canaanite deities, such as Baal (2.8, 13; 9.1; 11.2–3; cf. Pss 78.23–27; 81.9–10, 16, psalms of Asaph). The Lord is neither a specialized deity, relegating the realm of nature to the Baals, nor a Baal-like deity, immanent in nature. What is more, having covenanted to be vassals of the Lord, Israel cannot rely on human kings, with their frenetic plotting and alliance building, to preserve its national existence (1.4; 3.4; 7.3–7; 8.4, 10). Israel must regard the Lord alone as its suzerain and savior (10.3; 13.4, 9–11).

Hosea develops the theme of love as an expression of the relationship between God and Israel. He daringly co-opts the love language of his syncretistic milieu, but equates Israel's covenant with a binding and exclusive marital love. A marriage can be devastated by adultery, and Israel's fertility religion and idolatry have meant agonizing sorrow for God. Yet God's heartbreak and the coming demise of Israel's promiscuity are not the end of the story, for Hosea prophesies a new beginning, a renewed covenant, and a new gift of the land in a second history of reconciliation and regeneration. [JAMES LUTHER MAYS, revised by STEPHEN L. COOK]

1 The word of the LORD that came to Hosea son of Beeri, in the days of Kings Uzziah, Jotham, Ahaz, and Hezekiah of Judah, and in the days of King Jeroboam son of Joash of Israel.

The Family of Hosea

2 When the LORD first spoke through Hosea, the LORD said to Hosea, "Go, take for yourself a wife of whoredom and have children of whoredom, for the land commits great whoredom by forsaking the LORD." [3] So he went and took Gomer daughter of Diblaim, and she conceived and bore him a son.

4 And the LORD said to him, "Name him Jezreel;[a] for in a little while I will punish the house of Jehu for the blood of Jezreel, and I will put an end to the kingdom of the house of Israel. [5] On that day I will break the bow of Israel in the valley of Jezreel."

6 She conceived again and bore a daughter. Then the LORD said to him, "Name her Lo-ruhamah,[b] for I will no longer have pity on the house of Israel or forgive them. [7] But I will have pity on the house of Judah, and I will save them by the LORD their God; I will not save them by bow, or by sword, or by war, or by horses, or by horsemen."

8 When she had weaned Lo-ruhamah, she conceived and bore a son. [9] Then the LORD said, "Name him Lo-ammi,[c] for you are not my people and I am not your God."[d]

---

a That is God sows   b That is Not pitied   c That is Not my people   d Heb I am not yours

---

1.1 Word of the LORD . . . came, an editorial formula introducing Hosea's prophetic collection and emphatically declaring its divine origins. For the kings mentioned, see 2 Kings 15–18. **1.2–3.5** Israel as a promiscuous wife and a land of whoredom. **1.2–2.1** As a dramatic symbolic action, God commissions Hosea to marry a wife prone to adultery and to have her children bear ominous names. Her propensity toward whoredom will dramatically act out Israel's involvement with fertility deities and sexual rites (4.13–14; 9.1; cf. Ex 32.6, E). **1.2** The second and third children are of whoredom in a literal sense, since only with respect to the first son is it said that Hosea's wife bore him a child (v. 3; cf. vv. 6, 8). Further, the daughter's name, Lo-ruhamah ("Not pitied," v. 6), is specifically associated with prostitution in 2.4, and the second boy's name, Lo-ammi, can be taken to mean "No kin of mine." **1.4–5** Jezreel, an emblem of bloodshed, as it was the locale of a bloody coup perpetrated by Jehu in 843/2 BCE (2 Kings 9–10). Hosea's prophecy of doom for Jehu's dynasty would have scandalized the reigning king, Jeroboam II, a descendant of Jehu. Later in the book, Jezreel takes on new meaning (see v. 11; 2.22, text note a). **1.5** Break the bow, destroy a state's military power (Jer 49.35; Ezek 39.3). **1.6** The name Lo-ruhamah, also translated "No compassion," publicly signals the withdrawal of the divine mercy emphasized in Ex 33.19 (E); 2 Kings 13.23 (but see note on 2.1). **1.7** Judean editors interject that God's compassion is still available to the Southern Kingdom (cf. the editorial work in Ps 78.67–69, a psalm of Asaph). **1.9** Lo-ammi, "Not my people," negates a formulaic expression of the Sinai covenant (cf. Deut 29.13; Jer 7.23; 11:3–4). I am not your God, read literally in the Hebrew, is a reversal

The Restoration of Israel

10[a] Yet the number of the people of Israel
shall be like the sand of the sea, which can be
neither measured nor numbered; and in the
place where it was said to them, "You are not
my people," it shall be said to them, "Children
of the living God." 11 The people of Judah and
the people of Israel shall be gathered together,
and they shall appoint for themselves one
head; and they shall take possession of[b] the
land, for great shall be the day of Jezreel.

2[c] Say to your brother,[d] Ammi,[e] and to your
sister,[f] Ruhamah.[g]

Israel's Infidelity, Punishment, and Redemption

2   Plead with your mother, plead—
        for she is not my wife,
        and I am not her husband—
    that she put away her whoring from her
            face,
        and her adultery from between her
            breasts,
3   or I will strip her naked
        and expose her as in the day she was
            born,
    and make her like a wilderness,
        and turn her into a parched land,
        and kill her with thirst.
4   Upon her children also I will have no pity,
        because they are children of
            whoredom.
5   For their mother has played the whore;
        she who conceived them has acted
            shamefully.
    For she said, "I will go after my lovers;
        they give me my bread and my water,
        my wool and my flax, my oil and my
            drink."
6   Therefore I will hedge up her[h] way with
            thorns;
        and I will build a wall against her,
        so that she cannot find her paths.
7   She shall pursue her lovers,
        but not overtake them;
    and she shall seek them,
        but shall not find them.
    Then she shall say, "I will go
        and return to my first husband,
        for it was better with me then than
            now."
8   She did not know
        that it was I who gave her
        the grain, the wine, and the oil,
    and who lavished upon her silver
        and gold that they used for Baal.
9   Therefore I will take back
        my grain in its time,
        and my wine in its season;
    and I will take away my wool and my flax,
        which were to cover her nakedness.
10 Now I will uncover her shame
        in the sight of her lovers,

---

a Ch 2.1 in Heb   b Heb rise up from   c Ch 2.3 in Heb
d Gk: Heb brothers   e That is My people   f Gk Vg: Heb sisters
g That is Pitied   h Gk Syr: Heb your

---

of Ex 3.14 (E), God's self-presentation as the great "I
AM." **1.10–2.1** Judah and Israel will be restored as the
dear *children of the living God.* **1.10** *Like the sand of the
sea.* Cf. Gen 22.17; 1 Kings 3.8. Given Hosea's levitical
background, *the place* where he announced the name
Not my people (v. 9) was likely an Israelite shrine.
1.11 Israel and Judah shall be *gathered together* as one
tribal people (cf. Mic 5.3). *Head* (tribal leader) is used
instead of "king," because the restored Israel is to be as
it was before the time of the monarchy. In contrast to
its use in 1.4–5, *Jezreel* here connotes bounty (see note
on 2.22). **2.1** The foreboding meanings of the symbolic names in 1.9 and 1.6 are here revoked by removing the initial Hebrew negative, *Lo-* (see also 2.23).
Ruhamah has strong connotations of maternal compassion, like that of an expectant mother for her unborn child.
   2.2–23 The condemnation for covenant infidelity
in vv. 2–13 slips back and forth between the metaphor
of a husband confronting an adulterous wife and more
straightforward words about the fate of the land of Israel. This literary slippage creates a danger, which

readers must studiously avoid, of seeing a sanction for
domestic violence in this chapter. Although it does describe God inflicting devastation on Israel's land, the
text never describes Hosea physically abusing Gomer.
2.2 Individual Israelites should join God's legal action
against their mother, corporate Israel. The aim is settling the conflict, not a divorce. On cultic jewelry, see
note on 2.13. **2.3** *Strip her,* shocking—not porno-
graphic—language, forcing its original audience to
contemplate a coming humiliation and stripping as
war prisoners (cf. Isa 20.3–4; and Assyria's own depictions of its prisoners). Applied to the arable land, the
reference is to agricultural failure (v. 9). **2.5** *My lovers,*
the fertility deities, thought by Hosea's audience to
control the land's fruitfulness. **2.6–7** Frustration over
access to a beloved is a motif of ancient love poetry (cf.
Song 5.6). A call to *return* (i.e., repent) is key to Hosea's
message (3.5; 5.4; 7.10; 11.5; 12.6; 14.1; cf. 5.15; 10.12).
2.8–13 Hosea's traditions emphasized the Lord's control of the land's fertility (Pss 78.23–27; 81.9–10, 16,
psalms of Asaph; Deut 11.11–12; Jer 5.24; 14.22).
Withholding the produce of the land will demonstrate

and no one shall rescue her out of my
    hand.
11 I will put an end to all her mirth,
    her festivals, her new moons, her
       sabbaths,
    and all her appointed festivals.
12 I will lay waste her vines and her fig trees,
    of which she said,
    "These are my pay,
      which my lovers have given me."
    I will make them a forest,
      and the wild animals shall devour
       them.
13 I will punish her for the festival days of
      the Baals,
    when she offered incense to them
    and decked herself with her ring and
       jewelry,
    and went after her lovers,
    and forgot me, says the Lord.

14 Therefore, I will now allure her,
    and bring her into the wilderness,
    and speak tenderly to her.
15 From there I will give her her vineyards,
    and make the Valley of Achor a door of
      hope.
    There she shall respond as in the days of
      her youth,
    as at the time when she came out of
      the land of Egypt.
16 On that day, says the Lord, you will call me,
"My husband," and no longer will you call me,
"My Baal."[a] 17For I will remove the names of

the Baals from her mouth, and they shall be
mentioned by name no more. 18I will make
for you[b] a covenant on that day with the wild
animals, the birds of the air, and the creeping
things of the ground; and I will abolish[c] the
bow, the sword, and war from the land; and I
will make you lie down in safety. 19And I will
take you for my wife forever; I will take you for
my wife in righteousness and in justice, in
steadfast love, and in mercy. 20I will take you
for my wife in faithfulness; and you shall know
the Lord.
21 On that day I will answer, says the Lord,
    I will answer the heavens
      and they shall answer the earth;
22 and the earth shall answer the grain, the
      wine, and the oil,
      and they shall answer Jezreel;[d]
23 and I will sow him[e] for myself in the
      land.
    And I will have pity on Lo-ruhamah,[f]
      and I will say to Lo-ammi,[g] "You are
       my people";
    and he shall say, "You are my God."

Further Assurances of God's Redeeming Love

3 The Lord said to me again, "Go, love a
woman who has a lover and is an adulteress, just as the Lord loves the people of Israel,
though they turn to other gods and love raisin

---

a That is, *"My master"*   *b* Heb *them*   *c* Heb *break*   *d* That is *God sows*   *e* Cn: Heb *her*   *f* That is *Not pitied*   *g* That is *Not my people*

---

who its real giver is (cf. 1 Kings 17.1). **2.11** *Festivals.* See Ex 23.14–17; 34.22–24. *New moons.* See 2 Kings 4.23; Am 8.5. **2.13** *Baals* (plural), the deity's various manifestations at local shrines (cf. Gen 35.7; Num 25.3). On sacred *jewelry,* cf. 2.2; Gen 35.3–4; and the pendant amulets of the goddess Asherah unearthed at Tell el-'Ajjul. On the idiom *forgot me,* cf. Ps 50.22, a psalm of Asaph. **2.14–23** A plan for Israel's rehabilitation (vv. 14–15) that is then developed in a series of promises (vv. 16–23). **2.14** In the *wilderness,* after the exodus, Israel was truly dependent on the Lord, and the corrupting influences of the monarchy were unknown (cf. 9.10; 12.9; Jer 2.2). **2.15** The Lord will recapitulate the original gift of the divine manor. *The Valley of Achor,* Israel's "Heartbreak Valley" (cf. Josh 7.22–26), now becomes a gateway of *hope,* a route into the heart of the land. **2.16–17** In Hebrew *Baal* is both a divine name and a term for "master" (text note *a*). Israel apparently was using *Baal* as a title for Yahweh, running the risk of confusing the Lord with Canaan's storm deity. My *husband* (Hebrew *'ishi*), God's title of preference here, is a more intimate and personal title

than "Baal." **2.18** The gift of *safety* (cf. Mic 4.4). **2.19–20** The new marriage. The five virtues listed are either qualities imparted to Israel as a betrothal gift (cf. Gen 24.22, 53) or a display of divine affection understood metaphorically as a payment of the bride-price (cf. 1 Sam 18.25). **2.20** *Know the Lord,* be faithful to the covenant (cf. 4.1, 6; 5.4; 6.6; Deut 7.9), which includes both obedience to the law (*torah;* cf. Jer 22.16) and loving intimacy with God (see, e.g., Gen 19.8; 24.16). **2.21–23** The repetition of *answer* connects the Lord with every phase of fertility. **2.22** *Jezreel* means "God sows!" Israel's God, not Baal, sows the crops; and in v. 23 God also sows Israel back into its land (see Ps 80.8–10, 15, a psalm of Asaph; Ex 15.17). **2.23** The names *Lo-ruhamah* (1.6) and *Lo-ammi* (1.9) are revoked, as already in 2.1.

3.1–5 Hosea's marriage is restored. Ch. 3—at least in the book's present canonical form—picks up where 1.9 left off. God's first instructions (1.2) to Hosea are clearly not the end of the story. **3.1** Hosea is to retrieve his lost wife, just as God is determined to retrieve Israel (2.19–20). *Lover* echoes the Hebrew wording of

cakes." ²So I bought her for fifteen shekels of silver and a homer of barley and a measure of wine.ᵃ ³And I said to her, "You must remain as mine for many days; you shall not play the whore, you shall not have intercourse with a man, nor I with you." ⁴For the Israelites shall remain many days without king or prince, without sacrifice or pillar, without ephod or teraphim. ⁵Afterward the Israelites shall return and seek the LORD their God, and David their king; they shall come in awe to the LORD and to his goodness in the latter days.

God Accuses Israel

4 Hear the word of the LORD, O people of Israel;
for the LORD has an indictment against the inhabitants of the land.
There is no faithfulness or loyalty,
and no knowledge of God in the land.
² Swearing, lying, and murder,
and stealing and adultery break out;
bloodshed follows bloodshed.
³ Therefore the land mourns,
and all who live in it languish;
together with the wild animals

and the birds of the air,
even the fish of the sea are perishing.

⁴ Yet let no one contend,
and let none accuse,
for with you is my contention, O priest.ᵇ
⁵ You shall stumble by day;
the prophet also shall stumble with you by night,
and I will destroy your mother.
⁶ My people are destroyed for lack of knowledge;
because you have rejected knowledge,
I reject you from being a priest to me.
And since you have forgotten the law of your God,
I also will forget your children.

⁷ The more they increased,
the more they sinned against me;
they changedᶜ their glory into shame.
⁸ They feed on the sin of my people;
they are greedy for their iniquity.

ᵃ Gk: Heb *a homer of barley and a lethech of barley*
ᵇ Cn: Meaning of Heb uncertain   ᶜ Ancient Heb tradition: MT *I will change*

Lev 20.10. *Raisin cakes,* offerings shaped like a fertility goddess (cf. Jer 7.18; 44.19; and the terra-cotta cake mold unearthed in Cyprus). **3.2** Payment of a price implies that the woman has lost her freedom, perhaps through a vow to a deity, falling into debt slavery, or committing a crime. Hosea paid half in money and half in produce. **3.4** Israel must live without its monarchy and all the other false stand-ins for its covenant Lord. *Prince* means royal officer—Hosea consistently lambastes Israel's current hierarchically based organization (5.1; 8.4; 13.10–11). *Sacrifice* has become a problem according to 4.13, 19; 8.11–13; 10.1–2. *Pillar,* a sacred standing stone (see 10.2; Mic 5.13; Deut 7.5; 2 Kings 17.10; 23.14). *Ephod,* a box for divinatory instruments (Judg 8.27; 17.5); to believe such instruments can compel God's guidance is idolatrous. *Teraphim,* religious images also used in divination (Judg 17.5; 18.14; 2 Kings 23.24; Zech 10.2). Again, the Lord of the covenant resists being tamed by any such instrument. **3.5** Cf. 1.11; 2.7, 15. *Return.* See note on 2.6–7. The mention of *David* is a Judean addition; cf. 1.7.
4.1–14.8 Prophetic sayings of judgment and promise. **4.1–11.11** An unfaithful people, their coming punishment, and their parent's love. **4.1–3** A legal indictment introducing chs. 4–11. **4.1** *Indictment* (Hebrew *riv*), a divine lawsuit against the people for breach of the covenant (cf. Ps 50.7, a psalm of Asaph; Mic 6.1–2); for additional courtroom language, see 2.2 (*plead*); 4.4 (*contention*); 12.2. *Faithfulness* entails firm commitment to the Lord (Josh 24.14; Jer 2.21).

Loyalty (Hebrew *chesed*)—a crucial term in Hosea's theology—is the quality of life required in covenantal relation with God. It also appears translated as (*steadfast) love* (2.19; 6.4, 6; 10.12; 12.6). On *knowledge of God,* another crucial term in Hosea (2.8, 20; 4.6; 5.4; 6.6), see note on 2.20. Knowledge of God issues from covenant instruction (*torah*), the special responsibility of Israel's priests (see note on 4.6). **4.2** Israel is transgressing basic covenantal commandments (cf. Ps 50.18–20, a psalm of Asaph). **4.3** *The land,* a gift of the Lord for the life of the people, suffers from the sins of its inhabitants. **4.4–19** Both priests (vv. 4–11) and those in their care (vv. 12–19) are guilty of cultic heresy. **4.4** The entire royally sanctioned priesthood is addressed in the following verses (cf. 5.1; Jer 2.26; 4.9; 23.11); the singular *priest* may refer to a chief priest (cf. Amaziah in Am 7.10–17). **4.5–6** Levites such as Hosea valued a priesthood's genealogical continuity. *Destroy your mother* (or "destroy your kindred") and *forget your children* refer to disruption of the priests' lineage. **4.6** The prophet also upholds the duty of levitical priests to transmit and authoritatively apply the law (*torah*) given at Mount Sinai (Deut 17.9–12, 18; 31.9; 33.10; 2 Kings 17.27–28; Jer 2.8; 18.18; Mal 2.6–7). In Hosea's traditions, the Sinai covenant entailed specific, binding regulations on Israel (*torah*). **4.7** *Changed their glory.* Cf. Ps 106.19–21; Jer 2.11. **4.8** Priests *feed on the sin* of the people as they delight in profiting from the many sin offerings brought to their shrines (cf. 1 Sam 2.12–17). Contrary to some scholarly opinion, sacrifices in Hosea's period aimed to atone for *sin*

9 And it shall be like people, like priest;
  I will punish them for their ways,
  and repay them for their deeds.
10 They shall eat, but not be satisfied;
   they shall play the whore, but not
     multiply;
   because they have forsaken the LORD
     to devote themselves to [11]whoredom.

The Idolatry of Israel

Wine and new wine
  take away the understanding.
12 My people consult a piece of wood,
   and their divining rod gives them
     oracles.
   For a spirit of whoredom has led them
     astray,
   and they have played the whore,
     forsaking their God.
13 They sacrifice on the tops of the
     mountains,
   and make offerings upon the hills,
   under oak, poplar, and terebinth,
     because their shade is good.

   Therefore your daughters play the whore,
     and your daughters-in-law commit
       adultery.
14 I will not punish your daughters when
     they play the whore,
   nor your daughters-in-law when they
     commit adultery;
   for the men themselves go aside with
     whores,
   and sacrifice with temple prostitutes;
   thus a people without understanding
     comes to ruin.

15 Though you play the whore, O Israel,
   do not let Judah become guilty.

Do not enter into Gilgal,
  or go up to Beth-aven,
  and do not swear, "As the LORD lives."
16 Like a stubborn heifer,
   Israel is stubborn;
   can the LORD now feed them
   like a lamb in a broad pasture?

17 Ephraim is joined to idols—
   let him alone.
18 When their drinking is ended, they
     indulge in sexual orgies;
   they love lewdness more than their
     glory.[a]
19 A wind has wrapped them[b] in its
     wings,
   and they shall be ashamed because of
     their altars.[c]

Impending Judgment on Israel and Judah

5 Hear this, O priests!
  Give heed, O house of Israel!
  Listen, O house of the king!
  For the judgment pertains to you;
  for you have been a snare at Mizpah,
    and a net spread upon Tabor,
2 and a pit dug deep in Shittim;[d]
  but I will punish all of them.

3 I know Ephraim,
  and Israel is not hidden from me;
  for now, O Ephraim, you have played the
    whore;
  Israel is defiled.
4 Their deeds do not permit them
  to return to their God.

---

a Cn Compare Gk: Meaning of Heb uncertain   b Heb her
c Gk Syr: Heb sacrifices   d Cn: Meaning of Heb uncertain

---

and *iniquity* (see also 8.11; Mic 6.7). **4.10–11a** "Futility curses," a known component of West Semitic treaties, also figure significantly in the Sinai covenant (cf. 8.7; 9.12, 16; Mic 6.14). *Play the whore,* worship Baal and other fertility deities (1.2; 2.5; Deut 31.16; Ps 78.57–58, a psalm of Asaph). **4.12** *Piece of wood,* possibly a religious symbol of the goddess Asherah (see Ex 34.13; Deut 16.21; Mic 5.14). *Spirit of whoredom,* an inner disposition toward fertility religion (cf. 5.4). **4.13** Israel's popular cultic sites included hilltop precincts, sometimes with sacred standing stones and groves of sacred trees (Deut 12.2; 2 Kings 17.10; Jer 3.6, 13; Ezek 6.13; 20.28). *Daughters* of Israelites seem to have been involved informally in promiscuous sex and debauchery, which were thought to "jump-start"

agricultural fecundity (cf. Ex 32.6; Num 25.1–5; 31.13–20). **4.14** *Temple prostitutes.* Hebrew *qedeshah* means either a simple harlot (as in Gen 38.15, 21) or perhaps a woman who had vowed to donate her fee for prostitution to a shrine (see Prov 7.14). **4.15** *Beth-aven,* Hebrew, "house of wrong," a pejorative name for Bethel (cf. Am 5.5). *Gilgal* (cf. Josh 4.19–20; Am 5.5) and Bethel (12.4; Gen 35.1–4) were cities with once holy shrines that became places of apostasy with the rise of the monarchical state. **4.16** *Stubborn heifer.* See 10.11; Jer 31.18; cf. Ps 78.8, a psalm of Asaph. **4.17** *Ephraim,* name for the Northern Kingdom, Israel. **5.1–7** New leaders have misled the Israelites into the trap of Baal worship. **5.1–2** *Mizpah, Tabor,* and *Shittim,* towns with shrines of the Baal cult. **5.4** *Spirit*

For the spirit of whoredom is within them,
  and they do not know the LORD.

5 Israel's pride testifies against him;
  Ephraim[a] stumbles in his guilt;
  Judah also stumbles with them.
6 With their flocks and herds they shall go
    to seek the LORD,
  but they will not find him;
  he has withdrawn from them.
7 They have dealt faithlessly with the LORD;
    for they have borne illegitimate children.
  Now the new moon shall devour them
    along with their fields.

8 Blow the horn in Gibeah,
    the trumpet in Ramah.
  Sound the alarm at Beth-aven;
    look behind you, Benjamin!
9 Ephraim shall become a desolation
    in the day of punishment;
  among the tribes of Israel
    I declare what is sure.
10 The princes of Judah have become
    like those who remove the landmark;
  on them I will pour out
    my wrath like water.
11 Ephraim is oppressed, crushed in
      judgment,
  because he was determined to go after
      vanity.[b]
12 Therefore I am like maggots to Ephraim,
    and like rottenness to the house of
      Judah.
13 When Ephraim saw his sickness,
    and Judah his wound,

then Ephraim went to Assyria,
  and sent to the great king.[c]
But he is not able to cure you
  or heal your wound.
14 For I will be like a lion to Ephraim,
    and like a young lion to the house of
      Judah.
  I myself will tear and go away;
    I will carry off, and no one shall
      rescue.
15 I will return again to my place
    until they acknowledge their guilt and
      seek my face.
  In their distress they will beg my favor:

A Call to Repentance

6 "Come, let us return to the LORD;
    for it is he who has torn, and he will
      heal us;
  he has struck down, and he will bind
      us up.
2 After two days he will revive us;
    on the third day he will raise us up,
    that we may live before him.
3 Let us know, let us press on to know the
      LORD;
    his appearing is as sure as the dawn;
  he will come to us like the showers,
    like the spring rains that water the
      earth."

Impenitence of Israel and Judah

4 What shall I do with you, O Ephraim?
    What shall I do with you, O Judah?

---

a Heb Israel and Ephraim   b Gk: Meaning of Heb uncertain
c Cn: Heb to a king who will contend

---

of whoredom. See note on 4.12. Do not know. See note on 2.20. **5.5–6** For the people to seek the LORD at shrines with sacrifices from their flocks is useless, since they do not acknowledge their guilt and turn to God wholeheartedly (v. 15). **5.7** The Hebrew may mean that the Lord, not the moon, is the devourer (as in 13.8)—either a devourer of Israel's new moon festival itself (as at 2.11) or one wielding destruction at the time of the festival. **5.8–6.6** The historical setting for this unit is the Syro-Ephraimite war (2 Kings 15.37; 16.5–9; Isa 7.1–9). **5.8–10** These verses presuppose a counterattack by Judah during the Syro-Ephraimite war. **5.8** Gibeah, Ramah, and Beth-aven (Bethel; see note on 4.15), towns in Benjamin's tribal territory along the path of invasion of the Judean army. **5.10** Judah's invasion of Ephraim is compared to altering boundaries between farm plots, a crime forbidden in the Sinai covenant (Deut 19.14; 27.17; Prov 22.28; Mic 2.2). Princes. See note on 3.4. **5.11** Go

after vanity, Ephraim's alliance with Syria. **5.13** After the Syro-Ephraimite initiative failed and Assyria invaded the land in 733 BCE, Israel surrendered territory and paid tribute to Assyria (cf. 2 Kings 15.19–20; 17.3). Assyria is not able to cure the people, because only the Lord is their suzerain and savior (10.3; 13.4, 9–11; 14.3). **5.14** Hosea takes this metaphorical language from the psalms of Asaph (Ps 50.22). **5.15** Mention of the Lord's place initially conjures the image of a lion's den (cf. v. 14; Jer 4.7), but the reference is to God's heavenly temple (cf. Mic 1.3). Until stresses the possibility of repentance (see note on 2.6–7). Seek my face, revive the traditional rites of the Lord (cf. Pss 24.6; 27.8; 105.4). **6.1–3** Hosea presents a parody of the people's current insufficient gestures at penitence. The song uses some right words but mixes in language from the fertility cult (e.g., v. 3b). **6.2** Revive us and raise us up reflect the mythology of the fertility cult, in which Baal's rising from death restored both people

Your love is like a morning cloud,
  like the dew that goes away early.
5 Therefore I have hewn them by the
      prophets,
  I have killed them by the words of my
      mouth,
  and my[a] judgment goes forth as the
      light.
6 For I desire steadfast love and not
      sacrifice,
  the knowledge of God rather than
      burnt offerings.

7 But at[b] Adam they transgressed the
      covenant;
  there they dealt faithlessly with me.
8 Gilead is a city of evildoers,
  tracked with blood.
9 As robbers lie in wait[c] for someone,
  so the priests are banded together;[d]
  they murder on the road to Shechem,
  they commit a monstrous crime.
10 In the house of Israel I have seen a
      horrible thing;
  Ephraim's whoredom is there, Israel is
      defiled.

11 For you also, O Judah, a harvest is
      appointed.

  When I would restore the fortunes of my
      people,

7 1 when I would heal Israel,
  the corruption of Ephraim is revealed,
  and the wicked deeds of Samaria;

for they deal falsely,
  the thief breaks in,
  and the bandits raid outside.
2 But they do not consider
  that I remember all their wickedness.
  Now their deeds surround them,
  they are before my face.
3 By their wickedness they make the king
      glad,
  and the officials by their treachery.
4 They are all adulterers;
  they are like a heated oven,
  whose baker does not need to stir the fire,
  from the kneading of the dough until
      it is leavened.
5 On the day of our king the officials
  became sick with the heat of wine;
  he stretched out his hand with
      mockers.
6 For they are kindled[e] like an oven, their
      heart burns within them;
  all night their anger smolders;
  in the morning it blazes like a flaming
      fire.
7 All of them are hot as an oven,
  and they devour their rulers.
  All their kings have fallen;
  none of them calls upon me.

8 Ephraim mixes himself with the peoples;
  Ephraim is a cake not turned.
9 Foreigners devour his strength,

---

a Gk Syr: Heb *your*   b Cn: Heb *like*   c Cn: Meaning of Heb
uncertain   d Syr: Heb *are a company*   e Gk Syr: Heb *brought
near*

---

and nature to new life. **6.4–6** The Lord's soliloquy,
though reflecting inner heartbreak, rejects Israel's attempt at rapprochement (cf. 5.6; Jer 14.7–12). The
people's penitence does not pass the tests of authenticity and constancy (v. 4b); neither Israel nor Judah
maintains a devoted *love* (Hebrew *chesed*, v. 6) for
God. **6.4** *O Ephraim . . . O Judah* reflects Hosea's understanding of the unity of the covenant people (cf.
5.12–14; Mic 1.5); traditional priests such as Hosea
advocate intertribal solidarity. **6.5** Hosea had predecessors, also mediators of the covenant, who announced God's punishment. **6.6** On *steadfast love*
(Hebrew *chesed*) and *knowledge of God*, see note on
4.1. God's statement is not aimed against sacrifices
but stresses the relative importance of integrity of life
under the covenant over mere rituals and shows of
piety (cf. Mic 6.6–8; 1 Sam 15.22; Jer 7.22–23).
  6.7–7.16 Covenant loyalty to the Lord is lacking in
Israel. **6.7–7.2** A catalog of treachery. **6.7** On the Sinai
covenant, see notes on 1.9; 4.1; 4.6; 4.10–11a; 8.1. *Adam*,

See Josh 3.16. **6.8** On the incident at *Gilead*, see 2 Kings
15.24–25. **6.9** *Shechem*, location of an ancient sanctuary
of Israel's covenant God (Gen 33.18–20, E; Josh 24);
priests of the new regime (1 Kings 12.31; 13.33–34)
now harass pilgrims who visit it. **7.1** *Samaria*, capital of
the Northern Kingdom (*Ephraim*). **7.3–7** The passions
behind political intriguing in Israel are as constant as
an oven fire, banked (v. 6) as the dough is prepared
for baking (v. 4). **7.3** *King*, possibly Hoshea, who
gained the throne through *treachery* (2 Kings 15.30).
7.4 *Adulterers*, politically treasonous evildoers. **7.5** *The
day of our king*, the time of the coronation festival.
7.7 Israel saw four royal murders within just twelve
years (ca. 745–732 BCE); see 2 Kings 15.8–10, 13–14,
23–25, 30. **7.8–12** Israel allies itself with other nations,
violating its covenantal oath of sole allegiance to the
Lord. **7.8** The metaphor of a *cake* made up of foreign
ingredients and half baked. **7.9** *Foreigners*, Egypt and
Assyria (see v. 11), between whom Israel alternates in
seeking a protecting ally (2 Kings 15.19–20; 17.3–4).

but he does not know it;
gray hairs are sprinkled upon him,
but he does not know it.

10 Israel's pride testifies against[a] him;
yet they do not return to the LORD
their God,
or seek him, for all this.

Futile Reliance on the Nations

11 Ephraim has become like a dove,
silly and without sense;
they call upon Egypt, they go to
Assyria.
12 As they go, I will cast my net over them;
I will bring them down like birds of the
air;
I will discipline them according to the
report made to their assembly.[b]
13 Woe to them, for they have strayed from
me!
Destruction to them, for they have
rebelled against me!
I would redeem them,
but they speak lies against me.

14 They do not cry to me from the heart,
but they wail upon their beds;
they gash themselves for grain and wine;
they rebel against me.
15 It was I who trained and strengthened
their arms,
yet they plot evil against me.
16 They turn to that which does not profit;[c]
they have become like a defective bow;
their officials shall fall by the sword

because of the rage of their tongue.
So much for their babbling in the land of
Egypt.

Israel's Apostasy

8 Set the trumpet to your lips!
One like a vulture[b] is over the house of
the LORD,
because they have broken my covenant,
and transgressed my law.
2 Israel cries to me,
"My God, we—Israel—know you!"
3 Israel has spurned the good;
the enemy shall pursue him.

4 They made kings, but not through me;
they set up princes, but without my
knowledge.
With their silver and gold they made idols
for their own destruction.
5 Your calf is rejected, O Samaria.
My anger burns against them.
How long will they be incapable of
innocence?
6 For it is from Israel,
an artisan made it;
it is not God.
The calf of Samaria
shall be broken to pieces.[d]

7 For they sow the wind,
and they shall reap the whirlwind.

---

a Or *humbles*   *b* Meaning of Heb uncertain   *c* Cn: Meaning
of Heb uncertain   *d* Or *shall go up in flames*

7.10 Cf. 5.5. *Return.* See note on 2.6–7. **7.11** *Silly* dove, allowing itself to be easily snared. **7.13** The Lord is frustrated in his desire to *redeem,* i.e., rescue or reclaim, the people (also 13.14; cf. Ps 78.42, a psalm of Asaph; Mic 6.4; Deut 7.8). **7.14** Wailing and self-mutilation (cf. Deut 14.1; 1 Kings 18.28) treat the Lord like a Canaanite god. **7.16** Turning to useless allies treats the Lord as a god who cannot save. The metaphor of a *defective bow* is also found in the psalms of Asaph (Ps 78.57).
8.1–14 Israel has broken the *covenant* (vv. 1–3): through the monarchy's policies (vv. 4–7), through its foreign relations (vv. 8–10), and through its hypocritical rites (vv. 11–13). **8.1** *Vulture,* Assyria. *House of the Lord,* the whole land of Israel (cf. 9.15). *Broken my covenant,* a distinctive idiom (cf. Deut 17.2; Josh 23.16; Judg 2.20; 2 Kings 18.12). The word pair *covenant* and *law* (i.e., covenantal stipulations) is paralleled in the psalms of Asaph (Ps 78.10). On Hosea's stress on these concepts, see notes on 4.6; 6.7. **8.3** *The good,* the cov-

enant's "good" legal standards (cf. Mic 6.8; 1 Sam 12.23). **8.4** On *kings* and *princes* (representatives of Israel's new centralized polity), see note on 3.4. Hosea held that God must be involved in appointing Israel's leaders (see Deut 17.15, "God will choose"). **8.5–6** Hosea observes that Israel's monarchy is bound up with idolatry (cf. 1 Sam 8.7–8). *Calf of Samaria,* the golden bull that Jeroboam I placed in Bethel (10.5; 1 Kings 12.26–33). Samaria, the monarchical capital, is the sponsor of the image (cf. Am 7.13). **8.6** Hosea does not agree that the bull image was a mere divine pedestal. His declaration, *it is not God,* counters actual worship of the bull (as shown in 1 Kings 12.28; cf. Ex 32.4, 8, E). In 13.2, Hosea calls the image an *idol* (cf. 10.6). Among similar finds, a bull-calf statuette, dating to ca. 1600 BCE and probably representing Baal, has been recovered from a small temple at Ashkelon. Cross-culturally, the bull is a symbol of virility, the roaring thundercloud, and fertility. **8.7** A covenantal "futility curse" as in 4.10 (cf. Mic 6.15; Deut 28.38).

The standing grain has no heads,
it shall yield no meal;
if it were to yield,
foreigners would devour it.
8 Israel is swallowed up;
now they are among the nations
as a useless vessel.
9 For they have gone up to Assyria,
a wild ass wandering alone;
Ephraim has bargained for lovers.
10 Though they bargain with the nations,
I will now gather them up.
They shall soon writhe
under the burden of kings and
princes.

11 When Ephraim multiplied altars to
expiate sin,
they became to him altars for sinning.
12 Though I write for him the multitude of
my instructions,
they are regarded as a strange thing.
13 Though they offer choice sacrifices,[a]
though they eat flesh,
the Lord does not accept them.
Now he will remember their iniquity,
and punish their sins;
they shall return to Egypt.
14 Israel has forgotten his Maker,
and built palaces;
and Judah has multiplied fortified cities;
but I will send a fire upon his cities,
and it shall devour his strongholds.

Punishment for Israel's Sin

9 Do not rejoice, O Israel!
Do not exult[b] as other nations do;
for you have played the whore, departing
from your God.
You have loved a prostitute's pay
on all threshing floors.

2 Threshing floor and wine vat shall not
feed them,
and the new wine shall fail them.
3 They shall not remain in the land of the
Lord;
but Ephraim shall return to Egypt,
and in Assyria they shall eat unclean
food.

4 They shall not pour drink offerings of
wine to the Lord,
and their sacrifices shall not please
him.
Such sacrifices shall be like mourners'
bread;
all who eat of it shall be defiled;
for their bread shall be for their hunger
only;
it shall not come to the house of the
Lord.

5 What will you do on the day of appointed
festival,
and on the day of the festival of the
Lord?
6 For even if they escape destruction,
Egypt shall gather them,
Memphis shall bury them.
Nettles shall possess their precious things
of silver;[c]
thorns shall be in their tents.

7 The days of punishment have come,
the days of recompense have come;
Israel cries,[d]
"The prophet is a fool,
the man of the spirit is mad!"
Because of your great iniquity,

---

a Cn: Meaning of Heb uncertain   b Gk: Heb To exultation
c Meaning of Heb uncertain   d Cn Compare Gk: Heb shall know

Sow the wind. Cf. 12.1. 8.9 Wild ass, figurative of will-fulness and lust (cf. Jer 2.24). Bargained for lovers, made frantic deals with Syria, Egypt, and Assyria (e.g., 2 Kings 15.19; 17.3). 8.12 Multitude of my instructions, requirements of the covenant (cf. 4.6; 8.1). 8.13 Remember their iniquity. Cf. Ps 79.8, a psalm of Asaph. A return to Egypt (cf. 9.3, 6; 11.5, 11) would reverse the Lord's historical way with Israel (cf. Ex 13.17, E; Deut 17.16).

9.1–9 Hosea condemns a harvest festival (vv. 1–6) and finds himself denounced (vv. 7–9). 9.1 Festival pilgrims (see v. 5) encamp and celebrate near threshing floors, venues exuding fertility and sexuality (cf. Ruth

3.14). The harvest is prostitute's pay (cf. 2.12; Mic 1.7; Deut 23.18), because Israel takes it as the gift of Baal in return for her service. 9.3 Hosea's expression land of the Lord makes plain that Yahweh alone is the owner of the land and the one who determines the people's tenancy (cf. 8.1; 9.15; Ps 78.54, a psalm of Asaph; Ex 32.13, E). 9.4 In exile, there is no produce of God's land for sacrifices. Mourners' bread. See Deut 26.14. 9.5 A sarcastic, rhetorical question. Festival of the Lord, the Feast of Tabernacles (Sukkoth). 9.6 Memphis, an Egyptian city with mortuary associations. Nettles and thorns. Cf. Mic 3.12. Tents, pilgrims' camps. 9.7 Hosea reports the taunt of his opposition

your hostility is great.
8 The prophet is a sentinel for my God over
    Ephraim,
yet a fowler's snare is on all his ways,
    and hostility in the house of his God.
9 They have deeply corrupted themselves
    as in the days of Gibeah;
he will remember their iniquity,
    he will punish their sins.

10 Like grapes in the wilderness,
    I found Israel.
Like the first fruit on the fig tree,
    in its first season,
    I saw your ancestors.
But they came to Baal-peor,
    and consecrated themselves to a thing
      of shame,
    and became detestable like the thing
      they loved.
11 Ephraim's glory shall fly away like a
      bird—
    no birth, no pregnancy, no conception!
12 Even if they bring up children,
    I will bereave them until no one is left.
Woe to them indeed
    when I depart from them!
13 Once I saw Ephraim as a young palm
      planted in a lovely meadow,[a]
but now Ephraim must lead out his
      children for slaughter.
14 Give them, O LORD—
    what will you give?
Give them a miscarrying womb
    and dry breasts.

15 Every evil of theirs began at Gilgal;
    there I came to hate them.
Because of the wickedness of their deeds
    I will drive them out of my house.

I will love them no more;
    all their officials are rebels.

16 Ephraim is stricken,
    their root is dried up,
    they shall bear no fruit.
Even though they give birth,
    I will kill the cherished offspring of
      their womb.

17 Because they have not listened to him,
    my God will reject them;
they shall become wanderers among
    the nations.

Israel's Sin and Captivity

10 Israel is a luxuriant vine
    that yields its fruit.
The more his fruit increased
    the more altars he built;
as his country improved,
    he improved his pillars.
2 Their heart is false;
    now they must bear their guilt.
The LORD[b] will break down their altars,
    and destroy their pillars.

3 For now they will say:
    "We have no king,
for we do not fear the LORD,
    and a king—what could he do for us?"
4 They utter mere words;
    with empty oaths they make
      covenants;
so litigation springs up like poisonous
      weeds
    in the furrows of the field.
5 The inhabitants of Samaria tremble
    for the calf[c] of Beth-aven.

---

a Meaning of Heb uncertain   b Heb he   c Gk Syr: Heb calves

(cf. Jer 20.7–8; 29.26; 2 Kings 2.23; 9.11). **9.8** *Sentinel.* Cf. Jer 6.17; Ezek 3.17. *The house of his God,* either the whole land (cf. 8.1) or a formerly holy shrine (cf. 9.4) where Levites like Hosea are no longer welcome (see 1 Kings 12.31). **9.9** *The days of Gibeah* (cf. 10.9) probably refers to the ancient atrocity perpetrated against a Levite's concubine and recorded in Judg 19–21. *Remember their iniquity.* Cf. 8.13; Ps 79.8. **9.10–17** The guilt of Baal-peor and Gilgal still marks the present. **9.10** At *Baal-peor,* the last station of its wilderness journey, Israel embraced Baal (Num 25.1–5). *Thing of shame* (Hebrew *boshet*), a derogatory name for Baal (cf. Jer 11.13). **9.15** Kingship for Israel was inaugurated at *Gilgal* (1 Sam 11.14–15); Israel's kings were

responsible for religious apostasy and political instability. *Out of my house,* out of God's manor land (cf. 8.1), where tenancy is conditional based on covenant faithfulness (cf. 9.3, 17; Mic 4.10).

10.1–8 God will sweep away cultic sites (vv. 1–2, 8), golden calf (vv. 5–6), and king (vv. 3–4, 7). **10.1–2** Hosea's theology links satiety with apostasy (cf. 4.7; 13.6; Deut 6.10–15; 8.12–14). On God's removal of *altars* and *pillars,* see note on 3.4. **10.3** In Hosea's tradition, kingship is an abortive mistake (cf. 13.11; Judg 8.23; 1 Sam 8.7–8). **10.5** *Beth-aven.* See note on 4.15. On Samaria's sponsorship of the *calf* image there, see note on 8.5–6. The monarchy has replaced Bethel's Levites with *idolatrous priests* (Hebrew *kemarim*).

Its people shall mourn for it,
and its idolatrous priests shall wail[a]
over it,
over its glory that has departed from it.
6 The thing itself shall be carried to Assyria
as tribute to the great king.[b]
Ephraim shall be put to shame,
and Israel shall be ashamed of his idol.[c]

7 Samaria's king shall perish
like a chip on the face of the waters.
8 The high places of Aven, the sin of Israel,
shall be destroyed.
Thorn and thistle shall grow up
on their altars.
They shall say to the mountains, Cover us,
and to the hills, Fall on us.

9 Since the days of Gibeah you have sinned,
O Israel;
there they have continued.
Shall not war overtake them in Gibeah?
10 I will come[d] against the wayward people
to punish them;
and nations shall be gathered against
them
when they are punished[e] for their
double iniquity.

11 Ephraim was a trained heifer
that loved to thresh,
and I spared her fair neck;
but I will make Ephraim break the
ground;
Judah must plow;
Jacob must harrow for himself.
12 Sow for yourselves righteousness;
reap steadfast love;
break up your fallow ground;
for it is time to seek the LORD,
that he may come and rain
righteousness upon you.

13 You have plowed wickedness,
you have reaped injustice,
you have eaten the fruit of lies.
Because you have trusted in your power
and in the multitude of your
warriors,
14 therefore the tumult of war shall rise
against your people,
and all your fortresses shall be
destroyed,
as Shalman destroyed Beth-arbel on the
day of battle
when mothers were dashed in pieces
with their children.
15 Thus it shall be done to you, O Bethel,
because of your great wickedness.
At dawn the king of Israel
shall be utterly cut off.

God's Compassion Despite Israel's Ingratitude

11 When Israel was a child, I loved him,
and out of Egypt I called my son.
2 The more I[f] called them,
the more they went from me;[g]
they kept sacrificing to the Baals,
and offering incense to idols.

3 Yet it was I who taught Ephraim to
walk,
I took them up in my[h] arms;
but they did not know that I healed
them.
4 I led them with cords of human kindness,
with bands of love.
I was to them like those
who lift infants to their cheeks.[i]
I bent down to them and fed them.

a Cn: Heb exult   b Cn: Heb to a king who will contend
c Cn: Heb counsel   d Cn Compare Gk: Heb In my desire
e Gk: Heb bound   f Gk: Heb they   g Gk: Heb them
h Gk Syr Vg: Heb his   i Or who ease the yoke on their jaws

10.8 *High places*, sacral installations for ritual sacrifices (cf. Ps 78.58, a psalm of Asaph; 2 Kings 17.9; 23.8); the Mesha Stele mentions one in Moab's capital. **10.9–15** Israel has plowed wickedness. **10.9** *Days of Gibeah*. See note on 9.9. **10.10** Gibeah is associated with a *double iniquity*, because, just as its gruesome crime in the village era resulted in large-scale fratricide (Judg 19–21), so also in Hosea's era fratricide raged in the Syro-Ephraimite war near the same locale (see note on 5.8–6.6). **10.11–13a** The metaphor of a heifer (4.16) set to plowing: *sow, reap,* and *break up.* Israel must "cultivate" *righteousness* and *steadfast love* (see note on 4.1) to receive *righteousness* as a blessing. **10.14** *Shalman*, perhaps Shalmaneser V, king of Assyria. His destruction of *Beth-arbel* is as yet unattested, but 2 Kings 17.3 may provide the general context. **11.1–11** Divine compassion overcomes divine anger at betrayal. **11.1** For Israel as God's *child*, see Ex 4.22–23; Deut 1.31; 8.5; 32.6; Jer 2.14; 31.9. *Called* signifies God's election of Israel as a vassal people. **11.2** *I called them*, as, e.g., in Ps 81.8–10, a psalm of Asaph. *Baals.* See note on 2.13. *Idols,* sculpted divine images; see Ps 78.58, a psalm of Asaph; Mic 1.7; 5.13. **11.3–4** The Lord's way is like the tender care of a new parent

5 They shall return to the land of Egypt,
   and Assyria shall be their king,
   because they have refused to return to
      me.
6 The sword rages in their cities,
   it consumes their oracle-priests,
   and devours because of their schemes.
7 My people are bent on turning away from
      me.
   To the Most High they call,
   but he does not raise them up at all. *a*

8 How can I give you up, Ephraim?
   How can I hand you over, O Israel?
   How can I make you like Admah?
   How can I treat you like Zeboiim?
   My heart recoils within me;
   my compassion grows warm and
      tender.
9 I will not execute my fierce anger;
   I will not again destroy Ephraim;
   for I am God and no mortal,
   the Holy One in your midst,
   and I will not come in wrath. *a*

10 They shall go after the LORD,
   who roars like a lion;
   when he roars,
   his children shall come trembling from
      the west.
11 They shall come trembling like birds
      from Egypt,
   and like doves from the land of
      Assyria;
   and I will return them to their homes,
   says the LORD.

12 *b* Ephraim has surrounded me with lies,
   and the house of Israel with deceit;

but Judah still walks *c* with God,
   and is faithful to the Holy One.

12 Ephraim herds the wind,
   and pursues the east wind all day long;
they multiply falsehood and violence;
   they make a treaty with Assyria,
   and oil is carried to Egypt.

The Long History of Rebellion

2 The LORD has an indictment against Judah,
   and will punish Jacob according to his
      ways,
   and repay him according to his deeds.
3 In the womb he tried to supplant his
      brother,
   and in his manhood he strove with
      God.
4 He strove with the angel and prevailed,
   he wept and sought his favor;
   he met him at Bethel,
   and there he spoke with him. *d*
5 The LORD the God of hosts,
   the LORD is his name!
6 But as for you, return to your God,
   hold fast to love and justice,
   and wait continually for your God.

7 A trader, in whose hands are false
      balances,
   he loves to oppress.
8 Ephraim has said, "Ah, I am rich,
   I have gained wealth for myself;
   in all of my gain
   no offense has been found in me
   that would be sin." *a*
9 I am the LORD your God

---

a Meaning of Heb uncertain   *b* Ch 12.1 in Heb   *c* Heb *roams* or *rules*   *d* Gk Syr: Heb *us*

(cf. 7.15). **11.5** On the threatened *return to . . . Egypt,* cf. 8.13; 9.3, 6; 11.11. *Return to me.* See note on 2.6–7. **11.8** God begins an intense self-questioning. *Admah* and *Zeboiim* were totally destroyed (Deut 29.23). God's burning tenderness parallels that of the mother in 1 Kings 3.26. **11.9** *Again destroy,* or "turn to destroy" (Hebrew). *No mortal.* The traditions behind Hosea stress God's mysterious otherness and freedom; see Ps 50.21, a psalm of Asaph; Ex 3.14, E; Num 23.19, E; Mic 7.18; Deut 4.15–24. **11.10–11** Catastrophe does finally strike Israel in 722 BCE, but, unlike Admah and Zeboiim, God's people can look forward to a future, resettled in God's land. **11.11** The returnees from exile flutter home to their dovecote (cf. Isa 60.8). **11.12–14.8** Death and new life for Israel. **11.12–12.14** God's indictments of the descendants of Jacob. **12.1** *Herds the wind,* is obsessed with the ephemeral (cf. 8.7; Ps 78.39), referring here to political intrigue (cf. 2 Kings 15.19–20;17.3–4). **12.2–6** Jacob's return to the Lord, especially his abandonment of foreign gods at Bethel (Gen 35.1–8, E), should be an example for his descendants. **12.4** On how Jacob *strove with the angel,* see Gen 32.24–32, E. Tradition held that Jacob founded the *Bethel* shrine (Gen 35.1–8, E), a formerly holy site where God used to instruct Israel (see text note *d*). **12.6** In old Israel instruction at Bethel had emphasized core covenantal values such as *love* and *justice* (Hebrew *chesed* and *mishpat;* cf. 2.19; Mic 6.8; Jer 9.24). **12.7** *Trader* can be translated "Canaanite"; the term is a double taunt. **12.9** *I am the LORD . . . Egypt,* the opening of a covenant instruction (see note on 13.4) like those cultivated of old by Levites like Hosea at periodic festal assemblies of the tribes

from the land of Egypt;
I will make you live in tents again,
as in the days of the appointed
festival.

10 I spoke to the prophets;
it was I who multiplied visions,
and through the prophets I will bring
destruction.
11 In Gilead[a] there is iniquity,
they shall surely come to nothing.
In Gilgal they sacrifice bulls,
so their altars shall be like stone heaps
on the furrows of the field.
12 Jacob fled to the land of Aram,
there Israel served for a wife,
and for a wife he guarded sheep.[b]
13 By a prophet the LORD brought Israel up
from Egypt,
and by a prophet he was guarded.
14 Ephraim has given bitter offense,
so his Lord will bring his crimes down
on him
and pay him back for his insults.

Relentless Judgment on Israel

13 When Ephraim spoke, there was
trembling;
he was exalted in Israel;
but he incurred guilt through Baal and
died.
2 And now they keep on sinning
and make a cast image for themselves,
idols of silver made according to their
understanding,
all of them the work of artisans.
"Sacrifice to these," they say.[c]
People are kissing calves!
3 Therefore they shall be like the morning
mist

or like the dew that goes away early,
like chaff that swirls from the threshing
floor
or like smoke from a window.

4 Yet I have been the LORD your God
ever since the land of Egypt;
you know no God but me,
and besides me there is no savior.
5 It was I who fed[d] you in the wilderness,
in the land of drought.
6 When I fed[e] them, they were satisfied;
they were satisfied, and their heart was
proud;
therefore they forgot me.
7 So I will become like a lion to them,
like a leopard I will lurk beside the
way.
8 I will fall upon them like a bear robbed of
her cubs,
and will tear open the covering of their
heart;
there I will devour them like a lion,
as a wild animal would mangle them.

9 I will destroy you, O Israel;
who can help you?[f]
10 Where now is[g] your king, that he may
save you?
Where in all your cities are your
rulers,
of whom you said,
"Give me a king and rulers"?
11 I gave you a king in my anger,
and I took him away in my wrath.

---

a Compare Syr: Heb *Gilead*   b Heb lacks *sheep*
c Cn Compare Gk: Heb *To these they say sacrifices of people*
d Gk Syr: Heb *knew*   e Cn: Heb *according to their pasture*
f Gk Syr: Heb *for in me is your help*   g Gk Syr Vg: Heb *I will be*

(cf. Judg 21.19). God plans to return Israel to those *days of the appointed festival* (cf. 2.14–15; 3.4). **12.11** *Gilead.* See note on 6.8. Expensive offerings of *bulls* at *Gilgal* (cf. 4.15; 9.15) were a poor substitute for covenant faithfulness (cf. Mic 6.6–8). **12.12–14** *Jacob* tended *sheep,* but Moses tended God's human flock (see Ps 77.20, a psalm of Asaph). Since Hosea now has Moses' role (see Deut 18.15–19), Jacob's descendants should heed him. **12.14** *Given bitter offense,* an idiom from Hosea's traditions for breaking the covenant and worshiping foreign gods (1 Kings 14.9; Ps 78.58, a psalm of Asaph).
　13.1–16 Israel is headed for death. **13.1** *Ephraim.* See note on 4.17. *Exalted.* Cf. 12.8. *Guilt through Baal,* because of violation of the covenant. *Died,* because Israel had become detestable (9.10) and lost independence (2 Kings 17.3). **13.2** *Keep on sinning.* Cf. Ps. 78.17, a psalm of Asaph. The *cast image* refers to Bethel's bull image (8.5; 10.5); on *kissing calves,* see 1 Kings 19.18. *Work of artisans.* Cf. Deut 27.15; Jer 10.3–4, 9. **13.3** *Smoke from a window.* Israelite houses had no chimneys to vent interior fire pits, so smoke escaped through glass-free openings in the walls. **13.4** A core tradition behind Hosea's prophecy (see 12.9; Ex 20.2–3; Ps 81.9–10, a psalm of Asaph; Deut 5.6–7), forbidding any gods other than the Lord. **13.6** On the theme of satiety, see note on 10.1–2. **13.10** Cf. Mic 4.9. The background is likely Assyria's imprisonment of King Hoshea (2 Kings 17.4). *Give me a king.* Cf. 1 Sam 8.6, 19; 12.13, 17. **13.11** An indictment of societal centralization and monarchy; see notes on 3.4; 8.4; 10.3.

12 Ephraim's iniquity is bound up;
   his sin is kept in store.
13 The pangs of childbirth come for him,
   but he is an unwise son;
for at the proper time he does not present
   himself
   at the mouth of the womb.

14 Shall I ransom them from the power of
   Sheol?
   Shall I redeem them from Death?
O Death, where are[a] your plagues?
   O Sheol, where is[a] your destruction?
   Compassion is hidden from my eyes.

15 Although he may flourish among rushes,[b]
   the east wind shall come, a blast from
   the LORD,
   rising from the wilderness;
and his fountain shall dry up,
   his spring shall be parched.
It shall strip his treasury
   of every precious thing.
16 [c] Samaria shall bear her guilt,
   because she has rebelled against her God;
they shall fall by the sword,
   their little ones shall be dashed in
   pieces,
   and their pregnant women ripped
   open.

A Plea for Repentance

14 Return, O Israel, to the LORD your
   God,
   for you have stumbled because of your
   iniquity.
2 Take words with you
   and return to the LORD;
say to him,
   "Take away all guilt;

accept that which is good,
   and we will offer
   the fruit[d] of our lips.
3 Assyria shall not save us;
   we will not ride upon horses;
we will say no more, 'Our God,'
   to the work of our hands.
In you the orphan finds mercy."

Assurance of Forgiveness

4 I will heal their disloyalty;
   I will love them freely,
   for my anger has turned from them.
5 I will be like the dew to Israel;
   he shall blossom like the lily,
   he shall strike root like the forests of
   Lebanon.[e]
6 His shoots shall spread out;
   his beauty shall be like the olive tree,
   and his fragrance like that of Lebanon.
7 They shall again live beneath my[f] shadow,
   they shall flourish as a garden;[g]
they shall blossom like the vine,
   their fragrance shall be like the wine of
   Lebanon.

8 O Ephraim, what have I[h] to do with idols?
   It is I who answer and look after you.[i]
I am like an evergreen cypress;
   your faithfulness[j] comes from me.
9 Those who are wise understand these
   things;
   those who are discerning know them.
For the ways of the LORD are right,
   and the upright walk in them,
   but transgressors stumble in them.

---

a Gk Syr: Heb I will be   b Or among brothers   c Ch 14.1 in
Heb   d Gk Syr: Heb bulls   e Cn: Heb like Lebanon   f Heb his
g Cn: Heb they shall grow grain   h Or What more has Ephraim
i Heb him   j Heb your fruit

13.14 *O Death, where are your plagues? O Sheol, where is
your destruction?* The Hebrew may entail a divine summons to effect punishment: "O Death, bring on your
plagues. O Grave, bring on your destruction." Alternatively, the sense may be one of hope (see the Septuagint;
1 Cor 15.55).
   14.1–8 A summons to repentance (vv. 1–3) and a
divine promise of renewal (vv. 4–8). **14.2** Above and
beyond animal sacrifice, Israel is bid to bring *words* of

genuine repentance (see note on 6.6; cf. Ps 50.13–15, a
psalm of Asaph). **14.3** Turning to *Assyria* (see notes on
5.13; 12.1) and worshiping idols (8.6; 10.6; 11.2; 13.2)
were basic betrayals of the covenant. *The orphan finds
mercy.* See Ex 22.22–23; Deut 27.19; Pss 10.14; 68.5.
14.9 Conclusion in the style of wisdom writings, such
as Proverbs and Ps 1. Study of Hosea's book reveals
God's path to life, even for those living long after the
prophet's era.

JOEL

Content and Structure

THE BOOK OF JOEL is the second book in the Masoretic version of the book of the Twelve Prophets. The superscription of the book in 1.1 simply tells us that the word of the Lord, YHWH [editor's note: Some scholars write the Divine Name without vowels as a sign of respect, while others spell and pronounce it Yahweh], came to the prophet, Joel ben Pethuel, without providing further details concerning the prophet's identity or the historical background. The body of the book first presents the prophet's call for the people to lament (1.2–2.14), employing the metaphor of a swarm of locusts (1.2–20) to portray the threat of an enemy invasion of Jerusalem (2.1–14). It then turns to the prophet's announcement of YHWH's response to the people that they will be protected from the threat (2.15–3.21). It reports YHWH's response to the people (2.15–20) and reassures them that the fertility of the land will be restored and the nations that threaten Jerusalem will be defeated (2.21–3.8). It concludes with the prophet's call to the nations to assemble for judgment as YHWH carries out the divine promise to restore the land and the nation (3.9–21).

Historical Background

THE BOOK OF JOEL is notoriously difficult to date since it lacks clear historical references. Interpreters have suggested dates ranging from the ninth through the fourth centuries BCE. Earlier proposals associate Joel's condemnation of Egypt with Pharaoh Shishak's campaign against Israel following the death of Solomon (1 Kings 14.25–29) and the condemnation of Edom with the Edomite revolt against King Jehoram of Judah (2 Kings 8.20–22). Most interpreters date Joel to the fifth and fourth centuries BCE based largely on its allusions to earlier biblical literature, such as 1.15 (Isa 13.6; Ezek 30.2–3); 3.10 (Mic 4.1–4; Isa 2.2–4); 2.1–2 (Zeph 1.14–15); 3.2, 12 (2 Chr 20.20–26); 3.16, 18 (Am 1.2; 9.13), and the many references to Obadiah throughout ch. 3.

Message

JOEL IS FREQUENTLY VIEWED as a protoapocalyptic book owing to its correlation of natural and human events. Indeed, its portrayal of the portents in heaven and earth on the "day of YHWH," i.e., the darkened sun and stars, the moon turned to blood, and the pouring out of the "divine spirit" on all flesh prior to the judgment of the nations, suggests an apocalyptic scenario. Nevertheless, readers must be aware that Joel's scenario does not constitute a portrayal of the end of time. The imagery is associated with the *Hamsin* (Arabic) or *Sharav* (Hebrew), the dry desert wind—much like the Santa Ana winds of southern California—that fills the sky with blowing dust and marks the transitions between the dry summer and rainy winter seasons in both ancient and modern Israel. Although the prophet employs this imagery to portray the threat of enemy invasion against Jerusalem, the use of earlier biblical traditions points to YHWH's deliverance of the city. Altogether, the book of Joel presents YHWH's response of mercy to Judah's pleas for help. [RICHARD A. HENSHAW, revised by MARVIN A. SWEENEY]

1 The word of the LORD that came to Joel son of Pethuel:

Lament over the Ruin of the Country

2 Hear this, O elders,
> give ear, all inhabitants of the land!
> Has such a thing happened in your days,
> or in the days of your ancestors?
3 Tell your children of it,
> and let your children tell their children,
> and their children another generation.

4 What the cutting locust left,
> the swarming locust has eaten.
> What the swarming locust left,
> the hopping locust has eaten,
> and what the hopping locust left,
> the destroying locust has eaten.

5 Wake up, you drunkards, and weep;
> and wail, all you wine-drinkers,
> over the sweet wine,
> for it is cut off from your mouth.
6 For a nation has invaded my land,

> powerful and innumerable;
> its teeth are lions' teeth,
> and it has the fangs of a lioness.
7 It has laid waste my vines,
> and splintered my fig trees;
> it has stripped off their bark and thrown
> it down;
> their branches have turned white.

8 Lament like a virgin dressed in sackcloth
> for the husband of her youth.
9 The grain offering and the drink offering
> are cut off
> from the house of the LORD.
> The priests mourn,
> the ministers of the LORD.
10 The fields are devastated,
> the ground mourns;
> for the grain is destroyed,
> the wine dries up,
> the oil fails.

11 Be dismayed, you farmers,
> wail, you vinedressers,

1.1 The superscription simply identifies the following materials as a prophetic oracle from YHWH that came to the prophet Joel ben Pethuel. It provides neither further identification of the prophet nor any information concerning the historical background for Joel's message. **1.2–2.14** The prophet calls for communal lamentation based on the impending threat of a plague of locusts that metaphorically describes an enemy invasion. **1.1–12** The prophet calls for the people to assemble in the Jerusalem temple to appeal to YHWH for deliverance from a locust plague, which threatens to destroy Judah's crops and livelihood. The imagery of locusts draws heavily on the portrayal of the locust plague against Egypt in the exodus traditions (Ex 10.1–20), but this time the victims of the locusts are Judah and Jerusalem (cf. Am 7.1–3). **1.2–4** Opening, scene-setting verses, such as occur often in the prophetic books, call upon the people to *hear;* see Hos 4.1; Isa 1.2; Mic 1.2. **1.2** The prophet's rhetorical question in v. 2b heightens the importance of the situation to his Judean audience, i.e., such a thing has never happened before. **1.4** Four kinds of *locust* symbolize four different invasions, according to some commentators. The type translated *cutting locust* appears also in Am 4.9, one of the many contacts between this presumably later book and Amos. **1.5–7** The prophet turns to the specific effects of the locust plague, i.e., the destruction of the grape crop and the wine it would produce. Grapes and wine were dietary staples in ancient Judah, together with grain and oil (Deut 14.23; 18.4). The threat to the grape harvest suggests that the setting for the prophet's message is the festival of Sukkoth, "Booths" or "Tabernacles," which commemorates the conclusion of the fruit harvest (Ex 23.16; 34.22; Lev 23.33–36; 39.44; Num 28.12–39; Deut 16.13–15). **1.8–10** *Lament* was often done in the ancient Near East by women (see Jer 9.17–22). In Ezek 8.14 women weep for Tammuz, a Babylonian god. In Jer 31.15 Rachel, no doubt an eponym for lamenting women, laments for the captured Israelites. **1.9** The invasion of the army (a *nation*, v. 6), both symbolic and actual, has caused the temple services to cease. **1.11–**

over the wheat and the barley;
  for the crops of the field are ruined.
12 The vine withers,
  the fig tree droops.
Pomegranate, palm, and apple—
  all the trees of the field are dried up;
surely, joy withers away
  among the people.

A Call to Repentance and Prayer

13 Put on sackcloth and lament, you priests;
  wail, you ministers of the altar.
Come, pass the night in sackcloth,
  you ministers of my God!
Grain offering and drink offering
  are withheld from the house of your
    God.

14 Sanctify a fast,
  call a solemn assembly.
Gather the elders
  and all the inhabitants of the land
to the house of the Lord your God,
  and cry out to the Lord.

15 Alas for the day!
For the day of the Lord is near,
  and as destruction from the Almighty[a]
    it comes.
16 Is not the food cut off
  before our eyes,
joy and gladness
  from the house of our God?

17 The seed shrivels under the clods,[b]
  the storehouses are desolate;
the granaries are ruined
  because the grain has failed.
18 How the animals groan!
  The herds of cattle wander about
because there is no pasture for them;
  even the flocks of sheep are dazed.[c]

19 To you, O Lord, I cry.
  For fire has devoured

  the pastures of the wilderness,
and flames have burned
  all the trees of the field.
20 Even the wild animals cry to you
  because the watercourses are dried up,
and fire has devoured
  the pastures of the wilderness.

2 Blow the trumpet in Zion;
  sound the alarm on my holy mountain!
Let all the inhabitants of the land
    tremble,
  for the day of the Lord is coming, it is
    near—
2 a day of darkness and gloom,
  a day of clouds and thick darkness!
Like blackness spread upon the
    mountains
  a great and powerful army comes;
their like has never been from of old,
  nor will be again after them
in ages to come.

3 Fire devours in front of them,
  and behind them a flame burns.
Before them the land is like the garden of
    Eden,
  but after them a desolate wilderness,
  and nothing escapes them.

4 They have the appearance of horses,
  and like war-horses they charge.
5 As with the rumbling of chariots,
  they leap on the tops of the mountains,
like the crackling of a flame of fire
  devouring the stubble,
like a powerful army
  drawn up for battle.

6 Before them peoples are in anguish,
  all faces grow pale.[b]
7 Like warriors they charge,

---

a Traditional rendering of Heb *Shaddai*   b Meaning of Heb
uncertain   c Compare Gk Syr Vg: Meaning of Heb uncertain

---

12 The prophet calls upon the *farmers* to be *dismayed* and to lament at the loss of their grain crops and fruit harvests. **1.13–20** A ritual lament that appeals for fasting and mourning on the *day of the Lord* (v. 15). **1.13–14** The lament is led by *priests* and includes *the elders*, indeed *all the inhabitants*, and calls for *fasting, blowing the trumpet* (2.1), and *crying out* to YHWH. Archaeology has recovered many prayers of lamentation from ancient Babylonia. **1.15** *The day of the Lord* is a major

theme in Joel and an often used prophetic motif, very close to themes in, e.g., Am 5.18–20; Isa 2.11–22; 13.6–19; Zeph 1.2–2.13.
  2.1–14 The prophet's call for the nation to lament concerning the threat of invasion by an enemy army. **2.2** *Darkness and gloom,* the thrust also of the "day" passage in Am 5.18. **2.5** *Rumbling . . . crackling.* Those who have experienced locust plagues remark on the accompanying noise, which is like a roar or an onrush-

like soldiers they scale the wall.
Each keeps to its own course,
they do not swerve from[a] their paths.
8 They do not jostle one another,
each keeps to its own track;
they burst through the weapons
and are not halted.
9 They leap upon the city,
they run upon the walls;
they climb up into the houses,
they enter through the windows like a
thief.

10 The earth quakes before them,
the heavens tremble.
The sun and the moon are darkened,
and the stars withdraw their shining.
11 The LORD utters his voice
at the head of his army;
how vast is his host!
Numberless are those who obey his
command.
Truly the day of the LORD is great;
terrible indeed—who can endure it?

12 Yet even now, says the LORD,
return to me with all your heart,
with fasting, with weeping, and with
mourning;
13 rend your hearts and not your clothing.
Return to the LORD, your God,
for he is gracious and merciful,
slow to anger, and abounding in steadfast
love,
and relents from punishing.
14 Who knows whether he will not turn and
relent,
and leave a blessing behind him,
a grain offering and a drink offering
for the LORD, your God?

15 Blow the trumpet in Zion;
sanctify a fast;
call a solemn assembly;
16 gather the people.
Sanctify the congregation;
assemble the aged;
gather the children,
even infants at the breast.
Let the bridegroom leave his room,
and the bride her canopy.

17 Between the vestibule and the altar
let the priests, the ministers of the
LORD, weep.
Let them say, "Spare your people,
O LORD,
and do not make your heritage a
mockery,
a byword among the nations.
Why should it be said among the peoples,
'Where is their God?' "

God's Response and Promise

18 Then the LORD became jealous for his
land,
and had pity on his people.
19 In response to his people the LORD said:
I am sending you
grain, wine, and oil,
and you will be satisfied;
and I will no more make you
a mockery among the nations.

20 I will remove the northern army far from
you,
and drive it into a parched and
desolate land,
its front into the eastern sea,

---

a Gk Syr Vg: Heb *they do not take a pledge along*

ing fire. **2.8–9** No way has ever been discovered of stopping the ongoing rush of a locust horde. **2.10–11** The effect of the locusts, now with YHWH at their head, is that of the *day of the LORD* described in more detail in 2.30–31. **2.12–14** YHWH appeals for the people to return and avoid the projected consequences of the *day of the LORD* (1.15). **2.12** *Fasting . . . weeping,* a further description of the lamentation theme of 1.13–14. **2.13** *Gracious . . . relents from punishing.* This concatenation of epithets is as deeply religious as anything in all of prophetic literature; each of these elements is found elsewhere (see Ex 34.6; Ps 103.8–9). **2.15–3.21** The prophet's announcement of YHWH's response to the people's lament. YHWH promises to protect the people from threats. **2.15–20** The prophet summons the people to a holy assembly in the temple so that they can appeal for protection to YHWH. YHWH responds that the people will have crops and deliverance from an oppressor who comes from the north. **2.17** *The vestibule and the altar.* The prophet knows quite a bit about the temple and its practices. The vestibule was at the entrance and the altar was at the extreme front, so this is another way of saying the whole temple. We can picture a procession here or the description of the places where prayer was offered. **2.20** *Northern army.* Other than from Egypt, almost all of Israel's invasions came from the north. The *eastern sea* is the Persian (Arabian) Gulf, and the *western sea* is

and its rear into the western sea;
 its stench and foul smell will rise up.
  Surely he has done great things!

21 Do not fear, O soil;
  be glad and rejoice,
   for the Lord has done great things!
22 Do not fear, you animals of the field,
  for the pastures of the wilderness are
    green;
 the tree bears its fruit,
  the fig tree and vine give their full
    yield.

23 O children of Zion, be glad
  and rejoice in the Lord your God;
 for he has given the early rain*a* for your
    vindication,
 he has poured down for you abundant
    rain,
 the early and the later rain, as before.
24 The threshing floors shall be full of grain,
  the vats shall overflow with wine and
    oil.

25 I will repay you for the years
  that the swarming locust has eaten,
 the hopper, the destroyer, and the cutter,
  my great army, which I sent against
    you.

26 You shall eat in plenty and be satisfied,
  and praise the name of the Lord your
    God,

 who has dealt wondrously with you.
  And my people shall never again be put
    to shame.
27 You shall know that I am in the midst of
    Israel,
  and that I, the Lord, am your God and
    there is no other.
 And my people shall never again be put
    to shame.

God's Spirit Poured Out

28 *b* Then afterward
  I will pour out my spirit on all flesh;
 your sons and your daughters shall
    prophesy,
  your old men shall dream dreams,
  and your young men shall see visions.
29 Even on the male and female slaves,
  in those days, I will pour out my spirit.

30 I will show portents in the heavens and
on the earth, blood and fire and columns of
smoke. 31 The sun shall be turned to darkness,
and the moon to blood, before the great and
terrible day of the Lord comes. 32 Then everyone who calls on the name of the Lord shall
be saved; for in Mount Zion and in Jerusalem
there shall be those who escape, as the Lord
has said, and among the survivors shall be
those whom the Lord calls.

3 *c* For then, in those days and at that time,
  when I restore the fortunes of Judah and

---

a Meaning of Heb uncertain *b* Ch 3.1 in Heb *c* Ch 4.1 in Heb

---

the Mediterranean. *Stench.* Victims of present-day locust swarms describe the fetid odor from the millions
of dead insects remaining when the plague is over.
2.21–3.8 YHWH reassures the people that creation
will be restored and the nation delivered from oppressors. **2.21–27** The crops will grow again, the *army* (v.
20) will go away; indeed there will be a reversal in that
the people will have abundance and they will praise
YHWH's name (v. 26). Then they will know that
YHWH is in their *midst* (v. 27; cf. Isa 7.14). **2.25** The
reversal of fortune refers to the *locusts,* now an *army,* in
the same terms as in 1.4. **2.27** This assurance of
YHWH's presence has the tone of an ending, delineat-
ing one of the several divisions in the book. *Never
again.* The invasions will not occur over and over
again, as in the past, but will come to an end. The
theme is repeated in 3.17. **2.28–32** Joel's announcement concerning YHWH's signs and wonders on the
day of the Lord (1.15). **2.28–29** The *spirit* (or "wind";
the Hebrew word can mean either) *poured out* employs the metaphor of the *Hamsin* (Arabic) or *Sharav*
(Hebrew), the dry desert wind that marks the change

of seasons and the same wind that divides the Red Sea in
the exodus traditions (Ex 14–15), to describe a
prophetic fervor, a kind of ecstasy, as in Num 11.25. But
unlike anything seen before, the spirit will fall on all
human beings, irrespective of their social status or class.
This will occur *afterward . . . in those days,* a "day of
YHWH" motif, sometime in the future. **2.30–31** Cf.
2.10; 3.15. With these apocalyptic elements, the text
slips into a different "language." The *portents* in the sky,
and the *blood, fire, and columns of smoke* recall the imagery of the exodus, when a pillar of smoke and fire,
employing the symbolism of the temple altar in operation, led the people through the wilderness to the promised land (Ex 13.21–22; 40.36–38). The *sun . . . turned to
darkness* and the *moon turned to blood* likewise use Exodus motifs but rely on the natural imagery of the *Ham-
sin/Sharav* (see note on 2.28–29), which darkens the sky
and makes the moon appear blood red due to the large
amount of dust and dirt blown through the sky.
2.32 *Everyone who calls* must by context mean Judeans.
3.1–8 Now the *nations* who were cruel toward Judah
will be judged (see Zeph 2). **3.2** The location of the *val-*

Jerusalem, 2I will gather all the nations and bring them down to the valley of Jehoshaphat, and I will enter into judgment with them there, on account of my people and my heritage Israel, because they have scattered them among the nations. They have divided my land, 3and cast lots for my people, and traded boys for prostitutes, and sold girls for wine, and drunk it down.

4 What are you to me, O Tyre and Sidon, and all the regions of Philistia? Are you paying me back for something? If you are paying me back, I will turn your deeds back upon your own heads swiftly and speedily. 5For you have taken my silver and my gold, and have carried my rich treasures into your temples.*a* 6You have sold the people of Judah and Jerusalem to the Greeks, removing them far from their own border. 7But now I will rouse them to leave the places to which you have sold them, and I will turn your deeds back upon your own heads. 8I will sell your sons and your daughters into the hand of the people of Judah, and they will sell them to the Sabeans, to a nation far away; for the LORD has spoken.

Judgment in the Valley of Jehoshaphat

9 Proclaim this among the nations:
   Prepare war,*b*
      stir up the warriors.
   Let all the soldiers draw near,
      let them come up.
10 Beat your plowshares into swords,
      and your pruning hooks into spears;
      let the weakling say, "I am a warrior."

11 Come quickly,*c*
      all you nations all around,
      gather yourselves there.
   Bring down your warriors, O LORD.

12 Let the nations rouse themselves,
      and come up to the valley of
         Jehoshaphat;
   for there I will sit to judge
      all the neighboring nations.

13 Put in the sickle,
      for the harvest is ripe.
   Go in, tread,
      for the wine press is full.
   The vats overflow,
      for their wickedness is great.

14 Multitudes, multitudes,
      in the valley of decision!
   For the day of the LORD is near
      in the valley of decision.

15 The sun and the moon are darkened,
      and the stars withdraw their shining.

16 The LORD roars from Zion,
      and utters his voice from Jerusalem,
      and the heavens and the earth shake.
   But the LORD is a refuge for his people,
      a stronghold for the people of Israel.

The Glorious Future of Judah

17 So you shall know that I, the LORD your
         God,
      dwell in Zion, my holy mountain.
   And Jerusalem shall be holy,
      and strangers shall never again pass
         through it.

18 In that day
      the mountains shall drip sweet wine,
      the hills shall flow with milk,

---

a Or *palaces*   *b* Heb *sanctify war*   *c* Meaning of Heb uncertain

---

ley of Jehoshaphat is unknown, although there could have been a valley named for this early Judean king. It was undoubtedly chosen in this prophecy for its symbolic meaning: "YHWH judges." YHWH defeated the Edomites, Moabites, and Ammonites during the reign of Jehoshaphat in the Valley of Beracah (2 Chr 20.20–26). **3.3** For the imagery of casting lots and drunkenness, see Ob 11; 16. **3.4–6** Criticism of *Tyre and Sidon* and *Philistia* for plundering and *selling the people . . . to the Greeks* is a historical note unattested elsewhere. The Greeks here are the Ionian Greeks, who inhabited the western coast of Asia Minor, as the Hebrew term for them, *Yavan*, indicates. The Greeks and Phoenicians were well known for slave trading in the fifth and fourth centuries BCE. **3.8** *Sabeans,* an important trad-

ing and caravan people whose homeland was on the western side of the tip of the Arabian Peninsula, part of today's Yemen.

3.9–21 The prophet summons the nations to judgment by YHWH. **3.10a** An ironic reversal of Mic 4.3 and Isa 2.4, so that an idyllic image of the nation's recognition of YHWH now becomes a scenario of divine judgment against them. **3.12** YHWH will judge them in the *valley* called "YHWH judges" (see 3.2). **3.14** *Valley of decision,* again an unknown place, but apparently an echo of the valley of Jehoshaphat of vv. 2, 12. **3.15** *Sun . . . moon are darkened.* Like 2.10, 31, one of the several cases in which the book quotes itself. Again, the imagery presupposes the *Hamsin/Sharav* (see note on 2.30–31). **3.16** An almost exact replica of half of the opening

and all the stream beds of Judah
　　shall flow with water;
a fountain shall come forth from the
　　house of the LORD
　　and water the Wadi Shittim.

19　Egypt shall become a desolation
　　　and Edom a desolate wilderness,
　　because of the violence done to the
　　　people of Judah,

in whose land they have shed innocent
　　blood.
20　But Judah shall be inhabited forever,
　　　and Jerusalem to all generations.
21　I will avenge their blood, and I will not
　　　clear the guilty,*ª*
　　for the LORD dwells in Zion.

---

a Gk Syr: Heb *I will hold innocent their blood that I have not held
innocent*

---

prophetic verse of Am 1.2. *Shake,* the same Hebrew
word as that of Am 1.1. **3.18–21** An ideal, utopian ending. The passage starts with an *in that day* verse, matching the themes of the ends of other prophetic books
(Am 9.11–15; Hos 14.4–9; Mic 7.11–20; Zeph 3.14–20;
Isa 66.10–14). **3.18** *Wine . . . milk . . . water.* The people's
deliverance from threat will be symbolized by material
forms: drinking wine in Am 9.14, flourishing gardens in
Hos 14.7, and fortunes restored in Zeph 3.20. *Fountain
. . . from the house of the LORD,* like the water from the

temple in Ezek 47.1–12. *Wadi Shittim,* a place in Moab
where the people sinned (Num 25.1); that sin will be
overcome by this water. **3.19** Under Pharaoh Neco
Egypt controlled and exploited Judah (see 2 Kings
23.31–35). The tradition that *Edom* plundered
Jerusalem when it was being overrun by others appears
in many places in the Bible, e.g., Ezek 25.12–14; Obadiah; Am 1.11; Mal 1.4; Ps 137.7. **3.21** The book concludes with YHWH's dwelling in Zion, i.e., the Jerusalem temple (cf. Pss 2; 46; 47; 48; 89).

AMOS

OF THE FOUR PROPHETIC BOOKS that originated with eighth-century BCE figures—Amos, Hosea, Isaiah, and Micah—Amos is possibly the earliest one. But Amos was by no means the earliest prophet in ancient Israel. The historical books of the OT allude to the existence of other prophets since the eleventh century BCE (see 1 Sam 9.9–13; 2 Sam 12).

Historical Circumstances

THE SUPERSCRIPTION (1.1) LOCATES AMOS in the reigns of two kings, Uzziah of Judah (783–742 BCE) and Jeroboam II of Israel (786–746 BCE). Allusions elsewhere in the book, especially in 7.9–10, confirm this and also verify that the prophet was a native of the Southern Kingdom, Judah, who came to the Northern Kingdom, Israel, to proclaim the word of God. Although the earthquake by which Amos is dated (1.1) cannot be identified, the report that the prophet spoke "two years before the earthquake" suggests that Amos was active for only a short time.

More precisely, the circumstances assumed by the prophet's message place Amos in the last decade or so of the reign of Jeroboam II, about 760 BCE. The reigns of Jeroboam II and Uzziah were long and relatively peaceful. There had been no major threats to the small states from major Near Eastern powers such as Egypt or Assyria, and peace seems to have been accompanied by prosperity, at least for a few and—according to Amos—at the expense of many. There seems to have been a breakdown in the old tribal and family systems of land ownership and the emergence of a wealthy class at the top of the society.

But Israel and Judah would not be left on their own much longer. At about the time the long reigns of Uzziah and Jeroboam ended, a new and aggressive king came to the throne in Assyria. He was Tiglath-pileser III (745–727 BCE), whose goal was to incorporate the little states in Syria and Palestine into his empire. He would not live to conquer Israel, but his successors would invade the Northern Kingdom, destroy its cities, and carry the people into exile. Samaria, the capital city, fell to the Assyrian kings Shalmaneser V and Sargon II in 722/21 BCE (2 Kings 17.1–6), and the history of Israel came to an end. The prophecies of Amos thus were fulfilled some forty years after he uttered them.

Only a few details are preserved concerning the life of Amos. His home, Tekoa, is in the Judean hills south of Bethlehem, and by trade he was "a herdsman, and a dresser of sycamore trees" (7.14) who was called to prophesy in Israel. Since Amos addressed his words particularly to those who lived in Samaria and Bethel, it is reasonable to conclude that he was active in those two Northern cities.

The Book of Amos

THE BOOK OF AMOS is a collection of the words of and traditions concerning the prophet. The material is sometimes organized carefully, but at other points the logic of the collection is difficult to discern. Most of the book consists of speeches attributed to the prophet, and most of his speeches are prophetic announcements; i.e., he speaks in the name of the Lord concerning the immediate future. Some of his speeches were reports of his threatening visions. Although it is possible that Amos himself later dictated his speeches to someone, or even wrote them down himself, it is more likely that the addresses were collected and recorded by others. In addition to speeches there are reports about the prophet's activities (1.1; 7.10–17) and three fragments of hymns (4.13; 5.8–9; 9.5–6).

Not everything in the book comes from the prophet or even from his time. The first verse looks back on the prophet's activity and talks about him. Likewise the story of the prophet's clash with Amaziah the priest of Bethel (7.10–17) speaks of Amos from the perspective of a third party. A few other passages possibly reflect a perspective considerably after the Northern Kingdom fell and may have been added later as the book was saved and then circulated in Judah. According to scholars these include the prophecy against Judah (2.4–5), the hymnic passages, the concluding prophecies of hope (9.8c–15), and a few others.

The Message of the Prophet and of the Book

THE MESSAGE OF AMOS is direct and uncompromising. Over and over he announces to the people of Israel that, because of their social injustice and religious arrogance, the Lord will punish them by means of a total military disaster. His addresses typically make a logical connection between Israel's unjust actions—past and present—and the Lord's coming judgment. Rarely does the prophet call for the people to change their behavior.

The words of Amos are so startling and dramatic that they might appear to be unprecedented, but the message of the prophet did not arise out of thin air. Rather, Amos over and over again appeals to traditions that he and his hearers held in common. Among these is the belief that the Lord brought Israel out of Egypt and granted the people the land of Canaan (2.9–10; 3.1–2; 9.7–8). The prophet also takes for granted that the people of Israel had always known that the Lord expected of them justice and righteousness. Consequently, he is not introducing any new moral or legal expectations, but draws disturbing implications from them in holding the people accountable for their transgressions. In this respect Amos is not radical, but conservative, calling Israel back to what had been revealed from the beginning of its history.

Although Amos relies upon earlier beliefs and traditions, he does introduce some new perspectives. First, he seems to have been the first to stress that Israel's election itself may be a reason for judgment (3.1–2) and that Israel is not the only people the Lord has chosen (9.7–8). Second, Amos is the first one we know of who announced total and complete judgment upon Israel.

Just as Amos depended upon tradition, so his words became part of tradition, being collected and handed down in Judah after Israel fell to Assyria. In the process of centuries additions were made to the scroll, generally with a view toward applying the old prophetic message to new circumstances. This is one way to account for the references to Judah in the book. For example, Amos may not have spoken against Judah, yet an announcement against Judah (2.4–5) was subsequently added, to apply the now validated words of judgment also to the Southern Kingdom. [GENE M. TUCKER, revised by J. ANDREW DEARMAN]

1 The words of Amos, who was among the shepherds of Tekoa, which he saw concerning Israel in the days of King Uzziah of Judah and in the days of King Jeroboam son of Joash of Israel, two years *a* before the earthquake.

Judgment on Israel's Neighbors

2 And he said:

The LORD roars from Zion,
  and utters his voice from Jerusalem;
the pastures of the shepherds wither,
  and the top of Carmel dries up.

3 Thus says the LORD:
For three transgressions of Damascus,
  and for four, I will not revoke the
    punishment; *b*
because they have threshed Gilead
  with threshing sledges of iron.
4 So I will send a fire on the house of Hazael,
  and it shall devour the strongholds of
    Ben-hadad.
5 I will break the gate bars of Damascus,
  and cut off the inhabitants from the
    Valley of Aven,
and the one who holds the scepter from
    Beth-eden;
  and the people of Aram shall go into
    exile to Kir,
          says the LORD.

6 Thus says the LORD:
For three transgressions of Gaza,
  and for four, I will not revoke the
    punishment; *b*
because they carried into exile entire
    communities,
  to hand them over to Edom.
7 So I will send a fire on the wall of Gaza,
  fire that shall devour its strongholds.
8 I will cut off the inhabitants from
    Ashdod,
  and the one who holds the scepter
    from Ashkelon;
I will turn my hand against Ekron,
  and the remnant of the Philistines shall
    perish,
          says the Lord GOD.

9 Thus says the LORD:
For three transgressions of Tyre,
  and for four, I will not revoke the
    punishment; *b*
because they delivered entire
    communities over to Edom,
  and did not remember the covenant of
    kinship.
10 So I will send a fire on the wall of Tyre,
  fire that shall devour its strongholds.

a Or *during two years* *b* Heb *cause it to return*

1.1–2 An introduction to the whole book. 1.1 The superscription to the book, providing its title, *The words of Amos,* and information concerning the background of the prophet, the object of his words, and the date of his activity. In addition to locating Amos in the reigns of *Uzziah* (783–742 BCE) and *Jeroboam* (786–746 BCE), the editor provides a specific date, *two years before the earthquake.* 1.2 The motto summarizes the message of the book: the word of the Lord through the Judean prophet *roars* northward to bring destruction.

1.3–2.16 Seven similar prophecies against foreign nations are followed by a prophecy against Israel. The foreigners are not judged because they are Israel's enemies but because of violations against other neighbors and an international moral code overseen by the Lord. The sequence of condemning foreigners, then Judah, and finally Israel would have been rhetorically power-

ful before an Israelite audience, but there is no reason to doubt the seriousness of those judgments, as well as that against Israel. 1.3 The phrase *for three transgressions of X and for four,* a refrain in the series of announcements (e.g., vv. 3, 6, 9, 11, 13; 2.1, 4, 6), probably means an indefinite but finally decisive number of violations. The meaning of the Hebrew phrase translated *I will not revoke the punishment,* lit. "I will not cause it to return," is uncertain, but it likely refers to the Lord's promise not to stop the effects of the transgressions. 1.4 The Aramean king *Hazael* established a dynasty by assassinating a certain *Ben-hadad* (2 Kings 8.15). Likewise one of his descendants was named Ben-hadad (2 Kings 13.3). 1.6 *Gaza* was one of the Philistine city-states. Three others are listed in v. 8. 1.9 Since *covenant of kinship,* lit. "covenant of brothers," does not occur elsewhere in the OT, its meaning is uncertain. It probably refers to a political treaty that Tyre violated. 2.4 The

11 Thus says the LORD:
For three transgressions of Edom,
    and for four, I will not revoke the
        punishment;[a]
because he pursued his brother with the
    sword
    and cast off all pity;
he maintained his anger perpetually,[b]
    and kept his wrath[c] forever.

12 So I will send a fire on Teman,
    and it shall devour the strongholds of
        Bozrah.

13 Thus says the LORD:
For three transgressions of the
    Ammonites,
    and for four, I will not revoke the
        punishment;[a]
because they have ripped open pregnant
    women in Gilead
    in order to enlarge their territory.

14 So I will kindle a fire against the wall of
    Rabbah,
    fire that shall devour its strongholds,
with shouting on the day of battle,
    with a storm on the day of the
        whirlwind;

15 then their king shall go into exile,
    he and his officials together,
                                says the LORD.

2 Thus says the LORD:
For three transgressions of Moab,
    and for four, I will not revoke the
        punishment;[a]
because he burned to lime
    the bones of the king of Edom.

2 So I will send a fire on Moab,
    and it shall devour the strongholds of
        Kerioth,
and Moab shall die amid uproar,
    amid shouting and the sound of the
        trumpet;

3 I will cut off the ruler from its midst,

and will kill all its officials with him,
                                says the LORD.

Judgment on Judah

4 Thus says the LORD:
For three transgressions of Judah,
    and for four, I will not revoke the
        punishment;[a]
because they have rejected the law of the
    LORD,
    and have not kept his statutes,
but they have been led astray by the same
    lies
    after which their ancestors walked.

5 So I will send a fire on Judah,
    and it shall devour the strongholds of
        Jerusalem.

Judgment on Israel

6 Thus says the LORD:
For three transgressions of Israel,
    and for four, I will not revoke the
        punishment;[a]
because they sell the righteous for silver,
    and the needy for a pair of sandals—

7 they who trample the head of the poor
        into the dust of the earth,
    and push the afflicted out of the way;
father and son go in to the same girl,
    so that my holy name is profaned;

8 they lay themselves down beside every
        altar
    on garments taken in pledge;
and in the house of their God they drink
    wine bought with fines they imposed.

9 Yet I destroyed the Amorite before them,
    whose height was like the height of
        cedars,
    and who was as strong as oaks;
I destroyed his fruit above,
    and his roots beneath.

---

a Heb *cause it to return*   b Syr Vg: Heb *and his anger tore
perpetually*   c Gk Syr Vg: Heb *and his wrath kept*

---

indictment of *Judah* is quite different from the preceding ones, all of which had listed violations of standards
of international conduct as reasons for Yahweh's judgment. The language of the accusation, *law of the LORD
. . . his statutes . . . after which their ancestors walked,* is
that of Deuteronomy, perhaps indicating that the judgment against Judah was added after the time of Amos,
and possibly even after Jerusalem had fallen to the
Babylonians. **2.6–8** Israel is accused of injustice against
the poor and of several forms of religious corruption.

2.6 *Sell the righteous,* a reference to enslavement for
nonpayment of debts. **2.7** *Push the afflicted out,* probably the denial of legal due process in the courts. *Father
and son . . . same girl.* The accusation may refer to the
violation of laws concerning incest, although there is
no law that exactly parallels this situation (but see Lev
18.15; 20.12), or the offense may be the exploitation of
the girl. **2.9–11** As further foundation for the announcement of judgment Yahweh reminds Israel of his
saving acts on their behalf. **2.9** *Amorite.* See Num

10 Also I brought you up out of the land of
       Egypt,
    and led you forty years in the
       wilderness,
    to possess the land of the Amorite.
11 And I raised up some of your children to
       be prophets
    and some of your youths to be
       nazirites. *a*
    Is it not indeed so, O people of Israel?
                                   says the LORD.

12 But you made the nazirites*a* drink wine,
    and commanded the prophets,
    saying, "You shall not prophesy."

13 So, I will press you down in your place,
    just as a cart presses down
    when it is full of sheaves. *b*
14 Flight shall perish from the swift,
    and the strong shall not retain their
       strength,
    nor shall the mighty save their lives;
15 those who handle the bow shall not
       stand,
    and those who are swift of foot shall
       not save themselves,
    nor shall those who ride horses save
       their lives;
16 and those who are stout of heart among
       the mighty
    shall flee away naked in that day,
                                   says the LORD.

Israel's Guilt and Punishment

3 Hear this word that the LORD has spoken
    against you, O people of Israel, against the
whole family that I brought up out of the land
of Egypt:
2 You only have I known
    of all the families of the earth;

therefore I will punish you
    for all your iniquities.

3 Do two walk together
    unless they have made an
       appointment?
4 Does a lion roar in the forest,
    when it has no prey?
    Does a young lion cry out from its den,
    if it has caught nothing?
5 Does a bird fall into a snare on the earth,
    when there is no trap for it?
    Does a snare spring up from the ground,
    when it has taken nothing?
6 Is a trumpet blown in a city,
    and the people are not afraid?
    Does disaster befall a city,
    unless the LORD has done it?
7 Surely the Lord GOD does nothing,
    without revealing his secret
    to his servants the prophets.
8 The lion has roared;
    who will not fear?
    The Lord GOD has spoken;
    who can but prophesy?

9 Proclaim to the strongholds in Ashdod,
    and to the strongholds in the land of
       Egypt,
    and say, "Assemble yourselves on Mount *c*
       Samaria,
    and see what great tumults are within it,
    and what oppressions are in its midst."
10 They do not know how to do right, says
       the LORD,
    those who store up violence and
       robbery in their strongholds.
11 Therefore thus says the Lord GOD:

---

a That is, *those separated* or *those consecrated*   *b* Meaning of
Heb uncertain   *c* Gk Syr: Heb *the mountains of*

21.21–31. **2.11** The *nazirites,* "separated or consecrated
ones," took vows that included abstinence from wine
and strong drink (see v. 12; Num 6.1–21). The only
person specifically named as a Nazirite was Samson
(see Judg 13.4–7), whose consecration included the
vow that his hair would never be cut. **2.13–16** The Lord
announces judgment against Israel in the form of a
military catastrophe in which the army is routed and
even the most courageous *flee away naked.* **2.16** *That
day,* the day of the Lord (see 5.18–20).

3.1–6.14 A collection of oracles against Israel. **3.1–
2** Ironically, because the people of Israel were the Lord's
elect, saved from Egypt, they will be held particularly

accountable for their actions. **3.2** *Therefore . . . iniquities,* lit. "therefore I will visit your sins upon you." **3.3–
8** A series of sayings in the form of rhetorical questions
(vv. 3–6) establishes the principle that every effect has
its cause, arguing in support of the conclusion that the
Lord GOD (Lord Yahweh) is the one who causes someone to *prophesy* (v. 8; see 7.10–17). **3.7** A later addition
from the point of view of Deuteronomy, asserting far
more than the original prophetic saying, namely, that
Yahweh does not act at all without confiding in the
prophets. **3.9–15** Sayings concerning Samaria, the capital of Israel. **3.9** The prophetic voice calls for the Philistines (*Ashdod*) and the Egyptians to serve as witnesses

An adversary shall surround the land,
    and strip you of your defense;
    and your strongholds shall be plundered.

12 Thus says the LORD: As the shepherd rescues from the mouth of the lion two legs, or a piece of an ear, so shall the people of Israel who live in Samaria be rescued, with the corner of a couch and part*a* of a bed.

13 Hear, and testify against the house of Jacob,
    says the Lord GOD, the God of hosts:
14 On the day I punish Israel for its
        transgressions,
    I will punish the altars of Bethel,
    and the horns of the altar shall be cut off
        and fall to the ground.
15 I will tear down the winter house as well
        as the summer house;
    and the houses of ivory shall perish,
    and the great houses*b* shall come to an end,
                    says the LORD.

4 Hear this word, you cows of Bashan
    who are on Mount Samaria,
who oppress the poor, who crush the
        needy,
    who say to their husbands, "Bring
        something to drink!"
2 The Lord GOD has sworn by his holiness:
    The time is surely coming upon you,
    when they shall take you away with hooks,
        even the last of you with fishhooks.
3 Through breaches in the wall you shall
        leave,
    each one straight ahead;
    and you shall be flung out into
        Harmon,*a*
                    says the LORD.

4 Come to Bethel—and transgress;
    to Gilgal—and multiply transgression;
    bring your sacrifices every morning,
    your tithes every three days;
5 bring a thank offering of leavened bread,
    and proclaim freewill offerings, publish
        them;
    for so you love to do, O people of
        Israel!
                    says the Lord GOD.

Israel Rejects Correction

6 I gave you cleanness of teeth in all your
        cities,
    and lack of bread in all your places,
    yet you did not return to me,
                    says the LORD.

7 And I also withheld the rain from you
    when there were still three months to
        the harvest;
    I would send rain on one city,
    and send no rain on another city;
    one field would be rained upon,
    and the field on which it did not rain
        withered;
8 so two or three towns wandered to one
        town
    to drink water, and were not satisfied;
    yet you did not return to me,
                    says the LORD.

9 I struck you with blight and mildew;
    I laid waste*c* your gardens and your
        vineyards;

---

a Meaning of Heb uncertain   *b* Or *many houses*   *c* Cn: Heb *the multitude of*

---

to Samaria's corruption. **3.11** Yahweh addresses Samaria directly, announcing a military defeat. **3.12** A simile of disaster. When the day of trouble comes, all that will be left of Israel will be broken fragments (see 5.3). **3.13–15** Judgment against Israel will include destruction of two types of buildings, the sanctuaries (*altars of Bethel*) and the houses of those wealthy enough to have both a summer and a winter place.

4.1–3 A prophecy of punishment against the wealthy women of Samaria, ridiculed as *cows of Bashan*. Bashan was a region in northern Transjordan known for its sleek cattle (cf. Deut 32.14; Ps 22.12). Typically, the prophecy includes a summons to attention (v. 1a), an indictment (v. 1b), and an announcement of punishment (vv. 2–3). **4.1** The women are guilty of social injustice and arrogance, epitomized by

what they say to their husbands. **4.4–5** Through ironic calls to worship or parodies of pilgrim songs to the traditional sanctuaries at *Bethel* and *Gilgal* (Gen 28.10–22; Josh 5.2–9; Am 7.10–17), Amos asserts that worship and *transgression* have become synonymous (see 5.21–24). **4.6–13** Because a series of disasters sent by the Lord has failed to persuade Israel to *return* to its God, the people will now *meet* (v. 12) that God directly. The meaning of the refrain that links the series, *yet you did not return to me*, is not self-evident. In some instances the expression refers to obedience to God generally (Deut 4.30; 30.2), but elsewhere "to return" or "to turn" to the Lord refers specifically to acts of confession and repentance (Isa 19.22; Hos 14.2; Joel 2.12). **4.6** *Cleanness of teeth . . . and lack of bread,* hunger, resulting from famine. **4.7–8** Drought did not

the locust devoured your fig trees and
your olive trees;
yet you did not return to me,
says the LORD.

10 I sent among you a pestilence after the
manner of Egypt;
I killed your young men with the
sword;
I carried away your horses;[a]
and I made the stench of your camp go
up into your nostrils;
yet you did not return to me,
says the LORD.

11 I overthrew some of you,
as when God overthrew Sodom and
Gomorrah,
and you were like a brand snatched
from the fire;
yet you did not return to me,
says the LORD.

12 Therefore thus I will do to you, O Israel;
because I will do this to you,
prepare to meet your God, O Israel!

13 For lo, the one who forms the mountains,
creates the wind,
reveals his thoughts to mortals,
makes the morning darkness,
and treads on the heights of the
earth—
the LORD, the God of hosts, is his
name!

A Lament for Israel's Sin

5 Hear this word that I take up over you in
lamentation, O house of Israel:

2 Fallen, no more to rise,
is maiden Israel;
forsaken on her land,
with no one to raise her up.

3 For thus says the Lord GOD:
The city that marched out a thousand
shall have a hundred left,
and that which marched out a hundred
shall have ten left.[b]

4 For thus says the LORD to the house of
Israel:
Seek me and live;
5 but do not seek Bethel,
and do not enter into Gilgal
or cross over to Beer-sheba;
for Gilgal shall surely go into exile,
and Bethel shall come to nothing.

6 Seek the LORD and live,
or he will break out against the house
of Joseph like fire,
and it will devour Bethel, with no one
to quench it.

7 Ah, you that turn justice to wormwood,
and bring righteousness to the ground!

8 The one who made the Pleiades and
Orion,
and turns deep darkness into the
morning,
and darkens the day into night,
who calls for the waters of the sea,
and pours them out on the surface of
the earth,

a Heb *with the captivity of your horses*   b Heb adds *to the house of Israel*

lead Israel to its God. **4.9** Crops were destroyed by disease and insects. **4.10** *A pestilence after the manner of Egypt.* The prophet alludes to the tradition of the plagues against Egypt (Ex 5–11, esp. 9.3–7, 15). The remainder of the verse refers to a military disaster. **4.11** By the time of Amos, *Sodom and Gomorrah* were synonymous with total and divinely sent destruction (Gen 19.12–29; Isa 1.9; Jer 49.18). **4.12** Although the verse is cryptic, the *therefore* that links it to the recital of Israel's failure to return indicates that *prepare to meet your God* is an announcement of judgment. The encounter with God will not be pleasant. **4.13** Words from a hymn that probably once functioned in worship conclude the announcement against Israel (see also 5.8–9; 9.5–6).
5.1–3 The prophet calls for the people (*house of Is-*

rael) to hear a *lamentation,* i.e., a dirge or funeral song. **5.2** Since it is *maiden Israel* that has died, the song announces the death of the nation. **5.3** The military forces will be decimated. **5.4–7** Exhortations to *seek the Lord* as the path to life. See also 5.14–15. **5.4** *Seek* is probably a technical term for inquiring of God or turning to God in a service of prayer. **5.5** Seeking the Lord is contrasted with making pilgrimages to the famous religious centers at *Bethel* (see 3.14; 4.4; 7.10–17), *Gilgal,* and *Beer-sheba* (see 8.14; Gen 21.14, 32–33; 26.23–25), which are destined for *exile* and destruction. **5.6** *House of Joseph,* the Northern Kingdom, Israel. **5.7** *Justice . . . righteousness.* See 5.24. **5.8–9** Like many of the psalms, this hymn extols the Lord as the creator of the cosmos. **5.8** The Lord made the constellations (*Pleiades and Orion*), causes day and night, and

the LORD is his name,

9 who makes destruction flash out against
the strong,
so that destruction comes upon the
fortress.

10 They hate the one who reproves in the
gate,
and they abhor the one who speaks the
truth.

11 Therefore because you trample on the
poor
and take from them levies of grain,
you have built houses of hewn stone,
but you shall not live in them;
you have planted pleasant vineyards,
but you shall not drink their wine.

12 For I know how many are your
transgressions,
and how great are your sins—
you who afflict the righteous, who take a
bribe,
and push aside the needy in the gate.

13 Therefore the prudent will keep silent in
such a time;
for it is an evil time.

14 Seek good and not evil,
that you may live;
and so the LORD, the God of hosts, will be
with you,
just as you have said.

15 Hate evil and love good,
and establish justice in the gate;
it may be that the LORD, the God of
hosts,
will be gracious to the remnant of
Joseph.

16 Therefore thus says the LORD, the God of
hosts, the Lord:
In all the squares there shall be wailing;
and in all the streets they shall say,
"Alas! alas!"
They shall call the farmers to mourning,
and those skilled in lamentation, to
wailing;

17 in all the vineyards there shall be wailing,
for I will pass through the midst of
you,
says the LORD.

The Day of the LORD a Dark Day

18 Alas for you who desire the day of the
LORD!
Why do you want the day of the LORD?
It is darkness, not light;

19 as if someone fled from a lion,
and was met by a bear;
or went into the house and rested a hand
against the wall,
and was bitten by a snake.

20 Is not the day of the LORD darkness, not
light,
and gloom with no brightness in it?

21 I hate, I despise your festivals,
and I take no delight in your solemn
assemblies.

22 Even though you offer me your burnt
offerings and grain offerings,
I will not accept them;
and the offerings of well-being of your
fatted animals
I will not look upon.

23 Take away from me the noise of your
songs;

---

brings rain from the sea. **5.9** The one who controls natural forces also acts in history to destroy. **5.10–13** Accusations of injustice against the wealthy and powerful members of the community who take advantage of the poor (v. 11) and the needy (v. 12). **5.10** *They* are the ones addressed as *you* in v. 11, i.e., the prophet's audience. The *gate* is the location of the law court. **5.11** Ironically, the wealthy will lose the very things they have acquired unjustly. **5.12** *Push aside the needy in the gate,* use the legal process to take advantage of the poor. **5.13** The prophet refers enigmatically to the time of judgment (*evil time*). **5.14–15** Further exhortations to seek the Lord. See 5.4–7. **5.15** It is possible that it is not too late to change and avert the coming disaster. *Be gracious,* pardon. *Remnant of Joseph,* what is left of the Northern Kingdom, Israel. **5.16–20** Contrary to popular expectations, a day of death

and destruction lies ahead. **5.16–17** As in vv. 1–2, mourning songs announce the death of Israel. *Those skilled in lamentation* are professional mourners (Jer 9.17–19; Ezek 8.14; 2 Chr 35.25). **5.18–20** The *day of the LORD* will be a dark day of judgment. In this earliest prophetic reference to the expectation, Amos repudiates and reverses the false hopes of his hearers through the use of rhetorical questions and metaphorical language. For subsequent understandings of the "day of the LORD" see Ezek 30.1–4; Joel 2.1–2; Zeph 1.14–18. **5.21–27** The prophet has the Lord speaking in the strongest terms (*I hate, I despise,* v. 21) to reject all kinds of religious practices and to call instead for *justice* and *righteousness* (v. 24; see Isa 1.10–17; Mic 6.6–8). **5.21** *Festivals* and *solemn assemblies* include both regular and unscheduled gatherings for prayer, sacrifice, and celebration. **5.22** Three common types of sac-

I will not listen to the melody of your
harps.
24 But let justice roll down like waters,
and righteousness like an ever-flowing
stream.

25 Did you bring to me sacrifices and offerings the forty years in the wilderness, O house
of Israel? 26 You shall take up Sakkuth your
king, and Kaiwan your star-god, your images, *a*
which you made for yourselves; 27 therefore I
will take you into exile beyond Damascus, says
the LORD, whose name is the God of hosts.

Complacent Self-Indulgence Will Be Punished

6 Alas for those who are at ease in Zion,
and for those who feel secure on Mount
Samaria,
the notables of the first of the nations,
to whom the house of Israel resorts!
2 Cross over to Calneh, and see;
from there go to Hamath the great;
then go down to Gath of the
Philistines.
Are you better *b* than these kingdoms?
Or is your *c* territory greater than their *d*
territory,
3 O you that put far away the evil day,
and bring near a reign of violence?

4 Alas for those who lie on beds of ivory,
and lounge on their couches,
and eat lambs from the flock,
and calves from the stall;
5 who sing idle songs to the sound of the
harp,

and like David improvise on
instruments of music;
6 who drink wine from bowls,
and anoint themselves with the finest
oils,
but are not grieved over the ruin of
Joseph!
7 Therefore they shall now be the first to go
into exile,
and the revelry of the loungers shall
pass away.

8 The Lord GOD has sworn by himself
(says the LORD, the God of hosts):
I abhor the pride of Jacob
and hate his strongholds;
and I will deliver up the city and all
that is in it.

9 If ten people remain in one house, they
shall die. 10 And if a relative, one who burns
the dead, *e* shall take up the body to bring it out
of the house, and shall say to someone in the
innermost parts of the house, "Is anyone else
with you?" the answer will come, "No." Then
the relative *f* shall say, "Hush! We must not
mention the name of the LORD."

11 See, the LORD commands,
and the great house shall be shattered
to bits,
and the little house to pieces.
12 Do horses run on rocks?
Does one plow the sea with oxen? *g*

---

a Heb *your images, your star-god*   *b* Or *Are they better*
c Heb *their*   *d* Heb *your*   *e* Or *who makes a burning for him*
f Heb *he*   *g* Or *Does one plow them with oxen*

---

rifice are rejected. **5.23** The Lord considers sacred
music to be *noise* (see 8.10). **5.24** Amos frequently
speaks of *justice* and *righteousness* in tandem (see also
v. 7; 6.12). *Justice* is the establishment of the right, and
of the person in the right, through fair legal procedures (v. 15; Deut 25.1), in accordance with the will of
the Lord. *Righteousness* is that quality of life in relationship with others in the community that gives rise
to justice. **5.25** Contrary to the pentateuchal account
of Israel's history (Ex 19–Num 10), Amos asserts that
sacrifices and offerings were not given during the
wandering in the wilderness (see also Jer 7.21–26).
5.26 *Sakkuth* and *Kaiwan* were Mesopotamian deities.
5.27 *Exile beyond Damascus*, i.e., to Assyria.

6.1–7 Indictments of a self-indulgent society conclude (v. 7) with an announcement of judgment. **6.1–
3** The powerful and wealthy (*notables*) are accused of
arrogant self-satisfaction. **6.1** Although the message of

Amos is to the Northern Kingdom (Israel) and its capital (*Samaria*) in particular, here he includes the leaders of Jerusalem (*Zion*) as well. **6.2** *Calneh* and *Hamath* were Syrian cities to the north of Israel, perhaps
taken by Assyria in 738 BCE; *Gath* was one of the five
Philistine cities to the west. **6.4–6** The upper classes,
including the political leadership, indulge themselves
with rich food, drink, and entertainment, but have no
concern for the troubles of the nation (*ruin of Joseph,*
v. 6). **6.4** *Alas* does not appear in the Hebrew text.
6.7 The leaders will lead the way into exile. **6.8–14** Diverse materials have been combined to advance the
common theme of the Lord's judgment on *the city* (v.
8), presumably Samaria. **6.8** The Lord solemnly swears
(see 4.2; 8.7) to hand over (*deliver up*) the city and its
inhabitants to its enemies. **6.9–10** A narrative sketches
a mysterious and ominous little scene of survivors
hiding among the ruins and the bodies of the slain.

But you have turned justice into poison
and the fruit of righteousness into
wormwood—
13 you who rejoice in Lo-debar,[a]
who say, "Have we not by our own
strength
taken Karnaim[b] for ourselves?"
14 Indeed, I am raising up against you a
nation,
O house of Israel, says the LORD, the
God of hosts,
and they shall oppress you from Lebo-
hamath
to the Wadi Arabah.

Locusts, Fire, and a Plumb Line

7 This is what the Lord GOD showed me: he
was forming locusts at the time the latter
growth began to sprout (it was the latter
growth after the king's mowings). 2When they
had finished eating the grass of the land, I said,
"O Lord GOD, forgive, I beg you!
How can Jacob stand?
He is so small!"
3 The LORD relented concerning this;
"It shall not be," said the LORD.

4 This is what the Lord GOD showed me:
the Lord GOD was calling for a shower of fire,[c]
and it devoured the great deep and was eating
up the land. 5Then I said,
"O Lord GOD, cease, I beg you!
How can Jacob stand?
He is so small!"

6 The LORD relented concerning this;
"This also shall not be," said the Lord
GOD.

7 This is what he showed me: the Lord was
standing beside a wall built with a plumb line,
with a plumb line in his hand. 8And the LORD
said to me, "Amos, what do you see?" And I
said, "A plumb line." Then the Lord said,
"See, I am setting a plumb line
in the midst of my people Israel;
I will never again pass them by;
9 the high places of Isaac shall be made
desolate,
and the sanctuaries of Israel shall be
laid waste,
and I will rise against the house of
Jeroboam with the sword."

Amaziah Complains to the King

10 Then Amaziah, the priest of Bethel, sent to
King Jeroboam of Israel, saying, "Amos has
conspired against you in the very center of the
house of Israel; the land is not able to bear all
his words. 11For thus Amos has said,
'Jeroboam shall die by the sword,
and Israel must go into exile
away from his land.'"
12And Amaziah said to Amos, "O seer, go, flee
away to the land of Judah, earn your bread
there, and prophesy there; 13but never again

a Or in a thing of nothingness b Or horns c Or for a
judgment by fire

6.12 The prophet employs proverbial sayings to show
that Israel's sins are unnatural and ridiculous behavior. 6.13 Israel boasts that its military conquests were
achieved through its own *strength*. The names of cities
in the Transjordan conquered by Jeroboam II (2 Kings
14.25) are turned into puns, "not a thing" and "horns,"
the sarcastic use of a symbol of strength. 6.14 The
Lord promises to bring an unnamed enemy to oppress
the people from one end of the land to the other.
7.1–9.4 Five vision reports organize this section of
the book. 7.1–9 Amos reports three visions of divine
judgment against Israel. In the first two (7.1–3, 4–6)
he intercedes on behalf of the people and the Lord relents, but in the third (7.7–9), as in the fourth and fifth
(8.1–3; 9.1–4), he does not intercede and the sentence
is not lifted. 7.1 *Showed me*, technical language in autobiographical style for the introduction of a vision report (7.4, 7; 8.1). *Locusts* were a familiar threat to crops
and therefore to the lives of the people. 7.3 *Relented*, or
"repented." Reports that God repented or reversed a
decision are not uncommon in the Hebrew scriptures

(see esp. Jon 3.9–10; 4.2; Joel 2.14, 18–19). 7.4 *Shower
of fire*, better "judgment by fire." Since it devoured the
great deep, the waters believed to surround the earth
and heavens (see Gen 1.2), as well as the *land*, this was
no ordinary flame but a cosmic fire. 7.7 The Hebrew
word translated *plumb line* appears only in this context
and therefore its meaning is uncertain. 7.9 The *high
places* were the locations of sanctuaries for legitimate
worship and sacrifice until they were outlawed in the
time of Josiah (2 Kings 23.8). *Isaac* as a name for the
land of Israel is unusual. 7.10–17 Conflict between
prophet and priest. The report from the perspective of
a third person first gives the background (vv. 10–11)
and then reports the dialogue between Amos and Amaziah (vv. 12–15) that concludes with the prophet's
announcement of judgment against the priest, his
family, and his people (vv. 16–17). 7.10–11 Amos is
accused of conspiracy against the state because of
words of judgment such as those found in v. 9. 7.12–
13 Amaziah does not challenge the right of Amos to
prophesy, but only his authority to speak at the royal

prophesy at Bethel, for it is the king's sanctuary, and it is a temple of the kingdom."

14 Then Amos answered Amaziah, "I am[a] no prophet, nor a prophet's son; but I am[a] a herdsman, and a dresser of sycamore trees, 15and the LORD took me from following the flock, and the LORD said to me, 'Go, prophesy to my people Israel.'

16 "Now therefore hear the word of the LORD.
You say, 'Do not prophesy against Israel,
    and do not preach against the house of
        Isaac.'
17 Therefore thus says the LORD:
'Your wife shall become a prostitute in
    the city,
    and your sons and your daughters shall
        fall by the sword,
    and your land shall be parceled out by
        line;
you yourself shall die in an unclean land,
    and Israel shall surely go into exile
        away from its land.' "

The Basket of Fruit

8 This is what the Lord GOD showed me—a basket of summer fruit.[b] 2He said, "Amos, what do you see?" And I said, "A basket of summer fruit."[b] Then the LORD said to me,
"The end[c] has come upon my people
    Israel;
I will never again pass them by.
3 The songs of the temple[d] shall become
    wailings in that day,"
                            says the Lord GOD;
"the dead bodies shall be many,
    cast out in every place. Be silent!"

4 Hear this, you that trample on the needy,
    and bring to ruin the poor of the land,
5 saying, "When will the new moon be over
    so that we may sell grain;
and the sabbath,

so that we may offer wheat for sale?
We will make the ephah small and the
    shekel great,
    and practice deceit with false balances,
6 buying the poor for silver
    and the needy for a pair of sandals,
    and selling the sweepings of the wheat."

7 The LORD has sworn by the pride of Jacob:
Surely I will never forget any of their
    deeds.
8 Shall not the land tremble on this account,
    and everyone mourn who lives in it,
and all of it rise like the Nile,
    and be tossed about and sink again,
        like the Nile of Egypt?

9 On that day, says the Lord GOD,
    I will make the sun go down at noon,
    and darken the earth in broad daylight.
10 I will turn your feasts into mourning,
    and all your songs into lamentation;
I will bring sackcloth on all loins,
    and baldness on every head;
I will make it like the mourning for an
    only son,
    and the end of it like a bitter day.

11 The time is surely coming, says the Lord
    GOD,
    when I will send a famine on the land;
not a famine of bread, or a thirst for water,
    but of hearing the words of the LORD.
12 They shall wander from sea to sea,
    and from north to east;
they shall run to and fro, seeking the
    word of the LORD,
    but they shall not find it.

13 In that day the beautiful young women
    and the young men

---

a Or was   b Heb qayits   c Heb qets   d Or palace

sanctuary and, by implication, in the kingdom of Israel. **7.14** *I am no prophet.* The Hebrew clause could be translated "I was no prophet." *Prophet's son,* member of a prophetic guild (see 2 Kings 2.3; 4.1). **7.15** Amos asserts the authority of his divine vocation against the authority of the priest. **7.16–17** Judgment is announced upon Amaziah and his household because he has opposed the word of God.

8.1–3 The fourth vision report parallels the third one (7.7–9) in form and effect: divine judgment upon Israel. **8.2** The Hebrew for *basket of summer fruit* (qayits)

is a pun on the word for *end* (qets). **8.4–8** Because of Israel's corrupt business practices that oppress the needy and the poor (vv. 4–6), the Lord will intervene against the *land* (vv. 7–8). **8.5** The *new moon* was obviously a monthly religious festival day when business was suspended (see 2.6). **8.6** *Buying the poor,* a reference to debt slavery (see 2.6). **8.8** *Land,* the earth. **8.9–14** The coming day of the Lord (5.18–20) will be a time of darkness, mourning, famine, and thirst. **8.9** The imagery of a solar eclipse is a portent of the darkness of death. **8.11–12** Worse than a *famine* will be the Lord's withdrawal of his *word.*

shall faint for thirst.

14 Those who swear by Ashimah of Samaria,
    and say, "As your god lives, O Dan,"
    and, "As the way of Beer-sheba lives"—
    they shall fall, and never rise again.

The Destruction of Israel

9 I saw the LORD standing beside[a] the altar,
    and he said:
Strike the capitals until the thresholds
    shake,
    and shatter them on the heads of all
      the people;[b]
and those who are left I will kill with the
    sword;
    not one of them shall flee away,
    not one of them shall escape.

2 Though they dig into Sheol,
    from there shall my hand take them;
though they climb up to heaven,
    from there I will bring them down.
3 Though they hide themselves on the top
    of Carmel,
    from there I will search out and take
      them;
and though they hide from my sight at
    the bottom of the sea,
    there I will command the sea-serpent,
    and it shall bite them.
4 And though they go into captivity in
    front of their enemies,
    there I will command the sword, and it
      shall kill them;
and I will fix my eyes on them
    for harm and not for good.

5 The Lord, GOD of hosts,
    he who touches the earth and it melts,
    and all who live in it mourn,

and all of it rises like the Nile,
    and sinks again, like the Nile of
      Egypt;
6 who builds his upper chambers in the
    heavens,
    and founds his vault upon the earth;
who calls for the waters of the sea,
    and pours them out upon the surface
      of the earth—
the LORD is his name.

7 Are you not like the Ethiopians[c] to me,
    O people of Israel? says the LORD.
Did I not bring Israel up from the land of
    Egypt,
    and the Philistines from Caphtor and
      the Arameans from Kir?
8 The eyes of the Lord GOD are upon the
    sinful kingdom,
    and I will destroy it from the face of
      the earth
    —except that I will not utterly destroy
      the house of Jacob,
                              says the LORD.

9 For lo, I will command,
    and shake the house of Israel among all
      the nations
as one shakes with a sieve,
    but no pebble shall fall to the ground.
10 All the sinners of my people shall die by
    the sword,
    who say, "Evil shall not overtake or
      meet us."

The Restoration of David's Kingdom

11 On that day I will raise up
    the booth of David that is fallen,

---

a Or on   b Heb all of them   c Or Nubians; Heb Cushites

8.14 *Ashimah* and *the way of Beer-sheba* are either the names of gods or pejorative titles applied to gods. **9.1–4** The fifth vision report is unlike the previous ones in form, lacking the introductory formula and dialogue between the prophet and the Lord; it is the vision of the most severe judgment. **9.1** The prophet sees the Lord himself and hears him giving orders for the total destruction of the people. **9.2–4** There is no escape from the Lord, not even in death or captivity. **9.2** *Sheol*, the underworld realm of the dead. **9.3** *Sea-serpent*, the dragon of chaos, well known in Near Eastern mythology. **9.5–6** The third hymnic passage or doxology of judgment in the book (4.13; 5.8–9). The Lord is the name of the one who created the world and

whose touch can cause it to melt or toss about. **9.7–8** Against people who had come to view their election by God arrogantly, the prophet points out that the Lord had been concerned for and had brought up other nations as well. **9.8** The Israelites election has become the occasion for their self-satisfaction and therefore for their judgment (see 3.1–2). In a later addition to the book, an exception is made for Judah (*house of Jacob*). **9.9–10** Typically in the book of Amos judgment is announced on the people as a whole, but these verses restrict it to certain sinners. **9.9** The simile of a *sieve* suggests the process of separating the sinners from the others. **9.11–15** Announcements of salvation. Since the prophecies presume that the nation has been destroyed

and repair its^a breaches,
  and raise up its^b ruins,
  and rebuild it as in the days of old;
12 in order that they may possess the
    remnant of Edom
  and all the nations who are called by
    my name,
  says the LORD who does this.

13 The time is surely coming, says the LORD,
  when the one who plows shall overtake
    the one who reaps,
  and the treader of grapes the one who
    sows the seed;
  the mountains shall drip sweet wine,
  and all the hills shall flow with it.

14 I will restore the fortunes of my people
    Israel,
  and they shall rebuild the ruined cities
    and inhabit them;
  they shall plant vineyards and drink their
    wine,
  and they shall make gardens and eat
    their fruit.
15 I will plant them upon their land,
  and they shall never again be plucked
    up
  out of the land that I have given them,
    says the LORD your God.

---

a Gk: Heb *their* *b* Gk: Heb *his*

and the people exiled, they probably come from the time of the Babylonian exile (597–539 BCE). **9.11–12** The Lord promises to restore the Davidic kingdom, rebuild its cities, and restore its territory, a theme one encounters elsewhere in the prophets (see, e.g., Isa 9.1–7; 11.1–9; Jer 23.5–6; Ezek 37.24–28). **9.11** *That day.*

Unlike other texts in Amos (5.18–21; 2.16; 8.3), here the day of the Lord is a time of salvation for God's people. **9.13–15** In the new age, nature will be incredibly fruitful and the people will be secure in their land. Those who experienced the judgment announced by Amos now see God acting to save and restore.

OBADIAH

THE SHORTEST BOOK OF THE OT, Obadiah is associated with a prophetic figure whose name means "slave/servant of Yah (i.e., Yahweh, the LORD)." Only the name of the prophet is given; nothing is said about his time, town, profession, or even the name of his father. Some consider this laconic presentation an invitation to readers to fill the gaps. The time of composition is unknown, though internal evidence suggests an early postexilic date. The title verse characterizes the book as a "vision" (cf. Isa 1.1), a term that here carries a meaning similar to "prophecy," since visual elements do not figure prominently (the same holds true for Isa 1.1).

Structure and Content

OBADIAH USES MUCH OF THE TERMINOLOGY of the better-known prophetic books, and its theology is on the whole similar. There is no general agreement about the structure of the book, though most scholars would agree that vv. 1b/2–7 (sometimes divided into 1b/2–4 and 5–7), vv. 8–18 (sometimes divided into 8–15 and 16–18 or 8–11, 12–15, and 16–18), and vv. 19–21 are the primary blocks. The book focuses on judgment against Edom (Mount Esau) and a utopian image of Judah (Mount Zion) that will be fulfilled in the future. It assumes the destruction of Jerusalem. There is some debate on whether "Edom" here stands only for the historical nation of Edom or is also a type for "the nations" (v. 15). The text certainly emphasizes that "Edom" is Israel's (Jacob's) "brother" and that this status entails obligations and expectations. If the latter are not met, then the Lord will judge and punish "Edom." In fact, the book's conclusion includes a reference to the contrasting future fates of Mount Zion and Mount Esau. The utopian future is imagined by Obadiah as a period of reversal in which the dispossessed will take possession of those who dispossessed them, saviors will ascend Mount Zion (and judge Mount Esau), and the kingdom (or the kingship) will be the Lord's.

Message

EDOM (ESAU) IS CHARACTERIZED as an enemy of the Lord. It has been proud and so will be brought "down to the ground" (v. 3). Moreover, Edom (Esau) has done "violence" to its "brother Jacob" (v. 10, the same theme found in Am 1.11), rejoicing when Judah was in distress, even looting it (v. 13). One of the leading terms in the book is "the day" (vv. 8, 11, 12, 13, 14, 15). It closely associates images of the disaster and suffering of Judah in the past with the activities of Edom (Esau) at the very same time and with the future punishment of the nations, including Edom (Esau; vv. 8, 15). Among the main operative concepts in the book are images of reversals of fate and wrongful deeds returning to affect those who perform them. The latter are taken to be collective groups (e.g., Edom/Esau), not individuals (i.e., the particular Edomites who did violence against Israel, not even necessarily their entire generation).

The utopian future portrayed in the book does not refer to a Davidic king, but to human saviors (cf. the judges) and above all to the Lord's kingship. Mount Zion plays a central role in that future. Significantly, the book explicitly states that Mount Zion shall be sacred at that time, but avoids referring to the remnant of Israel as sacred (v. 17). [RICHARD A. HENSHAW, revised by EHUD BEN ZVI]

Proud Edom Will Be Brought Low

1 The vision of Obadiah.

Thus says the Lord GOD concerning Edom:
We have heard a report from the LORD,
  and a messenger has been sent among
    the nations:
"Rise up! Let us rise against it for battle!"
2 I will surely make you least among the
    nations;
  you shall be utterly despised.
3 Your proud heart has deceived you,
  you that live in the clefts of the rock,[a]
  whose dwelling is in the heights.
You say in your heart,
  "Who will bring me down to the
    ground?"
4 Though you soar aloft like the eagle,
  though your nest is set among the stars,
  from there I will bring you down,
    says the LORD.

Pillage and Slaughter Will Repay Edom's Cruelty

5 If thieves came to you,
  if plunderers by night

—how you have been destroyed!—
  would they not steal only what they
    wanted?
If grape-gatherers came to you,
  would they not leave gleanings?
6 How Esau has been pillaged,
  his treasures searched out!
7 All your allies have deceived you,
  they have driven you to the border;
your confederates have prevailed against
    you;
  those who ate[b] your bread have set a
    trap for you—
  there is no understanding of it.
8 On that day, says the LORD,
  I will destroy the wise out of Edom,
  and understanding out of Mount Esau.
9 Your warriors shall be shattered,
  O Teman,
  so that everyone from Mount Esau will
    be cut off.

Edom Mistreated His Brother

10 For the slaughter and violence done to
    your brother Jacob,

a Or clefts of Sela b Cn: Heb lacks those who ate

1–7 The Hebrew text shows very detailed similarities to Jer 49.7a, 14, 16, 9, 10. It is unclear whether one text was composed on the basis of the other, or both share a common source. 1 Edom, a nation directly east of the Arabah whose inhabitants were considered "brothers" by the biblical authors (see Gen 25.23–26; Am 1.1; Ob 12). Edomites eventually settled in much of what was southern Judah during the monarchical period. Their settlement area was called Idumea during the Second Temple period. Esau is Edom's eponymous ancestor in the tale in Genesis; the name is sometimes used in this book for Edom to emphasize the (failed) brotherhood of Esau/Edom. 3–7 Confidence in one's power, intelligence, allies, or the topographical features of one's territory is often mentioned as an attribute of those who foolishly confront the Lord and are consequently punished. 3 The rock (Hebrew sela'), a pun, as it refers both to the rocks in whose clefts the Edomites dwell according to the speaker and to Sela, a major Edomite city. 4 Soar aloft . . . bring you down. There is no escape from the Lord, a theme also found in Am 9.2–3. 5 Grape-gatherers. Another pun. The Hebrew word sounds very similar to Bozrah, another main city in Edom (cf. Isa 34.6; 63.1; Jer 49.13, 22; Am 1.12). 7 Ate your bread. Commensality (i.e., the act of eating together) was a very important social practice in the ancient Near East, including Israel. Table fellowship reflected and symbolized social fellowship, closeness, and solidarity. Edom, legendary for its wisdom (v. 8), is presented as deceived. There is

shame shall cover you,
and you shall be cut off forever.

11 On the day that you stood aside,
on the day that strangers carried off his
wealth,
and foreigners entered his gates
and cast lots for Jerusalem,
you too were like one of them.

12 But you should not have gloated[a] over[b]
your brother
on the day of his misfortune;
you should not have rejoiced over the
people of Judah
on the day of their ruin;
you should not have boasted
on the day of distress.

13 You should not have entered the gate of
my people
on the day of their calamity;
you should not have joined in the
gloating over Judah's[c] disaster
on the day of his calamity;
you should not have looted his goods
on the day of his calamity.

14 You should not have stood at the
crossings
to cut off his fugitives;
you should not have handed over his
survivors
on the day of distress.

15 For the day of the LORD is near against all
the nations.
As you have done, it shall be done to
you;
your deeds shall return on your own
head.

16 For as you have drunk on my holy
mountain,
all the nations around you shall drink;
they shall drink and gulp down,[d]
and shall be as though they had never
been.

Israel's Final Triumph

17 But on Mount Zion there shall be those
that escape,
and it shall be holy;
and the house of Jacob shall take
possession of those who
dispossessed them.

18 The house of Jacob shall be a fire,
the house of Joseph a flame,
and the house of Esau stubble;
they shall burn them and consume
them,
and there shall be no survivor of the
house of Esau;
for the LORD has spoken.

19 Those of the Negeb shall possess Mount
Esau,
and those of the Shephelah the land of
the Philistines;
they shall possess the land of Ephraim
and the land of Samaria,
and Benjamin shall possess Gilead.

20 The exiles of the Israelites who are in
Halah[e]
shall possess[f] Phoenicia as far as
Zarephath;

---

a Heb *But do not gloat* (and similarly through verse 14)
b Heb *on the day of* c Heb *his* d Meaning of Heb uncertain
e Cn: Heb *in this army* f Cn: Meaning of Heb uncertain

---

no understanding of it, better "there is no understanding in it." **9** *Teman*, another important city in Edom (cf. Jer 49.7, 20; Ezek 25.13; Am 1.12), here a synecdoche standing for the whole country. **10–13** *The day* refers to the fall of Jerusalem in 587/6 BCE. 2 Kings 24.20–25.21 and 2 Chr 36.11–21 give accounts of the event, its causes, and aftermath. Edomites are not mentioned in either, but cf. Ps 137.7; Lam 4.21–22; Ezek 35.12–14. Notice the association of Edom with Babylon in Ps 137.7–8. **15–16** *The day of the LORD*, a common term in the prophets indicating not a twenty-four-hour period but a promised time when the Lord will finally display an awesome power, whether for punishment or reward. Here the day is characterized by requital against the nations, as their wrongful deeds will be turned back on them. The *day* is close and its coming certain, but the time of its fulfillment is not stipulated. **16–17** The motif of reversal

is emphasized and culminates with the *house of Jacob* taking *possession of those who dispossessed them.* **17** *Mount Zion . . . holy.* The mount shall be holy. The term *Mount Zion* is picked up again in v. 21, where it is explicitly contrasted with *Mount Esau. Those that escape* (cf. Joel 2.32; Ezra 9.8, 13, 15). The Hebrew word may be translated "remnant," as it is by the NRSV in Ezra. The notion of a remnant looms large in prophetic texts; cf. Am 3.12; 5.3; 6.9; 9.1; Isa 7.3; 10.20–22; Zeph 3.12–13. **20** *Halah*, an emendation of the Hebrew text (see text note *e*), refers to a place of uncertain location in northern Mesopotamia to which Israelites had been exiled by the Assyrians (see 2 Kings 17.6; 18.11). *Phoenicia*, lit. "the Canaanites." *Zarephath*, a coastal town in southern Phoenicia. *Sepharad*, not the medieval word for Spain or for the Sephardic branch of Judaism, but a place where, according to the text but not found elsewhere, the people from

and the exiles of Jerusalem who are in
　　Sepharad
　　shall possess the towns of the Negeb.
21　Those who have been saved[a] shall go up
　　　to Mount Zion

_____

a Or *Saviors*

Jerusalem were exiled. Some identify it with the city of
Sardis in Asia Minor. **21** *Those who have been saved,* a
proposed emendation of the Hebrew text (see text
note *a*). The Hebrew reads, "Saviors shall go up to
Mount Zion to judge (rule?) Mount Esau." *The king-*

to rule Mount Esau;
and the kingdom shall be the LORD's.

dom (or "kingship") *shall be the LORD's,* an emphatic
statement of hope for a community that, through its
reading of or listening to the text, vicariously experiences the suffering of its ancestors at the time of the
fall of Jerusalem.

JONAH

THE JONAH STORY is quite different from all the other prophetic books, whose primary focus is on Israel and Judah. Although those prophets had only minimal success, their books are filled with oracles passionately urging the people to observe Israel's covenant obligations to God. Jonah, on the other hand, is the story of a prophet sent to the Assyrians in Nineveh—a people whose brutal actions had made their name a byword among the people of Israel (cf. Nahum). Unable to resist God's commission, Jonah delivered a one-verse oracle (3.4) and succeeded marvelously, despite his best efforts to run away and fail. The story is a satire, giving us a hero who says the right things in a context in which his actions belie his words (1.9; 2.2–9; 4.2). The result is a unique piece of prophetic literature with universal appeal.

Setting and Purpose

SATIRE ENTERTAINS, but it also has a polemical purpose, addressing major issues faced by the writer's contemporaries. Because of its language and allusive style, most scholars date this work to the postexilic period (after 539 BCE). This was a time of great trauma but also of regeneration within the Jewish community. Diaspora Jews, scattered among gentile populations throughout the Middle East and beyond, faced a new array of pressures as they were forced to rethink earlier traditions within vastly different historical and cultural contexts. If we keep in mind the book's likely postexilic background, several different interpretations of Jonah present themselves. Since during the fifth century BCE many Jews felt they could remain holy only by strict separation from gentile culture, some scholars interpret the story's appeal for a universal God as a satire. Jonah is a xenophobic Jew who understands the Lord as a supreme national god, a god who should stand with his people against his and their gentile enemies. He should save Israel by bringing judgment on Nineveh. Another view points to the earlier prophets, who had envisioned a new age of peace and justice in which the Lord would rule over the nations from Zion through the line of David, and the fact that their oracles had not been realized. This view says the issue is the failure of the prophetic word, both in postexilic times and in this story. Jonah's anger that the word God had given him to speak did not come to pass made the prophet feel foolish and inconsequential. A third interpretation considers the justice of God. To Jews living in the Diaspora the gentile lifestyle was more abhorrent than theirs had ever been, yet Nineveh, the ultimate sinful city, was spared and Israel was destroyed. More than a century later proud Babylon would destroy Jerusalem. Why did God not bring judgment on Gentiles as well? Is the Lord really a just god?

This Introduction holds with those scholars who argue that the central issue in the book of Jonah is God's justice and mercy. Why does Jonah not want to let the Ninevites hear God's word of doom, thus giving them an outside chance to change? Jonah wants God to make them like Sodom and Gomorrah because Nineveh has been the archetypal wicked city for generations, not because it is a gentile city. This is Jonah's challenge to God in ch. 4. Should one all-out repentance ceremony that includes sincere adults along with innocent children and animals warrant God's "changing his mind" concerning the judgment planned for the city (3.10)? This is not justice, thinks Jonah; this is divine caprice. There is something beyond repentance and covenant justice, however, that Jonah and readers must learn. God speaks of "pity" for a world he has created—a world that is full of ignorant humans and animals—leaving Jonah with a question about the role of divine mercy within the created order. Yet the God who judges "to the third and the fourth generation" lurks in the background (Ex 34.7). The earliest readers of Jonah knew that Nineveh (612 BCE) and Jerusalem (587 BCE) had both been destroyed. In this story we encounter a God who is indeed concerned about social injustice, but who, in the mystery of God's ways, permits the sovereignty of the divine heart to overrule the requirements of divine justice. By challenging Jonah (and the community of the writer's contemporaries) to emulate the idealized Ninevites by repentance and reform, God (and the writer) reminds readers of the strong biblical tradition of divine compassion that will welcome and bless the day when the original community of readers is itself thus overthrown (i.e., transformed; see note on 3.4–5). [JAMES S. ACKERMAN]

Jonah Tries to Run Away from God

1 Now the word of the LORD came to Jonah son of Amittai, saying, 2 "Go at once to Nineveh, that great city, and cry out against it; for their wickedness has come up before me." 3 But Jonah set out to flee to Tarshish from the presence of the LORD. He went down to Joppa and found a ship going to Tarshish; so he paid his fare and went on board, to go with them to Tarshish, away from the presence of the LORD.

4 But the LORD hurled a great wind upon the sea, and such a mighty storm came upon the sea that the ship threatened to break up.

5 Then the mariners were afraid, and each cried to his god. They threw the cargo that was in the ship into the sea, to lighten it for them. Jonah, meanwhile, had gone down into the hold of the ship and had lain down, and was fast asleep. 6 The captain came and said to him, "What are you doing sound asleep? Get up, call on your god! Perhaps the god will spare us a thought so that we do not perish."

7 The sailors[a] said to one another, "Come, let us cast lots, so that we may know on whose account this calamity has come upon us." So they cast lots, and the lot fell on Jonah. 8 Then

_____
a Heb *They*

1.1–16 Jonah's call and flight. **1.1** In 2 Kings 14.25 we learn that *Jonah son of Amittai* from Gath-hepher was a court prophet who told Jeroboam II (786–746 BCE) that God would extend his reign in the Northern Kingdom (Israel) from the Dead Sea to the entrance of Hamath in Syria (see Num 34.7–9). **1.2** *Nineveh,* a major city in Assyria, the nation to the east that conquered the Northern Kingdom in 722 BCE. Although many biblical prophets gave oracles against foreign nations, only Elisha (and the Jonah of this story) journeyed from Israel to another land to deliver a message from God (2 Kings 8.7–15). **1.3** *Tarshish,* a western seaport possibly to be identified with Tartessus in Spain—on the outer edge of the then known world. Many biblical prophets resisted their initial call from God (e.g., Ex 3.11; 4.10–17; Jer 1.6). Jonah resists even more strenuously, moving in a direction exactly opposite to the one commanded by God. His flight from *the presence of the LORD* is described as a series of descents, down from his village and down into the Tarshish-bound ship. Later in the story he will descend even deeper! **1.7** See Josh 7.16–18; 1 Sam

they said to him, "Tell us why this calamity has come upon us. What is your occupation? Where do you come from? What is your country? And of what people are you?" 9 "I am a Hebrew," he replied. "I worship the LORD, the God of heaven, who made the sea and the dry land." 10 Then the men were even more afraid, and said to him, "What is this that you have done!" For the men knew that he was fleeing from the presence of the LORD, because he had told them so.

11 Then they said to him, "What shall we do to you, that the sea may quiet down for us?" For the sea was growing more and more tempestuous. 12 He said to them, "Pick me up and throw me into the sea; then the sea will quiet down for you; for I know it is because of me that this great storm has come upon you." 13 Nevertheless the men rowed hard to bring the ship back to land, but they could not, for the sea grew more and more stormy against them. 14 Then they cried out to the LORD, "Please, O LORD, we pray, do not let us perish on account of this man's life. Do not make us guilty of innocent blood; for you, O LORD, have done as it pleased you." 15 So they picked Jonah up and threw him into the sea; and the sea ceased from its raging. 16 Then the men feared the LORD even more, and they offered a sacrifice to the LORD and made vows.

17 *a* But the LORD provided a large fish to swallow up Jonah; and Jonah was in the belly of the fish three days and three nights.

A Psalm of Thanksgiving

2 Then Jonah prayed to the LORD his God from the belly of the fish, 2 saying,
"I called to the LORD out of my distress,
    and he answered me;
out of the belly of Sheol I cried,
    and you heard my voice.
3 You cast me into the deep,
    into the heart of the seas,
    and the flood surrounded me;
all your waves and your billows
    passed over me.
4 Then I said, 'I am driven away
    from your sight;
how *b* shall I look again
    upon your holy temple?'
5 The waters closed in over me;
    the deep surrounded me;
weeds were wrapped around my head
6   at the roots of the mountains.
I went down to the land
    whose bars closed upon me forever;
yet you brought up my life from the Pit,
    O LORD my God.
7 As my life was ebbing away,
    I remembered the LORD;
and my prayer came to you,
    into your holy temple.
8 Those who worship vain idols
    forsake their true loyalty.
9 But I with the voice of thanksgiving

a Ch 2.1 in Heb   *b* Theodotion: Heb *surely*

14.40–42. **1.9** Jonah's pious confession of faith in God as creator of *the sea and the dry land* underscores the futility of his attempt to escape from God's presence. **1.15** The Lord *hurled* the great wind (v. 4), which prompted first the hurling overboard of the ship's cargo (v. 5) and then finally the hurling (the same word is used in Hebrew) of Jonah. **1.16** The sailors have changed from fearing the storm and crying to their gods (v. 5) to crying to (v. 14) and fearing the Lord.

1.17–2.10 God judges and delivers Jonah by means of a fish. **1.17** The Hebrew verb translated *to swallow up* always has a negative meaning in the Bible (Ex 15.12; Num 16.30–33). To readers the fish may appear as an instrument of divine judgment taking the prophet down to Sheol, but Jonah's prayer, if taken literally and sequentially, seems to indicate that the prophet had already gone down to the city of death and been rescued there by the fish. *Three days and three nights* is the traditional time for travel to or from the underworld. **2.1** Since the Hebrew verb translated *prayed* always refers to asking for help not yet rendered, many scholars conclude that Jonah's song of thanksgiving in vv. 2–9 was added by a later writer or editor. If the song is read as an integral part of the story, however, we again find Jonah saying words that do not accord with the action (cf. 1.9). It is thus possible to read the prayer ironically as false piety, since Jonah is eager to return to the temple even though he has not repented for having disobeyed God's command. **2.3–6** Other biblical texts depict the underworld as a walled city located under the waters and below the mountains that were thought to support the cosmos (see Job 38.16–17; Pss 9.13–14; 107.18). This city is the antipole of Zion and its temple as well as of God's temple in the heavens. **2.6** City gates were secured with *bars* in the ancient world (Deut 3.5; Judg 16.3; Nah 3.13). **2.8–9** Jonah perceives pagans as forsakers of *true loyalty* (Hebrew *chesed*) and vows to make a proper *sacrifice* when he returns, while the gentile sailors in the ship above him have already completed their sacrificial vows to the Lord (1.16).

will sacrifice to you;
what I have vowed I will pay.
Deliverance belongs to the LORD!"
10 Then the LORD spoke to the fish, and it spewed Jonah out upon the dry land.

Conversion of Nineveh

3 The word of the LORD came to Jonah a second time, saying, 2 "Get up, go to Nineveh, that great city, and proclaim to it the message that I tell you." 3 So Jonah set out and went to Nineveh, according to the word of the LORD. Now Nineveh was an exceedingly large city, a three days' walk across. 4 Jonah began to go into the city, going a day's walk. And he cried out, "Forty days more, and Nineveh shall be overthrown!" 5 And the people of Nineveh believed God; they proclaimed a fast, and everyone, great and small, put on sackcloth.

6 When the news reached the king of Nineveh, he rose from his throne, removed his robe, covered himself with sackcloth, and sat in ashes. 7 Then he had a proclamation made in Nineveh: "By the decree of the king and his nobles: No human being or animal, no herd or flock, shall taste anything. They shall not feed, nor shall they drink water. 8 Human beings and animals shall be covered with sackcloth, and they shall cry mightily to God. All shall turn from their evil ways and from the violence that is in their hands. 9 Who knows? God may relent and change his mind; he may turn from his fierce anger, so that we do not perish."

10 When God saw what they did, how they turned from their evil ways, God changed his mind about the calamity that he had said he would bring upon them; and he did not do it.

Jonah's Anger

4 But this was very displeasing to Jonah, and he became angry. 2 He prayed to the LORD and said, "O LORD! Is not this what I said while I was still in my own country? That is why I fled to Tarshish at the beginning; for I knew that you are a gracious God and merciful, slow to anger, and abounding in steadfast love, and ready to relent from punishing. 3 And now, O LORD, please take my life from me, for it is better for me to die than to live." 4 And the LORD said, "Is it right for you to be angry?" 5 Then Jonah went out of the city and sat down east of the city, and made a booth for himself there. He sat under it in the shade, waiting to see what would become of the city.

6 The LORD God appointed a bush,[a] and made it come up over Jonah, to give shade over his head, to save him from his discomfort; so Jonah was very happy about the bush. 7 But when dawn came up the next day, God appointed a worm that attacked the bush, so that it withered. 8 When the sun rose, God prepared a sultry east wind, and the sun beat down on the head of Jonah so that he was faint

---

a Heb qiqayon, possibly the castor bean plant

2.10 God's response to Jonah's song is to have the fish spew Jonah out; a better translation would be "vomit" (see Lev 18.28; Prov 23.8; Jer 25.27).
3.1–10 A second group of Gentiles turns to God; here the king and Ninevites replace the captain and sailors of ch. 1. Jonah's great success with the king in Nineveh should be contrasted with the prophets' repeated failure with kings in Jerusalem (e.g., Jer 36.9–32). 3.3 An exceedingly large city, in Hebrew lit. "a great city to God," thus contrasting it with the city of death that Jonah had almost entered during the fish episode (2.3–6). The three days it takes to traverse Nineveh recalls Jonah's three days in the belly of the fish (1.17). 3.4–5 Overthrown renders the same Hebrew verb that describes the overturning of Sodom and Gomorrah (Gen 19.21, 25, 29), but Jonah here uses the passive-reflexive voice, which can mean "turned around" or "transformed" (Ex 7.17, 20; 1 Sam 10.6). 3.6 Covered... with sackcloth, sat in ashes, traditional acts of repentance in response to personal and national crises; see Job 42.6; Dan 9.3; Neh 9.1. 3.10 Changed his mind. See Ex 32.14; Jer 18.8, 10; Am 7.3, 6; cf. Num 23.19; 1 Sam 15.29.

4.1–11 Ch. 4 juxtaposes Jonah's response to the sparing of Nineveh with God's reason for that action. 4.2 Citing part of God's self-description before Moses on Mount Sinai (Ex 34.6–7), Jonah accuses God of having too much steadfast love (Hebrew chesed; cf. note on 2.8–9). Readers will note, however, that Jonah skips the ending of 34.7 about God "by no means clearing the guilty . . . to the third and the fourth generation." 4.3 Returning to the death/descent theme of chs. 1–2, the prophet prefers death to living in a world with no recognizable order of justice. 4.5 Certain that Nineveh will return to its evil ways, Jonah finds solace in a secure shelter (booth, Hebrew sukkah) that he builds for himself. 4.6–7 Reinforcing the shelter theme, God appoints a bush to save Jonah (cf. 1 Kings 19.4–18) and then destroys it to bring the prophet to his senses. 4.8–9 The scorching wind (Hebrew ruach) playfully recalls the divine spirit (ruach) that traditionally inspired the prophets (Num 11.24–29; 2 Kings 2.9, 15). Jonah's reaction to the loss of the protective bush is the same as his reaction to the sparing of Nineveh (v. 3). Back then he was angry at God's mercy; now he misses God's pro-

and asked that he might die. He said, "It is better for me to die than to live."

Jonah Is Reproved

9 But God said to Jonah, "Is it right for you to be angry about the bush?" And he said, "Yes, angry enough to die." 10Then the LORD said, "You are concerned about the bush, for which you did not labor and which you did not grow; it came into being in a night and perished in a night. 11And should I not be concerned about Nineveh, that great city, in which there are more than a hundred and twenty thousand persons who do not know their right hand from their left, and also many animals?"

---

tective care. **4.10–11** In vv. 2–3 Jonah confronted God with thirty-nine words (in Hebrew) of complaint. Here God gets the last thirty-nine words. The Lord emphasizes his sovereignty over and care for the whole creation rather than Nineveh's repentance. The bush *perished* in a night; both the sea captain and the king were desperate to keep their people from perishing (1.6; 3.9). God, we learn, is attentive to their concern. **4.11** The Jonah of 2 Kings had prophesied the expansion of the Northern Kingdom's borders even though its king had done wrong in God's eyes. The writer continues, "For the LORD saw that the distress of Israel was very bitter; there was no one left, bond or free, and no one to help Israel" (14.26). The Lord's pity on Israel's helplessness elicited divine intervention despite the king's wickedness. Could the writer of this story have selected Jonah as (anti-) hero in order to develop his theme of God's merciful care for the helpless of the earth?

MICAH

The Prophet

VERY LITTLE IS KNOWN about Micah, whose name, which means "Who is like the LORD?" was common in ancient Israel. The prophet is distinguished from his namesakes by being identified with his hometown Moresheth, a pastoral village that was most likely a military and administrative outpost of Jerusalem. Together with Amos, Isaiah, and Hosea, Micah was one of Israel's four great eighth-century BCE prophets. His rural roots in the Southern Kingdom, Judah, enabled him to understand how the overbearing policies of the political, social, and religious leaders of his time affected the peasant class. A prophet more of the marketplace and town square than the temple or its sanctuary, Micah addressed injustice with passion and poetic eloquence.

Historical Situation

THE SUPERSCRIPTION (1.1) SUGGESTS that Micah prophesied during the reigns of three Judahite kings: Jotham (742–735), Ahaz (735–715), and Hezekiah (715–687/6 BCE). More precisely, Micah's prophetic career probably spanned the last quarter of the eighth century during the reigns of Ahaz and Hezekiah.

A vigorous ruler, Hezekiah initiated several religious reforms. He took many precautions to safeguard Judah against the threat of an Assyrian invasion, including forming a coalition with Phoenicia and Philistia against Sennacherib, Assyria's king, the successor of Sargon II. Under Hezekiah, Judah experienced an economic revolution. Wealth, invested in the land, led to the growth of vast estates and the collapse of small holdings. Wealthy landowners thrived at the expense of small peasant farmers. The shift from a bartering to a monetary, mercantile economy increased the gap between the rich and the poor. Furthermore, many priests and prophets viewed their ministry as a business rather than a vocation and acted accordingly. Thus, Micah preached during a time when Judah was experiencing radical internal change while living under the threat of a foreign military invasion.

International Setting

IN 732 ASSYRIAN ARMIES under Tiglath-pileser III conquered Damascus along with part of Israel, and in 722 they besieged Samaria, Israel's capital. The Philistine city Ashdod fell in 711. Under Ahaz, Judah became a vassal state of the Assyrian Empire. Under Hezekiah, Judah entered into a coalition with Phoenicia and Philistia (Ashkelon and Ekron) against Sennacherib. When Sennacherib attacked the Southern Kingdom in 701, forty-six fortified towns fell. Although Jerusalem was left unharmed, Judah remained a dominated land and a captive people.

Structure

THE BOOK OF MICAH IS, for the most part, well preserved. Scholars generally accept chs. 1–3, apart from 2.12–13, as authentic. The remainder of the book appears to be a compilation of later additions, though 6.1–7.6 may also be authentic. Scholars are divided over the general structure of the book, but the proclamations form an overarching thematic scheme: judgment (1.1–2.11), salvation (2.12–13), judgment (3.1–12), salvation (4.1–5.15), judgment (6.1–16), lament (7.1–7), and hope and confidence (7.8–20). The historical circumstances of Micah's proclamations invite further study.

The Message

MICAH UNDERSTOOD HIS TASK to be a preacher of truth—to expose injustice and inequity, to offer a word of hope and salvation, and to make known a vision of a new and transformed way of life for his community and his world. Deeply concerned with ethical issues, Micah railed against the political and religious leaders of his day because they had abandoned their divinely ordained responsibility of exercising and maintaining justice throughout the land. The common good was being usurped by personal self-interest on the part of Judean law courts, large landowners, and merchants. Micah's biting proclamations made clear God's disdain for apostasy, idolatry, hypocrisy, and disregard for Torah. He condemned the break in covenant relationship that led to grave injustices and much suffering. Micah warned leaders about their self-reliant attitudes and smug spiritual pride. He foresaw the Assyrian invasion; he made known the devastation that an empire greater than Israel and Judah would bring on the community. His words were not heeded, and the inevitable invasion did occur, leaving many cities in ruins.

Doom, however, was not Micah's overriding message. In the midst of a long judgment speech (chs. 1–3) is a word of hope (2.12–13); this theme continues throughout chs. 4–5 and 6–7. The book ends with an expression of confidence in God, who is merciful and who will exercise justice for the sake of the salvation of all peoples. Micah makes known to his people, and to later readers of the text, that God is indeed a God of righteousness whose compassion outweighs justice and whose love for all remains steadfast. [PHILIP J. KING, revised by CAROL J. DEMPSEY]

1 The word of the LORD that came to Micah of Moresheth in the days of Kings Jotham, Ahaz, and Hezekiah of Judah, which he saw concerning Samaria and Jerusalem.

Judgment Pronounced against Samaria

2 Hear, you peoples, all of you;
    listen, O earth, and all that is in it;
  and let the Lord GOD be a witness against
      you,
    the Lord from his holy temple.
3 For lo, the LORD is coming out of his
      place,
  and will come down and tread upon
      the high places of the earth.
4 Then the mountains will melt under him
    and the valleys will burst open,

like wax near the fire,
    like waters poured down a steep place.
5 All this is for the transgression of Jacob
    and for the sins of the house of Israel.
  What is the transgression of Jacob?
    Is it not Samaria?
  And what is the high place *a* of Judah?
    Is it not Jerusalem?
6 Therefore I will make Samaria a heap in
      the open country,
    a place for planting vineyards.
  I will pour down her stones into the
      valley,
    and uncover her foundations.
7 All her images shall be beaten to pieces,

_____
a Heb *what are the high places*

1.1 Superscription. This editorial convention, written later than the time of Micah, provides information about the prophet, the period of his activity, the mode of divine revelation, and the subject matter of the prophecy. It is similar to the titles of the three other eighth-century BCE prophetic books and suggests a common editorial policy and possibly the same editorial pen. *The word of the LORD*, a phrase used repeatedly in the OT to denote a personal utterance of God, lending authority to the prophet's words. This phrase stands in the same position in Hos 1.1; Joel 1.1; Zeph 1.1 and appears at a later point in Jer 1.2; Ezek 1.3; Hag 1.1; Zech 1.1; Mal 1.1. *Came* indicates that the prophetic word comes to the prophet as a gift. It is not something a prophet can attain through personal effort, nor is it at the disposal of a prophet. *Micah* means "Who is like Yahweh?" The name exists in several forms and was borne by several persons in the Bible. *Moresheth*, or Moresheth-gath (v. 14), Micah's place of origin, by which he is identified (cf. mention of Hosea's father, Hos. 1.1). Moresheth was a small village of uncertain location, but it may have been on the road linking Azekah and Lachish. The site is generally identified with the modern village Tell-el-Judeideh, two kilometers north of Eleutheropolis, ten kilometers from Lachish, and twenty-five miles southwest of Jerusalem. If this is correct, then the village was strategically situated on the vital north-south route that skirts the mountain country of Samaria and Judah through the Shephelah, linking the valley of Aijalon with Lachish. *Jotham, Ahaz, and Hezekiah*, three kings of Judah, indicating the time of Micah's ministry (see Introduction). *Samaria and Jerusalem*, the capital cities of the Northern Kingdom, Israel, and the Southern Kingdom, Judah, respectively. Micah's attention is focused on the cities but extends to Israel as a whole. King Omri (ca. 876–869 BCE) established *Samaria* as the capital of Israel. The region where Samaria was located was fertile, and the city itself was easily defensible since it was situated on a hill about three hundred feet above the valley. It was also close to trade routes.

Jerusalem, about forty miles south of Samaria, became the religious and political capital of Judah after David (ca. 1000–970 BCE) captured it from the Jebusites. The Jerusalem of David, known as the City of David, occupied only the southeast section of present-day Jerusalem. **1.2–7** Judgment speech attesting to the power and sovereignty of God. Micah calls listeners and readers to attention (v. 2), describes God's impending coming and its effects (vv. 3–4), states God's accusation against Israel (v. 5), and proclaims God's forthcoming chastisement upon Samaria (vv. 6–7). **1.2** *Listen . . . in it*, a statement of direct address whereby Micah calls all earthly creation to be attentive to his proclamation. *Let the Lord . . . against you*, a common petition in the OT. God is often called upon to act as a witness (Gen 31.50; 1 Sam 12.5; Jer 42.5). Here Micah calls on God to be a witness among the earth's inhabitants. *Holy temple*, God's heavenly dwelling place (Ps 11.4). **1.3–4** An impending theophany—a manifestation of God—depicted in poetic language. Here the theophany highlights the transcendent nature of God, who is perceived as being beyond the created world. **1.3** *High places*, artificially constructed elevations (Jer 48.35) serving as shrines, found particularly in Samaria (1 Kings 13.32; 2 Kings 19.9–11; 23.19). Associated with apostasy (2 Kings 23.5–9), they incited God's wrath (Lev 26.30; 2 Kings 17.7–23; Ps 78.58). Here the *high places of the earth* refers not only to shrines where illicit religious rites were practiced, but also to Jerusalem and, by implication, to Samaria (cf. v. 5). The illicit religious rites were associated with Canaanite religious practice as well as popular Israelite religion. Only from the eighth century on were the high places condemned. **1.5** Micah refers to *Jacob* eleven times. The first use here, in synonymous parallelism with *Israel*, refers to all of Israel, both the Northern and Southern Kingdoms; the second use, in synonymous parallelism with *Samaria*, refers to the Northern Kingdom, contrasting with the parallelism of *Judah/Jerusalem* at the end of the verse. **1.7** A polemic

all her wages shall be burned with fire,
and all her idols I will lay waste;
for as the wages of a prostitute she
gathered them,
and as the wages of a prostitute they
shall again be used.

The Doom of the Cities of Judah

8 For this I will lament and wail;
I will go barefoot and naked;
I will make lamentation like the jackals,
and mourning like the ostriches.
9 For her wound*a* is incurable.
It has come to Judah;
it has reached to the gate of my people,
to Jerusalem.

10 Tell it not in Gath,
weep not at all;
in Beth-leaphrah
roll yourselves in the dust.
11 Pass on your way,
inhabitants of Shaphir,
in nakedness and shame;

the inhabitants of Zaanan
do not come forth;
Beth-ezel is wailing
and shall remove its support from you.
12 For the inhabitants of Maroth
wait anxiously for good,
yet disaster has come down from the
LORD
to the gate of Jerusalem.
13 Harness the steeds to the chariots,
inhabitants of Lachish;
it was the beginning of sin
to daughter Zion,
for in you were found
the transgressions of Israel.
14 Therefore you shall give parting gifts
to Moresheth-gath;
the houses of Achzib shall be a deception
to the kings of Israel.
15 I will again bring a conqueror upon you,
inhabitants of Mareshah;
the glory of Israel

----

a Gk Syr Vg: Heb *wounds*

against idolatry. Idolatrous worship is described as harlotry or prostitution. Sacred prostitution was sometimes practiced at religious shrines called high places (see note on 1.3). **1.8–16** Composed of three subunits (vv. 8–9, 10–15, 16), this unit is a dirge-lament, i.e., a mourning song sung over one envisaged as already dead. For this form, see also Isa 32.9–15; Ezek 26.15–18; 32.19–32; Am 5.1–3. **1.8** *For this*, a pivotal phrase that links vv. 2–7 with vv. 8–16. *Barefoot and naked* signifies mourning (cf. Isa 20.2–4; Ezek 24.17–23). Nakedness also functions symbolically insofar as it is associated with sin (cf. Gen 3.10; 9.20–23). Micah's nakedness is a prophetic statement to and about his community—it is guilty of sin. *Jackals*, scavengers with a distinctive wailing howl that often prowl around ruins and desertlike areas. *Ostriches* are also often associated with desertlike or uninhabited areas (Job 30.29; Isa 13.21; 43.20; Jer 50.39). **1.10–15** Micah's dirge-lament. Resembling the form of a funeral song for one who has already died, this block of material is rich in wordplays and puns on place-names. The historical setting is most likely the Assyrian invasion by Sennacherib in 701 BCE. All the towns mentioned in this section are situated in Judah, southwest of Jerusalem, the region of the country best known to Micah. Except for those of Beth-leaphrah, Shaphir, Zaanan, and Maroth, their locations have been identified in the Shephelah, the lowlands or valley region. **1.10** *Gath*, one of the five Philistine cities, has not been identified with certainty, but it probably is located at Tell es-Safi (Tel Zafit), twelve miles east of the Philistine city of Ashdod. Gath was one of the places to which the ark of the covenant was taken by the Philis-

tines (1 Sam 5.8); it was also connected with David (1 Sam 27; 1 Chr 18.1). *Beth-leaphrah*, Hebrew "house of dust," may be identified with et-Taiyibeh, northwest of Hebron in the hill country of Judah. Rolling in the dust (*'aphar*) was a way of expressing grief or mourning. *Roll yourselves* (*hitpallashti*) may be a pun on "Philistines." **1.11** *Shaphir* means "beautiful"; by calling the inhabitants of the "Beautiful City" to roll themselves in nakedness and shame, Micah reverses the image of the city. Shaphir may be located at Khirbet el-Qom, a hill west of Hebron. The sound of the name *Zaanan* suggests the Hebrew word "going out," which, ironically, the city is said not to do, contradicting its own name. *Beth-ezel* may be modern Deir el-Asal, in the vicinity of Hebron. **1.12** The site of *Maroth* has not been identified, but the wordplay consists in the sharp contrast between Maroth, meaning "to be bitter," and the adjective *good*. **1.13** *Lachish*, situated thirty miles southwest of Jerusalem in the Judean hills, the most important city in Judah after Jerusalem. In the reign of Hezekiah two massive city walls fortified Lachish. Stratum III of Lachish, dating to 701 BCE, is an indisputable witness to Sennacherib's devastation of the city. Micah reproaches the people of Lachish for relying on horses and chariots. The wordplay is on the name Lachish and the phrase (to) *the steeds* (Hebrew *larekesh*). *Daughter Zion* personifies Jerusalem. **1.14** *Achzib*, tentatively identified with Tell el-Beida, northeast of Lachish. The pun focuses on the Hebrew root *kzb* ("to lie"), found both in the name Achzib and *deception* (*'akzab*). **1.15** *Mareshah*, modern Tell Sandahanna, one mile southeast of Beit Jibrin (Eleutheropolis). Famous as an underground city because of its caves, it is known in Greek as

shall come to Adullam.

16 Make yourselves bald and cut off your hair
        for your pampered children;
    make yourselves as bald as the eagle,
        for they have gone from you into exile.

Social Evils Denounced

2 Alas for those who devise wickedness
        and evil deeds[a] on their beds!
    When the morning dawns, they perform it,
        because it is in their power.
2 They covet fields, and seize them;
        houses, and take them away;
    they oppress householder and house,
        people and their inheritance.
3 Therefore thus says the LORD:
    Now, I am devising against this family an
        evil
        from which you cannot remove your
            necks;
    and you shall not walk haughtily,
        for it will be an evil time.
4 On that day they shall take up a taunt
            song against you,
        and wail with bitter lamentation,
    and say, "We are utterly ruined;
        the LORD[b] alters the inheritance of my
            people;
    how he removes it from me!
        Among our captors[c] he parcels out our
            fields."
5 Therefore you will have no one to cast the
            line by lot
        in the assembly of the LORD.

6 "Do not preach"—thus they preach—
        "one should not preach of such things;
        disgrace will not overtake us."
7 Should this be said, O house of Jacob?
        Is the LORD's patience exhausted?
        Are these his doings?
    Do not my words do good
        to one who walks uprightly?
8 But you rise up against my people[d] as an
            enemy;
        you strip the robe from the peaceful,[e]
    from those who pass by trustingly
        with no thought of war.
9 The women of my people you drive out
        from their pleasant houses;
    from their young children you take away
        my glory forever.
10 Arise and go;
        for this is no place to rest,
    because of uncleanness that destroys
        with a grievous destruction.[f]
11 If someone were to go about uttering
            empty falsehoods,
        saying, "I will preach to you of wine
            and strong drink,"
    such a one would be the preacher for
        this people!

A Promise for the Remnant of Israel

12 I will surely gather all of you, O Jacob,
        I will gather the survivors of Israel;

---

a Cn: Heb work evil   b Heb he   c Cn: Heb the rebellious
d Cn: Heb But yesterday my people rose   e Cn: Heb from before
a garment   f Meaning of Heb uncertain

Marisa (1 Macc 5.66; 2 Macc 12.35). The play is on the name Mareshah and the Hebrew participle *yoresh*, "to possess," although not obvious in the translation *conqueror*. Mareshah belonged to the tribe of Judah (Josh 15.44), was settled by Calebites (1 Chr 2.42), and was fortified by Rehoboam (2 Chr 11.5–10). *Adullam* may be located at Tell Khirbet esh-Sheikh Madkur, five miles south of Beth-shemesh. It was a fortress town (2 Chr 11.7). David took refuge from Saul in a cave near Adullam (1 Sam 22.1; 2 Sam 23.13). It was also the hometown of Judah's friend Hirah (Gen 38.12). **1.16** The lament concludes with a description of mourning rites. Although artificial baldness was prohibited (Lev 19.27; Deut 14.1), shaving the head was sometimes practiced as a sign of mourning.

2.1–5 Woe proclamation announcing doom upon those Israelites who plan and carry out injustices (vv. 1–2) and presenting God's response to the situation (vv. 3–5). The focus is on land monopoly by the greedy rich at the expense of the defenseless poor. **2.2** *Inheritance*, land belonging to God and given to Is-

rael as a gift, which Israel is commanded to respect. To lose one's *inheritance* was to lose one's independence. **2.3** *Against this family*. Referent uncertain, perhaps Judah or the whole of Israel. The metaphor of a yoked ox describes the punishment for expropriation of land. **2.4** A mocking song that predicts disaster. **2.5** Those guilty of covetousness and amassing property not their own are destined to lose everything. *Assembly of the LORD*, the religious community of Israel. **2.6–11** Disputation prophecy addressed to all of Israel. Here Micah quotes God, who quotes some members within the community (vv. 6, 11). **2.8** The *enemy* who rises up against the Israelites is, ironically, from their own household. **2.10** *Arise and go*, a double command spoken by God through Micah that makes a clear ethical point: just as the oppressors drove out others (v. 9), so they too are driven out. Expulsion from the land foreshadows the Assyrian invasion and resultant exile. **2.11** God, through Micah, states sarcastically that the people would prefer corrupt prophets to those who tell the truth. **2.12–13** Salvation procla-

I will set them together
  like sheep in a fold,
like a flock in its pasture;
  it will resound with people.
13 The one who breaks out will go up before
    them;
  they will break through and pass the
    gate,
  going out by it.
Their king will pass on before them,
  the LORD at their head.

Wicked Rulers and Prophets

3 And I said:
  Listen, you heads of Jacob
    and rulers of the house of Israel!
  Should you not know justice?—
2   you who hate the good and love the
      evil,
  who tear the skin off my people,[a]
    and the flesh off their bones;
3 who eat the flesh of my people,
    flay their skin off them,
  break their bones in pieces,
    and chop them up like meat[b] in a kettle,
    like flesh in a caldron.

4 Then they will cry to the LORD,
    but he will not answer them;
  he will hide his face from them at that
    time,
  because they have acted wickedly.

5 Thus says the LORD concerning the
    prophets

who lead my people astray,
who cry "Peace"
  when they have something to eat,
but declare war against those
  who put nothing into their mouths.
6 Therefore it shall be night to you, without
    vision,
  and darkness to you, without
    revelation.
The sun shall go down upon the
    prophets,
  and the day shall be black over them;
7 the seers shall be disgraced,
    and the diviners put to shame;
  they shall all cover their lips,
    for there is no answer from God.
8 But as for me, I am filled with power,
    with the spirit of the LORD,
    and with justice and might,
  to declare to Jacob his transgression
    and to Israel his sin.

9 Hear this, you rulers of the house of
    Jacob
    and chiefs of the house of Israel,
  who abhor justice
    and pervert all equity,
10 who build Zion with blood
    and Jerusalem with wrong!
11 Its rulers give judgment for a bribe,
    its priests teach for a price,
    its prophets give oracles for money;
  yet they lean upon the LORD and say,

---

a Heb *from them* b Gk: Heb *as*

---

mation dated to the Babylonian exile (587–539 BCE) by some and claimed as authentic material from Micah by others. The Lord who is shepherd-king speaks (Jer 23.1–4; Ezek 34). The promised restoration is described in terms of a new exodus (Isa 49.9–12). **2.12** *Survivors,* those who will be redeemed.

3.1–12 A prophetic judgment speech presenting a gruesome picture of Israel's social injustice and political and religious decay, along with an insight into the character and mission of the prophet (v. 8). It is composed of four subunits: vv. 1–4, 5–7, 8, 9–12. **3.1–4** Address to Israel's political and religious leaders. With a brutal metaphor (vv. 2b–3), Micah compares Israel's leaders to savage butchers and voracious cannibals who treat people like animals to be consumed. The metaphor stresses the extent of injustice within the community, by its leadership in particular. Silence and hiddenness are the divine responses to such atrocities. **3.5–7** Proclamation *concerning the prophets.* Here Micah confronts those who have corrupted their

prophetic office for the sake of personal gain. **3.5** *Peace* (Hebrew *shalom*) means wholeness, well-being, integrity. **3.6–7** Imagery of darkness communicates a single message: neither legitimate nor illegitimate prophecy will continue. **3.7** *Covering their lips,* a sign of deep mourning (Ezek 24.17, 22). **3.8** Interlude: statement of confidence. Micah lists four gifts with which he has been divinely endowed to enable him to exercise his prophetic office and mission. In stark contrast to those who have corrupted their prophetic office, Micah becomes a sign of hope for the poor and oppressed. **3.9–12** Second address to Israel's leadership. Micah enumerates the crimes of *Jacob/Israel,* while now citing the priests along with the corrupt leaders, rulers, and prophets. **3.10** Archaeology testifies to the building activities underway in Jerusalem at that time, obviously done at the expense of the poor. **3.11** *"Surely the LORD . . . upon us."* Secular and religious leaders flaunt their piety while continuing their blatant injustices. They are guilty of spiritual pride and

"Surely the Lord is with us!
  No harm shall come upon us."
12 Therefore because of you
    Zion shall be plowed as a field;
  Jerusalem shall become a heap of ruins,
    and the mountain of the house a
      wooded height.

Peace and Security through Obedience

4 In days to come
    the mountain of the Lord's house
  shall be established as the highest of the
      mountains,
    and shall be raised up above the hills.
  Peoples shall stream to it,
2   and many nations shall come and say:
  "Come, let us go up to the mountain of
      the Lord,
    to the house of the God of Jacob;
  that he may teach us his ways
    and that we may walk in his paths."
  For out of Zion shall go forth instruction,
    and the word of the Lord from
      Jerusalem.
3 He shall judge between many peoples,
    and shall arbitrate between strong
      nations far away;
  they shall beat their swords into
      plowshares,
    and their spears into pruning hooks;
  nation shall not lift up sword against
      nation,
    neither shall they learn war any more;

4 but they shall all sit under their own vines
    and under their own fig trees,
    and no one shall make them afraid;
  for the mouth of the Lord of hosts has
      spoken.

5 For all the peoples walk,
    each in the name of its god,
  but we will walk in the name of the Lord
      our God
    forever and ever.

Restoration Promised after Exile

6 In that day, says the Lord,
    I will assemble the lame
  and gather those who have been driven
      away,
    and those whom I have afflicted.
7 The lame I will make the remnant,
    and those who were cast off, a strong
      nation;
  and the Lord will reign over them in
      Mount Zion
    now and forevermore.

8 And you, O tower of the flock,
    hill of daughter Zion,
  to you it shall come,
    the former dominion shall come,
    the sovereignty of daughter Jerusalem.

9 Now why do you cry aloud?
    Is there no king in you?

---

smug confidence. **3.12** The severest of all judgments. What is most precious to God is about to be destroyed; what happened to Samaria (1.6) will also happen to Jerusalem. This stunning announcement is the one least expected by the political and religious leaders, who had put their confidence in the Zion tradition with its message of the inviolability of Jerusalem. Here Micah shatters the leaders' religious pride.
4.1–5 A prophetic vision that promises peace for the future, closely paralleled in Isa 2.2–4, but in marked contrast to Mic 3.12. Scholars disagree on the relationship between these texts, and some have posited dependence on a common source. **4.1** The mountain of the Lord's house, Mount Zion. **4.2** Three times each year on the major feasts (Passover, Pentecost, and Tabernacles) pilgrims went up to Jerusalem (Ps 122.1, 4). Instruction (Hebrew torah), in the sense of divine teachings. **4.3** Micah describes a vision of world peace that God as just ruler and judge will bring about in a nonviolent way through arbitration. This vision would fulfill one of the sovereign's main responsibilities, namely, to bring peace and tranquility

to all nations (1 Kings 5.4; Isa 9.7; 11.1–9; Jer 23.5–6; 33.15–16). **4.4** Peace among nations leads to individual peace, symbolized by an agrarian image of security and stability. Vines and fig trees represent long-term stability, peace, and prosperity. **4.5** We, the congregation in Judah. **4.6–8** A divine promise. God will act positively on behalf of the remnant, and both sovereignty and noble dignity will be restored to Jerusalem. **4.7** The dispersed will be brought back to Jerusalem, where the Lord will exercise dominion on their behalf from the Temple Mount. **4.8** Tower of the flock, translation of the Hebrew place-name Migdal Eder, situated between Bethlehem and Hebron, where Jacob tented after burying Rachel (Gen 35.21). Towers were sometimes erected to protect pastures. Here tower of the flock designates Mount Zion. Hill (Hebrew 'ophel) refers to the fortified upper sector of capital cities where the palace and other royal buildings stood. In Jerusalem, Ophel designated the area lying between the Temple Mount and the City of David on the southeast hill. **4.9–10** Prophetic announcement of salvation. God's suffering people will be consoled and re-

Has your counselor perished,
    that pangs have seized you like a
        woman in labor?
10 Writhe and groan,*a* O daughter Zion,
    like a woman in labor;
for now you shall go forth from the city
    and camp in the open country;
        you shall go to Babylon.
There you shall be rescued,
    there the LORD will redeem you
        from the hands of your enemies.

11 Now many nations
    are assembled against you,
saying, "Let her be profaned,
    and let our eyes gaze upon Zion."
12 But they do not know
    the thoughts of the LORD;
they do not understand his plan,
    that he has gathered them as sheaves to
        the threshing floor.
13 Arise and thresh,
    O daughter Zion,
for I will make your horn iron
    and your hoofs bronze;
you shall beat in pieces many peoples,
    and shall*b* devote their gain to the
        LORD,
    their wealth to the Lord of the whole
        earth.

5 *c* Now you are walled around with a wall;*d*
    siege is laid against us;
with a rod they strike the ruler of Israel
    upon the cheek.

The Ruler from Bethlehem

2 *e* But you, O Bethlehem of Ephrathah,
    who are one of the little clans of Judah,
from you shall come forth for me
    one who is to rule in Israel,
whose origin is from of old,
    from ancient days.
3 Therefore he shall give them up until the
        time
    when she who is in labor has brought
        forth;
then the rest of his kindred shall return
    to the people of Israel.
4 And he shall stand and feed his flock in
        the strength of the LORD,
    in the majesty of the name of the LORD
        his God.
And they shall live secure, for now he
        shall be great
    to the ends of the earth;
5 and he shall be the one of peace.

If the Assyrians come into our land
    and tread upon our soil,*f*
we will raise against them seven shepherds
    and eight installed as rulers.
6 They shall rule the land of Assyria with
        the sword,
    and the land of Nimrod with the
        drawn sword;*g*

---

a Meaning of Heb uncertain   *b* Gk Syr Tg: Heb *and I will*
c Ch 4.14 in Heb   *d* Cn Compare Gk: Meaning of Heb
uncertain   *e* Ch 5.1 in Heb   *f* Gk: Heb *in our palaces*
g Cn: Heb *in its entrances*

---

deemed from their suffering. The references to childbirth suggest new life. At this juncture the people are in a state of transition as they move from devastation to reprieve to restoration. **4.10–11** *Like a woman in labor,* an image that, although not fully developed in these verses, is suggestive of the birth pangs necessary for new life. The simile conveys a message of hope, but one not without its dangers. **4.11–13** Prophetic announcement of salvation. The nations are coming to wage war against Zion, but Zion, according to God's divine plan, will prevail against them. **4.13** *Iron, bronze,* symbols of strength and hardness, respectively (cf. Jer 1.18). *Gain,* legitimate plunder as well as ill-gotten treasures, including bribes. *Wealth,* legitimate gain.

5.1–6 Prophetic announcement of salvation. The passage strengthens the hope of the people as they anticipate a new royal messiah, the ideal leader, promised by the prophet, who will usher in a time of strength, justice, and peace. **5.1** *They strike . . . upon the cheek,* an act of humiliation expressing contempt for the king. It may refer to King Hezekiah, who in 701 BCE was cowed by Sennacherib. **5.2** *Bethlehem,* a small town five miles south of Jerusalem. David, a native of Bethlehem, was anointed there by Samuel (1 Sam 16.1–13). *Ephrathah* is identified with Bethlehem. The relationship between Bethlehem and Ephrathah is unclear. Ephrathah may have been the ancient name of Bethlehem, or it may have been absorbed into Bethlehem. This undistinguished town was paradoxically to be the source of salvation. *Me,* God. *Whose origin . . . ancient days,* the Davidic covenant (2 Sam 7). **5.4** A description, comparable to that in the royal psalms (e.g., Pss 2; 72), of the ideal shepherd-king, who will bring security and peace. **5.5–6** A picture of victory over the unrelenting Assyrians to be accomplished by Israel's own leaders. **5.5** *Seven . . . eight,* a numerical progression, as in Am 1.3, signifying an indefinite number. The reference is to an alliance of rulers defeating the Assyrians. **5.6** *Land of Nimrod,* a poetic term for Assyria, is in parallel with *land of Assyria.*

they[a] shall rescue us from the Assyrians
  if they come into our land
  or tread within our border.

The Future Role of the Remnant

7 Then the remnant of Jacob,
    surrounded by many peoples,
  shall be like dew from the LORD,
    like showers on the grass,
  which do not depend upon people
    or wait for any mortal.
8 And among the nations the remnant of
      Jacob,
    surrounded by many peoples,
  shall be like a lion among the animals of
      the forest,
    like a young lion among the flocks of
      sheep,
  which, when it goes through, treads down
    and tears in pieces, with no one to
      deliver.
9 Your hand shall be lifted up over your
      adversaries,
    and all your enemies shall be cut off.

10 In that day, says the LORD,
    I will cut off your horses from among
      you
    and will destroy your chariots;
11 and I will cut off the cities of your land
    and throw down all your strongholds;
12 and I will cut off sorceries from your
      hand,
    and you shall have no more
      soothsayers;
13 and I will cut off your images
    and your pillars from among you,
  and you shall bow down no more
    to the work of your hands;
14 and I will uproot your sacred poles[b] from
      among you

and destroy your towns.
15 And in anger and wrath I will execute
      vengeance
    on the nations that did not obey.

God Challenges Israel

6 Hear what the LORD says:
    Rise, plead your case before the
      mountains,
    and let the hills hear your voice.
2 Hear, you mountains, the controversy of
      the LORD,
    and you enduring foundations of the
      earth;
  for the LORD has a controversy with his
      people,
    and he will contend with Israel.

3 "O my people, what have I done to you?
    In what have I wearied you? Answer me!
4 For I brought you up from the land of
      Egypt,
    and redeemed you from the house of
      slavery;
  and I sent before you Moses,
    Aaron, and Miriam.
5 O my people, remember now what King
      Balak of Moab devised,
    what Balaam son of Beor answered
      him,
  and what happened from Shittim to
      Gilgal,
    that you may know the saving acts of
      the LORD."

What God Requires

6 "With what shall I come before the LORD,
    and bow myself before God on high?

---

a Heb he   b Heb Asherim

Nimrod, renowned as a hunter, was an ancient Mesopotamian king (Gen 10.8–12). **5.7–9** Prophetic announcement of salvation. The theme of victory introduced in vv. 5–6 continues in these verses, but now the remnant itself will be victorious over its adversaries. **5.10–15** Continued proclamation of salvation. As part of the messianic restoration, Israel will be stripped of all those things that have caused alienation from the Lord, including military armament, sorcery, and idolatrous worship. **5.13** *Images,* carved or sculpted from stone, metal, or wood. Representations of God were forbidden to the Israelites (Ex 20.4; Deut 5.8). *Pillars,* standing stone monuments with a variety of functions; they may have been symbols of the male deity (Deut 16.22;

1 Kings 14.23). *Work of your hands,* sardonic reference to idols. **5.14** *Sacred poles,* wooden cult symbols of the Canaanite mother goddess Asherah.
  6.1–5 A covenant lawsuit (Hebrew *riv*). The prophet, acting as an attorney, represents God's case against an ungrateful people. **6.1–2** The natural elements are invoked as witnesses (cf. 1.2). **6.3–5** God, acting as a plaintiff, now puts forth the charge against the people. The repeated use of the vocative *O my people* (vv. 3, 5) adds a note of poignancy. **6.4** God's complaint contains allusions to the exodus. **6.5** *King Balak* tried unsuccessfully to persuade the prophet Balaam to curse the Israelite armies (Num 22–24). *From Shittim to Gilgal,* from the east to the west side of the Jordan. *Shittim*

Shall I come before him with burnt
    offerings,
  with calves a year old?
7 Will the LORD be pleased with thousands
    of rams,
  with ten thousands of rivers of oil?
Shall I give my firstborn for my
    transgression,
  the fruit of my body for the sin of my
    soul?"
8 He has told you, O mortal, what is good;
  and what does the LORD require of you
but to do justice, and to love kindness,
  and to walk humbly with your God?

Cheating and Violence to Be Punished

9 The voice of the LORD cries to the city
    (it is sound wisdom to fear your name):
  Hear, O tribe and assembly of the city! *a*
10   Can I forget *b* the treasures of
        wickedness in the house of the
        wicked,
    and the scant measure that is accursed?
11 Can I tolerate wicked scales
    and a bag of dishonest weights?
12 Your *c* wealthy are full of violence;
    your *d* inhabitants speak lies,
    with tongues of deceit in their mouths.
13 Therefore I have begun *e* to strike you down,
    making you desolate because of your
        sins.
14 You shall eat, but not be satisfied,
    and there shall be a gnawing hunger
        within you;
  you shall put away, but not save,
    and what you save, I will hand over to
        the sword.
15 You shall sow, but not reap;
    you shall tread olives, but not anoint
        yourselves with oil;

you shall tread grapes, but not drink
    wine.
16 For you have kept the statutes of Omri *f*
    and all the works of the house of Ahab,
    and you have followed their counsels.
Therefore I will make you a desolation,
    and your *g* inhabitants an object of
        hissing;
  so you shall bear the scorn of my people.

The Total Corruption of the People

7 Woe is me! For I have become like one
      who,
  after the summer fruit has been
      gathered,
  after the vintage has been gleaned,
finds no cluster to eat;
  there is no first-ripe fig for which I
      hunger.
2 The faithful have disappeared from the
      land,
    and there is no one left who is upright;
  they all lie in wait for blood,
    and they hunt each other with nets.
3 Their hands are skilled to do evil;
    the official and the judge ask for a bribe,
  and the powerful dictate what they desire;
    thus they pervert justice. *h*
4 The best of them is like a brier,
    the most upright of them a thorn hedge.
  The day of their *i* sentinels, of their *i*
      punishment, has come;
  now their confusion is at hand.
5 Put no trust in a friend,
    have no confidence in a loved one;

---

a Cn Compare Gk: Heb *tribe, and who has appointed it yet?*
b Cn: Meaning of Heb uncertain *c* Heb *Whose* *d* Heb *whose*
e Gk Syr Vg: Heb *have made sick* *f* Gk Syr Vg Tg: Heb *the
statutes of Omri are kept* *g* Heb *its* *h* Cn: Heb *they weave it*
i Heb *your*

---

was the site of Israel's camp under Joshua east of the
Jordan River; *Gilgal* was the site of the Israelite camp
after crossing the Jordan (Josh 3–5). **6.6–8** Torah
liturgy. In vv. 6–7 Micah speaks on behalf of the community for whom he responds to God's complaint. In v.
8 he offers a response to the people's questions posed in
vv. 6–7. **6.6** *Burnt offerings*, holocausts in which the entire victim is burned and is thus totally dedicated to
God. **6.7** *Give my firstborn.* Human sacrifice may have
been practiced in Judah under Kings Ahaz (2 Kings
16.3) and Manasseh (2 Kings 21.6). **6.8** Acts of justice,
kindness, and right relationship with God, symbolized
by a humble walk, are preferred to ritual sacrifices. The
verse summarizes the prophetic teaching on true religion. **6.9–16** Judgment speech. The people of Jerusalem

are indicted by God because of their social sins, and they
will be chastised accordingly. **6.10–11** A rhetorical
question introduces the charge of cheating with fraudulent weights and measures (Lev 19.35–36; Deut 25.13–
16). **6.14–15** Curses, based on the old covenant curses
(Deut 28.30–31, 38–40), are invoked on the people as a
response to their unjust ways. **6.16** *Omri* and his son
Ahab, ninth-century BCE kings of Israel guilty of syncretism and apostasy (1 Kings 16.25–26, 30–33).

7.1–6 A lament uttered by the prophet, who feels
alone and abandoned as he undertakes the futile task of
finding a good person. **7.2–4** In the absence of honorable people, only the treacherous, including the civil
leaders, remain. **7.5–6** Normal human relations, even
among family members, have ceased for lack of trust.

guard the doors of your mouth
  from her who lies in your embrace;
6 for the son treats the father with contempt,
  the daughter rises up against her
    mother,
  the daughter-in-law against her mother-
    in-law;
  your enemies are members of your
    own household.
7 But as for me, I will look to the Lord,
  I will wait for the God of my salvation;
  my God will hear me.

Penitence and Trust in God

8 Do not rejoice over me, O my enemy;
  when I fall, I shall rise;
  when I sit in darkness,
    the Lord will be a light to me.
9 I must bear the indignation of the Lord,
  because I have sinned against him,
  until he takes my side
    and executes judgment for me.
  He will bring me out to the light;
    I shall see his vindication.
10 Then my enemy will see,
  and shame will cover her who said
    to me,
  "Where is the Lord your God?"
  My eyes will see her downfall;[a]
  now she will be trodden down
    like the mire of the streets.

A Prophecy of Restoration

11 A day for the building of your walls!
  In that day the boundary shall be far
    extended.
12 In that day they will come to you
  from Assyria to[b] Egypt,
  and from Egypt to the River,
  from sea to sea and from mountain to
    mountain.
13 But the earth will be desolate

because of its inhabitants,
  for the fruit of their doings.

14 Shepherd your people with your staff,
  the flock that belongs to you,
  which lives alone in a forest
    in the midst of a garden land;
  let them feed in Bashan and Gilead
    as in the days of old.
15 As in the days when you came out of the
    land of Egypt,
  show us[c] marvelous things.
16 The nations shall see and be ashamed
    of all their might;
  they shall lay their hands on their mouths;
    their ears shall be deaf;
17 they shall lick dust like a snake,
  like the crawling things of the earth;
  they shall come trembling out of their
    fortresses;
  they shall turn in dread to the Lord
    our God,
  and they shall stand in fear of you.

God's Compassion and Steadfast Love

18 Who is a God like you, pardoning iniquity
  and passing over the transgression
  of the remnant of your[d] possession?
  He does not retain his anger forever,
  because he delights in showing
    clemency.
19 He will again have compassion upon us;
  he will tread our iniquities under foot.
  You will cast all our[e] sins
    into the depths of the sea.
20 You will show faithfulness to Jacob
  and unswerving loyalty to Abraham,
  as you have sworn to our ancestors
    from the days of old.

---

a Heb lacks *downfall*   b One Ms: MT *Assyria and cities of*
c Cn: Heb *I will show him*   d Heb *his*   e Gk Syr Vg Tg: Heb *their*

7.7–20 A prophetic liturgy of hope, petition, and confidence spoken by the prophet on behalf of the community. **7.7** *But as for me.* In Hebrew, this clause is grammatically unrelated to the main sentence, which serves to separate Micah from the rest of his dishonorable community members. The repeated reference to the Lord and God (twice) attests to Micah's steadfast faith. **7.8–10** The prophet speaks on behalf of those of his community who, confident of their deliverance, confess their sins. **7.11–13** The prophetic vision describes restoration and repopulation in the future. **7.12** *River,* the Euphrates in Mesopotamia (modern Iraq). **7.14–17** With this prayer of petition Micah, on behalf of his community, asks God to act as a shepherd as in days past and to govern the people with strength as in the days of the exodus, so that enemy nations will be put to shame and stand in fear of Israel's God. **7.14** *Bashan,* the fertile plateau northeast of the Jordan River. *Gilead,* a highland region with rich pastures lying east of the Jordan. Both symbolize abundance. **7.15** *You,* God. **7.16–17** The nations other than Israel will be humiliated. **7.18–20** Micah, on behalf of the community, makes a confession of faith. The image of a loving and forgiving God echoes Ex 34.6–7.

NAHUM

Historical Context

NAHUM IS THE ONLY PROPHETIC ACCOUNT to name itself a "book." The poetic images vividly express the Lord's coming judgment against Nineveh, the capital city of the Assyrians and a city in northern Iraq near the modern city of Mosul. The title of the "book of vision" (1.1) gives no specific date for Nahum's activity, but it is reasonable to assume that the oracles were delivered after the fall of Thebes (663 BCE), alluded to in 3.8, and shortly before the fall of Nineveh (612 BCE). Since there is no mention of the sins of Judah, as is so frequently found in earlier and later prophetic accounts, Nahum's activity is best located at the height of Josiah's reformation (622– 609 BCE), when attention was directed to reform and not the past ills of God's people.

Message

THE ANNOUNCEMENT OF NINEVEH'S IMPENDING FALL is placed in the context of the initial psalm (1.2–8), which pictures a God of awesome power who sees Judah's need for assurance that the Lord will deliver it. After one hundred and twenty-five years of brutal Assyrian domination of many small countries, including Judah, and the destruction of the Northern Kingdom (Israel) in 722 BCE, Judah heard these oracles as both reassuring and terrifying. To know that the Lord "is slow to anger but great in power" (1.3) and "a stronghold in a day of trouble" (1.7) gives profound assurance in the face of a terrible enemy like Assyria. On the other hand, Judah knows that there are those in its midst who question the Lord's resolve to destroy the enemy (1.9–10). Nahum's oracles do not call the Judahites to account for their transgressions but remind them that their God above all else will not permit oppression and "will by no means clear the guilty" (1.3). The utterances collected in the book of Nahum encompass both judgment and salvation. Judgment will come for all who would subvert God's justice. Salvation will come to Judah as a result of God's judgment on Nineveh (1.12), thus making possible once again the joyous celebration of sacred festivals (1.15).

Canonical Context

THE BOOK OF NAHUM has often been criticized as vengeful and lacking in the strong moral tone of a book like Amos. Some have suggested that Nahum does not present the breadth and depth of a book like Isaiah or Jeremiah. We do not know what else Nahum may have spoken, but this "account" regarding Nineveh yields unforgettably powerful poetic words. Others have said that Nahum would be complemented by reading it with Jonah to highlight God's compassion. These concerns about the religious and theological perspectives of Nahum, along with a series of literary and historical issues, continue all too often to impede the reading of the book. One must, however, place Nahum among his contemporaries, such as Habakkuk, Jeremiah, and Zephaniah, to hear the interplay between God's judgment and salvation and the strong word of assurance in Nahum that the Lord will prevail against evil. [KENT HAROLD RICHARDS]

1 An oracle concerning Nineveh. The book of the vision of Nahum of Elkosh.

The Consuming Wrath of God

2 A jealous and avenging God is the LORD,
    the LORD is avenging and wrathful;
the LORD takes vengeance on his
    adversaries
and rages against his enemies.
3 The LORD is slow to anger but great in
    power,
and the LORD will by no means clear
    the guilty.

His way is in whirlwind and storm,
    and the clouds are the dust of his feet.
4 He rebukes the sea and makes it dry,
    and he dries up all the rivers;
Bashan and Carmel wither,
    and the bloom of Lebanon fades.
5 The mountains quake before him,

    and the hills melt;
the earth heaves before him,
    the world and all who live in it.

6 Who can stand before his indignation?
    Who can endure the heat of his anger?
His wrath is poured out like fire,
    and by him the rocks are broken in
      pieces.
7 The LORD is good,
    a stronghold in a day of trouble;
he protects those who take refuge in him,
8   even in a rushing flood.
He will make a full end of his
    adversaries,[a]
and will pursue his enemies into
    darkness.
9 Why do you plot against the LORD?
    He will make an end;

_____
a Gk: Heb of her place

1.1 The title, or superscription, identifies Nahum as an *oracle*, or message (lit. "burden," used frequently in prophetic accounts; cf. Isa 13.1; Hab 1.1; Zech 9.1; Mal 1.1), against Nineveh and as a *book of the vision.* No other superscription of a prophetic book refers to the contents as a *book,* although Hab 2.2 refers to the Lord instructing the prophet to "write the vision." *Vision* is used in prophetic superscriptions (Isa 1.1; Ob 1) and also in parallel with "dream" (Job 33.15). The distinction between dream and vision is not always made in Hebrew. *Nahum,* not mentioned anyplace else in the Bible, means "comfort" and is related to the name Nehemiah. *Elkosh,* also not mentioned anyplace else in the Bible, is not known precisely but most likely is in the southwestern part of Judah. 1.2–8 (9) An alphabetic (acrostic) psalm (cf. Pss 9–10; 25; 34; 37; 111; 112; 119; 145; Prov 31.10–31; Lam 1–4). It contains only the first half (eleven of twenty-two) of the letters of the Hebrew alphabet. The psalm expresses in awesome, theophanic terms the Lord's protection of *those who take refuge* (v. 7; cf. Pss 27.1; 31.4) in the God who is creator and judge of all adversaries. No mention of Nineveh occurs in these verses. The use of nature to describe God's power is reminiscent of Pss 18.7–12; 97.1–5; Mic 1.3–4 and serves as a prelude to the verses that follow. 1.2 *God.* The Hebrew uses *El* and not the more common *Elohim. Wrathful,* lit. "a baal of wrath." That the Hebrew uses terms such as *baal* and *El,* which were divine names in the Canaanite religion, suggests Canaanite mythic images, as do the terms *sea* and *rivers* (v. 4) and the images of storm and fire throughout the psalm (see Ps 29). *Avenging* and *vengeance* arise from a legal sense of justifiable vindication and not rancorous retaliation (see Ps 94). The repetition of the avenging terms in three of the four lines reinforces God's intolerance for injustice. 1.3 *Slow to anger* (lit. "long of nostril") is frequently found with the additional phrase "of great mercy" (Neh 9.17; Pss 86.15; 103.8; Joel 2.13; Jon 4.2). The latter is not included here to reinforce the legal sense of justifiable vindication. 1.4 *Bashan, Carmel,* and *Lebanon* are especially noted for their fertility, so their drying up enforces the power of the theophanic images (cf. Isa 19.5–7; 33.9). 1.5 *World and all who live in it* reinforces the enormity of the impact: both inhabited and uninhabited lands are affected. 1.8 *Flood* may refer to the flood in Noah's time (Gen 6–9). 1.9–15 The prophet's promise and assurance of Judah's deliverance. The addressee is am-

no adversary will rise up twice.
10 Like thorns they are entangled,
　　like drunkards they are drunk;
　　they are consumed like dry straw.
11 From you one has gone out
　　who plots evil against the LORD,
　　one who counsels wickedness.

Good News for Judah

12 Thus says the LORD,
"Though they are at full strength and
　　many,[a]
　　they will be cut off and pass away.
Though I have afflicted you,
　　I will afflict you no more.
13 And now I will break off his yoke from you
　　and snap the bonds that bind you."

14 The LORD has commanded concerning
　　you:
"Your name shall be perpetuated no
　　longer;
from the house of your gods I will cut off
　　the carved image and the cast image.
I will make your grave, for you are
　　worthless."

15[b] Look! On the mountains the feet of one
　　who brings good tidings,
　　who proclaims peace!
Celebrate your festivals, O Judah,
　　fulfill your vows,
for never again shall the wicked invade
　　you;
　　they are utterly cut off.

The Destruction of the Wicked City

2 A shatterer[c] has come up against you.
　　Guard the ramparts;
　　watch the road;
gird your loins;
　　collect all your strength.

2 (For the LORD is restoring the majesty of
　　Jacob,
　　as well as the majesty of Israel,
though ravagers have ravaged them
　　and ruined their branches.)

3 The shields of his warriors are red;
　　his soldiers are clothed in crimson.
The metal on the chariots flashes
　　on the day when he musters them;
　　the chargers[d] prance.
4 The chariots race madly through the
　　streets,
　　they rush to and fro through the
　　squares;
their appearance is like torches,
　　they dart like lightning.
5 He calls his officers;
　　they stumble as they come forward;
they hasten to the wall,
　　and the mantelet[e] is set up.
6 The river gates are opened,
　　the palace trembles.
7 It is decreed[e] that the city[f] be exiled,

---

a Meaning of Heb uncertain　*b* Ch 2.1 in Heb　*c* Cn: Heb
scatterer　*d* Cn Compare Gk Syr: Heb *cypresses*　*e* Meaning of
Heb uncertain　*f* Heb *it*

---

biguous, not only because the English language does
not distinguish gender and number in the second person, "you," but also because the Hebrew text uses diverse second-person grammatical forms. Judah and
Jerusalem seem to be addressed in vv. 9–10, 11–13 and
are specifically cited in v. 15. The second masculine
singular of v. 14 is best understood as an address to the
king of Assyria. **1.10** A difficult Hebrew sentence. The
NRSV presents the best solution: *thorns* are consumed
as are the *drunkards*. Enemies are frequently referred
to as *thorns* (2 Sam 23.6). **1.11** *You,* Nineveh, the place
from which the evil comes. **1.12** *They,* the Assyrians.
You, God's people. **1.15** The import of this section is
clear; namely, the one bringing *good tidings* and *peace*
has arrived, and *Judah* may *celebrate* because the end
of Nineveh has come. According to 2 Kings 23.21–25,
the public celebration of Passover was possible after
the Assyrian domination was concluded during the
reign of Josiah (640–609 BCE). **2.1–3.19** Oracles concerning the king of Assyria

and Nineveh, the capital of Assyria. The *king of Assyria*
is specifically addressed in 3.18; and in 2.1 *you* seems
to be the city Nineveh. *Nineveh* (2.8), *city of bloodshed*
(3.1), is spoken of extensively between the addresses to
the king at the beginning and end. These diverse oracles declare to Judah that the Assyrians will no longer
be the oppressor. The tone of these oracles is ironic,
expectantly exulting, and gloating in the potential victory. **2.1–13** A succession of diverse and powerful images depicting the fall of Nineveh. **2.1** Nahum urges
Nineveh in an ironic way to prepare to do battle
(*guard, watch, gird, collect*). **2.2** Parentheses indicate a
later insertion. The verse draws on earlier prophetic
motifs and connects this chapter with the assurance of
deliverance in the previous chapter. **2.3–5** The images
continue the description begun in v. 1 and are reminiscent of the warrior imagery in 1.2–8. **2.6–8** The
water/flood images of 1.4, 8 are revisited with convincing power given the location of Nineveh near the Tigris River. *Moaning like doves,* an expression of sorrow

its slave women led away,
　　moaning like doves
　　　and beating their breasts.
8 Nineveh is like a pool
　　whose waters[a] run away.
　"Halt! Halt!"—
　　but no one turns back.
9 "Plunder the silver,
　　plunder the gold!
　There is no end of treasure!
　　An abundance of every precious
　　　　thing!"

10 Devastation, desolation, and destruction!
　　Hearts faint and knees tremble,
　all loins quake,
　　all faces grow pale!
11 What became of the lions' den,
　　the cave[b] of the young lions,
　where the lion goes,
　　and the lion's cubs, with no one to
　　　disturb them?
12 The lion has torn enough for his whelps
　　and strangled prey for his lionesses;
　he has filled his caves with prey
　　and his dens with torn flesh.

13 See, I am against you, says the LORD of
hosts, and I will burn your[c] chariots in smoke,
and the sword shall devour your young lions; I
will cut off your prey from the earth, and the
voice of your messengers shall be heard no
more.

Ruin Imminent and Inevitable

3 Ah! City of bloodshed,
　　utterly deceitful, full of booty—
　　no end to the plunder!
2　The crack of whip and rumble of wheel,
　　galloping horse and bounding chariot!

3 Horsemen charging,
　　flashing sword and glittering spear,
　piles of dead,
　　heaps of corpses,
　dead bodies without end—
　　they stumble over the bodies!
4 Because of the countless debaucheries of
　　　　the prostitute,
　　gracefully alluring, mistress of sorcery,
　who enslaves[d] nations through her
　　　　debaucheries,
　　and peoples through her sorcery,
5 I am against you,
　　says the LORD of hosts,
　　and will lift up your skirts over your
　　　　face;
　and I will let nations look on your
　　　　nakedness
　　and kingdoms on your shame.
6 I will throw filth at you
　　and treat you with contempt,
　　and make you a spectacle.
7 Then all who see you will shrink from
　　　　you and say,
　"Nineveh is devastated; who will bemoan
　　　　her?"
　　Where shall I seek comforters for you?

8 Are you better than Thebes[e]
　　that sat by the Nile,
　with water around her,
　　her rampart a sea,
　　water her wall?
9 Ethiopia[f] was her strength,
　　Egypt too, and that without limit;
　　Put and the Libyans were her[g] helpers.

---

a Cn Compare Gk: Heb *a pool, from the days that she has
become, and they*　b Cn: Heb *pasture*　c Heb *her*　d Heb *sells*
e Heb *No-amon*　f Or *Nubia*; Heb *Cush*　g Gk: Heb *your*

(Isa 38.14; 59.11). **2.9** Nahum addresses those attacking the city, telling them to take everything in sight; the
defenders are on the run and victory is anticipated.
2.10 The translation mimics the mocking alliteration
(repeated *d* sound) of the Hebrew. **2.11–13** The taunting image of the *lion* concludes the section. The lion,
associated with Assyria's ferocious strength even in Assyrian reliefs, succumbs. The taunt is reinforced by
virtue of the frequent identification of the Lord with
the power of the lion (Hos 5.14; 13.8; Am 3.8).
2.13 The only prose verse in the book of Nahum connects chs. 2 and 3 (*lions* in 2.11–12 and the LORD of
hosts in 3.5). **3.1–17** A woe oracle addressed to Nineveh. **3.1–3** The oracle commences with the war im-

agery begun in 2.3–5. **3.4–7** A new image of Nineveh
as the *prostitute, gracefully alluring* (v. 4) all nations to
her in order to plunder them. Her seduction will be no
more. The Lord will *lift up* her *skirts* and expose her
nakedness (v. 5; cf. Jer 13.22, 26), just as an enemy handles a conquered city (cf. Isa 47.1–3). **3.8–10** A rhetorical question (v. 8) and extended answer (vv. 9–10)
compare Nineveh with the extensively fortified
Thebes, capital of Upper Egypt captured by the Assyrians under Ashurbanipal in 663 BCE. Thebes is located
on the Nile about 350 miles south of modern Cairo.
Ethiopia's twenty-fifth dynasty controlled Egypt during this period. The listing of *Egypt, Put* (precise location unknown), and the *Libyans* illustrates the in-

10 Yet she became an exile,
        she went into captivity;
    even her infants were dashed in pieces
        at the head of every street;
    lots were cast for her nobles,
        all her dignitaries were bound in fetters.
11 You also will be drunken,
        you will go into hiding;[a]
    you will seek
        a refuge from the enemy.
12 All your fortresses are like fig trees
        with first-ripe figs—
    if shaken they fall
        into the mouth of the eater.
13 Look at your troops:
        they are women in your midst.
    The gates of your land
        are wide open to your foes;
    fire has devoured the bars of your gates.

14 Draw water for the siege,
        strengthen your forts;
    trample the clay,
        tread the mortar,
        take hold of the brick mold!
15 There the fire will devour you,
        the sword will cut you off.
    It will devour you like the locust.

    Multiply yourselves like the locust,
        multiply like the grasshopper!
16 You increased your merchants
        more than the stars of the heavens.
    The locust sheds its skin and flies
        away.
17 Your guards are like grasshoppers,
        your scribes like swarms[b] of locusts
    settling on the fences
        on a cold day—
    when the sun rises, they fly away;
        no one knows where they have gone.

18 Your shepherds are asleep,
        O king of Assyria;
        your nobles slumber.
    Your people are scattered on the
        mountains
        with no one to gather them.
19 There is no assuaging your hurt,
        your wound is mortal.
    All who hear the news about you
        clap their hands over you.
    For who has ever escaped
        your endless cruelty?

_____
a Meaning of Heb uncertain

domitability of Thebes. **3.11–13** Even more than Thebes, Nineveh will fall like the *first-ripe figs*. **3.14–15a** Each of the commands (v. 14) evokes irony, as the conclusion suggests (v. 15a). **3.14–17** The oracle concludes with a multileveled comparison of Nineveh and its leaders with the *locust*. First, the comparison concerns the way they both *devour* (v. 15a), then ironically suggests that Nineveh must *multiply* (vv. 15b–16a) as rapidly as the locust, and concludes with the notion of the ephemeral quality of Nineveh's *guards* and *scribes* (v. 17), who, like the locust, will disappear. **3.18–19** The tone shifts to exultation at the defeat of Nin-

eveh. From the leaders in the preceding verses the book turns to address the *king of Assyria*, who is so bewildered with the destruction that he must be told his leaders are *asleep*, most probably meaning they are dead (see Ps 13.3; Jer 51.39; 57). *All who hear the news*, presumably even those beyond Judah, will *clap their hands*. They will rejoice at knowing the Assyrian king finally will get what he has given to so many neighboring people, death and suffering. The book ends with a rhetorical question, just as does the book of Jonah, which also is concerned with Nineveh. The answer is that everyone will rejoice.

HABAKKUK

Traditional Interpretations

THE BOOK OF HABAKKUK gives little direct information about the prophet even though in later Jewish tradition Habakkuk is identified as a Levite. The lack of specific information has led to diverse understandings of the book and the prophet. In Jewish tradition the prayer of Habakkuk in ch. 3 is associated with the giving of the Torah at Sinai. An addition to Daniel entitled Bel and the Dragon from the second century BCE refers to the prophet Habakkuk, and some versions attribute the addition to Habakkuk. The members of the Qumran community related chs. 1–2 to their own time (first century BCE) in a commentary (the *Pesher Habakkuk*), which has been preserved among the Dead Sea Scrolls. The apostle Paul built his notion of "justification by faith" on Hab 2.4b (cf. Rom 1.17; Gal 3.11).

Historical Background and Message

THE ORACLES COME FROM DIFFERENT OCCASIONS during the last quarter of the seventh century and the first decade of the sixth century BCE. No dates are cited in the book. To a large extent dating hinges on the interpretation of ch. 1, that is, determining whether the evil people referred to in vv. 2–4 and vv. 12–17 are the people of Judah or foreign enemies. The most plausible interpretation is to understand the people spoken of in vv. 2–4 as those within Judah during the time of the Judean king Jehoiakim (609–598 BCE). Because vv. 6–10 clearly refer to the Chaldeans, a people who bring God's judgment on Judah in 597 BCE, the wicked people spoken of in vv. 12–17 are thought to be the same as those identified in vv. 6–10, namely, the Chaldeans. Whatever its precise historical background, Habakkuk, unlike most prophetic books, confronts God rather than presents the deity confronting the people. The message centers on the question of how the violence and evil of the world can serve God's purposes. In the concluding prayer the prophet sees God's intervention portrayed in cosmic, theophanic terms. Habakkuk's repeated complaints and questions find their answer in the affirmation "GOD, the Lord, is my strength" (3.19).

Literary Character

THE BOOK USES DIVERSE LITERARY DEVICES to convey its message. Dominant among these is the first-person, almost autobiographical dialogue between the prophet and God (1.2–2.5).

1254

Habakkuk raises two questions (1.2–4; 1.12–17) and the Lord responds (1.5–11; 2.2–5). This exchange is further elaborated in the prayer of ch. 3, which ends on the high note of confidence so frequently found in individual thanksgivings. Because of the numerous musical and liturgical elements, especially in the last chapter, and the dialogical shaping of the first two chapters, some interpreters have claimed that the book is shaped by liturgical concerns. Yet no single type of literature provides a key to the book, which is shaped by the powerful images of justice and injustice, confidence and doubt, salvation and judgment, God and humankind. [KENT HAROLD RICHARDS]

1 The oracle that the prophet Habakkuk saw.

The Prophet's Complaint

2 O LORD, how long shall I cry for help,
    and you will not listen?
  Or cry to you "Violence!"
    and you will not save?
3 Why do you make me see wrongdoing
    and look at trouble?
  Destruction and violence are before me;
    strife and contention arise.
4 So the law becomes slack
    and justice never prevails.
  The wicked surround the righteous—
    therefore judgment comes forth
      perverted.

5 Look at the nations, and see!
    Be astonished! Be astounded!
  For a work is being done in your days
    that you would not believe if you were
      told.
6 For I am rousing the Chaldeans,
    that fierce and impetuous nation,
  who march through the breadth of the
      earth
    to seize dwellings not their own.
7 Dread and fearsome are they;

their justice and dignity proceed from
      themselves.
8 Their horses are swifter than leopards,
    more menacing than wolves at dusk;
    their horses charge.
  Their horsemen come from far away;
    they fly like an eagle swift to devour.
9 They all come for violence,
    with faces pressing[a] forward;
    they gather captives like sand.
10 At kings they scoff,
    and of rulers they make sport.
  They laugh at every fortress,
    and heap up earth to take it.
11 Then they sweep by like the wind;
    they transgress and become guilty;
    their own might is their god!

12 Are you not from of old,
    O LORD my God, my Holy One?
    You[b] shall not die.
  O LORD, you have marked them for
      judgment;
    and you, O Rock, have established
      them for punishment.
13 Your eyes are too pure to behold evil,
    and you cannot look on wrongdoing;

___

a Meaning of Heb uncertain   b Ancient Heb tradition: MT We

1.1 The title, or superscription, identifies Habakkuk as an *oracle* (lit. "burden"; cf. Isa 13.1; Nah 1.1; Zech 9.1; Mal 1.1) from a *prophet*. *Prophet* is only used in the titles of two other books, Haggai and Zechariah. This title is for chs. 1–2, since ch. 3 begins with another superscription (see 3.1). **1.2–2.20** A series of exchanges between the prophet and God. **1.2–4** At the beginning of the exchange with God, Habakkuk uses language typical of the complaint (see Job 19.1–7; Ps 13) to question *how long* and *why* injustice within Judah, perpetrated by the *wicked,* will persist. **1.2** *"Violence!"* shouts Habakkuk. The term appears six times in Habakkuk (cf. 1.3, 9; 2.8, 17), always signifying confusion and the disruption of order (cf. Gen 6.11, 13). **1.4** *Law* (Hebrew *torah*) refers to all that would maintain order, including prophetic oracle and priestly instruction. **1.5–11** The speaker is not explicitly identified and does not directly answer the question asked in vv. 2–4. The speaker seems to be God. The response somewhat unexpectedly comes in an oracle of judgment, which will be brought by the *Chaldeans* (i.e., Babylonians), an enemy of extraordinary might. This motif of God's judgment being carried out by an enemy of God's people, emphasizing the unexpectedness of divine action, is not uncommon (e.g., Isa 5.26–30; Jer 32.4–5, 24–25, 28–29). **1.12–17** Habakkuk's second complaint implies that he has heard God's answer. Nevertheless Habakkuk registers shock that God could use the *enemy* (v. 15) to bring judgment on the people, since God's *eyes are too pure to behold evil* (v. 13). **1.12** *Holy*

why do you look on the treacherous,
    and are silent when the wicked swallow
        those more righteous than they?
14 You have made people like the fish of the
        sea,
    like crawling things that have no ruler.

15 The enemy[a] brings all of them up with a
        hook;
    he drags them out with his net,
he gathers them in his seine;
    so he rejoices and exults.
16 Therefore he sacrifices to his net
    and makes offerings to his seine;
for by them his portion is lavish,
    and his food is rich.
17 Is he then to keep on emptying his net,
    and destroying nations without mercy?

God's Reply to the Prophet's Complaint

2 I will stand at my watchpost,
    and station myself on the rampart;
I will keep watch to see what he will say
        to me,
    and what he[b] will answer concerning
        my complaint.
2 Then the LORD answered me and said:
Write the vision;
    make it plain on tablets,
    so that a runner may read it.
3 For there is still a vision for the appointed
        time;
    it speaks of the end, and does not lie.
If it seems to tarry, wait for it;
    it will surely come, it will not delay.
4 Look at the proud!
    Their spirit is not right in them,
    but the righteous live by their faith.[c]
5 Moreover, wealth[d] is treacherous;

the arrogant do not endure.
They open their throats wide as Sheol;
    like Death they never have enough.
They gather all nations for themselves,
    and collect all peoples as their own.

The Woes of the Wicked

6 Shall not everyone taunt such people and,
with mocking riddles, say about them,
    "Alas for you who heap up what is not
        your own!"
    How long will you load yourselves with
        goods taken in pledge?
7 Will not your own creditors suddenly
        rise,
    and those who make you tremble wake
        up?
    Then you will be booty for them.
8 Because you have plundered many nations,
    all that survive of the peoples shall
        plunder you—
because of human bloodshed, and
    violence to the earth,
    to cities and all who live in them.

9 "Alas for you who get evil gain for your
        house,
    setting your nest on high
    to be safe from the reach of harm!"
10 You have devised shame for your house
    by cutting off many peoples;
    you have forfeited your life.
11 The very stones will cry out from the
        wall,
    and the plaster[e] will respond from the
        woodwork.

---

a Heb He   b Syr: Heb I   c Or faithfulness   d Other Heb Mss
read wine   e Or beam

One, used widely in Isaiah (e.g., Isa 1.4; 5.19, 24) and
later in Hab 3.3. **1.14–17** The Babylonians are figuratively described. This leads to the question posed in v.
17. **1.14** You have made . . . of the sea begins a comparison of people to fish and crawling things that have no
ruler. This is in stark opposition to the views expressed
in Ps 8, where humans are slightly less than God and
provide order for the entire natural world. **1.15** Moreover, the enemy who is bringing the judgment treats
the people merely as fish. **1.16** Sacrifices to his net emphasizes the value the Babylonians placed on those
implements with which they attained their power.
2.1–4 The prophet takes his watchpost (see Isa 21.8;
Ezek 33.1–9) to await God's response to his second
complaint, which comes in v. 4. **2.2** Write the vision is
indicative of the connection in Habakkuk and other

prophetic traditions between hearing and seeing (see
Am 1.1; Mic 1.1). The vision is put in writing to preserve it for the appropriate time of fulfillment (see Isa
30.8). **2.4** Contrasted with the proud are the righteous
who live by their faith and trust in the reliability of
God's fulfilling the vision. **2.5–20** A series of five woe
oracles expands on the meaning of vv. 1–4. **2.5** The arrogant are the same as the proud (v. 4). Gather, a bringing together in a negative sense like the gathering in
1.15. **2.6** The taunt of the Babylonians by everyone
who has suffered at their hands. Alas (also vv. 9, 12, 15,
17) sets off each of the following five woe oracles directed toward the various crimes of the Babylonians.
2.6b–8 The first woe oracle is directed toward plundering. **2.8** Repeated in v. 17b. **2.9–11** The second woe
oracle indicates that even the buildings constructed

12 "Alas for you who build a town by
          bloodshed,
    and found a city on iniquity!"
13 Is it not from the LORD of hosts
          that peoples labor only to feed the
          flames,
    and nations weary themselves for
          nothing?
14 But the earth will be filled
    with the knowledge of the glory of the
          LORD,
    as the waters cover the sea.

15 "Alas for you who make your neighbors
          drink,
    pouring out your wrath*a* until they are
          drunk,
    in order to gaze on their nakedness!"
16 You will be sated with contempt instead
          of glory.
    Drink, you yourself, and stagger!*b*
    The cup in the LORD's right hand
    will come around to you,
    and shame will come upon your glory!
17 For the violence done to Lebanon will
          overwhelm you;
    the destruction of the animals will
          terrify you—*c*
    because of human bloodshed and
          violence to the earth,
    to cities and all who live in them.

18 What use is an idol
    once its maker has shaped it—
    a cast image, a teacher of lies?

For its maker trusts in what has been
          made,
    though the product is only an idol that
          cannot speak!
19 Alas for you who say to the wood, "Wake
          up!"
    to silent stone, "Rouse yourself!"
    Can it teach?
    See, it is gold and silver plated,
    and there is no breath in it at all.

20 But the LORD is in his holy temple;
    let all the earth keep silence before him!

3 A prayer of the prophet Habakkuk ac-
    cording to Shigionoth.

The Prophet's Prayer

2 O LORD, I have heard of your renown,
    and I stand in awe, O LORD, of your
          work.
    In our own time revive it;
    in our own time make it known;
    in wrath may you remember mercy.
3 God came from Teman,
    the Holy One from Mount Paran. *Selah*
    His glory covered the heavens,
    and the earth was full of his praise.
4 The brightness was like the sun;
    rays came forth from his hand,
    where his power lay hidden.
5 Before him went pestilence,

---

a Or *poison* *b* Q Ms Gk: MT *be uncircumcised* *c* Gk Syr:
Meaning of Heb uncertain

---

for safety by the Babylonians will *cry out* (cf. 1.2)
against the injustices. **2.12–14** The third woe oracle
suggests that those who *build a town by bloodshed* will
be punished, and this will become visible when the
glory of the LORD fills the earth (cf. Isa 11.9). **2.15–
17** The metaphor of drinking is used in this fourth
woe oracle to speak of how the oppressor degraded the
oppressed (see Jer 51.7) by forcing them to drink and
how the *cup in the LORD's right hand* will be turned on
the oppressor in like manner (see Jer 25.15–27). *Violence.* See note on 1.2. **2.18–20** The final woe oracle
decries idolatry, namely, the inability to recognize the
true God. The woe oracles conclude with the simple
request, among all the clatter of these words, to *keep silence* before the Lord (cf. Ps 46.10).
      3.1–19 The so-called prayer of Habakkuk consists of
a request (v. 2), a theophanic vision report (vv. 3–15),
the prophet's prayerful declaration of trust in God (vv.
16–19a), and an editorial superscription and postscript
(vv. 1, 19b). Some psalms have a similar title (Pss 86; 90;

102). **3.1, 3** *Shigionoth* (see Ps 7.1), *Selah* (also vv. 9, 13;
see Ps 3), musical terms possibly indicating that the
prayer may have been used in the temple. **3.2** An introduction to the prayer requesting that the Lord's *work*
(cf. 1.5) be renewed. The request is that this new work
bring salvation. **3.3–15** Description of the new work in
a theophanic vision that causes both people and the
earth to shake (cf. Judg 5.4–5; Nah 1.3–5). God's appearing here uses the traditional language of nature so
frequently found elsewhere in the OT (Ex 19.16–18; Pss
18.7–15; 29.3–10; Mic 1.3–4; Nah 1.3b–5). **3.3–7** Description of God coming from the southern mountains
near Sinai (cf. Deut 33.2) and through *Cushan* (a term
not found elsewhere in the OT) and *Midian* (east side of
the Gulf of Aqaba). *Teman* was a district of Edom, an
area to the southeast of Judah. *Mount Paran* is a desolate
mountainous area on the Sinai Peninsula to the west of
the Gulf of Aqaba. **3.3** *Holy One.* Cf. 1.12. *Selah.* See
note on 3.1. **3.5** *Pestilence* and *plague* were frequently
used by the Lord against enemies (see Ex 5.3; 9.15; Deut

and plague followed close behind.

6 He stopped and shook the earth;
    he looked and made the nations
        tremble.
The eternal mountains were shattered;
    along his ancient pathways
    the everlasting hills sank low.

7 I saw the tents of Cushan under
        affliction;
    the tent-curtains of the land of Midian
        trembled.

8 Was your wrath against the rivers,[a]
    O LORD?
Or your anger against the rivers,[a]
    or your rage against the sea,[b]
when you drove your horses,
    your chariots to victory?

9 You brandished your naked bow,
    sated[c] were the arrows at your
        command.[d]   *Selah*
You split the earth with rivers.

10 The mountains saw you, and writhed;
    a torrent of water swept by;
the deep gave forth its voice.
    The sun[e] raised high its hands;

11 the moon[f] stood still in its exalted place,
    at the light of your arrows speeding by,
    at the gleam of your flashing spear.

12 In fury you trod the earth,
    in anger you trampled nations.

13 You came forth to save your people,
    to save your anointed.
You crushed the head of the wicked
        house,
    laying it bare from foundation to roof.[d]
                 Selah

14 You pierced with their[g] own arrows the
    head[h] of his warriors,[i]
who came like a whirlwind to scatter
    us,[j]
gloating as if ready to devour the poor
    who were in hiding.

15 You trampled the sea with your horses,
    churning the mighty waters.

16 I hear, and I tremble within;
    my lips quiver at the sound.
Rottenness enters into my bones,
    and my steps tremble[k] beneath me.
I wait quietly for the day of calamity
    to come upon the people who attack us.

Trust and Joy in the Midst of Trouble

17 Though the fig tree does not blossom,
    and no fruit is on the vines;
though the produce of the olive fails,
    and the fields yield no food;
though the flock is cut off from the fold,
    and there is no herd in the stalls,

18 yet I will rejoice in the LORD;
    I will exult in the God of my salvation.

19 GOD, the Lord, is my strength;
    he makes my feet like the feet of a deer,
    and makes me tread upon the heights.[l]

To the leader: with stringed[m] instruments.

---

a Or *against River* *b* Or *against Sea* *c* Cn: Heb *oaths*
d Meaning of Heb uncertain *e* Heb *It* *f* Heb *sun, moon*
g Heb *his* *h* Or *leader* *i* Vg Compare Gk Syr: Meaning of
Heb uncertain *j* Heb *me* *k* Cn Compare Gk: Meaning of
Heb uncertain *l* Heb *my heights* *m* Heb *my stringed*

32.24). **3.8** *Was your wrath against the rivers?* asks the prophet, only to return to the theophanic description. *Rivers* and *sea* (also v. 15) are allusions, along with *the deep* (v. 10), to God's victory over the cosmic forces of chaos. **3.13** *You . . . save your people* is the answer to the question posed in v. 8, namely, that the salvation has come forth. *Anointed* refers to a Davidic king. *Crushed . . . the wicked house* brings to mind the earlier allusions to the *wicked* (1.4, 13), who are now defeated. **3.16–**

19a These verses describe the prophet's response to the vision he just "heard" (v. 16; cf. v. 2). Although deeply shaken by it, he vows that despite agricultural failings and hardships (v. 17), he will rejoice in the Lord, who alone is the source of his confidence (vv. 18–19a). **3.19b** *To the leader: with stringed instruments,* a concluding musical and liturgical notation much like those found in the superscriptions to many psalms (see, e.g., Pss 4; 6; 54; 61; 76).

ZEPHANIAH

Historical Context

THE WORDS IN ZEPHANIAH reflect a time early in the reign of the Judahite king Josiah (640–609 BCE) before his reforms were fully developed. As reported in Kings (2 Kings 22.1–23.25), Josiah came to the throne when he was eight years old, and not until he was eighteen is there mention of the beginning of his reforming activities. Zephaniah, who may have been born during the reign of Manasseh (2 Kings 21), condemns the religious and political leadership, but says little about Josiah, who proved to be one of the few kings since David and Solomon to provide strong moral leadership.

Message

IN VIEW OF THE AWARENESS IN ZEPHANIAH of the corruption and injustice rampant in Judah, which provides a link with earlier prophetic traditions, some have suggested that Zephaniah may have been a disciple of Isaiah. The "day of the LORD" tradition is used to bring a message of judgment against Judah, but not a judgment void of promise and hope. The promise seems to have rested with a just remnant, who were among the humble rather than the corrupt and disobedient leaders with whom Zephaniah must have been intimately familiar, since he was undoubtedly from a prominent family. The restoration of salvation among God's people (3.9–20) may stem in part from later editors of the Zephaniah tradition. Nevertheless, it is abundantly clear that God's announcement of judgment brought by Zephaniah was inextricably bound to an anticipated return of fortune for God's people. The words of the book are woven together through repetitions, parallel expressions, and aesthetic devices that lead readers forward yet remind them of earlier allusions. The message leaves no doubt about the forthcoming judgment, just as it leaves no doubt about the restoration of fortune.

Canonical Context

THE BOOK OF ZEPHANIAH stands as an evocative call for renewal. It has never, however, attained the stature of the books of Isaiah, Amos, or any of the prophetic traditions on which Zephaniah relied. Nevertheless, the book, which employs traditional announcements of judgment and salvation, is a vital link in prophetic traditions. Zephaniah develops the "day of the LORD" tradition, which gave rise to the medieval hymn *Dies Irae.* More important, it serves as a reminder of the need for religious renewal—not otherworldly renewal, but one through which this world will come to reflect God's vision of a world without violence, injustice, and oppression, a world where even God may sing in response to human song (3.14–17). [KENT HAROLD RICHARDS]

1 The word of the LORD that came to Zephaniah son of Cushi son of Gedaliah son of Amariah son of Hezekiah, in the days of King Josiah son of Amon of Judah.

The Coming Judgment on Judah

2 I will utterly sweep away everything
   from the face of the earth, says the
      LORD.
3 I will sweep away humans and animals;
   I will sweep away the birds of the air
   and the fish of the sea.
   I will make the wicked stumble.*a*
   I will cut off humanity
   from the face of the earth, says the
      LORD.
4 I will stretch out my hand against Judah,
   and against all the inhabitants of
      Jerusalem;
   and I will cut off from this place every
      remnant of Baal
   and the name of the idolatrous
      priests;*b*
5 those who bow down on the roofs
   to the host of the heavens;

those who bow down and swear to the
      LORD,
   but also swear by Milcom;*c*
6 those who have turned back from
      following the LORD,
   who have not sought the LORD or
      inquired of him.

7 Be silent before the Lord GOD!
   For the day of the LORD is at hand;
   the LORD has prepared a sacrifice,
   he has consecrated his guests.
8 And on the day of the LORD's sacrifice
   I will punish the officials and the king's
      sons
   and all who dress themselves in foreign
      attire.
9 On that day I will punish
   all who leap over the threshold,
   who fill their master's house
   with violence and fraud.

---

a Cn: Heb *sea, and those who cause the wicked to stumble*
b Compare Gk: Heb *the idolatrous priests with the priests*
c Gk Mss Syr Vg: Heb *Malcam* (or, *their king*)

1.1 Using a frequently found title for a prophetic book, the superscription identifies the account as a revelation from the Lord, names the recipient with genealogical information, and concludes with historical information (cf. Hos 1.1; Joel 1.1; Mic 1.1). The long genealogy suggests that the prophet came from a prominent family (cf. Jer 36.14). If the *Hezekiah* mentioned here is the well-known king, Zephaniah would have been a relative of Josiah. Zephaniah, however, is a fairly common Hebrew name meaning "the LORD hides or protects." *In the days of King Josiah,* 640–609 BCE.
1.2–2.3 A variety of individual announcements of judgment from different occasions that develop older prophetic traditions, especially the "day of the LORD" motif. **1.2–3** An announcement of judgment against all humans and animals sets a universal context, which is developed throughout the book. *I will sweep away* occurs three times to emphasize the totality of the destruction (cf. Ps 26.9). *From the face of the earth* begins and ends this judgment, forming a literary device known as an *inclusio.* The phrase calls to mind the threefold repetition of it in the flood story (cf. Gen 6.7; 7.4; 8.8). *Says the LORD,* a formulaic identification of an oracle of the Lord used extensively in Zephaniah and other prophetic literature. **1.4–6** The

beginning of the series of specific announcements of judgment against Judah and Jerusalem. *Stretch out my hand* typically announces an action against an enemy (see Ezek 14.9, 13; 25.13) instead of toward the Lord's people. *Idolatrous priests* translates a rare Hebrew word that refers to pagan priests banned by Josiah (see 2 Kings 23.5; Hos 10.5). The list of those who will be *cut off* in vv. 5–6 includes syncretists who worship the heavenly bodies (cf. Deut 4.19) and *Milcom,* an Ammonite deity (cf. 2 Kings 23.13), as well as those who were unfaithful (*turned back;* see Ps 78.57). **1.7–13** A direct address to the prophet begins this section. **1.7** The *day of the LORD* is a major motif known widely in Judah and Israel. The expectation was that the Lord would appear one day to destroy all enemies, and that this day would be one of great victory for the Lord's people. Yet, just as Amos does (Am 5.17–20), Zephaniah announces that the day will bring punishment and not rescue for the Lord's people. *Sacrifice* plays further on the unexpected, since Judah will become the offering. **1.8** *I will punish* continues the direct address of the Lord and is repeated two more times (vv. 9, 12) to emphasize the message of judgment. *Foreign attire* continues the objection to syncretism (1.4–5). **1.9** *All who . . . threshold.* See 1 Sam

10 On that day, says the LORD,
     a cry will be heard from the Fish Gate,
   a wail from the Second Quarter,
     a loud crash from the hills.
11 The inhabitants of the Mortar wail,
     for all the traders have perished;
   all who weigh out silver are cut off.
12 At that time I will search Jerusalem with
       lamps,
     and I will punish the people
   who rest complacently[a] on their dregs,
     those who say in their hearts,
   "The LORD will not do good,
     nor will he do harm."
13 Their wealth shall be plundered,
     and their houses laid waste.
   Though they build houses,
     they shall not inhabit them;
   though they plant vineyards,
     they shall not drink wine from them.

The Great Day of the LORD

14 The great day of the LORD is near,
     near and hastening fast;
   the sound of the day of the LORD is bitter,
     the warrior cries aloud there.
15 That day will be a day of wrath,
     a day of distress and anguish,
   a day of ruin and devastation,
     a day of darkness and gloom,
   a day of clouds and thick darkness,
16   a day of trumpet blast and battle cry
   against the fortified cities
     and against the lofty battlements.

17 I will bring such distress upon people
     that they shall walk like the blind;
   because they have sinned against the
       LORD,
   their blood shall be poured out like dust,
     and their flesh like dung.
18 Neither their silver nor their gold
     will be able to save them
   on the day of the LORD's wrath;
   in the fire of his passion
     the whole earth shall be consumed;
   for a full, a terrible end
     he will make of all the inhabitants of
       the earth.

Judgment on Israel's Enemies

2 Gather together, gather,
     O shameless nation,
2 before you are driven away
     like the drifting chaff,[b]
   before there comes upon you
     the fierce anger of the LORD,
   before there comes upon you
     the day of the LORD's wrath.
3 Seek the LORD, all you humble of the
       land,
     who do his commands;
   seek righteousness, seek humility;
     perhaps you may be hidden
   on the day of the LORD's wrath.
4 For Gaza shall be deserted,

---

a Heb *who thicken*   b Cn Compare Gk Syr: Heb *before a decree*
is born; like chaff a day has passed away

5.5. **1.10** *Fish Gate.* See Neh 12.38–39. **1.11** *Mortar,* a district in Jerusalem. **1.12** *At that time,* in parallel with *On that day* in vv. 9–10. *I will punish,* in parallel with the same phrase in v. 9. **1.14–18** These verses develop with even greater anticipation (*hastening fast*) the coming of the *day of the LORD.* Although Judah and Jerusalem are not mentioned in this section, given the immediate context it is apparent that they are the recipients of the announcement of utter desolation. **1.15** *A day of darkness and gloom.* See Joel 2.2. **1.16** *Trumpet blast.* See Judg 3.27. **1.17–18** The deity again speaks in the first person. *Walk like the blind.* See Deut 28.29; Isa 59.10. **1.18** *The whole earth . . . consumed* returns to the broader context of vv. 2–3 and serves to underscore the comprehensiveness of the destruction. **2.1–3** A hint that the people might avoid the "day of the LORD's" wrath. **2.1** *Gather together.* The Hebrew term is used for the gathering of straw or sticks (see Ex 5.7–12; Num 15.32), contrasting with the gathering of people for rejoicing in 3.20. The *shameless nation* is Judah. The Hebrew term translated *shameless*

is unusual; the phrase is lit. a "nation not longing for [God]" (see Ps 84.2). The Hebrew word used for *nation* is one used for non-Israelite people, further emphasizing that God's people have become no different than any other nation. **2.3** *Perhaps* indicates only a hope, not an assurance, that judgment is avoidable. **2.4–15** The threat now expands to foreign nations, following the familiar movement in prophetic books from threats against Judah and Jerusalem to threats against foreign nations. **2.4** *For* links these judgments with those against Judah, serves to underscore the totality of God's judgment, and provides an additional motivation for the possibility given Judah in vv. 1–3. **2.4–7** *Philistines* occupied the area to the west. Four of the five major Philistine cities are mentioned (*Gaza, Ashkelon, Ashdod, Ekron*) from south to north; and the fifth, Gath, was already destroyed by the Assyrian king Sargon II. The destruction of this ancient enemy of the Hebrew people would have delighted them, had they not already heard in the previous chapter of their own demise. *Cherethites* (v. 5), a group within the Philis-

and Ashkelon shall become a
      desolation;
Ashdod's people shall be driven out at
      noon,
      and Ekron shall be uprooted.

5   Ah, inhabitants of the seacoast,
      you nation of the Cherethites!
The word of the LORD is against you,
      O Canaan, land of the Philistines;
      and I will destroy you until no
      inhabitant is left.
6   And you, O seacoast, shall be pastures,
      meadows for shepherds
      and folds for flocks.
7   The seacoast shall become the possession
      of the remnant of the house of Judah,
      on which they shall pasture,
      and in the houses of Ashkelon
      they shall lie down at evening.
For the LORD their God will be mindful
      of them
      and restore their fortunes.

8   I have heard the taunts of Moab
      and the revilings of the Ammonites,
how they have taunted my people
      and made boasts against their territory.
9   Therefore, as I live, says the LORD of
      hosts,
      the God of Israel,
Moab shall become like Sodom
      and the Ammonites like Gomorrah,
a land possessed by nettles and salt pits,
      and a waste forever.
The remnant of my people shall plunder
      them,
      and the survivors of my nation shall
      possess them.
10 This shall be their lot in return for their
      pride,
      because they scoffed and boasted

against the people of the LORD of
      hosts.
11 The LORD will be terrible against them;
      he will shrivel all the gods of the earth,
and to him shall bow down,
      each in its place,
      all the coasts and islands of the nations.

12 You also, O Ethiopians,ᵃ
      shall be killed by my sword.

13 And he will stretch out his hand against
      the north,
      and destroy Assyria;
and he will make Nineveh a desolation,
      a dry waste like the desert.
14 Herds shall lie down in it,
      every wild animal;ᵇ
the desert owlᶜ and the screech owlᶜ
      shall lodge on its capitals;
the owlᵈ shall hoot at the window,
      the ravenᵉ croak on the threshold;
      for its cedar work will be laid bare.
15 Is this the exultant city
      that lived secure,
that said to itself,
      "I am, and there is no one else"?
What a desolation it has become,
      a lair for wild animals!
Everyone who passes by it
      hisses and shakes the fist.

The Wickedness of Jerusalem

3   Ah, soiled, defiled,
      oppressing city!
2   It has listened to no voice;
      it has accepted no correction.
It has not trusted in the LORD;
      it has not drawn near to its God.

---

a Or *Nubians*; Heb *Cushites*   *b* Tg Compare Gk: Heb *nation*
c Meaning of Heb uncertain   *d* Cn: Heb *a voice*   *e* Gk Vg:
Heb *desolation*

---

tines (2 Sam 8.18). **2.7** *Remnant of the house of Judah,*
those who have been judged (1.4–16). **2.8–11** Judgment against *Moab* and the *Ammonites,* who lived to
the east. The direct address of the deity in vv. 8–9 is
followed by a prophetic comment in vv. 10–11.
2.9 *Therefore as I live* indicates the beginning of an
oath. LORD *of hosts, the God of Israel* comes from the
earlier Zion theology (2 Sam 7.27) and may hint at the
hope of reuniting Israel and Judah. **2.12** *Ethiopians.*
The location of judgment now moves to the south,
probably indicating a remote region as well as the extent of the Lord's power, which includes even the most

faraway places. **2.13–15** After the threats have been issued to the areas west, east, and south, Zephaniah
turns to the north with judgment against *Assyria* and
Nineveh. Stretch out his hand recalls the same words
used against Judah and Jerusalem in 1.4. *Exultant city,*
Nineveh.

3.1–13 The city addressed is not identified, but it is
generally agreed to be Jerusalem. This is confirmed by
v. 4. **3.2–5** Every type of political and religious leader
in the city (cf. Ezek 22.23–29) is contrasted with the
Lord (v. 5). **3.2** Jerusalem has not heeded or paid any
attention to the Lord, which was first mentioned in 1.6

3 The officials within it
    are roaring lions;
  its judges are evening wolves
    that leave nothing until the morning.
4 Its prophets are reckless,
    faithless persons;
  its priests have profaned what is sacred,
    they have done violence to the law.
5 The LORD within it is righteous;
    he does no wrong.
  Every morning he renders his
      judgment,
    each dawn without fail;
  but the unjust knows no shame.

6 I have cut off nations;
    their battlements are in ruins;
  I have laid waste their streets
    so that no one walks in them;
  their cities have been made desolate,
    without people, without inhabitants.
7 I said, "Surely the city*a* will fear me,
    it will accept correction;
  it will not lose sight*b*
    of all that I have brought upon it."
  But they were the more eager
    to make all their deeds corrupt.

Punishment and Conversion of the Nations

8 Therefore wait for me, says the LORD,
    for the day when I arise as a witness.
  For my decision is to gather nations,
    to assemble kingdoms,
  to pour out upon them my indignation,
    all the heat of my anger;
  for in the fire of my passion
    all the earth shall be consumed.

9 At that time I will change the speech of
      the peoples
    to a pure speech,

that all of them may call on the name of
    the LORD
  and serve him with one accord.
10 From beyond the rivers of Ethiopia*c*
    my suppliants, my scattered ones,
  shall bring my offering.

11 On that day you shall not be put to
      shame
    because of all the deeds by which you
        have rebelled against me;
  for then I will remove from your
      midst
    your proudly exultant ones,
  and you shall no longer be haughty
    in my holy mountain.
12 For I will leave in the midst of you
    a people humble and lowly.
  They shall seek refuge in the name of the
    LORD—
13   the remnant of Israel;
  they shall do no wrong
    and utter no lies,
  nor shall a deceitful tongue
    be found in their mouths.
  Then they will pasture and lie down,
    and no one shall make them afraid.

A Song of Joy

14 Sing aloud, O daughter Zion;
    shout, O Israel!
  Rejoice and exult with all your heart,
    O daughter Jerusalem!
15 The LORD has taken away the judgments
      against you,
    he has turned away your enemies.
  The king of Israel, the LORD, is in your
      midst;
    you shall fear disaster no more.

---

a Heb it   *b* Gk Syr: Heb *its dwelling will not be cut off*
c Or *Nubia*; Heb *Cush*

(see Jer 7.28). **3.4** *Prophets.* See Mic 3.5–7. *Priests.* See Hos 4.6–9; 6.9. Priests are to discern for the people (Lev 10.10; Hag 2.10–13; Ezek 22.26). **3.6–13** A shift back to a direct quotation of the Lord. Here begins a section suggesting that there will exist among the people a *remnant* (2.7, 9; 3.13) who will listen to the Lord. **3.8** A return to the general judgment (see 1.2–3, 17–18). *Wait* often suggests that something positive will follow (see Ps 33.20; Isa 8.17; Hab 2.3). **3.9** *I will change...pure speech*, lit. "I will give the speech of peoples lips that are clean" (see Isa 6.5). **3.11** *On that day* refers back to v. 9 and connects with 1.9 and 3.16.

Proudly exultant ones alludes to the leaders in vv. 2–4. **3.12–13** *I will leave* plays on the same Hebrew word as *remnant* (v. 13) and contrasts with the negative remnants left in the land by other religions (see 1.4). **3.14–20** The call to sing sets a new tone for Zephaniah and assumes the restoration spoken of in vv. 8–13. From v. 14 through the first line of v. 18 (*as on a day of festival*) the prophet calls the remnant to rejoice (Isa 52.7–10; Zech 2.10; 9.9). The remainder of the chapter gives the promise spoken directly by the Lord. **3.14** *Sing aloud*, a public invitation to respond to the salvation that has come. **3.15** The reason for the people to sing.

16 On that day it shall be said to Jerusalem:
   Do not fear, O Zion;
      do not let your hands grow weak.
17 The LORD, your God, is in your midst,
      a warrior who gives victory;
   he will rejoice over you with gladness,
      he will renew you*a* in his love;
   he will exult over you with loud singing
18   as on a day of festival.*b*
   I will remove disaster from you,*c*
      so that you will not bear reproach for it.
19 I will deal with all your oppressors
      at that time.

And I will save the lame
   and gather the outcast,
and I will change their shame into praise
   and renown in all the earth.
20 At that time I will bring you home,
   at the time when I gather you;
for I will make you renowned and praised
   among all the peoples of the earth,
when I restore your fortunes
   before your eyes, says the LORD.

---

a Gk Syr: Heb *he will be silent*   *b* Gk Syr: Meaning of Heb uncertain   *c* Cn: Heb *I will remove from you; they were*

3.16 *On that day* no longer refers to the day on which punishment arises (1.9–10), but a day on which it can be said *Do not fear,* an introduction to words of salvation (see Isa 10.24). **3.17** *With loud singing.* The same Hebrew word used to call the people to *sing aloud* (v. 14) now has the Lord responding in kind. **3.19** *Oppres-* sors includes those within Judah and those in other nations. **3.20** *Gather* no longer carries the irony of gathering straw (see note on 2.1) but is more like the gathering a shepherd does of lambs (Isa 40.11; Jer 23.3). The restoration of *fortunes* envisaged is much like that described in Deut 30.1–4.

HAGGAI

Name

THE BOOK OF HAGGAI gives us no personal information about the seer whose name it bears. Later tradition obviously regards "the prophets Haggai and Zechariah son of Iddo" as contemporary figures (Ezra 5.1; 6.14). Neither prophet ever mentions the other, however, though their shared mission surely brought them together in the small town that Jerusalem was early in the Persian period. Perhaps Haggai's name, which is derived from the Hebrew verbal root *hgg*, "to make a pilgrimage," comes from his single-minded effort to bring about the reconstruction of that destination of ancient Judean pilgrims, the temple in Jerusalem.

Date, Content, and Message

IN CONTRAST TO the person of the author, information about the date of the book of Haggai is unusually precise. The chronological notices attached to the four oracles of the book place Haggai's work between mid-August and mid-December, 520 BCE, early in the reign of Darius I (the Great), who ruled the Persian Empire from 522 to 486 BCE. In the decades after 539 BCE, when the Persian king Cyrus freed the Judean exiles from their Babylonian captivity, modest prosperity had evidently begun to return to the land. A start may even have been made at rebuilding the ruined temple in Jerusalem (see Ezra 5.14–16). Work must have stopped, however, for in 520 the prophet Haggai warns that until the temple is up and running, normal living will elude the Judean community (see note on 2.15).

Only a minimal story line ties together the sequence of sermons in the book, which moves chronologically from the prophet's initial exhortation to Zerubbabel the governor and Joshua the high priest, through the beginning of the reconstruction project, to the blessings that began to flow on the occasion of the consecration of the still unfinished structure. The actual completion of the work in 516/5 BCE (see Ezra 6.15) evidently lay outside Haggai's purview. But what he saw under way moved him deeply, for he understood it to be the prelude to the coming messianic age. [W. SIBLEY TOWNER]

The Command to Rebuild the Temple

1 In the second year of King Darius, in the sixth month, on the first day of the month, the word of the LORD came by the prophet Haggai to Zerubbabel son of Shealtiel, governor of Judah, and to Joshua son of Jehozadak, the high priest: ²Thus says the LORD of hosts: These people say the time has not yet come to rebuild the LORD's house. ³Then the word of the LORD came by the prophet Haggai, saying: ⁴Is it a time for you yourselves to live in your paneled houses, while this house lies in ruins? ⁵Now therefore thus says the LORD of hosts: Consider how you have fared. ⁶You have sown much, and harvested little; you eat, but you never have enough; you drink, but you never have your fill; you clothe yourselves, but no one is warm; and you that earn wages earn wages to put them into a bag with holes.

7 Thus says the LORD of hosts: Consider how you have fared. ⁸Go up to the hills and bring wood and build the house, so that I may take pleasure in it and be honored, says the LORD. ⁹You have looked for much, and, lo, it came to little; and when you brought it home, I blew it away. Why? says the LORD of hosts. Because my house lies in ruins, while all of you hurry off to your own houses. ¹⁰Therefore the heavens above you have withheld the dew, and the earth has withheld its produce. ¹¹And I have called for a drought on the land and the hills, on the grain, the new wine, the oil, on what the soil produces, on human beings and animals, and on all their labors.

12 Then Zerubbabel son of Shealtiel, and Joshua son of Jehozadak, the high priest, with all the remnant of the people, obeyed the voice of the LORD their God, and the words of the prophet Haggai, as the LORD their God had sent him; and the people feared the LORD. ¹³Then Haggai, the messenger of the LORD, spoke to the people with the LORD's message, saying, I am with you, says the LORD. ¹⁴And the LORD stirred up the spirit of Zerubbabel son of Shealtiel, governor of Judah, and the spirit of Joshua son of Jehozadak, the high priest, and the spirit of all the remnant of the people; and they came and worked on the house of the LORD of hosts, their God, ¹⁵on the twenty-fourth day of the month, in the sixth month.

The Future Glory of the Temple

2 In the second year of King Darius, ¹in the seventh month, on the twenty-first day of the month, the word of the LORD came by the prophet Haggai, saying: ²Speak now to Zerubbabel son of Shealtiel, governor of Judah, and to Joshua son of Jehozadak, the high priest, and to the remnant of the people, and say, ³Who is left among you that saw this house in its former glory? How does it look to you now? Is it not in your sight as nothing? ⁴Yet now take courage, O Zerubbabel, says the LORD;

1.1–15 The prophet speaks to Zerubbabel. **1.1** *Sixth month . . . first day,* August 29, 520 BCE. *Zerubbabel son of Shealtiel,* the grandson of Jehoiachin (Jeconiah), the Judean king who enjoyed royal favor in Babylonian captivity (2 Kings 25.27–30; 1 Chr 3.17–19). He was presumably made *governor of Judah* by Darius, known simply (and favorably) as "the king." *Joshua son of Jehozadak,* the first person to bear the title *high priest* in the OT (see Zech 3.8; 6.11). His father was a priest among the exiles in Babylon (1 Chr 6.15). Evidently Haggai was in a position to direct the Lord's word to the leading people of the land. **1.2** *These people,* either the entire Judean community or *the remnant* (see v. 12) who had returned from Babylonian exile more than two decades earlier; however, the reference to *paneled houses* in v. 4 suggests that the message of the prophet was directed to the more affluent community leaders. The same contrast between *the LORD's house* and the houses of the human authorities is present in 2 Sam 7.1–17. On the eve of Babylonian captivity, the prophet Jeremiah too had railed against the cedar paneling of the king's house (Jer 22.13–17). **1.9** The forms of productivity listed in v. 11 were considered blessings by the ancient Judahites, but they lacked all of them. Haggai identifies the cause: God's house is neglected while individuals *hurry off* uncaringly to their own houses. It is noteworthy that, although earlier prophets found the cultic worship of their own day corrupt and repugnant (e.g., Am 5.21–24; Isa 1.10–15; Mic 6.6–8), Haggai and Zechariah focus on a different community abuse: the failure to restore the temple and its ritual system. **1.13–15a** The simple but reassuring word brought by *the messenger of the LORD* (see Mal 3.1) results in *stirred up* spirits. In this case, prophecy works; however, more than three weeks elapse after Haggai's first oracle before the reconstruction of the temple gets under way.

1.15b–2.9 Second address to Zerubbabel. **2.1** *Seventh month . . . twenty-first day,* October 17, 520 BCE. **2.3** Persons old enough to remember the appearance of the First Temple prior to its destruction in 587 would have to have been at least seventy-three years of age when Haggai said these words. **2.4–5** *I am with you . . . Egypt.* Haggai compares the spirit of God in the midst of the community of his day to the manifestation of God's presence in the pillars of cloud and fire

take courage, O Joshua, son of Jehozadak, the high priest; take courage, all you people of the land, says the LORD; work, for I am with you, says the LORD of hosts, [5]according to the promise that I made you when you came out of Egypt. My spirit abides among you; do not fear. [6]For thus says the LORD of hosts: Once again, in a little while, I will shake the heavens and the earth and the sea and the dry land; [7]and I will shake all the nations, so that the treasure of all nations shall come, and I will fill this house with splendor, says the LORD of hosts. [8]The silver is mine, and the gold is mine, says the LORD of hosts. [9]The latter splendor of this house shall be greater than the former, says the LORD of hosts; and in this place I will give prosperity, says the LORD of hosts.

A Rebuke and a Promise

10 On the twenty-fourth day of the ninth month, in the second year of Darius, the word of the LORD came by the prophet Haggai, saying: [11]Thus says the LORD of hosts: Ask the priests for a ruling: [12]If one carries consecrated meat in the fold of one's garment, and with the fold touches bread, or stew, or wine, or oil, or any kind of food, does it become holy? The priests answered, "No." [13]Then Haggai said, "If one who is unclean by contact with a dead body touches any of these, does it become unclean?" The priests answered, "Yes, it becomes unclean." [14]Haggai then said, So is

it with this people, and with this nation before me, says the LORD; and so with every work of their hands; and what they offer there is unclean. [15]But now, consider what will come to pass from this day on. Before a stone was placed upon a stone in the LORD's temple, [16]how did you fare?[a] When one came to a heap of twenty measures, there were but ten; when one came to the wine vat to draw fifty measures, there were but twenty. [17]I struck you and all the products of your toil with blight and mildew and hail; yet you did not return to me, says the LORD. [18]Consider from this day on, from the twenty-fourth day of the ninth month. Since the day that the foundation of the LORD's temple was laid, consider: [19]Is there any seed left in the barn? Do the vine, the fig tree, the pomegranate, and the olive tree still yield nothing? From this day on I will bless you.

God's Promise to Zerubbabel

20 The word of the LORD came a second time to Haggai on the twenty-fourth day of the month: [21]Speak to Zerubbabel, governor of Judah, saying, I am about to shake the heavens and the earth, [22]and to overthrow the throne of kingdoms; I am about to destroy the strength of the kingdoms of the nations, and overthrow the chariots and their riders; and the horses and their riders shall fall, every one

---

a Gk: Heb since they were

during the exodus from Egypt (Ex 13.21–22). *Do not fear.* The admonition that was addressed to Abram at the beginning of Israelite history (Gen 15.1) continues late in the canon to be a vital word of encouragement (see also Zech 8.13, 15). From the poverty, despair, and factionalism of the restored *people of the land* the Lord promises deliverance. **2.6–9** God will take such powerful action against all the nations that, because of their tribute in gold and silver, the splendor of the Second Temple will eclipse that of the First. The notion that the "wealth of nations" would flow to the future restored Jerusalem is a favorite theme of another late sixth-century BCE prophet, so-called Third Isaiah (Isa 56–66; see Isa 60.11; 61.6; 66.12).

2.10–14 An indictment of the people in dialogue form. **2.10** *Twenty-fourth day . . . ninth month,* December 18, 520 BCE. **2.12** Even though the temple had not yet resumed its function as the source of holiness in Judah, the priests remember that *consecrated meat* cannot make other foodstuffs *holy* by contact (cf. Lev 6.26–27). **2.13** Things can, however, become *unclean* through contact with what is ritually unclean. **2.14** Now the point of these priestly rulings becomes

clear: like a corpse, the Judean people are themselves unclean. Thus, they cannot make offerings acceptable to God because *every work of their hands* (i.e., agricultural produce; see v. 17) is *unclean.* The source of their uncleanness is not identified, but the desecration of the temple and the consequent loss of its atoning and purifying functions seems likely to be the cause. **2.15–19** The prophet promises a new era. **2.15** *From this day on* (see v. 10) suggests that a milestone has been reached in the temple reconstruction project. Whereas in 1.14 the people *came and worked on the house of the LORD,* here they have placed *stone . . . upon stone,* suggesting that a foundation deposit ceremony or consecration took place. The blessing that now begins to flow (v. 19) hints that the prophet regarded this day of dedication as the prelude to the "day of the LORD," beyond which lay the blessed new age of peace and plenty foreseen by the earlier prophets (e.g., Am 9.11–15). **2.17** See Am 4.9. **2.20–23** On the same day that he spoke the words of vv. 10–19, Haggai addressed a final oracle directly to Zerubbabel. **2.21–22** The Lord's imminent intervention means cosmic quakes (see v. 6; Joel 3.16) and military disaster for the *kingdoms of the*

by the sword of a comrade. [23] On that day, says the LORD of hosts, I will take you, O Zerubbabel my servant, son of Shealtiel, says the LORD,

and make you like a signet ring; for I have chosen you, says the LORD of hosts.

---

nations (see Ex 15.1–10). **2.23** Consistent with the promise to David in 2 Sam 7.16, Zerubbabel, the descendant of David, is *chosen* to be the Lord's *signet ring* (see Sir 49.11). Just as the bearer of the king's signet ring enjoyed the authority of the king (see Esth 3.10; 8.2; Jer 22.24), so also the chosen one acted on behalf

of the Lord (cf. Isa 42.1; 43.10; see also the attribution of future cosmic authority to Zerubbabel in Zech 4.6–10). Earlier prophets such as Jeremiah spoke words of judgment against the kings of their day. In contrast, the words of Haggai culminate in an apparent effort to exalt the Judean monarchy.

ZECHARIAH

Date, Authorship, and Context

THE BOOK OF ZECHARIAH is generally agreed to have been written by more than one person. The eight visions and numerous prophetic oracles that make up so-called First Zechariah, chs. 1–8, begin in October/November 520 (1.1) and end in December 518 BCE (7.1). There seems no reason to question this chronological framework, nor for that matter the attribution of the first part of the book to one of the exiles returned from Babylon (see note on 1.1). The meaning of the name Zechariah, "Yahweh has remembered," suggests that his role was to weave memories and traditions of the First Temple period into the new directions taken after the exile.

The Judean exiles began to return from Babylonian captivity after 539 BCE, armed with the so-called edict of Cyrus (Ezra 6.3–5), which permitted them to rebuild the holy sanctuary in Jerusalem. Perhaps they were guided as well by the visionary plan of restoration put forth in Ezek 40–48; certainly they were animated by the stunning promises of the great prophet of the exile, the author of Isa 40–55 (Second Isaiah). Reconstruction work began rather quickly under Sheshbazzar, the descendant of David appointed by the Persians to be the governor of Judah, but then for unknown reasons it stopped (see Ezra 4.4–5; 5.13–16). More than a decade later, during the tension stirred up throughout the Persian Empire by the accession of Darius I in 522 BCE, first Haggai, then Zechariah sprang into prophetic action. Haggai stresses the importance of rebuilding the temple so that the elect and restored community of Judah might enjoy the divine blessings that flow from right worship. In contrast to this practical program for restoration, Zech 1–6 offers cosmic visions of the world at peace and foresees pivotal roles for Zerubbabel, the Davidic governor (nephew of Sheshbazzar), and Joshua, the high priest. Even the nonvisionary prophetic oracles collected together in chs. 7–8 sound a strong note of hope for the Jerusalem of the future. In short, First Zechariah aims to provide a theological rationale for the emerging new order of Israel.

First and Second Zechariah Contrasted

THE VISIONS AND ORACLES of Zech 1–8 reflect the essentially hierocratic, or priestly, outlook of a "central prophet," i.e., one who belonged to temple circles and who linked Israel's salvation with worship and priestly leadership. An individual or a school with a more peripheral or so-

1269

cially marginal point of view speaks in Zech 9–14. This so-called Second (Deutero-) Zechariah does not display the editorial unity of the first eight chapters of the book. It reveals a pattern of steadily increasing disillusionment with the postexilic polity and a sense that the glorious vision of a just society put forward by Isaiah of the exile (chs. 40–55) and by his visionary successor in Zech 1–8 was not going to be achieved by a priestly-Davidic establishment centered in Jerusalem.

Nevertheless, Second Zechariah offers images of a coming new age of holiness and peace, brought in by Yahweh alone, that are even more powerful than those of First Zechariah. An editor has collected into the first "oracle" (chs. 9–11) vivid poetic portrayals of Yahweh as victorious Divine Warrior. In the second collection of mostly prose vision reports (chs. 12–14), an ever more urgent sense of the impending "day of the LORD" suggests that the author(s) worked over a number of decades. The culminating vision of ch. 14 may have occurred late in the fifth century BCE. This would place these chapters in the company of such other protoapocalyptic texts as Joel 2.28–3.21; Isa 24–27. [W. SIBLEY TOWNER]

Israel Urged to Repent

1 In the eighth month, in the second year of Darius, the word of the LORD came to the prophet Zechariah son of Berechiah son of Iddo, saying: 2The LORD was very angry with your ancestors. 3Therefore say to them, Thus says the LORD of hosts: Return to me, says the LORD of hosts, and I will return to you, says the LORD of hosts. 4Do not be like your ancestors, to whom the former prophets proclaimed, "Thus says the LORD of hosts, Return from your evil ways and from your evil deeds." But they did not hear or heed me, says the LORD. 5Your ancestors, where are they? And the prophets, do they live forever? 6But my words and my statutes, which I commanded my servants the prophets, did they not overtake your ancestors? So they repented and said, "The LORD of hosts has dealt with us according to our ways and deeds, just as he planned to do."

First Vision: The Horsemen

7 On the twenty-fourth day of the eleventh month, the month of Shebat, in the second year of Darius, the word of the LORD came to the prophet Zechariah son of Berechiah son of Iddo; and Zechariah*a* said, 8In the night I saw a man riding on a red horse! He was standing among the myrtle trees in the glen; and behind him were red, sorrel, and white horses. 9Then I said, "What are these, my lord?" The angel who talked with me said to me, "I will show you what they are." 10So the man who was standing among the myrtle trees answered, "They are those whom the LORD has sent to patrol the earth." 11Then they spoke to the angel of the LORD who was standing among the myrtle trees, "We have patrolled the earth, and lo, the whole earth remains at peace." 12Then the

_____
a Heb *and he*

1.1–8.23 First Zechariah. 1.1–6 Prologue. 1.1 *Eighth month . . . second year,* October/November 520 BCE. *Zechariah son of Berechiah son of Iddo.* Neh 12.16 establishes that Zechariah was of a priestly family. According to Ezra 5.1; 6.14, he was the son and not the grandson of Iddo. 1.6 *So they repented,* lit. "they returned." "Return" is the theme of this opening oracle (vv. 3, 4, 6). Though the prophets often called for return or repentance (e.g., Jer 18.11; 25.5; 35.15; Ezek 14.6; Am 5.14–15), it is not often reported that repentance occurred.
1.7–13 First vision. 1.7 *Twenty-fourth day . . . eleventh month,* February 15, 519 BCE. *Shebat* here and *Chislev* in 7.1 are the earliest uses in the Hebrew Bible of the Babylonian names of the months. Eventually these names were accepted in the Hebrew calendar.

1.8 *In the night.* The uninterrupted sequence of vision reports in vv. 8–13 suggests that they all came to Zechariah in a single night, perhaps in the form of dreams. Visions and dreams are, of course, media of divine revelation for Hebrew seers. *A man,* one of the angelic host (v. 11). Angelic interpreters provide vital explanations for several of the prophet's visions, so that the weird, symbolic sights become conveyors of deeper understanding, i.e., *word* (v. 7). In Second Isaiah, *myrtle* is a feature of the restored Israel (see Isa 41.19; 55.13). The red, sorrel, and white colors of the horses might have symbolic values; however, they probably simply reflect the colors of horses known in the ancient Near East. 1.10–11 The horses have been sent out from the heavenly court on reconnaissance of the earth (see 6.1–8). 1.12 The angel's cry, *O LORD of*

angel of the LORD said, "O LORD of hosts, how long will you withhold mercy from Jerusalem and the cities of Judah, with which you have been angry these seventy years?" 13Then the LORD replied with gracious and comforting words to the angel who talked with me. 14So the angel who talked with me said to me, Proclaim this message: Thus says the LORD of hosts; I am very jealous for Jerusalem and for Zion. 15And I am extremely angry with the nations that are at ease; for while I was only a little angry, they made the disaster worse. 16Therefore, thus says the LORD, I have returned to Jerusalem with compassion; my house shall be built in it, says the LORD of hosts, and the measuring line shall be stretched out over Jerusalem. 17Proclaim further: Thus says the LORD of hosts: My cities shall again overflow with prosperity; the LORD will again comfort Zion and again choose Jerusalem.

Second Vision: The Horns and the Smiths

18*ª* And I looked up and saw four horns. 19I asked the angel who talked with me, "What are these?" And he answered me, "These are the horns that have scattered Judah, Israel, and Jerusalem." 20Then the LORD showed me four blacksmiths. 21And I asked, "What are they coming to do?" He answered, "These are the horns that scattered Judah, so that no head could be raised; but these have come to terrify them, to strike down the horns of the nations

that lifted up their horns against the land of Judah to scatter its people."*ᵇ*

Third Vision: The Man with a Measuring Line

2*ᶜ* I looked up and saw a man with a measuring line in his hand. 2Then I asked, "Where are you going?" He answered me, "To measure Jerusalem, to see what is its width and what is its length." 3Then the angel who talked with me came forward, and another angel came forward to meet him, 4and said to him, "Run, say to that young man: Jerusalem shall be inhabited like villages without walls, because of the multitude of people and animals in it. 5For I will be a wall of fire all around it, says the LORD, and I will be the glory within it."

Interlude: An Appeal to the Exiles

6 Up, up! Flee from the land of the north, says the LORD; for I have spread you abroad like the four winds of heaven, says the LORD. 7Up! Escape to Zion, you that live with daughter Babylon. 8For thus said the LORD of hosts (after his glory*ᵈ* sent me) regarding the nations that plundered you: Truly, one who touches you touches the apple of my eye.*ᵉ* 9See now, I am going to raise*ᶠ* my hand against them, and they shall become plunder for their own slaves.

---

a Ch 2.1 in Heb   *b* Heb *it*   *c* Ch 2.5 in Heb   *d* Cn: Heb *after glory he*   *e* Heb *his eye*   *f* Or *wave*

---

hosts, how long? draws on the language of the psalms of lament (e.g., Pss 6.3; 13.2; 79.5) to press God about the duration of human suffering. *Seventy years,* a conventional figure applied to various spans of time. In Jer 25.11; 29.10 it refers to the seventy-plus years in which the Neo-Babylonian Empire flourished (612–539 BCE); here it refers to the period of the devastation and exile of Jerusalem and Judah (587, the year of the destruction of the temple, to the approximate time of this oracle, 519 BCE). **1.14–17** Angelic oracle of interpretation. In *gracious and comforting words* (v. 13), the Lord speaks through the angel to announce the end of Zion's woes. **1.14** *Jealous.* See note on 8.2. **1.16** *Measuring line,* an image drawn from carpentry (Isa 44.13), can refer to judgment (see Isa 34.11; Lam 2.8) or, as in this case, restoration (see also Jer 31.38–39). **1.17** *The LORD will . . . choose Jerusalem.* No other prophet ever claims that God "chose" Jerusalem (see also 2.12; 3.2), but the theme is sounded in Deut 12.1–28; 1 Kings 8.44–48; 11.13.

   1.18–21 Second vision. **1.19** *Horns,* the foreign nations that had oppressed Israel since the days of the Divided Monarchy (cf. Dan 7.19–27). They are not identified; the number *four* may simply represent to-

tality (cf. 2.6), i.e., all of Israel's historic enemies. **1.20–21** *Four blacksmiths,* all the divine agents who will destroy the oppressive foreign powers (see Isa 54.16–17).
   2.1–5 Third vision. **2.1** *Measuring line,* used here to find the limits of the extant Jerusalem (cf. Am 7.17; Mic 2.4–5), producing dimensions that are immediately pronounced obsolete. **2.4** The restored city will have a *multitude* of human and animal inhabitants. Second Isaiah (chs. 40–55) also envisions restored Israel as "too crowded for your inhabitants" (Isa 49.19; see 54.3; Zech 14.11). The resulting ecological crisis is addressed in 11.1–3. **2.5** The priestly theme of the return of God's glory to the rebuilt temple is set forth in Ezek 43.1–5. In Zechariah's vision, God's presence is manifested even more dramatically as *a wall of fire all around* Jerusalem. **2.6–13** An oracle of the Lord. **2.6** *North,* the generic location of the enemies of Israel and the place of its exile (see Jer 6.22; 10.22). The return of exiles from the Diaspora to Zion is a frequent feature of OT renditions of the culmination of history (e.g., Jer 31.10–17). **2.9** The prophet imagines that the returning exiles will *plunder* their captors (see Ex 12.35–36). Such a reversal of fortunes leads to a formula suitable for the recognition of God's work in his-

Then you will know that the LORD of hosts has sent me. [10]Sing and rejoice, O daughter Zion! For lo, I will come and dwell in your midst, says the LORD. [11]Many nations shall join themselves to the LORD on that day, and shall be my people; and I will dwell in your midst. And you shall know that the LORD of hosts has sent me to you. [12]The LORD will inherit Judah as his portion in the holy land, and will again choose Jerusalem.

13 Be silent, all people, before the LORD; for he has roused himself from his holy dwelling.

Fourth Vision: Joshua and Satan

3 Then he showed me the high priest Joshua standing before the angel of the LORD, and Satan[a] standing at his right hand to accuse him. [2]And the LORD said to Satan,[a] "The LORD rebuke you, O Satan![a] The LORD who has chosen Jerusalem rebuke you! Is not this man a brand plucked from the fire?" [3]Now Joshua was dressed with filthy clothes as he stood before the angel. [4]The angel said to those who were standing before him, "Take off his filthy clothes." And to him he said, "See, I

have taken your guilt away from you, and I will clothe you with festal apparel." [5]And I said, "Let them put a clean turban on his head." So they put a clean turban on his head and clothed him with the apparel; and the angel of the LORD was standing by.

6 Then the angel of the LORD assured Joshua, saying [7]"Thus says the LORD of hosts: If you will walk in my ways and keep my requirements, then you shall rule my house and have charge of my courts, and I will give you the right of access among those who are standing here. [8]Now listen, Joshua, high priest, you and your colleagues who sit before you! For they are an omen of things to come: I am going to bring my servant the Branch. [9]For on the stone that I have set before Joshua, on a single stone with seven facets, I will engrave its inscription, says the LORD of hosts, and I will remove the guilt of this land in a single day. [10]On that day, says the LORD of hosts, you shall invite each other to come under your vine and fig tree."

a Or the Accuser; Heb the Adversary

tory: *you will know . . . sent me* (see also v. 11; 4.9; 6.15; see also Ezek 33.33, where the prophet is validated by historical events). This slogan and its variations are thematic in Ezekiel, where they are used more than seventy times. **2.10** *Daughter Zion* often receives good news of her rescue (see 9.9; also Isa 12.6; 52.2; 62.11; Mic 4.8; Zeph 3.14–15). The familial term is one of endearment. **2.11** The notion that on the "day of the LORD" the gentile nations *shall be* God's *people* has many precedents in prophetic literature (e.g., Isa 19.24–25; 56.6–8; 60.3). **2.12** *Holy land,* used nowhere else in the OT, though it can be found in Wis 12.3; 2 Macc 1.7. **2.13** Awed silence is appropriate for all peoples as God prepares to act. Cf. Hab 2.20.

3.1–5 Fourth vision. The cleansing and reconsecration of the high priest is accomplished in the divine council. **3.1** *The high priest Joshua.* See note on Hag 1.1. *Satan.* The use of the article before *satan* in Hebrew makes clear that this is a title or a function, not a personal name—"the *satan*," not "Satan" (see text note *a*). The *satan* is a member of the divine council whose task it is to discover and indict malefactors (see Job 1.6–12). The OT treats *satan* as a proper name only in 1 Chr 21.1, where "Satan" assumes the function of testing that the Lord plays in the parallel text in 2 Sam 24.1. The picture of the divine council given in 1 Kings 22.19–23 shows spirits performing various functions in God's court, including that of testing and provoking sinners. **3.2–3** In Isa 4.3–4, the filthiness of Jerusalem is purged by burning. Here Joshua has already emerged as *a brand plucked from the fire,* and his filthiness derives not from his sin but from his fiery ordeal. **3.4–**

5 These verses anticipate the consecration of the high priest in *festal apparel* and *clean turban* to his function of taking upon himself the guilt of the people, so that they may be acceptable before the Lord (see Ex 28.31–38). **3.6–10** Oracular responses to the vision. **3.7** *Right of access.* Formerly, prophets were the only human beings to have enjoyed observer status at meetings of the divine court (1 Kings 22; Isa 6; Jer 23.18). In postexilic times, as prophecy recedes, the priesthood achieves higher standing. **3.8** *My servant the Branch.* In Isa 11.1, the coming Davidic ruler is described as a "branch" (see also Jer 23.5; 33.15). In this verse, the *Branch* is someone other than Joshua and his colleagues, since Joshua was not of the royal dynasty of David. Most likely to be this messianic figure is Zerubbabel, who, as Hag 2.20–23 indicates, embodied the hopes for a political future for Judah under a descendant of David. See also note on 6.12. **3.9** *A single stone with seven facets* may refer to the engraved "rosette of pure gold" (Ex 28.36–38), which was fastened to the front of the turban of the high priest. The mysterious engraving on the seven sides of the stone might be the Hebrew words for "Holy to the LORD" (Ex 28.36), which could be written in seven letters. In this verse, the ornament is not fabricated by any human hand but is given to Joshua by the Lord. For Zechariah, divine intervention alone could solve the problems of contamination and deconsecration that confounded efforts at worship in the temple in the early postexilic Judean community. When the priestly mediator is purified, the system of atonement can function and the entire community can be cleansed *in a single day.*

Fifth Vision: The Lampstand and Olive Trees

4 The angel who talked with me came again, and wakened me, as one is wakened from sleep. ²He said to me, "What do you see?" And I said, "I see a lampstand all of gold, with a bowl on the top of it; there are seven lamps on it, with seven lips on each of the lamps that are on the top of it. ³And by it there are two olive trees, one on the right of the bowl and the other on its left." ⁴I said to the angel who talked with me, "What are these, my lord?" ⁵Then the angel who talked with me answered me, "Do you not know what these are?" I said, "No, my lord." ⁶He said to me, "This is the word of the LORD to Zerubbabel: Not by might, nor by power, but by my spirit, says the LORD of hosts. ⁷What are you, O great mountain? Before Zerubbabel you shall become a plain; and he shall bring out the top stone amid shouts of 'Grace, grace to it!' "

8 Moreover the word of the LORD came to me, saying, ⁹"The hands of Zerubbabel have laid the foundation of this house; his hands shall also complete it. Then you will know that the LORD of hosts has sent me to you. ¹⁰For whoever has despised the day of small things shall rejoice, and shall see the plummet in the hand of Zerubbabel.

"These seven are the eyes of the LORD, which range through the whole earth." ¹¹Then I said to him, "What are these two olive trees on the right and the left of the lampstand?" ¹²And a second time I said to him, "What are these two branches of the olive trees, which pour out the oil[a] through the two golden pipes?" ¹³He said to me, "Do you not know what these are?" I said, "No, my lord." ¹⁴Then he said, "These are the two anointed ones who stand by the Lord of the whole earth."

Sixth Vision: The Flying Scroll

5 Again I looked up and saw a flying scroll. ²And he said to me, "What do you see?" I answered, "I see a flying scroll; its length is twenty cubits, and its width ten cubits." ³Then he said to me, "This is the curse that goes out over the face of the whole land; for everyone who steals shall be cut off according to the writing on one side, and everyone who swears falsely[b] shall be cut off according to the writ-

---

a Cn: Heb *gold*   *b* The word *falsely* added from verse 4

4.1–14 Fifth vision. This apparently complex vision is made much clearer when the two oracles to Zerubbabel embedded within it (vv. 6–7, 8–10a) are treated separately. **4.2** *Lampstand,* not the familiar seven-branched candelabrum of Ex 25.31–40; 37.17–24. Archaeological evidence now confirms that the object envisioned here could be a bowl-shaped oil reservoir surmounting a golden base and fitted around the rim with seven (not forty-nine!) protruding spouts to serve as lamps. **4.5** Angelic question. If vv. 6–7, 8–10a are construed as a pair of embedded oracles, v. 10b flows perfectly as the angel's response to this question. **4.6** *Zerubbabel.* See note on Hag 1.1. **4.7** *O great mountain,* possibly the Temple Mount, cluttered with ruins that would need to be removed. Perhaps the *top stone* should be understood as a stone from the former temple incorporated into the foundation deposit of the new structure. Mesopotamian sources attest to similar efforts to ensure sacral continuity. **4.9** *You will know . . . sent me.* See note on 2.9. **4.10a** *Day of small things.* This assurance seems to be addressed to those who have found the pace of restoration too feeble. The leadership of Zerubbabel promises renewed action. Now he is pictured at the end of the temple reconstruction process with *plummet* in hand. Recent commentators understand this object to be not a builders' tool but rather an inscribed metallic tablet to be deposited in the finished structure. Such a practice is well attested in Babylonian and Persian texts. **4.10b** *These seven . . .*

eyes of the LORD returns us to the angelic question of v. 5. If the lamps are the eyes of the Lord, then the lampstand must represent the Lord's person. The image of the all-seeing eyes of the Lord is common in biblical tradition (see 2 Chr 16.9; Job 34.21; Pss 14.2; 66.7; Prov 15.3). **4.14** At last the two olive trees are identified as *the two anointed ones* (lit. "sons of the oil") and no doubt represent Joshua and Zerubbabel, the two heroes of the temple reconstruction effort in both Zech 1–8 and Haggai. In Zechariah's vision for the polity of the emerging Judean community, royal and priestly "messiahs" (*anointed ones*) stand on either side of God, sharing leadership. The "oil" referred to here is not that used for consecration of priest or king but rather that used for food and lamp fuel. If the lamp burns this very oil, then there is an exquisite interrelationship between the human and divine worlds, since human abundance would help feed the divine light.

5.1–4 Sixth vision. For the first time the prophet envisions curse and judgment rather than blessing. **5.2** Since a *cubit* is about 18 inches in length, this visionary scroll was 30 by 15 feet. Such a scroll would be impossible to unroll or handle, but this is a *flying scroll* (v. 1), not held by human hands. **5.3** The scroll flies about directing the *curse* against violators of the eighth and ninth commandments, which forbid theft and false oaths (see Ex 20.15–16; Deut 5.19–20). Zechariah demonstrates that life and blessing depend on obedience to the ancient covenant requirements.

ing on the other side. [4]I have sent it out, says the LORD of hosts, and it shall enter the house of the thief, and the house of anyone who swears falsely by my name; and it shall abide in that house and consume it, both timber and stones."

Seventh Vision: The Woman in a Basket

5 Then the angel who talked with me came forward and said to me, "Look up and see what this is that is coming out." [6]I said, "What is it?" He said, "This is a basket[a] coming out." And he said, "This is their iniquity[b] in all the land." [7]Then a leaden cover was lifted, and there was a woman sitting in the basket![a] [8]And he said, "This is Wickedness." So he thrust her back into the basket,[a] and pressed the leaden weight down on its mouth. [9]Then I looked up and saw two women coming forward. The wind was in their wings; they had wings like the wings of a stork, and they lifted up the basket[a] between earth and sky. [10]Then I said to the angel who talked with me, "Where are they taking the basket?"[a] [11]He said to me, "To the land of Shinar, to build a house for it; and when this is prepared, they will set the basket[a] down there on its base."

Eighth Vision: Four Chariots

6 And again I looked up and saw four chariots coming out from between two mountains—mountains of bronze. [2]The first chariot had red horses, the second chariot black horses, [3]the third chariot white horses, and the fourth chariot dappled gray[c] horses. [4]Then I

said to the angel who talked with me, "What are these, my lord?" [5]The angel answered me, "These are the four winds[d] of heaven going out, after presenting themselves before the Lord of all the earth. [6]The chariot with the black horses goes toward the north country, the white ones go toward the west country,[e] and the dappled ones go toward the south country." [7]When the steeds came out, they were impatient to get off and patrol the earth. And he said, "Go, patrol the earth." So they patrolled the earth. [8]Then he cried out to me, "Lo, those who go toward the north country have set my spirit at rest in the north country."

The Coronation of the Branch

9 The word of the LORD came to me: [10]Collect silver and gold[f] from the exiles—from Heldai, Tobijah, and Jedaiah—who have arrived from Babylon; and go the same day to the house of Josiah son of Zephaniah. [11]Take the silver and gold and make a crown,[g] and set it on the head of the high priest Joshua son of Jehozadak; [12]say to him: Thus says the LORD of hosts: Here is a man whose name is Branch: for he shall branch out in his place, and he shall build the temple of the LORD. [13]It is he that shall build the temple of the LORD; he shall bear royal honor, and shall sit upon his throne and rule. There shall be a priest by his throne, with peaceful un-

---

a Heb *ephah*   *b* Gk Compare Syr: Heb *their eye*   *c* Compare Gk: Meaning of Heb uncertain   *d* Or *spirits*   *e* Cn: Heb *go after them*   *f* Cn Compare verse 11: Heb lacks *silver and gold*   *g* Gk Mss Syr Tg: Heb *crowns*

5.5–11 Seventh vision. **5.6** *A basket,* in Hebrew an *ephah,* a container of about two-thirds of a bushel in dry measure, typically used for such commodities as flour (Lev 5.11) and barley (Ruth 2.17). **5.8–9** *This is Wickedness.* Israel's sin is personified as a woman who could somehow fit into a basket. The female imagery for evil is somewhat offset in this vision by the cleansing power of the *two women* with *wind . . . in their wings* who carry the basket away. **5.11** *The land of Shinar,* Babylon, the place of Israel's exile (see Isa 11.11; Dan 1.2). Shinar was also the place of the primeval sin of the Tower of Babel (Gen 11.2). Placing the basket in the *house* (temple) built for it suggests that the cleansing of Judah through the reconstruction of the temple causes a corresponding desecration of worship in the land of the oppressor. **6.1–8** Eighth vision. **6.1** The patrol sent forth from divine headquarters is equipped with *chariots* drawn in all directions by teams of various colored horses (see notes on 1.8; 1.10–11). The first vision (1.7–13), with which this last vision forms a kind of bookend, also pictured an angelic horse patrol, but without chariots. **6.6** Presumably the red

team heads eastward. **6.8** *My spirit . . . in the north country.* God has extended right order throughout the world, even in the north, the traditional land of the enemy (see note on 2.6).

6.9–15 A political oracle. From this point through ch. 8, the prophet of First Zechariah ceases to function as a visionary and assumes the more typical role of an intermediary for divine instructions for the right ordering of the restored Judean community. **6.12–13** *A man whose name is Branch.* See note on 3.8. Even though the oracles of 4.6–7, 8–10a hail Zerubbabel as the rebuilder of the temple, the crown of silver and gold is placed on the head of the priestly figure, Joshua son of Jehozadak, and not on the head of the royal figure (v. 11). Perhaps this text was edited toward a more priestly bias after the final disappearance of any vestige of the house of David. **6.13** *A priest by his throne,* however, still suggests the kind of bicameral polity in the postexilic community described in Hag 1.1–15, in which priest and civil governor worked side by side. The shared leadership foreseen in 4.14 is now further elaborated: it is carried out in *peaceful understanding.* The

derstanding between the two of them. [14]And the crown[a] shall be in the care of Heldai,[b] Tobijah, Jedaiah, and Josiah[c] son of Zephaniah, as a memorial in the temple of the LORD.

15 Those who are far off shall come and help to build the temple of the LORD; and you shall know that the LORD of hosts has sent me to you. This will happen if you diligently obey the voice of the LORD your God.

Hypocritical Fasting Condemned

7 In the fourth year of King Darius, the word of the LORD came to Zechariah on the fourth day of the ninth month, which is Chislev. [2]Now the people of Bethel had sent Sharezer and Regem-melech and their men, to entreat the favor of the LORD, [3]and to ask the priests of the house of the LORD of hosts and the prophets, "Should I mourn and practice abstinence in the fifth month, as I have done for so many years?" [4]Then the word of the LORD of hosts came to me: [5]Say to all the people of the land and the priests: When you fasted and lamented in the fifth month and in the seventh, for these seventy years, was it for me that you fasted? [6]And when you eat and when you drink, do you not eat and drink only for yourselves? [7]Were not these the words that the LORD proclaimed by the former prophets, when Jerusalem was inhabited and in prosperity, along with the towns around it, and when the Negeb and the Shephelah were inhabited?

Punishment for Rejecting God's Demands

8 The word of the LORD came to Zechariah, saying: [9]Thus says the LORD of hosts: Render true judgments, show kindness and mercy to one another; [10]do not oppress the widow, the orphan, the alien, or the poor; and do not devise evil in your hearts against one another. [11]But they refused to listen, and turned a stubborn shoulder, and stopped their ears in order not to hear. [12]They made their hearts adamant in order not to hear the law and the words that the LORD of hosts had sent by his spirit through the former prophets. Therefore great wrath came from the LORD of hosts. [13]Just as, when I[d] called, they would not hear, so, when they called, I would not hear, says the LORD of hosts, [14]and I scattered them with a whirlwind among all the nations that they had not known. Thus the land they left was desolate, so that no one went to and fro, and a pleasant land was made desolate.

God's Promises to Zion

8 The word of the LORD of hosts came to me, saying: [2]Thus says the LORD of hosts: I am jealous for Zion with great jealousy, and I am jealous for her with great wrath. [3]Thus says the LORD: I will return to Zion, and will dwell in the midst of Jerusalem; Jerusalem shall be called the faithful city, and the mountain of the LORD of hosts shall be called the holy mountain. [4]Thus says the LORD of hosts: Old men and old women shall again sit in the streets of Jerusalem, each with staff in hand because of their great age. [5]And the streets of the city shall be full of boys and girls playing in its streets.

---

a Gk Syr: Heb crowns b Syr Compare verse 10: Heb Helem c Syr Compare verse 10: Heb Hen d Heb he

---

Branch now seems to be someone other than Joshua. **6.15** You shall know . . . sent me. See note on 2.9.
7.1–14 Question and answer on the utility of fasting. **7.1** Fourth year . . . ninth month, December 7, 518 BCE. Chislev. See note on 1.7. Nearly two years have passed since the prophet's night of eight visions. **7.3** Mention of the priests of the house of the LORD suggests that the temple staff was back in action after the temple was reconsecrated, even though it was not yet fully reconstructed (see Hag 2.10–19). The number of years during which the people of Bethel have maintained their discipline of fasting and mourning is said by the prophet to be seventy (v. 5), the traditional length of the exile (e.g., Jer 25.11–12; 29.10; Zech 1.12). The fast of the fifth month may have been established in memory of the destruction of the First Temple (2 Kings 25.8–9; Jer 52.12–13). The Bethel question has significance for religious practice, then: Do we continue to mourn for the temple when it has been rebuilt? **7.7** The

words . . . by the former prophets. The preexilic prophets criticized Israel's public piety as hypocritical (e.g., Isa 1.16–17; Am 5.14–15; fasting itself is mentioned only in Jer 14.12). Their criticism came at a time when Jerusalem was inhabited, namely, when no evidence of the Lord's displeasure at the shallowness of such practice had as yet been manifested in destruction and dispersal. **7.9–10** The true acts of piety before God are true judgments . . . kindness and mercy and the other righteous acts enumerated here. The covenant tradition stands front and center (cf. Deut 14.29; 24.19–21). The words are reminiscent of the great teaching of Mic 6.8 and also of the social ethics of the former prophets (v. 12; e.g., Isa 1.16–17; Am 5.14–15; 21–24).
8.1–17 Oracles and exhortations on the restoration of Zion. **8.2** God's jealousy is zeal for achieving justice for Zion (see also 1.14). **8.3** See 1.16; also Isa 11.9; 65.25; Jer 31.23. **8.4–5** The delightful vision of streets full of boys and girls as well as old men and women ech-

⁶Thus says the LORD of hosts: Even though it seems impossible to the remnant of this people in these days, should it also seem impossible to me, says the LORD of hosts? ⁷Thus says the LORD of hosts: I will save my people from the east country and from the west country; ⁸and I will bring them to live in Jerusalem. They shall be my people and I will be their God, in faithfulness and in righteousness.

9 Thus says the LORD of hosts: Let your hands be strong—you that have recently been hearing these words from the mouths of the prophets who were present when the foundation was laid for the rebuilding of the temple, the house of the LORD of hosts. ¹⁰For before those days there were no wages for people or for animals, nor was there any safety from the foe for those who went out or came in, and I set them all against one another. ¹¹But now I will not deal with the remnant of this people as in the former days, says the LORD of hosts. ¹²For there shall be a sowing of peace; the vine shall yield its fruit, the ground shall give its produce, and the skies shall give their dew; and I will cause the remnant of this people to possess all these things. ¹³Just as you have been a cursing among the nations, O house of Judah and house of Israel, so I will save you and you shall be a blessing. Do not be afraid, but let your hands be strong.

14 For thus says the LORD of hosts: Just as I purposed to bring disaster upon you, when your ancestors provoked me to wrath, and I did not relent, says the LORD of hosts, ¹⁵so again I have purposed in these days to do good to Jerusalem and to the house of Judah; do not be afraid. ¹⁶These are the things that you shall do: Speak the truth to one another, render in your gates judgments that are true and make for peace, ¹⁷do not devise evil in your hearts against one another, and love no false oath; for all these are things that I hate, says the LORD.

Joyful Fasting

18 The word of the LORD of hosts came to me, saying: ¹⁹Thus says the LORD of hosts: The fast of the fourth month, and the fast of the fifth, and the fast of the seventh, and the fast of the tenth, shall be seasons of joy and gladness, and cheerful festivals for the house of Judah: therefore love truth and peace.

Many Peoples Drawn to Jerusalem

20 Thus says the LORD of hosts: Peoples shall yet come, the inhabitants of many cities; ²¹the inhabitants of one city shall go to another, saying, "Come, let us go to entreat the favor of the LORD, and to seek the LORD of hosts; I myself am going." ²²Many peoples and strong nations shall come to seek the LORD of hosts in Jerusalem, and to entreat the favor of the LORD. ²³Thus says the LORD of hosts: In those days ten men from nations of every language shall take hold of a Jew, grasping his garment and saying, "Let us go with you, for we have heard that God is with you."

---

oes the blessing for age and youth alike in the coming new Jerusalem envisioned in Isa 65.20. Significantly, the prophet uses language not of power and glory, but of rest and play, to capture the ethos of the city of the future. **8.6** In Isaiah too the restored community of Judah is typically referred to as the *remnant* (Isa 10.22–23; 11.11; 37.31–32). **8.7–8** *I will bring them.* Again, a hallmark of the new age is the gathering of the exiles to Jerusalem (see note on 2.6; also 6.15). *They shall . . . their God,* a refrain heard frequently in Jeremiah (24.7; 31.33; 32.38) and Ezekiel (11.20; 14.11; 37.23, 27). The covenant stipulated that this right relationship would come into existence when Israel was faithful. **8.9–13** *Words from . . . the prophets,* e.g., Hag 1.6–11; 2.4–9, 15–19. **8.13** The exiled and dispersed Judah and Israel have been objects of hissing and cursing (see Jer 25.18; 29.18; Mic 6.16), but all that is to be reversed in a restoration era characterized by agricultural productivity and peace. **8.14–17** The prophet continues to think in terms of the covenant tradition, stressing truth and justice as the basis for a new community (see 7.9–10; Mic 6.12; Eph 4.25). **8.18–23** Three oracles on the future joy of Judah. **8.19** To the fasts mentioned in 7.5 are now added fasts of the *fourth* and *tenth* months. This verse answers the question raised by the elders of Bethel in 7.2–3: no, in the days to come fasts shall become *cheerful festivals.* No wonder! The new community is founded on the values of *truth and peace.* **8.20–22** *Many peoples and strong nations* are among the throngs envisioned as coming to the soon to be reconstructed temple to *entreat the favor of the LORD.* The universal scope of God's future work of blessing answers to the promise to Abram in Gen 12.3; it is also used to describe the work of God in Christ in such texts as Jn 12.32. **8.23** *Jew,* a term that comes into use only late in the OT period. It is common in Ezra, Nehemiah, and Esther, and used in Dan 3.8, 12. This is its only use in the prophetic canon, and it may be the earliest use of the term in the Bible. The vision of universal human harmony with Zion at the center responds fully to the earlier prophetic vision of the peaceable kingdom (Isa 11.6–9), the beating of swords into plowshares (Isa 2.4; Mic 4.3), the love of God for other nations mediated through the faithful prophets of Israel (Isa 19.23–25; Jonah), and the work of the servant of the Lord (Isa 42.4; 49.1–6).

Judgment on Israel's Enemies

9   An Oracle.

The word of the LORD is against the land
    of Hadrach
    and will rest upon Damascus.
For to the LORD belongs the capital[a] of
        Aram,[b]
    as do all the tribes of Israel;
2   Hamath also, which borders on it,
        Tyre and Sidon, though they are very
            wise.
3   Tyre has built itself a rampart,
        and heaped up silver like dust,
        and gold like the dirt of the streets.
4   But now, the Lord will strip it of its
            possessions
        and hurl its wealth into the sea,
        and it shall be devoured by fire.

5   Ashkelon shall see it and be afraid;
        Gaza too, and shall writhe in anguish;
        Ekron also, because its hopes are
            withered.
    The king shall perish from Gaza;
        Ashkelon shall be uninhabited;
6   a mongrel people shall settle in Ashdod,
        and I will make an end of the pride of
            Philistia.
7   I will take away its blood from its mouth,
        and its abominations from between its
            teeth;
    it too shall be a remnant for our God;
        it shall be like a clan in Judah,
        and Ekron shall be like the Jebusites.

8   Then I will encamp at my house as a guard,
        so that no one shall march to and fro;
    no oppressor shall again overrun them,
        for now I have seen with my own eyes.

The Coming Ruler of God's People

9   Rejoice greatly, O daughter Zion!
        Shout aloud, O daughter Jerusalem!
    Lo, your king comes to you;
        triumphant and victorious is he,
    humble and riding on a donkey,
        on a colt, the foal of a donkey.
10 He[c] will cut off the chariot from Ephraim
        and the war-horse from Jerusalem;
    and the battle bow shall be cut off,
        and he shall command peace to the
            nations;
    his dominion shall be from sea to sea,
        and from the River to the ends of the
            earth.

11 As for you also, because of the blood of
            my covenant with you,
    I will set your prisoners free from the
            waterless pit.
12 Return to your stronghold, O prisoners
            of hope;
        today I declare that I will restore to you
            double.
13 For I have bent Judah as my bow;
        I have made Ephraim its arrow.
    I will arouse your sons, O Zion,
        against your sons, O Greece,
        and wield you like a warrior's sword.

_____
a Heb eye   b Cn: Heb of Adam (or of humankind)   c Gk: Heb I

9.1–14.21 Second (Deutero-) Zechariah. 9.1–11.17 The Divine Warrior and the restoration of scattered Israel. 9.1–8 These verses picture the Lord as Divine Warrior moving triumphantly toward Jerusalem prior to the "day of the LORD" (cf. Joel 2.11; Isa 63.1–6). The list of cities mentioned in this passage works its way systematically from north to south, pausing for a siege of Tyre (v. 3). These enemies of Israel also belong to the Lord (v. 1), and God is sovereign over them. 9.1 An Oracle, an introductory formula, repeated in 12.1, uniting the two parts of Second Zechariah (chs. 9–11, 12–14; see Introduction). The ensuing booklet of Malachi is introduced by the same formula and perhaps should be viewed as an appendix to Zechariah. 9.5–7 The threats against the Philistines may include resettlement of non-natives, a mongrel people, in Ashdod. The remnant of Philistia is not a favored group, like the "remnant" of Israel in Isa 1–39, but consists merely of the survivors of the Lord's attack. Their separate identity will cease for they will be dedicated for our God. 9.9 Daughter Zion. See note on 2.10. The triumphant king arrives humble and riding on a . . . donkey, thereby demonstrating his peaceful intentions. Two Gospels (Mt 21.2–7; Jn 12.14–15) cite this text in their accounts of Palm Sunday, but the Matthean version fails to take into consideration the parallelism of the Hebrew poetry (donkey is equivalent to colt), so it has Jesus riding on two donkeys at once. 9.10 The Divine Warrior demilitarizes the nations within the vast sweep of his dominion from the River (the Euphrates) to the ends of the earth (see Ps 46.8–9). 9.11 Blood of my covenant, the conventional way of referring to the sacrificially sealed covenant relationship between the Lord and the people (see Ex 24.8; Mt 26.28; Heb 9.15–22). 9.13 God will rescue the long-vanished Northern Kingdom, Ephraim (Israel), along with Judah (see 10.7). Greece, probably the earliest reference in the Bible to that emerging western superpower, though

14 Then the LORD will appear over them,
 and his arrow go forth like lightning;
 the Lord GOD will sound the trumpet
 and march forth in the whirlwinds of
  the south.
15 The LORD of hosts will protect them,
 and they shall devour and tread down
  the slingers;*ᵃ*
 they shall drink their blood*ᵇ* like wine,
 and be full like a bowl,
 drenched like the corners of the altar.

16 On that day the LORD their God will save
  them
 for they are the flock of his people;
 for like the jewels of a crown
 they shall shine on his land.
17 For what goodness and beauty are his!
 Grain shall make the young men
  flourish,
 and new wine the young women.

Restoration of Judah and Israel

10 Ask rain from the LORD
 in the season of the spring rain,
 from the LORD who makes the storm
  clouds,
 who gives showers of rain to you,*ᶜ*
 the vegetation in the field to everyone.
2 For the teraphim*ᵈ* utter nonsense,
 and the diviners see lies;
 the dreamers tell false dreams,
 and give empty consolation.
 Therefore the people wander like sheep;
 they suffer for lack of a shepherd.

3 My anger is hot against the shepherds,
 and I will punish the leaders;*ᵉ*
 for the LORD of hosts cares for his flock,
  the house of Judah,

and will make them like his proud
  war-horse.
4 Out of them shall come the cornerstone,
 out of them the tent peg,
 out of them the battle bow,
 out of them every commander.
5 Together they shall be like warriors in
  battle,
 trampling the foe in the mud of the
  streets;
 they shall fight, for the LORD is with them,
 and they shall put to shame the riders
  on horses.

6 I will strengthen the house of Judah,
 and I will save the house of Joseph.
 I will bring them back because I have
  compassion on them,
 and they shall be as though I had not
  rejected them;
 for I am the LORD their God and I will
  answer them.
7 Then the people of Ephraim shall become
  like warriors,
 and their hearts shall be glad as with
  wine.
 Their children shall see it and rejoice,
 their hearts shall exult in the LORD.

8 I will signal for them and gather them in,
 for I have redeemed them,
 and they shall be as numerous as they
  were before.
9 Though I scattered them among the
  nations,
 yet in far countries they shall
  remember me,

---

a Cn: Heb *the slingstones*   *b* Gk: Heb *shall drink*   *c* Heb *them*
d Or *household gods*   *e* Or *male goats*

---

the late prophet Joel also refers to "the Greeks" (Joel 3.6). By the time of the book of Daniel (early second century BCE), Hellenistic kingdoms are the only enemies of Israel. **9.14** In classic Divine Warrior guise, *the LORD will appear over them*, with the heavenly hosts. God does all the fighting on the "day of the LORD"; God's people simply reap the fruits of victory. **9.15** *Devour . . . drink their blood* suggests not only the triumph of the Lord's human allies but also a sacral ceremony comparable to the sacrifice of an animal on an altar (Ex 24.8). **9.17** *Grain shall . . . young women* (see Jer 31.12–14; Am 9.13–14; Joel 3.18). In the aftermath of victory peace and plenitude are the hallmarks of the new age that lies beyond the terrible intervention of

the "day of the LORD." **10.1** The bounty of agriculture is attributed to the Lord, the giver of rain. Yahweh need not be manipulated to send the rain: the people need only to *ask*. **10.2** *Teraphim*, part of the apparatus of prophetic prognosticators. They were evidently amulets, metallic images, or statues of gods (see Judg 18.14–20; Ezek 21.21; Hos 3.4). The great prophets of the previous century were particularly incensed about the perversion of the prophetic office by false prophets (see Jer 14.14; 23.23–32; Ezek 13.8–16; 22.28). Zechariah agrees (cf. 13.2–6). **10.3** Because of the failure of Israel's human *leaders,* the Lord will personally be the shepherd of the house of Judah, displacing the male goats (see text note *e;* cf. Ezek 34.11–24,

and they shall rear their children and
  return.
10 I will bring them home from the land of
    Egypt,
  and gather them from Assyria;
  I will bring them to the land of Gilead
    and to Lebanon,
  until there is no room for them.
11 They[a] shall pass through the sea of
    distress,
  and the waves of the sea shall be struck
    down,
  and all the depths of the Nile dried up.
  The pride of Assyria shall be laid low,
    and the scepter of Egypt shall depart.
12 I will make them strong in the LORD,
    and they shall walk in his name,
                        says the LORD.

11

Open your doors, O Lebanon,
  so that fire may devour your cedars!
2 Wail, O cypress, for the cedar has fallen,
    for the glorious trees are ruined!
  Wail, oaks of Bashan,
    for the thick forest has been felled!
3 Listen, the wail of the shepherds,
    for their glory is despoiled!
  Listen, the roar of the lions,
    for the thickets of the Jordan are
      destroyed!

Two Kinds of Shepherds

4 Thus said the LORD my God: Be a shepherd
of the flock doomed to slaughter. 5 Those who
buy them kill them and go unpunished; and
those who sell them say, "Blessed be the LORD,

for I have become rich"; and their own shepherds have no pity on them. 6 For I will no
longer have pity on the inhabitants of the
earth, says the LORD. I will cause them, every
one, to fall each into the hand of a neighbor,
and each into the hand of the king; and they
shall devastate the earth, and I will deliver no
one from their hand.

7 So, on behalf of the sheep merchants, I became the shepherd of the flock doomed to
slaughter. I took two staffs; one I named Favor,
the other I named Unity, and I tended the
sheep. 8 In one month I disposed of the three
shepherds, for I had become impatient with
them, and they also detested me. 9 So I said, "I
will not be your shepherd. What is to die, let it
die; what is to be destroyed, let it be destroyed;
and let those that are left devour the flesh of
one another!" 10 I took my staff Favor and
broke it, annulling the covenant that I had
made with all the peoples. 11 So it was annulled
on that day, and the sheep merchants, who
were watching me, knew that it was the word of
the LORD. 12 I then said to them, "If it seems
right to you, give me my wages; but if not, keep
them." So they weighed out as my wages thirty
shekels of silver. 13 Then the LORD said to me,
"Throw it into the treasury"[b]—this lordly
price at which I was valued by them. So I took
the thirty shekels of silver and threw them into
the treasury[b] in the house of the LORD. 14 Then
I broke my second staff Unity, annulling the
family ties between Judah and Israel.

15 Then the LORD said to me: Take once

---

a Gk: Heb He   b Syr: Heb it to the potter

---

where the leaders of the people are also called "goats").
10.10–12 As it was in First Zechariah (2.4; 6.15; 8.7–
8), the theme of the gathering in of the exiles is
sounded. In a veritable new exodus, they will come
from Egypt and Assyria *until there is no room for them*
(see note on 2.4). **11.1–3** In an ironic way Lebanon is
invited to lay itself open to destruction, in contrast to
the invitation to Judah to make itself open to divine
nurture (10.1). The deforestation lamented by trees,
animals, and rural people themselves seems to be the
negative result of the overpopulation resulting from
the return of numberless exiles (2.4; 10.8–12).

11.4–17 This strange passage defies crisp explanation, though it seems to continue the polemic against
the corrupt religious and political leadership (10.3)
that existed in Judea prior to the Lord's promised day
of purging and renewal. Following the Lord's indictment of the false shepherds (vv. 4–6), the prophet tells
about his sign-acts of judgment (vv. 7–14). The text

concludes with the Lord's decision to raise up a worthless antishepherd (vv. 15–17). **11.7** *So . . . I became
the shepherd.* An unknown individual, perhaps the
prophet himself, undertakes to do acts symbolic of the
recalcitrance of the Judean community. It is difficult to
say who *the sheep merchants* for whom he is working
are. **11.10** *I took my staff Favor and broke it* no doubt
reflects the prophetic indictment of the leadership of
the Judean community, perhaps in the years immediately following the reconstruction of the temple.
11.12–13 *Thirty shekels of silver,* the figure assigned in
Ex 21.32 as indemnity for a slave who had been gored
by an ox. This was the fee paid to the traitor Judas (Mt
26.15; 27.9–10). The Gospel writers surely allude to
these verses in reporting that Judas threw down the silver coins in the temple and that the money was used to
buy the Potter's Field as a burial place (see text note *b*).
11.14 *I broke my second staff Unity* suggests despair for
the restoration of both the Northern and Southern

more the implements of a worthless shepherd. 16For I am now raising up in the land a shepherd who does not care for the perishing, or seek the wandering,ᵃ or heal the maimed, or nourish the healthy,ᵇ but devours the flesh of the fat ones, tearing off even their hoofs.

17 Oh, my worthless shepherd,
    who deserts the flock!
May the sword strike his arm
    and his right eye!
Let his arm be completely withered,
    his right eye utterly blinded!

Jerusalem's Victory

12 An Oracle.

The word of the LORD concerning Israel: Thus says the LORD, who stretched out the heavens and founded the earth and formed the human spirit within: 2See, I am about to make Jerusalem a cup of reeling for all the surrounding peoples; it will be against Judah also in the siege against Jerusalem. 3On that day I will make Jerusalem a heavy stone for all the peoples; all who lift it shall grievously hurt themselves. And all the nations of the earth shall come together against it. 4On that day, says the LORD, I will strike every horse with panic, and its rider with madness. But on the house of Judah I will keep a watchful eye, when I strike every horse of the peoples with blindness. 5Then the clans of Judah shall say to themselves, "The inhabitants of Jerusalem have strength through the LORD of hosts, their God."

6 On that day I will make the clans of Judah like a blazing pot on a pile of wood, like a flaming torch among sheaves; and they shall devour to the right and to the left all the surrounding peoples, while Jerusalem shall again be inhabited in its place, in Jerusalem.

7 And the LORD will give victory to the tents of Judah first, that the glory of the house of David and the glory of the inhabitants of Jerusalem may not be exalted over that of Judah. 8On that day the LORD will shield the inhabitants of Jerusalem so that the feeblest among them on that day shall be like David, and the house of David shall be like God, like the angel of the LORD, at their head. 9And on that day I will seek to destroy all the nations that come against Jerusalem.

Mourning for the Pierced One

10 And I will pour out a spirit of compassion and supplication on the house of David and the inhabitants of Jerusalem, so that, when they look on the oneᶜ whom they have pierced, they shall mourn for him, as one mourns for an only child, and weep bitterly over him, as one weeps over a firstborn. 11On that day the mourning in Jerusalem will be as

---

a Syr Compare Gk Vg: Heb *the youth* *b* Meaning of Heb uncertain *c* Heb *on me*

Kingdoms (cf. 9.13; 10.6–7). **11.15–17** An expansion of these verses is in 13.7–9. **11.17** God raises up a *worthless shepherd* so vicious that he is placed under the terrible curse of maiming and blinding. Presumably this figure is a ruler in Judea (cf. Ezek 34.1–10).

12.1–14.21 The use of the formulas *on that day* and *day of the LORD* seventeen times in these three chapters provides them with a strong thematic unity. Now the focus will be on the culminating day of God's victory as Divine Warrior and on the paradisiacal aftermath of that victory. **12.1–13.6** The purge of Jerusalem. This section may be datable to the middle of the fifth century BCE when tensions between early apocalyptic visionary circles and the Jerusalem priests were beginning to grow acute. **12.1–9** These verses presuppose Jerusalem's conflict not only with the nations around it but with Judah itself. **12.1** *An oracle.* See note on 9.1. The introduction of the Lord as the creator of the cosmos suggests that God can also effect the new creation that is coming. **12.2** *A cup of reeling.* See Ps 75.8; Isa 51.17, 22. Nations that drink it are doomed (Jer 25.15–29). **12.3** Like the stone not cut by human hands of Dan 2.34–45, God's elect city becomes a *heavy stone for all the peoples* on the "day of the LORD." The older

motifs of the election of Jerusalem (3.2; cf. Isa 31.4–5) and of the house of David (2 Sam 7.16; Ps 132.11–18; Isa 9.1–7; 11.1–10) recur in the thinking of Second Zechariah. **12.8–9** The motif of the great battle against the nations gathered before Jerusalem is a favorite one in late prophetic eschatology (Isa 63.1–6; Ezek 38.14–23) and is taken up again in apocalyptic texts (see Joel 3.11–14; Rev 14.14–20). As he envisions the future status of Jerusalem and Judah, the prophet's enthusiasm peaks: *the house of David shall be like God* (v. 8). Presumably this reflects the leading role to be played by the Jews in God's victory over *all the nations* (v. 9). **12.10** *The one . . . pierced.* The Hebrew text (see text note *c*) suggests that the prophet himself (see 13.6) might be this "suffering servant" (see Isa 52.13–53.12; Mt 23.37; Jn 19.34–37). Other ancient versions point to an unknown victim of intracommunity strife. **12.11** The martyrdom of the prophetic/messianic figure leads to a *day of mourning in Jerusalem.* If *Hadadrimmon* is taken as the name of a place in the region of *Megiddo,* and not that of a Canaanite fertility god as some commentators prefer, it should probably be identified with the Rimmon of Josh 19.13 (not that of Zech 14.10). The mourning alluded to in that case

great as the mourning for Hadad-rimmon in the plain of Megiddo. ¹²The land shall mourn, each family by itself; the family of the house of David by itself, and their wives by themselves; the family of the house of Nathan by itself, and their wives by themselves; ¹³the family of the house of Levi by itself, and their wives by themselves; the family of the Shimeites by itself, and their wives by themselves; ¹⁴and all the families that are left, each by itself, and their wives by themselves.

13 On that day a fountain shall be opened for the house of David and the inhabitants of Jerusalem, to cleanse them from sin and impurity.

Idolatry Cut Off

2 On that day, says the LORD of hosts, I will cut off the names of the idols from the land, so that they shall be remembered no more; and also I will remove from the land the prophets and the unclean spirit. ³And if any prophets appear again, their fathers and mothers who bore them will say to them, "You shall not live, for you speak lies in the name of the LORD"; and their fathers and their mothers who bore them shall pierce them through when they prophesy. ⁴On that day the prophets will be ashamed, every one, of their visions when they prophesy; they will not put on a hairy mantle in order to deceive, ⁵but each of them will say, "I am no prophet, I am a tiller of the soil; for the land has been my possession*a* since my youth." ⁶And if anyone asks them, "What are these wounds on your chest?"*b* the answer will be "The wounds I received in the house of my friends."

The Shepherd Struck, the Flock Scattered

7 "Awake, O sword, against my shepherd,
　　against the man who is my associate,"
　　　　　　says the LORD of hosts.
　Strike the shepherd, that the sheep may
　　be scattered;
　I will turn my hand against the little
　　ones.
8 In the whole land, says the LORD,
　　two-thirds shall be cut off and perish,
　　and one-third shall be left alive.
9 And I will put this third into the fire,
　　refine them as one refines silver,
　　and test them as gold is tested.
　They will call on my name,
　　and I will answer them.
　I will say, "They are my people";
　　and they will say, "The LORD is our
　　　God."

Future Warfare and Final Victory

14 See, a day is coming for the LORD, when the plunder taken from you will be divided in your midst. ²For I will gather all the nations against Jerusalem to battle, and the city shall be taken and the houses looted and the women raped; half the city shall go

---

a Cn: Heb *for humankind has caused me to possess*
b Heb *wounds between your hands*

---

might be that for the Judean king Josiah, killed on the plain of Megiddo in 609 BCE, which was made customary by the prophet Jeremiah and the singers (see 2 Chr 35.20–27). **13.1** *Fountain,* the first of two references in Zechariah to the river of God that flows from the Jerusalem sanctuary for the cleansing of the people (14.8; see also Ps 46.4; Ezek 47.1–12; Joel 3.18; Rev 22.1–2; in Jn 4.14; 7.37–38, Jesus compares himself to this life-giving stream). **13.2–3** The *unclean spirit* of the prophets condemned by Zechariah is a direct descendant of the "lying spirit" that possessed false prophets in the days of the kings (1 Kings 22.13–28). Zechariah goes so far as to foresee that parents will kill their own children if they prophesy. **13.4** *Hairy mantle.* None of the usual tricks of the prophetic trade will find favor on the "day of the LORD." Perhaps vv. 2–6 are intended to be a rejection of prophetic guilds associated with the temple; however, the denial by prophets that the wounds visible on their chests are evidences of ecstatic self-flagellation (v. 6) hints at a rejection of all forms of prophecy. **13.5** *I am no prophet.* Here, near the end of

the prophetic period, the words of Amos, the very first writing prophet, are echoed (Am 7.14). Evidently false prophets were a destructive element in Israel from start to finish of the prophetic era (see also 10.2). **13.7–9** A resumption of the theme of 11.15–17. The purging of *my shepherd . . . my associate,* the dispersal and death of two-thirds of the people, and the fiery purification of the rest (cf. Isa 48.10; Mal 3.2–4) lead in the end to the mutual confessions of trust of v. 9b. Jesus perceives the same process of refining at work when he uses this text to predict that his disciples will abandon him during his Passion (Mk 14.27).

14.1–21 Because this chapter achieves the most radical, even cosmic, vision of change on the "day of the LORD," it is thought to be the latest in the ongoing series of oracles and visions in Second Zechariah. It may be as late as 420 BCE. **14.1** On the "day of the LORD," *plunder* will be taken and *divided.* This is not the motif of the despoiling of the oppressor nations by Israel (see 2.9; Ex 12.36; Ezek 38–39; Nah 2.9; Hag 2.7–8), but rather one of the details of the terror to be experienced by those Judeans who will have to endure

into exile, but the rest of the people shall not be cut off from the city. ³Then the LORD will go forth and fight against those nations as when he fights on a day of battle. ⁴On that day his feet shall stand on the Mount of Olives, which lies before Jerusalem on the east; and the Mount of Olives shall be split in two from east to west by a very wide valley; so that one half of the Mount shall withdraw northward, and the other half southward. ⁵And you shall flee by the valley of the LORD's mountain,ᵃ for the valley between the mountains shall reach to Azal;ᵇ and you shall flee as you fled from the earthquake in the days of King Uzziah of Judah. Then the LORD my God will come, and all the holy ones with him.

6 On that day there shall not beᶜ either cold or frost.ᵈ ⁷And there shall be continuous day (it is known to the LORD), not day and not night, for at evening time there shall be light.

8 On that day living waters shall flow out from Jerusalem, half of them to the eastern sea and half of them to the western sea; it shall continue in summer as in winter.

9 And the LORD will become king over all the earth; on that day the LORD will be one and his name one.

10 The whole land shall be turned into a plain from Geba to Rimmon south of Jerusalem. But Jerusalem shall remain aloft on its site from the Gate of Benjamin to the place of the former gate, to the Corner Gate, and from the Tower of Hananel to the king's wine presses. ¹¹And it shall be inhabited, for never again shall it be doomed to destruction; Jerusalem shall abide in security.

12 This shall be the plague with which the LORD will strike all the peoples that wage war against Jerusalem: their flesh shall rot while they are still on their feet; their eyes shall rot in their sockets, and their tongues shall rot in their mouths. ¹³On that day a great panic from the LORD shall fall on them, so that each will seize the hand of a neighbor, and the hand of the one will be raised against the hand of the other; ¹⁴even Judah will fight at Jerusalem. And the wealth of all the surrounding nations shall be collected—gold, silver, and garments in great abundance. ¹⁵And a plague like this plague shall fall on the horses, the mules, the camels, the donkeys, and whatever animals may be in those camps.

16 Then all who survive of the nations that have come against Jerusalem shall go up year after year to worship the King, the LORD of hosts, and to keep the festival of booths.ᵉ ¹⁷If any of the families of the earth do not go up to Jerusalem to worship the King, the LORD of hosts, there will be no rain upon them. ¹⁸And if the family of Egypt do not go up and present themselves, then on them shallᶠ come the plague that the LORD inflicts on the nations that do not go up to keep the festival of booths.ᵉ ¹⁹Such shall be the punishment of Egypt and the punishment of all the nations that do not go up to keep the festival of booths.ᵉ

---

a Heb *my mountains*   *b* Meaning of Heb uncertain
c Cn: Heb *there shall not be light*   *d* Compare Gk Syr Vg Tg: Meaning of Heb uncertain   *e* Or *tabernacles*; Heb *succoth*
f Gk Syr: Heb *shall not*

---

the purge that precedes God's victory (13.7–9). **14.3** See note on 12.8–9. Now the Divine Warrior turns the terror against Israel's enemies. **14.4** *Mount of Olives . . . in two.* The cosmic dimension of this last vision of Zechariah implies changes in the very structure of the earth itself. Perhaps by their hugeness and weight, the divine feet are sufficient to alter the landscape around Jerusalem (cf. Mic 1.2–4). **14.5** *All the holy ones with him.* The Lord engages in divine warfare with a full complement of angelic forces (cf. Dan 7.22). **14.6–7** The displacement of the sun by the glory of God is a motif used by the nearly contemporary "Isaiah Apocalypse" (Isa 24–27; see also Isa 60.19–20; Rev 22.5). Light was the first of God's creations (Gen 1.3). With that light came night and day, i.e., time. In the new creation, time ceases because the divine glory is perpetual. **14.8** *Living waters.* See note on 13.1. **14.9** *The LORD will be one and his name one* suggests the achievement of that utter undividedness of loyalty

anticipated in the Shema (Deut 6.4). **14.10** *Aloft on its site.* The altered topography of the new age leaves Jerusalem standing high and alone. The image has roots in Near Eastern mythology, which would understand the holy city and the Temple Mount as the cosmic mountain where earth and heaven meet and where God dwells. **14.11** *Shall be inhabited.* See 2.4; Joel 3.20. The lifting of the curse pronounced in 11.6 leads to the blessing of progeny promised to a people obedient to the covenant in Deut 28.11. **14.14** A motif in the prophetic vision of the future is the flow of the *wealth of . . . nations* to preeminent Jerusalem (e.g., Isa 60.5–7; 61.6; 66.12). **14.15** Those who fight against Jerusalem will experience disease and death like those who oppose the covenant of God (Deut 28.20–22). **14.16–19** In the new age that lies beyond the "day of the LORD" the now Judaized remnants of the other nations are obliged to observe the annual pilgrimage *festival of booths* (v. 16; see Lev 23.39–43) on pain of

20 On that day there shall be inscribed on the bells of the horses, "Holy to the LORD." And the cooking pots in the house of the LORD shall be as holy as*a* the bowls in front of the altar; 21and every cooking pot in Jerusalem and Judah shall be sacred to the LORD of hosts, so that all who sacrifice may come and use them to boil the flesh of the sacrifice. And there shall no longer be traders*b* in the house of the LORD of hosts on that day.

_____

a Heb *shall be like*   *b* Or *Canaanites*

_____

drought or the *plague* (v. 18). **14.20–21** *Bells, cooking pots,* and *bowls* will all achieve ritual purity through the direct activity of God rather than through priestly consecration (cf. Lev 27.30–33). Holiness spreads everywhere! In contrast to Joel 3.17, this vision anticipates the gathering of all nations to Jerusalem with the exception that *there shall no longer be traders* (Hebrew, "Canaanites") *in the house of the LORD* (see Mk 11.15–17 and parallels; Jn 2.13–17). Thus did the visionaries who gave us Second Zechariah imagine that the temple, the restoration of which was a major concern of Zechariah son of Berechiah, will in the new age finally become fit to serve as the worship center for the whole world.

MALACHI

Date and Historical Context

THE BOOK OF MALACHI must have been written after Haggai and Zech 1–8, and after the temple was rededicated in 516/5 BCE (see Ezra 6.15). The fact that the sacrificial worship of the temple had had time to fall into disorder (1.6–14; 2.11) coupled with the writer's deep concern about intermarriage with foreign women (2.10–17), which this book shares with Ezra and Nehemiah, both suggest that it was written shortly before Nehemiah's first return in 445/4 BCE during the reign of the Persian king Artaxerxes I (465–424 BCE).

Name, Authorship, and Message

LIKE THE BOOK OF HAGGAI, Malachi gives us no personal information about its author. Even the name Malachi may not be a personal name at all, but simply a title, "My messenger." The name is appropriate, however, for it is the task of this late prophetic book to bring two messages: God is displeased with the lack of piety in the community gathered around the temple (1.6–2.16; 3.6–12); and God is about to send a messenger who will reunite and purify all of Israel prior to the "great and terrible day of the LORD" (4.5). The book ends on that eschatological note; in the Protestant canon it is followed immediately by the Gospel announcement of the birth of Jesus. The earliest Gospel, Mark, even opens with the preaching of the "messenger," John the Baptist, whom Jesus called "Elijah who is to come" (Mt 11.14; see also Mk 9.13). This juxtaposition suggests that in early Christian eyes the advent of the Christ was the first of the culminating events of history promised by the prophet "Malachi."

Social Location

UNLIKE SUCH EARLY PROPHETS as Amos and Hosea, the late prophetic book of Malachi is not simply the voice of one of the observant believers raised against a corrupt priesthood, though it resoundingly indicts the priesthood for its failures (1.6–2.9). In fact, the writer may actually have been a priest himself who put on the prophetic mantle of the Lord's messenger. The book identifies itself with levitical priestly circles (2.4–6) and believes deeply in the temple, true worship, and the payment of tithes as the means for obtaining the blessing of the land (3.10–12). Like Haggai and Zech 1–8 in the previous century, it may be the work of a "temple" prophet who worked among the ruling circles of Judah rather than at the periphery. [W. SIBLEY TOWNER]

1
An oracle. The word of the LORD to Israel by Malachi.*

Israel Preferred to Edom

2 I have loved you, says the LORD. But you say, "How have you loved us?" Is not Esau Jacob's brother? says the LORD. Yet I have loved Jacob ³but I have hated Esau; I have made his hill country a desolation and his heritage a desert for jackals. ⁴If Edom says, "We are shattered but we will rebuild the ruins," the LORD of hosts says: They may build, but I will tear down, until they are called the wicked country, the people with whom the LORD is angry forever. ⁵Your own eyes shall see this, and you shall say, "Great is the LORD beyond the borders of Israel!"

Corruption of the Priesthood

6 A son honors his father, and servants their master. If then I am a father, where is the honor due me? And if I am a master, where is the respect due me? says the LORD of hosts to you, O priests, who despise my name. You say, "How have we despised your name?" ⁷By offering polluted food on my altar. And you say, "How have we polluted it?"ᵇ By thinking that the LORD's table may be despised. ⁸When you offer blind animals in sacrifice, is that not wrong? And when you offer those that are lame or sick, is that not wrong? Try presenting that to your governor; will he be pleased with you or show you favor? says the LORD of hosts.

⁹And now implore the favor of God, that he may be gracious to us. The fault is yours. Will he show favor to any of you? says the LORD of hosts. ¹⁰Oh, that someone among you would shut the templeᶜ doors, so that you would not kindle fire on my altar in vain! I have no pleasure in you, says the LORD of hosts, and I will not accept an offering from your hands. ¹¹For from the rising of the sun to its setting my name is great among the nations, and in every place incense is offered to my name, and a pure offering; for my name is great among the nations, says the LORD of hosts. ¹²But you profane it when you say that the Lord's table is polluted, and the food for itᵈ may be despised. ¹³"What a weariness this is," you say, and you sniff at me,ᵉ says the LORD of hosts. You bring what has been taken by violence or is lame or sick, and this you bring as your offering! Shall I accept that from your hand? says the LORD. ¹⁴Cursed be the cheat who has a male in the flock and vows to give it, and yet sacrifices to the Lord what is blemished; for I am a great King, says the LORD of hosts, and my name is reverenced among the nations.

2
And now, O priests, this command is for you. ²If you will not listen, if you will not lay it to heart to give glory to my name, says the LORD of hosts, then I will send the curse on you and I will curse your blessings; indeed I

---

a Or *by my messenger*   *b* Gk: Heb *you*   *c* Heb lacks *temple*
d Compare Syr Tg: Heb *its fruit, its food*   *e* Another reading is *at it*

1.1 Superscription. *Oracle,* lit. "burden." See note on Zech 9.1. **1.2–5** First oracle. This section introduces the question-and-answer style of Malachi, a form of disputation also found quite prominently in Haggai (Hag 1.4–6, 7–11; 2.3–5, 15–16). The opening affirmation of the Lord's love of Jacob/Israel underlies all that follows. **1.2** *Esau Jacob's brother.* See Gen 25.24–34. Esau is identified as the ancestor of the Edomites in Gen 36.1. For other prophetic oracles against Edom, see Isa 34; 63.1–6; Jer 49.7–22; Ezek 25.12–14; and most of the book of Obadiah. In Rom 9.13 Paul cites this verse as evidence that God's preference for Jacob/Israel over Esau/Edom is unrelated to any special merit on Israel's part, but derives solely from God's mercy. By the time of Malachi, the ancient enemy was apparently *a desolation* (v. 3). **1.5** The Lord's sovereignty even *beyond the borders of Israel* is a theme beloved of the exilic and postexilic prophets (e.g., Isa 19.23–25; 46.1–2; Ezek 1.1–3; Zech 9.1–8;

Jon 3–4). The aim of this oracle about the rejection of Edom is to elicit from Malachi's Judean audience this exclamation of trust.

1.6–2.9 Second oracle. An indictment of the Jerusalemite priesthood for its failures (1.6–14), followed by a curse (2.1–9). **1.8** *Blind animals* and those that are *lame or sick* were not acceptable for sacrifice (see Lev 22.17–30; Deut 15.21). Deficient offerings showed disrespect to the Lord. **1.10** *Shut the temple doors* suggests that no worship at all would be preferable to stingy, grudging offerings. **1.11** In a universal vision of the worship of Israel's Lord, even the gentile *nations* are said to be able to worship the Lord in holiness (see also v. 14; Ps 50.1). *Pure offering* may refer to the manner of worship carried on by Jews living in exile, which contrasts sharply with the corruption of worship at the temple itself (v. 12). **2.2** It is the task of priests to pronounce blessings (Num 6.22–27). Malachi's curse against the priests turns their benedictions into anath-

have already cursed them,^a because you do not lay it to heart. ³I will rebuke your offspring, and spread dung on your faces, the dung of your offerings, and I will put you out of my presence.^b

4 Know, then, that I have sent this command to you, that my covenant with Levi may hold, says the LORD of hosts. ⁵My covenant with him was a covenant of life and wellbeing, which I gave him; this called for reverence, and he revered me and stood in awe of my name. ⁶True instruction was in his mouth, and no wrong was found on his lips. He walked with me in integrity and uprightness, and he turned many from iniquity. ⁷For the lips of a priest should guard knowledge, and people should seek instruction from his mouth, for he is the messenger of the LORD of hosts. ⁸But you have turned aside from the way; you have caused many to stumble by your instruction; you have corrupted the covenant of Levi, says the LORD of hosts, ⁹and so I make you despised and abased before all the people, inasmuch as you have not kept my ways but have shown partiality in your instruction.

The Covenant Profaned by Judah

10 Have we not all one father? Has not one God created us? Why then are we faithless to one another, profaning the covenant of our ancestors? ¹¹Judah has been faithless, and abomination has been committed in Israel and in Jerusalem; for Judah has profaned the sanctuary of the LORD, which he loves, and has married the daughter of a foreign god. ¹²May

the LORD cut off from the tents of Jacob anyone who does this—any to witness^c or answer, or to bring an offering to the LORD of hosts.

13 And this you do as well: You cover the LORD's altar with tears, with weeping and groaning because he no longer regards the offering or accepts it with favor at your hand. ¹⁴You ask, "Why does he not?" Because the LORD was a witness between you and the wife of your youth, to whom you have been faithless, though she is your companion and your wife by covenant. ¹⁵Did not one God make her?^d Both flesh and spirit are his.^e And what does the one God^f desire? Godly offspring. So look to yourselves, and do not let anyone be faithless to the wife of his youth. ¹⁶For I hate^g divorce, says the LORD, the God of Israel, and covering one's garment with violence, says the LORD of hosts. So take heed to yourselves and do not be faithless.

17 You have wearied the LORD with your words. Yet you say, "How have we wearied him?" By saying, "All who do evil are good in the sight of the LORD, and he delights in them." Or by asking, "Where is the God of justice?"

The Coming Messenger

3 See, I am sending my messenger to prepare the way before me, and the Lord whom you seek will suddenly come to his temple. The messenger of the covenant in

a Heb it   b Cn Compare Gk Syr: Heb and he shall bear you to it
c Cn Compare Gk: Heb arouse   d Or Has he not made one?
e Cn: Heb and a remnant of spirit was his   f Heb he
g Cn: Heb he hates

---

emas. **2.3** *I will rebuke your offspring.* The Septuagint reads "I will cut off your arm," perhaps as a way of stressing that the priests will not be able to perform their duty of pronouncing blessings with upraised hands. The *dung* of offerings was supposed to be burned outside the camp (see Ex 29.14). **2.4–6** Because the priestly tribe of *Levi* supported Moses against the Aaronites in the incident of the golden calf and were immediately ordained to divine service (Ex 32.25–29), the Levites were always held in esteem by the prophets. **2.4** The *covenant with Levi* is nowhere described, but its existence is affirmed in Jer 33.21–22. **2.7** Lev 10.11 underscores the duty of priests to teach the covenant tradition, but this is the only place in the Hebrew Bible where the priest is described as *the messenger of the LORD of hosts.* The entire book of Malachi stands at the junction of prophetic oracle and priestly pronouncement.
    2.10–16 Third oracle. An indictment of the people

for their infidelity. **2.11** Marriage to foreign women threatens the very identity of Israel, which has been reduced to one of the many minor subject peoples within the Persian Empire (see also Ezra 10.44; Neh 13.23–27). **2.13–16** This is the strongest condemnation of divorce expressed anywhere in the Hebrew Bible. Although divorce is permitted by Deut 24.1–4, the Bible always regards marriage as a holy covenant (Gen 2.24; 31.50; Prov 2.17; Eph 5.21–33).
    2.17–3.5 Fourth oracle. The judgment day to come. **2.17** In words reminiscent of the skepticism of Eccl 7.15; 8.14–15, the questioners challenge God's intention to vindicate goodness and to be just. Yet they themselves have been neither good nor just. **3.1–4** Before the Lord *suddenly* comes *to his temple, the messenger of the covenant* will fully cleanse the levitical priests so that they will at last be able to perform the priestly office *in righteousness* (v. 3). This will open the way for blessings to flow, just as was promised by Haggai at the time of

whom you delight—indeed, he is coming, says the LORD of hosts. 2But who can endure the day of his coming, and who can stand when he appears?

For he is like a refiner's fire and like fullers' soap; 3he will sit as a refiner and purifier of silver, and he will purify the descendants of Levi and refine them like gold and silver, until they present offerings to the LORD in righteousness.ᵃ 4Then the offering of Judah and Jerusalem will be pleasing to the LORD as in the days of old and as in former years.

5 Then I will draw near to you for judgment; I will be swift to bear witness against the sorcerers, against the adulterers, against those who swear falsely, against those who oppress the hired workers in their wages, the widow and the orphan, against those who thrust aside the alien, and do not fear me, says the LORD of hosts.

6 For I the LORD do not change; therefore you, O children of Jacob, have not perished. 7Ever since the days of your ancestors you have turned aside from my statutes and have not kept them. Return to me, and I will return to you, says the LORD of hosts. But you say, "How shall we return?"

Do Not Rob God

8 Will anyone rob God? Yet you are robbing me! But you say, "How are we robbing you?" In your tithes and offerings! 9You are cursed with a curse, for you are robbing me—the whole nation of you! 10Bring the full tithe into the storehouse, so that there may be food in my house, and thus put me to the test, says the LORD of hosts; see if I will not open the windows of heaven for you and pour down for you an overflowing blessing. 11I will rebuke the locustᵇ for you, so that it will not destroy the produce of your soil; and your vine in the field shall not be barren, says the LORD of hosts. 12Then all nations will count you happy, for you will be a land of delight, says the LORD of hosts.

13 You have spoken harsh words against me, says the LORD. Yet you say, "How have we spoken against you?" 14You have said, "It is vain to serve God. What do we profit by keeping his command or by going about as mourners before the LORD of hosts? 15Now we count the arrogant happy; evildoers not only prosper, but when they put God to the test they escape."

The Reward of the Faithful

16 Then those who revered the LORD spoke with one another. The LORD took note and listened, and a book of remembrance was written before him of those who revered the LORD and thought on his name. 17They shall be mine, says the LORD of hosts, my special pos-

---

a Or *right offerings to the* LORD   *b* Heb *devourer*

the reconsecration of the temple (Hag 2.19). **3.5** God promises to *be swift to bear witness* (see Zeph 3.8) against all those who violate the covenant tradition. The list of sins is typical of the prophetic indictment of evildoers (see Jer 7.9; note on Zech 7.9–10). Because God is "Father of orphans and protector of widows" (Ps 68.5), the "day of the LORD" brings retribution to any who abuse the marginalized (Zeph 3.1–5). **3.6–12** Fifth oracle. Repentance issuing in right action will restore God's blessings. **3.6** The very existence of sinful Israel is grounded in the Lord's constancy. **3.8** The law required that God receive the first tenth of the produce of the land (see Lev 27.30; Num 18.21–24). In Deut 14.28 the tithe due every third year is designated for the support of resident aliens, widows, orphans, and levitical priests. Failure to pay up amounts to robbing God. **3.10** At the waters of Meribah the people "tested" God in the matter of the manna, causing God to be angry (Ps 95.8–11). Here, however, God invites Israel to *put me to the test.* The Lord makes a direct causal connection between covenant obedience and showers of blessing. **3.12** Judah is assured that the test will vindicate God and that *all nations will count it happy* (see Pss 41.2; 72.17; Isa 61.6–9; 62.4). The

charge that the Lord delights in evildoers (2.17) is here refuted by the nations, who once again prove to be authentic witnesses to the truth about God's blessing (cf. 1.14).

3.13–4.3 Sixth oracle. God takes note of the faithful and will save them on the day of judgment. **3.14–15** See note on 2.17. Conventional wisdom held that the righteous prosper and evildoers fail (Ps 1.3; Prov 28.13). Yet the tragedy of exile (see Lam 1.5), the ambivalence of the Preacher (see Eccl 8.10–13), and the pessimism of the apocalyptic writers about history (see Dan 8.25; 11.36) all concede that the wicked may prosper. Malachi tacitly concedes this as well, but their success is only temporary. **3.16** Biblical tradition knows of three heavenly record books. The book hinted at in Ps 139.16 seems to be a book of destiny in which the fate of the individual was written down before the beginning of time (cf. Dan 10.21; Rev 13.8; 20.15; 21.27). Here, however, the *book of remembrance* is juridical in character. In it the obedient deeds done by individuals during their lifetimes are recorded (see Ex 32.32–33; Ps 40.7 [cited in Heb 10.7]; 56.8; 69.28; Phil 4.3; Rev 3.5). Two references to "the books" in Dan 7.10; 12.1 could be read either way; and in the great judgment scene of Rev 20.12 a

session on the day when I act, and I will spare them as parents spare their children who serve them. ¹⁸Then once more you shall see the difference between the righteous and the wicked, between one who serves God and one who does not serve him.

The Great Day of the LORD

4ᵃ See, the day is coming, burning like an oven, when all the arrogant and all evildoers will be stubble; the day that comes shall burn them up, says the LORD of hosts, so that it will leave them neither root nor branch. ²But for you who revere my name the sun of righteousness shall rise, with healing in its wings. You shall go out leaping like calves from the

stall. ³And you shall tread down the wicked, for they will be ashes under the soles of your feet, on the day when I act, says the LORD of hosts.

4 Remember the teaching of my servant Moses, the statutes and ordinances that I commanded him at Horeb for all Israel.

5 Lo, I will send you the prophet Elijah before the great and terrible day of the LORD comes. ⁶He will turn the hearts of parents to their children and the hearts of children to their parents, so that I will not come and strike the land with a curse.ᵇ

---

a Ch 4.1-6 are Ch 3.19-24 in Heb   *b* Or *a ban of utter destruction*

---

third "book of life" is mentioned. **3.17** A *special possession* is the title given Israel in one of the most famous election scenes in the Bible, Ex 19.5. To be recorded in God's book ensures salvation on the coming *day* when God will *act*. **4.1** See Mt 3.10–12. **4.2** *Sun of righteousness.* See Ps 84.11. One of the most familiar symbols of deity in Egyptian and Mesopotamian religion is the winged solar disk. Although God is not directly described here as a winged disk, the implication is that God will rise on the "day of the LORD" to effect *healing* for the righteous (see also Job 38.12–15; Ps 46.5).

4.4–6 Two of Israel's greatest covenant mediators are mentioned in the concluding postscripts to the book. **4.4** In Deuteronomy, on the high scarp of Moab

Moses preached the *statutes and ordinances* that God gave at Horeb/Sinai. They were to be the foundation of life in the promised land. **4.5–6** The "messenger" of 3.1 is now identified with Elijah the prophet, who also encountered the Lord at Horeb (1 Kings 19.4–18). Because he did not die but was carried into heaven (2 Kings 2.11), he becomes a figure of the future, poised to return as the harbinger of the "day of the LORD." In the Gospel tradition the identification is carried further to John the Baptist (see Mt 11.13; 17.9–13; Mk 6.14–15; Lk 1.17). Malachi predicts that the returned Elijah will effect reconciliation within families, undoing the alienation of kindred that stretches back to the beginning of the biblical narrative.

THE APOCRYPHAL/

DEUTEROCANONICAL BOOKS

of The Old Testament

NEW REVISED STANDARD VERSION

Apocryphal/Deuterocanonical Books in Various Bibles

BOOKS INCLUDED IN ALL ORTHODOX AND CATHOLIC BIBLES

Tobit
Judith
Additions to Esther
Wisdom of Solomon
Ecclesiasticus, or the Wisdom of Jesus Son of Sirach
Baruch
Letter of Jeremiah
Additions to Daniel (Prayer of Azariah and the Song of the Three Jews, Susanna,
Bel and the Dragon)
1 Maccabees
2 Maccabees

GREEK ORTHODOX BIBLE	SLAVONIC ORTHODOX BIBLES
Prayer of Manasseh	Prayer of Manasseh
Psalm 151	Psalm 151
1 Esdras	2 Esdras
3 Maccabees	3 Esdras
4 Maccabees (in appendix)	3 Maccabees

Designations for Books Asssociated with Ezra and Nehemiah

NRSV	GREEK BIBLE (SEPTUAGINT)	LATIN BIBLE (VULGATE)	SLAVONIC BIBLE
Ezra	2 Esdras	1 Ezra	1 Esdras
Nehemiah	2 Esdras	2 Ezra	Nehemiah
1 Esdras	1 Esdras	3 Ezra	2 Esdras
2 Esdras	(not included)	4 Ezra*	3 Esdras

*4 Ezra is sometimes used for chs. 3–14 specifically; chs. 1–2 are then designated 5 Ezra and chs.
15–16 designated 6 Ezra.

TOBIT

TOBIT, A MULTIFACETED PIECE OF HISTORICAL FICTION about the sufferings and healing of a pious Israelite and his family, is one of the most remarkable texts to have survived from Jewish antiquity. In complex ways it offers precious evidence about the religious, intellectual, and social worlds of the people of Israel in the last centuries before the common era.

A Religious Text

THEODICY, THE VINDICATION OF GOD'S JUSTICE, is the book's central motif. Tobit, the story's protagonist, is by every account a pious and righteous Israelite who does not deserve the intense suffering he experiences. Nor does his young relative Sarah. The situation is different for the nation as a whole; Israel has been exiled because of its apostasy, and the prophets' predictions that the nation will return to the land promised to Abraham and his descendants remain unfulfilled. The author offers a twofold explanation of unjust suffering. In some cases, an unseen demonic realm causes the innocent to suffer; in others, God sends suffering to those who are righteous, but not perfect, as a temporary means of chastisement. The author solves the problem of suffering by appealing to the future. As in Job, things end well for the righteous sufferer. For Israel, the prophecies will be fulfilled when the nation's chastisement at the hands of more sinful nations is complete. But in everything a sovereign and just God is active, orchestrating human events for the good of those who are pious and righteous.

The author makes these points by means of a worldview in which visible and invisible realms interpenetrate. Readers are allowed to see activity in both realms and can also empathize with the real-life characters, who are oblivious to God's beneficent presence and activity.

Tobit appropriates and modifies elements in the religious traditions that were then becoming Israel's scripture. Details in the narrative recall the patriarchal stories of Genesis (Sarah's altercation with Hagar, Gen 21; Eliezer's journey for Isaac's bride, Gen 24). Tobit's piety is based on commandments and injunctions in the Torah and a wisdom tradition (attested also in Sirach) spun out of the Torah. The books of the prophets, especially Second and Third Isaiah (Isa 40–66), are considered reliable forecasts of God's future for the nation. Events and themes in chs. 1–2 echo the Mesopotamian court tales preserved in Dan 1–6 as well as the pagan story of Ahikar, which Jews and Christians adopted as their own. With its demons and archangels, its view of divine sovereignty and predestination, and its appeal to the future revelation of God's

1293

justice, Tobit's narrative also employs motifs and devices at home in apocalypses like Daniel and *1 Enoch*.

A Window into a Social World

BECAUSE IT IS A NARRATIVE about real-life characters rather than an apocalypse, the book offers a window into its author's world and some of its customs relating to family life, marriage, burial, the eating of meals, relationships between parents and children, inequalities between the sexes, elements of religious ritual, and the obligations of the rich to the poor.

Literary Aspects

THE COMPLEXITY OF TOBIT is most obvious in its use of literary genres and themes. As a whole it is a fictional narrative about life in biblical times. It differs from its sketchier narrative counterparts in the Bible in that its characters are developed with some attention to the complexity of their emotions and motivations. Narrative tension is maintained as scenes alternate between Nineveh and Ecbatana. An element of humor that runs through the story holds readers' attention and reminds them that there is a fine line between the sublime and the ridiculous. The narrative is nuanced by its use of other genres familiar from biblical and related literature: prayers and hymns, an account of the appearance of a divine being (epiphany), two testaments containing proverbial wisdom, and a prediction of future events similar to historical apocalypses. These genres enrich the narrative and embody elements from the author's social, intellectual, and religious worlds.

Complicating an assessment of this sophisticated piece of literature are a few narrative details that suggest knowledge of Homer's *Odyssey* and some folkloric motifs found elsewhere in ancient tales about the "dangerous bride" and the "grateful dead." These folkloric elements, including a playful touch of magic, stand in tension with the story's theological reflections and the intellectual strains of its wisdom tradition. The mix reminds one that this story about a wealthy member of the royal court is also about ordinary people—their experiences and expectations, woes and worries, superstitions and naïveté. In this complexity and the artistry with which it is presented lies the story's appeal.

Date, Place of Origin, and Language

THE MANY HISTORICAL INACCURACIES in the story indicate that it is a pseudonymous text written long after the time it portrays. The date of its composition is limited by its mention of the rebuilding of the temple (515 BCE) and its omission of any reference to the persecution of the Jews under Antiochus IV Epiphanes (168 BCE). Tobit was most likely composed between the mid-third century and early second century BCE.

The diaspora setting of the story, which underlies its many concerns about interactions between Israelites and Gentiles, suggests that it was written either in the Diaspora or in a predominantly gentile setting.

Tobit was composed in a Semitic language. Textual fragments of one Hebrew and four Aramaic manuscripts were found among the Dead Sea Scrolls. The story in its entirety has been preserved in manuscripts of the Greek OT.

Function

THE STORY'S USE OF WISDOM GENRES and its repeated assertions that God acts for good even in adverse circumstances indicate that the author wishes to encourage readers to trust in and hope for God's mercy in their personal lives, in the gathering of the Jewish people from the Diaspora, and in the realization of God's reign over all humanity. [GEORGE W. E. NICKELSBURG]

1 This book tells the story of Tobit son of Tobiel son of Hananiel son of Aduel son of Gabael son of Raphael son of Raguel of the descendants[a] of Asiel, of the tribe of Naphtali, 2who in the days of King Shalmaneser[b] of the Assyrians was taken into captivity from Thisbe, which is to the south of Kedesh Naphtali in Upper Galilee, above Asher toward the west, and north of Phogor.

Tobit's Youth and Virtuous Life

3 I, Tobit, walked in the ways of truth and righteousness all the days of my life. I performed many acts of charity for my kindred and my people who had gone with me in exile to Nineveh in the land of the Assyrians. 4When I was in my own country, in the land of Israel, while I was still a young man, the whole tribe of my ancestor Naphtali deserted the house of David and Jerusalem. This city had been chosen from among all the tribes of Israel, where all the tribes of Israel should offer sacrifice and where the temple, the dwelling of God, had been consecrated and established for all generations forever.

5 All my kindred and our ancestral house of Naphtali sacrificed to the calf[c] that King Jeroboam of Israel had erected in Dan and on all the mountains of Galilee. 6But I alone went often to Jerusalem for the festivals, as it is pre-

scribed for all Israel by an everlasting decree. I would hurry off to Jerusalem with the first fruits of the crops and the firstlings of the flock, the tithes of the cattle, and the first shearings of the sheep. 7I would give these to the priests, the sons of Aaron, at the altar; likewise the tenth of the grain, wine, olive oil, pomegranates, figs, and the rest of the fruits to the sons of Levi who ministered at Jerusalem. Also for six years I would save up a second tenth in money and go and distribute it in Jerusalem. 8A third tenth[d] I would give to the orphans and widows and to the converts who had attached themselves to Israel. I would bring it and give it to them in the third year, and we would eat it according to the ordinance decreed concerning it in the law of Moses and according to the instructions of Deborah, the mother of my father Tobiel,[e] for my father had died and left me an orphan. 9When I became a man I married a woman,[f] a member of our own family, and by her I became the father of a son whom I named Tobias.

---

a Other ancient authorities lack *of Raphael son of Raguel of the descendants* b Gk *Enemessaros* c Other ancient authorities read *heifer* d *A third tenth* added from other ancient authorities e Lat: Gk *Hananiel* f Other ancient authorities add *Anna*

1.1–2 This title provides the protagonist with a genealogy and place of origin. Cf. Zeph 1.1. **1.1** *Tobit,* the Greek form of the Hebrew *Tobi* ("my good"), which may be an abbreviation for *Tobiah* ("Yahweh is my good"), the name of Tobit's son (*Tobias* in Greek), or *Tobiel* ("God is my good"), the name of Tobit's father. The name is appropriate to the story. **1.2** *Thisbe, Phogor,* locations uncertain. *Asher,* probably Hazor. **1.3–9** Tobit is a faithful and righteous exception among his compatriots, who continue Jeroboam's apostasy (1 Kings 12.25–33). **1.3** Israelite wisdom tradition describes human conduct as walking *in the ways of truth and righteousness* or *in the ways of wrongdoing* (4.5). The Northern Kingdom, Israel, was exiled to *the land of the Assyrians* in 732 BCE under Tiglath-Pileser III and 722 BCE under Sargon II. **1.4–5** Because God

had *chosen* Jerusalem as the unique site for Israelite worship (Deut 12.5–7), Jeroboam's sin was apostasy. **1.5** *Dan* lies eleven miles from Kedesh (v. 2), not far from Tobit's home. It continued to be a site of religious activity long after the exile; cf. *1 Enoch* 13.7–10, a text contemporary with the book of Tobit. **1.6–8** Tobit's faithfulness to the Torah is evident in his festival pilgrimages to *Jerusalem* (Deut 16.16–17; cf. Lk 2.41) and his presentation to the priests of *first fruits of the crops* (Deut 26.1–11), *firstlings* (Ex 13.12), *tithes of the cattle* (Lev 27.32), *first shearings* (Deut 18.4), a *tenth* of his crops (Lev 27.30; Deut 14.22–23), a *second tenth* turned to money (Deut 14.25), and a *third tenth,* which he distributed *to the orphans and widows and to the converts* (Deut 14.28–29). **1.9** Endogamy, marriage to *a member of* one's *own family* (not just to an Israel-

Taken Captive to Nineveh

10 After I was carried away captive to Assyria and came as a captive to Nineveh, everyone of my kindred and my people ate the food of the Gentiles, 11but I kept myself from eating the food of the Gentiles. 12Because I was mindful of God with all my heart, 13the Most High gave me favor and good standing with Shalmaneser,[a] and I used to buy everything he needed. 14Until his death I used to go into Media, and buy for him there. While in the country of Media I left bags of silver worth ten talents in trust with Gabael, the brother of Gabri. 15But when Shalmaneser[a] died, and his son Sennacherib reigned in his place, the highways into Media became unsafe and I could no longer go there.

Courage in Burying the Dead

16 In the days of Shalmaneser[a] I performed many acts of charity to my kindred, those of my tribe. 17I would give my food to the hungry and my clothing to the naked; and if I saw the dead body of any of my people thrown out behind the wall of Nineveh, I would bury it. 18I also buried any whom King Sennacherib put to death when he came fleeing from Judea in those days of judgment that the king of heaven executed upon him because of his blasphemies. For in his anger he put to death many Israelites; but I would secretly remove the bodies and bury them. So when Sennacherib looked for them he could not find them. 19Then one of the Ninevites went and informed the king about me, that I was burying them; so I hid myself. But when I realized that the king knew about me and that I was being searched for to be put to death, I was afraid and ran away. 20Then all my property was confiscated; nothing was left to me that was not taken into the royal treasury except my wife Anna and my son Tobias.

21 But not forty[b] days passed before two of Sennacherib's[c] sons killed him, and they fled to the mountains of Ararat, and his son Esar-haddon[d] reigned after him. He appointed Ahikar, the son of my brother Hanael[e] over all the accounts of his kingdom, and he had authority over the entire administration. 22Ahikar interceded for me, and I returned to Nineveh. Now Ahikar was chief cupbearer, keeper of the signet, and in charge of administration of the accounts under King Sennacherib of Assyria; so Esar-haddon[d] reappointed him. He was my nephew and so a close relative.

2 Then during the reign of Esar-haddon[d] I returned home, and my wife Anna and my son Tobias were restored to me. At our festival of Pentecost, which is the sacred festival of weeks, a good dinner was prepared for me and I reclined to eat. 2When the table was set for me and an abundance of food placed before me, I said to my son Tobias, "Go, my child, and bring whatever poor person you may find of our people among the exiles in Nineveh,

---

a Gk *Enemessaros*   *b* Other ancient authorities read either *forty-five* or *fifty*   *c* Gk *his*   *d* Gk *Sacherdonos*   *e* Other authorities read *Hananael*

---

ite), is a major concern in Tobit; see 4.12–13. **1.10–22** Tobit's promotion in a Mesopotamian court, his persecution for pious acts, and his restoration echo Dan 1–6, Esther, and the story of Ahikar. **1.10** *Nineveh*, the Assyrian capital. **1.11–13** As in vv. 5–9, Tobit's piety is exceptional. Like Daniel, he is rewarded for avoiding unclean *food* (Dan 1.8–20; Lev 11). **1.14** On *Media* as a site of Israelite settlement, cf. 2 Kings 17.6. The deposit of silver with *Gabael* is one of several providential events in the story and prepares the way for a major turn in the plot (4.1). **1.15** This section is marked by a number of historical inaccuracies. *Shalmaneser* V died during the siege of Samaria; his successors were his brothers Sargon II (not mentioned here or in 2 Kings 17) and Sennacherib (cf. vv. 18–20). **1.16–20** Tobit's piety, like Daniel's, leads to his persecution (see Dan 3; 6). **1.17** On the obligation to *give . . . food to the hungry and . . . clothing to the naked,* cf. [Isa 58.]7; 16; Mt 25.35–36. **1.18** Sennacherib invaded [Judah (2] Kings 19.35–37) in 701 BCE, twenty years be-fore his death (cf. *forty days*, v. 21). Exposure of bodies was a common means of showing contempt (cf. 1 Kings 21.24; 2 Kings 9.30–37; Ps 79.2–3). Burial of the dead is a major motif in Tobit (2.3–8; 4.3–4; 6.15; 8.12; 14.10–13). **1.19** Punishment for burying the king's victims recalls Sophocles' *Antigone.* **1.21** *Ahikar,* the protagonist in a popular Mesopotamian story preserved by Jews and Christians; however, it makes no mention of Tobit. Other details of the story are reflected in v. 22; 2.10; 11.18; 14.10.

2.1–10 Tobit's pious concern for others—the poor and the unburied—again results in his suffering. **2.1** In addition to food laws (1.11), Tobit observes Israelite festivals, here the harvest *festival of Pentecost* (Deut 16.10). **2.2** On the obligation to feed the *poor,* cf. Lk 14.12–24; 16.19–31. For Tobit the festival must be shared with one *who is wholeheartedly mindful of God,* as he is (1.12). Wholehearted love of and obedience to God is a cliché; cf. Deut 30.2, 6; allusions to the Deuteronomic language in Bar 2.30–33; Jubilees 1.14–

who is wholeheartedly mindful of God,ᵃ and he shall eat together with me. I will wait for you, until you come back." ³So Tobias went to look for some poor person of our people. When he had returned he said, "Father!" And I replied, "Here I am, my child." Then he went on to say, "Look, father, one of our own people has been murdered and thrown into the market place, and now he lies there strangled." ⁴Then I sprang up, left the dinner before even tasting it, and removed the bodyᵇ from the squareᶜ and laid itᵇ in one of the rooms until sunset when I might bury it.ᵇ ⁵When I returned, I washed myself and ate my food in sorrow. ⁶Then I remembered the prophecy of Amos, how he said against Bethel,ᵈ

"Your festivals shall be turned into
        mourning,
    and all your songs into lamentation."

And I wept.

Tobit Becomes Blind

7 When the sun had set, I went and dug a grave and buried him. ⁸And my neighbors laughed and said, "Is he still not afraid? He has already been hunted down to be put to death for doing this, and he ran away; yet here he is again burying the dead!" ⁹That same night I washed myself and went into my courtyard and slept by the wall of the courtyard; and my face was uncovered because of the heat. ¹⁰I did not know that there were sparrows on the wall; their fresh droppings fell into my eyes and produced white films. I went to physicians to be healed, but the more they treated me with ointments the more my vision was obscured by the white films, until I became completely blind. For four years I remained unable to see. All my kindred were sorry for me, and Ahikar took care of me for two years before he went to Elymais.

Tobit's Wife Earns Their Livelihood

11 At that time, also, my wife Anna earned money at women's work. ¹²She used to send what she made to the owners and they would pay wages to her. One day, the seventh of Dystrus, when she cut off a piece she had woven and sent it to the owners, they paid her full wages and also gave her a young goat for a meal. ¹³When she returned to me, the goat began to bleat. So I called her and said, "Where did you get this goat? It is surely not stolen, is it? Return it to the owners; for we have no right to eat anything stolen." ¹⁴But she said to me, "It was given to me as a gift in addition to my wages." But I did not believe her, and told her to return it to the owners. I became flushed with anger against her over this. Then she replied to me, "Where are your acts of charity? Where are your righteous deeds? These things are known about you!"ᵉ

Tobit's Prayer

3 Then with much grief and anguish of heart I wept, and with groaning began to pray:
2 "You are righteous, O Lord,
        and all your deeds are just;
    all your ways are mercy and truth;
        you judge the world.ᶠ

ᵃ Lat: Gk *wholeheartedly mindful*   ᵇ Gk *him*   ᶜ Other ancient authorities lack *from the square*   ᵈ Other ancient authorities read *against Bethlehem*   ᵉ Or *to you*; Gk *with you*   ᶠ Other ancient authorities read *you render true and righteous judgment forever*

---

16. **2.4–9** The rationale for this sequence of events is unclear. Contact with a corpse rendered one impure (Num 19.11–19), which explains why Tobit sleeps in the *courtyard*; but why may he eat in his house? **2.6** The meal provides a setting in which Tobit can apply ironically to himself Am 8.10, "*Your festivals . . . into lamentation*," an oracle against those who trample on the poor and take their grain. **2.9–10** How does the author understand the cause of Tobit's blindness? Is it happenstance, or are the sparrows agents of a demon like Asmodeus (3.8; cf. *Jubilees* 11.11; Mk 4.4, 15)? In either case, the incident triggers the divinely directed scenario recounted through the rest of the story. Although Tobit and his family cannot predict the outcome, a providential God will dispose matters for them. **2.11–3.17** The destinies of two innocent sufferers are joined as reproach leads them to pray for

death. **2.11–14** The humiliation of the once wealthy public servant is complete, and the situation pits Tobit and his wife against each other. **2.12** *The seventh of Dystrus*, roughly mid-January in the Macedonian calendar. **2.13–14** Tobit's concern with righteousness has become an obsession. His distrust of Anna leads to her ironic rebuke; its gist is either to question the sincerity of his *righteous deeds* or to taunt him because they have gone unrewarded. **3.1–6** His neighbors' mockery and his wife's rebuke prompt Tobit to seek release in death. **3.2–5** The motifs in the first part of Tobit's prayer are common in Jewish prayers of confession (Dan 9.4–19; Bar 1.15–3.8; Prayer of Azariah) and may indicate that this is an excerpt or epitome of a traditional text. Vv. 2, 5 frame the section with the assertion that God's judgments are *righteous, just,* and *true* (cf. *Psalms of Solomon* 2.10, 15; 8.7, 26).

3 And now, O Lord, remember me
      and look favorably upon me.
  Do not punish me for my sins
      and for my unwitting offenses
      and those that my ancestors
            committed before you.
  They sinned against you,
4   and disobeyed your commandments.
  So you gave us over to plunder, exile, and
            death,
      to become the talk, the byword, and an
            object of reproach
      among all the nations among whom
            you have dispersed us.
5 And now your many judgments are
            true
      in exacting penalty from me for my
            sins.
  For we have not kept your
            commandments
      and have not walked in accordance
            with truth before you.
6 So now deal with me as you will;
      command my spirit to be taken from
            me,
      so that I may be released from the face
            of the earth and become dust.
  For it is better for me to die than to live,
      because I have had to listen to
            undeserved insults,
      and great is the sorrow within me.
  Command, O Lord, that I be released
            from this distress;
      release me to go to the eternal home,
      and do not, O Lord, turn your face
            away from me.
  For it is better for me to die
      than to see so much distress in my
            life
      and to listen to insults."

Sarah Falsely Accused

7 On the same day, at Ecbatana in Media, it also happened that Sarah, the daughter of Raguel, was reproached by one of her father's maids. 8For she had been married to seven husbands, and the wicked demon Asmodeus had killed each of them before they had been with her as is customary for wives. So the maid said to her, "You are the one who kills*a* your husbands! See, you have already been married to seven husbands and have not borne the name of*b* a single one of them. 9Why do you beat us? Because your husbands are dead? Go with them! May we never see a son or daughter of yours!"

Sarah's Prayer for Death

10 On that day she was grieved in spirit and wept. When she had gone up to her father's upper room, she intended to hang herself. But she thought it over and said, "Never shall they reproach my father, saying to him, 'You had only one beloved daughter but she hanged herself because of her distress.' And I shall bring my father in his old age down in sorrow to Hades. It is better for me not to hang myself, but to pray the Lord that I may die and not listen to these reproaches anymore." 11At that same time, with hands outstretched toward the window, she prayed and said,
  "Blessed are you, merciful God!
      Blessed is your name forever;
      let all your works praise you forever.
12   And now, Lord,*c* I turn my face to you,
      and raise my eyes toward you.
13   Command that I be released from the
            earth

---

a Other ancient authorities read *strangles*   *b* Other ancient authorities read *have had no benefit from*   *c* Other ancient authorities lack *Lord*

3.3 Though Tobit is righteous, he is not sinless; he is guilty of *sins* and *unwitting offenses,* and he does not have access to the sacrificial system to atone for them (Lev 5.17–19; *Psalms of Solomon* 3.8). He is also liable for the sins of his *ancestors* (Ex 20.5–6). On all these accounts, a just God is exacting judgment on him. On the manner of this judgment, see note on 11.15. **3.4** The idea that the *exile* is deserved punishment for Israel's sins is a common OT motif. **3.5** Tobit, the righteous exception, paradoxically acknowledges his solidarity with the sinful nation (cf. 2 Macc 7.18, 33). **3.6** Tobit seeks to *become dust* (Gen 3.19) and find release from Anna's *undeserved* (lit. "false") *insults.* **3.7–9** Tobit's relative Sarah is also an innocent victim of circumstances beyond her control and an ob-

ject of insults. **3.8–9** The meaning of the name *Asmodeus* is uncertain. The demon lover, a common motif in ancient folklore, also appears in *1 Enoch* 6–11. Here the demon who cannot satisfy his lust kills his rival each time before the marriage is consummated, thus leaving Sarah without the possibility of offspring and making her the object of reproach (cf. Gen 16.4–6, on another Sarah and her maid; 1 Sam 1.6). For an allusion to a story about marriage to seven brothers, see Mk 12.18–25. **3.10–15** Unfair reproach leads Sarah, like Tobit, to pray for death. **3.10** Sarah's rejection of suicide indicates a concern for her family lacking in Tobit's unmitigated self-pity. **3.11** Sarah adopts a common posture for prayer, *with hands outstretched* (Ezra 9.5; Dan 6.10). In spite of her

and not listen to such reproaches any
    more.
14 You know, O Master, that I am innocent
    of any defilement with a man,
15 and that I have not disgraced my name
    or the name of my father in the land of
      my exile.
I am my father's only child;
    he has no other child to be his heir;
and he has no close relative or other
      kindred
    for whom I should keep myself as wife.
Already seven husbands of mine have
    died.
Why should I still live?
But if it is not pleasing to you, O Lord, to
    take my life,
hear me in my disgrace."

An Answer to Prayer

16 At that very moment, the prayers of both of
them were heard in the glorious presence of
God. 17 So Raphael was sent to heal both of
them: Tobit, by removing the white films from
his eyes, so that he might see God's light with
his eyes; and Sarah, daughter of Raguel, by
giving her in marriage to Tobias son of Tobit,
and by setting her free from the wicked demon
Asmodeus. For Tobias was entitled to have her
before all others who had desired to marry
her. At the same time that Tobit returned from
the courtyard into his house, Sarah daughter
of Raguel came down from her upper room.

Tobit Gives Instructions to His Son

4 That same day Tobit remembered the
money that he had left in trust with
Gabael at Rages in Media, 2 and he said to himself, "Now I have asked for death. Why do I not
call my son Tobias and explain to him about
the money before I die?" 3 Then he called his
son Tobias, and when he came to him he said,
"My son, when I die,ᵃ give me a proper burial.
Honor your mother and do not abandon her
all the days of her life. Do whatever pleases
her, and do not grieve her in anything. 4 Remember her, my son, because she faced many
dangers for you while you were in her womb.
And when she dies, bury her beside me in the
same grave.

5 "Revere the Lord all your days, my son,
and refuse to sin or to transgress his commandments. Live uprightly all the days of
your life, and do not walk in the ways of
wrongdoing; 6 for those who act in accordance
with truth will prosper in all their activities. To
all those who practice righteousnessᵇ 7 give
alms from your possessions, and do not let
your eye begrudge the gift when you make it.
Do not turn your face away from anyone who
is poor, and the face of God will not be turned
away from you. 8 If you have many posses-

_____

a Lat b The text of codex Sinaiticus goes directly from verse 6
to verse 19, reading *To those who practice righteousness* 19 *the Lord
will give good counsel.* In order to fill the lacuna verses 7 to 18 are
derived from other ancient authorities

tragedy, she can bless a *merciful God* (cf. Pr Azar 3).
3.14–15 Unlike Tobit, Sarah does not confess her sins.
Her denial of sexual sin (cf. Sus 42–43) may be a
protest that the deaths of her husbands are unjust for
a chaste woman. Her marriages to seven relatives fulfilled levirate law (Deut 25.5–10; cf. Gen 38). Unaware of Tobias's existence, she sees no further options for marriage, but, unlike Tobit, she allows God
another option if her death is not *pleasing* to God.
3.16–17 God does have an unexpected solution to the
parallel problems in the Tobiad family. **3.16** In the
glorious presence of God, seven angels relay human
prayers and stand ready to implement God's responses (cf. Rev 1.4; 1 Enoch 20). **3.17** *Raphael* (Hebrew, "God has healed") is the appropriate agent to
heal Tobit's and Sarah's afflictions. Tobias's preeminent right *to marry* Sarah, his predestined bride
(6.18), has ironically been facilitated by the tragic
deaths of their seven kinsmen.
4.1–19 Certain that God will answer his prayer for
death, Tobit dispenses testamentary instruction to his
son. The testament was a well-defined literary genre in
biblical and early Jewish and Christian literature (Gen

49; 1 Enoch 81–82.3; 91; Jubilees 20–21; *Testaments of
the Twelve Patriarchs; Testament of Job*) in which a father anticipating death offered his children ethical instruction and information about the future. Tobit will
offer the latter in ch. 14 in connection with his actual
death. **4.1–2** One wonders why Tobit had not previously remembered the deposit of silver that would
solve his financial woes. Evidently God has jogged his
memory; Tobias will return from Media not only with
the silver, but with the wife God has destined for him.
4.3 On the son's responsibility to provide his parents *a
proper burial,* cf. Mt 8.21; Lk 9.59. **4.3–4** On the nuance in the allusion to the fourth (fifth) commandment (Ex 20.12), cf. Sir 7.27. **4.5** An admonition to act
righteously and avoid the *ways of wrongdoing* (cf. 1.3)
prefaces a section on the right use of money (vv. 6–
11), which is appropriate in light of Tobias's mission.
4.7 To *give alms* to the poor was an important element
of Jewish piety linked to biblical concerns about the
poor. Here and elsewhere in ch. 4 a principle of appropriate recompense governs God's reward of the righteous (*Do not turn your face away . . . and the face of
God will not be turned away from you*). **4.8** Cf. Mk

sions, make your gift from them in proportion; if few, do not be afraid to give according to the little you have. 9So you will be laying up a good treasure for yourself against the day of necessity. 10For almsgiving delivers from death and keeps you from going into the Darkness. 11Indeed, almsgiving, for all who practice it, is an excellent offering in the presence of the Most High.

12 "Beware, my son, of every kind of fornication. First of all, marry a woman from among the descendants of your ancestors; do not marry a foreign woman, who is not of your father's tribe; for we are the descendants of the prophets. Remember, my son, that Noah, Abraham, Isaac, and Jacob, our ancestors of old, all took wives from among their kindred. They were blessed in their children, and their posterity will inherit the land. 13So now, my son, love your kindred, and in your heart do not disdain your kindred, the sons and daughters of your people, by refusing to take a wife for yourself from among them. For in pride there is ruin and great confusion. And in idleness there is loss and dire poverty, because idleness is the mother of famine.

14 "Do not keep over until the next day the wages of those who work for you, but pay them at once. If you serve God you will receive payment. Watch yourself, my son, in everything you do, and discipline yourself in all your conduct. 15And what you hate, do not do

to anyone. Do not drink wine to excess or let drunkenness go with you on your way. 16Give some of your food to the hungry, and some of your clothing to the naked. Give all your surplus as alms, and do not let your eye begrudge your giving of alms. 17Place your bread on the grave of the righteous, but give none to sinners. 18Seek advice from every wise person and do not despise any useful counsel. 19At all times bless the Lord God, and ask him that your ways may be made straight and that all your paths and plans may prosper. For none of the nations has understanding, but the Lord himself will give them good counsel; but if he chooses otherwise, he casts down to deepest Hades. So now, my child, remember these commandments, and do not let them be erased from your heart.

Money Left in Trust with Gabael

20 "And now, my son, let me explain to you that I left ten talents of silver in trust with Gabael son of Gabrias, at Rages in Media. 21Do not be afraid, my son, because we have become poor. You have great wealth if you fear God and flee from every sin and do what is good in the sight of the Lord your God."

The Angel Raphael

5 Then Tobias answered his father Tobit, "I will do everything that you have commanded me, father; 2but how can I obtain the

---

12.41–44. **4.10** Tobit has practiced the *almsgiving* he preaches (1.3, 17), although his depressed situation seems to undercut the notion that God rewards the righteous. Deliverance *from death* does not mean eternal life, but avoidance of premature death. **4.11** In a diaspora situation, where Israelites could not engage in sacrificial practices, the atoning value of almsgiving as *an excellent offering* (cf. 12.9; Sir 35.1–2) was especially significant, as it again came to be after the destruction of the temple in 70 CE. **4.12–13** Returning to a concern about family (see vv. 3–4), and in keeping with his own example (1.9), Tobit advocates endogamy, recalling the patriarchal narratives (Gen 11.29; 24.3–4; 27.46–28.2; *Jubilees* 4.33). Israelite theory and practice on this subject varied. Mandating marriage to an Israelite are the Genesis passages just cited, Ezra 9–10, Neh 10.28–30, and many passages in *Jubilees*. Ruth attests a more liberal attitude. In a diaspora situation, the concern for preserving national and religious identity is understandable and the problem of finding the right spouse especially difficult. **4.14–19** These verses return to the topic of vv. 5–10. **4.14** For *do not keep . . . for you*, see Lev 19.13. **4.15** The Golden Rule, *what you hate, do not do to anyone*, was

widespread in the cultures of antiquity. In the Judeo-Christian tradition, its negative formulation is first attested here; it is also attributed to Rabbi Hillel (*Babylonian Talmud Shabbat* 31a), James (Acts 15.20, 29 in manuscripts of the "Western tradition"), and the Twelve (*Didache* 1.2). The positive form of the proverb is ascribed to Jesus in Mt 7.12; Lk 6.31. On the evils of *drunkenness*, cf. Prov 23.29–35; Sir 31.25–30; *Testament of Judah* 11–14, 16. **4.17** The practice alluded to here is obscure. The idea is that one should sustain the hungry, but that it is better to leave food at the grave of the righteous than to give it to sinners (cf. *Ahikar* 2.10, Syriac version). The restriction of charity to the righteous is noteworthy; cf. 2.2; Gal 6.10. **4.19** *At all times bless . . . God* may reflect Ps 34.1; the psalm describes the plight and fate of people like Tobit. That *none of the nations has understanding* (Deut 32.28) is an observation appropriate to the diaspora setting. On the concluding admonition, cf. *1 Enoch* 94.5. **4.20– 5.3** The conclusion of Tobit's instruction returns to the narrative that introduced it (4.1–2). **4.20** *Ten talents of silver* weighed about 750 pounds, worth a substantial sum. **5.1** Tobias's response to his father's instruction echoes Ex 19.8; 24.3; Josh 1.16.

money*a* from him, since he does not know me and I do not know him? What evidence*b* am I to give him so that he will recognize and trust me, and give me the money? Also, I do not know the roads to Media, or how to get there." [3]Then Tobit answered his son Tobias, "He gave me his bond and I gave him my bond. I*c* divided his in two; we each took one part, and I put one with the money. And now twenty years have passed since I left this money in trust. So now, my son, find yourself a trustworthy man to go with you, and we will pay him wages until you return. But get back the money from Gabael."*d*

4 So Tobias went out to look for a man to go with him to Media, someone who was acquainted with the way. He went out and found the angel Raphael standing in front of him; but he did not perceive that he was an angel of God. [5]Tobias*e* said to him, "Where do you come from, young man?" "From your kindred, the Israelites," he replied, "and I have come here to work." Then Tobias*f* said to him, "Do you know the way to go to Media?" [6]"Yes," he replied, "I have been there many times; I am acquainted with it and know all the roads. I have often traveled to Media, and would stay with our kinsman Gabael who lives in Rages of Media. It is a journey of two days from Ecbatana to Rages; for it lies in a mountainous area, while Ecbatana is in the middle of the plain." [7]Then Tobias said to him, "Wait for me, young man, until I go in and tell my father; for I do need you to travel with me, and I will pay you your wages." [8]He replied, "All right, I will wait; but do not take too long."

9 So Tobias*f* went in to tell his father Tobit and said to him, "I have just found a man who is one of our own Israelite kindred!" He replied, "Call the man in, my son, so that I may learn about his family and to what tribe he belongs, and whether he is trustworthy enough to go with you."

10 Then Tobias went out and called him, and said, "Young man, my father is calling for you." So he went in to him, and Tobit greeted him first. He replied, "Joyous greetings to you!" But Tobit retorted, "What joy is left for me any more? I am a man without eyesight; I cannot see the light of heaven, but I lie in darkness like the dead who no longer see the light. Although still alive, I am among the dead. I hear people but I cannot see them." But the young man*f* said, "Take courage; the time is near for God to heal you; take courage." Then Tobit said to him, "My son Tobias wishes to go to Media. Can you accompany him and guide him? I will pay your wages, brother." He answered, "I can go with him and I know all the roads, for I have often gone to Media and have crossed all its plains, and I am familiar with its mountains and all of its roads."

11 Then Tobit*f* said to him, "Brother, of what family are you and from what tribe? Tell me, brother." [12]He replied, "Why do you need to know my tribe?" But Tobit*f* said, "I want to be sure, brother, whose son you are and what your name is." [13]He replied, "I am Azariah, the son of the great Hananiah, one of your relatives." [14]Then Tobit said to him, "Welcome! God save you, brother. Do not feel bitter toward me, brother, because I wanted to be sure about your ancestry. It turns out that you are a kinsman, and of good and noble lineage. For I knew Hananiah and Nathan,*g* the two sons of Shemeliah,*h* and they used to go with me to Jerusalem and worshiped with me there, and were not led astray. Your kindred are good people; you come of good stock. Hearty welcome!"

15 Then he added, "I will pay you a drachma a day as wages, as well as expenses for yourself and my son. So go with my son, [16]and*i* I will add

a Gk *it*   *b* Gk *sign*   *c* Other authorities read *He*   *d* Gk *from him*   *e* Gk *He*   *f* Gk *he*   *g* Other ancient authorities read *Jathan* or *Nathaniah*   *h* Other ancient authorities read *Shemaiah*   *i* Other ancient authorities add *when you return safely*

5.4–17a Tobias's need for a traveling companion (see 1.15) is met by the angel Raphael, who is conveniently waiting outside the door. Stories about the appearance (epiphany) of a divine being are frequent in the Bible (e.g., Gen 18.1–15; Judg 13; Lk 1.8–23, 26–38) and elsewhere in antiquity (e.g., books 1–3 of the *Odyssey,* where Athena travels with Telemachus). The conversation between Raphael and the two Israelites is a storyteller's delight. The divine being cannot reveal his identity and must resort to double entendres, white lies, and half-truths, while Tobit is unaware of the real truth of some of his own utterances. **5.5** Given Raphael's real identity, his conversation with Tobias is a charade, although it is true that he has *come here to work.* **5.6** Raphael's angelic missions have doubtless taken him to Media. **5.10** *Take courage,* a typical admonition in epiphanies (*Joseph and Aseneth* 14.11; 15.2–5). **5.11–14** Tobit's queries are irrelevant, although his conclusion that "Azariah's" *kindred are good people* and he comes *of good stock* is true in a way he cannot imagine (cf. 5.22). **5.13** The names *Azariah* (Hebrew, "Yahweh has helped") and *Hananiah* ("Yahweh has had

something to your wages." Raphael[a] answered, "I will go with him; so do not fear. We shall leave in good health and return to you in good health, because the way is safe." [17]So Tobit[b] said to him, "Blessings be upon you, brother."

Then he called his son and said to him, "Son, prepare supplies for the journey and set out with your brother. May God in heaven bring you safely there and return you in good health to me; and may his angel, my son, accompany you both for your safety."

Before he went out to start his journey, he kissed his father and mother. Tobit then said to him, "Have a safe journey."

18 But his mother[c] began to weep, and said to Tobit, "Why is it that you have sent my child away? Is he not the staff of our hand as he goes in and out before us? [19]Do not heap money upon money, but let it be a ransom for our child. [20]For the life that is given to us by the Lord is enough for us." [21]Tobit[a] said to her, "Do not worry; our child will leave in good health and return to us in good health. Your eyes will see him on the day when he returns to you in good health. Say no more! Do not fear for them, my sister. [22]For a good angel will accompany him; his journey will be successful, and he will come back in good health." 6 [1]So she stopped weeping.

Journey to Rages

The young man went out and the angel went with him; [2]and the dog came out with him and went along with them. So they both journeyed along, and when the first night overtook them they camped by the Tigris river. [3]Then the young man went down to wash his feet in the Tigris river. Suddenly a large fish leaped up from the water and tried to swallow the young man's foot, and he cried out. [4]But the angel said to the young man, "Catch hold of the fish and hang on to it!" So the young man grasped the fish and drew it up on the land. [5]Then the angel said to him, "Cut open the fish and take out its gall, heart, and liver. Keep them with you, but throw away the intestines. For its gall, heart, and liver are useful as medicine." [6]So after cutting open the fish the young man gathered together the gall, heart, and liver; then he roasted and ate some of the fish, and kept some to be salted.

The two continued on their way together until they were near Media.[d] [7]Then the young man questioned the angel and said to him, "Brother Azariah, what medicinal value is there in the fish's heart and liver, and in the gall?" [8]He replied, "As for the fish's heart and liver, you must burn them to make a smoke in the presence of a man or woman afflicted by a demon or evil spirit, and every affliction will flee away and never remain with that person any longer. [9]And as for the gall, anoint a person's eyes where white films have appeared on them; blow upon them, upon the white films, and the eyes[e] will be healed."

Raphael's Instructions

10 When he entered Media and already was approaching Ecbatana,[f] [11]Raphael said to the young man, "Brother Tobias." "Here I am," he answered. Then Raphael[b] said to him, "We must stay this night in the home of Raguel. He is your relative, and he has a daughter named Sarah. [12]He has no male heir and no daughter except Sarah only, and you, as next of kin to her, have before all other men a hereditary claim on her. Also it is right for you to inherit her father's possessions. Moreover, the girl is sensible, brave, and very beautiful, and her fa-

---

a Gk *He* b Gk *he* c Other ancient authorities add *Anna*
d Other ancient authorities read *Ecbatana* e Gk *they* f Other ancient authorities read *Rages*

---

mercy") symbolize a situation Tobit does not understand. **5.17a** Readers are to smile at Tobit's wish that an angel accompany Tobias and "Azariah." **5.17b–6.1a** Tobit's and Anna's contrasting attitudes toward their son's departure are in character. Cf. 10.1–7.

6.1b–9 The journey to Rages has several functions. Most obviously, it is the narrative device that gets Tobias to his money, his bride, and the magical devices that will heal Sarah and Tobit. It also has symbolic overtones. Readers see how God literally makes the paths of the righteous prosper (cf. 4.19), and the presence of Raphael recalls the notion that a good angel guides one along the paths of righteousness (cf. Dead Sea Scrolls

Rule of the Community [1QS] 3.18–4.6; *Letter of Barnabas* 18; Hermas, *Mandates* 6.2). On the angelic guide, cf. Ex 23.20; *1 Enoch* 20–33. **6.3–6** Again God intervenes, this time by providing *a large fish* (cf. Jon 1.17). **6.10–18** The author now reveals the real purposes for the journey. In addition to finding the medicine to heal Tobit (v. 9), Tobias will rid Sarah of her demon, and each will find in the other the kind of spouse recommended by Tobit (4.12–13) and the very spouse foreordained by God. Recovering the money from Gabael is a bonus. The section is rich in psychological insight. **6.11** "Azariah" plays the marriage broker (cf. Gen 24, where the servant may be Eliezer, which means in He-

ther is a good man." [13]He continued, "You have every right to take her in marriage. So listen to me, brother; tonight I will speak to her father about the girl, so that we may take her to be your bride. When we return from Rages we will celebrate her marriage. For I know that Raguel can by no means keep her from you or promise her to another man without incurring the penalty of death according to the decree of the book of Moses. Indeed he knows that you, rather than any other man, are entitled to marry his daughter. So now listen to me, brother, and tonight we shall speak concerning the girl and arrange her engagement to you. And when we return from Rages we will take her and bring her back with us to your house."

14 Then Tobias said in answer to Raphael, "Brother Azariah, I have heard that she already has been married to seven husbands and that they died in the bridal chamber. On the night when they went in to her, they would die. I have heard people saying that it was a demon that killed them. [15]It does not harm her, but it kills anyone who desires to approach her. So now, since I am the only son my father has, I am afraid that I may die and bring my father's and mother's life down to their grave, grieving for me—and they have no other son to bury them."

16 But Raphael[a] said to him, "Do you not remember your father's orders when he commanded you to take a wife from your father's house? Now listen to me, brother, and say no more about this demon. Take her. I know that this very night she will be given to you in marriage. [17]When you enter the bridal chamber, take some of the fish's liver and heart, and put them on the embers of the incense. An odor will be given off; [18]the demon will smell it and flee, and will never be seen near her any more. Now when you are about to go to bed with her, both of you must first stand up and pray, imploring the Lord of heaven that mercy and safety may be granted to you. Do not be afraid,

for she was set apart for you before the world was made. You will save her, and she will go with you. I presume that you will have children by her, and they will be as brothers to you. Now say no more!" When Tobias heard the words of Raphael and learned that she was his kinswoman,[b] related through his father's lineage, he loved her very much, and his heart was drawn to her.

Arrival at Home of Raguel

7 Now when they[c] entered Ecbatana, Tobias[a] said to him, "Brother Azariah, take me straight to our brother Raguel." So he took him to Raguel's house, where they found him sitting beside the courtyard door. They greeted him first, and he replied, "Joyous greetings, brothers; welcome and good health!" Then he brought them into his house. [2]He said to his wife Edna, "How much the young man resembles my kinsman Tobit!" [3]Then Edna questioned them, saying, "Where are you from, brothers?" They answered, "We belong to the descendants of Naphtali who are exiles in Nineveh." [4]She said to them, "Do you know our kinsman Tobit?" And they replied, "Yes, we know him." Then she asked them, "Is he[d] in good health?" [5]They replied, "He is alive and in good health." And Tobias added, "He is my father!" [6]At that Raguel jumped up and kissed him and wept. [7]He also spoke to him as follows, "Blessings on you, my child, son of a good and noble father![e] O most miserable of calamities that such an upright and beneficent man has become blind!" He then embraced his kinsman Tobias and wept. [8]His wife Edna also wept for him, and their daughter Sarah likewise wept. [9]Then Raguel[a] slaughtered a ram from the flock and received them very warmly.

---

a Gk *he*   *b* Gk *sister*   *c* Other ancient authorities read *he*
d Other ancient authorities add *alive and*   *e* Other ancient authorities add *When he heard that Tobit had lost his sight, he was stricken with grief and wept. Then he said,*

---

brew "El is my help"). **6.14–18** Tobias's hesitation is not simply self-serving; it reflects concern for his parents, which Raphael cleverly parries by reference to his father's command. **6.18** The youth's acquiescence is remarkable, given that he is unaware of his companion's real identity, but his trust in the *Lord of Heaven* carries him through the dilemma. *Do not be afraid,* typical vocabulary of epiphanies (cf. Lk 1.13, 30).

7.1–9a The arrival of Tobias and "Azariah" at

Raguel's house is marked by a concern about family ties and well-being. **7.7** Raguel echoes a major motif in the story when he observes that Tobit's blindness is incongruous for one who is *upright and beneficent*. **7.9b–16** Raphael, Raguel, and Tobias now work out the details of the marriage. The narrative seems to reflect actual customs of hospitality: greetings, ablutions, and a sumptuous meal (cf. Gen 18.1–8; Lk 7.44) for males only (see vv. 12–13). **7.9b** One normally did

Marriage of Tobias and Sarah

When they had bathed and washed themselves and had reclined to dine, Tobias said to Raphael, "Brother Azariah, ask Raguel to give me my kinswoman*a* Sarah." [10]But Raguel overheard it and said to the lad, "Eat and drink, and be merry tonight. For no one except you, brother, has the right to marry my daughter Sarah. Likewise I am not at liberty to give her to any other man than yourself, because you are my nearest relative. But let me explain to you the true situation more fully, my child. [11]I have given her to seven men of our kinsmen, and all died on the night when they went in to her. But now, my child, eat and drink, and the Lord will act on behalf of you both." But Tobias said, "I will neither eat nor drink anything until you settle the things that pertain to me." So Raguel said, "I will do so. She is given to you in accordance with the decree in the book of Moses, and it has been decreed from heaven that she be given to you. Take your kinswoman;*a* from now on you are her brother and she is your sister. She is given to you from today and forever. May the Lord of heaven, my child, guide and prosper you both this night and grant you mercy and peace." [12]Then Raguel summoned his daughter Sarah. When she came to him he took her by the hand and gave her to Tobias,*b* saying, "Take her to be your wife in accordance with the law and decree written in the book of Moses. Take her and bring her safely to your father. And may the God of heaven prosper your journey with his peace." [13]Then he called her mother and told her to bring writing material; and he wrote out a copy of a marriage contract, to the effect that he gave her to him

as wife according to the decree of the law of Moses. [14]Then they began to eat and drink.

15 Raguel called his wife Edna and said to her, "Sister, get the other room ready, and take her there." [16]So she went and made the bed in the room as he had told her, and brought Sarah*c* there. She wept for her daughter.*c* Then, wiping away the tears,*d* she said to her, "Take courage, my daughter; the Lord of heaven grant you joy*e* in place of your sorrow. Take courage, my daughter." Then she went out.

Tobias Routs the Demon

8 When they had finished eating and drinking they wanted to retire; so they took the young man and brought him into the bedroom. [2]Then Tobias remembered the words of Raphael, and he took the fish's liver and heart out of the bag where he had them and put them on the embers of the incense. [3]The odor of the fish so repelled the demon that he fled to the remotest parts*f* of Egypt. But Raphael followed him, and at once bound him there hand and foot.

4 When the parents*g* had gone out and shut the door of the room, Tobias got out of bed and said to Sarah,*c* "Sister, get up, and let us pray and implore our Lord that he grant us mercy and safety." [5]So she got up, and they began to pray and implore that they might be kept safe. Tobias*h* began by saying,

"Blessed are you, O God of our ancestors,
and blessed is your name in all
generations forever.

---

a Gk *sister* *b* Gk *him* *c* Gk *her* *d* Other ancient authorities read *the tears of her daughter* *e* Other ancient authorities read *favor* *f* Or *fled through the air to the parts* *g* Gk *they* *h* Gk *He*

---

not discuss business before the meal; Tobias's breach of etiquette underscores the urgency of his request. **7.10** Raguel's suggestion to *eat and drink, and be merry* may be an ironic reformulation of the familiar aphorism. If past events are any indicator, tomorrow Sarah's new husband will be dead. See Lk 12.19–20 for a similar ironic reformulation. The narrative presumes throughout the law of levirate marriage (Deut 25.5–10). Although such marriage was a duty, honesty leads Raguel to offer Tobias the option to decline. **7.11–12** Raguel's assertion that *the Lord will act on behalf of . . . both* and his wish that the Lord *grant . . . mercy and peace* suggest that his pessimism, which will return in 8.9–10, is momentarily tempered. The titles *Lord of Heaven* and *God of Heaven* are typical of contemporary Mesopotamian documents (cf. Dan 2.19, 37, 44;

5.23). In Tobit the titles appear primarily in quasi-liturgical formulas of blessing (see 5.17; 6.18; 7.16; 8.15; 9.6; 10.11–13). **7.16** Edna also vacillates between sorrow and hope. Her repeated *take courage* may translate the same Aramaic phrase as Raphael's *do not be afraid* (6.18), spoken to Tobias on the same subject.

8.1–18 For most of the characters in the story the tension is unbearable: will Tobias suffer the fate of his kinsmen and Sarah's last hope be dashed? God, Raphael, and readers know better. **8.2–3** Tobias's humorous fumigation ritual may reflect some actual exorcistic technique. **8.3** *Binding* is a technical term for incapacitating a demon (cf. Mt 22.13; *1 Enoch* 10.4, also of Raphael). **8.5** The doxological character of Tobias's and Sarah's prayer, expressed in the repeated *blessed* and *bless*, contrasts with Raguel's pessimism and ludi-

Let the heavens and the whole creation
    bless you forever.
6 You made Adam, and for him you made
    his wife Eve
    as a helper and support.
  From the two of them the human race
    has sprung.
  You said, 'It is not good that the man
    should be alone;
    let us make a helper for him like
    himself.'
7 I now am taking this kinswoman of mine,
    not because of lust,
    but with sincerity.
  Grant that she and I may find mercy
    and that we may grow old together."
8And they both said, "Amen, Amen." 9Then
they went to sleep for the night.

But Raguel arose and called his servants to
him, and they went and dug a grave, 10for he
said, "It is possible that he will die and we will
become an object of ridicule and derision."
11When they had finished digging the grave,
Raguel went into his house and called his wife,
12saying, "Send one of the maids and have her
go in to see if he is alive. But if he is dead, let us
bury him without anyone knowing it." 13So
they sent the maid, lit a lamp, and opened the
door; and she went in and found them sound
asleep together. 14Then the maid came out
and informed them that he was alive and that
nothing was wrong. 15So they blessed the God
of heaven, and Raguel^a said,

  "Blessed are you, O God, with every pure
    blessing;
    let all your chosen ones bless you.^b
  Let them bless you forever.
16 Blessed are you because you have made
    me glad.
  It has not turned out as I expected,
    but you have dealt with us according to
    your great mercy.
17 Blessed are you because you had
    compassion
    on two only children.
  Be merciful to them, O Master, and keep
    them safe;

bring their lives to fulfillment
    in happiness and mercy."
18Then he ordered his servants to fill in the
grave before daybreak.

Wedding Feast

19 After this he asked his wife to bake many
loaves of bread; and he went out to the herd
and brought two steers and four rams and ordered them to be slaughtered. So they began to
make preparations. 20Then he called for Tobias and swore on oath to him in these words:^c
"You shall not leave here for fourteen days, but
shall stay here eating and drinking with me;
and you shall cheer up my daughter, who has
been depressed. 21Take at once half of what I
own and return in safety to your father; the
other half will be yours when my wife and I
die. Take courage, my child. I am your father
and Edna is your mother, and we belong to
you as well as to your wife^d now and forever.
Take courage, my child."

The Money Recovered

9 Then Tobias called Raphael and said to
  him, 2"Brother Azariah, take four servants and two camels with you and travel to
Rages. Go to the home of Gabael, give him the
bond, get the money, and then bring him with
you to the wedding celebration. 4For you
know that my father must be counting the
days, and if I delay even one day I will upset
him very much. 3You are witness to the oath
Raguel has sworn, and I cannot violate his
oath."^e 5So Raphael with the four servants and
two camels went to Rages in Media and stayed
with Gabael. Raphael^f gave him the bond and
informed him that Tobit's son Tobias had
married and was inviting him to the wedding
celebration. So Gabael^g got up and counted
out to him the money bags, with their seals intact; then they loaded them on the camels.^h
6In the morning they both got up early and

---

a Gk *they* **b** Other ancient authorities lack this line **c** Other
ancient authorities read *Tobias and said to him* **d** Gk *sister*
e In other ancient authorities verse 3 precedes verse 4 **f** Gk *He*
g Gk *he* **h** Other ancient authorities lack *on the camels*

---

crous grave digging (vv. 9–11). **8.6** Tobias and Sarah
appeal to God's intention in creation (Gen 2.20).
8.15 When Raguel ascertains that Tobias is alive, he utters a blessing parallel to that of Tobias and Sarah (v. 5).
8.19–21 The apprehension felt during the meal of welcome is replaced by joy. **8.20** Raguel's invitation to eat,

drink, and *cheer up* his *daughter* contrasts with 7.10.
8.21 Raguel's twofold *take courage*, spoken to Tobias,
parallels Edna's words to Sarah (7.16). *I am . . . forever*
reads almost like a formula of adoption. Cf. 10.12.
9.6 Gabael is welcomed as a member of the family and
his meeting with Tobias parallels the scene in 7.1–8.

went to the wedding celebration. When they came into Raguel's house they found Tobias reclining at table. He sprang up and greeted Gabael,[a] who wept and blessed him with the words, "Good and noble son of a father good and noble, upright and generous! May the Lord grant the blessing of heaven to you and your wife, and to your wife's father and mother. Blessed be God, for I see in Tobias the very image of my cousin Tobit."

Anxiety of the Parents

10 Now, day by day, Tobit kept counting how many days Tobias[b] would need for going and for returning. And when the days had passed and his son did not appear, 2he said, "Is it possible that he has been detained? Or that Gabael has died, and there is no one to give him the money?" 3And he began to worry. 4His wife Anna said, "My child has perished and is no longer among the living." And she began to weep and mourn for her son, saying, 5"Woe to me, my child, the light of my eyes, that I let you make the journey." 6But Tobit kept saying to her, "Be quiet and stop worrying, my dear;[c] he is all right. Probably something unexpected has happened there. The man who went with him is trustworthy and is one of our own kin. Do not grieve for him, my dear;[c] he will soon be here." 7She answered him, "Be quiet yourself! Stop trying to deceive me! My child has perished." She would rush out every day and watch the road her son had taken, and would heed no one.[d] When the sun had set she would go in and mourn and weep all night long, getting no sleep at all.

Tobias and Sarah Start for Home

Now when the fourteen days of the wedding celebration had ended that Raguel had sworn to observe for his daughter, Tobias came to him and said, "Send me back, for I know that my father and mother do not believe that they will see me again. So I beg of you, father, to let me go so that I may return to my own father. I have already explained to you how I left him." 8But Raguel said to Tobias, "Stay, my child, stay with me; I will send messengers to your father Tobit and they will inform him about you." 9But he said, "No! I beg you to send me back to my father." 10So Raguel promptly gave Tobias his wife Sarah, as well as half of all his property: male and female slaves, oxen and sheep, donkeys and camels, clothing, money, and household goods. 11Then he saw them safely off; he embraced Tobias[a] and said, "Farewell, my child; have a safe journey. The Lord of heaven prosper you and your wife Sarah, and may I see children of yours before I die." 12Then he kissed his daughter Sarah and said to her, "My daughter, honor your father-in-law and your mother-in-law,[c] since from now on they are as much your parents as those who gave you birth. Go in peace, daughter, and may I hear a good report about you as long as I live." Then he bade them farewell and let them go. Then Edna said to Tobias, "My child and dear brother, the Lord of heaven bring you back safely, and may I live long enough to see children of you and of my daughter Sarah before I die. In the sight of the Lord I entrust my daughter to you; do nothing to grieve her all the days of your life. Go in peace, my child. From now on I am your mother and Sarah is your beloved wife.[c] May we all prosper together all the days of our lives." Then she kissed them both and saw them safely off. 13Tobias parted from Raguel with happiness and joy, praising the Lord of heaven and earth, King over all, because he had made his journey a success. Finally, he blessed Raguel and his wife Edna, and said, "I have been commanded by the Lord to honor you all the days of my life."[f]

---

a Gk him b Gk he c Gk sister d Other ancient authorities read *and she would eat nothing* e Other ancient authorities lack parts of *Then . . . mother-in-law* f Lat: Meaning of Gk uncertain

---

10.1–11.18 Tobias completes his journey, and Tobit's healing solves the problem that led to the development of the plot. **10.1–7a** In contrast to the joy of the wedding celebration, gloom pervades the Tobiad home. Unaware of events in Ecbatana, Tobit and Anna, last seen in 5.17–22, engage in an increasingly bitter dispute. Anna grieves and mourns over her son as if he were dead. **10.7b–13** This farewell scene between children and parents is a more extensive counterpart of 5.17. Family concerns govern the discourse. **10.7b–** **9** As in 6.15, Tobias expresses concern for his parents. **10.10** Sarah's dowry is a down payment on the full inheritance of her family's wealth, which Raphael has predicted (6.12). **10.12** *Honor . . . your mother-in-law*, a paraphrase of the fourth (fifth) commandment, parallels 4.3. *They are . . . your parents* parallels 8.21, where Tobias is accepted as the son of Raguel and Edna. **10.13** With an allusion to the fourth (fifth) commandment, *I have . . . my life*, Tobias acknowledges that he is the son of Raguel and Edna.

Homeward Journey

11 When they came near to Kaserin, which is opposite Nineveh, Raphael said, 2"You are aware of how we left your father. 3Let us run ahead of your wife and prepare the house while they are still on the way." 4As they went on together Raphael*a* said to him, "Have the gall ready." And the dog*b* went along behind them.

5 Meanwhile Anna sat looking intently down the road by which her son would come. 6When she caught sight of him coming, she said to his father, "Look, your son is coming, and the man who went with him!"

Tobit's Sight Restored

7 Raphael said to Tobias, before he had approached his father, "I know that his eyes will be opened. 8Smear the gall of the fish on his eyes; the medicine will make the white films shrink and peel off from his eyes, and your father will regain his sight and see the light."

9 Then Anna ran up to her son and threw her arms around him, saying, "Now that I have seen you, my child, I am ready to die." And she wept. 10Then Tobit got up and came stumbling out through the courtyard door. Tobias went up to him, 11with the gall of the fish in his hand, and holding him firmly, he blew into his eyes, saying, "Take courage, father." With this he applied the medicine on his eyes, 12and it made them smart.*c* 13Next, with both his

hands he peeled off the white films from the corners of his eyes. Then Tobit*a* saw his son and*d* threw his arms around him, 14and he wept and said to him, "I see you, my son, the light of my eyes!" Then he said,

"Blessed be God,
　and blessed be his great name,
　and blessed be all his holy angels.
May his holy name be blessed*e*
　throughout all the ages.
15 Though he afflicted me,
　he has had mercy upon me.*f*
　Now I see my son Tobias!"

So Tobit went in rejoicing and praising God at the top of his voice. Tobias reported to his father that his journey had been successful, that he had brought the money, that he had married Raguel's daughter Sarah, and that she was, indeed, on her way there, very near to the gate of Nineveh.

16 Then Tobit, rejoicing and praising God, went out to meet his daughter-in-law at the gate of Nineveh. When the people of Nineveh saw him coming, walking along in full vigor and with no one leading him, they were amazed. 17Before them all, Tobit acknowledged that God had been merciful to him and had restored his sight. When Tobit met Sarah the wife of his son Tobias, he blessed her say-

---

a Gk he   *b* Codex Sinaiticus reads *And the Lord*   *c* Lat: Meaning of Gk uncertain   *d* Other ancient authorities lack *saw his son and*   *e* Codex Sinaiticus reads *May his great name be upon us and blessed be all the angels*   *f* Lat: Gk lacks this line

---

11.1–6 Unlike the journey to Rages (6.1–9), the journey home is not described; the author focuses on the arrival in Nineveh and the events to come. **11.4** Tobias's *dog* has been mentioned previously only in 6.2, at the beginning of the journey. The significance of this narrative device framing the journey account is obscure; however, the detail here is reminiscent of Odysseus's dog's recognition of its master upon his return (*Odyssey* 17.290–327). Cf. note on 5.4–17a on the journey of Telemachus and Athena. The Bible does not generally describe dogs as pets (but cf. Mk 7.27–28) and often portrays them as carnivorous scavengers. **11.7–15** The problem that triggered the plot is now resolved. The scene has some striking parallels (and echoes?) in Lk 15.20–24. **11.9** Anna's speech momentarily delays the account of Tobit's healing and maintains narrative tension. On her words, cf. Lk 2.29–30. **11.11–13** The cause and cure of Tobit's blindness make some anatomical sense. Acid on the cornea can discolor its epithelium, which sometimes can be peeled off like a film. Cf. Acts 9.18. The healing has a miraculous element: fish gall is effective where physicians failed (2.10). Of course, that failure faci-

tated both the recovery of Tobit's money and Tobias's marriage. **11.14** Tobit's ability to see *the light of* his *eyes* fulfills Raphael's prediction that he will *see the light* (v. 8). **11.14–15** Like Tobias, Sarah, and Raguel before him (8.5–7, 15–17), Tobit appropriately breaks into a doxology, which is a foil to his earlier prayer of lament (3.2–6). Cf. the contrast between the Prayer of Azariah and the Song of the Three Jews. Tobit's reference to God's *holy angels* is to the point, though he does not know this. **11.15** The word pair *afflicted* (lit. "scourged") / *had mercy* recurs in 13.2, 5 with reference to Israel. These are technical terms for the manner in which God deals with the righteous. God will judge the wicked (or the nations) with full fury; in contrast, God scourges, chastises, or disciplines the righteous (or Israel), so that when they repent they will be shown mercy. Cf. 2 Macc 6.12–16; *Psalms of Solomon* 3, 13. **11.16–17** Elements in this scene—visible evidence of the cure, the people's amazement, and Tobit's acknowledgment of God's activity—recur in the later miracle stories in the Gospels. **11.17** Tobit now meets the wife he had hoped Tobias would find (4.12–13). The reference to *the Jews* (Judeans) is odd

ing, "Come in, my daughter, and welcome. Blessed be your God who has brought you to us, my daughter. Blessed be your father and your mother, blessed be my son Tobias, and blessed be you, my daughter. Come in now to your home, and welcome, with blessing and joy. Come in, my daughter." So on that day there was rejoicing among all the Jews who were in Nineveh. 18 Ahikar and his nephew Nadab were also present to share Tobit's joy. With merriment they celebrated Tobias's wedding feast for seven days, and many gifts were given to him.*a*

Raphael's Wages

12 When the wedding celebration was ended, Tobit called his son Tobias and said to him, "My child, see to paying the wages of the man who went with you, and give him a bonus as well." 2 He replied, "Father, how much shall I pay him? It would do no harm to give him half of the possessions brought back with me. 3 For he has led me back to you safely, he cured my wife, he brought the money back with me, and he healed you. How much extra shall I give him as a bonus?" 4 Tobit said, "He deserves, my child, to receive half of all that he brought back." 5 So Tobias*b* called him and said, "Take for your wages half of all that you brought back, and farewell."

Raphael's Exhortation

6 Then Raphael*b* called the two of them privately and said to them, "Bless God and acknowledge him in the presence of all the living

for the good things he has done for you. Bless and sing praise to his name. With fitting honor declare to all people the deeds*c* of God. Do not be slow to acknowledge him. 7 It is good to conceal the secret of a king, but to acknowledge and reveal the works of God, and with fitting honor to acknowledge him. Do good and evil will not overtake you. 8 Prayer with fasting*d* is good, but better than both is almsgiving with righteousness. A little with righteousness is better than wealth with wrongdoing.*e* It is better to give alms than to lay up gold. 9 For almsgiving saves from death and purges away every sin. Those who give alms will enjoy a full life, 10 but those who commit sin and do wrong are their own worst enemies.

Raphael Discloses His Identity

11 "I will now declare the whole truth to you and will conceal nothing from you. Already I have declared it to you when I said, 'It is good to conceal the secret of a king, but to reveal with due honor the works of God.' 12 So now when you and Sarah prayed, it was I who brought and read*f* the record of your prayer before the glory of the Lord, and likewise whenever you would bury the dead. 13 And that time when you did not hesitate to get up and leave your dinner to go and bury the dead, 14 I was sent to you to test you. And at the same time God sent me to heal you and Sarah your

---

a Other ancient authorities lack parts of this sentence *b* Gk *he* *c* Gk *words*; other ancient authorities read *words of the deeds* *d* Codex Sinaiticus *with sincerity* *e* Lat *f* Lat: Gk lacks *and read*

---

in a document about a Northern family in exile in Assyria, but note the close identification with Jerusalem in 1.3–7 and ch. 13. **12.1–22** Stories about epiphanies traditionally end with the divine being revealing its identity and suddenly disappearing. **12.1–5** Because Raphael has exceeded expectations, Tobit and Tobias, still acting in accordance with their misperceptions, offer the angel a 50 percent commission (cf. 5.15–16), an act of generosity consonant with the book's attitude about the use of money. **12.6–10** Raphael's self-revelation and instruction occur privately to the men of the story. Throughout the narrative, there has been no contact or proximity between the angel and the women (cf. 1 Cor 11.10; 1 Enoch 6–11). **12.6** The admonition to praise God *in the presence of all the living* anticipates ch. 13 and its universalistic tone (13.3–4, 11; see also 14.6–7). **12.7a** Raphael's admonition that *it is good . . . to acknowledge him* presupposes Tobit's former position in the royal court and seems to presume God's status as

king (see 13.6–7, 10–11, 15–16). **12.7b–10** Complementary proverbs in vv. 7b and 10 frame a section on almsgiving that reiterates 4.6–11. **12.8** The combined references to *prayer, fasting, almsgiving,* and *laying up gold* parallel Mt 6.1–21, which is itself based on Jewish wisdom teaching. **12.9** *Almsgiving saves from death.* In light of subsequent events the truth of 4.10 is now evident, although Tobit's assertion there that *almsgiving delivers from death* seemed ironic. **12.11–22** Raphael reveals to Tobit and Tobias what readers have known since 3.16–17. **12.12** On the notion that angels *read the record* of human prayers and deeds in God's presence, cf. *1 Enoch* 8.4–9.11; 89.76; 97.3–6; 99.3; 104.1. **12.14** Raphael's having been sent to *test* Tobit may suggest divine initiative in the events described in 2.1–10. More likely, it reflects the widespread belief that Satan originates testing or tempting and that God witnesses human responses and provides help, sometimes through an angel; cf. Mt 4.1–10; 6.13; 1 Cor 10.13; Dead Sea Scrolls *Rule of the Community* (1QS) 3.20, 24;

daughter-in-law. ¹⁵I am Raphael, one of the seven angels who stand ready and enter before the glory of the Lord."

16 The two of them were shaken; they fell face down, for they were afraid. ¹⁷But he said to them, "Do not be afraid; peace be with you. Bless God forevermore. ¹⁸As for me, when I was with you, I was not acting on my own will, but by the will of God. Bless him each and every day; sing his praises. ¹⁹Although you were watching me, I really did not eat or drink anything—but what you saw was a vision. ²⁰So now get up from the ground,ᵃ and acknowledge God. See, I am ascending to him who sent me. Write down all these things that have happened to you." And he ascended. ²¹Then they stood up, and could see him no more. ²²They kept blessing God and singing his praises, and they acknowledged God for these marvelous deeds of his, when an angel of God had appeared to them.

Tobit's Thanksgiving to God

13 Then Tobitᵇ said:
"Blessed be God who lives forever,
  because his kingdomᶜ lasts throughout
    all ages.
2 For he afflicts, and he shows mercy;

he leads down to Hades in the lowest
  regions of the earth,
and he brings up from the great abyss,ᵈ
  and there is nothing that can escape his
    hand.
3 Acknowledge him before the nations,
  O children of Israel;
for he has scattered you among them.
4 He has shown you his greatness even
  there.
Exalt him in the presence of every living
  being,
because he is our Lord and he is our
  God;
he is our Father and he is God forever.
5 He will afflictᵉ you for your iniquities,
  but he will again show mercy on all of
    you.
He will gather you from all the nations
  among whom you have been scattered.
6 If you turn to him with all your heart and
  with all your soul,
to do what is true before him,

---

a Other ancient authorities read *now bless the Lord on earth*
b Gk *he*   *c* Other ancient authorities read *forever, and his kingdom*   *d* Gk *from destruction*   *e* Other ancient authorities read *He afflicted*

Jubilees 17.15–18.16. **12.16** This imagery and vocabulary are traditional in epiphany accounts; cf. Dan 10.1–12; *1 Enoch* 14.24–15.1. **12.19** That angels do not eat human food is a traditional idea (cf. Lk 24.36–43; *Testament of Abraham* 4, recension A). **12.20–22** The formula *I am ascending to him who sent me* recurs in Jn 16.5. John shares with Tobit the pattern of a descending and ascending savior figure. The command to *write* a book is also consonant with the commissioning function in such stories about heavenly messengers on earth; cf. Rev 1.9–20. It is to be a doxological book, and the commands to *bless* God (vv. 17–18) and *acknowledge* God's merciful activity resonate with the frequent blessing of God throughout the narrative and in the hymn that follows (see 13.1, 3, 6, 10, 15, 17).
13.1–17 Tobit's hymn of praise, a much-expanded counterpart to 11.14–15, epitomizes the book's many exhortations to praise God. Very possibly a version of a liturgical composition, it reflects real usage in the author's time and lends verisimilitude to this portrait of a pious Israelite. Although its vocabulary is reminiscent of the Psalter (esp. Pss 92–118), its themes reflect the concerns of the author's time. **13.1–2** The introduction establishes the hymn's theme of divine justice and mercy. **13.1** An opening blessing and explication ("Blessed are you . . . because . . .") is formulaic in prayers of this period (cf. Dead Sea Scrolls *Thanksgiving Hymns* [1QH] 13[5].20; 18[10].14). V. 1b implies the title *King of the ages* (vv. 6, 10). **13.2** On

the word pair *afflicts / shows mercy* (see also v. 5), see note on 11.15. Tobit's situation is inseparable from the nation's; see note on 3.2–5. Sickness and healing were, in Israelite thought, descent to and return from Sheol (Greek *Hades*), the realm of the dead. The complex of ideas here echoes Deut 32.39; 1 Sam 2.6; Wis 16.13–15; 2 Macc 7.35. For death, Sheol, and resurrection as metaphors for exile and return, cf. Ezek 34; Bar 2.17; 3.4–8. **13.3–7** The first of two major sections of the hymn. Its vocabulary echoes Deut 30.2, and it presumes the importance of Deut 28–33 as a prediction of Israel's situation in exile and Diaspora. The Deuteronomic scheme of sin, punishment, repentance, and salvation predominates in Jewish literature of the Greco-Roman period. Cf. *Testament of Moses*; Baruch; 2 Macc 3–8; *Jubilees* 23.14–31. **13.3** This section of the hymn is addressed to the *children of Israel . . . scattered* in exile. Like the blessing in v. 1, "I acknowledge you, O Lord . . . for . . ." is formulaic in contemporary hymns (cf. Dead Sea Scrolls *Thanksgiving Hymns* [1QH] 11[3].19; 12[4].5). **13.5** Return to the promised land is the solution for the Diaspora and exile faced by the author. **13.6** Such a restoration requires that Israel repent (*turn to God with all your heart and with all your soul*). Tobit's acknowledgment of God *to a nation of sinners* reflects a concern that the enemy not draw unwarranted conclusions about its power and the weakness of Israel's God, who is described throughout the hymn with ti-

then he will turn to you
and will no longer hide his face from
you.
So now see what he has done for you;
acknowledge him at the top of your
voice.
Bless the Lord of righteousness,
and exalt the King of the ages.[a]
In the land of my exile I acknowledge him,
and show his power and majesty to a
nation of sinners:
'Turn back, you sinners, and do what is
right before him;
perhaps he may look with favor upon
you and show you mercy.'
7 As for me, I exalt my God,
and my soul rejoices in the King of
heaven.
8 Let all people speak of his majesty,
and acknowledge him in Jerusalem.
9 O Jerusalem, the holy city,
he afflicted[b] you for the deeds of your
hands,[c]
but will again have mercy on the
children of the righteous.
10 Acknowledge the Lord, for he is good,[d]
and bless the King of the ages,
so that his tent[e] may be rebuilt in you
in joy.
May he cheer all those within you who
are captives,
and love all those within you who are
distressed,
to all generations forever.
11 A bright light will shine to all the ends of
the earth;
many nations will come to you from
far away,
the inhabitants of the remotest parts of
the earth to your holy name,
bearing gifts in their hands for the
King of heaven.
Generation after generation will give
joyful praise in you;
the name of the chosen city will endure
forever.

12 Cursed are all who speak a harsh word
against you;
cursed are all who conquer you
and pull down your walls,
all who overthrow your towers
and set your homes on fire.
But blessed forever will be all who
revere you.[f]
13 Go, then, and rejoice over the children of
the righteous,
for they will be gathered together
and will praise the Lord of the ages.
14 Happy are those who love you,
and happy are those who rejoice in
your prosperity.
Happy also are all people who grieve with
you
because of your afflictions;
for they will rejoice with you
and witness all your glory forever.
15 My soul blesses[g] the Lord, the great King!
16 For Jerusalem will be built[h] as his
house for all ages.
How happy I will be if a remnant of my
descendants should survive
to see your glory and acknowledge the
King of heaven.
The gates of Jerusalem will be built with
sapphire and emerald,
and all your walls with precious stones.
The towers of Jerusalem will be built with
gold,
and their battlements with pure gold.
The streets of Jerusalem will be paved
with ruby and with stones of Ophir.
17 The gates of Jerusalem will sing hymns of
joy,
and all her houses will cry, 'Hallelujah!
Blessed be the God of Israel!'
and the blessed will bless the holy
name forever and ever."

a The lacuna in codex Sinaiticus, verses 6b to 10a, is filled in
from other ancient authorities   b Other ancient authorities
read *will afflict*   c Other ancient authorities read *your children*
d Other ancient authorities read *Lord worthily*   e Or *tabernacle*
f Other ancient authorities read *who build you up*   g Or *O my
soul, bless*   h Other ancient authorities add *for a city*

tles that emphasize the divine *power, majesty,* and sovereignty. On this concern, cf. Deut 32.27–31; Dan 1–6. **13.8–17** Although Tobit is a Galilean, the second major part of the hymn focuses on *Jerusalem* as the locus of salvation; cf. 1.6–8; 14.5–7. The direct address to Jerusalem and the joyful anticipation of Jerusalem's deliverance parallel a number of contemporary compositions (Bar 4.36–5.9; *Psalms of* Solomon 11; Dead Sea Scrolls *Psalms Scroll* [11QPs[a]] 22.1–15; cf. Sir 36.1–17). Like other contemporary texts influenced by Isa 40–66 (the chief source for the hope of Zion's restoration), these verses do not foresee a restoration of the Davidic dynasty. God will rule as *King* without an earthly agent. **13.16–17** Cf. Isa 54.11–14 and the even bolder allusion to the new Jerusalem in Rev 21.9–27.

Tobit's Final Counsel

14 So ended Tobit's words of praise. 2 Tobit[a] died in peace when he was one hundred twelve years old, and was buried with great honor in Nineveh. He was sixty-two[b] years old when he lost his eyesight, and after regaining it he lived in prosperity, giving alms and continually blessing God and acknowledging God's majesty.

3 When he was about to die, he called his son Tobias and the seven sons of Tobias[c] and gave this command: "My son, take your children 4and hurry off to Media, for I believe the word of God that Nahum spoke about Nineveh, that all these things will take place and overtake Assyria and Nineveh. Indeed, everything that was spoken by the prophets of Israel, whom God sent, will occur. None of all their words will fail, but all will come true at their appointed times. So it will be safer in Media than in Assyria and Babylon. For I know and believe that whatever God has said will be fulfilled and will come true; not a single word of the prophecies will fail. All of our kindred, inhabitants of the land of Israel, will be scattered and taken as captives from the good land; and the whole land of Israel will be desolate, even Samaria and Jerusalem will be desolate. And the temple of God in it will be burned to the ground, and it will be desolate for a while.[d]

5 "But God will again have mercy on them, and God will bring them back into the land of Israel; and they will rebuild the temple of God, but not like the first one until the period when the times of fulfillment shall come. After this they all will return from their exile and will rebuild Jerusalem in splendor; and in it the temple of God will be rebuilt, just as the prophets of Israel have said concerning it. 6Then the nations in the whole world will all be converted and worship God in truth. They will all abandon their idols, which deceitfully have led them into their error; 7and in righteousness they will praise the eternal God. All the Israelites who are saved in those days and are truly mindful of God will be gathered together; they will go to Jerusalem and live in safety forever in the land of Abraham, and it will be given over to them. Those who sincerely love God will rejoice, but those who commit sin and injustice will vanish from all the earth. 8,9So now, my children, I command you, serve God faithfully and do what is pleasing in his sight. Your children are also to be commanded to do what is right and to give alms, and to be mindful of God and to bless his name at all times with sincerity and with all their strength. So now, my son, leave Nineveh; do not remain here. 10On whatever day you bury your mother beside me, do not stay overnight within the confines of the city. For I see that there is much wickedness within it, and that

---

a Gk *He* *b* Other ancient authorities read *fifty-eight* *c* Lat: Gk lacks *and the seven sons of Tobias* *d* Lat: Other ancient authorities read *of God will be in distress and will be burned for a while*

14.1–11a The final chapter centers on the events relating to Tobit's death, especially his second testament (vv. 3–11a), which, unlike the first (ch. 4), focuses on predictions about the future (vv. 4–7). 14.2–3a The narrative introduction contrasts with the setting of Tobit's first testament and affirms that Tobit's piety has been rewarded; his almsgiving and praise of God have led to a long, prosperous life. 14.4–7 Tobit supports his predictions by appealing to *everything...spoken by the prophets of Israel* (v. 4); cf. 2.6; 14.5. These references attest the authority of the biblical prophetic corpus in at least some circles during the author's time. Vv. 4–5 are the earliest extant testimony to the belief that the events of history are fixed and must occur *at their appointed times* (v. 4) in accordance with prophetic predictions. Later apocalyptic speculation lays out detailed scenarios based on this idea; cf. Dan 10–12; *1 Enoch* 85–90; 93.1–10 + 91.11–17. A number of NT texts also presume that future events are fixed and must occur according to the prophetic word (Mk 8.31; 9.11; 13.7, 10; Rev 1.1; cf. Acts 1.7). Identifiable historical events in Tobit's scenario for the future begin with the destruction of Nineveh (612 BCE), predicted by the prophet *Nahum* (v. 4), and end with the return from the Babylonian exile and the rebuilding of *Jerusalem in splendor* (515 BCE; v. 5), as foreseen in Isa 40–66. In vv. 5b–7, the recitation of historical events gives way to a picture of the future that transcends the author's experience: a glorified temple, the conversion of the nations and their abandoning of their idols, the full return of the Diaspora, and the removal of sin from the earth. Elements in this scenario are predicted in the books of the prophets, notably Isa 40–66, but the best parallel is *1 Enoch* 91.11–14. 14.7 A return from the Diaspora to the land of Israel is a common topic in texts of the Greco-Roman period (cf. Sir 36.11; Bar 4.21–5.9; *Psalms of Solomon* 11; *1 Enoch* 90.33). In keeping with a major emphasis in the patriarchal narratives (Gen 12.1; 13.14–18; 15.7, 18–19), Israel is identified as *the land of Abraham*. 14.8–11a Tobit's testament concludes with a summary of ethical instruction that reiterates motifs in ch. 4 and 12.8–10. Here Tobit's example is supplemented by those of *Nadab* and *Ahikar* (v. 10); on Ahikar's alms-

much deceit is practiced within it, while the people are without shame. See, my son, what Nadab did to Ahikar who had reared him. Was he not, while still alive, brought down into the earth? For God repaid him to his face for this shameful treatment. Ahikar came out into the light, but Nadab went into the eternal darkness, because he tried to kill Ahikar. Because he gave alms, Ahikar[a] escaped the fatal trap that Nadab had set for him, but Nadab fell into it himself, and was destroyed. [11]So now, my children, see what almsgiving accomplishes, and what injustice does—it brings death! But now my breath fails me."

Death of Tobit and Anna

Then they laid him on his bed, and he died; and he received an honorable funeral. [12]When Tobias's mother died, he buried her beside his father. Then he and his wife and children[b] returned to Media and settled in Ecbatana with

Raguel his father-in-law. [13]He treated his parents-in-law[c] with great respect in their old age, and buried them in Ecbatana of Media. He inherited both the property of Raguel and that of his father Tobit. [14]He died highly respected at the age of one hundred seventeen[d] years. [15]Before he died he heard[e] of the destruction of Nineveh, and he saw its prisoners being led into Media, those whom King Cyaxares[f] of Media had taken captive. Tobias[g] praised God for all he had done to the people of Nineveh and Assyria; before he died he rejoiced over Nineveh, and he blessed the Lord God forever and ever. Amen.[h]

a Gk he; other ancient authorities read Manasses b Codex Sinaiticus lacks and children c Gk them d Other authorities read other numbers e Codex Sinaiticus reads saw and heard f Cn: Codex Sinaiticus Ahikar; other ancient authorities read Nebuchadnezzar and Ahasuerus g Gk He h Other ancient authorities lack Amen

giving, see 2.10. **14.11b–15** The honorable funeral of Tobit (v. 11b) and the reference to Tobias's inheritance (v. 13) are final reminders that this is a story about the wealthy. For this author, the pious rich deserve splendid burials. Cf. Lk 16.19–31; 1 Enoch 103.5–8.

14.13 Tobias's responsibility as a son extends to the burial of his parents-in-law. **14.15** The destruction of Nineveh guarantees the fulfillment of the other predictions in Tobit's testament. Not surprisingly, the book ends with Tobias blessing the Lord.

JUDITH

WRITTEN IN GREEK and found only in the Septuagint, Judith is excluded from the Hebrew canon as an "outside book." Protestants regard Judith as part of the Apocrypha. Roman Catholic and Eastern Orthodox Christians designate Judith as one of the deuterocanonical books in the OT, listing it as one of the historical books.

The story is extant in four Greek recensions (Septuagint codices Vaticanus, Sinaiticus, Alexandrinus, and Basiliano-Vaticanus), four translations (Old Latin, Syriac, Sahidic, and Ethiopic), and other relatively late abridged and modified Hebrew versions. Despite Jerome's claim in the Vulgate to have translated an Aramaic text, no ancient Aramaic or Hebrew manuscripts have been found. The oldest extant text of Judith is likely a third-century CE potsherd on which Jdt 15.1–7 is preserved.

Setting and Date

JUDITH IS AN ANONYMOUS BOOK, likely written by a Palestinian Jew. Nothing is known about its author, except what can be surmised from the story itself, which is written in Greek that imitates Hebrew idiom and syntax. The story imaginatively intermingles references to well-known geographic sites with uncertain and even imaginary ones. Judith shows familiarity with Palestinian, Assyrian, Babylonian, Persian, and Greek history and geography, and most especially Jewish religious customs of the second and first centuries BCE.

Judith is replete with conflated details drawn from at least five centuries. There are historical references to Nineveh (1.1; 2.21), the Assyrian capital destroyed in the seventh century (612 BCE); Nebuchadnezzar (1.1), a sixth-century Babylonian ruler (605/4–562 BCE); the Second Temple (4.3), rebuilt by 515 BCE; two characters with Persian names, Holofernes and Bagoas (12.10–11), who appear together in the fourth century in the campaigns of Artaxerxes III Ochus (358–338 BCE); as well as references associated with the second century BCE when Antiochus IV Epiphanes required that the Jews forsake their God (cf. 3.8) and when the Jews were governed by a high priest (cf. 4.6) with military and religious responsibilities (cf. 1 Macc 14.41–49).

A reference to Judith in the *First Letter of Clement* of Rome in the first century CE makes it clear that the story was composed before this time. Most likely Judith was composed late in the second or early in the first century BCE, during the late Hasmonean period.

The story would fit well in the reign of John Hyrcanus (134–104 BCE), who served as both king and high priest of Jerusalem. Early in Hyrcanus's reign, after Jerusalem had been under siege for a year, he agreed to pay a heavy tribute to the Seleucid king Antiochus VII Sidetes. On the death of Antiochus in 129 BCE, Hyrcanus ceased paying the indemnity and expanded the borders of his territory. He forced the Idumeans (Edomites) to become Jews. Similar issues related to the fear of military domination and disputes over which god should be served figure in the story of Judith.

Narrative Character and Structure

THERE CAN BE NO DOUBT that Judith was composed as didactic fiction, not factual history. Not only are historical and geographical details of the story conflated, but its most important scene and star character are otherwise unknown. Most of the story takes place during two fateful months in 587 BCE in the little town Bethulia, described as strategically located to the north of Jerusalem in the region of Samaria, but otherwise unknown in Palestinian geography. For thirty-four days Bethulia is under attack (7.20); for four days Judith, the otherwise unknown courageous woman who delivers her people, is in the enemy camp (12.10); and for thirty days the Israelites go out from this town to plunder the Assyrians (15.11).

The sixteen chapters of Judith divide into two balanced and proportional parts. Each is structured internally by a threefold chiastic pattern that repeats certain narrative components in reverse order. Part 1 (1.1–7.32) narrates a military and religious struggle that begins in Persia and makes its way across the western nations to the little Israelite town of Bethulia. Nebuchadnezzar's political sovereignty over all the nations of the western world and God's divine sovereignty over Israel come into direct conflict. Judging themselves guilty of some sin (7.28), the besieged Bethulians lose faith and declare that God has abandoned them (7.25). Crisis makes apostasy and slavery look appealing, and they ask their leaders to surrender. Uzziah, a town official, suggests a compromise that gives God five days to deliver them. As Part 1 ends, the Bethulians, "in great misery" (7.32), have temporarily postponed what seems inevitable surrender, destruction of their sanctuary, and worship of Nebuchadnezzar.

Part 2 (8.1–16.25) tells how the God-fearing woman Judith destroys the enemies of Israel. This "beautiful" widow of Manasseh (8.7) lays aside the sackcloth of her widowhood in order to make herself "very beautiful, to entice the eyes of all the men who might see her" (10.4). The elders of Bethulia (10.7), the Assyrian patrol (10.14), the entire Assyrian camp (10.19), and, most important, Holofernes, the Assyrian general (10.23), marvel at her "beauty." Holofernes and his servants acclaim her as "beautiful" and "wise in speech" (11.21, 23). Holofernes is so aroused that he instructs his eunuch, Bagoas, to persuade her to eat and drink with them so that he might have an opportunity for sexual intercourse with her (12.13). Judith, who "fears God with great devotion" (8.8), takes advantage of his drunkenness to cut off his head. The Assyrian army flees in panic. The Israelites plunder the camp, and Judith is hailed as the "glory of Jerusalem" and the "great boast of Israel" (15.9).

Together the two parts convey a message similar to what we find in the book of Judges. God delivers his people when they cry to him and can bring low an arrogant king, even by the hand of a woman. [TONI CRAVEN, revised by JOHN J. COLLINS]

Arphaxad Fortifies Ecbatana

1 It was the twelfth year of the reign of Nebuchadnezzar, who ruled over the Assyrians in the great city of Nineveh. In those days Arphaxad ruled over the Medes in Ecbatana. [2]He built walls around Ecbatana with hewn stones three cubits thick and six cubits long; he made the walls seventy cubits high and fifty cubits wide. [3]At its gates he raised towers one hundred cubits high and sixty cubits wide at the foundations. [4]He made its gates seventy cubits high and forty cubits wide to allow his armies to march out in force and his infantry to form their ranks. [5]Then King Nebuchadnezzar made war against King Arphaxad in the great plain that is on the borders of Ragau. [6]There rallied to him all the people of the hill country and all those who lived along the Euphrates, the Tigris, and the Hydaspes, and, on the plain, Arioch, king of the Elymeans. Thus, many nations joined the forces of the Chaldeans. [a]

Nebuchadnezzar Issues Ultimatum

7 Then Nebuchadnezzar, king of the Assyrians, sent messengers to all who lived in Persia and to all who lived in the west, those who lived in Cilicia and Damascus, Lebanon and Antilebanon, and all who lived along the seacoast, [8]and those among the nations of Carmel and Gilead, and Upper Galilee and the great plain of Esdraelon, [9]and all who were in Samaria and its towns, and beyond the Jordan as far as Jerusalem and Bethany and Chelous and Kadesh and the river of Egypt, and Tahpanhes and Raamses and the whole land of Goshen, [10]even beyond Tanis and Memphis, and all who lived in Egypt as far as the borders of Ethiopia. [11]But all who lived in the whole region disregarded the summons of Nebuchadnezzar, king of the Assyrians, and refused to join him in the war; for they were not afraid of him, but regarded him as only one man. [b] So they sent back his messengers empty-handed and in disgrace.

12 Then Nebuchadnezzar became very angry with this whole region, and swore by his throne and kingdom that he would take revenge on the whole territory of Cilicia and Damascus and Syria, that he would kill with his sword also all the inhabitants of the land of Moab, and the people of Ammon, and all Judea, and every one in Egypt, as far as the coasts of the two seas.

Arphaxad Is Defeated

13 In the seventeenth year he led his forces against King Arphaxad and defeated him in battle, overthrowing the whole army of Arphaxad and all his cavalry and all his chariots. [14]Thus he took possession of his towns and came to Ecbatana, captured its towers, plundered its markets, and turned its glory into disgrace. [15]He captured Arphaxad in the mountains of Ragau and struck him down with his spears, thus destroying him once and for all. [16]Then he returned to Nineveh, he and all his combined forces, a vast body of troops; and there he and his forces rested and feasted for one hundred twenty days.

The Expedition against the West

2 In the eighteenth year, on the twenty-second day of the first month, there was talk in the palace of Nebuchadnezzar, king of the

_____
a Syr: Gk *Cheleoudites*   b Or *a man*

1.1–7.32 Part 1. 1.1–16 Introduction to Nebuchadnezzar and his campaign against Arphaxad. Arphaxad and his strongly fortified capital city, Ecbatana, are destroyed. Vassal nations who do and do not join Nebuchadnezzar are listed. 1.1 *Nebuchadnezzar* (605/4–562 BCE), the most famous Neo-Babylonian king, ruled from Babylon, not Nineveh, and destroyed Jerusalem in 586 BCE (2 Kings 24–25). His father, Nabopolassar, together with Cyaxares, the king of the Medes, destroyed the Assyrian capital Nineveh in 612. Nebuchadnezzar is described as a military aggressor against the invented character *Arphaxad* in his Median capital. *Ecbatana*, modern Hamadan, three hundred miles northeast of Babylon and three hundred and twenty-five southeast of Nineveh, a favorite summer palace of the Persian King Cyrus; the city figures in Tob 3.7 as the home of Sarah, the daughter of Edna and Raguel, and in Ezra 6.2 as the place where the edict permitting the Babylonian exiles to return home was preserved. 1.5 *Ragau*, two hundred miles northeast of Ecbatana, mentioned in v. 15 as the place where Arphaxad is slain. 1.6 *Chaldeans*, Neo-Babylonians. 1.11 *The whole region* of the west corresponds to Syria, Lebanon, Palestine, and Egypt; see note on 2.1. 1.12 *The two seas*, unclear, possibly the Mediterranean and the Red Sea. 1.13 In the *seventeenth year* (588 BCE), without the help of the nations of the west, Nebuchadnezzar defeats Arphaxad. 2.1–13 Nebuchadnezzar commissions Holofernes to take vengeance on the disobedient vassal nations. 2.1 Most of the story (2.1–16.20) is imagined as having occurred in the *eighteenth year*, the catastrophic year 587/6 BCE, when Jerusalem actually fell

Assyrians, about carrying out his revenge on the whole region, just as he had said. 2He summoned all his ministers and all his nobles and set before them his secret plan and recounted fully, with his own lips, all the wickedness of the region.[a] 3They decided that every one who had not obeyed his command should be destroyed.

4 When he had completed his plan, Nebuchadnezzar, king of the Assyrians, called Holofernes, the chief general of his army, second only to himself, and said to him, 5"Thus says the Great King, the lord of the whole earth: Leave my presence and take with you men confident in their strength, one hundred twenty thousand foot soldiers and twelve thousand cavalry. 6March out against all the land to the west, because they disobeyed my orders. 7Tell them to prepare earth and water, for I am coming against them in my anger, and will cover the whole face of the earth with the feet of my troops, to whom I will hand them over to be plundered. 8Their wounded shall fill their ravines and gullies, and the swelling river shall be filled with their dead. 9I will lead them away captive to the ends of the whole earth. 10You shall go and seize all their territory for me in advance. They must yield themselves to you, and you shall hold them for me until the day of their punishment. 11But to those who resist show no mercy, but hand them over to slaughter and plunder throughout your whole region. 12For as I live, and by the power of my kingdom, what I have spoken I will accomplish by my own hand. 13And you—take care not to transgress any of your lord's commands, but carry them out exactly as I have ordered you; do it without delay."

Campaign of Holofernes

14 So Holofernes left the presence of his lord, and summoned all the commanders, generals, and officers of the Assyrian army. 15He mustered the picked troops by divisions as his lord had ordered him to do, one hundred twenty thousand of them, together with twelve thousand archers on horseback, 16and he organized them as a great army is marshaled for a campaign. 17He took along a vast number of camels and donkeys and mules for transport, and innumerable sheep and oxen and goats for food; 18also ample rations for everyone, and a huge amount of gold and silver from the royal palace.

19 Then he set out with his whole army, to go ahead of King Nebuchadnezzar and to cover the whole face of the earth to the west with their chariots and cavalry and picked foot soldiers. 20Along with them went a mixed crowd like a swarm of locusts, like the dust[b] of the earth—a multitude that could not be counted.

21 They marched for three days from Nineveh to the plain of Bectileth, and camped opposite Bectileth near the mountain that is to the north of Upper Cilicia. 22From there Holofernes[c] took his whole army, the infantry, cavalry, and chariots, and went up into the hill country. 23He ravaged Put and Lud, and plun-

---

a Meaning of Gk uncertain *b* Gk *sand* *c* Gk *he*

---

to the historical Nebuchadnezzar. Revenge is planned against the *whole region*, meaning all the nations west of Persia as far as Egypt. These nations are mentioned nine times in chs. 1–2: 1.7–10 specifies the nations; *the whole region* (or *the region*) appears again in 1.11; 1.12; 2.1; 2.2; 2.11; *all the land to the west* in 2.6; *the whole face of the earth to the west* in 2.19; and 2.23–28 details the ravaging of specific western nations. **2.2** Ironically Nebuchadnezzar fully recounts *his secret plan . . . with his own lips,* but in 8.34 Judith keeps her plan secret. **2.5–13** Calling himself *the Great King, the lord of the whole earth,* Nebuchadnezzar, in his only speech, declares that all the rebel lands must surrender. **2.10–13** Nebuchadnezzar specifically instructs Holofernes to seize the disobedient territory and hold it, killing with *no mercy* (v. 11) only those who refuse to surrender.
    2.14–7.32 Holofernes attacks the western nations. The confrontation between the various nations who refused to aid Nebuchadnezzar is told in a threefold

chiastic structure—similar episodes are repeated in reverse order. Each unit is defined by a major shift of scene, alternation between the nations of Assyria and Israel, and a temporal clause. In the following notes, the scenes are labeled A, B, C, and their counterparts, C′, B′, A′. In domino-like fashion, the nations fall to Assyria as "terror" sweeps across the empire at large (2.28), then Judea (4.1), and finally Bethulia (7.4). **2.14–3.10** In Section A of the first chiastic unit (see note on 2.14–7.32), Holofernes leads the campaign against the disobedient nations; the vassals surrender. The line of advance is from Nineveh to Damascus; all the vassals are ravaged, plundered, burned, and destroyed. **2.21** *The plain of Bectileth,* an unidentified plain opposite Upper Cilicia, a distance of three hundred miles from Nineveh, which would be impossible to cover in three days. **2.23** *Put and Lud, Rassisites, Chelleans,* unknown locations and peoples here in proximity to Cilicia (a large and important area in the southeastern coastal zone of Asia Minor, divided into

dered all the Rassisites and the Ishmaelites on the border of the desert, south of the country of the Chelleans. [24]Then he followed[a] the Euphrates and passed through Mesopotamia and destroyed all the fortified towns along the brook Abron, as far as the sea. [25]He also seized the territory of Cilicia, and killed everyone who resisted him. Then he came to the southern borders of Japheth, facing Arabia. [26]He surrounded all the Midianites, and burned their tents and plundered their sheepfolds. [27]Then he went down into the plain of Damascus during the wheat harvest, and burned all their fields and destroyed their flocks and herds and sacked their towns and ravaged their lands and put all their young men to the sword.

[28] So fear and dread of him fell upon all the people who lived along the seacoast, at Sidon and Tyre, and those who lived in Sur and Ocina and all who lived in Jamnia. Those who lived in Azotus and Ascalon feared him greatly.

Entreaties for Peace

3 They therefore sent messengers to him to sue for peace in these words: [2]"We, the servants of Nebuchadnezzar, the Great King, lie prostrate before you. Do with us whatever you will. [3]See, our buildings and all our land and all our wheat fields and our flocks and herds and all our encampments[b] lie before you; do with them as you please. [4]Our towns and their inhabitants are also your slaves; come and deal with them as you see fit."

[5] The men came to Holofernes and told him all this. [6]Then he went down to the seacoast with his army and stationed garrisons in the fortified towns and took picked men from them as auxiliaries. [7]These people and all in the countryside welcomed him with garlands and dances and tambourines. [8]Yet he demolished all their shrines[c] and cut down their sacred groves; for he had been commissioned to destroy all the gods of the land, so that all nations should worship Nebuchadnezzar alone, and that all their dialects and tribes should call upon him as a god.

[9] Then he came toward Esdraelon, near Dothan, facing the great ridge of Judea; [10]he camped between Geba and Scythopolis, and remained for a whole month in order to collect all the supplies for his army.

Judea on the Alert

4 When the Israelites living in Judea heard of everything that Holofernes, the general of Nebuchadnezzar, the king of the Assyrians, had done to the nations, and how he had plundered and destroyed all their temples, [2]they were therefore greatly terrified at his approach; they were alarmed both for Jerusalem and for the temple of the Lord their God. [3]For they had only recently returned from exile, and all the people of Judea had just now gath-

---

a Or crossed *b* Gk all the sheepfolds of our tents *c* Syr: Gk borders

---

western and eastern parts by the Lamus River). *Ishmaelites,* Arabs. **2.24** *Then he followed the Euphrates,* geographically impossible without backtracking. *Abron,* unknown. **2.25** *Seized . . . Cilicia* seems better after v. 21. *Japheth,* the youngest of Noah's three sons, ancestor of the Indo-European family of nations whose area stretched from the south coast of Europe to Persia (Gen 5.32; 10.2–5). *Facing Arabia,* facing the Syrian desert (1 Macc 11.16). **2.26** *Midianites,* nomads identified in the annals of Tiglath-pileser III (ca. 732 BCE) as Haiappu, perhaps located in northwest Arabia. **2.27** *Damascus,* capital of Syria. **2.28** *People who lived along the seacoast.* Seven peoples are listed in the Phoenician maritime and commercial centers. *Sidon,* a city on the Mediterranean coast. *Tyre,* originally an island twenty-five miles south of Sidon, difficult to subdue because of its protected location. Nebuchadnezzar besieged Tyre for thirteen years; Alexander attacked it by building a mole half a mile long and 200 feet wide from the mainland. *Sur, Ocina,* both unknown. *Jamnia,* nine miles north of Azotus, about four miles inland. *Azotus,* formerly Ashdod, one of the five principal cities of the Philistines. *Ascalon,* also one of the five

Philistine cities, destroyed by Nebuchadnezzar in 609 BCE. **3.1–4** The seven cities in 2.28 surrender. **3.8** Violating the instruction of 2.10–13, Holofernes *demolishes all their shrines,* claiming that Nebuchadnezzar is the sovereign god (6.2) whom all must worship. Ptolemy V of Egypt (203–181 BCE) was the first king to present himself as "God Manifest." No Assyrian, Babylonian, or Persian king is known to have claimed divinity. **3.9** *Esdraelon,* the western portion of the Valley of Jezreel. *Dothan,* fifteen miles southeast of Scythopolis, is mentioned also in 4.6; 7.3, 18; 8.3, leading some to suggest that this was the author's home. **3.10** *Geba,* uncertain. *Scythopolis,* the only city in Judith given its Greek name, strategically guarded the eastern end of the Valley of Jezreel and was the chief city of the Decapolis; in Hebrew, Beth-Shan. Cf. 1 Sam 31.10–12; 1 Kings 4.12.

4.1–15 In Section B (see note on 2.14–7.32) the scene shifts to Judea and what is happening there. Israel hears and is greatly terrified; Joakim orders preparations for war. **4.3** *Recently returned from exile,* a reference to 539 BCE, inconsistent with 2.1. The issue is further complicated by the phrase *consecrated after*

ered together, and the sacred vessels and the altar and the temple had been consecrated after their profanation. 4So they sent word to every district of Samaria, and to Kona, Beth-horon, Belmain, and Jericho, and to Choba and Aesora, and the valley of Salem. 5They immediately seized all the high hilltops and fortified the villages on them and stored up food in preparation for war—since their fields had recently been harvested.

6 The high priest, Joakim, who was in Jerusalem at the time, wrote to the people of Bethulia and Betomesthaim, which faces Esdraelon opposite the plain near Dothan, 7ordering them to seize the mountain passes, since by them Judea could be invaded; and it would be easy to stop any who tried to enter, for the approach was narrow, wide enough for only two at a time to pass.

Prayer and Penance

8 So the Israelites did as they had been ordered by the high priest Joakim and the senate of the whole people of Israel, in session at Jerusalem. 9And every man of Israel cried out to God with great fervor, and they humbled themselves with much fasting. 10They and their wives and their children and their cattle and every resident alien and hired laborer and purchased slave—they all put sackcloth around their waists. 11And all the Israelite men, women, and children living at Jerusalem prostrated themselves before the temple and put ashes on their heads and spread out their sackcloth before the Lord. 12They even draped the altar with sackcloth and cried out in unison, praying fervently to the God of Israel not to allow their infants to be carried off and

their wives to be taken as booty, and the towns they had inherited to be destroyed, and the sanctuary to be profaned and desecrated to the malicious joy of the Gentiles.

13 The Lord heard their prayers and had regard for their distress; for the people fasted many days throughout Judea and in Jerusalem before the sanctuary of the Lord Almighty. 14The high priest Joakim and all the priests who stood before the Lord and ministered to the Lord, with sackcloth around their loins, offered the daily burnt offerings, the votive offerings, and freewill offerings of the people. 15With ashes on their turbans, they cried out to the Lord with all their might to look with favor on the whole house of Israel.

Council against the Israelites

5 It was reported to Holofernes, the general of the Assyrian army, that the people of Israel had prepared for war and had closed the mountain passes and fortified all the high hilltops and set up barricades in the plains. 2In great anger he called together all the princes of Moab and the commanders of Ammon and all the governors of the coastland, 3and said to them, "Tell me, you Canaanites, what people is this that lives in the hill country? What towns do they inhabit? How large is their army, and in what does their power and strength consist? Who rules over them as king and leads their army? 4And why have they alone, of all who live in the west, refused to come out and meet me?"

Achior's Report

5 Then Achior, the leader of all the Ammonites, said to him, "May my lord please lis-

---

their profanation, referring to the rededication of the temple. The event envisioned in the narrative would have occurred sometime after 515 BCE in the rebuilt temple, but the description is more appropriate for the rededication of the temple that took place in 164 BCE after its profanation by Antiochus Epiphanes. 4.4 Of the eight cities listed, only Samaria, Beth-horon, and Jericho can be located. 4.6 The high priest Joakim (see also 4.8, 14; 15.8) exercises both military and religious authority (on this role of the high priest, see Jonathan in 1 Macc 10.18–21; on the name, see Neh 12.26). Bethulia. The site is perhaps to be identified with Bethel or Shechem. Betomesthaim, unknown. 4.7 Wide enough . . . pass, dramatic exaggeration. 4.8 Senate. A supreme Jewish council was not known until the Maccabean period (see 2 Macc 11.27). The Greek term used here, gerousia, "council of elders," is also used in

11.14; 15.8. 4.10 Wearing sackcloth was a traditional act of mourning, penitence, and supplication. 4.13 The Lord heard their prayers, an important detail in the later development of the story when the people believe God has abandoned them (7.25).

5.1–6.13 In Section C (see note on 2.14–7.32) the scene shifts to the Assyrian camp outside Bethulia. Holofernes talks with Achior; Achior is expelled from the camp for suggesting that the Assyrians may fail to capture Bethulia because of the power of its God. 5.2 Moab, Ammon. The Moabites, east of the Dead Sea, and the Ammonites, in Transjordan north of Moab, were Semitic peoples who were traditional enemies of Israel (see 2 Kings 24.2). 5.5 Achior, a righteous Gentile. His name may mean in Hebrew "brother of light" or may be derived from Ahihud, meaning "brother of Judah." 5.5–21 Achior recites Israel's history from

ten to a report from the mouth of your servant, and I will tell you the truth about this people that lives in the mountain district near you. No falsehood shall come from your servant's mouth. 6 These people are descended from the Chaldeans. 7 At one time they lived in Mesopotamia, because they did not wish to follow the gods of their ancestors who were in Chaldea. 8 Since they had abandoned the ways of their ancestors, and worshiped the God of heaven, the God they had come to know, their ancestors[a] drove them out from the presence of their gods. So they fled to Mesopotamia, and lived there for a long time. 9 Then their God commanded them to leave the place where they were living and go to the land of Canaan. There they settled, and grew very prosperous in gold and silver and very much livestock. 10 When a famine spread over the land of Canaan they went down to Egypt and lived there as long as they had food. There they became so great a multitude that their race could not be counted. 11 So the king of Egypt became hostile to them; he exploited them and forced them to make bricks. 12 They cried out to their God, and he afflicted the whole land of Egypt with incurable plagues. So the Egyptians drove them out of their sight. 13 Then God dried up the Red Sea before them, 14 and he led them by the way of Sinai and Kadesh-barnea. They drove out all the people of the desert, 15 and took up residence in the land of the Amorites, and by their might destroyed all the inhabitants of Heshbon; and crossing over the Jordan they took possession of all the hill country. 16 They drove out before them the Canaanites, the Perizzites, the Jebusites, the Shechemites, and all the Gergesites, and lived there a long time.

17 "As long as they did not sin against their God they prospered, for the God who hates iniquity is with them. 18 But when they departed from the way he had prescribed for them, they were utterly defeated in many battles and were led away captive to a foreign land. The temple of their God was razed to the ground, and their towns were occupied by their enemies.

19 But now they have returned to their God, and have come back from the places where they were scattered, and have occupied Jerusalem, where their sanctuary is, and have settled in the hill country, because it was uninhabited.

20 "So now, my master and lord, if there is any oversight in this people and they sin against their God and we find out their offense, then we can go up and defeat them. 21 But if they are not a guilty nation, then let my lord pass them by; for their Lord and God will defend them, and we shall become the laughingstock of the whole world."

22 When Achior had finished saying these things, all the people standing around the tent began to complain; Holofernes' officers and all the inhabitants of the seacoast and Moab insisted that he should be cut to pieces. 23 They said, "We are not afraid of the Israelites; they are a people with no strength or power for making war. 24 Therefore let us go ahead, Lord Holofernes, and your vast army will swallow them up."

Achior Handed over to the Israelites

6 When the disturbance made by the people outside the council had died down, Holofernes, the commander of the Assyrian army, said to Achior[b] in the presence of all the foreign contingents:
2 "Who are you, Achior and you mercenaries of Ephraim, to prophesy among us as you have done today and tell us not to make war against the people of Israel because their God will defend them? What god is there except Nebuchadnezzar? He will send his forces and destroy them from the face of the earth. Their God will not save them; 3 we the king's[c] servants will destroy them as one man. They cannot resist the might of our cavalry. 4 We will overwhelm them;[d] their mountains will be drunk with their blood, and their fields will be full of their dead. Not even their footprints will survive our attack; they will utterly perish.

---

a Gk they b Other ancient authorities add and to all the Moabites c Gk his d Other ancient authorities add with it

---

Abraham to the exile and affirms God's special protection of the covenant people if they do not sin. **5.8** *God of heaven,* also in 6.19; 11.17 (cf. 7.28; 9.12; 13.18); the title is more common in Persian times (see Gen 24.3, 7; 2 Chr 36.23; Ezra 1.2; 5.11, 12; 6.9, 10; 7.12, 21; Dan 2.37; Jon 1.9; Tob 10.11–12). **5.16** Cf. other lists of dispossessed peoples in Gen 15.19–21, Ex 3.8, 17; Deut 7.1; Josh 11.3. The inclusion of the *Shechemites* is unusual and perhaps anticipates the allusion to revenge on the Shechemites by Simeon (Gen 34) in Judith's prayer (9.2). **6.2** *Who are you? What god is there except Nebuchadnezzar?* Holofernes asks important identity questions that constitute one of the corresponding symmetries in the two halves of the book. In 8.12, Ju-

So says King Nebuchadnezzar, lord of the whole earth. For he has spoken; none of his words shall be in vain.

5 "As for you, Achior, you Ammonite mercenary, you have said these words in a moment of perversity; you shall not see my face again from this day until I take revenge on this race that came out of Egypt. 6Then at my return the sword of my army and the spear[a] of my servants shall pierce your sides, and you shall fall among their wounded. 7Now my slaves are going to take you back into the hill country and put you in one of the towns beside the passes. 8You will not die until you perish along with them. 9If you really hope in your heart that they will not be taken, then do not look downcast! I have spoken, and none of my words shall fail to come true."

10 Then Holofernes ordered his slaves, who waited on him in his tent, to seize Achior and take him away to Bethulia and hand him over to the Israelites. 11So the slaves took him and led him out of the camp into the plain, and from the plain they went up into the hill country and came to the springs below Bethulia. 12When the men of the town saw them,[b] they seized their weapons and ran out of the town to the top of the hill, and all the slingers kept them from coming up by throwing stones at them. 13So having taken shelter below the hill, they bound Achior and left him lying at the foot of the hill, and returned to their master.

14 Then the Israelites came down from their town and found him; they untied him and brought him into Bethulia and placed him before the magistrates of their town, 15who in those days were Uzziah son of Micah, of the tribe of Simeon, and Chabris son of Gothoniel,

and Charmis son of Melchiel. 16They called together all the elders of the town, and all their young men and women ran to the assembly. They set Achior in the midst of all their people, and Uzziah questioned him about what had happened. 17He answered and told them what had taken place at the council of Holofernes, and all that he had said in the presence of the Assyrian leaders, and all that Holofernes had boasted he would do against the house of Israel. 18Then the people fell down and worshiped God, and cried out:

19 "O Lord God of heaven, see their arrogance, and have pity on our people in their humiliation, and look kindly today on the faces of those who are consecrated to you."

20 Then they reassured Achior, and praised him highly. 21Uzziah took him from the assembly to his own house and gave a banquet for the elders; and all that night they called on the God of Israel for help.

The Campaign against Bethulia

7 The next day Holofernes ordered his whole army, and all the allies who had joined him, to break camp and move against Bethulia, and to seize the passes up into the hill country and make war on the Israelites. 2So all their warriors marched off that day; their fighting forces numbered one hundred seventy thousand infantry and twelve thousand cavalry, not counting the baggage and the foot soldiers handling it, a very great multitude. 3They encamped in the valley near Bethulia, beside the spring, and they spread

a Lat Syr: Gk *people*   b Other ancient authorities add *on the top of the hill*

dith asks the magistrates of Bethulia, *Who are you to put God to the test today?* **6.5–9** Holofernes declares that Achior will *not see* his *face again* until revenge is taken against the Israelites; this verse anticipates the reversal of 14.6.

6.14–21 In Section C′, which begins the second half of the chiastic structure for Part 1 of the book (see note on 2.14–7.32), the scene shifts back to Israel. From this point on the narrative in Part 1 inverts its scenes and actions. Achior who was expelled from the Assyrian camp is now brought into Bethulia; conversation with the Assyrian Holofernes corresponds to conversation with the Israelite magistrates of Bethulia. **6.15** *Uzziah . . . of the tribe of Simeon.* The tribe of Simeon first settled in the general vicinity of Shechem (Gen 34; Deut 27.12) but later moved to the most southerly border of the cultivated land in the vicinity of Beer-sheba with

the capture the town Zephath/Hormah (Judg 1.17); it is not mentioned in the Song of Deborah (Judg 5) or the blessing of Moses (Deut 33). Judith is also from the tribe of Simeon (9.2). *Chabris, Charmis,* invented characters. **6.18** *Then the people . . . worshiped God.* As in 4.12, the people turn to God in their distress. **6.19** *God of heaven.* See note on 5.8.

7.1–5 In Section B′ (see note on 2.14–7.32) the scene shifts to the Assyrian camp (vv. 1–3) and then back to the Bethulia (vv. 4–5). Holofernes orders war preparations; Israel sees this and is greatly terrified. **7.2** The forces of Holofernes have grown from one hundred twenty thousand (2.5, 15) to *one hundred seventy thousand* infantry. **7.3** As in 6.11 *Bethulia* is described as atop a hill with its water supply below it. If the writer had Shechem in mind as a model for Bethulia, then perhaps the spring is the so-called Well of

out in breadth over Dothan as far as Balbaim and in length from Bethulia to Cyamon, which faces Esdraelon.

4 When the Israelites saw their vast numbers, they were greatly terrified and said to one another, "They will now strip clean the whole land; neither the high mountains nor the valleys nor the hills will bear their weight." 5Yet they all seized their weapons, and when they had kindled fires on their towers, they remained on guard all that night.

6 On the second day Holofernes led out all his cavalry in full view of the Israelites in Bethulia. 7He reconnoitered the approaches to their town, and visited the springs that supplied their water; he seized them and set guards of soldiers over them, and then returned to his army.

8 Then all the chieftains of the Edomites and all the leaders of the Moabites and the commanders of the coastland came to him and said, 9"Listen to what we have to say, my lord, and your army will suffer no losses. 10This people, the Israelites, do not rely on their spears but on the height of the mountains where they live, for it is not easy to reach the tops of their mountains. 11Therefore, my lord, do not fight against them in regular formation, and not a man of your army will fall. 12Remain in your camp, and keep all the men in your forces with you; let your servants take possession of the spring of water that flows from the foot of the mountain, 13for this is where all the people of Bethulia get their water. So thirst will destroy them, and they will surrender their town. Meanwhile, we and our people will go up to the tops of the nearby mountains and camp there to keep watch to see that no one gets out of the town. 14They and their wives and children will waste away with famine, and before the sword reaches them they will be strewn about in the streets where they live. 15Thus you will pay them back with evil, because they rebelled and did not receive you peaceably."

16 These words pleased Holofernes and all his attendants, and he gave orders to do as they had said. 17So the army of the Ammonites moved forward, together with five thousand Assyrians, and they encamped in the valley and seized the water supply and the springs of the Israelites. 18And the Edomites and Ammonites went up and encamped in the hill country opposite Dothan; and they sent some of their men toward the south and the east, toward Egrebeh, which is near Chusi beside the Wadi Mochmur. The rest of the Assyrian army encamped in the plain, and covered the whole face of the land. Their tents and supply trains spread out in great number, and they formed a vast multitude.

The Distress of the Israelites

19 The Israelites then cried out to the Lord their God, for their courage failed, because all their enemies had surrounded them, and there was no way of escape from them. 20The whole Assyrian army, their infantry, chariots, and cavalry, surrounded them for thirty-four days, until all the water containers of every inhabitant of Bethulia were empty; 21their cisterns were going dry, and on no day did they have enough water to drink, for their drinking water was rationed. 22Their children were listless, and the women

---

Jacob, first mentioned in the story of the Samaritan woman (Jn 4.6). Tradition supports identification of this ancient site with a deep cistern or spring located at Shechem, near the foot of Mount Gerizim, where roads from Jerusalem and the Jordan Valley join. *Dothan.* See note on 3.9. *Balbaim, Cyamon,* unknown. **7.4–5** Despair overcomes the Bethulians when they see the enormous size of the enemy. Nonetheless, they seize their weapons and prepare to defend their town.

7.6–32 In Section A´, which completes the first chiasm (see note on 2.14–7.32), the scene shifts between the Assyrian camp (vv. 6–18) and Bethulia (vv. 19–32). Holofernes leads the campaign against Bethulia; the Bethulians want to surrender. **7.7** Holofernes seizes the *springs* (v. 3) that supplied Bethulia's water. **7.8** *Edomites* (mentioned here for first time) and *Moabites* propose a scheme to cut off the water supply so that thirst and famine will destroy the Bethulians. **7.10** The leaders point out that the Israelites depend *on the height of the mountains where they live* for protection. **7.12** *Take possession of the spring* is redundant, given that the springs were taken and put under guard in v. 7. **7.13** Thirst will devastate the Bethulians, but the plan to surround the town in order *to see that no one gets out of the town* ultimately fails because it is not enforced to stop the two women—Judith and her female servant—from leaving the city (10.9b–10) and saving it. **7.16** Holofernes orders the town surrounded, but either his order is ignored or understood to refer to men only. **7.18** *Egrebeh . . . Mochmur,* likely Acraba, near Sychar's well, twenty-five miles north of Jerusalem. **7.19–32** The final scene in Part 1 takes the people of Bethulia to the threshold of surrender. **7.20** After being surrounded for *thirty-four days,* the Bethulians lose heart. In Part 2, Judith spends four days in the Assyrian camp (12.10) and the Israelites plunder the enemy

and young men fainted from thirst and were collapsing in the streets of the town and in the gateways; they no longer had any strength.

23 Then all the people, the young men, the women, and the children, gathered around Uzziah and the rulers of the town and cried out with a loud voice, and said before all the elders, 24"Let God judge between you and us! You have done us a great injury in not making peace with the Assyrians. 25For now we have no one to help us; God has sold us into their hands, to be strewn before them in thirst and exhaustion. 26Now summon them and surrender the whole town as booty to the army of Holofernes and to all his forces. 27For it would be better for us to be captured by them.*a* We shall indeed become slaves, but our lives will be spared, and we shall not witness our little ones dying before our eyes, and our wives and children drawing their last breath. 28We call to witness against you heaven and earth and our God, the Lord of our ancestors, who punishes us for our sins and the sins of our ancestors; do today the things that we have described!"

29 Then great and general lamentation arose throughout the assembly, and they cried out to the Lord God with a loud voice. 30But Uzziah said to them, "Courage, my brothers and sisters!*b* Let us hold out for five days more; by that time the Lord our God will turn his mercy to us again, for he will not forsake us utterly. 31But if these days pass by, and no help comes for us, I will do as you say."

32 Then he dismissed the people to their various posts, and they went up on the walls and towers of their town. The women and children he sent home. In the town they were in great misery.

The Character of Judith

8 Now in those days Judith heard about these things: she was the daughter of Merari son of Ox son of Joseph son of Oziel son of Elkiah son of Ananias son of Gideon son of Raphain son of Ahitub son of Elijah son of Hilkiah son of Eliab son of Nathanael son of Salamiel son of Sarasadai son of Israel. 2Her husband Manasseh, who belonged to her tribe and family, had died during the barley harvest. 3For as he stood overseeing those who were binding sheaves in the field, he was overcome by the burning heat, and took to his bed and died in his town Bethulia. So they buried him with his ancestors in the field between Dothan and Balamon. 4Judith remained as a widow for three years and four months 5at home where she set up a tent for herself on the roof of her house. She put sackcloth around her waist and dressed in widow's clothing. 6She fasted all the days of her widowhood, except the day before the sabbath and the sabbath itself, the day before the new moon and the day of the new moon, and the festivals and days of rejoicing of the house of Israel. 7She was beautiful in appearance, and was very lovely to behold. Her husband Manasseh had left her gold and silver, men and women slaves, livestock, and fields; and she maintained this estate. 8No one spoke ill of her, for she feared God with great devotion.

a Other ancient authorities add *than to die of thirst*
b Gk *Courage, brothers*

camp for thirty days (15.11). **7.25** In despair, the people claim they have *no one to help* them, that *God has sold* them into the Assyrians' *hands;* cf. Esth 7.4. According to 4.13, God *heard their prayers and had regard for their distress,* but the people are not convinced. **7.27** Crisis and confusion make slavery to Assyria look appealing. **7.28** The people judge themselves guilty, for God *punishes* them for their *sins* and the *sins* of their *ancestors.* In 8.18–27 Judith will deny that their suffering is the result of sinfulness. **7.30–31** Uzziah urges courage, but does not address the theological confusion that has made the people believe their suffering results from sin. He asks for a compromise to give God *five days more* before surrender. **7.32** Part 1 ends on the bleak note that the people return to their various posts and homes in *great misery.* Surrender, destruction of the sanctuary, and worship of Nebuchadnezzar seem inevitable, granted the five-day wait.

8.1–16.25 Part 2. These chapters are organized ac- cording to a threefold chiastic pattern, in which narrative elements are repeated in reverse order (A, B, C, C′, B′, A′), with the climactic scene of the beheading of Holofernes at its center (D). **8.1–8** Section A of Part 2 (see note on 8.1–16.25) introduces Judith. **8.1** *Judith* is named for the first time in the story; according to her genealogy her father, Merari, was a descendant of Israel/Jacob of the fourteenth generation. The Greek name *Judith* (Hebrew *yehudit*) is the feminine of "Jew" or "Judean." *Now in those days Judith heard* links Part 2 to all that has gone before. **8.2–3** *Manasseh,* Judith's husband, is dead as the result of sunstroke (cf. 2 Kings 4.19). The last reference to *Dothan.* See note on 3.9. **8.4–8** No longer a wife, apparently never a mother, Judith is pious, beautiful, wealthy, and lives alone on her estate (cf. 16.21). **8.6** *New moon.* Cf. Num 28.11–15. **8.8** *No one spoke ill of her, for she feared God.* Notice about her effect on the people is repeated in the story's conclusion (16.25). Judith fears no one in the story save God.

Judith and the Elders

9 When Judith heard the harsh words spoken by the people against the ruler, because they were faint for lack of water, and when she heard all that Uzziah said to them, and how he promised them under oath to surrender the town to the Assyrians after five days, 10 she sent her maid, who was in charge of all she possessed, to summon Uzziah and[a] Chabris and Charmis, the elders of her town. 11 They came to her, and she said to them:

"Listen to me, rulers of the people of Bethulia! What you have said to the people today is not right; you have even sworn and pronounced this oath between God and you, promising to surrender the town to our enemies unless the Lord turns and helps us within so many days. 12 Who are you to put God to the test today, and to set yourselves up in the place of[b] God in human affairs? 13 You are putting the Lord Almighty to the test, but you will never learn anything! 14 You cannot plumb the depths of the human heart or understand the workings of the human mind; how do you expect to search out God, who made all these things, and find out his mind or comprehend his thought? No, my brothers, do not anger the Lord our God. 15 For if he does not choose to help us within these five days, he has power to protect us within any time he pleases, or even to destroy us in the presence of our enemies. 16 Do not try to bind the purposes of the Lord our God; for God is not like a human being, to be threatened, or like a mere mortal, to be won over by pleading. 17 Therefore, while we wait for his deliverance, let us call upon him to help us, and he will hear our voice, if it pleases him.

18 "For never in our generation, nor in these present days, has there been any tribe or family or people or town of ours that worships gods made with hands, as was done in days gone by. 19 That was why our ancestors were handed over to the sword and to pillage, and so they suffered a great catastrophe before our enemies. 20 But we know no other god but him, and so we hope that he will not disdain us or any of our nation. 21 For if we are captured, all Judea will be captured and our sanctuary will be plundered; and he will make us pay for its desecration with our blood. 22 The slaughter of our kindred and the captivity of the land and the desolation of our inheritance—all this he will bring on our heads among the Gentiles, wherever we serve as slaves; and we shall be an offense and a disgrace in the eyes of those who acquire us. 23 For our slavery will not bring us into favor, but the Lord our God will turn it to dishonor.

24 "Therefore, my brothers, let us set an example for our kindred, for their lives depend upon us, and the sanctuary—both the temple and the altar—rests upon us. 25 In spite of everything let us give thanks to the Lord our God, who is putting us to the test as he did our ancestors. 26 Remember what he did with Abraham, and how he tested Isaac, and what happened to Jacob in Syrian Mesopotamia, while he was tending the sheep of Laban, his mother's brother. 27 For he has not tried us with fire, as he did them, to search their hearts, nor has he taken vengeance on us; but the Lord scourges those who are close to him in order to admonish them."

28 Then Uzziah said to her, "All that you have said was spoken out of a true heart, and

---

a Other ancient authorities lack Uzziah and (see verses 28 and 35)   b Or above

---

8.9–10.8 Section B (see note on 8.1–16.25) tells how Judith plans to save Israel. 8.9–36 Judith and the elders. 8.9 When Judith heard. The narrative resumes with repetition of the opening words of Part 2 (v. 1). 8.10 Judith's first act in the story is to send the unnamed woman (maid, lit. "graceful one"; see also 8.33; 10.2, 5, 17; 13.9; 16.23) who was in charge of all she possessed (cf. Gen 15.2; 24.2; 39.4) to summon the town officials, Uzziah and Chabris and Charmis (see 6.15). 8.12 Judith reprimands the leaders for putting God to the test (cf. Deut 6.16); in vv. 25–27 Judith will argue that to God alone belongs the right to test. 8.15 Judith defends God's freedom to deliver or destroy (cf. Job 1.21; 2.10). 8.16 God is not like a human being and cannot be won over by threat (cf. the actions of the Assyrians, 2.1–13) or pleading (cf. the actions of Israel, 7.23–29). 8.17 Faith is waiting for deliverance, calling upon God for help, and being heard if it pleases God. Judith defends the innocence of her people (vv. 18–23). 8.24 Let us set an example. Judith includes herself in the solution she proposes. 8.26 Abraham, Isaac, Jacob. See Gen 13–31. 8.27 Tried us with fire may allude especially to the Aqedah, or binding of Isaac, in Gen 22. Together the patriarchs will model belief that God scourges those who are close to him (wisdom reminiscent of Ps 94.10, 12; Prov 3.12). 8.28 Uzziah responds and acknowledges her true heart (because of this verse, Judith has been the queen of hearts in French playing

there is no one who can deny your words. [29]Today is not the first time your wisdom has been shown, but from the beginning of your life all the people have recognized your understanding, for your heart's disposition is right. [30]But the people were so thirsty that they compelled us to do for them what we have promised, and made us take an oath that we cannot break. [31]Now since you are a God-fearing woman, pray for us, so that the Lord may send us rain to fill our cisterns. Then we will no longer feel faint from thirst."

32 Then Judith said to them, "Listen to me. I am about to do something that will go down through all generations of our descendants. [33]Stand at the town gate tonight so that I may go out with my maid; and within the days after which you have promised to surrender the town to our enemies, the Lord will deliver Israel by my hand. [34]Only, do not try to find out what I am doing; for I will not tell you until I have finished what I am about to do."

35 Uzziah and the rulers said to her, "Go in peace, and may the Lord God go before you, to take vengeance on our enemies." [36]So they returned from the tent and went to their posts.

The Prayer of Judith

9 Then Judith prostrated herself, put ashes on her head, and uncovered the sackcloth she was wearing. At the very time when the evening incense was being offered in the house of God in Jerusalem, Judith cried out to the Lord with a loud voice, and said,

2 "O Lord God of my ancestor Simeon, to whom you gave a sword to take revenge on those strangers who had torn off a virgin's clothing[a] to defile her, and exposed her thighs to put her to shame, and polluted her womb to

disgrace her; for you said, 'It shall not be done'—yet they did it; [3]so you gave up their rulers to be killed, and their bed, which was ashamed of the deceit they had practiced, was stained with blood, and you struck down slaves along with princes, and princes on their thrones. [4]You gave up their wives for booty and their daughters to captivity, and all their booty to be divided among your beloved children who burned with zeal for you and abhorred the pollution of their blood and called on you for help. O God, my God, hear me also, a widow.

5 "For you have done these things and those that went before and those that followed. You have designed the things that are now, and those that are to come. What you had in mind has happened; [6]the things you decided on presented themselves and said, 'Here we are!' For all your ways are prepared in advance, and your judgment is with foreknowledge.

7 "Here now are the Assyrians, a greatly increased force, priding themselves in their horses and riders, boasting in the strength of their foot soldiers, and trusting in shield and spear, in bow and sling. They do not know that you are the Lord who crushes wars; the Lord is your name. [8]Break their strength by your might, and bring down their power in your anger; for they intend to defile your sanctuary, and to pollute the tabernacle where your glorious name resides, and to break off the horns[b] of your altar with the sword. [9]Look at their pride, and send your wrath upon their heads. Give to me, a widow, the strong hand to do what I plan. [10]By the deceit of my lips strike down the slave with the prince and the prince with his servant; crush their arrogance by the hand of a woman.

a Cn: Gk *loosed her womb*   b Syr: Gk *horn*

cards since the fourteenth century). **8.29** Uzziah claims that Judith is recognized for her *understanding* and that her *heart's disposition is right*, although he did not think earlier to seek her counsel. **8.30** Uzziah argues that he was forced to take an *oath* that he *cannot break* (on other foolish vows, see Judg 11.30–31, 35; on the blaming of others, see Gen 3.12–13; Ex 32.22–24). **8.31** *Pray for us . . . rain*. Uzziah wants a face-saving miracle. **8.32–34** Judith protests that, within the five days allowed by the compromise, the Lord will *deliver Israel* by her hand. Judith refuses to explain the details of what she will do to accomplish God's purpose (cf. Nebuchadnezzar's full explanation of his secret plan in 2.2), but asks the leaders to meet her and her maid that night at the town gate. *Listen to me*. Note the verb changes from the reported *Judith heard* in 8.1, 8 to the

imperative *listen to me* in 8.11, 32 to the petition *hear me* in 9.4, 12. **9.1–14** Alone, Judith prays that God grant her success by hearing her prayer (v. 4), breaking the strength of the Assyrians (v. 8), and defeating the enemy by the *deceit of* her *lips* (v. 10; *deceitful words*, v. 13) and *the hand of a woman* (v. 10). **9.2** *My ancestor Simeon*. Cf. the story of the revenge of the sons of Jacob for the rape of Dinah in Gen 34.25–31. **9.10, 13** Twice Judith specifies *deceit* as her weapon for success. The law required that a person's public testimony have constancy and reliability (see Ex 20.16; Deut 5.20). Lev 19.11 prohibits lying, and other texts express negative sentiments about deceit (Ps 15.2; Prov 6.17; 12.22). Yet there are many biblical stories in which "private" lies are told for the preservation of the community (e.g., the lies told by Abraham, Gen 12.13;

11 "For your strength does not depend on numbers, nor your might on the powerful. But you are the God of the lowly, helper of the oppressed, upholder of the weak, protector of the forsaken, savior of those without hope. 12 Please, please, God of my father, God of the heritage of Israel, Lord of heaven and earth, Creator of the waters, King of all your creation, hear my prayer! 13 Make my deceitful words bring wound and bruise on those who have planned cruel things against your covenant, and against your sacred house, and against Mount Zion, and against the house your children possess. 14 Let your whole nation and every tribe know and understand that you are God, the God of all power and might, and that there is no other who protects the people of Israel but you alone!"

Judith Prepares to Go to Holofernes

10 When Judith[a] had stopped crying out to the God of Israel, and had ended all these words, 2 she rose from where she lay prostrate. She called her maid and went down into the house where she lived on sabbaths and on her festal days. 3 She removed the sackcloth she had been wearing, took off her widow's garments, bathed her body with water, and anointed herself with precious ointment. She combed her hair, put on a tiara, and dressed herself in the festive attire that she used to wear while her husband Manasseh was living. 4 She put sandals on her feet, and put on her anklets, bracelets, rings, earrings, and all her other jewelry. Thus she made herself very beautiful, to entice the eyes of all the men who might see her. 5 She gave her maid a skin of wine and a flask of oil, and filled a bag with roasted grain, dried fig cakes, and fine bread;[b] then she wrapped up all her dishes and gave them to her to carry.

6 Then they went out to the town gate of Bethulia and found Uzziah standing there with the elders of the town, Chabris and Charmis. 7 When they saw her transformed in appearance and dressed differently, they were very greatly astounded at her beauty and said to her, 8 "May the God of our ancestors grant you favor and fulfill your plans, so that the people of Israel may glory and Jerusalem may be exalted." She bowed down to God.

9 Then she said to them, "Order the gate of the town to be opened for me so that I may go out and accomplish the things you have just said to me." So they ordered the young men to open the gate for her, as she requested. 10 When they had done this, Judith went out, accompanied by her maid. The men of the town watched her until she had gone down the mountain and passed through the valley, where they lost sight of her.

Judith Is Captured

11 As the women[c] were going straight on through the valley, an Assyrian patrol met her 12 and took her into custody. They asked her, "To what people do you belong, and where are you coming from, and where are you going?" She replied, "I am a daughter of the Hebrews, but I am fleeing from them, for they are about to be handed over to you to be devoured. 13 I am on my way to see Holofernes the commander of your army, to give him a true report; I will show him a way by which he can go and capture all the hill country without losing one of his men, captured or slain."

14 When the men heard her words, and observed her face—she was in their eyes mar-

---

a Gk *she*   *b* Other ancient authorities add *and cheese*
c Gk *they*

20.2; Isaac, Gen 26.7; Rebekah, Gen 27–28; Tamar, Gen 38; the midwives, mother, and sister of Moses and the princess, Ex 1–2; Rahab, Josh 2; and the woman of Tekoa, 2 Sam 14). **9.10** *Woman,* Greek *theleia* ("female") rather than the more common *gyne* ("woman"); see also 13.15; 16.5. To be killed by a female was a special disgrace according to Judg 9.53–54. Cf. also Judg 4.17–22; 5.24–27. **10.1–8** Judith readies herself to carry out her plan. **10.3** That Judith *bathed her body with water* does not fit with the short supply of water in Bethulia. **10.4** Judith dresses beautifully *to entice the eyes of all the men.* Her motivation is not vanity—her plan is to smash the enemy. In Part 2, Judith's beauty influences all who meet her (8.7; 10.7, 14, 19, 23; 11.21, 23; 12.13).

10.5 Judith prepares ritually pure food for the journey (cf. Dan 1.8–16).

10.9–10 In Section C (see note on 8.1–16.25), Judith and her maid leave Bethulia. The order to open the gate begins a journey down the mountain and through the valley to the Assyrian camp, a journey that will be repeated in reverse in 13.10b–11.

10.11–13.10a In this climactic and central section (D; see note on 8.1–16.25), Judith overcomes Holofernes. **10.11–19** A patrol meets Judith and takes her to Holofernes. **10.12–13** Judith's first words to the patrol are a mixture of truth and lies: she is a *daughter of the Hebrews,* but she does not plan to give Holofernes a *true report* about how to capture the hill country without any

velously beautiful—they said to her, [15]"You have saved your life by hurrying down to see our lord. Go at once to his tent; some of us will escort you and hand you over to him. [16]When you stand before him, have no fear in your heart, but tell him what you have just said, and he will treat you well."

17 They chose from their number a hundred men to accompany her and her maid, and they brought them to the tent of Holofernes. [18]There was great excitement in the whole camp, for her arrival was reported from tent to tent. They came and gathered around her as she stood outside the tent of Holofernes, waiting until they told him about her. [19]They marveled at her beauty and admired the Israelites, judging them by her. They said to one another, "Who can despise these people, who have women like this among them? It is not wise to leave one of their men alive, for if we let them go they will be able to beguile the whole world!"

Judith Is Brought before Holofernes

20 Then the guards of Holofernes and all his servants came out and led her into the tent. [21]Holofernes was resting on his bed under a canopy that was woven with purple and gold, emeralds and other precious stones. [22]When they told him of her, he came to the front of the tent, with silver lamps carried before him. [23]When Judith came into the presence of Holofernes[a] and his servants, they all marveled at the beauty of her face. She prostrated herself and did obeisance to him, but his slaves raised her up.

11 Then Holofernes said to her, "Take courage, woman, and do not be afraid in your heart, for I have never hurt anyone who chose to serve Nebuchadnezzar, king of all the earth. [2]Even now, if your people who live in the hill country had not slighted me, I would never have lifted my spear against them. They have brought this on themselves. [3]But now tell me why you have fled from them and have come over to us. In any event, you

have come to safety. Take courage! You will live tonight and ever after. [4]No one will hurt you. Rather, all will treat you well, as they do the servants of my lord King Nebuchadnezzar."

Judith Explains Her Presence

5 Judith answered him, "Accept the words of your slave, and let your servant speak in your presence. I will say nothing false to my lord this night. [6]If you follow out the words of your servant, God will accomplish something through you, and my lord will not fail to achieve his purposes. [7]By the life of Nebuchadnezzar, king of the whole earth, and by the power of him who has sent you to direct every living being! Not only do human beings serve him because of you, but also the animals of the field and the cattle and the birds of the air will live, because of your power, under Nebuchadnezzar and all his house. [8]For we have heard of your wisdom and skill, and it is reported throughout the whole world that you alone are the best in the whole kingdom, the most informed and the most astounding in military strategy.

9 "Now as for Achior's speech in your council, we have heard his words, for the people of Bethulia spared him and he told them all he had said to you. [10]Therefore, lord and master, do not disregard what he said, but keep it in your mind, for it is true. Indeed our nation cannot be punished, nor can the sword prevail against them, unless they sin against their God.

11 "But now, in order that my lord may not be defeated and his purpose frustrated, death will fall upon them, for a sin has overtaken them by which they are about to provoke their God to anger when they do what is wrong. [12]Since their food supply is exhausted and their water has almost given out, they have planned to kill their livestock and have determined to use all that God by his laws has forbidden them to eat. [13]They have decided to

---

a Gk him

---

loss. **10.14** The men observe that she is *marvelously beautiful* (see note on 10.4). **10.18–19** Judith's beauty causes the whole camp to marvel (as it will Holofernes and his servants in v. 23). **10.20–12.9** During their first meeting, Judith and Holofernes deceive each other. Only in 11.9–10; 12.2, 4 does Judith speak the whole truth; otherwise her statements are lies or at best mixtures of truth and lie or words with double meanings (as in 11.6).

11.1 Holofernes' first lie, given his destruction of the worship places of the nations who pledged they were servants of Nebuchadnezzar (3.2). **11.3** *You will live tonight and ever after.* Holofernes ironically proclaims a truth that will not be of his doing. **11.5** Judith's words have a double meaning. Is *my lord* Holofernes or God? **11.11** Judith lies that *a sin has overtaken* her people (8.18–20 is her statement to the contrary). **11.17** Judith's plan (which is

consume the first fruits of the grain and the tithes of the wine and oil, which they had consecrated and set aside for the priests who minister in the presence of our God in Jerusalem—things it is not lawful for any of the people even to touch with their hands. 14Since even the people in Jerusalem have been doing this, they have sent messengers there in order to bring back permission from the council of the elders. 15When the response reaches them and they act upon it, on that very day they will be handed over to you to be destroyed.

16 "So when I, your slave, learned all this, I fled from them. God has sent me to accomplish with you things that will astonish the whole world wherever people shall hear about them. 17Your servant is indeed God-fearing and serves the God of heaven night and day. So, my lord, I will remain with you; but every night your servant will go out into the valley and pray to God. He will tell me when they have committed their sins. 18Then I will come and tell you, so that you may go out with your whole army, and not one of them will be able to withstand you. 19Then I will lead you through Judea, until you come to Jerusalem; there I will set your throne.ᵃ You will drive them like sheep that have no shepherd, and no dog will so much as growl at you. For this was told me to give me foreknowledge; it was announced to me, and I was sent to tell you."

20 Her words pleased Holofernes and all his servants. They marveled at her wisdom and said, 21"No other woman from one end of the earth to the other looks so beautiful or speaks so wisely!" 22Then Holofernes said to her, "God has done well to send you ahead of the people, to strengthen our hands and bring destruction on those who have despised my lord. 23You are not only beautiful in appearance, but wise in speech. If you do as you have said, your God shall be my God, and you shall live in the palace of King Nebuchadnezzar and be renowned throughout the whole world."

Judith as a Guest of Holofernes

12 Then he commanded them to bring her in where his silver dinnerware was kept, and ordered them to set a table for her with some of his own delicacies, and with some of his own wine to drink. 2But Judith said, "I cannot partake of them, or it will be an offense; but I will have enough with the things I brought with me." 3Holofernes said to her, "If your supply runs out, where can we get you more of the same? For none of your people are here with us." 4Judith replied, "As surely as you live, my lord, your servant will not use up the supplies I have with me before the Lord carries out by my hand what he has determined."

5 Then the servants of Holofernes brought her into the tent, and she slept until midnight. Toward the morning watch she got up 6and sent this message to Holofernes: "Let my lord now give orders to allow your servant to go out and pray." 7So Holofernes commanded his guards not to hinder her. She remained in the camp three days. She went out each night to the valley of Bethulia, and bathed at the spring in the camp.ᵇ 8After bathing, she prayed the Lord God of Israel to direct her way for the triumph of hisᶜ people. 9Then she returned purified and stayed in the tent until she ate her food toward evening.

Judith Attends Holofernes' Banquet

10 On the fourth day Holofernes held a banquet for his personal attendants only, and did not invite any of his officers. 11He said to Bagoas, the eunuch who had charge of his personal affairs, "Go and persuade the Hebrew woman who is in your care to join us and to eat and drink with us. 12For it would be a disgrace if we let such a woman go without having intercourse with her. If we do not seduce her, she will laugh at us."

13 So Bagoas left the presence of Holofernes,

---

a Or *chariot*   *b* Other ancient authorities lack *in the camp*
c Other ancient authorities read *her*

---

sealed in 12.5–7) to go out into the valley each night sets up her escape. **11.23** *Your God shall be my God.* Holofernes' offer is unlikely given his insistence that Nebuchadnezzar alone is god (3.8); cf. Ruth 1.16. **12.2** *Offense,* Greek *skandalon,* something that would cause someone to stumble or take offense. Judith shows special sensitivity around dietary prohibitions. Her strength resides in her resolute adherence to the distinctive signs of

the covenant people. **12.9** *Purified.* Judith's concern for proper food is matched by her attention to ritual cleanliness. Her daily bath in the spring may reflect the increasing use of the *mikveh,* or ritual bath, in the Second Temple period. **12.10–20** The banquet. **12.10** *On the fourth day* of the five allotted before the people of Bethulia surrender, Holofernes plans a banquet. **12.12** The purpose of the evening is for Holofernes to have *intercourse with*

and approached her and said, "Let this pretty girl not hesitate to come to my lord to be honored in his presence, and to enjoy drinking wine with us, and to become today like one of the Assyrian women who serve in the palace of Nebuchadnezzar." [14]Judith replied, "Who am I to refuse my lord? Whatever pleases him I will do at once, and it will be a joy to me until the day of my death." [15]So she proceeded to dress herself in all her woman's finery. Her maid went ahead and spread for her on the ground before Holofernes the lambskins she had received from Bagoas for her daily use in reclining.

16 Then Judith came in and lay down. Holofernes' heart was ravished with her and his passion was aroused, for he had been waiting for an opportunity to seduce her from the day he first saw her. [17]So Holofernes said to her, "Have a drink and be merry with us!" [18]Judith said, "I will gladly drink, my lord, because today is the greatest day in my whole life." [19]Then she took what her maid had prepared and ate and drank before him. [20]Holofernes was greatly pleased with her, and drank a great quantity of wine, much more than he had ever drunk in any one day since he was born.

Judith Beheads Holofernes

13 When evening came, his slaves quickly withdrew. Bagoas closed the tent from outside and shut out the attendants from his master's presence. They went to bed, for they all were weary because the banquet had lasted so long. [2]But Judith was left alone in the tent, with Holofernes stretched out on his bed, for he was dead drunk.

3 Now Judith had told her maid to stand outside the bedchamber and to wait for her to come out, as she did on the other days; for she said she would be going out for her prayers.

She had said the same thing to Bagoas. [4]So everyone went out, and no one, either small or great, was left in the bedchamber. Then Judith, standing beside his bed, said in her heart, "O Lord God of all might, look in this hour on the work of my hands for the exaltation of Jerusalem. [5]Now indeed is the time to help your heritage and to carry out my design to destroy the enemies who have risen up against us."

6 She went up to the bedpost near Holofernes' head, and took down his sword that hung there. [7]She came close to his bed, took hold of the hair of his head, and said, "Give me strength today, O Lord God of Israel!" [8]Then she struck his neck twice with all her might, and cut off his head. [9]Next she rolled his body off the bed and pulled down the canopy from the posts. Soon afterward she went out and gave Holofernes' head to her maid, [10]who placed it in her food bag.

Judith Returns to Bethulia

Then the two of them went out together, as they were accustomed to do for prayer. They passed through the camp, circled around the valley, and went up the mountain to Bethulia, and came to its gates. [11]From a distance Judith called out to the sentries at the gates, "Open, open the gate! God, our God, is with us, still showing his power in Israel and his strength against our enemies, as he has done today!"

12 When the people of her town heard her voice, they hurried down to the town gate and summoned the elders of the town. [13]They all ran together, both small and great, for it seemed unbelievable that she had returned. They opened the gate and welcomed them. Then they lit a fire to give light, and gathered around them. [14]Then she said to them with a loud voice, "Praise God, O praise him! Praise

---

her. **12.14** *Who am I to refuse?* Judith's identity is not at stake as she accepts Bagoas's invitation to the banquet (cf. 6.2; 8.12). **12.16** Holofernes is waiting *to seduce her;* Judith is there to deceive him. **12.18** *Greatest day in my whole life,* another highly ironic comment. See 11.3. **13.1–10a** Holofernes loses his head. **13.2–8** Judith is alone with Holofernes who is *dead drunk.* She prays twice (vv. 4–5, 7) and *strikes his neck twice* (v. 8) with his own sword. **13.9–10a** The reason for her actions, taking the head and pulling the canopy down, appear later (v. 15). **13.10b–11** In Section C′, which begins the second half of Part 2 (see note on 8.1–16.25), Judith and her maid retrace their steps (see 10.9–10) to Bethulia through the valley and up the mountain. **13.11** Judith proclaims that God is with them, in contrast to the

people's cry that God has abandoned them (7.25).

13.12–16.20 Judith plans the destruction of Israel's enemy. This section, B′, repeats elements found in B of Part 2 (8.9–10.8; see note on 8.1–16.25). Both open with a meeting with Judith: she summons the town officials (8.10); the people assemble when they "hear" (13.12) her voice asking that the gate be opened (13.13). (Cf. the uses of the important verb variously translated as *hear* or *listen* in 4.1, 13; 5.5; 7.9; 8.1, 9 [twice], 11, 17, 32; 9.4, 12; 10.14; 11.8, 9, 16; 13.12; 14.1, 7, 19; 15.1, 5.) B and B′ contain an instruction from Judith that begins with the words *listen to me* (8.11; 14.1). She prays for success in 9.1–14 and announces it in 13.14–16. Uzziah blesses her in 8.35 and again in 13.18–20. **13.12–14.10** Judith now speaks to

God, who has not withdrawn his mercy from the house of Israel, but has destroyed our enemies by my hand this very night!"

15 Then she pulled the head out of the bag and showed it to them, and said, "See here, the head of Holofernes, the commander of the Assyrian army, and here is the canopy beneath which he lay in his drunken stupor. The Lord has struck him down by the hand of a woman. 16 As the Lord lives, who has protected me in the way I went, I swear that it was my face that seduced him to his destruction, and that he committed no sin with me, to defile and shame me."

17 All the people were greatly astonished. They bowed down and worshiped God, and said with one accord, "Blessed are you our God, who have this day humiliated the enemies of your people."

18 Then Uzziah said to her, "O daughter, you are blessed by the Most High God above all other women on earth; and blessed be the Lord God, who created the heavens and the earth, who has guided you to cut off the head of the leader of our enemies. 19 Your praise[a] will never depart from the hearts of those who remember the power of God. 20 May God grant this to be a perpetual honor to you, and may he reward you with blessings, because you risked your own life when our nation was brought low, and you averted our ruin, walking in the straight path before our God." And all the people said, "Amen. Amen."

Judith's Counsel

14 Then Judith said to them, "Listen to me, my friends. Take this head and hang it upon the parapet of your wall. 2 As soon as day breaks and the sun rises on the earth, each of you take up your weapons, and let every able-bodied man go out of the town; set a captain over them, as if you were going down to the plain against the Assyrian out-

post; only do not go down. 3 Then they will seize their arms and go into the camp and rouse the officers of the Assyrian army. They will rush into the tent of Holofernes and will not find him. Then panic will come over them, and they will flee before you. 4 Then you and all who live within the borders of Israel will pursue them and cut them down in their tracks. 5 But before you do all this, bring Achior the Ammonite to me so that he may see and recognize the man who despised the house of Israel and sent him to us as if to his death."

6 So they summoned Achior from the house of Uzziah. When he came and saw the head of Holofernes in the hand of one of the men in the assembly of the people, he fell down on his face in a faint. 7 When they raised him up he threw himself at Judith's feet, and did obeisance to her, and said, "Blessed are you in every tent of Judah! In every nation those who hear your name will be alarmed. 8 Now tell me what you have done during these days."

So Judith told him in the presence of the people all that she had done, from the day she left until the moment she began speaking to them. 9 When she had finished, the people raised a great shout and made a joyful noise in their town. 10 When Achior saw all that the God of Israel had done, he believed firmly in God. So he was circumcised, and joined the house of Israel, remaining so to this day.

Holofernes' Death Is Discovered

11 As soon as it was dawn they hung the head of Holofernes on the wall. Then they all took their weapons, and they went out in companies to the mountain passes. 12 When the Assyrians saw them they sent word to their commanders, who then went to the generals and the captains and to all their other officers.

a Other ancient authorities read *hope*

---

the people of Bethulia. **13.15** *By the hand of a woman.* See note on 9.10. Judith gives God full credit for the triumph (see also v. 4; 16.5). **13.17** *Blessed,* Greek *eulogetos,* appears only seven times in Judith, and all its occurrences are in B′ (13.17; 13.18 [twice]; 14.7; 15.9; 15.10; 15.12). **14.1–5** *Listen to me* is used three times in this form; cf. the imperatives in 8.11, 32. Judith instructs the people to hang the head of Holofernes *upon the parapet* and to display themselves in ranks before the enemy at daybreak. Her strategy is that the Assyrians will then discover that Holofernes is dead and flee in panic.

14.5–6 *Achior* is brought to Judith so that Holofernes' head can be verified. Achior collapses at the sight. **14.7** *Blessed . . . in . . . Judah,* reminiscent of the praise of Jael in Judg 5.24. **14.10** *So he was circumcised.* The author is not concerned with the prohibition of Deut 23.3 that no Ammonite or Moabite shall enter the assembly, even to the tenth generation. Since Judith is more than ten generations removed from Jacob (8.1), so also is Achior and perhaps this law was not judged pertinent. Some suggest that this verse accounts for the exclusion of this book from the Hebrew canon. **14.11–15.7** The

13 They came to Holofernes' tent and said to the steward in charge of all his personal affairs, "Wake up our lord, for the slaves have been so bold as to come down against us to give battle, to their utter destruction."

14 So Bagoas went in and knocked at the entry of the tent, for he supposed that he was sleeping with Judith. 15 But when no one answered, he opened it and went into the bedchamber and found him sprawled on the floor dead, with his head missing. 16 He cried out with a loud voice and wept and groaned and shouted, and tore his clothes. 17 Then he went to the tent where Judith had stayed, and when he did not find her, he rushed out to the people and shouted, 18 "The slaves have tricked us! One Hebrew woman has brought disgrace on the house of King Nebuchadnezzar. Look, Holofernes is lying on the ground, and his head is missing!"

19 When the leaders of the Assyrian army heard this, they tore their tunics and were greatly dismayed, and their loud cries and shouts rose up throughout the camp.

The Assyrians Flee in Panic

15 When the men in the tents heard it, they were amazed at what had happened. 2 Overcome with fear and trembling, they did not wait for one another, but with one impulse all rushed out and fled by every path across the plain and through the hill country. 3 Those who had camped in the hills around Bethulia also took to flight. Then the Israelites, everyone that was a soldier, rushed out upon them. 4 Uzziah sent men to Betomasthaim[a] and Choba and Kola, and to all the frontiers of Israel, to tell what had taken place and to urge all to rush out upon the enemy to destroy them. 5 When the Israelites heard it, with one accord they fell upon the enemy,[b] and cut them down as far as Choba. Those in Jerusalem and all the hill country also came,

for they were told what had happened in the camp of the enemy. The men in Gilead and in Galilee outflanked them with great slaughter, even beyond Damascus and its borders. 6 The rest of the people of Bethulia fell upon the Assyrian camp and plundered it, acquiring great riches. 7 And the Israelites, when they returned from the slaughter, took possession of what remained. Even the villages and towns in the hill country and in the plain got a great amount of booty, since there was a vast quantity of it.

The Israelites Celebrate Their Victory

8 Then the high priest Joakim and the elders of the Israelites who lived in Jerusalem came to witness the good things that the Lord had done for Israel, and to see Judith and to wish her well. 9 When they met her, they all blessed her with one accord and said to her, "You are the glory of Jerusalem, you are the great boast of Israel, you are the great pride of our nation! 10 You have done all this with your own hand; you have done great good to Israel, and God is well pleased with it. May the Almighty Lord bless you forever!" And all the people said, "Amen."

11 All the people plundered the camp for thirty days. They gave Judith the tent of Holofernes and all his silver dinnerware, his beds, his bowls, and all his furniture. She took them and loaded her mules and hitched up her carts and piled the things on them.

12 All the women of Israel gathered to see her, and blessed her, and some of them performed a dance in her honor. She took ivy-wreathed wands in her hands and distributed them to the women who were with her; 13 and she and those who were with her crowned themselves with olive wreaths. She went before all the people in the dance, leading all the

---

a Other ancient authorities add and Bebai   b Gk them

---

effect of Judith's strategy on the Assyrian camp. **14.19** When the Assyrians hear Holofernes is dead, they are greatly dismayed; cf. the description of Israel in 4.1–2. **15.2** Here the Assyrians experience the fear and trembling they caused in 2.28. **15.4** Betomasthaim and Choba and Kola, unidentified locations. **15.8–16.20** A victory celebration in Bethulia with Joakim, the high priest of Jerusalem (15.8–10); a thirty-day interlude (15.11); and a triumphal procession of dance and song to Jerusalem for a three-month celebration (15.12–16.17). **15.11** The Israelites plun-

der the enemy camp for thirty days; added to the four days Judith spent in the Assyrian camp, the time balances the thirty-four days Bethulia was under siege (7.20). **15.12** Ivy-wreathed wands were regularly associated with the cult of the Greek deity Dionysos. Cf. 3 Macc 2.29. Their use by Judith here is another ironic touch that suggests that she is more than a match for Bacchantes, the female devotees of Dionysos who in frenzy could tear apart opponents of the god. **15.13** The wearing of olive wreaths was another Greek custom. Judith led the women in dance (like Miriam in

women, while all the men of Israel followed, bearing their arms and wearing garlands and singing hymns.

Judith Offers Her Hymn of Praise

14 Judith began this thanksgiving before all Israel, and all the people loudly sang this song of praise. [1] And Judith said,

16 Begin a song to my God with tambourines,
sing to my Lord with cymbals.
Raise to him a new psalm; [a]
exalt him, and call upon his name.

2 For the Lord is a God who crushes wars;
he sets up his camp among his people;
he delivered me from the hands of my pursuers.

3 The Assyrian came down from the mountains of the north;
he came with myriads of his warriors;
their numbers blocked up the wadis,
and their cavalry covered the hills.

4 He boasted that he would burn up my territory,
and kill my young men with the sword,
and dash my infants to the ground,
and seize my children as booty,
and take my virgins as spoil.

5 But the Lord Almighty has foiled them by the hand of a woman. [b]

6 For their mighty one did not fall by the hands of the young men,
nor did the sons of the Titans strike him down,
nor did tall giants set upon him;
but Judith daughter of Merari
with the beauty of her countenance undid him.

7 For she put away her widow's clothing to exalt the oppressed in Israel.
She anointed her face with perfume;

8 she fastened her hair with a tiara
and put on a linen gown to beguile him.

9 Her sandal ravished his eyes,
her beauty captivated his mind,
and the sword severed his neck!

10 The Persians trembled at her boldness,
the Medes were daunted at her daring.

11 Then my oppressed people shouted;
my weak people cried out, [c] and the enemy [d] trembled;
they lifted up their voices, and the enemy [d] were turned back.

12 Sons of slave-girls pierced them through
and wounded them like the children of fugitives;
they perished before the army of my Lord.

13 I will sing to my God a new song:
O Lord, you are great and glorious,
wonderful in strength, invincible.

14 Let all your creatures serve you,
for you spoke, and they were made.
You sent forth your spirit, [e] and it formed them; [f]
there is none that can resist your voice.

15 For the mountains shall be shaken to their foundations with the waters;
before your glance the rocks shall melt like wax.
But to those who fear you
you show mercy.

16 For every sacrifice as a fragrant offering is a small thing,
and the fat of all whole burnt offerings to you is a very little thing;
but whoever fears the Lord is great forever.

17 Woe to the nations that rise up against my people!
The Lord Almighty will take vengeance on them in the day of judgment;

---

a Other ancient authorities read *a psalm and praise* b Other ancient authorities add *he has confounded them* c Other ancient authorities read *feared* d Gk *they* e Or *breath* f Other ancient authorities read *they were created*

Ex 15.20). **15.14–16.17** Judith's hymn of praise is most likely modeled on the Song of Moses (Ex 15.1–18). This liturgical poem opens with a hymnic introduction in which Judith calls the people to worship and proclaims God victor and deliverer (16.1–2). There follows in vv. 3–12 a narration of the epic event in which Judith describes the Assyrian threat (vv. 3–5) and another voice tells of her triumph (vv. 6–10). In the hymnic conclusion (vv. 13–17) Judith praises God with a *new song* (v. 13) and summons all creation to join her song of praise. **16.5** *By the hand of a woman* emphasizes a key theme of the whole work. **16.15–16** *Fear* of God is entitlement to mercy and true greatness. Judith constantly demonstrated her piety, which guaranteed her success. **16.17** Ruin is the fate of those who arise against God's people.

he will send fire and worms into their flesh;
they shall weep in pain forever.

18 When they arrived at Jerusalem, they
worshiped God. As soon as the people were
purified, they offered their burnt offerings,
their freewill offerings, and their gifts. 19 Judith
also dedicated to God all the possessions of
Holofernes, which the people had given her;
and the canopy that she had taken for herself
from his bedchamber she gave as a votive offering. 20 For three months the people continued feasting in Jerusalem before the sanctuary,
and Judith remained with them.

The Renown and Death of Judith

21 After this they all returned home to their
own inheritances. Judith went to Bethulia,
and remained on her estate. For the rest of her
life she was honored throughout the whole
country. 22 Many desired to marry her, but she
gave herself to no man all the days of her life
after her husband Manasseh died and was
gathered to his people. 23 She became more
and more famous, and grew old in her husband's house, reaching the age of one hundred five. She set her maid free. She died in
Bethulia, and they buried her in the cave of
her husband Manasseh; 24 and the house of Israel mourned her for seven days. Before she
died she distributed her property to all those
who were next of kin to her husband Manasseh, and to her own nearest kindred. 25 No one
ever again spread terror among the Israelites
during the lifetime of Judith, or for a long
time after her death.

16.21–25 Section A´ (see note on 8.1–16.25), conclusion about Judith. The narrative closes with elements found in Section A (8.1–8). Both passages include the information that Judith was the widow of
Manasseh (8.2; 16.22), that she lived alone in Bethulia
on her estate (8.4; 16.22), and that she had servants
and property (8.7; 16.21, 24). Both tell of a death: Manasseh dies and is buried (8.2–3); Judith dies and is
buried (16.23–24). Both conclude with the public effect of Judith's faith (8.8; 16.25). **16.22** *Many desired to
marry her, but she gave herself to no man,* better "Many
men wanted her, but no man had intercourse with
her." Judith practiced celibacy. The motivations of the
men are unclear. What is certain is that she chose to
continue living in solitude for the rest of her life.
16.23 *One hundred five* years, the length of the Maccabean period (168–63 BCE). *She set her maid free.* Judith's last act balances her first, in which she sent the
maid to summon Uzziah, Chabris, and Charmis
(8.10). **16.24** *Seven days,* the customary period of
mourning for the dead (1 Sam 31.13; 1 Chr 10.12; Sir
22.12). **16.25** *No one ever again spread terror among the
Israelites.* The book ends with a note of utopian finality. Unfortunately, history was not so benign.

ESTHER

(The Greek Version Containing the Additional Chapters)

NOTE: The deuterocanonical portions of the book of Esther are several additional passages found in the Greek translation of the Hebrew book of Esther, a translation that differs also in other respects from the Hebrew text (the latter is translated in the NRSV OT). The disordered chapter numbers come from the displacement of the additions to the end of the canonical book of Esther by Jerome in his Latin translation and from the subsequent division of the Bible into chapters by Stephen Langton, who numbered the additions consecutively as though they formed a direct continuation of the Hebrew text. So that the additions may be read in their proper context, the whole of the Greek version is here translated, though certain familiar names are given according to their Hebrew rather than their Greek form, e.g., Mordecai and Vashti instead of Mardocheus and Astin. The order followed is that of the Greek text, but the chapter and verse numbers conform to those of the King James, or Authorized Version. The additions, conveniently indicated by the letters A–F, are located as follows: A, before 1.1; B, after 3.13; C and D, after 4.17; E, after 8.12; F, after 10.3.

The Two Books Compared

THE BOOK OF ESTHER AS FOUND IN THE GREEK BIBLE (the Septuagint) is significantly longer than the book of Esther in Hebrew. The Greek version contains subtle changes from its Hebrew original as well as blocks of material that are referred to as Additions to Esther. This designation suggests that the material was added to an earlier form of Esther to deal with concerns of Jews whose sensibilities were disturbed by qualities of the older Hebrew story. According to the postscript found in the Septuagint Esther, this version of the book was brought to Egypt sometime in the mid-first century BCE (Addition F, 11.1). It was composed in the late second or early first century BCE.

Contention has surrounded the book of Esther and its canonical status. Perhaps most striking in the Hebrew is the absence of any direct mention of God, especially in a story about dangers confronting Jews in an alien setting. Also striking is the apparent neglect, especially by Esther, of aspects of Jewish Torah that came to define what it meant to be a Jew. A number of points in the story stretch historical credulity, and the strong note of harsh vengeance wrought by the Jews on their enemies has disturbed some readers. Noteworthy is the central role played by a woman, for spheres of influence and action for women in postexilic Judaism were quite circumscribed.

Additions A–F

FROM THE OPENING OF THE GREEK ESTHER, God is very present as the author of Mordecai's dream (Addition A). Not only does the righteous nation cry out to God in its affliction, but we are told that what Mordecai saw was "what God had determined to do" (11.12). At the end of the story Mordecai recalls his dream, recognizes its point-by-point fulfillment, and attributes the rescue of his people to God (Addition F). This sense of providential shaping of events in human history, along with imagery envisioning a return of created order to chaos, envelops the story in an apocalyptic interpretative frame that creates a setting of cosmic conflict rather than a purely local political contest. This beginning and conclusion also highlight the importance of Mordecai, as does the account of how he uncovered a plot against the king, was rewarded with service in the court, and earned thereby the enmity of Haman.

Copies of the decrees written in the king's name (Additions B and E) provide historical verisimilitude. The first authorizes the pogrom planned by Haman (Addition B), while the second counters the first by allowing Jews to defend themselves and calls on Persians to support them against their enemies (Addition E). These appear to be the only Additions originally composed in Greek. They serve to characterize both the villain Haman and the malleable king in fine counterpoint. In the first Haman is lauded as "second father" (13.6) to the king, the Jews and their Torah are slandered, and the king's motives are said to be the peace of his kingdom. In the second Haman is vilified, the Jews and Torah are praised, the king's motives are defended, and credit for his enlightenment, Haman's defeat, and the Jews' salvation is attributed to "the living God" (16.16).

Prayers by Mordecai and Esther seeking divine aid (Addition C) assert God's power to save now as in the past. Mordecai is also able to justify his failure to bow before Haman by saying he would grant such respect only to God, and Esther is able to lament her marriage to a Gentile and her difficulties in observing Jewish dietary practices and to express her abhorrence of her present royal estate.

Esther's reception when she appears unbidden before the king (Addition D) is more dramatic than in the Hebrew Esther. The Greek version also attributes the king's change of spirit to God; and 6.1 states that "the Lord took sleep from the king," making the deity the force behind these climaxes on the road to salvation for the Jews.

The cumulative effect of the Additions and the small changes from the Hebrew make the Greek Esther a much more dramatic, emotional book. God and the Jewish covenant tradition are at the center of the story, while the importance of the Purim festival is lessened. Thus in both the Additions and in its other small variations, the Greek Esther represents a distinct story that differs qualitatively from the Hebrew. Within Christian tradition the Additions took on something of a life of their own, being either set at the end of a translation of the Hebrew Esther or gathered separately in the Protestant Apocrypha.

The notes focus on the Additions and on differences between the Greek and Hebrew versions. For fuller notes on the common material, see Esther in the OT. [W. LEE HUMPHREYS, revised by SIDNIE WHITE CRAWFORD]

ADDITION A
Mordecai's Dream

11 [a] [2]In the second year of the reign of Artaxerxes the Great, on the first day of Nisan, Mordecai son of Jair son of Shimei[b] son of Kish, of the tribe of Benjamin, had a dream. [3]He was a Jew living in the city of Susa, a great man, serving in the court of the king. [4]He was one of the captives whom King Nebuchadnezzar of Babylon had brought from Jerusalem with King Jeconiah of Judea. And this was his dream: [5]Noises[c] and confusion, thunders and earthquake, tumult on the earth! [6]Then two great dragons came forward, both ready to fight, and they roared terribly. [7]At their roaring every nation prepared for war, to fight against the righteous nation. [8]It was a day of darkness and gloom, of tribulation and distress, affliction and great tumult on the earth! [9]And the whole righteous nation was troubled; they feared the evils that threatened them,[d] and were ready to perish. [10]Then they cried out to God; and at their outcry, as though from a tiny spring, there came a great river, with abundant water; [11]light came, and the sun rose, and the lowly were exalted and devoured those held in honor.

[12]Mordecai saw in this dream what God had determined to do, and after he awoke he had it on his mind, seeking all day to understand it in every detail.

A Plot against the King

12 Now Mordecai took his rest in the courtyard with Gabatha and Tharra, the two eunuchs of the king who kept watch in the courtyard. [2]He overheard their conversation and inquired into their purposes, and learned that they were preparing to lay hands on King Artaxerxes; and he informed the king concerning them. [3]Then the king examined the two eunuchs, and after they had confessed it, they were led away to execution. [4]The king made a permanent record of these things, and Mordecai wrote an account of them. [5]And the king ordered Mordecai to serve in the court, and rewarded him for these things. [6]But Haman son of Hammedatha, a Bougean, who was in great honor with the king, determined to injure Mordecai and his people because of the two eunuchs of the king.

END OF ADDITION A

Arataxerxes' Banquet

1 It was after this that the following things happened in the days of Artaxerxes, the same Artaxerxes who ruled over one hundred twenty-seven provinces from India to Ethiopia.[e] [2]In those days, when King Artax-

---

a Chapters 11.2—12.6 correspond to chapter A 1-17 in some translations. *b* Gk *Semeios* *c* Or *Voices* *d* Gk *their own evils* *e* Other ancient authorities lack *to Ethiopia*

11.2–12 Mordecai's dream (Addition A) provides a divine but cryptic preview of what will take place. Mordecai is presented as a visionary, like Joseph or Daniel. **11.2** *Artaxerxes,* called Ahasuerus in the Hebrew Esther, is fully introduced in 1.1–9. *Nisan* (March–April), the first month of the Jewish year, the month of Passover. *Mordecai* is introduced as a Benjaminite of the line of Saul, Israel's first king. For *Shimei,* see 2 Sam 16.5–14; 19.16–23; 1 Kings 2.8, 36–46. For *Kish,* Saul's father, see 1 Sam 9.1, 14.51. Generations are telescoped, as *son of* can mean "descendant of." Mordecai is introduced again in 2.5. **11.3** In the Greek Esther Mordecai is an important figure in the royal court from the outset. Cf. the Hebrew, which says he "was sitting at the king's gate" (2.19; 3.2). **11.4** To have Mordecai exiled by *Nebuchadnezzar* in 597 BCE along with *Jeconiah* (2 Kings 24.6–17), elsewhere called Jehoiachin, poses chronological problems, for Artaxerxes I reigned from 465 to 424 BCE, and Artaxerxes II even later. **11.5–6** A potential return of created order to chaos is tersely presented here. What in the Hebrew Esther is a conflict sparked by contention between court officials is in this dream transposed into a cosmic conflict between Israel

and all other nations, indeed between righteous order and chaos. **11.7** The *righteous nation* is clearly Israel. **11.8** Comparison with Joel 2.2, 10–11 gives this dream an apocalyptic quality. **11.10** *God,* the first of many references to the deity in the Greek Esther, in marked contrast to the Hebrew, which makes no direct mention of the deity. *Tiny spring,* Esther. **11.12** The general import of this dream, stressing God's shaping of human history, seems clear to Mordecai, but the details will be apparent only at the end (10.4–12). **12.1–6** A plot against the king. **12.1** *Eunuchs,* men who had been castrated, were ever-present functionaries in the Persian court. **12.5** Cf. 2.21–23, a doublet of this episode, where the events are noted, but Mordecai is not *rewarded.* **12.6** *Haman,* the villain of this story, is motivated to act against Mordecai because of links with the executed eunuchs. The meaning of *Bougean* is unclear; the substitution of "Macedonian" in some Greek texts (see also 16.10) and the Hebrew's use of "Agagite" (3.1), linking him with Israel's enemies the Amalakites, suggest the term is derogatory. Haman is here presented as the enemy both of Mordecai and the Jews and of the king.

1.1–9 The king and his banquets, along with de-

erxes was enthroned in the city of Susa, 3in the third year of his reign, he gave a banquet for his Friends and other persons of various nations, the Persians and Median nobles, and the governors of the provinces. 4After this, when he had displayed to them the riches of his kingdom and the splendor of his bountiful celebration during the course of one hundred eighty days, 5at the end of the festivity[a] the king gave a drinking party for the people of various nations who lived in the city. This was held for six days in the courtyard of the royal palace, 6which was adorned with curtains of fine linen and cotton, held by cords of purple linen attached to gold and silver blocks on pillars of marble and other stones. Gold and silver couches were placed on a mosaic floor of emerald, mother-of-pearl, and marble. There were coverings of gauze, embroidered in various colors, with roses arranged around them. 7The cups were of gold and silver, and a miniature cup was displayed, made of ruby, worth thirty thousand talents. There was abundant sweet wine, such as the king himself drank. 8The drinking was not according to a fixed rule; but the king wished to have it so, and he commanded his stewards to comply with his pleasure and with that of the guests.

9 Meanwhile, Queen Vashti[b] gave a drinking party for the women in the palace where King Artaxerxes was.

Dismissal of Queen Vashti

10 On the seventh day, when the king was in good humor, he told Haman, Bazan, Tharra, Boraze, Zatholtha, Abataza, and Tharaba, the seven eunuchs who served King Artaxerxes, 11to escort the queen to him in order to proclaim her as queen and to place the diadem on her head, and to have her display her beauty to all the governors and the people of various nations, for she was indeed a beautiful woman. 12But Queen Vashti[b] refused to obey him and would not come with the eunuchs. This offended the king and he became furious. 13He said to his Friends, "This is how Vashti[b] has answered me.[c] Give therefore your ruling and judgment on this matter." 14Arkesaeus, Sarsathaeus, and Malesear, then the governors of the Persians and Medes who were closest to the king—Arkesaeus, Sarsathaeus, and Malesear, who sat beside him in the chief seats—came to him 15and told him what must be done to Queen Vashti[b] for not obeying the order that the king had sent her by the eunuchs. 16Then Muchaeus said to the king and the governors, "Queen Vashti[b] has insulted not only the king but also all the king's governors and officials" 17(for he had reported to them what the queen had said and how she had defied the king). "And just as she defied King Artaxerxes, 18so now the other ladies who are wives of the Persian and Median governors, on hearing what she has said to the king, will likewise dare to insult their husbands. 19If therefore it pleases the king, let him issue a royal decree, inscribed in accordance with the laws of the Medes and Persians so that it may not be altered, that the queen may no longer come into his presence; but let the king give her royal rank to a woman better than she. 20Let whatever law the king enacts be proclaimed in his kingdom, and thus all women will give honor to their husbands, rich and poor alike." 21This speech pleased the king and the governors, and the king did as Muchaeus had recommended. 22The king sent the decree into all his kingdom, to every province in its own language, so that in every house respect would be shown to every husband.

Esther Becomes Queen

2 After these things, the king's anger abated, and he no longer was concerned about Vashti[b] or remembered what he had said and how he had condemned her. 2Then the king's servants said, "Let beautiful and virtuous girls be sought out for the king. 3The king shall appoint officers in all the provinces of his kingdom, and they shall select beautiful young virgins to be brought to the harem in Susa, the capital. Let them be entrusted to the king's eu-

---

a Gk marriage feast b Gk Astin c Gk Astin has said thus and so

---

scriptions of the palace and extent of the empire, set an opulent stage for this story of court intrigue. The king in the Hebrew Esther is Xerxes (486–465 BCE); the king here is identified as Artaxerxes, either I (465–424) or II (404–358). **1.10–22** Dismissal of Queen Vashti. Although summoned not only to display her beauty, as in the Hebrew version, but also to be proclaimed queen and crowned with the diadem, Vashti disobeys the king, sparking a potential crisis from the males' point of view. Her disappearance clears the stage for Esther. **2.1–18** Esther becomes queen. **2.1** In the Hebrew the king's remembering Vashti launches the

nuch who is in charge of the women, and let ointments and whatever else they need be given them. [4]And the woman who pleases the king shall be queen instead of Vashti."[a] This pleased the king, and he did so.

5 Now there was a Jew in Susa the capital whose name was Mordecai son of Jair son of Shimei[b] son of Kish, of the tribe of Benjamin; [6]he had been taken captive from Jerusalem among those whom King Nebuchadnezzar of Babylon had captured. [7]And he had a foster child, the daughter of his father's brother, Aminadab, and her name was Esther. When her parents died, he brought her up to womanhood as his own. The girl was beautiful in appearance. [8]So, when the decree of the king was proclaimed, and many girls were gathered in Susa the capital in custody of Gai, Esther also was brought to Gai, who had custody of the women. [9]The girl pleased him and won his favor, and he quickly provided her with ointments and her portion of food,[c] as well as seven maids chosen from the palace; he treated her and her maids with special favor in the harem. [10]Now Esther had not disclosed her people or country, for Mordecai had commanded her not to make it known. [11]And every day Mordecai walked in the courtyard of the harem, to see what would happen to Esther.

12 Now the period after which a girl was to go to the king was twelve months. During this time the days of beautification are completed—six months while they are anointing themselves with oil of myrrh, and six months with spices and ointments for women. [13]Then she goes in to the king; she is handed to the person appointed, and goes with him from the harem to the king's palace. [14]In the evening she enters and in the morning she departs to the second harem, where Gai the king's eunuch is in charge of the women; and she does not go in to the king again unless she is summoned by name.

15 When the time was fulfilled for Esther daughter of Aminadab, the brother of Mordecai's father, to go in to the king, she neglected none of the things that Gai, the eunuch in charge of the women, had commanded. Now Esther found favor in the eyes of all who saw her. [16]So Esther went in to King Artaxerxes in the twelfth month, which is Adar, in the seventh year of his reign. [17]And the king loved Esther and she found favor beyond all the other virgins, so he put on her the queen's diadem. [18]Then the king gave a banquet lasting seven days for all his Friends and the officers to celebrate his marriage to Esther; and he granted a remission of taxes to those who were under his rule.

The Plot Discovered

19 Meanwhile Mordecai was serving in the courtyard. [20]Esther had not disclosed her country—such were the instructions of Mordecai; but she was to fear God and keep his laws, just as she had done when she was with him. So Esther did not change her mode of life.

21 Now the king's eunuchs, who were chief bodyguards, were angry because of Mordecai's advancement, and they plotted to kill King Artaxerxes. [22]The matter became known to Mordecai, and he warned Esther, who in turn revealed the plot to the king. [23]He investigated the two eunuchs and hanged them. Then the king ordered a memorandum to be deposited in the royal library in praise of the goodwill shown by Mordecai.

Mordecai Refuses to Do Obeisance

3 After these events King Artaxerxes promoted Haman son of Hammedatha, a Bougean, advancing him and granting him precedence over all the king's[d] Friends. [2]So all who were at court used to do obeisance to

---

a Gk *Astin* *b* Gk *Semeios* *c* Gk lacks *of food* *d* Gk *all his*

---

search for a replacement; here he forgets her. **2.5–6** A second introduction of Mordecai; see 11.2–4. **2.7** The Greek names Esther's father *Aminadab* (cf. the Hebrew's Abihail, 2.15) and fails to mention her Jewish name Hadassah. **2.9** Presumably the *portion of food* was not kosher (cf. 14.17). **2.18** This second in a series of banquets marking critical events in the story celebrates Esther's appointment as queen (see 1.10). **2.19–23** The plot discovered. This may be a second plot, not a repetition of 12.1–6, although the second episode is

an almost exact repetition of the first. **2.20** Unlike in the Hebrew, Mordecai's instructions to Esther include that she is *to fear God and keep his laws* (see 2.10; 14.17). **2.21–23** Mordecai's previous advancement sparks this plot by the chief bodyguards. His role is noted in a *memorandum*, but he is not rewarded (see 6.1–3). **3.1–15** Mordecai's disobedience endangers the Jews. **3.1** The villain *Haman* was first met in 12.6, allied with those involved in the first plot against the king. **3.2–4** Mordecai's refusal is explained in his prayer in

Haman,[a] for so the king had commanded to be done. Mordecai, however, did not do obeisance. [3] Then the king's courtiers said to Mordecai, "Mordecai, why do you disobey the king's command?" [4] Day after day they spoke to him, but he would not listen to them. Then they informed Haman that Mordecai was resisting the king's command. Mordecai had told them that he was a Jew. [5] So when Haman learned that Mordecai was not doing obeisance to him, he became furiously angry, [6] and plotted to destroy all the Jews under Artaxerxes' rule.

[7] In the twelfth year of King Artaxerxes Haman[b] came to a decision by casting lots, taking the days and the months one by one, to fix on one day to destroy the whole race of Mordecai. The lot fell on the fourteenth[c] day of the month of Adar.

Decree against the Jews

[8] Then Haman[b] said to King Artaxerxes, "There is a certain nation scattered among the other nations in all your kingdom; their laws are different from those of every other nation, and they do not keep the laws of the king. It is not expedient for the king to tolerate them. [9] If it pleases the king, let it be decreed that they are to be destroyed, and I will pay ten thousand talents of silver into the king's treasury." [10] So the king took off his signet ring and gave it to Haman to seal the decree[d] that was to be written against the Jews. [11] The king told Haman, "Keep the money, and do whatever you want with that nation."

[12] So on the thirteenth day of the first month the king's secretaries were summoned, and in accordance with Haman's instructions they wrote in the name of King Artaxerxes to the magistrates and the governors in every province from India to Ethiopia. There were one hundred twenty-seven provinces in all, and the governors were addressed each in his own language. [13] Instructions were sent by couriers throughout all the empire of Artaxerxes to destroy the Jewish people on a given day of the twelfth month, which is Adar, and to plunder their goods.

Addition B

The King's Letter

13 [e] This is a copy of the letter: "The Great King, Artaxerxes, writes the following to the governors of the hundred twenty-seven provinces from India to Ethiopia and to the officials under them:

[2] "Having become ruler of many nations and master of the whole world (not elated with presumption of authority but always acting reasonably and with kindness), I have determined to settle the lives of my subjects in lasting tranquility and, in order to make my kingdom peaceable and open to travel throughout all its extent, to restore the peace desired by all people.

[3] "When I asked my counselors how this might be accomplished, Haman—who excels among us in sound judgment, and is distinguished for his unchanging goodwill and steadfast fidelity, and has attained the second place in the kingdom— [4] pointed out to us that among all the nations in the world there is scattered a certain hostile people, who have laws contrary to those of every nation and continually disregard the ordinances of kings, so that the unifying of the kingdom that we honorably intend cannot be brought about. [5] We understand that this people, and it alone, stands constantly in opposition to every nation, perversely following a strange manner of life and laws, and is ill-disposed to our government, doing all the harm they can so that our kingdom may not attain stability.

[6] "Therefore we have decreed that those indicated to you in the letters written by Haman,

a Gk him   b Gk he   c Other ancient witnesses read thirteenth; see 8.12   d Gk lacks the decree   e Chapter 13.1-7 corresponds to chapter B 1-7 in some translations.

13.12–13; later Jewish tradition said it was because Haman had affixed a small idol to his garment, so that anyone bowing down to him was effectively worshiping an idol. 3.8–13 Just as the king did not earlier investigate the case of Vashti, so now he accepts Haman's presentation of the situation without inquiring into his charges. V. 10 mentions the Jews directly.
13.1–7 The bombastic quality of the king's letter (Addition B) and its claims contrast with the opaque-

ness shown by him up to now. The letter is actually written by Haman. 13.3 I asked . . . accomplished. The king here assumes the initiative in seeking advice leading to the pogrom. This description of Haman contrasts with how readers will experience him and how the king will in time describe him in 16.1–14. 13.4–5 Jewish Torah is said here not only to set Jews apart from others but to set them against other nations. 13.6 On Haman as the king's second father, cf. Joseph's relationship to Pharaoh

who is in charge of affairs and is our second father, shall all—wives and children included—be utterly destroyed by the swords of their enemies, without pity or restraint, on the fourteenth day of the twelfth month, Adar, of this present year, [7] so that those who have long been hostile and remain so may in a single day go down in violence to Hades, and leave our government completely secure and untroubled hereafter."

END OF ADDITION B

---

3 [14] Copies of the document were posted in every province, and all the nations were ordered to be prepared for that day. [15] The matter was expedited also in Susa. And while the king and Haman caroused together, the city of Susa[a] was thrown into confusion.

Mordecai Seeks Esther's Aid

4 When Mordecai learned of all that had been done, he tore his clothes, put on sackcloth, and sprinkled himself with ashes; then he rushed through the street of the city, shouting loudly: "An innocent nation is being destroyed!" [2] He got as far as the king's gate, and there he stopped, because no one was allowed to enter the courtyard clothed in sackcloth and ashes. [3] And in every province where the king's proclamation had been posted there was a loud cry of mourning and lamentation among the Jews, and they put on sackcloth and ashes. [4] When the queen's[b] maids and eunuchs came and told her, she was deeply troubled by what she heard had happened, and sent some clothes to Mordecai to put on instead of sackcloth; but he would not consent. [5] Then Esther summoned Hachratheus, the eunuch who attended her, and ordered him to get accurate information for her from Mordecai.[c]

7 So Mordecai told him what had happened and how Haman had promised to pay ten thousand talents into the royal treasury to bring about the destruction of the Jews. [8] He also gave him a copy of what had been posted in Susa for their destruction, to show to Esther; and he told him to charge her to go in to the king and plead for his favor in behalf of the people. "Remember," he said, "the days when you were an ordinary person, being brought up under my care—for Haman, who stands next to the king, has spoken against us and demands our death. Call upon the Lord; then speak to the king in our behalf, and save us from death."

9 Hachratheus went in and told Esther all these things. [10] And she said to him, "Go to Mordecai and say, [11] 'All nations of the empire know that if any man or woman goes to the king inside the inner court without being called, there is no escape for that person. Only the one to whom the king stretches out the golden scepter is safe—and it is now thirty days since I was called to go to the king.' "

12 When Hachratheus delivered her entire message to Mordecai, [13] Mordecai told him to go back and say to her, "Esther, do not say to yourself that you alone among all the Jews will escape alive. [14] For if you keep quiet at such a time as this, help and protection will come to the Jews from another quarter, but you and your father's family will perish. Yet, who knows whether it was not for such a time as this that you were made queen?" [15] Then Esther gave the messenger this answer to take back to Mordecai: [16] "Go and gather all the Jews who are in Susa and fast on my behalf; for three days and nights do not eat or drink, and my maids and I will also go without food. After that I will go to the king, contrary to the law, even if I must die." [17] So Mordecai went away and did what Esther had told him to do.

ADDITION C

Mordecai's Prayer

13 [8 d] Then Mordecai[e] prayed to the Lord, calling to remembrance all the works of the Lord.

---

a Gk *the city*   *b* Gk *When her*   *c* Other ancient witnesses add *[6] So Hachratheus went out to Mordecai in the street of the city opposite the city gate.*   *d* Chapters 13.8—15.16 correspond to chapters C 1-30 and D 1-16 in some translations.   *e* Gk *he*

---

in Gen 45.8. The Jews are to be *utterly destroyed,* lit. "destroyed with root and branch." **13.7** *Hades,* the place of the dead, not necessarily of eternal punishment.

4.1–17 Mordecai seeks Esther's aid. **4.8** Unlike in the Hebrew, Mordecai's actual words to Esther are cited, including his request that she *call upon the Lord* as well as approach the king. **4.11** Whether or not this ban on unsummoned appearances reflects actual Persian custom, it serves to heighten the narrative tension. **4.16** Initiative now passes to Esther, but not before Mordecai and she each offer prayers to their God.

13.8–18 Mordecai's prayer (Addition C). After ap-

9 He said, "O Lord, Lord, you rule as King over all things, for the universe is in your power and there is no one who can oppose you when it is your will to save Israel, 10for you have made heaven and earth and every wonderful thing under heaven. 11You are Lord of all, and there is no one who can resist you, the Lord. 12You know all things; you know, O Lord, that it was not in insolence or pride or for any love of glory that I did this, and refused to bow down to this proud Haman; 13for I would have been willing to kiss the soles of his feet to save Israel! 14But I did this so that I might not set human glory above the glory of God, and I will not bow down to anyone but you, who are my Lord; and I will not do these things in pride. 15And now, O Lord God and King, God of Abraham, spare your people; for the eyes of our foes are upon us*a* to annihilate us, and they desire to destroy the inheritance that has been yours from the beginning. 16Do not neglect your portion, which you redeemed for yourself out of the land of Egypt. 17Hear my prayer, and have mercy upon your inheritance; turn our mourning into feasting that we may live and sing praise to your name, O Lord; do not destroy the lips*b* of those who praise you."

18 And all Israel cried out mightily, for their death was before their eyes.

Esther's Prayer

14 Then Queen Esther, seized with deadly anxiety, fled to the Lord. 2She took off her splendid apparel and put on the garments of distress and mourning, and instead of costly perfumes she covered her head with ashes and dung, and she utterly humbled her body; every part that she loved to adorn she covered with her tangled hair. 3She prayed to the Lord God of Israel, and said: "O my Lord, you only are our king; help me, who am alone and have no helper but you, 4for my danger is in my hand. 5Ever since I was born I have heard in the tribe of my family that you, O Lord, took Israel out of all the nations, and our ancestors from among all their forebears, for an everlasting inheritance, and that you did for them all that you promised. 6And now we have sinned before you, and you have handed us over to our enemies 7because we glorified their gods. You are righteous, O Lord! 8And now they are not satisfied that we are in bitter slavery, but they have covenanted with their idols 9to abolish what your mouth has ordained, and to destroy your inheritance, to stop the mouths of those who praise you and to quench your altar and the glory of your house, 10to open the mouths of the nations for the praise of vain idols, and to magnify forever a mortal king.

11 "O Lord, do not surrender your scepter to what has no being; and do not let them laugh at our downfall; but turn their plan against them, and make an example of him who began this against us. 12Remember, O Lord; make yourself known in this time of our affliction, and give me courage, O King of the gods and Master of all dominion! 13Put eloquent speech in my mouth before the lion, and turn his heart to hate the man who is fighting against us, so that there may be an end of him and those who

a Gk for they are eying us *b* Gk mouth

---

pearing twice in this introduction, the word *Lord* appears eight times in the prayer, underscoring its themes of divine power to save and human reliance on that power. **13.9–11** The prayer opens with praise of the deity as *King*, Creator, able to *save Israel*, one whom none can *resist.* **13.12–14** A confession of innocence follows in which Mordecai explains why he did not bow down to Haman. Elsewhere in the Bible Jews are depicted bowing down before kings and others (Gen 23.7; 42.6; 2 Sam 14.4; 1 Kings 1.16), and in the Diaspora Jews, like others, showed respect in this way before authorities. **13.15–17** Petition follows, in which the deity's relationship with Abraham, the election of Israel, and the exodus are all recalled. **14.1–19** Esther's prayer. Esther's deeds, like her words, are more dramatic and given in fuller detail than Mordecai's, as is appropriate for the one who now acts to save her people. Praise and petition intermix in Esther's prayer.

14.2 *Ashes and dung* nicely contrasts Esther's present distress with her royal estate. **14.5** Israel's special relationship and history with God is the basis for its hope. **14.6–7** These sins are specified only here and are formulaic; they play no part in the story. According to 4.1 the people are *innocent.* **14.8–10** This issue of worshiping God or pagan idols, even mortal kings, also appears in Judith, recalling a basic theme in Isa 40–55 and other diaspora literature. **14.9** Jews in the Diaspora as well as the homeland were concerned for the welfare of the temple in Jerusalem. **14.11** *What has no being.* Pagan gods are not simply ineffective—they do not exist. **14.12–19** From prayer for her people Esther now turns to prayer for herself, seeking support and strength in what she is about to do and understanding for her difficult position as a Jew in this foreign court. **14.12** Referring to God as *King* and *Master,* she seeks aid in going before the Persian king and master of the empire.

agree with him. [14]But save us by your hand, and help me, who am alone and have no helper but you, O Lord. [15]You have knowledge of all things, and you know that I hate the splendor of the wicked and abhor the bed of the uncircumcised and of any alien. [16]You know my necessity—that I abhor the sign of my proud position, which is upon my head on days when I appear in public. I abhor it like a filthy rag, and I do not wear it on the days when I am at leisure. [17]And your servant has not eaten at Haman's table, and I have not honored the king's feast or drunk the wine of libations. [18]Your servant has had no joy since the day that I was brought here until now, except in you, O Lord God of Abraham. [19]O God, whose might is over all, hear the voice of the despairing, and save us from the hands of evildoers. And save me from my fear!"

END OF ADDITION C

ADDITION D

Esther Is Received by the King

15 On the third day, when she ended her prayer, she took off the garments in which she had worshiped, and arrayed herself in splendid attire. [2]Then, majestically adorned, after invoking the aid of the all-seeing God and Savior, she took two maids with her; [3]on one she leaned gently for support, [4]while the other followed, carrying her train. [5]She was radiant with perfect beauty, and she looked happy, as if beloved, but her heart was frozen with fear. [6]When she had gone through all the doors, she stood before the king. He was seated on his royal throne, clothed in the full array of his majesty, all covered with gold and precious stones. He was most terrifying.

[7]Lifting his face, flushed with splendor, he looked at her in fierce anger. The queen faltered, and turned pale and faint, and collapsed on the head of the maid who went in front of her. [8]Then God changed the spirit of the king to gentleness, and in alarm he sprang from his throne and took her in his arms until she came to herself. He comforted her with soothing words, and said to her, [9]"What is it, Esther? I am your husband.[a] Take courage; [10]You shall not die, for our law applies only to our subjects.[b] Come near."

[11]Then he raised the golden scepter and touched her neck with it; [12]he embraced her, and said, "Speak to me." [13]She said to him, "I saw you, my lord, like an angel of God, and my heart was shaken with fear at your glory. [14]For you are wonderful, my lord, and your countenance is full of grace." [15]And while she was speaking, she fainted and fell. [16]Then the king was agitated, and all his servants tried to comfort her.

END OF ADDITION D

5[c] [3]The king said to her, "What do you wish, Esther? What is your request? It shall be given you, even to half of my kingdom." [4]And Esther said, "Today is a special day for me. If it pleases the king, let him and Haman come to the dinner that I shall prepare today." [5]Then the king said, "Bring Haman quickly, so that we may do as Esther desires." So they both came to the dinner that Esther had spoken about. [6]While they were drinking wine, the king said to Esther, "What is it, Queen Esther?

---

a Gk *brother*　*b* Meaning of Gk uncertain　*c* In Greek, Chapter D replaces verses 1 and 2 in Hebrew.

14.13 *The lion,* Artaxerxes. **14.15** Esther gives a defense of her violation of strictures against marriage to non-Jews as in Deut 7.3–4; such strictures are especially characteristic of the reforms of Ezra and Nehemiah (Ezra 10.2; Neh 13.23–27). **14.16** *Filthy rag,* lit. "menstruous rag," expressing in a strikingly sexist image the uncleanness of Esther's royal attire (see Lev 15.19–24). **14.17** *Not eaten at Haman's table.* Esther does all she can to avoid nonkosher food (cf. Dan 1.8–16).

15.1–5.8 Esther is received by the king. The Greek Esther presents this initial climax in a much more dramatic manner than the Hebrew, contrasting Esther's inner fear with her outer calm and radiance and her vulnerability with the terrifying splendor of the king.

15.7 In the face of the king's initial anger Esther's fainting need not be a clever act on her part to change his attitude (see v. 15). **15.8** *God . . . to gentleness.* As earlier in the Greek form of the story, God is the ultimate mover of events and even the hearts of kings (cf. 11.12). **15.9–14** The king's willingness to accept and align Esther with himself provokes her laudatory praise of him, echoing what one might say of a deity. Cf. what she said in her prayer (14.10). *Like an angel of God,* also said of David (1 Sam 29.9; 2 Sam 14.17, 20; 19.27). **5.3–8** The motive for Esther's delay in requesting that her people be saved, even though she clearly has won royal favor, is not clear, but it heightens the tension and allows space for further complications.

It shall be granted you." 7She said, "My petition and request is: 8if I have found favor in the sight of the king, let the king and Haman come to the dinner that I shall prepare them, and tomorrow I will do as I have done today."

Haman's Plot against Mordecai

9 So Haman went out from the king joyful and glad of heart. But when he saw Mordecai the Jew in the courtyard, he was filled with anger. 10Nevertheless, he went home and summoned his friends and his wife Zosara. 11And he told them about his riches and the honor that the king had bestowed on him, and how he had advanced him to be the first in the kingdom. 12And Haman said, "The queen did not invite anyone to the dinner with the king except me; and I am invited again tomorrow. 13But these things give me no pleasure as long as I see Mordecai the Jew in the courtyard." 14His wife Zosara and his friends said to him, "Let a gallows be made, fifty cubits high, and in the morning tell the king to have Mordecai hanged on it. Then, go merrily with the king to the dinner." This advice pleased Haman, and so the gallows was prepared.

Mordecai's Reward from the King

6 That night the Lord took sleep from the king, so he gave orders to his secretary to bring the book of daily records, and to read to him. 2He found the words written about Mordecai, how he had told the king about the two royal eunuchs who were on guard and sought to lay hands on King Artaxerxes. 3The king said, "What honor or dignity did we bestow on Mordecai?" The king's servants said, "You have not done anything for him." 4While the king was inquiring about the goodwill shown by Mordecai, Haman was in the courtyard. The king asked, "Who is in the courtyard?" Now Haman had come to speak to the king about hanging Mordecai on the gallows that he had prepared. 5The servants of the king answered, "Haman is standing in the courtyard." And the king said, "Summon him." 6Then the king said

to Haman, "What shall I do for the person whom I wish to honor?" And Haman said to himself, "Whom would the king wish to honor more than me?" 7So he said to the king, "For a person whom the king wishes to honor, 8let the king's servants bring out the fine linen robe that the king has worn, and the horse on which the king rides, 9and let both be given to one of the king's honored Friends, and let him robe the person whom the king loves and mount him on the horse, and let it be proclaimed through the open square of the city, saying, 'Thus shall it be done to everyone whom the king honors.' " 10Then the king said to Haman, "You have made an excellent suggestion! Do just as you have said for Mordecai the Jew, who is on duty in the courtyard. And let nothing be omitted from what you have proposed." 11So Haman got the robe and the horse; he put the robe on Mordecai and made him ride through the open square of the city, proclaiming, "Thus shall it be done to everyone whom the king wishes to honor." 12Then Mordecai returned to the courtyard, and Haman hurried back to his house, mourning and with his head covered. 13Haman told his wife Zosara and his friends what had befallen him. His friends and his wife said to him, "If Mordecai is of the Jewish people, and you have begun to be humiliated before him, you will surely fall. You will not be able to defend yourself, because the living God is with him."

Haman at Esther's Banquet

14 While they were still talking, the eunuchs arrived and hurriedly brought Haman to the 7 banquet that Esther had prepared. 1So the king and Haman went in to drink with the queen. 2And the second day, as they were drinking wine, the king said, "What is it, Queen Esther? What is your petition and what is your request? It shall be granted to you, even to half of my kingdom." 3She answered and said, "If I have found favor with the king, let my life be granted me at my petition, and my people at my request. 4For we have been sold, I

5.9–14 Haman's plot against Mordecai. The apparent honor of being included in Esther's dinner clouds Haman's judgment, causing him to seek to hasten Mordecai's destruction and later to misconstrue the king's intent (6.6). 5.14 The exaggerated height of the gallows (*fifty cubits,* 75 feet!) accents Haman's hatred.
  6.1–13 Mordecai's reward from the king. 6.1 *The Lord took sleep from the king.* Unlike in the Hebrew,

royal insomnia is clearly caused by the deity. 6.2 The reference is to the second plot of 2.21–23, not 12.1–6. 6.13 Wise after the events, Haman's wife and friends interpret this second climactic reversal as God's work and a clear sign of Haman's fall. 6.14–7.6 Haman at Esther's banquet. Any hopes that Haman's fortunes might turn again at Esther's second dinner are quickly dashed as Esther reveals to the king both her people's

and my people, to be destroyed, plundered, and made slaves—we and our children—male and female slaves. This has come to my knowledge. Our antagonist brings shame on[a] the king's court." [5]Then the king said, "Who is the person that would dare to do this thing?" [6]Esther said, "Our enemy is this evil man Haman!" At this, Haman was terrified in the presence of the king and queen.

Punishment of Haman

7 The king rose from the banquet and went into the garden, and Haman began to beg for his life from the queen, for he saw that he was in serious trouble. [8]When the king returned from the garden, Haman had thrown himself on the couch, pleading with the queen. The king said, "Will he dare even assault my wife in my own house?" Haman, when he heard, turned away his face. [9]Then Bugathan, one of the eunuchs, said to the king, "Look, Haman has even prepared a gallows for Mordecai, who gave information of concern to the king; it is standing at Haman's house, a gallows fifty cubits high." So the king said, "Let Haman be hanged on that." [10]So Haman was hanged on the gallows he had prepared for Mordecai. With that the anger of the king abated.

Royal Favor Shown the Jews

8 On that very day King Artaxerxes granted to Esther all the property of the persecutor[b] Haman. Mordecai was summoned by the king, for Esther had told the king[c] that he was related to her. [2]The king took the ring that had been taken from Haman, and gave it to Mordecai; and Esther set Mordecai over everything that had been Haman's.

3 Then she spoke once again to the king and, falling at his feet, she asked him to avert all the evil that Haman had planned against the Jews. [4]The king extended his golden scepter to Esther, and she rose and stood before the king. [5]Esther said, "If it pleases you, and if I have found favor, let an order be sent rescinding the letters that Haman wrote and

sent to destroy the Jews in your kingdom. [6]How can I look on the ruin of my people? How can I be safe if my ancestral nation[d] is destroyed?" [7]The king said to Esther, "Now that I[e] have granted all of Haman's property to you and have hanged him on a tree because he acted against the Jews, what else do you request? [8]Write in my name what you think best and seal it with my ring; for whatever is written at the king's command and sealed with my ring cannot be contravened."

9 The secretaries were summoned on the twenty-third day of the first month, that is, Nisan, in the same year; and all that he commanded with respect to the Jews was given in writing to the administrators and governors of the provinces from India to Ethiopia, one hundred twenty-seven provinces, to each province in its own language. [10]The edict was written[f] with the king's authority and sealed with his ring, and sent out by couriers. [11]He ordered the Jews in every city to observe their own laws, to defend themselves, and to act as they wished against their opponents and enemies [12]on a certain day, the thirteenth of the twelfth month, which is Adar, throughout all the kingdom of Artaxerxes.

ADDITION E

The Decree of Artaxerxes

16 [g] The following is a copy of this letter: "The Great King, Artaxerxes, to the governors of the provinces from India to Ethiopia, one hundred twenty-seven provinces, and to those who are loyal to our government, greetings.

2 "Many people, the more they are honored with the most generous kindness of their benefactors, the more proud do they become, [3]and not only seek to injure our subjects, but in their inability to stand prosperity, they even

---

a Gk *is not worthy of*   b Gk *slanderer*   c Gk *him*
d Gk *country*   e Gk *If I*   f Gk *It was written*   g Chapter 16.1–24 corresponds to chapter E 1-24 in some translations.

---

plight and its cause. **7.7–10** Punishment of Haman. **7.8** Ironically, Haman's intent is here misunderstood by the king. **7.9–10** Ironic reversal of intent and result continues as measure-for-measure justice is executed when Haman is *hanged on the gallows he had prepared for Mordecai.* **8.1–17** Royal favor shown the Jews. The reversals are completed as Mordecai (through Esther) assumes the position and estate of Haman, and, in language that recalls 3.12–14, a decree allowing the Jews to defend themselves counters the decree issued by Haman. The Jews are ordered *to observe their own laws* (v. 11), i.e., the Torah.

16.1–24 The decree of Artaxerxes (Addition E). The earlier decree lauded Haman and vilified the Jews; this decree, written by Mordecai, reverses this characterization of each. **16.2–6** The decree opens with a general

undertake to scheme against their own bene-factors. [4]They not only take away thankfulness from others, but, carried away by the boasts of those who know nothing of goodness, they even assume that they will escape the evil-hating justice of God, who always sees everything. [5]And often many of those who are set in places of authority have been made in part responsible for the shedding of innocent blood, and have been involved in irremediable calamities, by the persuasion of friends who have been entrusted with the administration of public affairs, [6]when these persons by the false trickery of their evil natures beguile the sincere goodwill of their sovereigns.

[7]"What has been wickedly accomplished through the pestilent behavior of those who exercise authority unworthily can be seen, not so much from the more ancient records that we hand on, as from investigation of matters close at hand.[a] [8]In the future we will take care to render our kingdom quiet and peaceable for all, [9]by changing our methods and always judging what comes before our eyes with more equitable consideration. [10]For Haman son of Hammedatha, a Macedonian (really an alien to the Persian blood, and quite devoid of our kindliness), having become our guest, [11]enjoyed so fully the goodwill that we have for every nation that he was called our father and was continually bowed down to by all as the person second to the royal throne. [12]But, unable to restrain his arrogance, he undertook to deprive us of our kingdom and our life,[b] [13]and with intricate craft and deceit asked for the destruction of Mordecai, our savior and perpetual benefactor, and of Esther, the blameless partner of our kingdom, together with their whole nation. [14]He thought that by

these methods he would catch us undefended and would transfer the kingdom of the Persians to the Macedonians.

[15]"But we find that the Jews, who were consigned to annihilation by this thrice-accursed man, are not evildoers, but are governed by most righteous laws [16]and are children of the living God, most high, most mighty,[c] who has directed the kingdom both for us and for our ancestors in the most excellent order.

[17]"You will therefore do well not to put in execution the letters sent by Haman son of Hammedatha, [18]since he, the one who did these things, has been hanged at the gate of Susa with all his household—for God, who rules over all things, has speedily inflicted on him the punishment that he deserved.

[19]"Therefore post a copy of this letter publicly in every place, and permit the Jews to live under their own laws. [20]And give them reinforcements, so that on the thirteenth day of the twelfth month, Adar, on that very day, they may defend themselves against those who attack them at the time of oppression. [21]For God, who rules over all things, has made this day to be a joy for his chosen people instead of a day of destruction for them.

[22]"Therefore you shall observe this with all good cheer as a notable day among your commemorative festivals, [23]so that both now and hereafter it may represent deliverance for you[d] and the loyal Persians, but that it may be a reminder of destruction for those who plot against us.

[24]"Every city and country, without exception, that does not act accordingly shall be de-

---

a Gk *matters beside* (your) *feet*   b Gk *our spirit*   c Gk *greatest*
d Other ancient authorities read *for us*

---

lesson drawn from this experience about pride, loyalty, gratitude, and deceit. **16.4** Even the king now acknowledges that human plans stand under divine judgment. **16.5–6** So far the king asserts his own innocence: he was deceived by one he trusted as friend. **16.7–16** The general lesson of vv. 1–16 is now brought to the immediate events at hand. **16.7** *Ancient records,* possibly monuments and inscriptions available for all to consult. **16.8–9** The king almost admits his guilt, or at least his negligence. His motives remain, as he stated in 13.2, the welfare and peace of the kingdom. **16.10** *Macedonian,* a reproach; cf. *Bougean* in 12.6. **16.11–13** The alien Haman, who was valued as father to the king (13.6), but plotted to kill him, is contrasted with the aliens Mordecai, who acted truly as royal *benefactor* and *savior,* and Esther, who is recognized as

a *blameless partner* in the rule of the empire (see 15.9). **16.14** That treason, not revenge for slighted honor, might have motivated Haman suggests that this is the king's view of matters, in contrast to how Mordecai and Esther would perceive Haman's plot against their co-religionists. **16.15–16** Here and in vv. 18, 21 the king again acknowledges the guiding hand of the living God, who rules all things (cf. Nebuchadnezzar in Dan 4.34–37; Cyrus in Ezra 1.2). The Torah of the Jews is declared most righteous, anticipating permission granted to the Jews (v. 19) to live by it. **16.17** The king cannot annul the earlier decree but can align himself with the Jews and allow them to defend themselves. **16.21** The designation *chosen people* carries echoes of the exodus. **16.22–23** Commemoration of the day of deliverance entails celebration for Jews and a sign to

stroyed in wrath with spear and fire. It shall be made not only impassable for human beings, but also most hateful to wild animals and birds for all time.

END OF ADDITION E

8 13"Let copies of the decree be posted conspicuously in all the kingdom, and let all the Jews be ready on that day to fight against their enemies."

14 So the messengers on horseback set out with all speed to perform what the king had commanded; and the decree was published also in Susa. 15Mordecai went out dressed in the royal robe and wearing a gold crown and a turban of purple linen. The people in Susa rejoiced on seeing him. 16And the Jews had light and gladness 17in every city and province wherever the decree was published; wherever the proclamation was made, the Jews had joy and gladness, a banquet and a holiday. And many of the Gentiles were circumcised and became Jews out of fear of the Jews.

Victory of the Jews

9 Now on the thirteenth day of the twelfth month, which is Adar, the decree written by the king arrived. 2On that same day the enemies of the Jews perished; no one resisted, because they feared them. 3The chief provincial governors, the princes, and the royal secretaries were paying honor to the Jews, because fear of Mordecai weighed upon them. 4The king's decree required that Mordecai's name be held in honor throughout the kingdom.*a* 6Now in the city of Susa the Jews killed five hundred people, 7including Pharsannestain, Delphon, Phasga, 8Pharadatha, Barea, Sarbacha, 9Marmasima, Aruphaeus, Arsaeus, Zabutheus, 10the ten sons of Haman son of Hammedatha, the Bougean, the enemy of the Jews—and they indulged*b* themselves in plunder.

11 That very day the number of those killed in Susa was reported to the king. 12The king said to Esther, "In Susa, the capital, the Jews have destroyed five hundred people. What do you suppose they have done in the surrounding countryside? Whatever more you ask will be done for you." 13And Esther said to the king, "Let the Jews be allowed to do the same tomorrow. Also, hang up the bodies of Haman's ten sons." 14So he permitted this to be done, and handed over to the Jews of the city the bodies of Haman's sons to hang up. 15The Jews who were in Susa gathered on the fourteenth and killed three hundred people, but took no plunder.

16 Now the other Jews in the kingdom gathered to defend themselves, and got relief from their enemies. They destroyed fifteen thousand of them, but did not engage in plunder. 17On the fourteenth day they rested and made that same day a day of rest, celebrating it with joy and gladness. 18The Jews who were in Susa, the capital, came together also on the fourteenth, but did not rest. They celebrated the fifteenth with joy and gladness. 19On this account then the Jews who are scattered around the country outside Susa keep the fourteenth of Adar as a joyful holiday, and send presents of food to one another, while those who live in the large cities keep the fifteenth day of Adar as their joyful holiday, also sending presents to one another.

The Festival of Purim

20 Mordecai recorded these things in a book, and sent it to the Jews in the kingdom of Artaxerxes both near and far, 21telling them that they should keep the fourteenth and fifteenth days of Adar, 22for on these days the Jews got relief from their enemies. The whole month

---

a Meaning of Gk uncertain. Some ancient authorities add verse 5, *So the Jews struck down all their enemies with the sword, killing and destroying them, and they did as they pleased to those who hated them.*   *b* Other ancient authorities read *did not indulge*

Persians, both loyal and otherwise, of the fate of those who plot against the Jews and thereby the king.

8.13 The Greek version's *fight against* is less harsh than the Hebrew's "take revenge." **8.17** Many Persians not only supported the Jews but actually *were circumcised and became Jews;* cf. the Hebrew version's "professed to be Jews." **9.1–19** Victory of the Jews. The Jews treat their enemies as they would have been treated by them. V. 5 is omitted, lessening the harshness of the original. The Greek reduces the number of dead from

seventy-five thousand to a more plausible fifteen thousand (v. 16). **9.20–10.3** The Festival of Purim. The name *Purim* (9.26) is based on the Hebrew word *Pur,* which is related to the Akkadian word for *lots,* used by Haman to determine the day for his pogrom. The emphasis on keeping the feast throughout the generations seems designed to regularize and secure a place in the Jewish calendar for a celebration that was not authorized by Torah and whose legitimacy might therefore be doubted.

(namely, Adar), in which their condition had been changed from sorrow into gladness and from a time of distress to a holiday, was to be celebrated as a time for feasting[a] and gladness and for sending presents of food to their friends and to the poor.

23 So the Jews accepted what Mordecai had written to them [24]—how Haman son of Hammedatha, the Macedonian,[b] fought against them, how he made a decree and cast lots[c] to destroy them, [25]and how he went in to the king, telling him to hang Mordecai; but the wicked plot he had devised against the Jews came back upon himself, and he and his sons were hanged. [26]Therefore these days were called "Purim," because of the lots (for in their language this is the word that means "lots"). And so, because of what was written in this letter, and because of what they had experienced in this affair and what had befallen them, Mordecai established this festival,[d] [27]and the Jews took upon themselves, upon their descendants, and upon all who would join them, to observe it without fail.[e] These days of Purim should be a memorial and kept from generation to generation, in every city, family, and country. [28]These days of Purim were to be observed for all time, and the commemoration of them was never to cease among their descendants.

29 Then Queen Esther daughter of Aminadab along with Mordecai the Jew wrote down what they had done, and gave full authority to the letter about Purim.[f] [31]And Mordecai and Queen Esther established this decision on their own responsibility, pledging their own well-being to the plan.[e] [32]Esther established it by a decree forever, and it was written for a memorial.

10 The king levied a tax upon his kingdom both by land and sea. [2]And as for his power and bravery, and the wealth and glory of his kingdom, they were recorded in the annals of the kings of the Persians and the Medes. [3]Mordecai acted with authority on behalf of King Artaxerxes and was great in the kingdom, as well as honored by the Jews. His way of life was such as to make him beloved to his whole nation.

ADDITION F

Mordecai's Dream Fulfilled

4[g] And Mordecai said, "These things have come from God; [5]for I remember the dream that I had concerning these matters, and none of them has failed to be fulfilled. [6]There was the little spring that became a river, and there was light and sun and abundant water—the river is Esther, whom the king married and made queen. [7]The two dragons are Haman and myself. [8]The nations are those that gathered to destroy the name of the Jews. [9]And my nation, this is Israel, who cried out to God and was saved. The Lord has saved his people; the Lord has rescued us from all these evils; God has done great signs and wonders, wonders that have never happened among the nations. [10]For this purpose he made two lots, one for the people of God and one for all the nations, [11]and these two lots came to the hour and moment and day of decision before God and among all the nations. [12]And God remembered his people and vindicated his inheritance. [13]So they will observe these days in the month of Adar, on the fourteenth and fifteenth[h] of that month, with an assembly and

---

a Gk of weddings   b Other ancient witnesses read the Bougean   c Gk a lot   d Gk he established (it)   e Meaning of Gk uncertain   f Verse 30 in Heb is lacking in Gk: Letters were sent to all the Jews, to the one hundred twenty-seven provinces of the kingdom of Ahasuerus, in words of peace and truth.   g Chapter 10.4-13 and 11.1 correspond to chapter F 1-11 in some translations.   h Other ancient authorities lack and fifteenth

---

10.4–13 Mordecai's dream stands fulfilled. 10.4–5 Recalling his dream, Mordecai underscores God's action. No part of what was predicted failed to be fulfilled, as he briefly details. 10.9 Signs and wonders links this story with God's saving events in the history of the Jews and especially the exodus. 10.10–11 Lots can refer to the fate set by God for Israel and the nations, fulfilled in the time appointed. According to Deut 32.9, Israel is God's lot, or portion, among the nations. 11.1 Postscript. Greek texts sometimes contained postscripts or colophons presenting date, author, and assertions of authenticity. This could be especially important for Esther, which existed in different Greek as well as Hebrew forms. Many suggest the Ptolemy referred to here is Ptolemy XII (ca. 78 BCE), although two other Ptolemies were married to a Cleopatra and ruled for at least four years. Dositheus, Ptolemy, and Lysimachus are common Greek names, although these figures are Jews; nothing specific can be added to what is claimed here about them. The designation a priest and a Levite is unusual, since they are distinct categories (cf. Lk 10.29–37). The reference to the preceding Letter about Purim refers not just to the document mentioned in 9.29 but to the Greek Esther to which this postscript is attached.

joy and gladness before God, from generation to generation forever among his people Israel."

Postscript

11 ¹In the fourth year of the reign of Ptolemy and Cleopatra, Dositheus, who said that he was a priest and a Levite,ᵃ and his son Ptolemy brought to Egyptᵇ the preced-

ing Letter about Purim, which they said was authentic and had been translated by Lysimachus son of Ptolemy, one of the residents of Jerusalem.

END OF ADDITION F

---

a Or *priest, and Levitas*   *b* Cn: Gk *brought in*

WISDOM OF SOLOMON

THE WISDOM OF SOLOMON is a hortatory discourse featuring a highly enthusiastic and eulogistic invocation of wisdom. The book is divided into three main parts. The first (1.1–6.21) is an exhortation to rulers to pursue wisdom and justice. Its central section is an exemplary story about the oppression of the just by the wicked and the ultimate triumph of the just through God's judgment. The second part (6.22–10.21), written in the first-person singular, is about the nature of wisdom as a gift from God. The final part (11.1–19.22) is an elaborate account of events in the exodus in which God uses elements of the cosmos to save the Israelites and punish the Egyptians. The final sections of the first and second parts (6.12–21; 10.1–21) serve as transitions to the following parts. As is clearly the case in 1.1–6.21 and 6.22–10.21, the fictive speaker in 11.1–19.22 is King Solomon.

Authorship, Language, and Style

THE WISDOM OF SOLOMON was written in Greek by a learned and profoundly hellenized Jew. The strongest argument for the unity of the book is based on its language and style. In spite of some Hebrew coloring, such as parallelism, Hebraisms, and the simple connection of clauses by conjunctions, the author's Greek is rich and spontaneous, and Jerome's judgment that his style is "redolent of Greek eloquence" is completely justified. The author's writing at times has the light touch of Greek lyric poetry, and he employs a wide array of Greek rhetorical figures. These characteristics, in addition to his many favorite theme words and expressions that recur throughout the book, argue for unity of authorship. The hypothesis that the Wisdom of Solomon is a translation of a Hebrew original is untenable.

Place and Date of Composition

MOST COMMENTATORS HAVE CORRECTLY ASSUMED an Egyptian origin for the book. The author's hostility toward the Egyptians (chs. 11–19), their idolatry (chs. 13–15), and worship of animals (11.15; 12.24; 13.14; 15.18–19) fits well into an Egyptian context. The level of the author's literary and philosophical education points more specifically to Alexandria as the place of composition. There is no consensus, however, regarding the date of the book, and various scholars have placed it anywhere between 250 BCE and 150 CE. The date of composition is difficult to determine because the book evinces no clear allusions to specific events. The presence

1348

of vocabulary that first appears in secular Greek literature only in the first century CE points to a period not earlier than that of Augustus (30 BCE), but the comparative paucity of Greek literature from the first century BCE makes this argument suggestive rather than probative. The desire to flatter a distant ruler (14.17) also points to the early Roman period, as does the use of the term "dominion" (*kratesis*) in 6.3, frequently used in papyri to refer to the capture of Alexandria by Augustus. The composition of the book, then, is most plausibly dated to the period between 30 BCE and 70 CE, although a date earlier in the first century BCE cannot be excluded.

Purpose and Situation

THE AUTHOR IS PRIMARILY ADDRESSING his fellow Jews in an effort to encourage them to take pride in their faith. He maintains that Jewish monotheism and morality are philosophically and ethically superior to the religious beliefs and practices of the Greeks and Egyptians. By presenting Judaism in this way, he seeks to shore up his people's faith in the face of the increasing tensions between Jews and non-Jews in Alexandria following the Roman conquest of the city in 30 BCE, tensions that broke out in violence during the anti-Jewish riots in 38 CE. He also writes for the educated Jews who were attracted by Greek culture and tempted to assimilate fully and give up their Judaism.

Although the author's attitude toward Egyptian religion and culture is clearly hostile, his attitude toward Greek culture is ambivalent. On the one hand, he himself is deeply hellenized and has internalized many of the viewpoints of Greek philosophy. His emphasis on the universal character of Judaism and its philosophical and ethical superiority (6.22–9.18) reflects Greek values. On the other hand, he is deeply committed to Judaism and the Jewish people. He implies that, as God protected the Jewish people at the time of the exodus (chs. 11–19), so too will he protect the Jewish community in their present situation.

Religious Ideas

THE CENTRALITY OF THE TEACHING on the immortality of the soul rather than on the resurrection of the dead represents a new emphasis in Jewish thought. It is a Greek idea and, as formulated by Plato, was a natural characteristic of the soul (*Phaedrus* 245C–E). Plato also held to the preexistence of souls, which were periodically joined to appropriate bodies (*Republic* 617E). The author of Wisdom does mention such a preexistence (8.19–20), but his emphasis lies elsewhere. Immortality is not a natural attribute of the soul but rather a gift of God granted as a reward only to the righteous (2.23–24; 3.4; 5.15; 6.17–19; 8.13, 17; 15.3).

A central figure in the Wisdom of Solomon is *Sophia,* or Woman Wisdom. Although Wisdom appears in the first and third parts of the book, she dominates the central part of the book (6.22–10.21). In her role in the creation and ordering of the cosmos and in the providential guidance of the events of history she is no innovation; rooted in ancient Near Eastern myth, she has already appeared in Prov 8.22–31 and Sir 24.1–22. New here is the strongly philosophical way in which the author describes her. Her attraction as a mediating principle was clear. She was the perfect bridge between the particular traditions of Israel and the Greek universalist philosophical tradition that appealed so strongly to the author and to other educated Jews of Alexandria.

In sketching his own spiritual odyssey, the author confesses to a passion for Sophia that had gripped him from early youth and had led him to cast his lot with her forever. One has the impression here of more than mere literary artifice; readers are confronting a genuine religious experience that has enveloped the author's mind and soul and filled him with the divine presence (8.2–3). His unbridled love for Wisdom is vividly reflected in his magnificent fivefold description of her essence, in which she is conceived as an eternal emanation of God's power and glory (7.25–26, 29–30).

Moreover, the author is convinced that this experience is open to all and offers himself as a living paradigm for others to follow. In thus detailing his spiritual odyssey, he strikes a religious chord new to Hebrew wisdom writings, echoing a type of religiosity characteristic of the contemporary Isis mysteries in the pagan world and the Dead Sea sect within the Jewish world. In contrast to both, however, he disdains the path of esotericism, conveying instead the openness of wisdom's path, which requires neither secret initiations nor entry into the community of a holy elect. [DAVID WINSTON, revised by THOMAS H. TOBIN]

Exhortation to Uprightness

1 Love righteousness, you rulers of the earth,
  think of the Lord in goodness
  and seek him with sincerity of heart;
2 because he is found by those who do not put him to the test,
  and manifests himself to those who do not distrust him.
3 For perverse thoughts separate people from God,
  and when his power is tested, it exposes the foolish;
4 because wisdom will not enter a deceitful soul,
  or dwell in a body enslaved to sin.
5 For a holy and disciplined spirit will flee from deceit,
  and will leave foolish thoughts behind,
  and will be ashamed at the approach of unrighteousness.

6 For wisdom is a kindly spirit,
  but will not free blasphemers from the guilt of their words;
  because God is witness of their inmost feelings,
  and a true observer of their hearts, and a hearer of their tongues.
7 Because the spirit of the Lord has filled the world,
  and that which holds all things together knows what is said,
8 therefore those who utter unrighteous things will not escape notice,
  and justice, when it punishes, will not pass them by.
9 For inquiry will be made into the counsels of the ungodly,
  and a report of their words will come to the Lord,
  to convict them of their lawless deeds;
10 because a jealous ear hears all things,
  and the sound of grumbling does not go unheard.
11 Beware then of useless grumbling,
  and keep your tongue from slander;
  because no secret word is without result,[a]
  and a lying mouth destroys the soul.

a Or will go unpunished

1.1–6.21 The first part of the book has a chiastic, or concentric, structure: 1.1–15 (A) and 6.1–21 (A′) are exhortations to rulers to seek uprightness (A) and wisdom (A′); 1.16–2.24 (B) and 4.20–5.23 (B′) contain the defense by the ungodly of their decision to persecute the just (B) and their confession of their error in doing this (B′); 3.1–4.19 (C) is the central section and contains disproof of that defense and proof of the integrity of the just. It draws heavily on the scriptural motif of the persecution and vindication of the just person (Pss 27; 35; 37; 38; 86; 109; Isa 52.13–53.12; Dan 12.1–3). 1.1–15 This exhortation (A; see note on 1.1–6.21) introduces many of the key themes and motifs of the book: righteousness assures wisdom and immortality; wickedness leads to death. 1.1 The author writes as if he were King Solomon (9.7–8, 12) addressing fellow kings, *you rulers of the earth*; in fact, the book is addressed to the author's Jewish audience. 1.3–10 *Power* (v. 3), *wisdom* (v. 4), *holy . . . spirit*, the divine tutor (v. 5), *spirit of the Lord* (v. 7), *justice* (v. 8), and *jealous ear* (v. 10) all speak of differing aspects of God. 1.6 *Kindly spirit*, lit. "lover of humanity," a Greek expression. 1.7 *That which holds all things together*, a Stoic expression adopted here to describe the spirit that holds the cosmos in existence (Diogenes Laertius, *Lives of Eminent Philosophers* 7.148). 1.10 *Grumbling* recalls the rebellion of Israel in

12 Do not invite death by the error of your
　　life,
　or bring on destruction by the works of
　　your hands;
13 because God did not make death,
　and he does not delight in the death of
　　the living.
14 For he created all things so that they
　　might exist;
　the generative forces[a] of the world are
　　wholesome,
　and there is no destructive poison in
　　them,
　and the dominion[b] of Hades is not on
　　earth.
15 For righteousness is immortal.

Life as the Ungodly See It

16 But the ungodly by their words and deeds
　　summoned death;[c]
　considering him a friend, they pined away
　and made a covenant with him,
　because they are fit to belong to his
　　company.

2 For they reasoned unsoundly, saying to
　　themselves,
　"Short and sorrowful is our life,
　and there is no remedy when a life comes
　　to its end,
　and no one has been known to return
　　from Hades.
2 For we were born by mere chance,
　and hereafter we shall be as though we
　　had never been,
　for the breath in our nostrils is smoke,
　and reason is a spark kindled by the
　　beating of our hearts;

3 when it is extinguished, the body will
　　turn to ashes,
　and the spirit will dissolve like empty air.
4 Our name will be forgotten in time,
　and no one will remember our works;
　our life will pass away like the traces of a
　　cloud,
　and be scattered like mist
　that is chased by the rays of the sun
　and overcome by its heat.
5 For our allotted time is the passing of a
　　shadow,
　and there is no return from our death,
　because it is sealed up and no one turns
　　back.

6 "Come, therefore, let us enjoy the good
　　things that exist,
　and make use of the creation to the full as
　　in youth.
7 Let us take our fill of costly wine and
　　perfumes,
　and let no flower of spring pass us by.
8 Let us crown ourselves with rosebuds
　　before they wither.
9 Let none of us fail to share in our revelry;
　everywhere let us leave signs of
　　enjoyment,
　because this is our portion, and this our
　　lot.
10 Let us oppress the righteous poor man;
　let us not spare the widow
　or regard the gray hairs of the aged.
11 But let our might be our law of right,
　for what is weak proves itself to be useless.

_____

a Or *the creatures*　*b* Or *palace*　*c* Gk *him*

_____

the desert (Ex 15–17; Num 17.5–10), which epitomizes all rebellion against God. **1.12–13** *Death,* the lot of the sinner, is eternal separation from God; the author of Wisdom pays little attention to the reality of physical death. **1.14** *Hades* is personified (Job 38.17; Rev 6.8; 20.14). **1.15** Immortality is not a natural quality, but dependent on living in conformity with God's will, i.e., according to righteousness (v. 1). **1.16–2.24** In this section (B; see note on 1.1–6.21), the author allows the wicked to speak for themselves in the manner of the Hellenistic diatribe, a popular philosophical discourse often making use of an imaginary adversary. The pessimistic tone is a frequent feature of the popular thought and poetry of Hellenistic and Imperial times. **1.16** The wicked *covenant* with Death (Isa 28.15). Their *pining* for Death is exemplified in *Apocalypse of Abraham* 13, 23, and in the Dead Sea Scrolls *War Scroll* (1QM) it is repeatedly stated that the wicked are at-

tached to Belial (Satan) because their desire is for him (13.12; 15.9; 17.4). **2.1** *Short and sorrowful is our life,* a commonplace human lament (Job 14.1–2; Lucretius, *On the Nature of Things* 3.914–15). **2.2** *Chance* played an important role in Epicurean cosmology. In a Greek epitaph from the third century BCE we read, "Like animals we are pulled hither and thither by chance, in life as in death." A similar thought is prominent in Ecclesiastes, where the Hebrew word *miqreh* ("fate") refers to the common fate awaiting all, death, the timing of which is utterly concealed from human understanding (Eccl 2.14; 3.19; 9.2). The Stoics conceived of the soul as *a spark,* a fiery breath. **2.4** Plato refers to the childish fear that, when the soul leaves the body, it will be blown away and *scattered* by the wind (*Phaedo* 77D). **2.6** *Let us enjoy,* a popular motif (Isa 22.13; Eccl 9.7; Horace, *Odes* 1.11.8, *carpe diem,* Latin, "seize the day"). **2.9** *Our portion,* a prominent motif in Ecclesiastes (2.10; 3.22; 9.9).

12 "Let us lie in wait for the righteous man,
    because he is inconvenient to us and
        opposes our actions;
    he reproaches us for sins against the law,
    and accuses us of sins against our
        training.
13 He professes to have knowledge of God,
    and calls himself a child[a] of the Lord.
14 He became to us a reproof of our
        thoughts;
15 the very sight of him is a burden to us,
    because his manner of life is unlike that
        of others,
    and his ways are strange.
16 We are considered by him as something
        base,
    and he avoids our ways as unclean;
    he calls the last end of the righteous happy,
    and boasts that God is his father.
17 Let us see if his words are true,
    and let us test what will happen at the
        end of his life;
18 for if the righteous man is God's child, he
        will help him,
    and will deliver him from the hand of his
        adversaries.
19 Let us test him with insult and torture,
    so that we may find out how gentle he is,
    and make trial of his forbearance.
20 Let us condemn him to a shameful death,
    for, according to what he says, he will be
        protected."

Error of the Wicked

21 Thus they reasoned, but they were led
        astray,
    for their wickedness blinded them,

22 and they did not know the secret
        purposes of God,
    nor hoped for the wages of holiness,
    nor discerned the prize for blameless souls;
23 for God created us for incorruption,
    and made us in the image of his own
        eternity,[b]
24 but through the devil's envy death
        entered the world,
    and those who belong to his company
        experience it.

The Destiny of the Righteous

3 But the souls of the righteous are in the
        hand of God,
    and no torment will ever touch them.
2 In the eyes of the foolish they seemed to
        have died,
    and their departure was thought to be a
        disaster,
3 and their going from us to be their
        destruction;
    but they are at peace.
4 For though in the sight of others they
        were punished,
    their hope is full of immortality.
5 Having been disciplined a little, they will
        receive great good,
    because God tested them and found them
        worthy of himself;
6 like gold in the furnace he tried them,
    and like a sacrificial burnt offering he
        accepted them.
7 In the time of their visitation they will
        shine forth,

---

a Or servant   b Other ancient authorities read nature

2.12–20 The description of the suffering and vindication of the *child of the Lord* (v. 13) is based on the fourth servant song in Isaiah (52.13–53.12). The early church fathers saw in this description a prophecy of Christ's Passion. **2.17** When Joseph's brothers plot his death, they similarly say, "Let us kill him . . . and we shall see what will become of his dreams" (Gen 37.20). **2.22** *The secret purposes of God.* The doctrine of the afterlife is referred to as a mystery in 1 Cor 4.1–5; 15.51; *1 Enoch* 103.2; and in the Dead Sea Scrolls *Book of Mysteries* (1Q27) 1.3–4.

3.1–4.19 The central section of this part of the book (C; see note on 1.1–6.21) contains three antithetical portraits, or diptychs, contrasting the righteous with the ungodly. The first diptych (3.1–13a) contrasts the destinies of the righteous and the ungodly; the second (3.13b–4.6) deals with the issue of sterility and progeny; and the third (4.7–19) deals with the issue of pre-

mature death. All three contrasts show the superiority of the righteous over the wicked. **3.1–13a** The first contrast (see note on 3.1–4.19) is between the destinies of the righteous (3.1–9) and the ungodly (3.10–13a). The author is deliberately vague about the precise timing and location of the postmortem events he describes. He may have envisaged the temporary abode of all souls in Sheol until the final judgment, as in *1 Enoch* 22, or else thought that the judgment takes place immediately after death. **3.1** The Greek doctrine of the immortality of the soul is already found in *1 Enoch* 102–105; and later in 4 Macc 18.23; Philo, *On Abraham* 258; Josephus, *War* 3.372; 7.343–50. **3.5** The notion of brief chastisement followed by *great good* (Isa 54.7–8) is elaborated by the author of 2 Maccabees (6.12) to justify the calamities of the persecution by Antiochus IV Epiphanes. **3.7** *Shine forth.* The future starlike brilliance of the righteous and their judging and governing

and will run like sparks through the
      stubble.
8 They will govern nations and rule over
      peoples,
   and the Lord will reign over them forever.
9 Those who trust in him will understand
      truth,
   and the faithful will abide with him in love,
   because grace and mercy are upon his
      holy ones,
   and he watches over his elect.[a]

The Destiny of the Ungodly

10 But the ungodly will be punished as their
      reasoning deserves,
   those who disregarded the righteous[b]
   and rebelled against the Lord;
11 for those who despise wisdom and
      instruction are miserable.
   Their hope is vain, their labors are
      unprofitable,
   and their works are useless.
12 Their wives are foolish, and their children
      evil;
13 their offspring are accursed.

On Childlessness

   For blessed is the barren woman who is
      undefiled,
   who has not entered into a sinful union;
   she will have fruit when God examines
      souls.
14 Blessed also is the eunuch whose hands
      have done no lawless deed,
   and who has not devised wicked things
      against the Lord;
   for special favor will be shown him for
      his faithfulness,
   and a place of great delight in the temple
      of the Lord.

15 For the fruit of good labors is renowned,
   and the root of understanding does not
      fail.
16 But children of adulterers will not come
      to maturity,
   and the offspring of an unlawful union
      will perish.
17 Even if they live long they will be held of
      no account,
   and finally their old age will be without
      honor.
18 If they die young, they will have no hope
   and no consolation on the day of
      judgment.
19 For the end of an unrighteous generation
      is grievous.

4 Better than this is childlessness with
      virtue,
   for in the memory of virtue[c] is
      immortality,
   because it is known both by God and by
      mortals.
2 When it is present, people imitate[d] it,
   and they long for it when it has gone;
   throughout all time it marches, crowned
      in triumph,
   victor in the contest for prizes that are
      undefiled.
3 But the prolific brood of the ungodly will
      be of no use,
   and none of their illegitimate seedlings
      will strike a deep root
   or take a firm hold.
4 For even if they put forth boughs for a
      while,

---

a Text of this line uncertain; omitted by some ancient
authorities. Compare 4.15 b Or what is right c Gk it
d Other ancient authorities read honor

---

of the nations (v. 8) is a common conception in Jewish
apocalyptic (Dan 7.22; 12.3; 2 Esd 9.97; 1 Enoch 104.2;
Testament of Abraham 1–4; Dead Sea Scrolls Commentary on Habakkuk [1QpHab] 5.4; cf. Sifre Deuteronomy
10). 3.13b–4.6 The second contrast (see note on 3.1–
4.19) shows the paradoxical superiority of virtue with
sterility (3.13b–15; 4.1–2) over wickedness with progeny (3.16–19; 4.3–6). Status in the ancient Near East
was deeply affected by the number of one's progeny.
Sexual sin was believed to result in sterility (Gen 30.23;
Ps 128; Lk 1.25; 1 Enoch 98.5; Ps.-Philo, Biblical Antiquities 50.5; Genesis Rabbah 45.4). The Wisdom of
Solomon, however, emphatically denies any necessary
connection between sin and sterility. Sterility, if pure,
will be redeemed by spiritual fertility. 3.14 The eunuch.

See Isa 56.3–5, in which the prophet refers to the Jewish
youth who were castrated at the hands of the Babylonians and consequently despaired of sharing in Israel's
future redemption (Deut 23.1). Isaiah gives them the
divine assurance of a monument and a name better
than sons or daughters. 3.16 It was believed that illegitimate children would not live long (Sir 23.25; 1 Enoch
10.9; Babylonian Talmud Yebamot 78b). 4.1 Better . . . is
childlessness with virtue strikes a Platonic note. The life
of the soul is paramount, so that physical childlessness
is of little moment, provided the soul is productive
(Plato, Symposium 208E). 4.2 The sage's contest for
virtue is contrasted with unholy athletic contests (see
4 Macc 17.11–16; Plato, Phaedrus 256B; Philo, On Husbandry 113). 4.3 Strike a deep root. See Sir 23.25.

standing insecurely they will be shaken by
    the wind,
and by the violence of the winds they will
    be uprooted.

5 The branches will be broken off before
    they come to maturity,
and their fruit will be useless,
not ripe enough to eat, and good for
    nothing.

6 For children born of unlawful unions
are witnesses of evil against their parents
    when God examines them.[a]

7 But the righteous, though they die early,
    will be at rest.

8 For old age is not honored for length of
    time,
or measured by number of years;

9 but understanding is gray hair for anyone,
and a blameless life is ripe old age.

10 There were some who pleased God and
    were loved by him,
and while living among sinners were
    taken up.

11 They were caught up so that evil might
    not change their understanding
or guile deceive their souls.

12 For the fascination of wickedness
    obscures what is good,
and roving desire perverts the innocent
    mind.

13 Being perfected in a short time, they
    fulfilled long years;

14 for their souls were pleasing to the Lord,
therefore he took them quickly from the
    midst of wickedness.

15 Yet the peoples saw and did not
    understand,
or take such a thing to heart,

that God's grace and mercy are with his
    elect,
and that he watches over his holy ones.

The Triumph of the Righteous

16 The righteous who have died will
    condemn the ungodly who are
    living,
and youth that is quickly perfected[b] will
    condemn the prolonged old age
    of the unrighteous.

17 For they will see the end of the wise,
and will not understand what the Lord
    purposed for them,
and for what he kept them safe.

18 The unrighteous[c] will see, and will have
    contempt for them,
but the Lord will laugh them to scorn.
After this they will become dishonored
    corpses,
and an outrage among the dead forever;

19 because he will dash them speechless to
    the ground,
and shake them from the foundations;
they will be left utterly dry and barren,
and they will suffer anguish,
and the memory of them will perish.

The Final Judgment

20 They will come with dread when their
    sins are reckoned up,
and their lawless deeds will convict them
    to their face.

5 Then the righteous will stand with great
    confidence
in the presence of those who have
    oppressed them

---

a Gk *at their examination* b Or *ended* c Gk *They*

4.6 *Witnesses . . . against their parents,* a widespread motif (see *Leviticus Rabbah* 23.12; Ps.-Phocylides, *The Sentences* 178; Horace, *Odes* 4.5.23; *Gospel of Philip* 78). **4.7–19** The third contrast (see note on 3.1–4.19) shows the superiority of a short life marked by virtue (4.7–15) over a long life filled with wickedness (4.16–19). Premature death is justified by viewing it as a token of God's care. The author employs the popular philosophical conceit that one's true age is not measured chronologically, but by maturity of intellect and character (see Cicero, *Tusculan Disputations* 5.5; Seneca, *Epistles* 93.2), and further resorts to a Jewish tradition that Enoch had been removed by God early to forestall the imminent perversion of his character (*Genesis Rabbah* 25.1). **4.10** *Some who . . . loved by him,*

lit. "being well pleasing to God he was dearly loved." The reference is to Enoch (Gen 5.24). We have here the first example of the author's deliberate avoidance of proper names, revealing his lack of interest in the historical differences among the biblical figures to whom he alludes; his concern is only for the manifestations of universal types such as the righteous and the wicked. The same technique is employed in Philo, *On the Virtues* 199–219, and the *Testament of Orpheus* 27–32, 41–42. **4.11** Seneca similarly consoles Marcia for the loss of her sons by noting that even noble natures do not maintain into old age the expectations of their youth (*To Marcia* 22). **4.12** *Roving desire,* a Greek expression, most likely a Stoic coinage (Marcus Aurelius, *Meditations* 2.7). **4.18** *Laugh them to scorn.* See Prov

and those who make light of their labors.

2 When the unrighteous[a] see them, they
    will be shaken with dreadful fear,
and they will be amazed at the
    unexpected salvation of the
    righteous.

3 They will speak to one another in
    repentance,
and in anguish of spirit they will groan,
    and say,

4 "These are persons whom we once held
    in derision
and made a byword of reproach—fools
    that we were!
We thought that their lives were madness
and that their end was without honor.

5 Why have they been numbered among
    the children of God?
And why is their lot among the saints?

6 So it was we who strayed from the way of
    truth,
and the light of righteousness did not
    shine on us,
and the sun did not rise upon us.

7 We took our fill of the paths of
    lawlessness and destruction,
and we journeyed through trackless
    deserts,
but the way of the Lord we have not
    known.

8 What has our arrogance profited us?
And what good has our boasted wealth
    brought us?

9 "All those things have vanished like a
    shadow,
and like a rumor that passes by;

10 like a ship that sails through the billowy
    water,
and when it has passed no trace can be
    found,
no track of its keel in the waves;

11 or as, when a bird flies through the air,
no evidence of its passage is found;
the light air, lashed by the beat of its
    pinions
and pierced by the force of its rushing
    flight,
is traversed by the movement of its wings,
and afterward no sign of its coming is
    found there;

12 or as, when an arrow is shot at a target,
the air, thus divided, comes together at
    once,
so that no one knows its pathway.

13 So we also, as soon as we were born,
    ceased to be,
and we had no sign of virtue to show,
but were consumed in our wickedness."

14 Because the hope of the ungodly is like
    thistledown[b] carried by the
    wind,
and like a light frost[c] driven away by a
    storm;
it is dispersed like smoke before the wind,
and it passes like the remembrance of a
    guest who stays but a day.

The Reward of the Righteous

15 But the righteous live forever,
and their reward is with the Lord;
the Most High takes care of them.

16 Therefore they will receive a glorious
    crown
and a beautiful diadem from the hand of
    the Lord,
because with his right hand he will cover
    them,
and with his arm he will shield them.

17 The Lord[d] will take his zeal as his whole
    armor,

---

a Gk *they* b Other ancient authorities read *dust* c Other
ancient authorities read *spider's web* d Gk *He*

1.26; Ps 2.4; *1 Enoch* 94.10; *Sifre Numbers* 117. **4.20–
5.23** A tableau of the final judgment, colored especially by the language and imagery of Isa 52.13–15;
59.16–17. This section (B′; see note on 1.1–6.21) parallels 1.16–2.24 (B), and the speech of the wicked in
5.4–13 confesses the foolishness of their speech in
2.1–20. Although this section uses imagery found in
apocalyptic literature, there is no mention of the resurrection of the dead, only the immortality of the soul.
5.1 The *great confidence* of the righteous contrasts
with the speechlessness of the wicked (4.19). **5.5** *Children of God*, lit. "sons of God," a reference to the an-

gelic host. **5.9–14** Multiple similes illustrate the author's point. Similarly, in 7.25–8.1 he employs five
metaphors to describe wisdom's origin. **5.10** *Like a
ship*. The image is of a light skiff gliding over the
water's surface and leaving no impression, like the reed
boats in Job 9.26. **5.14** *Like . . . a guest who stays but a
day*, a vivid image of the transitoriness of the wicked
(cf. Jer 14.8). **5.17–20** These verses are modeled on Isa
59.17, where God is presented as a warrior arming
himself with his own attributes for chastisement of the
wicked and deliverance of the godly. Similar imagery
appears in Rom 13.12; 2 Cor 6.7; Eph 6.14–17; *Testa-*

and will arm all creation to repel[a] his
enemies;

18 he will put on righteousness as a
breastplate,
and wear impartial justice as a helmet;

19 he will take holiness as an invincible shield,

20 and sharpen stern wrath for a sword,
and creation will join with him to fight
against his frenzied foes.

21 Shafts of lightning will fly with true aim,
and will leap from the clouds to the
target, as from a well-drawn bow,

22 and hailstones full of wrath will be hurled
as from a catapult;
the water of the sea will rage against
them,
and rivers will relentlessly overwhelm
them;

23 a mighty wind will rise against them,
and like a tempest it will winnow them
away.
Lawlessness will lay waste the whole earth,
and evildoing will overturn the thrones of
rulers.

Kings Should Seek Wisdom

6 Listen therefore, O kings, and
understand;
learn, O judges of the ends of the earth.

2 Give ear, you that rule over multitudes,
and boast of many nations.

3 For your dominion was given you from
the Lord,
and your sovereignty from the Most High;
he will search out your works and inquire
into your plans.

4 Because as servants of his kingdom you
did not rule rightly,
or keep the law,
or walk according to the purpose of God,

5 he will come upon you terribly and
swiftly,
because severe judgment falls on those in
high places.

6 For the lowliest may be pardoned in
mercy,
but the mighty will be mightily tested.

7 For the Lord of all will not stand in awe
of anyone,
or show deference to greatness;
because he himself made both small and
great,
and he takes thought for all alike.

8 But a strict inquiry is in store for the
mighty.

9 To you then, O monarchs, my words are
directed,
so that you may learn wisdom and not
transgress.

10 For they will be made holy who observe
holy things in holiness,
and those who have been taught them
will find a defense.

11 Therefore set your desire on my words;
long for them, and you will be
instructed.

Description of Wisdom

12 Wisdom is radiant and unfading,
and she is easily discerned by those who
love her,
and is found by those who seek her.

13 She hastens to make herself known to
those who desire her.

14 One who rises early to seek her will have
no difficulty,
for she will be found sitting at the gate.

15 To fix one's thought on her is perfect
understanding,
and one who is vigilant on her account
will soon be free from care,

16 because she goes about seeking those
worthy of her,
and she graciously appears to them in
their paths,
and meets them in every thought.

_____

a Or punish

---

ment of Levi 8.2. **5.20** _Creation will join with him,_ a favorite thought of the author (see also 16.17, 24; 19.6).
Similarly, in Judg 5.20 the stars join the battle against
Sisera (cf. Sir 39.28–31). **5.23** _Lawlessness_ and _evildo-_
ing, like the elements of nature just mentioned, will be
causes of great chaos and destruction.
6.1–21 An exhortation to kings to seek wisdom
with its gifts of immortality and sovereignty. This section (A´; see note on 1.1–6.21) parallels the exhortation to righteousness in 1.1–15 (A). **6.1** _Judges of the_
ends of the earth may refer to the spreading power of
Roman rule. **6.3** _Dominion_ translates a Greek term
(_kratesis_) frequently used in papyri to date the capture
of Alexandria by Augustus Caesar. **6.4–8** The mighty
will be judged more severely than the lowly because
they are God's servants and their dominion has been
given to them by God (vv. 3–4). **6.4** _The law,_ not Mosaic law, but the natural principles of justice. **6.12–**
21 This praise of wisdom serves as an appropriate
transition to the second part of the book (6.22–10.21).

17 The beginning of wisdom[a] is the most
        sincere desire for instruction,
    and concern for instruction is love of her,
18 and love of her is the keeping of her laws,
    and giving heed to her laws is assurance
        of immortality,
19 and immortality brings one near to God;
20 so the desire for wisdom leads to a
        kingdom.

21 Therefore if you delight in thrones and
        scepters, O monarchs over the
        peoples,
    honor wisdom, so that you may reign
        forever.
22 I will tell you what wisdom is and how
        she came to be,
    and I will hide no secrets from you,
    but I will trace her course from the
        beginning of creation,
    and make knowledge of her clear,
    and I will not pass by the truth;
23 nor will I travel in the company of sickly
        envy,
    for envy[b] does not associate with wisdom.
24 The multitude of the wise is the salvation
        of the world,
    and a sensible king is the stability of any
        people.

25 Therefore be instructed by my words, and
        you will profit.

Solomon Like Other Mortals

7 I also am mortal, like everyone else,
    a descendant of the first-formed child of
        earth;
    and in the womb of a mother I was
        molded into flesh,
2   within the period of ten months,
        compacted with blood,
    from the seed of a man and the pleasure
        of marriage.
3   And when I was born, I began to breathe
        the common air,
    and fell upon the kindred earth;
    my first sound was a cry, as is true of all.
4   I was nursed with care in swaddling
        cloths.
5   For no king has had a different beginning
        of existence;
6   there is for all one entrance into life, and
        one way out.

Solomon's Respect for Wisdom

7   Therefore I prayed, and understanding
        was given me;

a Gk Her beginning   b Gk this

6.17–20 A six-part chain syllogism (in Greek *sorites*) in which statements proceed step by step to a climactic conclusion, each successive statement picking up the last key word or phrase from the one before. This stylistic device is common in Greco-Roman, Indian, and Chinese literature and also occurs in ancient Egyptian and Semitic wisdom writings. 6.22–10.21 The central part of the book, written in the first-person singular (see Introduction). Although his name is never mentioned, the fictive speaker is clearly Solomon, and his speech in 7.1–8.21 has its roots in 1 Kings 3.3–15; 2 Chr 1.7–13. Wisdom is a much more prominent and complex figure in this part of the book than in either the preceding or the following part. See Prov 8.22–31; Sir 24.1–29. 6.22–25 The speaker's intention is to reveal wisdom's mysteries. In *1 Enoch* 51.3 the Elect One is said to pour forth all the secrets of wisdom, and a favorite Qumran expression is "to give knowledge in the marvelous mysteries of God" (Dead Sea Scrolls *Thanksgiving Hymns* [1QH] 4.27; 7.27; 11.9). 6.23 *Envy* is personified (as in Ovid, *Metamorphoses* 2.770–80). That *envy does not associate with wisdom* is a well-known Platonic motif (*Phaedrus* 247A; *Timaeus* 29E); it is also very prominent in Philo (*Every Good Man Is Free* 13). 6.24 This vocation of the wise to be the *salvation of the world* is frequently referred to by Philo and the rabbis. 7.1–8.21 Solomon's

speech. Like 1.1–6. 21, this section has a chiastic, or concentric, structure: 7.1–6 (A) and 8.17–21 (A′) emphasize Solomon's humanity; 7.7–14 (B) and 8.9–16 (B′) emphasize the gifts that come with wisdom; 7.15–22a (C) and 8.2–8 (C′) emphasize the connection between wisdom and knowledge; 7.22b–8.1 (D) is the central section emphasizing the cosmic characteristics of wisdom. 7.1–6 The speaker is like other human beings (A; see note on 7.1–8.21). In keeping with the Jewish view, the author emphasizes the human side of the king, unlike pagan writers, who often treated the king as divine (cf. *Letter of Aristeas* 352–63; 282). 7.1 *First-formed,* a standard epithet of Adam (cf. 1 Tim 2.13; *Testament of Abraham* A 11.9; Philo, *Questions on Exodus* 2.46; Ps.-Philo, *Biblical Antiquities* 13.8). 7.2 A widespread view in the ancient world was that pregnancy lasted *ten months.* According to Roman law, ten lunar months made up the full period of gestation. *Compacted with blood,* better "curdled"; cf. Job 10.10; Aristotle, *Generation of Animals* 739b21. That the menstrual blood is the material from which the seminal fluid produces the embryo was a common concept in ancient Greek science. *Pleasure,* part of the author's scientific description. See Aristotle, *Generation of Animals* 728a10. 7.3 *Kindred,* better "that suffers the same from all," i.e., mother earth, which all both use and misuse. 7.7–14 The speaker prays for wisdom (B; see

I called on God, and the spirit of wisdom
    came to me.
8 I preferred her to scepters and thrones,
    and I accounted wealth as nothing in
       comparison with her.
9 Neither did I liken to her any priceless
       gem,
    because all gold is but a little sand in her
       sight,
    and silver will be accounted as clay before
       her.
10 I loved her more than health and beauty,
    and I chose to have her rather than light,
    because her radiance never ceases.
11 All good things came to me along with
       her,
    and in her hands uncounted wealth.
12 I rejoiced in them all, because wisdom
       leads them;
    but I did not know that she was their
       mother.
13 I learned without guile and I impart
       without grudging;
    I do not hide her wealth,
14 for it is an unfailing treasure for mortals;
    those who get it obtain friendship with
       God,
    commended for the gifts that come from
       instruction.

Solomon Prays for Wisdom

15 May God grant me to speak with
       judgment,
    and to have thoughts worthy of what I
       have received;

for he is the guide even of wisdom
    and the corrector of the wise.
16 For both we and our words are in his
       hand,
    as are all understanding and skill in crafts.
17 For it is he who gave me unerring
       knowledge of what exists,
    to know the structure of the world and
       the activity of the elements;
18 the beginning and end and middle of
       times,
    the alternations of the solstices and the
       changes of the seasons,
19 the cycles of the year and the
       constellations of the stars,
20 the natures of animals and the tempers of
       wild animals,
    the powers of spirits *a* and the thoughts of
       human beings,
    the varieties of plants and the virtues of
       roots;
21 I learned both what is secret and what is
       manifest,
22 for wisdom, the fashioner of all things,
       taught me.

The Nature of Wisdom

There is in her a spirit that is intelligent,
       holy,
unique, manifold, subtle,
mobile, clear, unpolluted,
distinct, invulnerable, loving the good,
       keen,

a Or *winds*

note on 7.1–8.21). A passage reflecting Philo's position in its more moderate mood: one should seek wisdom for its own sake, but all other goods will inevitably follow. **7.7** *Prayed.* See 1 Kings 3.6–15; 8.12–53; Sir 51.13. **7.11** *Came to me along with her.* Cf. 1 Kings 3.13; Mt 6.33; *Song of Songs Rabbah* 1.1.9. **7.13** *Without grudging.* See Plato, *Symposium* 210A; Ps.-Aristotle, *On the Cosmos* 391a17; Xenophon, *Symposium* 4.43. **7.15–22a** The relationship of wisdom to other kinds of knowledge (C; see note on 7.1–8.21). Divine wisdom is here identified with the full range of human science and philosophy. Cf. Aeschylus, *Prometheus Bound* 436–506 and the striking parallel in Ps.-Plato, *Axiochus* 370B, where it is argued that it is only through the divine breath in the soul that such knowledge can be attained and immortality be assured. The passage is inspired by the Greek philosophical argument from design, in which God's works are seen as a manifestation of his existence and wise regime. **7.15** God is the source of wisdom, and wisdom is subordinate to God.

7.17–20 God is also the source of the human sciences and philosophy. **7.18** *Beginning and end and middle,* a phrase deriving from the Orphic theogony and one that recurs in the Hellenistic-Jewish poem *Orphica,* v. 39. **7.22a** *Fashioner.* The Stoics defined nature as "an artistically working fire going on its way to create" (Diogenes Laertius, *Lives of Eminent Philosophers* 7.156). Although clearly subordinate to God, wisdom as the "fashioner of all things" also seems to be a distinct divine reality.

7.22b–8.1 In this central section (D; see note on 7.1–8.21) the author lists the characteristics of wisdom, the relation of wisdom to God, and the relation of wisdom to creation. It is the most densely philosophical section of the Wisdom of Solomon. **7.22b–24** The characteristics of wisdom are listed in a series of twenty-one epithets borrowed largely from Greek philosophy, especially Stoic philosophy. There are numerous parallels for such serial lists in the ancient world. **7.22b** Anaxagoras (Fragment 12) describes the cosmic

irresistible, 23beneficent, humane,
steadfast, sure, free from anxiety,
all-powerful, overseeing all,
and penetrating through all spirits
    that are intelligent, pure, and altogether
        subtle.
24 For wisdom is more mobile than any
        motion;
    because of her pureness she pervades and
        penetrates all things.
25 For she is a breath of the power of God,
    and a pure emanation of the glory of the
        Almighty;
    therefore nothing defiled gains entrance
        into her.
26 For she is a reflection of eternal light,
    a spotless mirror of the working of God,
    and an image of his goodness.
27 Although she is but one, she can do all
        things,
    and while remaining in herself, she
        renews all things;
    in every generation she passes into holy
        souls
    and makes them friends of God, and
        prophets;
28 for God loves nothing so much as the
        person who lives with wisdom.
29 She is more beautiful than the sun,
    and excels every constellation of the
        stars.

Compared with the light she is found to
    be superior,
30 for it is succeeded by the night,
    but against wisdom evil does not prevail.

8 She reaches mightily from one end of the
    earth to the other,
and she orders all things well.

Solomon's Love for Wisdom

2 I loved her and sought her from my
        youth;
    I desired to take her for my bride,
    and became enamored of her beauty.
3 She glorifies her noble birth by living
        with God,
    and the Lord of all loves her.
4 For she is an initiate in the knowledge of
        God,
    and an associate in his works.
5 If riches are a desirable possession in life,
    what is richer than wisdom, the active
        cause of all things?
6 And if understanding is effective,
    who more than she is fashioner of what
        exists?
7 And if anyone loves righteousness,
    her labors are virtues;
    for she teaches self-control and prudence,
        justice and courage;
    nothing in life is more profitable for
        mortals than these.

---

mind as the most *subtle* of all things. **7.24** *Pervades and penetrates,* technical Stoic phraseology reflecting the principle of "body going through body." **7.25–26** The author employs a fivefold metaphor to emphasize the notion that wisdom is an emanation from God's power and glory—a bold move for one writing within the biblical tradition; even the more philosophically ambitious Philo backs off from such explicit terminology in describing the origin of the Logos. The use of these terms in Philo and in later Neo-Platonism may indicate that their use here reflects influence from early Middle Platonism. **7.25** *Emanation,* the earliest attestation of the explicit application of this Greek term (*aporroia*) to Sophia as an effluence from God. **7.26** Heb 1.3 refers to Christ as a *reflection* of God's glory. *Image,* a favorite Platonic metaphor. Philo speaks of the Logos as the image of God. **7.27–8.1** The relation of wisdom to creation and especially to *holy souls.* **7.27** *Remaining in herself.* Anaxagoras's cosmic mind similarly remains unmixed and motionless while moving all things (cf. Plato, *Timaeus* 42E). **7.29** According to Philo, the *sun* is only an image of wisdom, and according to his precursor Aristobulus, "All light comes from wisdom." In Ps.-Philo's *Biblical Antiquities* we read that Moses came down from the mountain covered with an invisible

light that overcame the brightness of sun and moon (12.1–3). **8.1** *From one end of the earth to the other.* Cf. the similar description in Sir 24.3–6.

8.2–8 This section (C′; see note on 7.1–8.21) parallels 7.15–22a (C) in its emphasis on the connection of wisdom with other kinds of knowledge. Solomon sought to make wisdom his bride. In rabbinic literature, Torah is imaged as the daughter of God, a bride, and a mother. The bride image is based on a midrashic reading of the Hebrew word *morashah,* "possession," in Deut 33.4 as *me'orasah,* "betrothed." This feminine depiction is connected in some texts to the metaphorical depiction of the Sinai theophany as a wedding day. Cf. Prov 7.4; Sir 15.2. Similar sexual imagery is found in Philo's *On the Preliminary Studies,* where he develops an allegory in which Abraham, the Soul, is married to Sarah, Wisdom. **8.2** *Sought her.* Cf. Ps.-Plato, *Epinomis* 989A, "For I have sought this wisdom high and low." **8.3** *Living with God.* Philo similarly writes: "With his knowledge God had union, not as men have it, and begat created being" (*On Sobriety* 30). **8.5–8** The four successive clauses beginning with *if* are an example of the author's striving for rhetorical effect. **8.7** *Self-control and prudence, justice and courage.* The four cardinal virtues go back to Plato (*Phaedo* 69C).

8 And if anyone longs for wide experience,
    she knows the things of old, and infers
        the things to come;
    she understands turns of speech and the
        solutions of riddles;
    she has foreknowledge of signs and
        wonders
    and of the outcome of seasons and times.

Wisdom Indispensible to Rulers

9 Therefore I determined to take her to live
        with me,
    knowing that she would give me good
        counsel
    and encouragement in cares and grief.
10 Because of her I shall have glory among
        the multitudes
    and honor in the presence of the elders,
        though I am young.
11 I shall be found keen in judgment,
    and in the sight of rulers I shall be
        admired.
12 When I am silent they will wait for me,
    and when I speak they will give heed;
    if I speak at greater length,
    they will put their hands on their mouths.
13 Because of her I shall have immortality,
    and leave an everlasting remembrance to
        those who come after me.
14 I shall govern peoples,
    and nations will be subject to me;
15 dread monarchs will be afraid of me
        when they hear of me;
    among the people I shall show myself
        capable, and courageous in war.
16 When I enter my house, I shall find rest
        with her;
    for companionship with her has no
        bitterness,

and life with her has no pain, but
    gladness and joy.
17 When I considered these things inwardly,
    and pondered in my heart
    that in kinship with wisdom there is
        immortality,
18 and in friendship with her, pure delight,
    and in the labors of her hands, unfailing
        wealth,
    and in the experience of her company,
        understanding,
    and renown in sharing her words,
    I went about seeking how to get her for
        myself.
19 As a child I was naturally gifted,
    and a good soul fell to my lot;
20 or rather, being good, I entered an
        undefiled body.
21 But I perceived that I would not possess
        wisdom unless God gave her to
        me—
    and it was a mark of insight to know
        whose gift she was—
    so I appealed to the Lord and implored
        him,
    and with my whole heart I said:

Solomon's Prayer for Wisdom

9 "O God of my ancestors and Lord of
        mercy,
    who have made all things by your word,
2 and by your wisdom have formed
        humankind
    to have dominion over the creatures you
        have made,
3 and rule the world in holiness and
        righteousness,
    and pronounce judgment in uprightness
        of soul,

Cf. 4 Macc 1.18. **8.9–16** This section (B´; see note on 7.1–8.21) parallels 7.7–14 (B). Both emphasize what comes with wisdom. Here the emphasis is on the capacity to rule nations wisely and well and the honor and glory among other rulers that come with it. **8.16** *Find rest,* the same idea in Sir 6.28 and a central theme in Philo. Cf. Plato, *Republic* 490B. **8.17–21** This section (A´; see note on 7.1–8.21), which parallels 7.1–6 (A), is again concerned with Solomon's humanity, but here especially with his natural endowments of soul and body. Yet even so, wisdom remains a sheer gift of God's grace. **8.17** *Kinship* with wisdom is a characteristic teaching of Plato (*Timaeus* 90A) and the Stoics. Philo takes up the theme with equal vigor. **8.19** Moses too, according to Philo, had a *naturally gifted* soul (*Life of Moses* 1.9), and in general "God drops from above

the ethereal wisdom upon minds that are naturally well endowed" (*On Flight and Finding* 138). **8.20** *I entered an undefiled body* clearly implies the notion of the soul's preexistence. Cf. *2 Enoch* 23.4–5; *2 Apocalypse of Baruch* 23.5; Philo, *On Dreams* 1.135–41. In *Testament of Naphtali* 2.2 it is said that God implants the spirit according to the capacity of the body. **8.21** *Unless God gave her to me.* So too in Ps.-Plato, *Epinomis* 989D even those naturally gifted "cannot get this teaching either, unless God gives his guidance."

9.1–18 The prayer consists of three strophes (vv. 1–6, 7–12, 13–18) chiastically arranged. The author presents his own version of Solomon's prayer (1 Kings 3.6–9; 2 Chr 1.8–10). **9.1** *By your word.* Cf. Ps 33.6; Sir 39.17; *Sibylline Oracles* 3.20. **9.2** *By your wisdom,* an emphatic theme in the Dead Sea Scrolls (cf. *2 Enoch* A 30.8).

4 give me the wisdom that sits by your
  throne,
and do not reject me from among your
  servants.
5 For I am your servant[a] the son of your
  serving girl,
a man who is weak and short-lived,
with little understanding of judgment
  and laws;
6 for even one who is perfect among
  human beings
will be regarded as nothing without the
  wisdom that comes from you.
7 You have chosen me to be king of your
  people
and to be judge over your sons and
  daughters.
8 You have given command to build a
  temple on your holy mountain,
and an altar in the city of your
  habitation,
a copy of the holy tent that you prepared
  from the beginning.
9 With you is wisdom, she who knows your
  works
and was present when you made the
  world;
she understands what is pleasing in your
  sight
and what is right according to your
  commandments.
10 Send her forth from the holy heavens,
and from the throne of your glory send
  her,
that she may labor at my side,
and that I may learn what is pleasing to
  you.

11 For she knows and understands all things,
and she will guide me wisely in my
  actions
and guard me with her glory.
12 Then my works will be acceptable,
and I shall judge your people justly,
and shall be worthy of the throne[b] of my
  father.
13 For who can learn the counsel of God?
Or who can discern what the Lord wills?
14 For the reasoning of mortals is worthless,
and our designs are likely to fail;
15 for a perishable body weighs down the
  soul,
and this earthy tent burdens the
  thoughtful[c] mind.
16 We can hardly guess at what is on earth,
and what is at hand we find with labor;
but who has traced out what is in the
  heavens?
17 Who has learned your counsel,
unless you have given wisdom
and sent your holy spirit from on high?
18 And thus the paths of those on earth were
  set right,
and people were taught what pleases you,
and were saved by wisdom."

The Work of Wisdom from Adam to Moses

10 Wisdom[d] protected the first-formed
father of the world, when he alone
had been created;
she delivered him from his transgression,
2 and gave him strength to rule all things.

_____

a Gk slave   b Gk thrones   c Or anxious   d Gk She

9.4 _Wisdom . . . sits by your throne._ In Greek literature Justice is pictured as sitting with Zeus, and the same image is frequent in Philo. **9.5** _Weak and short-lived._ Cf. 1 Chr 29.15; Philo, _Who Is the Heir_ 58. **9.6** Philo also never tires of insisting that without divine help we could accomplish nothing. **9.8** _Your holy mountain,_ Mount Moriah, which became identified with the place where Abraham was commanded to sacrifice Isaac; see 2 Chr 3.1. According to rabbinic tradition even before the creation of the world there already existed a supernal temple of which the earthly temple is a _copy_. The same notion is found in the Dead Sea Scrolls and in Heb 8–10 and is also widespread in the Pseudepigrapha. Philo too tells us that the tabernacle is a representation and copy of wisdom (_Who Is the Heir_ 112). **9.9** _When you made the world._ Cf. Prov 8.22, a verse cited both by Aristobulus and Philo. **9.10** In his famous _Hymn to Zeus,_ the Stoic philosopher Cleanthes prays that Zeus

bestow the wisdom by which he steers all things in justice. **9.13** _For who can learn._ Cf. Prov 30.2–4; Isa 40.13–14; Sir 1.1–10; Bar 3.29–37; 2 Esd 4; _1 Enoch_ 93.11–14. A similar note is already found in the Babylonian poem I Will Praise the Lord of Wisdom 36–38. **9.15** The adverse influence of the _body_ on the soul is emphatically taught by Plato in _Phaedo_ (66B). That the body _weighs down the soul_ is another widespread Platonic motif (_Phaedo_ 81C) and fairly common in Philo and the Roman Stoics. _Earthy tent,_ a Greek expression for the body, very frequent in Neo-Pythagorean writings. **9.16** This verse expresses a widespread literary conceit (Jdt 8.14; 2 Esd 4.11; Jn 3.12; _Testament of Job_ 38.5; _Babylonian Talmud Sanhedrin_ 39a).

10.1–21 Wisdom's saving and punishing power is illustrated by the enumeration of seven righteous heroes and their wicked counterparts. Events in Genesis and Exodus are reinterpreted as the providential or-

3 But when an unrighteous man departed
      from her in his anger,
he perished because in rage he killed his
      brother.
4 When the earth was flooded because of
      him, wisdom again saved it,
steering the righteous man by a paltry
      piece of wood.

5 Wisdom[a] also, when the nations in
      wicked agreement had been put
      to confusion,
recognized the righteous man and
      preserved him blameless before
      God,
and kept him strong in the face of his
      compassion for his child.

6 Wisdom[a] rescued a righteous man when
      the ungodly were perishing;
he escaped the fire that descended on the
      Five Cities.[b]
7 Evidence of their wickedness still
      remains:
a continually smoking wasteland,
plants bearing fruit that does not ripen,
and a pillar of salt standing as a
      monument to an unbelieving
      soul.
8 For because they passed wisdom by,
they not only were hindered from
      recognizing the good,
but also left for humankind a reminder of
      their folly,

so that their failures could never go
      unnoticed.
9 Wisdom rescued from troubles those who
      served her.
10 When a righteous man fled from his
      brother's wrath,
she guided him on straight paths;
she showed him the kingdom of God,
and gave him knowledge of holy things;
she prospered him in his labors,
and increased the fruit of his toil.
11 When his oppressors were covetous,
she stood by him and made him rich.
12 She protected him from his enemies,
and kept him safe from those who lay in
      wait for him;
in his arduous contest she gave him the
      victory,
so that he might learn that godliness is
      more powerful than anything else.
13 When a righteous man was sold, wisdom[c]
      did not desert him,
but delivered him from sin.
She descended with him into the
      dungeon,
14 and when he was in prison she did not
      leave him,
until she brought him the scepter of a
      kingdom
and authority over his masters.

---

a Gk She   b Or on Pentapolis   c Gk she

---

dering of Israel's history through wisdom's continuous election of righteous servants. Because he mentions no names, the author emphasizes the exemplary nature of the stories. His ode to wisdom is constructed by the use of anaphora, repetition of the same word at the beginning of successive verses. He thus introduces wisdom throughout the chapter with the emphatic Greek pronoun *haute* ("she"), which marks off six sections each of which contains the word *righteous* once (vv. 1–4, 5, 6–8, 9–12, 13–14, 15–21). See the similar use of anaphora in Acts 7.35–38; Cicero's hymn to philosophy in *Tusculan Disputations* 5.5; Seneca, *To Marcia* 20.2; and the Hellenistic aretalogies, or hymns of praise, discovered in Egypt. **10.1** *Father of the world,* Adam. See Gen 2–3. **10.3** *An unrighteous man,* Cain. *Killed his brother.* Philo thrice applies the adjective "fratricidal" to Cain. See Gen 4.3–16. **10.4** *Because of him.* As the first murderer Cain serves as a paradigm of wickedness, so that the cause of the flood can be ascribed to him. The verb translated *steering* here is also employed by Stoics to describe the guiding power of

reason. According to the midrash *Genesis Rabbah* 34.8, the stars did not function during the flood, implying that Noah's ark was piloted by God. *The righteous man,* here Noah. See Gen 6.9–8.22. **10.5** *The righteous man,* Abraham. According to *Genesis Rabbah* 38.6, Abraham was a contemporary of the generation of the Tower of Babel. See Gen 11.1–9. *His child,* Isaac. See Gen 22.1–19. **10.6** *A righteous man,* Lot. See Gen 19.1–29. **10.7** *Evidence . . . still remains.* See Gen 19.26, 28. Both Philo and Josephus speak of vestiges of the divine fire as still visible. *Fruit that does not ripen.* See Josephus, *War* 4.484; Tacitus, *Histories* 5.7. *A pillar of salt.* Josephus writes: "I have seen this pillar of salt which remains to this day" (*Antiquities* 1.203–4). The erosion of the salt mountain along the south end of the Dead Sea has caused pinnacles to stand out, which many writers have likened to Lot's wife. **10.10** *A righteous man,* Jacob. See Gen 27.41–45. *Showed him . . . holy things,* Jacob's dream at Bethel (Gen 28.10–17). **10.12** *Arduous contest,* a reference to Jacob's struggle with the angel (Gen 32.25–33). *So that he might learn.*

Those who accused him she showed to be
false,
and she gave him everlasting honor.

Wisdom Led the Israelites out of Egypt

15 A holy people and blameless race
wisdom delivered from a nation of
oppressors.
16 She entered the soul of a servant of the
Lord,
and withstood dread kings with wonders
and signs.
17 She gave to holy people the reward of
their labors;
she guided them along a marvelous way,
and became a shelter to them by day,
and a starry flame through the night.
18 She brought them over the Red Sea,
and led them through deep waters;
19 but she drowned their enemies,
and cast them up from the depth of the
sea.
20 Therefore the righteous plundered the
ungodly;
they sang hymns, O Lord, to your holy
name,
and praised with one accord your
defending hand;
21 for wisdom opened the mouths of those
who were mute,
and made the tongues of infants speak
clearly.

Wisdom Led the Israelites through the Desert

11 Wisdom[a] prospered their works by
the hand of a holy prophet.
2 They journeyed through an uninhabited
wilderness,
and pitched their tents in untrodden
places.
3 They withstood their enemies and fought
off their foes.
4 When they were thirsty, they called upon
you,
and water was given them out of flinty
rock,
and from hard stone a remedy for their
thirst.
5 For through the very things by which
their enemies were punished,
they themselves received benefit in their
need.
6 Instead of the fountain of an ever-flowing
river,
stirred up and defiled with blood
7 in rebuke for the decree to kill the
infants,
you gave them abundant water
unexpectedly,
8 showing by their thirst at that time
how you punished their enemies.

_____
a Gk She

Jacob's struggle is given a symbolic meaning. **10.13** *A righteous man*, Joseph. See Gen 37; 39–50. **10.15–21** A reinterpretation of Ex 1–15 emphasizing the role of wisdom. **10.16** *Servant of the Lord*, Moses (see Isa 63.11–14). **10.17** *The reward of their labors*, the objects of silver and gold "borrowed" by the Israelites from the Egyptians before leaving Egypt (Ex 11.2; 12.35–36; cf. Ps 105.37; *Jubilees* 48.18; Ezekiel the Tragedian, *Exagoge* 165; Philo, *Life of Moses* 1.140–42). *Shelter, starry flame*. The pillar of cloud and of fire (Ex 13.21–22) is allegorized as wisdom. **10.20** *Plundered the ungodly.* Demetrius, the earliest known Greco-Jewish writer, had already attempted to answer the question raised as to how the Israelites, who left Egypt unarmed, managed to obtain arms (cf. Josephus, *Antiquities* 2.349). *With one accord.* Cf. *2 Enoch* 19.6; *Ascension of Isaiah* 7.15; *Testament of Solomon* 18.2; *Song of Songs Rabbah* 8.15. **10.21** *Tongues of infants* alludes to an early Jewish tradition that even the infants sang God's praises (*Tosefta Sota* 6.4).

11.1–19.22 After an introduction (11.1–5), the third part of the book (see Introduction) is an elaborate *synkrisis*, or comparison, in which the author employs seven antitheses (11.6–14; 11.15–16.4; 16.5–14;

16.15–29; 17.1–18.4; 18.5–25; 19.1–9) to illustrate his theme that Egypt was punished measure for measure and Israel was benefited by the very things with which Egypt was punished. Already in the biblical account, the contrast between the fate of the Egyptians and the Israelites is clearly spelled out in five of the ten plagues. In general this part addresses God in the second-person singular. Because the author uses no proper names, the narrative has a typical or exemplary quality to it. **11.1–5** A brief narrative of the successful advance of the Israelites through the desert followed by a statement of the theme of the comparison (the Israelites are benefited by the very things that punish the Egyptians). **11.1** Better, "Their works prospered by the hand of a holy prophet." Wisdom does not play an important role in this part of the book. **11.6–14** The first antithesis (see note on 11.1–19.22): the Nile water changed to blood, but the Israelites obtained water from a desert rock. See Ex 1.15–16; 7.7–24; 17.1–7; Num 20.2–13. **11.6** *An ever-flowing river*, the Nile. **11.7** *In rebuke.* The same notion appears in *Pirke Rabbi Eliezer* 19, where it is stated that God plagued the waters of the Nile because the Egyptians had cast the children of the Israelites into it. **11.8** The author here

9 For when they were tried, though they
    were being disciplined in mercy,
they learned how the ungodly were
    tormented when judged in
    wrath.

10 For you tested them as a parent[a] does in
    warning,
but you examined the ungodly[b] as a stern
    king does in condemnation.

11 Whether absent or present, they were
    equally distressed,

12 for a twofold grief possessed them,
and a groaning at the memory of what
    had occurred.

13 For when they heard that through their
    own punishments
the righteous[c] had received benefit, they
    perceived it was the Lord's
    doing.

14 For though they had mockingly rejected
    him who long before had been
    cast out and exposed,
at the end of the events they marveled at
    him,
when they felt thirst in a different way
    from the righteous.

Punishment of the Wicked

15 In return for their foolish and wicked
    thoughts,
which led them astray to worship
    irrational serpents and worthless
    animals,

you sent upon them a multitude of
    irrational creatures to punish
    them,

16 so that they might learn that one is
    punished by the very things by
    which one sins.

17 For your all-powerful hand,
which created the world out of formless
    matter,
did not lack the means to send upon
    them a multitude of bears, or
    bold lions,

18 or newly-created unknown beasts full of
    rage,
or such as breathe out fiery breath,
or belch forth a thick pall of smoke,
or flash terrible sparks from their eyes;

19 not only could the harm they did destroy
    people,[d]
but the mere sight of them could kill by
    fright.

20 Even apart from these, people[c] could fall
    at a single breath
when pursued by justice
and scattered by the breath of your power.
But you have arranged all things by
    measure and number and weight.

God Is Powerful and Merciful

21 For it is always in your power to show
    great strength,

---

a Gk *a father*   b Gk *those*   c Gk *they*   d Gk *them*

---

enunciates a principle that recurs in 16.4, that it was pedagogically necessary that the Israelites have a taste of their enemies' punishments. **11.9** *Tried.* See Deut 8.2–5. **11.11** The Egyptians suffered both when the Israelites were *present* with them in Egypt (they were afflicted by the plagues) and when the Israelites were *absent* from them in the wilderness (they were overwhelmed in the sea). **11.12** They were pained *twofold,* both at their own calamity and by the fact that it brought deliverance to the Israelites.

11.15–16.4 The second antithesis (see note on 11.1–19.22): the Egyptians hunger through animal plagues, but Israel enjoys exotic quail food. See Ex 8.1–19; 9.1–7; Num 11. This section is interrupted by two excursuses (11.17–12.22; 13.1–15.19). **11.15–16** A restatement of 11.5 referring to the role of irrational animals. **11.15** *Irrational serpents and worthless animals.* Cf. *Letter of Aristeas* 138; Philo, *On the Decalogue* 76–80. Roman ridicule of Egyptian animal worship is best illustrated by Octavian's remark when he was asked if he would like to visit the Apis bull: "My custom is to worship gods, not cattle" (Dio Cassius, *Roman History* 51.16.5). **11.16** The law of retaliation occurs three times in the

Pentateuch (Ex 21.23–25; Lev 24.18–20; Deut 19.21) and appears frequently in the Pseudepigrapha. The rabbis were equally fond of elaborating this principle (*Tosefta Sota* 3–4). **11.17–12.22** The first excursus (see note on 11.15–16.4) deals with the nature and purpose of divine mercy. The Egyptians could have been smashed with one blow, but God never acts arbitrarily. His omnipotence guarantees his all-embracing love, and his very act of creation is a manifestation of this love, precluding the possibility of hatred toward any of his creatures. This section includes an attempt to justify the Israelite conquest of Canaan (12.3–18). **11.17** The doctrine is Platonic, but for the terminology of *formless matter,* see Aristotle, *Physics* 191a10; Posidonius Fragment 92. Philo raises the same question as this author about whether God *lacks the means* to create, and his first answer is similar to that given in v. 23 (*Life of Moses* 1.109–12). **11.20** *By measure and number and weight.* God's actions always follow the mathematical laws by which he governs the entire cosmos. Disproportionate punishments such as those described in vv. 17–19 are therefore ruled out. Cf. Job 28.25; Isa 40.12; 2 Esd 4.36–37; *Testament of Naphtali* 2.3. Philo placed special em-

and who can withstand the might of your
    arm?
22 Because the whole world before you is
    like a speck that tips the scales,
    and like a drop of morning dew that falls
      on the ground.
23 But you are merciful to all, for you can do
    all things,
    and you overlook people's sins, so that
      they may repent.
24 For you love all things that exist,
    and detest none of the things that you
      have made,
    for you would not have made anything if
      you had hated it.
25 How would anything have endured if you
    had not willed it?
    Or how would anything not called forth
      by you have been preserved?
26 You spare all things, for they are yours,
    O Lord, you who love the living.

12 For your immortal spirit is in all
    things.
2 Therefore you correct little by little those
    who trespass,
    and you remind and warn them of the
      things through which they sin,
    so that they may be freed from
      wickedness and put their trust in
      you, O Lord.

The Sins of the Canaanites

3 Those who lived long ago in your holy
    land
4 you hated for their detestable practices,
    their works of sorcery and unholy rites,
5 their merciless slaughter*a* of children,
    and their sacrificial feasting on human
      flesh and blood.

These initiates from the midst of a
    heathen cult,*b*
6 these parents who murder helpless lives,
    you willed to destroy by the hands of our
      ancestors,
7 so that the land most precious of all to you
    might receive a worthy colony of the
      servants*c* of God.
8 But even these you spared, since they
    were but mortals,
    and sent wasps*d* as forerunners of your
      army
    to destroy them little by little,
9 though you were not unable to give the
      ungodly into the hands of the
      righteous in battle,
    or to destroy them at one blow by dread
      wild animals or your stern word.
10 But judging them little by little you gave
      them an opportunity to repent,
    though you were not unaware that their
      origin*e* was evil
    and their wickedness inborn,
    and that their way of thinking would
      never change.
11 For they were an accursed race from the
      beginning,
    and it was not through fear of anyone
      that you left them unpunished for
      their sins.

God Is Sovereign

12 For who will say, "What have you done?"
    or will resist your judgment?
    Who will accuse you for the destruction
      of nations that you made?

a Gk *slaughterers* *b* Meaning of Gk uncertain *c* Or *children*
d Or *hornets* *e* Or *nature*

---

phasis on this notion (*On Dreams* 2.193; cf. Plato, *Laws* 575B). **11.22** Cf. Isa 40.15. **11.24** *Detest none . . . that you have made.* Cf. Sir 15.11. This view is in sharp contrast with that of the Dead Sea sect.

12.3–18 An attempt to justify the Israelite conquest of Canaan. In Jewish-Hellenistic apologetics, this issue occupied no small place. The author of *Jubilees* rewrote Genesis to prove that the land of Canaan was originally allotted to Shem and illegally seized by Canaan (8.8–11; 9.14–15; 10.29–34; cf. *Genesis Rabbah* 56.14), and Philo's account of the conquest of Canaan is openly apologetic (*Hypothetica* 6.5; *Special Laws* 2.170). **12.3** *Holy land.* For this designation, see Zech 2.12; 2 Macc 1.7; 2 Esd 13.48; Ps.-Philo, *Biblical Antiquities* 19.20; *2 Apocalypse of Baruch* 63.10; *Testament of Job* 33.5, where it is a metaphor for heaven.

12.5 *Slaughter of children.* The sacrifices of Molech described in the Bible (Lev 18.21; 20.2–5) are identical with the *molk* sacrifices in North Africa and were kept up for a very long time. There is also evidence of human sacrifice in Egypt during the Roman period. *Sacrificial,* lit. "entrail-devouring." The charge of *feasting on human flesh and blood* appears to be an exaggeration and turns the tables on those who, like Damocritus and Apion, had hurled the charge of cannibalism against the Jews. **12.8** *Wasps.* See text note *d; see also* Ex 23.28, text note *a.* **12.10** *Their origin was evil.* A similar notion is found in 2 Esd 4.30. **12.11** *Accursed race* refers to the curse laid upon Canaan (Gen 9.25–27), but there is no hint in the biblical text of a curse that entails moral degeneracy. Cf. Wis 3.12–13; Sir 33.12; *Jubilees* 22.20–21. **12.12** See Job 9.12; Eccl 8.4; Dan

Or who will come before you to plead as
    an advocate for the unrighteous?

13 For neither is there any god besides you,
        whose care is for all people,[a]
to whom you should prove that you have
        not judged unjustly;

14 nor can any king or monarch confront
        you about those whom you have
        punished.

15 You are righteous and you rule all things
        righteously,
deeming it alien to your power
to condemn anyone who does not
        deserve to be punished.

16 For your strength is the source of
        righteousness,
and your sovereignty over all causes you
        to spare all.

17 For you show your strength when people
        doubt the completeness of your
        power,
and you rebuke any insolence among
        those who know it.[b]

18 Although you are sovereign in strength,
        you judge with mildness,
and with great forbearance you govern us;
for you have power to act whenever you
        choose.

God's Lessons for Israel

19 Through such works you have taught
        your people
that the righteous must be kind,
and you have filled your children with
        good hope,
because you give repentance for sins.

20 For if you punished with such great care
        and indulgence[c]
the enemies of your servants[d] and those
        deserving of death,
granting them time and opportunity to
        give up their wickedness,

21 with what strictness you have judged
        your children,
to whose ancestors you gave oaths and
        covenants full of good promises!

22 So while chastening us you scourge our
        enemies ten thousand times
        more,
so that, when we judge, we may meditate
        upon your goodness,
and when we are judged, we may expect
        mercy.

The Punishment of the Egyptians

23 Therefore those who lived unrighteously,
        in a life of folly,
you tormented through their own
        abominations.

24 For they went far astray on the paths of
        error,
accepting as gods those animals that even
        their enemies[e] despised;
they were deceived like foolish infants.

25 Therefore, as though to children who
        cannot reason,
you sent your judgment to mock them.

26 But those who have not heeded the
        warning of mild rebukes
will experience the deserved judgment of
        God.

27 For when in their suffering they became
        incensed
at those creatures that they had thought
        to be gods, being punished by
        means of them,
they saw and recognized as the true God
        the one whom they had before
        refused to know.
Therefore the utmost condemnation
        came upon them.

The Foolishness of Nature Worship

13 For all people who were ignorant of
        God were foolish by nature;
and they were unable from the good
        things that are seen to know the
        one who exists,

---

a Or all things   b Meaning of Gk uncertain   c Other ancient
authorities lack and indulgence; others read and entreaty
d Or children   e Gk they

4.32; Rom 9.20; Genesis Rabbah 1.2. **12.23–27** These
verses return to the second antithesis and the idea of
measure for measure found in 11.15–16. The emphasis is on the foolishness of Egyptian animal worship.
    13.1–15.19 The theme of Egyptian animal worship
leads the author to a second, long excursus (see note
on 11.15–16.4) on idolatry, whose major components
are clearly discernible in the analogous passages in

Philo (On the Decalogue 52–81; Special Laws 1.13–31).
Both accounts probably derive from a common Jewish-Hellenistic apologetic tradition. See Rom 1.18–32.
13.1–9 Worship of nature rather than of nature's creator. **13.1** The one who exists, lit. "he who exists," derived from Ex 3.14. Unlike Philo, who uses both the
personal masculine form (Greek ho on) and the im-
personal neuter (to on), the author of the Wisdom of

nor did they recognize the artisan while
　　paying heed to his works;
2　but they supposed that either fire or wind
　　　or swift air,
　or the circle of the stars, or turbulent
　　　water,
　or the luminaries of heaven were the gods
　　　that rule the world.
3　If through delight in the beauty of these
　　　things people assumed them to be
　　　gods,
　let them know how much better than
　　　these is their Lord,
　for the author of beauty created them.
4　And if people[a] were amazed at their
　　　power and working,
　let them perceive from them
　how much more powerful is the one who
　　　formed them.
5　For from the greatness and beauty of
　　　created things
　comes a corresponding perception of
　　　their Creator.
6　Yet these people are little to be blamed,
　for perhaps they go astray
　while seeking God and desiring to find
　　　him.
7　For while they live among his works, they
　　　keep searching,
　and they trust in what they see, because
　　　the things that are seen are
　　　beautiful.
8　Yet again, not even they are to be excused;
9　for if they had the power to know so much
　that they could investigate the world,
　how did they fail to find sooner the Lord
　　　of these things?

The Foolishness of Idolatry

10　But miserable, with their hopes set on
　　　dead things, are those

who give the name "gods" to the works of
　　　human hands,
gold and silver fashioned with skill,
and likenesses of animals,
or a useless stone, the work of an ancient
　　　hand.
11　A skilled woodcutter may saw down a
　　　tree easy to handle
and skillfully strip off all its bark,
and then with pleasing workmanship
make a useful vessel that serves life's needs,
12　and burn the cast-off pieces of his work
to prepare his food, and eat his fill.
13　But a cast-off piece from among them,
　　　useful for nothing,
a stick crooked and full of knots,
he takes and carves with care in his
　　　leisure,
and shapes it with skill gained in
　　　idleness;[b]
he forms it in the likeness of a human
　　　being,
14　or makes it like some worthless animal,
giving it a coat of red paint and coloring
　　　its surface red
and covering every blemish in it with
　　　paint;
15　then he makes a suitable niche for it,
and sets it in the wall, and fastens it there
　　　with iron.
16　He takes thought for it, so that it may not
　　　fall,
because he knows that it cannot help
　　　itself,
for it is only an image and has need of
　　　help.
17　When he prays about possessions and his
　　　marriage and children,

---

a Gk *they*　　*b* Other ancient authorities read *with intelligent skill*

Solomon uses only the former. **13.5** This is a well-known Stoic argument (already used by Plato and Aristotle and repeated by Philo): we form the concept of divinity from our awareness of the world's beauty, since no beautiful thing happens by chance but is the product of creative art. **13.6** *While seeking God,* a widespread motif (Philo, *On Abraham* 124–30; *Bhagavad Gita* 7.16). **13.7** Nature worshipers are overly impressed by *what they see,* whereas the ultimate reality is invisible (cf. Heb 11.3; Plato, *Sophist* 246A–B; Philo, *On Abraham* 69; *Testament of Orpheus* 4–5). **13.9** *Investigate the world,* better "infer the universe." **13.10–15.17** This satire of idolatry seems to have a chiastic, or

concentric, structure: 13.10–14.2 (A) and 15.7–13 (A′) are respectively about the carpenter and wooden images and the potter and clay images; 14.3–11 (B) and 15.1–6 (B′) both begin as apostrophes to God; 14.12–31 (C) is the central section describing the origins and evil consequences of idolatry. **13.10–14.2** The carpenter and wooden image making (A; see note on 13.10–15.17). See Isa 44.13–17. **13.10** *Useless stone.* Philo of Byblos defined the bethels, rough stones regarded as the residence of a god, as "animate stones"; the animate quality referred to is magnetism, very common in meteorites. **13.12** *To prepare his food.* See Isa 44.16; *Apocalypse of Abraham* 5; *Mekilta* on Ex 20.3.

he is not ashamed to address a lifeless
    thing.
18 For health he appeals to a thing that is
    weak;
for life he prays to a thing that is dead;
for aid he entreats a thing that is utterly
    inexperienced;
for a prosperous journey, a thing that
    cannot take a step;
19 for money-making and work and success
    with his hands
he asks strength of a thing whose hands
    have no strength.

Folly of a Navigator Praying to an Idol

14 Again, one preparing to sail and about
    to voyage over raging waves
calls upon a piece of wood more fragile
    than the ship that carries him.
2 For it was desire for gain that planned
    that vessel,
and wisdom was the artisan who built it;
3 but it is your providence, O Father, that
    steers its course,
because you have given it a path in the sea,
and a safe way through the waves,
4 showing that you can save from every
    danger,
so that even a person who lacks skill may
    put to sea.
5 It is your will that works of your wisdom
    should not be without effect;
therefore people trust their lives even to
    the smallest piece of wood,
and passing through the billows on a raft
    they come safely to land.
6 For even in the beginning, when arrogant
    giants were perishing,

the hope of the world took refuge on a raft,
and guided by your hand left to the world
    the seed of a new generation.
7 For blessed is the wood by which
    righteousness comes.

8 But the idol made with hands is accursed,
    and so is the one who made it—
he for having made it, and the perishable
    thing because it was named a god.
9 For equally hateful to God are the
    ungodly and their ungodliness;
10 for what was done will be punished
    together with the one who did it.
11 Therefore there will be a visitation also
    upon the heathen idols,
because, though part of what God
    created, they became an
    abomination,
snares for human souls
and a trap for the feet of the foolish.

The Origin and Evils of Idolatry

12 For the idea of making idols was the
    beginning of fornication,
and the invention of them was the
    corruption of life;
13 for they did not exist from the beginning,
    nor will they last forever.
14 For through human vanity they entered
    the world,
and therefore their speedy end has been
    planned.

15 For a father, consumed with grief at an
    untimely bereavement,
made an image of his child, who had
    been suddenly taken from him;

14.1 *Calls upon a piece of wood.* The divine twins, Castor and Pollux, the youths of Zeus (Dioscuri), were especially popular as rescuers from danger at sea. St. Elmo's fire, the electric discharge from the ship's mast during a thunderstorm, was regarded as their corporeal epiphany. According to Cyril of Alexandria (commenting on Acts 28.11), it was especially an Alexandrian custom to have pictures of the twins to right and left of the ship's prow. **14.3–11** Apostrophe to God and the evil of idol worship (B; see note on 13.10–15.17). **14.3** *Your providence . . . that steers,* Platonic/Stoic terminology. **14.5** *Works of your wisdom should not be without effect.* God wishes to allow for a better distribution of nature's products (cf. Euripides, *Suppliant Women* 209; Philo, *On Providence* 2.65). **14.6** *The hope of the world,* Noah and his family (cf. 4 Macc 15.31). **14.7** *Wood,* Noah's ark. The church fathers applied this verse either directly or symbolically to the

cross. **14.12–31** The origins (vv. 12–21) and evil consequences (vv. 22–31) of idolatry (C; see note on 13.10–15.17). To bolster his attack on idolatry, the author argues that it did not exist from the beginning but arose in the course of time through human error. The two explanations adduced for its origins probably derive from a pagan Hellenistic source, a highly rationalized euhemeristic account of the origins of the idol cult. **14.13** Idols will not *last forever.* See Isa 2.18; Ezek 30.13; Mic 5.12; Zech 13.2; Let Jer 50–73. **14.14** *Human vanity,* better "empty imagining," an Epicurean term. Since the origin of idols is rooted in total emptiness, *their speedy end has been planned,* i.e., the moment their vacuous character is disclosed, idolatry will evaporate into thin air and completely disappear (cf. Jer 16.19; *Gospel of Truth* 26.25). **14.15** Fulgentius provides an Egyptian analogue to the explanation given in this verse, and we have a refer-

he now honored as a god what was once a
dead human being,
and handed on to his dependents secret
rites and initiations.

16 Then the ungodly custom, grown strong
with time, was kept as a law,
and at the command of monarchs carved
images were worshiped.

17 When people could not honor monarchs[a]
in their presence, since they lived
at a distance,
they imagined their appearance far away,
and made a visible image of the king
whom they honored,
so that by their zeal they might flatter the
absent one as though present.

18 Then the ambition of the artisan impelled
even those who did not know the king to
intensify their worship.

19 For he, perhaps wishing to please his ruler,
skillfully forced the likeness to take more
beautiful form,

20 and the multitude, attracted by the charm
of his work,
now regarded as an object of worship the
one whom shortly before they
had honored as a human being.

21 And this became a hidden trap for
humankind,
because people, in bondage to misfortune
or to royal authority,
bestowed on objects of stone or wood the
name that ought not to be shared.

22 Then it was not enough for them to err
about the knowledge of God,
but though living in great strife due to
ignorance,
they call such great evils peace.

23 For whether they kill children in their
initiations, or celebrate secret
mysteries,
or hold frenzied revels with strange
customs,

24 they no longer keep either their lives or
their marriages pure,
but they either treacherously kill one
another, or grieve one another by
adultery,

25 and all is a raging riot of blood and murder,
theft and deceit, corruption,
faithlessness, tumult, perjury,

26 confusion over what is good,
forgetfulness of favors,
defiling of souls, sexual perversion,
disorder in marriages, adultery, and
debauchery.

27 For the worship of idols not to be named
is the beginning and cause and end of
every evil.

28 For their worshipers[b] either rave in
exultation,
or prophesy lies, or live unrighteously, or
readily commit perjury;

29 for because they trust in lifeless idols
they swear wicked oaths and expect to
suffer no harm.

30 But just penalties will overtake them on
two counts:
because they thought wrongly about God
in devoting themselves to idols,
and because in deceit they swore
unrighteously through contempt
for holiness.

31 For it is not the power of the things by
which people swear,[c]
but the just penalty for those who sin,
that always pursues the transgression of
the unrighteous.

Benefits of Worshiping the True God

15 But you, our God, are kind and true,
patient, and ruling all things[d] in mercy.
2 For even if we sin we are yours, knowing
your power;

---

a Gk *them* *b* Gk *they* *c* Or *of the oaths people swear*
d Or *ruling the universe*

---

ence to it in *Mekilta* on Ex 12.30 (cf. Cicero, *To Atticus*
12.35–36). **14.17** Perhaps a reference to the cult of the
distant Roman emperor. **14.21** *Ought not to be shared.*
See Isa 42.8. **14.22** *Call such great evils peace.* Cf. Jer 6.14;
Tacitus, *Agricola* 30. The theme of war-in-peace was
common in the Cynic-Stoic philosophical discourses of
the first century CE (see Ps.-Heraclitus, *Epistle* 7).
14.26 *Sexual perversion*, lit. "alteration of generation," i.e.,
all nonprocreative sexual activities. See Rom 1.26–27.

15.1–6 An apostrophe to God and Israel's immunity
from idolatry (B′; see note on 13.10–15.17). The writer
is thinking of his own period. The consensus among
the rabbis of the third century was that all idolatrous
impulses had been eradicated from Israel as early as the
beginning of the Second Temple period (*Babylonian
Talmud Yoma* 69b; cf. Jdt 8.18; Tacitus, *Histories* 5.5).
15.1 For the four divine attributes enumerated here,
see Ex 34.6. **15.2** *We are yours.* According to Rabbi Meir

but we will not sin, because we know that
    you acknowledge us as yours.
3 For to know you is complete
        righteousness,
    and to know your power is the root of
        immortality.
4 For neither has the evil intent of human
        art misled us,
    nor the fruitless toil of painters,
    a figure stained with varied colors,
5 whose appearance arouses yearning in
        fools,
    so that they desire*a* the lifeless form of a
        dead image.
6 Lovers of evil things and fit for such
        objects of hope*b*
    are those who either make or desire or
        worship them.

The Foolishness of Worshiping Clay Idols

7 A potter kneads the soft earth
    and laboriously molds each vessel for our
        service,
    fashioning out of the same clay
    both the vessels that serve clean uses
    and those for contrary uses, making all
        alike;
    but which shall be the use of each of
        them
    the worker in clay decides.
8 With misspent toil, these workers form a
        futile god from the same clay—
    these mortals who were made of earth a
        short time before
    and after a little while go to the earth
        from which all mortals are
        taken,
    when the time comes to return the souls
        that were borrowed.

9 But the workers are not concerned that
        mortals are destined to die
    or that their life is brief,
    but they compete with workers in gold
        and silver,
    and imitate workers in copper;
    and they count it a glorious thing to
        mold counterfeit gods.
10 Their heart is ashes, their hope is cheaper
        than dirt,
    and their lives are of less worth than clay,
11 because they failed to know the one who
        formed them
    and inspired them with active souls
    and breathed a living spirit into them.
12 But they considered our existence an idle
        game,
    and life a festival held for profit,
    for they say one must get money however
        one can, even by base means.
13 For these persons, more than all others,
        know that they sin
    when they make from earthy matter
        fragile vessels and carved images.

14 But most foolish, and more miserable
        than an infant,
    are all the enemies who oppressed your
        people.
15 For they thought that all their heathen
        idols were gods,
    though these have neither the use of their
        eyes to see with,
    nor nostrils with which to draw breath,
    nor ears with which to hear,
    nor fingers to feel with,
    and their feet are of no use for walking.

_____
a Gk *and he desires* *b* Gk *such hopes*

(*Sifre Deuteronomy* 96), whether the Jews sin or do not sin, they are God's children (cf. Philo, *Special Laws* 4.180–81). **15.4** The choice of the Greek word *skiagraphos*—here translated *painter*—is deliberate, since it refers to "painting with the shadows" so as to produce an illusion of solidity at a distance and is frequently used to indicate that which is illusory. The fourth-century Christian bishop Epiphanius connected the beginnings of idolatry with painting or shadow sketching (*Panarion* 3.4–5; *Ancoratus* 102.1; cf. Pliny, *Natural History* 35.151). **15.5** See Ovid, *Metamorphoses* 10.243–97 for the story of Pygmalion, who, having fashioned an ivory statue of a woman, fell in love with it. **15.7–13** The potter and clay images (A′; see note on 13.10–15.17). **15.7** *Clean uses . . . contrary uses.* This theme is reminiscent of the story about Amasis (often quoted by

Christian writers), who made an image of a god out of his golden footbath (Herodotus, *History* 2.172; cf. Philo, *Contemplative Life* 7). **15.8** *When the time . . . borrowed,* a very popular Platonic image (*Timaeus* 42E; cf. Ps.-Phocylides, *Sentences* 106; Josephus, *War* 3.372–74; Philo, *On Abraham* 257 and frequently; Lk 12.20). **15.12** For the metaphor of *an idle game,* cf. Plato, *Laws* 644D; Cicero, *On Duties* 1.103; Qur'an 57.19. Life as a *festival* is another widespread motif (Epictetus, *Discourses* 4.1.105; Cicero, *Tusculan Disputations* 5.9). *However one can, even by base means,* another commonplace (Sophocles, *Antigone* 312; Horace, *Epistles* 1.1.65; Philo, *Every Good Man Is Free* 65). **15.14–19** Conclusion on the idolatry of the Egyptians. The emphasis is on the lifelessness of the idols and the foolishness of human beings worshiping objects inferior to

16 For a human being made them,
    and one whose spirit is borrowed formed
       them;
    for none can form gods that are like
       themselves.
17 People are mortal, and what they make
       with lawless hands is dead;
    for they are better than the objects they
       worship,
    since*a* they have life, but the idols*b* never
       had.

Serpents in the Desert

18 Moreover, they worship even the most
       hateful animals,
    which are worse than all others when
       judged by their lack of
       intelligence;
19 and even as animals they are not so
       beautiful in appearance that one
       would desire them,
    but they have escaped both the praise of
       God and his blessing.

16 Therefore those people*c* were
       deservedly punished through such
       creatures,
    and were tormented by a multitude of
       animals.
2 Instead of this punishment you showed
       kindness to your people,
    and you prepared quails to eat,
    a delicacy to satisfy the desire of
       appetite;
3 in order that those people, when they
       desired food,
    might lose the least remnant of appetite*d*
    because of the odious creatures sent to
       them,
    while your people,*e* after suffering want a
       short time,
    might partake of delicacies.
4 For it was necessary that upon those
       oppressors inescapable want
       should come,

    while to these others it was merely shown
       how their enemies were being
       tormented.

5 For when the terrible rage of wild
       animals came upon your people*e*
    and they were being destroyed by the
       bites of writhing serpents,
    your wrath did not continue to the end;
6 they were troubled for a little while as a
       warning,
    and received a symbol of deliverance to
       remind them of your law's
       command.

7 For the one who turned toward it was
       saved, not by the thing that was
       beheld,
    but by you, the Savior of all.
8 And by this also you convinced our
       enemies
    that it is you who deliver from every evil.
9 For they were killed by the bites of locusts
       and flies,
    and no healing was found for them,
    because they deserved to be punished by
       such things.
10 But your children were not conquered
       even by the fangs of venomous
       serpents,
    for your mercy came to their help and
       healed them.
11 To remind them of your oracles they were
       bitten,
    and then were quickly delivered,
    so that they would not fall into deep
       forgetfulness
    and become unresponsive*f* to your
       kindness.
12 For neither herb nor poultice cured
       them,

---

a Other ancient authorities read *of which*   *b* Gk *but they*
c Gk *they*   *d* Gk *loathed the necessary appetite*   *e* Gk *them*
f Meaning of Gk uncertain

---

themselves. This section serves as a transition back to the second antithesis (see note on 11.1–19.22).

16.1–4 The author returns to complete the second antithesis (see note on 11.1–19.22) with a description of the Israelites being fed by God with quail. He has adapted the biblical version of this event (Num 11) to serve his own purposes by omitting all mention of the people's murmuring and gluttony and the divine anger that culminated in the destruction of many of them. **16.5–14** The third antithesis (see note on 11.1–

19.22): the Egyptians are slain by flies and locusts, but Israel survives a serpent attack in the desert. See Ex 8.20–32; 10.3–20; Num 21.4–9. **16.6** *A symbol of deliverance,* the bronze serpent (Num 21.9). Philo similarly interprets the serpent of Moses as a symbol of steadfast endurance (*On Husbandry* 98). Cf. Jn 3.14; Justin, *First Apology* 60. **16.7** The author replaces the principle of homeopathic magic that appears to be operative in Num 21.8–9 with a spiritual conception (a similar interpretation is in *Mishnah Rosh Hashanah* 3.8).

but it was your word, O Lord, that heals
    all people.

13 For you have power over life and death;
you lead mortals down to the gates of
    Hades and back again.

14 A person in wickedness kills another,
but cannot bring back the departed spirit,
or set free the imprisoned soul.

Disastrous Storms Strike Egypt

15 To escape from your hand is impossible;
16 for the ungodly, refusing to know you,
were flogged by the strength of your arm,
pursued by unusual rains and hail and
    relentless storms,
and utterly consumed by fire.

17 For—most incredible of all—in water,
    which quenches all things,
the fire had still greater effect,
for the universe defends the righteous.

18 At one time the flame was restrained,
so that it might not consume the
    creatures sent against the ungodly,
but that seeing this they might know
that they were being pursued by the
    judgment of God;

19 and at another time even in the midst of
    water it burned more intensely
    than fire,
to destroy the crops of the unrighteous
    land.

The Israelites Receive Manna

20 Instead of these things you gave your
    people food of angels,
and without their toil you supplied them
    from heaven with bread ready to
    eat,
providing every pleasure and suited to
    every taste.

21 For your sustenance manifested your
    sweetness toward your children;
and the bread, ministering[a] to the desire
    of the one who took it,

was changed to suit everyone's liking.

22 Snow and ice withstood fire without
    melting,
so that they might know that the crops of
    their enemies
were being destroyed by the fire that
    blazed in the hail
and flashed in the showers of rain;

23 whereas the fire,[b] in order that the
    righteous might be fed,
even forgot its native power.

24 For creation, serving you who made it,
exerts itself to punish the unrighteous,
and in kindness relaxes on behalf of those
    who trust in you.

25 Therefore at that time also, changed into
    all forms,
it served your all-nourishing bounty,
according to the desire of those who had
    need,[c]

26 so that your children, whom you loved,
    O Lord, might learn
that it is not the production of crops that
    feeds humankind
but that your word sustains those who
    trust in you.

27 For what was not destroyed by fire
was melted when simply warmed by a
    fleeting ray of the sun,

28 to make it known that one must rise
    before the sun to give you thanks,
and must pray to you at the dawning of
    the light;

29 for the hope of an ungrateful person will
    melt like wintry frost,
and flow away like waste water.

Terror Strikes the Egyptians at Night

17 Great are your judgments and hard to
    describe;

---

a Gk *and it, ministering*   *b* Gk *this*   *c* Or *who made
supplication*

16.13 Cf. 1 Sam 2.6; Tob 13.2. 16.15–29 The fourth antithesis (see note on 11.1–19.22): the Egyptians are
plagued by thunderstorms (Ex 9.13–26), but Israel is fed
by manna from heaven (Ex 16; Num 11.7–9). 16.18 *At
one time.* The author appears to assume that the plagues
of frogs, flies, gnats, locusts, and hail were simultaneous,
thus contradicting the biblical narrative. There is no
known parallel to our author's particular scheme.
16.20 *Food of angels* reflects the unusual phrase *lechem
'abbirim* (lit. "bread of the mighty ones"), which in Ps

78.25 is translated by the Septuagint as "bread of angels"
(cf. *Babylonian Talmud Yoma* 75b). *Suited to every taste.*
See *Mekilta* on Ex 16.23; *Babylonian Talmud Yoma* 75a.
16.26 An adaptation of Deut 8.3. 16.28 *To make it
known,* another example of the author's eagerness to uncover the symbolic meaning behind the physical events
narrated in scripture; see also note on 10.12. *At the
dawning of the light.* Cf. *Babylonian Talmud Berakot* 9b;
Josephus, *War* 2.128; Philo, *Contemplative Life* 89.
   17.1–18.4 The fifth antithesis (see note on 11.1–

therefore uninstructed souls have gone
    astray.
2 For when lawless people supposed that
    they held the holy nation in their
    power,
they themselves lay as captives of
    darkness and prisoners of long
    night,
shut in under their roofs, exiles from
    eternal providence.
3 For thinking that in their secret sins they
    were unobserved
behind a dark curtain of forgetfulness,
they were scattered, terribly*a* alarmed,
and appalled by specters.
4 For not even the inner chamber that held
    them protected them from fear,
but terrifying sounds rang out around
    them,
and dismal phantoms with gloomy faces
    appeared.
5 And no power of fire was able to give light,
nor did the brilliant flames of the stars
avail to illumine that hateful night.
6 Nothing was shining through to them
except a dreadful, self-kindled fire,
and in terror they deemed the things that
    they saw
to be worse than that unseen appearance.
7 The delusions of their magic art lay
    humbled,
and their boasted wisdom was scornfully
    rebuked.
8 For those who promised to drive off the
    fears and disorders of a sick soul
were sick themselves with ridiculous fear.
9 For even if nothing disturbing frightened
    them,

yet, scared by the passing of wild animals
    and the hissing of snakes
10 they perished in trembling fear,
refusing to look even at the air, though it
    nowhere could be avoided.
11 For wickedness is a cowardly thing,
    condemned by its own
    testimony;*b*
distressed by conscience, it has always
    exaggerated*c* the difficulties.
12 For fear is nothing but a giving up of the
    helps that come from reason;
13 and hope, defeated by this inward
    weakness,
prefers ignorance of what causes the
    torment.
14 But throughout the night, which was
    really powerless
and which came upon them from the
    recesses of powerless Hades,
they all slept the same sleep,
15 and now were driven by monstrous
    specters,
and now were paralyzed by their souls'
    surrender;
for sudden and unexpected fear
    overwhelmed them.
16 And whoever was there fell down,
and thus was kept shut up in a prison not
    made of iron;
17 for whether they were farmers or
    shepherds
or workers who toiled in the wilderness,
they were seized, and endured the
    inescapable fate;

---

a Other ancient authorities read *unobserved, they were darkened behind a dark curtain of forgetfulness, terribly* *b* Meaning of Gk uncertain *c* Other ancient authorities read *anticipated*

19.22): the Egyptians are terrified by darkness, but the Israelites are led by light from the pillar of fire. The author employs all his rhetorical skill to provide readers with a living impression of the psychological terror occasioned by the plague of darkness (Ex 10.21–23). He deftly moves from the physical contrast between darkness and light to the spiritual one that sees in the Egyptians moral villains obsessed with a bad conscience and in Israel ethical heroes destined to illumine the world with the light of the Torah. He was undoubtedly influenced by the literary genre of the "descent into Hades." The rabbis similarly identified the darkness that plagued the Egyptians as coming from Gehenna (*Exodus Rabbah* 14.2). **17.2** *Lawless people,* the Egyptians. **17.3** Another example of the principle of talion (see note on Deut 19.19–21): the Egyptians sought to conceal their sins in darkness and were therefore

plagued by darkness. *Appalled by specters.* Cf. Sir 40.5–7. **17.10** *The air,* better "the dark haze." The haze (Greek *aer*) in which Apollo hides Hector is described in the *Iliad* (20.446) as thick, and Achilles strikes it three times with his spear. **17.11** *Distressed by conscience.* The same phrase appears in *Testament of Reuben* 4.3. The notion of conscience (*syneidesis*) appears in the writings of the Greek poets and popular moralists, such as Euripides and Menander, and above all in the Epicurean stress on the pangs of conscience suffered by the guilty (Lucretius, *On the Nature of Things* 3.1018). **17.12** As in much Greek philosophy, *fear* is understood as an irrational passion. **17.14** *From the recesses of powerless Hades.* Cf. Apollonius of Rhodes, *Argonautica* 4.1694–1700. **17.17** *Workers who toiled in the wilderness,* better, "troubled laborer in the wilderness." Egyptian peasants crushed by taxes often with-

for with one chain of darkness they all
    were bound.

18 Whether there came a whistling wind,
    or a melodious sound of birds in wide-
        spreading branches,
    or the rhythm of violently rushing
        water,

19 or the harsh crash of rocks hurled down,
    or the unseen running of leaping
        animals,
    or the sound of the most savage roaring
        beasts,
    or an echo thrown back from a hollow of
        the mountains,
    it paralyzed them with terror.

20 For the whole world was illumined with
        brilliant light,
    and went about its work unhindered,

21 while over those people alone heavy night
        was spread,
    an image of the darkness that was
        destined to receive them;
    but still heavier than darkness were they
        to themselves.

Light Shines on the Israelites

18 But for your holy ones there was very
        great light.
Their enemies[a] heard their voices but did
    not see their forms,
    and counted them happy for not having
        suffered,

2 and were thankful that your holy ones,[b]
        though previously wronged, were
        doing them no injury;
    and they begged their pardon for having
        been at variance with them.[b]

3 Therefore you provided a flaming pillar
        of fire
    as a guide for your people's[c] unknown
        journey,
    and a harmless sun for their glorious
        wandering.

4 For their enemies[d] deserved to be
        deprived of light and imprisoned
        in darkness,
    those who had kept your children
        imprisoned,
    through whom the imperishable light of
        the law was to be given to the
        world.

The Death of the Egyptian Firstborn

5 When they had resolved to kill the infants
        of your holy ones,
    and one child had been abandoned and
        rescued,
    you in punishment took away a
        multitude of their children;
    and you destroyed them all together by a
        mighty flood.

6 That night was made known beforehand
        to our ancestors,
    so that they might rejoice in sure
        knowledge of the oaths in which
        they trusted.

7 The deliverance of the righteous and the
        destruction of their enemies
    were expected by your people.

8 For by the same means by which you
        punished our enemies
    you called us to yourself and glorified us.

9 For in secret the holy children of good
        people offered sacrifices,
    and with one accord agreed to the divine
        law,
    so that the saints would share alike the
        same things,
    both blessings and dangers;
    and already they were singing the praises
        of the ancestors.[e]

10 But the discordant cry of their enemies
        echoed back,

---

a Gk *They*   *b* Meaning of Gk uncertain   *c* Gk *their*
d Gk *those persons*   *e* Other ancient authorities read *dangers,
the ancestors already leading the songs of praise*

---

drew into the desert, where they led the life of outlaws.
These flights became especially frequent under the Romans. **18.4** In Jewish-Hellenistic and rabbinic writings
Israel's acceptance of the Torah is understood to include an obligation to spread its teachings among the
Gentiles (see 2 Esd 7.20–24; *Testament of Levi* 14.4;
2 Apocalypse of Baruch 48.40; Ps.-Philo, *Biblical Antiquities* 11.1–2; *Mekilta* on Ex 20.2; Philo, *Questions on
Exodus* 2.41–42).   **18.5–25** The sixth antithesis (see note on 11.1–
19.22): the Egyptian firstborn are destroyed (Ex 11.1–

12.32), but Israel is protected and glorified. **18.5** *One
child,* Moses (Ex 1.22–2.10). *By a mighty flood.* The author returns to his favorite theme of measure for measure (cf. *Mekilta* on Ex 14.26; *Jubilees* 48.14). **18.6** *That
night,* the well-known night on which the firstborn of
the Egyptians were slain. *The oaths.* Cf. Ps 105.42–43.
18.9 *Singing the praises of the ancestors.* The writer attributes to those who partook of the first Passover a
practice that developed in later days; see 2 Chr 30.21;
Jubilees 49.6. **18.10** *The discordant cry ... back.* The
rabbis draw the same contrast (*Mekilta* on Ex 13.4;

of the Hebrew scriptures, Sirach has been assigned to the Apocrypha by Protestants and to the deuterocanonical writings by the Roman Catholic and Orthodox Churches. The NRSV translation is based on a critical comparison of the Hebrew manuscripts with the Greek text edited by Joseph Ziegler in the Göttingen edition of the Septuagint.

Date and Times

BEN SIRA, A TEACHER IN JERUSALEM, wrote sometime between 200 and 180 BCE, in the shadow of the shift in hegemony that occurred in 198 BCE when the Seleucid successors to Alexander the Great in Antioch wrested control of Judea from the Ptolemies of Egypt. In ch. 50 Ben Sira mentions the high priest Simon son of Onias (50.1) as if he were a contemporary who had recently died, and in the prologue his grandson reports that he moved to Egypt in the thirty-eighth year of the reign of (Ptolemy) Euergetes ("Benefactor"). Simon II, "the Just," was high priest from 219 to 196 BCE, and the grandson's arrival in Egypt can be dated at 132; thus he finished his translation around 117 after Ptolemy's death. Since Sirach contains no allusions to the Maccabean-Seleucid conflict that broke out under Antiochus IV in 175–164, Ben Sira must have completed his writings by 180 BCE.

At that time trouble was already brewing for the Jews in Jerusalem. The Seleucid victory aggravated two issues that had been threatening the Jewish social system: the hegemony of foreign kings and the social, cultural, and religious tensions that resulted from the introduction of Hellenistic culture. Combined with internal conflicts arising from the aspirations of leading priestly families who jockeyed between the Ptolemies and the Seleucids for patronage, these threats set the stage for the wars and bloody intrigues that soon broke out under Antiochus IV.

Parts of his work clearly reflect Ben Sira's assessment of what he perceived as threats to the Jewish temple system and way of life, but he does not address them directly. Instead, he offers a book of instruction that assumes the integrity and glory of the Jewish way of life, a way of life to which he was fully committed and to which he devoted his life as a scholar and teacher. Social and cultural threats are handled obliquely by allusion, repeated emphasis upon injunctions related to critical social relations, and warnings about foreign rulers and strangers.

Content and Achievement

BEN SIRA'S ACHIEVEMENT WAS to combine the learning typical of the ancient Near Eastern and Israelite wisdom traditions with the commandments of Moses found in the Torah (Hebrew, "instruction," regularly translated "law"), although he does not quote the Torah explicitly. He did this, moreover, in the interest of supporting the Second Temple system of governance with its priestly codes of law and sacrifice. The term he uses to combine the wisdom of Proverbs with the law of Moses is the "fear of the Lord," a term capable of naming an ethical piety appropriate to the culture of Second Temple Judaism.

Ben Sira's intellectual achievement is demonstrated by his knowledge and employment of a large literature. In the prologue to the Greek translation his grandson mentions his study of the Hebrew scriptures. Allusions to this literature throughout Sirach indicate a familiarity with all of the books now contained in the Hebrew Bible except Ezra, Daniel, Esther, and Ruth. He also shows knowledge of Greek and Egyptian literature and thought. His achievement was to draw upon this learning to create a conceptual framework in support of an ethic of Jewish piety for Second Temple times.

Literary Forms

BEN SIRA COMBINES PROVERBS AND PRECEPTS in compositions typical of Hebrew poetry. He uses parallel lines (or bicola) creatively in various combinations to yield units of poetry with thematic and rhetorical coherence. He also wrote hymns of praise on the model of Hebrew psalms and prayers as well as narrative, autobiographical, and exegetical poems on a wide range of topics. Among his more famous accomplishments are a number of poems in praise of the personified figure of wisdom, especially ch. 24, and the long epic poem in chs. 44–50 in praise of the ancestors.

The book as a whole is loosely constructed. The wisdom poem in ch. 1 works well as an introduction, however, and the first several chapters show signs of deliberate design and sequence. There also seems to be some design to the sequence and placement of the wisdom poems in the first half of the book, through ch. 24, as well as purpose to the position of the hymn in praise of the ancestors at the end of the book. Many smaller units are highly crafted and arranged in sequences to form larger coherent sections, but the nature of the material in this large collection of wisdom proverbs and poetry prohibits neat organization and frustrates prolonged linear reading. It is doubtful that the book was meant to be read from beginning to end as if it developed a narrative or logical theme. It was a resource of instructional material that perhaps was intended for use as a handbook to consult in the preparation of lessons.

[BURTON L. MACK, revised by BENJAMIN G. WRIGHT III]

THE PROLOGUE

Many great teachings have been given to us through the Law and the Prophets and the others[a] that followed them, and for these we should praise Israel for instruction and wisdom. Now, those who read the scriptures must not only themselves understand them, but must also as lovers of learning be able through the spoken and written word to help the outsiders. So my grandfather Jesus, who had devoted himself especially to the reading of the Law and the Prophets and the other books of our ancestors, and had acquired considerable proficiency in them, was himself also led to write something pertaining to instruction and wisdom, so that by becoming familiar also with his book[b] those who love learning might make even greater progress in living according to the law.

You are invited therefore to read it with goodwill and attention, and to be indulgent in cases where, despite our diligent labor in translating, we may seem to have rendered some phrases imperfectly. For what was originally expressed in Hebrew does not have exactly the same sense when translated into another language. Not only this book, but even the Law itself, the Prophecies, and the rest of the books differ not a little when read in the original.

When I came to Egypt in the thirty-eighth year of the reign of Euergetes and stayed for some time, I found opportunity for no little instruction.[c] It seemed highly necessary that I should myself devote some diligence and labor to the translation of this book. During that time I have applied my skill day and night to complete and publish the book for those living abroad who wished to gain learning and are disposed to live according to the law.

---

a Or *other books*   *b* Gk *with these things*   *c* Other ancient authorities read *I found a copy affording no little instruction*

Prologue The prologue was written by Ben Sira's grandson, who explains the importance of the book, the relationship of his translation to Ben Sira's Hebrew, and the circumstances of its publication for those living abroad. *The Law and the Prophets and the other books,* the Hebrew scriptures; this is the earliest clear reference to such a threefold classification. *Instruction and wisdom,* perhaps the combination of Torah instruction and proverbial wisdom characteristic of his grandfather's book. There may be an allusion to Deut 4.6. *Living according to the law,* a Greek formulation of the Jewish idiom "to keep (observe, or obey) the law."

has anyone trusted in the Lord and
  been disappointed?
Or has anyone persevered in the fear of
  the Lord[a] and been forsaken?
Or has anyone called upon him and
  been neglected?

11 For the Lord is compassionate and
  merciful;
  he forgives sins and saves in time of
  distress.

12 Woe to timid hearts and to slack hands,
  and to the sinner who walks a double
  path!
13 Woe to the fainthearted who have no trust!
  Therefore they will have no shelter.
14 Woe to you who have lost your nerve!
  What will you do when the Lord's
  reckoning comes?

15 Those who fear the Lord do not disobey
  his words,
  and those who love him keep his ways.
16 Those who fear the Lord seek to please
  him,
  and those who love him are filled with
  his law.
17 Those who fear the Lord prepare their
  hearts,
  and humble themselves before him.
18 Let us fall into the hands of the Lord,
  but not into the hands of mortals;
  for equal to his majesty is his mercy,
  and equal to his name are his works.[b]

Duties toward Parents

3 Listen to me your father, O children;
  act accordingly, that you may be kept in
  safety.
2 For the Lord honors a father above his
  children,
  and he confirms a mother's right over
  her children.
3 Those who honor their father atone for
  sins,
4 and those who respect their mother are
  like those who lay up treasure.
5 Those who honor their father will have
  joy in their own children,
  and when they pray they will be heard.
6 Those who respect their father will have
  long life,
  and those who honor[c] their mother
  obey the Lord;
7 they will serve their parents as their
  masters.[d]
8 Honor your father by word and deed,
  that his blessing may come upon you.
9 For a father's blessing strengthens the
  houses of the children,
  but a mother's curse uproots their
  foundations.
10 Do not glorify yourself by dishonoring
  your father,

---

a Gk of him b Syr: Gk lacks this line c Heb: Other ancient
authorities read comfort d In other ancient authorities this line
is preceded by Those who fear the Lord honor their father,

2.11 Compassionate and merciful, taken from Ex 34.6–
7. The theme of the Lord's compassion is common in
Psalms and the prophets. See Pss 86.5, 15; 103.3–4;
145.8–9; Joel 2.13. That the Lord saves in time of distress those who call upon him is another theme common to Psalms that recurs in Sirach. See 4.6; 11.12–13,
22; 21.5; 33.1; 34.15; 35.16–26; 39.33; 48.20; Ex 22.23;
Pss 34; 57; 61; 81.7. Wisdom also rescues those in trouble (Wis 10.9). 2.12–14 Woe to, a prophetic formula.
Although a "wisdom teacher," Ben Sira perceives his
activity as akin to that of the prophets; cf. 24.30–34.
2.14 The Lord's reckoning, times in life when accounts
will be settled, usually in chastisement or punishment
for wrongdoing. This is a traditional notion about divine rewards and punishment in support of piety and
in answer to the question of why sinners prosper; it
does not refer to a day of divine judgment after life or
at the end of history. See 5.1–8; 16.5–23. 2.18 Equal to
his name, a play on the Hebrew term "Merciful One,"
referring to the Lord in Ex 34.6.
  3.1–16 A poem in three stanzas elaborates on the

commandment to honor father and mother (Ex 20.12;
Deut 5.16). Its position suggests that the preceding
poem may have been written with the first commandment in mind. The connection between the "fear of
the Lord" (see 2.15–17) and the honor of one's parents
is made in vv. 1–4 and recurs as a conclusion, or period, in v. 16. 3.2 The curious formulation of this verse
results from the desire to keep the Lord in view as the
ultimate author of the commandment to honor parents. It nevertheless expresses the ranking basic to ancient Jewish family structure and ethic. 3.3 To atone for
sins, or for failures to keep the law, one could offer a
sacrifice or perform an act of mercy such as almsgiving. Cf. notes on 4.1–10; 28.5; 35.1–13. 3.4 Lay up
treasure. See note on 29.11. In v. 14 such a kindness to
a father will be credited . . . against one's sins; see note
on 3.14. 3.6 Long life, an allusion to the reward for
honoring parents in Ex 20.12; Deut 5.16 as well as a
recollection of the long life promised by wisdom
in 1.12, 20. 3.9 For examples of a father's blessing, see
Gen 27.27–29 (Isaac); 48.15–16, 20; 49.8–12 (Jacob).

for your father's dishonor is no glory
to you.

11 The glory of one's father is one's own glory,
and it is a disgrace for children not to
respect their mother.

12 My child, help your father in his old age,
and do not grieve him as long as he
lives;

13 even if his mind fails, be patient with
him;
because you have all your faculties do
not despise him.

14 For kindness to a father will not be
forgotten,
and will be credited to you against
your sins;

15 in the day of your distress it will be
remembered in your favor;
like frost in fair weather, your sins will
melt away.

16 Whoever forsakes a father is like a
blasphemer,
and whoever angers a mother is cursed
by the Lord.

Humility

17 My child, perform your tasks with
humility;[a]
then you will be loved by those whom
God accepts.

18 The greater you are, the more you must
humble yourself;
so you will find favor in the sight of the
Lord.[b]

20 For great is the might of the Lord;
but by the humble he is glorified.

21 Neither seek what is too difficult for you,
nor investigate what is beyond your
power.

22 Reflect upon what you have been
commanded,
for what is hidden is not your
concern.

23 Do not meddle in matters that are
beyond you,
for more than you can understand has
been shown you.

24 For their conceit has led many astray,
and wrong opinion has impaired their
judgment.

25 Without eyes there is no light;
without knowledge there is no
wisdom.[c]

26 A stubborn mind will fare badly at the
end,
and whoever loves danger will perish
in it.

27 A stubborn mind will be burdened by
troubles,
and the sinner adds sin to sins.

28 When calamity befalls the proud, there is
no healing,
for an evil plant has taken root in him.

29 The mind of the intelligent appreciates
proverbs,
and an attentive ear is the desire of the
wise.

Alms for the Poor

30 As water extinguishes a blazing fire,
so almsgiving atones for sin.

31 Those who repay favors give thought to
the future;
when they fall they will find support.

a Heb: Gk meekness   b Other ancient authorities add as verse
19, Many are lofty and renowned, but to the humble he reveals his
secrets.   c Heb: Other ancient authorities lack verse 25

3.14 Credited . . . against your sins. God keeps an account of one's sins and transgressions as well as one's deeds of mercy. See note on 28.1. **3.16** This harsh conclusion may allude to the death penalty prescribed for one who curses father or mother (cf. Ex 21.17; Lev 20.9; Prov 19.26). It may also be Ben Sira's attempt to integrate an ethic of honor (wisdom) with his religious piety (fear of the Lord). **3.17–4.10** A longer poetic unit on humility and almsgiving brings the needy and society into view. It completes the triad of relationships under consideration in the first major section of the book (1.1–4.10): duties to God, family, and society. **3.17–29** Humility is the essential virtue, an attitude appropriate to all three traditions of thought combined in Ben Sira's ethical system: wisdom, Mosaic law, and temple worship. Cf. 2 Chr 7.14; Job 22.29; Prov 15.33; Mic 6.8. **3.21** What is beyond your power draws upon the theme of hidden wisdom as a way to express human limitation. See 18.4–7; Ps 131; Eccl 7.24. In vv. 22–24, Ben Sira may be warning against Jewish apocalyptic speculation (like that found in 1 Enoch) or possibly Greek philosophy. **3.27** Adds sin to sins, a reference to the (sinful) presumption that sins make no difference. See 5.5. **3.30–31** Almsgiving atones for sin, the statement of a basic theme elaborated in the next section (4.1–10); but also note Ben Sira's use of cultic language. On almsgiving, see 7.10, 32–36; 12.3–7; 14.13; 17.22; 18.15; 29.1–20; 35.4; 40.17. Almsgiving was the cornerstone of Jewish social ethic at this time. See Tob 4.10–11.

Duties toward the Poor and the Oppressed

4 My child, do not cheat the poor of their
living,
and do not keep needy eyes waiting.

2 Do not grieve the hungry,
or anger one in need.

3 Do not add to the troubles of the
desperate,
or delay giving to the needy.

4 Do not reject a suppliant in distress,
or turn your face away from the poor.

5 Do not avert your eye from the needy,
and give no one reason to curse you;

6 for if in bitterness of soul some should
curse you,
their Creator will hear their prayer.

7 Endear yourself to the congregation;
bow your head low to the great.

8 Give a hearing to the poor,
and return their greeting politely.

9 Rescue the oppressed from the oppressor;
and do not be hesitant in giving a
verdict.

10 Be a father to orphans,
and be like a husband to their mother;
you will then be like a son of the Most
High,
and he will love you more than does
your mother.

The Rewards of Wisdom

11 Wisdom teaches[a] her children
and gives help to those who seek her.

12 Whoever loves her loves life,
and those who seek her from early
morning are filled with joy.

13 Whoever holds her fast inherits glory,
and the Lord blesses the place she[b]
enters.

14 Those who serve her minister to the Holy
One;
the Lord loves those who love her.

15 Those who obey her will judge the
nations,
and all who listen to her will live
secure.

16 If they remain faithful, they will inherit
her;
their descendants will also obtain her.

17 For at first she will walk with them on
tortuous paths;
she will bring fear and dread upon
them,
and will torment them by her discipline
until she trusts them,[c]
and she will test them with her
ordinances.

18 Then she will come straight back to them
again and gladden them,
and will reveal her secrets to them.

19 If they go astray she will forsake them,
and hand them over to their ruin.

20 Watch for the opportune time, and
beware of evil,

---

a Heb Syr: Gk *exalts* *b* Or *he* *c* Or *until they remain faithful
in their heart*

4.1–10 An ancient standard for social justice lies behind this section: the care of widows, orphans, aliens, and the poor. This covenantal standard was used to measure the righteousness of a king's rule, the health of a society, and the piety of an individual Jew. It was basic for prophetic social critique. See Ex 22.22; Lev 19.9–10; 23.22; Deut 10.18; 24.17–22; 27.19; Job 29.11–16; 31.13–22; Isa 1.17; Am 5.10–15; Zech 7.10; Tob 1.3, 8; Jas 1.27. See also Sir 35.16–19. **4.9** *Giving a verdict,* an indication that Ben Sira's students were being prepared for a scribal vocation that might include rendering judgments. See 38.31–33. This unit completes the section of the book (1.1–4.10) concerned with the programmatic relation of wisdom to ethical piety. **4.10** *More than does your mother,* a touching image of how God loves those who care for the marginalized. **4.11–31** A poem on wisdom, personified as a female teacher (vv. 11–19), introduces the topic of considered speech (vv. 20–31) and prepares for much of the material in chs. 5–6. **4.11–19** The

poem echoes the speech of personified wisdom in Prov 1.20–9.6. **4.13** *The place she enters,* possibly the temple (24.10–11) as her "house." Cf. Prov 9.1–6. **4.15** To *judge the nations* was a widespread hope, namely, that the righteous wise ones would rule the world. Cf. Prov 8.15–16; 29.9; Wis 3.8; 9.12; Lk 22.30; 1 Cor 6.2. In the Greek tradition of popular philosophy the wise were the true kings. **4.17** *At first,* the first of two stages in education: wisdom's *tortuous* discipline results in accomplishment (v. 18). The Hebrew *musar* can be translated "discipline" or "education." In Greek tradition the standard metaphors for education (*paideia,* meaning both "education" and "culture") were sowing seed and cultivating vines. The labor of farming occurs as the metaphor of wisdom's discipline in 6.18–31. Here in vv. 17–18 the metaphor of the *path* is used. Cf. Wis 6.13–16. The phrase *her ordinances* merges wisdom instruction with the commandments of the Torah as if the commandments were ordained by personified wisdom. Cf. Wis 6.18. **4.19** *She will for-*

and do not be ashamed to be yourself.

21 For there is a shame that leads to sin,
   and there is a shame that is glory and
      favor.

22 Do not show partiality, to your own harm,
   or deference, to your downfall.

23 Do not refrain from speaking at the
      proper moment,[a]
   and do not hide your wisdom.[b]

24 For wisdom becomes known through
      speech,
   and education through the words of
      the tongue.

25 Never speak against the truth,
   but be ashamed of your ignorance.

26 Do not be ashamed to confess your sins,
   and do not try to stop the current of a
      river.

27 Do not subject yourself to a fool,
   or show partiality to a ruler.

28 Fight to the death for truth,
   and the Lord God will fight for you.

29 Do not be reckless in your speech,
   or sluggish and remiss in your deeds.

30 Do not be like a lion in your home,
   or suspicious of your servants.

31 Do not let your hand be stretched out to
      receive
   and closed when it is time to give.

Precepts for Everyday Living

5 Do not rely on your wealth,
   or say, "I have enough."

2 Do not follow your inclination and
      strength
   in pursuing the desires of your heart.

3 Do not say, "Who can have power over
      me?"
   for the Lord will surely punish you.

4 Do not say, "I sinned, yet what has
      happened to me?"
   for the Lord is slow to anger.

5 Do not be so confident of forgiveness[c]
   that you add sin to sin.

6 Do not say, "His mercy is great,
   he will forgive[d] the multitude of my
      sins,"
   for both mercy and wrath are with him,
   and his anger will rest on sinners.

7 Do not delay to turn back to the Lord,
   and do not postpone it from day to
      day;
   for suddenly the wrath of the Lord will
      come upon you,
   and at the time of punishment you will
      perish.

8 Do not depend on dishonest wealth,
   for it will not benefit you on the day of
      calamity.

9 Do not winnow in every wind,
   or follow every path.[e]

10 Stand firm for what you know,
   and let your speech be consistent.

11 Be quick to hear,
   but deliberate in answering.

12 If you know what to say, answer your
      neighbor;
   but if not, put your hand over your
      mouth.

13 Honor and dishonor come from speaking,
   and the tongue of mortals may be their
      downfall.

14 Do not be called double-tongued[f]

---

a Heb: Gk *at a time of salvation*   b So some Gk Mss and Heb Syr
Lat: Other Gk Mss lack *and do not hide your wisdom*   c Heb: Gk
atonement   d Heb: Gk *he* (or *it*) *will atone for*   e Gk adds *so it is
with the double-tongued sinner* (see 6.1)   f Heb: Gk *a slanderer*

---

sake them, reminiscent of Prov 1.24–32. **4.20–31** Negative injunctions appear as an appropriate form of instruction. The common theme is considered speech, the goal of ancient education in both the Near East and Greece. See v. 24. The theme continues in chs. 5–6, interwoven with the codes of honor/shame and sin. **4.20** Watching for the *opportune time* refers to knowing when to speak, what to say on a specific occasion, and when to keep silent. See 1.23; 4.23; 20.7, 20. Proverbs were formulated as general statements, but in fact were observations on particular sets of circumstances ("cases"). Knowing when a proverb applied was also a mark of wisdom. See 20.20. **4.29** *Speech* and *deeds,* the two modes of human behavior that must correspond in a person of integrity.

5.1–6.4 A twenty-two-line poetic arrangement of warnings on the ruinous consequences of mistaken presumptions, wrong speech, and shameful behavior. **5.4** *Slow to anger,* a reference to Ex 34.6, a verse basic to a commonly held understanding of the relationship between the Lord's wrath and mercy. **5.7** *The time of punishment,* any experience of ruin, shame, or destruction as a moment of divine retribution; see 16.5–23. *Suddenly* contrasts with *slow* in v. 4. **5.9** Metaphors of behavior without principle. **5.12** *Put your hand over your mouth,* an idiomatic gesture common to Egypt and Israel indicating discretionary silence, whether out of respect, admission of ignorance, or regret. See Job 21.5; Prov 30.32; Wis 8.12. **5.14** *Double-tongued,* a common idiom for deceitful speech, slander, and gos

and do not lay traps with your tongue;
for shame comes to the thief,
and severe condemnation to the
double-tongued.

15 In great and small matters cause no harm,[a]

6 1 and do not become an enemy instead
of a friend;
for a bad name incurs shame and
reproach;
so it is with the double-tongued sinner.

2 Do not fall into the grip of passion,[b]
or you may be torn apart as by a bull.[c]
3 Your leaves will be devoured and your
fruit destroyed,
and you will be left like a withered tree.
4 Evil passion destroys those who have it,
and makes them the laughingstock of
their enemies.

Friendship, False and True

5 Pleasant speech multiplies friends,
and a gracious tongue multiplies
courtesies.
6 Let those who are friendly with you be
many,
but let your advisers be one in a
thousand.
7 When you gain friends, gain them
through testing,
and do not trust them hastily.
8 For there are friends who are such when
it suits them,
but they will not stand by you in time
of trouble.
9 And there are friends who change into
enemies,
and tell of the quarrel to your disgrace.
10 And there are friends who sit at your
table,

but they will not stand by you in time
of trouble.
11 When you are prosperous, they become
your second self,
and lord it over your servants;
12 but if you are brought low, they turn
against you,
and hide themselves from you.
13 Keep away from your enemies,
and be on guard with your friends.

14 Faithful friends are a sturdy shelter:
whoever finds one has found a
treasure.
15 Faithful friends are beyond price;
no amount can balance their worth.
16 Faithful friends are life-saving medicine;
and those who fear the Lord will find
them.
17 Those who fear the Lord direct their
friendship aright,
for as they are, so are their neighbors
also.

Blessings of Wisdom

18 My child, from your youth choose
discipline,
and when you have gray hair you will
still find wisdom.
19 Come to her like one who plows and
sows,
and wait for her good harvest.
For when you cultivate her you will toil
but little,
and soon you will eat of her produce.
20 She seems very harsh to the
undisciplined;

---

a Heb Syr: Gk *be ignorant*   b Heb: Meaning of Gk uncertain
c Meaning of Gk uncertain

---

sip. See 28.13. *The thief,* one who "robs" another's good
reputation, i.e., a slanderer. **6.1** *A bad name incurs
shame* connects reputation with social status. **6.2** *Passion,* sexual passion. **6.4** *Laughingstock* alludes to
shame.

6.5–17 A unit that contrasts true and false friends
shifts the preceding reflections on integrity away from
students and to associates. Friendship was an important concept in social relations during the Hellenistic
period. See 9.10; 11.29–14.2; 22.19–26; 37.1–6; cf.
Prov. 17.17; 18.24; 27. 6, 10. In Greek literature of the
time, a friend was one who remained true in times of
distress and could therefore be trusted with one's official or private interests and affairs. This unit completes
a section of instructions and admonitions concerned

with situations that test one's resolve, integrity, and capacity for making judgments in keeping with wisdom
piety (4.11–6.17). Note the sets of three in vv. 8–10
and 14–16. **6.18–37** A twenty-two-line poem on personified wisdom elaborating on the theme of discipline at first, honors at last. Cf. 4.17–19. The first
stanza (vv. 18–22) emphasizes the harshness of wisdom's discipline; the second (vv. 23–31) promises rewards for those who accept it; and the last (vv. 32–37)
applies the metaphors to the teacher-student relationship. **6.19** *Toil . . . eat of her produce* parallels the common Greek maxim: "The root of education is bitter,
but the fruit is sweet"—the toil is unpleasant, but the
honor and accomplishment are sweet. On toiling with
wisdom, cf. Wis 8.7; 9.10. On toiling but little, see

fools cannot remain with her.

21 She will be like a heavy stone to test them,
and they will not delay in casting her
aside.

22 For wisdom is like her name;
she is not readily perceived by many.

23 Listen, my child, and accept my
judgment;
do not reject my counsel.

24 Put your feet into her fetters,
and your neck into her collar.

25 Bend your shoulders and carry her,
and do not fret under her bonds.

26 Come to her with all your soul,
and keep her ways with all your might.

27 Search out and seek, and she will become
known to you;
and when you get hold of her, do not
let her go.

28 For at last you will find the rest she gives,
and she will be changed into joy for you.

29 Then her fetters will become for you a
strong defense,
and her collar a glorious robe.

30 Her yoke[a] is a golden ornament,
and her bonds a purple cord.

31 You will wear her like a glorious robe,
and put her on like a splendid crown.[b]

32 If you are willing, my child, you can be
disciplined,
and if you apply yourself you will
become clever.

33 If you love to listen you will gain
knowledge,
and if you pay attention you will
become wise.

34 Stand in the company of the elders.
Who is wise? Attach yourself to such a
one.

35 Be ready to listen to every godly
discourse,
and let no wise proverbs escape you.

36 If you see an intelligent person, rise early
to visit him;
let your foot wear out his doorstep.

37 Reflect on the statutes of the Lord,
and meditate at all times on his
commandments.
It is he who will give insight to[c] your
mind,
and your desire for wisdom will be
granted.

Miscellaneous Advice

7 Do no evil, and evil will never overtake
you.

2 Stay away from wrong, and it will turn
away from you.

3 Do[d] not sow in the furrows of injustice,
and you will not reap a sevenfold crop.

4 Do not seek from the Lord high office,
or the seat of honor from the king.

5 Do not assert your righteousness before
the Lord,
or display your wisdom before the
king.

6 Do not seek to become a judge,
or you may be unable to root out
injustice;
you may be partial to the powerful,

---

a Heb: Gk *Upon her* *b* Heb: Gk *crown of gladness* *c* Heb: Gk
will confirm *d* Gk *My child, do*

51.27. **6.22** *Like her name,* a wordplay on the Hebrew
musar, meaning "instruction," which can also mean
"withdrawn," a subtle reference to the hiddenness of
personified wisdom. The twofold reference to wisdom
and instruction (or discipline) in vv. 18, 22 forms a poetic unit, or period. **6.23–31** The two stages of education are described. Faithful toil in wisdom's yoke and
fetters (vv. 23–27) turns those constraints into the garments of a royal priest (vv. 28–31). **6.24** On wisdom's
collar, or yoke (vv. 24–25, 29–30), see 51.26; Mt 11.29–
30. **6.26** *With all your soul . . . and might.* Cf. Deut 6.5.
6.30–31 For *a purple cord,* cf. Num 15.38–39. On the
glorious *robe* and *crown,* see 50.11; Prov 4.8–9. Cf. the
description of Aaron's vestments, 45.7–12. **6.32–
37** This stanza applies the preceding metaphors to enrollment as a student in the *company of the elders,* wise
teachers whose intelligence encompasses both prover-

bial wisdom and the law. On the elders as sages, cf. 8.8–
9. **6.34** *Attach yourself to such a one* is reminiscent of
later rabbinic practice. This may be early evidence for
such a practice in formative Judaism and may also reflect the Greek custom of becoming a student of a particular teacher. See note on 51.23. **6.37** Cf. Ps 1.2.

7.1–9.16 A long section of warnings and advice
characterized by negative injunctions (*Do not . . .*), frequently interspersed with motive clauses (*For . . .* in the
sense of "because"). The structure is loose, but generally consists of small units organized around relationships to particular classes of people. **7.4–7** This admonition against seeking high office in the court of a king
or as a judge is most curious, since both offices were
traditional goals of scribal education. It cautions
against presumption, as in Prov 25.6–7, but may also
reflect the political circumstances of Ben Sira's day; cf.

and so mar your integrity.

7 Commit no offense against the public,
  and do not disgrace yourself among
    the people.

8 Do not commit a sin twice;
  not even for one will you go
    unpunished.

9 Do not say, "He will consider the great
      number of my gifts,
  and when I make an offering to the
      Most High God, he will accept it."

10 Do not grow weary when you pray;
   do not neglect to give alms.

11 Do not ridicule a person who is
     embittered in spirit,
   for there is One who humbles and
     exalts.

12 Do not devise[a] a lie against your brother,
   or do the same to a friend.

13 Refuse to utter any lie,
   for it is a habit that results in no good.

14 Do not babble in the assembly of the
     elders,
   and do not repeat yourself when you
     pray.

15 Do not hate hard labor
   or farm work, which was created by the
     Most High.

16 Do not enroll in the ranks of sinners;
   remember that retribution does not
     delay.

17 Humble yourself to the utmost,
   for the punishment of the ungodly is
     fire and worms.[b]

Relations with Others

18 Do not exchange a friend for money,
   or a real brother for the gold of Ophir.

19 Do not dismiss[c] a wise and good wife,
   for her charm is worth more than gold.

20 Do not abuse slaves who work faithfully,
   or hired laborers who devote
     themselves to their task.

21 Let your soul love intelligent slaves;[d]
   do not withhold from them their
     freedom.

22 Do you have cattle? Look after them;
   if they are profitable to you, keep them.

23 Do you have children? Discipline them,
   and make them obedient[e] from their
     youth.

24 Do you have daughters? Be concerned for
     their chastity,[f]
   and do not show yourself too
     indulgent with them.

25 Give a daughter in marriage, and you
     complete a great task;
   but give her to a sensible man.

26 Do you have a wife who pleases you?[g] Do
     not divorce her;
   but do not trust yourself to one whom
     you detest.

27 With all your heart honor your father,
   and do not forget the birth pangs of
     your mother.

28 Remember that it was of your parents[h]
     you were born;
   how can you repay what they have
     given to you?

29 With all your soul fear the Lord,
   and revere his priests.

---

a Heb: Gk *plow* *b* Heb *for the expectation of mortals is worms*
c Heb: Gk *deprive yourself of* *d* Heb *Love a wise slave as
yourself* *e* Gk *bend their necks* *f* Gk *body* *g* Heb Syr *lack
who pleases you* *h* Gk *them*

11.9. **7.8–14** Admonitions concerning careless performance of basic ritual and ethical prescriptions. On offerings, prayers, and alms, see note on 35.1–13. **7.15–17** A set of three bicola on the virtue of labor. The translation follows the Greek text, which has partially obscured the logic of the Hebrew, especially in v. 16, where to *enroll in the ranks of sinners* is unclear. The original point was not to esteem oneself better than those who do manual labor (v. 16), but to practice humility in one's own (scribal, bureaucratic, or managerial) vocation (v. 17). **7.15** *Work* was considered good in the wisdom tradition and by Ben Sira. See 38.24–34. Labor is mentioned neutrally in the Decalogue (Deut 5.13), but cf. Gen 2.15, where labor is a result of sin.

Created translates the Greek; the Hebrew reads "assigned" or "allotted." Both terms indicate human occupations that have their place in the world as God intended it to be. See 31.27; 38.1; 39.25; 40.1; 44.2. **7.17** The Hebrew does not contain any allusion to postmortem punishment or fire; the references to *the punishment of the ungodly* and *fire* reveal the influence of Hellenistic eschatologies on the translator. **7.18–28** Advice on managing one's household, a frequent theme in Sirach. **7.18** *Ophir,* a region on the lower western shore of the Red Sea famous for its gold. See 1 Kings 9.28; Job 28.16. **7.21** On giving *slaves* their *freedom,* see Ex 21.2; Deut 15.12. **7.29–31** Wisdom piety includes honoring the *priests* who serve at the altar.

30 With all your might love your Maker,
and do not neglect his ministers.
31 Fear the Lord and honor the priest,
and give him his portion, as you have
been commanded:
the first fruits, the guilt offering, the gift
of the shoulders,
the sacrifice of sanctification, and the
first fruits of the holy things.

32 Stretch out your hand to the poor,
so that your blessing may be complete.
33 Give graciously to all the living;
do not withhold kindness even from
the dead.
34 Do not avoid those who weep,
but mourn with those who mourn.
35 Do not hesitate to visit the sick,
because for such deeds you will be loved.
36 In all you do, remember the end of your
life,
and then you will never sin.

Prudence and Common Sense

8 Do not contend with the powerful,
or you may fall into their hands.
2 Do not quarrel with the rich,
in case their resources outweigh yours;
for gold has ruined many,
and has perverted the minds of kings.
3 Do not argue with the loud of mouth,
and do not heap wood on their fire.

4 Do not make fun of one who is ill-bred,
or your ancestors may be insulted.
5 Do not reproach one who is turning away
from sin;
remember that we all deserve
punishment.
6 Do not disdain one who is old,
for some of us are also growing old.
7 Do not rejoice over anyone's death;
remember that we must all die.

8 Do not slight the discourse of the
sages,
but busy yourself with their maxims;
because from them you will learn
discipline
and how to serve princes.
9 Do not ignore the discourse of the aged,
for they themselves learned from their
parents;[a]
from them you learn how to understand
and to give an answer when the need
arises.

10 Do not kindle the coals of sinners,
or you may be burned in their flaming
fire.
11 Do not let the insolent bring you to your
feet,
or they may lie in ambush against your
words.
12 Do not lend to one who is stronger than
you;
but if you do lend anything, count it as
a loss.
13 Do not give surety beyond your means;
but if you give surety, be prepared to
pay.

14 Do not go to law against a judge,
for the decision will favor him because
of his standing.
15 Do not go traveling with the reckless,
or they will be burdensome to you;
for they will act as they please,
and through their folly you will perish
with them.
16 Do not pick a fight with the quick-
tempered,
and do not journey with them through
lonely country,

---

a Or ancestors

Ben Sira was a fervent supporter of the Jerusalem priestly authorities for whom he worked. *With all your soul . . . might.* Cf. Deut 6.5. **7.31** On the priest's *portion,* see Ex 29.27; Lev 7.31–34; Deut 18.3; Num 18.8–20. **7.32–36** The wisdom ethic focuses on helping the socially marginalized. **7.33** The meaning of *kindness* toward the *dead* is unclear. It may refer to burial of the poor, a pious act. See Tob 1.17.
8.1–19 Cautionary advice on dangerous relationships with a long list of character types and social roles. Here is evidence of Ben Sira's and his students'

social status. Although they must contend with the wealthy classes who presumably employ them, they are not reckoned among the poor and marginalized. Caution is a constant theme underlying much of the advice in Sirach, and many cautionary sayings have parallels in Egyptian wisdom literature. **8.3** *Heap wood on their fire,* a common metaphor for "fueling the flame" of a hothead, or person given to anger, a character type just the opposite of the "cool" person of wisdom. See 8.10; 28.10; cf. the Egyptian Instruction of Amenemope. **8.11** *Lie in ambush,* a common

because bloodshed means nothing to
　　them,
　　and where no help is at hand, they will
　　　　strike you down.
17 Do not consult with fools,
　　for they cannot keep a secret.
18 In the presence of strangers do nothing
　　　that is to be kept secret,
　　for you do not know what they will
　　　　divulge.*a*
19 Do not reveal your thoughts to anyone,
　　or you may drive away your
　　　　happiness.*b*

Advice concerning Women

9 Do not be jealous of the wife of your
　　bosom,
　　or you will teach her an evil lesson to
　　　your own hurt.
2 Do not give yourself to a woman
　　and let her trample down your
　　　strength.
3 Do not go near a loose woman,
　　or you will fall into her snares.
4 Do not dally with a singing girl,
　　or you will be caught by her tricks.
5 Do not look intently at a virgin,
　　or you may stumble and incur
　　　penalties for her.
6 Do not give yourself to prostitutes,
　　or you may lose your inheritance.
7 Do not look around in the streets of a city,
　　or wander about in its deserted
　　　sections.
8 Turn away your eyes from a shapely
　　　woman,
　　and do not gaze at beauty belonging to
　　　another;

many have been seduced by a woman's
　　beauty,
　　and by it passion is kindled like a fire.
9 Never dine with another man's wife,
　　or revel with her at wine;
or your heart may turn aside to her,
　　and in blood*c* you may be plunged into
　　　destruction.

Choice of Friends

10 Do not abandon old friends,
　　for new ones cannot equal them.
A new friend is like new wine;
　　when it has aged, you can drink it with
　　　pleasure.

11 Do not envy the success of sinners,
　　for you do not know what their end
　　　will be like.
12 Do not delight in what pleases the
　　　ungodly;
　　remember that they will not be held
　　　guiltless all their lives.

13 Keep far from those who have power to
　　kill,
　　and you will not be haunted by the fear
　　　of death.
But if you approach them, make no
　　　misstep,
　　or they may rob you of your life.
Know that you are stepping among
　　　snares,
　　and that you are walking on the city
　　　battlements.

---

a Or *it will bring forth*　　*b* Heb: Gk *and let him not return a favor to you*　　*c* Heb: Gk *by your spirit*

---

metaphor for entrapment. **8.18** To keep a *secret* refers to keeping a confidence, the mark of a true friend. The problem of betrayal by strangers and fools was of great concern to Ben Sira. See 1.30; 13.12; 19.7–12; 22.22; 27.16–21; 37.10; 42.1.

9.1–9 Warnings about seduction and sexual promiscuity. The male point of view prevails. The topic was both ancient and timely, given the Jews' heightened concern during this period for stable families and ethnic purity as ways to guarantee their distinctive social identity. **9.3** *A loose woman,* mentioned in Prov 2.16–19; 5.3–6; 7.5–27; 9.13–18. **9.4** *A singing girl* suggests an entertainer, customarily viewed as a prostitute in the Greek tradition of the banquet. Cf. Isa 23.15–16. **9.6** *Lose your inheritance* is unclear but may mean "squander." Cf. Prov 29.3. **9.9** To *dine with another man's wife* was considered risky. Greek prac-

tice frowned upon the presence of wives at meals where guests were present. Ben Sira knew about the Greek convention of the banquet and its after-dinner symposium. He does not include warnings about women in attendance in his description of mealtime etiquette in 31.12–32.13. *Plunged into destruction* may refer to the death penalty for adultery (Lev 20.10; Deut 22.22). **9.10–16** Advice on associations with various classes of people serves as a subtle introduction to the discourse on those in positions of power in ch. 10. **9.10** On the theme of friendship and its social and political significance, see note on 6.5–17. **9.11–12** *Sinners* and the *ungodly,* possibly foreigners as a class as well as Jews who assimilate gentile ways. Cf. the picture of the ungodly in Wis 1.16–4.20 and the contrast between Jews and "gentile sinners" in Gal 2.15. **9.13** *Those who have power to kill,* rulers and kings. Cf.

14 As much as you can, aim to know your
        neighbors,
        and consult with the wise.
15 Let your conversation be with intelligent
        people,
        and let all your discussion be about the
        law of the Most High.
16 Let the righteous be your dinner
        companions,
        and let your glory be in the fear of the
        Lord.

Concerning Rulers

17 A work is praised for the skill of the
        artisan;
        so a people's leader is proved wise by
        his words.
18 The loud of mouth are feared in their
        city,
        and the one who is reckless in speech is
        hated.

10 A wise magistrate educates his people,
        and the rule of an intelligent person is
        well ordered.
2 As the people's judge is, so are his officials;
        as the ruler of the city is, so are all its
        inhabitants.
3 An undisciplined king ruins his people,
        but a city becomes fit to live in through
        the understanding of its rulers.
4 The government of the earth is in the
        hand of the Lord,
        and over it he will raise up the right
        leader for the time.
5 Human success is in the hand of the Lord,
        and it is he who confers honor upon
        the lawgiver. *a*

The Sin of Pride

6 Do not get angry with your neighbor for
        every injury,

and do not resort to acts of insolence.
7 Arrogance is hateful to the Lord and to
        mortals,
        and injustice is outrageous to both.
8 Sovereignty passes from nation to nation
        on account of injustice and insolence
        and wealth. *b*
9 How can dust and ashes be proud?
        Even in life the human body decays. *c*
10 A long illness baffles the physician; *d*
        the king of today will die tomorrow.
11 For when one is dead
        he inherits maggots and vermin *e* and
        worms.
12 The beginning of human pride is to
        forsake the Lord;
        the heart has withdrawn from its
        Maker.
13 For the beginning of pride is sin,
        and the one who clings to it pours out
        abominations.
Therefore the Lord brings upon them
        unheard-of calamities,
        and destroys them completely.
14 The Lord overthrows the thrones of
        rulers,
        and enthrones the lowly in their place.
15 The Lord plucks up the roots of the
        nations, *f*
        and plants the humble in their place.
16 The Lord lays waste the lands of the
        nations,
        and destroys them to the foundations
        of the earth.
17 He removes some of them and destroys
        them,

a Heb: Gk *scribe*   *b* Other ancient authorities add here or after
verse 9a, *Nothing is more wicked than one who loves money, for
such a person puts his own soul up for sale.*   *c* Heb: Meaning of
Gk uncertain   *d* Heb Lat: Meaning of Gk uncertain   *e* Heb:
Gk *wild animals*   *f* Other ancient authorities read *proud nations*

Dan 2.5; 3.29; Lk 12.4. **9.17–10.5** This description of
the ideal ruler has roots in traditional wisdom and in
the OT. Perhaps it serves as a veiled critique of Ptole-
maic-Seleucid hegemony. It breaks the pattern of negative injunctions and cautionary advice that predominates in chs. 7–9.
        10.6–18 A discourse on the sin of pride directed to-
ward those in power. A first stanza shows pride to be
foolish in the light of human mortality (vv. 6–11). A
second stanza forms a poetic unit on the consequences
of pride because of its close relationship to sin (vv. 12–
18). **10.8** *Insolence,* the Greek notion of arrogance and
violence (*hubris*), is added to the Jewish concern for

justice and a social critique of wealth as factors in the
rise and fall of kingdoms. Insolence may be an oblique
reference to Hellenistic ideologies of kings as gods.
10.10 For the counterproposition that *the king . . . will
die,* cf. Wis 7.5–6 in tension with Wis 8.19–20.
10.13 *Pride* and *sin* are joined to form a vicious cycle.
Because pride stems from sin, which then produces
abominations, it suffers the divine response to sin.
10.14–16 The motif of humiliation/exaltation as
found in Psalms and the wisdom stories of the pious
righteous one (Gen 39–50; Dan 1–6; Wis 2–5) is
merged with a theology of divine judgment and applied to the fall and rise of nations. This section antici-

and erases the memory of them from
the earth.

18 Pride was not created for human beings,
or violent anger for those born of
women.

Persons Deserving Honor

19 Whose offspring are worthy of honor?
Human offspring.
Whose offspring are worthy of honor?
Those who fear the Lord.
Whose offspring are unworthy of honor?
Human offspring.
Whose offspring are unworthy of honor?
Those who break the commandments.

20 Among family members their leader is
worthy of honor,
but those who fear the Lord are worthy
of honor in his eyes.*a*

22 The rich, and the eminent, and the poor—
their glory is the fear of the Lord.

23 It is not right to despise one who is
intelligent but poor,
and it is not proper to honor one who
is sinful.

24 The prince and the judge and the ruler
are honored,
but none of them is greater than the
one who fears the Lord.

25 Free citizens will serve a wise servant,
and an intelligent person will not
complain.

Concerning Humility

26 Do not make a display of your wisdom
when you do your work,
and do not boast when you are in need.

27 Better is the worker who has goods in
plenty
than the boaster who lacks bread.

28 My child, honor yourself with humility,
and give yourself the esteem you
deserve.

29 Who will acquit those who condemn*b*
themselves?
And who will honor those who
dishonor themselves?*c*

30 The poor are honored for their knowledge,
while the rich are honored for their
wealth.

31 One who is honored in poverty, how
much more in wealth!
And one dishonored in wealth, how
much more in poverty!

The Deceptiveness of Appearances

11 The wisdom of the humble lifts their
heads high,
and seats them among the great.

2 Do not praise individuals for their good
looks,
or loathe anyone because of
appearance alone.

3 The bee is small among flying creatures,
but what it produces is the best of
sweet things.

4 Do not boast about wearing fine clothes,
and do not exalt yourself when you are
honored;
for the works of the Lord are wonderful,
and his works are concealed from
humankind.

5 Many kings have had to sit on the ground,
but one who was never thought of has
worn a crown.

6 Many rulers have been utterly disgraced,

---

a Other ancient authorities add as verse 21, *The fear of the Lord
is the beginning of acceptance; obduracy and pride are the
beginning of rejection.*   *b* Heb: Gk *sin against*   *c* Heb Lat: Gk
their own life

---

pates and encapsulates 35.22–36.22. **10.18** *Created*
translates "allotted," or "assigned," Ben Sira's term for
divine intention, agency, and will. Cf. note on 7.15.
The point is that God is not responsible for sin and its
effects, an issue with which Ben Sira struggles in chs.
15–17. **10.19–11.6** A section on the honor due those
who fear the Lord. It contrasts with the preceding section on the pride of those who do not fear the Lord
(9.17–10.18). **10.19–25** Four riddles establish the
theme that only those who fear the Lord are truly honorable (v. 19). Vv. 22–25 establish that one who fears
the Lord occupies a station higher than any human social category. **10.25** To *serve a wise servant* draws upon
a topic common in the Hellenistic period, namely, that
slaves may be more learned than their masters. This

was frequently the case because of the widespread enslavement of peoples by conquest. **10.26–31** A small
collection of proverbs concerned with the problem of
relating the notion of honor to humility, a cultural
code and an ethic of piety at odds with one another.
11.1–6 A cluster of warnings and proverbs about pre-
tension and false appearances supports the suggestion
that the tables will be turned on the proud and mighty
(10.14) and that the humble (pious) will be vindicated
by the Lord. Cf. 1 Sam 2.7–8; Ps 113.7–8. **11.4** On the
wonder of God's *works*, see 42.15–43.26. **11.5** Possibly
an allusion to the story of David's selection to be king
(1 Sam 16.6–13). **11.6** *Handed over*, a common idiom
for defeat in war, related to "falling into the hands of"
one who gains power over another.

and the honored have been handed
over to others.

Deliberation and Caution

7 Do not find fault before you investigate;
examine first, and then criticize.

8 Do not answer before you listen,
and do not interrupt when another is
speaking.

9 Do not argue about a matter that does
not concern you,
and do not sit with sinners when they
judge a case.

10 My child, do not busy yourself with many
matters;
if you multiply activities, you will not
be held blameless.
If you pursue, you will not overtake,
and by fleeing you will not escape.

11 There are those who work and struggle
and hurry,
but are so much the more in want.

12 There are others who are slow and need
help,
who lack strength and abound in
poverty;
but the eyes of the Lord look kindly upon
them;
he lifts them out of their lowly condition

13 and raises up their heads
to the amazement of the many.

14 Good things and bad, life and death,
poverty and wealth, come from the
Lord. *a*

17 The Lord's gift remains with the devout,
and his favor brings lasting success.

18 One becomes rich through diligence and
self-denial,
and the reward allotted to him is this:

19 when he says, "I have found rest,
and now I shall feast on my goods!"
he does not know how long it will be
until he leaves them to others and dies.

20 Stand by your agreement and attend to it,
and grow old in your work.

21 Do not wonder at the works of a sinner,
but trust in the Lord and keep at your
job;
for it is easy in the sight of the Lord
to make the poor rich suddenly, in an
instant.

22 The blessing of the Lord is *b* the reward of
the pious,
and quickly God causes his blessing to
flourish.

23 Do not say, "What do I need,
and what further benefit can be mine?"

24 Do not say, "I have enough,
and what harm can come to me now?"

25 In the day of prosperity, adversity is
forgotten,
and in the day of adversity, prosperity
is not remembered.

26 For it is easy for the Lord on the day of
death
to reward individuals according to
their conduct.

27 An hour's misery makes one forget past
delights,
and at the close of one's life one's deeds
are revealed.

28 Call no one happy before his death;
by how he ends, a person becomes
known. *c*

Care in Choosing Friends

29 Do not invite everyone into your home,
for many are the tricks of the crafty.

30 Like a decoy partridge in a cage, so is the
mind of the proud,
and like spies they observe your
weakness; *d*

31 for they lie in wait, turning good into
evil,
and to worthy actions they attach
blame.

32 From a spark many coals are kindled,
and a sinner lies in wait to shed blood.

33 Beware of scoundrels, for they devise evil,
and they may ruin your reputation
forever.

34 Receive strangers into your home and
they will stir up trouble for you,
and will make you a stranger to your
own family.

12 If you do good, know to whom you
do it,
and you will be thanked for your good
deeds.

---

a Other ancient authorities add as verses 15 and 16, *15Wisdom,
understanding, and knowledge of the law come from the Lord;
affection and the ways of good works come from him. 16Error and
darkness were created with sinners; evil grows old with those who
take pride in malice.* *b* Heb: Gk is in *c* Heb: Gk and through
his children a person becomes known *d* Heb: Gk downfall

2 Do good to the devout, and you will be
  repaid—
    if not by them, certainly by the Most
    High.
3 No good comes to one who persists in evil
  or to one who does not give alms.
4 Give to the devout, but do not help the
  sinner.
5 Do good to the humble, but do not
    give to the ungodly;
  hold back their bread, and do not give it
    to them,
    for by means of it they might subdue
    you;
  then you will receive twice as much evil
    for all the good you have done to them.
6 For the Most High also hates sinners
    and will inflict punishment on the
    ungodly.ᵃ
7 Give to the one who is good, but do not
  help the sinner.
8 A friend is not knownᵇ in prosperity,
  nor is an enemy hidden in adversity.
9 One's enemies are friendlyᶜ when one
    prospers,
  but in adversity even one's friend
    disappears.
10 Never trust your enemy,
  for like corrosion in copper, so is his
  wickedness.
11 Even if he humbles himself and walks
    bowed down,
  take care to be on your guard against
    him.
  Be to him like one who polishes a mirror,
    to be sure it does not become
    completely tarnished.
12 Do not put him next to you,
  or he may overthrow you and take
  your place.

Do not let him sit at your right hand,
  or else he may try to take your own
  seat,
and at last you will realize the truth of my
  words,
  and be stung by what I have said.
13 Who pities a snake charmer when he is
    bitten,
  or all those who go near wild animals?
14 So no one pities a person who associates
    with a sinner
  and becomes involved in the other's
  sins.
15 He stands by you for a while,
  but if you falter, he will not be there.
16 An enemy speaks sweetly with his lips,
  but in his heart he plans to throw you
    into a pit;
  an enemy may have tears in his eyes,
  but if he finds an opportunity he will
    never have enough of your blood.
17 If evil comes upon you, you will find him
    there ahead of you;
  pretending to help, he will trip you up.
18 Then he will shake his head, and clap his
    hands,
  and whisper much, and show his true
  face.

Caution Regarding Associates

13 Whoever touches pitch gets dirty,
  and whoever associates with a proud
  person becomes like him.
2 Do not lift a weight too heavy for you,
  or associate with one mightier and
  richer than you.

---

a Other ancient authorities add *and he is keeping them for the
day of their punishment* *b* Other ancient authorities read
punished *c* Heb: Gk *grieved*

11.7–28 A reflection on patience aimed at instilling
confidence that the Lord will reward piety in his time.
11.14 On God as the source of all human conditions,
cf. Job 1.21; Isa 45.7. **11.17** Ben Sira accepts the
Deuteronomic view that the faithful prosper. See, e.g.,
Deut 6.1–3, 17–19. **11.19** On leaving one's goods to
others, cf. Ps 49.10; Eccl 2.18–23; Lk 12.19. **11.26** This
is Ben Sira's solution to the problem of individual
theodicy, or the assurance that accounts will be balanced so that the righteous will be rewarded and sinners punished. Since he did not imagine life after
death, the *day of death* is the last earthly moment for
the "appointed time" of rewards and judgments. The
reward will be to have one's good name remembered

and the strength and confidence to bless the next generation. See 1.13; 2.3; 3.26; 6.18, 28; 7.17, 36; 8.7; 9.11–
12; 14.12–19; 17.27–32; 18.24; 19.3; 21.10; 28.6; 29.21;
33.24; 37.25; 38.21–23; 39.11; 41.1–10. **11.28** A saying
proverbial among the Greeks. **11.29–12.18** Cautionary advice on close relationships with scoundrels,
strangers, sinners, and enemies. They are not to be
trusted, since they can do material and physical harm
as well as compromise one's honor. **12.4–5** *Do not help
. . . them.* For a contrasting view, see Mt 5.42.

13.1–24 Ben Sira gives cautionary advice to
prospective scribes who have to negotiate relationships
with their wealthy patrons/employers. **13.1a** A proverb
with a long history that can be traced from Theognis

How can the clay pot associate with the
    iron kettle?
    The pot will strike against it and be
      smashed.

3 A rich person does wrong, and even adds
    insults;
    a poor person suffers wrong, and must
      add apologies.

4 A rich person*a* will exploit you if you can
    be of use to him,
    but if you are in need he will abandon
      you.

5 If you own something, he will live with
    you;
    he will drain your resources without a
      qualm.

6 When he needs you he will deceive you,
    and will smile at you and encourage
      you;
    he will speak to you kindly and say,
      "What do you need?"

7 He will embarrass you with his delicacies,
    until he has drained you two or three
      times,
    and finally he will laugh at you.
    Should he see you afterwards, he will pass
      you by
    and shake his head at you.

8 Take care not to be led astray
    and humiliated when you are enjoying
      yourself.*b*

9 When an influential person invites you,
    be reserved,
    and he will invite you more insistently.

10 Do not be forward, or you may be
    rebuffed;
    do not stand aloof, or you will be
      forgotten.

11 Do not try to treat him as an equal,
    or trust his lengthy conversations;
    for he will test you by prolonged talk,
    and while he smiles he will be
      examining you.

12 Cruel are those who do not keep your
    secrets;
    they will not spare you harm or
      imprisonment.

13 Be on your guard and very careful,
    for you are walking about with your
      own downfall.*c*

15 Every creature loves its like,
    and every person the neighbor.

16 All living beings associate with their own
    kind,
    and people stick close to those like
      themselves.

17 What does a wolf have in common with a
    lamb?
    No more has a sinner with the devout.

18 What peace is there between a hyena and
    a dog?
    And what peace between the rich and
      the poor?

19 Wild asses in the wilderness are the prey
    of lions;
    likewise the poor are feeding grounds
      for the rich.

20 Humility is an abomination to the proud;
    likewise the poor are an abomination
      to the rich.

21 When the rich person totters, he is
    supported by friends,
    but when the humble*d* falls, he is
      pushed away even by friends.

22 If the rich person slips, many come to the
    rescue;
    he speaks unseemly words, but they
      justify him.
    If the humble person slips, they even
      criticize him;
    he talks sense, but is not given a
      hearing.

23 The rich person speaks and all are silent;
    they extol to the clouds what he says.
    The poor person speaks and they say,
      "Who is this fellow?"
    And should he stumble, they even push
      him down.

24 Riches are good if they are free from sin;
    poverty is evil only in the opinion of
      the ungodly.

25 The heart changes the countenance,
    either for good or for evil.*e*

26 The sign of a happy heart is a cheerful
    face,
    but to devise proverbs requires painful
      thinking.

14 Happy are those who do not blunder
    with their lips,

---

a Gk *He*   *b* Other ancient authorities read *in your folly*
c Other ancient authorities add as verse 14, *When you hear these
things in your sleep, wake up! During all your life love the Lord,
and call on him for your salvation.*   *d* Other ancient authorities
read *poor*   *e* Other ancient authorities add *and a glad heart
makes a cheerful countenance*

and need not suffer remorse for sin.

2 Happy are those whose hearts do not
      condemn them,
   and who have not given up their hope.

Responsible Use of Wealth

3 Riches are inappropriate for a small-
      minded person;
   and of what use is wealth to a miser?

4 What he denies himself he collects for
      others;
   and others will live in luxury on his
      goods.

5 If one is mean to himself, to whom will
      he be generous?
   He will not enjoy his own riches.

6 No one is worse than one who is
      grudging to himself;
   this is the punishment for his
      meanness.

7 If ever he does good, it is by mistake;
   and in the end he reveals his meanness.

8 The miser is an evil person;
   he turns away and disregards people.

9 The eye of the greedy person is not
      satisfied with his share;
   greedy injustice withers the soul.

10 A miser begrudges bread,
    and it is lacking at his table.

11 My child, treat yourself well, according to
      your means,
    and present worthy offerings to the
      Lord.

12 Remember that death does not tarry,
    and the decree[a] of Hades has not been
      shown to you.

13 Do good to friends before you die,
    and reach out and give to them as
      much as you can.

14 Do not deprive yourself of a day's
      enjoyment;
    do not let your share of desired good
      pass by you.

15 Will you not leave the fruit of your labors
      to another,
    and what you acquired by toil to be
      divided by lot?

16 Give, and take, and indulge yourself,
    because in Hades one cannot look for
      luxury.

17 All living beings become old like a
      garment,
    for the decree[b] from of old is, "You
      must die!"

18 Like abundant leaves on a spreading tree
      that sheds some and puts forth others,
    so are the generations of flesh and blood:
      one dies and another is born.

19 Every work decays and ceases to exist,
    and the one who made it will pass
      away with it.

The Happiness of Seeking Wisdom

20 Happy is the person who meditates on[c]
      wisdom
    and reasons intelligently,

21 who[d] reflects in his heart on her ways
    and ponders her secrets,

22 pursuing her like a hunter,
    and lying in wait on her paths;

23 who peers through her windows
    and listens at her doors;

24 who camps near her house
    and fastens his tent peg to her walls;

25 who pitches his tent near her,

---

a Heb Syr: Gk *covenant*   b Heb: Gk *covenant*   c Other ancient
authorities read *dies in*   d The structure adopted in verses 21–
27 follows the Heb

---

through Sirach and Shakespeare to the present time.
13.5 *He will live with you* may have the sense of "moving in on you." **13.19** *Feeding grounds,* a particularly
striking image for social predation. Preying upon the
poor was a major concern for the prophets of social justice; see Am 5.11–13; cf. Isaiah's vision of a society
without predation (Isa 11.6–9). **13.24** An exception to
the preceding statements about the rich is made for
wealth that is *free from sin.* This probably refers to almsgiving; see 3.30–4.6. Ben Sira does not criticize the rich
simply for being rich, nor are the poor sinful for being
poor. **13.25–14.2** A short meditation on happiness.
The *heart* (v. 25) was understood as the seat of sentiment, desire, thought, and will. **14.3–19** Reflections on

mortality and the proper use of wealth. **14.3–10** A poetic unit on the miser as a contrast to a wise user of
wealth. **14.11** *According to your means* allows for enjoyment of one's resources. See also v. 14. **14.12** *The decree
of Hades* may refer either to death's appointed time or
to the decree that one must die as expressed in v. 17.
14.15 *Divided by lot,* a method for distributing an inheritance. **14.16** *Indulge yourself,* reminiscent of Eccl
7.14; 9.7–10. **14.17** An allusion to Gen 3.3, 19.
   14.20–15.10 A poem on personified wisdom in two
stanzas developing the theme of seeking (14.20–27)
and finding (15.1–10). **14.21–22** On wisdom's *ways,*
or path, cf. 51.15; Prov 3.17; 8.20, 32. **14.23–25** On the
metaphor of approaching wisdom's *house,* cf. 51.13–

and so occupies an excellent lodging
  place;
26 who places his children under her
  shelter,
  and lodges under her boughs;
27 who is sheltered by her from the heat,
  and dwells in the midst of her glory.

15 Whoever fears the Lord will do this,
  and whoever holds to the law will
  obtain wisdom. ^a
2 She will come to meet him like a mother,
  and like a young bride she will
  welcome him.
3 She will feed him with the bread of
  learning,
  and give him the water of wisdom to
  drink.
4 He will lean on her and not fall,
  and he will rely on her and not be put
  to shame.
5 She will exalt him above his neighbors,
  and will open his mouth in the midst
  of the assembly.
6 He will find gladness and a crown of
  rejoicing,
  and will inherit an everlasting name.
7 The foolish will not obtain her,
  and sinners will not see her.
8 She is far from arrogance,
  and liars will never think of her.
9 Praise is unseemly on the lips of a sinner,
  for it has not been sent from the Lord.
10 For in wisdom must praise be uttered,
  and the Lord will make it prosper.

Freedom of Choice

11 Do not say, "It was the Lord's doing that I
  fell away";
  for he does not do ^b what he hates.
12 Do not say, "It was he who led me astray";
  for he has no need of the sinful.
13 The Lord hates all abominations;
  such things are not loved by those who
  fear him.
14 It was he who created humankind in the
  beginning,
  and he left them in the power of their
  own free choice.
15 If you choose, you can keep the
  commandments,
  and to act faithfully is a matter of your
  own choice.
16 He has placed before you fire and water;
  stretch out your hand for whichever
  you choose.
17 Before each person are life and death,
  and whichever one chooses will be
  given.
18 For great is the wisdom of the Lord;
  he is mighty in power and sees
  everything;
19 his eyes are on those who fear him,
  and he knows every human action.
20 He has not commanded anyone to be
  wicked,
  and he has not given anyone
  permission to sin.

_____
a Gk *her*   b Heb: Gk *you ought not to do*

14; Prov 8.34; 9.1–6. **14.26–27** On wisdom as a tree, cf. 1.20; 24.13–17; Prov 3.18. **15.1** On the connection of wisdom and Torah, see ch. 24. **15.2** On wisdom as *mother* and *bride*, cf. Prov 7.4; Wis 7.12; 8.2. **15.3** On receiving *bread* and *water* (or wine) from wisdom, cf. 1.16; 24.19–21; Prov 9.5. **15.5** On the *assembly* as the place for speech and praise, see 21.17; 24.2; 31.11; 33.19; 38.32–33; 39.10; 44.15; Wis 8.10–12.

15.11–20 A diatribe, or fictional debate, introduces the question of responsibility for sin in the light of its devastating consequences, a theme that has surfaced with increasing frequency in the preceding chapters. The position argued against is that God ultimately must be responsible because he created the world in such a way as to make sin possible. Ben Sira argues that God is not responsible because humans have free choice. This is a theodicy similar to that argued by the friends of Job, but quite different from that proposed by the author of Job. **15.14** *Free choice* translates the Hebrew *yetser,* a term for the "design," "plan," or "intention" one has in

mind when preparing to form, craft, or create something. *Yetser* is used of evil design or imagination in Gen 6.5; 8.21, and of good design in 1 Chr 29.28; Isa 26.3. Sirach documents an early use of the term to define human nature. Cf. 17.6; 21.11; 27.6; 37.3. Later rabbinic tradition sometimes refers to two *yetsers,* meaning that each person has both a good and an evil "inclination." The Greek is *diaboulion,* meaning "deliberation." V. 15 and the context show that *free choice* is an appropriate translation. Cf. 6.32. **15.16** *Fire and water,* metaphors for destruction and the generation of life. **15.17** *Life and death.* Cf. Deut 30.19. The image of choosing between "two ways," one of life and one of death, is a common theme in Jewish and early Christian literature as well as in the Greek tradition. **15.18** That the Lord *sees everything* is a notion essential to Ben Sira's theodicy with its insistence upon divine reward (or rescue) for the righteous and punishment for sinners. See 16.17–23; 17.15–19; 23.19–21; 34.19–20; 39.19–20; 42.16–20; cf. Job 34.21–22; Pss 33.13–15; 90.8; Prov 5.21; 15.3; Heb 4.13.

God's Punishment of Sinners

16 Do not desire a multitude of worthless[a] children,
and do not rejoice in ungodly offspring.

2 If they multiply, do not rejoice in them,
unless the fear of the Lord is in them.

3 Do not trust in their survival,
or rely on their numbers;[b]
for one can be better than a thousand,
and to die childless is better than to have ungodly children.

4 For through one intelligent person a city can be filled with people,
but through a clan of outlaws it becomes desolate.

5 Many such things my eye has seen,
and my ear has heard things more striking than these.

6 In an assembly of sinners a fire is kindled,
and in a disobedient nation wrath blazes up.

7 He did not forgive the ancient giants who revolted in their might.

8 He did not spare the neighbors of Lot,
whom he loathed on account of their arrogance.

9 He showed no pity on the doomed nation,
on those dispossessed because of their sins;[c]

10 or on the six hundred thousand foot soldiers
who assembled in their stubbornness.[d]

11 Even if there were only one stiff-necked person,
it would be a wonder if he remained unpunished.
For mercy and wrath are with the Lord;[e]
he is mighty to forgive—but he also pours out wrath.

12 Great as is his mercy, so also is his chastisement;
he judges a person according to his or her deeds.

13 The sinner will not escape with plunder,
and the patience of the godly will not be frustrated.

14 He makes room for every act of mercy;
everyone receives in accordance with his or her deeds.[f]

17 Do not say, "I am hidden from the Lord,
and who from on high has me in mind?

---

a Heb: Gk *unprofitable* *b* Other ancient authorities add *For you will groan in untimely mourning, and will know of their sudden end.* *c* Other ancient authorities add *All these things he did to the hard-hearted nations, and by the multitude of his holy ones he was not appeased.* *d* Other ancient authorities add *Chastising, showing mercy, striking, healing, the Lord persisted in mercy and discipline.* *e* Gk *him* *f* Other ancient authorities add [15]*The Lord hardened Pharaoh so that he did not recognize him, in order that his works might be known under heaven.* [16]*His mercy is manifest to the whole of creation, and he divided his light and darkness with a plumb line.*

16.1–23 A set of three arguments for the certainty of divine recompense: that the large number of the ungodly does not count (vv. 1–4); that history provides examples of the destruction of sinners (vv. 5–14); and that the Lord sees everything (vv. 17–23). **16.1–4** A challenge to the traditional view that many children are a blessing: this is not so if they are *worthless* or *ungodly.* To Sirach one's good memory after death, especially through one's children, constitutes immortality; see 39.9. **16.3** This radical view of the acceptability of childlessness is an indication of social distress. It is repeated in Wis 4.1–3. **16.4** The importance of *one intelligent person* for the well-being of a city recurs as a theme in the writings of Philo of Alexandria; cf. Eccl 9.15. *Filled with people* may be an allusion to Abraham's blessing (Gen 17.5–6; 22.17–18). He was considered a wise man in such legendary accounts as Philo's *De Abrahamo. Desolate* may be an allusion to the Sodomites (Gen 18.16–32). **16.5–14** A series of examples from the epic history of Israel prepares for a programmatic statement about the Lord's mercy and wrath (vv. 11–12). **16.6** An *assembly of sin-* ners, an allusion to the rebellion of Korah's company (Num 16); cf. Num 11.1–3; see Sir 45.18–19. **16.7** *Giants.* See Gen 6.1–4; the legend of the fall of the Watchers in *1 Enoch* 6–16. **16.8** *The neighbors of Lot* alludes to Gen 19; cf. Ezek 16.49–50. **16.9** *Doomed nation* may be an allusion to the Canaanites. **16.10** An allusion to Israel in the wilderness (Ex 12.37); cf. Sir 46.8. **16.12** The Hebrew word for *chastisement* also means "punishment." The Greek term is *elengchos,* "conviction," in the sense of instructional correction. At a somewhat later time chastisement for the godly was distinguished from punishment for the ungodly, as in the Wisdom of Solomon. The mention of mercy in vv. 11–12 and the shift to a consideration of rewards and punishments according to one's deeds in this section as a whole may have called for a Greek term other than "punishment" and probably lie behind the additions in some manuscripts to v. 10 that emphasize chastising and discipline (text note *d*). Cf. 18.13. **16.17–23** The theme of hidden wisdom is used ironically to characterize the speech of the foolish person who draws the wrong conclusion from the inscrutabil-

Among so many people I am unknown,
  for what am I in a boundless creation?

18 Lo, heaven and the highest heaven,
      the abyss and the earth, tremble at his
        visitation!^{a}

19 The very mountains and the foundations
      of the earth
    quiver and quake when he looks upon
      them.

20 But no human mind can grasp this,
      and who can comprehend his ways?

21 Like a tempest that no one can see,
      so most of his works are concealed.^{b}

22 Who is to announce his acts of justice?
    Or who can await them? For his
      decree^c is far off."^{d}

23 Such are the thoughts of one devoid of
      understanding;
    a senseless and misguided person
      thinks foolishly.

God's Wisdom Seen in Creation

24 Listen to me, my child, and acquire
      knowledge,
    and pay close attention to my words.

25 I will impart discipline precisely^e
      and declare knowledge accurately.

26 When the Lord created^f his works from
      the beginning,
    and, in making them, determined their
      boundaries,

27 he arranged his works in an eternal order,
    and their dominion^g for all
      generations.
    They neither hunger nor grow weary,

    and they do not abandon their tasks.

28 They do not crowd one another,
      and they never disobey his word.

29 Then the Lord looked upon the earth,
      and filled it with his good things.

30 With all kinds of living beings he covered
      its surface,
    and into it they must return.

17 The Lord created human beings out
      of earth,
    and makes them return to it again.

2 He gave them a fixed number of days,
    but granted them authority over
      everything on the earth.^{h}

3 He endowed them with strength like his
      own,^{i}
    and made them in his own image.

4 He put the fear of them^j in all living
      beings,
    and gave them dominion over beasts
      and birds.^{k}

6 Discretion and tongue and eyes,
    ears and a mind for thinking he gave
      them.

7 He filled them with knowledge and
      understanding,
    and showed them good and evil.

---

a Other ancient authorities add *The whole world past and present
is in his will.* b Meaning of Gk uncertain: Heb Syr *If I sin, no
eye can see me, and if I am disloyal all in secret, who is to know?*
c Heb *the decree:* Gk *the covenant* d Other ancient authorities
add *and a scrutiny for all comes at the end* e Gk *by weight*
f Heb: Gk *judged* g Or *elements* h Lat: Gk *it* i Lat: Gk
proper to them j Syr: Gk *him* k Other ancient authorities add
as verse 5, *They obtained the use of the five faculties of the Lord; as
sixth he distributed to them the gift of mind, and as seventh,
reason, the interpreter of one's faculties.*

---

ity of God's ways. **16.18** *Visitation,* an important concept for Jewish theodicies of the time. It refers to a time
when God "visits" the earth and looks upon it to render judgment. See 18.20. Cf. Ps 104.32; Wis 3.7; 14.11.
  16.24–18.14 A long didactic poem on the Lord's
creation with a focus upon the creation of human beings, their capacity to know and keep the law, and their
ability to repent should they fall into sin. **16.24–30** An
account of creation emphasizing the stability, order,
and "obedience" of God's works; see 42.15–25. Cf. Gen
1.1–31; Ps 104. **16.29** *Good things,* an allusion to the repeated statement in Gen 1 that "God saw that it was
good." To affirm that God's creation is good was a
characteristic of the wisdom tradition. Cf. Wis 1.14.
Among the Greeks, and especially with the Stoics, *good
things* was a common technical term for beneficial
goods and human values. **16.30** *Must return.* Cf. Gen
3.19. **17.1–24** A poem in praise of the Lord for the creation of humankind. This is an early interpretation of

the Genesis account. **17.1** *Out of earth.* Cf. Gen 2.7.
17.2 For a *fixed number of days,* see 18.9; cf. Gen 6.3; Ps
90.10. **17.3** *His own image.* Cf. Gen 1.26–27. **17.4** *Dominion.* Cf. Gen 1.28. Ben Sira combines the two accounts of the creation of humankind (Gen 1.26–27;
2.7) and interprets the image of God as authority (v. 2),
strength (v. 3), and dominion (v. 4), thus developing a
hierarchy of power: God, humans, living beings. Cf.
10.4 (God, rulers, people); 3.2 (God, fathers, children).
In Philo's works and later literature a distinction between the two creation accounts led to elaborate, speculative anthropologies. Cf. 1 Cor 15.45–49. **17.6** This
list of faculties for perception is similar to that common to the Stoic tradition. See the addition in v. 5,
(text note *k*), which is clearly a reference to Stoic psy-
chologies; the "five faculties" were sight, touch, smell,
hearing, and taste. *Discretion* probably translates *yetser*
(the Hebrew text is missing at this point); see note on
15.14. **17.7** *Showed them good and evil.* Cf. Gen 2.17;

8 He put the fear of him into[a] their hearts
   to show them the majesty of his works.[b]
10 And they will praise his holy name,
9   to proclaim the grandeur of his works.
11 He bestowed knowledge upon them,
   and allotted to them the law of life.[c]
12 He established with them an eternal
      covenant,
   and revealed to them his decrees.
13 Their eyes saw his glorious majesty,
   and their ears heard the glory of his
      voice.
14 He said to them, "Beware of all evil."
   And he gave commandment to each of
      them concerning the neighbor.
15 Their ways are always known to him;
   they will not be hid from his eyes.[d]
17 He appointed a ruler for every nation,
   but Israel is the Lord's own portion.[e]
19 All their works are as clear as the sun
      before him,
   and his eyes are ever upon their ways.
20 Their iniquities are not hidden from him,
   and all their sins are before the Lord.[f]
22 One's almsgiving is like a signet ring with
      the Lord,[g]
   and he will keep a person's kindness
      like the apple of his eye.[h]
23 Afterward he will rise up and repay them,
   and he will bring their recompense on
      their heads.
24 Yet to those who repent he grants a return,
   and he encourages those who are
      losing hope.

A Call to Repentance

25 Turn back to the Lord and forsake your
      sins;
   pray in his presence and lessen your
      offense.

26 Return to the Most High and turn away
      from iniquity,[i]
   and hate intensely what he abhors.
27 Who will sing praises to the Most High in
      Hades
   in place of the living who give thanks?
28 From the dead, as from one who does not
      exist, thanksgiving has ceased;
   those who are alive and well sing the
      Lord's praises.
29 How great is the mercy of the Lord,
   and his forgiveness for those who
      return to him!
30 For not everything is within human
      capability,
   since human beings are not immortal.
31 What is brighter than the sun? Yet it can
      be eclipsed.
   So flesh and blood devise evil.
32 He marshals the host of the height of
      heaven;
   but all human beings are dust and
      ashes.

The Majesty of God

18 He who lives forever created the
   whole universe;

a Other ancient authorities read *He set his eye upon*   b Other
ancient authorities add *and he gave them to boast of his marvels
forever*   c Other ancient authorities add *so that they may know
that they who are alive now are mortal*   d Other ancient
authorities add 16*Their ways from youth tend toward evil, and
they are unable to make for themselves hearts of flesh in place of
their stony hearts.* 17*For in the division of the nations of the whole
earth, he appointed*   e Other ancient authorities add as verse 18,
*whom, being his firstborn, he brings up with discipline, and
allotting to him the light of his love, he does not neglect him.*
f Other ancient authorities add as verse 21, *But the Lord, who is
gracious and knows how they are formed, has neither left them nor
abandoned them, but has spared them.*   g Gk *him*   h Other
ancient authorities add *apportioning repentance to his sons and
daughters*   i Other ancient authorities add *for he will lead you
out of darkness to the light of health.*

3.5, 22. Sirach overlooks the transgression in the Genesis story that led to this knowledge. But cf. 25.24. **17.11** *The law of life*, Mosaic law, which is included in the endowments that God "allotted" to humankind, thus collapsing the time between creation and Sinai. **17.13** *Their eyes saw.* Cf. Ex 19.16–19; 24.15–17. **17.14** *Commandment*, the duties to one's neighbors outlined in the Ten Commandments (Ex 20.13–17; Deut 5.17–21). **17.17** For Israel as *the Lord's own portion*, see Deut 32.8–9. **17.22** *Signet ring.* Cf. 49.11; Jer 22.24; Hag 2.23. *Apple of his eye.* Cf. Deut 32.10. **17.24** *A return* to those who repent accords with the tradition of Deuteronomy and the prophets. **17.25–32** One should repent in order to sing praises to the

Most High. **17.27** *Sing praises*, for Ben Sira, humanity's highest achievement. See 15.9–10; 17.10; 18.4–7; 39.8, 15, 35; 43.28–30; 51.1, 22; cf. the same theme in Psalms; Wis 10.20–21; 18.1. **17.30** A clear statement of Ben Sira's position against the Greek idea of immortality, an idea that was later found attractive by Jewish thinkers. See the addition to Sirach in 19.19 (text note *e* on p. 1403); cf. Wis 8.13. **17.32** *Dust and ashes*, an allusion to the makeup of humans at creation. See Gen 2.7, 3.19.

18.1–14 An assurance of God's mercy. The frailty of humans, demonstrated by their inability to understand fully and to praise God's creation (vv. 2–7), their inability to understand themselves (v. 8), and by mortality (vv. 9–10), is the reason for God's mercy and

2 the Lord alone is just. [a]

4 To none has he given power to proclaim
       his works;
    and who can search out his mighty
       deeds?

5 Who can measure his majestic power?
    And who can fully recount his mercies?

6 It is not possible to diminish or increase
       them,
    nor is it possible to fathom the
       wonders of the Lord.

7 When human beings have finished, they
       are just beginning,
    and when they stop, they are still
       perplexed.

8 What are human beings, and of what use
       are they?
    What is good in them, and what is evil?

9 The number of days in their life is great if
       they reach one hundred years. [b]

10 Like a drop of water from the sea and a
       grain of sand,
    so are a few years among the days of
       eternity.

11 That is why the Lord is patient with
       them
    and pours out his mercy upon them.

12 He sees and recognizes that their end is
       miserable;
    therefore he grants them forgiveness all
       the more.

13 The compassion of human beings is for
       their neighbors,
    but the compassion of the Lord is for
       every living thing.
    He rebukes and trains and teaches them,
    and turns them back, as a shepherd his
       flock.

14 He has compassion on those who accept
       his discipline
    and who are eager for his precepts.

The Right Spirit in Giving Alms

15 My child, do not mix reproach with your
       good deeds,
    or spoil your gift by harsh words.

16 Does not the dew give relief from the
       scorching heat?
    So a word is better than a gift.

17 Indeed, does not a word surpass a good
       gift?
    Both are to be found in a gracious
       person.

18 A fool is ungracious and abusive,

and the gift of a grudging giver makes
    the eyes dim.

The Need of Reflection and Self-control

19 Before you speak, learn;
    and before you fall ill, take care of your
       health.

20 Before judgment comes, examine yourself;
    and at the time of scrutiny you will
       find forgiveness.

21 Before falling ill, humble yourself;
    and when you have sinned, repent.

22 Let nothing hinder you from paying a
       vow promptly,
    and do not wait until death to be
       released from it.

23 Before making a vow, prepare yourself;
    do not be like one who puts the Lord
       to the test.

24 Think of his wrath on the day of death,
    and of the moment of vengeance when
       he turns away his face.

25 In the time of plenty think of the time of
       hunger;
    in days of wealth think of poverty and
       need.

26 From morning to evening conditions
       change;
    all things move swiftly before the Lord.

27 One who is wise is cautious in
       everything;
    when sin is all around, one guards
       against wrongdoing.

28 Every intelligent person knows wisdom,
    and praises the one who finds her.

29 Those who are skilled in words become
       wise themselves,
    and pour forth apt proverbs. [c]

SELF-CONTROL [d]

30 Do not follow your base desires,
    but restrain your appetites.

31 If you allow your soul to take pleasure in
       base desire,
    it will make you the laughingstock of
       your enemies.

---

a Other ancient authorities add *and there is no other beside him;*
3he steers the world with the span of his hand, and all things obey his
will; for he is king of all things by his power, separating among them
the holy things from the profane. b Other ancient authorities add
but the death of each one is beyond the calculation of all c Other
ancient authorities add *Better is confidence in the one Lord than*
clinging with a dead heart to a dead one. d This heading is
included in the Gk text.

³² Do not revel in great luxury,
    or you may become impoverished by
        its expense.
³³ Do not become a beggar by feasting with
        borrowed money,
    when you have nothing in your purse.ᵃ

19 The one who does thisᵇ will not
        become rich;
    one who despises small things will fail
        little by little.
² Wine and women lead intelligent men
        astray,
    and the man who consorts with
        prostitutes is reckless.
³ Decay and worms will take possession of
        him,
    and the reckless person will be
        snatched away.

Against Loose Talk

⁴ One who trusts others too quickly has a
        shallow mind,
    and one who sins does wrong to himself.
⁵ One who rejoices in wickednessᶜ will be
        condemned,ᵈ
⁶ but one who hates gossip has less evil.
⁷ Never repeat a conversation,
    and you will lose nothing at all.
⁸ With friend or foe do not report it,
    and unless it would be a sin for you, do
        not reveal it;
⁹ for someone may have heard you and
        watched you,
    and in time will hate you.
¹⁰ Have you heard something? Let it die
        with you.
    Be brave, it will not make you burst!
¹¹ Having heard something, the fool suffers
        birth pangs
    like a woman in labor with a child.
¹² Like an arrow stuck in a person's thigh,
    so is gossip inside a fool.

¹³ Question a friend; perhaps he did not
        do it;
    or if he did, so that he may not do it
        again.
¹⁴ Question a neighbor; perhaps he did not
        say it;
    or if he said it, so that he may not
        repeat it.
¹⁵ Question a friend, for often it is slander;
    so do not believe everything you hear.
¹⁶ A person may make a slip without
        intending it.
    Who has not sinned with his tongue?
¹⁷ Question your neighbor before you
        threaten him;
    and let the law of the Most High take
        its course.ᵉ

True and False Wisdom

²⁰ The whole of wisdom is fear of the Lord,
    and in all wisdom there is the
        fulfillment of the law.ᶠ
²² The knowledge of wickedness is not
        wisdom,
    nor is there prudence in the counsel of
        sinners.
²³ There is a cleverness that is detestable,
    and there is a fool who merely lacks
        wisdom.
²⁴ Better are the God-fearing who lack
        understanding

a Other ancient authorities add *for you will be plotting against your own life* b Heb: Gk *A worker who is a drunkard* c Other ancient authorities read *heart* d Other ancient authorities add *but one who withstands pleasures crowns his life.* ⁶*One who controls the tongue will live without strife,* e Other ancient authorities add *and do not be angry.* ¹⁸*The fear of the Lord is the beginning of acceptance, and wisdom obtains his love.* ¹⁹*The knowledge of the Lord's commandments is life-giving discipline; and those who do what is pleasing to him enjoy the fruit of the tree of immortality.* f Other ancient authorities add *and the knowledge of his omnipotence.* ²¹*When a slave says to his master, "I will not act as you wish," even if later he does it, he angers the one who supports him.*

compassion (vv. 11–12). Ben Sira emphasizes the contrast of human beings' fleeting existence and God's compassion for them. **18.8** The rhetorical questions are reminiscent of Ps 8. **18.13** That the Lord *turns them back* by rebuke, training, and teaching contrasts with the exercise of his punishment upon sinners. *As a shepherd* draws upon a common image for kings and gods. Cf. Isa 40.11; Ezek 34.23.
    18.15–19.17 Practical advice on almsgiving (18.15–18), self-criticism (18.19–21), vows (18.22–23), eventualities (18.24–29), desires (18.30–19.3), and gossip (19.4–17), with the topic of speech sprin-

kled throughout. **18.23** The standard example of *putting the Lord to the test* was the story of the murmuring of the people in the wilderness (Ex 17.1–7; Deut 6.16). **18.27** *Cautious in everything,* a succinct statement of Ben Sira's ethic of caution. See 8.1–19. **19.3** *Decay and worms,* the proverbial description of a sinner's death; e.g., that of Antiochus IV (2 Macc 9.9); Herod Agrippa (Acts 12.23). *Snatched away,* an idiom for untimely death. **19.20–30** A contrast between true wisdom and cleverness. **19.20** *Wisdom is fear of the Lord,* a connection fundamental to Sirach that is established at the very beginning of the book. See 1.14–16.

than the highly intelligent who
  transgress the law.
25 There is a cleverness that is exact but
  unjust,
    and there are people who abuse favors
    to gain a verdict.
26 There is the villain bowed down in
  mourning,
  but inwardly he is full of deceit.
27 He hides his face and pretends not to
  hear,
    but when no one notices, he will take
    advantage of you.
28 Even if lack of strength keeps him from
  sinning,
    he will nevertheless do evil when he
    finds the opportunity.
29 A person is known by his appearance,
    and a sensible person is known when
    first met, face to face.
30 A person's attire and hearty laughter,
    and the way he walks, show what he is.

Silence and Speech

20 There is a rebuke that is untimely,
    and there is the person who is wise
    enough to keep silent.
2 How much better it is to rebuke than to
  fume!
3 And the one who admits his fault will be
  kept from failure.
4 Like a eunuch lusting to violate a girl
    is the person who does right under
    compulsion.
5 Some people keep silent and are thought
  to be wise,
    while others are detested for being
    talkative.
6 Some people keep silent because they
  have nothing to say,
    while others keep silent because they
    know when to speak.
7 The wise remain silent until the right
  moment,
    but a boasting fool misses the right
    moment.
8 Whoever talks too much is detested,
    and whoever pretends to authority is
    hated.ᵃ

Paradoxes

9 There may be good fortune for a person
  in adversity,
    and a windfall may result in a loss.

10 There is the gift that profits you nothing,
    and the gift to be paid back double.
11 There are losses for the sake of glory,
    and there are some who have raised
    their heads from humble
    circumstances.
12 Some buy much for little,
    but pay for it seven times over.
13 The wise make themselves beloved by
  only few words,ᵇ
    but the courtesies of fools are wasted.
14 A fool's gift will profit you nothing,ᶜ
    for he looks for recompense
    sevenfold.ᵈ
15 He gives little and upbraids much;
    he opens his mouth like a town crier.
  Today he lends and tomorrow he asks it
  back;
    such a one is hateful to God and
    humans.ᵉ
16 The fool says, "I have no friends,
    and I get no thanks for my good deeds.
  Those who eat my bread are evil-
  tongued."
17 How many will ridicule him, and how
  often!ᶠ

Inappropriate Speech

18 A slip on the pavement is better than a
  slip of the tongue;
    the downfall of the wicked will occur
    just as speedily.
19 A coarse person is like an inappropriate
  story,
    continually on the lips of the ignorant.
20 A proverb from a fool's lips will be
  rejected,
    for he does not tell it at the proper time.

21 One may be prevented from sinning by
  poverty;
    so when he rests he feels no remorse.
22 One may lose his life through shame,
    or lose it because of human respect.ᵍ
23 Another out of shame makes promises to
  a friend,
    and so makes an enemy for nothing.

ᵃ Other ancient authorities add *How good it is to show repentance
when you are reproved, for so you will escape deliberate sin!*
ᵇ Heb: Gk *by words* ᶜ Other ancient authorities add *so it is with
the envious who give under compulsion* ᵈ Syr: Gk *he has many
eyes instead of one* ᵉ Other ancient authorities lack *to God and
humans* ᶠ Other ancient authorities add *for he has not honestly
received what he has, and what he does not have is unimportant to
him* ᵍ Other ancient authorities read *his foolish look*

Lying

24 A lie is an ugly blot on a person;
   it is continually on the lips of the
   ignorant.
25 A thief is preferable to a habitual liar,
   but the lot of both is ruin.
26 A liar's way leads to disgrace,
   and his shame is ever with him.

PROVERBIAL SAYINGS a

27 The wise person advances himself by his
   words,
   and one who is sensible pleases the
   great.
28 Those who cultivate the soil heap up their
   harvest,
   and those who please the great atone
   for injustice.
29 Favors and gifts blind the eyes of the wise;
   like a muzzle on the mouth they stop
   reproofs.
30 Hidden wisdom and unseen treasure,
   of what value is either?
31 Better are those who hide their folly
   than those who hide their wisdom. b

Various Sins

21 Have you sinned, my child? Do so no
   more,
   but ask forgiveness for your past sins.
2 Flee from sin as from a snake;
   for if you approach sin, it will bite you.
   Its teeth are lion's teeth,
   and can destroy human lives.
3 All lawlessness is like a two-edged sword;
   there is no healing for the wound it
   inflicts.

4 Panic and insolence will waste away riches;
   thus the house of the proud will be laid
   waste. c

5 The prayer of the poor goes from their
   lips to the ears of God, d
   and his judgment comes speedily.
6 Those who hate reproof walk in the
   sinner's steps,
   but those who fear the Lord repent in
   their heart.
7 The mighty in speech are widely known;
   when they slip, the sensible person
   knows it.
8 Whoever builds his house with other
   people's money
   is like one who gathers stones for his
   burial mound. e
9 An assembly of the wicked is like a
   bundle of tow,
   and their end is a blazing fire.
10 The way of sinners is paved with smooth
   stones,
   but at its end is the pit of Hades.

Wisdom and Foolishness

11 Whoever keeps the law controls his
   thoughts,
   and the fulfillment of the fear of the
   Lord is wisdom.
12 The one who is not clever cannot be
   taught,
   but there is a cleverness that increases
   bitterness.
13 The knowledge of the wise will increase
   like a flood,
   and their counsel like a life-giving
   spring.
14 The mind f of a fool is like a broken jar;
   it can hold no knowledge.

---

a This heading is included in the Gk text.   b Other ancient
authorities add 32Unwearied endurance in seeking the Lord is
better than a masterless charioteer of one's own life.   c Other
ancient authorities read uprooted   d Gk his ears   e Other
ancient authorities read for the winter   f Syr Lat: Gk entrails

---

20.1–31 A loosely connected set of sayings on the
topic of timely and appropriate speech using the frequent contrast of the wise and the foolish.
21.1–10 A loose collection of sayings on sin.
21.5 That the prayer of the poor will be heard is a form
of the common theme about the cry of the righteous
in distress. See Sir 2.10–11; 35.16–26. That God hears
such prayers is based on Ex 22.21–23. Ben Sira, however, does not think that the poor are preferred by God
because of their poverty. 21.8 Builds his house, probably meant literally, but "building a house" was also a
metaphor for amassing wealth. 21.10 Paved with

smooth stones indicates the easy way that sinners take
and may be an oblique reference to Greco-Roman
roads. 21.11–28 A loosely connected set of sayings
contrasting the wise and the foolish. 21.11 Thoughts
probably translates the Hebrew yetser, thus "impulses"
or "designs"; see note on 15.14. The fear of the Lord is
closely connected with ethical piety, or obedience to
the law, and thus can be "fulfilled." Cf. 1.28, where the
fear of the Lord can be obeyed or disobeyed; also
19.20. 21.13 The fluvial image of wisdom contrasts
with v. 14, in which the broken jar of a foolish
mind holds nothing. See also the image in 22.9.

15 When an intelligent person hears a wise
         saying,
    he praises it and adds to it;
    when a fool[a] hears it, he laughs at[b] it
         and throws it behind his back.
16 A fool's chatter is like a burden on a
         journey,
    but delight is found in the speech of
         the intelligent.
17 The utterance of a sensible person is
         sought in the assembly,
    and they ponder his words in their
         minds.

18 Like a house in ruins is wisdom to a fool,
    and to the ignorant, knowledge is talk
         that has no meaning.
19 To a senseless person education is fetters
         on his feet,
    and like manacles on his right hand.
20 A fool raises his voice when he laughs,
    but the wise[c] smile quietly.
21 To the sensible person education is like a
         golden ornament,
    and like a bracelet on the right arm.

22 The foot of a fool rushes into a house,
    but an experienced person waits
         respectfully outside.
23 A boor peers into the house from the
         door,
    but a cultivated person remains outside.
24 It is ill-mannered for a person to listen at
         a door;
    the discreet would be grieved by the
         disgrace.

25 The lips of babblers speak of what is not
         their concern,[d]
    but the words of the prudent are
         weighed in the balance.
26 The mind of fools is in their mouth,
    but the mouth of the wise is in[e] their
         mind.
27 When an ungodly person curses an
         adversary,[f]

    he curses himself.
28 A whisperer degrades himself
    and is hated in his neighborhood.

The Idler

22 The idler is like a filthy stone,
      and every one hisses at his disgrace.
2 The idler is like the filth of dunghills;
    anyone that picks it up will shake it off
         his hand.

Degenerate Children

3 It is a disgrace to be the father of an
         undisciplined son,
    and the birth of a daughter is a loss.
4 A sensible daughter obtains a husband of
         her own,
    but one who acts shamefully is a grief
         to her father.
5 An impudent daughter disgraces father
         and husband,
    and is despised by both.
6 Like music in time of mourning is ill-
         timed conversation,
    but a thrashing and discipline are at all
         times wisdom.[g]

Wisdom and Folly

9 Whoever teaches a fool is like one who
         glues potsherds together,
    or who rouses a sleeper from deep
         slumber.
10 Whoever tells a story to a fool tells it to a
         drowsy man;
    and at the end he will say, "What is it?"
11 Weep for the dead, for he has left the light
         behind;
    and weep for the fool, for he has left
         intelligence behind.
    Weep less bitterly for the dead, for he is at
         rest;

a Syr: Gk *reveler*   b Syr: Gk *dislikes*   c Syr Lat: Gk *clever*
d Other ancient authorities read *of strangers speak of these things*
e Other ancient authorities omit *in*   f Or *curses Satan*   g Other
ancient authorities add [7]*Children who are brought up in a good life,
conceal the lowly birth of their parents.* [8]*Children who are
disdainfully and boorishly haughty stain the nobility of their kindred.*

21.15 *Throws it behind his back,* disregards it.
21.17 *Ponder his words,* a reference to deliberation in
an assembly charged with making decisions. See
notes on 15.5; 38.32–33; cf. Wis 8.10–12. 21.19 *Fetters,*
here a negative image of enslavement. Cf. the metaphor connected with personified wisdom in 6.24.
21.21 *Golden ornament,* a metaphor connected with
personified wisdom in 6.30. 21.22–28 The topic of

manners is important for Ben Sira's students in their
prospective scribal careers.
   22.3–6 A small set of sayings on the need to discipline one's children. 22.3 A common view in antiquity was that *the birth of a daughter is a loss.* For Ben
Sira's views on daughters, see 42.9–14. 22.6 *Thrash-
ing,* the commonly accepted approach to *discipline* in
antiquity, both at home and in the Hellenistic class-

but the life of the fool is worse than
death.

12 Mourning for the dead lasts seven days,
but for the foolish or the ungodly it
lasts all the days of their lives.

13 Do not talk much with a senseless person
or visit an unintelligent person.[a]
Stay clear of him, or you may have
trouble,
and be spattered when he shakes
himself off.
Avoid him and you will find rest,
and you will never be wearied by his
lack of sense.

14 What is heavier than lead?
And what is its name except "Fool"?

15 Sand, salt, and a piece of iron
are easier to bear than a stupid person.

16 A wooden beam firmly bonded into a
building
is not loosened by an earthquake;
so the mind firmly resolved after due
reflection
will not be afraid in a crisis.

17 A mind settled on an intelligent thought
is like stucco decoration that makes a
wall smooth.

18 Fences[b] set on a high place
will not stand firm against the wind;
so a timid mind with a fool's resolve
will not stand firm against any fear.

The Preservation of Friendship

19 One who pricks the eye brings tears,
and one who pricks the heart makes
clear its feelings.

20 One who throws a stone at birds scares
them away,
and one who reviles a friend destroys a
friendship.

21 Even if you draw your sword against a
friend,
do not despair, for there is a way back.

22 If you open your mouth against your
friend,

do not worry, for reconciliation is
possible.
But as for reviling, arrogance, disclosure
of secrets, or a treacherous
blow—
in these cases any friend will take to
flight.

23 Gain the trust of your neighbor in his
poverty,
so that you may rejoice with him in his
prosperity.
Stand by him in time of distress,
so that you may share with him in his
inheritance.[c]

24 The vapor and smoke of the furnace
precede the fire;
so insults precede bloodshed.

25 I am not ashamed to shelter a friend,
and I will not hide from him.

26 But if harm should come to me because
of him,
whoever hears of it will beware of him.

A Prayer for Help against Sinning

27 Who will set a guard over my mouth,
and an effective seal upon my lips,
so that I may not fall because of them,
and my tongue may not destroy me?

23 O Lord, Father and Master of my life,
do not abandon me to their designs,
and do not let me fall because of them!

2 Who will set whips over my thoughts,
and the discipline of wisdom over my
mind,
so as not to spare me in my errors,
and not overlook my[d] sins?

3 Otherwise my mistakes may be
multiplied,
and my sins may abound,
and I may fall before my adversaries,
and my enemy may rejoice over me.[e]

---

a Other ancient authorities add *For being without sense he will
despise everything about you*   b Other ancient authorities read
Pebbles   c Other ancient authorities add *For one should not
always despise restricted circumstances, or admire a rich person
who is stupid.*   d Gk *their*   e Other ancient authorities add
From them the hope of your mercy is remote

---

room. See 30.1–13; Prov 13.24. **22.9–18** On watching out for the fool, a character type common to wisdom discourse. **22.12** *Seven days,* the traditional period of mourning. See Gen 50.10; Jdt 16.24; but cf. Sir
38.17. **22.13** *Shakes himself off,* unclear. The Hebrew
is missing, but the Syriac reads "pig" for the *unintelli-*

gent person, which means that the Hebrew may have
used a derogatory label such as "dog," an animal that
shakes itself off. **22.14** On the *fool* as a heavy burden,
see 21.16. **22.19–26** A cluster of sayings on insults
and their effect upon friendship. **22.27–23.6** A
prayer of petition that the Lord be a guardian or

4 O Lord, Father and God of my life,
  do not give me haughty eyes,
5   and remove evil desire from me.
6 Let neither gluttony nor lust overcome
  me,
  and do not give me over to shameless
  passion.

DISCIPLINE OF THE TONGUE [a]

7 Listen, my children, to instruction
  concerning the mouth;
  the one who observes it will never be
  caught.
8 Sinners are overtaken through their lips;
  by them the reviler and the arrogant
  are tripped up.
9 Do not accustom your mouth to oaths,
  nor habitually utter the name of the
  Holy One;
10 for as a servant who is constantly under
  scrutiny
  will not lack bruises,
  so also the person who always swears and
  utters the Name
  will never be cleansed [b] from sin.
11 The one who swears many oaths is full of
  iniquity,
  and the scourge will not leave his house.
  If he swears in error, his sin remains on
  him,
  and if he disregards it, he sins doubly;
  if he swears a false oath, he will not be
  justified,
  for his house will be filled with
  calamities.

Foul Language

12 There is a manner of speaking
  comparable to death; [c]
  may it never be found in the
  inheritance of Jacob!
  Such conduct will be far from the godly,
  and they will not wallow in sins.
13 Do not accustom your mouth to coarse,
  foul language,

for it involves sinful speech.
14 Remember your father and mother
  when you sit among the great,
  or you may forget yourself in their
  presence,
  and behave like a fool through bad
  habit;
  then you will wish that you had never
  been born,
  and you will curse the day of your
  birth.
15 Those who are accustomed to using
  abusive language
  will never become disciplined as long
  as they live.

Concerning Sexual Sins

16 Two kinds of individuals multiply sins,
  and a third incurs wrath.
  Hot passion that blazes like a fire
  will not be quenched until it burns
  itself out;
  one who commits fornication with his
  near of kin
  will never cease until the fire burns
  him up.
17 To a fornicator all bread is sweet;
  he will never weary until he dies.
18 The one who sins against his marriage
  bed
  says to himself, "Who can see me?
  Darkness surrounds me, the walls hide
  me,
  and no one sees me. Why should I
  worry?
  The Most High will not remember
  sins."
19 His fear is confined to human eyes
  and he does not realize that the eyes of
  the Lord
  are ten thousand times brighter than
  the sun;

---

a This heading is included in the Gk text. b Syr be free
c Other ancient authorities read clothed about with death

---

teacher to help one control one's speech, thoughts, and desires.
23.7–11 Advice against swearing oaths. **23.9** *The Holy One*, an epithet, not a proper name, occurring frequently in Isaiah, e.g., Isa 1.4. **23.10** It is unclear whether the problem is the habitual practice of swearing, a misuse of taking an oath, or the breaking of a taboo against uttering the divine name. On taking God's name "in vain," see Ex 20.7; Lev 19.12; Deut 5.11.

23.11 *Sins doubly* may refer to Lev 5.4. **23.12–15** Advice against the use of course speech. **23.12** *Comparable to death*, unclear. It may mean "rivaling death" or "meriting death" and so intend a reference to blasphemy, the punishment for which was death. See Lev 24.11–16. **23.16–27** A narrative poem on the sexual license of a man (vv. 16–21) and a woman (vv. 22–27), introduced by a numerical proverb (*Two kinds . . . and a third*). For other numerical proverbs in Sirach, see 25.1–2, 7; 26.5,

they look upon every aspect of human
behavior
and see into hidden corners.
20 Before the universe was created, it was
known to him,
and so it is since its completion.
21 This man will be punished in the streets
of the city,
and where he least suspects it, he will
be seized.

22 So it is with a woman who leaves her
husband
and presents him with an heir by
another man.
23 For first of all, she has disobeyed the law
of the Most High;
second, she has committed an offense
against her husband;
and third, through her fornication she
has committed adultery
and brought forth children by another
man.
24 She herself will be brought before the
assembly,
and her punishment will extend to her
children.
25 Her children will not take root,

and her branches will not bear fruit.
26 She will leave behind an accursed
memory
and her disgrace will never be blotted
out.
27 Those who survive her will recognize
that nothing is better than the fear of
the Lord,
and nothing sweeter than to heed the
commandments of the Lord. *a*

THE PRAISE OF WISDOM *b*

24 Wisdom praises herself,
and tells of her glory in the midst of
her people.
2 In the assembly of the Most High she
opens her mouth,
and in the presence of his hosts she
tells of her glory:
3 "I came forth from the mouth of the
Most High,
and covered the earth like a mist.
4 I dwelt in the highest heavens,
and my throne was in a pillar of cloud.
5 Alone I compassed the vault of heaven

---

a Other ancient authorities add as verse 28, *It is a great honor to
follow God, and to be received by him is long life.* *b* This heading
is included in the Gk text.

---

28. **23.21** *Punished in the streets* means that his sin will
become public knowledge. *In the streets* may refer to
the marketplace or the city gates, where trials took
place. According to Lev 20.10; Deut 22.22–24, the
penalty for adultery was death. Ben Sira does not allude
to that, so the penalty referred to is probably dishonor.
23.24 *Brought before the assembly,* a court hearing. As
with the case of the man (v. 21), it is not clear what the
woman's punishment would have been. That *her punishment will extend to her children* seems to imply disgrace, the point made in the following lines. For a
similar picture, see Wis 4.3–6. **23.26** On memory, immortality, and children, see note on 16.1–4.

24.1–22 A poem of twenty-two lines in praise of
personified wisdom, with three stanzas (vv. 3–7, 8–12,
13–17) plus introduction (vv. 1–2) and conclusion
(vv. 19–22). The three stanzas tell the story of wisdom
from creation, through Israel's epic history, to her
flourishing in Jerusalem. The poem is tightly constructed, and the narrative logic is controlled and
complete. The last line of each stanza introduces an
image that prepares for the next stanza. The poem
stands in the tradition of Job 28; Prov 8.22–31 (cf. Bar
3.9–37) and brings to a climax the wisdom poems in
Sirach: 1.1–20; 4.11–19; 6.18–37; 14.20–15.10. These
poems respond to problem of hidden wisdom by
imagining God's wisdom in creation to be present and
available in Israel's tradition with its covenants and

Mosaic law. Ch. 24 expands upon this claim by locating wisdom in the temple society of Ben Sira's time.
This distinguishes the poem and prepares for the express identification of wisdom with the books of
Moses in 24.23 as well as her location in the vocation
of the scribe in 39.1–11, the history of Israel's leaders
in chs. 44–49, and the office of the high priest in ch.
50. **24.1–2** An introduction of the speaker. **24.1** *Praises
herself,* Ben Sira's acknowledgment of the distinctive
characteristic of the poem, called an aretalogy (a
recital of one's virtues or achievements), a genre associated primarily with the Egyptian goddess Isis.
24.2 *The assembly of the Most High,* a curious formulation, suggesting that both *her people* (v. 1) and *his*
(heavenly) *hosts* (v. 2) are present as she speaks. *His
hosts* are the heavenly bodies and court of the Most
High; see 17.32; cf. Pss 82; 103.19–22. **24.3–7** The first
stanza (see note on 24.1–22) tells of Wisdom's origin
(v. 3), her part in the creation of the world (vv. 4–6),
and her quest for rest and residence (v. 7). **24.3** *From
the mouth,* an image common in Egyptian poems of
creation; here it perhaps alludes to Gen 1 ("And God
said"). Cf. Pss 29.2; 33.6. *Like a mist,* an image common to Egyptian mythologies of creation, here perhaps alluding to the spirit of God in Gen 1.2.
24.4 *Throne . . . in a pillar of cloud,* an allusive interpretation of Ex 13.21–22. **24.5** That wisdom traversed the
great circle and so "described" (created) the world is an

and traversed the depths of the abyss.

6 Over waves of the sea, over all the earth,
and over every people and nation I
have held sway.[a]

7 Among all these I sought a resting place;
in whose territory should I abide?

8 "Then the Creator of all things gave me a
command,
and my Creator chose the place for my
tent.
He said, 'Make your dwelling in Jacob,
and in Israel receive your inheritance.'

9 Before the ages, in the beginning, he
created me,
and for all the ages I shall not cease to be.

10 In the holy tent I ministered before him,
and so I was established in Zion.

11 Thus in the beloved city he gave me a
resting place,
and in Jerusalem was my domain.

12 I took root in an honored people,
in the portion of the Lord, his heritage.

13 "I grew tall like a cedar in Lebanon,
and like a cypress on the heights of
Hermon.

14 I grew tall like a palm tree in En-gedi,[b]
and like rosebushes in Jericho;
like a fair olive tree in the field,
and like a plane tree beside water[c] I
grew tall.

15 Like cassia and camel's thorn I gave forth
perfume,

and like choice myrrh I spread my
fragrance,
like galbanum, onycha, and stacte,
and like the odor of incense in the tent.

16 Like a terebinth I spread out my branches,
and my branches are glorious and
graceful.

17 Like the vine I bud forth delights,
and my blossoms become glorious and
abundant fruit.[d]

19 "Come to me, you who desire me,
and eat your fill of my fruits.

20 For the memory of me is sweeter than
honey,
and the possession of me sweeter than
the honeycomb.

21 Those who eat of me will hunger for
more,
and those who drink of me will thirst
for more.

22 Whoever obeys me will not be put to
shame,
and those who work with me will not
sin."

Wisdom and the Law

23 All this is the book of the covenant of the
Most High God,

---

a Other ancient authorities read *I have acquired a possession*
b Other ancient authorities read *on the beaches* c Other
ancient authorities omit *beside water* d Other ancient
authorities add as verse 18, *I am the mother of beautiful love, of
fear, of knowledge, and of holy hope; being eternal, I am given to all
my children, to those who are named by him.*

---

image common in Egyptian mythology. Cf. Prov 8.27–
29. **24.6** *Held sway,* ruled as queen. The Egyptian goddess Isis makes a similar claim in one of her aretalogies: "I am the queen of every land." Cf. Wis 8.1.
24.7 That Wisdom *sought a resting place* is reminiscent
of Isis mythologies. Wisdom's quest for recognition
and habitation among humans complements the
human quest for wisdom, thus making the theme of
seeking and finding capable of inversion. In contrast,
see *1 Enoch* 42, where Wisdom finds no place to dwell
among humans and so returns to heaven. **24.8–12** The
second stanza (see note on 24.1–22) tells of Wisdom
finding a resting place in Jerusalem. **24.8** *My Creator*
domesticates the preceding mythological imagery by
using the preferred language of creation. Cf. 1.4; Prov
8.22. *My tent,* the tabernacle in the wilderness (Ex
25.8–9); cf. v. 10. **24.9** Cf. Prov 8.22. **24.10** *Ministered
before him* as priest is a rare attribution and shows Ben
Sira's support of the Judean temple state. The traditional social location of wisdom was the palace or the
school; but see 4.13. *Zion,* a designation for Jerusalem

as the location for God's house and presence in Israel;
see 36.18–19. **24.13–17** The third stanza (see note on
24.1–22) tells of Wisdom "taking root" in Jerusalem,
flourishing like a tree. Most of the trees mentioned
were prized for their beauty, utility, and fragrance, and
some were symbolic of the grandeur of their districts
from Lebanon in the north (cedar) to Judea in the
south (olive). Several were used in the preparation of
perfumes and incense, suggesting a connection to the
temple ritual mentioned in v. 15. The addition of the
vine and its fruit in v. 17 enables a shift to the
metaphor of cultivation and prepares for the concluding invitation that follows in vv. 19–22. **24.18** In some
ancient manuscripts this verse describes Wisdom as a
mother (see text note *d*); cf. Prov 8.32; Wis 7.12; Lk
13.34; it also occurs in Philo's writings and in Gnostic
texts. **24.19–22** Wisdom's invitation to her feast. On
Wisdom's fruit, see 1.16–17; 6.19; 15.3; Prov 8.19; 9.2,
5. **24.22** *Will not be put to shame.* This verse is the culmination of the preceding honor/shame discourses.
24.23–34 Ben Sira acknowledges that personified wis-

the law that Moses commanded us
  as an inheritance for the congregations
  of Jacob.*a*

25 It overflows, like the Pishon, with
      wisdom,
    and like the Tigris at the time of the
      first fruits.

26 It runs over, like the Euphrates, with
      understanding,
    and like the Jordan at harvest time.

27 It pours forth instruction like the Nile,*b*
    like the Gihon at the time of vintage.

28 The first man did not know wisdom*c*
      fully,
    nor will the last one fathom her.

29 For her thoughts are more abundant than
      the sea,
    and her counsel deeper than the great
      abyss.

30 As for me, I was like a canal from a river,
    like a water channel into a garden.

31 I said, "I will water my garden
      and drench my flower-beds."
    And lo, my canal became a river,
      and my river a sea.

32 I will again make instruction shine forth
      like the dawn,
    and I will make it clear from far away.

33 I will again pour out teaching like
      prophecy,
    and leave it to all future generations.

34 Observe that I have not labored for
      myself alone,
    but for all who seek wisdom.*c*

Those Who Are Worthy of Praise

25 I take pleasure in three things,
    and they are beautiful in the sight of
      God and of mortals:*d*
  agreement among brothers and sisters,
    friendship among neighbors,
    and a wife and a husband who live in
      harmony.

2 I hate three kinds of people,
    and I loathe their manner of life:
  a pauper who boasts, a rich person who
    lies,
    and an old fool who commits adultery.

3 If you gathered nothing in your youth,
    how can you find anything in your old
      age?

4 How attractive is sound judgment in the
    gray-haired,
    and for the aged to possess good
      counsel!

5 How attractive is wisdom in the aged,

---

a Other ancient authorities add as verse 24, "Do not cease to be
strong in the Lord, cling to him so that he may strengthen you; the
Lord Almighty alone is God, and besides him there is no savior."
b Syr: Gk It makes instruction shine forth like light *c* Gk her
d Syr Lat: Gk In three things I was beautiful and I stood in beauty
before the Lord and mortals.

---

dom is a metaphor for the wisdom available in both
the Mosaic law (vv. 23–29) and his own instruction
(vv. 30–34). **24.23–29** The wisdom of the Torah is unfathomable. **24.23** The express identification of Wisdom with the Torah is given in prose, not poetry, an
extremely odd feature of this transition between the
poem and its interpretation. It is the earliest statement
of this kind in Jewish literature; but cf. Deut 4.5–8. In
later rabbinic tradition the identification of wisdom
and Torah was common and even the mythology of
personified wisdom was transferred to the Torah. The
reference to the *book of the covenant* is uncertain, but
cf. Ex 24.7. For *the law that Moses commanded,* see
Deut 33.4. **24.25–27** The rivers are those flowing from
the garden of Eden (Gen 2.10–14), plus the Jordan
and the Nile. **24.27** *Pours forth like the Nile,* a simile derived from Egyptian lore about the first cataract (Elephantine, modern Aswan) as the "source" of the Nile
and its periodic inundations. The principal temple of
Isis was located at Philae, an island at the first cataract.
See 24.30–31 and the image of *pour out* in 24.33. The
metaphor is used of wisdom (1.9), the scribe (39.6),
the Lord's blessing (39.22), Solomon's wisdom
(47.14–15), and Ben Sira's own instruction (50.27).

24.28–29 On the limits of human understanding, a
theme related to that of hidden wisdom, see 1.6.
24.28 *The first man,* a continuation of the image of
Eden from vv. 25–26. **24.30–34** Ben Sira assumes the
voice of personified wisdom. **24.30–31** The fluvial
metaphor used also of Wisdom above connects Ben
Sira's teaching with Wisdom's. **24.32** *Make instruction
shine forth,* an expression of Ben Sira's desire, perhaps
in the awareness that his program was new. It counters
the skepticism expressed in works like Ecclesiastes. On
the Torah as light, cf. Ps 119.105; Prov 4.18; 6.23. On
wisdom as light, see Wis 7.26, 29. **24.33** *Pour out teaching like prophecy,* a novel notion that merges two concepts of effective speech, that of the sage, which leads
to understanding, and that of the prophet, which predicts or effects change in a political or social situation.
The combination is based on Ben Sira's conception of
personified wisdom as a source of enlightenment and
thus identifiable with the spirit (of God) as the agent
of prophetic inspiration. On *pour out,* see note on
24.27. On prophecy as wisdom, see notes on 39.1; 39.6.
24.34 Repeated in 33.18.

25.1–2 Two contrasting numerical proverbs on acceptable and unacceptable relationships. **25.3–6** A

and understanding and counsel in the
     venerable!

6 Rich experience is the crown of the
        aged,
     and their boast is the fear of the Lord.

7 I can think of nine whom I would call
        blessed,
     and a tenth my tongue proclaims:
   a man who can rejoice in his children;
     a man who lives to see the downfall of
        his foes.

8 Happy the man who lives with a sensible
        wife,
     and the one who does not plow with
        ox and ass together.ᵃ
   Happy is the one who does not sin with
        the tongue,
     and the one who has not served an
        inferior.

9 Happy is the one who finds a friend,ᵇ
     and the one who speaks to attentive
        listeners.

10 How great is the one who finds wisdom!
     But none is superior to the one who
        fears the Lord.

11 Fear of the Lord surpasses everything;
     to whom can we compare the one who
        has it?ᶜ

Some Extreme Forms of Evil

13 Any wound, but not a wound of the
        heart!
     Any wickedness, but not the
        wickedness of a woman!

14 Any suffering, but not suffering from
        those who hate!
     And any vengeance, but not the
        vengeance of enemies!

15 There is no venomᵈ worse than a snake's
        venom,ᵈ
     and no anger worse than a woman'sᵉ
        wrath.

The Evil of a Wicked Woman

16 I would rather live with a lion and a
        dragon
     than live with an evil woman.

17 A woman's wickedness changes her
        appearance,
     and darkens her face like that of a bear.

18 Her husband sitsᶠ among the neighbors,
     and he cannot help sighingᵍ bitterly.

19 Any iniquity is small compared to a
        woman's iniquity;
     may a sinner's lot befall her!

20 A sandy ascent for the feet of the aged—
     such is a garrulous wife to a quiet
        husband.

21 Do not be ensnared by a woman's
        beauty,
     and do not desire a woman for her
        possessions.ʰ

22 There is wrath and impudence and great
        disgrace
     when a wife supports her husband.

23 Dejected mind, gloomy face,
     and wounded heart come from an evil
        wife.
   Drooping hands and weak knees
     come from the wife who does not
        make her husband happy.

24 From a woman sin had its beginning,
     and because of her we all die.

25 Allow no outlet to water,
     and no boldness of speech to an evil
        wife.

26 If she does not go as you direct,
     separate her from yourself.

ᵃ Heb Syr: Gk lacks *and the one who does not plow with ox and ass together* ᵇ Lat Syr: Gk *good sense* ᶜ Other ancient authorities add as verse 12, *The fear of the Lord is the beginning of love for him, and faith is the beginning of clinging to him.* ᵈ Gk *head* ᵉ Other ancient authorities read *an enemy's* ᶠ Heb Syr: Gk *loses heart* ᵍ Other ancient authorities read *and listening he sighs* ʰ Heb Syr: Other Gk authorities read *for her beauty*

---

unit in praise of mature wisdom. **25.7–11** A numerical proverb introducing a series of beatitudes. **25.8** To *plow with ox and ass together* was a legal prohibition, used here as metaphor for an incompatible marriage or perhaps for two incompatible wives. See Deut 22.10; cf. Sir 26.6. *Served an inferior*, an act considered a disgrace. **25.10** *None is superior* encapsulates Ben Sira's idea that fear of the Lord enables one to transcend human social status. **25.13–26.27** A large collection of proverbs about bad and good wives. **25.13–15** Sayings about a woman's wrath. **25.14** *The*

vengeance of enemies may refer to two wives in a single household; see 26.6. **25.16–26** The bad wife was a topic traditional to proverbial wisdom. See Prov 21.19; 25.24; 27.15. **25.24** *From a woman sin had its beginning* alludes to Eve (Gen 3.1–24). Cf. 2 Cor 11.3; 1 Tim 2.14. Alternate interpretations of the Genesis story were that sin originated from the devil, as in Wis 2.24, or from Adam, as in Rom 5.12–14. Ben Sira does not mention the sin of either Adam or Eve in his interpretation of the Genesis account in 17.7. **25.26** *Separate her from yourself,* implying divorce; cf. Deut 24.1.

The Joy of a Good Wife

26 Happy is the husband of a good wife;
the number of his days will be
doubled.
2 A loyal wife brings joy to her husband,
and he will complete his years in peace.
3 A good wife is a great blessing;
she will be granted among the
blessings of the man who fears the
Lord.
4 Whether rich or poor, his heart is
content,
and at all times his face is cheerful.

The Worst of Evils: A Wicked Wife

5 Of three things my heart is frightened,
and of a fourth I am in great fear:[a]
Slander in the city, the gathering of a
mob,
and false accusation—all these are
worse than death.
6 But it is heartache and sorrow when a
wife is jealous of a rival,
and a tongue-lashing makes it known
to all.
7 A bad wife is a chafing yoke;
taking hold of her is like grasping a
scorpion.
8 A drunken wife arouses great anger;
she cannot hide her shame.
9 The haughty stare betrays an unchaste
wife;
her eyelids give her away.

10 Keep strict watch over a headstrong
daughter,
or else, when she finds liberty, she will
make use of it.
11 Be on guard against her impudent eye,
and do not be surprised if she sins
against you.
12 As a thirsty traveler opens his mouth
and drinks from any water near him,
so she will sit in front of every tent peg
and open her quiver to the arrow.

The Blessing of a Good Wife

13 A wife's charm delights her husband,
and her skill puts flesh on his bones.
14 A silent wife is a gift from the Lord,
and nothing is so precious as her self-
discipline.
15 A modest wife adds charm to charm,
and no scales can weigh the value of
her chastity.
16 Like the sun rising in the heights of the
Lord,
so is the beauty of a good wife in her
well-ordered home.
17 Like the shining lamp on the holy
lampstand,
so is a beautiful face on a stately figure.
18 Like golden pillars on silver bases,
so are shapely legs and steadfast feet.

Other ancient authorities add verses 19-27:

19 *My child, keep sound the bloom of your*
youth,
and do not give your strength to
strangers.
20 *Seek a fertile field within the whole plain,*
and sow it with your own seed, trusting
in your fine stock.
21 *So your offspring will prosper,*
and, having confidence in their good
descent, will grow great.
22 *A prostitute is regarded as spittle,*
and a married woman as a tower of
death to her lovers.
23 *A godless wife is given as a portion to a*
lawless man,
but a pious wife is given to the man who
fears the Lord.
24 *A shameless woman constantly acts*
disgracefully,
but a modest daughter will even be
embarrassed before her husband.

---

a Syr: Meaning of Gk uncertain

26.1–4 The good wife was also a traditional wisdom topic; see Prov 31.10–31. **26.5–12** Additional sayings about a bad wife. **26.6** *Jealous of a rival* may assume polygamy; cf. Gen 30.1. **26.10** The mention of a *daughter* interrupts the discourse on wives. Since the Syriac has "wife" and the Hebrew is missing, the saying was probably about a wife. **26.12** Euphemisms for sexual intercourse. **26.13–18** Six attributes of a good wife.

26.16 In both Jewish and Greek society, the woman's place was in the household for which she had the responsibility of maintaining order. **26.17** *The holy lampstand,* the menorah, a candelabrum located in the temple. **26.19–27** A miscellany on women, added later. **26.19–21** Mixed marriage was taboo in Second Temple times and violated the laws of ritual purity. Cf. Ezra 10.1–17; Neh 10.30; 13.23–27.

25 A headstrong wife is regarded as a dog,
   but one who has a sense of shame will
      fear the Lord.
26 A wife honoring her husband will seem
      wise to all,
   but if she dishonors him in her pride she
      will be known to all as ungodly.
   Happy is the husband of a good wife;
   for the number of his years will be
      doubled.
27 A loud-voiced and garrulous wife is like a
      trumpet sounding the charge,
   and every person like this lives in the
      anarchy of war.

Three Depressing Things

28 At two things my heart is grieved,
      and because of a third anger comes
         over me:
   a warrior in want through poverty,
      intelligent men who are treated
         contemptuously,
   and a man who turns back from
         righteousness to sin—
      the Lord will prepare him for the
         sword!

The Temptations of Commerce

29 A merchant can hardly keep from
      wrongdoing,
   nor is a tradesman innocent of sin.

27 Many have committed sin for gain,[a]
   and those who seek to get rich will
      avert their eyes.
2 As a stake is driven firmly into a fissure
      between stones,
   so sin is wedged in between selling and
      buying.
3 If a person is not steadfast in the fear of
      the Lord,
   his house will be quickly overthrown.

Tests in Life

4 When a sieve is shaken, the refuse appears;
   so do a person's faults when he speaks.

5 The kiln tests the potter's vessels;
   so the test of a person is in his
      conversation.
6 Its fruit discloses the cultivation of a tree;
   so a person's speech discloses the
      cultivation of his mind.
7 Do not praise anyone before he speaks,
   for this is the way people are tested.

Reward and Retribution

8 If you pursue justice, you will attain it
   and wear it like a glorious robe.
9 Birds roost with their own kind,
   so honesty comes home to those who
      practice it.
10 A lion lies in wait for prey;
   so does sin for evildoers.

Varieties of Speech

11 The conversation of the godly is always
      wise,
   but the fool changes like the moon.
12 Among stupid people limit your time,
   but among thoughtful people linger on.
13 The talk of fools is offensive,
   and their laughter is wantonly sinful.
14 Their cursing and swearing make one's
      hair stand on end,
   and their quarrels make others stop
      their ears.
15 The strife of the proud leads to bloodshed,
   and their abuse is grievous to hear.

Betraying Secrets

16 Whoever betrays secrets destroys
      confidence,
   and will never find a congenial friend.
17 Love your friend and keep faith with him;
   but if you betray his secrets, do not
      follow after him.
18 For as a person destroys his enemy,
   so you have destroyed the friendship of
      your neighbor.
19 And as you allow a bird to escape from
      your hand,

_____
a Other ancient authorities read a trifle

26.28–27.21 A collection of proverbs on violations of integrity. 26.29 An exceptionally harsh judgment about commerce, owing perhaps to the social and political situation of the time. The traditional warning was against dishonesty in dealing, not against trade itself. Cf. Prov 11.1; 20.10. 27.6 The cultivation of his mind combines concepts of the Hebrew yetser with the standard Greek metaphor for education, paideia; cf. 6.18–37; see notes on 4.17; 15.14. Integrity was measured by the correspondence of one's speech with one's actions. 27.16–21 A unit on betraying confidence. Cf. Prov 20.19; 25.8–10; see Sir 8.17–19. To

so you have let your neighbor go, and
    will not catch him again.
20 Do not go after him, for he is too far off,
    and has escaped like a gazelle from a
        snare.
21 For a wound may be bandaged,
    and there is reconciliation after abuse,
    but whoever has betrayed secrets is
        without hope.

Hypocrisy and Retribution

22 Whoever winks the eye plots mischief,
    and those who know him will keep
        their distance.
23 In your presence his mouth is all
        sweetness,
    and he admires your words;
    but later he will twist his speech
    and with your own words he will trip
        you up.
24 I have hated many things, but him above
        all;
    even the Lord hates him.
25 Whoever throws a stone straight up
        throws it on his own head,
    and a treacherous blow opens up many
        wounds.
26 Whoever digs a pit will fall into it,
    and whoever sets a snare will be caught
        in it.
27 If a person does evil, it will roll back
        upon him,
    and he will not know where it came
        from.
28 Mockery and abuse issue from the proud,
    but vengeance lies in wait for them like
        a lion.
29 Those who rejoice in the fall of the godly
        will be caught in a snare,
    and pain will consume them before
        their death.

Anger and Vengeance

30 Anger and wrath, these also are
        abominations,
    yet a sinner holds on to them.

28

The vengeful will face the Lord's
        vengeance,
    for he keeps a strict account of[a] their
        sins.
2 Forgive your neighbor the wrong he has
        done,
    and then your sins will be pardoned
        when you pray.
3 Does anyone harbor anger against
        another,
    and expect healing from the Lord?
4 If one has no mercy toward another like
        himself,
    can he then seek pardon for his own
        sins?
5 If a mere mortal harbors wrath,
    who will make an atoning sacrifice for
        his sins?
6 Remember the end of your life, and set
        enmity aside;
    remember corruption and death, and
        be true to the commandments.
7 Remember the commandments, and do
        not be angry with your neighbor;
    remember the covenant of the Most
        High, and overlook faults.

8 Refrain from strife, and your sins will be
        fewer;
    for the hot-tempered kindle strife,
9 and the sinner disrupts friendships
    and sows discord among those who are
        at peace.
10 In proportion to the fuel, so will the fire
        burn,
    and in proportion to the obstinacy, so
        will strife increase;[b]
    in proportion to a person's strength will
        be his anger,
    and in proportion to his wealth he will
        increase his wrath.
11 A hasty quarrel kindles a fire,
    and a hasty dispute sheds blood.

---

a Other ancient authorities read *for he firmly establishes*
b Other ancient authorities read *burn*

---

keep a confidence was a standard measure of true
friendship. **27.22–29** A description of the schemer
with warning. **27.22** On *winking* as a sign of duplicity,
cf. Prov 6.13; 10.10. **27.29** Since Ben Sira does not believe in postmortem rewards and punishments, he
maintains that sin is recompensed in this life; see note
on 11.26. **27.30–28.11** On anger and forgiveness.
28.1 That the Lord keeps a *strict account* of one's sins

(and deeds of mercy) occurs repeatedly in Sirach. See
2.14; 3.14, 31; 5.3–8; 11.26; 12.2; 16.14; 17.23; 18.20;
35.13, 24. **28.2** *Forgive your neighbor . . . when you pray.*
Cf. Mk 11.25; Lk 11.4. **28.5** Since one made sacrifice
for one's own sins, the implied answer to this question
(regarding the person who harbors wrath, vv. 2–5) is
no one. This puts an ethical condition upon the efficacy of sacrifice for sins. **28.7** *Do not be angry with your*

The Evil Tongue

12 If you blow on a spark, it will glow;
    if you spit on it, it will be put out;
    yet both come out of your mouth.

13 Curse the gossips and the double-
    tongued,
    for they destroy the peace of many.

14 Slander*a* has shaken many,
    and scattered them from nation to
    nation;
    it has destroyed strong cities,
    and overturned the houses of the great.

15 Slander*a* has driven virtuous women
    from their homes,
    and deprived them of the fruit of their
    toil.

16 Those who pay heed to slander*b* will not
    find rest,
    nor will they settle down in peace.

17 The blow of a whip raises a welt,
    but a blow of the tongue crushes the
    bones.

18 Many have fallen by the edge of the sword,
    but not as many as have fallen because
    of the tongue.

19 Happy is the one who is protected from it,
    who has not been exposed to its anger,
    who has not borne its yoke,
    and has not been bound with its fetters.

20 For its yoke is a yoke of iron,
    and its fetters are fetters of bronze;

21 its death is an evil death,
    and Hades is preferable to it.

22 It has no power over the godly;
    they will not be burned in its flame.

23 Those who forsake the Lord will fall into
    its power;
    it will burn among them and will not
    be put out.
    It will be sent out against them like a lion;
    like a leopard it will mangle them.

24a As you fence in your property with thorns,
25b   so make a door and a bolt for your
    mouth.
24b As you lock up your silver and gold,

25a   so make balances and scales for your
    words.
26 Take care not to err with your tongue,*c*
    and fall victim to one lying in wait.

On Lending and Borrowing

29 The merciful lend to their neighbors;
    by holding out a helping hand they
    keep the commandments.

2 Lend to your neighbor in his time of need;
    repay your neighbor when a loan falls
    due.

3 Keep your promise and be honest with
    him,
    and on every occasion you will find
    what you need.

4 Many regard a loan as a windfall,
    and cause trouble to those who help
    them.

5 One kisses another's hands until he gets a
    loan,
    and is deferential in speaking of his
    neighbor's money;
    but at the time for repayment he delays,
    and pays back with empty promises,
    and finds fault with the time.

6 If he can pay, his creditor*d* will hardly get
    back half,
    and will regard that as a windfall.
    If he cannot pay, the borrower*d* has
    robbed the other of his money,
    and he has needlessly made him an
    enemy;
    he will repay him with curses and
    reproaches,
    and instead of glory will repay him
    with dishonor.

7 Many refuse to lend, not because of
    meanness,
    but from fear*e* of being defrauded
    needlessly.

8 Nevertheless, be patient with someone in
    humble circumstances,

a Gk *A third tongue* *b* Gk *it* *c* Gk *with it* *d* Gk *he*
e Other ancient authorities read *many refuse to lend, therefore,
because of such meanness; they are afraid*

---

neighbor may be an interpretation of Lev 19.18. **28.12–
26** On slander. **28.22** *Burned in its flame,* a reference to
slander, the subject throughout this section, not to
Hades, mentioned in v. 21. On the fiery nature of the
tongue, see Jas 3.5b–6.
    29.1–20 A twenty-two-line poem on money mat-

ters. **29.1** That *the merciful lend to their neighbors* is a
merger of wisdom piety with the traditional code on
lending to fellow Jews; cf. Ex 22.25; Lev 25.35–37;
Deut 15.7–11; 23.20–21; Neh 5.10–11. In v. 20, this
advice is tempered with practicality. **29.8** Almsgiving
was the most emphasized of all the acts of piety; see

and do not keep him waiting for your alms.

9 Help the poor for the commandment's sake,
  and in their need do not send them away empty-handed.
10 Lose your silver for the sake of a brother or a friend,
  and do not let it rust under a stone and be lost.
11 Lay up your treasure according to the commandments of the Most High,
  and it will profit you more than gold.
12 Store up almsgiving in your treasury,
  and it will rescue you from every disaster;
13 better than a stout shield and a sturdy spear,
  it will fight for you against the enemy.

On Guaranteeing Debts

14 A good person will be surety for his neighbor,
  but the one who has lost all sense of shame will fail him.
15 Do not forget the kindness of your guarantor,
  for he has given his life for you.
16 A sinner wastes the property of his guarantor,
17 and the ungrateful person abandons his rescuer.
18 Being surety has ruined many who were prosperous,
  and has tossed them about like waves of the sea;
  it has driven the influential into exile,
  and they have wandered among foreign nations.
19 The sinner comes to grief through surety;
  his pursuit of gain involves him in lawsuits.
20 Assist your neighbor to the best of your ability,
  but be careful not to fall yourself.

Home and Hospitality

21 The necessities of life are water, bread, and clothing,
  and also a house to assure privacy.
22 Better is the life of the poor under their own crude roof
  than sumptuous food in the house of others.
23 Be content with little or much,
  and you will hear no reproach for being a guest. *a*
24 It is a miserable life to go from house to house;
  as a guest you should not open your mouth;
25 you will play the host and provide drink without being thanked,
  and besides this you will hear rude words like these:
26 "Come here, stranger, prepare the table;
  let me eat what you have there."
27 "Be off, stranger, for an honored guest is here;
  my brother has come for a visit, and I need the guest-room."
28 It is hard for a sensible person to bear scolding about lodging *b* and the insults of the moneylender.

CONCERNING CHILDREN *c*

30 He who loves his son will whip him often,
  so that he may rejoice at the way he turns out.
2 He who disciplines his son will profit by him,
  and will boast of him among acquaintances.
3 He who teaches his son will make his enemies envious,
  and will glory in him among his friends.

---

a Lat: Gk *reproach from your family*; other ancient authorities lack this line   *b* Or *scolding from the household*   *c* This heading is included in the Gk text.

3.30–4.6. **29.9** For the *commandment,* see Deut 15.7–11. **29.10** On treasure *rusting,* cf. Mt 6.19; Jas 5.2–3. **29.11** *Lay up . . . treasure,* an idiomatic expression for almsgiving, a way of adding credits to one's account. See v. 12; cf. Tob 4.9; Mt 6.20–21. **29.14** *Surety,* collateral. Giving surety is a topic common to wisdom texts. In Proverbs the advice is against giving surety (Prov 6.1–5; 11.15; 17.18; 22.26). See also 4QInstruction (1Q26, 4Q415–418, 423) from the Dead Sea Scrolls. **29.15** *Has given his life for you.* The guarantor risks property or livelihood and hence his "life." Cf. 33.31. **29.21–28** Supporting oneself is better than dependence upon others. **29.21** Another list of *the necessities of life* is given in 39.26. **29.25** *Play the host,* ironic; the host is being treated like a slave. **30.1–13** On the discipline of children. **30.1** *Whip him often* accords with the

4 When the father dies he will not seem to
     be dead,
       for he has left behind him one like
         himself,
5 whom in his life he looked upon with joy
     and at death, without grief.
6 He has left behind him an avenger against
     his enemies,
       and one to repay the kindness of his
         friends.

7 Whoever spoils his son will bind up his
     wounds,
       and will suffer heartache at every cry.
8 An unbroken horse turns out stubborn,
     and an unchecked son turns out
       headstrong.
9 Pamper a child, and he will terrorize you;
     play with him, and he will grieve you.
10 Do not laugh with him, or you will have
     sorrow with him,
       and in the end you will gnash your
         teeth.
11 Give him no freedom in his youth,
     and do not ignore his errors.
12 Bow down his neck in his youth,[a]
     and beat his sides while he is young,
   or else he will become stubborn and
     disobey you,
       and you will have sorrow of soul from
         him.[b]
13 Discipline your son and make his yoke
     heavy,[c]
       so that you may not be offended by his
         shamelessness.

14 Better off poor, healthy, and fit
     than rich and afflicted in body.

15 Health and fitness are better than any
     gold,
       and a robust body than countless
         riches.
16 There is no wealth better than health of
     body,
       and no gladness above joy of heart.
17 Death is better than a life of misery,
     and eternal sleep[d] than chronic
       sickness.

CONCERNING FOODS[e]

18 Good things poured out upon a mouth
     that is closed
       are like offerings of food placed upon a
         grave.
19 Of what use to an idol is a sacrifice?
     For it can neither eat nor smell.
   So is the one punished by the Lord;
20 he sees with his eyes and groans
     as a eunuch groans when embracing a
       girl.[f]

21 Do not give yourself over to sorrow,
     and do not distress yourself   ·
       deliberately.
22 A joyful heart is life itself,
     and rejoicing lengthens one's life span.
23 Indulge yourself[g] and take comfort,
     and remove sorrow far from you,
   for sorrow has destroyed many,
     and no advantage ever comes from it.

---

a Other ancient authorities lack this line and the preceding line
b Other ancient authorities lack this line c Heb: Gk take pains
with him d Other ancient authorities lack eternal sleep
e This heading is included in the Gk text; other ancient
authorities place the heading before verse 16 f Other ancient
authorities add So is the person who does right under compulsion
g Other ancient authorities read Beguile yourself

---

standard approach to discipline and education in antiquity. See 22.6; cf. Prov 13.24; 23.13–14. **30.4–6** The
ancient Jewish conception of survival after death was
the continuation of one's name in one's progeny, who
can enhance the father's reputation. *An avenger*, the
son who will defend the father's name and interests.
Honor, obligation, and the keeping of accounts were
trans-generational matters.
  30.14–25 A miscellany on attitudes in the face of illness. **30.18** *A mouth that is closed* probably refers to
one who is sick, but the language is suggestive of one
who has died; the Hebrew reads "one who cannot eat."
The hyperbole is followed by three examples of those
incapable of enjoying the pleasures of life: the dead (v.
18), idols (v. 19), and eunuchs (v. 20). *Offerings of food
placed upon a grave*, the Eastern Mediterranean custom of placing food and pouring out drink on the bur-

ial stones of the dead. See 7.33; Deut 4.28; 26.14; Ezek
24.17; Tob 4.7. **30.19** That sacrificial offerings are of
no *use to an idol* is ridicule. Criticism of idolatry was
characteristic of the Jews. The critique is based upon
the second commandment (Ex 20.4; Deut 5.8) and
phrased as a comparison between the Lord as the living God and idols, lifeless things made by human artisans. The ridicule is aimed at the way in which idols
were treated as if they were alive (clothed, served with
offerings of food and drink, conversed with, and handled) when in fact they were lifeless objects. Cf. Ps
115.4–7; Isa 44.9–11; 57.6; Wis 13; Let Jer 27; Bel 3–
22. **30.21** *Do not give yourself over to sorrow*, the language of mourning, used as a transition from the imagery of death (vv. 17–19) to the topic of enjoyment.
On mourning, see 38.17–20. **30.23** *Indulge yourself*,
advice also common to the Epicurean tradition. Cf.

24 Jealousy and anger shorten life,
    and anxiety brings on premature old
        age.
25 Those who are cheerful and merry at
        table
    will benefit from their food.

Right Attitude toward Riches

31 Wakefulness over wealth wastes away
    one's flesh,
    and anxiety about it drives away sleep.
2 Wakeful anxiety prevents slumber,
    and a severe illness carries off sleep. *a*
3 The rich person toils to amass a fortune,
    and when he rests he fills himself with
        his dainties.
4 The poor person toils to make a meager
        living,
    and if ever he rests he becomes needy.

5 One who loves gold will not be justified;
    one who pursues money will be led
        astray *b* by it.
6 Many have come to ruin because of gold,
    and their destruction has met them
        face to face.
7 It is a stumbling block to those who are
        avid for it,
    and every fool will be taken captive by it.

8 Blessed is the rich person who is found
        blameless,
    and who does not go after gold.
9 Who is he, that we may praise him?
    For he has done wonders among his
        people.
10 Who has been tested by it and been
        found perfect?
    Let it be for him a ground for boasting.
    Who has had the power to transgress and
        did not transgress,
    and to do evil and did not do it?
11 His prosperity will be established, *c*
    and the assembly will proclaim his acts
        of charity.

Table Etiquette

12 Are you seated at the table of the great? *d*
    Do not be greedy at it,
    and do not say, "How much food there
        is here!"
13 Remember that a greedy eye is a bad
        thing.
    What has been created more greedy
        than the eye?
    Therefore it sheds tears for any reason.

---

a Other ancient authorities read *sleep carries off a severe illness*
b Heb Syr: Gk *pursues destruction will be filled* *c* Other ancient
authorities add *because of this* *d* Heb Syr: Gk *at a great table*

14.11, 16; Eccl 2.24. **30.25** After the images of mourning and eating in vv. 17–23 *merry at table* is a weak attempt to return to the theme of gladness in vv.14–16.
The translation follows the Greek text, since the Hebrew is uncertain. V. 25 occurs at a break in the Greek
text where several pages of a Greek codex were mistakenly transposed; instead of continuing with ch. 31 (as
do the Hebrew and the NRSV), the Septuagint inserts
33.16–36.13 at this point, thus giving rise to messy
textual seams both here and at 36.13 (where see text
note d). The Greek of 30.25 may have been rephrased
after the transposition in the attempt to round off the
preceding proverbial unit.

31.1–11 A troubled set of sayings on acquiring, protecting, and using wealth. Two ethical considerations
underlie Ben Sira's attempt to deal with widespread critique of the rich: avarice is to be condemned (vv. 5–8);
almsgiving is to be commended (vv. 9–11). **31.2** Wakefulness commonly served both as a sign of anxiety and
as a sign of legitimate concern. Kings were expected to
stay awake out of concern for their people, and in the
case of impending crises wakefulness (as watchfulness)
was enjoined for all. Anxiety, on the other hand, was
usually thought detrimental (cf. Lk 12.22). The phrase
wakeful anxiety is a combination of the two terms
based on their occurrence in v. 1. **31.3–4** A common
form of couplet, used to compare two sets of opposing

categories (rich/poor; sufficiency/need) by relating
each to a third and common factor (toil). In this case,
the resulting observation is merely clever, not judgmental. **31.8** *Found blameless,* Ben Sira's notion of the
pious rich; cf. 13.24. The Greek word for *gold* translates
the Hebrew *mammon;* this is the earliest example of
this Aramaic loanword that also occurs in Mt 6.24; Lk
16.9, 11, 13. **31.9–11** The rhetorical questions may
be intended as irony, illustrating the difficulty of
amassing wealth and continuing free from sin. **31.12–
32.13** Comportment at a banquet, including moderation in eating (31.12–24) and drinking wine (31.25–
31) and knowing one's place (32.1–2), when to speak
(32.3–9), and when to depart (32.10–13). The banquet
in question corresponds to the Greek dinner with
guests followed by a symposium; in common are the
concern for reputation (31.23–24), the wine-drinking
contest (31.25–26), merrymaking (31.31; 32.2), a master of the feast (32.1), concern for rank (32.1–2; 32.3,
7), entertainment and a display of cleverness (32.4),
music (32.5–6), and a blessing at the conclusion of the
feast (32.13). Here Ben Sira advises his prospective
scribes on etiquette, so that they are equipped for success. Cf. Prov 23.1–8. **31.13** *Greedy eye,* a somewhat unusual reference to the eye as medium for desire and
lust; cf. 14.9; Job 31.1. *Tears for any reason* includes the
calculated kind, for purposes of deception, and the

14 Do not reach out your hand for
    everything you see,
    and do not crowd your neighbor[a] at
        the dish.
15 Judge your neighbor's feelings by your
    own,
    and in every matter be thoughtful.
16 Eat what is set before you like a well
    brought-up person,[b]
    and do not chew greedily, or you will
        give offense.
17 Be the first to stop, as befits good manners,
    and do not be insatiable, or you will
        give offense.
18 If you are seated among many persons,
    do not help yourself[c] before they do.

19 How ample a little is for a well-
    disciplined person!
    He does not breathe heavily when in
        bed.
20 Healthy sleep depends on moderate
    eating;
    he rises early, and feels fit.
    The distress of sleeplessness and of
        nausea
    and colic are with the glutton.
21 If you are overstuffed with food,
    get up to vomit, and you will have relief.
22 Listen to me, my child, and do not
    disregard me,
    and in the end you will appreciate my
        words.
    In everything you do be moderate,[d]
    and no sickness will overtake you.
23 People bless the one who is liberal with
    food,
    and their testimony to his generosity is
        trustworthy.
24 The city complains of the one who is
    stingy with food,
    and their testimony to his stinginess is
        accurate.

Temperance in Drinking Wine

25 Do not try to prove your strength by
    wine-drinking,

for wine has destroyed many.
26 As the furnace tests the work of the
    smith,[e]
    so wine tests hearts when the insolent
        quarrel.
27 Wine is very life to human beings
    if taken in moderation.
    What is life to one who is without wine?
    It has been created to make people
        happy.
28 Wine drunk at the proper time and in
    moderation
    is rejoicing of heart and gladness of
        soul.
29 Wine drunk to excess leads to bitterness
    of spirit,
    to quarrels and stumbling.
30 Drunkenness increases the anger of a fool
    to his own hurt,
    reducing his strength and adding
        wounds.
31 Do not reprove your neighbor at a
    banquet of wine,
    and do not despise him in his
        merrymaking;
    speak no word of reproach to him,
    and do not distress him by making
        demands of him.

Etiquette at a Banquet

32 If they make you master of the feast,
    do not exalt yourself;
    be among them as one of their
        number.
    Take care of them first and then sit down;
2 when you have fulfilled all your duties,
    take your place,
    so that you may be merry along with
        them
    and receive a wreath for your excellent
        leadership.

3 Speak, you who are older, for it is your
    right,

---

a Gk him   b Heb: Gk like a human being   c Gk reach out your
hand   d Heb Syr: Gk industrious   e Heb: Gk tests the
hardening of steel by dipping

---

natural kind, the result of emotion or desire. **31.23–
24** Their testimony . . . is trustworthy . . . accurate in the
sense of having a lasting effect. The point is reputation.
On being stingy, see 14.9–10. **31.25** Prove your strength,
in the drinking contest, a feature of the Greek symposium. See 32.5–6. On the thought that wine has de-

stroyed many, cf. Prov 23.29–35. **31.27** The phrase very
life may derive from a toast. It was common in Eastern
Mediterranean cultures to praise wine. Cf. Ps 104.15.
32.1 Master of the feast, a position of honor with responsibility for such things as seating arrangements,
courses, wines, and entertainment. **32.3** It is your right.

but with accurate knowledge, and do
　　not interrupt the music.
4 Where there is entertainment, do not
　　pour out talk;
　do not display your cleverness at the
　　wrong time.
5 A ruby seal in a setting of gold
　　is a concert of music at a banquet of
　　wine.
6 A seal of emerald in a rich setting of gold
　　is the melody of music with good wine.

7 Speak, you who are young, if you are
　　obliged to,
　but no more than twice, and only if
　　asked.
8 Be brief; say much in few words;
　be as one who knows and can still hold
　　his tongue.
9 Among the great do not act as their
　　equal;
　and when another is speaking, do not
　　babble.

10 Lightning travels ahead of the thunder,
　　and approval goes before one who is
　　modest.
11 Leave in good time and do not be the
　　last;
　go home quickly and do not linger.
12 Amuse yourself there to your heart's
　　content,
　but do not sin through proud speech.
13 But above all bless your Maker,
　　who fills you with his good gifts.

The Providence of God

14 The one who seeks God[a] will accept his
　　discipline,
　and those who rise early to seek him[b]
　　will find favor.
15 The one who seeks the law will be filled
　　with it,

but the hypocrite will stumble at it.
16 Those who fear the Lord will form true
　　judgments,
　and they will kindle righteous deeds
　　like a light.
17 The sinner will shun reproof,
　　and will find a decision according to
　　his liking.
18 A sensible person will not overlook a
　　thoughtful suggestion;
　an insolent[c] and proud person will
　　not be deterred by fear.[d]
19 Do nothing without deliberation,
　　but when you have acted, do not
　　regret it.
20 Do not go on a path full of hazards,
　　and do not stumble at an obstacle
　　twice.[e]
21 Do not be overconfident on a smooth[f]
　　road,
22 and give good heed to your paths.[g]
23 Guard[h] yourself in every act,
　　for this is the keeping of the
　　commandments.

24 The one who keeps the law preserves
　　himself,[i]
　and the one who trusts the Lord will
　　not suffer loss.

33 No evil will befall the one who fears
　　the Lord,
　but in trials such a one will be rescued
　　again and again.
2 The wise will not hate the law,
　　but the one who is hypocritical about
　　it is like a boat in a storm.

---

a Heb: Gk who fears the Lord　b Other ancient authorities lack
to seek him　c Heb: Gk alien　d Meaning of Gk uncertain.
Other ancient authorities add and after acting, with him, without
deliberation　e Heb: Gk stumble on stony ground　f Or an
unexplored　g Heb Syr: Gk and beware of your children
h Heb Syr: Gk Trust　i Heb: Gk who believes the law heeds the
commandments

In ancient Near Eastern custom older persons were
honored with the privilege of speaking first, a form of
ranking. The advice was not for the elders, who would
know this, but for youths being taught the rules of social etiquette and social advancement. Cf. 32.7–9.
32.14–33.6 A loosely connected set of sayings on
being deliberate in one's judgments. **32.14** *Rise early to
seek him,* a reference to prayers at sunrise, a sign of piety.
Cf. 39.5. **32.16–17** To *form true judgments* was the goal
of instruction in wisdom, meaning here instruction in
Mosaic law (32.15; 33.3–4). *The sinner,* in contrast, *will*

find a decision according to his liking (v. 17). On rendering
judgments as a judge, apparently one of the sage's social
roles and a goal of Ben Sira's instructions, see 38.31–33.
Righteous deeds, the thoughts and words of those who
seek the law and are filled with it (32.15). **32.23** A curious identification of the wisdom of caution with ethical
piety (obedience to the law), perhaps with an eye toward
Deut 4.9. On the wisdom of caution, see 8.1–19. **33.1** *No
evil will befall* reflects Ben Sira's Deuteronomic proclivi-
ties. On *rescue* as a theme, see 2.6–11; cf. Wis 10.1–21.
33.2 *Like a boat in a storm,* without rudder or control, a

3 The sensible person will trust in the law;
  for such a one the law is as dependable
    as a divine oracle.

4 Prepare what to say, and then you will be
    listened to;
  draw upon your training, and give
    your answer.

5 The heart of a fool is like a cart wheel,
  and his thoughts like a turning axle.

6 A mocking friend is like a stallion
  that neighs no matter who the rider is.

Differences in Nature and in Humankind

7 Why is one day more important than
    another,
  when all the daylight in the year is
    from the sun?

8 By the Lord's wisdom they were
    distinguished,
  and he appointed the different seasons
    and festivals.

9 Some days he exalted and hallowed,
  and some he made ordinary days.

10 All human beings come from the ground,
   and humankind*a* was created out of
     the dust.

11 In the fullness of his knowledge the Lord
     distinguished them
   and appointed their different ways.

12 Some he blessed and exalted,
   and some he made holy and brought
     near to himself;
   but some he cursed and brought low,
     and turned them out of their place.

13 Like clay in the hand of the potter,
     to be molded as he pleases,
   so all are in the hand of their Maker,
     to be given whatever he decides.

14 Good is the opposite of evil,
     and life the opposite of death;
   so the sinner is the opposite of the
     godly.

15 Look at all the works of the Most High;
     they come in pairs, one the opposite of
       the other.

16 Now I was the last to keep vigil;
     I was like a gleaner following the
       grape-pickers;

17 by the blessing of the Lord I arrived first,

---

a Heb: Gk *Adam*

---

very common metaphor in late antiquity. **33.3** *The law is as dependable as a divine oracle,* unclear. Oracles were predictive. Perhaps the saying refers to the blessings promised in the Torah (Lev 26.3–13; Deut 28.1–14), or the promises attached to the covenants in the biblical epic (see 44.21), or simply to the Torah is as being as trustworthy in its own way as a divine oracle; see 34.6. The oracle used by the priests was the casting of dice called Urim and Thummim. See Ex 28.30; Lev 8.8; Num 27.21; Deut 33.8; 1 Sam 14.41–42; Ezra 2.63; Neh 7.65. On attitudes toward divination, see Sir 34.1–20.

33.7–19 A striking list of ranked pairs in creation and history, including exalted and ordinary days (vv. 7–9); blessed and cursed human beings (vv. 10–13); good and evil, life and death, sinners and the godly, all the works of the Lord (vv. 14–15); and early and late arrivals in the "vineyard" of the scribal office (vv. 16–19). The logic behind this reflects both wisdom categories and Greek conceptuality with its penchant for classification into categories of opposition. These verses anticipate 42.24, where Ben Sira articulates his doctrine that creation is ordered by pairs of opposites. **33.7–9** *Exalted* and *ordinary days,* the Jewish calendar of weeks, months, and festivals based on the lunar year. See 43.6–8; cf. 39.12; 50.6; Gen 1.14; Ps 104.19. **33.12** *Some he blessed,* probably the blessing promised to Abraham (Gen 12.2–3; 15.5; 22.17; 24.60; 28.14; Ex 32.13; Deut 1.10); cf. Sir 44.20–23. *Some he made holy and brought near to himself,* probably the priests of Is-

rael whose privilege was to approach the Lord. Cf. Num 16.5; Ezek 40.46. Second Temple society was organized largely by orientation to priestly families and their genealogies. *Some he cursed . . . out of their place,* possibly the Canaanites. Cf. 16.9; Gen 9.25–27; 12.6–7; Ex 33.1–3; Deut 34.1–4. **33.13** *Clay in the hand of the potter,* a common metaphor for the divine determination of human destinies. Cf. Isa 29.16; 45.8; 64.8; Jer 18.4; Wis 15.7–8; Rom 9.21. The word *potter,* meaning "one who forms," is from the same Hebrew root as the word *yetser.* See note on 15.14. **33.14–15** The *works* of the Lord was a common idiom for creation, with particular reference to the sun, moon, and astrophysical and geophysical phenomena. See 42.15–43.33. That they *come in pairs* is a novel notion. See 42.24–25. The concept of pairs is probably taken from the ethical dualism of wise/foolish, righteous/sinner, good/bad, life/death, which has been transferred to "all the works" in the interest of a theodicy of divine power and judgment. See note on 33.7–19; also 34.14–20; 39.16–31; 40.8–10; cf. Wis 16.24–26; 17.20–21; 18.24–25; 19.6–22. **33.16** Ben Sira refers to himself by using the first person, a practice common in Greek literary traditions. On authorial self-reference in Sirach, cf. 24.30–34; 34.12–13; 39.12–15, 32–35; 41.16; 43.32; 50.25–29; 51.1–30. To be the *last to keep vigil* means to stand at the end of a line of teachers; vigil may imply an association with the prophets, who "watched out" for the well-being of the people. Cf. Ezek 3.17; 33.7;

and like a grape-picker I filled my wine
press.

18 Consider that I have not labored for
myself alone,
but for all who seek instruction.

19 Hear me, you who are great among the
people,
and you leaders of the congregation,
pay heed!

The Advantage of Independence

20 To son or wife, to brother or friend,
do not give power over yourself, as
long as you live;
and do not give your property to another,
in case you change your mind and
must ask for it.

21 While you are still alive and have breath
in you,
do not let anyone take your place.

22 For it is better that your children should
ask from you
than that you should look to the hand
of your children.

23 Excel in all that you do;
bring no stain upon your honor.

24 At the time when you end the days of
your life,
in the hour of death, distribute your
inheritance.

The Treatment of Slaves

25 Fodder and a stick and burdens for a
donkey;
bread and discipline and work for a
slave.

26 Set your slave to work, and you will find
rest;
leave his hands idle, and he will seek
liberty.

27 Yoke and thong will bow the neck,
and for a wicked slave there are racks
and tortures.

28 Put him to work, in order that he may
not be idle,

29 for idleness teaches much evil.

30 Set him to work, as is fitting for him,
and if he does not obey, make his
fetters heavy.
Do not be overbearing toward anyone,
and do nothing unjust.

31 If you have but one slave, treat him like
yourself,
because you have bought him with
blood.
If you have but one slave, treat him like a
brother,
for you will need him as you need your
life.

32 If you ill-treat him, and he leaves you and
runs away,

33 which way will you go to seek him?

Dreams Mean Nothing

34 The senseless have vain and false
hopes,
and dreams give wings to fools.

2 As one who catches at a shadow and
pursues the wind,
so is anyone who believes in[a] dreams.

3 What is seen in dreams is but a reflection,
the likeness of a face looking at itself.

4 From an unclean thing what can be
clean?
And from something false what can be
true?

5 Divinations and omens and dreams are
unreal,
and like a woman in labor, the mind
has fantasies.

6 Unless they are sent by intervention from
the Most High,
pay no attention to them.

---

a Syr: Gk *pays heed to*

Hab 2.1. **33.17** *I arrived first* implies privilege or
honor. Cf. "The last will be first" (Mt 19.30). *Filled my
wine press,* a metaphor for wisdom. Cf. 1.15; 24.17–21;
39.6; 51.15. **33.18** Repeated in 24.34. **33.20–24** A small
unit offers advice on controlling one's own property.
33.25–33 Advice on controlling one's slaves. For OT
laws on slavery, see Ex 21.2–6, 20–21, 26–27; Lev
25.46; Deut 15.12–18. **33.31** *Bought him with blood,*
an exaggeration based on the idea that "life" is one's
"livelihood." Cf. 29.15; 34.27.
34.1–8 A decidedly negative judgment on the predic-

tive value of dreams. In contrast, cf. the important role
of dreams in the stories of Joseph (Gen 37–50), Gideon
(Judg 7.13–15), Job (Job 33.15–18), and Daniel. During the Hellenistic period dreams were generally
thought to contain predictions, and dream interpretation was considered a critical and scientific occupation.
Ben Sira ranks dreams with omens and other forms of
divination as fantasies (v. 5). His criticism here may reflect a rejection of apocalyptic speculation about God's
secrets; cf. 3.21–24. **34.2** *Pursues the wind,* a metaphor
for impossible projects. Cf. Eccl 1.14; Hos 12.1. **34.6** *Un-*

7 For dreams have deceived many,
   and those who put their hope in them
      have perished.
8 Without such deceptions the law will be
      fulfilled,
   and wisdom is complete in the mouth
      of the faithful.

Experience as a Teacher

9 An educated[a] person knows many things,
   and one with much experience knows
      what he is talking about.
10 An inexperienced person knows few
      things,
11   but he that has traveled acquires much
         cleverness.
12 I have seen many things in my travels,
   and I understand more than I can
      express.
13 I have often been in danger of death,
   but have escaped because of these
      experiences.

Fear the Lord

14 The spirit of those who fear the Lord will
      live,
15   for their hope is in him who saves them.
16 Those who fear the Lord will not be
      timid,
   or play the coward, for he is their hope.
17 Happy is the soul that fears the Lord!
18   To whom does he look? And who is his
         support?
19 The eyes of the Lord are on those who
      love him,
   a mighty shield and strong support,
   a shelter from scorching wind and a
      shade from noonday sun,

a guard against stumbling and a help
   against falling.
20 He lifts up the soul and makes the eyes
      sparkle;
   he gives health and life and blessing.

Offering Sacrifices

21 If one sacrifices ill-gotten goods, the
      offering is blemished;[b]
22   the gifts[c] of the lawless are not
         acceptable.
23 The Most High is not pleased with the
      offerings of the ungodly,
   nor for a multitude of sacrifices does
      he forgive sins.
24 Like one who kills a son before his
      father's eyes
   is the person who offers a sacrifice
      from the property of the poor.
25 The bread of the needy is the life of the
      poor;
   whoever deprives them of it is a
      murderer.
26 To take away a neighbor's living is to
      commit murder;
27   to deprive an employee of wages is to
         shed blood.

28 When one builds and another tears
      down,
   what do they gain but hard work?
29 When one prays and another curses,
   to whose voice will the Lord listen?
30 If one washes after touching a corpse, and
      touches it again,

---

a Other ancient authorities read A traveled   b Other ancient
authorities read is made in mockery   c Other ancient authorities
read mockeries

---

less . . . sent . . . from the Most High. With this exception, Ben Sira hesitates to reject all dreams as evil or taboo according to Jewish standards. How one distinguished dreams that were sent from the Most High is not explained. Cf. the similar problem of true and false prophecy in Deut 18.15–22. **34.8** The law will be fulfilled echoes 33.3. Wisdom is complete. In Ben Sira's view wisdom, in addition to knowledge of the Lord's instructions, promises, and covenants, includes knowing the Lord's "ways," namely, that he will protect, rescue, and restore the righteous and Israel to states of well-being (cf. 24.33; 36.1–22; 39.33; 50.24); thus one does not need to pursue divination. **34.9–13** On the value of travel. **34.9** An educated person, better a traveled person (text note a) for the sense of this section. Learning through travel was a common idea in Hellenistic times, made famous by writers from

Herodotus to Pausanius. **34.13** In danger of death, idiomatic for lack of protection away from home, a common theme in entertaining literature such as the Joseph story (Gen 37–50) and the Hellenistic romance. See also Paul's list of dangers in 2 Cor 11.23–27. **34.14–20** On the protection of those who fear the Lord. **34.14** The spirit . . . will live does not refer to spiritual or postmortem destiny, but to a sense of courage that is "lively." **34.15** The Lord saves those who fear him from trouble or distress. Cf. 2.6–11. **34.19** On the eyes of the Lord, see 42.16–20. On the Lord as a shelter and a guard, cf. Ps 91.1–16. **34.21–31** A unit on ritual observances relates wisdom piety to temple worship. **34.21** That ill-gotten goods are blemished merges Ben Sira's ethic of acquisition (cf. 31.1–9) with the prescription that sacrificial offerings were to be made from "perfect," or "unblemished," animals or produce.

what has been gained by washing?
³¹ So if one fasts for his sins,
and goes again and does the same
things,
who will listen to his prayer?
And what has he gained by humbling
himself?

The Law and Sacrifices

35 The one who keeps the law makes
many offerings;
² one who heeds the commandments
makes an offering of well-being.
³ The one who returns a kindness offers
choice flour,
⁴ and one who gives alms sacrifices a
thank offering.
⁵ To keep from wickedness is pleasing to
the Lord,
and to forsake unrighteousness is an
atonement.
⁶ Do not appear before the Lord empty-
handed,
⁷ for all that you offer is in fulfillment of
the commandment.
⁸ The offering of the righteous enriches the
altar,
and its pleasing odor rises before the
Most High.
⁹ The sacrifice of the righteous is acceptable,
and it will never be forgotten.
¹⁰ Be generous when you worship the Lord,
and do not stint the first fruits of your
hands.
¹¹ With every gift show a cheerful face,
and dedicate your tithe with gladness.
¹² Give to the Most High as he has given to
you,
and as generously as you can afford.
¹³ For the Lord is the one who repays,
and he will repay you sevenfold.

Divine Justice

¹⁴ Do not offer him a bribe, for he will not
accept it;
¹⁵ and do not rely on a dishonest
sacrifice;
for the Lord is the judge,
and with him there is no partiality.
¹⁶ He will not show partiality to the poor;
but he will listen to the prayer of one
who is wronged.
¹⁷ He will not ignore the supplication of the
orphan,
or the widow when she pours out her
complaint.
¹⁸ Do not the tears of the widow run down
her cheek
¹⁹ as she cries out against the one who
causes them to fall?
²⁰ The one whose service is pleasing to the
Lord will be accepted,
and his prayer will reach to the clouds.
²¹ The prayer of the humble pierces the
clouds,
and it will not rest until it reaches its
goal;
it will not desist until the Most High
responds
²² and does justice for the righteous, and
executes judgment.
Indeed, the Lord will not delay,
and like a warrior[a] will not be patient
until he crushes the loins of the
unmerciful
²³ and repays vengeance on the nations;
until he destroys the multitude of the
insolent,
and breaks the scepters of the
unrighteous;

---

a Heb: Gk *and with them*

Cf. Lev 22.21. **34.24–25** Taking from the poor is the moral equivalent of murder. **34.30** *Touching a corpse* made one ritually impure. Cf. Num 19.11.

35.1–13 Advice concerning the offering of sacrifices. Ben Sira regards ethical piety (keeping the commandments, especially almsgiving) as effective as ritual observance (vv. 1–5), but does not conclude that the sacrificial system is therefore unimportant or ineffective (vv. 6–13). His recommended cultic practices include temple worship, support for the priests, tithes, sacrificial offerings, prayers, praise, and oaths. See 4.13–14; 7.9–10, 31; 14.11; 23.9–11; 28.5; 34.21–31; 35.14–26; 38.9–15; 45.6–22; 50.1–21. **35.6** *Appear be-*

fore the Lord, approach the temple with offerings. **35.14–26** A unit on divine justice that builds upon the ethic of helping the poor, the widow, and the orphan, confidence in the effectiveness of prayers of supplication from one in distress, and a theology of divine judgment in history. On the Lord's provision for the poor, the widow, and the orphan, see 4.1–10. For the cry of one in distress, see 2.10–11. The theme of divine intervention in history appears unexpectedly and prepares for the prayer to follow in 36.1–22. **35.22** The verse segues from God's protection of the marginalized in Israel to God's protection of Israel, culminating in chap 36.

24 until he repays mortals according to their
      deeds,
   and the works of all according to their
      thoughts;
25 until he judges the case of his people
   and makes them rejoice in his mercy.
26 His mercy is as welcome in time of
      distress
   as clouds of rain in time of drought.

A Prayer for God's People

36 Have mercy upon us, O God*a* of all,
   2 and put all the nations in fear of you.
3 Lift up your hand against foreign nations
   and let them see your might.
4 As you have used us to show your
      holiness to them,
   so use them to show your glory to us.
5 Then they will know,*b* as we have known,
   that there is no God but you, O Lord.
6 Give new signs, and work other wonders;
7   make your hand and right arm
      glorious.
8 Rouse your anger and pour out your
      wrath;
9   destroy the adversary and wipe out the
      enemy.
10 Hasten the day, and remember the
      appointed time,*c*
   and let people recount your mighty
      deeds.
11 Let survivors be consumed in the fiery
      wrath,
   and may those who harm your people
      meet destruction.

12 Crush the heads of hostile rulers
   who say, "There is no one but
      ourselves."
13 Gather all the tribes of Jacob,*d*
16   and give them their inheritance, as at
      the beginning.
17 Have mercy, O Lord, on the people called
      by your name,
   on Israel, whom you have named*e* your
      firstborn,
18 Have pity on the city of your sanctuary,*f*
   Jerusalem, the place of your dwelling.*g*
19 Fill Zion with your majesty,*h*
   and your temple*i* with your glory.
20 Bear witness to those whom you created
      in the beginning,
   and fulfill the prophecies spoken in
      your name.
21 Reward those who wait for you
   and let your prophets be found
      trustworthy.
22 Hear, O Lord, the prayer of your servants,
      according to your goodwill
      toward*j* your people,
   and all who are on the earth will know
      that you are the Lord, the God of the
      ages.

---

a Heb: Gk *O Master, the God*   *b* Heb: Gk *And let them know
you*   *c* Other ancient authorities read *remember your oath*
d Owing to a dislocation in the Greek Mss of Sirach, the verse
numbers 14 and 15 are not used in chapter 36, though no text is
missing.   *e* Other ancient authorities read *you have likened to*
f Or *on your holy city*   *g* Heb: Gk *your rest*   *h* Heb Syr: Gk *the
celebration of your wondrous deeds*   *i* Heb Syr: Gk Lat *people*
j Heb and two Gk witnesses: Lat and most Gk witnesses read
according to the blessing of Aaron for

36.1–22 A prayer for the deliverance of Jerusalem
and the people of Israel from foreign oppression. Such
a prayer comes as a surprise in a book of wisdom and
expresses political judgments and hopes extremely
veiled elsewhere in Sirach. In form it draws upon the
Psalms and shares many features with prayers and
poems found in other Second Temple Jewish texts.
Foreign nations (v. 3), *the enemy* (v. 9), *those who harm
your people* (v. 11), and the *hostile rulers* (v. 12) probably refer to the Seleucid overlords at the time.
36.4 *Show your holiness,* divine deliverance in the
idiom of cultic practices. Cf. Ezek 20.41; 28.25.
36.5 *Then they will know,* a common expression of
theodicy related to divine deliverance. See v. 22; cf.
1 Sam 17.46–47; 1 Kings 8.60; 1 Chr 17.20; Isa 45.14;
Wis 4.20–5.8; 12.26–27. **36.6–7** *Signs and . . . wonders,
hand and right arm,* common shorthand allusions to
the exodus story of deliverance from Egypt; cf. Ex 15.6;
Deut 4.34; 7.19; 11.3; Neh 9.10; Isa 63.12; Pss 78.43;
98.1. **36.16** *Their inheritance,* the land promised to the

children of Abraham (Gen 17.8). **36.17** *Called by your
name,* a common description of the people of Israel.
See Deut 28.10; Isa 63.19; Jer 14.9; 15.16. The name Israel means "God rules." That Israel was *named your
firstborn* evokes a common idea; see Ex 4.22; Jer 31.9;
Hos 11.1; Wis 18.13. **36.18–19** On Jerusalem as *Zion,*
the place where God dwells, cf. Ex 15.17; Isa 2.2–3; Jer
31.6; Mic 4.1–2. **36.20–21** This petition is an early occurrence of the idea that the *prophecies* of the *prophets*
refer to a divine deliverance of Jerusalem yet to be accomplished. It is unique in Sirach, though the idea became programmatic for the somewhat later Qumran
community, some Jewish authors of apocalyptic literature, and early Christian authors such as Mark. A
somewhat related idea occurs in Sir 48.10, where Elijah
is expected to return as *it is written.* Elsewhere in Sirach prophecies are referred to as a source of wisdom,
insight, and instruction. See 24.33. In chs. 44–50
prophets are those whose insights and words were effective agents in the events of their times that deter-

Concerning Discrimination

23 The stomach will take any food,
   yet one food is better than another.

24 As the palate tastes the kinds of game,
   so an intelligent mind detects false
      words.

25 A perverse mind will cause grief,
   but a person with experience will pay
      him back.

26 A woman will accept any man as a
      husband,
   but one girl is preferable to another.

27 A woman's beauty lights up a man's face,
   and there is nothing he desires more.

28 If kindness and humility mark her
      speech,
   her husband is more fortunate than
      other men.

29 He who acquires a wife gets his best
      possession,[a]
   a helper fit for him and a pillar of
      support.[b]

30 Where there is no fence, the property will
      be plundered;
   and where there is no wife, a man will
      become a fugitive and a wanderer.[c]

31 For who will trust a nimble robber
   that skips from city to city?
So who will trust a man that has no nest,
   but lodges wherever night overtakes
      him?

False Friends

37 Every friend says, "I too am a friend";
   but some friends are friends only in
      name.

2 Is it not a sorrow like that for death itself
   when a dear friend turns into an
      enemy?

3 O inclination to evil, why were you
      formed
   to cover the land with deceit?

4 Some companions rejoice in the
      happiness of a friend,
   but in time of trouble they are against
      him.

5 Some companions help a friend for their
      stomachs' sake,
   yet in battle they will carry his shield.

6 Do not forget a friend during the battle,[d]
   and do not be unmindful of him when
      you distribute your spoils.[e]

Caution in Taking Advice

7 All counselors praise the counsel they
      give,
   but some give counsel in their own
      interest.

8 Be wary of a counselor,
   and learn first what is his interest,
   for he will take thought for himself.
He may cast the lot against you

9 and tell you, "Your way is good,"
   and then stand aside to see what
      happens to you.

10 Do not consult the one who regards you
      with suspicion;
   hide your intentions from those who
      are jealous of you.

11 Do not consult with a woman about her
      rival
   or with a coward about war,
with a merchant about business
   or with a buyer about selling,
with a miser about generosity[f]
   or with the merciless about kindness,
with an idler about any work
   or with a seasonal laborer about
      completing his work,
with a lazy servant about a big task—
   pay no attention to any advice they
      give.

12 But associate with a godly person
      whom you know to be a keeper of the
         commandments,
   who is like-minded with yourself,
      and who will grieve with you if you
         fail.

13 And heed[g] the counsel of your own heart,

---

a Heb: Gk *enters upon a possession*   *b* Heb: Gk *rest*   *c* Heb: Gk
wander about and sigh   *d* Heb: Gk *in your heart*   *e* Heb: Gk
him in your wealth   *f* Heb: Gk *gratitude*   *g* Heb: Gk *establish*

---

mined the epic history of Israel. See 46.13. **36.23–31** A
cluster of loosely connected sayings on food and finding a wife. **36.29** *Helper fit for him* recalls Gen 2.18.
36.30 *A fugitive and a wanderer* recalls Cain's punishment in Gen 4.12. **37.1–6** A set of five sayings on the
difficulty of identifying a true friend (vv. 1–5) concludes with advice on how to treat such a friend in
both adversity and prosperity (v. 6); cf. 6.7–13.
37.3 *Inclination to evil.* See note on 15.14. **37.7–15** A
unit of nine sayings cautions against the advice of persons biased by self-interest (vv. 7–11) and recommends instead the counsel of godly persons, one's own

for no one is more faithful to you than
    it is.

14 For our own mind sometimes keeps us
    better informed
    than seven sentinels sitting high on a
    watchtower.

15 But above all pray to the Most High
    that he may direct your way in truth.

True and False Wisdom

16 Discussion is the beginning of every work,
    and counsel precedes every
    undertaking.

17 The mind is the root of all conduct;

18   it sprouts four branches,[a]
    good and evil, life and death;
    and it is the tongue that continually
    rules them.

19 Some people may be clever enough to
    teach many,
    and yet be useless to themselves.

20 A skillful speaker may be hated;
    he will be destitute of all food,

21 for the Lord has withheld the gift of charm,
    since he is lacking in all wisdom.

22 If a person is wise to his own advantage,
    the fruits of his good sense will be
    praiseworthy.[b]

23 A wise person instructs his own people,
    and the fruits of his good sense will
    endure.

24 A wise person will have praise heaped
    upon him,
    and all who see him will call him
    happy.

25 The days of a person's life are numbered,
    but the days of Israel are without
    number.

26 One who is wise among his people will
    inherit honor,[c]
    and his name will live forever.

Concerning Moderation

27 My child, test yourself while you live;
    see what is bad for you and do not give
    in to it.

28 For not everything is good for everyone,
    and no one enjoys everything.

29 Do not be greedy for every delicacy,
    and do not eat without restraint;

30 for overeating brings sickness,
    and gluttony leads to nausea.

31 Many have died of gluttony,
    but the one who guards against it
    prolongs his life.

Concerning Physicians and Health

38 Honor physicians for their services,
    for the Lord created them;

2 for their gift of healing comes from the
    Most High,
    and they are rewarded by the king.

3 The skill of physicians makes them
    distinguished,
    and in the presence of the great they
    are admired.

4 The Lord created medicines out of the
    earth,
    and the sensible will not despise them.

5 Was not water made sweet with a tree
    in order that its[d] power might be
    known?

6 And he gave skill to human beings
    that he[e] might be glorified in his
    marvelous works.

7 By them the physician[f] heals and takes
    away pain;

8   the pharmacist makes a mixture from
    them.

---

a Heb: Gk *As a clue to changes of heart four kinds of destiny appear*
b Other ancient witnesses read *trustworthy* c Other ancient
authorities read *confidence* d Or *his* e Or *they* f Heb: Gk *he*

---

heart, and the guidance of God (vv. 12–15). **37.16–
26** A set of reflections on deliberative speech in the
counsel chambers concludes with sayings on the
honor granted to a skillful speaker. **37.26** *His name will
live forever.* See note on 11.26. **37.27–31** Caution
about overindulgence introduces the theme of sickness as a preparation for the following sayings on the
value of physicians.

38.1–15 A meditation on physicians recommends
using their services (vv. 1–8) while not forgetting the
traditional approach to illness (vv. 9–15). The science
and practice of medicine, developed by the Greeks,
threatened the ancient Near Eastern view of illness as

caused by personal fault and its remedy by sacrifice for
sin and healing. Ben Sira struggled to find a place for
each approach, arguing that medicines are the works of
the Lord (vv. 4–8), that the physician should be consulted after offering sacrifice (vv. 9–12), and that the
physician also entreats the Lord (vv. 13–15). **38.1** The
statement that the Lord *created* physicians, both here
and in v. 12, translates the Greek; the Hebrew reads "allotted" with the sense that God ordained the profession
as part of his plan for human society. See note on 7.15.
38.4 *Medicines out of the earth,* medicinal plants, the
knowledge of which belonged to ancient Near Eastern
and Egyptian wisdom traditions. **38.5** *Water made sweet*

God's[a] works will never be finished;
and from him health[b] spreads over all
the earth.

9 My child, when you are ill, do not delay,
but pray to the Lord, and he will heal
you.

10 Give up your faults and direct your hands
rightly,
and cleanse your heart from all sin.

11 Offer a sweet-smelling sacrifice, and a
memorial portion of choice flour,
and pour oil on your offering, as much
as you can afford.[c]

12 Then give the physician his place, for the
Lord created him;
do not let him leave you, for you need
him.

13 There may come a time when recovery
lies in the hands of physicians,[d]

14 for they too pray to the Lord
that he grant them success in diagnosis[e]
and in healing, for the sake of
preserving life.

15 He who sins against his Maker,
will be defiant toward the physician.[f]

On Mourning for the Dead

16 My child, let your tears fall for the dead,
and as one in great pain begin the
lament.
Lay out the body with due ceremony,
and do not neglect the burial.

17 Let your weeping be bitter and your
wailing fervent;
make your mourning worthy of the
departed,
for one day, or two, to avoid criticism;
then be comforted for your grief.

18 For grief may result in death,

and a sorrowful heart saps one's
strength.

19 When a person is taken away, sorrow is
over;
but the life of the poor weighs down
the heart.

20 Do not give your heart to grief;
drive it away, and remember your own
end.

21 Do not forget, there is no coming back;
you do the dead[g] no good, and you
injure yourself.

22 Remember his[h] fate, for yours is like it;
yesterday it was his,[i] and today it is
yours.

23 When the dead is at rest, let his
remembrance rest too,
and be comforted for him when his
spirit has departed.

Trades and Crafts

24 The wisdom of the scribe depends on the
opportunity of leisure;
only the one who has little business
can become wise.

25 How can one become wise who handles
the plow,
and who glories in the shaft of a goad,
who drives oxen and is occupied with
their work,
and whose talk is about bulls?

26 He sets his heart on plowing furrows,
and he is careful about fodder for the
heifers.

27 So it is with every artisan and master
artisan

---

a Gk His b Or peace c Heb: Lat lacks as much as you can
afford; Meaning of Gk uncertain d Gk in their hands e Heb:
Gk rest f Heb: Gk may he fall into the hands of the physician
g Gk him h Heb: Gk my i Heb: Gk mine

---

with a tree alludes to the miracle in Ex 15.23–25.
38.10 *Faults* and *sin* were thought to be the cause of illness. See Deut 28.22; Job; Prov 3.7–8; Jn 9.2. **38.11** *Flour.*
The cereal offering is described in Lev 2.1–3. **38.16–23** Injunctions to observe the traditions of mourning and burial (vv. 16–17) yield to advice on appropriate attitudes and thoughts about death (vv. 18–23). The advice is remarkable in that it presents a realistic attitude toward death as an argument against excessive grief.
38.16 *The lament,* an ancient tradition; see 2 Sam 1.17; Jer 7.29; 9.9, 19; Ezek 19.1; 26.17; 27.32; 32.16; Am 5.1; 8.10. *Burial* was a religious duty; see Tob 1.17–18; 4.3–4; 6.15; 12.12; 14.12–13. **38.17** That one should mourn *one day or two* is a striking curtailment of the customary requirement of seven days. See 22.12. **38.24–34** A tightly

crafted poem describing those who work with their hands. The poem has been compared with the Egyptian Instruction of Duauf, sometimes called a "Satire on the Trades," which was written from the elitist perspective of the scribal vocation. Ben Sira's poem does not, however, engage in satire. The crafts are set in contrast to the vocation of the scribe (vv. 24, 32–33) without ridicule. In fact, he notes in v. 34a that craftsmen *maintain the fabric of the world.* The point of contrast is that artisans must concentrate their attention upon their handiwork and therefore have no time for the pursuit of learning, which requires leisure. The examples given, farmer, *artisan,* smith, and potter, when combined with the mention of rulers, judges, scribes, and public assemblies, provide a sketch of the productive society of Ben Sira's time.

who labors by night as well as by day;
those who cut the signets of seals,
  each is diligent in making a great
    variety;
they set their heart on painting a lifelike
  image,
and they are careful to finish their work.

28 So it is with the smith, sitting by the anvil,
  intent on his iron-work;
the breath of the fire melts his flesh,
  and he struggles with the heat of the
    furnace;
the sound of the hammer deafens his ears,*a*
  and his eyes are on the pattern of the
    object.
He sets his heart on finishing his
  handiwork,
  and he is careful to complete its
    decoration.

29 So it is with the potter sitting at his work
  and turning the wheel with his feet;
he is always deeply concerned over his
  products,
  and he produces them in quantity.

30 He molds the clay with his arm
  and makes it pliable with his feet;
he sets his heart to finish the glazing,
  and he takes care in firing*b* the kiln.

31 All these rely on their hands,
  and all are skillful in their own work.

32 Without them no city can be inhabited,
  and wherever they live, they will not go
    hungry.*c*
Yet they are not sought out for the
  council of the people,*d*
33   nor do they attain eminence in the
    public assembly.
They do not sit in the judge's seat,
  nor do they understand the decisions
    of the courts;
they cannot expound discipline or
  judgment,
  and they are not found among the
    rulers.*e*
34 But they maintain the fabric of the world,
  and their concern is for*f* the exercise of
    their trade.

The Activity of the Scribe

How different the one who devotes
  himself
  to the study of the law of the Most
    High!

39 He seeks out the wisdom of all the
  ancients,
  and is concerned with prophecies;
2 he preserves the sayings of the famous

a Cn: Gk *renews his ear* *b* Cn: Gk *cleaning* *c* Syr: Gk *and people can neither live nor walk there* *d* Most ancient authorities lack this line *e* Cn: Gk *among parables* *f* Syr: Gk *prayer is in*

38.32–33 *Rulers, courts,* and *public assemblies* indicate the social setting for the professional activity of the scribe, the one who can read, write, and speak well; see also 39.4. Missing is any mention of a school, Ben Sira's own social location. Cf. 51.23. The professional goal of instruction in wisdom, assumed in these verses, explains the emphasis throughout the book on effective speech, sound judgment, and knowledge of and consideration for conventional codes of law, piety, and ethics as well as the repeated references to the assembly as the place where praise and honor are won or lost. For references to the assembly, see note on 15.5. **38.34b** If the second line of the bicola in v. 34 is treated as an *inclusio* (a repetition signaling the beginning and end of a unit), returning to the theme announced in v. 24, the poem on the trades is composed of twenty-two lines framed by statements of contrast with the vocation of the scribe. V. 34b also serves as an introduction to the following poem on the scribe and so can be seen as a carefully crafted transitional statement intended both to sum up the previous unit and to lead into the following reflection. Transitional statements of this kind were common in literary compositions of the time. **38.34b–39.11** A poem on the activity of the scribe includes mention of his study (vv. 1–3), professional role (v. 4a), wide experience (v. 4b), piety (v. 5), inspiration (vv. 6–7), learned achievements (v. 8), and honor among the people, both in life and after death (vv. 9–11). **38.34b** *Law,* the Torah, or books of Moses. Cf. 24.23. **39.1** *The wisdom of all the ancients,* probably literature in general without respect to cultural constraints, rather than specifically the books of Moses. It was common in antiquity to trace the collective knowledge of a people to the discoveries and revelations of culture-bringers and sages who lived at the beginning of time. The scribe *seeks out* this wisdom both through an intellectual quest in general, which could include cross-cultural experience (v. 4), and concerted research in the literatures of the time. The genres of wisdom for which one looked appear in the following verses. *Prophecies* has been taken to refer specifically to the books of the Hebrew prophets, but a more probable reference is to prophecies, oracles, and omens wherever found. Ben Sira lists prophecies along with sayings, parables, and proverbs (vv. 2–3) as various formulations of wisdom (v. 1). In 44.3–5 prophecies are included in a list of scribal accomplishments, and in 24.33 Ben Sira promises to *pour out teaching like prophecy.* On prophets and prophecy, see 36.20–21; 46.13. **39.2–3** *Parables,* the metaphors,

and penetrates the subtleties of
    parables;
3 he seeks out the hidden meanings of
    proverbs
  and is at home with the obscurities of
    parables.
4 He serves among the great
    and appears before rulers;
  he travels in foreign lands
    and learns what is good and evil in the
      human lot.
5 He sets his heart to rise early
    to seek the Lord who made him,
    and to petition the Most High;
  he opens his mouth in prayer
    and asks pardon for his sins.

6 If the great Lord is willing,
    he will be filled with the spirit of
      understanding;
  he will pour forth words of wisdom of his
    own
    and give thanks to the Lord in prayer.
7 The Lord*a* will direct his counsel and
    knowledge,
    as he meditates on his mysteries.
8 He will show the wisdom of what he has
    learned,
    and will glory in the law of the Lord's
      covenant.
9 Many will praise his understanding;
    it will never be blotted out.
  His memory will not disappear,
    and his name will live through all
      generations.

10 Nations will speak of his wisdom,
    and the congregation will proclaim his
      praise.
11 If he lives long, he will leave a name
    greater than a thousand,
  and if he goes to rest, it is enough*b* for
    him.

A Hymn of Praise to God

12 I have more on my mind to express;
    I am full like the full moon.
13 Listen to me, my faithful children, and
    blossom
    like a rose growing by a stream of
      water.
14 Send out fragrance like incense,
    and put forth blossoms like a lily.
  Scatter the fragrance, and sing a hymn of
    praise;
    bless the Lord for all his works.
15 Ascribe majesty to his name
    and give thanks to him with praise,
  with songs on your lips, and with harps;
    this is what you shall say in
      thanksgiving:

16 "All the works of the Lord are very good,
    and whatever he commands will be
      done at the appointed time.
17 No one can say, 'What is this?' or 'Why is
    that?'—
    for at the appointed time all such
      questions will be answered.

———————
a Gk *He himself*   *b* Cn: Meaning of Gk uncertain

similes, and comparisons typical of wisdom discourse. The Hebrew is missing, but probably used the term *meshalim*, a general designation for wisdom sayings of all kinds, including proverbs, riddles, rhetorical questions, and maxims. **39.6** *Spirit of understanding*, an application of a prophetic idiom (speaking by the spirit of God) to the accomplished scribe. The wisdom he pours forth, however, is said to be *his own*. Cf. 24.27. **39.8–11** This small section anticipates Ben Sira's introduction to his famous praise of the ancestors in chaps. 44–50; see esp. 44.14–15. That *the congregation will proclaim* the speaker's *praise* refers to honor as the scribe's ultimate reward. Honor was the public recognition of one's status and of behavior and accomplishments appropriate to one's social position. Honor before the congregation or people is a theme in Sirach; see 1.24; 1.30 and note; 7.7, 14; 15.5–6; 21.17; 24.2; 33.19; 44.15. The last passage is a close parallel to 39.10. *Leave a name*, be remembered, the Jewish correlate to the Greek notion of immortality.

39.12–35 A lengthy poem in praise of the works of the Lord (vv. 16–31) introduced by an invitation to recite it (vv. 12–15) and concluded by a personal statement from the author (vv. 32–35). The poem follows upon the description of the scribe in vv. 1–11 as if to exemplify Ben Sira's own accomplishments. **39.12–15** The metaphors used to depict the author's thoughts and the congregation's recitation, being *full like the full moon*, sending out *fragrance*, and putting forth *blossoms*, are reminiscent of the flourishing of wisdom in 24.13–34. **39.16–31** The hymn of praise focuses upon the works of the Lord in both creation and history and argues that the works are good for the godly but turn to vengeance for sinners. **39.16** That the works are *very good* is a common view in the traditions of wisdom; see 16.26–29; Gen 1. *The appointed time*, a divine visitation as planned and in keeping with the calendrical ordering of natural and historical events; see 16.18; 36.10; 39.34; 48.10. **39.17** *The waters stood in a heap.* Cf. Ex 15.8.

At his word the waters stood in a heap,
and the reservoirs of water at the word
of his mouth.

18 When he commands, his every purpose is
fulfilled,
and none can limit his saving power.

19 The works of all are before him,
and nothing can be hidden from his
eyes.

20 From the beginning to the end of time he
can see everything,
and nothing is too marvelous for him.

21 No one can say, 'What is this?' or 'Why is
that?'—
for everything has been created for its
own purpose.

22 "His blessing covers the dry land like a
river,
and drenches it like a flood.

23 But his wrath drives out the nations,
as when he turned a watered land into
salt.

24 To the faithful his ways are straight,
but full of pitfalls for the wicked.

25 From the beginning good things were
created for the good,
but for sinners good things and bad.[a]

26 The basic necessities of human life
are water and fire and iron and salt
and wheat flour and milk and honey,
the blood of the grape and oil and
clothing.

27 All these are good for the godly,
but for sinners they turn into evils.

28 "There are winds created for vengeance,
and in their anger they can dislodge
mountains;[b]
on the day of reckoning they will pour
out their strength
and calm the anger of their Maker.

29 Fire and hail and famine and pestilence,
all these have been created for
vengeance;

30 the fangs of wild animals and scorpions
and vipers,
and the sword that punishes the
ungodly with destruction.

31 They take delight in doing his bidding,
always ready for his service on earth;
and when their time comes they never
disobey his command."

32 So from the beginning I have been
convinced of all this
and have thought it out and left it in
writing:

33 All the works of the Lord are good,
and he will supply every need in its
time.

34 No one can say, "This is not as good as
that,"
for everything proves good in its
appointed time.

35 So now sing praise with all your heart
and voice,
and bless the name of the Lord.

Human Wretchedness

40 Hard work was created for everyone,
and a heavy yoke is laid on the
children of Adam,
from the day they come forth from their
mother's womb
until the day they return to[c] the
mother of all the living.[d]

2 Perplexities and fear of heart are theirs,
and anxious thought of the day of their
death.

3 From the one who sits on a splendid
throne
to the one who grovels in dust and
ashes,

4 from the one who wears purple and a
crown
to the one who is clothed in burlap,

a Heb Lat: Gk *sinners bad things*   b Heb Syr: Gk *can scourge
mightily*   c Other Gk and Lat authorities read *are buried in*
d Heb: Gk *of all*

39.22 The image of inundation, which may allude to the
flooding of the Nile, also occurs in 24.25–27, 30–33.
39.23 *Land into salt* alludes to Sodom and Gomorrah.
Cf. Gen 13.10; 19.24–28; Deut 29.23; Ps 107.34; Wis
10.7. 39.28–31 A catalog of geophysical and natural
phenomena that obey their creator to punish the ungodly. The list is reminiscent of the exodus plagues. Cf. a
similar view in Wis 16.24–19.22. 39.32–35 A first-person signature that reveals Ben Sira's self-understanding

as a scribe on the model of vv. 1–11 and expressly mentions creative writing (in addition to collecting or copying) as a scribal accomplishment. This pride of authorship is a clear indication of Hellenistic influence.
40.1–11 A somber reflection on miseries that affect
all people, good and bad, with an attempt to see them
in the light of the theodicy proposed in 39.16–31.
40.1 *Work was created*, an allusion to Gen 3.17–19. Eve
is referred to as *the mother of all the living* in Gen 3.20;

5 there is anger and envy and trouble and
        unrest,
        and fear of death, and fury and strife.
    And when one rests upon his bed,
        his sleep at night confuses his mind.
6 He gets little or no rest;
        he struggles in his sleep as he did by
        day.[a]
    He is troubled by the visions of his mind
        like one who has escaped from the
        battlefield.
7 At the moment he reaches safety he
        wakes up,
        astonished that his fears were
        groundless.
8 To all creatures, human and animal,
        but to sinners seven times more,
9 come death and bloodshed and strife and
        sword,
        calamities and famine and ruin and
        plague.
10 All these were created for the wicked,
        and on their account the flood came.
11 All that is of earth returns to earth,
        and what is from above returns
        above.[b]

Injustice Will Not Prosper

12 All bribery and injustice will be blotted
        out,
        but good faith will last forever.
13 The wealth of the unjust will dry up like a
        river,
        and crash like a loud clap of thunder in
        a storm.
14 As a generous person has cause to
        rejoice,
        so lawbreakers will utterly fail.
15 The children of the ungodly put out few
        branches;
        they are unhealthy roots on sheer
        rock.
16 The reeds by any water or river bank
        are plucked up before any grass;
17 but kindness is like a garden of blessings,
        and almsgiving endures forever.

The Joys of Life

18 Wealth and wages make life sweet,[c]
        but better than either is finding a
        treasure.
19 Children and the building of a city
        establish one's name,
        but better than either is the one who
        finds wisdom.
    Cattle and orchards make one
        prosperous;[d]
        but a blameless wife is accounted
        better than either.
20 Wine and music gladden the heart,
        but the love of friends[e] is better than
        either.
21 The flute and the harp make sweet
        melody,
        but a pleasant voice is better than
        either.
22 The eye desires grace and beauty,
        but the green shoots of grain more
        than either.
23 A friend or companion is always
        welcome,
        but a sensible wife[f] is better than
        either.
24 Kindred and helpers are for a time of
        trouble,
        but almsgiving rescues better than
        either.
25 Gold and silver make one stand firm,
        but good counsel is esteemed more
        than either.
26 Riches and strength build up confidence,
        but the fear of the Lord is better than
        either.
    There is no want in the fear of the Lord,
        and with it there is no need to seek for
        help.

---

a Arm: Meaning of Gk uncertain   b Heb Syr: Gk Lat *from the
waters returns to the sea*   c Heb: Gk *Life is sweet for the self-
reliant worker*   d Heb Syr: Gk lacks *but better . . . prosperous*
e Heb: Gk *wisdom*   f Heb Compare Syr: Gk *wife with her
husband*

here the reference is to the earth, to which all must return (Gen 3.19; cf. Sir 16.30). **40.9** Ben Sira's Deuteronomic theology insists that sinners will have it worse
than the righteous; cf. 39.25. **40.10** *Flood* alludes to the
story in Gen 6–8; see Gen 6.7, 17. **40.11** *What is from
above returns above,* probably the life-breath of God.
Cf. Gen 2.7; Eccl 12.7. **40.12–17** An affirmation that
good faith (v. 12) and almsgiving (v. 17) are lasting values; it is only ungodliness that will come to naught. A
further reflection of Ben Sira's Deuteronomic viewpoint. **40.18–27** A reflection on the good things in life
composed as a unit of ten sayings that develop the
comparative degree, frequently called the "better than"
proverb, an ancient form of proverbial wisdom. The
poem comes to a climax in vv. 26–27 with the thought
that the fear of the Lord is better than any other good.

27 The fear of the Lord is like a garden of
        blessing,
      and covers a person better than any
        glory.

The Disgrace of Begging

28 My child, do not lead the life of a beggar;
      it is better to die than to beg.
29 When one looks to the table of another,
      one's way of life cannot be considered
        a life.
    One loses self-respect with another
        person's food,
      but one who is intelligent and well
        instructed guards against that.
30 In the mouth of the shameless begging is
        sweet,
      but it kindles a fire inside him.

Concerning Death

41 O death, how bitter is the thought of
        you
    to the one at peace among possessions,
    who has nothing to worry about and is
        prosperous in everything,
      and still is vigorous enough to enjoy
        food!
2   O death, how welcome is your sentence
      to one who is needy and failing in
        strength,
    worn down by age and anxious about
        everything;
      to one who is contrary, and has lost all
        patience!
3   Do not fear death's decree for you;
      remember those who went before you
        and those who will come after.
4   This is the Lord's decree for all flesh;
      why then should you reject the will of
        the Most High?
    Whether life lasts for ten years or a
        hundred or a thousand,
      there are no questions asked in Hades.

The Fate of the Wicked

5   The children of sinners are abominable
        children,
      and they frequent the haunts of the
        ungodly.
6   The inheritance of the children of sinners
        will perish,
      and on their offspring will be a
        perpetual disgrace.
7   Children will blame an ungodly father,
      for they suffer disgrace because of
        him.
8   Woe to you, the ungodly,
      who have forsaken the law of the Most
        High God!
9   If you have children, calamity will be
        theirs;
      you will beget them only for groaning.
    When you stumble, there is lasting joy;[a]
      and when you die, a curse is your lot.
10 Whatever comes from earth returns to
        earth;
      so the ungodly go from curse to
        destruction.

11 The human body is a fleeting thing,
      but a virtuous name will never be
        blotted out.[b]
12 Have regard for your name, since it will
        outlive you
      longer than a thousand hoards of
        gold.
13 The days of a good life are numbered,
      but a good name lasts forever.

14 My children, be true to your training and
        be at peace;
      hidden wisdom and unseen treasure—
        of what value is either?

---

a Heb: Meaning of Gk uncertain   *b* Heb: Gk *People grieve over the death of the body, but the bad name of sinners will be blotted out*

40.27 *Garden of blessing* (Greek), "Eden of blessing" (Hebrew), an allusion to Gen 2.15. **40.28–30** Several sayings warn against begging. It is improbable that the students of Ben Sira would need to be warned against leading the *life of a beggar* owing to economic exigency, given the elitist constituency of the profession. The poor might have meager possessions (cf. 29.21–22), but begging constituted a form of social death. **41.1–4** A meditation on the thought of dying recognizes its gravity (vv. 1–2) but recommends its acceptance without fear (vv. 3–4). **41.4** *The Lord's decree.* Cf. Gen 3.19.

41.5–14 A set of reflections on the fate of the ungodly (vv. 5–10) in contrast to the memorial of the godly (vv. 11–14). **41.6** That a *perpetual disgrace* rests upon sinners and their children was a very serious consideration in the light of Jewish concern for progeny, memorial, and honor. The thought that disgrace continues in one's children is developed in Wis 3.12–13, 16–19; 4.3–6. **41.13** To have a *good name,* or honorable reputation, and to be remembered by subsequent generations was the Jewish way of transcending death. See 39.11. **41.14** The thought seems to be that,

A Series of Contrasts

15 Better are those who hide their folly
   than those who hide their wisdom.
16 Therefore show respect for my words;
   for it is not good to feel shame in every
     circumstance,
   nor is every kind of abashment to be
     approved.[a]

17 Be ashamed of sexual immorality, before
     your father or mother;
   and of a lie, before a prince or a ruler;
18 of a crime, before a judge or magistrate;
   and of a breach of the law, before the
     congregation and the people;
   of unjust dealing, before your partner or
     your friend;
19 and of theft, in the place where you live.
   Be ashamed of breaking an oath or
     agreement,[b]
   and of leaning on your elbow at meals;
   of surliness in receiving or giving,
20 and of silence, before those who greet
     you;
   of looking at a prostitute,
21 and of rejecting the appeal of a relative;
   of taking away someone's portion or gift,
   and of gazing at another man's wife;
22 of meddling with his servant-girl—
   and do not approach her bed;
   of abusive words, before friends—
   and do not be insulting after making a
     gift.

42 Be ashamed of repeating what you hear,
   and of betraying secrets.
   Then you will show proper shame,
     and will find favor with everyone.

Of the following things do not be
   ashamed,
   and do not sin to save face:
2 Do not be ashamed of the law of the
     Most High and his covenant,
   and of rendering judgment to acquit
     the ungodly;
3 of keeping accounts with a partner or
     with traveling companions,
   and of dividing the inheritance of
     friends;
4 of accuracy with scales and weights,
   and of acquiring much or little;
5 of profit from dealing with merchants,
   and of frequent disciplining of children,
   and of drawing blood from the back of
     a wicked slave.
6 Where there is an untrustworthy wife, a
     seal is a good thing;
   and where there are many hands, lock
     things up.
7 When you make a deposit, be sure it is
     counted and weighed,
   and when you give or receive, put it all
     in writing.
8 Do not be ashamed to correct the stupid
     or foolish
   or the aged who are guilty of sexual
     immorality.
   Then you will show your sound training,
     and will be approved by all.

Daughters and Fathers

9 A daughter is a secret anxiety to her father,
   and worry over her robs him of sleep;

a Heb: Gk *and not everything is confidently esteemed by everyone*
b Heb: Gk *before the truth of God and the covenant*

in view of the previous reflections about death, one
need not do more to assure lasting honor than be *true*
to one's *training*. V. 14b is an exact quotation in Greek
of 20.30: one needs to use one's training for it to be
beneficial. **41.15–42.8** A poem in two stanzas on the
topic of shame, consisting of an introduction (41.15–
16), a stanza on shameful behavior (41.17–42.1a), and
a stanza on things about which one should not be
ashamed (42.1b–8). The poem uses the language of
honor and shame customary for the public recognition of shared values in ancient societies, but it mentions such a mixture of actions and attitudes that one
cannot be sure whose values Ben Sira had in mind. A
curious twist in the second stanza is that many of these
items may actually have been matters about which
many were ashamed. Most of the actions contained
here (sexual morality, business dealings, and speech)

are important subjects in the book. **42.1** To find *favor*
(honor) *with everyone* by *showing proper shame* is a
succinct definition of the honor/shame system. *To save
face* indicates that social forces may have been running
against Ben Sira and his students on the things about
which one should not be ashamed.

42.9–14 A reflection on the danger of falling into
public disfavor through a daughter's actions, with advice
on protecting her from promiscuity. The harsh measures recommended may indicate that traditional customs were being severely challenged by the social and
cultural forces of the time. Although the protection of a
daughter's virtue and the arrangement of a successful
marriage for her were essential for Jewish ethnic identity
and cultural independence (cf. Ezra 10), the basic concern here is with the manner in which a daughter affects
her father's honor and reputation in the Jewish commu-

when she is young, for fear she may not
　　marry,
　　or if married, for fear she may be
　　　disliked;

10　while a virgin, for fear she may be seduced
　　and become pregnant in her father's
　　　house;
　　or having a husband, for fear she may go
　　　astray,
　　or, though married, for fear she may be
　　　barren.

11　Keep strict watch over a headstrong
　　　daughter,
　　or she may make you a laughingstock
　　　to your enemies,
　　a byword in the city and the assembly of[a]
　　　the people,
　　and put you to shame in public
　　　gatherings.[b]
　　See that there is no lattice in her room,
　　　no spot that overlooks the approaches
　　　to the house.[c]

12　Do not let her parade her beauty before
　　　any man,
　　or spend her time among married
　　　women;[a]

13　for from garments comes the moth,
　　and from a woman comes woman's
　　　wickedness.

14　Better is the wickedness of a man than a
　　　woman who does good;
　　it is woman who brings shame and
　　　disgrace.

The Works of God in Nature

15　I will now call to mind the works of the
　　　Lord,
　　and will declare what I have seen.
　　By the word of the Lord his works are
　　　made;
　　and all his creatures do his will.[d]

16　The sun looks down on everything with
　　　its light,
　　and the work of the Lord is full of his
　　　glory.

17　The Lord has not empowered even his
　　　holy ones
　　to recount all his marvelous works,
　　which the Lord the Almighty has
　　　established
　　so that the universe may stand firm in
　　　his glory.

18　He searches out the abyss and the human
　　　heart;

he understands their innermost secrets.
For the Most High knows all that may be
　　known;
　　he sees from of old the things that are
　　　to come.[e]

19　He discloses what has been and what is
　　　to be,
　　and he reveals the traces of hidden
　　　things.

20　No thought escapes him,
　　and nothing is hidden from him.

21　He has set in order the splendors of his
　　　wisdom;
　　he is from all eternity one and the
　　　same.
　　Nothing can be added or taken away,
　　and he needs no one to be his
　　　counselor.

22　How desirable are all his works,
　　and how sparkling they are to see![f]

23　All these things live and remain forever;
　　each creature is preserved to meet a
　　　particular need.[g]

24　All things come in pairs, one opposite the
　　　other,
　　and he has made nothing incomplete.

25　Each supplements the virtues of the other.
　　Who could ever tire of seeing his glory?

The Splendor of the Sun

43　The pride of the higher realms is the
　　clear vault of the sky,
　　as glorious to behold as the sight of the
　　　heavens.

2　The sun, when it appears, proclaims as it
　　　rises
　　what a marvelous instrument it is, the
　　　work of the Most High.

3　At noon it parches the land,
　　and who can withstand its burning
　　　heat?

4　A man tending[h] a furnace works in
　　　burning heat,
　　but three times as hot is the sun
　　　scorching the mountains;
　　it breathes out fiery vapors,
　　and its bright rays blind the eyes.

5　Great is the Lord who made it;
　　at his orders it hurries on its course.

---

a Heb: Meaning of Gk uncertain　b Heb: Gk to shame before
the great multitude　c Heb: Gk lacks See . . . house　d Syr
Compare Heb: most Gk witnesses lack and all . . . will　e Heb:
Gk he sees the sign(s) of the age　f Meaning of Gk uncertain
g Heb: Gk forever for every need, and all are obedient　h Other
ancient authorities read blowing upon

The Splendor of the Moon

6 It is the moon that marks the changing
    seasons,[a]
    governing the times, their everlasting
      sign.
7 From the moon comes the sign for festal
    days,
    a light that wanes when it completes its
      course.
8 The new moon, as its name suggests,
    renews itself;[b]
    how marvelous it is in this change,
    a beacon to the hosts on high,
    shining in the vault of the heavens!

The Glory of the Stars and the Rainbow

9 The glory of the stars is the beauty of
    heaven,
    a glittering array in the heights of the
      Lord.
10 On the orders of the Holy One they stand
    in their appointed places;
    they never relax in their watches.
11 Look at the rainbow, and praise him who
    made it;
    it is exceedingly beautiful in its
      brightness.
12 It encircles the sky with its glorious arc;
    the hands of the Most High have
      stretched it out.

The Marvels of Nature

13 By his command he sends the driving snow
    and speeds the lightnings of his
      judgment.

14 Therefore the storehouses are opened,
    and the clouds fly out like birds.
15 In his majesty he gives the clouds their
    strength,
    and the hailstones are broken in pieces.
17a The voice of his thunder rebukes the
    earth;
16   when he appears, the mountains shake.
At his will the south wind blows;
17b   so do the storm from the north and the
    whirlwind.
He scatters the snow like birds flying
    down,
    and its descent is like locusts alighting.
18 The eye is dazzled by the beauty of its
    whiteness,
    and the mind is amazed as it falls.
19 He pours frost over the earth like salt,
    and icicles form like pointed thorns.
20 The cold north wind blows,
    and ice freezes on the water;
    it settles on every pool of water,
    and the water puts it on like a
      breastplate.
21 He consumes the mountains and burns
    up the wilderness,
    and withers the tender grass like fire.
22 A mist quickly heals all things;
    the falling dew gives refreshment from
      the heat.

23 By his plan he stilled the deep
    and planted islands in it.

---

a Heb: Meaning of Gk uncertain   b Heb: Gk The month is
named after the moon

---

nity. **42.15–43.33** A hymn of praise to the Lord and his
creation. It consists of a concise poem on the inscrutable
knowledge and power of the creator (42.15–21) followed by a lengthy poem on the wonders of the natural
order (42.22–43.26) and concludes with an invitation to
join the author in singing the Lord's praises (43.27–33).
42.15–21 The Lord is praised for his wisdom and power
as revealed in his works. **42.15** *By the word of the Lord* alludes to the account of creation in Gen 1.1–31. **42.17** *His
holy ones*, the members of his heavenly court, his angels.
If the Lord's angels cannot *recount all his marvelous
works*, how much more inscrutable are they to humans?
See 43.27–33. **42.18** *The Most High* knows everything
because he *sees* all. The notion was basic to the thought
of the Lord's wisdom and to Ben Sira's theodicy of divine
rewards and punishments. Cf. note on 15.18. It drew
upon the ancient Near Eastern system of governance, in
which the king's men were his "eyes and ears," as well as
upon a fascination with solar mythology, in which the

sun represented the eye of the high god. Note the importance and role of the sun in 42.16; 43.1–5. **42.19** Time
and future events are part of God's marvelous works.
42.22–43.33 The works of the Lord are arranged in a
list that begins with the *sun* as the highest visible creature, descends through *moon, stars,* and geophysical
phenomena (*rainbow, lightning, clouds, wind, snow,
frost, ice,* and *dew*), to end with a notice about the ocean
as *the deep*. This arrangement was typical of *onomas-
tica*, or lists of natural phenomena. Cf. the similar
arrangement in Job 38.1–38. In Job the list of astrophysical phenomena is complemented by a list of living
creatures in 38.39–41.34. **43.6** Ben Sira assumes a lunar
calendar. Cf. 33.8. **43.14** It was common in antiquity to
imagine *storehouses* in the heavens, beyond the horizon,
where the Lord kept the winds, clouds, and storms until
he needed them. He then opened the doors and sent
them out to perform their missions. **43.23** That the
Lord *stilled the deep* is derived from an ancient myth of

24 Those who sail the sea tell of its dangers,
     and we marvel at what we hear.
25 In it are strange and marvelous creatures,
     all kinds of living things, and huge
       sea-monsters.
26 Because of him each of his messengers
       succeeds,
     and by his word all things hold together.
27 We could say more but could never say
       enough;
     let the final word be: "He is the all."
28 Where can we find the strength to praise
       him?
     For he is greater than all his works.
29 Awesome is the Lord and very great,
     and marvelous is his power.
30 Glorify the Lord and exalt him as much
       as you can,

for he surpasses even that.
When you exalt him, summon all your
       strength,
     and do not grow weary, for you cannot
       praise him enough.
31 Who has seen him and can describe him?
     Or who can extol him as he is?
32 Many things greater than these lie
       hidden,
     for I*a* have seen but few of his works.
33 For the Lord has made all things,
     and to the godly he has given wisdom.

Hymn in Honor of Our Ancestors *b*

44 Let us now sing the praises of famous
     men,
   our ancestors in their generations.

a Heb: Gk *we*   *b* This title is included in the Gk text.

creation according to which God had to slay the monster of the deep, or still the chaotic waters, in order to let the dry land appear and construct upon it his house. Cf. Pss 104.24–26; 107.23–24. **43.26** This verse, which serves as a conclusion to the poem of praise for the natural order (42.22–43.26), brings together two cosmologies, mythical accounts of the ordering of the world. *Messengers*, all the natural phenomena as servants of the Lord who do his bidding *so that the universe may stand firm* (42.17). *His word* by which *all things hold together* may reflect the Stoic view of the *logos* (Greek, "word" or "logic") that permeates the natural world (*kosmos*) as a principle of cohesion and order. It is probable that Ben Sira had the Genesis account of creation in mind, according to which God spoke the world into being, and that both mythologies were understood as explications of God words, as commands (to his "messengers") and as expressions of rhyme and reason for the world he had in mind ("logos"). In somewhat later literatures, such as the works of Philo of Alexandria and the Gospel of John (Jn 1.1–18), the Stoic *logos* became the primary concept for interpreting the Genesis account. **43.27** *"He is the all"* may reflect Stoic philosophies of the world as an organism generated and held together by a single (divine) principle. **43.30** To *praise* and *glorify* the Lord is a demonstration of one's own wisdom, that one has come to see how marvelous his works are despite the limitations of human capacity to plumb their mysteries. According to 15.9–10, *in wisdom must praise be uttered*. **43.33** A transitional verse providing a summary for the hymn in praise of creation and pointing ahead to the hymn in praise of famous men to follow. It shows that Ben Sira intended the two poems to be taken together, *now* to call the works of the Lord to mind (42.15), *now* to sing the praises of famous men (44.1). The combination follows a recognizable pattern in certain psalms and other poems that begin with a meditation upon creation and come to focus upon the sweep of history. Cf. Pss 135; 136.

44.1–51.24 A long poem eulogizing the great leaders of the people throughout the epic history of Israel. It consists of an introductory poem in praise of all the ancestors, even those who left no name (44.1–15), a series of poetic units dedicated to specific figures from Enoch to Nehemiah (44.16–49.16), and a concluding *encomium*, or work of praise, on the high priest Simon from Ben Sira's own time (50.1–24). The epic is divided into three parts, the period during which the covenants were established, the period of the kings and their kingdoms, and the Second Temple period following the return from exile. The three periods of the epic are joined together by descriptions of the two transitional periods, one under the judges (46.1–12) and one under the leaders of the restoration (49.11–13). The hymn as a whole appears to be patterned on the model of Hellenistic *encomia*, eulogistic histories in commemoration of local shrines and cities, in this case with an eye toward the temple at Jerusalem. The individual units are patterned on the model of Hellenistic *encomia* in praise of famous persons and leaders. The *encomium* opened with an introduction and a mention of the person's birth and genealogy, then went on to describe the person's pursuits, virtues, accomplishments, and blessings, and concluded with acknowledgment of his death and memorial. Ben Sira modifies this pattern in keeping with Jewish culture and values. A leader's election to office is more important than an account of his genealogy and pursuits. Piety counts more than personal virtues. And a leader's deeds are not noted as heroic achievements. Instead, he is eulogized for correct performance of social and religious offices established by the covenants and consistently evaluated in keeping with the consequences of his performance as it affected the well-being of the people. His reward is the honor he received from both God (by election and favor) and the people (who sang his praises). **44.1–15** The ancestors are glorious because of their

2 The Lord apportioned to them[a] great glory,
    his majesty from the beginning.
3 There were those who ruled in their
        kingdoms,
    and made a name for themselves by
        their valor;
  those who gave counsel because they
        were intelligent;
    those who spoke in prophetic oracles;
4 those who led the people by their counsels
    and by their knowledge of the people's
        lore;
    they were wise in their words of
        instruction;
5 those who composed musical tunes,
    or put verses in writing;
6 rich men endowed with resources,
    living peacefully in their homes—
7 all these were honored in their
        generations,
    and were the pride of their times.
8 Some of them have left behind a name,
    so that others declare their praise.
9 But of others there is no memory;
    they have perished as though they had
        never existed;
  they have become as though they had
        never been born,
    they and their children after them.
10 But these also were godly men,

whose righteous deeds have not been
    forgotten;
11 their wealth will remain with their
        descendants,
    and their inheritance with their
        children's children.[b]
12 Their descendants stand by the
        covenants;
    their children also, for their sake.
13 Their offspring will continue forever,
    and their glory will never be blotted out.
14 Their bodies are buried in peace,
    but their name lives on generation
        after generation.
15 The assembly declares[c] their wisdom,
    and the congregation proclaims their
        praise.

Enoch

16 Enoch pleased the Lord and was taken up,
    an example of repentance to all
        generations.

Noah

17 Noah was found perfect and righteous;
    in the time of wrath he kept the race
        alive;[d]

---

a Heb: Gk *created*   b Heb Compare Lat Syr: Meaning of Gk
uncertain   c Heb: Gk *Peoples declare*   d Heb: Gk *was taken in
exchange*

---

recognition by God (v. 2), their honorable achievements (vv. 3–6), their recognition by their own generations (vv. 7–8), their godliness (vv. 9–10), their legacy to their children (vv. 11–12), and their lasting name and memory (vv. 13–14). **44.3–6** The list of social roles includes several offices traditional for ancient Hebrew society, such as king and prophet, that appear in the following verses. The purpose of the list, however, is not to present a full and balanced typology of the offices, but to create a general picture of glory and honor worthy of the ancestors and characteristic for the grand tradition Ben Sira wishes to claim for the Jews. These verses are heavily weighted toward the accomplishments of the wise, the intellectuals, the creative, and the wealthy; not all the leaders praised in the following verses have all these characteristics. The epic sections of the hymn (see note on 44.1–51.24) are more concerned with the covenants underlying the social structure of Israel, the failure of the kingdoms to actualize the ideal order, and the claim that a society organized around the temple and its systems is what God originally intended for Israel. Thus patriarchs, priests, kings, and prophets dominate the history. Scribes, teachers, and sages are hardly in view. **44.9** Despite the connection Ben Sira makes between a good memory and immortality, he recognizes that the

memory of many pious people has not persisted, and thus they have become *as though they had never been born*. **44.12** *The covenants*, contracts or agreements between God and the patriarchs or leaders of Israel who initiated institutions and offices constitutive for the social and religious structure of Israel. Most covenants were associated with ritual occasions and their stories therefore served as charters for contemporary ritual practices. In the poem to follow, covenants are mentioned for Noah, Abraham, Isaac, Jacob-Israel, Moses, Aaron, and Phinehas from the archaic period before the entrance into the land, when the plans for Israel were being formulated, and for David from the period of the kings after Israel is located in the land. **44.16** A single bicola, alluding to Gen 4.24, is dedicated to Enoch. His significance for the poem as a whole is unclear, since he does not represent a covenant (as do the next seven figures) and is set forth as an example (something not true of the other twenty-nine figures in the poem). V. 16 is missing in the earliest Hebrew fragments from Masada as well as in the Syriac text, but it may have dropped out by a copyist's error. Scholarly opinion is divided. Some think that the poem began with Enoch as an *inclusio* with 49.14. Others view him as disrupting the logic of the first part of the poem and argue that the original poem opened

therefore a remnant was left on the earth
    when the flood came.

18 Everlasting covenants were made with
    him
      that all flesh should never again be
        blotted out by a flood.

Abraham

19 Abraham was the great father of a
    multitude of nations,
      and no one has been found like him in
        glory.

20 He kept the law of the Most High,
      and entered into a covenant with
        him;
    he certified the covenant in his flesh,
      and when he was tested he proved
        faithful.

21 Therefore the Lord[a] assured him with an
    oath
      that the nations would be blessed
        through his offspring;
    that he would make him as numerous as
      the dust of the earth,
    and exalt his offspring like the stars,
      and give them an inheritance from sea to
        sea
      and from the Euphrates[b] to the ends of
        the earth.

Isaac and Jacob

22 To Isaac also he gave the same assurance
      for the sake of his father Abraham.
    The blessing of all people and the
      covenant

23   he made to rest on the head of Jacob;
    he acknowledged him with his blessings,
      and gave him his inheritance;
    he divided his portions,
      and distributed them among twelve
        tribes.

Moses

From his descendants the Lord[a] brought
    forth a godly man,
  who found favor in the sight of all

45 ¹and was beloved by God and people,
      Moses, whose memory is blessed.

2 He made him equal in glory to the holy
    ones,
      and made him great, to the terror of
        his enemies.

3 By his words he performed swift
    miracles;[c]
      the Lord[a] glorified him in the presence
        of kings.
    He gave him commandments for his
      people,
      and revealed to him his glory.

4 For his faithfulness and meekness he
    consecrated him,
      choosing him out of all humankind.

5 He allowed him to hear his voice,
      and led him into the dark cloud,
    and gave him the commandments face to
      face,
      the law of life and knowledge,
    so that he might teach Jacob the
      covenant,
      and Israel his decrees.

Aaron

6 He exalted Aaron, a holy man like Moses[d]
      who was his brother, of the tribe of
        Levi.

7 He made an everlasting covenant with
    him,
      and gave him the priesthood of the
        people.

a Gk he   b Syr: Heb Gk River   c Heb: Gk caused signs to cease
d Gk him

with Noah. **44.17–18** Noah survived the flood, and
God made a covenant with him never again to destroy
humankind. See Gen 6–9. That Noah was deemed
righteous derives from Gen 6.9; 7.1. For the *covenants*
and the rainbow as sign, see Gen 9.8–17. **44.19–
21** Abraham is praised as the blessed *father of a multitude of nations*. See Gen 17.4–8. **44.20** *Covenant in his
flesh*, circumcision. See Gen 17.9–14. *When he was
tested* alludes to the binding of Isaac (Gen 22.1–14).
44.21 For *oath* and *blessed*, see Gen 22.15–18. A blessing established legitimacy and involved a promise of
divine fulfillment. **44.22–23** The blessing passed
through Isaac to Jacob, the father of the children of Is-

rael. See Gen 17.19; 28.1–4. Jacob's *inheritance* was the
land (Gen 28.4). **44.23–45.5** Moses was chosen to receive the commandments and teach them to Israel.
45.2 *Holy Ones* are God's angels; see 42.17. **45.3** *Miracles . . . in the presence of kings*, the exodus. Cf. Ex 7.1–
11.10. *Gave him commandments*, the revelation of the
Ten Commandments to Moses. Cf. Ex 20.1–17; Deut
5.1–33. **45.4** *Faithfulness and meekness*. Cf. Num 12.3,
7. **45.5** Meeting God *face to face* in the *cloud* alludes to
the stories of Moses on the mountain; cf. Ex 19–20; 24;
34. *That he might teach* alludes to Deut 4.1–5.
    45.6–22 With Aaron the priesthood is established.
45.7 *Everlasting covenant*, the "perpetual priesthood"

He blessed him with stateliness,
and put a glorious robe on him.
8 He clothed him in perfect splendor,
and strengthened him with the
symbols of authority,
the linen undergarments, the long
robe, and the ephod.
9 And he encircled him with
pomegranates,
with many golden bells all around,
to send forth a sound as he walked,
to make their ringing heard in the
temple
as a reminder to his people;
10 with the sacred vestment, of gold and
violet
and purple, the work of an
embroiderer;
with the oracle of judgment, Urim and
Thummim;
11 with twisted crimson, the work of an
artisan;
with precious stones engraved like seals,
in a setting of gold, the work of a
jeweler,
to commemorate in engraved letters
each of the tribes of Israel;
12 with a gold crown upon his turban,
inscribed like a seal with "Holiness,"
a distinction to be prized, the work of an
expert,
a delight to the eyes, richly adorned.
13 Before him such beautiful things did not
exist.
No outsider ever put them on,
but only his sons
and his descendants in perpetuity.
14 His sacrifices shall be wholly burned
twice every day continually.
15 Moses ordained him,
and anointed him with holy oil;
it was an everlasting covenant for him
and for his descendants as long as the
heavens endure,

to minister to the Lord[a] and serve as
priest
and bless his people in his name.
16 He chose him out of all the living
to offer sacrifice to the Lord,
incense and a pleasing odor as a
memorial portion,
to make atonement for the[b] people.
17 In his commandments he gave him
authority and statutes and[c] judgments,
to teach Jacob the testimonies,
and to enlighten Israel with his law.
18 Outsiders conspired against him,
and envied him in the wilderness,
Dathan and Abiram and their followers
and the company of Korah, in wrath
and anger.
19 The Lord saw it and was not pleased,
and in the heat of his anger they were
destroyed;
he performed wonders against them
to consume them in flaming fire.
20 He added glory to Aaron
and gave him a heritage;
he allotted to him the best of the first
fruits,
and prepared bread of first fruits in
abundance;
21 for they eat the sacrifices of the Lord,
which he gave to him and his
descendants.
22 But in the land of the people he has no
inheritance,
and he has no portion among the
people;
for the Lord[d] himself is his[e] portion
and inheritance.

Phinehas

23 Phinehas son of Eleazar ranks third in
glory

---

a Gk him b Other ancient authorities read his or your
c Heb: Gk authority in covenants of d Gk he e Other ancient
authorities read your

---

promised in Ex 29.9; 40.15. Cf. Sir 45.13, 15. **45.8** *Clothed him in perfect splendor,* elaborated in vv. 8–13, derives from Ex 28. Cf. the description of Simon in Sir 50.5–11. **45.10** *Urim and Thummim.* See note on 33.3. **45.14** Twice daily burnt offerings were the practice in Ben Sira's time. Cf. Lev 6.8–15. **45.15** *Ordained* by Moses alludes to Lev 8.1–13; cf. Ex 28.41. *To bless . . . in his name,* possibly the blessing in Num 6.22–27; cf. Deut 10.8. **45.17** On the priest's *authority . . . to teach,* cf. Lev 10.11; Deut 33.10; Mal 2.7. **45.18** *The company*
of Korah alludes to the story in Num 16.1–17.15. **45.20–21** For the prescription that priests may *eat the sacrifices,* see Num 18.8–19. **45.22** On the Lord as Aaron's *portion,* see Num 18.20. **45.23–26** Phinehas is glorified as a priest in the line of Aaron with whom the covenant of friendship (Hebrew, "peace") was confirmed. Cf. Num 25.7–13. **45.23** *Third in glory* may refer to Phinehas's being third in the sequence of the poem after Moses and Aaron or his being third in the priestly line from Aaron; cf. Num 25.10.

for being zealous in the fear of the
Lord,
and standing firm, when the people
turned away,
in the noble courage of his soul;
and he made atonement for Israel.

24 Therefore a covenant of friendship was
established with him,
that he should be leader of the
sanctuary and of his people,
that he and his descendants should have
the dignity of the priesthood forever.

25 Just as a covenant was established with
David
son of Jesse of the tribe of Judah,
that the king's heritage passes only from
son to son,
so the heritage of Aaron is for his
descendants alone.

26 And now bless the Lord
who has crowned you with glory.*
May the Lord*b* grant you wisdom of mind
to judge his people with justice,
so that their prosperity may not vanish,
and that their glory may endure
through all their generations.

Joshua and Caleb

46 Joshua son of Nun was mighty in war,
and was the successor of Moses in the
prophetic office.
He became, as his name implies,
a great savior of God's*c* elect,
to take vengeance on the enemies that
rose against them,
so that he might give Israel its
inheritance.

2 How glorious he was when he lifted his
hands

and brandished his sword against the
cities!

3 Who before him ever stood so firm?
For he waged the wars of the Lord.

4 Was it not through him that the sun
stood still
and one day became as long as two?

5 He called upon the Most High, the
Mighty One,
when enemies pressed him on every
side,
and the great Lord answered him
with hailstones of mighty power.

6 He overwhelmed that nation in battle,
and on the slope he destroyed his
opponents,
so that the nations might know his
armament,
that he was fighting in the sight of the
Lord;
for he was a devoted follower of the
Mighty One.

7 And in the days of Moses he proved his
loyalty,
he and Caleb son of Jephunneh:
they opposed the congregation,*d*
restrained the people from sin,
and stilled their wicked grumbling.

8 And these two alone were spared
out of six hundred thousand infantry,
to lead the people*e* into their inheritance,
the land flowing with milk and honey.

9 The Lord gave Caleb strength,
which remained with him in his old
age,
so that he went up to the hill country,

---

a Heb: Gk lacks *And . . . glory*   *b* Gk *he*   *c* Gk *his*   *d* Other
ancient authorities read *the enemy*   *e* Gk *them*

45.25 Mention of the *covenant . . . with David* is out of
place here. Cf. 47.11. The point, however, is to link the
two covenants, of kingship and priesthood, as fundamental for the ideal structure of Israel's society. *For his
descendants alone* restricts priestly prerogatives to
Aaron's progeny and may indicate an ideological battle
for the priesthood in Ben Sira's time between the Oni-
ads and the Tobiads, two leading families who fought
for political control of Jerusalem during the shift from
Ptolemaic to Seleucid hegemony. **45.26** The sudden
shift to the plural *you* likely indicates Ben Sira's prayer
for the contemporary high priest, Simon II (see ch.
50), and his successors.
46.1–10 Joshua and Caleb are praised for leading
Israel into the land. **46.1** On the *successor of Moses*, see

Deut 34.9; Josh 1.1, 5; 3.7. The *prophetic office* is Ben
Sira's designation for the social role of teachers,
scribes, counselors, and prophets who instruct kings
and priests as well as the people in the law. *As his name
implies* refers to the meaning of Joshua in Hebrew,
"The Lord is salvation." **46.2** *He lifted his hands . . .
against*, an idiom for going to war, a reference to
Joshua taking the land (Josh 6–11). **46.4** *The sun stood
still.* See Josh 10.12–14. **46.5** *Hailstones.* See Josh
10.11. **46.7** *Proved his loyalty*, by the "good report" that
Joshua and Caleb brought when spying out the land
(Num 14.6–10; cf. 1 Macc 2.55–56). **46.8** Of the *six
hundred thousand* who were led out of Egypt, all perished in the wilderness except Joshua and Caleb, who
alone were spared and entered the land. See Num

and his children obtained it for an
   inheritance,
10 so that all the Israelites might see
   how good it is to follow the Lord.

The Judges

11 The judges also, with their respective
   names,
   whose hearts did not fall into idolatry
   and who did not turn away from the
   Lord—
   may their memory be blessed!
12 May their bones send forth new life from
   where they lie,
   and may the names of those who have
   been honored
   live again in their children!
13 Samuel was beloved by his Lord;
   a prophet of the Lord, he established
   the kingdom
   and anointed rulers over his people.
14 By the law of the Lord he judged the
   congregation,
   and the Lord watched over Jacob.
15 By his faithfulness he was proved to be a
   prophet,
   and by his words he became known as
   a trustworthy seer.
16 He called upon the Lord, the Mighty One,
   when his enemies pressed him on
   every side,
   and he offered in sacrifice a suckling
   lamb.
17 Then the Lord thundered from heaven,
   and made his voice heard with a
   mighty sound;
18 he subdued the leaders of the enemy[a]
   and all the rulers of the Philistines.
19 Before the time of his eternal sleep,
   Samuel[b] bore witness before the Lord
   and his anointed:
   "No property, not so much as a pair of
   shoes,

have I taken from anyone!"
   And no one accused him.
20 Even after he had fallen asleep, he
   prophesied
   and made known to the king his death,
   and lifted up his voice from the ground
   in prophecy, to blot out the wickedness
   of the people.

Nathan

47
After him Nathan rose up
to prophesy in the days of David.

David

2 As the fat is set apart from the offering of
   well-being,
   so David was set apart from the
   Israelites.
3 He played with lions as though they were
   young goats,
   and with bears as though they were
   lambs of the flock.
4 In his youth did he not kill a giant,
   and take away the people's disgrace,
   when he whirled the stone in the sling
   and struck down the boasting Goliath?
5 For he called on the Lord, the Most High,
   and he gave strength to his right arm
   to strike down a mighty warrior,
   and to exalt the power[c] of his people.
6 So they glorified him for the tens of
   thousands he conquered,
   and praised him for the blessings
   bestowed by the Lord,
   when the glorious diadem was given to
   him.
7 For he wiped out his enemies on every
   side,
   and annihilated his adversaries the
   Philistines;
   he crushed their power[c] to our own
   day.

---

a Heb: Gk *leaders of the people of Tyre*   *b* Gk *he*   *c* Gk *horn*

11.21; 14.38; 26.65. **46.9** On Caleb's *inheritance,* see Josh 14.6–14. **46.11–12** Some of the judges deserve to be honored, those who *did not fall into idolatry.* See Judg 8.27; 16.20. *New life* from their *bones* means drawing strength from their spiritual legacy through memory and memorial. Cf. 49.10. **46.13–20** Samuel is honored as the prophet who established kingship in Israel. See 1 Sam 1.1–16.13. **46.13** *Anointed rulers* (plural), both Saul and David (1 Sam 10.1; 16.13), though Saul is not mentioned in the poem by name.

46.16 *Offered in sacrifice.* See 1 Sam 7.9–11. **46.19** *Bore witness.* See 1 Sam 12.3. **46.20** *His voice from the ground.* See 1 Sam 28.8–19.

47.1 Nathan is mentioned as the prophet associated with David. See 2 Sam 7.2–17; 12.1; 1 Chr 17.1. **47.2–11** David is given a covenant of kingship. **47.2** *Set apart,* chosen by God to be king (1 Sam 16.1–12). **47.3** *Played with lions . . . and with bears,* a euphemism for the easy kill; see 1 Sam 17.34–36. **47.4** *Kill a giant, . . . Goliath.* See 1 Sam 17.48–51. **47.6** *Tens of thousands* alludes to

8 In all that he did he gave thanks
    to the Holy One, the Most High,
        proclaiming his glory;
he sang praise with all his heart,
    and he loved his Maker.
9 He placed singers before the altar,
    to make sweet melody with their
        voices.ᵃ
10 He gave beauty to the festivals,
    and arranged their times throughout
        the year,ᵇ
while they praised God'sᶜ holy name,
    and the sanctuary resounded from
        early morning.
11 The Lord took away his sins,
    and exalted his powerᵈ forever;
he gave him a covenant of kingship
    and a glorious throne in Israel.

Solomon

12 After him a wise son rose up
    who because of him lived in security:ᵉ
13 Solomon reigned in an age of peace,
    because God made all his borders
        tranquil,
so that he might build a house in his
        name
    and provide a sanctuary to stand
        forever.
14 How wise you were when you were
        young!
    You overflowed like the Nileᶠ with
        understanding.

15 Your influence spread throughout the
        earth,
    and you filled it with proverbs having
        deep meaning.
16 Your fame reached to far-off islands,
    and you were loved for your peaceful
        reign.
17 Your songs, proverbs, and parables,
    and the answers you gave astounded
        the nations.
18 In the name of the Lord God,
    who is called the God of Israel,
you gathered gold like tin
    and amassed silver like lead.
19 But you brought in women to lie at your
        side,
    and through your body you were
        brought into subjection.
20 You stained your honor,
    and defiled your family line,
so that you brought wrath upon your
        children,
    and they were grievedᵍ at your folly,
21 because the sovereignty was divided
    and a rebel kingdom arose out of
        Ephraim.
22 But the Lord will never give up his mercy,
    or cause any of his works to perish;

---

a Other ancient authorities add *and daily they sing his praises*
b Gk *to completion* *c* Gk *his* *d* Gk *horn* *e* Heb: Gk *in a broad place* *f* Heb: Gk *a river* *g* Other ancient authorities read *I was grieved*

---

1 Sam 18.7. **47.8–10** That David *sang praise,* installed *singers* in the temple, and arranged the *festivals* is an anachronism taken from Chronicles, which recasts the image of David to include care for the institution of the temple systems. See 1 Chr 16.4; 23.5, 31–32. It is this tradition that resulted in the attribution of the Psalms to David. **47.11** On David's *sins,* see 2 Sam 12.1–15. For the *covenant of kingship,* see 2 Sam 7.12–16; cf. Ps 89.28–29; Sir 45.25. **47.12–22** Solomon is praised for his wisdom and remembered for the consequences of his sin. See 1 Kings 1–11. **47.13** Solomon's reign was *an age of peace* in contrast to the wars of David. Cf. 1 Kings 4.20–21; 5.3–4. He was therefore privileged to *build a house* (for God), the famous temple of Solomon. See 1 Kings 5–8. **47.16** *Fame reached to far-off islands* (Hebrew, "distant coasts") may be an allusion to the queen of Sheba (1 Kings 10.1–12). **47.17** Solomon's wisdom was proverbial. See 1 Kings 3.3–14; 4.29–34; 10.1–10, 23–25. Attributed to him were the book of Proverbs, the Song of Solomon, the Wisdom of Solomon, a first-century BCE collection of prayers and meditations called the *Psalms of Solomon,* and a late first-century CE book of esoteric Christian devotions called the *Odes of* Solomon as well as other poems, prayers, riddles, and lore scattered through Jewish and early Christian literature of the Greco-Roman period. See Prov 1.1; Song 1.1; Wis 7–9; Lk 11.31. **47.18** On Solomon's *gold* and *silver,* see 1 Kings 10.21, 27. **47.20** *Stained your honor.* Solomon took foreign wives and built shrines to foreign gods, practices against which the Lord had warned him. See 1 Kings 11.1–11. **47.21** The Divided Kingdom was thought to be the result of Solomon's sin. Cf. 47.23–25; 1 Kings 11.9–11; 12.12–20. After Solomon there were two kingdoms: the Southern Kingdom (Judah), centered in Jerusalem; and the Northern Kingdom (Israel), centered at Shechem. *Ephraim,* another name for the Northern Kingdom, was used by writers loyal to Jerusalem to claim the name and traditions of Israel as their own heritage. **47.22** Despite Solomon's sin and the division of the kingdom, the promise to David remained in force. See 2 Sam 7.12–16; 1 Kings 11.12–13, 34–39. *Remnant* refers to a Jewish theology of survival: despite oppression, wars, and exile, some would remain true to the Lord and survive. *Root,* a metaphor for Davidic genealogy. Cf. 2 Kings 19.30; Isa 11.10; 37.31; 53.2. The combination of *rem-*

he will never blot out the descendants of
    his chosen one,
  or destroy the family line of him who
    loved him.
So he gave a remnant to Jacob,
  and to David a root from his own
    family.

Rehoboam and Jeroboam

23 Solomon rested with his ancestors,
    and left behind him one of his sons,
  broad in*a* folly and lacking in sense,
    Rehoboam, whose policy drove the
      people to revolt.
Then Jeroboam son of Nebat led Israel
    into sin
  and started Ephraim on its sinful ways.
24 Their sins increased more and more,
    until they were exiled from their land.
25 For they sought out every kind of
    wickedness,
  until vengeance came upon them.

Elijah

48 Then Elijah arose, a prophet like fire,
    and his word burned like a torch.
2 He brought a famine upon them,
    and by his zeal he made them few in
      number.
3 By the word of the Lord he shut up the
    heavens,
  and also three times brought down fire.
4 How glorious you were, Elijah, in your
    wondrous deeds!
  Whose glory is equal to yours?
5 You raised a corpse from death

and from Hades, by the word of the
    Most High.
6 You sent kings down to destruction,
    and famous men, from their sickbeds.
7 You heard rebuke at Sinai
    and judgments of vengeance at Horeb.
8 You anointed kings to inflict retribution,
    and prophets to succeed you.*b*
9 You were taken up by a whirlwind of fire,
    in a chariot with horses of fire.
10 At the appointed time, it is written, you
    are destined*c*
to calm the wrath of God before it
    breaks out in fury,
to turn the hearts of parents to their
    children,
  and to restore the tribes of Jacob.
11 Happy are those who saw you
    and were adorned*d* with your love!
  For we also shall surely live.*e*

Elisha

12 When Elijah was enveloped in the
    whirlwind,
  Elisha was filled with his spirit.
He performed twice as many signs,
    and marvels with every utterance of his
      mouth.*f*
Never in his lifetime did he tremble
    before any ruler,
  nor could anyone intimidate him at all.
13 Nothing was too hard for him,

---

a Heb (with a play on the name Rehoboam) Syr: Gk *the people's*
b Heb: Gk *him*   *c* Heb: Gk *are for reproofs*   *d* Other ancient
authorities read *and have died*   *e* Text and meaning of Gk
uncertain   *f* Heb: Gk lacks *He performed . . . mouth*

---

nant and *root* is Ben Sira's own interpretation and
hope. **47.23–25** The kingdom of David and Solomon
was divided between Rehoboam, Solomon's son at
Jerusalem, and Jeroboam, who established himself as
king at Shechem. There is manuscript evidence that
wordplays instead of proper names were originally
used to refer to each of them in v. 23. That would agree
with Ben Sira's care in the use of proper names
throughout the poem, a concern related to the importance of memory and memorial and governed by his
intention to praise only those worthy of honor.
47.23 *Rehoboam's folly* was an increase in forced labor
(1 Kings 12.1–24). The *sin of Jeroboam* was to set up
shrines at Dan and Bethel as rivals of the temple in
Jerusalem (1 Kings 12.25–33). **47.24** The kingdom divided in 922 BCE; the exile occurred in 722 BCE when
the Assyrians conquered Shechem/Samaria and deported the Israelites (2 Kings 17.6, 18–23).
48.1–11 Elijah is praised as the prophet of the

Northern Kingdom who prophesied in the name of
the Lord against King Ahab of the house of Omri (ca.
869 BCE) and countered the worship of Baal. For the
many exploits of Elijah mentioned by Ben Sira, see
1 Kings 17–19; 2 Kings 1–2. **48.10** *It is written.* The
text that prophesies Elijah's return is Mal 4.5–6. Cf.
Mt 11.14; 16.14; 17.10–12; Mk 6.15; 8.28; 9.11–13; Lk
9.8, 19. **48.11** The meaning of this verse is unclear because of divergent manuscript traditions. According to
2 Kings 2.10, Elisha was the fortunate (or happy) one
who *saw* Elijah taken up, but the Hebrew text seems to
refer to seeing Elijah upon his return. Later scribes,
likely interpreting Mal 4.5–6, apparently understood
Elijah's ascension to be a transformation and thus a
sign of translation to immortal status. Cf. Mt 17.3–4;
Mk 9.4–5; Lk 9.30–33. **48.12–16** The prophet Elisha is
praised for continuing the work in the spirit of Elijah.
See 2 Kings 2–13. **48.12** *Filled with his spirit* alludes to
2 Kings 2.9–15. **48.13** *His body prophesied.* See 2 Kings

and when he was dead, his body
    prophesied.

14 In his life he did wonders,
    and in death his deeds were marvelous.

15 Despite all this the people did not repent,
    nor did they forsake their sins,
    until they were carried off as plunder
        from their land,
    and were scattered over all the earth.
    The people were left very few in number,
        but with a ruler from the house of
        David.

16 Some of them did what was right,
    but others sinned more and more.

Hezekiah

17 Hezekiah fortified his city,
    and brought water into its midst;
    he tunneled the rock with iron tools,
    and built cisterns for the water.

18 In his days Sennacherib invaded the
        country;
    he sent his commander[a] and departed;
    he shook his fist against Zion,
    and made great boasts in his arrogance.

19 Then their hearts were shaken and their
        hands trembled,
    and they were in anguish, like women
        in labor.

20 But they called upon the Lord who is
        merciful,
    spreading out their hands toward him.
    The Holy One quickly heard them from
        heaven,
    and delivered them through Isaiah.

21 The Lord[b] struck down the camp of the
        Assyrians,
    and his angel wiped them out.

22 For Hezekiah did what was pleasing to
        the Lord,
    and he kept firmly to the ways of his
        ancestor David,
    as he was commanded by the prophet
        Isaiah,
    who was great and trustworthy in his
        visions.

Isaiah

23 In Isaiah's[c] days the sun went backward,
    and he prolonged the life of the king.

24 By his dauntless spirit he saw the future,
    and comforted the mourners in Zion.

25 He revealed what was to occur to the end
        of time,
    and the hidden things before they
        happened.

Josiah and Other Worthies

49 The name[d] of Josiah is like blended
        incense
    prepared by the skill of the perfumer;
    his memory[e] is as sweet as honey to every
        mouth,
    and like music at a banquet of wine.

2 He did what was right by reforming the
        people,
    and removing the wicked
        abominations.

---

a Other ancient authorities add *from Lachish*   b Gk *He*
c Gk *his*   d Heb: Gk *memory*   e Heb: Gk *it*

13.20–21. **48.15** That the people *were carried off* because they *did not repent* is stated in 2 Kings 18.11–12. That *the people were left very few in number* is a translation from the Greek. The Hebrew reads: "But Judah was left, a small people." The original point was that, despite the sorry end for the people of the Northern Kingdom, continuity with the earlier kingdom of David and Solomon was assured because Judah remained and had *a ruler from the house of David,* a reference to Hezekiah, whose praise immediately follows. **48.16** The reference is to the kings of Judah. In 1 and 2 Kings they are assessed according to Deuteronomic values with the result that only six receive commendation: Asa (1 Kings 15.11); Jehosaphat (22.43); Joash (2 Kings 12.2); Azariah (15.3); Hezekiah (18.3); and Josiah (22.2). Of these six, Ben Sira mentions only two, Hezekiah and Josiah, as worthy of praise along with David. Cf. 49.4. **48.17–22** Hezekiah is praised for his defense of Jerusalem and obedience to the Lord. His

reign (715–687 BCE) is recorded in 2 Kings 18–20; 2 Chr 29–32. **48.17** On Hezekiah's defense of the city, see 2 Kings 20.20; 2 Chr 32.5, 30. **48.18** The failure of Sennacherib to conquer Jerusalem is related in 2 Kings 18.13–37; 2 Chr 32.1–20. Cf. Isa 36.1–22. **48.20** That they *called upon the Lord* and were *delivered . . . through Isaiah* is related in 2 Kings 19.15–35. Cf. Isa 37.21–38. **48.23–25** Isaiah is praised for his prophetic role during Hezekiah's reign and for his trustworthy visions of the future (v. 22). Ben Sira may have had in mind not only the stories about Isaiah in 2 Kings 19–20, but the prophecies of restoration in the book of Isaiah (chs. 40–66). **48.23** That *the sun went backward* is related in 2 Kings 20.6–11. Cf. Isa 38.5–8. **48.24** *Comforted . . . Zion* may be an allusion to Isa 40.1.

49.1–3 Josiah is praised for reforming the people in lawless times. See 2 Kings 22.2–23.25; 2 Chr 34–35. Ben Sira does not mention the most remarkable feature of Josiah's reign, namely, that the reform was a cov-

3 He kept his heart fixed on the Lord;
    in lawless times he made godliness
        prevail.

4 Except for David and Hezekiah and Josiah,
    all of them were great sinners,
    for they abandoned the law of the Most
        High;
    the kings of Judah came to an end.
5 They*a* gave their power to others,
    and their glory to a foreign nation,
6 who set fire to the chosen city of the
        sanctuary,
    and made its streets desolate,
    as Jeremiah had foretold.*b*
7 For they had mistreated him,
    who even in the womb had been
        consecrated a prophet,
    to pluck up and ruin and destroy,
    and likewise to build and to plant.

8 It was Ezekiel who saw the vision of glory,
    which God*c* showed him above the
        chariot of the cherubim.
9 For God*d* also mentioned Job
    who held fast to all the ways of justice.*e*
10 May the bones of the Twelve Prophets
    send forth new life from where they lie,

for they comforted the people of Jacob
    and delivered them with confident
        hope.

11 How shall we magnify Zerubbabel?
    He was like a signet ring on the right
        hand,
12 and so was Jeshua son of Jozadak;
    in their days they built the house
    and raised a temple*f* holy to the Lord,
        destined for everlasting glory.
13 The memory of Nehemiah also is lasting;
    he raised our fallen walls,
    and set up gates and bars,
    and rebuilt our ruined houses.

Retrospect

14 Few have*g* ever been created on earth like
        Enoch,
    for he was taken up from the earth.
15 Nor was anyone ever born like Joseph;*h*
    even his bones were cared for.
16 Shem and Seth and Enosh were honored,*i*

---

a Heb *He* *b* Gk *by the hand of Jeremiah* *c* Gk *He* *d* Gk *he*
e Heb Compare Syr: Meaning of Gk uncertain *f* Other ancient
authorities read *people* *g* Heb Syr: Gk *No one has* *h* Heb Syr:
Gk adds *the leader of his brothers, the support of the people*
i Heb: Gk *Shem and Seth were honored by people*

---

enant to obey the book of the law, which was discovered during repair of the temple. **49.4–7** The end of the kings of Judah is attributed to a failure to keep the law, and the desolation of Jerusalem is said to have been foretold by Jeremiah. This reflects Ben Sira's ambivalent evaluation of the monarchy in favor of a priestly ruler over Israel; see his description of Simon in ch. 50. **49.5** The *foreign nation* that destroyed Jerusalem (586 BCE) was Babylon. See 2 Kings 25.1–15; 2 Chr 36.17–19. **49.6** For Jeremiah's prophecies concerning the fall of Jerusalem, see Jer 36–38. **49.7** For Jeremiah's call and mistreatment, see Jer 1.5, 10; 20; 37.13–15; 38.4–6. **49.8–10** Ezekiel and the twelve prophets are honored for their visions of restoration. **49.8** Ezekiel's *vision of glory* is a reference to Ezek 1.4–28 and is the earliest reference to what Ezekiel saw as the *merkebah*, or *chariot*. Later Jewish mystical speculation focused on ascents to God's chariot-throne. **49.9** *God . . . mentioned Job* to Ezekiel in an oracle (Ezek 14.14, 20). **49.10** The *Twelve Prophets* are the books of Hosea, Joel, Amos, Obadiah, Jonah, Micah, Nahum, Habakkuk, Zephaniah, Haggai, Zechariah, and Malachi. Their mention by Ben Sira is evidence that these books were classed together in his time and were regarded as a single corpus. That they *comforted the people* indicates that they were not being read for their prophecies of doom but for their promising predictions of restoration, a characteristic of the oracles with which most of the prophetic books end.

49.11–13 Three leaders of the return (537 BCE) and restoration are praised. **49.11–12** *Zerubbabel,* the governor of Judah when Cyrus, king of Persia, captured Babylon and gave his famous edict that the Jews could return to Jerusalem and rebuild their temple (537 BCE), and *Jeshua,* the high priest at the time, are mentioned in Hag 1.1–2, 8, 12; 2.2. Cf. Zech 3–4. The description of Zerubbabel as *like a signet ring* is taken from Hag 2.23. **49.13** *Nehemiah* is remembered for rebuilding the city walls. See Neh 2.17–7.3; 13.14, 22, 31. Somewhat curiously, Ben Sira does not mention Ezra the scribe. See Ezra 7–10. **49.14–16** Six additional figures are briefly mentioned as worthy of praise, four from the preflood period. The significance of the unit is unclear because it breaks the sequence of the epic history and ascribes honor for reasons not noted as glorious elsewhere in Sirach. It may have been a later addition to the poem. For *Enoch's* being *taken up,* see Gen 5.24; cf. Wis 4.10–14; Heb 11.5. For the burial of *Joseph,* see Gen 50.25–26; cf. Ex 13.9; Josh 24.32. Of the three sons of Noah, *Shem* was blessed as the forefather of Abraham. See Gen 9.18–27; 11.10–26. *Seth* and *Enosh* provide the first two genealogical links from Adam to Noah. See Gen 5.1–25; cf. Gen 4.25. That *Adam* is honored above all seems out of place in Sirach. Such an idealization is not otherwise documented until a somewhat later time. Cf. Wis 10.1; Lk 3.38; Philo of Alexandria, *On the Creation* 88.

but above every other created living
    being was Adam.

Simon Son of Onias

50 The leader of his brothers and the
    pride of his people[a]
was the high priest, Simon son of
    Onias,
who in his life repaired the house,
    and in his time fortified the temple.

2 He laid the foundations for the high
    double walls,
    the high retaining walls for the temple
      enclosure.

3 In his days a water cistern was dug,[b]
    a reservoir like the sea in
      circumference.

4 He considered how to save his people
    from ruin,
    and fortified the city against siege.

5 How glorious he was, surrounded by the
    people,
    as he came out of the house of the
      curtain.

6 Like the morning star among the clouds,
    like the full moon at the festal season;[b]

7 like the sun shining on the temple of the
    Most High,
    like the rainbow gleaming in splendid
      clouds;

8 like roses in the days of first fruits,
    like lilies by a spring of water,
    like a green shoot on Lebanon on a
      summer day;

9 like fire and incense in the censer,
    like a vessel of hammered gold
      studded with all kinds of precious
        stones;

10 like an olive tree laden with fruit,
    and like a cypress towering in the
      clouds.

11 When he put on his glorious robe
    and clothed himself in perfect
      splendor,
when he went up to the holy altar,
    he made the court of the sanctuary
      glorious.

12 When he received the portions from the
    hands of the priests,
    as he stood by the hearth of the altar
with a garland of brothers around him,
    he was like a young cedar on Lebanon
      surrounded by the trunks of palm
        trees.

13 All the sons of Aaron in their splendor
    held the Lord's offering in their hands
    before the whole congregation of Israel.

14 Finishing the service at the altars,[c]
    and arranging the offering to the Most
      High, the Almighty,

15 he held out his hand for the cup
    and poured a drink offering of the
      blood of the grape;
he poured it out at the foot of the altar,
    a pleasing odor to the Most High, the
      king of all.

16 Then the sons of Aaron shouted;
    they blew their trumpets of hammered
      metal;
    they sounded a mighty fanfare
    as a reminder before the Most High.

17 Then all the people together quickly

---

a Heb Syr: Gk lacks this line. Compare 49.15   b Heb: Meaning
of Gk uncertain   c Other ancient authorities read *altar*

50.1–24 Simon the high priest is praised for his
leadership (v. 1), fortification of the temple (vv. 1–4),
glorious appearance in the court of the temple (vv. 5–
11), performance of the daily sacrifice (vv. 12–19),
and pronouncement of the blessing (vv. 20–21).
50.1 *Simon son of Onias,* called Simon the Just in later
tradition, was high priest from 219 to 196 BCE That he
repaired the house (temple; cf. Josephus, *Antiquities*
12.141) following Seleucid-Ptolemaic struggles for
control of Judea is reminiscent of Hezekiah's glory
(48.17). This achievement subtly attributes royal functions to him and emphasizes Ben Sira's ideal of a high-
priestly ruler in Israel. **50.5–11** Simon's *glorious* appearance is described in terms reminiscent both of
Aaron's glory (45.8–13) and wisdom's flourishing
(24.13–17). **50.5** The *house of the curtain,* the temple;
Ben Sira recalls the tent, or tabernacle, in the wilder-

ness. The Hebrew for v. 5a reads "How glorious he was
as he looked out from the tent" (instead of the Greek
surrounded by the people), using the term that refers to
the tent in the wilderness (Ex 26.33). No curtain or veil
is mentioned for Solomon's temple in 1 Kings 6, but
was added to its description in 2 Chr 3.14. See also
1 Macc 1.21–23; Mk 15.38; Heb 10.20; Josephus, *Antiquities* 3.124–25. **50.11** The high priest's *robe* was frequently described at great length, and its symbols were
allegorized by later writers such as Philo of Alexandria;
cf. Ex 28.2–43; 39.1–31; Wis 18.24; Josephus, *Antiquities* 3.151–78. *Perfect splendor.* See 45.8. **50.12–
21** Simon's service at the altars closely parallels the description of the daily whole offering in *Mishnah Tamid*
6.3–7.3. **50.13** *Sons of Aaron,* the priests. **50.15** On the
drink offering as a libation, cf. Num 28.7; Josephus, *Antiquities* 3.234. **50.16** *Trumpets of hammered metal.*

fell to the ground on their faces
to worship their Lord,
the Almighty, God Most High.

18 Then the singers praised him with their
voices
in sweet and full-toned melody.[a]
19 And the people of the Lord Most High
offered
their prayers before the Merciful One,
until the order of worship of the Lord
was ended,
and they completed his ritual.
20 Then Simon[b] came down and raised his
hands
over the whole congregation of
Israelites,
to pronounce the blessing of the Lord
with his lips,
and to glory in his name;
21 and they bowed down in worship a
second time,
to receive the blessing from the Most
High.

A Benediction

22 And now bless the God of all,
who everywhere works great wonders,
who fosters our growth from birth,
and deals with us according to his mercy.
23 May he give us[c] gladness of heart,
and may there be peace in our[d] days
in Israel, as in the days of old.
24 May he entrust to us his mercy,
and may he deliver us in our[e] days!

Epilogue

25 Two nations my soul detests,
and the third is not even a people:

26 Those who live in Seir,[f] and the
Philistines,
and the foolish people that live in
Shechem.

27 Instruction in understanding and
knowledge
I have written in this book,
Jesus son of Eleazar son of Sirach[g] of
Jerusalem,
whose mind poured forth wisdom.
28 Happy are those who concern themselves
with these things,
and those who lay them to heart will
become wise.
29 For if they put them into practice, they
will be equal to anything,
for the fear[h] of the Lord is their path.

PRAYER OF JESUS SON OF SIRACH[i]

51 I give you thanks, O Lord and King,
and praise you, O God my Savior.
I give thanks to your name,
2 for you have been my protector and
helper
and have delivered me from destruction
and from the trap laid by a slanderous
tongue,
from lips that fabricate lies.
In the face of my adversaries
you have been my helper 3 and
delivered me,
in the greatness of your mercy and of
your name,

---

a Other ancient authorities read *in sweet melody throughout the
house* b Gk *he* c Other ancient authorities read *you* d Other
ancient authorities read *your* e Other ancient authorities read
his f Heb Compare Lat: Gk *on the mountain of Samaria*
g Heb: Meaning of Gk uncertain h Heb: Other ancient
authorities read *light* i This title is included in the Gk text.

See Num 10.2. **50.18** *Singers*. See 2 Chr 29.26–30.
50.20 The *blessing* of the high priest conferred peace in
the name of the Lord. Cf. Lev 9.22–23; Num 6.24–27.
50.22–24 Ben Sira adds his own benediction and
prayer for peace. The Hebrew differs from the Greek; it
includes a prayer for God's "lasting kindness toward
Simon" and for fulfillment of "the covenant with Phinehas" (cf. 45.23–25), items that may have been deleted
by the grandson as embarrassing or dangerous in the
light of the violent end to the Zadokite line of high
priests that had occurred in the meantime. Onias III,
Simon's son, had been deposed and murdered (2 Macc
4.34); Menelaus, who was not from a priestly family,
had been installed as high priest by Antiochus IV; and
the Maccabean wars had produced the Hasmonean
dynasty of priest-kings. Thus it was obvious that Ben

Sira's prayer had not been answered. **50.25–29** An epilogue and signature conclude Ben Sira's book of instruction. **50.26** The detested nations are those that
bordered Judea to the south (*Seir*), the west (*Philistines*), and the north (*Shechem*), but they are referred
to by archaic designations. *Those who live in Seir* were
the Edomites, known in Ben Sira's time as Idumeans.
Shechem was the old center of the Northern Kingdom
and a euphemism for Samaria in Ben Sira's time. The
Philistines were the ancient occupants of the land and
enemies during the time of the judges and the early
kings; Ben Sira probably alludes to the Hellenistic cities along the seacoast.
51.1–12 A psalm of thanksgiving for deliverance
from adversity is appended to the book of instruction.
Its authenticity has been questioned, but nothing

from grinding teeth about to devour me,
  from the hand of those seeking my
      life,
from the many troubles I endured,
4 from choking fire on every side,
  and from the midst of fire that I had
      not kindled,
5 from the deep belly of Hades,
  from an unclean tongue and lying
      words—
6 the slander of an unrighteous tongue
      to the king.
My soul drew near to death,
  and my life was on the brink of Hades
      below.
7 They surrounded me on every side,
  and there was no one to help me;
I looked for human assistance,
  and there was none.
8 Then I remembered your mercy,
      O Lord,
  and your kindness*a* from of old,
for you rescue those who wait for you
  and save them from the hand of their
      enemies.
9 And I sent up my prayer from the earth,
  and begged for rescue from death.
10 I cried out, "Lord, you are my Father;*b*
  do not forsake me in the days of
      trouble,
when there is no help against the
      proud.
11 I will praise your name continually,
  and will sing hymns of thanksgiving."
My prayer was heard,
12 for you saved me from destruction
  and rescued me in time of trouble.
For this reason I thank you and praise
      you,
  and I bless the name of the Lord.

Heb adds:
Give thanks to the LORD, for he is good,
  for his steadfast love endures forever;

Give thanks to the God of praises,
  for his steadfast love endures forever;

Give thanks to the guardian of Israel,
  for his steadfast love endures forever;

Give thanks to him who formed all things,
  for his steadfast love endures forever;

Give thanks to the redeemer of Israel,
  for his steadfast love endures forever;

Give thanks to him who gathers the
      dispersed of Israel,
  for his steadfast love endures forever;

Give thanks to him who rebuilt his city and
      his sanctuary,
  for his steadfast love endures forever;

Give thanks to him who makes a horn to
      sprout for the house of David,
  for his steadfast love endures forever;

Give thanks to him who has chosen the
      sons of Zadok to be priests,
  for his steadfast love endures forever;

Give thanks to the shield of Abraham,
  for his steadfast love endures forever;

Give thanks to the rock of Isaac,
  for his steadfast love endures forever;

Give thanks to the mighty one of Jacob,
  for his steadfast love endures forever;

Give thanks to him who has chosen Zion,
  for his steadfast love endures forever;

Give thanks to the King of the kings of
      kings,
  for his steadfast love endures forever;

He has raised up a horn for his people,
  praise for all his loyal ones.

For the children of Israel, the people close to
      him.
  Praise the LORD!

Autobiographical Poem on Wisdom

13 While I was still young, before I went on
      my travels,
  I sought wisdom openly in my
      prayer.
14 Before the temple I asked for her,
  and I will search for her until the end.

---

a Other ancient authorities read *work*   *b* Heb: Gk *the Father of my lord*

15 From the first blossom to the ripening
      grape
      my heart delighted in her;
  my foot walked on the straight path;
      from my youth I followed her steps.

16 I inclined my ear a little and received her,
      and I found for myself much
        instruction.
17 I made progress in her;
      to him who gives wisdom I will give
        glory.

18 For I resolved to live according to
      wisdom,*a*
    and I was zealous for the good,
    and I shall never be disappointed.
19 My soul grappled with wisdom,*a*
    and in my conduct I was strict;*b*

  I spread out my hands to the heavens,
    and lamented my ignorance of her.
20 I directed my soul to her,
    and in purity I found her.

  With her I gained understanding from
    the first;
    therefore I will never be forsaken.
21 My heart was stirred to seek her;
    therefore I have gained a prize
      possession.
22 The Lord gave me my tongue as a reward,
    and I will praise him with it.

23 Draw near to me, you who are
      uneducated,
    and lodge in the house of instruction.
24 Why do you say you are lacking in these
      things,*c*
    and why do you endure such great
      thirst?
25 I opened my mouth and said,
    Acquire wisdom*d* for yourselves
      without money.

26 Put your neck under her*e* yoke,
    and let your souls receive instruction;
    it is to be found close by.

27 See with your own eyes that I have
      labored but little
    and found for myself much serenity.
28 Hear but a little of my instruction,
    and through me you will acquire silver
      and gold.*f*

29 May your soul rejoice in God's*g* mercy,
    and may you never be ashamed to
      praise him.
30 Do your work in good time,
    and in his own time God*h* will give you
      your reward.

---

a Gk *her*   *b* Meaning of Gk uncertain   *c* Cn Compare Heb
Syr: Meaning of Gk uncertain   *d* Heb: Gk lacks *wisdom*
e Heb: other ancient authorities read *the*   *f* Syr Compare Heb:
Gk *Get instruction with a large sum of silver, and you will gain by
it much gold.*   *g* Gk *his*   *h* Gk *he*

about its form or content suggests that Ben Sira could not have written it. **Between 51.12 and 51.13** The hymn of praise positioned between vv. 12 and 13 is not included in the Greek or Syriac manuscripts and is therefore difficult to attribute to Ben Sira. It is composed as a litany in the style of Ps 136 and contains features that suggest Essene provenance. These include the epithet *God of praises*, designations in the banner style such as *shield of Abraham* and *rock of Isaac* and the notice of Zadokite loyalty. **51.13–30** An autobiographical poem with an erotic tinge on the author's quest for wisdom (vv. 13–22) leads to an invitation to join him in receiving her instruction (vv. 23–30). A manuscript containing the first half of the poem (vv. 13–20a) discovered among the Dead Sea Scrolls

(*Psalms Scroll* [11QPs^a]) shows that the original Hebrew was an acrostic, a feature that was obscured in later transcriptions and translations. The language of seeking and finding wisdom resonates with the poetry of personified wisdom in chs. 1, 4, 6, 14, 15, and 24. **51.13** The *prayer* for wisdom may allude to Solomon's request (1 Kings 3.7–9); cf. Sir 51.20; Wis 7.7; 8.21; 9.1–12. **51.23** The invitation is reminiscent of wisdom. Cf. 14.20–27; Prov 9.1–6. It is difficult to know whether the *house of instruction* is merely a poetic figure or whether it refers to a school. Given the form and content of Ben Sira's book of instruction, some formal setting for educational purposes has to be supposed. **51.26** For wisdom's *yoke*, see 6.23–31. For the idea that her instruction is *close by*, cf. Deut 30.11–14.

BARUCH

Authorship

THE NARRATIVE INTRODUCTION presents the book of Baruch as a letter sent by Baruch, the secretary and friend of Jeremiah, from exile in Babylon to the priests and people of Jerusalem in the early sixth century BCE. According to Jer 43.1–7, however, in 582 BCE Jeremiah and Baruch were taken from Jerusalem to Egypt, where they presumably remained until they died. A later tradition, reflected in Baruch and other Jewish sources (*Seder Olam Rabbah* 26; *Midrash Rabbah Song* 5.5; *Babylonian Talmud Megilla* 16b), assumes that Baruch went to Babylon. These sources are full of historical inaccuracies and belong to the realm of legend rather than history. It was a relatively common practice during the late Second Temple period to compose edifying works that expanded the biblical tradition (e.g., Prayer of Manasseh, *Jubilees*, Ps.-Philo, *Biblical Antiquities*), and it is within this context that Baruch should be situated.

Content

BARUCH CONSISTS OF THREE originally independent compositions, a prose prayer, a wisdom poem, and a poem of consolation, that have been joined together and given a narrative introduction. The narrative introduction (1.1–14) instructs the recipients to read the contents as a confessional liturgy "on the days of the festivals and at appointed seasons" (1.14). It is followed by a prose prayer (1.15–3.8) consisting of a preliminary confession (1.15–2.10) and the prayer itself (2.11–3.8). The confession and prayer are a pastiche of quotations from Daniel and Jeremiah; the relationship between Bar 1.15–2.19 and Dan 9.4–19 is especially close. The wisdom poem (3.9–4.4) speaks of the elusiveness of wisdom but also identifies wisdom with the Torah ("the book of the commandments of God," 4.1) as God's gift to Israel. Like the prose prayer, the wisdom poem is a pastiche of biblical phrases. Although no single text predominates, echoes of Deut 30; Job 28; and Sir 24 are easily identifiable. The last section of the book is a poem of consolation (4.5–5.9) that is strongly influenced by Isa 40–66. The poem begins with words of encouragement to the remnant of Israel (4.5–9a) and continues with an address of personified Zion to her neighbors (4.9b–16) and to her children (4.17–29). The poem concludes with words of encouragement to Zion (4.30–5.9), who will see the return of her children. The last part of the poem, 4.36–5.9, closely resembles the noncanonical *Psalms of Solomon* 11.1–7.

1452

Opinion is divided, however, as to whether *Psalms of Solomon* is dependent on Baruch or whether both draw on an earlier poem of restoration.

The distinctiveness of the sections is evident not only in their different styles and in the different biblical texts on which they draw but also in the terms used for God. In the prose introduction and prayer God is referred to most often as "Lord," in the wisdom poem as "God," and in the poem of consolation as "the Everlasting."

Language, Place, and Date of Composition

IT IS NOW GENERALLY AGREED that all of the parts of Baruch were originally composed in Hebrew, although no Hebrew text now exists. Of the translations, the Greek text is the most important. Versions in Syriac, Latin, Coptic, Ethiopic, Arabic, and Armenian are also known. Because the book was composed in Hebrew, Palestine is the most likely place of origin.

The dates of composition of the originally independent sections of Baruch are difficult to establish. Historical inaccuracies in the introduction suggest a time considerably later than the Babylonian exile. The dependence of the prose prayer on Dan 9 might point to a date after 165 BCE, the date of Daniel, but it is possible that the prayer in Dan 9 is an earlier composition than Daniel as a whole. If the wisdom poem does in fact allude to Sir 24, then a date after 180 BCE is indicated for that section. There are few clues to the date of the poem of consolation. Most scholars favor a date between 200 and 60 BCE for the compilation of the book as a whole.
[CAROL A. NEWSOM]

Baruch and the Jews in Babylon

1 These are the words of the book that Baruch son of Neriah son of Mahseiah son of Zedekiah son of Hasadiah son of Hilkiah wrote in Babylon, 2 in the fifth year, on the seventh day of the month, at the time when the Chaldeans took Jerusalem and burned it with fire.

3 Baruch read the words of this book to Jeconiah son of Jehoiakim, king of Judah, and to all the people who came to hear the book, 4 and to the nobles and the princes, and to the elders, and to all the people, small and great, all who lived in Babylon by the river Sud.

5 Then they wept, and fasted, and prayed before the Lord; 6 they collected as much money as each could give, 7 and sent it to Jerusalem to the high priest[a] Jehoiakim son of Hilkiah son of Shallum, and to the priests, and to all the people who were present with him in Jerusalem. 8 At the same time, on the tenth day of Sivan, Baruch[b] took the vessels of the house of the Lord, which had been carried away

_____
a Gk *the priest*   b Gk *he*

1.1–9 The first part of the narrative introduction, giving the circumstances of the letter. **1.1** *Baruch son of . . . Hilkiah.* Only Baruch's father and grandfather are named in the genealogy in Jer 32.12. **1.2** Whether the *fifth year* is calculated from the exile of 597 BCE (see 2 Kings 24.10–17) or of 586 BCE (see 2 Kings 25.8–12) is not stated. The reference to the burning of Jerusalem suggests the latter. Curiously, the date formula omits the name of the month (but see v. 8). 2 Kings 25.8 states that Nebuzaradan burned Jerusalem "in the fifth month, on the seventh day of the month." For penitential activity in Palestine on the anniversary of the destruction, see Zech 7.3–5. **1.3** *Jeconiah* is one of the names of Jehoiachin, the last king of Judah, who was exiled in 597 BCE. **1.4** *The river Sud* is otherwise unknown. Ezekiel also locates the community of exiles to which he belongs in relation to a river, the Chebar (Ezek 1.1). **1.5** The favorable reception given to Baruch's book by the exiled king and all the assembled people contrasts with the hostility Baruch received from Jeconiah's father, King Jehoiakim, when he read the scroll dictated by Jeremiah in 604 BCE (Jer 36). **1.6–9** The account of a collection for Jerusalem and the return of silver vessels is apparently modeled on Ezra 1, where a similar collection accompanies the return of gold and silver vessels by the Persian king Cyrus in 538 BCE. **1.7** No high priest by the name of *Jehoiakim* appears in the list of 1 Chr 6.13–15. **1.8–9** *Sivan,* the third month of the Jewish year (May/June). 2 Kings does not mention the making of *silver vessels* by *Zedekiah* to replace those taken by *Nebuchadnezzar* in the exile of 597 BCE (cf. 2 Kings 25.13–

from the temple, to return them to the land of Judah—the silver vessels that Zedekiah son of Josiah, king of Judah, had made, 9after King Nebuchadnezzar of Babylon had carried away from Jerusalem Jeconiah and the princes and the prisoners and the nobles and the people of the land, and brought them to Babylon.

A Letter to Jerusalem

10 They said: Here we send you money; so buy with the money burnt offerings and sin offerings and incense, and prepare a grain offering, and offer them on the altar of the Lord our God; 11and pray for the life of King Nebuchadnezzar of Babylon, and for the life of his son Belshazzar, so that their days on earth may be like the days of heaven. 12The Lord will give us strength, and light to our eyes; we shall live under the protection*a* of King Nebuchadnezzar of Babylon, and under the protection of his son Belshazzar, and we shall serve them many days and find favor in their sight. 13Pray also for us to the Lord our God, for we have sinned against the Lord our God, and to this day the anger of the Lord and his wrath have not turned away from us. 14And you shall read aloud this scroll that we are sending you, to make your confession in the house of the Lord on the days of the festivals and at appointed seasons.

Confession of Sins

15 And you shall say: The Lord our God is in the right, but there is open shame on us today, on the people of Judah, on the inhabitants of Jerusalem, 16and on our kings, our rulers, our priests, our prophets, and our ancestors, 17because we have sinned before the Lord. 18We have disobeyed him, and have not heeded the voice of the Lord our God, to walk in the statutes of the Lord that he set before us. 19From the time when the Lord brought our ancestors out of the land of Egypt until today, we have been disobedient to the Lord our God, and we have been negligent, in not heeding his voice. 20So to this day there have clung to us the calamities and the curse that the Lord declared through his servant Moses at the time when he brought our ancestors out of the land of Egypt to give to us a land flowing with milk and honey. 21We did not listen to the voice of the Lord our God in all the words of the prophets whom he sent to us, 22but all of us followed the intent of our own wicked hearts by serving other gods and doing what is evil in the sight of the Lord our God.

2 So the Lord carried out the threat he spoke against us: against our judges who ruled Israel, and against our kings and our rulers and the people of Israel and Judah. 2Under the whole heaven there has not been done the like of what he has done in Jerusalem, in accordance with the threats that were*b* written in the law of Moses. 3Some of us ate the flesh of their sons and others the flesh of their daughters. 4He made them subject to all the kingdoms around us, to be an object of scorn and a desolation among all the surrounding peoples, where the Lord has scattered them. 5They were brought down and not raised up, because our nation*c* sinned against the Lord our God, in not heeding his voice.

6 The Lord our God is in the right, but there is open shame on us and our ancestors this very day. 7All those calamities with which the Lord threatened us have come upon us. 8Yet we have not entreated the favor of the Lord by turning away, each of us, from the thoughts of our wicked hearts. 9And the Lord has kept the

---

a Gk *in the shadow*   *b* Gk *in accordance with what is*
c Gk *because we*

---

16). **1.10–14** The letter to the community in Jerusalem includes instructions for the use of the collection and requests for prayer and the public reading of the scroll. **1.10** The text assumes the continuation of sacrifices in Jerusalem. This does not necessarily imply a date before 586 BCE; see Jer 41.5. **1.11** *Belshazzar* was not the son of Nebuchadnezzar but of Nabonidus. Here the author of Baruch is influenced by Dan 5, which also erroneously calls Belshazzar Nebuchadnezzar's son. Prayer was offered for the Persian king and his children according to Ezra 6.10.

1.15–2.10 In preparation for prayer, the people confess their guilt before God. The passage is modeled closely on Dan 9.7–14, with significant influence also from Deuteronomy, Jeremiah, and the prayer in Neh 9. **1.15** Dan 9.7. **1.16–17** See Dan 9.8; Neh 9.33–34; Jer 32.32. **1.18** Dan 9.9–10; see Neh 9.26. **1.19** See Deut 9.7; Jer 7.25. **1.20** See Dan 9.11, 13; Deut 29.20; Jer 11.4–5. For the *curse*, see Lev 26.14–39; Deut 28.15–68. **1.21** Dan 9.10; see Deut 9.23; 28.15; Jer 26.5. **1.22** See Jer 7.24. **2.1–2** Dan 9.12–13. **2.3** Cannibalism of one's own children in time of siege is mentioned as one of the horrors of war in Lev 26.29; Deut 28.53; 2 Kings 6.24–31; Jer 19.9; Lam 2.20; 4.10. **2.4** Jer 29.18. **2.5** See Deut 28.13; Dan 9.8, 11. **2.6** Dan 9.7. **2.7** Dan 9.12. **2.8** Dan 9.13; see Jer 7.24. **2.9** See Dan 9.14.

calamities ready, and the Lord has brought them upon us, for the Lord is just in all the works that he has commanded us to do. 10 Yet we have not obeyed his voice, to walk in the statutes of the Lord that he set before us.

Prayer for Deliverance

11 And now, O Lord God of Israel, who brought your people out of the land of Egypt with a mighty hand and with signs and wonders and with great power and outstretched arm, and made yourself a name that continues to this day, 12 we have sinned, we have been ungodly, we have done wrong, O Lord our God, against all your ordinances. 13 Let your anger turn away from us, for we are left, few in number, among the nations where you have scattered us. 14 Hear, O Lord, our prayer and our supplication, and for your own sake deliver us, and grant us favor in the sight of those who have carried us into exile; 15 so that all the earth may know that you are the Lord our God, for Israel and his descendants are called by your name.

16 O Lord, look down from your holy dwelling, and consider us. Incline your ear, O Lord, and hear; 17 open your eyes, O Lord, and see, for the dead who are in Hades, whose spirit has been taken from their bodies, will not ascribe glory or justice to the Lord; 18 but the person who is deeply grieved, who walks bowed and feeble, with failing eyes and famished soul, will declare your glory and righteousness, O Lord.

19 For it is not because of any righteous deeds of our ancestors or our kings that we bring before you our prayer for mercy, O Lord our God. 20 For you have sent your anger and your wrath upon us, as you declared by your servants the prophets, saying: 21 Thus says the Lord: Bend your shoulders and serve the king of Babylon, and you will remain in the land that I gave to your ancestors. 22 But if you will not obey the voice of the Lord and will not serve the king of Babylon, 23 I will make to cease from the towns of Judah and from the region around Je-

rusalem the voice of mirth and the voice of gladness, the voice of the bridegroom and the voice of the bride, and the whole land will be a desolation without inhabitants.

24 But we did not obey your voice, to serve the king of Babylon; and you have carried out your threats, which you spoke by your servants the prophets, that the bones of our kings and the bones of our ancestors would be brought out of their resting place; 25 and indeed they have been thrown out to the heat of day and the frost of night. They perished in great misery, by famine and sword and pestilence. 26 And the house that is called by your name you have made as it is today, because of the wickedness of the house of Israel and the house of Judah.

God's Promise Recalled

27 Yet you have dealt with us, O Lord our God, in all your kindness and in all your great compassion, 28 as you spoke by your servant Moses on the day when you commanded him to write your law in the presence of the people of Israel, saying, 29 "If you will not obey my voice, this very great multitude will surely turn into a small number among the nations, where I will scatter them. 30 For I know that they will not obey me, for they are a stiff-necked people. But in the land of their exile they will come to themselves 31 and know that I am the Lord their God. I will give them a heart that obeys and ears that hear; 32 they will praise me in the land of their exile, and will remember my name 33 and turn from their stubbornness and their wicked deeds; for they will remember the ways of their ancestors, who sinned before the Lord. 34 I will bring them again into the land that I swore to give to their ancestors, to Abraham, Isaac, and Jacob, and they will rule over it; and I will increase them, and they will not be diminished. 35 I will make an everlasting covenant with them to be their God and they shall be my people; and I will never again remove my people Israel from the land that I have given them."

2.10 Dan 9.10. **2.11–35** Recalling God's activity in the exodus and confessing their sin, the people appeal to God's mercy. **2.11–18** These verses closely follow Dan 9.15–19. **2.11–12** See Dan 9.15; Jer 32.20–21. **2.13** See Dan 9.16; Deut 4.27; Jer 42.2. **2.14–15** See 2 Kings 19.19; Dan 9.16–17; See also Gen 39.21. **2.16** Dan 9.18; see Deut 26.15. **2.17–18** See 2 Kings 19.16; Dan 9.18. For the idea that the *dead* cannot praise God, see

Pss 30.9; 88.10–12; 115.17; Isa 38.18. **2.19–20** Dan 9.6, 18. **2.21–23** Not an exact quotation from Jeremiah but a pastiche of Jer 7.34; 27.9, 12; 48.9. **2.24–26** The *threats* are adapted from Jer 8.1; 11.17; 16.4; 32.36; 36.30; 44.6. **2.29–35** The quotation attributed to Moses is not attested in the Pentateuch but is largely a pastiche of phrases from Jeremiah, with some echoes of Deuteronomy. Cf. Deut 28.62; Jer 24.7, 9; 25.5; 29.6;

3 O Lord Almighty, God of Israel, the soul in anguish and the wearied spirit cry out to you. ²Hear, O Lord, and have mercy, for we have sinned before you. ³For you are enthroned forever, and we are perishing forever. ⁴O Lord Almighty, God of Israel, hear now the prayer of the people*a* of Israel, the children of those who sinned before you, who did not heed the voice of the Lord their God, so that calamities have clung to us. ⁵Do not remember the iniquities of our ancestors, but in this crisis remember your power and your name. ⁶For you are the Lord our God, and it is you, O Lord, whom we will praise. ⁷For you have put the fear of you in our hearts so that we would call upon your name; and we will praise you in our exile, for we have put away from our hearts all the iniquity of our ancestors who sinned against you. ⁸See, we are today in our exile where you have scattered us, to be reproached and cursed and punished for all the iniquities of our ancestors, who forsook the Lord our God.

In Praise of Wisdom

9 Hear the commandments of life, O Israel;
      give ear, and learn wisdom!
10 Why is it, O Israel, why is it that you are
      in the land of your enemies,
   that you are growing old in a foreign
      country,
   that you are defiled with the dead,
11   that you are counted among those in
      Hades?
12 You have forsaken the fountain of
      wisdom.
13 If you had walked in the way of God,
      you would be living in peace forever.
14 Learn where there is wisdom,
      where there is strength,

where there is understanding,
   so that you may at the same time discern
      where there is length of days, and life,
      where there is light for the eyes, and
      peace.

15 Who has found her place?
      And who has entered her storehouses?
16 Where are the rulers of the nations,
      and those who lorded it over the
      animals on earth;
17 those who made sport of the birds of the
      air,
      and who hoarded up silver and gold
   in which people trust,
      and there is no end to their getting;
18 those who schemed to get silver, and were
      anxious,
      but there is no trace of their works?
19 They have vanished and gone down to
      Hades,
      and others have arisen in their place.
20 Later generations have seen the light of
      day,
      and have lived upon the earth;
   but they have not learned the way to
      knowledge,
      nor understood her paths,
      nor laid hold of her.
21 Their descendants have strayed far from
      her*b* way.
22 She has not been heard of in Canaan,
      or seen in Teman;
23 the descendants of Hagar, who seek for
      understanding on the earth,
      the merchants of Merran and Teman,

_____
a Gk *dead*   *b* Other ancient authorities read *their*

30.3; 31.33; 32.40. Cf. also Lev 26.42–45; Deut 30.1–5. **3.1–8** Conclusion and final petition. The exiles' repentance and prayer conforms to the pattern of Lev 26.40–45; Deut 30.1–10; Jer 29.12–14. **3.7** See Jer 32.40. **3.8** The exiles are punished for the sins of their *ancestors* (Ex 3.7; Lam 5.7); but cf. Jer 31.29; Ezek 18.2–32.

3.9–4.4 A poem in the style of a wisdom discourse describes the elusiveness of wisdom but also God's gift of wisdom to Israel in the Torah. **3.9–14** Israel's experience of exile is used as an object lesson to motivate obedience to *the commandments of life* and *wisdom;* cf. Deut 30.15–20. **3.9** The address to Israel echoes Deut 4.1; 5.1; cf. also the command to hear in Prov 1.8; 4.1, 10. **3.10** An exilic setting is presumed, though *growing*

old in a foreign country suggests a different time than *the fifth year* mentioned in 1.2. **3.11** Ps 88.4. **3.12** See Prov 18.4; Sir 1.1, 5. **3.14** See Prov 3.13–18. **3.15–28** Neither the powerful, nor the wealthy, nor the nations with a reputation for wisdom, nor the ancient giants have been able to find wisdom. **3.15** See Job 28.12, 20. **3.16–17** Both the hunting and the collecting of exotic animals were symbols of royal power; cf. 1 Kings 10.22; Jer 27.6; Dan 2.38; Jdt 11.7. **3.22** The *Canaanite* (Phoenician) cities of Tyre and Sidon were associated with wisdom; cf. Ezek 28.4; Zech 9.2. For the wisdom of *Teman,* the capital of Edom, see Job 2.11; Jer 49.7; Ob 8. **3.23** *The descendants of Hagar,* the Ishmaelites (Gen 16.11–12), who appear as merchant travelers in Gen 37.25. *Merran* may be an error for Midian; see

the story-tellers and the seekers for
    understanding,
have not learned the way to wisdom,
    or given thought to her paths.

24 O Israel, how great is the house of God,
    how vast the territory that he
        possesses!
25 It is great and has no bounds;
    it is high and immeasurable.
26 The giants were born there, who were
        famous of old,
    great in stature, expert in war.
27 God did not choose them,
    or give them the way to knowledge;
28 so they perished because they had no
        wisdom,
    they perished through their folly.

29 Who has gone up into heaven, and taken
        her,
    and brought her down from the
        clouds?
30 Who has gone over the sea, and found
        her,
    and will buy her for pure gold?
31 No one knows the way to her,
    or is concerned about the path to her.
32 But the one who knows all things knows
        her,
    he found her by his understanding.
The one who prepared the earth for all
        time
    filled it with four-footed creatures;
33 the one who sends forth the light, and it
        goes;
    he called it, and it obeyed him,
        trembling;
34 the stars shone in their watches, and were
        glad;

he called them, and they said, "Here we
    are!"
They shone with gladness for him who
    made them.
35 This is our God;
    no other can be compared to him.
36 He found the whole way to knowledge,
    and gave her to his servant Jacob
    and to Israel, whom he loved.
37 Afterward she appeared on earth
    and lived with humankind.

4 She is the book of the commandments of
    God,
    the law that endures forever.
All who hold her fast will live,
    and those who forsake her will die.
2 Turn, O Jacob, and take her;
    walk toward the shining of her light.
3 Do not give your glory to another,
    or your advantages to an alien people.
4 Happy are we, O Israel,
    for we know what is pleasing to God.

Encouragement for Israel

5 Take courage, my people,
    who perpetuate Israel's name!
6 It was not for destruction
    that you were sold to the nations,
but you were handed over to your enemies
    because you angered God.
7 For you provoked the one who made you
    by sacrificing to demons and not to
        God.
8 You forgot the everlasting God, who
        brought you up,
    and you grieved Jerusalem, who reared
        you.
9 For she saw the wrath that came upon
        you from God,

Gen 37.28 for Midianite caravaners. Sir 39.4 associates
travel with wisdom. **3.24–25** Here the *house of God* is
not the temple but the whole cosmos. **3.26–28** According to ancient tradition, the *giants* (see Gen 6.1–
4) were the children of fallen angels, who communicated a corrupted form of heavenly wisdom to humans (*1 Enoch* 7). The giants perished in the deluge
(Wis 14.6). **3.29–37** Although no human can reach
Wisdom, God knows her and has given her to Israel.
3.29–30a Cf. Deut 30.12–13, which uses similar imagery to describe the accessibility of the divine commandments. **3.30b** See Job 28.12–19. **3.31–32** See Job
28.23–27. **3.33–34** See Job 38.35. **3.35** See Isa 43.10–
11; 45.18. **3.36–37** For the gift of wisdom to Israel, see
Sir 24.8. Although v. 37 has sometimes been regarded

as a Christian interpolation referring to the incarnation, the idea that Wisdom *lived with humankind* is attested in Prov 8.1–4, 31; Wis 9.10; Sir 24.10–12. **4.1–
4** Wisdom is explicitly identified with the Torah (cf. Sir
24.23). **4.4** See Wis 9.18.
4.5–5.9 In the poem of consolation the psalmist addresses the exiles (4.5–9a), quotes the words of personified Jerusalem (4.9b–29), and finally addresses
words of hope to Jerusalem (4.30–5.9). The composition draws extensively on phrases and images from Isa
40–66. **4.5–9a** The reason for the exile is identified as
the people's sin. **4.5** The call to *take courage* is repeated
in vv. 21, 30. **4.6** See Isa 50.1b. **4.7** *Sacrificing to
demons.* Cf. Deut 32.16–17. **4.8** Parental images of
God (Deut 32.18; Isa 1.2; Hos 11.4) and Jerusalem (see

and she said:
Listen, you neighbors of Zion,
  God has brought great sorrow upon
    me;
10 for I have seen the exile of my sons and
    daughters,
  which the Everlasting brought upon
    them.
11 With joy I nurtured them,
  but I sent them away with weeping and
    sorrow.
12 Let no one rejoice over me, a widow
  and bereaved of many;
  I was left desolate because of the sins of
    my children,
  because they turned away from the law
    of God.
13 They had no regard for his statutes;
  they did not walk in the ways of God's
    commandments,
  or tread the paths his righteousness
    showed them.
14 Let the neighbors of Zion come;
  remember the capture of my sons and
    daughters,
  which the Everlasting brought upon
    them.
15 For he brought a distant nation against
    them,
  a nation ruthless and of a strange
    language,
  which had no respect for the aged
  and no pity for a child.
16 They led away the widow's beloved
    sons,
  and bereaved the lonely woman of her
    daughters.

17 But I, how can I help you?
18 For he who brought these calamities
    upon you
  will deliver you from the hand of your
    enemies.
19 Go, my children, go;
  for I have been left desolate.
20 I have taken off the robe of peace
  and put on sackcloth for my
    supplication;

I will cry to the Everlasting all my
    days.
21 Take courage, my children, cry to God,
  and he will deliver you from the power
    and hand of the enemy.
22 For I have put my hope in the Everlasting
    to save you,
  and joy has come to me from the Holy
    One,
  because of the mercy that will soon come
    to you
  from your everlasting savior.[a]
23 For I sent you out with sorrow and
    weeping,
  but God will give you back to me with
    joy and gladness forever.
24 For as the neighbors of Zion have now
    seen your capture,
  so they soon will see your salvation by
    God,
  which will come to you with great glory
  and with the splendor of the
    Everlasting.
25 My children, endure with patience the
    wrath that has come upon you
    from God.
  Your enemy has overtaken you,
  but you will soon see their destruction
  and will tread upon their necks.
26 My pampered children have traveled
    rough roads;
  they were taken away like a flock
    carried off by the enemy.

27 Take courage, my children, and cry to
    God,
  for you will be remembered by the one
    who brought this upon you.
28 For just as you were disposed to go astray
    from God,
  return with tenfold zeal to seek him.
29 For the one who brought these calamities
    upon you
  will bring you everlasting joy with your
    salvation.

_a_ Or _from the Everlasting, your savior_

---

note on 4.9b–16) are combined. **4.9b–16** The personification of Zion as a grieving widow and mother is based on Isa 51.18–20; Lam 1.1, 16–18; 2.19–22. **4.15** Deut 28.49–50. **4.20** For _sackcloth_ as a garment of mourning, see Lam 1.10. In Isa 52.1 festive garments mark the end of mourning (see note on 5.1–2). **4.22** _Everlasting._ Cf. Isa 26.4; 40.28. _Holy One_ is a common epithet for God in Isa 40–55; see also Pss 71.22; 78.41; Hab 3.3. **4.23** See Ps 126.6; Isa 35.10; 51.11. **4.24** See Isa 60.1–3. **4.25** See Deut 33.29; cf. Isa 51.23.

Jerusalem Is Assured of Help

30 Take courage, O Jerusalem,
    for the one who named you will
        comfort you.
31 Wretched will be those who mistreated
        you
    and who rejoiced at your fall.
32 Wretched will be the cities that your
        children served as slaves;
    wretched will be the city that received
        your offspring.
33 For just as she rejoiced at your fall
        and was glad for your ruin,
    so she will be grieved at her own
        desolation.
34 I will take away her pride in her great
        population,
    and her insolence will be turned to
        grief.
35 For fire will come upon her from the
        Everlasting for many days,
    and for a long time she will be
        inhabited by demons.

36 Look toward the east, O Jerusalem,
    and see the joy that is coming to you
        from God.
37 Look, your children are coming, whom
        you sent away;
    they are coming, gathered from east
        and west,
    at the word of the Holy One,
        rejoicing in the glory of God.

5 Take off the garment of your sorrow and
    affliction, O Jerusalem,

and put on forever the beauty of the
    glory from God.
2 Put on the robe of the righteousness that
    comes from God;
    put on your head the diadem of the
        glory of the Everlasting;
3 for God will show your splendor
        everywhere under heaven.
4 For God will give you evermore the
        name,
    "Righteous Peace, Godly Glory."

5 Arise, O Jerusalem, stand upon the
        height;
    look toward the east,
    and see your children gathered from west
        and east
    at the word of the Holy One,
        rejoicing that God has remembered
        them.
6 For they went out from you on foot,
    led away by their enemies;
    but God will bring them back to you,
        carried in glory, as on a royal throne.
7 For God has ordered that every high
        mountain and the everlasting hills
        be made low
    and the valleys filled up, to make level
        ground,
    so that Israel may walk safely in the
        glory of God.
8 The woods and every fragrant tree
    have shaded Israel at God's command.
9 For God will lead Israel with joy,
    in the light of his glory,
    with the mercy and righteousness that
        come from him.

4.30–5.9 Three imperatives (*take courage*, 4.30; *look*, 4.36; *arise*, 5.5) divide the address to Jerusalem into its major parts. **4.30–35** The punishment of Babylon is part of the consolation of Jerusalem (cf. Isa 43.14; 47.1–15). Contrast the attitude expressed in 1.11–12. **4.30** See Isa 51.12; 62.2, 4. **4.31** Edom was especially blamed for having gloated over Jerusalem's destruction (Isa 34; 63.1–6; Lam 4.21; Ob 8–14; Mal 1.2–5). **4.35** *Fire.* Cf. Jer 50.32; 51.30, 58. *Inhabited by demons.* Cf. Isa 13.21. **4.36–5.4** Jerusalem's joy at seeing her exiled children return is described. **4.36** See Isa 40.9–11. **4.37** See Isa 43.5–6; Zech 8.7–8; cf. *Psalms of Solomon* 11.3. **5.1–2** These verses reverse the image of 4.20. See Isa 52.1; 61.10; cf. *Psalms of Solomon* 11.8. **5.4** New garments and a new name for Jerusalem are mentioned together in Isa 62.2–4. For other symbolic names of Zion, see Isa 1.26; 60.14; Jer 33.16; Ezek 48.35. **5.5–9** The return of the exiled children is described. **5.5** See Isa 40.9; 43.5; 51.17; 60.4; cf. *Psalms of Solomon* 11.3. **5.6** See Isa 49.22; 66.20. **5.7** See Isa 40.4–5; cf. *Psalms of Solomon* 11.5. **5.8** Cf. *Psalms of Solomon* 11.6–7. **5.9** See Isa 60.1–3.

THE LETTER OF
JEREMIAH

THE LETTER OF JEREMIAH is, according to its superscription, a copy of a letter sent by the seventh–sixth century BCE prophet to those Judeans soon to be exiled to Babylon by King Nebuchadnezzar, presumably in 597, though possibly in 586 BCE. It imitates the letter found in Jer 29.1–23, which informs those already in exile of their length of stay ("seventy years") and of their need, therefore, to establish themselves in their new homeland and to seek its welfare (Jer 29.5–7, 10). The Letter of Jeremiah similarly advises the exiles of their length of stay (now "up to seven generations," v. 3), but is more antagonistic toward the host nation, ridiculing it for its idolatry and warning the exiles not to participate in this apostasy.

Content

THE LETTER OF JEREMIAH is an extended diatribe against idolatry that draws heavily upon Jer 10.1–16 and related biblical passages (e.g., Deut 4.27–28; Pss 115.3–8; 135.15–18; Isa 40.18–20; 41.7; 44.9–20; 46.1–7; Hab 2.18–19). Although the relationship between statue and deity was more nuanced in ancient Near Eastern thought than these condemnations allow (the idol was a representation of, and could even be animated by, the deity but was not equivalent to the deity), for those committed to the supremacy of Israel's God (e.g., Isa 45) and the commandments against divine images (Ex 20.3–5; Deut 5.7–9), these idols were nothing more than the inanimate objects from which they were crafted (wood, gold, and silver). Indeed, that these idols required constant care and attention from their devotees proved their impotence, a point reiterated throughout the Letter (e.g., vv. 13, 24, 27, 48).

Date

BECAUSE THE LETTER OF JEREMIAH shows a clear dependence upon earlier polemics against idolatry from the Neo-Babylonian (626–539 BCE) and Persian (539–332 BCE) periods, most scholars date the Letter to the Hellenistic period (332–63 BCE). Taking the reference in v. 3 to "seven generations" literally yields a date of composition near the end of the fourth century BCE. "Seven generations" may, however, simply be a way of denoting a long period of time, in which case a later date may be intended. The Letter is likely alluded to by the author of 2 Macc 2.1–3, which was composed near the end of the second century BCE. A Greek fragment of vv. 43–44, dating to ca. 100 BCE, was discovered in Cave 7 at Qumran. Thus, the available evidence suggests a date of composition sometime between the late fourth and late second century BCE.

Setting

SINCE THE LETTER OF JEREMIAH is addressed to those heading into Babylonian exile (vv. 1–2) and describes cultic practices known from Babylonia (e.g., vv. 4, 40, 42, 43), many scholars argue for a Mesopotamian provenance. Yet the Letter is written from the perspective of one living in Israel, and the author's familiarity with Mesopotamian cultic practices could have come from biblical descriptions and other secondhand sources. Therefore, a Judean provenance is also possible. Some scholars have even argued for an Egyptian origin, though the main evidence for this remains highly speculative. Whatever the Letter's exact provenance, its descriptions of foreign cultic practices fit well the various manifestations of idolatry throughout the ancient Near East, and therefore it had broad appeal and applicability to the diverse Jewish communities of the Hellenistic era.

Structure

FOLLOWING THE INTRODUCTION (vv. 1–7), the Letter of Jeremiah divides most naturally into ten sections (vv. 8–16; 17–23; 24–29; 30–40a; 40b–44; 45–49; 50–52; 53–56; 57–65; 66–69) and a conclusion (vv. 70–73), each ending with a summary statement (indicated by "therefore," "then," or "so"). The introduction contains two such statements, corresponding to the Letter's two main themes: the duration of the exiles' stay (v. 3) and the need, therefore, to resist idolatry (v. 5). The summary statements for the ten sections in the body of the Letter emphasize the futility of idols, five times by negative assertion and five times by rhetorical question. The final section ends with an admonition that brings to denouement the Letter's main message: "Better, therefore, is someone upright who has no idols; such a person will be far above reproach" (v. 73).

Language and Place in the Canon

THE LETTER OF JEREMIAH survives only in Greek and in versions based upon the Septuagint, such as Syriac and Latin. Linguistic evidence suggests, however, that the Letter was originally composed in a Semitic language, perhaps Aramaic, though more likely Hebrew. In most Greek manuscripts the Letter appears adjacent to the book of Lamentations, which in Jewish and Christian tradition is also attributed to the prophet Jeremiah. In Latin manuscripts, including the Vulgate, the Letter is appended to the book of Baruch as its final chapter. The NRSV follows the Greek tradition of treating the Letter as a distinct work but follows the Latin tradition of placing it immediately after Baruch and numbering it as Baruch's sixth chapter. [RICHARD J. CLIFFORD, revised by JEFFREY G. GEOGHEGAN]

6 *a* A copy of a letter that Jeremiah sent to those who were to be taken to Babylon as exiles by the king of the Babylonians, to give them the message that God had commanded him.

The People Face a Long Captivity

2 Because of the sins that you have committed before God, you will be taken to Babylon as exiles by Nebuchadnezzar, king of the Babylonians. 3Therefore when you have come to Babylon you will remain there for many years, for a long time, up to seven generations; after that I will bring you away from there in peace. 4Now in Babylon you will see gods made of silver and gold and wood, which people carry on their shoulders, and which cause the heathen to fear. 5So beware of becoming at all like the foreigners or of letting fear for these gods *b* possess you 6when you see the multitude before and behind them worshiping them. But say in your heart, "It is you, O Lord, whom we must worship." 7For my angel is with you, and he is watching over your lives.

The Helplessness of Idols

8 Their tongues are smoothed by the carpenter, and they themselves are overlaid with gold and silver; but they are false and cannot speak. 9People *c* take gold and make crowns for the heads of their gods, as they might for a girl who loves ornaments. 10Sometimes the priests secretly take gold and silver from their gods and spend it on themselves, 11or even give some of it to the prostitutes on the terrace. They deck their gods *d* out with garments like human beings—these gods of silver and gold and wood 12that cannot save themselves from rust and corrosion. When they have been dressed in purple robes, 13their faces are wiped because of the dust from the temple, which is thick upon them. 14One of them holds a scepter, like a district judge, but is un-

---

a The King James Version (like the Latin Vulgate) prints The Letter of Jeremiah as Chapter 6 of the Book of Baruch, and the chapter and verse numbers are here retained. In the Greek Septuagint, the Letter is separated from Baruch by the Book of Lamentations. *b* Gk *for them* *c* Gk *They* *d* Gk *them*

1–7 Historical introduction and theme. **1** *A copy of a letter.* Cf. Jer 29.1–23, which records a letter sent by Jeremiah to those already in Babylonian exile. *Exiles,* presumably the deportees of 597 BCE (2 Kings 24.10–17), since the letter in Jer 29 is addressed to these same exiles. **2** *Because of the sins.* The Babylonian conquest of Jerusalem was recompense for human wrongdoing, not the result of divine impotence—an important point for the author, who will later deride idols for their inability to deliver their worshipers from calamity (vv. 36, 37, 48). Cf. Jer 16.10–13. **3** *Therefore,* Greek *oun,* a term also translated *then* (vv. 40a, 44, 49, 52, 56, 65) or *so* (vv. 5, 16, 23, 69) and indicating the summary statements for each section of the book (see Introduction). *Oun* is also translated *therefore* in v. 73 and left untranslated in v. 29. Taking *up to seven generations* literally, reckoning forty years to the generation (see Num 14.33; Ps 95.10), yields a date of ca. 317 BCE (597 minus 280). More likely, however, the phrase expands Jeremiah's projection of seventy years (Jer 25.12; 29.10) or three generations of Babylonian rulers (Jer 27.7) in order to accommodate those living in foreign lands long after the time suggested by Jeremiah's prophecies. Cf. Dan 9.24, where Jeremiah's "seventy years" becomes "seventy weeks (of years)." **4** *Gods made of silver and gold and wood.* Cf. Deut 4.28; Pss 115.4; 135.15. Idols were often crafted of wood and adorned with silver and gold. Cf. Isa 40.19; 41.6–7; 44.10–17; 46.6; Jer 10.3–4. *Which people carry on their shoulders,* perhaps an allusion to the Akitu or Babylonian New Year festival, during which idols were carried in procession by priests (cf. Jer 10.5). Similar processions are attested throughout the ancient Near East.

6 *It is you, O Lord, whom we must worship,* an affirmation expressing a central theme of the Letter and of the Bible: "You shall have no other gods before me" (Ex 20.3; Deut 5.7) and "The LORD is our God, the LORD alone" (Deut 6.4). For similar affirmations under pressure to commit idolatry, see Dan 3.17–18; 2 Macc 7. **7** *My angel,* a heavenly being commissioned by God to guide and protect individuals (Gen 16.7; 24.7; 48.16) and nations (e.g., Israel; Ex 23.20–23; 32.34). By the time of Daniel, Israel's protector is specifically identified as Michael (Dan 12.1; cf. Rev 12.7). *Watching over your lives,* for the purpose of protection (cf. Dan 3.28; 6.22), though the Greek verb can also denote "to search out" for the purpose of rendering judgment.

8–16 Though made with great care and at great cost, idols are unable to act on behalf of themselves or others. **8** *Tongues are smoothed.* The mouths of idols were important for ingesting sacrifices and declaring oracles. For the author of this letter, however, their mouths both are *false* (i.e., they cannot perform normal bodily functions, such as eating) and *cannot speak* (i.e., they are powerless to declare oracles). **9–10** The statues' authority and power, denoted by *crowns,* cannot prevent their own priests from plundering their gold. **11** *Prostitutes on the terrace,* perhaps a reference to the payment of cult prostitutes (cf. 1 Kings 14.24; Strabo, *Geography* 16.1.20; cf. Herodotus, *History* 1.199) or to the use of divine offerings for personal pleasure (see v. 10). Cf. Deut 23.17–18, which condemns the giving of money gained from prostitution to the temple. **12–13** *Purple robes* denote royal power (cf. Jer 10.9), yet the gods cannot even keep their faces clean. **14–15** Ancient Near Eastern deities were often

able to destroy anyone who offends it. [15]Another has a dagger in its right hand, and an ax, but cannot defend itself from war and robbers. [16]From this it is evident that they are not gods; so do not fear them.

17 For just as someone's dish is useless when it is broken, [18]so are their gods when they have been set up in the temples. Their eyes are full of the dust raised by the feet of those who enter. And just as the gates are shut on every side against anyone who has offended a king, as though under sentence of death, so the priests make their temples secure with doors and locks and bars, in order that they may not be plundered by robbers. [19]They light more lamps for them than they light for themselves, though their gods[a] can see none of them. [20]They are[b] just like a beam of the temple, but their hearts, it is said, are eaten away when crawling creatures from the earth devour them and their robes. They do not notice [21]when their faces have been blackened by the smoke of the temple. [22]Bats, swallows, and birds alight on their bodies and heads; and so do cats. [23]From this you will know that they are not gods; so do not fear them.

24 As for the gold that they wear for beauty—it[c] will not shine unless someone wipes off the tarnish; for even when they were being cast, they did not feel it. [25]They are bought without regard to cost, but there is no breath in them. [26]Having no feet, they are carried on the shoulders of others, revealing to humankind their worthlessness. And those who serve them are put to shame [27]because, if any of these gods falls[d] to the ground, they themselves must pick it up. If anyone sets it upright, it cannot move itself; and if it is tipped over, it cannot straighten itself. Gifts are placed before them just as before the dead. [28]The priests sell the sacrifices that are offered to these gods[e] and use the money themselves. Likewise their wives preserve some of the meat[f] with salt, but give none to the poor or helpless. [29]Sacrifices to them may even be touched by women in their periods or at childbirth. Since you know by these things that they are not gods, do not fear them.

30 For how can they be called gods? Women serve meals for gods of silver and gold and wood; [31]and in their temples the priests sit with their clothes torn, their heads and beards shaved, and their heads uncovered. [32]They howl and shout before their gods as some do at a funeral banquet. [33]The priests take some of the clothing of their gods[g] to clothe their wives and children. [34]Whether one does evil to

---

a Gk *they*   *b* Gk *It is*   *c* Lat Syr: Gk *they*   *d* Gk *if they fall*
e Gk *to them*   *f* Gk *of them*   *g* Gk *some of their clothing*

---

depicted wielding symbols of their authority (e.g., *scepter*) and power (e.g., *dagger, ax*). **16** A variant of this statement, posed five times as an assertion (vv. 16, 23, 29, 65, 69) and five times as a question (vv. 40, 44, 49, 52, 56), concludes each section of the body of the Letter (see Introduction). **17–23** Idols are useless and unseeing. **17** The *broken dish* is proverbial for uselessness (Jer 19.11; 22.28; Hos 8.8). **18** The gods are shut up within their temples like prisoners. **19** *Light . . . lamps.* Some scholars have suggested that this is an allusion to the Egyptian Festival of Lamps at Sais (cf. Herodotus, *History* 2.62). Lamps, however, are common to temples from all periods and places. *Can see none of them.* Cf. Ps 115.5. **20** Although the idols are no different from the beams supporting the temple, when the former succumb to insect infestation *it is said* (presumably by those maintaining the idols) that *their hearts* (i.e., their inward faculties of reason) *are eaten away,* even as *their robes* (i.e., their outward symbols of authority) are devoured. Cf. v. 55. **22** *Birds alight . . . and so do cats.* The Greek word rendered "alight" more accurately means "to fly over, to flit," which is not the behavior of cats. It is possible that the text originally listed another type of bird or even another type of divine emblem similarly vexed by flying creatures that was subsequently misunderstood by a later translator

or copyist. For the problem of bats in temples, see Strabo (*Geography* 16.1.7).

24–29 Idols are unfeeling and passive, and their food is plundered and ritually unclean. **25** *No breath in them.* Cf. Ps 135.17; Jer 10.14; Hab 2.19. **26** *Carried on the shoulders.* See v. 4. Cf. also Isa 46.7; Jer 10.5. **27** *Falls to the ground.* Cf. 1 Sam 5.1–5. *Before the dead.* Offerings for the dead were commonplace in the ancient Near East, though the practice is generally prohibited in the Bible (Deut 26.14; see also Sir 30.18–19; but cf. Tob 4.17). **28** *The poor or helpless.* True religion shows concern for the needy (Deut 15.11; 24.17–22; Ps 41.1; also Jas 1.27). **29** According to biblical law, women became ritually unclean *in their periods or at childbirth* (Lev 12.2–5; 15.19–30). **30–40a** The statues cannot do what people expect of a deity. **30** Offering food to statues made of *silver and gold and wood* epitomizes the foolishness of idolatry. Cf. Bel and the Dragon. **31–32** *Clothes torn, howl and shout,* behavior typical of ritual mourning, which in a cultic setting likely refers to the rites associated with a dying and rising god such as Tammuz (see Ezek 8.14). Israel's priests were forbidden to participate in mourning for the dead, except in the case of immediate relatives, as it made them ritually impure (Lev 21.1–6, 10). **33–34a** The gods are unable to prevent their own servants from plundering them

them or good, they will not be able to repay it. They cannot set up a king or depose one. 35Likewise they are not able to give either wealth or money; if one makes a vow to them and does not keep it, they will not require it. 36They cannot save anyone from death or rescue the weak from the strong. 37They cannot restore sight to the blind; they cannot rescue one who is in distress. 38They cannot take pity on a widow or do good to an orphan. 39These things that are made of wood and overlaid with gold and silver are like stones from the mountain, and those who serve them will be put to shame. 40Why then must anyone think that they are gods, or call them gods?

The Foolishness of Worshiping Idols

Besides, even the Chaldeans themselves dishonor them; for when they see someone who cannot speak, they bring Bel and pray that the mute may speak, as though Bel*a* were able to understand! 41Yet they themselves cannot perceive this and abandon them, for they have no sense. 42And the women, with cords around them, sit along the passageways, burning bran for incense. 43When one of them is led off by one of the passers-by and is taken to bed by him, she derides the woman next to her, because she was not as attractive as herself and her cord was not broken. 44Whatever is done for these idols*b* is false. Why then must anyone think that they are gods, or call them gods?

45 They are made by carpenters and goldsmiths; they can be nothing but what the arti-

sans wish them to be. 46Those who make them will certainly not live very long themselves; 47how then can the things that are made by them be gods? They have left only lies and reproach for those who come after. 48For when war or calamity comes upon them, the priests consult together as to where they can hide themselves and their gods.*b* 49How then can one fail to see that these are not gods, for they cannot save themselves from war or calamity? 50Since they are made of wood and overlaid with gold and silver, it will afterward be known that they are false. 51It will be manifest to all the nations and kings that they are not gods but the work of human hands, and that there is no work of God in them. 52Who then can fail to know that they are not gods?*c*

53 For they cannot set up a king over a country or give rain to people. 54They cannot judge their own cause or deliver one who is wronged, for they have no power; 55they are like crows between heaven and earth. When fire breaks out in a temple of wooden gods overlaid with gold or silver, their priests will flee and escape, but the gods*d* will be burned up like timbers. 56Besides, they can offer no resistance to king or enemy. Why then must anyone admit or think that they are gods?

57 Gods made of wood and overlaid with silver and gold are unable to save themselves from thieves or robbers. 58Anyone who can will strip them of their gold and silver and of

---

a Gk he   b Gk them   c Meaning of Gk uncertain   d Gk they

(cf. v. 10). **34b** *Cannot set . . . one.* Cf. Ps 2; Dan 2.21. **35** *Not able . . . money.* Cf. 1 Sam 2.7; Job 42.10. *Will not require it.* Cf. Deut 23.21. **36–37.** *Cannot save . . . cannot rescue.* Cf. Ex 20.2; 1 Sam 17.37. **38** *Cannot take pity.* Cf. Pss 68.5–6; 146.8–9. **39** *Put to shame.* Cf. Isa 44.11.

40b–44 Those who worship idols participate in senseless and dishonoring behavior. **40** *Chaldeans,* either people of the Babylonian Empire or, as here, professional diviners and wise men (see Dan 2.2; 4.7; 5.7). *Bel,* the Akkadian word for "lord" (corresponding to Hebrew *Baal*), a title of Marduk, chief of the Babylonian pantheon (cf. Jer 50.2; 51.44; Isa 46.1; Bel and the Dragon). His priests, supposedly wise, pray to an unhearing and mute god for the cure of the mute (cf. Hab 2.18–19). **42–43** *Women . . . taken to bed.* According to Herodotus (*History* 1.199), it was the obligation of every Babylonian woman once in her lifetime to sit in the temple precinct of Aphrodite (Ishtar) until selected for sexual intercourse by a stranger, presumably as part of the fertility rites associated with the goddess (see also Strabo, *Geography* 16.1.20). Herodotus makes no men-

tion of the *burning bran,* which may have been a form of grain offering or perhaps an aphrodisiac. **45–56** The statues of the gods are made by mortals. **45** *Made by carpenters and goldsmiths.* Cf. Ps 115.4; Isa 40.19; Jer 10.9. The statues represent human rather than divine will. **47** One generation was expected to hand on to *those who come after* the tradition of true worship (cf. Deut 6.7; Pss 48.13; 78.1–8), but the artisans hand on only shameful images. **48–50** The statues are only wooden cores *overlaid with gold and silver;* therefore, they will be unable to protect themselves from the ravages of war and time. **53–54** Among the tasks of gods in the ancient Near East were to establish kings (cf. Dan 2.21), give fertility (cf. Deut 11.14), and rescue the innocent poor (cf. 1 Sam 2.8), but these gods do nothing. **55** The difficult *crows* is sometimes corrected to "clouds" based on the assumption that the Greek translator mistook the graphically similar Hebrew word *k'bym* ("like clouds") for *k'rbym* ("like ravens"). If so, then the gods are powerless like clouds blown by the winds. **57–65** Idols are helpless and useless, unfit im-

the robes they wear, and go off with this booty, and they will not be able to help themselves. [59]So it is better to be a king who shows his courage, or a household utensil that serves its owner's need, than to be these false gods; better even the door of a house that protects its contents, than these false gods; better also a wooden pillar in a palace, than these false gods.

60 For sun and moon and stars are bright, and when sent to do a service, they are obedient. [61]So also the lightning, when it flashes, is widely seen; and the wind likewise blows in every land. [62]When God commands the clouds to go over the whole world, they carry out his command. [63]And the fire sent from above to consume mountains and woods does what it is ordered. But these idols[a] are not to be compared with them in appearance or power. [64]Therefore one must not think that they are gods, nor call them gods, for they are not able either to decide a case or to do good to anyone. [65]Since you know then that they are not gods, do not fear them.

66 They can neither curse nor bless kings; [67]they cannot show signs in the heavens for the nations, or shine like the sun or give light like the moon. [68]The wild animals are better than they are, for they can flee to shelter and help themselves. [69]So we have no evidence whatever that they are gods; therefore do not fear them.

70 Like a scarecrow in a cucumber bed, which guards nothing, so are their gods of wood, overlaid with gold and silver. [71]In the same way, their gods of wood, overlaid with gold and silver, are like a thornbush in a garden on which every bird perches; or like a corpse thrown out in the darkness. [72]From the purple and linen[b] that rot upon them you will know that they are not gods; and they will finally be consumed themselves, and be a reproach in the land. [73]Better, therefore, is someone upright who has no idols; such a person will be far above reproach.

---

a Gk these things   b Cn: Gk marble, Syr silk

---

ages of the one true God. **57–58** Cf. vv. 10, 28, 49, 56. **59** All things, noble and base, have their use, but not idols, which can do nothing. **60** *Sun and moon and stars . . . are obedient.* Cf. Job 38.24–38; Ps 8.3–4; Bar 3.33–34. The luminaries mark day and night and seasonal feasts (Gen 1.14–18). **61–63** These manifestations of storm, often the domain of the chief deities of the ancient Near East, are indicative of God's power and presence (Ex 19.16–19; 1 Kings 18.44–45; Ps 29). **64** *Not able . . . to decide a case,* in contrast to Israel's God (Ex 18.19; Ps 43.1; Isa 41.21). **66–69** The gods are passive, mute, and more helpless than wild animals. **66** *Neither*

curse nor bless. Cf. Num 22.12; Deut 11.26–28. **67** *Signs in the heavens,* perhaps astrological signs used for divination, though more likely astral phenomena in general. Cf. Jer 10.2; Joel 2.30. **70–72** Final metaphors of contempt for idols. **70** *Scarecrow in a cucumber bed.* Just as a scarecrow's ability to frighten depends upon its being perceived as a living being, so an idol's power to evoke fear (i.e., worship) requires human self-deception. Cf. Jer 10.5. **71** *Thornbush, corpse thrown out,* metaphors for things useless, even detrimental (cf. Judg 9.14–15; Am 8.3; Jer 14.16; Isa 34.3; Bar 2.25). **73** True honor belongs to the *upright person* who shuns idolatry.

THE PRAYER OF AZARIAH
and the Song of the Three Jews

THE GREEK AND LATIN VERSIONS OF DANIEL contain three additions that are not present in the Jewish and Protestant canons of the OT. These are collectively referred to as the Additions to Daniel and consist of the Prayer of Azariah and the Song of the Three Jews, Susanna, and Bel and the Dragon.

The first of these, the Prayer of Azariah and the Song of the Three Jews, is found inserted between Dan 3.23 and 3.24. Dan 3 recounts the story of Daniel's three companions who are thrown into a furnace by Nebuchadnezzar and survive unharmed. Although short prayers and doxologies are found in Daniel (2.20–23; 3.28; 4.3, 34–35, 37; 6.26–27), this addition is much longer, delaying the narrative considerably. It was a common practice in the editing of the OT to insert such poetic compositions into prose works (cf. 1 Sam 2; 2 Sam 22). This insertion falls into three parts: the Prayer of Azariah (vv. 1–22); a description of the furnace (vv. 23–27); and the Song of the Three Jews (vv. 28–68). The last section can also be divided further into vv. 28–34 and 35–68, based on differences in the poetic arrangement. This addition was probably inserted in the second or first century BCE. Although there is no evidence that the Prayer of Azariah or the Song of the Three Jews was used in Jewish liturgy, they were very popular among Christians and were included as numbers 7 and 8 in the section "Odes" in some manuscripts of the Greek Bible.

By form, the Prayer of Azariah is a national lament, similar to Pss 44; 74; 79; and 80, although the latter do not dwell as much on the speaker's confession of sin. The confession of sin was, however, a staple of the covenantal theology of the postexilic period (cf. Ezra 9.6–15; Neh 9.6–37; Dan 9.4–19; Bar 1.15–3.8).

The Song of the Three Jews was often divided in early Christian use at the same point where a division is suggested here, between vv. 34 and 35. In both parts this is a hymn of praise; the first part is similar to Pss 96 and 97 in its themes, while the second is similar to Ps 148 in content and to Ps 136 in its use of a repeated, antiphonal refrain.

Daniel 3.25 only hints at what is going on within the furnace, but this addition serves to record the prayers and blessings of the three men and to increase the sense of the miraculous by describing in detail how the angel is intervening. Readers thus enter more fully into the experience of the three pious and courageous Jews. [LAWRENCE WILLS]

(Additions to Daniel, inserted between
3.23 and 3.24)

The Prayer of Azariah in the Furnace

1 They[a] walked around in the midst of the
flames, singing hymns to God and blessing the
Lord. 2 Then Azariah stood still in the fire and
prayed aloud:

3   "Blessed are you, O Lord, God of our
            ancestors, and worthy of praise;
        and glorious is your name forever!
4   For you are just in all you have done;
        all your works are true and your ways
            right,
        and all your judgments are true.
5   You have executed true judgments in all
            you have brought upon us
        and upon Jerusalem, the holy city of
            our ancestors;
        by a true judgment you have brought
            all this upon us because of our
            sins.
6   For we have sinned and broken your law
            in turning away from you;
        in all matters we have sinned
            grievously.
7   We have not obeyed your
            commandments,
        we have not kept them or done what
            you have commanded us for our
            own good.
8   So all that you have brought upon us,
        and all that you have done to us,
            you have done by a true judgment.
9   You have handed us over to our enemies,
        lawless and hateful rebels,

and to an unjust king, the most wicked
    in all the world.
10   And now we cannot open our mouths;
        we, your servants who worship you,
            have become a shame and a
            reproach.
11   For your name's sake do not give us up
            forever,
        and do not annul your covenant.
12   Do not withdraw your mercy from us,
        for the sake of Abraham your beloved
        and for the sake of your servant Isaac
            and Israel your holy one,
13   to whom you promised
        to multiply their descendants like the
            stars of heaven
        and like the sand on the shore of the
            sea.
14   For we, O Lord, have become fewer than
            any other nation,
        and are brought low this day in all the
            world because of our sins.
15   In our day we have no ruler, or prophet,
            or leader,
        no burnt offering, or sacrifice, or
            oblation, or incense,
        no place to make an offering before
            you and to find mercy.
16   Yet with a contrite heart and a humble
            spirit may we be accepted,
17   as though it were with burnt offerings
            of rams and bulls,
        or with tens of thousands of fat lambs;

a That is, Hananiah, Mishael, and Azariah (Dan 2.17), the
original names of Shadrach, Meshach, and Abednego (Dan 1.6-7)

1–22 The Prayer of Azariah. Elements of the older
"national lament" psalms are combined here with the
confession of sin as a step toward reestablishing a covenant with God. The tone of penitence is totally lacking in Dan 1–6, and the three Jews are apparently
blameless before God; thus the prayer does not correspond to their circumstances but has been added to
the book of Daniel to introduce another dimension of
the religious life of Jews in the postexilic period. 2 Both
the Hebrew names of the three men and their adopted
Babylonian names are given in Dan 1.7, but only the
Babylonian names are used in Dan 3, and only the Hebrew names in the addition (vv. 2, 66). 5–10 The confession of sin, and the recognition that God's covenant
has been broken, which has resulted in the fall of
Jerusalem. 9 An unjust king, the most wicked. Although
Jewish tradition would naturally hurl this sort of invective at Nebuchadnezzar for capturing Jerusalem
and destroying the temple, Dan 1–4 presents a varied

portrait of this king. Later Jewish tradition condemned Daniel's cooperation with Nebuchadnezzar,
and this addition shares this negative view. The reference could also be taken to refer to Antiochus IV
Epiphanes (1 Macc 1.10). 11–22 Appeal to God's
mercy to reinstate the covenant. 12–13 God's covenant with *Abraham* is invoked (cf. Gen 15.1–6); *Isaac*
and *Israel* (Jacob) are also included (Gen 22.15–18;
Josh 24.3–4; Isa 41.8). 15 *No ruler . . . no place.* The
temple and the government have fallen, which fits
Daniel's situation, but it is possible that the lament
may have been written about the events surrounding
the Maccabean revolt. 16–17 Azariah's prayer takes up
the theme of Ps 51 that a *contrite heart* is a substitute
for *sacrifice*, but it goes further: the death of the Jews
by fire will be their *sacrifice.* The penitential theology
of Ezra 9.6–15; Neh 9.6–37; Dan 9.4–19; Bar 1.15–3.8
is reflected here, and although these Jews do not die,
the sentiment expressed is similar to that associated

such may our sacrifice be in your sight
    today,
and may we unreservedly follow you,[a]
    for no shame will come to those who
        trust in you.
18 And now with all our heart we follow
    you;
    we fear you and seek your presence.
19 Do not put us to shame,
    but deal with us in your patience
    and in your abundant mercy.
20 Deliver us in accordance with your
      marvelous works,
    and bring glory to your name, O Lord.
21 Let all who do harm to your servants be
      put to shame;
    let them be disgraced and deprived of
      all power,
    and let their strength be broken.
22 Let them know that you alone are the
      Lord God,
    glorious over the whole world."

The Song of the Three Jews

23 Now the king's servants who threw them in
kept stoking the furnace with naphtha, pitch,
tow, and brushwood. 24And the flames poured
out above the furnace forty-nine cubits, 25and
spread out and burned those Chaldeans who
were caught near the furnace. 26But the angel
of the Lord came down into the furnace to be
with Azariah and his companions, and drove
the fiery flame out of the furnace, 27and made
the inside of the furnace as though a moist
wind were whistling through it. The fire did
not touch them at all and caused them no pain
or distress.

28 Then the three with one voice praised
and glorified and blessed God in the furnace:
29   "Blessed are you, O Lord, God of our
      ancestors,
    and to be praised and highly exalted
      forever;
30   And blessed is your glorious, holy name,
    and to be highly praised and highly
      exalted forever.
31   Blessed are you in the temple of your
      holy glory,
    and to be extolled and highly glorified
      forever.
32   Blessed are you who look into the depths
      from your throne on the cherubim,
    and to be praised and highly exalted
      forever.

33   Blessed are you on the throne of your
      kingdom,
    and to be extolled and highly exalted
      forever.
34   Blessed are you in the firmament of heaven,
    and to be sung and glorified forever.
35   "Bless the Lord, all you works of the Lord;
    sing praise to him and highly exalt him
      forever.
36   Bless the Lord, you heavens;
    sing praise to him and highly exalt him
      forever.
37   Bless the Lord, you angels of the Lord;
    sing praise to him and highly exalt him
      forever.
38   Bless the Lord, all you waters above the
      heavens;
    sing praise to him and highly exalt him
      forever.
39   Bless the Lord, all you powers of the Lord;
    sing praise to him and highly exalt him
      forever.
40   Bless the Lord, sun and moon;
    sing praise to him and highly exalt him
      forever.
41   Bless the Lord, stars of heaven;
    sing praise to him and highly exalt him
      forever.
42   "Bless the Lord, all rain and dew;
    sing praise to him and highly exalt him
      forever.
43   Bless the Lord, all you winds;
    sing praise to him and highly exalt him
      forever.
44   Bless the Lord, fire and heat;
    sing praise to him and highly exalt him
      forever.
45   Bless the Lord, winter cold and summer
      heat;
    sing praise to him and highly exalt him
      forever.
46   Bless the Lord, dews and falling snow;
    sing praise to him and highly exalt him
      forever.
47   Bless the Lord, nights and days;
    sing praise to him and highly exalt him
      forever.
48   Bless the Lord, light and darkness;
    sing praise to him and highly exalt him
      forever.

_____

a Meaning of Gk uncertain

49 Bless the Lord, ice and cold;
    sing praise to him and highly exalt him
        forever.
50 Bless the Lord, frosts and snows;
    sing praise to him and highly exalt him
        forever.
51 Bless the Lord, lightnings and clouds;
    sing praise to him and highly exalt him
        forever.

52 "Let the earth bless the Lord;
    let it sing praise to him and highly
        exalt him forever.
53 Bless the Lord, mountains and hills;
    sing praise to him and highly exalt him
        forever.
54 Bless the Lord, all that grows in the ground;
    sing praise to him and highly exalt him
        forever.
55 Bless the Lord, seas and rivers;
    sing praise to him and highly exalt him
        forever.
56 Bless the Lord, you springs;
    sing praise to him and highly exalt him
        forever.
57 Bless the Lord, you whales and all that
        swim in the waters;
    sing praise to him and highly exalt him
        forever.
58 Bless the Lord, all birds of the air;
    sing praise to him and highly exalt him
        forever.
59 Bless the Lord, all wild animals and cattle;
    sing praise to him and highly exalt him
        forever.

60 "Bless the Lord, all people on earth;
    sing praise to him and highly exalt him
        forever.

61 Bless the Lord, O Israel;
    sing praise to him and highly exalt him
        forever.
62 Bless the Lord, you priests of the Lord;
    sing praise to him and highly exalt him
        forever.
63 Bless the Lord, you servants of the Lord;
    sing praise to him and highly exalt him
        forever.
64 Bless the Lord, spirits and souls of the
        righteous;
    sing praise to him and highly exalt him
        forever.
65 Bless the Lord, you who are holy and
        humble in heart;
    sing praise to him and highly exalt him
        forever.

66 "Bless the Lord, Hananiah, Azariah, and
        Mishael;
    sing praise to him and highly exalt him
        forever.
For he has rescued us from Hades and
        saved us from the power[a] of
        death,
and delivered us from the midst of the
        burning fiery furnace;
from the midst of the fire he has
        delivered us.
67 Give thanks to the Lord, for he is good,
    for his mercy endures forever.
68 All who worship the Lord, bless the God
        of gods,
    sing praise to him and give thanks to
        him,
    for his mercy endures forever."

_____
a Gk hand

with the martyrdoms of pious Jews in 2 Macc 6–7;
4 Macc 4–12. **23–27** Description of the furnace.
23 *Naphtha, pitch, tow, brushwood,* highly flammable
substances and kindling that are fed to the flames—
mere wood will not do! The miraculous element is
thus heightened in the addition, and the story made
more exciting by the inclusion of such details.
24 *Forty-nine cubits,* about 80 feet. **28–68** The Song of
the Three Jews. **29–34** First song, a royal enthronement hymn that celebrates God's rule of the universe
as king (cf. Pss 96; 97). **31** Some of the images seem to
presuppose a standing *temple* and ongoing worship
(cf. Azariah's prayer, v. 15), but the text refers directly
only to a heavenly temple. **32** *Cherubim,* mythical
creatures on which God rides in heaven; they were represented in the temple (cf. 1 Sam 4.4; 1 Kings 6.23–

28). **35–68** Second song. Praise is elicited from all of
God's creation beginning with the highest cosmological phenomena and the angels (vv. 36–41), descending
through the elements of the atmosphere (vv. 42–51) to
the earth and the creatures on it (vv. 52–59) and ending with worshipers of God (vv. 60–68; cf. Ps 148). The
first song addresses God directly and utilizes many
similar-sounding phrases to increase its poetic beauty,
but here the universe itself is summoned to give praise,
and the second line of each verse is not only similar,
but identical, likely an antiphonal community response to the first line (cf. Ps 136). The two songs
probably both existed separately before being inserted
here. **66** *Hananiah, Azariah, and Mishael,* probably an
addition to the hymn here, since in this verse the orderly structure is disrupted.

S U S A N N A

(Chapter 13 of the Greek Version of Daniel)

MANY STORIES AND VISIONS CONCERNING DANIEL, similar to the ones now contained in the OT book, circulated in ancient Judaism in the Second Temple period; fragments of some of these have been found at Qumran. Susanna and Bel and the Dragon are two such entertaining short stories that probably circulated independently and were later inserted into the book of Daniel. Theodotion's version of the OT places Susanna at the beginning of Daniel in order to introduce Daniel as a young man, while the Septuagint and Vulgate versions place Susanna at the end with Bel and the Dragon. The purpose of adding these two stories to the previously existing book was perhaps to bring it more in line with the novelistic literature of the period such as Tobit, Judith, and Esther (especially with its Greek additions).

Susanna and Bel and the Dragon are best read as edifying fictions; no real historical account is intended in either case. They are examples of a commonplace in Jewish literature, the persecution and vindication of the righteous hero or heroine (cf. Gen 37–50; Esther; Dan 3; 6; Wis 2–5). Susanna differs from Dan 1–6 and Bel and the Dragon (as well as Gen 37–50 and Esther) in that the action does not take place in the highest court in the land, but in the local, self-governing Jewish court.

Traditional folk motifs, such as the upright woman who is falsely accused of being promiscuous and the young boy who steps forward to render a just verdict, are reflected in the story. Susanna is also one of the first detective stories of world literature, or better, one of the first "courtroom dramas." It cannot be dated precisely but was probably composed between the third and first centuries BCE. The Greek text translated here is from Theodotion's version; the Septuagint version is quite different in a number of places (see note on v. 32). [LAWRENCE WILLS]

Susanna's Beauty Attracts Two Elders

1 There was a man living in Babylon whose name was Joakim. [2] He married the daughter of Hilkiah, named Susanna, a very beautiful woman and one who feared the Lord. [3] Her parents were righteous, and had trained their daughter according to the law of Moses. [4] Joakim was very rich, and had a fine garden adjoining his house; the Jews used to come to him because he was the most honored of them all.

5 That year two elders from the people were appointed as judges. Concerning them the Lord had said: "Wickedness came forth from Babylon, from elders who were judges, who were supposed to govern the people." [6] These men were frequently at Joakim's house, and all who had a case to be tried came to them there.

7 When the people left at noon, Susanna would go into her husband's garden to walk. [8] Every day the two elders used to see her, going in and walking about, and they began to lust for her. [9] They suppressed their consciences and turned away their eyes from looking to Heaven or remembering their duty to administer justice. [10] Both were overwhelmed with passion for her, but they did not tell each other of their distress, [11] for they were ashamed to disclose their lustful desire to seduce her. [12] Day after day they watched eagerly to see her.

13 One day they said to each other, "Let us go home, for it is time for lunch." So they both left and parted from each other. [14] But turning back, they met again; and when each pressed the other for the reason, they confessed their lust. Then together they arranged for a time when they could find her alone.

The Elders Attempt to Seduce Susanna

15 Once, while they were watching for an opportune day, she went in as before with only two maids, and wished to bathe in the garden, for it was a hot day. [16] No one was there except the two elders, who had hidden themselves and were watching her. [17] She said to her maids, "Bring me olive oil and ointments, and shut the garden doors so that I can bathe." [18] They did as she told them: they shut the doors of the garden and went out by the side doors to bring what they had been commanded; they did not see the elders, because they were hiding.

19 When the maids had gone out, the two elders got up and ran to her. [20] They said, "Look, the garden doors are shut, and no one can see us. We are burning with desire for you; so give your consent, and lie with us. [21] If you refuse, we will testify against you that a young man was with you, and this was why you sent your maids away."

22 Susanna groaned and said, "I am completely trapped. For if I do this, it will mean death for me; if I do not, I cannot escape your hands. [23] I choose not to do it; I will fall into your hands, rather than sin in the sight of the Lord."

24 Then Susanna cried out with a loud voice, and the two elders shouted against her. [25] And one of them ran and opened the garden doors. [26] When the people in the house heard the shouting in the garden, they rushed in at the side door to see what had happened to her. [27] And when the elders told their story, the servants felt very much ashamed, for nothing like this had ever been said about Susanna.

The Elders Testify against Susanna

28 The next day, when the people gathered at the house of her husband Joakim, the two elders came, full of their wicked plot to have Susanna put to death. In the presence of the people they said, [29] "Send for Susanna daughter of Hilkiah, the wife of Joakim." [30] So they sent for

---

1–14 Calm setting of the story and introduction of a threat to Susanna. **1** Since the story introduces the young man Daniel, the time must be during the exile. It is difficult to imagine Jews living lives of such genteel wealth during the exile in *Babylon,* but cf. Jer 29.4–7 and, from a much later period, 2 Esd 3.2. This story may reflect the actual social conditions of some Jews of a later century. *Joakim,* in Hebrew "the Lord will establish." This figure is not to be identified either with the Joakim of Jdt 4.6; 15.8 or with Jehoiachin in 2 Kings 24.15. **2** *Hilkiah,* in Hebrew "the Lord is my portion," a common priestly name. *Susanna,* in Hebrew "lily." *A* *very beautiful woman . . . the Lord.* Cf. Tob 6.12; Jdt 8.7–8; Esth 2.7, 20 (according to the Greek translation). **5** The quotation is unknown, but cf. Jer 23.14–15; 29.20–23. **9** *Heaven,* i.e., God. **15–27** The attempted coercion of Susanna. **17** *Olive oil,* used as a cosmetic and sometimes perfumed with myrrh to make fragrant *ointments;* cf. Esth 2.12; Ps 104.15. **21** *Was with you,* here a euphemism for sexual intercourse; merely being alone with a young man would not warrant death (cf. v. 37). **22** According to Mosaic law the punishment for adultery was *death* (Lev 20.10; Deut 22.22). **23** *I choose not to do it.* Central to many

her. And she came with her parents, her children, and all her relatives.

31 Now Susanna was a woman of great refinement and beautiful in appearance. 32As she was veiled, the scoundrels ordered her to be unveiled, so that they might feast their eyes on her beauty. 33Those who were with her and all who saw her were weeping.

34 Then the two elders stood up before the people and laid their hands on her head. 35Through her tears she looked up toward Heaven, for her heart trusted in the Lord. 36The elders said, "While we were walking in the garden alone, this woman came in with two maids, shut the garden doors, and dismissed the maids. 37Then a young man, who was hiding there, came to her and lay with her. 38We were in a corner of the garden, and when we saw this wickedness we ran to them. 39Although we saw them embracing, we could not hold the man, because he was stronger than we, and he opened the doors and got away. 40We did, however, seize this woman and asked who the young man was, 41but she would not tell us. These things we testify."

Because they were elders of the people and judges, the assembly believed them and condemned her to death.

42 Then Susanna cried out with a loud voice, and said, "O eternal God, you know what is secret and are aware of all things before they come to be; 43you know that these men have given false evidence against me. And now I am to die, though I have done none of the wicked things that they have charged against me!"

44 The Lord heard her cry. 45Just as she was being led off to execution, God stirred up the holy spirit of a young lad named Daniel, 46and he shouted with a loud voice, "I want no part in shedding this woman's blood!"

Daniel Rescues Susanna

47 All the people turned to him and asked, "What is this you are saying?" 48Taking his stand among them he said, "Are you such fools, O Israelites, as to condemn a daughter of Israel without examination and without learning the facts? 49Return to court, for these men have given false evidence against her."

50 So all the people hurried back. And the rest of the[a] elders said to him, "Come, sit among us and inform us, for God has given you the standing of an elder." 51Daniel said to them, "Separate them far from each other, and I will examine them."

52 When they were separated from each other, he summoned one of them and said to him, "You old relic of wicked days, your sins have now come home, which you have committed in the past, 53pronouncing unjust judgments, condemning the innocent and acquitting the guilty, though the Lord said, 'You shall not put an innocent and righteous person to death.' 54Now then, if you really saw this woman, tell me this: Under what tree did you see them being intimate with each other?" He answered, "Under a mastic tree."[b] 55And Daniel said, "Very well! This lie has cost you your head, for the angel of God has received the sentence from God and will immediately cut[b] you in two."

56 Then, putting him to one side, he ordered them to bring the other. And he said to him, "You offspring of Canaan and not of Judah, beauty has beguiled you and lust has perverted your heart. 57This is how you have been treating the daughters of Israel, and they

---

a Gk lacks rest of the   b The Greek words for mastic tree and cut are similar, thus forming an ironic wordplay

such Jewish stories is a moment of decision; cf. Gen 39.9. **28–46** The trial of Susanna. **32** The narrative presumes that a woman of position would be *veiled* in public; unveiling her face would violate her modesty. In the Septuagint version of Susanna, however, she is evidently stripped and exposed to the gaze of the crowd, a ritual punishment for adulterous women attested in Jewish law. Cf. Ezek 16.37–39; Hos 2.3–10; *Mishnah Sota* 1.5–6. **34** The gesture of laying *hands* on the *head* was used in various solemn rituals (cf. Gen 48.14; Lev 16.21; Num 8.10), but here it signifies the witnesses' role in testifying to a capital offense before the community carries out the execution (cf. Lev 24.14). **42–43** Susanna, who has *trusted in the Lord* (v. 35), testifies on her own behalf before God as a higher judge. She accuses the elders of bearing false witness, a violation of Jewish law (Deut 19.16–21). Her prayer for intercession, though quite short, is similar to the prayers of Jdt 9.2–14; Add Esth 14.3–19. **44–46** God as judge hears her testimony and inspires Daniel to come to her defense as a legal advocate. The *holy spirit* may be the spirit of prophecy, but it is associated with wisdom as well (cf. Dan 4.8, 18; 5.11–12; 6.3). **47–64** Vindication of Susanna. **48** Cross-examination of the two witnesses has been wrongly omitted (Deut 19.15–20). **53** See Ex 23.7. **56** The wicked elder is asso-

were intimate with you through fear; but a daughter of Judah would not tolerate your wickedness. 58 Now then, tell me: Under what tree did you catch them being intimate with each other?" He answered, "Under an evergreen oak."*a* 59 Daniel said to him, "Very well! This lie has cost you also your head, for the angel of God is waiting with his sword to split*a* you in two, so as to destroy you both."

60 Then the whole assembly raised a great shout and blessed God, who saves those who hope in him. 61 And they took action against the two elders, because out of their own mouths Daniel had convicted them of bearing false witness; they did to them as they had wickedly planned to do to their neighbor. 62 Acting in accordance with the law of Moses, they put them to death. Thus innocent blood was spared that day.

63 Hilkiah and his wife praised God for their daughter Susanna, and so did her husband Joakim and all her relatives, because she was found innocent of a shameful deed. 64 And from that day onward Daniel had a great reputation among the people.

---

a The Greek words for *evergreen oak* and *split* are similar, thus forming an ironic wordplay

---

ciated with the sexual sins of *Canaan* (Gen 9.20–27; Lev 18.24–28). **57** *Daughters of Israel, daughter of Judah.* Jews traced their descent through southern Judahites, not northern Israelites. **61–62** The punishment for bearing false witness is the same as the one that would have been applied to the charge falsely brought, in this case, *death.*

BEL AND THE
DRAGON
(Chapter 14 of the Greek Version of Daniel)

BEL AND THE DRAGON is found at the end of the book of Daniel in the Greek version as another story of Daniel's experiences in the great royal courts of the ancient Near East. Here Daniel serves the benevolent King Cyrus of Persia; conquered Babylonians are Daniel's competitors within the court. The two parts of Bel and the Dragon (vv. 1–22, 23–42) are composed of narratives that depict the folly of revering idols; they may have circulated independently before being added to Daniel. During the postexilic period, when Jews regularly encountered those who worshiped representations of various kinds, the theme of the parody of idols was developed into a literary commonplace (Pss 115.4–8; 135.15–18; Isa 40.18–20; 44.9–20; 46.6–7; Jer 10.3–9; Hab 2.18–19; Wis 13.1–15.17; Letter of Jeremiah). Daniel's uncovering of wrongdoing is similar to his courtroom heroics in Susanna. The entertaining motifs that begin Bel and the Dragon are given a more dramatic turn, however; the angry Babylonians force the king to throw Daniel into the lions' den. Daniel's fall from a position of honor and the threat to his life together with his vindication and restoration at the end are similar in plot outline to Dan 3 and 6 and also to Susanna, Gen 37–50, and Esther (see Introduction to Susanna).

Although Dan 6 and Bel and the Dragon evidently share a common history (the method of execution in both is to be thrown into a den of lions), it is unclear whether either is directly dependent on the other. Bel and the Dragon is more fantastic and miraculous than Dan 6—perhaps even whimsical—but in two details Bel and the Dragon is more realistic: the succession of kings here is correct ("Darius the Mede" of Dan 5.31; 6.28 is unhistorical), and the use of the signet ring here is more logical and better integrated into the narrative (cf. Dan 6.17).

Bel and the Dragon, like Susanna, was probably composed between the third and first centuries BCE. [LAWRENCE WILLS]

Daniel and the Priests of Bel

1 When King Astyages was laid to rest with his ancestors, Cyrus the Persian succeeded to his kingdom. 2 Daniel was a companion of the king, and was the most honored of all his Friends.

3 Now the Babylonians had an idol called Bel, and every day they provided for it twelve bushels of choice flour and forty sheep and six measures*a* of wine. 4 The king revered it and went every day to worship it. But Daniel worshiped his own God.

So the king said to him, "Why do you not worship Bel?" 5 He answered, "Because I do not revere idols made with hands, but the living God, who created heaven and earth and has dominion over all living creatures."

6 The king said to him, "Do you not think that Bel is a living god? Do you not see how much he eats and drinks every day?" 7 And Daniel laughed, and said, "Do not be deceived, O king, for this thing is only clay inside and bronze outside, and it never ate or drank anything."

8 Then the king was angry and called the priests of Bel*b* and said to them, "If you do not tell me who is eating these provisions, you shall die. 9 But if you prove that Bel is eating them, Daniel shall die, because he has spoken blasphemy against Bel." Daniel said to the king, "Let it be done as you have said."

10 Now there were seventy priests of Bel, besides their wives and children. So the king went with Daniel into the temple of Bel. 11 The priests of Bel said, "See, we are now going outside; you yourself, O king, set out the food and prepare the wine, and shut the door and seal it with your signet. 12 When you return in the morning, if you do not find that Bel has eaten it all, we will die; otherwise Daniel will, who is telling lies about us." 13 They were unconcerned, for beneath the table they had made a hidden entrance, through which they used to go in regularly and consume the provisions. 14 After they had gone out, the king set out the food for Bel. Then Daniel ordered his servants to bring ashes, and they scattered them throughout the whole temple in the presence of the king alone. Then they went out, shut the door and sealed it with the king's signet, and departed. 15 During the night the priests came as usual, with their wives and children, and they ate and drank everything.

16 Early in the morning the king rose and came, and Daniel with him. 17 The king said, "Are the seals unbroken, Daniel?" He answered, "They are unbroken, O king." 18 As soon as the doors were opened, the king looked at the table, and shouted in a loud voice, "You are great, O Bel, and in you there is no deceit at all!"

19 But Daniel laughed and restrained the king from going in. "Look at the floor," he said, "and notice whose footprints these are." 20 The king said, "I see the footprints of men and women and children."

21 Then the king was enraged, and he arrested the priests and their wives and children. They showed him the secret doors through which they used to enter to consume what was on the table. 22 Therefore the king put them to

---

a A little more than fifty gallons   *b* Gk *his priests*

1–22 Daniel uncovers the deceit of the priests of Bel. 1 *King Astyages* ruled the Medes from 585 to 550 BCE.; according to Herodotus (*History* 1.130), *Cyrus the Persian* took the kingdom of Astyages by force. In Dan 5.31; 6.28 Cyrus succeeds the unknown "Darius the Mede." 2 *Friends,* here a designation for those who held favored positions in the court; cf. Gen 26.26; 1 Kings 4.5; Jn 19.12. 3 When Cyrus captured Babylon in 539 BCE, the *Babylonians,* like the Jews, became a subject people whose interests—and deities—would be seen by Jews as competing with theirs. *Bel,* or Baal, was identified with the main Babylonian deity Marduk (Merodach); cf. Isa 46.1; Jer 50.2. Herodotus (*History* 1.183) provides a secondhand description of the idol of Bel in Babylon, a "figure of a man" 18 feet tall made of solid gold (cf. v. 7). According to inscriptions, Nebuchadnezzar supplied large quantities of food and drink to the god. 4 Cyrus claimed in an inscription to have been ordained by Bel to rule over Babylon. 5 *Idols made with hands,* a negative phrase that came into use in the postexilic period; cf. Jdt 8.18; Mk 14.58; Acts 7.48; Heb 9.11. *The living God,* who truly exists apart from all representations; cf. Deut 5.26; Jer 10.10; Acts 14.15; 1 Thess 1.9. 6 Cyrus ironically applies the lofty idea of *a living god* to a god who gorges on vast quantities of food and wine like a living being. Irony of various kinds can be found in the Bible (cf. Judg 5.28–30; Tob 5.3–21; Jdt 11.5–6), but what is ironic here (as in v. 24) is that lofty theological ideas are misconstrued as referring to the mundane level (cf. Jn 3.3–4; 4.10–15). 7 *Clay inside and bronze outside.* Cf. Isa 40.18–19. 18 The king ironically utters the cry *in you there is no deceit* just after readers are fully informed of the deceit involved (vv. 13, 15). 19 Daniel's boldness with Cyrus (cf. v. 14) is paralleled by the king's surprising sympathy for Daniel (vv. 30, 40). 22 A morally balanced pun-

death, and gave Bel over to Daniel, who destroyed it and its temple.

Daniel Kills the Dragon

23 Now in that place[a] there was a great dragon, which the Babylonians revered. 24 The king said to Daniel, "You cannot deny that this is a living god; so worship him." 25 Daniel said, "I worship the Lord my God, for he is the living God. 26 But give me permission, O king, and I will kill the dragon without sword or club." The king said, "I give you permission." 27 Then Daniel took pitch, fat, and hair, and boiled them together and made cakes, which he fed to the dragon. The dragon ate them, and burst open. Then Daniel said, "See what you have been worshiping!"

28 When the Babylonians heard about it, they were very indignant and conspired against the king, saying, "The king has become a Jew; he has destroyed Bel, and killed the dragon, and slaughtered the priests." 29 Going to the king, they said, "Hand Daniel over to us, or else we will kill you and your household." 30 The king saw that they were pressing him hard, and under compulsion he handed Daniel over to them.

Daniel in the Lions' Den

31 They threw Daniel into the lions' den, and he was there for six days. 32 There were seven lions in the den, and every day they had been given two human bodies and two sheep; but now they were given nothing, so that they would devour Daniel.

33 Now the prophet Habakkuk was in Judea; he had made a stew and had broken bread into a bowl, and was going into the field to take it to the reapers. 34 But the angel of the Lord said to Habakkuk, "Take the food that you have to Babylon, to Daniel, in the lions' den." 35 Habakkuk said, "Sir, I have never seen Babylon, and I know nothing about the den." 36 Then the angel of the Lord took him by the crown of his head and carried him by his hair; with the speed of the wind[b] he set him down in Babylon, right over the den.

37 Then Habakkuk shouted, "Daniel, Daniel! Take the food that God has sent you." 38 Daniel said, "You have remembered me, O God, and have not forsaken those who love you." 39 So Daniel got up and ate. And the angel of God immediately returned Habakkuk to his own place.

40 On the seventh day the king came to mourn for Daniel. When he came to the den he looked in, and there sat Daniel! 41 The king shouted with a loud voice, "You are great, O Lord, the God of Daniel, and there is no other besides you!" 42 Then he pulled Daniel[c] out, and threw into the den those who had attempted his destruction, and they were instantly eaten before his eyes.

---

a Other ancient authorities lack *in that place*   *b* Or *by the power of his spirit*   *c* Gk *him*

---

ishment for the villains typical of folk narrative: the priests are *put . . . to death* (with their families) in accord with their previous agreement (vv. 8–9) and by the same means of execution they had intended for Daniel. **23–30** Daniel cleverly kills the dragon. **23** *Great dragon*. In early OT passages a serpent is sometimes associated with Mosaic practice, but it was later excluded in Israel (Num 21.6–9; 2 Kings 18.4). A mythological serpent or chaos monster was said by the Babylonians to be destroyed by Bel/Marduk, and serpents appear elsewhere in ancient Near Eastern mythology (cf. Job 7.12; Ps 74.13–14; Isa 27.1). It is not clear whether the worship of a living snake is being parodied here or the mythological battle of Bel and the chaos monster is reduced to a humorous scale. **24** Once again Cyrus looks for evidence of *a living god* on a mundane level (cf. v. 6). **27** *Pitch, fat, and hair* are not magical ingredients, but

everyday substances. The absurdity of the story should not detract from its enjoyment; with suspension of disbelief, readers can accept that this clever concoction will swell up in the dragon's stomach and burst it open. The idol parody theme in postexilic literature looked to a naturalistic exposé of idolatry (see Introduction). **28** *The king has become a Jew*. Cf. Dan 2.47, 3.28–29, 4.37, 6.26–27; 2 Macc 9.17; Acts 26.29. **30** Cyrus is portrayed very favorably; it is the Babylonians who force the king's hand, so that he acts only *under compulsion*. Cyrus's actual authority over the Babylonians would have been absolute. **31–42** Daniel is thrown into the lions' den and survives unharmed. **33** *The prophet Habakkuk* is abruptly introduced to heighten the miraculous; vv. 33–39 may be an interpolation. **40** Daniel is in the lions' den for seven days, a holy number in Judaism. **41** Cf. Dan 3.28; 4.3, 34–35, 37; 6.26–27.

1 MACCABEES

Historical Setting

ALEXANDER THE GREAT'S CONQUEST of the Persian Empire brought a change of political masters to Judea and the whole land of Israel. With Alexander's death in 323 BCE there was great confusion and struggle among his generals, friends, and heirs, but by about 300 the political situation of the Near East had become clearer. Judea found itself between two powerful Hellenistic dynasties—the Seleucids in the north (Syria) and the Ptolemies in the south (Egypt). From 300 to 200 BCE Judea was under the Ptolemies. After defeating the Ptolemies in 198, Antiochus III brought the Jews of Palestine into the Seleucid Empire. His successor, Seleucus IV (187–175), was in turn replaced by Antiochus IV Epiphanes (175–164), who intervened more aggressively in Jewish affairs.

Content

THE FIRST BOOK OF MACCABEES tells the story of the revolt initiated by the Jewish priest Mattathias and carried on by his five sons and grandson. The family is known both as the Maccabees (from the nickname given to Judas, 2.4) and as the Hasmoneans (perhaps from Mattathias's grandfather Simeon, 2.1).

Covering the period from the reign of Antiochus IV to 134 BCE, 1 Maccabees describes how the God of Israel used this family to remove foreign political and cultural oppression and how the Jewish high priesthood came to reside in this family. After sketching the crisis caused by Antiochus IV and his Jewish supporters (ch. 1) and the resistance begun by Mattathias (ch. 2), it narrates in turn the exploits of Judas Maccabeus (3.1–9.22), his brothers Jonathan (9.23–12.53) and Simon (13.1–15.41), and Simon's son John (16.1–24). The book portrays the Maccabees as God's instruments for bringing about Jewish independence: "the family of those men through whom deliverance was given to Israel" (5.62).

Relation to Other Works

THE TEXT OF 1 MACCABEES exists in Greek and is part of the Septuagint. It is generally assumed that the work was composed in Hebrew (now lost) and translated into a "biblical" or "Semitic"

Greek, similar to the Greek versions of the early historical books (1–2 Samuel, 1–2 Kings) in language and style.

The book ends with the accession of Simon's son John Hyrcanus to the high priesthood in 134 BCE. The Hebrew original was probably composed during the reign of John Hyrcanus (134–104) or in the early first century BCE. The author, who is unknown, was surely a supporter of the Maccabean dynasty. The book undoubtedly served as "propaganda" for the Maccabean dynasty (whose legitimacy was suspect in some Jewish circles on political and religious grounds).

First Maccabees incorporates some "official" documents (8.23–32; 10.18–20; 10.25–45; 11.30–37; 11.57; 12.5–23; 13.36–40). The authenticity of these documents has long been debated, though current scholarship supports them at least in their basic content. Some of the battle reports (3.27–4.24; 6.18–63; 9.1–22) may depend on the eyewitness accounts of participants, though in many passages the numbers are inflated. A common source may underlie the material about Judas in 1 Macc 1–7 and 2 Macc 3–15. The poems, speeches, and prayers throughout the book are best interpreted as free compositions by the author (in accordance with the practices of ancient historians).

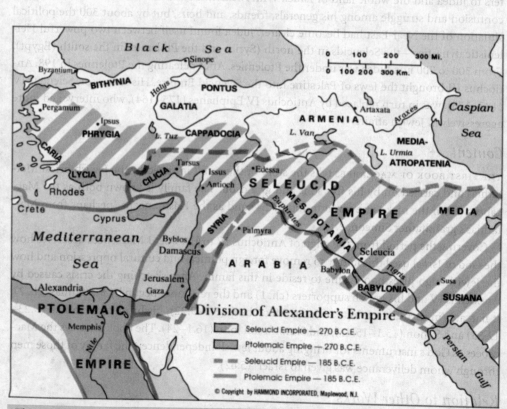

Division of Alexander's Empire

Seleucid Empire — 270 B.C.E.
Ptolemaic Empire — 270 B.C.E.
Seleucid Empire — 185 B.C.E.
Ptolemaic Empire — 185 B.C.E.

© Copyright by HAMMOND INCORPORATED, Maplewood, N.J.

The contest between the two kingdoms that divided Alexander the Great's legacy dominated Syro-Palestine in the third and early second centuries BCE. Ascendancy of the Seleucids set the stage for the struggle recounted in 1 and 2 Maccabees.

The three generations of the Maccabee family constitute the focus of 1 Maccabees. The book of Daniel, written shortly before the death of Antiochus IV Epiphanes, looked for imminent divine intervention to defeat Israel's enemies and to establish God's kingdom. 2 Maccabees stresses God's role as the defender of the Jerusalem temple. 1 Maccabees, however, presents the Maccabean family as bringing about Israel's "salvation" and emphasizes their military and political exploits as well as their religious observance. Those in the community responsible for the Qumran scrolls may have been early supporters of the Maccabean movement who fell away when the Maccabees took control of the high priesthood and the temple worship.

In literary style and evocations of biblical precedents, 1 Maccabees shows how the words and deeds of the Maccabean dynasty stood in line with those of earlier biblical heroes. It presents the Maccabees as exemplars of worldly activism and champions of Jewish religious freedom and national independence. It allows readers to follow the course of a Jewish revolutionary movement over the period of more than thirty years. It is considered canonical by Catholics and Orthodox, apocryphal/deuterocanonical by Protestants, and noncanonical by Jews (though Jews trace the origin of Hanukkah to the events described in 4.36–59). [DANIEL J. HARRINGTON]

The Maccabees: A Family Tree

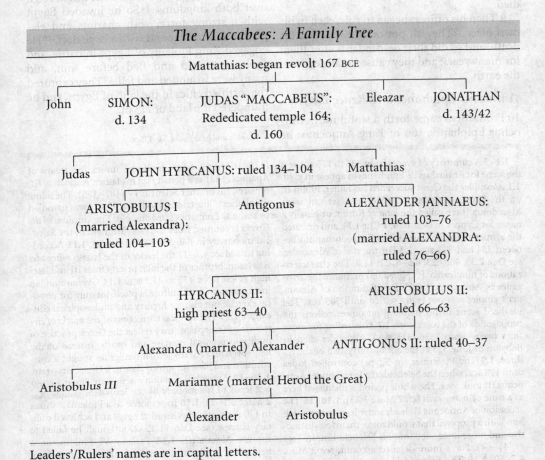

Mattathias: began revolt 167 BCE

John | SIMON: d. 134 | JUDAS "MACCABEUS": Rededicated temple 164; d. 160 | Eleazar | JONATHAN d. 143/42

Judas | JOHN HYRCANUS: ruled 134–104 | Mattathias

ARISTOBULUS I (married Alexandra): ruled 104–103 | Antigonus | ALEXANDER JANNAEUS: ruled 103–76 (married ALEXANDRA: ruled 76–66)

HYRCANUS II: high priest 63–40 | ARISTOBULUS II: ruled 66–63

Alexandra (married) Alexander | ANTIGONUS II: ruled 40–37

Aristobulus III | Mariamne (married Herod the Great)

Alexander | Aristobulus

Leaders'/Rulers' names are in capital letters.

Alexander the Great

1 After Alexander son of Philip, the Macedonian, who came from the land of Kittim, had defeated[a] King Darius of the Persians and the Medes, he succeeded him as king. (He had previously become king of Greece.) [2]He fought many battles, conquered strongholds, and put to death the kings of the earth. [3]He advanced to the ends of the earth, and plundered many nations. When the earth became quiet before him, he was exalted, and his heart was lifted up. [4]He gathered a very strong army and ruled over countries, nations, and princes, and they became tributary to him.

5 After this he fell sick and perceived that he was dying. [6]So he summoned his most honored officers, who had been brought up with him from youth, and divided his kingdom among them while he was still alive. [7]And after Alexander had reigned twelve years, he died.

8 Then his officers began to rule, each in his own place. [9]They all put on crowns after his death, and so did their descendants after them for many years; and they caused many evils on the earth.

Antiochus Epiphanes and Renegade Jews

10 From them came forth a sinful root, Antiochus Epiphanes, son of King Antiochus; he had been a hostage in Rome. He began to reign in the one hundred thirty-seventh year of the kingdom of the Greeks.[b]

11 In those days certain renegades came out from Israel and misled many, saying, "Let us go and make a covenant with the Gentiles around us, for since we separated from them many disasters have come upon us." [12]This proposal pleased them, [13]and some of the people eagerly went to the king, who authorized them to observe the ordinances of the Gentiles. [14]So they built a gymnasium in Jerusalem, according to Gentile custom, [15]and removed the marks of circumcision, and abandoned the holy covenant. They joined with the Gentiles and sold themselves to do evil.

Antiochus in Egypt

16 When Antiochus saw that his kingdom was established, he determined to become king of the land of Egypt, in order that he might reign over both kingdoms. [17]So he invaded Egypt with a strong force, with chariots and elephants and cavalry and with a large fleet. [18]He engaged King Ptolemy of Egypt in battle, and Ptolemy turned and fled before him, and many were wounded and fell. [19]They captured the fortified cities in the land of Egypt, and he plundered the land of Egypt.

---

a Gk adds *and he defeated*   b 175 B.C.

1.1–9 A summary of events from 336 to 175 BCE sets the scene for Antiochus IV Epiphanes to appear in v. 10. 1.1 *Alexander* the Great succeeded his father, Philip II, on the latter's assassination (336 BCE), set out from Macedonia (here called the *land of Kittim*, originally a name for Cyprus in Gen 10.4; 1 Chr 1.7), and defeated the armies of the Persian Darius III Codomannus between 334 and 331 BCE. 1.3 For the rise of Alexander, see Dan 2.33, 40; 7.23; 8.5–8, 21; 11.3. The characterizations of him (*exalted . . . lifted up*) prefigure the arrogance of Antiochus. 1.6 The configuration of Alexander's empire was not really settled until 305 BCE. The idealized scene of his handing on power reflects the propaganda of the successors. 1.7 After ruling for more than *twelve years* (336–323 BCE), Alexander died in Babylon in June 323 at the age of thirty-two or thirty-three. 1.9 The Ptolemies (in Egypt) controlled Judea until 198 BCE, when the Seleucids (in Syria) under Antiochus III took over. The whole period is dismissed here as a time of *many evils* (cf. 2 Macc 3.23). 1.10–15 The accession of Antiochus IV leads some Jews to approach him with a proposal that would make them less distinctive and more integrated into his Seleucid Empire (see vv. 41–64). For a more detailed account, see 2 Macc 4.7–50. 1.10 The Seleucid king *Antiochus Epiphanes*

(175–164 BCE), taken to Rome under the treaty of Apamea (188) as a penalty on his father, Antiochus III, replaced his brother Seleucus IV (187–175). The name Epiphanes ("illustrious, [god] manifest") was parodied by some as Epimanes ("madman"). The *kingdom of the Greeks* is counted from the establishment of the Seleucid monarchy in Babylon (312/311 BCE). 1.11 According to 2 Macc 4.7–17 the leader of the Jewish *renegades* was Jason, brother of the high priest Onias III and later high priest from 175 to 172 BCE. 1.14 *Gymnasium*, an institution of Greek culture, a place not only for physical exercise but also for literary and philosophical education. 1.15 The surgical correction of *the marks of circumcision* (epispasm) may reflect the Greek practice of nudity in physical exercise and sports. Instead of the *holy covenant* (Torah) Jewish renegades sought a constitution and lifestyle appropriate to a Greek city-state. 1.16–19 Antiochus's military action in Egypt in 169 BCE leads to his robbery of the Jerusalem temple. See 2 Macc 5.1–21. 1.16 In response to a Ptolemaic threat in 170 BCE Antiochus invaded *Egypt* and achieved military success (see Dan 11.25–27), though he failed to capture Alexandria. 1.18 *Ptolemy VI* Philometor, a nephew of Antiochus, remained ruler in Egypt from 180 to 145 BCE. 1.20–28 Like other ancient temples, the

Persecution of the Jews

20 After subduing Egypt, Antiochus returned in the one hundred forty-third year.[a] He went up against Israel and came to Jerusalem with a strong force. 21He arrogantly entered the sanctuary and took the golden altar, the lampstand for the light, and all its utensils. 22He took also the table for the bread of the Presence, the cups for drink offerings, the bowls, the golden censers, the curtain, the crowns, and the gold decoration on the front of the temple; he stripped it all off. 23He took the silver and the gold, and the costly vessels; he took also the hidden treasures that he found. 24Taking them all, he went into his own land.

He shed much blood,
    and spoke with great arrogance.
25 Israel mourned deeply in every
      community,
26   rulers and elders groaned,
    young women and young men became
      faint,

the beauty of the women faded.
27 Every bridegroom took up the lament;
    she who sat in the bridal chamber was
      mourning.
28 Even the land trembled for its inhabitants,
    and all the house of Jacob was clothed
      with shame.

The Occupation of Jerusalem

29 Two years later the king sent to the cities of Judah a chief collector of tribute, and he came to Jerusalem with a large force. 30Deceitfully he spoke peaceable words to them, and they believed him; but he suddenly fell upon the city, dealt it a severe blow, and destroyed many people of Israel. 31He plundered the city, burned it with fire, and tore down its houses and its surrounding walls. 32They took captive the women and children, and seized the livestock. 33Then they fortified the city of David with a great strong wall and strong towers, and

---

a 169 B.C.

Jerusalem temple had sacred vessels and served as a bank (see 2 Macc 3.10–11). To pay his mercenaries and probably to exact what had been promised him by the high priest Menelaus (2 Macc 5.15), Antiochus follows the example of Antiochus III (who died robbing a temple) and Seleucus IV (2 Macc 3). **1.21** For the furnishings and sacred vessels of the *sanctuary,* see 1 Kings 6.23–36; Ex 39.32–40.11. Whereas 2 Macc 5.11–21 places the robbery after Antiochus's second Egyptian campaign, 1 Maccabees agrees with Dan 11.28 in placing it after his first Egyptian campaign.

1.25–28 For other laments over Jerusalem, see 1.36–40; 2.7–13; 3.45. **1.29–40** A second Seleucid attack against Jerusalem (in 167 BCE) results in the establishment of a garrison (Akra) there. See 2 Macc 5.22–26. **1.29** *Chief collector of tribute,* Greek translation of the Hebrew *sar hammissim,* a misreading of *sar hammusim* ("chief of the Mysians"). In 2 Macc 5.24 he is named Apollonius, the "captain of the Mysians" (mercenaries from northwest Asia Minor). **1.33** The *citadel* served as a garrison for foreign troops and renegade Jews. Though its precise location is debated, it over-

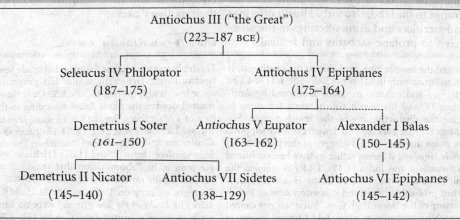

A Family Tree of Seleucid Rulers in the Maccabean Period

Antiochus III ("the Great")
(223–187 BCE)

Seleucus IV Philopator   Antiochus IV Epiphanes
(187–175)   (175–164)

Demetrius I Soter   Antiochus V Eupator   Alexander I Balas
(161–150)   (163–162)   (150–145)

Demetrius II Nicator   Antiochus VII Sidetes   Antiochus VI Epiphanes
(145–140)   (138–129)   (145–142)

-------- represents claim of sonship

it became their citadel. [34]They stationed there a sinful people, men who were renegades. These strengthened their position; [35]they stored up arms and food, and collecting the spoils of Jerusalem they stored them there, and became a great menace,

[36] for the citadel[a] became an ambush
        against the sanctuary,
    an evil adversary of Israel at all times.
[37] On every side of the sanctuary they shed
        innocent blood;
    they even defiled the sanctuary.
[38] Because of them the residents of
        Jerusalem fled;
    she became a dwelling of strangers;
    she became strange to her offspring,
        and her children forsook her.
[39] Her sanctuary became desolate like a
        desert;
    her feasts were turned into mourning,
    her sabbaths into a reproach,
        her honor into contempt.
[40] Her dishonor now grew as great as her
        glory;
    her exaltation was turned into
        mourning.

Installation of Gentile Cults

[41] Then the king wrote to his whole kingdom that all should be one people, [42]and that all should give up their particular customs. [43]All the Gentiles accepted the command of the king. Many even from Israel gladly adopted his religion; they sacrificed to idols and profaned the sabbath. [44]And the king sent letters by messengers to Jerusalem and the towns of Judah; he directed them to follow customs strange to the land, [45]to forbid burnt offerings and sacrifices and drink offerings in the sanctuary, to profane sabbaths and festivals, [46]to defile the sanctuary and the priests, [47]to build altars and sacred precincts and shrines for idols, to sacrifice swine and other unclean animals, [48]and to leave their sons uncircumcised. They were to make themselves abominable by everything unclean and profane, [49]so that they would forget the law and change all the ordinances. [50]He added,[b] "And whoever does not obey the command of the king shall die."

[51] In such words he wrote to his whole kingdom. He appointed inspectors over all the people and commanded the towns of Judah to offer sacrifice, town by town. [52]Many of the people, everyone who forsook the law, joined them, and they did evil in the land; [53]they drove Israel into hiding in every place of refuge they had.

[54] Now on the fifteenth day of Chislev, in the one hundred forty-fifth year,[c] they erected a desolating sacrilege on the altar of burnt offering. They also built altars in the surrounding towns of Judah, [55]and offered incense at the doors of the houses and in the streets. [56]The books of the law that they found they tore to pieces and burned with fire. [57]Anyone found possessing the book of the covenant, or anyone who adhered to the law, was condemned to death by decree of the king. [58]They kept using violence against Israel, against those who were found month after month in the towns. [59]On the twenty-fifth day of the month they offered sacrifice on the altar that was on top of the altar of burnt offering. [60]According to the decree, they put to death the women who had their children circumcised, [61]and their families and those who circumcised them; and they hung the infants from their mothers' necks.

---

a Gk *it*   *b* Gk lacks *He added*   *c* 167 B.C.

---

looked the temple area, probably to the northwest. It fell to Simon only in 141 BCE (13.49–50). **1.41–64** The religious and cultural program sponsored by Antiochus IV and his Jewish collaborators threatens to erase the distinctiveness of the Jewish people. See 2 Macc 6.1–11. **1.41** No non-Jewish evidence supports the claim that Antiochus IV imposed this policy on *his whole kingdom*; it seems rather to have been confined to Jerusalem and Judea (1.44). **1.43** *His religion,* the cult of Ba'al Shamen ("Lord of the Heavens"). Antiochus *probably* understood it as equivalent to Jewish worship of the "Most High God," but it was not viewed as such by everyone in Israel. **1.44** *Customs strange to the land.* Antiochus prohibited temple worship, celebration of sabbaths and holy days, circumcision, and Torah observance—those features that made Jews distinctive in the Hellenistic world. His program won some Jewish support (vv. 43, 52). **1.53** Only those who resisted deserve the name *Israel* according to the author of 1 Maccabees. For the fate of some Jews in *hiding,* see 2.29–38; 2 Macc 6.11. **1.54** *The fifteenth day of Chislev,* around the middle of December. The *desolating sacrilege* from Dan 11.31 (Hebrew *shiqquts meshomem,* lit. "abomination that makes desolate") reflects a pun on the title "Lord of Heaven" (Ba'al Shamen; see note on 1.43); see Mt 24.15; Mk 13.14. **1.56** The *books of the law* (Torah) were no longer to serve as Israel's constitution (see v. 15). **1.59** The *twenty-fifth day of the month* (December 167 BCE) coincided with the monthly celebration of Antio-

62 But many in Israel stood firm and were resolved in their hearts not to eat unclean food. 63 They chose to die rather than to be defiled by food or to profane the holy covenant; and they did die. 64 Very great wrath came upon Israel.

Mattathias and His Sons

2 In those days Mattathias son of John son of Simeon, a priest of the family of Joarib, moved from Jerusalem and settled in Modein. 2 He had five sons, John surnamed Gaddi, 3 Simon called Thassi, 4 Judas called Maccabeus, 5 Eleazar called Avaran, and Jonathan called Apphus. 6 He saw the blasphemies being committed in Judah and Jerusalem, 7 and said,

"Alas! Why was I born to see this,
  the ruin of my people, the ruin of the holy city,
and to live there when it was given over to the enemy,
  the sanctuary given over to aliens?
8 Her temple has become like a person without honor;[a]
9   her glorious vessels have been carried into exile.
Her infants have been killed in her streets,
  her youths by the sword of the foe.
10 What nation has not inherited her palaces[b]
  and has not seized her spoils?
11 All her adornment has been taken away;
  no longer free, she has become a slave.
12 And see, our holy place, our beauty,
  and our glory have been laid waste;
  the Gentiles have profaned them.
13   Why should we live any longer?"

14 Then Mattathias and his sons tore their clothes, put on sackcloth, and mourned greatly.

Pagan Worship Refused

15 The king's officers who were enforcing the apostasy came to the town of Modein to make them offer sacrifice. 16 Many from Israel came to them; and Mattathias and his sons were assembled. 17 Then the king's officers spoke to Mattathias as follows: "You are a leader, honored and great in this town, and supported by sons and brothers. 18 Now be the first to come and do what the king commands, as all the Gentiles and the people of Judah and those that are left in Jerusalem have done. Then you and your sons will be numbered among the Friends of the king, and you and your sons will be honored with silver and gold and many gifts."

19 But Mattathias answered and said in a loud voice: "Even if all the nations that live under the rule of the king obey him, and have chosen to obey his commandments, every one of them abandoning the religion of their ancestors, 20 I and my sons and my brothers will continue to live by the covenant of our ancestors. 21 Far be it from us to desert the law and the ordinances. 22 We will not obey the king's words by turning aside from our religion to the right hand or to the left."

23 When he had finished speaking these words, a Jew came forward in the sight of all to offer sacrifice on the altar in Modein, according to the king's command. 24 When Mattathias saw it, he burned with zeal and his heart was stirred. He gave vent to righteous anger; he ran and killed him on the altar. 25 At the same time he killed the king's officer who was forcing them to sacrifice, and he tore down the altar. 26 Thus he burned with zeal for the law, just as Phinehas did against Zimri son of Salu.

---

a Meaning of Gk uncertain   b Other ancient authorities read *has not had a part in her kingdom*

---

chus IV's birthday (see 2 Macc 6.7). **1.63** For those who *chose to die,* see 2.29–38; 2 Macc 6.18–7.42.

2.1–14 The main characters in the book are introduced: Mattathias (ch. 2), Judas (chs. 3–8), Jonathan (chs. 9–12), and Simon (chs. 13–16). **2.1** *Joarib.* See 1 Chr 9.10; 24.7. *Modein,* seven miles east of Lydda, seventeen miles northwest of Jerusalem. Mattathias may have been there for a short time (because of recent events in Jerusalem) or a long time before 167 BCE (see v. 70; 9.19). **2.2–5** The surnames of the five sons are mysterious, though *Maccabeus* most likely means "Hammerer." **2.7–13** The language echoes Lamentations and Pss 44; 74; 79. **2.14** For signs of *mourning,* see Gen

2.15–41 The revolt begins with Mattathias's refusal to participate in what he perceived as pagan worship. His zealous and aggressive resistance contrasts with the fate of a group that refuses to fight back on the sabbath (see vv. 29–38). **2.18** The rank of *Friends of the king* carried the privileges of members of the Seleucid royal court (see 10.65; 11.27). **2.26** According to Num 25.6–15, *Phinehas,* grandson of Aaron, showed his *zeal* by killing an Israelite man and a Midianite woman involved in the cult of Baal Peor, thus stopping a plague. Celebrated for his zeal for God's covenant and worship (Ps 106.28–31; Sir 45.23–24), Phinehas provides a model for Mattathias (v. 54). **2.28** *Hills,* most likely in

27 Then Mattathias cried out in the town with a loud voice, saying: "Let every one who is zealous for the law and supports the covenant come out with me!" 28 Then he and his sons fled to the hills and left all that they had in the town.

29 At that time many who were seeking righteousness and justice went down to the wilderness to live there, 30 they, their sons, their wives, and their livestock, because troubles pressed heavily upon them. 31 And it was reported to the king's officers, and to the troops in Jerusalem the city of David, that those who had rejected the king's command had gone down to the hiding places in the wilderness. 32 Many pursued them, and overtook them; they encamped opposite them and prepared for battle against them on the sabbath day. 33 They said to them, "Enough of this! Come out and do what the king commands, and you will live." 34 But they said, "We will not come out, nor will we do what the king commands and so profane the sabbath day." 35 Then the enemy[a] quickly attacked them. 36 But they did not answer them or hurl a stone at them or block up their hiding places, 37 for they said, "Let us all die in our innocence; heaven and earth testify for us that you are killing us unjustly." 38 So they attacked them on the sabbath, and they died, with their wives and children and livestock, to the number of a thousand persons.

39 When Mattathias and his friends learned of it, they mourned for them deeply. 40 And all said to their neighbors: "If we all do as our kindred have done and refuse to fight with the Gentiles for our lives and for our ordinances, they will quickly destroy us from the earth." 41 So they made this decision that day: "Let us fight against anyone who comes to attack us on the sabbath day; let us not all die as our kindred died in their hiding places."

Counter-Attack

42 Then there united with them a company of Hasideans, mighty warriors of Israel, all who offered themselves willingly for the law. 43 And all who became fugitives to escape their troubles joined them and reinforced them. 44 They organized an army, and struck down sinners in their anger and renegades in their wrath; the survivors fled to the Gentiles for safety. 45 And Mattathias and his friends went around and tore down the altars; 46 they forcibly circumcised all the uncircumcised boys that they found within the borders of Israel. 47 They hunted down the arrogant, and the work prospered in their hands. 48 They rescued the law out of the hands of the Gentiles and kings, and they never let the sinner gain the upper hand.

The Last Words of Mattathias

49 Now the days drew near for Mattathias to die, and he said to his sons: "Arrogance and scorn have now become strong; it is a time of ruin and furious anger. 50 Now, my children, show zeal for the law, and give your lives for the covenant of our ancestors.

51 "Remember the deeds of the ancestors, which they did in their generations; and you will receive great honor and an everlasting name. 52 Was not Abraham found faithful when tested,

a Gk *they*

the district of Gophna, northeast of Modein and bordering on Samaria. But 2 Macc 5.27 (which says nothing of the Modein incident) suggests the Judean desert. **2.29** The group is described in terms (*seeking righteousness and justice*) used also of the Qumran community. The Judean *wilderness* was a traditional place of refuge (see 1 Sam 23.14). **2.34** The group died because they refused to obey the king's decree to *profane the sabbath day.* They refused to fight even defensive wars as part of their strict code of piety, thus inviting martyrdom. See 2 Macc 6.11. **2.41** The Maccabees' decision to engage in defensive warfare on the *sabbath* was not necessarily a complete innovation in Israel; the problem surely had arisen previously. **2.42–48** The rebellion begun by Mattathias and his sons attracts Jewish support, especially from the Hasideans. **2.42** Unlike the group described in vv. 29–38, the *Hasideans* (Hebrew, "pious, loyal ones") join the military action with the Maccabees. See 7.12–13, which suggests a scribal aspect to their movement and a rift with the Maccabees. In 2 Macc 14.6, however, Judas appears as the leader of the Hasideans. **2.48** Seeking to *rescue the law,* the Maccabean rebels attack not only Gentiles but also Jewish collaborators (*sinners* and *renegades,* v. 44). Their goal was to end the program described in 1.41–50 and to reestablish traditional Judaism. **2.49–70** As he faces death in 166 BCE (v. 70) Mattathias gives a farewell speech as did Jacob (Gen 49), Moses (Deut 33), and Samuel (1 Sam 12). He appeals to biblical figures who underwent testing and so were rewarded by God: Abraham (Gen 22), Joseph (Gen 39–45), Phinehas (Num 25), Joshua (Josh 1), Caleb (Num 13), David (2 Sam 7), Elijah (1 Kings 18; 2 Kings 2), and Daniel and his three companions (Dan 1–6). Their rewards—priesthood, rulership, deliverance from danger, land—foreshadow the gains to be made by Judas, Jonathan, and Simon. **2.62** For *dung and worms* as the sin-

and it was reckoned to him as righteousness? [53]Joseph in the time of his distress kept the commandment, and became lord of Egypt. [54]Phinehas our ancestor, because he was deeply zealous, received the covenant of everlasting priesthood. [55]Joshua, because he fulfilled the command, became a judge in Israel. [56]Caleb, because he testified in the assembly, received an inheritance in the land. [57]David, because he was merciful, inherited the throne of the kingdom forever. [58]Elijah, because of great zeal for the law, was taken up into heaven. [59]Hananiah, Azariah, and Mishael believed and were saved from the flame. [60]Daniel, because of his innocence, was delivered from the mouth of the lions.

[61] "And so observe, from generation to generation, that none of those who put their trust in him will lack strength. [62]Do not fear the words of sinners, for their splendor will turn into dung and worms. [63]Today they will be exalted, but tomorrow they will not be found, because they will have returned to the dust, and their plans will have perished. [64]My children, be courageous and grow strong in the law, for by it you will gain honor.

[65] "Here is your brother Simeon who, I know, is wise in counsel; always listen to him; he shall be your father. [66]Judas Maccabeus has been a mighty warrior from his youth; he shall command the army for you and fight the battle against the peoples.[a] [67]You shall rally around you all who observe the law, and avenge the wrong done to your people. [68]Pay back the Gentiles in full, and obey the commands of the law."

[69] Then he blessed them, and was gathered to his ancestors. [70]He died in the one hundred forty-sixth year[b] and was buried in the tomb of his ancestors at Modein. And all Israel mourned for him with great lamentation.

The Early Victories of Judas

3 Then his son Judas, who was called Maccabeus, took command in his place. [2]All his brothers and all who had joined his father helped him; they gladly fought for Israel.

[3] He extended the glory of his people.
Like a giant he put on his breastplate;
he bound on his armor of war and waged battles,
protecting the camp by his sword.

[4] He was like a lion in his deeds,
like a lion's cub roaring for prey.

[5] He searched out and pursued those who broke the law;
he burned those who troubled his people.

[6] Lawbreakers shrank back for fear of him;
all the evildoers were confounded;
and deliverance prospered by his hand.

[7] He embittered many kings,
but he made Jacob glad by his deeds,
and his memory is blessed forever.

[8] He went through the cities of Judah;
he destroyed the ungodly out of the land;[c]
thus he turned away wrath from Israel.

[9] He was renowned to the ends of the earth;
he gathered in those who were perishing.

10 Apollonius now gathered together Gentiles and a large force from Samaria to fight against Israel. [11]When Judas learned of it, he went out to meet him, and he defeated and killed him. Many were wounded and fell, and the rest fled. [12]Then they seized their spoils; and Judas took the sword of Apollonius, and used it in battle the rest of his life.

13 When Seron, the commander of the Syrian army, heard that Judas had gathered a large company, including a body of faithful soldiers who stayed with him and went out to battle, [14]he said, "I will make a name for myself and win honor in the kingdom. I will make war on Judas and his companions, who scorn the king's command." [15]Once again a strong army of godless men went up with him to help him, to take vengeance on the Israelites.

---

a Or *of the people* *b* 166 B.C. *c* Gk *it*

ner's fate, see the description of Antiochus IV's death in 2 Macc 9.5–10, 28. **2.65** Only here is Simon called *Simeon.* Though an older son (see v. 3), Simon will exercise leadership only after Judas and Jonathan die.

3.1–26 A poem (vv. 3–9) summarizing Judas's exploits celebrates him as the legitimate leader of Israel (v. 2) and the enemy of renegade Jews and foreign kings. His first battles end in dramatic victories over Apollonius (vv. 10–12) and Seron (vv. 13–26). **3.7** The

many kings include Antiochus IV and Antiochus V as well as Demetrius I. **3.9** The *ends of the earth* extend at least to Rome (see ch. 8). **3.10** *Apollonius,* the military commander and governor of Samaria. Whether his force included Samaritans is uncertain. **3.12** Judas used the *sword of Apollonius* just as David used the sword of Goliath (1 Sam 17.51; 21.8–9). **3.13** *Commander of the Syrian army,* probably an exaggeration of Seron's rank and importance. **3.15** The *godless men*

16 When he approached the ascent of Beth-horon, Judas went out to meet him with a small company. [17] But when they saw the army coming to meet them, they said to Judas, "How can we, few as we are, fight against so great and so strong a multitude? And we are faint, for we have eaten nothing today." [18] Judas replied, "It is easy for many to be hemmed in by few, for in the sight of Heaven there is no difference between saving by many or by few. [19] It is not on the size of the army that victory in battle depends, but strength comes from Heaven. [20] They come against us in great insolence and lawlessness to destroy us and our wives and our children, and to despoil us; [21] but we fight for our lives and our laws. [22] He himself will crush them before us; as for you, do not be afraid of them."

23 When he finished speaking, he rushed suddenly against Seron and his army, and they were crushed before him. [24] They pursued them[a] down the descent of Beth-horon to the plain; eight hundred of them fell, and the rest fled into the land of the Philistines. [25] Then Judas and his brothers began to be feared, and terror fell on the Gentiles all around them. [26] His fame reached the king, and the Gentiles talked of the battles of Judas.

The Policy of Antiochus

27 When King Antiochus heard these reports, he was greatly angered; and he sent and gathered all the forces of his kingdom, a very strong army. [28] He opened his coffers and gave a year's pay to his forces, and ordered them to be ready for any need. [29] Then he saw that the money in the treasury was exhausted, and that the revenues from the country were small because of the dissension and disaster that he had caused in the land by abolishing the laws that had existed from the earliest days. [30] He feared that he might not have such funds as he had before for his expenses and for the gifts that he used to give more lavishly than preceding kings. [31] He was greatly perplexed in mind; then he determined to go to Persia and collect the revenues from those regions and raise a large fund.

32 He left Lysias, a distinguished man of royal lineage, in charge of the king's affairs from the river Euphrates to the borders of Egypt. [33] Lysias was also to take care of his son Antiochus until he returned. [34] And he turned over to Lysias[b] half of his forces and the elephants, and gave him orders about all that he wanted done. As for the residents of Judea and Jerusalem, [35] Lysias was to send a force against them to wipe out and destroy the strength of Israel and the remnant of Jerusalem; he was to banish the memory of them from the place, [36] settle aliens in all their territory, and distribute their land by lot. [37] Then the king took the remaining half of his forces and left Antioch his capital in the one hundred and forty-seventh year.[c] He crossed the Euphrates river and went through the upper provinces.

Preparations for Battle

38 Lysias chose Ptolemy son of Dorymenes, and Nicanor and Gorgias, able men among

---

a Other ancient authorities read *him*   *b* Gk *him*   *c* 165 B.C.

---

include renegade Jews. According to the author, Judas and his army constitute the real *Israelites*. **3.16** *The ascent of Beth-horon*, on the main road from the west to Jerusalem. About twelve miles northwest of Jerusalem travelers went through a narrow pass between Lower and Upper Beth-horon, which made the ambush by Judas and his army relatively easy. **3.18–19** Some of Judas's speech before battle echoes the words of Jonathan in 1 Sam 14.6. Instead of "Lord" or "God," 1 Maccabees often uses *Heaven* or personal pronouns (see v. 22). **3.24** *Eight hundred*, a modest number when compared with the figures for other battles. *Land of the Philistines*, hellenized cities in the southern coastal plain. **3.27–37** The importance of the Jewish rebellion is deliberately exaggerated to give the impression that it was determining all of Antiochus IV's policies. In fact he had to deal with serious rebellions and incursions in the eastern part of his empire as well. **3.28** *A year's pay*, not only a subsistence allowance but also the wages paid to mercenaries and regular troops. The unusual arrangement heightens the importance of the situation. **3.30** The historian Polybius and other ancient sources confirm that Antiochus IV was lavish in giving *gifts*. **3.31** *Persia*, the entire territory of historical Persia, not simply the eastern province of Persis. Antiochus IV died while plundering a temple in Elam, according to Polybius (*Histories* 31.9) and Appian (*Roman History* 11.66). **3.32** Prominent in the later battles at Beth-zur and Beth-zechariah (4.26–35; 6.28–63), *Lysias* held the highest title of Seleucid nobility ("King's Kinsman"). He became overseer in the western part of Antiochus IV's empire and guardian of Antiochus V (then a young boy). **3.34** The Greek text gives the impression that all the *elephants* remained with Lysias (see v. 37). **3.37** *Antioch* on the Orontes in Syria, the western Seleucid capital, built by Seleucus I in 300 BCE. **3.38–60** The defiled sanctuary in Jerusalem becomes the rallying point for the Jewish

the Friends of the king, 39and sent with them forty thousand infantry and seven thousand cavalry to go into the land of Judah and destroy it, as the king had commanded. 40So they set out with their entire force, and when they arrived they encamped near Emmaus in the plain. 41When the traders of the region heard what was said to them, they took silver and gold in immense amounts, and fetters,*a* and went to the camp to get the Israelites for slaves. And forces from Syria and the land of the Philistines joined with them.

42 Now Judas and his brothers saw that misfortunes had increased and that the forces were encamped in their territory. They also learned what the king had commanded to do to the people to cause their final destruction. 43But they said to one another, "Let us restore the ruins of our people, and fight for our people and the sanctuary." 44So the congregation assembled to be ready for battle, and to pray and ask for mercy and compassion.

45   Jerusalem was uninhabited like a
          wilderness;
      not one of her children went in or out.
   The sanctuary was trampled down,
      and aliens held the citadel;
      it was a lodging place for the Gentiles.
   Joy was taken from Jacob;
      the flute and the harp ceased to play.

46 Then they gathered together and went to Mizpah, opposite Jerusalem, because Israel formerly had a place of prayer in Mizpah. 47They fasted that day, put on sackcloth and sprinkled ashes on their heads, and tore their clothes. 48And they opened the book of the law to inquire into those matters about which the Gentiles consulted the likenesses of their gods. 49They also brought the vestments of the priesthood and the first fruits and the tithes, and they stirred up the nazirites*b* who had completed their days; 50and they cried aloud to Heaven, saying,

   "What shall we do with these?
      Where shall we take them?
51 Your sanctuary is trampled down and
          profaned,
      and your priests mourn in
          humiliation.
52 Here the Gentiles are assembled against
          us to destroy us;
      you know what they plot against us.
53 How will we be able to withstand them,
      if you do not help us?"

54 Then they sounded the trumpets and gave a loud shout. 55After this Judas appointed leaders of the people, in charge of thousands and hundreds and fifties and tens. 56Those who were building houses, or were about to be married, or were planting a vineyard, or were fainthearted, he told to go home again, according to the law. 57Then the army marched out and encamped to the south of Emmaus.

58 And Judas said, "Arm yourselves and be courageous. Be ready early in the morning to fight with these Gentiles who have assembled against us to destroy us and our sanctuary. 59It is better for us to die in battle than to see the misfortunes of our nation and of the sanctuary. 60But as his will in heaven may be, so shall he do."

The Battle at Emmaus

4 Now Gorgias took five thousand infantry and one thousand picked cavalry, and this

---

a Syr: Gk Mss, Vg *slaves*   *b* That is *those separated* or *those consecrated*

---

rebels. Judas takes care to evoke biblical precedents and observe biblical regulations for battle. See 2 Macc 8.9–23. **3.38** According to 2 Macc 8.8–9 *Gorgias* was a deputy to *Nicanor*, and *Ptolemy* was superior to Nicanor and ordered him and Gorgias into battle. **3.39** *Forty thousand*, twenty thousand according to 2 Macc 8.9. Both figures are exaggerated, perhaps on the basis of 1 Chr 18.4; 19.18. **3.40** *Emmaus*, about twenty miles west-northwest of Jerusalem. The Seleucid encampment attracted slave traders (v. 41), who expected an easy Seleucid victory. **3.45** *Jerusalem was uninhabited*, because no true Israelites, now equated with Judas and his army, were there. **3.46** *Mizpah*, eight miles north of Jerusalem, a place of assembly and prayer before battle in Judg 20.1; 1 Sam 7.5–9; 10.17. For fasting there, see 1 Sam 7.6. **3.48** The Jews consulted the *book of the law*

for guidance in battle. A Greek variant reading of the second part of the verse suggests that the scroll had been defiled with pagan pictures. **3.49** According to Num 6.1–21 *nazirites* took vows of (temporary) consecration to God. The completion of their period of special consecration was marked by rites at the temple (which were impossible because the temple was in the wrong hands). **3.55** For another division of the army, see 2 Macc 8.22–23. **3.56** The list of those exempted from battle follows Deut 20.5–8. Judas appears throughout as the ideal biblical warrior. **3.57** Emmaus was less appropriate than Mizpah as a site for Judas's prebattle speech (see Deut 20.3–4).

   4.1–25 Judas divides the army of Gorgias and defeats the main camp as well as Gorgias's expeditionary force. See 2 Macc 8.24–30. **4.1** *Five thousand . . . one*

division moved out by night [2]to fall upon the camp of the Jews and attack them suddenly. Men from the citadel were his guides. [3]But Judas heard of it, and he and his warriors moved out to attack the king's force in Emmaus [4]while the division was still absent from the camp. [5]When Gorgias entered the camp of Judas by night, he found no one there, so he looked for them in the hills, because he said, "These men are running away from us."

6 At daybreak Judas appeared in the plain with three thousand men, but they did not have armor and swords such as they desired. [7]And they saw the camp of the Gentiles, strong and fortified, with cavalry all around it; and these men were trained in war. [8]But Judas said to those who were with him, "Do not fear their numbers or be afraid when they charge. [9]Remember how our ancestors were saved at the Red Sea, when Pharaoh with his forces pursued them. [10]And now, let us cry to Heaven, to see whether he will favor us and remember his covenant with our ancestors and crush this army before us today. [11]Then all the Gentiles will know that there is one who redeems and saves Israel."

12 When the foreigners looked up and saw them coming against them, [13]they went out from their camp to battle. Then the men with Judas blew their trumpets [14]and engaged in battle. The Gentiles were crushed, and fled into the plain, [15]and all those in the rear fell by the sword. They pursued them to Gazara, and to the plains of Idumea, and to Azotus and Jamnia; and three thousand of them fell. [16]Then Judas and his force turned back from pursuing them,

[17]and he said to the people, "Do not be greedy for plunder, for there is a battle before us; [18]Gorgias and his force are near us in the hills. But stand now against our enemies and fight them, and afterward seize the plunder boldly."

19 Just as Judas was finishing this speech, a detachment appeared, coming out of the hills. [20]They saw that their army[a] had been put to flight, and that the Jews[a] were burning the camp, for the smoke that was seen showed what had happened. [21]When they perceived this, they were greatly frightened, and when they also saw the army of Judas drawn up in the plain for battle, [22]they all fled into the land of the Philistines. [23]Then Judas returned to plunder the camp, and they seized a great amount of gold and silver, and cloth dyed blue and sea purple, and great riches. [24]On their return they sang hymns and praises to Heaven— "For he is good, for his mercy endures forever." [25]Thus Israel had a great deliverance that day.

First Campaign of Lysias

26 Those of the foreigners who escaped went and reported to Lysias all that had happened. [27]When he heard it, he was perplexed and discouraged, for things had not happened to Israel as he had intended, nor had they turned out as the king had ordered. [28]But the next year he mustered sixty thousand picked infantry and five thousand cavalry to subdue them. [29]They came into Idumea and encamped at Beth-zur, and Judas met them with ten thousand men.

a Gk they

---

thousand. Whether so many troops would be able to carry out such a journey by night is dubious. As in 3.39, the numbers seem exaggerated. **4.2** The guides from the citadel in Jerusalem most likely included Jews familiar with the terrain. **4.5** Gorgias looked for Judas in the hills. Presumably it never occurred to him that Judas would attack the main camp at Emmaus. **4.8** Following the instruction in Deut 20.3–4, Judas the commander exhorts his troops to disregard the great disparity in numbers (see 3.39; 4.1, 6). See the precedent of Gideon (Judg 7), who triumphed with only three hundred men. **4.9** For Moses' victory at the Red Sea, see Ex 14. **4.10** Covenant, God's promises of the land and descendants (Gen 17) as well as the privilege of serving God according to the Torah (Ex 19)— precisely matters at stake in this rebellion (see 1.11). **4.15** Gazara (Gezer), the closest Seleucid fort in the district (see 7.45; 13.43–48). Azotus, biblical Ashdod. The three thousand slain enemy soldiers matches the

number of Judas's army (see 4.6). **4.18** Judas's military strategy splits Gorgias (v. 1) and a portion of his men off from his main force. **4.20** Burning the camp before seizing its plunder indicates that the battle was over and suggests that Judas had a very large army, thus demoralizing Gorgias and his troops. **4.23** The gold and silver and other plunder had been brought at least in part by the slave traders (see 3.41). **4.24–25** The victory is celebrated by singing Ps 136.1, thus marking God's deliverance of Israel from its enemies (see Judg 15.18; 1 Sam 14.45). **4.26–35** In 164 BCE Lysias tries a different battle approach to Judas and his army, but he too meets defeat. See 2 Macc 11.1–15. **4.26** Lysias was in charge of the western part of Antiochus IV's empire and served as guardian of Antiochus V (see 3.32). **4.28–29** Though exaggerated, the numbers suggest that, although still vastly outnumbered, Judas's army was growing larger (see v. 6). **4.29** Beth-zur, on the southern border of Judea and Idumea. Lysias ap-

30 When he saw that their army was strong, he prayed, saying, "Blessed are you, O Savior of Israel, who crushed the attack of the mighty warrior by the hand of your servant David, and gave the camp of the Philistines into the hands of Jonathan son of Saul, and of the man who carried his armor. 31 Hem in this army by the hand of your people Israel, and let them be ashamed of their troops and their cavalry. 32 Fill them with cowardice; melt the boldness of their strength; let them tremble in their destruction. 33 Strike them down with the sword of those who love you, and let all who know your name praise you with hymns."

34 Then both sides attacked, and there fell of the army of Lysias five thousand men; they fell in action.*a* 35 When Lysias saw the rout of his troops and observed the boldness that inspired those of Judas, and how ready they were either to live or to die nobly, he withdrew to Antioch and enlisted mercenaries in order to invade Judea again with an even larger army.

Cleansing and Dedication of the Temple

36 Then Judas and his brothers said, "See, our enemies are crushed; let us go up to cleanse the sanctuary and dedicate it." 37 So all the army assembled and went up to Mount Zion. 38 There they saw the sanctuary desolate, the altar profaned, and the gates burned. In the courts they saw bushes sprung up as in a thicket, or as on one of the mountains. They saw also the chambers of the priests in ruins. 39 Then they tore their clothes and mourned with great lamentation; they sprinkled themselves with ashes 40 and fell face down on the ground. And when the signal was given with the trumpets, they cried out to Heaven.

41 Then Judas detailed men to fight against those in the citadel until he had cleansed the sanctuary. 42 He chose blameless priests devoted to the law, 43 and they cleansed the sanctuary and removed the defiled stones to an unclean place. 44 They deliberated what to do about the altar of burnt offering, which had been profaned. 45 And they thought it best to tear it down, so that it would not be a lasting shame to them that the Gentiles had defiled it. So they tore down the altar, 46 and stored the stones in a convenient place on the temple hill until a prophet should come to tell what to do with them. 47 Then they took unhewn*b* stones, as the law directs, and built a new altar like the former one. 48 They also rebuilt the sanctuary and the interior of the temple, and consecrated the courts. 49 They made new holy vessels, and brought the lampstand, the altar of incense, and the table into the temple. 50 Then they offered incense on the altar and lit the lamps on the lampstand, and these gave light in the temple. 51 They placed the bread on the table and hung up the curtains. Thus they finished all the work they had undertaken.

52 Early in the morning on the twenty-fifth day of the ninth month, which is the month of Chislev, in the one hundred forty-eighth year,*c* 53 they rose and offered sacrifice, as the law directs, on the new altar of burnt offering that they had built. 54 At the very season and on the very day that the Gentiles had profaned it, it was dedicated with songs and harps and lutes and cymbals. 55 All the people fell on their faces and worshiped and blessed Heaven, who had prospered them. 56 So they celebrated the

a Or *and some fell on the opposite side*   *b* Gk *whole*   *c* 164 B.C.

proached from the south in a "fishhook" strategy to take advantage of the somewhat easier terrain and the political sympathies of the inhabitants. **4.30** In his prayer before battle (Deut 20.3–4) Judas invokes the examples of *David* (1 Sam 17) and *Jonathan* (1 Sam 14). **4.35** For Lysias's second invasion of *Judea*, see 6.28–31. **4.36–61** Having defeated the Seleucid forces, Judas restores the temple furnishings and reinstates the proper religious rituals there. See 2 Macc 10.1–8. **4.36** The immediate goal of the uprising was achieved when the Jews were able to *dedicate* the new altar in the temple. The term Hanukkah derives from the Hebrew word for "dedicate." In 2 Maccabees the theme of purification is stressed. **4.37** *Mount Zion*, the temple area. **4.38–40** Why the temple area was in such disrepair is not clear. Was the Seleucid "reform" a total failure? Is this merely the writer's judgment on it? Did Judas

delay in restoring the temple? **4.41** The *citadel* overlooking the temple area (1.33) was still under enemy control. **4.42–43** The *blameless priests* remained ritually pure (Lev 21.17–23) and did not participate in programs established under Antiochus IV (2 Macc 4.14–15). The *defiled stones* were associated with the desolating sacrilege (1.54). **4.44–46** Rather than destroy the defiled *altar of burnt offering,* Judas proposed waiting for illumination about it from a future *prophet* (see 14.41; Deut 18.15; Mal 4.5). **4.47–51** For building the altar with *unhewn stones,* see Ex 20.25; Deut 27.5–6. The temple furnishings, plundered by Antiochus IV (1.21–24), are restored in accord with Ex 25–27. **4.52–55** Proper temple worship was resumed on 14 December 164 BCE. See 2 Chr 7.1–10 for the dedication of the First Temple. **4.56** The Feast of Dedication (Hanukkah) lasted *eight days,* after the pattern of the Festival

dedication of the altar for eight days, and joyfully offered burnt offerings; they offered a sacrifice of well-being and a thanksgiving offering. 57 They decorated the front of the temple with golden crowns and small shields; they restored the gates and the chambers for the priests, and fitted them with doors. 58 There was very great joy among the people, and the disgrace brought by the Gentiles was removed.

59 Then Judas and his brothers and all the assembly of Israel determined that every year at that season the days of dedication of the altar should be observed with joy and gladness for eight days, beginning with the twenty-fifth day of the month of Chislev.

60 At that time they fortified Mount Zion with high walls and strong towers all around, to keep the Gentiles from coming and trampling them down as they had done before. 61 Judas[a] stationed a garrison there to guard it; he also fortified Beth-zur to guard it, so that the people might have a stronghold that faced Idumea.

Wars with Neighboring Peoples

5 When the Gentiles all around heard that the altar had been rebuilt and the sanctuary dedicated as it was before, they became very angry, 2 and they determined to destroy the descendants of Jacob who lived among them. So they began to kill and destroy among the people. 3 But Judas made war on the descendants of Esau in Idumea, at Akrabattene, because they kept lying in wait for Israel. He dealt them a heavy blow and humbled them and despoiled them. 4 He also remembered the wickedness of the sons of Baean, who were a trap and a snare to the people and ambushed them on the highways. 5 They were shut up by

him in their[b] towers; and he encamped against them, vowed their complete destruction, and burned with fire their towers and all who were in them. 6 Then he crossed over to attack the Ammonites, where he found a strong band and many people, with Timothy as their leader. 7 He engaged in many battles with them, and they were crushed before him; he struck them down. 8 He also took Jazer and its villages; then he returned to Judea.

Liberation of Galilean Jews

9 Now the Gentiles in Gilead gathered together against the Israelites who lived in their territory, and planned to destroy them. But they fled to the stronghold of Dathema, 10 and sent to Judas and his brothers a letter that said, "The Gentiles around us have gathered together to destroy us. 11 They are preparing to come and capture the stronghold to which we have fled, and Timothy is leading their forces. 12 Now then, come and rescue us from their hands, for many of us have fallen, 13 and all our kindred who were in the land of Tob have been killed; the enemy[c] have captured their wives and children and goods, and have destroyed about a thousand persons there."

14 While the letter was still being read, other messengers, with their garments torn, came from Galilee and made a similar report; 15 they said that the people of Ptolemais and Tyre and Sidon, and all Galilee of the Gentiles,[d] had gathered together against them "to annihilate us." 16 When Judas and the people heard these messages, a great assembly was called to determine what they should do for their kindred who were in distress and were being attacked by enemies.[e] 17 Then Judas said

---

a Gk He b Gk her c Gk they d Gk aliens e Gk them

---

of Booths (Tabernacles; see Lev 23.33–36; 2 Macc 1.9, 18) and earlier consecrations of the temple by Solomon (1 Kings 8) and Hezekiah (2 Chr 29). **4.60–61** Mount Zion, the temple area, was fortified against attacks from the citadel, and Beth-zur against approaches from the south (as in v. 29).

5.1–8 To secure the safety of other Jews sympathetic to the Maccabees, Judas and his brothers wage battles against allies of the Seleucids and other enemies (with David as their model; 2 Sam 8; 10). See 2 Macc 8.30–33; 10.14–17. **5.2** Descendants of Jacob, Jews living outside the area controlled by Judas. The Maccabees' success angered their non-Jewish neighbors. **5.3** Akrabattene, possibly the ascent of Akrabbim (Num 34.4), southwest of the Dead Sea, or (more likely) a place on

the eastern boundary of Judea and Samaria. **5.4** Sons of Baean, nomads who attacked caravans (see 2 Macc 10.14). **5.6** Timothy, possibly the local ruler of the Ammonites in Transjordan or the Syrian commander (2 Macc 8.30–33). **5.8** Jazer (Num 21.32), near Heshbon in Transjordan. **5.9–23** In response to pleas from Jews in Gilead and western Galilee, Judas sends Simon to Galilee and goes with Jonathan to Gilead. **5.9** Gilead, the territory east of the Jordan (Josh 22.9). Dathema. Location uncertain aside from the fact that it was a night's journey from Bozrah (5.29). **5.13** Land of Tob (Judg 11.3–5), modern et-Taiyibeh, twelve miles east and slightly north of Ramoth-gilead, across the Jordan. **5.15** All Galilee of the Gentiles (see Isa 9.1), the seacoast towns south of Ptolemais, Tyre, and Sidon.

to his brother Simon, "Choose your men and go and rescue your kindred in Galilee; Jonathan my brother and I will go to Gilead." [18]But he left Joseph, son of Zechariah, and Azariah, a leader of the people, with the rest of the forces, in Judea to guard it; [19]and he gave them this command, "Take charge of this people, but do not engage in battle with the Gentiles until we return." [20]Then three thousand men were assigned to Simon to go to Galilee, and eight thousand to Judas for Gilead.

21 So Simon went to Galilee and fought many battles against the Gentiles, and the Gentiles were crushed before him. [22]He pursued them to the gate of Ptolemais; as many as three thousand of the Gentiles fell, and he despoiled them. [23]Then he took the Jews[a] of Galilee and Arbatta, with their wives and children, and all they possessed, and led them to Judea with great rejoicing.

Judas and Jonathan in Gilead

24 Judas Maccabeus and his brother Jonathan crossed the Jordan and made three days' journey into the wilderness. [25]They encountered the Nabateans, who met them peaceably and told them all that had happened to their kindred in Gilead: [26]"Many of them have been shut up in Bozrah and Bosor, in Alema and Chaspho, Maked and Carnaim"—all these towns were strong and large— [27]"and some have been shut up in the other towns of Gilead; the enemy[b] are getting ready to attack the strongholds tomorrow and capture and destroy all these people in a single day."

28 Then Judas and his army quickly turned back by the wilderness road to Bozrah; and he took the town, and killed every male by the edge of the sword; then he seized all its spoils and burned it with fire. [29]He left the place at night, and they went all the way to the stronghold of Dathema.[c] [30]At dawn they looked out and saw a large company, which could not be counted, carrying ladders and engines of war to capture the stronghold, and attacking the Jews within.[d] [31]So Judas saw that the battle had begun and that the cry of the town went up to Heaven, with trumpets and loud shouts, [32]and he said to the men of his forces, "Fight today for your kindred!" [33]Then he came up behind them in three companies, who sounded their trumpets and cried aloud in prayer. [34]And when the army of Timothy realized that it was Maccabeus, they fled before him, and he dealt them a heavy blow. As many as eight thousand of them fell that day.

35 Next he turned aside to Maapha,[e] and fought against it and took it; and he killed every male in it, plundered it, and burned it with fire. [36]From there he marched on and took Chaspho, Maked, and Bosor, and the other towns of Gilead.

37 After these things Timothy gathered another army and encamped opposite Raphon, on the other side of the stream. [38]Judas sent men to spy out the camp, and they reported to him, "All the Gentiles around us have gathered to him; it is a very large force. [39]They also have hired Arabs to help them, and they are encamped across the stream, ready to come and fight against you." And Judas went to meet them.

40 Now as Judas and his army drew near to the stream of water, Timothy said to the officers of his forces, "If he crosses over to us first, we will not be able to resist him, for he will surely defeat us. [41]But if he shows fear and camps on the other side of the river, we will cross over to him and defeat him." [42]When

---

a Gk *those*   *b* Gk *they*   *c* Gk lacks *of Dathema*. See verse 9
d Gk *and they were attacking them*   *e* Other ancient authorities read *Alema*

5.18–19 For the results of the failure of *Joseph* and *Azariah* to obey, see 5.55–62. 5.22–23 *Ptolemais*, named after Ptolemy II of Egypt, who restored it; also known as Acco and Acre. *Arbatta* (or Narbatta), probably south of Mount Carmel. 5.24–44 Relying on information from the Nabateans, Judas and Jonathan rescue Jews under siege in Gilead and defeat Timothy decisively near Raphon. See 2 Macc 12.1–25. 5.25 *Nabateans*, caravan traders whose center was in southern Transjordan. Here and in 9.35 they appear friendly toward Judas and Jonathan. They may have shared the Jews' desire for independence from the Seleucids. 5.26 *Bozrah* (seventy miles south of Damascus) . . . *and Carnaim*, all cities east and north of the Yarmuk River in Transjordan. Their non-Jewish inhabitants probably identified with the Seleucids and thus opposed the Jews because of their recent victories over them. 5.29 That Jews had a *stronghold* or fortress at *Dathema* (see v. 9) or elsewhere (see v. 27) may exaggerate the actual situation. 5.30–32 The description of the siege echoes various biblical texts (1 Sam 4.5–6; 5.12; Jer 4.19; Ezek 4.23; 21.22; Joel 2.1). 5.35 *Maapha*, possibly Mizpah of Gilead (Judg 11.29). 5.37 *Timothy*, possibly not the same person as in vv. 6–8. 5.39 The Seleucids used *Arabs* as mercenaries (see 2 Macc 12.10). 5.40–43 Rather than looking for an omen or heavenly sign, Timothy sought to discover whether Judas's troops were sufficiently few for him to take the initiative in

Judas approached the stream of water, he stationed the officers[a] of the army at the stream and gave them this command, "Permit no one to encamp, but make them all enter the battle." [43] Then he crossed over against them first, and the whole army followed him. All the Gentiles were defeated before him, and they threw away their arms and fled into the sacred precincts at Carnaim. [44] But he took the town and burned the sacred precincts with fire, together with all who were in them. Thus Carnaim was conquered; they could stand before Judas no longer.

The Return to Jerusalem

[45] Then Judas gathered together all the Israelites in Gilead, the small and the great, with their wives and children and goods, a very large company, to go to the land of Judah. [46] So they came to Ephron. This was a large and very strong town on the road, and they could not go around it to the right or to the left; they had to go through it. [47] But the people of the town shut them out and blocked up the gates with stones.

[48] Judas sent them this friendly message, "Let us pass through your land to get to our land. No one will do you harm; we will simply pass by on foot." But they refused to open to him. [49] Then Judas ordered proclamation to be made to the army that all should encamp where they were. [50] So the men of the forces encamped, and he fought against the town all that day and all the night, and the town was delivered into his hands. [51] He destroyed every male by the edge of the sword, and razed and plundered the town. Then he passed through the town over the bodies of the dead.

[52] Then they crossed the Jordan into the large plain before Beth-shan. [53] Judas kept rallying the laggards and encouraging the people

all the way until he came to the land of Judah. [54] So they went up to Mount Zion with joy and gladness, and offered burnt offerings, because they had returned in safety; not one of them had fallen.

Joseph and Azariah Defeated

[55] Now while Judas and Jonathan were in Gilead and their[b] brother Simon was in Galilee before Ptolemais, [56] Joseph son of Zechariah, and Azariah, the commanders of the forces, heard of their brave deeds and of the heroic war they had fought. [57] So they said, "Let us also make a name for ourselves; let us go and make war on the Gentiles around us." [58] So they issued orders to the men of the forces that were with them and marched against Jamnia. [59] Gorgias and his men came out of the town to meet them in battle. [60] Then Joseph and Azariah were routed, and were pursued to the borders of Judea; as many as two thousand of the people of Israel fell that day. [61] Thus the people suffered a great rout because, thinking to do a brave deed, they did not listen to Judas and his brothers. [62] But they did not belong to the family of those men through whom deliverance was given to Israel.

[63] The man Judas and his brothers were greatly honored in all Israel and among all the Gentiles, wherever their name was heard. [64] People gathered to them and praised them.

Success at Hebron and Philistia

[65] Then Judas and his brothers went out and fought the descendants of Esau in the land to the south. He struck Hebron and its villages and tore down its strongholds and burned its towers on all sides. [66] Then he marched off to go into the land of the Philistines, and passed

---

a Or scribes b Gk his

5.43 *Carnaim,* which means "horns," suggests that the goddess Astarte, who was often represented with cow's horns, was worshiped there (cf. 2 Macc 12.21, 26). Timothy fled there in hope of protection from the pagan goddess or of asylum. 5.44 When Judas *took the town,* he did not respect the sanctity of the pagan shrine at Carnaim. 5.45–54 The Israelites in Gilead are brought to Judea and the Jerusalem temple by way of Ephron and Beth-shan. See 2 Macc 12.26–31. 5.46–51 *Ephron,* nine miles east of Jordan, opposite Beth-shan. Judas treats it in accord with Deut 20.10–15. 5.52 *Beth-shan,* also known as Scythopolis ("city of Scythians") and Nysa, was west of the Jordan.

5.54 According to 2 Macc 12.31–32 they arrived at *Mount Zion* in time to celebrate the Festival of Weeks/Pentecost. 5.55–64 The rout suffered by the two left in charge of Judea (5.18–19) is blamed on their failure to follow Judas's command (v. 61). See 2 Macc 12.32–35. 5.58–59 *Jamnia* (Yavneh), the capital of the province of Azotus (Ashdod) and a seat of opposition to the Jews (2 Macc 12.8–9). *Gorgias,* possibly not the same person as in 3.38; 4.1. 5.65–68 The account of Jewish victories closes with battles against Idumea (to the south) and Philistia (to the west). See 2 Macc 12.36–45. 5.65–66 The ancient names *Esau* and *Philistines* contribute to the portrayal of Judas as

through Marisa.[a] 67On that day some priests, who wished to do a brave deed, fell in battle, for they went out to battle unwisely. 68But Judas turned aside to Azotus in the land of the Philistines; he tore down their altars, and the carved images of their gods he burned with fire; he plundered the towns and returned to the land of Judah.

The Last Days of Antiochus Epiphanes

6 King Antiochus was going through the upper provinces when he heard that Elymais in Persia was a city famed for its wealth in silver and gold. 2Its temple was very rich, containing golden shields, breastplates, and weapons left there by Alexander son of Philip, the Macedonian king who first reigned over the Greeks. 3So he came and tried to take the city and plunder it, but he could not because his plan had become known to the citizens 4and they withstood him in battle. So he fled and in great disappointment left there to return to Babylon.

5 Then someone came to him in Persia and reported that the armies that had gone into the land of Judah had been routed; 6that Lysias had gone first with a strong force, but had turned and fled before the Jews;[b] that the Jews[c] had grown strong from the arms, supplies, and abundant spoils that they had taken from the armies they had cut down; 7that they had torn down the abomination that he had erected on the altar in Jerusalem; and that they had surrounded the sanctuary with high walls as before, and also Beth-zur, his town.

8 When the king heard this news, he was astounded and badly shaken. He took to his bed and became sick from disappointment, because things had not turned out for him as he had planned. 9He lay there for many days, because deep disappointment continually gripped him, and he realized that he was dying. 10So he called all his Friends and said to them, "Sleep has departed from my eyes and I am downhearted with worry. 11I said to myself, 'To what distress I have come! And into what a great flood I now am plunged! For I was kind and beloved in my power.' 12But now I remember the wrong I did in Jerusalem. I seized all its vessels of silver and gold, and I sent to destroy the inhabitants of Judah without good reason. 13I know that it is because of this that these misfortunes have come upon me; here I am, perishing of bitter disappointment in a strange land."

14 Then he called for Philip, one of his Friends, and made him ruler over all his kingdom. 15He gave him the crown and his robe and the signet, so that he might guide his son Antiochus and bring him up to be king. 16Thus King Antiochus died there in the one hundred forty-ninth year.[d] 17When Lysias learned that the king was dead, he set up Antiochus the king's[e] son to reign. Lysias[f] had brought him up from boyhood; he named him Eupator.

Renewed Attacks from Syria

18 Meanwhile the garrison in the citadel kept hemming Israel in around the sanctuary. They were trying in every way to harm them and strengthen the Gentiles. 19Judas therefore resolved to destroy them, and assembled all the people to besiege them. 20They gathered together and besieged the citadel[g] in the one hundred fiftieth year;[h] and he built siege tow-

---

a Other ancient authorities read Samaria　b Gk them　c Gk they
d 163 B.C.　e Gk his　f Gk He　g Gk it　h 162 B.C.

---

the ideal biblical warrior. **5.67** The *priests who ... fell in battle* failed to follow Judas's command (as in vv. 56–62); 2 Macc 12.32–45 may be another version of this episode. **5.68** *Azotus* (Ashdod), possibly the province, not just the city.

6.1–17 For other reports of Antiochus IV's death, cf. 2 Macc 1.13–17; 9.1–29; Dan 11.40–45. Antiochus died in late 164 BCE while plundering a pagan temple. The Jews interpreted his death as punishment for his outrages against them and their temple. **6.1** *Elymais* (Elam), the mountainous country west of Persia. *City,* possibly Persepolis. **6.5–7** To the report of the defeat of *Lysias* (3.32–4.35) is added a summary of events in 4.36–61 that occurred after the death of Antiochus IV. **6.10** *Friends,* the king's advisers, the lowest rank of nobility in the Seleucid aristocracy. **6.11–13** Antiochus

IV's description of himself as *kind and beloved* is affirmed by the name Eupator ("of a good father") given his son in v. 17. But 1 Maccabees looks at him mainly with regard to the effects of his policies on the Jews and presents him as cruel and hated. **6.14** *Philip* receives the same appointment Lysias had (3.32–33), and so the two become rivals. **6.16** *Antiochus* died in October or November 164 BCE, but news of his death may not have reached Jerusalem before the dedication of the temple in December (4.36–61). **6.18–31** Judas's attempt to seize the citadel in Jerusalem leads to renewed complaints against him and a new and massive Seleucid expedition. **6.18** The Seleucid *garrison in the citadel* (see 1.33–34; 4.41; 9.52; 10.6–9; 11.41; 14.36) continued harassment of Judas's people. Some were Jews (vv. 18, 21). **6.19–20** Judas took the confusion

ers and other engines of war. 21But some of the garrison escaped from the siege and some of the ungodly Israelites joined them. 22They went to the king and said, "How long will you fail to do justice and to avenge our kindred? 23We were happy to serve your father, to live by what he said, and to follow his commands. 24For this reason the sons of our people besieged the citadel*a* and became hostile to us; moreover, they have put to death as many of us as they have caught, and they have seized our inheritances. 25It is not against us alone that they have stretched out their hands; they have also attacked all the lands on their borders. 26And see, today they have encamped against the citadel in Jerusalem to take it; they have fortified both the sanctuary and Beth-zur; 27unless you quickly prevent them, they will do still greater things, and you will not be able to stop them."

28 The king was enraged when he heard this. He assembled all his Friends, the commanders of his forces and those in authority.*b* 29Mercenary forces also came to him from other kingdoms and from islands of the seas. 30The number of his forces was one hundred thousand foot soldiers, twenty thousand horsemen, and thirty-two elephants accustomed to war. 31They came through Idumea and encamped against Beth-zur, and for many days they fought and built engines of war; but the Jews*c* sallied out and burned these with fire, and fought courageously.

The Battle at Beth-zechariah

32 Then Judas marched away from the citadel and encamped at Beth-zechariah, opposite the camp of the king. 33Early in the morning the king set out and took his army by a forced march along the road to Beth-zechariah, and his troops made ready for battle and sounded their trumpets. 34They offered the elephants the juice of grapes and mulberries, to arouse them for battle. 35They distributed the animals among the phalanxes; with each elephant they stationed a thousand men armed with coats of mail, and with brass helmets on their heads; and five hundred picked horsemen were assigned to each beast. 36These took their position beforehand wherever the animal was; wherever it went, they went with it, and they never left it. 37On the elephants*d* were wooden towers, strong and covered; they were fastened on each animal by special harness, and on each were four*e* armed men who fought from there, and also its Indian driver. 38The rest of the cavalry were stationed on either side, on the two flanks of the army, to harass the enemy while being themselves protected by the phalanxes. 39When the sun shone on the shields of gold and brass, the hills were ablaze with them and gleamed like flaming torches.

40 Now a part of the king's army was spread out on the high hills, and some troops were on the plain, and they advanced steadily and in good order. 41All who heard the noise made by their multitude, by the marching of the multitude and the clanking of their arms, trembled, for the army was very large and strong. 42But Judas and his army advanced to the battle, and six hundred of the king's army fell. 43Now Eleazar, called Avaran, saw that one of the animals was equipped with royal armor. It was

---

a Meaning of Gk uncertain *b* Gk those over the reins
c Gk they *d* Gk them *e* Cn: Some authorities read thirty; others thirty-two

---

surrounding the death of Antiochus IV as the occasion for attacking the citadel. **6.21-27** The complaint of the *ungodly Israelites* (led by the high priest Menelaus according to 2 Macc 13.3) was that, despite their cooperation and support for the program of Antiochus IV, they were being abandoned in the face of Judas's growing power. **6.22** The *king*, Antiochus V Eupator, was only about eleven or twelve years old. Lysias was making policy, though the young king was probably involved in the events. **6.28-31** The size (probably exaggerated) of the Seleucid force indicates how seriously Judas was now taken. As in 4.29 the Seleucid army approached from the south, through *Idumea*. Beth-zur, which figured in the first battle with Lysias (4.29-35), had been fortified by Judas (4.61) as the southern outpost against attacks. **6.32-47** Perhaps based on an eyewitness account, this report is a remarkably vivid and generally accurate description of an ancient battle. That Judas was defeated is played down; the emphasis is on the superior numbers of the Seleucids and the bravery of Eleazar. See 2 Macc 13.18-20. **6.32** *Beth-zechariah*, south of Jerusalem and six miles north of Beth-zur, was chosen because its topography could be used to stop the enemy's advances. Apparently Beth-zur (v. 31) had already fallen (see vv. 49-50). **6.34-37** The *elephants* (the ancient equivalent of tanks) served as a rallying point for the Seleucid formations. That there were *thirty-two* elephants (v. 30) is unlikely. That number appears again in the Greek in v. 37; the conjecture *four* is more reasonable. **6.40-41** As the Seleucid army proceeds, some troops are dispatched to secure the *high hills*. **6.43-47** That the boy-king Antiochus V would have been riding on an elephant in battle is unlikely. *Eleazar* (2.5) may have wanted to

taller than all the others, and he supposed that the king was on it. [44]So he gave his life to save his people and to win for himself an everlasting name. [45]He courageously ran into the midst of the phalanx to reach it; he killed men right and left, and they parted before him on both sides. [46]He got under the elephant, stabbed it from beneath, and killed it; but it fell to the ground upon him and he died. [47]When the Jews[a] saw the royal might and the fierce attack of the forces, they turned away in flight.

The Siege of the Temple

48 The soldiers of the king's army went up to Jerusalem against them, and the king encamped in Judea and at Mount Zion. [49]He made peace with the people of Beth-zur, and they evacuated the town because they had no provisions there to withstand a siege, since it was a sabbatical year for the land. [50]So the king took Beth-zur and stationed a guard there to hold it. [51]Then he encamped before the sanctuary for many days. He set up siege towers, engines of war to throw fire and stones, machines to shoot arrows, and catapults. [52]The Jews[a] also made engines of war to match theirs, and fought for many days. [53]But they had no food in storage,[b] because it was the seventh year; those who had found safety in Judea from the Gentiles had consumed the last of the stores. [54]Only a few men were left in the sanctuary; the rest scattered to their own homes, for the famine proved too much for them.

Syria Offers Terms

55 Then Lysias heard that Philip, whom King Antiochus while still living had appointed to bring up his son Antiochus to be king, [56]had returned from Persia and Media with the forces that had gone with the king, and that he was trying to seize control of the government. [57]So he quickly gave orders to withdraw, and said to the king, to the commanders of the forces, and to the troops, "Daily we grow weaker, our food supply is scant, the place against which we are fighting is strong, and the affairs of the kingdom press urgently on us. [58]Now then let us come to terms with these people, and make peace with them and with all their nation. [59]Let us agree to let them live by their laws as they did before; for it was on account of their laws that we abolished that they became angry and did all these things."

60 The speech pleased the king and the commanders, and he sent to the Jews[c] an offer of peace, and they accepted it. [61]So the king and the commanders gave them their oath. On these conditions the Jews[a] evacuated the stronghold. [62]But when the king entered Mount Zion and saw what a strong fortress the place was, he broke the oath he had sworn and gave orders to tear down the wall all around. [63]Then he set off in haste and returned to Antioch. He found Philip in control of the city, but he fought against him, and took the city by force.

Expedition of Bacchides and Alcimus

7 In the one hundred fifty-first year[d] Demetrius son of Seleucus set out from Rome, sailed with a few men to a town by the sea, and there began to reign. [2]As he was entering the royal palace of his ancestors, the army seized Antiochus and Lysias to bring them to him. [3]But when this act became known to him,

a Gk they   b Other ancient authorities read in the sanctuary
c Gk them   d 161 B.C.

---

demonstrate that the elephants could be stopped. If so, his action had the opposite effect (6.47). **6.48–54** With the defeat at Beth-zechariah, the surrender of Beth-zur, the Temple Mount under siege, and low food supplies, the Maccabean movement is close to complete defeat. **6.48** The symbolic value of the Temple Mount (*Mount Zion;* see 4.36–61) explains both the Seleucid strategy and the Jewish resistance. **6.49** In a *sabbatical year* the land was not worked (Ex 23.11; Lev 25.3–7). The real food shortage would occur after the sabbatical year (see v. 53), since no store of food would be left. **6.55–63** Because Lysias has to return to Antioch to prevent Philip from taking control (see vv. 14–15), he makes a quick settlement with Judas. See 2 Macc 13.23–26. **6.57** The scant *food supply* caused by the sabbatical year (vv. 49,

53) threatened the Seleucid army too. **6.59** By agreeing to let the Jews *live by their laws as they did before* (i.e., by the Torah) Lysias effectively cancelled the decree of Antiochus IV (1.41–50). **6.61–62** The Temple Mount (Mount Zion), held by Judas's troops and fortified by a wall (4.60), functioned as a *stronghold.* The citadel remained in enemy hands.

7.1–25 After removing Antiochus V and Lysias, Demetrius I seeks to stabilize affairs in Judea by sending Bacchides' army there and by making Alcimus both high priest and political ruler. **7.1** *Demetrius I Soter, son of Seleucus* IV, escaped from being held hostage at Rome with the help of Polybius the historian and landed at Tripolis (*a town by the sea*) in 161 BCE. See 2 Macc 14.1–2. **7.2** The *royal palace* was in An-

he said, "Do not let me see their faces!" [4]So the army killed them, and Demetrius took his seat on the throne of his kingdom.

5 Then there came to him all the renegade and godless men of Israel; they were led by Alcimus, who wanted to be high priest. [6]They brought to the king this accusation against the people: "Judas and his brothers have destroyed all your Friends, and have driven us out of our land. [7]Now then send a man whom you trust; let him go and see all the ruin that Judas[a] has brought on us and on the land of the king, and let him punish them and all who help them."

8 So the king chose Bacchides, one of the king's Friends, governor of the province Beyond the River; he was a great man in the kingdom and was faithful to the king. [9]He sent him, and with him he sent the ungodly Alcimus, whom he made high priest; and he commanded him to take vengeance on the Israelites. [10]So they marched away and came with a large force into the land of Judah; and he sent messengers to Judas and his brothers with peaceable but treacherous words. [11]But they paid no attention to their words, for they saw that they had come with a large force.

12 Then a group of scribes appeared in a body before Alcimus and Bacchides to ask for just terms. [13]The Hasideans were first among the Israelites to seek peace from them, [14]for they said, "A priest of the line of Aaron has come with the army, and he will not harm us." [15]Alcimus[b] spoke peaceable words to them and swore this oath to them, "We will not seek to injure you or your friends." [16]So they trusted him; but he seized sixty of them and killed them in one day, in accordance with the word that was written,
[17]   "The flesh of your faithful ones and their blood

they poured out all around Jerusalem, and there was no one to bury them."
[18]Then the fear and dread of them fell on all the people, for they said, "There is no truth or justice in them, for they have violated the agreement and the oath that they swore."

19 Then Bacchides withdrew from Jerusalem and encamped in Beth-zaith. And he sent and seized many of the men who had deserted to him,[c] and some of the people, and killed them and threw them into a great pit. [20]He placed Alcimus in charge of the country and left with him a force to help him; then Bacchides went back to the king.

21 Alcimus struggled to maintain his high priesthood, [22]and all who were troubling their people joined him. They gained control of the land of Judah and did great damage in Israel. [23]And Judas saw all the wrongs that Alcimus and those with him had done among the Israelites; it was more than the Gentiles had done. [24]So Judas[a] went out into all the surrounding parts of Judea, taking vengeance on those who had deserted and preventing those in the city[d] from going out into the country. [25]When Alcimus saw that Judas and those with him had grown strong, and realized that he could not withstand them, he returned to the king and brought malicious charges against them.

Nicanor in Judea

26 Then the king sent Nicanor, one of his honored princes, who hated and detested Israel, and he commanded him to destroy the people. [27]So Nicanor came to Jerusalem with a large force, and treacherously sent to Judas

---

a Gk he   b Gk He   c Or many of his men who had deserted
d Gk and they were prevented

---

tioch, about 170 miles north of Tripolis. **7.5** *Alcimus* (*Yakim* in Hebrew), from a priestly family (7.14; 1 Chr 24.12), may have already been appointed as high priest under Antiochus V. He represented an Israelite faction favorable to the Seleucids (see 1.11–15; 2 Macc 14.3–4). **7.8** Since Demetrius I was busy putting down the rebellion of Timarchus in the east, he appointed *Bacchides* (governor of *Beyond the River* province—between the Euphrates and Egypt) to subdue Judea. **7.12–15** Deceived by peaceable words from Bacchides (v. 10) and Alcimus (v. 15) and impressed by the priestly lineage of Alcimus, the *Hasideans* (see 2.42) deserted the cause of Judas. **7.16–18** Why Alcimus had *sixty* Hasideans killed is not stated; perhaps it was because of their past opposition to the pro-Seleucid faction (2.42). The fate of these Hasideans is said to fulfill

Ps 79.2–3. **7.19** *Beth-zaith,* between Jerusalem and Beth-zur. *Pit,* probably a large cistern no longer used for saving water (see Jer 41.7). **7.20** Bacchides' plan in subduing Judea was to establish the high priest Alcimus as head of state (*in charge of the country*) as previous high priests (Onias, Jason, Menelaus) had been. **7.24** Judas was still strong enough to carry out guerilla warfare and thus prevent Alcimus from taking full control of Judea. **7.26–32** Sent to strengthen Alcimus and his party, Nicanor uses diplomatic and military strategies against Judas. See 2 Macc 14.11–36 for a different perspective on Nicanor. **7.26** *Nicanor,* possibly not the same Nicanor who helped Demetrius flee from Rome (see Josephus, *Antiquities* 12.402) or was part of the Emmaus campaign (3.38). **7.27** Whereas in 1 Maccabees Nicanor acts *treacherously* throughout, in

and his brothers this peaceable message, [28]"Let there be no fighting between you and me; I shall come with a few men to see you face to face in peace."

29 So he came to Judas, and they greeted one another peaceably; but the enemy were preparing to kidnap Judas. [30]It became known to Judas that Nicanor[a] had come to him with treacherous intent, and he was afraid of him and would not meet him again. [31]When Nicanor learned that his plan had been disclosed, he went out to meet Judas in battle near Caphar-salama. [32]About five hundred of the army of Nicanor fell, and the rest[b] fled into the city of David.

Nicanor Threatens the Temple

33 After these events Nicanor went up to Mount Zion. Some of the priests from the sanctuary and some of the elders of the people came out to greet him peaceably and to show him the burnt offering that was being offered for the king. [34]But he mocked them and derided them and defiled them and spoke arrogantly, [35]and in anger he swore this oath, "Unless Judas and his army are delivered into my hands this time, then if I return safely I will burn up this house." And he went out in great anger. [36]At this the priests went in and stood before the altar and the temple; they wept and said,

[37]   "You chose this house to be called by
      your name,
  and to be for your people a house of
      prayer and supplication.
[38] Take vengeance on this man and on his
      army,
  and let them fall by the sword;

remember their blasphemies,
  and let them live no longer."

The Death of Nicanor

39 Now Nicanor went out from Jerusalem and encamped in Beth-horon, and the Syrian army joined him. [40]Judas encamped in Adasa with three thousand men. Then Judas prayed and said, [41]"When the messengers from the king spoke blasphemy, your angel went out and struck down one hundred eighty-five thousand of the Assyrians.[c] [42]So also crush this army before us today; let the rest learn that Nicanor[a] has spoken wickedly against the sanctuary, and judge him according to this wickedness."

43 So the armies met in battle on the thirteenth day of the month of Adar. The army of Nicanor was crushed, and he himself was the first to fall in the battle. [44]When his army saw that Nicanor had fallen, they threw down their arms and fled. [45]The Jews[b] pursued them a day's journey, from Adasa as far as Gazara, and as they followed they kept sounding the battle call on the trumpets. [46]People came out of all the surrounding villages of Judea, and they outflanked the enemy[d] and drove them back to their pursuers,[e] so that they all fell by the sword; not even one of them was left. [47]Then the Jews[b] seized the spoils and the plunder; they cut off Nicanor's head and the right hand that he had so arrogantly stretched out, and brought them and displayed them just outside Jerusalem. [48]The people rejoiced greatly and celebrated that day as a day of great gladness. [49]They decreed that this day should be cele-

a Gk he   b Gk they   c Gk of them   d Gk them   e Gk these

---

2 Macc 14.18–25 he at first seems to develop a genuine friendship with Judas and tries to mediate between the Jewish factions. **7.31** *Caphar-salama.* Exact location unknown, but likely to the north of Jerusalem. **7.32** *City of David,* presumably the Seleucid-held citadel (Akra) in Jerusalem. **7.33–38** Nicanor's threat to destroy the temple unless Judas is handed over seems to have come more from frustration than from political realism. **7.33** The temple priests, probably loyal to Alcimus and the Seleucids, offered sacrifices and prayers on behalf of the Seleucid *king* (see Ezra 6.10). **7.34** *Defiled* them, perhaps spat on them, thus making them temporarily unfit for service. **7.37–38** The prayer echoes that of Solomon in 1 Kings 8 (see vv. 29–30, 33–34, 43). **7.39–50** Nicanor's threat against the temple ends in his defeat by Judas and the dismemberment of his body. See 2 Macc 15.1–37.

7.39–40 For an earlier battle near *Beth-horon,* see 3.13–26. *Adasa,* between Jerusalem and Beth-horon, though its exact location is uncertain. **7.41** The allusion to the expedition of Sennacherib in 701 BCE (2 Kings 19.35; Isa 37.36) suggests that Judas was vastly outnumbered. See also 2 Macc 8.19; 15.22. **7.42** Nicanor's threat *against the sanctuary* (vv. 33–35) became the rallying cry for Judas's supporters. **7.43–44** When the armies met in March (*Adar*) 161 or 160 BCE, Judas's strategy was to kill the commander Nicanor and so cause his troops to panic. **7.45** *Gazara* (Gezer), the closest Seleucid fort to the west. **7.47** Cutting off the *head and the right hand* was originally a Persian punishment. Here it is traced to Nicanor's threat against the Jerusalem temple. **7.49** *The thirteenth day of Adar,* celebrated as "Nicanor's Day" in the first century CE but later dropped from the Jewish cal-

brated each year on the thirteenth day of Adar. ⁵⁰So the land of Judah had rest for a few days.

A Eulogy of the Romans

8 Now Judas heard of the fame of the Romans, that they were very strong and were well-disposed toward all who made an alliance with them, that they pledged friendship to those who came to them, ²and that they were very strong. He had been told of their wars and of the brave deeds that they were doing among the Gauls, how they had defeated them and forced them to pay tribute, ³and what they had done in the land of Spain to get control of the silver and gold mines there, ⁴and how they had gained control of the whole region by their planning and patience, even though the place was far distant from them. They also subdued the kings who came against them from the ends of the earth, until they crushed them and inflicted great disaster on them; the rest paid them tribute every year. ⁵They had crushed in battle and conquered Philip, and King Perseus of the Macedonians,ᵃ and the others who rose up against them. ⁶They also had defeated Antiochus the Great, king of Asia, who went to fight against them with one hundred twenty elephants and with cavalry and chariots and a very large army. He was crushed by them; ⁷they took him alive and decreed that he and those who would reign after him should pay a heavy tribute and give hostages and surrender some of their best provinces, ⁸the countries of India, Media, and Lydia. These they took from him and gave to King Eumenes. ⁹The Greeks planned to come and destroy them, ¹⁰but this became known to them, and they sent a general against the Greeksᵇ and attacked them. Many of them were wounded and fell, and the Romansᶜ took captive their wives and children; they plundered them, conquered the land, tore down their strongholds, and enslaved them to this day. ¹¹The remaining kingdoms and islands, as many as ever opposed them, they destroyed and enslaved; ¹²but with their friends and those who rely on them they have kept friendship. They have subdued kings far and near, and as many as have heard of their fame have feared them. ¹³Those whom they wish to help and to make kings, they make kings, and those whom they wish they depose; and they have been greatly exalted. ¹⁴Yet for all this not one of them has put on a crown or worn purple as a mark of pride, ¹⁵but they have built for themselves a senate chamber, and every day three hundred twenty senators constantly deliberate concerning the people, to govern them well. ¹⁶They trust one man each year to rule over them and to control all their land; they all heed the one man, and there is no envy or jealousy among them.

An Alliance with Rome

17 So Judas chose Eupolemus son of John son of Accos, and Jason son of Eleazar, and sent them to Rome to establish friendship and alliance, ¹⁸and to free themselves from the yoke; for they saw that the kingdom of the Greeks was enslaving Israel completely. ¹⁹They went to Rome, a very long journey; and they entered the senate chamber and spoke as follows:

a Or *Kittim*   *b* Gk *them*   *c* Gk *they*

---

endar. **7.50** A formula familiar from Judges (e.g., 3.30; 5.31) is modified drastically (*for a few days*) to underline the ongoing Seleucid threat.

8.1–16 An idealized and sometimes inaccurate description of the Romans prepares for the treaty described in vv. 17–32. **8.2** The *Gauls* defeated by the Romans were most likely the Cisalpine Gauls, on the south side of the Alps. **8.3** After the defeat of the Carthaginians in the late third century BCE, *Spain* was increasingly under Roman control. **8.4** Mention of the *kings* introduces the episodes in vv. 5–13. **8.5** The Romans defeated *Philip* V of Macedon in 197 BCE and later his son *Perseus* in 168. **8.6–8** *Antiochus* III was defeated by the Romans at Magnesia in 190 BCE and was forced to cede some of his territories to *Eumenes* II of Pergamum. Among the *hostages* was Antiochus IV. Neither *India* nor *Media* was ceded to Eumenes; perhaps the text originally had "Ionia" and "Mysia." **8.9–**

10 In 146 BCE the Achaean League of Greece was defeated by Lucius Mummius, who in turn destroyed Corinth. These events happened fifteen years after the Jewish embassy to Rome described in vv. 17–32. **8.15** The senate had three hundred members, not *three hundred twenty,* and did not meet *every day.* **8.16** Two consuls, not *one,* were chosen every year. **8.17–32** Eager to extend their influence eastward, the Romans are displeased by the actions of Demetrius. The Jews need a powerful ally against the Seleucids. But in the period covered by 1 Maccabees nothing comes of the alliance until 14.16–24. Nevertheless, the author refers to it in 12.1, 3–4. **8.17** *Eupolemus,* from the priestly clan of Hakkoz (1 Chr 24.10), was the son of John, who gained concessions from Antiochus III (2 Macc 4.11). **8.19** Their *very long journey* to Rome (over a month) may have taken place in 161 BCE, when Demetrius arrived in Syria and before the defeat of Ni-

20"Judas, who is also called Maccabeus, and his brothers and the people of the Jews have sent us to you to establish alliance and peace with you, so that we may be enrolled as your allies and friends." 21The proposal pleased them, 22and this is a copy of the letter that they wrote in reply, on bronze tablets, and sent to Jerusalem to remain with them there as a memorial of peace and alliance:

23 "May all go well with the Romans and with the nation of the Jews at sea and on land forever, and may sword and enemy be far from them. 24If war comes first to Rome or to any of their allies in all their dominion, 25the nation of the Jews shall act as their allies wholeheartedly, as the occasion may indicate to them. 26To the enemy that makes war they shall not give or supply grain, arms, money, or ships, just as Rome has decided; and they shall keep their obligations without receiving any return. 27In the same way, if war comes first to the nation of the Jews, the Romans shall willingly act as their allies, as the occasion may indicate to them. 28And to their enemies there shall not be given grain, arms, money, or ships, just as Rome has decided; and they shall keep these obligations and do so without deceit. 29Thus on these terms the Romans make a treaty with the Jewish people. 30If after these terms are in effect both parties shall determine to add or delete anything, they shall do so at their discretion, and any addition or deletion that they may make shall be valid.

31 "Concerning the wrongs that King Demetrius is doing to them, we have written to him as follows, 'Why have you made your yoke heavy on our friends and allies the Jews? 32If now they appeal again for help against you, we will defend their rights and fight you on sea and on land.' "

Bacchides Returns to Judea

9 When Demetrius heard that Nicanor and his army had fallen in battle, he sent Bacchides and Alcimus into the land of Judah a second time, and with them the right wing of the army. 2They went by the road that leads to Gilgal and encamped against Mesaloth in Arbela, and they took it and killed many people. 3In the first month of the one hundred fifty-second year[a] they encamped against Jerusalem; 4then they marched off and went to Berea with twenty thousand foot soldiers and two thousand cavalry.

5 Now Judas was encamped in Elasa, and with him were three thousand picked men. 6When they saw the huge number of the enemy forces, they were greatly frightened, and many slipped away from the camp, until no more than eight hundred of them were left.

7 When Judas saw that his army had slipped away and the battle was imminent, he was crushed in spirit, for he had no time to assemble them. 8He became faint, but he said to those who were left, "Let us get up and go against our enemies. We may have the strength to fight them." 9But they tried to dissuade him, saying, "We do not have the strength. Let us rather save our own lives now, and let us come back with our kindred and fight them; we are too few." 10But Judas said, "Far be it from us to do such a thing as to flee from them. If our time has come, let us die bravely for our kindred, and leave no cause to question our honor."

---

a 160 B.C.

---

canor. **8.22** The original treaty is said to have been inscribed on *bronze tablets* and kept in Rome. The copy was presumably written in Latin or Greek, translated into Hebrew in the original version of 1 Maccabees, and translated into Greek in the extant text of 1 Maccabees. **8.23–30** The content of the treaty is regarded as basically authentic by most scholars today. After the opening (v. 23), there are parallel clauses stipulating that each side will come to the aid of the other if war breaks out (vv. 24–26, 27–28). **8.25** The clause *as the occasion may indicate to them* leaves a good deal of flexibility. **8.26** *Without receiving any return*, possibly a mistake in translation; see the parallel clause *without deceit* in v. 28, which corresponds to the usual treaty form. **8.30** Possible alterations had to be done by the common consent of *both parties*. **8.31–32** The threatening letter to

Demetrius I is cast in biblical idiom (*you made your yoke heavy*) and was never acted upon by the Romans. It may not have been part of the original treaty.

9.1–10 To avenge the defeat of Nicanor, Demetrius sends Bacchides, who confronts the vastly outnumbered army of Judas north of Jerusalem. **9.1** *Right wing*, the right flank of the army in battle formation (as in v. 12). **9.2** *Gilgal*, possibly an error for Galilee. *Mesaloth*, possibly a misreading of a Hebrew common noun meaning "trails, highways, ascents." **9.4** *Berea*, about ten miles north of Jerusalem, opposite *Elasa* (v. 5, precise location uncertain). **9.5–6** The number of deserters (from *three thousand* select troops to *eight hundred*) is large and may be exaggerated to explain Judas's defeat. **9.8–10** Judas hoped to seize the initiative and surprise his numerically superior opponents.

The Last Battle of Judas

11 Then the army of Bacchides[a] marched out from the camp and took its stand for the encounter. The cavalry was divided into two companies, and the slingers and the archers went ahead of the army, as did all the chief warriors. 12Bacchides was on the right wing. Flanked by the two companies, the phalanx advanced to the sound of the trumpets; and the men with Judas also blew their trumpets. 13The earth was shaken by the noise of the armies, and the battle raged from morning until evening.

14 Judas saw that Bacchides and the strength of his army were on the right; then all the stouthearted men went with him, 15and they crushed the right wing, and he pursued them as far as Mount Azotus. 16When those on the left wing saw that the right wing was crushed, they turned and followed close behind Judas and his men. 17The battle became desperate, and many on both sides were wounded and fell. 18Judas also fell, and the rest fled.

19 Then Jonathan and Simon took their brother Judas and buried him in the tomb of their ancestors at Modein, 20and wept for him. All Israel made great lamentation for him; they mourned many days and said,

21 "How is the mighty fallen,
        the savior of Israel!"

22Now the rest of the acts of Judas, and his wars and the brave deeds that he did, and his greatness, have not been recorded, but they were very many.

Jonathan Succeeds Judas

23 After the death of Judas, the renegades emerged in all parts of Israel; all the wrongdoers reappeared. 24In those days a very great famine occurred, and the country went over to their side. 25Bacchides chose the godless and put them in charge of the country. 26They made inquiry and searched for the friends of Judas, and brought them to Bacchides, who took vengeance on them and made sport of them. 27So there was great distress in Israel, such as had not been since the time that prophets ceased to appear among them.

28 Then all the friends of Judas assembled and said to Jonathan, 29"Since the death of your brother Judas there has been no one like him to go against our enemies and Bacchides, and to deal with those of our nation who hate us. 30Now therefore we have chosen you today to take his place as our ruler and leader, to fight our battle." 31So Jonathan accepted the leadership at that time in place of his brother Judas.

The Campaigns of Jonathan

32 When Bacchides learned of this, he tried to kill him. 33But Jonathan and his brother Simon and all who were with him heard of it, and they fled into the wilderness of Tekoa and camped by the water of the pool of Asphar. 34Bacchides found this out on the sabbath day, and he with all his army crossed the Jordan.

35 So Jonathan[b] sent his brother as leader of the multitude and begged the Nabateans, who

a Gk lacks *of Bacchides*   b Gk *he*

9.11–22 After a vivid description of the battle of Elasa, there is mourning over the fallen Judas, who is celebrated as a biblical hero. **9.12** *Phalanx* (see 6.35, 38, 45; 10.82), the heavy-infantry unit of soldiers carrying spears and shields. **9.14** Judas's plan was to destroy Bacchides and the *right* flank of his army, but he found himself trapped in a pincer maneuver on the part of the Seleucids (v. 16). **9.15** There is no *Mount Azotus* (Ashdod). The Hebrew original probably read "the mountain slopes." **9.19** For the Maccabean family tomb at *Modein*, see 2.70; 13.27–30. **9.21** The lament combines material from 2 Sam 1.25, 27; Judg 3.9. **9.22** The concluding formula (*the rest of the acts of Judas*) echoes the refrain in 1–2 Kings applied to the kings of Israel and Judah (e.g., 1 Kings 11.41). **9.23–31** With the death of Judas, the reemergence of renegade Jews, a famine, and the punishment of Judas's supporters, the Maccabean revolt reaches its lowest point. Jonathan is chosen to carry on the movement.

9.24 During a *famine* the Seleucid authorities could take control of the food supply and easily win people *over to their side*. **9.27** *Prophets*, probably the postexilic prophets Haggai and Zechariah or Malachi. See 4.46; 14.41 for hope of a new prophet arising. **9.28–31** Why *Jonathan* was preferred over the older Simon is not explained. As *ruler and leader* Jonathan acts like the judges of old (Judg 11.11). **9.32–49** Jonathan avenges the death of his brother John east of the Jordan and narrowly escapes from Bacchides at the Jordan. **9.33** The *wilderness of Tekoa* (fifteen miles southeast of Jerusalem) was a safe refuge for Jonathan (see 2 Sam 14.1–17; 2 Chr 20.20). *Pool of Asphar*, probably a cistern. **9.34** The report of Bacchides' movement is out of place here; it properly belongs in v. 43, where it is repeated. **9.35–36** For the *Nabateans* as *friends* of the Maccabean movement, see 5.25. It is not clear whether the family of *Jambri* from *Medeba* (near the northeastern tip of the Dead Sea) were Nabateans. That John

were his friends, for permission to store with them the great amount of baggage that they had. ³⁶But the family of Jambri from Medeba came out and seized John and all that he had, and left with it.

37 After these things it was reported to Jonathan and his brother Simon, "The family of Jambri are celebrating a great wedding, and are conducting the bride, a daughter of one of the great nobles of Canaan, from Nadabath with a large escort." ³⁸Remembering how their brother John had been killed, they went up and hid under cover of the mountain. ³⁹They looked out and saw a tumultuous procession with a great amount of baggage; and the bridegroom came out with his friends and his brothers to meet them with tambourines and musicians and many weapons. ⁴⁰Then they rushed on them from the ambush and began killing them. Many were wounded and fell, and the rest fled to the mountain; and the Jews*a* took all their goods. ⁴¹So the wedding was turned into mourning and the voice of their musicians into a funeral dirge. ⁴²After they had fully avenged the blood of their brother, they returned to the marshes of the Jordan.

43 When Bacchides heard of this, he came with a large force on the sabbath day to the banks of the Jordan. ⁴⁴And Jonathan said to those with him, "Let us get up now and fight for our lives, for today things are not as they were before. ⁴⁵For look! the battle is in front of us and behind us; the water of the Jordan is on this side and on that, with marsh and thicket; there is no place to turn. ⁴⁶Cry out now to Heaven that you may be delivered from the hands of our enemies." ⁴⁷So the battle began, and Jonathan stretched out his hand to strike Bacchides, but he eluded him and went to the rear. ⁴⁸Then Jonathan and the men with him leaped into the Jordan and swam across to the other side, and the enemy*a* did not cross the Jordan to attack them. ⁴⁹And about one thousand of Bacchides' men fell that day.

Bacchides Builds Fortifications

50 Then Bacchides*b* returned to Jerusalem and built strong cities in Judea: the fortress in Jericho, and Emmaus, and Beth-horon, and Bethel, and Timnath, and*c* Pharathon, and Tephon, with high walls and gates and bars. ⁵¹And he placed garrisons in them to harass Israel. ⁵²He also fortified the town of Beth-zur, and Gazara, and the citadel, and in them he put troops and stores of food. ⁵³And he took the sons of the leading men of the land as hostages and put them under guard in the citadel at Jerusalem.

54 In the one hundred and fifty-third year,*d* in the second month, Alcimus gave orders to tear down the wall of the inner court of the sanctuary. He tore down the work of the prophets! ⁵⁵But he only began to tear it down, for at that time Alcimus was stricken and his work was hindered; his mouth was stopped and he was paralyzed, so that he could no longer say a word or give commands concerning his house. ⁵⁶And Alcimus died at that time in great agony. ⁵⁷When Bacchides saw that Alcimus was dead, he returned to the king, and the land of Judah had rest for two years.

The End of the War

58 Then all the lawless plotted and said, "See! Jonathan and his men are living in quiet and confidence. So now let us bring Bacchides back, and he will capture them all in one

a Gk *they*   *b* Gk *he*   *c* Some authorities omit *and*   *d* 159 B.C.

(see 2.2) was killed is made clear in 9.42. **9.37** There is much speculation but no certainty about *Canaan* (code name for Nabatean traders? archaism? origin west of the Jordan?) and *Nadabath* (Nebo? Medeba?). **9.43–49** To discern from the text the places and strategies of the armies is difficult. The basic point is that in swampy area north of the Dead Sea Jonathan eluded the trap sprung by Bacchides. This is the first report of actual fighting on a sabbath (see 2.40–41). **9.49** *One thousand,* probably exaggerated. In fact, the encounter was probably a defeat for Jonathan, who was fortunate to escape alive. **9.50–57** The Seleucid triumph represented by Bacchides' fortifications and Alcimus's remodeling the temple is cut short by Alcimus's death, thus giving Jonathan a chance to regroup and gain power. **9.50–52** Bacchides secured key places in northern *Judea* and southern Samaria (*Timnath, Pharathon, Tephon*) against Jonathan. **9.53** To gain the cooperation of their parents, Bacchides held the sons of Jewish leaders in the citadel as *hostages.* **9.54** The *wall of the inner court* separated the holy of holies (reserved for Israelite priests) from the rest of the temple area. The *prophets* Haggai and Zechariah had encouraged and oversaw the building of the Second Temple. **9.55–56** The stroke and subsequent death of Alcimus were viewed as punishment for altering the temple architecture. **9.58–73** Setbacks for Bacchides and the renegade Jews result in peace with Jonathan, who takes on the role of "judge" at Michmash. The high priesthood was most likely vacant between 159 and 152 BCE.

night." 59And they went and consulted with him. 60He started to come with a large force, and secretly sent letters to all his allies in Judea, telling them to seize Jonathan and his men; but they were unable to do it, because their plan became known. 61And Jonathan's men[a] seized about fifty of the men of the country who were leaders in this treachery, and killed them.

62 Then Jonathan with his men, and Simon, withdrew to Bethbasi in the wilderness; he rebuilt the parts of it that had been demolished, and they fortified it. 63When Bacchides learned of this, he assembled all his forces, and sent orders to the men of Judea. 64Then he came and encamped against Bethbasi; he fought against it for many days and made machines of war.

65 But Jonathan left his brother Simon in the town, while he went out into the country; and he went with only a few men. 66He struck down Odomera and his kindred and the people of Phasiron in their tents. 67Then he[b] began to attack and went into battle with his forces; and Simon and his men sallied out from the town and set fire to the machines of war. 68They fought with Bacchides, and he was crushed by them. They pressed him very hard, for his plan and his expedition had been in vain. 69So he was very angry at the renegades who had counseled him to come into the country, and he killed many of them. Then he decided to go back to his own land.

70 When Jonathan learned of this, he sent ambassadors to him to make peace with him and obtain release of the captives. 71He agreed, and did as he said; and he swore to Jonathan[c] that he would not try to harm him as long as he lived. 72He restored to him the captives whom he had taken previously from the land of Judah; then he turned and went back to his own land, and did not come again

into their territory. 73Thus the sword ceased from Israel. Jonathan settled in Michmash and began to judge the people; and he destroyed the godless out of Israel.

Revolt of Alexander Epiphanes

10 In the one hundred sixtieth year[d] Alexander Epiphanes, son of Antiochus, landed and occupied Ptolemais. They welcomed him, and there he began to reign. 2When King Demetrius heard of it, he assembled a very large army and marched out to meet him in battle. 3Demetrius sent Jonathan a letter in peaceable words to honor him; 4for he said to himself, "Let us act first to make peace with him[e] before he makes peace with Alexander against us, 5for he will remember all the wrongs that we did to him and to his brothers and his nation." 6So Demetrius[f] gave him authority to recruit troops, to equip them with arms, and to become his ally; and he commanded that the hostages in the citadel should be released to him.

7 Then Jonathan came to Jerusalem and read the letter in the hearing of all the people and of those in the citadel. 8They were greatly alarmed when they heard that the king had given him authority to recruit troops. 9But those in the citadel released the hostages to Jonathan, and he returned them to their parents.

10 And Jonathan took up residence in Jerusalem and began to rebuild and restore the city. 11He directed those who were doing the work to build the walls and encircle Mount Zion with squared stones, for better fortification; and they did so. 12 Then the foreigners who were in the strongholds that Bacchides had built fled; 13all

---

a Gk they b Other ancient authorities read they c Gk him
d 152 B.C. e Gk them f Gk he

9.60 The plot to kill Jonathan in 157 BCE *became known* and was thus a defeat for the renegade Jews and an embarrassment for Bacchides. 9.62 *Bethbasi*, a fort south of Bethlehem (see 2 Chr 26.10), toward Tekoa. 9.66 *Odomera . . . Phasiron*, local people who allied themselves with Bacchides. 9.69 Bacchides' anger is now directed *at the renegades*, perhaps out of frustration at having been called on so often to resolve internal conflicts in Judea. 9.70–72 With *Jonathan* the only remaining significant political figure in Judea, Bacchides came to terms with him. 9.73 *Michmash*, seven miles north of Jerusalem, had been the base of an earlier Israelite kingdom (1 Sam 13.2) and the scene of the earlier Jonathan's victory (1 Sam 14.5–31). It was Jonathan's headquarters from 157 to 152 BCE.

10.1–17 The emergence of Alexander Balas in 152 BCE as claimant to the Seleucid throne enables Jonathan to gain concessions from him and Demetrius I. 10.1 *Alexander Epiphanes* (also called Balas) claimed to be the son of Antiochus IV Epiphanes. 10.3 *Demetrius* I recognized that Jonathan was the only remaining military and political force in Judea. 10.6 *Hostages*, sons of leading men in Judea (see 9.53). 10.11 The *walls* of Jerusalem had been destroyed on several occasions in

of them left their places and went back to their own lands. [14]Only in Beth-zur did some remain who had forsaken the law and the commandments, for it served as a place of refuge.

15 Now King Alexander heard of all the promises that Demetrius had sent to Jonathan, and he heard of the battles that Jonathan[a] and his brothers had fought, of the brave deeds that they had done, and of the troubles that they had endured. [16]So he said, "Shall we find another such man? Come now, we will make him our friend and ally." [17]And he wrote a letter and sent it to him, in the following words:

Jonathan Becomes High Priest

18 "King Alexander to his brother Jonathan, greetings. [19]We have heard about you, that you are a mighty warrior and worthy to be our friend. [20]And so we have appointed you today to be the high priest of your nation; you are to be called the king's Friend and you are to take our side and keep friendship with us." He also sent him a purple robe and a golden crown.

21 So Jonathan put on the sacred vestments in the seventh month of the one hundred sixtieth year,[b] at the festival of booths,[c] and he recruited troops and equipped them with arms in abundance. [22]When Demetrius heard of these things he was distressed and said, [23]"What is this that we have done? Alexander has gotten ahead of us in forming a friendship with the Jews to strengthen himself. [24]I also will write them words of encouragement and promise them honor and gifts, so that I may have their help." [25]So he sent a message to them in the following words:

A Letter from Demetrius to Jonathan

"King Demetrius to the nation of the Jews, greetings. [26]Since you have kept your agreement with us and have continued your friendship with us, and have not sided with our enemies, we have heard of it and rejoiced. [27]Now continue still to keep faith with us, and we will repay you with good for what you do for us. [28]We will grant you many immunities and give you gifts.

29 "I now free you and exempt all the Jews from payment of tribute and salt tax and crown levies, [30]and instead of collecting the third of the grain and the half of the fruit of the trees that I should receive, I release them from this day and henceforth. I will not collect them from the land of Judah or from the three districts added to it from Samaria and Galilee, from this day and for all time. [31]Jerusalem and its environs, its tithes and its revenues, shall be holy and free from tax. [32]I release also my control of the citadel in Jerusalem and give it to the high priest, so that he may station in it men of his own choice to guard it. [33]And everyone of the Jews taken as a captive from the land of Judah into any part of my kingdom, I set free without payment; and let all officials cancel also the taxes on their livestock.

34 "All the festivals and sabbaths and new moons and appointed days, and the three days before a festival and the three after a festival— let them all be days of immunity and release for all the Jews who are in my kingdom. [35]No one shall have authority to exact anything

---

a Gk he   b 152 B.C.   c Or tabernacles

---

recent times (1.31; 6.62). *Mount Zion*, the temple area. **10.14** Renegade Jews remained not only at *Beth-zur* (9.52), but also in Gazara (13.43). **10.15– 16** As Alexander made his move against Demetrius, he wanted to avoid having Jonathan as an enemy and a distraction. **10.18–25** When Alexander offers Jonathan the Jewish high priesthood, Jonathan seizes the opportunity. **10.20** The office of *high priest* had been vacant since the death of Alcimus. As Seleucid king, Alexander could appoint the Jewish high priest (2 Macc 4.7, 23–24). Jonathan was from a priestly family (1 Macc 2.1), but not from the right high-priestly family. The *purple robe* and *golden crown* symbolized Jonathan's new office as high priest and Friend of the king. **10.21** At the *festival of booths* (see Lev 23.39–43) in October 152 BCE, *Jonathan* assumed the office of Jewish high priest. Opposition to his claim may have been the occasion for the beginning

of the movement behind the Qumran community and the building of a rival temple by Onias IV at Leontopolis in Egypt (see 2 Macc 1.1–9). **10.25– 45** The letter from Demetrius to Jonathan may have originally sought to win the Jewish people away from Jonathan. In this context, however, it is used to confirm his privileges as high priest (10.32, 38). **10.25– 28** The letter is addressed to the *nation of the Jews* rather than to Jonathan directly. The claim that they *have not sided with* Demetrius's *enemies* overlooks Jonathan's acceptance of the high priesthood from Alexander Balas and his new status as Friend of the king. **10.29–45** The list of promises includes exemption from various taxes, recognition of Jerusalem as a holy city, release of Jewish captives, religious freedom for Jews, maintenance for Jewish soldiers, annexation of territory, subsidy for Jerusalem, right of asylum in Jerusalem, and money to rebuild Jerusalem.

from them or annoy any of them about any matter.

36 "Let Jews be enrolled in the king's forces to the number of thirty thousand men, and let the maintenance be given them that is due to all the forces of the king. [37]Let some of them be stationed in the great strongholds of the king, and let some of them be put in positions of trust in the kingdom. Let their officers and leaders be of their own number, and let them live by their own laws, just as the king has commanded in the land of Judah.

38 "As for the three districts that have been added to Judea from the country of Samaria, let them be annexed to Judea so that they may be considered to be under one ruler and obey no other authority than the high priest. [39]Ptolemais and the land adjoining it I have given as a gift to the sanctuary in Jerusalem, to meet the necessary expenses of the sanctuary. [40]I also grant fifteen thousand shekels of silver yearly out of the king's revenues from appropriate places. [41]And all the additional funds that the government officials have not paid as they did in the first years,[a] they shall give from now on for the service of the temple.[b] [42]Moreover, the five thousand shekels of silver that my officials[c] have received every year from the income of the services of the temple, this too is canceled, because it belongs to the priests who minister there. [43]And all who take refuge at the temple in Jerusalem, or in any of its precincts, because they owe money to the king or are in debt, let them be released and receive back all their property in my kingdom.

44 "Let the cost of rebuilding and restoring the structures of the sanctuary be paid from the revenues of the king. [45]And let the cost of rebuilding the walls of Jerusalem and fortifying it all around, and the cost of rebuilding the walls in Judea, also be paid from the revenues of the king."

Death of Demetrius

46 When Jonathan and the people heard these words, they did not believe or accept them, because they remembered the great wrongs that Demetrius[d] had done in Israel and how much he had oppressed them. [47]They favored Alexander, because he had been the first to speak peaceable words to them, and they remained his allies all his days.

48 Now King Alexander assembled large forces and encamped opposite Demetrius. [49]The two kings met in battle, and the army of Demetrius fled, and Alexander[e] pursued him and defeated them. [50]He pressed the battle strongly until the sun set, and on that day Demetrius fell.

Treaty of Ptolemy and Alexander

51 Then Alexander sent ambassadors to Ptolemy king of Egypt with the following message: [52]"Since I have returned to my kingdom and have taken my seat on the throne of my ancestors, and established my rule—for I crushed Demetrius and gained control of our country; [53]I met him in battle, and he and his army were crushed by us, and we have taken our seat on the throne of his kingdom— [54]now therefore let us establish friendship with one another; give me now your daughter as my wife, and I will become your son-in-law, and will make gifts to you and to her in keeping with your position."

55 Ptolemy the king replied and said, "Happy was the day on which you returned to the land of your ancestors and took your seat on the throne of their kingdom. [56]And now I will do for you as you wrote, but meet me at Ptolemais, so that we may see one another, and I will become your father-in-law, as you have said."

57 So Ptolemy set out from Egypt, he and his daughter Cleopatra, and came to Ptolemais in the one hundred sixty-second year.[f] [58]King Alexander met him, and Ptolemy[d] gave him his daughter Cleopatra in marriage, and celebrated her wedding at Ptolemais with great pomp, as kings do.

59 Then King Alexander wrote to Jonathan

---

a Meaning of Gk uncertain *b* Gk *house* *c* Gk *they* *d* Gk *he*
e Other ancient authorities read *Alexander fled, and Demetrius*
f 150 B.C.

10.46–50 Jonathan's distrust of Demetrius and his promises is borne out by the latter's defeat at the hands of Alexander. **10.47** As vv. 3–6, 15 indicate, Demetrius had been the *first* to offer peace. **10.50** Demetrius was killed in battle in 150 BCE. **10.51–66** A marriage alliance between the Ptolemies and Seleucids provides

Jonathan with still another opportunity for advancement. **10.51** *Ptolemy king of Egypt,* Ptolemy VI Philometor (see 1.18). **10.54** *Daughter,* Cleopatra Thea (v .58). Marriage alliances between the Seleucids and Ptolemies were sometimes unsuccessful (see Dan 2.43; 11.17). **10.56** *Ptolemais* (Acco), a neutral site on

to come and meet him. 60So he went with pomp to Ptolemais and met the two kings; he gave them and their Friends silver and gold and many gifts, and found favor with them. 61A group of malcontents from Israel, renegades, gathered together against him to accuse him; but the king paid no attention to them. 62The king gave orders to take off Jonathan's garments and to clothe him in purple, and they did so. 63The king also seated him at his side; and he said to his officers, "Go out with him into the middle of the city and proclaim that no one is to bring charges against him about any matter, and let no one annoy him for any reason." 64When his accusers saw the honor that was paid him, in accord with the proclamation, and saw him clothed in purple, they all fled. 65Thus the king honored him and enrolled him among his chief*a* Friends, and made him general and governor of the province. 66And Jonathan returned to Jerusalem in peace and gladness.

Apollonius Is Defeated by Jonathan

67 In the one hundred sixty-fifth year*b* Demetrius son of Demetrius came from Crete to the land of his ancestors. 68When King Alexander heard of it, he was greatly distressed and returned to Antioch. 69And Demetrius appointed Apollonius the governor of Coelesyria, and he assembled a large force and encamped against Jamnia. Then he sent the following message to the high priest Jonathan:

70 "You are the only one to rise up against us, and I have fallen into ridicule and disgrace because of you. Why do you assume authority against us in the hill country? 71If you now have confidence in your forces, come down to the plain to meet us, and let us match strength with each other there, for I have with me the power of the cities. 72Ask and learn who I am and who the others are that are helping us.

People will tell you that you cannot stand before us, for your ancestors were twice put to flight in their own land. 73And now you will not be able to withstand my cavalry and such an army in the plain, where there is no stone or pebble, or place to flee."

74 When Jonathan heard the words of Apollonius, his spirit was aroused. He chose ten thousand men and set out from Jerusalem, and his brother Simon met him to help him. 75He encamped before Joppa, but the people of the city closed its gates, for Apollonius had a garrison in Joppa. 76So they fought against it, and the people of the city became afraid and opened the gates, and Jonathan gained possession of Joppa.

77 When Apollonius heard of it, he mustered three thousand cavalry and a large army, and went to Azotus as though he were going farther. At the same time he advanced into the plain, for he had a large troop of cavalry and put confidence in it. 78Jonathan*c* pursued him to Azotus, and the armies engaged in battle. 79Now Apollonius had secretly left a thousand cavalry behind them. 80Jonathan learned that there was an ambush behind him, for they surrounded his army and shot arrows at his men from early morning until late afternoon. 81But his men stood fast, as Jonathan had commanded, and the enemy's*d* horses grew tired.

82 Then Simon brought forward his force and engaged the phalanx in battle (for the cavalry was exhausted); they were overwhelmed by him and fled, 83and the cavalry was dispersed in the plain. They fled to Azotus and entered Beth-dagon, the temple of their idol, for safety. 84But Jonathan burned Azotus and the surrounding towns and plundered them; and the temple of Dagon, and those who had

---

a Gk *first*　*b* 147 B.C.　*c* Gk *he*　*d* Gk *their*

---

the Palestinian coast. **10.60–61** Where Jonathan got these *gifts* is not said. His Jewish opponents, who are dismissed as *malcontents* and *renegades,* may have objected that he raised taxes from them or plundered them. **10.65** Jonathan is promoted from Friend to a *chief Friend* and made the military and political ruler in Judea. **10.67–89** A Seleucid plan to remove Jonathan fails and results in even greater honors for Jonathan when he defeats Apollonius. **10.67** *Demetrius* II was about fourteen in 147 BCE. **10.69** As governor of *Coelesyria* (originally the region between the Lebanon and Anti-Lebanon mountains, but later a political-ge-

ographical designation that included Palestine), *Apollonius* was officially Jonathan's superior. *Jamnia* (Yavneh) was on the coast. **10.72–73** Apollonius's taunt that the Jews had been *twice put to flight* alludes to Judas's defeats at Beth-zechariah (6.47) and Elasa (9.18). The *pebble* recalls the David and Goliath episode (1 Sam 17.40, 49–50). **10.75–76** By taking *Joppa* (north of Jamnia) Jonathan cut Apollonius off from Demetrius II. **10.77–83** By heading south to *Azotus* (Ashdod) Apollonius lured Jonathan onto more level ground (see vv. 71, 73). **10.84–85** For Judas's similar treatment of other pagan sanctuaries,

taken refuge in it, he burned with fire. 85The number of those who fell by the sword, with those burned alive, came to eight thousand.

86 Then Jonathan left there and encamped against Askalon, and the people of the city came out to meet him with great pomp.

87 He and those with him then returned to Jerusalem with a large amount of booty. 88When King Alexander heard of these things, he honored Jonathan still more; 89and he sent to him a golden buckle, such as it is the custom to give to the King's Kinsmen. He also gave him Ekron and all its environs as his possession.

Ptolemy Invades Syria

11 Then the king of Egypt gathered great forces, like the sand by the seashore, and many ships; and he tried to get possession of Alexander's kingdom by trickery and add it to his own kingdom. 2He set out for Syria with peaceable words, and the people of the towns opened their gates to him and went to meet him, for King Alexander had commanded them to meet him, since he was Alexander's*a* father-in-law. 3But when Ptolemy entered the towns he stationed forces as a garrison in each town.

4 When he*b* approached Azotus, they showed him the burnt-out temple of Dagon, and Azotus and its suburbs destroyed, and the corpses lying about, and the charred bodies of those whom Jonathan*c* had burned in the war, for they had piled them in heaps along his route. 5They also told the king what Jonathan had done, to throw blame on him; but the king kept silent. 6Jonathan met the king at Joppa with pomp, and they greeted one another and spent the night there. 7And Jonathan went with the king as far as the river called Eleutherus; then he returned to Jerusalem.

8 So King Ptolemy gained control of the coastal cities as far as Seleucia by the sea, and he kept devising wicked designs against Alexander. 9He sent envoys to King Demetrius, saying, "Come, let us make a covenant with each other, and I will give you in marriage my daughter who was Alexander's wife, and you shall reign over your father's kingdom. 10I now regret that I gave him my daughter, for he has tried to kill me." 11He threw blame on Alexander*d* because he coveted his kingdom. 12So he took his daughter away from him and gave her to Demetrius. He was estranged from Alexander, and their enmity became manifest.

13 Then Ptolemy entered Antioch and put on the crown of Asia. Thus he put two crowns on his head, the crown of Egypt and that of Asia. 14Now King Alexander was in Cilicia at that time, because the people of that region were in revolt. 15When Alexander heard of it, he came against him in battle. Ptolemy marched out and met him with a strong force, and put him to flight. 16So Alexander fled into Arabia to find protection there, and King Ptolemy was triumphant. 17Zabdiel the Arab cut off the head of Alexander and sent it to Ptolemy. 18But King Ptolemy died three days later, and his troops in the strongholds were killed by the inhabitants of the strongholds. 19So Demetrius became king in the one hundred sixty-seventh year.*e*

Jonathan's Diplomacy

20 In those days Jonathan assembled the Judeans to attack the citadel in Jerusalem, and he built many engines of war to use against it. 21But certain renegades who hated their na-

---

a Gk *his*   *b* Other ancient authorities read *they*   *c* Gk *he*
d Gk *him*   *e* 145 B.C.

---

see 5.44, 68. **10.86** *Askalon*, the harbor city south of Azotus, offered no resistance. **10.89** The *King's Kinsmen* fastened their purple cloaks with a golden buckle. *Ekron*, another ancient Philistine city, on the road from Jerusalem to the coast.

11.1–19 The attempt by Ptolemy VI Philometer (Alexander Balas's father-in-law) to annex the Seleucid kingdom ends in his death and that of Alexander Balas, thus allowing Demetrius II to take power in 145 BCE. **11.1** Other ancient sources cast doubt on the claim that Ptolemy's sole motive was *to get possession of Alexander's* (Seleucid) *kingdom* (see also v. 11). **11.3** The *garrisons* that Ptolemy VI established in the coastal towns were destroyed after his death (see v. 18). **11.4–5** For what Jonathan did at *Azotus*, see 10.83–85. **11.7** The

river *Eleutherus*, two hundred miles north of Joppa, marked the southern border of the Syrian territory of the Seleucids. **11.8** *Seleucia*, the port city of Antioch, was loyal to Demetrius II. **11.9–12** For the earlier marriage alliance between Ptolemy and Alexander, see 10.51–58. **11.15** The *battle* was fought at the river Oenoparus near Antioch in summer 145 BCE. Ptolemy VI died (v. 18) from wounds inflicted in this battle. **11.16** *Arabia*, here the northern desert east of Damascus. **11.20–37** After another failed attempt at taking control of the citadel, Jonathan meets Demetrius II at Ptolemais, where he gains important concessions and honors. **11.20–21** In light of the political confusion at Antioch Jonathan sought to attack the *citadel* in Jerusalem. There was opposition from other Jews (*ren-*

tion went to the king and reported to him that Jonathan was besieging the citadel. 22 When he heard this he was angry, and as soon as he heard it he set out and came to Ptolemais; and he wrote Jonathan not to continue the siege, but to meet him for a conference at Ptolemais as quickly as possible.

23 When Jonathan heard this, he gave orders to continue the siege. He chose some of the elders of Israel and some of the priests, and put himself in danger, 24 for he went to the king at Ptolemais, taking silver and gold and clothing and numerous other gifts. And he won his favor. 25 Although certain renegades of his nation kept making complaints against him, 26 the king treated him as his predecessors had treated him; he exalted him in the presence of all his Friends. 27 He confirmed him in the high priesthood and in as many other honors as he had formerly had, and caused him to be reckoned among his chief[a] Friends. 28 Then Jonathan asked the king to free Judea and the three districts of Samaria[b] from tribute, and promised him three hundred talents. 29 The king consented, and wrote a letter to Jonathan about all these things; its contents were as follows:

30 "King Demetrius to his brother Jonathan and to the nation of the Jews, greetings. 31 This copy of the letter that we wrote concerning you to our kinsman Lasthenes we have written to you also, so that you may know what it says. 32 'King Demetrius to his father Lasthenes, greetings. 33 We have determined to do good to the nation of the Jews, who are our friends and fulfill their obligations to us, because of the goodwill they show toward us. 34 We have confirmed as their possession both the territory of Judea and the three districts of Aphairema and Lydda and Rathamin; the latter, with all the region bordering them, were added to Judea from Samaria. To all those who

offer sacrifice in Jerusalem we have granted release from[c] the royal taxes that the king formerly received from them each year, from the crops of the land and the fruit of the trees. 35 And the other payments henceforth due to us of the tithes, and the taxes due to us, and the salt pits and the crown taxes due to us— from all these we shall grant them release. 36 And not one of these grants shall be canceled from this time on forever. 37 Now therefore take care to make a copy of this, and let it be given to Jonathan and put up in a conspicuous place on the holy mountain.' "

The Intrigue of Trypho

38 When King Demetrius saw that the land was quiet before him and that there was no opposition to him, he dismissed all his troops, all of them to their own homes, except the foreign troops that he had recruited from the islands of the nations. So all the troops who had served under his predecessors hated him. 39 A certain Trypho had formerly been one of Alexander's supporters; he saw that all the troops were grumbling against Demetrius. So he went to Imalkue the Arab, who was bringing up Antiochus, the young son of Alexander, 40 and insistently urged him to hand Antiochus[d] over to him, to become king in place of his father. He also reported to Imalkue[d] what Demetrius had done and told of the hatred that the troops of Demetrius[e] had for him; and he stayed there many days.

41 Now Jonathan sent to King Demetrius the request that he remove the troops of the citadel from Jerusalem, and the troops in the strongholds; for they kept fighting against Israel. 42 And Demetrius sent this message back to Jonathan: "Not only will I do these things

---

a Gk first   *b* Cn: Gk the three districts and Samaria
c Or Samaria, for all those who offer sacrifice in Jerusalem, in place of   *d* Gk him   *e* Gk his troops

---

egades) more closely allied to Seleucid interests. **11.23–29** At Ptolemais (Acco) Demetrius II confirmed many privileges granted or promised by Demetrius I and Alexander Balas (10.3–6, 15–20, 25–45, 59–66). **11.31–32** Lasthenes, the chief of Demetrius's Cretan mercenaries and his chief minister. His titles kinsman and father were honorary, expressing Lasthenes' powerful role in the court of Demetrius II. **11.34** For the three districts, see 10.30, 38; 11.28. Their revenues were to go to supporting the Jerusalem temple. **11.37** For another public display of the copy of a treaty, see 8.22. The holy mountain is the Temple Mount, also called

Mount Zion. **11.38–53** Although Jonathan helps Demetrius II put down a rebellion in Antioch, he is not rewarded properly. **11.38** Lasthenes convinced Demetrius II to dismiss all the native troops and retain only mercenary troops; thus Demetrius was freed from financial obligations and could exercise tighter control over his army. The Greek islands were the home of Lasthenes' mercenaries. **11.39–40** Diodotus Trypho ("the luxurious one") persuaded Imalkue to let him set up Alexander Balas's young son as Antiochus VI. For Antiochus VI's murder by Trypho, see 13.31–32. **11.41** Jonathan's earlier attack against the citadel (vv. 20–21) had

for you and your nation, but I will confer great honor on you and your nation, if I find an opportunity. ⁴³Now then you will do well to send me men who will help me, for all my troops have revolted." ⁴⁴So Jonathan sent three thousand stalwart men to him at Antioch, and when they came to the king, the king rejoiced at their arrival.

45 Then the people of the city assembled within the city, to the number of a hundred and twenty thousand, and they wanted to kill the king. ⁴⁶But the king fled into the palace. Then the people of the city seized the main streets of the city and began to fight. ⁴⁷So the king called the Jews to his aid, and they all rallied around him and then spread out through the city; and they killed on that day about one hundred thousand. ⁴⁸They set fire to the city and seized a large amount of spoil on that day, and saved the king. ⁴⁹When the people of the city saw that the Jews had gained control of the city as they pleased, their courage failed and they cried out to the king with this entreaty: ⁵⁰"Grant us peace, and make the Jews stop fighting against us and our city." ⁵¹And they threw down their arms and made peace. So the Jews gained glory in the sight of the king and of all the people in his kingdom, and they returned to Jerusalem with a large amount of spoil.

52 So King Demetrius sat on the throne of his kingdom, and the land was quiet before him. ⁵³But he broke his word about all that he had promised; he became estranged from Jonathan and did not repay the favors that Jonathan[a] had done him, but treated him very harshly.

Trypho Seizes Power

54 After this Trypho returned, and with him the young boy Antiochus who began to reign and put on the crown. ⁵⁵All the troops that Demetrius had discharged gathered around him; they fought against Demetrius,[b] and he fled and was routed. ⁵⁶Trypho captured the elephants[c] and gained control of Antioch. ⁵⁷Then the young Antiochus wrote to Jonathan, saying, "I confirm you in the high priesthood and set you over the four districts and make you one of the king's Friends." ⁵⁸He also sent him gold plates and a table service, and granted him the right to drink from gold cups and dress in purple and wear a gold buckle. ⁵⁹He appointed Jonathan's[d] brother Simon governor from the Ladder of Tyre to the borders of Egypt.

Campaigns of Jonathan and Simon

60 Then Jonathan set out and traveled beyond the river and among the towns, and all the army of Syria gathered to him as allies. When he came to Askalon, the people of the city met him and paid him honor. ⁶¹From there he went to Gaza, but the people of Gaza shut him out. So he besieged it and burned its suburbs with fire and plundered them. ⁶²Then the people of Gaza pleaded with Jonathan, and he made peace with them, and took the sons of their rulers as hostages and sent them to Jerusalem. And he passed through the country as far as Damascus.

63 Then Jonathan heard that the officers of Demetrius had come to Kadesh in Galilee with a large army, intending to remove him from office. ⁶⁴He went to meet them, but left his brother Simon in the country. ⁶⁵Simon encamped before Beth-zur and fought against it for many days and hemmed it in. ⁶⁶Then they asked him to grant them terms of peace, and he did so. He removed them from there, took possession of the town, and set a garrison over it.

67 Jonathan and his army encamped by the

---

a Gk he   b Gk him   c Gk animals   d Gk his

---

failed. For the other *strongholds*, see 9.50–51. **11.44–51** The role played by *Jews*, though substantial, was probably secondary to that of the Cretan mercenaries under Lasthenes. **11.53** Trusting in his mercenaries, Demetrius II felt bold enough to demand taxes from Judea going back to the "first kings." **11.54–59** Through Antiochus VI, Trypho gains Jonathan and Simon as allies. **11.55** Trypho exploited the unrest among the Seleucid *troops*, who had been sent away under Lasthenes (see v. 38). **11.58** For the *gold buckle* as a sign of the rank of the King's Kinsmen, see 10.89. **11.59** The appointment of *Simon* as governor of the coastal area from Syria to Egypt expanded Maccabean control westward. **11.60–74** Jonathan recruits soldiers for Antiochus VI and wins a surprising victory at Hazor, while Simon takes Beth-zur. **11.60–62** Jonathan traveled throughout *beyond the river* (the province west of the Euphrates) to gather troops against Demetrius II. **11.63** Because Jonathan was now supporting Antiochus VI, the *officers of Demetrius* sought to stop him from rallying troops. **11.65–66** Simon's capture of *Beth-zur* in 144 BCE (see 9.51; 10.14) gave the Maccabees a southern garrison again. **11.67** *Hazor*, captured by Joshua (Josh 11.10–11), was ten miles north of the Sea of Galilee (*the waters*

waters of Gennesaret. Early in the morning they marched to the plain of Hazor, 68and there in the plain the army of the foreigners met him; they had set an ambush against him in the mountains, but they themselves met him face to face. 69Then the men in ambush emerged from their places and joined battle. 70All the men with Jonathan fled; not one of them was left except Mattathias son of Absalom and Judas son of Chalphi, commanders of the forces of the army. 71Jonathan tore his clothes, put dust on his head, and prayed. 72Then he turned back to the battle against the enemy[a] and routed them, and they fled. 73When his men who were fleeing saw this, they returned to him and joined him in the pursuit as far as Kadesh, to their camp, and there they encamped. 74As many as three thousand of the foreigners fell that day. And Jonathan returned to Jerusalem.

Alliances with Rome and Sparta

12 Now when Jonathan saw that the time was favorable for him, he chose men and sent them to Rome to confirm and renew the friendship with them. 2He also sent letters to the same effect to the Spartans and to other places. 3So they went to Rome and entered the senate chamber and said, "The high priest Jonathan and the Jewish nation have sent us to renew the former friendship and alliance with them." 4And the Romans[b] gave them letters to the people in every place, asking them to provide for the envoys[a] safe conduct to the land of Judah.

5 This is a copy of the letter that Jonathan wrote to the Spartans: 6"The high priest Jonathan, the senate of the nation, the priests, and the rest of the Jewish people to their brothers the Spartans, greetings. 7Already in time past a letter was sent to the high priest Onias from

Arius,[c] who was king among you, stating that you are our brothers, as the appended copy shows. 8Onias welcomed the envoy with honor, and received the letter, which contained a clear declaration of alliance and friendship. 9Therefore, though we have no need of these things, since we have as encouragement the holy books that are in our hands, 10we have undertaken to send to renew our family ties and friendship with you, so that we may not become estranged from you, for considerable time has passed since you sent your letter to us. 11We therefore remember you constantly on every occasion, both at our festivals and on other appropriate days, at the sacrifices that we offer and in our prayers, as it is right and proper to remember brothers. 12And we rejoice in your glory. 13But as for ourselves, many trials and many wars have encircled us; the kings around us have waged war against us. 14We were unwilling to annoy you and our other allies and friends with these wars, 15for we have the help that comes from Heaven for our aid, and so we were delivered from our enemies, and our enemies were humbled. 16We therefore have chosen Numenius son of Antiochus and Antipater son of Jason, and have sent them to Rome to renew our former friendship and alliance with them. 17We have commanded them to go also to you and greet you and deliver to you this letter from us concerning the renewal of our family ties. 18And now please send us a reply to this."

19 This is a copy of the letter that they sent to Onias: 20"King Arius of the Spartans, to the high priest Onias, greetings. 21It has been found in writing concerning the Spartans and the Jews that they are brothers and are of the family of Abraham. 22And now that we have

a Gk *them*   *b* Gk *they*   *c* Vg Compare verse 20: Gk *Darius*

---

of Gennesaret). **11.71** Jonathan does what Joshua did according to Josh 7.6–9.

12.1–23 By confirming Jewish alliances with Rome and Sparta, Jonathan and Simon seek to take pressure off their own situation in 144 BCE. **12.1** For the earlier embassy to *Rome* and the friendship treaty, see 8.17–32. **12.2** With the Roman defeat of the Greek Achaean League in 146 BCE (see 8.9–10) the *Spartans* (who had not been part of that league) regained prominence. **12.3** The formula *the high priest Jonathan and the Jewish nation* implies an independent status beyond that claimed in 8.20; see also 12.6. **12.6** The *senate* (Greek *gerousia*) was the council of Jewish elders.

12.7 *Onias* I, the Jewish high priest around 300 BCE. *Arius* I, king of Sparta from 312 to 265. **12.8** The *letter* quoted in vv. 20–23 says nothing about an *alliance*. **12.9** For what constituted the *holy books* see the prologue to Sirach ("the Law and the Prophets and the other books of our ancestors"); see also 2 Macc 2.14. **12.14–15** The apparent failure of Onias I to respond to Arius I is explained as due to the Jews' unwillingness to *annoy* allies. **12.16** The ambassadors sent to *Rome* (see also 14.22, 24) stopped at Sparta on their return home. **12.21** The fiction that Spartans and Jews both descended from *Abraham* is an example of finding genealogical justification for an alliance.

learned this, please write us concerning your welfare; [23] we on our part write to you that your livestock and your property belong to us, and ours belong to you. We therefore command that our envoys[a] report to you accordingly."

Further Campaigns of Jonathan and Simon

24 Now Jonathan heard that the commanders of Demetrius had returned, with a larger force than before, to wage war against him. [25] So he marched away from Jerusalem and met them in the region of Hamath, for he gave them no opportunity to invade his own country. [26] He sent spies to their camp, and they returned and reported to him that the enemy[a] were being drawn up in formation to attack the Jews[b] by night. [27] So when the sun had set, Jonathan commanded his troops to be alert and to keep their arms at hand so as to be ready all night for battle, and he stationed outposts around the camp. [28] When the enemy heard that Jonathan and his troops were prepared for battle, they were afraid and were terrified at heart; so they kindled fires in their camp and withdrew.[c] [29] But Jonathan and his troops did not know it until morning, for they saw the fires burning. [30] Then Jonathan pursued them, but he did not overtake them, for they had crossed the Eleutherus river. [31] So Jonathan turned aside against the Arabs who are called Zabadeans, and he crushed them and plundered them. [32] Then he broke camp and went to Damascus, and marched through all that region.

33 Simon also went out and marched through the country as far as Askalon and the neighboring strongholds. He turned aside to Joppa and took it by surprise, [34] for he had heard that they were ready to hand over the stronghold to those whom Demetrius had sent. And he stationed a garrison there to guard it.

35 When Jonathan returned he convened the elders of the people and planned with them to build strongholds in Judea, [36] to build the walls of Jerusalem still higher, and to erect a high barrier between the citadel and the city to separate it from the city, in order to isolate it so that its garrison[a] could neither buy nor sell. [37] So they gathered together to rebuild the city; part of the wall on the valley to the east had fallen, and he repaired the section called Chaphenatha. [38] Simon also built Adida in the Shephelah; he fortified it and installed gates with bolts.

Trypho Captures Jonathan

39 Then Trypho attempted to become king in Asia and put on the crown, and to raise his hand against King Antiochus. [40] He feared that Jonathan might not permit him to do so, but might make war on him, so he kept seeking to seize and kill him, and he marched out and came to Beth-shan. [41] Jonathan went out to meet him with forty thousand picked warriors, and he came to Beth-shan. [42] When Trypho saw that he had come with a large army, he was afraid to raise his hand against him. [43] So he received him with honor and commended him to all his Friends, and he gave him gifts and commanded his Friends and his troops to obey him as they would himself. [44] Then he said to Jonathan, "Why have you put all these people to so much trouble when we are not at war? [45] Dismiss them now to their homes and choose for yourself a few men to stay with you, and come with me to Ptolemais. I will hand it over to you as well as the other strongholds and the remaining troops and all the officials, and will turn around and go home. For that is why I am here."

---

a Gk they   b Gk them   c Other ancient authorities omit and withdrew

---

12.24–38 Jonathan and Simon win additional military victories and set up their own garrisons. **12.25** Hamath, in the Orontes Valley between the Lebanon and Anti-Lebanon mountains. **12.31** The Zabadeans lived about thirty miles northwest of Damascus. There may be a connection with Zabdiel (11.17), who killed Alexander Balas. **12.33–34** Simon, now governor in the coastal district (11.59), puts down a planned rebellion in Joppa (10.76). **12.35–36** The strongholds probably included those fortified by Bacchides (9.50; 10.12). The Jerusalem citadel still escaped Maccabean control.

12.37 Chaphenatha, usually identified as the "Second Quarter," northwest of the temple area (see 2 Kings 22.14). **12.38** Adida, near Lydda, could serve as a stronghold between the coastal plain and the hill country of Judea. **12.39–53** At first Trypho is thwarted from capturing Jonathan but finally succeeds in doing so, thus leaving Israel without a leader or helper (v. 53). **12.39** Asia, a name for the Seleucid Empire. **12.40–41** Beth-shan (Scythopolis-Nysa), a strategic point in the Jordan Valley (see 5.52). Although forty thousand picked warriors is an exaggeration, it does seem that

46 Jonathan[a] trusted him and did as he said; he sent away the troops, and they returned to the land of Judah. 47 He kept with himself three thousand men, two thousand of whom he left in Galilee, while one thousand accompanied him. 48 But when Jonathan entered Ptolemais, the people of Ptolemais closed the gates and seized him, and they killed with the sword all who had entered with him.

49 Then Trypho sent troops and cavalry into Galilee and the Great Plain to destroy all Jonathan's soldiers. 50 But they realized that Jonathan had been seized and had perished along with his men, and they encouraged one another and kept marching in close formation, ready for battle. 51 When their pursuers saw that they would fight for their lives, they turned back. 52 So they all reached the land of Judah safely, and they mourned for Jonathan and his companions and were in great fear; and all Israel mourned deeply. 53 All the nations around them tried to destroy them, for they said, "They have no leader or helper. Now therefore let us make war on them and blot out the memory of them from humankind."

Simon Takes Command

13 Simon heard that Trypho had assembled a large army to invade the land of Judah and destroy it, 2 and he saw that the people were trembling with fear. So he went up to Jerusalem, and gathering the people together 3 he encouraged them, saying to them, "You yourselves know what great things my brothers and I and the house of my father have done for the laws and the sanctuary; you know also the wars and the difficulties that my brothers and I have seen. 4 By reason of this all my brothers have perished for the sake of Israel, and I alone am left. 5 And now, far be it from me to spare my life in any time of distress, for I am not better than my brothers. 6 But I will avenge my nation and the sanctuary and your wives and children, for all the nations have gathered together out of hatred to destroy us."

7 The spirit of the people was rekindled when they heard these words, 8 and they answered in a loud voice, "You are our leader in place of Judas and your brother Jonathan. 9 Fight our battles, and all that you say to us we will do." 10 So he assembled all the warriors and hurried to complete the walls of Jerusalem, and he fortified it on every side. 11 He sent Jonathan son of Absalom to Joppa, and with him a considerable army; he drove out its occupants and remained there.

Deceit and Treachery of Trypho

12 Then Trypho left Ptolemais with a large army to invade the land of Judah, and Jonathan was with him under guard. 13 Simon encamped in Adida, facing the plain. 14 Trypho learned that Simon had risen up in place of his brother Jonathan, and that he was about to join battle with him, so he sent envoys to him and said, 15 "It is for the money that your brother Jonathan owed the royal treasury, in connection with the offices he held, that we are detaining him. 16 Send now one hundred talents of silver and two of his sons as hostages, so that when released he will not revolt against us, and we will release him."

17 Simon knew that they were speaking deceitfully to him, but he sent to get the money and the sons, so that he would not arouse great hostility among the people, who might say, 18 "It was because Simon[b] did not send him the money and the sons, that Jonathan[a] perished." 19 So he sent the sons and the hundred talents, but Trypho[a] broke his word and did not release Jonathan.

20 After this Trypho came to invade the

a Gk he   b Gk I

Jonathan's large force frightened Trypho. **12.48** For earlier references to the hostility of *Ptolemais*, see 5.15, 22, 55. **12.49** *The Great Plain*, also called Esdraelon, the western section of the valleys and plains separating Galilee from Samaria. **12.50** As 13.23 shows, Jonathan had not yet *perished*.

13.1–11 As the only remaining brother (see 2.1–5), Simon takes over Jonathan's roles in Judea. **13.3–6** Simon's speech reminds the people of what the Maccabees fought for (*laws, sanctuary, Israel*) and how they died doing so: Eleazar (6.46), Judas (9.18), John (9.36–42), and Jonathan (13.23). **13.10–11** For fortifications

in *Jerusalem*, see 12.36–37. For problems at *Joppa*, see 12.33–34. *Jonathan son of Absalom*, possibly the brother of Mattathias (11.70). **13.12–24** Trypho deceives Simon and kills Jonathan but fails to capture Jerusalem. **13.13** *Adida*, recently fortified (12.38), blocked the road from Ptolemais to Jerusalem. **13.15–16** Although the reason Jonathan owed *money* to the royal treasury is not specified, the debt gave Trypho an excuse to exploit. Perhaps the independence shown by Jonathan was interpreted as a *revolt*, for the Seleucids still looked on the Maccabees as their clients. **13.20** Trypho tried to approach Jerusalem from the

country and destroy it, and he circled around by the way to Adora. But Simon and his army kept marching along opposite him to every place he went. 21 Now the men in the citadel kept sending envoys to Trypho urging him to come to them by way of the wilderness and to send them food. 22 So Trypho got all his cavalry ready to go, but that night a very heavy snow fell, and he did not go because of the snow. He marched off and went into the land of Gilead. 23 When he approached Baskama, he killed Jonathan, and he was buried there. 24 Then Trypho turned and went back to his own land.

Jonathan's Tomb

25 Simon sent and took the bones of his brother Jonathan, and buried him in Modein, the city of his ancestors. 26 All Israel bewailed him with great lamentation, and mourned for him many days. 27 And Simon built a monument over the tomb of his father and his brothers; he made it high so that it might be seen, with polished stone at the front and back. 28 He also erected seven pyramids, opposite one another, for his father and mother and four brothers. 29 For the pyramids[a] he devised an elaborate setting, erecting about them great columns, and on the columns he put suits of armor for a permanent memorial, and beside the suits of armor he carved ships, so that they could be seen by all who sail the sea. 30 This is the tomb that he built in Modein; it remains to this day.

Judea Gains Independence

31 Trypho dealt treacherously with the young King Antiochus; he killed him 32 and became king in his place, putting on the crown of Asia; and he brought great calamity on the land.

33 But Simon built up the strongholds of Judea and walled them all around, with high towers and great walls and gates and bolts, and he stored food in the strongholds. 34 Simon also chose emissaries and sent them to King Demetrius with a request to grant relief to the country, for all that Trypho did was to plunder. 35 King Demetrius sent him a favorable reply to this request, and wrote him a letter as follows, 36 "King Demetrius to Simon, the high priest and friend of kings, and to the elders and nation of the Jews, greetings. 37 We have received the gold crown and the palm branch that you[b] sent, and we are ready to make a general peace with you and to write to our officials to grant you release from tribute. 38 All the grants that we have made to you remain valid, and let the strongholds that you have built be your possession. 39 We pardon any errors and offenses committed to this day, and cancel the crown tax that you owe; and whatever other tax has been collected in Jerusalem shall be collected no longer. 40 And if any of you are qualified to be enrolled in our bodyguard,[c] let them be enrolled, and let there be peace between us."

41 In the one hundred seventieth year[d] the yoke of the Gentiles was removed from Israel, 42 and the people began to write in their documents and contracts, "In the first year of Simon the great high priest and commander and leader of the Jews."

The Capture of Gazara by Simon

43 In those days Simon[e] encamped against Gazara[f] and surrounded it with troops. He

a Gk For these b The word you in verses 37–40 is plural
c Or court d 142 B.C. e Gk he f Cn: Gk Gaza

---

south, as Lysias had done (4.29; 6.31). *Adora,* about five miles southwest of Hebron. **13.21** The garrison at the Jerusalem *citadel* urged Trypho to attack from the *wilderness* of Judah, from the south and southeast. **13.22–23** *Baskama.* Location uncertain. If it was in *Gilead* (rather than Galilee), Trypho made a large circle in his abortive attack on Jerusalem. He probably killed Jonathan's hostage sons also (vv. 16, 19) in the winter of 143/142 BCE. **13.25–30** The interment of Jonathan's bones becomes the occasion for Simon to build a monument to his family. **13.25–27** The family tomb at *Modein* (2.70; 9.19) was presumably a cave or chamber carved out of rock, with small recesses for corpses. The *monument* was built over it. **13.28** For the *pyramid* or pillar of Absalom, see 2 Sam 18.18. The seventh pyramid was for Simon. **13.29–30** The *ships* may have commemorated the capture of Joppa and expressed a Mac-

cabean claim to sea power. *Modein,* twelve miles from the sea. **13.31–42** Simon's support for Demetrius II wins Judea's freedom from the annual crown tax and a greater measure of independence. **13.31–32** Trypho deposed Antiochus VI in 142 BCE and had him killed in 139 BCE. For *putting on the crown of Asia,* see 8.6. **13.34** Simon went over to Demetrius II because Trypho had killed Jonathan and demanded heavy taxes (*plunder*). **13.37** *Gold crown, palm branch,* peace offerings. **13.39–40** The *errors and offenses* included supporting Trypho and fighting against Demetrius II (11.63–74; 12.24–32). *Crown tax,* the annual tribute from Jerusalem. For the royal *bodyguard,* see 11.47–48. **13.41–42** *Yoke of the Gentiles,* perhaps specifically the annual crown tax (v. 39). Its removal was taken as the start of a new era, that of Simon. **13.43–48** With Trypho and Demetrius II occupied with their own

made a siege engine, brought it up to the city, and battered and captured one tower. 44 The men in the siege engine leaped out into the city, and a great tumult arose in the city. 45 The men in the city, with their wives and children, went up on the wall with their clothes torn, and they cried out with a loud voice, asking Simon to make peace with them; 46 they said, "Do not treat us according to our wicked acts but according to your mercy." 47 So Simon reached an agreement with them and stopped fighting against them. But he expelled them from the city and cleansed the houses in which the idols were located, and then entered it with hymns and praise. 48 He removed all uncleanness from it, and settled in it those who observed the law. He also strengthened its fortifications and built in it a house for himself.

Simon Regains the Citadel at Jerusalem

49 Those who were in the citadel at Jerusalem were prevented from going in and out to buy and sell in the country. So they were very hungry, and many of them perished from famine. 50 Then they cried to Simon to make peace with them, and he did so. But he expelled them from there and cleansed the citadel from its pollutions. 51 On the twenty-third day of the second month, in the one hundred seventy-first year,[a] the Jews[b] entered it with praise and palm branches, and with harps and cymbals and stringed instruments, and with hymns and songs, because a great enemy had been crushed and removed from Israel. 52 Simon[c] decreed that every year they should celebrate this day with rejoicing. He strengthened the fortifications of the temple hill alongside the citadel, and he and his men lived there. 53 Simon saw that his son John had reached manhood, and so he made him commander of all the forces; and he lived at Gazara.

Capture of Demetrius

14 In the one hundred seventy-second year[d] King Demetrius assembled his forces and marched into Media to obtain help, so that he could make war against Trypho. 2 When King Arsaces of Persia and Media heard that Demetrius had invaded his territory, he sent one of his generals to take him alive. 3 The general[c] went and defeated the army of Demetrius, and seized him and took him to Arsaces, who put him under guard.

Eulogy of Simon

4   The land[e] had rest all the days of Simon.
        He sought the good of his nation;
    his rule was pleasing to them,
        as was the honor shown him, all his
            days.
5   To crown all his honors he took Joppa for
            a harbor,
        and opened a way to the isles of the
            sea.
6   He extended the borders of his nation,
        and gained full control of the country.
7   He gathered a host of captives;
        he ruled over Gazara and Beth-zur and
            the citadel,
    and he removed its uncleanness from it;
        and there was none to oppose him.
8   They tilled their land in peace;
        the ground gave its increase,
        and the trees of the plains their fruit.
9   Old men sat in the streets;
        they all talked together of good things,

---

a 141 B.C.   b Gk they   c Gk He   d 140 B.C.   e Other ancient authorities add of Judah

struggle, Simon captures Gaza (Gezer). 13.43 The reading Gaza in the Greek is surely incorrect; the capture of Gazara (Gezer) is assumed in 13.53; 14.7, 34; 15.28, 35; 16.1, 19, 21. Siege engine, a movable tower containing battering rams and catapults, able to accommodate many soldiers. 13.47–48 Simon made Gazara a Jewish city (thus ensuring its loyalty to him) and was also able to reward his soldiers and supporters with property there. 13.49–53 Simon's capture of the citadel at Jerusalem, the last symbol of anti-Maccabean power in Jerusalem, marks the final success of the revolt. There are parallels with the cleansing of the temple (4.41–61). 13.49–52 The citadel, founded under Antiochus IV in 167 BCE, fell in June 141 BCE. It was then fortified by Simon's troops. 13.53 John Hyrcanus I

succeeded his father, Simon, and ruled Judea from 134 to 104 BCE. 1 Maccabees may have been composed during his reign as a kind of dynastic history stretching from his grandfather Mattathias, through the brothers (Judas, Jonathan, Simon), to John Hyrcanus himself.

14.1–3 In 140 BCE Simon's ally Demetrius II was removed from power in his campaign against the Parthians. 14.2 Arsaces VI, the dynastic name of the Parthian king Mithridates I (171–138 BCE). He treated Demetrius well and even married his daughter to him. 14.4–15 A poem summarizes Simon's achievements (vv. 4–7) and celebrates them in biblical language (vv. 8–15). 14.5 The capture of Joppa (see 12.33; 13.11) gave Simon a Mediterranean port. 14.8–15 For biblical texts underlying this section, see Lev

and the youths put on splendid
    military attire.
10 He supplied the towns with food,
    and furnished them with the means of
        defense,
    until his renown spread to the ends of
        the earth.
11 He established peace in the land,
    and Israel rejoiced with great joy.
12 All the people sat under their own vines
        and fig trees,
    and there was none to make them
        afraid.
13 No one was left in the land to fight them,
    and the kings were crushed in those
        days.
14 He gave help to all the humble among his
        people;
    he sought out the law,
    and did away with all the renegades
        and outlaws.
15 He made the sanctuary glorious,
    and added to the vessels of the
        sanctuary.

Diplomacy with Rome and Sparta

16 It was heard in Rome, and as far away as Sparta, that Jonathan had died, and they were deeply grieved. 17 When they heard that his brother Simon had become high priest in his stead, and that he was ruling over the country and the towns in it, 18 they wrote to him on bronze tablets to renew with him the friendship and alliance that they had established with his brothers Judas and Jonathan. 19 And these were read before the assembly in Jerusalem.

20 This is a copy of the letter that the Spartans sent:

"The rulers and the city of the Spartans to the high priest Simon and to the elders and the priests and the rest of the Jewish people, our brothers, greetings. 21 The envoys who were sent to our people have told us about your glory and honor, and we rejoiced at their coming. 22 We have recorded what they said in our public decrees, as follows, 'Numenius son of Antiochus and Antipater son of Jason, envoys of the Jews, have come to us to renew their friendship with us. 23 It has pleased our people to receive these men with honor and to put a copy of their words in the public archives, so that the people of the Spartans may have a record of them. And they have sent a copy of this to the high priest Simon.' "

24 After this Simon sent Numenius to Rome with a large gold shield weighing one thousand minas, to confirm the alliance with the Romans.[a]

Official Honors for Simon

25 When the people heard these things they said, "How shall we thank Simon and his sons? 26 For he and his brothers and the house of his father have stood firm; they have fought and repulsed Israel's enemies and established its freedom." 27 So they made a record on bronze tablets and put it on pillars on Mount Zion.

This is a copy of what they wrote: "On the eighteenth day of Elul, in the one hundred seventy-second year,[b] which is the third year of the great high priest Simon, 28 in Asaramel,[c] in the great assembly of the priests and the people and the rulers of the nation and the elders of the country, the following was proclaimed to us:

29 "Since wars often occurred in the country, Simon son of Mattathias, a priest of the sons[d] of Joarib, and his brothers, exposed themselves to danger and resisted the enemies of their nation, in order that their sanctuary and the law might be preserved; and they brought great glory to their nation. 30 Jonathan rallied the[e] nation, became their high priest, and was gathered to his people. 31 When

---

a Gk *them* *b* 140 B.C. *c* This word resembles the Hebrew words for *the court of the people of God* or *the prince of the people of God* *d* Meaning of Gk uncertain *e* Gk *their*

26.3–4 (v. 8); Zech 8.4 (v. 9); Mic 4.4 (v. 12). **14.14** *Renegades and outlaws,* Jews who still supported the Seleucid program (1.11–15). **14.16–24** The alliances with Rome and Sparta are renewed under Simon. **14.18** It was customary to renew alliances when leadership changed. The renewal of the Roman alliance probably took place shortly after Simon's accession in 142 BCE. For *bronze tablets,* see 8.22. **14.22** Numenius and Antipater had served previously as Jonathan's ambassadors (12.16). **14.24** The report about the *gold shield* may belong before 14.16, since Numenius and Antipater had already visited Rome and Sparta (12.16, 22). **14.25–49** The official decree declaring Simon as benefactor of the Jewish people outlines his good deeds, confirms him as sole leader, and warns those who oppose him. **14.27** The decree is dated September 140 BCE. **14.29–40** A summary of events narrated elsewhere in the book, apart from the note that Simon spent *great sums of his own money* (v. 32). This fact has not been mentioned, unless 13.15–

their enemies decided to invade their country and lay hands on their sanctuary, [32] then Simon rose up and fought for his nation. He spent great sums of his own money; he armed the soldiers of his nation and paid them wages. [33] He fortified the towns of Judea, and Beth-zur on the borders of Judea, where formerly the arms of the enemy had been stored, and he placed there a garrison of Jews. [34] He also fortified Joppa, which is by the sea, and Gazara, which is on the borders of Azotus, where the enemy formerly lived. He settled Jews there, and provided in those towns[a] whatever was necessary for their restoration.

35 "The people saw Simon's faithfulness[b] and the glory that he had resolved to win for his nation, and they made him their leader and high priest, because he had done all these things and because of the justice and loyalty that he had maintained toward his nation. He sought in every way to exalt his people. [36] In his days things prospered in his hands, so that the Gentiles were put out of the[c] country, as were also those in the city of David in Jerusalem, who had built themselves a citadel from which they used to sally forth and defile the environs of the sanctuary, doing great damage to its purity. [37] He settled Jews in it and fortified it for the safety of the country and of the city, and built the walls of Jerusalem higher.

38 "In view of these things King Demetrius confirmed him in the high priesthood, [39] made him one of his Friends, and paid him high honors. [40] For he had heard that the Jews were addressed by the Romans as friends and allies and brothers, and that the Romans[d] had received the envoys of Simon with honor.

41 "The Jews and their priests have resolved that Simon should be their leader and high priest forever, until a trustworthy prophet should arise, [42] and that he should be governor over them and that he should take charge of the sanctuary and appoint officials over its tasks and over the country and the weapons and the strongholds, and that he should take charge of the sanctuary, [43] and that he should be obeyed

by all, and that all contracts in the country should be written in his name, and that he should be clothed in purple and wear gold.

44 "None of the people or priests shall be permitted to nullify any of these decisions or to oppose what he says, or to convene an assembly in the country without his permission, or to be clothed in purple or put on a gold buckle. [45] Whoever acts contrary to these decisions or rejects any of them shall be liable to punishment."

46 All the people agreed to grant Simon the right to act in accordance with these decisions. [47] So Simon accepted and agreed to be high priest, to be commander and ethnarch of the Jews and priests, and to be protector of them all.[e] [48] And they gave orders to inscribe this decree on bronze tablets, to put them up in a conspicuous place in the precincts of the sanctuary, [49] and to deposit copies of them in the treasury, so that Simon and his sons might have them.

Letter of Antiochus VII

15 Antiochus, son of King Demetrius, sent a letter from the islands of the sea to Simon, the priest and ethnarch of the Jews, and to all the nation; [2] its contents were as follows: "King Antiochus to Simon the high priest and ethnarch and to the nation of the Jews, greetings. [3] Whereas certain scoundrels have gained control of the kingdom of our ancestors, and I intend to lay claim to the kingdom so that I may restore it as it formerly was, and have recruited a host of mercenary troops and have equipped warships, [4] and intend to make a landing in the country so that I may proceed against those who have destroyed our country and those who have devastated many cities in my kingdom, [5] now therefore I confirm to you all the tax remissions that the kings before me have granted you, and a release from all the other payments from which they have released you. [6] I permit you to mint

---

a Gk them   b Other ancient authorities read conduct
c Gk their   d Gk they   e Or to preside over them all

19; 14.24 should be taken this way. **14.41–42** The people agree that Simon should have military (*leader*), religious (*high priest*), and political (*governor*) powers. The provision about a *trustworthy prophet* (see 4.46; 9.27) suggests some doubt about or opposition to Simon's high priesthood. **14.43** For dating *contracts*, see 13.42. For *purple* and *gold* as insignia of a high priest and a king's Friend, see 10.20, 89.

15.1–14 Antiochus VII makes promises to Simon and traps Trypho at Dor in 138 BCE. **15.1** Since *Antiochus* VII, the son of Demetrius I and younger brother of Demetrius II, grew up in Side in Pamphylia, he was known as Sidetes. **15.3** The *scoundrels* included Trypho, and perhaps Alexander Balas and Antiochus VI. **15.6** To the privileges already granted to Simon, Antiochus added the right to mint his own *coinage*.

your own coinage as money for your country, [7] and I grant freedom to Jerusalem and the sanctuary. All the weapons that you have prepared and the strongholds that you have built and now hold shall remain yours. [8] Every debt you owe to the royal treasury and any such future debts shall be canceled for you from henceforth and for all time. [9] When we gain control of our kingdom, we will bestow great honor on you and your nation and the temple, so that your glory will become manifest in all the earth."

10 In the one hundred seventy-fourth year[a] Antiochus set out and invaded the land of his ancestors. All the troops rallied to him, so that there were only a few with Trypho. [11] Antiochus pursued him, and Trypho[b] came in his flight to Dor, which is by the sea; [12] for he knew that troubles had converged on him, and his troops had deserted him. [13] So Antiochus encamped against Dor, and with him were one hundred twenty thousand warriors and eight thousand cavalry. [14] He surrounded the town, and the ships joined battle from the sea; he pressed the town hard from land and sea, and permitted no one to leave or enter it.

Rome Supports the Jews

15 Then Numenius and his companions arrived from Rome, with letters to the kings and countries, in which the following was written: [16] "Lucius, consul of the Romans, to King Ptolemy, greetings. [17] The envoys of the Jews have come to us as our friends and allies to renew our ancient friendship and alliance. They had been sent by the high priest Simon and by the Jewish people [18] and have brought a gold shield weighing one thousand minas. [19] We therefore have decided to write to the kings and countries that they should not seek their harm or make war against them and

their cities and their country, or make alliance with those who war against them. [20] And it has seemed good to us to accept the shield from them. [21] Therefore if any scoundrels have fled to you from their country, hand them over to the high priest Simon, so that he may punish them according to their law."

22 The consul[c] wrote the same thing to King Demetrius and to Attalus and Ariarathes and Arsaces, [23] and to all the countries, and to Sampsames,[d] and to the Spartans, and to Delos, and to Myndos, and to Sicyon, and to Caria, and to Samos, and to Pamphylia, and to Lycia, and to Halicarnassus, and to Rhodes, and to Phaselis, and to Cos, and to Side, and to Aradus and Gortyna and Cnidus and Cyprus and Cyrene. [24] They also sent a copy of these things to the high priest Simon.

Antiochus VII Threatens Simon

25 King Antiochus besieged Dor for the second time, continually throwing his forces against it and making engines of war; and he shut Trypho up and kept him from going out or in. [26] And Simon sent to Antiochus[e] two thousand picked troops, to fight for him, and silver and gold and a large amount of military equipment. [27] But he refused to receive them, and broke all the agreements he formerly had made with Simon, and became estranged from him. [28] He sent to him Athenobius, one of his Friends, to confer with him, saying, "You hold control of Joppa and Gazara and the citadel in Jerusalem; they are cities of my kingdom. [29] You have devastated their territory, you have done great damage in the land, and you have taken possession of many places in my kingdom. [30] Now then, hand over the cities

a 138 B.C.   b Gk he   c Gk He   d The name is uncertain
e Gk him

But there are no Jewish coins from Simon's time (see v. 27). **15.9** Despite the independence implied by the privileges, it appears that Antiochus VII regarded Judea as part of his own *kingdom.* **15.11** *Dor,* south of Mount Carmel and nine miles north of Caesarea Maritima. **15.15–24** The sequel to 14.16–24, this passage presents a letter (from the copy sent to Simon, v. 24) reaffirming friendship and alliance between Rome and the Jews. **15.15** *Numenius,* the Jewish envoy (12.16; 14.22, 24). **15.16** *Lucius* Caecilius Metellus (consul in 142 BCE) addresses *Ptolemy* VIII Euergetes II (146–116 BCE). The text sent to the Egyptian ruler was also sent to those listed in vv. 22–23. **15.22** *Demetrius* II of Syria

(see 14.3); *Attalus* II of Pergamum; *Ariarathes* V of Cappadocia; and *Arsaces* of Parthia (see 14.2). **15.23** *Countries . . . Cyrene,* mainly independent states in Asia Minor, Greece, and the Greek Isles. **15.25–36** Antiochus VII refuses Simon's aid, takes away all concessions, and demands indemnities from Simon. **15.25** The story of the siege of Dor broken off in v. 14 is rejoined with the awkward expression *for the second time.* **15.27** Antiochus VII *refused* Simon's help because victory was in his grasp and he did not need Simon. Therefore he retracted the promises made in vv. 5–9. **15.30** The places *outside the borders of Judea* probably included the Samaritan districts (11.34) as

that you have seized and the tribute money of the places that you have conquered outside the borders of Judea; [31]or else pay me five hundred talents of silver for the destruction that you have caused and five hundred talents more for the tribute money of the cities. Otherwise we will come and make war on you."

32 So Athenobius, the king's Friend, came to Jerusalem, and when he saw the splendor of Simon, and the sideboard with its gold and silver plate, and his great magnificence, he was amazed. When he reported to him the king's message, [33]Simon said to him in reply: "We have neither taken foreign land nor seized foreign property, but only the inheritance of our ancestors, which at one time had been unjustly taken by our enemies. [34]Now that we have the opportunity, we are firmly holding the inheritance of our ancestors. [35]As for Joppa and Gazara, which you demand, they were causing great damage among the people and to our land; for them we will give you one hundred talents."

Athenobius[a] did not answer him a word, [36]but returned in wrath to the king and reported to him these words, and also the splendor of Simon and all that he had seen. And the king was very angry.

Victory over Cendebeus

37 Meanwhile Trypho embarked on a ship and escaped to Orthosia. [38]Then the king made Cendebeus commander-in-chief of the coastal country, and gave him troops of infantry and cavalry. [39]He commanded him to encamp against Judea, to build up Kedron and fortify its gates, and to make war on the people; but the king pursued Trypho. [40]So Cendebeus came to Jamnia and began to provoke the people and invade Judea and take the people captive and kill them. [41]He built up Kedron and stationed horsemen and troops there, so that they might go out and make raids along the highways of Judea, as the king had ordered him.

16 John went up from Gazara and reported to his father Simon what Cendebeus had done. [2]And Simon called in his two eldest sons Judas and John, and said to them: "My brothers and I and my father's house have fought the wars of Israel from our youth until this day, and things have prospered in our hands so that we have delivered Israel many times. [3]But now I have grown old, and you by Heaven's[b] mercy are mature in years. Take my place and my brother's, and go out and fight for our nation, and may the help that comes from Heaven be with you."

4 So John[c] chose out of the country twenty thousand warriors and cavalry, and they marched against Cendebeus and camped for the night in Modein. [5]Early in the morning they started out and marched into the plain, where a large force of infantry and cavalry was coming to meet them; and a stream lay between them. [6]Then he and his army lined up against them. He saw that the soldiers were afraid to cross the stream, so he crossed over first; and when his troops saw him, they crossed over after him. [7]Then he divided the army and placed the cavalry in the center of the infantry, for the cavalry of the enemy were very numerous. [8]They sounded the trumpets, and Cendebeus and his army were put to flight; many of them fell wounded and the rest fled into the stronghold. [9]At that time Judas the brother of John was wounded, but John pursued them until Cendebeus[d] reached Kedron, which he had built. [10]They also fled into the towers that were in the fields of Azotus, and John[d] burned it with fire, and about two thousand of them fell. He then returned to Judea safely.

---

a Gk *He*   *b* Gk *his*   *c* Other ancient authorities read *he*
d Gk *he*

---

well as Adida, Beth-zur, and Akkaron. **15.33** The right to the *inheritance* of one's ancestors was based on Greek international law as well as (in the case of the Jews) the biblical promises of the Jews. **15.37–16.10** Simon's son John defeats the Seleucids under Cendebeus. **15.37** When Trypho escaped to *Orthosia* (a port north of Tripolis), Antiochus VII pursued him and had him killed in Apamea. **15.38–41** *Cendebeus,* governor of the coastal region appointed in the absence of Antiochus VII. *Kedron,* Cendebeus's base, four miles southeast of *Jamnia.* **16.1** The Maccabean fortress nearest to Cendebeus's activity was *Gazara,* where John Hyrcanus was in command (see 13.53). **16.2** For the fate of Simon's sons *Judas* and *Mattathias,* see vv. 14–16. **16.4** Jewish *cavalry* is mentioned here for the first time. *Modein* (see 2.1) had remained a center of Maccabean support. **16.6** For courage in crossing the *stream,* see Judas's action in 5.40–43. **16.7** Having the Jewish *cavalry* go up against the Seleucid *infantry* (not cavalry) confused the enemy's battle plan. **16.10** Jonathan had burned *Azotus* previously (10.84).

Murder of Simon and His Sons

11 Now Ptolemy son of Abubus had been appointed governor over the plain of Jericho; he had a large store of silver and gold, 12for he was son-in-law of the high priest. 13His heart was lifted up; he determined to get control of the country, and made treacherous plans against Simon and his sons, to do away with them. 14Now Simon was visiting the towns of the country and attending to their needs, and he went down to Jericho with his sons Mattathias and Judas, in the one hundred seventy-seventh year,[a] in the eleventh month, which is the month of Shebat. 15The son of Abubus received them treacherously in the little stronghold called Dok, which he had built; he gave them a great banquet, and hid men there. 16When Simon and his sons were drunk, Ptolemy and his men rose up, took their weapons, rushed in against Simon in the banquet hall and killed him and his two sons, as well as some of his servants. 17So he committed an act of great treachery and returned evil for good.

John Succeeds Simon

18 Then Ptolemy wrote a report about these things and sent it to the king, asking him to send troops to aid him and to turn over to him the towns and the country. 19He sent other troops to Gazara to do away with John; he sent letters to the captains asking them to come to him so that he might give them silver and gold and gifts; 20and he sent other troops to take possession of Jerusalem and the temple hill. 21But someone ran ahead and reported to John at Gazara that his father and brothers had perished, and that "he has sent men to kill you also." 22When he heard this, he was greatly shocked; he seized the men who came to destroy him and killed them, for he had found out that they were seeking to destroy him.

23 The rest of the acts of John and his wars and the brave deeds that he did, and the building of the walls that he completed, and his achievements, 24are written in the annals of his high priesthood, from the time that he became high priest after his father.

a 134 B.C.

16.11–17 In the winter of 134 BCE, Simon and his sons Judas and Mattathias are murdered near Jericho in an attempted coup by Simon's son-in-law Ptolemy. **16.11** *Abubus,* probably "beloved" (in Hebrew *chabub*). **16.15** *Dok,* a fortress near Jericho. **16.18–24** Simon's surviving son, John Hyrcanus, escapes his brother-in-law's plot and succeeds his father as high priest and military and political ruler. **16.18** Ptolemy's

report *to the king* suggests that he hoped to be appointed the official Seleucid ruler in Judea and environs. **16.19–22** John Hyrcanus escaped at Gazara only because an informant told him what happened to Simon and his two brothers at Dok. **16.23–24** Using a formula familiar from 1–2 Kings (see 1 Macc 9.22), the book ends by showing how John Hyrcanus inherited the Jewish high priesthood.

2 MACCABEES

Content

THE SECOND BOOK OF MACCABEES supplies important information about the events leading up to the revolt under Judas Maccabeus and recounts the subsequent exploits of Judas up to 161 BCE (his defeat of Nicanor). It describes the political intrigues surrounding the Jewish high priesthood and portrays Judas Maccabeus as the ideal Jewish warrior—one who prays before battles and gives thanks afterward, one who is careful to observe the sabbath and other Jewish rituals.

The body of 2 Maccabees (2.19–15.39) narrates three attacks on the Jerusalem temple by Israel's enemies and their defeats by supernatural agents or by Judas and his companions. The first attack (3.1–40) occurs under Seleucus IV when Heliodorus seeks to plunder the temple treasury. The second attack (4.1–10.9) takes place under Antiochus IV Epiphanes and ends with Judas's capture of the temple and its purification. The third attack (10.10–15.36) happens under Antiochus V Eupator and involves the defeat of his general Nicanor as he tries to kill Judas. Though this outline does not include everything in the book, it does bring out the events that were most important for the author and underlines his emphasis on the holiness and inviolability of the Jerusalem temple.

Literary Connections and Character

IN THE AUTHOR'S PREFACE (2.19–32) we are told that 2 Maccabees is the condensation of a five-volume work by Jason of Cyrene (2.23). Jason's work is no longer extant, and there is no way of being sure how closely the condenser/epitomator followed his source. The original language of both Jason's five-volume work and 2 Maccabees was Greek. The Greek is not nearly as "biblical" as that of 1 Maccabees. Jason may have written shortly after the events he described; at least the narrative breaks off before the death of Judas. The "author" of 2 Maccabees claims to rely on Jason for the facts and proposes to give a pleasurable and memorable account. The condensation may have been completed by 124 BCE, the date of the "cover letter" preserved in 1.1–9.

The major theme of 2 Maccabees is the Jerusalem temple and its Defender, the God of Israel, who is at work in angelic figures and especially in Judas Maccabeus. Because the book stresses the sanctity of the temple, it has been referred to as "temple propaganda." The book has also been described as "pathetic history" in that it speaks to and plays upon human emotions (Greek *pathe*). The two prefixed letters (1.1–9; 1.10–2.18) encourage Jews in Egypt and elsewhere to observe the festival of Hanukkah as it was being observed in Jerusalem. The letters appear to have been added to the main work when it was sent to Jews in the Diaspora.

As a historical source 2 Maccabees is especially valuable for information concerning the disputes among Jews regarding the high priesthood (held by Onias III, Jason, Menelaus) and the cultural-religious program of hellenization carried out under Antiochus IV (4.9–17; 6.1–9). These matters are treated more briefly in 1 Maccabees. When 2 Maccabees recounts the battles and other events described in 1 Maccabees, it tends to be less reliable about the facts and more concerned with religious matters. The two books share a tendency to inflate the numbers of enemy troops and casualties. The author of 2 Maccabees probably did not have access to 1 Maccabees, which may not have yet been written. It is possible that the two writers used a common source, but that is difficult to prove. The letters quoted in ch. 11 very likely reflect authentic documents, though they contain some confusions and obscurities.

Theological Ideas

BESIDES STRESSING THE INVIOLABILITY OF THE JERUSALEM TEMPLE, 2 Maccabees is noteworthy for its teachings about suffering (5.18–20; 6.12–17) and portrayals of martyrs (6.10–11, 18–31; 7.1–42; 14.37–46). The sufferings inflicted on the Jews are interpreted both as the consequence of their leaders' sins (Simon, Jason, Menelaus) and a sign of God's loving discipline toward the chosen people. There is an expectation that Israel's enemies will eventually be punished appropriately. The martyrs (especially Eleazar, the seven brothers and their mother, and Razis) willingly undergo torture and death rather than be unfaithful to the distinctive precepts of Judaism. In ch. 7 these two themes come together around the theme of the resurrection of the body. In the resurrection the martyrs will be rewarded with eternal life and the wicked (like King Antiochus IV) will be punished. The author's own strong belief in resurrection led him to interpret Judas's sin offering for his dead soldiers (12.39–45) as atonement on behalf of the sins of the dead. 2 Maccabees is canonical for Catholics and Orthodox, deuterocanonical/apocryphal for Protestants, and noncanonical for Jews (though it does recount the origin of Hanukkah). [DANIEL J. HARRINGTON]

A Letter to the Jews in Egypt

1 The Jews in Jerusalem and those in the land of Judea,
To their Jewish kindred in Egypt,
Greetings and true peace.

2 May God do good to you, and may he remember his covenant with Abraham and Isaac and Jacob, his faithful servants. 3 May he give you all a heart to worship him and to do his will with a strong heart and a willing spirit. 4 May he open your heart to his law and his commandments, and may he bring peace. 5 May he hear your prayers and be reconciled to you, and may he not forsake you in time of evil. 6 We are now praying for you here.

7 In the reign of Demetrius, in the one hundred sixty-ninth year,[a] we Jews wrote to you, in the critical distress that came upon us in those years after Jason and his company revolted from the holy land and the kingdom 8 and burned the gate and shed innocent blood. We prayed to the Lord and were heard, and we offered sacrifice and grain offering, and we lit the lamps and set out the loaves. 9 And now see that you keep the festival of booths in the month of Chislev, in the one hundred eighty-eighth year.[b]

A Letter to Aristobulus

10 The people of Jerusalem and of Judea and the senate and Judas,

---

a 143 B.C.   b 124 B.C.

To Aristobulus, who is of the family of the anointed priests, teacher of King Ptolemy, and to the Jews in Egypt,

Greetings and good health.

11 Having been saved by God out of grave dangers we thank him greatly for taking our side against the king,[a] 12for he drove out those who fought against the holy city. 13When the leader reached Persia with a force that seemed irresistible, they were cut to pieces in the temple of Nanea by a deception employed by the priests of the goddess[b] Nanea. 14On the pretext of intending to marry her, Antiochus came to the place together with his Friends, to secure most of its treasures as a dowry. 15When the priests of the temple of Nanea had set out the treasures and Antiochus had come with a few men inside the wall of the sacred precinct, they closed the temple as soon as he entered it. 16Opening a secret door in the ceiling, they threw stones and struck down the leader and his men; they dismembered them and cut off their heads and threw them to the people outside. 17Blessed in every way be our God, who has brought judgment on those who have behaved impiously.

Fire Consumes Nehemiah's Sacrifice

18 Since on the twenty-fifth day of Chislev we shall celebrate the purification of the temple, we thought it necessary to notify you, in order that you also may celebrate the festival of booths and the festival of the fire given when Nehemiah, who built the temple and the altar, offered sacrifices.

19 For when our ancestors were being led captive to Persia, the pious priests of that time took some of the fire of the altar and secretly hid it in the hollow of a dry cistern, where they took such precautions that the place was unknown to anyone. 20But after many years had passed, when it pleased God, Nehemiah, having been commissioned by the king of Persia, sent the descendants of the priests who had hidden the fire to get it. And when they reported to us that they had not found fire but only a thick liquid, he ordered them to dip it out and bring it. 21When the materials for the sacrifices were presented, Nehemiah ordered the priests to sprinkle the liquid on the wood and on the things laid upon it. 22When this had been done and some time had passed, and when the sun, which had been clouded over, shone out, a great fire blazed up, so that all marveled. 23And while the sacrifice was being consumed, the priests offered prayer—the priests and everyone. Jonathan led, and the rest responded, as did Nehemiah. 24The prayer was to this effect:

"O Lord, Lord God, Creator of all things, you are awe-inspiring and strong and just and merciful, you alone are king and are kind, 25you alone are bountiful, you alone are just and

---

a Cn: Gk as those who array themselves against a king
b Gk lacks the goddess

1.1–9 In 124 BCE the Jews of Jerusalem and Judea wrote to the Jews in Egypt to urge them to celebrate Hanukkah. The letter may have been composed to accompany the copy of 2 Maccabees sent to Egypt. **1.2–6** The prayer following the greeting may be criticizing the Jewish temple founded by Onias IV at Leontopolis in Egypt in about 160 BCE. **1.5** Time of evil, perhaps a persecution of Egyptian Jews under Ptolemy VIII. **1.7–8** Demetrius II (145–140 BCE). The letter referred to was written in 143 BCE and recounted the events described in 5.5–10. **1.9** The festival of booths was celebrated in the seventh month (Tishri), not the ninth month (Chislev). For Hanukkah as similar to the Festival of Booths, see 10.6. **1.10–17** A second letter begins the long explanation (reaching to 2.18) about Hanukkah's origins in Jewish history. It starts with an account of the death of Antiochus IV Epiphanes. **1.10** If the letter was from Judas Maccabeus, it must have been written between 164 (Antiochus's death) and 160 BCE (Judas's death). Aristobulus, the Jewish teacher of Ptolemy VI (180–145 BCE). **1.11–12** King, Antiochus IV (175–164 BCE). For the recovery of the holy city of Jerusalem, see 10.1. **1.13–17** Leader, Antiochus IV, though the story may first have been told about Antiochus III, his father. Nanea, originally a Sumerian goddess of love and fertility. For different accounts of the king's death, see ch. 9; 1 Macc 6.1–16; Dan 11.40–45. **1.17** From the Jewish perspective Antiochus died for behaving impiously against the Jerusalem temple, not the temple of Nanea. **1.18–36** The miracle of the fire is one precedent for the purification of the temple commemorated at Hanukkah. The strained search for precedents here and in 2.1–18 suggests that observing Hanukkah was still controversial. **1.18** For the date, see 6.7; 10.5; 1 Macc 1.59. The Second Temple and its altar were already built when Nehemiah came to Jerusalem as governor. **1.19** The Jews were exiled to Babylon, not Persia, but Babylon had become part of the Persian Empire by Nehemiah's time. **1.20** Thick liquid, a kind of highly flamable petroleum (naphtha; see v. 36) that burst into flames under the heat of the sun (v. 22). **1.23** Jonathan may be the same as Mattaniah "who was the leader to begin the thanksgiving in prayer" (Neh 11.17). Both names mean "God's gift" in Hebrew. **1.24–29** The prayer's emphases on monotheism, divine mercy, and Israel's

almighty and eternal. You rescue Israel from every evil; you chose the ancestors and consecrated them. 26 Accept this sacrifice on behalf of all your people Israel and preserve your portion and make it holy. 27 Gather together our scattered people, set free those who are slaves among the Gentiles, look on those who are rejected and despised, and let the Gentiles know that you are our God. 28 Punish those who oppress and are insolent with pride. 29 Plant your people in your holy place, as Moses promised."

30 Then the priests sang the hymns. 31 After the materials of the sacrifice had been consumed, Nehemiah ordered that the liquid that was left should be poured on large stones. 32 When this was done, a flame blazed up; but when the light from the altar shone back, it went out. 33 When this matter became known, and it was reported to the king of the Persians that, in the place where the exiled priests had hidden the fire, the liquid had appeared with which Nehemiah and his associates had burned the materials of the sacrifice, 34 the king investigated the matter, and enclosed the place and made it sacred. 35 And with those persons whom the king favored he exchanged many excellent gifts. 36 Nehemiah and his associates called this "nephthar," which means purification, but by most people it is called naphtha.*a*

Jeremiah Hides the Tent, Ark, and Altar

2 One finds in the records that the prophet Jeremiah ordered those who were being deported to take some of the fire, as has been mentioned, 2 and that the prophet, after giving them the law, instructed those who were being deported not to forget the commandments of the Lord, or to be led astray in their thoughts on seeing the gold and silver statues and their adornment. 3 And with other similar words he exhorted them that the law should not depart from their hearts.

4 It was also in the same document that the prophet, having received an oracle, ordered that the tent and the ark should follow with him, and that he went out to the mountain where Moses had gone up and had seen the inheritance of God. 5 Jeremiah came and found a cave-dwelling, and he brought there the tent and the ark and the altar of incense; then he sealed up the entrance. 6 Some of those who followed him came up intending to mark the way, but could not find it. 7 When Jeremiah learned of it, he rebuked them and declared: "The place shall remain unknown until God gathers his people together again and shows his mercy. 8 Then the Lord will disclose these things, and the glory of the Lord and the cloud will appear, as they were shown in the case of Moses, and as Solomon asked that the place should be specially consecrated."

9 It was also made clear that being possessed of wisdom Solomon*b* offered sacrifice for the dedication and completion of the temple. 10 Just as Moses prayed to the Lord, and fire came down from heaven and consumed the sacrifices, so also Solomon prayed, and the fire came down and consumed the whole burnt offerings. 11 And Moses said, "They were consumed because the sin offering had not been eaten." 12 Likewise Solomon also kept the eight days.

13 The same things are reported in the records and in the memoirs of Nehemiah, and also that he founded a library and collected the books about the kings and prophets, and the writings of David, and letters of kings about votive offerings. 14 In the same way Judas also collected all the books that had been lost on account of the war that had come upon us, and they are in our possession. 15 So if you have need of them, send people to get them for you.

16 Since, therefore, we are about to cele-

---

a Gk *nephthai*   *b* Gk *he*

---

election were very appropriate to the situation of Israel in the second century BCE, as was the plea that God rescue Israel and punish its enemies. **1.31–34** Fire was sacred to the *Persians*, who sometimes built temples around it. The event described in vv. 31–32 stresses the sacredness of the altar in the Jerusalem temple. **1.36** For the interpretation of Hanukkah as a *purification*, see 2.18; 10.3; 14.36. *Naphtha*. See note on 1.20.

2.1–18 More precedents for Hanukkah are found in connection with Jeremiah, Solomon, Moses, and Nehemiah. **2.2** For Jeremiah's warnings against idolatry, see the Letter of Jeremiah. **2.4** *Prophet*, again Jeremiah.

Mountain, Nebo (Deut 32.49), from which Moses viewed the promised land but did not enter it. **2.8** *Glory of the Lord, cloud*. See Ex 40.34–35 (Moses and the tent of meeting); 1 Kings 8.10–11 (Solomon's temple). **2.10–12** For *fire* from heaven, see Lev 9.23–24; 2 Chr 7.1. For the words of *Moses*, see Lev 10.16–19. *Eight days*. See 1 Kings 8.65–66; 2 Chr 7.9. **2.13** The "memoirs" in Neh 1–7, 11–13 do not mention the building of the temple or the fire. Nehemiah's *library* may have included historical books (1 Samuel through 2 Kings), Prophets, Psalms, and the royal decrees in Ezra 6.3–12; 7.12–26. **2.14** For Jewish *books . . . lost on*

brate the purification, we write to you. Will you therefore please keep the days? [17]It is God who has saved all his people, and has returned the inheritance to all, and the kingship and the priesthood and the consecration, [18]as he promised through the law. We have hope in God that he will soon have mercy on us and will gather us from everywhere under heaven into his holy place, for he has rescued us from great evils and has purified the place.

The Compiler's Preface

19 The story of Judas Maccabeus and his brothers, and the purification of the great temple, and the dedication of the altar, [20]and further the wars against Antiochus Epiphanes and his son Eupator, [21]and the appearances that came from heaven to those who fought bravely for Judaism, so that though few in number they seized the whole land and pursued the barbarian hordes, [22]and regained possession of the temple famous throughout the world, and liberated the city, and re-established the laws that were about to be abolished, while the Lord with great kindness became gracious to them— [23]all this, which has been set forth by Jason of Cyrene in five volumes, we shall attempt to condense into a single book. [24]For considering the flood of statistics involved and the difficulty there is for those who wish to enter upon the narratives of history because of the mass of material, [25]we have aimed to please those who wish to read, to make it easy for those who are inclined to memorize, and to profit all readers. [26]For us who have undertaken the toil of abbreviating, it is no light matter but calls for sweat and loss of sleep, [27]just as it is not easy for one who prepares a banquet and seeks the benefit of others. Nevertheless, to secure the gratitude of many we will gladly endure the uncomfortable

toil, [28]leaving the responsibility for exact details to the compiler, while devoting our effort to arriving at the outlines of the condensation. [29]For as the master builder of a new house must be concerned with the whole construction, while the one who undertakes its painting and decoration has to consider only what is suitable for its adornment, such in my judgment is the case with us. [30]It is the duty of the original historian to occupy the ground, to discuss matters from every side, and to take trouble with details, [31]but the one who recasts the narrative should be allowed to strive for brevity of expression and to forego exhaustive treatment. [32]At this point therefore let us begin our narrative, without adding any more to what has already been said; for it would be foolish to lengthen the preface while cutting short the history itself.

Arrival of Heliodorus in Jerusalem

3 While the holy city was inhabited in unbroken peace and the laws were strictly observed because of the piety of the high priest Onias and his hatred of wickedness, [2]it came about that the kings themselves honored the place and glorified the temple with the finest presents, [3]even to the extent that King Seleucus of Asia defrayed from his own revenues all the expenses connected with the service of the sacrifices.

4 But a man named Simon, of the tribe of Benjamin, who had been made captain of the temple, had a disagreement with the high priest about the administration of the city market. [5]Since he could not prevail over Onias, he went to Apollonius of Tarsus,[a] who at that time was governor of Coelesyria and Phoenicia, [6]and reported to him that the treasury in

---

a Gk Apollonius son of Tharseas

account of the war, see the reference to destroying "the books of the law," 1 Macc 1.56–57. **2.16–18** The call to observe Hanukkah (see 1.18, 36) as the *purification* of the temple alludes to Ex 19.6; Deut 30.3–5. **2.19–32** The body of 2 Maccabees is the digest of the five-volume work by Jason of Cyrene. Here the condenser explains his goals and procedures. **2.19–22** The summary of contents omits Seleucus IV (ch. 3) and Demetrius I (chs. 14–15). It contains the first extant use of the word *Judaism* (see 8.1; 14.38) and refers to *appearances* or epiphanies (see 3.24–26; 10.29–30; 11.8; 12.22; 15.27), which figure prominently in the main narrative. **2.23** *Cyrene*, a city in Cyrenaica (modern Libya) that had Jewish settlers from Egypt. *Jason* was undoubtedly Jewish and may have settled in

Judea. **2.24–28** Although relying on Jason for *exact details*, the writer wants to make the story pleasurable, memorable, and profitable (v. 25). **2.29** The author compares Jason to a builder and himself to a painter-decorator (see v. 25). See 15.38–39.

3.1–12 The first crisis involving *the sanctity and inviolability of the temple* in Jerusalem (v. 12) arises from rivalry between pro-Seleucid (Simon) and pro-Ptolemaic (Hyrcanus) factions among the Jews. **3.1** *Onias* III, the Jewish high priest until 175 BCE. **3.2** *The place*, frequent name for the temple in 2 Maccabees. **3.3** *Seleucus* IV Philopator (187–175 BCE), successor of Antiochus III and predecessor of Antiochus IV. **3.4** *Simon* was more likely from the priestly clan of Bilgah (Neh 12.5, 18; 1 Chr 24.14) than from the *tribe of Benjamin*. His broth-

Jerusalem was full of untold sums of money, so that the amount of the funds could not be reckoned, and that they did not belong to the account of the sacrifices, but that it was possible for them to fall under the control of the king. [7]When Apollonius met the king, he told him of the money about which he had been informed. The king[a] chose Heliodorus, who was in charge of his affairs, and sent him with commands to effect the removal of the reported wealth. [8]Heliodorus at once set out on his journey, ostensibly to make a tour of inspection of the cities of Coelesyria and Phoenicia, but in fact to carry out the king's purpose.

9 When he had arrived at Jerusalem and had been kindly welcomed by the high priest of[b] the city, he told about the disclosure that had been made and stated why he had come, and he inquired whether this really was the situation. [10]The high priest explained that there were some deposits belonging to widows and orphans, [11]and also some money of Hyrcanus son of Tobias, a man of very prominent position, and that it totaled in all four hundred talents of silver and two hundred of gold. To such an extent the impious Simon had misrepresented the facts. [12]And he said that it was utterly impossible that wrong should be done to those people who had trusted in the holiness of the place and in the sanctity and inviolability of the temple that is honored throughout the whole world.

Heliodorus Plans to Rob the Temple

13 But Heliodorus, because of the orders he had from the king, said that this money must in any case be confiscated for the king's treasury. [14]So he set a day and went in to direct the inspection of these funds.

There was no little distress throughout the whole city. [15]The priests prostrated themselves before the altar in their priestly vestments and called toward heaven upon him who had given the law about deposits, that he should keep them safe for those who had deposited them. [16]To see the appearance of the high priest was to be wounded at heart, for his face and the change in his color disclosed the anguish of his soul. [17]For terror and bodily trembling had come over the man, which plainly showed to those who looked at him the pain lodged in his heart. [18]People also hurried out of their houses in crowds to make a general supplication because the holy place was about to be brought into dishonor. [19]Women, girded with sackcloth under their breasts, thronged the streets. Some of the young women who were kept indoors ran together to the gates, and some to the walls, while others peered out of the windows. [20]And holding up their hands to heaven, they all made supplication. [21]There was something pitiable in the prostration of the whole populace and the anxiety of the high priest in his great anguish.

The Lord Protects His Temple

22 While they were calling upon the Almighty Lord that he would keep what had been entrusted safe and secure for those who had entrusted it, [23]Heliodorus went on with what had been decided. [24]But when he arrived at the treasury with his bodyguard, then and there the Sovereign of spirits and of all authority caused so great a manifestation that all who had been so bold as to accompany him were astounded by the power of God, and became faint with terror. [25]For there appeared to them a magnificently caparisoned horse, with a rider of frightening mien; it rushed furiously at Heliodorus and struck at him with its front hoofs. Its rider was seen to have armor and weapons of gold. [26]Two young men also appeared to him, remarkably strong, gloriously beautiful and splendidly dressed, who stood on either side of him and flogged him contin-

a Gk He   b Other ancient authorities read and

ers were Menelaus (4.23) and Lysimachus (4.29). **3.5** *Apollonius* is called *son of Menestheus* in 4.4, 21, and so the reading *son of Tharseas* (see text note *a* on p. 1523) is emended to *Tarsus*. His territory included Judea and all the area from the Euphrates to the Mediterranean except for Seleucis (the area of Greek cities in north Syria). **3.6** The temple *treasury* accepted money from private depositors (see vv. 10–11), a common practice in antiquity. **3.7** *Heliodorus* was raised with Seleucus IV and was involved in the plot that resulted in the king's death in 175 BCE. **3.11** *Hyrcanus*, son of Joseph and grandson of Tobias, was part of the Jewish family of Tobiads, known to be sympathetic to the Ptolemies. **3.13–21** Heliodorus's threat to the temple's security and sanctity elicits a highly emotional response from the people of Jerusalem. **3.15** *The law about deposits.* See Ex 22.7–13. Nothing is said about the gentile Heliodorus profaning the temple. **3.19** *Sackcloth,* a coarse material made from goats' hair worn as a sign of mourning (Esth 4.1; Neh 9.1; Jon 3.6). **3.22–28** The Lord defends the temple miraculously by striking down Heliodorus. **3.24–25** Other miraculous manifestations of *horse* and *rider* occur in

uously, inflicting many blows on him. [27]When he suddenly fell to the ground and deep darkness came over him, his men took him up, put him on a stretcher, [28]and carried him away—this man who had just entered the aforesaid treasury with a great retinue and all his bodyguard but was now unable to help himself. They recognized clearly the sovereign power of God.

Onias Prays for Heliodorus

[29] While he lay prostrate, speechless because of the divine intervention and deprived of any hope of recovery, [30]they praised the Lord who had acted marvelously for his own place. And the temple, which a little while before was full of fear and disturbance, was filled with joy and gladness, now that the Almighty Lord had appeared.

[31] Some of Heliodorus's friends quickly begged Onias to call upon the Most High to grant life to one who was lying quite at his last breath. [32]So the high priest, fearing that the king might get the notion that some foul play had been perpetrated by the Jews with regard to Heliodorus, offered sacrifice for the man's recovery. [33]While the high priest was making an atonement, the same young men appeared again to Heliodorus dressed in the same clothing, and they stood and said, "Be very grateful to the high priest Onias, since for his sake the Lord has granted you your life. [34]And see that you, who have been flogged by heaven, report to all people the majestic power of God." Having said this they vanished.

The Conversion of Heliodorus

[35] Then Heliodorus offered sacrifice to the Lord and made very great vows to the Savior of his life, and having bidden Onias farewell, he marched off with his forces to the king. [36]He bore testimony to all concerning the deeds of the supreme God, which he had seen

with his own eyes. [37]When the king asked Heliodorus what sort of person would be suitable to send on another mission to Jerusalem, he replied, [38]"If you have any enemy or plotter against your government, send him there, for you will get him back thoroughly flogged, if he survives at all; for there is certainly some power of God about the place. [39]For he who has his dwelling in heaven watches over that place himself and brings it aid, and he strikes and destroys those who come to do it injury." [40]This was the outcome of the episode of Heliodorus and the protection of the treasury.

Simon Accuses Onias

4 The previously mentioned Simon, who had informed about the money against[a] his own country, slandered Onias, saying that it was he who had incited Heliodorus and had been the real cause of the misfortune. [2]He dared to designate as a plotter against the government the man who was the benefactor of the city, the protector of his compatriots, and a zealot for the laws. [3]When his hatred progressed to such a degree that even murders were committed by one of Simon's approved agents, [4]Onias recognized that the rivalry was serious and that Apollonius son of Menestheus,[b] and governor of Coelesyria and Phoenicia, was intensifying the malice of Simon. [5]So he appealed to the king, not accusing his compatriots but having in view the welfare, both public and private, of all the people. [6]For he saw that without the king's attention public affairs could not again reach a peaceful settlement, and that Simon would not stop his folly.

Jason's Reforms

7 When Seleucus died and Antiochus, who was called Epiphanes, succeeded to the king-

a Gk and   b Vg Compare verse 21: Meaning of Gk uncertain

5.2–3; 10.29; 11.8. **3.26** *Two young men,* angelic figures. **3.28** Who *recognized* God's power—Heliodorus and his retinue or the Jewish bystanders? See also v. 30. **3.29–34** Lest the miraculous intervention be misinterpreted by Seleucus IV, the high priest Onias III prays for the healing of Heliodorus. **3.30** As in many biblical texts, there is no sharp line between the action of the *Almighty Lord* and the angelic figures. **3.33** The ability of Onias III to make *atonement* for a gentile sinner like Heliodorus places him with Moses (Ex 8.28–29) and Job (Job 42.7–10).**3.35–40** As a result of the miraculous in-

tervention Heliodorus recognizes the power of Israel's God to defend the temple. **3.35–36** Without becoming a Jew, Heliodorus *offered sacrifice* and acknowledged Israel's God as *supreme.* **3.38** The *power of God about the place* (the temple) is a major theme in 2 Maccabees.

4.1–6 The internal Jewish struggle between Simon and Onias III is intertwined with Seleucid affairs. **4.1** *Simon* was *previously mentioned* in 3.4–6. His slander may have been due to Onias's pro-Ptolemaic stance. **4.2** *Laws,* not only the Jewish Torah but also the Seleucid laws. **4.4** *Apollonius* was also Simon's collabo-

dom, Jason the brother of Onias obtained the high priesthood by corruption, [8]promising the king at an interview[a] three hundred sixty talents of silver, and from another source of revenue eighty talents. [9]In addition to this he promised to pay one hundred fifty more if permission were given to establish by his authority a gymnasium and a body of youth for it, and to enroll the people of Jerusalem as citizens of Antioch. [10]When the king assented and Jason[b] came to office, he at once shifted his compatriots over to the Greek way of life.

11 He set aside the existing royal concessions to the Jews, secured through John the father of Eupolemus, who went on the mission to establish friendship and alliance with the Romans; and he destroyed the lawful ways of living and introduced new customs contrary to the law. [12]He took delight in establishing a gymnasium right under the citadel, and he induced the noblest of the young men to wear the Greek hat. [13]There was such an extreme of Hellenization and increase in the adoption of foreign ways because of the surpassing wickedness of Jason, who was ungodly and no true[c] high priest, [14]that the priests were no longer intent upon their service at the altar. Despising the sanctuary and neglecting the sacrifices, they hurried to take part in the unlawful proceedings in the wrestling arena after the signal for the discus-throwing, [15]disdaining the honors prized by their ancestors and putting the highest value upon Greek forms of prestige. [16]For this reason heavy disaster overtook them, and those whose ways of living they admired and wished to imitate completely became their enemies and punished them. [17]It is no light thing to show irreverence to the divine laws—a fact that later events will make clear.

Jason Introduces Greek Customs

18 When the quadrennial games were being held at Tyre and the king was present, [19]the vile Jason sent envoys, chosen as being Antiochian citizens from Jerusalem, to carry three hundred silver drachmas for the sacrifice to Hercules. Those who carried the money, however, thought best not to use it for sacrifice, because that was inappropriate, but to expend it for another purpose. [20]So this money was intended by the sender for the sacrifice to Hercules, but by the decision of its carriers it was applied to the construction of triremes.

21 When Apollonius son of Menestheus was sent to Egypt for the coronation[d] of Philometor as king, Antiochus learned that Philometor[b] had become hostile to his government, and he took measures for his own security. Therefore upon arriving at Joppa he proceeded to Jerusalem. [22]He was welcomed magnificently by Jason and the city, and ushered in with a blaze of torches and with shouts. Then he marched his army into Phoenicia.

Menelaus Becomes High Priest

23 After a period of three years Jason sent Menelaus, the brother of the previously men-

---

a Or *by a petition*   *b* Gk *he*   *c* Gk lacks *true*   *d* Meaning of Gk uncertain

---

rator in 3.7. **4.7–17** The new high priest Jason introduces Greek institutions and customs to Jerusalem. See 1 Macc 1.11–15, where Jason is not named. **4.7** After *Seleucus IV* was killed in 175 BCE, he was succeeded (after a political struggle) by *Antiochus IV Epiphanes* (175–164 BCE), who appointed *Jason* the Jewish high priest in place of Onias III. **4.9** *Gymnasium,* a Greek institution concerned not only with physical exercise but also with education and general culture. Some Jews may have become honorary *citizens of Antioch* in Syria; or perhaps Jerusalem had been renamed Antioch and made a Greek city-state. **4.10** *The Greek way of life* contrasts with Judaism (2.21). Far more than 1 Maccabees, 2 Maccabees interprets the Jewish "reformers" as supporting a foreign culture and religion. **4.11** The *royal concessions to the Jews* included the right to be governed by their Torah rather than by Seleucid law. For Eupolemus's *mission* to Rome, see 1 Macc 8.17. **4.12** *Citadel,* the fort overlooking the temple area. *Greek hat* (Greek *petasos*), the wide-brimmed hat worn by Hermes, god of athletic skill. **4.13** As a brother of Onias III, Jason was from a proper priestly family. In the writer's eyes he was *no true high priest* because he obtained the office by corruption and carried out a program hostile to Judaism. **4.16–17** According to 2 Maccabees the evils that befell the Jewish people and the temple were the result of following the Greek way of life (see 6.12–17). **4.18–22** Participation in the games at Tyre and Jason's welcome of Antiochus IV to Jerusalem illustrate the bad results of the hellenization program. **4.18–19** *Games* were held at Tyre in honor of the god *Hercules* (Heracles, Melqart) every four years. *Antiochian citizens from Jerusalem.* See note on 4.9. **4.20** Rather than allow the money to be used for sacrifices to a pagan god, the Jews had it applied to the *construction of triremes,* Greek ships with three rows of oars on each side. **4.21** Through *Apollonius* (3.7; 4.4) Antiochus IV learned that his nephew Ptolemy VI *Philometor* had designs against his Seleucid kingdom. On his way down the coast to Egypt Antiochus went east to Jerusalem,

tioned Simon, to carry the money to the king and to complete the records of essential business. 24But he, when presented to the king, extolled him with an air of authority, and secured the high priesthood for himself, outbidding Jason by three hundred talents of silver. 25After receiving the king's orders he returned, possessing no qualification for the high priesthood, but having the hot temper of a cruel tyrant and the rage of a savage wild beast. 26So Jason, who after supplanting his own brother was supplanted by another man, was driven as a fugitive into the land of Ammon. 27Although Menelaus continued to hold the office, he did not pay regularly any of the money promised to the king. 28When Sostratus the captain of the citadel kept requesting payment—for the collection of the revenue was his responsibility—the two of them were summoned by the king on account of this issue. 29Menelaus left his own brother Lysimachus as deputy in the high priesthood, while Sostratus left Crates, the commander of the Cyprian troops.

The Murder of Onias

30 While such was the state of affairs, it happened that the people of Tarsus and of Mallus revolted because their cities had been given as a present to Antiochis, the king's concubine. 31So the king went hurriedly to settle the trouble, leaving Andronicus, a man of high rank, to act as his deputy. 32But Menelaus, thinking he had obtained a suitable opportunity, stole some of the gold vessels of the temple and gave them to Andronicus; other vessels, as it happened, he had sold to Tyre and the neighboring cities. 33When Onias became fully aware of these acts, he publicly exposed them, having first withdrawn to a place of sanctuary at Daphne near Antioch. 34Therefore Menelaus, taking Andronicus aside, urged him to kill Onias. Andronicus[a] came to Onias, and resorting to treachery, offered him sworn pledges and gave him his right hand; he persuaded him, though still suspicious, to come out from the place of sanctuary; then, with no regard for justice, he immediately put him out of the way.

Andronicus Is Punished

35 For this reason not only Jews, but many also of other nations, were grieved and displeased at the unjust murder of the man. 36When the king returned from the region of Cilicia, the Jews in the city[b] appealed to him with regard to the unreasonable murder of Onias, and the Greeks shared their hatred of the crime. 37Therefore Antiochus was grieved at heart and filled with pity, and wept because of the moderation and good conduct of the deceased. 38Inflamed with anger, he immediately stripped off the purple robe from Andronicus, tore off his clothes, and led him around the whole city to that very place where he had committed the outrage against Onias, and there he dispatched the bloodthirsty fellow. The Lord thus repaid him with the punishment he deserved.

Unpopularity of Lysimachus and Menelaus

39 When many acts of sacrilege had been committed in the city by Lysimachus with the connivance of Menelaus, and when report of them had spread abroad, the populace gathered against Lysimachus, because many of the gold vessels had already been stolen. 40Since the crowds were becoming aroused and filled

---

a Gk He   b Or in each city

---

where he was welcomed by Jason. **4.23–29** The *vile Jason* (v. 19) is replaced by the even worse Menelaus, the brother of Simon (3.4). **4.23–24** In 172 BCE Menelaus outbid Jason for the high priesthood, just as Jason had outbid Onias III (vv. 7–8). **4.26** Jason fled to *Ammon* in Transjordan, perhaps to the Nabateans (5.8) or to Hyrcanus (3.11). **4.28** *Sostratus* (a non-Jew) was in charge of the *citadel* (v. 12), which was held mainly by mercenaries from Cyprus (v. 29). **4.29** *Lysimachus.* See 4.39–42. **4.30–34** The evil character of Menelaus and Andronicus is made manifest in their treatment of the temple vessels and the murder of the rightful high priest, Onias III. **4.30** *Tarsus* and *Mallus,* cities in Cilicia, across the Syrian border to the northwest. **4.31–32** *Andronicus* had the young son of Seleucus IV mur-dered in 175 BCE. He was being bribed by Menelaus, who was plundering the Jerusalem temple. **4.33** Onias III denounced both Menelaus and Andronicus. *Place of sanctuary,* the temple of Apollo at *Daphne,* five miles from Antioch. **4.35–38** The revulsion of both Jews and non-Jews leads Antiochus IV to punish Andronicus. **4.36** There was a growing Jewish community in the *city* of Antioch, as the presence of Onias III indicates. **4.38** The *purple robe* was worn by Friends of the king (see 1 Macc 10.20). Antiochus IV may well have recognized the *bloodthirsty* Andronicus as a threat to his own rule. **4.39–50** A riot in Jerusalem leads to the death of Lysimachus, and Menelaus escapes by bribery. **4.39** *Lysimachus,* Menelaus's brother and assistant (v. 29), had joined in plundering the temple vessels at

with anger, Lysimachus armed about three thousand men and launched an unjust attack, under the leadership of a certain Auranus, a man advanced in years and no less advanced in folly. [41] But when the Jews[a] became aware that Lysimachus was attacking them, some picked up stones, some blocks of wood, and others took handfuls of the ashes that were lying around, and threw them in wild confusion at Lysimachus and his men. [42] As a result, they wounded many of them, and killed some, and put all the rest to flight; the temple robber himself they killed close by the treasury.

43 Charges were brought against Menelaus about this incident. [44] When the king came to Tyre, three men sent by the senate presented the case before him. [45] But Menelaus, already as good as beaten, promised a substantial bribe to Ptolemy son of Dorymenes to win over the king. [46] Therefore Ptolemy, taking the king aside into a colonnade as if for refreshment, induced the king to change his mind. [47] Menelaus, the cause of all the trouble, he acquitted of the charges against him, while he sentenced to death those unfortunate men, who would have been freed uncondemned if they had pleaded even before Scythians. [48] And so those who had spoken for the city and the villages[b] and the holy vessels quickly suffered the unjust penalty. [49] Therefore even the Tyrians, showing their hatred of the crime, provided magnificently for their funeral. [50] But Menelaus, because of the greed of those in power, remained in office, growing in wickedness, having become the chief plotter against his compatriots.

Jason Tries to Regain Control

5 About this time Antiochus made his second invasion of Egypt. [2] And it happened that, for almost forty days, there appeared over all the city golden-clad cavalry charging through the air, in companies fully armed with lances and drawn swords— [3] troops of cavalry drawn up, attacks and counterattacks made on this side and on that, brandishing of shields, massing of spears, hurling of missiles, the flash of golden trappings, and armor of all kinds. [4] Therefore everyone prayed that the apparition might prove to have been a good omen.

5 When a false rumor arose that Antiochus was dead, Jason took no fewer than a thousand men and suddenly made an assault on the city. When the troops on the wall had been forced back and at last the city was being taken, Menelaus took refuge in the citadel. [6] But Jason kept relentlessly slaughtering his compatriots, not realizing that success at the cost of one's kindred is the greatest misfortune, but imagining that he was setting up trophies of victory over enemies and not over compatriots. [7] He did not, however, gain control of the government; in the end he got only disgrace from his conspiracy, and fled again into the country of the Ammonites. [8] Finally he met a miserable end. Accused[c] before Aretas the ruler of the Arabs, fleeing from city to city, pursued by everyone, hated as a rebel against the laws, and abhorred as the executioner of his country and his compatriots, he was cast ashore in Egypt. [9] There he who had driven many from their own country into exile died in exile, having embarked to go to the Lacedaemonians in hope of finding protection because of their kinship. [10] He who had cast out many to lie unburied had no one to mourn for him; he had no funeral of any sort and no place in the tomb of his ancestors.

11 When news of what had happened reached the king, he took it to mean that Judea was in revolt. So, raging inwardly, he left Egypt and took the city by storm. [12] He commanded

a Gk they b Other ancient authorities read the people
c Cn: Gk Imprisoned

Jerusalem. **4.42** That the *temple robber* Lysimachus died at the place he was robbing was a sign to the writer of divine intervention. **4.45** *Ptolemy son of Dorymenes*, later governor of Coelesyria and Phoenicia (8.8; 1 Macc 3.38), sided with Menelaus against the delegates sent by the senate (Greek *gerousia*), the council of Jewish elders. **4.47** *Scythians*, people north of the Black Sea notorious for their cruelty and regarded as barbarians.

5.1–14 Jason's abortive coup results in a brutal attack on Jerusalem by a frustrated Antiochus IV. **5.1** Antiochus's *second invasion of Egypt* took place in 168 BCE (see Dan 11.29–30). Forced by the Romans to retreat, Antiochus vented his anger on Jerusalem. **5.2–4** In view of what follows in chs. 5–7, the apparition does not seem to have been a *good omen*. **5.5–6** Jason apparently took the report about the Romans' stopping of Antiochus in Egypt as including his death (see 5.11). His rival Menelaus joined the Cyprian mercenaries in the citadel. **5.7** For Jason's earlier flight to the *Ammonites*, see 4.26. **5.8** *Aretas*, Harith I, king of the Nabateans. As a rebel against the Seleucids Jason found refuge in *Egypt*. **5.9** *Lacedaemonians*, Spartans, in Greece. For their alleged kinship with the Jews, see 1 Macc 12.2–23. **5.10** The villain Jason suffers an ap-

his soldiers to cut down relentlessly everyone they met and to kill those who went into their houses. [13]Then there was massacre of young and old, destruction of boys, women, and children, and slaughter of young girls and infants. [14]Within the total of three days eighty thousand were destroyed, forty thousand in hand-to-hand fighting, and as many were sold into slavery as were killed.

Pillage of the Temple

15 Not content with this, Antiochus[a] dared to enter the most holy temple in all the world, guided by Menelaus, who had become a traitor both to the laws and to his country. [16]He took the holy vessels with his polluted hands, and swept away with profane hands the votive offerings that other kings had made to enhance the glory and honor of the place. [17]Antiochus was elated in spirit, and did not perceive that the Lord was angered for a little while because of the sins of those who lived in the city, and that this was the reason he was disregarding the holy place. [18]But if it had not happened that they were involved in many sins, this man would have been flogged and turned back from his rash act as soon as he came forward, just as Heliodorus had been, whom King Seleucus sent to inspect the treasury. [19]But the Lord did not choose the nation for the sake of the holy place, but the place for the sake of the nation. [20]Therefore the place itself shared in the misfortunes that befell the nation and afterward participated in its benefits; and what was forsaken in the wrath of the Almighty was restored again in all its glory when the great Lord became reconciled.

21 So Antiochus carried off eighteen hundred talents from the temple, and hurried away to Antioch, thinking in his arrogance that he could sail on the land and walk on the sea, because his mind was elated. [22]He left governors to oppress the people: at Jerusalem, Philip, by birth a Phrygian and in character more barbarous than the man who appointed him; [23]and at Gerizim, Andronicus; and besides these Menelaus, who lorded it over his compatriots worse than the others did. In his malice toward the Jewish citizens,[b] [24]Antiochus[a] sent Apollonius, the captain of the Mysians, with an army of twenty-two thousand, and commanded him to kill all the grown men and to sell the women and boys as slaves. [25]When this man arrived in Jerusalem, he pretended to be peaceably disposed and waited until the holy sabbath day; then, finding the Jews not at work, he ordered his troops to parade under arms. [26]He put to the sword all those who came out to see them, then rushed into the city with his armed warriors and killed great numbers of people.

27 But Judas Maccabeus, with about nine others, got away to the wilderness, and kept himself and his companions alive in the mountains as wild animals do; they continued to live on what grew wild, so that they might not share in the defilement.

The Suppression of Judaism

6 Not long after this, the king sent an Athenian[c] senator[d] to compel the Jews to forsake the laws of their ancestors and no longer to live by the laws of God; [2]also to pol-

a Gk he   b Or worse than the others did in his malice toward the Jewish citizens   c Other ancient authorities read Antiochian
d Or Geron an Athenian

---

propriate punishment (see 4.16, 38, 42). **5.14** As usual in 1–2 Maccabees, the numbers are inflated. Antiochus probably viewed events in Jerusalem as a full-scale rebellion that needed to be controlled. **5.15–27** The robbery by Antiochus with the help of Menelaus and the attack by Apollonius are softened only by the introduction of Judas Maccabeus in v. 27. See 1 Macc 1.21–40. **5.15–16** Non-Jews were forbidden to enter the most sacred parts of the temple complex and handle the sacred vessels. That Menelaus (the high priest!) served as Antiochus's guide outraged the writer. **5.17–18** According to 2 Maccabees God allowed the profanation because of the people's sins (see 6.12–17). But Antiochus's arrogance will eventually be punished (see 9.1–29). **5.21** Eighteen hundred talents, a very large sum, perhaps an exaggeration. For the "elation" of Antiochus, see Dan 11.36. **5.22–23** Philip the Phrygian

(from western Asia Minor) appears again in 6.11; 8.8. This Andronicus is not the same as the one in 4.31–38. **5.24–26** For another account of Apollonius, see 1 Macc 1.29–32. 2 Maccabees places the attack on the sabbath when Jews would not be prepared for warfare (see 1 Macc 2.29–38). **5.27** Judas Maccabeus and his nine companions observe the Jewish food laws by eating vegetation and refusing unclean animals. No mention is made of Judas's father or brothers (see 1 Macc 2.1–5). Judas reappears in 2 Macc 8.

6.1–11 The assimilation to Greek religion and customs is interpreted as a direct attack on Judaism. See 1 Macc 1.41–64. **6.1** In 167 BCE an Athenian elder (Greek geron) or senator, or Geron an Athenian, was sent to bring order to the religious and political affairs of the Jews. **6.2** Olympian Zeus, the Greek equivalent of Israel's Most High God, though pious Jews resented

lute the temple in Jerusalem and to call it the temple of Olympian Zeus, and to call the one in Gerizim the temple of Zeus-the-Friend-of-Strangers, as did the people who lived in that place.

3 Harsh and utterly grievous was the onslaught of evil. 4For the temple was filled with debauchery and reveling by the Gentiles, who dallied with prostitutes and had intercourse with women within the sacred precincts, and besides brought in things for sacrifice that were unfit. 5The altar was covered with abominable offerings that were forbidden by the laws. 6People could neither keep the sabbath, nor observe the festivals of their ancestors, nor so much as confess themselves to be Jews.

7 On the monthly celebration of the king's birthday, the Jews*a* were taken, under bitter constraint, to partake of the sacrifices; and when a festival of Dionysus was celebrated, they were compelled to wear wreaths of ivy and to walk in the procession in honor of Dionysus. 8At the suggestion of the people of Ptolemais*b* a decree was issued to the neighboring Greek cities that they should adopt the same policy toward the Jews and make them partake of the sacrifices, 9and should kill those who did not choose to change over to Greek customs. One could see, therefore, the misery that had come upon them. 10For example, two women were brought in for having circumcised their children. They publicly paraded them around the city, with their babies hanging at their breasts, and then hurled them down headlong from the wall. 11Others who had assembled in the caves nearby, in order to observe the seventh day secretly, were betrayed to Philip and were all burned together, because their piety kept them from defending themselves, in view of their regard for that most holy day.

Providential Significance of the Persecution

12 Now I urge those who read this book not to be depressed by such calamities, but to recognize that these punishments were designed not to destroy but to discipline our people. 13In fact, it is a sign of great kindness not to let the impious alone for long, but to punish them immediately. 14For in the case of the other nations the Lord waits patiently to punish them until they have reached the full measure of their sins; but he does not deal in this way with us, 15in order that he may not take vengeance on us afterward when our sins have reached their height. 16Therefore he never withdraws his mercy from us. Although he disciplines us with calamities, he does not forsake his own people. 17Let what we have said serve as a reminder; we must go on briefly with the story.

The Martyrdom of Eleazar

18 Eleazar, one of the scribes in high position, a man now advanced in age and of noble presence, was being forced to open his mouth to eat swine's flesh. 19But he, welcoming death with honor rather than life with pollution, went up to the rack of his own accord, spitting out the flesh, 20as all ought to go who have the courage to refuse things that it is not right to taste, even for the natural love of life.

21 Those who were in charge of that unlawful sacrifice took the man aside because of their long acquaintance with him, and privately urged him to bring meat of his own providing, proper for him to use, and to pretend that he was eating the flesh of the sacrificial meal that had been commanded by the king,

---

a Gk they   *b* Cn: Gk *suggestion of the Ptolemies* (or *of Ptolemy*)

---

this identification. **6.4** The description suggests temple prostitution (see Am 2.7; Ezek 23.36–49; Dan 11.31), a practice more common in Semitic than Greek religions. **6.5** Though it mentions *abominable offerings*, 2 Maccabees is silent about the "desolating sacrilege" (1 Macc 1.54; Dan 11.31). **6.7** Antiochus's *birthday* was celebrated on the twenty-fifth of every month (1 Macc 1.58–59). *Dionysus*, the Greek god of wine and harvest. **6.8** *Ptolemais*, probably a city on the coast, also known as Acco; or perhaps *Ptolemy*, mentioned in 4.45, should be read. **6.9** *Greek customs*, the general cultural program known as Hellenism. Not every feature came from Greece; there was a mixture of Greek and oriental elements. **6.10–11** Similar incidents appear in 1 Macc 1.60–61; 2.31–38. **6.12–17** The stories of Israel's martyrs are interpreted as a discipline applied by God in the short term. Nevertheless God's mercy to Israel remains firm and will prevail in the end. **6.14–15** The *other nations* are given the leeway to have their sins build up, with the result that their ultimate punishment will be worse than Israel's. **6.18–31** Eleazar refuses to compromise his Jewish religious principles in the face of suffering and death. He is thus a model of nobility and courage. **6.18** The story of *Eleazar* (otherwise unknown) is told at greater length in 4 Macc 5–7. Eating *swine's flesh* was prohibited by Lev 11.7–8; Deut 14.8. **6.19** The exact nature of the torture is uncertain; the *rack* is only one possibility.

²²so that by doing this he might be saved from death, and be treated kindly on account of his old friendship with them. ²³But making a high resolve, worthy of his years and the dignity of his old age and the gray hairs that he had reached with distinction and his excellent life even from childhood, and moreover according to the holy God-given law, he declared himself quickly, telling them to send him to Hades.

²⁴"Such pretense is not worthy of our time of life," he said, "for many of the young might suppose that Eleazar in his ninetieth year had gone over to an alien religion, ²⁵and through my pretense, for the sake of living a brief moment longer, they would be led astray because of me, while I defile and disgrace my old age. ²⁶Even if for the present I would avoid the punishment of mortals, yet whether I live or die I will not escape the hands of the Almighty. ²⁷Therefore, by bravely giving up my life now, I will show myself worthy of my old age ²⁸and leave to the young a noble example of how to die a good death willingly and nobly for the revered and holy laws."

When he had said this, he went^a at once to the rack. ²⁹Those who a little before had acted toward him with goodwill now changed to ill will, because the words he had uttered were in their opinion sheer madness.^b ³⁰When he was about to die under the blows, he groaned aloud and said: "It is clear to the Lord in his holy knowledge that, though I might have been saved from death, I am enduring terrible sufferings in my body under this beating, but in my soul I am glad to suffer these things because I fear him."

³¹So in this way he died, leaving in his death an example of nobility and a memorial of courage, not only to the young but to the great body of his nation.

The Martyrdom of Seven Brothers

7 It happened also that seven brothers and their mother were arrested and were being compelled by the king, under torture with whips and thongs, to partake of unlawful swine's flesh. ²One of them, acting as their spokesman, said, "What do you intend to ask and learn from us? For we are ready to die rather than transgress the laws of our ancestors."

³The king fell into a rage, and gave orders to have pans and caldrons heated. ⁴These were heated immediately, and he commanded that the tongue of their spokesman be cut out and that they scalp him and cut off his hands and feet, while the rest of the brothers and the mother looked on. ⁵When he was utterly helpless, the king^c ordered them to take him to the fire, still breathing, and to fry him in a pan. The smoke from the pan spread widely, but the brothers^d and their mother encouraged one another to die nobly, saying, ⁶"The Lord God is watching over us and in truth has compassion on us, as Moses declared in his song that bore witness against the people to their faces, when he said, 'And he will have compassion on his servants.' "^e

⁷After the first brother had died in this way, they brought forward the second for their sport. They tore off the skin of his head with the hair, and asked him, "Will you eat rather than have your body punished limb by limb?" ⁸He replied in the language of his ancestors and said to them, "No." Therefore he in turn underwent tortures as the first brother had done. ⁹And when he was at his last breath, he said, "You accursed wretch, you dismiss us from this present life, but the King of the universe will raise us up to an everlasting renewal of life, because we have died for his laws."

¹⁰After him, the third was the victim of their sport. When it was demanded, he quickly put out his tongue and courageously stretched forth his hands, ¹¹and said nobly, "I got these

---

a Other ancient authorities read *was dragged*   *b* Meaning of Gk uncertain   *c* Gk *he*   *d* Gk *they*   *e* Gk *slaves*

6.23 *Hades,* the abode of the dead, Sheol in the Hebrew scriptures. **6.26** Eleazar envisions the possibility of *punishment* from God after death. **6.29** For the (incorrect) assessment of the death of the righteous as *madness,* see Wis 3.1–4; 5.4. **6.30** *Holy knowledge,* God's ability to know why Eleazar underwent martyrdom. **7.1–42** The most famous part of 2 Maccabees contains statements by the seven brothers and their mother about the resurrection of the just and the punishment and annihilation of the wicked. **7.1** *King,* later identified as Antiochus (v. 24). *Swine's flesh.* See note on 6.18. **7.3–5** The punishments for the sons involved scalping, dismemberment, and roasting. **7.6** In Deut 32.36–38 trust in the Lord's *compassion* appears in the context of rejecting apostasy (as here). **7.8** *Language of his ancestors,* Hebrew (see also 7.21, 27; 12.37; 15.29). **7.9** The *King of the universe* (God) is superior to King Antiochus since only God can raise the faithful to eternal life (see Dan 12.1–3). **7.11** *Hope* in bodily resurrection is based on the power of God as creator, not on

from Heaven, and because of his laws I disdain them, and from him I hope to get them back again." 12 As a result the king himself and those with him were astonished at the young man's spirit, for he regarded his sufferings as nothing.

13 After he too had died, they maltreated and tortured the fourth in the same way. 14 When he was near death, he said, "One cannot but choose to die at the hands of mortals and to cherish the hope God gives of being raised again by him. But for you there will be no resurrection to life!"

15 Next they brought forward the fifth and maltreated him. 16 But he looked at the king,[a] and said, "Because you have authority among mortals, though you also are mortal, you do what you please. But do not think that God has forsaken our people. 17 Keep on, and see how his mighty power will torture you and your descendants!"

18 After him they brought forward the sixth. And when he was about to die, he said, "Do not deceive yourself in vain. For we are suffering these things on our own account, because of our sins against our own God. Therefore[b] astounding things have happened. 19 But do not think that you will go unpunished for having tried to fight against God!"

20 The mother was especially admirable and worthy of honorable memory. Although she saw her seven sons perish within a single day, she bore it with good courage because of her hope in the Lord. 21 She encouraged each of them in the language of their ancestors. Filled with a noble spirit, she reinforced her woman's reasoning with a man's courage, and said to them, 22 "I do not know how you came into being in my womb. It was not I who gave you life and breath, nor I who set in order the elements within each of you. 23 Therefore the Creator of the world, who shaped the beginning of humankind and devised the origin of all things, will in his mercy give life and breath back to you again, since you now forget yourselves for the sake of his laws."

24 Antiochus felt that he was being treated with contempt, and he was suspicious of her reproachful tone. The youngest brother being still alive, Antiochus[c] not only appealed to him in words, but promised with oaths that he would make him rich and enviable if he would turn from the ways of his ancestors, and that he would take him for his Friend and entrust him with public affairs. 25 Since the young man would not listen to him at all, the king called the mother to him and urged her to advise the youth to save himself. 26 After much urging on his part, she undertook to persuade her son. 27 But, leaning close to him, she spoke in their native language as follows, deriding the cruel tyrant: "My son, have pity on me. I carried you nine months in my womb, and nursed you for three years, and have reared you and brought you up to this point in your life, and have taken care of you.[d] 28 I beg you, my child, to look at the heaven and the earth and see everything that is in them, and recognize that God did not make them out of things that existed.[e] And in the same way the human race came into being. 29 Do not fear this butcher, but prove worthy of your brothers. Accept death, so that in God's mercy I may get you back again along with your brothers."

30 While she was still speaking, the young man said, "What are you[f] waiting for? I will not obey the king's command, but I obey the command of the law that was given to our ancestors through Moses. 31 But you,[g] who have contrived all sorts of evil against the Hebrews, will certainly not escape the hands of God. 32 For we are suffering because of our own sins. 33 And if our living Lord is angry for a little while, to rebuke and discipline us, he will again be reconciled with his own servants.[h] 34 But you, unholy wretch, you most defiled of all mortals, do not be elated in vain and puffed up by uncertain hopes, when you raise your

---

a Gk at him   b Lat: Other ancient authorities lack Therefore
c Gk he   d Or have borne the burden of your education
e Or God made them out of things that did not exist   f The Gk here for you is plural   g The Gk here for you is singular
h Gk slaves

---

human nature. **7.14** For the wicked there will be *no resurrection to life*; they will be annihilated. **7.17** Antiochus's *descendants* include Antiochus V Eupator, Alexander Balas, and Antiochus VI. **7.18–19** *Our sins*, the sins of the people as a whole (see also v. 32). The sixth son echoes what the author said in 6.12–17. **7.22–23** For God as the *origin* of human life and so lord over its destiny, see v. 11; Job 1.10–12; Ps 139.13–

16; Eccl 11.5. **7.24** *Friend*, an official title for the king's advisers (see 1 Macc 2.18). **7.28** The mother's confession that *God did not make them out of things that existed* echoes vv. 11, 22–23; it need not be taken as a philosophical or theological statement about "creation out of nothing" (Latin *creatio ex nihilo*). **7.32–33** For the same basic theology of suffering as a discipline, see 6.12–17; 7.18–19. *Sins*, of the people taken collec-

hand against the children of heaven. 35You have not yet escaped the judgment of the almighty, all-seeing God. 36For our brothers after enduring a brief suffering have drunk*a* of ever-flowing life, under God's covenant; but you, by the judgment of God, will receive just punishment for your arrogance. 37I, like my brothers, give up body and life for the laws of our ancestors, appealing to God to show mercy soon to our nation and by trials and plagues to make you confess that he alone is God, 38and through me and my brothers to bring to an end the wrath of the Almighty that has justly fallen on our whole nation."

39 The king fell into a rage, and handled him worse than the others, being exasperated at his scorn. 40So he died in his integrity, putting his whole trust in the Lord.

41 Last of all, the mother died, after her sons.

42 Let this be enough, then, about the eating of sacrifices and the extreme tortures.

The Revolt of Judas Maccabeus

8 Meanwhile Judas, who was also called Maccabeus, and his companions secretly entered the villages and summoned their kindred and enlisted those who had continued in the Jewish faith, and so they gathered about six thousand. 2They implored the Lord to look upon the people who were oppressed by all; and to have pity on the temple that had been profaned by the godless; 3to have mercy on the city that was being destroyed and about to be leveled to the ground; to hearken to the blood that cried out to him; 4to remember also the lawless destruction of the innocent babies and the blasphemies committed against his name; and to show his hatred of evil.

5 As soon as Maccabeus got his army organized, the Gentiles could not withstand him, for the wrath of the Lord had turned to mercy. 6Coming without warning, he would set fire

to towns and villages. He captured strategic positions and put to flight not a few of the enemy. 7He found the nights most advantageous for such attacks. And talk of his valor spread everywhere.

8 When Philip saw that the man was gaining ground little by little, and that he was pushing ahead with more frequent successes, he wrote to Ptolemy, the governor of Coelesyria and Phoenicia, to come to the aid of the king's government. 9Then Ptolemy*b* promptly appointed Nicanor son of Patroclus, one of the king's chief*c* Friends, and sent him, in command of no fewer than twenty thousand Gentiles of all nations, to wipe out the whole race of Judea. He associated with him Gorgias, a general and a man of experience in military service. 10Nicanor determined to make up for the king the tribute due to the Romans, two thousand talents, by selling the captured Jews into slavery. 11So he immediately sent to the towns on the seacoast, inviting them to buy Jewish slaves and promising to hand over ninety slaves for a talent, not expecting the judgment from the Almighty that was about to overtake him.

Preparation for Battle

12 Word came to Judas concerning Nicanor's invasion; and when he told his companions of the arrival of the army, 13those who were cowardly and distrustful of God's justice ran off and got away. 14Others sold all their remaining property, and at the same time implored the Lord to rescue those who had been sold by the ungodly Nicanor before he ever met them, 15if not for their own sake, then for the sake of the covenants made with their ancestors, and because he had called them by his holy and glorious name. 16But Maccabeus gathered his forces together, to the number six thousand,

---

a Cn: Gk *fallen*   *b* Gk *he*   *c* Gk *one of the first*

---

tively, as in vv. 18–19. **7.37–38** By dying *for the laws of his ancestors* the seventh son hopes to hasten both the end of the discipline placed on Israel and the just recompense owed to the wicked king.
8.1–11 Judas Maccabeus (the "Hammerer") arises as Israel's champion against the Seleucids and their Jewish collaborators. See 1 Macc 3.1–41. **8.1** The story of *Judas* begun in 5.27 continues. Most of the material in 1 Macc 2.1–3.26 is absent. **8.2–4** The prayer by the troops summarizes events described so far in the book. **8.5–7** Judas's success as a guerilla warrior is inter-

preted in accord with 6.12–17; 7.38: *the wrath of the Lord . . . turned to mercy.* **8.8–9** In 1 Macc 3.38–41 the major opponent is *Gorgias.* This *Nicanor* may not be the same as the figure in 2 Macc 14–15. **8.10** *Tribute due to the Romans,* perhaps the payment imposed on Antiochus III by the treaty of Apamea in 188 BCE. **8.11** *Ninety slaves for a talent,* a very low price, thus expressing contempt toward Jews. **8.12–20** Judas gathers his army and exhorts them to fight bravely despite the numerical odds against them. See 1 Macc 3.42–60. **8.13** In 1 Macc 3.56 the desertion is explained in the

and exhorted them not to be frightened by the enemy and not to fear the great multitude of Gentiles who were wickedly coming against them, but to fight nobly, [17]keeping before their eyes the lawless outrage that the Gentiles[a] had committed against the holy place, and the torture of the derided city, and besides, the overthrow of their ancestral way of life. [18]"For they trust to arms and acts of daring," he said, "but we trust in the Almighty God, who is able with a single nod to strike down those who are coming against us, and even, if necessary, the whole world."

[19] Moreover, he told them of the occasions when help came to their ancestors; how, in the time of Sennacherib, when one hundred eighty-five thousand perished, [20]and the time of the battle against the Galatians that took place in Babylonia, when eight thousand Jews[b] fought along with four thousand Macedonians; yet when the Macedonians were hard pressed, the eight thousand, by the help that came to them from heaven, destroyed one hundred twenty thousand Galatians[c] and took a great amount of booty.

Judas Defeats Nicanor

[21] With these words he filled them with courage and made them ready to die for their laws and their country; then he divided his army into four parts. [22]He appointed his brothers also, Simon and Joseph and Jonathan, each to command a division, putting fifteen hundred men under each. [23]Besides, he appointed Eleazar to read aloud[d] from the holy book, and gave the watchword, "The help of God"; then, leading the first division himself, he joined battle with Nicanor.

[24] With the Almighty as their ally, they killed more than nine thousand of the enemy, and wounded and disabled most of Nicanor's army, and forced them all to flee. [25]They captured the money of those who had come to buy them as slaves. After pursuing them for some distance, they were obliged to return because the hour was late. [26]It was the day before the sabbath, and for that reason they did not continue their pursuit. [27]When they had collected the arms of the enemy and stripped them of their spoils, they kept the sabbath, giving great praise and thanks to the Lord, who had preserved them for that day and allotted it to them as the beginning of mercy. [28]After the sabbath they gave some of the spoils to those who had been tortured and to the widows and orphans, and distributed the rest among themselves and their children. [29]When they had done this, they made common supplication and implored the merciful Lord to be wholly reconciled with his servants.[e]

Judas Defeats Timothy and Bacchides

[30] In encounters with the forces of Timothy and Bacchides they killed more than twenty thousand of them and got possession of some exceedingly high strongholds, and they divided a very large amount of plunder, giving to those who had been tortured and to the orphans and widows, and also to the aged, shares equal to their own. [31]They collected the arms of the enemy,[f] and carefully stored all of them in strategic places; the rest of the spoils they carried to Jerusalem. [32]They killed the commander of Timothy's forces, a most wicked man, and one who had greatly troubled the Jews. [33]While they were celebrating the victory in the city of their ancestors, they burned those who had set fire to the sacred gates, Callisthenes and some others, who had fled into one little house; so these received the proper reward for their impiety.[d]

a Gk they   b Gk lacks Jews   c Gk lacks Galatians
d Meaning of Gk uncertain   e Gk slaves   f Gk their arms

light of Deut 20.5–8. **8.16–18** For another version of Judas's exhortation, see 1 Macc 3.58–60. **8.19** For *Sennacherib's* defeat in 701 BCE, see 2 Kings 19.35–36; Isa 37.36. For other allusions to this incident, see 1 Macc 7.41; 2 Macc 15.22. **8.20** *Galatians* in Babylonia, Celtic mercenaries defeated by Jews and Seleucids (*Macedonians*). **8.21–29** In defeating Nicanor Judas emerges as an exemplary biblical warrior. See 1 Macc 4.1–25. **8.22–23** *Simon* and *Jonathan*, Judas's brothers. *Eleazar* may be Azariah (1 Macc 5.18, 55–62), the companion of *Joseph*. *The help of God*, the meaning of Eleazar in Hebrew. **8.24–25** For a fuller account, see 1 Macc 4.13–25. *Nine thousand*, three thousand in 1 Macc 4.15. **8.26–27** In 2 Maccabees Judas is very careful to observe the *sabbath*; 1 Macc 4.16–17 provides a different rationale for postponing the plundering. **8.28** For the division of *spoils*, see Num 31.25–47; 1 Sam 30.21–25. *Widows and orphans*. See Deut 26.12–13. **8.30–36** A summary of victories over Israel's enemies. **8.30–31** For the defeats of *Timothy* and *Bacchides*, see 1 Macc 5.6–7; 7.8–25. For the policy regarding *plunder*, see v. 28. **8.32** *Commander of Timothy's forces*, possibly the chief of the Arab mercenaries (see 1 Macc 5.37–44). **8.33** *Gates*. See 1 Macc 1.31. Nothing is

34 The thrice-accursed Nicanor, who had brought the thousand merchants to buy the Jews, 35having been humbled with the help of the Lord by opponents whom he regarded as of the least account, took off his splendid uniform and made his way alone like a runaway slave across the country until he reached Antioch, having succeeded chiefly in the destruction of his own army! 36So he who had undertaken to secure tribute for the Romans by the capture of the people of Jerusalem proclaimed that the Jews had a Defender, and that therefore the Jews were invulnerable, because they followed the laws ordained by him.

The Last Campaign of Antiochus Epiphanes

9 About that time, as it happened, Antiochus had retreated in disorder from the region of Persia. 2He had entered the city called Persepolis and attempted to rob the temples and control the city. Therefore the people rushed to the rescue with arms, and Antiochus and his army were defeated,[a] with the result that Antiochus was put to flight by the inhabitants and beat a shameful retreat. 3While he was in Ecbatana, news came to him of what had happened to Nicanor and the forces of Timothy. 4Transported with rage, he conceived the idea of turning upon the Jews the injury done by those who had put him to flight; so he ordered his charioteer to drive without stopping until he completed the journey. But the judgment of heaven rode with him! For in his arrogance he said, "When I get there I will make Jerusalem a cemetery of Jews."

5 But the all-seeing Lord, the God of Israel, struck him with an incurable and invisible blow. As soon as he stopped speaking he was seized with a pain in his bowels, for which there was no relief, and with sharp internal tortures— 6and that very justly, for he had tortured the bowels of others with many and strange inflictions. 7Yet he did not in any way stop his insolence, but was even more filled with arrogance, breathing fire in his rage against the Jews, and giving orders to drive even faster. And so it came about that he fell out of his chariot as it was rushing along, and the fall was so hard as to torture every limb of his body. 8Thus he who only a little while before had thought in his superhuman arrogance that he could command the waves of the sea, and had imagined that he could weigh the high mountains in a balance, was brought down to earth and carried in a litter, making the power of God manifest to all. 9And so the ungodly man's body swarmed with worms, and while he was still living in anguish and pain, his flesh rotted away, and because of the stench the whole army felt revulsion at his decay. 10Because of his intolerable stench no one was able to carry the man who a little while before had thought that he could touch the stars of heaven. 11Then it was that, broken in spirit, he began to lose much of his arrogance and to come to his senses under the scourge of God, for he was tortured with pain every moment. 12And when he could not endure his own stench, he uttered these words, "It is right to be subject to God; mortals should not think that they are equal to God."[b]

Antiochus Makes a Promise to God

13 Then the abominable fellow made a vow to the Lord, who would no longer have mercy on him, stating 14that the holy city, which he was hurrying to level to the ground and to make a cemetery, he was now declaring to be free; 15and the Jews, whom he had not considered

a Gk they were defeated b Or not think thoughts proper only to God

---

known about Callisthenes. **8.34–35** The story returns to Nicanor (see v. 24), who suffers an appropriate punishment: one who sought to enslave Israel flees like a runaway slave. **8.36** Defender, the God of Israel.

9.1–12 After undergoing various gruesome but appropriate punishments, Antiochus finally recognizes the power of Israel's God. For different accounts of his end, see 1 Macc 6.1–17; 2 Macc 1.13–17; Dan 11.40–45. **9.2–3** Persepolis, the old capital of the Persian Empire, founded by Darius I. Ecbatana, in Media, northwest of Persepolis. **9.4** The judgment of heaven (God) imposes the misfortunes that Antiochus undergoes:

pains in his bowels (v. 5–6), fall from the chariot (v. 7), and worms and stench (vv. 9–10). **9.8** For an earlier display of Antiochus's arrogance, see 5.21. Cf. Isa 40.12. **9.9** For worms as a punishment for the wicked, see Isa 14.11; 66.24; Jdt 16.17; Sir 7.17; Acts 12.23. **9.12** For a similar acknowledgment by King Nebuchadnezzar, see Dan 4.34–37. **9.13–18** No other ancient source verifies Antiochus's promises to the God of Israel, and they are historically unlikely. At any rate, God does not accept Antiochus's prayer. **9.14** Jerusalem was to be free of taxes (see 1 Macc 10.31). **9.15** Athens was not part of Antiochus's empire. To be

worth burying but had planned to throw out with their children for the wild animals and for the birds to eat, he would make, all of them, equal to citizens of Athens; 16and the holy sanctuary, which he had formerly plundered, he would adorn with the finest offerings; and all the holy vessels he would give back, many times over; and the expenses incurred for the sacrifices he would provide from his own revenues; 17and in addition to all this he also would become a Jew and would visit every inhabited place to proclaim the power of God. 18But when his sufferings did not in any way abate, for the judgment of God had justly come upon him, he gave up all hope for himself and wrote to the Jews the following letter, in the form of a supplication. This was its content:

Antiochus's Letter and Death

19 "To his worthy Jewish citizens, Antiochus their king and general sends hearty greetings and good wishes for their health and prosperity. 20If you and your children are well and your affairs are as you wish, I am glad. As my hope is in heaven, 21I remember with affection your esteem and goodwill. On my way back from the region of Persia I suffered an annoying illness, and I have deemed it necessary to take thought for the general security of all. 22I do not despair of my condition, for I have good hope of recovering from my illness, 23but I observed that my father, on the occasions when he made expeditions into the upper country, appointed his successor, 24so that, if anything unexpected happened or any unwelcome news came, the people throughout the realm would not be troubled, for they would know to whom the government was left. 25Moreover, I understand how the princes along the borders and the neighbors of my kingdom keep watching for opportunities and waiting to see what will happen. So I have appointed my son Antiochus to be king, whom I have often entrusted and commended to most of you when I hurried off to the upper provinces; and I have written to him what is written here. 26I therefore urge and beg you to remember the public and private services rendered to you and to maintain your present goodwill, each of you, toward me and my son. 27For I am sure that he will follow my policy and will treat you with moderation and kindness."

28 So the murderer and blasphemer, having endured the more intense suffering, such as he had inflicted on others, came to the end of his life by a most pitiable fate, among the mountains in a strange land. 29And Philip, one of his courtiers, took his body home; then, fearing the son of Antiochus, he withdrew to Ptolemy Philometor in Egypt.

Purification of the Temple

10 Now Maccabeus and his followers, the Lord leading them on, recovered the temple and the city; 2they tore down the altars that had been built in the public square by the foreigners, and also destroyed the sacred precincts. 3They purified the sanctuary, and made another altar of sacrifice; then, striking fire out of flint, they offered sacrifices, after a lapse of two years, and they offered incense and lighted lamps and set out the bread of the Presence. 4When they had done this, they fell prostrate and implored the Lord that they might never again fall into such misfortunes, but that, if they should ever sin, they might be disciplined by him with forbearance and not be handed over to blasphemous and barbarous nations. 5It happened that on the same

---

equal to citizens of Athens probably meant that Jews were to enjoy freedom and democracy. 9.19–29 The tone of the letter appointing Antiochus V as successor does not fit this context well, but its content is probably authentic. 9.19 Rather than addressed to his worthy Jewish citizens, the letter was more likely meant for the people of Antioch. 9.21 In view of vv. 5–12 an annoying illness is understatement and probably reflects Antiochus's true condition (exaggerated in vv. 5–12). 9.23 Antiochus's father, Antiochus III, appointed Seleucus IV as his successor. 9.25 My son, Antiochus V Eupator ("of a good father"), who was still a young boy and needed a regent (1 Macc 3.33; 6.14–15). 9.28 According to 2 Maccabees Antiochus died before the purification of the Jerusalem temple, whereas in 1 Mac-

cabees (6.1–17) he died afterward. In fact he died just about the same time, and both writers drew a connection. 9.29 When Philip tried to seize the government (1 Macc 6.55–56), he could not hold Antioch (6.63) and so he fled to Egypt.

10.1–9 2 Maccabees portrays Judas's restoration of the temple as a purification; 1 Macc 4.36–59 presents it more as a dedication. 10.1–2 1 Maccabees mentions neither the recovery of the city nor the altars . . . built in the public square. 10.3 For the fire, see 1.19–2.1, which gives a very different account; the use of flint guaranteed a new fire. Two years seems one year short (see 1 Macc 1.54; 4.52). 10.4 In accord with 6.12–17 the desecration of the temple is explained as punishment for Israel's sins (especially for following Jason and Menelaus) and as a

day on which the sanctuary had been profaned by the foreigners, the purification of the sanctuary took place, that is, on the twenty-fifth day of the same month, which was Chislev. 6They celebrated it for eight days with rejoicing, in the manner of the festival of booths, remembering how not long before, during the festival of booths, they had been wandering in the mountains and caves like wild animals. 7Therefore, carrying ivy-wreathed wands and beautiful branches and also fronds of palm, they offered hymns of thanksgiving to him who had given success to the purifying of his own holy place. 8They decreed by public edict, ratified by vote, that the whole nation of the Jews should observe these days every year.

9 Such then was the end of Antiochus, who was called Epiphanes.

Accession of Antiochus Eupator

10 Now we will tell what took place under Antiochus Eupator, who was the son of that ungodly man, and will give a brief summary of the principal calamities of the wars. 11This man, when he succeeded to the kingdom, appointed one Lysias to have charge of the government and to be chief governor of Coelesyria and Phoenicia. 12Ptolemy, who was called Macron, took the lead in showing justice to the Jews because of the wrong that had been done to them, and attempted to maintain peaceful relations with them. 13As a result he was accused before Eupator by the king's Friends. He heard himself called a traitor at every turn, because he had abandoned Cyprus, which Philometor had entrusted to him, and had gone over to Antiochus Epiphanes. Unable to command the respect due his office,[a] he took poison and ended his life.

Campaign in Idumea

14 When Gorgias became governor of the region, he maintained a force of mercenaries, and at every turn kept attacking the Jews. 15Besides this, the Idumeans, who had control of important strongholds, were harassing the Jews; they received those who were banished from Jerusalem, and endeavored to keep up the war. 16But Maccabeus and his forces, after making solemn supplication and imploring God to fight on their side, rushed to the strongholds of the Idumeans. 17Attacking them vigorously, they gained possession of the places, and beat off all who fought upon the wall, and slaughtered those whom they encountered, killing no fewer than twenty thousand.

18 When at least nine thousand took refuge in two very strong towers well equipped to withstand a siege, 19Maccabeus left Simon and Joseph, and also Zacchaeus and his troops, a force sufficient to besiege them; and he himself set off for places where he was more urgently needed. 20But those with Simon, who were money-hungry, were bribed by some of those who were in the towers, and on receiving seventy thousand drachmas let some of them slip away. 21When word of what had happened came to Maccabeus, he gathered the leaders of the people, and accused these men of having sold their kindred for money by setting their enemies free to fight against them. 22Then he killed these men who had turned traitor, and immediately captured the two towers. 23Having success at arms in everything he undertook, he destroyed more than twenty thousand in the two strongholds.

a Cn: Meaning of Gk uncertain

---

discipline. **10.5–6** For the date, see 1 Macc 4.52, 54. For the comparison with the *festival of booths,* see 2 Macc 1.9. For the allusion to Judas in the *mountains,* see 5.27. **10.7** Although the *ivy-wreathed wands* (Greek *thyrsoi*) were carried in processions honoring the god Dionysus (6.7), here they were probably not perceived as distinctively pagan. **10.8** The *whole nation of the Jews* was expected to observe the feast, though Jews in Egypt still needed encouragement to do so (see 1.1–9; 2.16–18). **10.10–13** On the death of Antiochus IV the Seleucid Empire passes to his son Antiochus V Eupator. **10.10** *Antiochus V Eupator* ("of a good father"); see 9.25, 29. He was about nine years old. He reigned until 162 BCE, when he was murdered by Demetrius I. **10.11** *Lysias* had been regent over the western territories

(1 Macc 3.32–33). Since Antiochus V was very young, Lysias was responsible for making policy. **10.12** *Ptolemy . . . Macron* ("large-headed") supported Antiochus IV when Antiochus's fleet invaded Cyprus in 168 BCE and so incurred suspicion from both Ptolemies and Seleucids. **10.14–23** In Idumea (see 1 Macc 5.1–54) Judas is successful. Whatever success he lacks is due to the treachery of some of his troops. **10.14** *Gorgias,* governor of Idumea (12.32). **10.15–17** For another account of the war against the *Idumeans,* see 1 Macc 5.3. **10.17–18, 23** *Twenty thousand, nine thousand,* and *twenty thousand,* exaggerated. **10.18–23** For Judas's attack on *towers* of the sons of Baean, see 1 Macc 5.4–5. **10.19** *Joseph.* See 1 Macc 5.18, 56; 2 Macc 8.22. Nothing is known of *Zacchaeus.* **10.24–38** In his battles with Timothy, Judas

Judas Defeats Timothy

24 Now Timothy, who had been defeated by the Jews before, gathered a tremendous force of mercenaries and collected the cavalry from Asia in no small number. He came on, intending to take Judea by storm. 25 As he drew near, Maccabeus and his men sprinkled dust on their heads and girded their loins with sackcloth, in supplication to God. 26 Falling upon the steps before the altar, they implored him to be gracious to them and to be an enemy to their enemies and an adversary to their adversaries, as the law declares. 27 And rising from their prayer they took up their arms and advanced a considerable distance from the city; and when they came near the enemy they halted. 28 Just as dawn was breaking, the two armies joined battle, the one having as pledge of success and victory not only their valor but also their reliance on the Lord, while the other made rage their leader in the fight.

29 When the battle became fierce, there appeared to the enemy from heaven five resplendent men on horses with golden bridles, and they were leading the Jews. 30 Two of them took Maccabeus between them, and shielding him with their own armor and weapons, they kept him from being wounded. They showered arrows and thunderbolts on the enemy, so that, confused and blinded, they were thrown into disorder and cut to pieces. 31 Twenty thousand five hundred were slaughtered, besides six hundred cavalry.

32 Timothy himself fled to a stronghold called Gazara, especially well garrisoned, where Chaereas was commander. 33 Then Maccabeus and his men were glad, and they besieged the fort for four days. 34 The men within, relying on the strength of the place, kept blaspheming terribly and uttering wicked words. 35 But at dawn of the fifth day, twenty young men in the army of Maccabeus, fired with anger because of the blasphemies, bravely stormed the wall and with savage fury cut down everyone they met. 36 Others who came up in the same way wheeled around against the defenders and set fire to the towers; they kindled fires and burned the blasphemers alive. Others broke open the gates and let in the rest of the force, and they occupied the city. 37 They killed Timothy, who was hiding in a cistern, and his brother Chaereas, and Apollophanes. 38 When they had accomplished these things, with hymns and thanksgivings they blessed the Lord who shows great kindness to Israel and gives them the victory.

Lysias Besieges Beth-zur

11 Very soon after this, Lysias, the king's guardian and kinsman, who was in charge of the government, being vexed at what had happened, 2 gathered about eighty thousand infantry and all his cavalry and came against the Jews. He intended to make the city a home for Greeks, 3 and to levy tribute on the temple as he did on the sacred places of the other nations, and to put up the high priesthood for sale every year. 4 He took no account whatever of the power of God, but was elated with his ten thousands of infantry, and his thousands of cavalry, and his eighty elephants. 5 Invading Judea, he approached Beth-zur, which was a fortified place about five stadia[a] from Jerusalem, and pressed it hard.

6 When Maccabeus and his men got word that Lysias[b] was besieging the strongholds, they and all the people, with lamentations and tears, prayed the Lord to send a good angel to save Israel. 7 Maccabeus himself was the first to take up arms, and he urged the others to risk their lives with him to aid their kindred. Then they eagerly rushed off together. 8 And there,

---

a Meaning of Gk uncertain   b Gk he

prays and gives thanks, and so gets additional victories. **10.24** For the defeat of Timothy *before,* see 8.30–33. **10.26** *As the law declares,* in Ex 23.22. **10.29** For other visions of *men on horses,* see 3.25–26; 5.2–3; 11.8. Here they protect Judas and send thunderbolts on the enemy—usually considered Greek features. **10.31** The numbers are exaggerated. **10.32** Simon captured *Gazara* (Gezer); see 1 Macc 13.43–48. The story originally concerned Jazer as in 1 Macc 5.8. *Chaereas,* identified as Timothy's brother in 10.37. **10.37** *Cistern,* a large pit with plastered walls, used for storing water during the rainy season.

11.1–12 1 Macc 4.28–35 places Lysias's siege of Bethzur before the death of Antiochus IV. **11.1** Lysias was named *guardian* of Antiochus V by Antiochus IV (see 1 Macc 3.32–33). *Kinsman,* an honorary title applied to the king's closest advisers. **11.2** *Eighty thousand.* According to 1 Macc 4.28 Lysias had sixty thousand infantry and five thousand cavalry. In both accounts the figures are exaggerated. **11.2–3** *The city,* Jerusalem. For the sale of the *high priesthood* (a common Hellenistic practice), see 4.7–8, 23–24. **11.4** For Lysias's *elephants,* see 1 Macc 3.34. **11.5** *Beth-zur,* about twenty miles south of Jerusalem. **11.8** For earlier visions of horse-

while they were still near Jerusalem, a horseman appeared at their head, clothed in white and brandishing weapons of gold. 9And together they all praised the merciful God, and were strengthened in heart, ready to assail not only humans but the wildest animals or walls of iron. 10They advanced in battle order, having their heavenly ally, for the Lord had mercy on them. 11They hurled themselves like lions against the enemy, and laid low eleven thousand of them and sixteen hundred cavalry, and forced all the rest to flee. 12Most of them got away stripped and wounded, and Lysias himself escaped by disgraceful flight.

Lysias Makes Peace with the Jews

13 As he was not without intelligence, he pondered over the defeat that had befallen him, and realized that the Hebrews were invincible because the mighty God fought on their side. So he sent to them 14and persuaded them to settle everything on just terms, promising that he would persuade the king, constraining him to be their friend.*a* 15Maccabeus, having regard for the common good, agreed to all that Lysias urged. For the king granted every request in behalf of the Jews which Maccabeus delivered to Lysias in writing.

16 The letter written to the Jews by Lysias was to this effect:

"Lysias to the people of the Jews, greetings. 17John and Absalom, who were sent by you, have delivered your signed communication and have asked about the matters indicated in it. 18I have informed the king of everything that needed to be brought before him, and he has agreed to what was possible. 19If you will maintain your goodwill toward the government, I will endeavor in the future to help promote your welfare. 20And concerning such matters and their details, I have ordered these

men and my representatives to confer with you. 21Farewell. The one hundred forty-eighth year,*b* Dioscorinthius twenty-fourth."

22 The king's letter ran thus:

"King Antiochus to his brother Lysias, greetings. 23Now that our father has gone on to the gods, we desire that the subjects of the kingdom be undisturbed in caring for their own affairs. 24We have heard that the Jews do not consent to our father's change to Greek customs, but prefer their own way of living and ask that their own customs be allowed them. 25Accordingly, since we choose that this nation also should be free from disturbance, our decision is that their temple be restored to them and that they shall live according to the customs of their ancestors. 26You will do well, therefore, to send word to them and give them pledges of friendship, so that they may know our policy and be of good cheer and go on happily in the conduct of their own affairs."

27 To the nation the king's letter was as follows:

"King Antiochus to the senate of the Jews and to the other Jews, greetings. 28If you are well, it is as we desire. We also are in good health. 29Menelaus has informed us that you wish to return home and look after your own affairs. 30Therefore those who go home by the thirtieth of Xanthicus will have our pledge of friendship and full permission 31for the Jews to enjoy their own food and laws, just as formerly, and none of them shall be molested in any way for what may have been done in ignorance. 32And I have also sent Menelaus to encourage you. 33Farewell. The one hundred forty-eighth year,*b* Xanthicus fifteenth."

34 The Romans also sent them a letter, which read thus:

a Meaning of Gk uncertain   *b* 164 B.C.

men, see 3.25–26; 5.2–3; 10.29–30. **11.11** According to 1 Macc 4.34, only five thousand of Lysias's men fell. **11.13–38** The peace negotiations between Lysias and the Jews are described by means of four letters. Their most likely historical sequence is vv. 16–21, 34–38, 27–33, 22–26. **11.13** The term *Hebrews* (7.31; 15.37) complements the emphasis on their divine protector (3.39; 8.36). **11.16–21** Lysias addressed the Jewish *people* (not Judas) and agreed to the peace described in v. 15, with the proviso *what was possible* (v. 18). **11.17** *John*, perhaps Judas's brother (1 Macc 2.2). *Absalom*. See 1 Macc 11.70; 13.11. **11.21** The name of the month *Dioscorinthius* is uncertain; the compiler thought it pre-

ceded March (Xanthicus) 164 BCE (see vv. 33, 38). **11.22–26** Antiochus V instructs Lysias (after his second campaign; see 1 Macc 6.28–63; 2 Macc 13.1–26) to give back to the Jews their temple (which they already possessed) and to let them live according to their ancestral laws (which Antiochus IV had already allowed; see v. 31). **11.27–33** In March 164 BCE Antiochus IV granted amnesty to Jews who stopped fighting before the end of the month. He also allowed them to return to observing the Torah. **11.29** *Menelaus* apparently went to the king (in Persia?) and convinced him that this strategy would weaken the Jewish opposition. **11.34–38** In March 164 BCE the Romans consented to the arrangement between

"Quintus Memmius and Titus Manius, envoys of the Romans, to the people of the Jews, greetings. ³⁵With regard to what Lysias the kinsman of the king has granted you, we also give consent. ³⁶But as to the matters that he decided are to be referred to the king, as soon as you have considered them, send some one promptly so that we may make proposals appropriate for you. For we are on our way to Antioch. ³⁷Therefore make haste and send messengers so that we may have your judgment. ³⁸Farewell. The one hundred forty-eighth year,ᵃ Xanthicus fifteenth."

Incidents at Joppa and Jamnia

12 When this agreement had been reached, Lysias returned to the king, and the Jews went about their farming.

2 But some of the governors in various places, Timothy and Apollonius son of Gennaeus, as well as Hieronymus and Demophon, and in addition to these Nicanor the governor of Cyprus, would not let them live quietly and in peace. ³And the people of Joppa did so ungodly a deed as this: they invited the Jews who lived among them to embark, with their wives and children, on boats that they had provided, as though there were no ill will to the Jews;ᵇ ⁴and this was done by public vote of the city. When they accepted, because they wished to live peaceably and suspected nothing, the people of Joppaᶜ took them out to sea and drowned them, at least two hundred. ⁵When Judas heard of the cruelty visited on his compatriots, he gave orders to his men ⁶and, calling upon God, the righteous judge, attacked the murderers of his kindred. He set fire to the harbor by night, burned the boats, and massacred those who had taken refuge there. ⁷Then, because the city's gates were closed, he withdrew, intending to come again and root out the whole community of Joppa. ⁸But learning that the people in Jamnia meant in the same

way to wipe out the Jews who were living among them, ⁹he attacked the Jamnites by night and set fire to the harbor and the fleet, so that the glow of the light was seen in Jerusalem, thirty milesᵈ distant.

The Campaign in Gilead

10 When they had gone more than a mileᵉ from there, on their march against Timothy, at least five thousand Arabs with five hundred cavalry attacked them. ¹¹After a hard fight, Judas and his companions, with God's help, were victorious. The defeated nomads begged Judas to grant them pledges of friendship, promising to give him livestock and to help his peopleᶠ in all other ways. ¹²Judas, realizing that they might indeed be useful in many ways, agreed to make peace with them; and after receiving his pledges they went back to their tents.

13 He also attacked a certain town that was strongly fortified with earthworksᵍ and walls, and inhabited by all sorts of Gentiles. Its name was Caspin. ¹⁴Those who were within, relying on the strength of the walls and on their supply of provisions, behaved most insolently toward Judas and his men, railing at them and even blaspheming and saying unholy things. ¹⁵But Judas and his men, calling upon the great Sovereign of the world, who without battering rams or engines of war overthrew Jericho in the days of Joshua, rushed furiously upon the walls. ¹⁶They took the town by the will of God, and slaughtered untold numbers, so that the adjoining lake, a quarter of a mileʰ wide, appeared to be running over with blood.

Judas Defeats Timothy's Army

17 When they had gone ninety-five milesⁱ from there, they came to Charax, to the Jews who are called Toubiani. ¹⁸They did not find

___
a 164 B.C. b Gk to them c Gk they d Gk two hundred forty stadia e Gk nine stadia f Gk them g Meaning of Gk uncertain h Gk two stadia i Gk seven hundred fifty stadia

___
Lysias and the Jews. **11.34** *Titus* Manilius (Torquatus) was consul in 165 BCE and in Egypt in 164. *Manius* Sergius was sent to Antiochus IV in 164. The two figures may be conflated here.

12.1–9 At Joppa and Jamnia, Judas emerges as the champion of all Jews, even those outside of Jerusalem and Judea. **12.2** *Timothy.* There may be more than one person bearing the name. See 8.30–33; 10.24–28; 12.10–31. **12.3** *Joppa,* an important harbor city on the Mediterranean coast, about thirty-two miles from Jerusalem. **12.8–9** *Jamnia,* about twelve miles south of

Joppa, somewhat inland; see 1 Macc 5.58. **12.10–16** For a fuller account of Judas's campaign in Gilead, see 1 Macc 5.9–36. **12.10** Gilead is east of the Jordan; *more than a mile* is awkward and erroneous, suggesting textual corruption. The *Arabs* were mercenaries (see 1 Macc 5.39); here they are assimilated to the Nabateans favorable to Judas's cause (1 Macc 5.25). **12.13** *Caspin,* probably the same as Chaspho in 1 Macc 5.26, 36. **12.14** For *blaspheming* by Judas's opponents, see 10.34, 36; Antiochus and Nicanor are called blasphemers (9.28; 15.24). **12.15** For the fall of *Jericho,* see

Timothy in that region, for he had by then left there without accomplishing anything, though in one place he had left a very strong garrison. [19]Dositheus and Sosipater, who were captains under Maccabeus, marched out and destroyed those whom Timothy had left in the stronghold, more than ten thousand men. [20]But Maccabeus arranged his army in divisions, set men[a] in command of the divisions, and hurried after Timothy, who had with him one hundred twenty thousand infantry and two thousand five hundred cavalry. [21]When Timothy learned of the approach of Judas, he sent off the women and the children and also the baggage to a place called Carnaim; for that place was hard to besiege and difficult of access because of the narrowness of all the approaches. [22]But when Judas's first division appeared, terror and fear came over the enemy at the manifestation to them of him who sees all things. In their flight they rushed headlong in every direction, so that often they were injured by their own men and pierced by the points of their own swords. [23]Judas pressed the pursuit with the utmost vigor, putting the sinners to the sword, and destroyed as many as thirty thousand.

24 Timothy himself fell into the hands of Dositheus and Sosipater and their men. With great guile he begged them to let him go in safety, because he held the parents of most of them, and the brothers of some, to whom no consideration would be shown. [25]And when with many words he had confirmed his solemn promise to restore them unharmed, they let him go, for the sake of saving their kindred.

Judas Wins Other Victories

26 Then Judas[b] marched against Carnaim and the temple of Atargatis, and slaughtered twenty-five thousand people. [27]After the rout and destruction of these, he marched also against Ephron, a fortified town where Lysias lived with multitudes of people of all nationalities.[c] Stalwart young men took their stand before the walls and made a vigorous defense; and great stores of war engines and missiles were there. [28]But the Jews[d] called upon the Sovereign who with power shatters the might of his enemies, and they got the town into their hands, and killed as many as twenty-five thousand of those who were in it.

29 Setting out from there, they hastened to Scythopolis, which is seventy-five miles[e] from Jerusalem. [30]But when the Jews who lived there bore witness to the goodwill that the people of Scythopolis had shown them and their kind treatment of them in times of misfortune, [31]they thanked them and exhorted them to be well disposed to their race in the future also. Then they went up to Jerusalem, as the festival of weeks was close at hand.

Judas Defeats Gorgias

32 After the festival called Pentecost, they hurried against Gorgias, the governor of Idumea, [33]who came out with three thousand infantry and four hundred cavalry. [34]When they joined battle, it happened that a few of the Jews fell. [35]But a certain Dositheus, one of Bacenor's men, who was on horseback and was a strong man, caught hold of Gorgias, and grasping his cloak was dragging him off by main strength, wishing to take the accursed man alive, when one of the Thracian cavalry bore down on him and cut off his arm; so Gorgias escaped and reached Marisa.

---

a Gk *them*   b Gk *he*   c Meaning of Gk uncertain   d Gk *they*
e Gk *six hundred stadia*

Josh 6.1–21. **12.17–25** For another account of Judas's defeat of Timothy, see 1 Macc 5.37–43. **12.17** *Charax,* perhaps a common noun ("pallisaded camp") rather than a place-name. *Toubiani,* the remnants of a military unit commanded by the Tobiad family. **12.21** *Carnaim* (see 1 Macc 5.43–44) means "horns"; it was site of a temple to Atargatis (see note on 12.26). **12.22** The reference to God as one *who sees all things* implies sins on Timothy's part (v. 2; see 1 Macc 5.10–13, 25–27). **12.25** *Their kindred,* the relatives of the Tobiad Jews (see 1 Macc 5.13). **12.26–31** For another account of Judas's victories, see 1 Macc 5.46–54. **12.26** In Hellenistic times *Atargatis,* the Syrian fish and grain goddess, consort of Hadad, was identified with Astarte and Artemis. **12.27** *Ephron* (see 1 Macc 5.46), east of the Jordan and opposite Beth-shan/Scythopolis. *Lysias* may not be the governor mentioned in 10.11. **12.28** For *the Sovereign* (Greek *dynastes*) as a divine title, see 12.15. **12.29** *Scythopolis,* the Greek name ("city of Scythians") for Beth-shan (see 1 Macc 5.52), west of the Jordan. **12.31** The *festival of weeks,* or Shavuoth in Hebrew (Ex 23.16; Lev 23.15–22), marked the beginning of the grain harvest; its Greek name is Pentecost (v. 32), meaning "fifty" (days after Passover). **12.32–37** For episodes similar to Judas's defeat of Gorgias, see 1 Macc 5.55–68. **12.32** Idumea, Edom in ancient times, south and east of Judea. For *Gorgias* and *Idumea,* see 10.14–15. **12.35** *Dositheus.* See 12.19, 24. *Marisa,* called Mareshah in ancient times, one of the major cities of Idumea; see 1 Macc

36 As Esdris and his men had been fighting for a long time and were weary, Judas called upon the Lord to show himself their ally and leader in the battle. 37 In the language of their ancestors he raised the battle cry, with hymns; then he charged against Gorgias's troops when they were not expecting it, and put them to flight.

Prayers for Those Killed in Battle

38 Then Judas assembled his army and went to the city of Adullam. As the seventh day was coming on, they purified themselves according to the custom, and kept the sabbath there.

39 On the next day, as had now become necessary, Judas and his men went to take up the bodies of the fallen and to bring them back to lie with their kindred in the sepulchres of their ancestors. 40 Then under the tunic of each one of the dead they found sacred tokens of the idols of Jamnia, which the law forbids the Jews to wear. And it became clear to all that this was the reason these men had fallen. 41 So they all blessed the ways of the Lord, the righteous judge, who reveals the things that are hidden; 42 and they turned to supplication, praying that the sin that had been committed might be wholly blotted out. The noble Judas exhorted the people to keep themselves free from sin, for they had seen with their own eyes what had happened as the result of the sin of those who had fallen. 43 He also took up a collection, man by man, to the amount of two thousand drachmas of silver, and sent it to Jerusalem to provide for a sin offering. In doing this he acted very well and honorably, taking account of the resurrection. 44 For if he were not expecting that those who had fallen would rise again, it would have been superfluous and foolish to pray for the dead. 45 But if he was looking to the splendid reward that is laid up for those who fall asleep in godliness, it was a holy and pious thought. Therefore he made atonement for the dead, so that they might be delivered from their sin.

Menelaus Is Put to Death

13 In the one hundred forty-ninth year[a] word came to Judas and his men that Antiochus Eupator was coming with a great army against Judea, 2 and with him Lysias, his guardian, who had charge of the government. Each of them had a Greek force of one hundred ten thousand infantry, five thousand three hundred cavalry, twenty-two elephants, and three hundred chariots armed with scythes.

3 Menelaus also joined them and with utter hypocrisy urged Antiochus on, not for the sake of his country's welfare, but because he thought that he would be established in office. 4 But the King of kings aroused the anger of Antiochus against the scoundrel; and when Lysias informed him that this man was to blame for all the trouble, he ordered them to take him to Beroea and to put him to death by the method that is customary in that place. 5 For there is a tower there, fifty cubits high, full of ashes, and it has a rim running around it that on all sides inclines precipitously into the ashes. 6 There they all push to destruction anyone guilty of sacrilege or notorious for other crimes. 7 By such a fate it came about that Menelaus the lawbreaker died, without even burial in the earth. 8 And this was eminently just; because he had committed many sins against the altar whose fire and ashes were holy, he met his death in ashes.

a 163 B.C.

5.66, where Judas is said to have passed through (the district of) Marisa. **12.36** *Esdris,* perhaps Eleazar/Azariah of 8.23. **12.37** *Language of their ancestors.* See note on 7.8. **12.38–45** Judas's perfect Torah observance in battle contrasts with that of the fallen soldiers. His sin offering for them receives a novel interpretation: it is proof of his belief in resurrection of the dead. **12.38** *Adullam,* about eight miles northeast of Marisa. The purification involved ritual bathing after battle. **12.40** *Sacred tokens,* perhaps amulets dedicated to foreign gods or other objects taken from pagan shrines, which were prohibited for Jews (see Deut 7.25–26). **12.43** Judas's *sin offering* was probably intended to ward off punishment against the living (see Josh 7), but the author of 2 Maccabees took it as applying to the dead and thus as proof of Judas's belief in *resurrection* (see ch. 7; Dan 12.1–3).

13.1–8 Menelaus, the Jewish high priest, receives just punishment for his evil deeds. **13.1–2** In 163 BCE *Antiochus* V succeeded his father, with Lysias serving as his chief adviser (1 Macc 6.17). The *Greek force* was composed of mercenaries. The *scythes* on the chariots kept infantry away. **13.3–4** The *King of kings* (God) aroused anger against *Menelaus,* who may have fallen behind on paying his taxes (4.27, 43–47). **13.4** *Beroea,* the name given to Aleppo in Syria by Seleucus I. **13.5–6** The method of execution was used by the Persians; the person died by suffocation (if the ashes were cold) or burning (if they were hot). **13.8** Menelaus's mode of death was *just,* since his punishment fit his crimes.

A Battle Near the City of Modein

9 The king with barbarous arrogance was coming to show the Jews things far worse than those that had been done[a] in his father's time. 10But when Judas heard of this, he ordered the people to call upon the Lord day and night, now if ever to help those who were on the point of being deprived of the law and their country and the holy temple, 11and not to let the people who had just begun to revive fall into the hands of the blasphemous Gentiles. 12When they had all joined in the same petition and had implored the merciful Lord with weeping and fasting and lying prostrate for three days without ceasing, Judas exhorted them and ordered them to stand ready.

13 After consulting privately with the elders, he determined to march out and decide the matter by the help of God before the king's army could enter Judea and get possession of the city. 14So, committing the decision to the Creator of the world and exhorting his troops to fight bravely to the death for the laws, temple, city, country, and commonwealth, he pitched his camp near Modein. 15He gave his troops the watchword, "God's victory," and with a picked force of the bravest young men, he attacked the king's pavilion at night and killed as many as two thousand men in the camp. He stabbed[b] the leading elephant and its rider. 16In the end they filled the camp with terror and confusion and withdrew in triumph. 17This happened, just as day was dawning, because the Lord's help protected him.

Antiochus Makes a Treaty with the Jews

18 The king, having had a taste of the daring of the Jews, tried strategy in attacking their positions. 19He advanced against Beth-zur, a strong fortress of the Jews, was turned back, attacked again,[c] and was defeated. 20Judas sent in to the garrison whatever was necessary. 21But Rhodocus, a man from the ranks of the Jews, gave secret information to the enemy; he was sought for, caught, and put in prison. 22The king negotiated a second time with the people in Beth-zur, gave pledges, received theirs, withdrew, attacked Judas and his men, was defeated; 23he got word that Philip, who had been left in charge of the government, had revolted in Antioch; he was dismayed, called in the Jews, yielded and swore to observe all their rights, settled with them and offered sacrifice, honored the sanctuary and showed generosity to the holy place. 24He received Maccabeus, left Hegemonides as governor from Ptolemais to Gerar, 25and went to Ptolemais. The people of Ptolemais were indignant over the treaty; in fact they were so angry that they wanted to annul its terms.[b] 26Lysias took the public platform, made the best possible defense, convinced them, appeased them, gained their goodwill, and set out for Antioch. This is how the king's attack and withdrawal turned out.

Alcimus Speaks against Judas

14 Three years later, word came to Judas and his men that Demetrius son of Seleucus had sailed into the harbor of Tripolis with a strong army and a fleet, 2and had taken possession of the country, having made away with Antiochus and his guardian Lysias.

3 Now a certain Alcimus, who had formerly been high priest but had willfully defiled himself in the times of separation,[d] realized that there was no way for him to be safe or to have

---

a Or the worst of the things that had been done   b Meaning of Gk uncertain   c Or faltered   d Other ancient authorities read of mixing

---

13.9–17 After appropriate preparations for battle, Judas engages the Seleucid army near Modein. **13.9** There is no explanation for Antiochus V's actions beyond his *barbarous arrogance* (see, however, 11.22–26). In any case, it was Lysias's policy, since Antiochus V was a boy. **13.10–12** For battle preparations, see 1 Macc 3.44–47. **13.14** *Modein*, the hometown of the Maccabees (1 Macc 2.1), allowed Judas to make a preemptive strike. **13.15** For Eleazar's heroic death while stabbing an *elephant*, see 1 Macc 6.43–46. **13.18–26** The peace treaty between Antiochus V and the Jews is due also to events back in Antioch. **13.18–22** For the siege of *Beth-zur*, see 1 Macc 6.31, 49–50. 2 Maccabees blames its fall on the treachery of

Rhodocus, a Jew with a Persian name. **13.23** *Philip* (see 9.29) was appointed by Antiochus IV (1 Macc 6.14–15) and took control of Antioch (1 Macc 6.63). **13.24** *From Ptolemais to Gerar*, i.e., the coastal plain from north to south. **13.25** For *Ptolemais* as hostile to Jews, see 6.8; 1 Macc 5.15.

14.1–14 For another account of Alcimus's criticism of Judas, see 1 Macc 7.1–7, 25–26. 2 Maccabees omits Bacchides (1 Macc 7.8–24). **14.1–2** In 161 BCE *Demetrius* I, son of *Seleucus* IV, arrived at *Tripolis*, a port city named "Three Cities" because merchants from three other cities controlled parts of it. For more vivid descriptions of the fates of *Antiochus* V and *Lysias*, see 1 Macc 7.1–4. **14.3–5** *Alcimus* had

access again to the holy altar, [4]and went to King Demetrius in about the one hundred fifty-first year,[a] presenting to him a crown of gold and a palm, and besides these some of the customary olive branches from the temple. During that day he kept quiet. [5]But he found an opportunity that furthered his mad purpose when he was invited by Demetrius to a meeting of the council and was asked about the attitude and intentions of the Jews. He answered:

[6] "Those of the Jews who are called Hasideans, whose leader is Judas Maccabeus, are keeping up war and stirring up sedition, and will not let the kingdom attain tranquility. [7]Therefore I have laid aside my ancestral glory—I mean the high priesthood—and have now come here, [8]first because I am genuinely concerned for the interests of the king, and second because I have regard also for my compatriots. For through the folly of those whom I have mentioned our whole nation is now in no small misfortune. [9]Since you are acquainted, O king, with the details of this matter, may it please you to take thought for our country and our hard-pressed nation with the gracious kindness that you show to all. [10]For as long as Judas lives, it is impossible for the government to find peace." [11]When he had said this, the rest of the king's Friends,[b] who were hostile to Judas, quickly inflamed Demetrius still more. [12]He immediately chose Nicanor, who had been in command of the elephants, appointed him governor of Judea, and sent him off [13]with orders to kill Judas and scatter his troops, and to install Alcimus as high priest of the great[c] temple. [14]And the Gentiles throughout Judea, who had fled before[d] Judas, flocked to join Nicanor, thinking that the misfortunes and calamities of the Jews would mean prosperity for themselves.

Nicanor Makes Friends with Judas

[15] When the Jews[e] heard of Nicanor's coming and the gathering of the Gentiles, they sprinkled dust on their heads and prayed to him who established his own people forever and always upholds his own heritage by manifesting himself. [16]At the command of the leader, they[f] set out from there immediately and engaged them in battle at a village called Dessau.[d] [17]Simon, the brother of Judas, had encountered Nicanor, but had been temporarily[g] checked because of the sudden consternation created by the enemy.

[18] Nevertheless Nicanor, hearing of the valor of Judas and his troops and their courage in battle for their country, shrank from deciding the issue by bloodshed. [19]Therefore he sent Posidonius, Theodotus, and Mattathias to give and receive pledges of friendship. [20]When the terms had been fully considered, and the leader had informed the people, and it had appeared that they were of one mind, they agreed to the covenant. [21]The leaders[h] set a day on which to meet by themselves. A chariot came forward from each army; seats of honor were set in place; [22]Judas posted armed men in readiness at key places to prevent sudden treachery on the part of the enemy; so they duly held the consultation.

[23] Nicanor stayed on in Jerusalem and did nothing out of the way, but dismissed the flocks of people that had gathered. [24]And he kept Judas always in his presence; he was warmly attached to the man. [25]He urged him to marry and have children; so Judas[f] married, settled down, and shared the common life.

---

a 161 B.C.   *b* Gk *of the Friends*   *c* Gk *greatest*   *d* Meaning of Gk uncertain   *e* Gk *they*   *f* Gk *he*   *g* Other ancient authorities read *slowly*   *h* Gk *They*

---

been appointed high priest by Antiochus V after Menelaus was executed. His "defilement" probably consisted in collaborating with the Seleucid regime. He seems to have had two meetings with Demetrius I (vv. 4–5). **14.6** In 1 Macc 2.42; 7.12–17 the *Hasideans* constitute a party separate from the Maccabees. Here Judas is portrayed as their leader. **14.7** For the *ancestral* claim to the high priesthood by Alcimus, see 1 Macc 7.14. **14.11** *The rest of the king's Friends* suggests that Alcimus was a member of the inner circle of royal advisers. **14.12** *Nicanor.* See 2 Macc 8.9–36. His appointment as *governor* was probably tempo-

rary until he cleared up matters in Judea. **14.14** These *Gentiles* may have been settled in Judea under Antiochus IV. **14.15–25** For another view of Nicanor's relationship with Judas, see 1 Macc 7.27–29. **14.16–17** *Dessau.* Location uncertain, though it seems to have been in Judea. The encounter with *Nicanor* appears to have been a defeat for *Simon.* **14.19** *Mattathias,* a Hebrew name. *Theodotus,* a Greek name often taken by Jews. Both mean "gift of God." **14.21–25** The private discussion between Nicanor and Judas issues in a warm friendship; see 1 Macc 7.27, where Nicanor is accused of treachery from the start.

Nicanor Turns against Judas

26 But when Alcimus noticed their goodwill for one another, he took the covenant that had been made and went to Demetrius. He told him that Nicanor was disloyal to the government, since he had appointed that conspirator against the kingdom, Judas, to be his successor. 27 The king became excited and, provoked by the false accusations of that depraved man, wrote to Nicanor, stating that he was displeased with the covenant and commanding him to send Maccabeus to Antioch as a prisoner without delay.

28 When this message came to Nicanor, he was troubled and grieved that he had to annul their agreement when the man had done no wrong. 29 Since it was not possible to oppose the king, he watched for an opportunity to accomplish this by a stratagem. 30 But Maccabeus, noticing that Nicanor was more austere in his dealings with him and was meeting him more rudely than had been his custom, concluded that this austerity did not spring from the best motives. So he gathered not a few of his men, and went into hiding from Nicanor. 31 When the latter became aware that he had been cleverly outwitted by the man, he went to the great[a] and holy temple while the priests were offering the customary sacrifices, and commanded them to hand the man over. 32 When they declared on oath that they did not know where the man was whom he wanted, 33 he stretched out his right hand toward the sanctuary, and swore this oath: "If you do not hand Judas over to me as a prisoner, I will level this shrine of God to the ground and tear down the altar, and build here a splendid temple to Dionysus."

34 Having said this, he went away. Then the priests stretched out their hands toward heaven and called upon the constant Defender of our nation, in these words: 35 "O Lord of all, though you have need of nothing, you were pleased that there should be a temple for your habitation among us; 36 so now, O holy One, Lord of all holiness, keep undefiled forever this house that has been so recently purified."

Razis Dies for His Country

37 A certain Razis, one of the elders of Jerusalem, was denounced to Nicanor as a man who loved his compatriots and was very well thought of and for his goodwill was called father of the Jews. 38 In former times, when there was no mingling with the Gentiles, he had been accused of Judaism, and he had most zealously risked body and life for Judaism. 39 Nicanor, wishing to exhibit the enmity that he had for the Jews, sent more than five hundred soldiers to arrest him; 40 for he thought that by arresting[b] him he would do them an injury. 41 When the troops were about to capture the tower and were forcing the door of the courtyard, they ordered that fire be brought and the doors burned. Being surrounded, Razis[c] fell upon his own sword, 42 preferring to die nobly rather than to fall into the hands of sinners and suffer outrages unworthy of his noble birth. 43 But in the heat of the struggle he did not hit exactly, and the crowd was now rushing in through the doors. He courageously ran up on the wall, and bravely threw himself down into the crowd. 44 But as they quickly drew back, a space opened and he fell in the middle of the empty space. 45 Still alive and aflame with anger, he rose, and though his blood gushed forth and his wounds were severe he ran through the crowd; and standing upon a steep rock, 46 with his blood now completely drained from him, he tore out his entrails, took them in both hands and hurled them at the crowd, calling upon the Lord of life and spirit to give them back to him again. This was the manner of his death.

a Gk greatest   b Meaning of Gk uncertain   c Gk he

14.26–36 For another version of Nicanor's change in attitude toward Judas, see 1 Macc 7.30–38. 14.26–27 It is possible that, in the interests of peace in Judea, Nicanor viewed Judas as his *successor* or deputy. *Alcimus* sought to wreck that plan by denouncing Nicanor and having Judas taken *prisoner*. 14.28–30 According to 1 Macc 7.30–32, Judas was informed about Nicanor's treacherous intent and defeated Nicanor in battle near Caphar-salama. 14.31–33 Cf. 1 Macc 7.33–38, where Nicanor threatens to burn the temple. His threat to turn the Jerusalem temple into *a splendid temple to Dionysus* may be the author's embellishment (see 6.7). 14.34 For God as Israel's *Defender*, see 8.36. 14.35–36 For the fulfillment of the prayer, see 15.34. 14.37–46 There is no parallel in 1 Maccabees to the martyrdom of Razis; see the other martyrdoms in 2 Macc 6–7. 14.37 *Razis* (Persian name), possibly a convert to Judaism (as v. 38 suggests). As an *elder* he may have been a member of the council; as *father of the Jews* he was acknowledged as their benefactor. 14.42 Razis's decision *to die nobly* rather than to fall into enemy hands had a biblical precedent in Saul (1 Sam 31.4). 14.46 Razis's voluntary death was based on the conviction that God would restore his body in the resurrection (see 7.11, 22–23).

Nicanor's Arrogance

15 When Nicanor heard that Judas and his troops were in the region of Samaria, he made plans to attack them with complete safety on the day of rest. 2When the Jews who were compelled to follow him said, "Do not destroy so savagely and barbarously, but show respect for the day that he who sees all things has honored and hallowed above other days," 3the thrice-accursed wretch asked if there were a sovereign in heaven who had commanded the keeping of the sabbath day. 4When they declared, "It is the living Lord himself, the Sovereign in heaven, who ordered us to observe the seventh day," 5he replied, "But I am a sovereign also, on earth, and I command you to take up arms and finish the king's business." Nevertheless, he did not succeed in carrying out his abominable design.

Judas Prepares the Jews for Battle

6 This Nicanor in his utter boastfulness and arrogance had determined to erect a public monument of victory over Judas and his forces. 7But Maccabeus did not cease to trust with all confidence that he would get help from the Lord. 8He exhorted his troops not to fear the attack of the Gentiles, but to keep in mind the former times when help had come to them from heaven, and so to look for the victory that the Almighty would give them. 9Encouraging them from the law and the prophets, and reminding them also of the struggles they had won, he made them the more eager. 10When he had aroused their courage, he issued his orders, at the same time pointing out the perfidy of the Gentiles and their violation of oaths. 11He armed each of them not so much with confidence in shields and spears as with the inspiration of brave words, and he cheered them all by relating a dream, a sort of vision,*a* which was worthy of belief.

12 What he saw was this: Onias, who had been high priest, a noble and good man, of modest bearing and gentle manner, one who spoke fittingly and had been trained from childhood in all that belongs to excellence, was praying with outstretched hands for the whole body of the Jews. 13Then in the same fashion another appeared, distinguished by his gray hair and dignity, and of marvelous majesty and authority. 14And Onias spoke, saying, "This is a man who loves the family of Israel and prays much for the people and the holy city—Jeremiah, the prophet of God." 15Jeremiah stretched out his right hand and gave to Judas a golden sword, and as he gave it he addressed him thus: 16"Take this holy sword, a gift from God, with which you will strike down your adversaries."

17 Encouraged by the words of Judas, so noble and so effective in arousing valor and awaking courage in the souls of the young, they determined not to carry on a campaign*b* but to attack bravely, and to decide the matter by fighting hand to hand with all courage, because the city and the sanctuary and the temple were in danger. 18Their concern for wives and children, and also for brothers and sisters*c* and relatives, lay upon them less heavily; their greatest and first fear was for the consecrated sanctuary. 19And those who had to remain in the city were in no little distress, being anxious over the encounter in the open country.

The Defeat and Death of Nicanor

20 When all were now looking forward to the coming issue, and the enemy was already close at hand with their army drawn up for battle, the elephants*d* strategically stationed and the cavalry deployed on the flanks, 21Maccabeus,

---

a Meaning of Gk uncertain   *b* Or *to remain in camp*   *c* Gk for *brothers*   *d* Gk *animals*

15.1–5 Nicanor's decision to attack Judas on the sabbath is portrayed as an attempt to claim divine sovereignty for himself. **15.1** From *Samaria* and the area around Modein Judas controlled the northern approaches to Jerusalem. Nicanor knew nothing of the Maccabees' decision to defend themselves on the sabbath (see 1 Macc 2.41). **15.3–5** The conversation between Nicanor and the Jewish collaborators revolved around who is the real *sovereign*—the God of Israel or Nicanor? **15.6–19** In contrast to Nicanor's arrogance, Judas displays exemplary piety and is encouraged by a vision of Onias III and Jeremiah. **15.6** The *public monument,* or trophy, was to be constructed with armor taken from Judas and other dead soldiers. **15.10** For Nicanor's *violation of oaths,* see 14.18–30. **15.12** For the intercessory prayer of *Onias* III, see 3.31–33. **15.13–16** For *Jeremiah,* see 2.1–8. The *sword* may allude to Jer 50.35–38. Both priest (Onias III) and prophet (Jeremiah) take up Judas's cause. **15.18** Defense of the *consecrated sanctuary* is the major theme of 2 Maccabees. **15.20–37** 1 Macc 7.40–50 locates the battle at Adasa. **15.20** The use of *elephants* suggests an open, level bat-

observing the masses that were in front of him and the varied supply of arms and the savagery of the elephants, stretched out his hands toward heaven and called upon the Lord who works wonders; for he knew that it is not by arms, but as the Lord[a] decides, that he gains the victory for those who deserve it. 22 He called upon him in these words: "O Lord, you sent your angel in the time of King Hezekiah of Judea, and he killed fully one hundred eighty-five thousand in the camp of Sennacherib. 23 So now, O Sovereign of the heavens, send a good angel to spread terror and trembling before us. 24 By the might of your arm may these blasphemers who come against your holy people be struck down." With these words he ended his prayer.

25 Nicanor and his troops advanced with trumpets and battle songs, 26 but Judas and his troops met the enemy in battle with invocations to God and prayers. 27 So, fighting with their hands and praying to God in their hearts, they laid low at least thirty-five thousand, and were greatly gladdened by God's manifestation.

28 When the action was over and they were returning with joy, they recognized Nicanor, lying dead, in full armor. 29 Then there was shouting and tumult, and they blessed the Sovereign Lord in the language of their ancestors. 30 Then the man who was ever in body and soul the defender of his people, the man who maintained his youthful goodwill toward his compatriots, ordered them to cut off Nicanor's head and arm and carry them to Jerusalem. 31 When he arrived there and had called his compatriots together and stationed the priests before the altar, he sent for those who were in the citadel. 32 He showed them the vile Nicanor's head and that profane man's arm, which had been boastfully stretched out against the holy house of the Almighty. 33 He cut out the tongue of the ungodly Nicanor and said that he would feed it piecemeal to the birds and would hang up these rewards of his folly opposite the sanctuary. 34 And they all, looking to heaven, blessed the Lord who had manifested himself, saying, "Blessed is he who has kept his own place undefiled!" 35 Judas[b] hung Nicanor's head from the citadel, a clear and conspicuous sign to everyone of the help of the Lord. 36 And they all decreed by public vote never to let this day go unobserved, but to celebrate the thirteenth day of the twelfth month—which is called Adar in the Aramaic language—the day before Mordecai's day.

37 This, then, is how matters turned out with Nicanor, and from that time the city has been in the possession of the Hebrews. So I will here end my story.

The Compiler's Epilogue

38 If it is well told and to the point, that is what I myself desired; if it is poorly done and mediocre, that was the best I could do. 39 For just as it is harmful to drink wine alone, or, again, to drink water alone, while wine mixed with water is sweet and delicious and enhances one's enjoyment, so also the style of the story delights the ears of those who read the work. And here will be the end.

_____

a Gk he   b Gk He

tlefield. **15.22** For the miraculous defeat of _Sennacherib_, see 2 Kings 18.13–19.35; Isa 36–37. The incident is part of Judas's prayer in 1 Macc 7.41–42; see also 2 Macc 8.19. **15.27** According to 1 Macc 7.40 Judas had three thousand men, hardly enough to kill _thirty-five thousand_ of the enemy. His victory is taken as _God's manifestation_. **15.29** _Language of their ancestors._ See note on 7.8. **15.31** The _citadel_, the garrison overlooking the temple area, was still in Seleucid control. **15.32–**

35 The gruesome disposition of _Nicanor's_ body climaxes the theme of appropriate punishments for evildoers. See Jdt 13–14. **15.36** For _Mordecai's day_, see Esth 3.7; 9.20–23; 10.3. **15.37** _The city_, Jerusalem. It remained in _possession of the Hebrews_ until the intervention of the Roman general Pompey in 63 BCE. **15.38–39** The narrator's epilogue takes up the tone and content of his preface in 2.19–32. **15.39** In antiquity _wine_ was often so strong that it had to be mixed with water.

1 ESDRAS

ESDRAS IS THE GREEK FORM of the Hebrew personal name Ezra. 1 Esdras as the name of the book derives from the Greek Bible (the Septuagint), where it is called Esdras A (*alpha*), while the combined book of Ezra and Nehemiah is called Esdras B (*beta*). In the Latin Bible (the Vulgate), 1 Esdras is called 3 Ezra.

Scope and Relation to Other Biblical Books

FIRST ESDRAS IS A SELECTIVE NARRATIVE of important religious events in the history of Judah from the Passover of Josiah, after the finding of the book of the law, to the reading of the law by Ezra and its imposition as the norm for Jewish life. For the most part, 1 Esdras simply parallels the relevant portions of 2 Chronicles, Ezra, and Nehemiah; the only extensive unparalleled material is 1 Esd 3.1–5.6, the debate of the three bodyguards. The detailed correspondences of 1 Esdras to other biblical texts are set out in the table on p. 1549, "The Relation of 1 Esdras to Other Biblical Books."

The exact relation of 1 Esdras to the other biblical texts in the table is a matter of some dispute. 1 Esdras is extant only in Greek and in other versions translated from the Greek (Latin, Syriac, Ethiopic, Armenian, and Arabic). There is no Hebrew version. Some have thought that it was originally written in Hebrew, its text being a variant of that of the Masoretic Text of the Hebrew Bible. Others have suggested that it is a fragment of a Greek translation of those books older than the Septuagint translation in the second century BCE. Perhaps the most common view is that 1 Esdras was compiled on the basis of the Septuagint version of the books of 2 Chronicles, Ezra, and Nehemiah. Occasionally it seems to preserve a reading preferable to that of the Hebrew Masoretic Text, which would suggest that its compiler used either a form of the Septuagint no longer attested or else a Hebrew original differing from the Masoretic Text.

Whatever the origins of the text of the book as a whole, the debate of the three bodyguards in chs. 3–4 should be treated separately, as a Hebrew or Aramaic composition, even if the rest of the book was originally composed in Greek.

Purpose

TO DISCERN THE PURPOSE for the compilation of 1 Esdras would be easier if we had the complete work. The ending has almost certainly been lost (the last sentence is incomplete), and the beginning is so abrupt as to raise suspicions that the book originally opened at a somewhat earlier point.

The temple appears in Josiah's Passover celebration in ch. 1, the restoration of the its treasures in ch. 2, its rebuilding in 5.56–7.9, the treasures brought for it by Ezra in ch. 8, and the settlement of the mixed marriages question in the square before the temple and the reading of the law in the same place in ch. 9. It would, however, be hazardous to argue that the temple is the theme of the work; there is too much material that has no connection at all with the temple.

Likewise, there is an obvious concentration on the two leaders of the postexilic community, Zerubbabel and Ezra. The work of Zerubbabel is more prominent than it is in the book of Ezra, and the figure of Ezra has entirely supplanted that of Nehemiah, but it would be unwise to regard the whole work as designed to rewrite the historical record about these characters, for the modifications to the books of Ezra and Nehemiah are relatively slight. It is more likely that 1 Esdras reflects the views of a group in postexilic Judaism that regarded Ezra and Nehemiah and their work quite differently (in 2 Macc 1.18–2.13 and Sir 49.13 Nehemiah is mentioned and Ezra is ignored).

The presence of the extensive narrative of the debate of the three bodyguards of Darius in chs. 3–4 further complicates the question of the purpose or theme of the book. The victor in the debate is Zerubbabel, and the narrative enhances his portrait, but no connection is drawn between the speeches in the debate and the events narrated in the rest of the book. The narrative seems to be told for its own sake, with only the weakest of links to the characters of the book.

It is hard for even a careful reader to resist the impression that the book has no clear theme. The very reason for its existence is not apparent, and the selection of material from the other biblical books has been carried out on principles no longer evident.

The Relation of 1 Esdras to Other Biblical Books

1 ESDRAS	PARALLEL BIBLICAL TEXTS
1.1–33	2 Chr 35.1–27
1.34–58	2 Chr 36.1–21
2.1–15	Ezra 1.1–11
2.16–30	Ezra 4.7–24a
5.7–46	Ezra 2.1–70 (Neh 7.6–73a)
5.47–65	Ezra 3.1–13
5.66–73	Ezra 4.1–5
6.1–22	Ezra 4.24b–5.17
6.23–34	Ezra 6.1–12
7.1–15	Ezra 6.13–22
8.1–27	Ezra 7.1–28
8.28–67	Ezra 8.1–36
8.68–90	Ezra 9.1–15
8.91–96	Ezra 10.1–5
9.1–36	Ezra 10.6–44
9.37–55	Neh 7.73b–8.13

Date

LACKING ANY IDEA OF THE PURPOSE OF THE BOOK, we are at a loss to date it with any accuracy, although most scholars would assign it to the second century BCE. We know that 1 Esdras, rather than the books of Ezra and Nehemiah, was the source used by Josephus in composing his *Antiquities of the Jews* toward the end of the first century CE. [DAVID J. A. CLINES]

Josiah Celebrates the Passover

1 Josiah kept the passover to his Lord in Jerusalem; he killed the passover lamb on the fourteenth day of the first month, 2having placed the priests according to their divisions, arrayed in their vestments, in the temple of the Lord. 3He told the Levites, the temple servants of Israel, that they should sanctify themselves to the Lord and put the holy ark of the Lord in the house that King Solomon, son of David, had built; 4and he said, "You need no longer carry it on your shoulders. Now worship the Lord your God and serve his people Israel; prepare yourselves by your families and kindred, 5in accordance with the directions of King David of Israel and the magnificence of his son Solomon. Stand in order in the temple according to the groupings of the ancestral houses of you Levites, who minister before your kindred the people of Israel, 6and kill the passover lamb and prepare the sacrifices for your kindred, and keep the passover according

to the commandment of the Lord that was given to Moses."

7 To the people who were present Josiah gave thirty thousand lambs and kids, and three thousand calves; these were given from the king's possessions, as he promised, to the people and the priests and Levites. 8Hilkiah, Zechariah, and Jehiel,[a] the chief officers of the temple, gave to the priests for the passover two thousand six hundred sheep and three hundred calves. 9And Jeconiah and Shemaiah and his brother Nethanel, and Hashabiah and Ochiel and Joram, captains over thousands, gave the Levites for the passover five thousand sheep and seven hundred calves.

10 This is what took place. The priests and the Levites, having the unleavened bread, stood in proper order according to kindred 11and the grouping of the ancestral houses, before the people, to make the offering to the Lord as it is written in the book of Moses; this

_____
a Gk *Esyelus*

NOTE: Since most of 1 Esdras is found elsewhere in the biblical text, the notes comment only on the differences between 1 Esdras and those other texts. **1.1–22** This account of the reign of Josiah is parallel to that in 2 Chr 35. An important concern of the book is introduced in the opening chapter: the Jerusalem temple and the worship carried out there. The Passover celebrations obviously symbolized for the author the reformation of the temple worship undertaken by Josiah. **1.1** *Josiah,* king of Judah 640–609 BCE. *Kept the passover.* Cf. 2 Chr 35.1–19; 2 Kings 23.21–23. *To his Lord.* The Hebrew in the parallel verse, 2 Chr 35.1, has "to the LORD," using the divine name YHWH; in Greek, however, the divine personal name is represented by the title "the Lord," to which the possessive pronoun "his" can be attached. **1.2** *Divisions,* the "courses," or teams, of priests rostered throughout the year for service in the temple; see 1 Chr 24.3–19. The detail that the priests were *arrayed in their vestments* is not in 2 Chr 35.2, but see Ezra 3.10. The author is attracted by the splendor of the temple officials (see also note on 1.10). **1.3** *The Levites, the temple servants.* In 2 Chr 35.3 the Levites are described as those who

"taught all Israel." Perhaps the author has less regard for the Levites than does the Chronicler (though 1 Esd 9.48–49 does depict them as teachers of the law). The temple servants are elsewhere a separate and inferior class, the Nethinim (cf. Ezra 2.43–54). **1.4** *Worship . . . and serve.* In the Hebrew of 2 Chr 35.3 there is only one verb, "serve," which can mean both "worship" (a deity) and "serve" (humans). **1.5** *Magnificence.* 2 Chr 35.4 has only "written directions," but 1 Esdras is stressing the importance of the temple. **1.7** *Calves,* or "young bulls"; 2 Chr 35.7 reads "bulls." **1.9** *Seven hundred calves,* in 2 Chr 35.9 "five hundred bulls." **1.10** *It* should be the *Levites* alone who are preparing the Passover for themselves and for the priests (1.13). *Unleavened bread,* perhaps a misreading of the Hebrew *mitswat,* "command" (2 Chr 35.10), as *matsot,* "unleavened bread." The Festival of Unleavened Bread followed Passover (cf. 1.19). *In proper order,* lit. "becomingly," stresses the attractive appearance of the clergy more than the Hebrew "in their divisions" (2 Chr 35.10). **1.11** *Morning,* a misreading of the Hebrew *baqar,* "cattle" (2 Chr 35.12), as *boqer,* "morning" (some Hebrew manuscripts have the same error).

they did in the morning. 12They roasted the passover lamb with fire, as required; and they boiled the sacrifices in bronze pots and caldrons, with a pleasing odor, 13and carried them to all the people. Afterward they prepared the passover for themselves and for their kindred the priests, the sons of Aaron, 14because the priests were offering the fat until nightfall; so the Levites prepared it for themselves and for their kindred the priests, the sons of Aaron. 15The temple singers, the sons of Asaph, were in their place according to the arrangement made by David, and also Asaph, Zechariah, and Eddinus, who represented the king. 16The gatekeepers were at each gate; no one needed to interrupt his daily duties, for their kindred the Levites prepared the passover for them.

17 So the things that had to do with the sacrifices to the Lord were accomplished that day: the passover was kept 18and the sacrifices were offered on the altar of the Lord, according to the command of King Josiah. 19And the people of Israel who were present at that time kept the passover and the festival of unleavened bread seven days. 20No passover like it had been kept in Israel since the times of the prophet Samuel; 21none of the kings of Israel had kept such a passover as was kept by Josiah and the priests and Levites and the people of Judah and all of Israel who were living in Jerusalem. 22In the eighteenth year of the reign of Josiah this passover was kept.

The End of Josiah's Reign

23 And the deeds of Josiah were upright in the sight of the Lord, for his heart was full of godliness. 24In ancient times the events of his

reign have been recorded—concerning those who sinned and acted wickedly toward the Lord beyond any other people or kingdom, and how they grieved the Lord*a* deeply, so that the words of the Lord fell upon Israel.

25 After all these acts of Josiah, it happened that Pharaoh, king of Egypt, went to make war at Carchemish on the Euphrates, and Josiah went out against him. 26And the king of Egypt sent word to him saying, "What have we to do with each other, O king of Judea? 27I was not sent against you by the Lord God, for my war is at the Euphrates. And now the Lord is with me! The Lord is with me, urging me on! Stand aside, and do not oppose the Lord."

28 Josiah, however, did not turn back to his chariot, but tried to fight with him, and did not heed the words of the prophet Jeremiah from the mouth of the Lord. 29He joined battle with him in the plain of Megiddo, and the commanders came down against King Josiah. 30The king said to his servants, "Take me away from the battle, for I am very weak." And immediately his servants took him out of the line of battle. 31He got into his second chariot; and after he was brought back to Jerusalem he died, and was buried in the tomb of his ancestors.

32 In all Judea they mourned for Josiah. The prophet Jeremiah lamented for Josiah, and the principal men, with the women,*b* have made lamentation for him to this day; it was ordained that this should always be done throughout the whole nation of Israel. 33These things are written in the book of the histories of the kings of Judea; and every one of the acts of Josiah, and

a Gk him   b Or their wives

1.12 At the beginning of this verse 2 Chr 35.11–12 has been omitted. *With a pleasing odor,* a misreading of "pans" (2 Chr 35.13).

1.23–33 The death of Josiah. **1.23–24** 1 Esdras makes this addition to 2 Chr 35 as an explanatory preface to the narrative of how, despite Josiah's piety, he meets an untimely death (1.25–31). The death of Josiah was obviously a theological problem. There may be some allusion to 2 Kings 23.24–27. It is strange that 1 Esdras omits the phrase from 2 Chr 35.20 "After all this, when Josiah had set the temple in order," since that would have suited its purposes well. **1.28** Instead of *the words of the prophet Jeremiah* the Hebrew has "the words of Neco" (2 Chr 35.22). Perhaps the author disapproved of depicting the Egyptian king as a vehicle for God's words. No specific words of Jeremiah on the subject are known, but the author may have felt Jo-

siah should have been warned by words like Jer 46.6. **1.32** *The principal men, with the women,* probably a misreading of the Hebrew *hasharim wehasharot,* "the singing men and singing women" (2 Chr 35.25), as *hasharim wesarot,* "the princes and princesses," which the Greek author further transformed by putting the women in a subordinate place. **1.33** *The book of the histories of the kings of Judea,* not the biblical Kings or Chronicles. 2 Chr 35.25 says their laments are "recorded in the Laments," but that does not refer to the biblical book of Lamentations. Josephus refers to such a lament (*Antiquities* 10.78–80), but we do not know his source. *His splendor, and his understanding of the law of the Lord,* in 2 Chr 35.26 simply "his faithful deeds in accordance with what is written in the law of the Lord." Josiah is more of a hero to the author of 1 Esdras.

his splendor, and his understanding of the law of the Lord, and the things that he had done before, and these that are now told, are recorded in the book of the kings of Israel and Judah.

The Last Kings of Judah

34 The men of the nation took Jeconiah[a] son of Josiah, who was twenty-three years old, and made him king in succession to his father Josiah. 35 He reigned three months in Judah and Jerusalem. Then the king of Egypt deposed him from reigning in Jerusalem, 36 and fined the nation one hundred talents of silver and one talent of gold. 37 The king of Egypt made his brother Jehoiakim king of Judea and Jerusalem. 38 Jehoiakim put the nobles in prison, and seized his brother Zarius and brought him back from Egypt.

39 Jehoiakim was twenty-five years old when he began to reign in Judea and Jerusalem; he did what was evil in the sight of the Lord. 40 King Nebuchadnezzar of Babylon came up against him; he bound him with a chain of bronze and took him away to Babylon. 41 Nebuchadnezzar also took some holy vessels of the Lord, and carried them away, and stored them in his temple in Babylon. 42 But the things that are reported about Jehoiakim,[b] and his uncleanness and impiety, are written in the annals of the kings.

43 His son Jehoiachin[c] became king in his place; when he was made king he was eighteen years old, 44 and he reigned three months and ten days in Jerusalem. He did what was evil in the sight of the Lord. 45 A year later Nebuchadnezzar sent and removed him to Babylon, with the holy vessels of the Lord, 46 and made Zedekiah king of Judea and Jerusalem.

The Fall of Jerusalem

Zedekiah was twenty-one years old, and he reigned eleven years. 47 He also did what was evil in the sight of the Lord, and did not heed the

words that were spoken by the prophet Jeremiah from the mouth of the Lord. 48 Although King Nebuchadnezzar had made him swear by the name of the Lord, he broke his oath and rebelled; he stiffened his neck and hardened his heart and transgressed the laws of the Lord, the God of Israel. 49 Even the leaders of the people and of the priests committed many acts of sacrilege and lawlessness beyond all the unclean deeds of all the nations, and polluted the temple of the Lord in Jerusalem—the temple that God had made holy. 50 The God of their ancestors sent his messenger to call them back, because he would have spared them and his dwelling place. 51 But they mocked his messengers, and whenever the Lord spoke, they scoffed at his prophets, 52 until in his anger against his people because of their ungodly acts he gave command to bring against them the kings of the Chaldeans. 53 These killed their young men with the sword around their holy temple, and did not spare young man or young woman,[d] old man or child, for he gave them all into their hands. 54 They took all the holy vessels of the Lord, great and small, the treasure chests of the Lord, and the royal stores, and carried them away to Babylon. 55 They burned the house of the Lord, broke down the walls of Jerusalem, burned their towers with fire, 56 and utterly destroyed all its glorious things. The survivors he led away to Babylon with the sword, 57 and they were servants to him and to his sons until the Persians began to reign, in fulfillment of the word of the Lord by the mouth of Jeremiah, 58 saying, "Until the land has enjoyed its sabbaths, it shall keep sabbath all the time of its desolation until the completion of seventy years."

Cyrus Permits the Exiles to Return

2 In the first year of Cyrus as king of the Persians, so that the word of the Lord by

---

a 2 Kings 23.30; 2 Chr 36.1 *Jehoahaz*   *b* Gk *him*
c Gk *Jehoiakim*   *d* Gk *virgin*

1.34–46a The last kings of Judah. **1.34** *Jeconiah*, an error for Jehoahaz (who appears in 2 Kings 23.30; 2 Chr 36.1). **1.35** 1 Chr 36.2 adds that Jehoahaz was twenty-three years old at his accession. **1.38** In having Jehoiakim *put the nobles in prison* (not in 2 Chr 36) and in having him, not the Egyptian Neco, deport his brother Zarius (Jehoahaz), 1 Esdras paints Jehoiakim as more of a villain than does 2 Chr 36. *From Egypt* should probably be "to Egypt" (as some manuscripts also have). **1.43** *Eighteen years old*, as in 2 Kings 24.8 and one Septuagint reading in 2 Chr 36.9; the Hebrew

of 2 Chr 36.9 has "eight years old." **1.45** *A year later.* The Greek perhaps means "at the end of the accession year" (which in this case would have lasted for only three months), and so "at the turn of the regnal year" or "in the spring" (as in 2 Chr 36.10). **1.46b–58** The fall of Jerusalem. **1.58** The quote is a combination of Jeremiah's prophecy of a seventy-year devastation of the land (Jer 25.11–12) with the idea of that period as a sabbatical rest for the land (Lev 26.34–35).

2.1–15 The return of the exiles. **2.1–5** These sentences are paralleled in both 2 Chr 36.22–23 and Ezra

the mouth of Jeremiah might be accomplished— 2the Lord stirred up the spirit of King Cyrus of the Persians, and he made a proclamation throughout all his kingdom and also put it in writing:

3 "Thus says Cyrus king of the Persians: The Lord of Israel, the Lord Most High, has made me king of the world, 4and he has commanded me to build him a house at Jerusalem, which is in Judea. 5If any of you, therefore, are of his people, may your Lord be with you; go up to Jerusalem, which is in Judea, and build the house of the Lord of Israel—he is the Lord who dwells in Jerusalem— 6and let each of you, wherever you may live, be helped by the people of your place with gold and silver, 7with gifts and with horses and cattle, besides the other things added as votive offerings for the temple of the Lord that is in Jerusalem."

8 Then arose the heads of families of the tribes of Judah and Benjamin, and the priests and the Levites, and all whose spirit the Lord had stirred to go up to build the house in Jerusalem for the Lord; 9their neighbors helped them with everything, with silver and gold, with horses and cattle, and with a very great number of votive offerings from many whose hearts were stirred.

10 King Cyrus also brought out the holy vessels of the Lord that Nebuchadnezzar had carried away from Jerusalem and stored in his temple of idols. 11When King Cyrus of the Persians brought these out, he gave them to Mithridates, his treasurer, 12and by him they were given to Sheshbazzar,[a] the governor of Judea. 13The number of these was: one thousand gold cups, one thousand silver cups, twenty-nine silver censers, thirty gold bowls, two thousand four hundred ten silver bowls, and one thousand other vessels. 14All the vessels were handed over, gold and silver, five thousand four hundred sixty-nine, 15and they were carried back by Sheshbazzar with the returning exiles from Babylon to Jerusalem.

Opposition to Rebuilding Jerusalem

16 In the time of King Artaxerxes of the Persians, Bishlam, Mithridates, Tabeel, Rehum, Beltethmus, the scribe Shimshai, and the rest of their associates, living in Samaria and other places, wrote him the following letter, against those who were living in Judea and Jerusalem:

17 "To King Artaxerxes our lord, your servants the recorder Rehum and the scribe Shimshai and the other members of their council, and the judges in Coelesyria and Phoenicia: 18Let it now be known to our lord the king that the Jews who came up from you to us have gone to Jerusalem and are building that rebellious and wicked city, repairing its market places and walls and laying the foundations for a temple. 19Now if this city is built and the walls finished, they will not only refuse to pay tribute but will even resist kings. 20Since the building of the temple is now going on, we think it best not to neglect such a matter, 21but to speak to our lord the king, in order that, if it seems good to you, search may be made in the records of your ancestors. 22You will find in the annals what has been written about them, and will learn that this city was rebellious, troubling both kings and other cities, 23and that the Jews were rebels and kept setting up blockades in it from of old. That is why this city was laid waste. 24Therefore we now make known to you, O lord and king, that if this city is built and its walls finished, you will no longer have access to Coelesyria and Phoenicia."

25 Then the king, in reply to the recorder Rehum, Beltethmus, the scribe Shimshai, and the others associated with them and living in Samaria and Syria and Phoenicia, wrote as follows:

26 "I have read the letter that you sent me. So I ordered search to be made, and it has been

a Gk Sanabassaros

1.1–3. 2.13–14 For the differences in the listing of the vessels, see Ezra 1.9–11. 2.16–30 The narrative now skips to Ezra 4.7, omitting notice that the building of the temple actually started (cf. Ezra 3.8–10), though v. 30 says that it stopped (the start of the work will be recounted much later, in 5.56–58). More important, the narrative becomes misleading by introducing here an episode from a much later period. We are now not in the time of the temple building (537–515 BCE), but in the days of Artaxerxes I (465–424 BCE), when the tem-

ple had long been finished and it was the rebuilding of the walls of Jerusalem (not the temple) that was being hindered. The author of 1 Esdras, however, confused the two building operations, inserting references to the temple in vv. 18, 20 where they do not belong (cf. Ezra 4.12, 14). 2.16 The names listed are a combination of two sets of signatories to separate letters in Ezra 4.7, 8. 2.17 Coelesyria, lit. "hollow Syria," the valleys and flatlands of inland Syria, reaching as far south as Judea, as distinct from Phoenicia, the eastern Mediterranean

found that this city from of old has fought against kings, 27that the people in it were given to rebellion and war, and that mighty and cruel kings ruled in Jerusalem and exacted tribute from Coelesyria and Phoenicia. 28Therefore I have now issued orders to prevent these people from building the city and to take care that nothing more be done 29and that such wicked proceedings go no further to the annoyance of kings."

30 Then, when the letter from King Artaxerxes was read, Rehum and the scribe Shimshai and their associates went quickly to Jerusalem, with cavalry and a large number of armed troops, and began to hinder the builders. And the building of the temple in Jerusalem stopped until the second year of the reign of King Darius of the Persians.

The Debate of the Three Bodyguards

3 Now King Darius gave a great banquet for all that were under him, all that were born in his house, and all the nobles of Media and Persia, 2and all the satraps and generals and governors that were under him in the hundred twenty-seven satrapies from India to Ethiopia. 3They ate and drank, and when they were satisfied they went away, and King Darius went to his bedroom; he went to sleep, but woke up again.

4 Then the three young men of the bodyguard, who kept guard over the person of the king, said to one another, 5"Let each of us state what one thing is strongest; and to the one whose statement seems wisest, King Darius

will give rich gifts and great honors of victory. 6He shall be clothed in purple, and drink from gold cups, and sleep on a gold bed,[a] and have a chariot with gold bridles, and a turban of fine linen, and a necklace around his neck; 7and because of his wisdom he shall sit next to Darius and shall be called Kinsman of Darius."

8 Then each wrote his own statement, and they sealed them and put them under the pillow of King Darius, 9and said, "When the king wakes, they will give him the writing; and to the one whose statement the king and the three nobles of Persia judge to be wisest the victory shall be given according to what is written." 10The first wrote, "Wine is strongest." 11The second wrote, "The king is strongest." 12The third wrote, "Women are strongest, but above all things truth is victor."[b]

13 When the king awoke, they took the writing and gave it to him, and he read it. 14Then he sent and summoned all the nobles of Persia and Media and the satraps and generals and governors and prefects, 15and he took his seat in the council chamber, and the writing was read in their presence. 16He said, "Call the young men, and they shall explain their statements." So they were summoned, and came in. 17They said to them, "Explain to us what you have written."

The Speech about Wine

Then the first, who had spoken of the strength of wine, began and said: 18"Gentlemen, how is

---

a Gk on gold   b Or but truth is victor over all things

---

coast. **2.27** *Cruel*, better "ruthless" or "stubborn" (there is nothing corresponding to this in the Aramaic of Ezra 4.20). **2.30** The addition of *cavalry . . . armed troops* gives the story a more dramatic touch than that in Ezra 4.23, which speaks more abstractly of "force and power."

3.1–4.63 The debate of the three bodyguards. This is the one lengthy section of 1 Esdras that has no equivalent in 2 Chronicles or in Ezra-Nehemiah. Its function is to introduce the governor Zerubbabel, explaining how this Jew came to be favored by the Persian king Darius. Zerubbabel proves to be the winner of the debate over what the strongest thing in the world is (4.13, 41), and he is rewarded by being given permission to rebuild the temple (4.42–57, 62–63). It seems likely that the story was popular long before it had the name of Zerubbabel attached to it, since it is found in other forms in different cultures. **3.1–17** This account of a banquet given by Darius (522–486 BCE) has probably been borrowed from Esth 1.1–2, where

the king is Ahasuerus. **3.1** *Media* had been an important part of the Persian Empire since Cyrus I conquered it in 550 BCE. **3.2** *Satraps,* governors of the satrapies, as the twenty provinces of the Persian Empire were called. **3.3** *But woke up again* contradicts v. 13; there may be a textual error. **3.4–11** The details lack plausibility. Why should the bodyguards suppose that the winner of a competition of their own devising and for their own amusement would be rewarded so handsomely by the king? And why should the answers be put under the king's pillow if *they* (his servants, presumably, v. 9) are going to give them to him? Josephus, not surprisingly, rewrites the story to have the king himself make the promise of reward (as does Herod in Mk 6.22–23). **3.12** Strangely, the third guard has two chances to win the competition! Also, how can women be strongest if truth is stronger still? *But above all things truth is victor,* an addition to an earlier form of the story. **3.18–24** The main point of this speech about wine is that it is "strong," but in it we can also de-

wine the strongest? It leads astray the minds of all who drink it. 19It makes equal the mind of the king and the orphan, of the slave and the free, of the poor and the rich. 20It turns every thought to feasting and mirth, and forgets all sorrow and debt. 21It makes all hearts feel rich, forgets kings and satraps, and makes everyone talk in millions.[a] 22When people drink they forget to be friendly with friends and kindred, and before long they draw their swords. 23And when they recover from the wine, they do not remember what they have done. 24Gentlemen, is not wine the strongest, since it forces people to do these things?" When he had said this, he stopped speaking.

The Speech about the King

4 Then the second, who had spoken of the strength of the king, began to speak: 2"Gentlemen, are not men strongest, who rule over land and sea and all that is in them? 3But the king is stronger; he is their lord and master, and whatever he says to them they obey. 4If he tells them to make war on one another, they do it; and if he sends them out against the enemy, they go, and conquer mountains, walls, and towers. 5They kill and are killed, and do not disobey the king's command; if they win the victory, they bring everything to the king— whatever spoil they take and everything else. 6Likewise those who do not serve in the army or make war but till the soil; whenever they sow and reap, they bring some to the king; and they compel one another to pay taxes to the king. 7And yet he is only one man! If he tells them to kill, they kill; if he tells them to release, they release; 8if he tells them to attack, they attack; if he tells them to lay waste, they lay waste; if he tells them to build, they build; 9if he tells them to cut down, they cut down; if he tells them to plant, they plant. 10All his people and his armies obey him. Furthermore, he reclines, he eats and drinks and sleeps, 11but they keep watch around him, and no one may go away to attend to his own affairs, nor do they disobey

him. 12Gentlemen, why is not the king the strongest, since he is to be obeyed in this fashion?" And he stopped speaking.

The Speech about Women

13 Then the third, who had spoken of women and truth (and this was Zerubbabel), began to speak: 14"Gentlemen, is not the king great, and are not men many, and is not wine strong? Who is it, then, that rules them, or has the mastery over them? Is it not women? 15Women gave birth to the king and to every people that rules over sea and land. 16From women they came; and women brought up the very men who plant the vineyards from which comes wine. 17Women make men's clothes; they bring men glory; men cannot exist without women. 18If men gather gold and silver or any other beautiful thing, and then see a woman lovely in appearance and beauty, 19they let all those things go, and gape at her, and with open mouths stare at her, and all prefer her to gold or silver or any other beautiful thing. 20A man leaves his own father, who brought him up, and his own country, and clings to his wife. 21With his wife he ends his days, with no thought of his father or his mother or his country. 22Therefore you must realize that women rule over you!

"Do you not labor and toil, and bring everything and give it to women? 23A man takes his sword, and goes out to travel and rob and steal and to sail the sea and rivers; 24he faces lions, and he walks in darkness, and when he steals and robs and plunders, he brings it back to the woman he loves. 25A man loves his wife more than his father or his mother. 26Many men have lost their minds because of women, and have become slaves because of them. 27Many have perished, or stumbled, or sinned because of women. 28And now do you not believe me?

"Is not the king great in his power? Do not all lands fear to touch him? 29Yet I have seen

---

a Gk talents

---

tect a note of praise for wine (cf. Ps 104.15; Sir 31.27–28) as well as a note of warning (cf. Prov 20.1; 23.29–35). **4.1–12** This speech about the power of the king portrays an absolute monarch who determines the lives of his subjects. There is at least a hint of sycophancy about this speech, which is (in the narrative) being delivered in the presence of the king. But the author no doubt also intends to criticize the despotism he describes. **4.13–32** This speech about women is put

in the mouth of the historical personage Zerubbabel, known as the governor of the province of Judea (cf. Ezra 3.2). The attitude taken toward women here is ambivalent, as is that toward wine and the king in the previous speeches. Although women can further men's interests (vv. 16–17), they also can be harmful to men (vv. 18–19, 26–27). Interestingly, women's power here is only in relation to individual men; they have no political or social power of their own. **4.29** No concu-

him with Apame, the king's concubine, the daughter of the illustrious Bartacus; she would sit at the king's right hand ³⁰and take the crown from the king's head and put it on her own, and slap the king with her left hand. ³¹At this the king would gaze at her with mouth agape. If she smiles at him, he laughs; if she loses her temper with him, he flatters her, so that she may be reconciled to him. ³²Gentlemen, why are not women strong, since they do such things?"

The Speech about Truth

33 Then the king and the nobles looked at one another; and he began to speak about truth: ³⁴"Gentlemen, are not women strong? The earth is vast, and heaven is high, and the sun is swift in its course, for it makes the circuit of the heavens and returns to its place in one day. ³⁵Is not the one who does these things great? But truth is great, and stronger than all things. ³⁶The whole earth calls upon truth, and heaven blesses it. All God's works[a] quake and tremble, and with him there is nothing unrighteous. ³⁷Wine is unrighteous, the king is unrighteous, women are unrighteous, all human beings are unrighteous, all their works are unrighteous, and all such things. There is no truth in them and in their unrighteousness they will perish. ³⁸But truth endures and is strong forever, and lives and prevails forever and ever. ³⁹With it there is no partiality or preference, but it does what is righteous instead of anything that is unrighteous or wicked. Everyone approves its deeds, ⁴⁰and there is nothing unrighteous in its judgment. To it belongs the strength and the kingship

and the power and the majesty of all the ages. Blessed be the God of truth!" ⁴¹When he stopped speaking, all the people shouted and said, "Great is truth, and strongest of all!"

Zerubbabel's Reward

42 Then the king said to him, "Ask what you wish, even beyond what is written, and we will give it to you, for you have been found to be the wisest. You shall sit next to me, and be called my Kinsman." ⁴³Then he said to the king, "Remember the vow that you made on the day when you became king, to build Jerusalem, ⁴⁴and to send back all the vessels that were taken from Jerusalem, which Cyrus set apart when he began[b] to destroy Babylon, and vowed to send them back there. ⁴⁵You also vowed to build the temple, which the Edomites burned when Judea was laid waste by the Chaldeans. ⁴⁶And now, O lord the king, this is what I ask and request of you, and this befits your greatness. I pray therefore that you fulfill the vow whose fulfillment you vowed to the King of heaven with your own lips."

47 Then King Darius got up and kissed him, and wrote letters for him to all the treasurers and governors and generals and satraps, that they should give safe conduct to him and to all who were going up with him to build Jerusalem. ⁴⁸And he wrote letters to all the governors in Coelesyria and Phoenicia and to those in Lebanon, to bring cedar timber from Lebanon to Jerusalem, and to help him build the city. ⁴⁹He wrote in behalf of all the Jews who were going up from his kingdom to Judea, in the in-

a Gk All the works   b Cn: Gk vowed

bine of a Persian king by the name *Apame* is known from other sources. The point would be made better if no reference were made to the woman's parentage. **4.33–41** This speech in praise of truth contains no ambivalence about its subject. *Truth* is here not freedom from error, but more like "virtue"; it is the opposite of *unrighteousness* (vv. 37, 39–40). It is hard to see any real argument in this speech that truth is "strong"; there is a claim that truth endures and prevails (4.38), but no evidence is brought forward. The speech about truth has not been well integrated into the story of the three-cornered contest, which apparently existed in an earlier version without Zerubbabel. **4.38** The origin of the aphorism "Great is truth and it prevails" (often quoted in the Vulgate version, *magna est veritas et praevalet*).
4.42–57 This account of the resumption of the rebuilding of the Jerusalem temple differs somewhat

from that of the other biblical books. **4.43** Ezra 1.7–8 (cf. 6.5; 1 Esd 3.10–12) says that it was Cyrus, not Darius, who restored the temple vessels. **4.45** No other biblical text says that the *Edomites* burned the temple, though Ob 11–14 has them involved in the destruction of the city. **4.47** Zerubbabel and Darius were not involved in the *building* of the city of *Jerusalem*; it was, rather, Nehemiah under Artaxerxes. **4.48** The letters of safe conduct and permission to take cedars from Lebanon were given to Nehemiah, not Zerubbabel (Neh 2.7–8). **4.49–56** The various rights given here to Zerubbabel and his community (freedom; privacy; tax-free status; removal of Idumeans; specific sums for temple worship; support of priests, Levites, and city guardkeepers) are not to be found in the decree of Cyrus in Ezra 6.6–12, though the provision of temple vessels, tax-free status for temple personnel, and specific sums for maintaining temple worship are prom-

terest of their freedom, that no officer or satrap or governor or treasurer should forcibly enter their doors; 50that all the country that they would occupy should be theirs without tribute; that the Idumeans should give up the villages of the Jews that they held; 51that twenty talents a year should be given for the building of the temple until it was completed, 52and an additional ten talents a year for burnt offerings to be offered on the altar every day, in accordance with the commandment to make seventeen offerings; 53and that all who came from Babylonia to build the city should have their freedom, they and their children and all the priests who came. 54He wrote also concerning their support and the priests' vestments in which*a* they were to minister. 55He wrote that the support for the Levites should be provided until the day when the temple would be finished and Jerusalem built. 56He wrote that land and wages should be provided for all who guarded the city. 57And he sent back from Babylon all the vessels that Cyrus had set apart; everything that Cyrus had ordered to be done, he also commanded to be done and to be sent to Jerusalem.

Zerubbabel's Prayer

58 When the young man went out, he lifted up his face to heaven toward Jerusalem, and praised the King of heaven, saying, 59"From you comes the victory; from you comes wisdom, and yours is the glory. I am your servant. 60Blessed are you, who have given me wisdom; I give you thanks, O Lord of our ancestors."

61 So he took the letters, and went to Babylon and told this to all his kindred. 62And they praised the God of their ancestors, because he had given them release and permission 63to go up and build Jerusalem and the temple that is called by his name; and they feasted, with music and rejoicing, for seven days.

List of the Returning Exiles

5 After this the heads of ancestral houses were chosen to go up, according to their tribes, with their wives and sons and daughters, and their male and female servants, and their livestock. 2And Darius sent with them a thousand cavalry to take them back to Jerusalem in safety, with the music of drums and flutes; 3all their kindred were making merry. And he made them go up with them.

4 These are the names of the men who went up, according to their ancestral houses in the tribes, over their groups: 5the priests, the descendants of Phinehas son of Aaron; Jeshua son of Jozadak son of Seraiah and Joakim son of Zerubbabel son of Shealtiel, of the house of David, of the lineage of Phares, of the tribe of Judah, 6who spoke wise words before King Darius of the Persians, in the second year of his reign, in the month of Nisan, the first month.

7 These are the Judeans who came up out of their sojourn in exile, whom King Nebuchad-

---

a Gk in what priestly vestments

---

ised by Artaxerxes to Ezra (Ezra 7.12–26). **4.58–63** Praise and celebration. **4.59–60** Zerubbabel's prayer of thanks combines many conventional OT phrases. **4.63** As before (e.g., v. 47), the *building* of the city *Jerusalem* is here ascribed to Zerubbabel rather than Nehemiah, whose work does not appear in 1 Esdras at all (the Nehemiah in 5.8 may or may not be the governor Nehemiah; see also note on 5.40).

5.1–6 These verses correspond to nothing in Ezra and are obviously designed as a link between the story of the three bodyguards in chs. 3–4 and the material from Ezra that resumes in 5.7. The book of Ezra has no account of a return of exiles in the time of Darius. **5.1** The idea that certain exiles were *chosen to go up*, to return to the land, is not found elsewhere. In Ezra 1.5 it is those "whose spirit God had stirred," and in Ezra 8.16–17 certain classes of exiles are prevailed upon to join Ezra's company. *Their livestock,* as in Ezra 1.4, 6. **5.2** The inclusion of *a thousand cavalry* is unparalleled elsewhere, though cf. Neh 2.9. *With the music of drums and flutes.* The picture is of a religious procession or

perhaps a military march. The music, however, might be simply for the farewell. **5.4** *These are the names . . . who went up.* What follows is not a full list of returnees, so there seems to be some problem with the text. **5.5** Something is amiss here, since *Joakim* is not one of the *sons of Zerubbabel* according to 1 Chr 3.19, and, more important, Zerubbabel is not a priest but a ruler from the *tribe of Judah.* There must be some error in the text. **5.6** *Who spoke wise words before King Darius,* Zerubbabel and his speech in 4.13–40. The author knows that the building of the temple was halted until *the second year of the reign of King Darius* (2.30), so the contest is dated to *the month of Nisan, the first month* of that year, to explain how Zerubbabel came to be appointed as director of the temple works. **5.7–46** This inventory of inhabitants of Judea at some unknown period in postexilic times is copied from Ezra 2.1–70 (Neh 7.6–73a) and assigned to the time of Zerubbabel, whose name is indeed the first in the list of leaders of returning exiles (v. 8). The number of the Judeans differs somewhat in the various lists: there are,

nezzar of Babylon had carried away to Babylon [8]and who returned to Jerusalem and the rest of Judea, each to his own town. They came with Zerubbabel and Jeshua, Nehemiah, Seraiah, Resaiah, Eneneus, Mordecai, Beelsarus, Aspharasus, Reeliah, Rehum, and Baanah, their leaders.

9 The number of those of the nation and their leaders: the descendants of Parosh, two thousand one hundred seventy-two. The descendants of Shephatiah, four hundred seventy-two. [10]The descendants of Arah, seven hundred fifty-six. [11]The descendants of Pahath-moab, of the descendants of Jeshua and Joab, two thousand eight hundred twelve. [12]The descendants of Elam, one thousand two hundred fifty-four. The descendants of Zattu, nine hundred forty-five. The descendants of Chorbe, seven hundred five. The descendants of Bani, six hundred forty-eight. [13]The descendants of Bebai, six hundred twenty-three. The descendants of Azgad, one thousand three hundred twenty-two. [14]The descendants of Adonikam, six hundred sixty-seven. The descendants of Bigvai, two thousand sixty-six. The descendants of Adin, four hundred fifty-four. [15]The descendants of Ater, namely of Hezekiah, ninety-two. The descendants of Kilan and Azetas, sixty-seven. The descendants of Azaru, four hundred thirty-two. [16]The descendants of Annias, one hundred one. The descendants of Arom. The descendants of Bezai, three hundred twenty-three. The descendants of Arsiphurith, one hundred twelve. [17]The descendants of Baiterus, three thousand five. The descendants of Bethlomon, one hundred twenty-three. [18]Those from Netophah, fifty-five. Those from Anathoth, one hundred fifty-eight. Those from Bethasmoth, forty-two. [19]Those from Kiriatharim, twenty-five. Those from Chephirah and Beeroth, seven hundred forty-three. [20]The Chadiasans and Ammidians, four hundred twenty-two. Those from Kirama and Geba, six hundred twenty-one. [21]Those from Macalon, one hundred twenty-two. Those from Betolio, fifty-two. The descendants of Niphish, one hundred fifty-six. [22]The descendants of the other Calamolalus and Ono, seven hundred twenty-five. The descendants of Jerechus, three hundred forty-five. [23]The descendants of Senaah, three thousand three hundred thirty.

24 The priests: the descendants of Jedaiah son of Jeshua, of the descendants of Anasib, nine hundred seventy-two. The descendants of Immer, one thousand and fifty-two. [25]The descendants of Pashhur, one thousand two hundred forty-seven. The descendants of Charme, one thousand seventeen.

26 The Levites: the descendants of Jeshua and Kadmiel and Bannas and Sudias, seventy-four. [27]The temple singers: the descendants of Asaph, one hundred twenty-eight. [28]The gatekeepers: the descendants of Shallum, the descendants of Ater, the descendants of Talmon, the descendants of Akkub, the descendants of Hatita, the descendants of Shobai, in all one hundred thirty-nine.

29 The temple servants: the descendants of Esau, the descendants of Hasupha, the descendants of Tabbaoth, the descendants of Keros, the descendants of Sua, the descendants of Padon, the descendants of Lebanah, the descendants of Hagabah, [30]the descendants of Akkub, the descendants of Uthai, the descendants of Ketab, the descendants of Hagab, the descendants of Subai, the descendants of Hana, the descendants of Cathua, the descendants of Geddur, [31]the descendants of Jairus, the descendants of Daisan, the descendants of Noeba, the descendants of Chezib, the descendants of Gazera, the descendants of Uzza, the descendants of Phinoe, the descendants of Hasrah, the descendants of Basthai, the descendants of Asnah, the descendants of Maani, the descendants of Nephisim, the descendants of Acuph,[a] the descendants of Hakupha, the descendants of Asur, the descendants of Pharakim, the descendants of Bazluth, [32]the descendants of Mehida, the descendants of Cutha, the descendants of Charea, the descendants of Barkos, the descendants of Serar, the descendants of Temah, the descendants of Neziah, the descendants of Hatipha.

33 The descendants of Solomon's servants: the descendants of Assaphioth, the descendants of Peruda, the descendants of Jaalah, the descendants of Lozon, the descendants of Isdael, the descendants of Shephatiah, [34]the descendants of Agia, the descendants of Pochereth-hazzebaim, the descendants of Sarothie, the descendants of Masiah, the descendants of Gas, the descendants of Addus, the descendants of Subas, the descendants of

---

a Other ancient authorities read Acub or Acum

Apherra, the descendants of Barodis, the descendants of Shaphat, the descendants of Allon.

35 All the temple servants and the descendants of Solomon's servants were three hundred seventy-two.

36 The following are those who came up from Tel-melah and Tel-harsha, under the leadership of Cherub, Addan, and Immer, 37though they could not prove by their ancestral houses or lineage that they belonged to Israel: the descendants of Delaiah son of Tobiah, and the descendants of Nekoda, six hundred fifty-two.

38 Of the priests the following had assumed the priesthood but were not found registered: the descendants of Habaiah, the descendants of Hakkoz, and the descendants of Jaddus who had married Agia, one of the daughters of Barzillai, and was called by his name. 39When a search was made in the register and the genealogy of these men was not found, they were excluded from serving as priests. 40And Nehemiah and Attharias*a* told them not to share in the holy things until a high priest should appear wearing Urim and Thummim.*b*

41 All those of Israel, twelve or more years of age, besides male and female servants, were forty-two thousand three hundred sixty; 42their male and female servants were seven thousand three hundred thirty-seven; there were two hundred forty-five musicians and singers. 43There were four hundred thirty-five camels, and seven thousand thirty-six horses, two hundred forty-five mules, and five thousand five hundred twenty-five donkeys.

44 Some of the heads of families, when they came to the temple of God that is in Jerusalem, vowed that, to the best of their ability, they would erect the house on its site, 45and that they would give to the sacred treasury for the work a thousand minas of gold, five thousand minas of silver, and one hundred priests' vestments.

46 The priests, the Levites, and some of the people*c* settled in Jerusalem and its vicinity; and the temple singers, the gatekeepers, and all Israel in their towns.

Worship Begins Again

47 When the seventh month came, and the Israelites were all in their own homes, they gathered with a single purpose in the square before the first gate toward the east. 48Then Jeshua son of Jozadak, with his fellow priests, and Zerubbabel son of Shealtiel, with his kinsmen, took their places and prepared the altar of the God of Israel, 49to offer burnt offerings upon it, in accordance with the directions in the book of Moses the man of God. 50And some joined them from the other peoples of the land. And they erected the altar in its place, for all the peoples of the land were hostile to them and were stronger than they; and they offered sacrifices at the proper times and burnt offerings to the Lord morning and evening. 51They kept the festival of booths, as it is commanded in the law, and offered the proper sacrifices every day, 52and thereafter the regular offerings and sacrifices on sabbaths and at new moons and at all the consecrated feasts. 53And all who had made any vow to God began to offer sacrifices to God, from the new moon of the seventh month, though the temple of God was not yet built. 54They gave money to the masons and the carpenters, and food and drink 55and carts*d* to the Sidonians and the Tyrians, to bring cedar logs from Lebanon and convey them in rafts to the harbor of Joppa,

a Or *the governor*   *b* Gk *Manifestation and Truth*   *c* Or *those who were of the people*   *d* Meaning of Gk uncertain

---

for example, 2,150 more inhabitants of Judea in 1 Esd 5 than in Ezra 2, and several names are missing from either list. The differences all seem to be due to scribal error. **5.40** *Nehemiah and Attharias.* Ezra 2.63 has simply "the governor" (in Hebrew *hattirshata*). This has been understood as a reference to Nehemiah (who is called by this term in Neh 8.9), and then the term has been misunderstood as a proper name, Attharias. *Urim and Thummim,* the sacred lots used by the priests to make decisions (see note on Ezra 2.63). **5.47–55** This account of the restoration of worship is largely identical with that in Ezra 3.1–7. **5.47** In this context (cf. 2.30; 5.6) this is *the seventh month* in the second year of Darius I (520 BCE). In Ezra 3.1, how-

ever, it is in the first year of Cyrus (538 BCE). The transference of the return and the resumption of worship to the reign of Darius serves to emphasize further the work of Zerubbabel. *In the square . . . the east,* i.e., in the vicinity of the temple. The phrase is not paralleled in the account in Ezra 3. **5.50** *Some joined them from the other peoples of the land* is an interesting addition to the narrative taken from Ezra. It may be due simply to a scribal error, for it is hard to see why some of the other inhabitants would have joined in the worship if *all the peoples of the land were hostile to them* (cf. also 5.66–71). **5.52** *Sacrifices on sabbaths,* an addition to the Ezra account perhaps reflecting the increasing prominence of the sabbath. **5.55** *Carts.* Ezra 3.7 reads

according to the decree that they had in writing from King Cyrus of the Persians.

The Foundations of the Temple Laid

56 In the second year after their coming to the temple of God in Jerusalem, in the second month, Zerubbabel son of Shealtiel and Jeshua son of Jozadak made a beginning, together with their kindred and the levitical priests and all who had come back to Jerusalem from exile; 57and they laid the foundation of the temple of God on the new moon of the second month in the second year after they came to Judea and Jerusalem. 58They appointed the Levites who were twenty or more years of age to have charge of the work of the Lord. And Jeshua arose, and his sons and kindred and his brother Kadmiel and the sons of Jeshua Emadabun and the sons of Joda son of Iliadun, with their sons and kindred, all the Levites, pressing forward the work on the house of God with a single purpose.

So the builders built the temple of the Lord. 59And the priests stood arrayed in their vestments, with musical instruments and trumpets, and the Levites, the sons of Asaph, with cymbals, 60praising the Lord and blessing him, according to the directions of King David of Israel; 61they sang hymns, giving thanks to the Lord, "For his goodness and his glory are forever upon all Israel." 62And all the people sounded trumpets and shouted with a great shout, praising the Lord for the erection of the house of the Lord. 63Some of the levitical priests and heads of ancestral houses, old men who had seen the former house, came to the building of this one with outcries and loud weeping, 64while many came with trumpets and a joyful noise, 65so that the people could not hear the trumpets because of the weeping of the people.

For the multitude sounded the trumpets loudly, so that the sound was heard far away; 66and when the enemies of the tribe of Judah and Benjamin heard it, they came to find out what the sound of the trumpets meant.

67They learned that those who had returned from exile were building the temple for the Lord God of Israel. 68So they approached Zerubbabel and Jeshua and the heads of the ancestral houses and said to them, "We will build with you. 69For we obey your Lord just as you do and we have been sacrificing to him ever since the days of King Esar-haddon[a] of the Assyrians, who brought us here." 70But Zerubbabel and Jeshua and the heads of the ancestral houses in Israel said to them, "You have nothing to do with us in building the house for the Lord our God, 71for we alone will build it for the Lord of Israel, as Cyrus, the king of the Persians, has commanded us." 72But the peoples of the land pressed hard[b] upon those in Judea, cut off their supplies, and hindered their building; 73and by plots and demagoguery and uprisings they prevented the completion of the building as long as King Cyrus lived. They were kept from building for two years, until the reign of Darius.

Work on the Temple Begins Again

6 Now in the second year of the reign of Darius, the prophets Haggai and Zechariah son of Iddo prophesied to the Jews who were in Judea and Jerusalem; they prophesied to them in the name of the Lord God of Israel. 2Then Zerubbabel son of Shealtiel and Jeshua son of Jozadak began to build the house of the Lord that is in Jerusalem, with the help of the prophets of the Lord who were with them.

3 At the same time Sisinnes the governor of Syria and Phoenicia and Sathrabuzanes and their associates came to them and said, 4"By whose order are you building this house and this roof and finishing all the other things? And who are the builders that are finishing these things?" 5Yet the elders of the Jews were dealt with kindly, for the providence of the Lord was over the captives; 6they were not prevented from building until word could be sent to Darius concerning them and a report made.

---

a Gk *Asbasareth* *b* Meaning of Gk uncertain

"oil." *Convey them in rafts,* a quite correct explanation of the mode of transport from the Lebanon. **5.56–73** The foundations of the temple. **5.62** *All the people sounded trumpets,* not in Ezra 3, is a strange comment, since trumpets were usually blown by priests (e.g., Num 10.2–10). **5.64–65** *Trumpets,* also not paralleled in Ezra 3. **5.73** *Kept from building for two years,* apparently a misunderstanding of the reference to "the sec-

ond year" of Darius in Ezra 4.24. The account in Ezra envisages cessation of work on the temple from about the second year of Cyrus (537 BCE) to the second year of Darius (520 BCE).

6.1–34 Work begins again. **6.4** *Finishing all the other things.* Perhaps the author of 1 Esdras has in mind that other buildings in addition to the temple were in progress (as in 2.18, where the building of the temple

7 A copy of the letter that Sisinnes the governor of Syria and Phoenicia, and Sathrabuzanes, and their associates the local rulers in Syria and Phoenicia, wrote and sent to Darius: 8 "To King Darius, greetings. Let it be fully known to our lord the king that, when we went to the country of Judea and entered the city of Jerusalem, we found the elders of the Jews, who had been in exile, 9building in the city of Jerusalem a great new house for the Lord, of hewn stone, with costly timber laid in the walls. 10These operations are going on rapidly, and the work is prospering in their hands and being completed with all splendor and care. 11Then we asked these elders, 'At whose command are you building this house and laying the foundations of this structure?' 12In order that we might inform you in writing who the leaders are, we questioned them and asked them for a list of the names of those who are at their head. 13They answered us, 'We are the servants of the Lord who created the heaven and the earth. 14The house was built many years ago by a king of Israel who was great and strong, and it was finished. 15But when our ancestors sinned against the Lord of Israel who is in heaven, and provoked him, he gave them over into the hands of King Nebuchadnezzar of Babylon, king of the Chaldeans; 16and they pulled down the house, and burned it, and carried the people away captive to Babylon. 17But in the first year that Cyrus reigned over the country of Babylonia, King Cyrus wrote that this house should be rebuilt. 18And the holy vessels of gold and of silver, which Nebuchadnezzar had taken out of the house in Jerusalem and stored in his own temple, these King Cyrus took out again from the temple in Babylon, and they were delivered to Zerubbabel and Sheshbazzar*a* the governor 19with the command that he should take all these vessels back and put them in the temple at Jerusalem, and that this temple of the Lord should be rebuilt on its site. 20Then this Sheshbazzar, after coming here, laid the foundations of the house of the Lord that is in Jerusalem. Although it has been in process of construction from that time until now, it has not yet reached completion.' 21Now therefore, O king, if it seems wise to do so, let search be made in the royal archives of our lord*b* the king that are in Babylon; 22if it is found that the building of the house of the Lord in Jerusalem was done with the consent of King Cyrus, and if it is approved by our lord the king, let him send us directions concerning these things."

Official Permission Granted

23 Then Darius commanded that search be made in the royal archives that were deposited in Babylon. And in Ecbatana, the fortress that is in the country of Media, a scroll*c* was found in which this was recorded: 24"In the first year of the reign of King Cyrus, he ordered the building of the house of the Lord in Jerusalem, where they sacrifice with perpetual fire; 25its height to be sixty cubits and its width sixty cubits, with three courses of hewn stone and one course of new native timber; the cost to be paid from the treasury of King Cyrus; 26and that the holy vessels of the house of the Lord, both of gold and of silver, which Nebuchadnezzar took out of the house in Jerusalem and carried away to Babylon, should be restored to the house in Jerusalem, to be placed where they had been."

27 So Darius*d* commanded Sisinnes the governor of Syria and Phoenicia, and Sathrabuzanes, and their associates, and those who were appointed as local rulers in Syria and Phoenicia, to keep away from the place, and to permit Zerubbabel, the servant of the Lord and governor of Judea, and the elders of the Jews to build this house of the Lord on its site. 28"And I command that it be built completely, and that full effort be made to help those who have returned from the exile of Judea, until the house of the Lord is finished; 29and that out of the tribute of Coelesyria and Phoenicia a portion be scrupulously given to

---

a Gk *Sanabassarus* *b* Other ancient authorities read *of Cyrus*
c Other authorities read *passage* *d* Gk *he*

---

and the building of the city are conflated). **6.18–20** *Zerubbabel*, an addition to Ezra 5.14; it is a curious feature of the Ezra account that Zerubbabel's name is missing, and the absence is probably significant in some way. Nevertheless, it is *Sheshbazzar*, not Zerubbabel, who lays the foundations of the temple (6.20); in the Hebrew of Ezra 3.6 it is not a matter of laying foundations but of repairing the building. **6.27** *Zerubbabel, the servant . . . Judea*. In Ezra 6.7 the reference is solely to "the governor of the Jews"; the naming of Zerubbabel and especially the title given to him are evidence of his importance in the eyes of the author of

these men, that is, to Zerubbabel the governor, for sacrifices to the Lord, for bulls and rams and lambs, 30and likewise wheat and salt and wine and oil, regularly every year, without quibbling, for daily use as the priests in Jerusalem may indicate, 31in order that libations may be made to the Most High God for the king and his children, and prayers be offered for their lives."

32 He commanded that if anyone should transgress or nullify any of the things herein written,[a] a beam should be taken out of the house of the perpetrator, who then should be impaled upon it, and all property forfeited to the king.

33 "Therefore may the Lord, whose name is there called upon, destroy every king and nation that shall stretch out their hands to hinder or damage that house of the Lord in Jerusalem.

34 "I, King Darius, have decreed that it be done with all diligence as here prescribed."

The Temple Is Dedicated

7 Then Sisinnes the governor of Coelesyria and Phoenicia, and Sathrabuzanes, and their associates, following the orders of King Darius, 2supervised the holy work with very great care, assisting the elders of the Jews and the chief officers of the temple. 3The holy work prospered, while the prophets Haggai and Zechariah prophesied; 4and they completed it by the command of the Lord God of Israel. So with the consent of Cyrus and Darius and Artaxerxes, kings of the Persians, 5the holy house was finished by the twenty-third day of the month of Adar, in the sixth year of King Darius. 6And the people of Israel, the priests, the Levites, and the rest of those who returned from exile who joined them, did according to what was written in the book of Moses. 7They offered at the dedication of the temple of the Lord one hundred bulls, two hundred rams, four hundred lambs, 8and twelve male goats for the sin of all Israel, according to the number of the twelve leaders of the tribes of Israel; 9and the priests and the Levites stood arrayed in their vestments, according to kindred, for the services of the Lord God of Israel in accordance with the book of Moses; and the gatekeepers were at each gate.

The Passover

10 The people of Israel who came from exile kept the passover on the fourteenth day of the first month, after the priests and the Levites were purified together. 11Not all of the returned captives were purified, but the Levites were all purified together,[b] 12and they sacrificed the passover lamb for all the returned captives and for their kindred the priests and for themselves. 13The people of Israel who had returned from exile ate it, all those who had separated themselves from the abominations of the peoples of the land and sought the Lord. 14They also kept the festival of unleavened bread seven days, rejoicing before the Lord, 15because he had changed the will of the king of the Assyrians concerning them, to strengthen their hands for the service of the Lord God of Israel.

Ezra Arrives in Jerusalem

8 After these things, when Artaxerxes, the king of the Persians, was reigning, Ezra came, the son of Seraiah, son of Azariah, son of Hilkiah, son of Shallum, 2son of Zadok, son of Ahitub, son of Amariah, son of Uzzi, son of Bukki, son of Abishua, son of Phineas, son of Eleazar, son of Aaron the high[c] priest. 3This Ezra came up from Babylon as a scribe skilled in the law of Moses, which was given by the God of Israel; 4and the king showed him honor, for he found favor before the king[d] in all his requests. 5There came up with him to Jerusalem some of the people of Israel and some of the priests and Levites and temple singers and gatekeepers and temple servants, 6in the seventh year of the reign of Artaxerxes, in the fifth month (this was the king's seventh year); for they left Babylon on the new moon of the first month and arrived in Jerusalem on the new moon of the fifth month, by the prosperous journey that the Lord gave them.[e] 7For Ezra possessed great knowledge, so that he omitted nothing from the law of the Lord or the commandments, but taught all Israel all the ordinances and judgments.

The King's Mandate

8 The following is a copy of the written commission from King Artaxerxes that was delivered to Ezra the priest and reader of the law of the Lord:

9 "King Artaxerxes to Ezra the priest and reader of the law of the Lord, greeting. 10In accordance with my gracious decision, I have

---

a Other authorities read *stated above* or *added in writing*
b Meaning of Gk uncertain   c Gk *the first*   d Gk *him*
e Other authorities add *for him* or *upon him*

given orders that those of the Jewish nation and of the priests and Levites and others in our realm, those who freely choose to do so, may go with you to Jerusalem. [11]Let as many as are so disposed, therefore, leave with you, just as I and the seven Friends who are my counselors have decided, [12]in order to look into matters in Judea and Jerusalem, in accordance with what is in the law of the Lord, [13]and to carry to Jerusalem the gifts for the Lord of Israel that I and my Friends have vowed, and to collect for the Lord in Jerusalem all the gold and silver that may be found in the country of Babylonia, [14]together with what is given by the nation for the temple of their Lord that is in Jerusalem, both gold and silver for bulls and rams and lambs and what goes with them, [15]so as to offer sacrifices on the altar of their Lord that is in Jerusalem. [16]Whatever you and your kindred are minded to do with the gold and silver, perform it in accordance with the will of your God; [17]deliver the holy vessels of the Lord that are given you for the use of the temple of your God that is in Jerusalem. [18]And whatever else occurs to you as necessary for the temple of your God, you may provide out of the royal treasury.

[19]"I, King Artaxerxes, have commanded the treasurers of Syria and Phoenicia that whatever Ezra the priest and reader of the law of the Most High God sends for, they shall take care to give him, [20]up to a hundred talents of silver, and likewise up to a hundred cors of wheat, a hundred baths of wine, and salt in abundance. [21]Let all things prescribed in the law of God be scrupulously fulfilled for the Most High God, so that wrath may not come upon the kingdom of the king and his sons. [22]You are also informed that no tribute or any other tax is to be laid on any of the priests or Levites or temple singers or gatekeepers or temple servants or persons employed in this temple, and that no one has authority to impose any tax on them.

[23]"And you, Ezra, according to the wisdom of God, appoint judges and justices to judge all those who know the law of your God, throughout all Syria and Phoenicia; and you shall teach it to those who do not know it. [24]All who transgress the law of your God or the law of the kingdom shall be strictly punished, whether by death or some other punishment, either fine or imprisonment."

Ezra Praises God

[25]Then Ezra the scribe said,[a] "Blessed be the Lord alone, who put this into the heart of the king, to glorify his house that is in Jerusalem, [26]and who honored me in the sight of the king and his counselors and all his Friends and nobles. [27]I was encouraged by the help of the Lord my God, and I gathered men from Israel to go up with me."

The Leaders Who Returned

[28]These are the leaders, according to their ancestral houses and their groups, who went up with me from Babylon, in the reign of King Artaxerxes: [29]Of the descendants of Phineas, Gershom. Of the descendants of Ithamar, Gamael. Of the descendants of David, Hattush son of Shecaniah. [30]Of the descendants of Parosh, Zechariah, and with him a hundred fifty men enrolled. [31]Of the descendants of Pahath-moab, Eliehoenai son of Zerahiah, and with him two hundred men. [32]Of the descendants of Zattu, Shecaniah son of Jahaziel, and with him three hundred men. Of the descendants of Adin, Obed son of Jonathan, and with him two hundred fifty men. [33]Of the descendants of Elam, Jeshaiah son of Gotholiah, and with him seventy men. [34]Of the descendants of Shephatiah, Zeraiah son of Michael, and with him seventy men. [35]Of the descendants of Joab, Obadiah son of Jehiel, and with him two hundred twelve men. [36]Of the descen-

a Other ancient authorities lack *Then Ezra the scribe said*

---

1 Esdras. **7.1–9** The temple is dedicated. **7.2** The account in Ezra 6.13 speaks only of the non-Jews doing what Darius had ordered—providing resources for the temple work. Here they are, strangely enough, actively involved in the rebuilding as they *supervised the holy work.* **7.5** *The twenty-third day of the month of Adar,* April 1, 515 BCE, a date perhaps to be preferred to that of Ezra 6.15, "the third day." **7.9** *And the gatekeepers were at each gate,* an addition to Ezra 6.18. **7.10–15** The Passover. **7.11** *Not all of the returned captives*

were purified, lacking in Ezra 6.20, is perhaps the result of a scribal error, though there may be an allusion to 2 Chr 30.18, where some unpurified Northerners nevertheless were able to celebrate Passover. **7.15** *King of the Assyrians,* an unusual and incorrect title for Darius, but borrowed from Ezra 6.22.

8.1–7 Ezra arrives. **8.1–2** The genealogy of Ezra is more concise than in Ezra 7.1–5. **8.7** *He omitted nothing from the law of the Lord,* wording that emphasizes, even more so than that of Ezra 7.10, Ezra's strict obser-

dants of Bani, Shelomith son of Josiphiah, and with him a hundred sixty men. 37Of the descendants of Bebai, Zechariah son of Bebai, and with him twenty-eight men. 38Of the descendants of Azgad, Johanan son of Hakkatan, and with him a hundred ten men. 39Of the descendants of Adonikam, the last ones, their names being Eliphelet, Jeuel, and Shemaiah, and with them seventy men. 40Of the descendants of Bigvai, Uthai son of Istalcurus, and with him seventy men.

41 I assembled them at the river called Theras, and we encamped there three days, and I inspected them. 42When I found there none of the descendants of the priests or of the Levites, 43I sent word to Eliezar, Iduel, Maasmas, 44Elnathan, Shemaiah, Jarib, Nathan, Elnathan, Zechariah, and Meshullam, who were leaders and men of understanding; 45I told them to go to Iddo, who was the leading man at the place of the treasury, 46and ordered them to tell Iddo and his kindred and the treasurers at that place to send us men to serve as priests in the house of our Lord. 47And by the mighty hand of our Lord they brought us competent men of the descendants of Mahli son of Levi, son of Israel, namely Sherebiah*a* with his descendants and kinsmen, eighteen; 48also Hashabiah and Annunus and his brother Jeshaiah, of the descendants of Hananiah, and their descendants, twenty men; 49and of the temple servants, whom David and the leaders had given for the service of the Levites, two hundred twenty temple servants; the list of all their names was reported.

Ezra Proclaims a Fast

50 There I proclaimed a fast for the young men before our Lord, to seek from him a prosperous journey for ourselves and for our children and the livestock that were with us. 51For I was ashamed to ask the king for foot soldiers and cavalry and an escort to keep us safe from our adversaries; 52for we had said to the king, "The power of our Lord will be with those who seek him, and will support them in every way." 53And again we prayed to our Lord about these things, and we found him very merciful.

The Gifts for the Temple

54 Then I set apart twelve of the leaders of the priests, Sherebiah and Hashabiah, and ten of their kinsmen with them; 55and I weighed out to them the silver and the gold and the holy vessels of the house of our Lord, which the king himself and his counselors and the nobles and all Israel had given. 56I weighed and gave to them six hundred fifty talents of silver, and silver vessels worth a hundred talents, and a hundred talents of gold, 57and twenty golden bowls, and twelve bronze vessels of fine bronze that glittered like gold. 58And I said to them, "You are holy to the Lord, and the vessels are holy, and the silver and the gold are vowed to the Lord, the Lord of our ancestors. 59Be watchful and on guard until you deliver them to the leaders of the priests and the Levites, and to the heads of the ancestral houses of Israel, in Jerusalem, in the chambers of the house of our Lord." 60So the priests and the Levites who took the silver and the gold and the vessels that had been in Jerusalem carried them to the temple of the Lord.

The Return to Jerusalem

61 We left the river Theras on the twelfth day of the first month; and we arrived in Jerusalem by the mighty hand of our Lord, which was upon us; he delivered us from every enemy on the way, and so we came to Jerusalem. 62When we had been there three days, the silver and the gold were weighed and delivered in the house of our Lord to the priest Meremoth son of Uriah; 63with him was Eleazar son of Phinehas, and with them were Jozabad son of Jeshua and Moeth son of Binnui,*b* the Levites. 64The whole was counted and weighed, and the weight of everything was recorded at that very time. 65And those who had returned from exile offered sacrifices to the Lord, the God of Israel, twelve bulls for all Israel, ninety-six rams, 66seventy-two lambs, and as a thank offering twelve male goats—all as a sacrifice to the Lord. 67They delivered the king's orders to the royal stewards and to the governors of Coelesyria and Phoenicia; and these officials*c* honored the people and the temple of the Lord.

Ezra's Prayer

68 After these things had been done, the leaders came to me and said, 69"The people of Israel and the rulers and the priests and the Levites have not put away from themselves the alien peoples of the land and their pollutions,

---

a Gk *Asbebias* *b* Gk *Sabannus* *c* Gk *they*

the Canaanites, the Hittites, the Perizzites, the Jebusites, the Moabites, the Egyptians, and the Edomites. 70For they and their descendants have married the daughters of these people,[a] and the holy race has been mixed with the alien peoples of the land; and from the beginning of this matter the leaders and the nobles have been sharing in this iniquity."

71 As soon as I heard these things I tore my garments and my holy mantle, and pulled out hair from my head and beard, and sat down in anxiety and grief. 72And all who were ever moved at[b] the word of the Lord of Israel gathered around me, as I mourned over this iniquity, and I sat grief-stricken until the evening sacrifice. 73Then I rose from my fast, with my garments and my holy mantle torn, and kneeling down and stretching out my hands to the Lord 74I said,

"O Lord, I am ashamed and confused before your face. 75For our sins have risen higher than our heads, and our mistakes have mounted up to heaven 76from the times of our ancestors, and we are in great sin to this day. 77Because of our sins and the sins of our ancestors, we with our kindred and our kings and our priests were given over to the kings of the earth, to the sword and exile and plundering, in shame until this day. 78And now in some measure mercy has come to us from you, O Lord, to leave to us a root and a name in your holy place, 79and to uncover a light for us in the house of the Lord our God, and to give us food in the time of our servitude. 80Even in our bondage we were not forsaken by our Lord, but he brought us into favor with the kings of the Persians, so that they have given us food 81and glorified the temple of our Lord, and raised Zion from desolation, to give us a stronghold in Judea and Jerusalem.

82 "And now, O Lord, what shall we say, when we have these things? For we have transgressed your commandments, which you gave by your servants the prophets, saying, 83'The land that you are entering to take possession of is a land polluted with the pollution of the aliens of the land, and they have filled it with their uncleanness. 84Therefore do not give your daughters in marriage to their descendants, and do not take their daughters for your descendants; 85do not seek ever to have peace with them, so that you may be strong and eat the good things of the land and leave it for an inheritance to your children forever.' 86And all that has happened to us has come about because of our evil deeds and our great sins. For you, O Lord, lifted the burden of our sins 87and gave us such a root as this; but we turned back again to transgress your law by mixing with the uncleanness of the peoples of the land. 88Were you not angry enough with us to destroy us without leaving a root or seed or name? 89O Lord of Israel, you are faithful; for we are left as a root to this day. 90See, we are now before you in our iniquities; for we can no longer stand in your presence because of these things."

The Plan for Ending Mixed Marriages

91 While Ezra was praying and making his confession, weeping and lying on the ground before the temple, there gathered around him a very great crowd of men and women and youths from Jerusalem; for there was great weeping among the multitude. 92Then Shecaniah son of Jehiel, one of the men of Israel, called out, and said to Ezra, "We have sinned against the Lord, and have married foreign women from the peoples of the land; but even now there is hope for Israel. 93Let us take an oath to the Lord about this, that we will put away all our foreign wives, with their children, 94as seems good to you and to all who obey the law of the Lord. 95Rise up[c] and take action, for it is your task, and we are with you to take strong measures." 96Then Ezra rose up and made the leaders of the priests and Levites of all Israel swear that they would do this. And they swore to it.

The Expulsion of Foreign Wives

9 Then Ezra set out and went from the court of the temple to the chamber of Je-

---

a Gk their daughters   b Or zealous for   c Other ancient authorities read as seems good to you." And all who obeyed the law of the Lord rose and said to Ezra, 95"Rise up

---

vance of the law. 8.42 None of the descendants . . . Levites. Ezra 8.15 says only that there were no Levites. 8.50 Young men, a misreading of nahar ("river," as in Ezra 8.21) as na'arim, "young men." 8.66 Ezra 8.35 has "seventy-seven lambs"; 1 Esdras may preserve the correct number, seventy-two, which is a multiple of twelve, symbolizing the twelve tribes of Israel. 8.71 My holy mantle. Ezra 9.3 has simply "my mantle," but Ezra is of course a priest, so his garments are holy. 8.80 Have given us food. Ezra 9.9 has a less literal phrase, "to give

hohanan son of Eliashib, [2]and spent the night there; and he did not eat bread or drink water, for he was mourning over the great iniquities of the multitude. [3]And a proclamation was made throughout Judea and Jerusalem to all who had returned from exile that they should assemble at Jerusalem, [4]and that if any did not meet there within two or three days, in accordance with the decision of the ruling elders, their livestock would be seized for sacrifice and the men themselves[a] expelled from the multitude of those who had returned from the captivity.

5 Then the men of the tribe of Judah and Benjamin assembled at Jerusalem within three days; this was the ninth month, on the twentieth day of the month. [6]All the multitude sat in the open square before the temple, shivering because of the bad weather that prevailed. [7]Then Ezra stood up and said to them, "You have broken the law and married foreign women, and so have increased the sin of Israel. [8]Now then make confession and give glory to the Lord the God of our ancestors, [9]and do his will; separate yourselves from the peoples of the land and from your foreign wives."

10 Then all the multitude shouted and said with a loud voice, "We will do as you have said. [11]But the multitude is great and it is winter, and we are not able to stand in the open air. This is not a work we can do in one day or two, for we have sinned too much in these things. [12]So let the leaders of the multitude stay, and let all those in our settlements who have foreign wives come at the time appointed, [13]with the elders and judges of each place, until we are freed from the wrath of the Lord over this matter."

14 Jonathan son of Asahel and Jahzeiah son of Tikvah[b] undertook the matter on these terms, and Meshullam and Levi and Shabbethai served with them as judges. [15]And those who had returned from exile acted in accordance with all this.

16 Ezra the priest chose for himself the leading men of their ancestral houses, all of them by name; and on the new moon of the tenth month they began their sessions to investigate the matter. [17]And the cases of the men who had foreign wives were brought to an end by the new moon of the first month.

18 Of the priests, those who were brought in and found to have foreign wives were: [19]of the descendants of Jeshua son of Jozadak and his kindred, Maaseiah, Eliezar, Jarib, and Jodan. [20]They pledged themselves to put away their wives, and to offer rams in expiation of their error. [21]Of the descendants of Immer: Hanani and Zebadiah and Maaseiah and Shemaiah and Jehiel and Azariah. [22]Of the descendants of Pashhur: Elioenai, Maaseiah, Ishmael, and Nathanael, and Gedaliah, and Salthas.

23 And of the Levites: Jozabad and Shimei and Kelaiah, who was Kelita, and Pethahiah and Judah and Jonah. [24]Of the temple singers: Eliashib and Zaccur.[c] [25]Of the gatekeepers: Shallum and Telem.[d]

26 Of Israel: of the descendants of Parosh: Ramiah, Izziah, Malchijah, Mijamin, and Eleazar, and Asibias, and Benaiah. [27]Of the descendants of Elam: Mattaniah and Zechariah, Jezrielus and Abdi, and Jeremoth and Elijah. [28]Of the descendants of Zamoth: Eliadas, Eliashib, Othoniah, Jeremoth, and Zabad and Zerdaiah. [29]Of the descendants of Bebai: Jehohanan and Hananiah and Zabbai and Emathis. [30]Of the descendants of Mani: Olamus, Mamuchus, Adaiah, Jashub, and Sheal and Jeremoth. [31]Of the descendants of Addi: Naathus and Moossias, Laccunus and Naidus, and Bescaspasmys and Sesthel, and Belnuus and Manasseas. [32]Of the descendants of Annan, Elionas and Asaias and Melchias and Sabbaias and Simon Chosamaeus. [33]Of the descendants of Hashum: Mattenai and Mattattah and Zabad and Eliphelet and Manasseh and Shimei. [34]Of the descendants of Bani: Jeremai, Momdius, Maerus, Joel, Mamdai and Bedeiah and Vaniah, Carabasion and Eliashib and Mamitanemus, Eliasis, Binnui, Elialis, Shimei, Shelemiah, Nethaniah. Of the descendants of Ezora: Shashai, Azarel, Azael, Samatus, Zambris, Joseph. [35]Of the descendants of Nooma: Mazitias, Zabad, Iddo, Joel, Benaiah. [36]All these had married foreign women, and they put them away together with their children.

Ezra Reads the Law to the People

37 The priests and the Levites and the Israelites settled in Jerusalem and in the country. On the new moon of the seventh month, when the people of Israel were in their settlements, [38]the whole multitude gathered with

---

a Gk he himself   b Gk Thocanos   c Gk Bacchurus
d Gk Tolbanes

one accord in the open square before the east gate of the temple; [39]they told Ezra the chief priest and reader to bring the law of Moses that had been given by the Lord God of Israel. [40]So Ezra the chief priest brought the law, for all the multitude, men and women, and all the priests to hear the law, on the new moon of the seventh month. [41]He read aloud in the open square before the gate of the temple from early morning until midday, in the presence of both men and women; and all the multitude gave attention to the law. [42]Ezra the priest and reader of the law stood on the wooden platform that had been prepared; [43]and beside him stood Mattathiah, Shema, Ananias, Azariah, Uriah, Hezekiah, and Baalsamus on his right, [44]and on his left Pedaiah, Mishael, Malchijah, Lothasubus, Nabariah, and Zechariah. [45]Then Ezra took up the book of the law in the sight of the multitude, for he had the place of honor in the presence of all. [46]When he opened the law, they all stood erect. And Ezra blessed the Lord God Most High, the God of hosts, the Almighty, [47]and the multitude answered, "Amen." They lifted up their hands, and fell to the ground and worshiped the Lord. [48]Jeshua and Anniuth and Sherebiah, Jadinus, Akkub, Shabbethai, Hodiah, Maiannas and Kelita, Azariah and Jozabad, Hanan, Pelaiah, the Levites, taught the law of the Lord,[a] at the same time explaining what was read.

49 Then Attharates[b] said to Ezra the chief priest and reader, and to the Levites who were teaching the multitude, and to all, [50]"This day is holy to the Lord"—now they were all weeping as they heard the law— [51]"so go your way, eat the fat and drink the sweet, and send portions to those who have none; [52]for the day is holy to the Lord; and do not be sorrowful, for the Lord will exalt you." [53]The Levites commanded all the people, saying, "This day is holy; do not be sorrowful." [54]Then they all went their way, to eat and drink and enjoy themselves, and to give portions to those who had none, and to make great rejoicing; [55]because they were inspired by the words which they had been taught. And they came together.[c]

---

a Other ancient authorities add *and read the law of the Lord to the multitude*   b Or *the governor*   c The Greek text ends abruptly: compare Neh 8.13

---

us new life." **9.4** *Seized for sacrifice.* The parallel in Ezra 10.8 has "forfeited," but the reference is to the ancient institution of the "ban," according to which objects were removed from secular use and devoted to God by sacrifice. **9.14** *Undertook the matter,* or perhaps "approved of this"; Ezra 10.15 suggests rather that these men opposed the proposal of the people. **9.36** *They put them . . . children,* more intelligible than the Hebrew text of the parallel in Ezra 10.44 and so perhaps the original Hebrew reading. **9.37–55** The narrative jumps to Nehemiah 7.73b–8.12, where the story of Ezra continues in the books of Ezra and Nehemiah. The work of Nehemiah is entirely omitted from the narrative of 1 Esdras. Historically, the events of these verses, set at the beginning of the seventh month (v. 37), probably occurred between Ezra's arrival in Jerusalem in the fifth month of the seventh year of Artaxerxes (8.6) and the twentieth day of the ninth month, when the assembly met to consider the question of the mixed marriages (9.5). See also Neh 7.73b–8.13. Narrating the reading of the law at the very end of 1 Esdras serves to make even more clear than in Ezra and Nehemiah that the reading and acceptance of the law was the goal of Ezra's mission. **9.49** *Attharates,* the transformation of the Hebrew title *tirshata,* "governor," into a personal name. The parallel in Neh 8.9 has "Nehemiah, who was the governor"; but 1 Esdras is ignoring the work of Nehemiah almost entirely (though cf. note on 5.40). Strangely, it is the governor here who tells Ezra and the Levites how the people should behave on the holy day. The reading of Neh 8.9 is more probable, where it is Ezra and the Levites (along with the governor Nehemiah, if indeed his name rightly belongs in the verse) who give the people directions. **9.55** *They were inspired by the words.* Neh 8.12 has, more prosaically, "they had understood the words." *And they came together.* These words clearly imply that a continuation of the narrative has been lost. They seem to be from Neh 8.13, and we may assume that 1 Esdras originally included at least the narrative of the celebration of the Festival of Booths found in Neh 8.13–18.

THE PRAYER OF
MANASSEH

THE PRAYER OF MANASSEH is included in Greek and Slavonic Bibles and, since the Council of Trent (1546), has been included with 3 and 4 Esdras in the appendix to the Vulgate. In two Septuagint manuscripts it appears as part of a collection entitled "Odes," a group of fifteen psalms or canticles that are also found in other canonical books (e.g., Ex 15; Deut 32; Lk 1).

Setting

MANASSEH, KING OF JUDAH of the house of David from about 698 to 642 BCE, reigned longer than any other monarch. In 2 Kings (21.1–18) he is portrayed as the worst possible offender of the laws set forth in the Torah and as the cause of the downfall of Judah. In 2 Chr 33.10–17, Manasseh, depicted as Judah's most sinful king before his deportation to Babylon, is reported to have humbly repented in exile and earnestly prayed to God, who restored him to kingship in Jerusalem, where he rectified his most serious idolatrous offenses. His prayer is further mentioned in the concluding record of his reign (2 Chr 33.18–19).

But Chronicles fails to include the prayer. Many ancient readers would have noted the lack, and one of them filled the void by piecing together familiar liturgical and psalmic phrases found elsewhere in the Bible as well as a few interesting nonbiblical expressions (vv. 8, 11, 13). Some scholars believe that the Prayer of Manasseh was originally composed in Greek late in the first century BCE. It was translated in antiquity into Latin and Syriac.

Style and Theology

THE PRAYER OF MANASSEH, though largely composed (like 1 Chr 16.8–36) of older biblical terms and phrases, is a classic of penitential intention with limited literary quality. The theology is resonant with that of early Judaism generally: God, though clearly the God of justice, is equally the God of mercy. He is especially the God of those who repent of their sinful ways (v. 13). The theme was important to the developing theology of exilic and postexilic Judaism, which constantly lived under repressive regimes throughout the eastern Mediterranean region. The consequences of Manasseh's sin devolved upon the whole kingdom of Judah and upon the following generations (see Ex 34.7). The scriptural base of the prayer's theology of repentance is found in the pivotal affirmations of individual responsibility within the covenant community found in Jer 31.29–30 and Ezek 18. Manasseh's repentance, although apparently efficacious for himself and his immediate generation (2 Chr 33.14–17), was limited to his personal restoration and did nothing to halt the demise of the kingdom of Judah.

Manasseh as king had the power to do the evil that, in the divine economy, brought about the destruction of Judah. In the Jewish mind of the period, however, Manasseh's exclusion from repentance and redemption would have raised questions about who could repent and doubt about God as the God of mercy as well as of justice. God is not only Creator and Sustainer (vv. 1–4) but also Redeemer, "of great compassion, long-suffering, and very merciful" (v. 7), who did not appoint repentance for the righteous, like Abraham, Isaac, and Jacob, but ordained it for all sinners (v. 8), even Manasseh. [JAMES A. SANDERS]

Ascription of Praise

1 O Lord Almighty,
    God of our ancestors,
    of Abraham and Isaac and Jacob
    and of their righteous offspring;
2 you who made heaven and earth
    with all their order;
3 who shackled the sea by your word of
        command,
    who confined the deep
    and sealed it with your terrible and
        glorious name;
4 at whom all things shudder,
    and tremble before your power,
5 for your glorious splendor cannot be
        borne,
    and the wrath of your threat to sinners is
        unendurable;
6 yet immeasurable and unsearchable
    is your promised mercy,
7 for you are the Lord Most High,
    of great compassion, long-suffering, and
        very merciful,
    and you relent at human suffering.
    O Lord, according to your great goodness
    you have promised repentance and
        forgiveness
    to those who have sinned against you,
    and in the multitude of your mercies
    you have appointed repentance for sinners,
    so that they may be saved. *a*

8 Therefore you, O Lord, God of the
        righteous,
    have not appointed repentance for the
        righteous,
    for Abraham and Isaac and Jacob, who
        did not sin against you,
    but you have appointed repentance for
        me, who am a sinner.

Confession of Sins

9 For the sins I have committed are more in
        number than the sand of the sea;
    my transgressions are multiplied, O Lord,
        they are multiplied!
    I am not worthy to look up and see the
        height of heaven
    because of the multitude of my iniquities.
10 I am weighted down with many an iron
        fetter,
    so that I am rejected *b* because of my sins,
    and I have no relief;
    for I have provoked your wrath
    and have done what is evil in your sight,
    setting up abominations and multiplying
        offenses.

Supplication for Pardon

11 And now I bend the knee of my heart,
    imploring you for your kindness.

---

a Other ancient authorities lack *O Lord, according . . . be saved*
b Other ancient authorities read *so that I cannot lift up my head*

1–7 An invocation to the *God of our ancestors* (Ex 3.6, 15; 1 Chr 29.18; Dan 2.23), the first and longest of the three strophes that make up the prayer. It lists the divine attributes starting with God's creation of *heaven and earth with all their order* (Gen 1.1; Gen 2.1 in the Septuagint). **3** *Who shackled the sea* recalls Job 38.8–11; Ps 104.7, 9. *Who confined the deep* expresses the power of God to control the forces of chaos and evil (e.g., Gen 1.2; 7.11; 8.2; Pss 63.9; 88.5–6). **7** *Of great compassion, long-suffering, and very merciful.* See Joel 2.13 (Septuagint). The second part of the verse, *O Lord, according . . . be saved,* reminding God of the divine promises, is preserved in the Latin and Syriac versions and in some late Greek manuscripts. **8–10** Manasseh's confession of sins more numerous than *the sand of the sea* (v. 9). The contrast between the righteous (Mk 2.17; Lk 5.32; 1 Tim 1.15) and sinners (Lk 15.7; 18.13) reflects first-century thinking like that found in the NT and the Dead Sea Scrolls. **11–15** Manasseh's petition for forgiveness. **11** *Bend the knee of*

12 I have sinned, O Lord, I have sinned,
    and I acknowledge my transgressions.
13 I earnestly implore you,
    forgive me, O Lord, forgive me!
    Do not destroy me with my
        transgressions!
    Do not be angry with me forever or store
        up evil for me;
    do not condemn me to the depths of the
        earth.

    For you, O Lord, are the God of those
        who repent,
14 and in me you will manifest your
        goodness;
    for, unworthy as I am, you will save me
        according to your great mercy,
15 and I will praise you continually all the
        days of my life.
    For all the host of heaven sings your praise,
        and yours is the glory forever. Amen.

---

my heart, an image not found elsewhere that well expresses the depth of sincerity of the truly penitent. **12–13** The twofold repetition *I have sinned* is matched in pathos by the double supplication *forgive me, O Lord, forgive me. Depths of the earth.* See note on v. 3. *God of those who repent,* like *God of the righteous* (v. 8), is not found in the Bible and should probably be neither generalized nor seen to conflict with biblical thinking; rather, it expresses the spirit of one who feels deeply the need to repent and be restored to the fold of the faithful. **15** The prayer closes with a doxology expressing the hope that the praise of God, which Manasseh vows *all the days of* his *life,* would be caught up into the praise of the whole *host of heaven* (see 2 Chr 18.18).

PSALM 151

PSALM 151 IS KNOWN in four ancient text forms: Hebrew, Greek, Latin, and Syriac. The oldest is the Hebrew, which is found in a scroll of biblical psalms discovered in 1956 at Qumran (11QPs^a); the manuscript dates to the first half of the first century CE. The Greek Psalm 151 was a recension of the original Hebrew. The Syriac (except for one verse), like the Latin, was translated from the Greek. As indicated in the accompanying notes, the psalm underwent revision as well as translation in antiquity.

The reason Psalm 151 is included in the apocryphal section of the NRSV is that it forms a part of the Bibles of communities of faith today, those revering Eastern Orthodox canons, including the Greek and Slavonic. Its discovery, therefore, in a Hebrew Psalter belonging to a pre-Christian Jewish community was notable indeed; it has never, to our knowledge, formed a part of any Jewish canon since that time.

It is called Psalm 151 not only because it follows Ps 150 in some Greek Psalter manuscripts but also because it is numbered Psalm 151 in what is probably the oldest and most reliable Greek manuscript (Sinaiticus) and in some medieval Syriac Psalters (one of which has four additional psalms specifically numbered 152–155).

The text of Greek Psalm 151 is straightforward, with few problems and only one important variant in v. 3. The text of the Hebrew at vv. 3–4 is by contrast highly multivalent, lending itself to different understandings. This was probably the reason the psalm was condensed in translation into Greek or had been condensed already in the Hebrew precursor of the Greek.

Although the Greek (and Latin and Syriac) version of the psalm appears to be a single unit of seven verses, the Hebrew text comprises two poetic units, each bearing a superscription in the manner of other psalms purporting to reflect events in David's life (e.g., Pss 3; 7; 18). Each is a poetic midrash (or commentary) on events reported in 1 Samuel, the first on 16.1–13 and the second on 17.17–54. The first unit was condensed into Greek vv. 1–5, and the second into vv. 6–7.

The date of the composition of Hebrew Psalm 151 is unknown; estimates vary from the sixth century BCE to sometime in the Hellenistic period (332–63 BCE), with the latter more likely. The translation into Greek was probably made by the beginning of the second century CE.

[JAMES A. SANDERS]

This psalm is ascribed to David as his own composition (though it is outside the number[a]), after he had fought in single combat with Goliath.

1 I was small among my brothers,
   and the youngest in my father's house;
   I tended my father's sheep.

2 My hands made a harp;
   my fingers fashioned a lyre.

3 And who will tell my Lord?
   The Lord himself; it is he who hears.[b]

4 It was he who sent his messenger[c]
   and took me from my father's sheep,

and anointed me with his anointing oil.

5 My brothers were handsome and tall,
   but the Lord was not pleased with them.

6 I went out to meet the Philistine,[d]
   and he cursed me by his idols.

7 But I drew his own sword;
   I beheaded him, and took away
      disgrace from the people of Israel.

---

a Other ancient authorities add *of the one hundred fifty* (psalms)
b Other ancient authorities add *everything*; others add *me*; others read *who will hear me*   c Or *angel*   d Or *foreigner*

---

1 *Small.* In Hebrew the same adjective is used to describe David in 1 Sam 16.11; 17.14 ("the youngest") and by Solomon in speaking of himself in 1 Kings 3.7 ("a little child"). *Youngest.* Gideon describes himself with the same adjective in Judg 6.15 ("the least"); see Ps 119.141. This verse in the Hebrew reads, "Smaller was I than my brothers and the youngest of the sons of my father, yet he made me shepherd of his flock and ruler over his kids" (on "shepherd," see 1 Sam 16.11; on "ruler," see Ps 105.21). Some Syriac manuscripts conclude v. 1 with "and I found a lion and a wolf and I killed and rent them." **2** The Hebrew concludes v. 2 with "and (so) have I rendered glory to the LORD, thought I within myself." **3** The Hebrew text here is both longer and multivalent:

The mountains do not witness to him,
   nor do the hills proclaim;
The trees have cherished my words
   and the flocks my works.
For who can proclaim and who can bespeak
   and who can recount the deeds of the Lord?
Everything has God seen,
   everything has he heard and he has heeded.

Greek manuscripts vary considerably in the reading *The Lord himself; it is he who hears*; one important Greek witness (Sinaiticus) reads "the Lord himself, he hears everything," reflecting, like the Hebrew, 1 Sam 16.7. The reason the Hebrew recensionist or Greek translator omitted most of the lines of the Hebrew was that they seem to contradict frequent biblical asser-

tions that nature does indeed proclaim the glory of God. In the context of the Hebrew poem the surrounding mountains and hills seem to be mute, while the solitary shepherd dedicates his musical gifts to the glorification of God by fashioning musical instruments, tunes, and words (2 Chr 29.26; cf. Am 6.5). **5** The first poetic unit of Psalm 151 in the Hebrew scroll concludes:

He sent his prophet to anoint me,
Samuel to make me great;
My brothers went out to meet him,
handsome of figure and appearance.
Though they were tall of stature
and handsome by their hair,
The Lord God chose
them not.
But he sent and took me from behind the flock
and anointed me with holy oil,
And he made me leader of his people
and ruler over the people of his covenant.

6 The second poetic unit in the original Hebrew, with its superscription, reads: "At the beginning of David's power after the prophet of God had anointed him. Then I [saw] a Philistine uttering defiances from the r[anks of the enemy]." *By his idols.* See 1 Sam 17.43. Some later Latin, Arabic, and Ethiopic manuscripts continue, "and I threw three stones at him in the middle of his forehead and felled him by the power of the Lord" (cf. "a stone" in 1 Sam 17.49–50). **7** *His own sword.* See 1 Sam 17.51.

3 MACCABEES

THE TITLE 3 MACCABEES is a misnomer, as the book has nothing to do with the Maccabees. It is found in some manuscripts of the Greek Bible (Alexandrinus and Venetus, but not Vaticanus or Sinaiticus). The title probably comes from the fact that this book follows 1 and 2 Maccabees in the manuscripts and is set in the Hellenistic period (332–63 BCE). Because it was not included in the Latin Vulgate, it is not one of the deuterocanonical books that are accepted by the Roman Catholic Church, nor is it among the traditional Protestant Apocrypha. It is, however, regarded as deuterocanonical in the Eastern Orthodox Churches.

Content and Historical Accuracy

THIRD MACCABEES DESCRIBES THREE EPISODES in the reign of Ptolemy IV Philopator, king of Egypt (221–204 BCE). Chapter 1.1–5 describes how an attempted assassination of Ptolemy was foiled by the intervention of an apostate Jew named Dositheus. An unsuccessful attempt by the king to enter the Jerusalem temple is recorded in 1.6–2.24; the main body of the book, 2.25–7.23, describes Ptolemy's persecution of the Egyptian Jews.

Although some scholars have accepted 3 Maccabees as either wholly or partly a historical account, the genre of the narrative raises grave doubts about its historical value. The story has strong legendary features and seems designed to edify and inspire wonder rather than to report accurately. The plot to assassinate Ptolemy (1.2) is also reported by the second-century BCE Greek historian Polybius, but without mention of the Jew Dositheus, whose role in 3 Maccabees is reminiscent of that of Mordecai in Esth 2.21–23. The unsuccessful attempt to enter the temple has a parallel in 2 Macc 3 in the story of Heliodorus. A variant of the longest episode, the persecution of the Egyptian Jews, is found in the tract *Against Apion* (2.53–55), written by the Jewish historian Josephus at the end of the first century CE. There, however, Ptolemy is identified not as Philopator but as Ptolemy VIII Euergetes II (Physcon, 144–117 BCE). This variation shows that the story became traditional and that historical accuracy was not the primary consideration in its transmission. It may, of course, refer to historical events (such as the battle of Raphia), but these references are incidental. The book is best viewed as a historical novel with a religious message.

Language, Place, and Date of Composition

THERE IS GENERAL AGREEMENT that 3 Maccabees was written in Greek, probably in Alexandria (in Egypt). It was most likely written during the Roman era (30 BCE–70 CE). It shows signs of dependence on the Greek editions of Esther and Daniel, which would require a date no earlier than the first century BCE. The most specific indication of date is the statement in 2.28 that "all Jews shall be subjected to a registration involving poll tax and to the status of slaves." The Greek word *laographia*, lit. "census," here translated "registration," acquired a special connotation in Roman times because of a poll tax introduced by Augustus in 24/23 BCE. Greeks were exempt from this tax, but Jews were not, so they suffered a de facto reduction in status. This tax bore directly on the issue of whether the Jews had "equal citizenship with the Alexandrians" (2.30).

A further indication of date lies in the book's peculiar combination of episodes that find parallels in different sources and may have circulated as independent stories. The decision of the author of 3 Maccabees to combine the story of a threat to the Jerusalem temple with that of the persecution of Egyptian Judaism brings to mind the reign of Caligula (37–41 CE). During that reign there was a pogrom in Alexandria and also an attempt to introduce a statue of Caligula into the Jerusalem temple (both incidents are described in the treatise *On the Embassy to Gaius* by the Jewish philosopher Philo of Alexandria). Though the stories in 3 Maccabees are traditional tales and were not composed as allegories for the crisis of the Roman era, that crisis may have been the occasion for their combination and edition in this book.

Some scholars, however, date the book to the early first century BCE, before the beginning of Roman rule in Egypt, mainly because of the author's accurate use of terminology relating to the Ptolemaic court.

Message and Outlook

THIRD MACCABEES IS REMINISCENT of the stories of Esther and Dan 1–6 as a description of life in the Jewish Diaspora. It describes a situation of divided loyalty. The Jews are loyal servants of the king but also strict observers of the Jewish law. Problems arise because of the arrogance, even madness, of the king and his bad advisers. But these problems are aberrations. In the end, the king comes to his senses and all is well for the Jews. 3 Maccabees also distinguishes sharply between the Alexandrians, who are hostile to the Jews, and "the Greeks," who are sympathetic. This distinction is of dubious historical value, as the Alexandrians were predominantly Greek, but it reflects the desire of the Jewish community to be accepted as Greek and its refusal to dignify its enemies with that name.

3 Maccabees can be seen as an illustration of the problems of a religious minority in an alien land, and as such it is relevant to situations that have recurred throughout history. The viewpoint of 3 Maccabees is optimistic. Evil is an aberration, and divine providence will prevail. The religious message of the book is that God responds to those who pray for deliverance (see 2.21; 5.28; 6.18). There is no appeal to the ideas of immortality or afterlife that were widely accepted in Hellenistic Judaism by this time. The optimistic theology of the book was still possible for Jews in the time of Caligula, but in the following century the Jewish community in Egypt was virtually destroyed. Unfortunately, subsequent history has more often reminded readers of the book's picture of Jews being rounded up for destruction (ch. 4) than of its picture of miraculous deliverance. [JOHN J. COLLINS]

The Battle of Raphia

1 When Philopator learned from those who returned that the regions that he had controlled had been seized by Antiochus, he gave orders to all his forces, both infantry and cavalry, took with him his sister Arsinoë, and marched out to the region near Raphia, where the army of Antiochus was encamped. [2]But a certain Theodotus, determined to carry out the plot he had devised, took with him the best of the Ptolemaic arms that had been previously issued to him,[a] and crossed over by night to the tent of Ptolemy, intending single-handed to kill him and thereby end the war. [3]But Dositheus, known as the son of Drimylus, a Jew by birth who later changed his religion and apostatized from the ancestral traditions, had led the king away and arranged that a certain insignificant man should sleep in the tent; and so it turned out that this man incurred the vengeance meant for the king.[b] [4]When a bitter fight resulted, and matters were turning out rather in favor of Antiochus, Arsinoë went to the troops with wailing and tears, her locks all disheveled, and exhorted them to defend themselves and their children and wives bravely, promising to give them each two minas of gold if they won the battle. [5]And so it came about that the enemy was routed in the action, and many captives also were taken. [6]Now that he had foiled the plot, Ptolemy[c] decided to visit the neighboring cities and encourage them. [7]By doing this, and by endowing their sacred enclosures with gifts, he strengthened the morale of his subjects.

Philopator Attempts to Enter the Temple

[8]Since the Jews had sent some of their council and elders to greet him, to bring him gifts of welcome, and to congratulate him on what had happened, he was all the more eager to visit them as soon as possible. [9]After he had arrived in Jerusalem, he offered sacrifice to the supreme God[d] and made thank offerings and did what was fitting for the holy place.[e] Then, upon entering the place and being impressed by its excellence and its beauty, [10]he marveled at the good order of the temple, and conceived a desire to enter the sanctuary. [11]When they said that this was not permitted, because not even members of their own nation were allowed to enter, not even all of the priests, but only the high priest who was pre-eminent over all—and he only once a year—the king was by no means persuaded. [12]Even after the law had been read to him, he did not cease to maintain that he ought to enter, saying, "Even if those men are deprived of this honor, I ought not to be." [13]And he inquired why, when he entered every other temple,[f] no one there had stopped him. [14]And someone answered thoughtlessly that it was wrong to take that as a portent.[g] [15]"But since this has happened," the king[c] said, "why should not I at least enter, whether they wish it or not?"

---

a Or the best of the Ptolemaic soldiers previously put under his command b Gk that one c Gk he d Gk the greatest God e Gk the place f Or entered the temple precincts g Or to boast of this

---

1.1–5 The battle of Raphia (217 BCE). The abrupt beginning suggests that this passage was adapted from a longer account. A full description of the battle is found in Polybius, Histories 5.79–86. **1.1** Philopator, Ptolemy IV, king of Egypt (221–204 BCE). Antiochus, Antiochus III, later called the Great, king of Syria (223–187 BCE). Raphia, a town in Palestine, three miles from Gaza, near the Egyptian border. **1.2** According to Polybius, Theodotus had been commander in chief of the Egyptian forces in Syria but had defected to Antiochus. Single-handed. Polybius says Theodotus took two soldiers with him. **1.3** Dositheus, the name of a Jewish general in Egypt in the mid-second century BCE. Dositheus son of Drimylus occurs as the name of a pagan priest in a papyrus from the third century BCE (Papyrus Hibeh 90), but there is no evidence that this individual was Jewish. Note that apostate Jews are held in abhorrence in 2.33. Polybius identifies the man who slept in the tent as Andreas, the

king's physician, who was not insignificant. The author of 3 Maccabees may have misread "Andreas" as andra (Greek, "man"). **1.5** According to Polybius, Antiochus lost nearly 10,000 foot soldiers and 300 cavalry, and 4,000 were taken prisoners, while Ptolemy lost 1,500 foot soldiers and 700 cavalry. **1.6–15** Ptolemy attempts to enter the Jerusalem temple. Cf. the story of Heliodorus in 2 Macc 3. **1.9** The supreme (lit. "greatest") God is mentioned often in 3 Maccabees and also in 2 Macc 3.36. Josephus claims that Alexander the Great also sacrificed to God in Jerusalem (Antiquities 11.336). **1.10** He marveled at . . . the temple. Philopator was known for his interest in architecture. **1.11** Only the high priest was allowed to enter the inner sanctuary, or most holy place (Ex 30.10; Lev 16.2, 11–12, 15, 34; Heb 9.7). In 63 BCE the Roman general Pompey outraged the Jews by entering the most holy place. In contrast, Antiochus the Great, in 198 BCE, decreed it unlawful for any foreigner to enter the temple enclo-

Jewish Resistance to Ptolemy

16 Then the priests in all their vestments prostrated themselves and entreated the supreme God[a] to aid in the present situation and to avert the violence of this evil design, and they filled the temple with cries and tears; 17 those who remained behind in the city were agitated and hurried out, supposing that something mysterious was occurring. 18 Young women who had been secluded in their chambers rushed out with their mothers, sprinkled their hair with dust,[b] and filled the streets with groans and lamentations. 19 Those women who had recently been arrayed for marriage abandoned the bridal chambers[c] prepared for wedded union, and, neglecting proper modesty, in a disorderly rush flocked together in the city. 20 Mothers and nurses abandoned even newborn children here and there, some in houses and some in the streets, and without a backward look they crowded together at the most high temple. 21 Various were the supplications of those gathered there because of what the king was profanely plotting. 22 In addition, the bolder of the citizens would not tolerate the completion of his plans or the fulfillment of his intended purpose. 23 They shouted to their compatriots to take arms and die courageously for the ancestral law, and created a considerable disturbance in the holy place;[d] and being barely restrained by the old men and the elders,[e] they resorted to the same posture of supplication as the others. 24 Meanwhile the crowd, as before, was engaged in prayer, 25 while the elders near the king tried in various ways to change his arrogant mind from the plan that he had conceived. 26 But he, in his arrogance, took heed of nothing, and began now to approach, determined to bring the aforesaid plan to a conclusion. 27 When those who were around him observed this, they turned, together with our people, to call upon him who has all power to defend them in the present trouble and not to overlook this unlawful and haughty deed. 28 The continuous, vehement, and concerted cry of the crowds[f] resulted in an immense uproar; 29 for it seemed that not only the people but also the walls and the whole earth around echoed, because indeed all at that time[g] preferred death to the profanation of the place.

The Prayer of the High Priest Simon

2 Then the high priest Simon, facing the sanctuary, bending his knees and extending his hands with calm dignity, prayed as follows:[h] 2 "Lord, Lord, king of the heavens, and sovereign of all creation, holy among the holy ones, the only ruler, almighty, give attention to us who are suffering grievously from an impious and profane man, puffed up in his audacity and power. 3 For you, the creator of all things and the governor of all, are a just Ruler, and you judge those who have done anything in insolence and arrogance. 4 You destroyed those who in the past committed injustice, among whom were even giants who trusted in their strength and boldness, whom you destroyed by bringing on them a boundless flood. 5 You consumed with fire and sulfur the people of Sodom who acted arrogantly, who were notorious for their vices;[i] and you made them an example to those who should come afterward. 6 You made known your mighty power by inflicting many and varied punishments on the audacious Pharaoh who had enslaved your holy people Israel. 7 And when he

---

a Gk the greatest God   b Other ancient authorities add and ashes   c Or the canopies   d Gk the place   e Other ancient authorities read priests   f Other ancient authorities read vehement cry of the assembled crowds   g Other ancient authorities lack at that time   h Other ancient authorities lack verse 1   i Other ancient authorities read secret in their vices

---

sure (Josephus, *Antiquities* 12.145). **1.16–29** The Jewish reaction to Philopator's effort to enter the temple. A very similar account is found in the story of Heliodorus in 2 Macc 3.15–22. There were comparable incidents in the first century CE when Pilate allowed military standards with images of the emperor to be brought into Jerusalem and when Caligula ordered the erection of his statue in the temple. **1.23** The Jews' resolve *to take arms and die courageously for the ancestral law* is comparable to the stand taken by Mattathias in 1 Macc 2. *Barely restrained by the . . . elders.* Josephus reports similar attempts to restrain the rebels at the outbreak of the Jewish War in 66 CE.

2.1–20 The high priest's prayer conforms to a type common in postexilic Judaism (Ezra 9; Neh 9; Dan 9; Bar 1.15–3.8) that reviews salvation history and emphasizes the righteousness of God and the sinfulness of Israel. This prayer differs from the others in that it does not relate the distress of Israel to the exile and that it places less emphasis on confession of sin. **2.1** *The high priest Simon*, Simon II, called "the Just." He is eulogized in Sir 50. **2.4** The connection between the *giants* (Gen 6.1–4) and the *flood* is more explicit in intertestamental writings such as *1 Enoch* 6–11 than it is in Genesis. **2.5** *The people of Sodom.* See Gen 19. **2.6** *Pharaoh.* See Ex 7–12. **2.7** *In the depths of the sea.* See Ex 14–15.

pursued them with chariots and a mass of troops, you overwhelmed him in the depths of the sea, but carried through safely those who had put their confidence in you, the Ruler over the whole creation. [8]And when they had seen works of your hands, they praised you, the Almighty. [9]You, O King, when you had created the boundless and immeasurable earth, chose this city and sanctified this place for your name, though you have no need of anything; and when you had glorified it by your magnificent manifestation,[a] you made it a firm foundation for the glory of your great and honored name. [10]And because you love the house of Israel, you promised that if we should have reverses and tribulation should overtake us, you would listen to our petition when we come to this place and pray. [11]And indeed you are faithful and true. [12]And because oftentimes when our fathers were oppressed you helped them in their humiliation, and rescued them from great evils, [13]see now, O holy King, that because of our many and great sins we are crushed with suffering, subjected to our enemies, and overtaken by helplessness. [14]In our downfall this audacious and profane man undertakes to violate the holy place on earth dedicated to your glorious name. [15]For your dwelling is the heaven of heavens, unapproachable by human beings. [16]But because you graciously bestowed your glory on your people Israel, you sanctified this place. [17]Do not punish us for the defilement committed by these men, or call us to account for this profanation, otherwise the transgressors will boast in their wrath and exult in the arrogance of their tongue, saying, [18]'We have trampled down the house of the sanctuary as the houses of the abominations are trampled down.' [19]Wipe away our sins and disperse our errors, and reveal your mercy at this hour. [20]Speedily let your mercies overtake us, and put praises in the mouth of those who are downcast and broken in spirit, and give us peace."

God's Punishment of Ptolemy

21 Thereupon God, who oversees all things, the first Father of all, holy among the holy ones, having heard the lawful supplication, scourged him who had exalted himself in insolence and audacity. [22]He shook him on this side and that as a reed is shaken by the wind, so that he lay helpless on the ground and, besides being paralyzed in his limbs, was unable even to speak, since he was smitten[b] by a righteous judgment. [23]Then both friends and bodyguards, seeing the severe punishment that had overtaken him, and fearing that he would lose his life, quickly dragged him out, panic-stricken in their exceedingly great fear. [24]After a while he recovered, and though he had been punished, he by no means repented, but went away uttering bitter threats.

Hostile Measures against the Jews

25 When he arrived in Egypt, he increased in his deeds of malice, abetted by the previously mentioned drinking companions and comrades, who were strangers to everything just. [26]He was not content with his uncounted licentious deeds, but even continued with such audacity that he framed evil reports in the various localities; and many of his friends, intently observing the king's purpose, themselves also followed his will. [27]He proposed to inflict public disgrace on the Jewish community,[c] and he set up a stone[d] on the tower in the courtyard with this inscription: [28]"None of those who do not sacrifice shall enter their sanctuaries, and all

a Or epiphany   b Other ancient authorities read pierced
c Gk the nation   d Gk stele

2.9 This place, Jerusalem. For your name. See Deut 12.11; 1 Kings 8.29. Your magnificent manifestation, the glory of the Lord. Cf. Isa 6; Ezek 1. **2.10** You would listen . . . this place. See 1 Kings 8.27–50. **2.13** Because of our many and great sins, a standard confession in prayers of this type, even though in this case the fault rests with the intruder. **2.15** Your dwelling is the heaven of heavens. See 1 Kings 8.27; Isa 66.1. **2.18** We have trampled down. See Isa 10.11; Dan 8.13. **2.21–24** The punishment of Ptolemy. **2.21** Scourged. Cf. 2 Macc 3.26, where two young men appeared and scourged Heliodorus, and 2 Macc 9.5, where the Lord struck Antiochus IV Epiphanes an incurable and unseen blow. **2.24** Ptolemy

by no means repented, though 2 Maccabees says that both Heliodorus and Antiochus IV Epiphanes repented (2 Macc 3.31–40; 9.11–29). Here the repentance of the king is deferred to a later point in the story. **2.25–33** The demand made on the Jews. **2.25** The previously mentioned drinking companions have not in fact been previously mentioned. Either the beginning of the book has been lost or this passage was excerpted from a more detailed source. **2.27** He set up a stone. Decrees were often displayed on palace walls. **2.28** Those who do not sacrifice can only refer to the Jews. A registration involving poll tax. See Introduction. The idea was probably inspired by the poll tax introduced by Augustus in

Jews shall be subjected to a registration involving poll tax and to the status of slaves. Those who object to this are to be taken by force and put to death; [29] those who are registered are also to be branded on their bodies by fire with the ivy-leaf symbol of Dionysus, and they shall also be reduced to their former limited status." [30] In order that he might not appear to be an enemy of all, he inscribed below: "But if any of them prefer to join those who have been initiated into the mysteries, they shall have equal citizenship with the Alexandrians."

31 Now some, however, with an obvious abhorrence of the price to be exacted for maintaining the religion of their city,[a] readily gave themselves up, since they expected to enhance their reputation by their future association with the king. [32] But the majority acted firmly with a courageous spirit and did not abandon their religion; and by paying money in exchange for life they confidently attempted to save themselves from the registration. [33] They remained resolutely hopeful of obtaining help, and they abhorred those who separated themselves from them, considering them to be enemies of the Jewish nation,[b] and depriving them of companionship and mutual help.

The Jews and Their Neighbors

3 When the impious king comprehended this situation, he became so infuriated that not only was he enraged against those Jews who lived in Alexandria, but was still more bitterly hostile toward those in the countryside; and he ordered that all should promptly be gathered into one place, and put to death by the most cruel means. [2] While these matters were being arranged, a hostile rumor was circulated against the Jewish nation by some who conspired to do them ill, a pretext being given by a report that they hindered others[c] from the observance of their customs. [3] The Jews, however, continued to maintain goodwill and unswerving loyalty toward the dynasty; [4] but because they worshiped God and conducted themselves by his law, they kept their separateness with respect to foods. For this reason they appeared hateful to some; [5] but since they adorned their style of life with the good deeds of upright people, they were established in good repute with everyone. [6] Nevertheless those of other races paid no heed to their good service to their nation, which was common talk among all; [7] instead they gossiped about the differences in worship and foods, alleging that these people were loyal neither to the king nor to his authorities, but were hostile and greatly opposed to his government. So they attached no ordinary reproach to them.

---

a Meaning of Gk uncertain   *b* Gk *the nation*   *c* Gk *them*

24/23 BCE. *Status of slaves.* The author may have confused branding in honor of Dionysus (2.29) with the branding of slaves. In the Maccabean wars, the Syrian commanders sold Jewish captives into slavery (1 Macc 3.41). **2.29** *Branded . . . with the ivy-leaf symbol of Dionysus.* Greeks and Romans often confused Judaism with the cult of Dionysus, because of the Festival of Tabernacles at the height of the vintage and the Jewish ritual use of wine (see Plutarch, *Table Talk* 4.6.1–2). During the persecution by Antiochus Epiphanes, Jews were compelled to walk in procession in honor of Dionysus wearing wreaths of ivy (2 Macc 6.7). Philopator was known for his devotion to Dionysus, and it is possible that he made some attempt to organize Judaism as a Dionysiac cult. The custom of branding or tattooing was associated with the cult of Dionysus from ancient times. *Their former limited status,* probably the condition of Jewish captives before their liberation by Ptolemy II Philadelphus (*Letter of Aristeas* 22). **2.30** The Jews in Egypt very much wanted equal status with the Alexandrians, but most were unwilling to perform the pagan religious acts that citizenship would have required. Cf. the offer in 1 Macc 2.18 to number Mattathias and his sons among the Friends of the king if they would perform the pagan sacrifice. **2.31** As in the Maccabean crisis, many Jews forsook the law (1 Macc 1.52). **2.32** *But the majority acted firmly.* Cf. Dan 11.32; 1 Macc 1.62. **2.33** *Those who separated themselves,* i.e., renegades, are singled out for special contempt.

3.1–10 The slander against the Jews. **3.1** *This situation,* the refusal of the Jews to submit to registration. *Enraged against those Jews.* Cf. Philo's comment on the situation under Caligula: "A vast and truceless war was prepared against the nation" (*On the Embassy to Gaius* 119). The following story deals initially with the threat to the Jews *in the countryside* (see note on 4.12). It would seem that this part of the story came from a distinct source. **3.2** There was a tradition of anti-Jewish polemic in Egypt beginning with the historian Manetho about 300 BCE and reaching a crescendo in the first century CE (see Josephus, *Against Apion*). Among the recurring charges were "atheism" and "inhospitality" because of the exclusivism of the Jewish religion. **3.3** The Jews in Egypt were known for their *goodwill and . . . loyalty* to the Ptolemies, and also at first to the Romans; this loyalty exacerbated their relations with the native Egyptians. **3.4** Jewish dietary laws that required *separateness with respect to foods* were incomprehensible to the Greeks, but were an essential marker of separate identity. *Letter of Aristeas* 128–66

8 The Greeks in the city, though wronged in no way, when they saw an unexpected tumult around these people and the crowds that suddenly were forming, were not strong enough to help them, for they lived under tyranny. They did try to console them, being grieved at the situation, and expected that matters would change; 9for such a great community ought not be left to its fate when it had committed no offense. 10And already some of their neighbors and friends and business associates had taken some of them aside privately and were pledging to protect them and to exert more earnest efforts for their assistance.

Ptolemy's Decree That All Jews Be Arrested

11 Then the king, boastful of his present good fortune, and not considering the might of the supreme God,[a] but assuming that he would persevere constantly in his same purpose, wrote this letter against them:

12 "King Ptolemy Philopator to his generals and soldiers in Egypt and all its districts, greetings and good health:

13 "I myself and our government are faring well. 14When our expedition took place in Asia, as you yourselves know, it was brought to conclusion, according to plan, by the gods' deliberate alliance with us in battle, 15and we considered that we should not rule the nations inhabiting Coelesyria and Phoenicia by the power of the spear, but should cherish them with clemency and great benevolence, gladly treating them well. 16And when we had granted very great revenues to the temples in the cities, we came on to Jerusalem also, and went up to honor the temple of those wicked people, who never cease from their folly. 17They accepted our presence by word, but insincerely by deed, because when we proposed to enter their inner temple and honor it with magnificent and most beautiful offerings, 18they were carried away by their traditional arrogance, and excluded us from entering; but they were spared the exercise of our power because of the benevolence that we have toward all. 19By maintaining their manifest ill-will toward us, they become the only people among all nations who hold their heads high in defiance of kings and their own benefactors, and are unwilling to regard any action as sincere.

20 "But we, when we arrived in Egypt victorious, accommodated ourselves to their folly and did as was proper, since we treat all nations with benevolence. 21Among other things, we made known to all our amnesty toward their compatriots here, both because of their alliance with us and the myriad affairs liberally entrusted to them from the beginning; and we ventured to make a change, by deciding both to deem them worthy of Alexandrian citizenship and to make them participants in our regular religious rites.[b] 22But in their innate malice they took this in a contrary spirit, and disdained what is good. Since they incline constantly to evil, 23they not only spurn the priceless citizenship, but also both by speech and by silence they abominate those few among them who are sincerely disposed toward us; in every situation, in accordance with their infamous way of life, they secretly suspect that we may soon alter our policy. 24Therefore, fully convinced by these indications that they are ill-disposed toward us in every way, we have taken precautions so that, if a sudden disorder later arises against us, we shall not have these impious people behind our backs as traitors and barbarous enemies. 25Therefore we have given

---

a Gk *the greatest God*   *b* Other ancient authorities read *partners of our regular priests*

---

defends the dietary laws but gives them an allegorical explanation. **3.8** The author insists that the enemies of the Jews were not *the Greeks in the city,* although the Friends of the king must surely have been Greeks. **3.11–30** Ptolemy's decree. Cf. the decree in Add Esth 13.1–7. **3.11** In *boasting* and *not considering the might of the supreme God,* the king is guilty of hubris, the typical sin of kings in both Greek tragedy and Hebrew prophecy (Isa 14; Ezek 28). **3.12** The Ptolemies did not use titles such as *Philopator* in their decrees until about 100 BCE. **3.17** *Insincerely by deed.* The refusal of admission to the temple is construed as a lack of genuine respect for the king. Similarly, Caligula failed to understand or accept the reasons for Jewish resistance to placing his statue in the temple. **3.21** *Myriad affairs ... beginning.* Jews were entrusted with military duties as early as the fifth century BCE at Elephantine in southern Egypt. *We ventured to make a change.* The king's claim that his actions were benevolent seemed hypocritical from a Jewish viewpoint. Note, however, that Gentiles such as the Roman historian Tacitus thought that Antiochus Epiphanes was trying to civilize the Jews by forcing them to adopt Greek customs. **3.23** *The priceless citizenship* was offered to the Jews of Alexandria, but the punishment falls on the Jews of the countryside. **3.25** Cf. Esth 3.13, where orders to kill the

orders that, as soon as this letter arrives, you are to send to us those who live among you, together with their wives and children, with insulting and harsh treatment, and bound securely with iron fetters, to suffer the sure and shameful death that befits enemies. 26 For when all of these have been punished, we are sure that for the remaining time the government will be established for ourselves in good order and in the best state. 27 But those who shelter any of the Jews, whether old people or children or even infants, will be tortured to death with the most hateful torments, together with their families. 28 Any who are willing to give information will receive the property of those who incur the punishment, and also two thousand drachmas from the royal treasury, and will be awarded their freedom.[a] 29 Every place detected sheltering a Jew is to be made unapproachable and burned with fire, and shall become useless for all time to any mortal creature." 30 The letter was written in the above form.

The Jews Deported to Alexandria

4 In every place, then, where this decree arrived, a feast at public expense was arranged for the Gentiles with shouts and gladness, for the inveterate enmity that had long ago been in their minds was now made evident and outspoken. 2 But among the Jews there was incessant mourning, lamentation, and tearful cries; everywhere their hearts were burning, and they groaned because of the unexpected destruction that had suddenly been decreed for them. 3 What district or city, or what habitable place at all, or what streets were not filled with mourning and wailing for them? 4 For with such a harsh and ruthless spirit were they being sent off, all together, by the generals in the several cities, that at the sight of their unusual punishments, even some of their enemies, perceiving the common object of pity before their eyes, reflected on the uncertainty of life and shed tears at the most miserable expulsion of these people. 5 For a multitude of gray-headed old men, sluggish and bent with age, was being led

away, forced to march at a swift pace by the violence with which they were driven in such a shameful manner. 6 And young women who had just entered the bridal chamber[b] to share married life exchanged joy for wailing, their myrrh-perfumed hair sprinkled with ashes, and were carried away unveiled, all together raising a lament instead of a wedding song, as they were torn by the harsh treatment of the heathen.[c] 7 In bonds and in public view they were violently dragged along as far as the place of embarkation. 8 Their husbands, in the prime of youth, their necks encircled with ropes instead of garlands, spent the remaining days of their marriage festival in lamentations instead of good cheer and youthful revelry, seeing death immediately before them.[d] 9 They were brought on board like wild animals, driven under the constraint of iron bonds; some were fastened by the neck to the benches of the boats, others had their feet secured by unbreakable fetters, 10 and in addition they were confined under a solid deck, so that, with their eyes in total darkness, they would undergo treatment befitting traitors during the whole voyage.

The Jews Imprisoned at Schedia

11 When these people had been brought to the place called Schedia, and the voyage was concluded as the king had decreed, he commanded that they should be enclosed in the hippodrome that had been built with a monstrous perimeter wall in front of the city, and that was well suited to make them an obvious spectacle to all coming back into the city and to those from the city[e] going out into the country, so that they could neither communicate with the king's forces nor in any way claim to be inside the circuit of the city.[f] 12 And when this had happened, the king, hearing that the Jews' compatriots from the city frequently went out in secret to lament bitterly the igno-

---

a Gk *crowned with freedom*   b Or *the canopy*   c Other ancient authorities read *as though torn by heathen whelps*   d Gk *seeing Hades already lying at their feet*   e Gk *those of them*   f Or *claim protection of the walls*; meaning of Gk uncertain

---

Jews were sent to all the provinces. In 3 Maccabees the Jews are to be gathered for destruction. **3.26** *The government will be established.* Cf. Add Esth 13.7. **3.28** The statement that informers will be *awarded their freedom* is presumably addressed to the native Egyptians.

4.1–21 The imprisonment of the Jews. The emotionalism of the account is typical of Greek historiography in this period. **4.1** *A feast at public expense.* Cf.

the feast of the Jews in Esth 8.17. **4.2** *Incessant mourning.* See Esth 4.3. **4.11** *Schedia,* a promontory about three miles from Alexandria. The *hippodrome* was located at the east, or Canobic, gate of the city. A canal joined Schedia and the Canobic gate (Strabo, *Geography* 17.1.10, 16). **4.12** Given that *the Jews' compatriots from the city frequently went out,* it is clear that only the Jews from the countryside were imprisoned initially.

ble misfortune of their kindred, [13]ordered in his rage that these people be dealt with in precisely the same fashion as the others, not omitting any detail of their punishment. [14]The entire race was to be registered individually, not for the hard labor that has been briefly mentioned before, but to be tortured with the outrages that he had ordered, and at the end to be destroyed in the space of a single day. [15]The registration of these people was therefore conducted with bitter haste and zealous intensity from the rising of the sun until its setting, coming to an end after forty days but still uncompleted.

[16] The king was greatly and continually filled with joy, organizing feasts in honor of all his idols, with a mind alienated from truth and with a profane mouth, praising speechless things that are not able even to communicate or to come to one's help, and uttering improper words against the supreme God.[a] [17]But after the previously mentioned interval of time the scribes declared to the king that they were no longer able to take the census of the Jews because of their immense number, [18]though most of them were still in the country, some still residing in their homes, and some at the place;[b] the task was impossible for all the generals in Egypt. [19]After he had threatened them severely, charging that they had been bribed to contrive a means of escape, he was clearly convinced about the matter [20]when they said and proved that both the paper[c] and the pens they used for writing had already given out. [21]But this was an act of the invincible providence of him who was aiding the Jews from heaven.

Execution of the Jews Is Twice Thwarted

5 Then the king, completely inflexible, was filled with overpowering anger and wrath;

so he summoned Hermon, keeper of the elephants, [2]and ordered him on the following day to drug all the elephants—five hundred in number—with large handfuls of frankincense and plenty of unmixed wine, and to drive them in, maddened by the lavish abundance of drink, so that the Jews might meet their doom. [3]When he had given these orders he returned to his feasting, together with those of his Friends and of the army who were especially hostile toward the Jews. [4]And Hermon, keeper of the elephants, proceeded faithfully to carry out the orders. [5]The servants in charge of the Jews[d] went out in the evening and bound the hands of the wretched people and arranged for their continued custody through the night, convinced that the whole nation would experience its final destruction. [6]For to the Gentiles it appeared that the Jews were left without any aid, [7]because in their bonds they were forcibly confined on every side. But with tears and a voice hard to silence they all called upon the Almighty Lord and Ruler of all power, their merciful God and Father, praying [8]that he avert with vengeance the evil plot against them and in a glorious manifestation rescue them from the fate now prepared for them. [9]So their entreaty ascended fervently to heaven.

[10] Hermon, however, when he had drugged the pitiless elephants until they had been filled with a great abundance of wine and satiated with frankincense, presented himself at the courtyard early in the morning to report to the king about these preparations. [11]But the Lord[e] sent upon the king a portion of sleep, that beneficence that from the beginning,

---

a Gk *the greatest God*   *b* Other ancient authorities read *on the way*   *c* Or *paper factory*   *d* Gk *them*   *e* Gk *he*

Perhaps the story originally concerned an attempt to register the Jews from the countryside by bringing them to one place. **4.14** *The entire race was to be registered individually,* presumably so that no one would escape, but the process seems unduly laborious. Again this may point to an original story concerned with registration rather than annihilation. **4.15** *Forty days,* a stereotypical figure. This is the length of time it took for Ezra to transcribe the law and the apocryphal books in 2 Esd 14.44. **4.16** *A profane mouth.* See Dan 7.8, 20. *Against the supreme God.* See Dan 11.36. **4.17** The failure of the scribes underlines the absurdity of the endeavor. For Israel as a people so numerous they cannot be numbered, see 1 Kings 3.8. **4.21** The failure of the census might be taken as proof of the king's folly, but

3 Maccabees draws a more theological lesson about *invincible providence.*

5.1–51 The frustration of the king's plans. **5.1** *Hermon* recalls Haman, the adversary of the Jews in Esther. **5.2** Drugging *the elephants* would have made little sense. War elephants were trained to trample and would have been more difficult to control if they were drugged. *Five hundred.* At the battle of Raphia, Philopator had only seventy-three elephants, still an impressive number. **5.3** The *Friends* of the king constituted a special honorific class in the Hellenistic age. **5.5** *Bound the hands.* According to 3.25, the Jews had been sent to Alexandria in fetters. Presumably they had been unbound in the meantime. **5.8** *Glorious manifestation.* Cf. 2 Macc 2.21. **5.11** Cf. Ps 127.2. *Sleep,*

night and day, is bestowed by him who grants it to whomever he wishes. [12] And by the action of the Lord he was overcome by so pleasant and deep a sleep[a] that he quite failed in his lawless purpose and was completely frustrated in his inflexible plan. [13] Then the Jews, since they had escaped the appointed hour, praised their holy God and again implored him who is easily reconciled to show the might of his all-powerful hand to the arrogant Gentiles.

14 But now, since it was nearly the middle of the tenth hour, the person who was in charge of the invitations, seeing that the guests were assembled, approached the king and nudged him. [15] And when he had with difficulty roused him, he pointed out that the hour of the banquet was already slipping by, and he gave him an account of the situation. [16] The king, after considering this, returned to his drinking, and ordered those present for the banquet to recline opposite him. [17] When this was done he urged them to give themselves over to revelry and to make the present[b] portion of the banquet joyful by celebrating all the more. [18] After the party had been going on for some time, the king summoned Hermon and with sharp threats demanded to know why the Jews had been allowed to remain alive through the present day. [19] But when he, with the corroboration of the king's[c] Friends, pointed out that while it was still night he had carried out completely the order given him, [20] the king,[d] possessed by a savagery worse than that of Phalaris, said that the Jews[e] were benefited by today's sleep, "but," he added, "tomorrow without delay prepare the elephants in the same way for the destruction of the lawless Jews!" [21] When the king had spoken, all those present readily and joyfully with one accord gave their approval, and all went to their own homes. [22] But they did not so much employ the duration of the night in sleep as in devising all sorts of insults for those they thought to be doomed.

23 Then, as soon as the cock had crowed in the early morning, Hermon, having equipped[f] the animals, began to move them along in the great colonnade. [24] The crowds of the city had been assembled for this most pitiful spectacle and they were eagerly waiting for daybreak. [25] But the Jews, at their last gasp—since the time had run out—stretched their hands toward heaven and with most tearful supplication and mournful dirges implored the supreme God[g] to help them again at once. [26] The rays of the sun were not yet shed abroad, and while the king was receiving his Friends, Hermon arrived and invited him to come out, indicating that what the king desired was ready for action. [27] But he, on receiving the report and being struck by the unusual invitation to come out—since he had been completely overcome by incomprehension—inquired what the matter was for which this had been so zealously completed for him. [28] This was the act of God who rules over all things, for he had implanted in the king's mind a forgetfulness of the things he had previously devised. [29] Then Hermon and all the king's Friends[h] pointed out that the animals and the armed forces were ready, "O king, according to your eager purpose."[i] [30] But at these words he was filled with an overpowering wrath, because by the providence of God his whole mind had been deranged concerning these matters; and with a threatening look he said, [31] "If your parents or children were present, I would have prepared them to be a rich feast for the savage animals instead of the Jews, who give me no ground for complaint and have exhibited to an extraordinary degree a full and firm loyalty to my ancestors. [32] In fact you would have been deprived of life instead of these, if it were not for an affection arising from our nurture in common and your usefulness." [33] So Hermon suffered an unexpected and dangerous threat, and his eyes wavered and his face fell. [34] The king's Friends one by one sullenly slipped away and dis-

a Other ancient authorities add *from evening until the ninth hour*
b Other ancient authorities read *delayed* (Gk *untimely*)
c Gk *his* d Gk *he* e Gk *they* f Or *armed* g Gk *the greatest God* h Gk *all the Friends* i Other ancient authorities read *pointed to the beasts and the armed forces, saying, "They are ready, O king, according to your eager purpose."*

often praised as a divine gift, especially in the classical tradition. **5.14** *The middle of the tenth hour,* mid-afternoon, at the end of siesta time. Elaborate banquets started early rather than finishing late. **5.20** *Phalaris,* tyrant of Agrigentum in the sixth century BCE. He was known for roasting people alive in his hollow brazen bull so that it would bellow realistically (Polybius, *His-* tories 12.25). *Tomorrow without delay.* The frustration of the first plan and the new beginning contribute to building suspense. **5.29** Some manuscripts have an interpolation at this point in which the king wants to release the Jews but Hermon persuades him to proceed. **5.30** *His whole mind had been deranged.* Cf. the madness of Nebuchadnezzar in Dan 4. **5.33** Hermon suf-

missed[a] the assembled people to their own occupations. 35 Then the Jews, on hearing what the king had said, praised the manifest Lord God, King of kings, since this also was his aid that they had received.

36 The king, however, reconvened the party in the same manner and urged the guests to return to their celebrating. 37 After summoning Hermon he said in a threatening tone, "How many times, you poor wretch, must I give you orders about these things? 38 Equip[b] the elephants now once more for the destruction of the Jews tomorrow!" 39 But the officials who were at table with him, wondering at his instability of mind, remonstrated as follows: 40 "O king, how long will you put us to the test, as though we are idiots, ordering now for a third time that they be destroyed, and again revoking your decree in the matter?[c] 41 As a result the city is in a tumult because of its expectation; it is crowded with masses of people, and also in constant danger of being plundered."

42 At this the king, a Phalaris in everything and filled with madness, took no account of the changes of mind that had come about within him for the protection of the Jews, and he firmly swore an irrevocable oath that he would send them to death[d] without delay, mangled by the knees and feet of the animals, 43 and would also march against Judea and rapidly level it to the ground with fire and spear, and by burning to the ground the temple inaccessible to him[e] would quickly render it forever empty of those who offered sacrifices there. 44 Then the Friends and officers departed with great joy, and they confidently posted the armed forces at the places in the city most favorable for keeping guard.

45 Now when the animals had been brought virtually to a state of madness, so to speak, by the very fragrant draughts of wine mixed with frankincense and had been equipped with frightful devices, the elephant keeper 46 entered at about dawn into the courtyard—the city now being filled with countless masses of people crowding their way into the hippodrome—and urged the king on to the matter at hand. 47 So he, when he had filled his impious mind with a deep rage, rushed out in full force along with the animals, wishing to witness, with invulnerable heart and with his own eyes, the grievous and pitiful destruction of the aforementioned people.

48 When the Jews saw the dust raised by the elephants going out at the gate and by the following armed forces, as well as by the trampling of the crowd, and heard the loud and tumultuous noise, 49 they thought that this was their last moment of life, the end of their most miserable suspense, and giving way to lamentation and groans they kissed each other, embracing relatives and falling into one another's arms[f]—parents and children, mothers and daughters, and others with babies at their breasts who were drawing their last milk. 50 Not only this, but when they considered the help that they had received before from heaven, they prostrated themselves with one accord on the ground, removing the babies from their breasts, 51 and cried out in a very loud voice, imploring the Ruler over every power to manifest himself and be merciful to them, as they stood now at the gates of death.[d]

The Prayer of Eleazar

6 Then a certain Eleazar, famous among the priests of the country, who had attained a ripe old age and throughout his life had been adorned with every virtue, directed the elders around him to stop calling upon the holy God, and he prayed as follows: 2 "King of great power, Almighty God Most High, governing all creation with mercy, 3 look upon the descendants of Abraham, O Father, upon the children of the sainted Jacob, a people of your

a Other ancient authorities read *he dismissed*   b Or *Arm*
c Other ancient authorities read *when the matter is in hand*
d Gk *Hades*   e Gk *us*   f Gk *falling upon their necks*

fers an unexpected reversal of royal favor, as Haman did in Esther. **5.41** The vacillation of the king again heightens the suspense (for the crowd and readers). **5.42–43** The double threat to the Alexandrian Jews and the Jerusalem temple is particularly reminiscent of the time of Caligula. **5.42** *An irrevocable oath.* Cf. the irrevocable decree of Darius in Dan 6.8. **5.45** Apparently *devices* such as scythes and knives were attached to the elephants as they were to war chariots.

6.1–15 The prayer of Eleazar further delays the climax and builds the suspense. It also balances the prayer of Simon in ch. 2. **6.1** *Eleazar,* the name of a high priest in *Letter of Aristeas* 41 and of a martyr in 2 Macc 6.18–31; 4 Macc 5–7. *Priests of the country,* perhaps the priests of the Jewish temple at Leontopolis. *A ripe old age.* See 2 Macc 6.18. **6.3** *Perishing as foreigners.* Cf. the assertion of Philo that Jews "severally hold that land as their fatherland in which they were

consecrated portion who are perishing as foreigners in a foreign land. 4 Pharaoh with his abundance of chariots, the former ruler of this Egypt, exalted with lawless insolence and boastful tongue, you destroyed together with his arrogant army by drowning them in the sea, manifesting the light of your mercy on the nation of Israel. 5 Sennacherib exulting in his countless forces, oppressive king of the Assyrians, who had already gained control of the whole world by the spear and was lifted up against your holy city, speaking grievous words with boasting and insolence, you, O Lord, broke in pieces, showing your power to many nations. 6 The three companions in Babylon who had voluntarily surrendered their lives to the flames so as not to serve vain things, you rescued unharmed, even to a hair, moistening the fiery furnace with dew and turning the flame against all their enemies. 7 Daniel, who through envious slanders was thrown down into the ground to lions as food for wild animals, you brought up to the light unharmed. 8 And Jonah, wasting away in the belly of a huge, sea-born monster, you, Father, watched over and restored[a] unharmed to all his family. 9 And now, you who hate insolence, all-merciful and protector of all, reveal yourself quickly to those of the nation of Israel[b]— who are being outrageously treated by the abominable and lawless Gentiles.

10 "Even if our lives have become entangled in impieties in our exile, rescue us from the hand of the enemy, and destroy us, Lord, by whatever fate you choose. 11 Let not the vain-minded praise their vanities[c] at the destruction of your beloved people, saying, 'Not even their god has rescued them.' 12 But you, O Eternal One, who have all might and all power, watch over us now and have mercy on us who by the senseless insolence of the lawless are being deprived of life in the manner of traitors. 13 And let the Gentiles cower today in fear of your invincible might, O honored One,

who have power to save the nation of Jacob. 14 The whole throng of infants and their parents entreat you with tears. 15 Let it be shown to all the Gentiles that you are with us, O Lord, and have not turned your face from us; but just as you have said, 'Not even when they were in the land of their enemies did I neglect them,' so accomplish it, O Lord."

Two Angels Rescue the Jews

16 Just as Eleazar was ending his prayer, the king arrived at the hippodrome with the animals and all the arrogance of his forces. 17 And when the Jews observed this they raised great cries to heaven so that even the nearby valleys resounded with them and brought an uncontrollable terror upon the army. 18 Then the most glorious, almighty, and true God revealed his holy face and opened the heavenly gates, from which two glorious angels of fearful aspect descended, visible to all but the Jews. 19 They opposed the forces of the enemy and filled them with confusion and terror, binding them with immovable shackles. 20 Even the king began to shudder bodily, and he forgot his sullen insolence. 21 The animals turned back upon the armed forces following them and began trampling and destroying them.

22 Then the king's anger was turned to pity and tears because of the things that he had devised beforehand. 23 For when he heard the shouting and saw them all fallen headlong to destruction, he wept and angrily threatened his Friends, saying, 24 "You are committing treason and surpassing tyrants in cruelty; and even me, your benefactor, you are now attempting to deprive of dominion and life by secretly devising acts of no advantage to the kingdom. 25 Who has driven from their homes those who faithfully kept our country's for-

---

a Other ancient authorities read *rescued and restored*; others, *mercifully restored*   *b* Other ancient authorities read *to the saints of Israel*   *c* Or *bless their vain gods*

---

born and reared" (*Flaccus* 46). **6.4** *By drowning them in the sea.* See Ex 14–15. **6.5** *Sennacherib.* See 2 Kings 18–19; Isa 36–37. **6.6** *The three companions.* See Dan 3. *Moistening the fiery furnace.* This detail is found only in the Additions to Daniel (Pr Azar 27). **6.7** *Daniel . . . wild animals.* See Dan 6; Bel 31–42. **6.10** *Even if our lives . . . impieties,* an even more minimal confession of sin than was found in the prayer of Simon (ch. 2). **6.11** See Ps 115.2. **6.15** *Not even . . . did I neglect them,* from Lev 26.44. **6.16–29** The reversal of fortune. The

story now moves to its climax. **6.17** *An uncontrollable terror.* See Ex 15.16. **6.18** *Two glorious angels.* See 2 Macc 3.26. The fact that the angels are not visible to everyone shows their supernatural character. **6.21** At the battle of Raphia, Philopator's elephants proved intractable and disrupted their own lines (Polybius, *Histories* 5.84.7). **6.22** *The king's anger was turned to pity.* This is the moment of reversal. **6.23** Philopator blames his *Friends* (see note on 5.3), though it is he who took the initiative. In Esther and Daniel, the counselors

tresses, and foolishly gathered every one of them here? [26]Who is it that has so lawlessly encompassed with outrageous treatment those who from the beginning differed from[a] all nations in their goodwill toward us and often have accepted willingly the worst of human dangers? [27]Loose and untie their unjust bonds! Send them back to their homes in peace, begging pardon for your former actions![b] [28]Release the children of the almighty and living God of heaven, who from the time of our ancestors until now has granted an unimpeded and notable stability to our government." [29]These then were the things he said; and the Jews, immediately released, praised their holy God and Savior, since they now had escaped death.

The Jews Celebrate Their Deliverance

30 Then the king, when he had returned to the city, summoned the official in charge of the revenues and ordered him to provide to the Jews both wines and everything else needed for a festival of seven days, deciding that they should celebrate their rescue with all joyfulness in that same place in which they had expected to meet their destruction. [31]Accordingly those disgracefully treated and near to death,[c] or rather, who stood at its gates, arranged for a banquet of deliverance instead of a bitter and lamentable death, and full of joy they apportioned to celebrants the place that had been prepared for their destruction and burial. [32]They stopped their chanting of dirges and took up the song of their ancestors, praising God, their Savior and worker of wonders.[d] Putting an end to all mourning and wailing, they formed choruses[e] as a sign of peaceful joy. [33]Likewise also the king, after convening a great banquet to celebrate these events, gave thanks to heaven unceasingly and lavishly for the unexpected rescue that he[f] had experienced. [34]Those who had previously believed that the Jews would be destroyed and become food for birds, and had joyfully registered them, groaned as they themselves were

overcome by disgrace, and their fire-breathing boldness was ignominiously[g] quenched.

35 The Jews, as we have said before, arranged the aforementioned choral group[h] and passed the time in feasting to the accompaniment of joyous thanksgiving and psalms. [36]And when they had ordained a public rite for these things in their whole community and for their descendants, they instituted the observance of the aforesaid days as a festival, not for drinking and gluttony, but because of the deliverance that had come to them through God. [37]Then they petitioned the king, asking for dismissal to their homes. [38]So their registration was carried out from the twenty-fifth of Pachon to the fourth of Epeiph,[i] for forty days; and their destruction was set for the fifth to the seventh of Epeiph,[j] the three days [39]on which the Lord of all most gloriously revealed his mercy and rescued them all together and unharmed. [40]Then they feasted, being provided with everything by the king, until the fourteenth day,[k] on which also they made the petition for their dismissal. [41]The king granted their request at once and wrote the following letter for them to the generals in the cities, magnanimously expressing his concern:

Ptolemy's Letter on Behalf of the Jews

7 "King Ptolemy Philopator to the generals in Egypt and all in authority in his government, greetings and good health:

2 "We ourselves and our children are faring well, the great God guiding our affairs according to our desire. [3]Certain of our friends, frequently urging us with malicious intent, persuaded us to gather together the Jews of the kingdom in a body and to punish them with barbarous penalties as traitors; [4]for they declared that our government would never be

---

a Or *excelled above*   b Other ancient authorities read *revoking your former commands*   c Gk *Hades*   d Other ancient authorities read *praising Israel and the wonder-working God*; or *praising Israel's Savior, the wonder-working God*   e Or *dances*   f Other ancient authorities read *they*   g Other ancient authorities read *completely*   h Or *dance*   i July 7—August 15   j August 16—18   k August 25

---

were primarily to blame. **6.25** *Those who faithfully kept our country's fortresses.* Jews already kept the fortress at Elephantine in the fifth century BCE. **6.28** *The children . . . heaven.* See Wis 18.13. **6.30–41** The celebration. **6.31** *A banquet of deliverance instead of . . . death* heavily emphasizes the reversal of fortune. **6.32** *The song of their ancestors,* perhaps Ps 136 (cf. 1 Chr 16.41; 2 Chr 5.13; 7.3; Ezra 3.11). **6.34** *Food for birds.* See Ezek 39.4;

2 Macc 9.15. **6.36** Cf. the establishment of Purim in Esth 9. Josephus says that the deliverance from the elephants was "the origin of the well-known feast which the Jews of Alexandria keep, with good reason, on this day" (*Against Apion* 2.55).

7.1–9 Ptolemy's letter. **7.2** *Our children.* Philopator had only one legitimate son, who later reigned as Ptolemy V Epiphanes. **7.3** Again the king puts the

firmly established until this was accomplished, because of the ill-will that these people had toward all nations. ⁵They also led them out with harsh treatment as slaves, or rather as traitors, and, girding themselves with a cruelty more savage than that of Scythian custom, they tried without any inquiry or examination to put them to death. ⁶But we very severely threatened them for these acts, and in accordance with the clemency that we have toward all people we barely spared their lives. Since we have come to realize that the God of heaven surely defends the Jews, always taking their part as a father does for his children, ⁷and since we have taken into account the friendly and firm goodwill that they had toward us and our ancestors, we justly have acquitted them of every charge of whatever kind. ⁸We also have ordered all people to return to their own homes, with no one in any place*a* doing them harm at all or reproaching them for the irrational things that have happened. ⁹For you should know that if we devise any evil against them or cause them any grief at all, we always shall have not a mortal but the Ruler over every power, the Most High God, in everything and inescapably as an antagonist to avenge such acts. Farewell."

The Jews Return Home with Joy

10 On receiving this letter the Jews*b* did not immediately hurry to make their departure, but they requested of the king that at their own hands those of the Jewish nation who had willfully transgressed against the holy God and the law of God should receive the punishment they deserved. ¹¹They declared that those who for the belly's sake had transgressed the divine commandments would never be favorably disposed toward the king's government. ¹²The king*c* then, admitting and approving the truth of what they said, granted them a general license so that freely, and without royal authority or supervision, they might destroy those everywhere in his kingdom who had transgressed the law of God. ¹³When they had applauded him in fitting manner, their priests and the whole multitude shouted the Hallelujah and joyfully departed. ¹⁴And so on their way they punished and put to a public and shameful death any whom they met of their compatriots who had become defiled. ¹⁵In that day they put to death more than three hundred men; and they kept the day as a joyful festival, since they had destroyed the profaners. ¹⁶But those who had held fast to God even to death and had received the full enjoyment of deliverance began their departure from the city, crowned with all sorts of very fragrant flowers, joyfully and loudly giving thanks to the one God of their ancestors, the eternal Savior*d* of Israel, in words of praise and all kinds of melodious songs.

17 When they had arrived at Ptolemais, called "rose-bearing" because of a characteristic of the place, the fleet waited for them, in accordance with the common desire, for seven days. ¹⁸There they celebrated their deliverance,*e* for the king had generously provided all things to them for their journey until all of them arrived at their own houses. ¹⁹And when they had all landed in peace with appropriate thanksgiving, there too in like manner they decided to observe these days as a joyous festival during the time of their stay. ²⁰Then, after inscribing them as holy on a pillar and dedicating a place of prayer at the site of the festival, they departed unharmed, free, and overjoyed, since at the king's command they had all of them been brought safely by land and sea and river to their own homes. ²¹They also possessed greater prestige among their enemies, being held in honor and awe; and they were

a Other ancient authorities read *way*   *b* Gk *they*   *c* Gk *He*
d Other ancient authorities read *the holy Savior*; others, *the holy one*   *e* Gk *they made a cup of deliverance*

---

blame on *certain . . . friends*, in blatant contradiction of the story. **7.5** The *Scythians* were proverbial for barbarism and cruelty. See 2 Macc 4.47; 4 Macc 10.7. **7.6** Jewish stories of this period often have the pagan king acknowledge the true God (Dan 2.47; 4.2, 37; 6.26; 2 Macc 9.12, 13). *God of heaven*, a title that might be used by both Jews and Gentiles. Philopator does not necessarily concede that Judaism is the only true religion, but he does concede that the universal God protects it. **7.10–16** Revenge on apostates. In Esther, the king authorized the Jews to slaughter their gentile ene-

mies (Esth 8.11–13; 9.1–17). Here there is no revenge on the Gentiles, but more than three hundred Jewish apostates are killed, even though they acted under duress. This reflects the tensions within the Jewish community in time of crisis. It is ironic that 3 Maccabees began with an exploit of the apostate Dositheus. **7.17–23** The departure. **7.17** *Ptolemais*, the one at the harbor near Cairo, not the better known Ptolemais in Upper Egypt. **7.20** The king is benevolent in the end. *Sea*, possibly Lake Moeris, or perhaps *by land and sea and river* is idiomatic and means "by whatever means

not subject at all to confiscation of their belongings by anyone. ²²Besides, they all recovered all of their property, in accordance with the registration, so that those who held any of it restored it to them with extreme fear.ᵃ So the

supreme God perfectly performed great deeds for their deliverance. ²³Blessed be the Deliverer of Israel through all times! Amen.

---

a Other ancient authorities read *with a very large supplement*

---

necessary." **7.22** The *registration* proves to have a providential purpose, as it enables the Jews to recover their

possessions. **7.23** *Blessed be the Deliverer of Israel.* Cf. the closing doxology in 4 Macc 18.24.

2 ESDRAS

THE BOOK WE KNOW AS 2 ESDRAS is made up of three works: *4 Ezra*, an apocalypse by a Jewish author (chs. 3–14), and two independent Christian supplements, 5 Ezra (chs. 1–2) and 6 Ezra (chs. 15–16). Esdras, the Greek form of the Hebrew name Ezra, is the seer who receives seven visions in the main portion of the book. The pseudepigraphical author writes as if he were the Ezra who figures in the books of Ezra and Nehemiah.

4 Ezra

FOURTH EZRA WAS WRITTEN in the aftermath of the Roman destruction of the Second Temple in 70 CE. On the basis of the identification of the heads in the fifth vision (chs. 11–12), its date can be set more precisely in the last decade of the first century CE. Other indications of date have been sought in the work, but no convincing argument can be made for them.

The original audience of *4 Ezra* consisted of Jews, probably living in the land of Israel, who were wrestling with the implications of the destruction of the temple. An indication of the author's prophetic status within his own community may be found in 12.42, but we have little indication of how *4 Ezra* functioned in that community or how it was used.

Scholars today almost universally hold that *4 Ezra* was composed in a Semitic language, most probably Hebrew. The original Hebrew text and the Greek primary translation of it have perished except for a few quotations from the Greek text by ancient authors. The text translated here is basically the Latin version, with some account taken of Syriac, Ethiopic, Arabic, Armenian, and Georgian versions. Previous theories of the composition of *4 Ezra* from five sources are no longer entertained. It is the work of one individual, who draws at points on older material. In 4.35–36a; 6.49–52; 13.1–20; 13.40–47, the author has included what seem to be preexisting blocks of material.

4 Ezra is composed of seven visions separated by fasts. The first three visions are unusual in form, composed of addresses, dialogues, and predictions. In the first two visions (3.1–6.34) the seer's problems in the addresses are partly answered in the predictive dialogues and direct predictions. The third vision (6.35–9.25) is very long and much more complex. The address of the first vision (3.4–36) indicts God the creator for the state of the world and of Israel. Israel's suffering under Rome raises for the author the question of God's justice. The angel's responses in the first three visions gradually lead Ezra from skepticism to acceptance of God's incomprehensible providence. Indeed, Ezra comes to embrace answers he rejected previously.

This acceptance provides the basis for the fourth vision (9.26–10.59), the seer's conversion followed by his waking experience of heavenly Jerusalem, after which he becomes a more conventional apocalyptic seer. In the fifth (11.1–12.51) and sixth (13.1–58) visions, we find symbolic dreams interpreted by an angel, as is customary in apocalypses. In the seventh vision (14.1–48), Ezra is granted a revelation of the ninety-four secret and public books of scripture. The visions are set within a narrative framework indicating the progression of the seer's experience.

4 Ezra was an influential writing, deeply imbued with the Hebrew scriptures and having an explicit relationship to the book of Daniel, which sets it in an apocalyptic tradition. Of ancient Jewish writing, it is extremely closely related to *2 Apocalypse of Baruch,* although scholars differ as to which work was written first. A number of later Christian apocalypses are fashioned on the form of *4 Ezra.* The chief such writings are 6 Ezra, the *Greek Esdras Apocalypse,* the *Apocalypse of Sedrach* (Greek), the *Revelation of Ezra* (Latin), and the *Questions of Ezra* (Armenian). *4 Ezra* had a deep and broad influence in both Eastern and Western Christianity. No impression on rabbinic or later Judaism has been discerned.

5 and 6 Ezra

FIFTH EZRA IS OF CHRISTIAN AUTHORSHIP; there are some indications that it was written in the second–third centuries CE, although this is not certain. 6 Ezra was probably written by a Christian and can be dated on internal grounds to the third century CE. Both works indicate how *4 Ezra* was read in the centuries after its composition. 5 Ezra seems to have been written as a separate literary unit. It comprises two parts of varied character, a prophetic indictment of God's people (1.4–2.9) and an assurance of redemption to a new people (2.10–48). 6 Ezra, composed of predictions, woes, and exhortations to God's people, was written to encourage a third-century Christian audience in time of oppression. Its original beginning (as well as the end of *4 Ezra*) was likely modified when it was combined with *4 Ezra.* Some dependence on the NT has been discerned in both works.

Scholars generally agree that 5 Ezra was originally written in Greek. A papyrus fragment of the Greek text of 6 Ezra has been identified, and there seems no reason to doubt its composition in that language. Both 5 Ezra and 6 Ezra survive in full only in Latin. The three Ezra books occur together only in the Latin version, sometimes in the order 5, 4, 6 Ezra (as is the case here) and sometimes as 4, 6, 5 Ezra. 5 Ezra had no known influence on Jewish literature, but it influenced the Roman church, particularly in the liturgy. 6 Ezra seems to have had no particular influence in Jewish or Christian circles.

Canonical Status

NO PART OF 2 ESDRAS HAS CANONICAL STATUS in the Jewish tradition. Except for a few quotations and its utilization in the Greek apocalypses mentioned above, it had no standing in the Greek church. The Western church was much attached to it, and it was often found in manuscripts of the Vulgate; however, the book did not form part of the Roman Catholic canon as defined by the Council of Trent (1546). In the Armenian church it has a semicanonical status, being mentioned in some canon lists and occurring exclusively in biblical manuscripts. In Ethiopic too it occurs in biblical manuscripts (though the concept of canon in the Ethiopic church is not always clear). The fact that there are only a few copies in Christian Arabic and Georgian indicates that it had no canonical role in these churches. [MICHAEL E. STONE]

Comprising what is sometimes called 5 Ezra (chapters 1–2), 4 Ezra (chapters 3–14), and 6 Ezra (chapters 15–16)

The Genealogy of Ezra

1 The book[a] of the prophet Ezra son of Seraiah, son of Azariah, son of Hilkiah, son of Shallum, son of Zadok, son of Ahitub, 2son of Ahijah, son of Phinehas, son of Eli, son of Amariah, son of Azariah, son of Meraimoth, son of Arna, son of Uzzi, son of Borith, son of Abishua, son of Phinehas, son of Eleazar, 3son of Aaron, of the tribe of Levi, who was a captive in the country of the Medes in the reign of Artaxerxes, king of the Persians.[b]

Ezra's Prophetic Call

4 The word of the Lord came to me, saying, 5"Go, declare to my people their evil deeds, and to their children the iniquities that they have committed against me, so that they may tell[c] their children's children 6that the sins of their parents have increased in them, for they have forgotten me and have offered sacrifices to strange gods. 7Was it not I who brought them out of the land of Egypt, out of the house of bondage? But they have angered me and despised my counsels. 8Now you, pull out the hair of your head and hurl[d] all evils upon them, for they have not obeyed my law—they are a rebellious people. 9How long shall I endure them, on whom I have bestowed such great benefits? 10For their sake I have overthrown many kings; I struck down Pharaoh with his servants and all his army. 11I destroyed all nations before them, and scattered in the east the peoples of two provinces,[e] Tyre and Sidon; I killed all their enemies.

God's Mercies to Israel

12 "But speak to them and say, Thus says the Lord: 13Surely it was I who brought you through the sea, and made safe highways for you where there was no road; I gave you Moses as leader and Aaron as priest; 14I provided light for you from a pillar of fire, and did great wonders among you. Yet you have forgotten me, says the Lord.

15 "Thus says the Lord Almighty:[f] The quails were a sign to you; I gave you camps for your protection, and in them you complained. 16You have not exulted in my name at the destruction of your enemies, but to this day you still complain.[g] 17Where are the benefits that I bestowed on you? When you were hungry and thirsty in the wilderness, did you not cry out to me, 18saying, 'Why have you led us into this wilderness to kill us? It would have been better for us to serve the Egyptians than to die in this wilderness.' 19I pitied your groanings and gave you manna for food; you ate the bread of angels. 20When you were thirsty, did I not split the rock so that waters flowed in abundance? Because of the heat I clothed you with the leaves of trees.[h] 21I divided fertile lands among you; I drove out the Canaanites, the Perizzites, and the Philistines[i] before you. What more can I do for you? says the Lord. 22Thus says the Lord Almighty:[f] When you were in the wilderness, at the bitter stream, thirsty and blaspheming my name, 23I did not send fire on you for your blasphemies, but threw a tree into the water and made the stream sweet.

Israel's Disobedience and Rejection

24 "What shall I do to you, O Jacob? You, Judah, would not obey me. I will turn to other

---

a Other ancient authorities read *The second book*   b Other ancient authorities, which place chapters 1 and 2 after 16.78, lack verses 1-3 and begin the chapter: *The word of the Lord that came to Ezra son of Chusi in the days of King Nebuchadnezzar, saying, "Go,*   c Other ancient authorities read *nourish*   d Other ancient authorities read *and shake out*   e Other ancient authorities read *Did I not destroy the city of Bethsaida because of you, and to the south burn two cities . . . ?*   f Other ancient authorities lack *Almighty*   g Other ancient authorities read verse 16, *Your pursuer with his army I sank in the sea, but still the people complain also concerning their own destruction.*   h Other ancient authorities read *I made for you trees with leaves*   i Other ancient authorities read *Perizzites and their children*

1.1–2.48 Chs. 1–2 form a separate, Christian work often entitled 5 Ezra (see Introduction). **1.1–3** Ezra is here described both as priest (cf. Ezra 7.1–5; 1 Esd 8.1–2) and *prophet*. The latter is unusual. In the biblical book Ezra is a scribe (Ezra 7.6). **1.4–23** The "exodus review" is common in the Hebrew scriptures and other Jewish literature; cf., e.g., Pss 78; 105; 106; Neh 9; the *Dayyenu* prayer in the Passover Haggadah. **1.4–11** A summary of God's gracious deeds and Israel's rejection of them. **1.4** Such prophetic calls are found in, e.g., Jer 1.4; Ezek 7.1. **1.8** *Pull out the hair of your head,* a sign of mourning; cf. Ezra 9.3. **1.10** See Ex 14.28; 20.2. **1.11** The verse is obscure; *Tyre and Sidon* are cities, not provinces, and are west, not east, of Media (cf. v. 3). **1.12–23** Similar to Neh 9; Ps 78. **1.14** *Pillar of fire.* Cf. Ex 13.21. **1.15** God's care in the desert. For the *quails,* see Ex 16.13. **1.18** See Ex 14.11–12. **1.19** *Bread of angels,* i.e., manna; see Ps 78.25. **1.20** *Split the rock.* See Num 20.11. The clothing with the *leaves of trees* is unknown. **1.22** A reference to the complaints at the Wa-

nations and will give them my name, so that they may keep my statutes. 25Because you have forsaken me, I also will forsake you. When you beg mercy of me, I will show you no mercy. 26When you call to me, I will not listen to you; for you have defiled your hands with blood, and your feet are swift to commit murder. 27It is not as though you had forsaken me; you have forsaken yourselves, says the Lord.

28 "Thus says the Lord Almighty: Have I not entreated you as a father entreats his sons or a mother her daughters or a nurse her children, 29so that you should be my people and I should be your God, and that you should be my children and I should be your father? 30I gathered you as a hen gathers her chicks under her wings. But now, what shall I do to you? I will cast you out from my presence. 31When you offer oblations to me, I will turn my face from you; for I have rejected your*a* festal days, and new moons, and circumcisions of the flesh.*b* 32I sent you my servants the prophets, but you have taken and killed them and torn their bodies*c* in pieces; I will require their blood of you, says the Lord.*d*

33 "Thus says the Lord Almighty: Your house is desolate; I will drive you out as the wind drives straw; 34and your sons will have no children, because with you*e* they have neglected my commandment and have done what is evil in my sight. 35I will give your houses to a people that will come, who without having heard me will believe. Those to whom I have shown no signs will do what I have commanded. 36They have seen no prophets, yet will recall their former state.*f* 37I call to witness the gratitude of the people that is to come, whose children rejoice with gladness;*g* though they do not see me with bodily eyes, yet with the spirit they will believe the things I have said.

38 "And now, father,*h* look with pride and see the people coming from the east; 39to them I will give as leaders Abraham, Isaac, and Jacob, and Hosea and Amos and Micah and Joel and Obadiah and Jonah 40and Nahum and Habakkuk, Zephaniah, Haggai, Zechariah and Malachi, who is also called the messenger of the Lord.*i*

God's Judgment on Israel

2 "Thus says the Lord: I brought this people out of bondage, and I gave them commandments through my servants the prophets; but they would not listen to them, and made my counsels void. 2The mother who bore them*j* says to them, 'Go, my children, because I am a widow and forsaken. 3I brought you up with gladness; but with mourning and sorrow I have lost you, because you have sinned before the Lord God and have done what is evil in my sight.*a* 4But now what can I do for you? For I am a widow and forsaken. Go, my children, and ask for mercy from the Lord.' 5Now I call upon you, father, as a wit-

---

a Other ancient authorities read *I have not commanded for you* *b* Other ancient authorities lack *of the flesh* *c* Other ancient authorities read *the bodies of the apostles* *d* Other ancient authorities add *Thus says the Lord Almighty: Recently you also laid hands on me, crying out before the judge's seat for him to deliver me to you. You took me as a sinner, not as a father who freed you from slavery, and you delivered me to death by hanging me on the tree; these are the things you have done. Therefore, says the Lord, let my Father and his angels return and judge between you and me; if I have not kept the commandment of the Father, if I have not nourished you, if I have not done these things my Father commanded, I will contend in judgment with you, says the Lord.* *e* Other ancient authorities lack *with you* *f* Other ancient authorities read *their iniquities* *g* Other ancient authorities read *The apostles bear witness to the coming people with joy* *h* Other ancient authorities read *brother* *i* Other ancient authorities read *and Jacob, Elijah and Enoch, Zechariah and Hosea, Amos, Joel, Micah, Obadiah, Zephaniah,* 40*Nahum, Jonah, Mattia (or Mattathias), Habakkuk, and twelve angels with flowers* *j* Other ancient authorities read *They begat for themselves a mother who*

---

ters of Marah (Hebrew, "bitterness"); see Ex 15.22–25. **1.24–40** Israel is replaced by *the people . . . from the east* (v. 38; cf. v. 24), which is usually taken to show the Christian origin of 5 Ezra. **1.29** God as parent of Israel is a frequent image in the Hebrew Bible; cf. Jer 3.19; 31.9. **1.30** *As a hen gathers her chicks.* See Mt 23.37; Lk 13.34. **1.32** Based on Mt 23.34–35; Lk 11.49–51. The rejection of prophets is found in the Hebrew Bible (e.g., 2 Chr 24.19; 36.16; Jer 2.3) and other Jewish writings (e.g., *Jubilees* 1.12; *1 Enoch* 89.51–53). **1.35** The transfer of Israel's position to the Christians. In particular, the gentile Christians are implied here. *Signs,* Christ's signs while alive. **1.36** Again the Gentiles are implied. The book of Jonah makes an analogous point from an intra-Israelite perspective. **1.37** *Though they*

do not see me. Cf. Jn 20.29. **1.38** *Father,* a unique title denoting Ezra (see also 2.5); also a prophetic title (2 Kings 2.12). Does *from the east* imply that the place of origin of 5 Ezra was Palestine? Is this a different group of Christians from those referred to in vv. 35–37? **1.39–40** *Leaders,* the three patriarchs of Israel and twelve minor prophets. **1.40** *Malachi,* in Hebrew "my messenger." Ezra is identified as Malachi by rabbinic sources. **2.1–9** God judges and rejects Israel as a mother rejects her children. **2.1** The laws are given through *prophets;* cf. Ezra 9.10–11; Dan 9.10. **2.2** Zion speaks as Israel's *mother,* a biblical idea (cf. esp. Bar 4.5–29; also 2 Esd 10.38–54). She is both widowed and deserted and rejects her children (v. 4). **2.5** The writer invokes the *father,* God (or perhaps Ezra), and the

ness in addition to the mother of the children, because they would not keep my covenant, [6]so that you may bring confusion on them and bring their mother to ruin, so that they may have no offspring. [7]Let them be scattered among the nations; let their names be blotted out from the earth, because they have despised my covenant.

8 "Woe to you, Assyria, who conceal the unrighteous within you! O wicked nation, remember what I did to Sodom and Gomorrah, [9]whose land lies in lumps of pitch and heaps of ashes.[b] That is what I will do to those who have not listened to me, says the Lord Almighty."

10 Thus says the Lord to Ezra: "Tell my people that I will give them the kingdom of Jerusalem, which I was going to give to Israel. [11]Moreover, I will take back to myself their glory, and will give to these others the everlasting habitations, which I had prepared for Israel.[c] [12]The tree of life shall give them fragrant perfume, and they shall neither toil nor become weary. [13]Go[d] and you will receive; pray that your days may be few, that they may be shortened. The kingdom is already prepared for you; be on the watch! [14]Call, O call heaven and earth to witness: I set aside evil and created good; for I am the Living One, says the Lord.

Exhortation to Good Works

15 "Mother, embrace your children; bring them up with gladness, as does a dove; strengthen their feet, because I have chosen you, says the Lord. [16]And I will raise up the dead from their places, and bring them out from their tombs, because I recognize my name

in them. [17]Do not fear, mother of children, for I have chosen you, says the Lord. [18]I will send you help, my servants Isaiah and Jeremiah. According to their counsel I have consecrated and prepared for you twelve trees loaded with various fruits, [19]and the same number of springs flowing with milk and honey, and seven mighty mountains on which roses and lilies grow; by these I will fill your children with joy.

20 "Guard the rights of the widow, secure justice for the ward, give to the needy, defend the orphan, clothe the naked, [21]care for the injured and the weak, do not ridicule the lame, protect the maimed, and let the blind have a vision of my splendor. [22]Protect the old and the young within your walls. [23]When you find any who are dead, commit them to the grave and mark it,[e] and I will give you the first place in my resurrection. [24]Pause and be quiet, my people, because your rest will come.

25 "Good nurse, nourish your children; strengthen their feet. [26]Not one of the servants[f] whom I have given you will perish, for I will require them from among your number. [27]Do not be anxious, for when the day of tribulation and anguish comes, others shall weep and be sorrowful, but you shall rejoice and have abundance. [28]The nations shall envy you, but they shall not be able to do anything against you, says the Lord. [29]My power will protect[g] you, so that your children may not see hell.[h]

30 "Rejoice, O mother, with your children, because I will deliver you, says the Lord. [31]Re-

---

[a] Other ancient authorities read *in his sight*   [b] Other ancient authorities read *Gomorrah, whose land descends to hell*   [c] Lat *for those*   [d] Other ancient authorities read *Seek*   [e] Or *seal it; or mark them and commit them to the grave*   [f] Or *slaves*   [g] Lat *hands will cover*   [h] Lat *Gehenna*

---

mother, Zion, to witness and pronounces doom on the children and ruin on the mother. The imagery of dual rejection is particularly powerful. **2.7** *Scattering,* an ultimate curse for disobedience (Lev 26.33). *Names . . . blotted out* expresses annihilation—Israel's very name will be forgotten. For the importance of name and memory as a form of immortality, see Sir 41.11–13. **2.8** *Assyria,* possibly a cognomen for Rome, replacing the more common "Babylon"; cf. 3.1. The Jews, and the Romans who harbored them, are cursed. **2.10–14** The reward for the new Israel. **2.11** In *habitations* the righteous Christians are to be rewarded and will be given glory; cf. 4.35; 7.98. **2.12** *Perfume.* Some thought the tree of life exuded a fragrance or oil rather than gave fruit; cf. *Life of Adam and Eve* 36.2, 40–42; *2 Enoch* 5.5. **2.13** Eschatological reward is created in advance. For the sense of urgency, cf., e.g., Mt 24.15–34; Mk 13.14–

20; Rom 13.11–14; 1 Cor 7.29–31; 1 Thess 4.13–5.11; Rev 1.3; 22.10–12, 20. **2.14** *Call heaven and earth to witness.* Cf. Deut 4.26 **2.15–32** The image of the mother is applied to the church. Resurrection is promised throughout this passage (e.g., vv. 16, 23, 29, 31). **2.18–19** A description of eschatological paradise. *Twelve trees.* Cf. Rev 22.2. *Milk and honey,* traditional symbols of fertility; cf. Ex 3.8. *Seven . . . mountains,* perhaps the mountains of paradise (*1 Enoch* 24–25); Rome is known later as the city of seven hills, so this might be an inversion of Rome's role. **2.20–23** The call to protect the weak and particularly to care for the dead is standard biblical exhortation; cf. Tob 1.17 and, indeed, the whole book of Tobit. On burial of the executed, see Deut 21.22–23. **2.24** *Rest,* eschatological reward; cf. 7.36; Heb 3.18–19; *1 Enoch* 11.2. **2.25–26** *Nurse,* the church. *Your number,* "the number given

member your children that sleep, because I will bring them out of the hiding places of the earth, and will show mercy to them; for I am merciful, says the Lord Almighty. 32 Embrace your children until I come, and proclaim mercy to them; because my springs run over, and my grace will not fail."

Ezra on Mount Horeb

33 I, Ezra, received a command from the Lord on Mount Horeb to go to Israel. When I came to them they rejected me and refused the Lord's commandment. 34 Therefore I say to you, O nations that hear and understand, "Wait for your shepherd; he will give you everlasting rest, because he who will come at the end of the age is close at hand. 35 Be ready for the rewards of the kingdom, because perpetual light will shine on you forevermore. 36 Flee from the shadow of this age, receive the joy of your glory; I publicly call on my savior to witness.ᵃ 37 Receive what the Lord has entrusted to you and be joyful, giving thanks to him who has called you to the celestial kingdoms. 38 Rise, stand erect and see the number of those who have been sealed at the feast of the Lord. 39 Those who have departed from the shadow of this age have received glorious garments from the Lord. 40 Take again your full number, O Zion, and close the list of your people who are clothed in white, who have fulfilled the law of the Lord. 41 The number of your children, whom you desired, is now complete; implore the Lord's authority that your people, who have been called from the beginning, may be made holy."

Ezra Sees the Son of God

42 I, Ezra, saw on Mount Zion a great multitude that I could not number, and they all were praising the Lord with songs. 43 In their midst was a young man of great stature, taller than any of the others, and on the head of each of them he placed a crown, but he was more exalted than they. And I was held spellbound. 44 Then I asked an angel, "Who are these, my lord?" 45 He answered and said to me, "These are they who have put off mortal clothing and have put on the immortal, and have confessed the name of God. Now they are being crowned, and receive palms." 46 Then I said to the angel, "Who is that young man who is placing crowns on them and putting palms in their hands?" 47 He answered and said to me, "He is the Son of God, whom they confessed in the world." So I began to praise those who had stood valiantly for the name of the Lord.ᵇ 48 Then the angel said to me, "Go, tell my people how great and how many are the wonders of the Lord God that you have seen."

Ezra's Prayer of Complaint

3 In the thirtieth year after the destruction of the city, I was in Babylon—I, Salathiel, who am also called Ezra. I was troubled as I lay on my bed, and my thoughts welled up in my heart, 2 because I saw the desolation of Zion and the wealth of those who lived in Babylon. 3 My spirit was greatly agitated, and I began to speak anxious words to the Most High, and said, 4 "O sovereign Lord, did you not speak at the beginning when you plantedᶜ the earth—and that without help—and commanded the dustᵈ 5 and it gave you Adam, a lifeless body?

---

a Other ancient authorities read *I testify that my savior has been commissioned by the Lord*   b Other ancient authorities read *to praise and glorify the Lord*   c Other ancient authorities read *formed*   d Syr Ethiop: Lat *people* or *world*

---

to you"; the phrase may derive from Jn 17.12. **2.31** *Sleep,* death, but resurrection is implied. **2.33–41** A first-person address by Ezra. **2.33** The depiction of Ezra on *Mount Horeb* (i.e., Mount Sinai) suggests a typological comparison of Ezra with Moses; see ch. 14. Israel is again rejected. **2.34** *Shepherd,* Christ. **2.35** *Light will shine* upon the righteous. Cf. Isa 60.19–20; Rev 21.23. **2.36** *Savior,* clearly Christ. **2.37** The soul is what is *entrusted;* see 1 Tim 6.20; 2 Tim 1.12, 14; Shepherd of Hermas, *Mandates* 3.2. **2.38** *Sealed.* See Ezek 9.4; Rev 7.2–8. **2.39** *Glorious garments,* the shining robes of the righteous at the end; cf. Rev 3.4–5. **2.40–41** The *number* of the righteous is fixed; cf. 4.36. **2.42–48** Christ confirms the predictions offered in the preceding passage. **2.42** *Mount Zion.* Cf. ch. 13; Rev

14.1. **2.43** For a similar description of the crowning, see Shepherd of Hermas, *Similitudes* 8.2.1; 8.3.6. **2.45** Victors receive *palms;* perhaps a reference to martyrs.

3.1–14.48 Chs. 3–14 form a separate work, a Jewish apocalypse containing seven visions; it is often called 4 Ezra (see Introduction). **3.1–5.15** First vision. **3.1–3** The introduction to the first vision. **3.1** Cf. Ezek 1.1. *Salathiel,* used only here; cf. Dan 4.5. Of course, *Ezra* is only a pseudonym. **3.3** The onset of inspiration. *Most High,* the usual title for God in this book. **3.4–36** Ezra's address falls into two parts. Vv. 4–27 are an indictment of God set as a historical review; vv. 28–36 set forth the specific charges. **3.4** *Speak, without help.* God creates alone (perhaps a polemical assertion) and by speech; cf. Ps 33.6, 9. **3.5** For God's

Yet he was the creation of your hands, and you breathed into him the breath of life, and he was made alive in your presence. 6 And you led him into the garden that your right hand had planted before the earth appeared. 7 And you laid upon him one commandment of yours; but he transgressed it, and immediately you appointed death for him and for his descendants. From him there sprang nations and tribes, peoples and clans without number. 8 And every nation walked after its own will; they did ungodly things in your sight and rejected your commands, and you did not hinder them. 9 But again, in its time you brought the flood upon the inhabitants of the world and destroyed them. 10 And the same fate befell all of them: just as death came upon Adam, so the flood upon them. 11 But you left one of them, Noah with his household, and all the righteous who have descended from him.

12 "When those who lived on earth began to multiply, they produced children and peoples and many nations, and again they began to be more ungodly than were their ancestors. 13 And when they were committing iniquity in your sight, you chose for yourself one of them, whose name was Abraham; 14 you loved him, and to him alone you revealed the end of the times, secretly by night. 15 You made an everlasting covenant with him, and promised him that you would never forsake his descendants; and you gave him Isaac, and to Isaac you gave Jacob and Esau. 16 You set apart Jacob for yourself, but Esau you rejected; and Jacob became a great multitude. 17 And when you led his descendants out of Egypt, you brought them to Mount Sinai. 18 You bent down the heavens and shook[a] the earth, and moved the world, and caused the depths to tremble, and troubled the times. 19 Your glory passed through the four gates of fire and earthquake and wind and ice, to give the law to the descendants of Jacob, and your commandment[a] to the posterity of Israel.

20 "Yet you did not take away their evil heart from them, so that your law might produce fruit in them. 21 For the first Adam, burdened with an evil heart, transgressed and was overcome, as were also all who were descended from him. 22 Thus the disease became permanent; the law was in the hearts of the people along with the evil root; but what was good departed, and the evil remained. 23 So the times passed and the years were completed, and you raised up for yourself a servant, named David. 24 You commanded him to build a city for your name, and there to offer you oblations from what is yours. 25 This was done for many years; but the inhabitants of the city transgressed, 26 in everything doing just as Adam and all his descendants had done, for they also had the evil heart. 27 So you handed over your city to your enemies.

Babylon Compared with Zion

28 "Then I said in my heart, Are the deeds of those who inhabit Babylon any better? Is that why it has gained dominion over Zion? 29 For when I came here I saw ungodly deeds without number, and my soul has seen many sinners during these thirty years.[b] And my heart failed me, 30 because I have seen how you endure those who sin, and have spared those who act wickedly, and have destroyed your people, and protected your enemies, 31 and have not shown to anyone how your way may be comprehended.[c] Are the deeds of Babylon

a Syr Ethiop Arab 1 Georg: Lat *set fast* b Ethiop Arab 1 Arm: Lat Syr *in this thirtieth year* c Syr; compare Ethiop: Lat *how this way should be forsaken*

---

hands, see also 8.7, 44; *2 Enoch* A 44.1. **3.6** Eden was created before the world, a common exegesis of Gen 2.8. **3.8** God did not prevent human sin; see also v. 20. **3.10** *Adam's* punishment is again evoked; cf. vv. 21, 26. **3.14** The night revelation is that of Gen 15.17; cf. *Apocalypse of Abraham.* It concerned secrets about the end of times also in many rabbinic sources. Cf. 14.5–6. **3.15** Cf. Gen 15.18–21; Josh 24.3–4. **3.16** See Mal 1.2–3. *Esau* may signify Rome. **3.17** Moses is not mentioned. **3.18** See Ex 19.18. *Times,* better "universe." **3.19** *Gates,* the storehouses of the weather; cf. Ps 78.23; *1 Enoch* 36.1; 76.1–14. **3.20–21** *Evil heart,* the inclination to sin; cf. 4.30; Sir 37.3; the Dead Sea Scrolls *Rule of the Community* (1QS) 3.13–4.26. Humans were created with it, transgressed as a result, and

became mortal. This accords generally with rabbinic ideas. *Fruit,* reward. **3.22** *Evil root.* Cf. 8.53; see Ps 155.13–14 in the Dead Sea Scrolls *Psalms Scroll* (11QPsa) 24. The view expressed in this verse differs from that in Rom 7 and is modified later in the book; see vv. 32–36; 7.116–31. **3.23–24** In 10.46 Solomon builds the city. **3.26** Israel's sin is parallel to *Adam's;* both lead to expulsion; cf. *Genesis Rabbah* 19.9. Thus Israel's exile results from the way God created the world. **3.28** *Then I said in my heart.* A reflective tone enters the address. The concern resembles that in Isa 10.5–8; Jer 25.8–14. **3.29** *Here,* Babylon. **3.30** The problem arises from comparing Israel's fate and that of the nations. **3.31** Ezra wishes to understand God's way of conducting the world. For *way of God,* see 4.2,

better than those of Zion? ³²Or has another nation known you besides Israel? Or what tribes have so believed the covenants as these tribes of Jacob? ³³Yet their reward has not appeared and their labor has borne no fruit. For I have traveled widely among the nations and have seen that they abound in wealth, though they are unmindful of your commandments. ³⁴Now therefore weigh in a balance our iniquities and those of the inhabitants of the world; and it will be found which way the turn of the scale will incline. ³⁵When have the inhabitants of the earth not sinned in your sight? Or what nation has kept your commandments so well? ³⁶You may indeed find individuals who have kept your commandments, but nations you will not find."

Limitations of the Human Mind

4 Then the angel that had been sent to me, whose name was Uriel, answered ²and said to me, "Your understanding has utterly failed regarding this world, and do you think you can comprehend the way of the Most High?" ³Then I said, "Yes, my lord." And he replied to me, "I have been sent to show you three ways, and to put before you three problems. ⁴If you can solve one of them for me, then I will show you the way you desire to see, and will teach you why the heart is evil."

5 I said, "Speak, my lord."

And he said to me, "Go, weigh for me the weight of fire, or measure for me a blast^a of wind, or call back for me the day that is past."

6 I answered and said, "Who of those that have been born can do that, that you should ask me about such things?"

7 And he said to me, "If I had asked you, 'How many dwellings are in the heart of the sea, or how many streams are at the source of the deep, or how many streams are above the

firmament, or which are the exits of Hades, or which are the entrances^b of paradise?' ⁸perhaps you would have said to me, 'I never went down into the deep, nor as yet into Hades, neither did I ever ascend into heaven.' ⁹But now I have asked you only about fire and wind and the day—things that you have experienced and from which you cannot be separated, and you have given me no answer about them." ¹⁰He said to me, "You cannot understand the things with which you have grown up; ¹¹how then can your mind comprehend the way of the Most High? And how can one who is already worn out^c by the corrupt world understand incorruption?"^d When I heard this, I fell on my face^e ¹²and said to him, "It would have been better for us not to be here than to come here and live in ungodliness, and to suffer and not understand why."

Parable of the Forest and the Sea

13 He answered me and said, "I went into a forest of trees of the plain, and they made a plan ¹⁴and said, 'Come, let us go and make war against the sea, so that it may recede before us and so that we may make for ourselves more forests.' ¹⁵In like manner the waves of the sea also made a plan and said, 'Come, let us go up and subdue the forest of the plain so that there also we may gain more territory for ourselves.' ¹⁶But the plan of the forest was in vain, for the fire came and consumed it; ¹⁷likewise also the plan of the waves of the sea was in vain,^f for the sand stood firm and blocked it. ¹⁸If now you

---

a Syr Ethiop Arab 1 Arab 2 Georg *a measure*   b Syr Compare Ethiop Arab 2 Arm: Lat lacks *of Hades, or which are the entrances*   c Meaning of Lat uncertain   d Syr Ethiop *the way of the incorruptible?*   e Syr Ethiop Arab 1: Meaning of Lat uncertain   f Lat lacks *was in vain*

11; Rom 11.33; Dead Sea Scrolls *Thanksgiving Hymns* (1QH) 7.31–32. God's action is unknowable; cf. Job 9.11–12; Isa 40.13. **3.32** Israel, though not perfect, is better than the others. **3.34** For the *scale* weighing human deeds, see *1 Enoch* 41.1; 61.8; *2 Enoch* 44.5. **3.35–36** These verses stress the injustice of God's punishment of Israel.

4.1–25 The seer and the angel argue. **4.1** *Uriel* appears without introduction. He often reveals secrets; cf. *1 Enoch* 19.1. **4.2** *Utterly failed*, better "quite confounded." **4.3** Uriel poses three riddles to Ezra, oddly called *ways.* **4.5–8** These questions and those in 5.36–37 imply a rejection of subjects commonly encountered in apocalypses; cf. *2 Apocalypse of Baruch* 59.5–

11. **4.7–8** The angel shows Ezra the limitations of his knowledge. The questions are patterned on Job 38.16–17. *Streams . . . above the firmament,* the orbits of the luminaries. **4.9** The angel's point resembles that in Job 37.14–39.30. **4.11** Instead of *one who is already worn out,* read "your vessel," i.e., your body; cf. 7.88; *Apocalypse of Moses* 31.4. **4.12** Understanding is stressed. *Suffer and not understand why.* See Job 6.24; 10.2. **4.13–18** A nature parable; other such nature parables are in 4.48–49; 7.3–9, *51–56*; 8.41–43; 10.9–13. **4.13** *I went into a forest of trees of the plain.* The best text reads: "Once upon a time the forests of trees of the plain set forth." **4.15** The conflict between land and sea may have mythical roots. **4.17** For *sand* as a

were a judge between them, which would you undertake to justify, and which to condemn?"

19 I answered and said, "Each made a foolish plan, for the land has been assigned to the forest, and the locale of the sea a place to carry its waves."

20 He answered me and said, "You have judged rightly, but why have you not judged so in your own case? 21 For as the land has been assigned to the forest and the sea to its waves, so also those who inhabit the earth can understand only what is on the earth, and he who is[a] above the heavens can understand what is above the height of the heavens."

The New Age Will Make All Things Clear

22 Then I answered and said, "I implore you, my lord, why[b] have I been endowed with the power of understanding? 23 For I did not wish to inquire about the ways above, but about those things that we daily experience: why Israel has been given over to the Gentiles in disgrace; why the people whom you loved has been given over to godless tribes, and the law of our ancestors has been brought to destruction and the written covenants no longer exist. 24 We pass from the world like locusts, and our life is like a mist,[c] and we are not worthy to obtain mercy. 25 But what will he do for his[d] name that is invoked over us? It is about these things that I have asked."

26 He answered me and said, "If you are alive, you will see, and if you live long,[e] you will often marvel, because the age is hurrying swiftly to its end. 27 It will not be able to bring the things that have been promised to the righteous in their appointed times, because this age is full of sadness and infirmities. 28 For the evil about which[f] you

ask me has been sown, but the harvest of it has not yet come. 29 If therefore that which has been sown is not reaped, and if the place where the evil has been sown does not pass away, the field where the good has been sown will not come. 30 For a grain of evil seed was sown in Adam's heart from the beginning, and how much ungodliness it has produced until now—and will produce until the time of threshing comes! 31 Consider now for yourself how much fruit of ungodliness a grain of evil seed has produced. 32 When heads of grain without number are sown, how great a threshing floor they will fill!"

When Will the New Age Come?

33 Then I answered and said, "How long?[f] When will these things be? Why are our years few and evil?" 34 He answered me and said, "Do not be in a greater hurry than the Most High. You, indeed, are in a hurry for yourself,[g] but the Highest is in a hurry on behalf of many. 35 Did not the souls of the righteous in their chambers ask about these matters, saying, 'How long are we to remain here?[h] And when will the harvest of our reward come?' 36 And the archangel Jeremiel answered and said, 'When the number of those like yourselves is completed;[i] for he has weighed the age in the balance, 37 and measured the times by measure, and numbered the times by number; and he will not move or arouse them until that measure is fulfilled.' "

38 Then I answered and said, "But, O sover-

a Or those who are b Syr Ethiop Arm: Meaning of Lat uncertain c Syr Ethiop Arab Georg: Lat a trembling d Ethiop adds holy e Syr: Lat live f Syr Ethiop: Meaning of Lat uncertain g Syr Ethiop Arab Arm: Meaning of Lat uncertain h Syr Ethiop Arab 2 Georg: Lat How long do I hope thus? i Syr Ethiop Arab 2: Lat number of seeds is completed for you

---

barrier, see Jer 5.22. **4.21** The moral of the parable emphasizes Ezra's constitutional inability to understand the way of the Most High and his place in the cosmos relative to God. **4.22–25** A rephrasing of the question of understanding; Ezra has not been convinced by the angel's argument. He is asking about an earthly matter that he should be able to understand. Israel's fate is incomprehensible in light of God's love for Israel. **4.23** The destruction of all of scripture is meant; cf. 14.21. **4.25** Cf. 2 Apocalypse of Baruch 21.21. **4.26–32** A transitional oracle. The author shifts from disputatious to predictive dialogue. **4.26** This verse implies the dominant idea of the imminence of the end and refers to the author's own time. Marvel (like wonders, 7.27; 13.14, 50, 56; 14.5), used almost exclusively of eschatological events. **4.27** Appointed times implies predestinarian ideas. **4.28** Harvest, the fruit of action, i.e., recompense. On the connection between

harvesting and judgment, see Jer 51.33; Hos 6.11; Joel 3.13; 2 Apocalypse of Baruch 70.2. **4.29** The harvest is both in the human heart and this world. There will be a new heart and a new world. **4.30** Threshing, a metaphor for eschatological separation and judgment. **4.33–52** Ezra continues to elicit information about the end by posing questions. **4.33** Why are our years few and evil, preferably "for our years are few and evil," expresses Ezra's sense of urgency. **4.34** Do not . . . Most High. Cf. 5.33, 44; 8.47. **4.35–36a** Possibly from another source. **4.35** Chambers, where souls repose after death; cf. v. 41; 7.32, 80. **4.36–37** Cf. Wis 11.20. The idea of foreordination of the times is prominent. **4.36** Jeremiel, i.e., Jerachmeel, appears also in the Coptic Apocalypses of Zephaniah and the Coptic Jeremiah Apocalypse. Number . . . is completed. The predestined number of the created occurs in 2 Apocalypse of Baruch 23.4–5; cf. 48.46. **4.38** Sovereign

eign Lord, all of us also are full of ungodliness. [39]It is perhaps on account of us that the time of threshing is delayed for the righteous—on account of the sins of those who inhabit the earth."

40 He answered me and said, "Go and ask a pregnant woman whether, when her nine months have been completed, her womb can keep the fetus within her any longer."

41 And I said, "No, lord, it cannot."

He said to me, "In Hades the chambers of the souls are like the womb. [42]For just as a woman who is in labor makes haste to escape the pangs of birth, so also do these places hasten to give back those things that were committed to them from the beginning. [43]Then the things that you desire to see will be disclosed to you."

How Much Time Remains?

44 I answered and said, "If I have found favor in your sight, and if it is possible, and if I am worthy, [45]show me this also: whether more time is to come than has passed, or whether for us the greater part has gone by. [46]For I know what has gone by, but I do not know what is to come."

47 And he said to me, "Stand at my right side, and I will show you the interpretation of a parable."

48 So I stood and looked, and lo, a flaming furnace passed by before me, and when the flame had gone by I looked, and lo, the smoke remained. [49]And after this a cloud full of water passed before me and poured down a heavy and violent rain, and when the violent rainstorm had passed, drops still remained in the cloud. [a]

50 He said to me, "Consider it for yourself; for just as the rain is more than the drops, and the fire is greater than the smoke, so the quantity that passed was far greater; but drops and smoke remained."

51 Then I prayed and said, "Do you think that I shall live until those days? Or who will be alive in those days?"

52 He answered me and said, "Concerning the signs about which you ask me, I can tell you in part; but I was not sent to tell you concerning your life, for I do not know.

Signs of the End

5 "Now concerning the signs: lo, the days are coming when those who inhabit the earth shall be seized with great terror,[b] and the way of truth shall be hidden, and the land shall be barren of faith. [2]Unrighteousness shall be increased beyond what you yourself see, and beyond what you heard of formerly. [3]And the land that you now see ruling shall be a trackless waste, and people shall see it desolate. [4]But if the Most High grants that you live, you shall see it thrown into confusion after the third period;[c]

and the sun shall suddenly begin to shine
　　at night,
　　and the moon during the day.
[5]　Blood shall drip from wood,
　　and the stone shall utter its voice;
　the peoples shall be troubled,
　　and the stars shall fall.[d]

[6]And one shall reign whom those who inhabit the earth do not expect, and the birds shall fly away together; [7]and the Dead Sea[e] shall cast up fish; and one whom the many do not know shall make his voice heard by night, and all shall hear his voice.[f] [8]There shall be chaos also in many places, fire shall often break out, the wild animals shall roam beyond their haunts, and menstruous women shall bring forth monsters. [9]Salt waters shall be found in the

---

a Lat *in it*　　*b* Syr Ethiop: Meaning of Lat uncertain
c Literally *after the third*; Ethiop *after three months*; Arm *after the third vision*; Georg *after the third day*　　*d* Ethiop Compare Syr and Arab: Meaning of Lat uncertain　　*e* Lat *Sea of Sodom*
f Cn: Lat *fish; and it shall make its voice heard by night, which the many have not known, but all shall hear its voice.*

Lord. As often, the angel is addressed as if he were God. **4.40** The simile of the *pregnant woman* also occurs elsewhere; cf. 5.46, 48. **4.41** *In Hades the chambers*, better "the underworld and its treasuries." **4.42** *Committed*. Cf. 1 Tim 6.20; 2 Tim 1.12, 14; Ps.-Philo, *Biblical Antiquities* 3.10. Souls are something entrusted to humans. On the impending eschaton compared to a woman in labor, see note on 16.38. **4.44–52** A double parable seen as a vision; cf. vv. 13–18; 7.3–9; Jer 1.11–14. **4.51** *Who will be alive*, better "what will take place." The two questions derive from v. 26. **4.52** *Signs*, those terrible events that will take place before the end; cf. 5.1, 13. *In part*. The description continues in 6.11–28.

5.1–13 Prediction of the woes that will precede the eschaton, i.e., the end of this world/age. The passage has poetic form and traditional content. **5.1** *Lo, the days* gives a prophetic flavor; cf. 6.18; 7.26; Isa 39.6. *Way*, better "portion" or "lot." **5.2** Evil is to peak before the Messiah comes; cf. Mt 24.12. **5.3** The destruction of Rome. **5.4** *Period*. This word is quite uncertain. The confusion of the natural order is part of the eschatological woes. **5.5** *Blood . . . wood*. Cf. *Letter of Barnabas* 12.1. **5.6** *One shall reign*, not a specific ruler, but the expected wicked future king; cf. *2 Apocalypse of Baruch* 40.1. **5.8** *Chaos*, better "chasms"; cf. Zech 14.4; *Sibylline Oracles* 3.341. **5.9** *Friends . . . conquer one another*. Conflict between friends or relatives is part of the messianic woes; cf. Isa

sweet, and all friends shall conquer one another; then shall reason hide itself, and wisdom shall withdraw into its chamber, [10]and it shall be sought by many but shall not be found, and unrighteousness and unrestraint shall increase on earth. [11]One country shall ask its neighbor, 'Has righteousness, or anyone who does right, passed through you?' And it will answer, 'No.' [12]At that time people shall hope but not obtain; they shall labor, but their ways shall not prosper. [13]These are the signs that I am permitted to tell you, and if you pray again, and weep as you do now, and fast for seven days, you shall hear yet greater things than these."

Conclusion of the Vision

14 Then I woke up, and my body shuddered violently, and my soul was so troubled that it fainted. [15]But the angel who had come and talked with me held me and strengthened me and set me on my feet.

16 Now on the second night Phaltiel, a chief of the people, came to me and said, "Where have you been? And why is your face sad? [17]Or do you not know that Israel has been entrusted to you in the land of their exile? [18]Rise therefore and eat some bread, and do not forsake us, like a shepherd who leaves the flock in the power of savage wolves."

19 Then I said to him, "Go away from me and do not come near me for seven days; then you may come to me."

He heard what I said and left me. [20]So I fasted seven days, mourning and weeping, as the angel Uriel had commanded me.

Ezra's Second Prayer of Complaint

21 After seven days the thoughts of my heart were very grievous to me again. [22]Then my soul recovered the spirit of understanding, and I began once more to speak words in the presence of the Most High. [23]I said, "O sovereign Lord, from every forest of the earth and from all its trees you have chosen one vine, [24]and from all the lands of the world you have chosen for yourself one region,[a] and from all the flowers of the world you have chosen for yourself one lily, [25]and from all the depths of the sea you have filled for yourself one river, and from all the cities that have been built you have consecrated Zion for yourself, [26]and from all the birds that have been created you have named for yourself one dove, and from all the flocks that have been made you have provided for yourself one sheep, [27]and from all the multitude of peoples you have gotten for yourself one people; and to this people, whom you have loved, you have given the law that is approved by all. [28]And now, O Lord, why have you handed the one over to the many, and dishonored[b] the one root beyond the others, and scattered your only one among the many? [29]And those who opposed your promises have trampled on those who believed your covenants. [30]If you really hate your people, they should be punished at your own hands."

Response to Ezra's Complaints

31 When I had spoken these words, the angel who had come to me on a previous night was sent to me. [32]He said to me, "Listen to me, and I will instruct you; pay attention to me, and I will tell you more."

33 Then I said, "Speak, my lord." And he said to me, "Are you greatly disturbed in mind

<hr/>

a Ethiop: Lat *pit* *b* Syr Ethiop Arab: Lat *prepared*

19.2; Mt 24.7; Mk 13.8; *1 Enoch* 56.7. On wisdom's withdrawal, cf. *1 Enoch* 42. **5.13** End of the vision. *Fasts* or limited food precede the second, third, fourth, and fifth visions. **5.14–15** Conclusion of the vision. **5.14** *Woke up* describes Ezra's leaving the trance; he is frightened and faints; cf. Zech 4.1; Dan 7.15. The angel functions similarly in Dan 8.18; 10.10–11. **5.16–22** Narrative transition to the second vision. The only similar narrative is 12.40–50. Vv. 20–22 resemble the other transitions; see 3.1–3. **5.16** *Phaltiel*, no known person; for the name, cf. Num 34.26; 2 Sam 3.15. **5.18** *Shepherds*, an image often used for the leaders of the people; see Acts 20.29; *1 Enoch* 89. **5.19** Add at the end of the verse "and I will tell you the matter." **5.22** *Recovered*, better "received." This is the onset of the seer's inspiration.

5.23–6.34 Second vision. **5.23–30** Ezra's address functions just like 3.4–36 in the first vision. Vv. 23–27 have a common rhetorical structure, *from all . . . you have chosen,* highlighting the election of Israel. **5.23** Cf. *Apocalypse of Sedrach* 8.2. Israel is a *vine;* see 9.21; Isa 5.7; Jer 2.21. **5.24** *From all the lands . . . one region,* the election of the land; see, e.g., Gen 12.1; *2 Apocalypse of Baruch* 40.2. *Lily.* See Hos 14.6; Song 2.1–2. **5.25** *River,* the Jordan. *Zion,* the site of the temple, is *consecrated* as a sacred place where sacrifices are offered. **5.26** *From all the birds . . . one dove,* based on an allegorical interpretation of Song 2.14; 5.2. *Sheep* and *flocks* evoke Israel's nomadic origins. **5.28** These questions focus the address on the problems arising from Israel's election and fate. **5.29** *Promises,* better "Torah." **5.30** Punishment should come from God, an old idea; see 2 Sam 24.14; Sir 2.18. **5.31–40** Dispute. **5.32** Similar invocations are

over Israel? Or do you love him more than his Maker does?"

34 I said, "No, my lord, but because of my grief I have spoken; for every hour I suffer agonies of heart, while I strive to understand the way of the Most High and to search out some part of his judgment."

35 He said to me, "You cannot." And I said, "Why not, my lord? Why then was I born? Or why did not my mother's womb become my grave, so that I would not see the travail of Jacob and the exhaustion of the people of Israel?"

36 He said to me, "Count up for me those who have not yet come, and gather for me the scattered raindrops, and make the withered flowers bloom again for me; 37 open for me the closed chambers, and bring out for me the winds shut up in them, or show me the picture of a voice; and then I will explain to you the travail that you ask to understand." [a]

38 I said, "O sovereign Lord, who is able to know these things except him whose dwelling is not with mortals? 39 As for me, I am without wisdom, and how can I speak concerning the things that you have asked me?"

40 He said to me, "Just as you cannot do one of the things that were mentioned, so you cannot discover my judgment, or the goal of the love that I have promised to my people."

Why Successive Generations Have Been Created

41 I said, "Yet, O Lord, you have charge of those who are alive at the end, but what will those do who lived before me, or we, ourselves, or those who come after us?"

42 He said to me, "I shall liken my judgment to a circle;[b] just as for those who are last there is no slowness, so for those who are first there is no haste."

43 Then I answered and said, "Could you not have created at one time those who have

been and those who are and those who will be, so that you might show your judgment the sooner?"

44 He replied to me and said, "The creation cannot move faster than the Creator, nor can the world hold at one time those who have been created in it."

45 I said, "How have you said to your servant that you[c] will certainly give life at one time to your creation? If therefore all creatures will live at one time[d] and the creation will sustain them, it might even now be able to support all of them present at one time."

46 He said to me, "Ask a woman's womb, and say to it, 'If you bear ten[e] children, why one after another?' Request it therefore to produce ten at one time."

47 I said, "Of course it cannot, but only each in its own time."

48 He said to me, "Even so I have given the womb of the earth to those who from time to time are sown in it. 49 For as an infant does not bring forth, and a woman who has become old does not bring forth any longer, so I have made the same rule for the world that I created."

When and How Will the End Come?

50 Then I inquired and said, "Since you have now given me the opportunity, let me speak before you. Is our mother, of whom you have told me, still young? Or is she now approaching old age?"

51 He replied to me, "Ask a woman who bears children, and she will tell you. 52 Say to her, 'Why are those whom you have borne recently not like those whom you bore before, but smaller in stature?' 53 And she herself will answer you, 'Those born in the strength of youth are different from those born during

---

a Lat see   b Or crown   c Syr Ethiop Arab 1: Meaning of Lat uncertain   d Lat lacks If . . . one time   e Syr Ethiop Arab 2 Arm: Meaning of Lat uncertain

---

found in Job 33.1; Prov 4.1. Cf. 2 Esd 7.49. **5.33** Cf. 4.34; 5.47. Ezra can no more exceed God's love than he can know God's way. **5.34** Ezra's mourning for Israel. **5.35** This sentiment is found elsewhere; cf. 1 Macc 2.7; 2 Apocalypse of Baruch 3.1–2; 10.6–7. **5.36–37** These seven riddles (see note on 5.37) complement those in 4.5–8 and are drawn from the same list. Cf. Sir 1.2; 2 Enoch 47.5. **5.37** Winds could also be translated "spirits." The better texts also have "or show me the appearance of him whom you have never seen" following shut up in them. **5.38** Cf. 4.6, 13–19, 21. **5.41–6.10** Predic-

tive dialogue concerning the last things. **5.41** Have charge of, perhaps "promise." **5.42** Circle, perhaps better crown (see text note b). The circularity of the crown implies identity of beginning and end. **5.44** The creation . . . Creator. Cf. 4.26–27, 34. The end cannot be forced. **5.45** Give life . . . to your creation. The resurrection is implied. **5.48** The earth is both mother and womb; cf. 10.9–14. **5.50** The senescence of the earth and consequent breakdown of order; cf. v. 55; 14.10. This implies an overall scheme of history. **5.52–55** Degeneration of offspring corresponds to degeneration of

the time of old age, when the womb is failing.' [54]Therefore you also should consider that you and your contemporaries are smaller in stature than those who were before you, [55]and those who come after you will be smaller than you, as born of a creation that already is aging and passing the strength of youth."

56 I said, "I implore you, O Lord, if I have found favor in your sight, show your servant through whom you will visit your creation."

6 He said to me, "At the beginning of the circle of the earth, before[a] the portals of the world were in place, and before the assembled winds blew, [2]and before the rumblings of thunder sounded, and before the flashes of lightning shone, and before the foundations of paradise were laid, [3]and before the beautiful flowers were seen, and before the powers of movements[b] were established, and before the innumerable hosts of angels were gathered together, [4]and before the heights of the air were lifted up, and before the measures of the firmaments were named, and before the footstool of Zion was established, [5]and before the present years were reckoned and before the imaginations of those who now sin were estranged, and before those who stored up treasures of faith were sealed— [6]then I planned these things, and they were made through me alone and not through another; just as the end shall come through me alone and not through another."

The Dividing of the Times

7 I answered and said, "What will be the dividing of the times? Or when will be the end of the first age and the beginning of the age that follows?"

8 He said to me, "From Abraham to Isaac,[c] because from him were born Jacob and Esau, for Jacob's hand held Esau's heel from the be-

ginning. [9]Now Esau is the end of this age, and Jacob is the beginning of the age that follows. [10]The beginning of a person is the hand, and the end of a person is the heel;[d] seek for nothing else, Ezra, between the heel and the hand, Ezra!"

More Signs of the End

11 I answered and said, "O sovereign Lord, if I have found favor in your sight, [12]show your servant the last of your signs of which you showed me a part on a previous night."

13 He answered and said to me, "Rise to your feet and you will hear a full, resounding voice. [14]And if the place where you are standing is greatly shaken [15]while the voice is speaking, do not be terrified; because the word concerns the end, and the foundations of the earth will understand [16]that the speech concerns them. They will tremble and be shaken, for they know that their end must be changed."

17 When I heard this, I got to my feet and listened; a voice was speaking, and its sound was like the sound of mighty[e] waters. [18]It said, "The days are coming when I draw near to visit the inhabitants of the earth, [19]and when I require from the doers of iniquity the penalty of their iniquity, and when the humiliation of Zion is complete. [20]When the seal is placed upon the age that is about to pass away, then I will show these signs: the books shall be opened before the face of the firmament, and all shall see my judgment[f] together. [21]Children a year old shall speak with their voices, and pregnant women

---

a Meaning of Lat uncertain: Compare Syr *The beginning by the hand of humankind, but the end by my own hands. For as before the land of the world existed there, and before;* Ethiop: *At first by the Son of Man, and afterwards I myself. For before the earth and the lands were created, and before* *b* Or *earthquakes* *c* Other ancient authorities read *to Abraham* *d* Syr: Meaning of Lat uncertain *e* Lat *many* *f* Syr: Lat lacks *my judgment*

---

the generations. **6.1** After *he said to me* should be added "The beginning is through a human being and the end is through myself." Instead of *at the beginning of,* read "for before." **6.2** Paradise was created before the world; cf. 3.6. **6.3** *Powers of movements,* probably angels; cf. Mt 24.29. **6.4** *Zion* is God's footstool; cf. Pss 99.5; 132.7. **6.5** Predetermination is stressed. **6.6** *Just as ... another should* be omitted; it is in the Latin but not in any of the other versions. God alone planned and created. **6.8–10** The answer to the double question of v. 7. *From Abraham to Isaac.* Read *From Abraham to Abraham* (text note *c*); i.e., there is no division of the times, yet the second *Abraham* denotes Esau and Jacob, who fol-

lowed one another immediately. So Rome (Esau) will be followed by Israel's kingdom. **6.11–29** A prediction of signs resembling 5.1–13 in form and continuing it. **6.13** *Rise to your feet,* for divine pronouncement. *A full, resounding voice.* Cf. the sound with Ezek 1.24; Dan 10.6. **6.14–16** The earth shakes when God appears (1 Kings 19.11–12; Joel 3.16); a cosmic change will happen. **6.18** God is speaking. *Visit,* punish; see 5.56. **6.19–20** *When* these measures are filled, *then* omens will be revealed. *Books,* of human deeds; see Dan 7.10; Rev 20.12; *2 Apocalypse of Baruch* 24.1. **6.21** The omen is a dramatic shortening of the normal life pattern. Cf. Gen 3.6; *Jubilees* 23.25. **6.22** The natural order is dis-

shall give birth to premature children at three and four months, and these shall live and leap about. 22 Sown places shall suddenly appear unsown, and full storehouses shall suddenly be found to be empty; 23 the trumpet shall sound aloud, and when all hear it, they shall suddenly be terrified. 24 At that time friends shall make war on friends like enemies, the earth and those who inhabit it shall be terrified, and the springs of the fountains shall stand still, so that for three hours they shall not flow.

25 "It shall be that whoever remains after all that I have foretold to you shall be saved and shall see my salvation and the end of my world. 26 And they shall see those who were taken up, who from their birth have not tasted death; and the heart of the earth's*a* inhabitants shall be changed and converted to a different spirit. 27 For evil shall be blotted out, and deceit shall be quenched; 28 faithfulness shall flourish, and corruption shall be overcome, and the truth, which has been so long without fruit, shall be revealed."

Conclusion of the Second Vision

29 While he spoke to me, little by little the place where I was standing began to rock to and fro.*b* 30 And he said to me, "I have come to show you these things this night.*c* 31 If therefore you will pray again and fast again for seven days, I will again declare to you greater things than these,*d* 32 because your voice has surely been heard by the Most High; for the Mighty One has seen your uprightness and has also observed the purity that you have maintained from your youth. 33 Therefore he sent me to show you all these things, and to say to you: 'Believe and do not be afraid! 34 Do not be quick to think vain thoughts concerning the former times; then you will not act hastily in the last times.'"

The Third Vision

35 Now after this I wept again and fasted seven days in the same way as before, in order to complete the three weeks that had been prescribed for me. 36 Then on the eighth night my heart was troubled within me again, and I began to speak in the presence of the Most High. 37 My spirit was greatly aroused, and my soul was in distress.

God's Work in Creation

38 I said, "O Lord, you spoke at the beginning of creation, and said on the first day, 'Let heaven and earth be made,' and your word accomplished the work. 39 Then the spirit was blowing, and darkness and silence embraced everything; the sound of human voices was not yet there.*e* 40 Then you commanded a ray of light to be brought out from your storechambers, so that your works could be seen.

41 "Again, on the second day, you created the spirit of the firmament, and commanded it to divide and separate the waters, so that one part might move upward and the other part remain beneath.

42 "On the third day you commanded the waters to be gathered together in a seventh part of the earth; six parts you dried up and kept so that some of them might be planted and cultivated and be of service before you. 43 For your word went forth, and at once the work was done. 44 Immediately fruit came forth in endless abundance and of varied appeal to the taste, and flowers of inimitable color, and odors of inexpressible fragrance. These were made on the third day.

---

a Syr Compare Ethiop Arab 1 Arm: Lat lacks *earth's*   *b* Syr Ethiop Compare Arab Arm: Meaning of Lat uncertain   *c* Syr Compare Ethiop: Meaning of Lat uncertain   *d* Syr Ethiop Arab 1 Arm: Lat adds *by day*   *e* Syr Ethiop: Lat *was not yet from you*

---

rupted. **6.24** *Friends . . . like enemies,* social disorder; cf. note on 5.9; *1 Enoch* 100.1. **6.25** The first prophecy of redemption. *See my salvation.* Cf. 7.27; 9.8; 13.48, 50; Ps 91.16; Dead Sea Scrolls *Damascus Document* (CD) 20.34. **6.26** *Who . . . have not tasted death.* Perhaps including Enoch (Gen 5.24) and Elijah (2 Kings 2.9–12). *Heart . . . shall be changed.* See Ezek 11.19; 36.26. **6.27– 28** An eschatological poem; cf. 7.33–35, 113–14; 14.18. *Corruption* designates this-worldly things. **6.29** The fulfillment of vv. 13–16. **6.30–34** Conclusion including injunctions (cf. 5.13) and statement of Ezra's worthiness (cf. 12.36; 14.45–46). **6.30** *This night,* better "on the night that has passed." **6.34** Oracular statements mark shifts in the revelatory dynamic. See 4.34.

6.35–9.25 Third vision. **6.35–37** Introduction. Cf. 3.1–3; 5.21–22. This vision is extremely long. **6.35** *Three weeks* of fasting, apparently taken from Dan 10.2–3. The first week is not mentioned before the first vision. **6.37** Ezra receives inspiration. **6.38–59** Address. Cf. 3.4– 36; 5.23–30. A narrative of creation, followed by inferences from it. **6.38** Cf. Gen 1.1; *Jubilees* 2.2. Creation through speech; see 3.4. **6.39** Cf. Gen 1.2. Primordial silence; see 7.30; Ps.-Philo, *Biblical Antiquities* 60.2. Speech is an essential attribute characterizing the creation of humans. **6.40** Cf. Gen 1.3; *Jubilees* 2.2. **6.41** Spirits of natural phenomena; see also *Jubilees* 2.2; *1 Enoch* 60.15. **6.42** Cf. Gen 1.9–10; *Jubilees* 2.5–6; a sevenfold division of the world is unknown elsewhere. **6.44** Note the *fra-*

45 "On the fourth day you commanded the brightness of the sun, the light of the moon, and the arrangement of the stars to come into being; and you commanded them to serve humankind, about to be formed.

46 the fifth day you commanded the [fourth] part, where the water had been gathered together, to bring forth living creatures, and fishes; and so it was done. 48The [dumb] and lifeless water produced living creatures, as it was commanded, so that therefore the nations might declare your wondrous works.

49 "Then you kept in existence two living creatures;[a] the one you called Behemoth[b] and the name of the other Leviathan. 50And you separated one from the other, for the seventh part where the water had been gathered together could not hold them both. 51And you gave Behemoth[b] one of the parts that had been dried up on the third day, to live in it, where there are a thousand mountains; 52but to Leviathan you gave the seventh part, the watery part; and you have kept them to be eaten by whom you wish, and when you wish.

53 "On the sixth day you commanded the earth to bring forth before you cattle, wild animals, and creeping things; 54and over these you placed Adam, as ruler over all the works that you had made; and from him we have all come, the people whom you have chosen.

Why Do God's People Suffer?

55 "All this I have spoken before you, O Lord, because you have said that it was for us that you created this world.[c] 56As for the other nations that have descended from Adam, you have said that they are nothing, and that they are like spittle, and you have compared their abundance to a drop from a bucket. 57And now, O Lord, these nations, which are reputed

to be as nothing, domineer over us and devour us. 58But we your people, whom you have called your firstborn, only begotten, zealous for you,[d] and most dear, have been given into their hands. 59If the world has indeed been created for us, why do we not possess our world as an inheritance? How long will this be so?"

Response to Ezra's Questions

7 When I had finished speaking these words, the angel who had been sent to me on the former nights was sent to me again. 2He said to me, "Rise, Ezra, and listen to the words that I have come to speak to you."

3 I said, "Speak, my lord." And he said to me, "There is a sea set in a wide expanse so that it is deep and vast, 4but it has an entrance set in a narrow place, so that it is like a river. 5If there are those who wish to reach the sea, to look at it or to navigate it, how can they come to the broad part unless they pass through the narrow part? 6Another example: There is a city built and set on a plain, and it is full of all good things; 7but the entrance to it is narrow and set in a precipitous place, so that there is fire on the right hand and deep water on the left. 8There is only one path lying between them, that is, between the fire and the water, so that only one person can walk on the path. 9If now the city is given to someone as an inheritance, how will the heir receive the inheritance unless by passing through the appointed danger?"

10 I said, "That is right, lord." He said to me, "So also is Israel's portion. 11For I made the world for their sake, and when Adam transgressed my statutes, what had been made was

---

a Syr Ethiop: Lat *two souls*   b Other Lat authorities read *Enoch*
c Syr Ethiop Arab 2: Lat *the firstborn world* Compare Arab 1 *first world*   d Meaning of Lat uncertain

---

grances; cf. *1 Enoch* 24.3–4; *2 Enoch* 8.3. **6.45** Cf. Gen 1.14–19; *Jubilees* 2.8–10. **6.47** Cf. Gen 1.20; *Jubilees* 2.11. **6.49–52** *Behemoth, Leviathan.* Cf. Job 40.15–41.11. These legendary animals developed from mythological origins. They will be the food at the eschatological banquet for the righteous, according to Jewish tradition; see *2 Apocalypse of Baruch* 29.4; *1 Enoch* 60.7–10. **6.55** The world was created for Israel's sake; see v. 59; 7.11; *Testament of Moses* 1.12; *Sifre Deuteronomy* 11.21; *Genesis Rabbah* 12.2. **6.56** Based on Isa 40.15, 17. **6.57** See 3.28; 5.28–29. **6.58** *Firstborn.* Cf. Ex 4.22; Jer 31.9; Sir 36.17. **6.59** *How long.* Cf. Pss 4.2; 13.2; *2 Apocalypse of Baruch* 81.3. **7.1–25** Ezra and

the angel begin a dialogic dispute. **7.1** Parallel to 4.1; 5.31. **7.2** *Rise.* On standing for solemn events, cf. 4.47; 6.13. **7.3–5** The origins of this parable are unclear. **7.5** *Navigate,* an emendation of "rule over." **7.6–9** A second similar parable follows, as in Mk 4.26–33. The plenteous *city* evokes Jerusalem with the righteous. Similar images occur in Shepherd of Hermas, *Similitudes* 9.12.5; *Testament of Job* 18.6. *Good things,* eschatological reward. **7.7** *Entrance,* possibly "way." The way, with dangers on both sides, occurs in Ps 66.12 (Septuagint, Vulgate); Sir 15.11, 15–17; *Avot de Rabbi Nathan* A 28. **7.9** Israel is to inherit the world; cf. 6.59. **7.11** See note on 6.55. This view of the result of

judged. 12And so the entrances of this world were made narrow and sorrowful and toilsome; they are few and evil, full of dangers and involved in great hardships. 13But the entrances of the greater world are broad and safe, and yield the fruit of immortality. 14Therefore unless the living pass through the difficult and futile experiences, they can never receive those things that have been reserved for them. 15Now therefore why are you disturbed, seeing that you are to perish? Why are you moved, seeing that you are mortal? 16Why have you not considered in your mind what is to come, rather than what is now present?"

The Fate of the Ungodly

17 Then I answered and said, "O sovereign Lord, you have ordained in your law that the righteous shall inherit these things, but that the ungodly shall perish. 18The righteous, therefore, can endure difficult circumstances while hoping for easier ones; but those who have done wickedly have suffered the difficult circumstances and will never see the easier ones."

19 He said to me, "You are not a better judge than the Lord,ᵃ or wiser than the Most High! 20Let many perish who are now living, rather than that the law of God that is set before them be disregarded! 21For the Lordᵇ strictly commanded those who came into the world, when they came, what they should do to live, and what they should observe to avoid punishment. 22Nevertheless they were not obedient, and spoke against him;

they devised for themselves vain thoughts,

23 and proposed to themselves wicked frauds;
they even declared that the Most High does not exist,
and they ignored his ways.
24 They scorned his law,
and denied his covenants;
they have been unfaithful to his statutes,
and have not performed his works.
25That is the reason, Ezra, that empty things are for the empty, and full things are for the full.

The Temporary Messianic Kingdom

26 "For indeed the time will come, when the signs that I have foretold to you will come to pass, that the city that now is not seen shall appear,ᶜ and the land that now is hidden shall be disclosed. 27Everyone who has been delivered from the evils that I have foretold shall see my wonders. 28For my son the Messiahᵈ shall be revealed with those who are with him, and those who remain shall rejoice four hundred years. 29After those years my son the Messiah shall die, and all who draw human breath.ᵉ 30Then the world shall be turned back to primeval silence for seven days, as it was at the first beginnings, so that no one shall be left. 31After seven days the world that is not yet awake shall be roused, and that which is corruptible shall perish. 32The earth shall give up

---

a Other ancient authorities read *God*; Ethiop Georg *the only One*
b Other ancient authorities read *God* *c* Arm: Lat Syr *that the bride shall appear, even the city appearing* *d* Syr Arab 1: Ethiop *my Messiah*; Arab 2 *the Messiah*; Arm *the Messiah of God*; Lat *my son Jesus* *e* Arm *all who have continued in faith and in patience*

Adam's sin is to be found in contemporary Judaism. **7.12–13** Note the contrast *this world*/age and the *greater* (or "coming") *world*/age, common terms in NT and rabbinic sources. The fruit gives immortality; cf. Gen 3.6, 22. **7.14** Difficulties precede reward. **7.15–16** Rebuke questions, implying an assertion of Ezra's future immortality. **7.17** *Sovereign Lord.* The angel is frequently addressed as God. The reference may be to Deut 8.1 or Ps 37.9. **7.18** Cf. vv. *117–18.* **7.19** Similar rebukes occur in 4.34; 5.33. **7.20** Alternately "let many perish . . . who disregarded the law of God." *Perish* implies eternal death. **7.21** *Commanded.* See Deut 30.15–18; cf. Sir 15.17. **7.23–24** The wicked are charged with overall unfaithfulness (also vv. 79, 81) and denying God's existence (also v. 37; 8.55–58; 9.10). Cf. Ps 14.1. **7.25** Oracular transitional statement; cf. note on 6.34. **7.26–44** The course of eschatological events is expounded. **7.26** *Indeed,* or "behold." The unseen *city* is heavenly Jerusalem; see the fourth vision (10.27–59).

For a new or heavenly Jerusalem, cf. the Dead Sea Scrolls *New Jerusalem* (2Q4; 4Q554–55; 5Q15; 11Q18); Tob 13.8–17; Rev 21.9–22.7. *Land,* the land of Israel; it is *hidden* since it was precreated. Cf. 6.14–16. **7.27** Those who survive the woes preceding the Messiah's advent shall see the wonders; cf. 6.25; 9.8. *Wonders* are eschatological events. **7.28** *My son the Messiah,* better "my Messiah." A kingdom with God or the Messiah living among its citizens is envisaged in *Psalms of Solomon* 17.32–36; *1 Enoch* 105.2. Its duration is limited; see 12.34. The Messiah's assumed companions are also mentioned in 13.52; 14.9; cf. 1 Thess 3.13. **7.29** *Son,* better "servant." That *the Messiah shall die* is not explicit elsewhere, but see *2 Apocalypse of Baruch* 30.1; cf. 1 Cor 15.28. **7.30** The world reverts to the primordial state. *Silence.* See 6.39. *Seven days* corresponds to the seven days of creation. **7.31** *After seven days . . . roused.* Cf. Ps.-Philo, *Biblical Antiquities* 3.10. **7.32** Omit the words *in silence.* For *chambers,* see

those who are asleep in it, and the dust those who rest there in silence; and the chambers shall give up the souls that have been committed to them. [33] The Most High shall be revealed on the seat of judgment, and compassion shall pass away, and patience shall be withdrawn. [a] [34] Only judgment shall remain, truth shall stand, and faithfulness shall grow strong. [35] Recompense shall follow, and the reward shall be manifested; righteous deeds shall awake, and unrighteous deeds shall not sleep. [b] [36] The pit [c] of torment shall appear, and opposite it shall be the place of rest; and the furnace of hell [d] shall be disclosed, and opposite it the paradise of delight. [37] Then the Most High will say to the nations that have been raised from the dead, 'Look now, and understand whom you have denied, whom you have not served, whose commandments you have despised. [38] Look on this side and on that; here are delight and rest, and there are fire and torments.' Thus he will [e] speak to them on the day of judgment— [39] a day that has no sun or moon or stars, [40] or cloud or thunder or lightning, or wind or water or air, or darkness or evening or morning, [41] or summer or spring or heat or winter [f] or frost or cold, or hail or rain or dew, [42] or noon or night, or dawn or shining or brightness or light, but only the splendor of the glory of the Most High, by which all shall see what has been destined. [43] It will last as though for a week of years. [44] This is my judgment and its prescribed order; and to you alone I have shown these things."

Only a Few Will Be Saved

[45] I answered and said, "O sovereign Lord, I said then and [g] I say now: Blessed are those who are alive and keep your commandments! [46] But what of those for whom I prayed? For who among the living is there that has not sinned, or who is there among mortals that has not transgressed your covenant? [47] And now I see that the world to come will bring delight to few, but torments to many. [48] For an evil heart has grown up in us, which has alienated us from God, [h] and has brought us into corruption and the ways of death, and has shown us the paths of perdition and removed us far from life—and that not merely for a few but for almost all who have been created."

[49] He answered me and said, "Listen to me, Ezra, [i] and I will instruct you, and will admonish you once more. [50] For this reason the Most High has made not one world but two. [51] Inasmuch as you have said that the righteous are not many but few, while the ungodly abound, hear the explanation for this.

[52] "If you have just a few precious stones, will you add to them lead and clay?" [j] [53] I said, "Lord, how could that be?" [54] And he said to me, "Not only that, but ask the earth and she will tell you; defer to her, and she will declare it to you. [55] Say to her, 'You produce gold and silver and bronze, and also iron and lead and clay; [56] but silver is more abundant than gold, and bronze than silver, and iron than bronze, and lead than iron, and clay than lead.' [57] Judge therefore which

---

a Lat *shall gather together*   b The passage from verse 36 to verse 105, formerly missing, has been restored to the text   c Syr Ethiop: Lat *place*   d Lat Syr Ethiop *Gehenna*   e Syr Ethiop Arab 1: Lat *you shall*   f Or *storm*   g Syr: Lat *And I answered*, "I said then, O Lord, and   h Cn: Lat Syr Ethiop *from these*   i Syr Arab 1 Georg: Lat Ethiop lack *Ezra*   j Arab 1: Meaning of Lat Syr Ethiop uncertain

---

note on 4.35. The reunion of soul and body in resurrection is described. For a connection between *chambers* and resurrection, see *1 Clement* 50.4. **7.33** God alone judges humans; for the *seat of judgment*, see Dan 7.9. The withdrawal of *compassion* in judgment comes from the full revelation of truth; see v. 104. **7.35** *Recompense* follows judgment. **7.36** *Torment*, a common term for eschatological punishment (vv. 38, 47, 67); *rest* (vv. 38, 75, 95), *delight* (the translation of Hebrew *Eden*), common terms for reward. **7.37** Despite the term *nations*, the contrast between the righteous and wicked dominates. *Midrash on Proverbs* 16.11 preserves a similar address. **7.39–42** Abolition of the divisions of times and seasons. The list derives from Gen 8.22; cf. Zech 14.6–7; *Sibylline Oracles* 3.88–92. **7.42** *Or noon . . . the Most High*, the development and eschatologization of Isa

60.19–20. *Glory* is connected with God's appearance on earth; see 3.19; 7.60, 112, 122. **7.43** *Week of years*, a seven-year period, used in apocalyptic reckonings; see Dan 9.24, 26. **7.45–74** Ezra's questions urge his point of view against the angel's. **7.45** *Blessed are . . . commandments*, a biblical commonplace; cf. Pss 1.1; 119.1; Lk 11.28; Rev 22.7. **7.46** The statement that all have sinned is ancient and widespread, e.g., 1 Kings 8.46; Prov 20.9. The book often takes extreme positions at the start of an argument. **7.47** In *the world to come* the righteous will be few; see 8.1–3. This issue of the few and the many pervades the rest of the third vision. **7.48** See 3.2–22. *Life*, eternal life. As in v. 47, sin is not quite universal. **7.51** *The ungodly abound*. The angel corrects Ezra's words in vv. 46–47. **7.52–57** A parable of precious and base metals. A similar image is the droplets and the wave (9.14–16).

things are precious and desirable, those that are abundant or those that are rare?"

58 I said, "O sovereign Lord, what is plentiful is of less worth, for what is more rare is more precious."

59 He answered me and said, "Consider within yourself[a] what you have thought, for the person who has what is hard to get rejoices more than the person who has what is plentiful. 60 So also will be the judgment[b] that I have promised; for I will rejoice over the few who shall be saved, because it is they who have made my glory to prevail now, and through them my name has now been honored. 61 I will not grieve over the great number of those who perish; for it is they who are now like a mist, and are similar to a flame and smoke—they are set on fire and burn hotly, and are extinguished."

Lamentation of Ezra, with Response

62 I replied and said, "O earth, what have you brought forth, if the mind is made out of the dust like the other created things? 63 For it would have been better if the dust itself had not been born, so that the mind might not have been made from it. 64 But now the mind grows with us, and therefore we are tormented, because we perish and we know it. 65 Let the human race lament, but let the wild animals of the field be glad; let all who have been born lament, but let the cattle and the flocks rejoice. 66 It is much better with them than with us; for they do not look for a judgment, and they do not know of any torment or salvation promised to them after death. 67 What does it profit us that we shall be preserved alive but cruelly tormented? 68 For all who have been born are entangled in[c] iniquities, and are full of sins and burdened with

transgressions. 69 And if after death we were not to come into judgment, perhaps it would have been better for us."

70 He answered me and said, "When the Most High made the world and Adam and all who have come from him, he first prepared the judgment and the things that pertain to the judgment. 71 But now, understand from your own words—for you have said that the mind grows with us. 72For this reason, therefore, those who live on earth shall be tormented, because though they had understanding, they committed iniquity; and though they received the commandments, they did not keep them; and though they obtained the law, they dealt unfaithfully with what they received. 73 What, then, will they have to say in the judgment, or how will they answer in the last times? 74 How long the Most High has been patient with those who inhabit the world!—and not for their sake, but because of the times that he has foreordained."

State of the Dead before Judgment

75 I answered and said, "If I have found favor in your sight, O Lord, show this also to your servant: whether after death, as soon as everyone of us yields up the soul, we shall be kept in rest until those times come when you will renew the creation, or whether we shall be tormented at once?"

76 He answered me and said, "I will show you that also, but do not include yourself with those who have shown scorn, or number yourself among those who are tormented. 77 For you have a treasure of works stored up with the Most High, but it will not be shown to you

---

a Syr Ethiop Arab 1: Meaning of Lat uncertain   *b* Syr Arab 1: Lat *creation*   *c* Syr *defiled with*

7.59 *What you have thought,* i.e., in the preceding verse. **7.60–61** The few and the many from the angel's perspective. *Name,* like *glory,* is a divine hypostasis; cf. *Apocalypse of Abraham* 29.17. *Mist, flame,* and *smoke* all convey impermanence in the Hebrew scriptures. **7.62** Apostrophe of the *earth;* see 4.40. This opens a lament over the mind comparable with 4.12–22. *Mind* seems to mean consciousness. **7.64** Punishment is related to mind; cf. v. 72; *2 Apocalypse of Baruch* 15.6; 55.2. **7.67** A special application of the idea of the survivors. **7.69** A recapitulation of v. 63, ending the lament with one of its opening themes. **7.70** *He first prepared the judgment.* A famous rabbinic dictum says paradise and Gehenna

were created before the world. **7.71** Ezra's words in v. 64 are quoted. **7.72** *Understanding, iniquity.* Cf. Rom 1.18–32. 2 Esdras uses terms like *commandments* and *covenants* (v. 83) for obligations placed on the Gentiles; cf. vv. 11, 21. **7.73** See Mt 25.37, 44. **7.74** The reasons for the delay of the end are discussed in 4.35–37. **7.75–99** A prediction of the postmortem state of the righteous and wicked unparalleled in ancient Jewish literature; it is set in corresponding sets of seven, the seventh being the greatest. **7.75** Will there be immediate recompense after death or only at the end of the age? **7.76** Ezra is repeatedly assured of his own righteousness; cf. 8.47–51, responding to 7.45–74. **7.77** *Treasure . . . stored up with the Most*

until the last times. 78 Now concerning death, the teaching is: When the decisive decree has gone out from the Most High that a person shall die, as the spirit leaves the body to return again to him who gave it, first of all it adores the glory of the Most High. 79 If it is one of those who have shown scorn and have not kept the way of the Most High, who have despised his law and hated those who fear God— 80 such spirits shall not enter into habitations, but shall immediately wander about in torments, always grieving and sad, in seven ways. 81 The first way, because they have scorned the law of the Most High. 82 The second way, because they cannot now make a good repentance so that they may live. 83 The third way, they shall see the reward laid up for those who have trusted the covenants of the Most High. 84 The fourth way, they shall consider the torment laid up for themselves in the last days. 85 The fifth way, they shall see how the habitations of the others are guarded by angels in profound quiet. 86 The sixth way, they shall see how some of them will cross over*a* into torments. 87 The seventh way, which is worse*b* than all the ways that have been mentioned, because they shall utterly waste away in confusion and be consumed with shame,*c* and shall wither with fear at seeing the glory of the Most High in whose presence they sinned while they were alive, and in whose presence they are to be judged in the last times.

88 "Now this is the order of those who have kept the ways of the Most High, when they shall be separated from their mortal body.*d* 89 During the time that they lived in it,*e* they laboriously served the Most High, and withstood danger every hour so that they might keep the law of the Lawgiver perfectly. 90 Therefore this is the teaching concerning

them: 91 First of all, they shall see with great joy the glory of him who receives them, for they shall have rest in seven orders. 92 The first order, because they have striven with great effort to overcome the evil thought that was formed with them, so that it might not lead them astray from life into death. 93 The second order, because they see the perplexity in which the souls of the ungodly wander and the punishment that awaits them. 94 The third order, they see the witness that he who formed them bears concerning them, that throughout their life they kept the law with which they were entrusted. 95 The fourth order, they understand the rest that they now enjoy, being gathered into their chambers and guarded by angels in profound quiet, and the glory waiting for them in the last days. 96 The fifth order, they rejoice that they have now escaped what is corruptible and shall inherit what is to come; and besides they see the straits and toil*e* from which they have been delivered, and the spacious liberty that they are to receive and enjoy in immortality. 97 The sixth order, when it is shown them how their face is to shine like the sun, and how they are to be made like the light of the stars, being incorruptible from then on. 98 The seventh order, which is greater than all that have been mentioned, because they shall rejoice with boldness, and shall be confident without confusion, and shall be glad without fear, for they press forward to see the face of him whom they served in life and from whom they are to receive their reward when glorified. 99 This is the order of the souls of the righteous, as henceforth is announced;*f* and the

---

a Cn: Meaning of Lat uncertain *b* Lat Syr Ethiop *greater* *c* Syr Ethiop: Meaning of Lat uncertain *d* Lat *the corruptible vessel* *e* Syr Ethiop: Lat *fullness* *f* Syr: Meaning of Lat uncertain

---

High. Cf. 8.32, 36. The same terminology is found in many Jewish sources; cf. Mt 6.20; Lk 12.33; Mt 19.21; Mk 10.21. **7.78** *Decree . . . death.* Cf. Sir 41.2–4. *The spirit . . . who gave it,* drawn from Eccl 12.7. **7.80** *Habitations,* better "chambers"; cf. 4.35. The righteous rest while the wicked *wander.* **7.82** After judgment starts there is no *repentance* (v. 33), an idea here applied to the intermediate state (cf. *1 Enoch* 63.5–9). **7.83** Part of punishment is seeing the reward of the righteous; cf. v. 93. **7.85** *Quiet.* Cf. *rest* in v. 95; such guardian *angels* are found in v. 95; *1 Enoch* 100.5. **7.87** Note the effect on the wicked souls of *seeing the glory* of God; cf. *Midrash on Psalms* 12.5. **7.88** *Mortal body,* better "mortal vessel"; cf. 4.11.

7.90–91 A later development of this passage is *Questions of Ezra* A 19. The wicked wander on *ways* (v. 80), but the righteous ascend through *orders.* **7.92** Righteousness is achieved *with great effort,* by struggle, the labor of v. 89. *Evil thought.* See note on 3.20–21. *Corruptible . . . immortality.* See 1 Cor 15.53–54. **7.93** The converse of v. 83, implying precreation of eschatological punishment. **7.94** *Witness . . . concerning them,* legal language. **7.95** *Chambers,* better "treasuries." **7.96** A reference predominantly to the eschatological state. **7.97** *Their face is to shine.* See v. 125. The righteous shine; see Dan 12.3; cf. Rev 1.16; 2 *Enoch* 1.5; 19.1. They resemble *stars;* see 4 Macc 17.5; 2 *Apocalypse of Baruch* 51.10.

previously mentioned are the ways of torment that those who would not give heed shall suffer hereafter."

100 Then I answered and said, "Will time therefore be given to the souls, after they have been separated from the bodies, to see what you have described to me?"

101 He said to me, "They shall have freedom for seven days, so that during these seven days they may see the things of which you have been told, and afterwards they shall be gathered in their habitations."

No Intercession for the Ungodly

102 I answered and said, "If I have found favor in your sight, show further to me, your servant, whether on the day of judgment the righteous will be able to intercede for the ungodly or to entreat the Most High for them— *103* fathers for sons or sons for parents, brothers for brothers, relatives for their kindred, or friends for those who are most dear."

104 He answered me and said, "Since you have found favor in my sight, I will show you this also. The day of judgment is decisive *a* and displays to all the seal of truth. Just as now a father does not send his son, or a son his father, or a master his servant, or a friend his dearest friend, to be ill *b* or sleep or eat or be healed in his place, *105* so no one shall ever pray for another on that day, neither shall anyone lay a burden on another; *c* for then all shall bear their own righteousness and unrighteousness."

36 106 I answered and said, "How then do we find that first Abraham prayed for the people of Sodom, and Moses for our ancestors who sinned in the desert, *37 107* and Joshua after him for Israel in the days of Achan, *38 108* and Samuel in the days of Saul, *d* and David for the plague, and Solomon for those at the dedication, *39 109* and Elijah for those who received the rain, and for the one who was dead, that he might live, *40 110* and Hezekiah for the people in the days of Sennacherib, and many others prayed for many? *41 111* ; and many, when corruption has increased and unrighteousness has multiplied, the righteous have prayed for the ungodly, why will it not be so now as well?"

42 112 He answered me and said, "The present world is not the end; the full glory does not *e* remain in it; *f* therefore those who were strong prayed for the weak. *43 113* But the day of judgment will be the end of this age and the beginning *g* of the immortal age to come, in which corruption has passed away, *44 114* sinful indulgence has come to an end, unbelief has been cut off, and righteousness has increased and truth has appeared. *45 115* Therefore no one will then be able to have mercy on someone who has been condemned in the judgment, or to harm *h* someone who is victorious."

Lamentation over the Fate of Most People

46 116 I answered and said, "This is my first and last comment: it would have been better if the earth had not produced Adam, or else, when it had produced him, had restrained him from sinning. *47 117* For what good is it to all that they live in sorrow now and expect punishment after death? *48 118* O Adam, what have you done? For though it was you who sinned, the fall was not yours alone, but ours also who are your descendants. *49 119* For what good is it to us, if an immortal time has been promised

---

a Lat *bold*　*b* Syr Ethiop Arm: Lat *to understand*　*c* Syr Ethiop: Lat lacks *on that . . . another*　*d* Syr Ethiop Arab 1: Lat Arab 2 Arm lack *in the days of Saul*　*e* Lat lacks *not*　*f* Or *the glory does not continuously abide in it*　*g* Syr Ethiop: Lat lacks *the beginning*　*h* Syr Ethiop: Lat *overwhelm*

7.98 *The face of him.* The climax is the vision of God's face; cf. Ex 33.20. **7.100–115** Dialogic prediction about intercession. **7.100** The reverse of v. 32. *Will time therefore be given?* means "How long will be given?" **7.102–3** Cf. Ps.-Philo, *Biblical Antiquities* 33.5. The question of intercession dominates. **7.104** *Seal of truth*, an expression strikingly paralleled in *Babylonian Talmud Shabbat* 55a; *Babylonian Talmud Yoma* 69b. **7.105** Individual responsibility. Cf. Deut 24.16; Jer 31.28–29; Ezek 18.20. **7.106** *Abraham*, Gen 18.23–33; *Moses*, Ex 32.11–14. On double verse numbering, see text note *b* at v. 35. **7.107** *Joshua*, Josh 7.6–9. **7.108** *Samuel*, 1 Sam 7.8–9; *David*, 2 Sam 24.17–25; *Solomon*, 1 Kings 8.22–53. **7.109** *Elijah*, for drought, 1 Kings 18.2–6, 36–46; for revival, 1 Kings 17.21–23. **7.110** *Hezekiah*, 2 Kings 19.15–19; Isa 37.16–20. **7.111** This is an argument *a fortiori*. **7.112** *This present world is not the end*, better "The end of this world has not yet come to pass." Since the world does not exhibit glory fully, intercession can be effective. **7.113–14** Cf. 6.27–28; 7.33–35. **7.116–8.3** A dispute composed of a lament (vv. *116–26*) and a midrash on the divine attributes (vv. *132–40*), punctuated by angelic responses. **7.116** A variant on the idea "Why was I born?"; cf. v. 62. The earth is here said to do what God does in ch. 3. **7.117** Pessimistic; cf. vv. *62, 67–68*; *2 Apocalypse of Baruch* 14.14. **7.118** Apostrophe to *Adam*, comparable to 3.20–22. *Fall*, better "misfortune." **7.119–25** Powerful

to us, but we have done deeds that bring death?
50 120 And what good is it that an everlasting
hope has been promised to us, but we have
51 121 Or that safe and health-
miserably have been reserved for us, but
ful had wickedly? 52 122 Or that the glory
we most High will defend those who have
of life, but we have walked in the most
ways? 53 123 Or that a paradise shall be
d, whose fruit remains unspoiled and in
are abundance and healing, but we shall
enter it 54 124 because we have lived in per-
se ways? 55 125 Or that the faces of those
who practiced self-control shall shine more
than the stars, but our faces shall be blacker
than darkness? 56 126 For while we lived and
committed iniquity we did not consider what
we should suffer after death."

57 127 He answered and said, "This is the
significance of the contest that all who are
born on earth shall wage: 58 128 if they are defeated they shall suffer what you have said, but
if they are victorious they shall receive what I
have said. 59 129 For this is the way of which
Moses, while he was alive, spoke to the people,
saying, 'Choose life for yourself, so that you
may live!' 60 130 But they did not believe him or
the prophets after him, or even myself who
have spoken to them. 61 131 Therefore there
shall not be grief at their destruction, so much
as joy over those to whom salvation is assured."

Ezra Appeals to God's Mercy

62 132 I answered and said, "I know, O Lord,
that the Most High is now called merciful, because he has mercy on those who have not yet
come into the world; 63 133 and gracious, because he is gracious to those who turn in repentance to his law; 64 134 and patient, because
he shows patience toward those who have
sinned, since they are his own creatures;

65 135 and bountiful, because he would rather
give than take away; 66 136 and abundant in
compassion, because he makes his compas-
sions abound more and more to those now
living and to those who are gone and to those
yet to come— 67 137 for if he did not make
them abound, the world with those who inhabit it would not have life— 68 138 and he is
called the giver, because if he did not give out
of his goodness so that those who have committed iniquities might be relieved of them,
not one ten-thousandth of humankind could
have life; 69 139 and the judge, because if he did
not pardon those who were created by his
word and blot out the multitude of their sins,
70 140 there would probably be left only very
few of the innumerable multitude."

8 He answered me and said, "The Most
High made this world for the sake of
many, but the world to come for the sake of
only a few. 2 But I tell you a parable, Ezra. Just
as, when you ask the earth, it will tell you that
it provides a large amount of clay from which
earthenware is made, but only a little dust
from which gold comes, so is the course of the
present world. 3 Many have been created, but
only a few shall be saved."

Ezra Again Appeals to God's Mercy

4 I answered and said, "Then drink your fill of
understanding, O my soul, and drink wisdom, O my heart. 5 For not of your own will
did you come into the world, and against
your will you depart, for you have been given
only a short time to live. 6 O Lord above us,
grant to your servant that we may pray before
you, and give us a seed for our heart and culti-

a Cn: Lat Syr places b Syr Ethiop Arab 1: Lat what I say
c Syr: Lat there was not d Or he is ready to give according to
requests e Lat contempts f Syr: Lat Then release understanding
g Syr: Meaning of Lat uncertain

rhetorical use of repetition and contrast. 7.119 Death,
eternal death. 7.120 Everlasting hope. Cf. 1 Pet 1.3.
7.121 Habitations, better "treasuries." 7.122 Glory as
advocate is comparable with glory as judgment; cf. vv.
112–15. 7.123 Fruit . . . abundance and healing. Cf.
Ezek 47.12. 7.125 For shining faces, see note on 7.97;
for blackened faces, see 1 Enoch 62.10. 7.127 The conflict of the good and evil inclinations in the human
heart. See v. 92; cf. Apocryphon of John 26.4–6.
7.128 vv. 59–61. 7.129 Quotations are rare; this is
Deut 30.19. Free will is asserted; cf. vv. 21–24, 72;
8.56–62; 14.34. The idea here stands in tension with
the idea elsewhere in the book of the evil root that inclines people to sin (3.22; 8.53). 7.130 The prophets

were rejected; cf. 2 Chr 36.15–16; Mt 5.17; 23.34–37.
7.131 See vv. 45–74; 1 Enoch 94.10. 7.132–40 A
midrash on Ex 34.6–7, verses often quoted in penitential prayers. 7.137 The world cannot survive without
compassion; cf. Genesis Rabbah 12.15. 7.139 Judge. Cf.
Ex 34.7; 2 Apocalypse of Baruch 84.11. 7.140 Cf. v. 48;
9.15–16. 8.2 The earth's response demanded by 7.55–
56. 8.3 A proverbial statement; cf. 9.15; Mt 22.14. 8.4–
19a A monologue, the third part of the third vision.
Issues are raised—God creates, nurtures, and brings
the end of humans (vv. 4–14)—and questions
posed—how is Israel's fate to be understood (vv. 15–
19a)? 8.4–5 Sapiential apostrophe to the soul. 8.5 Not
of your own will . . . into the world. Cf. 2 Apocalypse of

vation of our understanding so that fruit may be produced, by which every mortal who bears the likeness[a] of a human being may be able to live. 7For you alone exist, and we are a work of your hands, as you have declared. 8And because you give life to the body that is now fashioned in the womb, and furnish it with members, what you have created is preserved amid fire and water, and for nine months the womb[b] endures your creature that has been created in it. 9But that which keeps and that which is kept shall both be kept by your keeping.[c] And when the womb gives up again what has been created in it, 10you have commanded that from the members themselves (that is, from the breasts) milk, the fruit of the breasts, should be supplied, 11so that what has been fashioned may be nourished for a time; and afterwards you will still guide it in your mercy. 12You have nurtured it in your righteousness, and instructed it in your law, and reproved it in your wisdom. 13You put it to death as your creation, and make it live as your work. 14If then you will suddenly and quickly[d] destroy what with so great labor was fashioned by your command, to what purpose was it made? 15And now I will speak out: About all humankind you know best; but I will speak about your people, for whom I am grieved, 16and about your inheritance, for whom I lament, and about Israel, for whom I am sad, and about the seed of Jacob, for whom I am troubled. 17Therefore I will pray before you for myself and for them, for I see the failings of us who inhabit the earth; 18and now also[e] I have heard of the swiftness of the judgment that is to come. 19Therefore hear my voice and understand my words, and I will speak before you."

Ezra's Prayer

The beginning of the words of Ezra's prayer,[f] before he was taken up. He said: 20"O Lord, you who inhabit eternity,[g] whose eyes are exalted[h] and whose upper chambers are in the air, 21whose throne is beyond measure and whose glory is beyond comprehension, before whom the hosts of angels stand trembling 22and at whose command they are changed to wind and fire,[i] whose word is sure and whose utterances are certain; whose command is strong and whose ordinance is terrible, 23whose look dries up the depths and whose indignation makes the mountains melt away, and whose truth is established[j] forever— 24hear, O Lord, the prayer of your servant, and give ear to the petition of your creature; attend to my words. 25For as long as I live I will speak, and as long as I have understanding I will answer. 26O do not look on the sins of your people, but on those who serve you in truth. 27Do not take note of the endeavors of those who act wickedly, but of the endeavors of those who have kept your covenants amid afflictions. 28Do not think of those who have lived wickedly in your sight, but remember those who have willingly acknowledged that you are to be feared. 29Do not will the destruction of those who have the ways of cattle, but regard those who have gloriously taught your law.[k] 30Do not be angry with those who are deemed worse than wild animals, but love

a Syr: Lat place   b Lat what you have formed   c Syr: Meaning of Lat uncertain   d Syr: Lat will with a light command   e Syr: Lat but   f Syr Ethiop; Lat beginning of Ezra's words   g Or you who abide forever   h Another Lat text reads whose are the highest heavens   i Syr: Lat they whose service takes the form of wind and fire   j Arab 2: Other authorities read truth bears witness   k Syr have received the brightness of your law

Baruch 48.15; Mishnah Avot 4.21. **8.6** God is addressed. For the agricultural image, cf. 4.28–32. **8.7** *You alone exist,* the uniqueness of God; cf. Deut 4.35; 6.4. Humans were created by God's *hands;* see 3.5. **8.8–11** Wonder at God's creation; cf. Dead Sea Scrolls *Thanksgiving Hymns* (1QH) 9.29–31. *Fire and water,* unparalleled elsewhere. **8.9** *That which keeps . . . keeping,* a striking use of repetition. **8.11** God's responsibility extends to education, perhaps reflecting one of the roles that wisdom plays in Jewish wisdom literature such as Proverbs and Sirach. **8.12** *Law,* or Torah, is equated with *wisdom;* see Sir 24; Bar 4.1. **8.13** God's responsibility is reemphasized; cf. Deut 32.39; 1 Sam 2.6; 2 Kings 5.7. **8.14** Cf. *Greek Esdras Apocalypse* 3.9; *Apocalypse of Sedrach* 3.7. Note the apparent contradiction in God's action. **8.15** See 3.1–2, 28–32; 4.23. **8.16** Israel is God's *inheritance;* see 5.27–28; Deut 32.9. **8.19b–36** Ezra's prayer (cf. Ezra 9; Neh 9; Dan 9), including doxology, confession, and petition. **8.19b** Ezra's assumption; see 14.9, 49. This is a gloss. **8.20** *Eyes,* alternately "heavens." Ancient concepts of the deity's heavenly palace are reflected here. *Upper chambers.* Cf. Ps 104.3; Am 9.6. **8.21** God's fiery *throne* surrounded by ministering hosts; cf. 1 Kings 22.19; Isa 6; Dan 7. **8.22** *Wind and fire.* See Ps 104.4; cf. *2 Apocalypse of Baruch* 21.6; 48.8; *Genesis Rabbah* 78.1. **8.23** *Dries up* (cf. Ps 74.15; Isa 50.2; 51.10), *melt* (cf. Ps 97.5; Mic 1.4; *1 Enoch* 1.6), theophanic language. **8.25** Cf. *Greek Esdras Apocalypse* 2.7; 4.1, 4; 6.20. Ezra will speak whatever the consequences. **8.26–31** Intercession commences. Ezra asks God to do the reverse of 7.131. **8.27** On keeping of *covenants,* see 3.32, 35. **8.29** *Cattle.* The contrast is be-

those who have always put their trust in your glory. ³¹For we and our ancestors have passed our lives in ways that bring death;ᵃ but it is because of us sinners that you are called merciful. ³²For if you have desired to have pity on us, who have no works of righteousness, then you will be called merciful. ³³For the righteous, who have many works laid up with you, shall receive their reward in consequence of their own deeds. ³⁴But what are mortals, that you are angry with them; or what is a corruptible race, that you are so bitter against it? ³⁵For in truth there is no one among those who have been born who has not acted wickedly; among those who have existedᵇ there is no one who has not done wrong. ³⁶For in this, O Lord, your righteousness and goodness will be declared, when you are merciful to those who have no store of good works."

Response to Ezra's Prayer

37 He answered me and said, "Some things you have spoken rightly, and it will turn out according to your words. ³⁸For indeed I will not concern myself about the fashioning of those who have sinned, or about their death, their judgment, or their destruction; ³⁹but I will rejoice over the creation of the righteous, over their pilgrimage also, and their salvation, and their receiving their reward. ⁴⁰As I have spoken, therefore, so it shall be.

41 "For just as the farmer sows many seeds in the ground and plants a multitude of seedlings, and yet not all that have been sown will come upᶜ in due season, and not all that were planted will take root; so also those who have been sown in the world will not all be saved."

42 I answered and said, "If I have found favor in your sight, let me speak. ⁴³If the farmer's seed does not come up, because it has not received your rain in due season, or if it has been ruined by too much rain, it perishes.ᵈ ⁴⁴But people, who have been formed by your hands and are called your own image because they are made like you, and for whose sake you have formed all things—have you also made them like the farmer's seed? ⁴⁵Surely not, O Lordᵉ above! But spare your people and have mercy on your inheritance, for you have mercy on your own creation."

Ezra's Final Appeal for Mercy

46 He answered me and said, "Things that are present are for those who live now, and things that are future are for those who will live hereafter. ⁴⁷For you come far short of being able to love my creation more than I love it. But you have often compared yourselfᶠ to the unrighteous. Never do so! ⁴⁸But even in this respect you will be praiseworthy before the Most High, ⁴⁹because you have humbled yourself, as is becoming for you, and have not considered yourself to be among the righteous. You will receive the greatest glory, ⁵⁰for many miseries will affect those who inhabit the world in the last times, because they have walked in great pride. ⁵¹But think of your own case, and inquire concerning the glory of those who are like yourself, ⁵²because it is for you that paradise is opened, the tree of life is planted, the age to come is prepared, plenty is provided, a city is built, rest is appointed,ᵍ goodness is established and wisdom perfected beforehand.

---

a Syr Ethiop: Meaning of Lat uncertain   *b* Syr: Meaning of Lat uncertain   *c* Syr Ethiop *will live;* Lat *will be saved*
d Cn: Compare Syr Arab 1 Arm Georg 2: Meaning of Lat uncertain   *e* Ethiop Arab Compare Syr: Lat lacks *O Lord*   *f* Syr Ethiop: Lat *brought yourself near*   *g* Syr Ethiop: Lat *allowed*

---

tween domestic and wild animals; see v. 30; cf. 7.65–66; Ps 73.22. **8.31–36** Confession; cf. 7.119, 122; Dan 9.4–6. **8.32** Cf. Rom 3.19–26. **8.33** The sinners, not the righteous, need mercy; cf. Pr Man 8, 13–14. **8.34** *What are mortals?* a common theme in prayers; cf. Job 7.17; Ps 8.4. **8.35** Note the typical apparent contradiction with v. 33; cf. Rom 3.22–23. **8.37–62** Disputatious and predictive discourse. Two angelic addresses (vv. 37–41, 46–62) are separated by Ezra's response (vv. 42–45). **8.37** *Spoken*, i.e., in the preceding. **8.38** *Death, judgment, destruction*, eternal perdition. **8.39** *Pilgrimage, salvation, reward*, terms parallel to those in v. 38. *Pilgrimage* indicates the soul's ascent. **8.40** Emphatic conclusion of the long discussion. **8.41** A parable complete with interpretation; cf. Mk 4.1–9, 14–20.

8.43 *Your*, i.e., God's, stressing divine responsibility. **8.44** God's role in the creation of humans makes the last question more telling. *Your own image*. See Gen 1.26–27. **8.45** An appeal for mercy like 7.132–139; 8.32–36. **8.46** An antithesis resembling 4.21; 7.25. Mercy will be in the future world. **8.47** *You come far short . . . than I love it*. Ezra, though righteous (cf. 7.76), cannot love Israel more than God. **8.49** A common NT sentiment; cf. Mt 23.12; Lk 14.11. **8.50** *Miseries*, the troubles preceding the Messiah's advent. **8.51** *Your own case*. Attention is focused on Ezra, a paradigmatic righteous man. Cf. 2 Apocalypse of Baruch 48.48. **8.52** Features of the future world; cf. 7.117–25; Testament of Levi 18.9–10. *Paradise*, the place of eschatological reward. *City*, heavenly Jerusalem;

that received it; [37]the law, however, does not perish but survives in its glory."

The Vision of a Weeping Woman

38 When I said these things in my heart, I looked around,[a] and on my right I saw a woman; she was mourning and weeping with a loud voice, and was deeply grieved at heart; her clothes were torn, and there were ashes on her head. [39]Then I dismissed the thoughts with which I had been engaged, and turned to her [40]and said to her, "Why are you weeping, and why are you grieved at heart?"

41 She said to me, "Let me alone, my lord, so that I may weep for myself and continue to mourn, for I am greatly embittered in spirit and deeply distressed."

42 I said to her, "What has happened to you? Tell me."

43 And she said to me, "Your servant was barren and had no child, though I lived with my husband for thirty years. [44]Every hour and every day during those thirty years I prayed to the Most High, night and day. [45]And after thirty years God heard your servant, and looked upon my low estate, and considered my distress, and gave me a son. I rejoiced greatly over him, I and my husband and all my neighbors;[b] and we gave great glory to the Mighty One. [46]And I brought him up with much care. [47]So when he grew up and I came to take a wife for him, I set a day for the marriage feast.

10 "But it happened that when my son entered his wedding chamber, he fell down and died. [2]So all of us put out our lamps, and all my neighbors[b] attempted to console me; I remained quiet until the evening of the second day. [3]But when all of them had stopped consoling me, encouraging me to be quiet, I got up in the night and fled, and I came to this field, as you see. [4]And now I intend not to return to the town, but to stay here; I will neither eat nor drink, but will mourn and fast continually until I die."

5 Then I broke off the reflections with which I was still engaged, and answered her in anger and said, [6]"You most foolish of women, do you not see our mourning, and what has happened to us? [7]For Zion, the mother of us all, is in deep grief and great distress. [8]It is most appropriate to mourn now, because we are all mourning, and to be sorrowful, because we are all sorrowing; you are sorrowing for one son, but we, the whole world, for our mother.[c] [9]Now ask the earth, and she will tell you that it is she who ought to mourn over so many who have come into being upon her. [10]From the beginning all have been born of her, and others will come; and, lo, almost all go[d] to perdition, and a multitude of them will come to doom. [11]Who then ought to mourn the more, she who lost so great a multitude, or you who are grieving for one alone? [12]But if you say to me, 'My lamentation is not like the earth's, for I have lost the fruit of my womb, which I brought forth in pain and bore in sorrow; [13]but it is with the earth according to the way of the earth—the multitude that is now in it goes as it came';

---

a Syr Arab Arm: Lat I looked about me with my eyes   b Literally all my citizens   c Compare Syr: Meaning of Lat uncertain   d Literally walk

---

analogy in vv. 34–35. **9.38–10.4** Vision. The first-person narrative continues. The woman's tale may be an earlier piece incorporated by the author. Folk motifs resemble those in Tobit and 1 Sam 1–2. Cf. Luke 1.5–25. In general, the parallels between the Ezra of the first three visions and the woman here are notable. **9.38** On my right. Cf. 4.47. This is a waking vision; no trance or dream state is implied. **9.39** An attempt to account for the discrepancy that the vision is not a response to the address. The verse is repeated in 10.5 and may further indicate the abandonment of the issues motivating the first three visions. **9.41** Cf. 1 Sam 1.10. **9.43** An imitation of biblical style; cf. 12.8; 13.14; esp. 1 Sam 1.16. Thirty may evoke the period from the exile to Ezra's vision (3.1). **9.44** Cf. the role of prayer in 1 Sam 1.9–11. **9.45** Low estate, better "affliction." **9.47** The mother takes a wife for her son; cf. Gen 21.21; cf. Mishnah Kiddushin 2.1; 3.7–9. A feast celebrating a marriage was common in biblical times; cf. Mt 25.1–

10. **10.1** Cf. Tob 7.11; 8.10. **10.2** The night of the second day marked the end of the first period of mourning. Sitting in silence and extinguishing lamps are ancient Jewish mourning customs. **10.5–24** The second part of Ezra's vision; here Ezra dominates, as the woman did in the preceding section. Ezra takes on the angel's characteristics, and the woman takes on Ezra's. This is possible because Ezra has accepted the teachings contained in the angel's earlier speech, yet his pain persists. **10.5** See 9.39. **10.6** Our mourning . . . to us points ahead to the next part of the vision. Cf. the angel's reproach in 4.2; 5.33. **10.7** Zion, or Jerusalem, as mother is biblical, e.g., Isa 50.1; Jer 50.12; Gal 4.26. A striking parallel story is Pesiqta Rabbati 26. **10.8** But we . . . mother does not seem to be original; the verse's structure resembles v. 20. **10.9** This apostrophe quotes 7.54, which emphasizes Ezra's acceptance of the angel's perspective; cf. 4.40. The earth begets humans; cf. 5.48; 6.53. **10.10** This teaching Ezra rejected in the third vision. His perception has

14then I say to you, 'Just as you brought forth in sorrow, so the earth also has from the beginning given her fruit, that is, humankind, to him who made her.' 15Now, therefore, keep your sorrow to yourself, and bear bravely the troubles that have come upon you. 16For if you acknowledge the decree of God to be just, you will receive your son back in due time, and will be praised among women. 17Therefore go into the town to your husband."

18 She said to me, "I will not do so; I will not go into the city, but I will die here."

19 So I spoke again to her, and said, 20"Do not do that, but let yourself be persuaded—for how many are the adversities of Zion?—and be consoled because of the sorrow of Jerusalem. 21For you see how our sanctuary has been laid waste, our altar thrown down, our temple destroyed; 22our harp has been laid low, our song has been silenced, and our rejoicing has been ended; the light of our lampstand has been put out, the ark of our covenant has been plundered, our holy things have been polluted, and the name by which we are called has been almost profaned; our children[a] have suffered abuse, our priests have been burned to death, our Levites have gone into exile, our virgins have been defiled, and our wives have been ravished; our righteous men[b] have been carried off, our little ones have been cast out, our young men have been enslaved and our strong men made powerless. 23And, worst of all, the seal of Zion has been deprived of its glory, and given over into the hands of those that hate us. 24Therefore shake off your great sadness and lay aside your many sorrows, so that the Mighty One may be merciful to you again, and the Most High may give you rest, a respite from your troubles."

25 While I was talking to her, her face suddenly began to shine exceedingly; her countenance flashed like lightning, so that I was too frightened to approach her, and my heart was terrified. While[c] I was wondering what this meant, 26she suddenly uttered a loud and fearful cry, so that the earth shook at the sound. 27When I looked up, the woman was no longer visible to me, but a city was being built,[d] and a place of huge foundations showed itself. I was afraid, and cried with a loud voice and said, 28"Where is the angel Uriel, who came to me at first? For it was he who brought me into this overpowering bewilderment; my end has become corruption, and my prayer a reproach."

Uriel's Interpretation of the Vision

29 While I was speaking these words, the angel who had come to me at first came to me, and when he saw me 30lying there like a corpse, deprived of my understanding, he grasped my right hand and strengthened me and set me on my feet, and said to me, 31"What is the matter with you? And why are you troubled? And why are your understanding and the thoughts of your mind troubled?"

32 I said, "It was because you abandoned me. I did as you directed, and went out into the field, and lo, what I have seen and can still see, I am unable to explain."

33 He said to me, "Stand up like a man, and I will instruct you."

34 I said, "Speak, my lord; only do not forsake me, so that I may not die before my time.[e] 35For I have seen what I did not know, and I

---

a Ethiop *free men*   b Syr *our seers*   c Syr Ethiop Arab 1: Lat lacks *I was too . . . terrified. While*   d Lat: Syr Ethiop Arab 1 Arab 2 Arm *but there was an established city*   e Syr Ethiop Arab: Lat *die to no purpose*

---

changed. **10.12** *Pain* and *sorrow*. Cf. Gen 3.16. **10.14** *The earth* also undergoes a sort of travail. **10.16** This focuses Ezra's earlier concern with justice. Here he asserts what he rejected previously. The return of the son may be an element of the older folk tale. *Due time* implies predestination. **10.17** The *husband*'s role is secondary. **10.21–22** Note this poetic lament; cf. 1 Macc 1.36–40; 2.7–13, relating to the desecration of the temple; also cf. Lam 1.10; 2.7. This is the last lament in *4 Ezra*. The destruction of the temple and the ensuing issue of theodicy are central in ancient Judaism. **10.22** This verse mentions temple-related features and different groups of the population. **10.23** *Seal*, meaning unclear, but the point is that Zion is in enemy hands. **10.25–28** Transformation. Nothing had hinted that the woman was other than what she seemed. The description of her transforma-

tion is unparalleled in apocalyptic literature. Ezra is terrified and faints; he undergoes an intense emotional experience. **10.25** *Face . . . began to shine*. See note on 7.97. **10.26** The earth shakes at portentous events and cries accompany them; see 3.18; 6.13–15. **10.27** *But a city was being built* should be read as *but there was an established city* (text note d). See 7.26; 8.52; 13.36. *Foundations*. Cf. Heb 11.10; Rev 21.14, 19. **10.28** *Uriel*, the usual interpreting angel in the book. **10.29–37** The angel's role as interpreter here differs from that in 5.31; 7.1 and is more traditional. A strong sense of Ezra's turmoil is conveyed. **10.30** *Lying there like a corpse*. Fainting is described; cf. 5.14. **10.31** Cf. 4.2. **10.32** *And can still see* implies that the vision has not passed. *Unable to explain*, different from 2 Cor 12.4. **10.33** *Stand up*. Cf. 4.47; 6.13; 7.2. **10.34** Danger accompanies such experiences.

hear[a] what I do not understand 36—or is my mind deceived, and my soul dreaming? 37 Now therefore I beg you to give your servant an explanation of this bewildering vision."

38 He answered me and said, "Listen to me, and I will teach you, and tell you about the things that you fear; for the Most High has revealed many secrets to you. 39 He has seen your righteous conduct, and that you have sorrowed continually for your people and mourned greatly over Zion. 40 This therefore is the meaning of the vision. 41 The woman who appeared to you a little while ago, whom you saw mourning and whom you began to console 42 (you do not now see the form of a woman, but there appeared to you a city being built)[b] 43 and who told you about the misfortune of her son—this is the interpretation: 44 The woman whom you saw is Zion, which you now behold as a city being built.[c] 45 And as for her telling you that she was barren for thirty years, the reason is that there were three thousand[d] years in the world before any offering was offered in it.[e] 46 And after three thousand[f] years Solomon built the city, and offered offerings; then it was that the barren woman bore a son. 47 And as for her telling you that she brought him up with much care, that was the period of residence in Jerusalem. 48 And as for her saying to you, 'My son died as he entered his wedding chamber,' and that misfortune had overtaken her,[g] this was the destruction that befell Jerusalem. 49 So you saw her likeness, how she mourned for her son, and you began to console her for what had happened.[h] 50 For now the Most High, seeing that you are sincerely grieved and profoundly distressed for her, has shown you the brilliance of her glory, and the loveliness of her beauty. 51 Therefore I told you to remain in the field where no house had been built, 52 for I knew that the Most High would reveal these things to you. 53 Therefore I told you to go into the field where there was no foundation of any building, 54 because no work of human construction could endure in a place where the city of the Most High was to be revealed.

55 "Therefore do not be afraid, and do not let your heart be terrified; but go in and see the splendor or[i] the vastness of the building, as far as it is possible for your eyes to see it, 56 and afterward you will hear as much as your ears can hear. 57 For you are more blessed than many, and you have been called to be with[j] the Most High as few have been. 58 But tomorrow night you shall remain here, 59 and the Most High will show you in those dream visions what the Most High will do to those who inhabit the earth in the last days."

So I slept that night and the following one, as he had told me.

The Vision of the Eagle

11 On the second night I had a dream: I saw rising from the sea an eagle that had twelve feathered wings and three heads. 2 I saw it spread its wings over[k] the whole earth, and all

---

a Other ancient authorities read *have heard*   *b* Lat: Syr Ethiop Arab 1 Arab 2 Arm *an established city*   *c* Cn: Lat *an established city*   *d* Most Lat Mss read *three*   *e* Cn: Lat Syr Arab Arm *her*   *f* Syr Ethiop Arab Arm: Lat *three*   *g* Or *him*   *h* Most Lat Mss and Arab 1 add *These were the things to be opened to you*   *i* Other ancient authorities read *and*   *j* Or *been named by*   *k* Arab 2 Arm: Lat Syr Ethiop *in*

10.35 *Hear,* better *have heard* (text note *a*). Cf. Job 42.3–5. A sense of numinous awe is conveyed; Ezra has seen the ineffable. **10.36** Cf. Sir 34.1–8. **10.38–54** Interpretation of the vision; cf. 12.10; 13.25. The detailed interpretation of the vision's symbols (vv. 44–48) is followed by an explanation of Ezra's experience (vv. 49–54). The center stage is held by the woman, and the son's role is quite passive. **10.38** *Secrets* indicates the special nature of the ensuing. **10.39** Cf. v. 50. **10.40** General introduction to the interpretation; cf. 4.47. *Meaning of the vision,* lit. "word." **10.42** *A city being built,* better *an established city* (text note *b*), and similarly in v. 44. Cf. 10.27. **10.43** This verse marks the shift from relating the symbol to offering its interpretation. **10.45** Metaphorical barrenness; see 5.1; 6.28. Temple offerings are central; cf. 3.24. A millennial reckoning from the creation of the world may be used here, but it would be unusual. **10.46** *Solomon.* David builds the city in 3.24. Both David and Solomon in fact expanded it. **10.47** Cf. 9.45–46. The son's marriage is attributed no significance. **10.48** Cf. vv. 1–2. **10.49** Cf. 9.38–40; 10.6–24. *Likeness,* appearance. **10.50** *For her* indicates the shift from signifying the woman to signifying Zion. On *glory,* see 3.19; 7.42. **10.51** *Field.* Cf. 9.24. **10.54** See note on 7.26. **10.55–59** Concluding injunctions of the fourth vision. **10.55** *Go in and see* implies that the city is still standing; cf. v. 32. **10.56** *Afterward,* after you enter the building. Ezra's experience in the city is not related. *As much as* stresses the limits of human knowledge. **10.57** *Called,* better "named"; cf. 14.35; Isa 45.4. Only *few* resemble Ezra. **10.59** The preparation for the fifth vision differs from preceding visions: only two nights' wait, no fast, and *dream visions* are promised, which are a new type in the book.

11.1–12.39, 51 Fifth vision. **11.1–12.3a** This long vision is a dream the writer had at night. It resembles other apocalypses and is related to them by 11.40,

the winds of heaven blew upon it, and the clouds were gathered around it.[a] 3I saw that out of its wings there grew opposing wings; but they became little, puny wings. 4But its heads were at rest; the middle head was larger than the other heads, but it too was at rest with them. 5Then I saw that the eagle flew with its wings, and it reigned over the earth and over those who inhabit it. 6And I saw how all things under heaven were subjected to it, and no one spoke against it—not a single creature that was on the earth. 7Then I saw the eagle rise upon its talons, and it uttered a cry to its wings, saying, 8"Do not all watch at the same time; let each sleep in its own place, and watch in its turn; 9but let the heads be reserved for the last."

10 I looked again and saw that the voice did not come from its heads, but from the middle of its body. 11I counted its rival wings, and there were eight of them. 12As I watched, one wing on the right side rose up, and it reigned over all the earth. 13And after a time its reign came to an end, and it disappeared, so that even its place was no longer visible. Then the next wing rose up and reigned, and it continued to reign a long time. 14While it was reigning its end came also, so that it disappeared like the first. 15And a voice sounded, saying to it, 16"Listen to me, you who have ruled the earth all this time; I announce this to you before you disappear. 17After you no one shall rule as long as you have ruled, not even half as long."

18 Then the third wing raised itself up, and held the rule as the earlier ones had done, and it also disappeared. 19And so it went with all the wings; they wielded power one after another and then were never seen again. 20I kept looking, and in due time the wings that followed[b] also rose up on the right[c] side, in order to rule. There were some of them that ruled, yet disappeared suddenly; 21and others of them rose up, but did not hold the rule.

22 And after this I looked and saw that the twelve wings and the two little wings had disappeared, 23and nothing remained on the eagle's body except the three heads that were at rest and six little wings.

24 As I kept looking I saw that two little wings separated from the six and remained under the head that was on the right side; but four remained in their place. 25Then I saw that these little wings[d] planned to set themselves up and hold the rule. 26As I kept looking, one was set up, but suddenly disappeared; 27a second also, and this disappeared more quickly than the first. 28While I continued to look the two that remained were planning between themselves to reign together; 29and while they were planning, one of the heads that were at rest (the one that was in the middle) suddenly awoke; it was greater than the other two heads. 30And I saw how it allied the two heads with itself, 31and how the head turned with those that were with it and devoured the two little wings[d] that were planning to reign. 32Moreover this head gained control of the whole earth, and with much oppression dominated its inhabitants; it had greater power over the world than all the wings that had gone before.

33 After this I looked again and saw the head in the middle suddenly disappear, just as the wings had done. 34But the two heads remained, which also in like manner ruled over the earth and its inhabitants. 35And while I looked, I saw the head on the right side devour the one on the left.

A Lion Roused from the Forest

36 Then I heard a voice saying to me, "Look in front of you and consider what you see." 37When I looked, I saw what seemed to be a

a Syr: Compare Ethiop Arab: Lat lacks *the clouds* and *around it*
b Syr Arab 2 *the little wings*   c Some Ethiop Mss read *left*
d Syr: Lat *underwings*

---

which recalls Dan 7; cf. 2 Esd 12.11. The vision is composed of the description of the eagle, which symbolizes Rome (11.1–35), the judgment scene (11.36–46), and the execution of judgment (12.1–3a). **11.1** General description of the eagle. The eagle was the symbol found on the standards of the Roman legions. *Feathered,* probably secondary. **11.2–4** Initial stance of the eagle. **11.2** *Spread.* Cf. Ex 19.4; Deut 32.11. **11.3** The *puny wings* have particular significance. **11.5–6** The eagle's rule extended over the whole earth. **11.6** *Creature* may signify "human being." **11.7–11** Preparation for sequence of rulers. **11.8** *Watch,* i.e., "be awake."

11.9 *The last,* an eschatological term. **11.12–19** Rule of right-hand wings. The right side is dominant and favorable. **11.13** *And after a time,* text uncertain. *The next wing* is treated in detail because of its importance; cf. 12.15. **11.22–23** Summary. **11.24–27** Rule of four little wings. **11.25** *These little wings,* better "these four little wings." **11.26–27** Brief rule of first two wings. **11.28–32** Fate of next two wings. They did not achieve even a brief rule. **11.33–35** Fate of the heads. **11.35** The Dead Sea Scrolls *Pesher on Habakkuk* (1QpHab) 3.11 refers to the Kittim (understood to be Romans), which *devour* like an eagle. **11.36–38** The

lion roused from the forest, roaring; and I heard how it uttered a human voice to the eagle, and spoke, saying, 38"Listen and I will speak to you. The Most High says to you, 39'Are you not the one that remains of the four beasts that I had made to reign in my world, so that the end of my times might come through them? 40You, the fourth that has come, have conquered all the beasts that have gone before; and you have held sway over the world with great terror, and over all the earth with grievous oppression; and for so long you have lived on the earth with deceit.*a 41You have judged the earth, but not with truth, 42for you have oppressed the meek and injured the peaceable; you have hated those who tell the truth, and have loved liars; you have destroyed the homes of those who brought forth fruit, and have laid low the walls of those who did you no harm. 43Your insolence has come up before the Most High, and your pride to the Mighty One. 44The Most High has looked at his times; now they have ended, and his ages have reached completion. 45Therefore you, eagle, will surely disappear, you and your terrifying wings, your most evil little wings, your malicious heads, your most evil talons, and your whole worthless body, 46so that the whole earth, freed from your violence, may be refreshed and relieved, and may hope for the judgment and mercy of him who made it.'"

12 While the lion was saying these words to the eagle, I looked 2and saw that the remaining head had disappeared. The two wings that had gone over to it rose up and*b set themselves up to reign, and their reign was brief and full of tumult. 3When I looked again,

they were already vanishing. The whole body of the eagle was burned, and the earth was exceedingly terrified.

Then I woke up in great perplexity of mind and great fear, and I said to my spirit, 4"You have brought this upon me, because you search out the ways of the Most High. 5I am still weary in mind and very weak in my spirit, and not even a little strength is left in me, because of the great fear with which I have been terrified tonight. 6Therefore I will now entreat the Most High that he may strengthen me to the end."

The Interpretation of the Vision

7 Then I said, "O sovereign Lord, if I have found favor in your sight, and if I have been accounted righteous before you beyond many others, and if my prayer has indeed come up before your face, 8strengthen me and show me, your servant, the interpretation and meaning of this terrifying vision so that you may fully comfort my soul. 9For you have judged me worthy to be shown the end of the times and the last events of the times."

10 He said to me, "This is the interpretation of this vision that you have seen: 11The eagle that you saw coming up from the sea is the fourth kingdom that appeared in a vision to your brother Daniel. 12But it was not explained to him as I now explain to you or have explained it. 13The days are coming when a kingdom shall rise on earth, and it shall be more terrifying than all the kingdoms that have been

---

a Syr Arab Arm: Lat Ethiop *The fourth came, however, and conquered . . . and held sway . . . and for so long lived*   b Ethiop: Lat lacks *rose up and*

---

appearance of a lion. **11.36** I. Ezra becomes personally involved. **11.37** The *lion* symbolizes the Messiah. The *voice* is a human attribute. **11.38–43** Indictment of the eagle. These verses have a clearly legal character. **11.39** *My times,* better "the times." This verse establishes the identification of the eagle; cf. *2 Apocalypse of Baruch* 39.7. Kings and empires are foreordained by God; the eagle's domination is the zenith of evil, preceding the end. **11.40** A parallel structure is in *2 Apocalypse of Baruch* 39.8. **11.42** *Meek, peaceable.* Cf. Mt 5.5, 9. **11.43** *Pride,* typical of the wicked kingdom. **11.44–46** Sentencing of the eagle. **11.46** *Whole earth, freed . . . refreshed and relieved* apparently hints at the messianic kingdom. **12.1–3a** Execution of the sentence. Enemies of God are often destroyed by fire and terror; cf. Mal 3.19. **12.3b–9** In function, this section resembles 10.5–24; 13.13b–20a, describing the seer's reaction to the vision: fear, perplexity of mind, and

prayer. **12.3b** The seer's state of mind is similarly described in 5.33. **12.4** An apostrophe to his spirit or mind; cf. 7.62. The frightening dream is precipitated by his mind's search for understanding. **12.5** Cf. Dan 7.15; *mind,* like *spirit,* indicates the seer's consciousness. **12.7** *O sovereign Lord.* God is addressed. **12.8** Similar requests for interpretation may be seen in Dan 2.26; 5.26. **12.9** The revelation is of a special nature; cf. 3.14; 14.5. **12.10–36** Interpretation of the vision by the angel. Note the recapitulation of the symbol, followed by its meaning. The vision is related to apocalyptic tradition and explicitly to Dan 7.11. It also provides a date for the book. The vision and interpretation cohere closely, giving information about particular stages of the eschatological process. **12.10** Cf. 10.40; 13.25. **12.11** *Eagle,* the fourth kingdom (cf. Dan 7) and, implicitly, Rome. This vision and explanation supersede Daniel's. **12.13** *Terrifying.* Cf. Dan 7.7, 19,

before it. [14]And twelve kings shall reign in it, one after another. [15]But the second that is to reign shall hold sway for a longer time than any other one of the twelve. [16]This is the interpretation of the twelve wings that you saw.

[17]"As for your hearing a voice that spoke, coming not from the eagle's[a] heads but from the midst of its body, this is the interpretation: [18]In the midst of[b] the time of that kingdom great struggles shall arise, and it shall be in danger of falling; nevertheless it shall not fall then, but shall regain its former power.[c] [19]As for your seeing eight little wings[d] clinging to its wings, this is the interpretation: [20]Eight kings shall arise in it, whose times shall be short and their years swift; [21]two of them shall perish when the middle of its time draws near; and four shall be kept for the time when its end approaches, but two shall be kept until the end.

[22]"As for your seeing three heads at rest, this is the interpretation: [23]In its last days the Most High will raise up three kings,[e] and they[f] shall renew many things in it, and shall rule the earth [24]and its inhabitants more oppressively than all who were before them. Therefore they are called the heads of the eagle, [25]because it is they who shall sum up his wickedness and perform his last actions. [26]As for your seeing that the large head disappeared, one of the kings[g] shall die in his bed, but in agonies. [27]But as for the two who remained, the sword shall devour them. [28]For the sword of one shall devour him who was with him; but he also shall fall by the sword in the last days.

[29]"As for your seeing two little wings[h] passing over to[i] the head which was on the right side, [30]this is the interpretation: It is these whom the Most High has kept for the eagle's[j] end; this was the reign which was brief and full of tumult, as you have seen.

[31]"And as for the lion whom you saw rousing up out of the forest and roaring and speaking to the eagle and reproving him for his unrighteousness, and as for all his words that you have heard, [32]this is the Messiah[k] whom the Most High has kept until the end of days, who will arise from the offspring of David, and will come and speak[l] with them. He will denounce them for their ungodliness and for their wickedness, and will display before them their contemptuous dealings. [33]For first he will bring them alive before his judgment seat, and when he has reproved them, then he will destroy them. [34]But in mercy he will set free the remnant of my people, those who have been saved throughout my borders, and he will make them joyful until the end comes, the day of judgment, of which I spoke to you at the beginning. [35]This is the dream that you saw, and this is its interpretation. [36]And you alone were worthy to learn this secret of the Most High. [37]Therefore write all these things that you have seen in a book, put it[m] in a hidden place; [38]and you shall teach them to the wise among your people, whose hearts you know are able to comprehend and keep these secrets. [39]But as for you, wait here seven days more, so that you may be shown whatever it pleases the Most High to show you." Then he left me.

The People Come to Ezra

40 When all the people heard that the seven days were past and I had not returned to the city, they all gathered together, from the least to the greatest, and came to me and spoke to

---

a Lat *his*   *b* Syr Arm: Lat *After*   *c* Ethiop Arab 1 Arm: Lat Syr *its beginning*   *d* Syr: Lat *underwings*   *e* Syr Ethiop Arab Arm: Lat *kingdoms*   *f* Syr Ethiop Arm: Lat *he*   *g* Lat *them*   *h* Arab 1: Lat *underwings*   *i* Syr Ethiop: Lat lacks *to*   *j* Lat *his*   *k* Literally *anointed one*   *l* Syr: Lat lacks *of days . . . and speak*   *m* Ethiop Arab 1 Arab 2 Arm: Lat Syr *them*

---

23. **12.14** *Twelve kings* are expected. **12.15** The king with a long rule is Augustus (27 BCE–14 CE). **12.23** The idea is that evil will peak with the rule of the heads. **12.25** *Sum up,* better "be the heads of," making the wordplay evident. **12.26** The author adds information from contemporary events. The head is Vespasian (69–79 CE). **12.27–28** *The two,* Titus (79–81 CE) and Domitian (81–96 CE). The vision was written in the time of Domitian. **12.29–30** The *little wings* are part of the eschatological events. **12.31** Cf. *2 Apocalypse of Baruch* 39.8–40.3. *Lion.* The Messiah is associated with Judah and David. His activity is basically legal in character. **12.32** Indictment by the Messiah. *Them,* the Roman emperors. **12.33** *Before his judgment seat,* better "in judgment." The Messiah executes judgment. **12.34** Description of the messianic kingdom; cf. 9.8; 13.48. *Remnant,* those who survive the terrible "woes"; see 5.1–13. The day of judgment will follow the messianic kingdom. *Borders.* Note the role of the Holy Land here; cf. 13.48. **12.35** Cf. Dan 2.45. **12.36** The special *secret* status of the revealed information is stressed; cf. 10.38–39. **12.37–39** Conclusion. **12.37** The command to write the revelation in a *book* is new in *4 Ezra*; cf. Dan 12.4, 9. **12.38** The transmission of secret books to the *wise* is a prominent feature in ch. 14. A change has taken place in Ezra's role and in the vision's content. **12.40–50** A narrative interlude and transition comparable to 5.16–22. **12.40** The *days* of the first six visions add up to forty, corresponding to the forty days of Ezra's new revela-

me, saying, [41]"How have we offended you, and what harm have we done you, that you have forsaken us and sit in this place? [42]For of all the prophets you alone are left to us, like a cluster of grapes from the vintage, and like a lamp in a dark place, and like a haven for a ship saved from a storm. [43]Are not the disasters that have befallen us enough? [44]Therefore if you forsake us, how much better it would have been for us if we also had been consumed in the burning of Zion. [45]For we are no better than those who died there." And they wept with a loud voice.

Then I answered them and said, [46]"Take courage, O Israel; and do not be sorrowful, O house of Jacob; [47]for the Most High has you in remembrance, and the Mighty One has not forgotten you in your struggle. [48]As for me, I have neither forsaken you nor withdrawn from you; but I have come to this place to pray on account of the desolation of Zion, and to seek mercy on account of the humiliation of our[a] sanctuary. [49]Now go to your homes, every one of you, and after these days I will come to you." [50]So the people went into the city, as I told them to do. [51]But I sat in the field seven days, as the angel[b] had commanded me; and I ate only of the flowers of the field, and my food was of plants during those days.

The Man from the Sea

13 After seven days I dreamed a dream in the night. [2]And lo, a wind arose from the sea and stirred up[c] all its waves. [3]As I kept looking the wind made something like the figure of a man come up out of the heart of the sea. And I saw[d] that this man flew[e] with the clouds of heaven; and wherever he turned his face to look, everything under his gaze trembled, [4]and whenever his voice issued from his mouth, all who heard his voice melted as wax melts[f] when it feels the fire.

[5]After this I looked and saw that an innumerable multitude of people were gathered together from the four winds of heaven to make war against the man who came up out of the sea. [6]And I looked and saw that he carved out for himself a great mountain, and flew up on to it. [7]And I tried to see the region or place from which the mountain was carved, but I could not.

[8]After this I looked and saw that all who had gathered together against him, to wage war with him, were filled with fear, and yet they dared to fight. [9]When he saw the onrush of the approaching multitude, he neither lifted his hand nor held a spear or any weapon of war; [10]but I saw only how he sent forth from his mouth something like a stream of fire, and from his lips a flaming breath, and from his tongue he shot forth a storm of sparks.[g] [11]All these were mingled together, the stream of fire and the flaming breath and the great storm, and fell on the onrushing multitude that was prepared to fight, and burned up all of them, so that suddenly nothing was seen of the innumerable multitude but only the dust of ashes and the smell of smoke. When I saw it, I was amazed.

[12]After this I saw the same man come down from the mountain and call to himself another multitude that was peaceable. [13]Then many people[h] came to him, some of whom were joyful and some sorrowful; some of them were bound, and some were bringing others as offerings.

---

a Syr Ethiop: Lat *your*   b Literally *he*   c Other ancient authorities read *I saw a wind arise from the sea and stir up*   d Syr: Lat lacks *the wind . . . I saw*   e Syr Ethiop Arab Arm: Lat *grew strong*   f Syr: Lat *burned as the earth rests*   g Meaning of Lat uncertain   h Lat Syr Arab 2 literally *the faces of many people*

---

tion in ch. 14. *City,* presumably Babylon. **12.42** Ezra is called *prophet* for the first time in *4 Ezra* and this is his first "ordinary" apocalyptic revelation. He accepts this role. *Grapes* indicate election; see 9.21–22. *Lamp.* See *2 Apocalypse of Baruch* 77.13. **12.44** Reapplication of an old idea, stated in 4.12 of Ezra himself. **12.47** *In your struggle,* or else "forever." God's relationship to Israel is inalienable. **12.48** Cf. 12.38. Ezra keeps the revelation secret and says he was praying for the people, as a prophet should. **12.51** A second conclusion to the fifth vision. This injunction belongs with vv. 37–39.

13.1–58 Sixth vision. **13.1–13a** This vision is much simpler than the fifth. The closeness of the end is not mentioned. **13.1** *Seven days.* See 12.51. This is explicitly a dream; Ezra is prostrate (cf. v. 57). **13.2** *Wind,* better "great wind." Cf. Dan 7.2. **13.3** Cf. Dan 7.13; the *figure of a man* is a redeemer. **13.4** *Melting* of enemies is a divine characteristic; cf. Ps 97.5; Mic 1.4. The superhuman nature of the figure is strongly suggested. **13.5** The eschatological attack (see Rev 16.12–15), an idea originating in Deut 28.49; Joel 2.1–10. **13.6** *Carved out . . . a great mountain.* Cf. Dan 2.34, 45. **13.7** The dreamer intervenes here. **13.9** *Nor . . . any weapon of war.* Cf. *Psalms of Solomon* 17.33–34. Fire (v. 10) is God's chief weapon; cf. Ps 97.3. **13.10** This perhaps hints at God's effective word; see Ps 2.9; Isa 11.4; *Psalms of Solomon* 17.35. **13.11** Again the dreamer intervenes. **13.13a** The ingathering of converted Gentiles. See Isa 66.20; Rom 11.25; 15.16. **13.13b–20a** The response functions like

The Interpretation of the Vision

Then I woke up in great terror, and prayed to the Most High, and said, 14"From the beginning you have shown your servant these wonders, and have deemed me worthy to have my prayer heard by you; 15now show me the interpretation of this dream also. 16For as I consider it in my mind, alas for those who will be left in those days! And still more, alas for those who are not left! 17For those who are not left will be sad 18because they understand the things that are reserved for the last days, but cannot attain them. 19But alas for those also who are left, and for that very reason! For they shall see great dangers and much distress, as these dreams show. 20Yet it is better*a* to come into these things,*b* though incurring peril, than to pass from the world like a cloud, and not to see what will happen in the last days."

He answered me and said, 21"I will tell you the interpretation of the vision, and I will also explain to you the things that you have mentioned. 22As for what you said about those who survive, and concerning those who do not survive,*c* this is the interpretation: 23The one who brings the peril at that time will protect those who fall into peril, who have works and faith toward the Almighty. 24Understand therefore that those who are left are more blessed than those who have died.

25 "This is the interpretation of the vision: As for your seeing a man come up from the heart of the sea, 26this is he whom the Most High has been keeping for many ages, who will himself deliver his creation; and he will direct those who are left. 27And as for your seeing wind and fire and a storm coming out of his mouth, 28and as for his not holding a spear or weapon of war, yet destroying the onrushing multitude that came to conquer him, this is the interpretation: 29The days are coming when the Most High will deliver those who are on the earth. 30And bewilderment of mind shall come over those who inhabit the earth. 31They shall plan to make war against one another, city against city, place against place, people against people, and kingdom against kingdom. 32When these things take place and the signs occur that I showed you before, then my Son will be revealed, whom you saw as a man coming up from the sea.*d*

33 "Then, when all the nations hear his voice, all the nations shall leave their own lands and the warfare that they have against one another; 34and an innumerable multitude shall be gathered together, as you saw, wishing to come and conquer him. 35But he shall stand on the top of Mount Zion. 36And Zion shall come and be made manifest to all people, prepared and built, as you saw the mountain carved out without hands. 37Then he, my Son, will reprove the assembled nations for their ungodliness (this was symbolized by the storm), 38and will reproach them to their face with their evil thoughts and the torments with which they are to be tortured (which were symbolized by the flames), and will destroy them without effort by means of the law*e* (which was symbolized by the fire).

39 "And as for your seeing him gather to himself another multitude that was peaceable, 40these are the nine*f* tribes that were taken away from their own land into exile in the days of King Hoshea, whom Shalmaneser, king of the Assyrians, made captives; he took them across the river, and they were taken into an-

---

a Ethiop Compare Arab 2: Lat *easier*   b Syr: Lat *this*   c Syr Arab 1: Lat lacks *and . . . not survive*   d Syr and most Lat Mss lack *from the sea*   e Syr: Lat *effort and the law*   f Other Lat Mss ten; Syr Ethiop Arab 1 Arm *nine and a half*

12.3b–9. **13.14** Ezra asserts his own worthiness; cf. 12.7–9. *Wonders,* the eschatological revelation in the book. **13.16** Woe pronouncement: survivors live on after the woes; see v. 19. **13.18** The seeing of reward or punishment is part of recompense; see 7.66, 83, 93. **13.20** *Yet it is better . . . in the last days,* the reversal of the idea that death is better; cf. 4.12. Ezra, now a prophet, no longer despairs. **13.20b–55** The interpretation of the dream is unclear and repetitive. The author may have composed the interpretation for a previously existing vision he took over. **13.21** God interprets Ezra's dream and prayer without angelic mediation. **13.24** Ezra's view in v. 20 is confirmed. **13.26** *Who will himself,* better "through whom he will." The Messiah is precreated. *Those who are left,* after the messianic woes.

13.27–28 A restatement of vv. 10–11, but the interpretation comes only in vv. 36–38. **13.29** *The days are coming.* A predictive passage starts, relating to the woes. **13.30** Cf. *2 Apocalypse of Baruch* 25.3; 70.2. *Bewilderment of mind* leads to internecine strife; see 5.9; 6.24; 9.3–4. **13.32** *Son,* better either "servant" or "son" (no capital letter). The *man* (v. 3) is the servant. **13.33** *Voice.* See v. 4. **13.34** The evil nations' final assault on Zion; it will be repulsed by the Messiah. **13.35** See vv. 6–7; cf. Ps 2.6; Isa 31.4. **13.36** Cf. Dan 2.34, 45. *The mountain,* Zion. *Without hands* explicitly contradicts v. 6. **13.37** See vv. 10–11. The man's breath is both fire and judgment. **13.38** *Reproach,* the Messiah's judgmental word. **13.40** *Nine and a half* tribes (text note *f*) is the preferred reading here, and not *nine* or *ten*. This num-

other land. ⁴¹But they formed this plan for themselves, that they would leave the multitude of the nations and go to a more distant region, where no human beings had ever lived, ⁴²so that there at least they might keep their statutes that they had not kept in their own land. ⁴³And they went in by the narrow passages of the Euphrates river. ⁴⁴For at that time the Most High performed signs for them, and stopped the channels of the river until they had crossed over. ⁴⁵Through that region there was a long way to go, a journey of a year and a half; and that country is called Arzareth.ᵃ

46 "Then they lived there until the last times; and now, when they are about to come again, ⁴⁷the Most High will stopᵇ the channels of the river again, so that they may be able to cross over. Therefore you saw the multitude gathered together in peace. ⁴⁸But those who are left of your people, who are found within my holy borders, shall be saved.ᶜ ⁴⁹Therefore when he destroys the multitude of the nations that are gathered together, he will defend the people who remain. ⁵⁰And then he will show them very many wonders."

51 I said, "O sovereign Lord, explain this to me: Why did I see the man coming up from the heart of the sea?"

52 He said to me, "Just as no one can explore or know what is in the depths of the sea, so no one on earth can see my Son or those who are with him, except in the time of his day.ᵈ ⁵³This is the interpretation of the dream that you saw. And you alone have been enlightened about this, ⁵⁴because you have forsaken your own ways and have applied your-

self to mine, and have searched out my law; ⁵⁵for you have devoted your life to wisdom, and called understanding your mother. ⁵⁶Therefore I have shown you these things; for there is a reward laid up with the Most High. For it will be that after three more days I will tell you other things, and explain weighty and wondrous matters to you."

57 Then I got up and walked in the field, giving great glory and praise to the Most High for the wonders that he doesᵉ from time to time, ⁵⁸and because he governs the times and whatever things come to pass in their seasons. And I stayed there three days.

The Lord Commissions Ezra

14 On the third day, while I was sitting under an oak, suddenly a voice came out of a bush opposite me and said, "Ezra, Ezra!" ²And I answered, "Here I am, Lord," and I rose to my feet. ³Then he said to me, "I revealed myself in a bush and spoke to Moses when my people were in bondage in Egypt; ⁴and I sent him and ledᶠ my people out of Egypt; and I led him up on Mount Sinai, where I kept him with me many days. ⁵I told him many wondrous things, and showed him the secrets of the times and declared to himᵍ the end of the times. Then I commanded him, saying, ⁶'These words you shall publish openly, and these you shall keep secret.' ⁷And now I say to you: ⁸Lay up in your heart the

---

ᵃ That is Another Land   ᵇ Syr: Lat stops   ᶜ Syr: Lat lacks shall be saved   ᵈ Syr: Ethiop except when his time and his day have come. Lat lacks his   ᵉ Lat did   ᶠ Syr Arab 1 Arab 2 he led   ᵍ Syr Ethiop Arab Arm: Lat lacks declared to him

---

ber is also mentioned in 2 Apocalypse of Baruch 77.17, 19; 78.1. **13.41** Cf. Josephus, Antiquities 11.133. **13.44** Based on the miracle of the Red Sea, Ex 14.21–31. Cf. also the Israelites' crossing of the Jordan in Josh 3.14–17. **13.45** Arzareth, enigmatic; perhaps cf. Deut 29.28 for Hebrew 'erets 'acheret, "another land." **13.46** The end is close. **13.47** The Most High . . . to cross over. Eschatological redemption is associated with the exodus. **13.48** See 9.8; 12.34, where similar events are foretold. **13.49** The Messiah will protect the survivors. **13.50** Wonders, the Messiah's action; cf. 4.26; 7.27. See also "signs and wonders" in connection with the exodus, Ex 7.3, 9. **13.51** A repetitive question. Cf. vv. 25–26. **13.52** See v. 3. Depths of the sea. See 4.7. Those who are with him, those taken alive to heaven, like Elijah and Enoch. **13.54** Ezra's wisdom is praised; Torah (law) and wisdom are often connected; see 8.12. **13.55** Wisdom, the tradition of eschatological teaching; see 14.40, 47. **13.56–58** Conclusion and injunctions. This stands in

deliberate contrast to the start of the first vision. **13.56** Reward is precreated; see 8.52–53, 59. **13.57** Then I got up. In 3.1 Ezra lies on his bed in Babylon. **13.58** Because he governs . . . in their seasons. God's governance of the world had been questioned in ch. 3.

14.1–48 The seventh vision, the revelation of scripture to Ezra, concludes 4 Ezra. God speaks directly in this chapter. **14.1–2** Narrative introduction and call. **14.1** Third day. The preceding six visions total forty days. Oak. See Gen 18.1; Judg 4.5; 2 Apocalypse of Baruch 6.1; 77.18. Bush. See Ex 3.2–4.17. Ezra resembles Moses here. **14.2** See 6.13–15; Ex 3.5. **14.3–18** Address to Ezra before his assumption. **14.3–4** Cf. Ex 3.2–12. **14.4** See Ex 24.15–18; 34.1–35. **14.5** Cf. 3.14; 12.36–37. Moses also received a secret revelation; cf. 2 Apocalypse of Baruch 59.4. **14.6** A double revelation; this command is apocryphal, cf. 9.29–31; 12.37. Also cf. 14.45. **14.7** 12.9, 36–37 link Ezra's revelation to Moses' and Abraham's. **14.8** Ezra has only secret revelation in

signs that I have shown you, the dreams that you have seen, and the interpretations that you have heard; 9for you shall be taken up from among humankind, and henceforth you shall live with my Son and with those who are like you, until the times are ended. 10The age has lost its youth, and the times begin to grow old. 11For the age is divided into twelve parts, and nine*a* of its parts have already passed, 12as well as half of the tenth part; so two of its parts remain, besides half of the tenth part.*b* 13Now therefore, set your house in order, and reprove your people; comfort the lowly among them, and instruct those that are wise.*c* And now renounce the life that is corruptible, 14and put away from you mortal thoughts; cast away from you the burdens of humankind, and divest yourself now of your weak nature; 15lay to one side the thoughts that are most grievous to you, and hurry to escape from these times. 16For evils worse than those that you have now seen happen shall take place hereafter. 17For the weaker the world becomes through old age, the more shall evils be increased upon its inhabitants. 18Truth shall go farther away, and falsehood shall come near. For the eagle*d* that you saw in the vision is already hurrying to come."

Ezra's Concern to Restore the Scriptures

19 Then I answered and said, "Let me speak*e* in your presence, Lord. 20For I will go, as you have commanded me, and I will reprove the people who are now living; but who will warn those who will be born hereafter? For the world lies in darkness, and its inhabitants are without light. 21For your law has been burned, and so no one knows the things which have been done or will be done by you. 22If then I have found favor with you, send the holy spirit into me, and I will write everything that has happened in the world from the beginning, the things that were written in your law, so that people may be able to find the path, and that those who want to live in the last days may do so."

23 He answered me and said, "Go and gather the people, and tell them not to seek you for forty days. 24But prepare for yourself many writing tablets, and take with you Sarea, Dabria, Selemia, Ethanus, and Asiel—these five, who are trained to write rapidly; 25and you shall come here, and I will light in your heart the lamp of understanding, which shall not be put out until what you are about to write is finished. 26And when you have finished, some things you shall make public, and some you shall deliver in secret to the wise; tomorrow at this hour you shall begin to write."

Ezra's Last Words to the People

27 Then I went as he commanded me, and I gathered all the people together, and said, 28"Hear these words, O Israel. 29At first our ancestors lived as aliens in Egypt, and they were liberated from there 30and received the law of life, which they did not keep, which you also have transgressed after them. 31Then land was given to you for a possession in the land of Zion; but you and your ancestors committed iniquity and did not keep the ways that the

---

a Cn: Lat Ethiop *ten*   *b* Syr lacks verses 11, 12: Ethiop *For the world is divided into ten parts, and has come to the tenth, and half of the tenth remains. Now . . .*   *c* Lat lacks *and . . . wise*   *d* Syr Ethiop Arab Arm: Meaning of Lat uncertain   *e* Most Lat Mss lack *Let me speak*

---

the first six visions; cf. 14.6. **14.9** *Son,* better "servant." Ezra's assumption is prophesied; cf. 6.26; 13.52. **14.10** The waning of this world/age; see v. 17; also 4.45–50; 5.55. **14.11** Many such divisions of history exist; the actual basis of the reckoning here is obscure. See (note on) 13.40, where nine and a half tribes are exiled. **14.13** *Set your house . . . that are wise.* These commands, using wisdom terms, are executed in vv. 27–36, although the wise are not instructed. That which is *corruptible* dies. **14.14** Ezra is not to be assumed in the body. **14.15** Ezra will escape the toilsomeness of the age. **14.17** See vv. 10–11. The senescence of the earth brings evils. **14.18** The author here refers to his own times, not those of Ezra. **14.19–22** Ezra already has esoteric knowledge. Now he asks for exoteric revelation in order to become like Moses. **14.20** *Who will warn . . . hereafter?* Cf. 5.41. On *light,*

see Pss 36.10; 119.105; Prov 6.23. **14.21** The Torah (*law*) was lost; cf. 4.23. For its contents here, cf. *Jubilees* 1.29. **14.22** This request is unparalleled in the book. *Holy spirit.* See Ps 51.13; Isa 63.10; Wis 1.5; *Jubilees* 1.21. *Live,* i.e., have eternal life. **14.23–26** Injunctions. **14.23** *Forty days,* the length of time Moses was on the mountain (Ex 24.19). The first six visions also took a total of forty days. **14.24** *Ethanus,* alternately "Elkana." *Five* men. See 2 *Apocalypse of Baruch* 5.5. **14.25** *Is finished,* better "you finish." The nature of the inspiration is described. Ezra will remember the revelation until he finishes writing. **14.26** *Some . . . public, and some . . . to the wise.* The revelation is both exoteric and esoteric, like Moses' (v. 6). **14.27–36** Ezra's speech to the people stating the reasons for exile and the hope of eternal life. Zion's fate is not mentioned. **14.27** See v. 23. Ezra's admonition is prophetic. **14.28** Cf. 9.30. **14.30** *Law of*

Most High commanded you. ³²And since he is a righteous judge, in due time he took from you what he had given. ³³And now you are here, and your people[a] are farther in the interior.[b] ³⁴If you, then, will rule over your minds and discipline your hearts, you shall be kept alive, and after death you shall obtain mercy. ³⁵For after death the judgment will come, when we shall live again; and then the names of the righteous shall become manifest, and the deeds of the ungodly shall be disclosed. ³⁶But let no one come to me now, and let no one seek me for forty days."

The Restoration of the Scriptures

37 So I took the five men, as he commanded me, and we proceeded to the field, and remained there. ³⁸And on the next day a voice called me, saying, "Ezra, open your mouth and drink what I give you to drink." ³⁹So I opened my mouth, and a full cup was offered to me; it was full of something like water, but its color was like fire. ⁴⁰I took it and drank; and when I had drunk it, my heart poured forth understanding, and wisdom increased in my breast, for my spirit retained its memory, ⁴¹and my mouth was opened and was no longer closed. ⁴²Moreover, the Most High gave understanding to the five men, and by turns they wrote what was dictated, using characters that they did not know.[c] They sat forty days; they wrote during the daytime, and ate their bread at night. ⁴³But as for me, I spoke in the daytime and was not silent at night. ⁴⁴So during the forty days, ninety-four[d] books were written. ⁴⁵And when the forty days were ended, the Most High spoke to me, saying, "Make public the twenty-four[e] books that you wrote first, and let the worthy and the unworthy read

them; ⁴⁶but keep the seventy that were written last, in order to give them to the wise among your people. ⁴⁷For in them is the spring of understanding, the fountain of wisdom, and the river of knowledge." ⁴⁸And I did so.[f]

Vengeance on the Wicked

15 ⁸ Speak in the ears of my people the words of the prophecy that I will put in your mouth, says the Lord, ²and cause them to be written on paper; for they are trustworthy and true. ³Do not fear the plots against you, and do not be troubled by the unbelief of those who oppose you. ⁴For all unbelievers shall die in their unbelief.[h]

5 Beware, says the Lord, I am bringing evils upon the world, the sword and famine, death and destruction, ⁶because iniquity has spread throughout every land, and their harmful doings have reached their limit. ⁷Therefore, says the Lord, ⁸I will be silent no longer concerning their ungodly acts that they impiously commit, neither will I tolerate their wicked practices. Innocent and righteous blood cries out to me, and the souls of the righteous cry out continually. ⁹I will surely avenge them, says the Lord, and will receive to myself all the in-

a Lat *brothers*　b Syr Ethiop Arm: Lat *are among you*　c Syr Compare Ethiop Arab 2 Arm: Meaning of Lat uncertain　d Syr Ethiop Arab 1 Arm: Meaning of Lat uncertain　e Syr Arab 1: Lat lacks *twenty-four*　f Syr adds *in the seventh year of the sixth week, five thousand years and three months and twelve days after creation. At that time Ezra was caught up, and taken to the place of those who are like him, after he had written all these things. And he was called the scribe of the knowledge of the Most High for ever and ever.* Ethiop Arab 1 Arm have a similar ending　g Chapters 15 and 16 (except 15.57-59, which has been found in Greek) are extant only in Lat　h Other ancient authorities add *and all who believe shall be saved by their faith*

---

life. See Sir 17.11; 45.5. **14.32** General conclusion of the historical recital. **14.33** See 13.40–41. **14.35** Resurrection is intended and judgment is disclosed. **14.37–48** Revelation of the exoteric and esoteric books to Ezra, who has achieved prophetic status, and his translation. **14.37** *Five men.* See v. 24. **14.38** Cf. v. 25. This is a waking experience. **14.39** He passes from audition to vision. The *cup* contains the holy spirit. **14.40** *Drinking* denotes inspiration. *Poured forth understanding.* Cf. *Odes of Solomon* 36.7. **14.42** The scribes are also inspired, which guarantees the accuracy of their writing. Similarly, Philo of Alexandria, claims that the translators of the Septuagint were inspired (*Life of Moses* 2.25–44). **14.45–46** Cf. v. 26. *Twenty-four* is a traditional number of books in the Hebrew Bible. *Seventy*, perhaps the apocalyptic books; they are to be trans-

mitted secretly. **14.47** Cf. Prov 18.4; *1 Enoch* 48.1. The esoteric books contain saving knowledge. **14.49** Conclusion. The additional material, found in text note *f*, should be regarded as original; cf. vv. 9, 14–15.

15.1–16.78 Chs. 15–16 are a Christian addition to the Jewish apocalypse that concluded in 14.49. They are known as 6 Ezra. **15.1–4** The author is made a prophet. **15.1** *Put in your mouth.* Cf. Isa 51.16; Jer 1.9. The author is unnamed, but is presumably Ezra. **15.2** Is this related to ch. 14? If so, 6 Ezra was written to supplement *4 Ezra.* *Paper,* papyrus. **15.3** Cf. Jer 1.7–8. **15.5–27** Prediction of doom directed to the wicked. Egypt is mentioned specifically. **15.5** Cf. Isa 51.19; Jer 14.12. **15.6** There is a fixed measure of evil. **15.8** *Blood cries out.* Cf. Gen 4.10; reminiscent of Rev 6.9–10; *1 Enoch* 9.3–5. **15.9** *I will . . . avenge them, says the Lord.* See Deut 32.43. *Blood is life;*

nocent blood from among them. [10]See, my people are being led like a flock to the slaughter; I will not allow them to live any longer in the land of Egypt, [11]but I will bring them out with a mighty hand and with an uplifted arm, and will strike Egypt with plagues, as before, and will destroy all its land.

12 Let Egypt mourn, and its foundations, because of the plague of chastisement and castigation that the Lord will bring upon it. [13]Let the farmers that till the ground mourn, because their seed shall fail to grow[a] and their trees shall be ruined by blight and hail and by a terrible tempest. [14]Alas for the world and for those who live in it! [15]For the sword and misery draw near them, and nation shall rise up to fight against nation, with swords in their hands. [16]For there shall be unrest among people; growing strong against one another, they shall in their might have no respect for their king or the chief of their leaders. [17]For a person will desire to go into a city, and shall not be able to do so. [18]Because of their pride the cities shall be in confusion, the houses shall be destroyed, and people shall be afraid. [19]People shall have no pity for their neighbors, but shall make an assault upon[b] their houses with the sword, and plunder their goods, because of hunger for bread and because of great tribulation.

20 See how I am calling together all the kings of the earth to turn to me, says God, from the rising sun and from the south, from the east and from Lebanon; to turn and repay what they have given them. [21]Just as they have done to my elect until this day, so I will do, and will repay into their bosom. Thus says the Lord God: [22]My right hand will not spare the sinners, and my sword will not cease from those who shed innocent blood on earth.

[23]And a fire went forth from his wrath, and consumed the foundations of the earth and the sinners, like burnt straw. [24]Alas for those who sin and do not observe my commandments, says the Lord;[c] [25]I will not spare them. Depart, you faithless children! Do not pollute my sanctuary. [26]For God[d] knows all who sin against him; therefore he will hand them over to death and slaughter. [27]Already calamities have come upon the whole earth, and you shall remain in them; God[d] will not deliver you, because you have sinned against him.

A Terrifying Vision of Warfare

28 What a terrifying sight, appearing from the east! [29]The nations of the dragons of Arabia shall come out with many chariots, and from the day that they set out, their hissing shall spread over the earth, so that all who hear them will fear and tremble. [30]Also the Carmonians, raging in wrath, shall go forth like wild boars[e] from the forest, and with great power they shall come and engage them in battle, and with their tusks they shall devastate a portion of the land of the Assyrians with their teeth. [31]And then the dragons,[f] remembering their origin, shall become still stronger; and if they combine in great power and turn to pursue them, [32]then these shall be disorganized and silenced by their power, and shall turn and flee.[g] [33]And from the land of the Assyrians an enemy in ambush shall attack them and destroy one of them, and fear and trembling shall come upon their army, and indecision upon their kings.

a Lat lacks to grow   b Cn: Lat shall empty   c Other ancient authorities read God   d Other ancient authorities read the Lord   e Other ancient authorities lack like wild boars   f Cn: Lat dragon   g Other ancient authorities read turn their face to the north

cf. Lev 17.14. **15.10** Flock to the slaughter. Cf. Ps 44.22; Isa 53.7. The historical context remains obscure; some consider it the famine and plague in Alexandria sometime between 260 and 268 CE (Eusebius, Ecclesiastical History 7.21–22). **15.11** The exodus is invoked; cf. Deut 4.34. **15.13** Hail. Cf. Ex 9.25. **15.14** Troubles will come upon the whole earth. **15.15** Internecine strife; see 13.31; Mt 24.7. **15.16** The social order breaks down, part of the woes; cf. 5.1–13. **15.17–19** Civil order is overturned. Famine is also part of this chaos. **15.20** The kings are discussed here. Rising sun. The text is uncertain here. **15.21** Just as . . . so I will do. There is a relationship between punishment and the offense committed. **15.23** For fire as God's weapon, cf. Deut 32.22; Ezek 22.21. God's wrath affects the very underpinnings of the earth. Burnt straw, a common biblical image; cf. Ex

15.7; Mt 3.12. **15.24** A woe statement; cf. Isa 3.11; 1 Enoch 100.7–9. **15.25** Sanctuary may refer to a community. **15.26–27** The calamities that will befall the earth are foretold. **15.28–33** This passage has been thought to refer to the Sasanian Persian attack under Shapur of the mid-third century CE, which was eventually repulsed by Palmyrene forces under Odenathus, who was murdered in 267. Palmyra was an oasis between Syria and Babylonia and an important military and political force in the latter part of the third century. **15.29** Dragons of Arabia, the Palmyrene forces. The desert (i.e., Arabia) is a land of serpents (hissing); see Isa 30.6. **15.30** Carmonians, usually interpreted as Persians from Kirman province. Land of the Assyrians, Syria. **15.31–32** Shapur's defeat described. **15.33** Destroy one of them, perhaps the murder of Odenathus. **15.34–**

Judgment on Babylon

34 See the clouds from the east, and from the north to the south! Their appearance is exceedingly threatening, full of wrath and storm. 35 They shall clash against one another and shall pour out a heavy tempest on the earth, and their own tempest;[a] and there shall be blood from the sword as high as a horse's belly 36 and a man's thigh and a camel's hock. 37 And there shall be fear and great trembling on the earth; those who see that wrath shall be horror-stricken, and they shall be seized with trembling. 38 After that, heavy storm clouds shall be stirred up from the south, and from the north, and another part from the west. 39 But the winds from the east shall prevail over the cloud that was[b] raised in wrath, and shall dispel it; and the tempest[a] that was to cause destruction by the east wind shall be driven violently toward the south and west. 40 Great and mighty clouds, full of wrath and tempest, shall rise and destroy all the earth and its inhabitants, and shall pour out upon every high and lofty place[c] a terrible tempest, 41 fire and hail and flying swords and floods of water, so that all the fields and all the streams shall be filled with the abundance of those waters. 42 They shall destroy cities and walls, mountains and hills, trees of the forests, and grass of the meadows, and their grain. 43 They shall go on steadily to Babylon and blot it out. 44 They shall come to it and surround it; they shall pour out on it the tempest[a] and all its fury;[d] then the dust and smoke shall reach the sky, and all who are around it shall mourn for it. 45 And those who survive shall serve those who have destroyed it.

Judgment on Asia

46 And you, Asia, who share in the splendor of Babylon and the glory of her person— 47 woe to you, miserable wretch! For you have made yourself like her; you have decked out your daughters for prostitution to please and glory in your lovers, who have always lusted after you. 48 You have imitated that hateful one in all her deeds and devices.[e] Therefore God[f] says, 49 I will send evils upon you: widowhood, poverty, famine, sword, and pestilence, bringing ruin to your houses, bringing destruction and death. 50 And the glory of your strength shall wither like a flower when the heat shall rise that is sent upon you. 51 You shall be weakened like a wretched woman who is beaten and wounded, so that you cannot receive your mighty lovers. 52 Would I have dealt with you so violently, says the Lord, 53 if you had not killed my chosen people continually, exulting and clapping your hands and talking about their death when you were drunk?

54 Beautify your face! 55 The reward of a prostitute is in your lap; therefore you shall receive your recompense. 56 As you will do to my chosen people, says the Lord, so God will do to you, and will hand you over to adversities. 57 Your children shall die of hunger, and you shall fall by the sword; your cities shall be wiped out, and all your people who are in the open country shall fall by the sword. 58 Those who are in the mountains and highlands[g] shall perish of hunger, and they shall eat their own flesh in hunger for bread and drink their own blood in thirst for water. 59 Unhappy above all others, you shall come and suffer fresh miseries. 60 As they pass by they shall crush the hateful[h] city, and shall destroy a part of your land and abolish a portion of your glory, when they return from devastated Babylon. 61 You

---

a Meaning of Lat uncertain   b Literally that he   c Or eminent person   d Other ancient authorities add until they destroy it to its foundations   e Other ancient authorities read devices, and you have followed after that one about to gratify her magnates and leaders so that you may be made proud and be pleased by her fornications   f Other ancient authorities read the Lord   g Gk: Lat omits and highlands   h Another reading is idle or unprofitable

---

45 This passage is interpreted by some as the invasion of the Goths into the Roman Empire in the mid-third century CE; it could also be taken as a future prophecy. 15.34 For clouds in a symbolic vision, see also 2 Apocalypse of Baruch 53. 15.35 Blood . . . as high. Cf. Rev 14.20; 1 Enoch 100.3. 15.38–40 If the historical interpretation is taken, the events referred to here still are unclear, but the third century was very unsettled. 15.41 Flying swords. Cf. Sibylline Oracles 3.672. 15.43 Babylon means Rome; cf. 3.1; Rev 14.8; 2 Apocalypse of Baruch 11.1. 15.44–45 The attack reaches Rome itself. 15.46–63 Some have interpreted this passage as referring to the fate of Palmyra under Odenathus and Zenobia, while others see it as purely future prophecy. 15.47–48 Derived from Rev 17.4–6; Asia is the wicked harlot's daughter. 15.49 Cf. 15.5; see also Rev 18.7–8. 15.53 6 Ezra refers throughout to my . . . people, e.g., v. 10, but their identification is uncertain. Drunk. Cf. Dan 5.2. 3 Apocalypse of Baruch 4.17 is strongly opposed to alcoholic drink. 15.55 In biblical legislation the harlot's recompense is death (Gen 38.24; Lev 21.9). 15.56 See v. 21. 15.58 People fled to mountains in troubled times; see Isa 2.10, 19, 21; Mk 13.14; Mt 24.15–16; Rev 6.15–16. Eat their own flesh. Cf. Jer 19.9. 15.60 See vv. 43–44.

shall be broken down by them like stubble,[a] and they shall be like fire to you. 62They shall devour you and your cities, your land and your mountains; they shall burn with fire all your forests and your fruitful trees. 63They shall carry your children away captive, plunder your wealth, and mar the glory of your countenance.

Further Denunciations

16 Woe to you, Babylon and Asia! Woe to you, Egypt and Syria! 2Bind on sackcloth and cloth of goats' hair,[b] and wail for your children, and lament for them; for your destruction is at hand. 3The sword has been sent upon you, and who is there to turn it back? 4A fire has been sent upon you, and who is there to quench it? 5Calamities have been sent upon you, and who is there to drive them away? 6Can one drive off a hungry lion in the forest, or quench a fire in the stubble once it has started to burn?[c] 7Can one turn back an arrow shot by a strong archer? 8The Lord God sends calamities, and who will drive them away? 9Fire will go forth from his wrath, and who is there to quench it? 10He will flash lightning, and who will not be afraid? He will thunder, and who will not be terrified? 11The Lord will threaten, and who will not be utterly shattered at his presence? 12The earth and its foundations quake, the sea is churned up from the depths, and its waves and the fish with them shall be troubled at the presence of the Lord and the glory of his power. 13For his right hand that bends the bow is strong, and his arrows that he shoots are sharp and when they are shot to the ends of the world will not miss once. 14Calamities are sent forth and shall not return until they come over the earth. 15The fire is kindled, and shall not be put out until it consumes the foundations of

the earth. 16Just as an arrow shot by a mighty archer does not return, so the calamities that are sent upon the earth shall not return. 17Alas for me! Alas for me! Who will deliver me in those days?

The Horror of the Last Days

18 The beginning of sorrows, when there shall be much lamentation; the beginning of famine, when many shall perish; the beginning of wars, when the powers shall be terrified; the beginning of calamities, when all shall tremble. What shall they do, when the calamities come? 19Famine and plague, tribulation and anguish are sent as scourges for the correction of humankind. 20Yet for all this they will not turn from their iniquities, or ever be mindful of the scourges. 21Indeed, provisions will be so cheap upon earth that people will imagine that peace is assured for them, and then calamities shall spring up on the earth—the sword, famine, and great confusion. 22For many of those who live on the earth shall perish by famine; and those who survive the famine shall die by the sword. 23And the dead shall be thrown out like dung, and there shall be no one to console them; for the earth shall be left desolate, and its cities shall be demolished. 24No one shall be left to cultivate the earth or to sow it. 25The trees shall bear fruit, but who will gather it? 26The grapes shall ripen, but who will tread them? For in all places there shall be great solitude; 27a person will long to see another human being, or even to hear a human voice. 28For ten shall be left out of a city; and two, out of the field, those who have hidden themselves in thick groves and clefts in the rocks. 29Just as in

---

a Other ancient authorities read *like dry straw*   b Other ancient authorities lack *cloth of goats' hair*   c Other ancient authorities read *fire when dry straw has been set on fire*

15.61–63 According to the historical interpretation, this is Zenobia's defeat.

16.1–17 Judgment is irrevocable on the four nations that represent the Roman Empire. No historical situation can be envisaged. 16.1 *Syria.* See note on 15.30. 16.2 Signs of mourning. See 2 Sam 3.31; Am 8.10. 16.3 *Sword . . . upon you.* Cf. Ezek 21.8–11. 16.6 *Lion.* Cf. Am 3.8. *Stubble.* Cf. Isa 5.24; 47.14. 16.9 For *fire* as God's instrument, see 13.9; 15.23; Jer 4.4. 16.10 For *lightning* as God's instrument, see 2 Sam 22.15. 16.12 *The earth and its foundations quake.* Cf. 2 Sam 22.8, 16. The very underpinnings of the creation are shaken. *Fish.* Cf. Ezek 38.20. 16.13 *Arrows . . . he shoots.*

Cf. vv. 7, 16. This image is not frequent, though it appears in 2 Sam 22.15. 16.14 Cf. Jer 30.24. 16.15 At judgment the earth will be destroyed by fire; cf. 2 Pet 3.10; Josephus, *Antiquities* 1.70. 16.17 Cf. Isa 50; Jer 4.19–26; 15.10–18; Mic 7.1. 16.18–34 The eschatological desolation emerges from the discussion of judgment. 16.19 *Correction.* See Prov 3.11–12; Am 4.6–12. 16.21 *Provisions . . . assured for them.* Cf. *1 Enoch* 96.4–6. Plenty, regarded as a sign of virtue, will give false confidence. 16.22 *Famine, sword.* See 15.5, 57–58. 16.23 See 5.3. 16.24 See 6.22. 16.25–26 Cf. the covenant curses in Lev 26.16, 20. 16.27 Cf. 5.3. 16.28 *Ten . . . left out of a city.* Cf. Am 5.3. *Two, out of the field.* Cf.

an olive orchard three or four olives may be left on every tree, 30or just as, when a vineyard is gathered, some clusters may be left*a* by those who search carefully through the vineyard, 31so in those days three or four shall be left by those who search their houses with the sword. 32The earth shall be left desolate, and its fields shall be plowed up,*b* and its roads and all its paths shall bring forth thorns, because no sheep will go along them. 33Virgins shall mourn because they have no bridegrooms; women shall mourn because they have no husbands; their daughters shall mourn, because they have no help. 34Their bridegrooms shall be killed in war, and their husbands shall perish of famine.

God's People Must Prepare for the End

35 Listen now to these things, and understand them, you who are servants of the Lord. 36This is the word of the Lord; receive it and do not disbelieve what the Lord says.*c* 37The calamities draw near, and are not delayed. 38Just as a pregnant woman, in the ninth month when the time of her delivery draws near, has great pains around her womb for two or three hours beforehand, but when the child comes forth from the womb, there will not be a moment's delay, 39so the calamities will not delay in coming upon the earth, and the world will groan, and pains will seize it on every side.

40 Hear my words, O my people; prepare for battle, and in the midst of the calamities be like strangers on the earth. 41Let the one who sells be like one who will flee; let the one who buys be like one who will lose; 42let the one who does business be like one who will not make a profit; and let the one who builds a house be like one who will not live in it; 43let the one who sows be like one who will not reap; so also the one who prunes the vines, like one who will not gather the grapes; 44those who marry, like those who will have no children; and those who do not marry, like those who are widowed. 45Because of this, those who labor, labor in vain; 46for strangers shall gather their fruits, and plunder their goods, overthrow their houses, and take their children captive; for in captivity and famine they will produce their children.*d* 47Those who conduct business, do so only to have it plundered; the more they adorn their cities, their houses and possessions, and their persons, 48the more angry I will be with them for their sins, says the Lord. 49Just as a respectable and virtuous woman abhors a prostitute, 50so righteousness shall abhor iniquity, when she decks herself out, and shall accuse her to her face when he comes who will defend the one who searches out every sin on earth.

The Power and Wisdom of God

51 Therefore do not be like her or her works. 52For in a very short time iniquity will be removed from the earth, and righteousness will reign over us. 53Sinners must not say that they have not sinned;*e* for God*f* will burn coals of fire on the head of everyone who says, "I have not sinned before God and his glory." 54The Lord*g* certainly knows everything that people do; he knows their imaginations and their thoughts and their hearts. 55He said, "Let the earth be made," and it was made, and "Let the heaven be made," and it was made. 56At his word the stars were fixed in their places, and he knows the number of the stars. 57He

---

a Other ancient authorities read *a cluster may remain exposed* *b* Other ancient authorities read *be for briers* *c* Cn: Lat *do not believe the gods of whom the Lord speaks* *d* Other ancient authorities read *therefore those who are married may know that they will produce children for captivity and famine* *e* Other ancient authorities add *or the unjust done injustice* *f* Lat *for he* *g* Other ancient authorities read *Lord God*

Mt 24.40–41. *Clefts.* Cf. Isa 2.10; Rev 6.15–16. **16.29–31** Cf. Isa 17.4–6. *Clusters.* See 12.42. **16.32** Cf. Isa 7.23–25. Note the different application of the same image. **16.33** *Virgins . . . husbands.* Cf. Jer 7.34. **16.35–52** The eschatological woes are to come, and God's people must separate themselves from this-worldly concerns such as property. **16.35** The elect people are addressed again; see note on 15.53. **16.36** Prophetic opening: the Latin text is odd here and is emended. **16.37** *Calamities,* like those just prophesied; see 15.27. **16.38** The image of the *pregnant woman* is frequent in 2 Esdras and is used in similar contexts; e.g., 4.40–43. The troubles preceding the Messiah are called "birth pangs"; cf. Mt 24.8; Rom 8.22; 1 Thess 5.3. **16.40** The idea of the eschatological *battle* is greatly developed in the Dead Sea Scrolls *War Scroll* (1QM). *Strangers,* as in Heb 11.13; 1 Pet 2.11. **16.41–44** Advice to regard the present world as temporary; cf. 1 Cor 7.29–31. **16.45** Cf. 5.12. **16.47–48** God's anger at possessions, an ascetic dimension of the writer's views. **16.49** Iniquity as a *prostitute,* a widely used image. **16.50** *He comes who . . . every sin on earth.* God and his agent, Jesus, are intended. **16.52** Eschatological *righteousness.* **16.53–67** The sinner must not deny sinning because God the creator will know. **16.53** Cf. 1 Jn 1.8. **16.54** That *the Lord . . . knows everything* is a common biblical theme; cf. Sir 15.19. **16.55–62** Loosely based on Gen 1. **16.56** God's power in creating and numbering or nam-

searches the abyss and its treasures; he has measured the sea and its contents; [58]he has confined the sea in the midst of the waters;[a] and by his word he has suspended the earth over the water. [59]He has spread out the heaven like a dome and made it secure upon the waters; [60]he has put springs of water in the desert, and pools on the tops of the mountains, so as to send rivers from the heights to water the earth. [61]He formed human beings and put a heart in the midst of each body, and gave each person breath and life and understanding [62]and the spirit[b] of Almighty God,[c] who surely made all things and searches out hidden things in hidden places. [63]He knows your imaginations and what you think in your hearts! Woe to those who sin and want to hide their sins! [64]The Lord will strictly examine all their works, and will make a public spectacle of all of you. [65]You shall be put to shame when your sins come out before others, and your own iniquities shall stand as your accusers on that day. [66]What will you do? Or how will you hide your sins before the Lord and his glory? [67]Indeed, God[d] is the judge; fear him! Cease from your sins, and forget your iniquities, never to commit them again; so God[d] will lead you forth and deliver you from all tribulation.

Impending Persecution of God's People

68 The burning wrath of a great multitude is kindled over you; they shall drag some of you away and force you to eat what was sacrificed to idols. [69]And those who consent to eat shall be held in derision and contempt, and shall be trampled under foot. [70]For in many places[e] and in neighboring cities there shall be a great uprising against those who fear the Lord. [71]They shall[f] be like maniacs, sparing no one, but plundering and destroying those who continue to fear the Lord.[g] [72]For they shall destroy and plunder their goods, and drive them out of house and home. [73]Then the tested quality of my elect shall be manifest, like gold that is tested by fire.

Promise of Divine Deliverance

74 Listen, my elect ones, says the Lord; the days of tribulation are at hand, but I will deliver you from them. [75]Do not fear or doubt, for God[d] is your guide. [76]You who keep my commandments and precepts, says the Lord God, must not let your sins weigh you down, or your iniquities prevail over you. [77]Woe to those who are choked by their sins and overwhelmed by their iniquities! They are like a field choked with underbrush and its path[h] overwhelmed with thorns, so that no one can pass through. [78]It is shut off and given up to be consumed by fire.

---

a Other ancient authorities read *confined the world between the waters and the waters*   b Or *breath*   c Other ancient authorities read *of the Lord Almighty*   d Other ancient authorities read *the Lord*   e Meaning of Lat uncertain   f Other ancient authorities read *For people, because of their misfortunes, shall*   g Other ancient authorities read *fear God*   h Other ancient authorities read *seed*

16.64 The idea of the public character of judgment is found prominently in *7.37*. **16.65** *Put to shame.* Cf. *7.87.* **16.66** Glory as the revealing element; see *7.112.* **16.67** Exhortation. **16.68–73** An attack to test the righteous is foreseen. **16.68** Cf. Acts 15.20; 1 Cor 8; 2 Macc 6.7–8. **16.73** See Isa 48.10; Zech 13.9; 1 Pet 1.7.

---

ing the stars; cf. Isa 40.26; Ps 147.4. **16.57** See Job 38.16. **16.58** *Confined the sea.* See Jer 5.22; Pr Man 3; *1 Enoch* 69.19. *Suspended.* See Ps 136.6. **16.59** See Gen 1.6–8; Isa 44.24. **16.60** *Water in the desert.* Cf. Isa 40.22 (Septuagint); Ps 107.35. **16.61** *Formed human beings.* See Gen 2.8; 2 Esd 8.8–13. **16.62** Cf. Deut 29.29; Ps 44.21.

(d) The following book appears in an appendix to the Greek Bible.

4 MACCABEES

THE BOOK OF 4 MACCABEES is found as an appendix to some manuscripts of the Septuagint, although it was never considered canonical. It is also found in some manuscripts of the works of the first-century CE Jewish historian Flavius Josephus, although Josephus's authorship of 4 Maccabees is now universally rejected.

Content and Purpose

FOURTH MACCABEES IS DIVIDED INTO TWO PARTS. The first part (1.1–3.18) is a philosophical discourse demonstrating the supremacy of "devout reason" over the emotions and the compatibility of reason with Mosaic law. This compatibility is illustrated by several biblical examples. The second and much longer part (3.19–18.24) gives three examples to support the thesis of the supremacy of religious reason over the emotions. After an introductory narrative that sets the scene (3.19–4.26), the author tells the stories of the torture and martyrdom by the Seleucid ruler Antiochus IV Epiphanes of the elderly priest Eleazar (5.1–7.23), seven brothers (8.1–14.10), and their mother (14.11–17.6). These examples are followed by a loosely organized peroration (17.7–18.24). The author's purpose was, through the use of Greek rhetorical and philosophical conventions, to persuade his fellow diaspora Jews to continue to observe the Mosaic law strictly in the face of the pressures and attractions from the surrounding world to desert observance of the law and assimilate to a Greek way of life.

Literary Genre, Occasion, and Sources

FOURTH MACCABEES WAS COMPOSED IN GREEK, and its author was familiar with Greek rhetorical conventions and, to some extent, Greek philosophical viewpoints. The style of 4 Maccabees reflects the florid, elaborate "Asiatic" style of Greek rhetoric rather than the classical, Attic style. The book is an example of epideictic rhetoric (the rhetoric of praise and blame). More specifically, it is a combination of two literary genres: moral instruction and funeral oration, but it also contains elements drawn from Greek rhetorical historiography and Greek tragedy in its descriptions of the suffering and death of the main characters. The genre of moral instruction, with its emphasis on the domination of devout reason over the emotions, is most prominent in 1.1–3.18 but is also found scattered throughout the book (e.g., 6.31–35; 13.1–5). The genre of funeral oration dominates the rest of 4 Maccabees, which covers the actual descriptions of the suffering and death of Eleazar, the seven brothers, and their mother. Greek funeral orations, such as Pericles' funeral oration for the Athenian dead (Thucydides, *Peloponnesian Wars* 2.35–46) and Plato's *Menexemus*, have many thematic elements in common with 4 Maccabees. These themes include praise of the noble birth, education, courage, piety, and endurance of those who have fallen, praise of their opposition to a tyrannical king, and praise of the ancestral land for which they died. Both Greek funeral orations and 4 Maccabees were intended to encourage the living to show similar virtues.

It has been suggested that 4 Maccabees was written as a synagogue homily, a lecture, or a genuine funeral oration commemorating the anniversary of the deaths of the martyrs. Given its combination of literary genres and its ornate style, it was more likely composed as a fictive oration unconnected with any particular occasion, similar to the oration in Plato's *Menexemus*.

The source of the stories in 4 Maccabees is 2 Maccabees. 4 Macc 3.19–4.14 derives from 2 Macc 3.1–40, 4 Macc 4.15–26 from 2 Macc 4.7–6.11, 4 Macc 5.1–6.35 from 2 Macc 6.18–31, and 4 Macc 8.1–18.19 from 2 Macc 7.1–42. Although the author of 4 Maccabees may have been acquainted with the work of Jason of Cyrene, of which 2 Maccabees is a "summary," it is much more likely that the differences between 4 Maccabees and 2 Maccabees are due to reinterpretations and rhetorical expansions by the author of 4 Maccabees himself.

Author, Place, and Date of Composition

THE IDENTITY OF THE AUTHOR of 4 Maccabees is unknown, but he was certainly an observant Jew of the Hellenistic Diaspora who had a Greek rhetorical education. Although he makes use of Greek philosophical concepts and vocabulary (such as the cardinal virtues and the supremacy of reason over the emotions), his knowledge of Greek philosophy is limited and reflects an eclectic Stoicism that was common during this period. It is the philosophical knowledge someone would have obtained as part of a rhetorical rather than an extensive philosophical education. In the end it serves exclusively to support his views about the importance of the faithful observance of Mosaic law.

The precise date and place of composition of 4 Maccabees are unclear. It was almost certainly composed in the Hellenistic-Jewish Diaspora, i.e., outside of Palestine. Antioch in Syria and several of the coastal cities in Asia Minor, all of which had significant Jewish communities, have been suggested as places of composition. Since later Jewish and Christian tradition located the tombs of these martyrs at Antioch, that city may be the most plausible suggestion, although the others cannot be ruled out. Various dates of composition have been suggested, from the middle of the first century BCE through the early second century CE. The most plausible range of dates, however, is from the middle of the first century to the early second century CE.

Religious Ideas

FROM A THEOLOGICAL POINT OF VIEW, 4 Maccabees is notable for its belief in the immortality of the soul (e.g., 9.22; 14.5; 15.3; 16.13; 17.12; 18.23), a viewpoint it shares with the Wisdom of Solomon (ca. 30 BCE –70 CE) and the writings of Philo of Alexandria (ca. 10 BCE –50 CE). The pure and immortal soul will enter into the incorruption of everlasting life. There is also a strong belief in divine reward (e.g., 5.37; 9.8; 15.3; 17.12) and retribution (e.g., 4.10–12; 9.9, 32; 10.11, 15, 21; 11.3; 12.12, 18; 18.5, 22). God will reward those who die for the sake of Mosaic law and will punish both in this life and after death those who torture and execute them. Finally, there is the belief that the suffering and death of these martyrs have a redemptive efficacy and have secured God's pardon for Israel (6.28–29; 17.21–22; see also 1.11; 9.24; 12.17; 17.10; 18.4). The idea of vicarious atonement was also used in the NT to explain the efficacy of Jesus' suffering and death (e.g., Mt 20.28; Mk 10.45; Rom 3.24–26; 5.9–10; 8.3; 1 Tim 2.6; Heb 9.11–14). Though it is possible that some NT writers took this concept from 4 Maccabees, it is much more likely that both 4 Maccabees and the NT writers shared a belief that, although not widespread, was present in Judaism during this period (see also the Dead Sea Scrolls *Rule of the Community* [1QS] 5.6; 8.3–4, 6, 10; 9.4). [THOMAS. H. TOBIN]

The Author's Definition of His Task

1 The subject that I am about to discuss is most philosophical, that is, whether devout reason is sovereign over the emotions. So it is right for me to advise you to pay earnest attention to philosophy. 2For the subject is essential to everyone who is seeking knowledge, and in addition it includes the praise of the highest virtue—I mean, of course, rational judgment. 3If, then, it is evident that reason rules over those emotions that hinder self-control, namely, gluttony and lust, 4it is also clear that it masters the emotions that hinder one from justice, such as malice, and those that stand in the way of courage, namely anger, fear, and pain. 5Some might perhaps ask, "If reason rules the emotions, why is it not sovereign over forgetfulness and ignorance?" Their attempt at argument is ridiculous!*a* 6For reason does not rule its own emotions, but those that are opposed to justice, courage, and self-control;*b* and it is not for the purpose of destroying them, but so that one may not give way to them.

7 I could prove to you from many and various examples that reason*c* is dominant over the emotions, 8but I can demonstrate it best from the noble bravery of those who died for the sake of virtue, Eleazar and the seven brothers and their mother. 9All of these, by despising sufferings that bring death, demonstrated that reason controls the emotions. 10On this anniversary*d* it is fitting for me to praise for their virtues those who, with their mother, died for the sake of nobility and goodness, but I would also call them blessed for the honor in which they are held. 11All people, even their torturers, marveled at their courage and endurance, and they became the cause of the downfall of tyranny over their nation. By their endurance they conquered the tyrant, and thus their native land was purified through them. 12I shall shortly have an opportunity to speak of this; but, as my custom is, I shall begin by stating my main principle, and then I shall turn to their story, giving glory to the all-wise God.

---

a Or *They are attempting to make my argument ridiculous!*
b Other ancient authorities add *and rational judgment* *c* Other ancient authorities read *devout reason* *d* Gk *At this time*

1.1–3.18 In a lengthy philosophical introduction, the author develops his thesis about the supremacy of devout reason over the emotions and its harmony with Mosaic law. He then offers the conduct of Joseph, Moses, Jacob, and especially David as examples. **1.1–12** Rhetorical exordium (prologue). The author states the philosophical thesis that *devout reason is sovereign over the emotions* (vv. 1–6) and promises to prove this thesis by the examples of Eleazar and the seven brothers and their mother (vv. 7–12). **1.2–4** *Rational judgment* (or prudence), *self-control* (or temperance), *justice,* and *courage* are the four cardinal virtues commonly discussed in both the Platonic (Plato, *Republic* 427E–448E) and Stoic (Diogenes Laertius, *Lives of Eminent Philosophers* 7.92) schools of Greek philosophy. They are also discussed in Wis 8.7 and frequently in the works of Philo of Alexandria (e.g., *Allegories on the Law* 1.63–73). See v. 18; 5.23–24; 15.10. **1.5–6** See

2.24–3.5 for a fuller answer to the objection that reason is *not sovereign over forgetfulness and ignorance.* Though Stoics generally held that reason was able to eradicate the emotions, that position was not universal. The Stoic Posidonius (ca. 135–51 BCE) held that emotions could be controlled but not eradicated. See also vv. 28–29; 3.2–5. **1.8** *Eleazar and the seven brothers and their mother* serve as examples not only of the dominance of reason over the emotions but also of the virtues of courage and endurance, which led to the downfall of the tyrant (the Seleucid king Antiochus IV) and the purification of their native land. This second element is more prominent in 3.19–18.24 than the first. **1.10** *On this anniversary* (lit. *at this time;* see text note *d*) has led some (probably incorrectly) to believe that 4 Maccabees may have been composed in connection with some sort of commemoration of the deaths of Eleazar and the seven brothers and their

The Supremacy of Reason

13 Our inquiry, accordingly, is whether reason is sovereign over the emotions. 14We shall decide just what reason is and what emotion is, how many kinds of emotions there are, and whether reason rules over all these. 15Now reason is the mind that with sound logic prefers the life of wisdom. 16Wisdom, next, is the knowledge of divine and human matters and the causes of these. 17This, in turn, is education in the law, by which we learn divine matters reverently and human affairs to our advantage. 18Now the kinds of wisdom are rational judgment, justice, courage, and self-control. 19Rational judgment is supreme over all of these, since by means of it reason rules over the emotions. 20The two most comprehensive types*a* of the emotions are pleasure and pain; and each of these is by nature concerned with both body and soul. 21The emotions of both pleasure and pain have many consequences. 22Thus desire precedes pleasure and delight follows it. 23Fear precedes pain and sorrow comes after. 24Anger, as a person will see by reflecting on this experience, is an emotion embracing pleasure and pain. 25In pleasure there exists even a malevolent tendency, which is the most complex of all the emotions. 26In the soul it is boastfulness, covetousness, thirst for honor, rivalry, and malice; 27in the body, indiscriminate eating, gluttony, and solitary gormandizing.

28 Just as pleasure and pain are two plants growing from the body and the soul, so there are many offshoots of these plants,*b* 29each of which the master cultivator, reason, weeds and prunes and ties up and waters and thoroughly irrigates, and so tames the jungle of habits and emotions. 30For reason is the guide of the virtues, but over the emotions it is sovereign.

Observe now, first of all, that rational judgment is sovereign over the emotions by virtue of the restraining power of self-control. 31Self-control, then, is dominance over the desires. 32Some desires are mental, others are physical, and reason obviously rules over both. 33Otherwise, how is it that when we are attracted to forbidden foods we abstain from the pleasure to be had from them? Is it not because reason is able to rule over appetites? I for one think so. 34Therefore when we crave seafood and fowl and animals and all sorts of foods that are forbidden to us by the law, we abstain because of domination by reason. 35For the emotions of the appetites are restrained, checked by the temperate mind, and all the impulses of the body are bridled by reason.

Compatibility of the Law with Reason

2 And why is it amazing that the desires of the mind for the enjoyment of beauty are rendered powerless? 2It is for this reason, certainly, that the temperate Joseph is praised, because by mental effort*c* he overcame sexual desire. 3For when he was young and in his prime for intercourse, by his reason he nullified the frenzy*d* of the passions. 4Not only is reason proved to rule over the frenzied urge of sexual desire, but also over every desire.*e* 5Thus the law says, "You shall not covet your neighbor's wife or anything that is your neighbor's." 6In fact, since the law has told us not to covet, I could prove to you all the more that reason is able to control desires.

Just so it is with the emotions that hinder one from justice. 7Otherwise how could it be that someone who is habitually a solitary gor-

---

a Or *sources*   *b* Other ancient authorities read *these emotions*
c Other ancient authorities add *in reasoning*   *d* Or *gadfly*
e Or *all covetousness*

---

mother. See also 3.19; 14.9. **1.13–30a** A series of definitions and distinctions intended to show more specifically how reason dominates various emotions. Making such distinctions is common in most schools of Greco-Roman philosophy. This discussion is then connected with Mosaic law (vv. 17, 33–34). **1.16** This definition of wisdom was commonplace in Greek philosophy and was used by both Stoics and Platonists (Cicero, *Tusculan Disputations* 4.26.57; Philo, *On the Preliminary Studies* 79). **1.17** The author has reformulated the Greek notion of wisdom and identified it with *education in the law*. **1.18–27** This exposition of the virtues and their relationship to various vices is filled with philosophical commonplaces, but it cannot be identified exclusively with any one philosophical

school. **1.18** See vv. 2–4. **1.26–27** A catalog of vices; such catalogs were common in Greco-Roman ethics. See also Rom 1.28–32; Gal 5.19–23. **1.30b–2.23** An expansion on particular virtues and vices using biblical examples to illustrate the harmony between reason and Mosaic law. **1.30b–2.6a** The power of rational judgment as seen in the restraining power of self-control. **1.33** *Forbidden foods.* The author once again brings in Mosaic law, which then becomes more prominent in the rest of the philosophical introduction. **1.34** *Seafood and . . . animals.* For the various kinds of unclean creatures, see Lev 11.1–47; Deut 14.3–21; Acts 10.10–14. **2.2–3** The patriarch *Joseph* is used as an example of self-control. See Gen 39.7–12. **2.5** See Ex 20.17; Deut 5.21. **2.6b–9a** The power of

mandizer, a glutton, or even a drunkard can learn a better way, unless reason is clearly lord of the emotions? 8Thus, as soon as one adopts a way of life in accordance with the law, even though a lover of money, one is forced to act contrary to natural ways and to lend without interest to the needy and to cancel the debt when the seventh year arrives. 9If one is greedy, one is ruled by the law through reason so that one neither gleans the harvest nor gathers the last grapes from the vineyard.

In all other matters we can recognize that reason rules the emotions. 10For the law prevails even over affection for parents, so that virtue is not abandoned for their sakes. 11It is superior to love for one's wife, so that one rebukes her when she breaks the law. 12It takes precedence over love for children, so that one punishes them for misdeeds. 13It is sovereign over the relationship of friends, so that one rebukes friends when they act wickedly. 14Do not consider it paradoxical when reason, through the law, can prevail even over enmity. The fruit trees of the enemy are not cut down, but one preserves the property of enemies from marauders and helps raise up what has fallen. *a*

15 It is evident that reason rules even *b* the more violent emotions: lust for power, vainglory, boasting, arrogance, and malice. 16For the temperate mind repels all these malicious emotions, just as it repels anger—for it is sovereign over even this. 17When Moses was angry with Dathan and Abiram, he did nothing against them in anger, but controlled his anger by reason. 18For, as I have said, the temperate mind is able to get the better of the emotions, to

correct some, and to render others powerless. 19Why else did Jacob, our most wise father, censure the households of Simeon and Levi for their irrational slaughter of the entire tribe of the Shechemites, saying, "Cursed be their anger"? 20For if reason could not control anger, he would not have spoken thus. 21Now when God fashioned human beings, he planted in them emotions and inclinations, 22but at the same time he enthroned the mind among the senses as a sacred governor over them all. 23To the mind he gave the law; and one who lives subject to this will rule a kingdom that is temperate, just, good, and courageous.

24 How is it then, one might say, that if reason is master of the emotions, it does not control forgetfulness and ignorance? 3 1But this argument is entirely ridiculous; for it is evident that reason rules not over its own emotions, but over those of the body. 2No one of us *c* can eradicate that kind of desire, but reason can provide a way for us not to be enslaved by desire. 3No one of us can eradicate anger from the mind, but reason can help to deal with anger. 4No one of us can eradicate malice, but reason can fight at our side so that we are not overcome by malice. 5For reason does not uproot the emotions but is their antagonist.

King David's Thirst

6 Now this can be explained more clearly by the story of King David's thirst. 7David had been attacking the Philistines all day long, and

a Or *the beasts that have fallen* *b* Other ancient authorities read *through* *c* Gk *you*

---

reason as seen in the practice of justice. **2.8** On *lending without interest* (to fellow Jews), see Ex 22.25; Lev 25.35–37; Deut 23.19–20; on *canceling the debt when the seventh year arrives,* see Deut 15.1–11. **2.9a** On leaving gleanings for the poor, see Lev 19.9–10; 23.22; Deut 24.21. **2.9b–14** Reason/law prevails over all other natural affections, even love for parents, wife, and children. This discussion foreshadows the stories of Eleazar, the mother, and her seven sons, which form the main part of 4 Maccabees. See 14.1. *2.14 Fruit trees . . . not cut down.* Cutting down enemies' fruit trees is forbidden by Deut 20.19 (see Josephus, *Against Apion* 2.211–12). **2.15–23** The examples of Moses and Jacob show that reason/law rules over even violent emotions such as anger. **2.17** On *Dathan and Abiram,* see Num 16.12–15, 23–35; Sir 45.18–19. **2.19** On the rape of Dinah, the sister of Simeon and Levi, the slaughter of the Shechemites, and Jacob's rebuke, see Gen 34; 49.7. **2.21** God's *planting* of various emotions (both good

and evil) in human beings is discussed in the Dead Sea Scrolls (*Rule of the Community* [1QS] 3.13–4.26), in Philo (*On the Creation of the World* 153, 154; *Allegories on the Laws* 1.43–52), and in rabbinic literature (*Babylonian Talmud Berakot* 61a). **2.23** That the wise man is a king is a Stoic commonplace (Diogenes Laertius, *Lives of Eminent Philosophers* 7.122) and is also found in Philo (*On the Migration of Abraham* 197). See 14.2. **2.24–3.18** Reason cannot eradicate the emotions, but it can control them, an argument illustrated by an incident from the life of King David. **2.24–3.5** A fuller refutation of the objection raised in 1.5–6. The argument, however, is murky. The point seems to be that reason does not rule over those emotions (passions) internal to itself (e.g., forgetfulness or ignorance) but only over those in some way connected with the body. Reason can control these latter emotions, but not eradicate them. The inability of reason to master forgetfulness is discussed in Philo, *On the Migration of*

together with the soldiers of his nation had killed many of them. [8]Then when evening fell, he[a] came, sweating and quite exhausted, to the royal tent, around which the whole army of our ancestors had encamped. [9]Now all the rest were at supper, [10]but the king was extremely thirsty, and though springs were plentiful there, he could not satisfy his thirst from them. [11]But a certain irrational desire for the water in the enemy's territory tormented and inflamed him, undid and consumed him. [12]When his guards complained bitterly because of the king's craving, two staunch young soldiers, respecting[b] the king's desire, armed themselves fully, and taking a pitcher climbed over the enemy's ramparts. [13]Eluding the sentinels at the gates, they went searching throughout the enemy camp [14]and found the spring, and from it boldly brought the king a drink. [15]But David,[c] though he was burning with thirst, considered it an altogether fearful danger to his soul to drink what was regarded as equivalent to blood. [16]Therefore, opposing reason to desire, he poured out the drink as an offering to God. [17]For the temperate mind can conquer the drives of the emotions and quench the flames of frenzied desires; [18]it can overthrow bodily agonies even when they are extreme, and by nobility of reason spurn all domination by the emotions.

An Attempt on the Temple Treasury

[19] The present occasion now invites us to a narrative demonstration of temperate reason.

[20] At a time when our ancestors were enjoying profound peace because of their observance of the law and were prospering, so that even Seleucus Nicanor, king of Asia, had both appropriated money to them for the temple service and recognized their commonwealth— [21]just at that time certain persons attempted a revolution against the public harmony and caused many and various disasters.

4 Now there was a certain Simon, a political opponent of the noble and good man, Onias, who then held the high priesthood for life. When despite all manner of slander he was unable to injure Onias in the eyes of the nation, he fled the country with the purpose of betraying it. [2]So he came to Apollonius, governor of Syria, Phoenicia, and Cilicia, and said, [3]"I have come here because I am loyal to the king's government, to report that in the Jerusalem treasuries there are deposited tens of thousands in private funds, which are not the property of the temple but belong to King Seleucus." [4]When Apollonius learned the details of these things, he praised Simon for his service to the king and went up to Seleucus to inform him of the rich treasure. [5]On receiving authority to deal with this matter, he proceeded quickly to our country accompanied by the accursed Simon and a very strong military force. [6]He said that he had come with the king's authority to seize the private funds in

---

a Other ancient authorities read *he hurried and*
b Or *embarrassed because of* c Gk *he*

Abraham 206. **3.6–18** The example of David's thirst, a story, with some differences in detail, found in 2 Sam 23.13–17; 1 Chr 11.15–19. The author uses the story as the prime example of how reason, the temperate mind, can overcome irrational, frenzied desires. **3.11** That David's desire is *irrational* is emphasized.
3.19–18.24 The narratives of the martyrdoms. Two introductory narratives that set the scene (3.19–4.26) are followed first by the narratives of the martyrdoms of Eleazar (5.1–7.23), the seven brothers (8.1–14.10), and their mother (14.11–17.6) and then by a conclusion (17.7–18.24). These narratives emphasize specific virtues such as courage, patient endurance for the sake of religion, and commitment to observance of the law as well as the dominance of devout reason over the emotions. **3.19–4.14** A shortened version of 2 Macc 3.1–40. **3.19** *The present occasion*, the time at which the speech was purportedly delivered, probably a rhetorical fiction. See also 1.10; 14.9. **3.20–21** Peace and prosperity, which are connected with observance of the law, are endangered by those who seek to disturb

public harmony by breaking the law. In v. 20 as well as in 4.3, 13, 20 the author has omitted the references to sacrifices found in 2 Macc 3.3, 6, 32–33, 35; 4.14. **3.20** *Seleucus Nicanor* (311–281 BCE), an author error for Seleucus IV Philopator (187–175 BCE), who is the actual Seleucid king in this story. **4.1** *Simon*, the captain of the Jerusalem temple according to 2 Macc 3.4. Onias III, the son of the high priest Simon II the Just, praised in Sir 50.1–21. The practice of *life* tenure for the high priest was often disregarded, as in this case, by those in political power (Josephus, *Antiquities* 17.339; 18.34–35; 20.224–51). **4.2** *Cilicia* was attached to Syria and Phoenicia from 20 CE until the Roman emperor Vespasian made it a separate province in 72 CE. The connection in this verse may be a historical anachronism rather than a clue to the date of the composition of 4 Maccabees. **4.3** *In the . . . treasuries . . . private funds.* The temple treasury served as, among other things, a kind of bank (Josephus, *War* 6.282). **4.4–5** In 2 Macc 3.7 another official, Heliodorus, not *Apollonius*, was put in command of the expedition. The

the treasury. 7The people indignantly protested his words, considering it outrageous that those who had committed deposits to the sacred treasury should be deprived of them, and did all that they could to prevent it. 8But, uttering threats, Apollonius went on to the temple. 9While the priests together with women and children were imploring God in the temple to shield the holy place that was being treated so contemptuously, 10and while Apollonius was going up with his armed forces to seize the money, angels on horseback with lightning flashing from their weapons appeared from heaven, instilling in them great fear and trembling. 11Then Apollonius fell down half dead in the temple area that was open to all, stretched out his hands toward heaven, and with tears begged the Hebrews to pray for him and propitiate the wrath of the heavenly army. 12For he said that he had committed a sin deserving of death, and that if he were spared he would praise the blessedness of the holy place before all people. 13Moved by these words, the high priest Onias, although otherwise he had scruples about doing so, prayed for him so that King Seleucus would not suppose that Apollonius had been overcome by human treachery and not by divine justice. 14So Apollonius,[a] having been saved beyond all expectations, went away to report to the king what had happened to him.

Antiochus' Persecution of the Jews

15 When King Seleucus died, his son Antiochus Epiphanes succeeded to the throne, an arrogant and terrible man, 16who removed Onias from the priesthood and appointed Onias's[b] brother Jason as high priest. 17Jason[c] agreed that if the office were conferred on him

he would pay the king three thousand six hundred sixty talents annually. 18So the king appointed him high priest and ruler of the nation. 19Jason[c] changed the nation's way of life and altered its form of government in complete violation of the law, 20so that not only was a gymnasium constructed at the very citadel[d] of our native land, but also the temple service was abolished. 21The divine justice was angered by these acts and caused Antiochus himself to make war on them. 22For when he was warring against Ptolemy in Egypt, he heard that a rumor of his death had spread and that the people of Jerusalem had rejoiced greatly. He speedily marched against them, 23and after he had plundered them he issued a decree that if any of them were found observing the ancestral law they should die. 24When, by means of his decrees, he had not been able in any way to put an end to the people's observance of the law, but saw that all his threats and punishments were being disregarded 25— even to the extent that women, because they had circumcised their sons, were thrown headlong from heights along with their infants, though they had known beforehand that they would suffer this— 26when, I say, his decrees were despised by the people, he himself tried through torture to compel everyone in the nation to eat defiling foods and to renounce Judaism.

Antiochus's Encounter with Eleazar

5 The tyrant Antiochus, sitting in state with his counselors on a certain high place, and with his armed soldiers standing around him, 2ordered the guards to seize each and every

---

a Gk he b Gk his c Gk He d Or high place

---

author of 4 Maccabees has simplified the story. **4.15–26** A much-shortened version of 2 Macc 4.7–6.11. **4.15** *Antiochus IV Epiphanes* (175–164 BCE), the brother, not the *son*, of Seleucus IV. Both were sons of Antiochus III. **4.16** *Jason*, the Jewish high priest ca. 175–172 BCE. **4.20** The *gymnasium*, a place where the Greek way of life, in addition to physical training, was imparted to young men. The gymnasium was not actually built on the *citadel* but under it (2 Macc 4.12). **4.22** On *Ptolemy* VI Philomator (180–145 BCE), see 1 Macc 1.16–19. *People of Jerusalem* suggests that the events described in 4 Maccabees took place in Jerusalem, although the city is not mentioned again until 18.5. Later Jewish and Christian traditions placed the tombs of the martyrs in Antioch. **4.24–26** The author emphasizes the extent to which Jews would go to con-

tinue observing their law. **4.26** *Defiling foods*, esp. pork. See 5.2.

5.1–7.23 The source of the story of the death of Eleazar is 2 Macc 6.18–31. The story has been significantly expanded in 4 Maccabees, especially by means of speeches by Eleazar and Antiochus. **5.1–38** The emphasis in the encounter between Antiochus and Eleazar is on two speeches, one by Antiochus (vv. 5–13) and the other by Eleazar (vv. 14–38). Antiochus's speech is meant to exemplify arguments used to persuade Jews to forgo observance of the law and assimilate to the Greek way of life. Eleazar's speech is meant to demonstrate why Jews should continue to observe the law strictly and not assimilate. **5.1** *Tyrant*, for the Greeks a ruler unlimited by either law or a constitution, usually with a negative connotation. **5.2** During

Hebrew and to compel them to eat pork and food sacrificed to idols. [3]If any were not willing to eat defiling food, they were to be broken on the wheel and killed. [4]When many persons had been rounded up, one man, Eleazar by name, leader of the flock, was brought[a] before the king. He was a man of priestly family, learned in the law, advanced in age, and known to many in the tyrant's court because of his philosophy.[b]

[5]When Antiochus saw him he said, [6]"Before I begin to torture you, old man, I would advise you to save yourself by eating pork, [7]for I respect your age and your gray hairs. Although you have had them for so long a time, it does not seem to me that you are a philosopher when you observe the religion of the Jews. [8]When nature has granted it to us, why should you abhor eating the very excellent meat of this animal? [9]It is senseless not to enjoy delicious things that are not shameful, and wrong to spurn the gifts of nature. [10]It seems to me that you will do something even more senseless if, by holding a vain opinion concerning the truth, you continue to despise me to your own hurt. [11]Will you not awaken from your foolish philosophy, dispel your futile reasonings, adopt a mind appropriate to your years, philosophize according to the truth of what is beneficial, [12]and have compassion on your old age by honoring my humane advice? [13]For consider this: if there is some power watching over this religion of yours, it will excuse you from any transgression that arises out of compulsion."

[14]When the tyrant urged him in this fashion to eat meat unlawfully, Eleazar asked to have a word. [15]When he had received permission to speak, he began to address the people as follows: [16]"We, O Antiochus, who have been persuaded to govern our lives by the divine law, think that there is no compulsion more powerful than our obedience to the law. [17]Therefore we consider that we should not transgress it in any respect. [18]Even if, as you suppose, our law were not truly divine and we had wrongly held it to be divine, not even so would it be right for us to invalidate our reputation for piety. [19]Therefore do not suppose that it would be a petty sin if we were to eat defiling food; [20]to transgress the law in matters either small or great is of equal seriousness, [21]for in either case the law is equally despised. [22]You scoff at our philosophy as though living by it were irrational, [23]but it teaches us self-control, so that we master all pleasures and desires, and it also trains us in courage, so that we endure any suffering willingly; [24]it instructs us in justice, so that in all our dealings we act impartially,[c] and it teaches us piety, so that with proper reverence we worship the only living God.

[25]"Therefore we do not eat defiling food; for since we believe that the law was established by God, we know that in the nature of things the Creator of the world in giving us the law has shown sympathy toward us. [26]He has permitted us to eat what will be most suitable for our lives,[d] but he has forbidden us to eat

---

a Or *was the first of the flock to be brought*   *b* Other ancient authorities read *his advanced age*   *c* Or *so that we hold in balance all our habitual inclinations*   *d* Or *souls*

---

the Maccabean period and later, the refusal to *eat pork* became a touchstone to Jews for observance of the law in a hostile environment and as important as not eating *food sacrificed to idols.* **5.4** *Eleazar,* in Hebrew "God has helped." **5.5–13** Antiochus tries to persuade Eleazar to eat pork first on the basis of philosophical arguments (vv. 8–12) and then by claiming that compulsion is a legitimate excuse for transgressing a law (v. 13). Antiochus's philosophical arguments are based on the Stoic precept of "living according to nature." **5.7** The Greek word *threskeia* usually means religious cult or practice, but here it means something more general, i.e., *religion.* For a similar usage, see Wis 14.18, 27. **5.13** The idea of God *watching over* human beings is a Greek philosophical concept frequently found also in the works of Jewish writers (2 Macc 7.35; 9.5; 3 Macc 2.21; Philo, *Against Flaccus* 121). The same argument that *compulsion* is an excuse is found in 8.14, 25. **5.14–38** Eleazar's speech emphasizes not only his absolute commitment to observance of the law but also that this commitment is a rational one and in accordance with nature. Eleazar uses Stoic viewpoints to refute Antiochus's Stoic arguments. **5.20–21** The author seems to espouse the Stoic position that all transgressions are *of equal seriousness.* A similar position is found in Philo (*Allegories on the Laws* 3.241). **5.23–24** *Self-control, courage, justice,* three of the four cardinal virtues. Eleazar substitutes *piety* (Greek *eusebeia*), i.e., proper reverence toward God, for the usual fourth, rational judgment (Greek *phronesis;* see 1.2–4, 18; 15.10). The substitution of piety for one of the cardinal virtues is also found in Xenophon (*Memorabilia* 4.6), Josephus (*Against Apion* 2.170), and Philo (*On the Cherubim* 96). **5.26** Eleazar claims that eating certain foods and refraining from eating others has its basis in what is *suitable for our lives* (lit. *souls;* see text note *d*). A similar approach to the purity regulations is found in the *Letter of Aristeas* (128–71) and often in

meats that would be contrary to this. 27It would be tyrannical for you to compel us not only to transgress the law, but also to eat in such a way that you may deride us for eating defiling foods, which are most hateful to us. 28But you shall have no such occasion to laugh at me, 29nor will I transgress the sacred oaths of my ancestors concerning the keeping of the law, 30not even if you gouge out my eyes and burn my entrails. 31I am not so old and cowardly as not to be young in reason on behalf of piety. 32Therefore get your torture wheels ready and fan the fire more vehemently! 33I do not so pity my old age as to break the ancestral law by my own act. 34I will not play false to you, O law that trained me, nor will I renounce you, beloved self-control. 35I will not put you to shame, philosophical reason, nor will I reject you, honored priesthood and knowledge of the law. 36You, O king,*a* shall not defile the honorable mouth of my old age, nor my long life lived lawfully. 37My ancestors will receive me as pure, as one who does not fear your violence even to death. 38You may tyrannize the ungodly, but you shall not dominate my religious principles, either by words or through deeds."

Martyrdom of Eleazar

6 When Eleazar in this manner had made eloquent response to the exhortations of the tyrant, the guards who were standing by dragged him violently to the instruments of torture. 2First they stripped the old man, though he remained adorned with the gracefulness of his piety. 3After they had tied his arms on each side they flogged him, 4while a herald who faced him cried out, "Obey the king's commands!" 5But the courageous and noble man, like a true Eleazar, was unmoved, as though being tortured in a dream; 6yet while the old man's eyes were raised to heaven, his flesh was being torn by scourges, his blood flowing, and his sides were being cut to pieces. 7Although he fell to the ground because his

body could not endure the agonies, he kept his reason upright and unswerving. 8One of the cruel guards rushed at him and began to kick him in the side to make him get up again after he fell. 9But he bore the pains and scorned the punishment and endured the tortures. 10Like a noble athlete the old man, while being beaten, was victorious over his torturers; 11in fact, with his face bathed in sweat, and gasping heavily for breath, he amazed even his torturers by his courageous spirit.

12 At that point, partly out of pity for his old age, 13partly out of sympathy from their acquaintance with him, partly out of admiration for his endurance, some of the king's retinue came to him and said, 14"Eleazar, why are you so irrationally destroying yourself through these evil things? 15We will set before you some cooked meat; save yourself by pretending to eat pork."

16 But Eleazar, as though more bitterly tormented by this counsel, cried out: 17"Never may we, the children of Abraham,*b* think so basely that out of cowardice we feign a role unbecoming to us! 18For it would be irrational if having lived in accordance with truth up to old age and having maintained in accordance with law the reputation of such a life, we should now change our course 19and ourselves become a pattern of impiety to the young by setting them an example in the eating of defiling food. 20It would be shameful if we should survive for a little while and during that time be a laughingstock to all for our cowardice, 21and be despised by the tyrant as unmanly by not contending even to death for our divine law. 22Therefore, O children of Abraham, die nobly for your religion! 23And you, guards of the tyrant, why do you delay?"

24 When they saw that he was so courageous in the face of the afflictions, and that he had not been changed by their compassion, the guards brought him to the fire. 25There

---

a Gk lacks O king   *b* Or O children of Abraham

Philo's interpretations. See Lev 11.1–23. **5.37** *My ancestors will receive me.* See 13.17; 17.12, which indicate the immortality of the martyrs more clearly. **6.1–35** This account of Eleazar's death is marked by its graphic description of Eleazar's tortures and his speeches (vv. 16–23, 27–29) during the tortures. Cf. 2 Macc 6.28–29. **6.5** *A true Eleazar,* a worthy successor to his namesake Eleazar, the third and most prominent son of Aaron, who became high priest at Aaron's death

(Num 20.25–28). **6.10** *A noble athlete,* an image also used in 9.8; 11.20–21; 14.5; 15.29; 16.16; 17.11–16 about the seven brothers and their mother, was also popular in Christian martyrdom literature. **6.16–23** In reply to the suggestion that he pretend to eat pork, Eleazar emphasizes that it would be *irrational* for him (v. 18), after a long life of observing the law, now to eat defiled food and thus give an example of *impiety to the young* and become a *laughingstock to all* (vv. 19–

they burned him with maliciously contrived instruments, threw him down, and poured stinking liquids into his nostrils. 26When he was now burned to his very bones and about to expire, he lifted up his eyes to God and said, 27"You know, O God, that though I might have saved myself, I am dying in burning torments for the sake of the law. 28Be merciful to your people, and let our punishment suffice for them. 29Make my blood their purification, and take my life in exchange for theirs." 30After he said this, the holy man died nobly in his tortures; even in the tortures of death he resisted, by virtue of reason, for the sake of the law.

31 Admittedly, then, devout reason is sovereign over the emotions. 32For if the emotions had prevailed over reason, we would have testified to their domination. 33But now that reason has conquered the emotions, we properly attribute to it the power to govern. 34It is right for us to acknowledge the dominance of reason when it masters even external agonies. It would be ridiculous to deny it.[a] 35I have proved not only that reason has mastered agonies, but also that it masters pleasures and in no respect yields to them.

An Encomium on Eleazar

7 For like a most skillful pilot, the reason of our father Eleazar steered the ship of religion over the sea of the emotions, 2and though buffeted by the stormings of the tyrant and overwhelmed by the mighty waves of tortures, 3in no way did he turn the rudder of religion until he sailed into the haven of immortal victory. 4No city besieged with many ingenious war machines has ever held out as did that most holy man. Although his sacred life was consumed by tortures and racks, he conquered the besiegers with the shield of his devout reason. 5For in setting his mind firm like a jutting cliff, our father Eleazar broke the maddening waves of the emotions. 6O priest, worthy of the priesthood, you neither defiled your sacred teeth nor profaned your stomach, which had room only for reverence and purity, by eating defiling foods. 7O man in harmony with the law and philosopher of divine life! 8Such should be those who are administrators of the law, shielding it with their own blood and noble sweat in sufferings even to death. 9You, father, strengthened our loyalty to the law through your glorious endurance, and you did not abandon the holiness that you praised, but by your deeds you made your words of divine[b] philosophy credible. 10O aged man, more powerful than tortures; O elder, fiercer than fire; O supreme king over the passions, Eleazar! 11For just as our father Aaron, armed with the censer, ran through the multitude of the people and conquered the fiery[c] angel, 12so the descendant of Aaron, Eleazar, though being consumed by the fire, remained unmoved in his reason. 13Most amazing, indeed, though he was an old man, his body no longer tense and firm,[d] his muscles flabby, his sinews feeble, he became young again 14in spirit through reason; and by reason like that of Isaac he rendered the many-headed rack ineffective. 15O man of blessed age and of venerable gray hair and of law-abiding life, whom the faithful seal of death has perfected!

16 If, therefore, because of piety an aged man despised tortures even to death, most certainly devout reason is governor of the emotions. 17Some perhaps might say, "Not all have full command of their emotions, because not all have prudent reason." 18But as many as attend to religion with a whole heart, these alone are able to control the passions of the flesh, 19since they believe that they, like our patriarchs Abraham and Isaac and Jacob, do

a Syr: Meaning of Gk uncertain   b Other ancient authorities lack divine   c Other ancient authorities lack fiery   d Gk the tautness of the body already loosed

20) because of his cowardice. **6.27–29** Eleazar's final speech emphasizes the significance of his death for the sake of the law. The notion that the martyr's death was a vicarious atonement is found especially in 17.22 (see also 12.17; 17.10, 21–22; Introduction). **6.31–35** The author again emphasizes that devout reason is sovereign over the emotions. This emphasis is further developed in 7.1–23. See also 13.1–5, which closely parallels this passage. **7.1–23** In this encomium the author lavishes praise on Eleazar as an example of how devout reason can dominate the emotions only through observance of Mosaic law. **7.1–3** The metaphor of the pilot and the ship is common in Greek literature and recurs in 13.6–7; 15.31–32. See 1 Pet 3.20. **7.7–10** Eleazar's ability to control his emotions is linked to his loyalty to the law. **7.11** Aaron averted a plague (Num 16.46–50). In Wis 18.22 the plague is connected to an "avenger" similar to the angel in this verse. **7.14** An allusion to Gen 22.1–19. See note on 13.12. **7.16–23** Not everyone can dominate emotions with reason, but only those who attend to religion (v. 18) and live as philosophers by the whole rule of philosophy (v. 21), i.e.,

not die to God, but live to God. [20]No contradiction therefore arises when some persons appear to be dominated by their emotions because of the weakness of their reason. [21]What person who lives as a philosopher by the whole rule of philosophy, and trusts in God, [22]and knows that it is blessed to endure any suffering for the sake of virtue, would not be able to overcome the emotions through godliness? [23]For only the wise and courageous are masters of their emotions.

Seven Brothers Defy the Tyrant

8 For this is why even the very young, by following a philosophy in accordance with devout reason, have prevailed over the most painful instruments of torture. [2]For when the tyrant was conspicuously defeated in his first attempt, being unable to compel an aged man to eat defiling foods, then in violent rage he commanded that others of the Hebrew captives be brought, and that any who ate defiling food would be freed after eating, but if any were to refuse, they would be tortured even more cruelly.

3 When the tyrant had given these orders, seven brothers—handsome, modest, noble, and accomplished in every way—were brought before him along with their aged mother. [4]When the tyrant saw them, grouped about their mother as though a chorus, he was pleased with them. And struck by their appearance and nobility, he smiled at them, and summoned them nearer and said, [5]"Young men, with favorable feelings I admire each and every one of you, and greatly respect the beauty and the number of such brothers. Not only do I advise you not to display the same madness as that of the old man who has just been tortured, but I also exhort you to yield to me and enjoy my friendship. [6]Just as I am able

to punish those who disobey my orders, so I can be a benefactor to those who obey me. [7]Trust me, then, and you will have positions of authority in my government if you will renounce the ancestral tradition of your national life. [8]Enjoy your youth by adopting the Greek way of life and by changing your manner of living. [9]But if by disobedience you rouse my anger, you will compel me to destroy each and every one of you with dreadful punishments through tortures. [10]Therefore take pity on yourselves. Even I, your enemy, have compassion for your youth and handsome appearance. [11]Will you not consider this, that if you disobey, nothing remains for you but to die on the rack?"

12 When he had said these things, he ordered the instruments of torture to be brought forward so as to persuade them out of fear to eat the defiling food. [13]When the guards had placed before them wheels and joint-dislocators, rack and hooks[a] and catapults[b] and caldrons, braziers and thumbscrews and iron claws and wedges and bellows, the tyrant resumed speaking: [14]"Be afraid, young fellows; whatever justice you revere will be merciful to you when you transgress under compulsion."

15 But when they had heard the inducements and saw the dreadful devices, not only were they not afraid, but they also opposed the tyrant with their own philosophy, and by their right reasoning nullified his tyranny. [16]Let us consider, on the other hand, what arguments might have been used if some of them had been cowardly and unmanly. Would they not have been the following? [17]"O wretches that we are and so senseless! Since the king has

---

a Meaning of Gk uncertain   b Here and elsewhere in 4 Macc an instrument of torture

---

the law. **7.19** See 16.25; Ex 3.6; Mk 12.26; Rom 6.10; 14.8; Gal 2.19.

8.1–9.9 An expansion of 2 Macc 7.1–2 with speeches by the tyrant Antiochus (8.5–11) and the brothers (9.1–9) as well as a description of what the brothers could have said had they given in (8.17–26). These speeches present to the author's audience both the spurious arguments for assimilation and the appropriate reasons for remaining faithful to the observance of Mosaic law. **8.1** *Philosophy in accordance with devout reason,* Mosaic law. **8.4–11** Antiochus attempts to persuade the brothers to give up their *ancestral tradition of . . . national life* (v. 7) and to adopt the *Greek*

way of life (v. 8) by threatening them with severe tortures and death and by promising them his *friendship* and benefaction (vv. 5–6), two things highly sought after from autocratic Hellenistic rulers. **8.4** The *chorus,* which was important in Greek plays, usually spoke its lines in unison. See v. 29; 13.8–18; 14.7; 18.23. **8.12** Most of the *instruments of torture* cannot be described precisely. **8.14** See 5.13; 8.25. **8.16–26** By presenting this imaginary speech listing all the possible reasons for giving in, the author highlights the strength of the brothers' character in refusing to submit. The brothers' actual speech follows (9.1–9). The same technique is used in the story of the mother; an

summoned and exhorted us to accept kind treatment if we obey him, [18]why do we take pleasure in vain resolves and venture upon a disobedience that brings death? [19]O men and brothers, should we not fear the instruments of torture and consider the threats of torments, and give up this vain opinion and this arrogance that threatens to destroy us? [20]Let us take pity on our youth and have compassion on our mother's age; [21]and let us seriously consider that if we disobey we are dead! [22]Also, divine justice will excuse us for fearing the king when we are under compulsion. [23]Why do we banish ourselves from this most pleasant life and deprive ourselves of this delightful world? [24]Let us not struggle against compulsion[a] or take hollow pride in being put to the rack. [25]Not even the law itself would arbitrarily put us to death for fearing the instruments of torture. [26]Why does such contentiousness excite us and such a fatal stubbornness please us, when we can live in peace if we obey the king?"

27 But the youths, though about to be tortured, neither said any of these things nor even seriously considered them. [28]For they were contemptuous of the emotions and sovereign over agonies, [29]so that as soon as the tyrant had ceased counseling them to eat defiling food, all with one voice together, as from one mind, said:

9 "Why do you delay, O tyrant? For we are ready to die rather than transgress our ancestral commandments; [2]we are obviously putting our forebears to shame unless we should practice ready obedience to the law and to Moses[b] our counselor. [3]Tyrant and counselor of lawlessness, in your hatred for us do not pity us more than we pity ourselves.[c] [4]For we consider this pity of yours, which insures our safety through transgression of the law, to be more grievous than death itself. [5]You are trying to terrify us by threatening us with death by torture, as though a short time ago you learned nothing from Eleazar. [6]And if the aged men of the Hebrews because of their religion lived piously[d] while enduring torture, it would be even more fitting that we young men should die despising your coercive tortures, which our aged instructor also overcame. [7]Therefore, tyrant, put us to the test; and if you take our lives because of our religion, do not suppose that you can injure us by torturing us. [8]For we, through this severe suffering and endurance, shall have the prize of virtue and shall be with God, on whose account we suffer; [9]but you, because of your bloodthirstiness toward us, will deservedly undergo from the divine justice eternal torment by fire."

The Torture of the First and Second Brothers

10 When they had said these things, the tyrant was not only indignant, as at those who are disobedient, but also infuriated, as at those who are ungrateful. [11]Then at his command the guards brought forward the eldest, and having torn off his tunic, they bound his hands and arms with thongs on each side. [12]When they had worn themselves out beating him with scourges, without accomplishing anything, they placed him upon the wheel. [13]When the noble youth was stretched out around this, his limbs were dislocated, [14]and with every member disjointed he denounced the tyrant, saying, [15]"Most abominable tyrant, enemy of heavenly justice, savage of mind, you are mangling me in this manner, not because I

---

a Or fate   b Other ancient authorities read knowledge
c Meaning of Gk uncertain   d Other ancient authorities read died

imaginary speech in 16.6–11 is followed by her actual speech in 16.16–23. **8.22** The law would not condemn *fearing* the instruments of torture and death, but it would condemn submitting to the tyrant by committing idolatry, even in these circumstances. See 5.13; 8.14, 25. **8.27–9.9** In their actual speech the brothers defy the tyrant and refuse to shame their ancestors by transgressing the law. **9.5** See 5.4–6.30. **9.6** *Aged men of the Hebrews,* perhaps the prophets who, according to some Jewish traditions, were martyred. See *The Lives of the Prophets* (first century CE). **9.8–9** The brothers will be rewarded with immortality with God; the tyrant will suffer eternal torment. These are constant themes throughout 4 Maccabees.

9.10–12.19 In comparison to 2 Macc 7.3–40, the account of the tortures and deaths of the seven brothers has been significantly expanded by graphic descriptions of the tortures and by speeches from each of the brothers. Rhetorically these serve to increase the pathos of the scene. The speeches also comment on the significance of the events and bring out the themes the author wants to emphasize. In good rhetorical fashion, the descriptions of the tortures and deaths of the first brother (9.10–25) and the last brother (12.1–19) are the most elaborate. **9.10–25** In the story of the first brother, tyranny is contrasted to endurance for the sake of the law. **9.14** Opposition to tyranny was a common theme in funeral orations. **9.15–18** In the

am a murderer, or as one who acts impiously, but because I protect the divine law." [16]And when the guards said, "Agree to eat so that you may be released from the tortures," [17]he replied, "You abominable lackeys, your wheel is not so powerful as to strangle my reason. Cut my limbs, burn my flesh, and twist my joints; [18]through all these tortures I will convince you that children of the Hebrews alone are invincible where virtue is concerned." [19]While he was saying these things, they spread fire under him, and while fanning the flames[a] they tightened the wheel further. [20]The wheel was completely smeared with blood, and the heap of coals was being quenched by the drippings of gore, and pieces of flesh were falling off the axles of the machine. [21]Although the ligaments joining his bones were already severed, the courageous youth, worthy of Abraham, did not groan, [22]but as though transformed by fire into immortality, he nobly endured the rackings. [23]"Imitate me, brothers," he said. "Do not leave your post in my struggle[b] or renounce our courageous family ties. [24]Fight the sacred and noble battle for religion. Thereby the just Providence of our ancestors may become merciful to our nation and take vengeance on the accursed tyrant." [25]When he had said this, the saintly youth broke the thread of life.

[26] While all were marveling at his courageous spirit, the guards brought in the next eldest, and after fitting themselves with iron gauntlets having sharp hooks, they bound him to the torture machine and catapult. [27]Before torturing him, they inquired if he were willing to eat, and they heard his noble decision.[c] [28]These leopard-like beasts tore out his sinews with the iron hands, flayed all his flesh up to his chin, and tore away his scalp. But he steadfastly endured this agony and said, [29]"How sweet is any kind of death for the religion of our ancestors!" [30]To the tyrant he said, "Do you not think, you most savage tyrant, that you are being tortured more than I, as you see the arrogant design of your tyranny being defeated by our endurance for the sake of religion? [31]I lighten my pain by the joys that come from virtue, [32]but you suffer torture by the threats that come from impiety. You will not escape, you most abominable tyrant, the judgments of the divine wrath."

The Torture of the Third and Fourth Brothers

10 When he too had endured a glorious death, the third was led in, and many repeatedly urged him to save himself by tasting the meat. [2]But he shouted, "Do you not know that the same father begot me as well as those who died, and the same mother bore me, and that I was brought up on the same teachings? [3]I do not renounce the noble kinship that binds me to my brothers."[d] [5]Enraged by the man's boldness, they disjointed his hands and feet with their instruments, dismembering him by prying his limbs from their sockets, [6]and breaking his fingers and arms and legs and elbows. [7]Since they were not able in any way to break his spirit,[e] they abandoned the instruments[f] and scalped him with their fingernails in a Scythian fashion. [8]They immediately brought him to the wheel, and while his vertebrae were being dislocated

---

a Meaning of Gk uncertain   b Other ancient authorities read post forever   c Other ancient authorities read having heard his noble decision, they tore him to shreds   d Other ancient authorities add verse 4, So if you have any instrument of torture, apply it to my body; for you cannot touch my soul, even if you wish."   e Gk to strangle him   f Other ancient authorities read they tore off his skin

---

speech of the first brother, the themes of commitment to Mosaic law, the power of reason, and the *invincible . . . virtue* of the Hebrews are emphasized. **9.18** *Virtue*, also a standard theme in funeral orations. **9.21** *Worthy of Abraham*. The connection with ancestors was yet another common theme in funeral orations. **9.22** *Immortality*, lit. "incorruption." See also 14.5; 16.13; 17.12; 18.23. The purifying power of fire is a common biblical metaphor, especially in sacrificial contexts (e.g., Lev 1.9, 13; 2.2; 3.5; see also Mal 3.2). **9.24** *Religion*, lit. "piety." *Providence*, a Stoic theme found in the works of Greek historians and Josephus (see also 13.19; 17.22). Note also the themes of reward and punishment and the belief that the brothers' deaths will lead God to be *merciful* to the Jewish people. **9.26–**

11.27 The tortures of the second through the sixth brothers are told more briefly. **9.29** A similar theme can be found in the Latin poet Horace's *Ode* 3.2.13 ("How sweet and noble to die for one's fatherland"). **9.30–32** Again the themes of opposition to *tyranny*, *endurance for the sake of religion* (lit. "piety"), *virtue*, and eventual punishment of the tyrant recur. **10.1–11** In the story of the third brother, the themes of noble kinship (vv. 2–3), suffering for virtue (v. 10), and eventual punishment of the tyrant (v. 11) remain prominent. **10.4** The verse in text note *d* is not found in one of the most important manuscripts (Codex Alexandrinus) and may be an interpolation. **10.7** *Scythian fashion*. The Scythians were known for scalping their slain enemies (Herodotus, *Histories* 4.64; Pliny, *Natural His-*

by this, he saw his own flesh torn all around and drops of blood flowing from his entrails. [9]When he was about to die, he said, [10]"We, most abominable tyrant, are suffering because of our godly training and virtue, [11]but you, because of your impiety and bloodthirstiness, will undergo unceasing torments."

12 When he too had died in a manner worthy of his brothers, they dragged in the fourth, saying, [13]"As for you, do not give way to the same insanity as your brothers, but obey the king and save yourself." [14]But he said to them, "You do not have a fire hot enough to make me play the coward. [15]No—by the blessed death of my brothers, by the eternal destruction of the tyrant, and by the everlasting life of the pious, I will not renounce our noble family ties. [16]Contrive tortures, tyrant, so that you may learn from them that I am a brother to those who have just now been tortured." [17]When he heard this, the bloodthirsty, murderous, and utterly abominable Antiochus gave orders to cut out his tongue. [18]But he said, "Even if you remove my organ of speech, God hears also those who are mute. [19]See, here is my tongue; cut it off, for in spite of this you will not make our reason speechless. [20]Gladly, for the sake of God, we let our bodily members be mutilated. [21]God will visit you swiftly, for you are cutting out a tongue that has been melodious with divine hymns."

The Torture of the Fifth and Sixth Brothers

11 When he too died, after being cruelly tortured, the fifth leaped up, saying, [2]"I will not refuse, tyrant, to be tortured for the sake of virtue. [3]I have come of my own accord, so that by murdering me you will incur punishment from the heavenly justice for even more crimes. [4]Hater of virtue, hater of humankind, for what act of ours are you destroying us in this way? [5]Is it because[a] we revere the Creator of all things and live according to his virtuous law? [6]But these deeds deserve honors, not tortures."[b] [9]While he was saying these things, the guards bound him and dragged him to the catapult; [10]they tied him to it on his knees, and fitting iron clamps on them, they twisted his back[c] around the wedge on the wheel,[d] so that he was completely curled back like a scorpion, and all his members were disjointed. [11]In this condition, gasping for breath and in anguish of body, [12]he said, "Tyrant, they are splendid favors that you grant us against your will, because through these noble sufferings you give us an opportunity to show our endurance for the law."

13 When he too had died, the sixth, a mere boy, was led in. When the tyrant inquired whether he was willing to eat and be released, he said, [14]"I am younger in age than my brothers, but I am their equal in mind. [15]Since to this end we were born and bred, we ought likewise to die for the same principles. [16]So if you intend to torture me for not eating defiling foods, go on torturing!" [17]When he had said this, they led him to the wheel. [18]He was carefully stretched tight upon it, his back was broken, and he was roasted[e] from underneath. [19]To his back they applied sharp spits that had been heated in the fire, and pierced his ribs so that his entrails were burned through. [20]While being tortured he said, "O contest befitting holiness, in which so many of us brothers have been summoned to an arena of sufferings for religion, and in which we have not been defeated! [21]For religious knowledge, O tyrant, is invincible. [22]I also, equipped with nobility, will die with my brothers, [23]and I myself will bring a great avenger upon you, you inventor of tortures and enemy of those who are truly devout. [24]We six boys have paralyzed your tyranny. [25]Since you have not been able to persuade us to change our mind or to force us

a Other ancient authorities read *Or does it seem evil to you that*
b Other ancient authorities add verses 7 and 8, [7]*If you but understood human feelings and had hope of salvation from God—* [8]*but, as it is, you are a stranger to God and persecute those who serve him."*
c Gk *loins*   *d* Meaning of Gk uncertain   *e* Other ancient authorities add *by fire*

---

tory 7.11) and in general for their cruelty (2 Macc 4.47; 3 Macc 7.5). **10.12–21** In the narrative of the fourth brother the themes are quite similar to those in 10.1–11. **10.19–20** See Isa 53.7–12, the suffering of the servant. **10.21** See Isa 35.6. **11.1–12** The fifth brother also suffers for the sake of virtue, but he adds that he does it so that the tyrant will be punished. **11.7–8** The verses in text note *b* are missing from Codex Sinaiticus and are probably interpolations. **11.12** The fifth brother

claims, with some irony, that suffering for the law is not simply a necessity, but an *opportunity*. **11.13–27** The speeches of the sixth brother become more elaborate as the author builds toward a climax. **11.13** The pathos is heightened by the fact that the sixth brother is *a mere boy*. **11.20–21** The last words of the sixth brother are filled with images of an athletic *contest* in which he and his brothers are victorious because *religious knowledge . . . is invincible.* See note on

to eat defiling foods, is not this your downfall? [26]Your fire is cold to us, and the catapults painless, and your violence powerless. [27]For it is not the guards of the tyrant but those of the divine law that are set over us; therefore, unconquered, we hold fast to reason."

The Torture of the Seventh Brother

12 When he too, thrown into the caldron, had died a blessed death, the seventh and youngest of all came forward. [2]Even though the tyrant had been vehemently reproached by the brothers, he felt strong compassion for this child when he saw that he was already in fetters. He summoned him to come nearer and tried to persuade him, saying, [3]"You see the result of your brothers' stupidity, for they died in torments because of their disobedience. [4]You too, if you do not obey, will be miserably tortured and die before your time, [5]but if you yield to persuasion you will be my friend and a leader in the government of the kingdom." [6]When he had thus appealed to him, he sent for the boy's mother to show compassion on her who had been bereaved of so many sons and to influence her to persuade the surviving son to obey and save himself. [7]But when his mother had exhorted him in the Hebrew language, as we shall tell a little later, [8]he said, "Let me loose, let me speak to the king and to all his friends that are with him." [9]Extremely pleased by the boy's declaration, they freed him at once. [10]Running to the nearest of the braziers, [11]he said, "You profane tyrant, most impious of all the wicked, since you have received good things and also your kingdom from God, were you not ashamed to murder his servants and torture on the wheel those who practice religion? [12]Because of this, justice has laid up for you intense and eternal fire and tortures, and these throughout all time[a] will never let you go. [13]As a man, were you not ashamed, you most savage beast, to cut out the tongues of men who have feelings like yours and are made of the same elements as you, and to maltreat and torture them in this way? [14]Surely they by dying nobly fulfilled their service to God, but you will wail bitterly for having killed without cause the contestants for virtue." [15]Then because he too was about to die, he said, [16]"I do not desert the excellent example[b] of my brothers, [17]and I call on the God of our ancestors to be merciful to our nation;[c] [18]but on you he will take vengeance both in this present life and when you are dead." [19]After he had uttered these imprecations, he flung himself into the braziers and so ended his life.[d]

Reason's Sovereignty in the Seven

13 Since, then, the seven brothers despised sufferings even unto death, everyone must concede that devout reason is sovereign over the emotions. [2]For if they had been slaves to their emotions and had eaten defiling food, we would say that they had been conquered by these emotions. [3]But in fact it was not so. Instead, by reason, which is praised before God, they prevailed over their emotions. [4]The supremacy of the mind over these cannot be overlooked, for the brothers[e] mastered both emotions and pains. [5]How then can one fail to confess the sovereignty of right reason over

---

a Gk *throughout the whole age*   b Other ancient authorities read *the witness*   c Other ancient authorities read *my race*   d Gk *and so gave up*; other ancient authorities read *gave up his spirit* or *his soul*   e Gk *they*

6.10. **12.1–19** The dramatic character of the torture of the seventh and youngest brother is enhanced by the tyrant's apparent compassion for him and for his mother (vv. 2, 6), by the mother's exhortation to her son (v. 7), and by the son's asking to speak (v. 8). For a moment the catastrophe seems avoidable. **12.7** The mother exhorts her son in *Hebrew*, which emphasizes the sacred nature of the exhortation and also allows for dramatic tension in the minds of the hearers about what she is saying. The promise that the words of this speech will be given *later* seems to be fulfilled in 18.6–19. **12.8** *Friends*, a title for the king's courtiers. **12.11–18** The youngest brother's speech sums up a number of the themes found in the other speeches but emphasizes especially the injustice and savagery of the tyrant and the punishment awaiting him for all eternity. **12.13** *Who have feelings . . . as you*, a Stoic common-place about the unity of all human beings, also found in Wis 7.1–6. **12.14** For a similar lamentation by the wicked for their persecution of the pious, see Wis 5.1–13. **12.17** *To be merciful to our nation*, perhaps an allusion to the notion that the martyrdoms were an atonement for the nation (see note on 6.27–29). **12.19** See 17.1. Both Stoicism and Judaism allowed for suicide in some circumstances. See Josephus's description of the suicide of the remaining Jewish defenders at Masada in *War* 7.320–401.

13.1–14.10 After the graphic and emotionally charged description of the deaths of the seven brothers, the author returns to the theme that reason is sovereign over the emotions and then goes on to praise the brothers' courage, piety, and endurance for the sake of religion. See 1.1–3.18; 6.31–35. **13.1–5** A close parallel to 6.31–35 in both content and its position immediately

emotion in those who were not turned back by fiery agonies? [6]For just as towers jutting out over harbors hold back the threatening waves and make it calm for those who sail into the inner basin, [7]so the seven-towered right reason of the youths, by fortifying the harbor of religion, conquered the tempest of the emotions. [8]For they constituted a holy chorus of religion and encouraged one another, saying, [9]"Brothers, let us die like brothers for the sake of the law; let us imitate the three youths in Assyria who despised the same ordeal of the furnace. [10]Let us not be cowardly in the demonstration of our piety." [11]While one said, "Courage, brother," another said, "Bear up nobly," [12]and another reminded them, "Remember whence you came, and the father by whose hand Isaac would have submitted to being slain for the sake of religion." [13]Each of them and all of them together looking at one another, cheerful and undaunted, said, "Let us with all our hearts consecrate ourselves to God, who gave us our lives,[a] and let us use our bodies as a bulwark for the law. [14]Let us not fear him who thinks he is killing us, [15]for great is the struggle of the soul and the danger of eternal torment lying before those who transgress the commandment of God. [16]Therefore let us put on the full armor of self-control, which is divine reason. [17]For if we so die,[b] Abraham and Isaac and Jacob will welcome us, and all the fathers will praise us." [18]Those who were left behind said to each of the brothers who were being dragged away, "Do not put us to shame, brother, or betray the brothers who have died before us."

19 You are not ignorant of the affection of family ties, which the divine and all-wise Providence has bequeathed through the fathers to their descendants and which was implanted in the mother's womb. [20]There each of the brothers spent the same length of time and was shaped during the same period of time; and growing from the same blood and through the same life, they were brought to the light of day. [21]When they were born after an equal time of gestation, they drank milk from the same fountains. From such embraces brotherly-loving souls are nourished; [22]and they grow stronger from this common nurture and daily companionship, and from both general education and our discipline in the law of God.

23 Therefore, when sympathy and brotherly affection had been so established, the brothers were the more sympathetic to one another. [24]Since they had been educated by the same law and trained in the same virtues and brought up in right living, they loved one another all the more. [25]A common zeal for nobility strengthened their goodwill toward one another, and their concord, [26]because they could make their brotherly love more fervent with the aid of their religion. [27]But although nature and companionship and virtuous habits had augmented the affection of family ties, those who were left endured for the sake of religion, while watching their brothers being maltreated and tortured to death.

14 Furthermore, they encouraged them to face the torture, so that they not only despised their agonies, but also mastered the emotions of brotherly love.

2 O reason,[c] more royal than kings and freer than the free! [3]O sacred and harmonious

---

[a] Or souls   [b] Other ancient authorities read *suffer*
[c] Or O *minds*

---

after a description of martyrdom. **13.6** The metaphor of *towers jutting out over harbors* is similar to the nautical imagery in 7.1–3, esp. 7.5. **13.7** *Seven-towered right reason.* See Prov 9.1 (the seven pillars of wisdom). **13.8–18** The imagery of the *chorus* is again used (see note on 8.4). The author breaks up the chorus into short phrases uttered by individual members; some Greek tragedies do the same (see Aeschylus, *Agamemnon* 1346–71). **13.9** See Dan 3, the story of the three youths in the fiery furnace who also endured great trials for the sake of religion. **13.12** *Remember whence you came.* See Isa 51.1–2. *The father . . . slain.* See Gen 22.1–19. The binding of Isaac is alluded to also in 7.14; 14.20; 15.28; 16.20; 17.6; 18.11. See also Wis 10.5; Heb 11.17–19. **13.13** *All of them together.* After speaking separately, the brothers unite, again as in a Greek chorus, for the climactic closing lines. **13.14–15** See Mt 10.28.

13.16 *Armor.* See Eph 6.11–14. **13.17** See 5.37. **13.19–14.1** Praise of the family ties, education, and affection that encouraged the brothers to endure their trials together. Such praises were rhetorical commonplaces, especially in funeral orations. **13.19** *Divine and all-wise Providence,* a Stoic concept also found in 9.24; 17.22. A close parallel to the view that brotherly affection is instilled through the mother and father is found in Xenophon, *Cyropedia* 8.7.14. **13.22, 24** Note the emphasis on the brothers' education and training in Mosaic law, which nurtured both their companionship and their striving after virtue. **14.1** *Mastered the emotions of brotherly love,* a somewhat different viewpoint in which brotherly love is seen as an obstacle to be overcome, similar to the viewpoint in 2.9b–12, 19–20. **14.2–10** An apostrophe to reason followed by praise for the seven brothers. **14.2** *More royal than kings.*

concord of the seven brothers on behalf of religion! [4]None of the seven youths proved coward or shrank from death, [5]but all of them, as though running the course toward immortality, hastened to death by torture. [6]Just as the hands and feet are moved in harmony with the guidance of the mind, so those holy youths, as though moved by an immortal spirit of devotion, agreed to go to death for its sake. [7]O most holy seven, brothers in harmony! For just as the seven days of creation move in choral dance around religion, [8]so these youths, forming a chorus, encircled the sevenfold fear of tortures and dissolved it. [9]Even now, we ourselves shudder as we hear of the suffering of these young men; they not only saw what was happening, not only heard the direct word of threat, but also bore the sufferings patiently, and in agonies of fire at that. [10]What could be more excruciatingly painful than this? For the power of fire is intense and swift, and it consumed their bodies quickly.

An Encomium on the Mother of the Seven

[11]Do not consider it amazing that reason had full command over these men in their tortures, since the mind of woman despised even more diverse agonies, [12]for the mother of the seven young men bore up under the rackings of each one of her children.

[13]Observe how complex is a mother's love for her children, which draws everything toward an emotion felt in her inmost parts. [14]Even unreasoning animals, as well as human beings, have a sympathy and parental love for their offspring. [15]For example, among birds, the ones that are tame protect their young by building on the housetops, [16]and the others, by building at the tops of mountains and the depths of chasms, in holes of trees, and on treetops, hatch the nestlings and ward off the intruder. [17]If they are not able to keep the intruder[a] away, they do what they can to help their young by flying in circles around them in the anguish of love, warning them with their own calls. [18]And why is it necessary to demonstrate sympathy for children by the example of unreasoning animals, [19]since even bees at the time for making honeycombs defend themselves against intruders and, as though with an iron dart, sting those who approach their hive and defend it even to the death? [20]But sympathy for her children did not sway the mother of the young men; she was of the same mind as Abraham.

15 O reason of the children, tyrant over the emotions! O religion, more desirable to the mother than her children! [2]Two courses were open to this mother, that of religion, and that of preserving her seven sons for a time, as the tyrant had promised. [3]She loved religion more, the religion that preserves them for eternal life according to God's promise.[b] [4]In what manner might I express the emo-

a Gk it　b Gk according to God

See 2.23. **14.5** *Running the course,* another athletic metaphor. See note on 6.10. *Immortality,* lit. "deathlessness." See note on 9.22. **14.6** The seven brothers are *moved by an immortal spirit of devotion* (or piety). This goes beyond the ordinary Stoic notion that the members of the body are moved by the mind. **14.7** The importance of *seven* in connection with creation was emphasized by Philo in *On the Creation of the World 89–128.* **14.9** *Even now, we . . . shudder as we hear,* perhaps an indication that the speech was actually delivered, but more likely part of the rhetorical fiction of 4 Maccabees meant to draw the audience in. See also 1.10; 3.19.
14.11–17.6 The death of the mother, which is simply mentioned in 2 Macc 7.41, is transformed in 4 Maccabees into the climax of the oration. Writing in a highly rhetorical style, the author emphasizes the mother's terrible torments in being forced to watch the torture and death of all her seven sons. Through her commitment to religion and the law, her reason overcomes the weakness of her gender and even her maternal affection.
14.11–12 The author's assumption, a common one in the ancient world, was that reason is less dominant in

women than in men. Consequently, if the mother could endure her agonies, it is not amazing that *reason had full command* over the seven sons in theirs. This theme also occurs in 15.5, 23, 30; 16.1–2, 14. **14.13–20** The power of parental love in human beings is compared to that in *unreasoning animals* (v. 14). The examples of *birds* (vv. 15–17) and *bees* (v. 19) demonstrate that the parental instinct to protect one's young is extremely powerful. Yet *sympathy for her children did not sway* the mother's mind (v. 20). This combination of natural history and sentimentality is not uncommon in writings of this period. See Plutarch, *On the Love of Offspring 1–2.*
14.20 Abraham's willingness to sacrifice his own son is the prime example of someone overcoming parental affection for the sake of religion. See note on 13.12. **15.1–32** Both the power of maternal affection and the mother's ability to overcome it for the sake of religion are emphasized. **15.2–3** The mother's choice was between *religion* and *preserving her seven sons for a time.* She chose the former. See vv. 24–28, where the same theme occurs. **15.4** *Likeness both of mind and of form,* a Stoic doctrine that held that children are like their parents both in soul and in body. See Plutarch, *On the*

tions of parents who love their children? We impress upon the character of a small child a wondrous likeness both of mind and of form. Especially is this true of mothers, who because of their birth pangs have a deeper sympathy toward their offspring than do the fathers. 5Considering that mothers are the weaker sex and give birth to many, they are more devoted to their children.*a 6The mother of the seven boys, more than any other mother, loved her children. In seven pregnancies she had implanted in herself tender love toward them, 7and because of the many pains she suffered with each of them she had sympathy for them; 8yet because of the fear of God she disdained the temporary safety of her children. 9Not only so, but also because of the nobility of her sons and their ready obedience to the law, she felt a greater tenderness toward them. 10For they were righteous and self-controlled and brave and magnanimous, and loved their brothers and their mother, so that they obeyed her even to death in keeping the ordinances.

11 Nevertheless, though so many factors influenced the mother to suffer with them out of love for her children, in the case of none of them were the various tortures strong enough to pervert her reason. 12But each child separately and all of them together the mother urged on to death for religion's sake. 13O sacred nature and affection of parental love, yearning of parents toward offspring, nurture and indomitable suffering by mothers! 14This mother, who saw them tortured and burned one by one, because of religion did not change her attitude. 15She watched the flesh of her children being consumed by fire, their toes and fingers scattered*b on the ground, and the flesh of the head to the chin exposed like masks.

16 O mother, tried now by more bitter pains than even the birth pangs you suffered for them!

17O woman, who alone gave birth to such complete devotion! 18When the firstborn breathed his last, it did not turn you aside, nor when the second in torments looked at you piteously nor when the third expired; 19nor did you weep when you looked at the eyes of each one in his tortures gazing boldly at the same agonies, and saw in their nostrils the signs of the approach of death. 20When you saw the flesh of children burned upon the flesh of other children, severed hands upon hands, scalped heads upon heads, and corpses fallen on other corpses, and when you saw the place filled with many spectators of the torturings, you did not shed tears. 21Neither the melodies of sirens nor the songs of swans attract the attention of their hearers as did the voices of the children in torture calling to their mother. 22How great and how many torments the mother then suffered as her sons were tortured on the wheel and with the hot irons! 23But devout reason, giving her heart a man's courage in the very midst of her emotions, strengthened her to disregard, for the time, her parental love.

24 Although she witnessed the destruction of seven children and the ingenious and various rackings, this noble mother disregarded all these*c because of faith in God. 25For as in the council chamber of her own soul she saw mighty advocates—nature, family, parental love, and the rackings of her children— 26this mother held two ballots, one bearing death and the other deliverance for her children. 27She did not approve the deliverance that would preserve the seven sons for a short time, 28but as the daughter of God-fearing Abraham she remembered his fortitude.

29 O mother of the nation, vindicator of

---

a Or *For to the degree that mothers are weaker and the more children they bear, the more they are devoted to their children.*
b Or *quivering*   *c* Other ancient authorities read *having bidden them farewell, surrendered them*

Opinions of the Philosophers 7.11.3. **15.4b–7** That parental affection is especially strong in mothers because they bear their children in their wombs was a common view in the Greco-Roman world. See Aristotle, *Nicomachean Ethics* 1161b26–27. **15.5** See note on 14.11–12. **15.9** The sons' *nobility* and *obedience to the law* only increased their mother's affection for them. **15.10** *Righteous . . . self-controlled . . . brave*, three of the four cardinal virtues. Magnanimity is substituted for rational judgment. See 1.2–4, 18; 5.23–24. **15.11–23** The pathos of the situation is emphasized by calling to mind the sons' tortures, which the mother was forced to witness but which did not pervert her reason. **15.16–20** An apostrophe to the mother lends vividness to the scene (see also vv. 29–32; 16.14–15; 17.2–6). **15.21** *Melodies of sirens,* the songs by which the sirens sought to lure Odysseus and his companions to their deaths (*Odyssey* 12.39–58, 154–200). *Songs of swans,* the plaintive cries of swans, which they are proverbially said to utter as they are about to die. **15.23** *A man's courage.* See note on 14.11–12. **15.24–28** The author returns to the mother's choice between dying for religion and temporary deliverance (see vv. 1–3). **15.25–26** The imagery is that of balloting in the Greek assembly. **15.29–32** Another apostrophe to the mother (see note on 15.16–20). Note also the imagery of the athletic contest (see note on

the law and champion of religion, who carried away the prize of the contest in your heart! [30]O more noble than males in steadfastness, and more courageous than men in endurance! [31]Just as Noah's ark, carrying the world in the universal flood, stoutly endured the waves, [32]so you, O guardian of the law, overwhelmed from every side by the flood of your emotions and the violent winds, the torture of your sons, endured nobly and withstood the wintry storms that assail religion.

16 If, then, a woman, advanced in years and mother of seven sons, endured seeing her children tortured to death, it must be admitted that devout reason is sovereign over the emotions. [2]Thus I have demonstrated not only that men have ruled over the emotions, but also that a woman has despised the fiercest tortures. [3]The lions surrounding Daniel were not so savage, nor was the raging fiery furnace of Mishael so intensely hot, as was her innate parental love, inflamed as she saw her seven sons tortured in such varied ways. [4]But the mother quenched so many and such great emotions by devout reason.

[5]Consider this also: If this woman, though a mother, had been fainthearted, she would have mourned over them and perhaps spoken as follows: [6]"O how wretched am I and many times unhappy! After bearing seven children, I am now the mother of none! [7]O seven childbirths all in vain, seven profitless pregnancies, fruitless nurturings and wretched nursings! [8]In vain, my sons, I endured many birth pangs for you, and the more grievous anxieties of your upbringing. [9]Alas for my children, some unmarried, others married and without offspring.[a] I shall not see your children or have the happiness of being called grandmother. [10]Alas, I who had so many and beautiful children am a widow and alone, with many sorrows.[b] [11]And when I die, I shall have none of my sons to bury me."

[12]Yet that holy and God-fearing mother did not wail with such a lament for any of them, nor did she dissuade any of them from dying, nor did she grieve as they were dying. [13]On the contrary, as though having a mind like adamant and giving rebirth for immortality to the whole number of her sons, she implored them and urged them on to death for the sake of religion. [14]O mother, soldier of God in the cause of religion, elder and woman! By steadfastness you have conquered even a tyrant, and in word and deed you have proved more powerful than a man. [15]For when you and your sons were arrested together, you stood and watched Eleazar being tortured, and said to your sons in the Hebrew language, [16]"My sons, noble is the contest to which you are called to bear witness for the nation. Fight zealously for our ancestral law. [17]For it would be shameful if, while an aged man endures such agonies for the sake of religion, you young men were to be terrified by tortures. [18]Remember that it is through God that you have had a share in the world and have enjoyed life, [19]and therefore you ought to endure any suffering for the sake of God. [20]For his sake also our father Abraham was zealous to sacrifice his son Isaac, the ancestor of our nation; and when Isaac saw his father's hand wielding a knife[c] and descending upon him, he did not cower. [21]Daniel the righteous was thrown to the lions, and Hananiah, Azariah, and Mishael were hurled into the fiery furnace and endured it for the sake of God. [22]You too must have the same faith in God and not be grieved. [23]It is unrea-

---

a Gk *without benefit*   *b* Or *much to be pitied*   *c* Gk *sword*

6.10). **15.30** See note on 14.11–12. **15.31** See Gen 6.5–8.22. **16.1–4** The author returns to the theme with which he began this section in 15.1: *reason is sovereign over the emotions.* **16.3** On *Daniel* in the lions' den, see Dan 6; on the three youths in the *fiery furnace*, see Dan 3. **16.5–23** As in 8.16–9.9 regarding the seven brothers, the author contrasts a speech that the mother could have given had she been fainthearted (vv. 6–11) with the one that she actually gave (vv. 16–23). **16.6–11** The speech emphasizes the sorrows of a mother whose children all die before her. **16.10** *A widow and alone.* The place of a widow in the ancient world was always a precarious one. **16.11** To have no children to give one a proper burial was considered tragic in the ancient world among both Jews and Greeks. **16.12–15** Instead of grieving over the deaths of her sons, she urges them on to *rebirth for immortality* (see note on 9.22) for the sake of *religion* and to victory over the *tyrant.* **16.14–15** Another apostrophe to the mother (see note on 15.16–20). **16.14** See note on 14.11–12. **16.15** This speech was supposedly delivered when *Eleazar* was being tortured. This seems, however, to be inconsistent with 5.4; 8.3, which indicate that the mother and her sons were brought in only after the death of Eleazar. *Hebrew language.* See 12.7. **16.16–22** The initial imagery is that of an athletic *contest* in which the seven sons are to *fight zealously* for Mosaic law (see note on 6.10). This is followed by appeals to the examples of Eleazar (5.1–7.23), Abraham's willingness to sacrifice his son Isaac (Gen 22.1–19; see note on 13.12), Daniel in the lions' den (Dan 6), and the three youths in the fiery furnace (Dan 3). **16.23** Because reason (Greek *logismos*) can dominate the emotions, it

sonable for people who have religious knowledge not to withstand pain."

24 By these words the mother of the seven encouraged and persuaded each of her sons to die rather than violate God's commandment. 25They knew also that those who die for the sake of God live to God, as do Abraham and Isaac and Jacob and all the patriarchs.

17 Some of the guards said that when she also was about to be seized and put to death she threw herself into the flames so that no one might touch her body.

2 O mother, who with your seven sons nullified the violence of the tyrant, frustrated his evil designs, and showed the courage of your faith! 3Nobly set like a roof on the pillars of your sons, you held firm and unswerving against the earthquake of the tortures. 4Take courage, therefore, O holy-minded mother, maintaining firm an enduring hope in God. 5The moon in heaven, with the stars, does not stand so august as you, who, after lighting the way of your star-like seven sons to piety, stand in honor before God and are firmly set in heaven with them. 6For your children were true descendants of father Abraham. [a]

The Effect of the Martyrdoms

7 If it were possible for us to paint the history of your religion as an artist might, would not those who first beheld it have shuddered as they saw the mother of the seven children enduring their varied tortures to death for the sake of religion? 8Indeed it would be proper to inscribe on their tomb these words as a reminder to the people of our nation: [b]

9 "Here lie buried an aged priest and an aged woman and seven sons, because of the violence of the tyrant who wished to destroy the way of life of the Hebrews. 10They vindicated their nation, looking to God and enduring torture even to death."

11 Truly the contest in which they were engaged was divine, 12for on that day virtue gave the awards and tested them for their endurance. The prize was immortality in endless life. 13Eleazar was the first contestant, the mother of the seven sons entered the competition, and the brothers contended. 14The tyrant was the antagonist, and the world and the human race were the spectators. 15Reverence for God was victor and gave the crown to its own athletes. 16Who did not admire the athletes of the divine[c] legislation? Who were not amazed?

17 The tyrant himself and all his council marveled at their[d] endurance, 18because of which they now stand before the divine throne and live the life of eternal blessedness. 19For Moses says, "All who are consecrated are under your hands." 20These, then, who have been consecrated for the sake of God,[e] are honored, not only with this honor, but also by the fact that because of them our enemies did not rule over our nation, 21the tyrant was punished, and the homeland purified—they having become, as it were, a ransom for the sin of our nation. 22And through the blood of those de-

---

a Gk For your childbearing was from Abraham the father; other ancient authorities read For . . . Abraham the servant b Or as a memorial to the heroes of our people c Other ancient authorities read true d Other ancient authorities add virtue and e Other ancient authorities lack for the sake of God

---

would be *unreasonable* (Greek *alogiston*) not to endure pain for the sake of religion. **16.25** See note on 7.19. **17.1** See 2 Macc 7.41. The mother here throws herself into the flames rather than let the guards violate her chastity by touching her. On the question of suicide, see note on 12.19. **17.2–6** A final apostrophe to the mother (see note on 15.16–20). **17.2** A short summary of some of the principal themes of 4 Maccabees. **17.5** See Dan 12.3; *Testament of Job* 39.9–40.5. Plato and the Stoics thought of the stars as living beings.

17.7–18.24 A somewhat loosely organized peroration describing the effects of the martyrdoms on the martyrs themselves, on the tyrant, his council, and his soldiers, and, the author hopes, on his fellow Jews. The mother's final speech is in the climactic position (18.6–19). **17.7** *Paint . . . as an artist might.* Descriptions of artworks and their effects were common in Greek literature. **17.8–10** The mention of epitaphs is a classical rhetorical device; their mention here does not mean

that 4 Maccabees was delivered as an actual oration at the martyrs' tomb. **17.10** *They vindicated their nation,* perhaps another allusion to some sort of vicarious atonement for the nation (see note on 6.27–29). **17.11–16** The most fully developed metaphor of the martyrs' torture and death as an athletic contest in which the prize for a life tested by *virtue* is *immortality* (see notes on 6.10; 9.22). **17.14** *The world and the human race* gives a universal significance to the contest. **17.17–24** Descriptions of the amazement of Antiochus and his council (vv. 17–18, 23–24) precede and follow a summary of the effects of the martyrdoms on the Jewish people (vv. 19–22). **17.19** The quotation, from Deut 33.3, indicates that the martyrs are protected by God. **17.20–22** A summary of the results of the martyrs' deaths that credits them with the purification of the homeland and eventual defeat of Antiochus. **17.21–22** The most developed imagery in 4 Maccabees of vicarious atonement (see note on 6.27–29), drawing on

vout ones and their death as an atoning sacrifice, divine Providence preserved Israel that previously had been mistreated.

23 For the tyrant Antiochus, when he saw the courage of their virtue and their endurance under the tortures, proclaimed them to his soldiers as an example for their own endurance, 24and this made them brave and courageous for infantry battle and siege, and he ravaged and conquered all his enemies.

18 O Israelite children, offspring of the seed of Abraham, obey this law and exercise piety in every way, 2knowing that devout reason is master of all emotions, not only of sufferings from within, but also of those from without.

3 Therefore those who gave over their bodies in suffering for the sake of religion were not only admired by mortals, but also were deemed worthy to share in a divine inheritance. 4Because of them the nation gained peace, and by reviving observance of the law in the homeland they ravaged the enemy. 5The tyrant Antiochus was both punished on earth and is being chastised after his death. Since in no way whatever was he able to compel the Israelites to become pagans and to abandon their ancestral customs, he left Jerusalem and marched against the Persians.

The Mother's Address to Her Children

6 The mother of seven sons expressed also these principles to her children: 7"I was a pure virgin and did not go outside my father's house; but I guarded the rib from which woman was made.[a] 8No seducer corrupted me on a desert plain, nor did the destroyer, the deceitful serpent, defile the purity of my virginity. 9In the time of my maturity I remained with my husband, and when these sons had grown up their father died. A happy man was he, who lived out his life with good children, and did not have the grief of bereavement. 10While he was still with you, he taught you the law and the prophets. 11He read to you about Abel slain by Cain, and Isaac who was offered as a burnt offering, and about Joseph in prison. 12He told you of the zeal of Phinehas, and he taught you about Hananiah, Azariah, and Mishael in the fire. 13He praised Daniel in the den of the lions and blessed him. 14He reminded you of the scripture of Isaiah, which says, 'Even though you go through the fire, the flame shall not consume you.' 15He sang to you songs of the psalmist David, who said, 'Many are the afflictions of the righteous.' 16He recounted to you Solomon's proverb, 'There is a tree of life for those who do his will.' 17He confirmed the query of Ezekiel, 'Shall these dry bones live?' 18For he did not forget to teach you the song that Moses taught, which says, 19'I kill and I make alive: this is your life and the length of your days.' "

20 O bitter was that day—and yet not bitter—when that bitter tyrant of the Greeks quenched fire with fire in his cruel caldrons, and in his burning rage brought those seven sons of the daughter of Abraham to the catapult and back again to more[b] tortures, 21pierced the pupils of their eyes and cut out their tongues, and put them to death with various tortures. 22For these crimes divine justice pursued and will pursue the accursed tyrant. 23But the sons of Abraham with their victorious mother are gathered together into the chorus of the fathers, and have received pure and immortal[c] souls from God, 24to whom be glory forever and ever. Amen.

---

a Gk the rib that was built   b Other ancient authorities read to all his   c Other ancient authorities read victorious

---

the description of the ritual of the Day of Atonement in Lev 16.1–34. The Greek term for atoning sacrifice (hilasterion) also occurs in Rom 3.25. See also Heb 9.11–15; 1 Pet 1.18–19; 1 Jn 1.7. **17.23–24** The tyrant Antiochus is so amazed by the martyrs' courage that he uses them as examples for his soldiers. **18.1–5** A concluding exhortation to the author's fellow Jews emphasizing the values of obeying the law, mastering the emotions with reason, and suffering for the sake of religion. **18.5** Jerusalem. See 4.22, the only other place in 4 Maccabees that Jerusalem is mentioned. **18.6–19** The address promised in 12.7; it is placed here for greater rhetorical effect. Though emotional, it is not bombastic. It emphasizes the mother's chastity and the father's proper education of his sons in the heroic examples of the Jewish past, the law, and the prophets. See 2 Macc 7.22–29. **18.7** Rib. See Gen 2.22. **18.8** An allusion to Gen 3.1–7; Deut 22.25–27. **18.11** Abel . . . Cain. See Gen 4.2–15. Isaac. See Gen 22.1–19; note on 13.12. Joseph. See Gen 39.7–23. **18.12** Phinehas. See Num 25.7–13. Hananiah, Azariah, and Mishael. See Dan 3. **18.13** Daniel . . . lions. See Dan 6. **18.14** See Isa 43.2. **18.15** Ps 34.19. **18.16** Prov 3.18 (modified). **18.17** See Ezek 37.2–3. **18.19** Deut 32.39; see Deut 30.20. **18.20–24** The section serves as the conclusion of the whole work. The themes of punishment of the tyrant and the reward of immortality for the martyrs are once again emphasized. **18.23** Chorus. See note on 8.4. Immortal. See note on 9.22; Wis 8.19. **18.24** See Rom 11.36; 16.27; 2 Tim 4.18; Heb 13.21.

THE NEW COVENANT

Commonly Called

THE NEW TESTAMENT

of Our Lord and Savior Jesus Christ

NEW REVISED STANDARD VERSION

A Table of Parallel Passages in the Four Gospels

This table indicates where equivalent or similar passages occur in the four Gospels. Roman type indicates consecutive passages. Italic type signifies that the passages occur in a different order in the Gospel represented by that column.

	MATTHEW	MARK	LUKE	JOHN
JESUS' BIRTH AND CHILDHOOD				
Prologue	1.1	1.1	1.1–4	1.1–18
John's birth promised			1.5–25	
The annunciation			1.26–38	
Mary's visit to Elizabeth			1.39–56	
John's birth			1.57–80	
Jesus' lineage	1.2–17		3.23–28	
The birth of Jesus	1.18–25		2.1–7	
Adoration of the infant Jesus	2.1–12		2.8–20	
Jesus presented in the temple			2.21–38	
The flight into Egypt and return	2.13–21			
Jesus' childhood in Nazareth	2.22–23		2.39–40	
The child Jesus in the temple			2.41–52	
THE MINISTRY OF JOHN THE BAPTIST				
John the Baptist introduced	3.1–6	1.2–6	3.1–6	1.19–23
John preaches repentance	3.7–10		3.7–9	
John responds to questions			3.10–14	
John announces the Messiah	3.11–12	1.7–8	3.15–18	1.24–28
The imprisonment of John	14.3–4	6.17–18	3.19–20	
Jesus is baptized	3.13–17	1.9–11	3.21–22	1.29–34
Jesus' lineage	1.1–17		3.23–38	
Jesus is tempted	4.1–11	1.12–13	4.1–13	
THE BEGINNING OF JESUS' PUBLIC MINISTRY (according to John)				
Jesus call the first disciples				1.35–51
The wedding at Cana				2.1–11
The interlude at Capernaum				2.12
The first trip to Jerusalem				2.13
Jesus cleanses the temple	21.12–13	11.15–17	19.45–46	2.14–22

Based on *Synopsis Quattuor Evangeliorum*, 13th rev. ed., edited by Kurt Aland. Stuttgart: German Bible Society, 1990. Used with permission of German Bible Society.

	MATTHEW	MARK	LUKE	JOHN
The discussion with Nicodemus				2.23–3.21
Jesus' ministry in Judea				3.22
John testifies of the Messiah				3.23–36
JESUS' MINISTRY IN GALILEE				
The journey to Galilee	4.12	1.14a	4.14a	4.1–3
The discussion with the Samaritan woman				4.4–42
Jesus' ministry in Galilee	4.13–17	1.14b–15	4.14b–15	4.43–46a
Jesus' preaching at Nazareth	13.53–58	6.1–6a	4.16–30	
Jesus calls the disciples	4.18–22	1.16–20		
Teaching in the Capernaum synagogue		1.21–22	4.31–32	
Jesus heals a man with an unclean spirit		1.23–28	4.33–37	
The healing of Peter's mother-in-law	8.14–15	1.29–31	4.38–39	
Jesus heals various diseases	8.16–17	1.32–34	4.40–41	
Jesus leaves Capernaum		1.35–38	4.42–43	
Jesus' initial preaching in Galilee	4.23	1.39	4.44	
The miraculous catch of fish			5.1–11	
Jesus cures the leper	8.1–4	1.40–45	5.12–16	
Jesus heals the paralytic	9.1–8	2.1–12	5.17–26	5.1–9a
Jesus calls Levi (Matthew)	9.9–13	2.13–17	5.27–32	
The question about fasting	9.14–17	2.18–22	5.33–39	
Plucking grain on the sabbath	12.1–8	2.23–28	6.1–5	
Jesus heals the withered hand	12.9–14	3.1–6	6.6–11	
Jesus heals many	4.24–25	3.7–12	6.17–19	
	12.15–16			
Jesus chooses the Twelve	10.1–4	3.13–19a	6.12–16	
The Sermon on the Mount (according to Matthew)				
The setting of the sermon	5.1–2	3.7–13a	6.17–20a	
The Beatitudes	5.3–12		6.20b–23	
The salt of the earth	5.13	9.49–50	14.34–35	
The light of the world	5.14–16	4.21	8.16	
The law and the prophets	5.17–20		16.16–17	
On murder and anger	5.21–24			
On reconciliation and judgment	5.25–26		12.57–59	
On adultery and divorce	5.27–32	9.43–48	16.18	
On oaths	5.33–37			
On retaliation	5.38–42		6.29–30	

	MATTHEW	MARK	LUKE	JOHN
On love of enemies	5.43–48		6.27–28	
			6.32–36	
On giving alms	6.1–4			
On prayer	6.5–6			
The Lord's Prayer	6.7–15	11.25 [26]	11.1–4	
On fasting	6.16–18			
On treasures	6.19–21		12.33–34	
The healthy eye	6.22–23		11.34–36	
Serving two masters	6.24		16.13	
On anxiety	6.25–34		12.22–32	
On judging	7.1–5	4.24–25	6.37–42	
On profaning the holy	7.6			
That God answers prayer	7.7–11		11.9–13	
The Golden Rule	7.12		6.31	
The two ways	7.13–14		13.23–24	
Prophets known by their fruits	7.15–20		6.43–45	
	12.33–35			
Those who say, "Lord, Lord"	7.21–23		6.46	
The house built on the rock	7.24–27		6.47–49	
Response to the sermon	7.28–29	1.21–22		

The Sermon on the Plain
(according to Luke)

	MATTHEW	MARK	LUKE	JOHN
Occasion of the sermon	5.1–2	3.7–13a	6.17–20a	
The Beatitudes	5.3–12		6.20b–23	
The Woes			6.24–26	
On love of enemies	5.38–48		6.27–36	
On judging	7.1–5	4.24–25	6.37–42	
People known by their fruits	7.15–20		6.43–45	
	12.33–35			
The house built on the rock	7.21–27		6.46–49	
Jesus cures the leper	8.1–4	1.40–45	5.12–16	
The centurion of Capernaum	8.5–13	7.1–10	4.46b–54	
		7.30	13.28–29	
The widow's son at Nain			7.11–17	
The healing of Peter's mother-in-law	8.14–15	1.29–31	4.38–39	
The sick healed at evening	8.16–17	1.32–34	4.40–41	
On following Jesus	8.18–22		9.57–62	
Stilling the storm	8.23–27	4.35–41	8.22–25	
The Gadarene demoniacs	8.28–34	5.1–20	8.26–39	
The healing of the paralytic	9.1–8	2.1–12	5.17–26	5.1–9a
The call of Levi (Matthew)	9.9–13	2.13–17	5.27–32	

	MATTHEW	MARK	LUKE	JOHN
The question about fasting	9.14–17	2.18–22	5.33–39	
Jairus's daughter and the woman with a hemorrhage	9.18–26	5.21–43	8.40–56	
Two blind men	9.27–31	10.46–52	18.35–43	
	20.29–34			
The mute demoniac	9.32–34	3.22	11.14–15	
	12.22–24			
The harvest is great	9.35–38	6.6b	8.1	4.35
		6.34	10.2	
Commissioning of the Twelve	10.1–16	6.7	9.1	
		3.13–19	6.12–16	
		6.8–11	9.2–5	
			10.3	
The fate of the disciples	10.17–25		12.11–12	13.16
	24.9–14	13.9–13	21.12–19	
Exhortation to courage	10.26–33		12.2–9	
Households divided by the gospel	10.34–36		12.51–53	
The conditions of discipleship	10.37–39		14.25–27	
			17.33	12.25
The rewards of discipleship	10.40–42	9.41	10.16	13.20
Continuation of the journey	11.1			
Jesus answers John the Baptist	11.2–6		7.18–23	
Jesus praises John	11.7–19		7.24–35	
			16.16	
Woes on Galilean cities	11.20–24		10.13–15	
Jesus thanks the Father	11.25–27		10.21–22	
"Come to me"	11.28–30			
Plucking grain on the sabbath	12.1–8	2.23–28	6.1–5	
Healing the withered hand	12.9–14	3.1–6	6.6–11	
Jesus heals many by the sea	12.15–21	3.7–12	6.17–19	
The woman with the ointment	26.6–13	14.3–9	7.36–50	12.1–8
Women minister to Jesus			8.1–3	
Jesus thought to be out of his mind		3.19b–21		
Jesus accused of using Satan's power	12.22–30	3.22–27	11.14–15	
	9.32–34		11.17–23	
The sin against the Holy Spirit	12.31–32	3.28–30	12.10	
Tree and fruit	12.33–37			
	7.16–20	6.43–45		
The sign of Jonah	12.38–42	8.11–12	11.16	
	16.1–2a, 4		11.29–32	
The return of the unclean spirit	12.43–45		11.24–26	
Jesus' true family	12.46–50	3.31–35	8.19–21	15.14

	MATTHEW	MARK	LUKE	JOHN
The parable of the seed	13.1–9	4.1–9	8.4–8	
Jesus' rationale for the parables	13.10–17	4.10–12	8.9–10	
		4.25	8.18b	
Jesus explains the parable of the seed	13.18–23	4.13–20	8.11–15	
The one who has ears to hear	5.15	4.21–25	8.16–18	
	10.26			
	7.2			
	13.12			
The parable of the growing seed		4.26–29		
The parable of the weeds	13.24–30			
The parable of the mustard seed	13.31–32	4.30–32	13.18–19	
The parable of the yeast	13.33		13.20–21	
Jesus' use of parables	13.34–35	4.33–34		
Jesus explains the parable of the weeds	13.36–43			
The hidden treasure and the pearl	13.44–46			
The parable of the net	13.47–50			
Treasures new and old	13.51–52			
Jesus' true family	12.46–50	3.31–35	8.19–21	15.14
The stilling of the storm	8.23–27	4.35–41	8.22–25	
The Gerasene demoniac	8.28–34	5.1–20	8.26–39	
Jairus's daughter and the woman with a hemorrhage	9.18–26	5.21–43	8.40–56	
Jesus is rejected in Nazareth	13.53–58	6.1–6a	4.16–30	
Jesus' second journey to Jerusalem				5.1
The healing at the pool				5.2–47
Jesus commissions the Twelve	9.35	6.6b–13	9.1–6	
	10.1, 7–11, 14	3.13–15		
Jesus' identity discussed	14.1–2	6.14–16	9.7–9	
The death of John the Baptist	14.3–12	6.17–29	3.19–20	
The apostles' return		6.30–31	9.10a	
Jesus feeds the five thousand	14.13–21	6.32–44	9.10b–17	6.1–15
Jesus walks on the water	14.22–33	6.45–52		6.16–21
The healings at Gennesaret	14.34–36	6.53–56		6.22–25
The Bread of Life				6.26–59
On defilement	15.1–20	7.1–23	11.37–41	
			6.39	
The Syrophoenician woman	15.21–28	7.24–30		
Jesus heals a deaf mute	15.29–31	7.31–37		
Jesus feeds the four thousand	15.32–39	8.1–10		
The Pharisees seek a sign	16.1–4	8.11–13	11.16	
	12:38–39		12.54–56	
			11.29	

	MATTHEW	MARK	LUKE	JOHN
The yeast of the Pharisees	16.5–12	8.14–21	*12.1*	
A blind man is healed at Bethsaida		8.22–26		
Many take offense at Jesus				6.60–66
Peter's confession	16.13–20	8.27–30	9.18–21	6.67–71
First passion prediction	16.21–23	8.31–33	9.22	
The cost of discipleship	16.24–28	8.34–9.1	9.23–27	12.25
The transfiguration	17.1–9	9.2–10	9.28–36	
The coming of Elijah	17.10–13	9.11–13		
Jesus heals a possessed boy	17.14–21	9.14–29	9.37–43a	
			17.6	
Second passion prediction	17.22–23	9.30–32	9.43b–45	
On the temple tax	17.24–27			
True greatness	18.1–5	9.33–37	9.46–48	*13.20*
The outside exorcist	*10.42*	9.38–41	9.49–50	
Warnings concerning temptations	18.6–9	9.42–50	*17.1–2*	
	5.13		*14.34–35*	
The parable of the lost sheep	18.10–14		*15.3–7*	
On discipline in the community	18.15–18		*17.3*	20.23
"Where two or three are gathered"	18.19–20			
On reconciliation	18.21–22		*17.4*	
The parable of the unforgiving servant	18.23–35			
JOURNEY TO JERUSALEM (according to Luke)				
The departure for Jerusalem	19.1–2	10.1	9.51	
Rejection by Samaritans			9.52–56	
The demands of discipleship	*8.18–22*		9.57–62	
Jesus sends seventy before him	*9.37–38;*		10.1–16	
	10.7–16;			
	11.20–24;			
	10.40			13.20
The Seventy return	*11.25–27;*		10.17–24	
	13.16–17			
A lawyer's question	*22.34–40*	12.28–34	10.25–28	
The parable of the good Samaritan			10.29–37	
Mary and Martha			10.38–42	
The Lord's Prayer	*6.9–13*		11.1–4	
The parable of the importunate friend	*7.7–11*		11.5–13	
The Beelzebul controversy	*12.22–30*	*3.22–27*	11.14–23	
The return of the unclean spirit	*12.43–45*		11.24–26	
On those truly blessed			11.27–28	

	MATTHEW	MARK	LUKE	JOHN
The sign of Jonah	12.38–42	8.11–12	11.29–32	
On light and darkness	5.15; 6.22–23	4.21	11.33–36	
Jesus dines with a Pharisee	15.1–9	7.1–9	11.37–54	
One hypocrisy	16.5–6	8.14–15	12.1–3	
On fear and confession	10.26–33; 12.31–32	3.28–30	12.4–10	
The Holy Spirit's aid	10.19–20	13.11	12.11–12	
			21.14–15	
On riches	6.25–34, 19–21		12.13–34	
Exhortation to watch	24.42–51		12.35–48	13.4–5
Division in households	10.34–36		12.49–53	
On interpreting the present time	16.2–3		12.54–56	
On settling with one's accuser	5.25–26		12.57–59	
Repent or perish			13.1–9	
The healing of the crippled woman			13.10–17	
The parable of the mustard seed	13.31–32	4.30–32	13.18–19	
The parable of the yeast	13.33		13.20–21	
The narrow door to the kingdom	7.13–14, 22–23; 8.11–12 19.30	10.31	13.22–30	
The third day			13.31–33	
The lament of Jerusalem	23.37–39		13.34–35	
The healing of a man with dropsy			14.1–6	
On humility			14.7–14	
The parable of the great dinner	22.1–14		14.15–24	
On the costs of discipleship	10.37–38; 5.13	9.49–50	14.25–35	
The parable of the lost sheep	18.12–14		15.1–7	
The parable of the lost coin			15.8–10	
The parable of the prodigal son			15.11–32	
The parable of the dishonest manager and teaching about riches	6.24		16.1–15	
On the Torah	11.12–13; 5.18		16.16–17	
On divorce	19.9; 5.32	10.11–12	16.18	
The parable of the rich man and Lazarus			16.19–31	
On occasions for stumbling	18.6–7	9.42	17.1–3a	
On forgiveness	18.15, 21–22		17.3b–4	

	MATTHEW	MARK	LUKE	JOHN
On faith	*17.19–21*	*9.28–29*	17.5–6	
	21.21	*11.22–23*		
Worthless slaves			17.7–10	
Cleansing of ten lepers			17.11–19	
On the coming of God's kingdom			17.20–21	
The day of the Son of Man	*24.23, 26–27*	*13.19–23*	17.22–37	
	24.37–39,	*13.14–16*		
	17–18			
	10.39;			12.25
	24.40–41,			
	28			
The parable of the unjust judge			18.1–8	
The parable of the Pharisee and the tax collector	*23.12*		18.9–14	
JESUS AT THE FEAST OF TABERNACLES (according to John)				
A private pilgrimage				7.1–13
Jesus teaches in the temple				7.14–39
The crowd is divided over Jesus				7.40–52
[The woman caught in adultery				7.53–8.11]
The Light of the World				8.12–20
Discussion with the Jews: "Before Abraham was, I am"				8.21–59
Healing of a man born blind				9.1–41
The Good Shepherd				10.1–18
Renewed division among the Jews				10.19–21
JESUS' MINISTRY IN JUDEA				
The departure for Jerusalem	19.1–2	10.1	*9.51*	
On divorce and celibacy	19.3–12	10.2–12	*16.18*	
Jesus blesses the children	19.13–15	10.13–16	18.15–17	
The rich youth	19.16–22	10.17–22	18.18–23	
On riches and rewards	19.23–30	10.23–31	18.24–30	
			22.28–30	
The laborers in the vineyard	20.1–16	*10.31*	*13.30*	
Jesus at the Feast of Dedication				10.22–39
Jesus departs across the Jordan				10.40–42
The raising of Lazarus				11.1–14
The chief priests and Pharisees conspire against Jesus				11.45–53
Jesus withdraws to Ephraim				11.54–57

	MATTHEW	MARK	LUKE	JOHN
Third prediction of the Passion	20.17–19	10.32–34	18.31–34	
Preeminence among the disciples	20.20–28	10.35–45	22.24–27	
The healing of the blind	20.29–34	10.46–52	18.35–43	
	9.27–31			
Zacchaeus			19.1–10	
The parable of the pounds	25.14–30	13.34	19.11–27	
Mary anoints Jesus at Bethany	26.6–13	14.3–9	7.36–50	12.1–8
The priests plot against Lazarus				12.9–11

THE FINAL WEEK IN JERUSALEM

	MATTHEW	MARK	LUKE	JOHN
Triumphal entry	21.1–11; 17	11.1–11	19.28–40	12.12–19
Jesus weeps over Jerusalem			19.41–44	
The cursing of the fig tree	21.18–19	11.12–14		
The cleansing of the temple	21.12–16	11.15–17	19.45–46	2.13–17
The chief priests and scribes conspire against Jesus		11.18–19	19.47–48	
The withered fig tree	21.20–22	11.20–26		
	6.14–15			
Jesus' authority and the Baptist's	21.23–27	11.27–33	20.1–8	
The parable of two sons	21.28–32			
The parable of the wicked tenants	21.33–46	12.1–12	20.9–19	
The parable of the wedding banquet	22.1–14		14.15–24	
On paying taxes to the emperor	22.15–22	12.13–17	20.20–26	
On the resurrected life	22.23–33	12.18–27	20.27–40	
The Great Commandment	22.34–40	12.28–34	10.25–28	
On the Son of David	22.41–46	12.35–37a	20.41–44	
Woe to the scribes and the Pharisees	23.1–36	12.37b–40	20.45–47	
Jesus laments over Jerusalem	23.37–39		13.34–35	
The widow's copper coins		12.41–44	21.1–4	

The Eschatological Discourse

	MATTHEW	MARK	LUKE	JOHN
"Not one stone upon another"	24.1–2	13.1–2	21.5–6	
Signs of the end	24.3–8	13.3–8	21.7–11	
Persecutions foretold	24.9–14	13.9–13	21.12–19	
	10.17–22a		12.11–12	
The desolating sacrilege	24.15–22	13.14–20	21.20–24	
False messiahs and false prophets	24.23–28	13.21–23	17.23–24, 37b	
The coming of the Son of Man	24.29–31	13.24–27	21.25–28	
The parable of the fig tree	24.32–36	13.28–32	21.29–33	
Summons to watchfulness	25.13–15	13.33–37	21.34–36	
	24.42			

	MATTHEW	MARK	LUKE	JOHN
Example of the flood	24.37–44		*17.26–36*	
The parable of good and wicked slaves	24.45–51		*12.41–46*	
The parable of the ten bridesmaids	25.1–13			
The parable of the talents	25.14–30	*13.34*	*19.11–27*	
The final judment	25.31–46			
Summary: Jesus in Jerusalem			21.37–38	
Greeks wish to see Jesus				12.20–36
Blindness and judgment by the light				12.37–50
The chief priests conspire	26.1–5	14.1–2	22.1–2	
Anointing in Bethany	26.6–13	14.3–9	*7.36–50*	12.1–8
Judas conspires to betray Jesus	26.14–16	14.10–11	22.3–6	
Preparations for the Passover	26.17–20	14.12–17	22.7–14	
Jesus washes the disciples' feet				13.1–20
Judas' betrayal predicted	26.21–25	14.18–21	*22.21–23*	13.21–30
The Last Supper	26.26–29	14.22–25	22.15–20	
Preeminence among the disciples	20.24–28; 19.28	10.41–45	22.24–30	
The new commandment of love				13.31–35
Peter's denial predicted	26.30–35	14.26–31	22.31–34	13.36–38
The two swords			22.35–38	
Jesus' farewell discourses				14.1–16.33
Prayer with the disciples	26.36–46	14.32–42	22.39–46	17.1–26
The arrest of Jesus	26.47–56	14.43–52	22.47–53	18.1–12
Jesus before the council	26.57–68	14.53–65	22.54–55, 63–71	18.13–24
Peter's denial	26.69–75	14.66–72	22.56–62	18.25–27
Jesus handed over to Pilate	27.1–2	15.1	23.1	18.28
The death of Judas	27.3–10		*Acts 1.16–20*	
Jesus tried before Pilate	27.11–14	15.2–5	23.2–5	18.29–38
Jesus before Herod			23.6–12	
Pilate acquits Jesus of wrong			23.13–16	
Jesus or Barabbas	27.15–23	15.6–14	23.17–23	18.39–40
Jesus handed over to be crucified	27.24–26	15.15	23.24–25	19.1, 4–16
The soldiers mock Jesus	27.27–31a	15.16–20a		*19.2–3*
Jesus takes up his cross	27.31b–32	15.20b–21	23.26–32	19.17a
The crucifixion	27.33–37	15.22–26	23.33–34	19.17b–27
Jesus derided on the cross	27.38–43	15.27–32a	23.35–38	*19.18*
The two bandits	27.33–37	15.22–26	23.33–34	19.17b–27
The death of Jesus	27.45–54	15.33–39	23.44–48	19.28–30
Witnesses of the crucifixion	27.55–56	15.40–41	23.49	*19.25–27*

	MATTHEW	MARK	LUKE	JOHN
Piercing of Jesus' side				19.31–37
Jesus' burial	27.57–61	15.42–47	23.50–56	19.38–42
The guard at the tomb	27.62–66			
THE RESURRECTION OF JESUS				
The women at the tomb	28.1–8	16.1–8	24.1–12	20.1–13
Jesus appears to the women	28.9–10		*24.10–11*	20.14–18
The guards report	28.11–15			
Appearance to two disciples at Emmaus			24.13–35	
Appearance to the Eleven	28.16–17		24.36–43	20.19–29
The Eleven commissioned to preach	28.18–20		24.44–53	
Conclusion to the body of John's Gospel				20.30–31
Second appearance to disciples				21.1–14
Discussion with Peter				21.15–23
Seal of the beloved disciple				21.24–25

The Gospel According to
MATTHEW

THE FIRST GOSPEL resists neat genre classification. One might think that the work's title names the genre as "Gospel," but the titles (superscriptions) of such works were not original. Moreover, when titles were first inserted into these ancient manuscripts for the purposes of identification (second-century CE), they did not contain the words "The Gospel," only "According to X." Furthermore, the term "Gospel" referring to a literary genre appears nowhere in the NT or in surviving Greek and Roman literature. It seems to have appeared as a description of writings in the late second century, perhaps derived from Mark 1.1 ("The beginning of the *gospel* of Jesus Christ . . ."), which probably does not refer to the book but to the "good news" (the etymological sense of the Greek word for "gospel") that it contains.

In short, no genre called "Gospel" seems to have existed, but there were types of ancient literature with generic similarities to the Gospel. The most closely related type is the ancient Hellenistic "biography" (Greek *bios,* "life"). This genre praises a hero believed to have had divine and human origins who exercised special gifts such as teaching, recruiting followers, and miracle-working and who sometimes died an unusual death.

Most scholars maintain that the Gospel According to Mark was written first and that the author of Matthew transformed the Markan version of the *bios* further by heightening Israelite ("Jewish") features such as poetic parallelism; scribal argument; an emphasis on the law, religious practice, and piety; symbolic numbers; scriptural quotation and fulfillment; genealogy; baptism as a rite of entry; a special meal related to Passover; communal discipline; and prayer. In this transformation, Jesus became the authoritative interpreter of Moses, but also the promised messianic king of Israel. In the story he transferred his authority to a prominent disciple, Peter, and then appeared after his death, promising his followers that he would continue to be present with them until the end of the age. These special features of this genre transformation had a profound impact on the developing institutional church. Thus, it is not surprising that the Gospel According to Matthew was placed first in collections of the four Gospels and then in the NT itself.

Authorship and Date

EARLY CHURCH WRITERS CLAIMED that the author of this Gospel, Matthew the tax collector, a disciple of Jesus (10.3; 9.9), collected Jesus' sayings in the Hebrew dialect for others to translate

(Papias, early second century), or wrote the Gospel in the 50s or early 60s (Irenaeus, late second century), or wrote it in Judea in the decades following Jesus' death (Jerome, fifth century).

Various considerations cast serious doubt on those ancient views. First, the Gospel of Matthew contains, but is not itself, a collection of sayings. Second, a Hebrew version of this Gospel exists, but it is medieval, and scholars argue that the Gospel was originally written in Greek; thus it is not a translation. Third, the author of Matthew was almost certainly aware of the destruction of Jerusalem and the temple in 70 CE (see 21.41; 22.7; 24.15–16). Fourth, Jesus' main opponents in the story are the Pharisees, whose authority developed predominantly in the late first century. Fifth, according to widely held scholarly opinion (the "Two-Source Theory"), the major sources for the author were the Greek Gospel of Mark (late 60s or early 70s) and a sayings source in Greek that has been lost (designated "Q," probably composed pre-70) along with some special traditions ("M," also pre-70). These factors suggest a date after 70, probably between 80 and 90; composition by Jesus' Galilean tax-collecting disciple at mid-century is therefore extremely unlikely. More certain is the probability that it was written by a multilingual man, probably an Israelite, with a rather sophisticated command of Israelite traditions and scribal argumentation (see 13.52) in the late first century.

The Gospel's place of origin is debated. Suggestions include Alexandria in Egypt, Caesarea on the eastern Mediterranean coast, Galilee, southern Syria, and some town east of the Jordan River (19.1; 4.15), but the most common theory places its composition in Antioch of Syria. One good reason is that it was a Hellenistic city with a large Israelite population, which fits the Gospel; a more specific reason is that it was quoted by Bishop Ignatius of Antioch within a generation of its composition (ca. 110).

Since anonymous works in antiquity were often attributed to prominent persons, a plausible conclusion is that an unknown Greek-speaking Israelite male, probably a scribe, composed this Gospel about 80–90 CE. Its place of composition was perhaps Antioch, Syria.

Circumstances of Writing

THE GOSPEL OF MATTHEW was written by a subject of the Roman Empire, which can be described as a hierarchically ordered, commercialized, advanced agrarian (peasant) society with no middle class. A few powerful men and their families ruled; they were supported by bureaucrats, slaves, official priests, and a sophisticated military establishment. Those at the bottom of the socioeconomic pyramid were local business-people, artisans, and—the vast majority—peasant farmers and fishermen. There were also a few "expendables," e.g., bandits, beggars, and prostitutes. With few exceptions, women always ranked below men, and children below both. This structure was typical not only of Roman Italy but also of the Roman provinces. Not surprisingly, these social strata appear throughout the Gospel: provincial governors, centurions, "client" kings, priests, local aristocrats, peasant farmers, artisans, fishermen, lepers, bandits, and beggars. Jesus is portrayed as an advocate of the lower strata and thus in tension with the ruling aristocracy subject to Rome. Despite several important stories about women (9.18–26; 15.21–28; 26.6–13; 27.55–56, 61; 28.1–10), the Gospel was written by a man for men (see, e.g., 5.27–32; 18.15; 23.8).

Political resistance to Rome in the Gospel is not overt, but nonetheless suggestively implied: Jesus descends from King David through a long line of kings (1.6b–12) and is the promised Messiah; his name recalls Joshua, "the Savior" (1.21); his birth is marked by a heavenly star

(2.2); he is a threat to Rome's official ruling Herodian kings (ch. 2); his message is about the kingdom of heaven (4.17), which is in contrast to the "kingdom" of Rome; his predecessor, the prophet John the Baptizer, is executed by Rome's appointed representative, Herod Antipas, tetrarch of Galilee (14.1–12); he opposes the Jerusalem temple's priestly hierarchy, who must collaborate with Rome; he is condemned by a vacillating Roman governor, Pilate (27.2–26); and, most important, his execution is by crucifixion (27.32–56), a Roman penalty mainly for political rebels. In short, though the Matthean plot is not overtly political, economic and political issues of the larger Roman Empire are not far under the surface and should not be ignored in considering the circumstances of the Gospel's composition.

Other circumstances are more specifically religious. This Gospel expands on the Pharisees as Jesus' major Galilean opponents (9.11, 34; 12.2; 27.62); accuses them of being "hypocrites" (ch. 23); emphasizes a "righteousness" that exceeds theirs (5.17–20); and speaks of "their scribes" (7.29) and "their synagogues" (4.23; 9.35). These attacks suggest that the author represented a group of mainly Israelite messianic believers who were no longer aligned with post-70, Pharisee-led Israelites (see 21.28–23.39). At the same time, there is evidence that the Matthean group was disrupted internally. The narrative mentions a mixed body of good and bad (13.24–30, 47–50; 22.1–14); there are "false prophets," and Christ-believers who want freedom from Torah obedience altogether (7.15–23); and there are some who threaten the faith of others (18.6–7, 10–14). The disciples themselves are characterized by "little faith" (6.30; 8.26; 14.31; 16.8), although they evince understanding (13.51). In this connection, only in this Gospel among the four is the word "church" (Greek *ekklesia*) used, first in relation to the transferal of authority to Peter (16.17–19) and later in relation to the assembled group's power to ban errant members (18.17). The Sadducees, who were mainly priests, become the major opponents in Jerusalem, along with the Romans.

Structure and Composition

THE GOSPEL ACCORDING TO MATTHEW generally follows the largely geographical outline of Mark from Galilee to Jerusalem, but adds the birth stories at the beginning (chs. 1–2) and the resurrection appearance and final commissioning scene at the end (28.9–20) as well as material from other sources, especially in chs. 5–11. The narrative is marked by temporal statements in 4.17 and 16.21 ("From that time Jesus began . . ."), but its most striking structural feature is the sequence of five major discourses (5.1–7.27; 10.5–42; 13.1–52; 18.1–35; 24.3–25.46), each concluded by a similar formula, "When Jesus had finished saying these things . . ." (7.28; 11.1; 13.53; 19.1; 26.1). These discourses may be intended to recall the five books of the Torah, attributed to Moses, since the author seems to have viewed Jesus as a new, more authoritative Moses offering a new Torah that fulfills, yet supersedes, the old (see 2.13–18; 13.52). The Gospel also contains fourteen special "formula quotations" showing that events fulfill the holy scriptures construed as prophecy (see note on 1.22–23).

This Gospel contains subtle anti-Romanism, opposition to a religious establishment, a sharp anti-Pharisaism, moral stringency, and apocalyptic severity. Yet it has a marvelous vision of Jesus as the Moses-like teacher; the compassionate, healing Messiah/Son of David; the royal Son of God; and the apocalyptic Son of Man. It also claims that he is the fulfillment of the Torah and the prophets (5.17–20) and one who calls his followers to spread the good news of the kingdom of heaven to the whole world (28.16–20). [DENNIS C. DULING]

The Genealogy of Jesus the Messiah

1 An account of the genealogy[a] of Jesus the Messiah,[b] the son of David, the son of Abraham.

2 Abraham was the father of Isaac, and Isaac the father of Jacob, and Jacob the father of Judah and his brothers, 3 and Judah the father of Perez and Zerah by Tamar, and Perez the father of Hezron, and Hezron the father of Aram, 4 and Aram the father of Aminadab, and Aminadab the father of Nahshon, and Nahshon the father of Salmon, 5 and Salmon the father of Boaz by Rahab, and Boaz the father of Obed by Ruth, and Obed the father of Jesse, 6 and Jesse the father of King David.

And David was the father of Solomon by the wife of Uriah, 7 and Solomon the father of Rehoboam, and Rehoboam the father of Abijah, and Abijah the father of Asaph,[c] 8 and Asaph[c] the father of Jehoshaphat, and Jehoshaphat the father of Joram, and Joram the father of Uzziah, 9 and Uzziah the father of Jotham, and Jotham the father of Ahaz, and Ahaz the father of Hezekiah, 10 and Hezekiah

the father of Manasseh, and Manasseh the father of Amos,[d] and Amos[d] the father of Josiah, 11 and Josiah the father of Jechoniah and his brothers, at the time of the deportation to Babylon.

12 And after the deportation to Babylon: Jechoniah was the father of Salathiel, and Salathiel the father of Zerubbabel, 13 and Zerubbabel the father of Abiud, and Abiud the father of Eliakim, and Eliakim the father of Azor, 14 and Azor the father of Zadok, and Zadok the father of Achim, and Achim the father of Eliud, 15 and Eliud the father of Eleazar, and Eleazar the father of Matthan, and Matthan the father of Jacob, 16 and Jacob the father of Joseph the husband of Mary, of whom Jesus was born, who is called the Messiah.[e]

17 So all the generations from Abraham to David are fourteen generations; and from David to the deportation to Babylon, fourteen generations; and from the deportation to Babylon to the Messiah,[e] fourteen generations.

---

a Or birth b Or Jesus Christ c Other ancient authorities read Asa d Other ancient authorities read Amon e Or the Christ

---

1.1–2.23 The author presents Jesus' twofold "origin" (Greek *genesis*). First, he is human, having the legitimate prerequisites to be Israel's Messiah, with hints of his role as a new, but superior, Moses. Second, he is divine, born from a virgin by the Spirit of God. **1.1–17** Cf. Lk 3.23–38. Jesus' genealogical descent from patriarchs, kings, and four women who have unusual sexual histories but are part of God's plan. **1.1** *Genealogy,* lit. "origin" (Greek *genesis,* see text note *a*; translated *birth* in v. 18; cf. Gen 5.1). In this mainly linear genealogy the author emphasizes King David (first!) and the patriarch Abraham. *Jesus.* See note on 1.21. *Messiah,* lit. "Anointed [One]." In Israel, kings and priests were anointed with oils (see, e.g., 26.6–13; Lev 21.10–12; 1 Sam 10.1; 16.1–13; Ps 18.50; Lk 7.36–50). *Son of,* i.e., descended from (see, however, note on 9.27). *David,* Israel's greatest king (1 Sam 16.1–1 Kings 2.12). *Abraham,* ancestral patriarch of the Israelites, but also "ancestor of a multitude of nations (peoples, Gentiles)" (Gen 17.4–5, but see notes on 3.9; 25.32); see 10.5–6; 15.24; 28.19; see also Gal 3–4; Rom 4. **1.2–6a** The first of three divisions of the genealogy (with vv. 6b–11, 12–16); see v. 17; see also 1 Chr 2.1–15; Ruth 4.18–22. Four women (vv. 3, 5, 6) in a male line of descent is extraordinary; three (and perhaps the fourth, Bathsheba) are certainly Gentiles; three and *perhaps the fourth* (Ruth) had improper sexual relations but were later admired in Israelite legend and considered important for God's plan. Their inclusion may answer opponents' accusations about Mary's unusual pregnancy or foreshadow the disciples' commission to "all nations," including Gentiles (28.19). For interest in the number three, see the triadic arrangements of 5.21–48; 6.1–18; 6.19–24, and the explicit references to *three* in 12.40; 13.33; 15.32; 17.4; 26.34, 61; 27.40. **1.3** *Tamar,* a Canaanite who played the prostitute with her father-in-law, Judah (Gen 38; see 1 Chr 2.4); Philo of Alexandria attributed "virginal" beauty to her (*On Mating with the Preliminary Studies* 124). **1.5** *Rahab,* a Canaanite prostitute who helped Joshua's spies to escape (Josh 2.1–21; 6.22–25) and who was remembered for her faith (Heb 11.31) and hospitality (Jas 2.25); nowhere else is she mentioned as Boaz's mother or David's ancestor. *Ruth,* a sexually aggressive widow from Moab; see Ruth 2–4. **1.6a** *Jesse.* See Isa 11.1, 10. In relation to Jesus, see Rom 15.12; Rev 5.5; 22.16. **1.6b–11** The second division (see v. 17) traces Jesus' genealogy through the Davidic kings (1–2 Kings). **1.6b** *Wife of Uriah,* the very beautiful Bathsheba, with whom David committed adultery; perhaps she was a Hittite, like Uriah (but her name is Hebrew; see 2 Sam 11–12, esp. 12.9; 1 Kings 15.5). **1.11** *Deportation to Babylon,* i.e., the Babylonian exile (597–539 BCE). **1.12–16a** The third division contains mostly unknown names. **1.12** *Zerubbabel.* See Ezra 3.2, 8; Neh 12.1; Hag 1–2; cf. 1 Chr 3.17–19. **1.16** *Joseph the husband of Mary,* not "Joseph the father of Jesus," as expected from the linear genealogical pattern; there are alternatives in the ancient manuscripts; see note on 1.18–25. **1.17** The primary function of linear genealogies is to ascribe honor to a person by tracing ancestry to heroic ancestors; in oral cultures, mnemonic devices and telescoping genealogical units (omitting names) are common. *Fourteen,* the numeri-

The Birth of Jesus the Messiah

18 Now the birth of Jesus the Messiah[a] took place in this way. When his mother Mary had been engaged to Joseph, but before they lived together, she was found to be with child from the Holy Spirit. 19Her husband Joseph, being a righteous man and unwilling to expose her to public disgrace, planned to dismiss her quietly. 20But just when he had resolved to do this, an angel of the Lord appeared to him in a dream and said, "Joseph, son of David, do not be afraid to take Mary as your wife, for the child conceived in her is from the Holy Spirit. 21She will bear a son, and you are to name him Jesus, for he will save his people from their sins." 22All this took place to fulfill what had been spoken by the Lord through the prophet:

23 "Look, the virgin shall conceive and bear a son,

and they shall name him Emmanuel,"

which means, "God is with us." 24When Joseph awoke from sleep, he did as the angel of the Lord commanded him; he took her as his wife, 25but had no marital relations with her until she had borne a son;[b] and he named him Jesus.

The Visit of the Wise Men

2 In the time of King Herod, after Jesus was born in Bethlehem of Judea, wise men[c] from the East came to Jerusalem, 2asking, "Where is the child who has been born king of the Jews? For we observed his star at its rising,[d] and have come to pay him homage." 3When King Herod heard this, he was frightened, and all Jerusalem with him; 4and calling together all the chief priests and scribes of the people, he inquired of them where the Messiah[e] was to be born. 5They told him, "In Bethlehem of Judea; for so it has been written by the prophet:

6 'And you, Bethlehem, in the land of Judah, are by no means least among the rulers of Judah;

---

a Or Jesus Christ b Other ancient authorities read her firstborn son c Or astrologers; Gk magi d Or in the East e Or the Christ

---

cal value of David's name in Hebrew ($d = 4$ [twice]; v or $w = 6$), may be mnemonic; it symbolizes David, whose royal line is the second of three generations of fourteen. The three divisions of unequal length (about 750, 400, and 600 years each) involve telescoping; four kings and a queen are omitted in the second.

1.18–25 Cf. Lk 1.26–38. Jesus' second, or divine, origin, which also interprets v. 16. **1.18** *Birth.* See note on 1.1. *Engaged.* Marriage was not based on romantic love, but on a contract between families in which family status and economics played a role (e.g., dowry; bride-price). Marriageable age for girls was normally puberty, at which time the girl was contracted to her future husband (v. 19; see Deut 20.7). *Before they lived together,* the betrothal period. *To be with child* before marriage dishonored the families, especially the males, and was grounds for Joseph's dismissing her (see v. 19; ancient law even permitted her execution by stoning; cf. Deut 22.13–21). *The Holy Spirit,* creative divine agency (see v. 20; 3.16; 22.43; 28.19; Lk 1.35). **1.19** *Husband.* See note on 1.18. Henceforth *Joseph* (the man) dominates the story (cf. Lk 1–2). *Righteous,* here meaning "law (Torah) abiding," and *righteousness* (3.15) are favorite Matthean terms (see note on 3.15; 13.17, 43; Lk 1.6). *Dismiss.* See note on 1.18; 5.31–32; 19.7. **1.20** *Dream* (see also 2.12, 13, 19, 22), a means of divine communication, recalls Joseph the dreamer (Gen 37.5–11) and dream interpreter (Gen 40–41). *Son of David.* See v. 1. **1.21** *Jesus,* from the Greek form of a common Hebrew name (Joshua) derived from *yasha'*, "he saves" (see 8.25); thus *he will save his people from their sins.* **1.22–23** The quotation is from Isa 7.14 (Septuagint) and is the first of fourteen quotations introduced with almost identical formulas; see 2.5b–6;

2.15b; 2.17–18; 2.23b; 3.3; 4.14–16; 8.17; 12.17–21; 13.14–15; 13.35; 21.4–5; 26.56 (see 26.54); 27.9–10. These formula quotations emphasize that events fulfill prophecy, and thus God's will. *Virgin,* based on the Greek Septuagint; the Hebrew *'almah* normally means "young woman." **1.25** *Until.* The author's birth narrative does not seem to imply the perpetual virginity of Mary (see also 13.55). *Named,* accepted the child.

2.1–23 The infant Jesus is linked with Bethlehem, Egypt, and Nazareth. **2.1–12** Gentiles pay homage to the true king, not Rome's client king, Herod. **2.1** Rome allowed certain native client kings such as *Herod* (Herod the Great) to rule (37–4 BCE); see note on 2.22; Lk 3.1. *Bethlehem,* David's hometown, five miles south of Jerusalem (1 Sam 16.1–13; see note on 2.5–6; cf. Lk 1.26). *Wise men* (Greek *magoi*) *from the East,* court priests, perhaps from Parthia, who practiced magic and astrology (see text note c). **2.2** *King of the Jews* (see also 27.11, 29, 37, 42) contrasts with King Herod (2.1; see Introduction). The title "king" was granted only by Rome; thus the story has potentially subversive implications. *His star.* See Num 24.17. A famous leader of an Israelite messianic rebellion (132–135 CE) was called Bar Kochba, "Son of the Star." *Pay him homage,* i.e., bow down in respect or worship (see vv. 8, 11; 14.33; 28.9, 17; see also Ps 72.10–11). **2.4** *Chief priests,* high-ranking aristocratic temple priests who performed sacrifices and purification rites (see note on 21.15). *Scribes,* writing bureaucrats and scholars, usually viewed as in league with inimical Pharisees in Matthew (but cf. 8.19; 13.52; 17.10; 23.2–3). *The people* are occasionally viewed negatively; see 13.15; 15.8; 21.23; 26.3, 47; esp. 27.24–25; cf. 1.21; 4.23; 9.35. **2.5b–6** The second formula quotation (see note on 1.22–23) com-

for from you shall come a ruler
who is to shepherd[a] my people
Israel.' "

7 Then Herod secretly called for the wise men[b] and learned from them the exact time when the star had appeared. [8]Then he sent them to Bethlehem, saying, "Go and search diligently for the child; and when you have found him, bring me word so that I may also go and pay him homage." [9]When they had heard the king, they set out; and there, ahead of them, went the star that they had seen at its rising,[c] until it stopped over the place where the child was. [10]When they saw that the star had stopped,[d] they were overwhelmed with joy. [11]On entering the house, they saw the child with Mary his mother; and they knelt down and paid him homage. Then, opening their treasure chests, they offered him gifts of gold, frankincense, and myrrh. [12]And having been warned in a dream not to return to Herod, they left for their own country by another road.

The Escape to Egypt

13 Now after they had left, an angel of the Lord appeared to Joseph in a dream and said, "Get up, take the child and his mother, and flee to Egypt, and remain there until I tell you; for Herod is about to search for the child, to destroy him." [14]Then Joseph[e] got up, took the child and his mother by night, and went to Egypt, [15]and remained there until the death of Herod. This was to fulfill what had been spoken by the Lord through the prophet, "Out of Egypt I have called my son."

The Massacre of the Infants

16 When Herod saw that he had been tricked by the wise men,[b] he was infuriated, and he sent and killed all the children in and around Bethlehem who were two years old or under, according to the time that he had learned from the wise men.[b] [17]Then was fulfilled what had been spoken through the prophet Jeremiah:

18 "A voice was heard in Ramah,
wailing and loud lamentation,
Rachel weeping for her children;
she refused to be consoled, because
they are no more."

The Return from Egypt

19 When Herod died, an angel of the Lord suddenly appeared in a dream to Joseph in Egypt and said, [20]"Get up, take the child and his mother, and go to the land of Israel, for those who were seeking the child's life are dead." [21]Then Joseph[e] got up, took the child and his mother, and went to the land of Israel. [22]But when he heard that Archelaus was ruling over Judea in place of his father Herod, he was afraid to go there. And after being warned in a dream, he went away to the district of Galilee. [23]There he made his home in a town called Nazareth, so that what had been spoken through the prophets might be fulfilled, "He will be called a Nazorean."

---

a Or rule b Or astrologers; Gk magi c Or in the East
d Gk saw the star e Gk he

---

bines a modified Mic 5.2 with 2 Sam 5.2, giving Bethlehem geographic precision, prominence, and relevance (see note on 2.1). **2.11** *Frankincense*, a fragrant resin. See Ps 72.15; Isa 60.5–6. *Myrrh*, a resin used for anointing (Ex 30.23–32) and embalming (Jn 19.39–40). The author reports three gifts, but not three kings (a medieval expansion). **2.12** *Dream*. See note on 1.20. **2.13–15** Escape to and return from Egypt echo the stories of Joseph (Gen 37), Moses, the exodus, and thus Passover, a festival that remembers freedom from slavery with all of its political implications. **2.15b** The third formula quotation (see note on 1.22–23) cites Hos 11.1, where "son" refers to Israel (Ex 4.22–23; Deut 1.31); but see note on 3.17. **2.16–18** The massacre echoes Pharaoh's ruling at the birth of Moses (Ex 1.15–22), suggesting that Jesus is like Moses; see notes on 1.1–2.23; 2.13–15; 4.2; 4.8; 5.1–7.29; 7.28; 8.1–9.34; 8.4; 11.9; 17.1–8; 19.7; 22.24; 23.2. See note on Wis 11.7. **2.17–18** The fourth formula quotation (see note on 1.22–23) cites Jer 31.15, which originally referred to the exile of the Northern tribes to Assyria (722/1 BCE). **2.19–23** The final place of origin of the Messiah is identified as *Nazareth* (cf. vv. 4–5, 15). **2.19** *Dream*. See note on 1.20. **2.22** Herod's kingdom was divided among his three sons: *Archelaus* (ethnarch, ruled Judea, Samaria, and Idumea, 4 BCE–6 CE); Herod Antipas (tetrarch, ruled Galilee and Perea, 4 BCE–39 CE); and Philip (tetrarch, ruled the region northeast of the Sea of Galilee, 4 BCE–33/34 CE). See 14.3–4; Mk 6.17–18; Lk 3.1. **2.23a** *Nazareth*, an insignificant agricultural village fifteen miles west of the Sea of Galilee, unmentioned in the Hebrew Bible and other contemporary sources (see Lk 2.4; Jn 1.46; 7.41, 52). **2.23b** No known OT passage corresponds to this fifth formula quotation (see note on 1.22–23), but *Nazorean* perhaps alludes to the messianic "Branch" (Hebrew *netzer*) of David's line (Isa 11.1; see Zech 3.8; 6.12) or to a Nazirite, a "holy one" who vowed to abstain from wine and cutting his hair (Num 6; Judg 13.5–7; Acts 18.18; 21.17–26; cf. Mt 11.18–19).

The Proclamation of John the Baptist

3 In those days John the Baptist appeared in the wilderness of Judea, proclaiming, 2"Repent, for the kingdom of heaven has come near."[a] 3This is the one of whom the prophet Isaiah spoke when he said,

"The voice of one crying out in the
wilderness:
'Prepare the way of the Lord,
make his paths straight.' "

4Now John wore clothing of camel's hair with a leather belt around his waist, and his food was locusts and wild honey. 5Then the people of Jerusalem and all Judea were going out to him, and all the region along the Jordan, 6and they were baptized by him in the river Jordan, confessing their sins.

7 But when he saw many Pharisees and Sadducees coming for baptism, he said to them, "You brood of vipers! Who warned you to flee from the wrath to come? 8Bear fruit worthy of repentance. 9Do not presume to say to yourselves, 'We have Abraham as our ancestor'; for I tell you, God is able from these stones to raise up children to Abraham. 10Even now the ax is lying at the root of the trees; every tree therefore that does not bear good fruit is cut down and thrown into the fire.

11 "I baptize you with[b] water for repentance, but one who is more powerful than I is coming after me; I am not worthy to carry his sandals. He will baptize you with[b] the Holy Spirit and fire. 12His winnowing fork is in his hand, and he will clear his threshing floor and will gather his wheat into the granary; but the chaff he will burn with unquenchable fire."

The Baptism of Jesus

13 Then Jesus came from Galilee to John at the Jordan, to be baptized by him. 14John would have prevented him, saying, "I need to be baptized by you, and do you come to me?" 15But Jesus answered him, "Let it be so now;

_____
a Or is at hand   b Or in

3.1–4.25 The author follows the Markan outline for the accounts of John the Baptist, Jesus' baptism, the temptation, and Jesus' first public ministry, occasionally adding material from Q and M (see Introduction). 3.1–6 Cf. Mk 1.2–6; Lk 3.1–6; Jn 1.19–23. 3.1 John the Baptist. See also vv. 7–17; 11.2–19; 14.1–12; 16.14; 17.10–13; 21.23–27; Josephus, Antiquities 18.117. Wilderness, near where the Jordan empties into the Dead Sea. A traditional site is the Wadi el-Kharrar, east of the Jordan River opposite Jericho (cf. 20.29), also associated with Elijah stories (see notes on 3.3; 3.4; 4.11; 11.7–19). 3.2 Repent, change one's mind for the better. Kingdom . . . has come near. Only in Matthew does John proclaim Jesus' central message (see note on 4.17; cf. Mk 1.4). 3.3 Cf. Mark 1.2–3; Lk 3. 4–6; Jn 1.23. The sixth formula quotation (see note on 1.22–23) cites Isa 40.3. In the Dead Sea Scrolls Community Rule this Isaian verse is the rationale for the Qumran community's preparing for the way of the Lord (God) in the wilderness near the Dead Sea (1QS 8.12–16); cf. note on 20.29. The Lord, here meaning Jesus. See notes on 3.4; 7.21. 3.4 John's clothing recalls Elijah (see 2 Kings 1.8; Zech 13.4; note on 3.1), who reportedly did not die a natural death, but ascended into heaven and was expected to return before the "day of the LORD (God)" (see 2 Kings 2.1, 11; Mal 4.5–6; note on 11.5). 3.7–10 Cf. Lk 3.7–9. The author inserts into the Markan outline apocalyptic warnings from Q and adds Pharisees and Sadducees.

3.7 Pharisees, a contemporary Israelite group that rigorously applied the law to everyday living (see, e.g., 15.1–20). They are Jesus' major opponents in Matthew, especially in Galilee (see Introduction; see also 2.4; 5.20; 16.6, 11; 23). Sadducees, a group of powerful Jerusalem aristocrats, mainly priests, usually hostile to the Pharisees, but in Matthew sometimes linked with the Pharisees as Jesus' opponents; see 16.1–12; 22.23, 34–40. Vipers, an insulting label meaning poisonous snakes; see 12.34; 23.33. 3.8 Bear fruit, i.e., by doing good works (see v. 10; 5.17–20; 7.15–20; 12.33; 13.8, 23; 21.43; cf. Mk 10.17–22). See note on 25.31–46. 3.9 Raising up children to Abraham, the great eponymous ancestor, from stones appears to be an anti-ethnic statement; it may allude to Gentiles as outsiders (but see note on 1.1). 3.10 Thrown into the fire, a metaphor for eternal punishment (see v. 12; 5.22; 7.15–20; see also Mal 4.1). 3.11–12 Cf. Mk 1.7–8; Lk 3.15–18; Jn 1.24–28. 3.11 Repentance. See vv. 2, 6, 8. One . . . coming after me, a messianic allusion (see 11.3; 21.5, 9). Carry, i.e., as a slave carries (see 10.24). Holy Spirit and fire. See Acts 2.3; 19.1–7. 3.12 Winnowing fork, used to toss grain in the air so the wind would blow away the chaff. On other images contrasting the fates of the good and the evil, see 7.24–27; 13.47–50; 25.31–46; see also note on 5.45. 3.13–17 Cf. Mk 1.9–11; Lk 3.21–22; Jn 1.29–34. The author inserts into his rewriting of Mark an explanation for the apparent anomaly that a superior (Jesus) submits to baptism by his inferior (John), especially when baptism is for repentance for sins. Baptism and the Lord's Supper were practiced in Matthean communities; cf. 28.19; 26.26–30. 3.15 Righteousness, a favorite term of "Matthew." Here it means right conduct, correct observance, in accord with God's will as revealed in scripture (see notes on 1.19; 5.10; 5.17–20). To fulfill all righteousness, a distinctive phrase in this Gospel; its appearance in Ignatius of Antioch (Smyrnaeans 1.1), suggests that the Gospel might have been composed at Antioch, Syria.

for it is proper for us in this way to fulfill all righteousness." Then he consented. 16And when Jesus had been baptized, just as he came up from the water, suddenly the heavens were opened to him and he saw the Spirit of God descending like a dove and alighting on him. 17And a voice from heaven said, "This is my Son, the Beloved,*a* with whom I am well pleased."

The Temptation of Jesus

4 Then Jesus was led up by the Spirit into the wilderness to be tempted by the devil. 2He fasted forty days and forty nights, and afterwards he was famished. 3The tempter came and said to him, "If you are the Son of God,

a Or my beloved Son

3.16 *The heavens,* the sky dome covering the flat earth (Gen 1.6–8, 16–17). Above it sat God enthroned (see 22.44; 23.22; Acts 7.49). *He came up,* i.e., Jesus had been standing (immersed?) in the water. *Opened.* See Acts 7.55–56; Rev 4.1. *Spirit of God.* See Gen 1.2, text note *b*; Isa 61.1. **3.17** *My Son, the Beloved.* See Ps 2.7; Isa 42.1; see also Mt 17.5. The Davidic kings of Israel were called "Son of God" (see, e.g., 2 Sam 7.14); for

Jesus, cf. Lk 1.32; Rom 1.3–4; Mt 2.15; 4.3, 6; 8.29; 11.27; 16.16; 26.63; 28.19; esp. 14.33; 16.16.

4.1–11 Cf. Mk 1.12–13; Lk 4.1–13. The author expands Mark with stories of three temptations (from Q; see Introduction). Quotations from Deuteronomy in Q suggest a legend based on the testing of Israel in the wilderness. **4.1** *The Spirit.* See note on 3.16. *The devil,* Hebrew Satan (see v. 10), also called *the tempter* (see v. 3;

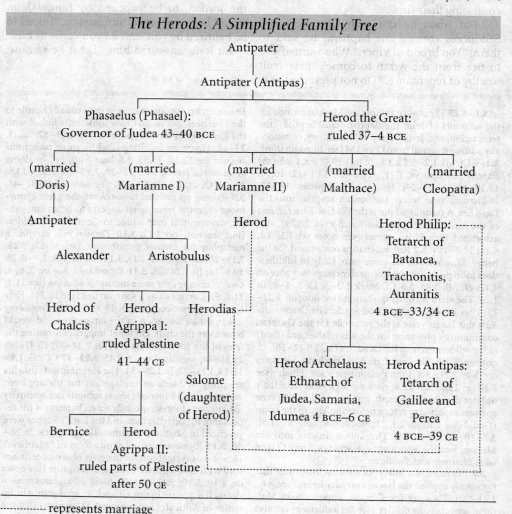

The Herods: A Simplified Family Tree

-------------- represents marriage

command these stones to become loaves of bread." [4]But he answered, "It is written,

'One does not live by bread alone,
    but by every word that comes from the mouth of God.' "

5 Then the devil took him to the holy city and placed him on the pinnacle of the temple, [6]saying to him, "If you are the Son of God, throw yourself down; for it is written,

'He will command his angels concerning you,'
and 'On their hands they will bear you up,
    so that you will not dash your foot against a stone.' "

[7]Jesus said to him, "Again it is written, 'Do not put the Lord your God to the test.' "

8 Again, the devil took him to a very high mountain and showed him all the kingdoms of the world and their splendor; [9]and he said to him, "All these I will give you, if you will fall down and worship me." [10]Jesus said to him, "Away with you, Satan! for it is written,

'Worship the Lord your God,
    and serve only him.' "

[11]Then the devil left him, and suddenly angels came and waited on him.

Jesus Begins His Ministry in Galilee

12 Now when Jesus[a] heard that John had been arrested, he withdrew to Galilee. [13]He left Nazareth and made his home in Capernaum by the sea, in the territory of Zebulun and Naphtali, [14]so that what had been spoken through the prophet Isaiah might be fulfilled:

[15] "Land of Zebulun, land of Naphtali,
    on the road by the sea, across the Jordan, Galilee of the Gentiles—
[16] the people who sat in darkness
    have seen a great light,
and for those who sat in the region and shadow of death
    light has dawned."

[17]From that time Jesus began to proclaim, "Repent, for the kingdom of heaven has come near."[b]

Jesus Calls the First Disciples

18 As he walked by the Sea of Galilee, he saw two brothers, Simon, who is called Peter, and Andrew his brother, casting a net into the sea—for they were fishermen. [19]And he said

a Gk he b Or is at hand

Job 1–2) and *the evil one* (see 6.13). **4.2** *Forty days and forty nights,* like Moses and Elijah (see Ex 24.18; 34.28; Deut 9.9; 1 Kings 19.8). Israel was tested in the wilderness forty years; see Deut 8.2; note on 2.16–18. **4.3** *Son of God.* See note on 3.17. Loaves *of bread* recall Israel's miraculous feeding with manna in the wilderness; see Ex 16; cf. Mt 14.13–21; 15.32–39; Jn 6.41. **4.4** Jesus quotes Deut 8.3. **4.6** The devil quotes Ps 91.11–12. **4.7** Jesus' quotation is from Deut 6.16. Jesus, unlike Israel, does not test God. **4.8** The first of several references to a *mountain* (see 5.1; 8.1; 14.23; 15.29; 17.1, 9; 24.3; 28.16), often in Matthew a sacred place of revelation suggesting that Jesus is like Moses (see Ex 19; Deut 34.1–4). See note on 2.16–18. **4.9** *Worship.* See note on 2.2. **4.10** Jesus quotes Deut 6.13. *Satan.* See note on 4.1. **4.11** Jesus is fed by *angels* like Elijah (see 1 Kings 19.5–8); cf. notes on 3.1; 28.2. **4.12–17** Cf. Mk 1.14–15; Lk 4.14–15. **4.12** *John had been arrested.* See 14.3–4. **4.13** *Capernaum,* a fishing, farming, and trading village on the northwest coast of the Sea of Galilee associated with Peter's house and several healing stories (8.5–13; 8.14–15; 9.1–8; 9.18–26), as well as the call of Matthew the toll collector (9.9–13). The traditional sites of Jesus' recruitment of his first disciples (4.18–22), the Mount of the Beatitudes (5.1–12), and a fish with a coin in its mouth (17.24–27) are near Capernaum. Jesus condemned Chorazin, Bethsaida, and Capernaum for failing to repent (11.21–24 [Q]). A Roman milestone has been discovered not far away. Some archaeologists think that they have evidence for

Peter's house at a traditional pilgrimage site (covered by a church). There are ruins of a later synagogue where one might have stood in the first century. **4.14–16** The seventh formula quotation (see note on 1.22–23) cites Isa 9.1–2. *Galilee* is the main location of Jesus' activity (but see Jn 1.46; 7.41–42, 52). *Of the Gentiles,* perhaps suggesting the mission to the Gentiles. See notes on 1.2–6a; 3.9; 28.19. **4.17** *From that time,* a phrase signaling a shift in the narrative (see Introduction; 16.21). *Repent.* See 3.2. *Kingdom* (Greek *basileia*), perhaps "rule," "reign," but also "empire." The contrast of God's empire with the Roman Empire would have had serious political implications (see Introduction). The *kingdom* is Jesus' central teaching (see, e.g., chs. 5–7, 13, 18–20). *Heaven,* lit. "the heavens," a spatial term (see note on 3.16) that avoids using the divine name, usually preferred by the author "kingdom of God" (but see 6.33; 12.28; 21.31, 43; cf. Mk 1.15). *Has come near.* Though the kingdom is present in some way with the coming of Jesus (see 11.12; 12.28), it remains primarily future. See, e.g., 5.20; 6.10; 21.31. **4.18–22** Cf. Mk 1.16–20; Lk 5.1–11. Jesus recruits his first disciples, two sets of two brothers. The author likes the number two (cf., e.g., 6.24; 8.28; 9.27; 10.10, 29; 14.17, 19; 18.8–9, 15–20; 20.21, 24, 30; 21.1, 28; 22.40; 24.40–41; 25.15, 17, 22; 26.60; 27.38) and will give two accounts of essentially the same story ("doublets"; cf. 9.27–31 = 20.29–34; 9.32–34 = 12.22–24). **4.18** On the naming of *Simon* as *Peter,* see 16.17–19. Peter is the most prominent disciple in the author's

to them, "Follow me, and I will make you fish for people." [20]Immediately they left their nets and followed him. [21]As he went from there, he saw two other brothers, James son of Zebedee and his brother John, in the boat with their father Zebedee, mending their nets, and he called them. [22]Immediately they left the boat and their father, and followed him.

Jesus Ministers to Crowds of People

[23] Jesus[a] went throughout Galilee, teaching in their synagogues and proclaiming the good news[b] of the kingdom and curing every disease and every sickness among the people. [24]So his fame spread throughout all Syria, and they brought to him all the sick, those who were afflicted with various diseases and pains, demoniacs, epileptics, and paralytics, and he cured them. [25]And great crowds followed him from Galilee, the Decapolis, Jerusalem, Judea, and from beyond the Jordan.

The Beatitudes

5 When Jesus[c] saw the crowds, he went up the mountain; and after he sat down, his disciples came to him. [2]Then he began to speak, and taught them, saying:

[3] "Blessed are the poor in spirit, for theirs is the kingdom of heaven.

[4] "Blessed are those who mourn, for they will be comforted.

[5] "Blessed are the meek, for they will inherit the earth.

[6] "Blessed are those who hunger and thirst for righteousness, for they will be filled.

[7] "Blessed are the merciful, for they will receive mercy.

[8] "Blessed are the pure in heart, for they will see God.

[9] "Blessed are the peacemakers, for they will be called children of God.

[10] "Blessed are those who are persecuted for righteousness' sake, for theirs is the kingdom of heaven.

[11] "Blessed are you when people revile you and persecute you and utter all kinds of evil against you falsely[d] on my account. [12]Rejoice

---

a Gk He   b Gk gospel   c Gk he   d Other ancient authorities lack falsely

---

story. *Fishermen* were from among the lower social strata (but cf. Mk 1.20). **4.19** *Follow me.* True discipleship; see also 8.22; 9.9; 10.38; 16.24; 19.21. *Fish for people.* See 13.47–50; cf. Jer 16.16. See note on 5.1. **4.21** *James son of Zebedee* (see also 10.2; 17.1; 20.20–23; 26.37; cf. Lk 9.51–56; Jn 21.1–8; Acts 1.13), not to be confused with Jesus' brother (cf. 13.55; Gal 1.19; 2.9, 12; 1 Cor 9.5; 15.7), was martyred by Herod Agrippa I; see Acts 12.1–3. *John* (see also 10.2; 17.1), his brother, became a Jerusalem church "pillar"; see Gal 2.9. **4.23–25** Cf. Mk 1.39. The author's first major summary of Jesus' acts (see also 8.16; 9.35; 14.35–36; 15.29–31; 19.1–2). It introduces the teachings and miracles of chs. 5–9. **4.23** The substance of this verse is repeated in 9.35, providing a summary beginning and ending, or framework ("bookends"), for chs. 5–9. *Their synagogues,* usually those of the Pharisees (see 9.35; 10.17; 12.9; see also *their scribes,* 7.29; note on 2.4; Introduction). The *good news* of the advent of the kingdom (see v. 17) is made concrete through Jesus' merciful and compassionate healings. **4.24** *Syria.* See Introduction. **4.25** *Crowds* appear often in Matthew. Although sometimes unperceptive (13.13), they are mainly neutral or sympathetic to Jesus (see, e.g., 7.28; 9.33; 12.23; 14.13; 21.45–46) until swayed by Jerusalem's religious leaders (see 26.47; 27.20; cf. 27.25).

5.1–7.29 Cf. Lk 6.20–49. "The Sermon on the Mount," the first of Jesus' five great discourses (see Introduction), inserted, partly from Q, into a Markan outline. Jesus both reinterprets the old law and offers a new law, recalling the revelation of the law to Moses on Mount Sinai (see Ex 19–24). See note on 2.16–18.

5.1–12 Cf. Mk 3.13; Lk 6.17, 20–23; Jn 6.3. The author's nine beatitudes (see also 11.6; 13.16; 16.17; 24.46) focus on both the future and present ethics. **5.1** *Crowds.* See note on 4.25. *Mountain.* See note on 4.8; but cf. Lk 6.17. *He sat down,* teaching like a rabbi (see 23.2; 24.3), or, according to contemporary Israelite interpretations of Deut 9.9, like Moses (see note on 2.16–18). *Disciples,* lit. "learners," those who are willing to sacrifice everything to follow Jesus and his teachings (see esp. 4.18–22; 8.19–23; 9.9; see also 12.49–50). **5.3** *Blessed,* "happy" or "fortunate" (see Ps 1.1–2; Prov 8.32, 34). *Poor,* or "broken," *in spirit,* a Matthean interpretation (softening?) of the literal poor; cf. Lk 6.20 ("you poor"); *Gospel of Thomas* 54 ("the poor"); Polycarp, *Philippians* 2.3 ("the poor"); Jas 2.5; cf. Isa 61.1; Lk 4.18. Yet the author criticizes worldly wealth; cf. 6.19–34; 10.9–10. For disdain of wealth among the Essenes, see, e.g., Philo, *Every Good Man Is Free* 12.76–77; Josephus, *Antiquities* 18.20–22; *War* 2.122; Pliny the Elder, *Natural History* 5.15.4 (73); cf. Dead Sea Scrolls, *Community Rule* (1QS) 6.22; 9.22. *Kingdom of heaven.* See note on 4.17. For social ranking in the Roman Empire, see Introduction. **5.4** *Mourn.* See Isa 61.2–3. **5.5** *Meek,* "humble" or "powerless"; see 11.29; 18.4; 21.5. *Earth,* or "land"; see Deut 4.1; 16.20. **5.6** *Righteousness.* See note on 3.15; cf. Lk 6.21; *Gospel of Thomas* 69; Polycarp, *Philippians* 2.3.

5.7 *Merciful.* See 9.13; 12.7; 18.21–35. **5.8** *Heart,* considered the region of thought, intention, and moral disposition; see 9.4; 11.29; 12.34; Ps 24.3–4; Isa 61.1. In the Bible one hears but does not usually *see God;* but cf. Job 19.26. **5.9** *Peacemakers.* See vv. 38–48;

and be glad, for your reward is great in heaven, for in the same way they persecuted the prophets who were before you.

Salt and Light

13 "You are the salt of the earth; but if salt has lost its taste, how can its saltiness be restored? It is no longer good for anything, but is thrown out and trampled under foot.

14 "You are the light of the world. A city built on a hill cannot be hid. 15No one after lighting a lamp puts it under the bushel basket, but on the lampstand, and it gives light to all in the house.

16In the same way, let your light shine before others, so that they may see your good works and give glory to your Father in heaven.

The Law and the Prophets

17 "Do not think that I have come to abolish the law or the prophets; I have come not to abolish but to fulfill. 18For truly I tell you, until heaven and earth pass away, not one letter,^{*a*} not one stroke of a letter, will pass from the law until all is accomplished. 19Therefore,

---

a Gk *one iota*

---

cf. 10.34. *Children,* lit. "sons" (see 3.17). **5.10** *Persecuted for righteousness' sake.* See note on 3.15; 5.11–12; 10.16–31; 23.34–35; 1 Pet 3.14; 4.14; *Gospel of Thomas* 68; 69; Polycarp, *Philippians* 2.3. **5.11–12** The final beatitude has an unusual, long form (see Lk 6.22–23). *Reward . . . in heaven.* See, e.g., vv. 19–20; 10.32–33. *Persecuted the prophets.* See note on 23.29–36. **5.13–16** Cf. Mk 9.50; 4.21; Lk 14.34–35; 8.16; 11.33. Three short sayings stress conduct. **5.14** *A city . . . on a hill.* See Isa 2.2–4; *Gospel of Thomas* 32. **5.15** *Lamp . . . under the bushel basket.* See *Gospel of Thomas* 33. **5.16** *Your Father in heaven.* See v. 48; 6.1, 9; note on 3.16. **5.17–20** Cf. Lk 16.17. This strong statement shows readers/hearers of the story that Jesus' teachings

are pro-law and pro-prophets despite the following antitheses (see note on 5.21–48); observance of the law should be stricter than among the writer's opponents (cf. 3.15). **5.17** *The law, the prophets,* two of the three Israelite divisions of scripture; see 7.12; 11.13; 22.40. *To fulfill,* to realize, complete. **5.18** *Truly I tell you,* a frequent introduction to Jesus' authoritative teaching; see also note on 5.21–48. *Letter,* lit. a Greek *iota* (corresponding to *i*) and *one stroke of a letter* (a serif, or ending brush stroke, on certain Hebrew letters). Either mark would be very small. *Until all is accomplished,* i.e., the end of the age; see 28.20; Isa 65.17. **5.19** On the correlation of God's final judgment with present conduct, see also 6.14–15; 7.1–2; 12.32. *Least,*

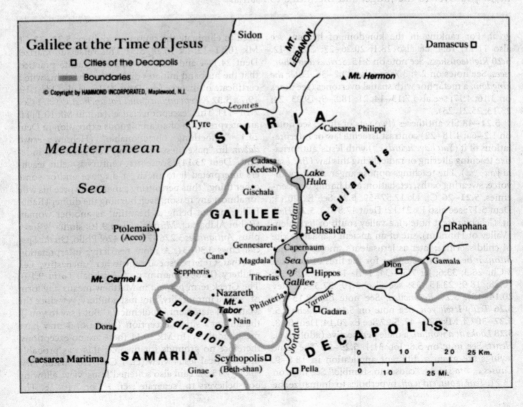

Galilee at the Time of Jesus
- ☐ Cities of the Decapolis
- ▬ Boundaries
- © Copyright by HAMMOND INCORPORATED, Maplewood, N.J.

whoever breaks[a] one of the least of these commandments, and teaches others to do the same, will be called least in the kingdom of heaven; but whoever does them and teaches them will be called great in the kingdom of heaven. 20For I tell you, unless your righteousness exceeds that of the scribes and Pharisees, you will never enter the kingdom of heaven.

Concerning Anger

21 "You have heard that it was said to those of ancient times, 'You shall not murder'; and 'whoever murders shall be liable to judgment.' 22But I say to you that if you are angry with a brother or sister,[b] you will be liable to judgment; and if you insult[c] a brother or sister,[d] you will be liable to the council; and if you say, 'You fool,' you will be liable to the hell[e] of fire. 23So when you are offering your gift at the altar, if you remember that your brother or sister[f] has something against you, 24leave your gift there before the altar and go; first be reconciled to your brother or sister,[f] and then come and offer your gift. 25Come to terms quickly with your accuser while you are on the way to court[g] with him, or your accuser may hand you over to the judge, and the judge to the guard, and you will be thrown into prison. 26Truly I tell you, you will never get out until you have paid the last penny.

Concerning Adultery

27 "You have heard that it was said, 'You shall not commit adultery.' 28But I say to you that everyone who looks at a woman with lust has already committed adultery with her in his heart. 29If your right eye causes you to sin, tear it out and throw it away; it is better for you to lose one of your members than for your whole body to be thrown into hell.[e] 30And if your right hand causes you to sin, cut it off and throw it away; it is better for you to lose one of your members than for your whole body to go into hell.[e]

Concerning Divorce

31 "It was also said, 'Whoever divorces his wife, let him give her a certificate of divorce.' 32But I say to you that anyone who divorces his wife, except on the ground of unchastity,

---

a Or annuls b Gk a brother; other ancient authorities add without cause c Gk say Raca to (an obscure term of abuse) d Gk a brother e Gk Gehenna f Gk your brother g Gk lacks to court

---

great. For ranking in the kingdom of heaven, see also 11.11; 18.4; cf. also 18.1; 20.26–27; 23.11, 12. **5.20** Righteousness. See note on 3.15. Scribes and Pharisees. See notes on 2.4; 3.7; see also 23.2–36. Enter the kingdom, a metaphor with spatial overtones (see notes on 3.16; 4.17; see also 7.13–14, 21; 18.8–9; 19.23–24; 23.13; 25.21, 23).

5.21–48 Six antitheses (two sets of three; see notes on 1.2–6a; 4.18–22) contrast Israelite law or interpretations of it (You have heard . . .) with Jesus' authoritative teaching altering or radicalizing this law (But I say to you . . .). The teachings oppose anger, adultery, divorce, swearing oaths, retaliation, and hating one's enemies. **5.21–26** Cf. Lk 12.57–59. **5.21** See Ex 20.13; Deut 5.17; see also Ex 21.12; Deut 17.8–13. **5.22** Hell, lit. Gehenna (text note e), a valley south of Jerusalem (Valley of Hinnom), site of an ancient Canaanite rite of child sacrifice; later as Jerusalem's smoldering city dump it became a metaphor for the fires of hell (see 2 Chr 28.3; 33.6; Jer 7.30–34; 19.1–15; Mt. 5.29, 30; 10.28; 18.9; 23.15, 33; see also 3.10; 27.3–10; Rev 20.14–15). **5.24** Reconciled. See note on 18.15–20. **5.26** Truly I tell you. See note on 5.18; Didache 1.5. **5.27–30** Cf. Mk 9.43–47. **5.27** See Ex 20.14; Deut 5.18. **5.28** Looks at a woman, a male perspective (adultery?). Heart. See note on 5.8; Job 31.1. **5.29–30** The same sayings are given a different application in 18.8–9. Causes . . . to sin, lit. "causes to stumble." See note on 13.21. Tear it out, cut it off, hyperboles to dramatize the need to eliminate the causes of adultery. **5.31–32** Cf. Mk 10.11–12; Lk 16.18. **5.31** This verse summarizes Deut 24.1–4 and assumes current Israelite practice, that the husband initiates divorce by giving his wife a certificate of divorce (see Deut 24.1; see also Mt 1.19; 19.7). **5.32** Except on the ground of unchastity (cf. 1 Cor 7.10–11). This "exception clause" (not in Mk 10.11) is an interpretation of an ambiguous expression in Deut 24.1, "something objectionable" (Hebrew 'erwat dabar, lit. "nakedness of a thing"; cf. "anything indecent," Deut 23.14). Some first-century Israelite teachers interpreted it to mean "a disgrace and/or some other thing," thus permitting a man to divorce his wife for almost any reason, even burning the dinner (Rabbi Hillel) or not being as beautiful as another woman (Rabbi Akiba); cf. Mishnah Gitin 9.10; similarly Josephus, Antiquities 3.276–77; Life 426; Philo, On the Special Laws 3.30–31. A more restrictive interpretation was that it referred specifically to her "unchastity," i.e., adultery (Rabbi Shammai; cf. Mishnah Gitin 9.10). The Greek term porneia in Matthew means any form of "sexual immorality," not just adultery; yet, since the Matthean statement is polemical ("But I say to you"), the author's single exception (unchastity) may have meant adultery. In Mk 10.11 there are no exceptions, therefore no grounds for divorce; this was probably the historical Jesus' view (cf. 1 Cor 7.10; Justin, First Apology 15.3). Paul also softened Jesus' view, allowing non-believers to "separate"; cf. 1 Cor 7.10–16. The

causes her to commit adultery; and whoever marries a divorced woman commits adultery.

Concerning Oaths

33 "Again, you have heard that it was said to those of ancient times, 'You shall not swear falsely, but carry out the vows you have made to the Lord.' 34But I say to you, Do not swear at all, either by heaven, for it is the throne of God, 35or by the earth, for it is his footstool, or by Jerusalem, for it is the city of the great King. 36And do not swear by your head, for you cannot make one hair white or black. 37Let your word be 'Yes, Yes' or 'No, No'; anything more than this comes from the evil one. *a*

Concerning Retaliation

38 "You have heard that it was said, 'An eye for an eye and a tooth for a tooth.' 39But I say to you, Do not resist an evildoer. But if anyone strikes you on the right cheek, turn the other also; 40and if anyone wants to sue you and take your coat, give your cloak as well; 41and if anyone forces you to go one mile, go also the second mile. 42Give to everyone who begs from you, and do not refuse anyone who wants to borrow from you.

Love for Enemies

43 "You have heard that it was said, 'You shall love your neighbor and hate your enemy.' 44But I say to you, Love your enemies and pray for those who persecute you, 45so that you may be children of your Father in heaven; for he makes his sun rise on the evil and on the good, and sends rain on the righteous and on the unrighteous. 46For if you love those who love you, what reward do you have? Do not even the tax collectors do the same? 47And if you greet only your brothers and sisters, *b* what more are you doing than others? Do not even the Gentiles do the same? 48Be perfect, therefore, as your heavenly Father is perfect.

Concerning Almsgiving

6 "Beware of practicing your piety before others in order to be seen by them; for then you have no reward from your Father in heaven.

2 "So whenever you give alms, do not sound a trumpet before you, as the hypocrites do in the synagogues and in the streets, so that they may be praised by others. Truly I tell you, they have received their reward. 3But when you give alms, do not let your left hand know what your right hand is doing, 4so that your alms may be done in secret; and your Father who sees in secret will reward you. *c*

Concerning Prayer

5 "And whenever you pray, do not be like the hypocrites; for they love to stand and pray in

---

a Or *evil*   *b* Gk *your brothers*   *c* Other ancient authorities add *openly*

Matthean author apparently preferred the position of Shammai. **5.33–37** Jesus prohibits oaths altogether; cf. 23.16–22; Jas 5.12. **5.33** See Ex 20.7, 13–17; Lev 19.12; Num 30.2; Deut 23.21; *Didache* 2.3. **5.35** A *great King* reigns over a great territory, like an emperor; here it metaphorically refers to God (see Ps 48.2). **5.37** *"Yes, Yes" or "No, No."* See Jas 5.12. **5.38–42** Cf. Lk 6.29–30. **5.38** See Ex 21.24; Lev 24.20; Deut 19.21; see also Mt 7.2. The saying permitted proportional retaliation, but was a legal deterrent to excessive retaliation. **5.39** See also Lam 3.30; 1 Pet 3.9; *Didache* 1.4. **5.40–41** *Coat* (Greek *chiton*), the tunic worn next to the skin. *Cloak,* the outer garment or robe. See *Didache* 1.4. **5.42** Cf. Lk 6.30, 34, 35. See also *Gospel of Thomas* 95; *Didache* 1.5; cf. Prov 22.7. **5.43–48** Cf. Lk 6.27–28, 32–33, 36. **5.43** *Love your neighbor.* See Lev 19.18; see also Mt 22.39; Rom 13.9; Gal 5.14; Jas 2.8. *Hate your enemy,* not scriptural, but see Ps 139.19–22; Dead Sea Scrolls, *Community Rule* (1QS) 9.21–22. **5.44** Advice to *love your enemies* was rare, but not unknown in antiquity, e.g., Prov 25.21–22; see also Polycarp, *Philippians* 12.3; *Didache* 1.3. *Your enemies . . . persecute you.* See *Didache* 1.3. **5.45** The author usually contrasts the fate of the good and the evil; see 3.12; 7.11, 16–20; 12.33–35;

20.15; 22.10; 25.21–26; see also note on 3.12. **5.46** *Reward.* See vv. 12, 19; 6.1–18. *Tax collectors,* usually native subjects of the Roman Empire, were hated by their compatriots; see 9.9; 11.19; 21.31. **5.47** *Greet.* Cf. 10.12–14. The Gospel's usual positive attitude toward the *Gentiles* (see, e.g., notes on 1.1; 3.9) is missing here, as also in 6.7; 18.17; see *Didache* 1.3. **5.48** *Perfect,* whole, complete, mature; see Lev 19.2; cf. 1 Cor 14.20; Heb 5.14; *Didache* 1.4. Perfection for Jesus' closest disciples also involves voluntary poverty and following Jesus (see 19.21). *Heavenly father.* See note on 6.9.

6.1–18 A contrast between the piety of the hypocrites and the piety rewarded by the Father in heaven; on alms, prayer, and fasting see *Gospel of Thomas* 6; 14; 27; 104. For the number three, see note on 1.2–6a. **6.1** *Practicing . . . piety,* lit. "doing righteousness"; see note on 3.15; see also 23.5. **6.2** *Alms,* or charitable gifts, were given in synagogues on the sabbath. *Hypocrites,* a frequent charge in Matthew leveled mostly against the Pharisees; see also vv. 5, 16; 7.5; 22.18; 23.13–21; but see note on 7.5. *Truly I tell you.* See note on 5.18. For other advice on giving, see *Didache* 1.5–6. **6.4** *Your Father who sees in secret.* See vv. 6, 18; 10.26; Rom 2.16; 1 Cor 4.5. **6.5** Adult Israelite males were expected to

the synagogues and at the street corners, so that they may be seen by others. Truly I tell you, they have received their reward. 6But whenever you pray, go into your room and shut the door and pray to your Father who is in secret; and your Father who sees in secret will reward you.[a]

7 "When you are praying, do not heap up empty phrases as the Gentiles do; for they think that they will be heard because of their many words. 8Do not be like them, for your Father knows what you need before you ask him.

9 "Pray then in this way:
Our Father in heaven,
   hallowed be your name.
10   Your kingdom come.
      Your will be done,
         on earth as it is in heaven.
11   Give us this day our daily bread.[b]
12   And forgive us our debts,
         as we also have forgiven our debtors.
13   And do not bring us to the time of trial,[c]
         but rescue us from the evil one.[d]

14For if you forgive others their trespasses, your heavenly Father will also forgive you; 15but if you do not forgive others, neither will your Father forgive your trespasses.

Concerning Fasting

16 "And whenever you fast, do not look dismal, like the hypocrites, for they disfigure their faces so as to show others that they are fasting. Truly I tell you, they have received their reward. 17But when you fast, put oil on your head and wash your face, 18so that your fasting may be seen not by others but by your Father who is in secret; and your Father who sees in secret will reward you.[a]

Concerning Treasures

19 "Do not store up for yourselves treasures on earth, where moth and rust[e] consume and where thieves break in and steal; 20but store up for yourselves treasures in heaven, where neither moth nor rust[e] consumes and where thieves do not break in and steal. 21For where your treasure is, there your heart will be also.

The Sound Eye

22 "The eye is the lamp of the body. So, if your eye is healthy, your whole body will be full of light; 23but if your eye is unhealthy, your whole body will be full of darkness. If then the light in you is darkness, how great is the darkness!

Serving Two Masters

24 "No one can serve two masters; for a slave will either hate the one and love the other, or

a Other ancient authorities add openly   b Or our bread for tomorrow   c Or us into temptation   d Or from evil. Other ancient authorities add, in some form, For the kingdom and the power and the glory are yours forever. Amen.   e Gk eating

pray morning and evening in the direction of Jerusalem (cf. note on 6.9b–13) and before and after meals, bowing down or, as here, standing (see Mk 11.25). For examples of prayer in this Gospel, see 7.7–11; 9.37–38; 15.21–28; 17.14–20; 18.18–20; 21.18–22; 26.36–46; 27.46. Truly I tell you. See note on 5.18. 6.7 For other criticism of long-winded prayers, see Eccl 5.2; Isa 1.15. 6.8 Your Father knows what you need. See vv. 9, 32. 6.9b–13 Cf. Mk 11.25; Lk 11.2–4; Didache 8.2. The author inserts a model prayer, revised from Q, perhaps in the light of a liturgy familiar to him. The prayer contains an address (v. 9b), three "God petitions" (vv. 9c–10), and four "human petitions" (vv. 11–13). Didache 8.3 says this prayer should be prayed three times a day (cf. note on 6.5). 6.9 The term Father (Aramaic 'Abba) suggests familial intimacy, but also respect and obedience when used by sons and daughters. Hallowed, honored as holy. 6.10 Your kingdom come. Cf. 4.17. Your will . . . heaven, probably added by the author; cf. Lk 11.2; see Mt 7.21; 12.50; 18.14; 21.31; 26.42. 6.11 Daily translates a rare Greek word that probably means (bread) "in the morning for the rest of the day" or "for tomorrow" (see text note b); see v. 34; 10.10. 6.12 Debts, lit. "what is owed"; but cf. Lk 11.4 ("sins"). As we . . . have forgiven. See vv. 14–15; 18.23–35. Polycarp, Phi-lippians 6.2. 6.13 The time of trial, a time of persecution; see 13.21; 26.39. Rescue us from the evil one, probably added by the author. See note on 4.1. Other ancient but less reliable manuscripts add a final doxology (see text note d); see also 24.30; for a related variant doxology, see Didache 8.2 (cf. 1 Chr 29.11–13). 6.14 Trespasses, rather than debts (v. 12), refers more directly to ethical transgressions. 6.16 The Day of Atonement was the only fast day prescribed by Israelite law (Lev 16.29–30), but cf. Neh 1.4; Dan 9.3; Zech 8.19; Mt 4.2; Didache 8.1 recommends fasting on Wednesdays and Fridays in contrast to the non-believing Israelites who fast on Mondays and Thursdays. Look dismal, i.e., with bowed head, sackcloth, and ashes; see 11.21; Isa 58.5. Hypocrites. See note on 6.2. Truly I tell you. See note on 5.18. 6.19–34 Sayings modified from Q (see Introduction) contrast right orientation to God with wrong orientation to worldly wealth; see also 13.22; 21.12–13; 23.25; 27.3–10; 28.11, 15. For social ranking of the poor in the Roman Empire, see Introduction. 6.19–21 Cf. Lk 12.33–34. Three kinds of destruction. See note on 1.2–6a. 6.20 Treasures in heaven. See Mk 10.21; 1 Tim 6.17–19; Jas 5.1–3; Gospel of Thomas 76; see also Sir 29.11; Tob 4.9. 6.21 Heart. See note on 5.8. 6.22–23 Cf. Lk 11.34–36. 6.23 Unhealthy, lit. "evil." The

be devoted to the one and despise the other. You cannot serve God and wealth.[a]

Do Not Worry

25 "Therefore I tell you, do not worry about your life, what you will eat or what you will drink,[b] or about your body, what you will wear. Is not life more than food, and the body more than clothing? 26Look at the birds of the air; they neither sow nor reap nor gather into barns, and yet your heavenly Father feeds them. Are you not of more value than they? 27And can any of you by worrying add a single hour to your span of life?[c] 28And why do you worry about clothing? Consider the lilies of the field, how they grow; they neither toil nor spin, 29yet I tell you, even Solomon in all his glory was not clothed like one of these. 30But if God so clothes the grass of the field, which is alive today and tomorrow is thrown into the oven, will he not much more clothe you—you of little faith? 31Therefore do not worry, saying, 'What will we eat?' or 'What will we drink?' or 'What will we wear?' 32For it is the Gentiles who strive for all these things; and indeed your heavenly Father knows that you need all these things. 33But strive first for the kingdom of God[d] and his[e] righteousness, and all these things will be given to you as well.

34 "So do not worry about tomorrow, for tomorrow will bring worries of its own. Today's trouble is enough for today.

Judging Others

7 "Do not judge, so that you may not be judged. 2For with the judgment you make you will be judged, and the measure you give will be the measure you get. 3Why do you see the speck in your neighbor's[f] eye, but do not notice the log in your own eye? 4Or how can you say to your neighbor,[g] 'Let me take the speck out of your eye,' while the log is in your own eye? 5You hypocrite, first take the log out of your own eye, and then you will see clearly to take the speck out of your neighbor's[f] eye.

Profaning the Holy

6 "Do not give what is holy to dogs; and do not throw your pearls before swine, or they will trample them under foot and turn and maul you.

Ask, Search, Knock

7 "Ask, and it will be given you; search, and you will find; knock, and the door will be opened for you. 8For everyone who asks receives, and everyone who searches finds, and for everyone who knocks, the door will be opened. 9Is there anyone among you who, if your child asks for bread, will give a stone? 10Or if the child asks for a fish, will give a snake? 11If you then, who are evil, know how to give good gifts to your children, how much more will your Father in heaven give good things to those who ask him!

The Golden Rule

12 "In everything do to others as you would have them do to you; for this is the law and the prophets.

---

a Gk mammon b Other ancient authorities lack or what you will drink c Or add one cubit to your height d Other ancient authorities lack of God e Or its f Gk brother's g Gk brother

---

"evil eye" was a metaphor for envy; see note on 20.15. **6.24** Cf. Lk 16.13. The retention of the Aramaic word *mammon* in the Greek text (see text note *a*) highlights wealth (personified) as an evil master. See *Gospel of Thomas* 47; *2 Clement* 6.1. *Two.* See note on 4.18–22. **6.25–34** Cf. Lk 12.22–32; 10.41; 12.11. **6.25** *Wear.* See *Gospel of Thomas* 36. **6.26** *Heavenly Father.* See note on 6.9. *More value.* An exegetical argument from the lesser or more obvious point to the greater or more difficult point (associated with Rabbi Hillel); see v. 30; 7.11; 10.25; 12.12. **6.29** For the glory or splendor of the reign of Solomon, see 1 Kings 10. **6.30** *Much more.* See note on 6.26. *You of little faith,* the author's stereotyped expression (known also in rabbinic literature) for the disciples (see 8.26; 14.31; 16.8; 17.20). **6.33** *Kingdom of God.* See note on 4.17. *Righteousness.* See note on 3.15.

7.1–12 Sayings (mainly from Q; see Introduction) about human conduct, based on images of family, household, neighborhood, and village. **7.1–2** Cf. Mk 4.24; Lk 6.37–38. **7.1** *Do not judge,* a prohibition of hypocritical judging; see Rom 2.1; Jas 4.11–12. *Be judged,* i.e., by God; see also 5.19; 6.14–15; Polycarp, *Philippians* 2.3. **7.3–5** Cf. Lk 6.41–42. A parable in the form of rhetorical questions illustrates vv. 1–2. See *Gospel of Thomas* 26. **7.5** *Hypocrite,* here a "brother" (see text note *f*), not a Pharisee (see note on 6.2). **7.6** *Dogs,* an insult; see 15.26–27; Deut 23.18; Phil 3.2; Rev 22.15. *Swine,* considered unclean by Israelites; see 8.31; Lev 11.7–8; Isa 65.4; 2 Pet 2.22; *Gospel of Thomas* 93; *Didache* 9.5. **7.7–11** Cf. Lk 11.9–13. **7.7** *Ask.* See also 18.19; *Gospel of Thomas* 2; 92; 94. **7.11** *How much more.* See note on 6.26. *Father in heaven.* See note on 6.9. **7.12** Cf. Lk 6.31. The "Golden Rule" was known in many versions (and religions!) in antiquity; see, e.g., Tob 4.15; Sir 31.15; Dead Sea Scrolls, *The Two Ways* (4Q473); *Babylonian Talmud Shabbat* 31a (Rabbi Hil-

The Narrow Gate

13 "Enter through the narrow gate; for the gate is wide and the road is easy*a* that leads to destruction, and there are many who take it. 14For the gate is narrow and the road is hard that leads to life, and there are few who find it.

A Tree and Its Fruit

15 "Beware of false prophets, who come to you in sheep's clothing but inwardly are ravenous wolves. 16You will know them by their fruits. Are grapes gathered from thorns, or figs from thistles? 17In the same way, every good tree bears good fruit, but the bad tree bears bad fruit. 18A good tree cannot bear bad fruit, nor can a bad tree bear good fruit. 19Every tree that does not bear good fruit is cut down and thrown into the fire. 20Thus you will know them by their fruits.

Concerning Self-Deception

21 "Not everyone who says to me, 'Lord, Lord,' will enter the kingdom of heaven, but only the one who does the will of my Father in heaven. 22On that day many will say to me, 'Lord, Lord, did we not prophesy in your name, and cast out demons in your name, and do many deeds of power in your name?' 23Then I will declare to them, 'I never knew you; go away from me, you evildoers.'

Hearers and Doers

24 "Everyone then who hears these words of mine and acts on them will be like a wise man who built his house on rock. 25The rain fell, the floods came, and the winds blew and beat on that house, but it did not fall, because it had been founded on rock. 26And everyone who hears these words of mine and does not act on them will be like a foolish man who built his house on sand. 27The rain fell, and the floods came, and the winds blew and beat against that house, and it fell—and great was its fall!"

28 Now when Jesus had finished saying these things, the crowds were astounded at his teaching, 29for he taught them as one having authority, and not as their scribes.

Jesus Cleanses a Leper

8 When Jesus*b* had come down from the mountain, great crowds followed him; 2and there was a leper*c* who came to him and knelt before him, saying, "Lord, if you choose, you can make me clean." 3He stretched out his hand and touched him, saying, "I do choose. Be made clean!" Immediately his leprosy*c* was

---

a Other ancient authorities read *for the road is wide and easy* *b* Gk *he* *c* The terms *leper* and *leprosy* can refer to several diseases

---

lel); *Didache* 1.2. *The law and the prophets.* See note on 5.17. **7.13–29** A series of warnings concludes the sermon. **7.13–14** *Road,* or "way." Cf. Lk 13.23–24. Instruction on the "Two Ways" was widespread in antiquity (see Prov 28.18; Wis 5.6–7; *Didache* 1–6; *Letter of Barnabas* 18–20). *Many, few.* See also 22.14. To enter *life* (18.8–9) parallels entering the kingdom (see 5.20; 7.21; 23.13). **7.15–20** Cf. Lk 6.43–44. **7.15** A warning against *false prophets* indicates the occasional presence of wandering prophets in the author's communities (see also v. 22; 10.5–15; 23.34; *Didache* 11; 16.3). **7.17** *Good fruit, bad fruit.* Cf. Lk 6.43–45. See note on 3.8; see also Jas 3.12; *Gospel of Thomas* 45; Sir 27.6. **7.19** *Thrown into the fire.* See notes on 3.10; 5.22. **7.21–23** Cf. Lk 6.46; 13.25–27. **7.21** *Lord,* a respectful address by an inferior to a superior (see 10.24) roughly equivalent to "Sir." It is used of God in scripture and, linked with terms of worship (see 14.30–33; Jn 9.38), it hints at Jesus' divinity. On doing the *will* of God, see note on 6.10. **7.22** See note on 7.15. The acts performed are otherwise praiseworthy (see 10.5–15); the issue is obedience to God's will. *That day,* the day of judgment; see 24.36, 42, 44; 25.31–46; see also Zech 14. *In your name,* i.e., by Jesus' authority. Jesus' name was also invoked as a source of power; see Acts 4.7; 19.13–17; Jas 5.14. **7.23** *I never knew you.* See 25.11–

12. *Evildoers,* lit. "workers of lawlessness" (see 13.41; 23.28; 24.12; see also note on 5.17–20). **7.24–27** Cf. Lk 6.47–49. **7.24** On hearing and acting or doing, see Rom 2.13; Jas 1.22–25. **7.27** *Great was its fall.* See Prov 14.11. **7.28** *When Jesus had finished.* Each of the five great discourses in Matthew is concluded by a similar closing formula reminiscent of Moses' words in Deut 31.1; 32.45. See Mt 11.1; 13.53; 19.1; 26.1. On the likeness to Moses, see Introduction; note on 2.16–18. *Crowds.* See note on 4.25. **7.29** *Authority.* See 28.18. *Not as their scribes.* See 5.20; note on 2.4.

8.1–9.34 From Mark and Q (see Introduction) the author creates a collection of ten miracles, recalling the ten miracles of Moses in Egypt (Ex 7.8–11.10). See note on 2.16–18. The stories are associated with locations on and around the Sea of Galilee and recall Elijah and Elisha; cf. note on 11.5. For Jesus' social ranking in the Roman Empire, which he as healer ignores or reverses, see Introduction. **8.1–17** The first three healings, concluding with a "formula quotation" (see note on 1.22–23). **8.1–4** Cf. Mk 1.40–44; Lk 5.12–14. **8.1** *Great crowds.* See note on 4.25. **8.2** *A leper* (see text note c) was considered ritually unclean and was excluded from the community; see Lev 13–14; 2 Kings 5.1–14. *Lord.* See note on 7.21. **8.3** *Touched . . . "Be made clean!"* The author avoids words or actions that

cleansed. 4Then Jesus said to him, "See that you say nothing to anyone; but go, show yourself to the priest, and offer the gift that Moses commanded, as a testimony to them."

Jesus Heals a Centurion's Servant

5 When he entered Capernaum, a centurion came to him, appealing to him 6and saying, "Lord, my servant is lying at home paralyzed, in terrible distress." 7And he said to him, "I will come and cure him." 8The centurion answered, "Lord, I am not worthy to have you come under my roof; but only speak the word, and my servant will be healed. 9For I also am a man under authority, with soldiers under me; and I say to one, 'Go,' and he goes, and to another, 'Come,' and he comes, and to my slave, 'Do this,' and the slave does it." 10When Jesus heard this, he was amazed and said to those who followed him, "Truly I tell you, in no one*a* in Israel have I found such faith. 11I tell you, many will come from east and west and will eat with Abraham and Isaac and Jacob in the kingdom of heaven, 12while the heirs of the kingdom will be thrown into the outer darkness, where there will be weeping and gnashing of teeth." 13And to the centurion Jesus said, "Go; let it be done for you according to your faith." And the servant was healed in that hour.

Jesus Heals Many at Peter's House

14 When Jesus entered Peter's house, he saw his mother-in-law lying in bed with a fever; 15he touched her hand, and the fever left her, and she got up and began to serve him. 16That evening they brought to him many who were possessed with demons; and he cast out the spirits with a word, and cured all who were sick. 17This was to fulfill what had been spoken through the prophet Isaiah, "He took our infirmities and bore our diseases."

Would-Be Followers of Jesus

18 Now when Jesus saw great crowds around him, he gave orders to go over to the other side. 19A scribe then approached and said, "Teacher, I will follow you wherever you go." 20And Jesus said to him, "Foxes have holes, and birds of the air have nests; but the Son of Man has nowhere to lay his head." 21Another of his disciples said to him, "Lord, first let me go and bury my father." 22But Jesus said to him, "Follow me, and let the dead bury their own dead."

Jesus Stills the Storm

23 And when he got into the boat, his disciples followed him. 24A windstorm arose on the sea,

---

a Other ancient authorities read *Truly I tell you, not even*

---

would suggest that Jesus was a magician, as later rabbinic tradition charged; see v. 16; 9.34. **8.4** *Say nothing,* a frequent command in Mark (see note on Mk 1.34), but less prominent in Matthew (but see 9.30). *Gift that Moses commanded.* See Lev 14.4, 10. Moses was believed to be the author of the Pentateuch. **8.5–13** Cf. Lk 7.1–10; 13.28–29; Jn 4.46–54. **8.5** *Capernaum.* See note on 4.13. A *centurion* commanded one hundred Roman infantry (see v. 9). **8.6** *Lord.* See note on 7.21. **8.10** *Truly I tell you.* See note on 5.18. For another instance of a Gentile's *faith,* see 15.28. **8.11** *Many . . . from east and west* includes Gentiles; see 2.1; note on 3.9; also Isa 2.2–4; 25.6; Mic 4.1–4; Zech 8.20–23. *Will eat,* at a future heavenly "messianic banquet"; see, e.g., 11.19; 22.1–14; 26.29; Ps 107.1–9; Isa 25.6–8; 62.1–9; Rev 19.9. *Kingdom of heaven.* See note on 4.17. **8.12** *Heirs,* Israelites, or more specifically Pharisees; see 23.29–36. *Weeping and gnashing of teeth,* the author's favorite expression to evoke the horror of the final punishment; see 13.42, 50; 22.13; 24.51; 25.30; Ps 112.10. **8.14–15** Cf. Mk 1.29–31; Lk 4.38–41. **8.14** *Peter's house.* See note on 4.13. *Mother-in-law.* Paul also indicates that Peter ("Cephas") was married; see 1 Cor 9.5. **8.15** *Touched.* See note on 8.3. **8.16–17** Cf. Mk 1.32–34; Lk 4.40–41. **8.16** Another summary statement; see note on 4.23–25. *With a word,* i.e., without magical

manipulation; see note on 8.3. *Cured all.* See 4.23; 9.35; 10.1; 12.15; 15.29–31. **8.17** The eighth formula quotation (see note on 1.22–23), Isa 53.4.

8.18–9.8 The second group of three miracles. **8.18–22** Cf. Mk 4.35; Lk 9.57–60. **8.19** Usually in Matthew, *scribes* rank among Jesus' opponents (see note on 2.4; but cf., e.g., 13.52; 23.34). Jesus is often addressed hypocritically or mockingly as *teacher* by his opponents (see 9.11; 12.38; 17.24; 22.15–18, 24, 36; cf. 23.8). **8.20** *Foxes, birds.* See *Gospel of Thomas* 86. Jesus frequently refers to himself as *Son of Man* in one of three different senses: as the final judge, usually reflecting Dan 7.13–14 (see, e.g., 24.30–31); as the one who must suffer, usually from prophecies in Mark about his death (see 16.21); or, as here, with reference to his present circumstances, from an Aramaic idiom for speaking about oneself as human, perhaps with humility, modesty, or allusion to danger or death (see Ezek 2.1, text note *a*). **8.21** *Lord.* See note on 7.21. **8.22** *Follow me* introduces vv. 23–27. See note on 4.19. *Let the dead bury their own dead.* Jesus' words challenge the traditional and honorable duty to bury one's parents (see, e.g., Tob 4.3–4). **8.23–27** Cf. Mk 4.35–41; Lk 8.22–25. The author's handling of this miracle shows that he interprets it as an allegory for following Jesus; see notes on 8.22; 8.23. **8.23** *His disciples.* See notes on 4.19; 5.1.

so great that the boat was being swamped by the waves; but he was asleep. 25And they went and woke him up, saying, "Lord, save us! We are perishing!" 26And he said to them, "Why are you afraid, you of little faith?" Then he got up and rebuked the winds and the sea; and there was a dead calm. 27They were amazed, saying, "What sort of man is this, that even the winds and the sea obey him?"

Jesus Heals the Gadarene Demoniacs

28 When he came to the other side, to the country of the Gadarenes,ᵃ two demoniacs coming out of the tombs met him. They were so fierce that no one could pass that way. 29Suddenly they shouted, "What have you to do with us, Son of God? Have you come here to torment us before the time?" 30Now a large herd of swine was feeding at some distance from them. 31The demons begged him, "If you cast us out, send us into the herd of swine." 32And he said to them, "Go!" So they came out and entered the swine; and suddenly, the whole herd rushed down the steep bank into the sea and perished in the water. 33The swineherds ran off, and on going into the town, they told the whole story about what had happened to the demoniacs. 34Then the whole town came out to meet Jesus; and when they saw him, they begged him to leave their neighborhood.

9 1And after getting into a boat he crossed the sea and came to his own town.

Jesus Heals a Paralytic

2 And just then some people were carrying a paralyzed man lying on a bed. When Jesus saw their faith, he said to the paralytic, "Take heart, son; your sins are forgiven." 3Then some of the scribes said to themselves, "This man is blaspheming." 4But Jesus, perceiving their thoughts, said, "Why do you think evil in your hearts? 5For which is easier, to say, 'Your sins are forgiven,' or to say, 'Stand up and walk'? 6But so that you may know that the Son of Man has authority on earth to forgive sins"—he then said to the paralytic—"Stand up, take your bed and go to your home." 7And he stood up and went to his home. 8When the crowds saw it, they were filled with awe, and they glorified God, who had given such authority to human beings.

The Call of Matthew

9 As Jesus was walking along, he saw a man called Matthew sitting at the tax booth; and he said to him, "Follow me." And he got up and followed him.

10 And as he sat at dinnerᵇ in the house, many tax collectors and sinners came and were sittingᶜ with him and his disciples. 11When the Pharisees saw this, they said to his disciples, "Why does your teacher eat with tax collectors and sinners?" 12But when he heard this, he said, "Those who are well have no need of a physician, but those who are sick. 13Go and learn what this means, 'I desire mercy, not sacrifice.' For I have come to call not the righteous but sinners."

ᵃ Other ancient authorities read *Gergesenes*; others, *Gerasenes*
ᵇ Gk *reclined*   ᶜ Gk *were reclining*

8.24 A *windstorm* often represented the evil waters of chaos (see Gen 1.1; Jon 1.4–16). **8.25** *Lord.* See note on 7.21. *Save us.* See note on 1.21. **8.26** *You of little faith.* See note on 6.30; cf. 8.10, 13. Here, as elsewhere, the author softens Mark's criticism of the disciples (Mk 4.40); see also Mt 13.10–11; 28.16–20. *Rebuked*, a word also used to exorcise demons (see, e.g., 17.18). On stilling *the sea*, see Job 26.11–12; Ps 89.8–9; Isa 51.9–10. **8.28–9.1** Cf. Mk 5.1–17; Lk 8.26–37. **8.28** *Gadarenes.* Gadara lay not on the edge of but six miles southeast of the Sea of Galilee; hence other locations appear in the manuscripts; cf. text note *a* (the traditional site, Gergesa, modern Kursi, on the east coast would be more appropriate). *Two.* See note on 4.18–22. *Tombs*, thought to be the habitations of demons. **8.29** *Son of God.* See note on 3.17. Here Jesus is recognized by a supernatural power; cf. 16.16. To name someone was thought to provide power over that person; thus the demoniacs seek here to gain power over the exorcist. **8.30** *Swine.* See note on 7.6. **8.32** *Water.* Demons were usually associated with arid regions; see 4.1. **9.1** *His own town,* Capernaum; see note on 4.13. **9.2–8** Cf. Mk 2.1–12; Lk 5.17–26. **9.2** *Their faith* precedes the miracle; see 8.10–13; 9.22, 28. **9.3** *Scribes.* See note on 2.4. *Blaspheming* usually involved dishonoring God's name (see Ex 20.7; Lev 24.16); here Jesus' implied claim to be able to forgive sins evokes the charge (see Mk 2.7; see also Mt 26.65). **9.4** *Hearts.* See note on 5.8. **9.6** *Son of Man.* See note on 8.20. *Authority . . . to forgive sins.* See 1.21; 28.18. **9.8** *Crowds.* See note on 4.25; see also 7.28–29. **9.9** *Matthew.* See 10.3; cf. Mk 2.14; Lk 5.27. *Follow me.* See note on 4.19. **9.10–13** Cf. Mk 2.15–17; Lk 5.29–32. **9.10** *Tax collectors and sinners,* i.e., social and moral outcasts; see note on 5.46; see also 11.19; 18.17; 21.31–32. **9.11** *Your teacher.* See note on 8.19. **9.12** Similar sayings are found in Greek literature. **9.13** *I desire mercy, not sacrifice* (repeated in 12.7). See Hos 6.6

The Question about Fasting

14 Then the disciples of John came to him, saying, "Why do we and the Pharisees fast often,[a] but your disciples do not fast?" 15 And Jesus said to them, "The wedding guests cannot mourn as long as the bridegroom is with them, can they? The days will come when the bridegroom is taken away from them, and then they will fast. 16 No one sews a piece of unshrunk cloth on an old cloak, for the patch pulls away from the cloak, and a worse tear is made. 17 Neither is new wine put into old wineskins; otherwise, the skins burst, and the wine is spilled, and the skins are destroyed; but new wine is put into fresh wineskins, and so both are preserved."

A Girl Restored to Life and a Woman Healed

18 While he was saying these things to them, suddenly a leader of the synagogue[b] came in and knelt before him, saying, "My daughter has just died; but come and lay your hand on her, and she will live." 19 And Jesus got up and followed him, with his disciples. 20 Then suddenly a woman who had been suffering from hemorrhages for twelve years came up behind him and touched the fringe of his cloak, 21 for she said to herself, "If I only touch his cloak, I will be made well." 22 Jesus turned, and seeing her he said, "Take heart, daughter; your faith has made you well." And instantly the woman was made well. 23 When Jesus came to the leader's house and saw the flute players and the crowd making a commotion, 24 he said, "Go away; for the girl is not dead but sleeping." And they laughed at him. 25 But when the crowd had been put outside, he went in and took her by the hand, and the girl got up. 26 And the report of this spread throughout that district.

Jesus Heals Two Blind Men

27 As Jesus went on from there, two blind men followed him, crying loudly, "Have mercy on us, Son of David!" 28 When he entered the house, the blind men came to him; and Jesus said to them, "Do you believe that I am able to do this?" They said to him, "Yes, Lord." 29 Then he touched their eyes and said, "According to your faith let it be done to you." 30 And their eyes were opened. Then Jesus sternly ordered them, "See that no one knows of this." 31 But they went away and spread the news about him throughout that district.

Jesus Heals One Who Was Mute

32 After they had gone away, a demoniac who was mute was brought to him. 33 And when the

---

a Other ancient authorities lack *often* *b* Gk lacks *of the synagogue*

(Septuagint). *The righteous.* See note on 1.19. **9.14–17** Cf. Mk 2.18–22; Lk 5.33–39. **9.14–15** See *Gospel of Thomas* 104. **9.14** *Disciples of John* (the Baptist). See 11.2; Acts 18.25. *Your disciples do not fast.* See 11.19. **9.15** *Wedding guests,* lit. "the sons of the bridegroom," his attendants who joyfully celebrate with him. Jesus is often described as a *bridegroom;* see notes on 25.1; 25.5; 25.10; see also Jn 3.29; 2 Cor 11.2; Rev 19.7. *Then they will fast.* These words provide a rationale for fasting in the early churches after Jesus' death; see also 6.16–18; *Didache* 7.4–8.1. **9.16–17** Two sayings interpret v. 15 and stress that the old cannot contain the new; see also 13.52; *Gospel of Thomas* 47. **9.18–34** Four healings conclude the section begun in 8.1. **9.18–26** Cf. Mk 5.21–43; Lk 8.40–56). The author incorporates a Markan technique of placing one story inside another (intercalation); a woman healed (vv. 20–22) interrupts a girl restored to life (vv. 18–19, 23–25). For women in Matthew, see Introduction; other stories are 15.21–28; 26.6–13; 27.55–56, 61; 28.1–10; see also notes on 1.2–6a; 1.3; 1.5; 1.6b; 1.16; 1.18–25; 23.37. **9.18** *Leader of the synagogue,* probably a civil administrator (the text does not mention the synagogue; see text note *b*); see note on 4.13. **9.20** *Hemorrhages,* i.e., a continuous flow. If menstrual (that is

not explicit), the woman is unclean and should not be touched. See Lev 15.19–30; Ezek 36.17; Dead Sea Scrolls, *Damascus Document* (CD) 4.12–5.17; *Temple Scroll* (11Q19) 48.15–17; Josephus, *War* 5.227; *Against Apion* 2.103–4; *Mishnah Niddah; Mishnah Zabim* 4.1; cf. *Acts of Pilate* 7 (named Bernice). *Fringe,* the tassels of Jesus' outer garment, a customary part of the dress of Israelite men in Palestine; see Num 15.37–41; Mt 23.5. **9.21** *If I only touch his cloak.* Healing power resided even in the healer's clothing; see 14.36; Acts 5.15; 19.12. **9.22** *Faith.* See note on 8.10. **9.23** *Flute players* accompanied professional mourners (see 11.17). **9.25** See note on 8.3. **9.27–31** The author creates this version of the miracle story; cf. 20.29–34; Mk 10.46–52; Lk 18.35–43; see note on 9.32–34. *Two.* See note on 4.18–22. **9.27** *Have mercy on us, Son of David!* This request and title, expanded from Mk 10.47–48, is usual in the Gospel's healing miracles; see 12.23; 15.22; 17.15; 20.30–31; cf. 21.9. *Mercy.* See v. 13; 12.7. **9.28** *Lord.* See note on 7.21. **9.29** *Faith.* See note on 8.10. **9.30** *See that no one knows.* See note on 8.4. **9.32–34** The author creates this miracle story; cf. 12.22–24; Mk 3.22; Lk 11.14–15. **9.32** *Mute.* Demons we˼ thought to attack specific parts of the body; se˼ 12.22–24. **9.33** *Crowds.* See note on 4.25; see a˼

demon had been cast out, the one who had been mute spoke; and the crowds were amazed and said, "Never has anything like this been seen in Israel." 34But the Pharisees said, "By the ruler of the demons he casts out the demons." *a*

The Harvest Is Great, the Laborers Few

35 Then Jesus went about all the cities and villages, teaching in their synagogues, and proclaiming the good news of the kingdom, and curing every disease and every sickness. 36When he saw the crowds, he had compassion for them, because they were harassed and helpless, like sheep without a shepherd. 37Then he said to his disciples, "The harvest is plentiful, but the laborers are few; 38therefore ask the Lord of the harvest to send out laborers into his harvest."

The Twelve Apostles

10 Then Jesus *b* summoned his twelve disciples and gave them authority over unclean spirits, to cast them out, and to cure every disease and every sickness. 2These are the names of the twelve apostles: first, Simon, also known as Peter, and his brother Andrew; James son of Zebedee, and his brother John; 3Philip and Bartholomew; Thomas and Matthew the tax collector; James son of Alphaeus, and Thaddaeus; *c* 4Simon the Cananaean, and Judas Iscariot, the one who betrayed him.

The Mission of the Twelve

5 These twelve Jesus sent out with the following instructions: "Go nowhere among the Gentiles, and enter no town of the Samaritans, 6but go rather to the lost sheep of the house of Israel. 7As you go, proclaim the good news, 'The kingdom of heaven has come near.' *d* 8Cure the sick, raise the dead, cleanse the lepers, *e* cast out demons. You received without payment; give without payment. 9Take no gold, or silver, or copper in your belts, 10no bag for your journey, or two tunics, or sandals, or a staff; for laborers deserve their food.

---

a Other ancient authorities lack this verse *b* Gk *he* *c* Other ancient authorities read *Lebbaeus*, or *Lebbaeus called Thaddaeus* *d* Or *is at hand* *e* The terms *leper* and *leprosy* can refer to several diseases

---

9.8. **9.34** *Pharisees.* See note on 3.7. *Ruler of the demons,* i.e., Satan, also called Beelzebul (see note on 4.1; 10.25; 12.24). **9.35–38** Cf. Mk 6.6b, 34; Lk 8.1; 10.2; Jn 4.35. See *Gospel of Thomas* 73. **9.35** The author's summary. See note on 4.23–25. **9.36** *Compassion.* See 14.14; 15.32; 18.27; 20.34. *Sheep without a shepherd.* See 10.6; 15.24; 18.10–14; 26.31; Num 27.16–17; Isa 40.11; Ezek 34.1–6; Jud 11.19; Dead Sea Scrolls, *Damascus Document* (CD) 13.9. **9.37** Cf. Lk 10.2. *Harvest,* a common image for the final end-time judgment (see 3.12; 13.30, 39; Rev 14.14–20; also 2 Esd 4.39; *2 Baruch* 70.2). *Laborers* anticipates the mission charge to the disciples (10.5–42). See Jn 4.35; *Gospel of Thomas* 73.
  10.1–11.1 The "Missionary Discourse," the fourth of Jesus' five great discourses (see Introduction), developing Mark with Q and M. The Twelve are commanded to follow Jesus' way, that of the wandering beggar, preacher, and healer. **10.1–4** Cf. Mk 6.7; 3.16–19; Lk 9.1; 6.13–16; see also Acts 1.13. **10.1** *Twelve* symbolizes a new Israel (twelve tribes of Israel); see 19.28; Gen 35.22–26; 49.1–28; Josh 4.2–9. *Authority,* to carry out the same deeds as Jesus, their teacher, except teaching; see 4.23; 9.35; 23.8; cf. 28.20. **10.2** *Apostles,* lit. "those sent out," on a mission in the name of someone. See vv. 40–42; 28.16–20. *Peter,* the first recruited and most prominent in the Gospel (4.18; 16.17–19; 17.24–27), always comes first in lists of the twelve disciples (Mk 3.16; Lk 6.14; Acts 1.13). *Andrew, James,* and *John* are always listed next (see 4.18–22). **10.3** *Philip.* See Jn 1.43–51; 6.5; 12.20–22; 14.8. *Thomas.* See Jn 11.16; 14.5; 20.24–29; 21.2; *Gospel of*

Thomas incipit. Matthew. See note on 9.9. *James son of Alphaeus.* Cf. Mk 2.14. **10.4** *The Cananaean,* probably from the Aramaic *qan'an,* "the zealot" (see Lk 6.15, "who was called the Zealot"; cf. Gal 1.14), and thus possibly a (former?) rebel (see 1 Macc 2.54; Josephus, *War* 2.651; 4.158–61). *Iscariot,* meaning uncertain, perhaps "from Kerioth" (southern Judea) or derived from the Latin *sicarius* ("dagger man," i.e., assassin); see notes on 26.55; 27.38. *Who betrayed him,* or "who handed him over," a prominent theme of the passion narrative in Mark (Mk 3.19; 9.31; 10.33; 14.21; 15.1; cf. Mt 17.22; 20.18; 26.2, 14–16, 24, 47–56); cf. also Acts 1.15–26. **10.5–15** Cf. Mk 6.8–11; Lk 9.2–5. **10.5** *Go nowhere among the Gentiles.* Cf. 8.5–13; 15.21–28; 28.19; see also notes on 1.1; 1.2–6a; 3.9. Jews avoided *Samaritans,* whom they regarded with animosity (see Jn 4.9; 8.48). **10.6** *To the lost sheep of the house of Israel.* See note on 15.24; see also 9.36; 18.12–14. **10.7** *The kingdom of heaven has come near.* See 3.2; 4.17. **10.8** *Cure the sick . . . cast out demons.* See 4.23–24; 11.5; 15.30–31. **10.9–15** Perhaps part of an early missionary "handbook." Cf. Mk 6.8–11; Lk 9.3–5. **10.9** *No gold, or silver, or copper.* The ideal of voluntary poverty is similar to that of the wandering Cynic philosophers but is rooted in the ethos of 6.25–34; see *Gospel of Thomas* 14; *Didache* 11–13; 1 Tim 5.18. For the usual social ranking in the Roman Empire, see Introduction. **10.10** *No bag.* Wandering Cynic philosopher-preachers carried a begging bag to symbolize their self-sufficiency. *Or two tunics, or sandals, or a staff.* Josephus (*War* 2.125–26), says traveling Essenes did not replace clothing or sandals until they were worn out, but car-

11Whatever town or village you enter, find out who in it is worthy, and stay there until you leave. 12As you enter the house, greet it. 13If the house is worthy, let your peace come upon it; but if it is not worthy, let your peace return to you. 14If anyone will not welcome you or listen to your words, shake off the dust from your feet as you leave that house or town. 15Truly I tell you, it will be more tolerable for the land of Sodom and Gomorrah on the day of judgment than for that town.

Coming Persecutions

16 "See, I am sending you out like sheep into the midst of wolves; so be wise as serpents and innocent as doves. 17Beware of them, for they will hand you over to councils and flog you in their synagogues; 18and you will be dragged before governors and kings because of me, as a testimony to them and the Gentiles. 19When they hand you over, do not worry about how you are to speak or what you are to say; for what you are to say will be given to you at that time; 20for it is not you who speak, but the Spirit of your Father speaking through you. 21Brother will betray brother to death, and a father his child, and children will rise against parents and have them put to death; 22and you will be hated by all because of my name. But the one who endures to the end will be saved. 23When they persecute you in one town, flee to the next; for truly I tell you, you will not have gone through all the towns of Israel before the Son of Man comes.

24 "A disciple is not above the teacher, nor a slave above the master; 25it is enough for the disciple to be like the teacher, and the slave like the master. If they have called the master of the house Beelzebul, how much more will they malign those of his household!

Whom to Fear

26 "So have no fear of them; for nothing is covered up that will not be uncovered, and nothing secret that will not become known. 27What I say to you in the dark, tell in the light; and what you hear whispered, proclaim from the housetops. 28Do not fear those who kill the body but cannot kill the soul; rather fear him who can destroy both soul and body in hell.[a] 29Are not two sparrows sold for a penny? Yet not one of them will fall to the ground apart from your Father. 30And even the hairs of your head are all counted. 31So do not be afraid; you are of more value than many sparrows.

32 "Everyone therefore who acknowledges me before others, I also will acknowledge before my Father in heaven; 33but whoever denies me before others, I also will deny before my Father in heaven.

Not Peace, but a Sword

34 "Do not think that I have come to bring peace to the earth; I have not come to bring peace, but a sword.

a Gk Gehenna

---

ried something (perhaps a staff) to ward off robbers. *Laborers deserve their food,* a missionary principle; see 1 Cor 9.3–18; *Didache* 13. Paul received support from the Philippians (Phil 4.14–20) but normally supported himself with his trade, for which he received criticism from rival missionaries; cf. 2 Cor 12.13–16. **10.12** In the author's day the *house* would have included the house church, where the faithful met to worship and socialize; cf., e.g., 1 Cor 16.15, 19. **10.13** A typical greeting was "*Peace* (Hebrew *shalom*) to this house"; see also Isa 52.7. **10.14** *Welcome.* See vv. 40–42; 18.5. *Shake off the dust from your feet,* a strong gesture of rejection; see Acts 13.51; 18.6. **10.15** *Truly I tell you.* See note on 5.18. *Sodom and Gomorrah,* proverbially wicked cities destroyed by judgment fire; see 11.24; Gen 19.1–28; Ezek 16.46–50; 2 Pet 2.6; Jude 7. **10.16–25** Cf. Mk 13.9–13; Lk 12.11–12; 6.40; 21.12–19. As the teacher will be persecuted, so will his followers. **10.16** See *Gospel of Thomas* 39. **10.17** *Councils,* probably local Israelite courts, not the supreme Jerusalem council (cf. 5.22; 26.59). *Flog.* See Deut 25.1–3; see also Mt 20.19; 23.34; 27.26; 2 Cor 11.23–24. *Their syna-*

gogues. See note on 4.23. **10.18** *Before governors.* See 27.11–14. **10.19** *Do not worry.* See 6.25–34. *What you are to say.* See Ex 4.10–17; Jer 1.6–10. **10.20** *The Spirit . . . speaking through you.* See Jn 14.26; 1 Cor 2.4; Phil 1.19. **10.21** See vv. 34–37. **10.22** *Hated . . . because of my name.* See 5.10–12. *Endures to the end,* until the end of the age; see v. 23; 24.13; 28.20. **10.23** *Truly I tell you.* See note on 5.18. *Son of Man.* See note on 8.20. **10.24** See Jn 13.16; 15.20. **10.25** *Beelzebul,* the prince of demons (i.e., Satan); see 9.34; 12.24. *How much more.* See note on 6.26. **10.26–33** Cf. Mk 4.22; Lk 12.2–9; 8.17. **10.26–27** See *Gospel of Thomas* 5; 6; 33; see also Mt 5.14–16; 1 Cor 4.5. **10.28** *Soul,* the true self. The one *who can destroy both soul and body* is God. *Hell.* See note on 5.22. **10.29–31** See 6.26; Ps 84.3. *Two.* See note on 4.18–22. **10.32–33** A direct correlation of present behavior with future judgment; see note on 5.19; see also Ps 62.12; Prov 24.12; Rom 2.6. **10.33** *Denies me before others,* like Peter; see 26.70; but cf. 28.16–20. **10.34–39** Cf. Mk 8.34–35; Lk 12.51–53; 14.26–27; 17.33. **10.34–36** See *Gospel of Thomas* 16. **10.34** *Not . . . peace, but a sword,* "cutting" old family

35 For I have come to set a man against his
     father,
   and a daughter against her mother,
   and a daughter-in-law against her
     mother-in-law;
36 and one's foes will be members of one's
     own household.

37 Whoever loves father or mother more than
me is not worthy of me; and whoever loves son
or daughter more than me is not worthy of me;
38 and whoever does not take up the cross and
follow me is not worthy of me. 39 Those who
find their life will lose it, and those who lose
their life for my sake will find it.

Rewards

40 "Whoever welcomes you welcomes me,
and whoever welcomes me welcomes the one
who sent me. 41 Whoever welcomes a prophet
in the name of a prophet will receive a
prophet's reward; and whoever welcomes a
righteous person in the name of a righteous
person will receive the reward of the righteous; 42 and whoever gives even a cup of cold
water to one of these little ones in the name of
a disciple—truly I tell you, none of these will
lose their reward."

11 Now when Jesus had finished instructing his twelve disciples, he went on
from there to teach and proclaim his message
in their cities.

Messengers from John the Baptist

2 When John heard in prison what the Messiah*a* was doing, he sent word by his*b* disciples
3 and said to him, "Are you the one who is to
come, or are we to wait for another?" 4 Jesus
answered them, "Go and tell John what you
hear and see: 5 the blind receive their sight, the
lame walk, the lepers*c* are cleansed, the deaf
hear, the dead are raised, and the poor have
good news brought to them. 6 And blessed is
anyone who takes no offense at me."

Jesus Praises John the Baptist

7 As they went away, Jesus began to speak to
the crowds about John: "What did you go out
into the wilderness to look at? A reed shaken
by the wind? 8 What then did you go out to
see? Someone*d* dressed in soft robes? Look,
those who wear soft robes are in royal palaces.
9 What then did you go out to see? A prophet?*e*
Yes, I tell you, and more than a prophet. 10 This
is the one about whom it is written,

   'See, I am sending my messenger ahead of
     you,
   who will prepare your way before you.'
11 Truly I tell you, among those born of women
no one has arisen greater than John the Bap-

a Or the Christ   *b* Other ancient authorities read two of his
c The terms leper and leprosy can refer to several diseases
d Or Why then did you go out? To see someone   *e* Other ancient
authorities read Why then did you go out? To see a prophet?

---

ties; see vv. 35–36. **10.35–36** An allusion to Mic 7.6.
10.37–39 See 16.24–25; Mk. 8.34–35; Lk 14.26–27.
Gospel of Thomas 55; 101. **10.38** *Take up the cross,* literally in 27.32; here, figuratively in self-denying discipleship. *Follow me.* See notes on 4.19; 5.1. **10.39** *Life,* lit.
"soul," the center of life or self. A paradox: giving up
physical or material life for the sake of the Messiah
leads to true life (see 16.26). **10.40–42** Cf. Mk 9.37, 41;
Lk 10.16; Jn 12.44; 13.20; see *Didache* 11.7–11.
10.40 *Welcomes,* shows hospitality (see vv. 11–14).
10.41 *Prophet,* i.e., a wandering prophet (see also
7.15–20; 13.17, 57; 21.11; 23.29–39; *Didache* 11–13).
A prophet's reward, perhaps defined in v. 32. *Righteous
person.* See note on 1.19; see also 13.17, 43, 49; 23.29;
cf. 23.28. *The reward of the righteous.* See 13.43; 25.34–
46. **10.42** *Little ones,* usually children (see 18.1–4;
19.13–15), but here probably adult missionaries (see
note on 18.6). *Truly I tell you.* See note on 5.18.
11.1 *When Jesus had finished,* a formulaic ending; see
notes on 7.28; 10.1–11.1; Introduction. *Twelve.* See
note on 10.1.
11.2–12.50 Drawing on Q and Mark (see Introduction), the author portrays Jesus as the healing Messiah,
Servant, and Son of Man, who continues his mission to

Israel even as the opposition of Israelite leaders intensifies. **11.2–6** Cf. Lk 7.18–23. **11.2** *In prison.* See 14.1–3.
What the Messiah was doing, lit. "the deeds of the Messiah," i.e., the healing miracles in chs. 8–9; see note on
11.5. *His,* John's; see 14.12. **11.3** *The one who is to come,*
the Messiah; see 3.11; 21.5, 9. **11.5** The deeds of chs. 8–
9 are summarized in language from Isa 35.5–6; see also
Isa 26.19; 29.18; 42.7, 18; 61.1. Elijah and Elisha performed similar healings; see 1 Kings 17.17–24; 2 Kings
5.1–14. *The poor.* See 5.3. *Good news.* See note on 4.23.
11.6 *Blessed.* See note on 5.3. *Anyone who takes no offense at me.* Cf. 15.12; see note on 13.21. **11.7–19** Cf. Lk
7.24–35; 16.16. John is identified as the expected Elijah; see notes on 3.4; 4.2; 4.11. **11.7–8.** *Wilderness.* See
3.1. *Soft robes.* Cf. 3.4. *Royal palaces,* perhaps an allusion to Herod Antipas, who placed the image of a reed
on his coins; see 14.1–12; note on 2.22; *Gospel of
Thomas* 78. **11.9** *Prophet,* a title that can be given to
miracle workers (like Elijah; Mal 4.5; note on 3.4); law-
givers (like Moses; Deut 18.15–18); classical prophets,
who had visions, spoke oracles, and pronounced judgment; and popular "charismatics" (see note on Acts
5.36). **11.10** The quotation is derived from Mal 3.1; see
Mt 3.3. **11.11** See *Gospel of Thomas* 46. *Truly I tell you.*

tist; yet the least in the kingdom of heaven is greater than he. [12]From the days of John the Baptist until now the kingdom of heaven has suffered violence,[a] and the violent take it by force. [13]For all the prophets and the law prophesied until John came; [14]and if you are willing to accept it, he is Elijah who is to come. [15]Let anyone with ears[b] listen!

16 "But to what will I compare this generation? It is like children sitting in the marketplaces and calling to one another,

[17] 'We played the flute for you, and you did not dance;
　　we wailed, and you did not mourn.'

[18]For John came neither eating nor drinking, and they say, 'He has a demon'; [19]the Son of Man came eating and drinking, and they say, 'Look, a glutton and a drunkard, a friend of tax collectors and sinners!' Yet wisdom is vindicated by her deeds."[c]

Woes to Unrepentant Cities

20 Then he began to reproach the cities in which most of his deeds of power had been done, because they did not repent. [21]"Woe to you, Chorazin! Woe to you, Bethsaida! For if the deeds of power done in you had been done in Tyre and Sidon, they would have repented long ago in sackcloth and ashes. [22]But I tell you, on the day of judgment it will be more tolerable for Tyre and Sidon than for you. [23]And you, Capernaum,

will you be exalted to heaven?
　　No, you will be brought down to Hades.

For if the deeds of power done in you had been done in Sodom, it would have remained until this day. [24]But I tell you that on the day of judgment it will be more tolerable for the land of Sodom than for you."

Jesus Thanks His Father

25 At that time Jesus said, "I thank[d] you, Father, Lord of heaven and earth, because you have hidden these things from the wise and the intelligent and have revealed them to infants; [26]yes, Father, for such was your gracious will.[e] [27]All things have been handed over to me by my Father; and no one knows the Son except the Father, and no one knows the Father except the Son and anyone to whom the Son chooses to reveal him.

28 "Come to me, all you that are weary and are carrying heavy burdens, and I will give you rest. [29]Take my yoke upon you, and learn from

---

a Or *has been coming violently*　*b* Other ancient authorities add *to hear*　*c* Other ancient authorities read *children*　*d* Or *praise*　*e* Or *for so it was well-pleasing in your sight*

See note on 5.18. *Least in the kingdom.* See notes on 5.19; 18.4. **11.12** *Has suffered violence,* has experienced the suffering and death of John, Jesus, and potentially Jesus' disciples (see 10.16–23). **11.13** *Prophets and the law.* See note on 5.17. **11.14** *Elijah . . . to come.* See note on 3.4; see also 16.14; 17.10–13. **11.15** *Anyone with ears,* i.e., to hear deeper meanings (see text note *b*); see 13.9, 14–16, 43; see also Isa 6.10; *Gospel of Thomas* 24; 63; 65; 96. **11.16–19** Cf. Lk 7.31–35. **11.16** *This generation,* a faithless and corrupt one, led by Pharisees; see Introduction; 12.38–45; 16.4; 17.17; 23.29–36; see also Deut 1.35. **11.17** *Played the flute . . . dance,* wedding games, i.e., the ministry of Jesus (see 9.15). *Wailed . . . mourn,* funeral games, i.e., the ministry of John (see 3.7–12; 9.14). **11.19** *Son of Man.* See note on 8.20. *Eating and drinking.* See 9.14–15; cf. John in 3.4. *A glutton and a drunkard.* Cf. the rebellious son in Deut 21.20. On *tax collectors and sinners,* see note on 9.10. Jesus seems to be identified with *wisdom,* although the latter was mythologized as female (see Prov 8–9; Wis 7.22–8.21). Thus *her deeds* are actually his; see vv. 2, 20–21. **11.20–24** Cf. Lk 10.13–15. The woes derive from Q. See Introduction. **11.20** *Deeds.* See notes on 11.2; 11.19. *Repent.* See 3.2; 4.17. **11.21** *Woe* introduces a prophetic oracle of lament or condemnation (see, e.g., Jer 13.27; 48.46; Hos 7.13), here the latter, approximating a curse; see also 18.7; 23.13–36; 26.24; cf. 11.6.

Chorazin and *Bethsaida* were Galilean towns not far from Capernaum; see note on 4.13; 11.23; Jn 1.44. *Tyre and Sidon* were gentile cities on the Mediterranean coast; see 15.21. *Sackcloth,* a dark garment of goats' or camels' hair (see Gen 37.34; Rev 6.12), and *ashes* were associated with rites of mourning, fasting, and repentance; see 6.16; Isa 58.5. **11.22** *But I tell you.* See note on 5.21–48. **11.23** *Capernaum.* See notes on 4.13; 11.21. Jesus' words against the city echo Isa 14.13, 15. *Hades,* Greek equivalent to Hebrew Sheol, realm of the departed dead. *Sodom.* See notes on 10.15; Tob 13.2. **11.25–27** Cf. Lk 10.21–22. **11.25** *Father.* See note on 6.9. *Lord of heaven and earth.* See 5.34–35; 6.10; 28.18; Acts 17.24; note on Tob 7.11–12. *Infants,* Jesus' followers; see 21.16 (cf. 21.9); note on 18.6; *Gospel of Thomas* 4. *Will.* See 6.10. **11.27** The use of *Father* and *Son* without modifiers (see also 24.36) and the theme of mutual knowledge are common in the Gospel of John (see Jn 3.35; 10.14–15; 13.3; 17.25). *The Son.* See note on 3.17; cf. *Gospel of Thomas* 61. **11.28–30** Cf. *Gospel of Thomas* 90. **11.28** *Come to me.* Personified wisdom speaks similar words in Sir 24.19; 51.23; cf. Mt 11.19. *Rest.* See Ex 33.14; Ps 95.11; Heb 4.1–11. **11.29** *Yoke,* a rabbinic metaphor for the difficult but joyous task of obedience to the Torah (see also 23.4; Jer 5.5; Acts 15.10). *Humble.* See 5.5; 21.5. *Rest for your souls.* See Jer 6.16; see also Sir 51.23–27.

me; for I am gentle and humble in heart, and you will find rest for your souls. ³⁰For my yoke is easy, and my burden is light."

Plucking Grain on the Sabbath

12 At that time Jesus went through the grainfields on the sabbath; his disciples were hungry, and they began to pluck heads of grain and to eat. ²When the Pharisees saw it, they said to him, "Look, your disciples are doing what is not lawful to do on the sabbath." ³He said to them, "Have you not read what David did when he and his companions were hungry? ⁴He entered the house of God and ate the bread of the Presence, which it was not lawful for him or his companions to eat, but only for the priests. ⁵Or have you not read in the law that on the sabbath the priests in the temple break the sabbath and yet are guiltless? ⁶I tell you, something greater than the temple is here. ⁷But if you had known what this means, 'I desire mercy and not sacrifice,' you would not have condemned the guiltless. ⁸For the Son of Man is lord of the sabbath."

The Man with a Withered Hand

9 He left that place and entered their synagogue; ¹⁰a man was there with a withered hand, and they asked him, "Is it lawful to cure on the sabbath?" so that they might accuse him. ¹¹He said to them, "Suppose one of you has only one sheep and it falls into a pit on the sabbath; will you not lay hold of it and lift it out? ¹²How much more valuable is a human being than a sheep! So it is lawful to do good on the sabbath." ¹³Then he said to the man, "Stretch out your hand." He stretched it out, and it was restored, as sound as the other. ¹⁴But the Pharisees went out and conspired against him, how to destroy him.

God's Chosen Servant

15 When Jesus became aware of this, he departed. Many crowds[a] followed him, and he cured all of them, ¹⁶and he ordered them not to make him known. ¹⁷This was to fulfill what had been spoken through the prophet Isaiah:

18   "Here is my servant, whom I have chosen,
       my beloved, with whom my soul is well
          pleased.
     I will put my Spirit upon him,
       and he will proclaim justice to the
          Gentiles.
19   He will not wrangle or cry aloud,
       nor will anyone hear his voice in the
          streets.
20   He will not break a bruised reed
       or quench a smoldering wick
          until he brings justice to victory.
21   And in his name the Gentiles will hope."

Jesus and Beelzebul

22 Then they brought to him a demoniac who was blind and mute; and he cured him, so that

---

a Other ancient authorities lack crowds

12.1–14 Two stories from Mark show that Jesus, in contrast to the Pharisees, stresses human need over sabbath observance. **12.1–8** Cf. Mk 2.23–28; Lk 6.1–5. **12.1** According to Deut 23.25, it was permissible *to pluck heads of grain* from a neighbor's field; see also Lev 19.9–10. **12.2** *Pharisees.* See note on 3.7. It was *not lawful* to harvest grain on the sabbath; Ex 20.10; 34.21; cf. Deut 5.14. **12.3** *Have you not read,* i.e., with understanding; a rebuke, not an inquiry; see also v. 5; 19.4; 21.16, 42; 22.31. On Jesus' literacy, cf. Lk 4.16. *What David did.* See 1 Sam 21.1–6. **12.4** *The bread of the Presence,* twelve consecrated loaves set out in the temple and replaced weekly; see Lev 24.5–9. **12.5** *Priests . . . break the sabbath;* priests perform duties even on the sabbath; see Num 28.9–10. **12.6** *I tell you.* See note on 5.18. *Something greater than the temple,* either Jesus himself or the kingdom of God; see note on 4.17. **12.7** *I desire mercy and not sacrifice,* Hos 6.6, quoted also in 9.13. Mercy is more important than sacrifices; and sacrifices are more important than sabbath observance (the implication of v. 5); thus, mercy is greater than the sabbath. **12.8** Mark's sharp sabbath critique is omitted (cf. Mk 2.27). *Son of Man.* See note on 8.20.

12.9–14 Cf. Mk 3.1–6; Lk 6.6–11. **12.9** *Their synagogue,* the Pharisees'; see note on 3.7. **12.10** *Is it lawful.* Later Israelite law allowed breaking the sabbath law in cases of immediate danger to life, but the specifics were debated. **12.11** Cf. Lk 14.5. See Ex 23.5; Deut 22.4 for helping animals. However, if an animal fell into a pit *on the sabbath,* the sabbath law took precedence. The animal could be fed or, as later rabbis said, devices could be set up to assist it in climbing out, but one should not *lift it out;* similarly Dead Sea Scrolls, *Damascus Document* (CD) 11.13–14. **12.12** *How much more.* See note on 6.26. **12.13** *Stretch out your hand.* See note on 8.3; see also 1 Kings 13.1–10. **12.14** *Pharisees . . . conspired.* The author omits "with the Herodians" (Mk 3.6); cf. notes on 2.22; 3.7.

12.15–21 Cf. Mk 3.7–12; Lk 6.17–19. **12.15** A summary of Jesus' healing ministry; see note on 4.23–25. **12.16** See note on 8.4. **12.17–21** The ninth formula quotation (see note on 1.22–23). Isa 42.1–4 is here freely rendered from Hebrew, emphasizing major themes in Matthew. **12.18** *My beloved.* See 3.17; 17.5. **12.19** *Not wrangle.* See 26.63; 27.12. **12.20** *Not break a bruised reed.* See 11.29; 21.5. **12.21** *Gentiles will hope.*

the one who had been mute could speak and see. 23All the crowds were amazed and said, "Can this be the Son of David?" 24But when the Pharisees heard it, they said, "It is only by Beelzebul, the ruler of the demons, that this fellow casts out the demons." 25He knew what they were thinking and said to them, "Every kingdom divided against itself is laid waste, and no city or house divided against itself will stand. 26If Satan casts out Satan, he is divided against himself; how then will his kingdom stand? 27If I cast out demons by Beelzebul, by whom do your own exorcists*a* cast them out? Therefore they will be your judges. 28But if it is by the Spirit of God that I cast out demons, then the kingdom of God has come to you. 29Or how can one enter a strong man's house and plunder his property, without first tying up the strong man? Then indeed the house can be plundered. 30Whoever is not with me is against me, and whoever does not gather with me scatters. 31Therefore I tell you, people will be forgiven for every sin and blasphemy, but blasphemy against the Spirit will not be forgiven. 32Whoever speaks a word against the Son of Man will be forgiven, but whoever speaks against the Holy Spirit will not be forgiven, either in this age or in the age to come.

A Tree and Its Fruit

33 "Either make the tree good, and its fruit good; or make the tree bad, and its fruit bad; for the tree is known by its fruit. 34You brood of vipers! How can you speak good things, when you are evil? For out of the abundance of the heart the mouth speaks. 35The good person brings good things out of a good trea-

sure, and the evil person brings evil things out of an evil treasure. 36I tell you, on the day of judgment you will have to give an account for every careless word you utter; 37for by your words you will be justified, and by your words you will be condemned."

The Sign of Jonah

38 Then some of the scribes and Pharisees said to him, "Teacher, we wish to see a sign from you." 39But he answered them, "An evil and adulterous generation asks for a sign, but no sign will be given to it except the sign of the prophet Jonah. 40For just as Jonah was three days and three nights in the belly of the sea monster, so for three days and three nights the Son of Man will be in the heart of the earth. 41The people of Nineveh will rise up at the judgment with this generation and condemn it, because they repented at the proclamation of Jonah, and see, something greater than Jonah is here! 42The queen of the South will rise up at the judgment with this generation and condemn it, because she came from the ends of the earth to listen to the wisdom of Solomon, and see, something greater than Solomon is here!

The Return of the Unclean Spirit

43 "When the unclean spirit has gone out of a person, it wanders through waterless regions looking for a resting place, but it finds none. 44Then it says, 'I will return to my house from which I came.' When it comes, it finds it empty, swept, and put in order. 45Then it goes and

---

a Gk sons

See 28.19. **12.22–32** Cf. Mk 3.22–29; Lk 11.14–23; 12.10. **12.22–24** See note on 9.32–34. **12.23** *Crowds.* See note on 4.25. *Son of David.* See note on 9.27. **12.24** *Beelzebul.* See notes on 9.34; 10.25. **12.27** *Exorcists.* See text note *a;* cf. "exorcists" and "sons" in Acts 19.13–14. Cf. also 7.22; the author omits Mk 9.38. **12.28** *The kingdom of God.* See note on 4.17. **12.29** See Isa 49.24; *Gospel of Thomas* 35. The *strong man,* Satan, is overcome by one even stronger. Jesus' exorcisms are seen as evidence of this victory. *Tying up* (binding), a common way to thwart demons; see 16.19; Rev 20.2. **12.31–32** See *Gospel of Thomas* 44; *Didache* 11.7. *Blasphemy against the Spirit,* i.e., attributing Jesus' Spirit-derived power to Satan (see note on 9.3). *Son of Man,* Jesus (see note on 8.20). **12.33–37** Cf. Lk 6.43–45. Warnings to the Pharisees; see *Gospel of Thomas* 45. **12.33** *Good, bad.* See notes on 3.12; 5.45; 7.17. See Ignatius *Ephesians* 14.2 **12.34** *Brood of vipers.* See 3.7;

23.33. *Heart.* See note on 5.8. *Mouth.* See 15.11, 18. **12.36** *Every careless word.* See 5.21–25. **12.38–42** Cf. Mk 8.11–12; Lk 11.16, 29–32. See *Didache* 11.7–11. **12.38** *Teacher.* See note on 8.19. **12.39** *An evil and adulterous generation.* See note on 11.16; 16.4. Adultery (cf. 5.27–30) was a prophetic metaphor for infidelity to God; see Isa 57.3–13; Hos 3.1. The author provides two interpretations of *the sign of the prophet Jonah:* Jesus' death and resurrection (12.40; see Jon 1.17–2.10) and Jesus' preaching of repentance (12.41; see 3.2; 4.17; also Lk 11.30–32; Jon 3.4–10). **12.40** *Three.* See note on 1.2–6a. **12.42** *The queen of the South,* the queen of Sheba; see 1 Kings 10.1–13; 2 Chr 9.1–12. According to Israelite interpretations of 1 Kings 4.29–34, the *wisdom of Solomon* included magic. **12.43–45** Cf. Lk 11.24–26. **12.43** *Unclean spirit,* a demon. *Waterless regions,* favored haunts of demons; see note on 8.32. **12.44** *My house,* the person within whom the demon

brings along seven other spirits more evil than itself, and they enter and live there; and the last state of that person is worse than the first. So will it be also with this evil generation."

The True Kindred of Jesus

46 While he was still speaking to the crowds, his mother and his brothers were standing outside, wanting to speak to him. 47 Someone told him, "Look, your mother and your brothers are standing outside, wanting to speak to you."[a] 48 But to the one who had told him this, Jesus[b] replied, "Who is my mother, and who are my brothers?" 49 And pointing to his disciples, he said, "Here are my mother and my brothers! 50 For whoever does the will of my Father in heaven is my brother and sister and mother."

The Parable of the Sower

13 That same day Jesus went out of the house and sat beside the sea. 2 Such great crowds gathered around him that he got into a boat and sat there, while the whole crowd stood on the beach. 3 And he told them many things in parables, saying: "Listen! A sower went out to sow. 4 And as he sowed, some seeds fell on the path, and the birds came and ate them up. 5 Other seeds fell on rocky ground, where they did not have much soil, and they sprang up quickly, since they had no depth of soil. 6 But when the sun rose, they were scorched; and since they had no root, they withered away. 7 Other seeds fell among thorns, and the thorns grew up and choked them.

8 Other seeds fell on good soil and brought forth grain, some a hundredfold, some sixty, some thirty. 9 Let anyone with ears[c] listen!"

The Purpose of the Parables

10 Then the disciples came and asked him, "Why do you speak to them in parables?" 11 He answered, "To you it has been given to know the secrets[d] of the kingdom of heaven, but to them it has not been given. 12 For to those who have, more will be given, and they will have an abundance; but from those who have nothing, even what they have will be taken away. 13 The reason I speak to them in parables is that 'seeing they do not perceive, and hearing they do not listen, nor do they understand.' 14 With them indeed is fulfilled the prophecy of Isaiah that says:

'You will indeed listen, but never
        understand,
    and you will indeed look, but never
        perceive.
15   For this people's heart has grown dull,
        and their ears are hard of hearing,
        and they have shut their eyes;
        so that they might not look with
            their eyes,
    and listen with their ears,
    and understand with their heart and
        turn—
    and I would heal them.'
16 But blessed are your eyes, for they see, and your ears, for they hear. 17 Truly I tell you,

---

a Other ancient authorities lack verse 47   *b* Gk *he*   *c* Other ancient authorities add *to hear*   *d* Or *mysteries*

---

dwells; see vv. 28–29. **12.45** *This evil generation.* See notes on 11.16; 12.39. *Seven,* a favorite number of the author; cf. 15.34, 36, 37; 16.10; 18.21, 22; 22.25, 28; see also seven parables in ch. 13 and seven woes against the Pharisees in ch. 23; see note on 18.21–22. **12.46–50** Cf. Mk 3.31–35; Lk 8.19–21. On Jesus' *mother and . . . brothers,* see 1.18–25; 13.55. *Outside.* In Mark, the setting for this scene is inside Jesus' house (see 13.1; Mk 3.19). **12.49** *Disciples* (see note on 5.1)—those who do the will of God (12.50)—are Jesus' true kin; see 10.34–39; 23.9. **12.50** *Whoever.* The circle of the twelve disciples is widened. *The will of my Father.* See note on 6.10.

13.1–53 Jesus' third discourse (see Introduction), expanded from Mark's four parables (Mk 4.1–34) to seven (cf. note on 12.45), establishes the special position of the disciples, who, in contrast to their portrayal in Mark's Gospel, understand Jesus' words. **13.1–9** Cf. Mk 4.1–9; Lk 8.4–8. See *Gospel of Thomas* 9. **13.1** *Sat,* i.e., for teaching (see note on 5.1). *The sea,* of Galilee.

13.2 *Crowds.* See note on 4.25. **13.3** *Parables,* brief comparison stories, drawn from nature or everyday life, that tease the imagination, challenge accepted values, or illustrate a point. **13.8** *Grain,* lit. "fruit," a metaphor for deeds (see note on 3.8). **13.9** *Anyone with ears.* See note on 11.15. **13.10–17** Cf. Mk 4.10–12, 25; Lk 8.9–10, 18. Private teaching to disciples. **13.11** *The secrets of the kingdom* concern Jesus' words and deeds; see 4.17; 10.1, 6–7; 11.25; 16.17; see also Dan 2.27–28. **13.12** See 25.29 (doublet); *Gospel of Thomas* 41. The reference here is to *those who have* knowledge about the kingdom. **13.13** The description of the crowds' faulty *seeing, hearing,* and ability to *understand* paraphrases Isa 6.9–10; Mk 4.11–12. See notes on 4.25; 11.15. **13.14–15** The tenth formula quotation (see note on 1.22–23) introduces Isa 6.9–10; see also Jn 12.40; Acts 28.26–27; Rom 11.8. *Their heart.* See note on 5.8. **13.16–17** Cf. Lk 10.23–24. **13.16** *Blessed.* See note on 5.3. *Your eyes . . . see.* See v. 51; see also 11.4–5, 14–15. **13.17** See *Gospel of Thomas*

many prophets and righteous people longed to see what you see, but did not see it, and to hear what you hear, but did not hear it.

The Parable of the Sower Explained

18 "Hear then the parable of the sower. [19]When anyone hears the word of the kingdom and does not understand it, the evil one comes and snatches away what is sown in the heart; this is what was sown on the path. [20]As for what was sown on rocky ground, this is the one who hears the word and immediately receives it with joy; [21]yet such a person has no root, but endures only for a while, and when trouble or persecution arises on account of the word, that person immediately falls away.[a] [22]As for what was sown among thorns, this is the one who hears the word, but the cares of the world and the lure of wealth choke the word, and it yields nothing. [23]But as for what was sown on good soil, this is the one who hears the word and understands it, who indeed bears fruit and yields, in one case a hundredfold, in another sixty, and in another thirty."

The Parable of Weeds among the Wheat

24 He put before them another parable: "The kingdom of heaven may be compared to someone who sowed good seed in his field; [25]but while everybody was asleep, an enemy came and sowed weeds among the wheat, and then went away. [26]So when the plants came up and bore grain, then the weeds appeared as well. [27]And the slaves of the householder came and said to him, 'Master, did you not sow good seed in your field? Where, then, did these weeds come from?' [28]He answered, 'An enemy has done this.' The slaves said to him, 'Then do you want us to go and gather them?' [29]But he replied, 'No; for in gathering the weeds you would uproot the wheat along with them. [30]Let both of them grow together until the harvest; and at harvest time I will tell the reapers, Collect the weeds first and bind them in bundles to be burned, but gather the wheat into my barn.' "

The Parable of the Mustard Seed

31 He put before them another parable: "The kingdom of heaven is like a mustard seed that someone took and sowed in his field; [32]it is the smallest of all the seeds, but when it has grown it is the greatest of shrubs and becomes a tree, so that the birds of the air come and make nests in its branches."

The Parable of the Yeast

33 He told them another parable: "The kingdom of heaven is like yeast that a woman took and mixed in with[b] three measures of flour until all of it was leavened."

The Use of Parables

34 Jesus told the crowds all these things in parables; without a parable he told them nothing. [35]This was to fulfill what had been spoken through the prophet:[c]

"I will open my mouth to speak in
        parables;
    I will proclaim what has been hidden
        from the foundation of the
        world."[d]

Jesus Explains the Parable of the Weeds

36 Then he left the crowds and went into the house. And his disciples approached him, say-

---

a Gk *stumbles*   *b* Gk *hid in*   *c* Other ancient authorities read *the prophet Isaiah*   *d* Other ancient authorities lack *of the world*

17; 38; 1 Cor 2.9; *1 Clement* 34.8. *Truly I tell you.* See note on 5.18. *Prophets,* here probably the OT prophets; cf. 10.41. *Righteous people.* See note on 1.19. **13.18–23** Cf. Mk 4.13–20; Lk 8.11–15. The allegorical interpretation explains why most of Israel does not accept Jesus. **13.18** *Hear then.* Cf. Mk 4.13. **13.19** *The evil one,* Satan or the devil (see note on 4.1; 6.13). *The heart.* See note on 5.8. **13.21** On *persecution,* see 5.10–12; 10.17–20. *Falls away.* The same Greek word (*skandalizein*) can be translated *take offense* (see 11.6; 13.57; 15.12), *stumble* (see 18.6), or *desert* (see 26.31, 33). See also 24.10. **13.22** The *lure of wealth.* See 6.19–21, 24. **13.23** *Fruit.* See notes on 3.8; 13.8. **13.24–30** This parable is explained in vv. 36–43. See also *Gospel of Thomas* 57. **13.24** *May be compared,* i.e., to all that follows. A typical parable introduction; see 18.23; 22.2.

13.30 *Harvest.* See v. 39. **13.31–32** Cf. Mk 4.30–32; Lk 13.18–19. See *Gospel of Thomas* 20. Though small, the *mustard seed* is not actually the *smallest of all the seeds* (cf. 17.20). The point of the parable is the contrast between small beginnings and great endings. **13.32** *Nests in its branches.* See Ezek 17.22–23; Dan 4.10–12. **13.33** Cf. Lk 13.20–21. See *Gospel of Thomas* 96. *Yeast,* a leavening agent, a small amount of which causes dough to rise and expand. *Three.* See note on 1.2–6a. *Three measures,* about 50 pounds of flour, enough for over a hundred loaves of bread. **13.34–35** Cf. Mk 4.33–34. **13.34** *In parables.* See vv. 10–13. **13.35** The eleventh formula quotation (see note on 1.22–23) introduces Ps 78.2. David, the presumed author of the Psalms, was thought to have written them while inspired by the Spirit, thus as *the prophet;* see Mt 22.43;

ing, "Explain to us the parable of the weeds of the field." 37He answered, "The one who sows the good seed is the Son of Man; 38the field is the world, and the good seed are the children of the kingdom; the weeds are the children of the evil one, 39and the enemy who sowed them is the devil; the harvest is the end of the age, and the reapers are angels. 40Just as the weeds are collected and burned up with fire, so will it be at the end of the age. 41The Son of Man will send his angels, and they will collect out of his kingdom all causes of sin and all evildoers, 42and they will throw them into the furnace of fire, where there will be weeping and gnashing of teeth. 43Then the righteous will shine like the sun in the kingdom of their Father. Let anyone with ears*a* listen!

Three Parables

44 "The kingdom of heaven is like treasure hidden in a field, which someone found and hid; then in his joy he goes and sells all that he has and buys that field.

45 "Again, the kingdom of heaven is like a merchant in search of fine pearls; 46on finding one pearl of great value, he went and sold all that he had and bought it.

47 "Again, the kingdom of heaven is like a net that was thrown into the sea and caught fish of every kind; 48when it was full, they drew it ashore, sat down, and put the good into baskets but threw out the bad. 49So it will be at the end of the age. The angels will come out and separate the evil from the righteous 50and throw them into the furnace of fire, where there will be weeping and gnashing of teeth.

Treasures New and Old

51 "Have you understood all this?" They answered, "Yes." 52And he said to them, "Therefore every scribe who has been trained for the kingdom of heaven is like the master of a household who brings out of his treasure what is new and what is old." 53When Jesus had finished these parables, he left that place.

The Rejection of Jesus at Nazareth

54 He came to his hometown and began to teach the people*b* in their synagogue, so that they were astounded and said, "Where did this man get this wisdom and these deeds of power? 55Is not this the carpenter's son? Is not his mother called Mary? And are not his brothers James and Joseph and Simon and Judas? 56And are not all his sisters with us? Where then did this man get all this?" 57And they took offense at him. But Jesus said to

a Other ancient authorities add *to hear*   *b* Gk *them*

Acts 2.30–31; 4.25–26. **13.36–43** The allegorical interpretation of the parable of the weeds (vv. 24–30). **13.36** *He . . . went into the house.* The interpretation is given as private instruction. **13.37** *Son of Man.* See note on 8.20. **13.38** *Children of the kingdom,* here those destined to inherit the kingdom of heaven (see 5.3, 10; 25.34; cf. 8.12). *The evil one.* See v. 19; note on 4.1. **13.39** *Harvest.* See note on 9.37. *The end of the age.* See 24.3; 28.20. On *angels* as end-time reapers and participants in the final judgment, see v. 49; 16.27; 24.31; 25.31–46; Rev 14.17. **13.40** *Fire.* See notes on 3.10; 5.22. **13.41** The concept of a *kingdom* of the Son of Man (see also 16.28; 20.21; 25.31–34), containing both good and evil, is found only in Matthew. It could refer to the world (see v. 38) or perhaps to the church (see vv. 47–50; 22.10–14). *Causes of sin,* lit. "stumbling blocks." See notes on 13.21; 18.6; see also 16.23; 18.6–7. **13.42** See v. 50. *Weeping and gnashing of teeth.* See note on 8.12. **13.43** *The righteous.* See notes on 1.19; 3.15; see also 10.41. *Shine like the sun.* See 17.2; Dan 12.3. *Anyone with ears.* See note on 11.15. **13.44–46** Twin parables liken the kingdom to a great treasure, worth risking all one has; see also *Gospel of Thomas* 76; 109. **13.47–50** See *Gospel of Thomas* 8. **13.48** On separating *good* and *bad*, see note on 3.12. **13.49–50** See notes 13.39; 13.40; 13.41; 13.42. **13.51–53** The cli-

max of the parable chapter. **13.51** *Have you understood?* See vv. 11, 13–16, 23; cf. vv. 13, 19. *Yes.* Cf. Mk 4.13; note on 13.1–53. **13.52** *Scribe,* here a reference to the disciples as well as to scribes in the Matthean groups (cf. note on 2.4). *Trained,* lit. "discipled." Both the *old* scriptures and their *new* fulfillment in Jesus' ministry are valued; see 5.17–20; 9.16–17. **13.53** See note on 7.28; Introduction.

13.54–17.27 The author rejoins the Markan outline. Rejection of Jesus in his hometown, misunderstanding by "Israel," and growing opposition by Pharisees lead Jesus to stress teaching to the disciples. **13.54–58** Cf. Mk 6.1–6; Lk 4.16–30. **13.54** *Hometown,* Nazareth (see 2.23). *Their synagogue.* See note on 4.23. *Wisdom . . . deeds of power.* See 11.19; 12.42. **13.55** Calling Jesus a *carpenter's son* may be more honorable than "son of Mary" (cf. Mk 6.3), but is still probably an implied insult. *His brothers,* though interpreted in various ways (e.g., as stepbrothers or cousins), probably refers to Jesus' natural siblings; see 1.25; 12.46; Jn 2.12; 7.5; Acts 1.14; 1 Cor 9.5. *James* became a leader of the Jerusalem church; see Acts 12.17; 15.13; 21.18; 1 Cor 15.7; Gal 1.19; 2.9, 12; Jas 1.1. *Joseph and Simon* are otherwise unattested (see note on 27.56). *Judas.* See Jude 1. **13.56** *All his sisters.* Cf. Mk 6.3 ("his sisters"). They are not mentioned by name. The Markan view

them, "Prophets are not without honor except in their own country and in their own house." 58And he did not do many deeds of power there, because of their unbelief.

The Death of John the Baptist

14 At that time Herod the ruler[a] heard reports about Jesus; 2and he said to his servants, "This is John the Baptist; he has been raised from the dead, and for this reason these powers are at work in him." 3For Herod had arrested John, bound him, and put him in prison on account of Herodias, his brother Philip's wife,[b] 4because John had been telling him, "It is not lawful for you to have her." 5Though Herod[c] wanted to put him to death, he feared the crowd, because they regarded him as a prophet. 6But when Herod's birthday came, the daughter of Herodias danced before the company, and she pleased Herod 7so much that he promised on oath to grant her whatever she might ask. 8Prompted by her mother, she said, "Give me the head of John the Baptist here on a platter." 9The king was grieved, yet out of regard for his oaths and for the guests, he commanded it to be given; 10he sent and had John beheaded in the prison. 11The head was brought on a platter and given to the girl, who brought it to her mother. 12His disciples came and took the body and buried it; then they went and told Jesus.

Feeding the Five Thousand

13 Now when Jesus heard this, he withdrew from there in a boat to a deserted place by himself. But when the crowds heard it, they followed him on foot from the towns. 14When he went ashore, he saw a great crowd; and he had compassion for them and cured their sick. 15When it was evening, the disciples came to him and said, "This is a deserted place, and the hour is now late; send the crowds away so that they may go into the villages and buy food for themselves." 16Jesus said to them, "They need not go away; you give them something to eat." 17They replied, "We have nothing here but five loaves and two fish." 18And he said, "Bring them here to me." 19Then he ordered the crowds to sit down on the grass. Taking the five loaves and the two fish, he looked up to heaven, and blessed and broke the loaves, and gave them to the disciples, and the disciples gave them to the crowds. 20And all ate and were filled; and they took up what was left over of the broken pieces, twelve baskets full. 21And those who ate were about five thousand men, besides women and children.

Jesus Walks on the Water

22 Immediately he made the disciples get into the boat and go on ahead to the other side, while he dismissed the crowds. 23And after he had dismissed the crowds, he went up the mountain by himself to pray. When evening came, he was there alone, 24but by this time the boat, battered by the waves, was far from the

---

a Gk *tetrarch* *b* Other ancient authorities read *his brother's wife* *c* Gk *he*

---

suggests at least two; the Matthean view perhaps more (*all*). **13.57** *Took offense.* See 11.6; 15.12; note on 13.21. *Prophets . . . in their own house,* a widespread proverb (see Lk 4.24; Jn 4.44; *Gospel of Thomas* 31; note on Mt 11.9). **14.1–12** Cf. Mk 6.14–29; Lk 9.7–9. The death of John the Baptist serves as a portent of Jesus' death. **14.1** *Herod* Antipas, a son of Herod the Great, ruled Galilee and Perea and built capitals at Sepphoris near Nazareth and Tiberias on the Sea of Galilee. See note on 2.22. *Ruler,* lit. *tetrarch* (text note *a*), Antipas's actual rank, which was considerably below that of king (cf. v. 9). **14.2** *This is John the Baptist.* See also 16.13–14. A different interpretation of the source of Jesus' powers is given by the Pharisees (see 12.24). **14.3–4** *Herodias* was never Philip's wife (see text note *b*), but her second husband, Herod Antipas, was her half uncle, and therefore the marriage was not lawful (see Lev 18.6–16; 20.21). **14.5** *He feared the crowd.* According to Josephus, John was executed because Herod feared that John's popularity might lead to rebellion (*Antiquities* 18.118–19). *Prophet.* See 11.9; 17.12–13; 21.26, 46; note on 3.4. See

also 5.12; 23.29–36. **14.12** *His disciples.* See 11.2; cf. 27.57–60. **14.13–21** Cf. Mk 6.32–44; Lk 9.10–17; Jn 6.1–13. The first of two scenes (see 15.32–39) in which the compassionate Jesus addresses physical hunger. Both contain echoes of the early sacred meal (26.26–29) and of the stories of Elijah and Elisha (see 1 Kings 17.8–16; 2 Kings 4.42–44). **14.13** *Withdrew.* Jesus increasingly withdraws from the crowds (see also v. 23), although they continue to follow. **14.14** *Compassion.* See notes on 9.36; 4.23. **14.16** *Give them something to eat.* See 2 Kings 4.42–43. **14.17** *Two.* See note on 4.18–22. **14.19** *Up to heaven.* See note on 3.16; Ps 123.1; Jn 11.41; 17.1. *Blessed and broke the loaves.* These actions were common to Israelite meals, but also echoed the sacred meal in the early church; see 26.26; Acts 27.35; 1 Cor 11.23–24. **14.20** See 2 Kings 4.42–44; see also Deut 8.10. *Twelve* probably symbolizes Israel (see 10.1, 2; 19.28). **14.21** *Women and children* were not normally counted (cf. Mk 6.44); see Introduction. **14.22–33** Cf. Mk 6.45–52; Jn 6.16–21. **14.22** *Other side,* i.e., of the Sea of Galilee. **14.23** *Mountain.* See note on 4.8. *Alone.* See note on 14.13. **14.24** *Bat-*

land,[a] for the wind was against them. 25 And early in the morning he came walking toward them on the sea. 26 But when the disciples saw him walking on the sea, they were terrified, saying, "It is a ghost!" And they cried out in fear. 27 But immediately Jesus spoke to them and said, "Take heart, it is I; do not be afraid."

28 Peter answered him, "Lord, if it is you, command me to come to you on the water." 29 He said, "Come." So Peter got out of the boat, started walking on the water, and came toward Jesus. 30 But when he noticed the strong wind,[b] he became frightened, and beginning to sink, he cried out, "Lord, save me!" 31 Jesus immediately reached out his hand and caught him, saying to him, "You of little faith, why did you doubt?" 32 When they got into the boat, the wind ceased. 33 And those in the boat worshiped him, saying, "Truly you are the Son of God."

Jesus Heals the Sick in Gennesaret

34 When they had crossed over, they came to land at Gennesaret. 35 After the people of that place recognized him, they sent word throughout the region and brought all who were sick to him, 36 and begged him that they might touch even the fringe of his cloak; and all who touched it were healed.

The Tradition of the Elders

15 Then Pharisees and scribes came to Jesus from Jerusalem and said, 2 "Why do your disciples break the tradition of the el-

ders? For they do not wash their hands before they eat." 3 He answered them, "And why do you break the commandment of God for the sake of your tradition? 4 For God said,[c] 'Honor your father and your mother,' and, 'Whoever speaks evil of father or mother must surely die.' 5 But you say that whoever tells father or mother, 'Whatever support you might have had from me is given to God,'[d] then that person need not honor the father.[e] 6 So, for the sake of your tradition, you make void the word[f] of God. 7 You hypocrites! Isaiah prophesied rightly about you when he said:

8   'This people honors me with their lips,
        but their hearts are far from me;
9   in vain do they worship me,
        teaching human precepts as
            doctrines.' "

Things That Defile

10 Then he called the crowd to him and said to them, "Listen and understand: 11 it is not what goes into the mouth that defiles a person, but it is what comes out of the mouth that defiles." 12 Then the disciples approached and said to him, "Do you know that the Pharisees took offense when they heard what you said?" 13 He answered, "Every plant that my heavenly Father has not planted will be uprooted. 14 Let

---

a Other ancient authorities read *was out on the sea*   b Other ancient authorities read *the wind*   c Other ancient authorities read *commanded, saying*   d Or *is an offering*   e Other ancient authorities add *or the mother*   f Other ancient authorities read *law*; others, *commandment*

---

tered . . . waves. See note on 8.24. **14.25** *Early in the morning,* lit. "the fourth watch," from 3:00 to 6:00 A.M. *Walking . . . on the sea.* See Job 9.8; Ps 77.19. **14.27** *It is I,* lit., "I am." Jesus' words suggest the name of God or his mysterious divine presence (see Ex 3.14; Isa 43.10; Jn 18.2–9). Israelite literature mentions magical clubs engraved with "I am" to beat back storms. **14.28** *Peter* increasingly represents the disciples (see also 15.15; 16.16). *Lord.* See note on 7.21. **14.30** *Save me!* See Ps 69.1–3; note on 1.21. **14.31** *Reached out his hand.* See Ps 18.15–16. *You of little faith.* See note on 6.30. Their *doubt* is apparently reversed in v. 33; see 28.17. **14.33** *Worshiped him.* See note on 2.2; cf. Mk 6.51. *The Son of God.* See notes on 3.17; 16.16. **14.34–36** Cf. Mk 6.53–56; Jn 6.22–25. **14.34** *Gennesaret,* a region or town on the northwest shore of the Sea of Galilee. **14.35–36** See note on 4.23–25. **14.36** *Touch . . . fringe of his cloak.* See notes on 9.20; 9.21.

15.1–9 Cf. Mk 7.1–13. **15.1** *Pharisees.* See note on 3.7. *Scribes.* See note on 2.4. **15.2** *Tradition of the elders,* the Pharisees' traditional interpretation of the Is-

raelite law, passed on orally and believed by them to have been given with the written law on Mount Sinai. The latter does not require Israelites to *wash their hands before they eat* (cf. Ex 30.17–21; Lev 15.11). **15.4** For the first command, see Ex 20.12; Deut 5.16; for the second, see Lev 20.9. **15.7** *Hypocrites,* here for the first time used to address opponents directly (cf. 6.1–18; see note on 7.5; 23.13–36). **15.8–9** Isa 29.13. *Hearts.* See note on 5.8. **15.10–20** Cf. Mk 7.14–23. **15.10** *Crowd.* See note on 4.25. *Listen and understand.* See 13.10–23, 43; Introduction. **15.11** See *Gospel of Thomas* 14. *What goes into the mouth.* See v. 2. It was widely debated in the early churches whether Israelite dietary laws were binding on those who believed in Jesus as Messiah; see Acts 10.14–15; Rom 14.19–21; Gal 2.11–14. *What comes out of the mouth.* See, e.g., 5.21–26, 33–37. *Defiles,* makes ritually unclean. **15.12** *Pharisees.* See note on 3.7. *Took offense.* See note on 13.21. **15.13** A *plant* was a common metaphor for righteous Israel; see Isa 60.21; *1 Enoch* 10.16; *Jubilees* 1.16. *My heavenly Father.* See note on 6.9. **15.14** *Blind guides.* See 23.16, 24; cf. Rom 2.19; *Gospel of Thomas* 34.

them alone; they are blind guides of the blind.[a] And if one blind person guides another, both will fall into a pit." 15 But Peter said to him, "Explain this parable to us." 16 Then he said, "Are you also still without understanding? 17 Do you not see that whatever goes into the mouth enters the stomach, and goes out into the sewer? 18 But what comes out of the mouth proceeds from the heart, and this is what defiles. 19 For out of the heart come evil intentions, murder, adultery, fornication, theft, false witness, slander. 20 These are what defile a person, but to eat with unwashed hands does not defile."

The Canaanite Woman's Faith

21 Jesus left that place and went away to the district of Tyre and Sidon. 22 Just then a Canaanite woman from that region came out and started shouting, "Have mercy on me, Lord, Son of David; my daughter is tormented by a demon." 23 But he did not answer her at all. And his disciples came and urged him, saying, "Send her away, for she keeps shouting after us." 24 He answered, "I was sent only to the lost sheep of the house of Israel." 25 But she came and knelt before him, saying, "Lord, help me." 26 He answered, "It is not fair to take the children's food and throw it to the dogs." 27 She said, "Yes, Lord, yet even the dogs eat the crumbs that fall from their masters' table." 28 Then Jesus answered her, "Woman, great is your faith! Let it be done for you as you wish." And her daughter was healed instantly.

Jesus Cures Many People

29 After Jesus had left that place, he passed along the Sea of Galilee, and he went up the mountain, where he sat down. 30 Great crowds came to him, bringing with them the lame, the maimed, the blind, the mute, and many others. They put them at his feet, and he cured them, 31 so that the crowd was amazed when they saw the mute speaking, the maimed whole, the lame walking, and the blind seeing. And they praised the God of Israel.

Feeding the Four Thousand

32 Then Jesus called his disciples to him and said, "I have compassion for the crowd, because they have been with me now for three days and have nothing to eat; and I do not want to send them away hungry, for they might faint on the way." 33 The disciples said to him, "Where are we to get enough bread in the desert to feed so great a crowd?" 34 Jesus asked them, "How many loaves have you?" They said, "Seven, and a few small fish." 35 Then ordering the crowd to sit down on the ground, 36 he took the seven loaves and the fish; and after giving thanks he broke them and gave them to the disciples, and the disciples gave them to the crowds. 37 And all of them ate and were filled; and they took up the broken pieces left over, seven baskets full. 38 Those who had eaten were four thousand men, besides women and children. 39 After

a Other ancient authorities lack of the blind

15.15 Peter. See note on 14.28. **15.16** Without understanding. Cf. note on 13.1–53. **15.17** Sewer, possibly "latrine." **15.18** Heart. See note on 5.8. **15.19** A vice list, widespread in ancient moral discourse (see, e.g., 1 Cor 6.9–10; Gal 5.19–21; Didache 5.1). **15.21–28** Cf. Mk 7.24–30. A pivotal story about women; see note on 9.18–26. **15.21** That place, probably Gennesaret (see 14.34). District of Tyre and Sidon, gentile territory (see 11.21). **15.22** Canaanite, a scriptural term for ancient Israel's pagan enemies (see, e.g., Deut 7.1; cf. Mk 7.26) here used to designate a Gentile. Woman. See notes on 9.18–26; 27.55. The Canaanite woman is doubly marginal, a woman and a Gentile. Lord. See note on 7.21. Have mercy . . . Son of David. See note on 9.27. **15.24** Lost sheep of the house of Israel, either a group within Israel or all of Israel (see also 9.36; 10.6; cf. 28.19). **15.25** She . . . knelt, implying worship (see note on 2.2). Lord, help me. Cf. notes on 9.27; 14.30. **15.26** Children, the Israelites (see, e.g., Deut 14.1; Isa 1.2). **15.27** The woman persists, controlling the action. Dogs, lit. "small dogs," i.e.,

puppies or house dogs, but still a very uncomplimentary term, often used for Gentiles or opponents (cf. Phil 3.2). Masters', lit. "lords" (see note on 7.21). **15.28** For another Gentile's faith, see 8.10. Healed instantly. See note on 8.3. **15.29–31** Cf. Mk 7.31–37. A major healing summary (see note on 4.23–25). **15.29** Mountain. See note on 4.8. He sat down. See note on 5.1. **15.30** See 8.17; 11.5. **15.31** They praised the God of Israel. The description of the crowd's response suggests that they were not Israelites, but Jesus has returned to Israelite territory (v. 29). **15.32–39** Cf. Mk 8.1–10; Jn 6.1–13. The second feeding miracle; see 14.13–21. **15.32** Compassion. See note on 9.36. Three. See note on 1.2–6a. **15.34, 37** Seven, a favorite number of the author (see note on 12.45), here perhaps symbolizing Gentiles (cf. 14.19–20; see Acts 6.1–6). **15.36** See note on 14.19. **15.38** Besides women and children. See note on 14.21; cf. Mk 8.9. **15.39** Magadan. Location unknown; it may be Magdala/Magdalan on the western shore of the Sea of Galilee (text note a); cf. 27.56, 61; 28.1.

sending away the crowds, he got into the boat and went to the region of Magadan.[a]

The Demand for a Sign

16 The Pharisees and Sadducees came, and to test Jesus[b] they asked him to show them a sign from heaven. 2He answered them, "When it is evening, you say, 'It will be fair weather, for the sky is red.' 3And in the morning, 'It will be stormy today, for the sky is red and threatening.' You know how to interpret the appearance of the sky, but you cannot interpret the signs of the times.[c] 4An evil and adulterous generation asks for a sign, but no sign will be given to it except the sign of Jonah." Then he left them and went away.

The Yeast of the Pharisees and Sadducees

5 When the disciples reached the other side, they had forgotten to bring any bread. 6Jesus said to them, "Watch out, and beware of the yeast of the Pharisees and Sadducees." 7They said to one another, "It is because we have brought no bread." 8And becoming aware of it, Jesus said, "You of little faith, why are you talking about having no bread? 9Do you still not perceive? Do you not remember the five loaves for the five thousand, and how many baskets you gathered? 10Or the seven loaves for the four thousand, and how many baskets you gathered? 11How could you fail to perceive that I was not speaking about bread? Beware of the yeast of the Pharisees and Sadducees!" 12Then they understood that he had not told them to beware of the yeast of bread, but of the teaching of the Pharisees and Sadducees.

Peter's Declaration about Jesus

13 Now when Jesus came into the district of Caesarea Philippi, he asked his disciples, "Who do people say that the Son of Man is?" 14And they said, "Some say John the Baptist, but others Elijah, and still others Jeremiah or one of the prophets." 15He said to them, "But who do you say that I am?" 16Simon Peter answered, "You are the Messiah,[d] the Son of the living God." 17And Jesus answered him, "Blessed are you, Simon son of Jonah! For flesh and blood has not revealed this to you, but my Father in heaven. 18And I tell you, you are Peter,[e] and on this rock[f] I will build my church, and the gates of Hades will not prevail against it. 19I will give you the keys of the kingdom of heaven, and whatever you bind on earth will be bound in heaven, and whatever you loose on earth will be loosed in heaven." 20Then he sternly ordered the disciples not to tell anyone that he was[g] the Messiah.[d]

Jesus Foretells His Death and Resurrection

21 From that time on, Jesus began to show his disciples that he must go to Jerusalem and un-

---

a Other ancient authorities read *Magdala* or *Magdalan* *b* Gk *him* *c* Other ancient authorities lack *2When it is . . . of the times* *d* Or *the Christ* *e* Gk *Petros* *f* Gk *petra* *g* Other ancient authorities add *Jesus*

16.1–4 Cf. Mk 8.11–13; Lk 12.54–56. See 12.38–42. **16.1** *Pharisees and Sadducees.* See note on 3.7. The desire *to test* suggests hostile intent (see, e.g., 4.1; 12.14; 19.3; 22.15, 35). **16.2–3** See *Gospel of Thomas* 91. *Signs of the times.* See 11.3–5; see also 24.3. **16.4** See 12.38–42. **16.5–12** Cf. Mk 8.14–21; Lk 12.1. **16.5** Only *disciples* are present with Jesus through 17.14. **16.6** *Yeast,* here a metaphor for evil influence (see v. 12; cf. 13.33). **16.8** *Little faith.* See note on 6.30. **16.9** *Do you still not perceive?* See note on 15.16; cf. Mk 8.17–18. *The five thousand.* See 14.13–21. **16.10** *The four thousand.* See 15.32–39. *Seven.* See note on 12.45. **16.12** *They understood.* See note on 13.1–53. **16.13–20** Cf. Mk 8.27–30; Lk 9.18–21. **16.13** *Caesarea Philippi,* a city twenty miles north of the Sea of Galilee. *Son of Man.* See note on 8.20. **16.14** *John the Baptist.* See 14.1–2. Jesus' miracles resembled those of *Elijah* (see notes on 11.5; 14.13–21; also note on 3.4). *Jeremiah or one of the prophets.* See, e.g., 13.57; 21.11; see note on 11.9. Deut 18.15–18 fueled the expectation of the appearance of a prophet, but the origin of the specific expectation of Jeremiah is unknown (see, however, 2.17; 27.9). **16.16** *Simon Peter.* See notes on 4.18; 10.2; 14.28. *Messiah.* See note on 1.1. *Son of the living God.* Cf. 14.33; see note on 3.17; cf. Rom 9.26 (Hos 1.10 Septuagint); *Jubilees* 1.25. **16.17** *Blessed.* See note on 5.3. *Son of Jonah.* Cf. Jn 1.42. *Flesh and blood,* human beings. **16.18** *And I tell you.* See note on 5.18. *Peter,* from the Greek *petros* (*Cephas,* Aramaic *kepha;* see note on 1 Cor 1.12) for *rock* or "stone," thus a symbolic renaming, "Rocky." *Church,* common in most of the NT, is found only here and in 18.17 (twice) in the four Gospels. *Gates of Hades* (see notes on 11.23; Tob 13.2), the power of death (see Isa 5.14; 38.10; Wis 16.13–14; Rev 1.18; 6.8) or of the evil underworld (see Rev 9.1). **16.19** *Keys of the kingdom,* here given to Peter, symbolize the authority to control entry (cf. *lock . . . out,* 23.13; see also Isa 22.22; Rev 3.7). In 18.18 the power to *bind* and *loose* is given to the communities (see also Jn 20.23). This could be the power to forgive sin (26.28; cf. Jn 20.23), exorcise demons (12.29), or ban persons from the communities (18.17–18), but most likely it is the power to teach authoritatively (28.20). **16.20** See note on 8.4. **16.21–23** Cf. Mk 8.31–

dergo great suffering at the hands of the elders and chief priests and scribes, and be killed, and on the third day be raised. 22And Peter took him aside and began to rebuke him, saying, "God forbid it, Lord! This must never happen to you." 23But he turned and said to Peter, "Get behind me, Satan! You are a stumbling block to me; for you are setting your mind not on divine things but on human things."

The Cross and Self-Denial

24 Then Jesus told his disciples, "If any want to become my followers, let them deny themselves and take up their cross and follow me. 25For those who want to save their life will lose it, and those who lose their life for my sake will find it. 26For what will it profit them if they gain the whole world but forfeit their life? Or what will they give in return for their life?

27 "For the Son of Man is to come with his angels in the glory of his Father, and then he will repay everyone for what has been done. 28Truly I tell you, there are some standing here who will not taste death before they see the Son of Man coming in his kingdom."

The Transfiguration

17 Six days later, Jesus took with him Peter and James and his brother John and led them up a high mountain, by themselves. 2And he was transfigured before them, and his face shone like the sun, and his clothes became dazzling white. 3Suddenly there appeared to them Moses and Elijah, talking with him. 4Then Peter said to Jesus, "Lord, it is good for us to be here; if you wish, I*a* will make three dwellings*b* here, one for you, one for Moses, and one for Elijah." 5While he was still speaking, suddenly a bright cloud overshadowed them, and from the cloud a voice said, "This is my Son, the Beloved;*c* with him I am well pleased; listen to him!" 6When the disciples heard this, they fell to the ground and were overcome by fear. 7But Jesus came and touched them, saying, "Get up and do not be afraid." 8And when they looked up, they saw no one except Jesus himself alone.

9 As they were coming down the mountain, Jesus ordered them, "Tell no one about the vision until after the Son of Man has been raised from the dead." 10And the disciples asked him, "Why, then, do the scribes say that Elijah must come first?" 11He replied, "Elijah is indeed coming and will restore all things; 12but I tell you that Elijah has already come, and they did not recognize him, but they did to him whatever they pleased. So also the Son of Man is about to suffer at their hands." 13Then the disciples understood that he was speaking to them about John the Baptist.

a Other ancient authorities read *we*   *b* Or *tents*   *c* Or *my beloved Son*

33; Lk 9.22. The first of four passion predictions (see also 17.22–23; 20.17–19; 26.1–2). **16.21** *He must.* The words suggest a divine plan, perhaps in fulfillment of Isa 52–53 (see 26.54; note on 1.22–23). *Elders,* Israelite leaders who, with the chief priests, constitute the primary opposition to Jesus during the final days in Jerusalem (see 26.3, 47, 57). *Chief priests and scribes.* See notes on 2.4; 21.15. *On the third day.* See also 1 Cor 15.4. *Be raised,* i.e., by God (see Acts 2.24; 4.10). **16.22** *Lord.* See note on 7.21. **16.23** *Satan.* See note on 4.1; cf. vv. 17–19. *Stumbling block.* See note on 13.41. *Divine things,* i.e., God's plan. **16.24–28** Cf. Mk 8.34–9.1; Lk 9.23–27. **16.24** *Disciples.* See notes on 4.18–22; 10.2; 16.5. *Take up their cross and follow me.* See 10.16–23, 38. **16.25** See 10.39. **16.26** *Gain the whole world.* See 4.8–9. **16.27** *Son of Man.* See note on 8.20. *With his angels.* See note on 13.39. *Repay . . . for what has been done.* Judgment according to one's deeds is prominent in Matthew (see 5.17–20; 7.15–20; see also Rom 2.6; 1 Cor 4.5; 2 Cor 5.10). Cf. note on 3.8. **16.28** *Truly I tell you.* See note on 5.18. *Some standing here.* The coming of the Son of Man was expected within the lifetime of that generation (see 10.23; 13.41; 24.34).

17.1–8 Cf. Mk 9.2–8; Lk 9.28–36. The transfiguration echoes the appearance of God to Moses on Mount Sinai. See note on 2.16–18. **17.1** *Peter, James,* and *John* form an inner circle of disciples (see 4.18–22; 26.37; see also Ex 24.13–14). *High mountain.* See note on 5.1; see also Ex 24.15; note on 4.8. **17.2** *Transfigured,* transformed to reveal his future glory (see 16.27; see also 2 Cor 3.18). *His face shone like the sun,* like that of Moses (see Ex 34.29; cf. note on 2.16–18) and like that of the heavenly Son of Man (see Rev 1.16). *Clothes . . . dazzling white.* See 28.3; Dan 7.9; Rev 1.12–16; 3.4–5. **17.3** *Moses* and *Elijah* could represent the law and the prophets (5.17; 7.12) or two prophets (see note on 11.9). **17.4** *Lord.* See note on 7.21. *Three.* See note on 1.2-6a. *Dwellings,* or *tents* (see text note b), perhaps recall the Festival of Booths (see Lev 23.42). Peter's strange suggestion may be intended to prolong the vision. **17.5** The *bright cloud* represents the presence of God (see Ex 24.15–18; see also Rev 14.14). *This is my Son.* See notes on 3.17; 16.16. *With him I am well pleased.* See 12.18, citing Isa 42.1; see also 2 Pet 1.17–18. *Listen to him.* See Deut 18.15, 18; Acts 3.22. **17.6** *Overcome by fear.* See 8.25–26; 14.26; 28.8–10; Ex 34.30. **17.9–13** Cf. Mk 9.9–13. **17.11** *Elijah . . . will restore all things.* See Mal 4.5–6. **17.12** *Elijah has already come.* See notes on 3.4; 11.14; 14.1–12. **17.13** *Disciples understood.* See note on 13.1–53.

Jesus Cures a Boy with a Demon

14 When they came to the crowd, a man came to him, knelt before him, 15and said, "Lord, have mercy on my son, for he is an epileptic and he suffers terribly; he often falls into the fire and often into the water. 16And I brought him to your disciples, but they could not cure him." 17Jesus answered, "You faithless and perverse generation, how much longer must I be with you? How much longer must I put up with you? Bring him here to me." 18And Jesus rebuked the demon,*a* and it*b* came out of him, and the boy was cured instantly. 19Then the disciples came to Jesus privately and said, "Why could we not cast it out?" 20He said to them, "Because of your little faith. For truly I tell you, if you have faith the size of a*c* mustard seed, you will say to this mountain, 'Move from here to there,' and it will move; and nothing will be impossible for you."*d*

Jesus Again Foretells His Death and Resurrection

22 As they were gathering*e* in Galilee, Jesus said to them, "The Son of Man is going to be betrayed into human hands, 23and they will kill him, and on the third day he will be raised." And they were greatly distressed.

Jesus and the Temple Tax

24 When they reached Capernaum, the collectors of the temple tax*f* came to Peter and said, "Does your teacher not pay the temple tax?"*f* 25He said, "Yes, he does." And when he came home, Jesus spoke of it first, asking, "What do you think, Simon? From whom do kings of the earth take toll or tribute? From their children or from others?" 26When Peter*g* said, "From others," Jesus said to him, "Then the children are free. 27However, so that we do not give offense to them, go to the sea and cast a hook; take the first fish that comes up; and when you open its mouth, you will find a coin;*h* take that and give it to them for you and me."

True Greatness

18 At that time the disciples came to Jesus and asked, "Who is the greatest in the kingdom of heaven?" 2He called a child, whom he put among them, 3and said, "Truly I tell you, unless you change and become like children, you will never enter the kingdom of

a Gk *it* or *him*   *b* Gk *the demon*   *c* Gk *faith as a grain of*
d Other ancient authorities add verse 21, *But this kind does not come out except by prayer and fasting*   *e* Other ancient authorities read *living*   *f* Gk *didrachma*   *g* Gk *he*
h Gk *stater*; the stater was worth two didrachmas

17.14–20 Cf. Mk 9.14–29; Lk 9.37–42. **17.15** *Lord, have mercy.* See note on 9.27. **17.16** *Disciples . . . could not cure him.* Cf. 10.1. **17.17** *Faithless and perverse generation.* Jesus' exasperated response is surprising, but see 11.16; 16.4; 23.36; see also Deut 32.5. **17.19** *Privately.* See 13.10, 36; note on 16.5. **17.20** *Little faith.* See note on 6.30. *Truly I tell you.* See note on 5.18. On the power of *faith*, see 21.21–22; Mk 11.22–23; Lk 17.6. *Mustard seed.* See 13.31–32. **17.22–23** Cf. Mk 9.30–32; Lk 9.43b–45. The second passion prediction (see note on 16.21–23). **17.22** *Son of Man.* See note on 8.20. *Betrayed,* or "handed over"; see note on 10.4. **17.24–27** Probably composed by the author to address the question of Christ-believing Israelites' obligations to the temple (and to Rome?). **17.24** *Capernaum.* See note on 4.13. The *temple tax* in Jesus' day was a drachma or denarius (cf. 22.19). The tax was levied annually on adult Israelite males to support temple sacrifices (see Ex 30.11–16; 38.26; 2 Chr 24.4–14; Neh 10.32). After the destruction of the Jerusalem temple (70 CE), the Romans doubled it to two drachmas (a didrachma) or two denarii, i.e., a half-shekel, and used it to support the temple of Jupiter Capitolinus in Rome. *Your teacher.* See note on 8.19. **17.25** *What do you think?* See also 18.12; 21.28. *Simon,* the representative disciple (see note on 4.18). **17.26** *The children are free* implies that the Son

of God (v. 5) and true children of God (5.45) do not need to contribute to the support of God's temple in Jerusalem—and in the author's day, the temple of Jupiter in Rome? See notes on 17.24; 17.27. **17.27** The conclusion, deriving from folklore, seems to soften the radical nature of the initial response in v. 26; cf. 22.19. The *coin*, a Greek stater, was worth a full shekel, or two didrachmas (four drachmas, four denarii), twice the temple tax after 70 CE, i.e., in the author's, not Jesus', day (see note on 17.24), and is thus enough for two (*for you and me*). In the author's time the passage may imply paying, but not really owing, taxes to Rome. The *fish* with the coin in its mouth was influential in later artistic portrayals of Jesus' Last Supper.

18.1–35 The fourth of Jesus' five great discourses, based on Mark and Q plus a parable from M (see Introduction), is inserted here to emphasize community discipline within a context of childlike humility and unbounded forgiveness. **18.1–5** Cf. Mk 9.33–37; Lk 9.46–48. **18.1** *Greatest.* See 5.19; *Gospel of Thomas* 12. *Kingdom of heaven.* See note on 4.17. **18.2** *Child,* here meant literally, but cf. vv. 6–14. **18.3** *Truly I tell you.* See note on 5.18. *Change,* i.e., repent (see 3.2). *Become like children,* i.e., without concern for social status (see Mk 10.15; *Gospel of Thomas* 22; 46). Children, like women, were considered of lower status (see Introduc-

heaven. [4] Whoever becomes humble like this child is the greatest in the kingdom of heaven. [5] Whoever welcomes one such child in my name welcomes me.

Temptations to Sin

[6] "If any of you put a stumbling block before one of these little ones who believe in me, it would be better for you if a great millstone were fastened around your neck and you were drowned in the depth of the sea. [7] Woe to the world because of stumbling blocks! Occasions for stumbling are bound to come, but woe to the one by whom the stumbling block comes!

[8] "If your hand or your foot causes you to stumble, cut it off and throw it away; it is better for you to enter life maimed or lame than to have two hands or two feet and to be thrown into the eternal fire. [9] And if your eye causes you to stumble, tear it out and throw it away; it is better for you to enter life with one eye than to have two eyes and to be thrown into the hell[a] of fire.

The Parable of the Lost Sheep

[10] "Take care that you do not despise one of these little ones; for, I tell you, in heaven their angels continually see the face of my Father in heaven.[b] [12] What do you think? If a shepherd has a hundred sheep, and one of them has gone astray, does he not leave the ninety-nine on the mountains and go in search of the one that went astray? [13] And if he finds it, truly I tell you, he rejoices over it more than over the ninety-nine that never went astray. [14] So it is not the will of your[c] Father in heaven that one of these little ones should be lost.

Reproving Another Who Sins

[15] "If another member of the church[d] sins against you,[e] go and point out the fault when the two of you are alone. If the member listens to you, you have regained that one.[f] [16] But if you are not listened to, take one or two others along with you, so that every word may be confirmed by the evidence of two or three witnesses. [17] If the member refuses to listen to them, tell it to the church; and if the offender refuses to listen even to the church, let such a one be to you as a Gentile and a tax collector. [18] Truly I tell you,

---

a Gk Gehenna   b Other ancient authorities add verse 11, For the Son of Man came to save the lost   c Other ancient authorities read my   d Gk If your brother   e Other ancient authorities lack against you   f Gk the brother

---

tion). **18.4** *Whoever becomes humble . . . is the greatest.* Reversal of status characterizes the kingdom (see 20.26–27; 23.11–12; Mk 10.43–44; Lk 14.11; 18.14; 22.26; Jas 4.6, 10; 1 Pet 5.5). For social ranking in the Roman Empire, see Introduction; in the kingdom of heaven, see note on 5.19. **18.5** *Child* here represents low status, not necessarily humility. For Jesus' humility, see 11.29; 21.5. **18.6–9** Cf. Mk 9.42–47; Lk 17.1–2. **18.6** *Put a stumbling block before,* lit. "cause to stumble." See notes on 13.21; 13.41. The term is repeated several times in this passage and is thus a catchword. *Little ones who believe in me,* no longer the literal children of vv. 1–4, but believers. It is not clear whether they are missionaries (see 10.42), disciples, recent converts, those of low social or economic status (see note on 18.3), or those weak in faith. *Millstone,* a large, circular stone driven by a donkey and used for grinding grain (see Rev 18.21). **18.7** *Woe.* See note on 11.21. **18.8–9** See note on 5.29–30. Here the sayings refer to the banning of errant members from the community. *Life,* the kingdom of heaven (see v. 3). **18.9** *Hell of fire.* See note on 5.22. **18.10–14** Cf. Lk 15.3–7. **18.10** *Little ones.* See note on 18.6. In Zech 13.7 (partially cited in Mt 26.31) "little ones" are also scattered sheep (see vv. 12–13). *I tell you.* See v. 13; note on 5.18. *Their angels,* guardian angels (see Tob 5.22). *See the face of my Father,* have constant access to God. **18.12–13** See Ezek 34.11–16; *Gospel of Thomas* 107. *What do you think?* See note on 17.25. *Gone astray.* See 24.4–5, 11, 24. **18.14** *The will of your Father.* See note on 6.9. **18.15–**

20 The author expands Q (see Lk 17.3; Introduction) into a formal procedure for settling disputes within the church. Reproof was based on interpretations of Lev 19.17–18: one should not allow anger to simmer inside, but confront one's "brother," friend, or neighbor openly. See, e.g., Sir 18.13–14; 19.13–17; *Testament of Gad* 4.1–4; 6.1–6; *4 Ezra* 14.13–22; rabbinic texts (*Sifra* Lev 9.17; *Babylonian Talmud Bava Mezi'a* 31a, emphasizing unending forgiveness, as in Mt 18.21–22; *Targum Ps.-Jonathan* Lev 19.17); Dead Sea Scrolls, *Community Rule* (1QS) 9.2–8; 5.24–6.1; 7.2–3, which stipulates that reproof is required on the same day; *Damascus Document* (CD) 9.6; 9.16b–22. Cf. also Heb 3.13. On God's sole right of vengeance, see Deut 32.35; Nah 1.2; Rom 12.19. Frank speech was thought by Hellenistic philosophers to improve friendship (e.g., Philodemus, *Concerning Frank Speech*). Formal procedures for expulsion are also found in Greco-Roman voluntary associations. **18.15** *Member of the church,* lit. "brother" (text notes *d, f*), kinship language (see also 12.49–50; see Lev 19.15–18). **18.16** *Two or three witnesses,* a legal requirement (see Deut 19.15; see also Mt 18.19–20; 26.60). According to later Israelite law, ca. 200 CE, neither slaves nor women could be witnesses in court (cf. 28.1, 9–10). **18.17** *As a Gentile and a tax collector,* i.e., an outsider; but see 8.10; 9.10; 11.19; 15.26; note on 1.1. *Church.* See 16.18. **18.18** *Truly I tell you.* See note on 5.18. The plural *you* points to the gathered assembly's authority to ban errant members (cf. note on 16.19; see Jn 20.23; 1 Cor 5.1–5; 2 Thess

whatever you bind on earth will be bound in heaven, and whatever you loose on earth will be loosed in heaven. 19Again, truly I tell you, if two of you agree on earth about anything you ask, it will be done for you by my Father in heaven. 20For where two or three are gathered in my name, I am there among them."

Forgiveness

21 Then Peter came and said to him, "Lord, if another member of the church[a] sins against me, how often should I forgive? As many as seven times?" 22Jesus said to him, "Not seven times, but, I tell you, seventy-seven[b] times.

The Parable of the Unforgiving Servant

23 "For this reason the kingdom of heaven may be compared to a king who wished to settle accounts with his slaves. 24When he began the reckoning, one who owed him ten thousand talents[c] was brought to him; 25and, as he could not pay, his lord ordered him to be sold, together with his wife and children and all his possessions, and payment to be made. 26So the slave fell on his knees before him, saying, 'Have patience with me, and I will pay you everything.' 27And out of pity for him, the lord of that slave released him and forgave him the debt. 28But that same slave, as he went out, came upon one of his fellow slaves who owed him a hundred denarii;[d] and seizing him by the throat, he said, 'Pay what you owe.' 29Then his fellow slave fell down and pleaded with him, 'Have patience with me, and I will pay you.' 30But he refused; then he went and threw him into prison until he would pay the debt. 31When his fellow slaves saw what had happened, they were greatly distressed, and they

went and reported to their lord all that had taken place. 32Then his lord summoned him and said to him, 'You wicked slave! I forgave you all that debt because you pleaded with me. 33Should you not have had mercy on your fellow slave, as I had mercy on you?' 34And in anger his lord handed him over to be tortured until he would pay his entire debt. 35So my heavenly Father will also do to every one of you, if you do not forgive your brother or sister[e] from your heart."

Teaching about Divorce

19 When Jesus had finished saying these things, he left Galilee and went to the region of Judea beyond the Jordan. 2Large crowds followed him, and he cured them there.

3 Some Pharisees came to him, and to test him they asked, "Is it lawful for a man to divorce his wife for any cause?" 4He answered, "Have you not read that the one who made them at the beginning 'made them male and female,' 5and said, 'For this reason a man shall leave his father and mother and be joined to his wife, and the two shall become one flesh'? 6So they are no longer two, but one flesh. Therefore what God has joined together, let no one separate." 7They said to him, "Why then did Moses command us to give a certificate of dismissal and to divorce her?" 8He said to them, "It was because you were so hardhearted that Moses allowed you to divorce your wives, but from the beginning it was not so. 9And I say to you, whoever divorces his

---

a Gk *if my brother*   *b* Or *seventy times seven*   *c* A talent was worth more than fifteen years' wages of a laborer *d* The denarius was the usual day's wage for a laborer *e* Gk *brother*

3.6–15; 2 Jn 10). **18.19** *Ask.* See 7.7–11. **18.20** *Where two or three are gathered,* here as a court of discipline. *In my name* (see also 7.22; 10.22) implies the vicarious presence and authority of the resurrected Jesus (see 28.20; 1 Cor 5.3–4). *Two.* See note on 4.18–22. **18.21– 22** Cf. Lk 17.4. The number *seven* (see note on 12.45) suggests completeness (see Gen 4.15; Lev 26.18; Lk 17.4; Rev 1.4, 12, 16). **18.21** *Peter.* See note on 14.28. *Another member.* See note on 18.15. **18.22** *I tell you.* See note on 5.18. **18.23–35** An allegorical parable. **18.23** *Kingdom of heaven.* See note on 4.17. *May be compared.* See note on 13.24. *King* (a thinly veiled allusion to God), a frequent figure in the author's parables (see, e.g., 22.2; 25.34). **18.24** *Ten thousand talents,* an unimaginable amount (see text note *c*); note on 25.15. **18.27** *Pity.* See 9.36. *The lord.* See note on 7.21; see also 10.24–25. **18.28** *A hundred denarii.* See text note *d*.

18.33 *Mercy.* See 9.13; 12.7. **18.35** On the need to *forgive,* see 6.14–15; 8.21–22.

19.1–20.34 The author rejoins the Markan outline (cf. note on 18.1–35). Jesus, with his disciples and the crowd(s), moves from Galilee to Jerusalem. **19.1– 12** Cf. Mk 10.1–12. **19.1** *When Jesus had finished.* See note on 7.28. *Left Galilee.* See note on 4.23–25. **19.3** *Pharisees.* See note on 3.7. *To test.* See notes on 12.14; 16.1; 22.15. **19.4** *Have you not read?* See note on 12.3. *Male and female.* See Gen 1.27. **19.5** Gen 2.24, quoted also in 1 Cor 6.16; Eph 5.31. **19.7** On Moses' *command,* see note on 8.4. *Certificate of dismissal.* See note on 5.31; Deut 24.1. **19.8** *Hard-hearted,* stubborn or obstinate. Paul also argues that the law of Moses cannot annul what was established earlier, in this case *from the beginning* (Gal 3.17). **19.9** *And I say to you.* See note on 5.18. *Except for unchastity.* See note on 5.32.

wife, except for unchastity, and marries another commits adultery."[a]

10 His disciples said to him, "If such is the case of a man with his wife, it is better not to marry." [11]But he said to them, "Not everyone can accept this teaching, but only those to whom it is given. [12]For there are eunuchs who have been so from birth, and there are eunuchs who have been made eunuchs by others, and there are eunuchs who have made themselves eunuchs for the sake of the kingdom of heaven. Let anyone accept this who can."

Jesus Blesses Little Children

13 Then little children were being brought to him in order that he might lay his hands on them and pray. The disciples spoke sternly to those who brought them; [14]but Jesus said, "Let the little children come to me, and do not stop them; for it is to such as these that the kingdom of heaven belongs." [15]And he laid his hands on them and went on his way.

The Rich Young Man

16 Then someone came to him and said, "Teacher, what good deed must I do to have eternal life?" [17]And he said to him, "Why do you ask me about what is good? There is only one who is good. If you wish to enter into life, keep the commandments." [18]He said to him, "Which ones?" And Jesus said, "You shall not murder; You shall not commit adultery; You shall not steal; You shall not bear false witness;

[19]Honor your father and mother; also, You shall love your neighbor as yourself." [20]The young man said to him, "I have kept all these;[b] what do I still lack?" [21]Jesus said to him, "If you wish to be perfect, go, sell your possessions, and give the money[c] to the poor, and you will have treasure in heaven; then come, follow me." [22]When the young man heard this word, he went away grieving, for he had many possessions.

23 Then Jesus said to his disciples, "Truly I tell you, it will be hard for a rich person to enter the kingdom of heaven. [24]Again I tell you, it is easier for a camel to go through the eye of a needle than for someone who is rich to enter the kingdom of God." [25]When the disciples heard this, they were greatly astounded and said, "Then who can be saved?" [26]But Jesus looked at them and said, "For mortals it is impossible, but for God all things are possible."

27 Then Peter said in reply, "Look, we have left everything and followed you. What then will we have?" [28]Jesus said to them, "Truly I tell you, at the renewal of all things, when the Son of Man is seated on the throne of his glory, you who have followed me will also sit on twelve thrones, judging the twelve tribes of Israel. [29]And everyone who has left houses or

a Other ancient authorities read *except on the ground of unchastity, causes her to commit adultery*; others add at the end of the verse *and he who marries a divorced woman commits adultery* b Other ancient authorities add *from my youth* c Gk lacks *the money*

19.11 *This teaching*, either Jesus' teaching on divorce (vv. 3–9), the disciples' comment on not marrying (v. 10), or the eunuch saying in v. 12. *Not everyone... but only those*, an inner core. **19.12** *Eunuchs*, emasculated males, were often keepers of the royal harem (see Esth 2.3, 14; Acts 8.27); in early Israel they were excluded from the community (see Deut 23.1). *Have made themselves eunuchs*, probably hyperbole for practicing celibacy (see also 22.30; 1 Cor 7.8, 25–40). *Kingdom of heaven*. Cf. note on 4.17. **19.13–15** Cf. Mk 10.13–16; Lk 18.15–17. See *Gospel of Thomas* 22; 46. **19.13** *Little children*, here actual children (but see 18.3–4; 18.6–10). *Lay his hands on them*, i.e., to impart a blessing (see Gen 48.8–16). **19.14** *To such as these*, to those of humble status (see note on 18.4). *Kingdom of heaven*. See note on 4.17. **19.16–30** Cf. Mk 10.17–31; Lk 18.18–30. **19.16** *What good deed must I do?* See note on 3.8. **19.17** *Enter into life*, i.e., enter the kingdom; see vv. 23–24; note on 4.17. **19.18–19** See Ex 20.12–16; Lev 19.18; Deut 5.16–20; see also Mt 5.21–37; *Didache* 2.2–3. *Honor your fa-*

ther and mother. Cf. 12.46–50. *Neighbor.* See notes on 18.15–20; 22.39. **19.21** *Perfect.* See note on 5.48. *Give ... to the poor.* See 26.9–11. *Treasure in heaven.* See 6.19–21. For social ranking in the Roman Empire, see Introduction. **19.23–26** Cf. Mk 10.23–27; Lk 18.24–27. **19.23** *Truly I tell you.* See note on 5.18. *Hard for a rich person.* See 1 Tim 6.9–10, 17–19; Jas 5.1–6. **19.24** *Camel... through the eye of a needle*, hyperbole suggesting virtual impossibility. **19.26** *All things are possible.* See also Gen 18.14; Mk 14.36; Lk 1.37. **19.27–30** Cf. Mk 10.28–31; Lk 13.30; 18.28–30; 22.28–30. **19.27** *Peter.* See note on 14.28. *Followed.* See 4.18–22. **19.28** *Truly I tell you.* See note on 5.18. *Renewal*, a revitalized creation following the final judgment (see also 2 Pet 3.10–13; Rev 21.1–22.5). *Son of Man... on the throne.* See note on 8.20; see also 16.27; 25.31–46. *Twelve thrones, judging the twelve tribes.* See note on 10.1; see also 1 Cor 6.2; Rev 3.21; 4.4. **19.29** On leaving family and possessions, see 8.20–22; 10.21–23, 37; 12.46–50. The church provides a *hundredfold* of brothers and sisters (see 12.50).

brothers or sisters or father or mother or children or fields, for my name's sake, will receive a hundredfold,ᵃ and will inherit eternal life. ³⁰But many who are first will be last, and the last will be first.

The Laborers in the Vineyard

20 "For the kingdom of heaven is like a landowner who went out early in the morning to hire laborers for his vineyard. ²After agreeing with the laborers for the usual daily wage,ᵇ he sent them into his vineyard. ³When he went out about nine o'clock, he saw others standing idle in the marketplace; ⁴and he said to them, 'You also go into the vineyard, and I will pay you whatever is right.' So they went. ⁵When he went out again about noon and about three o'clock, he did the same. ⁶And about five o'clock he went out and found others standing around; and he said to them, 'Why are you standing here idle all day?' ⁷They said to him, 'Because no one has hired us.' He said to them, 'You also go into the vineyard.' ⁸When evening came, the owner of the vineyard said to his manager, 'Call the laborers and give them their pay, beginning with the last and then going to the first.' ⁹When those hired about five o'clock came, each of them received the usual daily wage.ᵇ ¹⁰Now when the first came, they thought they would receive more; but each of them also received the usual daily wage.ᵇ ¹¹And when they received it, they grumbled against the landowner, ¹²saying, 'These last worked only one hour, and you have made them equal to us who have borne the burden of the day and the scorching heat.' ¹³But he replied to one of them, 'Friend, I am doing you no wrong; did you not agree with me for the usual daily wage?ᵇ ¹⁴Take what belongs to you and go; I choose to give to this last the same as I give to you. ¹⁵Am I not allowed to do what I choose with what belongs to me? Or are you envious because I am generous?'ᶜ ¹⁶So the last will be first, and the first will be last."ᵈ

A Third Time Jesus Foretells His Death and Resurrection

17 While Jesus was going up to Jerusalem, he took the twelve disciples aside by themselves, and said to them on the way, ¹⁸"See, we are going up to Jerusalem, and the Son of Man will be handed over to the chief priests and scribes, and they will condemn him to death; ¹⁹then they will hand him over to the Gentiles to be mocked and flogged and crucified; and on the third day he will be raised."

The Request of the Mother of James and John

20 Then the mother of the sons of Zebedee came to him with her sons, and kneeling before him, she asked a favor of him. ²¹And he said to her, "What do you want?" She said to him, "Declare that these two sons of mine will sit, one at your right hand and one at your left, in your kingdom." ²²But Jesus answered, "You

---

a Other ancient authorities read *manifold*   *b* Gk *a denarius*
c Gk *is your eye evil because I am good?*   *d* Other ancient authorities add *for many are called but few are chosen*

19.30 *First . . . last* here and the same terms in 20.16 frame the following allegorical parable. See note on 18.4; see also Lk 13.30; *Gospel of Thomas* 4.
   20.1–16 A general illustration of reversal: "the last will be first" (cf. 19.30; 20.16). **20.1** *Early in the morning,* about 6:00 A.M. **20.2** *Daily wage.* A denarius (see text note *b*) was about enough to feed a large peasant family for one day. **20.3** Poor day laborers gathered in the *marketplace* hoping to find work; for social ranking in the Roman Empire, see Introduction. **20.4** *Whatever is right,* i.e., whatever is just. No precise wage is stated (cf. v. 2). **20.8** *Evening.* The poor must be paid on the working day before sunset (see Lev 19.13; Deut 24.15). *The owner,* lit. "the lord." See note on 7.21; see also 21.40. *Beginning with the last.* See 19.30; 20.16. **20.13** *Friend,* intended sarcastically (see 22.12; 26.50). *Agree.* See v. 2. **20.15** *Envious,* lit. having an "evil eye" (see text note *c*; see also note on 6.23), a powerful and evil-causing look often associated with envy and resentment, here contrasted with the good "lord."

20.16 *Last . . . first.* See v. 8; note on 19.30; *Gospel of Thomas* 4. **20.17–19** Cf. Mk 10.32–34; Lk 18.31–33. The third passion prediction (see note on 16.21–23). **20.17** *Twelve disciples.* See 10.1. **20.18** *Son of Man.* See note on 8.20. *Handed over.* See note on 10.4. **20.19** Specificity of content characterizes the third prediction (cf. 16.21; 17.22–23). For fulfillment of the predictions, see 27.26–31. **20.20–23** Cf. Mk 10.35–40. **20.20** *The mother of the sons of Zebedee* (James and John; see note on 4.21) later observes the crucifixion and was apparently a follower of Jesus (see 27.55–56). **20.21** *Seats* at the *right hand* and at the *left* were the second and third positions of power and honor (see 22.44; cf. 25.33; 27.38). The scene envisioned is probably the judgment court (see 19.28). *Your kingdom,* i.e., the kingdom of the Son of Man (see note on 13.41). *Two.* See note on 4.18–22. **20.22** *You,* plural; therefore Jesus responds directly to James and John. *The cup* symbolizes one's destiny (see Pss 11.6; 16.5; 23.5), here suffering and death (see Mt 26.39).

do not know what you are asking. Are you able to drink the cup that I am about to drink?"[a] They said to him, "We are able." 23 He said to them, "You will indeed drink my cup, but to sit at my right hand and at my left, this is not mine to grant, but it is for those for whom it has been prepared by my Father."

24 When the ten heard it, they were angry with the two brothers. 25 But Jesus called them to him and said, "You know that the rulers of the Gentiles lord it over them, and their great ones are tyrants over them. 26 It will not be so among you; but whoever wishes to be great among you must be your servant, 27 and whoever wishes to be first among you must be your slave; 28 just as the Son of Man came not to be served but to serve, and to give his life a ransom for many."

Jesus Heals Two Blind Men

29 As they were leaving Jericho, a large crowd followed him. 30 There were two blind men sitting by the roadside. When they heard that Jesus was passing by, they shouted, "Lord,[b] have mercy on us, Son of David!" 31 The crowd sternly ordered them to be quiet; but they shouted even more loudly, "Have mercy on us, Lord, Son of David!" 32 Jesus stood still and called them, saying, "What do you want me to do for you?" 33 They said to him, "Lord, let our eyes be opened." 34 Moved with compassion, Jesus touched their eyes. Immediately they regained their sight and followed him.

Jesus' Triumphal Entry into Jerusalem

21 When they had come near Jerusalem and had reached Bethphage, at the Mount of Olives, Jesus sent two disciples, 2 saying to them, "Go into the village ahead of you, and immediately you will find a donkey tied, and a colt with her; untie them and bring them to me. 3 If anyone says anything to you, just say this, 'The Lord needs them.' And he will send them immediately.'"[c] 4 This took place to fulfill what had been spoken through the prophet, saying,

5   "Tell the daughter of Zion,
   Look, your king is coming to you,
       humble, and mounted on a donkey,
   and on a colt, the foal of a donkey."
6 The disciples went and did as Jesus had directed them; 7 they brought the donkey and the colt, and put their cloaks on them, and he sat on them. 8 A very large crowd[d] spread their cloaks on the road, and others cut branches from the trees and spread them on the road. 9 The crowds that went ahead of him and that followed were shouting,

   "Hosanna to the Son of David!
   Blessed is the one who comes in the
       name of the Lord!
   Hosanna in the highest heaven!"

---

a Other ancient authorities add *or to be baptized with the baptism that I am baptized with?* b Other ancient authorities lack *Lord* c Or *'The Lord needs them and will send them back immediately.'* d Or *Most of the crowd*

20.23 *You will indeed drink my cup.* Cf. v. 22. James was later martyred (see Acts 12.2) and various legends report John's death. *Not mine to grant.* Here the author subordinates the Son to the Father (cf. 11.27). **20.24–28** Cf. Mk 10.41–45; Lk 22.24–27. **20.27** See note on 18.4. **20.28** *Son of Man.* See note on 8.20. *Ransom,* the cost of freeing a prisoner or slave; see Titus 2.14 ("redeem"); 1 Pet 1.18–19. *For many.* See Isa 53.12. **20.29–34** A doublet of 9.27–31; cf. Mk 10.46–52; Lk 18.35–43. **20.29** *Jericho,* city about ten miles east of Jerusalem in the Jordan Valley north of the Dead Sea where Herod the Great had a winter retreat and built three Hellenistic-Roman palaces. The region is associated with John the Baptist and Khirbet Qumran; cf. note on 3.3; Zacchaeus in Lk 19.1–9. **20.30** *Lord, have mercy on us, Son of David.* See notes on 7.21; 9.27. **20.34** *Compassion.* See notes on 9.36; 25.35–36. *Touched.* See note on 8.3. "Seeing" leads to "following" (see notes on 4.19; 5.1).

21.1–23.39 Jesus enters Jerusalem; the conflict with the Israelite religious leaders intensifies. **21.1–11** Cf. Mk 11.1–11a; Lk 19.28–38; Jn 12.12–19. **21.1** *Beth-* *phage,* a small village near Jerusalem. *Mount of Olives.* See note on 24.3. **21.2** *Village,* probably Bethany (see note on 21.17). **21.3** *The Lord,* God or Jesus; the wording is ambiguous (see also note on 7.21). **21.4–5** The twelfth quotation formula (see note on 1.22–23) introduces a composite quote from Isa 62.11; Zech 9.9. **21.5** *Daughter of Zion,* the city of Jerusalem and its inhabitants. *Humble.* See 11.29; 20.28. In the poetic text of Zechariah, the same thought is often expressed in successive lines and *on a colt* is simply a repetition of *on a donkey.* The author interprets them as two different animals (see v. 7; cf. Mk 11.7). **21.8** *Spread . . . cloaks.* See 2 Kings 9.13. At the Feast of Booths, worshipers formed a procession around the temple altar carrying *branches* woven of myrtle, willow, and palm (see Lev 23.39–43; Jn 12.13). **21.9** *Hosanna,* lit. "save us" in Hebrew, but here just a shout of praise (see also v. 15; cf. Ps 118.25a). *Blessed . . . in the name of the Lord* (see also 23.39) is from Ps 118.26, a verse of the Hallel (Pss 113–118), which was chanted at the great Israelite festivals (see note on 26.30). *Son of David.* See notes on 1.1; 9.27; *Didache* 10.6. The author interprets *the one*

10 When he entered Jerusalem, the whole city was in turmoil, asking, "Who is this?" 11 The crowds were saying, "This is the prophet Jesus from Nazareth in Galilee."

Jesus Cleanses the Temple

12 Then Jesus entered the temple[a] and drove out all who were selling and buying in the temple, and he overturned the tables of the money changers and the seats of those who sold doves. 13 He said to them, "It is written,

'My house shall be called a house of
     prayer';

but you are making it a den of
     robbers."

14 The blind and the lame came to him in the temple, and he cured them. 15 But when the chief priests and the scribes saw the amazing things that he did, and heard[b] the children crying out in the temple, "Hosanna to the Son of David," they became angry 16 and said to him, "Do you hear what these are saying?" Jesus said to them, "Yes; have you never read,

'Out of the mouths of infants and
     nursing babies
you have prepared praise for
     yourself'?"

17 He left them, went out of the city to Bethany, and spent the night there.

Jesus Curses the Fig Tree

18 In the morning, when he returned to the city, he was hungry. 19 And seeing a fig tree by the side of the road, he went to it and found nothing at all on it but leaves. Then he said to it,

"May no fruit ever come from you again!" And the fig tree withered at once. 20 When the disciples saw it, they were amazed, saying, "How did the fig tree wither at once?" 21 Jesus answered them, "Truly I tell you, if you have faith and do not doubt, not only will you do what has been done to the fig tree, but even if you say to this mountain, 'Be lifted up and thrown into the sea,' it will be done. 22 Whatever you ask for in prayer with faith, you will receive."

The Authority of Jesus Questioned

23 When he entered the temple, the chief priests and the elders of the people came to him as he was teaching, and said, "By what authority are you doing these things, and who gave you this authority?" 24 Jesus said to them, "I will also ask you one question; if you tell me the answer, then I will also tell you by what authority I do these things. 25 Did the baptism of John come from heaven, or was it of human origin?" And they argued with one another, "If we say, 'From heaven,' he will say to us, 'Why then did you not believe him?' 26 But if we say, 'Of human origin,' we are afraid of the crowd; for all regard John as a prophet." 27 So they answered Jesus, "We do not know." And he said to them, "Neither will I tell you by what authority I am doing these things.

The Parable of the Two Sons

28 "What do you think? A man had two sons; he went to the first and said, 'Son, go and work

---

a Other ancient authorities add of God   b Gk lacks heard

---

who comes as a title for the messianic healer-king (see 3.11; 11.2; 21.5). **21.11** Crowds. See note on 4.25; see also 21.46. Prophet, an important but insufficient title for Jesus (see note on 11.9; 16.14–16). Jesus from Nazareth. See notes on 1.21; 2.23. **21.12–17** Cf. Mk 11.15–17; Lk 19.45–46; Jn 2.13–17. The author logically places the temple cleansing on the same day as the entry (but cf. Mk 11.11). **21.12** The selling and buying of animals for sacrifice and the presence of money changers were necessary adjuncts of temple sacrifices (see, e.g., Lev 1–7; Num 3.47). Doves were the sacrifices of the poor (Lev 5.7). **21.13** See Isa 56.7; Jer 7.11; see also Zech 14.21. **21.14** See note on 4.23–25. The blind and the lame were unclean and presumably should not have been in the temple (see Lev 21.16–20; 2 Sam 5.8). **21.15** The chief priests and the scribes, together with the elders (see v. 23), formed Jesus' Jerusalem opponents (see note on 2.4). Children, apparently to be understood literally (see notes on 18.2; 18.6). Hosanna to the Son of David. See v. 9. **21.16** Have

you never read. See note on 12.3. The text cited is Ps 8.2 (Septuagint). **21.17** Bethany, a village about two miles from Jerusalem on the eastern slope of the Mount of Olives (see vv. 1–2; 26.6–13). **21.18–22** Cf. Mk 11.12–14, 20–24. The only cursing miracle in the Gospels emphasizes the power of faith and foreshadows the coming destruction of Israel (cf. 3.10). **21.21** Truly I tell you. See note on 5.18. On the power of faith to move a mountain, see 17.20; Gospel of Thomas 48; 106. **21.22** See 7.7–11. **21.23–27** Cf. Mk 11.27–33; Lk 20.1–8. The Jerusalem leaders challenge Jesus' actions. **21.23** Chief priests, elders. See notes on 16.21; 21.15. **21.25** Baptism of John. See 3.1–6. From heaven, i.e., from God. On those who did not believe him, see v. 32. **21.26** Regard John as a prophet. See note on 14.5; see also 3.4; 11.7–15; 17.9–13; cf. 21.46.

21.28–22.14 Four allegorical parables illustrate the rejection of Israel's leaders and warn God's new people against self-righteous arrogance. **21.28–32** The first parable is given an immediate application. **21.28** What

in the vineyard today.' 29He answered, 'I will not'; but later he changed his mind and went. 30The father*a* went to the second and said the same; and he answered, 'I go, sir'; but he did not go. 31Which of the two did the will of his father?" They said, "The first." Jesus said to them, "Truly I tell you, the tax collectors and the prostitutes are going into the kingdom of God ahead of you. 32For John came to you in the way of righteousness and you did not believe him, but the tax collectors and the prostitutes believed him; and even after you saw it, you did not change your minds and believe him.

The Parable of the Wicked Tenants

33 "Listen to another parable. There was a landowner who planted a vineyard, put a fence around it, dug a wine press in it, and built a watchtower. Then he leased it to tenants and went to another country. 34When the harvest time had come, he sent his slaves to the tenants to collect his produce. 35But the tenants seized his slaves and beat one, killed another, and stoned another. 36Again he sent other slaves, more than the first; and they treated them in the same way. 37Finally he sent his son to them, saying, 'They will respect my son.' 38But when the tenants saw the son, they said to themselves, 'This is the heir; come, let us kill him and get his inheritance.' 39So they seized him, threw him out of the vineyard, and killed him. 40Now when the owner of the vineyard comes, what will he do to those tenants?" 41They said to him, "He will put those

wretches to a miserable death, and lease the vineyard to other tenants who will give him the produce at the harvest time."

42 Jesus said to them, "Have you never read in the scriptures:

'The stone that the builders rejected
    has become the cornerstone;*b*
this was the Lord's doing,
    and it is amazing in our eyes'?

43Therefore I tell you, the kingdom of God will be taken away from you and given to a people that produces the fruits of the kingdom.*c* 44The one who falls on this stone will be broken to pieces; and it will crush anyone on whom it falls."*d*

45 When the chief priests and the Pharisees heard his parables, they realized that he was speaking about them. 46They wanted to arrest him, but they feared the crowds, because they regarded him as a prophet.

The Parable of the Wedding Banquet

22 Once more Jesus spoke to them in parables, saying: 2"The kingdom of heaven may be compared to a king who gave a wedding banquet for his son. 3He sent his slaves to call those who had been invited to the wedding banquet, but they would not come. 4Again he sent other slaves, saying, 'Tell those who have been invited: Look, I have prepared my dinner, my oxen and my fat calves have been slaugh-

---

a Gk He *b* Or keystone *c* Gk the fruits of it *d* Other ancient authorities lack verse 44

---

do you think? Used also in 17.25; 18.12. Two sons. See note on 4.18–22. **21.31** Will of his father. See note on 6.10. Truly I tell you. See note on 5.18. The tax collectors and the prostitutes. See notes on 5.46; 9.10. Into the kingdom of God. See note on 4.17. **21.32** The way of righteousness. See note on 3.15. You did not believe him. See v. 25. **21.33–46** Cf. Mk 12.1–12; Lk 20.9–19. The second parable is strongly allegorical already in the Markan source. See also Gospel of Thomas 65. **21.33** Isa 5.1–7, an allegory, forms the basis of this allegorical parable and provides the key to its interpretation. Landowner, God. Vineyard, Israel. Tenants, the Israelite leaders. **21.34** Produce, lit. "fruits," i.e., good conduct; see note on 3.8. **21.35** Slaves, probably Israelite prophets (see 22.3, 6; 23.29–36). **21.36** Other slaves, probably later Israelite prophets or perhaps prophets and apostles in the churches (see 23.34–35). **21.37** His son, Jesus (see 3.17; 17.5). **21.39** Out of the vineyard, perhaps suggesting the crucifixion outside the Jerusalem walls; see the note on 27.33; cf. Heb 13.12–13. **21.40** Owner, lit. "lord"; see notes on 7.21; 20.8. **21.41** Miserable death, either the final judgment or the

destruction of Jerusalem in 70 CE, probably the latter (see note on 22.7; see also Isa 5.24–25). Other tenants, Christ-believers. **21.42** Have you never read. See note on 12.3. The text cited is Ps 118.22–23 from the Hallel (see note on 21.9). It is also applied to Jesus in Acts 4.11; 1 Pet 2.7. **21.43** Therefore I tell you. See note on 5.18. Kingdom of God. See note on 4.17. A people, here implying a group of Christ-believers (cf. 28.19; see 1 Pet 2.9). The fruits of the kingdom, righteous conduct (see note on 3.8; cf. 23.2–3). **21.44** The one who falls on this stone, probably an allusion to Isa 8.14 (see also Dan 2.34–35, 44–45). **21.45** Chief priests. See note on 2.4. Pharisees. See note on 3.7; see also 22.15, 34, 41. The reaction of the crowds is distinguished from that of the religious leaders (see note on 4.25; but cf. 27.25). **21.46** Prophet. See v. 11. **22.1–10** Cf. Lk 14.16–24. See also Gospel of Thomas 64. The third allegorical parable repeats many aspects of the second. **22.2** Kingdom of heaven. See note on 4.17. May be compared. See note on 13.24. King. See note on 18.23. Wedding banquet. See note on 8.11. **22.3** Slaves, probably Israelite prophets (see note on 21.35). Those . . . invited, the Israelites.

tered, and everything is ready; come to the wedding banquet.' ⁵But they made light of it and went away, one to his farm, another to his business, ⁶while the rest seized his slaves, mistreated them, and killed them. ⁷The king was enraged. He sent his troops, destroyed those murderers, and burned their city. ⁸Then he said to his slaves, 'The wedding is ready, but those invited were not worthy. ⁹Go therefore into the main streets, and invite everyone you find to the wedding banquet.' ¹⁰Those slaves went out into the streets and gathered all whom they found, both good and bad; so the wedding hall was filled with guests.

11 "But when the king came in to see the guests, he noticed a man there who was not wearing a wedding robe, ¹²and he said to him, 'Friend, how did you get in here without a wedding robe?' And he was speechless. ¹³Then the king said to the attendants, 'Bind him hand and foot, and throw him into the outer darkness, where there will be weeping and gnashing of teeth.' ¹⁴For many are called, but few are chosen."

The Question about Paying Taxes

15 Then the Pharisees went and plotted to entrap him in what he said. ¹⁶So they sent their disciples to him, along with the Herodians, saying, "Teacher, we know that you are sincere, and teach the way of God in accordance with truth, and show deference to no one; for you do not regard people with partiality. ¹⁷Tell us, then, what you think. Is it lawful to pay taxes to the emperor, or not?" ¹⁸But Jesus, aware of their malice, said, "Why are you putting me to the test, you hypocrites? ¹⁹Show me the coin used for the tax." And they brought him a denarius. ²⁰Then he said to them, "Whose head is this, and whose title?" ²¹They answered, "The emperor's." Then he said to them, "Give therefore to the emperor the things that are the emperor's, and to God the things that are God's." ²²When they heard this, they were amazed; and they left him and went away.

The Question about the Resurrection

23 The same day some Sadducees came to him, saying there is no resurrection;ᵃ and they asked him a question, saying, ²⁴"Teacher, Moses said, 'If a man dies childless, his brother shall marry the widow, and raise up children

---

a Other ancient authorities read *who say that there is no resurrection*

22.4 *Other slaves,* probably apostles or prophets in the churches (see note on 21.36). **22.6** On the persecution and martyrdom of Israelite prophets and apostles in the churches, see 10.16–23; 21.35–36; 23.29–35. **22.7** The graphic description of the punishment (cf. 21.41) seems to be a reference to the destruction of Jerusalem by Titus in 70 CE. **22.10** *Both good and bad* are within the author's communities (see note on 13.41), leading to the comments in vv. 11–14. **22.11–14** A fourth allegorical parable, added by the author to the preceding one. **22.11** A *wedding robe* would not be expected of someone summoned off the streets (vv. 9–10); it may symbolize a new way of life; see Rom 13.14; Gal 3.27–28; Col 3.11–12; *Gospel of Thomas* 37. **22.12** *Friend,* intended sarcastically (see 20.13; 26.50). **22.13** *Weeping and gnashing of teeth.* See note on 8.12. **22.14** The final words of the parable serve as a warning against self-righteous arrogance among God's new people (see also 7.13–14; Rom 11.13–24; 2 Esd 8.3, 41; 9.15; *Gospel of Thomas* 23).

22.15–46 Three more attempts by the Jerusalem authorities to entrap Jesus intensify the conflict. **22.15–22** Cf. Mk 12.13–17; Lk 20.20–26. **22.15** *Pharisees.* See note on 3.7. On the plot of the Pharisees to *entrap,* see 12.14; 16.1; 19.3; 22.35. **22.16** *Herodians,* probably the supporters of Herod Antipas (see 14.1) or the Herodian dynasty (see note on 2.1). The group is mentioned nowhere outside the Gospels (see also Mk 3.6; 12.13). *Teacher.* The opening words are insincere flattery. *Do not regard . . . with partiality,* do not show favoritism, especially toward people of high social status (see, e.g., Jas 2.1–9; cf. Mt 23.5–7). **22.17** Since census *taxes* were demanded by the Romans and despised by the Israelites, the trap (v. 15) was to force Jesus to make a statement that was either treasonous (to Rome) or offensive (to Israelites). **22.18** *Hypocrites.* See note on 15.7. **22.19–20** A silver *denarius,* the amount of the temple tax in Jesus' day (not the author's; cf. note on 17.24), bore an image of the emperor's *head* (see Ex 20.4; Deut 5.8) and, if recent, presumably had the *title* "TIBERIUS CAESAR, SON OF THE DIVINE AUGUSTUS, AUGUSTUS." **22.21** Jesus as portrayed here appears to support the state (see also 17.24–27; Rom 13.1–7; 1 Pet 2.13–17), but his lifestyle (e.g., 10.9–15) and the political implications of his religious, social, and economic teachings in the Gospel (e.g., 2.2; 4.17) were revolutionary and he was crucified by the Romans. **22.23–33** Cf. Mk 12.18–27; Lk 20.27–39. **22.23** *Sadducees* (see note on 3.7) did not believe in the *resurrection* because it is not attested in the Pentateuch, their textual authority (see Acts 23.8); but cf. note on 22.32. **22.24** *Moses,* the presumed author of the Pentateuch (see note on 8.4). The quotation derives from Deut 25.5–6. The purpose of this legislation (levirate law) was to preserve the deceased male's family line and name (see Gen 38.8; Ruth 4.10).

for his brother.' 25Now there were seven brothers among us; the first married, and died childless, leaving the widow to his brother. 26The second did the same, so also the third, down to the seventh. 27Last of all, the woman herself died. 28In the resurrection, then, whose wife of the seven will she be? For all of them had married her."

29 Jesus answered them, "You are wrong, because you know neither the scriptures nor the power of God. 30For in the resurrection they neither marry nor are given in marriage, but are like angels*a* in heaven. 31And as for the resurrection of the dead, have you not read what was said to you by God, 32'I am the God of Abraham, the God of Isaac, and the God of Jacob'? He is God not of the dead, but of the living." 33And when the crowd heard it, they were astounded at his teaching.

The Greatest Commandment

34 When the Pharisees heard that he had silenced the Sadducees, they gathered together, 35and one of them, a lawyer, asked him a question to test him. 36"Teacher, which commandment in the law is the greatest?" 37He said to him, " 'You shall love the Lord your God with all your heart, and with all your soul, and with all your mind.' 38This is the greatest and first commandment. 39And a second is like it: 'You shall love your neighbor as yourself.' 40On these two commandments hang all the law and the prophets."

The Question about David's Son

41 Now while the Pharisees were gathered together, Jesus asked them this question: 42"What do you think of the Messiah?*b* Whose son is he?" They said to him, "The son of David." 43He said to them, "How is it then that David by the Spirit*c* calls him Lord, saying,
44   'The Lord said to my Lord,
    "Sit at my right hand,
      until I put your enemies under your feet" '?
45If David thus calls him Lord, how can he be his son?" 46No one was able to give him an answer, nor from that day did anyone dare to ask him any more questions.

Jesus Denounces Scribes and Pharisees

23 Then Jesus said to the crowds and to his disciples, 2"The scribes and the Pharisees sit on Moses' seat; 3therefore, do whatever they teach you and follow it; but do not do as they do, for they do not practice what they teach. 4They tie up heavy burdens, hard to bear,*d* and lay them on the shoulders of others; but they themselves are unwilling to lift a finger to move them. 5They do all their deeds to be seen by others; for they make their phylacteries broad and their fringes long. 6They love to have the place of honor at ban-

---

a Other ancient authorities add *of God*   *b* Or *Christ*   *c* Gk *in spirit*   *d* Other ancient authorities lack *hard to bear*

22.25, 28 *Seven.* Cf. Tob 3.8, 15; 7.11; note on 12.45. **22.30** *Angels,* immortal beings who neither marry nor procreate (see 1 Cor 15.42–44); cf. note on 13.39. **22.31** *Have you not read.* See note on 12.3. **22.32** The quotation is from Ex 3.6. The present tense (*I am*) is here taken to imply that the deceased patriarchs were still *living,* i.e., resurrected. Evidence for the doctrine of resurrection is thus found in the Pentateuch (see note on 22.23). **22.34–40** Cf. Mk 12.28–31; Lk 10.25–28. **22.35** *Lawyer,* one learned in Mosaic law. *To test.* See note on 22.15. **22.37** Deut 6.5; this text was central to Israelite liturgy and life. **22.39** Lev 19.18; also cited in Mt 19.19. On Lev 19.17–19, see note on 18.15–20; *Didache* 1.2. **22.40** *The law and the prophets.* See note on 5.17. *Two.* See note on 4.18–22. **22.41–46** Cf. Mk 12.35–37; Lk 20.41–44. A fourth and final question is posed by Jesus (see note on 22.15–46). **22.42** *The Messiah.* See note on 1.1. *The Son of David.* See notes on 1.1; 9.27; see also Isa 11.1–9; Jer 23.5; 33.15; Jn 7.41–42; Acts 2.29–36; 13.22–23; Rom 1.3–4. **22.43** *By the Spirit.* It was assumed that David, the presumed author of Psalms, spoke under inspiration and thus prophetically (see Acts 2.30–31; 4.25). **22.44** Ps 110.1;

see also Ps 8.6b. *The Lord,* here God. *My Lord,* originally the Israelite king, here understood to be the promised Messiah (see note on 7.21). At the *right hand* was a position of power (see 20.21; 25.33; 26.64). **22.45** Fathers never address their sons as "lord," but only sons their fathers or inferiors their superiors. Since the author actually stresses Jesus' Davidic sonship elsewhere (see 1.1, 6, 17; note on 9.27), this saying probably suggests that Son of God, Son of Man, and Lord are more accurate titles.

23.1–36 A vitriolic attack on the leaders of Israel. **23.1–12** Cf. Mk 12.37–39; Lk 11.46; 20.45–46. **23.1** *Crowds.* See note on 4.25. **23.2** *Scribes.* See note on 2.4. *Pharisees.* See note on 3.7. *Sit on Moses' seat,* succeed Moses as authoritative teachers (see notes on 5.1; 2.16–18). **23.3** The command to *do whatever they teach* is surprising (cf. 5.21–48; 15.1–20; 16.5–12; 19.3–9), yet it is integral to the hypocrisy charges that follow. *Not . . . as they do.* See 5.20; 7.15–20. **23.4** *Heavy burdens,* the burden of Israelite law (cf. 11.28–30; see 12.9–14; 15.1–20; Acts 15.10; Gal 5.1). **23.5** *To be seen by others.* See also 6.1–18. *Phylacteries* (the Greek word can also be translated "amulets"), two small, square,

quets and the best seats in the synagogues, [7]and to be greeted with respect in the market-places, and to have people call them rabbi. [8]But you are not to be called rabbi, for you have one teacher, and you are all students.[a] [9]And call no one your father on earth, for you have one Father—the one in heaven. [10]Nor are you to be called instructors, for you have one instructor, the Messiah.[b] [11]The greatest among you will be your servant. [12]All who exalt themselves will be humbled, and all who humble themselves will be exalted.

[13] "But woe to you, scribes and Pharisees, hypocrites! For you lock people out of the kingdom of heaven. For you do not go in yourselves, and when others are going in, you stop them.[c] [15]Woe to you, scribes and Pharisees, hypocrites! For you cross sea and land to make a single convert, and you make the new convert twice as much a child of hell[d] as yourselves.

[16] "Woe to you, blind guides, who say, 'Whoever swears by the sanctuary is bound by nothing, but whoever swears by the gold of the sanctuary is bound by the oath.' [17]You blind fools! For which is greater, the gold or the sanctuary that has made the gold sacred? [18]And you say, 'Whoever swears by the altar is bound by nothing, but whoever swears by the gift that is on the altar is bound by the oath.' [19]How blind you are! For which is greater, the

gift or the altar that makes the gift sacred? [20]So whoever swears by the altar, swears by it and by everything on it; [21]and whoever swears by the sanctuary, swears by it and by the one who dwells in it; [22]and whoever swears by heaven, swears by the throne of God and by the one who is seated upon it.

[23] "Woe to you, scribes and Pharisees, hypocrites! For you tithe mint, dill, and cummin, and have neglected the weightier matters of the law: justice and mercy and faith. It is these you ought to have practiced without neglecting the others. [24]You blind guides! You strain out a gnat but swallow a camel!

[25] "Woe to you, scribes and Pharisees, hypocrites! For you clean the outside of the cup and of the plate, but inside they are full of greed and self-indulgence. [26]You blind Pharisee! First clean the inside of the cup,[e] so that the outside also may become clean.

[27] "Woe to you, scribes and Pharisees, hypocrites! For you are like whitewashed tombs, which on the outside look beautiful, but inside they are full of the bones of the dead and of all kinds of filth. [28]So you also on the outside

a Gk brothers b Or the Christ c Other authorities add here (or after verse 12) verse 14, Woe to you, scribes and Pharisees, hypocrites! For you devour widows' houses and for the sake of appearance you make long prayers; therefore you will receive the greater condemnation d Gk Gehenna e Other ancient authorities add and of the plate

leather boxes containing scripture verses, worn on the forehead and left arm by Israelite males while at prayer (see Ex 13.9, 16; Deut 6.8; 11.18). *Fringes.* See note on 9.20. **23.6** *Place of honor.* See Lk 14.1, 7–11. **23.7** *Rabbi,* lit. "my great one," a title for honored teachers increasingly used in later generations by the Pharisees (see also 26.25, 49). **23.8** *One teacher,* i.e., Jesus (see 7.28–29; 8.19). *You are all students,* lit. "you are all brothers." The issue here is sibling equality (see 12.48–50). **23.9** *One Father,* i.e., God (see Mal 2.10; cf. 5.16, 48; 6.9; 1 Cor 4.15). Fathers are not mentioned in the redefined "family" of disciples (see 12.48–50). **23.10** *Instructors,* academic teachers. **23.11** Cf. Mk 10.43–44; Lk 22.26; see also Mt 20.25–28. **23.12** For status, see Introduction; for status reversal, see note on 18.4.

23.13–36 A series of seven prophetic "woes" against scribes and Pharisees. *Seven.* See note on 12.45. **23.13** *Woe.* See note on 11.21; cf. 5.3–12. *Scribes and Pharisees.* See v. 2; notes on 2.4; 3.7. *Hypocrites!* See note on 6.2. *Lock people out of the kingdom of heaven* (cf. 16.19, *keys*), probably by opposing Jesus and his message. Cf. Lk 11.52; *Gospel of Thomas* 39; 102. **23.15** *Convert,* lit. "proselyte." See also Acts 2.10; 6.5; 13.43. *Hell.* See note on 5.22. **23.16–22** The argument highlights the absurdity of regarding a lesser oath

(e.g., swearing by the gold of the sanctuary or temple) as binding while regarding a greater oath (e.g., swearing by the sanctuary or temple itself) as not binding (cf. 5.33–37; Ex 20.7). **23.16** *Blind guides.* See note on 15.14. On *gold of the sanctuary,* see 1 Kings 6.20–22. **23.21** *The one who dwells in it,* i.e., God. **23.22** *By the throne of God.* See note on 3.16. **23.23** *Tithe,* a tenth of agricultural produce given to support the temple and its priests (see Lev 27.30–33; Num 18.8–32; Deut 14.22–29; 25.1–15; Tob 1.7–8). *Mint, dill, and cummin,* the smallest herbs (see also Lk 11.42). *Justice.* See 12.18, 20; see also Mic 6.8; Zech 7.9–10. *Mercy.* See 5.7; 6.12; 9.13; 12.7; 18.23–25. *Faith.* See 21.18–22. *Without neglecting the others.* See 5.17–20. **23.24** *Gnat,* an unclean insect (see Lev 11.41–44). *Camel,* also unclean (see Lev 11.4). **23.25–26** Cf. Lk 11.39–41; *Gospel of Thomas* 89. A then current debate about the correct sequence for ritual washing of the *cup* and the *plate* (see Mk 7.3–4) provided metaphors for criticizing the performance of external rituals without first cleansing the "heart" (see 15.1–20; also 6.1–18; 23.27–28). **23.27** Tombs were *whitewashed* before Passover to warn against defiling contact with unclean *bones of the dead* (see Lev 21.11; Num 5.2; 6.6–8; 19.11–20; cf. Lk 11.44). The emphasis here, however, is on the contrast

look righteous to others, but inside you are full of hypocrisy and lawlessness.

29 "Woe to you, scribes and Pharisees, hypocrites! For you build the tombs of the prophets and decorate the graves of the righteous, 30and you say, 'If we had lived in the days of our ancestors, we would not have taken part with them in shedding the blood of the prophets.' 31Thus you testify against yourselves that you are descendants of those who murdered the prophets. 32Fill up, then, the measure of your ancestors. 33You snakes, you brood of vipers! How can you escape being sentenced to hell?[a] 34Therefore I send you prophets, sages, and scribes, some of whom you will kill and crucify, and some you will flog in your synagogues and pursue from town to town, 35so that upon you may come all the righteous blood shed on earth, from the blood of righteous Abel to the blood of Zechariah son of Barachiah, whom you murdered between the sanctuary and the altar. 36Truly I tell you, all this will come upon this generation.

The Lament over Jerusalem

37 "Jerusalem, Jerusalem, the city that kills the prophets and stones those who are sent to it! How often have I desired to gather your children together as a hen gathers her brood under her wings, and you were not willing! 38See, your house is left to you, desolate.[b] 39For I tell you, you will not see me again until you say, 'Blessed is the one who comes in the name of the Lord.' "

The Destruction of the Temple Foretold

24 As Jesus came out of the temple and was going away, his disciples came to point out to him the buildings of the temple. 2Then he asked them, "You see all these, do you not? Truly I tell you, not one stone will be left here upon another; all will be thrown down."

Signs of the End of the Age

3 When he was sitting on the Mount of Olives, the disciples came to him privately, saying, "Tell us, when will this be, and what will be the sign of your coming and of the end of the age?" 4Jesus answered them, "Beware that no one leads you astray. 5For many will come in my name, saying, 'I am the Messiah!'[c] and they will lead many astray. 6And you will hear of

---

a Gk Gehenna **b** Other ancient authorities lack *desolate*
c Or *the Christ*

---

between inner and outer purity (see also vv. 25–26). **23.29–36** Cf. Lk 11.47–51. **23.30** On the *blood of the prophets*, see 1 Kings 18.13; 19.14. Later legends recount the martyrdom of Isaiah and Jeremiah (see also Acts 7.52; 1 Thess 2.14–15; Heb 11.36–38). **23.32** *Fill up . . . the measure.* The statement assumes a quota of evil that must be completed before the end; see also Rev 6.9–11. **23.33** *You brood of vipers.* See 3.7; 12.34. *Hell.* See note on 5.22. **23.34** *Prophets, sages, and scribes,* authoritative emissaries from the Matthean communities (see notes on 10.41; 13.52). The Gospel frequently alludes to the persecution of Christ-believers (see 5.11–12; 10.16–23; 20.19; 21.35–36; 22.6; 24.9–14). **23.35** *Righteous blood* anticipates the righteous suffering and dying Jesus, another martyr, and perhaps the Field of Blood (cf. note on 27.8). On *righteous Abel,* see Gen 4.8–11. On *Zechariah* the martyr, see 2 Chr 24.20–22. The one called the *son of Barachiah* was another Zechariah, the later (postexilic) prophet (see Zech 1.1). The author has apparently confused the two Zechariahs; cf. vv. 30, 37. **23.36** *Truly I tell you.* See note on 5.18. *This generation.* See note on 11.16. **23.37–39** Cf. Lk 13.34–35. The lament over Jerusalem (from Q) is transitional: it looks back to Jesus' entry into Jerusalem (21.1–11) and forward to Jesus' future coming as judge, the theme of the fifth discourse in chs. 24–25. **23.37** *Under her wings,* a maternal image. Cf. Deut 32.10–12; Pss 36.7; 61.4. **23.38** *House,* the temple, from which Jesus departs (see 24.1; cf. Ezek 10.18). **23.39** *For I tell you.* See note on 5.18. *Blessed.* The quotation from Ps 118.26 (see also 21.9) probably alludes here to Jesus' coming as future judge (see 24.3).

24.1–25.46 The fifth discourse (see Introduction) is an expansion of Mark's "little apocalypse" (Mk 13) using material that is from Q with material found only in Matthew. **24.1–2** Cf. Mk 13.1–2; Lk 21.5–6. **24.2** *Truly I tell you.* See note on 5.18. *All will be thrown down.* The Gospel was written after the temple had been destroyed (see Introduction; note on 22.7). Later in the story Jesus is accused of threatening to destroy the temple himself (see 26.60–61; 27.40; Acts 6.14). **24.3–8** Cf. Mk 13.3–8; Lk 21.7–11. **24.3** *Sitting.* See note on 5.1. *Mount of Olives,* located east of the Jerusalem Temple Mount across the Kidron Valley (see note on 4.8; 21.1; 26.30; Acts 1.12), was the place where, according to tradition, the temple-departing glory of God went (Ezek 10.18; 11.23; see 24.1) and where the Messiah was expected to appear (based on Zech 14.1–10). *This,* the destruction of the temple, which is distinguished from the *sign* of Jesus' coming for final judgment at the end of the age; cf. Mk 13.4. **24.4** *Leads you astray.* See vv. 11, 24; *Didache* 6.1. **24.5** According to Josephus, several figures in first-century Palestine claimed to be the *Messiah* (*Antiquities* 17.271–85; see also Mt 24.23–27; Acts 5.35–39; 21.38); cf. note on 24.26. **24.6–8** The view was wide-

wars and rumors of wars; see that you are not alarmed; for this must take place, but the end is not yet. [7]For nation will rise against nation, and kingdom against kingdom, and there will be famines[a] and earthquakes in various places: [8]all this is but the beginning of the birth pangs.

Persecutions Foretold

9 "Then they will hand you over to be tortured and will put you to death, and you will be hated by all nations because of my name. [10]Then many will fall away,[b] and they will betray one another and hate one another. [11]And many false prophets will arise and lead many astray. [12]And because of the increase of lawlessness, the love of many will grow cold. [13]But the one who endures to the end will be saved. [14]And this good news[c] of the kingdom will be proclaimed throughout the world, as a testimony to all the nations; and then the end will come.

The Desolating Sacrilege

15 "So when you see the desolating sacrilege standing in the holy place, as was spoken of by the prophet Daniel (let the reader understand), [16]then those in Judea must flee to the mountains; [17]the one on the housetop must not go down to take what is in the house; [18]the one in the field must not turn back to get a coat. [19]Woe to those who are pregnant and to those who are nursing infants in those days! [20]Pray that your flight may not be in winter or on a sabbath. [21]For at that time there will be great suffering, such as has not been from the beginning of the world until now, no, and never will be. [22]And if those days had not been cut short, no one would be saved; but for the sake of the elect those days will be cut short. [23]Then if anyone says to you, 'Look! Here is the Messiah!'[d] or 'There he is!'—do not believe it. [24]For false messiahs[e] and false prophets will appear and produce great signs and omens, to lead astray, if possible, even the elect. [25]Take note, I have told you beforehand. [26]So, if they say to you, 'Look! He is in the wilderness,' do not go out. If they say, 'Look! He is

---

a Other ancient authorities add *and pestilences*   b Or *stumble*   c Or *gospel*   d Or *the Christ*   e Or *christs*

---

spread that just as *birth pangs* precede birth, so a series of earthly catastrophes would precede the coming of the Messiah or the messianic age (see Isa 26.17–21; 42.14–16; 1 Thess 5.2–3; Rev 12.2; see also 2 Esd 13.31–32; *2 Baruch* 27). **24.9–14** Cf. Mk 13.9a, 13; Lk 21.12a, 17–19. The author omits most of Mk 13.9b–12, having used it earlier in 10.17–22. **24.9** *All nations.* Here persecution from outside the Israelite communities is envisioned, probably in connection with the gentile mission (see v. 14; 28.19; cf. 10.17). **24.10** *Fall away.* See note on 13.21; *Didache* 16.5. **24.11** *False prophets.* See v. 4; also 7.15–23; *Didache* 16.3. **24.12** *Love,* perhaps love within the communities (see v. 10; see also 5.43–46) or love of, i.e., fidelity to, God (see 13.20–21; 22.37–39; see also 2 Tim 3.1–5). **24.13** See 10.22. *Endures . . . saved.* See *Didache* 16.5. **24.14** *This good news of the kingdom* (see also 4.23; 9.35; 26.13), i.e., Jesus' teachings and deeds and perhaps also the author's Gospel. *To all the nations.* The mission, including the Gentiles, will precede the end (see 26.13; 28.19; but see also 10.5–15). **24.15–28** Cf. Mk 13.14–23; Lk 17.23–24, 37; 21.20–24. **24.15** *The desolating sacrilege,* from Dan 9.27; 11.31; 12.11 (see also 1 Macc 1.54; 2 Macc 8.17), where it referred to an offensive altar to the Greek god Zeus set up in the Jerusalem temple in 167 BCE by the Seleucid king Antiochus IV. The author of Matthew adds *spoken of by the prophet Daniel* and changes "set up where it ought not to be" (Mk 13.14) to *standing in the holy place.* The saying might once have referred to the emperor Caligula's unfulfilled plan to set up his statue in the Jerusalem temple in 40 CE, but the author probably understood it

as a reference to the presence of the Roman general Titus standing in the temple in 70 CE (see note on 22.7). *(Let the reader understand.)* This interruption, taken from Mk 13.14, signaled the importance of the mysterious symbol to the reader, who in antiquity normally read aloud, often to an assembly, e.g., a church. **24.16** *Those in Judea must flee to the mountains.* See 1 Macc 2.28. A tradition (whose accuracy is much debated) claims that Christians from Jerusalem obeyed an oracle to flee to Pella (a city east of the Jordan) when the Roman armies threatened the city (Eusebius, *Ecclesiastical History* 3.5.3). **24.19** *Woe,* here a lament (see note on 11.21). **24.20** Travel on the *sabbath* was restricted by Israelite law (see Ex 16.29–30; 20.8–11; Acts 1.12). This saying suggests that the author's communities still observed the sabbath (see 12.8; Rom 14.5–6). For a possible shift from the last to the first day of the week, probably in honor of Jesus' resurrection, see Acts 20.7; cf. also 1 Cor 16.2; note on Rev 1.10 ("the Lord's day"). **24.21** *Suffering,* Greek *thlipsis,* a word that became a technical term for end-time affliction (see v. 29; Dan 12.1; Rom 5.3; 8.35). **24.22** *The elect,* God's chosen, righteous people (see Deut 7.6–11; Rom 8.33; Col 3.12). **24.24** *False messiahs.* See note on 24.5. *Signs and omens.* See 12.38; 16.1; 2 Thess 2.9; *Didache* 16.4. According to Josephus, false prophets claimed there would be signs of deliverance from the Romans (*War* 6.285–309). See note on 24.16. **24.26** Cf. Lk 17.23; *Gospel of Thomas* 3; 51; 113. The isolated *wilderness* was a favorite hiding place for bandits and insurrectionists; see Acts 21.38; Josephus, *Antiquities* 20.97–99; 20.167–72; *War* 2.258–63; 7.437–

in the inner rooms,' do not believe it. 27 For as the lightning comes from the east and flashes as far as the west, so will be the coming of the Son of Man. 28 Wherever the corpse is, there the vultures will gather.

The Coming of the Son of Man

29 "Immediately after the suffering of those days

the sun will be darkened,
and the moon will not give its light;
the stars will fall from heaven,
and the powers of heaven will be shaken.

30 Then the sign of the Son of Man will appear in heaven, and then all the tribes of the earth will mourn, and they will see 'the Son of Man coming on the clouds of heaven' with power and great glory. 31 And he will send out his angels with a loud trumpet call, and they will gather his elect from the four winds, from one end of heaven to the other.

The Lesson of the Fig Tree

32 "From the fig tree learn its lesson: as soon as its branch becomes tender and puts forth its leaves, you know that summer is near. 33 So also, when you see all these things, you know that he[a] is near, at the very gates. 34 Truly I tell you, this generation will not pass away until all these things have taken place. 35 Heaven and earth will pass away, but my words will not pass away.

The Necessity for Watchfulness

36 "But about that day and hour no one knows, neither the angels of heaven, nor the Son,[b] but only the Father. 37 For as the days of Noah were, so will be the coming of the Son of Man. 38 For as in those days before the flood they were eating and drinking, marrying and giving in marriage, until the day Noah entered the ark, 39 and they knew nothing until the flood came and swept them all away, so too will be the coming of the Son of Man. 40 Then two will be in the field; one will be taken and one will be left. 41 Two women will be grinding meal together; one will be taken and one will be left. 42 Keep awake therefore, for you do not know on what day[c] your Lord is coming. 43 But understand this: if the owner of the house had known in what part of the night the thief was coming, he would have stayed awake and would not have let his house be broken into. 44 Therefore you also must be ready, for the Son of Man is coming at an unexpected hour.

The Faithful or the Unfaithful Slave

45 "Who then is the faithful and wise slave, whom his master has put in charge of his household, to give the other slaves[d] their allowance of food at the proper time? 46 Blessed is that slave whom his master will find at work when he arrives. 47 Truly I tell you, he will put that one in charge of all his possessions. 48 But if that wicked slave says to himself, 'My master is delayed,' 49 and he begins to beat his fellow slaves, and eats and drinks with drunkards, 50 the master of that slave will come on a day when he does not expect him and at an hour

---

a Or it b Other ancient authorities lack nor the Son c Other ancient authorities read at what hour d Gk to give them

---

41. **24.27** The coming (Greek parousia), i.e., to execute the final judgment at the end of the age (see vv. 3, 37, 39, 44, 50; 25.31–46). Son of Man. See note on 8.20. **24.28** This grisly proverb emphasizes that the coming of the Son of Man will be obvious to all. **24.29–31** Cf. Mk 13.24–27; Lk 21.25–28. The Parousia, or (second) coming, of the Son of Man. **24.29** The language echoes Isa 13.10, 13; 34.4; Ezek 32.7–8; Joel 2.10; Am 8.9; see also Rev 6.12–13. **24.30** The sign, perhaps the Son of Man himself or some cosmic sign (see v. 27; see also Isa 11.12; 49.22). All the tribes . . . will mourn, an allusion to Zech 12.10 (see also Rev 1.7). The Son of Man . . . clouds of heaven. See note on Mt 8.20; see also 26.64; Didache 16.6. **24.31** Angels. Cf. 13.41. On the gathering of the elect (see note on 24.22); see Isa 27.12–13; 1 Thess 4.16. Four winds, i.e., the whole world; see Ezek 37.9; Zech 2.6; Rev 7.1; Didache 10.5. **24.32–36** Cf. Mk 13.28–32; Lk 21.29–33. **24.33** You know that he is near. Cf. vv. 36, 48–50; 25.5. **24.34** Truly I tell you. See note on 5.18. This generation will not pass away. See 10.23; 16.28; cf. 24.36, 48; 25.5. **24.36** That day. See note on 7.22. Only the Father. Cf. 11.27. **24.37–44** Cf. Lk 17.26–27, 34–35; 12.39–40. The emphasis here is on the unexpectedness of the flood, which caught people unprepared. **24.40–41** Taken . . . left. Cf. Gospel of Thomas 61. Two. See note on 4.18–22. **24.42–44** Cf. Lk 12.39–40; 1 Thess 5.2; 2 Pet 3.10; Rev 3.3; 16.15; Gospel of Thomas 21; 103; Didache 16.1. **24.42** Keep awake. See 25.1–13; 26.36–46; 1 Thess 5.6–8. **24.43** The unexpectedness of a thief provides an apt metaphor for the coming of the Son of Man (see 1 Thess 5.2, 4; 2 Pet 3.10; Rev 3.3; 16.15). **24.45–51** Cf. Lk 12.42–46. An allegorically interpreted slave parable warns about a delay in Jesus' return. **24.46** Blessed. See note on 5.3. **24.47** Truly I tell you. See note on 5.18. **24.48** My master, lit. "my lord," Jesus (see note on 7.21). Delayed. See also 25.5, 19; 2 Pet 3.1–13. **24.50** An hour that he does not know. See vv. 36, 44; 25.13.

that he does not know. [51]He will cut him in pieces[a] and put him with the hypocrites, where there will be weeping and gnashing of teeth.

The Parable of the Ten Bridesmaids

25 "Then the kingdom of heaven will be like this. Ten bridesmaids[b] took their lamps and went to meet the bridegroom.[c] [2]Five of them were foolish, and five were wise. [3]When the foolish took their lamps, they took no oil with them; [4]but the wise took flasks of oil with their lamps. [5]As the bridegroom was delayed, all of them became drowsy and slept. [6]But at midnight there was a shout, 'Look! Here is the bridegroom! Come out to meet him.' [7]Then all those bridesmaids[b] got up and trimmed their lamps. [8]The foolish said to the wise, 'Give us some of your oil, for our lamps are going out.' [9]But the wise replied, 'No! there will not be enough for you and for us; you had better go to the dealers and buy some for yourselves.' [10]And while they went to buy it, the bridegroom came, and those who were ready went with him into the wedding banquet; and the door was shut. [11]Later the other bridesmaids[b] came also, saying, 'Lord, lord, open to us.' [12]But he replied, 'Truly I tell you, I do not know you.' [13]Keep awake therefore, for you know neither the day nor the hour.[d]

The Parable of the Talents

[14]"For it is as if a man, going on a journey, summoned his slaves and entrusted his property to them; [15]to one he gave five talents,[e] to another two, to another one, to each according to his ability. Then he went away. [16]The one who had received the five talents went off at once and traded with them, and made five more talents. [17]In the same way, the one who had the two talents made two more talents. [18]But the one who had received the one talent went off and dug a hole in the ground and hid his master's money. [19]After a long time the master of those slaves came and settled accounts with them. [20]Then the one who had received the five talents came forward, bringing five more talents, saying, 'Master, you handed over to me five talents; see, I have made five more talents.' [21]His master said to him, 'Well done, good and trustworthy slave; you have been trustworthy in a few things, I will put you in charge of many things; enter into the joy of your master.' [22]And the one with the two talents also came forward, saying, 'Master, you handed over to me two talents; see, I have made two more talents.' [23]His master said to him, 'Well done, good and trustworthy slave; you have been trustworthy in a few things, I will put you in charge of many things; enter into the joy of your master.' [24]Then the one who had received the one talent also came forward, saying, 'Master, I knew that you were a harsh man, reaping where you did not sow, and gathering where you did not scatter seed; [25]so I was afraid, and I went and hid your talent in the ground. Here you have what is yours.' [26]But his master replied, 'You wicked

---

a Or *cut him off*   *b* Gk *virgins*   *c* Other ancient authorities add *and the bride*   *d* Other ancient authorities add *in which the Son of Man is coming*   *e* A talent was worth more than fifteen years' wages of a laborer

---

24.51 *Cut him in pieces,* particularly savage imagery (see also 18.34). *With the hypocrites.* See, e.g., 23.29–33. *Weeping and gnashing of teeth.* See note on 8.12.

25.1–46 Three major parables about the coming (Greek *parousia*) of the Son of Man for final judgment. The first and third are found only in Matthew. **25.1–13** Parable of the ten bridesmaids, an allegory about readiness for the unexpected Parousia. **25.1** *Then,* at the Parousia (see 24.50). *Kingdom of heaven.* See note on 4.17. *Went to meet the bridegroom.* The setting is the return of the groom (with his new bride) to his father's house (see 22.2). The task of the bridesmaids (lit. *virgins,* text note *b*) is to welcome the bride and groom into the household; see note on 9.15. **25.5** *The bridegroom was delayed,* i.e., the delay of Jesus' return. See 24.36–51; 25.19. **25.6** *Midnight,* lit., "in the middle of the night," an unexpected time. **25.10** On the *wedding banquet* as a metaphor for the kingdom of heaven, see 22.1–10. *The door was shut.* See 22.11–14;

also 5.20; Lk 13.24–27. **25.11** *Lord, lord.* See 7.21–23. **25.12** *Truly I tell you.* See note on 5.18. **25.13** *Keep awake.* See note on 24.42. **25.14–30** Cf. Lk 19.12–27. Parable of the talents, an allegory for responsibility during the period before Jesus' return. **25.14** *Going on a journey.* The story suggests a temporary absence, as of the resurrected Son of Man. *Entrusted his property to them.* Household slaves often had positions of authority; see 24.45. **25.15** *Talent,* not human ability, but an unusually large amount of money (see text note *e*; 18.24). **25.16** *Traded with them.* The action suggests a willingness to take risks, possibly representing missionizing apostles (see 10.5–15). **25.18** *A hole in the ground,* a safe, risk-free way to save (see 13.44). *Master's,* lit. "lord's" (see note on 7.21). **25.19** *After a long time* suggests the delay of the Parousia (see 24.48; 25.5). *Settled accounts* suggests the last judgment (see 18.23). **25.21** *Enter into the joy of your master* suggests entering the kingdom (see vv. 10, 34).

and lazy slave! You knew, did you, that I reap where I did not sow, and gather where I did not scatter? 27Then you ought to have invested my money with the bankers, and on my return I would have received what was my own with interest. 28So take the talent from him, and give it to the one with the ten talents. 29For to all those who have, more will be given, and they will have an abundance; but from those who have nothing, even what they have will be taken away. 30As for this worthless slave, throw him into the outer darkness, where there will be weeping and gnashing of teeth.'

The Judgment of the Nations

31 "When the Son of Man comes in his glory, and all the angels with him, then he will sit on the throne of his glory. 32All the nations will be gathered before him, and he will separate people one from another as a shepherd separates the sheep from the goats, 33and he will put the sheep at his right hand and the goats at the left. 34Then the king will say to those at his right hand, 'Come, you that are blessed by my Father, inherit the kingdom prepared for you from the foundation of the world; 35for I was hungry and you gave me food, I was thirsty and you gave me something to drink, I was a stranger and you welcomed me, 36I was naked and you gave me clothing, I was sick and you took care of me, I was in prison and you visited me.' 37Then the righteous will answer him, 'Lord, when was it that we saw you hungry and gave

you food, or thirsty and gave you something to drink? 38And when was it that we saw you a stranger and welcomed you, or naked and gave you clothing? 39And when was it that we saw you sick or in prison and visited you?' 40And the king will answer them, 'Truly I tell you, just as you did it to one of the least of these who are members of my family,^{a} you did it to me.' 41Then he will say to those at his left hand, 'You that are accursed, depart from me into the eternal fire prepared for the devil and his angels; 42for I was hungry and you gave me no food, I was thirsty and you gave me nothing to drink, 43I was a stranger and you did not welcome me, naked and you did not give me clothing, sick and in prison and you did not visit me.' 44Then they also will answer, 'Lord, when was it that we saw you hungry or thirsty or a stranger or naked or sick or in prison, and did not take care of you?' 45Then he will answer them, 'Truly I tell you, just as you did not do it to one of the least of these, you did not do it to me.' 46And these will go away into eternal punishment, but the righteous into eternal life."

The Plot to Kill Jesus

26 When Jesus had finished saying all these things, he said to his disciples, 2"You know that after two days the Passover is coming, and the Son of Man will be handed over to be crucified."

---

a Gk these my brothers

25.29 See 13.12 (doublet). **25.30** *Weeping and gnashing of teeth.* See note on 8.12. **25.31–46** The criteria of the final judgment, the author's most powerful and dramatic ethical statement (vv. 35–36). **25.31** *When the Son of Man comes,* i.e., the Parousia (see note on 13.41; 16.27–28; 24.29–31). *The angels with him.* See Deut 33.2; Zech 14.5; note on 13.39. *Throne of his glory,* his glorious throne (see also 19.28; 26.64; Dan 7.13–14; Rev 3.21). **25.32** *Nations.* Greek *ethne* can mean groups of almost any kind, but especially "peoples" or "nations" (see also 24.9, 14; 28.19). It most often refers to groups other than one's own (see note on 1.1), thus also "Gentiles" (see 4.15; 6.32; 10.5, 18; 12.18, 21; 20.19, 25). The group is the object of missionary activity between the death of Jesus and his return (see 28.19; see also Isa 66.18; Rev 21.22–22.5). *Separate . . . sheep from the goats.* See Ezek 34.17–22; see note on 3.12. **25.33** *Right hand.* See note on 20.44. **25.34** In Jesus' parables the *king* usually represents God (see 18.23; 22.2), but here the king is the Son of Man (see note on 13.41; see also 21.5; 27.11; Rev 17.14). **25.35–36** The criteria are whether a person has performed works of mercy to those in great need in

the present world; cf. 9.13a. **25.37** *Righteous,* here those who innocently do good works (see 13.43; cf. 1.19). *Lord.* See note on 7.21. **25.40** *Truly I tell you.* See note on 5.18. *The least of these,* here probably believers (see 10.40–42; 18.6, 14). **25.41** *Prepared for the devil.* See Rev 20.10.

26.1–28.20 The passion and resurrection narratives follow the Markan outline and, like Mark, contain many allusions to the psalms of lament and to the suffering servant of Isa 52.13–53.12. **26.1–5** Cf. Mk 14.1–2; Lk 22.1–2; also cf. Jn 11.47–53. **26.1** *When Jesus had finished.* The closing formula to Jesus' fifth discourse (see note on 7.28). **26.2** *Passover,* a seven-day Israelite spring festival combined with the Feast of Unleavened Bread (see v. 17), celebrating the exodus from Egyptian slavery to freedom (see Ex 12.14–27; 34.18; see also note on 2.13–15). The term also refers especially to the period extending from the evening of the first day, the day of Preparation (27.62), when the lamb was slaughtered at the temple (Ex 12.6), to the ensuing evening when the meal was eaten, and to the meal itself (see 26.17). *Son of Man.* See notes on 8.20; 16.21–23. *Handed over,* or "betrayed," a key theme; see note on

3 Then the chief priests and the elders of the people gathered in the palace of the high priest, who was called Caiaphas, 4 and they conspired to arrest Jesus by stealth and kill him. 5 But they said, "Not during the festival, or there may be a riot among the people."

The Anointing at Bethany

6 Now while Jesus was at Bethany in the house of Simon the leper,*a* 7 a woman came to him with an alabaster jar of very costly ointment, and she poured it on his head as he sat at the table. 8 But when the disciples saw it, they were angry and said, "Why this waste? 9 For this ointment could have been sold for a large sum, and the money given to the poor." 10 But Jesus, aware of this, said to them, "Why do you trouble the woman? She has performed a good service for me. 11 For you always have the poor with you, but you will not always have me. 12 By pouring this ointment on my body she has prepared me for burial. 13 Truly I tell you, wherever this good news*b* is proclaimed in the whole world, what she has done will be told in remembrance of her."

Judas Agrees to Betray Jesus

14 Then one of the twelve, who was called Judas Iscariot, went to the chief priests 15 and said, "What will you give me if I betray him to you?" They paid him thirty pieces of silver. 16 And from that moment he began to look for an opportunity to betray him.

The Passover with the Disciples

17 On the first day of Unleavened Bread the disciples came to Jesus, saying, "Where do you want us to make the preparations for you to eat the Passover?" 18 He said, "Go into the city to a certain man, and say to him, 'The Teacher says, My time is near; I will keep the Passover at your house with my disciples.' " 19 So the disciples did as Jesus had directed them, and they prepared the Passover meal.

20 When it was evening, he took his place with the twelve;*c* 21 and while they were eating, he said, "Truly I tell you, one of you will betray me." 22 And they became greatly distressed and began to say to him one after another, "Surely not I, Lord?" 23 He answered, "The one who has dipped his hand into the bowl with me will betray me. 24 The Son of Man goes as it is written of him, but woe to that one by whom the Son of Man is betrayed! It would have been better for that one not to have been born." 25 Judas,

---

a The terms *leper* and *leprosy* can refer to several diseases
b Or *gospel*   *c* Other ancient authorities add *disciples*

10.4. **26.3** *Chief priests.* See notes on 2.4; 21.15. *Elders of the people.* See note on 16.21. The *palace* (lit. "courtyard"; cf. vv. 69–75) of *Caiaphas*, mentioned only in Matthew, is of uncertain location, but was probably in the wealthy quarter of the Upper City of Jerusalem. Caiaphas held the office of *high priest* from 18 to 36/7 CE (see vv. 57–66; Lk 3.2; Jn 11.49–53; Acts 4.6; Josephus, *Antiquities* 18.26, 35, 95), a lengthy term that suggests cooperation with the Romans. A family tomb with several chambers containing ossuaries (boxes for reburial of bones), including one with the inscription "Joseph son of Caiaphas" (i.e., Joseph Caiaphas; see Josephus, *Antiquities* 18.34), was discovered in the Peace Forest south of the old city of Jerusalem in 1990. It is probably the tomb of Caiaphas's family (called "Caiaphas's Tomb"). *Conspired.* Jerusalem authorities replace Pharisees in the plot (cf. 3.7; 12.14); *Festival,* e.g., Passover. **26.5** *Riots,* common at festivals (see 27.24; Josephus, *War* 1.88). **26.6–13** Cf. Mk 14.3–9; Lk 7.36–50; Jn 12.1–8. On women, see Introduction; note on 9.18–26. **26.6** *Bethany.* See note on 21.17. *Simon the leper,* otherwise unmentioned in Matthew, but see 8.2–4. **26.7** *Alabaster,* a soft cream-colored, marble-like stone. *Jar,* "flask" (archaeology). *Poured it on his head,* probably an act of hospitality (see Lk 7.46), but perhaps an allusion to the coronation ritual for a king (see note on 1.1; cf. 26.12). **26.9** On concern for the *poor,* see 19.21;

25.31–46; see note on 5.3; for social ranking in the Roman Empire, see Introduction. **26.11** *Always have the poor with you,* perhaps echoing Deut 15.11. **26.12** *Burial.* See 27.57–61. **26.13** *Truly I tell you.* See vv. 21, 29, 34; note on 5.18. *This good news* (see text note *b*) perhaps includes the author's written Gospel (see 24.14; see also 4.23; 9.35). *The whole world.* See 24.14; 28.19. The story (vv. 6–12) is *told in remembrance of her,* yet she is unnamed. **26.14–16** Cf. Mk 14.10–11; Lk 22.3–6; Jn 11.57. **26.14** *Judas Iscariot.* The betrayer's membership in the inner circle of the Twelve is emphasized (see 10.1–4; 26.20–25, 47–50). **26.15** *Betray.* See note on 17.22. *Thirty pieces of silver,* the value of an injured slave (Ex 21.32), but clearly an allusion to Zech 11.12–13 (see also Mt 27.3–10). **26.17–25** Cf. Mk 14.12–21; Lk 22.7–14, 21–23; Jn 13.21–26. **26.17** *First day,* the day of Preparation (see note on 26.2). *Unleavened Bread,* an alternate name for Passover. Leaven was left out of bread during the entire festival (see Ex 12.15–20; 13.3–10). **26.20** *The twelve.* See note on 10.1. **26.21** *Betray.* See note on 17.22. **26.22** *Lord.* See note on 7.21. **26.23** *Dipped.* The practice was common; it is mentioned here to emphasize that the betrayer broke the bond of those who eat together (see Ps 41.9). **26.24** *As is written of him.* The text referred to here is not known (cf. 16.21–23; Mk 8.31; see also Isa 52.13–53.12). *Woe,* here a curse oracle (see note on 11.21).

who betrayed him, said, "Surely not I, Rabbi?" He replied, "You have said so."

The Institution of the Lord's Supper

26 While they were eating, Jesus took a loaf of bread, and after blessing it he broke it, gave it to the disciples, and said, "Take, eat; this is my body." 27Then he took a cup, and after giving thanks he gave it to them, saying, "Drink from it, all of you; 28for this is my blood of the*a* covenant, which is poured out for many for the forgiveness of sins. 29I tell you, I will never again drink of this fruit of the vine until that day when I drink it new with you in my Father's kingdom."

30 When they had sung the hymn, they went out to the Mount of Olives.

Peter's Denial Foretold

31 Then Jesus said to them, "You will all become deserters because of me this night; for it is written,

'I will strike the shepherd,
    and the sheep of the flock will be
        scattered.'

32But after I am raised up, I will go ahead of you to Galilee." 33Peter said to him, "Though all become deserters because of you, I will never desert you." 34Jesus said to him, "Truly I tell you, this very night, before the cock crows, you will deny me three times." 35Peter said to him, "Even though I must die with you, I will not deny you." And so said all the disciples.

Jesus Prays in Gethsemane

36 Then Jesus went with them to a place called Gethsemane; and he said to his disciples, "Sit here while I go over there and pray." 37He took with him Peter and the two sons of Zebedee, and began to be grieved and agitated. 38Then he said to them, "I am deeply grieved, even to death; remain here, and stay awake with me." 39And going a little farther, he threw himself on the ground and prayed, "My Father, if it is possible, let this cup pass from me; yet not what I want but what you want." 40Then he came to the disciples and found them sleeping; and he said to Peter, "So, could you not stay awake with me one hour? 41Stay awake and pray that you may not come into the time of trial;*b* the spirit indeed is willing, but the flesh is weak." 42Again he went away for the second time and prayed, "My Father, if this cannot pass unless I drink it, your will be done." 43Again he came and found them sleeping, for their eyes were heavy. 44So leaving them again, he went away and prayed for the third time, saying the same words. 45Then he came to the disciples and said to them, "Are you still sleeping and taking your rest? See, the hour is at hand, and the Son of Man is betrayed into the hands of sinners. 46Get up, let us be going. See, my betrayer is at hand."

The Betrayal and Arrest of Jesus

47 While he was still speaking, Judas, one of the twelve, arrived; with him was a large crowd with swords and clubs, from the chief priests and the elders of the people. 48Now the betrayer had given them a sign, saying, "The one I will kiss is the man; arrest him." 49At once he

---

a Other ancient authorities add *new*   *b* Or *into temptation*

26.25 *Rabbi,* a title used of Jesus only by opponents and Judas (see v. 49; note on 23.7). *You have said so,* a cryptic answer probably meaning "yes," but with a qualification (see v. 64; 27.11). **26.26–30** Cf. Mk 14.22–26; Lk 22.15–20, 39; see also 1 Cor 11.23–25. **26.26** *Took bread . . . blessing . . . broke . . . gave,* the acts and words of the head of the household before Israelite meals and before the main meal at Passover (see also 14.19). *This is my body.* See 1 Cor 10.16–17. **26.28** Israelites were forbidden to drink *blood* (see Lev 17.10–14; Acts 15.20), but blood was used to ratify a *covenant* (see Ex 24.6–8; Zech 9.11; see also Jer 31.31–34). *Poured out for many* denotes a view of Jesus' death as sacrificial atonement (see Lev 16.21; Isa 53.10–12; Mk 10.45; Rom 3.25; 5.9; *Didache* 14.1 for the Eucharist as sacrifice). *Forgiveness of sins.* See 1.21; 6.12, 14–15; 9.6; 18.21–35. **26.29** *That day,* i.e., of the future messianic banquet (see note on 8.11). **26.30** *The hymn,* probably from the Hallel (see note on 21.9). *Mount of Olives.* See note on 24.3.

26.31–35 Cf. Mk 14.27–31; Lk 22.31–34; Jn 13.36–38. **26.31** *All become deserters.* See v. 56; see also note on 13.21. The quotation is from Zech 13.7; see also Isa 53.6. **26.32** The prediction is restated in 28.7, fulfilled in 28.16–20. **26.34** The prediction is fulfilled in vv. 69–75. On three denials, see note on 1.2–6a. **26.36–46** Cf. Mk 14.32–42; Lk 22.40–46; see also Jn 18.1. **26.36** *Gethsemane* (Hebrew for "oil press"), an unknown site somewhere on the west side of the Mount of Olives (see v. 30). **26.37** *Peter and . . . two sons of Zebedee.* See notes on 4.21; 17.1. **26.38** *Stay awake.* See 24.42; 25.13; 26.40–41. *This cup.* See note on 20.22. **26.40** *Sleeping.* See also vv. 43, 45. **26.41** *Time of trial.* See 6.13. **26.42** *Your will be done.* See 6.10. **26.45** *The Son of Man is betrayed.* See notes on 8.20; 10.4. **26.47–56** Cf. Mk 14.43–50; Lk 22.47–53; Jn 18.3–11. **26.47** *A large crowd,* here obviously hostile (see note on 4.25). *Chief priests . . . elders of the people.* See v. 3. **26.48** *Kiss,* a form of greeting; cf. Lk 15.20. **26.49** *Rabbi.* See note on

came up to Jesus and said, "Greetings, Rabbi!" and kissed him. 50Jesus said to him, "Friend, do what you are here to do." Then they came and laid hands on Jesus and arrested him. 51Suddenly, one of those with Jesus put his hand on his sword, drew it, and struck the slave of the high priest, cutting off his ear. 52Then Jesus said to him, "Put your sword back into its place; for all who take the sword will perish by the sword. 53Do you think that I cannot appeal to my Father, and he will at once send me more than twelve legions of angels? 54But how then would the scriptures be fulfilled, which say it must happen in this way?" 55At that hour Jesus said to the crowds, "Have you come out with swords and clubs to arrest me as though I were a bandit? Day after day I sat in the temple teaching, and you did not arrest me. 56But all this has taken place, so that the scriptures of the prophets may be fulfilled." Then all the disciples deserted him and fled.

Jesus before the High Priest

57 Those who had arrested Jesus took him to Caiaphas the high priest, in whose house the scribes and the elders had gathered. 58But Peter was following him at a distance, as far as the courtyard of the high priest; and going inside, he sat with the guards in order to see how this would end. 59Now the chief priests and the whole council were looking for false testimony against Jesus so that they might put him to death, 60but they found none, though many

false witnesses came forward. At last two came forward 61and said, "This fellow said, 'I am able to destroy the temple of God and to build it in three days.' " 62The high priest stood up and said, "Have you no answer? What is it that they testify against you?" 63But Jesus was silent. Then the high priest said to him, "I put you under oath before the living God, tell us if you are the Messiah,a the Son of God." 64Jesus said to him, "You have said so. But I tell you,

> From now on you will see the Son of Man
> seated at the right hand of Power
> and coming on the clouds of heaven."

65Then the high priest tore his clothes and said, "He has blasphemed! Why do we still need witnesses? You have now heard his blasphemy. 66What is your verdict?" They answered, "He deserves death." 67Then they spat in his face and struck him; and some slapped him, 68saying, "Prophesy to us, you Messiah!a Who is it that struck you?"

Peter's Denial of Jesus

69 Now Peter was sitting outside in the courtyard. A servant-girl came to him and said, "You also were with Jesus the Galilean." 70But he denied it before all of them, saying, "I do not know what you are talking about." 71When he went out to the porch, another servant-girl saw him, and she said to the bystanders, "This man was with Jesus of Nazareth."b 72Again he denied it with an oath, "I do

---

a Or Christ   b Gk the Nazorean

26.25. **26.50** *Friend,* probably sarcastic (see 20.13; 22.12; note on 26.23). **26.51** The *one* with Jesus is apparently a disciple (cf. Mk 14.47; Jn 18.10). **26.53** *Twelve legions.* A Roman legion was 6,000 infantry plus 120 cavalry. The saying reflects the myth of the warrior God leading heavenly angelic armies (see, e.g., 2 Kings 6.15–17; Ps 24.8–10; Rev 19.14). **26.55** *Bandit,* or rebel leader (see notes on 2.2; 10.4; 24.24; 27.35; 27.38). **26.56** The thirteenth quotation formula (see note on 1.22–23) does not introduce a specific text. *All the disciples . . . fled.* See v. 31. **26.57–68** Cf. Mk 14.53–65; Lk 22.54–55, 63–71; Jn 18.13–24. **26.57** *Caiaphas.* See note on 26.3; cf. Jn 18.12–14, 24. *Scribes.* See note on 2.4. *Elders.* See v. 3; note on 16.21. **26.59** *The whole council,* lit. "the Sanhedrin," a supreme Israelite court to handle internal affairs, controlled by priests. The session described here raises many questions, because trials during Passover, night trials, and single sessions for capital offenses were forbidden by Israelite law codified about 200 CE. Moreover, capital punishment may have been illegal for Jews to perform in Jesus' day (see also 27.2; note on Jn 18.31). **26.60** *Two*

witnesses were required by Israelite law (see note on 18.16). **26.61** See 24.2; 27.40. *In three days,* hinting at Jesus' resurrection (see also 12.40; 16.21). See note on 1.2–6a. **26.63** *Silent.* See Isa 53.7; 1 Pet 2.22–23. *Messiah.* See note on 1.1. *Son of God.* See note on 3.17. **26.64** *You have said so* replaces Mark's "I am" (14.62). See note on 26.25; 27.11. The vision of the *Son of Man* derives from Dan 7.13–14 (see Mt 24.30; note on 8.20). *Seated at the right hand of Power* (i.e., of God). For believers, this was the place of the resurrected, exalted Messiah (see Ps 110.1; see also Acts 2.32–36; 7.56; Rom 8.34; Eph 1.20; Col 3.1; Heb 1.3, 13; 8.1; 10.12). *Coming,* i.e., for the final judgment (see 24.29–31). **26.65** *Tore his clothes,* a gesture of distress (see 2 Kings 18.37–19.3; Acts 14.14). *Blasphemy,* normally dishonoring God's name (see note on 12.31–32), here used loosely to describe Jesus' messianic affirmation. **26.66** *Death,* the punishment for blasphemy (see Lev 24.10–23). **26.67** See Isa 50.6. **26.69–75** Cf. Mk 14.66–72; Lk 22.55–62; Jn 18.25–27. **26.69** *Peter,* the representative disciple (see note on 14.28). **26.71** *Jesus of Nazareth.* See 2.23; 21.11. **26.72** The *oath* suggests

not know the man." [73]After a little while the bystanders came up and said to Peter, "Certainly you are also one of them, for your accent betrays you." [74]Then he began to curse, and he swore an oath, "I do not know the man!" At that moment the cock crowed. [75]Then Peter remembered what Jesus had said: "Before the cock crows, you will deny me three times." And he went out and wept bitterly.

Jesus Brought before Pilate

27 When morning came, all the chief priests and the elders of the people conferred together against Jesus in order to bring about his death. [2]They bound him, led him away, and handed him over to Pilate the governor.

The Suicide of Judas

[3] When Judas, his betrayer, saw that Jesus[a] was condemned, he repented and brought back the thirty pieces of silver to the chief priests and the elders. [4]He said, "I have sinned by betraying innocent[b] blood." But they said, "What is that to us? See to it yourself." [5]Throwing down the pieces of silver in the temple, he departed; and he went and hanged himself. [6]But the chief priests, taking the pieces of silver, said, "It is not lawful to put them into the treasury, since they are blood money." [7]After conferring together, they used them to buy the potter's field as a place to bury foreigners. [8]For this reason that field has been called the Field

of Blood to this day. [9]Then was fulfilled what had been spoken through the prophet Jeremiah,[c] "And they took[d] the thirty pieces of silver, the price of the one on whom a price had been set,[e] on whom some of the people of Israel had set a price, [10]and they gave[f] them for the potter's field, as the Lord commanded me."

Pilate Questions Jesus

[11] Now Jesus stood before the governor; and the governor asked him, "Are you the King of the Jews?" Jesus said, "You say so." [12]But when he was accused by the chief priests and elders, he did not answer. [13]Then Pilate said to him, "Do you not hear how many accusations they make against you?" [14]But he gave him no answer, not even to a single charge, so that the governor was greatly amazed.

Barabbas or Jesus?

[15] Now at the festival the governor was accustomed to release a prisoner for the crowd, anyone whom they wanted. [16]At that time they had a notorious prisoner, called Jesus[g] Barabbas. [17]So after they had gathered, Pilate said to them, "Whom do you want me to release for you, Jesus[g] Barabbas or Jesus who is called the Messiah?"[h] [18]For he realized that it

---

a Gk *he*   *b* Other ancient authorities read *righteous*   *c* Other ancient authorities read *Zechariah* or *Isaiah*   *d* Or *I took*   *e* Or *the price of the precious One*   *f* Other ancient authorities read *I gave*   *g* Other ancient authorities lack *Jesus*   *h* Or *the Christ*

Peter's dishonesty (on oaths, see 5.33–37; 23.16–22; cf. 26.63). **26.75** *What Jesus had said.* See note on 26.34.
   27.1–2 Cf. Mk 15.1; Lk 22.66; 23.1; Jn 18.28. **27.1** *Chief priests and the elders.* See 26.3. **27.2** *Pilate* was the fifth Roman *governor* of the province of Judea (26–36 CE). A Latin inscription discovered in 1961 at Caesarea by the Sea, his headquarters in Palestine, shows that Pontius Pilate, "prefect of Judea" (procurator was a later title), dedicated a temple to honor the emperor Tiberius (14–37 CE). Prefects who came to Jerusalem at festival times normally stayed in Herod's palace along the western wall; cf. notes on 27.24–26; 27.27. On capital punishment, see note on Jn 18.31. **27.3–10** The story of Judas's suicide is found only in Matthew in the gospels and is based on several OT texts; cf. Acts 1.18–20 for a nonsuicide story. **27.3** *Thirty pieces of silver,* alluding to Zech 11.12–13; see note on 26.15. **27.4** Shedding *innocent blood* pollutes the land and brings "bloodguilt" on the people (see Num 35.33–34; Deut 19.10). Cf. note on 23.35. **27.5** *Throwing down the . . . silver,* an allusion to Zech 11.13 (see also Mt 27.6). *Hanged himself.* Cf. Acts 1.18; see Deut 21.23.

27.7 *Potter's field.* Cf. Acts 1.18. **27.8** *Field of Blood,* Hakeldama (cf. note on Acts 1.18–19), in the Valley of Hinnom (cf. note on 5.22). **27.9–10** The fourteenth quotation formula (see note on 1.22–23) introduces a text based loosely on Zech 11.13. *Jeremiah* is inaccurately mentioned as the source (see text note *c*), but the name is probably suggested by Jeremiah's purchase of land (Jer 32.6–15) and visit to the potter (Jer 18.1–3; 19.1–13). **27.11–14** Cf. Mk 15.2–5; Lk 23.2–3; Jn 18.29–38. Cf. note on 27.24–26. **27.11** *Before the governor.* See 10.18–20. To claim the title *King of the Jews* (see also 2.2), corresponding roughly to "Messiah" (see note on 1.1), would be treasonable (see notes on 2.2; 4.17). *You say so.* See notes on 26.25; 26.64. **27.14** *No answer.* See 26.63; Isa 53.7. *Greatly amazed.* See Isa 52.14–15. **27.15–23** Cf. Mk 15.6–14; Lk 23.18–23; Jn 18.39–40. **27.15** *Festival,* Passover (see 26.2). *Release . . . anyone . . . they wanted.* Evidence for such a custom is weak at best (see Josephus, *Antiquities* 20.215). **27.16** *Jesus Barabbas.* The author may have seen heavy irony in the name, which means in Aramaic "Jesus, son of the father" (cf. text note *g*). **27.17** *Messiah.* See note on 1.1.

was out of jealousy that they had handed him over. [19]While he was sitting on the judgment seat, his wife sent word to him, "Have nothing to do with that innocent man, for today I have suffered a great deal because of a dream about him." [20]Now the chief priests and the elders persuaded the crowds to ask for Barabbas and to have Jesus killed. [21]The governor again said to them, "Which of the two do you want me to release for you?" And they said, "Barabbas." [22]Pilate said to them, "Then what should I do with Jesus who is called the Messiah?" [a] All of them said, "Let him be crucified!" [23]Then he asked, "Why, what evil has he done?" But they shouted all the more, "Let him be crucified!"

Pilate Hands Jesus over to Be Crucified

24 So when Pilate saw that he could do nothing, but rather that a riot was beginning, he took some water and washed his hands before the crowd, saying, "I am innocent of this man's blood; [b] see to it yourselves." [25]Then the people as a whole answered, "His blood be on us and on our children!" [26]So he released Barabbas for them; and after flogging Jesus, he handed him over to be crucified.

The Soldiers Mock Jesus

27 Then the soldiers of the governor took Jesus into the governor's headquarters, [c] and they gathered the whole cohort around him. [28]They stripped him and put a scarlet robe on him, [29]and after twisting some thorns into a crown, they put it on his head. They put a reed in his right hand and knelt before him and mocked him, saying, "Hail, King of the Jews!" [30]They spat on him, and took the reed and struck him on the head. [31]After mocking him, they stripped him of the robe and put his own clothes on him. Then they led him away to crucify him.

The Crucifixion of Jesus

32 As they went out, they came upon a man from Cyrene named Simon; they compelled this man to carry his cross. [33]And when they came to a place called Golgotha (which means Place of a Skull), [34]they offered him wine to drink, mixed with gall; but when he tasted it, he would not drink it. [35]And when they had

---

a Or *the Christ* *b* Other ancient authorities read *this righteous blood*, or *this righteous man's blood* *c* Gk *the praetorium*

27.19 *Judgment seat*, a raised platform where magistrates judged (see also Jn 19.13; Acts 12.21). Only Matthew contains the tradition about Pilate's *wife*. *Innocent man*, lit. "righteous man." See Isa 53.8–9; notes on 1.19; 23.35. A *dream* often communicates a divine revelation (see 1.20); thus, Pilate's wife seems to be portrayed somewhat positively. **27.20** *Crowds*. See note on 4.25. **27.22** *Crucified*. See note on 27.35. **27.24–26** Cf. Mk 15.15; Lk 23.24–25; Jn 19.16. The author's insertion diminishes Pilate's legal liability. In the Gospels Pilate vacillates but is more positively portrayed than the Israelite leaders (e.g., v. 25); he is progressively exonerated in early church literature (e.g., *Gospel of Peter*; Tertullian, *Apology* 21.24; *Acts of Pilate*), ending up as a saint in the Coptic and Ethiopian churches. In contrast, ancient Israelite accounts accuse him of corruption, rape, murder, and contempt for the people of Israel (Philo, *Embassy to Gaius*; Josephus, *Antiquities* 18.55–62); cf. also Lk 13.1. The Roman Tacitus (*Annals* 15.44) mentions Jesus' death under Pilate. Cf. note on 27.2. **27.24** *Riot*. See note on 26.5. *Washed his hands*. See Deut 21.6–7; Pss 26.6; 73.13. **27.25** *The people as a whole*, more inclusive than the *crowd* (v. 24). *His blood be on us and on our children*. This familiar formula for accepting responsibility for a death (see Lev 20.9–16; 2 Sam 1.16; Jer 26.15) climaxes the author's condemnation of Israel (see also 21.43; 22.7; 23.29–36). **27.26** *Flogging* was done as punishment (see 10.17; Acts 5.40; 16.22–23; 22.24–25; 2 Cor 11.23) or to weaken a person prior to crucifixion (see also

20.19; Isa 50.6). Romans used a whip of knotted cord or leather, sometimes weighted with sharp bone or metal. **27.27–31** Cf. Mk 15.16–20; Jn 19.2–3. **27.27** The location of the *governor's headquarters* (Latin *praetorium*; see text note *c*) is uncertain, but it could have been Herod's palace (cf. v. 2) or the Antonia Fortress next to the temple (Roman troops were garrisoned there). The Roman *cohort* was the tenth part of a legion. In Palestine it comprised 760 infantry and 240 cavalry. **27.28** *Scarlet robe*, a cape indicating a Roman officer's rank, here mimicking a royal purple robe (cf. Mk 15.17; Jn 19.2). **27.29** *Reed in his right hand*, mimicking a royal scepter (see, e.g., Gen 49.10). *Knelt before him.* Cf. 2.11. *King of the Jews.* See note on 27.11. **27.30** *Spat*, a universal act of disrespect (see Num 12.14; Deut 25.9; Isa 50.6). **27.31** *Mocking*. See 20.19; Ps 22.7; see also Ps 69.19–20. **27.32–44** Cf. Mk 15.21–32; Lk 23.26–43; Jn 19.17–27. The crucifixion is described using the language of Pss 22; 69. **27.32** *Cyrene*, capital city of the Roman province of Cyrenaica (modern Libya); see Acts 2.10; 6.9; 11.20; 13.1. *Simon*, otherwise unknown. **27.33** *Golgotha* (Latin *calvaria*) means "skull," not "Place of a Skull" (see Lk 23.33), perhaps a small hill resembling a skull outside the city wall (Jn 19.20; Heb 13.12–13; see also note on Mt 21.39). The traditional site is now within the expanded city wall in the Church of the Holy Sepulchre. **27.34** *Gall*, a bitter and poisonous herb (see Ps 69.21). **27.35** *Crucified*. Crucifixion was a slow, painful execution by binding or nailing a victim to a cross, stake, or

crucified him, they divided his clothes among themselves by casting lots;[a] 36then they sat down there and kept watch over him. 37Over his head they put the charge against him, which read, "This is Jesus, the King of the Jews."

38 Then two bandits were crucified with him, one on his right and one on his left. 39Those who passed by derided[b] him, shaking their heads 40and saying, "You who would destroy the temple and build it in three days, save yourself! If you are the Son of God, come down from the cross." 41In the same way the chief priests also, along with the scribes and elders, were mocking him, saying, 42"He saved others; he cannot save himself.[c] He is the King of Israel; let him come down from the cross now, and we will believe in him. 43He trusts in God; let God deliver him now, if he wants to; for he said, 'I am God's Son.' " 44The bandits who were crucified with him also taunted him in the same way.

The Death of Jesus

45 From noon on, darkness came over the whole land[d] until three in the afternoon. 46And about three o'clock Jesus cried with a loud voice, "Eli, Eli, lema sabachthani?" that is, "My God, my God, why have you forsaken me?" 47When some of the bystanders heard it, they said, "This man is calling for Elijah." 48At once one of them ran and got a sponge, filled it with sour wine, put it on a stick, and gave it to him to drink. 49But the others said, "Wait, let us see whether Elijah will come to save him."[e] 50Then Jesus cried again with a loud voice and breathed his last.[f] 51At that moment the curtain of the temple was torn in two, from top to bottom. The earth shook, and the rocks were split. 52The tombs also were opened, and many bodies of the saints who had fallen asleep were raised. 53After his resurrection they came out of the tombs and entered the holy city and appeared to many. 54Now when the centurion and those with him, who were keeping watch over Jesus, saw the earthquake and what took place, they were terrified and said, "Truly this man was God's Son!"[g]

55 Many women were also there, looking on from a distance; they had followed Jesus from Galilee and had provided for him. 56Among them were Mary Magdalene, and Mary the mother of James and Joseph, and the mother of the sons of Zebedee.

---

a Other ancient authorities add in order that what had been spoken through the prophet might be fulfilled, "They divided my clothes among themselves, and for my clothing they cast lots." b Or blasphemed c Or is he unable to save himself? d Or earth e Other ancient authorities add And another took a spear and pierced his side, and out came water and blood f Or gave up his spirit g Or a son of God

---

tree. It was adopted by the Romans especially for those convicted of violent crime, slave revolt, army desertion, or rebellion against the state. In 1968, a heel bone with a spike through it was discovered in a burial cave ossuary of a certain Jehohanan in a north Jerusalem suburb; it is the only surviving first-century Palestinian evidence for crucifixion. *They divided his clothes . . . by casting lots.* See Ps 22.18. **27.36** *Kept watch.* See v. 54. **27.37** *The charge* was customarily put over the head of the victim as a deterrent to others. *King of the Jews* suggests seditious activity (see notes on 2.2; 4.17; 14.5; 26.55; 27.11), but contains a different, ironic truth for Christ-believers. **27.38** *Bandits* (see also 21.13; 26.55), perhaps rebel leaders (see notes on 2.2; 10.4; 26.55; 27.35; see also Isa 53.12). *Two.* See note on 4.18–22. **27.39** *Shaking their heads,* a gesture of derision (see Ps 22.7; see also Ps 109.25; Lam 2.15). **27.40** *You who would destroy the temple.* Cf. 26.61. *If you are the Son of God.* See 3.17; 4.3, 6; 26.63. *Three.* See note on 1.2 –6a. **27.41** *Chief priests . . . scribes . . . elders.* See 2.4; 16.21; 21.15; 23.13–36; 26.3, 57. **27.42** *He saved others.* See 1.21. *King of Israel,* the Israelite form of "King of the Jews" (cf. 2.2; 27.29, 37; see also Jn 1.49; 12.13). **27.43** *Let God deliver him.* See Ps 22.8; Wis 2.18. **27.45–56** Cf. Mk 15.33–41; Lk 23.44–49; Jn 19.25–30. **27.45** *Dark-* ness, for Amos a sign of the "day of the LORD" (see Am 5.18–20; 8.9). **27.46** Jesus' cry, given in transliteration of Hebrew (Mk 15.34, of Aramaic), is from Ps 22.1. *Eli,* a link with v. 47. **27.47** *Elijah.* See notes on 3.4; 27.46. **27.48** *Sour wine,* the cheap wine of the lower social classes; also an allusion to Ps 69.21. **27.49** According to popular Israelite belief, Elijah was the helper of the oppressed. **27.51** *Curtain,* probably the veil that hung at the entrance of the "most holy place" of the temple (Ex 26.31–35), where the divine presence dwelt. *Torn in two,* probably symbolizing access to God for all (see Heb 9.1–14; 10.19–22). **27.52** *Tombs . . . were opened,* foreshadowing the general resurrection. *Saints,* lit. "holy ones," is the usual term for Christ-believers (see Rom 15.25–26; 1 Cor 1.2). Here perhaps it refers to devout Israelites (see Ezek 37.12). *Fallen asleep,* i.e., died (see, e.g., 1 Cor 15.20). **27.54** *Centurion.* See note on 8.5. *God's Son.* See text note g; note on 3.17. **27.55** *Many women,* not heretofore mentioned (see notes on 9.18–26; 20.20; see also 27.61; 28.1–11). *Provided.* See Lk 8.1–3. **27.56** *Mary Magdalene,* i.e., from Magdala (see note on 15.39; see also 27.61; 28.1; Lk 8.2; Jn 20.1–18). *Mary.* See v. 61; 28.1. *James and Joseph,* probably not Jesus' brothers (but cf. 13.55); if so, the identity of this Mary is unknown. *Mother of the sons of Zebedee.* See 20.20.

The Burial of Jesus

57 When it was evening, there came a rich man from Arimathea, named Joseph, who was also a disciple of Jesus. 58 He went to Pilate and asked for the body of Jesus; then Pilate ordered it to be given to him. 59 So Joseph took the body and wrapped it in a clean linen cloth 60 and laid it in his own new tomb, which he had hewn in the rock. He then rolled a great stone to the door of the tomb and went away. 61 Mary Magdalene and the other Mary were there, sitting opposite the tomb.

The Guard at the Tomb

62 The next day, that is, after the day of Preparation, the chief priests and the Pharisees gathered before Pilate 63 and said, "Sir, we remember what that impostor said while he was still alive, 'After three days I will rise again.' 64 Therefore command the tomb to be made secure until the third day; otherwise his disciples may go and steal him away, and tell the people, 'He has been raised from the dead,' and the last deception would be worse than the first." 65 Pilate said to them, "You have a guard*a* of soldiers; go, make it as secure as you can."*b* 66 So they went with the guard and made the tomb secure by sealing the stone.

The Resurrection of Jesus

28 After the sabbath, as the first day of the week was dawning, Mary Magdalene and the other Mary went to see the tomb. 2 And suddenly there was a great earthquake; for an angel of the Lord, descending from heaven, came and rolled back the stone and sat on it. 3 His appearance was like lightning, and his clothing white as snow. 4 For fear of him the guards shook and became like dead men. 5 But the angel said to the women, "Do not be afraid; I know that you are looking for Jesus who was crucified. 6 He is not here; for he has been raised, as he said. Come, see the place where he*c* lay. 7 Then go quickly and tell his disciples, 'He has been raised from the dead,*d* and indeed he is going ahead of you to Galilee; there you will see him.' This is my message for you." 8 So they left the tomb quickly with fear and great joy, and ran to tell his disciples. 9 Suddenly Jesus met them and said, "Greetings!" And they came to him, took hold of his feet, and worshiped him. 10 Then Jesus said to them, "Do not be afraid; go and tell my brothers to go to Galilee; there they will see me."

The Report of the Guard

11 While they were going, some of the guard went into the city and told the chief priests everything that had happened. 12 After the priests*e* had assembled with the elders, they devised a plan to give a large sum of money to the soldiers, 13 telling them, "You must say, 'His

a Or Take a guard　*b* Gk you know how　*c* Other ancient authorities read the Lord　*d* Other ancient authorities lack from the dead　*e* Gk they

---

27.57–61 Cf. Mk 15.42–47; Lk 23.50–56; Jn 19.38–42. 27.57 Rich man. Cf. 19.24; see Isa 53.9. Arimathea, a Israelite town twenty miles east of Joppa (modern Jaffa). Joseph, the only named individual apart from the Twelve who is explicitly called a disciple (see 10.2–4; cf. 26.6; 27.55–56; 28.1). 27.58 The body of an executed person was not to remain exposed overnight (see Deut 21.22–23; for "hung on a tree" interpreted with reference to Jesus' crucifixion, cf. Gal 3.13). 27.59 Linen cloth. Israelites did not mummify, but washed, anointed, perfumed, and clothed the body (see 2 Chr 16.14; Jn 19.40). 27.61 Mary Magdalene and . . . Mary. See note on 27.56. 27.62–66 With 28.11–15, a defense against the charge that Jesus' body was stolen. 27.62 The day of Preparation, i.e., for the sabbath (see 28.1; Mk 15.42; Jn 19.31), not for Passover (see 26.2). The Pharisees reenter the narrative (see Introduction; notes on 3.7; 12.14; 26.3). Pilate. See vv. 2, 24–26. 27.63 After three days I will rise again. See 16.21; 17.23; 20.19; see also 12.40. 27.64 Ironically, the last deception is the opponents' (see 28.11–15; see also note on 28.13). 27.65 Guard, probably the temple police, under the high priest's command (see 28.11; Lk 22.4, 52; Jn 18.3, 12, 22).

28.1–10 Cf. Mk 16.1–8; Lk 24.1–12; Jn 20.1–18. 28.1 Mary Magdalene and the other Mary. See note on 27.56; 27.61. 28.2 The great earthquake highlights the end-time character of this event (see 24.7; 27.51, 54; Rev 6.12; 11.13; 16.18; see also Ex 19.18; 1 Kings 19.11). Angel. See also 1.20; 2.13, 19; 4.11; 13.39; 16.27; 18.10; 22.30; 24.31; 25.31; 26.53; cf. Mk 16.5. 28.3 White, the color of heavenly garments (see 17.2; Jn 20.12; Acts 1.10; Rev 19.14). 28.5 Do not be afraid. Cf. v. 10; also Gen 15.1; Lk 1.30. 28.6 As he said. See 16.21. 28.7 He is going ahead of you to Galilee. See 26.32; fulfilled in 28.16–20. 28.8 And ran to tell his disciples. Cf. Mk 16.8. 28.9 The two Marys are the first witnesses to Jesus' resurrection (see Jn 20.11–18; cf. Lk 24.13–35; 1 Cor 15.4–8). Worshiped him. See note on 2.2; see also 14.33; 28.17. 28.10 Do not be afraid. See v. 5. My brothers, the disciples (see v. 7; notes on 12.49; 18.15). 28.11–15 See note on 27.62–66. 28.11 Chief priests. See note on 26.3. 28.12 Money. See 6.19–24. 28.13 The real "deception" (see note on 27.64).

disciples came by night and stole him away while we were asleep.' [14]If this comes to the governor's ears, we will satisfy him and keep you out of trouble." [15]So they took the money and did as they were directed. And this story is still told among the Jews to this day.

The Commissioning of the Disciples

[16] Now the eleven disciples went to Galilee, to the mountain to which Jesus had directed them. [17]When they saw him, they worshiped him; but some doubted. [18]And Jesus came and said to them, "All authority in heaven and on earth has been given to me. [19]Go therefore and make disciples of all nations, baptizing them in the name of the Father and of the Son and of the Holy Spirit, [20]and teaching them to obey everything that I have commanded you. And remember, I am with you always, to the end of the age."[a]

_____

a Other ancient authorities add *Amen*

28.15 *To this day.* The story was in circulation when the Gospel was written (see also 26.13; 27.8). **28.16–20** The concluding episode highlights prominent Matthean themes. **28.16** *Eleven,* the Twelve minus Judas (see 27.3–10; note on 10.1; Acts 1.12–26). *Galilee.* See 26.32; 28.7, 10. *Mountain.* See note on 4.8. **28.17** *Worshiped him.* See 2.2; 28.9. *But some doubted.* The mixed response is typical of the disciples (see 14.31–33); cf. Jn 20.24–29. **28.18** *All authority . . . given to me,* an echo of the Son of Man tradition in Dan 7.13–14 (see note on 8.20). **28.19–20** New functions for the Eleven (cf. 10.1, 5–8; 15.24). **28.19** *All nations.* See notes on 1.1; 25.32; see also 24.9, 14; 26.13. Emphases elsewhere in the Gospel suggest the translation "all Gentiles" here (see, e.g., 2.1–12; 3.9; 4.15; 8.10; 15.21–28; 21.28–22.10 [esp. 21.43]; 27.25). *Baptizing.* Baptism in the early churches derives from John the Baptist (see 3.11; Acts 11.16). *The Father and . . . the Son and . . . the Holy Spirit.* This explicit trinitarian formula is rare in the NT and probably derives from early worship in the Matthean church; see *Didache* 7.1. **28.20** *Teaching.* Heretofore in Matthew only Jesus teaches (see 7.28–29; 23.8). *I am with you,* probably in fulfillment of 1.23 (see also 18.20). *To the end of the age,* i.e., to the coming of Jesus as the Son of Man for judgment (see chs. 24–25).

The Gospel According to
MARK

THE GOSPEL ACCORDING TO MARK was probably the first Gospel to be written. It is thus the first narrative interpretation of the oral proclamation of the "good news" and the first extended narrative presentation of the traditions about Jesus.

Authorship

THE EARLIEST REFERENCE TO MARK is a statement of Papias, written in the early second century CE, but surviving only in a quotation by Eusebius (*Ecclesiastical History* 3.39). Papias says that Mark was the interpreter of Peter and that he wrote down what Peter said, accurately but not in order. Some modern scholars accept this tradition as reliable. Many of these identify the "Mark" mentioned by Papias with the "John Mark" of Acts 12.12, 25; 15.37–39 and with the "Mark" of Col 4.10; Philem 24; 2 Tim 4.11; 1 Pet 5.13. Others argue that this Gospel was written anonymously, like the other canonical Gospels, and only attributed to Mark in the second century. Since the name "Mark" was not uncommon in the first century, it is uncertain whether all the references given here refer to the same person. Nevertheless, it is likely that those who first copied this Gospel for circulation knew who the author was and that therefore the traditional name of the author is reliable.

Setting, Date, and Occasion

THE TEXT DOES NOT PROVIDE clear evidence of the place of writing or of the audience. An old Latin preface to Mark states that it was written in the regions of Italy. Clement of Alexandria, according to Eusebius, wrote that Mark was written in Rome for the Christian community there (*Ecclesiastical History* 6.14.5–6). John Chrysostom says that Mark was written in Egypt (*Homilies on Matthew* 1.7). Some modern scholars conclude that Mark was written in Rome, citing the tradition about Mark's relationship with Peter and the influence of Latin on Mark's Greek as well as Christian tradition. Others locate the composition in Palestine or Syria because of the many references to localities in Syro-Palestine and the interest in Jerusalem and the Jewish war. These scholars attribute the influence of Latin to Roman cultural presence in the region. The use of Aramaic terms and whole sentences, along with translations of these in Greek, suggests that the author was aware that some in his intended audience knew Aramaic and some did not. It is clear from ch. 13 that Mark was written during or soon after the first

Jewish war with Rome, which began in 66 CE and reached its climax in the destruction of the temple in 70 CE. The occasion of the Gospel may well have been that war and the appearance of Jewish claimants to the role of Messiah. In that situation the author wished to reassert and interpret the claim of Jesus' followers that he was and is the Messiah.

Sources

THE SOURCES USED IN COMPOSING MARK are difficult to discern. The author was surely familiar with oral traditions about Jesus. He may have used a written collection of anecdotes or pronouncement stories in writing ch. 2 and one or two collections of parables in 4.1–34. It is likely that he used two collections of miracle stories in composing 4.35–8.26 and a written account of the Passion of Jesus in 14.32–15.38.

Style, Composition, and Conclusion

THE STYLE OF MARK is simple and effective. The simplicity of the style may be an indication of the level of education of the author or of the intended audience or both. Sentences and even paragraphs are often connected with a simple "and," and the narrative is episodic. The most coherent portion is the passion narrative. Although no consensus exists on the structure of the Gospel as a whole, interpreters agree that the central section (8.27–10.52) is carefully composed. The pattern of passion prediction (8.31; 9.31; 10.33–34), inappropriate response on the part of the disciples (8.32–33; 9.33–34; 10.35–41), and teaching by Jesus on discipleship (8.34–9.1; 9.35–50; 10.42–45) is repeated three times in that portion. A number of important manuscripts present Mark as ending with 16.8, with no indication that this ending is not the original or that any further material continuing the narrative is known; their existence is a strong indication that the Gospel originally ended at that point. Once Matthew, Luke, and John became well known, however, and the four Gospels were collected and copied into the same codex, the ending of Mark began to appear abrupt and inadequate. For this reason, various scribes added material to Mark: a shorter (additional) ending, a longer ending (16.9–20), and an expanded longer ending (with additional material after 16.14). Some scholars argue that 16.8 is not the original ending and that the original ending was either incorporated in the longer ending or lost.

Genre

THE GENRE OF MARK has been defined in three basic ways. The form critics and their heirs have argued that Mark is the first instance of a new Christian genre called "Gospel," an account of the "good news" that centers on the life, death, and resurrection of Jesus Christ. In their view this account, like a sermon, has as its primary function the evocation of repentance and faith. The literary type "Gospel" grew out of early Christian preaching and was practical in nature, not literary in the proper sense. The Gospels belong to the history of dogma and worship, not literature. Since 1977, the argument that Mark belongs to the genre of ancient "biography" has won increasing support. Mark has affinities with the subtype "didactic biography," written to instruct the audience about the life of a religious or philosophical leader and the way of life that he founded. Like such literature, Mark contains extensive teaching of Jesus, and discipleship is a major theme. The story of Jesus is told in part to instruct the audience about Christian teaching and the Christian way of life. Mark is also similar to the historical subtype of ancient biographies in that the story of Jesus is told primarily because his life was at the center of a crucial period of history from the point of view of Christian proclamation; his life is not told primarily to illustrate his character or cultural achievement. The third view is that Mark is close to some types of ancient historiography, not critical or positivistic history, but engaged, interpretative history. The author of Mark took up the genre of biblical, sacred history and transformed it, first by infusing it with an eschatological and apocalyptic perspective, and second by adapting it to Hellenistic historiographical and biographical conventions.

Emphases

IN KEEPING WITH ITS LIKELY OCCASION, the first Jewish war with Rome, an important emphasis of Mark is the reinterpretation of messiahship. The earthly Jesus is presented more as a prophet, teacher, and miracle worker than as a military leader and political king. Furthermore, the Gospel emphasizes that a primary element in the mission of the earthly Jesus was to suffer and die. In 10.45 and 14.24 this suffering and death is interpreted as effective for others. The suffering servant of Isa 52.13–53.12 and Greek ideas about vicarious suffering are likely models for this interpretation. In the passion narrative, on the assumption that David was the author of the Psalms, the psalms of individual lament are used to present Jesus as a suffering king. In the time between the inauguration (1.14–15) and the consummation (13.24–27) of the kingdom of God, discipleship is characterized, in imitation of Jesus, as self-sacrificial service to God and other members of the community for the sake of the gospel (8.34–9.1; 9.33–50; 10.35–45).

Relation to Other Gospels

THE BEST (THOUGH NOT PERFECT) EXPLANATION for the relationships between Mark, Matthew, and Luke (the Synoptic Gospels) is the Two-Source Theory: that the authors of Matthew and Luke used (in addition to oral tradition and perhaps other written sources peculiar to each Evangelist) two written sources, Mark and a collection of Jesus' sayings and brief anecdotes concerning him. The latter is known as "Q" from the German word for "source" (*Quelle*). Matthew and Luke expanded Mark's outline with traditions about the genealogy, conception, birth, and childhood of Jesus at the beginning of their Gospels and with traditions about appearances of the risen Jesus at the end. By means of Q (and perhaps other sources), they expanded the amount of Jesus' teaching provided by Mark. The relationship between Mark and John is disputed. Many American scholars argue that John is independent of Mark, whereas many Europeans conclude that John is dependent on Mark or on Matthew and/or Luke. On the one hand, John includes much that has no close relation to the Synoptic Gospels, although a good portion of that material is similar to the formal types found in the Synoptics (e.g., parables and miracle stories). On the other hand, Mark and John are quite similar with respect to their passion narratives. The best solution may be that Mark and John had different, though similar, sources and that some of the similarity between them may be due to the oral transmission of material from Mark. In other words, although the author of John may not have used Mark as a written source, he was familiar with the content of Mark as a widely used Christian text. [C. CLIFTON BLACK, revised by ADELA YARBRO COLLINS]

The Proclamation of John the Baptist

1 The beginning of the good news[a] of Jesus Christ, the Son of God.[b] 2 As it is written in the prophet Isaiah,[c]

"See, I am sending my messenger ahead
    of you,[d]
who will prepare your way;
3 the voice of one crying out in the
    wilderness:
'Prepare the way of the Lord,
    make his paths straight,' "

4 John the baptizer appeared[e] in the wilderness, proclaiming a baptism of repentance for the forgiveness of sins. 5 And people from the whole Judean countryside and all the people of Jerusalem were going out to him, and were baptized by him in the river Jordan, confessing their sins. 6 Now John was clothed with camel's hair, with a leather belt around his waist, and he ate locusts and wild honey. 7 He proclaimed, "The one who is more powerful than I is coming after me; I am not worthy to stoop down and untie the thong of his sandals. 8 I have baptized you with[f] water; but he will baptize you with[f] the Holy Spirit."

The Baptism of Jesus

9 In those days Jesus came from Nazareth of Galilee and was baptized by John in the Jordan. 10 And just as he was coming up out of the water, he saw the heavens torn apart and the Spirit descending like a dove on him. 11 And a voice came from heaven, "You are my Son, the Beloved;[g] with you I am well pleased."

The Temptation of Jesus

12 And the Spirit immediately drove him out into the wilderness. 13 He was in the wilderness forty days, tempted by Satan; and he was with the wild beasts; and the angels waited on him.

The Beginning of the Galilean Ministry

14 Now after John was arrested, Jesus came to Galilee, proclaiming the good news[a] of God,[h] 15 and saying, "The time is fulfilled, and the kingdom of God has come near;[i] repent, and believe in the good news."[a]

Jesus Calls the First Disciples

16 As Jesus passed along the Sea of Galilee, he saw Simon and his brother Andrew casting a net into the sea—for they were fishermen.

---

a Or gospel   b Other ancient authorities lack the Son of God   c Other ancient authorities read in the prophets   d Gk before your face   e Other ancient authorities read John was baptizing   f Or in   g Or my beloved Son   h Other ancient authorities read of the kingdom   i Or is at hand

---

1.1–15 The prologue of Mark, in which the introduction to Jesus (vv. 9–15) is grounded in the OT and prefaced by the ministry of John the Baptizer (vv. 1–8). **1.1–8** Cf. Mt 3.1–12; Lk 3.1–20; Jn 1.19–28. **1.1** As in Isa 40.9; 52.7; 61.1, good news (gospel; see text note a) suggests glad tidings of salvation (see also vv. 14–15; Mt 11.5; Rom 1.1; 1 Cor 15.1; 2 Cor 11.7; 1 Thess 2.2, 8–9). Christ, lit. "anointed one," i.e., "messiah," usually appears in Mark as an honorific title (see 8.29; 12.35; 13.21; 14.61; 15.32), though it can function as a proper name for Jesus (9.41). Son of God, a significant title for Jesus in Mark (1.11; 3.11; 5.7; 9.7; 12.6; 14.61; 15.39), is synonymous with "Christ (Messiah)." It thus has the connotation of being God's authoritative agent (cf. 2 Sam 7.13–14; Ps 2.7). **1.2–3** The quotation conflates material from Isa 40.3 with Ex 23.20; Mal 3.1. **1.4** The wilderness (see also vv. 3, 12, 13), though not specifically located (cf. Mt 3.1; Lk 3.3), recalls an earlier deliverance by God (e.g., Ex 6; 13.17–22; 16–24; Isa 41.18–20; 43.19–21; Hos 2.14–15). On the prophets' concern for repentance and forgiveness, see Isa 1.10–20; 55.7; Jer 31.34; Hos 6.1; Joel 2.12–13; Zech 1.4. The association of those concepts with immersion in water may signify a fulfillment of Ezek 36.25–28. **1.5** The whole Judean countryside suggests the region of southern Palestine around Judea's capital, Jerusalem. **1.6** John's attire recalls that of Elijah (2 Kings 1.8; but cf. Zech 13.4), whose return was sometimes regarded as a sign of the end of the age (Mal 4.5–6; see also Mk 9.11–13; Lk 1.17). **1.8** Holy Spirit. Israel's reinfusion with God's Spirit was expected in the last days (cf. Ezek 36.27; Joel 2.28–32; Acts 2.17–22). **1.9–11** Cf. Mt 3.13–17; Lk 3.21–22; Jn 1.29–34. **1.9** Galilee, a region of northern Palestine. **1.10** The heavens torn apart, an apocalyptic image signifying divine disclosure. See Isa 64.1; Ezek 1.1; Jn 1.51; Acts 7.56; Rev 4.1; cf. Mk 15.38. Like a dove may suggest the Spirit's hovering motion (cf. Gen 1.2). **1.11** The heavenly acclamation combines elements of Ps 2.7; Isa 42.1; see also Mk 9.7; Mt 12.18; 2 Pet 1.17. **1.12–13** Cf. Mt 4.1–11; Lk 4.1–13. **1.13** Forty days, reminiscent of Ex 34.28; 1 Kings 19.8. Tempted, i.e., tested, by Satan, God's adversary. See Job 2.1–8; see also Mk 3.23, 26; 4.15; 8.33. Jesus' being with the wild beasts evokes Ps 91.13, a psalm associated with the need for defense against Satan and demons in the Dead Sea Scrolls. **1.14–15** Cf. Mt 4.12–17; Lk 4.14–15. An introductory summary of Jesus' proclamation and teaching. **1.14** Arrested, lit. "handed over." See 6.17. Language of "handing over" is frequent in Mark, especially with regard to Jesus, and may echo the Greek version of Isa 53.6, 12. **1.15** The time, a decisive moment appointed by God, is fulfilled. See 11.13; 12.2; see also Ezek 7.12; Dan 7.22; Gal 4.4; Eph 1.10; 1 Pet 1.11; Rev 1.3. The kingdom of God, God's sovereign power or active reign, has come near. See 4.11; 9.1; 15.43.

17 And Jesus said to them, "Follow me and I will make you fish for people." 18 And immediately they left their nets and followed him. 19 As he went a little farther, he saw James son of Zebedee and his brother John, who were in their boat mending the nets. 20 Immediately he called them; and they left their father Zebedee in the boat with the hired men, and followed him.

The Man with an Unclean Spirit

21 They went to Capernaum; and when the sabbath came, he entered the synagogue and taught. 22 They were astounded at his teaching, for he taught them as one having authority, and not as the scribes. 23 Just then there was in their synagogue a man with an unclean spirit, 24 and he cried out, "What have you to do with us, Jesus of Nazareth? Have you come to destroy us? I know who you are, the Holy One of God." 25 But Jesus rebuked him, saying, "Be silent, and come out of him!" 26 And the unclean spirit, convulsing him and crying with a loud voice, came out of him. 27 They were all amazed, and they kept on asking one another, "What is this? A new teaching—with authority! He[a] commands even the unclean spirits, and they obey him." 28 At once his fame began to spread throughout the surrounding region of Galilee.

Jesus Heals Many at Simon's House

29 As soon as they[b] left the synagogue, they entered the house of Simon and Andrew, with James and John. 30 Now Simon's mother-in-law was in bed with a fever, and they told him about her at once. 31 He came and took her by the hand and lifted her up. Then the fever left her, and she began to serve them.

32 That evening, at sunset, they brought to him all who were sick or possessed with demons. 33 And the whole city was gathered around the door. 34 And he cured many who were sick with various diseases, and cast out many demons; and he would not permit the demons to speak, because they knew him.

A Preaching Tour in Galilee

35 In the morning, while it was still very dark, he got up and went out to a deserted place, and there he prayed. 36 And Simon and his companions hunted for him. 37 When they found him, they said to him, "Everyone is searching for you." 38 He answered, "Let us go on to the neighboring towns, so that I may proclaim the message there also; for that is what I came out to do." 39 And he went throughout Galilee, proclaiming the message in their synagogues and casting out demons.

Jesus Cleanses a Leper

40 A leper[c] came to him begging him, and kneeling[d] he said to him, "If you choose, you can make me clean." 41 Moved with pity,[e] Jesus[f] stretched out his hand and touched him, and

---

a Or A new teaching! With authority he   b Other ancient authorities read he   c The terms leper and leprosy can refer to several diseases   d Other ancient authorities lack kneeling   e Other ancient authorities read anger   f Gk he

---

1.16–45 Jesus' authoritative ministry in Galilee. **1.16–20** Cf. Mt 4.18–22; Lk 5.1–11; Jn 1.35–51; see also 1 Kings 19.19–21. **1.16** Sea of Galilee, actually an inland fresh-water lake. Fishermen enjoyed a lucrative business (note the reference to hired men in v. 20). **1.21–28** Cf. Mt 7.28–29; Lk 4.31–37. The first of four exorcisms (see also 5.1–20; 7.24–30; 9.14–29). **1.21–22** See note on 1.14–15. **1.21** Capernaum, a town on the northwestern shore of the Sea of Galilee. **1.22** They were astounded, a recurrent response to Jesus' activity in Mark (see also v. 27; 2.12; 5.20, 42; 6.2; 7.37; 11.18; 12.17). In Mark the scribes (here professional interpreters of Jewish law) are typically included among Jesus' opponents (e.g., 2.6, 16). The scribes in chs. 11–15 are officials of the temple in Jerusalem. **1.23** An unclean spirit, i.e., a demon (cf., e.g., 3.22, 30). **1.24** Us, perhaps a comprehensive reference to the demonic world. I know who you are. In antiquity, knowledge of someone's name or identity was thought to provide power over that one (see also Gen 2.19–20; 32.27–29; Ex 3.13–15; Judg 13.17–18). The Holy One of God. See also Jn 6.69. **1.25** Jesus' command accords with ancient methods of exorcism. **1.29–31** Cf.

Mt 8.14–15; Lk 4.38–39. **1.30** Simon's mother-in-law. Paul also indicates that Simon (also called Cephas; see note on 3.16) was married; see 1 Cor 9.5. **1.31** Took her by the hand and lifted her up, a gesture found elsewhere in Mark's healing stories (see 5.41; 9.27); see also note on 5.23. **1.32–34** Cf. Mt 8.16–17; Lk 4.40–41. The first transitional "summary report"; cf. the note on 1.14–15. **1.32** At sunset, when sabbath restrictions were lifted (cf. v. 21). **1.33** The whole city, a characteristically Markan exaggeration (see also all, v. 32; everyone, v. 37). **1.34** Not permit the demons to speak. This is the first injunction to silence about Jesus' identity; v. 25 prepares for it. See also 3.11–12; 8.30; 9.30. These commands are related to the reinterpretation of messiahship in Mark. **1.35–39** Cf. Mt 4.23; Lk 4.42–44. **1.35** A deserted place (see also 6.31, 32, 35), a setting for prayer in Mark (6.46). See also Lk 5.16; 6.12. **1.40–45** Cf. Mt 8.1–4; Lk 5.12–16. **1.40** Leprosy was regarded as a contagious, ritual impurity (Lev 13–14), curable only by divine power (2 Kings 5.7; cf. Mt 11.5; Lk 7.22); a leper was subject to banishment (2 Kings 7.3–10; 2 Chr 26.19–21). **1.41** Pity (see also 6.34; 9.22) appears in most ancient manuscripts,

said to him, "I do choose. Be made clean!" [42]Immediately the leprosy[a] left him, and he was made clean. [43]After sternly warning him he sent him away at once, [44]saying to him, "See that you say nothing to anyone; but go, show yourself to the priest, and offer for your cleansing what Moses commanded, as a testimony to them." [45]But he went out and began to proclaim it freely, and to spread the word, so that Jesus[b] could no longer go into a town openly, but stayed out in the country; and people came to him from every quarter.

Jesus Heals a Paralytic

2 When he returned to Capernaum after some days, it was reported that he was at home. [2]So many gathered around that there was no longer room for them, not even in front of the door; and he was speaking the word to them. [3]Then some people[c] came, bringing to him a paralyzed man, carried by four of them. [4]And when they could not bring him to Jesus because of the crowd, they removed the roof above him; and after having dug through it, they let down the mat on which the paralytic lay. [5]When Jesus saw their faith, he said to the paralytic, "Son, your sins are forgiven." [6]Now some of the scribes were sitting there, questioning in their hearts, [7]"Why does this fellow speak in this way? It is blasphemy! Who can forgive sins but God

alone?" [8]At once Jesus perceived in his spirit that they were discussing these questions among themselves; and he said to them, "Why do you raise such questions in your hearts? [9]Which is easier, to say to the paralytic, 'Your sins are forgiven,' or to say, 'Stand up and take your mat and walk'? [10]But so that you may know that the Son of Man has authority on earth to forgive sins"—he said to the paralytic— [11]"I say to you, stand up, take your mat and go to your home." [12]And he stood up, and immediately took the mat and went out before all of them; so that they were all amazed and glorified God, saying, "We have never seen anything like this!"

Jesus Calls Levi

13 Jesus[d] went out again beside the sea; the whole crowd gathered around him, and he taught them. [14]As he was walking along, he saw Levi son of Alphaeus sitting at the tax booth, and he said to him, "Follow me." And he got up and followed him.

15 And as he sat at dinner[e] in Levi's[f] house, many tax collectors and sinners were also sitting[g] with Jesus and his disciples—for there were many who followed him. [16]When the scribes of[h] the Pharisees saw that he was eating

a The terms *leper* and *leprosy* can refer to several diseases
b Gk *he*　c Gk *they*　d Gk *He*　e Gk *reclined*　f Gk *his*
g Gk *reclining*　h Other ancient authorities read *and*

though the harder variant reading *anger* (text note *d* on p. 1726) may be the original. **1.43** *Sternly warning.* Cf. 14.5; Mt 9.30; Jn 11.33, 38. **1.44** *Say nothing to anyone,* probably not an injunction to silence but an indication of the urgency and importance of the instruction to go to the priest. *Show yourself to the priest.* See also Lev 14.2–32; Lk 17.12–14. **1.45** *The word,* perhaps an allusion to early Christian preaching (see also 2.2; 4.14–20, 33; Acts 6.4; Gal 6.6; Col 4.3).

2.1–3.6 Conflict between Jesus and other religious leaders and authorities. **2.1–12** Cf. Mt 9.1–8; Lk 5.17–26. The first in a series of five controversy narratives (see also 2.13–17, 18–22, 23–28; 3.1–6), this passage embeds a story of conflict (vv. 6–10) within a story of healing (vv. 1–5, 11–12). Such narrative intertwinings are characteristic of Mark (see also 3.1–6, 19–35; 5.21–43; 6.7–30; 11.12–25; 14.1–11, 53–72; 15.6–32). **2.4** In Palestinian house design, the *roof* consisted of crossbeams covered with thatch and hardened mud (cf. Lk 5.19). **2.5** Here, as in other Markan miracle stories (see also 5.34, 36; 9.23–34; 10.52), *faith* suggests confidence in Jesus' healing power. For the correlation of healing with being *forgiven,* see Lk 7.48; see also 2 Sam 12.13; 2 Chr 7.14; Pss 41.4; 103.3; Isa 38.17; 57.17–19; Jer 3.22; Hos 14.4. **2.6–7** The accusation by

the *scribes* (see note on 1.22) of *blasphemy,* a theoretically capital offense (Lev 24.15–16; Mk 14.64), presumes that forgiveness was exclusively God's prerogative (see Ex 34.6–7; Isa 43.25; 44.22). It may also be an indirect condemnation of Jesus' bypassing the commandments regarding atonement that involved the temple. **2.10** *The Son of Man* in Mark sometimes clearly alludes to Dan 7.13–14 (8.38; 13.26; 14.62), but here it is ambiguous, as in v. 28. The scribes, as characters in the narrative, find the phrase confusing, but the audience would understand it as a title for Jesus based on a particular interpretation of Dan 7.13–14. Whatever its precise meaning, it focuses here on Jesus' earthly authority (see also v. 28; Mt 8.20; 11.19; 12.32; Lk 6.22; 7.34; 9.58; 12.10). **2.12** *Amazed.* See note on 1.22. **2.13–17** Cf. Mt 9.9–13; Lk 5.27–32. **2.14** *Levi son of Alphaeus* does not appear among Mark's listing of the Twelve (3.16–19; cf. Mt 9.9; 10.3). *Tax booth,* perhaps a roadside tollhouse. **2.15** *Tax* (or toll) *collectors* were despised by Jews for their presumed dishonesty and collaboration with Roman authorities. *Sinners,* the notoriously wicked who flouted Jewish law (in contrast with *the righteous;* see v. 17). On Jesus' association with social outcasts, see also Mt 11.19; Lk 7.34; 15.1–2. **2.16** *The Pharisees,* leaders of a popular re-

with sinners and tax collectors, they said to his disciples, "Why does he eat[a] with tax collectors and sinners?" [17]When Jesus heard this, he said to them, "Those who are well have no need of a physician, but those who are sick; I have come to call not the righteous but sinners."

The Question about Fasting

18 Now John's disciples and the Pharisees were fasting; and people[b] came and said to him, "Why do John's disciples and the disciples of the Pharisees fast, but your disciples do not fast?" [19]Jesus said to them, "The wedding guests cannot fast while the bridegroom is with them, can they? As long as they have the bridegroom with them, they cannot fast. [20]The days will come when the bridegroom is taken away from them, and then they will fast on that day.

21 "No one sews a piece of unshrunk cloth on an old cloak; otherwise, the patch pulls away from it, the new from the old, and a worse tear is made. [22]And no one puts new wine into old wineskins; otherwise, the wine will burst the skins, and the wine is lost, and so are the skins; but one puts new wine into fresh wineskins."[c]

Pronouncement about the Sabbath

23 One sabbath he was going through the grainfields; and as they made their way his disciples began to pluck heads of grain. [24]The Pharisees said to him, "Look, why are they doing what is not lawful on the sabbath?" [25]And he said to them, "Have you never read what David did when he and his companions were hungry and in need of food? [26]He entered the house of God, when Abiathar was high priest, and ate the bread of the Presence, which it is not lawful for any but the priests to eat, and he gave some to his companions." [27]Then he said to them, "The sabbath was made for humankind, and not humankind for the sabbath; [28]so the Son of Man is lord even of the sabbath."

The Man with a Withered Hand

3 Again he entered the synagogue, and a man was there who had a withered hand. [2]They watched him to see whether he would cure him on the sabbath, so that they might accuse him. [3]And he said to the man who had the withered hand, "Come forward." [4]Then he said to them, "Is it lawful to do good or to do harm on the sabbath, to save life or to kill?" But they were silent. [5]He looked around at them with anger; he was grieved at their hardness of heart and said to the man, "Stretch out your hand." He stretched it out, and his hand was restored. [6]The Pharisees went out and im-

---

a Other ancient authorities add *and drink* b Gk *they*
c Other ancient authorities lack *but one puts new wine into fresh wineskins*

---

form movement among ancient Jews, interpreted the law in the cultural context of the time and favored obedience to the commandments in all walks of life. Like the *scribes* (see note on 1.22), Pharisees are typically ranged among Jesus' adversaries in Mark (v. 24; 3.6; 7.1, 5; 8.11, 15; 10.2; 12.13). **2.17** A similar proverb is attributed to ancient philosophers. **2.18–22** Cf. Mt 9.14–17; Lk 5.33–39. **2.18–20** *John's disciples.* See also Mt 11.2–6; Lk 7.18–23; 11.1; Jn 1.35; 3.25–30. *Fasting,* originally a sign of contrition, was prescribed as an annual practice (Lev 16.29; Zech 7.5) and also undertaken on specific occasions (Ezra 8.21–23; Jon 3.7–9); see also Lk 18.12. In the Second Temple period, it was also practiced as an act of piety. V. 20 probably reflects the practice of fasting in the early church. **2.19** *Wedding guests* (or "the groomsmen"), *bridegroom,* imagery used in portraying God's saving covenant elsewhere in the NT (Mt 22.1–14; 25.1–13; 2 Cor 11.2; Eph 5.32; Rev 19.7; 21.2), in the OT (Isa 54.4–8; 62.4–5; Ezek 16.1–63; Hos 2.19), and among the rabbis. **2.23–28** Cf. Mt 12.1–8; Lk 6.1–5. **2.24** *What is not lawful,* evidently a reference to the prohibition of reaping on the sabbath in Ex 34.21. The legality of activities on the sabbath (Ex 20.8–11; Deut 5.12–15) was extensively debated among Jews in the Second Temple period and among the rabbis; see also Lk 14.1–6. **2.25** A counterquestion typical of ancient dialogues and debates. **2.26** It was not the son *Abiathar* (1 Sam 22.20) who was high priest, but the father, Ahimelech (1 Sam 21.1–6; cf. Mt 12.4; Lk 6.4). On the *bread of the Presence,* see Ex 25.30; Lev 24.5–9. **2.27–28** *Humankind,* lit. "man," referring to Adam. Thus, on one level, the *Son of Man* is the generic "human being" or "humankind" (cf. Ps 8.4). The informed members of the audience, however, know that the term is Jesus' authoritative self-designation (see note on 2.10). **3.1–6** Cf. Mt 12.9–14; Lk 6.6–11. Healing and controversy are entwined, again raising the issue of what is permitted on the sabbath, as in 2.23–28 (see Lk 13.10–17; 14.1–6; Jn 5.1–18; see also note on 2.1–12). **3.4** *Is it lawful.* See note on 2.24. This anecdote presupposes that healing was defined as work by some leaders at the time of Jesus, e.g., the Pharisees. Jesus' contemporaries would have accepted a violation of the sabbath *to save life* but probably would have questioned its relevance in this case. The Markan Jesus claims that healing work ought to take priority over observance of the sabbath. **3.5** *Hardness of heart,* or stubborn obtuseness

mediately conspired with the Herodians against him, how to destroy him.

A Multitude at the Seaside

7 Jesus departed with his disciples to the sea, and a great multitude from Galilee followed him; 8hearing all that he was doing, they came to him in great numbers from Judea, Jerusalem, Idumea, beyond the Jordan, and the region around Tyre and Sidon. 9He told his disciples to have a boat ready for him because of the crowd, so that they would not crush him; 10for he had cured many, so that all who had diseases pressed upon him to touch him. 11Whenever the unclean spirits saw him, they fell down before him and shouted, "You are the Son of God!" 12But he sternly ordered them not to make him known.

Jesus Appoints the Twelve

13 He went up the mountain and called to him those whom he wanted, and they came to him. 14And he appointed twelve, whom he also named apostles,ᵃ to be with him, and to be sent out to proclaim the message, 15and to have authority to cast out demons. 16So he appointed the twelve:ᵇ Simon (to whom he gave the name Peter); 17James son of Zebedee and John the brother of James (to whom he gave the name Boanerges, that is, Sons of Thunder); 18and Andrew, and Philip, and Bartholomew, and Matthew, and Thomas, and James son of Alphaeus, and Thaddaeus, and Simon the Cananaean, 19and Judas Iscariot, who betrayed him.

Jesus and Beelzebul

Then he went home; 20and the crowd came together again, so that they could not even eat. 21When his family heard it, they went out to restrain him, for people were saying, "He has gone out of his mind." 22And the scribes who came down from Jerusalem said, "He has Beelzebul, and by the ruler of the demons he casts out demons." 23And he called them to

---

a Other ancient authorities lack *whom he also named apostles*
b Other ancient authorities lack *So he appointed the twelve*

(see 6.52; 8.17; 10.5; see also Ex 9.34–35; 1 Sam 6.6; 2 Chr 36.13; Ps 95.8; Eph 4.18). **3.6** *Pharisees.* See note on 2.16. *Herodians,* "those belonging to Herod," i.e., partisans of Herod or, more likely in this context, Galilean officials appointed by Herod Antipas. This is the first of Mark's four references to a conspiracy to *destroy* Jesus (see also 11.18; 12.12; 14.1).

3.7–35 Portrayal of Jesus as the Son of God. **3.7–12** Cf. Mt 4.24–25; 12.15–16; Lk 6.17–19. A second transitional "summary report" (see note on 1.32–34) underscoring Jesus' popularity (see also 1.28, 35–37, 45) and foreshadowing his ministry beyond Palestine (see 7.24–31). **3.8** *Judea, Jerusalem.* See note on 1.5. *Idumea* ("Edom," Gen 32.3), a region southeast of Judea. *Beyond the Jordan* (Perea), an area northeast of Judea and southeast of Galilee. *Tyre and Sidon,* cities northwest of Galilee. **3.10** *To touch him.* See also 5.27–28; 6.56. **3.11** *Unclean spirits,* or demons (see also 1.23; 3.30), *fell down before him* in submission (see also 5.22, 33; 7.25); they, not humans, recognize Jesus as the *Son of God* (see also 1.24; 5.7; cf. 15.39). **3.12** On Jesus' injunctions to silence about his identity, see note on 1.34. **3.13–19a** Cf. Mt 10.1–4; Lk 6.12–16. **3.13** As in the OT (e.g., Ex 19.3–25; 1 Kings 19.8), the *mountain* (or "hill country") may symbolize a place of divine disclosure (see also 9.2–13), but such usage is not consistent throughout Mark (cf. 5.5, 11; 6.46; 11.1, 23; 13.3, 14; 4.26). **3.14** *Appointed,* lit. "made" (see also v. 16; 1 Kings 13.33; 2 Chr 2.18; Heb 3.2). *Twelve,* probably a symbolic representation of the twelve tribes of Israel (see Num 1.4–16; 13.1–16; Mt 19.28; Lk 22.30). *Apostles,* if original here, probably refers to emissaries authorized to discharge a specific commission (see 6.7–

13); rare in Mark (elsewhere only in 6.30). **3.16–19a** For variation in the names and ordering of the Twelve, cf. Mt 10.2–4; Lk 6.14–16; Jn 1.40–49; 21.2; Acts 1.13. **3.16** *Peter,* perhaps from the Greek for "stone" or "rock" (Mt 16.18–19); in Aramaic, Cephas (e.g., Jn 1.42; 1 Cor 1.12; Gal 1.18). **3.17** *Boanerges,* derivation and meaning obscure. "Boane-" may derive from the Hebrew meaning "sons of"; "-rges" may come from the Hebrew meaning "agitation" or "tumult," e.g., "thunder." **3.18** *Cananaean* probably derives from an Aramaic term denoting religious zeal (see Lk 6.15; Acts 1.13). **3.19a** *Iscariot,* probably meaning "a man from Kerioth," a city of Judea (see Josh 15.25; cf. Jer 48.24). On language about Jesus being *betrayed,* lit. "handed over," see note on 1.14. **3.19b–35** A controversy about exorcism (vv. 22–30; see also Mt 12.22–32; Lk 11.14–23; 12.10) is inserted into an episode about Jesus' family (vv. 19b–21, 31–35; see Mt 12.46–50; Lk 8.19–21; see also note on 2.1–12). **3.19b** *Home,* a typical site for much of Jesus' ministry in Mark (see, e.g., 1.29, 32–33; 2.1). **3.20** *They could not even eat.* See also 6.31. **3.21** *His family,* translation of an ambiguous phrase based on the people mentioned in v. 31. *Out of his mind.* As implied by v. 22, insanity in the ancient world was attributed to demonic possession (see also Jn 7.20; 8.48–52; 10.20). **3.22** See note on 1.22. *Jerusalem.* See 10.32–34. *Beelzebul,* related to "Baal Zabul," "Baal the Prince," the probable name of the Semitic deity mocked by the name "Baal Zebul" ("Lord of the Flies") in 2 Kings 1.2. By Mark's time, this Canaanite deity had been demoted to the status of the ruler of the demons, equivalent to Satan. **3.23** *Parables,* enigmatic proverbs or riddling stories that are provocative if not always il-

him, and spoke to them in parables, "How can Satan cast out Satan? 24If a kingdom is divided against itself, that kingdom cannot stand. 25And if a house is divided against itself, that house will not be able to stand. 26And if Satan has risen up against himself and is divided, he cannot stand, but his end has come. 27But no one can enter a strong man's house and plunder his property without first tying up the strong man; then indeed the house can be plundered.

28 "Truly I tell you, people will be forgiven for their sins and whatever blasphemies they utter; 29but whoever blasphemes against the Holy Spirit can never have forgiveness, but is guilty of an eternal sin"— 30for they had said, "He has an unclean spirit."

The True Kindred of Jesus

31 Then his mother and his brothers came; and standing outside, they sent to him and called him. 32A crowd was sitting around him; and they said to him, "Your mother and your brothers and sisters*a* are outside, asking for you." 33And he replied, "Who are my mother and my brothers?" 34And looking at those who sat around him, he said, "Here are my mother and my brothers! 35Whoever does the will of God is my brother and sister and mother."

The Parable of the Sower

4 Again he began to teach beside the sea. Such a very large crowd gathered around him that he got into a boat on the sea and sat there,

while the whole crowd was beside the sea on the land. 2He began to teach them many things in parables, and in his teaching he said to them: 3"Listen! A sower went out to sow. 4And as he sowed, some seed fell on the path, and the birds came and ate it up. 5Other seed fell on rocky ground, where it did not have much soil, and it sprang up quickly, since it had no depth of soil. 6And when the sun rose, it was scorched; and since it had no root, it withered away. 7Other seed fell among thorns, and the thorns grew up and choked it, and it yielded no grain. 8Other seed fell into good soil and brought forth grain, growing up and increasing and yielding thirty and sixty and a hundredfold." 9And he said, "Let anyone with ears to hear listen!"

The Purpose of the Parables

10 When he was alone, those who were around him along with the twelve asked him about the parables. 11And he said to them, "To you has been given the secret*b* of the kingdom of God, but for those outside, everything comes in parables; 12in order that

'they may indeed look, but not perceive,
    and may indeed listen, but not
        understand;
    so that they may not turn again and be
        forgiven.' "

13 And he said to them, "Do you not understand this parable? Then how will you under-

---

a Other ancient authorities lack *and sisters*   *b* Or *mystery*

luminating (3.24–27; 4.3–9, 21–32; 7.14–17; 12.1–12; 13.28; see also Ps 78.2; Prov 1.6; Ezek 17.2; Hab 2.6; Sir 47.17). **3.27** Cf. Isa 49.24–25. **3.28** *Truly I tell you,* a recurrent introductory formula (e.g., 8.12; 9.1, 41) emphasizing prophetic assurance. *People,* "the sons of men" (see 2.28; Ps 8.4). *Blasphemies.* See note on 2.6–7. **3.29** To link the Holy Spirit (see 1.8, 10, 12) or the Spirit's agent (3.30; Lk 11.20) with demons is to be *guilty of an eternal sin* (cf. 1 Jn 5.16). **3.31** See note on 3.21. The absence of Jesus' father with *his mother and his brothers* is of disputed significance; as in 6.3 (see also Jn 2.12; 7.3, 5, 10; Acts 1.14; 1 Cor 9.5; Gal 1.19), reference to *his brothers* suggests Mark's ignorance of the later doctrine of Mary's perpetual virginity. **3.35** *Will of God,* a phrase common in Paul's Letters (e.g., Rom 1.10; 12.2; 1 Cor 1.1; Gal 1.4), but appearing only here in Mark (but cf. 14.36; see also Jn 7.16–17). **4.1–34** Jesus teaches in parables. **4.1–9** Cf. Mt 13.1–9; Lk 8.4–8. The first in a series of parables. **4.1** *A very large crowd,* perhaps an enlarging of the audience suggested by 3.7, 9, 20. **4.2** *Parables.* See note on 3.23. **4.3** *Listen!* lit. "Look!" (see also vv. 9, 12; Deut 6.4; Judg 9.7; Isa 28.23; Ezek 20.47). **4.4–8** The metaphors of sow-

ing, planting, and growth occur in Jewish and Christian apocalyptic texts (see 2 Esd 4.26–32; cf. 1 Cor 3.6–8). **4.8** A *hundredfold* yield was astonishing, though not unheard of (see Gen 26.12). **4.9** An exhortation commonly attributed to Jesus (see, e.g., v. 23; Mt 11.15; 13.43; Lk 14.35; Rev 2.7, 11). **4.10–12** The purpose of the parables. **4.10** Jesus' followers extend to *those . . . around him along with the twelve* (see also 3.31–35). Private explanation often follows public instruction in Mark (4.34; 7.17; 9.28; 10.10; 13.3). **4.11** *The secret,* or "mystery," God's cosmic purposes, graciously disclosed to a select few; also Dan 2.18–19, 27–30, 47; Rom 11.25; 1 Cor 2.1, 7; 4.1; Rev 1.20; 10.7; 17.5, 7; Dead Sea Scrolls. *Kingdom of God.* See note on 1.15. *For those outside.* Cf. 3.31–32. *In parables.* See note on 3.23. **4.12** As elsewhere (Jn 12.40; Acts 28.26–27; cf. Rom 11.1–10), Isa 6.9–10 has been adapted to interpret disbelief of the Christian proclamation. Mark's harsh view of parables, told *in order that* perception and forgiveness may not occur, is softened in Mt 13.13; Lk 8.10. **4.13–20** The interpretation of the parable of the sower. It is probably a later Christian interpretation accentuating missionary hardships and the difficulty of discipleship (see also Rom 8.35; 2 Cor 4.8–

stand all the parables? 14The sower sows the word. 15These are the ones on the path where the word is sown: when they hear, Satan immediately comes and takes away the word that is sown in them. 16And these are the ones sown on rocky ground: when they hear the word, they immediately receive it with joy. 17But they have no root, and endure only for a while; then, when trouble or persecution arises on account of the word, immediately they fall away.*a* 18And others are those sown among the thorns: these are the ones who hear the word, 19but the cares of the world, and the lure of wealth, and the desire for other things come in and choke the word, and it yields nothing. 20And these are the ones sown on the good soil: they hear the word and accept it and bear fruit, thirty and sixty and a hundredfold."

A Lamp under a Bushel Basket

21 He said to them, "Is a lamp brought in to be put under the bushel basket, or under the bed, and not on the lampstand? 22For there is nothing hidden, except to be disclosed; nor is anything secret, except to come to light. 23Let anyone with ears to hear listen!" 24And he said to them, "Pay attention to what you hear; the measure you give will be the measure you get, and still more will be given you. 25For to those who have, more will be given; and from those who have nothing, even what they have will be taken away."

The Parable of the Growing Seed

26 He also said, "The kingdom of God is as if someone would scatter seed on the ground, 27and would sleep and rise night and day, and the seed would sprout and grow, he does not know how. 28The earth produces of itself, first the stalk, then the head, then the full grain in the head. 29But when the grain is ripe, at once he goes in with his sickle, because the harvest has come."

The Parable of the Mustard Seed

30 He also said, "With what can we compare the kingdom of God, or what parable will we use for it? 31It is like a mustard seed, which, when sown upon the ground, is the smallest of all the seeds on earth; 32yet when it is sown it grows up and becomes the greatest of all shrubs, and puts forth large branches, so that the birds of the air can make nests in its shade."

The Use of Parables

33 With many such parables he spoke the word to them, as they were able to hear it; 34he did not speak to them except in parables, but he explained everything in private to his disciples.

Jesus Stills a Storm

35 On that day, when evening had come, he said to them, "Let us go across to the other side." 36And leaving the crowd behind, they took him with them in the boat, just as he was. Other boats were with him. 37A great windstorm arose, and the waves beat into the boat, so that the boat was already being swamped.

---

a Or *stumble*

9; 2 Thess 1.4). **4.13** *Do you not understand,* a recurring criticism of the disciples (see, e.g., 6.52; 8.17, 21). **4.14** The seed of the parable is interpreted as *the word,* i.e., the gospel (vv. 14, 15b; see note on 1.45), and various responses to the word (vv. 15a, 16–20). Cf. 2 Esd 8.41–44; 9.31. **4.15** *Satan.* See note on 1.13; see also 8.31–33. **4.17** *They fall away,* lit. "they are scandalized," to the point of apostasy (see also 9.42–47; 14.27). **4.19** On pitfalls associated with *wealth,* see 10.23–25; Lk 12.15–21. **4.21–25** Cf. Mt 5.15; 7.2; 10.26; 13.12; 25.29; Lk 6.38; 8.16–18; 11.33; 12.2; 19.26. These sayings about disclosure and reception are linked by the catchwords *lamp, light* (vv. 21–22); *hear* (vv. 23–24); and *more, given* (vv. 24–25); see also vv. 10–12. **4.21** *Lamp,* a flexible metaphor in the OT (2 Sam 21.17; 22.29; Ps 119.105; Zech 4.2; Wis 18.4). *Bushel basket,* a dry measure of about 2 gallons. *Pay attention to what you hear.* See also vv. 3, 9, 12. **4.25** For a kindred proverb, see 2 Esd 7.25. **4.26–29** A second narrative parable. It is the only parable in Mark without parallel in the other Gospels (cf. Mt 13.24–30). **4.26** *Kingdom of God* (also v. 30). See note on 1.15. **4.29** *Sickle, harvest,* sometimes associated with the final judgment (Joel 3.13; Rev 14.14–20). **4.30–32** Cf. Mt 13.31–32; Lk 13.18–19. The third and final narrative parable in the section. **4.31** Though in fact not the smallest, the *mustard seed* may have been figuratively so regarded (see also Mt 17.20; Lk 17.6). **4.32** *Birds . . . make nests in its shade,* an allusion to a common OT image that suggests protection (Ezek 17.23; 31.6; Dan 4.12, 21). **4.33–34** A concluding summary. Cf. Mt 13.34–35. **4.33** *The word.* See note on 1.45. *As they were able to hear it,* ambiguous, suggesting that Jesus' parables were told either to relieve or to heighten his listeners incomprehension (see note on 4.12). **4.34** *In private to his disciples.* See notes on 4.10; 4.11.

4.35–6.6a Epiphanies of divine power. **4.35–41** Cf. Mt 8.23–27; Lk 8.22–25. **4.36** *Just as he was,* implying that Jesus was still in the boat as described in v. 1 (cf. Mt

38But he was in the stern, asleep on the cushion; and they woke him up and said to him, "Teacher, do you not care that we are perishing?" 39He woke up and rebuked the wind, and said to the sea, "Peace! Be still!" Then the wind ceased, and there was a dead calm. 40He said to them, "Why are you afraid? Have you still no faith?" 41And they were filled with great awe and said to one another, "Who then is this, that even the wind and the sea obey him?"

Jesus Heals the Gerasene Demoniac

5 They came to the other side of the sea, to the country of the Gerasenes.*a* 2And when he had stepped out of the boat, immediately a man out of the tombs with an unclean spirit met him. 3He lived among the tombs; and no one could restrain him any more, even with a chain; 4for he had often been restrained with shackles and chains, but the chains he wrenched apart, and the shackles he broke in pieces; and no one had the strength to subdue him. 5Night and day among the tombs and on the mountains he was always howling and bruising himself with stones. 6When he saw Jesus from a distance, he ran and bowed down before him; 7and he shouted at the top of his voice, "What have you to do with me, Jesus, Son of the Most High God? I adjure you by God, do not torment me." 8For he had said to

him, "Come out of the man, you unclean spirit!" 9Then Jesus*b* asked him, "What is your name?" He replied, "My name is Legion; for we are many." 10He begged him earnestly not to send them out of the country. 11Now there on the hillside a great herd of swine was feeding; 12and the unclean spirits*c* begged him, "Send us into the swine; let us enter them." 13So he gave them permission. And the unclean spirits came out and entered the swine; and the herd, numbering about two thousand, rushed down the steep bank into the sea, and were drowned in the sea.

14 The swineherds ran off and told it in the city and in the country. Then people came to see what it was that had happened. 15They came to Jesus and saw the demoniac sitting there, clothed and in his right mind, the very man who had had the legion; and they were afraid. 16Those who had seen what had happened to the demoniac and to the swine reported it. 17Then they began to beg Jesus*d* to leave their neighborhood. 18As he was getting into the boat, the man who had been possessed by demons begged him that he might be with him. 19But Jesus*b* refused, and said to him, "Go home to your friends, and tell them how much the Lord has done for you, and

a Other ancient authorities read *Gergesenes*; others, *Gadarenes*
b Gk *he*   *c* Gk *they*   *d* Gk *him*

8.23; Lk 8.22). **4.37** *Windstorm, waves, boat . . . being swamped* recall Ps 107.23–25; Jon 1.4. **4.38** *Asleep,* a typical posture of trust in God (Job 11.18–19; Pss 3.5; 4.8; but cf. Jon 1.5). Even in its stridency (Pss 35.23; 44.23–24; 59.4b; Isa 51.9a; cf. Mt 8.25; Lk 8.24), the disciples' plea for deliverance echoes the OT (Pss 69.1–2, 14–15; 107.26–28a). **4.39** Like the unclean spirit (1.25), the *wind* is *rebuked* and "silenced" (*Be still!* See also Ps 104.6–7). **4.40** The tension between being *afraid* (here, "cowardly") and having *faith* recurs in Mark (5.33–34, 36; 6.50). **4.41** *Great awe* or fear is characteristic of human response to divine manifestations (see, e.g., 6.51; 9.15; 16.8; Ex 3.1–6; Isa 6.1–5; Jon 1.10, 16; Lk 2.9). The quelling of chaotic waters implies divine power (Gen 1.2, 6–9; Job 38.8–11; Pss 65.5–8; 74.12–14; 89.8–10; 93.3–4; 107.28b–30; Isa 51.10; Jer 5.22; 2 Esd 6.41–43). **5.1–20** Cf. Mt 8.28–34; Lk 8.26–39. The second of four exorcisms (see also 1.21–28; 7.24–30; 9.14–29), detailing a contest (vv. 1–13) and its consequences (vv. 14–20). **5.1** *The other side of the sea,* the east bank of the Sea of Galilee (see note on 1.16). Over thirty miles from the sea, *the country of the Gerasenes* (modern Jerash) seems an unlikely setting for the action described in vv. 2, 13; alternative locations of "Gergesa" and "Gadara" (Mt 8.28) in other

versions reflect this problem (see text note *a*). **5.2** *Tombs,* the realm of the dead and of social outcasts (see also Isa 65.1–7). *An unclean spirit.* See note on 1.23. **5.6** *Bowed down before him.* See note on 3.11. **5.7** *The Most High God,* a title applied to Israel's God by Gentiles (Gen 14.18–20; Num 24.16; Isa 14.14; Dan 3.26; 4.2; cf. Lk 1.32; 6.35). *I adjure you by God,* an attempt to repel the exorcist (see note on 1.24). **5.9** *What is your name?* See note on 1.24. *Legion,* a Roman regiment of approximately six thousand soldiers. The term may also simply refer to a large number. **5.11** *Swine,* like tombs and demonic spirits, regarded by Jews as unclean (Lev 11.7–8; Deut 14.8; Isa 65.4; 66.17). **5.13** *Two thousand,* possibly another instance of exaggeration by the author or his source (see note on 1.33). *The sea.* See note on 4.41. **5.15** *They were afraid,* either awestruck in the presence of the supernatural (see note on 4.41) or fearful of Jesus' power (see v. 17). **5.19** *Tell them.* Cf. 1.44; 3.12; 5.43; 7.36. Elsewhere (Acts 26.20; 1 Cor 14.25; Heb 2.12; 1 Jn 1.2, 3), though not everywhere (cf. Mk 5.14; 1 Thess 1.9), the verb translated "tell" signifies Christian missionary proclamation. *The Lord,* i.e., God (thus 1.3[?]; 11.9; 12.11, 29–30, 36; 13.20; cf. Lk 8.39), although the title is occasionally used of Jesus (5.20; see also 2.28; 7.28;

what mercy he has shown you." 20 And he went away and began to proclaim in the Decapolis how much Jesus had done for him; and everyone was amazed.

A Girl Restored to Life and a Woman Healed

21 When Jesus had crossed again in the boat*a* to the other side, a great crowd gathered around him; and he was by the sea. 22 Then one of the leaders of the synagogue named Jairus came and, when he saw him, fell at his feet 23 and begged him repeatedly, "My little daughter is at the point of death. Come and lay your hands on her, so that she may be made well, and live." 24 So he went with him.

And a large crowd followed him and pressed in on him. 25 Now there was a woman who had been suffering from hemorrhages for twelve years. 26 She had endured much under many physicians, and had spent all that she had; and she was no better, but rather grew worse. 27 She had heard about Jesus, and came up behind him in the crowd and touched his cloak, 28 for she said, "If I but touch his clothes, I will be made well." 29 Immediately her hemorrhage stopped; and she felt in her body that she was healed of her disease. 30 Immediately aware that

power had gone forth from him, Jesus turned about in the crowd and said, "Who touched my clothes?" 31 And his disciples said to him, "You see the crowd pressing in on you; how can you say, 'Who touched me?' " 32 He looked all around to see who had done it. 33 But the woman, knowing what had happened to her, came in fear and trembling, fell down before him, and told him the whole truth. 34 He said to her, "Daughter, your faith has made you well; go in peace, and be healed of your disease."

35 While he was still speaking, some people came from the leader's house to say, "Your daughter is dead. Why trouble the teacher any further?" 36 But overhearing*b* what they said, Jesus said to the leader of the synagogue, "Do not fear, only believe." 37 He allowed no one to follow him except Peter, James, and John, the brother of James. 38 When they came to the house of the leader of the synagogue, he saw a commotion, people weeping and wailing loudly. 39 When he had entered, he said to them, "Why do you make a commotion and weep? The child is not dead but sleeping." 40 And they laughed at him. Then he put them

a Other ancient authorities lack *in the boat*   *b* Or *ignoring*; other ancient authorities read *hearing*

11.3; 12.37; 13.35). See also note on 11.3. **5.20** *Decapolis,* a group of ten cities. One, Scythopolis (Beth-shan), was west of the Jordan River, the rest east of it. Their populations were primarily gentile, although each was also home to a Jewish minority (see also 7.31). **5.21–43** Cf. Mt 9.18–26; Lk 8.40–56. The raising of Jairus's daughter (vv. 21–24a, 35–43; cf. 1 Kings 17.17–24; 2 Kings 4.18–37; Lk 7.11–17; Jn 11.1–44; Acts 9.36–43) frames the healing of a woman with an abnormal discharge (flow of blood; vv. 24b–34; see note on 2.1–12). **5.21** *To the other side,* presumably west of the Sea of Galilee. **5.22** *Leaders of the synagogue* were responsible for arranging and perhaps conducting worship as well as for building maintenance (see also Lk 13.14; Acts 13.15; 18.8, 17). *Fell at his feet.* See note on 3.11. **5.23** *At the point of death.* Cf. Mt 9.18. *Lay your hands on her,* an action rare in Jewish stories of healing but recurrent in Mark (6.5; 7.32; 8.22, 25; see also 3.10; 5.28; 6.56). *Made well,* lit. "saved" (see also 3.4; 5.28, 34; 6.56; 10.52). **5.25** *Hemorrhages,* better "a flow of blood," i.e., an abnormal discharge producing a state of ritual impurity that theoretically entailed social restriction or exclusion (Lev 12.1–8; 15.19–30); see also note on 1.40–45. The issue of ritual impurity is not mentioned in this story. **5.26** Criticism of *physicians* is commonplace in some ancient Near Eastern texts (e.g., Tob 2.10; Sir 38.15). **5.27–28** Popular belief in the magical power (v. 30) of holy people prompts the

woman's desire to *touch* Jesus' clothes (see note on 5.23; see also 3.10; Lk 6.19; Acts 5.15; 19.11–12). The Markan Jesus interprets her attitude as *faith* (v. 34). **5.31** The disciples' words here (cf. Mt 9.20–22; Lk 8.45–46) recall their protest in 4.38. **5.33** The woman's *fear and trembling* were in reaction to *what had happened to her* (see notes on 4.41; 5.15), not in response to having been found out (cf. Lk 8.47). *Fell down before him.* See also 3.11; 5.22. **5.34** *Daughter* (see also vv. 23, 35), *your faith has made you well.* See notes on 2.5; 5.23. *Go in peace,* a common Semitic farewell (Judg 18.6; 1 Sam 1.17; 20.42; Lk 7.50; Acts 16.36; Jas 2.16), suggests the wholeness associated with being healed. **5.36** *Do not fear, only believe* recalls a similar shift in vv. 33–34 (cf. 4.40). **5.37** Seclusion from the public is a conventional feature of some ancient miracle stories (see also v. 40; 7.33; 8.23; 1 Kings 17.19; 2 Kings 4.4, 33; Acts 9.40). Along with Andrew (1.16–20, 29; 13.3), *Peter, James, and John* are prominent among the Twelve (3.16–17; 9.2; 14.33). **5.38** *Weeping and wailing.* The mourners here may have been hired professionals. **5.39** Partly because *sleeping* is a common euphemism for death in the NT (e.g., Eph 5.14; 1 Thess 5.10), Jesus' assessment of the child's condition is ambiguous. The context, however, suggests that the girl was really dead and that Jesus' remark indicates the ease with which he will bring her back to life. **5.40** *They laughed at him,* i.e., skeptically (see also vv. 31, 35; 2 Kings 5.11; Jn

all outside, and took the child's father and mother and those who were with him, and went in where the child was. 41He took her by the hand and said to her, "Talitha cum," which means, "Little girl, get up!" 42And immediately the girl got up and began to walk about (she was twelve years of age). At this they were overcome with amazement. 43He strictly ordered them that no one should know this, and told them to give her something to eat.

The Rejection of Jesus at Nazareth

6 He left that place and came to his hometown, and his disciples followed him. 2On the sabbath he began to teach in the synagogue, and many who heard him were astounded. They said, "Where did this man get all this? What is this wisdom that has been given to him? What deeds of power are being done by his hands! 3Is not this the carpenter, the son of Mary*a* and brother of James and Joses and Judas and Simon, and are not his sisters here with us?" And they took offense*b* at him. 4Then Jesus said to them, "Prophets are not without honor, except in their hometown, and among their own kin, and in their own house." 5And he could do no deed of power there, except that he

laid his hands on a few sick people and cured them. 6And he was amazed at their unbelief.

The Mission of the Twelve

Then he went about among the villages teaching. 7He called the twelve and began to send them out two by two, and gave them authority over the unclean spirits. 8He ordered them to take nothing for their journey except a staff; no bread, no bag, no money in their belts; 9but to wear sandals and not to put on two tunics. 10He said to them, "Wherever you enter a house, stay there until you leave the place. 11If any place will not welcome you and they refuse to hear you, as you leave, shake off the dust that is on your feet as a testimony against them." 12So they went out and proclaimed that all should repent. 13They cast out many demons, and anointed with oil many who were sick and cured them.

The Death of John the Baptist

14 King Herod heard of it, for Jesus'*c* name had become known. Some were*d* saying, "John

---

a Other ancient authorities read *son of the carpenter and of Mary* *b* Or *stumbled* *c* Gk *his* *d* Other ancient authorities read *He was*

11.39). **5.41** *He took her by the hand* (see also 1.31; Acts 3.7; notes on 5.23; 5.25). *Talitha cum,* one of several Semitic expressions interpreted by Mark (3.17; 7.11, 34; 11.9–10; 14.36; 15.22, 34, 42), is reminiscent of the use of foreign phrases in ancient miracle stories. The different Greek words for the child's arising (vv. 41–42) were also used by Jews and Christians with reference to resurrection (e.g., 6.14, 16; 8.31; 12.23, 25–26; 16.6; Acts 2.24; 1 Cor 15.12–20). **5.42** The girl's *age* is probably mentioned simply to indicate that she was old enough to walk, though note the oblique correspondence with v. 25. *Overcome with amazement.* See note on 1.22. **5.43** Jesus' injunction to silence does not seem to be related to the secret of his identity. Rather, it makes the point that a mysterious and overwhelming event, a raising from the dead, should not be spoken about casually. **6.1–6a** Cf. Mt 13.53–58; Lk 4.16–30. Jesus' rejection in his homeland concludes the section on epiphanies of divine power in a way that recalls the resistance to him in 2.1–3.6. **6.2** *Astounded.* See note on 1.22. *Where did this man get all this?* See also 3.22; Jn 7.15. Jesus' *wisdom* likely refers to his teaching, represented in 4.1–34. *Deeds of power.* See 4.35–5.43. **6.3** The Greek word translated here as *carpenter* (cf. Mt 13.55) can also refer to an artisan in stone, metal, or wood. Because Jewish lineage was traced through one's father (cf. Jn 6.42), *the son of Mary* is an unexpected phrase of debatable significance; see also notes on 3.31; 3.35. *They took offense,* lit. "they were scandalized"; see also note on 4.17 (cf. 1 Cor 1.23; Gal 5.11). **6.4** This saying appears in various forms in Lk 4.24; Jn 4.44, and some noncanonical Gospels. *Among their own kin . . . in their own house.* See also 3.21, 31–32. **6.5** *He could do no deed of power there.* Cf. Mt 13.58. *Laid his hands on . . . cured them.* See note on 5.23. **6.6a** *Unbelief,* or "lack of faith." Cf. 5.34, 36; see also note on 2.5.

6.6b–8.26 The extension of Jesus' mission within and beyond Galilee (6.6b–13; 6.30–51; 6.53–8.13; 8.22–26), the increasing enmity of secular rulers (6.14–29), and the growing blindness of the disciples (6.52; 8.14–21). **6.6b** Cf. Mt 9.35. A transitional "summary report" (see note on 1.32–34). **6.7–30** Cf. Mt 10.1, 9–14; 14.1–12; Lk 9.1–10a. The death of John (vv. 14–29) is bracketed by the dispatch and return of the Twelve (vv. 7–13, 30; see note on 2.1–12). **6.7–9** Here the summonses in 1.17, 20; 3.13–15 are intensified. **6.7** *Two by two.* See also Lk 10.1; Acts 13.2–3; cf. Deut 17.6; 19.15; Mt 18.16; Jn 8.17; 2 Cor 13.1; 1 Tim 5.19. *Unclean spirits.* See note on 1.23. **6.8–9** Cynic preachers of antiquity carried *bread* and a beggar's *bag;* even *staff* and *sandals* are prohibited in Mt 10.10; Lk 9.3; 10.4. **6.10** *The place,* i.e., the village or region in which a hospitable *house* was located. **6.11** *Shake off the dust . . . on your feet.* On one level, this gesture shames those who refused to grant hospitality to the missionaries. On another, it is *testimony against them,* leading to condemnation of such people at the final judgment. **6.12** See also 1.4, 14–15. **6.13** *Anointed with oil.* See also Jas 5.14. **6.14** *Herod* Antipas, son of Herod the Great and tetrarch of Galilee and Perea (4 BCE–

the baptizer has been raised from the dead; and for this reason these powers are at work in him." [15]But others said, "It is Elijah." And others said, "It is a prophet, like one of the prophets of old." [16]But when Herod heard of it, he said, "John, whom I beheaded, has been raised."

17 For Herod himself had sent men who arrested John, bound him, and put him in prison on account of Herodias, his brother Philip's wife, because Herod[a] had married her. [18]For John had been telling Herod, "It is not lawful for you to have your brother's wife." [19]And Herodias had a grudge against him, and wanted to kill him. But she could not, [20]for Herod feared John, knowing that he was a righteous and holy man, and he protected him. When he heard him, he was greatly perplexed;[b] and yet he liked to listen to him. [21]But an opportunity came when Herod on his birthday gave a banquet for his courtiers and officers and for the leaders of Galilee. [22]When his daughter Herodias[c] came in and danced, she pleased Herod and his guests; and the king said to the girl, "Ask me for whatever you wish, and I will give it." [23]And he solemnly swore to her, "Whatever you ask me, I will give you, even half of my kingdom." [24]She went out and said to her mother, "What should I ask for?" She replied, "The head of John the baptizer." [25]Immediately she rushed back to the king and requested, "I want you to give me at once the head of John the Baptist on a platter." [26]The king was deeply grieved; yet out of regard for his oaths and for the guests, he did not want to refuse her. [27]Immediately the king sent a soldier of the guard with orders to bring John's[d] head. He went and beheaded him in the prison, [28]brought his head on a platter, and gave it to the girl. Then the girl gave it to her mother. [29]When his disciples heard about it, they came and took his body, and laid it in a tomb.

Feeding the Five Thousand

30 The apostles gathered around Jesus, and told him all that they had done and taught. [31]He said to them, "Come away to a deserted place all by yourselves and rest a while." For many were coming and going, and they had no leisure even to eat. [32]And they went away in the boat to a deserted place by themselves. [33]Now many saw them going and recognized them, and they hurried there on foot from all the towns and arrived ahead of them. [34]As he went ashore, he saw a great crowd; and he had compassion for them, because they were like sheep without a shepherd; and he began to teach them many things. [35]When it grew late, his disciples came to him and said, "This is a deserted place, and the hour is now very late; [36]send them away so that they may go into the surrounding country and villages and buy something for themselves to eat." [37]But he answered them, "You give them something to eat." They said to him, "Are we to go and buy two hundred denarii[e] worth of bread, and give

a Gk he   b Other ancient authorities read he did many things
c Other ancient authorities read the daughter of Herodias herself
d Gk his   e The denarius was the usual day's wage for a laborer

---

39 CE; see also 3.6; 8.15; Lk 1.5; 3.1), was apparently referred to as king by ordinary people. *John the baptizer.* See 1.4–9. *Powers.* See 5.30; 6.2; cf. Jn 10.41. **6.15** *Elijah,* harbinger of the "day of the LORD" in Mal 3.1–2; 4.5–6. Cf. Mk 1.2; 9.9–13; see also note on 1.6. *A prophet.* Cf. Deut 18.15–22. Public speculation about Jesus is similarly described in 8.28; cf. Jn 1.19–21. **6.17** Jesus' own ministry commenced after *John* had been arrested (1.14). According to the Jewish historian Josephus, *Herodias* had not been married to Philip but to another brother of Antipas, whose name was Herod (*War* 2.182; *Antiquities* 18.240–44). **6.18** The illegality of such marriage is stipulated in Lev 18.16; 20.21. **6.19–20** John's reaction recalls that of Eleazar (2 Macc 6.18–31; 4 Macc 5.1–7.23); Herodias's recalls that of Jezebel (1 Kings 19.1–3). Like Ahab (1 Kings 21.1–16), Herod is portrayed as a weak governor, manipulated by his wife (v. 26). .**22** Herod's daughter (named Salome, according to Josephus) is identified as *Herodias* here. This identification was amended in some manuscripts of Mark (cf. Mt 14.6; see also text note *c*). **6.23** *I will give . . . kingdom.* See Esth 5.3, 6; 7.2. **6.27** *Soldier of the guard,* translation of a Greek term that came to refer to an "executioner." **6.29** *Took his body, laid it in a tomb.* Cf. 15.45–46. **6.30** *Apostles.* See note on 3.14. **6.31–56** Renewed teaching and more mighty deeds. **6.31–44** Cf. Mt 14.13–21; Lk 9.10–17; Jn 6.1–13. The feeding of the five thousand recalls Israel's miraculous sustenance by God (Ex 16.13–35; Num 11.1–35; Neh 9.15; Ps 78.17–31; Isa 49.8–13) as well as Jewish expectations of an end-time feast for God's elect (Isa 25.6–8; Mt 22.1–14; Lk 14.15–24). **6.31** *A deserted place* (also vv. 32, 35). See note on 1.35. *No leisure even to eat.* See also 3.20. **6.33** *All the towns,* another instance of Markan exaggeration (see, e.g., 1.32). **6.34** *Sheep without a shepherd.* See Num 27.15–17; 1 Kings 22.17; 2 Chr 18.16; Ezek 34.1–31; Jdt 11.19; Mt 9.36. **6.37** *Two hundred denarii,* a sum beyond reach. A denarius represented a laborer's daily wage (Mt 20.2, 9, 13),

it to them to eat?" [38] And he said to them, "How many loaves have you? Go and see." When they had found out, they said, "Five, and two fish." [39] Then he ordered them to get all the people to sit down in groups on the green grass. [40] So they sat down in groups of hundreds and of fifties. [41] Taking the five loaves and the two fish, he looked up to heaven, and blessed and broke the loaves, and gave them to his disciples to set before the people; and he divided the two fish among them all. [42] And all ate and were filled; [43] and they took up twelve baskets full of broken pieces and of the fish. [44] Those who had eaten the loaves numbered five thousand men.

Jesus Walks on the Water

[45] Immediately he made his disciples get into the boat and go on ahead to the other side, to Bethsaida, while he dismissed the crowd. [46] After saying farewell to them, he went up on the mountain to pray.

[47] When evening came, the boat was out on the sea, and he was alone on the land. [48] When he saw that they were straining at the oars against an adverse wind, he came towards them early in the morning, walking on the sea. He intended to pass them by. [49] But when they saw him walking on the sea, they thought it was a ghost and cried out; [50] for they all saw him and were terrified. But immediately he spoke to them and said, "Take heart, it is I; do not be afraid." [51] Then he got into the boat with them and the wind ceased. And they were utterly astounded, [52] for they did not understand about the loaves, but their hearts were hardened.

Healing the Sick in Gennesaret

[53] When they had crossed over, they came to land at Gennesaret and moored the boat. [54] When they got out of the boat, people at once recognized him, [55] and rushed about that whole region and began to bring the sick on mats to wherever they heard he was. [56] And wherever he went, into villages or cities or farms, they laid the sick in the marketplaces, and begged him that they might touch even the fringe of his cloak; and all who touched it were healed.

The Tradition of the Elders

7 Now when the Pharisees and some of the scribes who had come from Jerusalem gathered around him, [2] they noticed that some of his disciples were eating with defiled hands, that is, without washing them. [3] (For the Pharisees, and all the Jews, do not eat unless they thoroughly wash their hands,[a] thus observing the tradition of the elders; [4] and they do not

---

a Meaning of Gk uncertain

6.39 *Groups*, lit. "symposia," suggesting a banquet's conviviality. **6.40** Companies *of hundreds and of fifties* were prescribed for aspects of community life among the Dead Sea sectarians (see also Ex 18.21, 25). **6.41** *He looked up to heaven.* See also 7.34; Job 22.26; Ps 121.1; Lk 18.13; Jn 11.41. Jesus' actions (*taking, blessed, broke, gave;* cf. 8.6) were customary for a host at a Jewish meal; see also 14.22. **6.42–44** The multitude's satisfaction and the abundant leftovers confirm the miracle (see also 2 Kings 4.42–44). The symbolic significance, if any, of the numbers *twelve* and *five thousand* is unclear (also *five* and *two* in v. 38). **6.45–52** Cf. Mt 14.22–33; Jn 6.15–21. Another epiphany of Jesus on the sea (see also 4.35–41; Jn 21.1–14). **6.45** *Bethsaida,* on the north-northeast shore of the Sea of Galilee. **6.46** *He went up on the mountain to pray.* See notes on 1.35; 3.13. **6.48** *Early in the morning,* lit. "around the fourth watch of the night" (between 3:00 and 6:00 A.M.). *Walking on the sea.* See notes on 4.37; 4.41. *He intended to pass them by,* a remark typical of theophanies; it alludes to God's veiled self-disclosure to Moses (Ex 33.18–23) and Elijah (1 Kings 19.11–12). **6.50** *It is I,* lit. "I am," an expression of divine self-revelation in the OT (Ex 3.13–15; Isa 41.4; 43.10–11; see also, e.g., Jn 4.26; 6.20, 35). *Take heart . . . do not be afraid.* See note on 4.40. **6.51** *The wind ceased.* See 4.39. *Astounded.* See note on 4.41. **6.52** *They did not understand.* See note on 4.13. *Loaves.* See vv. 37–38, 41, 44. *Their hearts were hardened.* See note on 3.5. **6.53–56** Cf. Mt 14.34–36. A transitional "summary report" (see note on 1.32–34). **6.53** Oddly, *they came to land at Gennesaret,* on the northwest shore of the Sea of Galilee (cf. v. 45); see also note on 5.1. **6.56** *The fringe of his cloak,* possibly the tassel that Jewish males were required to wear (Num 15.37–41; Deut 22.12; see also Mt 9.20; Lk 8.44). *All . . . healed.* See note on 5.27–28.

7.1–23 Cf. Mt 15.1–20. A dispute between Jesus and the Pharisees. **7.1** *Pharisees and . . . scribes . . . from Jerusalem.* See notes on 1.5; 1.22; 2.16. **7.2** *Eating,* lit. "eating the loaves," a Semitic expression that effectively recalls 6.41, 44. *With defiled hands* refers to ritual uncleanness (Acts 10.14; 11.8; cf. Mk 2.23–28); its interpretation (*that is, without washing them;* see Lev 15.11) and the explanations in vv. 3–4, 11, 19b presume that some members of the audience may be unfamiliar with Jewish customs. **7.3** That *all the Jews* observed hand washing has often been taken as historically inaccurate, but the practice was indeed widespread among Jews of the time and not confined to the Pharisees. *Thoroughly,* lit. "with a fist," probably means "up to the

eat anything from the market unless they wash it;*a* and there are also many other traditions that they observe, the washing of cups, pots, and bronze kettles.*b*) 5So the Pharisees and the scribes asked him, "Why do your disciples not live*c* according to the tradition of the elders, but eat with defiled hands?" 6He said to them, "Isaiah prophesied rightly about you hypocrites, as it is written,

'This people honors me with their lips,
    but their hearts are far from me;
7 in vain do they worship me,
    teaching human precepts as doctrines.'

8You abandon the commandment of God and hold to human tradition."

9 Then he said to them, "You have a fine way of rejecting the commandment of God in order to keep your tradition! 10For Moses said, 'Honor your father and your mother'; and, 'Whoever speaks evil of father or mother must surely die.' 11But you say that if anyone tells father or mother, 'Whatever support you might have had from me is Corban' (that is, an offering to God*d*)— 12then you no longer permit doing anything for a father or mother, 13thus making void the word of God through your tradition that you have handed on. And you do many things like this."

14 Then he called the crowd again and said to them, "Listen to me, all of you, and understand: 15there is nothing outside a person that by going in can defile, but the things that come out are what defile."*e*

17 When he had left the crowd and entered the house, his disciples asked him about the parable. 18He said to them, "Then do you also fail to understand? Do you not see that whatever goes into a person from outside cannot defile, 19since it enters, not the heart but the stomach, and goes out into the sewer?" (Thus he declared all foods clean.) 20And he said, "It is what comes out of a person that defiles. 21For it is from within, from the human heart, that evil intentions come: fornication, theft, murder, 22adultery, avarice, wickedness, deceit, licentiousness, envy, slander, pride, folly. 23All these evil things come from within, and they defile a person."

The Syrophoenician Woman's Faith

24 From there he set out and went away to the region of Tyre.*f* He entered a house and did not want anyone to know he was there. Yet he could not escape notice, 25but a woman whose little daughter had an unclean spirit immediately heard about him, and she came and bowed down at his feet. 26Now the woman was a Gentile, of Syrophoenician origin. She begged him to cast the demon out of her daughter. 27He said to her, "Let the children be fed first, for it is not fair to take the children's food and throw it to the dogs." 28But she answered him, "Sir,*g* even the dogs under the table eat the children's crumbs." 29Then he said to her, "For saying that, you may go—the

a Other ancient authorities read *and when they come from the marketplace, they do not eat unless they purify themselves*
b Other ancient authorities add *and beds*   *c* Gk *walk*
d Gk lacks *to God*   *e* Other ancient authorities add verse 16, *"Let anyone with ears to hear listen"*   *f* Other ancient authorities add *and Sidon*   *g* Or *Lord*; other ancient authorities prefix *Yes*

---

elbows." *The tradition of the elders,* oral interpretation, considered by Pharisees to be legally binding (see also Gal 1.14). **7.6–7** Isa 29.13 (Septuagint). Prophetic condemnation of empty worship was common; see, e.g., Isa 1.10–20; 58.1–14; Am 5.21–24. **7.8** Cf. Col 2.20–22. **7.10** See Ex 20.12; 21.17; Lev 20.9; Deut 5.16; see also Mk 10.19; Eph 6.2. **7.11** *Corban,* an offering dedicated to God (see Lev 1.2) and thereby withdrawn from secular uses such as parental support. What the Markan Jesus criticizes here is the practice of making pseudo-vows, i.e., declaring something an offering to God only if and when someone else, e.g., one's parents, attempted to make use of it. **7.13** *The word of God,* i.e., the written law. **7.15** On what can and cannot *defile,* see vv. 18–19; Acts 10.9–16; Rom 14.14; Gal 2.11–14; cf. Lev 11.1–47; see also notes on 1.40–45; 5.25; 5.41. V. 16 (see text note *e*) is probably a later textual addition, modeled after 4.9, 23. **7.17** *The house.* See note on 3.19b. *His disciples . . . parable.* See 4.10, 33–34; see also note on 3.23. **7.18** *Fail to understand.* See also 4.13;

6.52. **7.19** *The heart,* metaphorically regarded as the seat of moral and religious conduct (e.g., 1 Sam 12.20, 24; Ps 24.4–5; Jer 32.39–40; Mt 5.8). **7.21–22** Lists of vices are common in early Christian exhortation (e.g., Rom 1.29–31; Gal 5.19–21; 2 Tim 3.2–5). **7.22** *Envy,* or stinginess, lit. "an evil eye"; see Deut 15.9; Tob 4.7; Sir 14.10; 31.13. **7.24–30** Cf. Mt 15.21–28. The third of four exorcisms (see also 1.21–28; 5.1–20; 9.14–29). **7.24** *The region of Tyre* (see also 3.8), northwest of Galilee, largely gentile. *A house.* See note on 3.19b. On the recurring tension between Jesus' seclusion and disclosure, see also 1.44–45; 2.1–2; 3.19b–20; 6.31–33; 7.36. **7.25** *An unclean spirit,* or demon (vv. 26, 29, 30; see also 1.23). *Bowed down at his feet.* See note on 3.11. **7.26** *A Gentile,* lit. "a Greek" (see also Rom 1.16; 2.9–10; 1 Cor 1.24; 10.32; Gal 3.28; Col 3.11), whose specific nationality was *Syrophoenician*. **7.27** The saying implies the superiority of Israel's claim upon God's blessing (*food,* lit. "bread") over that of Gentiles, slandered as *dogs* (1 Sam 17.43; 24.14; Prov 26.11; Phil 3.2; Rev 22.15).

demon has left your daughter." ³⁰So she went home, found the child lying on the bed, and the demon gone.

Jesus Cures a Deaf Man

31 Then he returned from the region of Tyre, and went by way of Sidon towards the Sea of Galilee, in the region of the Decapolis. ³²They brought to him a deaf man who had an impediment in his speech; and they begged him to lay his hand on him. ³³He took him aside in private, away from the crowd, and put his fingers into his ears, and he spat and touched his tongue. ³⁴Then looking up to heaven, he sighed and said to him, "Ephphatha," that is, "Be opened." ³⁵And immediately his ears were opened, his tongue was released, and he spoke plainly. ³⁶Then Jesus[a] ordered them to tell no one; but the more he ordered them, the more zealously they proclaimed it. ³⁷They were astounded beyond measure, saying, "He has done everything well; he even makes the deaf to hear and the mute to speak."

Feeding the Four Thousand

8 In those days when there was again a great crowd without anything to eat, he called his disciples and said to them, ²"I have compassion for the crowd, because they have been with me now for three days and have nothing to eat. ³If I send them away hungry to their homes, they will faint on the way—and some of them have come from a great distance." ⁴His disciples replied, "How can one feed these people with bread here in the desert?" ⁵He asked

them, "How many loaves do you have?" They said, "Seven." ⁶Then he ordered the crowd to sit down on the ground; and he took the seven loaves, and after giving thanks he broke them and gave them to his disciples to distribute; and they distributed them to the crowd. ⁷They had also a few small fish; and after blessing them, he ordered that these too should be distributed. ⁸They ate and were filled; and they took up the broken pieces left over, seven baskets full. ⁹Now there were about four thousand people. And he sent them away. ¹⁰And immediately he got into the boat with his disciples and went to the district of Dalmanutha.[b]

The Demand for a Sign

11 The Pharisees came and began to argue with him, asking him for a sign from heaven, to test him. ¹²And he sighed deeply in his spirit and said, "Why does this generation ask for a sign? Truly I tell you, no sign will be given to this generation." ¹³And he left them, and getting into the boat again, he went across to the other side.

The Yeast of the Pharisees and of Herod

14 Now the disciples[c] had forgotten to bring any bread; and they had only one loaf with them in the boat. ¹⁵And he cautioned them, saying, "Watch out—beware of the yeast of the Pharisees and the yeast of Herod."[d] ¹⁶They said to one another, "It is because we have no

---

a Gk he   b Other ancient authorities read *Mageda* or *Magdala*
c Gk they   d Other ancient authorities read *the Herodians*

7.31–37 Cf. Mt 15.29–31. **7.31** The route is roundabout (see also notes on 5.1; 6.53): *Sidon* was twenty miles north of *Tyre* (see note on 7.24); *the region of the Decapolis* was east and southeast of *the Sea of Galilee* (see notes on 1.16; 5.20). **7.32** *Lay his hand on him.* See note on 5.23. **7.33** *In private, away from the crowd.* See note on 5.37. Jesus' healing technique, including the use of spittle, is common in ancient healing stories (see also Jn 9.6). **7.34** *Looking up to heaven.* See note on 6.41. *"Ephphatha," "Be opened."* See note on 5.41. **7.35** *His ears,* lit. "his hearing." **7.36** Similar commands or efforts are violated elsewhere; see 1.44–45; 7.24. **7.37** *Astounded beyond measure.* See note on 1.22. The acclamation echoes Isa 35.5–6; Wis 10.21.

  8.1–9 Cf. Mt 15.32–39. Another version of the feeding of the multitude (see note on 6.31–44). **8.4** *Desert,* or "wilderness"; see notes on 1.4; 1.35. **8.6** *Giving thanks, broke them.* See Acts 27.35; 1 Cor 11.24; see also note on 6.41. **8.8–9** See note on 6.42–44. Compared with 6.38, 43–44, the numbers of loaves (*seven,* v. 5),

baskets (*seven,* v. 8), and people (*four thousand,* v. 9) vary, yet their symbolism is equally indeterminate. **8.10–21** The question of a sign and bread. **8.10** *Dalmanutha.* Location unknown (cf. Mt 15.39; see also notes on 5.1; 6.53; 7.31). **8.11–13** Cf. Mt 16.1–4; Lk 11.29–32; cf. Mt 12.38–42; Lk 11.16; Jn 6.30. **8.11** *Pharisees.* See note on 2.16. *A sign from heaven,* i.e., verification of divine authority (see Ex 4.28, 30; Num 14.11; Deut 13.1–5; Isa 7.10–17). **8.12** *This generation* recalls OT terminology for human faithlessness (see Gen 7.1; Deut 32.5, 20; Ps 95.10; see also Mk 8.38; 9.19; 13.30). *Truly I tell you.* See note on 3.28. **8.14–21** Cf. Mt 16.5–12; Lk 12.1; Jn 6.32–36. An enigmatic passage highlighting the disciples' hardened hearts (v. 17); see notes on 3.5; 4.13. **8.14** Though ambiguous, a contrast between the disciples' need and their apparently insufficient resources may be intended (see also 6.37–38; 8.4–5). **8.15** *Yeast,* a symbol of pervasive corruption hidden within human beings (see also 1 Cor 5.6; Gal 5.9). *Pharisees.* See note on 2.16. *Herod.* See

bread." [17] And becoming aware of it, Jesus said to them, "Why are you talking about having no bread? Do you still not perceive or understand? Are your hearts hardened? [18] Do you have eyes, and fail to see? Do you have ears, and fail to hear? And do you not remember? [19] When I broke the five loaves for the five thousand, how many baskets full of broken pieces did you collect?" They said to him, "Twelve." [20] "And the seven for the four thousand, how many baskets full of broken pieces did you collect?" And they said to him, "Seven." [21] Then he said to them, "Do you not yet understand?"

Jesus Cures a Blind Man at Bethsaida

[22] They came to Bethsaida. Some people[a] brought a blind man to him and begged him to touch him. [23] He took the blind man by the hand and led him out of the village; and when he had put saliva on his eyes and laid his hands on him, he asked him, "Can you see anything?" [24] And the man[b] looked up and said, "I can see people, but they look like trees, walking." [25] Then Jesus[b] laid his hands on his eyes again; and he looked intently and his sight was restored, and he saw everything clearly. [26] Then he sent him away to his home, saying, "Do not even go into the village."[c]

Peter's Declaration about Jesus

[27] Jesus went on with his disciples to the villages of Caesarea Philippi; and on the way he asked his disciples, "Who do people say that I am?" [28] And they answered him, "John the Baptist; and others, Elijah; and still others, one of the prophets." [29] He asked them, "But who do you say that I am?" Peter answered him, "You are the Messiah."[d] [30] And he sternly ordered them not to tell anyone about him.

Jesus Foretells His Death and Resurrection

[31] Then he began to teach them that the Son of Man must undergo great suffering, and be rejected by the elders, the chief priests, and the scribes, and be killed, and after three days rise again. [32] He said all this quite openly. And Peter took him aside and began to rebuke him. [33] But turning and looking at his disciples, he rebuked Peter and said, "Get behind me, Satan! For you are setting your mind not on divine things but on human things."

[34] He called the crowd with his disciples, and said to them, "If any want to become my followers, let them deny themselves and take up their cross and follow me. [35] For those who want to save their life will lose it, and those who lose their life for my sake, and for the sake of the gospel,[e] will save it. [36] For what will it profit them to gain the whole world and forfeit their life? [37] Indeed, what can they give in

---

a Gk They   b Gk he   c Other ancient authorities add *or tell anyone in the village*   d Or *the Christ*   e Other ancient authorities read *lose their life for the sake of the gospel*

---

note on 6.14. **8.17–18** See also 4.11–12; Jer 5.21; Ezek 12.2. **8.19–20** See 6.41–44; 8.6–9. **8.22–26** Cf. Jn 9.1–7. The healing of the blind man of Bethsaida is transitional. It concludes 6.6b–8.26 and also introduces 8.27–10.45. It is another of the mighty deeds of Jesus portrayed in the preceding portion of the Gospel. As an instance of progressive relief from blindness, it is also symbolic of the disciples' symbolic blindness and partial understanding (cf. v. 18; 10.46–52). **8.22** *Bethsaida.* See note on 6.45; see also 6.53; 8.13. *To touch him.* See note on 5.23. **8.23** *Out of the village.* See note on 5.37. On the application of *saliva* and *hands,* see note on 7.33. **8.26** *Do not even go into the village.* See the similar prohibitions in 1.44–45; 5.43; 7.24, 36.

8.27–10.52 Jesus' anticipated suffering, the disciples' misunderstanding, and instruction in discipleship. **8.27–30** Cf. Mt 16.13–20; Lk 9.18–21. **8.27** *Caesarea Philippi,* a city in the district of Panias, part of the tetrarchy of Philip, situated near the southern slope of Mount Hermon. A grotto dedicated to the god Pan lay at the foot of the mountain from at least the third century BCE. Near this grotto Herod the Great built a temple dedicated to Roma and the emperor Augustus. **8.28** *John the Baptist.* See note on 6.14. *Elijah . . . one of*

the prophets. See note on 6.15. **8.29** Cf. Jn 1.49; 6.68–69. *The Messiah.* See note on 1.1. **8.30** *He sternly ordered,* or "rebuked" (see 1.25; 3.12; 4.39; 9.25; 10.13; see also note on 1.34). **8.31–9.1** Cf. Mt 16.21–28; Lk 9.22–27. The first set in a cycle of three predictions of Jesus' suffering and resurrection (8.31; see also 9.31; 10.33–34), three inappropriate responses by the disciples (8.32–33; see also 9.32–34; 10.35–41), and three discourses on discipleship (8.34–9.1; see also 9.35–50; 10.42–45). **8.31** *Son of Man,* Jesus' cryptic mode of self-reference (see note on 2.10), focused here on his sufferings. See also 9.12; 14.21, 41; Mt 8.20; 17.12; 26.2, 24, 45; Lk 9.58; 17.25; 22.22, 48; 24.7. *Must undergo,* i.e., in accordance with God's will (cf. Isa 53.4–6, 10). *The elders,* senior lay leaders (see also Lk 7.3; Acts 4.8), who with the *chief priests and the scribes* constitute the Sanhedrin, i.e., the council of the city of Jerusalem, and probably the supreme council of Judea according to Mark (14.43, 53–55; 15.1; see also note on 1.22). **8.32–33** *To rebuke.* See note on 8.30. *Satan.* See note on 1.13. **8.34** *Deny,* or "disown." See 14.30, 31, 72; see also Mt 10.38; Lk 14.27. *Cross,* an instrument of torturous execution (see 15.21, 30, 32). **8.35** *Gospel,* or "good news." See note on 1.1. See also Mt 10.39; Lk 17.33; Jn 12.25. **8.36** See also Lk 12.13–21.

return for their life? [38]Those who are ashamed of me and of my words[a] in this adulterous and sinful generation, of them the Son of Man will also be ashamed when he comes in the glory of his Father with the holy angels." [1]And he said to them, "Truly I tell you, there are some standing here who will not taste death until they see that the kingdom of God has come with[b] power."

The Transfiguration

2 Six days later, Jesus took with him Peter and James and John, and led them up a high mountain apart, by themselves. And he was transfigured before them, [3]and his clothes became dazzling white, such as no one[c] on earth could bleach them. [4]And there appeared to them Elijah with Moses, who were talking with Jesus. [5]Then Peter said to Jesus, "Rabbi, it is good for us to be here; let us make three dwellings,[d] one for you, one for Moses, and one for Elijah." [6]He did not know what to say, for they were terrified. [7]Then a cloud overshadowed them, and from the cloud there came a voice, "This is my Son, the Beloved;[e] listen to him!" [8]Suddenly when they looked around, they saw no one with them any more, but only Jesus.

The Coming of Elijah

9 As they were coming down the mountain, he ordered them to tell no one about what they had seen, until after the Son of Man had risen from the dead. [10]So they kept the matter to themselves, questioning what this rising from the dead could mean. [11]Then they asked him, "Why do the scribes say that Elijah must come first?" [12]He said to them, "Elijah is indeed coming first to restore all things. How then is it written about the Son of Man, that he is to go through many sufferings and be treated with contempt? [13]But I tell you that Elijah has come, and they did to him whatever they pleased, as it is written about him."

The Healing of a Boy with a Spirit

14 When they came to the disciples, they saw a great crowd around them, and some scribes

---

a Other ancient authorities read *and of mine* *b* Or *in* *c* Gk *no fuller* *d* Or *tents* *e* Or *my beloved Son*

8.38 See also Mt 10.33; Lk 12.9. *This adulterous and sinful generation.* See note on 8.12. Some Jews expected the figure described as "one like a human being" in Dan 7.13–14 to be the agent of God in the end time as king or judge. Christians identified this *Son of Man* with Jesus (see 13.26; 14.62; Mt 19.28; 24.37–44; Lk 12.40; 17.24–30; 18.8; 21.36; Acts 7.55–56); see also notes on 2.10; 8.31. *With the holy angels.* See also Mt 13.41; 25.31; Jn 1.51. **9.1** See also 13.30. *Truly I tell you.* See note on 3.28. *Taste death*, i.e., die; see also 2 Esd 6.26; Jn 8.52; Heb 2.9. *Kingdom of God.* See note on 1.15. **9.2–8** Cf. Mt 17.1–8; Lk 9.28–36. See also 2 Pet 1.17–18. **9.2** *Six days later*, an unusually precise setting (cf. Ex 24.15–16). *Peter and James and John.* See note on 5.37. *A high mountain.* The mention of Caesarea Philippi in 8.27 suggests that the mountain here is Mount Hermon. Cf. Ex 24.12–18; see also note on 3.13. *Apart, by themselves.* See 4.34; 6.31–32; 7.33; 9.28; 13.3. *Transfigured*, or "transformed," language rooted in Greek traditions about gods walking the earth in human form and then manifesting their divine glory or radiance. This Greek notion is adapted to accounts of theophany, the self-manifestation of God in the OT (Ex 24.15–17). **9.3** *His clothes became dazzling white*, an image connoting the radiance of a heavenly being or a glorified human being (see 16.5; Dan 7.9; 12.3; 2 Esd 7.97; Mt 13.43; 28.3; Lk 24.4; Rev 3.5; 4.4; 7.9, 13). *No one*, lit. *no fuller* (see text note *c*), one who whitens woolen cloth. **9.4** The appearance of *Elijah with Moses* recalls the traditions that they had been taken to heaven. Josephus provides evidence that at least some Jews of Mark's time believed that Moses (cf. Deut 34.5–6), like Elijah (2 Kings 2.9–12), was directly translated into heavenly life (*Antiquities* 4.326; cf. 2 Esd 6.26). See also note on 1.6. **9.5** Peter's suggestion that he, James, and John construct three tents, presumably related to Jesus, Elijah, and Moses, recalls Greek traditions implying that it was customary to build a shrine on the site of the epiphany of a deity. **9.6** *Terrified.* See note on 4.41. **9.7** OT theophanies are often accompanied by a *cloud* (see, e.g., Ex 24.15–18; Isa 4.5; Ezek 1.4). The heavenly voice recalls OT pronouncements (Deut 18.15; Ps 2.7; Isa 42.1); see note on 1.11. *My son.* See note on 1.1. **9.9–13** Cf. Mt 17.9–13. **9.9** *Tell no one*, less a command to conceal Jesus' identity than a signal to the disciples as characters in the narrative, and especially to the audience of Mark, that the transfiguration of Jesus is a preview of his resurrection. The account of the transfiguration in Mark fulfills the purpose of the resurrection appearances in the other canonical Gospels. *Son of Man* (also v. 12). See note on 8.31 (cf. 2.10; 8.38). **9.10** Resurrection was an intelligible concept for Jews; however, most Jewish traditions envisioned a collective rather than an individual resurrection. This unexpected difference leads to *questioning* (or "arguing") on the part of the disciples. **9.11** *Scribes.* See note on 1.22. The disciples' question implies the belief that the return of Elijah was expected to take place before the (general or collective) resurrection at the end. **9.12** The claim that it is written in scripture that the Son of Man is to *be treated with contempt* may be an allusion to Ps 22.7, which has similar wording in the Greek version. The divine necessity of Jesus' *many sufferings* is also expressed in 8.31 (cf. 14.21; Lk 18.31; 24.44, 46; Acts 13.29). **9.13** *Elijah has come.* See notes on 1.6; 6.15.

arguing with them. [15]When the whole crowd saw him, they were immediately overcome with awe, and they ran forward to greet him. [16]He asked them, "What are you arguing about with them?" [17]Someone from the crowd answered him, "Teacher, I brought you my son; he has a spirit that makes him unable to speak; [18]and whenever it seizes him, it dashes him down; and he foams and grinds his teeth and becomes rigid; and I asked your disciples to cast it out, but they could not do so." [19]He answered them, "You faithless generation, how much longer must I be among you? How much longer must I put up with you? Bring him to me." [20]And they brought the boy[a] to him. When the spirit saw him, immediately it convulsed the boy,[a] and he fell on the ground and rolled about, foaming at the mouth. [21]Jesus[b] asked the father, "How long has this been happening to him?" And he said, "From childhood. [22]It has often cast him into the fire and into the water, to destroy him; but if you are able to do anything, have pity on us and help us." [23]Jesus said to him, "If you are able!—All things can be done for the one who believes." [24]Immediately the father of the child cried out,[c] "I believe; help my unbelief!" [25]When Jesus saw that a crowd came running together, he rebuked the unclean spirit, saying to it, "You spirit that keeps this boy from speaking and hearing, I command you, come out of him, and never enter him again!" [26]After crying out and convulsing him terribly, it came out, and the boy was like a corpse, so that most of them said, "He is dead." [27]But Jesus took him by the hand and lifted him up, and he was able to stand. [28]When he had entered the house, his disciples asked him privately, "Why could we not cast it out?" [29]He said to them, "This kind can come out only through prayer."[d]

Jesus Again Foretells His Death and Resurrection

30 They went on from there and passed through Galilee. He did not want anyone to know it; [31]for he was teaching his disciples, saying to them, "The Son of Man is to be betrayed into human hands, and they will kill him, and three days after being killed, he will rise again." [32]But they did not understand what he was saying and were afraid to ask him.

Who Is the Greatest?

33 Then they came to Capernaum; and when he was in the house he asked them, "What were you arguing about on the way?" [34]But they were silent, for on the way they had argued with one another who was the greatest. [35]He sat down, called the twelve, and said to them, "Whoever wants to be first must be last of all and servant of all." [36]Then he took a little child and put it among them; and taking it in his arms, he said to them, [37]"Whoever welcomes one such child in my name welcomes

a Gk him   b Gk He   c Other ancient authorities add with tears   d Other ancient authorities add and fasting

9.14–29 Cf. Mt 17.14–20; Lk 9.37–43a. The last of four exorcisms (see also 1.21–28; 5.1–20; 7.24–30). **9.14** Scribes. See note on 1.22. **9.15** Overcome with awe, perhaps a muffled echo of Ex 34.30; see also note on 4.41. **9.17–18** The boy's symptoms suggest epilepsy. **9.18** But they could not do so. Cf. 6.13. **9.19** You faithless generation. See note on 8.12. **9.23** All things . . . believes. See note on 2.5; see also 11.22–23. **9.24** I believe; help my unbelief! See notes on 4.40; 6.6a. **9.25** The unclean spirit, i.e., a demon (see 1.23). **9.26–27** As in 5.41–42 (see note on 5.41), a healing is described with the language of resurrection. **9.28** Entered the house . . . privately. See notes on 4.10; 7.17. **9.29** On the power of faith through prayer, see also 11.24. **9.30–50** The second set in the cycle of three predictions of Jesus' suffering and resurrection, three misapprehensions by the disciples, and three sets of instruction on true discipleship (see note on 8.31–9.1). **9.30–32** Cf. Mt 17.22–23; Lk 9.43b–45. **9.30** Galilee. See note on 1.9. Not want anyone to know it. See note on 1.34. **9.31** Son of Man. See note on 8.31. Betrayed, also translated arrested in 1.14 and handed over in 3.19. See the note on 1.14. Into human hands, the simplest form of reference to the agents of Jesus' suffering (cf. 8.31; 10.33). **9.32** Characteristically in Mark (see notes on 4.13; 4.40), the disciples did not understand . . . and were afraid. **9.33** Capernaum. See note on 1.21. In the house. See note on 7.17. **9.34** Who was the greatest, a point of controversy within social groups of antiquity; see also Lk 22.24. **9.35** This saying appears in different forms and contexts in the Gospels (see 10.43–44; Mt 20.26–27; 23.11–12; Lk 9.48; 22.26). Here it signifies that humble service to the community is the norm, not distinguished rank. **9.36** Jesus' taking a little child and presenting it to the disciples together with his comment in v. 37 imply that the issue is the welcoming of actual children as members in the community and at communal gatherings. **9.37** Another saying whose variants are distributed throughout the Gospels (see 10.15; Mt 10.40; 18.5; Lk 9.48; 10.16; 18.17; Jn 12.44–45; 13.20). One such child in my name. Jesus identifies with actual children and teaches that whoever welcomes them wel-

me, and whoever welcomes me welcomes not me but the one who sent me."

Another Exorcist

38 John said to him, "Teacher, we saw some-one[a] casting out demons in your name, and we tried to stop him, because he was not following us." 39 But Jesus said, "Do not stop him; for no one who does a deed of power in my name will be able soon afterward to speak evil of me. 40 Whoever is not against us is for us. 41 For truly I tell you, whoever gives you a cup of water to drink because you bear the name of Christ will by no means lose the reward.

Temptations to Sin

42 "If any of you put a stumbling block before one of these little ones who believe in me,[b] it would be better for you if a great millstone were hung around your neck and you were thrown into the sea. 43 If your hand causes you to stumble, cut it off; it is better for you to enter life maimed than to have two hands and

to go to hell,[c] to the unquenchable fire.[d] 45 And if your foot causes you to stumble, cut it off; it is better for you to enter life lame than to have two feet and to be thrown into hell.[c,d] 47 And if your eye causes you to stumble, tear it out; it is better for you to enter the kingdom of God with one eye than to have two eyes and to be thrown into hell,[c] 48 where their worm never dies, and the fire is never quenched.

49 "For everyone will be salted with fire.[e] 50 Salt is good; but if salt has lost its saltiness, how can you season it?[f] Have salt in yourselves, and be at peace with one another."

Teaching about Divorce

10 He left that place and went to the region of Judea and[g] beyond the Jordan.

a Other ancient authorities add *who does not follow us*   b Other ancient authorities lack *in me*   c Gk *Gehenna*   d Verses 44 and 46 (which are identical with verse 48) are lacking in the best ancient authorities   e Other ancient authorities either add or substitute *and every sacrifice will be salted with salt*   f Or *how can you restore its saltiness?*   g Other ancient authorities lack *and*

comes Jesus. **9.38–40** Cf. Lk 9.49–50. This anecdote is probably placed here because of the association of *in your name* in v. 38 with *in my name* in v. 37. **9.38** Pagan magicians sometimes invoked a revered Jewish or Christian *name* (see also Acts 19.11–20). **9.40** This saying expresses openness in a context in which the Christ movement is spreading and becoming controversial (so also Lk 9.50). The related saying in Mt 12.30; Lk 11.23 (cf. Acts 19.13–17) reflects a stronger sense of communal boundaries and a desire to differentiate Christian healing from magic. **9.41** The giving of a cup of water may reflect hospitality in a missionary context (cf. Mt 10.40–42). *The name of Christ*, lit. "in the name that you belong to Christ." This phrase links the saying to the context by the association of the catchword "in the name of." See note on 9.38–40. **9.42–50** Cf. Mt 18.6–9; Lk 17.1–2. A chain of sayings linked by catchwords: *causes to stumble*, "scandalizes" or "trips up" (vv. 42–43, 45, 47; see also 4.17); *fire* (vv. 48–49); *salted* (vv. 49–50). **9.42–48** These sayings concern male sexuality in relation to the practice or the temptation to practice the sexual abuse of children and other sexual transgressions. **9.42** This saying picks up the theme of children from vv. 36–37 after a digression on outsiders (vv. 38–41). *A great millstone* was turned by a mule; cf. the hand-cranked mill implied by Mt 24.41; Lk 17.35. **9.43** See also Mt 5.30. *Hand*, probably an allusion to the Jewish prohibition of masturbation by males (see *Mishnah Niddah* 2.1; *Babylonian Talmud Niddah* 13a–b). *Life* (also v. 45), presumably eternal life (see note on 10.17). *Hell*, lit. Gehenna (text note *c*) or "valley of Hinnom" (also vv. 45, 47), a site associated with final punishment of the wicked (see Lk 12.5; Jas 3.6). **9.45** *Foot*, in biblical Hebrew sometimes a euphemism for the

male genitals (Isa 7.20; cf. Judg 3.24; Isa 6.2). The rabbis called masturbation "adultery with the hand" (because of the loss of seed) and adultery in the usual sense "adultery with the foot." **9.47** The idea of the eye causing one to stumble is related to the erotic gaze. See Mt 5.29 in relation to its context (5.27–28). *Kingdom of God.* See note on 1.15. **9.48** Undying *worm* and unquenchable *fire*, stock images for the destruction of evil (see Isa 66.24; Jdt 16.17; Sir 7.17). **9.49** This saying was probably placed in its present context because of the association of its reference to *fire* with the same word in v. 48. At least in its present context (vv. 43–48) it has an eschatological sense: each follower of Jesus will be tested by fire during the woes that end the old age or the birth pangs that usher in the full manifestation of the kingdom of God (cf. 1 Cor 3.13). What is worthless will be destroyed, and what is good will survive. Fire is analogous to salt, which preserves. **9.50** This group of sayings was placed here because, like v. 49, it uses the image of *salt. Salt is good* serves as an introduction to the other sayings. *If salt . . . season it?* Cf. Mt 5.13; Lk 14.34. *Have salt within yourselves,* cryptic, perhaps "Protect yourselves from corruption" (cf. Ignatius, *Magnesians* 10.2) or "Speak graciously and judiciously" (cf. Col 4.6). *Be at peace with one another* recalls the controversy disclosed in vv. 33–34. The members of the community are exhorted to avoid rivalry and self-assertion.

10.1–12 The question of divorce, an aspect of discipleship. Cf. Mt 19.1–9. **10.1** Jesus and his disciples continue on their journey southward to Jerusalem. *To the region of Judea and beyond the Jordan* seems to say that they went first to Judea and then to Perea, i.e., the region beyond the Jordan. The meaning, however, is

And crowds again gathered around him; and, as was his custom, he again taught them.

2 Some Pharisees came, and to test him they asked, "Is it lawful for a man to divorce his wife?" ³He answered them, "What did Moses command you?" ⁴They said, "Moses allowed a man to write a certificate of dismissal and to divorce her." ⁵But Jesus said to them, "Because of your hardness of heart he wrote this commandment for you. ⁶But from the beginning of creation, 'God made them male and female.' ⁷'For this reason a man shall leave his father and mother and be joined to his wife,ᵃ ⁸and the two shall become one flesh.' So they are no longer two, but one flesh. ⁹Therefore what God has joined together, let no one separate."

10 Then in the house the disciples asked him again about this matter. ¹¹He said to them, "Whoever divorces his wife and marries another commits adultery against her; ¹²and if she divorces her husband and marries another, she commits adultery."

Jesus Blesses Little Children

13 People were bringing little children to him in order that he might touch them; and the disciples spoke sternly to them. ¹⁴But when Jesus saw this, he was indignant and said to them, "Let the little children come to me; do not stop them; for it is to such as these that the kingdom of God belongs. ¹⁵Truly I tell you, whoever does not receive the kingdom of God as a little child will never enter it." ¹⁶And he took them up in his arms, laid his hands on them, and blessed them.

The Rich Man

17 As he was setting out on a journey, a man ran up and knelt before him, and asked him, "Good Teacher, what must I do to inherit eternal life?" ¹⁸Jesus said to him, "Why do you call me good? No one is good but God alone. ¹⁹You know the commandments: 'You shall not murder; You shall not commit adultery; You shall not steal; You shall not bear false witness; You shall not defraud; Honor your father and mother.' " ²⁰He said to him, "Teacher, I have kept all these since my youth." ²¹Jesus, looking at him, loved him and said, "You lack one thing; go, sell what you own, and give the moneyᵇ to the poor, and you will have treasure in heaven; then come, follow me." ²²When he heard this, he was shocked and went away grieving, for he had many possessions.

23 Then Jesus looked around and said to his

---

a Other ancient authorities lack *and be joined to his wife*
b Gk lacks *the money*

---

probably that they traveled through Perea to Judea (cf. 11.1, where the place arrived at last is also mentioned first). *Region of Judea.* See note on 1.5. **10.2** *Pharisees.* See note on 2.16. *Lawful,* what is "permitted" according to some interpretation of Jewish law. **10.3** See note on 2.25. **10.4** *A certificate of dismissal . . . to divorce her.* See Deut 24.1–4. **10.5** *Hardness of heart.* See note on 3.5. **10.6** Jesus quotes Gen 1.27; 5.2. **10.7–8** The quotation is from Gen 2.24; cf. Eph 5.31. **10.9** Absolute prohibition of divorce is relaxed elsewhere in the NT; cf. Mt 5.32; 19.9; 1 Cor 7.10–16. Divorce (without remarriage) seems allowable also in Mk 10.11–12. **10.10** *In the house.* See notes on 4.10; 7.17. **10.11** In contrast with Jesus' assertion here, Jewish law assumed that *adultery* was committed against a husband, not against a wife (see Lev 20.10; Deut 22.22; Sir 23.22–23). Greek and Roman law also defined adultery primarily as an offense against the husband's rights. **10.12** There is important evidence that Jewish women could initiate divorce, but Josephus claimed that it was against the Jewish law for women to do so. The wife could initiate divorce under Roman law, but different terms were used for the husband's and wife's activity in ending a marriage. Thus the use of the same terminology for both here is unusual. **10.13–16** Children and the kingdom of God. Cf. Mt 19.13–15; Lk 18.15–17. Children have a share in the kingdom of God.

10.13 *That he might touch them,* to convey some benefit (cf. 1.41; 3.10; 5.27–28; 6.56; 8.22). Blessing a person (v. 16) is also a way of conveying a benefit. **10.14** *Kingdom of God.* See note on 1.15. Children represent the type of character needed to enter the kingdom of God (cf. 9.33–37). **10.15** Cf. Mt 18.3; Jn 3.3–5. The connection between this passage and 9.33–37 suggests that receiving the kingdom as a child means receiving it without the ambition to be a figure of authority, but being content to be *last of all and servant of all* (9.35). **10.17–31** On property and the kingdom of God, cf. Mt 19.16–30; Lk 18.18–30. **10.17** *A man.* Cf. Mt 19.20 ("the young man"); Lk 18.18 ("a certain ruler"). *Knelt before him.* See note on 3.11. *Eternal life,* God's new creation in the age to come (Dan 12.2; 2 Macc 7.9; cf. Jn 3.15), comparable to the kingdom of God (vv. 23–25; see also 9.43, 45, 47; 10.30). **10.18** *No one is good.* Elsewhere Jesus' goodness or sinlessness is implied or affirmed; cf. Mt 19.17; Jn 8.46; 2 Cor 5.21; Heb 7.26; 1 Pet 2.22. Cf. Mt 3.14. **10.19** *The commandments.* See Ex 20.12–16; Deut 5.16–20. Though not in the Decalogue, *you shall not defraud* recalls Ex 20.17; Deut 24.14; Sir 4.1. **10.21** *Treasure in heaven.* See Mt 6.20; Lk 12.33. *Come, follow me.* See also 1.17–18; 10.28, 52. **10.22** *Shocked,* or appalled. **10.23** On *wealth* as jeopardizing spiritual health (also 4.18–19), see Job 22.23–26; Prov 28.11; Mt 6.24; 1 Tim 6.9–10.

disciples, "How hard it will be for those who have wealth to enter the kingdom of God!" 24And the disciples were perplexed at these words. But Jesus said to them again, "Children, how hard it is*a* to enter the kingdom of God! 25It is easier for a camel to go through the eye of a needle than for someone who is rich to enter the kingdom of God." 26They were greatly astounded and said to one another,*b* "Then who can be saved?" 27Jesus looked at them and said, "For mortals it is impossible, but not for God; for God all things are possible."

28 Peter began to say to him, "Look, we have left everything and followed you." 29Jesus said, "Truly I tell you, there is no one who has left house or brothers or sisters or mother or father or children or fields, for my sake and for the sake of the good news,*c* 30who will not receive a hundredfold now in this age—houses, brothers and sisters, mothers and children, and fields, with persecutions—and in the age to come eternal life. 31But many who are first will be last, and the last will be first."

A Third Time Jesus Foretells His Death and Resurrection

32 They were on the road, going up to Jerusalem, and Jesus was walking ahead of them; they were amazed, and those who followed were afraid. He took the twelve aside again and began to tell them what was to happen to him, 33saying, "See, we are going up to Jerusalem, and the Son of Man will be handed over to the chief priests and the scribes, and they will con-

demn him to death; then they will hand him over to the Gentiles; 34they will mock him, and spit upon him, and flog him, and kill him; and after three days he will rise again."

The Request of James and John

35 James and John, the sons of Zebedee, came forward to him and said to him, "Teacher, we want you to do for us whatever we ask of you." 36And he said to them, "What is it you want me to do for you?" 37And they said to him, "Grant us to sit, one at your right hand and one at your left, in your glory." 38But Jesus said to them, "You do not know what you are asking. Are you able to drink the cup that I drink, or be baptized with the baptism that I am baptized with?" 39They replied, "We are able." Then Jesus said to them, "The cup that I drink you will drink; and with the baptism with which I am baptized, you will be baptized; 40but to sit at my right hand or at my left is not mine to grant, but it is for those for whom it has been prepared."

41 When the ten heard this, they began to be angry with James and John. 42So Jesus called them and said to them, "You know that among the Gentiles those whom they recognize as their rulers lord it over them, and their great ones are tyrants over them. 43But it is not so among you; but whoever wishes to become great among you must be your servant, 44and whoever wishes to be first among you must be

---

a Other ancient authorities add *for those who trust in riches*
b Other ancient authorities read *to him*   *c* Or *gospel*

10.24 *Children,* the typical address in ancient times of a teacher to his pupils. **10.27** *For God all things are possible,* an idea prevalent in the OT (see Gen 18.14; Job 42.2; Zech 8.6). In non-Jewish contexts the idea that "all things are possible" only for the gods is widespread. **10.29** *Truly I tell you.* See note on 3.28. *Good news.* See note on 1.1. **10.30** *Now in this age.* Cf. more grandiose rewards promised in 2 Esd 7.88–99; Mt 19.28. The absence from this list of the father (cf. v. 29) is conspicuous, as is the added promise *with persecutions* (see 8.34–38). **10.31** This saying (cf. 9.35; 10.44) appears in different contexts in the Gospels (see Mt 19.30; 20.16; Lk 13.30). **10.32–45** Cf. Mt 20.17–28; Lk 18.31–34. The third and last set in the cycle of Jesus' three predictions, the three cases of the disciples' incomprehension, and the three teachings on discipleship (see note on 8.31–9.1). **10.32** *Jerusalem* (also v. 33), the Judean capital, from which hostility to Jesus has already come (3.22). *Amazed . . . afraid.* See notes on 4.13; 4.40. **10.33** *Son of Man.* See note on 8.31.

Handed over. See note on 9.31. *Chief priests, scribes.* See note on 8.31. **10.34** A capsule summary of 15.15–16.6. **10.35** *James and John, the sons of Zebedee.* See 1.19, 29; 3.17; 5.37; 9.2; 13.3; 14.33. Their request recalls Herod's impetuous offer in 6.22 (see 10.42). **10.37** *At your right hand,* the place of supreme honor (see, e.g., Ps 110.1). *In your glory.* See 8.38–9.1; 13.26. **10.38** In the OT the *cup* symbolizes either joy and salvation (e.g., Pss 23.5; 116.13) or the wrath of God (e.g., Ps 11.6; Isa 51.17, 22); the latter is intended here (see also Mk 14.36; Jn 18.11). Though ambiguous (and absent from Mt 20.22), the *baptism* undergone by Jesus and his followers seems to be death (cf. Lk 12.50; Rom 6.3–4). **10.42–44** See also 9.35; Mt 23.11; Lk 22.24–27. Jesus rejects the actual relations of power in the surrounding world. The ideal that the monarch should be the servant of the people is found in the OT (1 Kings 12.7) and in Greek and Roman treatments of kingship. **10.44** *Slave of all.* See also 1 Cor 9.19; 2 Cor 4.5; Gal 5.13. Greek and Roman populist or democratic leaders

slave of all. [45]For the Son of Man came not to be served but to serve, and to give his life a ransom for many."

The Healing of Blind Bartimaeus

[46]They came to Jericho. As he and his disciples and a large crowd were leaving Jericho, Bartimaeus son of Timaeus, a blind beggar, was sitting by the roadside. [47]When he heard that it was Jesus of Nazareth, he began to shout out and say, "Jesus, Son of David, have mercy on me!" [48]Many sternly ordered him to be quiet, but he cried out even more loudly, "Son of David, have mercy on me!" [49]Jesus stood still and said, "Call him here." And they called the blind man, saying to him, "Take heart; get up, he is calling you." [50]So throwing off his cloak, he sprang up and came to Jesus. [51]Then Jesus said to him, "What do you want me to do for you?" The blind man said to him, "My teacher,[a] let me see again." [52]Jesus said to him, "Go; your faith has made you well." Immediately he regained his sight and followed him on the way.

Jesus' Triumphal Entry into Jerusalem

11 When they were approaching Jerusalem, at Bethphage and Bethany, near the Mount of Olives, he sent two of his disciples [2]and said to them, "Go into the village ahead of you, and immediately as you enter it, you will find tied there a colt that has never been ridden; untie it and bring it. [3]If anyone says to you, 'Why are you doing this?' just say this, 'The Lord needs it and will send it back here immediately.' " [4]They went away and found a colt tied near a door, outside in the street. As they were untying it, [5]some of the bystanders said to them, "What are you doing, untying the colt?" [6]They told them what Jesus had said; and they allowed them to take it. [7]Then they brought the colt to Jesus and threw their cloaks on it; and he sat on it. [8]Many people spread their cloaks on the road, and others spread leafy branches that they had cut in the fields. [9]Then those who went ahead and those who followed were shouting,

---

a Aramaic *Rabbouni*

---

spoke about the ruler as a slave of the many. **10.45** *Son of Man.* See note on 8.31. *Ransom,* originally a compensation required to release (or "redeem") something or someone (see, e.g., Ex 21.8, 30; Lev 25.47–52; Num 3.45–51), was subsequently developed as a metaphor for the reclamation or redemption of God's people (Ex 6.6; 15.13; Isa 43.1–7; 44.21–23), particularly through Christ (e.g., Rom 3.23–25a; 1 Tim 2.5–6; 1 Pet 1.18–19). In certain Greek inscriptions somewhat later than Mark the term *ransom* is equivalent to "expiation" or "propitiation." *To give his life . . . for many.* See 14.24; and the portrayal of the servant in Isa 52.13–53.12. **10.46–52** Cf. Mt 20.29–34 (see also 9.27–31); Lk 18.35–43. The healing of Bartimaeus both concludes the central section (8.27–10.52) and introduces the next section (11.1–13.37). It corresponds to the two-stage healing of a blind man in 8.22–26, which is also transitional (see the note on 8.22–26). **10.46** *Jericho,* a city in the Jordan Valley about twenty miles northeast of Jerusalem. *Bartimaeus,* lit. *son of Timaeus.* The name Timaeus may have reminded some members of Mark's audience of Plato's praise of sight in his dialogue of that name. Other hearers may have recognized a wordplay on the Aramaic word for "unclean" and the Greek word for "highly prized." **10.47–48** *Son of David,* a title used by some Jews with expectant reference to a royal messiah (see 2 Sam 7.4–17; Ps 89.3–4). The Markan Jesus' challenge to the idea that the messiah is David's son (12.35–37) is part of the author's reinterpretation of messiahship. See Introduction; note on 1.34. **10.51** *What do . . . for you?* See also v. 36. **10.52** *Your faith has made you well.* See also 5.34; notes on 2.5; 5.23. *Followed him.* See also 1.18; 2.14.

11.1–13.37 Jesus' ministry in Jerusalem (11.1–12.44) and address to the disciples about the last days (13.1–37). **11.1–11** Compared with that in the other Gospels (Mt 21.1–11; Lk 19.28–40; Jn 12.12–19), the description of Jesus' arrival in the city is muted. **11.1** *Jerusalem.* See note on 10.32. Since Jesus and his disciples are coming from Jericho, the narrative presupposes that they are approaching Jerusalem from the east. The *Mount of Olives* is part of a ridge of hills, opposite Jerusalem across the Kidron Valley, that has three main summits, Mount Scopus in the north, the Mount of Olives directly across from the Temple Mount, and the Mount of Corruption (or Mount of Offense) on the south. The ancient road crossed the ridge south of Mount Scopus and north of the Mount of Olives. The location of *Bethphage* has been identified as south of the ancient road; *Bethany* was on the eastern slope of the ridge, southeast of Bethphage. The Mount of Olives was associated with both the city's defeat (2 Sam 15.13–30) and hope for God's end-time triumph (Zech 14.4). **11.2** The *colt* may be an allusion to the humble king's conveyance in Zech 9.9 (see Mt 21.5; Jn 12.15); its having *never been ridden* is reminiscent of unyoked, consecrated animals in the OT (Num 19.2; Deut 21.3; 1 Sam 6.7). **11.3** *The Lord,* the most exalted use of the title in Mark with direct reference to Jesus (apart from 16.19, which is part of a later addition to Mark). See also note on 5.19. **11.8** The spreading of *cloaks* and *leafy branches* on the road recalls Israel's royal or festal processions (2 Kings 9.13; 1 Macc 13.51; 2 Macc 10.7). **11.9–10** The acclamation approximates the wording of Ps 118.25–26. *Hosanna,* lit. "Save now!" (see note on 5.41), became a liturgical for-

"Hosanna!
 Blessed is the one who comes in the
     name of the Lord!
10   Blessed is the coming kingdom of our
     ancestor David!
 Hosanna in the highest heaven!"

11 Then he entered Jerusalem and went into the temple; and when he had looked around at everything, as it was already late, he went out to Bethany with the twelve.

Jesus Curses the Fig Tree

12 On the following day, when they came from Bethany, he was hungry. 13 Seeing in the distance a fig tree in leaf, he went to see whether perhaps he would find anything on it. When he came to it, he found nothing but leaves, for it was not the season for figs. 14 He said to it, "May no one ever eat fruit from you again." And his disciples heard it.

Jesus Cleanses the Temple

15 Then they came to Jerusalem. And he entered the temple and began to drive out those who were selling and those who were buying in the temple, and he overturned the tables of the money changers and the seats of those who sold doves; 16 and he would not allow anyone to carry anything through the temple. 17 He was teaching and saying, "Is it not written,

'My house shall be called a house of
     prayer for all the nations'?
 But you have made it a den of
     robbers."

18 And when the chief priests and the scribes heard it, they kept looking for a way to kill him; for they were afraid of him, because the whole crowd was spellbound by his teaching. 19 And when evening came, Jesus and his disciples[a] went out of the city.

The Lesson from the Withered Fig Tree

20 In the morning as they passed by, they saw the fig tree withered away to its roots. 21 Then Peter remembered and said to him, "Rabbi, look! The fig tree that you cursed has withered." 22 Jesus answered them, "Have[b] faith in God. 23 Truly I tell you, if you say to this moun-

---

a Gk *they*: other ancient authorities read *he*   *b* Other ancient authorities read *"If you have*

---

mula for the praise of God (v. 10). *Our ancestor David.* Cf. Mt. 21.9; Lk 1.32–33; see note on 10.47–48. **11.11** *The temple,* Israel's religious and political center, rebuilt by Herod the Great (37–4 BCE) and later razed by Roman military forces (70 CE; see Lk 19.41–44). This verse is anticlimactic. The honor paid to Jesus in the preceding verses leads the audience to expect his installation as king. Mark frustrates this expectation because of his redefinition of messiahship; see Introduction; notes on 1.34; 10.47–48. **11.12–25** Cf. Mt 21.12–22; Lk 19.45–48; Jn 2.13–22. The cursing of the fig tree (vv. 12–14, 20–25) and the cleansing of the temple (vv. 15–19) are interwoven; see note on 2.1–12. **11.13** As in Jer 8.13, the image of a fruitless *fig tree* is used to indict the leaders of the people. In the immediate context here the reason is that they failed to welcome Jesus as he entered Jerusalem. *It was not the season,* or "time appointed [by God]," *for figs.* See note on 1.15; cf. 13.28–29. This enigmatic saying may explain the anticlimactic character of Jesus' entry into Jerusalem. It was not yet the time appointed by God for Jesus' installation as king. **11.14** See also v. 20; though rare in the NT, destructive miracles are attributed to Jesus in some noncanonical literature. **11.15–17** The selling and buying of doves and other items for offerings and the changing of money were essential for carrying out the divine commandments regarding sacrifices. Jesus' deeds imply that these activities should not be conducted on the Temple Mount, but elsewhere, in order to maintain the sacred character of the whole temple complex, including the outer court.

This interpretation is supported by the prohibition against carrying things through the temple (v. 16). **11.15** *Temple.* See note on 11.11. *Selling* and *buying* of items related to offerings occurred in the outermost court. In Solomon's temple, the Second Temple, and Herod's remodeled temple, Gentiles were admitted to the outer court, which thus served as a secular civic center. In Ezekiel's model for the restoration of the temple (Ezek 40–48), Gentiles would not be admitted to any part of the temple, including the outer court. The Dead Sea Scrolls *Temple Scroll* also calls for the sacred, rather than profane, character of the outer court. **11.17** See Isa 56.7. On the temple as *a den of robbers,* or "bandits' lair," see Jer 7.1–11. In both Jeremiah and Mark *robbers,* or "bandits," is not meant literally but is a vivid term used to condemn the combination of worship in the temple with disobedience to God's will. In Mark, the issue is not political or economic exploitation of the people by the priests, but the rejection of Jesus and his message by the leaders of the people. **11.18** *Chief priests, scribes.* See notes on 1.22; 8.31. *They kept . . . kill him.* See note on 3.6. **11.21** *Then Peter remembered* picks up the statement in v. 14 that the disciples heard what Jesus said to the fig tree. **11.22–25** Some of these sayings may have circulated independently or in other contexts, e.g., vv. 23–25. They now seem to be connected by catchwords (see note on 9.42–50): *faith, believe* (or "have faith"; vv. 22–24); *prayer, praying* (vv. 24–25). **11.22** This initial saying serves as a heading or introduction to the rest. It may have been composed by Mark. **11.23** See 10.27; Mt

tain, 'Be taken up and thrown into the sea,' and if you do not doubt in your heart, but believe that what you say will come to pass, it will be done for you. 24So I tell you, whatever you ask for in prayer, believe that you have received[a] it, and it will be yours.

25 "Whenever you stand praying, forgive, if you have anything against anyone; so that your Father in heaven may also forgive you your trespasses."[b]

Jesus' Authority Is Questioned

27 Again they came to Jerusalem. As he was walking in the temple, the chief priests, the scribes, and the elders came to him 28and said, "By what authority are you doing these things? Who gave you this authority to do them?" 29Jesus said to them, "I will ask you one question; answer me, and I will tell you by what authority I do these things. 30Did the baptism of John come from heaven, or was it of human origin? Answer me." 31They argued with one another, "If we say, 'From heaven,' he will say, 'Why then did you not believe him?' 32But shall we say, 'Of human origin'?"—they were afraid of the crowd, for all regarded John as truly a prophet. 33So they answered Jesus, "We do not know." And Jesus said to them, "Neither will I tell you by what authority I am doing these things."

The Parable of the Wicked Tenants

12 Then he began to speak to them in parables. "A man planted a vineyard, put a fence around it, dug a pit for the wine press, and built a watchtower; then he leased it to tenants and went to another country. 2When the season came, he sent a slave to the tenants to collect from them his share of the produce of the vineyard. 3But they seized him, and beat him, and sent him away empty-handed. 4And again he sent another slave to them; this one they beat over the head and insulted. 5Then he sent another, and that one they killed. And so it was with many others; some they beat, and others they killed. 6He had still one other, a beloved son. Finally he sent him to them, saying, 'They will respect my son.' 7But those tenants said to one another, 'This is the heir; come, let us kill him, and the inheritance will be ours.' 8So they seized him, killed him, and threw him out of the vineyard. 9What then will the owner of the vineyard do? He will come and destroy the tenants and give the vineyard to others. 10Have you not read this scripture:

'The stone that the builders rejected
   has become the cornerstone;[c]
11 this was the Lord's doing,
   and it is amazing in our eyes'?"

12 When they realized that he had told this parable against them, they wanted to arrest him, but they feared the crowd. So they left him and went away.

---

a Other ancient authorities read *are receiving* b Other ancient authorities add verse 26, "But if you do not forgive, neither will your Father in heaven forgive your trespasses." c Or keystone

17.20; Lk 17.6; 1 Cor 13.2. *Truly I tell you.* See note on 3.28. **11.24** This saying shifts the topic from miracle working to prayer. See 9.28–29; Mt 18.19; Jn 14.13–14; 15.7; 16.23. **11.25** *Stand praying,* customary posture in Jewish worship (1 Kings 8.14; Neh 9.4; Ps 134.1; Mt 6.5; Lk 18.11, 13). The addition of v. 26 (see text note b) in some manuscripts was probably influenced by Mt 6.14–15. **11.27–33** Cf. Mt 21.23–27; Lk 20.1–8; cf. Mk 8.11–13. The first in a series of eight anecdotes set in the temple (see also 12.1–12, 13–17, 18–27, 28–34, 35–37, 38–40, 41–44); cf. 2.1–3.6. **11.27** *Chief priests, scribes, elders.* See 14.43, 53–55; 15.1; see also notes on 1.22; 8.31. **11.28** Cf. Jn 2.18. On Jesus' *authority,* see 1.22, 27; 2.10. **11.29** In rabbinic fashion Jesus counters with a *question;* see also 2.25–26; 10.3. **11.30** In emergent Christian reflection, the *baptism of John* was aligned with God's purposes (1.4–8; 6.14; Mt 21.32; Lk 7.28–30; Jn 1.33; Acts 13.24–25; 19.1–7). **11.31** *Argued with one another.* Cf. 9.10. **11.32** On regard for *John as truly a prophet,* see 6.15–16; 8.28; 9.13. **12.1–12** Cf. Mt 21.33–46; Lk 20.9–19. The non-canonical *Gospel of Thomas* presents a less allegorical version of this parable. Some argue that the version in *Thomas* is older than those of the Synoptic Gospels; others that oral transmission of the story in circles responsible for the *Gospel of Thomas* or an author or editor of the text eliminated the allegorical elements. **12.1** *Parables.* See note on 3.23. The planter's procedure recalls Isa 5.1–7, which identifies God's *vineyard* with Israel (see also Jer 2.21; Ezek 19.10–14; Hos 10.1). **12.2** *When the season came.* See notes on 1.15; 11.13. OT prophets were styled as God's servants, or *slaves* (see Jer 7.25; 25.4; Am 3.7; Zech 1.6). **12.3–5** OT prophets suffered similar brutality (see 1 Kings 19.1–3; 2 Chr 24.20–22; 36.15–16; Neh 9.26; see also Lk 13.34; Acts 7.52; 1 Thess 2.15; Rev 16.6). **12.6** *A beloved son.* See 1.11; 9.7; see also notes on 1.1; 1.11. **12.10–11** Here, as elsewhere in the NT (see Acts 4.11; Eph 2.20; 1 Pet 2.7), Ps 118.22–23 is cited to interpret the rejection of Jesus by Jewish leaders and to assert his vindication. **12.12** The religious leadership (see 11.27) *wanted* (lit. "sought") *to arrest him.* See note on 3.6.

The Question about Paying Taxes

13 Then they sent to him some Pharisees and some Herodians to trap him in what he said. 14And they came and said to him, "Teacher, we know that you are sincere, and show deference to no one; for you do not regard people with partiality, but teach the way of God in accordance with truth. Is it lawful to pay taxes to the emperor, or not? 15Should we pay them, or should we not?" But knowing their hypocrisy, he said to them, "Why are you putting me to the test? Bring me a denarius and let me see it." 16And they brought one. Then he said to them, "Whose head is this, and whose title?" They answered, "The emperor's." 17Jesus said to them, "Give to the emperor the things that are the emperor's, and to God the things that are God's." And they were utterly amazed at him.

The Question about the Resurrection

18 Some Sadducees, who say there is no resurrection, came to him and asked him a question, saying, 19"Teacher, Moses wrote for us that if a man's brother dies, leaving a wife but no child, the man*a* shall marry the widow and raise up children for his brother. 20There were seven brothers; the first married and, when he died, left no children; 21and the second married the widow*b* and died, leaving no children; and the third likewise; 22none of the seven left children. Last of all the woman herself died. 23In the resurrection*c* whose wife will she be? For the seven had married her."

24 Jesus said to them, "Is not this the reason you are wrong, that you know neither the scriptures nor the power of God? 25For when they rise from the dead, they neither marry nor are given in marriage, but are like angels in heaven. 26And as for the dead being raised, have you not read in the book of Moses, in the story about the bush, how God said to him, 'I am the God of Abraham, the God of Isaac, and the God of Jacob'? 27He is God not of the dead, but of the living; you are quite wrong."

The First Commandment

28 One of the scribes came near and heard them disputing with one another, and seeing that he answered them well, he asked him, "Which commandment is the first of all?" 29Jesus answered, "The first is, 'Hear, O Israel: the Lord our God, the Lord is one; 30you shall love the Lord your God with all your heart, and with all your soul, and with all your mind, and with all your strength.' 31The second is this, 'You shall love your neighbor as yourself.' There is no other commandment greater than these." 32Then the scribe said to him, "You are right, Teacher; you have truly said that 'he is

---

a Gk *his brother*   *b* Gk *her*   *c* Other ancient authorities add *when they rise*

12.13–17 Cf. Mt 22.15–22; Lk 20.20–26. **12.13** *Pharisees, Herodians.* See notes on 2.16; 3.6. **12.14** When Judea, Samaria, and Idumea became the Roman province of Judea in 6 CE, the governor of the province of Syria undertook a census of Judea to institute poll *taxes,* i.e., a tax on each individual. At that time an activist teacher, Judas (said to be from Galilee or from Gamala in Gaulanitis, now the Golan), led a movement of protest against taxes, arguing that God alone is the ruler of the Jewish people. The *trap* (v. 13) lay in an attempt to force Jesus into disloyalty toward the Romans or toward those Jews who resented the taxes. **12.15** *Denarius.* See note on 6.37. **12.16** *Head,* lit. "image." *Title,* lit. "inscription." *The emperor's,* lit. "Caesar's." The use of the simple name Caesar, which, without the addition of a specific name like Augustus or Tiberius, applied to all the emperors, allows the story to apply to Mark's audience as well as to those questioning Jesus and the crowd within the narrative. **12.17** *Give to the emperor.* See also Mt 17.24–27; Rom 13.1–7; 1 Pet 2.13–17. *Amazed.* See note on 1.22. **12.18–27** Cf. Mt 22.23–33; Lk 20.27–40. **12.18** *Sadducees,* a group within ancient Judaism depicted in the NT as associated with the priests of the temple in Jerusalem (Acts 4.1; 5.17) and as denying the *resurrection* (Acts 23.6–8). Their denial of resurrection (cf. Isa 26.19; Dan 12.2–3; 2 Macc 7.14, 23) is also attested by Josephus (*War* 2.165). **12.19** A conflation of Deut 25.5–6; Gen 38.8. **12.25** Jesus' answer implies that resurrection should not be understood as the revival of the earthly body, but as its transformation into a heavenly state like that of the angels (cf. 1 Cor 15.35–50). **12.26** Jesus' argument is based on Moses' description of God as "the God of Abraham, . . . Isaac, and . . . Jacob" (Ex 3.6, 15–16). Since God is not a God of the dead, but of the living (Ps 6.5; Isa 38.16–19; Sir 17.27–28), Abraham, Isaac, and Jacob must be living now (i.e., already risen from the dead) or will live again in the future (i.e., will rise from the dead in the end time). The argument resembles rabbinic exegesis. **12.28–34** Cf. Mt 22.34–40; Lk 10.25–28. **12.28** This scribe is portrayed as an interpreter of the law. *Scribes* typically oppose Jesus in Mark (see note on 1.22), but this one simply inquires about first principles, a question extensively debated among the rabbis. **12.29–30** An elaborated citation of Deut 6.4–5. *Heart* (also v. 33). See note on 7.19; see also 7.21–22. *Soul,* or "life" (so translated in 3.4; 8.35–37; 10.45). **12.31** Lev 19.18. See

one, and besides him there is no other'; [33]and 'to love him with all the heart, and with all the understanding, and with all the strength,' and 'to love one's neighbor as oneself,'—this is much more important than all whole burnt offerings and sacrifices." [34]When Jesus saw that he answered wisely, he said to him, "You are not far from the kingdom of God." After that no one dared to ask him any question.

The Question about David's Son

[35]While Jesus was teaching in the temple, he said, "How can the scribes say that the Messiah[a] is the son of David? [36]David himself, by the Holy Spirit, declared,

'The Lord said to my Lord,
"Sit at my right hand,
until I put your enemies under your
     feet." '

[37]David himself calls him Lord; so how can he be his son?" And the large crowd was listening to him with delight.

Jesus Denounces the Scribes

[38]As he taught, he said, "Beware of the scribes, who like to walk around in long robes,

and to be greeted with respect in the market-places, [39]and to have the best seats in the synagogues and places of honor at banquets! [40]They devour widows' houses and for the sake of appearance say long prayers. They will receive the greater condemnation."

The Widow's Offering

[41]He sat down opposite the treasury, and watched the crowd putting money into the treasury. Many rich people put in large sums. [42]A poor widow came and put in two small copper coins, which are worth a penny. [43]Then he called his disciples and said to them, "Truly I tell you, this poor widow has put in more than all those who are contributing to the treasury. [44]For all of them have contributed out of their abundance; but she out of her poverty has put in everything she had, all she had to live on."

The Destruction of the Temple Foretold

13 As he came out of the temple, one of his disciples said to him, "Look, Teacher,

a Or the Christ

---

also Rom 13.9; Gal 5.14; Jas 2.8. **12.32** *Besides him there is no other.* See Deut 4.35; Isa 45.5, 21. **12.33** *More important than . . . sacrifices.* See also 1 Sam 15.22; Hos 6.6. **12.34** *Kingdom of God.* See note on 1.15. **12.35–37** Cf. Mt 22.41–46; Lk 20.41–44. **12.35** Reference to the *scribes* links this passage with vv. 28–34, 38–40; see also notes on 9.42–50; 11.22–25. *The Messiah, the Son of David.* See notes on 1.1; 10.47–48. **12.36** Ps 110.1, traditionally attributed to *David himself,* was adopted by NT authors as a proof-text for Jesus' exaltation (see Acts 2.34–35; 1 Cor 15.25; Heb 1.13). *By the Holy Spirit,* i.e., with presumed prophetic force; see also Acts 1.16; 28.25; Heb 3.7; 10.15. **12.37** The Markan Jesus does not answer his own rhetorical question but leaves his audience to ponder the tension between the widespread idea that the messiah would be a descendant of David and the interpretation of Ps 110.1 according to which David calls the messiah "Lord." The Markan audience would of course identify Jesus with the messiah. The reference to God's putting Jesus' enemies under his feet expresses in a concrete way the kingship he is to exercise after the resurrection. The question about the messiah's being the son of David here is part of a complex and nuanced narrative reinterpretation of messiahship. **12.38–40** Cf. Lk 20.45–47. The contrast between the praise of the scribe in v. 34 and this condemnation may be explained by the inference that the scribes do not practice what they preach (cf. Mt 23.3). The denunciation of pretentious scribes (see note on 12.35) is directed against Pharisees in other Gospels (Mt 23.1–36; Lk 11.37–44).

12.39 *Places of honor at banquets.* See Lk 14.7–11. **12.40** The oppression of economically vulnerable *widows* is castigated in the OT (Ps 94.1–7; Isa 10.1–2; Zech 7.10; Mal 3.5). **12.41–44** Cf. Lk 21.1–4. Perhaps linked to the preceding passage by the catchword *widow* (vv. 40, 42). **12.41** Since Josephus says that the temple's treasury chambers were located in the inner court (*War* 5.200), it is unlikely that the scene described by Mark (Jesus watching people coming and going, depositing money) could have been set near the actual treasury chambers. Thus, the *treasury* must be a collection box or other kind of receptacle, probably in the outer court; see also Jn 8.20. **12.42** *Small copper coins,* i.e., the smallest coins minted in Judea at that time. Two of these were equivalent to a *penny,* lit., a Roman *quadrans* (see also Mt 5.26), the smallest denomination of Roman coinage. In Syria and Judea, Roman and local coinage coexisted, and local coins were understandable in terms of Roman denominations. The amount in question here was one sixty-fourth of a laborer's daily wage. **12.43** *Truly I tell you.* See note on 3.28. **12.44** *All she had to live on,* lit. "her whole life."

13.1–37 Cf. Mt 24.1–44; Lk 21.5–33. Introduced by a prophecy of the temple's destruction (vv. 1–4), Jesus' speech about the end of the age (vv. 5–37) has some similarities with the "farewell addresses" of the patriarchs to their sons and of biblical leaders to their followers (see Gen 49.1–33; Deut 33.1–29; Josh 23.1–24.30; Tob 14.3–11; Jn 14.1–17.26; Acts 20.18–35). **13.1** Josephus (*War* 5.184–227) corroborates the massive structure of the *temple;* see also note on 11.11.

what large stones and what large buildings!" ²Then Jesus asked him, "Do you see these great buildings? Not one stone will be left here upon another; all will be thrown down."

3 When he was sitting on the Mount of Olives opposite the temple, Peter, James, John, and Andrew asked him privately, ⁴"Tell us, when will this be, and what will be the sign that all these things are about to be accomplished?" ⁵Then Jesus began to say to them, "Beware that no one leads you astray. ⁶Many will come in my name and say, 'I am he!'ᵃ and they will lead many astray. ⁷When you hear of wars and rumors of wars, do not be alarmed; this must take place, but the end is still to come. ⁸For nation will rise against nation, and kingdom against kingdom; there will be earthquakes in various places; there will be famines. This is but the beginning of the birth pangs.

Persecution Foretold

9 "As for yourselves, beware; for they will hand you over to councils; and you will be beaten in synagogues; and you will stand before governors and kings because of me, as a testimony to them. ¹⁰And the good newsᵇ must first be proclaimed to all nations. ¹¹When they bring you to trial and hand you over, do not worry beforehand about what you are to say; but say whatever is given you at that time, for it is not you who speak, but the Holy Spirit. ¹²Brother will betray brother to death, and a father his child, and children will rise against parents and have them put to death; ¹³and you will be hated by all because of my name. But the one who endures to the end will be saved.

The Desolating Sacrilege

14 "But when you see the desolating sacrilege set up where it ought not to be (let the reader understand), then those in Judea must flee to the mountains; ¹⁵the one on the housetop must not go down or enter the house to take anything away; ¹⁶the one in the field must not turn back to get a coat. ¹⁷Woe to those who are pregnant and to those who are nursing infants in those days! ¹⁸Pray that it may not be in winter. ¹⁹For in those days there will be suffering, such as has not been from the beginning of the creation that God created until now, no, and never will be. ²⁰And if the Lord had not cut short those days, no one would be saved; but for the sake of the elect, whom he chose, he has cut short those days. ²¹And if anyone says to you at that time, 'Look! Here is the Messiah!'ᶜ or 'Look! There he is!'—do not believe it. ²²False messiahsᵈ and false prophets will appear and produce signs and omens, to lead

---

a Gk *I am*   *b* Gk *gospel*   *c* Or *the Christ*   *d* Or *christs*

13.2 Predictions of the earlier temple's ruin were made by ᴏᴛ prophets (Jer 26.6, 18; Mic 3.12). **13.3** *Mount of Olives opposite the temple.* See Ezek 11.23; see also note on 11.1. *Peter, James, John, and Andrew.* See note on 5.37. *Privately.* See note on 4.10. **13.5–6** The *many* who *will come* are either people claiming to be Jesus or, more likely, those who claim to be the messiah of Israel and to exercise the power and authority that, from the point of view of Mark, only the risen Jesus has. Such military leaders with royal aspirations appeared during the Jewish war with Rome in the late 60s ᴄᴇ. **13.7** By divine decree *this must take place* (see Dan 2.28–29; note on 8.31); *but the end is still to come* (see 2 Thess 2.1–12). **13.8** The images here are common in prophetic portents (2 Chr 15.6; Isa 13.13; 14.30; 19.2; Jer 22.23; Rev 6.8; 11.13; 16.18). **13.9** *Hand you over* (also v. 11), or *betray* (v. 12). See note on 9.31. *Councils,* lit. "sanhedrins," i.e., local Jewish courts; see Mt 10.17–18; cf. Mk 14.55. *Beaten.* See also Deut 25.1–3; 2 Cor 11.24. **13.10** *Good news.* See note on 1.1. *Proclaimed to all nations* (see also 11.17), an ᴏᴛ theme (Isa 49.6; 52.10) with ɴᴛ adaptations (Mk 16.20; Rom 1.5, 8–17; 11.11–32; Eph 3.1–10). **13.11** See also Mt 10.19–20; Lk 12.11–12; Jn 14.26. *At that time,* lit. "in that hour"; see note on 13.32. *Holy Spirit.* See notes on 1.8; 12.36. **13.12** A stock apocalyptic motif (cf. Mic 7.6; 2 Esd 6.24), yet such divisions within families apparently occurred among first-century Christians; see Jn 9.18–23; 16.2. **13.13** *Hated by all because of my name.* See also Mt 10.21–22; Jn 15.18–21. On *enduring to the end,* see Rev 2.10. **13.14** Mark implies that the prophecy of the *desolating sacrilege* in Dan 9.27; 11.31; 12.11 is about to be fulfilled. The expected event is probably the setting up of a statue of the emperor in the temple, i.e., that after their victory in the war, the Romans would actually do what Caligula had attempted in 39–40 ᴄᴇ. Fleeing to the *mountains* recalls the flight of Lot and his family from Sodom in Gen 19.17 (cf. Rev 11.8). **13.15–17** Cf. Lk 17.31; 23.29. **13.18** *In winter,* when travel was impeded by heavy rains. **13.19** Unparalleled tribulation was sometimes expected to precede the end; see Dan 12.1; Rev 7.14. **13.20** In the ᴏᴛ *the elect* (also vv. 22, 27), *whom he chose,* is Israel (Ps 105.6; Isa 42.1; 43.20; 65.9). In works of the Second Temple period, such as the book of *Enoch* and some of the Dead Sea Scrolls, the elect are the remnant of Israel, the few who have not turned away from God. The perspective of the ɴᴛ is analogous; the elect are the few who have responded to God's initiatives through John the Baptist and Jesus (Lk 18.7; Rom 8.33; Eph 1.4–5; Col 3.12; 2 Tim 2.10; 1 Pet 1.2; 2.9). **13.21** Cf. Lk 17.23. **13.22** *Signs and*

astray, if possible, the elect. 23But be alert; I have already told you everything.

The Coming of the Son of Man

24 "But in those days, after that suffering,
the sun will be darkened,
and the moon will not give its light,
25   and the stars will be falling from heaven,
and the powers in the heavens will be
shaken.
26Then they will see 'the Son of Man coming in clouds' with great power and glory. 27Then he will send out the angels, and gather his elect from the four winds, from the ends of the earth to the ends of heaven.

The Lesson of the Fig Tree

28 "From the fig tree learn its lesson: as soon as its branch becomes tender and puts forth its leaves, you know that summer is near. 29So also, when you see these things taking place, you know that he*a* is near, at the very gates. 30Truly I tell you, this generation will not pass away until all these things have taken place. 31Heaven and earth will pass away, but my words will not pass away.

The Necessity for Watchfulness

32 "But about that day or hour no one knows, neither the angels in heaven, nor the Son, but only the Father. 33Beware, keep alert;*b* for you do not know when the time will come. 34It is like a man going on a journey, when he leaves home and puts his slaves in charge, each with his work, and commands the doorkeeper to be on the watch. 35Therefore, keep awake—for you do not know when the master of the house will come, in the evening, or at midnight, or at cockcrow, or at dawn, 36or else he may find you asleep when he comes suddenly. 37And what I say to you I say to all: Keep awake."

The Plot to Kill Jesus

14 It was two days before the Passover and the festival of Unleavened Bread. The chief priests and the scribes were looking for a way to arrest Jesus*c* by stealth and kill him; 2for they said, "Not during the festival, or there may be a riot among the people."

---

a Or *it*   *b* Other ancient authorities add *and pray*   *c* Gk *him*

---

omens of *false prophets.* See also Deut 13.1–3; Mt 7.15–23; 2 Thess 2.9–10; Rev 19.20. **13.24–25** See 15.33; Isa 13.10; 34.4; 50.2–3; Ezek 32.7–8; Joel 2.10, 31; Am 8.9; 2 Esd 5.4–5; 2 Pet 3.12; Rev 6.12–14. **13.26** *The Son of Man coming in clouds.* Cf. Dan 7.13–14; Rev 1.7; see also notes on 2.10; 8.38. **13.27** The ingathering of God's dispersed elect is a pervasive biblical hope; see, e.g., Isa 11.11, 16; Ezek 39.25–29; Zech 10.6–12; Tob 13.13; Bar 5.5–9; 1 Thess 4.15–17. *From the ends . . . heaven.* Cf. Deut 13.7; 30.3–4. **13.28–37** The sayings in these verses are linked by catchwords (see notes on 9.42–50; 11.22–25): *these things* (vv. 29–30); *pass away* (vv. 30–31); *gates* (or "doors"), *doorkeeper* (vv. 29, 34); *beware, watch, keep awake* (vv. 33–35, 37). **13.28–31** An argument supporting imminent expectation. **13.28** *Fig tree.* Cf. 11.12–14, 20–21. *Lesson,* lit. "parable"; see note on 3.23. Here the "parable" is an illustration used in the service of an argument. **13.29** *He,* probably the Son of Man (v. 26), who is expected to come soon. **13.30** See also 9.1. *Truly I tell you.* See note on 3.28. *This generation.* See note on 8.12. **13.31** Variants of this saying are preserved in Mt 5.18; Lk 16.17. **13.32–36** An argument for watchfulness in light of the indefinite imminence of the coming of the Son of Man. **13.32** *That day* (also 14.25), the day of the coming of the Son of Man, which is presumably also "the day of the LORD"; see Isa 2.12; Jer 46.10; Ezek 30.2–3; Am 5.18–20; Zeph 1.14–18. *That . . . hour,* God's appointed time for the consummation of the age (see note on 1.15; see also 13.11; 14.35; Dan 8.17, 19; 11.35, 40, 45). Only here in Mark is Jesus called

simply *the Son* (cf. note on 1.1; see also Mt 11.27; Lk 10.22). **13.33–36** Several NT texts elaborate the themes of vigilance and accountability (14.32–42; Mt 24.37–51; 25.13–30; Lk 12.35–46; 19.11–27; see also Rom 13.11–14; 1 Thess 5.1–11). **13.35** The Romans reckoned four nocturnal watches: *evening, midnight, cockcrow,* and *dawn* (see also note on 6.48). **13.37** Here the Markan Jesus seems to address Markan audiences as well as the four disciples mentioned in v. 3. This saying concludes both the parable about the man going on a journey (vv. 34–36) as well as the speech of Jesus as a whole (vv. 5–37).

14.1–16.8 Jesus' apprehension (14.1–52); trials, execution, and burial (14.53–15.47); and resurrection (16.1–8). **14.1–11** Cf. Mt 26.1–16; Lk 22.1–6. The anointing of Jesus (vv. 3–9; cf. Lk 7.36–50; Jn 12.1–8) is illuminated against a conspiracy for his arrest (vv. 1–2, 10–11; see also note on 2.1–12). **14.1** *Two days before,* apparently 13 Nisan (the period March–April). *Passover,* the annual celebration of God's liberation of Israel from captivity (Ex 12.1–13.16) on 15 Nisan, was, by the first century CE, conjoined with the seven-day harvest *festival of Unleavened Bread* (2 Chr 35.17; Ezek 45.21–24). The plot, hinted at in 3.6 and desired in 11.18; 12.12, begins to unfold here, as instigated by the *chief priests and the scribes* (see notes on 1.22; 8.31; cf. Jn 11.45–57). **14.2** The concern of the chief priests and scribes was that Jesus' arrest happen *not during the festival,* i.e., not openly and publicly at a time when pilgrims crowded Jerusalem and its environs. Jesus' arrest does occur on Passover evening (vv. 12–50), but

The Anointing at Bethany

3 While he was at Bethany in the house of Simon the leper,[a] as he sat at the table, a woman came with an alabaster jar of very costly ointment of nard, and she broke open the jar and poured the ointment on his head. [4]But some were there who said to one another in anger, "Why was the ointment wasted in this way? [5]For this ointment could have been sold for more than three hundred denarii,[b] and the money given to the poor." And they scolded her. [6]But Jesus said, "Let her alone; why do you trouble her? She has performed a good service for me. [7]For you always have the poor with you, and you can show kindness to them whenever you wish; but you will not always have me. [8]She has done what she could; she has anointed my body beforehand for its burial. [9]Truly I tell you, wherever the good news[c] is proclaimed in the whole world, what she has done will be told in remembrance of her."

Judas Agrees to Betray Jesus

10 Then Judas Iscariot, who was one of the twelve, went to the chief priests in order to betray him to them. [11]When they heard it, they were greatly pleased, and promised to give him money. So he began to look for an opportunity to betray him.

The Passover with the Disciples

12 On the first day of Unleavened Bread, when the Passover lamb is sacrificed, his disciples said to him, "Where do you want us to go and make the preparations for you to eat the Passover?" [13]So he sent two of his disciples, saying to them, "Go into the city, and a man carrying a jar of water will meet you; follow him, [14]and wherever he enters, say to the owner of the house, 'The Teacher asks, Where is my guest room where I may eat the Passover with my disciples?' [15]He will show you a large room upstairs, furnished and ready. Make preparations for us there." [16]So the disciples set out and went to the city, and found everything as he had told them; and they prepared the Passover meal.

17 When it was evening, he came with the twelve. [18]And when they had taken their places and were eating, Jesus said, "Truly I tell you, one of you will betray me, one who is eating with me." [19]They began to be distressed and to say to him one after another, "Surely, not I?" [20]He said to them, "It is one of the twelve, one who is dipping bread[d] into the bowl[e] with me. [21]For the Son of Man goes as it is written of him, but woe to that one by whom the Son of Man is betrayed! It would have been better for that one not to have been born."

The Institution of the Lord's Supper

22 While they were eating, he took a loaf of bread, and after blessing it he broke it, gave it

---

a The terms *leper* and *leprosy* can refer to several diseases
b The denarius was the usual day's wage for a laborer
c Or *gospel*   d Gk lacks *bread*   e Other ancient authorities read *same bowl*

---

secretly or *by stealth.* **14.3** *Bethany.* See note on 11.1. *Leper.* See note on 1.40. *Nard,* spikenard, a fragrant ointment or perfume; see also Song 1.12; 4.13–14. *Poured the ointment on his head,* suggesting royal anointing (see 1 Sam 10.1; 2 Kings 9.6). **14.5** The disciples quite reasonably think of helping the poor (cf. 10.21). For a laborer, *more than three hundred denarii* was almost a full year's wages; see note on 6.37. *Scolded.* See note on 1.43, where the Greek word is translated *sternly warning.* **14.7** See also Deut 15.11; Mk 2.19–20. **14.8** *She has anointed . . . burial.* See 16.1; cf. Jn 19.38–40. **14.9** See also 13.10. *Truly I tell you.* See note on 3.28. **14.10** *Judas Iscariot.* See note on 3.19a. *Chief priests.* See note on 15.1. Though its content and motivation are unspecified in Mark, the plan to *betray* (or "hand over") Jesus and others is a recurring theme; see note on 9.31. **14.12–21** Cf. Mt 26.17–25; Lk 22.7–14; cf. Jn 13.21–30. Preparation for Passover (vv. 12–16) and prediction of betrayal (vv. 17–21). **14.12** *The first day of Unleavened Bread* (usually 15 Nisan) seems to be confused here with 14 Nisan, *when the Passover lamb is sacrificed.* The confusion may be due to differ-

ent ways of defining a "day." The biblical day, the day of ancient Israel, was reckoned from morning to morning. At some point in the Second Temple period, the day began to be calculated from evening to evening. Ordinary people everywhere in antiquity normally defined a day as from morning to evening, and Mark may be using the latter convention to communicate with as wide an audience as possible. See also note on 14.1; cf. Ex 12.1–20; Jn 18.28; 19.14, 31. **14.13–16** Similar wording and the motif of Jesus' foreknowledge also characterize 11.1–6; cf. 1 Sam 10.1–9. **14.18** *They had taken their places,* lit. "they were reclining," the customary posture at banquets (see, e.g., Lk 5.29). That they *were eating* the Passover is suggested only by the context (vv. 12–16), not by details of the meal itself; see note on 14.12. *Truly I tell you.* See note on 3.28. *Betray.* See note on 9.31. *One who is eating with me,* an echo of Ps 41.9 (cf. Jn 13.18). **14.21** *Son of Man.* See notes on 2.10; 8.31. *As it is written,* i.e., in accordance with the divine purpose. This saying may pick up the echo of Ps 41.9 in v. 18 and presuppose that the speaker of the psalm prefigures the Son of Man.

to them, and said, "Take; this is my body." ²³Then he took a cup, and after giving thanks he gave it to them, and all of them drank from it. ²⁴He said to them, "This is my blood of the*ᵃ covenant, which is poured out for many. ²⁵Truly I tell you, I will never again drink of the fruit of the vine until that day when I drink it new in the kingdom of God."

Peter's Denial Foretold

26 When they had sung the hymn, they went out to the Mount of Olives. ²⁷And Jesus said to them, "You will all become deserters; for it is written,

'I will strike the shepherd,
    and the sheep will be scattered.'

²⁸But after I am raised up, I will go before you to Galilee." ²⁹Peter said to him, "Even though all become deserters, I will not." ³⁰Jesus said to him, "Truly I tell you, this day, this very night, before the cock crows twice, you will deny me three times." ³¹But he said vehemently, "Even though I must die with you, I will not deny you." And all of them said the same.

Jesus Prays in Gethsemane

32 They went to a place called Gethsemane; and he said to his disciples, "Sit here while I pray." ³³He took with him Peter and James and John, and began to be distressed and agitated. ³⁴And he said to them, "I am deeply grieved, even to death; remain here, and keep awake."

³⁵And going a little farther, he threw himself on the ground and prayed that, if it were possible, the hour might pass from him. ³⁶He said, "Abba,ᵇ Father, for you all things are possible; remove this cup from me; yet, not what I want, but what you want." ³⁷He came and found them sleeping; and he said to Peter, "Simon, are you asleep? Could you not keep awake one hour? ³⁸Keep awake and pray that you may not come into the time of trial;ᶜ the spirit indeed is willing, but the flesh is weak." ³⁹And again he went away and prayed, saying the same words. ⁴⁰And once more he came and found them sleeping, for their eyes were very heavy; and they did not know what to say to him. ⁴¹He came a third time and said to them, "Are you still sleeping and taking your rest? Enough! The hour has come; the Son of Man is betrayed into the hands of sinners. ⁴²Get up, let us be going. See, my betrayer is at hand."

The Betrayal and Arrest of Jesus

43 Immediately, while he was still speaking, Judas, one of the twelve, arrived; and with him there was a crowd with swords and clubs, from the chief priests, the scribes, and the elders. ⁴⁴Now the betrayer had given them a sign, saying, "The one I will kiss is the man; arrest him

---

a Other ancient authorities add *new* *b* Aramaic for *Father*
c Or *into temptation*

See also 8.31; 1 Cor 15.3–4. **14.22–25** Cf. Mt 26.26–29; Lk 22.14–23; also cf. Jn 6.48–58; 1 Cor 11.23–25. **14.22** *Took, blessing, broke, gave*, reminiscent of Jesus' feeding the multitudes (see notes on 6.41; 8.6). In Greek, as in English, the *body* is a flexible metaphor; see also 1 Cor 10.16–17. **14.24** *Blood of the covenant*, an OT image for ratification; see Ex 24.6–8; Jer 31.31; Zech 9.11; cf. Heb 9.11–10.18. *Poured out for many.* See 10.45. **14.25** *Truly I tell you.* See note on 3.28. The new age (*that day . . . in the kingdom of God*) was sometimes imagined as a magnificent banquet; see notes on 1.15; 6.31–44. **14.26–31** Cf. Mt 26.30–35; Lk 22.31–34; Jn 13.36–38. Predictions of abandonment and denial. **14.26** *When they had sung the hymn*, lit. "when they had hymned"; the Greek text does not suggest a specific hymn. *Mount of Olives.* See note on 11.1. **14.27** *Become deserters* (also v. 29), or "fall away"; see note on 4.17. The quotation is from Zech 13.7; see also note on 14.21. *The sheep will be scattered.* See note on 6.34; cf. Jn 16.32. **14.28** *Galilee*, Jesus' homeland; see note on 1.9. **14.30** *Truly I tell you.* See note on 3.28. *The cock crows*, possibly a reference to one of the night watches; see note on 13.35. *Deny* (also v. 31). See note on 8.34. **14.31** See also Jn 11.16. **14.32–**

42 Cf. Mt 26.36–46; Lk 22.39–46; see also Heb 5.7–8. **14.32** *Gethsemane.* Cf. Lk 22.39–40; Jn 18.1. *While I pray.* See note on 1.35. **14.33** *Peter and James and John.* See note on 5.37. **14.34** *I am* (lit. "my soul is") *deeply grieved.* Cf. Pss 42.5, 11; 43.5; Jn 12.27. *Keep awake* (also vv. 37–38). See note on 13.33–36. **14.35** *The hour* (also vv. 37, 41). See note on 13.32. **14.36** *Abba* (Aramaic), a form used to address one's *Father* (see Rom 8.15; Gal 4.6; see also note on 5.41). *For you all things are possible.* See notes on 9.23; 10.27; see also 11.22–23. *This cup.* See note on 10.38. *Not what I want, but what you want.* See also Jn 5.30; 6.38. **14.38** *The time of trial.* See Sir 2.1; Mt 6.13; Lk 11.4; Jas 1.2; 1 Pet 1.6; Rev 2.10; 3.10; see also Mk 1.12–13. Here, the contrast between *spirit* and *flesh* suggests that one's intentions and promises are not always easy to accomplish. Cf. Peter's vehement assertion that he was ready to die with Jesus and that he would not deny him (v. 31) with his later denial of Jesus three times (vv. 66–72). **14.40** See also 9.6. **14.41** *The Son of Man . . . sinners.* See notes on 1.14; 8.31; 9.31. **14.43–52** Cf. Mt 26.47–56; Lk 22.47–53; Jn 18.3–12. **14.43** *Judas.* See 3.19; 14.10. *Chief priests, scribes, elders.* See note on 8.31. **14.44–45** A *rabbi* could be respectfully greeted by his disciples with

and lead him away under guard." ⁴⁵So when he came, he went up to him at once and said, "Rabbi!" and kissed him. ⁴⁶Then they laid hands on him and arrested him. ⁴⁷But one of those who stood near drew his sword and struck the slave of the high priest, cutting off his ear. ⁴⁸Then Jesus said to them, "Have you come out with swords and clubs to arrest me as though I were a bandit? ⁴⁹Day after day I was with you in the temple teaching, and you did not arrest me. But let the scriptures be fulfilled." ⁵⁰All of them deserted him and fled.

51 A certain young man was following him, wearing nothing but a linen cloth. They caught hold of him, ⁵²but he left the linen cloth and ran off naked.

Jesus before the Council

53 They took Jesus to the high priest; and all the chief priests, the elders, and the scribes were assembled. ⁵⁴Peter had followed him at a distance, right into the courtyard of the high priest; and he was sitting with the guards, warming himself at the fire. ⁵⁵Now the chief priests and the whole council were looking for testimony against Jesus to put him to death; but they found none. ⁵⁶For many gave false testimony against him, and their testimony did not agree. ⁵⁷Some stood up and gave false testimony against him, saying, ⁵⁸"We heard

him say, 'I will destroy this temple that is made with hands, and in three days I will build another, not made with hands.' " ⁵⁹But even on this point their testimony did not agree. ⁶⁰Then the high priest stood up before them and asked Jesus, "Have you no answer? What is it that they testify against you?" ⁶¹But he was silent and did not answer. Again the high priest asked him, "Are you the Messiah,ᵃ the Son of the Blessed One?" ⁶²Jesus said, "I am; and

'you will see the Son of Man
   seated at the right hand of the Power,'
and 'coming with the clouds of heaven.' "

⁶³Then the high priest tore his clothes and said, "Why do we still need witnesses? ⁶⁴You have heard his blasphemy! What is your decision?" All of them condemned him as deserving death. ⁶⁵Some began to spit on him, to blindfold him, and to strike him, saying to him, "Prophesy!" The guards also took him over and beat him.

Peter Denies Jesus

66 While Peter was below in the courtyard, one of the servant-girls of the high priest came by. ⁶⁷When she saw Peter warming himself, she stared at him and said, "You also were with

---

ᵃ Or the Christ

---

a *kiss;* being kissed by a *betrayer* is ironic (cf. Prov 27.6; Lk 7.38, 45; Rom 16.16; 1 Pet 5.14; see also notes on 14.10; 4.18). **14.47** *High priest,* presumably Caiaphas (18–36/7 CE; cf. Mt 26.3, 57; Jn 18.13, 24). **14.48–49** *Let the scriptures be fulfilled.* See notes on 14.21; 14.27. **14.50** See v. 27. **14.51–52** Various interpretations have been proposed for this mysterious incident, including allusions to the *young man* in 16.5, the *linen cloth* in 15.46, and *naked* flight in Gen 39.12; Am 2.16. The context suggests a contrast between Jesus' calm courage and a follower's desperate flight. **14.53–72** Cf. Mt 26.57–75; Lk 22.54–71; Jn 18.13–27. Interrogations of Peter (vv. 53–54, 66–72) and of Jesus (vv. 55–65) are interwoven (see note on 2.1–12). **14.53** *High priest.* See note on 14.47. *Chief priests, elders, scribes.* See notes on 1.22; 8.31; 11.27. **14.55** A formal, albeit irregular, trial by *the whole council* is suggested by Mark and Matthew (Mt 26.59–68; see also Mk 13.9; 15.1). **14.56–57** *False testimony . . . did not agree.* See also v. 59; cf. Deut 19.15; Pss 35.11–12; 109.2–3. **14.58** *Destroy this temple.* See 11.15–16; 13.1–2; 15.29; cf. Mt 26.61; Jn 2.19–21. Jewish texts from the Second Temple period express the idea that God would *build* a temple *not made with hands* (cf. 2 Sam 7.4–17) in the last days (*Jubilees,* Dead Sea Scrolls). The "men of holiness" who lived near Qumran spoke of themselves as a

metaphorical temple; members of the Christ movement also spoke of their communities in this way (1 Cor 3.16; 1 Pet 2.4–6; cf. 2 Cor 6.16). **14.61** *He was silent.* See Ps 38.12–14; Isa 53.7. The Markan high priest uses in his question the terms *Messiah* and *the Son of the Blessed One,* titles central to Christian proclamation; see 1.1; Mt 16.16; Jn 11.27; 20.31. **14.62** *I am.* See note on 6.50. The advent of a royal *Son of Man* combines imagery in Ps 110.1; Dan 7.13–14. See also notes on 8.38; 12.36; 13.26; 16.19. *The Power,* a reference to the deity that may reflect contemporary and later respectful avoidance of pronouncing God's name. **14.63** *Tore his clothes,* a gesture symbolizing grief or distress. See Gen 37.29; Jdt 14.16; Let Jer 6.31; Acts 14.14. **14.64** According to Josephus and the Mishnah, *blasphemy* involved pronouncing God's name. Philo provides evidence that some Jews of the late Second Temple period defined blasphemy more broadly, as speech that insults God, e.g., by compromising the Jewish affirmation that only God is divine. The language used by the Markan Jesus of himself in v. 62 could have been understood as claiming divinity and thus, from the point of view of the high priest and the council, as blasphemy (cf. Lev 24.16; Mk 2.7). **14.65** *Prophesy.* Cf. vv. 30, 66–72. The court's behavior is reminiscent of Isa 50.6; 53.3–5. **14.67** *With Jesus.* See

Jesus, the man from Nazareth." ⁶⁸But he denied it, saying, "I do not know or understand what you are talking about." And he went out into the forecourt.ᵃ Then the cock crowed.ᵇ ⁶⁹And the servant-girl, on seeing him, began again to say to the bystanders, "This man is one of them." ⁷⁰But again he denied it. Then after a little while the bystanders again said to Peter, "Certainly you are one of them; for you are a Galilean." ⁷¹But he began to curse, and he swore an oath, "I do not know this man you are talking about." ⁷²At that moment the cock crowed for the second time. Then Peter remembered that Jesus had said to him, "Before the cock crows twice, you will deny me three times." And he broke down and wept.

Jesus before Pilate

15 As soon as it was morning, the chief priests held a consultation with the elders and scribes and the whole council. They bound Jesus, led him away, and handed him over to Pilate. ²Pilate asked him, "Are you the King of the Jews?" He answered him, "You say so." ³Then the chief priests accused him of many things. ⁴Pilate asked him again, "Have you no answer? See how many charges they bring against you." ⁵But Jesus made no further reply, so that Pilate was amazed.

Pilate Hands Jesus over to Be Crucified

6 Now at the festival he used to release a prisoner for them, anyone for whom they asked. ⁷Now a man called Barabbas was in prison with the rebels who had committed murder during the insurrection. ⁸So the crowd came and began to ask Pilate to do for them according to his custom. ⁹Then he answered them, "Do you want me to release for you the King of the Jews?" ¹⁰For he realized that it was out of jealousy that the chief priests had handed him over. ¹¹But the chief priests stirred up the crowd to have him release Barabbas for them instead. ¹²Pilate spoke to them again, "Then what do you wish me to doᶜ with the man you callᵈ the King of the Jews?" ¹³They shouted back, "Crucify him!" ¹⁴Pilate asked them, "Why, what evil has he done?" But they shouted all the more, "Crucify him!" ¹⁵So Pilate, wishing to satisfy the crowd, released Barabbas for them; and after flogging Jesus, he handed him over to be crucified.

The Soldiers Mock Jesus

16 Then the soldiers led him into the courtyard of the palace (that is, the governor's headquartersᵉ); and they called together the whole cohort. ¹⁷And they clothed him in a purple cloak; and after twisting some thorns into a crown, they put it on him. ¹⁸And they began saluting him, "Hail, King of the Jews!" ¹⁹They struck his head with a reed, spat upon him, and knelt down in homage to him. ²⁰After mocking him, they stripped him of the purple cloak and put his own clothes on him. Then they led him out to crucify him.

---

a Or *gateway* *b* Other ancient authorities lack *Then the cock crowed* *c* Other ancient authorities read *what should I do* *d* Other ancient authorities lack *the man you call* *e* Gk *the praetorium*

3.14. **14.68** *I do not know or understand.* See note on 4.13; see also 6.52; 8.17, 21; 9.32; 14.71. **14.70** *A Galilean.* See note on 1.9. **14.72** *Then Peter remembered what Jesus had said* (v. 30).

15.1–15 Cf. Mt 27.1–2, 11–23; Lk 23.1–5, 13–25; Jn 18.28–40. **15.1** *As soon as it was morning,* the first of five temporal indicators (see also vv. 25, 33, 42). *The chief priests,* henceforth presented as Jesus' principal accusers (see vv. 3, 10, 11, 31). *Elders, scribes, whole council.* See notes on 1.22; 8.31; 13.9; 14.55. *Handed him over* (also vv. 10, 15). See notes on 1.14; 9.31. Jesus is interrogated by Pontius *Pilate,* fifth Roman prefect of Judea (26–36 CE; see also Acts 3.13–14; 13.28). **15.2** Appearing here for the first time in Mark, the title *King of the Jews* is also the first of five ironic acclamations of Jesus by the Roman governor and his agents (see also vv. 9, 12, 18, 26; cf. v. 32). **15.4** *Have you no answer?* See note on 14.61. **15.6** There is no evidence for this practice apart from the Gospels and writings dependent on them. **15.7** *Barabbas,* lit. "son of Abba," or

"son of the father." Barabbas, a violent man associated with armed rebellion against the Romans, is contrasted with Jesus the Son. It is not known which *insurrection* is meant; numerous Jewish revolts against Rome are indicated in Lk 13.1; Acts 5.36–37; and by Josephus. Mark's early audiences would think of the Jewish war with Rome that began in 66 CE. **15.9** *King of the Jews.* See note on 15.2. **15.10–11** Christian portrayal of Pilate as the reluctant pawn of manipulative Jews (which is highly unlikely from a historical point of view) is amplified in Mt 27.18–25; Lk 23.4–16; Jn 19.1–16; cf. Mk 6.14–29. **15.16–20** Cf. Mt 27.27–31; Jn 19.2–3. **15.16** *The whole cohort,* a detachment of two hundred to six hundred soldiers; see note on 1.33. **15.17** *Purple,* like the *crown,* suggests royal raiment (see 1 Macc 8.14; 10.20). **15.18** *Hail, King of the Jews!* Possibly a parody of the legionary salute, "Hail, Caesar, conqueror, emperor"; see also note on 15.2. **15.19–20** *They struck* and *spat, mocking.* See 10.34; cf. Isa 50.6; Mic 5.1. *In homage,* or "bowing in worship" (see Mt 2.11; Acts 10.25; Heb

The Crucifixion of Jesus

21 They compelled a passer-by, who was coming in from the country, to carry his cross; it was Simon of Cyrene, the father of Alexander and Rufus. 22 Then they brought Jesus[a] to the place called Golgotha (which means the place of a skull). 23 And they offered him wine mixed with myrrh; but he did not take it. 24 And they crucified him, and divided his clothes among them, casting lots to decide what each should take.

25 It was nine o'clock in the morning when they crucified him. 26 The inscription of the charge against him read, "The King of the Jews." 27 And with him they crucified two bandits, one on his right and one on his left.[b] 29 Those who passed by derided[c] him, shaking their heads and saying, "Aha! You who would destroy the temple and build it in three days, 30 save yourself, and come down from the cross!" 31 In the same way the chief priests, along with the scribes, were also mocking him among themselves and saying, "He saved others; he cannot save himself. 32 Let the Messiah,[d] the King of Israel, come down from the cross now, so that we may see and believe." Those who were crucified with him also taunted him.

The Death of Jesus

33 When it was noon, darkness came over the whole land[e] until three in the afternoon. 34 At three o'clock Jesus cried out with a loud voice, "Eloi, Eloi, lema sabachthani?" which means, "My God, my God, why have you forsaken me?"[f] 35 When some of the bystanders heard it, they said, "Listen, he is calling for Elijah." 36 And someone ran, filled a sponge with sour wine, put it on a stick, and gave it to him to drink, saying, "Wait, let us see whether Elijah will come to take him down." 37 Then Jesus gave a loud cry and breathed his last. 38 And the curtain of the temple was torn in two, from top to bottom. 39 Now when the centu-

---

a Gk him   b Other ancient authorities add verse 28, And the scripture was fulfilled that says, "And he was counted among the lawless."   c Or blasphemed   d Or the Christ   e Or earth   f Other ancient authorities read made me a reproach

---

11.21; Rev 5.14). **15.21–39** The crucifixion and death of Jesus, cf. Mt 27.32–54; Lk 23.26–48; Jn 19.16b–37. **15.21** A condemned prisoner carried only the crossbar, not *his cross* as a whole. *Cyrene* (see also Acts 6.9; 11.20; 13.1), a city in what is now Libya. The identification of *Rufus* with Paul's associate (Rom 16.13) is impossible to confirm. **15.22** Though it can no longer be located with certainty, *Golgotha* was evidently outside Jerusalem's city walls (see Jn 19.20); see note on 5.41. **15.23** *Wine mixed with myrrh,* spiced wine, a delicacy given to Jesus out of kindness, in mockery of his claim to be the messiah, or to reduce his pain (see Prov 31.6). **15.24** To be *crucified,* the victim's body was lashed or nailed to a stake and crossbar (see Jn 20.25). *Divided his clothes, casting lots.* It was customary for the executioners to take for themselves anything the condemned man had with him. The details, however, reflect subsequent reflection on Ps 22.18. **15.25** *Nine o'clock in the morning,* lit. "the third hour"; see note on 15.1. **15.26–27** A placard worn by the victim customarily bore *the inscription of the charge against him.* The charge, *the King of the Jews* (see note on 15.2), and identification of fellow victims as rebellious *bandits* (see also 14.48) suggest that Jesus' execution was on the grounds of imperial sedition. *One on his right . . . left.* Cf. 10.37. **15.29** *Derided.* A related Greek word is translated *blasphemy* in 14.64. The basic meaning of the word-group, however, is "to insult." *Shaking their heads.* See Pss 22.7; 109.25. On the substance of the jeer, see note on 14.58. **15.30** *Save yourself.* Cf. 8.35. **15.31** *Chief priests, scribes.* See note on 15.1. *Saved others, cannot save himself.* Cf. 10.45; 14.24. **15.32** *The Messiah, the King of Israel.* See notes on 1.1; 15.2. *So that we may see and believe.* See also Wis 2.17–18; cf. Mk 8.11–12. *Those . . . taunted him.* Cf. Lk 23.39–43. **15.33** *Noon,* lit. "the sixth hour"; *three in the afternoon,* "the ninth hour." See note on 15.1. Midday *darkness over the whole land* is an apocalyptic portrayal of divine judgment (see note on 13.24–25). Greeks and Romans would understand it as a portent signifying Jesus' greatness. **15.34** Translated from Aramaic (see note on 5.41), Jesus' cry (cf. v. 37) is a quotation from Ps 22.1; see also notes on 15.24; 15.29. **15.35** On those who *listen* (lit. "look") without understanding, see 4.12; 8.14–21. Evolving perhaps from 2 Kings 2.9–12, later Jewish folklore envisioned *Elijah* as rescuer of the righteous in distress, but cf. Mk 1.6; 9.11–13. **15.36** *Sour wine,* a common drink of the time, although an allusion to Ps 69.21 may be intended. **15.37** Cf. Lk 23.46; Jn 19.30. **15.38** *The curtain of the temple,* perhaps the veil of the holy of holies (see Ex 26.31–37), *was torn* (see note on 1.10). This event is ambiguous and probably symbolic. It may foreshadow the destruction of the temple, symbolize the rending of the barrier between humanity and God (like Heb 9.8; 10.19–20, it may suggest that the death of Jesus has made access to God possible for all humanity), or simply imply a divine self-revelation or theophany (God is revealed in the death of Jesus or God will vindicate Jesus). The interpretation of the rending of the veil in terms implying the supersession of Jewish ideas and practices by Christian ones became very popular during the patristic period, when Christians were attempting to forge a new identity vis-à-vis Jewish communities. **15.39** That Jesus was *God's Son* is finally confessed by a human (see notes on 1.1; 1.11; 3.11), a *centurion,* a Gentile (see also 3.8; 5.20; 7.24–31; 8.27; 11.17; 13.10).

rion, who stood facing him, saw that in this way he[a] breathed his last, he said, "Truly this man was God's Son!"[b]

40 There were also women looking on from a distance; among them were Mary Magdalene, and Mary the mother of James the younger and of Joses, and Salome. [41]These used to follow him and provided for him when he was in Galilee; and there were many other women who had come up with him to Jerusalem.

The Burial of Jesus

42 When evening had come, and since it was the day of Preparation, that is, the day before the sabbath, [43]Joseph of Arimathea, a respected member of the council, who was also himself waiting expectantly for the kingdom of God, went boldly to Pilate and asked for the body of Jesus. [44]Then Pilate wondered if he were already dead; and summoning the centurion, he asked him whether he had been dead for some time. [45]When he learned from the centurion that he was dead, he granted the body to Joseph. [46]Then Joseph[c] bought a linen cloth, and taking down the body,[d] wrapped it in the linen cloth, and laid it in a tomb that had been hewn out of the rock. He then rolled a stone against the door of the tomb. [47]Mary Magdalene and Mary the mother of Joses saw where the body[d] was laid.

The Resurrection of Jesus

16 When the sabbath was over, Mary Magdalene, and Mary the mother of James,

and Salome bought spices, so that they might go and anoint him. [2]And very early on the first day of the week, when the sun had risen, they went to the tomb. [3]They had been saying to one another, "Who will roll away the stone for us from the entrance to the tomb?" [4]When they looked up, they saw that the stone, which was very large, had already been rolled back. [5]As they entered the tomb, they saw a young man, dressed in a white robe, sitting on the right side; and they were alarmed. [6]But he said to them, "Do not be alarmed; you are looking for Jesus of Nazareth, who was crucified. He has been raised; he is not here. Look, there is the place they laid him. [7]But go, tell his disciples and Peter that he is going ahead of you to Galilee; there you will see him, just as he told you." [8]So they went out and fled from the tomb, for terror and amazement had seized them; and they said nothing to anyone, for they were afraid.[e]

THE SHORTER ENDING OF MARK

[[And all that had been commanded them they told briefly to those around Peter. And afterward Jesus himself sent out through them, from east to west, the sacred and imperishable proclamation of eternal salvation.[f]]]

---

a Other ancient authorities add *cried out and* *b* Or *a son of God* *c* Gk *he* *d* Gk *it* *e* Some of the most ancient authorities bring the book to a close at the end of verse 8. One authority concludes the book with the shorter ending; others include the shorter ending and then continue with verses 9-20. In most authorities verses 9-20 follow immediately after verse 8, though in some of these authorities the passage is marked as being doubtful. *f* Other ancient authorities add *Amen*

15.40–47 Cf. Mt 27.55–61; Lk 23.49–55; Jn 19.38–42. **15.40** *Women looking on from a distance* (cf. Ps 38.11; Jn 19.25), including *Mary Magdalene* (see also v. 47; 16.1). Whether *Mary the mother of James . . . and of Joses* is the same woman as Jesus' mother (see 6.3) is impossible to determine. *Salome*. Cf. Mt 27.56. **15.41** *Provided for*, lit. "served" or "ministered to." See also 1.31; 14.6. *Galilee*. See note on 1.9. *Other women*. See also Lk 8.1–3. **15.42** *Evening*. See note on 15.1. *The day of Preparation* for, thus *before, the sabbath*. **15.43** *Arimathea*, probably the same town as Ramathaim (1 Sam 1.1) or Rathamin (1 Macc 11.34), in northwest Judea. *The council* in which Joseph held membership is not identified; cf. Lk 23.50. *Kingdom of God*. See note on 1.15. **15.44–45** Pilate is surprised that Jesus had died so soon after crucifixion. The speedy death may be seen as a divine response to the lament of v. 34. **15.46** *Linen cloth*. See note on 14.51–52; cf. Jn 19.40. *Taking down the body, laid it in a tomb*. Cf. 6.29. **15.47** See v. 40.

16.1–8 Cf. Mt 28.1–8; Lk 24.1–12; Jn 20.1–10. Mark's epilogue, the announcement of Jesus' resurrec-

tion. **16.1–2** *When the sabbath was over*, after sundown on Saturday; specifically, *very early on* Sunday, *the first day of the week*. *Mary Magdalene, Mary, Salome*. See note on 15.40. *Anoint him*. See 14.8; cf. Jn 19.38–40. **16.3–4** The women's question and the sight of *the stone, which was very large* (see also 15.46), already *rolled back* create dramatic tension and arouse expectation of something extraordinary. **16.5** *A young man . . . in a white robe*. See notes on 9.3; 14.51–52. The young man should be understood as an angel; it was customary in Jewish texts of the Second Temple period to refer to what we would call an angel as "a man" (Dan 8.15–16; 9.21) or "a young man" (2 Macc 3.26, 33; Josephus, *Antiquities* 5.277). **16.6** *He has been raised*. See also 8.31; 9.9, 31; 10.34; Jn 5.21; Acts 4.10; 13.30; Rom 4.24; 1 Cor 15.3–4; 2 Tim 2.8. **16.7** *You will see him*. See also Jn 21.14; Acts 2.32; 3.15; 10.40–41; 1 Cor 9.1; 15.5–8. *Just as he told you*. See 14.28. **16.8** *Terror and amazement*. See also vv. 5–6; see note on 4.41.

THE SHORTER ENDING OF MARK. This was added not earlier than the fourth century CE. The phrase

THE LONGER ENDING OF MARK

Jesus Appears to Mary Magdalene

9 ⟦Now after he rose early on the first day of the week, he appeared first to Mary Magdalene, from whom he had cast out seven demons. 10She went out and told those who had been with him, while they were mourning and weeping. 11But when they heard that he was alive and had been seen by her, they would not believe it.

Jesus Appears to Two Disciples

12 After this he appeared in another form to two of them, as they were walking into the country. 13And they went back and told the rest, but they did not believe them.

Jesus Commissions the Disciples

14 Later he appeared to the eleven themselves as they were sitting at the table; and he upbraided them for their lack of faith and stubbornness, because they had not believed those who saw him after he had risen.[a] 15And he said to them, "Go into all the world and proclaim the good news[b] to the whole creation. 16The one who believes and is baptized will be saved; but the one who does not believe will be condemned. 17And these signs will accompany those who believe: by using my name they will cast out demons; they will speak in new tongues; 18they will pick up snakes in their hands,[c] and if they drink any deadly thing, it will not hurt them; they will lay their hands on the sick, and they will recover."

The Ascension of Jesus

19 So then the Lord Jesus, after he had spoken to them, was taken up into heaven and sat down at the right hand of God. 20And they went out and proclaimed the good news everywhere, while the Lord worked with them and confirmed the message by the signs that accompanied it.[d]⟧

---

a Other ancient authorities add, in whole or in part, And they excused themselves, saying, "This age of lawlessness and unbelief is under Satan, who does not allow the truth and power of God to prevail over the unclean things of the spirits. Therefore reveal your righteousness now"—thus they spoke to Christ. And Christ replied to them, "The term of years of Satan's power has been fulfilled, but other terrible things draw near. And for those who have sinned I was handed over to death, that they may return to the truth and sin no more, that they may inherit the spiritual and imperishable glory of righteousness that is in heaven." b Or gospel c Other ancient authorities lack in their hands d Other ancient authorities add Amen

---

from east to west presumes subsequent expansion of the Christian proclamation; cf. 13.10; Rom 15.22–29.

THE LONGER ENDING OF MARK. Though known as early as the late second century CE, the longer ending is missing from the earliest, most reliable Greek manuscripts and seems to mix motifs and phrases from the other Gospels. **16.9** Early on the first day of the week. See note on 16.1–2. He appeared first to Mary Magdalene. See Mt 28.9–10; Jn 20.11–18. From whom . . . demons. See Lk 8.2. **16.10–11** See Lk 24.9–11. **16.12–13** See Lk 24.13–35. **16.14** According to Luke-Acts, the risen Jesus appeared to early witnesses as they were sitting at the table. See Lk 24.30–31, 36–43; Acts 10.41. Lack of faith, or "unbelief"; see 6.6; 9.24. Stubbornness, lit. "hardness of heart"; see 3.5; 6.52; 8.17; 10.5. **16.15** Go into all the world and proclaim (also v. 20; cf. 13.10). See Mt 28.19; Lk 24.47; Jn 20.21; Acts 1.8. Good news. See note on 1.1. **16.16** The one . . . saved. See also Titus 3.5; 1 Pet 3.21; cf. Mt 28.19; Acts 2.38. The one . . . condemned. See also Jn 3.18. **16.17** On signs that accompany belief (also v. 20), see, e.g., Jn 2.23; 4.48; 6.30; cf. Mk 8.11–12; 13.22. By using my name. See 9.39; see also note on 1.24. Cast out demons. See 3.15; 6.7; 9.38. Speak in new tongues. See also Acts 2.4–11; 10.46; 19.6; 1 Cor 14. **16.18** Pick up snakes. See also Lk 10.19; Acts 28.3–6. Lay their hands on the sick . . . recover. See also Acts 3.1–10; 5.12–16; 9.12, 17–18; Jas 5.14–15. **16.19** The Lord. See notes on 5.19; 11.3. Taken up into heaven. See also Lk 24.51; Acts 1.2, 11, 22; 1 Tim 3.16; cf. 2 Kings 2.11. Sat down at the right hand of God (see Ps 110.1), a prevalent NT metaphor for Jesus' exaltation; see also Mk 14.62; Acts 2.33–34; 5.31; 7.55–56; Rom 8.34; Eph 1.20; Col 3.1; Heb 1.3; 8.1; 10.12; 12.2; 1 Pet 3.22. **16.20** Proclaimed the good news everywhere. See notes on 1.1; 13.10; 16.15. On divine cooperation with and confirmation of Christian believers, see also Acts 4.30; 6.8; 14.3; 15.12; Rom 15.19; Heb 2.3–4.

The Gospel According to
LUKE

THE GOSPEL ACCORDING TO LUKE presents a dramatic narrative of the birth, words and deeds, death, and resurrection of Jesus. Its author, identified by tradition as Luke, offers an "orderly account" to assure readers about "the truth" of their Christian instruction (1.3–4). A sequel, the Acts of the Apostles, picks up in Jerusalem where the Gospel leaves off and portrays the spread of early Christianity all the way to Rome. The manner in which Luke revises and incorporates preexisting Christian sources (e.g., Mark and the "sayings source" Q) into one long, continuous narrative displays considerable literary talent. The arrangement of the plot and attention to various details suggest that in addition to telling the story of Jesus, Luke's Gospel is also fundamentally concerned with addressing social and theological issues of crucial importance to the church of the author's own time. Key among these is the relation of Christian communities to the salvific legacy of Israel, on the one hand, and to the political, religious, and social milieu of the Roman-dominated world, on the other. At times, therefore, Luke's narrative decisions may be based more on the situation of the Christian community toward the end of the first century than on a presentation of historical events during the time of Jesus. Modern readers would do well to keep these two levels in mind when reading the Gospel.

Author

NOWHERE DOES THE AUTHOR reveal his identity. The prologue to the Gospel (1.1–4) makes it clear that the author is dependent on others and is not an eyewitness. The title "Gospel According to Luke" is found at the end of the oldest extant manuscript of the Gospel (P75, ca. 175–225 CE). The attribution to Luke may have been suggested by the presence of Luke's name in Paul's Letter to Philemon (v. 24) and in some Letters attributed to Paul (Col 4.14; 2 Tim 4.11) in light of the so-called "we" passages in Acts (16.10–17; 20.5–15; 21.8–18; 27.1–28.16), which give the impression that the author of Acts at times traveled with Paul. These first-person plural references may, however, have been inserted for literary effect and therefore not signal any firsthand knowledge of Paul on the part of the author. This assessment is confirmed by the overall portrait of Paul in Acts, which conflicts at numerous points with the self-testimony of Paul's own writings. The tone and perspective of Luke's two volumes fit a time removed from Paul and his concerns. The traditional identification of Luke as the author of Luke-Acts seems to have emerged during a time (the latter half of the second century) when it seemed important to trace the authoritative writings of the early church directly to the apostles or their associates.

Date and Place of Composition

MOST SCHOLARS DATE THE GOSPEL sometime after the destruction of Jerusalem by the Romans in 70 CE (19.41–44; 21.20–24) and before the end of the first century; between 85 and 95 is a good estimate. Some suggest that the date should be pushed into the early second century. Luke's geographical location is unknown, and scholars have suggested numerous possible sites ranging across the ancient Mediterranean world. Ancient tradition placed him in Antioch. Luke's obvious attachment to Paul and the Pauline tradition in Acts could indicate his connection to one of the cities of the Pauline mission around the Aegean.

Style and Genre

LUKE IS OFTEN IDENTIFIED as the first Christian historian, and there is truth in this claim, as long as one recognizes that crucial distinctions separate the methods and goals of ancient historiography from those of its modern counterpart. Luke's historical interests are clearly subordinate to his theological vision and pastoral agenda. For example, an especially noticeable structural difference compared to Mark and Matthew is found in Luke's extensive section 9.51–19.27, which portrays Jesus making his way to Jerusalem. This "travel narrative" is a creation of Luke, who has selected material of various origins and arranged it in the framework of a journey. Among other purposes it underlines the importance of Jerusalem in salvation history as the place where Jesus' destiny will be realized (9.30, 51; 13.33), and it develops the profile of discipleship, with particular attention to the proper use of possessions, that one must exhibit if one would follow him "on the way."

The Gospel reflects Luke's wide reading of the Septuagint, the Greek OT. He is capable of imitating its style when appropriate (e.g., chs. 1–2), employs a wide range of allusions to it, and even uses biblical prototypes (e.g., the Elijah-Elisha cycle) to construct entire scenes with regard to both the details of language and structural elements. Elsewhere Luke's stylistic ability betrays the marks of a Hellenistic education in his employment of rhetorical conventions, storytelling ability (e.g., 24.13–35), and the execution of a synthetic, narrative imagination.

Purpose

THE INTERNAL EVIDENCE OF THE GOSPEL AND ACTS suggests that Luke may have been a "God-fearer" (a sympathizer with Judaism) before becoming a Christian. Luke's ideal gentile convert is one who continues to practice Jewish piety (Acts 10.2; see also Lk 7.1–10), and gentile Christians are urged to adhere to behavior that would permit association with Jews (Acts 15.20). Luke's audience is obviously Greek-speaking, acquainted with scripture (i.e., the Greek OT), already Christian, and largely gentile. One of Luke's chief concerns is to demonstrate how God's faithful fulfillment of scriptural promises to Israel gives birth to a church that includes both Jews and Gentiles. The narrative of the Gospel and its sequel in Acts are designed to show how the church stands in continuity with the ancient people of God, yet also represents a new development that fulfills God's purpose of universalizing salvation (2.29–32). Another key goal is to address the relation of Christianity to its social environment. Luke portrays Christianity as an enlightened movement that is politically harmless to the Roman order—one can be both a Roman and a Christian. Thus the church emerges as a pluralistic community of Jews and Gentiles, Romans and non-Romans in the common people of God. [DAVID L. TIEDE, revised by CHRISTOPHER R. MATTHEWS]

Dedication to Theophilus

1 Since many have undertaken to set down an orderly account of the events that have been fulfilled among us, ²just as they were handed on to us by those who from the beginning were eyewitnesses and servants of the word, ³I too decided, after investigating everything carefully from the very first,ᵃ to write an orderly account for you, most excellent Theophilus, ⁴so that you may know the truth concerning the things about which you have been instructed.

The Birth of John the Baptist Foretold

5 In the days of King Herod of Judea, there was a priest named Zechariah, who belonged to the priestly order of Abijah. His wife was a descendant of Aaron, and her name was Elizabeth. ⁶Both of them were righteous before God, living blamelessly according to all the commandments and regulations of the Lord. ⁷But they had no children, because Elizabeth was barren, and both were getting on in years.

8 Once when he was serving as priest before God and his section was on duty, ⁹he was chosen by lot, according to the custom of the priesthood, to enter the sanctuary of the Lord and offer incense. ¹⁰Now at the time of the incense offering, the whole assembly of the people was praying outside. ¹¹Then there appeared to him an angel of the Lord, standing at the right side of the altar of incense. ¹²When Zechariah saw him, he was terrified; and fear overwhelmed him. ¹³But the angel said to him, "Do not be afraid, Zechariah, for your prayer has been heard. Your wife Elizabeth will bear you a son, and you will name him John. ¹⁴You will have joy and gladness, and many will rejoice at his birth, ¹⁵for he will be great in the sight of the Lord. He must never drink wine or strong drink; even before his birth he will be filled with the Holy Spirit. ¹⁶He will turn many of the people of Israel to the Lord their God. ¹⁷With the spirit and power of Eli-

---

a Or *for a long time*

1.1–4 Luke opens with a stylistically polished formal prologue (one sentence in Greek) that exhibits linguistic and structural parallels to other Jewish and Greco-Roman historical and learned works. **1.1** Luke sets about the task of providing an *orderly account* in light of previous attempts by *many* to narrate *the events that have been fulfilled* (see 24.26–27, 44). **1.2** *Eyewitnesses* (stressed by ancient historians), who are also *servants of the word*, have *handed on* traditions about Jesus. The author does not claim to be an eyewitness. **1.3** Luke stresses his careful investigation prior to writing an *orderly account* (a reference to the literary structure of the Gospel). *Theophilus* ("lover of God"; see also Acts 1.1), who bears a common Greek name also used by Jews, may be Luke's literary patron but is otherwise unknown. Some take the name to be symbolic of any interested reader. **1.4** *The truth* (Greek *asphaleia*), emphasized in Greek by its position at the end of the sentence, connotes the security offered by the narrative.
1.5–2.52 Luke's style abruptly shifts and imitates that of the Greek OT (the Septuagint). **1.5–25** The announcement of John's birth. **1.5** *Herod* the Great (see Mt 2; see also "The Herods: A Simplified Family Tree," p. 1672) ruled 37–4 BCE. *Abijah*, the eighth of the twenty-four classes of the priesthood (See 1 Chr 24.10). *Aaron*, the ancestor of Israel's priestly line (see

Ex 40.12–15). Thus John's parents both came from priestly families. **1.6** Zechariah and Elizabeth are portrayed as the epitome of faithful Israel. **1.7** *No children, on in years* recall the stories of Sarah and Abraham (Gen 18.11) and Hannah and Elkanah (1 Sam 1–2). See also Judg 13.2–25. **1.8** Each group of priests was probably *on duty* for a week twice each year. **1.9** Individuals *chosen by lot* were understood to be divinely appointed (see Acts 1.24–26). Only priests could *enter the sanctuary* and approach the divine presence. **1.10** *The people* share in the bloodless sacrifice of *incense* by *praying*. **1.11** The appearance of *an angel of the Lord* signals God's initiative. **1.12** *Fear*, a common human reaction to divine manifestations (Isa 6.5–6). **1.13** *Do not be afraid*, typical words of heavenly reassurance (see v. 30; 2.10; 5.10; 8.50; see also Gen 15.1; Dan 10.12; Acts 18.9; 27.24). Samuel's birth was also an answer to *prayer* in the temple (1 Sam 1.9–11). **1.15** John *will be great* (cf. v. 32). As Nazirites (see Num 6.2–4) Samson (Judg 13.4) and Samuel (1 Sam 1.11) were also children of divine promise, required to abstain from *wine or strong drink* so that only the Holy Spirit would fill them. On priestly abstinence, see also Lev 10.9. The Spirit will fill John *before his birth*, indicating his prophetic calling (see Jer 1.4–5). **1.16–17** *The spirit and power of Elijah* defines John's prophetic task of turning *many of the people of Israel* to

jah he will go before him, to turn the hearts of parents to their children, and the disobedient to the wisdom of the righteous, to make ready a people prepared for the Lord." 18 Zechariah said to the angel, "How will I know that this is so? For I am an old man, and my wife is getting on in years." 19 The angel replied, "I am Gabriel. I stand in the presence of God, and I have been sent to speak to you and to bring you this good news. 20 But now, because you did not believe my words, which will be fulfilled in their time, you will become mute, unable to speak, until the day these things occur."

21 Meanwhile the people were waiting for Zechariah, and wondered at his delay in the sanctuary. 22 When he did come out, he could not speak to them, and they realized that he had seen a vision in the sanctuary. He kept motioning to them and remained unable to speak. 23 When his time of service was ended, he went to his home.

24 After those days his wife Elizabeth conceived, and for five months she remained in seclusion. She said, 25 "This is what the Lord has done for me when he looked favorably on me and took away the disgrace I have endured among my people."

The Birth of Jesus Foretold

26 In the sixth month the angel Gabriel was sent by God to a town in Galilee called Nazareth, 27 to a virgin engaged to a man whose name was Joseph, of the house of David. The virgin's name was Mary. 28 And he came to her and said, "Greetings, favored one! The Lord is with you." [a] 29 But she was much perplexed by his words and pondered what sort of greeting this might be. 30 The angel said to her, "Do not be afraid, Mary, for you have found favor with God. 31 And now, you will conceive in your womb and bear a son, and you will name him Jesus. 32 He will be great, and will be called the Son of the Most High, and the Lord God will give to him the throne of his ancestor David. 33 He will reign over the house of Jacob forever, and of his kingdom there will be no end." 34 Mary said to the angel, "How can this be, since I am a virgin?" [b] 35 The angel said to her, "The Holy Spirit will come upon you, and the power of the Most High will overshadow you; therefore the child to be born [c] will be holy; he will be called Son of God. 36 And now, your relative Elizabeth in her old age has also conceived a son; and this is the sixth month for her who was said to be barren. 37 For nothing will be impossible with God." 38 Then Mary said, "Here am I, the servant of the Lord; let it be with me according to your word." Then the angel departed from her.

Mary Visits Elizabeth

39 In those days Mary set out and went with haste to a Judean town in the hill country, 40 where she entered the house of Zechariah and greeted Elizabeth. 41 When Elizabeth heard Mary's greeting, the child leaped in her womb. And Elizabeth was filled with the Holy

a Other ancient authorities add *Blessed are you among women* b Gk *I do not know a man* c Other ancient authorities add *of you*

---

repentance (3.3; Mal 4.5–6). **1.18** Zechariah's question expresses doubt (see also Sarah in Gen 18.12–14; cf. Mary in v. 34), though as a priest he should perhaps recall the biblical precedents pertinent to his situation. **1.19** *Gabriel*, an official emissary of God's court (see v. 26; Dan 8.16; 9.21; cf. Tob 12.15). **1.22** The people perceive that Zechariah has *seen a vision*, but his muteness keeps Gabriel's message a secret until Zechariah speaks prophetically (vv. 67–79). **1.25** Childlessness was considered a *disgrace* (see Gen 16.4; 30.23) requiring God's intervention. **1.26–38** Announcement of Jesus' blessed conception and birth (see also vv. 13–17). **1.26** This is the *sixth month* of Elizabeth's pregnancy (see vv. 24, 36). *Nazareth,* an unimportant village in Galilee, north of Judea (see Jn 1.46). **1.27** *Virgin* emphasizes Mary's youth and underlines the divine origin of Jesus (vv. 34–35; see also Isa 7.14; Mt 1.20–23). Jesus' royal lineage is traced through *Joseph* to *David* (see 2.4; 3.23; 2 Sam 7.12; 1 Chr 17.11). **1.31** *Jesus,* a common form of the name Joshua. Luke does not ex-

plain its meaning ("Yahweh saves"). **1.32** *Son of the Most High.* See v. 35; 8.28; 9.35; cf. v. 76; 6.35; Acts 16.17. **1.33** His *kingdom* with *no end* is the fulfillment of the promise to David (2 Sam 7.16; 1 Chr 17.14; Isa 9.7; see also Dan 7.14). **1.34** Mary's question, unlike Zechariah's (see note on 1.18), is not taken as doubt (see vv. 38, 45). **1.35** This verse interprets what is said in vv. 31–33. Luke uses *come upon* to describe the action of *the Holy Spirit* at Pentecost in Acts 1.8. In the OT God's presence is often conceived of as a light hidden in a cloud to *overshadow* mortals without harm (see Ex 16.10; 24.15–18; 40.34–35; see also Lk 9.34). This holy *Son of God,* i.e., conceived apart from natural means, surpasses David and his royal heirs, who were adopted sons of God (Ps 2.7). **1.37** Cf. God's word to Sarah in Gen 18.14; see also Job 42.2; Jer 32.17; Lk 18.27. **1.39–56** Mary and Elizabeth meet. **1.41** That *the child leaped in her womb* already signals John's role as forerunner to Jesus, as does Elizabeth's filling *with the Holy Spirit* and prophetic acclamation of Mary in vv. 42–45 (see v.

Spirit ⁴²and exclaimed with a loud cry, "Blessed are you among women, and blessed is the fruit of your womb. ⁴³And why has this happened to me, that the mother of my Lord comes to me? ⁴⁴For as soon as I heard the sound of your greeting, the child in my womb leaped for joy. ⁴⁵And blessed is she who believed that there would be*a* a fulfillment of what was spoken to her by the Lord."

Mary's Song of Praise

46 And Mary*b* said,

"My soul magnifies the Lord,
47   and my spirit rejoices in God my
          Savior,
48   for he has looked with favor on the
          lowliness of his servant.
       Surely, from now on all generations
          will call me blessed;
49   for the Mighty One has done great things
          for me,
       and holy is his name.
50   His mercy is for those who fear him
          from generation to generation.
51   He has shown strength with his arm;
          he has scattered the proud in the
          thoughts of their hearts.
52   He has brought down the powerful from
          their thrones,
          and lifted up the lowly;
53   he has filled the hungry with good things,
          and sent the rich away empty.
54   He has helped his servant Israel,
          in remembrance of his mercy,
55   according to the promise he made to our
          ancestors,

to Abraham and to his descendants
       forever."

56 And Mary remained with her about three months and then returned to her home.

The Birth of John the Baptist

57 Now the time came for Elizabeth to give birth, and she bore a son. ⁵⁸Her neighbors and relatives heard that the Lord had shown his great mercy to her, and they rejoiced with her.

59 On the eighth day they came to circumcise the child, and they were going to name him Zechariah after his father. ⁶⁰But his mother said, "No; he is to be called John." ⁶¹They said to her, "None of your relatives has this name." ⁶²Then they began motioning to his father to find out what name he wanted to give him. ⁶³He asked for a writing tablet and wrote, "His name is John." And all of them were amazed. ⁶⁴Immediately his mouth was opened and his tongue freed, and he began to speak, praising God. ⁶⁵Fear came over all their neighbors, and all these things were talked about throughout the entire hill country of Judea. ⁶⁶All who heard them pondered them and said, "What then will this child become?" For, indeed, the hand of the Lord was with him.

Zechariah's Prophecy

67 Then his father Zechariah was filled with the Holy Spirit and spoke this prophecy:
68   "Blessed be the Lord God of Israel,

a Or *believed, for there will be*   *b* Other ancient authorities read *Elizabeth*

67). **1.45** Mary is *blessed* because she *believed* the angel's message about her pregnancy (vv. 30–38; see also v. 42; cf. 11.27–28). **1.46–55** Mary's hymn of praise (traditionally called the Magnificat) interprets the events of the narrative theologically. It may be compared with various biblical hymns and prayers (e.g., Pss 34.1–3; 103.17; Hab 3.18; Sir 10.14), but especially echoes Hannah's song over Samuel's birth (1 Sam 2.1–10), in which God is also praised for salvation of the lowly and oppressed. Many phrases also recall psalms that celebrate God's victories. **1.49** *Holy is his name,* traditional Jewish words of praise (see Ps 111.9). **1.51** *Strength with his arm.* See Ps 89.10, 13; see also Ex 6.6; Acts 13.17. **1.52–53** The divine reversal announced here is a key theme of Luke's Gospel. **1.55** *The promise . . . to Abraham.* See Gen 17.6–8; 18.18; 22.17. The promise to David (2 Sam 7.11–16; 1 Chr 17.10–14) is also fulfilled. **1.57–80** John's birth and acclamation. **1.57** The episodes of ch. 1 are timed

by the months of Elizabeth's pregnancy (vv. 24, 26, 36). **1.58** The birth is seen as a sign of the Lord's *mercy* (see note on 1.25). **1.59** Regarding circumcision *on the eighth day,* see 2.21; Gen 17.12; 21.4; Lev 12.3; Acts 7.8. **1.60** In Luke the mothers, Mary (see v. 31) and Elizabeth, name the children (cf. Mt 1.21, 25). **1.62** Zechariah is portrayed as deaf as well as mute. **1.63** *His name is John.* Zechariah fulfills the angel's command (see v. 13). **1.65** The neighbors' *fear* expresses their awareness of divine action (see note on 1.12). *Throughout . . . Judea.* As here, Luke often indicates in summary fashion the wide circulation of news. See also note on 4.14–15. **1.67–79** Zechariah's inspired prophecy (traditionally called the Benedictus) answers the neighbors' question (v. 66) in the scriptural form of a prayer blessing God for what God has done (see 2.28; Pss 41.13; 72.18; 106.48). **1.68** *Looked favorably on,* or visited, as when a ruler makes an official visitation, here in an eschatological

for he has looked favorably on his
people and redeemed them.
69 He has raised up a mighty savior[a] for us
in the house of his servant David,
70 as he spoke through the mouth of his
holy prophets from of old,
71 that we would be saved from our
enemies and from the hand of all
who hate us.
72 Thus he has shown the mercy promised
to our ancestors,
and has remembered his holy covenant,
73 the oath that he swore to our ancestor
Abraham,
to grant us 74that we, being rescued
from the hands of our enemies,
might serve him without fear, 75in
holiness and righteousness
before him all our days.
76 And you, child, will be called the prophet
of the Most High;
for you will go before the Lord to
prepare his ways,
77 to give knowledge of salvation to his
people
by the forgiveness of their sins.
78 By the tender mercy of our God,
the dawn from on high will break
upon[b] us,

79 to give light to those who sit in darkness
and in the shadow of death,
to guide our feet into the way of
peace."
80 The child grew and became strong in
spirit, and he was in the wilderness until the
day he appeared publicly to Israel.

The Birth of Jesus

2 In those days a decree went out from Emperor Augustus that all the world should
be registered. 2This was the first registration
and was taken while Quirinius was governor
of Syria. 3All went to their own towns to be
registered. 4Joseph also went from the town
of Nazareth in Galilee to Judea, to the city of
David called Bethlehem, because he was
descended from the house and family of
David. 5He went to be registered with Mary,
to whom he was engaged and who was expecting a child. 6While they were there, the
time came for her to deliver her child. 7And
she gave birth to her firstborn son and
wrapped him in bands of cloth, and laid him
in a manger, because there was no place for
them in the inn.

a Gk a horn of salvation b Other ancient authorities read has broken upon

---

sense (see 7.16; 19.44; see also v. 78; Acts 15.14). His people indicates that more is involved than personal deliverance for John's parents (see note on 1.25). **1.69** *Savior,* lit. "a horn of salvation" (text note *a*), alluding to a Davidic ruler (see 1 Sam 2.10; Pss 18.2; 132.17; 148.14; see also Lk 1.31–33). **1.70** *Prophets.* See 10.24; 16.16, 31; 18.31; 24.25, 27, 44; see also v. 55. *From of old,* i.e., always. **1.72** Luke underlines the *covenant* with Abraham (see also Acts 3.25; 7.8). **1.73** On the oath to *Abraham,* see v. 55; Acts 3.25. **1.74** *Serve him without fear,* a reference to Israel's worship and life. **1.75** *Holiness and righteousness,* hallmarks of Israel's faithfulness to God's commands (see note on 1.6). **1.76** *The prophet of the Most High.* Cf. Jesus' title in v. 32. To *go before the Lord* (see also v. 17; 3.4; 7.27) recalls Mal 3.1. Luke stresses John's prophetic function over his baptizing activity. **1.77** The practical *knowledge of salvation* that John brings is focused on repentance for the *forgiveness of their sins* (see 3.3). **1.78** *Dawn,* a messianic metaphor (Num 24.17, Septuagint). **1.79** *Light,* a promised liberation from the *darkness* of captivity (see note on 22.53; Ps 107.10; Isa 9.2; 42.7; 60.1–3). *Peace.* See note on 2.14. **1.80** *The child grew.* See also 1 Sam 2.21, 26. John's strength *in spirit* (see also vv. 15, 17) anticipates that of Jesus (see 2.40; 4.14). *In the wilderness.* See also 3.2–4; Isa 40.3.

2.1–20 Cf. Mt 1.18–25; 2.1–12. Luke situates Jesus'

birth in the context of imperial edicts that affected occupied Israel (see also Acts 17.7). **2.1** A general *decree* of this sort is not otherwise attested. Gaius Octavius ruled as Caesar, or *Emperor,* from 31 BCE to 14 CE and was acclaimed *Augustus,* or "revered," in 27 BCE. *All the world,* probably Roman rhetoric for the whole empire. **2.2** A Roman *registration,* or census (see Acts 5.37), established control, especially for taxes and conscription. According to Josephus, *Quirinius* became *governor of Syria* (a Roman province that included Galilee and Judea) only in 6 CE, while Luke's story is still set in the time of Herod the Great, who died in 4 BCE (see 1.5; Mt 2.1). **2.3** A Roman census *registered* people in their places of residence, which for Mary and Joseph would have been Nazareth. **2.4** *Nazareth.* See note on 1.26. *Bethlehem,* south of Jerusalem, was the Judean village of King David's origin (1 Sam 16.1; 17.12; see also Mt 2.5–6; Jn 7.42). On Jesus' lineage from the *family of David,* see 1.27; 3.23–38. Luke interprets the decree of v. 1 to require registration in Bethlehem owing to its theological significance. **2.5** Luke says nothing about Joseph's understanding of this pregnancy (see 1.27; 2.33; cf. Mt 1.18–25). **2.6** The birth itself is not miraculous. **2.7** A *firstborn son* was considered a special blessing in Jewish families and had a privileged role (2.23; see also Ex 13.2; Num 3.12–13; 18.15; Deut 21.15–17). *Manger,* a feedbox for animals.

The Shepherds and the Angels

8 In that region there were shepherds living in the fields, keeping watch over their flock by night. 9 Then an angel of the Lord stood before them, and the glory of the Lord shone around them, and they were terrified. 10 But the angel said to them, "Do not be afraid; for see—I am bringing you good news of great joy for all the people: 11 to you is born this day in the city of David a Savior, who is the Messiah,*a* the Lord. 12 This will be a sign for you: you will find a child wrapped in bands of cloth and lying in a manger." 13 And suddenly there was with the angel a multitude of the heavenly host,*b* praising God and saying,

14 "Glory to God in the highest heaven,
     and on earth peace among those
          whom he favors!"*c*

15 When the angels had left them and gone into heaven, the shepherds said to one another, "Let us go now to Bethlehem and see this thing that has taken place, which the Lord has made known to us." 16 So they went with haste and found Mary and Joseph, and the child lying in the manger. 17 When they saw this, they made known what had been told them about this child; 18 and all who heard it were amazed at what the shepherds told them. 19 But Mary treasured all these words and pondered them in her heart. 20 The shepherds returned, glorifying and praising God for all they had heard and seen, as it had been told them.

Jesus Is Named

21 After eight days had passed, it was time to circumcise the child; and he was called Jesus, the name given by the angel before he was conceived in the womb.

Jesus Is Presented in the Temple

22 When the time came for their purification according to the law of Moses, they brought him up to Jerusalem to present him to the Lord 23 (as it is written in the law of the Lord, "Every firstborn male shall be designated as holy to the Lord"), 24 and they offered a sacrifice according to what is stated in the law of the Lord, "a pair of turtledoves or two young pigeons."

25 Now there was a man in Jerusalem whose name was Simeon;*d* this man was righteous and devout, looking forward to the consolation of Israel, and the Holy Spirit rested on him. 26 It had been revealed to him by the Holy Spirit that he would not see death before he had seen the Lord's Messiah.*e* 27 Guided by the Spirit, Simeon*f* came into the temple; and when the parents brought in the child Jesus, to do for him what was customary under the law,

---

a Or the Christ *b* Gk army *c* Other ancient authorities read peace, goodwill among people *d* Gk Symeon *e* Or the Lord's Christ *f* Gk In the Spirit, he

---

A formal *inn* is not in view here (as in 10.34), but rather a temporary lodging for travelers. **2.8** King David was also a *shepherd* (1 Sam 17.15; Ps 78.70–71). **2.9** This *angel of the Lord* is not named (cf. 1.19, 26), though Gabriel may be intended. *Glory of the Lord,* the blazing light of God's presence and power (Ex 16.7, 10; 24.17). **2.10** *Do not be afraid.* See notes on 1.12; 1.13. The mention of *good news* here in conjunction with *Savior* in v. 11 and *peace* in v. 14 suggests an implicit comparison with Roman imperial propaganda. **2.11** *This day,* or "today" (Greek *semeron*), in Luke often connotes the present inbreaking of salvation (see 4.21; 5.26; 13.32–33; 19.5, 9; 23.43). *City of David.* See v. 4. The title *Savior* is rare in the Gospels (see 1.47; Jn 4.42; see also Acts 5.31; 13.23), but was commonly used of the Roman emperor. Israel had long used this political title for God (see Isa 43.3, 11). *Lord* here may interpret the meaning of *Messiah* for Greek readers. Both titles are again combined in Peter's acclamation of Jesus in Acts 2.36. The *Messiah,* or Christ, is an anointed ruler (see Acts 10.38). **2.13** *Heavenly host,* the armies of heaven (see 1 Kings 22.19), whose testimony reveals the divine meaning of this birth. **2.14** A hymnic commentary on vv. 10–11. *Peace* as a benefit that the Roman emperor claimed to deliver is here implicitly juxtaposed to God's *glory,* which is emblematic of God's salvation (see note on 2.10). **2.16** The *sign* of a child in a manger (v. 12) is literally fulfilled. **2.19** Mary is represented as understanding the shepherd's report (see vv. 34–35, 51). **2.20** The shepherds' praise of God for what *they had heard and seen* echoes the praise of the angelic armies (vv. 13–14). **2.21–40** The presentation of Jesus in the temple. **2.21** *After eight days.* See also 1.59. On Jesus' *name,* see 1.31; cf. Mt 1.21, 25. **2.22–24** All the details of the *purification* of Mary are in close accord with Lev 12. Luke associates the redemption of the firstborn son with his mother's purification. **2.23** The quotation is from Ex 13.2. **2.24** A sacrifice of *turtledoves* or *pigeons* was acceptable for those who could not afford a sheep (see Lev 12.8). **2.25** Simeon is *righteous and devout,* i.e., faithful to the law (see note on 1.6; see also Acts 2.5; 8.2; 22.12). His expectation concerns *the consolation of Israel,* i.e., its deliverance (see Isa 40.1; 49.6; 61.2), now focused on the arrival of the Messiah. The presence of the *Holy Spirit* with Simeon (see also vv. 26–27) confirms the prophetic nature of his oracles. The language of "seeing" is prominent in these verses. **2.27** Simeon's recognition of the infant

28 Simeon[a] took him in his arms and praised God, saying,

29 "Master, now you are dismissing your
    servant[b] in peace,
    according to your word;
30 for my eyes have seen your salvation,
31   which you have prepared in the
       presence of all peoples,
32 a light for revelation to the Gentiles
    and for glory to your people Israel."

33 And the child's father and mother were amazed at what was being said about him. 34 Then Simeon[c] blessed them and said to his mother Mary, "This child is destined for the falling and the rising of many in Israel, and to be a sign that will be opposed 35 so that the inner thoughts of many will be revealed—and a sword will pierce your own soul too."

36 There was also a prophet, Anna[d] the daughter of Phanuel, of the tribe of Asher. She was of a great age, having lived with her husband seven years after her marriage, 37 then as a widow to the age of eighty-four. She never left the temple but worshiped there with fasting and prayer night and day. 38 At that moment she came, and began to praise God and to speak about the child[e] to all who were looking for the redemption of Jerusalem.

The Return to Nazareth

39 When they had finished everything required by the law of the Lord, they returned to Galilee, to their own town of Nazareth. 40 The child grew and became strong, filled with wisdom; and the favor of God was upon him.

The Boy Jesus in the Temple

41 Now every year his parents went to Jerusalem for the festival of the Passover. 42 And when he was twelve years old, they went up as usual for the festival. 43 When the festival was ended and they started to return, the boy Jesus stayed behind in Jerusalem, but his parents did not know it. 44 Assuming that he was in the group of travelers, they went a day's journey. Then they started to look for him among their relatives and friends. 45 When they did not find him, they returned to Jerusalem to search for him. 46 After three days they found him in the temple, sitting among the teachers, listening to them and asking them questions. 47 And all who heard him were amazed at his understanding and his answers. 48 When his parents[f] saw him they were astonished; and his mother said to him, "Child, why have you treated us like this? Look, your father and I have been searching for you in great anxiety." 49 He said to them, "Why were you searching for me? Did you not know that I must be in my Father's house?"[g] 50 But they did not understand what he said to them. 51 Then he went down with

a Gk he b Gk slave c Gk Symeon d Gk Hanna e Gk him
f Gk they g Or be about my Father's interests?

Jesus is *guided by the Spirit*. **2.28–32** Simeon's first oracle (traditionally called the Nunc Dimittis, Latin for *now you are dismissing*, v. 29) praises God and again declares God's saving purposes (see v. 11). **2.29** *Now* underlines a key moment in salvation history. **2.30** *Salvation*, here equivalent to *consolation* (v. 25) and *redemption* (v. 38). **2.31** *In the presence of all peoples* introduces a universalistic perspective; see Isa 40.3–5 (cited in Lk 3.6); 52.10. **2.32** The logic is that of Isa 49.6: i.e., Israel's *glory* is to be a *light for revelation to the Gentiles*. See also Isa 42.6; 46.13; 60.1–3. **2.34** Simeon's second oracle is directed to Mary and foreshadows what is to come. *The falling and the rising of many in Israel* is portrayed in the subsequent narrative and continues on in Acts. **2.35** *The inner thoughts of many* implies human resistance and rejection (see 5.22; 6.8; 7.39; 11.17). The *sword* of division will also cause pain for Mary and her family (see 8.19–21; 11.27–28; 12.51–53). **2.36–37** *Anna's* ancestry in Israel (*the tribe of Asher;* see Deut 33.24–25) and her credentials as a *prophet* (cf. Philip's daughters in Acts 21.9) and an aged *widow* (cf. Acts 6.1; 9.41; 1 Tim 5.3–16; Jdt 8.4–6) indicate her special status. Her piety is underlined by her constant presence in the *temple*. **2.38** Though not cited directly, Anna's words echo Simeon's prophetic speech insofar as the *redemption of Jerusalem* is analogous to the *consolation of Israel* (see notes on 2.25; 2.30). Luke is fond of juxtaposing male and female characters (see notes on 7.11–17; 8.40–56; 15.3–7). **2.39** In this chapter prophecy and fulfillment occur in the context of following the *law of the Lord* (see vv. 22–24, 25). *Nazareth*. See v. 4; note on 1.26. **2.40** *The child grew and became strong,* a summary of Jesus' boyhood. See note on 1.80. On the *favor of God,* see 1.30. **2.41–52** Only Luke provides a story of Jesus' boyhood. **2.41** The *Passover* festival was an observance of Israel's liberation from Egyptian bondage (Ex 12.1–27; 23.15; Num 9.2–14; Deut 16.16). **2.42** *Twelve years old.* Jesus' young age accents his superiority and explains the amazement of v. 47. **2.46** The *temple* is again the site (see vv. 22–38) where Israel's teachers of the law encounter the child of promise. **2.47** Though too young to have benefited from formal training in the law, Jesus demonstrates *understanding,* i.e., intellectual ability. **2.48** *Your father* sets up the opposition with *my Father's house* in v. 49. **2.49** That Jesus *must* be in the temple already is a necessity based on the divine plan of salvation that drives his mission (see 4.43; 9.22;

them and came to Nazareth, and was obedient to them. His mother treasured all these things in her heart.

52 And Jesus increased in wisdom and in years,[a] and in divine and human favor.

The Proclamation of John the Baptist

3 In the fifteenth year of the reign of Emperor Tiberius, when Pontius Pilate was governor of Judea, and Herod was ruler[b] of Galilee, and his brother Philip ruler[b] of the region of Ituraea and Trachonitis, and Lysanias ruler[b] of Abilene, 2during the high priesthood of Annas and Caiaphas, the word of God came to John son of Zechariah in the wilderness. 3He went into all the region around the Jordan, proclaiming a baptism of repentance for the forgiveness of sins, 4as it is written in the book of the words of the prophet Isaiah,

"The voice of one crying out in the
　　wilderness:
'Prepare the way of the Lord,
　　make his paths straight.
5　Every valley shall be filled,
　　　and every mountain and hill shall be
　　　　made low,
　　and the crooked shall be made straight,
　　　and the rough ways made smooth;
6　and all flesh shall see the salvation of
　　　God.'"

7 John said to the crowds that came out to be baptized by him, "You brood of vipers! Who warned you to flee from the wrath to come? 8Bear fruits worthy of repentance. Do not begin to say to yourselves, 'We have Abraham as our ancestor'; for I tell you, God is able from these stones to raise up children to Abraham. 9Even now the ax is lying at the root of the trees; every tree therefore that does not bear good fruit is cut down and thrown into the fire."

10 And the crowds asked him, "What then should we do?" 11In reply he said to them, "Whoever has two coats must share with anyone who has none; and whoever has food must do likewise." 12Even tax collectors came to be baptized, and they asked him, "Teacher, what should we do?" 13He said to them, "Collect no more than the amount prescribed for you." 14Soldiers also asked him, "And we, what should we do?" He said to them, "Do not extort money from anyone by threats or false accusation, and be satisfied with your wages."

15 As the people were filled with expectation, and all were questioning in their hearts concerning John, whether he might be the Messiah,[c] 16John answered all of them by saying, "I baptize you with water; but one who is more powerful than I is coming; I am not worthy to untie the thong of his sandals. He will baptize you with[d] the Holy Spirit and fire. 17His winnowing fork is in his hand, to clear

a Or in stature　b Gk tetrarch　c Or the Christ　d Or in

13.33; 17.25; 19.5; 22.37; 24.7, 26, 44). **2.50** *Treasured all these things.* See note on 2.19. **2.51–52** Jesus was *obedient* to his earthly mother and father as prescribed by the fifth commandment (Ex 20.12). The growth refrain (see also 1.80; 2.40) affirms both *divine and human favor.*

3.1–20 Cf. Mt 3.1–12; 14.3–4; Mk 1.2–8; 6.17–18. Luke locates the beginning of John's preaching by naming the contemporaneous political rulers and high priests (see 1.5; 2.1–2). **3.1** *Tiberius,* emperor during John's and Jesus' public activity (14–37 CE). *Pilate* (see also 13.1; 23.1–52), governor in Judea for most of that time (26–36 CE). *Herod* Antipas, the son of Herod the Great, whom the Romans had named "King of the Jews" (1.5; see Mt 2.1–12). Antipas unsuccessfully sought this title from Rome (perhaps accounting for the tension with Pilate in 23.12). *The fifteenth year of . . . Tiberius* places the call of John in 28/29 CE. **3.2** The high priests, *Annas and Caiaphas,* were subject to regulation and annual appointment by Rome. *The word of God came to John,* the call of a prophet (see Jer 1.4, 11; Hos 1.1; Joel 1.1). *Wilderness.* See note on 1.80. **3.3** *A baptism of repentance,* a ritual of cleansing signifying a return to God with the expectation of forgiveness (see 1.77). **3.4–6** The citation of Isa 40.3–5 serves to identify John with traditional hopes for Israel's restoration among the nations. **3.6** *All flesh* emphasizes the universal extent of God's plan (see note on 2.31). On the *salvation of God,* see notes on 2.11; 2.30. **3.8** *Abraham* is the father of Israel (16.23; see also Gen 17; Isa 51.2; Jn 8.33–40), but birth alone is no substitute for repentance. **3.9** *Even now* the judgment, the *wrath* of v. 7, is unfolding. *Tree . . . good fruit.* See 6.43–44. **3.11** The content of repentance is illustrated with a practical example (see also Acts 2.44–47; 4.32–35). **3.12–14** *Tax collectors* and *soldiers* do not appear in Matthew's or Mark's versions (see also Lk 5.27–30; 7.2–10, 29, 34; 15.1; 18.9–14). John's requirements fit the reputations of these groups (see note on 5.30). **3.15** *The people* (Greek *laos*), as opposed to the crowds (Greek *ochloi*) in need of repentance (v. 10), wait *with expectation* for the *Messiah,* Israel's Davidic king (see notes on 1.33; 2.11). **3.16** John declares the Messiah's baptism to be *with the Holy Spirit and fire* of judgment (vv. 9, 17). In Acts, however, the Holy Spirit and tongues of fire fall on the disciples at Pentecost as a sign of promise (Acts 2.1–21, 38–39). **3.17** The images of *threshing* and *winnowing,* or sepa-

his threshing floor and to gather the wheat into his granary; but the chaff he will burn with unquenchable fire."

18 So, with many other exhortations, he proclaimed the good news to the people. 19But Herod the ruler,*a* who had been rebuked by him because of Herodias, his brother's wife, and because of all the evil things that Herod had done, 20added to them all by shutting up John in prison.

The Baptism of Jesus

21 Now when all the people were baptized, and when Jesus also had been baptized and was praying, the heaven was opened, 22and the Holy Spirit descended upon him in bodily form like a dove. And a voice came from heaven, "You are my Son, the Beloved;*b* with you I am well pleased."*c*

The Ancestors of Jesus

23 Jesus was about thirty years old when he began his work. He was the son (as was thought) of Joseph son of Heli, 24son of Matthat, son of Levi, son of Melchi, son of Jannai, son of Joseph, 25son of Mattathias, son of Amos, son of Nahum, son of Esli, son of Naggai, 26son of Maath, son of Mattathias, son of Semein, son of Josech, son of Joda, 27son of Joanan, son of Rhesa, son of Zerubbabel, son of Shealtiel,*d* son of Neri, 28son of Melchi, son of Addi, son of Cosam, son of Elmadam, son of Er, 29son of Joshua, son of Eliezer, son of Jorim, son of Matthat, son of Levi, 30son of Simeon, son of Judah, son of Joseph, son of Jonam, son of Eliakim, 31son of Melea, son of Menna, son of Mattatha, son of Nathan, son of David, 32son of Jesse, son of Obed, son of Boaz, son of Sala,*e* son of Nahshon, 33son of Amminadab, son of Admin, son of Arni,*f* son of Hezron, son of Perez, son of Judah, 34son of Jacob, son of Isaac, son of Abraham, son of Terah, son of Nahor, 35son of Serug, son of Reu, son of Peleg, son of Eber, son of Shelah, 36son of Cainan, son of Arphaxad, son of Shem, son of Noah, son of Lamech, 37son of Methuselah, son of Enoch, son of Jared, son of Mahalaleel, son of Cainan, 38son of Enos, son of Seth, son of Adam, son of God.

The Temptation of Jesus

4 Jesus, full of the Holy Spirit, returned from the Jordan and was led by the Spirit in the wilderness, 2where for forty days he was tempted by the devil. He ate nothing at all during those days, and when they were over, he was famished. 3The devil said to him, "If you are the Son of God, command this stone to become a loaf of bread." 4Jesus answered him, "It is written, 'One does not live by bread alone.' "

5 Then the devil*g* led him up and showed him in an instant all the kingdoms of the world. 6And the devil*g* said to him, "To you I will give their glory and all this authority; for it has been given over to me, and I give it to anyone I please. 7If you, then, will worship me,

---

a Gk *tetrarch*　*b* Or *my beloved Son*　*c* Other ancient authorities read *You are my Son, today I have begotten you*　*d* Gk *Salathiel*　*e* Other ancient authorities read *Salmon*　*f* Other ancient authorities read *Amminadab, son of Aram*; others vary widely　*g* Gk *he*

---

rating, grain are commonly used for judgment (Isa 41.15–16; Jer 15.7; Rev 14.14–20). **3.19** *Herod* Antipas (see note on 3.1) is *rebuked* because of his unlawful marriage to *Herodias*. **3.20** The outcome of John's imprisonment is related in a flashback in 9.9. **3.21–22** Cf. Mt 3.13–17; Mk 1.9–11. Luke mentions Jesus' baptism only after reporting John's imprisonment. **3.22** The Spirit's descent is concretized *in bodily form* (cf. Mt 3.16; Mk 1.10). Jesus is acclaimed from heaven as God's *Son, the Beloved* (see Gen 22.2; Ps 2.7; Isa 42.1; see also Lk 4.1–13; Acts 4.27). **3.23–38** Cf. Mt 1.1–17. Jesus' ancestry is traced through Joseph's ostensible paternity. Names are taken from Gen 5.1–32; 11.10–32; Ruth 4.18–22; 1 Chr 1–3. **3.23** Jesus' age of *about thirty years* implies full maturity and fits with the middle of Tiberius's reign. David began to reign at age thirty (2 Sam 5.4); Joseph entered Pharaoh's service at thirty (Gen 41.46). **3.23b–31** Most of the persons in the genealogical list up to David are otherwise unknown. **3.31** *David*'s place in the genealogy is not highlighted (cf. Mt 1.6, 17); see, however, 1.32, 69; 18.38–39; cf. 20.41–44. **3.38** Matthew focuses on descent from Abraham, but Luke establishes Jesus as son of David in the line of *Adam, son of God* (see v. 22), thus emphasizing his significance for all humankind.

4.1–13 Cf. Mt 4.1–11; Mk 1.12–13. Jesus rebuffs Satan with scripture. **4.1–2** *Forty days* in the *wilderness* fits the pattern of Moses' and Elijah's fasts (Ex 34.28; Deut 9.9, 18; 1 Kings 19.8) and God's testing of Israel for forty years in the wilderness (Deut 8.2). There are also "forty days" between the resurrection and the ascension (Acts 1.3). **4.3** *If* here means "since" (see also 23.37), granting that Jesus is the Son of God (see 1.32, 35; 2.49; 4.41) but challenging how he will exercise that authority (4.6). **4.4** Jesus' three responses (also vv. 8, 12) refer to Deuteronomy, here Deut 8.3. **4.5** Luke transposes the second and third temptations compared to Mt 4.5–10 so that Jerusalem is accented in the

it will all be yours." ⁸Jesus answered him, "It is written,

'Worship the Lord your God,
and serve only him.'"

9 Then the devil*a* took him to Jerusalem, and placed him on the pinnacle of the temple, saying to him, "If you are the Son of God, throw yourself down from here, ¹⁰for it is written,

'He will command his angels concerning you,
to protect you,'

¹¹and

'On their hands they will bear you up,
so that you will not dash your foot
against a stone.'"

¹²Jesus answered him, "It is said, 'Do not put the Lord your God to the test.'" ¹³When the devil had finished every test, he departed from him until an opportune time.

The Beginning of the Galilean Ministry

14 Then Jesus, filled with the power of the Spirit, returned to Galilee, and a report about him spread through all the surrounding country. ¹⁵He began to teach in their synagogues and was praised by everyone.

The Rejection of Jesus at Nazareth

16 When he came to Nazareth, where he had been brought up, he went to the synagogue on the sabbath day, as was his custom. He stood up to read, ¹⁷and the scroll of the prophet Isaiah was given to him. He unrolled the scroll and found the place where it was written:

¹⁸ "The Spirit of the Lord is upon me,

because he has anointed me
to bring good news to the poor.
He has sent me to proclaim release to the captives
and recovery of sight to the blind,
to let the oppressed go free,
¹⁹ to proclaim the year of the Lord's favor."

²⁰And he rolled up the scroll, gave it back to the attendant, and sat down. The eyes of all in the synagogue were fixed on him. ²¹Then he began to say to them, "Today this scripture has been fulfilled in your hearing." ²²All spoke well of him and were amazed at the gracious words that came from his mouth. They said, "Is not this Joseph's son?" ²³He said to them, "Doubtless you will quote to me this proverb, 'Doctor, cure yourself!' And you will say, 'Do here also in your hometown the things that we have heard you did at Capernaum.'" ²⁴And he said, "Truly I tell you, no prophet is accepted in the prophet's hometown. ²⁵But the truth is, there were many widows in Israel in the time of Elijah, when the heaven was shut up three years and six months, and there was a severe famine over all the land; ²⁶yet Elijah was sent to none of them except to a widow at Zarephath in Sidon. ²⁷There were also many lepers*b* in Israel in the time of the prophet Elisha, and none of them was cleansed except Naaman the Syrian." ²⁸When they heard this, all in the synagogue were filled with rage. ²⁹They got up, drove him out of the town, and led him to the brow of the hill on which their

---

a Gk *he* *b* The terms *leper* and *leprosy* can refer to several diseases

---

final position of emphasis (and the sensitive issue of political authority is not). **4.7** *Worship me*, i.e., acknowledge my legitimate dominion. **4.8** Jesus quotes Deut 6.13. **4.10–11** The devil quotes Ps 91.11–12, which counsels trusting God, not testing. **4.12** Jesus quotes Deut 6.16. **4.13** On the *opportune time* of the devil's return, see 22.3–6. **4.14–30** Cf. Mt 13.53–58; Mk 6.1–6a. Jesus' appearance in Nazareth is paradigmatic for the plot of the rest of the Gospel. **4.14–15** Luke typically notes the wide-ranging impact of Jesus' activity (see v. 37; 5.15, 17; 6.17; 7.17; see also 8.39; 9.6). **4.14** The *Spirit* remains active at the beginning of Jesus' ministry (see also 3.22; 4.1, 18). **4.16** *As was his custom*. Jesus is faithful to Israel's practices, here observing synagogue worship on the sabbath (see also 2.21–38). The guest was invited to *read* from the prophetic scroll (v. 17) and comment (see Acts 13.15). **4.18–19** The reading includes portions of Isa 61.1–2; 58.6 (see also Lk 7.22). *The poor*. See 1.52; 6.20; 7.22;

14.13, 21; 16.20, 22. *The year of the Lord's favor*, a "year of jubilee" and restoration in Lev 25.8–12. **4.20** According to Jewish custom one stood to read scripture but *sat down* to teach (see also 5.3). **4.21** *Today* (see note on 2.11) indicates the actualization of the Isaiah text in vv. 18–19, though fulfillment *in your hearing* does not guarantee acceptance (see Isa 6.9–10; Acts 28.26–27). **4.22** *Joseph's son*. Cf. 2.48–49; 3.23. **4.23** This *proverb* (lit. "parable"; see note on 6.39) was common in Greek and Jewish lore. In Luke's story, Jesus arrives only later in *Capernaum* (v. 31). **4.24** Jesus proclaims the year of the Lord's *favor* (Greek *dektos*, v. 19) but is not *accepted* (*dektos*). **4.25–27** The stories of *Elijah* in *Sidon* (1 Kings 17.1–16) and *Elisha* and the *Syrian* (2 Kings 5.1–14) recall times of judgment on Israel in which the respective prophets turn to Gentiles and thus highlight the Lukan theme of the universalization of the gospel. The stories also anticipate Jesus' miracles in 5.12–14; 7.11–17. **4.29–30** *Hurl him off the cliff* may imply the stoning of a

town was built, so that they might hurl him off the cliff. 30But he passed through the midst of them and went on his way.

The Man with an Unclean Spirit

31 He went down to Capernaum, a city in Galilee, and was teaching them on the sabbath. 32They were astounded at his teaching, because he spoke with authority. 33In the synagogue there was a man who had the spirit of an unclean demon, and he cried out with a loud voice, 34"Let us alone! What have you to do with us, Jesus of Nazareth? Have you come to destroy us? I know who you are, the Holy One of God." 35But Jesus rebuked him, saying, "Be silent, and come out of him!" When the demon had thrown him down before them, he came out of him without having done him any harm. 36They were all amazed and kept saying to one another, "What kind of utterance is this? For with authority and power he commands the unclean spirits, and out they come!" 37And a report about him began to reach every place in the region.

Healings at Simon's House

38 After leaving the synagogue he entered Simon's house. Now Simon's mother-in-law was suffering from a high fever, and they asked him about her. 39Then he stood over her and rebuked the fever, and it left her. Immediately she got up and began to serve them.

40 As the sun was setting, all those who had any who were sick with various kinds of diseases brought them to him; and he laid his hands on each of them and cured them. 41Demons also came out of many, shouting, "You are the Son of God!" But he rebuked them and would not allow them to speak, because they knew that he was the Messiah.[a]

Jesus Preaches in the Synagogues

42 At daybreak he departed and went into a deserted place. And the crowds were looking for him; and when they reached him, they wanted to prevent him from leaving them. 43But he said to them, "I must proclaim the good news of the kingdom of God to the other cities also; for I was sent for this purpose." 44So he continued proclaiming the message in the synagogues of Judea.[b]

Jesus Calls the First Disciples

5 Once while Jesus[c] was standing beside the lake of Gennesaret, and the crowd was

a Or the Christ   b Other ancient authorities read Galilee
c Gk he

heretic, but somehow Jesus *went on* (Greek *poreuomai*) his determined *way* (see 13.31–35). The same verb (*poreuomai*) describes Jesus' journey to Jerusalem (see 9.51; 10.38; 17.11; 19.28). **4.31–37** Cf. Mt 4.13; 7.28–29; Mk 1.21–28. Luke now tells of Jesus' healings in Capernaum (see v. 23), which were narrated earlier in Mark's sequence. **4.32** *They were astounded*. The context is again sabbath teaching in the synagogue (see v. 16), but the astonishment of these hearers is evidently positive. **4.33** *With a loud voice*. See 8.28. **4.34** *The Holy One of God*. See 1.35; 2.23. For the evil spirits' recognition of Jesus as Son of God, see vv. 3, 9, 41; 8.28. **4.35** Jesus' *rebuke* of the demon is a power confrontation, demonstrating his dominion over evil and effecting liberation for those oppressed by demons (see v. 18; Acts 10.38). **4.36** Jesus' *authority and power* are demonstrated, but not on the devil's terms (see vv. 1–13). **4.37** *A report*. See note on 4.14–15. **4.38–44** Cf. Mt 8.14–17; 4.23; Mk 1.29–39. Additional Capernaum episodes illustrate a successful and popular ministry (cf. vv. 28–29). **4.38** In Luke's sequence, Jesus appears at *Simon's house* before Simon is called as a disciple (5.1–11; cf. Mk 1.16–20, 29–31). **4.39** Luke presents Jesus' rebuke of the high *fever* in the same terms as Jesus' confrontations with the demons (vv. 35, 41). *Immediately* signals the miraculous occurrence; see 5.25; 8.44, 47, 55 (*at once*); 13.13;

18.43; Acts 3.7; 5.10; 12.23; 13.11; 16.26. The healing of a woman follows the exorcism of a man (see note on 2.38). **4.40–41** These summary verses (see also vv. 14–15, 31–32) offer additional description of the promised liberation from physical and spiritual restraints (see vv. 18–19). Once again, the demons correctly recognize Jesus as *the Son of God* (see note on 4.34). **4.42–43** Luke's portrait of Jesus often includes retreats to *a deserted place* for solitude and prayer (see note on 5.16), balanced with the recurring theme of Jesus' determined *purpose* (see notes on 2.49; 9.51) to declare and inaugurate the kingdom of God. **4.43** The *kingdom* (or "reign") *of God* is the substance of Jesus' preaching (see, e.g., chs. 13, 18). It is made present in some sense by Jesus' person and deeds (11.20; 17.21), yet is also spoken of as a future hope (12.31; 22.16, 30). **4.44** Luke seems to use *Judea* here in a sense that includes Galilee (vv. 14, 16, 31; see text note b).
5.1–11 Cf. Mt 13.1–2; 4.18–22; Mk 4.1–2; 1.16–20; see Jn 21.1–11. This story echoes earlier scriptural accounts of the calls of Moses while tending sheep (Ex 3), Gideon while beating wheat (Judg 6), and Isaiah in the temple (Isa 6). These biblical call stories take mortals from their usual tasks and direct them toward God's mission to the people. **5.1** *Lake of Gennesaret*, a local name for the Sea of Galilee. The *crowd* is so great

pressing in on him to hear the word of God, ²he saw two boats there at the shore of the lake; the fishermen had gone out of them and were washing their nets. ³He got into one of the boats, the one belonging to Simon, and asked him to put out a little way from the shore. Then he sat down and taught the crowds from the boat. ⁴When he had finished speaking, he said to Simon, "Put out into the deep water and let down your nets for a catch." ⁵Simon answered, "Master, we have worked all night long but have caught nothing. Yet if you say so, I will let down the nets." ⁶When they had done this, they caught so many fish that their nets were beginning to break. ⁷So they signaled their partners in the other boat to come and help them. And they came and filled both boats, so that they began to sink. ⁸But when Simon Peter saw it, he fell down at Jesus' knees, saying, "Go away from me, Lord, for I am a sinful man!" ⁹For he and all who were with him were amazed at the catch of fish that they had taken; ¹⁰and so also were James and John, sons of Zebedee, who were partners with Simon. Then Jesus said to Simon, "Do not be afraid; from now on you will be catching people." ¹¹When they had brought their boats to shore, they left everything and followed him.

Jesus Cleanses a Leper

12 Once, when he was in one of the cities, there was a man covered with leprosy.ᵃ When he saw Jesus, he bowed with his face to the ground and begged him, "Lord, if you choose, you can make me clean." ¹³Then Jesusᵇ stretched out his hand, touched him, and said, "I do choose. Be made clean." Immediately the leprosyᵃ left him. ¹⁴And he ordered him to tell no one. "Go," he said, "and show yourself to the priest, and, as Moses commanded, make an offering for your cleansing, for a testimony to them." ¹⁵But now more than ever the word about Jesusᶜ spread abroad; many crowds would gather to hear him and to be cured of their diseases. ¹⁶But he would withdraw to deserted places and pray.

Jesus Heals a Paralytic

17 One day, while he was teaching, Pharisees and teachers of the law were sitting near by (they had come from every village of Galilee and Judea and from Jerusalem); and the power of the Lord was with him to heal.ᵈ ¹⁸Just then some men came, carrying a paralyzed man on a bed. They were trying to bring him in and lay him before Jesus;ᵉ ¹⁹but finding no way to bring him in because of the crowd, they went up on the roof and let him down with his bed through the tiles into the middle of the crowdᵉ in front of Jesus. ²⁰When he saw

---

a The terms *leper* and *leprosy* can refer to several diseases
b Gk *he*   *c* Gk *him*   *d* Other ancient authorities read *was present to heal them*   *e* Gk *into the midst*

---

it requires special arrangements to address them. *Word of God* occurs here for the first time and refers to Jesus' proclamation; in Acts it refers to the message about God's action in Jesus (Acts 6.7; 12.24; 19.20). **5.3** Jesus *sat down and taught.* See note on 4.20. **5.5** Though *Simon's* answer expresses hesitation, his address to Jesus as *Master* is deferential to his authority (see 8.24, 45; 9.33, 49; 17.13). **5.8** *Peter's* recognition of being a *sinful man* indicates his sense of divine presence (cf. Ex 3.6; Judg 6.22; Isa 6.5). **5.9** Their amazement is the mortal fear or awe evoked by an encounter with divine holiness (see notes on 1.12; 1.13; Acts 3.10). **5.10** On the image of fishing for *people*, see also Jer 16.16. **5.11** On leaving *everything*, see v. 28; 14.33; 18.22–23. *And followed.* To follow Jesus is a fundamental metaphor in Luke for discipleship (see vv. 27–28; 9.23, 49, 57, 59, 61; 18.22, 28, 43; 22.39, 54). **5.12–16** Cf. Mt 8.1–4; Mk 1.40–45. A cure of one who is ritually unclean marks the extension of Jesus' ministry to social outcasts. **5.12** Luke presents a person with an extensive condition of *leprosy* rather than a leper (but see 4.27; 7.22; 17.12). The term probably includes what modern diagnosis would identify as several diseases, but ancient Israel understood such unpleasant and disabling skin disorders to require measured separation from the community as much for reasons of ritual purity as hygiene (see Lev 13–14). **5.13** It is especially significant in this case that Jesus heals with a touch. **5.14** The *priest* certified a person clean, or healed, according to established standards (see also 17.14). *As Moses commanded.* Careful observance of the law is also noted in 1.6; 2.22–24. The *offering for your cleansing* provided a public testimony to the cure and led to reintegration into the community. **5.15** The clamor *to be cured* stands in tension with Jesus' command *tell no one* (v. 14; see also Mk 1.44–45). **5.16** On Jesus' retreat to *pray*, see note on 4.42–43; see also 3.21; 6.12; 9.18, 28, 29; 11.1; 22.32, 41, 44. **5.17–26** Cf. Mt 9.1–8; Mk 2.1–12. This healing story has a profound theological controversy about forgiveness at its center (vv. 20b–24a). **5.17** Jesus' teaching is being conducted in the midst of *Pharisees*, who were recognized authorities on the strict observance of the law (see Acts 26.5). The *teachers of the law* (see also Acts 5.34) may have been scribes of the Pharisaic party (see v. 21; 15.2) or associated with other official groups in Israel (see lists in 19.47; 20.1). The *power of the Lord*, i.e., of God (see 1.35; 4.14, 36; 6.19; 8.46; Acts 2.22; 10.38), enables Jesus to heal. *Every village . . . from Jerusalem* documents Jesus' impact on all of Israel (see note on 4.14–15). **5.19** Roof

their faith, he said, "Friend,*a* your sins are forgiven you." 21Then the scribes and the Pharisees began to question, "Who is this who is speaking blasphemies? Who can forgive sins but God alone?" 22When Jesus perceived their questionings, he answered them, "Why do you raise such questions in your hearts? 23Which is easier, to say, 'Your sins are forgiven you,' or to say, 'Stand up and walk'? 24But so that you may know that the Son of Man has authority on earth to forgive sins"—he said to the one who was paralyzed—"I say to you, stand up and take your bed and go to your home." 25Immediately he stood up before them, took what he had been lying on, and went to his home, glorifying God. 26Amazement seized all of them, and they glorified God and were filled with awe, saying, "We have seen strange things today."

Jesus Calls Levi

27 After this he went out and saw a tax collector named Levi, sitting at the tax booth; and he said to him, "Follow me." 28And he got up, left everything, and followed him.

29 Then Levi gave a great banquet for him in his house; and there was a large crowd of tax collectors and others sitting at the table*b* with them. 30The Pharisees and their scribes were complaining to his disciples, saying, "Why do you eat and drink with tax collectors and sinners?" 31Jesus answered, "Those who are well have no need of a physician, but those who are sick; 32I have come to call not the righteous but sinners to repentance."

The Question about Fasting

33 Then they said to him, "John's disciples, like the disciples of the Pharisees, frequently fast and pray, but your disciples eat and drink." 34Jesus said to them, "You cannot make wedding guests fast while the bridegroom is with them, can you? 35The days will come when the bridegroom will be taken away from them, and then they will fast in those days." 36He also told them a parable: "No one tears a piece from a new garment and sews it on an old garment; otherwise the new will be torn, and the piece from the new will not match the old. 37And no one puts new wine into old wineskins; otherwise the new wine will burst the skins and will be spilled, and the skins will be destroyed.

a Gk *Man*   *b* Gk *reclining*

---

tiles, rather than the usual mud roof (cf. Mk 2.4), may suggest a more elegant Hellenistic house (see Acts 10.9) and portray Jesus moving in an urban environment. **5.20** Jesus sees *their faith,* i.e., their decisive action. *Your sins are forgiven* (passive construction) implies that God is the one who has done so. **5.21** The official reaction is that Jesus is *speaking blasphemies* by daring to speak for God. **5.22–23** Jesus responds in the tradition of what is *easier* and "lighter" or harder and "heavier" (see 16.17; 18.24–25), increasing the tension even as the forgiven man lies paralyzed. **5.24** Jesus indirectly claims *authority on earth* to forgive by identifying himself as *the Son of Man* (see also 6.5; 7.34; 9.22, 26; 11.30; 12.8, 40; 17.22; 18.8; 19.10; 21.36). This title can refer to a prophetic figure (Ezek 2.1, 3), to the end-time judge expected to arrive on the clouds of heaven (Dan 7.13–14), or simply to a mortal human being. **5.25** *Immediately.* See note on 4.39. The visible event testifies to the reality of the forgiveness received. **5.26** *Filled with awe* reflects another experience of divine presence and power (see note on 5.9). *Strange things,* wonders or miracles beyond human understanding. **5.27–39** Cf. Mt 9.9–17; Mk 2.13–22. These verses set Jesus' fellowship and disciples apart from the standards of the recognized teachers of Israel. **5.27** On the particular role of *tax collectors* among Jesus' followers, see 3.12; 5.29, 30; 7.29, 34; 15.1; 18.10, 11, 13; 19.2. *Levi* does not appear among the Twelve (see 6.14–16), but in Mt 9.9 the tax collector is named

Matthew, who is listed among the Twelve. **5.28** On leaving everything to follow, see note on 5.11. **5.29** Although in tension with Levi's leaving everything (v. 28), the *great banquet* illustrates the meal fellowship of Jesus (see also 7.36–50; 9.12–17; 11.37–41; 14.1–15.2). On dinner guests *sitting at the table* in the kingdom of God, see 14.12–24. **5.30** To *eat and drink with tax collectors and sinners* was especially offensive in Israel, where food laws separated the properly observant from sinners (see also Acts 10.9–28; Gal 2.11–14). Tax collectors were suspect not only for collaborating with foreign powers but also for dishonesty (see 3.12–13). **5.31** Hellenistic teachers and rabbis were often described as *physicians* to sick souls. Recall the use of *doctor* in 4.23. **5.32** This saying explains the previous medical metaphor (v. 31). On *the righteous* who need no repentance, see 15.7. On calling *sinners to repentance,* see 3.3, 8; 15.7, 10; 24.47; Acts 2.38; 3.19. **5.33** *John's disciples.* See also 7.18–19; 11.1; Jn 1.35–40; 3.25–26; 4.1; Acts 18.25. Fasting and praying were common rituals of repentance, subject to criticism for hypocrisy (Mt 6.5–6, 16–18; see also Lk 18.9–14). **5.34** The images of the *bridegroom* and *wedding* banquet are common for the festivities of the dawn of God's reign (cf. Mt 22.1–14; 25.1–13; Rev 19.6–9). **5.35** *They will fast in those days.* See 22.16; Acts 13.2–3; 14.23. **5.36–39** Traditional proverbs, here called *parables,* emphasize the contrast between the old, or traditional, ways and the new time inaugurated by Jesus.

38But new wine must be put into fresh wine-skins. 39And no one after drinking old wine desires new wine, but says, 'The old is good.' "ᵃ

The Question about the Sabbath

6 One sabbathᵇ while Jesusᶜ was going through the grainfields, his disciples plucked some heads of grain, rubbed them in their hands, and ate them. 2But some of the Pharisees said, "Why are you doing what is not lawfulᵈ on the sabbath?" 3Jesus answered, "Have you not read what David did when he and his companions were hungry? 4He entered the house of God and took and ate the bread of the Presence, which it is not lawful for any but the priests to eat, and gave some to his companions?" 5Then he said to them, "The Son of Man is lord of the sabbath."

The Man with a Withered Hand

6 On another sabbath he entered the synagogue and taught, and there was a man there whose right hand was withered. 7The scribes and the Pharisees watched him to see whether he would cure on the sabbath, so that they might find an accusation against him. 8Even though he knew what they were thinking, he said to the man who had the withered hand, "Come and stand here." He got up and stood there. 9Then Jesus said to them, "I ask you, is it lawful to do good or to do harm on the sabbath, to save life or to destroy it?" 10After looking around at all of them, he said to him, "Stretch out your hand." He did so, and his hand was restored. 11But they were filled with fury and discussed with one another what they might do to Jesus.

Jesus Chooses the Twelve Apostles

12 Now during those days he went out to the mountain to pray; and he spent the night in prayer to God. 13And when day came, he called his disciples and chose twelve of them, whom he also named apostles: 14Simon, whom he named Peter, and his brother Andrew, and James, and John, and Philip, and Bartholomew, 15and Matthew, and Thomas, and James son of Alphaeus, and Simon, who was called the Zealot, 16and Judas son of James, and Judas Iscariot, who became a traitor.

Jesus Teaches and Heals

17 He came down with them and stood on a level place, with a great crowd of his disciples

a Other ancient authorities read better; others lack verse 39
b Other ancient authorities read On the second first sabbath
c Gk he d Other ancient authorities add to do

5.39 This verse may have been added later (see text note a). If original, it may concede that those who valued old ways were not attracted to Jesus' fellowship and practices (see also Sir 9.10).
6.1–16 Cf. Mt 12.1–14; 10.1–4; Mk 2.23–28; 3.1–6, 13–19. These first two sabbath conflicts (see also 13.10–17; 14.1–6) and the choosing of the Twelve occur in different contexts in Matthew. **6.1** Plucking a neighbor's grain with the *hands* (but not harvesting with a sickle) is explicitly allowed in Deut 23.25, but Ex 34.21 forbids harvesting on the sabbath. **6.2** The command to observe the *sabbath* by not working was foundational to Israel (Ex 20.8–11; Deut 5.12–15), but the debates about what was *lawful* divided interpreters. *Some of the Pharisees* (see also 13.31; 19.39; Acts 15.5) were stricter in defining work, agreeing with the later rabbinic tradition defining plucking as harvesting (*Mishnah Shabbat* 7.2). **6.3–4** Jesus appeals to the scriptural precedent of *David*'s behavior in an emergency where hunger relativized legal stipulations (1 Sam 21.1–6; see also Lk 1.32). Every sabbath, the *bread of the Presence* was placed on a table in the tabernacle or temple (Ex 25.30). The previous week's bread was removed and reserved for the priests to eat in the temple precincts (Lev 24.5–9). **6.5** The title *Son of Man* here points to Jesus' special authority (see note on 5.24). Luke does not repeat the saying on human freedom and the sabbath cited in Mk 2.27. **6.6** On

Jesus' practice of *sabbath* teaching in a synagogue, see 4.15–16, 31; 13.10. *Withered*, probably paralyzed. **6.7** *The Pharisees watched.* Their watching is adversarial (see also 14.1; 20.20) because they regarded curing *on the sabbath* as unlawful work (see vv. 1–2; 13.10–17; 14.1–6; see also Jn 5.9–16; 9.14). **6.8** On Jesus' discernment of *what they were thinking,* see 2.35; 5.22; 9.47; 11.17. Jesus takes the initiative in this case. **6.9–10** The question of what is *lawful* again receives only the indirect answer of a healing (see 5.23–25). **6.11** The *fury* and discussion reflect an escalating conflict over Jesus' claim to authority (see 20.19–20; 22.3–6). **6.12–16** The choosing of the Twelve sets the scene for the Sermon on the Plain (cf. Mk 3.7–19). **6.12** On Jesus at *prayer,* see note on 5.16; see also 11.1–13. Prayer through the *night* seems to signal a crucial decision (see 22.39–46). **6.13** *Twelve,* closely linked with the twelve tribes of Israel (see 22.30; Acts 7.8; 26.7). *Apostles,* delegates sent with authority (9.1–6; see also Acts 1.1–8); Luke limits the term to the Twelve. **6.14–16** See Acts 1.13. **6.14** *Simon . . . named Peter, James,* and *John* have already been called (5.1–11), but now they are chosen to be apostles. **6.15** In Luke *Matthew* is not identical with Levi (see note on 5.27). **6.16** On the replacement of *Judas* after he *became a traitor* (22.3–5, 47–48), see Acts 1.15–26. **6.17–49** Cf. Mt 4.23–5.12, 39–48; 7.1–5, 12a, 17–27; 12.33–35; Mk 3.7–13a; 4.24–25. Jesus' "Sermon on the Plain" (see v. 17), the

and a great multitude of people from all Judea, Jerusalem, and the coast of Tyre and Sidon. [18]They had come to hear him and to be healed of their diseases; and those who were troubled with unclean spirits were cured. [19]And all in the crowd were trying to touch him, for power came out from him and healed all of them.

Blessings and Woes

20 Then he looked up at his disciples and said:
"Blessed are you who are poor,
    for yours is the kingdom of God.
[21] "Blessed are you who are hungry now,
    for you will be filled.
"Blessed are you who weep now,
    for you will laugh.
22 "Blessed are you when people hate you, and when they exclude you, revile you, and defame you[a] on account of the Son of Man. [23]Rejoice in that day and leap for joy, for surely your reward is great in heaven; for that is what their ancestors did to the prophets.
[24] "But woe to you who are rich,
    for you have received your
        consolation.
[25] "Woe to you who are full now,
    for you will be hungry.
"Woe to you who are laughing now,
    for you will mourn and weep.
26 "Woe to you when all speak well of you, for that is what their ancestors did to the false prophets.

Love for Enemies

27 "But I say to you that listen, Love your enemies, do good to those who hate you, [28]bless those who curse you, pray for those who abuse you. [29]If anyone strikes you on the cheek, offer the other also; and from anyone who takes away your coat do not withhold even your shirt. [30]Give to everyone who begs from you; and if anyone takes away your goods, do not ask for them again. [31]Do to others as you would have them do to you.

32 "If you love those who love you, what credit is that to you? For even sinners love those who love them. [33]If you do good to those who do good to you, what credit is that to you? For even sinners do the same. [34]If you lend to those from whom you hope to receive, what credit is that to you? Even sinners lend to sinners, to receive as much again. [35]But love your enemies, do good, and lend, expecting nothing in return.[b] Your reward will be great, and you will be children of the Most High; for he is kind to the ungrateful and the wicked. [36]Be merciful, just as your Father is merciful.

Judging Others

37 "Do not judge, and you will not be judged; do not condemn, and you will not be condemned. Forgive, and you will be forgiven;

---

a Gk *cast out your name as evil*   *b* Other ancient authorities read *despairing of no one*

Messiah's second major address in Luke (see 4.16–30), closely parallels portions of the "Sermon on the Mount" in Matthew (Mt 5–7). **6.17–19** A typical summary statement sets the scene (see also 4.14–15, 40–41; 5.15, 17; 7.17). **6.17** *A level place.* Cf. Mt 5.1. *A great crowd of his disciples* indicates more than the twelve apostles (see v. 13). On the *multitude* from many places, see also 5.17; 7.9; 12.1. *All Judea* includes Galilee (see note on 4.44). **6.19** On Jesus' *touch* and *power* in healing stories, see 5.13, 17; 8.46. Here Jesus' deeds set the context for his words. **6.20** *Blessed,* i.e., happy or favored by God (see 7.23; 10.23; 11.27–28; 14.15; Deut 33.29; Pss 127.5; 128.1). *You.* Jesus' words in Luke are in the form of direct address to his disciples, who have left everything (5.11; cf. Mt 5.1–3). On the *poor* as a focus of Jesus' mission, see 4.18; 7.22; see also 14.13, 21; 16.20, 22; 18.22; 19.8; 21.2–3; cf. Mt 5.3. *Kingdom of God.* See note on 4.43. **6.21** *Hungry.* See 1.53; cf. Mt 5.6. *You who weep now.* Cf. Mt 5.4; see Ps 126.6; Isa 61.2–3; 65.18–19. **6.22** *Son of Man.* See notes on 5.24; 6.5. **6.23** To *leap for joy* is a prophetic fulfillment (Isa 35.6; Mal 4.2; see also Lk 1.41, 44; Acts

3.8). On the treatment of the *prophets,* see 11.47–51; 13.33–34; Acts 7.52. **6.24** Declarations of *woe,* or "alas," are common in oracles of prophetic judgment ("Ah," Isa 5.8–23; Am 6.1; Hab 2.6–19; see also Lk 10.13; 11.42–52; 17.1; 21.23; 22.22). Here the woes counterbalance the beatitudes of vv. 20–23. *You have received your consolation,* i.e., in your possessions (16.19–31). **6.26** Israel's prophets denounced as *false* those prophets who spoke what the people wanted to hear instead of the word of God (see Isa 30.9–11; Jer 5.30–31; 6.13–14; 23.16–17). **6.27–49** Addressed to a broader audience, *you that listen* (cf. v. 20). The behavior advocated alters usual practices. *Love your enemies.* See also v. 35; Mt 5.44. **6.29** *Coat,* the outer garment. *Shirt,* the garment worn next to the skin. **6.31** For various forms of this "golden rule," see Lev 19.18; Tob 4.15; Mt 7.12. **6.34** *Lend.* The language of finance makes forgiveness (vv. 37–38) concrete. **6.35** *Children of the Most High.* See Ps 82.6; see also Dan 3.26; 7.18–27; Lk 1.32; 8.28; Acts 16.17. **6.36** Human compassion is to imitate God's mercy (Lev 19.2; Deut 10.17–19; Mt 5.48). **6.37** The future passive verbs (*you will not be . . .*)

38 give, and it will be given to you. A good measure, pressed down, shaken together, running over, will be put into your lap; for the measure you give will be the measure you get back."

39 He also told them a parable: "Can a blind person guide a blind person? Will not both fall into a pit? 40 A disciple is not above the teacher, but everyone who is fully qualified will be like the teacher. 41 Why do you see the speck in your neighbor's*a* eye, but do not notice the log in your own eye? 42 Or how can you say to your neighbor,*b* 'Friend,*b* let me take out the speck in your eye,' when you yourself do not see the log in your own eye? You hypocrite, first take the log out of your own eye, and then you will see clearly to take the speck out of your neighbor's*a* eye.

A Tree and Its Fruit

43 "No good tree bears bad fruit, nor again does a bad tree bear good fruit; 44 for each tree is known by its own fruit. Figs are not gathered from thorns, nor are grapes picked from a bramble bush. 45 The good person out of the good treasure of the heart produces good, and the evil person out of evil treasure produces evil; for it is out of the abundance of the heart that the mouth speaks.

The Two Foundations

46 "Why do you call me 'Lord, Lord,' and do not do what I tell you? 47 I will show you what someone is like who comes to me, hears my words, and acts on them. 48 That one is like a man building a house, who dug deeply and laid the foundation on rock; when a flood arose, the river burst against that house but could not shake it, because it had been well built.*c* 49 But the one who hears and does not act is like a man who built a house on the ground without a foundation. When the river burst against it, immediately it fell, and great was the ruin of that house."

Jesus Heals a Centurion's Servant

7 After Jesus*d* had finished all his sayings in the hearing of the people, he entered Capernaum. 2 A centurion there had a slave whom he valued highly, and who was ill and close to death. 3 When he heard about Jesus, he sent some Jewish elders to him, asking him to come and heal his slave. 4 When they came to Jesus, they appealed to him earnestly, saying, "He is worthy of having you do this for him, 5 for he loves our people, and it is he who built our synagogue for us." 6 And Jesus went with them, but when he was not far from the house, the centurion sent friends to say to him, "Lord, do not trouble yourself, for I am not worthy to have you come under my roof; 7 therefore I did not presume to come to you. But only speak

---

a Gk *brother's*   *b* Gk *brother*   *c* Other ancient authorities read *founded upon the rock*   *d* Gk *he*

---

indicate God's action. **6.38** *A good measure . . . running over,* i.e., not leveled, generous. **6.39** In Luke, *parable* may be used quite precisely for a kind of comparison story (8.4; 12.16; 15.3; 18.1, 9; 19.11; 20.9) or, as in this text, more generally for a proverb (4.23; 5.36; 21.29). The *blind* guide is a common image of foolish behavior (see Eccl 2.14; Mt 15.14; 23.16–26; Rom 2.19). **6.42** *Hypocrite,* Jesus' frequent verdict on his opponents (see 12.1, 56; 13.15), but here the exaggerated tactic of a teacher. The term is used extensively in the controversies in Matthew, esp. Mt 23.13–15. **6.43–44** The image of the *tree* suggests that hypocritical behavior will be exposed by a person's *bad fruit* (see also 3.9; 13.6–9; Mt 7.16–20; 12.33–37). **6.45** On the disclosure of a person's *heart,* see 2.35; 5.22. **6.46** A follower may call Jesus *Lord* yet not possess the commitment necessary for discipleship (see 9.59, 61; 13.25). **6.47** On hearing and acting, see also Jas 2.14–26. **6.48** Houses in Palestine did not usually need an elaborate *foundation,* but this symbol of security was well understood (see Mt. 7.24–27; 1 Cor 3.10–15; Eph 2.19–20; Rev 21.14).
7.1–10 Cf. Mt 8.5–13; Jn 4.46b–54. This story of Jewish-gentile relations has a precedent in the tradi-

tions about Elisha (2 Kings 5.1–14; see also Lk 4.27). **7.1** *Capernaum.* See 4.31. **7.2** A *centurion* had charge over one hundred soldiers in the Roman army (see also 23.47; Acts 10.1–48; 22.25–26; 24.23; 27.1, 6, 11, 31, 43). Here a centurion is a benefactor of Jews (v. 5) and is declared to have faith (v. 9); in Acts the centurion Cornelius practices Jewish piety (Acts 10.1–2) and becomes the first gentile convert. **7.3** *Jewish elders,* here probably local synagogue leaders, but later the title will be linked closely with Jerusalem officials, especially from the temple, who opposed Jesus and the apostles (see 9.22; 20.1; 22.52; Acts 4.5, 8, 23; 6.12; 23.14; 24.1; 25.15). **7.4–5** *Worthy* implies acceptability by the standards of Jewish law as well as gratitude for the building of the synagogue. A Roman officer could be a "friend of the Jews" or one who "feared God" (see Acts 10.2, 22) but would not have been permitted by Rome to undergo circumcision as a convert. A Roman soldier who *loves* the Jewish *people* illustrates love of enemies (6.27). The centurion's address of Jesus as *Lord* implies respect for Jesus' authority (see v. 8). A Jew who came under a Gentile's *roof* would risk defilement (see Acts 10.28; 11.2–3). **7.7** The centurion is confident in the effectiveness of Jesus' *word* at a dis-

the word, and let my servant be healed. 8For I also am a man set under authority, with soldiers under me; and I say to one, 'Go,' and he goes, and to another, 'Come,' and he comes, and to my slave, 'Do this,' and the slave does it." 9When Jesus heard this he was amazed at him, and turning to the crowd that followed him, he said, "I tell you, not even in Israel have I found such faith." 10When those who had been sent returned to the house, they found the slave in good health.

Jesus Raises the Widow's Son at Nain

11 Soon afterwards[a] he went to a town called Nain, and his disciples and a large crowd went with him. 12As he approached the gate of the town, a man who had died was being carried out. He was his mother's only son, and she was a widow; and with her was a large crowd from the town. 13When the Lord saw her, he had compassion for her and said to her, "Do not weep." 14Then he came forward and touched the bier, and the bearers stood still. And he said, "Young man, I say to you, rise!" 15The dead man sat up and began to speak, and Jesus[b] gave him to his mother. 16Fear seized all of them; and they glorified God, saying, "A great prophet has risen among us!" and "God has looked favorably on his people!" 17This word about him spread throughout Judea and all the surrounding country.

Messengers from John the Baptist

18 The disciples of John reported all these things to him. So John summoned two of his disciples 19and sent them to the Lord to ask, "Are you the one who is to come, or are we to wait for another?" 20When the men had come to him, they said, "John the Baptist has sent us to you to ask, 'Are you the one who is to come, or are we to wait for another?' " 21Jesus[c] had just then cured many people of diseases, plagues, and evil spirits, and had given sight to many who were blind. 22And he answered them, "Go and tell John what you have seen and heard: the blind receive their sight, the lame walk, the lepers[d] are cleansed, the deaf hear, the dead are raised, the poor have good news brought to them. 23And blessed is anyone who takes no offense at me."

24 When John's messengers had gone, Jesus[c] began to speak to the crowds about John:[e] "What did you go out into the wilderness to look at? A reed shaken by the wind? 25What then did you go out to see? Someone[f] dressed in soft robes? Look, those who put on fine clothing and live in luxury are in royal palaces. 26What then did you go out to see? A prophet? Yes, I tell you, and more than a prophet. 27This is the one about whom it is written,

'See, I am sending my messenger ahead
　　of you,
who will prepare your way before you.'
28I tell you, among those born of women no one is greater than John; yet the least in the kingdom of God is greater than he." 29(And all

---

a Other ancient authorities read Next day　b Gk he　c Gk He
d The terms leper and leprosy can refer to several diseases
e Gk him　f Or Why then did you go out? To see someone

---

tance. 7.9 Jesus is amazed and defines the centurion's response as faith (see 5.20; 7.50; 8.25, 48; 17.19; 18.42). Not even in Israel, a prophetic reproach (see 4.25–27). 7.11–17 This story has a clear parallel in the Elijah traditions (1 Kings 17; see also 2 Kings 4) and was foreshadowed in 4.25–26. Luke juxtaposes healing stories focused on a high-status man (vv. 1–10) and a low-status woman. See note on 2.38. 7.11 Nain, a village near Nazareth. 7.12 The death of an only son was an economic catastrophe for a widow. She would have no legal inheritance and, deprived of her son's economic support, would be dependent upon charity (see Deut 26.12; 27.19; cf. Pss 68.5; 146.9). 7.13 Jesus' compassion is here depicted as a deep visceral response (Greek esplanchnisthe; see also 10.33; 15.20). It reflects God's compassion (see 6.36). 7.14 Touching the bier (or coffin) was a dramatic act, violating Jewish purity laws (Num 19.11, 16). Rise! Jesus' word is again efficacious (see v. 7; 1 Kings 17.22). 7.15 Jesus gave him to his mother, an exact quote from 1 Kings 17.23 (see also Lk 9.42). 7.16 Fear again denotes an awareness of a divine visitation (see notes on 1.12; 1.65; 2.10). On Jesus as a prophet, see 4.24–27; 7.39; 13.33; 24.19; Acts 3.22–23; 7.37; Deut 18.15–22. Looked favorably. See note on 1.68. God's action is identified with that of Jesus. 7.17 Judea. See note on 4.44; 6.17. 7.18–35 Cf. Mt 11.2–19. The relationship between the ministries of John the Baptist and Jesus is clarified. 7.18 Disciples of John. See note on 5.33. 7.19 The one who is to come. See John's announcement in 3.16; see also Acts 19.4. 7.22 In what John's disciples have now seen and heard, Jesus' earlier words are fulfilled (4.18–19; see also Deut 18.21–22; Isa 26.19; 29.18–19; 35.5–6; 61.1; see also Lk 14.13, 21). 7.23 On calling blessed those who take no offense (lit. "do not stumble") at Jesus, see also 2.34; 10.23. 7.24 Into the wilderness. See 1.80; 3.2, 4; Isa 40.3. 7.25 On John's clothing, see Mt 3.4; Mk 1.6. 7.26 More than a prophet. See 11.31–32. 7.27 The text cited is Mal 3.1; see also Lk 1.76; 3.4; Ex 23.20; Isa 40.3. 7.28 Since all are born of women, John is praised as the greatest

the people who heard this, including the tax collectors, acknowledged the justice of God,[a] because they had been baptized with John's baptism. 30 But by refusing to be baptized by him, the Pharisees and the lawyers rejected God's purpose for themselves.)

31 "To what then will I compare the people of this generation, and what are they like? 32 They are like children sitting in the marketplace and calling to one another,

'We played the flute for you, and you did not dance;
we wailed, and you did not weep.'

33 For John the Baptist has come eating no bread and drinking no wine, and you say, 'He has a demon'; 34 the Son of Man has come eating and drinking, and you say, 'Look, a glutton and a drunkard, a friend of tax collectors and sinners!' 35 Nevertheless, wisdom is vindicated by all her children."

A Sinful Woman Forgiven

36 One of the Pharisees asked Jesus[b] to eat with him, and he went into the Pharisee's house and took his place at the table. 37 And a woman in the city, who was a sinner, having learned that he was eating in the Pharisee's house, brought an alabaster jar of ointment. 38 She stood behind him at his feet, weeping, and began to bathe his feet with her tears and to dry them with her hair. Then she continued kissing his feet and anoint-

ing them with the ointment. 39 Now when the Pharisee who had invited him saw it, he said to himself, "If this man were a prophet, he would have known who and what kind of woman this is who is touching him—that she is a sinner." 40 Jesus spoke up and said to him, "Simon, I have something to say to you." "Teacher," he replied, "speak." 41 "A certain creditor had two debtors; one owed five hundred denarii,[c] and the other fifty. 42 When they could not pay, he canceled the debts for both of them. Now which of them will love him more?" 43 Simon answered, "I suppose the one for whom he canceled the greater debt." And Jesus[d] said to him, "You have judged rightly." 44 Then turning toward the woman, he said to Simon, "Do you see this woman? I entered your house; you gave me no water for my feet, but she has bathed my feet with her tears and dried them with her hair. 45 You gave me no kiss, but from the time I came in she has not stopped kissing my feet. 46 You did not anoint my head with oil, but she has anointed my feet with ointment. 47 Therefore, I tell you, her sins, which were many, have been forgiven; hence she has shown great love. But the one to whom little is forgiven, loves little." 48 Then he said to her, "Your sins are forgiven." 49 But those who were at the table with him began to say among them-

---

a Or praised God   b Gk him   c The denarius was the usual day's wage for a laborer   d Gk he

---

human until the era of the kingdom of God (see note on 16.16). **7.29** *Tax collectors.* See 3.12; notes on 5.27; 5.30. *Acknowledged the justice of God,* lit. "justified God," i.e., acknowledged the righteousness of God's plan of salvation and accepted it. **7.30** Luke's Gospel and Acts document a pattern of refusal and rejection (see 9.22; 17.25; 20.17; Acts 4.11; 7.35). The Deuteronomistic stubbornness motif is in the background (Deut 10.16; Ex 32.9; 33.3, 5; Acts 7.51–53). *Lawyers,* i.e., teachers of the law of Moses (see also 10.25; 11.45–52; 14.3), probably to be identified with scribes. *God's purpose.* See Acts 2.23; 4.27–28; 20.27. **7.31** On the *people of this generation* who have refused to repent, see also 9.41; 11.29–32, 49–51; 17.25; Acts 2.40; Deut 32.5, 20. **7.32** A childhood taunt to those who refuse to join a game functions as a prophetic accusation. **7.33** *Eating no bread,* a mark of extreme asceticism (see Mk 1.6). *Drinking no wine.* See 1.15. To accuse John of having a *demon* is to reject his divine call (see 1.68–79). A similar charge is leveled against Jesus in 11.14–20. **7.34** *Son of Man.* See notes on 5.24; 6.5. Jesus' meal fellowship offends Jewish sensibilities (see also 5.27–32; 14.12–24; 15.2). **7.35** *Wisdom,* a personified attribute of God, *is vindicated,* i.e., justified. See note on 7.29. Wisdom's *children* are those who hear

and follow God's instruction (see Prov 1–8). **7.36–50** Cf. Mt 26.6–13; Mk 14.3–9; Jn 12.1–7. A meal with a Pharisee provides an occasion to discuss who is acceptable in God's kingdom (see also 14.1–15.2). **7.36** No motive for the *Pharisee's* invitation is given (see also 11.37; 14.1), but it implies his interest in Jesus (cf. 5.30; 15.2). *Took his place at the table,* lit. "reclined." **7.37** The *woman's* sin is not identified. An *alabaster jar* would have been costly. *Ointment,* a perfumed oil. **7.38** Bathing the *feet* was a common sign of hospitality for guests (see v. 44; Gen 18.4; Jn 13.5; 1 Tim 5.10), but anointing the feet is unusual. Because Jesus is reclining (see v. 36) with his feet out away from the table, the woman can more easily anoint his feet than his head. **7.39** On Jesus as a *prophet,* see note on 7.16. A strict reading of Lev 5.1–5 indicates a risk of defilement upon even *touching* (or being touched by) a sinner. **7.40** Jesus' statement indicates that he knows Simon's thoughts (see note on 2.35). **7.41** The *denarius* was a day's wage. Both debts are significant. **7.42** *Love,* have gratitude toward. **7.44–46** The usual gestures of Near Eastern hospitality (*water for . . . feet,* a *kiss,* and *oil*) are extravagantly outdone by the woman. **7.47** That *she has shown great love* indicates that *her sins . . . have been forgiven.* **7.49** The scandal among the guests derives

selves, "Who is this who even forgives sins?" [50]And he said to the woman, "Your faith has saved you; go in peace."

Some Women Accompany Jesus

8 Soon afterwards he went on through cities and villages, proclaiming and bringing the good news of the kingdom of God. The twelve were with him, [2]as well as some women who had been cured of evil spirits and infirmities: Mary, called Magdalene, from whom seven demons had gone out, [3]and Joanna, the wife of Herod's steward Chuza, and Susanna, and many others, who provided for them[a] out of their resources.

The Parable of the Sower

[4]When a great crowd gathered and people from town after town came to him, he said in a parable: [5]"A sower went out to sow his seed; and as he sowed, some fell on the path and was trampled on, and the birds of the air ate it up. [6]Some fell on the rock; and as it grew up, it withered for lack of moisture. [7]Some fell among thorns, and the thorns grew with it and choked it. [8]Some fell into good soil, and when it grew, it produced a hundredfold." As he said this, he called out, "Let anyone with ears to hear listen!"

The Purpose of the Parables

[9]Then his disciples asked him what this parable meant. [10]He said, "To you it has been given to know the secrets[b] of the kingdom of God; but to others I speak[c] in parables, so that

'looking they may not perceive,
   and listening they may not
      understand.'

The Parable of the Sower Explained

[11]"Now the parable is this: The seed is the word of God. [12]The ones on the path are those who have heard; then the devil comes and takes away the word from their hearts, so that they may not believe and be saved. [13]The ones on the rock are those who, when they hear the word, receive it with joy. But these have no root; they believe only for a while and in a time of testing fall away. [14]As for what fell among the thorns, these are the ones who hear; but as they go on their way, they are choked by the cares and riches and pleasures of life, and their fruit does not mature. [15]But as for that in the good soil, these are the ones who, when they hear the word, hold it fast in an honest and good heart, and bear fruit with patient endurance.

A Lamp under a Jar

[16]"No one after lighting a lamp hides it under a jar, or puts it under a bed, but puts it on a lampstand, so that those who enter may see the light. [17]For nothing is hidden that will not be disclosed, nor is anything secret that will not become known and come to light. [18]Then pay attention to how you listen; for to those

---

a Other ancient authorities read *him*   *b* Or *mysteries*
c Gk lacks *I speak*

---

from Jesus' claim to speak for God in forgiving *sins* (see also 5.20–24). **7.50** On the saving power of *faith*, see 8.48; 17.19; 18.42. *Go in peace* (Hebrew *shalom*) are the traditional words of parting (see 8.48; 1 Sam 1.17; Acts 16.36), but peace is also the mark of God's reign or kingdom (see 1.79; 2.14; Isa 52.7).
   8.1–3 Transition verses stressing how Jesus' mission continues to cover Galilee (see 4.43–44). **8.1** *The twelve.* See note on 6.13. **8.2–3** *Women,* those named and *many others,* also accompany Jesus and later attend his burial and resurrection (23.49, 55; 24.10). *Evil spirits and infirmities,* afflictions to be healed, not sins to be forgiven. Magdala was on the western shore of Lake Gennesaret (see 5.1). *Seven demons* indicates the severity of the affliction (see 11.26). Joanna's connection to *Herod* contrasts her discipleship with the king's menace (see 9.9; 13.31; 23.8–11). *Provided* (Greek *diakoneo*) indicates "service" and is not limited to financial support. **8.4–15** Cf. Mt 13.1–23; Mk 4.1–20. A parable on the word of God (see Isa 55.10–11). **8.4** Luke again stresses the presence of a large *crowd* (see 5.1, 17; 6.17; 8.42; 9.18, 37; 11.29). *Parable.* See

note on 6.39. **8.8** Despite difficulties, a *hundredfold* yield results (see Gen 26.12), indicating the miraculous effect of God's word (see v. 11). *He called out* (lit. "he kept calling out"), emphasizing the message of the parable. The charge to *listen* raises the question of who has *ears to hear* (see 14.35; see also 8.10). **8.10** That the disciples are privy to the *secrets,* or *mysteries* (text note *b*), of the kingdom (here made concrete in vv. 9–15) highlights the division in Israel between those prepared to hear and accept Jesus' teaching and those unprepared to do so. *Parables* function here as prophetic speech (see Isa 6.9–10, partially cited here), further confounding the latter group (see also Acts 28.25–28; Wis 2.22). **8.12** On the activities of *the devil,* who works against belief and salvation, see 4.1–13; 10.17–20; 22.3, 31. **8.13** *A time of testing.* See 4.1–13; 21.12–19; 22.28–34, 39–46. **8.15** *Endurance,* perseverance in discipleship (see 9.23). **8.16–18** Cf. Mt 5.15; 10.26; 7.2; 13.12; Mk 4.21–25. Various sayings comment on the proper response to Jesus' preaching. **8.16** Wise and foolish behavior are contrasted (see 11.33). **8.17** See 2.35. **8.18** Luke focuses on *how you listen,* i.e., the lis-

who have, more will be given; and from those who do not have, even what they seem to have will be taken away."

The True Kindred of Jesus

19 Then his mother and his brothers came to him, but they could not reach him because of the crowd. 20And he was told, "Your mother and your brothers are standing outside, wanting to see you." 21But he said to them, "My mother and my brothers are those who hear the word of God and do it."

Jesus Calms a Storm

22 One day he got into a boat with his disciples, and he said to them, "Let us go across to the other side of the lake." So they put out, 23and while they were sailing he fell asleep. A windstorm swept down on the lake, and the boat was filling with water, and they were in danger. 24They went to him and woke him up, shouting, "Master, Master, we are perishing!" And he woke up and rebuked the wind and the raging waves; they ceased, and there was a calm. 25He said to them, "Where is your faith?" They were afraid and amazed, and said to one another, "Who then is this, that he commands even the winds and the water, and they obey him?"

Jesus Heals the Gerasene Demoniac

26 Then they arrived at the country of the Gerasenes,[a] which is opposite Galilee. 27As he stepped out on land, a man of the city who had demons met him. For a long time he had worn[b] no clothes, and he did not live in a house but in the tombs. 28When he saw Jesus, he fell down before him and shouted at the top of his voice, "What have you to do with me, Jesus, Son of the Most High God? I beg you, do not torment me"— 29for Jesus[c] had commanded the unclean spirit to come out of the man. (For many times it had seized him; he was kept under guard and bound with chains and shackles, but he would break the bonds and be driven by the demon into the wilds.) 30Jesus then asked him, "What is your name?" He said, "Legion"; for many demons had entered him. 31They begged him not to order them to go back into the abyss.

32 Now there on the hillside a large herd of swine was feeding; and the demons[d] begged Jesus[e] to let them enter these. So he gave them permission. 33Then the demons came out of the man and entered the swine, and the herd rushed down the steep bank into the lake and was drowned.

34 When the swineherds saw what had happened, they ran off and told it in the city and in the country. 35Then people came out to see what had happened, and when they came to

---

a Other ancient authorities read *Gadarenes*; others, *Gergesenes*
b Other ancient authorities read *a man of the city who had had demons for a long time met him. He wore*   *c* Gk *he*   *d* Gk *they*
e Gk *him*

---

tener's receptivity or attitude (see note on 8.8; cf. Mk 4.24) to the word of God (see vv. 15, 21). On the giving of more *to those who have,* see 19.26. **8.19–21** Cf. Mt 12.46–50; Mk 3.31–35. Jesus' family is defined in terms of obedience. Early Christian usage of "fictive kinship" language was distinctive (see, e.g., 1 Cor 1.10; 7.15; 15.6). **8.19** On Jesus' *mother,* see also 1.43; 2.33–51; Acts 1.14. Jesus' *brothers* are sometimes understood to be more distant blood relatives, but actual siblings are probably meant (see Mk 6.3; Jn 7.3–5; Acts 1.14; Gal 1.19). **8.20–21** See 11.27–28. **8.22–56** Three demonstrations of the power of the Messiah's word. **8.22–25** Cf. Mt 8.23–27; Mk 4.35–41. **8.22** Luke refers to the Sea of Galilee as a *lake* (see 5.1; 8.33), as does Josephus. **8.23** The *windstorm* evokes an eschatological trial (see Jer 25.32). **8.24** *Master.* See note on 5.5. Jesus *rebuked* the wind and water just as earlier he rebuked unclean spirits (4.35, 41), both times demonstrating authority over evil powers (see also Job 26.11–12; Ps 89.8–9). **8.25** *Where is your faith?* also a rebuke (see also 12.28; cf. 5.20; 7.9, 50; 8.48; 17.5–6, 19; 18.42; 22.32). *Afraid and amazed.* See notes on 1.12; 2.10. *Who then is this?* Jesus' identity is again a topic of discussion in 9.9, 18–22. **8.26–39** Cf. Mt 8.28–34; Mk 5.1–20.

8.26 *Gerasenes.* The exact spelling and location of their home are unclear (see text note *a*). Luke does not stress the fact that Jesus is now in non-Jewish territory. **8.27** For other confrontations with *demons,* see 4.33–34; 9.42; 11.14; see also 8.2. Living *in the tombs* implies perpetual uncleanness (see Num 19.11, 16; see also Isa 65.1–5) and separation from society. **8.28** The demons speak through the man's *voice.* On the demons' recognition of Jesus as *Son of the Most High God,* see 4.34, 41; Acts 16.17; see also 1.32. **8.29** The *wilds,* or wilderness areas, were thought to be favored haunts of demons (see 11.24). **8.30** Whereas in magical practice knowledge of the correct *name* was thought to provide controlling power over a person or demon, here the name underlines the extraordinary nature of this possession. A Roman *legion* was a battle force of four to six thousand soldiers. **8.31** *Abyss,* the bottomless pit reserved as a prison for God's enemies (see Rev 9.1–11; 11.7; 17.8; 20.1–3). **8.32** *Swine,* unclean animals according to Jewish law (Lev 11.7; Deut 14.8; see also Lk 15.15–16) and so fitting hosts for the *demons. Permission,* though granted, indicates Jesus' strong authority. **8.33** The implication is that, when the *herd* drowns, the demons go to the abyss (see v. 31). **8.35** A disciple

Jesus, they found the man from whom the demons had gone sitting at the feet of Jesus, clothed and in his right mind. And they were afraid. 36 Those who had seen it told them how the one who had been possessed by demons had been healed. 37 Then all the people of the surrounding country of the Gerasenes*e* asked Jesus*b* to leave them; for they were seized with great fear. So he got into the boat and returned. 38 The man from whom the demons had gone begged that he might be with him; but Jesus*c* sent him away, saying, 39 "Return to your home, and declare how much God has done for you." So he went away, proclaiming throughout the city how much Jesus had done for him.

A Girl Restored to Life and a Woman Healed

40 Now when Jesus returned, the crowd welcomed him, for they were all waiting for him. 41 Just then there came a man named Jairus, a leader of the synagogue. He fell at Jesus' feet and begged him to come to his house, 42 for he had an only daughter, about twelve years old, who was dying.

As he went, the crowds pressed in on him. 43 Now there was a woman who had been suffering from hemorrhages for twelve years; and though she had spent all she had on physicians,*d* no one could cure her. 44 She came up behind him and touched the fringe of his clothes, and immediately her hemorrhage stopped. 45 Then Jesus asked, "Who touched me?" When all denied it, Peter*e* said, "Master, the crowds surround you and press in on you."

46 But Jesus said, "Someone touched me; for I noticed that power had gone out from me." 47 When the woman saw that she could not remain hidden, she came trembling; and falling down before him, she declared in the presence of all the people why she had touched him, and how she had been immediately healed. 48 He said to her, "Daughter, your faith has made you well; go in peace."

49 While he was still speaking, someone came from the leader's house to say, "Your daughter is dead; do not trouble the teacher any longer." 50 When Jesus heard this, he replied, "Do not fear. Only believe, and she will be saved." 51 When he came to the house, he did not allow anyone to enter with him, except Peter, John, and James, and the child's father and mother. 52 They were all weeping and wailing for her; but he said, "Do not weep; for she is not dead but sleeping." 53 And they laughed at him, knowing that she was dead. 54 But he took her by the hand and called out, "Child, get up!" 55 Her spirit returned, and she got up at once. Then he directed them to give her something to eat. 56 Her parents were astounded; but he ordered them to tell no one what had happened.

The Mission of the Twelve

9 Then Jesus*c* called the twelve together and gave them power and authority over all demons and to cure diseases, 2 and he sent

---

a Other ancient authorities read *Gadarenes*; others, *Gergesenes*
b Gk *him*   *c* Gk *he*   *d* Other ancient authorities lack *and though she had spent all she had on physicians*   *e* Other ancient authorities add *and those who were with him*

---

sits *at the feet* of the teacher (see also Acts 22.3). *Clothed and in his right mind.* Cf. vv. 27, 29. *They were afraid.* See v. 37; note on 7.16. **8.39** The former demoniac declares what *God* has done in terms of what *Jesus* has done (see also 7.16). **8.40–56** Cf. Mt 9.18–26; Mk 5.21–43. Healing stories featuring a man and a woman of contrasting social status are intertwined (see note on 2.38). **8.41** The *leader of the synagogue* presided over meetings and enjoyed considerable status in the community (see also 13.14; Acts 13.15; 18.8, 17). **8.42** *An only daughter.* See 7.12. **8.43** *Hemorrhages for twelve years,* abnormal menstrual flow, making the woman constantly unclean and untouchable (Lev 15.25–30). Since impurity is contagious, she must be socially ostracized (see Lev 15.31). **8.44** *Fringe,* a required part of the Jewish male's clothes (see Num 15.38–39; Deut 22.12; Mt 23.5). **8.45** *Who touched me?* This touch would violate Jewish purity laws (see note on 8.43). *Master.* See note on 5.5. **8.46** On the *power* to

heal, see 5.17; 6.19; see also Acts 4.7. On healing by contact, see 5.13; 7.14; see also Acts 5.15–16; 19.11–12. **8.48** See note on 7.50. *Daughter.* See 13.16. **8.50** *Do not fear.* See note on 5.9. *Believe,* i.e., have trust, faith. *Saved* resonates with *made you well* in v. 48; the same Greek word (*sozo*) is used in both cases. **8.51** *Peter, John, and James,* the first disciples called (see 5.1–11), are singled out to witness special events (see also 9.28). Peter and John collaborate in Acts (see 3.1, 11; 4.13, 19; 8.14). **8.52** *Weeping and wailing* indicates the beginning of mourning (see also 23.27). **8.55** *Her spirit returned.* The belief that at death the spirit departed from the body is widely attested (see 23.46; Acts 7.59; see also 1 Kings 17.21–22). **8.56** *Tell no one.* See also 5.14.

9.1–50 Stories on Jesus' messianic mission and the nature of discipleship. **9.1–6** Cf. Mt 9.35; 10.1, 7–11, 14; Mk 6.6b–13; Lk 10.1–12. **9.1** Jesus gives *the Twelve* (see note on 6.13) *power and authority* to do what he has been doing. **9.2** *Sent . . . out* (Greek *apostellein*) in-

them out to proclaim the kingdom of God and to heal. 3He said to them, "Take nothing for your journey, no staff, nor bag, nor bread, nor money—not even an extra tunic. 4Whatever house you enter, stay there, and leave from there. 5Wherever they do not welcome you, as you are leaving that town shake the dust off your feet as a testimony against them." 6They departed and went through the villages, bringing the good news and curing diseases everywhere.

Herod's Perplexity

7 Now Herod the ruler[a] heard about all that had taken place, and he was perplexed, because it was said by some that John had been raised from the dead, 8by some that Elijah had appeared, and by others that one of the ancient prophets had arisen. 9Herod said, "John I beheaded; but who is this about whom I hear such things?" And he tried to see him.

Feeding the Five Thousand

10 On their return the apostles told Jesus[b] all they had done. He took them with him and withdrew privately to a city called Bethsaida. 11When the crowds found out about it, they followed him; and he welcomed them, and spoke to them about the kingdom of God, and healed those who needed to be cured.

12 The day was drawing to a close, and the twelve came to him and said, "Send the crowd away, so that they may go into the surrounding villages and countryside, to lodge and get pro-

visions; for we are here in a deserted place." 13But he said to them, "You give them something to eat." They said, "We have no more than five loaves and two fish—unless we are to go and buy food for all these people." 14For there were about five thousand men. And he said to his disciples, "Make them sit down in groups of about fifty each." 15They did so and made them all sit down. 16And taking the five loaves and the two fish, he looked up to heaven, and blessed and broke them, and gave them to the disciples to set before the crowd. 17And all ate and were filled. What was left over was gathered up, twelve baskets of broken pieces.

Peter's Declaration about Jesus

18 Once when Jesus[c] was praying alone, with only the disciples near him, he asked them, "Who do the crowds say that I am?" 19They answered, "John the Baptist; but others, Elijah; and still others, that one of the ancient prophets has arisen." 20He said to them, "But who do you say that I am?" Peter answered, "The Messiah[d] of God."

Jesus Foretells His Death and Resurrection

21 He sternly ordered and commanded them not to tell anyone, 22saying, "The Son of Man must undergo great suffering, and be rejected by the elders, chief priests, and scribes, and be killed, and on the third day be raised."

---

a Gk tetrarch   *b* Gk him   *c* Gk he   *d* Or The Christ

dicates the disciples' role as apostolic emissaries of the kingdom (see note on 6.13). *To proclaim . . . and to heal.* See 4.40–44; 6.18–19; 8.1; 10.9. **9.3** Taking *nothing* along requires reliance on local hospitality (10.4; see also Acts 9.43; 16.15). **9.4** *Whatever house.* See 10.5–7; note on 10.5. **9.5** *Shake the dust off your feet* indicates complete separation from those who reject them (see 10.10–11; Acts 13.51). **9.6** *Everywhere.* See note on 4.14–15. Acts 1.8 specifies another comprehensive mission for the apostles. **9.7–9** Cf. Mt 14.1–2; Mk 6.14–16. Herod's perplexity introduces an ominous note (see 13.31–35; 23.6–12; Acts 4.25–27). **9.8** The return of *Elijah* was promised in Mal 4.5 as a precursor to the impending judgment (see 1.17; see also 9.19, 30). **9.9** *John I beheaded.* This execution is not described in Luke (cf. 3.19–20; Mt 14.3–12; Mk 6.17–29). *Who is this?* Herod's question about Jesus recalls John's (see 7.19) and prepares for Peter's confession and Jesus' interpretation of it (see 9.18–20; see also 8.25). *He tried to see him,* and succeeded after Jesus' arrest (see 23.8; cf. 13.31). **9.10–17** Cf. Mt 14.13–21; Mk 6.30–44; Jn 6.1–14. **9.10** *Bethsaida,* on

the Sea of Galilee, had been recently elevated to the status of "city" by Herod Philip. **9.11** Another Lukan summary statement sets the scene (see 4.14–15, 40–41; 5.15, 17; 6.17–19). **9.12** *The twelve.* See note on 6.13. The *deserted place* recalls God's miraculous feeding of Israel in the wilderness (Ex 16; Ps 78.19–20). **9.13–17** See Elisha's feeding of one hundred people (2 Kings 4.42–44); see also Elijah's miracle of the unfailing meal and oil (1 Kings 17.8–16). **9.16** Jesus' actions in distributing the food (*taking, blessed, broke, gave*) replicate typical Jewish meal blessings and also anticipate the Last Supper (see 22.19). **9.17** *Twelve baskets* represent Israel and the apostles (see 22.30). **9.18–22** Cf. Mt 16.13–23; Mk 8.27–33. Peter's confession is set in contrast to the rumors that Herod heard (vv. 7–8). **9.20** *The Messiah of God,* God's anointed ruler (see 2.11, 26; 4.18, 41; see also 20.41; 22.67; 23.2, 35, 39). **9.21** The command *not to tell* is closely coupled with the first explicit passion prediction (see also 5.14; 8.56). **9.22** Jesus' indication of how the title Messiah is to be understood foreshadows a shift of emphasis in the narrative (see notes on 9.31; 9.51). The connection

23 Then he said to them all, "If any want to become my followers, let them deny themselves and take up their cross daily and follow me. 24 For those who want to save their life will lose it, and those who lose their life for my sake will save it. 25 What does it profit them if they gain the whole world, but lose or forfeit themselves? 26 Those who are ashamed of me and of my words, of them the Son of Man will be ashamed when he comes in his glory and the glory of the Father and of the holy angels. 27 But truly I tell you, there are some standing here who will not taste death before they see the kingdom of God."

The Transfiguration

28 Now about eight days after these sayings Jesus[a] took with him Peter and John and James, and went up on the mountain to pray. 29 And while he was praying, the appearance of his face changed, and his clothes became dazzling white. 30 Suddenly they saw two men, Moses and Elijah, talking to him. 31 They appeared in glory and were speaking of his departure, which he was about to accomplish at Jerusalem. 32 Now Peter and his companions were weighed down with sleep; but since they had stayed awake,[b] they saw his glory and the two men who stood with him. 33 Just as they were leaving him, Peter said to Jesus, "Master, it is good for us to be here; let us make three dwellings,[c] one for you, one for Moses, and one for Elijah"—not knowing what he said. 34 While he was saying this, a cloud came and overshadowed them; and they were terrified as they entered the cloud. 35 Then from the cloud came a voice that said, "This is my Son, my Chosen;[d] listen to him!" 36 When the voice had spoken, Jesus was found alone. And they kept silent and in those days told no one any of the things they had seen.

Jesus Heals a Boy with a Demon

37 On the next day, when they had come down from the mountain, a great crowd met him. 38 Just then a man from the crowd shouted, "Teacher, I beg you to look at my son; he is my only child. 39 Suddenly a spirit seizes him, and all at once he[e] shrieks. It convulses him until he foams at the mouth; it mauls him and will scarcely leave him. 40 I begged your disciples to cast it out, but they could not." 41 Jesus answered, "You faithless and perverse generation, how much longer must I be with you and bear with you? Bring your son here." 42 While he was coming, the demon dashed him to the ground in convulsions. But Jesus rebuked the unclean spirit, healed the boy, and gave him back to his father. 43 And all were astounded at the greatness of God.

a Gk *he* *b* Or *but when they were fully awake* *c* Or *tents*
d Other ancient authorities read *my Beloved* *e* Or *it*

of the *Son of Man* title (see note on 5.24) with a suffering figure is found only in the Gospels (see also v. 44; 18.31–33; cf. Isa 52.13–53.12). The same Son of Man would return in glory as judge (see v. 26; 21.27; Dan 7.13–14). *Must.* A theological necessity underlines Jesus' prediction (see note on 2.49; see also Acts 1.19; 3.21). *Elders, chief priests, and scribes,* the leaders of the Jerusalem council, or Sanhedrin (see 20.1; 22.2–4; note on 22.66). **9.23–27** Cf. Mt 16.24–28; Mk 8.34–9.1. **9.23** *All* now hear Jesus (see v. 18). *Take up their cross daily* stresses faithful endurance in the face of continuing trials (see 8.15; 21.19; Acts 14.22). **9.25** This saying is dramatized in 12.16–21. **9.26** *Ashamed of me.* The same thought is stated more positively in 12.8–9. **9.27** Luke drops Mark's reference to the *kingdom of God* "come with power" (Mk 9.1) and seems to refer loosely to the period after resurrection (see also 2.26). **9.28–36** Cf. Mt 17.1–9; Mk 9.2–10. **9.28** *Peter and John and James.* See note on 8.51. *To pray.* Prayer is often the setting of revelation (see 3.21–22; 22.39–46; note on 6.12). **9.29** *Dazzling white,* the color of heavenly garments (see 24.4; Acts 1.10; Rev 4.4; 7.9). **9.30** Both *Moses and Elijah* were expected to return before the final judgment (see Deut 18.15; Mal 4.5). Both also had visions of God on a mountain (Ex 24.15–18; 1 Kings 19.8–18). Here they represent the Law and the Prophets (see 24.27, 44; Acts 26.22). **9.31** *Glory,* a sign of divine presence (see Ex 24.17; 40.34). *Departure* (Greek *exodos*) probably Jesus' death, resurrection, and ascension, all of which will occur *at Jerusalem* (see esp. v. 51; 12.50; 24.50–51; Acts 1.9–11). **9.32** *Weighed down with sleep.* See also 22.45–46. **9.33** The *three dwellings* suggest the Festival of Booths, commemorating the exodus from Egypt (see v. 31; Deut 16). **9.34** The *cloud* signifies God's presence (see Ex 16.10; 19.9; 24.15–18). **9.35** *My Son, my Chosen.* See 3.22; 23.35; Isa 42.1. *Listen to him.* See Deut 18.15; Acts 3.22. **9.37–43a** Cf. Mt 17.14–21; Mk 9.14–29. **9.38** *Only child.* See 7.12; 8.42. **9.39** The boy's seizures and convulsions are viewed as evidence of a conflict with demonic powers (see 8.29). **9.40** On the disciples' inability to cast the demon out, see Mk 9.28–29; see also 2 Kings 4.31. **9.41** *Faithless and perverse generation.* See note on 7.31. **9.42** *Gave him back to his father.* See note on 7.15. **9.43a** That *all see the greatness of God* in Jesus' action is a concluding refrain for many healings (see 5.26; 7.16). **9.43b–45** Cf. Mt 17.22–23; Mk 9.30–32. Jesus' second prediction of the suffering of the Son of

Jesus Again Foretells His Death

While everyone was amazed at all that he was doing, he said to his disciples, 44"Let these words sink into your ears: The Son of Man is going to be betrayed into human hands." 45But they did not understand this saying; its meaning was concealed from them, so that they could not perceive it. And they were afraid to ask him about this saying.

True Greatness

46 An argument arose among them as to which one of them was the greatest. 47But Jesus, aware of their inner thoughts, took a little child and put it by his side, 48and said to them, "Whoever welcomes this child in my name welcomes me, and whoever welcomes me welcomes the one who sent me; for the least among all of you is the greatest."

Another Exorcist

49 John answered, "Master, we saw someone casting out demons in your name, and we tried to stop him, because he does not follow with us." 50But Jesus said to him, "Do not stop him; for whoever is not against you is for you."

A Samaritan Village Refuses to Receive Jesus

51 When the days drew near for him to be taken up, he set his face to go to Jerusalem. 52And he sent messengers ahead of him. On their way they entered a village of the Samari-

tans to make ready for him; 53but they did not receive him, because his face was set toward Jerusalem. 54When his disciples James and John saw it, they said, "Lord, do you want us to command fire to come down from heaven and consume them?"[a] 55But he turned and rebuked them. 56Then[b] they went on to another village.

Would-Be Followers of Jesus

57 As they were going along the road, someone said to him, "I will follow you wherever you go." 58And Jesus said to him, "Foxes have holes, and birds of the air have nests; but the Son of Man has nowhere to lay his head." 59To another he said, "Follow me." But he said, "Lord, first let me go and bury my father." 60But Jesus[c] said to him, "Let the dead bury their own dead; but as for you, go and proclaim the kingdom of God." 61Another said, "I will follow you, Lord; but let me first say farewell to those at my home." 62Jesus said to him, "No one who puts a hand to the plow and looks back is fit for the kingdom of God."

The Mission of the Seventy

10 After this the Lord appointed seventy[d] others and sent them on ahead of him in pairs to every town and place where he him-

---

a Other ancient authorities add *as Elijah did*   *b* Other ancient authorities read *rebuked them, and said, "You do not know what spirit you are of,* 56*for the Son of Man has not come to destroy the lives of human beings but to save them."* Then   *c* Gk *he*   *d* Other ancient authorities read *seventy-two*

Man (see v. 22; 18.31–34; see also 12.50; 13.32–33; 17.25). **9.44** *Let these words sink into your ears.* See 8.8; 14.35. See note on 24.6–7. **9.45** On the truth being *concealed from them* (i.e., by God), see 18.34; 24.16. **9.46–48** Cf. Mt 18.1–5; Mk 9.33–37. Luke gives the briefest version of the argument about greatness. **9.46** *Which . . . was the greatest.* See also 22.24–27. **9.47** *Aware of their inner thoughts.* See 2.35; 5.22; 6.8. **9.49–50** Cf. Mk 9.38–40. **9.49** *In your name,* i.e., by invoking Jesus' name as a source of power (see 10.17; Acts 3.6; 4.10, 30; 16.18; 19.13). Magical incantations of this period often contained the names of many gods. **9.50** *Whoever . . . for you.* See Num 11.24–30; cf. Lk 11.23; Acts 8.14–24.

9.51–19.27 The journey to Jerusalem is a major central section of Luke's narrative with few parallels to Mark. **9.51–56** These opening verses depict Jesus on a prophetic mission from Galilee toward Jerusalem. **9.51** This verse marks a major narrative shift. *Taken up* probably refers to all the events associated with Jesus' *departure* (see note on 9.31) but with special emphasis on the ascension (see 24.51; Acts 1.2, 11, 22; see also

2 Kings 2.10–11). *He set his face,* expressing determination or mission (see Isa 50.7; Ezek 21.1–2). *To Jerusalem.* Jesus' destination is repeatedly emphasized (see 13.22; 17.11; 18.31; 19.11, 28; see note on 4.5). **9.52** On sending *messengers ahead,* see 10.1; see also 7.27; Ex 23.20. The *Samaritans,* who traced their lineage to the old Northern Kingdom (Israel), were in Jewish eyes neither Jews nor Gentiles. Jewish-Samaritan relations were hostile (see Mt 10.5; Jn 4.9; 8.48). The Samaritans here reject Jesus' mission, though elsewhere in Luke-Acts they are positively portrayed (see 10.30–37; 17.11–19; Acts 1.8; 8.5–25). **9.54** *Fire . . . from heaven.* See 2 Kings 1.9–14; Lk 3.16–17; 12.49; 17.29. **9.57–62** Cf. Mt 8.18–22. Warnings on the cost of discipleship. **9.57** The *road,* or "way," to Jerusalem becomes symbolic of discipleship; see note on 5.11. An early name for the Christian movement was "the Way" (see Acts 9.2; 18.25; 19.23; 22.4; 24.22). **9.58** *Son of Man.* See note on 5.24. **9.59** A proper burial for one's *father* was a strong traditional obligation (Gen 50.5; Tob 4.3). **9.61** *Let me first say farewell.* See 1 Kings 19.19–21. **10.1–24** The mission of the Seventy moves

self intended to go. 2He said to them, "The harvest is plentiful, but the laborers are few; therefore ask the Lord of the harvest to send out laborers into his harvest. 3Go on your way. See, I am sending you out like lambs into the midst of wolves. 4Carry no purse, no bag, no sandals; and greet no one on the road. 5Whatever house you enter, first say, 'Peace to this house!' 6And if anyone is there who shares in peace, your peace will rest on that person; but if not, it will return to you. 7Remain in the same house, eating and drinking whatever they provide, for the laborer deserves to be paid. Do not move about from house to house. 8Whenever you enter a town and its people welcome you, eat what is set before you; 9cure the sick who are there, and say to them, 'The kingdom of God has come near to you.'*a* 10But whenever you enter a town and they do not welcome you, go out into its streets and say, 11'Even the dust of your town that clings to our feet, we wipe off in protest against you. Yet know this: the kingdom of God has come near.'*b* 12I tell you, on that day it will be more tolerable for Sodom than for that town.

Woes to Unrepentant Cities

13 "Woe to you, Chorazin! Woe to you, Bethsaida! For if the deeds of power done in you had been done in Tyre and Sidon, they would have repented long ago, sitting in sackcloth and ashes. 14But at the judgment it will be more tolerable for Tyre and Sidon than for you. 15And you, Capernaum,

will you be exalted to heaven?

No, you will be brought down to Hades.

16 "Whoever listens to you listens to me, and whoever rejects you rejects me, and whoever rejects me rejects the one who sent me."

The Return of the Seventy

17 The seventy*c* returned with joy, saying, "Lord, in your name even the demons submit to us!" 18He said to them, "I watched Satan fall from heaven like a flash of lightning. 19See, I have given you authority to tread on snakes and scorpions, and over all the power of the enemy; and nothing will hurt you. 20Nevertheless, do not rejoice at this, that the spirits submit to you, but rejoice that your names are written in heaven."

Jesus Rejoices

21 At that same hour Jesus*d* rejoiced in the Holy Spirit*e* and said, "I thank*f* you, Father, Lord of heaven and earth, because you have hidden these things from the wise and the in-

a Or is at hand for you *b* Or is at hand *c* Other ancient authorities read seventy-two *d* Gk he *e* Other authorities read in the spirit *f* Or praise

beyond the mission of the Twelve in 9.1–10. **10.1** *Seventy* may reflect the seventy nations in Gen 10 (seventy-two in the Septuagint; see text note *d* on p. 1783) or the seventy elders chosen by Moses from the twelve tribes (see Ex 24.1, 9; Num 11.16, 24). On traveling *in pairs*, see Acts 8.14; 13.2; 15.32, 39–40. The point may be connected to the testimony of two witnesses (Deut 19.15). **10.2** *Harvest*, the intended gathering of Israel (Isa 27.12), not primarily the judgment (cf. Mt 13.30, 39). **10.3** On *wolves* threatening the flock, see also Ezek 22.27; Jn 10.12; Acts 20.28–30. **10.4** See note on 9.3. *Greet no one on the road* implies an urgent journey (see also 2 Kings 4.29). **10.5** The early Christian mission was closely linked with private *houses* (see Acts 10.22; 11.12; 12.12; 16.15, 34; 18.7; 20.20; 21.8, 16; Rom 16.5; 1 Cor 16.19). *Peace*, though a traditional greeting (see note on 7.50; see also 24.36; 1 Sam 25.6), here signifies the peace of salvation (see 2.14; see also Gal 6.16). **10.6** *Shares in peace*, i.e., is receptive to the message (see v. 9). **10.7** *The laborer deserves to be paid.* See Mt 10.10b; 1 Cor 9.3–14; 1 Tim 5.18. **10.9** Like the word of peace (vv. 5–6), the proclamation of the *kingdom of God* (see note on 4.42–43) is a word of blessing to those who receive the disciples, but a word of judgment to those who reject them (v. 11). **10.11** *Dust . . .*

wipe off. See note on 9.5. **10.12** *That day,* i.e., the day of judgment (see also 21.34). For the fate of *Sodom,* see Gen 19.24–28. **10.13–16** Oracles against the cities in Galilee. See Mt 11.20–24. **10.13** *Chorazin.* Location unknown. *Bethsaida.* See note on 9.10. *Tyre and Sidon,* Phoenician (gentile) seacoast towns (see 6.17; cf. Mt 15.21–28; Mk 7.24–30). On the need to repent, see 3.3, 8; 11.32; 13.3, 5; 15.7, 10; 16.30. *Sackcloth and ashes* indicate deep repentance (see Jon 3.6). **10.15** *Capernaum.* See 4.23, 31; 7.1. *Hades* (Hebrew Sheol), originally the shadowy realm of all the dead (see Isa 38.10); here the place of eternal punishment for the wicked (see 16.22–26, 28). **10.17–24** Cf. Mt 11.25–27; 13.16–17. The return of the Seventy parallels the return of the Twelve in 9.10. **10.17** *Joy* characterizes the success of the mission (see 1.14, 44; 2.10; 8.13; 24.41, 52). **10.18–19** On the fall of *Satan* and the triumph of the kingdom over *the power of the enemy,* see 4.1–13; 11.14–20; 13.16; 22.31–32; cf. Rev 12.9–12; see also note on 8.12. *Snakes and scorpions* represent evil (see 11.11–12; see also Gen 3.1–14; Ps 58.3–4; Sir 21.2; Mk 16.18; Acts 28.1–6). **10.20** *Names . . . written in heaven.* See Ex 32.32–33; Ps 69.28; Isa 34.16; Dan 12.1; Mal 3.16–17; Phil 4.3; Heb 12.23; Rev 3.5; 13.8. **10.21** On contrasts between *hidden* and *revealed,* the *wise* and in-

telligent and have revealed them to infants; yes, Father, for such was your gracious will.[a] ²²All things have been handed over to me by my Father; and no one knows who the Son is except the Father, or who the Father is except the Son and anyone to whom the Son chooses to reveal him."

23 Then turning to the disciples, Jesus[b] said to them privately, "Blessed are the eyes that see what you see! ²⁴For I tell you that many prophets and kings desired to see what you see, but did not see it, and to hear what you hear, but did not hear it."

The Parable of the Good Samaritan

25 Just then a lawyer stood up to test Jesus.[c] "Teacher," he said, "what must I do to inherit eternal life?" ²⁶He said to him, "What is written in the law? What do you read there?" ²⁷He answered, "You shall love the Lord your God with all your heart, and with all your soul, and with all your strength, and with all your mind; and your neighbor as yourself." ²⁸And he said to him, "You have given the right answer; do this, and you will live."

29 But wanting to justify himself, he asked Jesus, "And who is my neighbor?" ³⁰Jesus replied, "A man was going down from Jerusalem to Jericho, and fell into the hands of robbers, who stripped him, beat him, and went away, leaving him half dead. ³¹Now by chance a priest was going down that road; and when he saw him, he passed by on the other side. ³²So likewise a Levite, when he came to the place and saw him, passed by on the other side. ³³But a Samaritan while traveling came near him; and when he saw him, he was moved with pity. ³⁴He went to him and bandaged his wounds, having poured oil and wine on them. Then he put him on his own animal, brought him to an inn, and took care of him. ³⁵The next day he took out two denarii,[d] gave them to the innkeeper, and said, 'Take care of him; and when I come back, I will repay you whatever more you spend.' ³⁶Which of these three, do you think, was a neighbor to the man who fell into the hands of the robbers?" ³⁷He said, "The one who showed him mercy." Jesus said to him, "Go and do likewise."

Jesus Visits Martha and Mary

38 Now as they went on their way, he entered a certain village, where a woman named Martha welcomed him into her home. ³⁹She had a sister named Mary, who sat at the Lord's feet and listened to what he was saying. ⁴⁰But Martha was distracted by her many tasks; so she came to him and asked, "Lord, do you not care that my sister has left me to do all the work by myself? Tell her then to help me." ⁴¹But the Lord answered her, "Martha, Martha, you are worried and distracted by many things; ⁴²there is need of only one thing.[e] Mary has chosen the better part, which will not be taken away from her."

The Lord's Prayer

11 He was praying in a certain place, and after he had finished, one of his disci-

---

a Or *for so it was well-pleasing in your sight* *b* Gk *he* *c* Gk *him* *d* The denarius was the usual day's wage for a laborer *e* Other ancient authorities read *few things are necessary, or only one*

---

fants, see 8.17. **10.22** No other portion of Luke explicates the relationship of the *Father* and the *Son* so directly (cf. v. 16; Jn 3.35; 6.65; 10.15; 13.3; 14.7–13; 17.25). **10.23** *Blessed are the eyes that see*. Though the disciples themselves have not yet fully seen (see 9.45; 18.34; 24.16), in Acts they are the key eye witnesses (see Acts 1.8, 21–22). **10.24** The *prophets* foretold, but did not see, the fulfillment of the messianic age (see 24.25, 44; Acts 2.16–21). **10.25–11.13** Jesus teaches the way of the kingdom. **10.25–37** Cf. Mt 22.34–40; Mk 12.28–34. The double love command leads to a teaching on being a neighbor. **10.25** *Lawyer*. See note on 7.30. **10.27** The text joins Deut 6.5 and Lev 19.18. **10.29** *Justify himself*. See 16.15. The question probes the limits of neighbor. **10.30** The road *down from Jerusalem to Jericho* descends about 3,200 feet; the distance between the two is about eighteen miles. See 18.35; 19.1. **10.31** *A priest*, perhaps returning home after temple service (see 1.23). **10.32** *Levite*, a temple functionary from the priestly tribe of Levi. Both he and the priest may have been concerned about impurity from contact with a corpse (see Num 5.2; 19.11–13). **10.33** The *Samaritan* in this setting is an outsider (see note on 9.52). *Moved with pity*. See note on 7.13. **10.34** *Oil and wine*, used for medicinal purposes (see Isa 1.6; Mk 6.13; Jas 5.14). **10.36** Jesus' question changes the definition of *neighbor* from one who is the object of kindness (cf. vv. 27, 29) to one who bestows it. **10.37** *Mercy*. See 1.72; 6.36; Mic 6.8. **10.38–42** See also Jn 11.1; 12.1–3. Interpreters find in the story of Martha and Mary conflicting messages on service and listening. **10.39** *Sat at the Lord's feet*. Mary is depicted as a disciple (see note on 8.35). This was exceptional for women. **10.40** *Many tasks*, lit. "much service." Discipleship is later defined in terms of service (see 22.24–27). For the active service of other women, see 8.2–3; 23.55–56; 24.1–3; Acts 9.36; 16.14–15; 18.2–3, 18. **10.42** *One thing* is

ples said to him, "Lord, teach us to pray, as John taught his disciples." ²He said to them, "When you pray, say:

Father,ᵃ hallowed be your name.
    Your kingdom come.ᵇ
3   Give us each day our daily bread.ᶜ
4   And forgive us our sins,
       for we ourselves forgive everyone
       indebted to us.
    And do not bring us to the time of
       trial."ᵈ

Perseverance in Prayer

5 And he said to them, "Suppose one of you has a friend, and you go to him at midnight and say to him, 'Friend, lend me three loaves of bread; ⁶for a friend of mine has arrived, and I have nothing to set before him.' ⁷And he answers from within, 'Do not bother me; the door has already been locked, and my children are with me in bed; I cannot get up and give you anything.' ⁸I tell you, even though he will not get up and give him anything because he is his friend, at least because of his persistence he will get up and give him whatever he needs.

9 "So I say to you, Ask, and it will be given you; search, and you will find; knock, and the door will be opened for you. ¹⁰For everyone who asks receives, and everyone who searches finds, and for everyone who knocks, the door will be opened. ¹¹Is there anyone among you who, if your child asks forᵉ a fish, will give a snake instead of a fish? ¹²Or if the child asks for an egg, will give a scorpion? ¹³If you then, who are evil, know how to give good gifts to your children, how much more will the heavenly Father give the Holy Spiritᶠ to those who ask him!"

Jesus and Beelzebul

14 Now he was casting out a demon that was mute; when the demon had gone out, the one who had been mute spoke, and the crowds were amazed. ¹⁵But some of them said, "He casts out demons by Beelzebul, the ruler of the demons." ¹⁶Others, to test him, kept demanding from him a sign from heaven. ¹⁷But he knew what they were thinking and said to them, "Every kingdom divided against itself becomes a desert, and house falls on house. ¹⁸If Satan also is divided against himself, how will his kingdom stand? —for you say that I cast out the demons by Beelzebul. ¹⁹Now if I cast out the demons by Beelzebul, by whom do your exorcistsᵍ cast them out? Therefore they will be your judges. ²⁰But if it is by the finger of God that I cast out the demons, then the kingdom of God has come to you. ²¹When a strong man, fully armed, guards his castle, his property is safe. ²²But when one stronger than he attacks him and overpowers him, he takes away his armor in which he trusted and divides his plunder. ²³Whoever is not with me is against me, and whoever does not gather with me scatters.

The Return of the Unclean Spirit

24 "When the unclean spirit has gone out of a person, it wanders through waterless regions

---

a Other ancient authorities read *Our Father in heaven* b A few ancient authorities read *Your Holy Spirit come upon us and cleanse us.* Other ancient authorities add *Your will be done, on earth as in heaven* c Or *our bread for tomorrow* d Or *us into temptation.* Other ancient authorities add *but rescue us from the evil one* (or *from evil*) e Other ancient authorities add *bread, will give a stone; or if your child asks for* f Other ancient authorities read *the Father give the Holy Spirit from heaven* g Gk *sons*

---

necessary, here listening to Jesus' teaching (see 18.22; see also 8.15, 21). **11.1–13** Cf. Mt 6.9–13; 7.7–11. A discourse on prayer appropriate to the time of the kingdom. **11.1** On *John*'s teaching, see 5.33. **11.2** *Father* (see 6.36; 9.26; 10.21; Deut 32.6; Ps 89.26–27; Mal 2.10; Sir 23.1, 4; 51.10) implies an intimate relationship (see Mk 14.36; Rom 8.15; Gal 4.6; cf. Acts 4.24). *Hallowed*, i.e., recognized as holy (see Ezek 36.22–23). *Your kingdom come.* See note on 4.43; see also 10.9; 17.20–21; 22.16. **11.3** *Daily bread* (see Ex 16.4), the bread necessary to live or bread for the future (see text note *c*). The phrase stresses constancy (see 9.23; Acts 6.1) or eschatological fulfillment (22.16). **11.4** *Trial*, or temptation, implies conflict with spiritual powers and human adversaries (4.1–13; 8.13; 22.28, 40, 46). **11.8** *His persistence*, i.e., his begging friend's shamelessness. On the application of persistence to prayer, see 18.1–8. **11.13** On the gift of the *Holy Spirit*, see

24.49; Acts 1.4–8; 2.1–13, 38; 4.31; 5.32; 10.44–47. **11.14–54** Jesus meets opposition. **11.14–28** Cf. Mt 12.22–30, 43–45; Mk 3.22–27. The Beelzebul controversy sharpens the question of where God's power is at work. **11.14** *Mute* (Greek *kophos*), or "deaf" (see 1.20, 62). **11.15** *Beelzebul*, a variant of the name of a Philistine god (see 2 Kings 1.2–16), here identical with Satan (v. 18). **11.16** On the *test* of Jesus' ability to produce a *sign*, see 4.9–12, 23; 11.29; 23.8. **11.17** *House falls on house*, warfare in households or dynasties (see 12.52–53). *Knew what they were thinking.* See note on 2.35. **11.20** *Finger of God*, an allusion to Ex 8.19, where Pharaoh's magicians recognized God's true power at work in Moses and Aaron. **11.21** *A strong man*, here Satan. **11.22** Jesus claims to be the *stronger* one who has invaded Satan's domain (see Isa 49.24–25). **11.23** In this conflict there is no middle ground (cf. 9.50). **11.24** *Waterless regions*, thought to be the pre-

looking for a resting place, but not finding any, it says, 'I will return to my house from which I came.' 25When it comes, it finds it swept and put in order. 26Then it goes and brings seven other spirits more evil than itself, and they enter and live there; and the last state of that person is worse than the first."

True Blessedness

27 While he was saying this, a woman in the crowd raised her voice and said to him, "Blessed is the womb that bore you and the breasts that nursed you!" 28But he said, "Blessed rather are those who hear the word of God and obey it!"

The Sign of Jonah

29 When the crowds were increasing, he began to say, "This generation is an evil generation; it asks for a sign, but no sign will be given to it except the sign of Jonah. 30For just as Jonah became a sign to the people of Nineveh, so the Son of Man will be to this generation. 31The queen of the South will rise at the judgment with the people of this generation and condemn them, because she came from the ends of the earth to listen to the wisdom of Solomon, and see, something greater than Solomon is here! 32The people of Nineveh will rise up at the judgment with this generation and condemn it, because they repented at the proclamation of Jonah, and see, something greater than Jonah is here!

The Light of the Body

33 "No one after lighting a lamp puts it in a cellar,[a] but on the lampstand so that those who enter may see the light. 34Your eye is the lamp of your body. If your eye is healthy, your whole body is full of light; but if it is not healthy, your body is full of darkness. 35Therefore consider whether the light in you is not darkness. 36If then your whole body is full of light, with no part of it in darkness, it will be as full of light as when a lamp gives you light with its rays."

Jesus Denounces Pharisees and Lawyers

37 While he was speaking, a Pharisee invited him to dine with him; so he went in and took his place at the table. 38The Pharisee was amazed to see that he did not first wash before dinner. 39Then the Lord said to him, "Now you Pharisees clean the outside of the cup and of the dish, but inside you are full of greed and wickedness. 40You fools! Did not the one who made the outside make the inside also? 41So give for alms those things that are within; and see, everything will be clean for you.

42 "But woe to you Pharisees! For you tithe mint and rue and herbs of all kinds, and neglect justice and the love of God; it is these you ought to have practiced, without neglecting the others. 43Woe to you Pharisees! For you love to have the seat of honor in the synagogues and to be greeted with respect in the marketplaces. 44Woe to you! For you are like unmarked graves, and people walk over them without realizing it."

45 One of the lawyers answered him,

a Other ancient authorities add or under the bushel basket

---

ferred haunts of demons (see 8.29; Lev 16.10). 11.26 To return with seven other spirits would mean infestation (see also 8.2, 30). 11.27 Blessed. See note on 6.20. The blessing pronounced by the woman conforms to Mary's prediction (1.48; see also 1.42; Gen 49.25). 11.28 Jesus redirects this blessing to those who hear the word of God and obey it (see 8.19–21; see also 6.47; 8.15). 11.29–32 Cf. Mt 12.38–42; Mk 8.12. A direct verdict on the preceding demand for a sign (v. 16). 11.29 An evil generation. See note on 7.31. 11.30 Sign of Jonah, in Mt 12.39–40 Jonah's three days and nights in the fish, here Jonah himself and his prophetic message (see Mt 12.41). Son of Man. See note on 5.24. 11.31 Queen of the South, the queen of Sheba (1 Kings 10.1–13; 2 Chr 9.1–12). 11.32 The Ninevites repented on hearing of impending judgment (see Jon 3.6–10). 11.33–36 Cf. Mt 5.15; 6.22–23; Mk 4.21. A series of loosely related sayings on light. 11.33 Lamp . . . lampstand. See 8.16. 11.34 Lamp of your body, the ancient notion that the eye emits light that enables one to see.

11.37–54 Cf. Mt 23.1–36; Mk 12.38–40. This second story of meal fellowship with a Pharisees (see 7.36–50) is structured around six "woes" (see also 6.24–26). 11.37 Pharisee. See note on 5.17. 11.38 Amazed, i.e., shocked. To wash before dinner was a matter of ritual cleanliness and obedience to the law, not mere hygiene (see Mk 7.1–5). 11.39 The contrast between outside and inside is a charge of hypocrisy (see Mt 23.25). 11.41 Alms, charitable donations to the poor, important in Jewish piety (Tob 4.7–11). The proper use of possessions is a major Lukan concern. Here almsgiving is recommended as a strategy for cleansing (see note on 12.33). 11.42 Woe. See note on 6.24. The Pharisees gave a tithe, or tenth part, of the harvest to the temple (see 18.12; Lev 27.30–33; Deut 14.22–29; 26.12–15; Mal 3.8–10). You . . . neglect justice, a classic prophetic indictment (see Isa 1.21–23; Am 5.21–24; Mic 3.9–12). 11.43 The seat of honor. See also 14.7; 20.46; Mt 23.6; Jas 2.1–7. 11.44 Unmarked graves could cause unwitting defilement (see Lev 21.11; Num

"Teacher, when you say these things, you insult us too." [46]And he said, "Woe also to you lawyers! For you load people with burdens hard to bear, and you yourselves do not lift a finger to ease them. [47]Woe to you! For you build the tombs of the prophets whom your ancestors killed. [48]So you are witnesses and approve of the deeds of your ancestors; for they killed them, and you build their tombs. [49]Therefore also the Wisdom of God said, 'I will send them prophets and apostles, some of whom they will kill and persecute,' [50]so that this generation may be charged with the blood of all the prophets shed since the foundation of the world, [51]from the blood of Abel to the blood of Zechariah, who perished between the altar and the sanctuary. Yes, I tell you, it will be charged against this generation. [52]Woe to you lawyers! For you have taken away the key of knowledge; you did not enter yourselves, and you hindered those who were entering."

53 When he went outside, the scribes and the Pharisees began to be very hostile toward him and to cross-examine him about many things, [54]lying in wait for him, to catch him in something he might say.

A Warning against Hypocrisy

12 Meanwhile, when the crowd gathered by the thousands, so that they trampled on one another, he began to speak first to his disciples, "Beware of the yeast of the Pharisees, that is, their hypocrisy. [2]Nothing is covered up that will not be uncovered, and nothing secret that will not become known. [3]Therefore whatever you have said in the dark will be heard in the light, and what you have whispered behind closed doors will be proclaimed from the housetops.

Exhortation to Fearless Confession

4 "I tell you, my friends, do not fear those who kill the body, and after that can do nothing more. [5]But I will warn you whom to fear: fear him who, after he has killed, has authority[a] to cast into hell.[b] Yes, I tell you, fear him! [6]Are not five sparrows sold for two pennies? Yet not one of them is forgotten in God's sight. [7]But even the hairs of your head are all counted. Do not be afraid; you are of more value than many sparrows.

8 "And I tell you, everyone who acknowledges me before others, the Son of Man also will acknowledge before the angels of God; [9]but whoever denies me before others will be denied before the angels of God. [10]And everyone who speaks a word against the Son of Man will be forgiven; but whoever blasphemes against the Holy Spirit will not be forgiven. [11]When they bring you before the synagogues, the rulers, and the authorities, do not worry about how[c] you are to defend yourselves or what you are to say; [12]for the Holy Spirit will teach you at that very hour what you ought to say."

a Or power   b Gk Gehenna   c Other ancient authorities add or what

19.11–22). **11.46** *Lawyers.* See notes on 7.30; 20.45–47. On the *burden* of keeping the law, see Acts 15.10; cf. Mt 11.30. **11.47** *Build the tombs of the prophets,* perhaps implying the sealing up of their testimony through complex interpretations (see note on 11.52). *Whom your ancestors killed.* See 13.34; Acts 7.52. **11.49** *The Wisdom of God* (see also 7.35) is closely identified with the Holy Spirit (see Acts 6.3, 10), but Matthew places Wisdom's words directly in Jesus' mouth (see Mt 23.34; see also 1 Cor 1.24). On the killing and persecution of *apostles,* see Acts 12.1–5. **11.50** *This generation.* See note on 7.31. **11.51** *Blood of Abel.* See Gen 4.8–11. *Blood of Zechariah.* See 2 Chr 24.20–22. **11.52** *Taken away the key,* i.e., controlled the scriptures through their interpretations rather than opening them by teaching (see note on 11.47). **11.53–54** The hostility of the religious leaders becomes a theme in the narrative (see esp. 19.47–48; 20.1–21.4). **12.1–13.21** More teaching on discipleship. **12.1–12** Cf. Mt 16.5–6; 10.26–33; Mk 8.14–15. Words of warning and encouragement. **12.1** Luke contrasts the reaction of the *crowd* with that of the religious leaders

(11.53–54; cf. 23.13–18). *Yeast,* actually sour or fermenting dough, suggesting hidden corruption (cf. 13.21). **12.2** On what is *covered up* and *uncovered,* see also 8.17; 10.21–22. **12.4** *My friends.* See Jn 15.13–15. **12.5** *Whom to fear,* i.e., God (see also Acts 9.31; 2 Cor 7.1; Phil 2.12; 1 Pet 1.17; 2.17). *Hell,* lit. *Gehenna* (text note *b*), originally the name of a valley near Jerusalem used at one time for human burnt sacrifices (Jer 19.4–6), then for burning rubbish. It became the name of the place of eternal punishment (Rev 9.1–2; 21.8). **12.6** *Two pennies,* a tiny sum. **12.7** *Are all counted,* i.e., known to God (see also 21.18; 1 Sam 14.45; 2 Sam 14.11; 1 Kings 1.52; Acts 27.34). **12.8** The wording is strange here, suggesting that the *Son of Man* was a figure different from Jesus (see also 9.26; 17.22–30). The issue is widely debated (see also note on 5.24). **12.10** In Luke-Acts, denial of Jesus can be forgiven (Lk 22.32, 54–62), but sins *against the Holy Spirit* risk dire judgment (Acts 5.1–11; 7.51; 8.18–24). **12.11** On trials *before the synagogues, the rulers, and the authorities,* see 21.12; Acts 4.1–22; 5.17–42; 17.1–9; 22.30–23.10; 24.1–21; 26.1–29. **12.12** *Will teach you.* Cf. 21.15; Jn

The Parable of the Rich Fool

13 Someone in the crowd said to him, "Teacher, tell my brother to divide the family inheritance with me." 14But he said to him, "Friend, who set me to be a judge or arbitrator over you?" 15And he said to them, "Take care! Be on your guard against all kinds of greed; for one's life does not consist in the abundance of possessions." 16Then he told them a parable: "The land of a rich man produced abundantly. 17And he thought to himself, 'What should I do, for I have no place to store my crops?' 18Then he said, 'I will do this: I will pull down my barns and build larger ones, and there I will store all my grain and my goods. 19And I will say to my soul, Soul, you have ample goods laid up for many years; relax, eat, drink, be merry.' 20But God said to him, 'You fool! This very night your life is being demanded of you. And the things you have prepared, whose will they be?' 21So it is with those who store up treasures for themselves but are not rich toward God."

Do Not Worry

22 He said to his disciples, "Therefore I tell you, do not worry about your life, what you will eat, or about your body, what you will wear. 23For life is more than food, and the body more than clothing. 24Consider the ravens: they neither sow nor reap, they have neither storehouse nor barn, and yet God feeds them. Of how much more value are you than the birds! 25And can any of you by worrying add a single hour to your span of life?[a] 26If then you are not able to do so small a thing as that, why do you worry about the rest? 27Consider the lilies, how they grow: they neither toil nor spin;[b] yet I tell you, even Solomon in all his glory was not clothed like one of these. 28But if God so clothes the grass of the field, which is alive today and tomorrow is thrown into the oven, how much more will he clothe you—you of little faith! 29And do not keep striving for what you are to eat and what you are to drink, and do not keep worrying. 30For it is the nations of the world that strive after all these things, and your Father knows that you need them. 31Instead, strive for his[c] kingdom, and these things will be given to you as well.

32 "Do not be afraid, little flock, for it is your Father's good pleasure to give you the kingdom. 33Sell your possessions, and give alms. Make purses for yourselves that do not wear out, an unfailing treasure in heaven, where no thief comes near and no moth destroys. 34For where your treasure is, there your heart will be also.

Watchful Slaves

35 "Be dressed for action and have your lamps lit; 36be like those who are waiting for their master to return from the wedding banquet, so that they may open the door for him as soon as he comes and knocks. 37Blessed are those slaves whom the master finds alert when he comes; truly I tell you, he will fasten his belt and have them sit down to eat, and he will come and serve them. 38If he comes during the middle of the night, or near dawn, and finds them so, blessed are those slaves.

39 "But know this: if the owner of the house had known at what hour the thief was coming, he[d] would not have let his house be broken

---

a Or add a cubit to your stature   b Other ancient authorities read Consider the lilies; they neither spin nor weave   c Other ancient authorities read God's   d Other ancient authorities add would have watched and

---

14.26. **12.13–21** The peril of wealth is demonstrated with a parable. See note on 9.25. **12.13** A *teacher*, or rabbi, could be expected to interpret the *inheritance* laws (Num 27.1–11; 36.7–9; Deut 21.15–17). **12.14** *Friend*, lit. "man" (Greek *anthrope*). See 22.58, 60. *Judge or arbitrator.* See Acts 7.27, 35. **12.17** *Thought to himself.* See vv. 19, 45; 15.17; 16.3–4; 18.4–5; 20.13. **12.19** *Eat, drink, be merry* was a common adage, though it often continues, "for tomorrow we die" (see Eccl 8.15; Tob 7.10; Sir 11.18–19; 1 Cor 15.32). **12.20** The *fool* leaves God out of the reckoning (see Ps 14.1). **12.21** *Rich toward God.* See notes on 11.41; 12.33; see also 16.13. **12.22–34** Cf. Mt 6.25–34, 19–21. The words on needless worrying serve as a commentary on the preceding parable (cf. Mt 6). **12.27** According to 1 Kings 3.10–14, wealth and power were given to Solomon because he did not seek them first (see also v. 31). **12.28** On human life as transitory as *grass*, see Job 8.12; Pss 37.2; 90.5–6; 102.11; 103.15–16; Isa 37.27; 40.6–8. **12.30** *The nations of the world*, the Gentiles, who are often negative examples (see 22.25; Mt 5.47; 6.7, 32; 18.17; 20.25). **12.32** *Do not be afraid.* See note on 1.13. *Little flock*, an image of care (see Ezek 34.11–31). **12.33** *Sell your possessions.* See 14.33; 18.22; Acts 2.44–45; 4.34–35. *Give alms.* See notes on 11.41; 12.21. **12.35–48** Cf. Mt 24.42–51; Mk 13.33–37. Admonitions on watchfulness. **12.35** *Dressed for action*, an OT image of readiness for service (e.g., 1 Kings 18.46; 2 Kings 4.29). **12.37** *Alert when he comes.* Cf. Jesus' disciples in 22.39–46. On the image of a master

into. 40 You also must be ready, for the Son of Man is coming at an unexpected hour."

The Faithful or the Unfaithful Slave

41 Peter said, "Lord, are you telling this parable for us or for everyone?" 42 And the Lord said, "Who then is the faithful and prudent manager whom his master will put in charge of his slaves, to give them their allowance of food at the proper time? 43 Blessed is that slave whom his master will find at work when he arrives. 44 Truly I tell you, he will put that one in charge of all his possessions. 45 But if that slave says to himself, 'My master is delayed in coming,' and if he begins to beat the other slaves, men and women, and to eat and drink and get drunk, 46 the master of that slave will come on a day when he does not expect him and at an hour that he does not know, and will cut him in pieces,ᵃ and put him with the unfaithful. 47 That slave who knew what his master wanted, but did not prepare himself or do what was wanted, will receive a severe beating. 48 But the one who did not know and did what deserved a beating will receive a light beating. From everyone to whom much has been given, much will be required; and from the one to whom much has been entrusted, even more will be demanded.

Jesus the Cause of Division

49 "I came to bring fire to the earth, and how I wish it were already kindled! 50 I have a baptism with which to be baptized, and what stress I am under until it is completed! 51 Do you think that I have come to bring peace to the earth? No, I tell you, but rather division! 52 From now on five in one household will be

divided, three against two and two against three; 53 they will be divided:

> father against son
> and son against father,
> mother against daughter
> and daughter against mother,
> mother-in-law against her daughter-in-
> law
> and daughter-in-law against mother-
> in-law."

Interpreting the Time

54 He also said to the crowds, "When you see a cloud rising in the west, you immediately say, 'It is going to rain'; and so it happens. 55 And when you see the south wind blowing, you say, 'There will be scorching heat'; and it happens. 56 You hypocrites! You know how to interpret the appearance of earth and sky, but why do you not know how to interpret the present time?

Settling with Your Opponent

57 "And why do you not judge for yourselves what is right? 58 Thus, when you go with your accuser before a magistrate, on the way make an effort to settle the case,ᵇ or you may be dragged before the judge, and the judge hand you over to the officer, and the officer throw you in prison. 59 I tell you, you will never get out until you have paid the very last penny."

Repent or Perish

13 At that very time there were some present who told him about the Galileans whose blood Pilate had mingled with their

ᵃ Or cut him off ᵇ Gk settle with him

---

who *serves*, see 22.24–27. *Blessed.* See note on 6.20. **12.40** On the coming of the *Son of Man* as judge, see note on 5.24; see also 17.22–37; 18.8; 21.27, 36. *An unexpected hour.* See also v. 46; 21.34–36; Acts 1.7. **12.41** *Peter's* role as spokesman will be central in Acts. **12.42–43** The household *manager* was usually a well-trained *slave* who was given significant responsibilities (see 16.1–8). **12.44** On the increased responsibility of those who have received, see also v. 48; 19.11–27. **12.49–59** Cf. Mt 10.34–36; 16.2–3; 5.25–26; Mk 10.38. Jesus defines his ministry in terms of division and judgment. **12.49** *Fire to the earth* suggests purification (3.16; Lev 13.52; Num 31.23) or judgment (9.54; 2 Kings 1.10–14). See also 1 Kings 18.36–40. **12.50** Jesus' *baptism,* here meant figuratively (cf. 3.21–22), probably refers to his death, which was earlier defined as his *departure* in (see note on) 9.31. *Stress* im-

plies a form of constraint like that of the prophets (see Jer 20.9; Am 3.8). **12.51** The promise of *peace* (see notes on 2.14; 7.50; 10.5; see also 1.79; 2.29; 8.48; 19.38; 24.36; Acts 9.31; 10.36) becomes a threat of *division* if the Messiah is rejected (see 2.34; 10.8–12; 19.41–44). **12.53** The promise to *turn the hearts of parents to their children* (1.17) is thwarted by rejection (see also Mic 7.6). **12.54–55** Contrast the weather pattern described here with Mt 16.2–3. **12.56** On *hypocrites,* especially as interpreters, see 6.39–42; 13.14–15; see also notes on 6.42; 12.1. *The present time,* i.e., the crucial time of Jesus' ministry. **13.1–9** Cf. Mt 21.18–19; Mk 11.12–14. Jesus repeats John's message of repentance. **13.1** *Pilate* was known for brutal reprisals and disdain for local religious practices (Josephus, *Antiquities* 18.85–89; *War* 2.169–77; see also Lk 3.1; 23.1–25). The incident mentioned in this verse is oth-

sacrifices. 2He asked them, "Do you think that because these Galileans suffered in this way they were worse sinners than all other Galileans? 3No, I tell you; but unless you repent, you will all perish as they did. 4Or those eighteen who were killed when the tower of Siloam fell on them—do you think that they were worse offenders than all the others living in Jerusalem? 5No, I tell you; but unless you repent, you will all perish just as they did."

The Parable of the Barren Fig Tree

6 Then he told this parable: "A man had a fig tree planted in his vineyard; and he came looking for fruit on it and found none. 7So he said to the gardener, 'See here! For three years I have come looking for fruit on this fig tree, and still I find none. Cut it down! Why should it be wasting the soil?' 8He replied, 'Sir, let it alone for one more year, until I dig around it and put manure on it. 9If it bears fruit next year, well and good; but if not, you can cut it down.' "

Jesus Heals a Crippled Woman

10 Now he was teaching in one of the synagogues on the sabbath. 11And just then there appeared a woman with a spirit that had crippled her for eighteen years. She was bent over and was quite unable to stand up straight. 12When Jesus saw her, he called her over and said, "Woman, you are set free from your ailment." 13When he laid his hands on her, immediately she stood up straight and began praising God. 14But the leader of the synagogue, indignant because Jesus had cured on the sabbath, kept saying to the crowd, "There

are six days on which work ought to be done; come on those days and be cured, and not on the sabbath day." 15But the Lord answered him and said, "You hypocrites! Does not each of you on the sabbath untie his ox or his donkey from the manger, and lead it away to give it water? 16And ought not this woman, a daughter of Abraham whom Satan bound for eighteen long years, be set free from this bondage on the sabbath day?" 17When he said this, all his opponents were put to shame; and the entire crowd was rejoicing at all the wonderful things that he was doing.

The Parable of the Mustard Seed

18 He said therefore, "What is the kingdom of God like? And to what should I compare it? 19It is like a mustard seed that someone took and sowed in the garden; it grew and became a tree, and the birds of the air made nests in its branches."

The Parable of the Yeast

20 And again he said, "To what should I compare the kingdom of God? 21It is like yeast that a woman took and mixed in with[a] three measures of flour until all of it was leavened."

The Narrow Door

22 Jesus[b] went through one town and village after another, teaching as he made his way to Jerusalem. 23Someone asked him, "Lord, will only a few be saved?" He said to them, 24"Strive to enter through the narrow door; for many, I tell you, will try to enter and will

---

a Gk hid in   b Gk He

---

erwise unattested. **13.2** Physical suffering was widely viewed as a consequence of sin (see Deut 28–30; Ezek 18.26–27; Jn 9.2–3). **13.3** *Repent.* See also John's preaching of repentance in 3.1–17. **13.4** The calamity with the *tower of Siloam* is otherwise unattested. The tower probably formed part of the defenses of Jerusalem. **13.6** *Fig tree,* a frequent metaphor for Israel or Judah (see Jer 8.13; Hos 9.10; Mic 7.1). *Looking for fruit.* Cf. Mt 21.19; Mk 11.13. **13.10–17** The third sabbath controversy (see also 6.1–5; 6.6–11; 14.1–6), here with Jesus teaching in the synagogue (see also 4.14–30, 31–38, 44). **13.11** For the perceived link between illness and an evil *spirit,* see note on 8.2–3; see also 9.42. **13.14** The objection to the healing is based on Ex 20.9–10; Deut 5.13–14. **13.15–16** Jesus argues from a lesser issue of care for the needs of animals (a point granted by the rabbis; see 14.5) to the greater issue of care for an afflicted woman. **13.16** *Daughter of Abra-*

ham identifies the woman as a Jew (Gen 12.2–3; 4 Macc 15.28; see also Lk 8.48; 19.9; cf. 3.8). *Satan.* See 10.18; 11.18; 22.3. The healing is presented as a conquest over evil powers (see also 4.39; 6.18; 7.21; 8.2; 9.1, 42). **13.18–21** Cf. Mt 13.31–33; Mk 4.30–32. Parables of remarkable growth. **13.19** A *tree* that provides shelter was a familiar metaphor for a kingdom (see Ezek 17.22–24; 31.2–9; Dan 4.10–12). **13.21** *Yeast,* here a positive metaphor for hidden growth (cf. 12.1; 1 Cor 5.6–8).

13.22–17.10 Jesus continues on his way to Jerusalem. **13.22–30** Cf. Mt 7.13–14, 22–23; 8.11–12; 19.30; Mk 10.31. Statements on salvation and rejection set the tone for this phase of the journey. **13.22** A summary statement noting progress toward Jerusalem (see note on 9.51). **13.23** The issue of whether many or *a few* would be *saved* was widely debated (see 2 Esd 7.47; 8.1; 9.15). **13.24** *Strive.* Luke emphasizes the struggle

not be able. 25When once the owner of the house has got up and shut the door, and you begin to stand outside and to knock at the door, saying, 'Lord, open to us,' then in reply he will say to you, 'I do not know where you come from.' 26Then you will begin to say, 'We ate and drank with you, and you taught in our streets.' 27But he will say, 'I do not know where you come from; go away from me, all you evildoers!' 28There will be weeping and gnashing of teeth when you see Abraham and Isaac and Jacob and all the prophets in the kingdom of God, and you yourselves thrown out. 29Then people will come from east and west, from north and south, and will eat in the kingdom of God. 30Indeed, some are last who will be first, and some are first who will be last."

The Lament over Jerusalem

31 At that very hour some Pharisees came and said to him, "Get away from here, for Herod wants to kill you." 32He said to them, "Go and tell that fox for me,*a* 'Listen, I am casting out demons and performing cures today and tomorrow, and on the third day I finish my work. 33Yet today, tomorrow, and the next day I must be on my way, because it is impossible for a prophet to be killed outside of Jerusalem.' 34Jerusalem, Jerusalem, the city that kills the prophets and stones those who are sent to it!

How often have I desired to gather your children together as a hen gathers her brood under her wings, and you were not willing! 35See, your house is left to you. And I tell you, you will not see me until the time comes when*b* you say, 'Blessed is the one who comes in the name of the Lord.' "

Jesus Heals the Man with Dropsy

14 On one occasion when Jesus*c* was going to the house of a leader of the Pharisees to eat a meal on the sabbath, they were watching him closely. 2Just then, in front of him, there was a man who had dropsy. 3And Jesus asked the lawyers and Pharisees, "Is it lawful to cure people on the sabbath, or not?" 4But they were silent. So Jesus*c* took him and healed him, and sent him away. 5Then he said to them, "If one of you has a child*d* or an ox that has fallen into a well, will you not immediately pull it out on a sabbath day?" 6And they could not reply to this.

Humility and Hospitality

7 When he noticed how the guests chose the places of honor, he told them a parable. 8"When you are invited by someone to a wedding ban-

---

a Gk lacks *for me*   *b* Other ancient authorities lack *the time comes when*   *c* Gk *he*   *d* Other ancient authorities read *a donkey*

---

the few must undertake to be saved, not merely their moral choice (cf. Mt 7.13–14). **13.25** The image shifts to one of limited time before the door to salvation is *shut.* **13.26** *We ate and drank with you,* a sign of community; see also 7.34; 14.12–14. **13.27** *Evildoers,* an allusion to Ps 6.8. **13.28** *Abraham, Isaac, Jacob,* the three patriarchs of Israel. See 20.37; Deut 1.8; Acts 3.13; 7.32. *Thrown out.* See also 16.22–31. **13.29** The *people* coming from every direction could be diaspora Jews or Gentiles (see Ps 107.2–3; Isa 43.5–6; 49.12). *Eat in the kingdom of God.* A common image for salvation (see 14.15; 22.16, 29–30; see note on 14.8; see also Isa 25.6–8; 65.13–14; Rev 3.20; 19.9). **13.31–35** Cf. Mt 23.37–39. Jesus links his fate with that of the prophets. **13.31** On Jesus' rejection of the counsel of *some Pharisees,* see also 19.39. *Herod* Antipas. See note on 3.1; 9.7–9; see also 3.19–20; 23.6–12. **13.32** To call Herod a *fox* is a dangerous insult; a lion would be the desired royal image (see 1 Kings 10.18–20; see also Rev 5.5). *The third day.* An allusion to the resurrection (see also 9.22; 18.33; 24.7, 21, 46; 1 Cor 15.4). *Finish my work.* See notes on 9.31; 9.51). **13.33** *I must.* In Luke, this necessity is not fate but obedience to God's will (see 4.43; 7.30; 22.42; Acts 2.23; 4.28; see also notes on 2.49 and 9.22). **13.34** *Jerusalem,* the focus of the impending confrontation (19.41–44). On the death of *prophets,*

see 11.49–51; 2 Chr 24.20–22; Jer 26.20–23; Acts 7.52. *I desired, you were not willing.* The conflict of wills is clear. The outstretched *wings* of the divine presence in the temple sheltered Israel (Deut 32.11; Pss 17.8; 57.1; 61.4). **13.35** The *house* forsaken is an image of judgment on the temple (see Jer 22.5–6). *Blessed . . . of the Lord,* a royal greeting from Ps 118.26, actually spoken in Lk 19.38. See also 7.19.

14.1–24 A meal with lawyers and Pharisees provides the backdrop for a healing controversy and several dinner-table teachings on the kingdom. **14.1–6** The fourth conflict over sabbath observance (see also 6.1–5; 6.6–11; 13.10–17) and the third meal with a Pharisee (7.36–50; 11.37–54; see also 5.29–32; 15.1–2). **14.1** The *watching* is unfriendly (see 11.53–54; 20.20). **14.2** *Dropsy,* a condition of severe fluid retention. **14.3** *Lawyers.* See note on 7.30. *Is it lawful?* The question concerns interpretation of Jewish law (see also 6.2, 9; 13.15–16). **14.5** On the required assistance to an *ox* or donkey (see text note *d*), see Ex 23.5; Deut 22.4. **14.7–14** Traditional wisdom about taking a modest place at a feast (Prov 25.6–7) illustrates a proverb (v. 11) about being humbled or exalted. **14.7** *Parable,* here sage advice (see note on 6.39). *Places of honor.* See note on 11.43. **14.8** *Wedding banquet,* an image of the heavenly feast (cf. Mt 22.1–10; see Lk

quet, do not sit down at the place of honor, in case someone more distinguished than you has been invited by your host; [9] and the host who invited both of you may come and say to you, 'Give this person your place,' and then in disgrace you would start to take the lowest place. [10] But when you are invited, go and sit down at the lowest place, so that when your host comes, he may say to you, 'Friend, move up higher'; then you will be honored in the presence of all who sit at the table with you. [11] For all who exalt themselves will be humbled, and those who humble themselves will be exalted."

12 He said also to the one who had invited him, "When you give a luncheon or a dinner, do not invite your friends or your brothers or your relatives or rich neighbors, in case they may invite you in return, and you would be repaid. [13] But when you give a banquet, invite the poor, the crippled, the lame, and the blind. [14] And you will be blessed, because they cannot repay you, for you will be repaid at the resurrection of the righteous."

The Parable of the Great Dinner

15 One of the dinner guests, on hearing this, said to him, "Blessed is anyone who will eat bread in the kingdom of God!" [16] Then Jesus[a] said to him, "Someone gave a great dinner and invited many. [17] At the time for the dinner he sent his slave to say to those who had been invited, 'Come; for everything is ready now.' [18] But they all alike began to make excuses. The first said to him, 'I have bought a piece of land, and I must go out and see it; please accept my regrets.' [19] Another said, 'I have bought five yoke of oxen, and I am going to try them out; please accept my regrets.' [20] Another said, 'I have just been married, and therefore I cannot come.' [21] So the slave returned and reported this to his master. Then the owner of the house became angry and said to his slave, 'Go out at once into the streets and lanes of the town and bring in the poor, the crippled, the blind, and the lame.' [22] And the slave said, 'Sir, what you ordered has been done, and there is still room.' [23] Then the master said to the slave, 'Go out into the roads and lanes, and compel people to come in, so that my house may be filled. [24] For I tell you,[b] none of those who were invited will taste my dinner.' "

The Cost of Discipleship

25 Now large crowds were traveling with him; and he turned and said to them, [26] "Whoever comes to me and does not hate father and mother, wife and children, brothers and sisters, yes, and even life itself, cannot be my disciple. [27] Whoever does not carry the cross and follow me cannot be my disciple. [28] For which of you, intending to build a tower, does not first sit down and estimate the cost, to see whether he has enough to complete it? [29] Otherwise, when he has laid a foundation and is not able to finish, all who see it will begin to ridicule him, [30] saying, 'This fellow began to build and was not able to finish.' [31] Or what king, going out to wage war against another king, will not sit down first and consider whether he is able with ten thousand to oppose the one who comes against him with twenty thousand? [32] If he cannot, then, while the other is still far away, he sends a delegation and asks for the terms of peace. [33] So therefore, none of you can become my disciple if you do not give up all your possessions.

About Salt

34 "Salt is good; but if salt has lost its taste, how can its saltiness be restored?[c] [35] It is fit neither

---

a Gk he   b The Greek word for you here is plural   c Or how can it be used for seasoning?

12.36; 14.14–15; see also note on 13.29). **14.11** See 18.14. **14.13** Inviting *the poor, crippled, lame, and blind,* i.e., social outcasts, goes against the customary etiquette of reciprocity, but it conforms to the priorities of the kingdom (see 4.18; 7.22; 14.21; see also Isa 29.18–19; 35.5–6; 61.1). **14.15–24** Cf. Mt 22.1–10. A final teaching set at the Pharisee's banquet (see v. 1) conveys a pointed warning about the consequences of refusing an invitation to enter the kingdom. **14.15** *Eat bread in the kingdom.* See note on 13.29. See also 22.16, 29–30. **14.18–20** See Deut 20.5–8; 24.5. **14.21** See note on 14.13. **14.23** *Roads and lanes* would be outside the town, probably an allusion to those "outside" Israel, i.e., the Gentiles (see 2.29–32; 3.8; Deut 32.21; Acts 13.46; 18.6; 28.23–28). **14.25–35** Cf. Mt 10.37–38; 5.13; Mk 9.49–50. The decision for discipleship must be seriously examined. **14.26** *Hate,* prophetic hyperbole for the uncompromising loyalty required toward Jesus and the true family of disciples (8.19–21; 9.57–62; see also 18.28–30). **14.27** *Carry the cross.* See 9.23–24. **14.33** *Give up all your possessions.* See 12.33; 18.22; see also Acts 5.1–11. **14.34** In its Lukan context, the saying on *salt* probably refers to the need for disciples to maintain their firm loyalty (cf. Mk 9.50). **14.35** On the warning to *listen,* see note on 8.8; see also 15.1.

for the soil nor for the manure pile; they throw it away. Let anyone with ears to hear listen!"

The Parable of the Lost Sheep

15 Now all the tax collectors and sinners were coming near to listen to him. 2And the Pharisees and the scribes were grumbling and saying, "This fellow welcomes sinners and eats with them."

3 So he told them this parable: 4"Which one of you, having a hundred sheep and losing one of them, does not leave the ninety-nine in the wilderness and go after the one that is lost until he finds it? 5When he has found it, he lays it on his shoulders and rejoices. 6And when he comes home, he calls together his friends and neighbors, saying to them, 'Rejoice with me, for I have found my sheep that was lost.' 7Just so, I tell you, there will be more joy in heaven over one sinner who repents than over ninety-nine righteous persons who need no repentance.

The Parable of the Lost Coin

8 "Or what woman having ten silver coins,ᵃ if she loses one of them, does not light a lamp, sweep the house, and search carefully until she finds it? 9When she has found it, she calls together her friends and neighbors, saying, 'Rejoice with me, for I have found the coin that I had lost.' 10Just so, I tell you, there is joy in the presence of the angels of God over one sinner who repents."

The Parable of the Prodigal and His Brother

11 Then Jesusᵇ said, "There was a man who had two sons. 12The younger of them said to his father, 'Father, give me the share of the property that will belong to me.' So he divided his property between them. 13A few days later the younger son gathered all he had and traveled to a distant country, and there he squandered his property in dissolute living. 14When he had spent everything, a severe famine took place throughout that country, and he began to be in need. 15So he went and hired himself out to one of the citizens of that country, who sent him to his fields to feed the pigs. 16He would gladly have filled himself withᶜ the pods that the pigs were eating; and no one gave him anything. 17But when he came to himself he said, 'How many of my father's hired hands have bread enough and to spare, but here I am dying of hunger! 18I will get up and go to my father, and I will say to him, "Father, I have sinned against heaven and before you; 19I am no longer worthy to be called your son; treat me like one of your hired hands."' 20So he set off and went to his father. But while he was still far off, his father saw him and was filled with compassion; he ran and put his arms around him and kissed him. 21Then the son said to him, 'Father, I have sinned against heaven and before you; I am no longer worthy to be called your son.'ᵈ 22But the father said to his slaves, 'Quickly, bring out a robe—the best one—and put it on him; put a ring on his finger and sandals on his feet. 23And get the fatted calf and kill it, and let us eat and celebrate; 24for this son of mine was dead and is alive

---

a Gk *drachmas*, each worth about a day's wage for a laborer
b Gk *he*   *c* Other ancient authorities read *filled his stomach with*
d Other ancient authorities add *Treat me like one of your hired servants*

15.1–32 Three parables on the lost and found. Only the first has a parallel in Matthew (see note on 15.3–7). **15.1–2** The audience for the parables and a definition of the "lost." **15.1** *Tax collectors and sinners.* See note on 5.30; see also 7.29–30. **15.2** On the Pharisees' *grumbling* about Jesus' meal fellowship, see 5.30; 7.39; 19.7; see also note on 15.25–30. **15.3–7** Cf. Mt 18.12–14. This parable featuring a well-off man closely parallels the next about a poor woman (vv. 8–10; see note on 2.38). **15.4** On concern for the *lost*, see vv. 6, 9, 24, 32; 19.10; see also Ezek 34.11–16; Jn 10.11–16. **15.6** The party with *friends and neighbors* is extravagant (*see also vv. 9, 22–24*). **15.7** *Joy in heaven.* See also vv. 10, 32. In Luke, *repentance* is not only an obligation (see 3.3, 8–9; 13.3, 5; see also Acts 2.38; 3.19; 8.22; 17.30; 26.20) but a gift or opportunity (5.31–32; 16.30; see also Acts 5.31; 11.18). **15.8–10** The second of the paired parables focuses on the intensity of the search. **15.11–32** Only Luke tells this story of the lost son and the loving father. **15.12** Traditional wisdom counseled against giving an inheritance before one's death (Sir 33.20–24). **15.13** *Dissolute living* is not defined except by the elder brother (v. 30). **15.15–16** It would be shameful for a Jewish boy to feed *pigs* and eat their food (see note on 8.32). **15.17–19** The younger son's sober speech to himself (see note on 12.17) begins his return, or repentance. **15.18** *Against heaven*, i.e., against God (see, e.g., Dan 4.26; cf. Ex 10.16). **15.19** The concept of being *worthy* is generally tied to observance of the law (see note on 7.4–5). **15.20** On the father's response of *compassion*, see 7.13; see also Jer 30.18; Hos 11.1–9. The father runs, contrary to the social expectations of the audience. **15.22** The father interrupts his son before he can present his proposal to work as a servant (see vv. 18–19). The festive clothes display the extravagance of the celebration (see Gen

again; he was lost and is found!' And they began to celebrate.

25 "Now his elder son was in the field; and when he came and approached the house, he heard music and dancing. 26 He called one of the slaves and asked what was going on. 27 He replied, 'Your brother has come, and your father has killed the fatted calf, because he has got him back safe and sound.' 28 Then he became angry and refused to go in. His father came out and began to plead with him. 29 But he answered his father, 'Listen! For all these years I have been working like a slave for you, and I have never disobeyed your command; yet you have never given me even a young goat so that I might celebrate with my friends. 30 But when this son of yours came back, who has devoured your property with prostitutes, you killed the fatted calf for him!' 31 Then the father *a* said to him, 'Son, you are always with me, and all that is mine is yours. 32 But we had to celebrate and rejoice, because this brother of yours was dead and has come to life; he was lost and has been found.' "

The Parable of the Dishonest Manager

16 Then Jesus *a* said to the disciples, "There was a rich man who had a manager, and charges were brought to him that this man was squandering his property. 2 So he summoned him and said to him, 'What is this that I hear about you? Give me an accounting of your management, because you cannot be my manager any longer.' 3 Then the manager said to himself, 'What will I do, now that my master is taking the position away from me? I am not strong enough to dig, and I am ashamed to beg. 4 I have decided what to do so that, when I am dismissed as manager, people may welcome me into their homes.' 5 So, summoning his master's debtors one by one, he asked the first, 'How much do you owe my master?' 6 He answered, 'A hundred jugs of olive oil.' He said to him, 'Take your bill, sit down quickly, and make it fifty.' 7 Then he asked another, 'And how much do you owe?' He replied, 'A hundred containers of wheat.' He said to him, 'Take your bill and make it eighty.' 8 And his master commended the dishonest manager because he had acted shrewdly; for the children of this age are more shrewd in dealing with their own generation than are the children of light. 9 And I tell you, make friends for yourselves by means of dishonest wealth *b* so that when it is gone, they may welcome you into the eternal homes. *c*

10 "Whoever is faithful in a very little is faithful also in much; and whoever is dishonest in a very little is dishonest also in much. 11 If then you have not been faithful with the dishonest wealth, *b* who will entrust to you the true riches? 12 And if you have not been faithful with what belongs to another, who will give you what is your own? 13 No slave can serve two masters; for a slave will either hate the one and love the other, or be devoted to the one

a Gk *he*   *b* Gk *mammon*   *c* Gk *tents*

41.42). **15.23** Meat was not often eaten, so killing the *fatted calf* was a sign of special celebration. **15.24** *Was dead.* See 9.60. *Lost . . . found.* See vv. 6, 9, 32. **15.25–30** The portrayal of the *elder son* and his resentment may be a subtle criticism of the grumbling Pharisees and scribes (vv. 1–2). **15.30** *This son of yours.* The elder son distances himself from both his brother and his father (cf. v. 32, *this brother of yours*). **15.31** The inheritance rights of the elder son are protected. **15.32** *We had to celebrate,* the obligation or necessity of mercy (see note on 2.49).

16.1–31 Jesus warns of the dangers of wealth. **16.1–13** Cf. Mt 6.24. An enigmatic parable is given several applications. **16.1** The audience is again the *disciples* (cf. 15.1–2). *Rich man,* probably an absentee landowner. *Manager.* See note on 12.42–43. *Squandering* could be merely inept management (see 15.13), but later the manager is called *dishonest* (vv. 8; see also vv. 9, 11). **16.2** *An accounting,* probably an inventory of possessions and transactions in anticipation of a new manager. **16.3** *Said to himself.* See note on 12.17. **16.5–7** The dishonest man uses his last opportunity as man-ager to obligate his *master's debtors* to himself (see also 7.41–43). The instructions to *make it fifty . . . make it eighty* eliminate the manager's personal commission from the debt. **16.8** *Commended.* The commendation is not for the manager's dishonesty but his prudent elimination of the commission, which showed his cleverness in dealing with an urgent situation. *Shrewd* (Greek *phronimos*), or "prudent" (see 12.42). *Children of light,* a term used in the NT for Christian disciples (see Jn 12.36; Eph 5.8; 1 Thess 5.5). **16.9** A second conclusion to the parable urging proper use of possessions, termed *dishonest wealth* (lit. "the mammon of wickedness") because of their corrupting influence (see 6.24; 16.25; 18.25). *Eternal homes* may be connected to the "treasure in heaven" that results from almsgiving (see notes on 11.41; 12.33). **16.10–12** A separate application focuses on the issue of responsible behavior. **16.11** On the value of the *true riches,* see also 12.33–34. **16.12** *What belongs to another, what is your own,* perhaps contrasting worldly goods with the disciples' true possession, the kingdom of God (see 6.20; 14.33). **16.13** A final, general application of the

and despise the other. You cannot serve God and wealth." [a]

The Law and the Kingdom of God

14 The Pharisees, who were lovers of money, heard all this, and they ridiculed him. 15So he said to them, "You are those who justify yourselves in the sight of others; but God knows your hearts; for what is prized by human beings is an abomination in the sight of God.

16 "The law and the prophets were in effect until John came; since then the good news of the kingdom of God is proclaimed, and everyone tries to enter it by force. [b] 17But it is easier for heaven and earth to pass away, than for one stroke of a letter in the law to be dropped.

18 "Anyone who divorces his wife and marries another commits adultery, and whoever marries a woman divorced from her husband commits adultery.

The Rich Man and Lazarus

19 "There was a rich man who was dressed in purple and fine linen and who feasted sumptuously every day. 20And at his gate lay a poor man named Lazarus, covered with sores, 21who longed to satisfy his hunger with what fell from the rich man's table; even the dogs would come and lick his sores. 22The poor man died and was carried away by the angels to be with Abraham. [c] The rich man also died and was buried. 23In Hades, where he was being tormented, he looked up and saw Abraham far away with Lazarus by his side. [d] 24He called out, 'Father Abraham, have mercy on me, and send Lazarus to dip the tip of his finger in water and cool my tongue; for I am in agony in these flames.' 25But Abraham said, 'Child, remember that during your lifetime you received your good things, and Lazarus in like manner evil things; but now he is comforted here, and you are in agony. 26Besides all this, between you and us a great chasm has been fixed, so that those who might want to pass from here to you cannot do so, and no one can cross from there to us.' 27He said, 'Then, father, I beg you to send him to my father's house— 28for I have five brothers—that he may warn them, so that they will not also come into this place of torment.' 29Abraham replied, 'They have Moses and the prophets; they should listen to them.' 30He said, 'No, father Abraham; but if someone goes to them from the dead, they will repent.' 31He said to him, 'If they do not listen to Moses and the prophets, neither will they be convinced even if someone rises from the dead.' "

Some Sayings of Jesus

17 Jesus [e] said to his disciples, "Occasions for stumbling are bound to come, but woe to anyone by whom they come! 2It would be better for you if a millstone were hung

---

[a] Gk mammon   [b] Or everyone is strongly urged to enter it
[c] Gk to Abraham's bosom   [d] Gk in his bosom   [e] Gk He

---

parable. *Serve.* The issue is not greed but idolatry (Ex 20.3; Deut 5.7; 6.13). **16.14–18** Cf. Mt 11.12–13; 5.18; 19.9; Mk 10.11–12. The Pharisees reemerge as the audience. **16.14** Luke accuses the Pharisees of being *lovers of money.* Grumbling (15.2) turns to ridicule. **16.15** *Justify yourselves.* See 10.29; cf. 18.14. *God knows your hearts.* See Prov 21.2; 24.12; Acts 1.24; 15.8. *What is prized by human beings,* here idolatrous love of money. *Abomination.* See Deut 7.25. **16.16** In Luke, John the Baptist stands at the apex of the age of *the law and the prophets* (see note on 7.28). The time of the proclamation of *the kingdom of God* is a new regime (4.43; 8.1; 9.2; 10.9; Acts 8.12). *Everyone tries to enter it by force.* This difficult phrase should probably be translated with emphasis on the passive force of the verb: "And everyone is constrained [Greek *biazesthai,* 'forced, compelled,' i.e., by God] to enter" (see text note *b; see also* 14.23). **16.18** Luke's version of this isolated statement presupposes Jewish customs that grant only the husband the right of divorce (see Deut 24.1–4; cf. Mk 10.11–12; 1 Cor 7.10–13). **16.19–31** The parable of the reversal of the states of the rich man and poor Lazarus recalls Jesus' statements in 6.20–25; see

also 1.53. It illustrates the failure to make prudent use of *dishonest wealth* (see note on 16.9; see also vv. 10–13). **16.19** The rich man *feasted sumptuously,* just as the rich fool in 12.19 "made merry" (Greek *euphrainein* in both cases). **16.21** *Dogs,* a sign of Lazarus's outcast status (see 1 Kings 21.19, 24; Ps 22.16; Mt 15.26–27; Mk 7.27–28). **16.22** On the honored place with *Abraham,* see 3.8; 13.28–29; see also Gen 15.15; 47.30; Deut 31.16. **16.23** *Hades.* See note on 10.15. **16.24** *Father Abraham.* See 3.8. *Have mercy.* See 17.13; 18.38–39. The rich man knows *Lazarus*'s name, revealing that his previous disregard was conscious. **16.27** *Send him,* i.e., in a dream or vision. **16.28** *Warn,* lit. "bear witness." See also Acts 2.40. **16.29** *Moses and the prophets* are sufficient to understand God's purpose (see 24.26–27, 44–48; see also 16.16). **16.31** *Even if someone rises from the dead,* an obvious allusion to Jesus' resurrection. See 9.22; Acts 1.22. **17.1–10** Cf. Mt 18.6–7, 21–22; Mk 9.42. Diverse sayings to the disciples. **17.1** *Occasions for stumbling,* i.e., apostasy (see 7.23; 8.13). *Woe.* Inevitability and divine necessity do not eliminate personal responsibility (see also 22.22). **17.2** *These little ones,* probably the disciples (see 10.21;

around your neck and you were thrown into the sea than for you to cause one of these little ones to stumble. ³Be on your guard! If another disciple*ª* sins, you must rebuke the offender, and if there is repentance, you must forgive. ⁴And if the same person sins against you seven times a day, and turns back to you seven times and says, 'I repent,' you must forgive."

5 The apostles said to the Lord, "Increase our faith!" ⁶The Lord replied, "If you had faith the size of a*ᵇ* mustard seed, you could say to this mulberry tree, 'Be uprooted and planted in the sea,' and it would obey you.

7 "Who among you would say to your slave who has just come in from plowing or tending sheep in the field, 'Come here at once and take your place at the table'? ⁸Would you not rather say to him, 'Prepare supper for me, put on your apron and serve me while I eat and drink; later you may eat and drink'? ⁹Do you thank the slave for doing what was commanded? ¹⁰So you also, when you have done all that you were ordered to do, say, 'We are worthless slaves; we have done only what we ought to have done.' "

Jesus Cleanses Ten Lepers

11 On the way to Jerusalem Jesus*ᶜ* was going through the region between Samaria and Galilee. ¹²As he entered a village, ten lepers*ᵈ* approached him. Keeping their distance, ¹³they called out, saying, "Jesus, Master, have mercy on us!" ¹⁴When he saw them, he said to them, "Go and show yourselves to the priests." And as they went, they were made clean. ¹⁵Then one of them, when he saw that he was healed, turned back, praising God with a loud voice.

¹⁶He prostrated himself at Jesus'*ᵉ* feet and thanked him. And he was a Samaritan. ¹⁷Then Jesus asked, "Were not ten made clean? But the other nine, where are they? ¹⁸Was none of them found to return and give praise to God except this foreigner?" ¹⁹Then he said to him, "Get up and go on your way; your faith has made you well."

The Coming of the Kingdom

20 Once Jesus*ᶜ* was asked by the Pharisees when the kingdom of God was coming, and he answered, "The kingdom of God is not coming with things that can be observed; ²¹nor will they say, 'Look, here it is!' or 'There it is!' For, in fact, the kingdom of God is among*ᶠ* you."

22 Then he said to the disciples, "The days are coming when you will long to see one of the days of the Son of Man, and you will not see it. ²³They will say to you, 'Look there!' or 'Look here!' Do not go, do not set off in pursuit. ²⁴For as the lightning flashes and lights up the sky from one side to the other, so will the Son of Man be in his day.*ᵍ* ²⁵But first he must endure much suffering and be rejected by this generation. ²⁶Just as it was in the days of Noah, so too it will be in the days of the Son of Man. ²⁷They were eating and drinking, and marrying and being given in marriage, until the day Noah entered the ark, and the flood came and destroyed all of them. ²⁸Likewise, just as it was in the days of Lot: they were eating and drinking, buying and selling, planting

---

a Gk *your brother*   *b* Gk *faith as a grain of*   *c* Gk *he*
d The terms *leper* and *leprosy* can refer to several diseases
e Gk *his*   *f* Or *within*   *g* Other ancient authorities lack *in his day*

12.32). **17.4** *Seven times a day,* i.e., continually. **17.5** *Apostles,* the twelve closest delegates (see 6.13). **17.10** *Worthless slaves,* those to whom nothing is owed. Cf. 12.37; 22.25–27.

17.11–19.27 The final stages of the journey to Jerusalem (see note on 9.51). **17.11–19** The healing of the ten lepers contains echoes of the healing in 5.12–14. See also 4.27. **17.11** Luke's reference to *the region between Samaria and Galilee* moves the journey along but the intended location is not at all clear. **17.12** *Keeping their distance,* as Jewish law required (see Lev 13.46; Num 5.2–3). **17.14** *Show yourselves to the priests,* i.e., for examination (see Lev 13.2–8; 14.2–3). **17.16** *A Samaritan.* See note on 9.52. See also 10.30–37. **17.18** *This foreigner.* See 7.9. **17.19** *Your faith has made you well.* See also 7.50; 8.48; 18.42. **17.20–37** The advent of the kingdom and the coming of the Son of Man are treated here and again in 21.7–36. **17.20** As in

Acts 1.6–7, the question of *when the kingdom of God was coming* is misguided and seeks signs (cf. 21.7). **17.21–22** Like the word of God in Deut 30.11–14, the kingdom is already present as it is announced *among you* (see note on 4.43; see also 6.20; 8.1; 9.2; 10.9, 11; 11.20; 12.32; 16.16). *The days of the Son of Man,* however, await the full revelation of the last judgment (17.30; see also Dan 7.9–14). **17.24** *As the lightning flashes.* The return of the Son of Man will be a sudden, highly visible appearance. See Acts 1.11. **17.25** See also 9.22; 24.26. *First* may imply a heavenly timetable that gives opportunity for repentance (see Acts 3.17–26). *This generation.* See note on 7.31. **17.26** *The days of Noah.* See Gen 6.5–8, 11. **17.27** *Eating . . . being given in marriage,* i.e., engaging in ordinary activities until the unexpected flood destroyed them (see Gen 7.21–23). **17.28** *The days of Lot.* See Gen 13.13; 19.15. *Eating . . . building.* The list depicts ordinary activities, not the

and building, 29but on the day that Lot left Sodom, it rained fire and sulfur from heaven and destroyed all of them 30—it will be like that on the day that the Son of Man is revealed. 31On that day, anyone on the housetop who has belongings in the house must not come down to take them away; and likewise anyone in the field must not turn back. 32Remember Lot's wife. 33Those who try to make their life secure will lose it, but those who lose their life will keep it. 34I tell you, on that night there will be two in one bed; one will be taken and the other left. 35There will be two women grinding meal together; one will be taken and the other left."a 37Then they asked him, "Where, Lord?" He said to them, "Where the corpse is, there the vultures will gather."

The Parable of the Widow and the Unjust Judge

18 Then Jesusb told them a parable about their need to pray always and not to lose heart. 2He said, "In a certain city there was a judge who neither feared God nor had respect for people. 3In that city there was a widow who kept coming to him and saying, 'Grant me justice against my opponent.' 4For a while he refused; but later he said to himself, 'Though I have no fear of God and no respect for anyone, 5yet because this widow keeps bothering me, I will grant her justice, so that she may not wear me out by continually coming.' "c 6And the Lord said, "Listen to what the unjust judge says. 7And will not God grant justice to his chosen ones who cry to him day and night? Will he delay long in helping them? 8I tell you, he will quickly grant justice to them. And yet, when the Son of Man comes, will he find faith on earth?"

The Parable of the Pharisee and the Tax Collector

9 He also told this parable to some who trusted in themselves that they were righteous and regarded others with contempt: 10"Two men went up to the temple to pray, one a Pharisee and the other a tax collector. 11The Pharisee, standing by himself, was praying thus, 'God, I thank you that I am not like other people: thieves, rogues, adulterers, or even like this tax collector. 12I fast twice a week; I give a tenth of all my income.' 13But the tax collector, standing far off, would not even look up to heaven, but was beating his breast and saying, 'God, be merciful to me, a sinner!' 14I tell you, this man went down to his home justified rather than the other; for all who exalt themselves will be humbled, but all who humble themselves will be exalted."

Jesus Blesses Little Children

15 People were bringing even infants to him that he might touch them; and when the disci-

---

a Other ancient authorities add verse 36, "Two will be in the field; one will be taken and the other left." *b* Gk he *c* Or so that she may not finally come and slap me in the face

---

corruption usually associated with Sodom (cf. Ezek 16.49–50). **17.29** *Fire . . . from heaven.* See Gen 19.24. See also Lk 9.54; 10.12. **17.32** The fate of *Lot's wife,* who looked back to view the destruction of Sodom (see Gen 19.26), serves as a warning not to *turn back* (v. 31). **17.33** See also 9.24; Mt 10.39; 16.25; Mk 8.35; Jn 12.25. **17.34** On the swift and unexpected judgment *on that night,* see also 12.38–40, 46; Mt 24.43–51. *Taken* (also v. 35), seemingly to safety. **17.37** This seems to say that to find those left one must look for the circling *vultures* (Prov 30.17; Hos 8.1).

18.1–8 This parable provides instruction on how to persevere until the eschaton. **18.1** *Not to lose heart.* On endurance in prayer, see 11.5–13. **18.2** One who has not *feared God* would lack the wisdom to judge equitably (see Prov 1.7; see also Acts 10.2, 22, 35; 13.16, 26). **18.3** A *widow* had a particular claim for justice in Israel (*Deut* 10.17–18; 24.17; 27.19; Sir 35.14–15; see also Lk 2.37; 4.25–26; 7.12; 20.47; 21.2–3; Acts 6.1; 9.39, 41). **18.5** See 11.8. *Wear me out,* lit. "hit under the eye," an image from boxing (see 1 Cor 9.27). **18.6** *Listen.* It is not the judge's indifference (v. 4) but his eventual yielding to the widow's complaint (v. 5) that is the point of the parable. **18.7** On God's granting *justice,* or vindication, see Deut 32.36; Ps 34.17–18. *Chosen ones.* See Ps 105.6, 43; Isa 43.20; 65.9, 22; see also Lk 9.35; 23.35. The questions suggest an awareness of a *delay* in the expected vindication (see also 12.38; Mt 24.48; 25.5, 19). **18.8b** The last half of the verse provides a second conclusion (see note on 16.9). *Will he find faith on earth?* Cf. 5.20; 7.9; 22.32. **18.9–14** The Pharisee and tax collector are stock examples of how contempt for others is the regular corollary of self-righteousness (see 5.29–32; 7.29–30; 15.1–2; see also 10.29; 16.15). **18.10** *Pharisee.* See note on 5.17. *Tax collector.* See note on 5.30. **18.11** *Praying,* lit. "praying to himself." See also 12.17–19. **18.12** *Fast.* See note on 5.33. On the *tenth,* or tithe, see note on 11.42. **18.13** *Beating his breast,* a sign of repentance (see 23.48). The plea for God to be *merciful* is a prayer for pardon (see Pss 25.11; 51.1; 65.3; see also Lk 6.36). **18.14** *Justified,* i.e., declared righteous by God. See 14.11. **18.15–17** Cf. Mt 19.13–15; Mk 10.13–16. The parallels with Mark's Gospel, broken off at 9.51, now resume. **18.15** *Sternly ordered,* lit. "rebuked." Cf. 9.55. The disciples have not learned from the incident with the children in 9.46–

ples saw it, they sternly ordered them not to do it. ¹⁶But Jesus called for them and said, "Let the little children come to me, and do not stop them; for it is to such as these that the kingdom of God belongs. ¹⁷Truly I tell you, whoever does not receive the kingdom of God as a little child will never enter it."

The Rich Ruler

18 A certain ruler asked him, "Good Teacher, what must I do to inherit eternal life?" ¹⁹Jesus said to him, "Why do you call me good? No one is good but God alone. ²⁰You know the commandments: 'You shall not commit adultery; You shall not murder; You shall not steal; You shall not bear false witness; Honor your father and mother.' " ²¹He replied, "I have kept all these since my youth." ²²When Jesus heard this, he said to him, "There is still one thing lacking. Sell all that you own and distribute the money*a* to the poor, and you will have treasure in heaven; then come, follow me." ²³But when he heard this, he became sad; for he was very rich. ²⁴Jesus looked at him and said, "How hard it is for those who have wealth to enter the kingdom of God! ²⁵Indeed, it is easier for a camel to go through the eye of a needle than for someone who is rich to enter the kingdom of God."

26 Those who heard it said, "Then who can be saved?" ²⁷He replied, "What is impossible for mortals is possible for God."

28 Then Peter said, "Look, we have left our homes and followed you." ²⁹And he said to

them, "Truly I tell you, there is no one who has left house or wife or brothers or parents or children, for the sake of the kingdom of God, ³⁰who will not get back very much more in this age, and in the age to come eternal life."

A Third Time Jesus Foretells His Death and Resurrection

31 Then he took the twelve aside and said to them, "See, we are going up to Jerusalem, and everything that is written about the Son of Man by the prophets will be accomplished. ³²For he will be handed over to the Gentiles; and he will be mocked and insulted and spat upon. ³³After they have flogged him, they will kill him, and on the third day he will rise again." ³⁴But they understood nothing about all these things; in fact, what he said was hidden from them, and they did not grasp what was said.

Jesus Heals a Blind Beggar Near Jericho

35 As he approached Jericho, a blind man was sitting by the roadside begging. ³⁶When he heard a crowd going by, he asked what was happening. ³⁷They told him, "Jesus of Nazareth*b* is passing by." ³⁸Then he shouted, "Jesus, Son of David, have mercy on me!" ³⁹Those who were in front sternly ordered him to be quiet; but he shouted even more loudly, "Son of David, have mercy on me!" ⁴⁰Jesus stood still and ordered the man to be brought to him; and when he came near, he asked him,

---

a Gk lacks *the money*   *b* Gk *the Nazorean*

---

48. **18.17** The qualities of openness, low status, and no claim to achievement characterize the *little child.* **18.18–30** Cf. Mt 19.16–30; Mk 10.17–31. An encounter with a rich ruler continues the teaching on how to inherit eternal life. **18.18** The ruler's question is the same as the lawyer's in 10.25. On Jesus as a *Teacher,* or interpreter of the law, see 7.40; 8.49; 9.38; 10.25; 11.45; 12.13; 19.39; 20.21, 28, 39; 21.7; 22.11. **18.19** *No one is good but God alone.* Jesus redirects attention away from himself and toward God's goodness (1 Chr 16.34; Pss 34.8; 106.1; 118.1, 29; see also Lk 11.13). **18.20** For the list of *commandments,* see Ex 20.12–16; Deut 5.16–20 (cf. Lk 10.27). **18.22** Discipleship to this teacher is not simply better observance of the law; the *one thing lacking* requires giving up *all* one's possessions (see also 14.33). On care for the *poor,* see note on 6.20. *Treasure in heaven.* See 12.33; note on 16.9. **18.24** See note on 16.9. See also 6.24; 16.10–13. **18.25** *A camel ... through the eye of a needle,* an image of extreme difficulty (see also 6.41–42). **18.26** *Who can be saved?* Cf. 13.23. **18.27** All is *possible for God* (see also 1.37; Gen 18.14);

thus even a rich person can enter the kingdom (see 19.1–10). **18.28** See 5.11. See note on 12.41. **18.29–30** A restatement of the assurances of 12.22–34. **18.31–34** Cf. Mt 20.17–19; Mk 10.32–34. The sixth prediction of the Passion (9.22, 44; 12.50; 13.32–34; 17.25). **18.31** Jesus' death is warranted as *written . . . by the prophets,* but without a clear reference to a particular prophetic text (see also 24.27, 44–46; Acts 3.18; 13.27; cf. Acts 4.25–28 [based on Ps 2.1–2]; 8.32–33 [based on Isa 53.7–8]). **18.32** *Handed over to the Gentiles.* See Acts 4.25–28; cf. Mt 20.18–19; Mk 10.33–34. *Mocked and insulted.* See 22.63; 23.11, 36. **18.34** The threefold emphasis on the disciples' ignorance echoes 9.45 (see also 2.50; 24.16). **18.35–43** Cf. Mt 20.29–34; 9.27–31; Mk 10.46–52. Jesus is announced as the Son of David before his royal entrance into Jerusalem (19.29–40). **18.35** Luke sets this story at Jesus' entrance to *Jericho* (see 19.1; see also 10.30), a city northeast of Jerusalem in the Jordan Valley (cf. Mk 10.46). The unnamed *blind man* perceives the Davidic ruler that others in the entourage do not recognize. **18.38** *Son of David.* See also

41"What do you want me to do for you?" He said, "Lord, let me see again." 42Jesus said to him, "Receive your sight; your faith has saved you." 43Immediately he regained his sight and followed him, glorifying God; and all the people, when they saw it, praised God.

Jesus and Zacchaeus

19 He entered Jericho and was passing through it. 2A man was there named Zacchaeus; he was a chief tax collector and was rich. 3He was trying to see who Jesus was, but on account of the crowd he could not, because he was short in stature. 4So he ran ahead and climbed a sycamore tree to see him, because he was going to pass that way. 5When Jesus came to the place, he looked up and said to him, "Zacchaeus, hurry and come down; for I must stay at your house today." 6So he hurried down and was happy to welcome him. 7All who saw it began to grumble and said, "He has gone to be the guest of one who is a sinner." 8Zacchaeus stood there and said to the Lord, "Look, half of my possessions, Lord, I will give to the poor; and if I have defrauded anyone of anything, I will pay back four times as much." 9Then Jesus said to him, "Today salvation has come to this house, because he too is a son of Abraham. 10For the Son of Man came to seek out and to save the lost."

The Parable of the Ten Pounds

11 As they were listening to this, he went on to tell a parable, because he was near Jerusalem, and because they supposed that the kingdom of God was to appear immediately. 12So he said, "A nobleman went to a distant country to get royal power for himself and then return. 13He summoned ten of his slaves, and gave them ten pounds,ᵃ and said to them, 'Do business with these until I come back.' 14But the citizens of his country hated him and sent a delegation after him, saying, 'We do not want this man to rule over us.' 15When he returned, having received royal power, he ordered these slaves, to whom he had given the money, to be summoned so that he might find out what they had gained by trading. 16The first came forward and said, 'Lord, your pound has made ten more pounds.' 17He said to him, 'Well done, good slave! Because you have been trustworthy in a very small thing, take charge of ten cities.' 18Then the second came, saying, 'Lord, your pound has made five pounds.' 19He said to him, 'And you, rule over five cities.' 20Then the other came, saying, 'Lord, here is your pound. I wrapped it up in a piece of cloth, 21for I was afraid of you, because you are a harsh man; you take what you did not deposit, and reap what you did not sow.' 22He said to him, 'I will judge you by your own words, you wicked slave! You knew, did you, that I was a harsh man, taking what I did not deposit and reaping what I did not sow? 23Why then did you not put my money into

---

a The mina, rendered here by *pound*, was about three months' wages for a laborer

---

1.27, 32, 69; 2.4, 11; 3.31; 20.41–44. **18.42** The command *receive your sight* recalls the reading in 4.18 (see also 7.21–22; Acts 9.17–18). *Your faith has saved you.* See 7.50; 8.48; 17.19; cf. 5.20. **18.43** *All the people . . . praised God.* See 5.26; 7.16; 13.17; see also 8.39; 17.15. **19.1–10** The story of Zacchaeus illustrates earlier statements about tax collectors (5.29–32), the rich (18.25–27), and the lost (ch. 15). **19.2** *Zacchaeus,* the Greek rendering of a common Hebrew name (Ezra 2.9; Neh 7.14; 2 Macc 10.19) meaning "innocent" or "clean." *A chief tax collector* played a role in the Roman bureaucracy that many Jews regarded as traitorous to their law (see 20.22; see also note on 5.30). **19.5** *I must stay at your house.* The comment implies divine necessity (see note on 2.49). *Today.* See note on 19.9. *19.7 The crowd's reaction recalls those in 5.30; 7.34, 39; 15.2. **19.8** Zacchaeus's promise to give *half* to the poor is voluntary (cf. 18.18–25). *Pay back four times as much,* fulfilling the strictest law of restitution (see Ex 22.1). *If I have defrauded.* See 3.14. Some scholars understand Zacchaeus's words to be a statement of his customary procedure (i.e., a defense) and not a sign of conversion, since the Greek verb behind *I will give* is in the present tense, lit. "I am giving." **19.9** *Today* (see 2.11; 4.21; 23.43; Deut 26.16–19) stresses the present reality of salvation (see note on 4.43). *Son of Abraham,* i.e., an Israelite (see also 3.8; 13.16; cf. Gal 3.29). **19.10** *To save the lost.* See note on 15.4. **19.11–27** Cf. Mt 25.14–30; Mk 13.34. This parable concludes the extended journey to Jerusalem (9.51–19.27) and again corrects misunderstandings about the present reality and future appearance of the kingdom of God (see 17.20–37; 21.7–36; Acts 1.6–7). **19.12** *To get royal power,* i.e., to acquire the status of a vassal king from an overlord (see note on 3.1). This allegorical detail alludes to Jesus' own imminent departure and exaltation (24.26; Acts 2.32–36). **19.13** The *pounds,* or "minas" (see text note *a*), are distributed equally (cf. Mt 25.15). Each was worth 100 drachmas (see 15.8, text note *a*). **19.14** Another allegorical detail seems to refer to Jesus' rejection (see 23.18). **19.17** *Take charge of ten cities.* The rewards are dispensed in direct proportion to performance.

the bank? Then when I returned, I could have collected it with interest.' 24He said to the by-standers, 'Take the pound from him and give it to the one who has ten pounds.' 25(And they said to him, 'Lord, he has ten pounds!') 26'I tell you, to all those who have, more will be given; but from those who have nothing, even what they have will be taken away. 27But as for these enemies of mine who did not want me to be king over them—bring them here and slaughter them in my presence.' "

Jesus' Triumphal Entry into Jerusalem

28 After he had said this, he went on ahead, going up to Jerusalem.

29 When he had come near Bethphage and Bethany, at the place called the Mount of Olives, he sent two of the disciples, 30saying, "Go into the village ahead of you, and as you enter it you will find tied there a colt that has never been ridden. Untie it and bring it here. 31If anyone asks you, 'Why are you untying it?' just say this, 'The Lord needs it.' " 32So those who were sent departed and found it as he had told them. 33As they were untying the colt, its owners asked them, "Why are you untying the colt?" 34They said, "The Lord needs it." 35Then they brought it to Jesus; and after throwing their cloaks on the colt, they set Jesus on it. 36As he rode along, people kept spreading their cloaks on the road. 37As he was now approaching the path down from the Mount of Olives, the whole multitude of the disciples began to praise God joyfully with a loud voice for all the deeds of power that they had seen, 38saying,

"Blessed is the king
    who comes in the name of the Lord!
Peace in heaven,
    and glory in the highest heaven!"

39Some of the Pharisees in the crowd said to him, "Teacher, order your disciples to stop." 40He answered, "I tell you, if these were silent, the stones would shout out."

Jesus Weeps over Jerusalem

41 As he came near and saw the city, he wept over it, 42saying, "If you, even you, had only recognized on this day the things that make for peace! But now they are hidden from your eyes. 43Indeed, the days will come upon you, when your enemies will set up ramparts around you and surround you, and hem you in on every side. 44They will crush you to the ground, you and your children within you, and they will not leave within you one stone upon another; because you did not recognize the time of your visitation from God."a

Jesus Cleanses the Temple

45 Then he entered the temple and began to drive out those who were selling things there; 46and he said, "It is written,

'My house shall be a house of prayer';
    but you have made it a den of robbers."

---

a Gk lacks from God

19.26 See also 8.18; Mt 13.12; 25.29; Mk 4.25. **19.27** The conclusion of the story portrays with harsh realism how oriental kings could treat their enemies (v. 14; see also 20.9–16). The detail may allude to the destruction of Jerusalem (see 21.20–24). **19.28–40** Cf. Mt 21.1–9; Mk 11.1–10; Jn 12.12–19. The journey that began in 9.51 now reaches its climax in Jerusalem. **19.28** *Going up.* See note on 10.30. **19.29** *Bethphage and Bethany* are villages about two miles from Jerusalem, on the lower slope of the *Mount of Olives* (see also 24.50; Mt 21.1; 26.6; Mk 11.1; 14.3; Jn 11.1, 18; 12.1). The Mount of Olives is just east of Jerusalem; God was expected to appear there on the "day of the LORD" and become "king over all the earth" (see Zech 14.4–9). The two *disciples* are advance agents preparing for a royal entrance (see also 9.52; 10.1). **19.30** The unridden *colt* marks a direct enactment of Zech 9.9 (see Mt 21.4–5; see also 1 Kings 1.33–35). **19.34** *The Lord needs it.* The colt is requisitioned as a royal prerogative. **19.36** Luke does not mention festal branches (cf. Mt 21.8; Mk 11.8; Jn 12.13), but *spreading their cloaks* has royal significance (cf. 2 Kings 9.13). **19.37** The *multitude of the disciples* again stresses Jesus' large following (see also 18.15, 36, 43; 19.3).

19.38 *Blessed . . . in the name of the Lord,* the usual greeting (from Ps 118.26) for Passover pilgrims (but with the word *king* added); and it also fulfills Jesus' royal prediction of 13.35. *Peace in heaven.* Cf. 2.14; 10.5–6; 12.51; 19.42. **19.39** The caution of *some of the Pharisees* recalls 13.31. This is the last appearance of the Pharisees in the Gospel. In Acts they almost serve as allies to the Christian cause (see Acts 5.33–42; 23.6–9). **19.40** Jesus' response (lit. "the stones will cry out") is prophetic (cf. Hab 2.11). **19.41–44** Jesus' lament over Jerusalem (see 13.34–35) is filled with allusions to oracles of destruction (2 Kings 8.11–12; Ps 137.9; Isa 29.3–10; 48.18; Jer 6.6–20; 8.18–21; 15.5; 23.38–40). **19.43** *Ramparts* implies siege warfare such as Titus used against Jerusalem in 70 CE, but also cf. Isa 29.3 (see also Introduction). **19.44** *Not . . . one stone upon another.* See also v. 40; 21.6. The fault lies in the failure to recognize Jesus as God's *visitation,* intended to save (1.68; 7.16) but now become judgment (Isa 29.6). **19.45–48** Cf. Mt 21.12–13; Mk 11.15–17; Jn 2.13–17. In a double visitation to the temple (see Mal 3.1–2), the Messiah drives merchants from it. **19.46** Restoring the temple as a *house of prayer* has prophetic precedent (Isa 56.7). *Den of robbers.* See

47 Every day he was teaching in the temple. The chief priests, the scribes, and the leaders of the people kept looking for a way to kill him; 48but they did not find anything they could do, for all the people were spellbound by what they heard.

The Authority of Jesus Questioned

20 One day, as he was teaching the people in the temple and telling the good news, the chief priests and the scribes came with the elders 2and said to him, "Tell us, by what authority are you doing these things? Who is it who gave you this authority?" 3He answered them, "I will also ask you a question, and you tell me: 4Did the baptism of John come from heaven, or was it of human origin?" 5They discussed it with one another, saying, "If we say, 'From heaven,' he will say, 'Why did you not believe him?' 6But if we say, 'Of human origin,' all the people will stone us; for they are convinced that John was a prophet." 7So they answered that they did not know where it came from. 8Then Jesus said to them, "Neither will I tell you by what authority I am doing these things."

The Parable of the Wicked Tenants

9 He began to tell the people this parable: "A man planted a vineyard, and leased it to tenants, and went to another country for a long time. 10When the season came, he sent a slave to the tenants in order that they might give him his share of the produce of the vineyard; but the tenants beat him and sent him away empty-handed. 11Next he sent another slave; that one also they beat and insulted and sent away empty-handed. 12And he sent still a third; this one also they wounded and threw out. 13Then the owner of the vineyard said, 'What shall I do? I will send my beloved son; perhaps they will respect him.' 14But when the tenants saw him, they discussed it among themselves and said, 'This is the heir; let us kill him so that the inheritance may be ours.' 15So they threw him out of the vineyard and killed him. What then will the owner of the vineyard do to them? 16He will come and destroy those tenants and give the vineyard to others." When they heard this, they said, "Heaven forbid!" 17But he looked at them and said, "What then does this text mean:

'The stone that the builders rejected
    has become the cornerstone'?[a]

18Everyone who falls on that stone will be broken to pieces; and it will crush anyone on whom it falls." 19When the scribes and chief priests realized that he had told this parable against them, they wanted to lay hands on him at that very hour, but they feared the people.

The Question about Paying Taxes

20 So they watched him and sent spies who pretended to be honest, in order to trap him

---

a Or keystone

Jer 7.11. **19.47–48** Jesus is *teaching in the temple* through ch. 21. Luke eliminates all the specific chronological references of Mark's "passion week" (e.g., Mk 14.1) and represents Jesus' time in Jerusalem as an extended time of teaching. On the efforts of the leaders to find *a way to kill him*, see 11.53–54; 22.2; see also 6.11. The constant presence of *the people* in Jerusalem serves as a buffer between Jesus and those who would do him harm (see 20.1, 6, 9, 19, 26, 45; 21.38; 22.2). **20.1–21.4** In a series of conflicts in the temple, Jesus' adversaries ask insincere questions to entrap or ridicule him, yet he still finds ways to teach with integrity. **20.1–8** Cf. Mt 21.23–27; Mk 11.27–33. **20.1** Jesus' daily teaching in the temple is linked with his "proclaiming," or *telling the good news* (see 4.18, 43; 7.22; 8.1; 9.6; 16.16). The *chief priests, scribes,* and *elders* are Jesus' primary adversaries in Jerusalem (see also 9.22; 19.47; 20.19; 22.52). **20.2** On the question of Jesus' *authority*, see 4.32, 36; 5.24; 11.14–23; see also 9.1; 10.19. **20.3** Jesus' *question* places his opponents on the horns of a dilemma. **20.4** *Baptism of John.* See 3.1–17; 7.24–35. **20.5–6** See 7.29–30; cf.

Acts 5.38–39. **20.9–19** Cf. Mt 21.33–46; Mk 12.1–12. Jesus' parable presses his adversaries beyond predictable scholastic questions (see also 10.25–26; 18.18–19). **20.9** *Vineyard.* See Isa 5.1–7. **20.10–12** The mistreatment of the slaves recalls the treatment of the prophets and apostles (11.49; Acts 7.52). **20.13** *What shall I do?* a common Lukan soliloquy (3.10, 14; 10.25; 12.17; 16.3; 18.18; Acts 2.37; 4.16; see also Isa 5.4). *My beloved son.* See 3.22; 9.35. **20.14** *Discussed it among themselves.* See v. 5; see also 19.47–48. **20.17** The text quoted is Ps 118.22, also quoted in Acts 4.11; 1 Pet 2.7. Another verse of this psalm is quoted in 13.35; 19.38. **20.18** The rejected but exalted *stone* (an allusion to Jesus' crucifixion and resurrection; see 9.22) will become an occasion for stumbling and judgment (see also 2.34; Isa 8.14–15; Dan 2.34–35, 44–45; 1 Pet 2.6–8). **20.19** The division continues between the *people* and the rulers (see note on 19.47–48). **20.20–26** Cf. Mt 22.15–22; Mk 12.13–17. The second controversy in the temple (see also vv. 1–8). **20.20** *They watched him.* See also 6.7; 14.1. *Spies* try to lay the groundwork for legal charges (see 23.2). *Governor,* Pilate (see 3.1; 23.1–25).

by what he said, so as to hand him over to the jurisdiction and authority of the governor. [21]So they asked him, "Teacher, we know that you are right in what you say and teach, and you show deference to no one, but teach the way of God in accordance with truth. [22]Is it lawful for us to pay taxes to the emperor, or not?" [23]But he perceived their craftiness and said to them, [24]"Show me a denarius. Whose head and whose title does it bear?" They said, "The emperor's." [25]He said to them, "Then give to the emperor the things that are the emperor's, and to God the things that are God's." [26]And they were not able in the presence of the people to trap him by what he said; and being amazed by his answer, they became silent.

The Question about the Resurrection

27 Some Sadducees, those who say there is no resurrection, came to him [28]and asked him a question, "Teacher, Moses wrote for us that if a man's brother dies, leaving a wife but no children, the man[a] shall marry the widow and raise up children for his brother. [29]Now there were seven brothers; the first married, and died childless; [30]then the second [31]and the third married her, and so in the same way all seven died childless. [32]Finally the woman also died. [33]In the resurrection, therefore, whose wife will the woman be? For the seven had married her."

34 Jesus said to them, "Those who belong to this age marry and are given in marriage; [35]but those who are considered worthy of a place in that age and in the resurrection from the dead neither marry nor are given in marriage. [36]Indeed they cannot die anymore, because they are like angels and are children of God, being children of the resurrection. [37]And the fact that the dead are raised Moses himself showed, in the story about the bush, where he speaks of the Lord as the God of Abraham, the God of Isaac, and the God of Jacob. [38]Now he is God not of the dead, but of the living; for to him all of them are alive." [39]Then some of the scribes answered, "Teacher, you have spoken well." [40]For they no longer dared to ask him another question.

The Question about David's Son

41 Then he said to them, "How can they say that the Messiah[b] is David's son? [42]For David himself says in the book of Psalms,

'The Lord said to my Lord,
"Sit at my right hand,
[43]　　until I make your enemies your
　　　　footstool." '

[44]David thus calls him Lord; so how can he be his son?"

Jesus Denounces the Scribes

45 In the hearing of all the people he said to the[c] disciples, [46]"Beware of the scribes, who like to walk around in long robes, and love to

---

a Gk his brother b Or the Christ c Other ancient authorities read his

---

20.21 The traditional compliments (see Lev 19.15; Deut 1.17; 16.19) are patently hypocritical. **20.22** The question was difficult for Jews because of the theological claims of the Roman order (see notes on 2.10; 2.11; 20.24) and the dangers of opposing Rome. **20.24** A Roman *denarius* of this era bore the engraved image of Tiberius Caesar (see 3.1; cf. Ex 20.4; Deut 5.8) and the inscription "SON OF THE DIVINE AUGUSTUS" (cf. Ex 20.23). **20.25** Jesus' answer changes the question from what one owes the emperor (i.e., coins with his image) to what belongs to God (people with God's image; Gen 1.26–27). See also Rom 13.6–7; 1 Pet 2.13–17. **20.27–40** Cf. Mt 22.23–33; Mk 12.18–27. The third controversy introduces new opponents (cf. vv. 1–8, 20–26). **20.27** The *Sadducees* denied the Pharisaic teachings of *resurrection* and angels (see also Acts 4.2; 23.6–10) and were closely linked with the temple leadership (Acts 4.1; 5.17). **20.28–33** The case cited by the Sadducees is absurd but refers to the law of levirate (brother-in-law) marriage, which kept a deceased husband's name alive (Deut 25.5–6; see also Gen 38.8). **20.34–36** *Marry*, i.e., to procreate. This is no longer necessary for those who inherit eternal life in the age to come. **20.37** *Moses himself.* Sadducees recognized only the authority of the books of Moses (the written Torah), which contain no explicit references to the resurrection. Jesus finds an implicit reference in Ex 3.6. **20.38** See 4 Macc 7.19. **20.41–44** Cf. Mt 22.41–46; Mk 12.35–37a. Jesus now poses a question to his former questioners. **20.41** *The Messiah is David's Son.* See notes on 1.55; 18.38. **20.42–43** See Ps 110.1. For a somewhat different use of this text, see Acts 2.32–36. **20.44** Since elsewhere the messianic title *son* of David is applied to Jesus (18.38–39; see also 1.32, 69), the meaning here is that this title, though correct, is not adequate, especially insofar as it suggests Jesus' subordination to David. Cf. 1.35. **20.45–47** Cf. Mt 23.1–36; Mk 12.37b–40. Jesus' concluding attack *in the hearing of all the people* on the scribes recalls his denouncement of the Pharisees in 11.37–52. **20.46** *Places of*

be greeted with respect in the marketplaces, and to have the best seats in the synagogues and places of honor at banquets. [47] They devour widows' houses and for the sake of appearance say long prayers. They will receive the greater condemnation."

The Widow's Offering

21 He looked up and saw rich people putting their gifts into the treasury; [2] he also saw a poor widow put in two small copper coins. [3] He said, "Truly I tell you, this poor widow has put in more than all of them; [4] for all of them have contributed out of their abundance, but she out of her poverty has put in all she had to live on."

The Destruction of the Temple Foretold

5 When some were speaking about the temple, how it was adorned with beautiful stones and gifts dedicated to God, he said, [6] "As for these things that you see, the days will come when not one stone will be left upon another; all will be thrown down."

Signs and Persecutions

7 They asked him, "Teacher, when will this be, and what will be the sign that this is about to take place?" [8] And he said, "Beware that you are not led astray; for many will come in my name and say, 'I am he!'[a] and, 'The time is near!'[b] Do not go after them.

9 "When you hear of wars and insurrections, do not be terrified; for these things must take place first, but the end will not follow immediately." [10] Then he said to them, "Nation will rise against nation, and kingdom against kingdom; [11] there will be great earthquakes, and in various places famines and plagues; and there will be dreadful portents and great signs from heaven.

12 "But before all this occurs, they will arrest you and persecute you; they will hand you over to synagogues and prisons, and you will be brought before kings and governors because of my name. [13] This will give you an opportunity to testify. [14] So make up your minds not to prepare your defense in advance; [15] for I will give you words[c] and a wisdom that none of your opponents will be able to withstand or contradict. [16] You will be betrayed even by parents and brothers, by relatives and friends; and they will put some of you to death. [17] You will be hated by all because of my name. [18] But not a hair of your head will perish. [19] By your endurance you will gain your souls.

The Destruction of Jerusalem Foretold

20 "When you see Jerusalem surrounded by armies, then know that its desolation has come near.[d] [21] Then those in Judea must flee to the mountains, and those inside the city must leave it, and those out in the country must not enter it; [22] for these are days of vengeance, as a fulfillment of all that is written. [23] Woe to those who are pregnant and to those who are nursing infants in those days! For there will be great distress on the earth and wrath against this people; [24] they will fall by the edge of the sword and be taken away as captives among all

---

a Gk *I am*　*b* Or *at hand*　*c* Gk *a mouth*　*d* Or *is at hand*

---

honor. See 14.7–11. **20.47** Widows. See note on 18.3; cf. 21.1–4.

21.1–4 Cf. Mk 12.41–44. The contrast between the abundance of the rich and the poverty of the widow is rehearsed three times in these verses (see also 6.20–26; 18.18–25; note on 7.12). **21.1** *Treasury,* i.e., offering box. **21.4** *All she had.* See 8.43. **21.5–36** Luke's version of the "Synoptic apocalypse" (cf. Mt 24; Mk 13) is located at the temple and rivals the Sermon on the Plain (6.20–49) for length and significance. **21.5–24** Cf. Mt 24.1–21; Mk 13.1–19. A collection of signs that will precede the destruction of Jerusalem. **21.6** *Not one stone . . . upon another.* See 19.44; Jer 7.1–15; 22.5. **21.7** Jesus continues to *speak as a Teacher,* interpreting tradition (see note on 18.18). On the request for a *sign,* see 11.16, 29–30. **21.8** False prophets declare the destruction of the temple to be *near,* but the divine plan has more phases. Cf. Acts 5.36–37; 21.38. **21.9** *Wars and insurrections.* See Dan 11.25, 44; Rev 6.3–4; 9.7–11. **21.10–11** On God's

judgment through cosmic struggle and warfare, see 2 Chr 15.6; Isa 19.2; Jer 4.13–22; 14.12; 21.6–7; Ezek 14.21; 38.19–23; 2 Esd 13.31. **21.12** Acts narrates the fulfillment of this prediction with stories of arrest, persecution, and imprisonment because of Jesus' *name* (see, e.g., Acts 4.1–22; 5.17–41; 12.1–11; 22–26; cf. Lk 6.22). **21.13** *An opportunity to testify.* See Acts 3.15; 4.33; 5.32; 26.22. **21.14** On not preparing a *defense in advance,* see also 12.11. **21.15** *A wisdom.* Cf. 12.12; Acts 6.10. **21.16** *Put . . . to death.* See Acts 7.54–60; 12.1–2. **21.17** *Hated by all* recalls Jesus' statement in 6.22 (cf. Acts 2.47). **21.18** *Hair.* See note on 12.7. **21.19** *Endurance,* faithful reliance on God to preserve life (see 8.15; 9.23–27). **21.20–24** The destruction of Jerusalem is described in language that echoes scriptural warnings of God's judgment (see also 13.34–35; 19.41–44). **21.20** *Desolation,* i.e., of Jerusalem. See Dan 9.26–27; see also Jer 26.9; cf. Mt 24.15; Mk 13.14. **21.22** *Days of vengeance.* See Deut 32.35; Hos 9.7. **21.23** *Woe.* See note

nations; and Jerusalem will be trampled on by the Gentiles, until the times of the Gentiles are fulfilled.

The Coming of the Son of Man

25 "There will be signs in the sun, the moon, and the stars, and on the earth distress among nations confused by the roaring of the sea and the waves. 26 People will faint from fear and foreboding of what is coming upon the world, for the powers of the heavens will be shaken. 27 Then they will see 'the Son of Man coming in a cloud' with power and great glory. 28 Now when these things begin to take place, stand up and raise your heads, because your redemption is drawing near."

The Lesson of the Fig Tree

29 Then he told them a parable: "Look at the fig tree and all the trees; 30 as soon as they sprout leaves you can see for yourselves and know that summer is already near. 31 So also, when you see these things taking place, you know that the kingdom of God is near. 32 Truly I tell you, this generation will not pass away until all things have taken place. 33 Heaven and earth will pass away, but my words will not pass away.

Exhortation to Watch

34 "Be on guard so that your hearts are not weighed down with dissipation and drunkenness and the worries of this life, and that day does not catch you unexpectedly, 35 like a trap. For it will come upon all who live on the face of the whole earth. 36 Be alert at all times, praying that you may have the strength to escape all these things that will take place, and to stand before the Son of Man."

37 Every day he was teaching in the temple, and at night he would go out and spend the night on the Mount of Olives, as it was called. 38 And all the people would get up early in the morning to listen to him in the temple.

The Plot to Kill Jesus

22 Now the festival of Unleavened Bread, which is called the Passover, was near. 2 The chief priests and the scribes were looking for a way to put Jesus*a* to death, for they were afraid of the people.

3 Then Satan entered into Judas called Iscariot, who was one of the twelve; 4 he went away and conferred with the chief priests and officers of the temple police about how he might betray him to them. 5 They were greatly pleased and agreed to give him money. 6 So he consented and began to look for an opportunity to betray him to them when no crowd was present.

The Preparation of the Passover

7 Then came the day of Unleavened Bread, on which the Passover lamb had to be sacrificed.

a Gk *him*

on 6.24. **21.24** *The edge of the sword.* See Jer 21.7; Sir 28.18. *Captives among all nations.* See Deut 28.64; Ezek 32.9. *Trampled on by the Gentiles.* See Zech 12.3; see also Dan 8.13; Rev 11.2. *Until the times of the Gentiles are fulfilled,* either the time when the gentile (i.e., Roman) triumph is complete or a divinely imposed limitation of the Gentiles' dominance (see also Rom 11.7–32). An expression of God's ultimate saving purpose for Israel has strong scriptural precedents (see Deut 32.26–27; Isa 45–47; Zech 12.1–6). **21.25–36** Cf. Mt 24.29–35; Mk 13.24–31. An apocalyptic vision of cosmic distress that will confuse the Gentiles and usher in the kingdom of God. **21.25** *Signs in the sun, the moon, and the stars,* common features of prophetic and apocalyptic pronouncements (see Joel 2.30–32, cited in Acts 2.19–21; see also Isa 13.10; 34.4; Ezek 32.7). On the *distress* of nations, see Isa 17.12–14. On the *sea and the waves,* see Pss 46.3; 89.9; 93.3–4. **21.26** See Isa 24.17–20. **21.27** The appearance of *the Son of Man* with *power and great glory* is the conferral of dominion for all to see (Dan 7.13–14; cf. Acts 1.11). **21.28** *Redemption* (see 1.68; 2.38; 24.21) and the kingdom of God (21.31; see also 10.9, 11) are now publicly imminent. **21.32** *This generation,* i.e., the

generation of the signs (see also 7.31; 9.41; 11.29–32, 50–51; 16.8; 17.25). **21.34** *That day,* i.e., the day of the Son of Man (see also 10.12; 17.22–37; see also 1 Thess 5.1–11). **21.36** *To stand before the Son of Man,* i.e., to face his judgment with confidence. **21.37–38** These verses and (see note on) 19.47–48 form a bracket around Luke's depiction of Jesus' teaching in the temple, which goes on for an indefinite period.

22.1–23.56 The story of Jesus' death. **22.1–13** Cf. Mt 26.1–5, 14–19; Mk 14.1–2, 10–16. Events at Passover reveal conflicting preparations by Jesus' adversaries (vv. 2–6) and his disciples (vv. 7–13). **22.1** *Passover.* See note on 2.41. *Was near.* Luke again provides a nonspecific chronological reference (see note on 19.47–48; cf. Mt 26.2; Mk 14.1). **22.2** The standoff between the leaders and *the people* continues (see note on 19.47–48; see also 22.6). **22.3** This is the *opportune time* (4.13) Satan has been awaiting since the temptation in 4.1–13 (see also vv. 31, 53; Jn 13.27; Acts 5.3). *Judas . . . Iscariot.* See 6.16; Acts 1.16–20. *The twelve.* See note on 6.13. **22.5** *Money.* See notes on 11.41; 16.9. **22.7** *The day of Unleavened Bread,* inexact usage. Unleavened bread was eaten all seven days of

8 So Jesus [a] sent Peter and John, saying, "Go and prepare the Passover meal for us that we may eat it." 9 They asked him, "Where do you want us to make preparations for it?" 10 "Listen," he said to them, "when you have entered the city, a man carrying a jar of water will meet you; follow him into the house he enters 11 and say to the owner of the house, 'The teacher asks you, "Where is the guest room, where I may eat the Passover with my disciples?" ' 12 He will show you a large room upstairs, already furnished. Make preparations for us there." 13 So they went and found everything as he had told them; and they prepared the Passover meal.

The Institution of the Lord's Supper

14 When the hour came, he took his place at the table, and the apostles with him. 15 He said to them, "I have eagerly desired to eat this Passover with you before I suffer; 16 for I tell you, I will not eat it [b] until it is fulfilled in the kingdom of God." 17 Then he took a cup, and after giving thanks he said, "Take this and divide it among yourselves; 18 for I tell you that from now on I will not drink of the fruit of the vine until the kingdom of God comes." 19 Then he took a loaf of bread, and when he had given thanks, he broke it and gave it to them, saying, "This is my body, which is given for you. Do this in remembrance of me." 20 And he did the same with the cup after supper, saying, "This cup that is poured out for you is the new covenant in my blood. [c] 21 But see, the one who be-

trays me is with me, and his hand is on the table. 22 For the Son of Man is going as it has been determined, but woe to that one by whom he is betrayed!" 23 Then they began to ask one another which one of them it could be who would do this.

The Dispute about Greatness

24 A dispute also arose among them as to which one of them was to be regarded as the greatest. 25 But he said to them, "The kings of the Gentiles lord it over them; and those in authority over them are called benefactors. 26 But not so with you; rather the greatest among you must become like the youngest, and the leader like one who serves. 27 For who is greater, the one who is at the table or the one who serves? Is it not the one at the table? But I am among you as one who serves.

28 "You are those who have stood by me in my trials; 29 and I confer on you, just as my Father has conferred on me, a kingdom, 30 so that you may eat and drink at my table in my kingdom, and you will sit on thrones judging the twelve tribes of Israel.

Jesus Predicts Peter's Denial

31 "Simon, Simon, listen! Satan has demanded [d] to sift all of you like wheat, 32 but I

a Gk he   b Other ancient authorities read never eat it again
c Other ancient authorities lack, in whole or in part, verses 19b–20 (which is given . . . in my blood)   d Or has obtained permission

the Passover festival (see Ex 12.14–20). **22.8** *Peter and John* are again singled out in the story (see note on 8.51). **22.13** *Found everything as he had told them.* Jesus' explicit instructions (vv. 10–12) are understood to have been prophetic (see also 19.32). **22.14–23** Cf. Mt 26.20, 26–29; Mk 14.17, 22–25. Jesus reinterprets the Passover meal in terms of his coming death and the coming kingdom. **22.14** *Hour,* the beginning of Passover; it also anticipates the dire hour of Jesus' arrest (v. 53). **22.15** *Suffer* (Greek *paschein*) refers here specifically to Jesus' death (see also 24.46; Acts 1.3; 3.18; 17.3; Heb 13.12; 1 Pet 2.21–23). **22.18** On the anticipation of the *kingdom* and its banquet, see 14.15–24. **22.19** *He broke it.* See 24.30, 35; Acts 2.42; 20.7, 11; 27.35. *In remembrance of me.* See 1 Cor 11.24–25. Passover was already a feast of remembrance (i.e., of God's deliverance of Israel from bondage in Egypt; see Ex 12.14). **22.20** Only Luke refers to a cup before (v. 17) and *after supper,* recalling the several cups of wine of the Passover feast (cf. 1 Cor 11.23–26). *New covenant.* See Jer 31.31–34; 1 Cor 11.25. *Blood* is treated as sacred to God because it is life (Gen 9.4; Deut 12.23) with atoning power (Lev 17.11; Heb 9.22). It was used

to seal the old covenant between God and Israel (see Ex 24.3–8). **22.21** *His hand is on the table.* See Ps 41.9. **22.22** Jesus' course as the Son of Man is *determined* by God's will as recorded in the scriptures (see 9.22; 18.31; 24.7, 25–27, 44–46), but the betrayer is still answerable for his actions (see also 17.1). **22.24–30** Cf. Mt 20.24–28; 19.28; Mk 10.41–45. Only Luke records the dispute about who is the greatest (see also 9.46) in the context of the betrayal, underscoring the apostles' lack of understanding (see also 9.45; 18.34). **22.25** *Benefactors,* a title often given to gods and kings in the Hellenistic world. **22.26** On the reversal of status that characterizes the kingdom, see also 6.20–26; 9.48. *Like one who serves.* See 12.37; see also Mk 10.45; Jn 13.1–17; Phil 2.6–11. **22.28** *Stood by me in my trials,* probably the apostles' presence during the rejections Jesus faced in his ministry (see, e.g., ch. 20; see also 23.49). Disciples will also experience trials (see 12.8–12; 21.12–19; 22.31–34). **22.29** *I confer on you . . . a kingdom.* See 12.32. **22.30** *You may eat . . . in my kingdom.* See note on 13.29. *Thrones.* See Ps 122.4–5. *Judging the twelve tribes.* See note on 6.13; cf. Rev 7.4–8. Judging connotes ruling, not simply passing judg-

have prayed for you that your own faith may not fail; and you, when once you have turned back, strengthen your brothers." 33 And he said to him, "Lord, I am ready to go with you to prison and to death!" 34 Jesus[a] said, "I tell you, Peter, the cock will not crow this day, until you have denied three times that you know me."

Purse, Bag, and Sword

35 He said to them, "When I sent you out without a purse, bag, or sandals, did you lack anything?" They said, "No, not a thing." 36 He said to them, "But now, the one who has a purse must take it, and likewise a bag. And the one who has no sword must sell his cloak and buy one. 37 For I tell you, this scripture must be fulfilled in me, 'And he was counted among the lawless'; and indeed what is written about me is being fulfilled." 38 They said, "Lord, look, here are two swords." He replied, "It is enough."

Jesus Prays on the Mount of Olives

39 He came out and went, as was his custom, to the Mount of Olives; and the disciples followed him. 40 When he reached the place, he said to them, "Pray that you may not come into the time of trial."[b] 41 Then he withdrew from them about a stone's throw, knelt down, and prayed, 42 "Father, if you are willing, remove this cup from me; yet, not my will but yours be done."〚 43 Then an angel from heaven appeared to him and gave him strength. 44 In his anguish he prayed more earnestly, and his sweat became like great drops of blood falling down on the ground.〛[c] 45 When he got up from prayer, he came to the disciples and found them sleeping because of grief, 46 and he said to them, "Why are you sleeping? Get up and pray that you may not come into the time of trial."[b]

The Betrayal and Arrest of Jesus

47 While he was still speaking, suddenly a crowd came, and the one called Judas, one of the twelve, was leading them. He approached Jesus to kiss him; 48 but Jesus said to him, "Judas, is it with a kiss that you are betraying the Son of Man?" 49 When those who were around him saw what was coming, they asked, "Lord, should we strike with the sword?" 50 Then one of them struck the slave of the high priest and cut off his right ear. 51 But Jesus said, "No more of this!" And he touched his ear and healed him. 52 Then Jesus said to the chief priests, the officers of the temple police, and the elders who had come for him, "Have you come out with swords and clubs as if I were a bandit? 53 When I was with you day after day in the temple, you did not lay hands on me. But this is your hour, and the power of darkness!"

a Gk He   b Or into temptation   c Other ancient authorities lack verses 43 and 44

ment. 22.31–34 Cf. Mt 26.30–35; Mk 14.27–31; Jn 13.36–38. Peter's imminent denial is defined in terms of Satan's activity. 22.31 On Satan claiming the right to test or try the apostles, see 4.1–13; cf. Job 1.6–12; 2.1–7. 22.32 Once you have turned back (i.e., repented). Jesus' prayer for Peter's endurance anticipates failure but is ultimately successful. 22.33 To prison. See Acts 5.18; 12.3. 22.34 Jesus' prophecy is fulfilled in vv. 54–62. 22.35–38 Jesus modifies his earlier advice on mission preparations (cf. 9.3; 10.4). 22.36 On the use of the sword, see vv. 49–51. 22.37 See Isa 53.12; see also Lk 23.32–33. 22.38 It is enough. Jesus' reply indicates that the apostles' have misunderstood the symbolic sense of his instruction, as vv. 49–51 make clear. 22.39–53 Cf. Mt 26.36–56; Mk 14.32–50; Jn 18.1–11. Luke's version of Jesus' garden agony and arrest highlights the need for prayer in the "hour of darkness." 22.39 Jesus' custom (see 21.37) is known to Judas (see 22.47). The disciples followed. See note on 5.11. 22.40 The time of trial (also v. 46) indicates spiritual struggle (see 4.1–13; 11.4; 22.31). 22.41 He . . . prayed. See notes on 5.16; 6.12. 22.42 If you are willing. The will of the Father is central to Jesus' mission (10.21; 11.13; 12.30–32; 24.49; Acts 21.14; 22.14). Cup, i.e.,

the cup of destiny (see Pss 11.6; 75.8; Isa 51.17; Jer 25.15; Lam 4.21; see also Lk 22.17, 20–22). 22.43–44 These verses were either added to some ancient manuscripts or omitted from others (see text note c; see also 23.34). 22.44 His anguish. See Heb 5.7. 22.45 Only Luke explains the disciples' sleep as because of grief. Cf. 9.32. 22.47 The crowd comprises the chief priests, the officers of the temple police, and the elders (see v. 52) and is not the crowd of the people who once protected Jesus (see note on 19.47–48; 22.2–6). Judas. See note on 6.16. The kiss was a common gesture of respectful greeting (7.45), but see Prov 27.6. It seems that Judas does not carry out the gesture. 22.48 Betraying (or "handing over") the Son of Man. See 9.44; 18.32; 20.20; 22.4, 6, 21–22; 24.7. 22.49 The disciples are willing to fight (cf. Mk 14.50). Sword. See vv. 36–38. 22.50 One of them. In Jn 18.10 Simon Peter strikes the slave. 22.51 Jesus repudiates violence and demonstrates love of enemies (6.27). 22.52 On treating Jesus as a bandit or insurrectionist, see the charges in 23.5, 14, 19, 25. 22.53 The hour of the adversaries is a limited moment in God's timetable (see, e.g., 21.24; Jn 19.11; Acts 4.27–28; Rom 13.11) and their power, or authority (Greek exousia), is the evil dominion of

Peter Denies Jesus

54 Then they seized him and led him away, bringing him into the high priest's house. But Peter was following at a distance. 55When they had kindled a fire in the middle of the courtyard and sat down together, Peter sat among them. 56Then a servant-girl, seeing him in the firelight, stared at him and said, "This man also was with him." 57But he denied it, saying, "Woman, I do not know him." 58A little later someone else, on seeing him, said, "You also are one of them." But Peter said, "Man, I am not!" 59Then about an hour later still another kept insisting, "Surely this man also was with him; for he is a Galilean." 60But Peter said, "Man, I do not know what you are talking about!" At that moment, while he was still speaking, the cock crowed. 61The Lord turned and looked at Peter. Then Peter remembered the word of the Lord, how he had said to him, "Before the cock crows today, you will deny me three times." 62And he went out and wept bitterly.

The Mocking and Beating of Jesus

63 Now the men who were holding Jesus began to mock him and beat him; 64they also blindfolded him and kept asking him, "Prophesy! Who is it that struck you?" 65They kept heaping many other insults on him.

Jesus before the Council

66 When day came, the assembly of the elders of the people, both chief priests and scribes, gathered together, and they brought him to their council. 67They said, "If you are the Messiah,[a] tell us." He replied, "If I tell you, you will not believe; 68and if I question you, you will not answer. 69But from now on the Son of Man will be seated at the right hand of the power of God." 70All of them asked, "Are you, then, the Son of God?" He said to them, "You say that I am." 71Then they said, "What further testimony do we need? We have heard it ourselves from his own lips!"

Jesus before Pilate

23 Then the assembly rose as a body and brought Jesus[b] before Pilate. 2They began to accuse him, saying, "We found this man perverting our nation, forbidding us to pay taxes to the emperor, and saying that he himself is the Messiah, a king."[c] 3Then Pilate asked him, "Are you the king of the Jews?" He answered, "You say so." 4Then Pilate said to the chief priests and the crowds, "I find no basis for an accusation against this man." 5But they were insistent and said, "He stirs up the people by teaching throughout all Judea,

a Or the Christ　*b* Gk him　*c* Or is an anointed king

darkness (4.6; 22.3; Eph 6.12; cf. Lk 1.79; Acts 26.18; 1 Thess 5.4–8). **22.54–71** Cf. Mt 26.57–75; Mk 14.53–72. Passion predictions begin to be fulfilled (see v. 34; 18.32; 9.22). **22.54** High priest's house, probably an official residence. Mt 26.57 identifies the high priest as Caiaphas. In following Jesus, Peter was keeping his promise (v. 33). **22.59** Mt 26.73 indicates that Peter's Galilean dialect gave him away. See Lk 23.6. **22.60** The cock crowed. See v. 34. **22.61** The Lord . . . looked at Peter. Only Luke mentions this direct gaze. **22.62** Peter's weeping shows that his predicted repentance (v. 32) has already begun. **22.63–64** Prophesy! The first mocking (see also 18.32; 23.11, 36) calls attention to Jesus as prophet (see 7.39; 13.34; 24.19). **22.65** Many other insults recalls other generalized summaries in 3.18; 8.3; Acts 15.35. **22.66** Council, i.e., the Sanhedrin, the supreme court of chief priests and elders in Jerusalem that interpreted and defended Jewish law (see also Acts 4.5–6, 23). In Luke the trial before this body occurs during the day (cf. Mt 26.57; Mk 14.53, where the phrase when day came is absent) and has none of the fierce charges or verdicts of Mt 26.61, 65–66; Mk 14.58, 63–64. **22.67** If you are the Messiah. See 23.35; cf. 4.41. **22.67b–69** Jesus' answer first rephrases Jeremiah's response to King Zedekiah (Jer 38.15), then

points to the heavenly Son of Man who will come in triumph and judgment (Ps 110.1; Dan 7.13; see also Lk 21.27; Acts 2.32–36). **22.70** You say that I am. Jesus' ambiguous answer (see also 23.3) implies an affirmative. **22.71** We have heard . . . own lips. With unintended irony, the council indicts itself (see v. 67).

23.1–5 Cf. Mt 27.1–2, 11–14; Mk 15.1–5. The Jewish authorities accuse Jesus before the local representative of the Roman government. **23.1** Pilate's seat of government, normally in Caesarea Maritima, was moved to Jerusalem during Passover to keep the peace. **23.2** The charges are phrased with political overtones to interest the Roman governor. The general accusation of perverting (or subverting) our nation (see also vv. 5, 14) highlights the risk of offending careful understandings between the Jews and Rome (see Jn 11.48) and could be understood as fomenting revolt. The specific charges concern forbidding . . . taxes, which was seditious (cf. 20.20–26), and the fact that only the Romans could appoint a king (see Jn 19.12; cf. Lk 19.38; 23.37–38). Cf. the charges brought against Paul in Acts 24.5–6. **23.3** Are you the king of the Jews? Later Pilate ironically confirms this title (v. 38). See also 22.70. **23.4** The first of a series of affirmations of Jesus' innocence by Rome (see vv. 14–15, 22, 41, 47; see

from Galilee where he began even to this place."

Jesus before Herod

6 When Pilate heard this, he asked whether the man was a Galilean. 7And when he learned that he was under Herod's jurisdiction, he sent him off to Herod, who was himself in Jerusalem at that time. 8When Herod saw Jesus, he was very glad, for he had been wanting to see him for a long time, because he had heard about him and was hoping to see him perform some sign. 9He questioned him at some length, but Jesus*a* gave him no answer. 10The chief priests and the scribes stood by, vehemently accusing him. 11Even Herod with his soldiers treated him with contempt and mocked him; then he put an elegant robe on him, and sent him back to Pilate. 12That same day Herod and Pilate became friends with each other; before this they had been enemies.

Jesus Sentenced to Death

13 Pilate then called together the chief priests, the leaders, and the people, 14and said to them, "You brought me this man as one who was perverting the people; and here I have examined him in your presence and have not found this man guilty of any of your charges against him. 15Neither has Herod, for he sent him back to us. Indeed, he has done nothing to deserve death. 16I will therefore have him flogged and release him."*b*

18 Then they all shouted out together, "Away with this fellow! Release Barabbas for

us!" 19(This was a man who had been put in prison for an insurrection that had taken place in the city, and for murder.) 20Pilate, wanting to release Jesus, addressed them again; 21but they kept shouting, "Crucify, crucify him!" 22A third time he said to them, "Why, what evil has he done? I have found in him no ground for the sentence of death; I will therefore have him flogged and then release him." 23But they kept urgently demanding with loud shouts that he should be crucified; and their voices prevailed. 24So Pilate gave his verdict that their demand should be granted. 25He released the man they asked for, the one who had been put in prison for insurrection and murder, and he handed Jesus over as they wished.

The Crucifixion of Jesus

26 As they led him away, they seized a man, Simon of Cyrene, who was coming from the country, and they laid the cross on him, and made him carry it behind Jesus. 27A great number of the people followed him, and among them were women who were beating their breasts and wailing for him. 28But Jesus turned to them and said, "Daughters of Jerusalem, do not weep for me, but weep for yourselves and for your children. 29For the days are surely coming when they will say, 'Blessed are the barren, and the wombs that never bore, and the breasts that never nursed.' 30Then they will begin to say to the mountains, 'Fall on us';

a Gk *he*   b Here, or after verse 19, other ancient authorities add verse 17, *Now he was obliged to release someone for them at the festival*

also Acts 3.14; 7.52). **23.5** *Judea.* See note on 4.44. This geographical summary brings the whole story *to this place* (i.e., Jerusalem), and Acts 1.8 moves it out from Jerusalem to the ends of the earth. **23.6–12** A hearing before Herod, found only in Luke, brings more mocking and another verdict of innocence (v. 15). **23.7** *Herod* Antipas, tetrarch of the northern regions of Galilee and Perea (see note on 3.1), perhaps in Jerusalem for Passover. **23.8** Herod's interest in Jesus is threatening (9.7–9; 13.31). On the desire for a *sign,* see 11.29. **23.11** The *elegant robe* suggests a royal mockery (see also 22.63; cf. Mk 15.16–20). **23.12** The friendship of *Herod and Pilate* is an unholy collusion (see Acts 4.26–28, citing Ps 2.2; cf. 1 Cor 2.8). **23.13–25** Cf. Mt 27.15–26; Mk 15.6–15. The final phase of the trial stresses Jesus' innocence and Pilate's capitulation. **23.13–14** The *people* are present to hear the charge that Jesus was *perverting the people* (see v. 2) and Pilate's *not . . . guilty.* See notes on 13.1; 23.4. **23.18** *Release Barabbas for us.* Mt 27.15–23; Mk 15.6–15 give a rationale for

the request. Nothing further is known of this custom or this individual. See also Acts 3.13–15. **23.21** *Crucify him.* Crucifixion was a brutal form of Roman execution, reserved for slaves and the worst criminals. **23.22** *A third time.* Luke continues to stress Pilate's desire to dismiss the charges. **23.23** *Their voices prevailed.* Luke construes Pilate's verdict as acquiescing to the crowd's will (see also *their demand,* v. 24; *as they wished,* v. 25). **23.26–56** Cf. Mt 27.31b–61; Mk 15.20b–47. The crucifixion, death, and burial of Jesus. **23.26** *Simon,* otherwise unknown (cf. Mk 15.21). *Cyrene,* a city on the coast of northern Africa, had a sizable Jewish colony (see Acts 2.10; 6.9; 11.20). **23.27** *Wailing for him,* perhaps an allusion to Zech 12.10–14 (see also 2 Sam 1.24; Jer 9.17–22). **23.28** *Daughters of Jerusalem,* a term often used in the OT (see Song 1.5; 2.7; 5.16; 8.4; Isa 37.22; Zeph 3.14; Zech 9.9). **23.29–30** Jesus' prophetic oracle of judgment compares closely with the dire effects of siege warfare described in 19.41–44. **23.29** *Blessed are the barren.* See also 21.23; Isa 54.1; cf.

and to the hills, 'Cover us.' ³¹For if they do this when the wood is green, what will happen when it is dry?"

32 Two others also, who were criminals, were led away to be put to death with him. ³³When they came to the place that is called The Skull, they crucified Jesus*a* there with the criminals, one on his right and one on his left. ⟦ ³⁴Then Jesus said, "Father, forgive them; for they do not know what they are doing."⟧*b* And they cast lots to divide his clothing. ³⁵And the people stood by, watching; but the leaders scoffed at him, saying, "He saved others; let him save himself if he is the Messiah*c* of God, his chosen one!" ³⁶The soldiers also mocked him, coming up and offering him sour wine, ³⁷and saying, "If you are the King of the Jews, save yourself!" ³⁸There was also an inscription over him,*d* "This is the King of the Jews."

39 One of the criminals who were hanged there kept deriding*e* him and saying, "Are you not the Messiah?*c* Save yourself and us!" ⁴⁰But the other rebuked him, saying, "Do you not fear God, since you are under the same sentence of condemnation? ⁴¹And we indeed have been condemned justly, for we are getting what we deserve for our deeds, but this man has done nothing wrong." ⁴²Then he said, "Jesus, remember me when you come into*f* your kingdom." ⁴³He replied, "Truly I tell you, today you will be with me in Paradise."

The Death of Jesus

44 It was now about noon, and darkness came over the whole land*g* until three in the afternoon, ⁴⁵while the sun's light failed;*h* and the curtain of the temple was torn in two. ⁴⁶Then Jesus, crying with a loud voice, said, "Father, into your hands I commend my spirit." Having said this, he breathed his last. ⁴⁷When the centurion saw what had taken place, he praised God and said, "Certainly this man was innocent."*i* ⁴⁸And when all the crowds who had gathered there for this spectacle saw what had taken place, they returned home, beating their breasts. ⁴⁹But all his acquaintances, including the women who had followed him from Galilee, stood at a distance, watching these things.

The Burial of Jesus

50 Now there was a good and righteous man named Joseph, who, though a member of the council, ⁵¹had not agreed to their plan and action. He came from the Jewish town of Arimathea, and he was waiting expectantly for the kingdom of God. ⁵²This man went to Pilate and asked for the body of Jesus. ⁵³Then he

a Gk *him* *b* Other ancient authorities lack the sentence *Then Jesus . . . what they are doing* *c* Or *the Christ* *d* Other ancient authorities add *written in Greek and Latin and Hebrew* (that is, *Aramaic*) *e* Or *blaspheming* *f* Other ancient authorities read *in* *g* Or *earth* *h* Or *the sun was eclipsed.* Other ancient authorities read *the sun was darkened* *i* Or *righteous*

Lk 11.27. **23.30** See Hos 10.8; Rev 6.16. **23.31** The saying is enigmatic, though a contrast seems to be drawn between the present relative prosperity and the harsh future days of the Roman destruction (see Ezek 20.47). **23.32** *Criminals.* See 22.37; Isa 53.12. **23.33** *The Skull,* a descriptive name for a prominent rock or hill marking the execution site. **23.34a** See note on 22.43–44. The theme of pardonable ignorance appears also in Acts 3.17; 7.60; 13.27; 17.30. **23.34b** See Ps 22.18. **23.35** The *people* are separated again from the *leaders* (cf. vv. 13–18). The leaders' mockery ignorantly speaks the truth of Jesus' identity as *Messiah of God, his chosen one* (see 2.11; 4.41; 9.20, 35; 24.26; Acts 2.36; 3.18; 4.27). **23.36** *Soldiers* are mentioned here for the first time in Luke's account; this is in line with other attempts in Luke-Acts to avoid portraying Romans as opposed to the Jesus movement (see Introduction; notes on 7.2; 23.4). *Mocked him.* See also 18.32; 22.63; 23.11. *Sour wine,* the common wine drunk by soldiers (see also Ps 69.21). **23.37–38** *King of the Jews.* The soldiers' mockery and Pilate's inscription ironically and publicly declare the truth. **23.39** The taunt *Save yourself* (see also vv. 35, 37) sharpens the question of how Jesus will be a Savior (2.11; 9.24; 19.10; Acts 5.31; 13.23).

23.41 *Nothing wrong.* See note on 23.4. **23.42** *Into your* (i.e., Jesus') *kingdom.* See 1.33; 22.29–30; cf. 24.26. **23.43** On *today* as the time of salvation (cf. the taunts in vv. 35, 37, 39), see notes on 2.11; 19.9. *Paradise,* originally a royal garden, the Garden of Eden in the Septuagint, and later, as here, a synonym for heaven (see also 2 Cor 12.4; Rev 2.7). **23.44** *Darkness,* a divine portent of the "day of the LORD" (see Joel 2.10, 31; Zeph 1.15). **23.45** The *curtain of the temple* veiled its holiest place (see Ex 26.31–35). Cf. the meditation in Heb 9.6–28. **23.46** Jesus' last words come from Ps 31.5 (see also Acts 7.59; cf. Mt 27.46, 50; Mk 15.34, 37). **23.47** *The centurion . . . praised God.* See note on 7.2. *Innocent.* See note on 23.4. **23.48** The *crowds* who have been watching (see v. 35) are now repentant (see 18.13; 23.27). **23.49** The *women* include those mentioned in 8.2–3 (see also 24.10). **23.50–51** *Joseph* is known only from the Gospels. The new tomb (v. 53) may reflect his wealth. His credentials as *good and righteous* and expectantly awaiting the *kingdom* recall the faithful people in the birth stories and their observance of the law (see 1.6; 2.22–27, 36–39). *Council.* See note on 22.66. **23.52** According to Jewish law, the *body* of an executed criminal was not allowed to remain exposed beyond sundown (see Deut 21.22–23).

took it down, wrapped it in a linen cloth, and laid it in a rock-hewn tomb where no one had ever been laid. 54It was the day of Preparation, and the sabbath was beginning.*a* 55The women who had come with him from Galilee followed, and they saw the tomb and how his body was laid. 56Then they returned, and prepared spices and ointments.

On the sabbath they rested according to the commandment.

The Resurrection of Jesus

24 But on the first day of the week, at early dawn, they came to the tomb, taking the spices that they had prepared. 2They found the stone rolled away from the tomb, 3but when they went in, they did not find the body.*b* 4While they were perplexed about this, suddenly two men in dazzling clothes stood beside them. 5The women*c* were terrified and bowed their faces to the ground, but the men*d* said to them, "Why do you look for the living among the dead? He is not here, but has risen.*e* 6Remember how he told you, while he was still in Galilee, 7that the Son of Man must be handed over to sinners, and be crucified, and on the third day rise again." 8Then they remembered his words, 9and returning from the tomb, they told all this to the eleven and to all the rest. 10Now it was Mary Magdalene, Joanna, Mary the mother of James, and the other women with them who told this to the apostles. 11But these words seemed to them an idle tale, and they did not believe them. 12But Peter got up and ran to the tomb; stooping and looking in, he saw the linen cloths by themselves; then he went home, amazed at what had happened.*f*

The Walk to Emmaus

13 Now on that same day two of them were going to a village called Emmaus, about seven miles*g* from Jerusalem, 14and talking with each other about all these things that had happened. 15While they were talking and discussing, Jesus himself came near and went with them, 16but their eyes were kept from recognizing him. 17And he said to them, "What are you discussing with each other while you walk along?" They stood still, looking sad.*h* 18Then one of them, whose name was Cleopas, answered him, "Are you the only stranger in Jerusalem who does not know the things that have taken place there in these days?" 19He asked them, "What things?" They replied, "The things about Jesus of Nazareth,*i* who was a prophet mighty in deed and word before God and all the people, 20and how our chief priests and leaders handed him over to be condemned to death and crucified him. 21But we had hoped that he was the one to redeem Israel.*j* Yes, and besides all this, it is now the third day since these things took place. 22Moreover, some women of our group astounded us. They were at the tomb early this morning, 23and when they did not find his body there, they came back and told us that they had indeed seen a vision of angels who said that he was alive. 24Some of those who

---

a Gk was dawning *b* Other ancient authorities add of the Lord Jesus *c* Gk They *d* Gk but they *e* Other ancient authorities lack He is not here, but has risen *f* Other ancient authorities lack verse 12 *g* Gk sixty stadia; other ancient authorities read a hundred sixty stadia *h* Other ancient authorities read walk along, looking sad?" *i* Other ancient authorities read Jesus the Nazorean *j* Or to set Israel free

---

23.53 See Acts 13.29. 23.54 *The day of Preparation,* i.e., for the sabbath. 23.56 *Spices and ointments,* used for burial (see 24.1; Jn 19.40).

24.1–12 Cf. Mt 28.1–8; Mk 16.1–6; Jn 20.1–10. The first news of the resurrection. 24.2 The *stone* would probably have been in the shape of a large wheel that rolled in a channel to seal the door of the tomb. 24.4 *Men in dazzling clothes,* identified as angels in v. 23 (see also Acts 1.10; 10.30; cf. Lk 9.29–31). 24.5 *The women were terrified.* See note on 1.12. 24.6–7 What the women are prompted to *remember* implies that they were present for the predictions given in 9.22, 44. See note on 8.2–3. Luke refers to Jesus' words in *Galilee,* but omits any mention of a meeting there (cf. Mt 28.10; Mk 16.7). 24.9 *The eleven,* i.e., the twelve apostles less Judas (Acts 1.16–20). 24.10 The first witnesses are all *women* (see also vv. 22–24), of whom three are named (see also 8.2–3). Cf. the tradi-

tion in 1 Cor 15.5. 24.11 The disbelief and amazement of the apostles anticipate later revelation and reprimand (vv. 25–27, 31). 24.12 The Gospel According to John also records a visit by *Peter* to the tomb (see Jn 20.3–10). 24.13–35 The appearance on the way to Emmaus. 24.13 The precise location of *Emmaus* is unknown but is consistent with Luke's understanding that all of the resurrection appearances happen in and around Jerusalem (see note on 24.6–7). 24.16 It is not clear who kept their eyes *from recognizing him,* but God may be the implied agent (see v. 31; see also 9.45; 18.34; cf. Jn 20.14–15). 24.18 *Cleopas* is otherwise unknown. 24.19 On Jesus as a *prophet,* see 7.16, 39; 9.8, 19; Acts 3.22. 24.20 The *chief priests and leaders* are held most accountable for Jesus' death (see also 22.52, 66; 23.1–2, 10, 13, 35). 24.21 The focus of hope remains on the redemption of *Israel* (see 1.68; 2.25, 38; 23.51; Acts 26.6–7, 23). *The third day.* See

were with us went to the tomb and found it just as the women had said; but they did not see him." 25Then he said to them, "Oh, how foolish you are, and how slow of heart to believe all that the prophets have declared! 26Was it not necessary that the Messiah*a* should suffer these things and then enter into his glory?" 27Then beginning with Moses and all the prophets, he interpreted to them the things about himself in all the scriptures.

28 As they came near the village to which they were going, he walked ahead as if he were going on. 29But they urged him strongly, saying, "Stay with us, because it is almost evening and the day is now nearly over." So he went in to stay with them. 30When he was at the table with them, he took bread, blessed and broke it, and gave it to them. 31Then their eyes were opened, and they recognized him; and he vanished from their sight. 32They said to each other, "Were not our hearts burning within us*b* while he was talking to us on the road, while he was opening the scriptures to us?" 33That same hour they got up and returned to Jerusalem; and they found the eleven and their companions gathered together. 34They were saying, "The Lord has risen indeed, and he has appeared to Simon!" 35Then they told what had happened on the road, and how he had been made known to them in the breaking of the bread.

Jesus Appears to His Disciples

36 While they were talking about this, Jesus himself stood among them and said to them,

"Peace be with you."*c* 37They were startled and terrified, and thought that they were seeing a ghost. 38He said to them, "Why are you frightened, and why do doubts arise in your hearts? 39Look at my hands and my feet; see that it is I myself. Touch me and see; for a ghost does not have flesh and bones as you see that I have." 40And when he had said this, he showed them his hands and his feet.*d* 41While in their joy they were disbelieving and still wondering, he said to them, "Have you anything here to eat?" 42They gave him a piece of broiled fish, 43and he took it and ate in their presence.

44 Then he said to them, "These are my words that I spoke to you while I was still with you—that everything written about me in the law of Moses, the prophets, and the psalms must be fulfilled." 45Then he opened their minds to understand the scriptures, 46and he said to them, "Thus it is written, that the Messiah*a* is to suffer and to rise from the dead on the third day, 47and that repentance and forgiveness of sins is to be proclaimed in his name to all nations, beginning from Jerusalem. 48You are witnesses*e* of these things. 49And see, I am sending upon you what my Father promised; so stay here in the city until you have been clothed with power from on high."

a Or the Christ *b* Other ancient authorities lack within us *c* Other ancient authorities lack and said to them, "Peace be with you." *d* Other ancient authorities lack verse 40 *e* Or nations. Beginning from Jerusalem 48you are witnesses

9.22; 13.32; 18.33; 24.7, 21, 46; Acts 10.40. **24.22–24** On the *women*, see vv. 1–11. **24.24** *Some . . . went to the tomb.* Only Peter is mentioned in v. 12. **24.26** Earlier passages have indicated that the Messiah's suffering was *necessary* to fulfill God's plan of salvation (see 9.22, 43b–45; 12.50; 13.32–33; 17.25; 18.31–34; see also Acts 3.18; 17.3; 26.23). **24.27** The risen Messiah introduces a new, christological interpretation of *Moses and all the prophets* (cf. 16.29, 31). No specific OT texts are indicated, but see Acts 2.25–36; 4.11, 25–28; 8.32–35; 13.32–41; 17.2–3. **24.30** See 9.16; 22.19; 24.35. In Acts, the "breaking of bread" is mentioned several times, perhaps with eucharistic overtones (see 2.42, 46; 20.7, 11; 27.35). **24.31** *Their eyes were opened.* See note on 24.16; see also 10.21–24. *He vanished.* Cf. Acts 8.39. **24.32** *On the road* (also v. 35). See note on 9.57. **24.34** The appearance to *Simon* (Peter) is not narrated (but see 1 Cor 15.5). **24.36–53** The third appearance of the risen Christ (see vv. 13–31, 34) recalls elements of John's narrative. **24.36** *Peace be with you.*

A conventional Jewish greeting but also a sign of the kingdom (see 1.79; 2.14, 29; 7.50; 8.48; 19.38, 42; Acts 10.36; see also Jn 20.19, 26). **24.37** *Startled and terrified.* See v. 5; note on 1.12. **24.39** *Touch me and see.* The command emphasizes the physical reality of Jesus' resurrection (see also Jn 20.25–29). He is not merely a *ghost* or spirit. Cf. 1 Cor 15.44. **24.42–43** Eating the *broiled fish* emphasizes again the reality of the resurrection (see also 8.55; Jn 21.9–14). **24.44–45** These verses again introduce the Messiah's interpretation of Israel's scriptures (see notes on 24.26; 24.27). **24.45** *He opened . . . scriptures.* Cf. 9.45; 18.34. **24.47** *Repentance and forgiveness of sins* is the substance of the mission in Acts 2.38. On going *to all nations, beginning from Jerusalem,* see Acts 1.8; see also Lk 2.32; Acts 13.46–48. **24.48** The role of the apostles is to be *witnesses* (see Acts 1.8, 22; 10.39–43). **24.49** *What my Father promised* proves to be the Holy Spirit. See Acts 1.4–5, 8; 2.4, 17–18 (citing Joel 2.28–29); 2.38; see also Isa 32.15; 44.3; Ezek 39.29.

The Ascension of Jesus

50 Then he led them out as far as Bethany, and, lifting up his hands, he blessed them. [51]While he was blessing them, he withdrew from them and was carried up into heaven.[a]

[52]And they worshiped him, and[b] returned to Jerusalem with great joy; [53]and they were continually in the temple blessing God.[c]

---

a Other ancient authorities lack *and was carried up into heaven*
b Other ancient authorities lack *worshiped him, and*   **c** Other ancient authorities add *Amen*

24.50 *Bethany.* See note on 19.29. **24.51** Jesus' exaltation into *heaven* is narrated in greater detail in Acts 1.1–11. **24.52–53** The return to *Jerusalem* again places the followers of Jesus at the *temple* (see 1.8–23; 2.22–51; 19.45–21.38; Acts 2.46; 3.1; 5.42), involved with the prayers of Israel.

The Gospel According to

JOHN

IT HAS LONG BEEN RECOGNIZED that the Gospel According to John differs significantly from the other Gospels. It has characters and events that the other three do not mention, and it lacks stories that are prominent in them. It uses language rich in symbolism and subtle shades of meaning. Irony and paradox are common in John; people often misunderstand what Jesus says, but in a way that opens up new levels of meaning. Instead of speaking in parables and short sayings about the kingdom of God, Jesus speaks in long, difficult monologues about himself, his relation to God, and the need to believe in him. Since the second century CE, it has been common to think of John as the "spiritual Gospel," more theological than historical. Recent study has, however, shown that John has a certain grounding in history.

Historical Setting

OF ALL THE NT GOSPELS, John presents by far the most hostile picture of relations between Jesus and the Jews. Throughout the book Jesus rebukes "the Jews" for their failure to recognize or understand him. For their part, they try to stone him, and people who confess him as the Messiah are put out of the synagogue so that his disciples are "afraid of the Jews" (9.22; 16.2; 20.19). Yet Jesus and his disciples were Jews themselves! It is not likely that Jewish Christians were expelled from synagogues before the 80s, and even then this did not happen everywhere.

It is now widely recognized that this state of affairs reflects the circumstances not of Jesus himself but of a Christian group some years after his death. The Gospel According to John seems to have been written late in the first century in a specific Christian community that was undergoing a painful separation from the Jewish society to which its members had belonged. Their claim that Jesus was the Messiah, and indeed the Son of God, brought disciplinary action from the synagogue authorities (who apparently belonged to the Pharisees; see 7.45–48; 12.42). For some, the punishment only emboldened their confession of belief. Others apparently sought to remain within the synagogue as secret Christians (12.42–43; 19.38).

It is important to remember, then, that when John speaks of "the Jews," it does not refer to the Jewish people as a whole. In some passages (e.g., chs. 7, 11) the translation "Judeans" is possible, perhaps reflecting tensions between Galileans and Judeans in the time of Jesus. Generally, however, the ultimate referent seems to be the synagogue authorities of a particular time and place who were inimical to the Christian movement, although another option might be those

Jewish believers whose faith, or their courage in expressing it, fell short in the writer's view. Most probably, the hostile debates between "the Jews" and Jesus in John indicate the intensity of the conflict between the synagogue authorities and the Jewish Christian community in which this Gospel was written.

Purpose

THE AIM OF THE GOSPEL is stated clearly in 20.31: to encourage its readers to believe that Jesus is the Messiah and the Son of God. Given the historical circumstances sketched above, this probably means that the book was intended to inspire members of the community to maintain their belief during a troubled time rather than to convert outsiders. Many things in John have meaning only for those who are Christians already. Yet even nonbelievers who are open to the Christian message may find John's powerful symbolic presentation of Jesus as the Light of the World and the Bread of Life moving and attractive.

Author and Sources

A TRADITION GOING BACK to the second century identifies the author of this Gospel as John the son of Zebedee, one of Jesus' disciples. Since the book also speaks of a "disciple whom Jesus loved" and seems to connect him with its writing (19.26, 35; 21.20–24), this "beloved disciple" has often been identified with John. Yet the Gospel itself does not make this identification and neither mentions John nor names its author. It may be that the author developed the book from traditions about Jesus that had been handed on by one of his disciples. The figure of the beloved disciple may allude to that individual, although the character clearly fulfills some important literary roles, exemplifying the dedication that should characterize an ideal disciple. It has also been suggested that an earlier document focusing on Jesus' miraculous "signs" (2.11) was incorporated into the Gospel. After its first writing, John was evidently further expanded: chs. 15–17 and 21 seem to have been added later, by the original author or by someone from the same circles.

John is thus a book with a complex history whose origins are not entirely clear to us. Yet even if its author can no longer be identified with certainty, its conception of Jesus remains important.

Date and Place of Writing

JOHN HAS ALWAYS BEEN RECOGNIZED as the latest of the four Gospels. Its references to expulsion of Christians from the synagogue and its highly developed theology suggest a date in the last decade of the first century or in the first decades of the second century. Second-century tradition placed the writing of John in Ephesus, and this remains quite possible, though other places have also been suggested.

Theology and Religious Background

JOHN LAYS MORE STRESS on the divinity of Jesus than do any of the other Gospels, so much so that Jesus is presented as being alien to this world (8.23). Such beliefs were the focus of the conflict between the Christian community and the synagogue authorities, which left the community itself feeling alienated from the world. A number of parallels to John's language and thought are found in other ancient religious writings, including the Dead Sea Scrolls and other Jewish writings, Greco-Roman texts such as the *Corpus hermeticum,* and speculative and esoteric texts from the second century associated with "gnostic" circles. Along with the synagogue conflict, influences from such traditions may have had a part in the development of this Gospel's distinctive traits. John states quite clearly that the community's ideas about Jesus changed after Jesus' lifetime and describes this development as the work of the Holy Spirit (12.16; 14.25–26; 16.12–13). By claiming that the divine Son of God truly "became flesh," i.e., was fully human, John presents the Christian belief that in Jesus God entered into human history to save human beings. Whatever other traditions it may appropriate, this belief is central to the symbolism and paradoxes of this Gospel. [DAVID K. RENSBERGER, revised by HAROLD W. ATTRIDGE]

The Word Became Flesh

1 In the beginning was the Word, and the Word was with God, and the Word was God. 2He was in the beginning with God. 3All things came into being through him, and without him not one thing came into being. What has come into being 4in him was life,*a* and the life was the light of all people. 5The light shines in the darkness, and the darkness did not overcome it.

6 There was a man sent from God, whose name was John. 7He came as a witness to testify to the light, so that all might believe through him. 8He himself was not the light, but he came to testify to the light. 9The true light, which enlightens everyone, was coming into the world.*b*

10 He was in the world, and the world came into being through him; yet the world did not know him. 11He came to what was his own,*c* and his own people did not accept him. 12But to all who received him, who believed in his name, he gave power to become children of God, 13who were born, not of blood or of the will of the flesh or of the will of man, but of God.

14 And the Word became flesh and lived among us, and we have seen his glory, the

---

a Or ³through him. And without him not one thing came into being that has come into being. ⁴In him was life   *b* Or He was the true light that enlightens everyone coming into the world   *c* Or to his own home

---

1.1–18 The prologue introduces the central theme of this Gospel: the divine Savior has come into the world, has been rejected by many, but has given eternal life to those who accepted him. Some hold that at least parts of the prologue (e.g., vv. 1–5, 10–11, 14, 16) were originally a separate poem, adapted for this purpose. In these verses a word in one clause often leads into the next clause. Also cf. 1 Jn 1.1–4, which is probably based on this prologue. **1.1** *In the beginning.* See Gen 1.1. *Word,* not simply a spoken word (like God's words of creation in Gen 1), but the *Logos,* in Greek thought the divine principle of reason that gives order to the universe and links the human mind to the mind of God. Jewish traditions about divine Wisdom (Prov 8.22) lie behind this image. The first-century Jewish philosopher Philo identified divine Wisdom and Word, evoking both biblical and Greek traditions. *With God . . . was God* succinctly expresses the sense of unity and distinction of divine Persons that undergirds classical expressions of Christian theism. **1.2–4** *He, him,* or possibly "it," i.e., the *Logos.* **1.4** A major part of John's message is that Jesus brought divine *life* into the world. Here this life is associated with creation; elsewhere it is described as "eternal life," the life of resurrection beyond death that is given now to those who believe in Jesus. See 3.16; 5.21–29; 6.32–40, 51–58; 11.25–26; 14.6; 17.1–3. **1.5** *Light, darkness.* See Gen 1.3–4; 1 Jn 2.8–11. *Overcome,* or "comprehend"; see also 12.35 (*overtake*). **1.6–8** The contrast with *John* the Baptist (also v. 15) links the prologue to the beginning of the story itself (vv. 19–34); see also 3.22–36. The strong insistence in all these places that John was not the Messiah suggests some rivalry between his followers and the Christian community for which this Gospel was written. **1.9** *Light.* See 3.18–19; 8.12; 9.5; 12.46; Isa 9.2; 42.6–7; 60.1–3. **1.10** *The world,* not simply the natural order, but the human beings who should have known their Creator in the coming of Christ. **1.11** *Did not accept him* foreshadows the opposition to Jesus that will run through the Gospel. **1.13** *Born . . . of God.* See 3.3–8; 1 Jn 2.29–3.1; 4.7; 5.1. **1.14–18** There are references here to events on Mount Sinai, where Moses desired to *see* God's *glory* but was told that *no one* could *see God;* however, God was revealed to Moses as full of steadfast love and faithfulness, concepts related to *grace and truth* (see Ex 33.18–34.8). **1.14** *Word.* See note on 1.1. *Flesh,* i.e., human, with all the limitations of mortality that this implies. Such a statement about the divine *Logos* would have seemed extraordinary in ancient religious thought. *Lived among us.* The OT speaks several times of God coming to live among the people of God (e.g., Ex 25.8; Ezek 37.27; Zech 2.10–11) and associates the presence of God with God's *glory* (Ex 16.10; 24.15–18; 29.43–46; 40.34–38; 1 Kings 8.10–11; Pss 26.8; 63.2; Ezek 11.22–23; 44.4). Many of these passages have to do with the tabernacle or the temple; cf. 2.18–22. *Lived,* literally "pitched a tent," an image used in Sir 24.8 for

glory as of a father's only son,[a] full of grace and truth. 15(John testified to him and cried out, "This was he of whom I said, 'He who comes after me ranks ahead of me because he was before me.' ") 16From his fullness we have all received, grace upon grace. 17The law indeed was given through Moses; grace and truth came through Jesus Christ. 18No one has ever seen God. It is God the only Son,[b] who is close to the Father's heart,[c] who has made him known.

The Testimony of John the Baptist

19 This is the testimony given by John when the Jews sent priests and Levites from Jerusalem to ask him, "Who are you?" 20He confessed and did not deny it, but confessed, "I am not the Messiah."[d] 21And they asked him, "What then? Are you Elijah?" He said, "I am not." "Are you the prophet?" He answered, "No." 22Then they said to him, "Who are you? Let us have an answer for those who sent us. What do you say about yourself?" 23He said,

"I am the voice of one crying out in the
        wilderness,
'Make straight the way of the Lord,' "
as the prophet Isaiah said.

24 Now they had been sent from the Pharisees. 25They asked him, "Why then are you baptizing if you are neither the Messiah,[d] nor Elijah, nor the prophet?" 26John answered them, "I baptize with water. Among you stands one whom you do not know, 27the one who is coming after me; I am not worthy to untie the thong of his sandal." 28This took place in Bethany across the Jordan where John was baptizing.

The Lamb of God

29 The next day he saw Jesus coming toward him and declared, "Here is the Lamb of God who takes away the sin of the world! 30This is he of whom I said, 'After me comes a man who ranks ahead of me because he was before me.' 31I myself did not know him; but I came baptizing with water for this reason, that he might be revealed to Israel." 32And John testified, "I saw the Spirit descending from heaven like a dove, and it remained on him. 33I myself did not know him, but the one who sent me to baptize with water said to me, 'He on whom you see the Spirit descend and remain is the one who baptizes with the Holy Spirit.' 34And I myself have seen and have testified that this is the Son of God."[e]

The First Disciples of Jesus

35 The next day John again was standing with two of his disciples, 36and as he watched Jesus walk by, he exclaimed, "Look, here is the Lamb of God!" 37The two disciples heard him say this, and they followed Jesus. 38When Jesus turned and saw them following, he said to them, "What are you looking for?" They said to him, "Rabbi" (which translated means Teacher), "where are

---

a Or the Father's only Son   b Other ancient authorities read It is an only Son, God, or It is the only Son   c Gk bosom   d Or the Christ   e Other ancient authorities read is God's chosen one

---

the dwelling of God's wisdom in Israel through the law. A father's only son, lit. "an only one from a [or the] father." **1.15** See vv. 27, 30; note on 1.6–8. **1.17** Came, or "came into existence." **1.18** No one has ever seen God. See also 1 Jn 4.12. God the only Son, lit. "the only God." Made him known. The primary function of Jesus is that of a revealer, although unlike other such figures in ancient religion he makes God known on the cross. **1.19–34** John the Baptist's testimony to Jesus is more developed in John than in the other Gospels (cf. Mt 3.1–12; Mk 1.2–8; Lk 3.1–18). Only Luke also includes speculation that John might be the Messiah, the anointed king expected at the end of time (cf. Jn 1.20; Lk 3.15; see also Acts 13.25; note on Jn 1.6–8). **1.19** The Jews, i.e., the Jewish authorities, identified in v. 24 as the Pharisees (see Introduction). Levites in NT times assisted the priests in the temple rituals and worked as administrators, guards, musicians, singers, etc. **1.21** Many Jews expected the return of Elijah (Mal 4.5–6; see also Mt 11.14; Mk 6.15; 8.28; 9.4–5, 11–13; Lk 1.17) or the rise of a prophet like Moses (Deut 18.15; see also Jn 6.14; 7.40, 52; Acts 3.22–24; 7.37) in

the last days. **1.23** John the Baptist quotes Isa 40.3. Cf. Mt 3.3; Mk 1.3; Lk 3.4. **1.26** Whom you do not know. See v. 10. **1.27** The one . . . coming after me. See v. 15. **1.28** Bethany across the Jordan (i.e., east of the Jordan River). Location unknown. **1.29** Lamb of God . . . world. Cf. 1 Jn 2.2. Why Jesus is called the Lamb is not quite clear. Bulls, goats, and sheep were used as sacrifices for sin (see Lev 4–5), but not lambs. John presents Jesus as the Passover lamb (see notes on 19.14; 19.36), but that lamb is not a sacrifice for sin. A reference to Isa 53.7 is possible but uncertain. **1.30** See v. 15. **1.32–34** Unlike in the other Gospels, Jesus' baptism itself is not described, only John's response to it; cf. Mt 3.13–17; Mk 1.9–11; Lk 3.21–22. The purpose of John's ministry is interpreted in strictly Christian terms. His baptism was not for repentance but that Jesus might be revealed (v. 31). **1.35–51** Only John says that Jesus' first disciples came from among the disciples of John the Baptist. They seem to increasingly recognize Jesus' special status (vv. 38, 41, 45, 49, 51), although Jesus finally tells them they will see something unexpected (v. 51). **1.36** Lamb of God. See v. 29.

you staying?" ³⁹He said to them, "Come and see." They came and saw where he was staying, and they remained with him that day. It was about four o'clock in the afternoon. ⁴⁰One of the two who heard John speak and followed him was Andrew, Simon Peter's brother. ⁴¹He first found his brother Simon and said to him, "We have found the Messiah" (which is translated Anointed*ᵃ*). ⁴²He brought Simon*ᵇ* to Jesus, who looked at him and said, "You are Simon son of John. You are to be called Cephas" (which is translated Peter*ᶜ*).

Jesus Calls Philip and Nathanael

43 The next day Jesus decided to go to Galilee. He found Philip and said to him, "Follow me." ⁴⁴Now Philip was from Bethsaida, the city of Andrew and Peter. ⁴⁵Philip found Nathanael and said to him, "We have found him about whom Moses in the law and also the prophets wrote, Jesus son of Joseph from Nazareth." ⁴⁶Nathanael said to him, "Can anything good come out of Nazareth?" Philip said to him, "Come and see." ⁴⁷When Jesus saw Nathanael coming toward him, he said of him, "Here is truly an Israelite in whom there is no deceit!" ⁴⁸Nathanael asked him, "Where did you get to know me?" Jesus answered, "I saw you under the fig tree before Philip called you." ⁴⁹Nathanael replied, "Rabbi, you are the Son of God! You are the King of Israel!" ⁵⁰Jesus answered, "Do you believe because I told you that I saw you under the fig tree? You will see

greater things than these." ⁵¹And he said to him, "Very truly, I tell you,*ᵈ* you will see heaven opened and the angels of God ascending and descending upon the Son of Man."

The Wedding at Cana

2 On the third day there was a wedding in Cana of Galilee, and the mother of Jesus was there. ²Jesus and his disciples had also been invited to the wedding. ³When the wine gave out, the mother of Jesus said to him, "They have no wine." ⁴And Jesus said to her, "Woman, what concern is that to you and to me? My hour has not yet come." ⁵His mother said to the servants, "Do whatever he tells you." ⁶Now standing there were six stone water jars for the Jewish rites of purification, each holding twenty or thirty gallons. ⁷Jesus said to them, "Fill the jars with water." And they filled them up to the brim. ⁸He said to them, "Now draw some out, and take it to the chief steward." So they took it. ⁹When the steward tasted the water that had become wine, and did not know where it came from (though the servants who had drawn the water knew), the steward called the bridegroom ¹⁰and said to him, "Everyone serves the good wine first, and then the inferior wine after the guests have become drunk. But you have kept the good wine until now." ¹¹Jesus did this, the first of his signs, in

a Or Christ *b* Gk him *c* From the word for rock in Aramaic (kepha) and Greek (petra), respectively *d* Both instances of the Greek word for you in this verse are plural

---

1.38 What are you looking for . . . Teacher. Cf. 20.15–16. **1.40** On Andrew and Simon Peter, cf. Mk 1.16–17. **1.42** On the naming of Peter, cf. Mt 16.17–18. **1.43** Philip appears in all the lists of the twelve apostles (e.g., Mk 3.18). He appears with Andrew in Jn 6.5–9; 12.21–22; and alone in 14.8. The calling of the disciples takes place in Bethany (see note on 1.28). **1.44** Bethsaida, a town near the northern end of the Sea of Galilee. **1.45** Nathanael appears only in John (here and in 21.2). Son of Joseph. Cf. v. 49. **1.46** Nazareth, a small secluded village. **1.47** An Israelite in whom there is no deceit. "Israel" was the name given to Jacob (Gen 32.28), who had been deceitful (Gen 27.34–36). **1.49** The Son of God, the King of Israel. In ancient Israel, the king might be thought of metaphorically as God's son (2 Sam 7.14; Pss 2.7; 89.26), but in John Jesus' sonship means his divinity. John also associates Jesus' messianic kingship with prophetic powers (see note on 6.14–15), here seen in Jesus' supernatural knowledge about Nathanael. **1.50** Greater things. See 5.20; 14.12. **1.51** Angels of God ascending and descending, another reference to Jacob/Israel (see note on 1.47), here to his dream of a ladder to heaven (Gen

28.12). Son of Man, a mysterious title that in the Gospels probably derives, at least in part, from Dan 7.13–14. In John, it often represents Jesus' role as a link between heaven and earth; see 3.13; 5.26–27; 6.62; 8.26–27; 12.32–33; see also Mk 14.62.
2.1–12 This miracle is found only in John. **2.1** The third day continues the series of days from 1.29, 35, 43. Wedding festivities usually lasted a week; those invited might be expected to contribute provisions such as wine. According to 21.2, Cana, in central Galilee, was the hometown of Nathanael (1.45). **2.4** What concern is that to you and to me, a negative response (cf. 2 Kings 3.13) but not necessarily a disrespectful one. Neither is it disrespectful for Jesus to call his mother woman; see 19.26. Jesus' hour means the hour of his death (see note on 7.30; cf. 4.21). **2.6** Rites of purification, e.g., washing of hands and vessels (see Mk 7.1–4). **2.8** Chief steward, perhaps a servant acting as headwaiter or one of the guests chosen as a master of ceremonies (Sir 32.1). **2.11** The first of his signs. A second sign is mentioned in 4.54 (though others happen in between; see 2.23) and other unrecorded signs in 20.30. This may suggest that John's Gospel is partly based on a source that focused

Cana of Galilee, and revealed his glory; and his disciples believed in him.

12 After this he went down to Capernaum with his mother, his brothers, and his disciples; and they remained there a few days.

Jesus Cleanses the Temple

13 The Passover of the Jews was near, and Jesus went up to Jerusalem. 14In the temple he found people selling cattle, sheep, and doves, and the money changers seated at their tables. 15Making a whip of cords, he drove all of them out of the temple, both the sheep and the cattle. He also poured out the coins of the money changers and overturned their tables. 16He told those who were selling the doves, "Take these things out of here! Stop making my Father's house a marketplace!" 17His disciples remembered that it was written, "Zeal for your house will consume me." 18The Jews then said to him, "What sign can you show us for doing this?" 19Jesus answered them, "Destroy this temple, and in three days I will raise it up." 20The Jews then said, "This temple has been under construction for forty-six years, and will you raise it up in three days?" 21But he was speaking of the temple of his body. 22After he was raised from the dead, his disciples remembered that he had said this; and they believed the scripture and the word that Jesus had spoken.

23 When he was in Jerusalem during the Passover festival, many believed in his name because they saw the signs that he was doing. 24But Jesus on his part would not entrust himself to them, because he knew all people 25and needed no one to testify about anyone; for he himself knew what was in everyone.

Nicodemus Visits Jesus

3 Now there was a Pharisee named Nicodemus, a leader of the Jews. 2He came to Jesus[a] by night and said to him, "Rabbi, we know that you are a teacher who has come from God; for no one can do these signs that you do apart from the presence of God." 3Jesus answered him, "Very truly, I tell you, no one can see the kingdom of God without being born from above."[b] 4Nicodemus said to him, "How can anyone be born after having grown old? Can one enter a second time into the mother's womb and be born?" 5Jesus answered, "Very truly, I tell you, no one can enter

---

a Gk *him*   b Or *born anew*

---

on miraculous signs of Jesus. In John such signs have a complex relation to *believing* (see 2.23–3.3; 4.48; 6.2, 14, 26, 30; 7.31; 9.16; 12.37). *Glory*. See note on 1.14. **2.12** *Capernaum*, a prosperous city near the northern end of the Sea of Galilee that Jesus made the center of his ministry (see 6.17, 24, 59; Mt 4.13; 11.23; Mk 2.1). *His brothers*. See also 7.3–5. **2.13–22** The cleansing of the temple is found at the end of Jesus' mission in the other Gospels (e.g., Mk 11.15–18); this is more likely to be correct historically, since it may have been one reason for his crucifixion. John uses the story here to introduce Jesus' confrontation with the Jewish authorities and also the theme that Jesus is the new temple. **2.13** *Passover* occurs in March or April (see Ex 12.1–13.10; Deut 16.1–8). As many as one hundred thousand people might make the pilgrimage to *Jerusalem* for this festival. **2.14** *Cattle, sheep, and doves*, animals used as sacrifices. *Money changers* converted foreign currency into the coins allowed in the temple. This activity took place in the outer area of the temple, where non-Jews were allowed. **2.15** Neither the *whip* nor the *sheep and cattle* are mentioned in the other Gospels. **2.16** *Stop making . . . marketplace*. See Zech 14.21. **2.17** The quotation is from Ps 69.9. **2.18** On the demand for a *sign*, see 6.30; Mk 11.27–33; see also Mt 12.38–39; Mk 8.11–13. **2.19–21** On the Jews' misunderstanding, see notes on 3.4; 7.33–36. In Mt 26.59–61; Mk 14.55–59 (cf. Acts 6.14), it is said that Jesus was falsely accused of making the claim in v. 19. **2.20** The *temple* here would have been the Second Temple, built in the sixth century BCE (Ezra 1; 3; 5–6; Hag 1–2; Zech 6.9–15). King Herod the Great began renovations and enlargements of it around 20 BCE, which were still in progress in Jesus' day. **2.21** Identification of the *temple* with Jesus' *body* precludes an accusation that he wanted to destroy the physical temple. It also suggests that Jesus is the true temple, where one abides with and worships God. Cf. 4.23; 14.20. **2.22** *His disciples remembered*. For other examples of remembrances, see 12.16; 14.25–26; 16.12–13; 20.9. **2.23–25** The mention of *signs* and believers to whom Jesus *would not entrust himself* makes a transition to the dialogue with Nicodemus in ch. 3. **2.23** *Signs*. See note on 2.11. **2.24–25** On the ability to discern *what was in everyone*, see also 1 Sam 16.7; 1 Chr 28.9; Ps 139.

3.1–21 Nicodemus is mentioned only in John (7.45–52; 19.38–42). He may stand for a group (*we*, v. 2; plural *you*, vv. 7, 11, 12) with inadequate faith based on signs (v. 2; cf. 2.23–25). See also 12.42–43; Introduction. **3.2** *Night*. The setting dramatizes the role of Jesus as the Light. Cf. 11.10; 13.30. **3.3** Cf. Mt 18.3–4; Mk 10.15. *Born from above*, i.e., born from God; see 1.12–13; cf. 3.31; 8.23; 19.11. **3.4** The Greek word translated *from above* in v. 3 can also mean *anew* (see text note b). This is the source of Nicodemus's misunderstanding. Such misunderstandings, cases of dramatic irony since readers know what the character in the story does not, are common in John; see, e.g., 2.19–21; 4.10–15, 31–38; 11.11–13; note on 7.33–36. **3.5** *Water*, i.e., baptism, associated with new birth and

the kingdom of God without being born of water and Spirit. 6What is born of the flesh is flesh, and what is born of the Spirit is spirit.*ᵃ* 7Do not be astonished that I said to you, 'You*ᵇ* must be born from above.'*ᶜ* 8The wind*ᵃ* blows where it chooses, and you hear the sound of it, but you do not know where it comes from or where it goes. So it is with everyone who is born of the Spirit." 9Nicodemus said to him, "How can these things be?" 10Jesus answered him, "Are you a teacher of Israel, and yet you do not understand these things?

11 "Very truly, I tell you, we speak of what we know and testify to what we have seen; yet you*ᵈ* do not receive our testimony. 12If I have told you about earthly things and you do not believe, how can you believe if I tell you about heavenly things? 13No one has ascended into heaven except the one who descended from heaven, the Son of Man.*ᵉ* 14And just as Moses lifted up the serpent in the wilderness, so must the Son of Man be lifted up, 15that whoever believes in him may have eternal life.*ᶠ*

16 "For God so loved the world that he gave his only Son, so that everyone who believes in him may not perish but may have eternal life. 17 "Indeed, God did not send the Son into the world to condemn the world, but in order that the world might be saved through him. 18Those who believe in him are not condemned; but those who do not believe are condemned already, because they have not believed in the name of the only Son of God. 19And this is the judgment, that the light has come into the world, and people loved darkness rather than light because their deeds were evil. 20For all who do evil hate the light and do not come to the light, so that their deeds may not be exposed. 21But those who do what is true come to the light, so that it may be clearly seen that their deeds have been done in God."*ᶠ*

a The same Greek word means both *wind* and *spirit*
b The Greek word for *you* here is plural   *c* Or *anew*
d The Greek word for *you* here and in verse 12 is plural
e Other ancient authorities add *who is in heaven*   *f* Some interpreters hold that the quotation concludes with verse 15

the *Spirit* in Rom 6.4; 1 Cor 6.11; 12.13; Titus 3.5. **3.6** On the contrast of *flesh* and *spirit*, see also 6.63. For the contrast of proper and improper births, cf. 1.13. **3.8** *You do not know . . . where it goes.* See 7.26–29; 8.14; 9.28–30. An old proverb may lie behind this remark. Cf. Eccl 11.5; Sir 16.21. **3.10** *A teacher*, lit. "the teacher." **3.11** On Jesus' *testimony*, see 8.13–18. **3.13** *Ascended, descended.* See 1.51; 6.62. **3.14** *Serpent.* See Num 21.9. *Lifted up* refers both to Jesus' glorification and to his crucifixion; see also 8.28; 12.32–34 (cf. Isa 52.13). Understanding the significance of the crucified Jesus is essential to the spiritual healing

that he provides. **3.16** See 5.24; 6.40, 47; 11.25–26; 20.31; 1 Jn 4.9. **3.17** See 1 Jn 4.14. *Condemn,* or "judge." See 5.24; 12.47–48. **3.19** *Light, darkness.* See 1.5, 9; 1 Jn 1.6–7; 2.9–11; Eph 5.11–14; Job 24.13–17. The notion of *judgment* is applied not to some future coming of Jesus but to his encounter with potential believers. **3.20** *All who do evil hate the light.* See 7.7; 15.22–24. The saying provides a rationale to explain why some people reject claims about Jesus. The sharp dichotomy of light and dark resembles the dualism in the Dead Sea Scrolls, *Rule of the Community* (1QS 3.15–4.1). **3.21** *Do what is true.* See 1 Jn 1.6.

Jewish Festivals in the Gospel of John

FESTIVAL	TIME OF YEAR	OCCURRENCE IN JOHN
Passover	March/April	John 2.13, 23; 4.45; 6.4; 11.55; 12.1, 12, 20; 13.1, 29; 18.28, 39; 19.14
Booths (Sukkoth)	October	John 7.1-14, 37
Dedication (Hanukkah)	December	John 10.22
An unnamed festival		John 5.1

Jesus and John the Baptist

22 After this Jesus and his disciples went into the Judean countryside, and he spent some time there with them and baptized. 23 John also was baptizing at Aenon near Salim because water was abundant there; and people kept coming and were being baptized 24— John, of course, had not yet been thrown into prison.

25 Now a discussion about purification arose between John's disciples and a Jew.[a] 26 They came to John and said to him, "Rabbi, the one who was with you across the Jordan, to whom you testified, here he is baptizing, and all are going to him." 27 John answered, "No one can receive anything except what has been given from heaven. 28 You yourselves are my witnesses that I said, 'I am not the Messiah,'[b] but I have been sent ahead of him.' 29 He who has the bride is the bridegroom. The friend of the bridegroom, who stands and hears him, rejoices greatly at the bridegroom's voice. For this reason my joy has been fulfilled. 30 He must increase, but I must decrease."[c]

The One Who Comes from Heaven

31 The one who comes from above is above all; the one who is of the earth belongs to the earth and speaks about earthly things. The one who comes from heaven is above all. 32 He testifies to what he has seen and heard, yet no one accepts his testimony. 33 Whoever has accepted his testimony has certified[d] this, that God is true. 34 He whom God has sent speaks the words of God, for he gives the Spirit without measure. 35 The Father loves the Son and has placed all things in his hands. 36 Whoever believes in the Son has eternal life; whoever disobeys the Son will not see life, but must endure God's wrath.

Jesus and the Woman of Samaria

4 Now when Jesus[e] learned that the Pharisees had heard, "Jesus is making and baptizing more disciples than John" 2—although it was not Jesus himself but his disciples who baptized— 3 he left Judea and started back to Galilee. 4 But he had to go through Samaria. 5 So he came to a Samaritan city called Sychar, near the plot of ground that Jacob had given to his son Joseph. 6 Jacob's well was there, and Jesus, tired out by his journey, was sitting by the well. It was about noon.

7 A Samaritan woman came to draw water, and Jesus said to her, "Give me a drink." 8 (His disciples had gone to the city to buy food.) 9 The Samaritan woman said to him, "How is it that you, a Jew, ask a drink of me, a woman of Samaria?" (Jews do not share things in common with Samaritans.)[f] 10 Jesus answered her, "If you knew the gift of God, and who it is that is saying to you, 'Give me a drink,' you would have asked him, and he would have given you living water." 11 The woman said to him, "Sir,

---

a Other ancient authorities read *the Jews*   b Or *the Christ*
c Some interpreters hold that the quotation continues through verse 36   d Gk *set a seal to*   e Other ancient authorities read *the Lord*   f Other ancient authorities lack this sentence

---

3.22–36 On the contrast between Jesus and John the Baptist, see notes on 1.6–8; 1.19–34. **3.22** Jesus is said to *baptize* only here and in 4.1 in the NT. **3.23** *Aenon, Salim.* Locations uncertain. **3.24** On the imprisonment of John, see Mt 11.2–3; Mk 6.17–18. **3.25** *Purification* might refer to John's and Jesus' baptizing. **3.27** See also 19.11. **3.28** *I am not the Messiah.* See 1.20. **3.29** For the image of God's people as a *bride,* see Isa 62.5; Jer 2.2; Hos 2.16–20; 2 Cor 11.2; Rev 19.6–8; 21.9–10; see also Mk 2.19–20. *Friend,* i.e., the "best man," who brought the bride to the groom. *Joy . . . fulfilled.* See 15.11; 16.24; 17.13; 1 Jn 1.4; 2 Jn 12. **3.31–36** Note the similarities to vv. 1–21 at several points: the superiority of the one who is *from above; testimony* that is rejected; and *eternal life* for those who *believe in the Son,* but condemnation for others. The passage is best construed as a narrator's summary of the story thus far. **3.31** *The one who comes from above.* See 8.23; 18.36; cf. 15.19; 17.14–16. **3.35** See 5.20. **3.36** See also 1 Jn 5.12. *God's wrath,* not simply divine emotion, but God's judgment; see, e.g., Rom 2.5–8; Col 3.6. The statement corrects a possible reading of v. 17 that would deny the reality of divine judgment.

4.1–6 This travel story brings Jesus to Samaria for his conversation with the woman at the well. **4.1** On Jesus' *baptizing,* see 3.22. **4.4** *Had to go through Samaria.* Other routes led from Judea to Galilee, but the most direct lay through Samaria. **4.5** *Sychar,* the OT city Shechem; see Gen 33.18–19; Josh 24.32. **4.6** *Jacob's well* is not mentioned in the OT. *Noon,* in the heat of the day, was an unusual time to draw water. **4.7–26** In her dialogue with Jesus, the woman gains an increasing recognition of who he is (vv. 9, 12, 19, 25). **4.9** Though both Jews and Samaritans were descended from ancient Israel and practiced similar religions, there was long-standing hostility between them. Thus it was also unusual for Jews to buy food (v. 8) from Samaritans. **4.10** *Living water.* See also 7.37–39. In Hebrew, the term means spring water (see Jer 2.13; Zech 14.8), although a metaphorical sense soon comes into view. **4.11–15** There is a similar dialogue in 6.30–35 contrasting what Jesus gives with what the ancestors had.

you have no bucket, and the well is deep. Where do you get that living water? 12Are you greater than our ancestor Jacob, who gave us the well, and with his sons and his flocks drank from it?" 13Jesus said to her, "Everyone who drinks of this water will be thirsty again, 14but those who drink of the water that I will give them will never be thirsty. The water that I will give will become in them a spring of water gushing up to eternal life." 15The woman said to him, "Sir, give me this water, so that I may never be thirsty or have to keep coming here to draw water."

16 Jesus said to her, "Go, call your husband, and come back." 17The woman answered him, "I have no husband." Jesus said to her, "You are right in saying, 'I have no husband'; 18for you have had five husbands, and the one you have now is not your husband. What you have said is true!" 19The woman said to him, "Sir, I see that you are a prophet. 20Our ancestors worshiped on this mountain, but you*a* say that the place where people must worship is in Jerusalem." 21Jesus said to her, "Woman, believe me, the hour is coming when you will worship the Father neither on this mountain nor in Jerusalem. 22You worship what you do not know; we worship what we know, for salvation is from the Jews. 23But the hour is coming, and is now here, when the true worshipers will worship the Father in spirit and truth, for the Father seeks such as these to worship him. 24God is spirit, and those who worship him must worship in spirit and truth." 25The woman said to

him, "I know that Messiah is coming" (who is called Christ). "When he comes, he will proclaim all things to us." 26Jesus said to her, "I am he,*b* the one who is speaking to you."

27 Just then his disciples came. They were astonished that he was speaking with a woman, but no one said, "What do you want?" or, "Why are you speaking with her?" 28Then the woman left her water jar and went back to the city. She said to the people, 29"Come and see a man who told me everything I have ever done! He cannot be the Messiah,*c* can he?" 30They left the city and were on their way to him.

31 Meanwhile the disciples were urging him, "Rabbi, eat something." 32But he said to them, "I have food to eat that you do not know about." 33So the disciples said to one another, "Surely no one has brought him something to eat?" 34Jesus said to them, "My food is to do the will of him who sent me and to complete his work. 35Do you not say, 'Four months more, then comes the harvest'? But I tell you, look around you, and see how the fields are ripe for harvesting. 36The reaper is already receiving*d* wages and is gathering fruit for eternal life, so that sower and reaper may rejoice together. 37For here the saying holds true, 'One sows and another reaps.' 38I sent you to reap that for which you did not labor. Others have labored, and you have entered into their labor."

a The Greek word for *you* here and in verses 21 and 22 is plural *b* Gk *I am* *c* Or *the Christ* *d* Or *35. . . the fields are already ripe for harvesting. 36The reaper is receiving*

See also Isa 55.1; Rev 21.6; 22.17. **4.12** *Are you greater.* See also 8.53. **4.15** The misunderstanding is a common Johannine technique; see notes on 3.4; 7.33–36. **4.16** *Husband.* Perhaps this subject is raised because, in the OT, the meeting of a man and a woman at a well often leads to marriage; see Gen 24.10–61; 29.1–20; Ex 2.15–21. **4.18** Though it is often suggested, *five husbands* probably does not refer to the five nations in the anti-Samaritan account in 2 Kings 17.24–41. Neither is an allegorical reading likely, such as that of Augustine, who suggested that the husbands symbolize the five senses. **4.19–20** The woman raises an issue suitable for a *prophet* to discuss. *Our ancestors*, i.e., the ancestors of both Jews and Samaritans. *You*, i.e., the Jews. *This mountain.* The Samaritans believed that Mount Gerizim, not Jerusalem, was the place designated by God for worship (see Deut 11.26–30; 27.1–13; Josh 8.30–35). They had once had a temple on the mountain, which was near Sychar (Shechem), where this story takes place. **4.23** John speaks several times of an *hour* that *is coming, and is now here* (5.25–29; 16.21, 32). See

also notes on 7.30; 12.23; 16.25. *Spirit and truth* are connected with Jesus and belief in him in John. See 1.14, 17, 33; 3.5–8; 6.63; 7.39; 8.31–32; 14.6; 17.17–19; 18.37; 20.22. **4.25** *Christ,* the Greek equivalent of the Hebrew word *Messiah.* Cf. 1.41. **4.26** *I am he.* See note on 8.24. **4.27–30** The Samaritans' movement toward Jesus (vv. 30, 39–40) forms the backdrop for his dialogue with the disciples (vv. 31–38). **4.27** It was against the social customs of that time for a Jewish religious teacher to be *speaking with a woman* in public. **4.29** *He cannot be the Messiah, can he?* or "Could he perhaps be the Messiah?" **4.31–38** Jesus has a better *food* (vv. 32, 34) than the disciples know (see note on 3.4), just as he had a better water than the woman thought (vv. 7–15). **4.34** *Food . . . work.* See 6.27–29; see also note on 5.19–20. **4.35–36** The harvest of people that is Jesus' work (cf. Lk 10.2) includes the Samaritans. The *sower* planted grain (see Mk 4.3–8) and the *reaper* harvested it several months later when it was ripe; but the time for this "harvest" has already come. **4.38** *Others,* perhaps Moses and the prophets, the teachers of the

39 Many Samaritans from that city believed in him because of the woman's testimony, "He told me everything I have ever done." 40 So when the Samaritans came to him, they asked him to stay with them; and he stayed there two days. 41 And many more believed because of his word. 42 They said to the woman, "It is no longer because of what you said that we believe, for we have heard for ourselves, and we know that this is truly the Savior of the world."

Jesus Returns to Galilee

43 When the two days were over, he went from that place to Galilee 44 (for Jesus himself had testified that a prophet has no honor in the prophet's own country). 45 When he came to Galilee, the Galileans welcomed him, since they had seen all that he had done in Jerusalem at the festival; for they too had gone to the festival.

Jesus Heals an Official's Son

46 Then he came again to Cana in Galilee where he had changed the water into wine. Now there was a royal official whose son lay ill in Capernaum. 47 When he heard that Jesus had come from Judea to Galilee, he went and begged him to come down and heal his son, for he was at the point of death. 48 Then Jesus said to him, "Unless you[a] see signs and wonders you will not believe." 49 The official said to him, "Sir, come down before my little boy dies." 50 Jesus said to him, "Go; your son will live." The man believed the word that Jesus spoke to him and started on his way. 51 As he was going down, his slaves met him and told him that his child was alive. 52 So he asked them the hour when he began to recover, and they said to him, "Yesterday at one in the afternoon the fever left him." 53 The father realized that this was the hour when Jesus had said to him, "Your son will live." So he himself believed, along with his whole household. 54 Now this was the second sign that Jesus did after coming from Judea to Galilee.

Jesus Heals on the Sabbath

5 After this there was a festival of the Jews, and Jesus went up to Jerusalem.

2 Now in Jerusalem by the Sheep Gate there is a pool, called in Hebrew[b] Beth-zatha,[c] which has five porticoes. 3 In these lay many invalids—blind, lame, and paralyzed.[d] 5 One man was there who had been ill for thirty-eight years. 6 When Jesus saw him lying there and knew that he had been there a long time,

---

a Both instances of the Greek word for *you* in this verse are plural *b* That is, *Aramaic* *c* Other ancient authorities read *Bethesda*, others *Bethsaida* *d* Other ancient authorities add, wholly or in part, *waiting for the stirring of the water;* 4*for an angel of the Lord went down at certain seasons into the pool, and stirred up the water; whoever stepped in first after the stirring of the water was made well from whatever disease that person had.*

Samaritans, or Christian missionaries. **4.39–42** Now the Samaritan "harvest" is reaped, first through *the woman's testimony,* then through direct contact with Jesus. The extent of contacts with Samaritans by Jesus is unclear. Mt 10.5 prohibits the disciples from going to them. Acts 8.4–13 places missionary activity to Samaria in the period of the early church. **4.42** *Savior of the world.* See 3.17; 12.47; 1 Jn 4.14. **4.43–45** Jesus finally reaches the goal for which he had set out in v. 3. **4.44** See Mk 6.4. Jesus' *own country* is Galilee (1.46; 7.41–42, 52); the claim that he *has no honor* there, though the Galileans welcome him (v. 45), may indicate doubts about their enthusiasm based on signs (see note on 2.11). **4.45** *Festival.* See 2.13, 23. **4.46–54** The story of the healing of the official's son is comparable to that of the centurion's servant (which also takes place at Capernaum) in Mt 8.5–13; Lk 7.1–10. **4.46** *Cana . . . water into wine.* See 2.1–11. *Royal official,* presumably in the service of Herod Antipas, the son of King Herod the Great (Mk 6.14; see "The Herods: A Simplified Family Tree," p. 1672). From Cana to *Capernaum* was fifteen or twenty miles. **4.48** On *signs* and *beliefs,* see 6.30; notes on 2.11; 11.40. **4.50** *Your son will live.* Cf. 1 Kings 17.23. **4.54** *Second sign.* See note on 2.11.

5.1–7.52 It has sometimes been suggested that ch. 5 belongs after ch. 6. This would make a good connection between ch. 5 and ch. 7, since the retreat in 7.1 would be directly caused by the dispute in ch. 5 (cf. also 7.19–24; 5.16–18). This arrangement would also make Jesus' travels clearer, since he would still be in Galilee to make the trip mentioned in 6.1. If, however, this were the original arrangement, it would be hard to explain the present order. **5.1–18** Though this miracle story is found only in John, other controversies over healing on the sabbath are found in Mt 12.9–14; Mk 3.1–6; Lk 13.10–17; 14.1–6. See also Jn 7.21–24; 9.13–17. **5.1** *Festival,* possibly Passover or Pentecost in the spring or the New Year or the Festival of Booths in the fall; or perhaps no specific festival was intended. (See "Jewish Festivals in the Gospel of John," p. 1820.) **5.2** *Sheep Gate,* probably a gate in the northern wall of Jerusalem, near the temple (see Neh 3.1). In that area are remains of a double pool, which may be *Beth-zatha.* The pools are surrounded by four *porticoes* (walkways with columns to support their roofs), and there is a fifth portico between the two pools. **5.3–5** Though v. 4 is striking, it is not found in the best manuscripts (see text note *d*), and its wording in Greek is unlike the rest of the Gospel of John. Therefore it was probably not originally part of this Gospel.

he said to him, "Do you want to be made well?" 7The sick man answered him, "Sir, I have no one to put me into the pool when the water is stirred up; and while I am making my way, someone else steps down ahead of me." 8Jesus said to him, "Stand up, take your mat and walk." 9At once the man was made well, and he took up his mat and began to walk.

Now that day was a sabbath. 10So the Jews said to the man who had been cured, "It is the sabbath; it is not lawful for you to carry your mat." 11But he answered them, "The man who made me well said to me, 'Take up your mat and walk.' " 12They asked him, "Who is the man who said to you, 'Take it up and walk'?" 13Now the man who had been healed did not know who it was, for Jesus had disappeared in*a* the crowd that was there. 14Later Jesus found him in the temple and said to him, "See, you have been made well! Do not sin any more, so that nothing worse happens to you." 15The man went away and told the Jews that it was Jesus who had made him well. 16Therefore the Jews started persecuting Jesus, because he was doing such things on the sabbath. 17But Jesus answered them, "My Father is still working, and I also am working." 18For this reason the Jews were seeking all the more to kill him, because he was not only breaking the sabbath, but was also calling God his own Father, thereby making himself equal to God.

The Authority of the Son

19 Jesus said to them, "Very truly, I tell you, the Son can do nothing on his own, but only what he sees the Father doing; for whatever the Father*b* does, the Son does likewise. 20The Father loves the Son and shows him all that he himself is doing; and he will show him greater works than these, so that you will be astonished. 21Indeed, just as the Father raises the dead and gives them life, so also the Son gives life to whomever he wishes. 22The Father judges no one but has given all judgment to the Son, 23so that all may honor the Son just as they honor the Father. Anyone who does not honor the Son does not honor the Father who sent him. 24Very truly, I tell you, anyone who hears my word and believes him who sent me has eternal life, and does not come under judgment, but has passed from death to life.

25 "Very truly, I tell you, the hour is coming, and is now here, when the dead will hear the voice of the Son of God, and those who hear will live. 26For just as the Father has life in himself, so he has granted the Son also to have life in himself; 27and he has given him authority to execute judgment, because he is the Son of Man. 28Do not be astonished at this; for the hour is coming when all who are in their graves will hear his voice 29and will come

a Or had left because of *b* Gk that one

5.8 *Stand up . . . and walk.* See also Mk 2.9, 11; Acts 3.6. 5.10 *The Jews,* as usual in John, the authorities, not the Jewish people in general; see Introduction. *Not lawful.* The law has few details about particular activities that are forbidden on the sabbath (see Ex 20.8–11; 31.12–17; 35.2–3; Lev 23.3; Deut 5.12–15); but carrying burdens on the sabbath is opposed in Neh 13.15–21; Jer 17.19–27, and this prohibition was accepted and developed in Jewish tradition. 5.14 *Do not sin any more.* See also Mk 2.5; Jn 8.11. 5.15 *Told the Jews.* See also 11.46. 5.17 *My Father is still working.* Cf. Gen 2.2. Jewish teachers held that God continued to "work" after creation, sustaining the world even on the sabbath. 5.18 *To kill him.* See 8.58–59; 10.30–39; see also 7.1, 19–20, 25; 8.37–40. *Making himself equal to God.* A theological claim, rather than breaking the sabbath, is now the heart of the dispute. 5.19–47 Jesus' first lengthy dispute with the Jewish authorities sets the stage for several more such disputes in chs. 6–10 by laying out themes that will be treated further in those chapters. 5.19–20 Cf. Mt 11.27. On the *works* of God and Jesus, see vv. 17, 36; see also 3.35; 4.34; 6.28–29; 9.3–4; 10.25, 37–38; 14.10–12; 17.4. *Be astonished.* See v. 28; 7.21; Hab 1.5. Jesus' defense initially suggests that

he is subordinate to the Father, but what he *sees the Father doing* is no ordinary human observation. 5.21 *Raises the dead,* i.e., at the resurrection on the last day. See note on 11.24. *Gives life.* See 6.33–35; 10.10, 28; 11.25; 14.6; 17.2. Jesus thus shares in the fundamental creative work of God, implying his functional equality with God. 5.22 Many Jews and early Christians expected God's final *judgment,* like the resurrection of the dead, at the end of time (Mt 12.36–37; Rom 2.1–16; 1 Jn 4.17–18; Rev 20.11–15). Here and in the following verses (vv. 23–30) this work of judgment, like that of resurrection, is transferred to Jesus (see also 3.17–19; 8.15–16; 9.39; 12.47–49). 5.23 Many passages state that to respond to Jesus is to respond to God, who sent him. See 12.44–45; 13.20; 14.7–9; Mt 10.40; Mk 9.37; Lk 10.16. 5.24 John asserts that for the believer eternal life does not wait until the end of time but is given now; see 11.25–26; 1 Jn 3.14; cf. Mk 10.30; Rom 2.5–7; Jude 21. 5.25–29 There may be a reference here to the raising of Lazarus (11.38–44); see also 6.39–40, 54. 5.25 *The hour.* See note on 4.23. 5.26 *The Son . . . to have life.* See also v. 21; 1.3–4. 5.27 *Son of Man.* See note on 1.51. 5.29 *Done good, done evil.* See also 3.19–21; Dan 12.2. *Resurrection of life,* in contrast

out—those who have done good, to the resurrection of life, and those who have done evil, to the resurrection of condemnation.

Witnesses to Jesus

30 "I can do nothing on my own. As I hear, I judge; and my judgment is just, because I seek to do not my own will but the will of him who sent me.

31 "If I testify about myself, my testimony is not true. 32 There is another who testifies on my behalf, and I know that his testimony to me is true. 33 You sent messengers to John, and he testified to the truth. 34 Not that I accept such human testimony, but I say these things so that you may be saved. 35 He was a burning and shining lamp, and you were willing to rejoice for a while in his light. 36 But I have a testimony greater than John's. The works that the Father has given me to complete, the very works that I am doing, testify on my behalf that the Father has sent me. 37 And the Father who sent me has himself testified on my behalf. You have never heard his voice or seen his form, 38 and you do not have his word abiding in you, because you do not believe him whom he has sent.

39 "You search the scriptures because you think that in them you have eternal life; and it is they that testify on my behalf. 40 Yet you refuse to come to me to have life. 41 I do not accept glory from human beings. 42 But I know that you do not have the love of God in *a* you. 43 I have come in my Father's name, and you do not accept me; if another comes in his own name, you will accept him. 44 How can you believe when you accept glory from one another and do not seek the glory that comes from the one who alone is God? 45 Do not think that I will accuse you before the Father; your accuser is Moses, on whom you have set your hope. 46 If you believed Moses, you would believe me, for he wrote about me. 47 But if you do not believe what he wrote, how will you believe what I say?"

Feeding the Five Thousand

6 After this Jesus went to the other side of the Sea of Galilee, also called the Sea of Tiberias. *b* 2 A large crowd kept following him, because they saw the signs that he was doing for the sick. 3 Jesus went up the mountain and sat down there with his disciples. 4 Now the Passover, the festival of the Jews, was near. 5 When he looked up and saw a large crowd coming toward him, Jesus said to Philip, "Where are we to buy bread for these people to eat?" 6 He said this to test him, for he himself knew what he was going to do. 7 Philip answered him, "Six months' wages *c* would not buy enough bread for each of them to get a little." 8 One of his disciples, Andrew, Simon Peter's brother, said to him, 9 "There is a boy here who has five barley loaves and two fish. But what are they among so many people?" 10 Jesus said, "Make the people sit down." Now there was a great deal of grass in the place; so

---

a Or *among*   *b* Gk *of Galilee of Tiberias*   *c* Gk *Two hundred denarii*; the denarius was the usual day's wage for a laborer

---

to v. 24, looks to a future resurrection. **5.30** *I can do nothing on my own.* See vv. 19–23; 8.15–16; note on 14.10. **5.31** Jewish law did not accept individuals' *testimony* about matters that concerned themselves; see also 8.13–18; 1 Jn 5.9. **5.33** See 1.19–28. **5.34** Jesus also explains why things are said in 11.42; 12.30. **5.35** That the Baptist was a *lamp* is a unique claim, which may recall a traditional saying such as Mt 5.14–16. **5.36** On the testimony of the *works,* see 10.25, 37–38; also note on 5.19–20. **5.37–38** The reference to the Father's testimony may mean the Jewish scriptures (vv. 39–40, 45–47), God's *word. Never heard his voice or seen his form.* See 1.18; 6.46; see also Ex 20.18–19; 33.18–20. **5.39** *You search* might also be translated as an ironic command, "Search the scriptures." In either case, eternal life is not in the scriptures, but in Jesus, to whom they testify. **5.41** Jesus does not seek *glory* for himself (cf. v. 18) but for God (see vv. 30, 44; 7.18; 8.50, 54; 12.43). **5.42** *Love of God,* probably love for God. **5.43** *In his own name,* perhaps like messianic pretenders. Cf. Mt 24.23–25;

Mk 13.21–23. **5.45–47** The point here is like that of vv. 39–40; see also Lk 16.29–31.

6.1–71 On the order of the chapters, see note on 5.1–7.52. **6.1–15** Cf. this story with the feeding of the five thousand in Mt 14.13–21; Mk 6.32–44; Lk 9.10–17; and the four thousand in Mt 15.32–39; Mk 8.1–10. John's version has some features that seem to come from a tradition independent of the other Gospels. **6.2** These *signs* may include those in 4.43–54 and others not narrated by John; see note on 2.11; cf. Mt 14.13; Lk 9.11. **6.3** *Mountain,* perhaps a particular unnamed mountain or "the hill country" more generally. **6.4** *Passover* (see also 2.13) is associated with unleavened bread and with the exodus, and thus with manna (vv. 31–35). Since Jesus' Last Supper was at or near Passover, the Christian Lord's Supper is also associated with Passover (see v. 11; "Jewish Festivals in the Gospel of John, p. 1820). **6.5** *Philip.* See note on 1.43. *Where are we to buy bread?* Cf. Num 11.13. **6.6** *He himself knew.* Cf. 11.42. **6.8** *Andrew.* See notes on 1.40; 1.43. **6.9** *Barley loaves.* Cf. 2 Kings 4.42–44.

they[a] sat down, about five thousand in all. [11]Then Jesus took the loaves, and when he had given thanks, he distributed them to those who were seated; so also the fish, as much as they wanted. [12]When they were satisfied, he told his disciples, "Gather up the fragments left over, so that nothing may be lost." [13]So they gathered them up, and from the fragments of the five barley loaves, left by those who had eaten, they filled twelve baskets. [14]When the people saw the sign that he had done, they began to say, "This is indeed the prophet who is to come into the world."

15 When Jesus realized that they were about to come and take him by force to make him king, he withdrew again to the mountain by himself.

Jesus Walks on the Water

16 When evening came, his disciples went down to the sea, [17]got into a boat, and started across the sea to Capernaum. It was now dark, and Jesus had not yet come to them. [18]The sea became rough because a strong wind was blowing. [19]When they had rowed about three or four miles,[b] they saw Jesus walking on the sea and coming near the boat, and they were terrified. [20]But he said to them, "It is I;[c] do not be afraid." [21]Then they wanted to take him into the boat, and immediately the boat reached the land toward which they were going.

The Bread from Heaven

22 The next day the crowd that had stayed on the other side of the sea saw that there had been only one boat there. They also saw that Jesus had not got into the boat with his disci-

ples, but that his disciples had gone away alone. [23]Then some boats from Tiberias came near the place where they had eaten the bread after the Lord had given thanks.[d] [24]So when the crowd saw that neither Jesus nor his disciples were there, they themselves got into the boats and went to Capernaum looking for Jesus.

25 When they found him on the other side of the sea, they said to him, "Rabbi, when did you come here?" [26]Jesus answered them, "Very truly, I tell you, you are looking for me, not because you saw signs, but because you ate your fill of the loaves. [27]Do not work for the food that perishes, but for the food that endures for eternal life, which the Son of Man will give you. For it is on him that God the Father has set his seal." [28]Then they said to him, "What must we do to perform the works of God?" [29]Jesus answered them, "This is the work of God, that you believe in him whom he has sent." [30]So they said to him, "What sign are you going to give us then, so that we may see it and believe you? What work are you performing? [31]Our ancestors ate the manna in the wilderness; as it is written, 'He gave them bread from heaven to eat.' " [32]Then Jesus said to them, "Very truly, I tell you, it was not Moses who gave you the bread from heaven, but it is my Father who gives you the true bread from heaven. [33]For the bread of God is that which[e] comes down from heaven and gives life to the world." [34]They said to him, "Sir, give us this bread always."

35 Jesus said to them, "I am the bread of

---

a Gk the men   b Gk about twenty-five or thirty stadia   c Gk I am   d Other ancient authorities lack after the Lord had given thanks   e Or he who

---

6.11 *Given thanks* translates the Greek word that is also the source of the term "Eucharist" (the Lord's Supper); cf. Jesus' actions here with those in Lk 22.19; 1 Cor 11.23–24. See also vv. 52–58; 21.13. **6.14–15** In the first century CE, a number of leaders who claimed to be the *prophet* (see note on 1.21) or the messianic *king* promised to do *signs* to prove that God had sent them to bring about the liberation of Israel from Roman control; see also 7.31; 9.17; 11.47–48; Acts 5.36–37; 21.38. **6.16–21** Jesus' walking on the sea is also connected with the feeding miracle in Mt 14.22–33; Mk 6.45–52. **6.18** Sudden violent storms are not uncommon on the Sea of Galilee. **6.20** *It is I* translates the same Greek words as *I am he* elsewhere in John; see note on 8.24. **6.22–24** A transitional passage. **6.23–24** *Tiberias* was on the southwest shore and *Capernaum* near the northern end of the Sea of Galilee.

6.25–34 From the very beginning of the discourse on the Bread of Life, Jesus seems critical of his audience. **6.26** *Not because you saw signs.* Cf. vv. 2, 14, 30, 36; see note on 2.11. **6.27–29** On *food* and *work*, see 4.32–34. **6.27** *Do not work for the food that perishes.* Cf. Mt 6.19–20. *His seal*, i.e., a mark of approval that sets the Son apart. **6.30–35** See the similar dialogue in 4.11–15 contrasting what Jesus gives with what the ancestors had. **6.31** *Manna.* See Ex 16. *Bread from heaven.* See Ex 16.4; Ps 78.23–25. Jesus' comments in what follows offer an interpretation of the scriptural verse applied to himself.

6.35–40 The ideas of *coming* to Jesus, *seeing* him and *believing* in him, and being *given* to him by God are closely associated in this passage. They are related to the situation of the early Christian community within the synagogue, where only some were coming

life. Whoever comes to me will never be hungry, and whoever believes in me will never be thirsty. 36But I said to you that you have seen me and yet do not believe. 37Everything that the Father gives me will come to me, and anyone who comes to me I will never drive away; 38for I have come down from heaven, not to do my own will, but the will of him who sent me. 39And this is the will of him who sent me, that I should lose nothing of all that he has given me, but raise it up on the last day. 40This is indeed the will of my Father, that all who see the Son and believe in him may have eternal life; and I will raise them up on the last day."

41 Then the Jews began to complain about him because he said, "I am the bread that came down from heaven." 42They were saying, "Is not this Jesus, the son of Joseph, whose father and mother we know? How can he now say, 'I have come down from heaven'?" 43Jesus answered them, "Do not complain among yourselves. 44No one can come to me unless drawn by the Father who sent me; and I will raise that person up on the last day. 45It is written in the prophets, 'And they shall all be taught by God.' Everyone who has heard and learned from the Father comes to me. 46Not that anyone has seen the Father except the one who is from God; he has seen the Father. 47Very truly, I tell you, whoever believes has eternal life. 48I am the bread of life. 49Your ancestors ate the manna in the wilderness, and they died. 50This is the bread that comes down from heaven, so that one may eat of it and not die. 51I am the living bread that came down from heaven. Whoever eats of this bread will live forever; and the bread that I will give for the life of the world is my flesh."

52 The Jews then disputed among themselves, saying, "How can this man give us his flesh to eat?" 53So Jesus said to them, "Very truly, I tell you, unless you eat the flesh of the Son of Man and drink his blood, you have no life in you. 54Those who eat my flesh and drink my blood have eternal life, and I will raise them up on the last day; 55for my flesh is true food and my blood is true drink. 56Those who eat my flesh and drink my blood abide in me, and I in them. 57Just as the living Father sent me, and I live because of the Father, so whoever eats me will live because of me. 58This is the bread that came down from heaven, not like that which your ancestors ate, and they died. But the one who eats this bread will live forever." 59He said these things while he was teaching in the synagogue at Capernaum.

The Words of Eternal Life

60 When many of his disciples heard it, they said, "This teaching is difficult; who can accept it?" 61But Jesus, being aware that his disciples

to join those who believed that Jesus was the Messiah (see Introduction). **6.35** *Bread of life,* like the *living water* (cf. 4.10, 14; 7.37–39), here symbolizes Jesus as the object of belief. **6.36** *I said to you,* perhaps a reference to v. 26; see also 3.12. On *seeing* and *believing,* see also vv. 30, 40. **6.37** *Everything . . . the Father gives me.* Cf. vv. 44–45; 10.28–29; 17.2, 6, 9. **6.38** *Not . . . my own will.* See 4.34; 5.30; 12.27; Lk 22.42. **6.39** *Raise it up on the last day.* Cf. 5.21–29; 11.23–26. **6.41–47** As in 3.1–15; 9.24–34, people resist the idea that God may act in an unexpected way (cf. v. 29); hence, as in vv. 35–40, it is those who are willing to hear and learn who are drawn by God. **6.41** The OT story of the manna (vv. 31, 49) is surrounded by incidents in which the people *complain* (Ex 15.22–17.7). **6.42** For the family of Jesus, see Mk 6.1–6; cf. Jn 7.27–28. **6.44** *Drawn.* See note on 6.35–40; cf. 12.32. **6.45** For the quotation, see Isa 54.13; see also Jer 31.34. The citation is part of the explication Ps 78 in v. 31, making clear that "eating" the bread from heaven is a metaphor for being *taught.* **6.46** *Seen the Father.* See 1.18; 3.13; 5.37; 1 Jn 4.12. **6.47** See v. 40; see also 3.16. **6.48–51** A summary of the discourse on the bread of life, emphasizing Jesus' role as the true giver of life. **6.49** See v. 31. *They died.* See Num 11.33; 14.26–35; Ps 78.30–31. **6.51** *My flesh,* both Jesus' sacrifice of his body on the cross, which is the heart of Jesus' wisdom, and the Lord's Supper, to which the language of "eating" will now refer. **6.52–58** John does not include Jesus' establishment of the Lord's Supper in ch. 13, where it would be expected. These verses, however, seem to refer to it and contain similarities to the words of Jesus at the Last Supper in chs. 14–17. Some scholars hold that the obvious sacramentalism of these verses contradicts the emphasis on belief in what preceded and v. 63 and therefore must be a later addition; others find the emphasis quite consistent with the Gospel's basic claim that *the Word became flesh* (1.14). **6.52–53** Cf. the form of these verses with 3.4–5 and with the "misunderstandings" discussed in the note on 7.33–36. **6.53** Jesus' *flesh* and *blood* are the bread and wine of the Lord's Supper. **6.54** *Eat,* here a more graphic verb (Greek *trogo*) than was used previously in the chapter. *The last day.* See vv. 39–40, 44. **6.55** *True food.* See also v. 27. **6.56** *Abide in me* introduces a key motif of the Last Supper discourses. See note on 14.20. **6.57** On living *because of* Jesus, see 14.19. On the parallel between God's relationship to Jesus and Jesus' relationship to the disciples, see 15.9; 17.18; 20.21. **6.58** See vv. 31, 49–50. **6.59** *Capernaum.* See note on

were complaining about it, said to them, "Does this offend you? [62]Then what if you were to see the Son of Man ascending to where he was before? [63]It is the spirit that gives life; the flesh is useless. The words that I have spoken to you are spirit and life. [64]But among you there are some who do not believe." For Jesus knew from the first who were the ones that did not believe, and who was the one that would betray him. [65]And he said, "For this reason I have told you that no one can come to me unless it is granted by the Father."

[66]Because of this many of his disciples turned back and no longer went about with him. [67]So Jesus asked the twelve, "Do you also wish to go away?" [68]Simon Peter answered him, "Lord, to whom can we go? You have the words of eternal life. [69]We have come to believe and know that you are the Holy One of God."[a] [70]Jesus answered them, "Did I not choose you, the twelve? Yet one of you is a devil." [71]He was speaking of Judas son of Simon Iscariot,[b] for he, though one of the twelve, was going to betray him.

The Unbelief of Jesus' Brothers

7 After this Jesus went about in Galilee. He did not wish[c] to go about in Judea because the Jews were looking for an opportunity to kill him. [2]Now the Jewish festival of Booths[d] was near. [3]So his brothers said to him, "Leave here and go to Judea so that your disciples also may see the works you are doing; [4]for no one who wants[e] to be widely known acts in secret. If you do these things, show yourself to the world." [5](For not even his brothers believed in him.) [6]Jesus said to them, "My time has not yet come, but your time is always here. [7]The world cannot hate you, but it hates me because I testify against it that its works are evil. [8]Go to the festival yourselves. I am not[f] going to this festival, for my time has not yet fully come." [9]After saying this, he remained in Galilee.

Jesus at the Festival of Booths

[10]But after his brothers had gone to the festival, then he also went, not publicly but as it were[g] in secret. [11]The Jews were looking for him at the festival and saying, "Where is he?" [12]And there was considerable complaining about him among the crowds. While some were saying, "He is a good man," others were saying, "No, he is deceiving the crowd." [13]Yet no one would speak openly about him for fear of the Jews.

[14]About the middle of the festival Jesus went up into the temple and began to teach. [15]The Jews were astonished at it, saying, "How does this man have such learning,[h] when he has never been taught?" [16]Then Jesus answered them, "My teaching is not mine but his who sent me. [17]Anyone who resolves to do the

---

a Other ancient authorities read *the Christ, the Son of the living God* b Other ancient authorities read *Judas Iscariot son of Simon;* others, *Judas son of Simon from Karyot* (Kerioth) c Other ancient authorities read *was not at liberty* d Or *Tabernacles* e Other ancient authorities read *wants it* f Other ancient authorities add *yet* g Other ancient authorities lack *as it were* h Or *this man know his letters*

2.12. **6.61** *Complaining.* See note on 6.41. **6.62** *Ascending.* See 3.13; note on 1.51. **6.63** On worship in *spirit,* cf. 4.23. *The flesh is useless.* The verse stands in tension with vv. 51, 53, although the emphasis on Jesus' *words* reinforces the importance of what he taught (cf. v. 45). **6.64** *One that would betray him,* i.e., Judas Iscariot; see note on 6.71. **6.65** See v. 44. **6.67–69** Cf. Mk 8.27–29. **6.71** *Judas.* See 12.4–6; 13.2, 11, 18, 21–30; 18.2–5.

7.1–52 On the order of the chapters, see note on 5.1–7.52. **7.1–10** Jesus' puzzling words and actions here may be meant to portray him as coming and going only when he is ready, since only he knows his *time* (vv. 6, 8), or *hour* (v. 30). **7.1** *Jews,* perhaps "Judeans," but more likely the Jewish authorities (see note on 7.13). On the Jews' efforts *to kill him,* see 5.18. **7.2** The *festival of Booths,* or Tabernacles (Hebrew Sukkoth), was a seven-day harvest festival observed in October (Lev 23.34–43; Deut 16.13–17; Neh 8.14–18; see "Jewish Festivals in the Gospel of John," p. 1820). The whole of chs. 7–8 is set during this festival, which drew many pilgrims to Jerusalem in the first century CE. It also included ceremonies involving the pouring out of water (see vv. 37–38) and the lighting of great lights (see 8.12) in the temple. **7.6** Jesus' *time,* his *hour* in (see note on) 7.30. **7.7** *The world . . . hates.* See 3.19–21; 15.18–19, 24–25. **7.8** It is conceivable that *not going* (lit. "not going up") *to this festival* also means that Jesus is not "going up" (i.e., returning to God; see 20.17) at this festival, because his *time has not yet fully come* (see notes on 7.6; 7.30). **7.10** *In secret.* See also v. 1; Jesus' hiding in 8.59; 11.54; 12.36. **7.11–15** Jesus' arrival at the festival causes division and uncertainty. **7.12** *Complaining,* or "whispering." Note the similar divisions among the crowds in vv. 30–31, 40–44; 8.30; 9.16; 10.19–21. **7.13** *For fear of the Jews.* See 9.22; 19.38; 20.19 (also 12.42). In all these places (as in 7.1, 11, 15, 35) *the Jews* means the authorities, since the people who are afraid are Jewish themselves. See also Introduction. **7.15** *Never been taught.* Cf. Acts 4.13. **7.16–24** This section has many parallels with ch. 5: cf. 7.16–17 with 5.19, 30; 7.18 with 5.31, 41–44; 7.19–23 with 5.16–18. **7.16–17** On the source of Jesus' *teach-*

1829

will of God will know whether the teaching is from God or whether I am speaking on my own. 18Those who speak on their own seek their own glory; but the one who seeks the glory of him who sent him is true, and there is nothing false in him.

19 "Did not Moses give you the law? Yet none of you keeps the law. Why are you looking for an opportunity to kill me?" 20The crowd answered, "You have a demon! Who is trying to kill you?" 21Jesus answered them, "I performed one work, and all of you are astonished. 22Moses gave you circumcision (it is, of course, not from Moses, but from the patriarchs), and you circumcise a man on the sabbath. 23If a man receives circumcision on the sabbath in order that the law of Moses may not be broken, are you angry with me because I healed a man's whole body on the sabbath? 24Do not judge by appearances, but judge with right judgment."

Is This the Christ?

25 Now some of the people of Jerusalem were saying, "Is not this the man whom they are trying to kill? 26And here he is, speaking openly, but they say nothing to him! Can it be that the authorities really know that this is the Messiah?[a] 27Yet we know where this man is from; but when the Messiah[a] comes, no one will know where he is from." 28Then Jesus cried out as he was teaching in the temple, "You know me, and you know where I am from. I have not come on my own. But the one who sent me is true, and you do not know him. 29I know him, because I am from him, and he sent me." 30Then they tried to arrest him, but no one laid hands on him, because his hour had not yet come. 31Yet many in the crowd believed in him and were saying, "When the Messiah[a] comes, will he do more signs than this man has done?"[b]

Officers Are Sent to Arrest Jesus

32 The Pharisees heard the crowd muttering such things about him, and the chief priests and Pharisees sent temple police to arrest him. 33Jesus then said, "I will be with you a little while longer, and then I am going to him who sent me. 34You will search for me, but you will not find me; and where I am, you cannot come." 35The Jews said to one another, "Where does this man intend to go that we will not find him? Does he intend to go to the Dispersion among the Greeks and teach the Greeks? 36What does he mean by saying, 'You will search for me and you will not find me' and 'Where I am, you cannot come'?"

Rivers of Living Water

37 On the last day of the festival, the great day, while Jesus was standing there, he cried out, "Let anyone who is thirsty come to me, 38and let the one who believes in me drink. As[c] the scripture has said, 'Out of the believer's heart[d]

---

a Or the Christ   b Other ancient authorities read is doing   c Or come to me and drink. 38The one who believes in me, as   d Gk out of his belly

---

ing, see 5.19–24; 8.26–28; note on 14.10. **7.18** On seeking glory, see 12.43. **7.20** The crowd (also vv. 12, 31, 40–44, 49) seems to be identical with neither the Jews (see note on 7.13) nor the people of Jerusalem (vv. 25–30). You have a demon. In ancient times insanity was often understood as demonic possession. Thus the crowd is claiming that Jesus is "out of his mind." See also 8.48–52; 10.20–21. **7.21** One work, i.e., the healing narrated in 5.1–9. Astonished. See 5.20; Hab 1.5. **7.22** Moses gave you circumcision. See Gen 17.9–14; Lev 12.3. Rules and procedures for circumcising on the sabbath had been developed in Jewish tradition. **7.23** For a similar defense of healing on the sabbath, cf. Mt 12.5. On controversies over the issue, see note on 5.1–18; see also 9.13–17. **7.24** Cf. 8.15.

7.25–44 Throughout the Festival of Booths Jesus' words continue to cause disputes among his hearers, and there are repeated attempts to arrest him. **7.26** The authorities. See v. 48. **7.27–29** Where this man is from, an important subject in John. The world's claim to know Jesus' origin (cf. vv. 41–42; see also 6.42) is in fact false (see 8.14; 9.29; cf. 3.8; 19.9). Jesus' retort (vv.

28–29) is therefore ironic or sarcastic. **7.28** I have not come on my own. See v. 17; see also 5.30; 8.28, 42; 12.49–50; note on 14.10. You do not know him. See 8.19, 55; 15.21; 16.3; 17.25. **7.30–31** On the division of opinions here, see note on 7.12. **7.30** Jesus' hour is that of his death and glorification (see note on 12.23; see also notes on 4.23; 16.25). Until that hour, no one can harm him (see vv. 6, 8, 44; see also 2.4; 8.20, 59; 10.31, 39). **7.31** Signs. See notes on 2.11; 6.14–15. **7.32** The combination chief priests and Pharisees refers to the Sanhedrin, or governing council (11.47), which had at its disposal a small force of police, mainly for keeping order in the temple (see 18.3). **7.33–36** This kind of misunderstanding (see also 8.21–22), which ironically proves to be more true than the speaker knows, is common in John (see 6.52; 8.53, 57; 11.51–52; 19.14; note on 3.4). **7.33** A little while. See also 14.19; 16.16. Going to him who sent me. See 13.1–3; 20.17. **7.34** See 8.21; 13.33. **7.35** The Greeks points to the later success of the Christian mission among Gentiles (cf. 12.20). **7.37** Festival. See note on 7.2. On Jesus' satisfaction of thirst, see 4.13–14; 6.35. **7.38** The scripture intended is

shall flow rivers of living water.' " 39 Now he said this about the Spirit, which believers in him were to receive; for as yet there was no Spirit,ᵃ because Jesus was not yet glorified.

Division among the People

40 When they heard these words, some in the crowd said, "This is really the prophet." 41 Others said, "This is the Messiah."ᵇ But some asked, "Surely the Messiahᵇ does not come from Galilee, does he? 42 Has not the scripture said that the Messiahᵇ is descended from David and comes from Bethlehem, the village where David lived?" 43 So there was a division in the crowd because of him. 44 Some of them wanted to arrest him, but no one laid hands on him.

The Unbelief of Those in Authority

45 Then the temple police went back to the chief priests and Pharisees, who asked them, "Why did you not arrest him?" 46 The police answered, "Never has anyone spoken like this!" 47 Then the Pharisees replied, "Surely you have not been deceived too, have you? 48 Has any one of the authorities or of the Pharisees believed in him? 49 But this crowd, which does not know the law—they are accursed." 50 Nicodemus, who had gone to Jesusᶜ before, and who was one of them, asked, 51 "Our law does not judge people without first giving them a hearing to find out what they are doing, does it?" 52 They replied, "Surely you are not also from Galilee, are you? Search and you will see that no prophet is to arise from Galilee."

The Woman Caught in Adultery

8 ⟦ 53 Then each of them went home, 1 while Jesus went to the Mount of Olives. 2 Early in the morning he came again to the temple. All the people came to him and he sat down and began to teach them. 3 The scribes and the Pharisees brought a woman who had been caught in adultery; and making her stand before all of them, 4 they said to him, "Teacher, this woman was caught in the very act of committing adultery. 5 Now in the law Moses commanded us to stone such women. Now what do you say?" 6 They said this to test him, so that they might have some charge to bring against him. Jesus bent down and wrote with his finger on the ground. 7 When they kept on questioning him, he straightened up and said to them, "Let anyone among you who is without sin be the first to throw a stone at her." 8 And once again he bent down and wrote on the ground.ᵈ 9 When they heard it, they went away, one by one, beginning with the elders; and Jesus was left alone with the woman standing before him. 10 Jesus straightened up and said to her, "Woman, where are they? Has no one condemned you?" 11 She said, "No one, sir."ᵉ And Jesus said, "Neither do I condemn you. Go your way, and from now on do not sin again."⟧ᶠ

ᵃ Other ancient authorities read *for as yet the Spirit* (others, *Holy Spirit*) *had not been given* ᵇ Or *the Christ* ᶜ Gk *him* ᵈ Other ancient authorities add *the sins of each of them* ᵉ Or *Lord* ᶠ The most ancient authorities lack 7.53—8.11; other authorities add the passage here or after 7.36 or after 21.25 or after Luke 21.38, with variations of text; some mark the passage as doubtful.

uncertain; cf. Isa 44.2–3; Zech 14.8 (Zech 14 is read at the Festival of Booths). *Out of the believer's heart*, lit. *out of his belly* (see text note *d* on p. 1829). *His* here may refer to Jesus rather than to the believer as the source of *living water*; see 4.10; 19.34. **7.39** *There was no Spirit*, i.e., no outpouring of the Spirit in the Christian community. *Glorified*. See note on 12.23. **7.40–41** *The prophet, the Messiah*. See notes on 1.21; 6.14–15. **7.42** *Bethlehem*. See 1 Sam 16.1–13; 2 Sam 7.12–16; Pss 89.3–4; 132.11–12; Mic 5.2. If John accepts the story of Jesus' birth in Bethlehem (Mt 2.1–12; Lk 2.4), the opponents' ignorance of Jesus' origin ironically fulfills their expectations (v. 27). **7.43** *Division*. See note on 7.12. **7.44** See note on 7.30. **7.45–52** The authorities, unable to arrest Jesus, ridicule those who believe in him. **7.47** *Deceived too*. See v. 12. **7.48–52** The question in v. 48 is intended to be ironic, but *Nicodemus*, who was *one of them*, i.e., an authority (leader) and a Pharisee, has shown tentative interest in Jesus (3.1–21). Whether John presents Nicodemus as one who truly believed in him, however, is in doubt.

Here Nicodemus begins to defend Jesus but goes no further than an appeal to the law (i.e., the Pharisees' law). See also notes on 3.1–21; 12.42–43; 19.39. **7.52** *Galilee* was regarded by many Pharisees as religiously lax; see also 1.46. *Search*, i.e., the scriptures. *No prophet is to arise*, or, with some manuscripts, "the prophet is not to arise" (see vv. 40–41).

7.53–8.11 On the basis of the best manuscripts and other ancient evidence (see text note *f*), scholars generally agree that this story was not originally part of the Gospel of John. It may, however, be based on early oral traditions about Jesus. **8.1–2** Cf. Lk 21.37–38. **8.3** Though the *scribes* are often named alongside the Pharisees in the other Gospels, they are not mentioned elsewhere in John. **8.5** *Such women*. In contrast, Lev 20.10; Deut 22.22 require that both offending parties be put to death. **8.6** *To test him*. See Mk 10.2; 12.14–15. What Jesus *wrote* (see also v. 8) is not known, despite many guesses. **8.7** Deut 17.7 requires that the witnesses be the first to stone a condemned person (cf. Acts 7.58). **8.9** *The elders*, or "the oldest." **8.11** *Do not*

Jesus the Light of the World

12 Again Jesus spoke to them, saying, "I am the light of the world. Whoever follows me will never walk in darkness but will have the light of life." 13 Then the Pharisees said to him, "You are testifying on your own behalf; your testimony is not valid." 14 Jesus answered, "Even if I testify on my own behalf, my testimony is valid because I know where I have come from and where I am going, but you do not know where I come from or where I am going. 15 You judge by human standards;[a] I judge no one. 16 Yet even if I do judge, my judgment is valid; for it is not I alone who judge, but I and the Father[b] who sent me. 17 In your law it is written that the testimony of two witnesses is valid. 18 I testify on my own behalf, and the Father who sent me testifies on my behalf." 19 Then they said to him, "Where is your Father?" Jesus answered, "You know neither me nor my Father. If you knew me, you would know my Father also." 20 He spoke these words while he was teaching in the treasury of the temple, but no one arrested him, because his hour had not yet come.

Jesus Foretells His Death

21 Again he said to them, "I am going away, and you will search for me, but you will die in your sin. Where I am going, you cannot come." 22 Then the Jews said, "Is he going to kill himself? Is that what he means by saying, 'Where I am going, you cannot come'?" 23 He said to them, "You are from below, I am from above; you are of this world, I am not of this world. 24 I told you that you would die in your sins, for you will die in your sins unless you believe that I am he."[c] 25 They said to him, "Who are you?" Jesus said to them, "Why do I speak to you at all?[d] 26 I have much to say about you and much to condemn; but the one who sent me is true, and I declare to the world what I have heard from him." 27 They did not understand that he was speaking to them about the Father. 28 So Jesus said, "When you have lifted up the Son of Man, then you will realize that I am he,[e] and that I do nothing on my own, but I speak these things as the Father instructed me. 29 And the one who sent me is with me; he has not left me alone, for I always do what is pleasing to him." 30 As he was saying these things, many believed in him.

True Disciples

31 Then Jesus said to the Jews who had believed in him, "If you continue in my word, you are truly my disciples; 32 and you will know the truth, and the truth will make you free." 33 They answered him, "We are descendants of Abraham and have never been slaves

a Gk according to the flesh   b Other ancient authorities read he   c Gk I am   d Or What I have told you from the beginning

sin again. See also 5.14. **8.12–20** On the themes of judgment and testimony that are prominent here, see esp. 5.22, 30–38; see also 12.47–49; 19.35; 21.24. **8.12** Light, darkness. See 1.4–5, 9; 3.19; 9.4–5; 11.9–10; 12.35–36, 46; cf. Mt 5.14; 1 Jn 1.5–7; 2.8–11. Originally (without 7.53–8.11), the author may have intended a connection between light here and Galilee in 7.52, based on Isa 9.1–2. See also Zech 14.7; notes on Jn 7.2; 7.37; 7.38. **8.13** See note on 5.31. **8.14** Where I have come from. See note on 7.27–29; cf. 3.8. **8.15** Cf. 7.24. **8.17** Two or more witnesses are required for a capital offense according to Num 35.30; Deut 17.6; Deut 19.15 also speaks of criminal charges. Here the principle of multiple witnesses is extended to another type of testimony. **8.18** On the testimony of the Father, see also 1 Jn 5.10. **8.19** You know . . . Father. See note on 7.28. If you knew . . . Father also. See 14.7–9. **8.20** His hour. See note on 7.30. **8.21–30** A dialogue in which Jesus' hearers repeatedly fail to understand his mysterious words; yet at the end, many believe in him. **8.21–22** On the ironic misunderstanding here, see note on 7.33–36. Jesus is not going to kill himself, but he is going to give up his life, and John makes clear that his death is fully under his control (10.17–18; 15.13;

18.4–8; 19.28–30). **8.23** I am from above. See also 3.3, 31; 19.11. I am not of this world. See also 18.36; note on 17.14–16. **8.24** I am he (lit. I am), part of Jesus' revelation of his divine identity in John. It functions virtually as a divine name, based on OT assertions of God's identity (see, e.g., Ex 3.14; Isa 43.10–11, 25; 51.12). Sometimes other predicates (such as light or bread) are added to the I am. See 4.26; 6.20, 35; 8.12, 28, 58; 10.11; 11.25; 13.19; 14.6; 15.1; 18.5–6. **8.26** The one who sent me is true. See 7.28–29. **8.28** Lifted up, i.e., both crucified and glorified; see notes on 3.14; 12.32; 12.34. I am he. See note on 8.24. I speak . . . as the Father instructed me. See v. 38; see also 3.11, 34; 5.19–20; 12.49–50.

8.31–59 This increasingly hostile dialogue involves Jews who had believed in Jesus (see Introduction). Jesus' word plays an important role throughout it; see also 14.23–24; 15.7. **8.32** The truth, Jesus himself (14.6); also that to which Jesus testifies (18.37), God's word, which he makes known (17.14, 17). See also 1 Jn 2.21; 2 Jn 1. **8.33** Never been slaves. By contrast, in Deuteronomy the people are frequently urged to remember that they were slaves in Egypt (Deut 6.20–21; 15.12–15; 16.12; 24.17–22). Many Jews in the first century also regarded Roman rule as a kind of slavery.

to anyone. What do you mean by saying, 'You will be made free'?"

34 Jesus answered them, "Very truly, I tell you, everyone who commits sin is a slave to sin. 35 The slave does not have a permanent place in the household; the son has a place there forever. 36 So if the Son makes you free, you will be free indeed. 37 I know that you are descendants of Abraham; yet you look for an opportunity to kill me, because there is no place in you for my word. 38 I declare what I have seen in the Father's presence; as for you, you should do what you have heard from the Father."[a]

Jesus and Abraham

39 They answered him, "Abraham is our father." Jesus said to them, "If you were Abraham's children, you would be doing[b] what Abraham did, 40 but now you are trying to kill me, a man who has told you the truth that I heard from God. This is not what Abraham did. 41 You are indeed doing what your father does." They said to him, "We are not illegitimate children; we have one father, God himself." 42 Jesus said to them, "If God were your Father, you would love me, for I came from God and now I am here. I did not come on my own, but he sent me. 43 Why do you not understand what I say? It is because you cannot accept my word. 44 You are from your father the devil, and you choose to do your father's desires. He was a murderer from the beginning and does not stand in the truth, because there is no truth in him. When he lies, he speaks according to his own nature, for he is a liar and the father of lies. 45 But because I tell the truth, you do not believe me. 46 Which of you convicts

me of sin? If I tell the truth, why do you not believe me? 47 Whoever is from God hears the words of God. The reason you do not hear them is that you are not from God."

48 The Jews answered him, "Are we not right in saying that you are a Samaritan and have a demon?" 49 Jesus answered, "I do not have a demon; but I honor my Father, and you dishonor me. 50 Yet I do not seek my own glory; there is one who seeks it and he is the judge. 51 Very truly, I tell you, whoever keeps my word will never see death." 52 The Jews said to him, "Now we know that you have a demon. Abraham died, and so did the prophets; yet you say, 'Whoever keeps my word will never taste death.' 53 Are you greater than our father Abraham, who died? The prophets also died. Who do you claim to be?" 54 Jesus answered, "If I glorify myself, my glory is nothing. It is my Father who glorifies me, he of whom you say, 'He is our God,' 55 though you do not know him. But I know him; if I would say that I do not know him, I would be a liar like you. But I do know him and I keep his word. 56 Your ancestor Abraham rejoiced that he would see my day; he saw it and was glad." 57 Then the Jews said to him, "You are not yet fifty years old, and have you seen Abraham?"[c] 58 Jesus said to them, "Very truly, I tell you, before Abraham was, I am." 59 So they picked up stones to throw at him, but Jesus hid himself and went out of the temple.

a Other ancient authorities read *you do what you have heard from your father* b Other ancient authorities read *If you are Abraham's children, then do* c Other ancient authorities read *has Abraham seen you?*

8.34 *A slave to sin.* See Rom 6.15–23; 2 Pet 2.19. **8.35** See Gen 21.9–10; Gal 4.1–7; Heb 3.5–6 (cf. Num 12.7). **8.37** *Look for an opportunity to kill me.* See 5.18; 7.1, 19. **8.38** *I declare . . . in the Father's presence.* See note on 8.28. *You should do what you have heard from the Father,* or "You are doing what you have heard from your father" (see text note *a*; vv. 41, 44). **8.39** *Abraham is our father.* Cf. Mt 3.9; Rom 4.1; Gal 3.16. **8.41** *Your father.* The identity of this "father" is indicated in v. 44. *Illegitimate children.* See Hos 1.2; 2.4. The language may reflect charges that Jesus was illegitimate. *One father, God himself.* See Ex 4.22; Deut 32.6; Isa 63.16; 64.8; Jer 3.4; 31.9, 20; Hos 11.1; Mal 2.10. **8.42** *I did not come on my own.* See 7.28. **8.43** *Accept my word.* See also 6.60. **8.44** *Your father the devil.* Cf. 1 Jn 3.8–15. This harsh language indicates the intensity of the conflict between the Jewish Christian community for which John was written and the synagogue authorities (see Introduction). **8.46** *Which of you convicts me of sin?* Cf. 2 Cor

5.21; Heb 4.15; 1 Jn 3.5. **8.47** Cf. 1 Jn 4.6. **8.48** *Samaritan.* See note on 4.9. *Demon.* See note on 7.20. **8.49** *You dishonor me.* See 5.23. **8.50** Seeking someone's *glory* is closely related to honoring them (v. 49). God seeks Jesus' glory by granting eternal life to those who keep his word (v. 51). See also 5.41–44; 7.18; 12.43. **8.51** See 5.24; 11.25–26; see also Deut 30.15–20. **8.53** *Are you greater?* Cf. 4.12. **8.55** *You do not know him.* See v. 19; note on 7.28. **8.56** There is no reference in Genesis to Abraham's vision of the Messiah. Heb 11.13 refers to Abraham's understanding of God's promises, and Heb 11.19 takes the binding of Isaac (Gen 22) as a prototype of resurrection. Similar traditions may be at work here. On Isaiah, cf. Jn 12.41. **8.57** *Not yet fifty years old.* This does not mean that Jesus was near fifty (Lk 3.23 suggests that he was in fact in his thirties), only that he was too young to have known Abraham. **8.58** *I am.* See note on 8.24. **8.59** On the attempt to *stone* Jesus, see 10.31; note on 7.30. *Hid himself.* See also 7.1, 10; 11.54; 12.36.

A Man Born Blind Receives Sight

9 As he walked along, he saw a man blind from birth. ²His disciples asked him, "Rabbi, who sinned, this man or his parents, that he was born blind?" ³Jesus answered, "Neither this man nor his parents sinned; he was born blind so that God's works might be revealed in him. ⁴We[a] must work the works of him who sent me[b] while it is day; night is coming when no one can work. ⁵As long as I am in the world, I am the light of the world." ⁶When he had said this, he spat on the ground and made mud with the saliva and spread the mud on the man's eyes, ⁷saying to him, "Go, wash in the pool of Siloam" (which means Sent). Then he went and washed and came back able to see. ⁸The neighbors and those who had seen him before as a beggar began to ask, "Is this not the man who used to sit and beg?" ⁹Some were saying, "It is he." Others were saying, "No, but it is someone like him." He kept saying, "I am the man." ¹⁰But they kept asking him, "Then how were your eyes opened?" ¹¹He answered, "The man called Jesus made mud, spread it on my eyes, and said to me, 'Go to Siloam and wash.' Then I went and washed and received my sight." ¹²They said to him, "Where is he?" He said, "I do not know."

The Pharisees Investigate the Healing

13 They brought to the Pharisees the man who had formerly been blind. ¹⁴Now it was a sabbath day when Jesus made the mud and opened his eyes. ¹⁵Then the Pharisees also began to ask him how he had received his sight. He said to them, "He put mud on my eyes. Then I washed, and now I see." ¹⁶Some of the Pharisees said, "This man is not from God, for he does not observe the sabbath." But others said, "How can a man who is a sinner perform such signs?" And they were divided. ¹⁷So they said again to the blind man, "What do you say about him? It was your eyes he opened." He said, "He is a prophet."

18 The Jews did not believe that he had been blind and had received his sight until they called the parents of the man who had received his sight ¹⁹and asked them, "Is this your son, who you say was born blind? How then does he now see?" ²⁰His parents answered, "We know that this is our son, and that he was born blind; ²¹but we do not know how it is that now he sees, nor do we know who opened his eyes. Ask him; he is of age. He will speak for himself." ²²His parents said this because they were afraid of the Jews; for the Jews had already agreed that anyone who confessed Jesus[c] to be the Messiah[d] would be put out of the synagogue. ²³Therefore his parents said, "He is of age; ask him."

24 So for the second time they called the man who had been blind, and they said to him, "Give glory to God! We know that this man is a sinner." ²⁵He answered, "I do not

---

a Other ancient authorities read I b Other ancient authorities read us c Gk him d Or the Christ

---

9.1–41 The blind man in this story may represent the Christian community in its struggle with the synagogue authorities (see Introduction). Like the Samaritan woman in 4.1–42, but unlike the sick man in 5.2–15, the blind man increasingly recognizes Jesus' identity (vv. 11, 17, 33, 38). The question of who is a sinner also runs through the entire chapter (see vv. 2–3, 16, 24–25, 31–33, 34, 41). 9.2 Cf. 5.14. Punishment of children for their parents' sins is spoken of in Ex 20.5; 34.7; Ps 109.13–15; Isa 65.6–7. In Ezek 18, on the other hand, the idea is condemned. 9.3 He was born blind, not actually in the Greek text of Jesus' reply. The point seems to be not to find a cause or a purpose for the man's blindness but to present it as an occasion for doing God's works of healing (see 4.34; 5.17–21, 36; 10.32–38; 14.10–12; 17.4). 9.4–5 The works of him who sent me. See 4.34. Day, night, light. See note on 8.12. Night . . . when no one can work. On one level, this refers to the end of Jesus' own life (v. 5), but the use of we (v. 4) extends it to Jesus' followers, who do even greater works than he (14.12) in the time available to them.

See also 11.9–10; 12.35–36. 9.6 See also Mk 8.23. 9.7 The pool of Siloam was fed by the waters of the spring Gihon running beneath the city of Jerusalem through a tunnel built by King Hezekiah (see 2 Kings 20.20; 2 Chr 32.30; Isa 22.11). Remains of the pool have been discovered recently in Jerusalem. 9.12 Cf. 5.12–13. 9.13–17 On controversies over healing on the sabbath, see note on 5.1–18; see also 7.21–24. 9.16 Divided. See note on 7.12. 9.17 He is a prophet. See note on 6.14–15. 9.18–23 The blind man's parents betray him to a fate they themselves fear; see also Lk 12.53; 21.16. 9.18 The Jews, here the same as the Pharisees in vv. 13–17, i.e., the synagogue authorities (see Introduction). 9.22 Afraid of the Jews. See note on 7.13. Jewish Christians were not put out of the synagogue until after Jesus' lifetime, perhaps the 80s CE; see 12.42; 16.2; Introduction. 9.24–34 The blind man's fearlessness is comparable to Jesus' own (see 18.19–24; cf. 18.15–18, 25–27). 9.24 Give glory to God, a command to tell the truth (Josh 7.19) but also related to ideas about martyrdom (see 21.19; note on 12.23).

know whether he is a sinner. One thing I do know, that though I was blind, now I see." 26They said to him, "What did he do to you? How did he open your eyes?" 27He answered them, "I have told you already, and you would not listen. Why do you want to hear it again? Do you also want to become his disciples?" 28Then they reviled him, saying, "You are his disciple, but we are disciples of Moses. 29We know that God has spoken to Moses, but as for this man, we do not know where he comes from." 30The man answered, "Here is an astonishing thing! You do not know where he comes from, and yet he opened my eyes. 31We know that God does not listen to sinners, but he does listen to one who worships him and obeys his will. 32Never since the world began has it been heard that anyone opened the eyes of a person born blind. 33If this man were not from God, he could do nothing." 34They answered him, "You were born entirely in sins, and are you trying to teach us?" And they drove him out.

Spiritual Blindness

35 Jesus heard that they had driven him out, and when he found him, he said, "Do you believe in the Son of Man?"[a] 36He answered, "And who is he, sir?[b] Tell me, so that I may believe in him." 37Jesus said to him, "You have seen him, and the one speaking with you is he." 38He said, "Lord,[b] I believe." And he worshiped him. 39Jesus said, "I came into this world for judgment so that those who do not see may see, and those who do see may become blind." 40Some of the Pharisees near him heard this and said to him, "Surely we are not blind, are we?" 41Jesus said to them, "If you were blind, you would not have sin. But now that you say, 'We see,' your sin remains.

Jesus the Good Shepherd

10 "Very truly, I tell you, anyone who does not enter the sheepfold by the gate but climbs in by another way is a thief and a bandit. 2The one who enters by the gate is the shepherd of the sheep. 3The gatekeeper opens the gate for him, and the sheep hear his voice. He calls his own sheep by name and leads them out. 4When he has brought out all his own, he goes ahead of them, and the sheep follow him because they know his voice. 5They will not follow a stranger, but they will run from him because they do not know the voice of strangers." 6Jesus used this figure of speech with them, but they did not understand what he was saying to them.

7 So again Jesus said to them, "Very truly, I tell you, I am the gate for the sheep. 8All who came before me are thieves and bandits; but the sheep did not listen to them. 9I am the gate. Whoever enters by me will be saved, and will come in and go out and find pasture. 10The thief comes only to steal and kill and destroy. I came that they may have life, and have it abundantly.

11 "I am the good shepherd. The good shepherd lays down his life for the sheep. 12The hired hand, who is not the shepherd and does not own the sheep, sees the wolf coming and leaves the sheep and runs away—and the wolf

a Other ancient authorities read *the Son of God*   b *Sir* and *Lord* translate the same Greek word

This man is a sinner. Cf. v. 16. **9.29** Where he comes from. See 8.14; note on 7.27–29. **9.31** God does not listen to sinners. See Pss 34.15; 66.18; Prov 15.29; Jas 5.16; 1 Jn 3.21–22. **9.34** Born entirely in sins. Cf. vv. 2–3. **9.35–41** Cf. 5.14–18. **9.37** See also 4.26. **9.38** Worshiped him, i.e., bowed down before him. **9.39** I came into this world for judgment. See 5.22, 27, 30; cf. 3.17; 8.15–16; 12.47. So that those . . . become blind. See also 12.39–40; Isa 6.9–10; Isa 35.5–6; 42.6–7, 16–20; Mt 11.25; 19.30. **9.41** If you were . . . sin. Cf. vv. 2–3; see also 15.22–24.

10.1–21 Jesus is apparently still speaking to the Pharisees (see 9.40). **10.1–5** This is the closest thing to a parable in the Gospel of John. It seems to present a highly realistic picture of Palestinian sheepherding in ancient times, and it hints at a plotline. The "parable" focuses first on the gate (vv. 1–2) and then on the shepherd (vv. 3–5). For another possible parabolic image, see ch. 15. **10.1** Sheepfold, an enclosure, often

with stone walls, where several shepherds could bring their flocks for safety at night. **10.3–4** Cf. Num 27.17. **10.6** They did not understand. Cf. Mt 13.13–15; Mk 4.11–12. **10.7–18** The explanation, like the "parable" itself, focuses first on Jesus as the gate (vv. 7–10) and then on Jesus as the shepherd (vv. 11–18). **10.8** Leaders of anti-Roman revolutionary movements, who sometimes made messianic claims (see note on 6.14–15), were occasionally called bandits. **10.10** I came that they may have life, a characteristic statement of Jesus' mission as John presents it; see v. 28; see also 3.16–17; 4.14; 5.21–29; 6.35; 11.25–26. **10.11–13** Cf. the good shepherd and the hired hand with OT images of God or the Messiah as good shepherd and Israel's leaders as bad shepherds (Jer 23.1–6; Ezek 34.1–16, 23–24; see also Isa 40.10–11; Zech 11.4–17). See Jn 21.15–17; Acts 20.28–29. **10.11** The good shepherd lays down his life. Cf. 1 Sam 17.34–35. On the significance of this ex-

snatches them and scatters them. 13 The hired hand runs away because a hired hand does not care for the sheep. 14 I am the good shepherd. I know my own and my own know me, 15 just as the Father knows me and I know the Father. And I lay down my life for the sheep. 16 I have other sheep that do not belong to this fold. I must bring them also, and they will listen to my voice. So there will be one flock, one shepherd. 17 For this reason the Father loves me, because I lay down my life in order to take it up again. 18 No one takes*a* it from me, but I lay it down of my own accord. I have power to lay it down, and I have power to take it up again. I have received this command from my Father."

19 Again the Jews were divided because of these words. 20 Many of them were saying, "He has a demon and is out of his mind. Why listen to him?" 21 Others were saying, "These are not the words of one who has a demon. Can a demon open the eyes of the blind?"

Jesus Is Rejected by the Jews

22 At that time the festival of the Dedication took place in Jerusalem. It was winter, 23 and Jesus was walking in the temple, in the portico of Solomon. 24 So the Jews gathered around him and said to him, "How long will you keep us in suspense? If you are the Messiah,*b* tell us plainly." 25 Jesus answered, "I have told you, and you do not believe. The works that I do in my Father's name testify to me; 26 but you do not believe, because you do not belong to my

sheep. 27 My sheep hear my voice. I know them, and they follow me. 28 I give them eternal life, and they will never perish. No one will snatch them out of my hand. 29 What my Father has given me is greater than all else, and no one can snatch it out of the Father's hand.*c* 30 The Father and I are one."

31 The Jews took up stones again to stone him. 32 Jesus replied, "I have shown you many good works from the Father. For which of these are you going to stone me?" 33 The Jews answered, "It is not for a good work that we are going to stone you, but for blasphemy, because you, though only a human being, are making yourself God." 34 Jesus answered, "Is it not written in your law,*d* 'I said, you are gods'? 35 If those to whom the word of God came were called 'gods'—and the scripture cannot be annulled— 36 can you say that the one whom the Father has sanctified and sent into the world is blaspheming because I said, 'I am God's Son'? 37 If I am not doing the works of my Father, then do not believe me. 38 But if I do them, even though you do not believe me, believe the works, so that you may know and understand*e* that the Father is in me and I am in the Father." 39 Then they tried to arrest him again, but he escaped from their hands.

a Other ancient authorities read *has taken* *b* Or *the Christ*
c Other ancient authorities read *My Father who has given them to me is greater than all, and no one can snatch them out of the Father's hand* *d* Other ancient authorities read *in the law*
e Other ancient authorities lack *and understand*; others read *and believe*

---

pression in John, see note on 15.13. **10.14–15** On the parallel between God's relationship to Jesus and Jesus' relationship to the disciples, see 14.20; 15.9–10; 17.21; 20.17. **10.16** *Other sheep,* probably the Gentiles; see 7.35; 11.52; 12.20–21, 32. *I must bring them.* Cf. Ezek 34.11–13. *Listen to my voice.* See vv. 3–5, 27; 18.37. *One shepherd.* Cf. Ezek 34.23; 37.24. **10.17** *The Father loves me.* See 15.10. **10.18** *No one takes it from me.* See note on 8.21–22; see also 15.13; 18.4–8; 19.28–30. **10.19** On the *division* among the Jews, see note on 7.12. **10.20** *Demon.* See note on 7.20. **10.21** *Open the eyes of the blind,* the healing in ch. 9. **10.22–39** Jesus' last controversy with "the Jews" in John. As elsewhere, this debate reflects the beliefs of the Christian community in its conflict with the synagogue authorities (see Introduction). **10.22** The last indication of *time* was in 7.37. The *festival of the Dedication* (Hebrew Hanukkah) takes place in December. It commemorates the rededication of the temple by Judas Maccabeus in 164 BCE (1 Macc 4.36–59; see "Jewish Festivals in the Gospel of John," p. 1820). **10.23** *Portico of Solomon,* a covered walkway on the eastern side of the temple area. There were similar porticoes around the other

three sides of the Court of the Gentiles, a rectangular area that surrounded the sanctuary itself. **10.24** *If you are the Messiah.* See 4.25–26; 7.25–31, 40–44; 9.22; 11.27; 12.34. **10.25** *I have told you.* Jesus has not explicitly told the Jews that he is the Messiah (though see 4.26; see also 8.25, text note *d*). He has, however, spoken of the works that attest his identity (5.36). *You do not believe.* See 6.36. **10.27** *Hear my voice.* See vv. 3–4, 16; 18.37. **10.29** On those *given* by the Father, see note on 6.35–40; 6.44–45; 17.2, 6, 9, 12. **10.30** *The Father and I are one.* See v. 38; see also 1.1; note on 14.10. On the other hand, 14.28; 20.17 suggest the Father's superiority to Jesus. **10.31** See 8.59; note on 7.30. **10.32** *Many good works from the Father.* See v. 25; see also 4.34; 5.20; 9.4. **10.33** In the other Gospels the accusation of *blasphemy* against Jesus appears at his trial (e.g., Mk 14.64). *Making yourself God.* See 5.18. **10.34** Jesus quotes Ps 82.6. *Law,* used loosely for the Jewish scriptures in general; also in 12.34; 15.25. **10.36** *Sanctified.* See 17.17–19. **10.37** *The works of my Father.* See notes on 10.25; 10.32. **10.38** On *works* and *belief,* see 14.10–11, which also speaks of Jesus being *in the Father* and vice versa, as do 14.20; 17.21. **10.39** See

40 He went away again across the Jordan to the place where John had been baptizing earlier, and he remained there. 41Many came to him, and they were saying, "John performed no sign, but everything that John said about this man was true." 42And many believed in him there.

The Death of Lazarus

11 Now a certain man was ill, Lazarus of Bethany, the village of Mary and her sister Martha. 2Mary was the one who anointed the Lord with perfume and wiped his feet with her hair; her brother Lazarus was ill. 3So the sisters sent a message to Jesus,ᵃ "Lord, he whom you love is ill." 4But when Jesus heard it, he said, "This illness does not lead to death; rather it is for God's glory, so that the Son of God may be glorified through it." 5Accordingly, though Jesus loved Martha and her sister and Lazarus, 6after having heard that Lazarusᵇ was ill, he stayed two days longer in the place where he was.

7 Then after this he said to the disciples, "Let us go to Judea again." 8The disciples said to him, "Rabbi, the Jews were just now trying to stone you, and are you going there again?" 9Jesus answered, "Are there not twelve hours of daylight? Those who walk during the day do not stumble, because they see the light of this world. 10But those who walk at night stumble, because the light is not in them." 11After saying this, he told them, "Our friend Lazarus has fallen asleep, but I am going there to awaken him." 12The disciples said to him, "Lord, if he has fallen asleep, he will be all right." 13Jesus, however, had been speaking about his death, but they thought that he was referring merely to sleep. 14Then Jesus told them plainly, "Lazarus is dead. 15For your sake I am glad I was not there, so that you may believe. But let us go to him." 16Thomas, who was called the Twin,ᶜ said to his fellow disciples, "Let us also go, that we may die with him."

Jesus the Resurrection and the Life

17 When Jesus arrived, he found that Lazarusᵇ had already been in the tomb four days. 18Now Bethany was near Jerusalem, some two milesᵈ away, 19and many of the Jews had come to Martha and Mary to console them about their brother. 20When Martha heard that Jesus was coming, she went and met him, while Mary stayed at home. 21Martha said to Jesus, "Lord, if you had been here, my brother would not have died. 22But even now I know that God will give you whatever you ask of him."

a Gk him   b Gk he   c Gk Didymus   d Gk fifteen stadia

note on 7.30; 7.44. **10.40–42** Jesus withdraws, as in 7.1; 8.59; 11.54; 12.36. **10.40** *Where John had been baptizing earlier,* i.e., Bethany *across the Jordan* (1.28), not John's later location at Aenon (3.23). **10.41** *Everything that John said.* See 1.19–34; 3.27–30.

11.1–44 Having spoken of himself as the good shepherd who lays down his life for the sheep (10.11–18), Jesus now risks his life to give life to his friend Lazarus (vv. 7–16; cf. 15.13). The result of this life-giving is Jesus' own death (vv. 45–53). Thus the story of the raising of Lazarus prepares readers for the passion narrative (chs. 18–19). **11.1** *Bethany,* not the same as Bethany across the Jordan, where John had baptized (see 1.28; note on 10.40). This Bethany lay just east of Jerusalem (v. 18), across the Kidron Valley and on the eastern side of the Mount of Olives. *Mary and her sister Martha,* perhaps the same women referred to in Lk 10.38–42, but this is uncertain. **11.2** *Anointed.* See 12.1–8. **11.4** *It is for God's glory.* Cf. 9.3. *Glory, glorified.* See v. 40; see also 2.11; 13.31–32; 14.13; 17.1. **11.6** Jesus seems deliberately to let Lazarus die (see also vv. 14–15, 21, 32, 37). Lazarus, however, might already have been dead by the time the message arrived, and Jesus' delay would have timed his arrival in Bethany after the finality of Lazarus's death had been confirmed (see note on 11.17). As elsewhere (2.3–4; 7.1–

10), Jesus acts at his own time. **11.8** *The Jews were . . . trying to stone you.* See 10.31; see also 8.59. *Jews,* possibly "Judeans" here and elsewhere in ch. 11. On the general issue of "the Jews" in John, see Introduction. **11.9** *Twelve hours of daylight.* Jesus apparently knows that his *hour* has not yet come (see note on 7.30), so that he can safely travel to Judea. *The light of this world.* See 8.12; 9.4–5; 12.35–36. **11.11** *Fallen asleep,* a common euphemism for death (see Mt 27.52; 1 Cor 15.6, text note *e* on p. 1952). **11.12–13** On the disciples' misunderstanding, see notes on 3.4; 7.33–36. **11.15** *I am glad I was not there.* See note on 11.6. **11.16** *Thomas.* See 14.5; 20.24–29; 21.2. *Die with him.* Cf. 13.36–38. **11.17** *In the tomb four days.* Jewish custom at that time required that burial take place the day of death, if possible. Jewish belief also held that the soul lingered near the body for three days, so that death was truly final on the fourth day. Jesus' two-day delay, plus one day's travel each way between Bethany and Jesus' location across the Jordan (10.40), would make four days if Lazarus died and was buried on the same day the messenger left Bethany to report his illness (see vv. 3–6). **11.18** *Bethany.* See note on 11.1. **11.20** *She went and met him.* People in mourning normally did not leave the house during the first seven days except to go to the tomb to grieve for the deceased (see note on 11.31).

23 Jesus said to her, "Your brother will rise again." 24 Martha said to him, "I know that he will rise again in the resurrection on the last day." 25 Jesus said to her, "I am the resurrection and the life. *a* Those who believe in me, even though they die, will live, 26 and everyone who lives and believes in me will never die. Do you believe this?" 27 She said to him, "Yes, Lord, I believe that you are the Messiah, *b* the Son of God, the one coming into the world."

Jesus Weeps

28 When she had said this, she went back and called her sister Mary, and told her privately, "The Teacher is here and is calling for you." 29 And when she heard it, she got up quickly and went to him. 30 Now Jesus had not yet come to the village, but was still at the place where Martha had met him. 31 The Jews who were with her in the house, consoling her, saw Mary get up quickly and go out. They followed her because they thought that she was going to the tomb to weep there. 32 When Mary came where Jesus was and saw him, she knelt at his feet and said to him, "Lord, if you had been here, my brother would not have died." 33 When Jesus saw her weeping, and the Jews who came with her also weeping, he was greatly disturbed in spirit and deeply moved. 34 He said, "Where have you laid him?" They said to him, "Lord, come and see." 35 Jesus began to weep. 36 So the Jews said, "See how he loved him!" 37 But some of them said, "Could not he who opened the eyes of the blind man have kept this man from dying?"

Jesus Raises Lazarus to Life

38 Then Jesus, again greatly disturbed, came to the tomb. It was a cave, and a stone was lying against it. 39 Jesus said, "Take away the stone." Martha, the sister of the dead man, said to him, "Lord, already there is a stench because he has been dead four days." 40 Jesus said to her, "Did I not tell you that if you believed, you would see the glory of God?" 41 So they took away the stone. And Jesus looked upward and said, "Father, I thank you for having heard me. 42 I knew that you always hear me, but I have said this for the sake of the crowd standing here, so that they may believe that you sent me." 43 When he had said this, he cried with a loud voice, "Lazarus, come out!" 44 The dead man came out, his hands and feet bound with strips of cloth, and his face wrapped in a cloth. Jesus said to them, "Unbind him, and let him go."

The Plot to Kill Jesus

45 Many of the Jews therefore, who had come with Mary and had seen what Jesus did, believed in him. 46 But some of them went to the Pharisees and told them what he had done. 47 So the chief priests and the Pharisees called a meeting of the council, and said, "What are we to do? This man is performing many signs. 48 If we let him go on like this, everyone will believe in him, and the Romans will come and destroy both our holy place *c* and our nation." 49 But one

a Other ancient authorities lack *and the life*   *b* Or *the Christ*
c Or *our temple*; Greek *our place*

11.21 See note on 11.6. 11.22 *Whatever you ask.* See also 14.13–14; 15.7, 16; 16.23–24. 11.23–27 Cf. 4.25–26. 11.24 Many Jews of that time believed that there would be a final *resurrection*, though others denied this (see Dan 12.2; Mk 12.18–27; Acts 23.6–8; 24.15, 21). 11.25–26 The difficulty of the logic in these verses may be deliberate; this is not a "logical" subject. As elsewhere (5.24–29; 6.40, 54; 8.51), Jesus brings the future *resurrection* and eternal *life* into the present. 11.27 Martha responds with belief not in Jesus' statement or its logic but in Jesus himself, and it is this belief that brings life (20.31). 11.31 *Going to the tomb.* See note on 11.20. *Weep,* not just tears, but wailing and lamentation for the dead person. 11.32 See note on 11.6. 11.33 *Disturbed . . . deeply moved.* A fully human Jesus experiences deep emotions. 11.37 *Opened the eyes of the blind man,* the healing event in ch. 9. 11.38 A *cave* with a *stone* over the entrance was a common burial place (see 20.1; Mk 15.46). 11.39 *Four days.* See note on 11.17. 11.40 Cf. the order of *believing* and see-

ing with that in v. 45; see also 4.48; 6.30; 20.24–29; note on 2.11. *Glory of God.* See note on 11.4. 11.42 Jesus also explains why things are said in 5.34; 12.30; see also 6.6. *So that . . . sent me.* See also 17.21. 11.43–44 Cf. 5.25, 28–29. *Binding* and *wrapping* were part of the Jewish burial customs of the day; see 20.6–7. *Let him go,* i.e., "let him walk." 11.45–53 The decision to put Jesus to death results from his giving life to Lazarus; cf. Mk 14.1–2. 11.46 See also 5.15. 11.47–48 *The council,* i.e., the Sanhedrin, the highest Jewish court and governing body (see note on 7.32). A man doing *signs* might intend to challenge the rule of the *Romans* and so bring on an attack; see note on 6.14–15. A generation after Jesus' time, the Jewish revolt of 66–70 CE resulted in the destruction of Jerusalem, including the temple (*holy place*), and in the death or captivity of thousands of Jews. 11.49 *That year.* The high-priesthood was theoretically a hereditary lifetime position (Num 25.10–13), but in the first century CE the office holder was subject to approval by the Roman

of them, Caiaphas, who was high priest that year, said to them, "You know nothing at all! 50You do not understand that it is better for you to have one man die for the people than to have the whole nation destroyed." 51He did not say this on his own, but being high priest that year he prophesied that Jesus was about to die for the nation, 52and not for the nation only, but to gather into one the dispersed children of God. 53So from that day on they planned to put him to death.

54 Jesus therefore no longer walked about openly among the Jews, but went from there to a town called Ephraim in the region near the wilderness; and he remained there with the disciples.

55 Now the Passover of the Jews was near, and many went up from the country to Jerusalem before the Passover to purify themselves. 56They were looking for Jesus and were asking one another as they stood in the temple, "What do you think? Surely he will not come to the festival, will he?" 57Now the chief priests and the Pharisees had given orders that anyone who knew where Jesus*a* was should let them know, so that they might arrest him.

Mary Anoints Jesus

12 Six days before the Passover Jesus came to Bethany, the home of Lazarus, whom he had raised from the dead. 2There they gave a dinner for him. Martha served, and Lazarus was one of those at the table with him. 3Mary took a pound of costly perfume made of pure nard, anointed Jesus' feet, and wiped them*b* with her hair. The house was filled with the fragrance of the perfume. 4But Judas Iscariot, one of his disciples (the one who was about to betray him), said, 5"Why was this perfume not sold for three hundred denarii*c* and the money given to the poor?" 6(He said this not because he cared about the poor, but because he was a thief; he kept the common purse and used to steal what was put into it.) 7Jesus said, "Leave her alone. She bought it*d* so that she might keep it for the day of my burial. 8You always have the poor with you, but you do not always have me."

The Plot to Kill Lazarus

9 When the great crowd of the Jews learned that he was there, they came not only because of Jesus but also to see Lazarus, whom he had raised from the dead. 10So the chief priests planned to put Lazarus to death as well, 11since it was on account of him that many of the Jews were deserting and were believing in Jesus.

Jesus' Triumphal Entry into Jerusalem

12 The next day the great crowd that had come to the festival heard that Jesus was coming to Jerusalem. 13So they took branches of palm trees and went out to meet him, shouting, "Hosanna!

a Gk *he*   *b* Gk *his feet*   *c* Three hundred denarii would be nearly a year's wages for a laborer   *d* Gk lacks *She bought it*

---

governor and the position changed hands frequently. *Caiaphas* in fact held office for eighteen years (18–36/7 CE); see 18.13; Mt 26.3; Lk 3.2; Acts 4.6. The high priest was a political as well as a religious leader and thus headed the Sanhedrin. See also 1 Macc 12.6; 14.41–45; Mk 14.60–64; Acts 5.17, 21; 23.1–5. **11.50** A cynical political judgment ironically contains a profound theological truth. **11.51** *He prophesied.* The high-priesthood was not generally regarded as carrying prophetic powers. John's point is that Caiaphas prophesied unconsciously; like other opponents of Jesus, he spoke more truly than he knew (see notes on 7.33–36; 19.14). **11.52** *To gather into one.* See also 10.16; 17.21. **11.54–57** Jesus in hiding; see also 7.1, 10; 8.59; 12.36. **11.54** *Ephraim.* Location uncertain. It may be the town mentioned in 2 Sam 13.23; 1 Macc 11.34 (Aphairema), perhaps near Bethel. **11.55** *Passover.* See notes on 2.13; 6.4. The last indication of time was in 10.22. *Purify themselves.* Num 9.10–11 requires those who are unclean to celebrate Passover a month late (cf. 18.28). **11.56** Cf. 7.11.

12.1–8 The anointing at Bethany is also found in Mk 14.3–9. A similar story is placed earlier in Jesus' career in Lk 7.37–38. **12.1** *Passover.* See note on 2.13. *Bethany.* See note on 11.1. *Lazarus . . . raised from the dead.* See 11.1–44. **12.2–3** *Martha, Mary.* See 11.1. **12.3** The Roman *pound* was about 12 ounces, or 340 grams. *Nard,* a perfumed ointment imported from the Himalayas; see Song 1.12; 4.13–14. **12.4** *Judas Iscariot.* See 13.2, 26–30; 18.2–5. **12.6** *Common purse,* actually a box in which Jesus and his disciples kept their shared funds. **12.7** This anointing of Jesus may foreshadow his impending death. Jewish *burial* customs included anointing the body with perfumed oil (see Lk 23.56). **12.9–11** Lazarus is also endangered because Jesus gave him life; see 11.45–53. **12.9** *Crowd.* See note on 2.13. **12.11** *Deserting,* or simply "going." **12.12–19** The triumphal entry. See Mt 21.1–11; Mk 11.1–10; Lk 19.28–40. **12.12** *Crowd.* See note on 2.13. **12.13** Only John mentions *branches of palm.* The words of the crowd come from Ps 118.25–26, and both palm branches and this psalm were used at the Festival of Booths (see note on 7.2). *Hosanna,* Hebrew,

Blessed is the one who comes in the name
of the Lord—
the King of Israel!"

14 Jesus found a young donkey and sat on it; as it is written:

15 "Do not be afraid, daughter of Zion.
Look, your king is coming,
sitting on a donkey's colt!"

16 His disciples did not understand these things at first; but when Jesus was glorified, then they remembered that these things had been written of him and had been done to him. 17 So the crowd that had been with him when he called Lazarus out of the tomb and raised him from the dead continued to testify. [a] 18 It was also because they heard that he had performed this sign that the crowd went to meet him. 19 The Pharisees then said to one another, "You see, you can do nothing. Look, the world has gone after him!"

Some Greeks Wish to See Jesus

20 Now among those who went up to worship at the festival were some Greeks. 21 They came to Philip, who was from Bethsaida in Galilee, and said to him, "Sir, we wish to see Jesus." 22 Philip went and told Andrew; then Andrew and Philip went and told Jesus. 23 Jesus answered them, "The hour has come for the Son of Man to be glorified. 24 Very truly, I tell you, unless a grain of wheat falls into the earth and dies, it remains just a single grain; but if it dies, it bears much fruit. 25 Those who love their life lose it, and those who hate their life in this world will keep it for eternal life. 26 Whoever serves me must follow me, and where I am, there will my servant be also. Whoever serves me, the Father will honor.

Jesus Speaks about His Death

27 "Now my soul is troubled. And what should I say—'Father, save me from this hour'? No, it is for this reason that I have come to this hour. 28 Father, glorify your name." Then a voice came from heaven, "I have glorified it, and I will glorify it again." 29 The crowd standing there heard it and said that it was thunder. Others said, "An angel has spoken to him." 30 Jesus answered, "This voice has come for your sake, not for mine. 31 Now is the judgment of this world; now the ruler of this world will be driven out. 32 And I, when I am lifted up from the earth, will draw all people [b] to myself." 33 He said this to indicate the kind of death he was to die. 34 The crowd answered him, "We have heard from the law that the Messiah [c] remains forever. How can you say that the Son of Man must be lifted up? Who is this Son of Man?" 35 Jesus said to them, "The light is with you for a little longer. Walk while you have the light, so that the darkness may not overtake you. If you walk in the darkness, you do not know where you are going. 36 While you have the light, believe in the light, so that you may become children of light."

The Unbelief of the People

After Jesus had said this, he departed and hid from them. 37 Although he had performed so many signs in their presence, they did not believe in him. 38 This was to fulfill the word spoken by the prophet Isaiah:

a Other ancient authorities read *with him began to testify that he had called . . . from the dead*   *b* Other ancient authorities read *all things*   *c* Or *the Christ*

"Save us, we beseech you!" **12.15** Zech 9.9. **12.16** *Did not understand . . . at first.* See also 2.17, 22; 20.9. John acknowledges that Christian ideas about Jesus developed after his resurrection (see also 14.25–26; 16.12–13). *Glorified.* See note on 12.23. **12.17–18** See 11.45–46; 12.9–11. Cf. the response to the feeding miracle in 6.26. **12.19** *The world has gone after him.* Cf. 11.48. **12.20–36** Jesus' last public dialogue in John, focused on his impending death. **12.20** *Greeks,* perhaps symbolic of the future mission of Christianity to the Gentiles (see 7.35–36), to take place after Jesus has been glorified (see vv. 23, 32). **12.22** *Philip.* See note on 1.43. *Andrew.* See notes on 1.40; 1.43. **12.23** The *hour* when Jesus is to be *glorified* is the hour of his death, resurrection, and ascension (see v. 32), which also glorifies God's name (v. 28) and provides a model for his followers (v. 26). See v. 16; see also 7.39; 13.1, 31–32; 17.1, 4–5; notes on 4.23; 7.30; 16.25. **12.24** Cf. 1 Cor 15.36–38. **12.25** See Mt 10.39;

Mk 8.35; Lk 17.33. **12.26** *Whoever serves . . . follow me.* See also 13.14–16; 15.18–16.4. Cf. Mk 8.34. *There will my servant be also.* See also 14.3; 17.24. **12.27** In the other Gospels, similar words are spoken in the garden of Gethsemane just before Jesus' arrest (e.g., Mk 14.33–36). **12.30** Jesus also explains why things are said in 5.34; 11.42. **12.31** *Ruler of this world,* i.e., the devil; see 14.30; 16.11. **12.32** *Lifted up from the earth,* both Jesus' crucifixion (v. 33) and his resurrection and ascension; see 3.14; 8.28 (cf. Isa 52.13). *Draw all people.* Cf. 6.44; 12.20. **12.34** *Law.* See note on 10.24. *The Messiah remains forever.* See Pss 89.3–4, 19–21, 28–29, 35–37; 110.4; Isa 9.6–7; Ezek 37.24–25; Dan 7.13–14. **12.35** *Light, darkness.* See 3.19–21; 8.12; 9.4–5; 11.9–10; 12.46. **12.36b** *Hid.* See also 7.10; 8.59; 11.54. **12.37–43** A reflection on the response to Jesus at the close of his public work. For a similar reflection, see 3.31–36. **12.37** On *signs* and *believing,* see note on 2.11. **12.38** The quota-

"Lord, who has believed our message,
and to whom has the arm of the Lord
been revealed?"
39 And so they could not believe, because Isaiah also said,
40 "He has blinded their eyes
and hardened their heart,
so that they might not look with their
eyes,
and understand with their heart and
turn—
and I would heal them."
41 Isaiah said this because *a* he saw his glory and spoke about him. 42 Nevertheless many, even of the authorities, believed in him. But because of the Pharisees they did not confess it, for fear that they would be put out of the synagogue; 43 for they loved human glory more than the glory that comes from God.

Summary of Jesus' Teaching

44 Then Jesus cried aloud: "Whoever believes in me believes not in me but in him who sent me. 45 And whoever sees me sees him who sent me. 46 I have come as light into the world, so that everyone who believes in me should not remain in the darkness. 47 I do not judge anyone who hears my words and does not keep them, for I came not to judge the world, but to save the world. 48 The one who rejects me and does not receive my word has a judge; on the

last day the word that I have spoken will serve as judge, 49 for I have not spoken on my own, but the Father who sent me has himself given me a commandment about what to say and what to speak. 50 And I know that his commandment is eternal life. What I speak, therefore, I speak just as the Father has told me."

Jesus Washes the Disciples' Feet

13 Now before the festival of the Passover, Jesus knew that his hour had come to depart from this world and go to the Father. Having loved his own who were in the world, he loved them to the end. 2 The devil had already put it into the heart of Judas son of Simon Iscariot to betray him. And during supper 3 Jesus, knowing that the Father had given all things into his hands, and that he had come from God and was going to God, 4 got up from the table, *b* took off his outer robe, and tied a towel around himself. 5 Then he poured water into a basin and began to wash the disciples' feet and to wipe them with the towel that was tied around him. 6 He came to Simon Peter, who said to him, "Lord, are you going to wash my feet?" 7 Jesus answered, "You do not know now what I am doing, but later you will understand." 8 Peter said to him, "You will never wash my feet." Jesus answered, "Unless I wash

a Other ancient witnesses read *when*   *b* Gk *from supper*

tion is from Isa 53.1 (see also Rom 10.16). **12.40** The quotation is from Isa 6.10 (see also Mt 13.15; Mk 4.12). **12.41** *Saw his glory* may refer to Isa 6.1–4 (see also Jn 8.56–58). **12.42–43** See Introduction. Nicodemus may be an example of such fearful believers; see notes on 3.1–21; 7.48–52; 19.38; 19.39. *Put out of the synagogue.* See notes on 9.22; 16.2. *Human glory.* See 5.41–44. **12.44–50** This somewhat detached speech serves to summarize and conclude all that Jesus has said in his public work. Hence it has many similarities to sayings earlier in John. **12.44–45** See 5.23; 13.20; 14.7–9; see also Mt 10.40; Mk 9.37; Lk 10.16. **12.46** See 8.12; see also 3.19–21; 9.4–5; 11.9–10; 12.35–36. **12.47–48** On Jesus and judgment, see 3.17–18; 5.24, 30, 45; 8.15–16, 50; 9.39. **12.49–50** See 5.31–34; 5.19, 30; 7.16–17, 28–29; 8.26–28, 38–42.

13.1–17.26 The story of the Last Supper in John is unlike that in any of the other Gospels. In them this supper is the Jewish Passover meal (Mt 26.17–19; Mk 14.12–16; Lk 22.7–13); in John the Passover was to be eaten on the following evening, after Jesus' crucifixion (13.1; 18.28; 19.14). Jesus' final words to the disciples in chs. 13–16 are also unique to John. A few sayings have parallels in the other Gospels, but not at the Last Supper. The lengthy prayer in ch. 17 has no equivalent

in the other Gospels. Most scholars conclude that these "farewell discourses," like the rest of John, reflect the understanding of Jesus developed in the Christian community for which John was written (see note on 14.25–26). The discourses also fit the category of "last words" or "testament," words of consolation and admonition spoken by a leader before dying (see also Gen 48–49; Deut 33; Josh 23–24; Acts 20.17–38; *Testaments of the Twelve Patriarchs*). **13.1–5** The story of Jesus washing the disciples' feet is found in no other Gospel. **13.1** An introduction to the final chapters of John. *Passover.* See notes on 2.13; 6.4. *Jesus knew.* See 18.4; 19.28. On Jesus' *hour,* see 17.1; notes on 7.30; 12.23. *He loved them to the end.* See v. 34; 15.12–13. **13.2** See vv. 26–30; Lk 22.3–4. **13.3** *He had come . . . to God.* See 16.28. **13.4–5** To offer guests water to wash their feet after a journey in sandals on dusty roads (Lk 7.44) was ordinary hospitality. A host was not expected to wash his guests' feet for them, but a slave might be assigned this task, or disciples might wash their teacher's feet. **13.6–11** This dialogue may transform the foot washing into a symbol of baptism. Or the foot washing may represent Jesus' death for the disciples, so that Peter's objection is similar to that in Mk 8.31–33. **13.7** See v. 36; see also 2.22; 12.16.

you, you have no share with me." 9Simon Peter said to him, "Lord, not my feet only but also my hands and my head!" 10Jesus said to him, "One who has bathed does not need to wash, except for the feet,*a* but is entirely clean. And you*b* are clean, though not all of you." 11For he knew who was to betray him; for this reason he said, "Not all of you are clean."

12 After he had washed their feet, had put on his robe, and had returned to the table, he said to them, "Do you know what I have done to you? 13You call me Teacher and Lord—and you are right, for that is what I am. 14So if I, your Lord and Teacher, have washed your feet, you also ought to wash one another's feet. 15For I have set you an example, that you also should do as I have done to you. 16Very truly, I tell you, servants*c* are not greater than their master, nor are messengers greater than the one who sent them. 17If you know these things, you are blessed if you do them. 18I am not speaking of all of you; I know whom I have chosen. But it is to fulfill the scripture, 'The one who ate my bread*d* has lifted his heel against me.' 19I tell you this now, before it occurs, so that when it does occur, you may believe that I am he.*e* 20Very truly, I tell you, whoever receives one whom I send receives me; and whoever receives me receives him who sent me."

Jesus Foretells His Betrayal

21 After saying this Jesus was troubled in spirit, and declared, "Very truly, I tell you, one of you will betray me." 22The disciples looked at one another, uncertain of whom he was speaking. 23One of his disciples—the one whom Jesus loved—was reclining next to him; 24Simon Peter therefore motioned to him to ask Jesus of whom he was speaking. 25So while reclining next to Jesus, he asked him, "Lord, who is it?" 26Jesus answered, "It is the one to whom I give this piece of bread when I have dipped it in the dish."*f* So when he had dipped the piece of bread, he gave it to Judas son of Simon Iscariot.*g* 27After he received the piece of bread,*h* Satan entered into him. Jesus said to him, "Do quickly what you are going to do." 28Now no one at the table knew why he said this to him. 29Some thought that, because Judas had the common purse, Jesus was telling him, "Buy what we need for the festival"; or, that he should give something to the poor. 30So, after receiving the piece of bread, he immediately went out. And it was night.

The New Commandment

31 When he had gone out, Jesus said, "Now the Son of Man has been glorified, and God has been glorified in him. 32If God has been glorified in him,*i* God will also glorify him in himself and will glorify him at once. 33Little children, I am with you only a little longer. You

a Other ancient authorities lack *except for the feet*   *b* The Greek word for *you* here is plural   *c* Gk *slaves*   *d* Other ancient authorities read *ate bread with me*   *e* Gk I am   *f* Gk *dipped it*   *g* Other ancient authorities read *Judas Iscariot son of Simon*; others, *Judas son of Simon from Karyot* (Kerioth)   *h* Gk *After the piece of bread*   *i* Other ancient authorities lack *If God has been glorified in him*

13.10 *Bathed,* possibly the Jewish ritual of purification (cf. 2.6); if this were done at home one would be *clean* and need only foot washing upon arriving for dinner. *You are clean.* See 15.3. **13.10–11** *Not all of you.* See vv. 18, 21–30; see also 6.64, 70–71; 17.12. **13.12–20** These verses both interpret the foot washing and introduce themes treated later in chs. 13–17. **13.14–15** It is not known whether the Christian community for which this Gospel was written practiced foot washing in the literal sense. If so, they probably also understood the action and this text as symbolizing humble service in love toward one another; see v. 34; 15.12–13. **13.15** *Do as I have done.* See also 14.12; 17.18; 20.21. **13.16** See 15.20; see also Mt 10.24–25. *Messengers,* or "apostles." **13.17** Cf. Jas 1.22–25. **13.18** *I am not speaking of all of you.* See note on 13.10–11. *Scripture,* i.e., Ps 41.9. *Ate my bread.* See v. 26. **13.19** See 14.29; 16.4, 33. *I am he.* See note on 8.24. **13.20** See also Mt 10.40 (Lk 10.16); Mk 9.37 (Lk 9.48). Similar relationships are spoken of in v. 34; 14.20; 15.9–12, 21, 23; 17.18; 20.21. **13.21–30** John's story of Jesus' final meal does not contain the institution of the Lord's Supper; cf. Mt 26.20–29; Lk 22.14–23. For Johannine reflection on the Eucharist, see 6.52–59. **13.23** *The one whom Jesus loved.* This beloved disciple is also mentioned in 19.26–27; 20.1–10; 21.7, 20–24. He may be referred to in 19.35 as well (and, although less likely, in 1.35–40; 18.15–16). He may symbolize the Christian community for which John was written or embody characteristics of an ideal follower of Jesus. See also Introduction. *Reclining.* On special occasions, meals were eaten while lying on couches around a low central table. Diners lay on their left sides; the disciple reclining *next* to Jesus would thus be to Jesus' right. **13.25** *While reclining next to Jesus,* lit. "while leaning on Jesus' chest"; see note on 13.23. **13.26** See v. 18. **13.27** *Satan entered into him.* Cf. v. 2. **13.29** *Common purse.* See note on 12.6. **13.30** *Night.* See 3.2; 9.4; 11.10; 12.35–36. **13.31–38** The beginning of John's "farewell discourses" (see note on 13.1–17.26) about Jesus' death and departure and their meaning for the disciples. **13.31–32** *Glorified.* See note on 12.23. The hour (see note on 7.30) is truly under way. **13.33** *As I said to the Jews.* See 7.34;

will look for me; and as I said to the Jews so now I say to you, 'Where I am going, you cannot come.' 34I give you a new commandment, that you love one another. Just as I have loved you, you also should love one another. 35By this everyone will know that you are my disciples, if you have love for one another."

Jesus Foretells Peter's Denial

36 Simon Peter said to him, "Lord, where are you going?" Jesus answered, "Where I am going, you cannot follow me now; but you will follow afterward." 37Peter said to him, "Lord, why can I not follow you now? I will lay down my life for you." 38Jesus answered, "Will you lay down your life for me? Very truly, I tell you, before the cock crows, you will have denied me three times.

Jesus the Way to the Father

14 "Do not let your hearts be troubled. Believe[a] in God, believe also in me. 2In my Father's house there are many dwelling places. If it were not so, would I have told you that I go to prepare a place for you?[b] 3And if I go and prepare a place for you, I will come again and will take you to myself, so that where I am, there you may be also. 4And you know the way to the place where I am going."[c] 5Thomas said to him, "Lord, we do not know where you are going. How can we know the way?" 6Jesus said to him, "I am the way, and the truth, and the life. No one comes to the Fa-

ther except through me. 7If you know me, you will know[d] my Father also. From now on you do know him and have seen him."

8 Philip said to him, "Lord, show us the Father, and we will be satisfied." 9Jesus said to him, "Have I been with you all this time, Philip, and you still do not know me? Whoever has seen me has seen the Father. How can you say, 'Show us the Father'? 10Do you not believe that I am in the Father and the Father is in me? The words that I say to you I do not speak on my own; but the Father who dwells in me does his works. 11Believe me that I am in the Father and the Father is in me; but if you do not, then believe me because of the works themselves. 12Very truly, I tell you, the one who believes in me will also do the works that I do and, in fact, will do greater works than these, because I am going to the Father. 13I will do whatever you ask in my name, so that the Father may be glorified in the Son. 14If in my name you ask me[e] for anything, I will do it.

The Promise of the Holy Spirit

15 "If you love me, you will keep[f] my commandments. 16And I will ask the Father, and he will give you another Advocate,[g] to be with you forever. 17This is the Spirit of truth, whom

---

a Or You believe   b Or If it were not so, I would have told you; for I go to prepare a place for you   c Other ancient authorities read Where I am going you know, and the way you know   d Other ancient authorities read If you had known me, you would have known   e Other ancient authorities lack me   f Other ancient authorities read me, keep   g Or Helper

---

8.21. **13.34–35** *A new commandment.* Cf. Mk 12.28–34, which quotes Lev 19.18. Cf. also Rom 13.9. In contrast to Mt 5.43–48; Lk 6.27–36, the love commandment in John is restricted to *one another,* i.e., the community of Jesus' *disciples. As I have loved you.* See v. 1; 15.12–13. **13.36–37** Precisely because they cannot in fact *lay down their lives* like Jesus (cf. 10.11–18; 15.13), the disciples *cannot follow* where he is going now. *Afterward.* See also v. 7. **13.38** The denial predicted here (cf. Mk 14.27–31; Lk 22.31–34) takes place in 18.15–18, 25–27.

14.1–3 Following the disturbing message in 13.36–38, these verses are comforting, for they introduce the subject of Jesus' return, which is then taken up and interpreted in several ways in the rest of ch. 14. Some scholars see these different conceptions as the work of different writers or editors. In any case, they render the actual second coming of Jesus, so important elsewhere in the NT, less significant in John. **14.3** *Where I am, there you may be also.* See also 12.26; 13.36. **14.4–11** The disciples' failure to know Jesus. **14.5** *Thomas.* See 11.16; 20.24–29; 21.2. **14.6** *Truth.* See also 6.55; 8.31–32; 17.17; 18.37. *Life.* See 6.35, 48; 11.25. **14.7** *If*

you know me, you will know. The reading found in other manuscripts, *If you had known me, you would have known* (see text note *d*), may correspond better to the disciples' lack of understanding (vv. 5, 8–11), which can only now, at Jesus' glorification, be cleared up. See also 7.28–29; 8.19; 15.21; 16.3. **14.9** *Whoever . . . the Father.* See 1.18; 6.46; 8.19; 12.44–45. **14.10** *I am in the Father and the Father is in me* (also v. 20; 10.30, 38; 17.11, 21–23), *I do not speak on my own* but speak the Father's words (also v. 24; 5.19–23, 30; 6.38; 7.16–18; 8.15–16, 28–29, 38; 12.49; 15.15; 17.7–8), two of Jesus' most characteristic claims in John. **14.11** *Believe . . . works themselves.* See 5.36; 10.37–38. **14.12–14** Believers are Jesus' successors and Jesus "returns" through their work (see note on 14.1–3). **14.13** *Whatever you ask in my name.* See 15.7–8, 16; 16.23–24; see also Mt 7.7–11; 18.19; 21.21–22; 1 Jn 3.22; 5.14–15. **14.15–17** The Holy Spirit is also Jesus' successor and in a sense represents his "return" (see note on 14.1–3). **14.15** *Keep my commandments.* See 15.9–15. **14.16** *Advocate* (Greek *paraclete,* also "Helper" or "Comforter"), i.e., the equivalent of a defense lawyer. Only John uses this term to speak of the

the world cannot receive, because it neither sees him nor knows him. You know him, because he abides with you, and he will be in[a] you.

18 "I will not leave you orphaned; I am coming to you. 19 In a little while the world will no longer see me, but you will see me; because I live, you also will live. 20 On that day you will know that I am in my Father, and you in me, and I in you. 21 They who have my commandments and keep them are those who love me; and those who love me will be loved by my Father, and I will love them and reveal myself to them." 22 Judas (not Iscariot) said to him, "Lord, how is it that you will reveal yourself to us, and not to the world?" 23 Jesus answered him, "Those who love me will keep my word, and my Father will love them, and we will come to them and make our home with them. 24 Whoever does not love me does not keep my words; and the word that you hear is not mine, but is from the Father who sent me.

25 "I have said these things to you while I am still with you. 26 But the Advocate,[b] the Holy Spirit, whom the Father will send in my name, will teach you everything, and remind you of all that I have said to you. 27 Peace I leave with you; my peace I give to you. I do not give to you as the world gives. Do not let your hearts be troubled, and do not let them be afraid. 28 You heard me say to you, 'I am going away, and I am coming to you.' If you loved me, you would rejoice that I am going to the Father, because the Father is greater than I. 29 And now I have told you this before it occurs, so that when it does occur, you may believe. 30 I will no longer talk much with you, for the ruler of this world is coming. He has no power over me; 31 but I do as the Father has commanded me, so that the world may know that I love the Father. Rise, let us be on our way.

Jesus the True Vine

15 "I am the true vine, and my Father is the vinegrower. 2 He removes every branch in me that bears no fruit. Every branch that bears fruit he prunes[c] to make it bear more fruit. 3 You have already been cleansed[c] by the word that I have spoken to you. 4 Abide in me as I abide in you. Just as the branch cannot bear fruit by itself unless it abides in the vine, neither can you unless you abide in me. 5 I am the vine, you are the branches. Those who abide in me and I in them bear much fruit, because apart from me you can do nothing. 6 Whoever does not abide in me is thrown away like a branch and withers; such branches are gathered, thrown into the fire, and burned. 7 If you abide in me, and my words abide in

---

a Or *among* *b* Or *Helper* *c* The same Greek root refers to pruning and cleansing

---

Holy Spirit (see v. 26; 15.26; 16.7; cf. 1 Jn 2.1). **14.17** *Spirit of truth*, another term for the Holy Spirit unique to John in the NT (see 15.26; 16.13), though it is used in the Dead Sea Scrolls. *The world cannot receive* or *know* the Spirit of truth because the Spirit is associated with Jesus (who is the truth; v. 6), whom the world also does not receive (1.11–12) or know (7.28; 8.19; 16.3). **14.18–24** Jesus' return as his abiding presence in the believers (see note on 14.1–3). For similar statements made about the Spirit, see vv. 15–17. **14.19** Or "In a little while the world will no longer see me; but you will see me, because I live and you will live." See also 6.57. *In a little while . . . see me.* See 7.33; 16.10, 16–22; cf. 14.17. **14.20** *I am in my Father.* See note on 14.10. *You in me, and I in you.* See 6.56; 14.23; 15.4–7; 17.21–23, 26; note on 1 Jn 2.6. **14.22** *Judas (not Iscariot)*, probably Judas son of James mentioned in Lk 6.16; Acts 1.13. **14.23** *Keep my word.* See 8.31, 43, 51, 55; 12.47; 15.7, 20; 17.6. **14.24** *The word . . . not mine.* See note on 14.10. **14.25–26** The work of the Holy Spirit, implying, as in 16.12–15, that the Spirit will lead the Christian community beyond Jesus' own teaching (see also note on 12.16; Introduction). **14.27–31** Conclusion. This rounds off the discourse in ch. 14 by echoing the words of vv. 1–3 and points forward to Jesus' arrest. **14.27** *Peace.* See 16.33; 20.19–21. **14.28** *The Father is greater than I.* See 20.17; also cf. 1.1; 10.30. **14.29** See 13.19; 16.4, 33. **14.30** *Ruler of this world*, i.e., the devil (see 12.31; 16.11; see also 13.2, 26–27). **14.31** Or "but this is so that the world may know that I love the Father, and do as the Father has commanded me. Rise . . . way." *I do as the Father has commanded me.* See also 8.29; 10.17–18; 12.49–50; 15.10.

15.1–17.26 The command *Rise, let us be on our way* in 14.31 and the statement that Jesus *will no longer talk much* in 14.30 lead most scholars to conclude that ch. 18 directly followed ch. 14 in the original edition of John and that chs. 15–17 were added later, either by the same author or by an editor from the same community. These chapters often take up themes from chs. 13–14 and develop them further. **15.1–6** In the OT the grapevine is a metaphor for Israel; God is the vinegrower, who tends it carefully but burns and destroys it if it is unfaithful. See Ps 80.8–16; Isa 5.1–7; 27.2–6; Jer 2.21; Ezek 15.1–6; 17.5–10; 19.10–14. **15.2–3** *Pruning* (the Greek root basically means *cleanse*) vine branches involves cutting back to the bare stem. *You have already been cleansed.* See also 13.10. **15.4–6** *Abide in me.* See note on 14.20. **15.7–17** Abiding in Jesus is discussed in relation to two themes, bearing fruit (vv. 7–

you, ask for whatever you wish, and it will be done for you. 8My Father is glorified by this, that you bear much fruit and become*a* my disciples. 9As the Father has loved me, so I have loved you; abide in my love. 10If you keep my commandments, you will abide in my love, just as I have kept my Father's commandments and abide in his love. 11I have said these things to you so that my joy may be in you, and that your joy may be complete.

12 "This is my commandment, that you love one another as I have loved you. 13No one has greater love than this, to lay down one's life for one's friends. 14You are my friends if you do what I command you. 15I do not call you servants*b* any longer, because the servant*c* does not know what the master is doing; but I have called you friends, because I have made known to you everything that I have heard from my Father. 16You did not choose me but I chose you. And I appointed you to go and bear fruit, fruit that will last, so that the Father will give you whatever you ask him in my name. 17I am giving you these commands so that you may love one another.

The World's Hatred

18 "If the world hates you, be aware that it hated me before it hated you. 19If you belonged to the world,*d* the world would love you as its own. Because you do not belong to the world, but I have chosen you out of the world—therefore the world hates you. 20Remember the word that I said to you,

'Servants*e* are not greater than their master.' If they persecuted me, they will persecute you; if they kept my word, they will keep yours also. 21But they will do all these things to you on account of my name, because they do not know him who sent me. 22If I had not come and spoken to them, they would not have sin; but now they have no excuse for their sin. 23Whoever hates me hates my Father also. 24If I had not done among them the works that no one else did, they would not have sin. But now they have seen and hated both me and my Father. 25It was to fulfill the word that is written in their law, 'They hated me without a cause.'

26 "When the Advocate*f* comes, whom I will send to you from the Father, the Spirit of truth who comes from the Father, he will testify on my behalf. 27You also are to testify because you have been with me from the beginning.

16 "I have said these things to you to keep you from stumbling. 2They will put you out of the synagogues. Indeed, an hour is coming when those who kill you will think that by doing so they are offering worship to God. 3And they will do this because they have not known the Father or me. 4But I have said these things to you so that when their hour comes you may remember that I told you about them.

---

a Or be *b* Gk slaves *c* Gk slave *d* Gk were of the world
e Gk Slaves *f* Or Helper

---

8) and abiding in his love by keeping his commandments (vv. 9–15), which are summed up in vv. 16–17. **15.7–8** See note on 14.12–14. **15.7** *My words abide in you.* Cf. 5.38; 8.31, 51; 14.23–24. **15.8** *Become my disciples.* See 13.35. **15.9** *As the Father . . . loved you.* See note on 13.20. **15.10** *Keep my commandments.* See v. 14; see also 14.15, 21–24. *Kept my Father's commandments.* See note on 14.31. **15.11** *That your joy may be complete.* See 3.29; 16.24; 17.13; 1 Jn 1.4; 2 Jn 12. **15.12** See 13.34. **15.13** *Lay down one's life,* an expression found only in the Gospel and Letters of John in the NT (see Jn 10.11, 15; 17; 13.37–38; 1 Jn 3.16). On the meaning of this expression within the Christian community, see 16.2. **15.15** *Everything . . . my Father.* See note on 14.10. **15.16** See vv. 7–8; note on 14.12–14. **15.17** Or "I am giving you this command, that you love one another"; see v. 12; see also 13.34.

15.18–16.4a This section on persecution is closely connected to the conflict between the synagogue authorities and the Christian community for which John was written (see Introduction). It is also similar at a number of points to sayings found in Mt 10; Mk 13.

15.18 See Mt 10.22; Mk 13.13. **15.19** *Not belong to the world.* See note on 17.14–16. **15.20** *Servants . . . master.* See 13.16; cf. Mt 10.24–25. *Kept my word.* See note on 14.23. **15.21** *Do not know him who sent me.* See 7.28–29; 8.19, 54–55; 16.3; note on 13.20. **15.22–24** Cf. 9.39–41. **15.23** See note on 13.20; see esp. Lk 10.16. *Hates me.* See also 3.20; 7.7. **15.24** *They have seen . . . my Father.* See note on 14.9. **15.25** Jesus quotes from Pss 35.19; 69.4. *Law.* See note on 10.34. **15.26–27** Cf. 16.7–11. **15.26** *Advocate.* See note on 14.16. *Spirit of truth.* See note on 14.17. *Testifying* under persecution is also mentioned in relation to the Spirit in Mt 10.17–20; Mk 13.9–11. **15.27** Cf. Acts 1.21–22. **16.1** *Stumbling,* or "falling away"; cf. Mt 24.9–10. **16.2** *Put you out of the synagogues.* See 9.22; 12.42; see also Mt 10.17; Mk 13.9. *An hour is coming.* See note on 16.25. *Kill you.* See Mt 10.21; Mk 13.12. See also Jn 15.13. **16.3** See 7.28–29; 8.19, 54–55; 14.9; 15.21. **16.4a** *I have said these things to you.* See 13.19; 14.29; 16.33.

16.4b–15 Further reflections on the work of the Spirit after Jesus' departure; cf. 14.16–17, 25–26;

The Work of the Spirit

"I did not say these things to you from the beginning, because I was with you. 5But now I am going to him who sent me; yet none of you asks me, 'Where are you going?' 6But because I have said these things to you, sorrow has filled your hearts. 7Nevertheless I tell you the truth: it is to your advantage that I go away, for if I do not go away, the Advocate*a* will not come to you; but if I go, I will send him to you. 8And when he comes, he will prove the world wrong about*b* sin and righteousness and judgment: 9about sin, because they do not believe in me; 10about righteousness, because I am going to the Father and you will see me no longer; 11about judgment, because the ruler of this world has been condemned.

12 "I still have many things to say to you, but you cannot bear them now. 13When the Spirit of truth comes, he will guide you into all the truth; for he will not speak on his own, but will speak whatever he hears, and he will declare to you the things that are to come. 14He will glorify me, because he will take what is mine and declare it to you. 15All that the Father has is mine. For this reason I said that he will take what is mine and declare it to you.

Sorrow Will Turn into Joy

16 "A little while, and you will no longer see me, and again a little while, and you will see me." 17Then some of his disciples said to one another, "What does he mean by saying to us, 'A little while, and you will no longer see me, and again a little while, and you will see me'; and 'Because I am going to the Father'?" 18They said, "What does he mean by this 'a little while'? We do not know what he is talking about." 19Jesus knew that they wanted to ask him, so he said to them, "Are you discussing among yourselves what I meant when I said, 'A little while, and you will no longer see me, and again a little while, and you will see me'? 20Very truly, I tell you, you will weep and mourn, but the world will rejoice; you will have pain, but your pain will turn into joy. 21When a woman is in labor, she has pain, because her hour has come. But when her child is born, she no longer remembers the anguish because of the joy of having brought a human being into the world. 22So you have pain now; but I will see you again, and your hearts will rejoice, and no one will take your joy from you. 23On that day you will ask nothing of me.*c* Very truly, I tell you, if you ask anything of the Father in my name, he will give it to you.*d* 24Until now you have not asked for anything in my name. Ask and you will receive, so that your joy may be complete.

Peace for the Disciples

25 "I have said these things to you in figures of speech. The hour is coming when I will no longer speak to you in figures, but will tell you

---

a Or *Helper*   *b* Or *convict the world of*   *c* Or *will ask me no question*   *d* Other ancient authorities read *Father, he will give it to you in my name*

15.26; see note on 15.1–17.26. **16.5** *None of you asks me.* Cf. 13.36; 14.5. **16.7** *Advocate.* See note on 14.16. **16.9** See 8.24; 15.22. **16.10** *Righteousness,* possibly that of Jesus, proven by his *going to the Father. See me no longer.* See vv. 16–22; see also 14.19. **16.11** *Judgment* and *condemned* come from the same Greek root (cf. 3.17–18 with 5.24; 12.47–48). *Ruler of this world,* i.e., the devil. See 12.31; 14.30. **16.12–15** See note on 14.25–26. **16.13** *Will speak whatever he hears,* just as Jesus spoke only what he had heard from the Father (see 8.26–28; 12.49; 14.10; 15.15; 17.7–8). **16.15** *All that . . . mine.* See also 17.10. **16.16–33** The disciples' pain and confusion at Jesus' departure are contrasted with the joy and clarity of the Christian community at his return. The disciples speak here for the first time since ch. 14, in which these themes are also addressed. **16.16–17** See vv. 5, 10; see also 7.33; 13.33; 14.19. **16.18** The question about the meaning of *a little while* may indicate debates within the Johannine community about Jesus' eschatological promises. **16.20** Cf. Mt 5.4; Lk 6.21. **16.21** Women's *labor* pains are frequently used by the OT prophets as a metaphor for times of cri-sis and trouble (Isa 13.7–8; 21.3; 26.17–18; Hos 13.13; Mic 4.9–10) and by the NT writers as a metaphor for the crisis of the end time (Mk 13.8; 1 Thess 5.3; Rev 12.1–6; cf. Rom 8.18–25). Here the metaphor applies to the experience of persecution by the community. **16.22** *I will see you again,* perhaps at both Jesus' resurrection and his second coming; see note on 14.1–3. **16.23–27** *On that day,* here apparently Jesus' resurrection (see 14.20), though elsewhere in the NT it refers to his second coming on the last day (Mt 7.22; Lk 10.12; 17.31; 2 Thess 1.10; 2 Tim 1.18; 4.8). After Jesus' resurrection, God answers prayers in Jesus' *name* (see 15.16; cf. 14.13–14). **16.24** *Ask and you will receive.* See Mt 7.7–8; Lk 11.9–10; note on 14.12–14. *Joy may be complete.* See note on 15.11. **16.25** John often speaks of an *hour* that *is coming* and has already come (see v. 32; notes on 4.23; 7.30; 12.23). Only here and in vv. 2–4 is there mention of an hour that is coming, but has not yet come. These passages therefore must be referring to a different "hour," the time of the Christian community after Jesus' death and resurrection. On the relation of speaking *plainly* to the coming of the Spirit, see vv.

plainly of the Father. 26On that day you will ask in my name. I do not say to you that I will ask the Father on your behalf; 27for the Father himself loves you, because you have loved me and have believed that I came from God.*ᵃ* 28I came from the Father and have come into the world; again, I am leaving the world and am going to the Father."

29 His disciples said, "Yes, now you are speaking plainly, not in any figure of speech! 30Now we know that you know all things, and do not need to have anyone question you; by this we believe that you came from God." 31Jesus answered them, "Do you now believe? 32The hour is coming, indeed it has come, when you will be scattered, each one to his home, and you will leave me alone. Yet I am not alone because the Father is with me. 33I have said this to you, so that in me you may have peace. In the world you face persecution. But take courage; I have conquered the world!"

Jesus Prays for His Disciples

17 After Jesus had spoken these words, he looked up to heaven and said, "Father, the hour has come; glorify your Son so that the Son may glorify you, 2since you have given him authority over all people,*ᵇ* to give eternal life to all whom you have given him. 3And this is eternal life, that they may know you, the only true God, and Jesus Christ whom you

have sent. 4I glorified you on earth by finishing the work that you gave me to do. 5So now, Father, glorify me in your own presence with the glory that I had in your presence before the world existed.

6 "I have made your name known to those whom you gave me from the world. They were yours, and you gave them to me, and they have kept your word. 7Now they know that everything you have given me is from you; 8for the words that you gave to me I have given to them, and they have received them and know in truth that I came from you; and they have believed that you sent me. 9I am asking on their behalf; I am not asking on behalf of the world, but on behalf of those whom you gave me, because they are yours. 10All mine are yours, and yours are mine; and I have been glorified in them. 11And now I am no longer in the world, but they are in the world, and I am coming to you. Holy Father, protect them in your name that you have given me, so that they may be one, as we are one. 12While I was with them, I protected them in your name that*ᶜ* you have given me. I guarded them, and not one of them was lost except the one destined to be lost,*ᵈ* so that the scripture might be fulfilled. 13But now I am coming to you, and I speak these things in the world so that they

---

a Other ancient authorities read *the Father*   *b* Gk *flesh*
c Other ancient authorities read *protected in your name those whom*   *d* Gk *except the son of destruction*

12–15; see also 14.25–26. **16.27–28** *I came from God.* See 3.2; 8.42; 13.3; 17.8. **16.29–30** The disciples are overconfident (as in 13.36–38), thinking mistakenly that *now* is the hour when Jesus will speak plainly (see note on 16.25) and they will *believe.* **16.32** *Scattered, each one to his home.* See also Zech 13.7; Mk 14.27, 50. *I am not alone.* See 8.29. **16.33** *I have said this to you.* See also 13.19; 14.29; 16.4. *Peace.* See 14.27. *In the world you face persecution.* See 15.18–16.4a. *I have conquered the world.* See 1 Jn 5.4–5.

17.1–26 Jesus' final prayer before his crucifixion (there is no prayer in the garden of Gethsemane in John). It has often been called a "high-priestly prayer," but it makes little reference to Jesus' sacrifice. Rather, it shows how the Savior might intercede for his disciples before his departure. There are some parallels to the Lord's Prayer (see notes on 17.11; 17.15; 17.17). **17.1–5** A summary of Jesus' mission and his relationship to God. **17.1** *The hour . . . glorify you.* See note on 12.23. **17.2** *To give eternal life . . . given him.* See 4.14; 6.27, 37–40; 10.28–29. **17.3** See 3.16; 5.24; 20.31. **17.4** *Finishing . . . to do.* See 4.34; 5.36. **17.5** *Before the world existed.* See v. 24. **17.6–19** Jesus' prayer for the unity of his disciples in a hostile world. Though these verses

speak only of the disciples of Jesus' lifetime, v. 20 suggests that the later Christian community saw itself in this prayer as well. **17.6** *I have made your name known,* because Jesus himself bears the divine name *I am* (see note on 8.24); see also vv. 11–12, 26. For other reflections on the special divine "name" that Christ bears, see Phil 2.9; Heb 1.5; Rev 19.12. The second-century *Gospel of Truth* develops an elaborate reflection on the theme. *Those . . . you gave me.* See vv. 2, 9; see also 10.29; note on 6.35–40. *Kept your word.* See 8.31, 51, 55. **17.8** *The words . . . I have given to them.* See note on 17.18. *I came from you.* See 13.3; 16.28–30. *Believed that you sent me.* Cf. vv. 21–23, 25; see also 11.42. **17.9** *Not asking on behalf of the world.* See note on 17.14–16. **17.10** *Yours are mine.* See 16.15. **17.11** *Holy Father . . . your name.* Cf. the Lord's Prayer (Mt 6.9; Lk 11.2). Since Jesus has God's *name* (see note on 17.6), he and God are *one* (see 10.30; note on 14.10), a unity based also on God's love (see 17.23–26). *So that they . . . one.* See vv. 21–23. **17.12** *One destined to be lost,* i.e., Judas; see 13.11. *Scripture . . . fulfilled.* In regard to Judas, see 13.18; Acts 1.16–20. Fulfillment of scripture is also a significant theme in the passion narrative (see 19.24, 28, 36–37). **17.13** *Joy made complete.* See note

may have my joy made complete in themselves.[a] 14I have given them your word, and the world has hated them because they do not belong to the world, just as I do not belong to the world. 15I am not asking you to take them out of the world, but I ask you to protect them from the evil one.[b] 16They do not belong to the world, just as I do not belong to the world. 17Sanctify them in the truth; your word is truth. 18As you have sent me into the world, so I have sent them into the world. 19And for their sakes I sanctify myself, so that they also may be sanctified in truth.

20 "I ask not only on behalf of these, but also on behalf of those who will believe in me through their word, 21that they may all be one. As you, Father, are in me and I am in you, may they also be in us,[c] so that the world may believe that you have sent me. 22The glory that you have given me I have given them, so that they may be one, as we are one, 23I in them and you in me, that they may become completely one, so that the world may know that you have sent me and have loved them even as you have loved me. 24Father, I desire that those also, whom you have given me, may be with me where I am, to see my glory, which you have given me because you loved me before the foundation of the world.

25 "Righteous Father, the world does not know you, but I know you; and these know that you have sent me. 26I made your name known to them, and I will make it known, so that the love with which you have loved me may be in them, and I in them."

The Betrayal and Arrest of Jesus

18 After Jesus had spoken these words, he went out with his disciples across the Kidron valley to a place where there was a garden, which he and his disciples entered. 2Now Judas, who betrayed him, also knew the place, because Jesus often met there with his disciples. 3So Judas brought a detachment of soldiers together with police from the chief priests and the Pharisees, and they came there with lanterns and torches and weapons. 4Then Jesus, knowing all that was to happen to him, came forward and asked them, "Whom are you looking for?" 5They answered, "Jesus of Nazareth."[d] Jesus replied, "I am he."[e] Judas, who betrayed him, was standing with them. 6When Jesus[f] said to them, "I am he,"[e] they stepped back and fell to the ground. 7Again he asked them, "Whom are you looking for?" And they said, "Jesus of Nazareth."[g] 8Jesus answered, "I told you that I am he.[e] So if you are looking for

a Or among themselves b Or from evil c Other ancient authorities read be one in us d Gk the Nazorean e Gk I am f Gk he g Gk the Nazorean

on 15.11. **17.14–16** *They do not belong to the world.* Despite 3.16, those in the Christian community for whom John was written seem to have felt alienated from the world. Their conflict with the synagogue authorities convinced them that *the world hated them* and that Jesus also *did not belong to the world* (3.31; 8.23). Indeed, John regards the *evil one* as the *ruler of this world* (12.31; 14.30; 16.11; 1 Jn 5.19). Despite this, they, like Jesus, are sent into the world (17.18), though they do not use the world's methods (18.36). The *world* refers not to the creation as such but to the human world that rejected God and the one whom God sent (see 1.10–11). See also 15.18–16.4a; Introduction. **17.15** *Protect . . . from the evil one.* Cf. the Lord's Prayer, Mt 6.13. **17.17** *Sanctify,* the same term as "hallow" in the Lord's Prayer (Mt 6.9; Lk 11.2); see also 10.36. *The truth* is God's *word,* but is also identified with Jesus himself in 14.6. **17.18** See 20.21; see also 3.17; 12.47; 13.20. **17.20–24** The prayer for the disciples is extended to the church beyond them, suggesting that the preceding prayer applies to that church as well. Cf. the *other sheep* of 10.16. **17.20** *Believe . . . word.* See also 4.39; 20.29. **17.21–23** See v. 11. *In me . . . in you . . . in us* (v. 21), *in them* (v. 23). See notes on 14.10; 14.20. **17.21** *So that the world . . . sent me.* See vv. 8, 25. **17.22** *Glory* implies the presence of God; see vv.

5, 24; note on 1.14. *As we are one.* See v. 11. **17.23** *Have loved them.* See v. 26; see also 14.21, 23; 16.27. **17.24** *Be with me where I am.* See 12.26; 14.3. *To see my glory.* See 1.14; 2.11. *Before the foundation of the world.* See v. 5; see also 1 Pet 1.20. **17.25–26** A concluding summary. **17.25** *The world does not know you.* See notes on 7.28; 17.14–16. **17.26** *I made your name known to them.* See vv. 6, 11–12. *The love . . . loved me.* See 15.9. *I in them.* See note on 14.20.

18.1–19.42 The passion narrative, i.e., the story of Jesus' trial and crucifixion. For John, this is the final act of the world's rejection of its redeemer (1.10–11; 3.19–21), yet it is also Jesus' glorification, his return to God (see note on 12.23). **18.1–11** The arrest (cf. Mt 26.30, 36, 47–56; Mk 14.26, 32, 43–52; Lk 22.39, 47–53). In John, Jesus virtually directs his own arrest; see 10.17–18. **18.1** The *Kidron valley* lies east of Jerusalem; by crossing it, one comes to the Mount of Olives. **18.3** *Detachment,* lit. "cohort," a unit of six hundred men, though it is debatable whether all of them would have been present. Only John mentions the presence of Roman soldiers at Jesus' arrest. He is also the only one to mention the *Pharisees* (on Pharisees, *chief priests,* and *police,* see note on 7.32). **18.4** *Knowing all . . . to him.* See 13.1–3; 19.28. *Whom are you looking for?* Cf. 20.15. **18.5–6** *I am he* is a divine reve-

me, let these men go." 9This was to fulfill the word that he had spoken, "I did not lose a single one of those whom you gave me." 10Then Simon Peter, who had a sword, drew it, struck the high priest's slave, and cut off his right ear. The slave's name was Malchus. 11Jesus said to Peter, "Put your sword back into its sheath. Am I not to drink the cup that the Father has given me?"

Jesus before the High Priest

12 So the soldiers, their officer, and the Jewish police arrested Jesus and bound him. 13First they took him to Annas, who was the father-in-law of Caiaphas, the high priest that year. 14Caiaphas was the one who had advised the Jews that it was better to have one person die for the people.

Peter Denies Jesus

15 Simon Peter and another disciple followed Jesus. Since that disciple was known to the high priest, he went with Jesus into the courtyard of the high priest, 16but Peter was standing outside at the gate. So the other disciple, who was known to the high priest, went out, spoke to the woman who guarded the gate, and brought Peter in. 17The woman said to Peter, "You are not also one of this man's disciples, are you?" He said, "I am not." 18Now the slaves and the police had made a charcoal fire because it was cold, and they were standing around it and warming themselves. Peter also was standing with them and warming himself.

The High Priest Questions Jesus

19 Then the high priest questioned Jesus about his disciples and about his teaching. 20Jesus answered, "I have spoken openly to the world; I have always taught in synagogues and in the temple, where all the Jews come together. I have said nothing in secret. 21Why do you ask me? Ask those who heard what I said to them; they know what I said." 22When he had said this, one of the police standing nearby struck Jesus on the face, saying, "Is that how you answer the high priest?" 23Jesus answered, "If I have spoken wrongly, testify to the wrong. But if I have spoken rightly, why do you strike me?" 24Then Annas sent him bound to Caiaphas the high priest.

Peter Denies Jesus Again

25 Now Simon Peter was standing and warming himself. They asked him, "You are not also one of his disciples, are you?" He denied it and said, "I am not." 26One of the slaves of the high priest, a relative of the man whose ear Peter had cut off, asked, "Did I not see you in the garden with him?" 27Again Peter denied it, and at that moment the cock crowed.

Jesus before Pilate

28 Then they took Jesus from Caiaphas to Pilate's headquarters.*a* It was early in the morning. They themselves did not enter the headquarters,*a* so as to avoid ritual defilement and

a Gk the praetorium

lation (see note on 8.24); hence they *fall to the ground.* **18.9** See 17.12; see also 6.39. **18.11** *Cup.* See Mk 14.36. **18.12–27** Jesus before the Jewish authorities (cf. Mt 26.57–75; Mk 14.53–72; Lk 22.54–71). Unlike the other Gospels, John does not have a trial before the Jewish Sanhedrin (see notes on 7.32; 11.47–48), perhaps because "the Jews" have already heard and condemned Jesus (see 10.24, 33). **18.12** *Officer,* lit. "tribune," commander of a Roman cohort (see note on 18.3; see also Acts 21.31–33; 22.22–29). **18.13** *Annas* had been high priest himself (6–15 CE) and remained influential. His sons also held the office, both before and after Caiaphas (see also Lk 3.2; Acts 4.6). *Caiaphas . . . high priest that year.* See note on 11.49. **18.14** See 11.50. **18.15** *Another disciple,* often identified with the disciple whom Jesus loved (see note on 13.23), though this is not certain. **18.18** The story of Peter's denial is continued in vv. 25–27. **18.19** *High priest,* apparently Annas, who retains the title in an honorary way (see note on 18.13). **18.20** See also Mk

14.49. **18.22–23** Cf. Acts 23.2–5. **18.27** *The cock crowed.* See 13.38.

18.28–19.16a Jesus' trial before Pilate (cf. Mt 27.1–31; Mk 15.1–20; Lk 23.1–25). This story is carefully arranged into seven scenes alternating between Pilate's dialogues with the Jewish leaders outside his headquarters and episodes involving Jesus inside them. In the trial scenes John emphasizes more than the other Gospels the political accusation that Jesus claims to be a king, in opposition to the Roman emperor. **18.28–32** Scene One: Jesus is handed over to Pilate (see note on 18.28–19.16a). **18.28** *Headquarters,* the praetorium, which included the governor's residence, military barracks, and an outdoor courtyard used as a court of judgment (19.13). The Roman governor of Judea resided in Caesarea, but because of the large crowds at Passover he came up to Jerusalem to help keep order. *To avoid ritual defilement.* Entering the house of a Gentile, where the law was never kept, would make a Jewish person religiously "unclean" and so unable to eat the

to be able to eat the Passover. 29 So Pilate went out to them and said, "What accusation do you bring against this man?" 30 They answered, "If this man were not a criminal, we would not have handed him over to you." 31 Pilate said to them, "Take him yourselves and judge him according to your law." The Jews replied, "We are not permitted to put anyone to death." 32 (This was to fulfill what Jesus had said when he indicated the kind of death he was to die.)

33 Then Pilate entered the headquarters*a* again, summoned Jesus, and asked him, "Are you the King of the Jews?" 34 Jesus answered, "Do you ask this on your own, or did others tell you about me?" 35 Pilate replied, "I am not a Jew, am I? Your own nation and the chief priests have handed you over to me. What have you done?" 36 Jesus answered, "My kingdom is not from this world. If my kingdom were from this world, my followers would be fighting to keep me from being handed over to the Jews. But as it is, my kingdom is not from here." 37 Pilate asked him, "So you are a king?" Jesus answered, "You say that I am a king. For this I was born, and for this I came into the world, to testify to the truth. Everyone who belongs to the truth listens to my voice." 38 Pilate asked him, "What is truth?"

Jesus Sentenced to Death

After he had said this, he went out to the Jews again and told them, "I find no case against him. 39 But you have a custom that I release

someone for you at the Passover. Do you want me to release for you the King of the Jews?" 40 They shouted in reply, "Not this man, but Barabbas!" Now Barabbas was a bandit.

19 Then Pilate took Jesus and had him flogged. 2 And the soldiers wove a crown of thorns and put it on his head, and they dressed him in a purple robe. 3 They kept coming up to him, saying, "Hail, King of the Jews!" and striking him on the face. 4 Pilate went out again and said to them, "Look, I am bringing him out to you to let you know that I find no case against him." 5 So Jesus came out, wearing the crown of thorns and the purple robe. Pilate said to them, "Here is the man!" 6 When the chief priests and the police saw him, they shouted, "Crucify him! Crucify him!" Pilate said to them, "Take him yourselves and crucify him; I find no case against him." 7 The Jews answered him, "We have a law, and according to that law he ought to die because he has claimed to be the Son of God."

8 Now when Pilate heard this, he was more afraid than ever. 9 He entered his headquarters*a* again and asked Jesus, "Where are you from?" But Jesus gave him no answer. 10 Pilate therefore said to him, "Do you refuse to speak to me? Do you not know that I have power to release you, and power to crucify you?" 11 Jesus answered him, "You would have no power over me unless it had been given you from above; therefore the one who handed me over to you

―――――――――――

a Gk *the praetorium*

Passover meal (see note on 11.55). **18.29** Pontius *Pilate*, the Roman governor of Judea 26–36 CE. Ancient Jewish authors, such as Josephus (*War* 2.169–180), represent him as harsh and unjust. Pilate is often thought of as willing to release Jesus but too weak to do so, but in John, Pilate's treatment of Jesus seems designed to ridicule Jewish kingship and to harass the Jews into accepting the emperor as their king. **18.31** *Not permitted to put . . . to death.* Opinions differ, but it is probable that the Romans seldom permitted the Jewish authorities to carry out death sentences. **18.32** See 12.32–33. **18.33–38a** Scene Two: Pilate's first interview with Jesus (see note on 18.28–19.16a). **18.33** On Pilate's question and Jesus' reply (v. 37), cf. Mk 15.2. On the significance of kingship, see note on 6.14–15. **18.36** *Kingdom,* or "kingship." *Not from this world,* i.e., "from above" (see 8.23; 19.11; note on 17.14–16). **18.37** *Listens to my voice.* See also 10.3–5, 16, 27. **18.38b–40** Scene Three: Barabbas is released instead of Jesus (cf. Mk 15.6–11; see note on 18.28–19.16a). **18.39** No mention of this *custom* has been found outside the Gospels. **18.40** *Bandit.* See note on 10.8. **19.1–3** Scene Four: Pilate's sol-

diers flog and mock Jesus (see note on 8.28–19.16a). **19.1** In Roman practice a prisoner was *flogged* only after he had been condemned to death (see Mt 27.26–31; Mk 15.15–20). Flogging whips often had bits of metal attached to them, producing severe wounds that sometimes proved fatal. Thus Jesus already has received a condemned person's beating (19.14–15) when he is presented by Pilate as King of the Jews, wearing the *purple robe* that was a symbol of royalty (see vv. 2, 5; see also Lk 23.11). Therefore, Pilate's declarations that Jesus is innocent may contain irony or sarcasm (see 18.38; 19.4, 6). See also note on 18.29. **19.4–7** Scene Five: Pilate presents Jesus to the Jewish authorities (cf. Mk 15.12–14; see note on 18.28–19.16a). **19.6** *Take him . . . and crucify him.* See note on 18.31. **19.7** See 10.33–38. **19.8–11** Scene Six: Pilate's second interview with Jesus (see note on 18.28–19.16a). **19.8** *More afraid than ever.* Pilate has not yet shown any fear; the Greek might also be translated "he became fearful than ever." **19.9** *Where are you from?* See also 7.27–29; 8.14; 9.29. *Jesus gave him no answer.* See also Mk 15.3–5; Lk 23.8–9. **19.11** *From above,* i.e., from God; see also 3.3, 31;

is guilty of a greater sin." [12]From then on Pilate tried to release him, but the Jews cried out, "If you release this man, you are no friend of the emperor. Everyone who claims to be a king sets himself against the emperor."

13 When Pilate heard these words, he brought Jesus outside and sat[a] on the judge's bench at a place called The Stone Pavement, or in Hebrew[b] Gabbatha. [14]Now it was the day of Preparation for the Passover; and it was about noon. He said to the Jews, "Here is your King!" [15]They cried out, "Away with him! Away with him! Crucify him!" Pilate asked them, "Shall I crucify your King?" The chief priests answered, "We have no king but the emperor." [16]Then he handed him over to them to be crucified.

The Crucifixion of Jesus

So they took Jesus; [17]and carrying the cross by himself, he went out to what is called The Place of the Skull, which in Hebrew[b] is called Golgotha. [18]There they crucified him, and with him two others, one on either side, with Jesus between them. [19]Pilate also had an inscription written and put on the cross. It read, "Jesus of Nazareth,[c] the King of the Jews." [20]Many of the Jews read this inscription, because the place where Jesus was crucified was near the city; and it was written in Hebrew,[b] in Latin, and in Greek. [21]Then the chief priests of the Jews said to Pilate, "Do not write, 'The King of the Jews,' but, 'This man said, I am King of the Jews.' " [22]Pilate answered, "What I have written I have written." [23]When the soldiers had crucified Jesus, they took his clothes and divided them into four parts, one for each soldier. They also took his tunic; now the tunic was seamless, woven in one piece from the top. [24]So they said to one another, "Let us not tear it, but cast lots for it to see who will get it." This was to fulfill what the scripture says,

"They divided my clothes among
  themselves,
and for my clothing they cast lots."

[25]And that is what the soldiers did.

Meanwhile, standing near the cross of Jesus were his mother, and his mother's sister, Mary the wife of Clopas, and Mary Magdalene. [26]When Jesus saw his mother and the disciple whom he loved standing beside her, he said to his mother, "Woman, here is your son." [27]Then he said to the disciple, "Here is your mother." And from that hour the disciple took her into his own home.

28 After this, when Jesus knew that all was

---

a Or *seated him*   *b* That is, *Aramaic*   *c* Gk *the Nazorean*

8.23. **19.12–16a** Scene Seven: Jesus is condemned to be crucified (see note on 18.28–19.16a). **19.12** *Friend of the emperor,* an official title that Pilate possibly had or desired. **19.13** The Aramaic name *Gabbatha* is not a translation of *Stone Pavement;* its precise meaning is uncertain. **19.14** On *the day of Preparation for the Passover* at *noon* the Passover lambs began to be slaughtered in the temple (since the large number of Passover pilgrims prevented Ex 12.6 from being followed literally). See notes on 1.29; 19.36. *Here is your King.* Like other characters in John, Pilate speaks more truly than he realizes (see notes on 7.33–36; 11.51). See also notes on 18.29; 19.1. **19.15** *No king but the emperor.* One of the hymns of Passover declares to God, "We have no king but you"; a similar motto was used by Jewish anti-Roman revolutionaries. **19.16a** *Them,* i.e., the Roman soldiers.

19.16b–30 The crucifixion (cf. Mt 27.32–56; Mk 15.21–41; Lk 23.26–49). Many of John's details are not found in the other Gospels. John shows a special interest here in the fulfillment of scripture (vv. 24, 28, 36–37). **19.17** *Carrying the cross by himself.* Cf. Mk 15.21. Only the crossbar was actually carried, the upright stake being already in place. *Golgotha,* Aramaic for "skull," so called, perhaps, because of the shape of the hill. **19.19** Roman authorities commonly displayed an *inscription* stating the charges against crucified crimi-

nals (though not usually on the cross itself). John's wording, *Jesus of Nazareth, the King of the Jews,* differs slightly from that in the other Gospels. The Latin version of it (*Iesus Nazarenus Rex Iudaeorum*) is the source of the acronym INRI commonly seen in paintings of the crucifixion. **19.20** *Greek* was widely used, alongside *Hebrew* (or Aramaic), spoken by Jews, and *Latin,* spoken by Romans. **19.22** On Pilate's declarations, see notes on 18.29; 19.14. **19.23** *Clothes,* i.e., the outer garment, a single long piece wrapped around one's body, which could be torn into pieces that could be used for something else. The *tunic* was an ankle-length, T-shaped garment, woven as a single piece and hemmed up the sides, which would be useless if torn. **19.24** *Scripture,* i.e., Ps 22.18. **19.25** Though the grammar is not precise, *Mary the wife of Clopas* is probably different from Jesus' *mother's sister.* **19.26–27** Jesus' *mother* is also mentioned in 2.1–5, 12; 6.42 (John never gives her name). *The disciple whom he loved.* See note on 13.23. Many suggestions have been made for a symbolic meaning for this incident (e.g., the church takes in the heritage of Israel; the church, or Mary herself, is mother to the Christian; there should be loving care within the church). None of them, however, can be confirmed with certainty. Whatever the symbolism, the scene accords a special status to the beloved disciple, who is now an adopted member of Jesus' family.

now finished, he said (in order to fulfill the scripture), "I am thirsty." 29 A jar full of sour wine was standing there. So they put a sponge full of the wine on a branch of hyssop and held it to his mouth. 30 When Jesus had received the wine, he said, "It is finished." Then he bowed his head and gave up his spirit.

Jesus' Side Is Pierced

31 Since it was the day of Preparation, the Jews did not want the bodies left on the cross during the sabbath, especially because that sabbath was a day of great solemnity. So they asked Pilate to have the legs of the crucified men broken and the bodies removed. 32 Then the soldiers came and broke the legs of the first and of the other who had been crucified with him. 33 But when they came to Jesus and saw that he was already dead, they did not break his legs. 34 Instead, one of the soldiers pierced his side with a spear, and at once blood and water came out. 35 (He who saw this has testified so that you also may believe. His testimony is true, and he knows*a* that he tells the truth.) 36 These things occurred so that the scripture might be fulfilled, "None of his bones shall be broken." 37 And again another passage of scripture says, "They will look on the one whom they have pierced."

The Burial of Jesus

38 After these things, Joseph of Arimathea, who was a disciple of Jesus, though a secret one because of his fear of the Jews, asked Pilate to let him take away the body of Jesus. Pilate gave him permission; so he came and removed his body. 39 Nicodemus, who had at first come to Jesus by night, also came, bringing a mixture of myrrh and aloes, weighing about a hundred pounds. 40 They took the body of Jesus and wrapped it with the spices in linen cloths, according to the burial custom of the Jews. 41 Now there was a garden in the place where he was crucified, and in the garden there was a new tomb in which no one had ever been laid. 42 And so, because it was the Jewish day of Preparation, and the tomb was nearby, they laid Jesus there.

The Resurrection of Jesus

20 Early on the first day of the week, while it was still dark, Mary Magdalene came

a Or there is one who knows

19.28 *When Jesus knew.* See 13.1–3; 18.4. *To fulfill the scripture.* See also 13.18; 17.12. The scripture referred to here is Ps 69.21. **19.29** *Sour wine,* i.e., wine vinegar, perhaps diluted in a drink popular among soldiers. *Hyssop,* a shrub whose branches are too short and flexible for the purpose named (see 1 Kings 4.33). Its use in purification rites (Lev 14.4–6, 49–52; Num 19.6, 18; Ps 51.7) and especially its connection with Passover (see Ex 12.22) may suggest a symbolic meaning. **19.30** *Finished,* i.e., "completed"; see 4.34; 5.36; 17.4. **19.31–37** Events after the death of Jesus. **19.31–33** *The day of Preparation,* i.e., for the sabbath. In contrast to the other Gospels, in John this sabbath was also Passover day (see notes on 19.14; 13.1–17.26). Lest the crucified men die on that sabbath, which would begin at sundown, and also because Deut 21.22–23 forbids hanged bodies to remain overnight, the Jews desired to hasten the men's death. Death by crucifixion could take several days. *Breaking the legs* prevented victims from pushing up to get their breath and led to swift suffocation. There was no need to break Jesus' legs, since *he was already dead.* **19.34** Why the soldier would *pierce* Jesus' *side* is not clear. Various suggestions have been made regarding the biological significance of the *blood and water,* but John's interest is theological, not medical. The flow of blood and water may be meant to demonstrate Jesus' true physical humanity (cf. 1 Jn 5.6) or, less probably, to symbolize the Lord's Supper and baptism. Whatever the symbolism, the "water" that

Jesus refers to (cf. 3.5; 4.14; 7.37–38) is now intimately bound up with the blood of the cross. **19.35** See also 21.24. The witness referred to here may be the "beloved disciple" (see v. 26; note on 13.23). **19.36** *Scripture,* possibly a combination of Ps 34.20 with Ex 12.46; Num 9.12. By referring to the last two, John presents Jesus as symbolizing the Passover lamb (see notes on 1.29; 19.14). **19.37** The quotation is from Zech 12.10. **19.38–42** The burial of Jesus. Cf. Mt 27.57–61; Mk 15.42–47; Lk 23.50–56. **19.38** *Arimathea,* a town about twenty miles northwest of Jerusalem. *A secret one . . . Jews.* See 9.22; 12.42–43; 20.19; note on 7.13; Introduction. **19.39** Only John associates *Nicodemus* with Joseph (see notes on 3.1–21; 7.48–52). The *myrrh and aloes* (the latter is an aromatic wood) would have been in powdered form and were meant to reduce the odor of decay. The *hundred* (Roman) *pounds* (about 75 English pounds or 34 kilograms) of burial spices is much more than was necessary. It may represent either great honor or inadequate faith in Jesus' resurrection. **19.41** The passion narrative ends, as it began, in a *garden* (18.1), which may also evoke the garden that began the story of human sin (Gen 2.8). **19.42** *Day of Preparation.* See note on 19.31–33.

20.1–31 The resurrection. Comparison with Mt 28; Mk 16; Lk 24 suggests that John has combined several sources, some of which may be related to sources used by the other Gospel writers. Mary Magdalene becomes a central figure. Her concern about where Jesus has

to the tomb and saw that the stone had been removed from the tomb. 2 So she ran and went to Simon Peter and the other disciple, the one whom Jesus loved, and said to them, "They have taken the Lord out of the tomb, and we do not know where they have laid him." 3 Then Peter and the other disciple set out and went toward the tomb. 4 The two were running together, but the other disciple outran Peter and reached the tomb first. 5 He bent down to look in and saw the linen wrappings lying there, but he did not go in. 6 Then Simon Peter came, following him, and went into the tomb. He saw the linen wrappings lying there, 7 and the cloth that had been on Jesus' head, not lying with the linen wrappings but rolled up in a place by itself. 8 Then the other disciple, who reached the tomb first, also went in, and he saw and believed; 9 for as yet they did not understand the scripture, that he must rise from the dead. 10 Then the disciples returned to their homes.

Jesus Appears to Mary Magdalene

11 But Mary stood weeping outside the tomb. As she wept, she bent over to look[a] into the tomb; 12 and she saw two angels in white, sitting where the body of Jesus had been lying, one at the head and the other at the feet. 13 They said to her, "Woman, why are you weeping?" She said to them, "They have taken away my Lord, and I do not know where they have laid him." 14 When she had said this, she turned around and saw Jesus standing there, but she did not know that it was Jesus. 15 Jesus said to her, "Woman, why are you weeping? Whom are you looking for?" Supposing him to be the gardener, she said to

him, "Sir, if you have carried him away, tell me where you have laid him, and I will take him away." 16 Jesus said to her, "Mary!" She turned and said to him in Hebrew,[b] "Rabbouni!" (which means Teacher). 17 Jesus said to her, "Do not hold on to me, because I have not yet ascended to the Father. But go to my brothers and say to them, 'I am ascending to my Father and your Father, to my God and your God.' " 18 Mary Magdalene went and announced to the disciples, "I have seen the Lord"; and she told them that he had said these things to her.

Jesus Appears to the Disciples

19 When it was evening on that day, the first day of the week, and the doors of the house where the disciples had met were locked for fear of the Jews, Jesus came and stood among them and said, "Peace be with you." 20 After he said this, he showed them his hands and his side. Then the disciples rejoiced when they saw the Lord. 21 Jesus said to them again, "Peace be with you. As the Father has sent me, so I send you." 22 When he had said this, he breathed on them and said to them, "Receive the Holy Spirit. 23 If you forgive the sins of any, they are forgiven them; if you retain the sins of any, they are retained."

Jesus and Thomas

24 But Thomas (who was called the Twin[c]), one of the twelve, was not with them when Jesus came. 25 So the other disciples told him, "We have seen the Lord." But he said to them,

---

a Gk lacks *to look*   *b* That is, *Aramaic*   *c* Gk *Didymus*

been laid (vv. 2, 13, 15) connects different parts of the story; no one gives her any help but Jesus. **20.1–2** Mary discovers the empty tomb (cf. Mk 16.1–4). **20.1** *Mary Magdalene* (see also 19.25) is described only in Lk 8.2 (there is no reason to identify her with the woman in Lk 7.36–50). "Magdalene" probably means she came from the town of Magdala on the western shore of the Sea of Galilee. The *stone* was not mentioned in 19.38–42; see note on 11.38. **20.2** On *the disciple . . . Jesus loved,* see note on 13.23. **20.3–10** Two disciples come to the tomb (cf. Lk 24.12). **20.5** *Linen wrappings.* See 19.40. **20.7** *The cloth . . . on Jesus' head.* Cf. 11.44. **20.9** Cf. 2.22; 12.16; Lk 24.25–27, 45–46. **20.11–13** Mary sees two angels in the tomb (cf. Mt 28.2–8; Mk 16.5–8; Lk 24.4–11). **20.14–18** Mary meets the risen Jesus (cf. Mt 28.9–10). **20.15** *Whom are you looking for?* See also 1.38; 18.4, 7. **20.16** Jesus' calling her by name, *Mary,* evokes the image of the good shepherd. Cf. 10.3, 14. *Rabbouni,* a variation on *rabbi,* which John uses elsewhere (e.g., 1.38).

20.17 *My Father and your Father.* See 1.12. *My God and your God.* Cf. the statements about Jesus' oneness with God in 1.1; 10.30, 38; 14.9–10; 20.28. **20.19–23** Jesus appears to the disciples (cf. Lk 24.36–49). **20.19** The disciples *fear . . . the Jews* like people of inadequate faith (see note on 7.13) despite having heard Mary's message of the resurrection (v. 18). *Peace be with you.* See also 14.27. **20.20** *Hands.* The Greek word can also include the forearm, where the nails were often driven in crucifixions. **20.21** *As the Father . . . send you.* Cf. 3.17; 6.57; 13.20; 17.18. **20.22** *He breathed on them.* See also Gen 2.7. *Receive the Holy Spirit.* See 14.15–17, 25–26; 15.26; 16.7–15. **20.23** Cf. Mt 16.19; 18.18. Here John indicates that the church's power to forgive and retain sins is part of its being "sent" as Jesus was and is related to its reception of the Spirit (cf. 1.29; 8.21, 24; 9.41; 15.22–24; 16.8–9. **20.24–29** The story of Jesus' appearance to Thomas has no parallels in the other Gospels. **20.24** *Thomas (the Twin).* See 11.16; 14.5; 21.2. **20.25** *Hands.* See note on

"Unless I see the mark of the nails in his hands, and put my finger in the mark of the nails and my hand in his side, I will not believe."

26 A week later his disciples were again in the house, and Thomas was with them. Although the doors were shut, Jesus came and stood among them and said, "Peace be with you." 27Then he said to Thomas, "Put your finger here and see my hands. Reach out your hand and put it in my side. Do not doubt but believe." 28Thomas answered him, "My Lord and my God!" 29Jesus said to him, "Have you believed because you have seen me? Blessed are those who have not seen and yet have come to believe."

The Purpose of This Book

30 Now Jesus did many other signs in the presence of his disciples, which are not written in this book. 31But these are written so that you may come to believe[a] that Jesus is the Messiah,[b] the Son of God, and that through believing you may have life in his name.

Jesus Appears to Seven Disciples

21 After these things Jesus showed himself again to the disciples by the Sea of Tiberias; and he showed himself in this way. 2Gathered there together were Simon Peter, Thomas called the Twin,[c] Nathanael of Cana in Galilee, the sons of Zebedee, and two others of his disciples. 3Simon Peter said to them, "I am going fishing." They said to him, "We will go with you." They went out and got into the boat, but that night they caught nothing.

4 Just after daybreak, Jesus stood on the beach; but the disciples did not know that it was Jesus. 5Jesus said to them, "Children, you have no fish, have you?" They answered him, "No." 6He said to them, "Cast the net to the right side of the boat, and you will find some." So they cast it, and now they were not able to haul it in because there were so many fish. 7That disciple whom Jesus loved said to Peter, "It is the Lord!" When Simon Peter heard that it was the Lord, he put on some clothes, for he was naked, and jumped into the sea. 8But the other disciples came in the boat, dragging the net full of fish, for they were not far from the land, only about a hundred yards[d] off.

9 When they had gone ashore, they saw a charcoal fire there, with fish on it, and bread. 10Jesus said to them, "Bring some of the fish that you have just caught." 11So Simon Peter went aboard and hauled the net ashore, full of large fish, a hundred fifty-three of them; and though there were so many, the net was not torn. 12Jesus said to them, "Come and have breakfast." Now none of the disciples dared to ask him, "Who are you?" because they knew it was the Lord. 13Jesus came and took the bread and gave it to them, and did the same with the fish. 14This was now the third time that Jesus appeared to the disciples after he was raised from the dead.

Jesus and Peter

15 When they had finished breakfast, Jesus said to Simon Peter, "Simon son of John, do you love me more than these?" He said to him, "Yes, Lord; you know that I love you." Jesus said to

---

a Other ancient authorities read may continue to believe
b Or the Christ   c Gk Didymus   d Gk two hundred cubits

20.20. **20.28** *My God.* See 1.1. **20.29** *Have not seen and yet . . . believe.* See also 17.20. **20.30–31** Probably the original conclusion of the book; see note on 21.1–25. **20.30** The reference to *signs* is sometimes thought to have come from one of John's sources (see note on 2.11). **20.31** *You,* plural. *Come to believe.* The alternate reading *continue to believe* (see text note *a*) may better reflect the purpose of the Gospel According to John as it stands, to strengthen the faith of an existing Christian community. **21.1–25** Differences in the language and style of ch. 21 and the fact that 20.30–31 sounds like the end of a book lead most scholars to believe that this chapter is an appendix or epilogue added on to the Gospel, perhaps by another member of the same Christian community and based on existing traditions. In Jn 20, as in Lk 24, all the appearances of Jesus were near Jerusalem; here, as in Mt 28.16–20; Mk 16.7, an appearance occurs in Galilee. **21.1–14** Jesus appears to the disciples by the Sea of Galilee. **21.1** *Sea of Tiberias.* See 6.1.

21.2 *Thomas . . . the Twin.* See 11.16; 14.5; 20.24–29. *Nathanael.* See 1.45–51. *The sons of Zebedee,* i.e., James and John (cf. Mk 1.19–20; 3.17; 10.35–45), not mentioned elsewhere in the Gospel of John. John the son of Zebedee has traditionally been identified with the disciple whom Jesus loved (vv. 7, 20–24; see note on 13.23). **21.3–11** On the miraculous catch of fish, cf. Lk 5.1–11. **21.4** *Did not know that it was Jesus.* Cf. Lk 24.15–16. **21.7** *That disciple whom Jesus loved.* See note on 13.23. *Put on some clothes,* or perhaps "belted his outer garment." *Naked.* Peter was perhaps wearing only a loincloth or a loose-fitting work smock and nothing else. **21.9** *Fish, bread.* Cf. 6.9. **21.11** *A hundred fifty-three.* Many suggestions have been made for a symbolic interpretation of this number, often centering on the fact that 153 is the sum of all numbers from 1 through 17. At any rate the large number may be meant to symbolize the expansion of the church. **21.13** See note on 6.11. **21.15–23** Jesus' dialogue with Peter. **21.15–17** Peter's

him, "Feed my lambs." 16A second time he said to him, "Simon son of John, do you love me?" He said to him, "Yes, Lord; you know that I love you." Jesus said to him, "Tend my sheep." 17He said to him the third time, "Simon son of John, do you love me?" Peter felt hurt because he said to him the third time, "Do you love me?" And he said to him, "Lord, you know everything; you know that I love you." Jesus said to him, "Feed my sheep. 18Very truly, I tell you, when you were younger, you used to fasten your own belt and to go wherever you wished. But when you grow old, you will stretch out your hands, and someone else will fasten a belt around you and take you where you do not wish to go." 19(He said this to indicate the kind of death by which he would glorify God.) After this he said to him, "Follow me."

Jesus and the Beloved Disciple

20 Peter turned and saw the disciple whom Jesus loved following them; he was the one who had reclined next to Jesus at the supper and had said, "Lord, who is it that is going to betray you?" 21When Peter saw him, he said to Jesus, "Lord, what about him?" 22Jesus said to him, "If it is my will that he remain until I come, what is that to you? Follow me!" 23So the rumor spread in the community[a] that this disciple would not die. Yet Jesus did not say to him that he would not die, but, "If it is my will that he remain until I come, what is that to you?"[b]

24 This is the disciple who is testifying to these things and has written them, and we know that his testimony is true. 25But there are also many other things that Jesus did; if every one of them were written down, I suppose that the world itself could not contain the books that would be written.

a Gk *among the brothers*   *b* Other ancient authorities lack *what is that to you*

---

threefold profession of his *love* parallels his threefold denial (18.15–18, 25–27). The first two times Jesus asks the question, the Greek verb for "love" is *agapan,* used, e.g., in 3.16; 13.34; 15.12. The third time, and in all of Peter's replies, the Greek verb for "love" is *philein,* sometimes said to represent a lesser type of love. The two may, however, be interchangeable: cf. 11.5; 14.21; 15.9; 21.7 (*agapan*) with 5.20; 11.3; 16.27; 20.2 (*philein*). *Feed my lambs,* and the variations on it, refer to Peter's leadership in the early church. **21.15** *Simon son of John.* See 1.42. **21.18–19** On the prediction of Peter's martyrdom, cf. 13.36–38. **21.18** *Stretch out your hands,* probably in death by crucifixion. **21.19** *Indicate the kind of death.* See 12.33; 18.32. *Glorify God.* See note on 12.23. *Follow me.* See also 12.25–26; Mk 1.17; Lk 5.11. **21.20** See 13.23–25. **21.23** According to legend, the apostle John (often identified with the disciple whom Jesus loved) lived to a great age. **21.24–25** The final verses address the writing of the Gospel. **21.24** See also 19.35. *Has written,* in Greek not necessarily "written with one's own hand." Thus the verse may mean only that the beloved disciple was responsible for the tradition on which this written Gospel is based (especially since v. 23 may imply that he was now dead). **21.25** *Many other things that Jesus did.* See also 20.30. On *the books that would be written,* cf. Eccl 12.12.

THE ACTS
of the Apostles

THE OPENING WORDS of the Acts of the Apostles ("In the first book") signal its uniqueness in the NT. Only here do we have a companion volume (to the Gospel of Luke), and only Acts contains stories about the early church. The traditional title inaccurately represents the content of Acts, since few of the apostles play prominent roles in the story; the most prominent figure is Paul, who is not an apostle by Luke's definition (see 1.21–22). Nevertheless, the title indicates the shift in content from Luke's Gospel, which is about Jesus, to Acts, which concerns the life and work of the church as it is brought into being and sustained by God.

Genre

PRECISELY BECAUSE IT DOES CONTAIN STORIES about the church, Acts is often referred to as a book of history. That identification, however, overlooks the number of genres within Acts, such as biography, homily, letter, and apology. To think of Acts exclusively as history can also obscure the way in which the author's theological convictions shape the story that unfolds. For these reasons, Acts is best regarded under the general category of theological narrative.

Authorship

EARLY CHURCH TRADITION ATTRIBUTES the writing of both the Third Gospel and Acts to Luke, a physician and associate of Paul (Col 4.14; 2 Tim 4.11; Philem 24). The dedications to Theophilus (Lk 1.3; Acts 1.1), a uniform literary style, and the shared perspectives of the two volumes make the common authorship of Luke and Acts certain. However, neither volume identifies an author, no physician or disciple named Luke appears in Acts, and such medical language as is employed reflects widespread convention rather than technical training. The author remains anonymous, although he will be referred to as "Luke" in deference to tradition. From indications within the two volumes, it appears that Luke may be a gentile Christian who has received a good education and has made careful study of Jewish scriptures.

Audience

LUKE ADDRESSES BOTH VOLUMES to Theophilus (in Greek, "Lover of God"), which has led readers to conclude that Acts is written for an individual, perhaps a recent convert asking for instruction or a Roman official whose tolerance the church seeks. Dedicating books was a common practice, however, even books intended for a wide audience, and Luke may well have offered the dedication in the hope that Theophilus would support the copying and distribution of the volumes.

Date and Location of Composition

LUKE PROBABLY WROTE BOTH VOLUMES between 80 and 90 CE, although no precision is possible on this question. Acts must have been written after the appointment of Festus as procurator, ca. 59 (Acts 24.27), and probably after the destruction of the Jerusalem temple in 70 (Lk 19.41–44; 21.20–24). Quotations from and allusions to Acts appear in Christian writings by the middle of the second century, which means it must have been completed before that time. Little in Acts helps to identify its place of composition, although various locations have been suggested, including Achaia, Macedonia, Antioch, Ephesus, Caesarea, and Rome.

Sources

IDENTIFYING THE NATURE AND EXTENT OF SOURCES Luke may have used in writing Acts is difficult. The existence of multiple Gospels enables readers to study their extensive similarities and draw tentative conclusions regarding their sources, but Acts stands without such parallels. Even the evidence that Luke possessed written sources for the composition of his Gospel does not require the assumption that he also had written sources for Acts. The sections of Acts written in the first-person plural ("we") often prompt the suggestion that Luke had a journal (his own or that of another of Paul's companions), but the use of the first-person plural may simply be a stylistic device. Stories about given locales, such as Antioch or Caesarea, have led to theories that Luke had access to written traditions of churches in those cities; the unity of theme and style throughout Acts makes identification of sources impossible, however. Whatever sources Luke used, written or oral, they lie beyond recovery.

Style and Language

GRIPPING INCIDENTS AND VIVID CHARACTERIZATIONS, including the dramatic punishment of Ananias and Sapphira (5.1–11), the speech of Paul before King Agrippa (26.2–23), and Paul's later adventure on the high seas (27.1–44), make Acts inviting reading. Luke's sophisticated use of the Greek language reflects the literary standards of his day. He also adjusts his style to make it suitable to particular contexts. In chs. 1–2, where he stresses the continuity of the church with Israel, he adopts a style imitative of the Septuagint, a Greek translation of the OT. When describing Paul's speech before the sophisticated Athenians (17.16–31), Luke refers to the pertinent philosophical schools and depicts the citizens in ways his contemporaries would have recognized. He often employs irony, as in his contrast between Peter, locked in prison by King Herod and yet freed by an angel, and Herod, free and yet destroyed by his own false pride (12.1–25).

Continuity with Luke's Gospel

BECAUSE THE GOSPELS WERE GROUPED together in the canon, Acts stands separate from Luke. Yet readers of Acts will be helped if they bear in mind its many connections with the Third Gospel. Among the most important Lukan themes is the fulfillment of God's promises in the ministry of Jesus and the life of the church. From the annunciation to Mary (Lk 1.35) to the mission of the church (Acts 1.8) to Paul's journey to Rome (Acts 27.24), Luke underscores the absolute reliability of God's word. Another overriding theme is the work of the Holy Spirit, which plays a prominent role in Jesus' ministry (Lk 4.1), in the empowering of the church (Acts 2.1–13), and in guiding the church's witness (15.28; 16.6–7). A third connection between the two volumes is that important figures in Acts duplicate aspects of Jesus' life, as when Peter raises the dead (Acts 9.36–43; cf. Lk 7.11–17) or when Paul's final journey to Jerusalem and Rome echoes that of Jesus to Jerusalem (Acts 19.21; cf. Lk 9.51–52). [BEVERLY ROBERTS GAVENTA]

The Promise of the Holy Spirit

1 In the first book, Theophilus, I wrote about all that Jesus did and taught from the beginning ²until the day when he was taken up to heaven, after giving instructions through the Holy Spirit to the apostles whom he had chosen. ³After his suffering he presented himself alive to them by many convincing proofs, appearing to them during forty days and speaking about the kingdom of God. ⁴While staying*a* with them, he ordered them not to leave Jerusalem, but to wait there for the promise of the Father. "This," he said, "is what you have heard from me; ⁵for John baptized with water, but you will be baptized with*b* the Holy Spirit not many days from now."

The Ascension of Jesus

6 So when they had come together, they asked him, "Lord, is this the time when you will restore the kingdom to Israel?" ⁷He replied, "It is not for you to know the times or periods that the Father has set by his own authority. ⁸But you will receive power when the Holy Spirit has come upon you; and you will be my witnesses in Jerusalem, in all Judea and Samaria, and to the ends of the earth." ⁹When he had said this, as they were watching, he was lifted up, and a cloud took him out of their sight. ¹⁰While he was going and they were gazing up toward heaven, suddenly two men in white robes stood by them. ¹¹They said, "Men of Galilee, why do you stand looking up toward heaven? This Jesus, who has been taken up from you into heaven, will come in the same way as you saw him go into heaven."

Matthias Chosen to Replace Judas

12 Then they returned to Jerusalem from the mount called Olivet, which is near Jerusalem, a sabbath day's journey away. ¹³When they had entered the city, they went to the room upstairs where they were staying, Peter, and John, and James, and Andrew, Philip and Thomas, Bartholomew and Matthew, James son of Alphaeus, and Simon the Zealot, and Judas son of*c* James. ¹⁴All these were constantly devoting themselves to prayer, together

a Or eating   *b* Or by   *c* Or the brother of

1.1–11 Acts opens with instruction of the apostles by the risen Jesus and three promises that precede his ascension: the gift of the Holy Spirit, the spread of their witness to the ends of the earth, and the eventual return of Jesus. **1.1** Following a literary custom of his day, Luke gives his work a formal dedication. *Theophilus,* lit. "lover of God" (see also Lk 1.3). **1.2–5** This scene repeats, but also conflicts with, the conclusion of Luke's Gospel (Lk 24.44–53). **1.3** Only here does the NT refer to a period of forty days between the resurrection and the ascension. In the synoptic Gospels, Jesus preaches about the *kingdom of God* as God's coming reign (see Lk 4.43; 9.27; 13.29); in Acts the phrase refers to the content of Christian preaching about Jesus (see, e.g., 8.12; 19.8; 28.23, 31). **1.5** *John baptized.* See Lk 3.1–20. **1.6** *Restore the kingdom to Israel,* i.e., restore Israel's political independence. **1.8** On the witness in *Jerusalem,* see 2.14–36; 3.12–26; in *Judea and Samaria,* see 8.1, 4–25. It is unclear whether *the ends of the earth* refers to the conversion of Gentiles (10.1–11.18), the arrival of Paul in Rome (28.16), or some event beyond the scope of Acts. **1.9** The *cloud* signifies the presence and activity of God (see Ex 24.15–18; Lk 9.34; 21.27). **1.10** *Two men in white robes,* probably to be understood as angels, indicate the importance of this event (see 5.19; Lk 1.11, 19; 24.4). **1.12–26** The apostles and other followers of Jesus return to Jerusalem, as they have been instructed to do (v. 4; Lk 24.49), and there a replacement for Judas is selected. **1.12** *The mount called Olivet* (the Mount of Olives) is located just east of Jerusalem (cf. Lk 24.50), which places the ascension in Bethany, a village along the eastern side of the mount. *A sabbath day's journey,* about a half mile. **1.13** The list of apostles coincides with the list in Lk 6.14–16 except for the omission of Judas Iscariot. **1.14** Luke frequently refers to *prayer* as an activity of the early church (e.g., 2.42; 6.4, 6; 10.9; 13.3; 28.8). This is the last reference to *Mary* in Luke-Acts. James, one of the *brothers* of Jesus, appears later in Acts (12.17; 15.13; 21.18), although Luke does not

with certain women, including Mary the mother of Jesus, as well as his brothers.

15 In those days Peter stood up among the believers[a] (together the crowd numbered about one hundred twenty persons) and said, [16]"Friends,[b] the scripture had to be fulfilled, which the Holy Spirit through David foretold concerning Judas, who became a guide for those who arrested Jesus— [17]for he was numbered among us and was allotted his share in this ministry." [18](Now this man acquired a field with the reward of his wickedness; and falling headlong,[c] he burst open in the middle and all his bowels gushed out. [19]This became known to all the residents of Jerusalem, so that the field was called in their language Hakeldama, that is, Field of Blood.) [20]"For it is written in the book of Psalms,

'Let his homestead become desolate,
    and let there be no one to live in it';
and

'Let another take his position of overseer.'
[21]So one of the men who have accompanied us during all the time that the Lord Jesus went in and out among us, [22]beginning from the baptism of John until the day when he was taken up from us—one of these must become a witness with us to his resurrection." [23]So they proposed two, Joseph called Barsabbas, who was also known as Justus, and Matthias. [24]Then they prayed and said, "Lord, you know everyone's heart. Show us which one of these two you have chosen [25]to take the place[d] in this ministry and apostleship from which

Judas turned aside to go to his own place." [26]And they cast lots for them, and the lot fell on Matthias; and he was added to the eleven apostles.

The Coming of the Holy Spirit

2 When the day of Pentecost had come, they were all together in one place. [2]And suddenly from heaven there came a sound like the rush of a violent wind, and it filled the entire house where they were sitting. [3]Divided tongues, as of fire, appeared among them, and a tongue rested on each of them. [4]All of them were filled with the Holy Spirit and began to speak in other languages, as the Spirit gave them ability.

5 Now there were devout Jews from every nation under heaven living in Jerusalem. [6]And at this sound the crowd gathered and was bewildered, because each one heard them speaking in the native language of each. [7]Amazed and astonished, they asked, "Are not all these who are speaking Galileans? [8]And how is it that we hear, each of us, in our own native language? [9]Parthians, Medes, Elamites, and residents of Mesopotamia, Judea and Cappadocia, Pontus and Asia, [10]Phrygia and Pamphylia, Egypt and the parts of Libya belonging to Cyrene, and visitors from Rome, both Jews and proselytes, [11]Cretans and Arabs—in our own languages we hear them

---

a Gk brothers b Gk Men, brothers c Or swelling up
d Other ancient authorities read the share

---

identify him as such (cf. Gal 1.19). **1.16** *The scripture had to be fulfilled.* For similar emphasis on divine necessity, see, e.g., 3.21; 9.16; Lk 24.44. It is not clear whether Luke refers to a specific passage of scripture or to scripture in a general sense. **1.18–19** On Judas's death, cf. Mt 27.3–10. *Hakeldama* transliterates an Aramaic expression. **1.20** The first quotation is adapted from Ps 69.25; the second from Ps 109.8. **1.21–22** In Luke's view, an apostle had to have been with Jesus *beginning from the baptism of John,* which means that Paul will not acquire that title (except in 14.14). The apostle's primary task is to *witness with us to his resurrection;* see, e.g., 2.32; 3.15; 4.33. **1.23** Neither *Justus* nor *Matthias* appears elsewhere in the NT. **1.26** On *casting lots* to determine God's will, see Prov 16.33.

2.1–13 The coming of the Holy Spirit has been anticipated by promises made in Lk 24.49; Acts 1.4–5. **2.1** The Jewish festival of *Pentecost* (lit. "fiftieth") derives its name from the fifty days that separate it from Passover (Lev 23.15–21). *All together in one place* may imply the presence of the full 120 mentioned in 1.15; Luke often refers to *all* believers being *together,* under-

scoring the unity of the community (e.g., v. 44; 4.24; 5.12). **2.3** On seeing *tongues, as of fire,* see Isa 5.24; *1 Enoch* 14.8–25; 71.5. Elsewhere in scripture fire accompanies the divine presence (Ex 19.18; Isa 66.15–16) and divine judgment (2 Thess 1.8). **2.4** *Other languages,* as the story that follows explains, refers to the gift of speaking in languages other than one's own and contrasts with the ecstatic speech to which Paul refers in 1 Cor 14.1–25 and which requires inspired interpretation. **2.5** *Devout Jews from every nation,* Jews from the Diaspora who either have come for Passover or have long-term business that keeps them in Jerusalem. Since the inclusion of Gentiles within the church comes only with the conversion of Cornelius in 10.1–11.18, those present at Pentecost are carefully identified as Jewish. Nevertheless, *every nation* hints at the larger reach of the gospel that is on the horizon. **2.9–11** The list of countries represented probably derives from similar lists found in ancient histories and geographies (e.g., Gen 10.2–31; *Sibylline Oracles* 3.156–95; 205–9; Philo, *Embassy* 281–83; *Flaccus* 45–46); it omits some locales that figure prominently in

speaking about God's deeds of power." 12All were amazed and perplexed, saying to one another, "What does this mean?" 13But others sneered and said, "They are filled with new wine."

Peter Addresses the Crowd

14 But Peter, standing with the eleven, raised his voice and addressed them, "Men of Judea and all who live in Jerusalem, let this be known to you, and listen to what I say. 15Indeed, these are not drunk, as you suppose, for it is only nine o'clock in the morning. 16No, this is what was spoken through the prophet Joel:

17 'In the last days it will be, God declares,

that I will pour out my Spirit upon all
     flesh,
  and your sons and your daughters shall
     prophesy,
  and your young men shall see visions,
     and your old men shall dream dreams.
18 Even upon my slaves, both men and
     women,
  in those days I will pour out my Spirit;
     and they shall prophesy.
19 And I will show portents in the heaven
     above
  and signs on the earth below,
     blood, and fire, and smoky mist.
20 The sun shall be turned to darkness
     and the moon to blood,

Acts, such as Macedonia and Achaia. **2.12–13** As in the Gospels, miraculous events prompt amazement and questioning; see, e.g., Lk 4.36–37; 5.17–26. *Wine* was sometimes viewed as an enhancement to prophetic speech; see Plutarch, *Oracles at Delphi* 406b; *Obsolescence of Oracles* 437d–e. **2.14–36** Peter's Pentecost speech signals the beginning of the Christian witness that was promised in 1.8; Lk 24.47–48. **2.14** *Men of Judea* and *all who live in Jerusalem* are not mutually exclusive groups; the repetition is for rhetorical effect. Similarly, *raised his voice, let this be known to you*, and

listen to what I say are all solemn assertions that underscore the importance of the speech that follows. **2.15** Several of the speeches of Acts have as their pretext a defense against some charge, in this case drunkenness in mid-morning; see also 4.5–12; 7.1–53; 11.2–18. **2.17–21** A quotation from the Septuagint of Joel 2.28–32, with small but significant alterations. Most important is the change from "afterward" (Joel 2.28) to *in the last days* (v. 17), emphasizing the eschatological context of the church. In v. 18, Luke adds the phrase *and they shall prophesy*, making explicit what the text

---

The Fulfillment of Acts 1.8 in the Following Narrative

"you will receive power when the Holy Spirit has come upon you"	At Pentecost the gift of the Holy Spirit fulfills this promise (2.1–13).
"you will be my witnesses in Jerusalem"	The preaching of Peter and others in Jerusalem brings about the witness there (2.14–8.3).
"in all Judea and Samaria"	Persecution in Jerusalem forces Christians out into Judea; the Samaritan mission follows (8.4–25).
"and to the ends of the earth"	The "ends of the earth" may refer to the Ethiopian, who comes from a great distance (8.26–40), or to Cornelius, the first acknowledged gentile convert (10.1–11.18), or to the arrival of Paul in Rome (28.14). It may even refer to some event beyond the scope of the narrative in Acts.

before the coming of the Lord's
great and glorious day.

21   Then everyone who calls on the name of
the Lord shall be saved.'

22 "You that are Israelites,[a] listen to what I
have to say: Jesus of Nazareth,[b] a man attested
to you by God with deeds of power, wonders,
and signs that God did through him among
you, as you yourselves know— 23this man,
handed over to you according to the definite
plan and foreknowledge of God, you crucified
and killed by the hands of those outside the
law. 24But God raised him up, having freed
him from death,[c] because it was impossible for
him to be held in its power. 25For David says
concerning him,

'I saw the Lord always before me,
    for he is at my right hand so that I will
        not be shaken;
26   therefore my heart was glad, and my
        tongue rejoiced;
    moreover my flesh will live in hope.
27   For you will not abandon my soul to
        Hades,
    or let your Holy One experience
        corruption.
28   You have made known to me the ways of
        life;
    you will make me full of gladness with
        your presence.'

29 "Fellow Israelites,[d] I may say to you confidently of our ancestor David that he both
died and was buried, and his tomb is with us
to this day. 30Since he was a prophet, he knew
that God had sworn with an oath to him that
he would put one of his descendants on his
throne. 31Foreseeing this, David[e] spoke of the
resurrection of the Messiah,[f] saying,

'He was not abandoned to Hades,
    nor did his flesh experience
        corruption.'

32This Jesus God raised up, and of that all of
us are witnesses. 33Being therefore exalted at[g]
the right hand of God, and having received
from the Father the promise of the Holy
Spirit, he has poured out this that you both see
and hear. 34For David did not ascend into the
heavens, but he himself says,

'The Lord said to my Lord,
    "Sit at my right hand,
35   until I make your enemies your
            footstool." '

36Therefore let the entire house of Israel know
with certainty that God has made him both
Lord and Messiah,[h] this Jesus whom you crucified."

The First Converts

37 Now when they heard this, they were cut to
the heart and said to Peter and to the other
apostles, "Brothers,[d] what should we do?"
38Peter said to them, "Repent, and be baptized
every one of you in the name of Jesus Christ so
that your sins may be forgiven; and you will
receive the gift of the Holy Spirit. 39For the
promise is for you, for your children, and for
all who are far away, everyone whom the Lord
our God calls to him." 40And he testified with
many other arguments and exhorted them,

---

a Gk Men, Israelites   b Gk the Nazorean   c Gk the pains of
death   d Gk Men, brothers   e Gk he   f Or the Christ
g Or by   h Or Christ

---

of Joel implies. **2.23** Luke consistently affirms both
human responsibility for the death of Jesus and the inevitability of that death in God's plan; see, e.g., 3.14–
18; 4.27–28; see also Lk 24.26, 44–48. The existence of
a divine *plan* for all is a prominent theme in Luke-Acts
(e.g., Acts 4.28; 20.27). **2.25a** *David* serves a dual role
in the speech: psalms ascribed to him become prophecies of Jesus, and he is the figure with whom Jesus is
compared. The resurrection signals Jesus' superiority
to David, whose tomb was thought to be well known
(see Josephus, *War* 1.61; *Antiquities* 7.393; 13.249).
2.25b–28 Peter quotes Ps 16.8–11. **2.29** Since David's
death is certain and even his burial place is known
(Neh 3.16), the psalm cannot refer to him. **2.30** On
God's *oath* to David, see Ps 132.11. **2.31** Peter quotes Ps
16.10. **2.32** Luke views *witnessing* as a defining characteristic of the apostolic task; see 1.22; 3.15; 4.33; 5.32;
10.41; 13.31. **2.33** Here the Holy Spirit is poured out
by the ascending Jesus, but earlier it is identified as

God's promise (1.4–5). **2.34–35** Peter quotes Ps 110.1;
see also 1 Cor 15.25. **2.36** The speech culminates in the
sharp contrast between human action (*this Jesus whom
you crucified*) and that of God (*God has made him both
Lord and Messiah*); see also vv. 23–24; 3.15; 4.10. **2.37–
47** The response to Peter's speech introduces central
Lukan themes regarding the church's life. **2.37** Speeches
in Acts are frequently interrupted at their climax (see,
e.g., 10.44; 17.32; 22.22). **2.38** The desired response to
Christian proclamation includes repentance, baptism, forgiveness of sins, and reception of the Holy
Spirit; these elements appear elsewhere in Acts, although not always in the same order (cf. 8.16; 10.44–
48; 19.1–6). **2.39** The *promise* extends to those distant
in time (*your children*) and in place (*all who are far
away*; see 22.21; Isa 57.19; Sir 24.32). What is promised
is, first of all, *the gift of the Holy Spirit* (v. 38; cf. 1.4–5;
2.33), but also more generally the salvation promised
to Israel (cf. 26.6) and offered by Jesus (13.23).

saying, "Save yourselves from this corrupt generation." 41So those who welcomed his message were baptized, and that day about three thousand persons were added. 42They devoted themselves to the apostles' teaching and fellowship, to the breaking of bread and the prayers.

Life among the Believers

43 Awe came upon everyone, because many wonders and signs were being done by the apostles. 44All who believed were together and had all things in common; 45they would sell their possessions and goods and distribute the proceeds*a* to all, as any had need. 46Day by day, as they spent much time together in the temple, they broke bread at home*b* and ate their food with glad and generous*c* hearts, 47praising God and having the goodwill of all the people. And day by day the Lord added to their number those who were being saved.

Peter Heals a Crippled Beggar

3 One day Peter and John were going up to the temple at the hour of prayer, at three o'clock in the afternoon. 2And a man lame from birth was being carried in. People would lay him daily at the gate of the temple called the Beautiful Gate so that he could ask for alms from those entering the temple. 3When he saw Peter and John about to go into the temple, he asked them for alms. 4Peter looked intently at him, as did John, and said, "Look at us." 5And

he fixed his attention on them, expecting to receive something from them. 6But Peter said, "I have no silver or gold, but what I have I give you; in the name of Jesus Christ of Nazareth,*d* stand up and walk." 7And he took him by the right hand and raised him up; and immediately his feet and ankles were made strong. 8Jumping up, he stood and began to walk, and he entered the temple with them, walking and leaping and praising God. 9All the people saw him walking and praising God, 10and they recognized him as the one who used to sit and ask for alms at the Beautiful Gate of the temple; and they were filled with wonder and amazement at what had happened to him.

Peter Speaks in Solomon's Portico

11 While he clung to Peter and John, all the people ran together to them in the portico called Solomon's Portico, utterly astonished. 12When Peter saw it, he addressed the people, "You Israelites,*e* why do you wonder at this, or why do you stare at us, as though by our own power or piety we had made him walk? 13The God of Abraham, the God of Isaac, and the God of Jacob, the God of our ancestors has glorified his servant*f* Jesus, whom you handed over and rejected in the presence of Pilate, though he had decided to release him. 14But you rejected the Holy and Righteous One and

---

a Gk them   *b* Or from house to house   *c* Or sincere   *d* Gk the Nazorean   *e* Gk Men, Israelites   *f* Or child

---

2.40 *Corrupt generation.* See Deut 32.5; Ps 78.8; Phil 2.15. **2.42–47** The first of several summaries in which Luke characterizes the life of the earliest Christian community as a fellowship involving worship, study, and shared possessions (see also 4.32–37; 5.12–16). Other ancient texts contain similar descriptions as demonstrations of the close friendships formed in philosophical or religious groups (Plato, *Republic* 449C; *Laws* 5.739C; Philo, *Abraham* 235; Seneca, *Epistles* 90.3; Strabo, *Geography* 7.3.9). **2.46** The *temple* continues as a place in which Christians worship; see also Lk 24.53. **2.47** Consistently Luke emphasizes the growth and divine guidance of the church; see, e.g., 6.7; 9.15–17, 31; 11.1–21; 12.24; 14.1). **3.1–10** This healing, which follows the same general pattern as healings in the Gospels, illustrates the *wonders and signs* done by the apostles (2.43) and prompts another speech by Peter. **3.1** It was customary to speak of *going up* when going to the temple (2 Kings 19.14; 20.5; Lk 18.10). *Three o'clock in the afternoon,* a regular time of prayer and the hour of the afternoon sacrifice (Dan 9.21; Jdt 9.1; Josephus, *Antiquities*

14.65; 3.237). **3.2** *Beautiful Gate,* puzzling, since ancient descriptions of the temple use no such title; it is generally identified with the Nicanor Gate, a gate made of bronze (Josephus, *War* 5.201; *Mishnah Middot* 1.4; 2.3). **3.4** *Looked intently.* See 13.9; 14.9. **3.6** Just as Peter urged repentance and baptism *in the name of Jesus* (2.38), so now the name is invoked and becomes the center of controversy when Peter and John are called before the council (4.5–20). **3.11–26** Peter's speech at the temple repeats themes of the Pentecost speech (2.14–36) concerning Jesus' place in Israel's history. **3.11** *The people,* Luke's characteristic way of referring to Israel (see v. 9; 4.10; 5.34; 10.41; Lk 2.10, 32; 7.29). *Solomon's Portico,* a colonnade on the east side of the temple enclosure. **3.12** As at Pentecost, the speech begins by addressing a misunderstanding; see 2.14–15. **3.13** *God of Abraham, . . . Isaac, . . . Jacob.* Luke connects God's action in Jesus to God's action in all of Israel's history (see Ex 3.6, 15–16; Lk 20.37). *His servant* (or *child*) *Jesus* recalls the servant of Isa 52.13–53.12 (see also Acts 4.27). On *Pilate*'s judgment, see Lk 23.13–16. **3.14** Calling Jesus *the Holy and Righteous One* (see also 7.52; 22.14; Lk 23.47) underscores the

asked to have a murderer given to you, [15]and you killed the Author of life, whom God raised from the dead. To this we are witnesses. [16]And by faith in his name, his name itself has made this man strong, whom you see and know; and the faith that is through Jesus[a] has given him this perfect health in the presence of all of you.

[17] "And now, friends,[b] I know that you acted in ignorance, as did also your rulers. [18]In this way God fulfilled what he had foretold through all the prophets, that his Messiah[c] would suffer. [19]Repent therefore, and turn to God so that your sins may be wiped out, [20]so that times of refreshing may come from the presence of the Lord, and that he may send the Messiah[d] appointed for you, that is, Jesus, [21]who must remain in heaven until the time of universal restoration that God announced long ago through his holy prophets. [22]Moses said, 'The Lord your God will raise up for you from your own people[b] a prophet like me. You must listen to whatever he tells you. [23]And it will be that everyone who does not listen to that prophet will be utterly rooted out of the people.' [24]And all the prophets, as many as have spoken, from Samuel and those after him, also predicted these days. [25]You are the descendants of the prophets and of the covenant that God gave to your ancestors, saying to Abraham, 'And in your descendants all the families of the earth shall be blessed.' [26]When God raised up his servant,[e] he sent him first to you, to bless you by turning each of you from your wicked ways."

Peter and John before the Council

4 While Peter and John[f] were speaking to the people, the priests, the captain of the temple, and the Sadducees came to them, [2]much annoyed because they were teaching the people and proclaiming that in Jesus there is the resurrection of the dead. [3]So they arrested them and put them in custody until the next day, for it was already evening. [4]But many of those who heard the word believed; and they numbered about five thousand.

[5] The next day their rulers, elders, and scribes assembled in Jerusalem, [6]with Annas the high priest, Caiaphas, John,[g] and Alexander, and all who were of the high-priestly family. [7]When they had made the prisoners[h] stand in their midst, they inquired, "By what power or by what name did you do this?" [8]Then Peter, filled with the Holy Spirit, said to them, "Rulers of the people and elders, [9]if we are questioned today because of a good deed done to someone who was sick and are asked how this man has been healed, [10]let it be known to all of you, and to all the people of Israel, that this man is standing before you in good health by the name of Jesus Christ of Nazareth,[i] whom you crucified, whom God raised from the dead. [11]This Jesus[j] is

---

a Gk him   b Gk brothers   c Or his Christ   d Or the Christ
e Or child   f Gk While they   g Other ancient authorities read
Jonathan   h Gk them   i Gk the Nazorean   j Gk This

---

moral contrast between him and the people, who preferred to have Pilate release the murderer Barabbas (Lk 23.18–19). **3.16** In the Gospels, the faith associated with healing is that of the person in need of healing (e.g., Mk 1.40–45; 10.46–52) or a bystander (Mk 5.22–43; 9.14–29). In this instance, the faith involved is that of the apostles themselves. **3.17–18** See note on 2.23. **3.20** *Times of refreshing,* either periods of relief during eschatological distress or the final restoration (see v. 21). **3.21** *Universal restoration,* not the restoration of Israel's kingdom (cf. 1.6), but roughly the equivalent of salvation itself. **3.22–23** See Deut 18.15–20. **3.25** See Gen 22.18; 26.4. **3.26** *First to you* underscores the priority of Israel (see 13.46) and anticipates another stage of proclamation, that to the Gentiles; see also Rom 1.16.

4.1–22 In contrast to the popular positive reaction to Peter's Pentecost speech (2.37–42), the speech at the temple (3.12–26) prompts the first official resistance to Christian preaching and sets the stage for Peter's defense (4.8–12). **4.1–2** Luke distinguishes *the people,* whom Peter and John address and who receive them gladly, from their rulers, who are hostile to the gospel.

The *captain of the temple* (see 5.24, 26; Lk 22.52) maintained order in the temple precinct and ranked just below the high priest in authority. In Acts, the *Sadducees* serve as foils for Christian preaching because they did not believe in the *resurrection of the dead* (see 23.6–10). Little information is available about this Jewish sect; sources consistently associate it with the aristocracy and temple priesthood (Josephus, *Antiquities* 13.297–298; 18.16–17; *War* 2.164–65), yet it did not have any particular authority in the area of the temple itself. **4.4** *Five thousand,* literally the number of males, suggesting that the number of believers was even larger. Since Luke often uses hyperbole for rhetorical impact (see, e.g., v. 16), any assessment of the accuracy of such figures is impossible. **4.6** *Annas,* high priest in 6–15 CE, well before the time of this story, probably included because of his prominence. *Caiaphas,* son-in-law to Annas and high priest in 18–36/7 CE; *John, Alexander,* otherwise unknown. **4.8** *Filled with the Holy Spirit* recalls Lk 12.11–12; Peter speaks not his own words but those given him by the Spirit. **4.10** Again Luke contrasts the responses to Jesus: the leaders crucified him, but God raised him

'the stone that was rejected by you, the
builders;
it has become the cornerstone.'[a]
12There is salvation in no one else, for there is
no other name under heaven given among
mortals by which we must be saved."

13 Now when they saw the boldness of
Peter and John and realized that they were
uneducated and ordinary men, they were
amazed and recognized them as companions
of Jesus. 14When they saw the man who had
been cured standing beside them, they had
nothing to say in opposition. 15So they ordered them to leave the council while they discussed the matter with one another. 16They
said, "What will we do with them? For it is obvious to all who live in Jerusalem that a notable sign has been done through them; we
cannot deny it. 17But to keep it from spreading
further among the people, let us warn them to
speak no more to anyone in this name." 18So
they called them and ordered them not to
speak or teach at all in the name of Jesus. 19But
Peter and John answered them, "Whether it is
right in God's sight to listen to you rather than
to God, you must judge; 20for we cannot keep
from speaking about what we have seen and
heard." 21After threatening them again, they
let them go, finding no way to punish them
because of the people, for all of them praised
God for what had happened. 22For the man on
whom this sign of healing had been performed was more than forty years old.

The Believers Pray for Boldness

23 After they were released, they went to their
friends[b] and reported what the chief priests
and the elders had said to them. 24When they
heard it, they raised their voices together to
God and said, "Sovereign Lord, who made the
heaven and the earth, the sea, and everything
in them, 25it is you who said by the Holy Spirit
through our ancestor David, your servant:[c]
'Why did the Gentiles rage,
and the peoples imagine vain things?
26 The kings of the earth took their stand,
and the rulers have gathered together
against the Lord and against his
Messiah.'[d]
27For in this city, in fact, both Herod and Pontius Pilate, with the Gentiles and the peoples
of Israel, gathered together against your holy
servant[c] Jesus, whom you anointed, 28to do
whatever your hand and your plan had predestined to take place. 29And now, Lord, look
at their threats, and grant to your servants[e] to
speak your word with all boldness, 30while
you stretch out your hand to heal, and signs
and wonders are performed through the name
of your holy servant[c] Jesus." 31When they had
prayed, the place in which they were gathered
together was shaken; and they were all filled
with the Holy Spirit and spoke the word of
God with boldness.

The Believers Share Their Possessions

32 Now the whole group of those who believed were of one heart and soul, and no one
claimed private ownership of any possessions,
but everything they owned was held in common. 33With great power the apostles gave
their testimony to the resurrection of the Lord
Jesus, and great grace was upon them all.
34There was not a needy person among them,
for as many as owned lands or houses sold
them and brought the proceeds of what was

a Or keystone   b Gk their own   c Or child   d Or his Christ
e Gk slaves

from the dead (see 2.36). **4.11** See Ps 118.22 and its use
in Lk 20.17; Mt 21.42; 1 Pet 2.7. **4.12** *Salvation*, both the
physical healing of the lame man and salvation from
judgment or from the service of false gods (see 13.26;
16.17). **4.13** Luke understands *boldness*, or forthright
speech, to be a hallmark of the apostles (see vv. 29–31;
18.26; 28.31). **4.16** *All who live in Jerusalem*, exaggeration to dramatize the authorities' dilemma. **4.19–
20** For comparable assertions about the necessity of
obedience to God, see Plato, *Apology* 29D; 2 Macc 7.2;
4 Macc 5.16–38; Josephus, *Antiquities* 17.158–59.
4.22 The subject's age underscores the significance of
the healing. **4.23–31** The community responds with
prayer to persecution and the release of Peter and John.
4.24 *Sovereign Lord*. See 3 Macc 2.2; Lk 2.29 (translated
"Master"); Rev 6.10. *Who made . . . everything in them.*
See 14.15; 17.24; see also Ex 20.11; Ps 146.6; Isa 37.16.
4.25b–26 Ps 2.1–2. Connecting the psalm both to
Jesus' death (v. 27) and to the persecution of the church
(v. 29) allows Luke to assert that both events serve
God's plan. **4.27** Cf. Lk 23.6–16, where *Herod* and *Pilate* seek to release Jesus. Perhaps they are included here
as counterparts to the psalm's *kings* and *rulers* (v. 26).
4.29 *Servants*, here those enslaved, a different Greek
word (*doulos*) than in vv. 25, 27, 30 (*pais*). **4.31** That the
place itself *was shaken* signals God's presence (Ex 19.18;
2 Esd 6.14–15, 29; Josephus, *Antiquities* 4.51). *All filled
with the Holy Spirit*. See 2.4. *Boldness*. See v. 13; 9.27–
28; 13.46; 28.31. **4.32–37** This second summary of the
common life of believers (cf. 2.42–47) emphasizes the
sharing of property in a way consistent with the Hellenistic ideal of friendship. **4.34** See Deut 15.4.

sold. [35]They laid it at the apostles' feet, and it was distributed to each as any had need. [36]There was a Levite, a native of Cyprus, Joseph, to whom the apostles gave the name Barnabas (which means "son of encouragement"). [37]He sold a field that belonged to him, then brought the money, and laid it at the apostles' feet.

Ananias and Sapphira

5 But a man named Ananias, with the consent of his wife Sapphira, sold a piece of property; [2]with his wife's knowledge, he kept back some of the proceeds, and brought only a part and laid it at the apostles' feet. [3]"Ananias," Peter asked, "why has Satan filled your heart to lie to the Holy Spirit and to keep back part of the proceeds of the land? [4]While it remained unsold, did it not remain your own? And after it was sold, were not the proceeds at your disposal? How is it that you have contrived this deed in your heart? You did not lie to us[a] but to God!" [5]Now when Ananias heard these words, he fell down and died. And great fear seized all who heard of it. [6]The young men came and wrapped up his body,[b] then carried him out and buried him.

[7] After an interval of about three hours his wife came in, not knowing what had happened. [8]Peter said to her, "Tell me whether you and your husband sold the land for such and such a price." And she said, "Yes, that was the price." [9]Then Peter said to her, "How is it that you have agreed together to put the Spirit of the Lord to the test? Look, the feet of those who have buried your husband are at the door, and they will carry you out." [10]Immediately

she fell down at his feet and died. When the young men came in they found her dead, so they carried her out and buried her beside her husband. [11]And great fear seized the whole church and all who heard of these things.

The Apostles Heal Many

[12] Now many signs and wonders were done among the people through the apostles. And they were all together in Solomon's Portico. [13]None of the rest dared to join them, but the people held them in high esteem. [14]Yet more than ever believers were added to the Lord, great numbers of both men and women, [15]so that they even carried out the sick into the streets, and laid them on cots and mats, in order that Peter's shadow might fall on some of them as he came by. [16]A great number of people would also gather from the towns around Jerusalem, bringing the sick and those tormented by unclean spirits, and they were all cured.

The Apostles Are Persecuted

[17] Then the high priest took action; he and all who were with him (that is, the sect of the Sadducees), being filled with jealousy, [18]arrested the apostles and put them in the public prison. [19]But during the night an angel of the Lord opened the prison doors, brought them out, and said, [20]"Go, stand in the temple and tell the people the whole message about this life." [21]When they heard this, they entered the temple at daybreak and went on with their teaching.

When the high priest and those with him

---

a Gk to men   b Meaning of Gk uncertain

4.35 That money from donated property is placed at the *apostles' feet* (see also v. 37; 5.2) suggests their authority over community life. **4.36** Whether *Barnabas* actually means "*son of encouragement*" is doubtful, but Barnabas's major role in Acts is encouraging the work of Paul (see, e.g., 9.27; 11.22–30). **4.37** This incident concretely illustrates the community's sharing of property and contrasts with the story that follows. **5.1–11** The story of the otherwise unknown Ananias and Sapphira underscores the importance of the community and especially of Peter, but the real focus here is on the lie to God involved in their actions; see Josh 7. **5.3** As with the betrayal of Jesus by Judas (Lk 22.3, 31), this event occurs at *Satan*'s instigation; nevertheless, Ananias and Sapphira are held responsible for their actions. **5.5** *He . . . died.* Following immediately on Peter's pronouncement that Ananias lied to God, this death enacts God's judgment. **5.7–11** The

fact that Luke describes Sapphira's death separately reflects both the significance of the story and Luke's customary attention to female characters; see, e.g., 9.36–43; 16.11–15; Lk 1.5–58; 2.36–38; 7.11–17, 36–50; 8.1–3, 43–48. **5.11** *Fear*, or awe, often accompanies the divine presence (see 2.43; 5.5; 9.31; 19.17; Lk 1.12; 2.9; 5.26; 7.16; 8.37; 21.26). The word *church* appears here for the first time in Luke-Acts. **5.12–16** The third summary of community life (see 2.42–47; 4.32–37) emphasizes the healings accomplished by the apostles in answer to the prayer of 4.30. **5.12** *Solomon's Portico.* See note on 3.11. **5.15** Like the fringe of Jesus' clothing (Lk 8.44) or Paul's handkerchief (19.12), even *Peter's shadow* can heal. **5.17–42** The series of miracles, speeches, and confrontations that begins in 3.1 culminates in this dramatic confrontation with the authorities. **5.17** *Sadducees.* See note on 4.1–2. **5.18** By characterizing this as a

arrived, they called together the council and the whole body of the elders of Israel, and sent to the prison to have them brought. 22But when the temple police went there, they did not find them in the prison; so they returned and reported, 23"We found the prison securely locked and the guards standing at the doors, but when we opened them, we found no one inside." 24Now when the captain of the temple and the chief priests heard these words, they were perplexed about them, wondering what might be going on. 25Then someone arrived and announced, "Look, the men whom you put in prison are standing in the temple and teaching the people!" 26Then the captain went with the temple police and brought them, but without violence, for they were afraid of being stoned by the people.

27 When they had brought them, they had them stand before the council. The high priest questioned them, 28saying, "We gave you strict orders not to teach in this name,ᵃ yet here you have filled Jerusalem with your teaching and you are determined to bring this man's blood on us." 29But Peter and the apostles answered, "We must obey God rather than any human authority.ᵇ 30The God of our ancestors raised up Jesus, whom you had killed by hanging him on a tree. 31God exalted him at his right hand as Leader and Savior that he might give repentance to Israel and forgiveness of sins. 32And we are witnesses to these things, and so is the Holy Spirit whom God has given to those who obey him."

33 When they heard this, they were enraged and wanted to kill them. 34But a Pharisee in the council named Gamaliel, a teacher of the law, respected by all the people, stood up and ordered the men to be put outside for a short time. 35Then he said to them, "Fellow Israelites,ᶜ consider carefully what you propose to do to these men. 36For some time ago Theudas rose up, claiming to be somebody, and a number of men, about four hundred, joined him; but he was killed, and all who followed him were dispersed and disappeared. 37After him Judas the Galilean rose up at the time of the census and got people to follow him; he also perished, and all who followed him were scattered. 38So in the present case, I tell you, keep away from these men and let them alone; because if this plan or this undertaking is of human origin, it will fail; 39but if it is of God, you will not be able to overthrow them—in that case you may even be found fighting against God!"

They were convinced by him, 40and when they had called in the apostles, they had them flogged. Then they ordered them not to speak in the name of Jesus, and let them go. 41As they left the council, they rejoiced that they were considered worthy to suffer dishonor for the sake of the name. 42And every day in the temple and at homeᵈ they did not cease to teach and proclaim Jesus as the Messiah.ᵉ

Seven Chosen to Serve

6 Now during those days, when the disciples were increasing in number, the Hellenists complained against the Hebrews be-

---

ᵃ Other ancient authorities read *Did we not give you strict orders not to teach in this name?*   ᵇ Gk *than men*   ᶜ Gk *Men, Israelites*   ᵈ Or *from house to house*   ᵉ Or *the Christ*

---

public act, Luke underscores the authorities' desire to intimidate and silence. **5.28–29** See 4.17–20. **5.34** Within the crowd of Sadducees (v. 17) the Pharisee Gamaliel seems to be a minority. In Acts, the *Pharisees* appear as natural allies of Christians because of their shared belief in resurrection (see 23.6–10). *Gamaliel,* referred to in Jewish writings as Gamaliel I or the Elder, is later identified as Paul's teacher (22.3), but little is known about him. Luke describes him favorably. **5.36** According to Josephus (*Antiquities* 20.97–98), *Theudas* declared himself a prophet and led a large group of people to the Jordan River, which he declared would part at his order. He was executed by the Romans ca. 44 CE, well after the time of Judas the Galilean (see v. 37) and after the time of Gamaliel's speech. Either Luke and Josephus refer to different persons, which seems unlikely, or one of them is incorrect. **5.37** *Judas the Galilean* led a revolt against the census of Quirinius ca. 6 CE. **5.41–42** The rejoicing of

the apostles and their continued preaching indicates already that persecution will not silence them; thus Gamaliel's warning in vv. 38–39 already proves prophetic.

6.1–7 This conflict between the Hellenists and the Hebrews raises a number of historical questions, since neither the groups nor their conflict has previously entered Luke's story. Luke appears less concerned with historical detail than with describing the way in which the church addresses a threat to its unity. **6.1** *Disciples,* the first use of the term since Lk 22.45; in Acts it refers to believers in general rather than to the apostles (e.g., 9.10; 15.10; 16.1). *Hellenists,* probably Jewish Christians from the Diaspora whose native language was Greek and who spoke little or no Aramaic. *Hebrews,* by contrast, Christians from among those Jews who spoke only or primarily Aramaic. Conflict could arise from their social and cultural differences and spill over into the *daily distribution of food* (see 4.35). In a cul-

cause their widows were being neglected in the daily distribution of food. ²And the twelve called together the whole community of the disciples and said, "It is not right that we should neglect the word of God in order to wait on tables.ᵃ ³Therefore, friends,ᵇ select from among yourselves seven men of good standing, full of the Spirit and of wisdom, whom we may appoint to this task, ⁴while we, for our part, will devote ourselves to prayer and to serving the word." ⁵What they said pleased the whole community, and they chose Stephen, a man full of faith and the Holy Spirit, together with Philip, Prochorus, Nicanor, Timon, Parmenas, and Nicolaus, a proselyte of Antioch. ⁶They had these men stand before the apostles, who prayed and laid their hands on them.

7 The word of God continued to spread; the number of the disciples increased greatly in Jerusalem, and a great many of the priests became obedient to the faith.

The Arrest of Stephen

8 Stephen, full of grace and power, did great wonders and signs among the people. ⁹Then some of those who belonged to the synagogue of the Freedmen (as it was called), Cyrenians,

Alexandrians, and others of those from Cilicia and Asia, stood up and argued with Stephen. ¹⁰But they could not withstand the wisdom and the Spiritᶜ with which he spoke. ¹¹Then they secretly instigated some men to say, "We have heard him speak blasphemous words against Moses and God." ¹²They stirred up the people as well as the elders and the scribes; then they suddenly confronted him, seized him, and brought him before the council. ¹³They set up false witnesses who said, "This man never stops saying things against this holy place and the law; ¹⁴for we have heard him say that this Jesus of Nazarethᵈ will destroy this place and will change the customs that Moses handed on to us." ¹⁵And all who sat in the council looked intently at him, and they saw that his face was like the face of an angel.

Stephen's Speech to the Council

7 Then the high priest asked him, "Are these things so?" ²And Stephen replied:

"Brothersᵉ and fathers, listen to me. The God of glory appeared to our ancestor Abraham when he was in Mesopotamia, before he lived

---

a Or keep accounts b Gk brothers c Or spirit d Gk the Nazorean e Gk Men, brothers

---

ture that allowed women little economic independence, widows, especially those of immigrants, would be among the most disadvantaged. This scene recalls the commands that Israel care for widow and orphan (Deut 14.28–29; 24.17–21; 26.12–13) as well as the sharp rebuke that follows when widow and orphan are neglected (Isa 10.1–3; Zech 7.10–12). **6.2** Luke only here refers to the apostles as *the twelve* (but cf. Lk 6.13; 1 Cor 15.5). Although the seven are assigned to *wait on tables*, Acts nowhere depicts them doing so. **6.5** All of the seven have Greek names, consistent with their identification with the Hellenists. Only *Stephen* (6.8–8.1) and *Philip* (8.4–13, 26–40; 21.8) enter the story again. That *Nicolaus* is identified as a proselyte, or convert, suggests that the others were born into Jewish families. **6.6** For the laying on of *hands* as a ritual of empowerment, see Num 27.23; 1 Tim 4.14; 5.22; 2 Tim 1.6. **6.7** *The word of God continued to spread,* one of several statements showing the church's growth in the face of dire threats, internal and external (see 5.14; 9.31; 11.21; 12.24; 16.5; 19.20). *Many of the priests,* a surprise, given the resistance of the chief priests in 4.5; 5.17. **6.8–15** Stephen's arrest expands the persecution of Christians to include diaspora Jews living in Jerusalem and escalates the actions beyond beating and imprisonment (5.17–42) to death. **6.8** Luke's emphasis on Stephen's holiness (see also vv. 5, 10, 15; 7.55–60) makes his persecution and death appear

more heinous. **6.9** Probably persons from at least two synagogues are involved in the dispute with Stephen: one group of *Freedmen* (i.e., former slaves) from Africa (Cyrene and Alexandria) and another group from Asia Minor (Cilicia and Asia). This is the first time diaspora Jews have been involved in resistance to Christian preaching. **6.11–14** The charges against Stephen are more specific than earlier charges against the apostles; he stands accused of threatening the temple and Mosaic law (cf. 21.28; 25.8). For similar charges against Jesus, see Mt 26.59–61; Mk 14.55–58; cf. Jn 2.19–22. **6.12** For the first time in Acts, the *people* side with the authorities against the church (cf. 2.47; 4.1–2). **6.15** That Stephen's face appears *like the face of an angel* confirms his innocence and anticipates the vision of 7.55–56.

7.1–53 Stephen's speech offers little direct response to the high priest's question, although it does deal at length with the topics of Moses and the temple. Rather than defend himself, Stephen recounts Israel's history, focusing on the figures of Abraham, Joseph, and Moses; for similar recitals, see Josh 24.2–13; Neh 9.6–37; Pss 78; 105; 106; 135. **7.2–8** The story of *Abraham* is here confined to God's actions of call, promise, and covenant, with little attention to the theme of Abraham's obedience and no reference to Sarah. **7.2** *The God of glory.* See Ps 29.3; cf. *the glory of God* in Acts 7.55. According to Gen 11.31, Abraham already lived

in Haran, [3]and said to him, 'Leave your country and your relatives and go to the land that I will show you.' [4]Then he left the country of the Chaldeans and settled in Haran. After his father died, God had him move from there to this country in which you are now living. [5]He did not give him any of it as a heritage, not even a foot's length, but promised to give it to him as his possession and to his descendants after him, even though he had no child. [6]And God spoke in these terms, that his descendants would be resident aliens in a country belonging to others, who would enslave them and mistreat them during four hundred years. [7]'But I will judge the nation that they serve,' said God, 'and after that they shall come out and worship me in this place.' [8]Then he gave him the covenant of circumcision. And so Abraham[a] became the father of Isaac and circumcised him on the eighth day; and Isaac became the father of Jacob, and Jacob of the twelve patriarchs.

9 "The patriarchs, jealous of Joseph, sold him into Egypt; but God was with him, [10]and rescued him from all his afflictions, and enabled him to win favor and to show wisdom when he stood before Pharaoh, king of Egypt, who appointed him ruler over Egypt and over all his household. [11]Now there came a famine throughout Egypt and Canaan, and great suffering, and our ancestors could find no food. [12]But when Jacob heard that there was grain in Egypt, he sent our ancestors there on their first visit. [13]On the second visit Joseph made himself known to his brothers, and Joseph's family became known to Pharaoh. [14]Then Joseph sent and invited his father Jacob and all his relatives to come to him, seventy-five in all; [15]so Jacob went down to Egypt. He himself died there as well as our ancestors, [16]and their bodies[b] were brought back to Shechem and laid in the tomb that Abraham had bought for a sum of silver from the sons of Hamor in Shechem.

17 "But as the time drew near for the fulfillment of the promise that God had made to Abraham, our people in Egypt increased and multiplied [18]until another king who had not known Joseph ruled over Egypt. [19]He dealt craftily with our race and forced our ancestors to abandon their infants so that they would die. [20]At this time Moses was born, and he was beautiful before God. For three months he was brought up in his father's house; [21]and when he was abandoned, Pharaoh's daughter adopted him and brought him up as her own son. [22]So Moses was instructed in all the wisdom of the Egyptians and was powerful in his words and deeds.

23 "When he was forty years old, it came into his heart to visit his relatives, the Israelites.[c] [24]When he saw one of them being wronged, he defended the oppressed man and avenged him by striking down the Egyptian. [25]He supposed that his kinsfolk would understand that God through him was rescuing them, but they did not understand. [26]The next day he came to some of them as they were quarreling and tried to reconcile them, saying, 'Men, you are brothers; why do you wrong each other?' [27]But the man who was wronging his neighbor pushed Moses[d] aside, saying, 'Who made you a ruler and a judge over us? [28]Do you want to kill me as you killed the Egyptian yesterday?' [29]When he heard this, Moses fled and became a resident alien in the land of Midian. There he became the father of two sons.

30 "Now when forty years had passed, an angel appeared to him in the wilderness of Mount Sinai, in the flame of a burning bush. [31]When Moses saw it, he was amazed at the sight; and as he approached to look, there

---

a Gk he   b Gk they   c Gk his brothers, the sons of Israel
d Gk him

---

in *Haran* when God called him. **7.3** The quotation is from Gen 12.1. **7.5** See Gen 13.15; 17.8; 48.4. **7.6–7** See Gen 15.13–14; see also Ex 2.22. **7.8** *Isaac* and *Jacob* receive scant attention here as Stephen moves quickly to Joseph (see Gen 21.1–4; 25.26; 29.31–30.24). **7.9–16** With *Joseph,* Stephen develops the theme of God's use of unlikely instruments for the salvation of Israel and Israel's rejection of those instruments. On Joseph's betrayal by his brothers, see Gen 37.11, 18–36. **7.14** *Seventy-five* agrees with the Septuagint text of Gen 46.27 over against the Hebrew text, which reads "seventy." **7.16** This account of the burial of the patri-

archs conflicts at several points with Genesis; see Gen 23.1–20; 25.9; 33.18–19; 50.13–14; Josh 24.32. *Shechem* may anticipate the inclusion of the Samaritans in 8.4–25, since Shechem was the center of Samaritan territory. **7.17–43** As the servant of God who is rejected by Israel, *Moses* receives the most detailed attention in Stephen's speech. **7.17–19** See Ex 1.7–10. **7.20–22** See Ex 2.2–10. **7.22** Luke's emphasis on Moses' *wisdom, power,* and role in God's plan (see v. 25) ties him to John the Baptist and Jesus (see Lk 1.68–80; 2.29–32, 40, 52) as well as to Stephen himself (6.5, 8, 10). **7.23–29** See Ex 2.11–22, where it is Pharaoh's

came the voice of the Lord: 32'I am the God of your ancestors, the God of Abraham, Isaac, and Jacob.' Moses began to tremble and did not dare to look. 33 Then the Lord said to him, 'Take off the sandals from your feet, for the place where you are standing is holy ground. 34 I have surely seen the mistreatment of my people who are in Egypt and have heard their groaning, and I have come down to rescue them. Come now, I will send you to Egypt.'

35 "It was this Moses whom they rejected when they said, 'Who made you a ruler and a judge?' and whom God now sent as both ruler and liberator through the angel who appeared to him in the bush. 36 He led them out, having performed wonders and signs in Egypt, at the Red Sea, and in the wilderness for forty years. 37 This is the Moses who said to the Israelites, 'God will raise up a prophet for you from your own people[a] as he raised me up.' 38 He is the one who was in the congregation in the wilderness with the angel who spoke to him at Mount Sinai, and with our ancestors; and he received living oracles to give to us. 39 Our ancestors were unwilling to obey him; instead, they pushed him aside, and in their hearts they turned back to Egypt, 40 saying to Aaron, 'Make gods for us who will lead the way for us; as for this Moses who led us out from the land of Egypt, we do not know what has happened to him.' 41 At that time they made a calf, offered a sacrifice to the idol, and reveled in the works of their hands. 42 But God turned away from them and handed them over to worship the host of heaven, as it is written in the book of the prophets:

'Did you offer to me slain victims and
    sacrifices

forty years in the wilderness, O house
    of Israel?
43 No; you took along the tent of Moloch,
    and the star of your god Rephan,
        the images that you made to worship;
    so I will remove you beyond Babylon.'

44 "Our ancestors had the tent of testimony in the wilderness, as God[b] directed when he spoke to Moses, ordering him to make it according to the pattern he had seen. 45 Our ancestors in turn brought it in with Joshua when they dispossessed the nations that God drove out before our ancestors. And it was there until the time of David, 46 who found favor with God and asked that he might find a dwelling place for the house of Jacob.[c] 47 But it was Solomon who built a house for him. 48 Yet the Most High does not dwell in houses made with human hands;[d] as the prophet says,
49 'Heaven is my throne,
    and the earth is my footstool.
What kind of house will you build for
    me, says the Lord,
    or what is the place of my rest?
50 Did not my hand make all these things?'

51 "You stiff-necked people, uncircumcised in heart and ears, you are forever opposing the Holy Spirit, just as your ancestors used to do. 52 Which of the prophets did your ancestors not persecute? They killed those who foretold the coming of the Righteous One, and now you have become his betrayers and murderers. 53 You are the ones that received the law as ordained by angels, and yet you have not kept it."

---

a Gk your brothers b Gk he c Other ancient authorities read for the God of Jacob d Gk with hands

anger that prompts Moses' flight. **7.30–34** See Ex 3.1–10. **7.35–43** Israel's rejection of Moses, and indeed of God, dominates Stephen's summary of the exodus and wilderness years as the account moves toward an indictment of Israel. **7.35** See Ex 2.14. **7.37** See Deut 18.15. **7.40** See Ex 32.1, 23. **7.42–43** See Am 5.25–27 (Septuagint). See also Rom 1.24, 26, 28, where God is said to have "given up" (or *handed . . . over*) humanity to sin because of its failure to acknowledge God. **7.44–53** The speech's final segment turns from key figures in Israel's history to the tent and temple as places of worship. **7.44** *Tent of testimony.* See Ex 33.7. On the *pattern* shown to Moses, see Ex 25.8–9. **7.45** See Josh 3.14–17. **7.46** On God's *favor* toward David, see 1 Sam 13.14; 2 Sam 15.25. On what David *asked* of God, see 2 Sam 7. **7.47** See 1 Kings 6. **7.48** That God does not dwell *in houses made with human hands* may be found already

in 1 Kings 8.27–30, and Stephen's audience would have agreed. **7.49–50** Having explained that God commanded the making of the tabernacle (v. 44) and having recalled Solomon's building of the temple (v. 47), Stephen, quoting from Isa 66.1–2, rejects not the temple as such but the assumption that humans have authority over it. See Jer 7.1–4; Mic 3.9–12. **7.51** *Stiff-necked people.* See Ex 33.3, 5. *Uncircumcised in heart and ears.* See Deut 10.16; Jer 6.10. *Forever opposing the Holy Spirit.* See 5.3; Isa 63.10; Lk 12.10. **7.52** The charge that the people of Jerusalem killed Jesus (see 2.23; 3.14–15; 4.10; 5.30) is here placed in the context of Israel's persecution of God's prophets, a claim hyperbolically asserted in v. 52a. **7.53** Paul employs the same tradition about *angels* to argue the law's inferiority (Gal 3.19; cf. Heb 2.2); here the angels confirm the law's importance. The tradition may be derived from

The Stoning of Stephen

54 When they heard these things, they became enraged and ground their teeth at Stephen.[a] 55But filled with the Holy Spirit, he gazed into heaven and saw the glory of God and Jesus standing at the right hand of God. 56"Look," he said, "I see the heavens opened and the Son of Man standing at the right hand of God!" 57But they covered their ears, and with a loud shout all rushed together against him. 58Then they dragged him out of the city and began to stone him; and the witnesses laid their coats at the feet of a young man named Saul. 59While they were stoning Stephen, he prayed, "Lord Jesus, receive my spirit." 60Then he knelt down and cried out in a loud voice, "Lord, do not hold this sin against them." When he had said 8 this, he died.[b] 1And Saul approved of their killing him.

Saul Persecutes the Church

That day a severe persecution began against the church in Jerusalem, and all except the apostles were scattered throughout the countryside of Judea and Samaria. 2Devout men buried Stephen and made loud lamentation over him. 3But Saul was ravaging the church by entering house after house; dragging off both men and women, he committed them to prison.

Philip Preaches in Samaria

4 Now those who were scattered went from place to place, proclaiming the word. 5Philip went down to the city[c] of Samaria and proclaimed the Messiah[d] to them. 6The crowds with one accord listened eagerly to what was said by Philip, hearing and seeing the signs that he did, 7for unclean spirits, crying with loud shrieks, came out of many who were possessed; and many others who were paralyzed or lame were cured. 8So there was great joy in that city.

9 Now a certain man named Simon had previously practiced magic in the city and amazed the people of Samaria, saying that he was someone great. 10All of them, from the least to the greatest, listened to him eagerly,

a Gk him b Gk fell asleep c Other ancient authorities read a city d Or the Christ

Deut 33.2; cf. Jubilees 1.27, 29; 2.1; Josephus, Antiquities 15.136. **7.54–8.1a** The narrative of Stephen's death dramatically contrasts Stephen with his attackers by emphasizing his innocence and their rage. The introduction of Saul, who becomes the ardent enemy of the church, completes the contrast. **7.54** Ground their teeth, a common depiction of God's enemies in the OT. See Lk 13.28; see also Job 16.9; Ps 35.16; 112.10. **7.55** The presence of the Holy Spirit and the vision of God's glory and of Jesus testify to Stephen's innocence (see also Lk 9.32). **7.56** Stephen's vision of the Son of Man recalls Jesus' earlier words to the council (see Lk 22.69; cf. Ps 110.1; Dan 7.13), although here the Son of Man is not seated but standing. **7.58** On stoning outside the city, see Lev 24.10–23; Num 15.32–36. Here again Stephen's story conforms to that of Jesus (Lk 4.28–29). Saul (or Paul; see 13.9) appears here for the first time and will shortly return as persecutor of the church (8.3); later he becomes a central figure in the church's mission (chs. 13–28). **7.59** Lord . . . receive my spirit. Cf. Jesus' words in Lk 23.46; see also Ps 31.5. **7.60** Do not hold this sin against them. Cf. Jesus' words in Lk 23.34. **8.1a** Saul's approval of Stephen's death sets the stage for the great persecution in Jerusalem (vv. 1b–3) and for Saul's persecution of Christians beyond Jerusalem (9.1–2).

8.1b–3 Persecution of the church provides an impetus to its growth as it forces the church into new territory. **8.1b** Since Acts has referred only to the church in Jerusalem, this reference to Jerusalem is superfluous except that, with the references to Judea and Samaria, it recalls the promise of 1.8. That all Christians except the apostles left Jerusalem seems highly improbable in view of later references to the Jerusalem church (11.2, 22). More likely, Jewish Christians from the Diaspora fled Jerusalem, leaving the Jerusalem church in the hands of local residents (see the Hebrews in 6.1–6). Luke's portrait of the flight of all except the apostles, who have already resisted persecution, underscores their importance for the Jerusalem community. **8.2** The devout men who bury Stephen may be Christians; given the flight described in v. 1, however, they could be non-Christian Jews who recognize the presence of God's activity in Stephen (by contrast with Saul). **8.4–25** Preaching in Samaria fulfills 1.8 and constitutes a significant movement in the church's development because of the long-standing animosity between Jews and Samaritans (see Lk 9.51–56; 10.29–37; Jn 4.1–42). **8.5** Philip. See 6.5. The city of Samaria, probably either Sebaste or Shechem (see 7.16). **8.6–8** The response in Samaria parallels the initial responses in Jerusalem (see 5.12–16). **8.9** Simon enters the story as the antithesis of Philip. That he practiced magic signals his corruption, since Jews were strictly forbidden any connection with magical practices (Lev 19.31, 20.6, 27; Deut 18.10–12). He appears in later Christian literature as Simon Magus (Magus is a title, derived from a Persian word for a priest, used in Greek for people who practiced "magic"), the archheretic. **8.10** Luke associates the power of God with Jesus and the work of the church. To equate Simon with this power constitutes blasphemy (see also 12.22–23).

saying, "This man is the power of God that is called Great." 11And they listened eagerly to him because for a long time he had amazed them with his magic. 12But when they believed Philip, who was proclaiming the good news about the kingdom of God and the name of Jesus Christ, they were baptized, both men and women. 13Even Simon himself believed. After being baptized, he stayed constantly with Philip and was amazed when he saw the signs and great miracles that took place.

14 Now when the apostles at Jerusalem heard that Samaria had accepted the word of God, they sent Peter and John to them. 15The two went down and prayed for them that they might receive the Holy Spirit 16(for as yet the Spirit had not come*a* upon any of them; they had only been baptized in the name of the Lord Jesus). 17Then Peter and John*b* laid their hands on them, and they received the Holy Spirit. 18Now when Simon saw that the Spirit was given through the laying on of the apostles' hands, he offered them money, 19saying, "Give me also this power so that anyone on whom I lay my hands may receive the Holy Spirit." 20But Peter said to him, "May your silver perish with you, because you thought you could obtain God's gift with money! 21You have no part or share in this, for your heart is not right before God. 22Repent therefore of this wickedness of yours, and pray to the Lord that, if possible, the intent of your heart may

be forgiven you. 23For I see that you are in the gall of bitterness and the chains of wickedness." 24Simon answered, "Pray for me to the Lord, that nothing of what you*c* have said may happen to me."

25 Now after Peter and John*d* had testified and spoken the word of the Lord, they returned to Jerusalem, proclaiming the good news to many villages of the Samaritans.

Philip and the Ethiopian Eunuch

26 Then an angel of the Lord said to Philip, "Get up and go toward the south*e* to the road that goes down from Jerusalem to Gaza." (This is a wilderness road.) 27So he got up and went. Now there was an Ethiopian eunuch, a court official of the Candace, queen of the Ethiopians, in charge of her entire treasury. He had come to Jerusalem to worship 28and was returning home; seated in his chariot, he was reading the prophet Isaiah. 29Then the Spirit said to Philip, "Go over to this chariot and join it." 30So Philip ran up to it and heard him reading the prophet Isaiah. He asked, "Do you understand what you are reading?" 31He replied, "How can I, unless someone guides me?" And he invited Philip to get in and sit beside him. 32Now the passage of the scripture that he was reading was this:

---

a Gk *fallen*   *b* Gk *they*   *c* The Greek word for *you* and the verb *pray* are plural   *d* Gk *after they*   *e* Or *go at noon*

8.13 Simon's *baptism* signals the superiority of Philip's ministry, although vv. 18–19 demonstrate that Simon's conversion is incomplete. **8.18** The gift of the *Spirit* does not depend on the *laying on of the apostles' hands* (see 9.17; 10.44), but the apostles' presence signals their cooperation with Philip's ministry and sets the stage for the confrontation between Peter and Simon. Magicians were widely viewed as people who plied their trade for *money;* Simon ascribes his own attitude to Peter. By contrast, Luke consistently depicts concern over money as threatening faith (e.g., Judas in 1.18; Ananias and Sapphira in 5.1–11; the owners of the girl with the gift of divination in 16.16–18; Demetrius the silversmith in 19.24–27). **8.23** *Gall of bitterness.* See Deut 29.18–20. **8.24** Ironically, the one earlier called *the power of God* (v. 10) now must seek Peter's intercession. **8.26–40** The conversion of the Ethiopian eunuch, from a region vastly removed from Jerusalem, signals the fulfillment of the promise to all those who are *far away* (2.39). The eunuch's receptivity (vv. 31, 34, 36, 39) exemplifies the attitude toward the gospel that Luke regards as appropriate for all. **8.26** Philip receives orders from *an angel*, underscoring that the initiative comes from God. He is to go *toward the south*,

or *at noon* (see text note *e*); the Greek may be translated either way (see 26.13, where Paul's conversion occurs at noon). **8.27** *Ethiopian*, in Luke's world anyone with dark skin, particularly persons from territories south of Egypt. Various ancient writers depict Ethiopia as the equivalent of the end of the world and its inhabitants as handsome people (e.g., Esth 1.1; 8.9; Ezek 29.10; Zeph 3.10; Homer, *Odyssey* 1.22–23; Herodotus, *History* 3.17–20; Strabo, *Geography* 17.2. 1–3). As a *eunuch,* he could not be a Jew or a proselyte to Judaism (Lev 21.20; Deut 23.1; Josephus, *Antiquities* 4.290–91; but cf. Isa 56.3–5; Wis 3.14), and thus his conversion foreshadows that of Cornelius (10.1–11.18), which formally opens the Christian mission to Gentiles. *Candace,* the title traditionally given to the queen of Meroe (a Nubian realm along the Upper Nile), making the eunuch's position one of considerable power. That he has been *to Jerusalem to worship* indicates his interest in Israel's religion, as does his reading of Isaiah. Gentiles could worship in the temple enclosure, although only in the outer court; see note on 21.28. **8.28** *Reading* was a customary activity during travel; here it sets the stage for Philip's approach. **8.29** The prompting of *the Spirit* suggests that God

"Like a sheep he was led to the slaughter,
 and like a lamb silent before its shearer,
 so he does not open his mouth.
33 In his humiliation justice was denied him.
 Who can describe his generation?
 For his life is taken away from the
 earth."

34The eunuch asked Philip, "About whom, may I ask you, does the prophet say this, about himself or about someone else?" 35Then Philip began to speak, and starting with this scripture, he proclaimed to him the good news about Jesus. 36As they were going along the road, they came to some water; and the eunuch said, "Look, here is water! What is to prevent me from being baptized?"ᵃ 38He commanded the chariot to stop, and both of them, Philip and the eunuch, went down into the water, and Philipᵇ baptized him. 39When they came up out of the water, the Spirit of the Lord snatched Philip away; the eunuch saw him no more, and went on his way rejoicing. 40But Philip found himself at Azotus, and as he was passing through the region, he proclaimed the good news to all the towns until he came to Caesarea.

The Conversion of Saul

9 Meanwhile Saul, still breathing threats and murder against the disciples of the Lord, went to the high priest 2and asked him for letters to the synagogues at Damascus, so that if he found any who belonged to the Way, men or women, he might bring them bound to Jerusalem. 3Now as he was going along and approaching Damascus, suddenly a light from heaven flashed around him. 4He fell to the ground and heard a voice saying to him, "Saul, Saul, why do you persecute me?" 5He asked, "Who are you, Lord?" The reply came, "I am Jesus, whom you are persecuting. 6But get up and enter the city, and you will be told what you are to do." 7The men who were traveling with him stood speechless because they heard the voice but saw no one. 8Saul got up from the ground, and though his eyes were open, he could see nothing; so they led him by the hand and brought him into Damascus. 9For three days he was without sight, and neither ate nor drank.

10 Now there was a disciple in Damascus named Ananias. The Lord said to him in a vision, "Ananias." He answered, "Here I am, Lord." 11The Lord said to him, "Get up and go to the street called Straight, and at the house of Judas look for a man of Tarsus named Saul. At this moment he is praying, 12and he has seen

a Other ancient authorities add all or most of verse 37, *And Philip said, "If you believe with all your heart, you may." And he replied, "I believe that Jesus Christ is the Son of God."* *b* Gk *he*

---

stands behind this overture (see 8.26). **8.32–33** The passage quoted is Isa 53.7–8. **8.35** Cf. Lk 24.27, where Jesus explains "things about himself" from scripture. **8.39** Later church tradition holds that the eunuch became the first Christian missionary to Africa, but Luke says nothing about his activity beyond *rejoicing* (see also 13.48; 15.31). **8.40** *Azotus,* a city about twenty-two miles north of Gaza near the Mediterranean coast. On Philip at *Caesarea,* see 21.8.

9.1–31 The conversion of Saul, the church's most ardent enemy, involves both an encounter with the risen Lord (vv. 3–6) and divine direction (vv. 10–16). Luke narrates this event again in 22.1–21; 26.2–23, indicating its importance for him. **9.1–2** *Breathing threats and murder* fulfills Stephen's words in 7.51–52 (and see 3 Macc 2.24; 5.18, 33; 4 Macc 4.8). The report of Saul's proposed trip to *Damascus,* about sixty miles northeast of the Sea of Galilee, assumes that Christianity has spread there; it also moves the persecution of the church well beyond Jerusalem. Historically, it is unclear how the *high priest* in Jerusalem would have had authority over *synagogues at Damascus,* which suggests that Luke may be exaggerating Paul's activity for dramatic effect. For other references to Paul's persecution, see also 22.4–5; 26.9–11; 1 Cor 15.9; Gal 1.13–14; Phil 3.6. *The Way,* the Christian faith; see 18.25–26; 19.9, 23; 22.4; 24.14, 22. **9.3–4** Saul's encounter contains several features often associated with divine appearances and commissions: *light* (4 Macc 4.10); falling *to the ground* (Ezek 1.28; Dan 10.9); the use of the double vocative, as in *Saul, Saul* (Gen 22.11; 46.2; Ex 3.4; 1 Sam 3.4, 10). *Why do you persecute me?* identifies Saul's persecution of disciples as persecution of Jesus himself (see Lk 10.16). In Acts, the verb *persecute* seldom appears except in reference to Saul (22.4, 7, 8; 26.11, 14, 15; see also 7.52; Lk 11.49; 21.12). **9.5** Saul's address of Jesus as *Lord* does not necessarily imply faith, since the Greek word *kyrios* can also function as the respectful address "sir." **9.8** Saul's blindness is consistent with Luke's use of sight and its absence elsewhere (see Lk 2.30; 4.18; 24.16, 31; Acts 13.11; 28.27). **9.10** Here Luke describes Ananias simply as *a disciple* (cf. 22.12); Saul will be aided by one of the disciples he set out to persecute (see 9.1). In Acts, surprising changes in mission are often set in motion by *visions* (e.g., 10.3; 16.9–10; 18.9–10; cf. 2.17). *Here I am, Lord.* See Gen 22.1; 1 Sam 3.6, 8. **9.11** *Straight* street was the major east-west corridor. For the first time, Saul is identified as being from *Tarsus,* the capital of the Roman province of Cilicia (see v. 30; note on 21.39). **9.12** Cf. the interconnected visions of Ananias and Saul with those of Cornelius and Peter in 10.1–16.

in a vision[a] a man named Ananias come in and lay his hands on him so that he might regain his sight." 13But Ananias answered, "Lord, I have heard from many about this man, how much evil he has done to your saints in Jerusalem; 14and here he has authority from the chief priests to bind all who invoke your name." 15But the Lord said to him, "Go, for he is an instrument whom I have chosen to bring my name before Gentiles and kings and before the people of Israel; 16I myself will show him how much he must suffer for the sake of my name." 17So Ananias went and entered the house. He laid his hands on Saul[b] and said, "Brother Saul, the Lord Jesus, who appeared to you on your way here, has sent me so that you may regain your sight and be filled with the Holy Spirit." 18And immediately something like scales fell from his eyes, and his sight was restored. Then he got up and was baptized, 19and after taking some food, he regained his strength.

Saul Preaches in Damascus

For several days he was with the disciples in Damascus, 20and immediately he began to proclaim Jesus in the synagogues, saying, "He is the Son of God." 21All who heard him were amazed and said, "Is not this the man who made havoc in Jerusalem among those who invoked this name? And has he not come here for the purpose of bringing them bound before the chief priests?" 22Saul became increasingly more powerful and confounded the Jews who lived in Damascus by proving that Jesus[c] was the Messiah.[d]

Saul Escapes from the Jews

23 After some time had passed, the Jews plotted to kill him, 24but their plot became known to Saul. They were watching the gates day and night so that they might kill him; 25but his disciples took him by night and let him down through an opening in the wall,[e] lowering him in a basket.

Saul in Jerusalem

26 When he had come to Jerusalem, he attempted to join the disciples; and they were all

---

a Other ancient authorities lack *in a vision* *b* Gk *him*
c Gk *that this* *d* Or *the Christ* *e* Gk *through the wall*

9.13–14 Ananias's resistance reinforces the identification of Saul as persecutor and prompts the new identification in vv. 15–16. **9.15** Paul's later audience does encompass *Gentiles* (17.22–31), *kings* (26.2–32), and *Israel* (13.16–41; 22.1–21). **9.16** *He must suffer for the sake of my name* (see 5.41; 15.26; 21.13) exactly reverses Ananias's statement regarding Saul in vv. 13–14. On the *name*, see 2.38; 3.6; 4.10; 5.28. **9.17** *Who appeared to you*, language elsewhere associated with the Easter appearances (see 1 Cor 15.5–8). **9.18** *Something like scales.* See Tob 3.17; 11.13. **9.19a** As in other miracles, the episode concludes with a demonstration of the healing, here through *taking some food* (see Lk 8.55). **9.19b–25** Saul's preaching provides further demonstration of his conversion. His increasing power as a proclaimer and the hostility toward him mirror vv. 1–2, where his power was directed against the church. **9.20** *Son of God* appears only here in Acts, but see 13.33; Lk 1.32, 35; 3.22; 4.3, 9, 41; 22.70. **9.25** Cf. 2 Cor 11.32–33, where Paul says he fled from the governor's attempt to seize

The spread of Christianity as described in Acts 1–8 was northward from Jerusalem through Judea and Samaria (see Acts 1.8). Early in the narrative Christians are found in urban centers like Damascus (9.1–22) and Joppa (10.5), and the establishing of Christianity in Caesarea Maritima (ch. 10) and Antioch (11.19–30) is described in some detail.

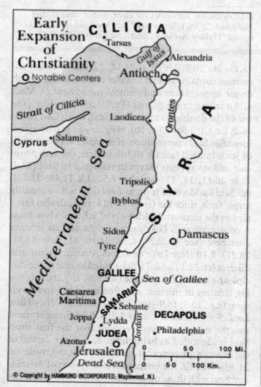

Early Expansion of Christianity
O Notable Centers

CILICIA
Tarsus
Gulf of Issus
Alexandria
Antioch
Strait of Cilicia
Laodicea
Cyprus · Salamis
Mediterranean Sea
Orontes
SYRIA
Tripolis
Byblos
Sidon
Damascus
Tyre
GALILEE   Sea of Galilee
Caesarea
Maritima   SAMARIA
Sebaste   Jordan
Joppa · Lydda   DECAPOLIS
JUDEA   · Philadelphia
Azotus ·
Jerusalem   0   50   100 Mi.
Dead Sea   0   50   100 Km.
© Copyright by HAMMOND INCORPORATED, Maplewood, N.J.

afraid of him, for they did not believe that he was a disciple. 27But Barnabas took him, brought him to the apostles, and described for them how on the road he had seen the Lord, who had spoken to him, and how in Damascus he had spoken boldly in the name of Jesus. 28So he went in and out among them in Jerusalem, speaking boldly in the name of the Lord. 29He spoke and argued with the Hellenists; but they were attempting to kill him. 30When the believers*a* learned of it, they brought him down to Caesarea and sent him off to Tarsus.

31 Meanwhile the church throughout Judea, Galilee, and Samaria had peace and was built up. Living in the fear of the Lord and in the comfort of the Holy Spirit, it increased in numbers.

The Healing of Aeneas

32 Now as Peter went here and there among all the believers,*b* he came down also to the saints living in Lydda. 33There he found a man named Aeneas, who had been bedridden for eight years, for he was paralyzed. 34Peter said to him, "Aeneas, Jesus Christ heals you; get up and make your bed!" And immediately he got up. 35And all the residents of Lydda and Sharon saw him and turned to the Lord.

Peter in Lydda and Joppa

36 Now in Joppa there was a disciple whose name was Tabitha, which in Greek is Dorcas.*c*

She was devoted to good works and acts of charity. 37At that time she became ill and died. When they had washed her, they laid her in a room upstairs. 38Since Lydda was near Joppa, the disciples, who heard that Peter was there, sent two men to him with the request, "Please come to us without delay." 39So Peter got up and went with them; and when he arrived, they took him to the room upstairs. All the widows stood beside him, weeping and showing tunics and other clothing that Dorcas had made while she was with them. 40Peter put all of them outside, and then he knelt down and prayed. He turned to the body and said, "Tabitha, get up." Then she opened her eyes, and seeing Peter, she sat up. 41He gave her his hand and helped her up. Then calling the saints and widows, he showed her to be alive. 42This became known throughout Joppa, and many believed in the Lord. 43Meanwhile he stayed in Joppa for some time with a certain Simon, a tanner.

Peter and Cornelius

10 In Caesarea there was a man named Cornelius, a centurion of the Italian Cohort, as it was called. 2He was a devout man who feared God with all his household; he gave alms generously to the people and prayed

a Gk brothers   *b* Gk all of them   *c* The name Tabitha in Aramaic and the name Dorcas in Greek mean *a gazelle*

---

him (see also Josh 2.15). **9.26–31** This incident is difficult to reconcile with Gal 1.18–24, where Paul insists that he saw only Cephas (Peter) and James, although his reputation as a persecutor is a factor in both texts (Gal 1.23). **9.27** How *Barnabas* knows about Saul's preaching remains unclear, but here he fulfills the name attributed to him in 4.36 (*son of encouragement*). **9.28** On *speaking boldly* as a characteristic of Christian proclamation, see note on 4.13. **9.29** The *Hellenists* are apparently Greek-speaking Jews who have not converted, but the same term is used of Christians in 6.1. **9.31** On the growth of the church, see note on 6.7. *Church* usually refers to a gathering in a single location (8.1; 13.1; 20.17), but here it refers to an entire region. *Galilee,* which has not been mentioned since 1.11, is striking, since nothing has been said in Acts about a mission there. **9.32–43** Two brief stories reintroduce Peter, recall the healings of Elijah, Elisha, and Jesus, and also prepare for the conversion of the first Gentile in 10.1–11.18. Lydda and Joppa (vv. 32, 26), towns west of Jerusalem, signal the movement of the gospel westward; it has already moved north as far as Damascus (v. 2). Luke does not indicate how the gospel came to these towns, but they could have been on Philip's route from Azotus to Caesarea (8.40). **9.34** Ear-

lier Peter heals in Jesus' name (3.6), but here he asserts that it is actually Jesus who carries out the healing. **9.35** *Sharon,* the plain on which *Lydda* was situated. *Turned to the Lord,* converted, most often used of Gentiles who turn to faith in the one God (see 11.21; 14.15; 15.19; 26.18, 20; Gal 4.9; 1 Thess 1.9). **9.36–43** Parallels to earlier stories concerning Elijah (1 Kings 17.17–24), Elisha (2 Kings 4.18–37), and Jesus (Lk 7.11–17; 8.41–42, 49–56) identify the prophetic power of the church with that of Israel's prophets and Jesus. **9.36** Only here in Acts is a woman explicitly called a *disciple;* the feminine noun for *disciple* appears nowhere else in the NT. **9.39** *Widows.* See 6.1; 1 Tim 5.3–16.

10.1–11.18 The story of the conversion of Cornelius and the church's acceptance of that event is narrated with considerable detail because it signals the opening of the mission to the Gentiles. (See note on 8.27.) The visions of both Cornelius and Peter (10.11–16), the repeated references to these visions (10.17, 19, 28, 30), and direct instructions from divine agents (10.7, 22, 32) demonstrate that this event occurs solely at God's initiative and under God's direction (as the Jerusalem community concludes in 11.18). **10.1** *Caesarea* Maritima, a largely gentile city north of Jerusalem

constantly to God. 3One afternoon at about three o'clock he had a vision in which he clearly saw an angel of God coming in and saying to him, "Cornelius." 4He stared at him in terror and said, "What is it, Lord?" He answered, "Your prayers and your alms have ascended as a memorial before God. 5Now send men to Joppa for a certain Simon who is called Peter; 6he is lodging with Simon, a tanner, whose house is by the seaside." 7When the angel who spoke to him had left, he called two of his slaves and a devout soldier from the ranks of those who served him, 8and after telling them everything, he sent them to Joppa.

9 About noon the next day, as they were on their journey and approaching the city, Peter went up on the roof to pray. 10He became hungry and wanted something to eat; and while it was being prepared, he fell into a trance. 11He saw the heaven opened and something like a large sheet coming down, being lowered to the ground by its four corners. 12In it were all kinds of four-footed creatures and reptiles and birds of the air. 13Then he heard a voice saying, "Get up, Peter; kill and eat." 14But Peter said, "By no means, Lord; for I have never eaten anything that is profane or unclean." 15The voice said to him again, a second time, "What God has made clean, you must not call profane." 16This happened three times, and the thing was suddenly taken up to heaven.

17 Now while Peter was greatly puzzled about what to make of the vision that he had seen, suddenly the men sent by Cornelius appeared. They were asking for Simon's house and were standing by the gate. 18They called out to ask whether Simon, who was called Peter, was staying there. 19While Peter was still thinking about the vision, the Spirit said to him, "Look, three *a* men are searching for you. 20Now get up, go down, and go with them without hesitation; for I have sent them." 21So Peter went down to the men and said, "I am the one you are looking for; what is the reason for your coming?" 22They answered, "Cornelius, a centurion, an upright and God-fearing man, who is well spoken of by the whole Jewish nation, was directed by a holy angel to send for you to come to his house and to hear what you have to say." 23So Peter *b* invited them in and gave them lodging.

The next day he got up and went with them, and some of the believers *c* from Joppa accompanied him. 24The following day they came to Caesarea. Cornelius was expecting them and had called together his relatives and close friends. 25On Peter's arrival Cornelius met him, and falling at his feet, worshiped him. 26But Peter made him get up, saying, "Stand up; I am only a mortal." 27And as he talked

a One ancient authority reads *two*; others lack the word
b Gk *he*   *c* Gk *brothers*

on the Mediterranean coast, was the location of the Roman government of Judea. *Centurion,* a Roman army officer in charge of one hundred men. *Italian Cohort,* a unit of the Roman army, possibly anachronistic, since its presence is first attested in Syria only ca. 69 CE, well after the time of this incident. **10.2** Although a Gentile, Cornelius is here described so as to emphasize his piety and make him a sympathetic character. Luke several times refers to Gentiles who *fear,* or worship, *God* (13.16, 26; 16.14; 18.7; see also Lk 7.1–9); it remains disputed whether this was a distinct group of Gentiles who worshiped God without becoming proselytes. *With all his household.* As the head of the household, Cornelius establishes the religious practices of his extended family, his slaves, and their families. *The people.* See note on 3.11. **10.3** *About three o'clock,* a traditional time for prayer; see 3.1. Like the preceding stories of the Ethiopian and Saul, this one also features a divine agent, *an angel of God.* **10.4** *As a memorial.* God has remembered Cornelius's piety (Ex 17.14; Tob 12.12; Sir 35.20–22). **10.5** For the first time in Acts, Peter is called *Simon* (see Lk 4.38; 5.3–5, 8; 6.14), perhaps to distinguish him from Simon the tanner (Acts 9.43). **10.6** *Whose house is by the seaside.* References to houses and hospitality abound in this story (vv. 17, 22–23, 30, 32, 33, 48), probably because Luke understands the gentile mission to include social interchange between Jews and Gentiles. **10.9–16** Since Peter's vision concerns food rather than people, it is sometimes suggested that the vision is an independent story about dietary restrictions inserted into an earlier story about Cornelius. In both the Bible and Hellenistic writings, however, narratives employ dreams that become meaningful only in retrospect (e.g., Gen 41.1–57; Dan 2.31–45; 4.1–27; 5.5–28; Plutarch, *Brutus* 20; *Cicero* 44). **10.11** *The heaven opened,* suggesting God's presence or some revelation from God (Ps 78.23; Isa 24.18; 64.1; Ezek 1.1; Mt 3.16; Lk 3.21; Rev 19.11). **10.12** A conventional classification of animals; see Gen 1.24; 6.20; Lev 11.46–47; Rom 1.23. A variety of animals is present; some but not all would be prohibited under Jewish dietary laws. **10.14–15** See Ezek 4.14. The dialogue concerns Peter's practice, but his assumption that he knows what is *profane or unclean.* **10.22** *The whole Jewish nation,* an additional testimony to Cornelius's righteousness; see v. 2. **10.25** *Falling at his feet,* a sign of respect or obeisance (Lk 5.12; Jn 11.32), would be highly unusual behavior

with him, he went in and found that many had assembled; 28and he said to them, "You yourselves know that it is unlawful for a Jew to associate with or to visit a Gentile; but God has shown me that I should not call anyone profane or unclean. 29So when I was sent for, I came without objection. Now may I ask why you sent for me?"

30 Cornelius replied, "Four days ago at this very hour, at three o'clock, I was praying in my house when suddenly a man in dazzling clothes stood before me. 31He said, 'Cornelius, your prayer has been heard and your alms have been remembered before God. 32Send therefore to Joppa and ask for Simon, who is called Peter; he is staying in the home of Simon, a tanner, by the sea.' 33Therefore I sent for you immediately, and you have been kind enough to come. So now all of us are here in the presence of God to listen to all that the Lord has commanded you to say."

Gentiles Hear the Good News

34 Then Peter began to speak to them: "I truly understand that God shows no partiality, 35but in every nation anyone who fears him and does what is right is acceptable to him. 36You know the message he sent to the people of Israel, preaching peace by Jesus Christ—he is Lord of all. 37That message spread throughout Judea, beginning in Galilee after the baptism that John announced: 38how God anointed Jesus of Nazareth with the Holy Spirit and with power; how he went about doing good and healing all who were oppressed by the devil, for God was with him. 39We are witnesses to all that he did both in Judea and in Jerusalem. They put him to death by hanging him on a tree; 40but God raised him on the third day and allowed him to appear, 41not to all the people but to us who were chosen by God as witnesses, and who ate and drank with him after he rose from the dead. 42He commanded us to preach to the people and to testify that he is the one ordained by God as judge of the living and the dead. 43All the prophets testify about him that everyone who believes in him receives forgiveness of sins through his name."

Gentiles Receive the Holy Spirit

44 While Peter was still speaking, the Holy Spirit fell upon all who heard the word. 45The circumcised believers who had come with Peter were astounded that the gift of the Holy Spirit had been poured out even on the Gentiles, 46for they heard them speaking in tongues and extolling God. Then Peter said, 47"Can anyone withhold the water for baptizing these people who have received the Holy Spirit just as we have?" 48So he ordered them to be baptized in the name of Jesus Christ. Then they invited him to stay for several days.

---

for a Roman centurion meeting a local resident in occupied territory. **10.26** On Peter's response, see 14.15; cf. 12.22–23. **10.28** Peter's statement that Jews were not allowed to *associate with . . . a Gentile* sharply exaggerates Jewish law, which, if observed, could render social interaction with Gentiles difficult but not impossible. Especially in the Diaspora, many Jews and Gentiles would have had extensive contact. Peter's conclusion that no one should be called *profane or unclean* solves the riddle of his dream (vv. 9–16) and paves the way for his sermon (vv. 34–43) and for the practice of full hospitality toward Gentiles. **10.34–43** Peter's speech succinctly summarizes the gospel in the context of his new understanding of God's impartiality, suggesting that Peter's conversion to the gentile mission is as central here as is Cornelius's conversion to Christian faith. **10.34** *That God shows no partiality,* an established concept meaning that God does not favor the rich or the powerful (see Lev 19.15; Deut 10.17–18; 2 Chr 19.7; Sir 35.15–16); here it takes on new meaning in the emergence of a gentile mission conducted without regard to social barriers (see also Rom 2.11). **10.35** See Ps 15.1–2. Cornelius has already been described as fearing God and doing right (see vv. 2, 22). **10.36** The message of *peace* was first proclaimed at Jesus' birth (Lk 1.79; also 2.14; Acts 9.31). *Lord of all,* elsewhere used of Zeus and Osiris (Plutarch, *Isis and Osiris* 355e); in the Septuagint the God of Israel is also declared "Lord of all the earth" (Josh 3.11, 13; Ps 97.5; Zech 6.5; Wis 6.7; 8.3). **10.37–43** This summation of Jesus' ministry replays some key Lukan themes: the ministry of John, the Spirit's presence in Jesus, the apostles as witnesses, the death and resurrection of Jesus, Jesus' postresurrection appearance to the apostles, the prophetic witness, and the forgiveness of sins. **10.44–48** The gift of the *Holy Spirit* provides final and irrefutable evidence that the inclusion of the Gentiles is indeed God's will. See also 11.15–18. **10.45–46** As at Pentecost, the Holy Spirit is *poured out* (see 2.17–18), accompanied by *speaking in tongues* (see 2.4–11) and prompting astonishment (see 2.12). **10.47–48** The normal order of baptism with water and then the Spirit is reversed, as the gift of the Holy Spirit justifies baptism with water (cf. 2.38). **10.48** *Invited him . . . several days.* The hospitality extended to Peter and his companions completes the breaking down of social barriers and prompts the investigation of 11.3.

Peter's Report to the Church at Jerusalem

11 Now the apostles and the believers*a* who were in Judea heard that the Gentiles had also accepted the word of God. ²So when Peter went up to Jerusalem, the circumcised believers*b* criticized him, ³saying, "Why did you go to uncircumcised men and eat with them?" ⁴Then Peter began to explain it to them, step by step, saying, ⁵"I was in the city of Joppa praying, and in a trance I saw a vision. There was something like a large sheet coming down from heaven, being lowered by its four corners; and it came close to me. ⁶As I looked at it closely I saw four-footed animals, beasts of prey, reptiles, and birds of the air. ⁷I also heard a voice saying to me, 'Get up, Peter; kill and eat.' ⁸But I replied, 'By no means, Lord; for nothing profane or unclean has ever entered my mouth.' ⁹But a second time the voice answered from heaven, 'What God has made clean, you must not call profane.' ¹⁰This happened three times; then everything was pulled up again to heaven. ¹¹At that very moment three men, sent to me from Caesarea, arrived at the house where we were. ¹²The Spirit told me to go with them and not to make a distinction between them and us.*c* These six brothers also accompanied me, and we entered the man's house. ¹³He told us how he had seen the angel standing in his house and saying, 'Send to Joppa and bring Simon, who is called Peter;

¹⁴he will give you a message by which you and your entire household will be saved.' ¹⁵And as I began to speak, the Holy Spirit fell upon them just as it had upon us at the beginning. ¹⁶And I remembered the word of the Lord, how he had said, 'John baptized with water, but you will be baptized with the Holy Spirit.' ¹⁷If then God gave them the same gift that he gave us when we believed in the Lord Jesus Christ, who was I that I could hinder God?" ¹⁸When they heard this, they were silenced. And they praised God, saying, "Then God has given even to the Gentiles the repentance that leads to life."

The Church in Antioch

19 Now those who were scattered because of the persecution that took place over Stephen traveled as far as Phoenicia, Cyprus, and Antioch, and they spoke the word to no one except Jews. ²⁰But among them were some men of Cyprus and Cyrene who, on coming to Antioch, spoke to the Hellenists*d* also, proclaiming the Lord Jesus. ²¹The hand of the Lord was with them, and a great number became believers and turned to the Lord. ²²News of this came to the ears of the church in Jerusalem, and they sent Barnabas to Antioch. ²³When he came and saw the grace of God, he rejoiced,

a Gk *brothers*   *b* Gk lacks *believers*   *c* Or *not to hesitate*
d Other ancient authorities read *Greeks*

11.1–18 The focus here is on the endorsement of Peter's actions by the Jerusalem community, while Peter recapitulates the Cornelius episode from his perspective. **11.2–3** *The circumcised believers* are mentioned not as a faction (cf. 15.5) but by contrast with the *uncircumcised men* to whom they object. *Why did you . . . eat with them?* The objection focuses on social interaction. **11.14** *By which you . . . will be saved.* Only here is Peter's message characterized as a means to salvation; cf. 10.4–5, 22, 31–33. **11.16** See Lk 3.16. In 10.44–48 no reference to John is made. **11.18** *The repentance that leads to life.* See 2.38; 5.31; 26.20. Nothing here restricts the inclusion of Gentiles to admirable people such as Cornelius. **11.19–30** Luke connects Antioch with the first intentional mission among Gentiles, the beginning of Saul's witness among Gentiles, the designation of believers as Christians, and the first Christian benevolence to Christians in other regions. Historically, the relationship between the origin of the gentile mission as portrayed here and as portrayed in 10.1–11.18 is probably beyond recovery. **11.19** *The persecution.* See 8.1b. The movement here is northward on the Mediterranean coast to *Phoenicia,* then northwest to the island of *Cyprus,* and finally northeast to *Antioch* on the

Orontes, third largest city in the Roman world and seat of the Roman government in Syria, which contained a large and strong Jewish community. Luke does not distinguish this Antioch from the several other cities of the same name, probably because he assumed its prominence. **11.20** *Men of Cyprus and Cyrene,* thus probably Hellenistic Christians, consistent with the suggestion that this is the group that fled Jerusalem (see 6.1–6; 8.1). Early manuscripts conflict here, with some reading *Hellenists* (i.e., probably Greek-speaking Jews; see 6.1), others *Greeks* (i.e., Gentiles); see text note *d.* Whatever the earliest reading, the context requires that the group at least include Gentiles even if it is not exclusively gentile. **11.21** See note on 6.7. *Turned to the Lord.* See note on 9.35. **11.22** As in Samaria (8.14) and the Cornelius episode (11.1–3), the *church in Jerusalem* investigates developments in the mission, even when the initiative arises elsewhere. For Luke, Jerusalem's continuing authority is important, and he may well exaggerate its actual role in the gentile mission. *Barnabas,* already introduced in connection with the sale of his property (4.36–37) and with the support of Saul (9.27), now enters as a major figure in the gentile mission. **11.25** *Tarsus.* See 9.30. **11.26** Reconciling this ac-

and he exhorted them all to remain faithful to the Lord with steadfast devotion; 24for he was a good man, full of the Holy Spirit and of faith. And a great many people were brought to the Lord. 25Then Barnabas went to Tarsus to look for Saul, 26and when he had found him, he brought him to Antioch. So it was that for an entire year they met with*a* the church and taught a great many people, and it was in Antioch that the disciples were first called "Christians."

27 At that time prophets came down from Jerusalem to Antioch. 28One of them named

Agabus stood up and predicted by the Spirit that there would be a severe famine over all the world; and this took place during the reign of Claudius. 29The disciples determined that according to their ability, each would send relief to the believers*b* living in Judea; 30this they did, sending it to the elders by Barnabas and Saul.

James Killed and Peter Imprisoned

12 About that time King Herod laid violent hands upon some who belonged

---

a Or *were guests of* *b* Gk *brothers*

---

count with Paul's words in Gal 1–2 is exceedingly difficult. *Christians,* possibly derogatory, indicating that outsiders see believers as a group that is somehow distinguished from other forms of Judaism. **11.27–30** Just as Christians in Jerusalem generously support those in need (see 2.45; 4.32–37), Christians in Antioch send relief to those in Judea. **11.28** *Agabus.* See 21.10. Josephus reports a famine in Judea ca. 45–48 CE (*Antiquities* 20.51–53, 101), and there are indications of food shortages in Rome during Claudius's rule, although a *famine over all the world* seems exaggerated, and relief sent

from Antioch to Jerusalem would be curious in that case. Luke may use Antioch's gift to signal both the church's charity and its indebtedness to Jerusalem. *Claudius,* Roman emperor 41–54 CE. **11.30** *Barnabas and Saul* are here confirmed as central figures in the Antiochene church. Correlating this trip with Paul's report in Gal 1.11–2.14 is extremely difficult.

12.1–25 Luke here drops the story of Antioch and returns to Jerusalem, vividly depicting a clash between the Christians (Peter) and their ostensibly powerful enemy (Herod). **12.1** *King Herod,* i.e., Herod Agrippa I,

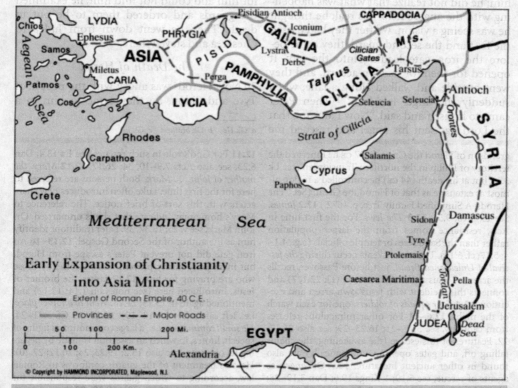

According to Acts the church in Antioch on the Orontes became an important base for Paul's missionary journeys westward through Asia Minor and into Europe (13.1–3; 14.24–28; 15.22–35; 18.22–23).

to the church. [2]He had James, the brother of John, killed with the sword. [3]After he saw that it pleased the Jews, he proceeded to arrest Peter also. (This was during the festival of Unleavened Bread.) [4]When he had seized him, he put him in prison and handed him over to four squads of soldiers to guard him, intending to bring him out to the people after the Passover. [5]While Peter was kept in prison, the church prayed fervently to God for him.

Peter Delivered from Prison

6 The very night before Herod was going to bring him out, Peter, bound with two chains, was sleeping between two soldiers, while guards in front of the door were keeping watch over the prison. [7]Suddenly an angel of the Lord appeared and a light shone in the cell. He tapped Peter on the side and woke him, saying, "Get up quickly." And the chains fell off his wrists. [8]The angel said to him, "Fasten your belt and put on your sandals." He did so. Then he said to him, "Wrap your cloak around you and follow me." [9]Peter[a] went out and followed him; he did not realize that what was happening with the angel's help was real; he thought he was seeing a vision. [10]After they had passed the first and the second guard, they came before the iron gate leading into the city. It opened for them of its own accord, and they went outside and walked along a lane, when suddenly the angel left him. [11]Then Peter came to himself and said, "Now I am sure that the Lord has sent his angel and rescued me from the hands of Herod and from all that the Jewish people were expecting."

12 As soon as he realized this, he went to the house of Mary, the mother of John whose other name was Mark, where many had gathered and were praying. [13]When he knocked at the outer gate, a maid named Rhoda came to answer. [14]On recognizing Peter's voice, she was so overjoyed that, instead of opening the gate, she ran in and announced that Peter was standing at the gate. [15]They said to her, "You are out of your mind!" But she insisted that it was so. They said, "It is his angel." [16]Meanwhile Peter continued knocking; and when they opened the gate, they saw him and were amazed. [17]He motioned to them with his hand to be silent, and described for them how the Lord had brought him out of the prison. And he added, "Tell this to James and to the believers."[b] Then he left and went to another place.

18 When morning came, there was no small commotion among the soldiers over what had become of Peter. [19]When Herod had searched for him and could not find him, he examined the guards and ordered them to be put to death. Then he went down from Judea to Caesarea and stayed there.

The Death of Herod

20 Now Herod[c] was angry with the people of Tyre and Sidon. So they came to him in a

---

a Gk He   b Gk brothers   c Gk he

grandson of Herod the Great. In 37 CE he inherited the territory of Philip in the northern Transjordan (see Lk 3.1), but at his death (44 CE) he controlled a region almost as extensive as that of Herod the Great. (See "The Herods: A Simplified Family Tree, p. 1672.) **12.2** *James.* See Lk 5.10; 9.54. **12.3** *The Jews.* For the first time in Acts, resistance comes from the larger population rather than the Sadducees or temple officials (e.g., 4.1–4; 5.17; cf. 6.12). That these events occur during *the festival of Unleavened Bread,* just before Passover, recalls the arrest of Jesus at the same season (Lk 22.1, 7) and connects this incident with Jesus' own arrest and execution. **12.4** *Four squads of soldiers,* one for each watch of the night. **12.6–11** For other miraculous releases from captivity, see 5.17–21; 16.23–29; see also 26.17, 22. Features of this escape (the awakening, the chains falling off, and gates opening automatically) are also found in other ancient literature. **12.7** On *angels* as agents of rescue, see 5.19; 1 Kings 19.5; Dan 3.19–28; Mt 18.10; cf. Acts 8.26; 10.3, 7, 22; 11.13; 27.23. The wording here is very close to that of Lk 2.9. *Light* accompanies the divine presence; see 9.3; 26.13.

12.11 For God's role in such rescues, see Ex 18.4; Dan 6.23; see also Acts 7.9–10, 34; 26.17. **12.12** *Mary, the mother of John . . . Mark.* Both persons are referred to here for the first time. Luke often introduces new characters with this sort of brief notice. The reference to Mary's home may indicate that she is unmarried. On John Mark, see v. 25; 15.37, 39. Later traditions identify him as the author of the Second Gospel. **12.13–16** An iron gate did not prevent Peter's escape from Herod, but incredulity nearly prevents his welcome by those who are praying for him. **12.17** *James,* the brother of Jesus, introduced here (see notes on 1.14; 12.12) and mentioned again in 15.13; 21.18. *Went to another place,* i.e., left safely (see vv. 18–19). **12.18–19** Cf. 5.21–24. *No small commotion,* i.e., a large commotion; a figure of speech, litotes, in which an assertion is made by negating its opposite (see also 15.2; 19.23, 24; 20.12; 27.20). Herod's treatment of the guards conforms to Roman law, according to which guards were responsible for their captives (see 16.27–28). **12.20–23** According to Josephus, Herod Agrippa I was greeted as a god, did not reject the title, and immediately saw an owl, which

body; and after winning over Blastus, the king's chamberlain, they asked for a reconciliation, because their country depended on the king's country for food. 21On an appointed day Herod put on his royal robes, took his seat on the platform, and delivered a public address to them. 22The people kept shouting, "The voice of a god, and not of a mortal!" 23And immediately, because he had not given the glory to God, an angel of the Lord struck him down, and he was eaten by worms and died.

24 But the word of God continued to advance and gain adherents. 25Then after completing their mission Barnabas and Saul returned to*a* Jerusalem and brought with them John, whose other name was Mark.

Barnabas and Saul Commissioned

13 Now in the church at Antioch there were prophets and teachers: Barnabas, Simeon who was called Niger, Lucius of Cyrene, Manaen a member of the court of Herod the ruler,*b* and Saul. 2While they were worshiping the Lord and fasting, the Holy Spirit said, "Set apart for me Barnabas and Saul for the work to which I have called them." 3Then after fasting and praying they laid their hands on them and sent them off.

The Apostles Preach in Cyprus

4 So, being sent out by the Holy Spirit, they went down to Seleucia; and from there they sailed to Cyprus. 5When they arrived at Salamis, they proclaimed the word of God in the synagogues of the Jews. And they had John also to assist them. 6When they had gone through the whole island as far as Paphos, they met a certain magician, a Jewish false prophet, named Bar-Jesus. 7He was with the proconsul, Sergius Paulus, an intelligent man, who summoned Barnabas and Saul and wanted to hear the word of God. 8But the magician Elymas (for that is the translation of his name) opposed them and tried to turn the proconsul away from the faith. 9But Saul, also known as Paul, filled with the Holy Spirit, looked intently at him 10and said, "You son of the devil, you enemy of all righteousness, full of all deceit and villainy, will you not stop making crooked the straight paths of the Lord? 11And now listen—the hand of the Lord is against

a Other ancient authorities read *from*   *b* Gk *tetrarch*

prompted him to recall earlier predictions about his death. He then declared his imminent death to be God's will, succumbed to severe abdominal pain, and died five days later (*Antiquities* 19.343–52). **12.21** Agrippa is said to have worn *royal robes* made entirely of silver; see Josephus, *Antiquities* 19.343–44. **12.22** See Ezek 28.2, 6, 9. **12.23** Unlike Peter, who praises God for his rescue (v. 11), Herod fails to praise God and is struck down. On death for blasphemy, see Sir 48.21; 1 Macc 7.41; on death *by worms,* see Jdt 16.17; 2 Macc 9.9. **12.24** This typical Lukan summary (see note on 6.7) contrasts with the outcome of Herod's story to comment wryly on the fate of the church's enemies. **12.25** A transitional verse prepares for the Antiochene mission and connects Antioch with Jerusalem by means of John Mark. Although the story requires that Barnabas and Saul return to Antioch from Jerusalem (see text note *a*), important early manuscripts read the opposite (*to* or *in* Jerusalem), creating logical confusion (cf. 11.29–30). Another suggested translation: "Barnabas and Saul returned, after completing their mission in Jerusalem." **13.1–12** The mission of the Antiochene church, like that of the Jerusalem church, begins with a confrontation with Satan in the form of his agent, a magician (see 8.4–25). **13.1** *Prophets and teachers.* See Rom 12.6–7; 1 Cor 12.28. *A member of the court of Herod the ruler,* i.e., a close friend of Herod Antipas. Herod Antipas is *the ruler* (or *tetrarch;* see text note *b,* as distinct from Herod Agrippa I, the *king* (see 12.1; also Lk 1.5).

13.2 Initiative for the new mission, here as elsewhere in Acts, comes from the *Spirit* rather than from human beings; this passage is distinctive in that only here does the Spirit direct the church collectively rather than individually (e.g., 8.29; 10.19–20; 21.11). **13.3** See 6.6, where prayer and the laying on of hands accompany the appointment of the Seven (see also 14.23). **13.4** *Seleucia,* seaport of Antioch. **13.5** *Salamis,* eastern port of the island of Cyprus (see 4.36; 11.19–20; 21.16). *John Mark's* role is presented as marginal; he is not identified with Barnabas and Saul when the Holy Spirit commissions them (vv. 2–3), and he soon returns to Jerusalem (v. 13; see also 15.37–38). **13.6** *Paphos,* on the southwest coast of the island of Cyprus. *A certain magician, a Jewish false prophet,* an identification revealing his character; not only is he a magician serving Satan, he is an apostate Jew (see note on 8.9). **13.7** *Sergius Paulus,* the *proconsul* or governor of the province, would have been a citizen of considerable standing. **13.8** *Elymas* does not translate Bar-Jesus. **13.9** *Saul, also known as Paul.* From this point on Luke employs only the Roman form of his name (except in 22.7, 13; 26.14), probably because the gentile mission predominates. *Filled with the Holy Spirit,* as were Peter (4.8) and Stephen (6.5). **13.10** *Making crooked the straight paths of the Lord* contrasts the false prophet (v. 6) with the true prophet, John (see Lk 3.4). Once again, as earlier in 5.3, resistance to God is identified with Satan. **13.11** Paul's blinding of Bar-Jesus proves the power of God over Satan, enacts the punishment for idolatry

you, and you will be blind for a while, unable to see the sun." Immediately mist and darkness came over him, and he went about groping for someone to lead him by the hand. 12When the proconsul saw what had happened, he believed, for he was astonished at the teaching about the Lord.

Paul and Barnabas in Antioch of Pisidia

13 Then Paul and his companions set sail from Paphos and came to Perga in Pamphylia. John, however, left them and returned to Jerusalem; 14but they went on from Perga and came to Antioch in Pisidia. And on the sabbath day they went into the synagogue and sat down. 15After the reading of the law and the prophets, the officials of the synagogue sent them a message, saying, "Brothers, if you have any word of exhortation for the people, give it." 16So Paul stood up and with a gesture began to speak:

"You Israelites,*a* and others who fear God, listen. 17The God of this people Israel chose

our ancestors and made the people great during their stay in the land of Egypt, and with uplifted arm he led them out of it. 18For about forty years he put up with*b* them in the wilderness. 19After he had destroyed seven nations in the land of Canaan, he gave them their land as an inheritance 20for about four hundred fifty years. After that he gave them judges until the time of the prophet Samuel. 21Then they asked for a king; and God gave them Saul son of Kish, a man of the tribe of Benjamin, who reigned for forty years. 22When he had removed him, he made David their king. In his testimony about him he said, 'I have found David, son of Jesse, to be a man after my heart, who will carry out all my wishes.' 23Of this man's posterity God has brought to Israel a Savior, Jesus, as he promised; 24before his coming John had already proclaimed a baptism of repentance to all the people of Israel. 25And as John was finishing his work, he said,

---

a Gk *Men*, *Israelites*   *b* Other ancient authorities read *cared for*

(Deut 28.28–29), and recalls Paul's own conversion (9.8). *Darkness,* the realm of separation from God (see 26.18; Lk 22.53). **13.12** *The teaching about the Lord* here concerns the power of God over Satan. **13.13– 52** Pisidian Antioch provides the venue for Paul's first speech in Acts. **13.13** Following the important victory over Satan's agent, Luke usually places Paul's name first (see vv. 43, 46, 50) rather than the earlier pattern of *Barnabas and Saul* (11.30; 12.25; 13.2, 7; but cf. 14.12,

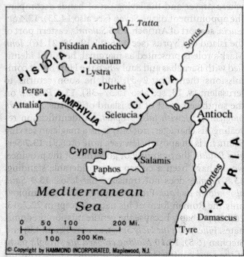

Acts 13–14 describes a missionary expedition by Paul and companions by way of Cyprus into Pamphylia and Pisidia.

14; 15.12), indicating that Paul has become the central figure. *Perga in Pamphylia.* The movement is north to the mainland of Asia Minor. **13.14** Pisidian *Antioch,* north of Perga (to be distinguished from Syrian Antioch, mentioned in v. 1; see note on 11.19). According to Luke, Paul's usual missionary practice is to go first to the *synagogue* (see, e.g., 14.1; 17.1–2; 18.4), although Paul's Letters do not suggest this pattern. **13.15** *Word of exhortation,* possibly a technical term for a sermon. Cf. Heb 13.22. **13.16a** The posture and gesture are those of a Greco-Roman orator. **13.16b–41** Paul's speech recalls earlier speeches in Acts; the speech traces God's saving actions on Israel's behalf and places Jesus in that tradition, concluding with a call to forgiveness. **13.16b–25** The first section moves from the exodus and conquest to the establishment of the kingship, identifying Jesus with the Davidic line. **13.16b** *Others who fear God,* i.e., Gentiles (see 10.2; 16.14; cf. 2.14; 3.12; 7.2). **13.17** On God's *choosing* of Israel, see Deut 4.37; 10.15. *With uplifted arm.* See Ex 6.1; Deut 4.34; 5.15. **13.18** The difference between *put up with* and *cared for* (see text note *b*) is one Greek letter. In the Septuagint of Deut 1.31, which is echoed here, the same text-critical problem exists. The evidence is so evenly divided that making a judgment is very difficult. **13.19** *Seven nations.* See Deut 7.1. On the *land as an inheritance,* see Josh 14.1–2. **13.20** *Four hundred fifty years,* apparently including the four hundred years prior to the exodus (Gen 15.13). **13.21** On the request for and granting of a *king,* see 1 Sam 8.5, 10; 10.21, 24. *Forty years.* See also Josephus, *Antiquities* 6.378; cf. 1 Sam 13.1. **13.22** See 1 Sam 13.14; 15.23; 16.1, 12–13. Jesus stands in David's line by virtue of both physical descent and obedience. **13.23** The connection between

'What do you suppose that I am? I am not he. No, but one is coming after me; I am not worthy to untie the thong of the sandals[a] on his feet.'

26 "My brothers, you descendants of Abraham's family, and others who fear God, to us[b] the message of this salvation has been sent. 27 Because the residents of Jerusalem and their leaders did not recognize him or understand the words of the prophets that are read every sabbath, they fulfilled those words by condemning him. 28 Even though they found no cause for a sentence of death, they asked Pilate to have him killed. 29 When they had carried out everything that was written about him, they took him down from the tree and laid him in a tomb. 30 But God raised him from the dead; 31 and for many days he appeared to those who came up with him from Galilee to Jerusalem, and they are now his witnesses to the people. 32 And we bring you the good news that what God promised to our ancestors 33 he has fulfilled for us, their children, by raising Jesus; as also it is written in the second psalm,

'You are my Son;
    today I have begotten you.'

34 As to his raising him from the dead, no more to return to corruption, he has spoken in this way,

'I will give you the holy promises made to David.'

35 Therefore he has also said in another psalm,

'You will not let your Holy One
    experience corruption.'

36 For David, after he had served the purpose of God in his own generation, died,[c] was laid beside his ancestors, and experienced corruption; 37 but he whom God raised up experienced no corruption. 38 Let it be known to you therefore, my brothers, that through this man forgiveness of sins is proclaimed to you; 39 by this Jesus[d] everyone who believes is set free from all those sins[e] from which you could not be freed by the law of Moses. 40 Beware, therefore, that what the prophets said does not happen to you:

41 'Look, you scoffers!
    Be amazed and perish,
    for in your days I am doing a work,
        a work that you will never believe, even
            if someone tells you.' "

42 As Paul and Barnabas[f] were going out, the people urged them to speak about these things again the next sabbath. 43 When the meeting of the synagogue broke up, many Jews and devout converts to Judaism followed Paul and Barnabas, who spoke to them and urged them to continue in the grace of God.

44 The next sabbath almost the whole city gathered to hear the word of the Lord.[g] 45 But when the Jews saw the crowds, they were filled with jealousy; and blaspheming, they contradicted what was spoken by Paul. 46 Then both Paul and Barnabas spoke out boldly, saying, "It was necessary that the word of God should

---

a Gk untie the sandals b Other ancient authorities read you c Gk fell asleep d Gk this e Gk all f Gk they g Other ancient authorities read God

David and Jesus runs throughout Luke's story; see 2.30; 13.34–37; Lk 1.32; 2.4. **13.25** See Lk 3.16. John's ministry connects David and Jesus, but Luke carefully places John the Baptist offstage when Jesus' ministry begins (see Lk 3.18–23; 16.16). **13.26–37** Direct address (*my brothers*) begins the second part of the speech, which interprets the death of Jesus as the fulfillment of scripture (vv. 27, 29) and God's promises (vv. 32–33). **13.26** *Others who fear God.* See v. 16. **13.27** Ironically, the ignorance of Jerusalem's residents brings about the fulfillment of scripture; see 3.17–18. **13.28** See 3.13–14; Lk 23.13–25. **13.29** In Luke, it is not the general populace that places Jesus in the tomb, but Joseph of Arimathea (Lk 23.50–53; see also Mt 27.57–60; Mk 15.42–47; Jn 19.38–42). **13.31** The apostles' primary task is to *witness;* see 1.8; Lk 24.48. **13.32** *We bring you the good news.* Even if Paul and Barnabas do not technically qualify as apostolic witnesses (see 1.21–22), they nevertheless function as proclaimers alongside the others. **13.33** The quotation from Ps 2.7 could imply that Jesus becomes God's Son by virtue of his resurrection (see also 2.36; Rom 1.4),

but cf. Lk 3.22. **13.34–37** For a similar contrast between David and Jesus, see 2.29–36. **13.34** The quotation is from Isa 55.3 (Septuagint). **13.35** Ps 16.10 is quoted; see also Acts 2.27, 31. **13.38** *Let it be known to you.* See note on 2.14. *My brothers.* Direct address marks the movement to the concluding call for repentance. *Forgiveness of sins.* See 2.38; 5.31; 10.43. **13.39** The implicit claim that Jesus brings freedom from the Mosaic law is new here in Acts and echoes themes from Paul's Letters (see, e.g., Gal 3.23–35; Rom 3.28; 8.3). **13.40–41** The prophetic warning, drawn from Hab 1.5, anticipates the Jews' rejection in vv. 44–47 (see also 28.23–28) and recalls the final words of Stephen's speech (7.51–53). **13.42–43** Like the initial preaching in Jerusalem, Paul's speech draws a receptive response; see 2.37–42. **13.44–52** For the first time, the theme of Jewish rejection of the gospel is joined with that of the gentile mission. **13.45** Jewish response here fulfills Paul's prophetic words in vv. 40–41. **13.46** *Boldly.* See note on 4.13. The geographical order of 1.8 also suggests that preaching moves from a Jewish audience (Jerusalem) *to the Gentiles (the ends of the*

be spoken first to you. Since you reject it and judge yourselves to be unworthy of eternal life, we are now turning to the Gentiles. [47]For so the Lord has commanded us, saying,

'I have set you to be a light for the Gentiles,
    so that you may bring salvation to the ends of the earth.' "

48 When the Gentiles heard this, they were glad and praised the word of the Lord; and as many as had been destined for eternal life became believers. [49]Thus the word of the Lord spread throughout the region. [50]But the Jews incited the devout women of high standing and the leading men of the city, and stirred up persecution against Paul and Barnabas, and drove them out of their region. [51]So they shook the dust off their feet in protest against them, and went to Iconium. [52]And the disciples were filled with joy and with the Holy Spirit.

Paul and Barnabas in Iconium

14 The same thing occurred in Iconium, where Paul and Barnabas[a] went into the Jewish synagogue and spoke in such a way that a great number of both Jews and Greeks became believers. [2]But the unbelieving Jews stirred up the Gentiles and poisoned their minds against the brothers. [3]So they remained for a long time, speaking boldly for the Lord, who testified to the word of his grace by granting signs and wonders to be done through

them. [4]But the residents of the city were divided; some sided with the Jews, and some with the apostles. [5]And when an attempt was made by both Gentiles and Jews, with their rulers, to mistreat them and to stone them, [6]the apostles[a] learned of it and fled to Lystra and Derbe, cities of Lycaonia, and to the surrounding country; [7]and there they continued proclaiming the good news.

Paul and Barnabas in Lystra and Derbe

8 In Lystra there was a man sitting who could not use his feet and had never walked, for he had been crippled from birth. [9]He listened to Paul as he was speaking. And Paul, looking at him intently and seeing that he had faith to be healed, [10]said in a loud voice, "Stand upright on your feet." And the man[b] sprang up and began to walk. [11]When the crowds saw what Paul had done, they shouted in the Lycaonian language, "The gods have come down to us in human form!" [12]Barnabas they called Zeus, and Paul they called Hermes, because he was the chief speaker. [13]The priest of Zeus, whose temple was just outside the city,[c] brought oxen and garlands to the gates; he and the crowds wanted to offer sacrifice. [14]When the apostles Barnabas and Paul heard of it, they tore their clothes and rushed out into the crowd, shouting, [15]"Friends,[d] why are you doing this? We

---

a Gk they   b Gk he   c Or The priest of Zeus-Outside-the-City
d Gk Men

---

earth, v. 47). **13.47** Isa 49.6 is quoted, recalling Simeon's words in Lk 2.32 and anticipating the statement in Paul's climactic speech before Agrippa (Acts 26.17–18). **13.48** The response of the *Gentiles* matches that of the Ethiopian eunuch (see 8.39). *Destined for eternal life.* See Lk 10.20; see also Ex 32.32–33; Ps 69.28; Isa 4.3; Dan 12.1. **13.51** *They shook the dust off.* See Lk 9.5; 10.11. *Iconium*, provincial capital of the district of Lycaonia, southeast of Pisidian Antioch.

14.1–7 Despite what 13.47 might lead one to expect, this brief transitional scene demonstrates that both Jews and Gentiles are among those who accept and who reject the Christian gospel. **14.1** *Greeks*, i.e., either proselytes to Judaism or Gentiles attracted to the synagogue (see note on 10.2). **14.2** Luke places responsibility for resistance on *Jews*. **14.3** *Speaking boldly.* See note on 4.13. *Signs and wonders*, a distinguishing characteristic of the Christian community; see 2.19, 22, 43; 4.30; 5.12; 6.8; 15.12; 2 Cor 12.12. **14.4** Only here and in v. 14 are Paul and Barnabas referred to as *apostles* (see note on 1.21–22). *Apostles* does not appear in the Greek text of 14.6. **14.6** *Lystra*, southwest of Iconium; *Derbe*, southeast of Lystra.

14.8–20 As at the outset of the Jerusalem mission, so also among Gentiles a miraculous event prompts misunderstanding, which then requires an explanation (see 2.1–4, 12–15; 3.1–13). **14.8** Lystra, popularly identified as a rustic and gullible backwater, is an ideal setting for this story. The detailed description of the man's disability enhances the miracle that follows; see also 3.2. **14.9** *Looking at him intently.* See 3.4; 13.9. *Faith to be healed.* See Lk 5.20. **14.11–12** The amazement typically generated by a miracle (see, e.g., Lk 5.26) here becomes blatant misunderstanding; cf. Ovid, *Metamorphoses* 8.611–725, where the gods *Zeus* and *Hermes* (Jupiter and Mercury) appear in the guise of two men. **14.14** The vehement rejection of this misunderstanding is fundamental to the service of God (cf. 12.22–23). Tearing of the clothing signals grief, as in Gen 37.29, 34; 2 Sam 1.2, 11; Jdt 14.16, 19; 1 Macc 2.14. **14.15–17** A brief speech provides the essentials of early Christian preaching to Gentiles (see also 17.22–31). The venue makes it meaningless to identify Jesus relative to Israel's history, so Paul and Barnabas begin with *the living God.* **14.15** *We are mortals.* See 10.26; Wis 7.1; Jas 5.17. *Turn . . . to the living God.* See

are mortals just like you, and we bring you good news, that you should turn from these worthless things to the living God, who made the heaven and the earth and the sea and all that is in them. 16In past generations he allowed all the nations to follow their own ways; 17yet he has not left himself without a witness in doing good—giving you rains from heaven and fruitful seasons, and filling you with food and your hearts with joy." 18Even with these words, they scarcely restrained the crowds from offering sacrifice to them.

19 But Jews came there from Antioch and Iconium and won over the crowds. Then they stoned Paul and dragged him out of the city, supposing that he was dead. 20But when the disciples surrounded him, he got up and went into the city. The next day he went on with Barnabas to Derbe.

The Return to Antioch in Syria

21 After they had proclaimed the good news to that city and had made many disciples, they returned to Lystra, then on to Iconium and Antioch. 22There they strengthened the souls of the disciples and encouraged them to continue in the faith, saying, "It is through many persecutions that we must enter the kingdom of God." 23And after they had appointed elders for them in each church, with prayer and fasting they entrusted them to the Lord in whom they had come to believe.

24 Then they passed through Pisidia and came to Pamphylia. 25When they had spoken the word in Perga, they went down to Attalia. 26From there they sailed back to Antioch, where they had been commended to the grace of God for the work *a* that they had completed. 27When they arrived, they called the church together and related all that God had done with them, and how he had opened a door of faith for the Gentiles. 28And they stayed there with the disciples for some time.

The Council at Jerusalem

15 Then certain individuals came down from Judea and were teaching the brothers, "Unless you are circumcised according to the custom of Moses, you cannot be saved." 2And after Paul and Barnabas had no small dissension and debate with them, Paul and Barnabas and some of the others were appointed to go up to Jerusalem to discuss this question with the apostles and the elders. 3So they were sent on their way by the church, and as they passed through both Phoenicia and Samaria, they reported the conversion of the Gentiles, and brought great joy to all the believers. *b* 4When they came to Jerusalem, they were welcomed by the church and the apostles and the elders, and they reported all that God had done with them. 5But some believers who belonged to the sect of the Pharisees stood up and said, "It is necessary for them to be circumcised and ordered to keep the law of Moses."

---

a Or committed in the grace of God to the work   *b* Gk brothers

note on 9.35. *Who made the heaven . . . in them.* See note on 4.24. **14.17** For a similar view that God should have been known from observation of the natural world, see Wis 13.1–9; Rom 1.20. **14.18–19** The fickleness of the crowd comes to light when it moves to sacrifice to Paul and Barnabas one moment and then attempts to stone Paul in the next. On *stoning,* see 2 Cor 11.25. **14.20** *Derbe.* See note on 14.6. **14.21–28** Paul and Barnabas return to Antioch, stopping along the way to encourage new believers and establish leaders in each congregation. **14.22** *To continue in the faith.* See 11.23. On *persecution* as an expected result of Christian faith, see 20.23; Mt 7.14; Phil 1.29; 1 Thess 3.3. **14.23** *Elders,* originally the title of important Jewish leaders (see Lk 7.3; 9.22), also figure in the Jerusalem church (see, e.g., 11.30; 15.1–6) and in the churches of the Pauline circle (1 Tim 5.17; Titus 1.5), although they are not mentioned in the undisputed Pauline Letters. *With prayer and fasting.* See 13.3. **14.24–26** The route leads southward to the harbor of *Attalia* and then back to Syrian *Antioch.* **14.27** Consistent with the narrative throughout Acts, *God* is cred-

ited with the success of the gentile mission (see, e.g., 11.18; 13.47; 15.7–8). *A door of faith.* See 1 Cor 16.9; 2 Cor 2.12.

15.1–35 The Jerusalem council presents the final defense of the gentile mission and resolves a bitter dispute concerning whether gentile Christians must conform to Mosaic law. The difficulty of reconciling Acts 15 with Paul's comments in Gal 2.1–14 suggests that Luke has shaped the story to reflect his own understanding of the emerging church. **15.1–5** For the first time in Acts, the question arises whether Gentiles who become Christians must be *circumcised* and keep Mosaic law. On circumcision, see Gen 17.9–14; Lev 12.3; cf. Rom 2.25–29; Gal 5.2–12. **15.1** Circumcision originates with God's command to Abraham, not with Mosaic law. See 7.8; Gen 17.9–14. **15.2** *No small dissension.* See note on 12.18–19. **15.3** *Phoenicia* has not previously been mentioned as a location of disciples. *Samaria.* See 8.1–24. **15.4** *All that God had done,* i.e., to effect the conversion of the Gentiles. See 14.27; 15.12; 21.19. **15.5** The demand to *keep the law of Moses* considerably expands the conflict beyond the issue of cir-

6 The apostles and the elders met together to consider this matter. [7]After there had been much debate, Peter stood up and said to them, "My brothers,[a] you know that in the early days God made a choice among you, that I should be the one through whom the Gentiles would hear the message of the good news and become believers. [8]And God, who knows the human heart, testified to them by giving them the Holy Spirit, just as he did to us; [9]and in cleansing their hearts by faith he has made no distinction between them and us. [10]Now therefore why are you putting God to the test by placing on the neck of the disciples a yoke that neither our ancestors nor we have been able to bear? [11]On the contrary, we believe that we will be saved through the grace of the Lord Jesus, just as they will."

12 The whole assembly kept silence, and listened to Barnabas and Paul as they told of all the signs and wonders that God had done through them among the Gentiles. [13]After they finished speaking, James replied, "My brothers,[a] listen to me. [14]Simeon has related how God first looked favorably on the Gentiles, to take from among them a people for his name. [15]This agrees with the words of the prophets, as it is written,

[16] 'After this I will return,
  and I will rebuild the dwelling of David,
    which has fallen;
  from its ruins I will rebuild it,
    and I will set it up,
[17] so that all other peoples may seek the
    Lord—
  even all the Gentiles over whom my
    name has been called.
  Thus says the Lord, who has been
    making these things [18]known
    from long ago.'[b]

[19]Therefore I have reached the decision that we should not trouble those Gentiles who are turning to God, [20]but we should write to them to abstain only from things polluted by idols and from fornication and from whatever has been strangled[c] and from blood. [21]For in every city, for generations past, Moses has had those who proclaim him, for he has been read aloud every sabbath in the synagogues."

The Council's Letter to Gentile Believers

22 Then the apostles and the elders, with the consent of the whole church, decided to choose

---

a Gk Men, brothers   b Other ancient authorities read things. [18]Known to God from of old are all his works.'   c Other ancient authorities lack and from whatever has been strangled

---

cumcision (see v. 1). **15.6–11** Peter's speech, the last reference to him in Acts (except for v. 14), appeals to the church's experience with the gentile mission and to an understanding of grace. **15.7** Much debate reveals the intense involvement of both parties. In the early days. See 10.1–11.18; whether Peter historically carried out this role is unclear (see 8.26–40; 11.19–26; Gal 2.7–8). **15.9** No distinction. See also Rom 3.22; 10.12. **15.10** Putting God to the test. See 5.9; Ex 17.2; Ps 78.41. Jewish writers sometimes spoke of the law as a yoke to be chosen (Mishnah Avot 3.5; Berakot 2.2; cf. Mt 11.29–30). **15.11** This statement reinterprets the conversion of Cornelius as a message not simply about the salvation of Gentiles, but also about the way in which salvation comes to all persons; see also Rom 3.24; 4.16; 5.21. **15.12–21** The report of Barnabas and Paul precedes James's speech, which interprets the gentile mission on the basis of scripture. **15.12** Signs and wonders. See note on 14.3. **15.13** James (the brother of Jesus) here reenters the narrative, having been referred to briefly in 12.17 (see 21.18). **15.14** Simeon, apparently Peter, although only here does Luke refer to him this way (cf. Simon in, e.g., 10.5; 11.13; Lk 22.31; but see also 2 Pet 1.1). A people for his name. The term reserved for Israel (see note on 3.11) now includes Gentiles also. **15.16–18** James quotes Am 9.11–12 to demonstrate that the inclusion of Gentiles has long been within God's plan. The quotation comes

from the Greek Septuagint, the use of which is incongruous with the portrait of James as the leader of Jerusalem Christianity, who would presumably speak Aramaic in this setting. I will rebuild. God is the one who restores Israel. See Lk 1.32–33; Acts 1.6. Instead of Israel constructing a house for God (7.47, 49), now God alone builds a house for all. **15.19** Turning to God. See note on 9.35. **15.20** See also v. 29; 21.25. In Lev 17.8–18.30 these regulations govern both Israel and outsiders who live within Israel; thus James proposes a law for gentile Christians in keeping with Mosaic law but without imposing circumcision (cf. Philo, Migration of Abraham 89–94; Josephus, Antiquities 20.38–48). Things polluted by idols include meat from animals sacrificed to idols; see Ex 34.15–16; 1 Cor 10.7, 14–22. Fornication. See Lev 18.6–30; 1 Cor 6.18. Whatever has been strangled, i.e., animals not slaughtered in accordance with Lev 17.3; 19.26; Deut 12.16, 23–27. From blood. See Lev 3.17; 17.10–14. All these prohibitions are associated with idolatry, directly or otherwise. **15.21** Moses, i.e., Mosaic law. See Josephus, Antiquities 16.43; Against Apion 2.175; Philo, Special Laws 2.61–64. **15.22–29** Including this letter from Jerusalem allows Luke to repeat the content of the agreement and emphasize the unanimity of the Jerusalem church. **15.22** Judas called Barsabbas, mentioned nowhere else. Silas accompanies Paul in 15.40–18.5 (Silas is probably "Silvanus" in 2 Cor 1.19; 1 Thess

men from among their members[a] and to send them to Antioch with Paul and Barnabas. They sent Judas called Barsabbas, and Silas, leaders among the brothers, 23with the following letter: "The brothers, both the apostles and the elders, to the believers[b] of Gentile origin in Antioch and Syria and Cilicia, greetings. 24Since we have heard that certain persons who have gone out from us, though with no instructions from us, have said things to disturb you and have unsettled your minds,[c] 25we have decided unanimously to choose representatives[d] and send them to you, along with our beloved Barnabas and Paul, 26who have risked their lives for the sake of our Lord Jesus Christ. 27We have therefore sent Judas and Silas, who themselves will tell you the same things by word of mouth. 28For it has seemed good to the Holy Spirit and to us to impose on you no further burden than these essentials: 29that you abstain from what has been sacrificed to idols and from blood and from what is strangled[e] and from fornication. If you keep yourselves from these, you will do well. Farewell."

30 So they were sent off and went down to Antioch. When they gathered the congregation together, they delivered the letter. 31When its members[f] read it, they rejoiced at the exhortation. 32Judas and Silas, who were themselves prophets, said much to encourage and strengthen the believers.[b] 33After they had been there for some time, they were sent off in peace by the believers[b] to those who had sent them.[g] 35But Paul and Barnabas remained in Antioch, and there, with many others, they taught and proclaimed the word of the Lord.

Paul and Barnabas Separate

36 After some days Paul said to Barnabas, "Come, let us return and visit the believers[b] in

every city where we proclaimed the word of the Lord and see how they are doing." 37Barnabas wanted to take with them John called Mark. 38But Paul decided not to take with them one who had deserted them in Pamphylia and had not accompanied them in the work. 39The disagreement became so sharp that they parted company; Barnabas took Mark with him and sailed away to Cyprus. 40But Paul chose Silas and set out, the believers[b] commending him to the grace of the Lord. 41He went through Syria and Cilicia, strengthening the churches.

Timothy Joins Paul and Silas

16 Paul[h] went on also to Derbe and to Lystra, where there was a disciple named Timothy, the son of a Jewish woman who was a believer; but his father was a Greek. 2He was well spoken of by the believers[b] in Lystra and Iconium. 3Paul wanted Timothy to accompany him; and he took him and had him circumcised because of the Jews who were in those places, for they all knew that his father was a Greek. 4As they went from town to town, they delivered to them for observance the decisions that had been reached by the apostles and elders who were in Jerusalem. 5So the churches were strengthened in the faith and increased in numbers daily.

Paul's Vision of the Man of Macedonia

6 They went through the region of Phrygia and Galatia, having been forbidden by the Holy Spirit to speak the word in Asia. 7When they had come opposite Mysia, they attempted

---

a Gk *from among them* *b* Gk *brothers* *c* Other ancient authorities add *saying, 'You must be circumcised and keep the law,'* *d* Gk *men* *e* Other ancient authorities lack *and from what is strangled* *f* Gk *When they* *g* Other ancient authorities add verse 34, *But it seemed good to Silas to remain there* *h* Gk *He*

1.1; 2 Thess 1.1). **15.24** *Though with no instructions from us* carefully distances the Jerusalem council from the demands for circumcision and law observance (see v. 1). **15.27** *By word of mouth.* The oral report of Judas and Silas, who accompany Paul and Barnabas as they deliver the letter, again reinforces the importance of this message. **15.28** Luke often highlights the role of the *Holy Spirit* (see, e.g., 2.1–13; 4.8, 31; 10.44–48). **15.29** See note on 15.20. **15.31** The Gentiles receive the church's decision with rejoicing, as they earlier received the gospel itself (see 13.48). **15.33** Silas later leaves with Paul (v. 40), as though this departure had not occurred (see text note g). **15.36–16.10** With new colleagues and after a false start, Paul is summoned to Macedonia and a significant

new witness there. **15.36–41** What later develops into a major mission trip begins with the simple plan to revisit the cities of their earlier preaching. **15.37–39** For another possible reason for the conflict between Paul and Barnabas, see Gal 2.11–14. **15.38** On John Mark's *desertion*, see 13.13. **15.40** *Silas.* See notes on 15.22; 15.33. **16.1–5** The addition of Timothy completes the team. **16.1** *Derbe, Lystra.* See note on 14.6. *Timothy.* See 17.14–15; 18.5; 19.22; 20.4. Paul's Letters give him a more substantial role in Paul's work than Luke indicates (see Rom 16.21; 1 Cor 4.17; 16.10; 2 Cor 1.1, 19; Phil 1.1; 2.19–22; 1 Thess 1.1; 3.2, 6; Philem 1). **16.3** By *circumcising* Timothy, Paul shows his awareness of Jewish sensitivities (see 21.17–26; 22.3; 24.14; 26.5; but cf. Gal 2.3). **16.5** See note on 6.7. **16.6–10** Consistent with

to go into Bithynia, but the Spirit of Jesus did not allow them; [8]so, passing by Mysia, they went down to Troas. [9]During the night Paul had a vision: there stood a man of Macedonia pleading with him and saying, "Come over to Macedonia and help us." [10]When he had seen the vision, we immediately tried to cross over to Macedonia, being convinced that God had called us to proclaim the good news to them.

The Conversion of Lydia

11 We set sail from Troas and took a straight course to Samothrace, the following day to Neapolis, [12]and from there to Philippi, which is a leading city of the district[a] of Macedonia and a Roman colony. We remained in this city for some days. [13]On the sabbath day we went outside the gate by the river, where we supposed there was a place of prayer; and we sat down and spoke to the women who had gathered there.

[14]A certain woman named Lydia, a worshiper of God, was listening to us; she was from the city of Thyatira and a dealer in purple cloth. The Lord opened her heart to listen eagerly to what was said by Paul. [15]When she and her household were baptized, she urged us, saying, "If you have judged me to be faithful to the Lord, come and stay at my home." And she prevailed upon us.

Paul and Silas in Prison

16 One day, as we were going to the place of prayer, we met a slave-girl who had a spirit of divination and brought her owners a great deal of money by fortune-telling. [17]While she followed Paul and us, she would cry out, "These men are slaves of the Most High God, who proclaim to you[b] a way of salvation."

---

a Other authorities read *a city of the first district*   *b* Other ancient authorities read *to us*

---

the picture elsewhere in Acts, a new phase in the mission arises only with divine guidance (see, e.g., 8.26; 10.9–16). Here Luke reinforces that theme by showing the rejection of human initiatives. **16.6–8** *Phrygia and Galatia.* The route is to the northwest, toward *Mysia*, the region abutting the Hellespont. Not permitted to go either south to *Asia* Minor or north to *Bithynia*, the group arrives by default in the harbor city of *Troas*. Probably the change from *the Holy Spirit* to the *Spirit of Jesus*, a phrase used nowhere else in Acts, reflects stylistic variation rather than a theological distinction. **16.9** On *visions* or dreams as a means of guidance, see 9.10–12; 10.3–6, 10–16; 11.5–10; 18.9–10. *Macedonia,*

a Roman province in the northern region of the Greek peninsula. **16.10** The shift here to the first-person plural narration (*we*) extends through v. 17 (see also 20.5–15; 21.1–18; 27.1–28.16). The change may result from stylistic considerations, or from the use of travel diaries only loosely reworked by Luke, or from the author's presence during this part of the journey. Given the uncertainty, little can be deduced from it regarding the historical accuracy of Acts or the identity of Luke. **16.11–40** Philippi signals an important new stage in the witness. **16.11–15** The mission in Philippi begins and ends with references to *Lydia* (see v. 40). **16.11–12** *Samothrace,* an island about halfway between Troas and *Neapolis,* port city of *Philippi.* **16.12** *Philippi,* a city in one of four districts within the province of *Macedonia* (see text note *a*). In this context, where Paul's status as a Roman citizen first appears (vv. 37–38), Luke identifies Philippi as a *Roman colony.* Pisidian Antioch (13.14), Lystra (14.6), Troas (16.8), and Corinth (18.1) were all colonies as well. **16.13** *A place of prayer,* either a synagogue or an informal place of worship. **16.14** *A worshiper of God,* i.e., a Gentile who worshiped Israel's God (see note on 10.2). *Thyatira* was in the district of Lydia, which had long been a center for the production of purple dye, a luxury good (Lk 16.19), although it is not clear that Lydia herself was wealthy. **16.15** References to the *household* of Lydia (her name is the same as that of the district) suggest that she is unmarried. Mistress of her own household and possibly a merchant, she may have had relatively high social and economic status. On the *baptism* of a household, see 10.24, 44–48; 11.14; 16.31–34. **16.16–24** As earlier in Acts (3.1–26; 14.8–18), a healing leads to a public confrontation. **16.16** *Spirit of divination,* lit. "a spirit of the Python," which was associated with the Delphic oracle. **16.17** *A way of salvation,* not only a major Lukan theme (see, e.g., 2.40; Lk 3.6), but also a preview of what will happen to both the slave-girl and the jailer. **16.18** On heal-

Acts 16 narrates the important expansion of the Pauline mission into Europe.

18 She kept doing this for many days. But Paul, very much annoyed, turned and said to the spirit, "I order you in the name of Jesus Christ to come out of her." And it came out that very hour.

19 But when her owners saw that their hope of making money was gone, they seized Paul and Silas and dragged them into the market-place before the authorities. 20 When they had brought them before the magistrates, they said, "These men are disturbing our city; they are Jews 21 and are advocating customs that are not lawful for us as Romans to adopt or observe." 22 The crowd joined in attacking them, and the magistrates had them stripped of their clothing and ordered them to be beaten with rods. 23 After they had given them a severe flogging, they threw them into prison and ordered the jailer to keep them securely. 24 Following these instructions, he put them in the innermost cell and fastened their feet in the stocks.

25 About midnight Paul and Silas were praying and singing hymns to God, and the prisoners were listening to them. 26 Suddenly there was an earthquake, so violent that the foundations of the prison were shaken; and immediately all the doors were opened and everyone's chains were unfastened. 27 When the jailer woke up and saw the prison doors wide open, he drew his sword and was about to kill himself, since he supposed that the prisoners had escaped. 28 But Paul shouted in a loud voice, "Do not harm yourself, for we are all here." 29 The jailer[a] called for lights, and rushing in, he fell down trembling before Paul and Silas. 30 Then he brought them outside and said, "Sirs, what must I do to be saved?" 31 They answered, "Believe on the Lord Jesus, and you will be saved, you and your household." 32 They spoke the word of the Lord[b] to him and to all who were in his house. 33 At the same hour of the night he took them and washed their wounds; then he and his entire family were baptized without delay. 34 He brought them up into the house and set food before them; and he and his entire household rejoiced that he had become a believer in God.

35 When morning came, the magistrates sent the police, saying, "Let those men go." 36 And the jailer reported the message to Paul, saying, "The magistrates sent word to let you go; therefore come out now and go in peace." 37 But Paul replied, "They have beaten us in public, uncondemned, men who are Roman citizens, and have thrown us into prison; and now are they going to discharge us in secret? Certainly not! Let them come and take us out themselves." 38 The police reported these words to the magistrates, and they were afraid when they heard that they were Roman citizens; 39 so they came and apologized to them. And they took them out and asked them to leave the city. 40 After leaving the prison they went to Lydia's home; and when they had seen and encouraged the brothers and sisters[c] there, they departed.

The Uproar in Thessalonica

17 After Paul and Silas[d] had passed through Amphipolis and Apollonia, they came to Thessalonica, where there was a synagogue of the Jews. 2 And Paul went in, as was his custom, and on three sabbath days argued with them from the scriptures, 3 explaining and proving that it was necessary for the Messiah[e] to suffer and to rise from the dead,

---

a Gk He   b Other ancient authorities read word of God
c Gk brothers   d Gk they   e Or the Christ

---

ing in the name of Jesus Christ, see 3.6, 16; 4.10. **16.19** See also note on 8.18. Cf. 19.25, where Luke draws attention to the economic motives of other potential competitors. Here the theme is underscored by false charges against Paul and Silas. **16.20** Magistrates, a popular designation for the chief officials of a Roman colony. **16.21** The charge against Paul and Silas manipulates opinion by characterizing them as outsiders. **16.22–24** See 2 Cor 11.23–25. **16.25–34** Unlike the two previous stories of prison release in Acts (5.19–21; 12.6–11), this one occasions a conversion. **16.27** See 12.19, where the guards are executed following Peter's miraculous escape. **16.30** What must I do to be saved? See 2.37. **16.32–34** As in the cases of Lydia (v. 15) and Cornelius (10.2, 24, 44; 11.14), this conversion involves the entire household. **16.37** Beaten . . . in public. Such treatment of a Roman citizen was against Roman law, but violations of this law occurred (see, e.g., Josephus, War 2.308). **16.40** See vv. 14–15.

17.1–15 The conflicting responses to Christian preaching in two cities prepare for Paul's important speech in Athens. **17.1** Paul and Silas travel the Via Egnatia, the main east-west road across Macedonia. Thessalonica, headquarters for the Roman governor and the leading city of the province of Macedonia. **17.2** As was his custom. In every city Paul goes first to Jews (see note on 13.14). From the scriptures. See Lk 4.16–21; 24.27, 32, 45, where Jesus interprets scripture about himself. **17.3** It was necessary. Luke often draws attention to divine necessity (see, e.g., 1.16; 3.21; 9.16; Lk 2.49; 24.7,

and saying, "This is the Messiah,[a] Jesus whom I am proclaiming to you." [4]Some of them were persuaded and joined Paul and Silas, as did a great many of the devout Greeks and not a few of the leading women. [5]But the Jews became jealous, and with the help of some ruffians in the marketplaces they formed a mob and set the city in an uproar. While they were searching for Paul and Silas to bring them out to the assembly, they attacked Jason's house. [6]When they could not find them, they dragged Jason and some believers[b] before the city authorities,[c] shouting, "These people who have been turning the world upside down have come here also, [7]and Jason has entertained them as guests. They are all acting contrary to the decrees of the emperor, saying that there is another king named Jesus." [8]The people and the city officials were disturbed when they heard this, [9]and after they had taken bail from Jason and the others, they let them go.

Paul and Silas in Beroea

[10]That very night the believers[b] sent Paul and Silas off to Beroea; and when they arrived, they went to the Jewish synagogue. [11]These Jews were more receptive than those in Thessalonica, for they welcomed the message very eagerly and examined the scriptures every day to see whether these things were so. [12]Many of them therefore believed, including not a few Greek women and men of high standing. [13]But when the Jews of Thessalonica learned that the word of God had been proclaimed by Paul in Beroea as well, they came there too, to stir up and incite the crowds. [14]Then the believers[b] immediately sent Paul away to the coast, but Silas and Timothy remained behind. [15]Those who conducted Paul brought him as far as Athens; and after receiving instructions to have Silas and Timothy join him as soon as possible, they left him.

Paul in Athens

[16]While Paul was waiting for them in Athens, he was deeply distressed to see that the city was full of idols. [17]So he argued in the synagogue with the Jews and the devout persons, and also in the marketplace[d] every day with those who happened to be there. [18]Also some Epicurean and Stoic philosophers debated with him. Some said, "What does this babbler want to say?" Others said, "He seems to be a proclaimer of foreign divinities." (This was because he was telling the good news about Jesus and the resurrection.) [19]So they took him and brought him to the Areopagus and asked him, "May we know what this new teaching is that you are presenting? [20]It sounds rather strange to us, so we would like to know what it means." [21]Now all the Athenians and the foreigners living there would spend their time in nothing but telling or hearing something new.

[22]Then Paul stood in front of the Areopa-

---

a Or *the Christ*   *b* Gk *brothers*   *c* Gk *politarchs*   *d* Or *civic center*; Gk *agora*

26, 46). **17.4–5** As earlier (13.43, 50; 14.1–2), both Jews and Greeks are among those who respond to the gospel and among those who reject it. The *ruffians* who are deployed here reveal the irony of the charge that it is Paul and Silas who are disturbing the peace. **17.6** *Turning the world upside down*, i.e., disturbing the peace, a highly inflammatory charge in the context of the Roman Empire (see also 16.20; 24.5, 12). **17.7** *Contrary to the decrees of the emperor.* See also 16.21. *Another king named Jesus.* See Lk 23.2–3, 37–38. **17.10** *Beroea*, a city south of the Via Egnatia (see note on 17.1). **17.15** *Athens*, a highly significant cultural center, offers an appropriate context for presenting Luke's understanding of a typical sermon to Gentiles. **17.16–34** Paul's speech at Athens, the only major speech in Acts to a pagan audience (although see 14.15–17), echoes important Lukan themes even as it differs from earlier speeches. References to the history of Israel are omitted here as meaningless to an audience composed entirely of Gentiles. **17.16** *The city was full of idols.* Ancient historians provide similar descriptions of the religious fervor of Athens. *Idols*, a derogatory

term that exposes Luke's thoroughly monotheistic perspective. **17.17** *In the synagogue.* See note on 13.14. **17.18** *Epicureans* ridiculed religious enthusiasm and argued against a fear of death and divine judgment. *Stoics* urged living in accord with nature, which they understood to be ruled by the divine *Logos.* In order to achieve this goal, they advocated the importance of reason and self-control. *Babbler,* lit. "one who picks up seeds," i.e., a person who gathers new ideas indiscriminately. *A proclaimer of foreign divinities,* a charge leveled also against Socrates (Plato, *Apology* 24B–C). *The resurrection* may have been understood by the Athenians as Resurrection, a female deity, Jesus' companion goddess. **17.19** *Areopagus,* either a place, the Hill of Ares, or an administrative council whose name derived from its location. **17.21** Ancient writers describe the Athenians in similar terms. See Sophocles, *Oedipus Coloneus* 260; Pausanias, *Description of Greece* 1.17.1; Josephus, *Against Apion* 2.130; Strabo, *Geography* 9.1.16; Livy, *History* 45.27.11). **17.22–31** Paul's speech begins with an acknowledgment of the religiosity of the Athenians (vv. 22–23),

gus and said, "Athenians, I see how extremely religious you are in every way. 23For as I went through the city and looked carefully at the objects of your worship, I found among them an altar with the inscription, 'To an unknown god.' What therefore you worship as unknown, this I proclaim to you. 24The God who made the world and everything in it, he who is Lord of heaven and earth, does not live in shrines made by human hands, 25nor is he served by human hands, as though he needed anything, since he himself gives to all mortals life and breath and all things. 26From one ancestor[a] he made all nations to inhabit the whole earth, and he allotted the times of their existence and the boundaries of the places where they would live, 27so that they would search for God[b] and perhaps grope for him and find him—though indeed he is not far from each one of us. 28For 'In him we live and move and have our being'; as even some of your own poets have said,

'For we too are his offspring.'

29Since we are God's offspring, we ought not to think that the deity is like gold, or silver, or stone, an image formed by the art and imagination of mortals. 30While God has overlooked the times of human ignorance, now he commands all people everywhere to repent, 31because he has fixed a day on which he will have the world judged in righteousness by a man whom he has appointed, and of this he has given assurance to all by raising him from the dead."

32 When they heard of the resurrection of the dead, some scoffed; but others said, "We will hear you again about this." 33At that point Paul left them. 34But some of them joined him and became believers, including Dionysius the Areopagite and a woman named Damaris, and others with them.

Paul in Corinth

18 After this Paul[c] left Athens and went to Corinth. 2There he found a Jew named Aquila, a native of Pontus, who had recently come from Italy with his wife Priscilla, because Claudius had ordered all Jews to leave Rome. Paul[d] went to see them, 3and, because he was of the same trade, he stayed with them, and they worked together—by trade they were tentmakers. 4Every sabbath he would argue in the synagogue and would try to convince Jews and Greeks.

5 When Silas and Timothy arrived from Macedonia, Paul was occupied with proclaiming the word,[e] testifying to the Jews that the Messiah[f] was Jesus. 6When they opposed and

a Gk From one; other ancient authorities read From one blood b Other ancient authorities read the Lord c Gk he d Gk He e Gk with the word f Or the Christ

moves to a sympathetic critique of idolatry (vv. 24–29), and concludes with a call for repentance (vv. 30–31). **17.22** *Extremely religious,* either in the pejorative sense of "superstitious" or as a straightforward description. Since speeches customarily began by praising the audience (see 26.2–3), the latter is preferable. **17.23** *To an unknown God.* No known inscription corresponds exactly to this one, but there is evidence of altars to unknown gods. **17.24–25** On God as creator, see 4.24; 14.15. That God does not live in buildings is a theme also of Stephen's speech; see 7.48. This philosophically inclined audience would have agreed. **17.26** *One ancestor.* See Lk 3.38, where Jesus' genealogy is traced back to Adam. *He allotted the times.* See 14.17. **17.27** On the notion that pagans *search for God,* see Wis 13.6. *He is not far from . . . us.* On God's nearness, see Ps 145.18; Jer 23.23; Josephus, *Antiquities* 8.108; Dio Chrysostom, *Discourses* 12, 28. **17.28** *In him we . . . have our being.* If a quotation (Greek uses no quotation marks), its source is unknown. *For we too are his offspring* is from Aratus (*Phaenomena* 5), a third-century BCE poet. **17.29** A conventional piece of Jewish polemic against idolatry; see 7.41–43; Isa 44.9–20; Wis 13.10; Rom 1.23. **17.30** Both Jewish and pagan *ignorance* is overlooked; see 3.17; 13.27. The call to *repent* is now universal; see 2.38; 3.19; 8.22; 11.18; 26.20. **17.31** Only here does the speech refer to Jesus. *Judged.* See 10.42; Rom 2.16. **17.32–34** As elsewhere in Acts, the speech is interrupted when it reaches its climactic point; see note on 2.37. Compared with earlier speeches, the response (both positive and negative) is mild (cf., e.g., 2.41; 13.43, 45).

18.1–17 Four brief scenes (vv. 1–4, 5–8, 9–11, 12–17) portray Paul's extended endeavors in Corinth. **18.1** *Corinth,* the Roman capital of Achaia, was well situated for commerce. **18.2** *Aquila* and *Priscilla* ("Prisca" in the Pauline Letters) are identified as Jews in order to explain the impact of Claudius's edict on them; evidently both converted to Christianity before Paul reached Corinth (see also Rom 16.3–4; 1 Cor 16.19). *Claudius,* Roman emperor 41–54 CE. *Ordered all Jews to leave Rome.* Since other sources indicate that a disturbance over Christian preaching caused this expulsion, it may well have targeted Jews who preached and taught about Jesus. **18.3** *Tentmakers,* the first reference in Acts to Paul's labor (but see 1 Cor 4.12), probably refers to leather working in general. **18.4** As elsewhere, Paul begins *in the synagogue;* see note on 13.14. **18.5** On the itinerary of Silas and Timothy, see 17.14. **18.6** *Shook the dust* recalls 13.51; Lk 9.5. *Your blood be on your own heads!* See also 5.28; 2 Sam 1.16; Ezek 33.4–5; cf. Mt 27.25. This is the second of three passages (13.46; 28.28) in which Paul announces that

reviled him, in protest he shook the dust from his clothes[a] and said to them, "Your blood be on your own heads! I am innocent. From now on I will go to the Gentiles." 7Then he left the synagogue[b] and went to the house of a man named Titius[c] Justus, a worshiper of God; his house was next door to the synagogue. 8Crispus, the official of the synagogue, became a believer in the Lord, together with all his household; and many of the Corinthians who heard Paul became believers and were baptized. 9One night the Lord said to Paul in a vision, "Do not be afraid, but speak and do not be silent; 10for I am with you, and no one will lay a hand on you to harm you, for there are many in this city who are my people." 11He stayed there a year and six months, teaching the word of God among them.

12 But when Gallio was proconsul of Achaia, the Jews made a united attack on Paul and brought him before the tribunal. 13They said, "This man is persuading people to worship God in ways that are contrary to the law." 14Just as Paul was about to speak, Gallio said to the Jews, "If it were a matter of crime or serious villainy, I would be justified in accepting the complaint of you Jews; 15but since it is a matter of questions about words and names and your own law, see to it yourselves; I do not wish to be a judge of these matters." 16And he dismissed them from the tribunal. 17Then all of them[d] seized Sosthenes, the official of the synagogue, and beat him in front of the tribunal. But Gallio paid no attention to any of these things.

Paul's Return to Antioch

18 After staying there for a considerable time, Paul said farewell to the believers[e] and sailed for Syria, accompanied by Priscilla and Aquila. At Cenchreae he had his hair cut, for he was under a vow. 19When they reached Ephesus, he left them there, but first he himself went into the synagogue and had a discussion with the Jews. 20When they asked him to stay longer, he declined; 21but on taking leave of them, he said, "I[f] will return to you, if God wills." Then he set sail from Ephesus.

22 When he had landed at Caesarea, he went up to Jerusalem[g] and greeted the church, and then went down to Antioch. 23After spending some time there he departed and went from place to place through the region of Galatia[h] and Phrygia, strengthening all the disciples.

Ministry of Apollos

24 Now there came to Ephesus a Jew named Apollos, a native of Alexandria. He was an elo-

a Gk reviled him, he shook out his clothes b Gk left there c Other ancient authorities read Titus d Other ancient authorities read all the Greeks e Gk brothers f Other ancient authorities read I must at all costs keep the approaching festival in Jerusalem, but I g Gk went up h Gk the Galatian region

he is going to the *Gentiles*. **18.7–8** Unlike earlier departures from the synagogue, Paul does not leave the area but remains very close by. Presumably *Titius Justus*, a Gentile who nevertheless worships God (see note on 10.2), has become a Christian. The conversion of *Crispus* (see 1 Cor 1.14) indicates that Paul continues to preach among Jews, despite v. 6, and that his proclamation meets with success even among synagogue leaders. On the conversion of *households*, see note on 10.2. **18.9** On *visions* as a means of divine guidance, see note on 9.10. **18.10** *I am with you.* See also Josh 1.9; Isa 41.10; 43.5; Jer 1.8, 19. *People* usually refers in Luke-Acts to Israel (see note on 3.11), but here, as in 15.14, it includes Gentiles as well. **18.12** An inscription at Delphi referring to *Gallio* allows his proconsulate in Corinth to be dated ca. 51–52 CE and thus may indicate that Paul began the church in Corinth during that period. Luke may have consolidated several of Paul's journeys to Corinth, however, making the connection between the reference to Gallio and Paul's activities uncertain. **18.13** The ambiguous charge could refer to either Jewish (see 6.13) or Roman law (16.21; 17.7). **18.14–15** Gallio's response, that this is an inter-Jewish quarrel, vindicates Paul and coheres with later claims (24.14–15; 25.19; 26.2–3). **18.17** Paul refers to a *Sosthenes* in 1 Cor 1.1, but identifying the two with one another seems unlikely since it is not clear that this Sosthenes is a Christian, much less a co-worker of Paul. Gallio's lack of concern about Jewish debates extends to a lack of concern when Sosthenes is beaten. **18.18–19.22** The mission in Ephesus is prepared for by Paul's travel (v. 19) and again in the story of Apollos (vv. 24–28). **18.18** *Priscilla and Aquila.* Placing the woman's name first is unusual and could suggest that Priscilla has a higher social or economic standing than Aquila (see v. 26; Rom 16.3; cf. 18.2; 1 Cor 16.19). *Cenchreae*, the eastern port of Corinth. On the Nazirite *vow*, see Num 6.1–21, although the requirement is that the hair not be cut until the end of the vow. As in 21.20–26, this action conveys continuity with Jewish practice. **18.19** *Ephesus*, a port in western Asia Minor, at this time the fourth largest city of the Roman Empire and capital of Asia. On Paul's practice of visiting *synagogues* first, see note on 13.14. **18.22–23** This sketchy description sets the stage for Paul's return to Ephesus (19.1) and reconnects Paul with the two central communities, Jerusalem and Antioch. **18.24** The description of *Apollos* is consistent with his origin in

quent man, well-versed in the scriptures. 25 He had been instructed in the Way of the Lord; and he spoke with burning enthusiasm and taught accurately the things concerning Jesus, though he knew only the baptism of John. 26 He began to speak boldly in the synagogue; but when Priscilla and Aquila heard him, they took him aside and explained the Way of God to him more accurately. 27 And when he wished to cross over to Achaia, the believers*a* encouraged him and wrote to the disciples to welcome him. On his arrival he greatly helped those who through grace had become believers, 28 for he powerfully refuted the Jews in public, showing by the scriptures that the Messiah*b* is Jesus.

Paul in Ephesus

19 While Apollos was in Corinth, Paul passed through the interior regions and came to Ephesus, where he found some disciples. 2 He said to them, "Did you receive the Holy Spirit when you became believers?" They replied, "No, we have not even heard that there is a Holy Spirit." 3 Then he said, "Into what then were you baptized?" They answered, "Into John's baptism." 4 Paul said, "John baptized with the baptism of repentance, telling the people to believe in the one who was to come after him, that is, in Jesus." 5 On hearing this, they were baptized in the name of the Lord Jesus. 6 When Paul had laid his hands on them, the Holy Spirit came upon them, and they spoke in tongues and prophesied— 7 altogether there were about twelve of them.

8 He entered the synagogue and for three months spoke out boldly, and argued persuasively about the kingdom of God. 9 When some stubbornly refused to believe and spoke evil of the Way before the congregation, he left them, taking the disciples with him, and argued daily in the lecture hall of Tyrannus.*c* 10 This continued for two years, so that all the residents of Asia, both Jews and Greeks, heard the word of the Lord.

The Sons of Sceva

11 God did extraordinary miracles through Paul, 12 so that when the handkerchiefs or aprons that had touched his skin were brought to the sick, their diseases left them, and the evil spirits came out of them. 13 Then some itinerant Jewish exorcists tried to use the name of the Lord Jesus over those who had evil spirits, saying, "I adjure you by the Jesus whom Paul proclaims." 14 Seven sons of a Jewish high priest named Sceva were doing this. 15 But the evil spirit said to them in reply, "Jesus I know,

---

a Gk *brothers*   *b* Or *the Christ*   *c* Other ancient authorities read *of a certain Tyrannus, from eleven o'clock in the morning to four in the afternoon*

Alexandria, the literary center of the Hellenistic world and home to a large Jewish population. **18.25** Where and how Apollos was converted is less important than the fact that his knowledge, though accurate, was incomplete. *The Way.* See note on 9.1–2. *With burning enthusiasm*, or "burning with the Spirit," which would explain how Apollos differs from the disciples in 19.1–7, who must be baptized and receive the Holy Spirit. **18.26** Speaking *boldly* further identifies Apollos with Christian preachers, even if he still requires instruction (see note on 4.13). *Priscilla and Aquila.* See notes on 18.2; 18.18; by their instruction of Apollos, they become the forerunners of Paul's Ephesian mission. *The Way.* See note on 9.1–2. **18.28** Like his predecessors in mission, Apollos argues from scripture (see, e.g., 8.35; 17.2–3; see also Lk 24.26–27, 45–46) about the messiahship of Jesus. **19.1–7** Paul's first encounter in Ephesus is with disciples who have been influenced by John the Baptist. **19.1** *Apollos . . . in Corinth.* See 1 Cor 1.12; 3.4–6, 22; 4.6; 16.12. *Some disciples,* Christians, but with incomplete education and experience. **19.2** *Receive the Holy Spirit.* See 1.5; 2.4; 8.17; 9.17; 10.44; Lk 3.16. **19.4** Cf. John's words in Lk 3.16–17. **19.5** On baptism *in the name*, see 2.38; 8.16; 10.48. **19.6** Peter and John conveyed the *Holy Spirit* to the Samaritans in

this same way; see 8.17. On speaking *in tongues*, see 2.4, 11; 10.46. **19.8** On *bold* speech, see note on 4.13. *Kingdom of God.* See note on 1.3. **19.9** As in Corinth (18.4–7), Paul's synagogue preaching is not well received. *The Way.* See note on 9.1–2. For the first time, Luke specifies that Paul takes believers with him when he separates from the synagogue. *The lecture hall of Tyrannus,* possibly a guild center or a place for philosophical instruction. Nothing is known of the individual after whom it is named. **19.10** *All the residents of Asia* surely exaggerates in order to underscore the importance of the Ephesian mission, which reaches *both Jews and Greeks* outside the synagogue; cf., e.g., 14.1; 17.1–4; 18.7, where Gentiles are reached within the synagogue setting. **19.11–12** Like those of his predecessors Peter (5.12–16) and Philip (8.4–8), Paul's ministry includes healing and exorcism; see also 2 Cor 12.12. **19.13–16** The humorous account of the defeat of seven exorcists contrasts sharply with the report of Paul's successful healings and exorcisms in 19.11–12. **19.13** *Jewish exorcists.* See Josephus, *Antiquities* 8.45–49; see also Acts 13.6–11; cf. Deut 18.10–14. It was a widespread assumption that having the *name* of a spirit allowed one to compel that spirit to act. **19.14** No high priest by the name of *Sceva* is known; a

and Paul I know; but who are you?" 16 Then the man with the evil spirit leaped on them, mastered them all, and so overpowered them that they fled out of the house naked and wounded. 17 When this became known to all residents of Ephesus, both Jews and Greeks, everyone was awestruck; and the name of the Lord Jesus was praised. 18 Also many of those who became believers confessed and disclosed their practices. 19 A number of those who practiced magic collected their books and burned them publicly; when the value of these books*a* was calculated, it was found to come to fifty thousand silver coins. 20 So the word of the Lord grew mightily and prevailed.

The Riot in Ephesus

21 Now after these things had been accomplished, Paul resolved in the Spirit to go through Macedonia and Achaia, and then to go on to Jerusalem. He said, "After I have gone there, I must also see Rome." 22 So he sent two of his helpers, Timothy and Erastus, to Macedonia, while he himself stayed for some time longer in Asia.

23 About that time no little disturbance broke out concerning the Way. 24 A man named Demetrius, a silversmith who made silver shrines of Artemis, brought no little business to the artisans. 25 These he gathered together, with the workers of the same trade, and said, "Men, you know that we get our wealth from this business. 26 You also see and hear that not only in Ephesus but in almost

the whole of Asia this Paul has persuaded and drawn away a considerable number of people by saying that gods made with hands are not gods. 27 And there is danger not only that this trade of ours may come into disrepute but also that the temple of the great goddess Artemis will be scorned, and she will be deprived of her majesty that brought all Asia and the world to worship her."

28 When they heard this, they were enraged and shouted, "Great is Artemis of the Ephesians!" 29 The city was filled with the confusion; and people*b* rushed together to the theater, dragging with them Gaius and Aristarchus, Macedonians who were Paul's travel companions. 30 Paul wished to go into the crowd, but the disciples would not let him; 31 even some officials of the province of Asia,*c* who were friendly to him, sent him a message urging him not to venture into the theater. 32 Meanwhile, some were shouting one thing, some another; for the assembly was in confusion, and most of them did not know why they had come together. 33 Some of the crowd gave instructions to Alexander, whom the Jews had pushed forward. And Alexander motioned for silence and tried to make a defense before the people. 34 But when they recognized that he was a Jew, for about two hours all of them shouted in unison, "Great is Artemis of the Ephesians!" 35 But when the town clerk had quieted the crowd, he said, "Citizens of Ephe-

---

a Gk them   *b* Gk they   *c* Gk some of the Asiarchs

Latin name, it would have been most remarkable for a high priest. **19.15** *Jesus I know.* See Jas 2.19. **19.17** As with the defeat of Bar-Jesus, the defeat of the seven prompts faith (see 13.6–11). **19.19** *Burned them publicly.* See the prohibitions in Deut 18.10–14. *Fifty thousand silver coins.* Because their possessors used them for financial gain, such books would command a high price. **19.20** See note on 6.7. **19.21** Unlike 16.6–8, where Paul's own mission initiatives are thwarted, here he makes his decision with the *Spirit's* aid. The motif of Paul's journey to *Jerusalem* and *Rome* recurs throughout the remainder of Acts (see 20.22; 21.13; 25.9–12; 28.14) and parallels Lk 9.51, where Jesus determines to go to Jerusalem. Paul *must also see Rome* because it is divine necessity; see note on 1.16; see also Rom 1.10, 15; 15.22–32. **19.22** *Timothy,* last referred to in 18.5; for references to Timothy's visit to Corinth, see 1 Cor 4.17; 16.10. An *Erastus* is mentioned in Rom 16.23; 2 Tim 4.20, but the name was common, making identification of these three persons with one another uncertain. **19.23–41** Paul's mission in Ephesus cul-

minates in a riot and in Paul's public vindication. **19.23** *No little disturbance.* See note on 12.18–19. *The Way.* See note on 9.1–2. **19.24** *Silver shrines of Artemis,* miniature versions of the temple of Artemis. *Artemis of the Ephesians* (vv. 28, 34), an ancient mother goddess widely worshiped in the Hellenistic world. Her temple in Ephesus, one of the Seven Wonders of the World, functioned as a cultural and financial center of Asia. *No little business.* See note on 12.18–19. **19.25** As in 16.16–21, Luke draws attention to the profit motive of competing groups. **19.26** See note on 17.29. **19.27** See 21.28 for parallel fears in Jerusalem regarding the people and the temple. **19.28** *Artemis of the Ephesians.* See v. 24. **19.29** See 7.57, where the crowd rushes against Stephen, and 21.30–31, where riot breaks out in Jerusalem. *Gaius.* See 20.4; see also Rom 16.23; 1 Cor 1.14; 3 Jn 1. *Aristarchus.* See 20.4; 27.2; Col 4.10; Philem 24. **19.33** Whether *Alexander* is a Christian is unclear. **19.35** *Temple keeper,* a title given cities that maintained temples honoring the emperor, but the term is also used of temples honoring gods or god-

sus, who is there that does not know that the city of the Ephesians is the temple keeper of the great Artemis and of the statue that fell from heaven?[a] 36Since these things cannot be denied, you ought to be quiet and do nothing rash. 37You have brought these men here who are neither temple robbers nor blasphemers of our[b] goddess. 38If therefore Demetrius and the artisans with him have a complaint against anyone, the courts are open, and there are proconsuls; let them bring charges there against one another. 39If there is anything further[c] you want to know, it must be settled in the regular assembly. 40For we are in danger of being charged with rioting today, since there is no cause that we can give to justify this commotion." 41When he had said this, he dismissed the assembly.

Paul Goes to Macedonia and Greece

20 After the uproar had ceased, Paul sent for the disciples; and after encouraging them and saying farewell, he left for Macedonia. 2When he had gone through those regions and had given the believers[d] much encouragement, he came to Greece, 3where he stayed for three months. He was about to set sail for Syria when a plot was made against him by the Jews, and so he decided to return through Macedonia. 4He was accompanied by Sopater son of Pyrrhus from Beroea, by Aristarchus and Secundus from Thessalonica, by Gaius from Derbe, and by Timothy, as well as by Tychicus and Trophimus from Asia. 5They

went ahead and were waiting for us in Troas; 6but we sailed from Philippi after the days of Unleavened Bread, and in five days we joined them in Troas, where we stayed for seven days.

Paul's Farewell Visit to Troas

7 On the first day of the week, when we met to break bread, Paul was holding a discussion with them; since he intended to leave the next day, he continued speaking until midnight. 8There were many lamps in the room upstairs where we were meeting. 9A young man named Eutychus, who was sitting in the window, began to sink off into a deep sleep while Paul talked still longer. Overcome by sleep, he fell to the ground three floors below and was picked up dead. 10But Paul went down, and bending over him took him in his arms, and said, "Do not be alarmed, for his life is in him." 11Then Paul went upstairs, and after he had broken bread and eaten, he continued to converse with them until dawn; then he left. 12Meanwhile they had taken the boy away alive and were not a little comforted.

The Voyage from Troas to Miletus

13 We went ahead to the ship and set sail for Assos, intending to take Paul on board there; for he had made this arrangement, intending to go by land himself. 14When he met us in Assos, we took him on board and went to Mit-

---

a Meaning of Gk uncertain   b Other ancient authorities read your   c Other ancient authorities read about other matters   d Gk given them

---

desses. *The statue that fell from heaven* refers to a legend about Artemis and counters Paul's assertion in v. 26. **19.37** Josephus says that Jews are not to blaspheme or destroy the gods of others (*Antiquities* 4.207; *Against Apion* 2.237); see also Rom 2.22; but cf. Deut 7.25. **19.38–40** By announcing that no formal charges have been made and that proper procedures have not been used, the town clerk offers an indirect defense of the Christian mission.

20.1–16 Paul's final trip to Jerusalem begins with pastoral visits to several cities. **20.1–2** *Encouragement* of believers is a constant refrain in Paul's journeys; see 14.22; 15.36, 41; 16.40. On the decision to go to *Macedonia* and *Greece*, see 19.21. **20.3** For earlier *plots*, see 9.24; 13.50; 14.5; 17.5, 13; 18.12–13; see also Lk 6.11; 19.47; 22.2. **20.4** *Sopater* and *Secundus*, mentioned only here. *Aristarchus.* See note on 19.29. Although in 19.29 *Gaius* is said to be a Macedonian, here he is said to be *from Derbe*, which is in Asia Minor. *Timothy.* See note on 16.3. *Tychicus.* See Eph 6.21; Col 4.7; 2 Tim 4.12; Titus 3.12. *Trophimus.* See 21.29; 2 Tim 4.20. **20.5** The use of

the first-person plural narration (*us, we*) resumes here and continues through 21.18, except for the speech in 20.17–38 (see note on 16.10). *Troas.* See 16.8–10. **20.6** *The days of Unleavened Bread*, originally a harvest festival, was combined with Passover; see Lk 22.1, which begins Jesus' passion narrative with the same reference. **20.7** *On the first day of the week*, i.e., the day after the sabbath. See Mark 16.2; 1 Cor 16.2. This is the first reference to *breaking bread* since 2.42, 46, and may recall Jesus' breaking bread just before his arrest (Lk 22.19). **20.8** *The room upstairs.* See 1.13. The rare detail about the *lamps* burning at midnight reflects Luke's frequent contrast between darkness and light, blindness and sight. See Lk 2.29–32; Acts 9.1–19; 13.4–12; 26.18. **20.9** *Eutychus* means "good fortune." On inappropriate sleepiness and the need for watchfulness, see v. 31; Lk 9.32; 12.35–38; 22.45–46. **20.10** Like Peter (9.36–42), Paul is here identified with Jesus' power to raise the dead (Lk 7.11–17; 8.41–42, 49–56). **20.12** *Not a little.* See note on 12.18–19. **20.13** *Assos*, a seaport in Mysia on the northwest coast of Asia Minor. **20.14** *Mitylene*, harbor

ylene. ¹⁵We sailed from there, and on the following day we arrived opposite Chios. The next day we touched at Samos, and*ᵃ the day after that we came to Miletus. ¹⁶For Paul had decided to sail past Ephesus, so that he might not have to spend time in Asia; he was eager to be in Jerusalem, if possible, on the day of Pentecost.

Paul Speaks to the Ephesian Elders

17 From Miletus he sent a message to Ephesus, asking the elders of the church to meet him. ¹⁸When they came to him, he said to them:

"You yourselves know how I lived among you the entire time from the first day that I set foot in Asia, ¹⁹serving the Lord with all humility and with tears, enduring the trials that came to me through the plots of the Jews. ²⁰I did not shrink from doing anything helpful, proclaiming the message to you and teaching you publicly and from house to house, ²¹as I testified to both Jews and Greeks about repentance toward God and faith toward our Lord Jesus. ²²And now, as a captive to the Spirit,ᵇ I am on my way to Jerusalem, not knowing what will happen to me there, ²³except that the Holy Spirit testifies to me in every city that imprisonment and persecutions are waiting for me. ²⁴But I do not count my life of any value to myself, if only I may finish my course and the ministry that I received from the Lord Jesus, to testify to the good news of God's grace.

25 "And now I know that none of you, among whom I have gone about proclaiming the kingdom, will ever see my face again. ²⁶Therefore I declare to you this day that I am not responsible for the blood of any of you, ²⁷for I did not shrink from declaring to you the whole purpose of God. ²⁸Keep watch over yourselves and over all the flock, of which the Holy Spirit has made you overseers, to shepherd the church of Godᶜ that he obtained with the blood of his own Son.ᵈ ²⁹I know that after I have gone, savage wolves will come in among you, not sparing the flock. ³⁰Some even from your own group will come distorting the truth in order to entice the disciples to follow them. ³¹Therefore be alert, remembering that for three years I did not cease night or day to warn everyone with tears. ³²And now I commend you to God and to the message of his grace, a message that is able to build you up and to give you the inheritance among all who are sanctified. ³³I coveted no one's silver or gold or clothing. ³⁴You know for yourselves that I worked with my own hands to support myself and my companions. ³⁵In all this I have given you an example that by such work we must support the weak, remembering the words of the Lord Jesus, for he himself said, 'It is more blessed to give than to receive.' "

36 When he had finished speaking, he knelt

---

a Other ancient authorities add *after remaining at Trogyllium*
b Or *And now, bound in the spirit*   c Other ancient authorities read *of the Lord*   d Or *with his own blood*; Gk *with the blood of his Own*

---

of the island of Lesbos in the Aegean. **20.15** *Chios,* an island in the Aegean south of Lesbos. *Samos,* an island in the Aegean southeast of Lesbos. *Miletus,* a large seaport in Ionia, on the southwest coast of Asia Minor. **20.16** On Paul's mission in *Ephesus,* see 18.18–19.41. See 19.21 for Paul's need to go to *Jerusalem. Pentecost* suggests Paul continues to observe Jewish customs. **20.17–38** Paul's farewell speech is his only speech to a Christian audience and his last speech prior to his arrest in Jerusalem. **20.17** *Elders of the church.* See 11.30; 14.23; 15.2; 16.4. **20.18–19** *Serving the Lord,* lit. "serving as a slave to the Lord." Paul describes his life among the Ephesians; see 19.1–41. **20.19** On *plots* against Paul, see note on 20.3. **20.20–21** A concise summary of Paul's mission. **20.22–23** Here *Jerusalem* appears for the first time to be a place of danger for Paul; cf. 19.21. Paul's imprisonment, like his ministry, occurs under the *Spirit's* guidance; see, e.g., 16.6–10; 19.21. *Imprisonment and persecutions.* See 9.16; 21.11, 33. **20.24** On Paul's willingness to die, see 21.13. The conversion accounts

(see 9.1–31; 22.3–21; 26.2–29) explain how Paul *received* his ministry. **20.25** The first clear indication that this is a farewell speech. **20.26** See note on 18.6. **20.28** *Overseers,* or "bishops" (see Phil 1.1; 1 Tim 3.1–7; Titus 1.7), but an activity, not an office, seems intended here. That the church came about through Jesus' *blood* is a new theme in Acts, but see Heb 9.12. **20.29–30** The threat of false teaching, whether from outside or inside the church, is a new theme in Acts, but see, e.g., Mt 7.15; 1 Tim 1.3–7; 4.1–3; 2 Tim 2.14–18. **20.29** In Lk 12.32, the disciples are the *flock;* cf. Jn 21.15–17; 1 Pet 5.2. **20.33** By contrast with others (e.g., 16.19; 19.25), Paul has no profit motive (see also 1 Cor 9). **20.34** On Paul's labor, see 18.2; his Letters reflect the same practice (1 Cor 4.12; 1 Thess 2.9). **20.35** *Support the weak* recalls 2.45; 4.32–35; 6.1–6. *It is more blessed to give than to receive.* The saying itself does not appear in the Gospels, but see Lk 6.38; see also Sir 4.31. Close parallels appear in Thucydides, *History of the Peloponnesian War* 2.97.4; Plutarch, *Moralia* 173d. **20.36–38** The emotional

down with them all and prayed. [37]There was much weeping among them all; they embraced Paul and kissed him, [38]grieving especially because of what he had said, that they would not see him again. Then they brought him to the ship.

Paul's Journey to Jerusalem

21 When we had parted from them and set sail, we came by a straight course to Cos, and the next day to Rhodes, and from there to Patara.[a] [2]When we found a ship bound for Phoenicia, we went on board and set sail. [3]We came in sight of Cyprus; and leaving it on our left, we sailed to Syria and landed at Tyre, because the ship was to unload its cargo there. [4]We looked up the disciples and stayed there for seven days. Through the Spirit they told Paul not to go on to Jerusalem. [5]When our days there were ended, we left and proceeded on our journey; and all of them, with wives and children, escorted us outside the city. There we knelt down on the beach and prayed [6]and said farewell to one another. Then we went on board the ship, and they returned home.

[7] When we had finished[b] the voyage from Tyre, we arrived at Ptolemais; and we greeted the believers[c] and stayed with them for one day. [8]The next day we left and came to Caesarea; and we went into the house of Philip the evangelist, one of the seven, and stayed with him. [9]He had four unmarried daughters[d] who had the gift of prophecy. [10]While we were staying there for several days, a prophet named Agabus came down from Judea. [11]He came to us and took Paul's belt, bound his own feet and hands with it, and said, "Thus says the Holy Spirit, 'This is the way the Jews in Jerusalem will bind the man who owns this belt and will hand him over to the Gentiles.' " [12]When we heard this, we and the people there urged him not to go up to Jerusalem. [13]Then Paul answered, "What are you doing, weeping and breaking my heart? For I am ready not only to be bound but even to die in Jerusalem for the name of the Lord Jesus." [14]Since he would not be persuaded, we remained silent except to say, "The Lord's will be done."

15 After these days we got ready and started to go up to Jerusalem. [16]Some of the disciples from Caesarea also came along and brought us to the house of Mnason of Cyprus, an early disciple, with whom we were to stay.

Paul Visits James at Jerusalem

17 When we arrived in Jerusalem, the brothers welcomed us warmly. [18]The next day Paul went with us to visit James; and all the elders were present. [19]After greeting them, he related one by one the things that God had done among the Gentiles through his ministry. [20]When they heard it, they praised God. Then they said to him, "You see, brother, how many thousands of believers there are among the

---

a Other ancient authorities add *and Myra*   *b* Or *continued*
c Gk *brothers*   *d* Gk *four daughters, virgins,*

---

farewell further anticipates Paul's death (see vv. 23–25). On the community at prayer, see 1.14; 2.42; 4.24–31; 13.3.
21.1–16 New anticipations of Paul's arrest mark the final stages of his journey to Jerusalem. **21.1–3** The route is around the southwestern perimeter of Asia Minor and then southeast to Tyre. *We.* See note on 16.10. **21.4** Nothing has been said of a mission in Tyre to account for the *disciples,* but see 11.19; 12.20; Lk 6.17; 10.13–14. Since Paul's decision to go to Jerusalem also came *through the Spirit* (19.21), this warning presumably reflects a fearful misinterpretation of the Spirit's message. **21.5–6** Cf. the farewell scene in 20.36–38. **21.7** *Ptolemais,* a major port city south of Tyre. Although nothing has been said of a mission there, see 11.19. **21.8** *Caesarea,* a port city south of Ptolemais, was the location of Cornelius's conversion (10.1, 24; 11.11; see also 9.30; 18.22). This is the first appearance of *Philip* since the conversion of the Ethiopian (8.26–40). **21.9** The detail about Philip's *daughters* is unusual, since they play no role in the story, but it recalls 2.17–18, the promise that both

women and men would prophesy. **21.10–11** *Agabus.* See 11.28; his dramatic action here recalls those of earlier prophets (see, e.g., Isa 20.2; Jer 13.1–11; Ezek 4.1–8). This prophecy contributes to the expectation that the trip to Jerusalem will have dire consequences for Paul (see note on 20.22–23). **21.13** On the trip to *Jerusalem,* see note on 19.21. Paul's declaration that he is prepared for death *for the name* recalls 9.16 as well as 2.21, 38; 3.6, 16; 4.7, 10; 5.41. **21.17–26** Paul receives a warm reception in Jerusalem, but also news of ominous charges against him that anticipate the fulfillment of 20.22–25, 38; 21.4, 11, 13. **21.18** The first reference to *James* since the Jerusalem council (15.13–21). **21.19** Luke consistently attributes the church's mission to *God;* see notes on 2.47; 8.26; 8.29; 10.1–11.18. **21.20–25** This brief speech prescribes a course of conduct to avert the charges against Paul. The charges themselves recall earlier charges against Stephen (6.11–14). **21.20** Paul here finds himself in conflict with Jewish Christians (cf. earlier conflicts with Jews and Gentiles; e.g., 13.45; 14.2; 16.20–21; 19.25–27). *Zealous for the law.* See 22.3; 1 Macc 2.27; Rom

Jews, and they are all zealous for the law. 21 They have been told about you that you teach all the Jews living among the Gentiles to forsake Moses, and that you tell them not to circumcise their children or observe the customs. 22 What then is to be done? They will certainly hear that you have come. 23 So do what we tell you. We have four men who are under a vow. 24 Join these men, go through the rite of purification with them, and pay for the shaving of their heads. Thus all will know that there is nothing in what they have been told about you, but that you yourself observe and guard the law. 25 But as for the Gentiles who have become believers, we have sent a letter with our judgment that they should abstain from what has been sacrificed to idols and from blood and from what is strangled*a* and from fornication." 26 Then Paul took the men, and the next day, having purified himself, he entered the temple with them, making public the completion of the days of purification when the sacrifice would be made for each of them.

Paul Arrested in the Temple

27 When the seven days were almost completed, the Jews from Asia, who had seen him in the temple, stirred up the whole crowd. They seized him, 28 shouting, "Fellow Israelites, help! This is the man who is teaching everyone everywhere against our people, our law, and this place; more than that, he has actually brought Greeks into the temple and has

defiled this holy place." 29 For they had previously seen Trophimus the Ephesian with him in the city, and they supposed that Paul had brought him into the temple. 30 Then all the city was aroused, and the people rushed together. They seized Paul and dragged him out of the temple, and immediately the doors were shut. 31 While they were trying to kill him, word came to the tribune of the cohort that all Jerusalem was in an uproar. 32 Immediately he took soldiers and centurions and ran down to them. When they saw the tribune and the soldiers, they stopped beating Paul. 33 Then the tribune came, arrested him, and ordered him to be bound with two chains; he inquired who he was and what he had done. 34 Some in the crowd shouted one thing, some another; and as he could not learn the facts because of the uproar, he ordered him to be brought into the barracks. 35 When Paul*b* came to the steps, the violence of the mob was so great that he had to be carried by the soldiers. 36 The crowd that followed kept shouting, "Away with him!"

Paul Defends Himself

37 Just as Paul was about to be brought into the barracks, he said to the tribune, "May I say something to you?" The tribune*c* replied, "Do you know Greek? 38 Then you are not the Egyptian who recently stirred up a revolt and led the four thousand assassins out into the

---

a Other ancient authorities lack *and from what is strangled*
b Gk *he*   *c* Gk *He*

10.2; Gal 1.14. **21.21** Unlike the dispute in Jerusalem, which concerned the demand that Gentiles obey the law, Jewish Christians claim that Paul dissuades Jews from observing the law. Although Paul's behavior in Acts does not support this claim, the question of Jewish-Christian law observance would inevitably arise as churches in the Diaspora incorporated both Jews and Gentiles (see note on 10.28). **21.23–24** Paul's own observance of the law, already established in the narrative (see 16.3; 18.18; 20.16), will serve as his defense. **21.25** See 15.20, 29. It is strange that the church leaders remind Paul of this decree, since he was present in Jerusalem, but repetition may remind Luke's audience that gentile Christians were liable to only a fraction of the law. **21.26** The *public* fulfillment of the vow enacts Paul's respect for Mosaic traditions, but it also sets the stage for the reaction that follows. **21.27–36** The events leading to Paul's arrest are not instigated by Jewish Christians, despite v. 20, but by the *Jews from Asia.* **21.28** The charges recall those against Stephen (6.13) and even those against Jesus (Mt 26.59–61; Mk 14.55–58; cf. Acts 18.13; 25.8). A Gentile who went be-

yond the temple's outer court could be put to death (Josephus, *War* 5.193–94; 6.124–26; *Antiquities* 15.417; Philo, *Embassy to Gaius* 212). The charge that Paul *brought Greeks into the temple* combines all the earlier charges (people, place, and law). **21.30–31** The mob's action recalls 7.57; 19.28–29, 32. The exaggerated references to *all the city* and *all Jerusalem* portray the danger. *Tribune of the cohort,* the military officer in charge. **21.33** *Two chains.* See 12.6; 21.11. The need to identify *what he had done* recurs in 22.30; 25.26. For the remainder of Acts, Paul is in custody. **21.34** On the crowd's confusion, see 19.32. **21.36** *Away with him!* See also 22.22; Lk 23.18; Jn 19.15.

21.37–22.21 A brief exchange with the tribune clarifies Paul's identity as an educated Jew and introduces his defense. **21.37** *Do you know Greek?* betrays the tribune's assumption that Paul is uneducated, since Greek was the *lingua franca.* **21.38** *The Egyptian,* the leader of a revolt against Rome ca. 52–59 CE; although the rebellion was quelled, the Egyptian leader escaped. Egyptians were often viewed with suspicion and condescension. See Strabo, *Geography* 17.1.12; Philo,

wilderness?" [39]Paul replied, "I am a Jew, from Tarsus in Cilicia, a citizen of an important city; I beg you, let me speak to the people." [40]When he had given him permission, Paul stood on the steps and motioned to the people for silence; and when there was a great hush, he addressed them in the Hebrew[a] language, saying:

22 "Brothers and fathers, listen to the defense that I now make before you."

2 When they heard him addressing them in Hebrew,[a] they became even more quiet. Then he said:

3 "I am a Jew, born in Tarsus in Cilicia, but brought up in this city at the feet of Gamaliel, educated strictly according to our ancestral law, being zealous for God, just as all of you are today. [4]I persecuted this Way up to the point of death by binding both men and women and putting them in prison, [5]as the high priest and the whole council of elders can testify about me. From them I also received letters to the brothers in Damascus, and I went there in order to bind those who were there and to bring them back to Jerusalem for punishment.

Paul Tells of His Conversion

6 "While I was on my way and approaching Damascus, about noon a great light from heaven suddenly shone about me. [7]I fell to the ground and heard a voice saying to me, 'Saul, Saul, why are you persecuting me?' [8]I answered, 'Who are you, Lord?' Then he said to me, 'I am Jesus of Nazareth[b] whom you are persecuting.' [9]Now those who were with me saw the light but did not hear the voice of the one who was speaking to me. [10]I asked, 'What am I to do, Lord?' The Lord said to me, 'Get up and go to Damascus; there you will be told everything that has been assigned to you to do.' [11]Since I could not see because of the brightness of that light, those who were with me took my hand and led me to Damascus.

12 "A certain Ananias, who was a devout man according to the law and well spoken of by all the Jews living there, [13]came to me; and standing beside me, he said, 'Brother Saul, regain your sight!' In that very hour I regained my sight and saw him. [14]Then he said, 'The God of our ancestors has chosen you to know his will, to see the Righteous One and to hear his own voice; [15]for you will be his witness to all the world of what you have seen and heard. [16]And now why do you delay? Get up, be baptized, and have your sins washed away, calling on his name.'

Paul Sent to the Gentiles

17 "After I had returned to Jerusalem and while I was praying in the temple, I fell into a trance [18]and saw Jesus[c] saying to me, 'Hurry and get out of Jerusalem quickly, because they will not accept your testimony about me.' [19]And I said, 'Lord, they themselves know that in every synagogue I imprisoned and beat

---

a That is, *Aramaic*   *b* Gk *the Nazorean*   *c* Gk *him*

Dreams 1.240; 2.255; *Allegorical Interpretation* 2.84; 3.13, 37–38, 81. **21.39** *I am . . . from Tarsus.* See note on 9.11; 22.3. It was possible to be a citizen of two cities, and Luke portrays Paul as a citizen of both Tarsus and Rome (see 16.37–38; 22.25). *The people.* See note on 3.11. **21.40** Motioning for *silence* is a characteristic gesture of an orator; see, e.g., 12.17; 13.16; 26.1. *In the Hebrew language,* i.e., in the Aramaic dialect. Paul's use of Aramaic signals his identification with this Jewish audience. **22.1–21** This account of Paul's conversion explains events from his own perspective (cf. 9.1–31) and, as part of his defense against Jewish accusers, Paul depicts himself as a loyal Jew who remains obedient to the God of Israel. **22.1** *Brothers and fathers* captures the audience's attention by signaling Paul's relationship to them (see 2.29; 7.2; 13.26; 15.7, 13). **22.2** *Hebrew.* See note on 21.40. **22.3** Paul identifies himself in terms congenial to this audience. *Born in Tarsus.* See notes on 9.11; 21.39. *Gamaliel.* See note on 5.34. *Zealous.* See note on 21.20. **22.4** *This Way.* See note on 9.1–2. **22.5** Cf. 9.2, which does not mention the *elders*.

22.6–11 See notes on 9.3–4; 9.5. **22.6** *About noon,* hence the light Paul saw was extremely bright (see 26.13; cf. 9.3). **22.9** Cf. 9.7, where Paul's companions do hear the voice; 26.14 could imply that they did not. **22.10** See 9.6; cf. 26.16–18, where the commission is more elaborate. **22.12–16** Ananias's objection to Paul, reported in 9.10–16, disappears here in favor of an additional statement concerning Paul's mission. **22.12** Paul describes Ananias in terms designed to appeal to a Jewish audience; cf. 9.10. **22.14** Even the expressions used for God and Jesus are calculated to win Jewish sympathy: *the God of our ancestors* (see Gen 43.23; 46.1; Ex 3.13; Deut 1.11) and *the Righteous One* (see 3.14; 7.52). **22.15** On *witness* as a prime characteristic of the church's activity, see note on 1.21–22. **22.16** See 2.38; cf. 9.18–19. **22.17–21** This scene, which appears in neither 9.1–31 nor 26.2–23, provides important confirmation of Paul's Jewish loyalty by situating him at prayer in the temple. **22.17** See 10.9–10, where Peter's vision comes while he is *praying.* **22.19** On Paul's activity as a persecutor, see 8.3;

those who believed in you. ²⁰And while the blood of your witness Stephen was shed, I myself was standing by, approving and keeping the coats of those who killed him.' ²¹Then he said to me, 'Go, for I will send you far away to the Gentiles.' "

Paul and the Roman Tribune

22 Up to this point they listened to him, but then they shouted, "Away with such a fellow from the earth! For he should not be allowed to live." ²³And while they were shouting, throwing off their cloaks, and tossing dust into the air, ²⁴the tribune directed that he was to be brought into the barracks, and ordered him to be examined by flogging, to find out the reason for this outcry against him. ²⁵But when they had tied him up with thongs,ᵃ Paul said to the centurion who was standing by, "Is it legal for you to flog a Roman citizen who is uncondemned?" ²⁶When the centurion heard that, he went to the tribune and said to him, "What are you about to do? This man is a Roman citizen." ²⁷The tribune came and asked Paul,ᵇ "Tell me, are you a Roman citizen?" And he said, "Yes." ²⁸The tribune answered, "It cost me a large sum of money to get my citizenship." Paul said, "But I was born a citizen." ²⁹Immediately those who were about to examine him drew back from him; and the tribune also was afraid, for he realized that Paul was a Roman citizen and that he had bound him.

Paul before the Council

30 Since he wanted to find out what Paulᶜ was being accused of by the Jews, the next day he released him and ordered the chief priests and the entire council to meet. He brought Paul down and had him stand before them.

23 While Paul was looking intently at the council he said, "Brothers,ᵈ up to this day I have lived my life with a clear conscience before God." ²Then the high priest Ananias ordered those standing near him to strike him on the mouth. ³At this Paul said to him, "God will strike you, you whitewashed wall! Are you sitting there to judge me according to the law, and yet in violation of the law you order me to be struck?" ⁴Those standing nearby said, "Do you dare to insult God's high priest?" ⁵And Paul said, "I did not realize, brothers, that he was high priest; for it is written, 'You shall not speak evil of a leader of your people.' "

6 When Paul noticed that some were Sadducees and others were Pharisees, he called out in the council, "Brothers, I am a Pharisee, a son of Pharisees. I am on trial concerning the hope of the resurrectionᵉ of the dead." ⁷When he said this, a dissension began between the Pharisees and the Sadducees, and the assembly was divided. ⁸(The Sadducees say that

---

a Or up for the lashes b Gk him c Gk he d Gk Men, brothers e Gk concerning hope and resurrection

---

9.1–2; 26.9–11. **22.20** See 7.58; 8.1. **22.21** For the first time the speech moves beyond the realm of the Jewish people and refers explicitly to Paul's mission among Gentiles (but see v. 15). **22.22–29** Apparently the reference to Gentiles (v. 21) triggers the repetition here of the cry in 21.36, this time intensified by the demand for Paul's death. **22.23** See 7.58; 22.20. **22.25** Paul dramatically invokes his *Roman* citizenship to prevent being flogged, but he also lays the foundation for his eventual confinement in Rome (see 25.10–12). Paul's question is rhetorical, as both Paul and the soldiers would have known the answer (see 16.37–39). **22.26–28** These exchanges reiterate Paul's status as a Roman citizen. **22.29** See 16.38.

22.30–23.11 Another attempt by the tribune to determine charges against Paul sets the stage for Paul's further defense of his Jewishness in his final speech in Jerusalem. **22.30** On the need to identify charges, see note on 21.33. That the tribune takes Paul before Jewish officials in order to arrive at charges suggests that the dispute is over internal Jewish concerns and not of interest to Rome (see 18.14–15; 26.30–31). There is little evidence on whether the tribune would have had authority to convene the chief priests and council, but

the scene places Paul before both Roman and Jewish audiences. **23.1** A concise summary of Paul's speech in 22.2–21. See 26.19; Phil 3.6. **23.2** *Ananias,* high priest beginning about 48 CE; he was assassinated at the outset of the Jewish revolt in 66 CE. **23.3** *Whitewashed wall.* See Ezek 13.10–16; Mt 23.27. Deut 19.16–19 requires that an accused person be confronted by an accuser directly and in the presence of a judge (see also Lev 19.15; Deut 1.16–17). **23.4–5** *I did not realize . . . he was high priest.* How Paul could have avoided recognizing the high priest is difficult to imagine. The question of v. 24 seems to dare Paul to speak openly of his contempt for the leadership, but he takes it instead as an opportunity to demonstrate his respect for scripture (he cites Ex 22.28). **23.6** That the council contained both *Sadducees* and *Pharisees* Paul would have known, but reference to this composition prompts a new phase in Paul's defense. Luke refers here for the first time to Paul's alignment with the Pharisees (see Phil 3.5); as in 5.33–39, they figure positively in the treatment of Christians. On one level, Paul's invoking Pharisaic belief in *the resurrection of the dead* (see v. 8) is a ploy that creates sympathy for himself; on a deeper level, however, reference to the resurrection is central to Chris-

there is no resurrection, or angel, or spirit; but the Pharisees acknowledge all three.) 9Then a great clamor arose, and certain scribes of the Pharisees' group stood up and contended, "We find nothing wrong with this man. What if a spirit or an angel has spoken to him?" 10When the dissension became violent, the tribune, fearing that they would tear Paul to pieces, ordered the soldiers to go down, take him by force, and bring him into the barracks.

11 That night the Lord stood near him and said, "Keep up your courage! For just as you have testified for me in Jerusalem, so you must bear witness also in Rome."

The Plot to Kill Paul

12 In the morning the Jews joined in a conspiracy and bound themselves by an oath neither to eat nor drink until they had killed Paul. 13There were more than forty who joined in this conspiracy. 14They went to the chief priests and elders and said, "We have strictly bound ourselves by an oath to taste no food until we have killed Paul. 15Now then, you and the council must notify the tribune to bring him down to you, on the pretext that you want to make a more thorough examination of his case. And we are ready to do away with him before he arrives."

16 Now the son of Paul's sister heard about the ambush; so he went and gained entrance to the barracks and told Paul. 17Paul called one of the centurions and said, "Take this young man to the tribune, for he has something to report to him." 18So he took him, brought him to the tribune, and said, "The prisoner Paul called me and asked me to bring this young man to you; he has something to tell you." 19The tribune took him by the hand, drew him aside privately, and asked, "What is it that you have to report to me?" 20He answered, "The Jews have agreed to ask you to bring Paul down to the council tomorrow, as though they were going to inquire more thoroughly into his case. 21But do not be persuaded by them, for more than forty of their men are lying in ambush for him. They have bound themselves by an oath neither to eat nor drink until they kill him. They are ready now and are waiting for your consent." 22So the tribune dismissed the young man, ordering him, "Tell no one that you have informed me of this."

Paul Sent to Felix the Governor

23 Then he summoned two of the centurions and said, "Get ready to leave by nine o'clock tonight for Caesarea with two hundred soldiers, seventy horsemen, and two hundred spearmen. 24Also provide mounts for Paul to ride, and take him safely to Felix the governor." 25He wrote a letter to this effect:

26 "Claudius Lysias to his Excellency the governor Felix, greetings. 27This man was seized by the Jews and was about to be killed by them, but when I had learned that he was a Roman citizen, I came with the guard and rescued him. 28Since I wanted to know the charge for which they accused him, I had him brought to their council. 29I found that he was accused concerning questions of their law, but was charged with nothing deserving death or imprisonment. 30When I was informed that there would be a plot against the man, I sent him to you at once, ordering his accusers also to state before you what they have against him.[a]"

31 So the soldiers, according to their in-

a Other ancient authorities add Farewell

---

tian preaching, and Paul introduces it as common ground. **23.8** Josephus confirms the dispute about resurrection but says nothing of a quarrel about the existence of angels or spirits (*War* 2.163–66; *Antiquities* 18.12–17). **23.11** *Jerusalem* and *Rome*. See note on 19.21. **23.12–35** Although there have been other plots against Paul (9.23–25, 29–30; 20.3, 19), this one is the most detailed, both in its planning and in the steps taken to overturn it. **23.16–22** Luke's elaboration of this scene (the report to Paul, calling the centurion, the full report to the tribune) enhances its dramatic impact. **23.16** Nothing else is known of the *son of Paul's sister*, nor is it clear how he might have been privy to the plot. **23.23** *Caesarea* is not only the capital of Judea but was prominent earlier in Acts. See 8.40; 10.1–

11.18; 12.19; 21.8, 16. *Two hundred soldiers . . . horsemen, and . . . spearmen*. This delegation, probably half the men at the tribune's command, seems improbably large, but tensions in first-century Palestine ran high. See Josephus, *Life* 200; *War* 2.224–31, 417–24; 4.128–34, 326–33; *Antiquities* 20.108–17. **23.24** *Felix the governor*, i.e., Antonius Felix, a freedman who governed Judea ca. 52–59 CE. Contemporary historians comment on his cruelty and immorality. See Tacitus, *History* 5.9. **23.26** *Claudius Lysias*, the tribune who has been unnamed to this point, delicately omits his involvement in Paul's mistreatment (see 21.31–38; 22.24–29). Although Lysias is protecting Paul from his enemies, he is also protecting himself. **23.28** On establishing the *charge* against Paul, see note on 21.33.

structions, took Paul and brought him during the night to Antipatris. 32The next day they let the horsemen go on with him, while they returned to the barracks. 33When they came to Caesarea and delivered the letter to the governor, they presented Paul also before him. 34On reading the letter, he asked what province he belonged to, and when he learned that he was from Cilicia, 35he said, "I will give you a hearing when your accusers arrive." Then he ordered that he be kept under guard in Herod's headquarters.*a*

Paul before Felix at Caesarea

24 Five days later the high priest Ananias came down with some elders and an attorney, a certain Tertullus, and they reported their case against Paul to the governor. 2When Paul*b* had been summoned, Tertullus began to accuse him, saying:

"Your Excellency,*c* because of you we have long enjoyed peace, and reforms have been made for this people because of your foresight. 3We welcome this in every way and everywhere with utmost gratitude. 4But, to detain you no further, I beg you to hear us briefly with your customary graciousness. 5We have, in fact, found this man a pestilent fellow, an agitator among all the Jews throughout the world, and a ringleader of the sect of the Nazarenes.*d* 6He even tried to profane the temple, and so we seized him.*e* 8By examining him yourself you will be able to learn from him concerning everything of which we accuse him."

9 The Jews also joined in the charge by asserting that all this was true.

Paul's Defense before Felix

10 When the governor motioned to him to speak, Paul replied:

"I cheerfully make my defense, knowing that for many years you have been a judge over this nation. 11As you can find out, it is not more than twelve days since I went up to worship in Jerusalem. 12They did not find me disputing with anyone in the temple or stirring up a crowd either in the synagogues or throughout the city. 13Neither can they prove to you the charge that they now bring against me. 14But this I admit to you, that according to the Way, which they call a sect, I worship the God of our ancestors, believing everything laid down according to the law or written in the prophets. 15I have a hope in God—a hope that they themselves also accept—that there will be a resurrection of both*f* the righteous and the unrighteous. 16Therefore I do my best always to have a clear conscience toward God and all people. 17Now after some years I came to bring alms to my nation and to offer sacrifices. 18While I was doing this, they found me in the temple, completing the rite of purification, without any crowd or disturbance. 19But there were some Jews from Asia—they ought to be here before you to make an accusation, if they have anything against me. 20Or let these men here tell what crime they had found when I stood before the council, 21unless it was this

a Gk praetorium   *b* Gk he   *c* Gk lacks Your Excellency
d Gk Nazoreans   *e* Other ancient authorities add *and we would have judged him according to our law.* 7But the chief captain Lysias came and with great violence took him out of our hands, 8commanding his accusers to come before you.   *f* Other ancient authorities read *of the dead, both of*

23.34 On *Cilicia* as Paul's home, see 22.3. **23.35** *Herod's headquarters,* i.e., the praetorium, the headquarters of the principal administrator of a region.

24.1–27 In a formal trial setting, Paul continues the defense begun in 22.3–21 by affirming both his innocence and his belief in the resurrection, this time for the Roman governor Felix. **24.1** *Ananias.* See note on 23.2. **24.2–4** Capturing the audience's attention by flattery was customary, but this introduction exceeds the norm (cf. v. 10; 26.2–3). Negative descriptions of Felix by ancient historians suggest that Tertullus's praise may be quite false (see note on 23.24). **24.5** Tertullus forcefully expresses charges already brought against Paul in a way calculated to play upon a Roman official's fear of rebellion (see 16.20; 17.6; 19.40; see also Lk 23.2–5). Only here in the NT are Christians referred to as *Nazarenes,* associating them with Jesus' home (see, e.g., 2.22; 3.6; 6.14; see also Mt 2.23).

24.6 See 21.28–29 for this erroneous charge. *And so we seized him* omits any reference to the riot in 21.27–36. **24.10–21** Paul's defense responds directly to the charges before returning to the themes of 22.3–21. **24.10** Like Tertullus, Paul also begins by flattering Felix (see note on 24.2–4). **24.12** On Paul's behavior in Jerusalem, see 21.17–30. **24.14** *Admit* can refer to a judicial confession or to a confession of faith; here Paul uses that ambiguity by offering what appears to be a confession of wrongdoing and then shifting the topic dramatically. What follows summarizes his remarks in 22.3–21; 23.6. *The Way.* See note on 9.1–2. **24.15** *Resurrection.* See note on 23.6. **24.16** *A clear conscience.* See note on 23.1. **24.17** *Alms to my nation* may allude to the collection Paul gathered for the Jerusalem church (see Rom 15.25–28; 1 Cor 16.1–4; 2 Cor 8–9; Gal 2.10), but this would be an unusual way to describe it. **24.19** *Some Jews from Asia.* See 21.27.

one sentence that I called out while standing before them, 'It is about the resurrection of the dead that I am on trial before you today.' "

22 But Felix, who was rather well informed about the Way, adjourned the hearing with the comment, "When Lysias the tribune comes down, I will decide your case." 23 Then he ordered the centurion to keep him in custody, but to let him have some liberty and not to prevent any of his friends from taking care of his needs.

Paul Held in Custody

24 Some days later when Felix came with his wife Drusilla, who was Jewish, he sent for Paul and heard him speak concerning faith in Christ Jesus. 25 And as he discussed justice, self-control, and the coming judgment, Felix became frightened and said, "Go away for the present; when I have an opportunity, I will send for you." 26 At the same time he hoped that money would be given him by Paul, and for that reason he used to send for him very often and converse with him.

27 After two years had passed, Felix was succeeded by Porcius Festus; and since he wanted to grant the Jews a favor, Felix left Paul in prison.

Paul Appeals to the Emperor

25 Three days after Festus had arrived in the province, he went up from Caesarea to Jerusalem 2 where the chief priests and the leaders of the Jews gave him a report against Paul. They appealed to him 3 and requested, as a favor to them against Paul,[a] to have him transferred to Jerusalem. They were, in fact, planning an ambush to kill him along

the way. 4 Festus replied that Paul was being kept at Caesarea, and that he himself intended to go there shortly. 5 "So," he said, "let those of you who have the authority come down with me, and if there is anything wrong about the man, let them accuse him."

6 After he had stayed among them not more than eight or ten days, he went down to Caesarea; the next day he took his seat on the tribunal and ordered Paul to be brought. 7 When he arrived, the Jews who had gone down from Jerusalem surrounded him, bringing many serious charges against him, which they could not prove. 8 Paul said in his defense, "I have in no way committed an offense against the law of the Jews, or against the temple, or against the emperor." 9 But Festus, wishing to do the Jews a favor, asked Paul, "Do you wish to go up to Jerusalem and be tried there before me on these charges?" 10 Paul said, "I am appealing to the emperor's tribunal; this is where I should be tried. I have done no wrong to the Jews, as you very well know. 11 Now if I am in the wrong and have committed something for which I deserve to die, I am not trying to escape death; but if there is nothing to their charges against me, no one can turn me over to them. I appeal to the emperor." 12 Then Festus, after he had conferred with his council, replied, "You have appealed to the emperor; to the emperor you will go."

Festus Consults King Agrippa

13 After several days had passed, King Agrippa and Bernice arrived at Caesarea to welcome

a Gk him

24.21 See note on 23.6. **24.22** Felix's response seems benign, even generous, although the promised decision is not forthcoming. *The Way.* See note on 9.1–2. *Lysias the tribune.* See note on 23.26. **24.23** Letting *his friends take care of his needs* is not an act of generosity, since prisoners routinely relied on outsiders even for basic necessities. **24.24** *Drusilla,* the daughter of Herod Agrippa I, had previously been married to the Syrian Azizus of Emesa but had left him for Felix, who reportedly pursued her for her great beauty. **24.25** Reports concerning Felix's corruption and immorality suggest why he might have found Paul's words frightening (see note on 23.24). **24.27** *Porcius Festus* succeeded Felix and governed ca. 59–61 CE (see 25.1–27; 26.24–32). Felix not only acts out of greed (v. 26) but grants political *favors* (see also 25.9).
25.1–12 The arrival of Festus prompts another plot, another cycle of accusation and defense, and fi-

nally Paul's appeal to the emperor. **25.1** By contrast with Felix (24.27), Festus acts promptly to resolve Paul's situation. **25.2–3** This plan replays the plot in 23.12–35. **25.6** *Tribunal,* the judgment seat or bench. **25.7** See the earlier *charges* in 21.28; 24.5–6. **25.8** See Paul's earlier defense in 22.1–21; 23.1, 6; 24.10–21. *Against the emperor* refers to the charge that Paul has threatened the civil order (24.5). **25.9** Like his predecessor, Festus wishes to appease the powerful Jewish leadership (see 24.27). **25.10** The details of the law governing appeals at this time are obscure. Here what is assumed is not the right to appeal a verdict but the right to be moved to another venue. **25.12** The solemn repetition of Paul's appeal underscores its importance. **25.13–27** The arrival of Agrippa and Bernice sets the stage for the climactic defense of Paul and the pronouncement of his innocence. **25.13** *King Agrippa,* Herod Agrippa II, son of Herod Agrippa I (see note on

Festus. [14]Since they were staying there several days, Festus laid Paul's case before the king, saying, "There is a man here who was left in prison by Felix. [15]When I was in Jerusalem, the chief priests and the elders of the Jews informed me about him and asked for a sentence against him. [16]I told them that it was not the custom of the Romans to hand over anyone before the accused had met the accusers face to face and had been given an opportunity to make a defense against the charge. [17]So when they met here, I lost no time, but on the next day took my seat on the tribunal and ordered the man to be brought. [18]When the accusers stood up, they did not charge him with any of the crimes[a] that I was expecting. [19]Instead they had certain points of disagreement with him about their own religion and about a certain Jesus, who had died, but whom Paul asserted to be alive. [20]Since I was at a loss how to investigate these questions, I asked whether he wished to go to Jerusalem and be tried there on these charges.[b] [21]But when Paul had appealed to be kept in custody for the decision of his Imperial Majesty, I ordered him to be held until I could send him to the emperor." [22]Agrippa said to Festus, "I would like to hear the man myself." "Tomorrow," he said, "you will hear him."

Paul Brought before Agrippa

23 So on the next day Agrippa and Bernice came with great pomp, and they entered the audience hall with the military tribunes and the prominent men of the city. Then Festus gave the order and Paul was brought in. [24]And Festus said, "King Agrippa and all here present with us, you see this man about whom the whole Jewish community petitioned me, both in Jerusalem and here, shouting that he ought not to live any longer. [25]But I found that he had done nothing deserving death; and when he appealed to his Imperial Majesty, I decided to send him. [26]But I have nothing definite to write to our sovereign about him. Therefore I have brought him before all of you, and especially before you, King Agrippa, so that, after we have examined him, I may have something to write— [27]for it seems to me unreasonable to send a prisoner without indicating the charges against him."

Paul Defends Himself before Agrippa

26 Agrippa said to Paul, "You have permission to speak for yourself." Then Paul stretched out his hand and began to defend himself:

[2] "I consider myself fortunate that it is before you, King Agrippa, I am to make my defense today against all the accusations of the Jews, [3]because you are especially familiar with all the customs and controversies of the Jews; therefore I beg of you to listen to me patiently.

[4] "All the Jews know my way of life from my youth, a life spent from the beginning among my own people and in Jerusalem. [5]They have known for a long time, if they are willing to testify, that I have belonged to the strictest sect of our religion and lived as a Pharisee. [6]And now I stand here on trial on account of my hope in the promise made by God to our ancestors, [7]a promise that our twelve tribes hope to attain, as they earnestly worship day and night. It is for this hope, your Excellency,[c] that I am accused by Jews! [8]Why is it thought incredible by any of you that God raises the dead?

---

a Other ancient authorities read *with anything*   b Gk *on them*   c Gk *O king*

12.1; "The Herods: A Simplified Family Tree," p. 1672). Because of his youth, Agrippa II did not succeed his father immediately, but by 50 CE he ruled the small region of Chalcis in Lebanon and later acquired considerable territory. His incestuous relationship with *Bernice*, his sister, was widely reported. Bernice later went to Rome in the company of the emperor Titus. **25.14–21** Festus's statement summarizes the events of 24.27–25.12, although with several changes: he states that the Jews asked for a verdict (25.15; cf. 25.2–3); he concedes the rightness of Paul's defense (25.18–19); and he omits his political reasons for proposing that Paul be tried in Jerusalem (25.20; cf. 25.9). **25.23** The formality of this setting prepares for Paul's final defense speech. **25.24** *The whole Jewish community*, another instance of Lukan hyperbole (see, e.g., 4.4, 16).

25.25 *Nothing deserving death*. See 23.29; 25.18; 26.31; see also Lk 23.15, 22. **25.26–27** On the need for specific *charges*, see note on 21.33.

26.1–32 Paul's final defense speech, combining themes from the speeches in 22.1–21; 24.10–21, begins with a claim to Jewish loyalty, rehearses once again Paul's conversion with special emphasis on his commission, and concludes with an assertion of Paul's obedience. **26.1** *Stretched out his hand*, a conventional orator's gesture (see 12.17; 13.16; 21.40). **26.2–3** On the tradition of opening a speech with praise for the audience, see note on 24.2–4. **26.4–5** See 22.3; 23.6. *My own people* and *our religion* imply that Paul does not regard Agrippa as one of those people (cf. 22.3). **26.6–8** See 23.6; 24.15. Resurrection is not simply the renewal of individual life but a symbol of all of God's

9 "Indeed, I myself was convinced that I ought to do many things against the name of Jesus of Nazareth.[a] 10 And that is what I did in Jerusalem; with authority received from the chief priests, I not only locked up many of the saints in prison, but I also cast my vote against them when they were being condemned to death. 11 By punishing them often in all the synagogues I tried to force them to blaspheme; and since I was so furiously enraged at them, I pursued them even to foreign cities.

Paul Tells of His Conversion

12 "With this in mind, I was traveling to Damascus with the authority and commission of the chief priests, 13 when at midday along the road, your Excellency,[b] I saw a light from heaven, brighter than the sun, shining around me and my companions. 14 When we had all fallen to the ground, I heard a voice saying to me in the Hebrew[c] language, 'Saul, Saul, why are you persecuting me? It hurts you to kick against the goads.' 15 I asked, 'Who are you, Lord?' The Lord answered, 'I am Jesus whom you are persecuting. 16 But get up and stand on your feet; for I have appeared to you for this purpose, to appoint you to serve and testify to the things in which you have seen me[d] and to those in which I will appear to you. 17 I will rescue you from your people and from the Gentiles—to whom I am sending you 18 to open their eyes so that they may turn from darkness to light and from the power of Satan to God, so that they may receive forgiveness of sins and a place among those who are sanctified by faith in me.'

Paul Tells of His Preaching

19 "After that, King Agrippa, I was not disobedient to the heavenly vision, 20 but declared first to those in Damascus, then in Jerusalem and throughout the countryside of Judea, and also to the Gentiles, that they should repent and turn to God and do deeds consistent with repentance. 21 For this reason the Jews seized me in the temple and tried to kill me. 22 To this day I have had help from God, and so I stand here, testifying to both small and great, saying nothing but what the prophets and Moses said would take place: 23 that the Messiah[e] must suffer, and that, by being the first to rise from the dead, he would proclaim light both to our people and to the Gentiles."

Paul Appeals to Agrippa to Believe

24 While he was making this defense, Festus exclaimed, "You are out of your mind, Paul! Too much learning is driving you insane!" 25 But Paul said, "I am not out of my mind, most excellent Festus, but I am speaking the sober truth. 26 Indeed the king knows about these things, and to him I speak freely; for I am certain that none of these things has escaped his notice, for this was not done in a corner. 27 King Agrippa, do you believe the prophets? I know that you believe." 28 Agrippa said to Paul, "Are you so quickly persuading me to become a Christian?"[f] 29 Paul replied, "Whether quickly or not, I pray to God that not only you but also all who are listening to me today might become such as I am—except for these chains."

30 Then the king got up, and with him the governor and Bernice and those who had been seated with them; 31 and as they were leaving, they said to one another, "This man is doing

---

a Gk the Nazorean   b Gk O king   c That is, Aramaic
d Other ancient authorities read the things that you have seen
e Or the Christ   f Or Quickly you will persuade me to play the Christian

---

promises to Israel and thus a theme throughout Luke-Acts. **26.9–11** This final depiction of Paul's activity as persecutor portrays it in much harsher terms than previously (cf. 8.1, 3; 9.1–2; 22.4–5). **26.13** See 9.3; 22.6. **26.14** In the Hebrew language, a detail not present in earlier accounts (cf. 9.4; 22.7). It hurts you to kick against the goads, also not present in earlier accounts, is from Euripides (Bacchae 794–95), although it had become a conventional proverb. **26.16–18** Here Paul receives his commission directly from Jesus (cf. 9.6, 15–16; 22.14–16). **26.17** I will rescue you. See 1 Chr 16.35; Jer 1.8, 19. **26.18** Turning from darkness to light, also a conventional expression for gentile conversion (see, e.g., 13.47; Lk 1.79; 2.32; note on 9.35). **26.20** See 9.19–22, 26–30; 13.46–49. **26.21** See 21.27–36. **26.22** Paul here resumes the argument of 26.6–8. **26.23** The Messiah must suffer. The necessity of the Messiah's death and resurrection is a key Lukan theme; see 3.18, 21–25; 8.32–35; Lk 24.26. Light plays a prominent role in this speech (vv. 13, 18), as it does elsewhere in Luke-Acts (e.g., 9.3; 12.7; 13.47; Lk 2.32; 8.16; 11.3). **26.24** You are out of your mind. Exactly what leads Festus to this conclusion is unclear, but his comment allows for the solemn assertion that follows. **26.26** Not done in a corner, i.e., these events have occurred in the open (see note on 12.18–19). **26.28** Agrippa's statement could be either an ironic insult or a straightforward comment on Paul's persuasiveness. **26.31** Agrippa, Bernice, and

nothing to deserve death or imprisonment." [32]Agrippa said to Festus, "This man could have been set free if he had not appealed to the emperor."

Paul Sails for Rome

27 When it was decided that we were to sail for Italy, they transferred Paul and some other prisoners to a centurion of the Augustan Cohort, named Julius. [2]Embarking on a ship of Adramyttium that was about to set sail to the ports along the coast of Asia, we put to sea, accompanied by Aristarchus, a Macedonian from Thessalonica. [3]The next day we put in at Sidon; and Julius treated Paul kindly, and allowed him to go to his friends to be cared for. [4]Putting out to sea from there, we sailed under the lee of Cyprus, because the winds were against us. [5]After we had sailed across the sea that is off Cilicia and Pamphylia, we came to Myra in Lycia. [6]There the centurion found an Alexandrian ship bound for Italy and put us on board. [7]We sailed slowly for a number of days and arrived with difficulty off Cnidus, and as the wind was against us, we sailed under the lee of Crete off Salmone. [8]Sailing past it with difficulty, we came to a place called Fair Havens, near the city of Lasea.

[9] Since much time had been lost and sailing was now dangerous, because even the Fast had already gone by, Paul advised them, [10]saying, "Sirs, I can see that the voyage will be with danger and much heavy loss, not only of the cargo and the ship, but also of our lives." [11]But the centurion paid more attention to the pilot and to the owner of the ship than to what Paul said. [12]Since the harbor was not suitable for spending the winter, the majority was in favor of putting to sea from there, on the chance that somehow they could reach Phoenix, where they could spend the winter. It was a harbor of Crete, facing southwest and northwest.

The Storm at Sea

[13] When a moderate south wind began to blow, they thought they could achieve their purpose; so they weighed anchor and began to sail past Crete, close to the shore. [14]But soon a violent wind, called the northeaster, rushed down from Crete.[a] [15]Since the ship was caught and could not be turned head-on into the wind, we gave way to it and were driven. [16]By running under the lee of a small island called Cauda[b] we were scarcely able to get the ship's boat under control. [17]After hoisting it up they took measures[c] to undergird the ship; then, fearing that they would run on the Syrtis, they lowered the sea anchor and so were driven. [18]We were being pounded by the storm so violently that on the next day they began to throw the cargo overboard, [19]and on the third day with their own hands they threw the ship's tackle overboard. [20]When neither sun nor stars appeared for many days, and no small tempest raged, all hope of our being saved was at last abandoned.

---

a Gk *it*   *b* Other ancient authorities read *Clauda*   *c* Gk *helps*

Festus together confirm the conclusion of Lysias (23.29). **26.32** The details of the law regarding appeals are obscure (see note on 25.10), but this pronouncement determines what lies ahead for Paul.

27.1–44 Paul's long-anticipated journey to Rome (see 19.21; 23.11) contains elements familiar from Greco-Roman literature: travel accounts, storms, shipwrecks, and the resulting preoccupation with safety. **27.1** The use of first-person plural narration (*we*) resumes and continues through 28.16; see note on 16.10. *Augustan Cohort*, named after the emperor Augustus, who died in 14 CE. **27.2** *Adramyttium*, a port on the northwest coast of Asia Minor, in the region of Mysia. *Aristarchus*. See note on 19.29. **27.3** *Sidon*, a Phoenician city north of Caesarea. **27.4** Sailing to the north and east of the island of Cyprus afforded protection from westerly winds. **27.5** The route moves west along the southern districts (Cilicia, Pamphylia, Lycia) of Asia Minor. **27.6** *Ship*, probably a grain ship (see v. 38); Rome imported much grain from Egypt. **27.7** *Cnidus*, a small island off the southwest coast of Asia Minor. *Salmone*, a cape at the northeastern extreme of Crete. **27.8** *Fair Havens* and *Lasea* are on the southern coast of Crete. After this point the ship would be in open waters without the protection of the island. **27.9** *The Fast*, the Day of Atonement, the tenth of Tishri (September/October). Voyages after mid-September were considered unwise because of the increased danger of bad weather. **27.10** It seems improbable that a prisoner would have been included in such deliberations. Together with the difficulties with the winds already noted in vv. 4–8, Paul's advice serves as a prophetic warning. **27.16** *Cauda*, south of Crete to the west of Fair Havens. *The ship's boat*, i.e., the lifeboat. **27.17** It is not clear what *undergirding* entailed. The *Syrtis*, two dangerous bays between Cyrene and Carthage on the northern coast of Africa. **27.20** With *neither sun nor stars*, the ship had no navigational guides. *No small tempest*. See note on 12.18–19. **27.21–26** Paul's brief

21 Since they had been without food for a long time, Paul then stood up among them and said, "Men, you should have listened to me and not have set sail from Crete and thereby avoided this damage and loss. 22I urge you now to keep up your courage, for there will be no loss of life among you, but only of the ship. 23For last night there stood by me an angel of the God to whom I belong and whom I worship, 24and he said, 'Do not be afraid, Paul; you must stand before the emperor; and indeed, God has granted safety to all those who are sailing with you.' 25So keep up your courage, men, for I have faith in God that it will be exactly as I have been told. 26But we will have to run aground on some island."

27 When the fourteenth night had come, as we were drifting across the sea of Adria, about midnight the sailors suspected that they were nearing land. 28So they took soundings and found twenty fathoms; a little farther on they took soundings again and found fifteen fathoms. 29Fearing that we might run on the rocks, they let down four anchors from the stern and prayed for day to come. 30But when the sailors tried to escape from the ship and had lowered the boat into the sea, on the pretext of putting out anchors from the bow, 31Paul said to the centurion and the soldiers, "Unless these men stay in the ship, you cannot be saved." 32Then the soldiers cut away the ropes of the boat and set it adrift.

33 Just before daybreak, Paul urged all of them to take some food, saying, "Today is the fourteenth day that you have been in suspense and remaining without food, having eaten nothing. 34Therefore I urge you to take some food, for it will help you survive; for none of you will lose a hair from your heads." 35After he had said this, he took bread; and giving thanks to God in the presence of all, he broke it and began to eat. 36Then all of them were encouraged and took food for themselves. 37(We were in all two hundred seventy-six[a]

persons in the ship.) 38After they had satisfied their hunger, they lightened the ship by throwing the wheat into the sea.

The Shipwreck

39 In the morning they did not recognize the land, but they noticed a bay with a beach, on which they planned to run the ship ashore, if they could. 40So they cast off the anchors and left them in the sea. At the same time they loosened the ropes that tied the steering-oars; then hoisting the foresail to the wind, they made for the beach. 41But striking a reef,[b] they ran the ship aground; the bow stuck and remained immovable, but the stern was being broken up by the force of the waves. 42The soldiers' plan was to kill the prisoners, so that none might swim away and escape; 43but the centurion, wishing to save Paul, kept them from carrying out their plan. He ordered those who could swim to jump overboard first and make for the land, 44and the rest to follow, some on planks and others on pieces of the ship. And so it was that all were brought safely to land.

Paul on the Island of Malta

28 After we had reached safety, we then learned that the island was called Malta. 2The natives showed us unusual kindness. Since it had begun to rain and was cold, they kindled a fire and welcomed all of us around it. 3Paul had gathered a bundle of brushwood and was putting it on the fire, when a viper, driven out by the heat, fastened itself on his hand. 4When the natives saw the creature hanging from his hand, they said to one another, "This man must be a murderer; though he has escaped from the sea, justice has not allowed him to live." 5He, however, shook off the creature into the fire and suffered no

a Other ancient authorities read *seventy-six*; others, *about seventy-six* b Gk *place of two seas*

speech recalls his earlier warning (v. 10) and interprets the ship's eventual safety as part of God's plan for Paul's mission (19.21; 23.11). **27.21** *Without food* refers to seasickness or fasting, as food was available (vv. 33–38). **27.23** *The God . . . I worship* identifies God for Paul's gentile fellow passengers. **27.24** *You must stand before the emperor.* See 9.15; 19.21; 23.11. Although Luke does not narrate Paul's trial before Caesar (see note on 28.30–31), he must have known that it occurred. **27.27** *The sea of Adria,* i.e., the Adriatic Sea.

27.33 *Take some food.* See note on 27.21. **27.34** See 1 Sam 14.45; 1 Kings 1.52; Lk 21.18. **27.35–36** There may be echoes of the Eucharist here (see Lk 22.19), although the separate meals of those present make any intentional reference unlikely. **27.39–44** Paul's earlier predictions are realized (see vv. 22, 24, 26, 34).

28.1–10 On Malta, Paul and his companions find exemplary hospitality and return it by healing the sick. **28.1** *Malta,* an island south of Sicily. **28.4** *Justice,* probably the Greek goddess, Dike, who personifies justice.

harm. 6They were expecting him to swell up or drop dead, but after they had waited a long time and saw that nothing unusual had happened to him, they changed their minds and began to say that he was a god.

7 Now in the neighborhood of that place were lands belonging to the leading man of the island, named Publius, who received us and entertained us hospitably for three days. 8It so happened that the father of Publius lay sick in bed with fever and dysentery. Paul visited him and cured him by praying and putting his hands on him. 9After this happened, the rest of the people on the island who had diseases also came and were cured. 10They bestowed many honors on us, and when we were about to sail, they put on board all the provisions we needed.

Paul Arrives at Rome

11 Three months later we set sail on a ship that had wintered at the island, an Alexandrian ship with the Twin Brothers as its figurehead. 12We put in at Syracuse and stayed there for three days; 13then we weighed anchor and came to Rhegium. After one day there a south wind sprang up, and on the second day we came to Puteoli. 14There we found believers*a* and were invited to stay with them for seven days. And so we came to Rome. 15The believers*a* from there, when they heard of us, came as far as the Forum of Appius and Three Taverns to meet us. On seeing them, Paul thanked God and took courage.

16 When we came into Rome, Paul was allowed to live by himself, with the soldier who was guarding him.

Paul and Jewish Leaders in Rome

17 Three days later he called together the local leaders of the Jews. When they had assembled, he said to them, "Brothers, though I had done nothing against our people or the customs of our ancestors, yet I was arrested in Jerusalem and handed over to the Romans. 18When they had examined me, the Romans*b* wanted to release me, because there was no reason for the death penalty in my case. 19But when the Jews objected, I was compelled to appeal to the emperor—even though I had no charge to bring against my nation. 20For this reason therefore I have asked to see you and speak with you,*c* since it is for the sake of the hope of Israel that I am bound with this chain." 21They replied, "We have received no letters from Judea about you, and none of the brothers coming here has reported or spoken anything evil about you. 22But we would like to hear from you what you think, for with regard to this sect we know that everywhere it is spoken against."

Paul Preaches in Rome

23 After they had set a day to meet with him, they came to him at his lodgings in great numbers. From morning until evening he explained the matter to them, testifying to the kingdom of God and trying to convince them about Jesus both from the law of Moses and from the prophets. 24Some were convinced by what he had said, while others refused to believe. 25So they disagreed with each other; and as they were leaving, Paul made one further statement: "The Holy Spirit was right in saying to your ancestors through the prophet Isaiah,
26 'Go to this people and say,
You will indeed listen, but never
     understand,
   and you will indeed look, but never
     perceive.

---

a Gk brothers *b* Gk they *c* Or I have asked you to see me and speak with me

---

28.11–16 The final part of Paul's journey to Rome recalls the much longer journey to Jerusalem in 20.1–21.17, with its travelogue and visits with believers. **28.11** *Three months later.* Sailing resumed in February or March (see note on 27.9). *An Alexandrian ship.* See note on 27.6. *Twin Brothers,* i.e., Castor and Pollux, sons of Zeus who are associated with safety on the *seas.* **28.12–13** The route (Syracuse to Rhegium to Puteoli) is along the eastern coast of Sicily and then along the western coast of Italy to the port of Puteoli, west of Naples. **28.14–15** The presence of *believers* in Puteoli and Rome indicates that Paul was not the first to preach the gospel there (see Rom 1.13). **28.15** The

Forum of Appius, a market town forty-three miles outside Rome. *Three Taverns,* a way station thirty-three miles from Rome along the Appian Way. **28.17–28** The final scene in Acts depicts Paul first defending himself before Roman Jews and then proclaiming to them the gospel. **28.17–20** Paul's speech recapitulates his earlier defense in Jerusalem: he had not violated the Jewish people or their customs (22.3–21; 24.11–13); he was charged with no capital crime (25.8, 11); he was compelled to appeal to the emperor (25.10–12); he acts only for the sake of Israel's hope (23.6; 24.14–15, 21; 26.6–8, 23). **28.23** *Kingdom of God.* See note on 1.3. *From the law of Moses and from the proph-*

27 For this people's heart has grown dull,
     and their ears are hard of hearing,
     and they have shut their eyes;
     so that they might not look with
       their eyes,
     and listen with their ears,
     and understand with their heart and
       turn—
     and I would heal them.'
28 Let it be known to you then that this salvation of God has been sent to the Gentiles; they
will listen." [a]

30 He lived there two whole years at his
own expense [b] and welcomed all who came to
him, 31 proclaiming the kingdom of God and
teaching about the Lord Jesus Christ with all
boldness and without hindrance.

---

a Other ancient authorities add verse 29, *And when he had said
these words, the Jews departed, arguing vigorously among
themselves*   *b* Or *in his own hired dwelling*

---

ets recalls Lk 24.27; see also Lk 24.44; Acts 3.18; 24.14;
26.22. **28.24** As elsewhere, Christian proclamation receives a mixed reaction; see, e.g., 13.43–45; 17.4–5.
28.26–27 See Isa 6.9–10 (Septuagint). **28.28** The announcement of God's *salvation* recalls the opening of
Luke-Acts (Lk 2.30–32; 3.6). This is the third time
Paul has announced that the gospel is for the *Gentiles*
(see 13.46–48; 18.5–6). Since this final statement
comes in the concluding lines of Acts, it may indeed
refer to the close of the Jewish mission; on the other
hand, the two earlier pronouncements are followed by
further preaching among Jews, and v. 30 indicates Paul
welcomed all who came to him, leaving open the possibility of further conversation. **28.30–31** Although
Luke does not narrate Paul's trial or death, he has provided ample indication that they lie ahead (see, e.g.,
19.21; 20.22–25; 23.11; 26.32; 27.24). He concludes
with a brief note about Paul's continued imprisonment, in which the gospel is nevertheless openly proclaimed. **28.31** *Kingdom of God.* See note on 1.3. On
boldness as a characteristic of Christian witness, see
note on 4.13.

Possible Chronology of the Pauline Letters

Letter	Date	Notes
1 Thessalonians	50–51 CE	
[2 Thessalonians]	[50–51, if authentic]	If pseudonymous, in the last decades of the first century.
Philippians	54–55	This dating assumes that the Letter was sent from Ephesus. If from Caesarea, three to four years later, and if from Rome, six to seven years later.
Philemon	54–55	This Letter seems to have been written under the same circumstances as Philippians, and the same uncertainties apply.
Galatians	50–56	Any closer dating depends in part on resolving the question of the location of the addressees.
1 Corinthians	54	
2 Corinthians	55–56	It is likely that different portions of the Letter were written and sent at different times within this period.
Romans	56–57	
[Colossians]	[57–61, if authentic]	Earlier in this period if from Caesarea, later if from Rome. If pseudonymous, sometime between 70 and 90.
[Ephesians]	[80–95]	Assuming pseudonymity.
[1–2 Timothy, Titus]	[90–110]	Assuming pseudonymity.

Brackets indicate that authorship by Paul is in question.

The Letter of Paul to the

ROMANS

BY 58 CE PAUL THOUGHT that his mission in the Aegean region was completed (15.23). Now only one thing remained: going to Jerusalem to deliver funds collected from his churches, as agreed at the Jerusalem council a decade before (Gal 2.1–10). Before leaving Greece he dictated this Letter to Tertius (16.22) and probably asked Phoebe, who was about to leave for Rome (16.1–2), to deliver it. He informed the readers that after going to Jerusalem he would stop in Rome on his way to Spain, where he would begin a new mission. Because of his foreboding about his reception in Jerusalem, he asked the recipients to support him with prayer; he also hinted that he would welcome their financial support for his work in Spain (1.8–15; 15.22–33).

The Roman Church

THE ORIGINS OF CHRISTIANITY in Rome are obscure, though some evidence suggests that it had arrived there by 50 CE. The historian Suetonius reports that in 49 the emperor Claudius expelled Jews from Rome because of disturbances over "Chrestus" (probably a mistake for "Christus," or Christ; *Life of Claudius* 25.3). According to Acts 18.1–3, in Corinth Paul met a Jewish Christian couple, Aquila and Priscilla, who were among those expelled. After the murder of Claudius in 54 CE, presumably the Jews returned, among them Aquila and Prisca (as Paul calls her; see Rom 16.3–4). Acts tells us nothing more about Roman Christianity, except that Christians from Rome met Paul as he neared that city as a prisoner (28.15–16)—the unforeseen result of going to Jerusalem (Acts 21.17–25.12).

Purposes

ALTHOUGH THE LETTER WAS SENT to people mostly still unknown to Paul, it provides clues about Christians in Rome that may indicate something about his purposes in writing. Apparently there were tensions between the Christian Gentiles and the returned Christian Jews—tensions that would inhibit the desired support for the new mission in Spain. In chs. 14–15 he addresses the "weak in faith" (the scrupulous in observing special days and diets) and "the strong" (the lax in such matters), but he does not say that the former are Jews and the latter Gentiles. So the extent to which Paul's counsels have in view the specific situation in Rome is not clear. More serious theologically was the danger that Paul's whole mission was being misinterpreted, on the one hand by Christian Jews who may have inferred that in going to Gentiles he was turning his back on his own people (see 10.1), and on the other by Christian Gentiles who apparently inferred that, because most Jews were rejecting the gospel, God had rejected the Jews (see 11.1–6). Thus when Paul sent this Letter, he faced opposite misunderstandings of the gospel: in Jerusalem he needed to defend the validity of his predominantly gentile churches, whose money he was bringing and who did not observe the Jewish law; in Rome he needed to defend the continuing validity of Israel in God's purpose (the current Jewish rejection of the gospel did not imply that Israel's election was now annulled, 11.13–24). His Letter, therefore, insists that there is one gospel for all humanity, albeit "to the Jew first" (1.16).

Character of the Letter

ROMANS—PAUL'S MOST SUSTAINED THEOLOGICAL ARGUMENT—is the work of a mature mind. Indeed, it might be the last Letter we have from Paul (assuming Philippians was written earlier and the Pastorals are pseudonymous). Behind it lie over two decades of teaching, preaching, and writing letters to deal with problems that had arisen in the churches he had founded. The Letter to the Galatians is closest to Romans, for it also emphasizes justification by faith, appeals to Abraham, and relies heavily on scripture. But the two Letters treat these topics somewhat differently; in Galatians Paul contends with rival interpretations of the gospel, whereas in Romans he presents the larger rationale of his gospel. Romans is not, however, a summary of Paul's thought. Important themes are either absent (e.g., the Lord's Supper) or mentioned only in passing (e.g., "church" appears only in ch. 16).

The Letter's opening (1.1–7) is followed by the customary paragraph of thanksgiving (1.8–15), which leads into a statement commonly seen as the theological theme (1.16–17). The theological argument (1.18–11.36) has two parts: 1.18–8.39 develops the meaning of God's righteousness, and chs. 9–11 focus on the meaning of Israel. Although chs. 9–11 are a discrete unit, they are neither an excursus nor an appendage, but an integral part of the argument in which Paul's view of God's righteousness is applied to the election of Israel. The admonitions (12.1–15.13) also have two parts. The first (chs. 12–13) discusses various matters; the second (14.1–15.13) addresses the "weak" and the "strong." The rest of ch. 15 reflects on Paul's work and travel plans. Thus the personal matters discussed in 1.1–15 and in 15.14–33 are a frame around the theological and ethical core (1.16–15.13). Ch. 16 consists mostly of greetings and the concluding doxology. Some have argued that the final chapter was a letter originally sent to Ephesus but later attached to Romans. Indeed, shorter editions of Romans did once exist. Rom 15.33 resembles a conclusion, and one manuscript actually has 16.25–27 at this point, while a number of others have it at the end of ch. 14. Rather than being a later addition, however, ch. 16 is more likely an original part of Romans that was omitted when a few manuscripts abbreviated the Letter for general church use (and omitted the reference to Rome in 1.7).

The study of Romans has concentrated on Paul's ideas (e.g., justification, grace, law), but recent work has turned also to his use of ancient rhetoric and to the ways in which the OT functions in his argument. Just as he uses conventions of ancient letter writing, so he uses Greco-Roman rhetorical techniques and Jewish exegetical methods to develop his argument, which is in effect a discourse intended to be read aloud. What gives Romans its depth and power, however, is the rigor of Paul's own thought, which these conventions help him to express effectively.

[LEANDER E. KECK]

Salutation

1 Paul, a servant[a] of Jesus Christ, called to be an apostle, set apart for the gospel of God, 2which he promised beforehand through his prophets in the holy scriptures, 3the gospel concerning his Son, who was descended from David according to the flesh 4and was declared to be Son of God with power according to the spirit[b] of holiness by resurrection from the dead, Jesus Christ our Lord, 5through whom we have received grace and apostleship to bring about the obedience of faith among all the Gentiles for the sake of his name, 6including yourselves who are called to belong to Jesus Christ,

7 To all God's beloved in Rome, who are called to be saints:

Grace to you and peace from God our Father and the Lord Jesus Christ.

Prayer of Thanksgiving

8 First, I thank my God through Jesus Christ for all of you, because your faith is proclaimed throughout the world. 9For God, whom I serve with my spirit by announcing the gospel[c] of his Son, is my witness that without ceasing I remember you always in my prayers, 10asking that by God's will I may somehow at last succeed in coming to you. 11For I am longing to see you so that I may share with you some spiritual gift to strengthen you— 12or rather so that we may be mutually encouraged by each other's faith, both yours and mine. 13I want you to know, brothers and sisters,[d] that I have often intended to come to you (but thus far have been prevented), in order that I may reap some harvest among you as I have among the rest of the Gentiles. 14I am a debtor both to Greeks and to barbarians, both to the wise and to the foolish 15—hence my eagerness to proclaim the gospel to you also who are in Rome.

The Power of the Gospel

16 For I am not ashamed of the gospel; it is the power of God for salvation to everyone who has faith, to the Jew first and also to the Greek. 17For in it the righteousness of God is revealed through faith for faith; as it is written, "The one who is righteous will live by faith."[e]

The Guilt of Humankind

18 For the wrath of God is revealed from heaven against all ungodliness and wickedness of those who by their wickedness suppress the

a Gk slave   b Or Spirit   c Gk my spirit in the gospel
d Gk brothers   e Or The one who is righteous through faith will live

1.1–7 To introduce himself, Paul expands the conventional salutation (writer, reader, greeting) with a summary of his gospel. **1.1** *Servant* (lit. "slave"). A slave is at the disposition of the owner, here *Christ;* see also 6.16–22; 12.11; 14.18; 16.18; Gal 1.10; Phil 1.1. *Apostle,* an emissary. **1.2** *Prophets,* probably generally the writers of the *scriptures,* which are the OT. **1.3–4** Paul probably quotes a confession, perhaps known in Rome, that viewed Jesus as the Son of David who was installed into the office of Son of God by his resurrection (see Acts 13.33); others think Paul simply uses traditional ideas. Paul himself believed that God's preexisting Son became Jesus; see 2 Cor 8.9; Phil 2.6–11. **1.4** *Spirit of holiness* (a phrase found only here in the NT), probably the Holy Spirit (see text note *b*). **1.5** *Obedience of faith,* obedience grounded in and shaped by faith. See 16.26. On Paul's mission to the *Gentiles,* see v. 13; 11.13; 15.16; Gal 2.1–10. **1.7** In the NT all Christians, not only outstanding ones, are *saints* (lit. "holy ones"). A few manuscripts omit "in Rome" (see Introduction). **1.8–15** A paragraph expressing gratitude to God for some aspect of the readers' faith and life is a standard element in Paul's Letters following the salutation. **1.8** *Faith,* here not the readers' personal trust in God but the presence of Christian faith in Rome. *Throughout the world* should not be taken literally. **1.13** See Acts 19.21–22. **1.14** *Greeks and . . . bar-barians,* a traditional Greek way of classifying people, means all people; *wise and . . . foolish* means the same. The language should not be pressed; Paul is simply establishing rapport with the readers. **1.16–17** The theme of the Letter. **1.16** *I am not ashamed,* probably a stylistic understatement meaning "I am proud of." On the *power of God,* see v. 20; 9.17; 1 Cor 1.18, 24; 2.5; 6.14. On the special status of *the Jew,* see 2.9–10; 3.1–2; chs. 9–11; cf. 3.9. *First* can refer to either a temporal or a theological priority. **1.17** *The righteousness* (or "justice") *of God,* a key theme in Romans; see 3.21–26; 10.3; see also Pss 31.1; 35.24; 71.2; Isa 45.8, 21; 46.13 ("deliverance"); 51.8. Here Paul understands it to mean the divine rectitude that rectifies (makes right) the relation between the Creator and the unrighteous person who believes the gospel. *Is revealed* (lit. "is being revealed"). The passive voice implies that God, not Paul, is doing the revealing. *Faith,* rendered *faithfulness* in 3.3, so its meaning here is not obvious. Perhaps *through faith* refers to God's faithfulness and *for faith* to the human response to it. The quotation (Hab 2.4) does not agree exactly with either the Hebrew or the Greek text; it may be Paul's own rendering (see text note *e*).

1.18–3.20 In this argument, carefully designed to lead up to the conclusion in 3.20, Paul shows that the gospel, which brings salvation to everyone who be-

truth. ¹⁹For what can be known about God is plain to them, because God has shown it to them. ²⁰Ever since the creation of the world his eternal power and divine nature, invisible though they are, have been understood and seen through the things he has made. So they are without excuse; ²¹for though they knew God, they did not honor him as God or give thanks to him, but they became futile in their thinking, and their senseless minds were darkened. ²²Claiming to be wise, they became fools; ²³and they exchanged the glory of the immortal God for images resembling a mortal human being or birds or four-footed animals or reptiles.

24 Therefore God gave them up in the lusts of their hearts to impurity, to the degrading of their bodies among themselves, ²⁵because they exchanged the truth about God for a lie and worshiped and served the creature rather than the Creator, who is blessed forever! Amen.

26 For this reason God gave them up to degrading passions. Their women exchanged natural intercourse for unnatural, ²⁷and in the same way also the men, giving up natural intercourse with women, were consumed with passion for one another. Men committed shameless acts with men and received in their own persons the due penalty for their error.

28 And since they did not see fit to acknowledge God, God gave them up to a debased mind and to things that should not be done. ²⁹They were filled with every kind of wickedness, evil, covetousness, malice. Full of envy, murder, strife, deceit, craftiness, they are gossips, ³⁰slanderers, God-haters,ᵃ insolent, haughty, boastful, inventors of evil, rebellious toward parents, ³¹foolish, faithless, heartless, ruthless. ³²They know God's decree, that those who practice such things deserve to die—yet they not only do them but even applaud others who practice them.

The Righteous Judgment of God

2 Therefore you have no excuse, whoever you are, when you judge others; for in passing judgment on another you condemn yourself, because you, the judge, are doing the very same things. ²You say,ᵇ "We know that God's judgment on those who do such things is in accordance with truth." ³Do you imagine, who-

a Or God-hated b Gk lacks You say

---

lieves it (v. 16), deals with a dilemma shared by all humans, whether they are Jews or Gentiles (see also 3.23; 10.12). **1.18–32** An indictment of Gentiles. **1.18** *The wrath of God,* God's rightful response to what humans have done; see also 2.5, 8; 3.5; 4.15; 5.9; 9.22; 12.19; 13.5. *Is revealed.* See note on 1.17. *Ungodliness* refers to the relationship between God and humans, *wickedness* (lit. "unrighteousness") to human relationships, as in the two tables of the Decalogue (see Ex 20.2–17). The *truth* about God's identity (see v. 19) is suppressed by wickedness because human behavior reflects what persons take God to be and stand for. **1.19** *Because God has shown it to them* nullifies an excuse of ignorance (v. 20). **1.20** That one could infer the *invisible* Creator from the created world was a familiar idea in Paul's time; see Wis 13.1–9. **1.21** The refusal to *honor* (lit. "glorify") God *as God* is humanity's root sin; cf. 15.6, 9; 1 Cor 6.20; 2 Cor 9.13. *They became futile,* lit. "they were made futile" (by God). **1.22–32** These verses clearly refer to Gentiles, as seen from the standpoint of Jewish horror of idolatry (Deut 4.16–18), but cf. Ps 106.20; Jer 2.11. **1.22** *They became fools,* lit. "they were made foolish" (by God). **1.24–25** The first of three expositions of the same point (see also vv. 26, 28): from idolatry follow all sorts of moral confusions (see Wis 13–15). *God gave them up* (lit. "handed them over") to those confusions, i.e., allowed immoralities to gain control. Thus the immoralities are themselves the symptoms of God's wrath, which is now disclosed by the gospel (see v. 18). **1.26–27** Some think that Paul here condemns homosexual acts by heterosexual people (i.e., *unnatural* means "unnatural for them"); others that he condemns pederasty (sexual activity between adult men and boys). It is questionable whether Paul thought of homosexuality as a condition or a disposition (see also 1 Cor 6.9). The repetition of the word *exchanged* (see v. 25) is deliberate: moral confusion follows idolatry, as Jewish thought had long maintained (see Wis 14.12). **1.28** *They did not see fit . . . a debased mind.* Paul's pun resists translation; reading *debased* as "unfit" conveys the idea. **1.29–31** Lists of vices (and of virtues) were common in Paul's day; see Gal 5.19–23; Col 3.5, 8; 1 Tim 1.9–10; 6.4; 2 Tim 3.2–4; Titus 3.3; 1 Pet 4.3. The order within the list is rhetorical. **1.32** The Greek word translated *decree* suggests "right verdict." On *deserve to die,* see 6.23; see also 5.12–21; Gen 3. Paul is not calling for capital punishment.

2.1–16 An indictment of the person who judges others (cf. 1.32). It is unlikely that here Paul thinks of the Jews, to whom he turns in v. 17. **2.1–5** Paul changes to the diatribe style, writing as if confronting an individual with a truth that demands a response. This was a well-established way of teaching used by philosophical schools as well as by traveling teachers such as Paul himself. **2.1** The judge is *doing the very same things* because all sins, whether gross or minor, express the same root sin (1.21). **2.2** The quotation

ever you are, that when you judge those who do such things and yet do them yourself, you will escape the judgment of God? 4Or do you despise the riches of his kindness and forbearance and patience? Do you not realize that God's kindness is meant to lead you to repentance? 5But by your hard and impenitent heart you are storing up wrath for yourself on the day of wrath, when God's righteous judgment will be revealed. 6For he will repay according to each one's deeds: 7to those who by patiently doing good seek for glory and honor and immortality, he will give eternal life; 8while for those who are self-seeking and who obey not the truth but wickedness, there will be wrath and fury. 9There will be anguish and distress for everyone who does evil, the Jew first and also the Greek, 10but glory and honor and peace for everyone who does good, the Jew first and also the Greek. 11For God shows no partiality.

12 All who have sinned apart from the law will also perish apart from the law, and all who have sinned under the law will be judged by the law. 13For it is not the hearers of the law who are righteous in God's sight, but the doers of the law who will be justified. 14When Gentiles, who do not possess the law, do instinctively what the law requires, these, though not having the law, are a law to themselves. 15They show that what the law requires is written on their hearts, to which their own conscience also bears witness; and their conflicting thoughts will accuse or perhaps excuse them 16on the day when, according to my gospel, God, through Jesus Christ, will judge the secret thoughts of all.

The Jews and the Law

17 But if you call yourself a Jew and rely on the law and boast of your relation to God 18and know his will and determine what is best because you are instructed in the law, 19and if you are sure that you are a guide to the blind, a light to those who are in darkness, 20a corrector of the foolish, a teacher of children, having in the law the embodiment of knowledge and truth, 21you, then, that teach others, will you not teach yourself? While you preach against stealing, do you steal? 22You that forbid adultery, do you commit adultery? You that abhor idols, do you rob temples? 23You that boast in the law, do you dishonor God by breaking the law? 24For, as it is written, "The name of God is blasphemed among the Gentiles because of you."

25 Circumcision indeed is of value if you obey the law; but if you break the law, your circumcision has become uncircumcision. 26So, if those who are uncircumcised keep the requirements of the law, will not their uncircumcision be regarded as circumcision? 27Then those who are physically uncircumcised but keep the law will condemn you that have the written code and circumcision but break the law. 28For a person is not a Jew who is one outwardly, nor is true circumcision something external and physical. 29Rather, a person is a Jew who is one inwardly, and real circumcision is a matter of the heart—it is spiritual and not literal. Such a person receives praise not from others but from God.

---

marks are inferred (see text note *b* on p. 1912). **2.4** One of Paul's rare references to *repentance;* see 2 Cor 7.9–10; 12.21. **2.5** The motif of *the day of wrath* ("the last judgment") is anchored deeply in the Bible; Paul refers to it often (5.9; 12.19; 13.4–5; 14.10; 1 Cor 4.4–5; 11.31–32; 2 Cor 5.10; 1 Thess 1.9–10). God's *judgment will be revealed* as the confirmation and final recompense of the wrath already being revealed (1.18). **2.6–16** Paul returns to the discursive style, which develops an idea in order to persuade. **2.6** This saying appears in various contexts; see Ps 62.12; Prov 24.12; Mt 16.27; 2 Cor 11.15; 2 Tim 4.14. **2.9–10** God will punish *the Jew first* (see also note on 1.16), because with priority in status goes priority in judgment. *The Greek,* i.e., the Gentile. **2.11** The impartiality of God's judgment is basic for the whole argument in 1.18–3.20. **2.12** The difference between *will . . . perish* and *will be judged* is more stylistic than substantial. Those who live *under the law* are the Jews. **2.13** To be *righteous in God's sight* and to be *justified* (declared to be in the right) are the same. See note

on 3.20. **2.14** *Instinctively* (lit. "by nature") interprets the Greek as the manner in which Gentiles obey the law; the wording more likely reflects the fact that Gentiles do not possess the Jewish law "by nature." **2.15** The idea of a *conscience,* an inner judge of one's deeds, implies a standard, a "law" to which Gentiles are accountable; whether Paul alludes to Jer 31.33 is debated. It is unlikely that here and in v. 14 Paul thinks of the Christian Gentiles. **2.17–29** Not an indictment of Judaism or all Jews, but of the arrogant Jew in vv. 17–24 who does not see the contradiction between privileged status and actual performance. In vv. 17–24 Paul uses the diatribe style. **2.24** See Isa 52.5; Ezek 36.20. **2.25** *Circumcision,* the sign of the Jews' covenant with God (see Gen 17.1–14). According to rabbinic thought, all Jews (except apostates) will share in the "world to come" because God honors the covenant commitment and has provided atonement for sins. God's impartiality (v. 11) underlies the argument in vv. 25–29. **2.29** *Circumcision . . . of the heart.* See Deut 10.16.

3 Then what advantage has the Jew? Or what is the value of circumcision? 2Much, in every way. For in the first place the Jews[a] were entrusted with the oracles of God. 3What if some were unfaithful? Will their faithlessness nullify the faithfulness of God? 4By no means! Although everyone is a liar, let God be proved true, as it is written,

"So that you may be justified in your words,
and prevail in your judging."[b]

5But if our injustice serves to confirm the justice of God, what should we say? That God is unjust to inflict wrath on us? (I speak in a human way.) 6By no means! For then how could God judge the world? 7But if through my falsehood God's truthfulness abounds to his glory, why am I still being condemned as a sinner? 8And why not say (as some people slander us by saying that we say), "Let us do evil so that good may come"? Their condemnation is deserved!

None Is Righteous

9 What then? Are we any better off?[c] No, not at all; for we have already charged that all, both Jews and Greeks, are under the power of sin, 10as it is written:

"There is no one who is righteous, not even one;
11   there is no one who has understanding,

there is no one who seeks God.
12 All have turned aside, together they have become worthless;
there is no one who shows kindness, there is not even one."
13 "Their throats are opened graves; they use their tongues to deceive."
"The venom of vipers is under their lips."
14 "Their mouths are full of cursing and bitterness."
15 "Their feet are swift to shed blood;
16   ruin and misery are in their paths,
17   and the way of peace they have not known."
18 "There is no fear of God before their eyes."

19 Now we know that whatever the law says, it speaks to those who are under the law, so that every mouth may be silenced, and the whole world may be held accountable to God. 20For "no human being will be justified in his sight" by deeds prescribed by the law, for through the law comes the knowledge of sin.

Righteousness through Faith

21 But now, apart from law, the righteousness of God has been disclosed, and is attested by the law and the prophets, 22the righteousness of God through faith in Jesus Christ[d] for all

a Gk they b Gk when you are being judged c Or at any disadvantage? d Or through the faith of Jesus Christ

---

3.1–8 Returning to the diatribe style, Paul responds to objections from the Jew portrayed in vv. 17–24. 3.2 The oracles of God, i.e., scripture. See 2.17–18. 3.4 Everyone is a liar. See Ps 116.11. The quotation is from Ps 51.4. 3.8 Some people. It is not known who is accusing Paul. 3.9–20 Paul concludes the indictment, supporting his claim by citing a chain of OT passages probably collected previously. 3.9 Are we any better off? The question paraphrases v. 1, though there is a tension between the answers provided. With the alternate translation (see text note c), Paul denies that the Jew is either better or worse off than the Gentile (see vv. 22–23). Under the power of sin (lit. "under sin") introduces a view of sin developed in chs. 6–7. 3.10 A paraphrase of Eccl 7.20. 3.11–12 See Ps 14.2–3. 3.13 See Pss 5.9; 140.3. 3.14 See Ps 10.7. 3.15–17 See Isa 59.7–8. 3.18 See Ps 36.1. 3.19 Under the law. See 2.12. So that expresses result, not intent. Every mouth may be silenced includes the Jew in the same situation as the Gentile (vv. 22–23; 10.12). 3.20 No human . . . his sight. See Ps 143.2, here paraphrased (see also Gal 2.16). Justified, here vindicated or acquitted, as in a trial. The tension between this verse and 2.13 is more apparent than real, because the fact of universal sin means that no one has

the righteousness required by the law. Knowledge of sin is explained in 7.7–12; law not only specifies what sin is but makes one aware of failure to achieve what is required. 3.21–31 Having indicted all humanity (1.18–3.20), Paul now states the solution: in Christ, God's righteousness itself rectifies the relationship between God and humans. 3.21–26 This passage is theologically dense and syntactically awkward (smoothed in translation), either because Paul cites and modifies a piece of Christian tradition (variously identified), or because he probably inserts a parenthesis, For there is no distinction . . . a gift (vv. 22–24), designed to recall 1.18–3.20. Apart from the parenthesis, God's righteousness has been disclosed (v. 21) in three ways: (a) through the faithfulness of Jesus Christ (see text note d; v. 22); (b) through the redemption (v. 24); (c) through ("by") the faithfulness (of Jesus) evidenced in his blood (i.e., his violent death, v. 25). The dual purpose of this disclosure is stated in v. 25 (show) and v. 26 (prove, lit. "for the demonstration of"). 3.21 Apart from law means not according to the reward-and-punishment logic of law. Attested (lit. "witnessed") by the law and the prophets. See, e.g., 1.2, 17. The law and the prophets, OT scripture as a whole. 3.22 Through faith in Jesus

who believe. For there is no distinction, [23]since all have sinned and fall short of the glory of God; [24]they are now justified by his grace as a gift, through the redemption that is in Christ Jesus, [25]whom God put forward as a sacrifice of atonement[a] by his blood, effective through faith. He did this to show his righteousness, because in his divine forbearance he had passed over the sins previously committed; [26]it was to prove at the present time that he himself is righteous and that he justifies the one who has faith in Jesus.[b]

27 Then what becomes of boasting? It is excluded. By what law? By that of works? No, but by the law of faith. [28]For we hold that a person is justified by faith apart from works prescribed by the law. [29]Or is God the God of Jews only? Is he not the God of Gentiles also? Yes, of Gentiles also, [30]since God is one; and he will justify the circumcised on the ground of faith and the uncircumcised through that same faith. [31]Do we then overthrow the law by this faith? By no means! On the contrary, we uphold the law.

The Example of Abraham

4 What then are we to say was gained by[c] Abraham, our ancestor according to the flesh? [2]For if Abraham was justified by works, he has something to boast about, but not before God. [3]For what does the scripture say? "Abraham believed God, and it was reckoned to him as righteousness." [4]Now to one who works, wages are not reckoned as a gift but as something due. [5]But to one who without works trusts him who justifies the ungodly, such faith is reckoned as righteousness. [6]So also David speaks of the blessedness of those to whom God reckons righteousness apart from works:

[7] "Blessed are those whose iniquities are
       forgiven,
   and whose sins are covered;
[8] blessed is the one against whom the Lord
       will not reckon sin."

9 Is this blessedness, then, pronounced only on the circumcised, or also on the uncircumcised? We say, "Faith was reckoned to Abraham as righteousness." [10]How then was it reckoned to him? Was it before or after he had been circumcised? It was not after, but before he was circumcised. [11]He received the sign of circumcision as a seal of the righteousness that he had by faith while he was still uncircumcised. The purpose was to make him the ancestor of all who believe without being circumcised and who thus have righteousness reckoned to them, [12]and likewise the ancestor of the circumcised who are not only circumcised but who also follow the example of the faith that our ancestor Abraham had before he was circumcised.

---

a Or *a place of atonement* *b* Or *who has the faith of Jesus*
c Other ancient authorities read *say about*

Christ. The alternate translation (text note *d* on p. 1914) is closer to the Greek, though "faithfulness" is preferable (see note on 1.17; see also note on 3.26). **3.23** In Jewish tradition the *glory of God* was taken from Adam after his sin; Paul implies that future salvation will restore it (see 5.2; 8.18). **3.24** *Redemption,* not a common word in Paul's writings, means the freeing of someone or something from being held hostage; see also Gal 3.13; 4.5. **3.25** *Sacrifice of atonement,* Greek *hilasterion,* rendered "the mercy seat" in Lev 16.13–15 (Septuagint), hence *place of atonement* in text note *a*. Cf. Heb 9.5. **3.26** *The one who has faith in Jesus,* or "the one who lives by the faithfulness of Jesus"; see note on 3.22. **3.27–31** Paul returns to the diatribe style (see 2.1–5). **3.27** *Boasting,* either pride in achieving what the law requires (see 4.1–2) or pride in the possession of the law as a sign of God's favor (2.17, 23). *The law of faith,* the principle or rationale of faith. **3.30** *God is one,* an allusion to Deut 6.4. Given God's impartiality (2.11), the same human plight calls for the same solution. **3.31** That justification by faith actually *upholds* the law (i.e., scripture) is argued in ch. 4.

4.1–25 The Abraham story (Gen 12–17) provides evidence that faith justifies, i.e., makes the relation to God right. In vv. 1–12 Abraham exemplifies the thesis stated in 3.28; in vv. 13–25 Paul applies this thesis to all who believe the gospel. **4.1** *Our ancestor* (lit. "father") *according to the flesh* acknowledges Abraham as the biological starting point of the Jewish people. **4.2** Abraham cannot boast *before God* (in accord with 2.29) because he did not earn his relation to God, which was the result of God's choice. **4.3** Gen 15.6 (used also in Gal 3.6; Jas 2.23 draws a different conclusion from the quotation). *Believed.* See note on 4.5. **4.4** *Reckoned,* a commercial term suggesting payment, here contrasted with justification as a *gift* (see 3.24). **4.5** *Trusts* renders the same Greek word translated *believed* in v. 3. *Him who justifies* (i.e., "rectifies") *the ungodly* expresses Paul's radical understanding of God; the *ungodly* includes everyone (3.19–20, 23). **4.6–8** Like Jewish interpreters who interpreted one passage by citing another using the same key word, here Paul supports his view of Genesis by quoting Ps 32.1–2, which also uses the word *reckon.* **4.9–12** Paul assumes that what is true of the ancestor is true of the descendants, here *all who believe without being circumcised* (v. 11). **4.9** See Gen 15.6. **4.10** *Before.* Abraham's circumcision is not mentioned until Gen 17.10–27, well after Gen 15.6.

God's Promise Realized through Faith

13 For the promise that he would inherit the world did not come to Abraham or to his descendants through the law but through the righteousness of faith. 14 If it is the adherents of the law who are to be the heirs, faith is null and the promise is void. 15 For the law brings wrath; but where there is no law, neither is there violation.

16 For this reason it depends on faith, in order that the promise may rest on grace and be guaranteed to all his descendants, not only to the adherents of the law but also to those who share the faith of Abraham (for he is the father of all of us, 17 as it is written, "I have made you the father of many nations")—in the presence of the God in whom he believed, who gives life to the dead and calls into existence the things that do not exist. 18 Hoping against hope, he believed that he would become "the father of many nations," according to what was said, "So numerous shall your descendants be." 19 He did not weaken in faith when he considered his own body, which was already*a* as good as dead (for he was about a hundred years old), or when he considered the barrenness of Sarah's womb. 20 No distrust made him waver concerning the promise of God, but he grew strong in his faith as he gave glory to God, 21 being fully convinced that God was able to do what he had promised. 22 Therefore his faith*b* "was reckoned to him as righteousness." 23 Now the words, "it was reckoned to him," were written not for his sake alone, 24 but for ours also. It will be reckoned to us who believe in him who raised Jesus our Lord from the dead, 25 who was handed over to death for our trespasses and was raised for our justification.

Results of Justification

5 Therefore, since we are justified by faith, we*c* have peace with God through our Lord Jesus Christ, 2 through whom we have obtained access*d* to this grace in which we stand; and we*e* boast in our hope of sharing the glory of God. 3 And not only that, but we*e* also boast in our sufferings, knowing that suffering produces endurance, 4 and endurance produces character, and character produces hope, 5 and hope does not disappoint us, because God's love has been poured into our hearts through the Holy Spirit that has been given to us.

6 For while we were still weak, at the right time Christ died for the ungodly. 7 Indeed, rarely will anyone die for a righteous person—though perhaps for a good person someone might actually dare to die. 8 But God proves his love for us in that while we still were sinners Christ died for us. 9 Much more surely then, now that we have been justified by his blood, will we be saved through him from the wrath of God.*f* 10 For if while we were enemies, we were reconciled to God through the death of his Son, much more surely, having been reconciled, will we be saved by his life. 11 But more than that, we even boast in God through our Lord Jesus Christ, through whom we have now received reconciliation.

---

a Other ancient authorities lack *already*   *b* Gk *Therefore it*   *c* Other ancient authorities read *let us*   *d* Other ancient authorities add *by faith*   *e* Or *let us*   *f* Gk *the wrath*

4.13 The idea that Abraham *would inherit the world* reflects Jewish interpretation of Gen 12.6–7. Sir 44.19–21 says he inherited the earth because he kept the law. **4.15** *Wrath.* See note on 1.18. For a different consequence of law, see 3.20. **4.17** *I . . . nations.* See Gen 17.5. *Who gives life to the dead* alludes to Jesus' resurrection (4.24) and to the birth of Isaac (4.19). *Calls into existence . . . do not exist.* The belief that God created out of nothing (*creatio ex nihilo*) was common in Hellenistic Judaism. See 2 Macc 7.28. **4.18** See Gen 15.5. **4.20** In giving *glory to God,* Abraham did the opposite of humanity's root sin (1.21). 1 Macc 2.61 also associates strength with trust. **4.22** Another quotation of Gen 15.6 (see vv. 3, 9). **4.25** Perhaps a known formulation in which *who* replaces an original "he."

5.1–11 A transitional passage linking 1.18–4.25 to the themes in chs. 6, 8. **5.2** *Boasting,* criticized in 2.17 and excluded by 3.27, is acceptable here because of what God has done; see also v. 11. *Hope* signals the fu- turity of salvation (see also v. 10), developed in 8.18–25. The *glory of God* is what humanity now lacks; see 3.23. **5.3** *In our sufferings* might mean in the midst of or because of present sufferings or allude to the sufferings expected at the end of history; see also 8.35; 12.12; 2 Cor 11.21–30. **5.5** *Does not disappoint,* lit. "does not make ashamed," i.e., at the final judgment. The *Holy Spirit* (see 1.4) is a major theme in ch. 8. **5.6** *The ungodly.* See note on 4.5. **5.7** *A good person,* or "a good thing." **5.8** Whereas key passages like 1.3–4 and 3.21–26 are complex because Paul may have used (and modified) traditions or traditional expressions, here he states his gospel in a simple sentence. *For us,* for our sakes or for our benefit, not in our place; similarly 5.6. **5.9** *By his blood* views Christ's death as a sacrifice (see 3.25). *The wrath of God* (lit. *the wrath;* see text note *f*). See notes on 1.18; 2.5. **5.10** *Reconciled,* virtually synonymous with "justified"; see also 2 Cor 5.18–19. **5.11** *Boast in God,* boast because of God; see note on

Adam and Christ

12 Therefore, just as sin came into the world through one man, and death came through sin, and so death spread to all because all have sinned— 13sin was indeed in the world before the law, but sin is not reckoned when there is no law. 14Yet death exercised dominion from Adam to Moses, even over those whose sins were not like the transgression of Adam, who is a type of the one who was to come.

15 But the free gift is not like the trespass. For if the many died through the one man's trespass, much more surely have the grace of God and the free gift in the grace of the one man, Jesus Christ, abounded for the many. 16And the free gift is not like the effect of the one man's sin. For the judgment following one trespass brought condemnation, but the free gift following many trespasses brings justification. 17If, because of the one man's trespass, death exercised dominion through that one, much more surely will those who receive the abundance of grace and the free gift of righteousness exercise dominion in life through the one man, Jesus Christ.

18 Therefore just as one man's trespass led to condemnation for all, so one man's act of righteousness leads to justification and life for all. 19For just as by the one man's disobedience the many were made sinners, so by the one man's obedience the many will be made righteous. 20But law came in, with the result that the trespass multiplied; but where sin increased, grace abounded all the more, 21so that, just as sin exercised dominion in death, so grace might also exercise dominion through justification*a* leading to eternal life through Jesus Christ our Lord.

Dying and Rising with Christ

6 What then are we to say? Should we continue in sin in order that grace may abound? 2By no means! How can we who died to sin go on living in it? 3Do you not know that all of us who have been baptized into Christ Jesus were baptized into his death? 4Therefore we have been buried with him by baptism into death, so that, just as Christ was raised from the dead by the glory of the Father, so we too might walk in newness of life.

5 For if we have been united with him in a death like his, we will certainly be united with him in a resurrection like his. 6We know that our old self was crucified with him so that the

_____
a Or righteousness

5.2. **5.12–21** A discussion of Adam and Christ as individuals whose acts had opposite consequences for humanity (see v. 18), and who therefore stand at the heads of the old and new creations. Thus the passage prepares for the discussions in chs. 6–8, which emphasize participation in Christ. Paul's interpretation of Gen 3 is similar to those in Wis 2.24; 2 Esd 3.21, 26; *2 Apocalypse of Baruch* 54.15. Paul writes of Adam and Christ somewhat differently in 1 Cor 15.20–24, 42–49. **5.12** *One man.* Paul ignores Eve and infers from Gen 3.3, 19 that Adam's *sin* brought *death*, which *spread*, i.e., became an unavoidable condition; see also 1 Cor 15.21–26. The Greek word here translated *because* was translated by the Vulgate as "in whom," implying "in Adam"; that translation became influential for the doctrine of original sin. **5.13** See 4.15. **5.14** *Type*, a person or thing seen—in retrospect—as a pattern or model for later persons or events (see, e.g., 1 Cor 10.6; Phil 3.17). *The one who was to come*, Christ. Adam was in the pattern for Christ insofar as he stood at the head of the old creation, as Christ stands at the head of the new (Gal 6.14–15). **5.15–17** *Not like*. The rest of the passage explains the difference Paul has in view (see esp. v. 16). **5.17** *Death* is a hostile tyrant because, due to Adam's acts, everyone must die; cf. 6.9; 1 Cor 15.54–55. **5.18** *One man's* (Christ's) *act of righteousness* is the same as *one man's obedience* (v. 19) and probably alludes to "the faithfulness of Jesus" in (see

notes on) 3.22; 3.26. **5.20** *Law came in.* It entered the world at Sinai (v. 13). *Trespass multiplied* because the law specifies transgressions; see 3.20; 4.15. In 7.7–25, Paul argues that law cannot control sin or overcome it. **5.21** Like death (see v. 14), *sin exercised dominion;* death, sin, and *grace* are domains of power. For Paul, sin is not simply something a person does; rather, sin does something to the person: makes one subject to death (6.23).

6.1–14 Participation in Christ's death and resurrection overcomes the tyranny of sin and death. **6.1** Using the diatribe style (see 2.1–5), Paul rejects a misunderstanding of 5.20. *Continue in sin*, i.e., remain within its domain (5.21). **6.2** *Died to sin*, explained in vv. 5–11. *Living in* sin means living within its sphere of power (see v. 14). **6.3** *Do you not know* (see also v. 16; 7.1). Paul appeals to what the Roman Christians already know, that baptism is *into Christ Jesus* (see also 1 Cor 12.13; Gal 3.27). Here Paul emphasizes that baptism is *into his death*, because this provides the rationale for vv. 5–14. **6.4** Paul distinguishes present solidarity with Christ's death from future solidarity with his resurrection (vv. 5, 8); the former makes possible a new moral life now (see 7.6). *Walk*, i.e., conduct one's life; see Deut 13.4–5; Isa 33.15. **6.5** *If*, "since," expressing not doubt but a fulfilled condition. **6.6** *Crucified with him*, the only explicit reference to Jesus' cross in Romans. *Body of sin. Body* probably means the actual self (as in

body of sin might be destroyed, and we might no longer be enslaved to sin. 7For whoever has died is freed from sin. 8But if we have died with Christ, we believe that we will also live with him. 9We know that Christ, being raised from the dead, will never die again; death no longer has dominion over him. 10The death he died, he died to sin, once for all; but the life he lives, he lives to God. 11So you also must consider yourselves dead to sin and alive to God in Christ Jesus.

12 Therefore, do not let sin exercise dominion in your mortal bodies, to make you obey their passions. 13No longer present your members to sin as instruments*a* of wickedness, but present yourselves to God as those who have been brought from death to life, and present your members to God as instruments*a* of righteousness. 14For sin will have no dominion over you, since you are not under law but under grace.

Slaves of Righteousness

15 What then? Should we sin because we are not under law but under grace? By no means! 16Do you not know that if you present yourselves to anyone as obedient slaves, you are slaves of the one whom you obey, either of sin, which leads to death, or of obedience, which leads to righteousness? 17But thanks be to God that you, having once been slaves of sin, have become obedient from the heart to the form of teaching to which you were entrusted, 18and that you, having been set free from sin,

have become slaves of righteousness. 19I am speaking in human terms because of your natural limitations.*b* For just as you once presented your members as slaves to impurity and to greater and greater iniquity, so now present your members as slaves to righteousness for sanctification.

20 When you were slaves of sin, you were free in regard to righteousness. 21So what advantage did you then get from the things of which you now are ashamed? The end of those things is death. 22But now that you have been freed from sin and enslaved to God, the advantage you get is sanctification. The end is eternal life. 23For the wages of sin is death, but the free gift of God is eternal life in Christ Jesus our Lord.

An Analogy from Marriage

7 Do you not know, brothers and sisters*c*— for I am speaking to those who know the law—that the law is binding on a person only during that person's lifetime? 2Thus a married woman is bound by the law to her husband as long as he lives; but if her husband dies, she is discharged from the law concerning the husband. 3Accordingly, she will be called an adulteress if she lives with another man while her husband is alive. But if her husband dies, she is free from that law, and if she marries another man, she is not an adulteress.

4 In the same way, my friends,*c* you have

---

a Or weapons *b* Gk the weakness of your flesh *c* Gk brothers

---

12.1), which is *enslaved to sin.* **6.7** This principle, together with v. 9, is essential for Paul's argument. **6.10** *He died to sin.* In death the power of sin was terminated; see v. 7; cf. 7.1–6. *Once for all,* once for all time. See Heb 7.27; 9.26–28. **6.12–14** The first explicit exhortation in the Letter shows that baptism entails a new moral life. **6.13** *Instruments,* or *weapons* (see text note *a*). Like philosophers of his day, Paul often describes the moral life as a military or athletic struggle; see 13.12; 2 Cor 6.7; 10.4; also Eph 6.11–17. **6.14** Everyone is under some *dominion,* either that of *sin* (see v. 6), *death* (see v. 9), and *law* (see 7.6; note on 7.1–6), or that of *grace* (see also 6.16). Paul analyzes *under law* in 7.7–24. For Paul, there is no autonomous self. **6.15–23** Again Paul uses the diatribe style to reject a wrong inference, now from v. 14. **6.16** *If,* when. **6.17** *The form of teaching,* probably the gospel tradition. The readers were *entrusted* to it, i.e., put in its charge, not vice versa (cf. 1 Tim 6.20). **6.18** *Slaves of righteousness,* i.e., under the dominion of God's rectifying power. See v. 22. **6.19** *In human terms.* Paul acknowledges that his language is unusual (see text note

b). *Impurity,* lit. "uncleanness." The language implies that Paul has gentile Christians in view. *Sanctification,* the process of making life holy, i.e., rightly aligned with God's will. See 12.1–2; also 1 Thess 4.3–7; 5.23. **6.20** *Free in regard to righteousness,* i.e., unable to "obey" righteousness. See vv. 16, 18. **6.22** *Enslaved to God.* See v. 18. **6.23** That *death* (both as the termination of life and as the tyrannous power during life) is the consequence of sin has been a theme since 5.12.

7.1–6 Also freedom from the law, seen as a power to which one is subject as one is to sin and death, comes through death (cf. 6.7–11). The argument is obscured, however, because in the illustration (vv. 1–3) the husband's death frees the wife, but in the application (vv. 4–6) it is the death of the wife (the believers who died with Christ in baptism; cf. 6.8) that is the point. **7.1–2** *Is binding,* lit. "lords it over," as do death (6.9) and sin (6.14), where the same verb is used. Accordingly *a married woman,* lit. "one under a man" (used also in the Greek of Prov 6.24; Sir 9.9, and in non-biblical texts) is subject to her husband while he lives. Concerned with the effect of death, Paul ignores divorce;

died to the law through the body of Christ, so that you may belong to another, to him who has been raised from the dead in order that we may bear fruit for God. ⁵While we were living in the flesh, our sinful passions, aroused by the law, were at work in our members to bear fruit for death. ⁶But now we are discharged from the law, dead to that which held us captive, so that we are slaves not under the old written code but in the new life of the Spirit.

The Law and Sin

7 What then should we say? That the law is sin? By no means! Yet, if it had not been for the law, I would not have known sin. I would not have known what it is to covet if the law had not said, "You shall not covet." ⁸But sin, seizing an opportunity in the commandment, produced in me all kinds of covetousness. Apart from the law sin lies dead. ⁹I was once alive apart from the law, but when the commandment came, sin revived ¹⁰and I died, and the very commandment that promised life proved to be death to me. ¹¹For sin, seizing an opportunity in the commandment, deceived me and through it killed me. ¹²So the law is holy, and the commandment is holy and just and good.

13 Did what is good, then, bring death to me? By no means! It was sin, working death in me through what is good, in order that sin

might be shown to be sin, and through the commandment might become sinful beyond measure.

The Inner Conflict

14 For we know that the law is spiritual; but I am of the flesh, sold into slavery under sin.ᵃ ¹⁵I do not understand my own actions. For I do not do what I want, but I do the very thing I hate. ¹⁶Now if I do what I do not want, I agree that the law is good. ¹⁷But in fact it is no longer I that do it, but sin that dwells within me. ¹⁸For I know that nothing good dwells within me, that is, in my flesh. I can will what is right, but I cannot do it. ¹⁹For I do not do the good I want, but the evil I do not want is what I do. ²⁰Now if I do what I do not want, it is no longer I that do it, but sin that dwells within me.

21 So I find it to be a law that when I want to do what is good, evil lies close at hand. ²²For I delight in the law of God in my inmost self, ²³but I see in my members another law at war with the law of my mind, making me captive to the law of sin that dwells in my members. ²⁴Wretched man that I am! Who will rescue me from this body of death? ²⁵Thanks be to God through Jesus Christ our Lord!

ᵃ Gk sold under sin

---

cf. 1 Cor 7.10–15. **7.4** *My friends,* lit. *my brothers* (see text note *c* on p. 1918). Paul never calls Christians his "friends," a common self-designation in certain philosophical schools. *Died to the law.* See also 6.14; cf. 6.10. *The body of Christ,* Christ's crucified body, not the church (cf. 12.5). *Another,* the resurrected Christ. *Bear fruit for God,* i.e., produce moral results. See 6.4, 13, 19; see also Col 1.10. **7.5** Like sin, law, and death, *flesh* is a controlling domain in which one lives (see v. 14; 8.4, 12); the term emphasizes weakness and corruptibility. How *passions* are *aroused by the law* is shown in vv. 7–25. **7.6** This verse restates the nature of Christian existence (see 6.4, 7, 11, 12–14, 17, 19). *Discharged from the law* reformulates 7.2; *dead to . . . captive* paraphrases 6.11. *New life of the Spirit,* lit. "in newness of Spirit," alludes to 6.4 and anticipates ch. 8. **7.7–13** Again Paul uses diatribe to reject the wrong inference from v. 6; the problem is not the law itself but its inability to curb sin; in fact, sin actually uses the law to provoke what it forbids. **7.7** *I,* probably stylistic rather than autobiographical (see Phil 3.4–6), a reference to the individual in the Adamic state (5.12–21). *Known sin.* See 3.20. *Covet,* lit. "desire." See Ex 20.17; Deut 5.21. **7.10** *I died.* See 6.23; see also 5.12–14. **7.11** *Deceived,* i.e., caused one to think law more powerful than sin. **7.13** The power of sin is so heinous because it

works even *through what is good.* **7.14–25** Why one cannot do the good that the law commands and that one intends to do. **7.14** *Flesh,* the physical self when, as the source of passions (e.g., covetousness; see v. 8), it becomes a dominant factor (see note on 7.5). The change to present tense suggests to some that Paul is now describing his Christian experience, but the words *sold into slavery under sin* make this unlikely (cf. 6.6, 11, 14, 17). Rather, Paul is expressing the frustration of the person defined by Adam (5.12–21). **7.17** Sin is a malign power residing in the self. There is no significant difference between "living in sin" (see note on 6.2) and sin residing in the self. **7.18** *Nothing good dwells within me,* lit. "the good does not dwell within me." **7.21** Paul calls the experience of being unable to do the good one desires *a law* because it is unavoidable. **7.22** *Inmost self,* the mind or heart, the seat of the will. **7.23** The inevitability of sin makes it *another law.* The self is not an achiever of the good but a *captive* (victim) of the inevitability (*law*) of sin. Paul uses the Jewish concept of "the evil impulse," which, implanted in the self along with "the good impulse," generates perpetual inner struggle; see Dead Sea Scrolls *Rule of the Community* (1QS) 3.13–4.26. For Paul, the law does not help one master the evil impulse but is itself thoroughly qualified by it. **7.24** *This body of*

So then, with my mind I am a slave to the law of God, but with my flesh I am a slave to the law of sin.

Life in the Spirit

8 There is therefore now no condemnation for those who are in Christ Jesus. ²For the law of the Spirit *a* of life in Christ Jesus has set you *b* free from the law of sin and of death. ³For God has done what the law, weakened by the flesh, could not do: by sending his own Son in the likeness of sinful flesh, and to deal with sin, *c* he condemned sin in the flesh, ⁴so that the just requirement of the law might be fulfilled in us, who walk not according to the flesh but according to the Spirit. *a* ⁵For those who live according to the flesh set their minds on the things of the flesh, but those who live according to the Spirit *a* set their minds on the things of the Spirit. *a* ⁶To set the mind on the flesh is death, but to set the mind on the Spirit *a* is life and peace. ⁷For this reason the mind that is set on the flesh is hostile to God; it does not submit to God's law—indeed it cannot, ⁸and those who are in the flesh cannot please God.

9 But you are not in the flesh; you are in the Spirit, *a* since the Spirit of God dwells in you. Anyone who does not have the Spirit of Christ does not belong to him. ¹⁰But if Christ is in you, though the body is dead because of sin, the Spirit *a* is life because of righteousness. ¹¹If the Spirit of him who raised Jesus from the dead dwells in you, he who raised Christ *d* from the dead will give life to your mortal bodies also through *e* his Spirit that dwells in you.

12 So then, brothers and sisters, *f* we are debtors, not to the flesh, to live according to the flesh— ¹³for if you live according to the flesh, you will die; but if by the Spirit you put to death the deeds of the body, you will live. ¹⁴For all who are led by the Spirit of God are children of God. ¹⁵For you did not receive a spirit of slavery to fall back into fear, but you have received a spirit of adoption. When we cry, "Abba! *g* Father!" ¹⁶it is that very Spirit bearing witness *h* with our spirit that we are children of God, ¹⁷and if children, then heirs, heirs of God and joint heirs with Christ—if, in fact, we suffer with him so that we may also be glorified with him.

Future Glory

18 I consider that the sufferings of this present time are not worth comparing with the glory about to be revealed to us. ¹⁹For the creation

a Or *spirit*   *b* Here the Greek word *you* is singular number; other ancient authorities read *me* or *us*   *c* Or *and as a sin offering*   *d* Other ancient authorities read *the Christ* or *Christ Jesus* or *Jesus Christ*   *e* Other ancient authorities read *on account of*   *f* Gk *brothers*   *g* Aramaic for *Father*   *h* Or *¹⁵a spirit of adoption, by which we cry, "Abba! Father!"* *¹⁶The Spirit itself bears witness*

death, the self, thoroughly qualified by and destined for death (see 6.16, 21, 23; cf. 6.9). **7.25** *With my mind . . . with my flesh* sums up the human condition. Some think this sentence either originally came before *thanks be to God* or was added by a copyist.

8.1–17 Paul explains that the solution to the dilemma exposed in 7.14–25 is the Spirit, whose dwelling in the self displaces the resident power of sin (see 7.17), making a new life possible. **8.1** *No condemnation,* the consequence of justification (see 5.16, 18). Being *in Christ Jesus* is the result of being baptized into Christ (6.3). **8.2** *The Spirit of life,* probably not *spirit* (as in text note *a*), but the Holy Spirit, which gives life (8.11). *In Christ Jesus,* here also a domain in which the Spirit is power. *Law of sin.* See 7.23. The law *of death* is the inevitability of death resulting from sin (6.23). **8.3** *Weakened by the flesh* alludes to the law's inability to deal decisively with sin as resident power (7.7–25). *Sending,* the incarnation of the preexistent Son of God; see Gal 4.4. *Likeness* suggests the Son's full identification with the human condition, but without becoming another instance of it. The additional phrase noted in text note *c* might allude to 3.25. **8.4** *The just requirement.* See 7.12. *Walk.* See note on 6.4. *Flesh* and *Spirit* are domains of power (see note on 8.2). **8.7** By definition, *flesh is hostile to God* (see note on 7.14). **8.8** *In the flesh,* i.e., within its domain, not simply in the body. **8.9–10** There is no difference between *you are in the Spirit* and *the Spirit . . . dwells in you,* nor between *the Spirit . . . dwells in you* and *Christ is in you.* **8.10** *Because of righteousness,* i.e., because of God's righteousness as saving, rectifying power. **8.11** *Will give life.* Paul again emphasizes the future resurrection of Christians; see also 5.10; 6.5, 8; 1 Cor 15.12–24, 50–57. The variant reading in text note *d* is probably preferable **8.13** *Will die* alludes to 6.23. *Deeds of the body,* not all bodily deeds but those of 7.19, 23, 25. Christians *will live* through *newness of life* now (6.4) and through future resurrection. **8.15** *Spirit of adoption,* i.e., the Spirit whose work is adopting. See also Gal 4.5–7. This adoption is both a present and a future reality; see v. 23. *When we cry, "Abba!"* This is probably not an allusion to the Lord's Prayer (see text note *h*). **8.17** Christians are *joint heirs* of the resurrection. See v. 29. **8.18–30** After comparing the consequences of Christ and Adam for persons (5.12–21), Paul turns to the consequences of Adam for creation, thus providing a wider perspective on present experiences. **8.18** *Sufferings.* See 5.3–4. *The glory,* completed salvation, expected soon. **8.19** *Creation* is spoken of as if it

waits with eager longing for the revealing of the children of God; 20for the creation was subjected to futility, not of its own will but by the will of the one who subjected it, in hope 21that the creation itself will be set free from its bondage to decay and will obtain the freedom of the glory of the children of God. 22We know that the whole creation has been groaning in labor pains until now; 23and not only the creation, but we ourselves, who have the first fruits of the Spirit, groan inwardly while we wait for adoption, the redemption of our bodies. 24For in*a* hope we were saved. Now hope that is seen is not hope. For who hopes*b* for what is seen? 25But if we hope for what we do not see, we wait for it with patience.

26 Likewise the Spirit helps us in our weakness; for we do not know how to pray as we ought, but that very Spirit intercedes*c* with sighs too deep for words. 27And God,*d* who searches the heart, knows what is the mind of the Spirit, because the Spirit*e* intercedes for the saints according to the will of God.*f*

28 We know that all things work together for good*g* for those who love God, who are called according to his purpose. 29For those whom he foreknew he also predestined to be conformed to the image of his Son, in order that he might be the firstborn within a large family.*h* 30And those whom he predestined he also called; and those whom he called he also justified; and those whom he justified he also glorified.

God's Love in Christ Jesus

31 What then are we to say about these things? If God is for us, who is against us? 32He who did not withhold his own Son, but gave him up for all of us, will he not with him also give us everything else? 33Who will bring any charge against God's elect? It is God who justifies. 34Who is to condemn? It is Christ Jesus, who died, yes, who was raised, who is at the right hand of God, who indeed intercedes for us.*i* 35Who will separate us from the love of Christ? Will hardship, or distress, or persecution, or famine, or nakedness, or peril, or sword? 36As it is written,

"For your sake we are being killed all day long;
we are accounted as sheep to be slaughtered."

37No, in all these things we are more than conquerors through him who loved us. 38For I am convinced that neither death, nor life, nor angels, nor rulers, nor things present, nor things to come, nor powers, 39nor height, nor depth,

a Or *by* *b* Other ancient authorities read *awaits* *c* Other ancient authorities add *for us* *d* Gk *the one* *e* Gk *he* or *it* *f* Gk *according to God* *g* Other ancient authorities read *God makes all things work together for good*, or *in all things God works for good* *h* Gk *among many brothers* *i* Or *Is it Christ Jesus . . . for us?*

---

were a person. *The revealing.* The truth to which the Spirit now witnesses (v. 16) is not yet manifest; see v. 23. **8.20** *Futility*, explained as *bondage to decay* in v. 21, alludes to the curse on the earth in Gen 3.17–19 and is regarded here as not permanent. **8.21** Just as humanity's forfeited *glory* will be restored (3.23; 5.2), so creation's original status will be restored. **8.22** The metaphor of birth *pains* was often used to describe the eschatological transition from the old to the new age; see Mk 13.8; 1 Thess 5.3; *1 Enoch* 62.4. **8.23** The *first fruits* of the harvest represent the whole, so the present experience of the Spirit is the pledge of its future work (see v. 11). Christians too *groan* because their salvation is not yet fully actualized (see 5.10). *Wait for adoption.* See v. 19. The whole self (i.e., the *body*; see note on 6.6) is destined for *redemption.* Because the body is part of creation, what is true of the part will be true also of the whole, i.e., creation too will be redeemed (released) from the inevitability of death. **8.24** *Hope.* See 5.3–5. **8.26** The Spirit not only speaks to us but also *intercedes* with God for us; in v. 34 Christ intercedes. **8.28** *Called*, chosen, as in 1.1, 7. **8.29** *Foreknew* and *predestined* reflect the view that what God knows and does in eternity appears to us as prior action; see also 11.2; Acts 2.23; 1 Pet 1.2, 20. *Conformed to the image*, another ex-

pression of the future solidarity of the Savior and the saved. See also v. 17; Phil 3.21. *Firstborn within a large family.* The children of God (v. 14) will be what the Son now is; see also Col 1.15; Heb 2.8–13. **8.30** *Glorified* is in the past tense because, although the glorification will occur in the future in human terms, it has occurred already in eternity (see note on 8.29). **8.31–39** This passage sums up with a flourish the import of the argument from 1.18 onward and ends on a triumphal note. **8.31** *For . . . against us.* The questions in this section are posed as if in a courtroom. **8.32** *Did not withhold his own Son*, a reformulation of 3.25; 5.8; 8.3–4. *With him* echoes 5.9–11; 8.11, 17. **8.33** *Justifies*, here pronounces one to be in the right, i.e., rightly related to God. **8.34** Text note *i* shows that the sentence might be a question. If so, it expects "No!" for an answer. *Intercedes.* As in vv. 9–10, what Paul says of the Spirit he can say also of the risen Christ (see 8.26). **8.35** *The love of Christ* coincides with God's love (5.8). *Hardship*, rendered *sufferings* in 5.3, often refers to the tribulations of the end time (see Mk 13.19; Rev 7.14). **8.36** Ps 44.22. **8.38** *Angels* contrast with *rulers*, who are probably earthly powers (cf. 1 Cor 15.24; Gal 4.8–11; Col 2.15). *Powers* are supernatural beings; see Mt 24.29; 1 Pet 3.22. **8.39** *Love of God.* See 5.8.

nor anything else in all creation, will be able to separate us from the love of God in Christ Jesus our Lord.

God's Election of Israel

9 I am speaking the truth in Christ—I am not lying; my conscience confirms it by the Holy Spirit— ²I have great sorrow and unceasing anguish in my heart. ³For I could wish that I myself were accursed and cut off from Christ for the sake of my own people,ᵃ my kindred according to the flesh. ⁴They are Israelites, and to them belong the adoption, the glory, the covenants, the giving of the law, the worship, and the promises; ⁵to them belong the patriarchs, and from them, according to the flesh, comes the Messiah,ᵇ who is over all, God blessed forever.ᶜ Amen.

6 It is not as though the word of God had failed. For not all Israelites truly belong to Israel, ⁷and not all of Abraham's children are his true descendants; but "It is through Isaac that descendants shall be named for you." ⁸This means that it is not the children of the flesh who are the children of God, but the children of the promise are counted as descendants. ⁹For this is what the promise said, "About this time I will return and Sarah shall have a son." ¹⁰Nor is that all; something similar happened to Rebecca when she had conceived children by one husband, our ancestor Isaac. ¹¹Even before they had been born or had done anything good or bad (so that God's purpose of election might continue, ¹²not by works but by his call) she was told, "The elder shall serve the younger." ¹³As it is written,

"I have loved Jacob,
    but I have hated Esau."

14 What then are we to say? Is there injustice on God's part? By no means! ¹⁵For he says to Moses,

"I will have mercy on whom I have
        mercy,
    and I will have compassion on whom I
        have compassion."

¹⁶So it depends not on human will or exertion, but on God who shows mercy. ¹⁷For the scripture says to Pharaoh, "I have raised you up for the very purpose of showing my power in you, so that my name may be proclaimed in all the earth." ¹⁸So then he has mercy on whomever he chooses, and he hardens the heart of whomever he chooses.

God's Wrath and Mercy

19 You will say to me then, "Why then does he still find fault? For who can resist his will?" ²⁰But who indeed are you, a human being, to argue with God? Will what is molded say to the one who molds it, "Why have you made me like this?" ²¹Has the potter no right over the clay, to make out of the same lump one object for special use and another for ordinary use? ²²What if God, desiring to show his wrath and to make known his power, has endured with much patience the objects of wrath that are made for destruction; ²³and what if he has done so in order to make known the riches of his glory for the objects of mercy, which he has prepared beforehand for glory— ²⁴including us whom he has called, not from the Jews only but also from the Gentiles? ²⁵As indeed he says in Hosea,

---

a Gk *my brothers* b Or *the Christ* c Or *Messiah, who is God over all, blessed forever*; or *Messiah. May he who is God over all be blessed forever*

9.1–11.28 See Introduction. In chs. 9–11 (which should be read as a unit) Paul probes the mysterious ways in which God shows freedom to be faithful to Israel. **9.1–18** The argument applies his theology of justification by faith (i.e., God's rectifying rectitude apart from the law, 3.21–26) to the election of Israel. **9.1** *I am not lying.* Paul's words almost constitute an oath (see also 2 Cor 11.31; Gal 1.20; 1 Tim 2.7). **9.3** *Accursed,* lit. "anathema"; see 1 Cor 16.22; Gal 1.8–9. **9.4** *Israelites.* The ancient biblical name reinforces the point: the distinctive items are the heritage of the Jewish people (see also 3.1–8). *Adoption,* the same word as in 8.15, 23. **9.5** *According to the flesh,* i.e., by human descent. See 1.3. **9.6–13** Paul appeals to what God said to the patriarchs in order to argue that the *word of God* (v. 6) is dependable. **9.6** *Not . . . failed* (v. 6). The rest of the passage demonstrates this. **9.7–8** Paul sees in Gen 21.12 the principle of the patriarchal story: being *children of God*

depends on promise and election (vv. 11–12), not on physical descent. **9.9** Gen 18.10, 14. **9.10–13** What was true in Abraham's time (vv. 6–9) was true also in the next generation. **9.12** Contrary to custom, *the elder shall serve the younger.* See Gen 25.23. **9.13** Mal 1.2–3. *Loved* and *hated,* chosen and not chosen. **9.14–15** God's freedom to choose does not imply that God is being unfair in the choice made, as God's word to Moses in Ex 33.19 shows. Mercy is not earned. **9.16** A reformulation of v. 12 in light of the quotation in v. 15. **9.17–18** God's word to Pharaoh in Ex 9.16 asserts God's freedom. *Hardens,* i.e., creates willful resistance in. See Ex 7.3, 13–14; 8.19; 9.12; 10.1, 20, 27; 11.10. **9.19–29** After defending God's freedom in election, Paul relates that freedom to the election of Gentiles as well as Jews. **9.21** The image of God as a *potter* was a popular one; see Isa 29.16; 45.9; Jer 18.1–11; Wis 15.7; Sir 33.13. Paul emphasizes God's freedom to divide *the same lump.* **9.23** *Prepared before-*

"Those who were not my people I will
        call 'my people,'
    and her who was not beloved I will call
        'beloved.' "
26 "And in the very place where it was said
        to them, 'You are not my people,'
    there they shall be called children of
        the living God."
27 And Isaiah cries out concerning Israel,
"Though the number of the children of Israel
were like the sand of the sea, only a remnant of
them will be saved; 28 for the Lord will execute
his sentence on the earth quickly and decisively." [a] 29 And as Isaiah predicted,
"If the Lord of hosts had not left
        survivors [b] to us,
    we would have fared like Sodom
        and been made like Gomorrah."

Israel's Unbelief

30 What then are we to say? Gentiles, who did
not strive for righteousness, have attained it,
that is, righteousness through faith; 31 but Israel, who did strive for the righteousness that
is based on the law, did not succeed in fulfilling that law. 32 Why not? Because they did not
strive for it on the basis of faith, but as if it
were based on works. They have stumbled
over the stumbling stone, 33 as it is written,
"See, I am laying in Zion a stone that will
        make people stumble, a rock that
        will make them fall,

and whoever believes in him [c] will not
        be put to shame."

10 Brothers and sisters, [d] my heart's desire
and prayer to God for them is that they
may be saved. 2 I can testify that they have a
zeal for God, but it is not enlightened. 3 For,
being ignorant of the righteousness that
comes from God, and seeking to establish
their own, they have not submitted to God's
righteousness. 4 For Christ is the end of the law
so that there may be righteousness for everyone who believes.

Salvation Is for All

5 Moses writes concerning the righteousness
that comes from the law, that "the person who
does these things will live by them." 6 But the
righteousness that comes from faith says, "Do
not say in your heart, 'Who will ascend into
heaven?' " (that is, to bring Christ down) 7 "or
'Who will descend into the abyss?' " (that is, to
bring Christ up from the dead). 8 But what
does it say?
"The word is near you,
    on your lips and in your heart"
(that is, the word of faith that we proclaim);
9 because [e] if you confess with your lips that
Jesus is Lord and believe in your heart that

---

a Other ancient authorities read *for he will finish his work and
cut it short in righteousness, because the Lord will make the
sentence shortened on the earth*   *b* Or *descendants*; Gk *seed*
c Or *trusts in it*   *d* Gk *Brothers*   *e* Or *namely, that*

---

hand, i.e., predestined (see 8.30). **9.25–26** See Hos 1.10;
2.23. Paul applies these texts, which refer to the restoration of Israel, to the inclusion of gentile Christians in
God's people. **9.27–28** See Isa 10.22–23. For Isaiah, the
remnant motif expressed hope of Israel's survival (Isa
28.5; 37.4, 31–32). Whereas the Hebrew of Isa 10.22
says "a remnant will return," the Greek used by Paul
reads "a remnant will be saved"—alluding, he believes,
to the few Jews who accept the gospel. *Only* is inserted
by the NRSV translators. **9.29** See Isa 1.9.
    9.30–10.4 Ironically, Gentiles (Christians) have
found God's righteousness through *faith*, but Israel has
missed it by wrongly relying on *works*. **9.31** *Righteousness . . . based on the law*, lit. "law of righteousness," the
law concerning/promising righteousness. *Fulfilling that
law* interprets what Paul actually wrote, "reaching the
law," probably meaning attaining to what the law is
about, righteousness. Here Paul uses the image of the
footrace. **9.32** *Based on works*. See 3.27–28; Gal 2.15–
16. *Have stumbled*, i.e., were offended. Whether the
stone refers to Christ or to the law is not obvious.
9.33 The quotation combines Isa 28.16; 8.14. For *stone*
as a reference to Christ, see, e.g., Mt 21.42; Acts 4.11;
1 Pet 2.6–8. **10.1** See 9.1–2. **10.2** In Phil 3.6, Paul recalls

his own *zeal*. **10.3** *The righteousness that comes from
God*, lit. "the righteousness of God," i.e., God's own rectifying righteousness (3.26). The verb *submitted* shows
that here God's righteousness is a power; see notes on
5.21; 6.14; 8.10. **10.4** It is not certain whether *end* means
termination or goal; the latter is the more probable, and
agrees with 8.3–4. **10.5–21** Paul develops the implications of v. 4. Those who think *end* in v. 4 means termination emphasize the contrast between what Moses
writes and what faith-based righteousness *says* (vv. 6–
8); those who think *end* means goal will see Moses'
words actualized in vv. 6–13. **10.5** As Gal 3.10–12 indicates, Paul's emphasis in citing the text from Lev 18.5
seems to be on the concept of "doing," i.e., works (see
9.32). *Will live by them*, will find life in them. **10.6–8** In
the quotations, Paul paraphrases Deut 30.12–14 (see
also Bar 3.29–30) as the appeal of *righteousness* itself.
He uses a common Jewish exegetical device (*that is . . .*)
to apply the text to Christ. **10.7** *Abyss* agrees with an Aramaic paraphrase of Deut 30.13 (see *Targum Neofiti* 1),
but Hebrew and Greek texts of Deuteronomy instead
refer to crossing the sea. Paul sees in *abyss* an allusion to
Christ's resurrection from the subterranean realm of
the dead. **10.9** *Confess* and *believe* are two aspects of one

God raised him from the dead, you will be saved. 10For one believes with the heart and so is justified, and one confesses with the mouth and so is saved. 11The scripture says, "No one who believes in him will be put to shame." 12For there is no distinction between Jew and Greek; the same Lord is Lord of all and is generous to all who call on him. 13For, "Everyone who calls on the name of the Lord shall be saved."

14 But how are they to call on one in whom they have not believed? And how are they to believe in one of whom they have never heard? And how are they to hear without someone to proclaim him? 15And how are they to proclaim him unless they are sent? As it is written, "How beautiful are the feet of those who bring good news!" 16But not all have obeyed the good news;ᵃ for Isaiah says, "Lord, who has believed our message?" 17So faith comes from what is heard, and what is heard comes through the word of Christ.ᵇ

18 But I ask, have they not heard? Indeed they have; for

"Their voice has gone out to all the earth,
    and their words to the ends of the
        world."

19Again I ask, did Israel not understand? First Moses says,

"I will make you jealous of those who are
    not a nation;
with a foolish nation I will make you
    angry."

20Then Isaiah is so bold as to say,

"I have been found by those who did not
    seek me;
I have shown myself to those who did
    not ask for me."

21But of Israel he says, "All day long I have held out my hands to a disobedient and contrary people."

Israel's Rejection Is Not Final

11 I ask, then, has God rejected his people? By no means! I myself am an Israelite, a descendant of Abraham, a member of the tribe of Benjamin. 2God has not rejected his people whom he foreknew. Do you not know what the scripture says of Elijah, how he pleads with God against Israel? 3"Lord, they have killed your prophets, they have demolished your altars; I alone am left, and they are seeking my life." 4But what is the divine reply to him? "I have kept for myself seven thousand who have not bowed the knee to Baal." 5So too at the present time there is a remnant, chosen by grace. 6But if it is by grace, it is no longer on the basis of works, otherwise grace would no longer be grace.ᶜ

7 What then? Israel failed to obtain what it was seeking. The elect obtained it, but the rest were hardened, 8as it is written,

"God gave them a sluggish spirit,
    eyes that would not see

---

a Or *gospel*   *b* Or *about Christ*; other ancient authorities read *of God*   *c* Other ancient authorities add *But if it is by works, it is no longer on the basis of grace, otherwise work would no longer be work*

---

act; the formulation reflects Deut 30.14 (cited in v. 8), which for Paul refers to the positive response to the gospel. **10.10** *Is saved*, lit. "for salvation," does not conflict with 5.9–10. **10.11** Isa 28.16; Rom 9.33. Not being *put to shame* means being vindicated (as in 5.5). **10.12** *No distinction* affirms the parity of *Jew and Greek* in salvation as in sin (3.22–23). *The same Lord*. See 3.29–30. *Call on*, i.e., look to, count on, or trust (see 1 Cor 1.2). **10.13** See Joel 2.32. **10.14–15** A chain of questions leads up to a shortened quotation of Isa 52.7; these verses state the rationale of the Christian mission and so set the stage for vv. 16–21. **10.16** *Obeyed* and *believed* are parallel verbs here; for faith as obedience, see 1.5. The quotation is from Isa 53.1. **10.17** *Word of Christ*, not Jesus' teaching but the proclamation whose content is Christ (see text note *b*). **10.18** *Have they not heard?* a rhetorical question answered in the affirmative by a quotation from Ps 19.4. *Their voice*, i.e., the voice of the Christian missionaries. **10.19** See Deut 32.21; in Greek this question clearly expects a negative answer. Thus Paul denies that Israel did not understand the

gospel. For Paul, *those who are not a nation* are the Christian Gentiles (see 9.25). **10.20** See Isa 65.1, here applied to Christian Gentiles. **10.21** See Isa 65.2, here applied to disobedient Israel (alluding to v. 16).

11.1–10 Using diatribal style (see note on 2.1–5), Paul argues that God did not, and does not now, annul Israel's election because the majority have disobeyed; see also 3.3–4; 9.6; 11.26, 29. **11.1** *I myself*. Paul's own Jewish identity shows that the whole people has not been rejected. **11.2** *Has not rejected*, perhaps an allusion to Ps 94.14, which uses the future tense. Paul's denial responds to those Christian Gentiles who thought otherwise. **11.3** See 1 Kings 19.10. **11.4** See 1 Kings 19.18, which uses the future tense. **11.5** *Remnant*, the few Christian Jews, like Paul; see 9.27–29. **11.6** *Grace* and *works* are mutually exclusive; see also 4.2–8; 9.11–16. The Christian Jewish remnant has no reason to boast, just as Abraham had none (cf. 4.2–5). **11.7** *Israel*, here empirical Israel as a whole. *What it was seeking*. See 9.31. *Elect*, the *remnant* (v. 5). *Hardened*. See 9.17–18; that the passive voice implies divine action is

and ears that would not hear,
　　down to this very day."
9 And David says,
　　"Let their table become a snare and a
　　　　trap,
　　a stumbling block and a retribution for
　　　　them;
10　let their eyes be darkened so that they
　　　　cannot see,
　　and keep their backs forever bent."

The Salvation of the Gentiles

11 So I ask, have they stumbled so as to fall? By no means! But through their stumbling[a] salvation has come to the Gentiles, so as to make Israel[b] jealous. 12 Now if their stumbling[a] means riches for the world, and if their defeat means riches for Gentiles, how much more will their full inclusion mean!

13 Now I am speaking to you Gentiles. Inasmuch then as I am an apostle to the Gentiles, I glorify my ministry 14 in order to make my own people[c] jealous, and thus save some of them. 15 For if their rejection is the reconciliation of the world, what will their acceptance be but life from the dead! 16 If the part of the dough offered as first fruits is holy, then the whole batch is holy; and if the root is holy, then the branches also are holy.

17 But if some of the branches were broken off, and you, a wild olive shoot, were grafted in their place to share the rich root[d] of the olive tree, 18 do not boast over the branches. If you do boast, remember that it is not you that support the root, but the root that supports you. 19 You will say, "Branches were broken off so that I might be grafted in." 20 That is true. They were broken off because of their unbelief, but you stand only through faith. So do not become proud, but stand in awe. 21 For if God did not spare the natural branches, perhaps he will not spare you.[e] 22 Note then the kindness and the severity of God: severity toward those who have fallen, but God's kindness toward you, provided you continue in his kindness; otherwise you also will be cut off. 23 And even those of Israel,[f] if they do not persist in unbelief, will be grafted in, for God has the power to graft them in again. 24 For if you have been cut from what is by nature a wild olive tree and grafted, contrary to nature, into a cultivated olive tree, how much more will these natural branches be grafted back into their own olive tree.

All Israel Will Be Saved

25 So that you may not claim to be wiser than you are, brothers and sisters,[g] I want you to understand this mystery: a hardening has come upon part of Israel, until the full number of the Gentiles has come in. 26 And so all Israel will be saved; as it is written,

---

a Gk transgression　*b* Gk them　*c* Gk my flesh　*d* Other ancient authorities read the richness　*e* Other ancient authorities read neither will he spare you　*f* Gk lacks of Israel　*g* Gk brothers

---

made explicit in 11.8. **11.8** The quotation is based roughly on Deut 29.4; Isa 29.10. **11.9–10** Ps 69.22–23, following the Greek version. There is no reason to think that *forever bent* predicts permanent punishment for Jews. **11.11–24** Paul now interprets the significance of Israel's response for the Gentiles. **11.11** *Stumbled* (being offended by the gospel and refusing it) is temporary, but *fall* suggests permanent loss, and so is rejected. *Salvation . . . to the Gentiles.* Paul notes that God uses the Jews' "no" to bring about the Gentiles' "yes." See Acts 13.44–48; 28.25–29. Israel is *jealous* because gentile Christians have what Israel lacks. **11.12** *Full inclusion* anticipates v. 26. **11.13** *I am speaking to you Gentiles.* See Introduction; note on 11.2. **11.15** *Rejection,* refusal in the sense of vv. 7–10, not complete repudiation. See v. 1. *Acceptance* here has the connotation of *full inclusion* (v. 12). God's ultimate acceptance of Israel is of the same order as a resurrection. **11.16** *Dough.* See Num 15.17–21. *First fruits.* See note on 8.23; the part (the remnant, the Jewish Christians in the present) implies the whole of Israel. **11.17–24** Paul uses metaphorical language to warn the Gentiles against arrogance. For a tree as an image of Israel, see Ps 92.12–14; Isa 61.3; Jer 11.16–17; *Psalms of Solomon* 14.3–4. **11.17** *Some of the branches,* the Jews who rejected the gospel. The *wild olive shoot,* i.e., Christian Gentiles. *Olive tree,* the people of God, not simply all descendants of Abraham (see 9.6). **11.19** Paul puts into perspective the view of arrogant Christian Gentiles. **11.20** *Unbelief,* lit. "unfaith," contrasting with *faith. Stand* is the opposite of *fall* in v. 11. *Awe,* lit. "fear." **11.22** *Fallen,* i.e., *broken off* (v. 17). **11.24** *Contrary to nature.* Paul knows that his allegory is inconsistent with horticultural practice, but the subject matter, consonant with resurrection (v. 15), requires such an image. **11.25–36** These verses resolve the problem of Israel and the Gentiles in relation to the gospel. **11.25** *Mystery* (see also 16.25; 1 Cor 2.1, 7; 15.51), a disclosed, divine secret plan, as in Dan 2.18–19, 27–30 and often in apocalyptic literature (see, e.g., 2 Esd 12.36–38; *1 Enoch* 103.2; *2 Apocalypse of Baruch* 81.4). *Hardening.* See 9.18; 11.7. *Until the full number* reflects the apocalyptic idea that God sets times and numbers in advance (see Dan 11.36; 2 Esd 4.36–37; Gal 4.4; Rev 6.11; *2 Apocalypse of Baruch* 23.4). **11.26a** *All Israel,* no longer a *remnant* (v. 5), *will be*

"Out of Zion will come the Deliverer;
    he will banish ungodliness from Jacob."
27 "And this is my covenant with them,
    when I take away their sins."
28As regards the gospel they are enemies of God[a] for your sake; but as regards election they are beloved, for the sake of their ancestors; 29for the gifts and the calling of God are irrevocable. 30Just as you were once disobedient to God but have now received mercy because of their disobedience, 31so they have now been disobedient in order that, by the mercy shown to you, they too may now[b] receive mercy. 32For God has imprisoned all in disobedience so that he may be merciful to all.

33 O the depth of the riches and wisdom and knowledge of God! How unsearchable are his judgments and how inscrutable his ways!
34 "For who has known the mind of the
    Lord?
    Or who has been his counselor?"
35 "Or who has given a gift to him,
    to receive a gift in return?"
36For from him and through him and to him are all things. To him be the glory forever. Amen.

The New Life in Christ

12 I appeal to you therefore, brothers and sisters,[c] by the mercies of God, to present your bodies as a living sacrifice, holy and acceptable to God, which is your spiritual[d] worship. 2Do not be conformed to this world,[e] but be transformed by the renewing of your minds, so that you may discern what is the will of God—what is good and acceptable and perfect.[f]

3 For by the grace given to me I say to everyone among you not to think of yourself more highly than you ought to think, but to think with sober judgment, each according to the measure of faith that God has assigned. 4For as in one body we have many members, and not all the members have the same function, 5so we, who are many, are one body in Christ, and individually we are members one of another. 6We have gifts that differ according to the grace given to us: prophecy, in proportion to faith; 7ministry, in ministering; the teacher, in teaching; 8the exhorter, in exhortation; the giver, in generosity; the leader, in diligence; the compassionate, in cheerfulness.

Marks of the True Christian

9 Let love be genuine; hate what is evil, hold fast to what is good; 10love one another with mutual affection; outdo one another in showing honor. 11Do not lag in zeal, be ardent in spirit, serve the Lord.[g] 12Rejoice in hope, be patient in suffering, persevere in prayer. 13Contribute to the needs of the saints; extend hospitality to strangers.

14 Bless those who persecute you; bless and do not curse them. 15Rejoice with those who rejoice, weep with those who weep. 16Live in harmony with one another; do not be haughty,

---

a Gk lacks *of God*   *b* Other ancient authorities lack *now*
c Gk *brothers*   *d* Or *reasonable*   *e* Gk *age*   *f* Or *what is the good and acceptable and perfect will of God*   *g* Other ancient authorities read *serve the opportune time*

---

saved on the same basis as Gentiles, i.e., by faith (v. 23). **11.26b–27** See Isa 59.20–21; see also Isa 27.9. Paul's quotation differs from the Hebrew and Greek of both passages. Some regard *the Deliverer* as Christ, others as God. *Zion*, a traditional name of Jerusalem. *Ungodliness* recalls its use in 1.18; 4.5. **11.28** *Of God* is an inference (see text note *a*); "of the gospel" is also possible. *Ancestors*, i.e., the patriarchs, especially Abraham. See 4.1–25. **11.29** See 9.6. It is the permanence of Israel's election that Paul defends throughout chs. 9–11. **11.32** See 3.19–20, 23; 5.12–21. God's mercy is as impartial as God's judgment (2.9–11). **11.34** See Isa 40.13 (Septuagint). **11.35** Based loosely on Job 41.11. **11.36a** *For . . . all things,* a typical Stoic formulation (*see* Marcus Aurelius, *Meditations* 4.23); see also 1 Cor 8.6. **11.36b** The discussion of Israel's fate closes with a doxology; see also 1.25; 9.5; 16.27.
12.1–8 The opening passage of the second part of the Letter (12.1–15.13), concerned with aspects of the Christian life. **12.1** *Bodies,* i.e., total selves. See 6.13, 16;

8.23; cf. 1.24. *Living sacrifice.* See 6.4; 8.13. *Spiritual,* lit. "rational" or *reasonable* (see text note *d*). What Paul calls for here is the opposite of what 1.18–32 describes. **12.2** *This world,* lit. *this age* (see text note *e*), an allusion to the apocalyptic contrast between "this age" and the age to come (see 1 Cor 2.6, 8). **12.3–8** Paul counsels church leaders how to exercise seven gifts of grace (vv. 6–7). See also 1 Cor 12.12–30. **12.9–21** A staccato series of imperatives for all Christians, drawing on the wisdom tradition and focusing on social relations. **12.12** *Suffering.* See 5.3. *Prayer.* See 8.26–27; 1 Thess 5.17. **12.13** *Contribute to the needs of the saints,* a general counsel, not referring to the funds Paul has collected for the Jerusalem church (see Introduction). Cf. 15.25–26. *Saints.* See note on 1.7. *Hospitality* was important, especially for traveling Christians like Phoebe (16.1–2). **12.14** See Lk 6.28; this may be one of Paul's rare allusions to Jesus' teaching; see also 1 Cor 4.12. **12.16** *Lowly.* Text note *a* recognizes that the Greek term can be either masculine (people) or neuter

but associate with the lowly;[a] do not claim to be wiser than you are. 17Do not repay anyone evil for evil, but take thought for what is noble in the sight of all. 18If it is possible, so far as it depends on you, live peaceably with all. 19Beloved, never avenge yourselves, but leave room for the wrath of God;[b] for it is written, "Vengeance is mine, I will repay, says the Lord." 20No, "if your enemies are hungry, feed them; if they are thirsty, give them something to drink; for by doing this you will heap burning coals on their heads." 21Do not be overcome by evil, but overcome evil with good.

Being Subject to Authorities

13 Let every person be subject to the governing authorities; for there is no authority except from God, and those authorities that exist have been instituted by God. 2Therefore whoever resists authority resists what God has appointed, and those who resist will incur judgment. 3For rulers are not a terror to good conduct, but to bad. Do you wish to have no fear of the authority? Then do what is good, and you will receive its approval; 4for it is God's servant for your good. But if you do what is wrong, you should be afraid, for the authority[c] does not bear the sword in vain! It is the servant of God to execute wrath on the wrongdoer. 5Therefore one must be subject,

not only because of wrath but also because of conscience. 6For the same reason you also pay taxes, for the authorities are God's servants, busy with this very thing. 7Pay to all what is due them—taxes to whom taxes are due, revenue to whom revenue is due, respect to whom respect is due, honor to whom honor is due.

Love for One Another

8 Owe no one anything, except to love one another; for the one who loves another has fulfilled the law. 9The commandments, "You shall not commit adultery; You shall not murder; You shall not steal; You shall not covet"; and any other commandment, are summed up in this word, "Love your neighbor as yourself." 10Love does no wrong to a neighbor; therefore, love is the fulfilling of the law.

An Urgent Appeal

11 Besides this, you know what time it is, how it is now the moment for you to wake from sleep. For salvation is nearer to us now than when we became believers; 12the night is far gone, the day is near. Let us then lay aside the works of darkness and put on the armor of light; 13let us live honorably as in the day, not

---

a Or *give yourselves to humble tasks*   *b* Gk *the wrath*   *c* Gk *it*

(things). *Wiser.* See 11.25; this counsel perhaps echoes Prov 3.7. **12.17** *Evil for evil.* See Mt 5.38–39; 1 Thess 5.15; 1 Pet 3.9; cf. Ex 21.23–25. *Noble in the sight of all.* See 2 Cor 8.21. **12.18** *Live peaceably.* See Mk 9.50; 2 Cor 13.11; 1 Thess 5.13; Heb 12.14; see also Ps 34.14. **12.19** *Never avenge yourselves.* See Prov 20.22; 24.29. *The wrath.* See 1.18; 2.5–11; 5.9. The quotation is from Deut 32.35; see also Heb 10.30 and the Qumran *Rule of the Community* (1QS) 10.17. **12.20** See Prov 25.21–22; see also Mt 5.44; 25.35; Lk 6.27.

13.1–7 Paul abruptly urges submission to civil authorities; a few scholars think the passage was added to what Paul wrote. See also 1 Pet 2.13–14; cf. 1 Tim 2.1–2. **13.1** This verse states the basic injunction that vv. 2–7 explain and justify. *Governing authorities,* most likely government officials and not angelic powers (cf. 8.37–39; 1 Cor 15.24–27; Gal 4.8–11). *Instituted by God,* a concept also expressed in the Jewish wisdom tradition (e.g., Prov 8.15–16; Wis 6.1–3; Sir 10.4–5) as well as in apocalyptic literature (e.g., Dan 2.37–38; 4.17, 25, 32; *1 Enoch* 46.5). **13.4** The *sword* represents the power to punish, ultimately by execution. **13.5** *Wrath.* See note on 1.18. *Conscience* (see 2.15), one's inner judge of right and wrong. **13.6** *Servants* renders a Greek word used for persons performing public functions, especially cultic activities; Paul uses it of himself in 15.16.

13.7 It is not clear whether Paul is alluding here to a teaching of Jesus (see Mk 12.13–17). *Taxes,* both customs duties or tolls and tribute. **13.8–10** Obeying the commandment to love fulfills the law. **13.8** *Owe* translates the same Greek word as *due* in v. 7. **13.9** The list of *commandments* is drawn from Ex 20.13–17; Deut 5.17–21; see also Rom 2.21–22; Mt 19.18–19; Mk 10.19. *Love . . . as yourself* is from Lev 19.18, which is cited also by Jesus in Mt 5.43; 19.19 (but not as a summary of the law); see also Gal 5.14; Jas 2.8. **13.10** *Love does no wrong.* See 1 Cor 13.4–6. On the *fulfilling of the law,* see 8.4; Gal 5.14. **13.11–14** Paul reminds the readers of the specifically Christian perspective from which the preceding injunctions must be viewed. **13.11** *Wake,* a term for summoning to moral action in view of the time (not a date but a significant *moment*). See also Mk 13.35–36; Eph 5.14; 1 Thess 5.6–7. *Salvation is nearer,* an allusion to the future coming of Christ, which is not otherwise mentioned explicitly in Romans. See 1 Cor 15.20–24; 2 Cor 5.1–5; 1 Thess 4.15–18; see also Mk 1.15; 13.28–29. **13.12** The metaphors of *darkness* and *light* suggest moral change from evil deeds to good; see 1 Thess 5.4–11; see also Prov 4.16–19; Wis 17.1–18.4. Changing clothes (here *armor*) was a common metaphor for replacing vices with virtues; see Job 29.14; Eph 4.22–24; 6.13–17; Col

in reveling and drunkenness, not in debauchery and licentiousness, not in quarreling and jealousy. 14Instead, put on the Lord Jesus Christ, and make no provision for the flesh, to gratify its desires.

Do Not Judge Another

14 Welcome those who are weak in faith,[a] but not for the purpose of quarreling over opinions. 2Some believe in eating anything, while the weak eat only vegetables. 3Those who eat must not despise those who abstain, and those who abstain must not pass judgment on those who eat; for God has welcomed them. 4Who are you to pass judgment on servants of another? It is before their own lord that they stand or fall. And they will be upheld, for the Lord[b] is able to make them stand.

5 Some judge one day to be better than another, while others judge all days to be alike. Let all be fully convinced in their own minds. 6Those who observe the day, observe it in honor of the Lord. Also those who eat, eat in honor of the Lord, since they give thanks to God; while those who abstain, abstain in honor of the Lord and give thanks to God.

7 We do not live to ourselves, and we do not die to ourselves. 8If we live, we live to the Lord, and if we die, we die to the Lord; so then, whether we live or whether we die, we are the Lord's. 9For to this end Christ died and lived again, so that he might be Lord of both the dead and the living.

10 Why do you pass judgment on your brother or sister?[c] Or you, why do you despise your brother or sister?[c] For we will all stand before the judgment seat of God.[d] 11For it is written,

"As I live, says the Lord, every knee shall
    bow to me,
    and every tongue shall give praise to[e]
    God."

12So then, each of us will be accountable to God.[f]

Do Not Make Another Stumble

13 Let us therefore no longer pass judgment on one another, but resolve instead never to put a stumbling block or hindrance in the way of another.[g] 14I know and am persuaded in the Lord Jesus that nothing is unclean in itself; but it is unclean for anyone who thinks it unclean. 15If your brother or sister[c] is being injured by what you eat, you are no longer walking in love. Do not let what you eat cause the ruin of one for whom Christ died. 16So do not let your good be spoken of as evil. 17For the kingdom of God is not food and drink but righteousness and peace and joy in the Holy Spirit. 18The one who thus serves Christ is acceptable to God and has human approval. 19Let us then pursue what makes for peace and for mutual

---

a Or conviction   b Other ancient authorities read for God
c Gk brother   d Other ancient authorities read of Christ
e Or confess   f Other ancient authorities lack to God   g Gk of
a brother

3.9–14; 1 Thess 5.8. **13.14** *Put on . . . Christ.* See Gal 3.27; being "clothed" with Christ is a vivid metaphor for being "in" Christ. On *desires* of the flesh, see 7.5; 8.5–8; Gal 5.16, 24.

14.1–12 Paul outlines his position regarding the tension between those who scrupulously observe religiously grounded regulations governing dietary matters and special days (the *weak*) and those who insist on their freedom in Christ to ignore those regulations (the *strong*). For a comparable discussion, see 1 Cor 8, 10. **14.1** *Weak in faith* (see text note *a*) is clearly not the group's self-designation but an epithet used by its opponents, the *strong* (see 15.1), to whom this exhortation is addressed. *Quarreling* ruptures the community whose unity Paul needs for his mission in Spain; see Introduction. **14.2** The strong eat *anything*, while the *weak* eat only *vegetables*. Although vegetarianism was practiced in some religious and philosophical circles, the origin of this Christian vegetarianism is unknown (but see Dan 1.1–17). **14.4** *Before their own lord . . . stand or fall.* Whether the behavior of both groups is deemed acceptable or unacceptable is for the Lord to decide. **14.5** *One day,* i.e., a holy day, probably not only

the sabbath. See Ex 20.8–11; Deut 5.12–15. **14.6** *In honor of the Lord.* The motivation of both groups is identical; cf. 1.21. **14.7–8** *Live to,* live for the sake of; *die to,* die for the sake of (see 2 Cor 5.15; Gal 2.19); for a different use of "dying to," see 6.10–11. **14.10** *Pass judgment.* See 14.4, 13. Paul can speak interchangeably of *the judgment seat of God* and that of Christ (see 2 Cor 5.10). **14.11** A composite quotation drawn primarily from Isa 45.23; see also Phil 2.10–11. **14.13–23** Paul, while implicitly agreeing with the *strong,* emphasizes their responsibility for the *weak.* **14.14** The emphatic *in the Lord Jesus* (see also Gal 5.10; 1 Thess 4.1) points to the authority of the risen Lord, not to the words of Jesus as reported in Mk 7.15–19. The distinction between clean and *unclean* (i.e., taboo) food is basic to Jewish dietary law (see Lev 11), but Gentiles too had food taboos. **14.15** *Injured,* lit. "grieved" or "offended." See 14.20–21. **14.17** *Kingdom of God,* one of Paul's rare uses of this phrase; see 1 Cor 4.20; 6.9–10; 15.50; Gal 5.21; 1 Thess 2.12. **14.19** *Pursue . . . peace.* See note on 12.18. *Upbuilding* the church is an ongoing Pauline concern; see 15.2; 1 Cor 8.1; 14.26; 2 Cor 10.8; 12.19; 13.10 (perhaps an echo of Jer 42.10);

upbuilding. [20]Do not, for the sake of food, destroy the work of God. Everything is indeed clean, but it is wrong for you to make others fall by what you eat; [21]it is good not to eat meat or drink wine or do anything that makes your brother or sister[a] stumble.[b] [22]The faith that you have, have as your own conviction before God. Blessed are those who have no reason to condemn themselves because of what they approve. [23]But those who have doubts are condemned if they eat, because they do not act from faith;[c] for whatever does not proceed from faith[c] is sin.[d]

Please Others, Not Yourselves

15 We who are strong ought to put up with the failings of the weak, and not to please ourselves. [2]Each of us must please our neighbor for the good purpose of building up the neighbor. [3]For Christ did not please himself; but, as it is written, "The insults of those who insult you have fallen on me." [4]For whatever was written in former days was written for our instruction, so that by steadfastness and by the encouragement of the scriptures we might have hope. [5]May the God of steadfastness and encouragement grant you to live in harmony with one another, in accordance with Christ Jesus, [6]so that together you may with one voice glorify the God and Father of our Lord Jesus Christ.

The Gospel for Jews and Gentiles Alike

7 Welcome one another, therefore, just as Christ has welcomed you, for the glory of God. [8]For I tell you that Christ has become a servant of the circumcised on behalf of the truth of God in order that he might confirm the promises given to the patriarchs, [9]and in order that the Gentiles might glorify God for his mercy. As it is written,

"Therefore I will confess[e] you among the Gentiles,
   and sing praises to your name";
[10]and again he says,
"Rejoice, O Gentiles, with his people";
[11]and again,
"Praise the Lord, all you Gentiles,
   and let all the peoples praise him";
[12]and again Isaiah says,
"The root of Jesse shall come,
   the one who rises to rule the Gentiles;
in him the Gentiles shall hope."
[13]May the God of hope fill you with all joy and peace in believing, so that you may abound in hope by the power of the Holy Spirit.

Paul's Reason for Writing So Boldly

14 I myself feel confident about you, my brothers and sisters,[f] that you yourselves are full of goodness, filled with all knowledge, and able to instruct one another. [15]Nevertheless on some points I have written to you rather boldly by way of reminder, because of the grace given me by God [16]to be a minister of Christ Jesus to the Gentiles in the priestly service of the gospel of God, so that the offering of the Gentiles may be acceptable, sanctified by the Holy Spirit. [17]In Christ Jesus, then, I

---

a Gk *brother* *b* Other ancient authorities add *or be upset or be weakened* *c* Or *conviction* *d* Other authorities, some ancient, add here 16.25-27 *e* Or *thank* *f* Gk *brothers*

Eph 4.29. **14.20** *Everything is . . . clean* (see also Mk 7.19; Acts 10.15), perhaps a slogan of the *strong,* here affirmed but qualified in favor of the community's well-being. Paul takes the same approach in 1 Cor 8.1, 8–9; 10.23. *Make others fall,* i.e., cause them to violate their faith by inducing them to do what they do not believe they are free to do. See 14.23; 1 Cor 8.7–13.

15.1–6 A plea for harmony based on an appeal to Christ's example. **15.1** Paul identifies himself with the *strong,* mentioned here for the first time. The wordplay is difficult to translate: *strong . . . failings of the weak,* lit. "the strong . . . weaknesses of the unstrong." **15.2** What is said in 14.8–10 is here applied to the tensions. **15.3b** Ps 69.9. **15.4** *Written for our instruction.* See 1 Cor 9.10; 10.11. **15.5** *Live in harmony.* See 12.16. **15.7–13** The conclusion of the counsel in which major themes in the Letter are recalled. **15.7** *Welcome one another.* Cf. 14.1; 15.5. *Christ has welcomed you.* Cf. 14.3. **15.8** Only here does Paul speak of Christ as a ser-

vant; cf. Mk 10.43–45. *The circumcised,* i.e., the Jews. *Promises.* See 4.13–25; 9.4; 11.29. **15.9–12** A string of quotations emphasizes the inclusion of *Gentiles.* **15.9b** Ps 18.49. **15.10** Deut 32.43 (Greek). *With,* present only in the Greek version, is essential for Paul's argument. **15.11** See Ps 117.1. **15.12** Isa 11.10 (Septuagint). *Root,* or "shoot," "offshoot." *Jesse* was the father of David (see Ruth 4.17; 1 Sam 17.17; Mt 1.6); hence the root of Jesse is the Son of David, the Messiah; see Isa 11.1; Rev 5.5; 22.16; cf. Jer 23.5; 33.15. *Rises* here probably alludes to Jesus' resurrection. **15.14–21** Paul's reflections on his past ministry provide a bridge to his future plans. **15.15** Aware that he has written to a Christian community not founded by him, Paul heads off resentment by referring to the Letter as a *reminder* (see also 6.3, 6, 9; 7.1; 8.22, 28; 13.11). *The grace given me,* i.e., Paul's apostleship; see 1.5. **15.16** Paul was not a priest; his ministry was *priestly* (sacral; see note on 13.6) because through it *the Gen-*

have reason to boast of my work for God. 18For I will not venture to speak of anything except what Christ has accomplished[a] through me to win obedience from the Gentiles, by word and deed, 19by the power of signs and wonders, by the power of the Spirit of God,[b] so that from Jerusalem and as far around as Illyricum I have fully proclaimed the good news[c] of Christ. 20Thus I make it my ambition to proclaim the good news,[c] not where Christ has already been named, so that I do not build on someone else's foundation, 21but as it is written,

> "Those who have never been told of him
>   shall see,
> and those who have never heard of
>   him shall understand."

Paul's Plan to Visit Rome

22 This is the reason that I have so often been hindered from coming to you. 23But now, with no further place for me in these regions, I desire, as I have for many years, to come to you 24when I go to Spain. For I do hope to see you on my journey and to be sent on by you, once I have enjoyed your company for a little while. 25At present, however, I am going to Jerusalem in a ministry to the saints; 26for Macedonia and Achaia have been pleased to share their resources with the poor among the saints at Jerusalem. 27They were pleased to do this, and indeed they owe it to them; for if the Gentiles have come to share in their spiritual blessings, they ought also to be of service to them in material things. 28So, when I have completed this, and have delivered to them what has been collected,[d] I will set out by way of you to Spain; 29and I know that when I come to you, I will come in the fullness of the blessing[e] of Christ.

30 I appeal to you, brothers and sisters,[f] by our Lord Jesus Christ and by the love of the Spirit, to join me in earnest prayer to God on my behalf, 31that I may be rescued from the unbelievers in Judea, and that my ministry[g] to Jerusalem may be acceptable to the saints, 32so that by God's will I may come to you with joy and be refreshed in your company. 33The God of peace be with all of you.[h] Amen.

Personal Greetings

16 I commend to you our sister Phoebe, a deacon[i] of the church at Cenchreae, 2so that you may welcome her in the Lord as is fitting for the saints, and help her in whatever she may require from you, for she has been a benefactor of many and of myself as well.

3 Greet Prisca and Aquila, who work with

---

a Gk speak of those things that Christ has not accomplished   b Other ancient authorities read of the Spirit or of the Holy Spirit   c Or gospel   d Gk have sealed to them this fruit   e Other ancient authorities add of the gospel   f Gk brothers   g Other ancient authorities read my bringing of a gift   h One ancient authority adds 16.25-27 here   i Or minister

---

tiles would be presented to God as an *offering* (see Isa 66.20). **15.17** Paul's *boast* stems from legitimate pride (see 1 Cor 15.31; 2 Cor 1.12–14; 7.4); it is not ironic, as in 2 Cor 10.8–12.10. See notes on 5.2; 5.11. **15.18** *Obedience.* See 1.5. **15.19** *Signs and wonders,* an OT phrase (e.g., Ex 7.3; Neh 9.10; Isa 8.18; Jer 32.20) used in the NT for the miraculous events marking the Christian mission. See Acts 4.30; 14.3; 2 Cor 12.12. An arc *from Jerusalem* to the eastern shore of the Adriatic Sea indicates the range of Paul's work; nothing is known of his activity in *Illyricum* itself. *Good news,* i.e., the gospel; see text note c. **15.20** See 2 Cor 10.15–16. **15.21** Paul uses Isa 52.15 (Greek) to express his sense of being the pioneer in preaching to Gentiles. **15.22–33** Paul announces his intent to stop in Rome en route to Spain and explains why he must first go to Jerusalem. **15.22** *Hindered.* See 1.13; the reference is obscure. **15.23** *No further place.* With v. 19, this implies that Paul has achieved his purpose of taking the gospel to *key* urban centers. **15.24** *Spain* has not been mentioned before by Paul; Acts is silent about Spain. *Sent on by you,* a hint that he would welcome support. See Acts 15.3; 1 Cor 16.6; 2 Cor 1.16. **15.25** *Ministry to the saints,* i.e., delivery of the collection for the Jerusalem church. See Introduction; note on 1.7; see also 1 Cor 16.1–4; 2 Cor 8–9. **15.26** The Roman province of *Macedonia* contained the cities of Thessalonica, Philippi, and Beroea. Corinth was in *Achaia.* **15.27** *Spiritual blessings,* the benefits of the gospel by which the Gentiles became members of God's people. See, e.g., 11.17–24. **15.30** *Love of the Spirit,* i.e., the love generated by the Spirit. See Gal 5.22. *Join me in earnest prayer,* lit. "struggle with me in prayers." Cf. Col 4.12. **15.31** *Rescued from the unbelievers.* Paul's fears for his life proved correct; see Acts 21.27–36. *Acceptable to the saints.* Paul fears that the collection might be refused. What actually happened is not known; Acts ignores the collection (24.17 is ambiguous).

16.1–16 Paul's greetings to friends and former associates provide important clues about early Christianity, though most of the people are otherwise unknown. For the relation of ch. 16 to the rest of the Letter, see Introduction. **16.1** *Phoebe,* probably the bearer of the Letter (see Introduction). *Deacon,* probably a recognized leadership role, though not yet a specific rank of clergy. See Phil 1.1; cf. 1 Tim 3.8–13. **16.2** *As benefactor* (lit. "patron"), Phoebe was evidently a woman of means (cf. Lk 8.3; Acts 16.14–15; 17.12); the patron-client pattern was common and basic in Hellenistic society. **16.3** *Prisca and Aquila.* See Acts 18; 1 Cor 16.19; also

me in Christ Jesus, [4]and who risked their necks for my life, to whom not only I give thanks, but also all the churches of the Gentiles. [5]Greet also the church in their house. Greet my beloved Epaenetus, who was the first convert[a] in Asia for Christ. [6]Greet Mary, who has worked very hard among you. [7]Greet Andronicus and Junia,[b] my relatives[c] who were in prison with me; they are prominent among the apostles, and they were in Christ before I was. [8]Greet Ampliatus, my beloved in the Lord. [9]Greet Urbanus, our co-worker in Christ, and my beloved Stachys. [10]Greet Apelles, who is approved in Christ. Greet those who belong to the family of Aristobulus. [11]Greet my relative[d] Herodion. Greet those in the Lord who belong to the family of Narcissus. [12]Greet those workers in the Lord, Tryphaena and Tryphosa. Greet the beloved Persis, who has worked hard in the Lord. [13]Greet Rufus, chosen in the Lord; and greet his mother—a mother to me also. [14]Greet Asyncritus, Phlegon, Hermes, Patrobas, Hermas, and the brothers and sisters[e] who are with them. [15]Greet Philologus, Julia, Nereus and his sister, and Olympas, and all the saints who are with them. [16]Greet one another with a holy kiss. All the churches of Christ greet you.

Final Instructions

17 I urge you, brothers and sisters,[e] to keep an eye on those who cause dissensions and offenses, in opposition to the teaching that you have learned; avoid them. [18]For such people do not serve our Lord Christ, but their own appetites,[f] and by smooth talk and flattery they deceive the hearts of the simple-minded. [19]For while your obedience is known to all, so that I rejoice over you, I want you to be wise in what is good and guileless in what is evil. [20]The God of peace will shortly crush Satan under your feet. The grace of our Lord Jesus Christ be with you.[g]

21 Timothy, my co-worker, greets you; so do Lucius and Jason and Sosipater, my relatives.[c]

22 I Tertius, the writer of this letter, greet you in the Lord.[h]

23 Gaius, who is host to me and to the whole church, greets you. Erastus, the city treasurer, and our brother Quartus, greet you.[i]

Final Doxology

25 Now to God[j] who is able to strengthen you according to my gospel and the proclamation of Jesus Christ, according to the revelation of the mystery that was kept secret for long ages [26]but is now disclosed, and through the prophetic writings is made known to all the Gentiles, according to the command of the eternal God, to bring about the obedience of faith— [27]to the only wise God, through Jesus Christ, to whom[k] be the glory forever! Amen.[l]

a Gk first fruits   b Or Junias; other ancient authorities read Julia   c Or compatriots   d Or compatriot   e Gk brothers   f Gk their own belly   g Other ancient authorities lack this sentence   h Or I Tertius, writing this letter in the Lord, greet you   i Other ancient authorities add verse 24, The grace of our Lord Jesus Christ be with all of you. Amen.   j Gk the one   k Other ancient authorities lack to whom. The verse then reads, to the only wise God be the glory through Jesus Christ forever. Amen.   l Other ancient authorities lack 16.25-27 or include it after 14.23 or 15.33; others put verse 24 after verse 27

2 Tim 4.19. **16.5** *Church in their house.* See 1 Cor 16.19; also Col 4.15; Philem 2. In Paul's day, all Christian groups met in homes (often tenements). **16.6** *Worked very hard,* Paul's terminology for efforts on behalf of the gospel and the church. See 1 Cor 15.10; Gal 4.11; Phil 2.16; see also 1 Cor 16.16. **16.7** *Junia,* a woman's name, *Junias* (see text note *b*) a man's. *Relatives,* perhaps simply fellow Jews (see text note *c*). *In Christ before I was,* i.e., before Paul's conversion, no later than 35 CE, and thus among the earliest Christians. When, where, or why they were imprisoned with Paul is unknown. The woman Junia, like Andronicus (her husband?) was a *prominent* apostle herself, not simply highly regarded by apostles. On what it meant for Paul to be an apostle, cf. 1 Cor 9.1–2; 2 Cor 11–12. **16.10** *The family of Aristobulus,* lit. "those of Aristobulus," i.e., his household. The reference is perhaps to the grandson of Herod the Great and brother of Agrippa I. (See "The Herods: A Simplified Family Tree," p. 1672.) **16.12** *Workers.* See note on 16.6. *Tryphaena and Tryphosa,* perhaps sisters. **16.13** *Rufus.* See Mk 15.21. **16.14–15** Paul greets those he knows in two house churches. **16.16** *Holy kiss,* a part of early Christian worship. See 1 Cor 16.20; 2 Cor 13.12; 1 Thess 5.26; 1 Pet 5.14. **16.17–20** Perhaps an addition reflecting later circumstances, not Paul's own postscript. **16.17** *Opposition to the teaching.* Cf. 15.14. *Avoid them.* See 1 Tim 6.20; 2 Tim 2.22; 3.5; Titus 3.9–10. **16.18** *Appetites,* lit. *belly* (see text note *f*). See also Phil 3.19. **16.20** *Satan,* mentioned only here in Romans; see 1 Cor 5.5; 7.5; 2 Cor 2.11; 11.14; 1 Thess 2.18; 2 Thess 2.9. **16.21–23** Greetings resumed, now from Paul's associates. *Timothy* greets but does not join in writing; cf. 2 Cor 1.1; Phil 1.1; 1 Thess 1.1; 2 Thess 1.1; Philem 1. *Lucius* and *Jason,* probably not those mentioned in Acts 13.1; 17.5–9. *Sosipater,* possibly the "Sopater" of Acts 20.4. **16.22** *Tertius,* Paul's scribe. **16.23** *Gaius* (see 1 Cor 1.14) hosted meetings of the *whole church,* i.e., the entire Christian community in Corinth. *Erastus.* See Acts 19.22; 2 Tim 4.20. **16.25–27** Romans and 2 Peter are the only NT Letters ending with a doxology, reflecting use in worship. This doxology is generally regarded as a later addition. It is uncertain where Paul himself ended the Letter (see text note *l*).

The First Letter of Paul to the
CORINTHIANS

THE FIRST LETTER OF PAUL to the Corinthians was written by the apostle Paul about 54 CE to a congregation he had founded several years earlier in the capital city of the Roman province of Achaia (Acts 18.1–18; see also 1 Cor 2.1–5; 2 Cor 1.19). Corinth was a large and prospering urban center with an ethnically, culturally, and religiously diverse population. Paul writes from Ephesus, where he intends to stay for a while before traveling to Macedonia and then on to Corinth (16.5–9; see also 4.19–21). Meanwhile, Timothy has been sent ahead (4.17; 16.10–11). The bearers of the present Letter may have been the Corinthians named in 16.17.

The Corinthian Congregation

PAUL'S CONGREGATION WAS PREDOMINANTLY GENTILE (12.2), and it probably mirrored the diversity of the city's population. Among its members were Prisca and Aquila (16.19; Rom 16.3–4; Acts 18.2), Achaicus, Fortunatus, and Stephanas (16.17; see also 1.16; 16.15), Crispus and Gaius (1.14; Acts 18.8; see also Rom 16.23), and Phoebe (Rom 16.1). Some, like the Erastus mentioned in Rom 16.23, must have been people of considerable prominence, but most were persons of lesser means and lower social standing (1.26). It is likely that there were small groups of believers situated in different quarters of the city who were organized into separate house churches. At some regular interval, apparently, all of these would "come together as an *ekklesia* (assembly, church)" for a common meal and worship (11.18; 14.26).

Occasion and Purpose

PAUL WRITES IN PART to answer a letter (which has not survived) from the Corinthians seeking his views about several disputed matters (7.1). In addition he is responding to reports, conveyed by word of mouth, about serious disorders within the congregation (1.11; 5.1; 11.18): the jockeying of rival groups for control (1.10–17), an indifference to cases of flagrant immorality (5.1–13), a disregard for those who are not fully enlightened about appropriate Christian conduct (8.1–11.1), and the marginalizing of the congregation's disadvantaged members (11.17–34; see also 12.20–26). In the midst of this, Paul's own apostolic authority seems to have been called into question (e.g., 1.12; 3.1–4.5; ch. 9). Overall, the Letter summons this fractious congregation to manifest the unity and concord that, in Paul's view, necessarily go along with their belonging to Christ. It opens with a call for unity (1.10–17), its central

counsels are informed by the view of love that is set out in 8.1–3 and ch. 13, and it closes with
an appeal to let love be the governing power in the life of the community (16.14).

The Views of the Corinthians

THE DISPUTES AND DISORDERS in the Corinthian congregation seem to have been nurtured by
particular religious views that, from the apostle's standpoint, departed in significant ways from
the gospel that he had preached in Corinth. Specifically, Paul is critical of those who boast that
they possess special religious "wisdom" or "knowledge" (1.17, 18–25; 2.6, 11; 3.18–20; 8.1–3)
and who regard certain spiritual gifts, particularly ecstatic speech, as evidence of a higher spiritual status (chs. 12–14). At least certain members of this congregation seem to believe that they
are in some sense already "reigning" with Christ in glory (4.8). Perhaps as a consequence of this
view, they hope for nothing beyond this present life (15.12–19).

Character and Style

THIS LETTER EXHIBITS many of the stylistic and rhetorical conventions of other ancient Hellenistic letters, yet Paul's sense of writing as an apostle to a Christian congregation of his own
founding has also left its mark. Broadly speaking, 1 Corinthians is a letter of exhortation and
pastoral counsel. In formulating and supporting his appeals and instructions, Paul invokes
scripture (e.g., 1.31; 14.21), specifically Christian traditions (e.g., 15.3–5), sayings attributed to

With its two ports, Lechaeon on the Gulf of Corinth and Cenchreae on the Saronic Gulf, Corinth was
a commercial center and a cosmopolitan city.

Jesus (7.10–11; 9.14), his own apostolic authority and example (e.g., 4.14–17), and also conventional practices and wisdom (e.g., 11.13–16; 15.33). In addition, he reinforces his argument with reprimands (e.g., 6.5; 11.22), irony (e.g., 4.8–13), threats (e.g., 3.17–18; 4.19–21; 6.9–10), and (less frequently) praise (e.g., 11.2). Primarily, however, he urges his readers to reflect on what it means to have been called by God from their pagan past into a new life "in Christ Jesus" (e.g., 1.30; 6.11, 12–20; 7.17–24; 12.12–13).

Relation to Other Letters

DESPITE THE HEADING GIVEN TO IT by the ancient editors of Paul's Letters, 1 Corinthians is at least the apostle's second letter to this congregation. An earlier one, mentioned in 5.9, seems to be lost (although some believe that a fragment survives in 2 Cor 6.14–7.1). What we know as 2 Corinthians, even if it is a composite, dates from a year or so later.

Significance

MORE THAN MOST OF PAUL'S LETTERS, 1 Corinthians shows how the apostle's missionary and pastoral experiences both required and nurtured his theological reflection. Here, underlying and shaping the specific appeals and counsels are seminal expositions of the saving power of the cross, the nature of the church, the "more excellent way" of love (12.31), and God's final victory. The result is a passionate yet reasoned call for the Corinthian Christians to understand the faith they profess and to become agents of God's love in the world. [VICTOR PAUL FURNISH]

Salutation

1 Paul, called to be an apostle of Christ Jesus by the will of God, and our brother Sosthenes,

2 To the church of God that is in Corinth, to those who are sanctified in Christ Jesus, called to be saints, together with all those who in every place call on the name of our Lord Jesus Christ, both their Lord*a* and ours:

3 Grace to you and peace from God our Father and the Lord Jesus Christ.

4 I give thanks to my*b* God always for you because of the grace of God that has been given you in Christ Jesus, 5for in every way you have been enriched in him, in speech and knowledge of every kind— 6just as the testimony of*c* Christ has been strengthened among you— 7so that you are not lacking in any spiritual gift as you wait for the revealing of our Lord Jesus Christ. 8He will also strengthen you to the end, so that you may be blameless on the day of our Lord Jesus Christ. 9God is faithful; by him you were called into the fellowship of his Son, Jesus Christ our Lord.

---

a Gk *theirs*   *b* Other ancient authorities lack *my*   *c* Or *to*

1.1–3 The salutations of Paul's Letters generally follow the conventional Hellenistic pattern: the name(s) of the sender(s), an indication of those addressed, and an apostolic blessing; see esp. 2 Cor 1.1–2. **1.1** *An apostle*, lit. "one who has been sent" (thus, commissioned); see 9.1–2; 15.9–10; Gal 1.13–17. The *Sosthenes* mentioned here as a *brother* (in Christ) and co-sender of the Letter is perhaps the same person named in Acts 18.17 as an official of the Corinthian synagogue. Paul refers to him nowhere else. **1.2** *The church of God . . . in Corinth.* Paul identifies this local Christian assembly (*ekklesia*) not only by its geographical location but also as a constituent part of God's church in its entirety. *Sanctified* (see v. 30; 6.11) and *saints* (see 6.1, 2) are from the same Greek root word meaning "to make

holy." In biblical usage, to be holy means primarily to be set apart for the service of the holy God (see Lev 22.32). **1.4–9** The thanksgiving paragraphs in Paul's Letters (see, e.g., Rom 1.8–15; Phil 1.3–11) usually introduce some of the topics that will come up later. **1.5** *Speech and knowledge of every kind* includes the spiritual gifts (see 1.7) of ecstatic speech and special religious wisdom, in which certain members of this congregation took inordinate pride. Paul will later seek to correct their views on these (see 1.18–3.4; chs. 12–14). **1.7–8** *Spiritual gift.* See 12.4. Christ's *revealing* will be when he returns on the last *day* to render judgment (3.12–15; 4.4–5; 5.5) and to take part in God's final victory (15.24–28). **1.9** *God is faithful.* See 10.13; 2 Cor 1.18; 1 Thess 5.24; also Heb 10.23; Deut 7.9; 32.4; Ps 145.13.

Divisions in the Church

10 Now I appeal to you, brothers and sisters,[a] by the name of our Lord Jesus Christ, that all of you be in agreement and that there be no divisions among you, but that you be united in the same mind and the same purpose. [11]For it has been reported to me by Chloe's people that there are quarrels among you, my brothers and sisters.[b] [12]What I mean is that each of you says, "I belong to Paul," or "I belong to Apollos," or "I belong to Cephas," or "I belong to Christ." [13]Has Christ been divided? Was Paul crucified for you? Or were you baptized in the name of Paul? [14]I thank God[c] that I baptized none of you except Crispus and Gaius, [15]so that no one can say that you were baptized in my name. [16](I did baptize also the household of Stephanas; beyond that, I do not know whether I baptized anyone else.) [17]For Christ did not send me to baptize but to proclaim the gospel, and not with eloquent wisdom, so that the cross of Christ might not be emptied of its power.

Christ the Power and Wisdom of God

18 For the message about the cross is foolishness to those who are perishing, but to us who are being saved it is the power of God. [19]For it is written,

"I will destroy the wisdom of the wise,
    and the discernment of the discerning
        I will thwart."

[20]Where is the one who is wise? Where is the scribe? Where is the debater of this age? Has not God made foolish the wisdom of the world? [21]For since, in the wisdom of God, the world did not know God through wisdom, God decided, through the foolishness of our proclamation, to save those who believe. [22]For Jews demand signs and Greeks desire wisdom, [23]but we proclaim Christ crucified, a stumbling block to Jews and foolishness to Gentiles, [24]but to those who are the called, both Jews and Greeks, Christ the power of God and the wisdom of God. [25]For God's foolishness is wiser than human wisdom, and God's weakness is stronger than human strength.

26 Consider your own call, brothers and sisters:[a] not many of you were wise by human standards,[d] not many were powerful, not many were of noble birth. [27]But God chose what is foolish in the world to shame the wise; God chose what is weak in the world to shame the strong; [28]God chose what is low and despised in the world, things that are not, to reduce to nothing things that are, [29]so that no one[e] might boast in the presence of God. [30]He is the source of your life in Christ Jesus, who became for us wisdom from God, and righteousness and sanctification and redemption, [31]in order that, as it is written, "Let the one who boasts, boast in[f] the Lord."

---

a Gk brothers   b Gk my brothers   c Other ancient authorities read I am thankful   d Gk according to the flesh   e Gk no flesh   f Or of

---

Fellowship, rendered sharing in 10.16. **1.10–17** The breakdown of community among the Corinthian Christians is one of Paul's chief concerns in this Letter; see also chs. 3–4; 8.1–11.1; 11.17–34; chs. 12–14. **1.11** Chloe's people, either members of Chloe's family, her slaves, or her business associates. She herself was likely a Christian woman of some prominence, in either Corinth or Ephesus. **1.12** Apollos seems to have spent time in Corinth (Acts 18.24–19.1) and to have been popular there; see also 3.4–6, 22; 4.6; 16.12. There is, however, no indication that Cephas (the Aramaic name by which Paul usually refers to Peter; see 3.22; 9.5; 15.5) had ever been in Corinth. Whether some actually boasted I belong to Christ is uncertain; and if they did, what they meant by the slogan remains unclear. **1.13** The questions presume the obvious answer, "No!" They point ahead to later discussions of Christ's crucifixion (vv. 18, 23) and baptism (in the name of Christ, 6.11) into the one body (12.12–13). **1.14–17** Paul does not mean to oppose the practice of baptism (see 12.12–13; Rom 6.3–4; Gal 3.27–28); he only opposes appealing to it to support factions. **1.14–16** Crispus, Gaius, and Stephanas. See Introduction. **1.17** As an apostle, Paul is obligated, above all, to proclaim the gospel (9.16) and in particular the cross of Christ; see also 1.18, 23; 2.2; Gal 3.1. **1.18–31** This passage, along with 2.1–16, supports the appeal of 1.10, which is resumed and continued in chs. 3–4. **1.18** Perishing and being saved describe nonbelievers (2 Cor 4.3) and believers (1 Cor 1.21), respectively; see also 2 Cor 2.15; Phil 1.28. The power of God. See v. 24; 2.4–5; Rom 1.16. **1.19** Isa 29.14. See also Ps 33.10. **1.20** This age, the world, the present historical order that is passing away (7.31). **1.22** Greeks, Gentiles (v. 23). **1.23** Stumbling block, lit. "scandal." **1.24** The called, those converted to the gospel; see also vv. 2, 26; Rom 8.28. Both Jews and Greeks. See 12.13; Rom 1.16. **1.26** Of noble birth, lit. "well-born," members of families privileged with wealth and status. **1.30** God's own righteousness is bestowed as believers are "justified" (put right with God) through Christ; see 6.11; Rom 3.21–26; 5.17–21. Sanctification. See v. 2. Redemption, to be reclaimed for one's appropriate relationship with God, as a slave is freed from a master or prisoners of war are freed from their captors (sometimes for a price, 6.19–20; 7.23); see also Rom 3.24; 8.23. **1.31** Jer 9.24. See also 15.31.

Proclaiming Christ Crucified

2 When I came to you, brothers and sisters,[a] I did not come proclaiming the mystery[b] of God to you in lofty words or wisdom. 2For I decided to know nothing among you except Jesus Christ, and him crucified. 3And I came to you in weakness and in fear and in much trembling. 4My speech and my proclamation were not with plausible words of wisdom,[c] but with a demonstration of the Spirit and of power, 5so that your faith might rest not on human wisdom but on the power of God.

The True Wisdom of God

6 Yet among the mature we do speak wisdom, though it is not a wisdom of this age or of the rulers of this age, who are doomed to perish. 7But we speak God's wisdom, secret and hidden, which God decreed before the ages for our glory. 8None of the rulers of this age understood this; for if they had, they would not have crucified the Lord of glory. 9But, as it is written,

"What no eye has seen, nor ear heard,
    nor the human heart conceived,
what God has prepared for those who
    love him"—

10these things God has revealed to us through the Spirit; for the Spirit searches everything, even the depths of God. 11For what human being knows what is truly human except the human spirit that is within? So also no one comprehends what is truly God's except the Spirit of God. 12Now we have received not the spirit of the world, but the Spirit that is from God, so that we may understand the gifts bestowed on us by God. 13And we speak of these things in words not taught by human wisdom but taught by the Spirit, interpreting spiritual things to those who are spiritual.[d]

14 Those who are unspiritual[e] do not receive the gifts of God's Spirit, for they are foolishness to them, and they are unable to understand them because they are spiritually discerned. 15Those who are spiritual discern all things, and they are themselves subject to no one else's scrutiny.

16 "For who has known the mind of the
        Lord
    so as to instruct him?"
But we have the mind of Christ.

On Divisions in the Corinthian Church

3 And so, brothers and sisters,[a] I could not speak to you as spiritual people, but rather as people of the flesh, as infants in Christ. 2I fed you with milk, not solid food, for you were not ready for solid food. Even now you are still not ready, 3for you are still of the flesh. For as long as there is jealousy and quarreling among you, are you not of the flesh, and behaving according to human inclinations? 4For when one says, "I belong to Paul," and another, "I belong to Apollos," are you not merely human?

---

a Gk brothers   b Other ancient authorities read testimony
c Other ancient authorities read the persuasiveness of wisdom
d Or interpreting spiritual things in spiritual language, or
comparing spiritual things with spiritual   e Or natural

2.1–5 Paul reminds the Corinthians of their first hearing of the gospel; see also 15.1–2. **2.1** When I came to you, at first; see Introduction. The mystery of God, the gospel, which seems like foolishness to nonbelievers (1.18–21; see also 2.6–8). **2.4** Paul's speech was not ornamented like that of the popular orators of the day; see 1.17; 2 Cor 10.10; also Ex 4.10–11 (Moses). With a demonstration of the Spirit and of power. Cf. 1.23–24; 1 Thess 1.5, 6. **2.6–16** The foolishness of the gospel (1.21) is now identified with the deepest wisdom. **2.6** The mature. Cf. Paul's description of the Corinthians as infants in 3.1–2. The rulers of this age, either earthly, political rulers or the cosmic powers hostile to God (see 15.24–26). **2.7** Secret and hidden, lit. "in a mystery, hidden," yet in some sense disclosed in the gospel; see v. 1; 4.1. Before the ages, before creation, from eternity. Our glory looks ahead to the fullness of salvation, which, according to Paul, will be granted only after this age has passed away; see, e.g., Rom 5.2; 8.18–21; 2 Cor 3.18; 1 Thess 2.12. **2.8** Paul refers to Christ as the Lord of glory only here. **2.9** The source of this quotation is not known; but see Isa 64.4; 52.15. Love him. See also 8.3. **2.12** We have received . . . the Spirit, either at the first hearing of the gospel (e.g., vv. 4–5; Gal 3.2–3) or at baptism (1 Cor 12.13; cf. 2 Cor 1.22), or perhaps both. The gifts bestowed on us by God, all that God has given (see 4.7), not just special gifts like speaking in tongues. **2.13** And we speak . . . by the Spirit. See v. 4. **2.14** The gifts of God's Spirit. See v. 12. **2.16** For who . . . instruct him? Isa 40.13, cited also in Rom 11.34; Wis 9.13. Paul speaks of the mind of Christ only here, but see Rom 8.9; Gal 4.6; Phil 1.19.

3.1–23 Paul now returns to the specific issue of disunity and rivalries within the congregation (see 1.10–17), a major concern throughout this Letter. **3.1** Spiritual people, those who are informed by the Spirit that is from God (2.12). People of the flesh, those who are misled by the spirit of the world (2.12). **3.2** With milk, perhaps as a nursing mother; see 1 Thess 2.7. Paul's concern is similarly expressed in 14.20 (see also 13.11).

5 What then is Apollos? What is Paul? Servants through whom you came to believe, as the Lord assigned to each. 6 I planted, Apollos watered, but God gave the growth. 7 So neither the one who plants nor the one who waters is anything, but only God who gives the growth. 8 The one who plants and the one who waters have a common purpose, and each will receive wages according to the labor of each. 9 For we are God's servants, working together; you are God's field, God's building.

10 According to the grace of God given to me, like a skilled master builder I laid a foundation, and someone else is building on it. Each builder must choose with care how to build on it. 11 For no one can lay any foundation other than the one that has been laid; that foundation is Jesus Christ. 12 Now if anyone builds on the foundation with gold, silver, precious stones, wood, hay, straw— 13 the work of each builder will become visible, for the Day will disclose it, because it will be revealed with fire, and the fire will test what sort of work each has done. 14 If what has been built on the foundation survives, the builder will receive a reward. 15 If the work is burned up, the builder will suffer loss; the builder will be saved, but only as through fire.

16 Do you not know that you are God's temple and that God's Spirit dwells in you?[a] 17 If anyone destroys God's temple, God will destroy that person. For God's temple is holy, and you are that temple.

18 Do not deceive yourselves. If you think that you are wise in this age, you should become fools so that you may become wise. 19 For the wisdom of this world is foolishness with God. For it is written,

"He catches the wise in their craftiness,"

20 and again,

"The Lord knows the thoughts of the wise, that they are futile."

21 So let no one boast about human leaders. For all things are yours, 22 whether Paul or Apollos or Cephas or the world or life or death or the present or the future—all belong to you, 23 and you belong to Christ, and Christ belongs to God.

The Ministry of the Apostles

4 Think of us in this way, as servants of Christ and stewards of God's mysteries. 2 Moreover, it is required of stewards that they be found trustworthy. 3 But with me it is a very small thing that I should be judged by you or by any human court. I do not even judge myself. 4 I am not aware of anything against myself, but I am not thereby acquitted. It is the Lord who judges me. 5 Therefore do not pronounce judgment before the time, before the Lord comes, who will bring to light the things now hidden in darkness and will disclose the purposes of the heart. Then each one will receive commendation from God.

6 I have applied all this to Apollos and my-

---

a In verses 16 and 17 the Greek word for *you* is plural

3.3 *Jealousy and quarreling.* See 1.10–11. **3.4** *I belong to Paul.* See 1.12. **3.5** *Servants,* of God, as in 2 Cor 6.4. Elsewhere the Greek word (*diakonos*) is translated as "minister(s)" (e.g., 2 Cor 3.6) or "deacon(s)" (Rom 16.1; Phil 1.1). *The Lord,* more likely God (see vv. 6, 9) rather than Christ. **3.6** *I planted,* a metaphor for Paul's missionary preaching in Corinth; see also 2.1–5; 4.15; 9.1–2, 11; 15.1. *Apollos watered.* See Acts 18.24–19.1. **3.8** The *wages* will be paid at the final judgment; see also vv. 12–15. **3.9** *Working together,* lit. "fellow workers" (NRSV has added the word *servants*), either fellow workers for God or fellow workers with God. **3.10** *The grace of God,* manifested in Paul's conversion and call to apostleship; see also 15.9–10; Rom 1.5; 12.3; 15.15; Gal 1.15; 2.9. *I laid a foundation,* a second metaphor for preaching the gospel in Corinth; see also note on 3.6. **3.13** *The Day,* of final judgment, as in 1.7–8; see also 5.5. *Revealed with fire,* an image for God's eschatological judgment, drawn from the apocalyptic tradition (e.g., Mal 3.2–3; cf. Mt 3.10–12). **3.14** *Reward,* rendered *wages* in v. 8. **3.15** *Only as through fire* probably means "just barely" (see Am 4.11; Zech 3.2; Jude 23). **3.16** *You are God's temple* describes the Corinthian congregation as a whole; see also 2 Cor 6.16; Ezek 37.26–28; cf. 1 Cor 6.19. **3.17** *Holy.* See note on 1.2. **3.18** This appeal is based on the argument developed in 1.18–25. **3.19** Paul quotes Job 5.12–13. **3.20** Ps 94.11. **3.22** *Paul or Apollos or Cephas.* See 1.12. *Life or death or the present or the future.* See also Rom 8.38. Paul envisions the ultimate destruction of death; see 1 Cor 15.26; see also 15.54–55. **3.23** *You belong to Christ.* See 6.19–20; 7.22–23; also 1.9. *Christ belongs to God.* See 11.3; 15.28.

4.1–13 Here, as in 1.10–17; ch. 3, Paul attempts to counteract the rivalries and jealousies that have developed in the Corinthian congregation. **4.1** *Servants,* or "helpers" ("attendant" in Lk 4.20). In 3.5 *servants* translates a different Greek word. *Stewards,* or "managers"; the word was often used, as in Lk 12.42–48, of the slave who supervised household business. See also Gal 4.2 (translated "guardians"); 1 Pet 4.10. *God's mysteries,* as disclosed in the gospel; see 2.1, 6–16; also 13.2. **4.4–5** *The Lord,* Christ. Concerning the final *judgment,* see esp. 3.12–15; 5.5, 13; 6.2, 9–10. *Disclose the purposes of the heart.* Cf. 14.25; 2 Cor 4.2; Rom 2.16. **4.6** *Apollos.* See 1.12. *Nothing beyond what is written.* How Paul wishes to apply the slogan remains unclear.

self for your benefit, brothers and sisters,[a] so that you may learn through us the meaning of the saying, "Nothing beyond what is written," so that none of you will be puffed up in favor of one against another. 7For who sees anything different in you?[b] What do you have that you did not receive? And if you received it, why do you boast as if it were not a gift?

8 Already you have all you want! Already you have become rich! Quite apart from us you have become kings! Indeed, I wish that you had become kings, so that we might be kings with you! 9For I think that God has exhibited us apostles as last of all, as though sentenced to death, because we have become a spectacle to the world, to angels and to mortals. 10We are fools for the sake of Christ, but you are wise in Christ. We are weak, but you are strong. You are held in honor, but we in disrepute. 11To the present hour we are hungry and thirsty, we are poorly clothed and beaten and homeless, 12and we grow weary from the work of our own hands. When reviled, we bless; when persecuted, we endure; 13when slandered, we speak kindly. We have become like the rubbish of the world, the dregs of all things, to this very day.

Fatherly Admonition

14 I am not writing this to make you ashamed, but to admonish you as my beloved children. 15For though you might have ten thousand guardians in Christ, you do not have many fathers. Indeed, in Christ Jesus I became your fa-

ther through the gospel. 16I appeal to you, then, be imitators of me. 17For this reason I sent[c] you Timothy, who is my beloved and faithful child in the Lord, to remind you of my ways in Christ Jesus, as I teach them everywhere in every church. 18But some of you, thinking that I am not coming to you, have become arrogant. 19But I will come to you soon, if the Lord wills, and I will find out not the talk of these arrogant people but their power. 20For the kingdom of God depends not on talk but on power. 21What would you prefer? Am I to come to you with a stick, or with love in a spirit of gentleness?

Sexual Immorality Defiles the Church

5 It is actually reported that there is sexual immorality among you, and of a kind that is not found even among pagans; for a man is living with his father's wife. 2And you are arrogant! Should you not rather have mourned, so that he who has done this would have been removed from among you?

3 For though absent in body, I am present in spirit; and as if present I have already pronounced judgment 4in the name of the Lord Jesus on the man who has done such a thing.[d] When you are assembled, and my spirit is present with the power of our Lord Jesus, 5you are to hand this man over to Satan for the de-

---

a Gk brothers *b* Or Who makes you different from another?
c Or am sending *d* Or on the man who has done such a thing in the name of the Lord Jesus

---

4.7 Everything, even life itself, is to be received as God's *gift;* see also 2.12; 3.21–22. **4.8–10** Paul writes with irony, critical of the Corinthians' presumptuous claims about their religious status. Cf. vv. 18–19; 5.2; 8.1; 13.4. **4.9** *Spectacle* evokes the image of prisoners of war being publicly vilified in an outdoor theater. **4.10** *Fools for the sake of Christ,* because they proclaim the cross, 1.18–25; 3.18–20. **4.11–13** Similar lists of hardships appear in 2 Cor 4.8–9; 6.4–5; 11.23–29; 12.10; Rom 8.35. **4.12** *When reviled, we bless* perhaps echoes the saying attributed to Jesus in Lk 6.28; see also Rom 12.14. **4.14–21** The appeals begun in 1.10 are concluded, and the Corinthians are alerted to Timothy's coming and to Paul's own later visit. **4.14–15** Paul can claim paternity because he had founded the church in Corinth (3.6; 9.1–2; see also 1 Thess 2.11–12). **4.16** *Be imitators of me.* See also 11.1; Gal 4.12; Phil 3.17; 4.9; 1 Thess 1.6–7; 2 Thess 3.6–13. **4.17** *Timothy,* one of Paul's closest associates (e.g., Acts 16.1–3; 1 Thess 3.2), had helped found the Corinthian church (2 Cor 1.19). He has probably been dispatched to Corinth in advance of this Letter (16.10–11); but if the verb *sent* is interpreted *am sending* (see text note *c*), Timothy is about to leave with

the Letter. **4.18–19** Paul nowhere names these *arrogant* people. He may actually have the whole congregation in mind. *I will come to you soon.* See 16.5–9. **4.20** *The kingdom of God.* See also 6.9–10; 15.24, 50; Rom 14.17; Gal 5.21; 1 Thess 2.12. **4.21** *With a stick,* as a disciplinarian; see also 2 Cor 10.2–6; 12.21; 13.1–3, 10. *With love in a spirit of gentleness.* See Gal 6.1.

5.1–8 The apostle now deals with a specific case involving a member (never named) of the Corinthian church. **5.1** *Reported,* lit. "it has been heard," as distinguished from received in writing. *Sexual immorality* translates a term sometimes rendered *fornication,* as in 6.13, 18; Gal 5.19; 1 Thess 4.3. *Pagans,* gentile nonbelievers. *Living with,* engaging in sex with. *Father's wife,* an idiom referring to one's stepmother. **5.2** *Mourned,* grieved over the immorality of a fellow Christian. **5.4** *Assembled,* perhaps for the weekly congregational meal and worship; see 11.17–22. **5.5** *Hand . . . over to Satan,* put out of the church (see vv. 2, 13). *Satan,* a name used by both Jews and Christians for the personification of evil; see also 7.5; Rom 16.20; 2 Cor 2.11; 11.14; 12.7; 1 Thess 2.18; 2 Thess 2.9. *The flesh,* either a literal reference to the immoral man's physical body or a figurative

struction of the flesh, so that his spirit may be saved in the day of the Lord.[a]

6 Your boasting is not a good thing. Do you not know that a little yeast leavens the whole batch of dough? 7Clean out the old yeast so that you may be a new batch, as you really are unleavened. For our paschal lamb, Christ, has been sacrificed. 8Therefore, let us celebrate the festival, not with the old yeast, the yeast of malice and evil, but with the unleavened bread of sincerity and truth.

Sexual Immorality Must Be Judged

9 I wrote to you in my letter not to associate with sexually immoral persons— 10not at all meaning the immoral of this world, or the greedy and robbers, or idolaters, since you would then need to go out of the world. 11But now I am writing to you not to associate with anyone who bears the name of brother or sister[b] who is sexually immoral or greedy, or is an idolater, reviler, drunkard, or robber. Do not even eat with such a one. 12For what have I to do with judging those outside? Is it not those who are inside that you are to judge? 13God will judge those outside. "Drive out the wicked person from among you."

Lawsuits among Believers

6 When any of you has a grievance against another, do you dare to take it to court be-

fore the unrighteous, instead of taking it before the saints? 2Do you not know that the saints will judge the world? And if the world is to be judged by you, are you incompetent to try trivial cases? 3Do you not know that we are to judge angels—to say nothing of ordinary matters? 4If you have ordinary cases, then, do you appoint as judges those who have no standing in the church? 5I say this to your shame. Can it be that there is no one among you wise enough to decide between one believer[b] and another, 6but a believer[b] goes to court against a believer[b]—and before unbelievers at that?

7 In fact, to have lawsuits at all with one another is already a defeat for you. Why not rather be wronged? Why not rather be defrauded? 8But you yourselves wrong and defraud—and believers[c] at that.

9 Do you not know that wrongdoers will not inherit the kingdom of God? Do not be deceived! Fornicators, idolaters, adulterers, male prostitutes, sodomites, 10thieves, the greedy, drunkards, revilers, robbers—none of these will inherit the kingdom of God. 11And this is what some of you used to be. But you were washed, you were sanctified, you were justified in the name of the Lord Jesus Christ and in the Spirit of our God.

---

a Other ancient authorities add *Jesus*   *b* Gk *brother*
c Gk *brothers*

---

reference to his evil desires. It is thus difficult to know what Paul expects will result from the punishment he is recommending. *The day of the Lord.* See 3.13. **5.6** *Yeast,* a metaphor for evil (see 5.8), as in Mt 16.6, 11–12; Mk 8.15; Lk 12.1; see also Gal 5.9. **5.7** *Paschal lamb,* the animal slaughtered for the Jewish celebration of Passover; see Ex 12.1–27. According to the Gospels, Jesus was put to death at Passover time (Mk 14–15). **5.8** Only *unleavened bread,* a symbol of purity, was to be eaten during Passover; see Ex 12.8, 15–20. **5.9–13** Paul's directions in a previous letter to Corinth, perhaps misunderstood, are now clarified. **5.9** The *letter* referred to either is lost or, as some believe, survives in fragmentary form in 2 Cor 6.14–7.1. **5.10–11** A similar list of evildoers is given in 6.9–10. **5.11** *Brother or sister,* a fellow Christian, as distinct from nonbelievers. The instruction to *not even eat* with immoral believers presumably includes barring them from participating in the Lord's Supper (see 10.16–17). **5.12** *Outside* and *inside,* where people are with reference to the Christian community. Paul's concern for how insiders should conduct themselves in relation to outsiders is apparent throughout 5.1–11.1 (see also 15.23–24). **5.13** *God will judge,* on judgment day (see 3.13). The quotation is from Deut 17.7.
6.1–11 Paul counsels against Christians asking Ro-

man courts to settle their disputes. Perhaps he has heard of some specific legal action initiated by one of the members of the congregation against another member of lower status and means. **6.1** *Unrighteous,* nonbelievers; *saints* (see 1.2), believers (see also 6.6). **6.2** *The world,* here nonbelievers. For the idea that the *saints* will assist with the final judgment, see Wis 3.8; 4.16; Sir 4.15; Lk 22.30; Mt 19.28; Rev 3.21; 20.4. **6.3** The expectation that *angels* are subject to final judgment is also envisioned in Isa 24.21–22; Jude 6 (see also 2 Pet 2.4), but not that any human agents will be their judges. **6.4** *Those . . . no standing in the church,* more likely nonbelievers than persons within the church, yet the latter interpretation is sometimes argued. **6.7** *Be wronged.* See also Mt 5.39–40; Lk 6.28–30. **6.8** *Defrauding.* See Mk 10.19. **6.9–10** The list of evildoers is similar to the one in 5.10–11. **6.9** *The kingdom of God.* See 4.20. *Fornicators,* persons who engage in sexual conduct regarded as immoral; see note on 5.1. *Male prostitutes,* adolescent boys who sold sexual favors to older males or, more generally, the more passive male in a homosexual act. *Sodomites,* Greek *arsenokoitai,* lit. "those who bed males," may be Paul's own coinage, for no earlier occurrence of the term is known. It seems to refer to the more active partner in a male homosexual act; see also Rom 1.27; 1 Tim 1.10. **6.11** *Washed,* proba-

Glorify God in Body and Spirit

12 "All things are lawful for me," but not all things are beneficial. "All things are lawful for me," but I will not be dominated by anything. [13]"Food is meant for the stomach and the stomach for food," [a] and God will destroy both one and the other. The body is meant not for fornication but for the Lord, and the Lord for the body. [14]And God raised the Lord and will also raise us by his power. [15]Do you not know that your bodies are members of Christ? Should I therefore take the members of Christ and make them members of a prostitute? Never! [16]Do you not know that whoever is united to a prostitute becomes one body with her? For it is said, "The two shall be one flesh." [17]But anyone united to the Lord becomes one spirit with him. [18]Shun fornication! Every sin that a person commits is outside the body; but the fornicator sins against the body itself. [19]Or do you not know that your body is a temple [b] of the Holy Spirit within you, which you have from God, and that you are not your own? [20]For you were bought with a price; therefore glorify God in your body.

Directions concerning Marriage

7 Now concerning the matters about which you wrote: "It is well for a man not to touch a woman." [2]But because of cases of sexual immorality, each man should have his own wife and each woman her own husband. [3]The husband should give to his wife her conjugal rights, and likewise the wife to her husband. [4]For the wife does not have authority over her own body, but the husband does; likewise the husband does not have authority over his own body, but the wife does. [5]Do not deprive one another except perhaps by agreement for a set time, to devote yourselves to prayer, and then come together again, so that Satan may not tempt you because of your lack of self-control. [6]This I say by way of concession, not of command. [7]I wish that all were as I myself am. But each has a particular gift from God, one having one kind and another a different kind.

8 To the unmarried and the widows I say that it is well for them to remain unmarried as I am. [9]But if they are not practicing self-control, they should marry. For it is better to marry than to be aflame with passion.

10 To the married I give this command— not I but the Lord—that the wife should not separate from her husband [11](but if she does separate, let her remain unmarried or else be reconciled to her husband), and that the husband should not divorce his wife.

---

a The quotation may extend to the word *other*   *b* Or *sanctuary*

---

bly baptized. *Sanctified.* See 1.2. *Justified.* See note on 1.30. *In the Spirit of our God.* See 12.13. **6.12–20** The apostle continues to criticize and correct the Corinthians' understanding of what it means to be faithful to the gospel. **6.12–13** Paul is quoting slogans popular in Corinth (see also 10.23), conceivably ones that some Corinthians have attributed to him. **6.13** *God will destroy,* either the ultimate destruction of all material things (see 7.31) or, more specifically, the last judgment (see 3.13). *The Lord,* here Christ (vv. 14–17). **6.14** See also 15.4, 12– 22; 2 Cor 4.14; 1 Thess 4.14; cf. Rom 8.11. **6.15** *Members of Christ.* See also 12.12–14, 27; Rom 12.4–5. **6.16** Paul quotes Gen 2.24. **6.17** *One spirit with him* refers to the spiritual character of communion with Christ. **6.19** *Temple of the Holy Spirit,* here used metaphorically of the individual believer's *body* (cf. 3.16). *Not your own.* See also Rom 14.7–8; 2 Cor 5.14–15. **6.20** *Bought with a price.* See also 7.23; note on 1.30. *Glorify God.* See also 10.31.

7.1–16 The issue to which Paul now turns has been raised with him in a letter from the Corinthians themselves, and the whole of ch. 7 is devoted to it. Their question is not just about marriage but, more generally, whether sexual intimacy is compatible with life in Christ. **7.1** *You wrote,* a reference to some (lost) letter to Paul from the Corinthians. Some scholars believe that

the quotation is another slogan current among the Corinthians (see 6.12–13); others believe it represents a view that Paul himself has expressed (perhaps in an earlier letter; see 5.9). Many translations do not mark it as a quotation at all. *Touch,* an idiom for "have sex with." **7.2** *Cases of sexual immorality.* See 5.1–5; 6.12–20. *Own wife . . . own husband* affirms monogamy and marital fidelity; see also 1 Thess 4.3–5. **7.3** *Give . . . conjugal rights.* This affirmation of sexual intimacy within a Christian marriage stands in contrast with the ascetic view quoted in v. 1. **7.4** A husband's authority over his wife was presupposed in the ancient world (see Eph 5.24; Col 3.18; 1 Pet 3.1, 6), but not a wife's authority over her husband. **7.5** *Do not deprive one another,* of conjugal rights. *Satan.* See 5.5. *Tempt you,* to marital infidelity. *Self-control.* Cf. v. 9; 9.25–27; Gal 5.23. **7.6** *Concession,* probably the provision for temporary abstinence from sexual intimacy (7.5). *Not of command.* See also v. 35; 2 Cor 8.8; Philem 8–9. **7.7** *As I myself am,* unmarried (see v. 8; 9.5, 15). Paul implies that celibacy is one *particular gift;* others are mentioned in ch. 12; Rom 12.6–8 (also 1 Pet 4.10). Cf. 1 Cor 3.5; 7.17. **7.8** *The unmarried,* perhaps widowers specifically (the expression is masculine). **7.9** *Aflame with passion,* a common metaphor; see Sir 9.8; 23.16. **7.10–11** *The Lord,* Jesus (see also 9.14). *Separate, divorce,* synonyms. The sayings about divorce attributed

12 To the rest I say—I and not the Lord—that if any believer*a* has a wife who is an unbeliever, and she consents to live with him, he should not divorce her. 13And if any woman has a husband who is an unbeliever, and he consents to live with her, she should not divorce him. 14For the unbelieving husband is made holy through his wife, and the unbelieving wife is made holy through her husband. Otherwise, your children would be unclean, but as it is, they are holy. 15But if the unbelieving partner separates, let it be so; in such a case the brother or sister is not bound. It is to peace that God has called you.*b* 16Wife, for all you know, you might save your husband. Husband, for all you know, you might save your wife.

The Life That the Lord Has Assigned

17 However that may be, let each of you lead the life that the Lord has assigned, to which God called you. This is my rule in all the churches. 18Was anyone at the time of his call already circumcised? Let him not seek to remove the marks of circumcision. Was anyone at the time of his call uncircumcised? Let him not seek circumcision. 19Circumcision is nothing, and uncircumcision is nothing; but obeying the commandments of God is everything. 20Let each of you remain in the condition in which you were called.

21 Were you a slave when called? Do not be concerned about it. Even if you can gain your freedom, make use of your present condition now more than ever.*c* 22For whoever was called in the Lord as a slave is a freed person belonging to the Lord, just as whoever was free when called is a slave of Christ. 23You were bought with a price; do not become slaves of human masters. 24In whatever condition you were called, brothers and sisters,*d* there remain with God.

The Unmarried and the Widows

25 Now concerning virgins, I have no command of the Lord, but I give my opinion as one who by the Lord's mercy is trustworthy.

a Gk brother   *b* Other ancient authorities read *us*   *c* Or *avail yourself of the opportunity*   *d* Gk *brothers*

to Jesus are found in one version in Mk 10.2–12 (see also Lk 16.18) and in other versions in Mt 5.31–32; 19.3–9. Paul's instructions here presume Roman law, according to which (in contrast to Deut 24.1–4) divorce could be initiated by either the husband or the wife (see also Mk 10.11–12); and they also presume that both partners are Christians (cf. vv. 12–16). See also v. 27; Rom 7.2. **7.12** *The rest,* persons who were already married when they were converted to the gospel, but whose spouses have remained nonbelievers. Such marriages are not addressed by the command of Jesus invoked in vv. 10–11. *I and not the Lord* (cf. v. 10). Paul now offers counsels on his own authority, without appealing to any teaching of Jesus. **7.14** *Made holy,* or "sanctified" (see 1.2), i.e., by God, not by the marriage as such. The overall point is that God's sanctifying power is stronger than unbelief. The exact meaning, however, is obscure, both here and when Paul describes the children in families where only one parent is Christian. Children seem to be regarded as *holy* so long as the Christian parent remains in the marriage, but as *unclean* when that parent leaves the marriage. **7.15** *Separates,* initiates a divorce. *To peace,* to a peaceful relationship with the non-Christian spouse. This counsel is consistent with the general directive about striving for peace with all people that Paul issues in Rom 12.18. **7.16** *Save,* here the conversion to Christianity of the non-Christian spouse (see also 1 Pet 3.1–2). Interpreters differ on whether Paul means that there is a good chance or only an outside chance of this happening. **7.17–24** Here Paul generalizes the particular counsels set forth in vv. 12–16. His basic principle, which he now illustrates with examples other than marriage, is that converts to Christianity should not ordi-

narily seek to change their situation in society. **7.17** *The Lord,* God. *All the churches,* the congregations founded by Paul; over those founded by others he exercised no authority. **7.18** *Call,* conversion to the gospel. Paul himself, like every male child born to devout Jews, had been circumcised as an infant (Phil 3.5) to signify his belonging to the covenant people (see Gen 17.9–14). Some Jews, seeking acceptance in gentile society, tried to *remove the marks of circumcision.* Paul's view that gentile converts should *not seek circumcision* differed from that of the Jerusalem church; see Gal 2.1–14. **7.19** See also Rom 2.25–29; Gal 5.6; 6.15. **7.20** *Condition,* lit. "calling," one's status and circumstances at the time of conversion. **7.21** Many converts were *slaves* (see 12.13; Gal 3.28; Philem 16; also Eph 6.5–9; Col 3.11, 22–4.1; 1 Tim 6.1–2; Titus 2.9–10; 1 Pet 2.18–25). The institution of slavery was fundamental to the social, economic, and political structures of imperial Rome. *Freedom* could be purchased by or for a slave for a price or could be granted for a variety of other reasons. *Make use . . . ever.* The translation in text note *c* is preferable. **7.22** *The Lord,* Christ. *A freed person,* an ex-slave; in this case, Paul is thinking of people who have been freed from the law, sin, and death for obedience to *the Lord;* see Rom 6.6–7.6; 8.15; Gal 4.7. *Whoever was free,* those who had been born free and remained so. A *slave of Christ,* belonging to Christ (3.23) as a committed, faithful Christian; see Rom 6.16–18, 22; 7.6 (also Rom 12.11; 14.18; 16.18; 1 Thess 1.9). **7.23** *Bought with a price.* See 6.20; note on 1.30. *Slaves of human masters,* a metaphor for yielding to merely human claims and values; see also Rom 8.12–17; Gal 5.1. **7.24** A reformulation of the principle stated in v. 20. **7.25–40** The discussion now returns to the spe-

26I think that, in view of the impending*a* crisis, it is well for you to remain as you are. 27Are you bound to a wife? Do not seek to be free. Are you free from a wife? Do not seek a wife. 28But if you marry, you do not sin, and if a virgin marries, she does not sin. Yet those who marry will experience distress in this life,*b* and I would spare you that. 29I mean, brothers and sisters,*c* the appointed time has grown short; from now on, let even those who have wives be as though they had none, 30and those who mourn as though they were not mourning, and those who rejoice as though they were not rejoicing, and those who buy as though they had no possessions, 31and those who deal with the world as though they had no dealings with it. For the present form of this world is passing away.

32 I want you to be free from anxieties. The unmarried man is anxious about the affairs of the Lord, how to please the Lord; 33but the married man is anxious about the affairs of the world, how to please his wife, 34and his interests are divided. And the unmarried woman and the virgin are anxious about the affairs of the Lord, so that they may be holy in body and spirit; but the married woman is anxious about the affairs of the world, how to please her husband. 35I say this for your own benefit, not to put any restraint upon you, but to promote good order and unhindered devotion to the Lord.

36 If anyone thinks that he is not behaving properly toward his fiancée,*d* if his passions are strong, and so it has to be, let him marry as he wishes; it is no sin. Let them marry. 37But if someone stands firm in his resolve, being under no necessity but having his own desire under control, and has determined in his own mind to keep her as his fiancée,*d* he will do well. 38So then, he who marries his fiancée*d* does well; and he who refrains from marriage will do better.

39 A wife is bound as long as her husband lives. But if the husband dies,*e* she is free to marry anyone she wishes, only in the Lord. 40But in my judgment she is more blessed if she remains as she is. And I think that I too have the Spirit of God.

Food Offered to Idols

8 Now concerning food sacrificed to idols: we know that "all of us possess knowl-

---

a Or *present*   *b* Gk *in the flesh*   *c* Gk *brothers*   *d* Gk *virgin*
e Gk *falls asleep*

---

cific issue of whether marriage is ever appropriate for Christians. **7.25** *Virgins,* women who have never been married, but whether Paul is thinking of them as engaged to be married is unclear (see vv. 36–38). *No command of the Lord.* Cf. v. 10; see also v. 12. *By the Lord's mercy,* a reference to God's calling Paul to apostleship; see 2 Cor 4.1; also 1 Cor 1.1. **7.26** *The impending crisis,* the tribulations traditionally expected to occur as the present age passes away (vv. 29–31; see Lk 21.23–24). The alternate translation, *present crisis* (see text note *a*), interprets Paul as referring to the troubles that Christians experience daily in society. *Remain as you are.* See vv. 17–24. **7.29** *The appointed time has grown short.* The time of Christ's return, the day of judgment, and the fulfillment of salvation is near; see 1.7–8; also Rom 13.11–12. *As though they had none.* See also Lk 14.26. Paul's counsel is not to abstain from conjugal relations (see vv. 3–5), but to realize that marriage too will pass away (see v. 31). **7.30** *As though they were not mourning . . . rejoicing.* Paul does not deny the reality of griefs and joys in this life, only their ultimate significance. *As though they had no possessions,* for all things belong to God (10.26; cf. 3.21–23). **7.31a** A generalizing counsel inclusive of those in vv. 29b–30. **7.31b** *The present form of this world,* the cosmos as it presently exists, not just its appearance. **7.32** *The Lord,* Christ (cf. Phil 2.21). **7.33** *The affairs of the world,* like those mentioned in vv. 29b–31a. **7.34** *Unmarried woman,* one previously mar-

ried, as distinguished from a *virgin,* who has never been married. **7.35** *Not to put any restraint.* See v. 6. **7.36–38** Interpreters differ on how these instructions relate to those about virgins in vv. 25–26, 28. Paul, however, is consistent in applying the twofold principle that it is better not to be married but no sin to be married (see vv. 7, 8, 25–28, 32–35). **7.39** *Bound . . . as long as her husband lives.* This is consistent with the Lord's command cited in vv. 10–11. The possibility of an exception should the husband not be a Christian (vv. 12–16) is probably taken for granted, even though it is not restated here. **7.40** *My judgment* (see also 7.12, 25; 2 Cor 8.10), the judgment of an apostle and one who has been informed by *the Spirit of God* (cf. 2.16, *we have the mind of Christ*).

8.1–13 From here through 11.1 Paul offers directives on a matter that has troubled his congregation: whether Christians may eat meat that has been left over from pagan sacrificial rites (cf. Rom 14). No agreement like the one reported in Acts 15.29 is in view. **8.1** *Now concerning* introduces a new topic. Perhaps, like the matter introduced by the same phrase in 7.1, it has been raised in a letter from Corinth, but this is not specifically indicated. *Food sacrificed to idols* translates one Greek word (lit. "things sacrificed to idols"), used only by Jews and Christians; the neutral term is "sacred food" (see note on 10.28). Both words refer to the meat of an animal that has been ritually

edge." Knowledge puffs up, but love builds up. [2] Anyone who claims to know something does not yet have the necessary knowledge; [3] but anyone who loves God is known by him.

[4] Hence, as to the eating of food offered to idols, we know that "no idol in the world really exists," and that "there is no God but one." [5] Indeed, even though there may be so-called gods in heaven or on earth—as in fact there are many gods and many lords— [6] yet for us there is one God, the Father, from whom are all things and for whom we exist, and one Lord, Jesus Christ, through whom are all things and through whom we exist.

[7] It is not everyone, however, who has this knowledge. Since some have become so accustomed to idols until now, they still think of the food they eat as food offered to an idol; and their conscience, being weak, is defiled. [8] "Food will not bring us close to God." [a] We are no worse off if we do not eat, and no better off if we do. [9] But take care that this liberty of yours does not somehow become a stumbling block to the weak. [10] For if others see you, who possess knowledge, eating in the temple of an idol, might they not, since their conscience is weak, be encouraged to the point of eating food sacrificed to idols? [11] So by your knowledge those weak believers for whom Christ died are destroyed. [b] [12] But when you thus sin against members of your family, [c] and wound their conscience when it is weak, you sin against Christ. [13] Therefore, if food is a cause of their falling, [d] I will never eat meat, so that I may not cause one of them [e] to fall.

The Rights of an Apostle

9 Am I not free? Am I not an apostle? Have I not seen Jesus our Lord? Are you not my work in the Lord? [2] If I am not an apostle to others, at least I am to you; for you are the seal of my apostleship in the Lord.

[3] This is my defense to those who would examine me. [4] Do we not have the right to our food and drink? [5] Do we not have the right to

---

a The quotation may extend to the end of the verse   *b* Gk *the weak brother . . . is destroyed*   *c* Gk *against the brothers*   *d* Gk *my brother's falling*   *e* Gk *cause my brother*

---

slaughtered. *All of us possess knowledge,* a slogan of some Corinthian Christians. *Knowledge puffs up,* not knowledge in general, but the kind of religious knowledge arrogantly flaunted by certain Corinthians; see 4.6, 18–19; 5.2; 13.4. *Love builds up* Christian community by uniting its members in the care of and service to one another; see 14.1–5, 12, 17, 26; also 10.23–24. Here and elsewhere in 1 Corinthians the Greek word used for *love* is *agape,* which is described in ch. 13 as utterly selfless; see also 4.21; 16.14, 24. **8.2** *Know something,* probably to be understood as "something about God," whereas the *necessary knowledge* is being *known by God* (v. 3). **8.3** *Loves God.* See 2.9; Rom 8.28; Jas 1.12; 2.5; also Deut 6.5. *Known by him.* See also 13.12; Gal 4.9. To be thus "known" is to be chosen and called by God; see Rom 8.29–30; also Gen 18.19; Ex 33.12, 17; Jer 1.5. **8.4** *No idol . . . really exists,* a fundamental tenet of Jewish and Christian teaching (Ex 20.4–5; Isa 46; Wis 13–14), with which the Corinthian Christians fully agree; see also 10.14; 12.2. *No God but one* echoes the affirmation of Deut 6.4—the Shema, often recited by Jews as a summary of their faith. **8.5** *Many gods and many lords,* the deities who were worshiped by gentile nonbelievers. Paul challenges their divine status (*so-called gods*), but does not deny their existence absolutely (*as in fact there are*); see also Gal 4.8. **8.6** An early Christian creed may lie behind this statement; see also 10.26; 11.12; 12.3; Rom 11.36; Col 1.16–17; Heb 2.10. **8.7** *Not everyone . . . some.* In both cases Paul is referring specifically to the Christian community. *Weak,* unenlightened, still under the illusion that pagan sacrifices have some kind of potency; see also vv. 10, 12; 10.27–29; Rom 14.1–2, 23; 15.1. *Defiled.*

The act prompts feelings of guilt; see also v. 12 (*wound*). **8.8** Paul is presumably quoting the Corinthians (so interpreted by NRSV) and does so with approval. What he then says about food he has said earlier about circumcision (7.19). **8.9** *Liberty,* or right, as in 9.4–6, 12, 18. *Stumbling block.* See also Rom 14.13, 20–21; 2 Cor 6.3. (The Greek word in 1.23 is different.) **8.10** *Knowledge.* See v. 1. *Eating in the temple of an idol.* Many pagan temples had a dining area where meat left over from the sacrifice was eaten at a communal meal. *Encouraged,* lit. "built up." **8.11** Christ's death for the *weak* is also invoked in Rom 14.15 (cf. Rom 5.6). **8.12** *Wound their conscience.* See note on 8.7. *Sin against Christ.* Cf. 11.17, 29; Mt 25.45; Heb 6.6. **8.13** *Meat,* left over from pagan rites.

9.1–27 Paul emphasizes that he has not exercised certain rights that are his as an apostle. His aim here is probably to support the counsels of ch. 8, although some interpreters believe that he is addressing a new topic. **9.1** Paul is *free* both to claim and to give up certain rights. *Apostle.* See 1.1. *Jesus our Lord,* the resurrected Christ, whom Paul beheld at his conversion and call; see 15.8–10. The Corinthian church was Paul's *work* because it had been founded by him. **9.2** The very existence of a church in Corinth attests (*seals*) Paul's *apostleship;* see also 2 Cor 3.2–3; 10.13–14. **9.3** *Those who would examine me,* perhaps specific adversaries, but they are never named. **9.4** *We,* apostles in general, including Paul. *Right,* translates a Greek word that sometimes means *liberty* (see 8.9) or "authority" (see 2 Cor 10.8). *Food and drink,* living expenses (or at least "board") while serving as an apostle. **9.5** *Brothers of the Lord,* Jesus' brothers (see Mk 6.3), of whom only James

be accompanied by a believing wife,[a] as do the other apostles and the brothers of the Lord and Cephas? 6Or is it only Barnabas and I who have no right to refrain from working for a living? 7Who at any time pays the expenses for doing military service? Who plants a vineyard and does not eat any of its fruit? Or who tends a flock and does not get any of its milk?

8 Do I say this on human authority? Does not the law also say the same? 9For it is written in the law of Moses, "You shall not muzzle an ox while it is treading out the grain." Is it for oxen that God is concerned? 10Or does he not speak entirely for our sake? It was indeed written for our sake, for whoever plows should plow in hope and whoever threshes should thresh in hope of a share in the crop. 11If we have sown spiritual good among you, is it too much if we reap your material benefits? 12If others share this rightful claim on you, do not we still more?

Nevertheless, we have not made use of this right, but we endure anything rather than put an obstacle in the way of the gospel of Christ. 13Do you not know that those who are employed in the temple service get their food from the temple, and those who serve at the altar share in what is sacrificed on the altar? 14In the same way, the Lord commanded that those who proclaim the gospel should get their living by the gospel.

15 But I have made no use of any of these rights, nor am I writing this so that they may be applied in my case. Indeed, I would rather die than that—no one will deprive me of my ground for boasting! 16If I proclaim the gospel, this gives me no ground for boasting, for an obligation is laid on me, and woe to me if I do not proclaim the gospel! 17For if I do this of my own will, I have a reward; but if not of my own will, I am entrusted with a commission. 18What then is my reward? Just this: that in my proclamation I may make the gospel free of charge, so as not to make full use of my rights in the gospel.

19 For though I am free with respect to all, I have made myself a slave to all, so that I might win more of them. 20To the Jews I became as a Jew, in order to win Jews. To those under the law I became as one under the law (though I myself am not under the law) so that I might win those under the law. 21To those outside the law I became as one outside the law (though I am not free from God's law but am under Christ's law) so that I might win those outside the law. 22To the weak I became weak, so that I might win the weak. I have become all things to all people, that I might by all means save some. 23I do it all for the sake of the gospel, so that I may share in its blessings.

24 Do you not know that in a race the runners all compete, but only one receives the prize? Run in such a way that you may win it. 25Athletes exercise self-control in all things; they do it to receive a perishable wreath, but we an imperishable one. 26So I do not run

a Gk a sister as wife

is ever named by Paul himself (see 15.7; Gal 1.19). *Cephas,* Peter (see 1.12), who, according to Mk 1.30, was married. **9.6** *Barnabas* (see Acts 4.36–37; Col 4.10) was apparently one of Paul's earliest associates (Gal 2.1–10; see also, e.g., Acts 9.27; 11.19–30), but he and Paul eventually had a falling out (Gal 2.13; see also Acts 15.36–41). *Working for a living,* in addition to apostolic labors; see Acts 18.1–4. **9.7** For the examples used here, see also Deut 20.6; 2 Tim 2.4. **9.9** Deut 25.4; see also 1 Tim 5.17–18. **9.11** *Spiritual good,* the gospel and all that follows from that; see also 3.6. **9.12** *Others,* conceivably Apollos and Peter (see 1.12). *Not made use of this right.* Paul has accepted no financial assistance from the Corinthians; see Acts 18.1–4; 2 Cor 11.7–11; 12.13, 14. **9.13** Jewish sacrifice (see also 10.18) and thus the Jerusalem temple are in view; see Num 18.8–32; Deut 18.1–5. **9.14** As in 7.10, Paul invokes a saying attributed to Jesus (Mt 10.10; Lk 10.7); see also 1 Tim 5.17–18. A similar principle is affirmed in Gal 6.6. **9.15** *These rights* are the ones mentioned in vv. 4–6, especially the right to a living; see also v. 12. Paul's

ground for boasting is that he had not burdened the Corinthians with his personal needs; see also 2 Cor 11.7–10. **9.16** On Paul's *obligation* to preach, see also 4.1–2; Acts 22.14–15; 26.14–18; Rom 1.1–6, 14–15; 15.18–21 (and Jer 20.9; Lk 17.10). **9.17** *Reward,* or "wage." Paul's *commission* was from God; related to the word translated as *steward* in 4.1–2. **9.19** *Though I am free* interprets the Greek clause as concessive, but it could equally well be taken as causal: "since I am free" (cf. v. 1). *A slave to all,* obligated to serve all; see v. 16; 2 Cor 4.5. *Win,* convert to, or perhaps also strengthen in, the gospel. **9.20** *I became as a Jew.* See Acts 16.3; 21.17–26. **9.21** *Those outside the law,* gentile nonbelievers. *Christ's law.* See also Gal 6.2. **9.22** *The weak,* probably not believers weak in faith (as in 8.9–12), but nonbelievers of lowly social status (as in 1.27), for the topic here is missionary preaching. **9.23** *That I may share in its blessings.* See also v. 27. **9.24** *Receives the prize.* See also Phil 3.12–16; 2 Tim 2.5. **9.25** *A perishable wreath.* At the Isthmian games, held near Corinth every two years, the winner's crown was made of with-

aimlessly, nor do I box as though beating the air; [27]but I punish my body and enslave it, so that after proclaiming to others I myself should not be disqualified.

Warnings from Israel's History

10 I do not want you to be unaware, brothers and sisters,[a] that our ancestors were all under the cloud, and all passed through the sea, [2]and all were baptized into Moses in the cloud and in the sea, [3]and all ate the same spiritual food, [4]and all drank the same spiritual drink. For they drank from the spiritual rock that followed them, and the rock was Christ. [5]Nevertheless, God was not pleased with most of them, and they were struck down in the wilderness.

6 Now these things occurred as examples for us, so that we might not desire evil as they did. [7]Do not become idolaters as some of them did; as it is written, "The people sat down to eat and drink, and they rose up to play." [8]We must not indulge in sexual immorality as some of them did, and twenty-three thousand fell in a single day. [9]We must not put Christ[b] to the test, as some of them did, and were destroyed by serpents. [10]And do not complain as some of them did, and were destroyed by the destroyer. [11]These things happened to them to serve as an example, and they were written down to instruct us, on

whom the ends of the ages have come. [12]So if you think you are standing, watch out that you do not fall. [13]No testing has overtaken you that is not common to everyone. God is faithful, and he will not let you be tested beyond your strength, but with the testing he will also provide the way out so that you may be able to endure it.

14 Therefore, my dear friends,[c] flee from the worship of idols. [15]I speak as to sensible people; judge for yourselves what I say. [16]The cup of blessing that we bless, is it not a sharing in the blood of Christ? The bread that we break, is it not a sharing in the body of Christ? [17]Because there is one bread, we who are many are one body, for we all partake of the one bread. [18]Consider the people of Israel;[d] are not those who eat the sacrifices partners in the altar? [19]What do I imply then? That food sacrificed to idols is anything, or that an idol is anything? [20]No, I imply that what pagans sacrifice, they sacrifice to demons and not to God. I do not want you to be partners with demons. [21]You cannot drink the cup of the Lord and the cup of demons. You cannot partake of the table of the Lord and the table of demons. [22]Or are we provoking the Lord to jealousy? Are we stronger than he?

---

a Gk brothers *b* Other ancient authorities read *the Lord* *c* Gk *my beloved* *d* Gk *Israel according to the flesh*

---

ered celery. The *imperishable* wreath stands for one's ultimate salvation; see Phil 4.1; 1 Thess 2.19; 2 Tim 4.8; 1 Pet 5.4; Rev 2.10. **9.27** *I punish my body and enslave it,* metaphors for, respectively, enduring hardships (4.11–13) and exercising self-control (v. 25); cf. 9.12b.
10.1–22 Paul now offers examples of the dangers of idolatry. The main topic, however, remains the question about eating meat that has come from pagan sacrifices (see vv. 19–20). **10.1** *Our ancestors,* the Israelites. On the *cloud* and the *sea,* see Ex 13.21–22; 14.22; Ps 105.39; Wis 19.7–8. **10.2** *Baptized,* an expression that derives from Christian practice, not from the Jewish scriptures on which Paul is drawing in this passage. **10.3** *Spiritual food,* i.e., manna; see Ex 16.4, 35; Deut 8.3; Ps 78.24–25. **10.4** On *spiritual drink,* see Ex 17.6; Num 20.7–11; Ps 78.15–16. Although the OT says nothing about a *rock that followed* the Israelites in the wilderness, a later rabbinic tradition did say this about a well (see Num 21.16–18). Since Paul identifies the rock with *Christ,* he probably views the Israelites' eating and drinking as a kind of Lord's Supper (see vv. 16–17). **10.5** On the punishment in the *wilderness,* see Num 14.16, 29–30; Ps 78.30–31; Heb 3.17; Jude 5. **10.6** *Desiring evil.* See Num 11.4–6, 34; Ps 106.14–15. **10.7** *The people . . . play.* Ex 32.6. **10.8** Cf. Num 25.1–9.

10.9 *To the test.* See Ps 78.18; also Deut 6.16; Isa 7.12; Ps 106.14; Bar 4.7; Mt 4.7; Lk 4.12; Acts 15.10. *Destroyed by serpents.* Cf. Num 21.5–6. **10.10** *Some of them* alludes to the Israelites who complained against Moses in the wilderness; e.g., Ex 16.2–3; Num 14.2, 36. *Destroyer,* some avenging angel; see also Ex 12.23; 2 Sam 24.16; 1 Chr 21.15; Wis 18.20–25; Heb 11.28. **10.11** *The ends of the ages,* the last days before the Lord's return; see 1.7–8; 2.7; 7.26, 29–31; also Dan 12.13; 2 Esd 11.44. **10.12** Addressed to those in Corinth who are heedless of the weak (e.g., 8.9–11). **10.13** *God is faithful.* See 1.9. **10.14** *Worship of idols.* See 8.4; 12.2; also 1 Jn 5.21. **10.15** *Judge for yourselves.* Cf. 11.13. **10.16–17** The Lord's Supper (see also 11.17–34) is described as a *sharing* both with Christ (see 1.9) and with other believers (see also Phil 1.5; Philem 6). *The blood of Christ.* Cf. 11.25, 27. *The body of Christ.* Cf. 11.24, 27, 29. *The bread that we break.* Cf. 11.24. Paul develops the image of the church as *one body* in 12.12–27 (see also Rom 12.4–8). **10.18** *Partners in the altar.* See 9.13; also Lev 7.6, 15. **10.20** *Demons,* the "so-called gods" (8.4–5) of which pagan idols are representations; see also Deut 32.17; Ps 106.37; Bar 4.7; Rev 9.20. **10.21** *The Lord,* Christ (as in v. 16); see also 2 Cor 6.15. **10.22** Given the statements in vv. 9, 21 (and despite an allusion to Deut

Do All to the Glory of God

23 "All things are lawful," but not all things are beneficial. "All things are lawful," but not all things build up. 24Do not seek your own advantage, but that of the other. 25Eat whatever is sold in the meat market without raising any question on the ground of conscience, 26for "the earth and its fullness are the Lord's." 27If an unbeliever invites you to a meal and you are disposed to go, eat whatever is set before you without raising any question on the ground of conscience. 28But if someone says to you, "This has been offered in sacrifice," then do not eat it, out of consideration for the one who informed you, and for the sake of conscience— 29I mean the other's conscience, not your own. For why should my liberty be subject to the judgment of someone else's conscience? 30If I partake with thankfulness, why should I be denounced because of that for which I give thanks?

31 So, whether you eat or drink, or whatever you do, do everything for the glory of God. 32Give no offense to Jews or to Greeks or to the church of God, 33just as I try to please everyone in everything I do, not seeking my own advantage, but that of many, so that they

11 may be saved. 1Be imitators of me, as I am of Christ.

Head Coverings

2 I commend you because you remember me in everything and maintain the traditions just as I handed them on to you. 3But I want you to understand that Christ is the head of every man, and the husband*a* is the head of his wife,*b* and God is the head of Christ. 4Any man who prays or prophesies with something on his head disgraces his head, 5but any woman who prays or prophesies with her head unveiled disgraces her head—it is one and the same thing as having her head shaved. 6For if a woman will not veil herself, then she should cut off her hair; but if it is disgraceful for a woman to have her hair cut off or to be shaved, she should wear a veil. 7For a man ought not to have his head veiled, since he is the image and reflection*c* of God; but woman is the reflection*c* of man. 8Indeed, man was not made from woman, but woman from man. 9Neither was man created for the sake of woman, but woman for the sake of man. 10For this reason a woman ought to have a symbol of*d* authority on her head,*e* because of the angels. 11Nevertheless, in the Lord woman is not

a The same Greek word means *man* or *husband*   *b* Or *head of the woman*   *c* Or *glory*   *d* Gk lacks *a symbol of*   *e* Or *have freedom of choice regarding her head*

32.21), *the Lord* almost certainly refers to Christ. **10.23–11.1** The discussion opened in 8.1 is brought to a conclusion. **10.23** As in 6.12–13 (see also 7.1), Paul cites and corrects Corinthian slogans. *Beneficial.* See also 6.12; 7.35; 10.33; 12.7. *Build up.* See 8.1. **10.24** Cf. 10.33; 13.5; Phil 2.3–4; Rom 15.1–3. **10.25** A *meat market* often sold cuts that had come from pagan temples. *Conscience.* See 8.7; 10.27–29. **10.26** Ps 24.1. See also Pss 50.12; 89.11; Ex 19.5; Deut 10.14. **10.27** *A meal,* either in a private home or in a public eating place (probably not in a pagan temple, as in 8.10). **10.28** *Someone.* Whether Paul thinks of another Christian or of a nonbeliever remains unclear. *This has been offered in sacrifice,* lit. "This is sacred food" (see note on 8.1). **10.29–30** Paul's questions (as translated here) seem to qualify the counsel of v. 28, but may represent objections by an imagined dialogue partner. Yet Paul's difficult logic has occasioned various interpretations. **10.30** *With thankfulness,* for what God has provided (10.26); see Rom 14.6; 1 Tim 4.3–4; but also 1 Cor 14.17. **10.31** *For the glory of God.* See also 6.20. **10.32** *Give no offense,* do not hinder anyone from coming to or growing in faith; see also 8.9, 13; Rom 14.13. **10.33** *Please everyone,* not in place of pleasing God (see 7.32–34; Gal 1.10; 1 Thess 2.4), but in place of seeking only one's *own advantage;* see v. 24; 9.19–23. *That they may be saved.* See 9.22. **11.1** *Be imitators of me.* See 4.16.

11.2–16 As in the following sections (vv. 17–34; chs. 12–14), Paul counsels the Corinthians about how to conduct themselves when assembled for worship. **11.3** *Christ is the head.* See also 3.23 (and Eph 1.22; 4.15; 5.23; Col 1.18; 2.10, 19). Some interpreters believe that *head* here connotes "source" (see v. 12) as well as (or rather than) superiority. *The husband is the head.* See also Gen 3.16; Eph 5.23. Paul may not be thinking specifically of marital relationships; see text notes *a* and *b. God is the head of Christ.* See also 3.23; 15.28. **11.4** *Prays or prophesies,* when the congregation is gathered for worship. On prophecy, see 12.10; 14.1–5. In Paul's day Jewish males did not wear any special *head* covering, even in the synagogue. **11.5** *Unveiled,* or more generally "uncovered," perhaps with loose, flowing hair (typically associated with promiscuous women or priestesses of pagan cults). **11.7** *Image . . . of God.* See Gen 1.26–27; 5.1; Wis 2.23; Sir 17.3; also 2 Cor 4.4, 6; Col 1.15; Heb 1.3. *Woman . . . of man* is explained in 11.8–9. **11.8** *Woman from man.* See Gen 2.21–23; see also 1 Tim 2.13. **11.9** *Woman for the sake of man.* See Gen 2.18. **11.10** There is no scholarly consensus about the translation of this verse (see text notes *d* and *e*) or about its interpretation. *The angels* (see also 4.9; 6.3; 13.1), probably not to be identified with the "sons of God" mentioned in Gen 6.2. **11.11** *In the Lord,* in Christ, thus among Christians. *Not inde-*

independent of man or man independent of woman. 12For just as woman came from man, so man comes through woman; but all things come from God. 13Judge for yourselves: is it proper for a woman to pray to God with her head unveiled? 14Does not nature itself teach you that if a man wears long hair, it is degrading to him, 15but if a woman has long hair, it is her glory? For her hair is given to her for a covering. 16But if anyone is disposed to be contentious—we have no such custom, nor do the churches of God.

Abuses at the Lord's Supper

17 Now in the following instructions I do not commend you, because when you come together it is not for the better but for the worse. 18For, to begin with, when you come together as a church, I hear that there are divisions among you; and to some extent I believe it. 19Indeed, there have to be factions among you, for only so will it become clear who among you are genuine. 20When you come together, it is not really to eat the Lord's supper. 21For when the time comes to eat, each of you goes ahead with your own supper, and one goes hungry and another becomes drunk.

22What! Do you not have homes to eat and drink in? Or do you show contempt for the church of God and humiliate those who have nothing? What should I say to you? Should I commend you? In this matter I do not commend you!

The Institution of the Lord's Supper

23 For I received from the Lord what I also handed on to you, that the Lord Jesus on the night when he was betrayed took a loaf of bread, 24and when he had given thanks, he broke it and said, "This is my body that is for*a* you. Do this in remembrance of me." 25In the same way he took the cup also, after supper, saying, "This cup is the new covenant in my blood. Do this, as often as you drink it, in remembrance of me." 26For as often as you eat this bread and drink the cup, you proclaim the Lord's death until he comes.

Partaking of the Supper Unworthily

27 Whoever, therefore, eats the bread or drinks the cup of the Lord in an unworthy manner will be answerable for the body and

---

a Other ancient authorities read *is broken for*

---

pendent of man . . . of woman suggests mutuality (see also 7.3–4), and some interpreters believe equality as well. **11.12** *Man comes through woman,* because women bear the children. *All things come from God.* See 3.21–23; 8.6; 10.26; Rom 11.36. **11.13** *Judge for yourselves.* Cf. 10.15. **11.14** *Nature,* perhaps what the culture of the day regarded as the created characteristics that differentiate male and female. **11.16** *The churches of God,* Paul's other congregations. **11.17–22** The discussion that begins here extends through v. 34. **11.17** *When you come together.* It is likely that there were several house churches in Corinth, and that they occasionally met together to observe the Lord's Supper. *The following instructions* are not about the conduct of the liturgy as such, but about the conduct of the congregation at the time of the liturgy. *I do not commend you.* Cf. v. 2. **11.18** *Divisions.* Some interpreters believe that these were caused by rivalries that had developed among the various Corinthian house churches (see note on 11.17; also 1.10–13; 12.25). **11.19** Paul's comment on *factions* may reflect the Jewish and early Christian expectation that the close of history would be preceded by various kinds of strife and suffering; see, e.g., 7.26; Mt 10.34–36; Mk 13; 2 Pet 2.1. **11.20–21** The Pauline congregations combined their ritual observance of Jesus' last supper (see Mk 14.17–26) with their own community meal. **11.20** *Not really to eat the Lord's supper.* Paul indicates in vv. 23–26 what a genuine Lord's Supper involves. **11.21** *Goes*

ahead with your own supper. Apparently some members of the congregation ate up the provisions they themselves had brought without waiting for all to arrive and then sharing with the assembly as a whole. **11.22** *The church of God.* See 1.2. *Those who have nothing,* the poorer members of the congregation (see 12.24–26; also Jas 2.6). **11.23–26** Paul repeats and comments on the words with which, according to tradition, Jesus at his last supper distributed bread and wine; see also 10.16–17; Mt 26.26–29; Mk 14.22–25; Lk 22.15–20. **11.23** *I received . . . what I also handed on* identifies the following as drawn *from the Lord* not directly, but by way of the church's tradition (see also 15.3). *Betrayed,* by Judas Iscariot (see Mk 14.43–46). **11.24** *Thanks.* Jewish meals customarily began with the blessing and distribution of the bread. *For you,* either "for your sake" or "in your place." **11.25** *The cup,* of wine (see 10.16). *After supper.* See also Lk 22.20. This phrase suggests that the ritual acts with bread and cup were customarily separated by an ordinary community meal. *New covenant.* See also Jer 31.31; 32.40; Lk 22.20; 2 Cor 3.6; Heb 8.6–13; 9.15–20. *Blood* seals and thus symbolizes the covenant; see Ex 24.8; Zech 9.11; Heb 9.12; 13.20; also Rom 3.25; 5.9. **11.26** Paul interprets the tradition he has just cited by accentuating Christ's saving death (see 15.3–5) and expected return (see 1.7–8). **11.27–34** The discussion begun in v. 17 is concluded with some sober warnings and earnest appeals. **11.27** *An unworthy manner.* See v. 29.

blood of the Lord. 28Examine yourselves, and only then eat of the bread and drink of the cup. 29For all who eat and drink*a* without discerning the body,*b* eat and drink judgment against themselves. 30For this reason many of you are weak and ill, and some have died.*c* 31But if we judged ourselves, we would not be judged. 32But when we are judged by the Lord, we are disciplined*d* so that we may not be condemned along with the world.

33 So then, my brothers and sisters,*e* when you come together to eat, wait for one another. 34If you are hungry, eat at home, so that when you come together, it will not be for your condemnation. About the other things I will give instructions when I come.

Spiritual Gifts

12 Now concerning spiritual gifts,*f* brothers and sisters,*e* I do not want you to be uninformed. 2You know that when you were pagans, you were enticed and led astray to idols that could not speak. 3Therefore I want you to understand that no one speaking by the Spirit of God ever says "Let Jesus be cursed!" and no one can say "Jesus is Lord" except by the Holy Spirit.

4 Now there are varieties of gifts, but the same Spirit; 5and there are varieties of services, but the same Lord; 6and there are varieties of activities, but it is the same God who activates all of them in everyone. 7To each is given the manifestation of the Spirit for the common good. 8To one is given through the Spirit the utterance of wisdom, and to another the utterance of knowledge according to the same Spirit, 9to another faith by the same Spirit, to another gifts of healing by the one Spirit, 10to another the working of miracles, to another prophecy, to another the discernment of spirits, to another various kinds of tongues, to another the interpretation of tongues. 11All these are activated by one and the same Spirit, who allots to each one individually just as the Spirit chooses.

a Other ancient authorities add *in an unworthy manner,* *b* Other ancient authorities read *the Lord's body* *c* Gk *fallen asleep* *d* Or *When we are judged, we are being disciplined by the Lord* *e* Gk *brothers* *f* Or *spiritual persons*

11.28 *Examine yourselves.* See also 2 Cor 13.5; Gal 6.4. **11.29** When believers neither discern nor are concerned for one another's needs, Christ's body (see 10.16–17; 12.12–13) is being disregarded and violated (cf. 8.12). **11.30** How many and who were *ill* or had *died* is unknown. These illnesses and deaths are interpreted as the consequence of disorders within the congregation. **11.31** *If we judged ourselves* involves a wordplay, since the Greek term translated *judged* can also be rendered *discerned,* as in v. 29. **11.32** *The Lord,* probably Christ, as in the liturgical tradition (v. 23). *The world,* non-Christians. **11.33–34** See vv. 21–22. **11.33** *Wait for one another* may suggest that the poorer members always had to arrive late for congregational meals; the verb here could also be translated "accept" or "welcome." Cf. 8.11–13; 12.25. **11.34** What *the other things* were is unknown. *When I come.* See 4.19–21; 16.5–9.

12.1–11 Paul's comments about spiritual gifts, introduced here, continue through ch. 14. In particular, he is concerned to correct the view that speaking in tongues somehow demonstrates the higher spiritual status of those who are thus graced. **12.1** *Now concerning.* See note on 8.1. *Spiritual gifts.* The form of the Greek word used here can mean either "spiritual things" or *spiritual persons* (see text note *f*). Which of these is adopted makes little difference; in either case Paul's focus in chs. 12–14 is on how gifts like "tongues" should be evaluated. **12.2** *Pagans,* gentile nonbelievers. *Idols that could not speak.* See 8.4–6; 10.6–14; also Pss 115.4–7; 135.15–17; Isa 46.7; Hab 2.18–19; 3 Macc 4.16. **12.3** *The Spirit of God.* See 2.12. It is unclear whether Paul actually knew of persons who said, *Let Jesus be cursed! Jesus is Lord* was one of the church's

earliest creedal affirmations; see also 8.6; Rom 10.9; 2 Cor 4.5; Phil 2.11. **12.4** *Gifts.* The Greek term here (and in 1.7; 7.7; 12.9, 28, 30, 31; Rom 1.11; 12.6) is *charisma,* not the one rendered *spiritual gifts* in v. 1. A *charisma* is a benefit with which one has been "graced." **12.5** *Services,* or "ministries," listed in v. 28; see also Rom 12.7. *The same Lord,* Christ; see also 8.6. **12.6** On God, who *activates,* or works, in everyone, see also Gal 2.8; Phil 2.13; 1 Thess 2.13; Eph 1.11. **12.7** *The common good,* or "the benefit of all," a major concern in this Letter; see 6.12; 7.35; 10.23, 33. **12.8–10** Similar (but not identical) lists of spiritual gifts appear in vv. 28, 29–30; Rom 12.6–8; see also Eph 4.11; 1 Pet 4.10–11. **12.8** *Utterance,* or "word" (an intelligible utterance). *Wisdom.* See 2.6–16. *Knowledge.* See 1.5; 8.1; 13.2, 8. **12.9** *Faith,* here the special ability, granted only to some believers, to do extraordinary things (see 13.2); not to be confused with the kind of faithfulness that is fundamental to the Christian life (see, e.g., 2.5; 16.13). *Healings* are attributed to Paul himself in Acts (e.g., 14.8–10). **12.10** *The working of miracles,* apparently regarded as a more comprehensive gift than those of "faith" and "healing"; see also v. 28; 2 Cor 12.12; Gal 3.5. *Prophecy.* See 11.4–5; 13.2, 8; ch. 14; 1 Thess 5.20. *Discernment of spirits,* perhaps the ability to distinguish between true and false prophecy, as in 14.29; 1 Thess 5.19–21; but see Acts 16.16–18; 1 Jn 4.1. *Tongues,* unintelligible utterance (in contrast to prophecy and the kinds of speech mentioned in v. 8); see 13.1, 8; ch. 14; Acts 10.46; 19.6. In Acts 2.4, 11 the same word is properly translated as "languages." *Interpretation of tongues.* See 14.5, 13, 26–28. **12.11** *Activated.* See v. 6. *As the Spirit chooses* expresses the sover-

One Body with Many Members

12 For just as the body is one and has many members, and all the members of the body, though many, are one body, so it is with Christ. 13For in the one Spirit we were all baptized into one body—Jews or Greeks, slaves or free—and we were all made to drink of one Spirit.

14 Indeed, the body does not consist of one member but of many. 15If the foot would say, "Because I am not a hand, I do not belong to the body," that would not make it any less a part of the body. 16And if the ear would say, "Because I am not an eye, I do not belong to the body," that would not make it any less a part of the body. 17If the whole body were an eye, where would the hearing be? If the whole body were hearing, where would the sense of smell be? 18But as it is, God arranged the members in the body, each one of them, as he chose. 19If all were a single member, where would the body be? 20As it is, there are many members, yet one body. 21The eye cannot say to the hand, "I have no need of you," nor again the head to the feet, "I have no need of you." 22On the contrary, the members of the body that seem to be weaker are indispensable, 23and those members of the body that we think less honorable we clothe with greater honor, and our less respectable members are treated with greater respect; 24whereas our more respectable members do not need this. But God has so arranged the body, giving the greater honor to the inferior member, 25that there may be no dissension within the body, but the members may have the same care for one another. 26If one member suffers, all suffer together with it; if one member is honored, all rejoice together with it.

27 Now you are the body of Christ and individually members of it. 28And God has appointed in the church first apostles, second prophets, third teachers; then deeds of power, then gifts of healing, forms of assistance, forms of leadership, various kinds of tongues. 29Are all apostles? Are all prophets? Are all teachers? Do all work miracles? 30Do all possess gifts of healing? Do all speak in tongues? Do all interpret? 31But strive for the greater gifts. And I will show you a still more excellent way.

The Gift of Love

13 If I speak in the tongues of mortals and of angels, but do not have love, I am a

eignty of divine grace; see also v. 18. **12.12–31** Paul now introduces (vv. 12–13) and elaborates (vv. 14–31) his metaphor of the church as Christ's body. Along with ch. 13, this provides a foundation for the more specific counsels that follow in ch. 14. **12.12–13** Like certain other ancient writers, Paul regards the human *body* as illustrating the point that unity and diversity are not incompatible (see also vv. 14–16). Applying this to the church, conceived as Christ's *body* (see v. 27), he alludes to an early Christian affirmation about the meaning of baptism into Christ; see also Gal 3.27–28; Col 3.11. *Jews or Greeks.* See 7.18–19; also 1.22, 24. *Slaves or free.* See 7.21–23. *Made to drink of one Spirit* may suggest that new believers become suffused with the Spirit at their baptism (cf. 10.3–4). **12.14–16** Paul stresses the diversity, thus interdependence, of the body's members; see also vv. 12, 20, 27; Rom 12.4–5; Eph 4.25; 5.30. **12.17–21** The body's diversity in unity is God's own doing (see also vv. 24, 28; cf. 15.38). **12.22** *The members . . . that seem to be weaker,* probably an allusion to the vulnerable but vital internal organs of a human body, thus by analogy the most vulnerable yet vital members of a Christian congregation. See also 8.7, 9–12; 9.22; 1 Thess 5.14. **12.23** *Less honorable . . . less respectable members,* the genitals, which in many cultures are covered to avoid shame (see Gen 3.7–10); by analogy the members of lower standing in society, who are nonetheless important to the congregation. **12.24** *More respectable members,* the parts of the body left uncovered; by analogy the congregational mem-

bers of higher standing in society. *The inferior member,* perhaps better "the needy member," which would include the *weaker,* the *less honorable,* and the *less respectable* (vv. 22–23). **12.25** *No dissension.* See also 1.10. *Care for one another.* See also 11.33. **12.26** Paul's conception of Christian community as sharing in the sufferings (e.g., 2 Cor 1.7; 11.28–29) and joys (e.g., 2 Cor 2.3; 7.13) of others departs from the ancient Greek and Roman ideal of dispassionate self-sufficiency; see also Rom 12.15; 15.1; Gal 6.2. **12.27** This description of the Corinthian church as *the body of Christ* makes explicit what seems implicit in v. 12 (if not already in 1.13; 6.15; 10.17). See also Rom 12.4–5. The metaphor is developed further in Colossians (e.g., 1.18, 24; 2.19; 3.15) and Ephesians (e.g., 4.4, 12; 5.23, 29–30). **12.28** See also the list of gifts in vv. 8–10. *Apostles.* See 1.1. *Teachers.* See 4.17; also Acts 13.1; Rom 12.7. *Deeds of power,* miracles, as in vv. 10, 29. *Assistance,* perhaps helpful deeds in general (see Rom 12.8; also 1 Tim 5.10). *Leadership.* The same Greek term is used in the Septuagint to refer to offering wise counsel (Prov 1.5; 11.14; 24.6). **12.30** *Do all interpret?* alludes to those who are able to interpret tongues; see 14.5, 13, 26–28. **12.31** *But strive for the greater gifts,* or "Do you strive for the greater gifts?" *The greater gifts* are, in Paul's view, those that build up the congregation; see 14.4–5. *A still more excellent way* than any spiritual gift is the kind of love described in ch. 13.

13.1–13 This chapter has been introduced by the last sentence of ch. 12. Although there is nothing ex-

noisy gong or a clanging cymbal. 2And if I have prophetic powers, and understand all mysteries and all knowledge, and if I have all faith, so as to remove mountains, but do not have love, I am nothing. 3If I give away all my possessions, and if I hand over my body so that I may boast,*a* but do not have love, I gain nothing.

4 Love is patient; love is kind; love is not envious or boastful or arrogant 5or rude. It does not insist on its own way; it is not irritable or resentful; 6it does not rejoice in wrongdoing, but rejoices in the truth. 7It bears all things, believes all things, hopes all things, endures all things.

8 Love never ends. But as for prophecies, they will come to an end; as for tongues, they will cease; as for knowledge, it will come to an end. 9For we know only in part, and we prophesy only in part; 10but when the complete comes, the partial will come to an end. 11When I was a child, I spoke like a child, I thought like a child, I reasoned like a child; when I became an adult, I put an end to childish ways. 12For now we see in a mirror, dimly,*b* but then we will see face to face. Now I know only in part; then I will know fully, even as I have been fully known. 13And now faith, hope,

and love abide, these three; and the greatest of these is love.

Gifts of Prophecy and Tongues

14 Pursue love and strive for the spiritual gifts, and especially that you may prophesy. 2For those who speak in a tongue do not speak to other people but to God; for nobody understands them, since they are speaking mysteries in the Spirit. 3On the other hand, those who prophesy speak to other people for their upbuilding and encouragement and consolation. 4Those who speak in a tongue build up themselves, but those who prophesy build up the church. 5Now I would like all of you to speak in tongues, but even more to prophesy. One who prophesies is greater than one who speaks in tongues, unless someone interprets, so that the church may be built up.

6 Now, brothers and sisters,*c* if I come to you speaking in tongues, how will I benefit you unless I speak to you in some revelation or knowledge or prophecy or teaching? 7It is the same way with lifeless instruments that pro-

a Other ancient authorities read *body to be burned*   *b* Gk *in a riddle*   *c* Gk *brothers*

plicitly theological here, Paul presupposes what he has already said about love in 8.1–3. Thus, along with ch. 12 this chapter lays the theological foundation for the counsels in ch. 14. **13.1** *I,* in this chapter either "anyone" or Paul himself. If the latter, the apostle is lifting up his own situation as exemplary. *The tongues of mortals and of angels.* The whole phrase may refer to the ecstatic utterance of those who speak in tongues, or else a distinction is intended between ordinary speech and tongues ("angelic" speech). **13.2** *Mysteries.* See 4.1; 14.2. *Faith . . . to remove mountains.* See 12.9; also Mk 11.22–23; Mt 21.21; Mt 17.20; also Isa 54.10. **13.3** *Giving away . . . possessions.* See Mt 6.2. Elsewhere Paul *boasts* in his weaknesses and sufferings; see 2 Cor 11.30; 12.5, 9–10. **13.4–7** Love's actions, as Paul identifies them here, stand in striking contrast to the prevailing pattern of conduct in the Corinthian congregation, of which he has been critical in earlier chapters. This description of love's way (12.31) matches his understanding of both God's love as disclosed in Christ (e.g., Rom 5.6, 8; 15.3, 7–8; 2 Cor 8.9; Phil 2.6–11) and what constitutes appropriate conduct for those who are in *Christ* (10.24, 32–33; Rom 15.1–2; 2 Cor 5.14–15; Phil 2.3–4). See also Rom 12.9–21; 13.8–10; Gal 5.13–14. **13.7** The declaration that love *believes all things, hopes all things* anticipates v. 13. **13.8–10** In emphasizing the limitations of *prophecies, tongues,* and *knowledge,* Paul seeks to correct the Corinthians' inflated claims about

these; see also 8.1; 13.2, 12–13. **13.8** Paul regards God's *love* as the ultimate and only enduring reality. See also v. 13; cf. 8.1–3; Rom 5.5; 8.35, 37–39. **13.10** *The complete,* an allusion to the promised eschatological fulfillment of salvation (see 1.7–8). **13.11–12** *I.* See note on 13.1. *Childish ways.* See also 3.1–4; 14.20. **13.12** *Now . . . then* distinguishes the present age from the age to come. Ancient *mirrors* were made of bronze, and those of Corinthian manufacture were noted for their excellence. *Dimly* perhaps describes the indirect, thus defective, view that one has of a mirrored object; see also 2 Cor 5.7. *Face to face.* See Ex 33.11 (also Deut 34.10); Num 12.8. *As I have been fully known,* by God; see 8.3; Gal 4.9. **13.13** *Faith, hope, and love.* This triad is also visible in v. 7; Rom 5.1–5; Gal 5.5–6; Col 1.4–5; 1 Thess 1.3; 5.8; Heb 10.22–24; 1 Pet 1.21–22. *The greatest.* According to 12.31b, love is a *still more excellent way* than even the greatest spiritual gifts.

14.1–25 The instructions about spiritual gifts offered in this chapter are based on what has been said in ch. 12 about Christ's body and on the teaching about love in 8.1–3 and ch. 13. **14.1** Because *love* is what matters most (ch. 13), those *spiritual gifts* (see 12.1) that build up the congregation are to be particularly valued (14.2–5); see 8.1; 14.12, 26; 16.14. **14.2** *Mysteries.* See 4.1; 13.2 (not the gospel, as in 2.1). **14.4** *Build up the church,* a special theme of this chapter; see also vv. 12, 17, 19, 26; cf. 8.7–11; 10.33–11.1. **14.5** *Even more to*

duce sound, such as the flute or the harp. If they do not give distinct notes, how will anyone know what is being played? 8And if the bugle gives an indistinct sound, who will get ready for battle? 9So with yourselves; if in a tongue you utter speech that is not intelligible, how will anyone know what is being said? For you will be speaking into the air. 10There are doubtless many different kinds of sounds in the world, and nothing is without sound. 11If then I do not know the meaning of a sound, I will be a foreigner to the speaker and the speaker a foreigner to me. 12So with yourselves; since you are eager for spiritual gifts, strive to excel in them for building up the church.

13 Therefore, one who speaks in a tongue should pray for the power to interpret. 14For if I pray in a tongue, my spirit prays but my mind is unproductive. 15What should I do then? I will pray with the spirit, but I will pray with the mind also; I will sing praise with the spirit, but I will sing praise with the mind also. 16Otherwise, if you say a blessing with the spirit, how can anyone in the position of an outsider say the "Amen" to your thanksgiving, since the outsider does not know what you are saying? 17For you may give thanks well enough, but the other person is not built up. 18I thank God that I speak in tongues more than all of you; 19nevertheless, in church I would rather speak five words with my mind, in order to instruct others also, than ten thousand words in a tongue.

20 Brothers and sisters,*a* do not be children in your thinking; rather, be infants in evil, but in thinking be adults. 21In the law it is written,

"By people of strange tongues
    and by the lips of foreigners
I will speak to this people;
    yet even then they will not listen to
        me,"

says the Lord. 22Tongues, then, are a sign not for believers but for unbelievers, while prophecy is not for unbelievers but for believers. 23If, therefore, the whole church comes together and all speak in tongues, and outsiders or unbelievers enter, will they not say that you are out of your mind? 24But if all prophesy, an unbeliever or outsider who enters is reproved by all and called to account by all. 25After the secrets of the unbeliever's heart are disclosed, that person will bow down before God and worship him, declaring, "God is really among you."

Orderly Worship

26 What should be done then, my friends?*a* When you come together, each one has a hymn, a lesson, a revelation, a tongue, or an interpretation. Let all things be done for building up. 27If anyone speaks in a tongue, let there be only two or at most three, and each in turn; and let one interpret. 28But if there is no one to interpret, let them be silent in church and speak to themselves and to God. 29Let two or three prophets speak, and let the others weigh what is said. 30If a revelation is made to someone else sitting nearby, let the first person be silent. 31For you can all prophesy one by one, so that all may learn and all be encouraged. 32And the spirits of prophets are subject

a Gk brothers

---

prophesy. See also Num 11.29. *Interprets.* See vv. 13, 26–28. **14.9** See vv. 2–5. *Into the air,* to no effect (cf. 9.26). **14.12** *Strive to excel.* See also 12.31; 14.1–5. **14.13** *The power to interpret,* a paraphrase of the Greek; perhaps better "the gift to interpret" (see 12.10, 30). **14.15** *With the spirit . . . with the mind* contrasts ordinary, intelligible speech with ecstatic utterances; see also Eph 5.18–19. **14.16** *Outsider.* Whether Paul means a nonbeliever or another Christian is unclear; see also vv. 23–24. *The "Amen,"* the traditional congregational response to prayer, whereby it is affirmed; see also 2 Cor 1.20. **14.18–19** Paul reformulates his primary appeal (vv. 1, 5) as a statement of personal resolve. **14.20** *Do not be children.* See also 3.1–4; 13.11. **14.21** Isa 28.11–12. **14.22** *Tongues . . . are . . . for unbelievers, prophecy is . . . for believers,* evidently because tongues do not edify while prophesying does (see vv. 23–25), but the exact point is unclear and scholarly in-

terpretations differ. **14.23** *Outsiders or unbelievers.* Whether Paul is using these terms synonymously is uncertain; see also v. 16. **14.25** *Secrets . . . disclosed.* See also 4.5; 2 Cor 4.2. *Bow down . . . and worship.* See Isa 45.14. *God is really among you.* See Zech 8.23. **14.26–40** Paul gives directives about what should happen when the congregation is assembled for worship. Who, if anyone, presided over the proceedings is unknown. **14.26** *Hymn,* lit. "psalm." *Lesson,* lit. "teaching" (probably not a "lesson" from scripture). *Revelation . . . tongue . . . interpretation.* See 12.7–10. *Let all things be done for building up,* another way of appealing for love (see v. 1; 16.14); see also 10.23; 14.12; Rom 14.19; 15.2; 2 Cor 12.19; Eph 4.12; 1 Thess 5.11. **14.29** *Let the others weigh what is said.* Every prophet's utterances are subject to critical analysis and evaluation (see also v. 32; 1 Thess 5.19–21). It is unclear whether *others* refers to all of the others present or only to the other prophets.

to the prophets, [33]for God is a God not of disorder but of peace.

(As in all the churches of the saints, [34]women should be silent in the churches. For they are not permitted to speak, but should be subordinate, as the law also says. [35]If there is anything they desire to know, let them ask their husbands at home. For it is shameful for a woman to speak in church.[a] [36]Or did the word of God originate with you? Or are you the only ones it has reached?)

[37]Anyone who claims to be a prophet, or to have spiritual powers, must acknowledge that what I am writing to you is a command of the Lord. [38]Anyone who does not recognize this is not to be recognized. [39]So, my friends,[b] be eager to prophesy, and do not forbid speaking in tongues; [40]but all things should be done decently and in order.

The Resurrection of Christ

15 Now I would remind you, brothers and sisters,[c] of the good news[d] that I proclaimed to you, which you in turn received, in which also you stand, [2]through which also you are being saved, if you hold firmly to the message that I proclaimed to you—unless you have come to believe in vain.

[3]For I handed on to you as of first importance what I in turn had received: that Christ died for our sins in accordance with the scriptures, [4]and that he was buried, and that he was raised on the third day in accordance with the scriptures, [5]and that he appeared to Cephas, then to the twelve. [6]Then he appeared to more than five hundred brothers and sisters[c] at one time, most of whom are still alive, though some have died.[e] [7]Then he appeared to James, then to all the apostles. [8]Last of all, as to one untimely born, he appeared also to me. [9]For I am the least of the apostles, unfit to be called an apostle, because I persecuted the church of God. [10]But by the grace of God I am what I am, and his grace toward me has not been in vain. On the contrary, I worked harder than any of them—though it was not I, but the grace of God that is with me. [11]Whether then it was I or they, so we proclaim and so you have come to believe.

The Resurrection of the Dead

[12]Now if Christ is proclaimed as raised from the dead, how can some of you say there is no

---

a Other ancient authorities put verses 34–35 after verse 40
b Gk my brothers   c Gk brothers   d Or gospel   e Gk fallen asleep

---

14.32 *The spirits of prophets.* See also Rev 22.6. **14.33** *God . . . of peace.* See also Rom 15.33; 16.20; 2 Cor 13.11; Phil 4.9; 1 Thess 5.23; 2 Thess 3.16; Heb 13.20. *As in all the churches of the saints,* sometimes seen as the closing phrase of the preceding sentence. **14.34–35** Some interpreters regard the instruction for women to be silent in churches as a later, non-Pauline addition to the Letter, more in keeping with the viewpoint of the Pastoral Letters (see 1 Tim 2.11–12; Titus 2.5) than of the certainly Pauline Letters. See also Eph 5.22–24; Col 3.18; 1 Pet 3.1–6. **14.36** Some interpreters who view vv. 34–35 as a non-Pauline addition include this verse as well. **14.37** *A command of the Lord,* not a reference to some specific saying of Jesus (as in 7.10; 9.14), but to all that Paul has said, as an apostle of Christ, about spiritual gifts. **14.38** *Not to be recognized.* See also Mt 7.23; 25.12; Mk 8.38. **14.40** Underlying this directive is the one in v. 26, and underlying both is the appeal to follow the more excellent way of love (12.31; 14.1; 16.14).

15.1–11 Here Paul lays the theological foundation for the last major topic of the Letter, the resurrection of the dead (see v. 12). **15.1** *I would remind you.* In what follows, Paul summarizes the message he had proclaimed in Corinth as a missionary (cf. 2 Cor 1.19). **15.3** *Handed on . . . received* identifies what follows (at least through v. 5) as the church's tradition (see also 11.23). *Christ died for our sins.* See also Rom 5.8; Gal

1.4; cf. Rom 3.25; 4.25; 6.10; 2 Cor 5.19, 21. *The scriptures,* what would later be called the Old Testament. Certain passages were interpreted as references to Christ's death, e.g., Ps 69.9 (see Rom 15.3); Isa 53.4–12 (see 1 Pet 2.22–25). **15.4** *Buried,* possibly an allusion to Isa 53.9. *Raised on the third day.* See Mt 16.21. Belief in Christ's resurrection is central to Paul's argument in vv. 12–34. *The scriptures.* It is uncertain what specific passage(s), if any, may be in mind (Hos 6.2? Jon 1.17?). **15.5** *Cephas,* Peter (as in 1.12); see Lk 24.34. *The twelve,* Jesus' disciples (even after Judas's defection); see Lk 24.36; Jn 20.19. **15.6** *More than five hundred,* perhaps on some occasion like that recounted in Acts 2.1–42. **15.7** *James,* Jesus' brother; see Mk 6.3; Gal 1.19. *All the apostles,* a more inclusive group than the Twelve. **15.8** *Untimely born,* some kind of unusual birth, possibly first used about Paul's conversion by his critics. *Appeared also to me,* at the apostle's conversion and call; see 9.1; Gal 1.15–16; Acts 9.3–6. **15.9** *Persecuted.* See Gal 1.13; Phil 3.6; Acts 8.3. **15.10** *The grace of God.* See 3.10. **15.11** Cf. vv. 1–3. *Whether . . . I or they.* What Paul proclaimed was not unique to him. **15.12–34** Paul argues that those who do not hope for the resurrection of the dead are in effect denying Christ's own resurrection and thus the gospel on which their faith rests (see vv. 1–11). **15.12** *Some of you.* If Paul knows who or how many, he never says; he could mean "most." *No resurrection of the dead.* Paul does not indi-

resurrection of the dead? [13]If there is no resurrection of the dead, then Christ has not been raised; [14]and if Christ has not been raised, then our proclamation has been in vain and your faith has been in vain. [15]We are even found to be misrepresenting God, because we testified of God that he raised Christ—whom he did not raise if it is true that the dead are not raised. [16]For if the dead are not raised, then Christ has not been raised. [17]If Christ has not been raised, your faith is futile and you are still in your sins. [18]Then those also who have died[a] in Christ have perished. [19]If for this life only we have hoped in Christ, we are of all people most to be pitied.

20 But in fact Christ has been raised from the dead, the first fruits of those who have died.[a] [21]For since death came through a human being, the resurrection of the dead has also come through a human being; [22]for as all die in Adam, so all will be made alive in Christ. [23]But each in his own order: Christ the first fruits, then at his coming those who belong to Christ. [24]Then comes the end,[b] when he hands over the kingdom to God the Father, after he has destroyed every ruler and every authority and power. [25]For he must reign until he has put all his enemies under his feet. [26]The last enemy to be destroyed is death. [27]For "God[c] has put all things in subjection under his feet." But when it says, "All things are put in subjection," it is plain that this does not include the one who put all things in subjection under him. [28]When all things are subjected to him, then the Son himself will also be subjected to the one who put all things in subjection under him, so that God may be all in all.

29 Otherwise, what will those people do who receive baptism on behalf of the dead? If the dead are not raised at all, why are people baptized on their behalf?

30 And why are we putting ourselves in danger every hour? [31]I die every day! That is as certain, brothers and sisters,[d] as my boasting of you—a boast that I make in Christ Jesus our Lord. [32]If with merely human hopes I fought with wild animals at Ephesus, what would I have gained by it? If the dead are not raised,

"Let us eat and drink,
   for tomorrow we die."

[33]Do not be deceived:

"Bad company ruins good morals."

[34]Come to a sober and right mind, and sin no more; for some people have no knowledge of God. I say this to your shame.

The Resurrection Body

35 But someone will ask, "How are the dead raised? With what kind of body do they come?" [36]Fool! What you sow does not come to life unless it dies. [37]And as for what you sow, you do not sow the body that is to be, but a bare seed, perhaps of wheat or of some other grain. [38]But God gives it a body as he has chosen, and to each kind of seed its own body. [39]Not all flesh is alike, but there is one flesh for human beings, another for animals, another for birds, and another for fish. [40]There are both heavenly bodies and earthly bodies, but the glory of the heavenly is one thing, and that of the earthly is another. [41]There is one glory of the sun, and another glory of the moon,

---

a Gk fallen asleep b Or Then come the rest c Gk he
d Gk brothers

---

cate the reasons alleged for this view. **15.13–14** See also vv. 15–16; the connection between Christ's resurrection and the resurrection of the dead has already been stated in 6.14, and will be explained in 15.20. **15.15** *Misrepresenting God.* See also 1 Jn 5.10. **15.17** *Sins.* See v. 3. **15.19** This verse may echo a Jewish proverb; see *2 Baruch* 21.13. **15.20** *Raised from the dead* echoes v. 4. In ancient Israel the *first fruits, the earliest produce of a season's harvest, were* dedicated to God; see Ex 23.19. **15.21–22** *Adam* and *Christ* are also compared in vv. 45–49; Rom 5.12–21. **15.23** *At his coming.* See 1.7–8; 1 Thess 4.13–17. **15.24** *The kingdom.* See 4.20; 15.50. *Every ruler . . . authority . . . power,* both earthly and heavenly; see also Rom 8.38; Eph 1.21; Col 2.10, 15; 1 Pet 3.22. **15.25–28** Interpreters disagree about which pronouns refer to God and which to Christ. **15.25** See Ps 110.1. **15.26** On the victory over *death,* see also vv. 54–55. **15.27** Ps 8.6. See also Phil 3.21. **15.28** *The Son . . . subjected.* See also 3.23; 11.3. **15.29** Why the Corinthians practiced *baptism on behalf of the dead* is unknown; see also 2 Macc 12.44–45. **15.30** For examples of this *danger,* see 4.11–13. **15.32** *Wild animals at Ephesus,* a figure of speech, perhaps alluding to the troubles mentioned in 2 Cor 1.8–9; see also 16.8–9. *Let us . . . we die.* Isa 22.13. **15.33** A proverbial saying, deriving from a lost play by the Athenian writer Menander (d. early third century BCE). **15.34** This verse epitomizes all of the appeals in this Letter. *No knowledge of God,* perhaps specifically that God raised Christ from the dead (v. 15). **15.35–58** Paul explains that at Christ's return the dead will be resurrected with "spiritual" bodies and that those who have not died will also be transformed. **15.38–39** See Gen 1.11–12, 20–25. **15.40–41** See Gen 1.14–18.

and another glory of the stars; indeed, star differs from star in glory.

42 So it is with the resurrection of the dead. What is sown is perishable, what is raised is imperishable. 43It is sown in dishonor, it is raised in glory. It is sown in weakness, it is raised in power. 44It is sown a physical body, it is raised a spiritual body. If there is a physical body, there is also a spiritual body. 45Thus it is written, "The first man, Adam, became a living being"; the last Adam became a life-giving spirit. 46But it is not the spiritual that is first, but the physical, and then the spiritual. 47The first man was from the earth, a man of dust; the second man is*a* from heaven. 48As was the man of dust, so are those who are of the dust; and as is the man of heaven, so are those who are of heaven. 49Just as we have borne the image of the man of dust, we will*b* also bear the image of the man of heaven.

50 What I am saying, brothers and sisters,*c* is this: flesh and blood cannot inherit the kingdom of God, nor does the perishable inherit the imperishable. 51Listen, I will tell you a mystery! We will not all die,*d* but we will all be changed, 52in a moment, in the twinkling of an eye, at the last trumpet. For the trumpet will sound, and the dead will be raised imperishable, and we will be changed. 53For this perishable body must put on imperishability, and this mortal body must put on immortality. 54When this perishable body puts on imperishability, and this mortal body puts on immortality, then the saying that is written will be fulfilled:

"Death has been swallowed up in
victory."

55 "Where, O death, is your victory?
Where, O death, is your sting?"
56The sting of death is sin, and the power of sin is the law. 57But thanks be to God, who gives us the victory through our Lord Jesus Christ.

58 Therefore, my beloved,*e* be steadfast, immovable, always excelling in the work of the Lord, because you know that in the Lord your labor is not in vain.

The Collection for the Saints

16 Now concerning the collection for the saints: you should follow the directions I gave to the churches of Galatia. 2On the first day of every week, each of you is to put aside and save whatever extra you earn, so that collections need not be taken when I come. 3And when I arrive, I will send any whom you approve with letters to take your gift to Jerusalem. 4If it seems advisable that I should go also, they will accompany me.

Plans for Travel

5 I will visit you after passing through Macedonia—for I intend to pass through Macedonia— 6and perhaps I will stay with you or even spend the winter, so that you may send me on my way, wherever I go. 7I do not want to see you now just in passing, for I hope to spend some time with you, if the Lord permits. 8But I will stay in Ephesus until Pentecost, 9for a wide door for effective work has opened to me, and there are many adversaries.

a Other ancient authorities add *the Lord*   *b* Other ancient authorities read *let us*   *c* Gk *brothers*   *d* Gk *fall asleep*
e Gk *beloved brothers*

15.43 *In glory . . . in power.* Cf. Phil 3.21. **15.45** *Adam became a living being.* Gen 2.7. *The last Adam,* Christ; see vv. 21–22. *Life-giving spirit,* in distinction from the first Adam, who was simply alive; see also v. 22. **15.47** Cf. Dan 7.13. **15.49** *Image.* See 11.7; Gen 1.26–27; 5.3; also Rom 8.29; 2 Cor 3.18; 4.4. **15.50** *Flesh and blood,* the physical body; see v. 44. *Kingdom of God.* See 4.20; 15.24. **15.51** *We will not all die.* Paul believes that at least some Christians (likely including himself) will survive until Christ's return; see also 1 Thess 4.15. **15.52** *The last trumpet.* See Mt 24.31; 1 Thess 4.16; Rev 8.2; also Isa 27.13. *We will be changed.* See also Phil 3.21; *2 Baruch* 51.1–6. **15.53** *Put on immortality.* See also 2 Cor 5.4. **15.54–55** *Death . . . sting* draws from Isa 25.8; Hos 13.14. **15.56** *Death* is understood to be the consequence of Adam's (humanity's) *sin* (vv. 21–22; Rom 5.12; see Gen 2.17), which is brought to life by *the law* (Rom 5.13; 7.9–13). **15.57** *Through our Lord Jesus*

Christ, who is the *life-giving spirit* (v. 45). **15.58** *The work of the Lord,* activities on behalf of the gospel; also 16.10. *Not in vain.* Cf. v. 10; Isa 49.4; 65.23.

16.1–4 These instructions presuppose that the Corinthians already know about Paul's collection project. **16.1** *Now concerning.* See note on 8.1. *The collection for the saints,* a fund for the Jerusalem church to which Paul had committed himself and his congregations; see Gal 2.10; also 2 Cor 8–9. **16.2** *First day of every week,* perhaps at a weekly meeting of the church or of its constituent house churches. **16.3–4** In the end, Paul does take the Corinthians' *gift to Jerusalem;* see Rom 15.25–29. **16.5–12** Paul informs the Corinthians of his travel plans and of the whereabouts of two others known to them. **16.5** *Macedonia,* the Roman province of which Thessalonica was the capital. **16.8** *Ephesus,* the capital city of the Roman province of Asia (see v. 19). *Pentecost,* a Jewish festival, also observed by Chris-

10 If Timothy comes, see that he has nothing to fear among you, for he is doing the work of the Lord just as I am; [11] therefore let no one despise him. Send him on his way in peace, so that he may come to me; for I am expecting him with the brothers.

12 Now concerning our brother Apollos, I strongly urged him to visit you with the other brothers, but he was not at all willing[a] to come now. He will come when he has the opportunity.

Final Messages and Greetings

13 Keep alert, stand firm in your faith, be courageous, be strong. [14]Let all that you do be done in love.

15 Now, brothers and sisters,[b] you know that members of the household of Stephanas were the first converts in Achaia, and they have devoted themselves to the service of the saints; [16]I urge you to put yourselves at the service of such people, and of everyone who works and toils with them. [17]I rejoice at the coming of Stephanas and Fortunatus and Achaicus, because they have made up for your absence; [18]for they refreshed my spirit as well as yours. So give recognition to such persons.

19 The churches of Asia send greetings. Aquila and Prisca, together with the church in their house, greet you warmly in the Lord. [20]All the brothers and sisters[b] send greetings. Greet one another with a holy kiss.

21 I, Paul, write this greeting with my own hand. [22]Let anyone be accursed who has no love for the Lord. Our Lord, come![c] [23]The grace of the Lord Jesus be with you. [24]My love be with all of you in Christ Jesus.[d]

---

a Or it was not at all God's will for him   b Gk brothers
c Gk Marana tha. These Aramaic words can also be read Maran atha, meaning Our Lord has come   d Other ancient authorities add Amen

---

tians, which took place each spring some weeks after Passover (see 2 Macc 12.32; Acts 2.1). **16.10** If Timothy comes, probably "whenever Timothy arrives," since he has been sent; see 4.17. **16.11** Whether the brothers are with Timothy or Paul is unclear. If the latter, they are perhaps the three named in v. 17. **16.12** Now concerning. See note on 8.1. Apollos. See 1.12. The other brothers, either persons traveling with Timothy or those named in v. 17. **16.13–24** Paul often precedes the closing benediction of a Letter, as he does here, with brief appeals, instructions, and comments on a variety of topics. **16.14** This appeal is implicit throughout the Letter (see 12.31–14.1). **16.15** Stephanas. See 1.16; 16.17. Achaia. See Introduction. Saints. See 1.2. **16.17–** 18 Fortunatus and Achaicus, like Stephanas, were probably Corinthians. **16.19** Asia. See note on 16.8. Aquila and Prisca, two of Paul's closest associates; see Acts 18.1–3; Rom 16.3–5. **16.20** Holy kiss, a form of Christian greeting; see also Rom 16.16; 1 Thess 5.26; 1 Pet 5.14. **16.21** With my own hand. The earlier portion of the Letter was dictated to a secretary; see also Gal 6.11; Col 4.18; 2 Thess 3.17; Philem 19. **16.22** Accursed. See also Rom 9.3; Gal 1.8–9. Our Lord, come! See also Rev 22.20. **16.23–24** An invocation of Christ's grace is found at the end of most of Paul's Letters, but only here does he add a comment about his love for the addressees (see, however, 1 Thess 3.12; cf. 2 Cor 2.4; 11.11; 12.15).

The Second Letter of Paul to the
CORINTHIANS

OF ALL PAUL'S LETTERS, 2 Corinthians is perhaps the most difficult to interpret. One contributing factor is the seemingly disjointed nature of its argument. 2 Cor 6.14–7.1 seems to be a digression from an appeal that begins in 6.11–13 and resumes in 7.2–4. The narration of Paul's journey from Asia Minor to Macedonia (2.12–13) is interrupted, only to resume five chapters later (7.5). In addition, the tone of the Letter varies widely. Ch. 7 is joyful and conciliatory, whereas chs. 10–13 are ironic and argumentative. Because of the digressions, abrupt transitions, and differences in tone, many scholars have argued that 2 Corinthians is composed of several fragments. Certainly it is a mixed Letter, containing different styles and various elements such as appeals, exhortations, rebukes, threats, attacks, counterattacks, self-defense, self-praise, and irony.

Nature and Sequence of the Corinthian Correspondence

AFTER PAUL ESTABLISHED THE CHURCH at Corinth, he carried on an extensive correspondence with the Christians in that city. They wrote him at least once (1 Cor 7.1), and he wrote them no fewer than four times. His first letter (Letter A) is mentioned in 1 Cor 5.9; the second (Letter B) is our 1 Corinthians, written from Ephesus (1 Cor 16.8). About the same time as Letter B, Paul sent his co-worker Timothy to Corinth (1 Cor 4.17; 16.10–11). According to most reconstructions, shortly thereafter a group of Jewish-Christian missionaries (2 Cor 11.22–23) arrived in Corinth and began to criticize the apostle. Timothy (1.1) apparently returned to Ephesus with a troubling report about the church, which prompted Paul to change his plans and to travel directly to Corinth. He later described this second visit as "painful" because some individual there wronged him (2.1–11; 7.12). Subsequent to this second visit and in lieu of a third visit, Paul wrote an emotionally charged letter, a "letter of tears" (1.23–2.4; 7.5–11). It was written either in Macedonia immediately after Paul's departure from Corinth (1.16) or upon his return to Ephesus. Instead of sending Timothy back to Corinth with this letter, Paul apparently sent Titus, another co-worker.

There are seven major theories about the nature and sequence of the correspondence following Timothy's return to Ephesus. According to the first and simplest theory, the "letter of tears" is Paul's third letter to Corinth (Letter C) and has been lost. 2 Corinthians as a whole is Paul's fourth letter (Letter D). Written from Macedonia after Titus's return, it contains no fragments of earlier letters. Although this theory, which typically explains differences within the Letter in terms of Paul's use of various rhetorical strategies, has been vigorously championed in recent years, most scholars regard it as inadequate to explain the complexities of the textual data. A second theory seeks to explain the sharp change in tone between chs. 1–9 and 10–13 by positing a change of situation for chs. 10–13. According to this hypothesis, 2 Corinthians is a literary unity, but whereas Paul wrote chs. 1–9 in response to Titus's optimistic report (7.5–16), he wrote chs. 10–13 after receiving new and troubling information about the situation in Corinth.

The third theory, like the second, assumes that Paul is addressing different situations in chs. 1–9 and 10–13. It too assumes that Letter C is the lost "letter of tears." It differs from the second theory by dividing 2 Corinthians into two originally independent letters. Paul's fourth letter (Letter D) is contained in chs. 1–9, and a fifth, later letter (Letter E) is partially preserved in chs. 10–13. Letters D and E both were written in Macedonia; Letter D was occasioned by Titus's optimistic report (7.5–16) and Letter E by a later, more pessimistic assessment of the state of affairs in the Corinthian church. A fourth theory differs from the third only by viewing ch. 9 as originally a separate letter about the collection. Advocates of this partition theory view chs. 1–8 as Letter D, ch. 9 as Letter E, and chs. 10–13 as Letter F.

The fifth theory, like the first four, maintains that the "letter of tears" is Paul's third letter (Letter C). It differs by identifying Letter C with chs. 10–13 and by usually assigning its place of composition to Ephesus (though Macedonia is favored in some reconstructions). Paul's fourth letter (Letter D) is equivalent to chs. 1–9; Titus's report is its occasion and Macedonia its place of composition. By making chs. 10–13 earlier than chs. 1–9, the fifth theory thus reverses the third theory's chronological sequence.

The sixth and seventh theories are the most complex. According to the sixth theory, Paul's third letter to Corinth (Letter C) is not the "letter of tears," but a letter (partially preserved in 2.14–6.13; 7.2–4) in which Paul defends himself against the verbal attacks of his opponents in Corinth. This letter, which preceded Paul's second visit to Corinth, was followed by another defensive letter (Letter D), partially preserved in chs. 10–13, which is probably, though not necessarily, the "letter of tears." Letters C and D were both composed in Ephesus. Paul's fifth letter (Letter E), occasioned by Titus's glowing report, is his "letter of reconciliation" with the Corinthian church. Written in Macedonia and completely preserved in 1.1–2.13; 7.5–16; 13.11–13, it provides the editorial frame for the entire canonical Letter. Chs. 8 and 9 (Letters F and G, respectively), which deal with the collection for the Jerusalem church, are chronologically the last of Paul's correspondence with the Christians of Achaia, though one of the chapters (probably 8) may originally have been attached to the "letter of reconciliation" (Letter E).

The seventh theory, like the sixth, divides 2 Corinthians into five different fragments, but it differs dramatically from all other reconstructions by viewing ch. 8, one of Paul's fund-raising missives, as Letter C. Instead of facilitating the collection, this deliberative appeal to the Corinthians backfired and created enormous problems for Paul, including angry charges that he was guilty of financial malfeasance and was usurping Corinthian prerogatives. This reaction led to Letter D (2.14–6.13; 7.2–4), in which the maligned apostle defended himself against these and other accusations. After his disastrous second visit to Corinth, Paul wrote Letter E (chs. 10–13), a sharp and often ironic self-defense of his apostolic legitimacy. Its success led to Letter F (1.1–2.13; 7.5–16; 13.11–13), which was written in order to effect a full reconciliation with the Corinthians, and Letter G (ch. 9), a final fund-raising missive directed to all believers in Achaia.

Date and Occasion of the Letter(s)

THE ARRIVAL OF PAUL'S OPPONENTS in Corinth, his unpleasant second visit to the city, his estrangement from part of the Corinthian church, the continuing problem of sin and impenitence in Corinth (12.20–21), the "letter of tears," the need for full reconciliation with both the church as a whole and Paul's offender (2.5–11; 7.12), Titus's glowing report, and possibly other, more negative reports provide the occasion for 2 Corinthians, either in part or as a whole. According to all seven reconstructions, Paul's later correspondence with Corinth belongs to the mid-50s of the first century (ca. 54–56 CE). This places it in the most theologically productive period of Paul's life, between 1 Thessalonians and Romans. Unquestionably Paul's interactions with the Corinthian church helped give both form and substance to his whole theology. [JOHN T. FITZGERALD]

Salutation

1 Paul, an apostle of Christ Jesus by the will of God, and Timothy our brother,

To the church of God that is in Corinth, including all the saints throughout Achaia:

2 Grace to you and peace from God our Father and the Lord Jesus Christ.

Paul's Thanksgiving after Affliction

3 Blessed be the God and Father of our Lord Jesus Christ, the Father of mercies and the God of all consolation, 4who consoles us in all our affliction, so that we may be able to console those who are in any affliction with the consolation with which we ourselves are consoled by God. 5For just as the sufferings of Christ are abundant for us, so also our consolation is abundant through Christ. 6If we are being afflicted, it is for your consolation and salvation; if we are being consoled, it is for your consolation, which you experience when you patiently endure the same sufferings that we are also suffering. 7Our hope for you is unshaken; for we know that as you share in our sufferings, so also you share in our consolation.

8 We do not want you to be unaware, brothers and sisters,[a] of the affliction we experienced in Asia; for we were so utterly, unbearably crushed that we despaired of life itself. 9Indeed, we felt that we had received the sentence of death so that we would rely not on ourselves but on God who raises the dead. 10He who rescued us from so deadly a peril will continue to rescue us; on him we have set our hope that he

a Gk brothers

1.1–2 The form of the salutation follows ancient letter-writing practice. 1.1 The co-sender of the Letter is Paul's protégé Timothy, who was with him when the church was established at Corinth (Acts 18.5; 2 Cor 1.19) and later returned there as his intermediary (Acts 19.22; 1 Cor 4.17; 16.10–11). Church of God collectively designates several groups of believers who met in the homes of various members (see 1 Cor 16.19). Saints, lit. "holy ones," a popular early designation of Christians as consecrated to God (see 1 Cor 1.2; 6.1–2). Since 27 BCE, Corinth had served as the capital of the Roman senatorial province of Achaia. 1.3–11 Instead of his customary thanksgiving (see Rom 1.8–15; 1 Cor 1.4–9), Paul uses here a benediction derived from ancient Jewish liturgical formulas such as "Blessed be the Lord" (see Gen 24.26–27; see also Eph 1.3–14; 1 Pet 1.3–9). 1.3 Father of mercies. See Ps 103.13; Lk 6.36; Rom 12.1. God of all consolation. See Rom 15.5. 1.4 Affliction and consolation are central themes both of the blessing and of the Letter as a whole; see 1.3–8; 2.4; 4.8, 17; 6.4; 7.4–7; 8.2, 13. 1.5 The sufferings of Christ indicates not only the afflictions Christ himself experienced, but also those his followers suffer in his name and on his behalf (4.10–11; Phil 3.10; 1 Pet 1.11; 4.13). 1.6 For Paul, divine consolation may occasionally take the form of deliverance from suffering (as in vv. 8–10), but it consists more fundamentally in the gift of divine power (4.7–9) that enables one to endure (see 6.4; Rom 5.3–5; 2 Thess 1.4; Rev 1.9) an abiding adverse circumstance (12.7–10). 1.7 Our hope for you is unshaken, one of several expressions of Paul's confidence in the Corinthians; see also v. 24; 7.4, 14, 16; 8.7. 1.8 We do not want you to be unaware, a disclosure formula frequently used by Paul to impart new or important information (see Rom 1.13; 11.25; 1 Cor 10.1; 12.1; 1 Thess 4.13). Asia, a Roman senatorial province located in Asia Minor. Nothing certain is known about the event Paul mentions; some conjecture that it was an otherwise unknown imprisonment in Ephesus during which he faced the possibility of execution (v. 9; see

will rescue us again, [11]as you also join in helping us by your prayers, so that many will give thanks on our[a] behalf for the blessing granted us through the prayers of many.

The Postponement of Paul's Visit

12 Indeed, this is our boast, the testimony of our conscience: we have behaved in the world with frankness[b] and godly sincerity, not by earthly wisdom but by the grace of God—and all the more toward you. [13]For we write you nothing other than what you can read and also understand; I hope you will understand until the end— [14]as you have already understood us in part—that on the day of the Lord Jesus we are your boast even as you are our boast.

15 Since I was sure of this, I wanted to come to you first, so that you might have a double favor;[c] [16]I wanted to visit you on my way to Macedonia, and to come back to you from Macedonia and have you send me on to Judea. [17]Was I vacillating when I wanted to do this? Do I make my plans according to ordinary human standards,[d] ready to say "Yes, yes" and "No, no" at the same time? [18]As surely as God is faithful, our word to you has not been "Yes and No." [19]For the Son of God, Jesus Christ, whom we proclaimed among you, Silvanus and Timothy and I, was not "Yes and No"; but in him it is always "Yes." [20]For in him every one of God's promises is a "Yes." For this reason it is through him that we say the "Amen," to the glory of God. [21]But it is God who establishes us with you in Christ and has anointed us, [22]by putting his seal on us and giving us his Spirit in our hearts as a first installment.

23 But I call on God as witness against me: it was to spare you that I did not come again to Corinth. [24]I do not mean to imply that we lord it over your faith; rather, we are workers with you for your joy, because you stand firm in the faith. 2 [1]So I made up my mind not to make you another painful visit. [2]For if I cause

---

a Other ancient authorities read *your*   b Other ancient authorities read *holiness*   c Other ancient authorities read *pleasure*   d Gk *according to the flesh*

---

also Phil 1.12–26). **1.12–14** Paul's personal integrity is a primary theme in 2 Corinthians. **1.12** The topic of Paul's *boast,* or self-commendation, is prominent in the Letters to Corinth; see 1 Cor 9.15; 2 Cor 3.1; 4.2; 5.12; 6.4; 10.8, 12–18; 11.10, 16–18, 30; 12.1, 5–6, 9, 11. The *conscience,* which plays an important role in the discussion of communal ethics in 1 Cor 8.7–13; 10.25–29, is invoked here in support of Paul's assertions about his own ethical conduct (see also Acts 23.1; 24.16; Rom 9.1; 2 Cor 4.2; 5.11). *Frankness.* The alternate reading *holiness* (see text note b) is preferred by many commentators. *Sincerity,* a term that Paul associates with "truthfulness" (see 1 Cor 5.8) and the divine (*godly;* see also 2 Cor 2.17). It thus stands in contrast to *earthly wisdom,* which uses duplicity and derives its power from rhetorical eloquence rather than the cross of Christ (see 1 Cor 1.17–25; 2.1–5). **1.13** *Until the end,* or "fully," yielding a contrast between partial (v. 14) and complete (v. 13) understanding (see 1 Cor 13.12). **1.14** *The day of the Lord Jesus,* i.e., the Second Coming (Greek *parousia*); see Phil 2.16. Paul's goal in 2 Corinthians is reconciliation and restoration of mutual pride between himself and the church. For Paul's pride in the Corinthians (*you are our boast*), see also 1 Cor 15.31; 2 Cor 7.4, 14; 8.24; 9.2–3; for the Corinthians' pride in Paul (*we are your boast*), see also 5.12. **1.15–2.4** An explanation for Paul's decision to send the Corinthians a grieving letter rather than revisit them. **1.15–16** For Paul's various travel plans in regard to Corinth, see also 1 Cor 4.18–21; 11.34; 16.3–9; 2 Cor 9.4; 12.14; 13.1. **1.16** *Macedonia,* the Roman senatorial province where both Philippi and Thessalonica were located. *Send me on,* i.e., provide financial assistance for the journey (see Rom 15.24; 1 Cor 16.6,

11; Titus 3.13; 3 Jn 6–8). *Judea,* the southern part of Palestine, where Jerusalem was located. For this destination, see also Rom 15.25; 1 Cor 16.3. **1.17** To some, Paul's departure from his announced itinerary (see 2.1) suggested he was *vacillating.* As a result, they accused him of base motives by alleging that he made and changed his travel plans *according to ordinary human standards* (see text note d; 10.2). *Yes and no.* Cf. Mt 5.37; Jas 5.12. **1.18** *God is faithful.* The OT theme of divine fidelity (see Deut 7.9), which appears frequently in the NT (1 Cor 1.9; 10.13; 1 Thess 5.24), functions here as an oath to confirm Paul's testimony (see also v. 23). **1.19** *Silvanus* (1 Thess 1.1; 2 Thess 1.1; 1 Pet 5.12), also known as Silas, was a prophet and leader in the Jerusalem church (Acts 15.22, 32) who accompanied Paul on his so-called second missionary journey (Acts 15.40–18.22). Consequently, he was with Paul and *Timothy* (see v. 1) when the church was established at Corinth (Acts 18.5). In Greek, the three men are mentioned in the order of importance: Paul, Silvanus, Timothy. **1.20** *Amen,* a Jewish and Christian liturgical acclamation meaning "So let it be" uttered by the congregation in response to benedictions and thanksgivings (see 1 Cor 14.16; Gal 1.5; Phil 4.20). **1.22** *First installment,* a commercial term rendered *guarantee* in 5.5 and "pledge" in Eph 1.14. The *Spirit,* whom believers receive at the time of conversion (see Gal 3.2–3), is the "down payment" that provides assurance that all God's saving promises (v. 20) will be fulfilled (see Rom 8.11; Eph 4.30). **1.23** For *God as witness* to Paul's oaths, see Rom 1.9; Phil 1.8; 1 Thess 2.5, 10. **1.24** Thematically, *joy* and pain (2.2) in 1.23–2.11 resume Paul's earlier discussion of affliction and consolation (1.3–11). *You stand firm in the faith.* See v. 7. **2.1** The *painful*

you pain, who is there to make me glad but the one whom I have pained? 3And I wrote as I did, so that when I came, I might not suffer pain from those who should have made me rejoice; for I am confident about all of you, that my joy would be the joy of all of you. 4For I wrote you out of much distress and anguish of heart and with many tears, not to cause you pain, but to let you know the abundant love that I have for you.

Forgiveness for the Offender

5 But if anyone has caused pain, he has caused it not to me, but to some extent—not to exaggerate it—to all of you. 6This punishment by the majority is enough for such a person; 7so now instead you should forgive and console him, so that he may not be overwhelmed by excessive sorrow. 8So I urge you to reaffirm your love for him. 9I wrote for this reason: to test you and to know whether you are obedient in everything. 10Anyone whom you forgive, I also forgive. What I have forgiven, if I have forgiven anything, has been for your sake

in the presence of Christ. 11And we do this so that we may not be outwitted by Satan; for we are not ignorant of his designs.

Paul's Anxiety in Troas

12 When I came to Troas to proclaim the good news of Christ, a door was opened for me in the Lord; 13but my mind could not rest because I did not find my brother Titus there. So I said farewell to them and went on to Macedonia.

14 But thanks be to God, who in Christ always leads us in triumphal procession, and through us spreads in every place the fragrance that comes from knowing him. 15For we are the aroma of Christ to God among those who are being saved and among those who are perishing; 16to the one a fragrance from death to death, to the other a fragrance from life to life. Who is sufficient for these things? 17For we are not peddlers of God's word like so many;*a* but in Christ we speak as

a Other ancient authorities read like the others

---

visit was Paul's second trip to Corinth; the next visit will be his third (see 12.14, 21; 13.1). **2.3** I wrote. See also v. 4, 9; 7.8, 12. For hypotheses concerning this "letter of tears," see Introduction. **2.5–11** A major goal of Paul is the reconciliation of the person who mistreated him during his second visit. **2.5** If anyone has caused pain (see also 7.12). Both the identity of this individual and the details of his actions are unknown. Earlier critics normally identified him with the "incestuous" man of 1 Cor 5, whereas most modern interpreters see him as either another member of the Corinthian church or someone from outside of Corinth. **2.6** Punishment, or "strong moral rebuke." **2.7** Forgive (see also Eph 4.32; Col 3.13), so that the church's action may be redemptive rather than destructive (7.10). **2.9** To be obedient (see also 10.6) entails recognition of Paul's apostolic authority (10.8; 13.10). His later praise of the Corinthians' obedience (7.15) indicates that they passed this test. **2.11** Satan is frequently mentioned not only in Paul's Letters to Corinth (1 Cor 5.5; 7.5; 2 Cor 6.15; 11.14; 12.7), but also in those written from that city (Rom 16.20; 1 Thess 2.18; 2 Thess 2.9). **2.12–13** Paul's anxiety over the effect of the letter carried by Titus (2.4; see Introduction). **2.12** The seaport city of Alexandria, Troas was a Roman colony located in the northwest corner of Asia Minor (see Acts 16.8, 11; 20.5–6; 2 Tim 4.13). A door was opened, a figurative expression indicating an opportunity for evangelization (see 1 Cor 16.9; Col 4.3; Rev 3.8). **2.13** Titus, like Silvanus and Timothy (1.19), was one of Paul's coworkers (7.6–7, 13–15; 8.6, 16–23; 12.18). A gentile Christian (Gal 2.3), he apparently was the bearer of the letter mentioned in 2.3–4, 9. To Macedonia. See 7.5 for

the resumption of Paul's discussion of this journey. **2.14–17** In this opening section of a lengthy discussion of his ministry (2.14–6.10), Paul emphasizes his God-given competence as a minister of the new covenant (see also 4.1–6). For the view that v. 14 marks the beginning of an earlier Pauline apologetic letter, partially preserved in 2.14–6.13; 7.2–4, see Introduction. **2.14** Thanks be to God. See Rom 6.17; 7.25; 1 Cor 15.57; 2 Cor 8.16; 9.15. Leads us in triumphal procession, an allusion to the famous Roman military parades in which victorious generals celebrated their triumphs along with their soldiers and in which their prisoners of war were compelled to march (see also Col 2.15). With this metaphor Paul is describing his itinerant apostolic ministry as directed by God, who through his envoy's proclamation of the gospel (fragrance) makes himself known. Fragrance that comes from knowing him, better "the aroma of the knowledge of him." **2.15–16** Continuing the use of olfactory imagery begun in v. 14 but shifting it in a striking way, Paul now identifies himself as the aroma of the Anointed One, thereby making the response to his apostolic activity identical to the reaction to the crucified Christ, whose messianic death led to radically different evaluations by the saved and the perishing (see also 1 Cor 1.18; 2 Cor 4.3). For the latter, Christ and Paul were an embalming unguent (a fragrance from death to death), whereas the former "smelled" in them the sweet scent of a healing balm that brings life. **2.16** Paul's question introduces the theme of his sufficiency, or competence (see also 3.5–6), as an apostle, which was a key issue in the dispute with his Corinthian opponents. **2.17** Here and in 4.2 Paul is

persons of sincerity, as persons sent from God and standing in his presence.

Ministers of the New Covenant

3 Are we beginning to commend ourselves again? Surely we do not need, as some do, letters of recommendation to you or from you, do we? [2]You yourselves are our letter, written on our[a] hearts, to be known and read by all; [3]and you show that you are a letter of Christ, prepared by us, written not with ink but with the Spirit of the living God, not on tablets of stone but on tablets of human hearts.

4 Such is the confidence that we have through Christ toward God. [5]Not that we are competent of ourselves to claim anything as coming from us; our competence is from God, [6]who has made us competent to be ministers of a new covenant, not of letter but of spirit; for the letter kills, but the Spirit gives life.

7 Now if the ministry of death, chiseled in letters on stone tablets,[b] came in glory so that the people of Israel could not gaze at Moses' face because of the glory of his face, a glory now set aside, [8]how much more will the ministry of the Spirit come in glory? [9]For if there was glory in the ministry of condemnation, much more does the ministry of justification abound in glory! [10]Indeed, what once had

glory has lost its glory because of the greater glory; [11]for if what was set aside came through glory, much more has the permanent come in glory!

12 Since, then, we have such a hope, we act with great boldness, [13]not like Moses, who put a veil over his face to keep the people of Israel from gazing at the end of the glory that[c] was being set aside. [14]But their minds were hardened. Indeed, to this very day, when they hear the reading of the old covenant, that same veil is still there, since only in Christ is it set aside. [15]Indeed, to this very day whenever Moses is read, a veil lies over their minds; [16]but when one turns to the Lord, the veil is removed. [17]Now the Lord is the Spirit, and where the Spirit of the Lord is, there is freedom. [18]And all of us, with unveiled faces, seeing the glory of the Lord as though reflected in a mirror, are being transformed into the same image from one degree of glory to another; for this comes from the Lord, the Spirit.

Treasure in Clay Jars

4 Therefore, since it is by God's mercy that we are engaged in this ministry, we do not

---

a Other ancient authorities read *your*   b Gk *on stones*   c Gk *of what*

---

probably denying his critics' accusations against him as well as making the counteraccusation that they, *like so many,* are hucksters and charlatans. *Sincerity.* See 1.12. For speech in the divine *presence,* see also 12.19.

3.1–18 Using a series of antitheses, Paul compares ministry under the old and new covenants. **3.1** *Commend ourselves.* See note on 1.12. *Letters of recommendation* were widely used in the Greco-Roman world to praise friends and acquaintances and to introduce them to others. Early Christians made frequent use of this ancient convention, especially for traveling missionaries (see Acts 18.27). **3.2–3** *Our letter.* Paul uses letter-writing imagery to describe the Corinthians' conversion, which he attributes to *Christ* by means of the *Spirit,* and his role as the one who "administered" (i.e., either *prepared* or, more likely, "delivered") the letter. **3.3** The Ten Commandments (Ex 20.1–17; Deut 5.6–21) were inscribed on *two tablets of stone* (Ex 24.12; 31.18; Deut 9.10). For *tablets of human hearts,* see Jer 31.33; also Prov 3.3; 7.3; Ezek 11.19; 36.26. **3.6** Both Paul and his rivals used *minister* and *apostle* (1.1) to depict themselves as the personal representatives of Christ (11.13–15, 23). *New covenant.* See Jer 31.31; also Lk 22.20; 1 Cor 11.25. *Letter.* Paul uses a different Greek word from that in vv. 1–3 and refers now to the law (see Rom 2.27; 7.6), which he often associates with death (v. 7) and condemnation (v. 9). By con-

trast, *the Spirit gives life* (see Rom 7.6–11; 8.2, 11; Gal 3.21). **3.7–18** Paul expounds the meaning of v. 6 by means of a two-part interpretation of Ex 34.29–35. **3.7** *Ministry of death* points to the lethal effects of the law (see Rom 7.10). **3.8** Paul employs here and in the following verses the rabbinic exegetical principle of arguing "from the lesser to the greater" (*how much more*) to assert that the new covenant and its ministry surpass the old in splendor. **3.12** *Boldness,* the manner of Paul's speaking, not his state of mind. In both Hellenistic philosophy and Pauline theology, frank speech was based on freedom (v. 17), confidence (v. 4), and competence (vv. 5–6), and it was appropriately used to foster moral improvement. **3.14** In contrast to the literal veil mentioned in v. 13 (see Ex 34.33–35), *veil* here and in vv. 15–16 is a metaphor for misunderstanding. **3.15** *Moses,* i.e., the book of Moses (the Torah or Pentateuch); see 2 Chr 25.4; Neh 13.1; Mk 12.26; Acts 15.21. **3.17** Paul apparently identifies "the LORD" mentioned in Ex 34.34 as *the Spirit* (see also v. 18). **3.18** Paul's statement reflects the widespread Hellenistic belief that humans are changed as a result of beholding the divine. On the metamorphosis to the divine *image,* see Rom 8.29; 1 Cor 15.49; Col 3.10; for Christ as the image of God, see 4.4.

4.1–6 The revelation of the glory of God in the apostolic proclamation of the gospel. **4.1** *Lose heart.* See v. 16.

lose heart. 2We have renounced the shameful things that one hides; we refuse to practice cunning or to falsify God's word; but by the open statement of the truth we commend ourselves to the conscience of everyone in the sight of God. 3And even if our gospel is veiled, it is veiled to those who are perishing. 4In their case the god of this world has blinded the minds of the unbelievers, to keep them from seeing the light of the gospel of the glory of Christ, who is the image of God. 5For we do not proclaim ourselves; we proclaim Jesus Christ as Lord and ourselves as your slaves for Jesus' sake. 6For it is the God who said, "Let light shine out of darkness," who has shone in our hearts to give the light of the knowledge of the glory of God in the face of Jesus Christ.

7 But we have this treasure in clay jars, so that it may be made clear that this extraordinary power belongs to God and does not come from us. 8We are afflicted in every way, but not crushed; perplexed, but not driven to despair; 9persecuted, but not forsaken; struck down, but not destroyed; 10always carrying in the body the death of Jesus, so that the life of Jesus may also be made visible in our bodies. 11For

while we live, we are always being given up to death for Jesus' sake, so that the life of Jesus may be made visible in our mortal flesh. 12So death is at work in us, but life in you.

13 But just as we have the same spirit of faith that is in accordance with scripture—"I believed, and so I spoke"—we also believe, and so we speak, 14because we know that the one who raised the Lord Jesus will raise us also with Jesus, and will bring us with you into his presence. 15Yes, everything is for your sake, so that grace, as it extends to more and more people, may increase thanksgiving, to the glory of God.

Living by Faith

16 So we do not lose heart. Even though our outer nature is wasting away, our inner nature is being renewed day by day. 17For this slight momentary affliction is preparing us for an eternal weight of glory beyond all measure, 18because we look not at what can be seen but at what cannot be seen; for what can be seen is temporary, but what cannot be seen is eternal.

5 For we know that if the earthly tent we live in is destroyed, we have a building from

---

4.2 Paul was accused both of being *cunning* (see 12.16; also 11.3; 1 Cor 3.19) and of *falsifying God's word* (see note on 2.17). *Conscience.* See 1.12. **4.3** *Veiled,* an enigmatic allusion to a criticism by Paul's opponents, who may have believed that he craftily distorted and hid his gospel by using rhetorical devices such as irony and covert allusion (see 1 Cor 4.6–8) or that Paul's sufferings veiled his message about God and led to its rejection. *Perishing.* See 2.15. **4.4** *The god of this world.* This sharply dualistic expression contains the only NT reference to Satan as "god"; but see Jn 12.31; 14.30; 16.11; Eph 2.2; also 1 Cor 2.6, 8. *Minds.* See 3.14. *Unbelievers,* either non-Christians (as in 1 Cor 6.6; 7.12–15; 10.27; 14.22–24) or Paul's adversaries, who are linked with Satan (11.13–15) and belong to the perishing (4.3; see also Phil 1.28; 3.18–19). *Image.* See 3.18; Col 1.15; also Heb 1.3. **4.5** *Jesus Christ as Lord* was a basic Christian confession; see Rom 10.9; 1 Cor 12.3; Phil 2.11; Col 2.6. **4.6** *Let light shine out of darkness.* These precise words do not appear in the OT; see, however, Gen 1.3; Ps 112.4; Isa 9.2. **4.7–5.10** The trials and triumph of Paul's ministry. **4.7–15** Apostolic weakness and divine power. **4.7** Earthenware was fragile and cheap; hence the paradox of precious *treasure* (his ministry and gospel) *in clay jars.* **4.8–9** Lists of hardships were commonly used to depict the ideal sage's own victory over adversity. Paul claims a similar superiority but *consistently* attributes it to God rather than himself (v. 7). Similar lists appear in 6.4–10; 11.23–28; 12.10; Rom 8.35–39; 1 Cor 4.9–13; Phil 4.11–12; 2 Tim 3.11. **4.9** *Not forsaken,* by God. **4.10** *Death,* lit. "necrosis," a graphic

word used by Greek medical writers of dead or dying tissue. Because God's power (v. 7) is displayed in Paul's sufferings, he *carries in the body* evidence of both Christ's death and his resurrection (*life of Jesus*). **4.11** *Being given up,* perhaps better "giving ourselves up," which would fit the emphasis found in both Hellenistic philosophy and Christian tradition on voluntary suffering (see Gal 2.20; Eph 5.2, 25). **4.13** The quotation is from Ps 115.1 in the Septuagint; cf. Ps 116.10 (Hebrew). **4.15** *For your sake.* See 2.10; also 1.6; 5.13; 8.23. On increased *thanksgiving,* see 1.11; 9.11–12. **4.16–5.10** A discussion of present affliction and future glory using terms and concepts drawn from both Hellenistic popular philosophy and Jewish apocalyptic. **4.16** *Lose heart.* See 4.1; Eph 3.13. The contrast between *inner nature* (lit. "person") and *outer nature* was common in Middle Platonism; see also Rom 7.22; Eph 3.16; 1 Pet 3.4. *Renewed.* See Rom 12.2; Col 3.10. **4.17** On *affliction* leading to *glory,* an apocalyptic concept, see Rom 8.18; 2 Thess 1.5. **4.18** The contrasts between visible and invisible, *temporary* and *eternal,* were common philosophical ones; see also Col 1.16; Heb 11.1, 3. **5.1–4** The difficulty of this passage is compounded by the striking manner in which Paul mixes residential imagery with terms involving clothing. **5.1** *Earthly tent,* a common Hellenistic term for the body; see vv. 6–10; see also Wis 9.15; 2 Pet 1.13. The tent/building contrast continues the temporary/permanent antithesis of 4.17–18. *Destroyed,* a reference to death. *We have,* either immediately after death or, more likely, at the Second Coming (as in 1 Cor 15.20–57; Phil 3.20–21;

God, a house not made with hands, eternal in the heavens. [2]For in this tent we groan, longing to be clothed with our heavenly dwelling— [3]if indeed, when we have taken it off[a] we will not be found naked. [4]For while we are still in this tent, we groan under our burden, because we wish not to be unclothed but to be further clothed, so that what is mortal may be swallowed up by life. [5]He who has prepared us for this very thing is God, who has given us the Spirit as a guarantee.

[6] So we are always confident; even though we know that while we are at home in the body we are away from the Lord— [7]for we walk by faith, not by sight. [8]Yes, we do have confidence, and we would rather be away from the body and at home with the Lord. [9]So whether we are at home or away, we make it our aim to please him. [10]For all of us must appear before the judgment seat of Christ, so that each may receive recompense for what has been done in the body, whether good or evil.

The Ministry of Reconciliation

[11] Therefore, knowing the fear of the Lord, we try to persuade others; but we ourselves are well known to God, and I hope that we are also well known to your consciences. [12]We are not commending ourselves to you again, but giving you an opportunity to boast about us, so that you may be able to answer those who boast in outward appearance and not in the heart. [13]For if we are beside ourselves, it is for God; if we are in our right mind, it is for you. [14]For the love of Christ urges us on, because we are convinced that one has died for all; therefore all have died. [15]And he died for all, so that those who live might live no longer for themselves, but for him who died and was raised for them.

[16] From now on, therefore, we regard no one from a human point of view;[b] even though we once knew Christ from a human point of view,[b] we know him no longer in that way. [17]So if anyone is in Christ, there is a new creation: everything old has passed away; see, everything has become new! [18]All this is from God, who reconciled us to himself through Christ, and has given us the ministry of reconciliation; [19]that is, in Christ God was reconcil-

---

a Other ancient authorities read *put it on*   b Gk *according to the flesh*

---

1 Thess 4.16–17). *Building from God,* either the resurrection body given each individual believer (see 1 Cor 15.44) or the apocalyptic concept of the new age with its heavenly temple in the new Jerusalem (see 2 Esd 10.40–57). *Not made with hands.* See Mk 14.58; Col 2.11, and text note *d;* Heb 9.11, 24. **5.2** *Groan.* See 5.4; Rom 8.23, 26. **5.3–4** According to many interpreters, Paul wishes to avoid death, which renders the soul *naked* and *unclothed;* he hopes instead to live until the Second Coming, so that he can be transformed and receive the resurrection body as *further clothing* (see 1 Cor 15.53–54). Others suggest that Paul is here contrasting himself and his destiny with that of his opponents. Whereas he will receive additional spiritual clothing, his rivals will be condemned at the judgment (see v. 10), stripped of their baptismal clothing (see Gal 3.27), and thus have nakedness as their final state. **5.5** *Guarantee.* See note on 1.22. **5.7** *Not by sight.* See 4.18; Rom 8.24–25; 1 Cor 13.12; 1 Pet 1.8. **5.8** On Paul's preference for death (*being away from the body*), see Phil 1.23. **5.10** On the (final) *judgment seat,* see Rom 2.16; 14.9–10. Even Christians face judgment over their *good or evil deeds; see 11.15;* Rom 2.6–10; 1 Cor 4.5, see also Eccl 12.14.
5.11–6.10 Apostolic existence as a ministry of reconciliation. **5.11** *The fear of the Lord* (see 7.1; Sir 1.30) does not suggest that Paul personally feared the judgment (see vv. 6–8) but that he took his ministry very seriously. **5.12** *Commending ourselves.* See note on 1.12. *Those who boast in outward appearance,* Paul's opponents, whom he describes with terms reminis-

cent of 1 Sam 16.7. **5.13** *Are beside ourselves.* Most interpreters see here a reference to mystical experiences (see 12.1–6), which, though praised by Paul's adversaries, were evaluated by him according to the same standard he applied to speaking in tongues (1 Cor 14.2, 19, 28). Others, however, believe that Paul is referring to the "letter of tears" (2.4) in which he depicted himself as mad with grief. **5.14** *Love of Christ,* i.e., Christ's love for us, expressed by his vicarious death (see v. 15; Gal 2.20; also Rom 5.8). **5.15** See Rom 7.4; 14.7–9; Gal 2.19–20. **5.16** To regard anyone— even Christ—*from a human point of view* (see also 1.17; 11.18) involves a judgment according to outward appearance (v. 12). **5.17** *New creation.* See Isa 43.18–19; 65.17; 66.22; Gal 6.15; Eph 2.15; 2 Pet 3.13; Rev 21.1–5. **5.18–20** In ancient thought, *reconciliation* (largely a secular term used for mending strained interpersonal and international relations) involved the removal of enmity and the establishment or restoration of friendship and within a political context was a task quintessentially entrusted to an *ambassador* (v. 20). Paul not only applies it to the divine-human relationship but also alters the way in which friendship with God is effected. The responsibility for reconciliation normally resided with those who were responsible for rupturing a relationship, but in contrast to normal expectations Paul presents God as the reconciler (Rom 5.10–11; also Col 1.20–22), not as the object of reconciliation (as in 2 Macc 1.5; 5.20; 7.33; 8.29). **5.19** *Not counting their trespasses against them.* Whereas human efforts at reconciliation were often thwarted by

ing the world to himself,[a] not counting their trespasses against them, and entrusting the message of reconciliation to us. [20]So we are ambassadors for Christ, since God is making his appeal through us; we entreat you on behalf of Christ, be reconciled to God. [21]For our sake he made him to be sin who knew no sin, so that in him we might become the righteousness of God.

6 As we work together with him,[b] we urge you also not to accept the grace of God in vain. [2]For he says,

> "At an acceptable time I have listened to
> you,
> and on a day of salvation I have helped
> you."

See, now is the acceptable time; see, now is the day of salvation! [3]We are putting no obstacle in anyone's way, so that no fault may be found with our ministry, [4]but as servants of God we have commended ourselves in every way: through great endurance, in afflictions, hardships, calamities, [5]beatings, imprisonments, riots, labors, sleepless nights, hunger; [6]by pu-

rity, knowledge, patience, kindness, holiness of spirit, genuine love, [7]truthful speech, and the power of God; with the weapons of righteousness for the right hand and for the left; [8]in honor and dishonor, in ill repute and good repute. We are treated as impostors, and yet are true; [9]as unknown, and yet are well known; as dying, and see—we are alive; as punished, and yet not killed; [10]as sorrowful, yet always rejoicing; as poor, yet making many rich; as having nothing, and yet possessing everything.

11 We have spoken frankly to you Corinthians; our heart is wide open to you. [12]There is no restriction in our affections, but only in yours. [13]In return—I speak as to children—open wide your hearts also.

The Temple of the Living God

14 Do not be mismatched with unbelievers. For what partnership is there between righ-

---

a Or *God was in Christ reconciling the world to himself*   *b* Gk *As we work together*

---

demands that the guilty be severely punished or that hefty reparations be made, Paul depicts God as magnanimously offering a blanket amnesty to humans. See Rom 4.8. **5.20** According to the standard paradigm for reconciliation, the apostle would have been sent as the world's (v. 19) *ambassador* to *appeal* to God, but Paul dramatically alters the imagery by depicting himself as God's emissary to humanity. **5.21** *Made him to be sin,* either in the sense that Christ assumed sinful human nature (see Rom 8.3), or that on the cross God treated the sinless Jesus as a sinner (see Gal 3.13), or that Jesus became a sacrifice for sin, either a guilt offering or a sin offering (see Isa 53.10; Rom 8.3, text note *c*). *Who knew no sin,* a traditional concept; see Jn 7.18; 8.46; Heb 4.15; 7.26; 1 Pet 1.19; 2.22; 3.18; 1 Jn 3.5. As Christ became God's righteousness for humans (1 Cor 1.30), so humans become in Christ *the righteousness of God;* the latter is an important Pauline phrase that denotes, depending on the context, either God's own righteousness or the righteousness that proceeds from God and justifies the believer (see Rom 1.17; 3.5, 21–22, 25–26; 10.3; Phil 3.9). **6.2** *At . . . helped you.* Isa 49.8. **6.3** *No obstacle.* See 1 Cor 9.12. **6.4** *Servants,* lit. "ministers"; see 3.6. *Commended ourselves.* See note on 1.12. **6.4–7** Adversity and virtue were closely linked in antiquity, so that the nine hardships given in vv. 4–5 (see also 4.8–9) function not only to magnify Paul's great endurance (v. 4), but also to prove that he is virtuous; the list of virtues (vv. 6–7) underscores the point. For other virtue lists, see Gal 5.22–23; Phil 4.8; Col 3.12; 1 Pet 3.8; 2 Pet 1.5–7. **6.8–10** The seven antithetic clauses that conclude this section contrast the outward appearance, which is false or deficient, with

the true and greater reality that belongs to Paul's heart (5.12; 6.11). In formulating these verses, Paul draws on Ps 118.17–18 as well as Greco-Roman paradoxes about the ideal sage. **6.10** *Poor, yet making many rich.* See 8.9.

6.11–7.16 After concluding the lengthy discussion of his reconciling ministry (2.14–6.10), Paul now makes an appeal for the church to be fully reconciled with him (6.11–7.4) and with the one who wronged him (7.5–16). **6.11** *We have spoken frankly to you.* For Paul's bold speech to the Corinthians, see notes on 3.12; 7.4. *Our heart is wide open to you,* a sign of Paul's affection for the Corinthians; see v. 12; 7.3. **6.13** *Children.* See 1 Cor 4.14; Gal 4.19; 1 Thess 2.11. **6.14–7.1** The origin and literary placement of this passage are highly problematic, because it contains a number of words not found elsewhere in Paul's Letter and appears to interrupt the appeal in 6.11–13; 7.2–4. Of the various solutions, five merit mention. The passage could be (1) a fragment from the letter mentioned in 1 Cor 5.9; (2) a digression in which Paul deliberately uses unusual and highly emotional language for rhetorical effect; (3) a passage, non-Pauline in origin, that Paul himself inserts here to provide moral exhortation and/or warn the Corinthians against associating with his opponents; (4) a non-Pauline passage, perhaps of Essene origin, inserted by a later editor; or (5) an originally anti-Pauline passage that reflects the theology of Paul's opponents. **6.14** *Mismatched,* lit. "yoked" (a common term for a close relationship such as friendship or marriage) to someone who is "different," in this case *unbelievers* (see 4.4). If the reference is to Paul's opponents, the passage functions to insist

teousness and lawlessness? Or what fellowship is there between light and darkness? 15What agreement does Christ have with Beliar? Or what does a believer share with an unbeliever? 16What agreement has the temple of God with idols? For we *a* are the temple of the living God; as God said,

"I will live in them and walk among
     them,
    and I will be their God,
    and they shall be my people.
17   Therefore come out from them,
    and be separate from them, says the
     Lord,
   and touch nothing unclean;
    then I will welcome you,
18   and I will be your father,
    and you shall be my sons and daughters,
    says the Lord Almighty."

7 Since we have these promises, beloved, let us cleanse ourselves from every defilement of body and of spirit, making holiness perfect in the fear of God.

Paul's Joy at the Church's Repentance

2 Make room in your hearts *b* for us; we have wronged no one, we have corrupted no one, we have taken advantage of no one. 3I do not say this to condemn you, for I said before that you are in our hearts, to die together and to live together. 4I often boast about you; I have great pride in you; I am filled with consolation; I am overjoyed in all our affliction.

5 For even when we came into Macedonia, our bodies had no rest, but we were afflicted in every way—disputes without and fears within. 6But God, who consoles the downcast, consoled us by the arrival of Titus, 7and not only by his coming, but also by the consolation with which he was consoled about you, as he told us of your longing, your mourning, your zeal for me, so that I rejoiced still more. 8For even if I made you sorry with my letter, I do not regret it (though I did regret it, for I see that I grieved you with that letter, though only briefly). 9Now I rejoice, not because you were grieved, but because your grief led to repentance; for you felt a godly grief, so that you were not harmed in any way by us. 10For godly grief produces a repentance that leads to salvation and brings no regret, but worldly grief produces death. 11For see what earnestness this godly grief has produced in you, what eagerness to clear yourselves, what indignation, what alarm, what longing, what zeal, what punishment! At every point you have proved yourselves guiltless in the matter. 12So although I wrote to you, it was not on account of the one who did the wrong, nor on account of the one who was wronged, but in order that your zeal for us might be made known to you before God. 13In this we find comfort.

In addition to our own consolation, we rejoiced still more at the joy of Titus, because his mind has been set at rest by all of you. 14For if I have been somewhat boastful about you to him, I was not disgraced; but just as everything we said to you was true, so our boasting to Titus has proved true as well. 15And his heart goes out all the more to you, as he remembers the obedience of all of you, and how you welcomed him with fear and trembling. 16I rejoice, because I have complete confidence in you.

---

a Other ancient authorities read *you*   *b* Gk lacks *in your hearts*

---

that full reconciliation with Paul entails a renunciation of the church's relationship with his rivals. **6.15** *Beliar,* a variant of Belial (Hebrew, "worthlessness"), one of the various Jewish names for Satan (see 2.11). **6.16** *The temple of the living God.* See 1 Cor 3.16. *As God said.* See 4.6. Three quotation formulas are used to introduce, connect, and conclude the chain of OT citations and paraphrases in vv. 16–18 (for similar chains, see Rom 3.10–18; 15.9–12). Lev 26.11–12; Ezek 37.27 are the sources used in v. 16. **6.17** See Isa 52.11 and the Septuagint of Ezek 20.34. **6.18** See 2 Sam 7.14; Isa 43.6. **7.2–4** Resumption of the appeal of vv. 11–13. **7.2** On the charge of *taking advantage* of the Corinthians, see 12.17–18. **7.3** *To die together and to live together,* a Christianized version of a traditional friendship formula (see 2 Sam 15.21). **7.4** *I often boast about you,* lit. "great is my bold speech toward you." Paul's candor is a sign of his friendship (v. 3) with the Corinthians; see 3.12; 6.11. *Pride . . . consolation . . . affliction,* a transitional verse that recalls the major themes of 1.3–14. **7.5–16** Resumption and conclusion of 1.15–2.13 (esp. 2.12–13); see Introduction. **7.6** *God, who consoles the downcast.* See 1.3–4; Isa 49.13. *Titus.* See 2.13; 7.13–15. **7.8** *Letter.* See 2.3. **7.9** *Godly grief,* i.e., grief that accords with God's will and results in repentance and salvation (v. 10). **7.12** *The one who did the wrong,* the offender discussed in 2.5–11, with whom the church is to be reconciled lest he be destroyed by worldly grief (2.7; 7.10). *The one who was wronged,* almost certainly Paul himself. **7.14** *Boastful.* See 1.14. **7.15** *Obedience.* See 2.9. **7.16** Expressions of *confidence* (see 1.7) serve to create a sense of responsibility on the part of the persons praised, making them more responsive to requests. V. 16 is thus transitional, not only concluding

Encouragement to Be Generous

8 We want you to know, brothers and sisters,[a] about the grace of God that has been granted to the churches of Macedonia; ²for during a severe ordeal of affliction, their abundant joy and their extreme poverty have overflowed in a wealth of generosity on their part. ³For, as I can testify, they voluntarily gave according to their means, and even beyond their means, ⁴begging us earnestly for the privilege[b] of sharing in this ministry to the saints— ⁵and this, not merely as we expected; they gave themselves first to the Lord and, by the will of God, to us, ⁶so that we might urge Titus that, as he had already made a beginning, so he should also complete this generous undertaking[c] among you. ⁷Now as you excel in everything—in faith, in speech, in knowledge, in utmost eagerness, and in our love for you[d]—so we want you to excel also in this generous undertaking.[c]

8 I do not say this as a command, but I am testing the genuineness of your love against the earnestness of others. ⁹For you know the generous act[e] of our Lord Jesus Christ, that though he was rich, yet for your sakes he became poor, so that by his poverty you might become rich. ¹⁰And in this matter I am giving my advice: it is appropriate for you who began last year not only to do something but even to desire to do something— ¹¹now finish doing it, so that your eagerness may be matched by completing it according to your means. ¹²For if the eagerness is there, the gift is acceptable according to what one has—not according to what one does not have. ¹³I do not mean that there should be relief for others and pressure on you, but it is a question of a fair balance between ¹⁴your present abundance and their need, so that their abundance may be for your need, in order that there may be a fair balance. ¹⁵As it is written,

> "The one who had much did not have
>   too much,
>   and the one who had little did not have
>   too little."

Commendation of Titus

16 But thanks be to God who put in the heart of Titus the same eagerness for you that I myself have. ¹⁷For he not only accepted our appeal, but since he is more eager than ever, he is going to you of his own accord. ¹⁸With him we are sending the brother who is famous among all the churches for his proclaiming the good news;[f] ¹⁹and not only that, but he has also been appointed by the churches to travel with us while we are administering this generous undertaking[c] for the glory of the Lord himself[g] and to show our goodwill. ²⁰We intend that no one should blame us about this generous gift that we are administering, ²¹for we intend to do what is right not only in the Lord's sight but also in the sight of others.

---

a Gk *brothers* b Gk *grace* c Gk *this grace* d Other ancient authorities read *your love for us* e Gk *the grace* f Or *the gospel* g Other ancient authorities lack *himself*

---

the discussion in vv. 5–16 but also laying the foundation for the requests made in chs. 8–9.

8.1–9.15 The collection for the Jerusalem church was intended not only to address its economic need but also to ratify the unity between Jewish and gentile Christians (Rom 15.25–32; 1 Cor 16.1–4; Gal 2.10; also Acts 24.17). (For the literary problems associated with 2 Cor 8–9, see Introduction.) **8.1** In chs. 8–9 Paul uses the Greek word *charis* to describe the beneficence of God and Christ as well as the human response to the divine action in both gratitude and giving. It is variously translated as *grace* (8.1; 9.14), *blessing* (9.8), *generous act* (8.9), *thanks* (8.16; 9.15), and, with reference to the collection, as *privilege* (8.4) and *generous undertaking* (8.6–7, 19). (For the hypothesis that ch. 8 was originally a deliberative letter written not long after *1 Corinthians*, see Introduction.) **8.2** This *affliction* is mentioned in Phil 1.29–30; 1 Thess 1.6; 2.14; 3.3–4. *Generosity.* See 9.11, 13; Rom 12.8. **8.3** *Voluntarily.* See v. 17; 9.7. **8.4** *Sharing*, applied here to the collection (see also 9.13; Rom 15.26), is also used by Paul to express the church's participation in Christ (1 Cor 1.9), especially in his body and blood (1 Cor 10.16) and in his sufferings (2 Cor 1.7; Phil 3.10), its communion with the Spirit (2 Cor 13.13), and its partnership in the gospel (Phil 1.5). *Ministry.* See 9.1, 12–13; also 8.19–20; Rom 15.31. *Saints,* here and in 9.1, 12 poor Jewish Christians in Jerusalem (Rom 15.25–26). **8.6** For the role of *Titus* in the collection, see also 8.16–24; 12.18. **8.7** For the abundance of *faith, speech, knowledge,* and other spiritual gifts in Corinth, see 1 Cor 1.5; 12.8–10; 13.1–2, 8. **8.8** *Command,* here the opposite of *advice* (v. 10; see 1 Cor 7.6, 25, 40). **8.9** *Though he was rich . . . became poor.* See Phil 2.6–8. *By his poverty . . . rich,* a clause that recalls Paul's self-description in 6.10. **8.10** *Last year.* See 9.2. **8.13–14** Paul advocates the ideals of both self-sufficiency (*having enough,* 9.8) and *fair balance:* people should have sufficient wealth not only to satisfy their own needs but also to share the excess with others, who are in turn obliged to reciprocate. **8.15** Ex 16.18. **8.16** *Thanks be to God.* See 2.14. **8.18–24** The identity of the two *brothers* (vv. 18, 22) who serve as the churches' envoys is unknown (but see 12.18; Acts 20.4–6). **8.20** *Blame.* See 6.3. **8.21** *In the*

22And with them we are sending our brother whom we have often tested and found eager in many matters, but who is now more eager than ever because of his great confidence in you. 23As for Titus, he is my partner and co-worker in your service; as for our brothers, they are messengers*a* of the churches, the glory of Christ. 24Therefore openly before the churches, show them the proof of your love and of our reason for boasting about you.

The Collection for Christians at Jerusalem

9 Now it is not necessary for me to write you about the ministry to the saints, 2for I know your eagerness, which is the subject of my boasting about you to the people of Macedonia, saying that Achaia has been ready since last year; and your zeal has stirred up most of them. 3But I am sending the brothers in order that our boasting about you may not prove to have been empty in this case, so that you may be ready, as I said you would be; 4otherwise, if some Macedonians come with me and find that you are not ready, we would be humiliated—to say nothing of you—in this undertaking.*b* 5So I thought it necessary to urge the brothers to go on ahead to you, and arrange in advance for this bountiful gift that you have promised, so that it may be ready as a voluntary gift and not as an extortion.

6 The point is this: the one who sows sparingly will also reap sparingly, and the one who sows bountifully will also reap bountifully. 7Each of you must give as you have made up your mind, not reluctantly or under compulsion, for God loves a cheerful giver. 8And God is able to provide you with every blessing in abundance, so that by always having enough of everything, you may share abundantly in every good work. 9As it is written,

"He scatters abroad, he gives to the poor;
    his righteousness*c* endures forever."
10He who supplies seed to the sower and bread for food will supply and multiply your seed for sowing and increase the harvest of your righteousness.*c* 11You will be enriched in every way for your great generosity, which will produce thanksgiving to God through us; 12for the rendering of this ministry not only supplies the needs of the saints but also overflows with many thanksgivings to God. 13Through the testing of this ministry you glorify God by your obedience to the confession of the gospel of Christ and by the generosity of your sharing with them and with all others, 14while they long for you and pray for you because of the surpassing grace of God that he has given you. 15Thanks be to God for his indescribable gift!

Paul Defends His Ministry

10 I myself, Paul, appeal to you by the meekness and gentleness of Christ—I who am humble when face to face with you, but bold toward you when I am away!— 2I ask that when I am present I need not show boldness by daring to oppose those who think we are acting according to human standards.*d* 3Indeed, we live as human beings,*e* but we do not wage war according to human standards;*d* 4for the weapons of our warfare are not

---

a Gk apostles   *b* Other ancient authorities add of boasting
c Or benevolence   *d* Gk according to the flesh   *e* Gk in the flesh

---

Lord's sight . . . sight of others. See Prov 3.4. **9.2** Eagerness. See 8.11. Macedonia. See 1.16. Achaia. See 1.1. Some believe that ch. 9 was originally part of a separate letter addressed to other Christians in Achaia (e.g., at Cenchreae; see Rom 16.1). **9.3** Brothers. See 8.16–23; 9.5. **9.5** Bountiful gift and voluntary gift are both translations of the same Greek word (eulogia); the word appears twice again in an expression translated bountifully in v. 6. **9.6** Sows . . . reap bountifully, an idea widespread in antiquity (see, e.g., Prov 11.24). **9.7** Not under compulsion. See 8.3; also Deut 15.10; Philem 14. God loves a cheerful giver virtually quotes the Septuagint of Prov 22.8. **9.8** Paul's attitude here toward possessions is positive: wealth is a gift, a financial blessing from God, provided that it leads to generosity (9.11); cf. 1 Tim 6.10. Good work. See Eph 2.10; Col 1.10; 2 Thess 2.17; 2 Tim 3.17; Titus 2.14. **9.9** Ps 112.9. **9.10** Seed . . . food. See Isa 55.10. Harvest of your righteousness, a phrase drawn from the Septuagint of Hos

10.12. **9.12** Rendering (Greek diakonia), translated ministry in 8.4; 9.1, 13. Ministry, here the standard term (leitourgia) for an act of public service that private citizens performed at their own expense (see Rom 15.27).

10.1–13.13 Paul's struggle with Satan's ministers and his appeal to the Corinthians. (For the literary issues involving these chapters, see Introduction.) **10.1–18** Paul's defense against criticism and attack on his critics. **10.1** Appeal (see also 2.8; 5.20; 6.1; also ask in 10.2) indicates that the ultimate goal of chs. 10–13 is exhortation. Meekness of Christ. See Mt 11.29. Gentleness as a quality stands in contrast to pugnacity (1 Tim 3.3). Humble when face to face. See v. 10. **10.2** On the charge of acting according to human standards, see 1.12, 17. **10.3** Wage war. The campaign is described in three successive stages: the demolishing of fortifications (vv. 4–5), the taking of captives (v. 5), and the punishing of resistance (v. 6). **10.4–5** Weapons, Paul's

merely human,[a] but they have divine power to destroy strongholds. We destroy arguments [5]and every proud obstacle raised up against the knowledge of God, and we take every thought captive to obey Christ. [6]We are ready to punish every disobedience when your obedience is complete.

7 Look at what is before your eyes. If you are confident that you belong to Christ, remind yourself of this, that just as you belong to Christ, so also do we. [8]Now, even if I boast a little too much of our authority, which the Lord gave for building you up and not for tearing you down, I will not be ashamed of it. [9]I do not want to seem as though I am trying to frighten you with my letters. [10]For they say, "His letters are weighty and strong, but his bodily presence is weak, and his speech contemptible." [11]Let such people understand that what we say by letter when absent, we will also do when present.

12 We do not dare to classify or compare ourselves with some of those who commend themselves. But when they measure themselves by one another, and compare themselves with one another, they do not show good sense. [13]We, however, will not boast beyond limits, but will keep within the field that God has assigned to us, to reach out even as far as you. [14]For we were not overstepping our limits when we reached you; we were the first to come all the way to you with the good news[b] of Christ. [15]We do not boast beyond limits, that is, in the labors of others; but our hope is

that, as your faith increases, our sphere of action among you may be greatly enlarged, [16]so that we may proclaim the good news[b] in lands beyond you, without boasting of work already done in someone else's sphere of action. [17]"Let the one who boasts, boast in the Lord." [18]For it is not those who commend themselves that are approved, but those whom the Lord commends.

Paul and the False Apostles

11 I wish you would bear with me in a little foolishness. Do bear with me! [2]I feel a divine jealousy for you, for I promised you in marriage to one husband, to present you as a chaste virgin to Christ. [3]But I am afraid that as the serpent deceived Eve by its cunning, your thoughts will be led astray from a sincere and pure[c] devotion to Christ. [4]For if someone comes and proclaims another Jesus than the one we proclaimed, or if you receive a different spirit from the one you received, or a different gospel from the one you accepted, you submit to it readily enough. [5]I think that I am not in the least inferior to these super-apostles. [6]I may be untrained in speech, but not in knowledge; certainly in every way and in all things we have made this evident to you.

7 Did I commit a sin by humbling myself so that you might be exalted, because I proclaimed God's good news[d] to you free of

___

a Gk fleshly   b Or the gospel   c Other ancient authorities lack and pure   d Gk the gospel of God

___

humble manner of life (v. 1), in which God's "divine power" is manifested (see also 4.7). Paul depicts the *strongholds* (defenses) of his opponents in terms typically used to describe the Stoic sage, who used reason (*arguments, thought*) as a defense. **10.6** Paul probably means that he will deal with the *disobedience* of his opponents once the Corinthians recognize his authority and give full *obedience* to his instructions (see 2.9). **10.7** Paul's critics probably claimed to *belong to Christ*. **10.8** *Boast.* See 1.12; another charge by Paul's critics is reflected here. *For building . . . down.* See v. 4; 12.19; 13.10; also Jer 1.10; 24.6. **10.10** *They say,* lit. "he says," which some identify with the individual to whom Paul refers in 2.5; 7.12. He continues by quoting here a charge made against him. **10.12** It was a standard laudatory technique to *compare and classify* someone with people of superior worth and to *measure* that person's achievements against those of others. For Paul's ironic use of the device, see 11.22–23. **10.13–16** Paul had strong views on the *limits* of his mission *field;* see Rom 15.17–21. **10.17** Jer 9.23–24, quoted also in 1 Cor 1.31. **10.18** *Commend themselves.* See v. 12.

11.1–12.10 A heavily ironic "fool's" speech; see 11.16–17, 19, 21; 12.11. **11.1–15** Paul's opponents as Satan's agents. **11.2–3** Paul as father (1 Cor 4.14–15) of the bride (i.e., the church) is responsible for safeguarding her purity between the time of the betrothal and the *marriage* at the Second Coming of Christ; see Mt 9.15; 25.1–13; Eph 5.26–32; Rev 19.7–9; 21.2, 9. **11.3** *Deceived.* See Gen 3.13; 1 Tim 2.14. Paul is probably thinking of the Jewish legend that Eve was sexually seduced by Satan (the serpent), who appeared to her disguised as an angel (see v. 14). **11.4** Unfortunately, Paul never discusses the *different gospel* of his opponents, and their identity is much debated. Some consider them Judaizers; others, Gnostics; still others, Hellenistic Jewish propagandists. **11.5** *Super-apostles* (see 12.11), probably a sarcastic reference to his opponents, but perhaps the Jerusalem apostles. **11.6** *Untrained in speech.* See 10.10. **11.7–11** Paul was criticized for refusing to accept support from the Corinthians; for his practice of supporting himself, see 1 Cor 9; 1 Thess 2.9; 2 Thess 3.7–9. **11.7** *Humbling myself,* by his voluntary manual labor, which he regarded as a demonstration of his love for his

charge? [8]I robbed other churches by accepting support from them in order to serve you. [9]And when I was with you and was in need, I did not burden anyone, for my needs were supplied by the friends[a] who came from Macedonia. So I refrained and will continue to refrain from burdening you in any way. [10]As the truth of Christ is in me, this boast of mine will not be silenced in the regions of Achaia. [11]And why? Because I do not love you? God knows I do!

[12] And what I do I will also continue to do, in order to deny an opportunity to those who want an opportunity to be recognized as our equals in what they boast about. [13]For such boasters are false apostles, deceitful workers, disguising themselves as apostles of Christ. [14]And no wonder! Even Satan disguises himself as an angel of light. [15]So it is not strange if his ministers also disguise themselves as ministers of righteousness. Their end will match their deeds.

Paul's Sufferings as an Apostle

[16] I repeat, let no one think that I am a fool; but if you do, then accept me as a fool, so that I too may boast a little. [17]What I am saying in regard to this boastful confidence, I am saying not with the Lord's authority, but as a fool; [18]since many boast according to human standards,[b] I will also boast. [19]For you gladly put up with fools, being wise yourselves! [20]For you put up with it when someone makes slaves of you, or preys upon you, or takes advantage of you, or puts on airs, or gives you a slap in the face. [21]To my shame, I must say, we were too weak for that!

But whatever anyone dares to boast of—I am speaking as a fool—I also dare to boast of

that. [22]Are they Hebrews? So am I. Are they Israelites? So am I. Are they descendants of Abraham? So am I. [23]Are they ministers of Christ? I am talking like a madman—I am a better one: with far greater labors, far more imprisonments, with countless floggings, and often near death. [24]Five times I have received from the Jews the forty lashes minus one. [25]Three times I was beaten with rods. Once I received a stoning. Three times I was shipwrecked; for a night and a day I was adrift at sea; [26]on frequent journeys, in danger from rivers, danger from bandits, danger from my own people, danger from Gentiles, danger in the city, danger in the wilderness, danger at sea, danger from false brothers and sisters;[a] [27]in toil and hardship, through many a sleepless night, hungry and thirsty, often without food, cold and naked. [28]And, besides other things, I am under daily pressure because of my anxiety for all the churches. [29]Who is weak, and I am not weak? Who is made to stumble, and I am not indignant?

[30] If I must boast, I will boast of the things that show my weakness. [31]The God and Father of the Lord Jesus (blessed be he forever!) knows that I do not lie. [32]In Damascus, the governor[c] under King Aretas guarded the city of Damascus in order to[d] seize me, [33]but I was let down in a basket through a window in the wall,[e] and escaped from his hands.

Paul's Visions and Revelations

12 It is necessary to boast; nothing is to be gained by it, but I will go on to visions and revelations of the Lord. [2]I know a person in

---

a Gk brothers   *b* Gk according to the flesh   *c* Gk ethnarch
d Other ancient authorities read and wanted to   *e* Gk through the wall

---

converts (v. 11; 12.15). **11.14** *Angel.* See note on 11.3. **11.16–12.10** Paul boastfully compares himself to his opponents in regard to both credentials and hardships (see 4.8–9; 6.4–10). **11.17–18** In what follows, Paul does not speak *in Christ* (2.17; 12.19) or *with the Lord's authority* (lit. "according to the Lord"), for his *boasting* is *according to human standards.* **11.20** The list of afflictions has the dual purpose of castigating Paul's opponents by describing their abusive acts and of shaming the Corinthians by means of mock praise (see 6.4; cf. 1 Cor 4.8). **11.22** Like Paul, his opponents are Jewish Christians, proud both that they are *Hebrews* (ethnic heritage) and that they are *Israelites* (religious heritage); see Rom 9.4; 11.1; Phil 3.5. **11.23–27** Few details are known about the hardships Paul mentions in this list. **11.23** *Imprisonments.* See Acts 16.22–40 for one of Paul's prior incarcerations; for later

instances, see Acts 24.27; 28.16. **11.23–25** Paul specifies two types of *floggings,* or beatings (see 6.5), a Roman one with *rods* (see Acts 16.22–23) and a Jewish one with *lashes* (see Deut 25.3). **11.25** *Stoning.* See Acts 14.19. *Shipwrecked.* For a later instance, see Acts 27.9–44. **11.26** *False brothers and sisters* would include the false apostles (v. 13). **11.32** *Damascus,* the Syrian city connected with Paul's conversion (Acts 9; Gal 1.17). *King Aretas* (IV), the ruler of the Arab kingdom of Nabatea from 9 BCE until his death (ca. 40 CE). The identity of the *governor* is unknown. **11.33** *Let down in a basket.* See Acts 9.23–25, where the plot is attributed to the Jews. **12.1–10** A continuation of the fool's speech, in which Paul presents himself in both ecstasy (vv. 1–7a) and agony (vv. 7b–10). **12.1** *Visions and revelations.* See 1 Cor 9.1; 15.8; Gal 1.12; 2.1–2. **12.2** *Person,* Paul himself, who in

Christ who fourteen years ago was caught up to the third heaven—whether in the body or out of the body I do not know; God knows. 3And I know that such a person—whether in the body or out of the body I do not know; God knows—4was caught up into Paradise and heard things that are not to be told, that no mortal is permitted to repeat. 5On behalf of such a one I will boast, but on my own behalf I will not boast, except of my weaknesses. 6But if I wish to boast, I will not be a fool, for I will be speaking the truth. But I refrain from it, so that no one may think better of me than what is seen in me or heard from me, 7even considering the exceptional character of the revelations. Therefore, to keep[a] me from being too elated, a thorn was given me in the flesh, a messenger of Satan to torment me, to keep me from being too elated.[b] 8Three times I appealed to the Lord about this, that it would leave me, 9but he said to me, "My grace is sufficient for you, for power[c] is made perfect in weakness." So, I will boast all the more gladly of my weaknesses, so that the power of Christ may dwell in me. 10Therefore I am content with weaknesses, insults, hardships, persecutions, and calamities for the sake of Christ; for whenever I am weak, then I am strong.

Paul's Concern for the Corinthian Church

11 I have been a fool! You forced me to it. Indeed you should have been the ones commending me, for I am not at all inferior to these super-apostles, even though I am nothing. 12The signs of a true apostle were performed among you with utmost patience, signs and wonders and mighty works. 13How have you been worse off than the other churches, except that I myself did not burden you? Forgive me this wrong!

14 Here I am, ready to come to you this third time. And I will not be a burden, because I do not want what is yours but you; for children ought not to lay up for their parents, but parents for their children. 15I will most gladly spend and be spent for you. If I love you more, am I to be loved less? 16Let it be assumed that I did not burden you. Nevertheless (you say) since I was crafty, I took you in by deceit. 17Did I take advantage of you through any of those whom I sent to you? 18I urged Titus to go, and sent the brother with him. Titus did not take advantage of you, did he? Did we not conduct ourselves with the same spirit? Did we not take the same steps?

19 Have you been thinking all along that we have been defending ourselves before you? We are speaking in Christ before God. Everything we do, beloved, is for the sake of building you up. 20For I fear that when I come, I may find you not as I wish, and that you may find me not as you wish; I fear that there may perhaps be quarreling, jealousy, anger, selfishness, slander, gossip, conceit, and disorder. 21I fear that when I come again, my God may humble me before you, and that I may have to mourn over many who previously sinned and have not repented of the impurity, sexual immorality, and licentiousness that they have practiced.

Further Warning

13 This is the third time I am coming to you. "Any charge must be sustained by the evidence of two or three witnesses." 2I warned those who sinned previously and all the others, and I warn them now while absent,

---

a Other ancient authorities read *To keep*   b Other ancient authorities lack *to keep me from being too elated*   c Other ancient authorities read *my power*

---

vv. 2–4 is describing one ecstatic experience. *Third heaven,* i.e., where Paradise (v. 4) is located. Heavenly journeys were a popular means of claiming divine authentication and were apparently used by Paul's opponents for this purpose. **12.7** The exact nature of the *thorn* is unknown; suggestions include physical or mental illness, spiritual trials, persecution, and opposition by adversaries. **12.10** For *hardship* lists, see note on 4.8–9. **12.11–13** The epilogue to the fool's speech. **12.11** *Super-apostles.* See 11.5. **12.12** *Signs and wonders and mighty works,* three different terms for miracles, which functioned in antiquity to validate wonder-workers and their claims; see Acts 2.22; 14.3; 15.12; Rom 15.19; Heb 2.4. **12.13** *I myself did not burden you,* i.e., by demanding payment for missionary activities as his rivals apparently did; see 11.7–11; 12.14.

12.14–13.10 Preparations for a third visit. **12.14** *Parents for their children.* Cf. Mt 15.5–6; 1 Tim 5.4, 8. **12.15** *Be spent for you.* See Phil 2.17. **12.16–18** Paul was charged with refusing support for himself while deceitfully enriching himself by means of the collection (see chs. 8–9). **12.18** For the role of *Titus* and *the brother,* see 8.16–9.5. Many scholars regard this verse as a retrospective reference to the same visit for the collection that is only anticipated in 8.6, 18. **12.19** *Building you up.* See 10.8. **12.20–21** For other vice lists, a traditional device used by both Jews and Greeks, see Mk 7.21–22; Rom 1.29–31; 13.13; 1 Cor 5.10–11; 6.9–10; Gal 5.19–21. **12.21** *Again* may modify *humble:* "my God may humble me again," i.e., by a repetition of what happened at the second visit; see 2.1–4. **13.1** *Any charge . . . witnesses.* Deut 19.15; used

as I did when present on my second visit, that if I come again, I will not be lenient— [3]since you desire proof that Christ is speaking in me. He is not weak in dealing with you, but is powerful in you. [4]For he was crucified in weakness, but lives by the power of God. For we are weak in him, [a] but in dealing with you we will live with him by the power of God.

5 Examine yourselves to see whether you are living in the faith. Test yourselves. Do you not realize that Jesus Christ is in you?—unless, indeed, you fail to meet the test! [6]I hope you will find out that we have not failed. [7]But we pray to God that you may not do anything wrong—not that we may appear to have met the test, but that you may do what is right, though we may seem to have failed. [8]For we cannot do anything against the truth, but only for the truth. [9]For we rejoice when we are weak and you are strong. This is what we pray for, that you may become perfect. [10]So I write these things while I am away from you, so that when I come, I may not have to be severe in using the authority that the Lord has given me for building up and not for tearing down.

Final Greetings and Benediction

11 Finally, brothers and sisters, [b] farewell. [c] Put things in order, listen to my appeal, [d] agree with one another, live in peace; and the God of love and peace will be with you. [12]Greet one another with a holy kiss. All the saints greet you.

13 The grace of the Lord Jesus Christ, the love of God, and the communion of [e] the Holy Spirit be with all of you.

---

a Other ancient authorities read *with him*   *b* Gk *brothers*
c Or *rejoice*   *d* Or *encourage one another*   *e* Or *and the sharing in*

---

also in Mt 18.16; 1 Tim 5.19. **13.2** Paul had canceled a previous trip out of *leniency;* see 1.23. **13.3** The ideas of testing and *proving* were important in Corinth; see, e.g., 1 Cor 11.28; 16.3; 2 Cor 8.8, 22; 9.13; see also 13.5–7. **13.5** *Christ is in you.* See Rom 8.10; Gal 2.20; Col 1.27. **13.9, 11** The words translated *perfect* and *put things in order* are related in Greek. **13.10** *I write these things.* This verse gives the ultimate purpose of 2 Cor 10–13; see also 10.8. **13.11–13** The closing of the Letter is typically Pauline; see, e.g., 1 Cor 16.20; 1 Thess 5.23–28. **13.13** The trinitarian formula is anticipated in 1.21–22; also Mt 28.19.

The Letter of Paul to the
GALATIANS

THE BITTERLY POLEMICAL Letter of Paul to the Galatians reflects a critical moment in the early Christian movement's struggle to define its mission and identity. The apostle Paul founded the churches of Galatia (1.2; 4.13–14), but he now finds his work challenged by unidentified Jewish-Christian teachers who are urging Paul's converts, formerly pagans (4.8–9), to be circumcised (5.2–12; 6.12–13). Apparently these teachers are also urging the Galatians to observe some other elements of Jewish law and ritual, such as the sabbath and festivals (4.10) and perhaps food laws (4.17, taken with 2.12). Paul discerns in this situation a threat to "the truth of the gospel" (2.5, 14) and composes an impassioned letter to dissuade the Galatians from adopting these religious practices.

Addressees and Date

HOW MANY "CHURCHES OF GALATIA" there were is unknown, and their exact location is a matter of long-standing debate. The term "Galatians" (3.1) originally designated a people of Celtic origin who migrated into central Asia Minor and settled in the region around Ancyra (modern Ankara); however, the Roman province of Galatia extended south toward the Mediterranean to include the cities of Iconium, Lystra, and Derbe, where Paul and Barnabas, according to Acts 14.1–23, founded churches (see map on p. 2060).

Some interpreters hold that the Letter was addressed to these "south Galatian" churches during the period prior to the "apostolic council" described in Acts 15; the council then addressed the controversy that Galatians exemplifies (see Acts 15.1) This reconstruction requires the assumption that the Jerusalem meeting mentioned in Gal 2.1–10 occurred during the "famine relief" visit of Acts 11.27–30. Majority scholarly opinion, however, identifies the council of Acts 15 with the meeting described in Gal 2.1–10, though the two accounts differ somewhat. Under this reading, the Galatian churches were probably in "north Galatia," and Paul's missionary activity there is identified with the brief references in Acts 16.6; 18.23.

Both reconstructions presuppose a positive view of Acts as a historical framework within which the Pauline Letters can be placed. The internal evidence of Galatians, however, offers no basis for determining either the geographical location of the churches or the Letter's date of composition. Some scholars regard Galatians as the earliest of Paul's Letters (perhaps 48–49 CE);

others place it during the mid-50s CE. The Letter's many thematic links with 2 Corinthians and Romans favor the latter view.

Rival Missionaries and Contested Issues

THE GALATIANS HAVE ENCOUNTERED "a different gospel" (1.6), proclaimed by missionaries whom Paul decries as agitators (5.12) and troublemakers who "want to pervert the gospel of Christ" (1.7). These rival missionaries are not Pharisaic Jews seeking to persuade Paul's converts to abandon their faith in Jesus; rather, they are Christian Jews who argue that the appropriate next step for Gentiles who have come to trust in Jesus as the Messiah is to undergo circumcision as a sign of their inclusion in God's covenant. Consequently, the Letter reflects an intra-Christian dispute over whether the marks of Jewish identity should be imposed upon gentile converts.

Even the categories "Christian" and "Jewish" are anachronistic here; the Letter was written before the irrevocable split of church and synagogue, and Paul, no less than the rival missionaries, understands himself as the true interpreter of the Jewish law (4.21; 5.14). Thus he contends that all who live under the cross of Christ in the "new creation" are members of "the Israel of God" (6.14–16).

It appears that the missionaries wanted gentile converts not just to be circumcised, but to adopt comprehensive observance of Jewish law—particularly if the quotation of Deuteronomy in 3.10 echoes the missionaries' message. The Antioch incident (2.11–16) shows that some Jewish Christians were adopting a "separate but equal" policy toward gentile Christians, which Paul regards as a manipulative tactic to force gentile Christians to observe Jewish law (2.14).

The rival missionaries must have spotlighted the figure of Abraham (regarded in rabbinic tradition as "the father of proselytes") and emphasized that God had commanded circumcision to him as a sign of the covenant (Gen 17.9–14). Paul's extended interpretation of the Abraham story (3.6–18; 4.21–5.1) is a rebuttal to their exegesis.

Paul's Response: Key Emphases

PAUL INSISTS THAT "RIGHTEOUSNESS" (right covenant relation with God) depends not on observance of Jewish law but on God's promise and its fulfillment through the death of Jesus Christ (2.21; 3.18, 29). It is debated whether the slogan *pistis Iesou Christou* (Greek, "faith of/in Jesus Christ"; see note on 2.16) refers to Jesus' faithful death or to the community's subsequent trust in him; despite venerable interpretive tradition, the former sense is more probable. Either way, Paul's emphasis falls consistently on God's initiative in setting human beings free from bondage to sin and to the norms and powers (Greek *stoicheia*) of the present age (1.4; 2.20–21; 3.13–14; 3.21–22; 4.3–9; 5.1). The crucifixion is an apocalyptic event that marks the end of the old age and the beginning of God's new creation (6.14–15). To require gentile believers to be circumcised would be to revert to the era "before faith came" and would render the death of Christ pointless (2.21; 3.23–25). Insisting on "works of the law" (2.16) as signs of covenant membership perpetuates a division that Christ's death was meant to destroy (3.28). That is why the message of the rival missionaries is, in Paul's eyes, no gospel (1.7).

Significance

GALATIANS OFFERS A WINDOW into formative Christianity and shows that the question of continuity with Jewish law and tradition was an urgent concern at this early date. Paul's statements about the law in Galatians created acute theological tensions that demanded further reflection (see Romans). His insistence on the radical character and universal scope of God's grace became a crucial factor in the early church's self-definition, and it has played a generative role in subsequent Christian theology. [RICHARD B. HAYS]

Salutation

1 Paul an apostle—sent neither by human commission nor from human authorities, but through Jesus Christ and God the Father, who raised him from the dead— 2and all the members of God's family*a* who are with me,

To the churches of Galatia:

3 Grace to you and peace from God our Father and the Lord Jesus Christ, 4who gave himself for our sins to set us free from the present evil age, according to the will of our God and Father, 5to whom be the glory forever and ever. Amen.

There Is No Other Gospel

6 I am astonished that you are so quickly deserting the one who called you in the grace of Christ and are turning to a different gospel— 7not that there is another gospel, but there are some who are confusing you and want to pervert the gospel of Christ. 8But even if we or an angel*b* from heaven should proclaim to you a gospel contrary to what we proclaimed to you, let that one be accursed! 9As we have said before, so now I repeat, if anyone proclaims to you a gospel contrary to what you received, let that one be accursed!

10 Am I now seeking human approval, or God's approval? Or am I trying to please people? If I were still pleasing people, I would not be a servant*c* of Christ.

Paul's Vindication of His Apostleship

11 For I want you to know, brothers and sisters,*d* that the gospel that was proclaimed by me is not of human origin; 12for I did not receive it from a human source, nor was I taught it, but I received it through a revelation of Jesus Christ.

13 You have heard, no doubt, of my earlier life in Judaism. I was violently persecuting the church of God and was trying to destroy it. 14I advanced in Judaism beyond many among my people of the same age, for I was far more zealous for the traditions of my ancestors. 15But when God, who had set me apart before I was born and called me through his grace, was pleased 16to reveal his Son to me,*e* so that I might proclaim him among the Gentiles, I did not confer with any human being, 17nor did I go up to Jerusalem to those who were already apostles before me, but I went away at once

---

a Gk *all the brothers*   *b* Or *a messenger*   *c* Gk *slave*
d Gk *brothers*   *e* Gk *in me*

1.1–5 Key themes of the Letter are introduced: Paul's apostolic authority and Christ's death as an act liberating his people from bondage. **1.2** No coauthor is named (cf., e.g., 1 Cor 1.1; 2 Cor 1.1), but Paul does present the Letter as coming from a group of believers (*all . . . with me*). **1.3–4** The naming of God as *Father* anticipates 4.6–7. **1.4** *Gave himself for our sins.* See 2.20; Mt 26.28; Rom 4.25; 5.8, 15–19; 8.3; 2 Cor 5.21; Titus 2.14; 1 Pet 2.24. According to Jewish apocalyptic thought, the *present evil age* would be supplanted by "the age to come," a messianic era in which God's justice would prevail (see Isa 60; 65.17–25; 2 Esd 7.50, 113; *1 Enoch* 91.15–17). Paul sees the death and resurrection of Jesus as a sign that this transformation has already begun (see 6.14–15; Rom 12.2; 1 Cor 7.31; 10.11). **1.6–9** Among Paul's Letters, only Galatians lacks an opening thanksgiving; instead, Paul rebukes his readers. **1.6** *The one who called you*, God, not Paul. See v. 15; Rom 8.30; 1 Cor 1.9; 7.17; 1 Thess 2.12; 5.24. **1.8** This shows that Paul is defending not his own personal authority but *the truth of the gospel* (2.14). **1.9** On the gospel they have *received*, see note on 3.1; 1 Cor 15.1–5. **1.10** A retort to the charge

that Paul is "soft" on observance of the Jewish law for reasons of expediency. **1.11–24** Responding to challenges, Paul tells the story of his own calling in a way that highlights God's initiative. **1.12** *Not . . . from a human source.* Elsewhere (1 Cor 11.23–25; 15.3–7) Paul shows his dependence on early Christian traditions. **1.13** *Persecuting the church.* See also Acts 8.3; 1 Cor 15.9; Phil 3.6; 1 Tim 1.12–14. **1.14** *Advanced*, a word commonly used by Stoic philosophers to describe progress in cultivating virtue. *Traditions of my ancestors*, the Jewish law and the oral traditions concerning its interpretation, as handed down in Pharisaic Judaism. See Acts 22.3; Phil 3.4–6. *Zealous* recalls the examples of Phinehas (Num 25.10–13), Elijah (1 Kings 19.10), and Mattathias (1 Macc 2.26–27), who employed violence to defend the purity of Israel's faith. **1.15** *God . . . his grace.* The language echoes OT prophetic call narratives; see Isa 49.1–6; Jer 1.5; Rom 1.1–2. **1.16** *Reveal his Son to me*, lit. *reveal his Son in me* (see text note *e*). Paul is to be the instrument of God's revelation to the Gentiles. **1.17** *Arabia*, perhaps the Nabatean kingdom, south of Damascus and east of the Jordan River; however, in 4.25 Paul

into Arabia, and afterwards I returned to Damascus.

18 Then after three years I did go up to Jerusalem to visit Cephas and stayed with him fifteen days; 19but I did not see any other apostle except James the Lord's brother. 20In what I am writing to you, before God, I do not lie! 21Then I went into the regions of Syria and Cilicia, 22and I was still unknown by sight to the churches of Judea that are in Christ; 23they only heard it said, "The one who formerly was persecuting us is now proclaiming the faith he once tried to destroy." 24And they glorified God because of me.

Paul and the Other Apostles

2 Then after fourteen years I went up again to Jerusalem with Barnabas, taking Titus along with me. 2I went up in response to a revelation. Then I laid before them (though only in a private meeting with the acknowledged leaders) the gospel that I proclaim among the Gentiles, in order to make sure that I was not running, or had not run, in vain. 3But even Titus, who was with me, was not compelled to be circumcised, though he was a Greek. 4But because of false believers[a] secretly brought in, who slipped in to spy on the freedom we have in Christ Jesus, so that they might enslave us—

5we did not submit to them even for a moment, so that the truth of the gospel might always remain with you. 6And from those who were supposed to be acknowledged leaders (what they actually were makes no difference to me; God shows no partiality)—those leaders contributed nothing to me. 7On the contrary, when they saw that I had been entrusted with the gospel for the uncircumcised, just as Peter had been entrusted with the gospel for the circumcised 8(for he who worked through Peter making him an apostle to the circumcised also worked through me in sending me to the Gentiles), 9and when James and Cephas and John, who were acknowledged pillars, recognized the grace that had been given to me, they gave to Barnabas and me the right hand of fellowship, agreeing that we should go to the Gentiles and they to the circumcised. 10They asked only one thing, that we remember the poor, which was actually what I was[b] eager to do.

Paul Rebukes Peter at Antioch

11 But when Cephas came to Antioch, I opposed him to his face, because he stood self-condemned; 12for until certain people came from James, he used to eat with the Gentiles.

a Gk false brothers   b Or had been

links Arabia with Mount Sinai. **1.18** It is debated whether the *three years* are to be counted from Paul's call experience (vv. 15–16) or from his return to Damascus (v. 17). *Cephas*, Aramaic, "rock." Paul uses Peter's Greek name (*Petros*) only in 2.7–8; cf. Jn 1.42; 1 Cor 1.12; 15.5. **1.19** *James*, the brother of Jesus (Mk 6.3), became a key leader in the Jerusalem church; see 2.9, 12; Acts 12.17; 15.13; 21.18. **1.21** *Syria and Cilicia,* the areas around Antioch and Tarsus; see Acts 15.23, 41.
2.1–10 These verses emphasize that even the Jerusalem church previously endorsed Paul's law-free gospel for Gentiles (see also Acts 15.1–29). **2.1** The *fourteen years* could be counted from Paul's first Jerusalem visit (1.18) or from his call (1.15–16). *Barnabas.* See Acts 4.36; 9.27; 11.22–30; 13.1–15.41. *Taking Titus,* an uncircumcised Gentile (v. 3), was a symbolic test of Jerusalem's acceptance of Paul's mission. **2.2** *In response to a revelation.* Cf. Acts 15.1–3; 1 Cor 14.26, 30. **2.4** The *false believers* (cf. Acts 15.5) are clearly distinguished from the Jerusalem leaders; Paul implicitly connects the former with his opponents in Galatia. **2.6** *God shows no partiality,* an OT maxim; see Deut 10.17; 2 Chr 19.7; Sir 35.15–16. In contrast to Acts 15.28–29, Paul says the Jerusalem leaders *contributed nothing* to his mission practice. **2.7** *Gospel . . . uncircumcised, gospel . . . circumcised,* not two different gospels (see 1.7) but two culturally distinct audiences.

2.9 *John,* son of Zebedee (Mk 1.19), is paired with Peter in Acts 3.1–4.22; 8.14–25. *Pillars,* metaphorically the supports of the church as a spiritual temple (see Mt 16.18; Eph 2.19–22; 1 Pet 2.4–5; Rev 3.12). In Second Temple Judaism, *pillar* was sometimes used of Abraham, Isaac, and Jacob. **2.10** Paul carried out his agreement to *remember the poor* (see Deut 15.7–11) by organizing a collection in his gentile mission churches (see Rom 15.25–27; 1 Cor 16.1–4; 2 Cor 8.1–9.15); however, *the poor* may also have been a religious self-designation of some early Jewish Christians. **2.11–21** Paul narrates his confrontation with Cephas (see note on 1.18) as a case that involves issues analogous to those now faced in Galatia. **2.11** *Antioch,* with a large Jewish population, became a major center of early Christian activity and, according to Acts 11.19–26; 13.1–3, the launching site for the preaching mission of Paul and Barnabas. **2.12** Observant Jews were forbidden to eat gentile meat and usually avoided gentile wine, but Jewish law did not prohibit eating *with the Gentiles;* presumably it was the food at the Antioch community's common meals that was objectionable. Or perhaps eating with Gentiles was frowned upon as dangerous, even if not strictly contrary to law (see the *Letter of Aristeas* 142; *Jubilees* 22.16; cf. Acts 10.28). The vacillation of Cephas and Barnabas shows that the Jerusalem agreement (vv. 7–10) had failed to address

But after they came, he drew back and kept himself separate for fear of the circumcision faction. 13And the other Jews joined him in this hypocrisy, so that even Barnabas was led astray by their hypocrisy. 14But when I saw that they were not acting consistently with the truth of the gospel, I said to Cephas before them all, "If you, though a Jew, live like a Gentile and not like a Jew, how can you compel the Gentiles to live like Jews?"*a*

Jews and Gentiles Are Saved by Faith

15 We ourselves are Jews by birth and not Gentile sinners; 16yet we know that a person is justified*b* not by the works of the law but through faith in Jesus Christ.*c* And we have come to believe in Christ Jesus, so that we might be justified by faith in Christ,*d* and not by doing the works of the law, because no one will be justified by the works of the law. 17But if, in our effort to be justified in Christ, we ourselves have been found to be sinners, is Christ then a servant of sin? Certainly not! 18But if I build up again the very things that I once tore down, then I demonstrate that I am a transgressor. 19For through the law I died to the law, so that I might live to God. I have been crucified with Christ; 20and it is no longer I

who live, but it is Christ who lives in me. And the life I now live in the flesh I live by faith in the Son of God,*e* who loved me and gave himself for me. 21I do not nullify the grace of God; for if justification*f* comes through the law, then Christ died for nothing.

Law or Faith

3 You foolish Galatians! Who has bewitched you? It was before your eyes that Jesus Christ was publicly exhibited as crucified! 2The only thing I want to learn from you is this: Did you receive the Spirit by doing the works of the law or by believing what you heard? 3Are you so foolish? Having started with the Spirit, are you now ending with the flesh? 4Did you experience so much for nothing?—if it really was for nothing. 5Well then, does God*g* supply you with the Spirit and work miracles among you by your doing the works of the law, or by your believing what you heard?

6 Just as Abraham "believed God, and it was

---

a Some interpreters hold that the quotation extends into the following paragraph *b* Or *reckoned as righteous;* and so elsewhere *c* Or *the faith of Jesus Christ* *d* Or *the faith of Christ* *e* Or *by the faith of the Son of God* *f* Or *righteousness* *g* Gk *he*

---

the problem of table fellowship. **2.14–16** Paul interprets Cephas's withdrawal as a tactic to pressure gentile converts into keeping the Jewish law. The direct quotation of Paul's address to Cephas probably extends to the end of v. 16, or even v. 21. **2.15** *Gentile sinners,* a traditional Jewish attitude, used with some irony here. **2.16** *Justified,* vindicated or placed in right relation to God. *Works of the law,* primarily practices commanded by the law (circumcision, dietary laws, sabbath observance) that distinctively mark Jewish ethnic identity; these symbolize comprehensive obedience to the law's covenant obligations. *Faith in Jesus Christ* ascribes saving efficacy to the believer's act of trusting in Christ. *The faith of Jesus Christ* (see text note *c;* see also 2.20; 3.22; Rom 3.22, 26; Phil 3.9) emphasizes Christ's faithful obedience to the point of death on a cross; see 1.4; Rom 5.18–19; Phil 2.8. *Have come to believe in,* or "placed our trust in." *No one will be justified* echoes Ps 143.2; see also Rom 3.20. **2.17** *Found to be sinners,* i.e., living like Gentiles (v. 15). **2.18** *The very things that I once tore down,* the Jewish commandments as a barrier between Jews and Gentiles (see also Eph 2.11–22; *Letter of Aristeas* 139). For Paul to rebuild the barrier would be to admit that he had been a transgressor by tearing it down in his missionary work. **2.19** The opposition between the *law* and living to God is a surprising reversal of Jewish tradition; see 4 Macc 16.24–25. *Crucified with Christ.* See

5.24; 6.14; Rom 6.5–11; 2 Cor 4.7–12. **2.20** *Christ . . . lives in me.* See Rom 8.9–11; 2 Cor 13.5; Col 1.27; also Jn 17.23. *Loved me and gave himself for me.* See note on 1.4. **2.21** Paul implies that his critics unwittingly *nullify the grace of God* (see 5.4) by adding observance of Jewish law to the *justification* or *righteousness* (right covenant relation to God; see text note *f;* also 3.6) that comes only through the death of Christ (see also 3.21).

3.1–5 Paul now addresses issues in Galatia directly; because of their experience of receiving the Spirit, the Galatians should know that they are already members of God's people. **3.1** *Publicly exhibited as crucified* refers to Paul's proclamation of the gospel in vivid images (see 1 Cor 2.1–5); the Galatians did not literally witness the crucifixion of Jesus. **3.2** On *receiving the Spirit,* see Acts 10–11. On *works of the law,* see 2.16; *doing* does not appear in the Greek. *By believing what you heard,* or "by the message of faith." **3.3** *Ending with the flesh,* an ironic double entendre, refers to circumcision (see 6.12–13) and also to mortal existence apart from God; see also 4.29; 5.16–26; 6.8; 1 Cor 3.3. **3.5** Paul thinks of the Galatians' experience of *the Spirit* and *miracles* as an ongoing aspect of their communal life; see also 1 Cor 12.4–11; 14.26–33a; 2 Cor 12.12. **3.6–14** Paul begins a complex argument from scripture to show that God always intended the salvation of Gentiles; see also Rom 3.27–4.25. **3.6** Gen 15.6; see also Rom 4.3. *Righteousness.* See note on 2.21.

reckoned to him as righteousness," [7]so, you see, those who believe are the descendants of Abraham. [8]And the scripture, foreseeing that God would justify the Gentiles by faith, declared the gospel beforehand to Abraham, saying, "All the Gentiles shall be blessed in you." [9]For this reason, those who believe are blessed with Abraham who believed.

10 For all who rely on the works of the law are under a curse; for it is written, "Cursed is everyone who does not observe and obey all the things written in the book of the law." [11]Now it is evident that no one is justified before God by the law; for "The one who is righteous will live by faith." [a] [12]But the law does not rest on faith; on the contrary, "Whoever does the works of the law [b] will live by them." [13]Christ redeemed us from the curse of the law by becoming a curse for us—for it is written, "Cursed is everyone who hangs on a tree"— [14]in order that in Christ Jesus the blessing of Abraham might come to the Gentiles, so that we might receive the promise of the Spirit through faith.

The Promise to Abraham

15 Brothers and sisters, [c] I give an example from daily life: once a person's will [d] has been ratified, no one adds to it or annuls it. [16]Now the promises were made to Abraham and to his offspring; [e] it does not say, "And to offsprings," [f] as of many; but it says, "And to your offspring," [e] that is, to one person, who is Christ. [17]My point is this: the law, which came four hundred thirty years later, does not annul a covenant previously ratified by God, so as to nullify the promise. [18]For if the inheritance comes from the law, it no longer comes from the promise; but God granted it to Abraham through the promise.

The Purpose of the Law

19 Why then the law? It was added because of transgressions, until the offspring [e] would come to whom the promise had been made; and it was ordained through angels by a mediator. [20]Now a mediator involves more than one party; but God is one.

21 Is the law then opposed to the promises of God? Certainly not! For if a law had been given that could make alive, then righteousness would indeed come through the law. [22]But the scripture has imprisoned all things under the power of sin, so that what was

---

a Or *The one who is righteous through faith will live*   *b* Gk *does them*   *c* Gk *Brothers*   *d* Or *covenant* (as in verse 17)   *e* Gk *seed*   *f* Gk *seeds*

3.8 *The gospel* spoken to Abraham (see Gen 12.3; 18.18; 22.18) focuses on the blessing of *the Gentiles.* **3.9** Paul's exegetical remark on the preceding quotation: the blessing pronounced on *Abraham who believed* (better "the faithful Abraham") includes those who later believe. **3.10** The quotation blends Deut 27.26 and 28.58. Those who enter the Deuteronomic covenant are subject to its conditional sanctions and curses; see esp. Deut 28.15–68. **3.11** The quotation is from Hab 2.4b. The Septuagint treats this text as a messianic prophecy; see Rom 1.17; cf. Heb 10.37–38. **3.12** The OT text quoted is Lev 18.5 (see also Rom 10.5). Paul does not argue that no one can keep the law; rather, he says that the law is unable to give the life it promises (see v. 21). **3.13** *Redeemed* refers to the emancipation of slaves. Christ's death effects redemption from the curse pronounced by the law (see Gen 12.3; Deut 27.15–26; 28.15–68), not from the law itself. *Becoming a curse for us.* Cf. 2 Cor 5.21. *Cursed is . . . a tree.* The proof-text (Deut 21.23) calls for the body of a hanged criminal to be buried immediately rather than left hanging to "defile the land." **3.14** *Blessing of Abraham.* See vv. 8–9; Paul sees the presence of *the Spirit* in gentile communities (see vv. 2–5) as a sign that the promised blessing has come to eschatological fulfillment. Both Isaiah and Ezekiel depict the promise of restoration through the outpouring of God's spirit (Isa 32.15–17; 44.1–5; 59.21; Ezek 36.22–27; 37.1–14). **3.15–18** *Will, covenant,* a wordplay. Greek

diatheke can mean either "covenant" or "last will and testament." Cf. Heb 9.15. Paul transfers the legal connotations of the latter to the story of God's covenant with Abraham. **3.15** *I give an example from daily life,* lit. "I speak in a human way." See Rom 6.19. **3.16** *Promises.* See Gen 12.2–3; 15.5; 17.8; 22.17–18. *Offspring,* lit. "seed" (see text note *e*). Paul employs a rabbinic exegetical convention, emphasizing the singular form of the collective noun. The identification of the "seed" as *Christ* (the Messiah) probably presupposes a link between Gen 17.8 and 2 Sam 7.12–14, a promise of an eternal kingdom for David's "seed." **3.17** *Four hundred thirty years.* See Ex 12.40; cf. Gen 15.13. **3.18** *Granted,* the verbal cognate of "grace" (see 1.6, 15; 2.21; 5.4). **3.19–25** The foregoing discussion raises the issue of why God gave the law at all; Paul argues that it was necessary but temporary. **3.19** It is disputed whether *because of transgressions* means "to increase transgressions" (see Rom 5.20) or "to restrain transgressions"; the argument of vv. 23–25 suggests the latter. *Ordained through angels* (see also Acts 7.53), a tradition developed from Deut 33.2; Ps 68.17. Philo's *Life of Moses* explicitly gives Moses the title of *mediator* (see Lev 26.46; Num 36.13). **3.20** This verse is notoriously obscure; apparently the point is that those who are in Christ have direct access to God's promise without mediation (see vv. 26–29; cf. 1 Tim 2.5). *God is one.* See Deut 6.4. **3.21** See 2.19–21; Rom 3.31; cf. Rom 7.7–13. **3.22** See also Rom 3.9–20; 11.32. Through faith in

promised through faith in Jesus Christ[a] might be given to those who believe.

23 Now before faith came, we were imprisoned and guarded under the law until faith would be revealed. [24]Therefore the law was our disciplinarian until Christ came, so that we might be justified by faith. [25]But now that faith has come, we are no longer subject to a disciplinarian, [26]for in Christ Jesus you are all children of God through faith. [27]As many of you as were baptized into Christ have clothed yourselves with Christ. [28]There is no longer Jew or Greek, there is no longer slave or free, there is no longer male and female; for all of you are one in Christ Jesus. [29]And if you belong to Christ, then you are Abraham's offspring,[b] heirs according to the promise.

4 My point is this: heirs, as long as they are minors, are no better than slaves, though they are the owners of all the property; [2]but they remain under guardians and trustees until the date set by the father. [3]So with us; while we were minors, we were enslaved to the elemental spirits[c] of the world. [4]But when the fullness of time had come, God sent his Son, born of a woman, born under the law, [5]in order to redeem those who were under the law, so that we might receive adoption as children. [6]And because you are children, God has

sent the Spirit of his Son into our[d] hearts, crying, "Abba![e] Father!" [7]So you are no longer a slave but a child, and if a child then also an heir, through God.[f]

Paul Reproves the Galatians

8 Formerly, when you did not know God, you were enslaved to beings that by nature are not gods. [9]Now, however, that you have come to know God, or rather to be known by God, how can you turn back again to the weak and beggarly elemental spirits?[g] How can you want to be enslaved to them again? [10]You are observing special days, and months, and seasons, and years. [11]I am afraid that my work for you may have been wasted.

12 Friends,[h] I beg you, become as I am, for I also have become as you are. You have done me no wrong. [13]You know that it was because of a physical infirmity that I first announced the gospel to you; [14]though my condition put you to the test, you did not scorn or despise me, but welcomed me as an angel of God, as Christ Jesus. [15]What has become of the goodwill you felt? For I testify that, had it been pos-

a Or *through the faith of Jesus Christ* *b* Gk *seed* *c* Or *the rudiments* *d* Other ancient authorities read *your* *e* Aramaic for *Father* *f* Other ancient authorities read *an heir of God through Christ* *g* Or *beggarly rudiments* *h* Gk *Brothers*

Jesus Christ. If *through the faith of Jesus Christ* (see text note *a*) is preferred, the phrase should modify *given* rather than *promised.* **3.23** See 4.4–5. **3.24** *Disciplinarian* (Greek *paidagogos*), not a teacher but a slave who guarded and supervised children. **3.26–29** Conclusion to the line of argument begun in vv. 6–14. **3.26** *Children of God.* See also Rom 8.14–17; Jn 1.12; Deut 14.1–2; *Jubilees* 1.23–25. **3.27** In early Christian baptismal liturgies, the newly baptized person was *clothed* in a new white garment; see also Rom 13.14; Eph 4.24. On baptism as union with Christ, see also Rom 6.3–5. **3.28** Probably a baptismal formula; see 1 Cor 12.13; Col 3.11. *No . . . male and female* echoes Gen 1.27; those in Christ have entered a *new creation* (see 6.15) where former social distinctions are replaced by unity. **3.29** *Offspring,* lit. "seed," is now interpreted corporately; cf. v. 16.

4.1–7 Paul links the inheritance metaphor to an apocalyptic story of redemption. **4.3** *Elemental spirits* (Greek *stoicheia*), a difficult term meaning either "basic principles" (as in Heb 5.12), such as the code of behavior *set forth in Jewish law,* or—as apparently here—quasi-demonic powers that oppress humankind (see 4.8; Col 2.8, 20). Either way, Paul's *we* includes Jews and Gentiles in a common state of slavery before Christ. **4.4** *Fullness of time.* See also Mk 1.15; Eph 1.10. God sent his Son. See 1.4; Jn 3.16–17; Rom

8.3–4; 1 Jn 4.9; see also Wis 9.9–18. *Born of a woman* emphasizes the Son's humanity (see Job 14.1; Mt 11.11); *born under the law,* his Jewishness. **4.5** *Redeem,* release from slavery, as in 3.13. On *adoption* and on vv. 5–7 as a whole, see also Rom 8.14–17; Eph 2.11–13. **4.6** *Abba.* See also Mk 14.36; Rom 8.15. **4.8–11** Paul characterizes the Galatians' interest in Jewish law as a return to bondage equivalent to their state as pagans. Perhaps he sees a parallel between pagan worship of natural elements (*stoicheia,* v. 9) and the belief that Israel's liturgical calendar (*days, months, seasons, years,* v. 10) regulated human religious observance in harmony with the divine ordering of the heavenly bodies (*Jubilees* 2.9; *1 Enoch* 82.7–9). See also Col 2.16. **4.11** *Wasted,* rendered *for nothing* in 3.4. See Phil 2.16; 1 Thess 3.5; see also Isa 49.4; 65.23. **4.12–20** Paul reminds the Galatians of his past relationship with them and appeals for its restoration. The passage employs motifs common in Hellenistic discussions of friendship. **4.12** *Become as I am.* See 1 Cor 4.16; 11.1; Phil 3.17; 1 Thess 1.6; Heb 6.12; 13.7. *I also have become as you are.* See 1 Cor 9.21. Paul has become like a Gentile, free from observing the commandments of Jewish law. **4.13** The character of Paul's *physical infirmity* is unknown; it may be related to persecutions suffered in his mission. See 6.17; 2 Cor 11.23–27; 12.7–10. **4.14** *Angel,* or "messenger." **4.15** *Torn out your eyes,*

sible, you would have torn out your eyes and given them to me. [16]Have I now become your enemy by telling you the truth? [17]They make much of you, but for no good purpose; they want to exclude you, so that you may make much of them. [18]It is good to be made much of for a good purpose at all times, and not only when I am present with you. [19]My little children, for whom I am again in the pain of childbirth until Christ is formed in you, [20]I wish I were present with you now and could change my tone, for I am perplexed about you.

The Allegory of Hagar and Sarah

21 Tell me, you who desire to be subject to the law, will you not listen to the law? [22]For it is written that Abraham had two sons, one by a slave woman and the other by a free woman. [23]One, the child of the slave, was born according to the flesh; the other, the child of the free woman, was born through the promise. [24]Now this is an allegory: these women are two covenants. One woman, in fact, is Hagar, from Mount Sinai, bearing children for slavery. [25]Now Hagar is Mount Sinai in Arabia[a] and corresponds to the present Jerusalem, for she is in slavery with her children. [26]But the other woman corresponds to the Jerusalem above; she is free, and she is our mother. [27]For it is written,

"Rejoice, you childless one, you who bear
    no children,
burst into song and shout, you who
    endure no birth pangs;

for the children of the desolate woman
    are more numerous
than the children of the one who is
    married."

[28]Now you,[b] my friends,[c] are children of the promise, like Isaac. [29]But just as at that time the child who was born according to the flesh persecuted the child who was born according to the Spirit, so it is now also. [30]But what does the scripture say? "Drive out the slave and her child; for the child of the slave will not share the inheritance with the child of the free woman." [31]So then, friends,[c] we are children, not of the slave but of the free woman. [1]For freedom Christ has set us free. Stand firm, therefore, and do not submit again to a yoke of slavery.

The Nature of Christian Freedom

2 Listen! I, Paul, am telling you that if you let yourselves be circumcised, Christ will be of no benefit to you. [3]Once again I testify to every man who lets himself be circumcised that he is obliged to obey the entire law. [4]You who want to be justified by the law have cut yourselves off from Christ; you have fallen away from grace. [5]For through the Spirit, by faith, we eagerly wait for the hope of righteousness. [6]For in Christ Jesus neither circumcision nor uncircumcision counts for anything; the only thing that counts is faith working[d] through love.

---

a Other ancient authorities read For Sinai is a mountain in Arabia b Other ancient authorities read we c Gk brothers d Or made effective

---

probably a proverbial expression for solidarity in friendship. **4.17** *Exclude you.* See also 2.12. **4.19** On Paul's churches as his *children,* see also 1 Cor 4.14; 2 Cor 6.13; 1 Thess 2.11–12. *Pain of childbirth,* a common image in Jewish apocalyptic texts for the suffering that accompanies the new age (*1 Enoch* 62.4; *2 Apocalypse of Baruch* 56.6; Mk 13.8; Rev 12.2). Apostolic suffering is one of the birth pangs of the new creation (see Rom 8.22–23; 1 Thess 5.3). *Christ . . . formed in you.* See Rom 8.29; note on 2.20. **4.21–5.1** An allegorical reading of Genesis that reverses Jewish tradition, according to which Isaac (circumcised on the eighth day, Gen 21.4) symbolizes Israel and Ishmael symbolizes Gentiles; cf. *Jubilees* 16.17–18. **4.21** *Law,* here, broadly, scripture. See, e.g., 1 Cor 14.21. **4.22–23** See Gen 16, 21; the rival missionaries may have emphasized this story. **4.24–25** The equation of Hagar with Mount Sinai has no basis in the Genesis story; apparently the link is posited by Paul to connect slavery with law. **4.24** The *two covenants* do not correspond to the OT and the NT, but more generally to the covenant

of promise and the covenant of law; according to Paul, the former is older than the latter (see 3.17). *Bearing children,* a metaphor for gaining converts through missionary preaching; see v. 19. **4.25** *Jerusalem . . . in slavery* may allude to the city's subjection to Rome; see Deut 28.49. **4.26** The image of a *Jerusalem above* appears in many Jewish apocalyptic texts (see 2 Esd 7.26; 10.25–28; *1 Enoch* 90.28–29; *2 Apocalypse of Baruch* 4.2–6) as well as in Heb 12.22; 13.14; Rev 3.12; 21.2, 9–27. Ps 86.5 in the Septuagint (Ps 87.5) acclaims "Mother Zion." **4.27** Isa 54.1; see also Isa 51.1–3. **4.29** The idea that Ishmael *persecuted* Isaac is found in rabbinic midrash, or commentary, based on Gen 21.9. *So it is now also.* See 5.11; 6.12. **4.30** Gen 21.10. **5.1** *Christ has set us free.* See 3.13; 4.4–5; cf. 2.4–5. For Jewish law as a *yoke,* see also Acts 15.10; the rabbis used the same image with positive connotations, as does Mt 11.29–30.

5.2–12 Paul drives home the Letter's aim: to dissuade the Galatians from accepting circumcision. **5.4** See 2.16, 21; 3.10–12. **5.5** See Rom 8.23–25. **5.6** See

7 You were running well; who prevented you from obeying the truth? 8Such persuasion does not come from the one who calls you. 9A little yeast leavens the whole batch of dough. 10I am confident about you in the Lord that you will not think otherwise. But whoever it is that is confusing you will pay the penalty. 11But my friends,[a] why am I still being persecuted if I am still preaching circumcision? In that case the offense of the cross has been removed. 12I wish those who unsettle you would castrate themselves!

13 For you were called to freedom, brothers and sisters;[a] only do not use your freedom as an opportunity for self-indulgence,[b] but through love become slaves to one another. 14For the whole law is summed up in a single commandment, "You shall love your neighbor as yourself." 15If, however, you bite and devour one another, take care that you are not consumed by one another.

The Works of the Flesh

16 Live by the Spirit, I say, and do not gratify the desires of the flesh. 17For what the flesh desires is opposed to the Spirit, and what the Spirit desires is opposed to the flesh; for these are opposed to each other, to prevent you from doing what you want. 18But if you are led by the Spirit, you are not subject to the law. 19Now the works of the flesh are obvious: fornication, impurity, licentiousness, 20idolatry, sorcery, enmities, strife, jealousy, anger, quarrels, dissensions, factions, 21envy,[c] drunkenness, carousing, and things like these. I am warning you, as I warned you before: those who do such things will not inherit the kingdom of God.

The Fruit of the Spirit

22 By contrast, the fruit of the Spirit is love, joy, peace, patience, kindness, generosity, faithfulness, 23gentleness, and self-control. There is no law against such things. 24And those who belong to Christ Jesus have crucified the flesh with its passions and desires. 25If we live by the Spirit, let us also be guided by the Spirit. 26Let us not become conceited, competing against one another, envying one another.

Bear One Another's Burdens

6 My friends,[d] if anyone is detected in a transgression, you who have received the Spirit should restore such a one in a spirit of gentleness. Take care that you yourselves are not tempted. 2Bear one another's burdens, and in this way you will fulfill[e] the law of Christ. 3For if those who are nothing think they are something, they deceive themselves. 4All must test their own work; then that work, rather than their neighbor's work, will become a cause for pride. 5For all must carry their own loads.

6 Those who are taught the word must share in all good things with their teacher.

a Gk brothers   b Gk the flesh   c Other ancient authorities add murder   d Gk Brothers   e Other ancient authorities read in this way fulfill

3.28; 6.15; 1 Cor 7.19. **5.7** *Prevented you,* lit. "cut in on you," as in a race. *Obeying the truth.* See 2.5, 14. **5.8** See 1.6. **5.9** See also 1 Cor 5.6–8. **5.10** See 1.7–9. **5.11** Paul is *being persecuted* neither by Rome nor by civil authorities, but by the synagogue (see 2 Cor 11.24) or perhaps by Jewish Christians (see 1.13; 4.29; 6.12). *Offense of the cross.* See 1 Cor 1.18–25. **5.13–26** Paul sketches a vision for a community led by the Spirit; he links the pressure for circumcision with rivalry and divisions. **5.13** See v. 1. **5.14** The quotation is from Lev 19.18; a saying of Rabbi Hillel sums up Jewish law in the command, "What is hateful to you, do not do to your neighbor." See also 6.2; Mk 12.28–34; Rom 8.3–4; 13.8–10. **5.16–18** See also v. 25; Rom 8.1–17; Eph 2.3. **5.16** *Live,* lit. "walk." *Desires of the flesh,* not just sexual impulses but all human self-seeking desires *apart from God; see* vv. 19–21. **5.17** *Prevent you ...want.* See Rom 7.15–24. **5.18** See also 3.23–25; Rom 6.14. **5.19–21** The list of vices is conventional; see, e.g., Mk 7.21–22; Rom 1.29–31; 1 Cor 6.9–10; 2 Cor 12.20. Paul highlights offenses against the unity of the community. **5.19** *Flesh.* See 1 Cor 3.3. **5.21** *Do such things.*

The verb is a present participle, indicating continuing action over time. *Inherit the kingdom of God.* See also Mt 5.5; 25.34; 1 Cor 6.9–10; 15.50; Rev 21.7. On inheritance, see also 3.15–18; 3.29–4.7; 4.30. **5.22–23** *Fruit of the Spirit.* See Rom 8.9–11; Phil 1.11; 1 Tim 6.11; 2 Pet 1.5–8; see also lists of "gifts" and "manifestations" of the Spirit in Rom 12.6–8; 1 Cor 12.7–11. **5.24** *Crucified the flesh,* perhaps an allusion to baptism; see also 2.19b; 6.14; Rom 6.6; 8.13. **5.25** See v. 16.

6.1–10 General exhortations stressing mutual responsibility within the church. **6.1** On *restoring* a transgressor, see also Lev 19.17; Mt 18.15–22; Lk 17.3–4; Jas 5.19–20; cf. 1 Cor 5.1–13; Titus 3.10–11; the Dead Sea Scrolls *Rule of the Community* (1QS) 5.24–6.1. **6.2** *Bear one another's burdens.* See also Rom 15.1–2. *Law of Christ,* either the law of love (5.14), the example of Christ, or the law of Moses as redefined by Christ; the phrase is perhaps borrowed ironically from the rival missionaries. See also Rom 15.1–7; 1 Cor 9.21; Jn 13.34. **6.4** See 2 Cor 13.5; Rom 12.3. **6.5** A reference to eschatological judgment; see 2 Esd 7.104–105. **6.6** A directive for financial support of Christian teachers (see also

7 Do not be deceived; God is not mocked, for you reap whatever you sow. 8If you sow to your own flesh, you will reap corruption from the flesh; but if you sow to the Spirit, you will reap eternal life from the Spirit. 9So let us not grow weary in doing what is right, for we will reap at harvest time, if we do not give up. 10So then, whenever we have an opportunity, let us work for the good of all, and especially for those of the family of faith.

Final Admonitions and Benediction

11 See what large letters I make when I am writing in my own hand! 12It is those who want to make a good showing in the flesh that try to compel you to be circumcised—only that they may not be persecuted for the cross of Christ. 13Even the circumcised do not

themselves obey the law, but they want you to be circumcised so that they may boast about your flesh. 14May I never boast of anything except the cross of our Lord Jesus Christ, by which[a] the world has been crucified to me, and I to the world. 15For[b] neither circumcision nor uncircumcision is anything; but a new creation is everything! 16As for those who will follow this rule—peace be upon them, and mercy, and upon the Israel of God.

17 From now on, let no one make trouble for me; for I carry the marks of Jesus branded on my body.

18 May the grace of our Lord Jesus Christ be with your spirit, brothers and sisters.[c] Amen.

---

a Or *through whom*   *b* Other ancient authorities add *in Christ Jesus*   *c* Gk *brothers*

---

1 Cor 9.3–14). **6.7** See Job 4.8; Prov 22.8. **6.8** See Rom 8.5–13; cf. 1 Cor 15.35–44. **6.9** *Not grow weary.* See 2 Cor 4.1, 16; also Lk 18.1. **6.10** *Family,* lit. "household"; see also Eph 2.19; 1 Tim 3.15. **6.11–18** A final summation underscoring the Letter's main points. **6.11** Paul writes the postscript in his *own hand,* an ancient epistolary convention; the body of the letter was taken down or copied by a secretary. See also Rom 16.22. **6.12–13** See also 2.3, 14; 4.17; 5.11. **6.13** *The circumcised.* Some manuscripts read "those who are being circumcised." *Boast.* See Rom 2.17–23; 3.27; 4.2; 1 Cor 4.7; 2 Cor 11.12–13, 18; Eph 2.9. **6.14** On *boasting* in God or Christ, see Rom 5.2–3, 11; 1 Cor 1.29–31; 2.2. On the *world* as *crucified,* see also 2.19–20; 5.24; 2 Cor 5.14, 17; Col 2.14–15. **6.15** See 3.28; 5.6; Eph 2.15–16. *New cre-*

ation echoes Isa 65.17–25; Paul understands salvation as God's remaking of the world (see Rom 8.19–23; 2 Cor 5.17–19; see also Rev 21.5). **6.16** This blessing stands in juxtaposition to the Letter's opening curse (1.8–9). A similar blessing is found in the peace benediction of the *Shemoneh Esreh,* a standard synagogue prayer. *This rule,* v. 16, or perhaps vv. 14–15. *Israel of God,* the church as the true Israel (see 3.7, 29; 4.28–31; Rom 9.6–8) or, alternatively, the Jewish people as a whole (see Rom 11.25–32); the argument of Galatians appears to support the former interpretation. **6.17** *The marks of Jesus,* Paul's scars (2 Cor 6.4–5; 11.23–25), incurred in his mission. The phrase may also suggest that Paul is branded by these scars as Christ's slave (see 1.10). **6.18** See also Phil 4.23; Philem 25.

The Letter of Paul to the
EPHESIANS

BECAUSE NO SINGLE EVENT or crisis can be discerned as its specific occasion and because of the general nature of its content, Ephesians is sometimes thought to have originated as a general letter intended for many churches, a notion reinforced by the lack of a place name in 1.1 in the best manuscripts. Clues within the Letter suggest its purpose. The readers are twice addressed as Gentiles (2.11; 3.1), but subsequently they are told to "no longer live as the Gentiles live" (4.17). Furthermore, they are reminded that "now in Christ Jesus" they are no longer "aliens from the commonwealth of Israel and strangers to the covenants of promise" (2.12–13). Thus, because of their response to the gospel, the readers are experiencing a radical transformation of their personal and social identity; they are being resocialized into God's purposes and family. Their new identity is in formation, and the Letter is designed to guide them from their baptism (4.5, 22, 24, 31; 6.11) toward their presentation as the unblemished bride of Christ.

Perhaps because of its general character and its arguing from the significance of believers' baptism to a sweeping portrayal of Christian behavior and unity, Ephesians, of all the Pauline and Paulinist Letters, propounds the most comprehensive and cohesive portrait of God's plans and purposes. What is said of God and Christ is applied to the community of believers and to members of their households (particularly in the last two chapters). Believers, communally and finally even individually, are instructed regarding their place and comportment in the world and before God.

Authorship

MARKED DIFFERENCES IN STYLE, phrasing, and viewpoint between this Letter and the seven un-questionably authentic Pauline Letters (Romans, 1 and 2 Corinthians, Galatians, Philippians, 1 Thessalonians, Philemon) have cast significant doubt on Pauline authorship of Ephesians. It is more likely that a disciple of Paul wrote the Letter in Paul's name, probably after the apostle's death. Complex sentences, relative clauses, distinctive terminology (e.g., "heavenly places," "to the praise of his glory"), and redundant expressions (e.g., "law with its commandments and ordinances," "strength of his power") appear frequently in Ephesians. Even more striking, how-ever, are the claims that believers already share in Christ's resurrection (2.6) and are saved (2.5, 8), assertions that lack parallels in the seven undisputed Letters. Also in this Letter, the church has become cosmic in function (3.10; cf. Philem 2) and now has Christ as its head (1.22–23; cf.

Rom 12.4–5; 1 Cor 12.12–26). Predominantly temporal categories in Paul's thought (see Rom 13.11–12) have been transposed into spatial conceptions (see 1.20; 2.6), perhaps as a way of dealing with the delay of Christ's return. Paul's understanding of sin as a hostile power and justification as deliverance from it (see Rom 5.6–11; 7.8, 11) is here replaced by an understanding of sins as individual trespasses and forgiveness as their removal (1.7; 2.1; 4.32).

Perspective

THE PERSPECTIVE OF EPHESIANS moves from a vastly cosmic picture of God's plan (1.3–23) and the believers' inclusion in it (2.1–22), to the role and mission of the church and life within it (3.1–5.20), to a depiction of relationships within the household (5.21–6.9), to a final description of how, with prayer, each believer stands battle-ready in God's power (6.10–20). This broad perspective binds the Letter together. God's power to enact the cosmic plan (1.3–23) is the same power available to the believer as armament (6.10–17). Relations of married persons mirror those between Christ and the church (5.21–33). Life within the church (4.1–13) reflects God's larger purpose in Christ, "to gather up all things in him, things in heaven and things on earth" (1.10).

Ephesians is especially concerned with power as ultimately grounded not in the "rulers and authorities" (1.21; 3.10; 6.12) but in God and enforced through Christ. It construes that power through metaphors of God as "Father" over "every family in heaven and on earth" (3.15) and Christ as "head" of the body (church) and by embracing traditional views of household arrangements (5.22–6.9). We have probably underestimated the social and political force of such a message in the first century when no one was more interested in power than Rome.

Date and Place of Writing

SEVERAL FEATURES OF EPHESIANS suggest a date in the last third of the first century CE. The author writes to a gentile church that seems to have little perception of being part of Israel and needs instructions regarding this connection (2.11–18). These features suggest that some time has passed since the original Pauline mission (cf. 1 Cor 16.3; Gal 6.16). Moreover, a late first-century date would also fit other features distinguishing this Letter from the seven undisputed Pauline Letters: the aforementioned transposition of Pauline eschatological fervor into spatial categories; the diminution of women's status (see 5.22–24); and the reaccommodation to long-standing cultural patterns of hierarchy and submission in the household (5.22–6.9). There are no clues within the Letter regarding its place of composition. [J. PAUL SAMPLEY]

Salutation

1 Paul, an apostle of Christ Jesus by the will of God,

To the saints who are in Ephesus and are faithful[a] in Christ Jesus:

2 Grace to you and peace from God our Father and the Lord Jesus Christ.

Spiritual Blessings in Christ

3 Blessed be the God and Father of our Lord Jesus Christ, who has blessed us in Christ with every spiritual blessing in the heavenly places, 4just as he chose us in Christ[b] before the foundation of the world to be holy and blameless before him in love. 5He destined us for adoption as his children through Jesus Christ, according to the good pleasure of his will, 6to the praise of his glorious grace that he freely bestowed on us in the Beloved. 7In him we have redemption through his blood, the forgiveness of our trespasses, according to the riches of his grace 8that he lavished on us. With all wisdom and insight 9he has made known to us the mystery of his will, according to his good pleasure that he set

---

a Other ancient authorities lack in Ephesus, reading saints who are also faithful   b Gk in him

forth in Christ, [10]as a plan for the fullness of time, to gather up all things in him, things in heaven and things on earth. [11]In Christ we have also obtained an inheritance,[a] having been destined according to the purpose of him who accomplishes all things according to his counsel and will, [12]so that we, who were the first to set our hope on Christ, might live for the praise of his glory. [13]In him you also, when you had heard the word of truth, the gospel of your salvation, and had believed in him, were marked with the seal of the promised Holy Spirit; [14]this[b] is the pledge of our inheritance toward redemption as God's own people, to the praise of his glory.

Paul's Prayer

15 I have heard of your faith in the Lord Jesus and your love[c] toward all the saints, and for this reason [16]I do not cease to give thanks for you as I remember you in my prayers. [17]I pray that the God of our Lord Jesus Christ, the Father of glory, may give you a spirit of wisdom and revelation as you come to know him, [18]so that, with the eyes of your heart enlightened, you may know what is the hope to which he has called you, what are the riches of his glorious inheritance among the saints, [19]and what is the immeasurable greatness of his power for us who believe, according to the working of his great power. [20]God[d] put this power to work in Christ when he raised him from the dead and seated him at his right hand in the heavenly places, [21]far above all rule and authority and power and dominion, and above every name that is named, not only in this age but also in the age to come. [22]And he has put all things under his feet and has made him the head over all things for the church, [23]which is his body, the fullness of him who fills all in all.

From Death to Life

2 You were dead through the trespasses and sins [2]in which you once lived, following

---

a Or *been made a heritage*   *b* Other ancient authorities read *who*   *c* Other ancient authorities lack *and your love*   *d* Gk *He*

1.1–2 The salutation takes the same form as most Pauline Letter openings. **1.1** Like Romans, but unlike most other Pauline letters, Ephesians is sent solely by *Paul.* On Paul's self-designation as *apostle,* see 2 Cor 1.1; Gal 1.1; Col 1.1. The frequent references to the *will of God* (see vv. 5, 9, 11; 5.17; 6.6) emphasize God's plan and power. The *saints,* i.e., those set apart for God, are the believers (see v. 18; 2.19; 3.8, 18; 4.12; 5.3; 6.18). The location of the addressees *in Ephesus* is lacking in the best Greek manuscripts (see text note *a*). **1.2** *Grace,* the foundation of life in Christ, has made *peace* possible (see Rom 5.1). *Father,* a favorite designation of God in Ephesians; see vv. 3, 17; 2.18; 3.14; 4.6; 5.20; 6.23. Family and household are primary social realities in Ephesians; in Roman times, the father had responsibility for all members of the household. **1.3–23** Where a formal thanksgiving might be expected (cf. Rom 1.8), there is an ancient Jewish prayer form (beginning *Blessed be the God;* see also 2 Cor 1.3; 1 Pet 1.3), which identifies the author with Jewish tradition. Vv. 15–23, however, incorporate many elements of a typical Pauline thanksgiving. **1.3** *Heavenly places,* an expression peculiar to Ephesians (see v. 20; 2.6; 3.10; 6.12). **1.4** *Chose* (see also *destined,* vv. 5, 11) stresses God's initiative. The *blameless* (lit. "without blemish") life expected of those set apart for God (see 5.27; Col 1.22) has its roots in the purity expected of sacrificial animals and of priests (see Lev 21–22). **1.5** *Adoption,* the means by which Gentiles are included in God's household. See 2.19; Gal 4.5. **1.6** *Grace* (Greek *charis*) echoes the salutation (v. 2) and is a technical term of benefaction that establishes reciprocity; God's unconditional and previous election, described in vv. 3–7, places all believers in God's debt. *The Beloved,* applied to Christ

as a title nowhere else in the NT, though it is found in second-century Christian writings (cf. *Letter of Barnabas* 3.6; 4.3; *Ascension of Isaiah* 3.13). **1.7** *Redemption,* the buying back of a slave or the freeing of a prisoner by ransom. See also v. 14; 4.30; Col 1.14. **1.9** The content of the *mystery,* a reference to God's previously hidden purposes, is given in 3.3–9; see also 5.32; 6.19. **1.10** *Fullness* denotes completeness; see v. 23; 3.19; 4.13; see also 4.10; 5.18; Col 1.19. God's *plan for the fullness of time* is linked with the previously hidden mystery in 3.2–9. *To gather up* (Greek, "to head up"). This image is developed later in the Letter where Christ is spoken of as the *head* of his body, the church (vv. 22–23; 4.15). **1.12** *For the praise of his glory* (see also vv. 6, 14) is distinctive in the NT and reflects liturgical tradition. **1.13** *The seal,* a sign of authentication or confirmation, designates ownership, and therefore protection, by the Holy Spirit; see 4.30. **1.14** *Pledge,* a down payment securing the entirety of what is promised. See 2 Cor 1.22; 5.5. On salvation as an *inheritance,* see Rom 8.17; Gal 4.7; Col 1.12. Adopted children (v. 5) share fully in the inheritance. **1.15** A nearly identical statement is Col 1.4. **1.18** All the saints, i.e., believers, have been *called* and are expected to live in accord with that calling; see 4.1, 4. **1.20** *At his right hand,* an echo of Ps 110.1. **1.21** *All rule and authority and power and dominion* includes all supposed rival powers, whether cosmic or mundane; see 3.10; 6.12; Rom 8.38; 1 Cor 15.24; Col 1.16; 2.10, 15; 1 Pet 3.22. **1.22** *Under his feet,* an echo of Ps 8.6. See also Ps 110.1; 1 Cor 15.25–28. Nowhere in the unquestionably authentic Pauline Letters is Christ called, as here, the *head* of the church (see also v. 10; 4.15; 5.23; cf. Rom 12.5; 1 Cor 12.12–27).

2.1–10 The believers' resurrection is linked with

the course of this world, following the ruler of the power of the air, the spirit that is now at work among those who are disobedient. 3All of us once lived among them in the passions of our flesh, following the desires of flesh and senses, and we were by nature children of wrath, like everyone else. 4But God, who is rich in mercy, out of the great love with which he loved us 5even when we were dead through our trespasses, made us alive together with Christ*a*—by grace you have been saved— 6and raised us up with him and seated us with him in the heavenly places in Christ Jesus, 7so that in the ages to come he might show the immeasurable riches of his grace in kindness toward us in Christ Jesus. 8For by grace you have been saved through faith, and this is not your own doing; it is the gift of God— 9not the result of works, so that no one may boast. 10For we are what he has made us, created in Christ Jesus for good works, which God prepared beforehand to be our way of life.

One in Christ

11 So then, remember that at one time you Gentiles by birth,*b* called "the uncircumcision" by those who are called "the circumcision"—a physical circumcision made in the flesh by human hands— 12remember that you were at that time without Christ, being aliens from the commonwealth of Israel, and strangers to the covenants of promise, having no hope and without God in the world. 13But now in Christ Jesus you who once were far off have been brought near by the blood of Christ. 14For he is our peace; in his flesh he has made both groups into one and has broken down the dividing wall, that is, the hostility between us. 15He has abolished the law with its commandments and ordinances, that he might create in himself one new humanity in place of the two, thus making peace, 16and might reconcile both groups to God in one body*c* through the cross, thus putting to death that hostility through it.*d* 17So he came and proclaimed peace to you who were far off and peace to those who were near; 18for through him both of us have access in one Spirit to the Father. 19So then you are no longer strangers and aliens, but you are citizens with the saints and also members of the household of God, 20built upon the foundation of the apostles and prophets, with Christ Jesus himself as the cornerstone.*e* 21In him the whole structure is joined together and grows into a holy temple in the Lord; 22in whom you also are built together spiritually*f* into a dwelling place for God.

Paul's Ministry to the Gentiles

3 This is the reason that I Paul am a prisoner for*g* Christ Jesus for the sake of you

a Other ancient authorities read *in Christ* *b* Gk *in the flesh*
c Or *reconcile both of us in one body for God* *d* Or *in him*, or *in himself* *e* Or *keystone* *f* Gk *in the Spirit* *g* Or *of*

that of Christ (see esp. v. 6). **2.2** *In which you once lived.* Different ways of living (lit. "walking") are described in 4.1–5.20; see 2.10; 4.1, 17; 5.2, 8, 15. *Ruler of the power of the air,* probably the devil (4.27; 6.11). The disobedient *spirit* associated with this figure stands in contrast with the promised Holy Spirit (1.13; 2.18, 22). **2.3** *Children of wrath,* powerless creatures subject to God's judgment. See 5.6; Col 3.6. **2.5** *By grace you have been saved* (see also 2.8). In the authentic letters, Paul views salvation as a future event (see Rom 5.9, 10; 13.11; 1 Thess 5.8). *Grace* (Greek *charis;* also v. 8). See note on 1.6. **2.6** *And raised us up with him* (see also Col 2.12; 3.1). In the authentic Letters, Paul is careful to speak of believers' resurrection as occurring in the future (see Rom 6.5; 1 Cor 15.21–23; Phil 3.10–11). **2.8–9** *By grace . . . not . . . works,* a concise summary of Paul's thought. See also Rom 3.21–31; 4.2–4, 16; 9.16; 11.6; Gal 2.16. **2.9** On the prohibition of improper *boasting,* see Rom 3.27; 4.2; 1 Cor 1.29–31. **2.10** *Good works* follow faith, never lead to it; see Col 1.10. **2.11–22** These verses discuss the unity of Gentiles and Jews in Christ and mark off a new identity with social and political implications. **2.12** On *aliens,* see 4.18; Col 1.21. *Strangers,* the opposite of citizens. See v. 19. *Cov-*enants of promise (see also 1.13; 3.6; Rom 9.4), possibly the covenants of Genesis, which also highlight God's promises (Gen 15.12–21; 17.1–8; 26.1–5; 35.11–12). **2.13** On *far off* and *near,* see also v. 17; Isa 57.19. *Blood of Christ,* an allusion to Christ's atoning death. See Lev 16; Rom 3.25; 5.9. **2.14** On *peace,* see also 1.2; 2.15, 17; 4.3; 6.15. *In his flesh* identifies Christ's physical body on the cross as the means of reconciliation between Gentiles and Jews and between both groups and God (see v. 16; Col 1.22). **2.19** *Strangers and aliens,* here reversed from v. 12 as a rhetorical *inclusio* (a repetition that signals the beginning and end of a unit). *Household of God,* a shift of image, but see note on 1.2; see 3.15; 5.21–6.4; see also 1 Tim 3.15; 1 Pet 4.17. **2.20** *Foundation of the apostles and prophets.* Cf. 1 Cor 3.11. The prophets could be those of ancient Israel (see Rom 3.21) or those of the early Christian church (3.5; 4.11; 1 Cor 11.4–5; 14.3–6, 24). *Cornerstone,* a scriptural image (see Ps 118.22; Isa 28.16) widely applied to Christ; see Mt 21.42; 1 Pet 2.6. **2.22** On believers collectively (the *you* is plural) as a *dwelling place for God,* see 1 Cor 3.16–17; 6.19; 1 Pet 2.4–6.

3.1–13 Paul's status and the church's mission are aligned with God's eternal plan. **3.1** Paul was a *prisoner*

Gentiles— 2for surely you have already heard of the commission of God's grace that was given me for you, 3and how the mystery was made known to me by revelation, as I wrote above in a few words, 4a reading of which will enable you to perceive my understanding of the mystery of Christ. 5In former generations this mystery*a* was not made known to humankind, as it has now been revealed to his holy apostles and prophets by the Spirit: 6that is, the Gentiles have become fellow heirs, members of the same body, and sharers in the promise in Christ Jesus through the gospel.

7 Of this gospel I have become a servant according to the gift of God's grace that was given me by the working of his power. 8Although I am the very least of all the saints, this grace was given to me to bring to the Gentiles the news of the boundless riches of Christ, 9and to make everyone see*b* what is the plan of the mystery hidden for ages in*c* God who created all things; 10so that through the church the wisdom of God in its rich variety might now be made known to the rulers and authorities in the heavenly places. 11This was in accordance with the eternal purpose that he has carried out in Christ Jesus our Lord, 12in whom we have access to God in boldness and confidence through faith in him.*d* 13I pray therefore that you*e* may not lose heart over my sufferings for you; they are your glory.

Prayer for the Readers

14 For this reason I bow my knees before the Father,*f* 15from whom every family*g* in heaven and on earth takes its name. 16I pray that, according to the riches of his glory, he may grant that you may be strengthened in your inner being with power through his Spirit, 17and that Christ may dwell in your hearts through faith, as you are being rooted and grounded in love. 18I pray that you may have the power to comprehend, with all the saints, what is the breadth and length and height and depth, 19and to know the love of Christ that surpasses knowledge, so that you may be filled with all the fullness of God.

20 Now to him who by the power at work within us is able to accomplish abundantly far more than all we can ask or imagine, 21to him be glory in the church and in Christ Jesus to all generations, forever and ever. Amen.

Unity in the Body of Christ

4 I therefore, the prisoner in the Lord, beg you to lead a life worthy of the calling to which you have been called, 2with all humility and gentleness, with patience, bearing with one another in love, 3making every effort to maintain the unity of the Spirit in the bond of peace. 4There is one body and one Spirit, just

---

a Gk *it*   *b* Other ancient authorities read *to bring to light*
c Or *by*   *d* Or *the faith of him*   *e* Or *I*   *f* Other ancient authorities add *of our Lord Jesus Christ*   *g* Gk *fatherhood*

---

on several occasions (see 2 Cor 6.5; 11.23; Phil 1.13–14; Col 4.3, 18; Philem 1, 9); it is not clear which imprisonment is intended here (see 6.20). **3.2** Paul had received a divinely appointed *commission* and was therefore a part of God's plan (see 1.10; 3.9; 1 Cor 9.17; Gal 1.15–16; 2.7–9; Col 1.25). **3.3** Conforming to the picture in the undisputed letters (2 Cor 12.1, 7; Gal 2.2), the author of Ephesians legitimates Paul's authority through the concept of *revelation*, for Paul was not one of the original disciples. **3.5** On the mystery *not made known* before but now revealed, see Rom 16.25. **3.6** Inclusion of *Gentiles* (echoing 2.19–22) in God's household or family. **3.7** On Paul as a *servant* (Greek *diakonos*), see 1 Cor 3.5. **3.8** *Least of all the saints.* See 1 Cor 15.9; 1 Tim 1.15; cf. 2 Cor 11.5. **3.9** *Plan, mystery,* and God's relationship to *all things* are treated once again (see 1.9–10; 3.3–5). **3.10** The *church has the cosmic* task of making the *wisdom of God* (either wisdom from God or wisdom about God) known in the *heavenly places;* cf. the references to localized house churches in the undisputed Letters (Rom 16.5, 15; Philem 2). *Rulers and authorities.* See 1.21; 6.12. **3.12** *Access to God,* a reprise of 2.18.

3.13 *Sufferings,* lit. "tribulations," a technical apocalyptic term for end-time afflictions; see Rom 5.3; 1 Thess 3.3, 7. **3.14–21** Prayer and doxology. **3.15** The Greek term for *family* is derived from the word "father"; see text note *g*. **3.16** *Riches of his glory,* an example of the effusive style of Ephesians. **3.17** On the notion that *Christ may dwell in* the faithful, see Gal 2.20. The *hearts* of the faithful as the dwelling place of Christ parallel the temple as the "dwelling place for God" (2.22). The doubled verbs (*rooted, grounded*) emphasize love and enlarge the metaphor to include growth. **3.18** *Breadth and length and height and depth,* expansive imagery that may refer to the cosmic vastness of God's plan and purpose; see Rom 8.38–39. **3.19** *Love of Christ,* either love for Christ or love from Christ; the Greek is ambiguous. **3.20–21** For similar doxologies, see Rom 16.25–27; Gal 1.5; 1 Tim 1.17; 2 Tim 4.18.

4.1–5.20 Counsels on behavior worthy of God's calling. **4.1–6** Believers' calling and comportment are grounded in their fundamental unity. **4.1** On the concern that believers live *worthy* lives, see Col 1.10; 1 Thess 2.12. **4.2–3** On the virtues of the worthy life, see Col 3.12–13; see also 1 Cor 13.4. **4.4–6** This strong

as you were called to the one hope of your calling, 5one Lord, one faith, one baptism, 6one God and Father of all, who is above all and through all and in all.

7 But each of us was given grace according to the measure of Christ's gift. 8Therefore it is said,

"When he ascended on high he made
     captivity itself a captive;
he gave gifts to his people."

9(When it says, "He ascended," what does it mean but that he had also descended*a* into the lower parts of the earth? 10He who descended is the same one who ascended far above all the heavens, so that he might fill all things.) 11The gifts he gave were that some would be apostles, some prophets, some evangelists, some pastors and teachers, 12to equip the saints for the work of ministry, for building up the body of Christ, 13until all of us come to the unity of the faith and of the knowledge of the Son of God, to maturity, to the measure of the full stature of Christ. 14We must no longer be children, tossed to and fro and blown about by every wind of doctrine, by people's trickery, by their craftiness in deceitful scheming. 15But speaking the truth in love, we must grow up in every way into him who is the head, into Christ, 16from whom the whole body, joined and knit together by every ligament with which it is equipped, as each part is working properly, promotes the body's growth in building itself up in love.

The Old Life and the New

17 Now this I affirm and insist on in the Lord: you must no longer live as the Gentiles live, in the futility of their minds. 18They are darkened in their understanding, alienated from the life of God because of their ignorance and hardness of heart. 19They have lost all sensitivity and have abandoned themselves to licentiousness, greedy to practice every kind of impurity. 20That is not the way you learned Christ! 21For surely you have heard about him and were taught in him, as truth is in Jesus. 22You were taught to put away your former way of life, your old self, corrupt and deluded by its lusts, 23and to be renewed in the spirit of your minds, 24and to clothe yourselves with the new self, created according to the likeness of God in true righteousness and holiness.

Rules for the New Life

25 So then, putting away falsehood, let all of us speak the truth to our neighbors, for we are members of one another. 26Be angry but do not sin; do not let the sun go down on your anger, 27and do not make room for the devil. 28Thieves must give up stealing; rather let them labor and work honestly with their own hands, so as to have something to share with the needy. 29Let no evil talk come out of your mouths, but only what is useful for building

a Other ancient authorities add *first*

emphasis on unity was anticipated in 1.22–23; 2.14–16, 18. **4.6** On God *above all and through all and in all,* see 1 Cor 15.28; cf. 1 Cor 8.6. **4.7–16** Grace equips the body of Christ with a variety of gifts (see 1 Cor 12.4–11). Responsibility for unity lies with all believers. **4.7** On individualized *measures,* see Rom 12.3. **4.8** The quotation is derived from Ps 68.18, which speaks, however, of God, not the people, receiving gifts. **4.9–11** An example of early Christian exegesis, focusing on key words in the quotation; see also Rom 10.6–10; Heb 2.6–9. **4.9** *Descended . . . earth.* See Mt 12.40; 1 Pet 3.19. **4.11** The list of *gifts* stresses leadership functions in the church. Is the list representative or complete? Rom 12.6–8; 1 Cor 12.28–30 suggest the former. **4.12** *Ministry* (Greek *diakonia*). As the cognate of this term, *servant,* was applied to Paul in 3.7, recipients of the Letter are invited to join with Paul in service to the gospel. **4.13** *Maturity* (lit. "mature person," reprising the "one new person" of 2.15, where the NRSV has *one new humanity,* as distinguished from childishness (v. 14); see Phil 3.12; Col 1.28. The Greek can be translated as "perfect person" (cf. Heb 6.1, which involves a

play on the two senses of maturity and perfection), but here such a translation is problematic both because Paul thinks of new believers as babies in faith (see Philem 10; Gal 4.19; 1 Cor 2.1; 4.15) and yearns for them to grow up in faith (Phil 3.12–15; 2 Cor 3.18) and because modern "perfectionism" is a serious malaise. **4.15–16** On Christ as *head* of the *body,* see 1.22–23; note on 1.22. **4.17–24** These verses address contrasting ways of life. **4.17** *Affirm and insist.* Doubling provides emphasis. Ironically in a letter written to Gentiles, *the Gentiles* denotes a rejected way of living. **4.20–24** Metaphors of teaching and learning are interlaced with references to putting garments off and on for baptism. To *learn Christ* (v. 20) means not only to learn *about him* (v. 21) but also to *put away* the old *way of life* (v. 22; see also Rom 6.6) and to be *clothed* with *the new self* (v. 24; see also Gal 3.27; Col 3.10). **4.25–32** Practical suggestions for the new life. **4.25** Putting away develops the theme of v. 22. *Speak the truth.* See Zech 8.16. **4.26** *Be angry but do not sin.* See Ps 4.4 (Septuagint). *Do not let the sun go down on your anger,* a maxim found in non-Christian writings

up,[a] as there is need, so that your words may give grace to those who hear. 30And do not grieve the Holy Spirit of God, with which you were marked with a seal for the day of redemption. 31Put away from you all bitterness and wrath and anger and wrangling and slander, together with all malice, 32and be kind to one another, tenderhearted, forgiving one another, as God in Christ has forgiven you.[b]

5 1Therefore be imitators of God, as beloved children, 2and live in love, as Christ loved us[c] and gave himself up for us, a fragrant offering and sacrifice to God.

Renounce Pagan Ways

3 But fornication and impurity of any kind, or greed, must not even be mentioned among you, as is proper among saints. 4Entirely out of place is obscene, silly, and vulgar talk; but instead, let there be thanksgiving. 5Be sure of this, that no fornicator or impure person, or one who is greedy (that is, an idolater), has any inheritance in the kingdom of Christ and of God.

6 Let no one deceive you with empty words, for because of these things the wrath of God comes on those who are disobedient. 7Therefore do not be associated with them. 8For once you were darkness, but now in the Lord you are light. Live as children of light— 9for the

fruit of the light is found in all that is good and right and true. 10Try to find out what is pleasing to the Lord. 11Take no part in the unfruitful works of darkness, but instead expose them. 12For it is shameful even to mention what such people do secretly; 13but everything exposed by the light becomes visible, 14for everything that becomes visible is light. Therefore it says,

"Sleeper, awake!
 Rise from the dead,
 and Christ will shine on you."

15 Be careful then how you live, not as unwise people but as wise, 16making the most of the time, because the days are evil. 17So do not be foolish, but understand what the will of the Lord is. 18Do not get drunk with wine, for that is debauchery; but be filled with the Spirit, 19as you sing psalms and hymns and spiritual songs among yourselves, singing and making melody to the Lord in your hearts, 20giving thanks to God the Father at all times and for everything in the name of our Lord Jesus Christ.

The Christian Household

21 Be subject to one another out of reverence for Christ.

---

a Other ancient authorities read *building up faith* b Other ancient authorities read *us* c Other ancient authorities read *you*

---

of this period (cf. Plutarch, *On Brotherly Love* 17, 488C). **4.30** Wrongful conduct risks alienation from the *Holy Spirit* by which readers were set apart for God (see 1.13–14). **4.32** An echo of v. 2. **5.1** The readers are to be *imitators of God* in forgiveness (4.32) and in love (5.2); this is a pivotal exhortation. Whereas calls to imitate Christ are widespread in the NT (see 5.25; see also Rom 15.7; 1 Cor 11.1), imitation of God is rare (see Mt 5.44–45, 48). *As beloved children*. In Roman times parents were role models (see also 1 Cor 4.14–17). **5.2** *Live in love* (lit. "walk in love"). See also vv. 8, 15. *Christ loved . . . for us*. See v. 25; also Gal 2.20. The image of Christ's self-sacrifice moves the author to describe believers as *a fragrant offering and sacrifice to God* (see, e.g., Ex 29.18; Ezek 20.14; see also Rom 12.1; Phil 4.18).

5.3–20 Counsels on how to live carefully and wisely. **5.3** On things that *must not even be mentioned*, much less done, see v. 12. **5.4–5** Lists of vices that imperil inheritance in the kingdom are also found in 1 Cor 6.9–10; Gal 5.19–21; Rev 22.14–15. On the connection between the *greedy* and the *idolater*, see Mt 6.24. **5.5** *Kingdom of Christ and of God*, an infrequent expression in the NT (but see 1 Cor 4.20; 6.9–10; 15.24, 50). **5.6** *Wrath of God*, a reference to God's final judgment. See Rom 1.18 (where God's *wrath* is also under-

stood as present); Col 3.6; Rev 19.15. **5.7** Being *associated* with unbelievers is also prohibited in 2 Cor 6.14; cf. 1 Cor 5.9–13; 7.12–16. **5.8** *Children of light*, a metaphor not found in Israel's scriptures, but common in the Dead Sea Scrolls and the NT. See Mt 5.16; Lk 16.8; Jn 12.36; 1 Thess 5.5. **5.9** *Fruit*, i.e., moral results. See Mt 7.16–20; Gal 5.22; cf. *unfruitful works* in v. 11. **5.10** *Try to find out*, lit. "find out," "discern." See Rom 12.2; Phil 1.10; see also v. 17. **5.13–14** On exposure by the *light*, see Jn 3.20–21. **5.14** The source of this quotation is uncertain. It may be a fragment of a Christian hymn; see also Isa 26.19. **5.16** *Making the most of the time*, lit. "buying up the time," but the meaning is uncertain. Cf. Col 4.5, where the same phrase bears on how believers relate to outsiders. *The days are evil*, a common apocalyptic perspective. See Mt 24.22; Acts 2.40; Gal 1.4. **5.17** *Understand . . . the will of the Lord*. See also v. 10. The contrast is with following sinful human wills (see 2.3, where the plural form of the Greek term here translated *will* is translated *desires*). **5.18** *Filled with the Spirit*, i.e., not with wine. See Acts 2.15–17. **5.20** *Giving thanks to God*. See 5.4; Col 3.17; 1 Thess 5.18.

5.21–6.9 The author introduces a discussion of relations within the household with an exhortation to mutual submission. **5.21** *Be subject to one another* (see

22 Wives, be subject to your husbands as you are to the Lord. 23 For the husband is the head of the wife just as Christ is the head of the church, the body of which he is the Savior. 24 Just as the church is subject to Christ, so also wives ought to be, in everything, to their husbands.

25 Husbands, love your wives, just as Christ loved the church and gave himself up for her, 26 in order to make her holy by cleansing her with the washing of water by the word, 27 so as to present the church to himself in splendor, without a spot or wrinkle or anything of the kind—yes, so that she may be holy and without blemish. 28 In the same way, husbands should love their wives as they do their own bodies. He who loves his wife loves himself. 29 For no one ever hates his own body, but he nourishes and tenderly cares for it, just as Christ does for the church, 30 because we are members of his body.[a] 31 "For this reason a man will leave his father and mother and be joined to his wife, and the two will become one flesh." 32 This is a great mystery, and I am applying it to Christ and the church. 33 Each of you, however, should love his wife as himself, and a wife should respect her husband.

Children and Parents

6 Children, obey your parents in the Lord,[b] for this is right. 2 "Honor your father and mother"—this is the first commandment with a promise: 3 "so that it may be well with you and you may live long on the earth."

4 And, fathers, do not provoke your children to anger, but bring them up in the discipline and instruction of the Lord.

Slaves and Masters

5 Slaves, obey your earthly masters with fear and trembling, in singleness of heart, as you obey Christ; 6 not only while being watched, and in order to please them, but as slaves of Christ, doing the will of God from the heart. 7 Render service with enthusiasm, as to the Lord and not to men and women, 8 knowing that whatever good we do, we will receive the same again from the Lord, whether we are slaves or free.

9 And, masters, do the same to them. Stop threatening them, for you know that both of you have the same Master in heaven, and with him there is no partiality.

The Whole Armor of God

10 Finally, be strong in the Lord and in the strength of his power. 11 Put on the whole armor of God, so that you may be able to stand against the wiles of the devil. 12 For our[c] struggle is not against enemies of blood and flesh, but against the rulers, against the authorities, against the cosmic powers of this present darkness, against the spiritual forces of evil in the heavenly places. 13 Therefore take up the whole armor of God, so that you may

a Other ancient authorities add of his flesh and of his bones
b Other ancient authorities lack in the Lord   c Other ancient authorities read your

1 Pet 5.5) was probably not originally part of the traditional material that follows, but derives from the author. It is debated whether the exhortation to mutual submission is applicable only to the section on wives and husbands or stands as the heading under which all the counsels in 5.22–6.9 are to be understood. **5.22–33** Wives and husbands (see Col 3.18–19). **5.23** For the *husband* as *head of the wife*, see 1 Cor 11.3; for *Christ* as *head of the church*, see 1.22; 4.15. **5.24** Subjection of wives to husbands is reaffirmed (see 5.22) and extended: *so also wives ought to be* subject *in everything*. Nowhere do the undisputed Pauline Letters call for the subjection of wives. **5.25** *As Christ loved the church.* See v. 2. **5.26** *Cleansing . . . washing,* a reference to baptism. See 4.22–24. **5.27** Usually Paul exhorts believers *to present* themselves to God or Christ (see Rom 6.13, 19; 12.1; 2 Cor 11.2); here the focus is entirely on Christ's action. *Without blemish.* See 1.4; Phil 1.10. **5.28** *He who loves his wife loves himself* (see also v. 33) echoes Lev 19.18. **5.31** Gen 2.24; see 1 Cor 6.15–17. **5.33** Mutuality of *husband* and *wife* is affirmed, despite the difference in verbs. **6.1–4** Children and parents (see Col 3.20–21). **6.2–3** See Deut 5.16; see also Ex 20.12. **6.4** On the *discipline* of children, see Heb 12.7–11. **6.5–9** Slaves and masters (see Col 3.22–4.1; 1 Tim 6.1–2; Titus 2.9–10; 1 Pet 2.18). **6.6** On *slaves of Christ,* see Rom 1.1; 1 Cor 7.22; Phil 1.1. *Will of God.* See 5.10, 17. **6.8** *Whether we are slaves or free* preserves the distinction between the two groups more than Gal 3.28 does (cf. 1 Cor 7.22). **6.9** That God shows *no partiality* was a traditional affirmation; see Deut 10.17; 1 Chr 19.7; Acts 10.34; Rom 2.11; 10.12.

6.10–20 The document's *peroratio,* or summary, passionate appeal such as a general might make before battle. **6.11** The exhortation to *put on* armor (see also v. 14) recalls the baptismal imagery of 4.24. To *stand against,* either to survive affliction and temptation (see 6.13) or to be found acceptable at the last judgment (see Rom 14.4; 1 Cor 10.12; Rev 6.17; see also Col 4.12). **6.12** The term translated *struggle* describes a wrestler's or soldier's close-quarter grappling. *Blood and flesh,* a Semitic phrase meaning human beings (see Mt 16.17). On *rulers, authorities,* and *powers,* see 1.21. The *cosmic* scope of the contention is foreshadowed in

be able to withstand on that evil day, and having done everything, to stand firm. [14]Stand therefore, and fasten the belt of truth around your waist, and put on the breastplate of righteousness. [15]As shoes for your feet put on whatever will make you ready to proclaim the gospel of peace. [16]With all of these,[a] take the shield of faith, with which you will be able to quench all the flaming arrows of the evil one. [17]Take the helmet of salvation, and the sword of the Spirit, which is the word of God.

18 Pray in the Spirit at all times in every prayer and supplication. To that end keep alert and always persevere in supplication for all the saints. [19]Pray also for me, so that when I speak, a message may be given to me to make known with boldness the mystery of the gospel,[b] [20]for which I am an ambassador in chains. Pray that I may declare it boldly, as I must speak.

Personal Matters and Benediction

21 So that you also may know how I am and what I am doing, Tychicus will tell you everything. He is a dear brother and a faithful minister in the Lord. [22]I am sending him to you for this very purpose, to let you know how we are, and to encourage your hearts.

23 Peace be to the whole community,[c] and love with faith, from God the Father and the Lord Jesus Christ. [24]Grace be with all who have an undying love for our Lord Jesus Christ.[d]

a Or *In all circumstances*   *b* Other ancient authorities lack *of the gospel*   *c* Gk *to the brothers*   *d* Other ancient authorities add *Amen*

1.20–21; 3.10; 4.9–10. **6.13–17** On identification of the *armor of God,* see Isa 11.5; 49.2; 59.17; Hos 6.5; Wis 5.17–20; 2 Cor 6.7; 1 Thess 5.8. The imagery is also found in the Dead Sea Scrolls *War Scroll* (1QM) and the writings of Hellenistic moral philosophers.

6.15 *The gospel of peace.* See Isa 52.7. **6.16** *Evil one,* the devil; see v. 11. **6.19** *Mystery of the gospel.* See 1.9. **6.20** *Chains,* a reminder of Paul's imprisonment (see 3.1). **6.21–22** Commendation of *Tychicus* (see Col 4.7–9). **6.23–24** Peace wish and final benediction.

The Letter of Paul to the
PHILIPPIANS

PAUL WROTE PHILIPPIANS to Christians in the city of Philippi, a Roman colony in the province of Macedonia. According to Acts 16.11–40, Paul, along with Timothy, Silas, and others, had visited this city some years before (ca. 50 CE) during his second missionary journey and founded a church there, Paul's first on European soil, whose members were predominantly gentile and whom Paul regarded with a special affection and deep longing (1.8; 2.19, 24).

Place and Date

PAUL WRITES THAT HE IS IN PRISON (1.7, 13–14, 17), but he does not say where. Imprisonment was not infrequent for Paul. He boasts vaguely of numerous imprisonments (2 Cor 11.23), but gives no locations. The author of *1 Clement* is more specific in claiming seven imprisonments for Paul (5.6), but again gives no locations. Acts identifies three: a brief one at Philippi at the founding of the church (Acts 16.23–40), another lasting two years at Caesarea (23.23–26.32) ca. 58–60 CE, and a third lasting at least two years at Rome (28.16–31) ca. 60–62. Traditionally, it has been assumed that Paul wrote this Letter from Rome, an assumption based on his references to the "imperial guard" (1.13) and the "emperor's household" (4.22).

These references, however, do not necessarily point to Rome (see notes on 1.13; 4.22). Scholars have thus proposed alternate sites, especially Caesarea and Ephesus. Ephesus has become an attractive option to scholars today, given the perils and even a death sentence that Paul faced in that city (2 Cor 1.8–9; Acts 19.23–41), not to mention his fighting with beasts there as well (1 Cor 15.32). Still, none of these sites is without problems. Consequently, it is prudent to keep the question of place open. Accordingly, the date for Philippians is either the mid-50s (if Ephesus), the late 50s (if Caesarea), or the early 60s (if Rome).

Occasion and Content

ALTHOUGH THE LOCATION OF PAUL'S IMPRISONMENT is difficult to identify, the role of that imprisonment in the Letter is not, for it determines the Letter's occasion and content. Paul is in prison, a circumstance that had become known to the Philippian Christians. They have responded by praying for his release (1.19) and then by sending one of their own, Epaphroditus, with gifts to supply his needs (2.25; 4.18). The Philippians have also learned that Epaphroditus, on delivering the gifts, had become seriously ill (2.26–27). Upon his recovery (2.28–29) Paul deems it necessary to send him back (2.25) along with the letter we know as Philippians.

Paul obviously needs to thank the Philippians for their concern and help, but aside from some brief acknowledgments (1.5; 2.25) he does not get around to doing so until late in the Letter (4.10–20). More pressing, it seems, is his concern, expressed at the start of the Letter, that the Philippians need to distinguish things that truly matter from those that do not (1.10). Paul's imprisonment, serious as it is, belongs to the latter category and should not cause the Philippians undue concern. Accordingly, Paul writes to console them by emphasizing his joy in this circumstance, for what truly matters is in fact going well: the gospel is advancing in spite of, or because of, his imprisonment (1.12–18); his special partnership with the Philippians is continuing (1.5; 4.15–18); Epaphroditus has recovered from his illness (2.28–29); and the coming day of Christ promises that the Philippians, should they live a life worthy of the gospel, will be saved (1.28; 2.12; 3.20) and he will receive a crown for his work (4.1).

Since these matters are going well, Paul is joyful and calls on the Philippians to rejoice with him. Indeed, "joy" is the principal theme of the Letter, occurring sixteen times: the word "joy" five times (1.4, 25; 2.2, 29; 4.1) and the verbs "rejoice" and "be glad" eleven (once in 2.28; 3.1; 4.10; and twice in 1.18; 2.17, 18; 4.4). A subsidiary theme of disappointment and worry, however, is also evident. Paul is disappointed at dissension among the Philippians (2.2–4; 4.2–3) and worried about certain people he calls "dogs," "evil workers," and "enemies of the cross of Christ" (3.2, 18). They espouse a righteousness based on law, especially on circumcision (3.2–3, 7–11, 19), which differs from his own view of righteousness based on Christ's crucifixion and resurrection (1.11; 2.6–11; 3.3, 9–11). Consequently, to the general exhortation to the Philippians to rejoice and live lives worthy of the gospel (1.27; see also 1.10; 2.3–5, 12, 15; 4.4–8), Paul adds that they should beware of these people (3.2), obey and imitate him (2.12; 3.17; 4.9), maintain unity (1.27; 2.2; 3.15; 4.2), and stand firm in the Lord (4.1). [RONALD F. HOCK]

Salutation

1 Paul and Timothy, servants[a] of Christ Jesus,

To all the saints in Christ Jesus who are in Philippi, with the bishops[b] and deacons:[c]

2 Grace to you and peace from God our Father and the Lord Jesus Christ.

Paul's Prayer for the Philippians

3 I thank my God every time I remember you, [4]constantly praying with joy in every one of my prayers for all of you, [5]because of your sharing in the gospel from the first day until now. [6]I am confident of this, that the one who began a good work among you will bring it to completion by the day of Jesus Christ. [7]It is right for me to think this way about all of you, because you hold me in your heart,[d] for all of you share in God's grace[e] with me, both in my imprisonment and in the defense and confirmation of the gospel. [8]For God is my witness,

how I long for all of you with the compassion of Christ Jesus. [9]And this is my prayer, that your love may overflow more and more with knowledge and full insight [10]to help you to determine what is best, so that in the day of Christ you may be pure and blameless, [11]having produced the harvest of righteousness that comes through Jesus Christ for the glory and praise of God.

Paul's Present Circumstances

12 I want you to know, beloved,[f] that what has happened to me has actually helped to spread the gospel, [13]so that it has become known throughout the whole imperial guard[g] and to everyone else that my imprisonment is for Christ; [14]and most of the brothers and sisters,[f] having been made confident in the Lord by

---

a Gk slaves   b Or overseers   c Or overseers and helpers
d Or because I hold you in my heart   e Gk in grace
f Gk brothers   g Gk whole praetorium

my imprisonment, dare to speak the word[a] with greater boldness and without fear.

15 Some proclaim Christ from envy and rivalry, but others from goodwill. 16 These proclaim Christ out of love, knowing that I have been put here for the defense of the gospel; 17 the others proclaim Christ out of selfish ambition, not sincerely but intending to increase my suffering in my imprisonment. 18 What does it matter? Just this, that Christ is proclaimed in every way, whether out of false motives or true; and in that I rejoice.

Yes, and I will continue to rejoice, 19 for I know that through your prayers and the help of the Spirit of Jesus Christ this will turn out for my deliverance. 20 It is my eager expectation and hope that I will not be put to shame in any way, but that by my speaking with all boldness, Christ will be exalted now as always

in my body, whether by life or by death. 21 For to me, living is Christ and dying is gain. 22 If I am to live in the flesh, that means fruitful labor for me; and I do not know which I prefer. 23 I am hard pressed between the two: my desire is to depart and be with Christ, for that is far better; 24 but to remain in the flesh is more necessary for you. 25 Since I am convinced of this, I know that I will remain and continue with all of you for your progress and joy in faith, 26 so that I may share abundantly in your boasting in Christ Jesus when I come to you again.

27 Only, live your life in a manner worthy of the gospel of Christ, so that, whether I come and see you or am absent and hear about you, I will know that you are standing firm in one

---

a Other ancient authorities read *word of God*

1.1–2 Naming the sender(s) and recipient(s) at the beginning is typical of Paul's Letters and of ancient letters generally. **1.1** *Timothy* is co-sender of this Letter, as also of 2 Corinthians, 1 Thessalonians, and Philemon. Paul's characterization of himself and Timothy as *servants* (lit. "slaves") *of Christ* (see also 2.22) reflects his emphasis on Christ's lordship (see notes on 2.10; 2.11). *Philippi*, originally named for the Macedonian king Philip II, the father of Alexander the Great, was a Roman military colony whose official name was *Colonia Augusta Julia Philippensis*. It lay about ten miles inland from the port city of Neapolis on the major Roman road, the Via Egnatia, which crossed the Greek mainland from the Aegean Sea to the Adriatic, and was thoroughly Roman, given the presence of retired Roman soldiers and Roman civic institutions, including the imperial cult. The precise meaning of *bishops and deacons* cannot be determined; they were leaders of the Philippian church. **1.3–11** After the salutation Paul typically expresses his gratitude for the conduct of the recipients; here he is grateful for the support of all the Philippians—note the emphatic repetition of the word *all* in vv. 4, 7 (twice), 8. **1.4** *With joy,* the first of many expressions of joy and rejoicing, which introduces the consolatory aim of the Letter (see Introduction). **1.5** *Sharing in the gospel.* The partnership between Paul and the Philippians involved several gifts from them in support of his missionary work, both previously and now that he is in prison (see 4.15–18). **1.6** *The day of Jesus Christ* (see also v. 10; 2.16). Paul expects Christ's return to save believers from God's wrathful judgment (see also Rom 2.5, 15–16; 1 Cor 1.8; 2 Cor 1.14; 1 Thess 1.10). **1.10** *What is best,* an inadequate rendering of *ta diapheronta,* a Stoic notion that means "the things that matter" (see Introduction). **1.11** *Righteousness . . . Jesus Christ.* See note on 3.9.

1.12–18 Despite his imprisonment and the questionable motives of some other Christian missionaries, Paul is joyful because the cause of Christ is advanc-

ing. **1.13** *Imperial guard* renders the Greek *praitorion* (from the Latin *praetorium;* see text note g on p. 1992) as if Paul were in Rome. The word, however, can also refer to any provincial governor's residence (as in Acts 23.35) and thus does not necessarily identify the place of Paul's imprisonment (see Introduction; note on 4.22). **1.19–26** Paul turns from his general circumstances to his upcoming trial. **1.19** *This will turn out for my deliverance,* a quotation from Job 13.16. *Deliverance* (lit. "salvation"), probably only Paul's acquittal and release from prison, not his eternal salvation. **1.20** *Put to shame,* i.e., be forced to deny Christ. *Whether by life or by death* leads to vv. 21–26, in which Paul ponders his own death using concepts deriving from ancient discussions of suicide. **1.21** *Living is Christ,* a difficult expression probably meaning that Paul has no life apart from his obligations to Christ (see also 2 Cor 4.11; Gal 2.20). *Dying is gain,* by contrast, is quite clear; it is a virtual refrain in ancient discussions of suicide. Death is a gain over a life of trouble and affliction, as Paul's was at this time owing to imprisonment (v. 17), struggles (v. 30), sorrows (2.27), hunger, and privation (4.12). **1.22** *Prefer,* more likely "choose," for it is clear what Paul prefers, even he does not know what he will choose. **1.23** On Paul's *desire . . . to . . . be with Christ,* see 2 Cor 5.1–9. **1.24** The appeal to what is *necessary* is often found in Stoic discussions of suicide. **1.27–30** Paul turns from his situation to that of the Philippians with an exhortation to live a life worthy of the gospel. **1.27** *Live your life,* a bland rendering of a word that comes from the political arena and means "live as citizens," perhaps even "engage in politics" (see also 3.20); this connotation would not have been lost on the Philippians, some of whom, by residing in a Roman colony, would have possessed Roman citizenship. **1.27–28** Paul presents the communal life of the Philippian Christians in military terms, assuming the role of a general and speaking of their *standing firm* in the line of battle, *striving* (better

spirit, striving side by side with one mind for the faith of the gospel, 28and are in no way intimidated by your opponents. For them this is evidence of their destruction, but of your salvation. And this is God's doing. 29For he has graciously granted you the privilege not only of believing in Christ, but of suffering for him as well— 30since you are having the same struggle that you saw I had and now hear that I still have.

Imitating Christ's Humility

2 If then there is any encouragement in Christ, any consolation from love, any sharing in the Spirit, any compassion and sympathy, 2make my joy complete: be of the same mind, having the same love, being in full accord and of one mind. 3Do nothing from selfish ambition or conceit, but in humility regard others as better than yourselves. 4Let each of you look not to your own interests, but to the interests of others. 5Let the same mind be in you that was[a] in Christ Jesus,

6 who, though he was in the form of God,
did not regard equality with God
as something to be exploited,
7 but emptied himself,
taking the form of a slave,
being born in human likeness.

And being found in human form,
8 he humbled himself
and became obedient to the point of
death—
even death on a cross.

9 Therefore God also highly exalted him
and gave him the name
that is above every name,
10 so that at the name of Jesus
every knee should bend,
in heaven and on earth and under the
earth,
11 and every tongue should confess
that Jesus Christ is Lord,
to the glory of God the Father.

Shining as Lights in the World

12 Therefore, my beloved, just as you have always obeyed me, not only in my presence, but much more now in my absence, work out your own salvation with fear and trembling; 13for it is God who is at work in you, enabling you both to will and to work for his good pleasure.

14 Do all things without murmuring and arguing, 15so that you may be blameless and innocent, children of God without blemish in

a Or that you have

"fighting") *side by side, in no way intimidated* (better "terrified" or "spooked," as a horse might be in the din of battle) by their *opponents* (better "by those arrayed opposite them"). Military language is appropriate when writing to Christians in a military colony like Philippi, but Paul uses such language rather frequently (see Rom 12.21; 13.12; 1 Cor 15.57–58; 16.13; 2 Cor 2.14; 10.3–6; 1 Thess 5.8).

2.1–11 Exhortations to unity and humility, as illustrated by Christ's life. **2.4** There is good manuscript evidence for adding "also" after *but. Others,* lit. "one another"; the Philippian Christians are to show humility toward one another, not necessarily toward people in general. **2.6–11** These verses, as their format shows, are widely regarded as a Christ hymn that Paul quotes here. There are several references to Christians singing hymns (see Acts 16.25; 1 Cor 14.26; Eph 5.19; Col 3.16), and other Letters associated with Paul quote hymns or at least fragments of them (see Eph 5.14; Col 1.15–20; 1 Tim 3.16; 2 Tim 2.11–13). This hymn, after an introductory statement about the preexistent Christ (v. 6), contains two stanzas: the first (vv. 7–8) speaks of Christ's life and death in terms of the obedience and humiliation characteristic of slaves, and the second (vv. 9–11) speaks of his resurrection in terms of the status and deference accorded a master. **2.6** *In the form of God,* puzzling; it may refer to Christ's di-

vine nature or to his divine glory or status. In any event the expression contrasts with *the form of a slave* in v. 7. *Exploited* (lit. "seized," as in robbery) is likewise problematic, but it too has a contrasting expression later in the hymn: what Christ could have seized is, by virtue of his refusal to do so and his subsequent humiliation, given to him by God (v. 9). **2.7** *The form of a slave.* See note on 2.6. **2.8** *Obedient,* presumably to God. *Death on a cross* was a cruel form of punishment reserved for slaves, brigands, and others of little or no status. **2.9** *The name that is above every name* is either *Jesus* (see v. 10) or, more likely, *Lord,* which denotes his status and power (see v. 11). **2.10** *Every knee should bend* was probably a liturgical signal for the whole congregation to bow down in recognition of Christ's present status as *Lord* (v. 11). **2.11** The title *Lord* (lit. "master") for Christ is central to this Letter (see 1.2, 14; 2.19, 29; 3.8, 20; 4.1, 2, 4, 10, 23). The hymn, comparing the resurrected Christ to a master, probably envisages a slave master, although some scholars think it compares Christ to the master par excellence, namely, the Roman emperor.

2.12–18 The hymn (vv. 6–11) grounds Paul's further exhortations. **2.12** *Obeyed.* The obedience shown by Christ (v. 8) is now expected of the Philippians. **2.15** *Crooked and perverse generation* recalls Deut 32.5. *You shine like stars in the world* has the same meaning

the midst of a crooked and perverse generation, in which you shine like stars in the world. [16]It is by your holding fast to the word of life that I can boast on the day of Christ that I did not run in vain or labor in vain. [17]But even if I am being poured out as a libation over the sacrifice and the offering of your faith, I am glad and rejoice with all of you— [18]and in the same way you also must be glad and rejoice with me.

Timothy and Epaphroditus

[19] I hope in the Lord Jesus to send Timothy to you soon, so that I may be cheered by news of you. [20]I have no one like him who will be genuinely concerned for your welfare. [21]All of them are seeking their own interests, not those of Jesus Christ. [22]But Timothy's[a] worth you know, how like a son with a father he has served with me in the work of the gospel. [23]I hope therefore to send him as soon as I see how things go with me; [24]and I trust in the Lord that I will also come soon.

[25] Still, I think it necessary to send to you Epaphroditus—my brother and co-worker and fellow soldier, your messenger[b] and minister to my need; [26]for he has been longing for[c] all of you, and has been distressed because you heard that he was ill. [27]He was indeed so ill that he nearly died. But God had mercy on him, and not only on him but on me also, so that I would not have one sorrow after another. [28]I am the more eager to send him, therefore, in order that you may rejoice at see-

ing him again, and that I may be less anxious. [29]Welcome him then in the Lord with all joy, and honor such people, [30]because he came close to death for the work of Christ,[d] risking his life to make up for those services that you could not give me.

3 Finally, my brothers and sisters,[e] rejoice[f] in the Lord.

Breaking with the Past

To write the same things to you is not troublesome to me, and for you it is a safeguard.

[2] Beware of the dogs, beware of the evil workers, beware of those who mutilate the flesh![g] [3]For it is we who are the circumcision, who worship in the Spirit of God[h] and boast in Christ Jesus and have no confidence in the flesh— [4]even though I, too, have reason for confidence in the flesh.

If anyone else has reason to be confident in the flesh, I have more: [5]circumcised on the eighth day, a member of the people of Israel, of the tribe of Benjamin, a Hebrew born of Hebrews; as to the law, a Pharisee; [6]as to zeal, a persecutor of the church; as to righteousness under the law, blameless.

[7] Yet whatever gains I had, these I have come to regard as loss because of Christ. [8]More than that, I regard everything as loss

---

a Gk his   b Gk apostle   c Other ancient authorities read longing to see   d Other ancient authorities read of the Lord   e Gk my brothers   f Or farewell   g Gk the mutilation   h Other ancient authorities read worship God in spirit

---

as the more familiar "You are the light of the world" (Mt 5.14). **2.16** *Run in vain,* an athletic image, used also in Gal 2.2. For Paul's use of athletic imagery, see esp. 1 Cor 9.24–27. **2.17** *Poured out as a libation,* a vivid image from sacrificial ritual. After the god's portion of the victim had been offered, the fire on the altar flared up when the priest poured wine on the fire, sending the aroma of the sacrifice to heaven. Here, the Philippian Christians are the priests, their faith the sacrifice, and Paul's blood the libation. **2.19–30** Paul announces, by way of digression, the coming visits of Timothy and Epaphroditus to Philippi. **2.19** *Timothy* (see 1.1) was well known to the Philippians (Acts 16.3, 12; 19.22). He was one of Paul's closest associates, which explains why Paul calls him his *son* (v. 22; see also 1 Cor 4.17; 1 Thess 3.1–6). **2.23** *How things go with me,* the outcome of Paul's trial. **2.25** *Epaphroditus* is introduced lavishly with three terms relating him to Paul and two to the Philippians. He is unlikely to be the Epaphras (a shortened form of Epaphroditus) of Col 1.17; Philem 23. *Fellow soldier* carries forward the military metaphor (see note on 1.27–28). **2.28** The tense of the verb translated *send* indicates that Epaph-

roditus, unlike Timothy, is leaving right away and will carry the Letter on his return to Philippi. **3.1a** *Rejoice* (see 2.18) functions as a transition back to the theme of the Letter after the digression of 2.19–30.

3.1b–11 The tone of the Letter changes as Paul warns the Philippians of dangerous persons and ideas. **3.2** *Dogs,* a reproach commonly used by Jews of non-Jews (see Mk 7.27–28; Rev 22.15). *Those who mutilate the flesh* is a harsh rejection of the literal circumcision of Christians; see also Gal 5.12. **3.3** *The circumcision,* now used only metaphorically, applies to Christians (see Rom 2.25–29; Eph 2.11). **3.5** For the custom of being *circumcised on the eighth day* after birth, see Gen 17.12; 21.4; Lev 12.3; Lk 1.59; 2.21; Acts 7.8. On Paul's descent from *the tribe of Benjamin,* see Rom 11.1. To judge from the distinction between Hebrews and Hellenists in Acts 6.1, *a Hebrew born of Hebrews* is probably Paul's claim to knowledge of Hebrew (see Acts 21.40; 22.2–3; Gal 1.14). On Paul as a *Pharisee,* see Acts 23.6; 26.5. **3.6** On Paul as a *persecutor,* see Acts 8.3; 9.1, 21; 22.4; 26.10–11; 1 Cor 15.9; Gal 1.13, 23. **3.8** *Rubbish* (lit. "garbage" or "human excrement"), a strong rejection of what Paul had earlier counted as

because of the surpassing value of knowing Christ Jesus my Lord. For his sake I have suffered the loss of all things, and I regard them as rubbish, in order that I may gain Christ ⁹and be found in him, not having a righteousness of my own that comes from the law, but one that comes through faith in Christ,ᵃ the righteousness from God based on faith. ¹⁰I want to know Christᵇ and the power of his resurrection and the sharing of his sufferings by becoming like him in his death, ¹¹if somehow I may attain the resurrection from the dead.

Pressing toward the Goal

12 Not that I have already obtained this or have already reached the goal;ᶜ but I press on to make it my own, because Christ Jesus has made me his own. ¹³Beloved,ᵈ I do not consider that I have made it my own;ᵉ but this one thing I do: forgetting what lies behind and straining forward to what lies ahead, ¹⁴I press on toward the goal for the prize of the heavenlyᶠ call of God in Christ Jesus. ¹⁵Let those of us then who are mature be of the same mind; and if you think differently about anything, this too God will reveal to you. ¹⁶Only let us hold fast to what we have attained.

17 Brothers and sisters,ᵈ join in imitating me, and observe those who live according to the example you have in us. ¹⁸For many live as enemies of the cross of Christ; I have often told you of them, and now I tell you even with tears. ¹⁹Their end is destruction; their god is the belly; and their glory is in their shame; their minds are set on earthly things. ²⁰But our citizenshipᵍ is in heaven, and it is from there that we are expecting a Savior, the Lord Jesus Christ. ²¹He will transform the body of our humiliationʰ that it may be conformed to the body of his glory,ⁱ by the power that also enables him to make all things subject to himself.

4 ¹Therefore, my brothers and sisters,ʲ whom I love and long for, my joy and crown, stand firm in the Lord in this way, my beloved.

Exhortations

2 I urge Euodia and I urge Syntyche to be of the same mind in the Lord. ³Yes, and I ask you also, my loyal companion,ᵏ help these women, for they have struggled beside me in the work of the gospel, together with Clement and the rest of my co-workers, whose names are in the book of life.

4 Rejoiceˡ in the Lord always; again I will say, Rejoice.ˡ ⁵Let your gentleness be known to everyone. The Lord is near. ⁶Do not worry about anything, but in everything by prayer and supplication with thanksgiving let your requests be made known to God. ⁷And the peace of God, which surpasses all understanding, will guard your hearts and your minds in Christ Jesus.

8 Finally, beloved,ᵐ whatever is true, whatever is honorable, whatever is just, whatever is pure, whatever is pleasing, whatever is commendable, if there is any excellence and if there is anything worthy of praise, think aboutⁿ these things. ⁹Keep on doing the things that you have learned and received and heard and seen in me, and the God of peace will be with you.

Acknowledgment of the Philippians' Gift

10 I rejoiceᵒ in the Lord greatly that now at last you have revived your concern for me; indeed,

---

a Or *through the faith of Christ* *b* Gk *him* *c* Or *have already been made perfect* *d* Gk *Brothers* *e* Other ancient authorities read *my own yet* *f* Gk *upward* *g* Or *commonwealth* *h* Or *our humble bodies* *i* Or *his glorious body* *j* Gk *my brothers* *k* Or *loyal Syzygus* *l* Or *Farewell* *m* Gk *brothers* *n* Gk *take account of* *o* Gk *I rejoiced*

---

dear. **3.9** Paul rejects a *righteousness of my own that comes from the law*—whether the individual righteousness of fulfilling the law or the corporate righteousness of being a member of the Jewish people—in favor of a righteousness *that comes through faith in Christ* (see 1.11; see also Rom 1–8; Gal 1–3). **3.12–4.1** Paul calls on the Philippians to remain united and to imitate him. **3.12** *This* is not in the Greek, but some object must be supplied from the context—resurrection (v. 11) or righteousness (v. 9). **3.13–14** Paul describes his life as a Christian using the athletic metaphor of a sprinter who ignores *what lies behind* him and looks only *forward, straining* toward the finish line in order to win the *prize*; see also note on 2.16. **3.17** On Paul's churches *imitating* him, see 1 Cor 4.16; 11.1; 1 Thess 1.6. *Us*, probably not only Paul, but also Timothy and Epaphroditus. **4.2–9** Specific and general exhortations. **4.2** Paul's earlier exhortation to the Philippians to be in agreement (2.2) is now directed specifically to two women, *Euodia* and *Syntyche*. The nature of their dispute is not known. **4.3** *Companion* (Greek *syzygos*). The Greek word may be a proper name (see text note *k*); if not, the referent is unknown. *The book of life.* See Ex 32.32; Ps 69.28; Dan 12.1. **4.10–20** Paul has already referred briefly to the gifts he has received from the Philippi-

you were concerned for me, but had no opportunity to show it.[a] 11Not that I am referring to being in need; for I have learned to be content with whatever I have. 12I know what it is to have little, and I know what it is to have plenty. In any and all circumstances I have learned the secret of being well-fed and of going hungry, of having plenty and of being in need. 13I can do all things through him who strengthens me. 14In any case, it was kind of you to share my distress.

15 You Philippians indeed know that in the early days of the gospel, when I left Macedonia, no church shared with me in the matter of giving and receiving, except you alone. 16For even when I was in Thessalonica, you sent me help for my needs more than once. 17Not that I seek the gift, but I seek the profit that accumulates to your account. 18I have been paid in full and have more than enough; I am fully satisfied, now that I have received from Epaphroditus the gifts you sent, a fragrant offering, a sacrifice acceptable and pleasing to God. 19And my God will fully satisfy every need of yours according to his riches in glory in Christ Jesus. 20To our God and Father be glory forever and ever. Amen.

Final Greetings and Benediction

21 Greet every saint in Christ Jesus. The friends[b] who are with me greet you. 22All the saints greet you, especially those of the emperor's household.

23 The grace of the Lord Jesus Christ be with your spirit.[c]

---

a Gk lacks to show it   b Gk brothers   c Other ancient authorities add Amen

---

ans through Epaphroditus (1.5; 2.25). Now he offers his full and formal thanks, although these expressions of gratitude alternate with those expressing his independence and even his indifference to privation. **4.11** *Learned to be content.* Being satisfied with whatever one's circumstances are is another Stoic concept in this Letter. See note on 1.10. **4.12** *Learned the secret* (lit. "have been initiated") reflects the language of religious initiation into mystery cults with their secret rites and revelations. **4.16** On Paul *in Thessalonica,* see Acts 17.1–9; 1 Thess 2.1–12. **4.17** *Not that I seek the gift* captures Paul's desire to be as independent as possible, e.g., through supporting himself by tentmaking (Acts 18.3; 1 Cor 4.12; 2 Cor 11.7–11; 12.14–15), an independence made more difficult because of imprisonment. **4.18** *I have been paid in full,* a commercial expression used in receipts. *Epaphroditus.* See note on 2.25. *A fragrant offering . . . to God,* language drawn again from sacrificial ritual (see note on 2.17), but here Paul speaks as though he were the priest reporting on the efficacy of the Philippians' gift/sacrifice. **4.21–23** Brief greetings conclude the Letter, again typical of Paul's Letters and ancient letters generally. **4.22** *The emperor's household* has been seen as evidence that Paul's imprisonment was in Rome. But that household included more than the emperor and his family; it embraced any number of slaves, freedmen, and soldiers who served the emperor in Rome or in the provinces. Accordingly, this phrase says less about the place of Paul's imprisonment than about the ties some of the Philippians had to Rome and its administrative apparatus, owing to Philippi's status as a Roman military colony (see Introduction).

The Letter of Paul to the
COLOSSIANS

COLOSSIANS, WHICH PURPORTS to be a Letter from Paul, was written to deal with a controversy that had developed in a gentile congregation (2.13) established not by Paul but probably by Epaphras (1.7–8; 2.1). Challenges to Pauline authorship of Colossians abound, for substantial reasons. Colossians makes claims that are not supported by the unquestionably authentic Letters (Romans, 1 and 2 Corinthians, Galatians, Philippians, 1 Thessalonians, and Philemon). Colossians asserts that believers already share Christ's resurrection (2.12–13; 3.1), while Paul scrupulously affirms that believers have died with Christ but have not yet been raised with him. Colossians states that Christ is the head of the church, his body, while Paul never extends the metaphor in that fashion (cf. Rom 12.4–5; 1 Cor 12.12–27). Colossians also says that through Christ there is "forgiveness of sins" (1.14; 2.13; 3.13), whereas Paul writes of freedom from sin defined in the singular and as a power. And Colossians, like Ephesians, but unlike the undisputed Pauline Letters, is composed of long, complex sentences that the NRSV breaks into shorter segments for clarity.

The Letter's strongest literary ties are with Ephesians, with which it shares various expressions (e.g., "fullness of God," Col 1.19; 2.9; Eph 1.23; 3.19), concepts (e.g., Christ's authority over rival powers, Col 2.10; Eph 1.21–22, and his headship over the church, 1.18; Eph 1.22), and tables of household admonitions (Col 3.18–4.1; Eph 5.21–6.9). Colossians has affinities with other documents of the late first century CE as well, sharing with them such concepts as the idea of Christ as the beginning or origin of creation (1.16, 18; see Heb 1.10; Rev 3.14), seated alongside God (3.1; see Acts 2.33–34; Heb 1.3, 13; 8.1; 10.12; 12.2; Rev 3.21), and the contrast between shadow and reality (2.17; see Heb 8.5; 10.1).

The Controversy

AT THE HEART OF COLOSSIANS is a christological dispute over whether what has already been accomplished in Christ has actually and completely liberated the believers from the powers of the universe and given them proper access to God. The opponents, whose position the author scornfully portrays as deceitful "philosophy" (2.8), seem to be urging asceticism (perhaps in order to achieve visions, 2.18), observance of special holy times (2.16), and worship of celestial powers (2.18) as means of gaining wisdom (2.23) and access to God.

By appealing to tradition (chiefly the Christ hymn of 1.15–20) and to the readers' clear experience of a new, full life in Christ inaugurated in their baptism, the author disputes the need for requirements beyond the "Christ in you" (1.27) that they already know. The author calls on the readers to show endurance and steadfastness while they live in a fashion appropriate to what they have already received. The Letter details the comportment appropriate to their status in Christ.

Baptism and the readers' experience of it ground the argument. Baptism is analogous to burial and resurrection (2.12–14; the death and rebirth motifs are developed in alternating paragraphs beginning in 2.20); it is a special circumcision (cf. Gen 17.9–14), signifying incorporation into a new body, God's people (2.11–14). With its disrobing and reclothing, baptism requires that believers "put off" their former way of life and "put on" a new and appropriate one (3.9–12).

The sufficiency of what believers have already received is affirmed throughout the Letter as a way of undermining the opponents' demand that they add special practices to support the adequacy of their standing before God. Accordingly we see a recurrent emphasis on "fullness" and "completeness" (1.19, 24; 2.3, 9–10), on what the Colossians already possess, including resurrection with Christ (2.12) and enthronement with God and Christ in the heavenly places (3.1–3). They already share in the riches (2.2), treasures (2.3), and inheritance (1.12) and are assured that they are already insiders, admitted to the previously hidden mystery of God that is "Christ himself" (1.26; 2.2).

The Christ hymn (1.15–20) is the bulwark of the Letter and its strains reverberate in later passages. Whether the opponents also used it to their ends is not clear. It buttresses several of the author's claims: Christ's close relationship to God (1.15, 19; 2.9); Christ's role in creating all things, including the celestial powers (1.16; 3.10); Christ's authority over the body (1.18; 2.19); and Christ's role in God's reconciling work (1.20; 3.11).

The Letter's recurrent wisdom terminology (1.9–10, 28; 2.2–3, 23; 3.10, 16; 4.5) reflects the dispute at its center. The author clings closely to tradition as an authority and to Christ as the means of access to wisdom, while the opponents, borrowing from various religious currents of the time, feature visions and special relationship to angels as the avenue to wisdom. While Paul was alive, he combined both tradition and visions (see 1 Cor 15.3–11; 2 Cor 12.1–5); the Pauline school, as represented in Colossians, has retained the former, but not the latter.

As a rhetorical strategy vilification is an ancient practice. The author does not aim for fairness but for triumph, so his opponents' positions are caricatured to his advantage. Accordingly any attempt to identify the opponents must at best be provisional and reserved.

Date and Place of Writing

THE DATE AND PLACE OF WRITING cannot be determined with certainty. Paul is portrayed as imprisoned (4.3, 10, 18; cf. Phil 1.12–14; Philem 1, 13, 23), but, as this document is probably by a follower writing after Paul's death, some date after the mid-60s CE must be supposed. In any case, Colossians was written at a post-Pauline time when women's roles were diminished (3.18; see also note on 3.11) and when relationships within the household were once again accommodated to the wider culture (3.18–4.1). [J. PAUL SAMPLEY]

Salutation

1 Paul, an apostle of Christ Jesus by the will of God, and Timothy our brother,

2 To the saints and faithful brothers and sisters[a] in Christ in Colossae:

Grace to you and peace from God our Father.

Paul Thanks God for the Colossians

3 In our prayers for you we always thank God, the Father of our Lord Jesus Christ, 4for we have heard of your faith in Christ Jesus and of the love that you have for all the saints, 5because of the hope laid up for you in heaven. You have heard of this hope before in the word of the truth, the gospel 6that has come to you. Just as it is bearing fruit and growing in the whole world, so it has been bearing fruit among yourselves from the day you heard it and truly comprehended the grace of God. 7This you learned from Epaphras, our beloved fellow servant.[b] He is a faithful minister of Christ on your[c] behalf, 8and he has made known to us your love in the Spirit.

9 For this reason, since the day we heard it, we have not ceased praying for you and asking that you may be filled with the knowledge of God's[d] will in all spiritual wisdom and understanding, 10so that you may lead lives worthy of the Lord, fully pleasing to him, as you bear fruit in every good work and as you grow in the knowledge of God. 11May you be made strong with all the strength that comes from his glorious power, and may you be prepared to endure everything with patience, while joyfully 12giving thanks to the Father, who has enabled[e] you[f] to share in the inheritance of the saints in the light. 13He has rescued us from the power of darkness and transferred us into the kingdom of his beloved Son, 14in whom we have redemption, the forgiveness of sins.[g]

The Supremacy of Christ

15 He is the image of the invisible God, the firstborn of all creation; 16for in[h] him all things in heaven and on earth were created, things visible and invisible, whether thrones or dominions or rulers or powers—all things have been created through him and for him. 17He himself is before all things, and in[h] him all things hold together. 18He is the head of the

a Gk brothers   b Gk slave   c Other ancient authorities read our   d Gk his   e Other ancient authorities read called   f Other ancient authorities read us   g Other ancient authorities add through his blood   h Or by

1.1–2 These verses formally resemble most Pauline Letter openings. **1.1** For Paul's self-designation as an *apostle,* see 2 Cor 1.1; Gal 1.1; Eph 1.1. **1.2** *Saints* (lit. "holy ones"; see also v. 22; 3.12), all believers, those who have been set apart for God and have an *inheritance* (v. 12). The designation of God as *Father* (see v. 12; 3.17) is consistent with the importance of the household in this Letter (see 3.18–4.1) and with the Pauline tradition (see, e.g., each of the Letter openings). **1.3–14** The thanksgiving, a feature of most Pauline Letters. **1.4–5** For the triad of *faith, love,* and *hope,* see 1 Cor 13.13; 1 Thess 1.3; 5.8. **1.4** See Eph 1.15. **1.5** Colossians emphasizes spatial concepts like *heaven* (see also vv. 16, 20; 3.1, 2, 5) instead of temporal ones like the "day of Jesus Christ" (Phil 1.6). **1.6** On *bearing fruit* (see also Mt 7.16–20; Rom 7.4–5) and *growing,* see v. 10; 2.19. **1.7** *Epaphras* was probably the founder of this church; see 4.12–13; Philem 23. **1.9** *Being filled* and coming to fullness (see also vv. 19, 25; 2.9–10) are ambivalent: the believers *have come to fullness in* Christ (2.10), yet here the author prays that they *may be filled* with proper wisdom. **1.10** *Lead lives worthy,* lit. "walk worthily," meaning conduct one's life appropriately. See also 2.6; 3.7–17; 4.5. **1.11** *His glorious power,* lit. "the power of his glory." Cf. the rival power in v. 13. **1.12** *Light* and darkness are ancient scriptural categories (Gen 1.4; Isa 42.16; Lam 3.2) that in the NT and the Dead Sea Scrolls designate opposing apocalyptic forces (1.13; 2 Cor 6.14; Eph 5.8; 1 Thess

5.5). **1.13** *The power of darkness,* the evil forces that bid to control the universe and worldly affairs, but whose ultimate defeat lies already in the crucifixion (2.15, 20). *Kingdom of his . . . Son.* Cf. 4.11; 1 Cor 15.24. **1.14** *Redemption,* the buying back of a slave or the freeing of a prisoner by ransom. See Rom 3.24; Eph 1.7, 14; 4.30. *Forgiveness of sins.* See 2.13; 3.13; Eph 1.7. In the undisputed Letters Paul views sin as an enslaving power, not a misdeed (see Rom 5.12; Gal 3.22).

1.15–23 A hymn, redolent with liturgical overtones, about Christ, followed by the author's application. The hymn (vv. 15–20), echoed in later parts of the Letter, is the heart of the author's argument. **1.15** On Christ as the *image* of God, see 2 Cor 3.18; 4.4; see also Phil 2.6; Heb 1.3. Describing God as *invisible* (see Jn 1.18; 1 Tim 1.17; Heb 11.27) was common in Hellenistic writings. *Firstborn of all creation.* See also Rom 8.29; Rev 3.14. Similar claims are made about Wisdom; see Prov 8.22–26; Sir 24.9. **1.16** The affirmation of Christ's active role in *creation* (see also Rom 11.36; 1 Cor 8.6; Heb. 1.2) corresponds to assertions made about Wisdom (Prov 8.27–30) and about the Word (Jn 1.1–3). *Thrones . . . powers,* either earthly or cosmic powers, or both; see also 2.10; Rom 8.38; 1 Cor 15.24; Eph 1.21; cf. Rev 2.13. In either case, the statement would have had political overtones. **1.18** On Christ as *head of the body, the church,* see 2.19; Eph 1.22–23. This precise image appears nowhere in the unquestionably authentic Pauline Letters (cf. Rom 12.5; 1 Cor 12.12). *Firstborn*

body, the church; he is the beginning, the first-born from the dead, so that he might come to have first place in everything. [19]For in him all the fullness of God was pleased to dwell, [20]and through him God was pleased to reconcile to himself all things, whether on earth or in heaven, by making peace through the blood of his cross.

21 And you who were once estranged and hostile in mind, doing evil deeds, [22]he has now reconciled[a] in his fleshly body[b] through death, so as to present you holy and blameless and irreproachable before him— [23]provided that you continue securely established and steadfast in the faith, without shifting from the hope promised by the gospel that you heard, which has been proclaimed to every creature under heaven. I, Paul, became a servant of this gospel.

Paul's Interest in the Colossians

24 I am now rejoicing in my sufferings for your sake, and in my flesh I am completing what is lacking in Christ's afflictions for the sake of his body, that is, the church. [25]I became its servant according to God's commission that was given to me for you, to make the word of God fully known, [26]the mystery that has been hidden throughout the ages and generations but has now been revealed to his saints. [27]To them God chose to make known how great among the Gentiles are the riches of the glory of this mystery, which is Christ in you, the hope of glory. [28]It is he whom we proclaim, warning everyone and teaching everyone in all wisdom, so that we may present everyone mature in Christ. [29]For this I toil and struggle with all the energy that he powerfully inspires within me.

2 For I want you to know how much I am struggling for you, and for those in Laodicea, and for all who have not seen me face to face. [2]I want their hearts to be encouraged and

---

a Other ancient authorities read *you have now been reconciled*
b Gk *in the body of his flesh*

---

from the dead, a reference to the resurrection. See Rev 1.5; cf. Rom 8.29; 1 Cor 15.20, 23. **1.19** The *fullness of God* that dwells in Christ (reaffirmed in 2.9; see also Eph 1.23; 4.10; cf. Jn 1.16) is available in him for all believers (see 2.10). **1.20** An expression of the author's confidence in *reconciliation* as a present reality. On Christ as its means, see 2 Cor 5.19; Eph 2.13–22. **1.22** *Present,* a technical term for bringing a sacrifice to an altar (see Rom 12.1) or an accused person before a judge (see 1.28). The same point, but with the image of a betrothal, is made in 2 Cor 11.2. **1.24–2.5** These verses establish Paul's trustworthiness and commitment to Christ and to the Colossians. **1.24** *Rejoicing in . . . sufferings.* See Rom 5.2–5; 2 Cor 6.9–10; Phil 1.12–18. *Completing . . . Christ's afflictions.* Believers' hardships and sufferings are seen as extensions of Christ's crucifixion; cf. 2 Cor 1.5. **1.27** On Gentiles' inclusion, see Eph 3.6. *Mystery, which is Christ in you* (see note on 2.2) refers to Christ's presence in the church because the *you* is plural (see Rom 8.10; 2 Cor 13.5; Gal 4.19; in each case the plural "you" implies a community rather than an individual). This present reality is the basis for the *hope of glory* in the future (see also Rom 5.2; 8.18). **1.28** *Warning* anticipates the author's treatment of the opponents in 2.4–23. *Mature,* i.e., complete, unshakable. See 4.12; Eph 4.13–14. **2.1** *Struggling* has the semantic range of "conflict," "fear," "care." The church at Colossae seems to have had strong ties with *Laodicea,* ten miles west; see 4.13–16. **2.2** *United,* rendered *held together* in v. 19. Here *Christ himself* is the content of

The cities of the Lycus Valley were important centers of Pauline Christianity. A special relation between churches at Laodicea and Colossae is suggested by Col 4.16.

united in love, so that they may have all the riches of assured understanding and have the knowledge of God's mystery, that is, Christ himself,[a] [3]in whom are hidden all the treasures of wisdom and knowledge. [4]I am saying this so that no one may deceive you with plausible arguments. [5]For though I am absent in body, yet I am with you in spirit, and I rejoice to see your morale and the firmness of your faith in Christ.

Fullness of Life in Christ

[6] As you therefore have received Christ Jesus the Lord, continue to live your lives[b] in him, [7]rooted and built up in him and established in the faith, just as you were taught, abounding in thanksgiving.

[8] See to it that no one takes you captive through philosophy and empty deceit, according to human tradition, according to the elemental spirits of the universe,[c] and not according to Christ. [9]For in him the whole fullness of deity dwells bodily, [10]and you have come to fullness in him, who is the head of every ruler and authority. [11]In him also you were circumcised with a spiritual circumcision,[d] by putting off the body of the flesh in the circumcision of Christ; [12]when you were

buried with him in baptism, you were also raised with him through faith in the power of God, who raised him from the dead. [13]And when you were dead in trespasses and the uncircumcision of your flesh, God[e] made you[f] alive together with him, when he forgave us all our trespasses, [14]erasing the record that stood against us with its legal demands. He set this aside, nailing it to the cross. [15]He disarmed[g] the rulers and authorities and made a public example of them, triumphing over them in it.

[16] Therefore do not let anyone condemn you in matters of food and drink or of observing festivals, new moons, or sabbaths. [17]These are only a shadow of what is to come, but the substance belongs to Christ. [18]Do not let anyone disqualify you, insisting on self-abasement and worship of angels, dwelling[h] on visions,[i] puffed up without cause by a human way of thinking,[j] [19]and not holding fast to the head, from whom the whole body, nourished and held together by its ligaments and sinews, grows with a growth that is from God.

a Other ancient authorities read *of the mystery of God, both of the Father and of Christ* *b* Gk *to walk* *c* Or *the rudiments of the world* *d* Gk *a circumcision made without hands* *e* Gk *he* *f* Other ancient authorities read *made us*; others, *made* *g* Or *divested himself of* *h* Other ancient authorities read *not dwelling* *i* Meaning of Gk uncertain *j* Gk *by the mind of his flesh*

the *mystery;* in 1.27 it is *Christ in you.* **2.4** The emphasis on *wisdom and knowledge* in vv. 2–3 suggests that the false but *plausible arguments* of the opponents have these as their goal as well; see v. 8; see also 1 Cor 1.18–2.5. **2.5** *Morale,* lit. "(good) order." See 1 Cor 14.40.

2.6–19 The proper grounding in Christ versus the opponents' *empty* demands. **2.8** *Philosophy and empty deceit* (see v. 4) is used to describe false teaching based on *human tradition* and on the erroneous assumption that power resides in the *elemental spirits of the universe.* This last phrase refers to the widespread Greco-Roman notion that the universe is composed of celestial powers that rule life; see 1.13, 16; 2.20; Gal 4.3. **2.9** *Fullness of deity.* See note on 1.19. **2.10** *You have come to fullness in him,* an emphatic identification of believers with Christ and therefore with his dominion over *every ruler and authority* (see v. 15; Eph 1.21–22). **2.11** *Circumcision,* the Jewish rite of inclusion in God's people, here a metaphor for the crucifixion and the believers' participation in it through baptism (cf. Rom 2.28–29; Phil 3.3). At baptism (see v. 12), new believers *put off* their old garments and afterwards were clothed in new ones; see also 3.9–10; Eph 4.22–24. **2.12** On baptism as *burial,* see Rom 6.3–5. Nowhere in the undisputed Pauline Letters are believers described as already *raised.* See 3.1; Eph 2.6; cf. Rom 6.3–5; 1 Cor 15.22–23; Phil 3.10–11. The evidence offered for the

power of God is Christ's resurrection. **2.13–15** Peace (cf. 3.15) won by military victory, with political implications for contemporary imperial aims. **2.13** *Uncircumcision of your flesh* identifies the audience as gentile; see 1.27. **2.14** *Record,* possibly a certificate of indebtedness or bond. *Legal demands,* lit. "requirements." There is no explicit reference to Israel's law here. **2.15** The image is of a triumphal military procession in which the conqueror leads the defeated powers (see 1.13; 2.10), publicly disgracing them. *Triumphing,* leading in triumph. See 2 Cor 2.14. *In it* refers to the cross (v. 14), but the Greek could be translated "in him," referring to Christ (see vv. 9–10). **2.16–23** These verses offer some insight into the opponents' requirements.

2.16 On *festivals, new moons, or sabbaths* as required observances, see Ezek 45.17. **2.18** *Disqualify you,* rob you of your prize (cf. *condemn you* in v. 16). Beyond a relationship to Christ, the opponents require *self-abasement,* i.e., through ascetic practices (see vv. 21, 23), and the *worship of angels,* which suggests either that angels could perform an intermediary function beyond what Christ offered or that self-mortification could grant access to worship *with* the angels. *Dwelling on visions,* a difficult phrase, possibly "the things seen when one entered [heaven? a place of oracles?]." *Human way of thinking,* an ironic put-down of the opponents' claims. **2.19** *Head,* a reference, through v. 10,

Warnings against False Teachers

20 If with Christ you died to the elemental spirits of the universe,[a] why do you live as if you still belonged to the world? Why do you submit to regulations, 21"Do not handle, Do not taste, Do not touch"? 22All these regulations refer to things that perish with use; they are simply human commands and teachings. 23These have indeed an appearance of wisdom in promoting self-imposed piety, humility, and severe treatment of the body, but they are of no value in checking self-indulgence.[b]

The New Life in Christ

3 So if you have been raised with Christ, seek the things that are above, where Christ is, seated at the right hand of God. 2Set your minds on things that are above, not on things that are on earth, 3for you have died, and your life is hidden with Christ in God. 4When Christ who is your[c] life is revealed, then you also will be revealed with him in glory.

5 Put to death, therefore, whatever in you is earthly: fornication, impurity, passion, evil desire, and greed (which is idolatry). 6On account of these the wrath of God is coming on those who are disobedient.[d] 7These are the ways you also once followed, when you were living that life.[e] 8But now you must get rid of all such things—anger, wrath, malice, slander, and abusive[f] language from your mouth. 9Do not lie to one another, seeing that you have stripped off the old self with its practices 10and have clothed yourselves with the new self, which is being renewed in knowledge according to the image of its creator. 11In that renewal[g] there is no longer Greek and Jew, circumcised and uncircumcised, barbarian, Scythian, slave and free; but Christ is all and in all!

12 As God's chosen ones, holy and beloved, clothe yourselves with compassion, kindness, humility, meekness, and patience. 13Bear with one another and, if anyone has a complaint against another, forgive each other; just as the Lord[h] has forgiven you, so you also must forgive. 14Above all, clothe yourselves with love, which binds everything together in perfect harmony. 15And let the peace of Christ rule in your hearts, to which indeed you were called in the one body. And be thankful. 16Let the word of Christ[i] dwell in you richly; teach and admonish one another in all wisdom; and with gratitude in your hearts sing psalms, hymns, and spiritual songs to God.[j] 17And whatever you do, in word or deed, do everything in the name of the Lord Jesus, giving thanks to God the Father through him.

Rules for Christian Households

18 Wives, be subject to your husbands, as is fitting in the Lord. 19Husbands, love your wives and never treat them harshly.

20 Children, obey your parents in every-

---

a Or *the rudiments of the world*   *b* Or *are of no value, serving only to indulge the flesh*   *c* Other authorities read *our*   *d* Other ancient authorities lack *on those who are disobedient* (Gk *the children of disobedience*)   *e* Or *living among such people*   *f* Or *filthy*   *g* Gk *its creator,* 11*where*   *h* Other ancient authorities read *just as Christ*   *i* Other ancient authorities read *of God,* or *of the Lord*   *j* Other ancient authorities read *to the Lord*

---

to the Christ hymn (see 1.18). *Growth.* See 1.6, 10. **2.20–23** The last explicit mention of the opponents and their teachings. **2.20** *If with Christ you died,* with reference to a present reality. **2.21** *Do not . . . touch,* regulations for self-abasement; see vv. 18, 23. **2.23** *Severe treatment of the body,* the ascetic rigors prescribed by the opponents as requisite to true piety (see vv. 16, 21).

3.1–17 How the readers should orient themselves and behave in light of their resurrection with Christ (see 2.12). **3.1** *At the right hand of God,* an echo of Ps 110.1. **3.4** For Christ as *life,* see Gal 2.20. On Christ and believers being *revealed* in the fullness of time, see Lk 17.30; Rom 8.19; 1 Jn 3.2. **3.5** Vice lists were a commonplace means of exhortation; see Rom 1.29–31; Gal 5.19–21. **3.6** On the *wrath of God,* an apocalyptic concept, see Rom 1.18; 2.5, 8; 3.5; Eph 5.6; see also Mt 3.7. **3.8–14** The language of disrobing (*get rid of, stripped off*) and being *clothed,* associated with baptism (see note on 2.11), is here applied to ethical behavior.

3.10 *Image of its creator,* i.e., the image of Christ. See 1.15; see also 2 Cor 4.4. **3.11** *No longer Greek . . . free,* a revised version of the baptismal formula in Gal 3.28. Missing is any reference to male and female (see also 1 Cor 12.13; cf. Col 3.18–19). *Scythians,* an ancient nomadic people widely viewed as the ultimate barbarians. **3.13** *Forgive . . . as the Lord has forgiven you,* in imitation of Christ. See 2.13; Eph 4.32; see also Mt 6.14. **3.15** *Called* has the same meaning as *chosen* in v. 12. **3.16** Believers are to *teach* each other as the author has taught them; see 1.28. *Singing psalms . . . and . . . songs.* See 1 Cor 14.26; Eph 5.19. **3.17** *Giving thanks.* See 1.12; see also Eph 5.20. **3.18–4.1** Guidelines for comportment within the household. **3.18** On the exhortation *Wives, be subject to your husbands,* a common notion in the Greco-Roman world, see 1 Cor 14.34; Eph 5.21, 22; Titus 2.3–5; 1 Pet 3.1–6; cf. 1 Cor 7.3–4; Gal 3.28. **3.19** On *love* for *wives,* see Eph 5.25; cf. 1 Pet 3.7. **3.20–21** On *children* and *fathers,* see Eph 6.1–4.

thing, for this is your acceptable duty in the Lord. [21] Fathers, do not provoke your children, or they may lose heart. [22] Slaves, obey your earthly masters[a] in everything, not only while being watched and in order to please them, but wholeheartedly, fearing the Lord.[a] [23] Whatever your task, put yourselves into it, as done for the Lord and not for your masters,[b] [24] since you know that from the Lord you will receive the inheritance as your reward; you serve[c] the Lord Christ. [25] For the wrongdoer will be paid back for whatever wrong has been done, and there is no partiality. [4] [1] Masters, treat your slaves justly and fairly, for you know that you also have a Master in heaven.

Further Instructions

[2] Devote yourselves to prayer, keeping alert in it with thanksgiving. [3] At the same time pray for us as well that God will open to us a door for the word, that we may declare the mystery of Christ, for which I am in prison, [4] so that I may reveal it clearly, as I should.

[5] Conduct yourselves wisely toward outsiders, making the most of the time.[d] [6] Let your speech always be gracious, seasoned with salt, so that you may know how you ought to answer everyone.

Final Greetings and Benediction

[7] Tychicus will tell you all the news about me; he is a beloved brother, a faithful minister, and a fellow servant[e] in the Lord. [8] I have sent him to you for this very purpose, so that you may know how we are[f] and that he may encourage your hearts; [9] he is coming with Onesimus, the faithful and beloved brother, who is one of you. They will tell you about everything here.

[10] Aristarchus my fellow prisoner greets you, as does Mark the cousin of Barnabas, concerning whom you have received instructions—if he comes to you, welcome him. [11] And Jesus who is called Justus greets you. These are the only ones of the circumcision among my co-workers for the kingdom of God, and they have been a comfort to me. [12] Epaphras, who is one of you, a servant[e] of Christ Jesus, greets you. He is always wrestling in his prayers on your behalf, so that you may stand mature and fully assured in everything that God wills. [13] For I testify for him that he has worked hard for you and for those in Laodicea and in Hierapolis. [14] Luke, the beloved physician, and Demas greet you. [15] Give my greetings to the brothers and sisters[g] in Laodicea, and to Nympha and the church in her house. [16] And when this letter has been read among you, have it read also in the church of the Laodiceans; and see that you read also the letter from Laodicea. [17] And say to Archippus, "See that you complete the task that you have received in the Lord."

[18] I, Paul, write this greeting with my own hand. Remember my chains. Grace be with you.[h]

---

a In Greek the same word is used for *master* and *Lord*
b Gk *not for men* c Or *you are slaves of,* or *be slaves of*
d Or *opportunity* e Gk *slave* f Other authorities read *that I may know how you are* g Gk *brothers* h Other ancient authorities add *Amen*

3.22–25 *Slaves* are also admonished in Eph 6.5–8; 1 Tim 6.1–2; Titus 2.9–10; 1 Pet 2.18–25; cf. 1 Cor 7.21–24. 3.25 On *no partiality,* see Eph 6.9; see also Rom 2.11; 3.22; 10.12. 4.1 On the just treatment of slaves by their *masters,* see Lev 25.43, 53; Eph 6.9.

4.2–6 Concluding admonitions. 4.2 On *prayer,* see 1.9; 4.3, 12. On *thanksgiving,* see 1.12; 2.7; 3.17. 4.3 *Mystery of Christ.* See 1.27; 2.2. *In prison.* It is not known which of Paul's many imprisonments is meant here; see vv. 10, 18; see also 2 Cor 6.5; 11.23. 4.5 On *making the most of the time,* see Eph 5.16. 4.6 If *seasoned with salt* is an echo of Ex 30.35, then all *speech* should be a thank offering to God. On *answering* the

questions of outsiders, see 1 Pet 3.15. 4.7–18 Greetings and instructions. 4.7 On the commendation of *Tychicus,* see Eph 6.21–22; see also Acts 20.4; 2 Tim 4.12; Titus 3.12. 4.9 On *Onesimus,* a Colossian, see Philem 10. 4.10–14 See Philem 23–24 for many of the same names. 4.11 *Kingdom of God.* Cf. 1.13; Eph 5.5. 4.12 On *standing* firm, see Eph 6.11–14. On *mature* status, see note on 1.28. 4.16 *Letter from Laodicea,* i.e., a letter from Paul to the Laodiceans, sent by them to Colossae; nothing is known of this letter. 4.18 Letters in antiquity were often dictated to a scribe (see Rom 16.22), but the author might append a *greeting* in his *own hand* (see 1 Cor 16.21; Gal 6.11).

The First Letter of Paul to the
THESSALONIANS

PAUL WROTE 1 THESSALONIANS, the oldest book in the NT, to the church in Thessalonica, a port located on the northern shore of the Aegean Sea. This city was the capital of the Roman province of Macedonia and was devoted to the imperial cult of Rome, but culturally it remained a Greek city governed by Greek law. Its location on the Via Egnatia, which ran from Byzantium to the Adriatic Sea, together with its commerce ensured commercial prosperity.

Circumstances of the Letter

AFTER A BAD EXPERIENCE in Philippi (2.2; Acts 16.11–40), Paul, Silvanus, and Timothy came to Thessalonica. Soon after they founded a church there, intense opposition from the Jewish community forced them to leave (Acts 17.1–10). They went on to Beroea, where Silvanus (called "Silas" in Acts) and Timothy stayed while Paul journeyed on to Athens (Acts 17.10–15). When Timothy joined Paul in Athens, Paul immediately sent him back to Thessalonica for information about the church (3.1–2) and then went on to Corinth, where Timothy and Silvanus met him later (Acts 18.1–5). Timothy reported favorably about the life of the community (3.6–7) but also, it seems, brought news of anxiety over Paul's failure to return (2.17–18).

Timothy's report stimulated Paul to write 1 Thessalonians from Corinth about 51 CE. In the Letter Paul responds to the Thessalonians' anxiety by reviewing his initial reception there (1.2–10) and his ongoing concern for the church (2.1–3.13). He reinforces his original teaching by describing how Christians should live in the face of the imminent return of Jesus the Lord (4.1–5.11) and how they should strengthen one another in their life together (5.12–22).

Authenticity and Integrity

ALTHOUGH NO SCHOLAR DOUBTS that Paul wrote 1 Thessalonians, a few argue that it contains fragments from two or three letters. Many regard 2.14–16 as a later insertion because of its severe language about Jewish persecution of Christians in Judea when there is little other evidence for such persecution. Scholars defending Paul's authorship of these verses argue that they reflect the tense situation described in Acts 17.5–13. If Paul wrote these verses, however, he later modified his position (see Rom 9.3–5; 11.17–31).

Stylistic Features and Significance

THE LETTER IS PASTORAL, warm in tone, and affectionate throughout. There is no evidence of disunity or theological debate in the community. The praise in 1.6–8 is unequaled in Paul's other Letters. Aware of the Thessalonians' Greek culture, Paul draws on language from Greek philosophy to discuss issues treated by many Greek writers: marriage, community life, engagement in civil life.

Some features are unique to this Letter. Because the Thessalonian converts were not Jewish, Paul does not refer explicitly (except in 2.14–16) to Judaism, to problems affecting Jewish Christians (e.g., Mosaic law), or to any OT person, institution, or event (e.g., Abraham, Moses, the temple, or sacrifice). He also does not quote the OT, though it often lies behind his language or thought, for Paul's Jewish heritage shaped him decisively. He names the recipients "Thessalonians," using the term for citizens of the city, a form of address repeated only in 2 Thessalonians.

1 Thessalonians gives us our earliest insight into Paul's missionary activity and continuing concern for his congregations. It reveals problems early Christians faced living in Greek society and lets us see the inner life of the early church. [EDGAR M. KRENTZ]

The first Christian groups established by Paul in Europe were at Philippi and Thessalonica. From there he traveled south through Beroea (Acts 17.10–15) to Athens (1 Thess 2.2–3.1) and finally to Corinth.

Salutation

1 Paul, Silvanus, and Timothy,
To the church of the Thessalonians in God the Father and the Lord Jesus Christ:
Grace to you and peace.

The Thessalonians' Faith and Example

2 We always give thanks to God for all of you and mention you in our prayers, constantly [3]remembering before our God and Father your work of faith and labor of love and steadfastness of hope in our Lord Jesus Christ. [4]For we know, brothers and sisters[a] beloved by God, that he has chosen you, [5]because our message of the gospel came to you not in word only, but also in power and in the Holy Spirit and with full conviction; just as you know what kind of persons we proved to be among you for your sake. [6]And you became imitators of us and of the Lord, for in spite of persecution you received the word with joy inspired by the Holy Spirit, [7]so that you became an example to all the believers in Macedonia and in Achaia. [8]For the word of the Lord has sounded forth from you not only in Macedonia and Achaia, but in every place your faith in God

has become known, so that we have no need to speak about it. [9]For the people of those regions[b] report about us what kind of welcome we had among you, and how you turned to God from idols, to serve a living and true God, [10]and to wait for his Son from heaven, whom he raised from the dead—Jesus, who rescues us from the wrath that is coming.

Paul's Ministry in Thessalonica

2 You yourselves know, brothers and sisters,[a] that our coming to you was not in vain, [2]but though we had already suffered and been shamefully mistreated at Philippi, as you know, we had courage in our God to declare to you the gospel of God in spite of great opposition. [3]For our appeal does not spring from deceit or impure motives or trickery, [4]but just as we have been approved by God to be entrusted with the message of the gospel, even so we speak, not to please mortals, but to please God who tests our hearts. [5]As you know and as God is our witness, we never came with words of flattery or with a pretext for greed; [6]nor did we seek praise from mortals, whether from

a Gk brothers   b Gk For they

1.1 A typical ancient letter opening with Christian modifications (see Rom 1.1–7). Formally there are three senders; *Paul*, however, is the writer, as 3.1 makes clear. *Silvanus* ("Silas" in Acts) and *Timothy* were trusted co-workers (see Acts 16.1–18.5; 2 Cor 1.19). **1.2–3.13** The first major section describes Paul's ongoing concern for the Thessalonians. **1.2–10** The Thessalonians' reception of Paul's preaching was ratified by what it produced: their experience of the Spirit and their own joyful proclamation. Paul uses emotional language (rhetorical *pathos*), designed to evoke a favorable response from the Thessalonians. **1.2–3** Ancient letters often begin with a prayer for the readers' well-being; Paul begins with thanks for the Thessalonians' present activity (see, e.g., Rom 1.8). **1.3** *Faith*, *hope*, and *love* occur together here for the first time in Paul's Letters; see also 5.8; Rom 5.1–5; 1 Cor 13.13; Gal 5.5–6. **1.4** *Chosen* implies a special relationship with God, like Israel's (see, e.g., Isa 41.8–10). **1.5** *Our message of the gospel* is not Paul's own creation but God's effective word that produces faith. *Word*, a philosophical term implying rational account and explanation; see also vv. 6, 8; 2.5; 4.18. To contrast speech and action was an ancient Greek philosophical convention. *Power*, the *Holy Spirit* (see also 1.6; 4.8; 5.19), and *full conviction* stress the effect on the Thessalonians of Paul's preaching. **1.6** Paul often uses himself (1 Cor 4.16; 11.1), other Christians (1 Thess 2.14), and the Lord (1 Cor 11.1) as models for *imitation*. *Persecution*

marked the founding of this church; see 2.2, 14–16; 3.3–4. **1.7** *Macedonia* (where Thessalonica lies) is northern mainland Greece; *Achaia* (where Corinth, from which Paul is writing, lies) is southern Greece. They are the two Roman provinces in European Greece. **1.8** *Sounded forth* stresses the Thessalonians' witnessing activity. **1.9–10** A terse summary of Paul's initial preaching to non-Jews; see also 1 Cor 8.6; 10.14. **1.9** *Idols*, i.e., statues. See also 1 Cor 8.4–13; 10.14–22. **1.10** *Wrath that is coming* from God (see also 2.16; 5.9), a feature of OT expectation (Isa 13.9; cf. Isa 2.10–22), here the final day of judgment; see also Rom 2.5, 8; 3.5; 5.9; 9.22.

2.1–16 Paul's fidelity to the gospel and concern for the Thessalonians determined his actions while in Thessalonica. He uses rhetorical *ethos*, language designed to impress the readers with his good character. **2.1** *You yourselves know*, a tactful invitation to recall Paul's ministry. See also 1.5; 2.2, 5, 11; 3.4; 4.2. **2.2** On events in *Philippi*, see Acts 16.11–40. *The gospel of God*, a revelation about God (see 1.9). **2.3–8** Using the language of philosophers of his day (*deceit, impure motives, trickery*, v. 3; *words of flattery, pretext for greed*, v. 5; *praise from mortals*, v. 6), Paul presents himself as an ideal philosopher whose way of life refutes the idea that he acted out of greed. For parallel language, see Dio Chrysostom, *Oration* 32.11–21 (to the Alexandrians). **2.3** *Appeal*, a philosophical term for moral exhortation such as that found in 4.1–5.22. **2.4** *To please*

you or from others, [7]though we might have made demands as apostles of Christ. But we were gentle[a] among you, like a nurse tenderly caring for her own children. [8]So deeply do we care for you that we are determined to share with you not only the gospel of God but also our own selves, because you have become very dear to us.

9 You remember our labor and toil, brothers and sisters;[b] we worked night and day, so that we might not burden any of you while we proclaimed to you the gospel of God. [10]You are witnesses, and God also, how pure, upright, and blameless our conduct was toward you believers. [11]As you know, we dealt with each one of you like a father with his children, [12]urging and encouraging you and pleading that you lead a life worthy of God, who calls you into his own kingdom and glory.

13 We also constantly give thanks to God for this, that when you received the word of God that you heard from us, you accepted it not as a human word but as what it really is, God's word, which is also at work in you believers. [14]For you, brothers and sisters,[b] became imitators of the churches of God in Christ Jesus that are in Judea, for you suffered the same things from your own compatriots as they did from the Jews, [15]who killed both the Lord Jesus and the prophets,[c] and drove us out; they displease God and oppose everyone [16]by hindering us from speaking to the Gentiles so that they may be saved. Thus they have constantly been filling up the measure of their sins; but God's wrath has overtaken them at last.[d]

Paul's Desire to Visit the Thessalonians Again

17 As for us, brothers and sisters,[b] when, for a short time, we were made orphans by being separated from you—in person, not in heart—we longed with great eagerness to see you face to face. [18]For we wanted to come to you—certainly I, Paul, wanted to again and again—but Satan blocked our way. [19]For what is our hope or joy or crown of boasting before our Lord Jesus at his coming? Is it not you? [20]Yes, you are our glory and joy!

3 Therefore when we could bear it no longer, we decided to be left alone in Athens; [2]and we sent Timothy, our brother and co-worker for God in proclaiming[e] the gospel of Christ, to strengthen and encourage you for the sake of your faith, [3]so that no one would be shaken by these persecutions. Indeed, you yourselves know that this is what we are destined for. [4]In fact, when we were with you, we told you beforehand that we were to suffer persecution; so it turned out, as you know. [5]For this reason, when I could bear it no longer, I sent to find out about your faith; I was afraid that somehow the tempter had tempted you and that our labor had been in vain.

Timothy's Encouraging Report

6 But Timothy has just now come to us from you, and has brought us the good news of your faith and love. He has told us also that you always remember us kindly and long to see us—just as we long to see you. [7]For this reason, brothers and sisters,[b] during all our distress and persecution we have been encouraged about you through your faith. [8]For we now live, if you continue to stand firm in the Lord. [9]How can we thank God enough for you in return for all the joy that we feel before our God

---

a Other ancient authorities read *infants*   b Gk *brothers*
c Other ancient authorities read *their own prophets*
d Or *completely* or *forever*   e Gk lacks *proclaiming*

God is Paul's fundamental moral criterion in this Letter (see 2.12; 4.1). **2.7** The only explicit reference to Paul's *apostleship* in the Letter. *Gentle . . . like a nurse.* For more maternal imagery, see Gal 4.19. **2.9** Like many contemporary philosophers, Paul *worked* to support himself; see Acts 18.3; 1 Cor 9.6–18; 2 Thess 3.7–10. **2.12** *Urging and encouraging . . . and pleading* are the opposite of making *demands* (v. 7). The three synonymous participles stress the importance of Christian life. **2.13–16** The second thanksgiving (see 1.2–3) for the Thessalonians' faith under opposition. **2.14–16** The authenticity of these verses is sometimes challenged; see Introduction. **2.15** On *killing . . . the prophets* (the only reference to the OT in the Letter), see Mt 23.31; Lk 11.49–51; Acts 7.52. **2.16** *Filling up the measure of their sins* (see also Dan 8.23; 2 Macc 6.14) reflects the apocalyptic concept that history moves in foreordained stages toward the end. *God's wrath.* See 1.10. *At last. Completely* or *forever* (see text note *d*) is preferable. **2.17–3.5** Paul expresses his concern for the Thessalonians while absent from them. **2.18** Paul's frustrated attempts to visit the Thessalonians are part of the apocalyptic struggle between God and *Satan;* see also Rom 16.20; 2 Cor 2.11; 11.14; 12.7. **2.19** *Crown of boasting.* The laurel wreath was a symbol of victory or praise. See Phil 2.16; 4.1. **3.5** *Tempter,* i.e., Satan (see 2.18). **3.6–13** Timothy's report (see v. 2) leads Paul to an exuberant response. **3.6** On *faith and love,* see 1.3;

because of you? [10]Night and day we pray most earnestly that we may see you face to face and restore whatever is lacking in your faith.

11 Now may our God and Father himself and our Lord Jesus direct our way to you. [12]And may the Lord make you increase and abound in love for one another and for all, just as we abound in love for you. [13]And may he so strengthen your hearts in holiness that you may be blameless before our God and Father at the coming of our Lord Jesus with all his saints.

A Life Pleasing to God

4 Finally, brothers and sisters,[a] we ask and urge you in the Lord Jesus that, as you learned from us how you ought to live and to please God (as, in fact, you are doing), you should do so more and more. [2]For you know what instructions we gave you through the Lord Jesus. [3]For this is the will of God, your sanctification: that you abstain from fornication; [4]that each one of you know how to control your own body[b] in holiness and honor, [5]not with lustful passion, like the Gentiles who do not know God; [6]that no one wrong or exploit a brother or sister[c] in this matter, because the Lord is an avenger in all these things, just as we have already told you beforehand and

solemnly warned you. [7]For God did not call us to impurity but in holiness. [8]Therefore whoever rejects this rejects not human authority but God, who also gives his Holy Spirit to you.

9 Now concerning love of the brothers and sisters,[a] you do not need to have anyone write to you, for you yourselves have been taught by God to love one another; [10]and indeed you do love all the brothers and sisters[a] throughout Macedonia. But we urge you, beloved,[a] to do so more and more, [11]to aspire to live quietly, to mind your own affairs, and to work with your hands, as we directed you, [12]so that you may behave properly toward outsiders and be dependent on no one.

The Coming of the Lord

13 But we do not want you to be uninformed, brothers and sisters,[a] about those who have died,[d] so that you may not grieve as others do who have no hope. [14]For since we believe that Jesus died and rose again, even so, through Jesus, God will bring with him those who have died.[d] [15]For this we declare to you by the word of the Lord, that we who are alive, who are left until the coming of the Lord, will by no means

a Gk brothers   b Or how to take a wife for himself
c Gk brother   d Gk fallen asleep

Paul reinforces hope in 4.13–18. **3.10** *Whatever is lacking in your faith* does not imply a rebuke (see 1.8) but refers to the teaching given in 4.1–5.22. **3.11–13** Paul's prayer, answered by later visits (1 Cor 16.5; 2 Cor 2.13; 7.5), repeats motifs found in 1.3–4. **3.13** *Saints* (lit. "holy ones"), an OT title for God's people (see Ex 19.6; Dan 7.18; *Psalms of Solomon* 17.26) or for angelic beings; here either significance makes sense.

4.1–5.24 In this second major section of the Letter, Paul gives practical instructions about Christian life in a non-Christian city. **4.1–12** Marriage, human relationships, and civic life—topics often discussed by philosophers—were significant for Christian life in a Greek city. **4.1–2** General introduction to 4.1–5.24. **4.1** *Finally*, better "therefore," marks the transition to 4.1–5.24. *Urge*, or "encourage," a technical term of ancient ethics, also found in 2.12; 3.2; 4.10; 5.11, 14. Some hold that the entire Letter is a letter of moral encouragement. **4.3** Reference to the *will of God* anticipates the strong theological emphasis in vv. 6–8. Greco-Roman sexual laxity scandalized Jews (see v. 5), so Paul often warns against *fornication* (see 1 Cor 5.1; 6.13, 18; Gal 5.19). **4.4** *How to control your own body* (see 1 Cor 7.2). *How to take a wife for himself* (text note b; lit. "how to possess a vessel or implement") is preferable. Both translations are possible, but Paul is discussing relationships here. *Holiness and honor*. Paul

evaluates marital sex positively (see also 1 Cor 7.3–6). **4.6** On *wronging . . . a brother or sister,* see Rom 14.13–23; 1 Cor 8.9–13. Paul describes God as an *avenger,* an OT motif (Ps 94.1), to stress the eschatological significance of what he teaches; see also 1.10; Rom 2.16; 12.19. **4.8** *Holy Spirit,* mentioned in 1.6; 5.19; not as prominent here as in 1 Corinthians and Romans. **4.9** *Love of the brothers and sisters* (Greek *philadelphia*) was a virtue in Epicurean philosophy; Paul uses the term only once more (Rom 12.10). *Taught by God,* a common Stoic idea. The term is not found elsewhere in the NT. **4.11** *Aspire to live quietly* corresponds to the Epicurean maxim "Escape notice as you live." *Mind your own affairs,* an Epicurean attitude that excluded participation in civic affairs (minding the common affairs). *Work with your hands* emphasizes self-sufficiency, a major Stoic goal (see 2.9; 1 Cor 4.12; 2 Thess 3.6–12). **4.13–18** Paul describes Jesus' return in language that has points of contact both with the Roman imperial cult and Jewish apocalyptic expectations. **4.13** *No hope* reflects a common Greco-Roman view, especially in Epicurean philosophy, that there is no resurrection. A Latin tomb inscription reads: "I was not, I was; I am not; I care not." **4.15** *By the* (better "a") *word of the Lord,* probably a special revelation from the risen Christ; no such saying of Jesus survives in the Gospels. *We who are alive.* Paul does not expect to die

precede those who have died.[a] 16For the Lord himself, with a cry of command, with the archangel's call and with the sound of God's trumpet, will descend from heaven, and the dead in Christ will rise first. 17Then we who are alive, who are left, will be caught up in the clouds together with them to meet the Lord in the air; and so we will be with the Lord forever. 18Therefore encourage one another with these words.

5 Now concerning the times and the seasons, brothers and sisters,[b] you do not need to have anything written to you. 2For you yourselves know very well that the day of the Lord will come like a thief in the night. 3When they say, "There is peace and security," then sudden destruction will come upon them, as labor pains come upon a pregnant woman, and there will be no escape! 4But you, beloved,[b] are not in darkness, for that day to surprise you like a thief; 5for you are all children of light and children of the day; we are not of the night or of darkness. 6So then let us not fall asleep as others do, but let us keep awake and be sober; 7for those who sleep sleep at night, and those who are drunk get drunk at night. 8But since we belong to the day, let us be sober, and put on the breastplate of faith and love, and for a helmet the hope of salvation. 9For God has destined us not for wrath but for obtaining salvation through our Lord Jesus Christ, 10who died for us, so that whether we are awake or asleep we may live with him. 11Therefore encourage one another and build up each other, as indeed you are doing.

Final Exhortations, Greetings, and Benediction

12 But we appeal to you, brothers and sisters,[b] to respect those who labor among you, and have charge of you in the Lord and admonish you; 13esteem them very highly in love because of their work. Be at peace among yourselves. 14And we urge you, beloved,[b] to admonish the idlers, encourage the fainthearted, help the weak, be patient with all of them. 15See that none of you repays evil for evil, but always seek to do good to one another and to all. 16Rejoice always, 17pray without ceasing, 18give thanks in all circumstances; for this is the will of God in Christ Jesus for you. 19Do not quench the Spirit. 20Do not despise the words of prophets,[c] 21but test everything; hold fast to what is good; 22abstain from every form of evil.

23 May the God of peace himself sanctify you entirely; and may your spirit and soul and body be kept sound[d] and blameless at the coming of our Lord Jesus Christ. 24The one who calls you is faithful, and he will do this.

25 Beloved,[e] pray for us.

26 Greet all the brothers and sisters[b] with a holy kiss. 27I solemnly command you by the Lord that this letter be read to all of them.[f]

28 The grace of our Lord Jesus Christ be with you.[g]

---

a Gk *fallen asleep*   *b* Gk *brothers*   *c* Gk *despise prophecies*   *d* Or *complete*   *e* Gk *Brothers*   *f* Gk *to all the brothers*   *g* Other ancient authorities add *Amen*

---

before Jesus' coming (see also 1 Cor 15.51–52). Later, however, he seems to reflect on the possibility of death; see 2 Cor 5.1–5; Phil 1.20–23. *Coming* (Greek *parousia*; see also 2.19; 3.13; 5.23), a technical term for a ruler's state visit. Cf. Mt 24.3; 1 Cor 15.23. **4.16** A *cry of command*, a herald's *call*, and a *trumpet* (see Isa 27.13; Joel 2.1; Zech 9.14) announce the ruler's arrival. ot texts and ruler cults both use such language. **4.17** Paul identifies Jesus as the *Lord* (an imperial title) of the universe, whom believers will welcome as city officials would *meet* and welcome a visiting ruler. Note that the Lord is coming to the earth, not going to heaven.

5.1–11 Paul draws out the implications of the hope of Jesus' coming with repeated calls for vigilance. **5.2** *Day of the Lord,* the day of judgment. See Isa 2.9–19; Am 5.18–20. **5.3** Roman imperial coins used *peace and security* as a propaganda legend; see also Jer 6.14; Ezek 13.10. *Labor pains.* See Isa 13.6–8; Hos 13.13; Rom 8.22. **5.6** *Let us not fall asleep.* See Mt 25.13; Mk 13.34–37; this exhortation to moral alertness is clari-

fied by *keep awake* and *be sober.* **5.8** Imagery of armor (*breastplate, helmet*) underscores the need to struggle; see also Rom 13.12; 2 Cor 6.7; 10.4; Eph 6.13–17; Phil 1.27–30. On *hope,* see 1.3; note on 3.6. Paul understands *salvation* to lie in the future; see Rom 5.9; Phil 2.12; 3.20. **5.10** *Who died for us,* a terse allusion to Jesus' death as a sacrifice for sin. See Rom 4.25; 1 Cor 15.3. Paul returns to his earlier use of *sleep* as a metaphor for death (see 4.13–15, text note *d*). **5.12–24** Exhortations to good relationships within the Christian community. **5.12** *Those who labor among you,* i.e., in ad hoc leadership roles. Formal clergy did not yet exist. **5.16–21** These commands may reflect a description of early Christian worship. **5.21** *Test everything,* i.e., using *what is good* as a criterion (see also Rom 12.2). **5.23–24** A concluding benediction stresses the faithfulness of God. **5.25–28** The conclusion of the Letter. **5.26** The *holy kiss* was a part of worship; see Rom 16.16; 1 Cor 16.20; 2 Cor 13.12. **5.27** The Letter is probably to be *read* in the recipients' worship assembly.

The Second Letter of Paul to the
THESSALONIANS

THOUGH 2 THESSALONIANS resembles other Letters of the Pauline corpus, especially 1 Thessalonians, questions have been raised about its authorship. The tone seems formal and stilted, especially in contrast to the warmth of 1 Thessalonians, and there are strange hints of forgery (2.2; 3.17), which have no parallel in other Pauline Letters. The second letter reproduces the wording and structure of the first to a remarkable extent, yet presents a radically different perspective on the end time. Scholars disagree over how to interpret this. Some assume that Paul wrote the second letter soon after the first to correct some misunderstandings that had arisen and to address a new crisis in the community. Others assume that an unknown author borrowed Paul's name and authority and used the model of 1 Thessalonians to construct a pseudonymous letter.

Occasion

ONE OF PAUL'S CONCERNS in writing 1 Thessalonians was to reassure his readers that Jesus' Second Coming (Greek *parousia*) could occur at any moment and to urge them to remain vigilant (1 Thess 5.1–11). The situation seems to be one of faltering apocalyptic hope. In 2 Thessalonians the author seeks to refute the view that the day of Jesus' return had already arrived and to remind the church of the numerous events that must precede it (2.1–12). The situation now seems to be one of keen apocalyptic expectations fueled by persecution (1.4). Indeed, the author of 2 Thessalonians (whether Paul or someone else) may have felt that 1 Thessalonians, with its eager anticipation of the Second Coming, had contributed to the new problem.

The author draws on a rich reservoir of apocalyptic traditions to buttress the arguments that the church's present affliction will be reversed on the "day of the Lord" (1.5–10), that that climactic day has not yet arrived (2.1–12), and that therefore actions in the present continue to be important (2.15–3.16).

Date and Place

IF 2 THESSALONIANS WAS WRITTEN BY PAUL, it was written shortly after 1 Thessalonians and to the same church. If not, it is impossible to date it with any precision. [JOUETTE M. BASSLER]

Salutation

1 Paul, Silvanus, and Timothy,
To the church of the Thessalonians in God our Father and the Lord Jesus Christ:

2 Grace to you and peace from God our[a] Father and the Lord Jesus Christ.

Thanksgiving

3 We must always give thanks to God for you, brothers and sisters,[b] as is right, because your faith is growing abundantly, and the love of every one of you for one another is increasing. 4Therefore we ourselves boast of you among the churches of God for your steadfastness and faith during all your persecutions and the afflictions that you are enduring.

The Judgment at Christ's Coming

5 This is evidence of the righteous judgment of God, and is intended to make you worthy of the kingdom of God, for which you are also suffering. 6For it is indeed just of God to repay with affliction those who afflict you, 7and to give relief to the afflicted as well as to us, when the Lord Jesus is revealed from heaven with his mighty angels 8in flaming fire, inflicting vengeance on those who do not know God and on those who do not obey the gospel of our Lord Jesus. 9These will suffer the punish-

ment of eternal destruction, separated from the presence of the Lord and from the glory of his might, 10when he comes to be glorified by his saints and to be marveled at on that day among all who have believed, because our testimony to you was believed. 11To this end we always pray for you, asking that our God will make you worthy of his call and will fulfill by his power every good resolve and work of faith, 12so that the name of our Lord Jesus may be glorified in you, and you in him, according to the grace of our God and the Lord Jesus Christ.

The Man of Lawlessness

2 As to the coming of our Lord Jesus Christ and our being gathered together to him, we beg you, brothers and sisters,[b] 2not to be quickly shaken in mind or alarmed, either by spirit or by word or by letter, as though from us, to the effect that the day of the Lord is already here. 3Let no one deceive you in any way; for that day will not come unless the rebellion comes first and the lawless one[c] is revealed, the one destined for destruction.[d] 4He opposes and exalts himself above every so-called god or object of worship, so that he

---

a Other ancient authorities read *the*   b Gk *brothers*   c Gk *the man of lawlessness*; other ancient authorities read *the man of sin*   d Gk *the son of destruction*

1.1–2 The brief opening of the Letter is nearly identical to that of 1 Thessalonians. **1.3–12** The apocalyptic content of the rather formal thanksgiving (cf. Rom 1.8–15; 1 Cor 1.4–9; 1 Thess 1.2–10) anticipates the argument of ch. 2. **1.4** Because *persecutions and . . . afflictions* were widely regarded as signs of the end of the age (see 2.2; Mk 13.19–27), they required careful interpretation; see vv. 5–10; 2.1–12; cf. Rom 5.3; 2 Cor 1.6–7; 1 Thess 1.6; 3.3, 7. **1.5–10** An apparent digression introduces a central theme of the Letter: the Second Coming of the Lord Jesus (see also 2.1–12). The author uses OT language about God to describe this event; see also *1 Enoch* 1.3–9. **1.5** The *evidence* (lit. "sign") of the *righteous judgment of God* is either the steadfastness and faith of the church (v. 4; see Phil 1.28) or its afflictions, which will make them *worthy of the kingdom of God* (see 1 Pet 4.17–18). **1.7b** On the retinue of *angels*, see Zech 14.5; Mt 25.31; Mk 8.38; Jude 14–15. **1.8** *Fire* is associated with God (Ex 3.2; Ezek 1.4, 13, 27) and with the final judgment (Isa 66.15–16; Mt 3.12; 1 Cor 3.13–15). **1.9** *From the presence . . . his might,* a refrain used in Isa 2.10, 19, 21 (Septuagint), where the day of God's terrible judgment is described. **1.10** *Saints* (lit. "holy ones"), the usual NT epithet for believers; here it may refer to the *mighty angels* (v. 7; see Zech 14.5). *That day,* i.e.,

the day of the Lord (see 2.2; Isa 2.11). **1.11–12** An intercessory prayer (see also 2.16–17; 3.5, 16) closes the thanksgiving. **1.11** *Work of faith.* See 1 Thess 1.3.

2.1–12 A major concern of this Letter is to refute the view that *the day of the Lord is already here* (v. 2). **2.1** The *coming* (Greek *parousia*) of Jesus in judgment (see 1.7–8) marks the *day of the Lord* (v. 2; see also 1.10; 1 Thess 5.1–11). **2.2** This *spirit* is a lying prophetic spirit; see 1 Cor 2.10–13; 1 Thess 5.19–21; 1 Jn 4.1. *By word,* i.e., by nonprophetic oral speech; see 1 Thess 1.5. *Letter as though from us* suggests a forged letter (see 3.17); however, the author (if pseudonymous) may intend to discredit 1 Thessalonians with this phrase. Since the *day of the Lord* was expected to be a dramatic and highly visible cosmic event, the meaning of the statement that it is *already here* is not clear. It probably refers to a spiritualized interpretation of the day (with no external signs), though some suggest that it means the day (traditionally understood) is very near. **2.3** It was widely believed that a *rebellion* (Greek *apostasia*) would precede the day of the Lord; see Mt 24.6–14; 2 Tim 3.1–5. The *lawless one* (see v. 8), a blasphemous antichrist figure whose revelation would be the last sign preceding the day of the Lord; see also Mt 24.23–24; 1 Jn 2.18; Rev 13. **2.4** The description of the lawless one echoes various OT passages; see Isa 14.13–

takes his seat in the temple of God, declaring himself to be God. 5Do you not remember that I told you these things when I was still with you? 6And you know what is now re-straining him, so that he may be revealed when his time comes. 7For the mystery of law-lessness is already at work, but only until the one who now restrains it is removed. 8And then the lawless one will be revealed, whom the Lord Jesus*a* will destroy*b* with the breath of his mouth, annihilating him by the manifesta-tion of his coming. 9The coming of the lawless one is apparent in the working of Satan, who uses all power, signs, lying wonders, 10and every kind of wicked deception for those who are perishing, because they refused to love the truth and so be saved. 11For this reason God sends them a powerful delusion, leading them to believe what is false, 12so that all who have not believed the truth but took pleasure in un-righteousness will be condemned.

Chosen for Salvation

13 But we must always give thanks to God for you, brothers and sisters*c* beloved by the Lord, because God chose you as the first fruits*d* for salvation through sanctification by the Spirit and through belief in the truth. 14For this pur-pose he called you through our proclamation of the good news,*e* so that you may obtain the glory of our Lord Jesus Christ. 15So then, brothers and sisters,*c* stand firm and hold fast to the traditions that you were taught by us, ei-ther by word of mouth or by our letter.

16 Now may our Lord Jesus Christ himself and God our Father, who loved us and through grace gave us eternal comfort and good hope, 17comfort your hearts and strengthen them in every good work and word.

Request for Prayer

3 Finally, brothers and sisters,*c* pray for us, so that the word of the Lord may spread rapidly and be glorified everywhere, just as it is among you, 2and that we may be rescued from wicked and evil people; for not all have faith. 3But the Lord is faithful; he will strengthen you and guard you from the evil one.*f* 4And we have confidence in the Lord concerning you, that you are doing and will go on doing the things that we command. 5May the Lord direct your hearts to the love of God and to the steadfastness of Christ.

Warning against Idleness

6 Now we command you, beloved,*c* in the name of our Lord Jesus Christ, to keep away from believers who are*g* living in idleness and not according to the tradition that they*h* re-ceived from us. 7For you yourselves know how you ought to imitate us; we were not idle when we were with you, 8and we did not eat anyone's bread without paying for it; but with toil and

---

a Other ancient authorities lack *Jesus*   *b* Other ancient authorities read *consume*   *c* Gk *brothers*   *d* Other ancient authorities read *from the beginning*   *e* Or *through our gospel*   *f* Or *from evil*   *g* Gk *from every brother who is*   *h* Other ancient authorities read *you*

14; Ezek 28.1–10; Dan 11.21–45. **2.6** The author does not say *what* (and *who;* see v. 7) *is now restraining him.* Suggestions include the Roman Empire and emperor, God and a divine decree, and Paul and his preaching; but the ambiguity may be intentional. The restraining force emphasizes the necessary delay of the day of the Lord. **2.7** The *mystery of lawlessness,* i.e., the already present power of the coming lawless one (see 1 Jn 4.3). **2.8** The OT image of the powerful *breath of* God's *mouth* is transferred to Jesus; see Job 4.9; Ps 33.6; Isa 11.4; cf. Rev 19.15. **2.9** The same Greek word (*parou-sia*) describes the *coming* of both the lawless one and the Lord Jesus (vv. 1, 8). *Signs* and *wonders* mark the coming of both true and false messiahs (1.7; Mk 13.22–25; Rev 13.13–14). **2.11** *God sends them a pow-erful delusion.* This is affirmed also in 1 Kings 22.23; Isa 6.10; Ezek 14.9; Mk 4.11–12; Rom 9.18–23. **2.13–14** The abrupt resumption of the thanksgiving (see 1.3; see also 1 Thess 1.2; 2.13) creates a stark contrast between the condemned and the saved. **2.13** On God's having *chosen,* or called, the readers, see 1 Thess 1.4–5;

4.7; 5.9. On *first fruits,* see Deut 26.1–2; here it means first converts (see Rom 16.5).
    2.15–3.16 Exhortations alternate with intercessory prayers. **2.15** *Stand firm.* See 1 Thess 3.8. The *traditions* include ethical (see 3.6) and doctrinal (see 2.5–6) teachings able to refute the erroneous views shaking the church. *Our letter* (cf. v. 2), probably the present Letter (see 3.14). **3.2** *Wicked and evil people* may be the source of the affliction of 1.6–8. **3.3** *Evil one,* Satan (2.9; see also Eph 6.16). If the reading in text note *f* is correct, the reference is to the *evil* conditions of the time (1.4; 2.7). **3.6** The final *command* is particularly emphatic (see also v. 12). On *idleness,* see 1 Thess 5.14; the Greek word can also mean "disorderliness." On ei-ther reading, the problem addressed may be the result of the conviction that the day of the Lord had arrived. **3.7** Paul frequently admonished others to *imitate* him (see 1 Cor 4.16; 11.1; Phil 3.17; 4.9; 1 Thess 1.6). It was a common mode of moral exhortation, not a sign of arrogance. **3.8** Paul was proud of not imposing a finan-cial *burden* on his churches; see 1 Thess 2.9; 2 Cor 11.7–

labor we worked night and day, so that we might not burden any of you. [9]This was not because we do not have that right, but in order to give you an example to imitate. [10]For even when we were with you, we gave you this command: Anyone unwilling to work should not eat. [11]For we hear that some of you are living in idleness, mere busybodies, not doing any work. [12]Now such persons we command and exhort in the Lord Jesus Christ to do their work quietly and to earn their own living. [13]Brothers and sisters,[a] do not be weary in doing what is right.

14 Take note of those who do not obey what we say in this letter; have nothing to do with them, so that they may be ashamed. [15]Do not regard them as enemies, but warn them as believers.[b]

Final Greetings and Benediction

16 Now may the Lord of peace himself give you peace at all times in all ways. The Lord be with all of you.

17 I, Paul, write this greeting with my own hand. This is the mark in every letter of mine; it is the way I write. [18]The grace of our Lord Jesus Christ be with all of you.[c]

---

a Gk Brothers   b Gk a brother   c Other ancient authorities add Amen

---

11; 12.14–15. **3.9** On Paul's *right* to receive payment, see 1 Cor 9.4–15. **3.12** *Work quietly.* See 1 Thess 4.11–12. **3.17–18** Paul often wrote Letter closings with his own hand (see 1 Cor 16.21; Gal 6.11; Col 4.18; Philem 19); the emphasis here, however, is striking and difficult to interpret according to any theory of authorship.

The First Letter of Paul to
TIMOTHY

THE LETTERS TO TIMOTHY and Titus are distinctive within the Pauline collection. They are very similar to each other in style, vocabulary, theology, and content and very different in those regards from the other Letters. Since the eighteenth century they have been marked out as a unit by a collective name, the Pastoral Letters (or the Pastorals), and since the early nineteenth century questions have been raised about their authorship.

Authorship

THESE LETTERS PRESENT PAUL as their author, but very few scholars now accept that claim. In addition to their distinctive vocabulary and style, key Pauline concepts such as faith, righteousness, and being "in Christ" are treated quite differently. Moreover, there is a new emphasis on sound teaching, apostolic tradition, culturally acceptable patterns of behavior, church order, and a level of church organization that far surpasses anything found in the undisputed Letters (Romans, 1–2 Corinthians, Galatians, Philippians, 1 Thessalonians, and Philemon). Though a few scholars continue to affirm Pauline authorship, often by placing them very late in Paul's career or by ascribing their un-Pauline features to a secretary, most assume that an unknown author—probably the same author for all three Letters—used Paul's name to give authority to his attempt to address problems in some post-Pauline churches.

Language and Sources

THOUGH THERE ARE CLEAR ECHOES of Paul's thought, the Letters often use the language of Hellenistic philosophy to define the Christian life and that of the imperial cult to describe God's actions. The author knew at least some of the authentic Pauline Letters and employed a variety of other sources as well: rules about church order, rules of conduct for various groups of people, liturgical fragments, and vice and virtue lists.

Date, Addressees, and Sequence

THE AUTHOR SEEMS TO KNOW the book of Acts (see 2 Tim 3.11), which was probably written about 90 CE, and Polycarp seems to refer to these Letters in his own *Letter to the Philippians*, written about 120. Thus the Letters were probably written early in the second century during the reign of Trajan (98–117) and probably, but not certainly, in Asia Minor. By that time

Paul's co-workers, Timothy and Titus, would have been dead, so the addressees of the Letters are part of their epistolary fiction. References to Timothy and Titus within the Letters serve the author's rhetorical goals, for these men are presented as ideal church leaders whose sound doctrine and morals stand in sharp contrast to the corrupt lives and words of the false teachers. It is likely that the three Pastoral Letters were conceived as a unit and intended to be read together, but in which sequence it is impossible to say. The canonical order was probably based simply on length, from longest to shortest, as was the case for the other Pauline Letters.

Occasion

1 TIMOTHY SUGGESTS A SITUATION in which Paul has left Ephesus, leaving Timothy behind to deal with false teachers (1.3) and to provide ethical instructions to the church (3.14–15). The actual situation was somewhat more complex. There was a problem with people who had once been part of the church but now taught a different doctrine. They are denounced with stock accusations, which makes identification difficult, but they seem to have gnosticizing tendencies (1 Tim 6.20) that are reflected in their belief in a spiritual, and therefore already accomplished, resurrection (2 Tim 2.18) and in their rejection of marriage (1 Tim 4.3). Their influence threatened the theological and social fabric of the church, especially regarding the role of women. The political climate added further difficulties. It was characterized by suspicion of groups that might disrupt cultural norms and social stability (see Pliny, *Epistle* 10).

The Eastern Mediterranean

Though the actual recipients are unknown, churches in Ephesus and Crete provide the setting for the pseudonymous Letters to Timothy and Titus.

This created a need, reflected in these Letters, to adapt to the prevailing social expectations in order to avoid persecution. Paul's sense of immediacy about the return of Christ is no longer evident. Instead, the author seeks to provide enduring structure and regulations for the church. [JOUETTE M. BASSLER]

Salutation

1 Paul, an apostle of Christ Jesus by the command of God our Savior and of Christ Jesus our hope,

2 To Timothy, my loyal child in the faith:

Grace, mercy, and peace from God the Father and Christ Jesus our Lord.

Warning against False Teachers

3 I urge you, as I did when I was on my way to Macedonia, to remain in Ephesus so that you may instruct certain people not to teach any different doctrine, 4and not to occupy themselves with myths and endless genealogies that promote speculations rather than the divine training*a* that is known by faith. 5But the aim of such instruction is love that comes from a pure heart, a good conscience, and sincere faith. 6Some people have deviated from these and turned to meaningless talk, 7desiring to be teachers of the law, without understanding either what they are saying or the things about which they make assertions.

8 Now we know that the law is good, if one uses it legitimately. 9This means understanding that the law is laid down not for the innocent but for the lawless and disobedient, for the godless and sinful, for the unholy and profane, for those who kill their father or mother,

for murderers, 10fornicators, sodomites, slave traders, liars, perjurers, and whatever else is contrary to the sound teaching 11that conforms to the glorious gospel of the blessed God, which he entrusted to me.

Gratitude for Mercy

12 I am grateful to Christ Jesus our Lord, who has strengthened me, because he judged me faithful and appointed me to his service, 13even though I was formerly a blasphemer, a persecutor, and a man of violence. But I received mercy because I had acted ignorantly in unbelief, 14and the grace of our Lord overflowed for me with the faith and love that are in Christ Jesus. 15The saying is sure and worthy of full acceptance, that Christ Jesus came into the world to save sinners—of whom I am the foremost. 16But for that very reason I received mercy, so that in me, as the foremost, Jesus Christ might display the utmost patience, making me an example to those who would come to believe in him for eternal life. 17To the King of the ages, immortal, invisible, the only God, be honor and glory forever and ever.*b* Amen.

18 I am giving you these instructions, Timothy, my child, in accordance with the prophecies

---

a Or plan   *b* Gk to the ages of the ages

1.1–2 The opening of the Letter follows Paul's conventions. **1.1** Both God and Christ are called *Savior* in the Pastorals; see 2.3; 4.10; 2 Tim 1.10; Titus 1.3–4. The title is rare in the NT but is frequently applied to God in the OT (Isa 45.15), to various gods in the Greco-Roman world, and to the emperor himself. **1.2** Timothy is Paul's *loyal* (lit. "legitimate") *child*, in contrast to the heretics, who have abandoned the faith (v. 6); see Titus 1.4; see also 1 Cor 4.17; Phil 2.19–22; 4.3. **1.3–7** The opening charge to Timothy addresses the problem of false teachers. Opponents are also mentioned in 4.1–3; 6.3–5, 20–21; 2 Tim 2.16–18, 23–26; 3.1–9, 13; 4.3–4; Titus 1.10–16; 3.9–11. **1.3** Two of these *certain people* are named in v. 20, but the opponents are often left anonymous; see v. 6; 4.1; 5.24; 6.10, 21. **1.4** *Myths* and *genealogies,* perhaps portions of the OT (see, e.g., Gen 4–5) or Gnostic speculations; see also 4.7; 2 Tim 4.4; Titus 1.14; 3.9. **1.7** *Law,* probably Jewish law, but that is not emphasized; cf. Titus 1.14. **1.8–11** This digression on the legitimate use of the law reflects aspects of Paul's

thought (cf. Rom 7–8; Gal 3–4). **1.8** On the law as *good,* see Rom 7.12, 16. **1.9** On the notion that the law is intended to curb *sinful* actions, see Gal 3.19, 23–26. **1.9–10** These verses contain vice and virtue lists, which were common devices for moral teaching; see, e.g., 6.4–5; 2 Tim 3.2–5; Titus 3.3; see also Rom 1.29–31; Gal 5.19–23. **1.10** The *sound* (lit. "healthy") *teaching* emphasized in these Letters (see, e.g., v. 3; 4.6; 6.3; 2 Tim 1.13; 4.3; Titus 1.9, 13; 2.1–2) is a bulwark against the false, diseased teaching of the opponents (2 Tim 2.17). **1.12–17** A statement of gratitude contains a lengthy biographical passage that presents Paul as an example of divine grace and mercy (cf. 1 Cor 15.9–10; Gal 1.13–17). This seems to convey an important message about the false teachers, who are also depicted as the *foremost* of sinners (6.3–5). **1.15** *The saying is sure,* a formula appearing four more times in these Letters and emphasizing statements about salvation: 3.1; 4.9; 2 Tim 2.11; Titus 3.8. **1.18–20** The author resumes the charge to Timothy. **1.18** The *instructions* include those in vv. 3–5

made earlier about you, so that by following them you may fight the good fight, [19]having faith and a good conscience. By rejecting conscience, certain persons have suffered shipwreck in the faith; [20]among them are Hymenaeus and Alexander, whom I have turned over to Satan, so that they may learn not to blaspheme.

Instructions concerning Prayer

2 First of all, then, I urge that supplications, prayers, intercessions, and thanksgivings be made for everyone, [2]for kings and all who are in high positions, so that we may lead a quiet and peaceable life in all godliness and dignity. [3]This is right and is acceptable in the sight of God our Savior, [4]who desires everyone to be saved and to come to the knowledge of the truth. [5]For

there is one God;
there is also one mediator between
God and humankind,
Christ Jesus, himself human,
[6]   who gave himself a ransom for all

—this was attested at the right time. [7]For this I was appointed a herald and an apostle (I am telling the truth,[a] I am not lying), a teacher of the Gentiles in faith and truth.

[8]I desire, then, that in every place the men should pray, lifting up holy hands without anger or argument; [9]also that the women should dress themselves modestly and decently in suitable clothing, not with their hair braided, or with gold, pearls, or expensive clothes, [10]but with good works, as is proper for women who profess reverence for God. [11]Let a woman[b] learn in silence with full submission. [12]I permit no woman[b] to teach or to have authority over a man;[c] she is to keep silent. [13]For Adam was formed first, then Eve; [14]and Adam was not deceived, but the woman was deceived and became a transgressor. [15]Yet she will be saved through childbearing, provided they continue in faith and love and holiness, with modesty.

Qualifications of Bishops

3 The saying is sure:[d] whoever aspires to the office of bishop[e] desires a noble task. [2]Now a bishop[f] must be above reproach, married only once,[g] temperate, sensible, re-

---

a Other ancient authorities add in Christ   b Or wife   c Or her husband   d Some interpreters place these words at the end of the previous paragraph. Other ancient authorities read The saying is commonly accepted   e Or overseer   f Or an overseer   g Gk the husband of one wife

---

and in chs. 2–6. Prophecies, probably part of an ordination ceremony; see 4.14; Acts 13.1–3. The good fight, a traditional phrase in Hellenistic moral philosophy, gains special significance here in the struggle against false teachers; see 6.12; 2 Tim 4.7; see also 2 Cor 10.3–5; Phil 1.27–30. 1.20 Hymenaeus. See 2 Tim 2.17. Alexander. See 2 Tim 4.14. Turning over to Satan probably involved expulsion from the church; see also Titus 3.10; 1 Cor 5.3–5.

2.1–3.16 A series of instructions addresses aspects of the church's life and leadership. 2.1–7 For everyone . . . for all. The theme of inclusive universality dominates the opening instructions on prayer; see also 4.10; Titus 2.11. 2.2 The author's response to the emperor cult (see also 1 Pet 2.17) is that prayers are to be made for kings, not to them. Godliness, the most prominent of the many terms used in these Letters to characterize the ideal Christian life; see, e.g., 4.7–8; 6.3; 2 Tim 3.5; Titus 1.1. It was never used by Paul, but it was a prominent virtue in Hellenistic philosophy. 2.4 Knowledge of the truth is crucial to this author in the context of false teaching; see 6.20; 2 Tim 2.25; 3.7; Titus 1.1. 2.5–6a For there is . . . ransom for all, probably a liturgical fragment. 2.5 Christ is here presented as a human mediator between the one invisible and transcendent God (1.17; 6.15–16) and all humans, not just the covenant people (cf. Heb 8.6). 2.6 Ransom, one of only two references to Jesus' death in these Letters (see also 2 Tim 2.8, 11). 2.8–15 A concern for women's behavior dom-

inates this discussion of worship. 2.9 Criticism of women's clothing, jewelry, and elaborate (braided) hairstyles was traditional in Greco-Roman culture; see 1 Pet 3.3. 2.10 Good works are stressed in these Letters; see 5.10, 25; 6.18; Titus 2.7, 14; 3.8, 14. Paul's concern was with works of the law. 2.11–12 Women's silence is also demanded in 1 Cor 14.34–35; cf. 1 Cor 11.5. Submission of wives to husbands is demanded in Eph 5.22; Col 3.18; Titus 2.5; 1 Pet 3.1; see also Gen 3.16. Here the demand is probably not limited to married couples (cf. text notes b and c). 2.13 The author's assumption is that the one formed first (see Gen 2; cf. Gen 1.27) has natural dominance. Adam's culpability (Gen 3.6, 17–19) is ignored in this argument (cf. Rom 5.12–21). 2.14 On Eve's being deceived, see Gen 3.13; 2 Cor 11.3. False teachers posed anew the threat of deception; see 4.1; 2 Tim 3.13; Titus 1.10. 2.15 The emphasis on childbearing may be a response to the false teachers' rejection of marriage (4.3); see also 5.10, 14. They, perhaps children, though the shift in subject is then abrupt. 3.1–13 The virtues that dominate the list of qualifications for bishops and deacons emphasize moderation and respectability. 3.1 The saying is sure may refer not to 3.1 but to 2.15 (see text note d; note on 1.15). Bishops (or "overseers") are mentioned in Acts 20.28; Phil 1.1; Titus 1.7–9. The relationship between bishops, deacons (see 3.8), and elders (see 5.17) is not clear in these Letters, nor are their respective tasks (but see note on Titus 1.5–9). 3.2 The require-

spectable, hospitable, an apt teacher, [3]not a drunkard, not violent but gentle, not quarrelsome, and not a lover of money. [4]He must manage his own household well, keeping his children submissive and respectful in every way— [5]for if someone does not know how to manage his own household, how can he take care of God's church? [6]He must not be a recent convert, or he may be puffed up with conceit and fall into the condemnation of the devil. [7]Moreover, he must be well thought of by outsiders, so that he may not fall into disgrace and the snare of the devil.

Qualifications of Deacons

[8]Deacons likewise must be serious, not double-tongued, not indulging in much wine, not greedy for money; [9]they must hold fast to the mystery of the faith with a clear conscience. [10]And let them first be tested; then, if they prove themselves blameless, let them serve as deacons. [11]Women[a] likewise must be serious, not slanderers, but temperate, faithful in all things. [12]Let deacons be married only once,[b] and let them manage their children and their households well; [13]for those who serve well as deacons gain a good standing for themselves and great boldness in the faith that is in Christ Jesus.

The Mystery of Our Religion

[14]I hope to come to you soon, but I am writing these instructions to you so that, [15]if I am delayed, you may know how one ought to behave in the household of God, which is the church of the living God, the pillar and bulwark of the truth. [16]Without any doubt, the mystery of our religion is great:

He[c] was revealed in flesh,
　vindicated[d] in spirit,[e]
　　seen by angels,
proclaimed among Gentiles,
　believed in throughout the world,
　　taken up in glory.

False Asceticism

4 Now the Spirit expressly says that in later[f] times some will renounce the faith by paying attention to deceitful spirits and teachings of demons, [2]through the hypocrisy of liars whose consciences are seared with a hot iron. [3]They forbid marriage and demand abstinence from foods, which God created to be received with thanksgiving by those who believe and know the truth. [4]For everything cre-

---

a Or *Their wives,* or *Women deacons*　*b* Gk *be husbands of one wife*　*c* Gk *Who;* other ancient authorities read *God;* others, *Which*　*d* Or *justified*　*e* Or *by the Spirit*　*f* Or *the last*

---

ment that bishops be *married only once,* lit. "husband of one wife," excludes polygamists (who were rare in that culture anyway), remarried widowers, and remarried divorced men. It also excludes unmarried men and all women. **3.3** The warning about *love of money* is conventional but emphasized by its repetition; see v. 8; 6.9–10, 17–19; 2 Tim 3.2; Titus 1.7. **3.4** *Household,* the basic unit of and metaphor for the church; see note on 3.15; see also 2 Tim 3.6; Titus 1.11. As described in these Letters, it was a very patriarchal and hierarchical entity. **3.6** The first specifically Christian requirement for a bishop is that he *not be a recent convert. Puffed up with conceit* may refer instead to being deluded, i.e., by the false teachers; see also 6.4; 2 Tim 3.4. *Devil,* lit. "slanderer," possibly a human slanderer (see v. 11; 2 Tim 3.3). **3.7** The concern for the opinion of *outsiders* probably reflects the difficulty of the church's situation (see Introduction; also 5.14; 6.1; Titus 2.5, 8, 10; 1 Cor 14.15–17; Col 4.5; 1 Thess 4.12). **3.8** *Deacons,* "servants" or "ministers," only here and in Rom 16.1; Phil 1.1 designating a church office. The requirements for deacons closely parallel those for bishops. **3.9** The *mystery of the faith* is defined in 3.16; *the faith* is thus equivalent here to *our religion* (v. 16). **3.11** It is not clear whether the *women* are wives of deacons or deacons themselves (see text note *a*). Paul knew women deacons (Rom 16.1), but the many restrictions

placed on women in these Letters make the first option more likely here. **3.14–16** The section closes with a statement of the Letter's purpose. **3.15** The image of the church as the *household of God* informs many of the instructions in these Letters; see, e.g., vv. 4–5, 12; 5.1–2; 2 Tim 2.20–21; see also Eph 2.19–22; Heb 3.6; 1 Pet 2.5; 4.17. *Pillar and bulwark* suggests a defensive stance; see Jer 1.18. **3.16** A hymnic fragment summarizes the content of the faith, here called the *mystery of our religion.* The emphasis is on revelation (*revealed, seen, proclaimed;* see also 2 Tim 1.10; Titus 1.3) that is attested in both the heavenly and earthly realms. Notably absent here and elsewhere in these Letters is any reference to the cross. *Vindicated* probably refers to the resurrection. *Angels,* possibly those at the tomb (Mt 28.2–7) or, more likely, those who witnessed Jesus' exaltation (1 Pet 3.22). He was *taken up* at the ascension; see Acts 1.11, 22.

4.1–5 This description of false teachers (see 1.3–7) contains both stock and concrete charges. **4.1** The author does not say how the *Spirit* speaks; perhaps it was through Christian prophets (see 1 Cor 12.4–11). The *later times* probably correspond to the author's present; see also 2 Tim 3.1; 4.3; 2 Pet 3.3; Jude 18. Paul also linked his opponents with *demons* or worse; see 2 Cor 11.13–15; see also Jn 8.44; Jas 3.15; 1 Jn 3.8–10. **4.3** This verse and 2 Tim 2.18 provide the only con-

ated by God is good, and nothing is to be rejected, provided it is received with thanksgiving; [5]for it is sanctified by God's word and by prayer.

A Good Minister of Jesus Christ

6 If you put these instructions before the brothers and sisters,[a] you will be a good servant[b] of Christ Jesus, nourished on the words of the faith and of the sound teaching that you have followed. [7]Have nothing to do with profane myths and old wives' tales. Train yourself in godliness, [8]for, while physical training is of some value, godliness is valuable in every way, holding promise for both the present life and the life to come. [9]The saying is sure and worthy of full acceptance. [10]For to this end we toil and struggle,[c] because we have our hope set on the living God, who is the Savior of all people, especially of those who believe.

11 These are the things you must insist on and teach. [12]Let no one despise your youth, but set the believers an example in speech and conduct, in love, in faith, in purity. [13]Until I arrive, give attention to the public reading of scripture,[d] to exhorting, to teaching. [14]Do not neglect the gift that is in you, which was given to you through prophecy with the laying on of hands by the council of elders.[e] [15]Put these things into practice, devote yourself to them, so that all may see your progress. [16]Pay close attention to yourself and to your teaching; continue in these things, for in doing this you will save both yourself and your hearers.

Duties toward Believers

5 Do not speak harshly to an older man,[f] but speak to him as to a father, to younger men as brothers, [2]to older women as mothers, to younger women as sisters—with absolute purity.

3 Honor widows who are really widows. [4]If a widow has children or grandchildren, they should first learn their religious duty to their own family and make some repayment to their parents; for this is pleasing in God's sight. [5]The real widow, left alone, has set her hope on God and continues in supplications and prayers night and day; [6]but the widow[g] who lives for pleasure is dead even while she lives. [7]Give these commands as well, so that they may be above reproach. [8]And whoever does not provide for relatives, and especially for family members, has denied the faith and is worse than an unbeliever.

9 Let a widow be put on the list if she is not less than sixty years old and has been married only once;[h] [10]she must be well attested for her good works, as one who has brought up children, shown hospitality, washed the saints' feet, helped the afflicted, and devoted herself to doing good in every way. [11]But refuse to put younger widows on the list; for when their sensual desires alienate them from Christ, they want to marry, [12]and so they incur condemnation for having violated their first pledge.

a Gk brothers b Or deacon c Other ancient authorities read suffer reproach d Gk to the reading e Gk by the presbytery f Or an elder, or a presbyter g Gk she h Gk the wife of one husband

---

crete information about the message of the opposing teachers. **4.6–16** The positive picture of Timothy in these verses stands in deliberate contrast to the preceding description of the false teachers. **4.6** *Sound teaching.* See note on 1.10. **4.7** *Myths.* See note on 1.4. *Godliness.* See note on 2.2. **4.8** *Physical training,* perhaps a reference to the opponents' asceticism (v. 3), though the image of the athlete was common in moral exhortation; see also 2 Tim 2.5; 4.7–8. **4.9** *Saying,* probably v. 8. **4.10** On God's saving concern for *all people,* see 2.1–7. **4.14** Paul identifies a number of spiritual gifts (Rom 12.6–8; 1 Cor 12.4–11, 28–31); here the single *gift* mentioned is that of ministry, which is linked to ordination and the rite of *laying on of hands;* see 2 Tim 1.6; see also Acts 6.6; 13.3. *Prophecy.* See note on 1.18. *Elders.* See note on 3.1.

5.1–6.2 Commonplace advice relating to age groups opens a series of more specific instructions concerning other groups within the congregation:

widows (5.3–16), elders (5.17–22), and slaves (6.1–2); see also Titus 2.2–10. **5.3** *Honor* probably implies financial support; see vv. 16, 17–18; Acts 6.1. Concern for *real widows* pervades the text (see vv. 5, 16), but see note on 5.9. There is a long tradition of support for widows; see, e.g., Ex 22.22; Deut 24.17–22; Isa 1.17; Acts 6.1–6; 9.36–42. **5.9** It is debated whether the widows *on the list* are identical with the real widows or constitute a separate group, an office within the church; cf., e.g., the requirements for widows (vv. 9–10) with those for bishops (3.2–4). If it is an office, the women's duties are difficult to discern in this passage. **5.10** The author wishes to associate the widows with proper female activities. *Washed the saints' feet,* a gesture demonstrating humility and hospitality; see Gen 18.4; 1 Sam 25.41; Lk 7.44; Jn 13.1–17. **5.11–12** The *pledge* the widows took was to Christ. Since they would break it if they were *to marry,* it was also a pledge to celibacy. The false teachers promoted a similar ideal

13Besides that, they learn to be idle, gadding about from house to house; and they are not merely idle, but also gossips and busybodies, saying what they should not say. 14So I would have younger widows marry, bear children, and manage their households, so as to give the adversary no occasion to revile us. 15For some have already turned away to follow Satan. 16If any believing woman*a* has relatives who are really widows, let her assist them; let the church not be burdened, so that it can assist those who are real widows.

17 Let the elders who rule well be considered worthy of double honor,*b* especially those who labor in preaching and teaching; 18for the scripture says, "You shall not muzzle an ox while it is treading out the grain," and, "The laborer deserves to be paid." 19Never accept any accusation against an elder except on the evidence of two or three witnesses. 20As for those who persist in sin, rebuke them in the presence of all, so that the rest also may stand in fear. 21In the presence of God and of Christ Jesus and of the elect angels, I warn you to keep these instructions without prejudice, doing nothing on the basis of partiality. 22Do not ordain*c* anyone hastily, and do not participate in the sins of others; keep yourself pure.

23 No longer drink only water, but take a little wine for the sake of your stomach and your frequent ailments.

24 The sins of some people are conspicuous and precede them to judgment, while the sins of others follow them there. 25So also good works are conspicuous; and even when they are not, they cannot remain hidden.

6 Let all who are under the yoke of slavery regard their masters as worthy of all honor, so that the name of God and the teaching may not be blasphemed. 2Those who have believing masters must not be disrespectful to them on the ground that they are members of the church;*d* rather they must serve them all the more, since those who benefit by their service are believers and beloved.*e*

False Teaching and True Riches

Teach and urge these duties. 3Whoever teaches otherwise and does not agree with the sound words of our Lord Jesus Christ and the teaching that is in accordance with godliness, 4is conceited, understanding nothing, and has a morbid craving for controversy and for disputes about words. From these come envy, dissension, slander, base suspicions, 5and wrangling among those who are depraved in mind and bereft of the truth, imagining that godliness is a means of gain.*f* 6Of course, there is great gain in godliness combined with contentment; 7for we brought nothing into the world, so that*g* we can take nothing out of it; 8but if we have food and clothing, we will be content with these. 9But those who want to be rich fall into temptation and are trapped by many senseless and harmful desires that plunge people into ruin and destruction. 10For the love of money is a

a Other ancient authorities read *believing man or woman*; others, *believing man* *b* Or *compensation* *c* Gk *Do not lay hands on* *d* Gk are *brothers* *e* Or *since they are believers and beloved, who devote themselves to good deeds* *f* Other ancient authorities add *Withdraw yourself from such people* *g* Other ancient authorities read *world—it is certain that*

(4.3). **5.13** *Gadding about* may be the author's view of pastoral visits (if "the widows" constitute an office; see note on 5.9). **5.14** Roman marriage laws promoted *bearing children* (cf. 2.15; 4.3). Domestic roles for women (like *managing their households*) are also emphasized in 2.15; 5.10; Titus 2.4–5. The *adversary,* lit. "the one opposed [to us]," probably refers to hostile outsiders; see Introduction. **5.15** *Follow Satan*, probably following the false teachers (see 4.1). **5.16** The Greek text does not refer to having *relatives* who are widows, but simply to "having widows." The author seems to have in mind the situation of a relatively wealthy woman supporting several widows, perhaps in her home (see, e.g., Acts 9.39). **5.17** *Elders*. See note on 3.1. *Double honor*. See note on 5.3. **5.18** The Gospels are regarded here as *scripture* alongside the OT. The first text quoted is Deut 25.4; the second is Lk 10.7. **5.22** *Ordain,* lit. *lay hands on* (see text note *c*). The laying on of hands is a rite that transmits the Spirit and

the Spirit's gifts (see 4.14; 2 Tim 1.6; Acts 8.17; 19.6). Here it may signify ordination (see also Acts 6.6; 13.3) or restitution after repentance. **5.23** *Take a little wine* reflects the author's message of moderation. The false teachers insisted on abstinence (4.3). **6.1–2** This advice on the relationship of slaves to masters was a standard piece of early Christian exhortation; see Eph 6.5–9; Col 3.22–4.1; Titus 2.9–10; 1 Pet 2.18–21; cf. 1 Cor 7.21–24. **6.1** Here *honor* has no financial significance; cf. 5.3, 17. God will *be blasphemed* when outsiders use the behavior of Christian slaves to defame the church; see note on 3.7.

6.3–16 The final contrast between false (vv. 3–5) and legitimate (vv. 11–15) leadership. **6.3** *Sound words*. See note on 1.10. *Godliness*. See note on 2.2. **6.6** The *gain* from godliness is described in 4.8. **6.9** *Ruin and destruction*, a reference to eschatological judgment; see 1 Thess 5.3; 2 Thess 1.9. **6.10** *The love of money . . . evil*, a common maxim in popular Hellenis-

root of all kinds of evil, and in their eagerness to be rich some have wandered away from the faith and pierced themselves with many pains.

The Good Fight of Faith

11 But as for you, man of God, shun all this; pursue righteousness, godliness, faith, love, endurance, gentleness. 12Fight the good fight of the faith; take hold of the eternal life, to which you were called and for which you made*a* the good confession in the presence of many witnesses. 13In the presence of God, who gives life to all things, and of Christ Jesus, who in his testimony before Pontius Pilate made the good confession, I charge you 14to keep the commandment without spot or blame until the manifestation of our Lord Jesus Christ, 15which he will bring about at the right time—he who is the blessed and only Sovereign, the King of kings and Lord of lords. 16It is he alone who has immortality and dwells in unapproachable light, whom no one has ever seen or can see; to him be honor and eternal dominion. Amen.

17 As for those who in the present age are rich, command them not to be haughty, or to set their hopes on the uncertainty of riches, but rather on God who richly provides us with everything for our enjoyment. 18They are to do good, to be rich in good works, generous, and ready to share, 19thus storing up for themselves the treasure of a good foundation for the future, so that they may take hold of the life that really is life.

Personal Instructions and Benediction

20 Timothy, guard what has been entrusted to you. Avoid the profane chatter and contradictions of what is falsely called knowledge; 21by professing it some have missed the mark as regards the faith.

Grace be with you.*b*

a Gk *confessed*   *b* The Greek word for *you* here is plural; in other ancient authorities it is singular. Other ancient authorities add *Amen*

---

tic philosophy. **6.11** The title *man of God* (translated "everyone who belongs to God" in 2 Tim 3.17) appears frequently in the OT to designate someone with a special commission from God; see Deut 33.1; 1 Sam 9.6–10; 1 Kings 17.18; 2 Kings 4.7; Neh 12.24. Here it refers to the ordained church leader. **6.12** *The good fight*. See note on 1.18. *The good confession* was made at baptism or, more probably, ordination (see 2 Tim 2.2). **6.13–16** The formal style and language suggest that this section was a liturgical fragment. **6.13** The content of Jesus' *good confession* is not stressed; see, e.g., Mt 27.11; Jn 18.33–37. **6.14** *Manifestation* (Greek *epiphaneia*), often used in Greco-Roman religions for the appearance of a god or savior, is applied frequently in these Letters to Christ. Here it refers to Jesus' future coming (also in 2 Tim 4.8; Titus 2.13). A related verb is used to refer to his birth in 3.16; 2 Tim 1.10. **6.17–19** A more negative view of the *rich* is given in vv. 7–10; see also Lk 12.16–21; Jas 1.10. **6.20–21** The final charge to Timothy. **6.20** *What has been entrusted to you,* i.e., the apostolic traditions summarized in these Letters; see 1.18; 2 Tim 1.14. *Falsely called knowledge* (Greek *gnosis*), a final reference to false teachers; see note on 2.4.

The Second Letter of Paul to

TIMOTHY

THE SECOND LETTER TO TIMOTHY differs in significant ways from both 1 Timothy and Titus. According to the latter two, Paul was a free apostle, but 2 Timothy assumes that he is in prison (1.8; 2.9), probably in Rome (1.16–17; cf. Acts 28.16), abandoned by all but a few of his friends (4.9–16) and facing imminent death (4.6–8). The Letter thus assumes many aspects of a final testament, a thoroughly pseudepigraphical genre in which a dying patriarch exhorts and blesses a faithful child, warning him of problems to come (see, e.g., 3.1–5; 4.1–5; cf. Acts 20.17–35; see also 2 Peter). Concern for church order is thus less important in this Letter than are personal exhortations. In particular, the example of Paul's faithful endurance in the face of suffering is used to encourage Timothy—and through him all Christians—to similar endurance.

The many personal elements in the Letter (e.g., 1.15–18; 4.10–16) are viewed by some interpreters as authentic fragments of (lost) Pauline letters, but they could equally well have been crafted to lend pathos and concreteness to the Letter's warnings and exhortations. For a further discussion of the Letter's authorship, date, and purpose, see the Introduction to 1 Timothy.

[JOUETTE M. BASSLER]

Salutation

1 Paul, an apostle of Christ Jesus by the will of God, for the sake of the promise of life that is in Christ Jesus,

2 To Timothy, my beloved child:

Grace, mercy, and peace from God the Father and Christ Jesus our Lord.

Thanksgiving and Encouragement

3 I am grateful to God—whom I worship with a clear conscience, as my ancestors did—when I remember you constantly in my prayers night and day. 4Recalling your tears, I long to see you so that I may be filled with joy. 5I am reminded of your sincere faith, a faith that lived first in your grandmother Lois and your mother Eunice and now, I am sure, lives in you. 6For this reason I remind you to rekindle the gift of God that is within you through the laying on of my hands; 7for God did not give us a spirit of cowardice, but rather a spirit of power and of love and of self-discipline.

8 Do not be ashamed, then, of the testimony about our Lord or of me his prisoner, but join with me in suffering for the gospel, relying on the power of God, 9who saved us and called us with a holy calling, not according to our works but according to his own purpose and grace. This grace was given to us in Christ Jesus before the ages began, 10but it has now been revealed through the appearing of our Savior Christ Jesus, who abolished death and brought life and immortality to light through the gospel. 11For this gospel I was appointed a herald and an apostle and a teacher,[a] 12and for this reason I suffer as I do. But I am not ashamed, for I know the one in whom I have put my trust, and I am sure that he is able to guard until that day what I have entrusted to him.[b] 13Hold to the standard of sound teaching that you have heard from me, in the faith and love that are in Christ Jesus. 14Guard the good treasure entrusted to you, with the help of the Holy Spirit living in us.

15 You are aware that all who are in Asia have turned away from me, including Phygelus and Hermogenes. 16May the Lord grant mercy to the household of Onesiphorus, because he often refreshed me and was not ashamed of my chain; 17when he arrived in Rome, he eagerly[c] searched for me and found me 18—may the Lord grant that he will find mercy from the Lord on that day! And you know very well how much service he rendered in Ephesus.

A Good Soldier of Christ Jesus

2 You then, my child, be strong in the grace that is in Christ Jesus; 2and what you have heard from me through many witnesses en-

---

a Other ancient authorities add *of the Gentiles*   b Or *what has been entrusted to me*   c Or *promptly*

1.1–2 The brief salutation is very similar to that of 1 Timothy. **1.1** The *promise of life* (see also 1 Tim 4.8) opens a Letter that focuses on Paul's impending death (see 4.6–8). **1.3–5** Like many of the Pauline Letters, 2 Timothy begins with a statement of gratitude or thanksgiving. **1.3** The reference to Paul's *ancestors* suggests the antiquity of the Christian religion. The Romans were suspicious of new cults but held ancient religions in high esteem. **1.5** According to Acts 16.1, Timothy's *mother* was a believer; the reference to *Lois* pushes this matrilineal line of faith back another generation. See also 3.15. **1.6–14** A series of exhortations to strengthen Timothy in the face of afflictions. **1.6** On the *gift of God* and *laying on of . . . hands*, see 1 Tim 4.14. Here the emphasis is on Paul's personal role in this event. **1.7** *Self-discipline,* one of the four cardinal virtues of Stoic philosophy. Various forms of the word (translated "decent," "prudent," or "temperate") appear frequently in the exhortations of these Letters; see, e.g., Titus 1.8; 2.5, 6. **1.8** Timothy might be *ashamed* of the disgrace associated with imprisonment (see 2.9). The author returns several times to this theme (see vv. 12, 16; 2.15). On *suffering for the gospel,* see 1 Cor 4.9–13; 2 Cor 4.7–12; Phil 1.27–30. **1.9–**

10 A liturgical fragment conveying a strong sense of election summarizes the gospel (see v. 11). **1.9** That salvation is *not according to our works* (see also Titus 3.5) resembles Paul's assertions. Paul, however, speaks of justification, not salvation, and of works of the law, not simply works; see Rom 3.28; Gal 2.16; cf. Eph 2.8–9. **1.10** *Appearing.* See note on 1 Tim 6.14. *Savior.* See 1 Tim 1.1. *Abolished death,* i.e., abolished the power of death. See Rom 8.38–39; 1 Cor 15.54–55. **1.12** *That day* (see also v. 18), the day of judgment; see 4.8. *What I have entrusted to him.* The reading in text note b, *what has been entrusted to me,* is better; see v. 14; 1 Tim 6.20. The reference is to the apostolic teaching, regarded as a deposit that must be guarded against corruption. **1.13** *Sound teaching.* See 1 Tim 1.10. **1.15–18** Contrasting examples of cowardice and strength. **1.15** *Asia,* a Roman province in Asia Minor. *All . . . turned away.* The motif of abandonment is strong in 2 Timothy; see 4.10, 16. *Phygelus and Hermogenes.* Opponents and friends are frequently named in this Letter (see 2.17; 4.10–15); these two men are not otherwise known. **1.16** *Onesiphorus.* See 4.19.

2.1–7 Renewed exhortations to Timothy. **2.2** *Through many witnesses,* better "before many witnesses"; see

trust to faithful people who will be able to teach others as well. [3]Share in suffering like a good soldier of Christ Jesus. [4]No one serving in the army gets entangled in everyday affairs; the soldier's aim is to please the enlisting officer. [5]And in the case of an athlete, no one is crowned without competing according to the rules. [6]It is the farmer who does the work who ought to have the first share of the crops. [7]Think over what I say, for the Lord will give you understanding in all things.

8 Remember Jesus Christ, raised from the dead, a descendant of David—that is my gospel, [9]for which I suffer hardship, even to the point of being chained like a criminal. But the word of God is not chained. [10]Therefore I endure everything for the sake of the elect, so that they may also obtain the salvation that is in Christ Jesus, with eternal glory. [11]The saying is sure:

If we have died with him, we will also live
     with him;
[12] if we endure, we will also reign with him;
     if we deny him, he will also deny us;
[13] if we are faithless, he remains faithful—
     for he cannot deny himself.

A Worker Approved by God

14 Remind them of this, and warn them before God[a] that they are to avoid wrangling over words, which does no good but only ruins those who are listening. [15]Do your best to present yourself to God as one approved by him, a worker who has no need to be ashamed, rightly explaining the word of truth. [16]Avoid profane chatter, for it will lead people into more and more impiety, [17]and their talk will spread like gangrene. Among them are Hymenaeus and Philetus, [18]who have swerved from the truth by claiming that the resurrection has already taken place. They are upsetting the faith of some. [19]But God's firm foundation stands, bearing this inscription: "The Lord knows those who are his," and, "Let everyone who calls on the name of the Lord turn away from wickedness."

20 In a large house there are utensils not only of gold and silver but also of wood and clay, some for special use, some for ordinary. [21]All who cleanse themselves of the things I have mentioned[b] will become special utensils, dedicated and useful to the owner of the house, ready for every good work. [22]Shun youthful passions and pursue righteousness, faith, love, and peace, along with those who call on the Lord from a pure heart. [23]Have nothing to do with stupid and senseless controversies; you know that they breed quarrels. [24]And the Lord's servant[c] must not be quarrelsome but kindly to everyone, an apt teacher, patient, [25]correcting opponents with gentleness. God may perhaps grant that they will repent and come to know the truth, [26]and that they may escape from the snare of the devil, having been held captive by him to do his will.[d]

Godlessness in the Last Days

3 You must understand this, that in the last days distressing times will come. [2]For people will be lovers of themselves, lovers of

a Other ancient authorities read the Lord   b Gk of these things
c Gk slave   d Or by him, to do his (that is, God's) will

---

1 Tim 6.12. *Entrust to faithful people.* The need to preserve the apostolic traditions from distortion by false teachers lies behind this concern for reliable successors. **2.8–13** The theological basis of Paul's endurance. **2.8** This summary of the *gospel* resembles Rom 1.3–4. **2.11** *The saying is sure* (see 1 Tim 1.15) introduces a hymnic fragment. *If we have died with him.* Paul links this dying with baptism and interprets it as a death to sin (see Rom 6.3–11). The context here seems to link dying with Christ to suffering like him. **2.12** One *denies* Christ through one's actions; see Titus 1.16. It is the opposite of endurance. **2.13** The *faithfulness* of God and Christ is the cornerstone of Christian hope; see Rom 3.3–4; 1 Cor 10.13; 1 Thess 5.24; Rev 19.11. **2.14–26** Renewed exhortations and warnings. **2.14** *Wrangling over words* characterizes the fruitless debate with false teachers; see v. 23; 1 Tim 6.4; Titus 3.9. **2.17** *Hymenaeus.* See 1 Tim 1.20. *Philetus* is mentioned nowhere else. **2.18** The false teachers claim that the *resurrection* is a present spiritual reality, not a future hope. The author of this Letter does not refute this claim with a theological argument, but he emphasizes future resurrection life in 1.1; 2.10–11; 4.8. **2.19** The first quotation is from Num 16.5; the second vaguely recalls a number of texts (see Job 36.10; Isa 26.13). **2.20** *For special use* or *ordinary* use, lit. for "honor" or "dishonor." The author probably has in mind the distinction between faithful ministers (v. 1) and false teachers (vv. 16–18). **2.24** *The Lord's servant* (see Titus 1.1), one engaged in ministry; cf. the qualities of the bishop in 1 Tim 3.2–3. **2.25** On *correcting opponents,* see Titus 1.9, 13. **2.26** *Snare of the devil.* Also in 1 Tim 3.7; see note on 1 Tim 3.6.

3.1–9 The author uses a prediction about the last days (see Mk 13) to attack the false teachers; see also 1 Tim 4.1–5. **3.2–4** This list of vices constitutes a

money, boasters, arrogant, abusive, disobedient to their parents, ungrateful, unholy, [3]inhuman, implacable, slanderers, profligates, brutes, haters of good, [4]treacherous, reckless, swollen with conceit, lovers of pleasure rather than lovers of God, [5]holding to the outward form of godliness but denying its power. Avoid them! [6]For among them are those who make their way into households and captivate silly women, overwhelmed by their sins and swayed by all kinds of desires, [7]who are always being instructed and can never arrive at a knowledge of the truth. [8]As Jannes and Jambres opposed Moses, so these people, of corrupt mind and counterfeit faith, also oppose the truth. [9]But they will not make much progress, because, as in the case of those two men,[a] their folly will become plain to everyone.

Paul's Charge to Timothy

10 Now you have observed my teaching, my conduct, my aim in life, my faith, my patience, my love, my steadfastness, [11]my persecutions, and my suffering the things that happened to me in Antioch, Iconium, and Lystra. What persecutions I endured! Yet the Lord rescued me from all of them. [12]Indeed, all who want to live a godly life in Christ Jesus will be persecuted. [13]But wicked people and impostors will go from bad to worse, deceiving others and being deceived. [14]But as for you, continue in what you have learned and firmly believed, knowing from whom you learned it, [15]and how from childhood you have known the sacred writings that are able to instruct you for salvation through faith in Christ Jesus. [16]All scripture is inspired by God and is[b] useful for teaching, for reproof, for correction, and for training in righteousness, [17]so that everyone who belongs to God may be proficient, equipped for every good work.

4 In the presence of God and of Christ Jesus, who is to judge the living and the dead, and in view of his appearing and his kingdom, I solemnly urge you: [2]proclaim the message; be persistent whether the time is favorable or unfavorable; convince, rebuke, and encourage, with the utmost patience in teaching. [3]For the time is coming when people will not put up with sound doctrine, but having itching ears, they will accumulate for themselves teachers to suit their own desires, [4]and will turn away from listening to the truth and wander away to myths. [5]As for you, always be sober, endure suffering, do the work of an evangelist, carry out your ministry fully.

6 As for me, I am already being poured out as a libation, and the time of my departure has come. [7]I have fought the good fight, I have finished the race, I have kept the faith. [8]From now on there is reserved for me the crown of righteousness, which the Lord, the righteous judge, will give me on that day, and not only to me but also to all who have longed for his appearing.

Personal Instructions

9 Do your best to come to me soon, [10]for Demas, in love with this present world, has

_____

a Gk lacks *two men*   b Or *Every scripture inspired by God is also*

---

broadside against the opponents, not an accurate description of them (see also 1 Tim 1.9–10). **3.5–7** The description of the opponents may become more specific here, for the focus on women in these Letters suggests that they may indeed have been targeted by the false teachers. **3.5** *Godliness.* See 1 Tim 2.2. **3.6** The author belittles the false teachers and reflects a cultural stereotype by describing their students as *silly women* (lit. the diminutive "little women"). **3.7** *Knowledge of the truth.* See 1 Tim 2.4. **3.8** *Jannes and Jambres,* the names given to Pharaoh's anonymous magicians (Ex 7.11, 22) in later Jewish sources (Dead Sea Scrolls, *Damascus Document* [CD] 5.18–19). **3.10–13** Paul's behavior stands in deliberate contrast to that of the false teachers. Suffering and endurance are again highlighted. **3.11** Acts 13–14 describes events in *Antioch, Iconium, and Lystra.* **3.13** The false teachers are frequently linked with *deceiving;* see note on 1 Tim 2.14. **3.14–4.8** The final charge to Timothy. **3.15** *Sacred writings,* the Jewish scriptures. **3.16** *Inspired by God,* lit. "god-breathed." See 2 Pet 1.21. The reading given in text note *b* is equally possible and changes significantly the extent of the claim for scriptural inspiration. **3.17** *Everyone who belongs to God* (lit. "the man [person] of God"). In 1 Tim 6.11, the phrase refers to the ordained church leader, and it may do so here as well. *Good work.* See 1 Tim 2.10. **4.1–2** The charge here assumes a particularly solemn note; see also 1 Tim 5.21. **4.1** *His appearing,* the Second Coming; see also 1.10; Titus 2.13. **4.3** *The time is coming.* The author regarded this prediction as being fulfilled in his time; see 3.1. *Sound doctrine.* See 1.13. **4.4** *Myths.* See 1 Tim 1.4. **4.5** *The work of an evangelist* (see Eph 4.11) is described in v. 2. **4.6–8** A reference to Paul's circumstances concludes the charge. **4.6** *Poured out as a libation* (see Phil 2.17) interprets Paul's impending death (*departure*) as a cultic drink offering; see Num 28.7. **4.7** *The good fight.* See 1 Tim 1.18, though the Greek words are different, there suggesting warfare, here an athletic contest. **4.8** *That day.* See 1.12. **4.9–22** Per-

deserted me and gone to Thessalonica; Crescens has gone to Galatia,[a] Titus to Dalmatia. [11]Only Luke is with me. Get Mark and bring him with you, for he is useful in my ministry. [12]I have sent Tychicus to Ephesus. [13]When you come, bring the cloak that I left with Carpus at Troas, also the books, and above all the parchments. [14]Alexander the coppersmith did me great harm; the Lord will pay him back for his deeds. [15]You also must beware of him, for he strongly opposed our message.

16 At my first defense no one came to my support, but all deserted me. May it not be counted against them! [17]But the Lord stood by me and gave me strength, so that through me the message might be fully proclaimed and all the Gentiles might hear it. So I was rescued from the lion's mouth. [18]The Lord will rescue me from every evil attack and save me for his heavenly kingdom. To him be the glory forever and ever. Amen.

Final Greetings and Benediction

19 Greet Prisca and Aquila, and the household of Onesiphorus. [20]Erastus remained in Corinth; Trophimus I left ill in Miletus. [21]Do your best to come before winter. Eubulus sends greetings to you, as do Pudens and Linus and Claudia and all the brothers and sisters.[b]

22 The Lord be with your spirit. Grace be with you.[c]

---

a Other ancient authorities read *Gaul*   b Gk *all the brothers*
c The Greek word for *you* here is plural. Other ancient authorities add *Amen*

sonal instructions and concluding greetings. The emphasis is on the desertion of Paul by his former companions (see also 1.15), yet a strong network of support remains. Some of these people are mentioned elsewhere in the Pauline corpus (see Col 4.7, 10, 14; Titus 3.12; Philem 24). **4.14** *Alexander.* See 1 Tim 1.20. A man with this name is also mentioned in Acts 19.33. **4.16** *First defense,* perhaps an earlier trial (see, e.g., Acts 23.1–11) or an earlier portion of Paul's current trial. **4.17** *Lion's mouth,* probably a metaphor. **4.19** *Prisca and Aquila.* See Acts 18.2, 18 and note at v. 18; Rom 16.3; 1 Cor 16.19. *Onesiphorus.* See 1.16–18.

The Letter of Paul to

TITUS

THE OSTENSIBLE ADDRESSEE of this Letter, Titus, is one of Paul's known co-workers (2 Cor 8.23). He accompanied Paul to an important meeting in Jerusalem (Gal 2.1–10), worked on the collection for that church (2 Cor 8.6, 16–24), and served as Paul's emissary during his troubled relations with the Corinthians (2 Cor 2.13; 7.5–16). The Letter assumes that Titus has been left in Crete to organize some churches that Paul had recently established (1.5) and provides instructions for this work. Neither Acts nor Paul's other Letters, however, mention a mission to Crete.

The form and content of this Letter duplicate in many regards those of 1 Timothy, though the false teachers are more clearly linked with Judaism (1.10, 14) and the church offices are not as fully developed. For a discussion of authorship, date, and purpose, see the Introduction to 1 Timothy. [JOUETTE M. BASSLER]

Salutation

1 Paul, a servant[a] of God and an apostle of Jesus Christ, for the sake of the faith of God's elect and the knowledge of the truth that is in accordance with godliness, 2in the hope of eternal life that God, who never lies, promised before the ages began— 3in due time he revealed his word through the proclamation with which I have been entrusted by the command of God our Savior,

4 To Titus, my loyal child in the faith we share:

Grace[b] and peace from God the Father and Christ Jesus our Savior.

Titus in Crete

5 I left you behind in Crete for this reason, so that you should put in order what remained to be done, and should appoint elders in every town, as I directed you: 6someone who is blameless, married only once,[c] whose children are believers, not accused of debauchery and not rebellious. 7For a bishop,[d] as God's steward, must be blameless; he must not be arrogant or quick-tempered or addicted to wine or violent or greedy for gain; 8but he must be hospitable, a lover of goodness, prudent, upright, devout, and self-controlled. 9He must have a firm grasp of the word that is trustworthy in accordance with the teaching, so that he may be able both to preach with sound doctrine and to refute those who contradict it.

10 There are also many rebellious people, idle talkers and deceivers, especially those of the circumcision; 11they must be silenced, since they are upsetting whole families by teaching for sordid gain what it is not right to teach. 12It was one of them, their very own prophet, who said,

"Cretans are always liars, vicious brutes, lazy gluttons."

13That testimony is true. For this reason rebuke them sharply, so that they may become sound in the faith, 14not paying attention to Jewish myths or to commandments of those who reject the truth. 15To the pure all things are pure, but to the corrupt and unbelieving nothing is pure. Their very minds and consciences are corrupted. 16They profess to know God, but they deny him by their actions. They are detestable, disobedient, unfit for any good work.

Teach Sound Doctrine

2 But as for you, teach what is consistent with sound doctrine. 2Tell the older men to be temperate, serious, prudent, and sound in faith, in love, and in endurance.

3 Likewise, tell the older women to be reverent in behavior, not to be slanderers or slaves to drink; they are to teach what is good, 4so that they may encourage the young women to love their husbands, to love their children, 5to be self-controlled, chaste, good managers of the household, kind, being submissive to their husbands, so that the word of God may not be discredited.

a Gk *slave* *b* Other ancient authorities read *Grace, mercy,* *c* Gk *husband of one wife* *d* Or *an overseer*

1.1–4 The opening of the Letter repeats many elements found in 1 Tim 1.1–2, with a new, lengthy emphasis on the purpose of Paul's apostleship (see also Rom 1.1–6). **1.1** The OT concepts *servant of God* (see 2 Sam 7.5; Jer 7.25) and *God's elect* (see Isa 65.9) were appropriated by Christians; see, e.g., Rom 1.1; 8.33; Phil 1.1; Col 3.12; 2 Tim 2.10. *Knowledge of truth.* See 1 Tim 2.4. *Godliness.* See 1 Tim 2.2. **1.2–3** *Before the ages* defines the antiquity of God's recently *revealed* plan of salvation; see 2 Tim 1.9–10; see also Rom 16.25–26. **1.5–9** The qualifications for elders (*see also* 1 Tim 4.14; 5.17–22) *resemble those for bishops and deacons; see 1 Tim 3.1–13*. Here the bishop (v. 7) seems to come from the council of elders. **1.9** *Sound* ("healthy") *doctrine*, or "teaching." See note on 1 Tim 1.10. **1.10–16** A lengthy description of the false teachers; see also 1 Tim 1.3–7. **1.10** *Circumcision* is an issue Paul dwells on at length in Galatians and Romans; here it is mentioned but not discussed. *Deceivers*, in the author's eyes, are particularly dangerous; see 1 Tim 2.14. **1.11** The Pastoral Letters show a pervasive concern for the structure and stability of *families;* see 2.4–5, 9–10; 1 Tim 2.15; 3.4–5, 12; 5.4, 8, 14. **1.12** This ethnic slur is attributed by later writers to Epimenides of Crete (600 BCE). **1.14** *Myths,* here specifically identified as Jewish (cf. 1 Tim 1.4; 4.7; 2 Tim 4.4). **1.15** *All things are pure,* perhaps a rebuttal of asceticism; see 1 Tim 4.3–5. **1.16** *Profess to know God.* See 1 Tim 6.20–21.

2.1–10 Various groups in the church are exhorted to conduct that reflects contemporary virtues and the specific concerns of these Letters; see also 1 Tim 5.1–6.2. **2.1** *Sound doctrine.* See note on 1 Tim 1.10. **2.2** The virtues of the *older men* resemble those of bishops and deacons; see 1 Tim 3.2, 8. **2.3** The instructions about *older women* resemble those concerning deacons' wives (or women deacons); see 1 Tim 3.11. **2.4** On the behavior of *young women,* see 1 Tim 2.11–15; 5.14. The behavior cultivated is that of the ideal Roman wife. **2.5** *Discredited,* i.e., by outsiders offended by their behavior. See vv.

6 Likewise, urge the younger men to be self-controlled. 7Show yourself in all respects a model of good works, and in your teaching show integrity, gravity, 8and sound speech that cannot be censured; then any opponent will be put to shame, having nothing evil to say of us.

9 Tell slaves to be submissive to their masters and to give satisfaction in every respect; they are not to talk back, 10not to pilfer, but to show complete and perfect fidelity, so that in everything they may be an ornament to the doctrine of God our Savior.

11 For the grace of God has appeared, bringing salvation to all,*a* 12training us to renounce impiety and worldly passions, and in the present age to live lives that are self-controlled, upright, and godly, 13while we wait for the blessed hope and the manifestation of the glory of our great God and Savior,*b* Jesus Christ. 14He it is who gave himself for us that he might redeem us from all iniquity and purify for himself a people of his own who are zealous for good deeds.

15 Declare these things; exhort and reprove with all authority.*c* Let no one look down on you.

Maintain Good Deeds

3 Remind them to be subject to rulers and authorities, to be obedient, to be ready for every good work, 2to speak evil of no one, to avoid quarreling, to be gentle, and to show every courtesy to everyone. 3For we ourselves were once foolish, disobedient, led astray, slaves to various passions and pleasures, passing our days in malice and envy, despicable, hating one another. 4But when the goodness and loving kindness of God our Savior appeared, 5he saved us, not because of any works of righteousness that we had done, but according to his mercy, through the water*d* of rebirth and renewal by the Holy Spirit. 6This Spirit he poured out on us richly through Jesus Christ our Savior, 7so that, having been justified by his grace, we might become heirs according to the hope of eternal life. 8The saying is sure.

I desire that you insist on these things, so that those who have come to believe in God may be careful to devote themselves to good works; these things are excellent and profitable to everyone. 9But avoid stupid controversies, genealogies, dissensions, and quarrels about the law, for they are unprofitable and worthless. 10After a first and second admonition, have nothing more to do with anyone who causes divisions, 11since you know that

a Or has appeared to all, bringing salvation *b* Or of the great God and our Savior *c* Gk commandment *d* Gk washing

8, 10; 1 Tim 3.7. **2.9** *Slaves* are also exhorted in 1 Tim 6.1–2. There are no instructions to masters in either passage (cf. Eph 6.5–9; Col 3.22–4.1). **2.11–15** This passage, which may contain a liturgical fragment (vv. 11–14), provides a theological basis for the Letter's exhortations (see also 3.4–7). **2.11–13** Two appearances or manifestations of Jesus mark God's plan of salvation: the incarnation is a manifestation of God's *grace* (see also 3.4; 1 Tim 3.16; 2 Tim 1.10) and the *parousia*, or Second Coming, is a manifestation of God's *glory* (see also 1 Tim 6.14). *Salvation to all.* See note on 1 Tim 2.1–7. **2.12** The Christian life is described in the language of Hellenistic moral philosophy. *Impiety* is the mark of the false teachers; see 2 Tim 2.16. *Worldly passions* are described in 3.3. *Self-controlled, upright, and godly* lives embody essential virtues of Hellenistic moral philosophy. **2.13** Where Paul speaks of Christ's "coming" (Greek *parousia;* see 1 Cor 15.23; 1 Thess 4.15), these Letters borrow the terminology of the imperial cult and speak of his *manifestation* (Greek *epiphaneia*). NT writers rarely speak of Christ as God (but see Jn 20.28; Heb 1.8). This text may *do so,* but the translation given in textual note *b,* which does not refer to Christ as God, is equally possible. Elsewhere in these Letters Jesus' humanity is stressed (see 1 Tim 2.5).
3.1–8a Brief instructions are buttressed with a lengthy description of God's mercy. **3.1** *Be subject,* rendered *be submissive* in 2.5, 9; see also 1 Tim 2.11; 3.4. On submission to *rulers,* see Rom 13.1–7; 1 Pet 2.13–17; see also 1 Tim 2.1–2. *Good work.* See 2.7; 3.8; 1 Tim 2.10. **3.3–7** The contrast between life prior to grace and life transformed by it is typical of Christian exhortation (see Rom 6.17–19; 1 Cor 6.9–11; Eph 2.1–10). The dense theological content of these verses suggests a liturgical or creedal origin (see also 2.11–14). **3.4** *Goodness and loving kindness.* God is described with the humanitarian attributes of an ideal ruler. These attributes *appeared* at the incarnation. **3.5** The rejection of the attaining of righteousness by *works* is very Pauline, though Paul specifies works of the law; see Rom 3.28; Gal 2.16; see also 2 Tim 1.9. *Water* (lit. *washing;* see text note *d*) *of rebirth,* i.e., baptism. See Eph 5.26. The language of *rebirth* is not found in Paul's Letters, but see Jn 3.3, 5; 1 Pet 1.3. **3.6** The *Spirit* was *poured out* at Pentecost; see Acts 2.14–18. **3.7** *Justified by his grace,* a very Pauline statement (see Rom 3.24). On the *hope of eternal life,* see Rom 5.2–5; see also Titus 1.2. **3.8a** *The saying is sure* refers back to vv. 4–7; see 1 Tim 1.15. **3.8b–11** A final warning about the false teachers emphasizes their divisiveness (cf. vv. 1–2); see also 1.10–16; 1 Tim 1.4–7; 2 Tim 2.16–23. **3.9** On the tactic of *avoidance,* see 1 Tim 4.7; 2 Tim

such a person is perverted and sinful, being self-condemned.

Final Messages and Benediction

12 When I send Artemas to you, or Tychicus, do your best to come to me at Nicopolis, for I have decided to spend the winter there. 13 Make every effort to send Zenas the lawyer and Apollos on their way, and see that they lack nothing. 14 And let people learn to devote themselves to good works in order to meet urgent needs, so that they may not be unproductive.

15 All who are with me send greetings to you. Greet those who love us in the faith. Grace be with all of you.[a]

_____

a Other ancient authorities add *Amen*

2.16, 23; cf. Titus 1.9. **3.12–15** Final instructions and greetings. **3.12** *Tychicus.* See Acts 20.4; Eph 6.21; Col 4.7–9; 2 Tim 4.12. *Nicopolis* is on the western coast of Epirus (Greece); no other NT writings mention a visit by Paul to this city. Sea travel was not possible in *winter;* see 2 Tim 4.21. **3.13** *Apollos.* See Acts 18.24–28; 1 Cor 3.4–9; 16.12. **3.14** A final exhortation to *good works;* see 1 Tim 2.10.

The Letter of Paul to

PHILEMON

ALTHOUGH PAUL'S LETTER to Philemon is generally comprehensible, his unusually deferential and indirect language and the very nature of a letter as only one half of a conversation make it difficult for later readers to know its occasion and content as precisely as the first ones did.

Place and Date

PAUL WRITES FROM PRISON (vv. 1, 9, 10, 13, 23) to a Christian living in Colossae in Asia Minor. The Letter does not say where he was imprisoned, though some manuscripts add a postscript saying that Paul wrote it "from Rome," i.e., during his Roman imprisonment of 60–62 CE (Acts 28.16–31). But Rome is problematic: it involves a long distance for the slave Onesimus to travel to be with Paul; and it causes problems with Pauline chronology, for Paul's plans after Rome were to travel westward to Spain (Rom 15.22–24) and not eastward to Colossae, as he promises Philemon (v. 22). Other imprisonments—e.g., at Philippi (Acts 16.23–40) or Caesarea (Acts 23.35)—are also problematic, so that it is best to leave open the place of Paul's imprisonment. Once Rome is ruled out, so is a precise dating, leaving a period from the mid to the late 50s as most likely.

Occasion and Content

THE SLAVE ONESIMUS IS WITH PAUL and during his stay has not only served him but has also been converted by him. In fact, Paul has come to regard him as his child (v. 10) and wants him to continue in his service (v. 13). He has decided, however, to send him back to his master, Philemon (v. 12), so as to obtain Philemon's approval (v. 14) and possibly Onesimus's freedom (v. 16). Paul's problem is that Onesimus, quite possibly a runaway, may have also wronged his master or stolen something from him (v. 18), so that his requests for Onesimus's continued stay and possible emancipation are directed to a master who was more likely to be angry than amenable. To deflect this anger Paul writes cautiously, speaking deferentially to Philemon and indirectly about Onesimus. The result is a masterpiece of church diplomacy, but equally a Letter that speaks so obliquely of Onesimus's situation—e.g., his being "separated" from Philemon (v. 15)—that it is far from certain whether Onesimus was a runaway. Likewise, the Letter speaks so disarmingly of Philemon's responsibility toward Onesimus—e.g., his being asked to treat him as "more than a slave" (v. 16)—that it is unclear what Paul's intentions for Philemon really were. [RONALD F. HOCK]

Salutation

1 Paul, a prisoner of Christ Jesus, and Timothy our brother,[a]

To Philemon our dear friend and co-worker, [2]to Apphia our sister,[b] to Archippus our fellow soldier, and to the church in your house:

3 Grace to you and peace from God our Father and the Lord Jesus Christ.

Philemon's Love and Faith

4 When I remember you[c] in my prayers, I always thank my God [5]because I hear of your love for all the saints and your faith toward the Lord Jesus. [6]I pray that the sharing of your faith may become effective when you perceive all the good that we[d] may do for Christ. [7]I have indeed received much joy and encouragement from your love, because the hearts of the saints have been refreshed through you, my brother.

Paul's Plea for Onesimus

8 For this reason, though I am bold enough in Christ to command you to do your duty, [9]yet I would rather appeal to you on the basis of love—and I, Paul, do this as an old man, and now also as a prisoner of Christ Jesus.[e] [10]I am appealing to you for my child, Onesimus, whose father I have become during my imprisonment. [11]Formerly he was useless to you, but now he is indeed useful[f] both to you and to me. [12]I am sending him, that is, my own heart, back to you. [13]I wanted to keep him with me, so that he might be of service to me in your place during my imprisonment for the gospel; [14]but I preferred to do nothing without your consent, in order that your good deed might be voluntary and not something forced. [15]Perhaps this is the reason he was separated from you for a while, so that you might have him back forever, [16]no longer as a slave but more than a slave, a beloved brother—especially to me but how much more to you, both in the flesh and in the Lord.

17 So if you consider me your partner, welcome him as you would welcome me. [18]If he has wronged you in any way, or owes you anything, charge that to my account. [19]I, Paul, am

---

a Gk *the brother* b Gk *the sister* c From verse 4 through verse 21, *you* is singular d Other ancient authorities read *you* (plural) e Or *as an ambassador of Christ Jesus, and now also his prisoner* f The name Onesimus means *useful* or (compare verse 20) *beneficial*

1–3 Identifying the sender(s) and recipient(s) at the beginning of a letter is typical of Paul and of ancient letter writers generally. **1** *Timothy,* co-sender of the Letter (as also of 2 Corinthians, Philippians, 1 Thessalonians), is one of Paul's closest associates in his missionary work (see 1 Cor 4.17; Phil 2.19–24; 1 Thess 3.1–6). **2** *Apphia* and *Archippus* (see also Col 4.17) may be Philemon's wife and son. The characterization *fellow soldier* (used also of Epaphroditus in Phil 2.25) is figurative, meaning co-worker. If not family members, they are at least leaders along with Philemon in the *church* that meets in Philemon's *house.* Using domestic structures for church meetings was typical in the NT period (see also Rom 16.5; 1 Cor 16.15, 19; Col 4.15). **4–7** Typical of Paul's Letters is a statement of gratitude to God for something commendable in the recipients' conduct. Here Paul's gratitude is aimed specifically at Philemon (see text note c). **5** *Love, faith.* For the combination, see 1 Cor 13.13 (with hope); Gal 5.6; 1 Thess 3.6; 1 Tim 1.14; 2 Tim 1.13; 2.22; Titus 2.2. **7** *Refreshed through you,* vague, though it may refer to some act of hospitality, perhaps toward traveling missionaries (see 3 Jn 5–8). Note Paul's similar expression in v. 20.

8–22 In the body of the Letter Paul turns to the matter at hand: asking for Onesimus's continued service and possibly his freedom. In vv. 8–16 Paul delicately prepares Philemon for the requests in vv. 17–22. **8** *Bold enough.* The Greek term connotes that Paul feels free to exercise frank and direct speech, as would be appropriate among good friends. **9.** *Love,* without the definite article, suggests love in general, but the Greek has the article and thus may refer to Philemon's specific acts of love (vv. 5, 7). **10** *Child* and *father,* metaphors Paul uses elsewhere of his converts and himself (e.g., 1 Cor 4.15; Gal 4.19; 1 Thess 2.11). **11** *Useless,* a standard term for bad slaves. *Useful,* which plays on the etymology of the name Onesimus (see text note f), is a term for good slaves and shows how much Onesimus has changed since he left. **12** *Heart.* The translation captures the flavor of the Greek, although the connotations of the word, which might be rendered "guts," are more graphic. See also v. 20. **15** *Was separated,* probably a tactful way of referring to Onesimus's having run away; the passive form of the verb also makes Onesimus less accountable for his action and may even suggest the working of providence. **16** *More than a slave,* vague, but may imply release from slavery (see also *do even more than I say,* v. 21). Paul considers the possibility of liberation from slavery also in 1 Cor 7.20–24. His basic advice to "remain as you were called" suggests that one's status as a member of the body of Christ is more important than one's social standing. His advice for those who have the opportunity for freedom is ambiguous. See the note on 1 Cor 7.21. **17** Paul also calls Titus his *partner* (2 Cor 8.23) but otherwise speaks of whole churches—especially the Philippians—as partners (2 Cor 8.4; Phil 4.15). **19** Paul often writes a portion of his Letters in his *own hand* (see 1 Cor 16.21; Gal 6.11; see also

writing this with my own hand: I will repay it. I say nothing about your owing me even your own self. 20 Yes, brother, let me have this benefit from you in the Lord! Refresh my heart in Christ. 21 Confident of your obedience, I am writing to you, knowing that you will do even more than I say.

22 One thing more—prepare a guest room for me, for I am hoping through your prayers to be restored to you.

Final Greetings and Benediction

23 Epaphras, my fellow prisoner in Christ Jesus, sends greetings to you,[a] 24 and so do Mark, Aristarchus, Demas, and Luke, my fellow workers.

25 The grace of the Lord Jesus Christ be with your spirit.[b]

---

a Here *you* is singular   b Other ancient authorities add *Amen*

---

2 Thess 3.17). *I will repay it.* Paul dramatically reemphasizes (see v. 18) his assumption of whatever financial burdens Onesimus may have caused Philemon. *Owing me even your own self* doubtlessly refers to Paul's having converted Philemon, perhaps at Ephesus (Acts 19.10). **21** *Obedience.* Although Paul has not formally commanded anything, he obviously expects his

admonitions to be respected. **23–24** An exchange of greetings often closes ancient letters. *Epaphras, Mark, Aristarchus, Demas,* and *Luke* are all included in the closing greetings of Colossians (4.10–14). Onesimus is also mentioned in Col 4.9. Mark (Acts 12.12, 25; 13.5) and Luke are the persons later credited with writing Gospels.

The Letter to the
HEBREWS

THE LETTER TO THE HEBREWS forcefully argues that through Christ, faithful Christians have direct access to God. The text urges the faithful, confident of their covenant relationship with God, to follow Christ's example and live as he did, faithful, hopeful, loving, and patient in the face of persecution.

Author and Date

ALTHOUGH HEBREWS WAS TRADITIONALLY attributed to Paul, even early Christian readers such as Origen (185–254 CE) recognized that its style is quite different from that of Paul's Letters. Scholars have proposed attributing Hebrews to various early Christian figures such as Barnabas, Apollos, or Priscilla, but solid evidence for such suggestions is lacking. The work thus remains anonymous.

The elaborate reflections on Christ in Hebrews took some decades to develop. Hence the text was probably composed after 60 and before 95 CE, the approximate date of *1 Clement,* a letter written from Rome that uses several portions of Hebrews.

Genre and Sources

ALTHOUGH CLASSED WITH THE LETTERS of the New Testament, Hebrews is really an extended sermon or, as its conclusion labels it, a "word of exhortation" (13.22). Hebrews does, however, end like a letter (13.19–25), and the final paragraphs suggest that the homily was sent to a distant congregation.

The most important source for Hebrews is the OT in its Greek form, the Septuagint, interpreted in light of belief in Jesus. Texts from all portions of Israel's scriptures come into play: the Pentateuch, Prophets, Psalms, and other Writings. Nonbiblical traditions also play a role. The comparison of Christ and Melchizedek in ch. 7, for example, resembles speculation widespread in first-century Judaism about the shadowy figure of Melchizedek, mentioned only in Gen 14 and Ps 110.

Audience

THE REFERENCE TO "HEBREWS" in the title represents a conjecture about the identity of the audience made by early Christian scribes on the basis of the content of the homily. Yet the audience, though possibly including people of Jewish background, clearly shares with the author a Christian commitment (3.1; 4.14; 10.23).

The location of the audience is not known with certainty. The farewell (13.24) contains greetings from "those from Italy," suggesting that the author's companions are saluting friends at home. This fact, plus the early attestation of Hebrews by Clement of Rome, points to a destination in Rome, where Christians continued to speak Greek until well into the second century.

The audience, members of the church's "second generation" (2.3), had experienced persecution (10.32–34) and had perhaps become disappointed that God's promised kingdom had not yet come. Some members may even have begun to abandon the community (10.25). The author confronts this situation with a combination of exhortations to be faithful and warnings not to fall away (see, e.g., 6.4–8).

Language and Style

THE GREEK OF HEBREWS is among the most sophisticated in the NT, involving a broad vocabulary knit into complex sentences and balanced, sometimes rhythmic cadences. The author also uses all the devices of contemporary orators to embellish the argument, though many of these effects, such as the repetition of similar sounds, cannot be reproduced in translation. Imagery from various spheres of activity, including education (5.12–14; 12.7–11), agriculture (6.7–8; 12.11), seafaring (6.19), and athletics (5.14; 12.1–3), illustrates the argument. The author delights in teasing out the meaning of individual words (3.1–6; 9.15–17). All of this serves the sermon's goal of reflection on the One through whom God has definitively spoken (1.1–2).

[HAROLD W. ATTRIDGE]

God Has Spoken by His Son

1 Long ago God spoke to our ancestors in many and various ways by the prophets, [2]but in these last days he has spoken to us by a Son,[a] whom he appointed heir of all things, through whom he also created the worlds. [3]He is the reflection of God's glory and the exact imprint of God's very being, and he sustains[b] all things by his powerful word. When he had made purification for sins, he sat down at the right hand of the Majesty on high, [4]having be-

come as much superior to angels as the name he has inherited is more excellent than theirs.

The Son Is Superior to Angels

5 For to which of the angels did God ever say,
    "You are my Son;
        today I have begotten you"?
Or again,
    "I will be his Father,
        and he will be my Son"?

_____
a Or the Son   b Or bears along

1.1–4 An introduction, with elaborate rhetorical devices of assonance and alliteration, celebrates the Christian confession that the exalted Jesus is God's eternal Son. **1.1** *Ancestors* includes all the faithful men and women in biblical history, many of whom appear in ch. 11. **1.2** For the widespread Christian belief that the faithful were living in the *last days,* see Mt 24.32–35; Mk 13.28–31; 1 Thess 4.13–18. Christ's status as *heir* gives assurance to his followers and fellow heirs (1.14; 6.12, 17); see also Rom 8.17. That God created *through* Christ is affirmed in Jn 1.3; 1 Cor 8.6; Col 1.16. *Worlds* (see also 11.3), either this world and the world to come (2.5) or the multiplicity of heavenly realms through which Christ has ascended (4.14; 9.11). **1.3** Divine Wisdom is also described as the *reflection* and

image of God; see Wis 7.26. *Purification* from sin is the effect of Christ's sacrificial death; see 9.14. The image of Christ seated *at the right hand,* from Ps 110.1, appears throughout Hebrews (1.13; 8.1; 10.12; 12.2) and in other references to Christ's exaltation (Mt 22.44; Acts 2.34–35; Eph 1.20; 1 Pet 3.22). *Majesty,* a reverent way of referring to God; see 8.1. **1.4** Christ's special *name,* received at his exaltation, is mentioned in Phil 2.9–10. Here the name is probably "Son." **1.5–14** A series of scriptural verses, mostly from royal psalms, illustrate Christ's lofty status; see also Eph 1.21; Col 1.16; 1 Pet 3.22. The verses may have been traditionally linked. **1.5** Ps 2.7. *Today,* in the psalm the day of the king's enthronement, when he was adopted, hence "begotten," as God's son; here either the day of Christ's exaltation

6And again, when he brings the firstborn into the world, he says,

"Let all God's angels worship him."

7Of the angels he says,

"He makes his angels winds,
    and his servants flames of fire."

8But of the Son he says,

"Your throne, O God, is*a* forever and ever,
    and the righteous scepter is the scepter
        of your*b* kingdom.
9 You have loved righteousness and hated
        wickedness;
    therefore God, your God, has anointed you
        with the oil of gladness beyond your
            companions."

10And,

"In the beginning, Lord, you founded the
        earth,
    and the heavens are the work of your
        hands;
11 they will perish, but you remain;
    they will all wear out like clothing;
12 like a cloak you will roll them up,
    and like clothing*c* they will be changed.
But you are the same,
    and your years will never end."

13But to which of the angels has he ever said,

"Sit at my right hand
    until I make your enemies a footstool
        for your feet"?

14Are not all angels*d* spirits in the divine service, sent to serve for the sake of those who are to inherit salvation?

Warning to Pay Attention

2 Therefore we must pay greater attention to what we have heard, so that we do not drift away from it. 2For if the message declared

through angels was valid, and every transgression or disobedience received a just penalty, 3how can we escape if we neglect so great a salvation? It was declared at first through the Lord, and it was attested to us by those who heard him, 4while God added his testimony by signs and wonders and various miracles, and by gifts of the Holy Spirit, distributed according to his will.

Exaltation through Abasement

5 Now God*e* did not subject the coming world, about which we are speaking, to angels. 6But someone has testified somewhere,

"What are human beings that you are
        mindful of them,*f*
    or mortals, that you care for them?*g*
7 You have made them for a little while
        lower*h* than the angels;
    you have crowned them with glory and
        honor,*i*
8   subjecting all things under their feet."

Now in subjecting all things to them, God*e* left nothing outside their control. As it is, we do not yet see everything in subjection to them, 9but we do see Jesus, who for a little while was made lower*j* than the angels, now crowned with glory and honor because of the suffering of death, so that by the grace of God*k* he might taste death for everyone.

10 It was fitting that God,*e* for whom and

_____

a Or *God is your throne*   *b* Other ancient authorities read *his*
c Other ancient authorities lack *like clothing*   *d* Gk *all of them*
e Gk *he*   *f* Gk *What is man that you are mindful of him?*
g Gk *or the son of man that you care for him?* In the Hebrew of Psalm 8.4-6 both *man* and *son of man* refer to all humankind
h Or *them only a little lower*   *i* Other ancient authorities add *and set them over the works of your hands*   *j* Or *who was made a little lower*   *k* Other ancient authorities read *apart from God*

─────────────────────────────

or God's heavenly generation of the Son. The verse is cited again in 5.5. For God's promise to be a *Father* to the son of David, see 2 Sam 7.14. **1.6** *Firstborn*, here perhaps a messianic title; cf. Rom 8.29; Col 1.15, 18; Rev 1.5. The verse appears in Deut 32.43 in the Septuagint. *Him*, here the Son. **1.7** Ps 104.4. The psalm portrays God as using natural elements, *winds* and *flames*, as messengers (Greek *angelos*). The author of Hebrews uses the verse to emphasize the transitoriness of the angels in contrast to the eternal Son (v. 8). **1.8–9** Ps 45.6–7. As the alternative reading (text note *a*) suggests, the psalm may have assured the Israelite king that his reign was secure because God was his throne. The author of Hebrews understands the psalm to address the Son as *God*. The eternal *throne*, then, is where the anointed Son sits; see 4.16. **1.10–12** Ps 102.25–27. **1.13** Ps 110.1. V. 4 of this psalm, cited in 5.6, will form the basis for ch. 7.

1.14 *Salvation* will occur when Christ comes again; see 9.28.

2.1–4 The author interrupts the exposition of scripture to warn against neglecting the Son's message; see also 3.12; 4.11; 6.4–8; 10.26–31; 12.16–17. **2.4** For some spiritual *gifts*, see 1 Cor 12.4–11. **2.5–18** The exposition continues with a new focus on the Son's solidarity with all humanity. **2.6a** *Someone*. Similar vague allusions are found in first-century writers such as Philo; see also 4.4. **2.6b–8** Ps 8.4–6 celebrates the lofty status of all human beings. The author of Hebrews reads the text as a prophetic account of the Son; see also 1 Cor 15.27. The preferred text is found in text notes *f* and *g*. All the plural pronouns here (*them*, *their*) are actually masculine singular ("him," "his") in the Greek; this facilitates a christological reading of the psalm. **2.10** The title *pioneer* reappears in 12.2. On

through whom all things exist, in bringing many children to glory, should make the pioneer of their salvation perfect through sufferings. [11]For the one who sanctifies and those who are sanctified all have one Father.[a] For this reason Jesus[b] is not ashamed to call them brothers and sisters,[c] [12]saying,

"I will proclaim your name to my
brothers and sisters,[c]
in the midst of the congregation I will
praise you."

[13]And again,

"I will put my trust in him."

And again,

"Here am I and the children whom God
has given me."

14 Since, therefore, the children share flesh and blood, he himself likewise shared the same things, so that through death he might destroy the one who has the power of death, that is, the devil, [15]and free those who all their lives were held in slavery by the fear of death. [16]For it is clear that he did not come to help angels, but the descendants of Abraham. [17]Therefore he had to become like his brothers and sisters[c] in every respect, so that he might be a merciful and faithful high priest in the service of God, to make a sacrifice of atonement for the sins of the people. [18]Because he himself was tested by what he suffered, he is able to help those who are being tested.

Moses a Servant, Christ a Son

3 Therefore, brothers and sisters,[c] holy partners in a heavenly calling, consider that Jesus, the apostle and high priest of our confession, [2]was faithful to the one who appointed him, just as Moses also "was faithful in all[d] God's[e] house." [3]Yet Jesus[f] is worthy of more glory than Moses, just as the builder of a house has more honor than the house itself. [4](For every house is built by someone, but the builder of all things is God.) [5]Now Moses was faithful in all God's[e] house as a servant, to testify to the things that would be spoken later. [6]Christ, however, was faithful over God's[e] house as a son, and we are his house if we hold firm[g] the confidence and the pride that belong to hope.

Warning against Unbelief

7 Therefore, as the Holy Spirit says,
"Today, if you hear his voice,
[8] do not harden your hearts as in the
rebellion,
as on the day of testing in the
wilderness,
[9] where your ancestors put me to the test,
though they had seen my works [10]for
forty years.
Therefore I was angry with that
generation,
and I said, 'They always go astray in their
hearts,
and they have not known my ways.'
[11] As in my anger I swore,
'They will not enter my rest.' "

a Gk are all of one b Gk he c Gk brothers d Other ancient authorities lack all e Gk his f Gk this one g Other ancient authorities add to the end

Jesus made *perfect* by suffering, see vv. 17–18; 5.8–10; 7.28; see also 10.14; 11.40; 12.2, 23. **2.12** Ps 22.22. **2.13** Isa 8.17–18. **2.17** Later (4.15) the author excludes sin from the ways in which Christ *became like* human beings. *High priest,* a special title for Christ appearing here for the first time; see 3.1; 4.14–15; 5.5, 10; 6.20; 7.26–28; 8.1, 3; 9.11, 25. **2.18** That Christ *himself was tested* makes him qualified to be a sympathetic intercessor and advocate for his people. Cf. 5.7–10; 6.19; 7.25.

3.1–6 A comparison between Jesus and Moses introduces the theme of fidelity, which continues to 4.13. It will reappear in ch. 11. **3.1** Only here in the NT is the title *apostle* given to Jesus. It conveys the notion, prominent in John (4.34; 5.24, 30, 37; 6.38, 44; 7.16, 28; 8.16, 29; 12.44, 49), that Jesus was sent by the Father. *Confession,* the faith in God and Christ professed by the author and the audience; see 4.14; 10.23. **3.2** That Moses was *faithful* derives from Num 12.7, cited again in v. 5. **3.3** The description of Jesus as *builder* of God's house alludes to Christ's role in either creation (1.2) or redemption (2.12–13). **3.5** Moses' designation as *servant* derives from Num 12.7, where it served to exalt him; here it makes Moses inferior to the Son. For similar contrasts, see Jn 8.35; Gal 4.7. For Moses as an example of faith, see 11.23–28. **3.6** *We are his house.* See also 1 Cor 3.16–17; 1 Tim 3.15; Heb 10.21; 1 Pet 2.5; 4.17. *Confidence,* elsewhere rendered *boldness* in confessing and living the faith; see 4.16; 10.19–24, 35. For appeals to retain *hope,* see 6.11, 18; 7.19; 10.23. **3.7–4.11** A little sermon, interpreting elements of Ps 95, urges fidelity by pointing to the dire consequences of faithlessness. **3.7–11** Ps 95.7–11. **3.7** For the *Holy Spirit* speaking in scripture, see 9.8; 10.15. **3.8** *Rebellion,* the Greek translation of the Hebrew place-name Meribah. *Of testing* translates the Hebrew place-name Massah. The author of Hebrews would thus have found the Septuagint particularly useful for his homiletic point. For both places, see Ex 17.7; Num 20.1–13; Deut 33.8. **3.10** *Forty years,* in the original psalm, associated with the period of wrath mentioned in the following verse. Its association

¹²Take care, brothers and sisters,[a] that none of you may have an evil, unbelieving heart that turns away from the living God. ¹³But exhort one another every day, as long as it is called "today," so that none of you may be hardened by the deceitfulness of sin. ¹⁴For we have become partners of Christ, if only we hold our first confidence firm to the end. ¹⁵As it is said,

"Today, if you hear his voice,
   do not harden your hearts as in the
      rebellion."

¹⁶Now who were they who heard and yet were rebellious? Was it not all those who left Egypt under the leadership of Moses? ¹⁷But with whom was he angry forty years? Was it not those who sinned, whose bodies fell in the wilderness? ¹⁸And to whom did he swear that they would not enter his rest, if not to those who were disobedient? ¹⁹So we see that they were unable to enter because of unbelief.

The Rest That God Promised

4 Therefore, while the promise of entering his rest is still open, let us take care that none of you should seem to have failed to reach it. ²For indeed the good news came to us just as to them; but the message they heard did not benefit them, because they were not united by faith with those who listened.[b] ³For

we who have believed enter that rest, just as God[c] has said,

"As in my anger I swore,
   'They shall not enter my rest,' "

though his works were finished at the foundation of the world. ⁴For in one place it speaks about the seventh day as follows, "And God rested on the seventh day from all his works." ⁵And again in this place it says, "They shall not enter my rest." ⁶Since therefore it remains open for some to enter it, and those who formerly received the good news failed to enter because of disobedience, ⁷again he sets a certain day—"today"—saying through David much later, in the words already quoted,

"Today, if you hear his voice,
   do not harden your hearts."

⁸For if Joshua had given them rest, God[c] would not speak later about another day. ⁹So then, a sabbath rest still remains for the people of God; ¹⁰for those who enter God's rest also cease from their labors as God did from his. ¹¹Let us therefore make every effort to enter that rest, so that no one may fall through such disobedience as theirs.

12 Indeed, the word of God is living and ac-

a Gk brothers   b Other ancient authorities read it did not meet with faith in those who listened   c Gk he

---

here with the period of testing of God by the Israelites of the desert generation highlights their rebelliousness. **3.11** *Rest,* in the psalm the land of Canaan as Israel's resting place. The author will find a deeper sense in the word in 4.1–11. **3.12** The admonition to *take care* (see also 12.25) is common in the NT. For the danger of *turning away,* or apostasizing, see Num 14.9, which treats the desert generation, and Mt 24.10–12. A Greek wordplay links *turning away* (*apostenai*) and the *unbelieving* (*apistias*) heart. The traditional phrase *living God* (see, e.g., Deut 5.26) reappears in 9.14; 10.31; 12.22. **3.14** *Partners.* See 3.1. The term translated *confidence* (*hypostasis*) is the same as that used in 1.3 for the *very being* of God. The author may be playing on different senses of the word, here calling the audience to hold on to the "reality" that Christ provides. Cf. the use of the same word in 11.1. **3.16** See Num 14.22. **3.17** See Num 14.33. **3.18** See Num 14.43.

4.1–11 The sermonette reaches its climax in a demonstration of the way in which *rest* remains a possibility for the audience. **4.1** Attention shifts to the final verse of the psalm citation (Heb 3.7–11) and the *promise* it implies. For this motif, see 6.12, 15, 17; 7.6; 8.6; 9.15; 10.36; 11.9, 13, 17, 33, 39. **4.2** The conviction that the same *good news* has come throughout salvation history is fundamental to Hebrews; see 1.1; 11.39–40. **4.3–5** Comparison of two verses that in

Greek use forms of the word *rest.* (Such an argument is common in rabbinic literature.) **4.3** Ps 95.11, already cited in 3.11, supports the claim that God's promise remains open. That God's *works were finished* at creation implies that "rest" was available long before the Israelites approached Canaan. **4.4** Gen 2.2, with its note that God *rested,* confirms that "rest" was a reality already present at the creation of the world. The verbal connection between Ps 95 and Gen 2 is not apparent in the Hebrew but works in the Greek, where forms of the same word for "rest" are used in both verses. **4.5** The author takes the phrase *my rest* in Ps 95.11 to refer precisely to the "rest" into which God entered on the seventh day. That rest was obviously not the land of Canaan but a heavenly reality. **4.6** *It remains open* summarizes the argument of vv. 1–5. The remark that the Israelites *failed to enter* summarizes 3.12–19. **4.7** The Greek version of the OT explicitly attributes Ps 95 to *David. Much later,* the interval between the conquest of Canaan and the time of David. **4.8** The author argues, despite the contrary affirmation of Josh 21.44, that the conquest generation, under the leadership of Joshua did not attain rest, for true "rest" is not to be found in the land of Canaan but is of a different order. **4.9** The description of the promise as a *sabbath rest* implies not simple inactivity, but joyous celebration characteristic of the weekly holy day. **4.12–13** A reflec-

tive, sharper than any two-edged sword, piercing until it divides soul from spirit, joints from marrow; it is able to judge the thoughts and intentions of the heart. 13 And before him no creature is hidden, but all are naked and laid bare to the eyes of the one to whom we must render an account.

Jesus the Great High Priest

14 Since, then, we have a great high priest who has passed through the heavens, Jesus, the Son of God, let us hold fast to our confession. 15 For we do not have a high priest who is unable to sympathize with our weaknesses, but we have one who in every respect has been tested[a] as we are, yet without sin. 16 Let us therefore approach the throne of grace with boldness, so that we may receive mercy and find grace to help in time of need.

5 Every high priest chosen from among mortals is put in charge of things pertaining to God on their behalf, to offer gifts and sacrifices for sins. 2 He is able to deal gently with the ignorant and wayward, since he himself is subject to weakness; 3 and because of this he must offer sacrifice for his own sins as well as for those of the people. 4 And one does not presume to take this honor, but takes it only when called by God, just as Aaron was.

5 So also Christ did not glorify himself in becoming a high priest, but was appointed by the one who said to him,

"You are my Son,
today I have begotten you";

6 as he says also in another place,

"You are a priest forever,
according to the order of Melchizedek."

7 In the days of his flesh, Jesus[b] offered up prayers and supplications, with loud cries and tears, to the one who was able to save him from death, and he was heard because of his reverent submission. 8 Although he was a Son, he learned obedience through what he suffered; 9 and having been made perfect, he became the source of eternal salvation for all who obey him, 10 having been designated by God a high priest according to the order of Melchizedek.

Warning against Falling Away

11 About this[c] we have much to say that is hard to explain, since you have become dull in understanding. 12 For though by this time you ought to be teachers, you need someone to teach you again the basic elements of the oracles of God. You need milk, not solid food; 13 for everyone who lives on milk, being still an infant, is unskilled in the word of righteousness. 14 But solid food is for the mature, for

a Or *tempted* *b* Gk *he* *c* Or *him*

tion on the power of God's word forms an epilogue to the sermon; see also 1.3. **4.12** For God's word as a *sword,* see Eph 6.17; Rev 1.16; 2.12. For the image of the word as a warrior carrying a sword, cf. Wis 18.15–16. Divine Wisdom also has power to *pierce* the spirit; see Wis 7.23. **4.13** That nothing is *hidden* before God's eyes is a commonplace; see Jer 11.20; Rom 8.27; 1 Cor 4.5; 1 Thess 2.4. In Greek the term for *account* is the same as that for God's word (*logos*). **4.14–5.10** Discussion of Christ's role resumes with the theme of the merciful high priest, whose heavenly presence guarantees help. **4.14** Christ's passage *through the heavens* refers to his exaltation; see 1.3, 13; 2.9; 9.11. **4.15** On Christ's role as a *tested* high priest, see 2.17–18. That Christ was *without sin* is a common assumption; see 7.26; Jn 8.46; 2 Cor 5.21; 1 Pet 1.19; 2.22; 3.18; 1 Jn 3.5. **4.16** The Son's heavenly *throne* (see 1.8) is now specified as one *of grace,* since from it issues help; see 2.18. **5.2** The concern for sinners who are *ignorant and wayward* is apparently based upon the scriptural texts that treat "unintentional" sins" (Lev 4.2; 5.15–16; Num 15.22–31). **5.3** The high priest's sacrifices *for his own sins* and *for those of the people* recall the Day of Atonement; see 7.27; Lev 9.7. That solemn day's ritual dominates chs. 9–10. **5.4** For the call of *Aaron,* see Ex 28.1; Lev 8.1–9; Num 16–18. **5.5** Ps 2.7, also cited in 1.5.

5.6 Ps 110.4. The psalm's first verse was cited in 1.13. *Melchizedek,* who appears in the OT only in Ps 110.4 and Gen 14, is discussed at length in ch. 7. **5.7** *Prayers and supplications* vaguely recalls Gethsemane (Mt 26.36–46; Mk 14.32–43; Lk 22.40–46), but the overall portrait is different. *Loud cries and tears* suggests the pious prayers of such psalms as 22.1–2; 116.8–11. **5.8** The *obedience* that Jesus learned is a model for his followers; see v. 9; 12.1–3. To learn through what one has *suffered* is a Greek proverb (*pathei mathos*). **5.9** For Christ *made perfect,* see 2.10. The notion that Christ was perfected has to do not with his moral character, but with his qualifications to be a sympathetic high priest. Cf. 2.10; 7.28. His sacrificial act in turn perfects his followers; see 10.14. **5.10** *Order of Melchizedek* echoes Ps 110.4, cited in v. 6, and anticipates ch. 7. **5.11–14** Common sermonic imagery serves as a warning. **5.11** The subject that is lengthy and *hard to explain* is the interpretation of Christ as heavenly high priest given in chs. 8–10. **5.12** *Oracles of God,* Israel's scriptures; see Acts 7.38; Rom 3.2; 1 Pet 4.11. *Milk* and *solid food* commonly symbolize levels of teaching, as in 1 Cor 3.1–3. **5.13** Those who *live on milk* receive only elementary instruction, presumably grammar and rhetoric, and have not yet advanced to the *word of righteousness,* or ethics. **5.14** The *mature* have mas-

those whose faculties have been trained by practice to distinguish good from evil.

The Peril of Falling Away

6 Therefore let us go on toward perfection,[a] leaving behind the basic teaching about Christ, and not laying again the foundation: repentance from dead works and faith toward God, 2instruction about baptisms, laying on of hands, resurrection of the dead, and eternal judgment. 3And we will do[b] this, if God permits. 4For it is impossible to restore again to repentance those who have once been enlightened, and have tasted the heavenly gift, and have shared in the Holy Spirit, 5and have tasted the goodness of the word of God and the powers of the age to come, 6and then have fallen away, since on their own they are crucifying again the Son of God and are holding him up to contempt. 7Ground that drinks up the rain falling on it repeatedly, and that produces a crop useful to those for whom it is cultivated, receives a blessing from God. 8But if it produces thorns and thistles, it is worthless and on the verge of being cursed; its end is to be burned over.

9 Even though we speak in this way, beloved, we are confident of better things in your case, things that belong to salvation. 10For God is not unjust; he will not overlook your work and the love that you showed for his sake[c] in serving the saints, as you still do. 11And we want each one of you to show the same diligence so as to realize the full assurance of hope to the very end, 12so that you may not become sluggish, but imitators of those who through faith and patience inherit the promises.

The Certainty of God's Promise

13 When God made a promise to Abraham, because he had no one greater by whom to swear, he swore by himself, 14saying, "I will surely bless you and multiply you." 15And thus Abraham,[d] having patiently endured, obtained the promise. 16Human beings, of course, swear by someone greater than themselves, and an oath given as confirmation puts an end to all dispute. 17In the same way, when God desired to show even more clearly to the heirs of the promise the unchangeable character of his purpose, he guaranteed it by an oath, 18so that through two unchangeable things, in which it is impossible that God would prove false, we who have taken refuge might be strongly encouraged to seize the hope set before us. 19We have this hope, a sure and stead-

---

a Or toward maturity   b Other ancient authorities read let us do   c Gk for his name   d Gk he

---

tered ethical matters and are ready for yet more "advanced" teaching that involves properly understanding Jesus. On being *trained by practice*, see 12.11; 1 Tim 4.7; 2 Pet 2.14.

6.1–12 A more severe warning (vv. 1–8) precedes encouragement (vv. 9–12). **6.1** The same Greek term (*teleiotes*) means both *perfection*, the result of Christ's suffering (2.10; 5.9), and *maturity*, to which the audience is called (5.14). *Dead works* are not works of the law, but actions that lead to or are sin (see 9.14). **6.2** For various *baptisms*, see perhaps Acts 18.25; 19.3–5. For ritual *laying on of hands*, see Acts 8.17; 19.6. **6.3** *This*, the movement on to perfection (v. 1). **6.4** For other *impossible* things, see v. 18; 10.4; 11.6. Like some other early Christian writers, the author of Hebrews takes a rigorous stand against the possibility of repentance after baptism. This condemnation of apostasy is similar to the notion of the unforgivable sin "against the Holy Spirit" of Mt 12.32; Mk 3.29; Lk 12.10 or the "mortal sin" of 1 Jn 5.16. To be *enlightened* refers generally to accepting the truth (10.32; see also 2 Cor 4.4–6; Eph 1.18) but may also allude to baptism. *Heavenly gift*, possibly the Eucharist, although a more general reference to God's saving love is likely. For similar gifts, see Acts 2.38; 10.45; Rom 5.15; 2 Cor 9.15; Eph 3.7. **6.7** *Ground that drinks up the rain* recalls the promised

land of Deut 11.11. **6.8** *Thorns and thistles* characterize the cursed land of Gen 3.18. Fields choked with weeds are *burned over*, but the fiery end here alludes to final judgment. **6.9** The address *beloved*, common in sermons and letters (see, e.g., 1 Cor 10.14; 15.58; 1 Jn 2.7), begins the message of encouragement. **6.11** For the *full assurance of hope*, see 10.22. For holding on *to the very end*, see 3.14. **6.12** Paul frequently calls for *imitators*; see 1 Cor 4.16; 11.1; 1 Thess 1.6; 2.14. For those who *inherit the promises*, see 11.1–12.3. **6.13–20** Assurance of God's fidelity reinforces the encouraging tone of the previous verses. **6.13** The *promise* that Abraham would be the father of a great people is repeated in Gen 12.2–3; 15.5; 17.5. In Gen 22.16, God, to confirm the promise, *swore* an oath on God's own name. **6.14** Gen 22.17. **6.15** *Abraham*. See also 11.17–19. **6.17** The first-century Jewish interpreter Philo (*On Abraham* 273) similarly holds that God took oaths in order to help human beings accept God's promises. **6.18** *Two unchangeable things*, most likely God's promise and the oath that confirms it. The author may have in mind Ps 2.7, cited in 5.5, as the basic promise and Ps 110.4, cited in 5.6, as the confirming oath. **6.19** The *anchor* as a symbol of hope is not scriptural but was common in Greco-Roman culture. *Inner shrine*, the most sacred part of the tabernacle; it lies behind the *curtain*; see Ex 26.31–

fast anchor of the soul, a hope that enters the inner shrine behind the curtain, [20]where Jesus, a forerunner on our behalf, has entered, having become a high priest forever according to the order of Melchizedek.

The Priestly Order of Melchizedek

7 This "King Melchizedek of Salem, priest of the Most High God, met Abraham as he was returning from defeating the kings and blessed him"; [2]and to him Abraham apportioned "one-tenth of everything." His name, in the first place, means "king of righteousness"; next he is also king of Salem, that is, "king of peace." [3]Without father, without mother, without genealogy, having neither beginning of days nor end of life, but resembling the Son of God, he remains a priest forever.

4 See how great he is! Even[a] Abraham the patriarch gave him a tenth of the spoils. [5]And those descendants of Levi who receive the priestly office have a commandment in the law to collect tithes[b] from the people, that is, from their kindred,[c] though these also are descended from Abraham. [6]But this man, who does not belong to their ancestry, collected tithes[b] from Abraham and blessed him who had received the promises. [7]It is beyond dispute that the inferior is blessed by the superior. [8]In the one case, tithes are received by those who are mortal; in the other, by one of whom it is testified that he lives. [9]One might even say that Levi himself, who receives tithes, paid tithes through Abraham, [10]for he was still in the loins of his ancestor when Melchizedek met him.

Another Priest, Like Melchizedek

11 Now if perfection had been attainable through the levitical priesthood—for the people received the law under this priesthood—what further need would there have been to speak of another priest arising according to the order of Melchizedek, rather than one according to the order of Aaron? [12]For when there is a change in the priesthood, there is necessarily a change in the law as well. [13]Now the one of whom these things are spoken belonged to another tribe, from which no one has ever served at the altar. [14]For it is evident that our Lord was descended from Judah, and in connection with that tribe Moses said nothing about priests.

15 It is even more obvious when another priest arises, resembling Melchizedek, [16]one who has become a priest, not through a legal requirement concerning physical descent, but through the power of an indestructible life. [17]For it is attested of him,

"You are a priest forever,
     according to the order of
          Melchizedek."

[18]There is, on the one hand, the abrogation of an earlier commandment because it was weak and ineffectual [19](for the law made nothing

---

a Other ancient authorities lack Even   b Or a tenth
c Gk brothers

33; 40.3; Mt 27.51. The imagery anticipates the discussion of the tabernacle in chs. 8–10. To enter into the most sacred space behind the curtain is the right only of the high priest, once yearly, on the most solemn festival of the Day of Atonement. **6.20** *Forerunner* recalls *pioneer* in 2.10.

7.1–28 The author explores the significance of applying Ps 110.4 to Christ. In interpreting the psalm, the author relies heavily on the only other reference to Melchizedek in the OT, the account in Gen 14 of his meeting with Abraham. **7.1** See Gen 14.18–19. For the significance of this action, see v. 7. **7.2** *One-tenth of everything.* Abraham's tithe appears in Gen 14.20. The explanations of the names are understandable but technically incorrect. Melchizedek means not *king of righteousness,* but "Zedek [a Canaanite deity] is my king." *Salem* is not "peace" (Hebrew *shalom*). Philo (*Allegorical Interpretation* 3.79) offers an etymological analysis of the name similar to that of Hebrews. **7.3** *Without father* and other characteristics listed here are deduced from scripture's silence. *A priest forever.* For eternality as the central feature of the "order of Melchizedek," see v. 24. **7.5** For the priestly *tithe,* see Num 18.21–32. **7.8** It is *testified that he lives,* because the scriptures do not report Melchizedek's death; see v. 3. Some first-century Jewish texts, such as the Dead Sea Scrolls *Melchizedek* (11Q13), speculate about an angelic Melchizedek, perhaps on similar grounds. Philo (*Allegorical Interpretation* 82) provides an allegorical interpretation of Melchizedek as the Logos, or Divine Word/Reason. **7.11** *Perfection* involves effective forgiveness of sin; see 9.14; 10.14, 17–18. **7.12** *Necessarily* suggests that there is an intimate connection between priesthood and covenant law. For other cases of "necessity," see 8.3; 9.16, 23. **7.13** *Another tribe,* specified in the next verse, is one distinct from the priestly tribe of Levi. **7.14** As a descendant of David (Mt. 1.1; 9.27; 15.22; Mk 10.47; Lk 1.32; Rom 1.3; 2 Tim 2.8; Rev 22.16), Jesus was of the tribe of *Judah.* **7.15** What is *even more obvious* is that a new priest has come in place of the old order. **7.17** Ps 110.4. **7.19** That the law made nothing *perfect* contrasts with the perfect cleansing of conscience effected by Christ; see 9.9; 10.1, 14. *Hope* is grounded in the forerunner's exaltation; see

perfect); there is, on the other hand, the introduction of a better hope, through which we approach God.

20 This was confirmed with an oath; for others who became priests took their office without an oath, 21but this one became a priest with an oath, because of the one who said to him,

"The Lord has sworn
    and will not change his mind,
'You are a priest forever' "—
22accordingly Jesus has also become the guarantee of a better covenant.

23 Furthermore, the former priests were many in number, because they were prevented by death from continuing in office; 24but he holds his priesthood permanently, because he continues forever. 25Consequently he is able for all time to save*a* those who approach God through him, since he always lives to make intercession for them.

26 For it was fitting that we should have such a high priest, holy, blameless, undefiled, separated from sinners, and exalted above the heavens. 27Unlike the other*b* high priests, he has no need to offer sacrifices day after day, first for his own sins, and then for those of the people; this he did once for all when he offered himself. 28For the law appoints as high priests those who are subject to weakness, but the word of the oath, which came later than the law, appoints a Son who has been made perfect forever.

Mediator of a Better Covenant

8 Now the main point in what we are saying is this: we have such a high priest, one who is seated at the right hand of the throne of the Majesty in the heavens, 2a minister in the sanctuary and the true tent*c* that the Lord, and not any mortal, has set up. 3For every high priest is appointed to offer gifts and sacrifices; hence it is necessary for this priest also to have something to offer. 4Now if he were on earth, he would not be a priest at all, since there are priests who offer gifts according to the law. 5They offer worship in a sanctuary that is a sketch and shadow of the heavenly one; for Moses, when he was about to erect the tent,*c* was warned, "See that you make everything according to the pattern that was shown you on the mountain." 6But Jesus*d* has now obtained a more excellent ministry, and to that degree he is the mediator of a better covenant, which has been enacted through better promises. 7For if that first covenant had been faultless, there would have been no need to look for a second one.

8 God*e* finds fault with them when he says:
"The days are surely coming, says the
    Lord,
    when I will establish a new covenant
        with the house of Israel
    and with the house of Judah;
9   not like the covenant that I made with
        their ancestors,
    on the day when I took them by the
        hand to lead them out of the land
        of Egypt;

---

a Or *able to save completely*   *b* Gk lacks *other*   *c* Or *tabernacle*   *d* Gk *he*   *e* Gk *He*

6.19–20. His *approach* to God enables others to follow; see 10.19–22. **7.20** The importance of another *oath* was indicated in 6.17. **7.21** Ps 110.4. **7.22** Christ is the new covenant's *guarantee* as one whose status is assured by God's oath. *A better covenant* anticipates chs. 8–10. **7.24** That Christ *continues forever* (see v. 3) reflects Christian claims (Jn 12.34) perhaps based on Ps 89.36. **7.25** For Christ's *intercession,* see 9.24; Jn 17.9; Rom 8.34; 1 Jn 2.1. **7.26** For Christ as *holy,* see Ps 16.10 as cited in Acts 2.27; 13.35. The adjectives applied here recall Christ's sinlessness; see 4.15. **7.27** The *once for all* character of Christ's sacrifice indicates its decisive function; see 9.12, 25–28; 10.10; see also Rom 6.10; 1 Pet 3.18. **7.28** *Word of the oath,* Ps 110.4, as in v. 21. It came *later than the law* since it is in a psalm of David. For a similar argument about relative dating of scriptures, see 4.7; see also Gal 3.17.

8.1–13 The central section of Hebrews, extending to 10.18, begins with a summary of Christ's role as the heavenly high priest followed by a prophecy of a new covenant. The antithesis of heaven and earth established here will echo through the following chapters until in 10.1–10 the "heavenly" act of Christ will finally be firmly anchored in his very human and very physical sacrificial death. **8.1** *Seated at the right hand* alludes to Ps 110.1; see Heb 1.3, 13. On *Majesty,* see 1.3. **8.2** For a heavenly counterpart to the earthly sanctuary, see Wis 9.8; Rev 3.12; 7.15; 11.19; 14.15; 15.5; *1 Enoch* 14.10–20; *Testament of Levi* 3.2–4; *2 Baruch* 4.5. **8.5** Ex 25.40. **8.6** *Better promises* involve effective forgiveness (10.16–18) in the context of an eternal covenant, mediated by an eternal priest (7.20–22). **8.8–12** The citation of Jer 31.31–34 introduces several contrasts to be developed in chs. 9–10, particularly the antitheses of new/old and interior/exterior. Jeremiah envisioned a renewal of the Sinai covenant, but the author of Hebrews envisions its replacement. **8.8** The promise of a *new covenant* leads to criticism of the old (v. 13; 9.9–10) and to confidence in what Christ made

for they did not continue in my covenant,
and so I had no concern for them, says
the Lord.

10 This is the covenant that I will make with
the house of Israel
after those days, says the Lord:
I will put my laws in their minds,
and write them on their hearts,
and I will be their God,
and they shall be my people.

11 And they shall not teach one another
or say to each other, 'Know the Lord,'
for they shall all know me,
from the least of them to the greatest.

12 For I will be merciful toward their
iniquities,
and I will remember their sins no
more."

13 In speaking of "a new covenant," he has
made the first one obsolete. And what is obsolete and growing old will soon disappear.

The Earthly and the Heavenly Sanctuaries

9 Now even the first covenant had regulations for worship and an earthly sanctuary. 2For a tent[a] was constructed, the first one,
in which were the lampstand, the table, and
the bread of the Presence;[b] this is called the
Holy Place. 3Behind the second curtain was a
tent[a] called the Holy of Holies. 4In it stood the
golden altar of incense and the ark of the covenant overlaid on all sides with gold, in which
there were a golden urn holding the manna,
and Aaron's rod that budded, and the tablets
of the covenant; 5above it were the cherubim

of glory overshadowing the mercy seat.[c] Of
these things we cannot speak now in detail.

6 Such preparations having been made, the
priests go continually into the first tent[a] to
carry out their ritual duties; 7but only the high
priest goes into the second, and he but once a
year, and not without taking the blood that he
offers for himself and for the sins committed
unintentionally by the people. 8By this the
Holy Spirit indicates that the way into the
sanctuary has not yet been disclosed as long as
the first tent[a] is still standing. 9This is a symbol[d] of the present time, during which gifts
and sacrifices are offered that cannot perfect
the conscience of the worshiper, 10but deal
only with food and drink and various baptisms, regulations for the body imposed until
the time comes to set things right.

11 But when Christ came as a high priest of
the good things that have come,[e] then through
the greater and perfect[f] tent[a] (not made with
hands, that is, not of this creation), 12he entered once for all into the Holy Place, not with
the blood of goats and calves, but with his own
blood, thus obtaining eternal redemption.
13For if the blood of goats and bulls, with the
sprinkling of the ashes of a heifer, sanctifies
those who have been defiled so that their flesh
is purified, 14how much more will the blood of
Christ, who through the eternal Spirit[g] offered
himself without blemish to God, purify our[a]

---

a Or tabernacle   b Gk the presentation of the loaves   c Or the
place of atonement   d Gk parable   e Other ancient authorities
read good things to come   f Gk more perfect   g Other ancient
authorities read Holy Spirit

---

available (10.19–22). The antithesis of new and old
parallels that of heaven and earth in vv. 1–6. **8.12** That
God will remember their sins no more is central to the
new covenant; see 10.17–18.

9.1–22 The author reflects on the themes of ch. 8
and considers how Christ's "heavenly" sacrifice inau-
gurates a new covenant. **9.1** The description of the
earthly sanctuary relies on the accounts of the desert
tabernacle in Ex 25.1–31.11; 36.1–40.38, with some
modifications. **9.2** Lampstand. See Ex 25.31–39;
37.17–24; 40.4. Table. See Ex 25.23–28; 37.10–15;
40.4. Bread. See Ex 25.30; 40.23; Mt 12.4. **9.4** Altar of
incense. See Ex 30.1–10; 37.25–28; 40.5. Ark. See Ex
25.10–15; 37.1–5; 40.3. Manna. See Ex 16.33–34.
Aaron's rod. See Num 17.1–11. Tablets of the covenant.
See Ex 25.16. **9.5** Cherubim, mercy seat. See Ex 25.17–
22; 37.6–9; Lev 16.15. The Greek word for the latter,
hilasterion, also appears in Rom 3.25. **9.6** Ritual duties
included trimming lamps (Ex 27.20–21) and placing
rows of "showbread" (Lev 24.5–9). **9.7** Once a year,

i.e., on the Day of Atonement, as specified in Lev
16.29–34. On the blood of the sin offering, see Lev
16.11–19. It is alluded to again in Heb 9.12. **9.8** The
way to where God dwells is opened by Christ; see 10.9–
20. The first, or outer, tent stands for the whole cultic
system. **9.10** Concern with food reappears in 13.9.
Baptisms, here cleansing rituals; cf. 6.2. The time to set
things right came with the inauguration of the new
covenant. **9.11** The greater and perfect tent is heavenly;
see 8.2. **9.12** Goats and calves alludes to the Day of
Atonement offerings; see Lev 16.5–15. The disdainful
tone imitates prophetic criticism of the sacrificial system; see Ps 50.13; Isa 1.11. **9.13** The ashes of a heifer
were used in purifying rituals; see Num 19. **9.14** Eternal Spirit, probably not the Holy Spirit (the term probably should not be capitalized) but the spiritual aspect
of Christ's sacrifice, which stands in contrast to the
Jewish temple sacrifices. The significance of that spiritual aspect will become clear in 10.5–10. Human conscience is the inner sanctuary where Christ's atoning

conscience from dead works to worship the living God!

15 For this reason he is the mediator of a new covenant, so that those who are called may receive the promised eternal inheritance, because a death has occurred that redeems them from the transgressions under the first covenant.[b] 16Where a will[b] is involved, the death of the one who made it must be established. 17For a will[b] takes effect only at death, since it is not in force as long as the one who made it is alive. 18Hence not even the first covenant was inaugurated without blood. 19For when every commandment had been told to all the people by Moses in accordance with the law, he took the blood of calves and goats,[c] with water and scarlet wool and hyssop, and sprinkled both the scroll itself and all the people, 20saying, "This is the blood of the covenant that God has ordained for you." 21And in the same way he sprinkled with the blood both the tent[d] and all the vessels used in worship. 22Indeed, under the law almost everything is purified with blood, and without the shedding of blood there is no forgiveness of sins.

Christ's Sacrifice Takes Away Sin

23 Thus it was necessary for the sketches of the heavenly things to be purified with these rites, but the heavenly things themselves need better sacrifices than these. 24For Christ did not enter a sanctuary made by human hands, a mere copy of the true one, but he entered into heaven itself, now to appear in the presence of God on our behalf. 25Nor was it to offer himself again and again, as the high priest enters the Holy Place year after year with blood that is not his own; 26for then he would have had to suffer again and again since the foundation of the world. But as it is, he has appeared once for all at the end of the age to remove sin by the sacrifice of himself. 27And just as it is appointed for mortals to die once, and after that the judgment, 28so Christ, having been offered once to bear the sins of many, will appear a second time, not to deal with sin, but to save those who are eagerly waiting for him.

Christ's Sacrifice Once for All

10 Since the law has only a shadow of the good things to come and not the true form of these realities, it[e] can never, by the same sacrifices that are continually offered year after year, make perfect those who approach. 2Otherwise, would they not have ceased being offered, since the worshipers, cleansed once for all, would no longer have any consciousness of sin? 3But in these sacrifices there is a reminder of sin year after year. 4For it is impossible for the blood of bulls and goats to take away sins. 5Consequently, when Christ[f] came into the world, he said,

---

a Other ancient authorities read *your*   *b* The Greek word used here means both *covenant* and *will*   *c* Other ancient authorities lack *and goats*   *d* Or *tabernacle*   *e* Other ancient authorities read *they*   *f* Gk *he*

---

sacrifice has its effect; see 8.10. For similar affirmations of the cleansing effect of Christ's death, see Acts 15.9; Eph 5.26; Titus 2.14; 1 Pet 3.21; 1 Jn 1.7, 9. *Dead works, sins* (see 6.1), which contrast with deeds of love (10.24). *Worship* involves Christian prayer (13.15), but also the "sacrifices" of good works (10.24; 13.6). **9.15** For Christians as *called,* see Rom 1.6; 1 Cor 1.2; Jude 1; Rev 17.14. *Inheritance.* See also 1.14; 6.12, 17. **9.15–17** *Covenant, will.* For a similar wordplay (see text note *b*), see Gal 3.15–18. The play on the two senses of the Greek *diatheke* suggests that the heavenly inheritance awaiting Christians is promised to them in the *covenant,* which is a "testament" that Christ left for them. **9.18** The sacrifice concluding the covenant's ratification in Ex 24.3–8 foreshadows Christ's death. **9.19** Various rituals are conflated. *Water, hyssop.* See Num 19.9, 18, 20. *Scarlet wool.* See Lev 14.2–6. **9.20** Ex 24.8. **9.23–28** Further consideration of Christ's sacrifice emphasizes its unique character. **9.23** *Heavenly things* probably symbolize the consciences (v. 14) of the faithful. **9.24** For Christ's entry *into heaven,* see

4.14; 8.1–2; 9.11–12. *On our behalf* reemphasizes Christ's intercessory role; see 7.25. **9.25** *Year after year* recalls the high priest's action on the annual Day of Atonement; see v. 7. For the *blood,* see vv. 12–14. **9.26** For the *once for all* quality of Christ's sacrifice, see 7.27; 9.12; 10.10. **9.27** The notion of final *judgment* (Dan 7.26; Mt 25.31–46; 2 Thess 2.12; Rev 20.12) is applied to the individual. **9.28** For the *sins of many,* see Isa 53.12; Mk 10.45; Rom 5.19. Christ's coming a *second time* was a common expectation; see Mk 13.24–27; Acts 1.10–11; 1 Cor 15.23–24; Rev 1.7.

10.1–18 A final reflection on Christ's sacrifice indicates how it inaugurated Jeremiah's promised covenant: as an act of conformity to God's will. **10.1** For the old as a *shadow* of the heavenly, see 8.5. That the law was unable to *make perfect* was argued in 7.11, 19. **10.3** *Year after year.* See 9.7, 25. **10.4** *Bulls and goats.* See 9.12–13. **10.5a** The *world,* not some heavenly realm, is where Christ made his decisive sacrifice. **10.5b–7** Ps 40.6–8. Similar sentiments appear in 1 Sam 15.22; Pss 50.8–15; 51.16–19; Isa 1.10–17; Jer 7.21–26; Hos 6.6. For

"Sacrifices and offerings you have not
desired,
but a body you have prepared for me;
6 in burnt offerings and sin offerings
you have taken no pleasure.
7 Then I said, 'See, God, I have come to do
your will, O God'
(in the scroll of the book[a] it is written
of me).'"

8When he said above, "You have neither desired nor taken pleasure in sacrifices and offerings and burnt offerings and sin offerings"
(these are offered according to the law), 9then
he added, "See, I have come to do your will."
He abolishes the first in order to establish the
second. 10And it is by God's will[b] that we have
been sanctified through the offering of the
body of Jesus Christ once for all.

11 And every priest stands day after day at
his service, offering again and again the same
sacrifices that can never take away sins. 12But
when Christ[c] had offered for all time a single
sacrifice for sins, "he sat down at the right
hand of God," 13and since then has been waiting "until his enemies would be made a footstool for his feet." 14For by a single offering he
has perfected for all time those who are sanctified. 15And the Holy Spirit also testifies to us,
for after saying,

16 "This is the covenant that I will make
with them
after those days, says the Lord:

I will put my laws in their hearts,
and I will write them on their minds,"
17he also adds,
"I will remember[d] their sins and their
lawless deeds no more."
18Where there is forgiveness of these, there is
no longer any offering for sin.

A Call to Persevere

19 Therefore, my friends,[e] since we have confidence to enter the sanctuary by the blood of
Jesus, 20by the new and living way that he
opened for us through the curtain (that is,
through his flesh), 21and since we have a great
priest over the house of God, 22let us approach
with a true heart in full assurance of faith, with
our hearts sprinkled clean from an evil conscience and our bodies washed with pure water.
23Let us hold fast to the confession of our hope
without wavering, for he who has promised is
faithful. 24And let us consider how to provoke
one another to love and good deeds, 25not neglecting to meet together, as is the habit of
some, but encouraging one another, and all the
more as you see the Day approaching.

26 For if we willfully persist in sin after having received the knowledge of the truth, there
no longer remains a sacrifice for sins, 27but a
fearful prospect of judgment, and a fury of fire

a Meaning of Gk uncertain b Gk by that will c Gk this one
d Gk on their minds and I will remember e Gk Therefore,
brothers

other OT passages attributed to Christ, see 2.12–13.
10.5b The reading *body you have prepared* follows the
Septuagint. **10.9** Real sacrifice is conformity to the *will*
of God. **10.10** On God's will that believers be *sanctified*, see 1 Thess 4.3. The composite name *Jesus Christ*
here appears for the first time in Hebrews (see also
13.8). For the name Jesus alone, see 2.9; 3.1; cf. 4.14.
The double name probably emphasizes that Christ's
obedience to God's will involved his whole being, including his body (see v. 5b), the reality that can cast a
shadow (see v. 1). The play on "body"/"shadow" imagery offers a surprising twist on the dichotomy previously deployed between the "heavenly" reality and the
"earthly" shadow. **10.11** The weakness of the old sacrificial system is emphasized for the last time; see 7.11,
19; 9.9–10; 10.1–4. **10.12** Ps 110.1, last encountered in
8.1. **10.13** For this portion of Ps 110.1, see 1.13. The
full effects of Christ's sacrifice are yet to be felt.
10.14 That Christ's death, which made him perfect
(2.10; 5.9; 7.28), has *perfected* worshipers is the key
point of contrast with old sacrifices; see 7.19; 9.9; 10.1.
10.15 For the testimony of the *Holy Spirit*, see 3.7.
10.16 A modified citation of Jer 31.33, cited in 8.10.
Here *with them* replaces "the house of Israel." **10.17** Jer

31.34b, cited in 8.12, here with the addition of *and
their lawless deeds*. **10.19–39** The author applies the
reflections on Christ to the audience, emphasizing
faith (v. 22), hope (v. 23), and love (v. 24). For the
triad, see 1 Cor 13.13. **10.19** For the recommended
confidence, see 3.6; 4.16. **10.20** On the opening of the
new . . . way, see 9.8. In Acts, Christianity is called the
"Way"; see Acts 9.2; 18.25; 24.14. The *curtain* (6.19;
9.3) through which the high priest passes (9.7) to approach God's presence is identified with Christ's *flesh*,
a synonym for his "body" (10.10). **10.21** For the high
priest and *house of God*, see 3.1–6. **10.22** For cultic *approach*, see 4.16. The reference to *hearts* being *sprinkled* recalls 9.13–14 and perhaps Ezek 36.25–26.
10.23 For holding to the *confession*, see 3.1–6; 4.14. On
hope, see 3.6. For God being *faithful*, see Deut 7.9; Ps
145.13. **10.24** For more loving *deeds*, see 13.1–16.
10.25 Israelite prophets (Isa 2.12; Joel 1.15; 3.14; Am
5.18; 8.9; Zeph 1.14; Zech 14.1) expected the *Day* of
the Lord, as did early Christians; see Mt 10.15; 1 Cor
1.8; 3.13; 5.5; 2 Cor 1.14; 1 Thess 5.2, 4; 2 Thess 2.2;
2 Pet 3.10; 1 Jn 4.17. **10.26** Stern language repeats the
warning of 6.4–8. **10.27** For consuming *fire*, see Isa
26.11; 66.15–16, 24; Zeph 1.18; 2 Thess 1.7–8; Rev

that will consume the adversaries. 28 Anyone who has violated the law of Moses dies without mercy "on the testimony of two or three witnesses." 29 How much worse punishment do you think will be deserved by those who have spurned the Son of God, profaned the blood of the covenant by which they were sanctified, and outraged the Spirit of grace? 30 For we know the one who said, "Vengeance is mine, I will repay." And again, "The Lord will judge his people." 31 It is a fearful thing to fall into the hands of the living God.

32 But recall those earlier days when, after you had been enlightened, you endured a hard struggle with sufferings, 33 sometimes being publicly exposed to abuse and persecution, and sometimes being partners with those so treated. 34 For you had compassion for those who were in prison, and you cheerfully accepted the plundering of your possessions, knowing that you yourselves possessed something better and more lasting. 35 Do not, therefore, abandon that confidence of yours; it brings a great reward. 36 For you need endurance, so that when you have done the will of God, you may receive what was promised. 37 For yet

"in a very little while,
    the one who is coming will come and
        will not delay;
38 but my righteous one will live by faith.
    My soul takes no pleasure in anyone
        who shrinks back."

39 But we are not among those who shrink back and so are lost, but among those who have faith and so are saved.

The Meaning of Faith

11 Now faith is the assurance of things hoped for, the conviction of things not seen. 2 Indeed, by faith a our ancestors received approval. 3 By faith we understand that the worlds were prepared by the word of God, so that what is seen was made from things that are not visible. b

The Examples of Abel, Enoch, and Noah

4 By faith Abel offered to God a more acceptable c sacrifice than Cain's. Through this he received approval as righteous, God himself giving approval to his gifts; he died, but through his faith d he still speaks. 5 By faith Enoch was taken so that he did not experience death; and "he was not found, because God had taken him." For it was attested before he was taken away that "he had pleased God." 6 And without faith it is impossible to please God, for whoever would approach him must believe that he exists and that he rewards those who seek him. 7 By faith Noah, warned by God about events as yet unseen, respected the warning and built an ark to save his household; by this he condemned the world and became an heir to the righteousness that is in accordance with faith.

The Faith of Abraham

8 By faith Abraham obeyed when he was called to set out for a place that he was to re-

---

a Gk by this b Or was not made out of visible things
c Gk greater d Gk through it

11.5; 20.14. **10.28** Anyone generalizes from the punishment for cases such as blasphemy (Lev 24.14–16) and idolatry (Deut 17.2–5). The general requirement of two or three witnesses (Deut 19.15) applies explicitly to idolatry in Deut 17.6. **10.30a** The citation is from Deut 32.35, in a form attested in Rom 12.19. **10.30b** The citation is from Deut 32.36 or Ps 135.14. **10.32** On being enlightened, see 6.4. **10.36** The concern with endurance dominates the remaining chapters; see 11.27; 12.2, 7; 13.13. To do the will of God is the essence of covenant fidelity; see v. 9; 13.21. **10.37–38** A composite citation of Isa 26.20 ("a little while") and Hab 2.3–4, the latter in its Greek form. Hab 2.4 is also cited in Rom 1.17; Gal 3.11. The one who is coming, i.e., Christ. **11.1–3** The definition of faith, which involves both belief and fidelity, is compact and evocative. **11.1** The word translated by assurance (Greek hypostasis) appears in 1.3, where it is translated very being, and in 3.14, where it is translated confidence. Conviction is not simply a subjective attitude; unseen realities are tested

and "proved" by experience. The following catalogue provides biblical examples of such experiences. Hopes and things not seen are paralleled in Rom 8.24. **11.3** The plural worlds appears in 1.2. For creation by God's word, see Gen 1.3; Ps 33.6; Wis 9.1; Jn 1.1–3. For creation from things that are not visible, see 2 Macc 7.28; Rom 4.17; 2 Enoch 24.2. **11.4–7** Various patriarchs exemplify hopeful belief and fidelity. **11.4** For Abel's sacrifice, see Gen 4.4. That Abel still speaks derives from Gen 4.10; see Heb 12.24. **11.5** For Enoch's removal to heaven, see Gen 5.24; Sir 44.16. That Enoch had pleased God relies on the Septuagint of Gen 5.22. **11.6** On the importance of belief that God exists, see Wis 13.1; 2 Esd 7.23; 8.58. God rewards those who seek him in Pss 14.2; 34.10; 53.2; 119.2; Am 9.12 as cited in Acts 15.17. **11.7** Noah. See Gen 6.8–9.17; Sir 44.17. **11.8–22** For other appeals to Abraham and his family, see Wis 10.5; Sir 44.19–21; 1 Macc 2.52; 4 Macc 16.20. In the NT, see Acts 7.2–8; Rom 4; Gal 3.6–9. **11.8** Abraham set out from Ur to Canaan; see Gen 11.31–12.4.

ceive as an inheritance; and he set out, not knowing where he was going. 9By faith he stayed for a time in the land he had been promised, as in a foreign land, living in tents, as did Isaac and Jacob, who were heirs with him of the same promise. 10For he looked forward to the city that has foundations, whose architect and builder is God. 11By faith he received power of procreation, even though he was too old—and Sarah herself was barren—because he considered him faithful who had promised.ᵃ 12Therefore from one person, and this one as good as dead, descendants were born, "as many as the stars of heaven and as the innumerable grains of sand by the seashore."

13 All of these died in faith without having received the promises, but from a distance they saw and greeted them. They confessed that they were strangers and foreigners on the earth, 14for people who speak in this way make it clear that they are seeking a homeland. 15If they had been thinking of the land that they had left behind, they would have had opportunity to return. 16But as it is, they desire a better country, that is, a heavenly one. Therefore God is not ashamed to be called their God; indeed, he has prepared a city for them.

17 By faith Abraham, when put to the test, offered up Isaac. He who had received the promises was ready to offer up his only son, 18of whom he had been told, "It is through Isaac that descendants shall be named for you." 19He considered the fact that God is able even to raise someone from the dead—and figuratively speaking, he did receive him back. 20By faith Isaac invoked blessings for the future on Jacob and Esau. 21By faith Jacob, when dying, blessed each of the sons of Joseph, "bowing in worship over the top of his staff." 22By faith Joseph, at the end of his life, made mention of the exodus of the Israelites and gave instructions about his burial.ᵇ

The Faith of Moses

23 By faith Moses was hidden by his parents for three months after his birth, because they saw that the child was beautiful; and they were not afraid of the king's edict.ᶜ 24By faith Moses, when he was grown up, refused to be called a son of Pharaoh's daughter, 25choosing rather to share ill-treatment with the people of God than to enjoy the fleeting pleasures of sin. 26He considered abuse suffered for the Christᵈ to be greater wealth than the treasures of Egypt, for he was looking ahead to the reward. 27By faith he left Egypt, unafraid of the king's anger; for he persevered as thoughᵉ he saw him who is invisible. 28By faith he kept the Passover and the sprinkling of blood, so that the destroyer of the firstborn would not touch the firstborn of Israel.ᶠ

The Faith of Other Israelite Heroes

29 By faith the people passed through the Red Sea as if it were dry land, but when the Egyptians attempted to do so they were drowned. 30By faith the walls of Jericho fell after they

---

a Or *By faith Sarah herself, though barren, received power to conceive, even when she was too old, because she considered him faithful who had promised.*   *b* Gk *his bones*   *c* Other ancient authorities add *By faith Moses, when he was grown up, killed the Egyptian, because he observed the humiliation of his people* (Gk *brothers*)   *d* Or *the Messiah*   *e* Or *because*   *f* Gk *would not touch them*

11.10 The city with divine *foundations* was traditionally Jerusalem; see Ps 87.1; Isa 54.11. Hebrews reinterprets such language in terms of a "heavenly" reality; see 12.22. **11.11** For the birth of Isaac, see Gen 18.1–15; 21.1–7. **11.12** *As good as dead* also describes Abraham in Rom 4.19. For *stars* and *sand*, see Gen 22.17. **11.13** For the status of being *strangers and foreigners*, see Gen 23.4; 47.4, 9; Lev 25.23; 1 Chr 29.15; Ps 39.12; Eph 2.19; 1 Pet 1.1; 2.11. **11.16** God is the God of the patriarchs in Gen 28.13; Ex 3.6; Mt 22.32; Mk 12.26–27. **11.17** For the episode when Abraham *offered up* his son, see Gen 22.1–14; Wis 10.5; Sir 44.20; 1 Macc 2.52; 4 Macc 16.18–20; Jubilees 17.15–18. **11.18** Gen 21.12. **11.19** *Figuratively speaking*, or "as a figure," i.e., of Christ's resurrection. **11.20** For Isaac's *blessings*, see Gen 27.27–40. **11.21** The *sons of Joseph*, Ephraim and Manasseh, receive Jacob's blessing in Gen 48.8–22. Jacob *bowed in worship* in Gen 47.31, following the Septuagint. **11.22** For the prophecy of the *exodus*, see Gen 50.24. **11.23–28** For other appeals to Moses, see Sir 45.1–5; Acts 7.20–34. Hebrews contrasts Moses with Christ in 3.1–6. **11.23** For the infancy of *Moses*, see Ex 2.1–10; Acts 7.20–22. **11.25** For Moses' decision to share the fate of the Israelites, see Ex 2.11–12; Acts 7.23–24. **11.26** How Moses understood his sufferings to have been *for the Christ* is obscure; perhaps he did so as a visionary (v. 27) forerunner of Christ. A connection between Moses and Christ could be based on Deut 18.15–20, cited in Acts 3.22–23, which speaks of a "prophet like Moses" who is to come. **11.27** Moses *left Egypt* for Midian in Ex 2.15; see also Acts 7.29. Moses *saw* God face to face according to Ex 33.11; Num 12.8; Deut 34.10; Sir 45.5. **11.28** For the first *Passover*, see Ex 12.1–28. **11.29–40** The catalogue of the faithful moves more rapidly. **11.29** For crossing the *Red Sea*, see Ex 14. **11.30** For

had been encircled for seven days. [31]By faith Rahab the prostitute did not perish with those who were disobedient,[a] because she had received the spies in peace.

32 And what more should I say? For time would fail me to tell of Gideon, Barak, Samson, Jephthah, of David and Samuel and the prophets— [33]who through faith conquered kingdoms, administered justice, obtained promises, shut the mouths of lions, [34]quenched raging fire, escaped the edge of the sword, won strength out of weakness, became mighty in war, put foreign armies to flight. [35]Women received their dead by resurrection. Others were tortured, refusing to accept release, in order to obtain a better resurrection. [36]Others suffered mocking and flogging, and even chains and imprisonment. [37]They were stoned to death, they were sawn in two,[b] they were killed by the sword; they went about in skins of sheep and goats, destitute, persecuted, tormented— [38]of whom the world was not worthy. They wandered in deserts and mountains, and in caves and holes in the ground.

39 Yet all these, though they were commended for their faith, did not receive what was promised, [40]since God had provided something better so that they would not, apart from us, be made perfect.

The Example of Jesus

12 Therefore, since we are surrounded by so great a cloud of witnesses, let us also lay aside every weight and the sin that clings so closely,[c] and let us run with perseverance the race that is set before us, [2]looking to Jesus the pioneer and perfecter of our faith, who for the sake of[d] the joy that was set before him endured the cross, disregarding its shame, and has taken his seat at the right hand of the throne of God.

3 Consider him who endured such hostility against himself from sinners,[e] so that you may not grow weary or lose heart. [4]In your struggle against sin you have not yet resisted to the point of shedding your blood. [5]And you have forgotten the exhortation that addresses you as children—

"My child, do not regard lightly the
    discipline of the Lord,
  or lose heart when you are punished by
    him;
[6] for the Lord disciplines those whom he
    loves,
  and chastises every child whom he
    accepts."

[7]Endure trials for the sake of discipline. God is treating you as children; for what child is there whom a parent does not discipline? [8]If you do not have that discipline in which all children share, then you are illegitimate and not his children. [9]Moreover, we had human parents to discipline us, and we respected them. Should we not be even more willing to be subject to the Father of spirits and live? [10]For they disciplined us for a short time as seemed best to them, but he disciplines us for our good, in order that we may share his holiness. [11]Now, discipline always seems painful rather than pleasant at the time, but later it yields the peaceful fruit of righteousness to those who have been trained by it.

---

a Or *unbelieving*   b Other ancient authorities add *they were tempted*   c Other ancient authorities read *sin that easily distracts*   d Or *who instead of*   e Other ancient authorities read *such hostility from sinners against themselves*

---

the fall of *Jericho,* see Josh 6. **11.31** *Rahab.* See Josh 2.1; 6.17. **11.32** *Gideon.* See Judg 6–8. *Barak.* See Judg 4–5. *Samson.* See Judg 13–16. *Jephthah.* See Judg 11–12. *David and Samuel.* See 1 and 2 Sam. **11.33** For shutting *mouths of lions,* see Judg 14.6; 1 Sam 17.34–35; Dan 6.19–23. **11.34** For quenching *fire,* see Dan 3, and the Septuagint addition, Pr Azar 26–27, 66. *Strength out of weakness* may allude to Gideon (Judg 6.15), Samson (Judg 16.17), or heroines such as Esther. **11.35** For cases of *resurrection,* see 1 Kings 17.17–24; 2 Kings 4.18–37. Those *tortured* were martyrs such as Eleazar in 2 Macc 6.18–31 or the youths of 2 Macc 7. **11.36** *Chains and imprisonment* may refer to Jeremiah; see Jer 20.2; 29.26; 37.15. **11.37** Zechariah was *stoned,* according to 2 Chr 24.21. Legend attributes the same fate to Jeremiah. Legend also relates that Isaiah was *sawn in two.*

12.1–13 Jesus is the prime example of the faithful endurance to which the audience is called (10.36). **12.1** For the image of the *race,* see Acts 20.24; 1 Cor 9.24–27; Gal 2.2; Phil 2.16; 2 Tim 4.7. **12.2** For Jesus as *pioneer,* see 2.10. The *perfecter* of faith is the one who was perfected by suffering (2.10; 5.8–9; 7.28). The combination of pioneer (*archegos*) and perfecter (*teleiotes*) involves a wordplay in Greek on "first" (*arch-*) and "last" (*tel-*). *Taken his seat,* the last allusion to Ps 110.1; see Heb 1.3, 13; 8.1; 10.12. **12.4** The *struggle* is now described with imagery that may evoke a boxing match or a military conflict. **12.5–6** Prov 3.11–12, Septuagint. **12.7** For suffering as divine *discipline,* see Prov 6.23; 2 Macc 6.12–17; 2 Cor 6.9; Eph 6.4. **12.9** The description of God as *Father of spirits* resembles traditional expressions for God's sovereignty over the world of spirits; see 2 Macc 3.24; Rev 22.6; *1 Enoch*

12 Therefore lift your drooping hands and strengthen your weak knees, 13and make straight paths for your feet, so that what is lame may not be put out of joint, but rather be healed.

Warnings against Rejecting God's Grace

14 Pursue peace with everyone, and the holiness without which no one will see the Lord. 15See to it that no one fails to obtain the grace of God; that no root of bitterness springs up and causes trouble, and through it many become defiled. 16See to it that no one becomes like Esau, an immoral and godless person, who sold his birthright for a single meal. 17You know that later, when he wanted to inherit the blessing, he was rejected, for he found no chance to repent,[a] even though he sought the blessing[b] with tears.

18 You have not come to something[c] that can be touched, a blazing fire, and darkness, and gloom, and a tempest, 19and the sound of a trumpet, and a voice whose words made the hearers beg that not another word be spoken to them. 20(For they could not endure the order that was given, "If even an animal touches the mountain, it shall be stoned to death." 21Indeed, so terrifying was the sight that Moses said, "I tremble with fear.") 22But you have come to Mount Zion and to the city of the living God, the heavenly Jerusalem, and to innumerable angels in festal gathering, 23and to the assembly[d] of the firstborn who are enrolled in heaven, and to God the judge of all, and to the spirits of the righteous made perfect, 24and to Jesus, the mediator of a new covenant, and to the sprinkled blood that speaks a better word than the blood of Abel.

25 See that you do not refuse the one who is speaking; for if they did not escape when they refused the one who warned them on earth, how much less will we escape if we reject the one who warns from heaven! 26At that time his voice shook the earth; but now he has promised, "Yet once more I will shake not only the earth but also the heaven." 27This phrase, "Yet once more," indicates the removal of what is shaken—that is, created things—so that what cannot be shaken may remain. 28Therefore, since we are receiving a kingdom that cannot be shaken, let us give thanks, by which we offer to God an acceptable worship with reverence and awe; 29for indeed our God is a consuming fire.

Service Well-Pleasing to God

13 Let mutual love continue. 2Do not neglect to show hospitality to strangers, for by doing that some have entertained angels without knowing it. 3Remember those who are in prison, as though you were in prison with them; those who are being tortured, as though you yourselves were being tortured.[e] 4Let marriage be held in honor by all, and let

---

a Or no chance to change his father's mind   b Gk it   c Other ancient authorities read a mountain   d Or angels, and to the festal gathering 23and assembly   e Gk were in the body

---

37.2–4; 38.4; 39.2, 7. **12.12** Drooping hands and weak knees derive from Isa 35.3. **12.13** For the call to make straight paths, see Prov 4.26. The promise to be healed may echo Prov 4.22. **12.14–29** A final warning. **12.14** Admonitions to pursue peace are common; see, e.g., Ps 34.14, cited in 1 Pet 3.11. Pursuit of peace as a means to see the Lord recalls the Beatitudes of Mt 5.8–9. **12.15** The root of bitterness, inspired by Deut 29.18; is probably idolatry or apostasy. **12.16** On Esau's sale of his birthright, see Gen 25.29–34. **12.17** Esau may have sought the blessing as the translation suggests, but the Greek is ambiguous (see text note b) and the author may be suggesting that Esau sought repentance, which was not open to him. For the denial of the possibility of second repentance, see 6.4–8; 10.26–31. For Esau's tears, see Gen 27.30–38. **12.18** Fire and darkness and gloom and a tempest recalls the descent of God on Mount Sinai; see Deut 4.11–12; 5.22–25. **12.19** Trumpet. See Ex 19.16. **12.20** Ex 19.12–13. **12.21** Moses found the golden calf terrifying; see Deut 9.19. **12.22** Zion, the holy mountain in Jerusalem, is the place where God is present; see Pss 2.6; 48.1; Isa 8.18. **12.23** Assembly of the firstborn, possibly the angels mentioned in the previous verse, but more likely the humans who are associated with the Firstborn One; see 1.6. **12.24** For Jesus as mediator, see 8.6; for his blood, 9.14. The better word spoken by the blood of Jesus is a message of true and lasting remission of sin; see 9.14; 10.16–18. Abel. See 11.4. **12.25** The one who is speaking, certainly God, whose "speech" has been of concern throughout Hebrews; see 1.1. The one who warned them, perhaps Moses or, more likely, God on Mount Sinai. **12.26** Hag 2.6. The global destruction recalls Heb 1.10–12. **12.27** What cannot be shaken includes the various heavenly realities made accessible by Christ. These include "rest" (4.1–11), the better possession (10.34), and the heavenly city (12.22; 13.14). **12.29** For God as fire, see Deut 4.24.

13.1–29 A series of admonitions, some specific, some general and symbolic, conclude the homily. **13.1** Mutual love. See Rom 12.10; 1 Thess 4.9; 1 Pet 1.22; 2 Pet 1.7. **13.2** Hospitality. See Mt 25.35; Rom 12.13; 1 Tim 3.2; Titus 1.8; 1 Pet 4.9. Various OT figures entertained angels; see Gen 18.2–15; 19.1–14; Judg 6.11–24; 13.3–23. **13.3** The audience had already supported those in prison; see 10.34. **13.4** For similar admonitions

the marriage bed be kept undefiled; for God will judge fornicators and adulterers. 5Keep your lives free from the love of money, and be content with what you have; for he has said, "I will never leave you or forsake you." 6So we can say with confidence,

"The Lord is my helper;
    I will not be afraid.
What can anyone do to me?"

7 Remember your leaders, those who spoke the word of God to you; consider the outcome of their way of life, and imitate their faith. 8Jesus Christ is the same yesterday and today and forever. 9Do not be carried away by all kinds of strange teachings; for it is well for the heart to be strengthened by grace, not by regulations about food,ᵃ which have not benefited those who observe them. 10We have an altar from which those who officiate in the tentᵇ have no right to eat. 11For the bodies of those animals whose blood is brought into the sanctuary by the high priest as a sacrifice for sin are burned outside the camp. 12Therefore Jesus also suffered outside the city gate in order to sanctify the people by his own blood. 13Let us then go to him outside the camp and bear the abuse he endured. 14For here we have no lasting city, but we are looking for the city that is to come. 15Through him, then, let us continually offer a sacrifice of praise to God, that is, the fruit of lips that confess his name. 16Do not neglect to do good and to share what you have, for such sacrifices are pleasing to God.

17 Obey your leaders and submit to them, for they are keeping watch over your souls and will give an account. Let them do this with joy and not with sighing—for that would be harmful to you.

18 Pray for us; we are sure that we have a clear conscience, desiring to act honorably in all things. 19I urge you all the more to do this, so that I may be restored to you very soon.

Benediction

20 Now may the God of peace, who brought back from the dead our Lord Jesus, the great shepherd of the sheep, by the blood of the eternal covenant, 21make you complete in everything good so that you may do his will, working among usᶜ that which is pleasing in his sight, through Jesus Christ, to whom be the glory forever and ever. Amen.

Final Exhortation and Greetings

22 I appeal to you, brothers and sisters,ᵈ bear with my word of exhortation, for I have written to you briefly. 23I want you to know that our brother Timothy has been set free; and if he comes in time, he will be with me when I see you. 24Greet all your leaders and all the saints. Those from Italy send you greetings. 25Grace be with all of you.ᵉ

a Gk not by foods b Or tabernacle c Other ancient authorities read you d Gk brothers e Other ancient authorities add Amen

to chastity, see 1 Cor 5.1–13; Eph 5.3–5; 1 Thess 4.3–7. **13.5** For warnings against *love of money,* see Mt 6.19–21, 24–34; Lk 12.22–34; 1 Tim 6.10; Jas 5.1–5. For God's promise not to *forsake,* see Deut 31.6, 8; Josh 1.5. **13.6** Ps 118.6, Septuagint. Up to this point God and Jesus have been in dialogue using the words of Psalms. See 1.5–13; 2.12–13; 5.5–6; 10.5–7. Now the followers of Jesus respond to God's call, again using the words of a psalm. **13.7** *Leaders* are also mentioned in 13.17. **13.8** For Jesus as ever the *same,* see 1.12. **13.9** For concern with improper *teachings,* see Eph 4.14; Col. 2.8; 1 Tim 1.3–7. For criticism of concern with *food,* see 9.10. **13.10** The *altar* probably refers to Christ's sacrificial death, not to a Christian altar or church building. **13.11** For bodies *burned outside the camp,* see Lev 16.27; for the sacrifice of the red heifer, see Num 19.2–3.

13.12 For the crucifixion *outside the city gate,* see Jn 19.17–20 and perhaps Mt 21.39; Lk 20.15. **13.14** Expectation of the *city that is to come* repeats the experience of Abraham; see 11.13–16. **13.15** *Sacrifices of praise* were a specific form of offering (Lev 7.11–18), but the term is also used as a metaphor for prayer; see Pss 50.14, 23; 107.22. To *confess* or thank God's *name* is common in Psalms; see Pss 44.8; 54.6; 99.3. **13.16** For right living as *sacrifice,* see Rom 12.1–2; Phil 2.17; 1 Pet 2.5. **13.17** For the call to *submit* to leaders, see 13.7; 1 Pet 5.5. **13.20–25** The epistolary conclusion has many standard features; see Rom 16.20–27; Phil 4.20–23; 1 Thess 5.23–28. **13.22** *Word of exhortation,* which may be a technical term for a sermon as in Acts 13.15, describes the whole of Hebrews. **13.23** *Timothy* is probably Paul's companion; see Acts 16.1–3; 17.14–15.

The Letter of
JAMES

THE LETTER OF JAMES was accepted as scripture by the church in Alexandria in the third century CE, by the Western church in the fourth century, and by the Syrian church in the fifth century. Thereafter it has remained in the NT canon of all churches, though at the time of the Reformation Martin Luther questioned its status because it appeared to contradict Paul's teaching on justification by faith, which Luther held to be of central importance. More recent interpreters have come to appreciate James's distinctive theological perspective and impassioned practical concern.

Author, Date, and Place

THE "JAMES" of the opening address has traditionally been identified as James the brother of Jesus (Gal 1.19), who became the leader of the church in Jerusalem (Acts 15.13; 21.18) and who was martyred before the outbreak of the Jewish war of 66–70 CE (see Josephus, *Antiquities* 20.200). The author's proficiency with Greek, however, and use of the Septuagint have suggested to some that the brother of Jesus probably did not write this text. The memory of James was widely revered in the early church, and his name may have been used by another writer to preserve his legacy. At any rate, the Letter's lack of references to developed ecclesiastical structures, its practical OT morality, and its echoes of the teachings of Jesus, probably drawn from oral tradition, are all consistent with an early, Palestinian origin. Its critical interaction with what appears to be a misuse of Paul's teachings (2.14–16) shows that different interpretations of Christianity were already current.

Genre, Audience, and Message

THE TEXT OPENS with typical epistolary greetings but has no comparable ending, indicating that it may be a letter in literary form only, not a real piece of correspondence. It is ostensibly addressed to "the twelve tribes in the Dispersion" (1.1), i.e., Jews scattered outside Palestine. Most likely this is symbolic language for the Christian community and signifies both its indebtedness to Israel and its members' need to return from spiritual "wandering" (5.19–20).

The text has often been described as Christian wisdom literature because, like Proverbs and Sirach, it consists largely of moral exhortations and precepts of a traditional and eclectic nature. By the same token, the author's antagonism toward the rich and emphasis on repentance are reminiscent of prophetic discourse. Taken as a whole, the Letter projects a religious outlook notable for its polarized character. The author is especially concerned to show how the perfect righteousness and generosity of God are utterly irreconcilable with "the world" and its selfish, corrupt ways (e.g., 4.4). In society, this antagonism manifests itself in the oppression of the faithful poor by the rich and the proud (2.5–7), who most embody "earthly" vices like envy, greed, and violence (3.14–16). Assurances are made that sin and oppression do not go unnoticed, but will be brought to an end when God comes as judge (5.1–6). In the meantime, the faithful are called upon to endure testing without complaint (5.7–11) and to live in solidarity with the world's social outcasts (1.27). It is in this regard that we can perhaps best understand James's emphasis on fulfilling "the perfect law" (1.25), referring not to dietary regulations or rituals like circumcision (cf. Gal 2.11–12), but to concrete acts of service that "complete" one's faith commitments (2.22). This contrasts with the comportment of "double-minded" doubters, whose faith has been compromised by a desire to befriend the world (1.8; 4.8).

[SOPHIE LAWS, revised by WALTER T. WILSON]

Salutation

1 James, a servant*a* of God and of the Lord Jesus Christ,
To the twelve tribes in the Dispersion: Greetings.

Faith and Wisdom

2 My brothers and sisters,*b* whenever you face trials of any kind, consider it nothing but joy, 3because you know that the testing of your faith produces endurance; 4and let endurance have its full effect, so that you may be mature and complete, lacking in nothing.

5 If any of you is lacking in wisdom, ask God, who gives to all generously and ungrudgingly, and it will be given you. 6But ask in faith, never doubting, for the one who doubts is like a wave of the sea, driven and tossed by the wind; 7, 8for the doubter, being double-minded and unstable in every way, must not expect to receive anything from the Lord.

Poverty and Riches

9 Let the believer*c* who is lowly boast in being raised up, 10and the rich in being brought low, because the rich will disappear like a flower in the field. 11For the sun rises with its scorching heat and withers the field; its flower falls, and its beauty perishes. It is the same way with the rich; in the midst of a busy life, they will wither away.

Trial and Temptation

12 Blessed is anyone who endures temptation. Such a one has stood the test and will receive the crown of life that the Lord*d* has promised to those who love him. 13No one, when tempted, should say, "I am being tempted by God"; for God cannot be tempted by evil and he himself tempts no one. 14But one is tempted by one's own desire, being lured and

a Gk *slave* *b* Gk *brothers* *c* Gk *brother* *d* Gk *he*; other ancient authorities read *God*

1.1 This is unlikely to be an address to Jews, since the historical *twelve tribes* ceased to exist after the invasion of the kingdom of Israel by Assyria in 721 BCE. Probably James is addressing Christians as the spiritual Israel (cf. 1 Pet 2.9–10; Rev 7.4–8). For Jews the *Dispersion* meant the Jewish people living outside Palestine, but Christians might also see themselves as exiles in the world (1 Pet 1.1; 2.11). **1.2–27** The first chapter presents miscellaneous precepts that anticipate themes to be developed later in the text, such as testing, wisdom, prayer, the law, and the fortunes of the rich and the poor. **1.2–4** A similar pattern of ethical teaching, where one virtue leads on to another, is found in Rom 5.3–4; 1 Pet 1.6–7. **1.5** James echoes the teaching of Jesus in Mt 7.7–11; Lk 11.9–13, though instead of Matthew's "good things" or Luke's "Holy Spirit" he specifies *wisdom* as the object of prayer (see also Jas 3.13–18). **1.8** *Double-minded*, an unusual word perhaps expressing the Jewish idea of competing impulses, for good and evil, in the human personality (see also 4.8; for another explanation of unanswered prayer, see 4.3). **1.9–10** The contrast between the humble *believer* and the doomed *rich* seems to assume that a rich person cannot also be a believer (see also 2.6–7; 5.1–6; cf. 1 Tim 6.17–19). **1.10** *Flower in the field.* See Isa 40.6–8. **1.12–15** The same word is used in

enticed by it; [15]then, when that desire has conceived, it gives birth to sin, and that sin, when it is fully grown, gives birth to death. [16]Do not be deceived, my beloved.[a]

17 Every generous act of giving, with every perfect gift, is from above, coming down from the Father of lights, with whom there is no variation or shadow due to change.[b] [18]In fulfillment of his own purpose he gave us birth by the word of truth, so that we would become a kind of first fruits of his creatures.

Hearing and Doing the Word

19 You must understand this, my beloved:[a] let everyone be quick to listen, slow to speak, slow to anger; [20]for your anger does not produce God's righteousness. [21]Therefore rid yourselves of all sordidness and rank growth of wickedness, and welcome with meekness the implanted word that has the power to save your souls.

22 But be doers of the word, and not merely hearers who deceive themselves. [23]For if any are hearers of the word and not doers, they are like those who look at themselves[c] in a mirror; [24]for they look at themselves and, on going away, immediately forget what they were like. [25]But those who look into the perfect law, the law of liberty, and persevere, being not hearers who forget but doers who act—they will be blessed in their doing.

26 If any think they are religious, and do not bridle their tongues but deceive their hearts, their religion is worthless. [27]Religion that is pure and undefiled before God, the Father, is this: to care for orphans and widows in their distress, and to keep oneself unstained by the world.

Warning against Partiality

2 My brothers and sisters,[d] do you with your acts of favoritism really believe in our glorious Lord Jesus Christ?[e] [2]For if a person with gold rings and in fine clothes comes into your assembly, and if a poor person in dirty clothes also comes in, [3]and if you take notice of the one wearing the fine clothes and say, "Have a seat here, please," while to the one who is poor you say, "Stand there," or, "Sit at my feet,"[f] [4]have you not made distinctions among yourselves, and become judges with evil thoughts? [5]Listen, my beloved brothers and sisters.[g] Has not God chosen the poor in the world to be rich in faith and to be heirs of the kingdom that he has promised to those who love him? [6]But you have dishonored the poor. Is it not the rich who oppress you? Is it not they who drag you into court? [7]Is it not they who blaspheme the excellent name that was invoked over you?

8 You do well if you really fulfill the royal

a Gk my beloved brothers b Other ancient authorities read variation due to a shadow of turning c Gk at the face of his birth d Gk My brothers e Or hold the faith of our glorious Lord Jesus Christ without acts of favoritism f Gk Sit under my footstool g Gk brothers

---

Greek for trial as an external test (see 1.2) and trial as temptation, an internal prompting. 1.17 Lights, stars or angels; see 5.4. Variation, shadow, and change are terms in Greek astronomy. 1.18 The reference could be to the creation of humankind by the word of God (see Gen 1.26) or more probably to the re-birth of Christians by the word of the gospel (see Jn 3.3–7; 1 Pet 1.23). The birth described here contrasts with that of v. 15. 1.21 Implanted word, perhaps the gospel (see v. 18), though the flow of the argument suggests some relationship with the law of liberty (v. 25) as well. 1.25 Law of liberty. See also 2.12. Jewish teachers also argued that the law is not a constraint, but rather gives true freedom. 1.26 Bridle their tongues. See also 3.2–5. 1.27 In the OT orphans and widows are the objects of special care, both human and divine; see Ex 22.22–24; Ps 68.5. Where 2 Pet 2.20 thinks of contamination by the physical world in terms of sexual vice, James thinks of corruption by selfish worldly values; see also 4.4.
2.1–7 James dramatizes the readers' failure to follow the precepts he has just issued. 2.1 Favoritism is frequently condemned in the OT (see Lev 19.15; Ps 82.2) and seen to be wholly contrary to God's charac-

ter (Job 34.17–19; see also Acts 10.34). Our glorious Jesus Christ, a very awkward Greek construction; the name may have been inserted into an original reference to God; another translation could be "our Lord Jesus Christ, the glory" (see Jn 1.14; 2 Cor 4.6; Heb 1.3). 2.2 The rich person is probably a visitor to the Christian meeting rather than a regular member; the gold rings may indicate the person's status in the Roman social order. The Greek word for assembly is also used for "synagogue," perhaps indicating the Jewish-Christian character of this community. 2.5 This verse may echo Jesus' blessing on the poor; see Mt 5.3; Lk 6.20. 2.6 Christians may have been taken into court because of allegations made against them by hostile fellow citizens; see, e.g., Acts 16.19; 26.11; 1 Pet 3.15–17; 4.14–16. 2.7 Christians were baptized in the name of Jesus (see Acts 2.38; 1 Cor 6.11), which was probably invoked over them as part of the baptismal ritual. 2.8–13 James's rejection of favoritism (v. 1) in social relations leads to a rejection of partiality (v. 9) in observing the law. 2.8 Jesus identified Lev 19.18 as the second commandment (Mt 22.39; Mk 12.31; see also Lk 10.27). It may be called royal law because of the im-

law according to the scripture, "You shall love your neighbor as yourself." 9But if you show partiality, you commit sin and are convicted by the law as transgressors. 10For whoever keeps the whole law but fails in one point has become accountable for all of it. 11For the one who said, "You shall not commit adultery," also said, "You shall not murder." Now if you do not commit adultery but if you murder, you have become a transgressor of the law. 12So speak and so act as those who are to be judged by the law of liberty. 13For judgment will be without mercy to anyone who has shown no mercy; mercy triumphs over judgment.

Faith without Works Is Dead

14 What good is it, my brothers and sisters,*a* if you say you have faith but do not have works? Can faith save you? 15If a brother or sister is naked and lacks daily food, 16and one of you says to them, "Go in peace; keep warm and eat your fill," and yet you do not supply their bodily needs, what is the good of that? 17So faith by itself, if it has no works, is dead.

18 But someone will say, "You have faith and I have works." Show me your faith apart from your works, and I by my works will show you my faith. 19You believe that God is one; you do well. Even the demons believe—and shudder. 20Do you want to be shown, you senseless person, that faith apart from works is barren? 21Was not our ancestor Abraham justified by works when he offered his son Isaac on the altar? 22You see that faith was active

along with his works, and faith was brought to completion by the works. 23Thus the scripture was fulfilled that says, "Abraham believed God, and it was reckoned to him as righteousness," and he was called the friend of God. 24You see that a person is justified by works and not by faith alone. 25Likewise, was not Rahab the prostitute also justified by works when she welcomed the messengers and sent them out by another road? 26For just as the body without the spirit is dead, so faith without works is also dead.

Taming the Tongue

3 Not many of you should become teachers, my brothers and sisters,*a* for you know that we who teach will be judged with greater strictness. 2For all of us make many mistakes. Anyone who makes no mistakes in speaking is perfect, able to keep the whole body in check with a bridle. 3If we put bits into the mouths of horses to make them obey us, we guide their whole bodies. 4Or look at ships: though they are so large that it takes strong winds to drive them, yet they are guided by a very small rudder wherever the will of the pilot directs. 5So also the tongue is a small member, yet it boasts of great exploits.

How great a forest is set ablaze by a small fire! 6And the tongue is a fire. The tongue is placed among our members as a world of iniquity; it stains the whole body, sets on fire the cycle of nature,*b* and is itself set on fire by hell.*c*

a Gk brothers   *b* Or wheel of birth   *c* Gk Gehenna

---

portance he gave to it or because it was seen as the law of the kingdom he preached. **2.10–11** Jews would similarly have insisted that their law must be kept *whole* and intact. James cites only the Decalogue (Ex 20.13–14; Deut 5.17–18), though, which suggests that he may be working here with a more focused view of the "whole law." **2.14–26** James's contrast of *faith* and *works* echoes Paul's arguments in Rom 3.19–5.1; Gal 2.11–3.24, but James, unlike Paul, is thinking of works of charity, not ritual commands like circumcision. **2.16** The verbs *keep warm* and *eat your fill* are passive in Greek, expressing a pious belief that God will relieve the needs of the poor. **2.19** *God is one,* the central statement of Jewish faith; see Deut 6.4. The demons' belief includes the knowledge that the one God is their enemy (see Mk 1.23–24); hence they *shudder,* a verb used in magical texts for the effect of an exorcism. **2.21** Gen 22.1–19; Paul demonstrates the faith of *Abraham* from his acceptance of God's promise rather than from his willingness to sacrifice *Isaac* (see Rom 4; Gal 3.6–18). **2.23** Gen 15.6, quoted by Paul in Rom 4.9; Gal 3.6. The OT does not use

the expression *friend of God* for Abraham, but it became popular in later Jewish writings and is used by other early Christian authors. **2.24** Cf. Rom 2.13; 3.28; Gal 2.16. **2.25** *Rahab.* See Josh 2.1–21; Heb 11.31.

3.1–12 James's attack on sins of speech, personified in an attack on the tongue (see 1.26), is highly rhetorical in tone. The concern for such sins is also prominent in wisdom literature (e.g., Sir 14.1; 19.16; 28.17–26). **3.1** *Teachers* were recognized figures in early Christian communities (e.g., Acts 13.1; 1 Cor 12.28); with James's warning about them, cf. Mt 23.8. **3.3–4** The metaphor of *ships* has no biblical parallel, but, like that of *horses,* is commonplace in Hellenistic writing. **3.6** The whole verse is very difficult. The *tongue* may be a *world of iniquity* because of its peculiar destructive force, which brings the corruption of the world to the human body (see 1.26–27) or because the tongue, with its special potential for sin, is a microcosm of the totality of human sin. *The cycle of nature,* the totality of life in all its phases and vicissitudes. For *hell* James uses the Jewish term "Gehenna"; see also Mt 5.30; Mk 9.45; Lk 12.5.

[7]For every species of beast and bird, of reptile and sea creature, can be tamed and has been tamed by the human species, [8]but no one can tame the tongue—a restless evil, full of deadly poison. [9]With it we bless the Lord and Father, and with it we curse those who are made in the likeness of God. [10]From the same mouth come blessing and cursing. My brothers and sisters,[a] this ought not to be so. [11]Does a spring pour forth from the same opening both fresh and brackish water? [12]Can a fig tree, my brothers and sisters,[b] yield olives, or a grapevine figs? No more can salt water yield fresh.

Two Kinds of Wisdom

[13]Who is wise and understanding among you? Show by your good life that your works are done with gentleness born of wisdom. [14]But if you have bitter envy and selfish ambition in your hearts, do not be boastful and false to the truth. [15]Such wisdom does not come down from above, but is earthly, unspiritual, devilish. [16]For where there is envy and selfish ambition, there will also be disorder and wickedness of every kind. [17]But the wisdom from above is first pure, then peaceable, gentle, willing to yield, full of mercy and good fruits, without a trace of partiality or hypocrisy. [18]And a harvest of righteousness is sown in peace for[c] those who make peace.

Friendship with the World

4 Those conflicts and disputes among you, where do they come from? Do they not come from your cravings that are at war within you? [2]You want something and do not have it; so you commit murder. And you covet[d] something and cannot obtain it; so you engage in disputes and conflicts. You do not have, because you do not ask. [3]You ask and do not receive, because you ask wrongly, in order to spend what you get on your pleasures. [4]Adulterers! Do you not know that friendship with the world is enmity with God? Therefore whoever wishes to be a friend of the world becomes an enemy of God. [5]Or do you suppose that it is for nothing that the scripture says, "God[e] yearns jealously for the spirit that he has made to dwell in us"? [6]But he gives all the more grace; therefore it says,

"God opposes the proud,
　　but gives grace to the humble."

[7]Submit yourselves therefore to God. Resist the devil, and he will flee from you. [8]Draw near to God, and he will draw near to you. Cleanse your hands, you sinners, and purify your hearts, you double-minded. [9]Lament and mourn and weep. Let your laughter be turned into mourning and your joy into dejection. [10]Humble yourselves before the Lord, and he will exalt you.

Warning against Judging Another

11 Do not speak evil against one another, brothers and sisters.[f] Whoever speaks evil

---

a Gk My brothers　b Gk my brothers　c Or by　d Or you murder and you covet　e Gk He　f Gk brothers

---

3.7 See Gen 1.26. **3.9** The ethical principle that human persons should be treated with the reverence appropriate to those *made in the likeness of God* (Gen 1.26) was familiar in Judaism and finds biblical precedent in Gen 9.6. **3.12** See also Mt 7.16–17; Lk 6.43–44; but the idea and the imagery of *tree* and fruit were also commonplace in Hellenistic teaching. **3.13–18** As in the OT wisdom literature, *wisdom* is associated with practical good behavior, not speculative thought. **3.15** *Unspiritual* (lit. "physical") is used by Paul to contrast the physical and the spiritual (1 Cor 15.44, 46). Here the contrast is between human wisdom and the wisdom that is given by God. **3.17** In Prov 8.22–31; Wis 9.9–10, 17 wisdom is portrayed as a heavenly being, alongside God at creation; *here it is the gift given from above* in answer to prayer; see 1.5.

4.1–12 James examines the causes and effects of divisions in the community. **4.1** *Within you,* lit. "in your members." The passage might describe disputes within the community as the body of Christ (Rom

12.4–5; 1 Cor 12.12–26), but it more probably recalls James's familiar theme of division within an individual, now seen as leading to communal strife (see 1.8, 14; Rom 7.21–23). **4.2** *Murder* and *disputes and conflicts,* the latter lit. "you fight and make war," are both hyperbole; see Mt 5.21–22. **4.3** For another example of improper and thus unanswered prayer, see 1.6–8. **4.4** *Adulterers.* The noun is feminine; some texts add a masculine to yield "adulterers and adulteresses" (cf. Jer 3.6–10). **4.5** A notoriously difficult verse. The *scripture* quotation is not found in the OT; *God* does not appear in the text (see text note e); *the spirit* could be the subject or object of the verb and understood as either the Holy Spirit or the human spirit. James could be quoting an otherwise unknown text or alluding to a passage like Ps 42.1 to make the point that the God-given human spirit should yearn after God, not after jealous desires. **4.6–8** A similar sequence of thought is found in 1 Pet 5.5–9. **4.6** Prov 3.34. **4.8** To be *double-minded* seems to be the essence of sin; see also 1.8. **4.9** Cf. Joel 1.8–12.

against another or judges another, speaks evil against the law and judges the law; but if you judge the law, you are not a doer of the law but a judge. 12There is one lawgiver and judge who is able to save and to destroy. So who, then, are you to judge your neighbor?

Boasting about Tomorrow

13 Come now, you who say, "Today or tomorrow we will go to such and such a town and spend a year there, doing business and making money." 14Yet you do not even know what tomorrow will bring. What is your life? For you are a mist that appears for a little while and then vanishes. 15Instead you ought to say, "If the Lord wishes, we will live and do this or that." 16As it is, you boast in your arrogance; all such boasting is evil. 17Anyone, then, who knows the right thing to do and fails to do it, commits sin.

Warning to Rich Oppressors

5 Come now, you rich people, weep and wail for the miseries that are coming to you. 2Your riches have rotted, and your clothes are moth-eaten. 3Your gold and silver have rusted, and their rust will be evidence against you, and it will eat your flesh like fire. You have laid up treasure*a* for the last days. 4Listen! The wages of the laborers who mowed your fields, which you kept back by fraud, cry out, and the cries of the harvesters have reached the ears of the Lord of hosts. 5You have lived on the earth in luxury and in pleasure; you have fattened

your hearts in a day of slaughter. 6You have condemned and murdered the righteous one, who does not resist you.

Patience in Suffering

7 Be patient, therefore, beloved,*b* until the coming of the Lord. The farmer waits for the precious crop from the earth, being patient with it until it receives the early and the late rains. 8You also must be patient. Strengthen your hearts, for the coming of the Lord is near.*c* 9Beloved,*d* do not grumble against one another, so that you may not be judged. See, the Judge is standing at the doors! 10As an example of suffering and patience, beloved,*b* take the prophets who spoke in the name of the Lord. 11Indeed we call blessed those who showed endurance. You have heard of the endurance of Job, and you have seen the purpose of the Lord, how the Lord is compassionate and merciful.

12 Above all, my beloved,*b* do not swear, either by heaven or by earth or by any other oath, but let your "Yes" be yes and your "No" be no, so that you may not fall under condemnation.

The Prayer of Faith

13 Are any among you suffering? They should pray. Are any cheerful? They should sing songs of praise. 14Are any among you sick? They

---

a Or will eat your flesh, since you have stored up fire
b Gk brothers   *c* Or is at hand

4.11 On *doer of the law,* see 1.22–25. The warning against judgment echoes Mt 7.1. **4.12** *Lawgiver and judge,* God; cf. 5.9. **4.13–17** A new attack on the rich; the message is the same as that of Jesus' parable of the rich fool (Lk 12.16–21). **4.15** The pious formula does not come from the OT but was familiar in the pagan Hellenistic world; see also 1 Cor 4.19; 16.7.

5.1–6 The attack on the rich now recalls prophetic denunciations like Jer 5.5–6; Mal 3.5. **5.1** See 1.10–11; also the woe to the *rich* in Lk 6.24. **5.3** *For the last days,* or "in the last days"; see v. 5. James shares the early Christian conviction that the end of the age is very near and will be accompanied by judgment; see v. 8. **5.4** To deprive *laborers* of their *wages* is a prime example of oppression in the OT; see, e.g., Lev 19.13; Deut 24.14–15. *Lord of hosts,* lit. "Lord Sabaoth," an OT title; see Isa 5.7. *Hosts,* stars or angels; see 1.17. **5.6** *The righteous one,* perhaps Jesus, so described in Acts 3.14; 7.52; see also 1 Pet 3.18; 1 Jn 2.1. More probably James echoes the familiar OT theme that God's righteous ones are the poor and oppressed; see, e.g., Ps 140.12–13; Wis 2.12–20. James of Jerusalem, who became a martyr, was also called "the Just" (i.e., "the Righ-

teous"). **5.7–12** An encouragement to endure in hope of a final reward. **5.7** These *rains* are characteristic of Palestine and Syria and are sometimes taken as a pointer to the Letter's place of origin, but they are also known from the OT (see Deut 11.14; Jer 5.24). **5.8** For the *coming,* or return, of Jesus, see, e.g., Mt 24.3; 1 Cor 15.23; 2 Pet 1.16. **5.10** Prophecy and martyrdom became closely associated in Jewish tradition, though in the OT only two *prophets* met violent deaths (see 2 Chr 24.20–21; Jer 26.20–23). Jeremiah is, however, an obvious example of a prophet who endured hardship and humiliation; see Jer 20.1–2; 38.6. **5.11** The suffering of *Job* is the subject of that book, though his *endurance* of it is hardly an example of patience. *Purpose,* or "the end," God's final restoration of Job. **5.12** A clear echo of the teaching of Jesus, whose prohibition of any *oath* was highly unusual; see Mt 5.33–37. **5.13–20** James concludes by encouraging practices that foster communal solidarity. **5.13** See Eph 5.19. **5.14** Some leaders of Christian communities are called *elders,* perhaps following the model of Jewish synagogue organization; see, e.g., Acts 14.23; 20.17; 1 Tim 5.17–19; Titus 1.5. For the gift of healing, see 1 Cor 12.27–30;

should call for the elders of the church and have them pray over them, anointing them with oil in the name of the Lord. [15]The prayer of faith will save the sick, and the Lord will raise them up; and anyone who has committed sins will be forgiven. [16]Therefore confess your sins to one another, and pray for one another, so that you may be healed. The prayer of the righteous is powerful and effective. [17]Elijah was a human being like us, and he prayed fervently that it might not rain, and for three

years and six months it did not rain on the earth. [18]Then he prayed again, and the heaven gave rain and the earth yielded its harvest.

19 My brothers and sisters,[a] if anyone among you wanders from the truth and is brought back by another, [20]you should know that whoever brings back a sinner from wandering will save the sinner's[b] soul from death and will cover a multitude of sins.

---

a Gk *My brothers* b Gk *his*

---

here it is exercised by the community's leaders. *Oil* was a common remedy for pain throughout the ancient world; see Lk 10.34. Christian healing was performed in the *name* of Jesus; see, e.g., Mk 16.17–18; Acts 3.6. **5.15** It was commonly assumed that sickness was in some measure a punishment for *sins,* so that healing

was both physical and spiritual or moral; see Mk 2.3–12; Jn 5.14; but cf. Jn 9.1–3. **5.17–18** See 1 Kings 17.1; 18.41–45. **5.20** The text simply has a possessive pronoun (see text note *b*), so it could be read as offering a double blessing, salvation of the *soul* and forgiveness of sins, to either the converter or the converted.

The First Letter of
PETER

THE SALUTATION (1.1–2) and final greeting (5.12–14) of 1 Peter give information concerning the Letter's origin and addressees and provide clues about its author and date. These verses say it was sent by the apostle Peter from Rome to Christians in five areas of Asia Minor whose names approximate those of Roman provinces there. The author calls Rome "Babylon" (5.13), a name frequently used for that city in Jewish and Christian tradition after the Roman destruction of Jerusalem in 70 CE. The salutation and 5.9 indicate that Christianity was widespread in Asia Minor when the Letter was written; this was probably the result of Paul's preaching there in the 60s.

Although the readers are suffering for their faith, there is no hint of current or impending martyrdom as there is, for example, in Revelation, a document often dated in the late 90s. If 1 Peter represents the earlier stages of such eventually lethal suffering, it would point to a date in the late 80s. This date and the high quality of the Greek suggest that 1 Peter is pseudonymous.

Purpose

THE SOCIAL TENSIONS AND the suffering reflected in 2.19–24; 3.14–15; 4.1–4, 12–19; 5.10 are best explained by the conversion of Gentiles who were at home in Greco-Roman culture (see 1.4, 18; 2.10; 4.3–4) to Christianity, which was a despised, foreign religion (see 4.14–16), and by the negative response of the converts' own families (see 3.1). Roman society was hierarchical, and suspicions about foreign religions included the fear that conversion would impair such established hierarchical relationships and cause slaves and women, for example, to misbehave (see, e.g., Cicero, *Laws* 2.1–15). Romans expected foreign religions to cause immorality (especially adultery), insubordination within the household, and sedition against the state. 1 Peter counters these expectations. The author emphasizes that those converted are to imitate Christ (2.21; 4.1) by, among other things, doing good (2.12, 15, 20; 3.16; 4.19; see Lk 6.27–28) and not retaliating against those who slander their community (2.18, 20–23; 3.9, 14–16).

Social Context

PLACED IN A SOCIAL CONTEXT whose core values were to be rejected (1.18; 4.3–4), Christians faced the problem of slander and misunderstanding from their neighbors, former friends, and families. Christians were not to go out of their way to be offensive or condemnatory (see

3.15b–16a), but in the final analysis, when Christian values conflicted with those of the society around them, Christians were to remain faithful to their core convictions, even when that entailed suffering, however undeserved it may have seemed. Their example was Christ, who also suffered unjustly. Yet as Christ did not abandon the world, neither were his followers to do that. Faithful Christian conduct could effect changes even within pagan society (2.15), and with such hope Christians were to live out their faith even when persecuted for it. Unlike Paul (see, e.g., Rom 9–10), the author of 1 Peter does not discuss the problem posed by an unbelieving Israel. Rather, adopting OT language to describe the new community grounded in God's redeeming act in Christ, the author makes clear that God's new chosen people is to be a unity comprising all people, Gentiles as well as Jews.

Genre and Sources

1 PETER IS A SINGLE, real letter, not, as some claim, a baptismal homily or portions of a baptismal liturgy shaped as or later incorporated into a letter. Rather, it is intended as a circular letter addressed to Christian communities scattered over the northern half of Asia Minor. There are allusions to materials contained in the Gospels, but the author's sources seem earlier than the written Gospels (cf. 4.14; Mt 5.10; Lk 6.22). Christian catechetical traditions are also employed (e.g., the household code), and 1.20; 3.18–22 may contain elements from early Christian hymns. [DAVID L. BALCH, revised by PAUL J. ACHTEMEIER]

The five provinces mentioned in the address of 1 Peter (1.1) make up a large proportion of Asia Minor.

Salutation

1 Peter, an apostle of Jesus Christ,
  To the exiles of the Dispersion in Pontus, Galatia, Cappadocia, Asia, and Bithynia, 2who have been chosen and destined by God the Father and sanctified by the Spirit to be obedient to Jesus Christ and to be sprinkled with his blood:

May grace and peace be yours in abundance.

A Living Hope

3 Blessed be the God and Father of our Lord Jesus Christ! By his great mercy he has given us a new birth into a living hope through the resurrection of Jesus Christ from the dead, 4and into an inheritance that is imperishable, undefiled, and unfading, kept in heaven for you, 5who are being protected by the power of God through faith for a salvation ready to be revealed in the last time. 6In this you rejoice,*a* even if now for a little while you have had to suffer various trials, 7so that the genuineness of your faith—being more precious than gold that, though perishable, is tested by fire—may be found to result in praise and glory and honor when Jesus Christ is revealed. 8Although you have not seen*b* him, you love him; and even though you do not see him now, you believe in him and rejoice with an indescribable and glorious joy, 9for you are receiving the outcome of your faith, the salvation of your souls.

10 Concerning this salvation, the prophets who prophesied of the grace that was to be yours made careful search and inquiry, 11inquiring about the person or time that the Spirit of Christ within them indicated when it testified in advance to the sufferings destined for Christ and the subsequent glory. 12It was revealed to them that they were serving not themselves but you, in regard to the things that have now been announced to you through those who brought you good news by the Holy Spirit sent from heaven—things into which angels long to look!

A Call to Holy Living

13 Therefore prepare your minds for action;*c* discipline yourselves; set all your hope on the grace that Jesus Christ will bring you when he is revealed. 14Like obedient children, do not be conformed to the desires that you formerly had in ignorance. 15Instead, as he who called you is holy, be holy yourselves in all your conduct; 16for it is written, "You shall be holy, for I am holy."

17 If you invoke as Father the one who judges all people impartially according to their deeds, live in reverent fear during the time of your exile. 18You know that you were ransomed from the futile ways inherited from your ancestors, not with perishable things like silver or gold, 19but with the precious blood of Christ, like that of a lamb without defect or

---

a Or *Rejoice in this*   *b* Other ancient authorities read *known*
c Gk *gird up the loins of your mind*

1.1–2 The salutation includes the author's self-introduction, a lengthy designation of addressees, and a prayer that replaces the usual greeting. **1.1** *Exiles of the Dispersion.* The author describes the negative social experience of these primarily gentile Christians in language derived from the OT account of the Jews being exiled from Israel to Babylon, thus beginning the identification of the Christian community as the (new) chosen people. **1.2** Being *chosen* by God (see 2.9; 5.13) marks out Christians as the new chosen people and thus alienates them religiously and socially from their contemporaries (see 2.11). *Sprinkled with his blood,* recalling the blood of the covenant (Ex 24.3–8), implies a similar covenant established through Christ. Cf. Heb 9.20–26. **1.3–12** Instead of an opening thanksgiving, a long blessing introduces some of the themes of the Letter (see also 2 Cor 1.3). **1.3** On *new birth* by hearing (and accepting) God's word, see v. 23. **1.5** *Salvation,* including judgment, is primarily God's future act (see vv. 13, 17; cf. v. 9). **1.10–11** Christians understood Israel's *prophets* to have been inspired by the *Spirit of Christ* and to have foretold events in the life of Jesus and in the history of the early church; see Lk 24.25–27. Such continuity between Israel and the Christian community justified the author's appropriation of the language of Israel to describe that Christian community. **1.13–21** The author shifts from reflection on the gospel to ethical exhortation. **1.13** *Prepare,* lit. "gird up your loins," i.e., gather your robes (see Ex 12.11). At Passover Jews gird themselves for action; here the metaphor is applied to Christian eschatological hope. *Hope,* introduced in v. 3, is central in vv. 13–21. **1.14** *Do not be conformed.* See Rom 12.2. The gentile addressees formerly lived in *ignorance* (see also v. 18; 2.10; 4.2–3). **1.16** Lev 19.2. **1.17** For God as one who *judges all people impartially,* see Deut 10.17; Acts 10.34; Rom 2.11. *Reverent fear.* See 2.17. *Exile.* See 1.1; 2.11. **1.18** *Ransomed* (see Isa 52.3; Mk 10.45; Rom 3.24–25; Gal 3.13), purchased by Christ, as a slave's freedom is purchased from a Roman master. *Futile ways inherited from . . . ancestors* again characterizes the readers as converted Gentiles (see note on 1.14). **1.19** *Lamb* may recall Isa 53.7 or Ex 12.5, but the Greek word used suggests the OT sacrificial system in which only perfect animals were acceptable to God. Cf. Jn 1.29;

blemish. [20]He was destined before the foundation of the world, but was revealed at the end of the ages for your sake. [21]Through him you have come to trust in God, who raised him from the dead and gave him glory, so that your faith and hope are set on God.

22 Now that you have purified your souls by your obedience to the truth[a] so that you have genuine mutual love, love one another deeply[b] from the heart.[c] [23]You have been born anew, not of perishable but of imperishable seed, through the living and enduring word of God.[d] [24]For

"All flesh is like grass
      and all its glory like the flower of grass.
The grass withers,
      and the flower falls,
25 but the word of the Lord endures forever."
That word is the good news that was announced to you.

The Living Stone and a Chosen People

2 Rid yourselves, therefore, of all malice, and all guile, insincerity, envy, and all slander. [2]Like newborn infants, long for the pure, spiritual milk, so that by it you may grow into salvation— [3]if indeed you have tasted that the Lord is good.

4 Come to him, a living stone, though rejected by mortals yet chosen and precious in God's sight, and [5]like living stones, let yourselves be built[e] into a spiritual house, to be a holy priesthood, to offer spiritual sacrifices acceptable to God through Jesus Christ. [6]For it stands in scripture:

"See, I am laying in Zion a stone,

a cornerstone chosen and precious;
and whoever believes in him[f] will not be
      put to shame."
[7]To you then who believe, he is precious; but for those who do not believe,

"The stone that the builders rejected
      has become the very head of the corner,"
[8]and

"A stone that makes them stumble,
      and a rock that makes them fall."
They stumble because they disobey the word, as they were destined to do.

9 But you are a chosen race, a royal priesthood, a holy nation, God's own people,[g] in order that you may proclaim the mighty acts of him who called you out of darkness into his marvelous light.
10 Once you were not a people,
      but now you are God's people;
once you had not received mercy,
      but now you have received mercy.

Live as Servants of God

11 Beloved, I urge you as aliens and exiles to abstain from the desires of the flesh that wage war against the soul. [12]Conduct yourselves honorably among the Gentiles, so that, though they malign you as evildoers, they may see your honorable deeds and glorify God when he comes to judge.[a]

13 For the Lord's sake accept the authority of

a Other ancient authorities add through the Spirit
b Or constantly c Other ancient authorities read a pure heart
d Or through the word of the living and enduring God e Or you yourselves are being built f Or it g Gk a people for his possession

Rev 5.6. **1.20** Destined . . . revealed. The contrast may be from an early Christian hymn. The author assumes that events of the end of the ages have already happened. **1.22–25** Christians' ethics are grounded in their new birth through the word of God. **1.22** Genuine mutual love (Greek philadelphia), a term more common in Greco-Roman ethics than in the NT (but see 3.8; 1 Thess 4.9). Love one another deeply. An ethic based on love is at the heart of the Christian faith. **1.23** For another use of seed as metaphor for the word of God, see Mk 4.14–20. **1.24–25a** Isa 40.6–8. **1.25b** The continuity of Israel and the Christian community is again emphasized: Isaiah's word becomes the Christian gospel.

2.1–3 The author returns to exhortation, urging all Christian readers to grow into salvation. **2.2** The author employs the feminine metaphor of a mother's milk for the word of Christ. **2.3** Tasted, a reference to Ps 34.8. The author returns to this psalm in 3.10–12. **2.4– 10** The author quotes Isa 28.16, then links it to two

other texts that also describe stones, Ps 118.22; Isa 8.14. See also Mt 21.42; Mk 12.10; Acts 4.11; Rom 9.33; Eph 2.20. **2.5** Spiritual sacrifices include worship and social ethics (see Rom 12.1; Heb 13.15–16). **2.6** Isa 28.16. Stone, Christ, as in vv. 7–8. **2.7** The quotation is from Ps 118.22. **2.8** Isa 8.14. **2.9** A chosen race . . . God's own people, four honorific titles taken from Ex 19.6; Isa 43.20–21. What in the OT describes Israel is here applied to the Christian community, as also v. 10. **2.10** Hos 1.9; 2.23. **2.11–3.12** Beloved, I urge you. A first-person address begins a major new section treating Christian conduct among gentile unbelievers. **2.11** Aliens and exiles is drawn from Greek Gen 23.4; Ps 38.13 and describes the status of Christians in their surrounding pagan society; see note on 1.1. **2.12** The readers' honorable conduct is meant to counter pagan gossip, not legal charges (see Introduction; Mt 5.11, 16; see also notes on 3.15; 3.16). **2.13–3.7** Elements of a household code (see also Eph 5.21–6.9; Col 3.18–

every human institution,[b] whether of the emperor as supreme, [14]or of governors, as sent by him to punish those who do wrong and to praise those who do right. [15]For it is God's will that by doing right you should silence the ignorance of the foolish. [16]As servants[c] of God, live as free people, yet do not use your freedom as a pretext for evil. [17]Honor everyone. Love the family of believers.[d] Fear God. Honor the emperor.

The Example of Christ's Suffering

18 Slaves, accept the authority of your masters with all deference, not only those who are kind and gentle but also those who are harsh. [19]For it is a credit to you if, being aware of God, you endure pain while suffering unjustly. [20]If you endure when you are beaten for doing wrong, what credit is that? But if you endure when you do right and suffer for it, you have God's approval. [21]For to this you have been called, because Christ also suffered for you, leaving you an example, so that you should follow in his steps.
[22] "He committed no sin,
        and no deceit was found in his mouth."
[23]When he was abused, he did not return abuse; when he suffered, he did not threaten; but he entrusted himself to the one who judges justly. [24]He himself bore our sins in his body on the cross,[e] so that, free from sins, we might live for righteousness; by his wounds[f] you have been healed. [25]For you were going

astray like sheep, but now you have returned to the shepherd and guardian of your souls.

Wives and Husbands

3 Wives, in the same way, accept the authority of your husbands, so that, even if some of them do not obey the word, they may be won over without a word by their wives' conduct, [2]when they see the purity and reverence of your lives. [3]Do not adorn yourselves outwardly by braiding your hair, and by wearing gold ornaments or fine clothing; [4]rather, let your adornment be the inner self with the lasting beauty of a gentle and quiet spirit, which is very precious in God's sight. [5]It was in this way long ago that the holy women who hoped in God used to adorn themselves by accepting the authority of their husbands. [6]Thus Sarah obeyed Abraham and called him lord. You have become her daughters as long as you do what is good and never let fears alarm you.

7 Husbands, in the same way, show consideration for your wives in your life together, paying honor to the woman as the weaker sex,[g] since they too are also heirs of the gracious gift of life—so that nothing may hinder your prayers.

a Gk God on the day of visitation b Or every institution ordained for human beings c Gk slaves d Gk Love the brotherhood e Or carried up our sins in his body to the tree f Gk bruise g Gk vessel

---

4.1) focusing on slaves and wives, whose lowly social status serves as a metaphor for the similarly low social status accorded Christians by Greco-Roman society. **2.13** On submission to governing *authorities,* see Rom 13.1–7; 1 Tim 2.1–2. **2.14** See Rom 13.3–4. **2.15** Christian behavior even under stress is the best defense against false charges brought against Christians. See 3.16. **2.16** The readers are *free* from ignorance and darkness, and, paradoxically, they are *servants* (more accurately *slaves;* see text note *c*) exhorted to accept others' legitimate authority. **2.17** The author differentiates the *fear* (reverent awe) due to God (see 1.17) from the *honor* due *everyone,* including the *emperor. Love* is again seen as a primary Christian virtue (see note on 1.22). **2.18–25** Because the slaves' Christian identity and behavior are metaphorical for those of all Christians, Christ's example and sacrifice are relevant for all readers. **2.18** The direct address to *slaves* is unusual in Greco-Roman ethical literature; it is a Jewish and Christian innovation. As 2.15; 3.16 indicate, the author hopes the slaves' behavior will affect even harsh, non-Christian masters; see also 1 Tim 6.1; Titus 2.9–10. **2.19–20** On *credit* (lit. "grace") for enduring wrongs, see 3.14; see also Lk 6.32–34. *Being aware of God* implies that their punishment results from their Christian

behavior or belief. **2.21–25** Many detect an early Christian hymn here; others see simply an interpretation of Isa 53. **2.22** Isa 53.9b. **2.23** See 3.9. **2.24** Christ's redeeming work is expressed by Isa 53.4–5. **2.25** *Astray like sheep.* See Isa 53.6; see also note on 5.2.

3.1–7 The household code continues with direct addresses to wives and husbands. Whereas other household codes (cf. Col 3–4) address other household members in pairs, only the wife/husband pair occurs in 1 Peter. **3.1** As is typical in patriarchal Greco-Roman culture, *wives* are exhorted to be subordinate in the household, although here the goal is to win over the unbelieving *husbands* to following Christ. **3.3–4** The contrast between external and internal adornment was common in both Jewish and Greco-Roman writings (e.g., Isa 3.18–24; *1 Enoch* 8.1; see also 1 Tim 2.9–10). **3.6** Sarah calls Abraham *lord* (or "husband") in Gen 18.12. To *do what is good* is a key idea in 1 Peter (see 2.15, 20; 3.17). *Fears* include wives' fear of their unbelieving husbands; the admonition not to fear is a reinterpretation of Prov 3.25. **3.7** The advice to husbands in light of the absence of a similar admonition to masters of slaves points to the importance of mutual respect between husbands and wives in early Christian communities. **3.7b** Failure by husbands to be considerate of their

Suffering for Doing Right

8 Finally, all of you, have unity of spirit, sympathy, love for one another, a tender heart, and a humble mind. 9 Do not repay evil for evil or abuse for abuse; but, on the contrary, repay with a blessing. It is for this that you were called—that you might inherit a blessing. 10 For

"Those who desire life
     and desire to see good days,
  let them keep their tongues from evil
     and their lips from speaking deceit;
11 let them turn away from evil and do
          good;
  let them seek peace and pursue it.
12 For the eyes of the Lord are on the
          righteous,
  and his ears are open to their prayer.
  But the face of the Lord is against those
          who do evil."

13 Now who will harm you if you are eager to do what is good? 14 But even if you do suffer for doing what is right, you are blessed. Do not fear what they fear,[a] and do not be intimidated, 15 but in your hearts sanctify Christ as Lord. Always be ready to make your defense to anyone who demands from you an accounting for the hope that is in you; 16 yet do it with gentleness and reverence.[b] Keep your conscience clear, so that, when you are maligned, those who abuse you for your good conduct in Christ may be put to shame. 17 For it is better to suffer for doing good, if suffering should be God's will, than to suffer for doing evil. 18 For Christ also suffered[c] for sins once for all, the righteous for the unrighteous, in order to bring you[d] to God. He was put to death in the flesh, but made alive in the spirit, 19 in which also he went and made a proclamation to the spirits in prison, 20 who in former times did not obey, when God waited patiently in the days of Noah, during the building of the ark, in which a few, that is, eight persons, were saved through water. 21 And baptism, which this prefigured, now saves you—not as a removal of dirt from the body, but as an appeal to God for[e] a good conscience, through the resurrection of Jesus Christ, 22 who has gone into heaven and is at the right hand of God, with angels, authorities, and powers made subject to him.

Good Stewards of God's Grace

4 Since therefore Christ suffered in the flesh,[f] arm yourselves also with the same intention (for whoever has suffered in the flesh

a Gk *their fear*   b Or *respect*   c Other ancient authorities read *died*   d Other ancient authorities read *us*   e Or *a pledge to God from*   f Other ancient authorities add *for us*; others, *for you*

wives will mean the husbands' prayers may be unheeded by God. **3.8–12** A summary of exhortations closes this section (2.11–3.12). **3.8** *Unity of spirit*, a central domestic and political concern of Greco-Roman society, was also highly important in early Christian tradition (see, e.g., Phil 2.1–4; Rom 12.16). On *love for one another* (lit. "brotherly love"), see 1.22; 2.17. **3.9** On not returning *abuse*, see 2.23; see also Lk 6.28; Rom 12.17. **3.10–12** Ps 34.12–16. The psalm includes terms and ideas central to this Letter, such as the warning against evil speech in v. 10b (see 2.22–23) and the emphasis on doing good in v. 11a. To *seek peace* (v. 11b) and harmony in household relationships and with society was one purpose of the household code. **3.13–17** The psalm quoted in vv. 10–12 provides a transition to this section, which is focused on doing good. **3.14** On the idea that those who suffer are *blessed*, see Mt 5.10. V. 14b quotes and interprets Isa 8.12. **3.15** *Defense* (Greek *apologia*) could refer technically to a legal defense but instead concerns the reputation of Christ and Christian exiles in Greco-Roman society (see Introduction). Jews also had to defend themselves (including their wives and slaves) against accusations (see Josephus, *Against Apion*). **3.16** Concern for outsiders who *malign* these Christians frames the household code; see note on 2.12. By the behavior recommended in the code, these *aliens and exiles* (2.11) indirectly address outsiders' objections. **3.17** On *suffering for doing good*, see 2.20. **3.18–22** The ascent of Christ, who had suffered, gives victory to the baptized. *Went* in v. 19 and *has gone* in v. 22 are the same verb, implying a description here of the one ascent by Christ. **3.18** Greek and Jewish heroes suffered for other worthy persons and for the law (see 2 Macc 6.28; 7.37; 4 Macc 6.27; see also Rom 5.7–8), but Christ *suffered for sins* (see 2.21). Many scholars perceive an early Christian tradition embodied in vv. 18, 22. **3.19** *The spirits in prison*, perhaps those "sons of God" who corrupted human women and were destroyed by the flood (see Gen 6.1–4; *1 Enoch* 10.4–6). The point is that the cosmic Lord is victorious over all the disobedient (see v. 22). **3.20** To establish a parallel with baptism, the author argues that Noah and his family were saved from a corrupted world *through water*, i.e., by means of the flood waters (see Gen 6–8). **3.21** *Dirt from the body*, lit. "filth of the flesh," i.e., desires of the flesh (see 2.11; 4.2). The reading of text note *e* is better, seeing baptism as *a pledge to God* out of a good consciousness or awareness of God. **3.22** On Jesus' seat at *the right hand of God*, see Ps 110.1; see also Eph 1.20–22; Heb 1.3–4, 13.

4.1–6 Exhortations to the moral life that distinguishes Christians from outsiders. **4.1** See 3.18. *Has fin-*

has finished with sin), [2]so as to live for the rest of your earthly life[a] no longer by human desires but by the will of God. [3]You have already spent enough time in doing what the Gentiles like to do, living in licentiousness, passions, drunkenness, revels, carousing, and lawless idolatry. [4]They are surprised that you no longer join them in the same excesses of dissipation, and so they blaspheme.[b] [5]But they will have to give an accounting to him who stands ready to judge the living and the dead. [6]For this is the reason the gospel was proclaimed even to the dead, so that, though they had been judged in the flesh as everyone is judged, they might live in the spirit as God does.

7 The end of all things is near;[c] therefore be serious and discipline yourselves for the sake of your prayers. [8]Above all, maintain constant love for one another, for love covers a multitude of sins. [9]Be hospitable to one another without complaining. [10]Like good stewards of the manifold grace of God, serve one another with whatever gift each of you has received. [11]Whoever speaks must do so as one speaking the very words of God; whoever serves must do so with the strength that God supplies, so that God may be glorified in all things through Jesus Christ. To him belong the glory and the power forever and ever. Amen.

Suffering as a Christian

12 Beloved, do not be surprised at the fiery ordeal that is taking place among you to test you, as though something strange were happening to you. [13]But rejoice insofar as you are sharing Christ's sufferings, so that you may also be glad and shout for joy when his glory is revealed. [14]If you are reviled for the name of Christ, you are blessed, because the spirit of glory,[d] which is the Spirit of God, is resting on you.[e] [15]But let none of you suffer as a murderer, a thief, a criminal, or even as a mischief maker. [16]Yet if any of you suffers as a Christian, do not consider it a disgrace, but glorify God because you bear this name. [17]For the time has come for judgment to begin with the household of God; if it begins with us, what will be the end for those who do not obey the gospel of God? [18]And

> "If it is hard for the righteous to be saved,
>   what will become of the ungodly and
>   the sinners?"

[19]Therefore, let those suffering in accordance with God's will entrust themselves to a faithful Creator, while continuing to do good.

Tending the Flock of God

5 Now as an elder myself and a witness of the sufferings of Christ, as well as one who shares in the glory to be revealed, I exhort the elders among you [2]to tend the flock of God that is in your charge, exercising the over-

---

ished with sin means either that those baptized are freed from sin's power (see Rom 6.7) or that Christ by carrying sins to the cross has dealt with them once for all (see Heb 7.27; 9.28), not that whoever has suffered no longer sins. **4.3** The Jewish-Christian author designates those outside the (primarily gentile) Christian community as Gentiles in keeping with the use of OT language to describe the Christian community. See Introduction; notes on 1.1; 1.10–11. **4.4** Those who slander the new Christians' lifestyle blaspheme God. **4.5** The tables will be turned on those who call Christians to give an accounting. See 3.15; see also Mt 7.1–2; Rom 2.3. **4.6** The gospel was proclaimed even to the dead. This means either that the righteous of Hebrew history share the faith of Christians (see Heb 4.2; 11) or that the Christian dead heard the gospel while they were still alive. **4.7–11** The focus of the exhortations shifts from relations with outsiders to the ways Christians should treat each other. **4.7** The end of all things, God's universal judgment (see v. 5). The expectation that this event was near was widespread in early Christianity; see Rom 13.12; 1 Cor 10.11; Rev 22.20; cf. 2 Pet 3.3. Prayers. See 3.7, 12. **4.8** Love for one another (see also 1.22; 2.17) is being

tested by persecution (see v. 12). **4.10** On the allotment of various gifts, see Rom 12.3–8; 1 Cor 12.4–11. **4.11** To him belong . . . Amen, a doxology repeated in 5.11. **4.12–19** The repetition of the address beloved signals a new section of the letter (see 2.11) that restates the themes of 1.6–8; 3.13–17. **4.12** Fiery ordeal. See 1.6–7. **4.13** Rejoice. See 1.6, 8. Sharing Christ's sufferings. See 2 Cor 1.3–11; Phil 3.10–11. Christ's glory is revealed at the last judgment. **4.14** Reviled . . . blessed. See the beatitude in Mt 5.11; Lk 6.22. **4.16** The name Christian was apparently originally employed by outsiders to designate followers of Christ; see Acts 11.26. **4.17** Household of God (see also Eph 2.19; 1 Tim 3.15; Heb 3.6), points to the close relationship among Christians; see 5.14. **4.18** Prov 11.31. **4.19** The author encourages readers by identifying the judge of all (see vv. 5, 7) as the faithful Creator. Entrust(ing) themselves to God is accomplished by doing good, a point that sums up the thrust of this section.

5.1–5 To elements of a household code (2.13–3.7) are added elements of a congregational code. **5.1** An elder myself, a rare self-reference by the author (see 1.1; 2.11). Elders were authoritative persons whose presence is noted in many early Christian writings.

sight,[a] not under compulsion but willingly, as God would have you do it[b]—not for sordid gain but eagerly. [3]Do not lord it over those in your charge, but be examples to the flock. [4]And when the chief shepherd appears, you will win the crown of glory that never fades away. [5]In the same way, you who are younger must accept the authority of the elders.[c] And all of you must clothe yourselves with humility in your dealings with one another, for

"God opposes the proud,
    but gives grace to the humble."

[6] Humble yourselves therefore under the mighty hand of God, so that he may exalt you in due time. [7]Cast all your anxiety on him, because he cares for you. [8]Discipline yourselves, keep alert.[d] Like a roaring lion your adversary the devil prowls around, looking for someone to devour. [9]Resist him, steadfast in your faith, for you know that your brothers and sisters[e] in all the world are undergoing the same kinds of suffering. [10]And after you have suffered for a little while, the God of all grace, who has called you to his eternal glory in Christ, will himself restore, support, strengthen, and establish you. [11]To him be the power forever and ever. Amen.

Final Greetings and Benediction

[12] Through Silvanus, whom I consider a faithful brother, I have written this short letter to encourage you and to testify that this is the true grace of God. Stand fast in it. [13]Your sister church[f] in Babylon, chosen together with you, sends you greetings; and so does my son Mark. [14]Greet one another with a kiss of love.

Peace to all of you who are in Christ.[g]

---

a Other ancient authorities lack *exercising the oversight*
b Other ancient authorities lack *as God would have you do it*
c Or *of those who are older*   d Or *be vigilant*   e Gk *your brotherhood*   f Gk *She who is*   g Other ancient authorities add *Amen*

5.2 *Tend the flock.* See Jn 21.16, Jesus' command to Peter. Proper tending is described by three pairs of contrasts (*not . . . but*) here and in v. 3. **5.3** The command not to *lord it over* others prohibits the kind of harsh authority some have experienced from outsiders (see 2.18). **5.4** *You will win* (lit. "you will receive payment"). This eschatological reward stands in contrast to the greed forbidden in v. 2. **5.5** *Younger,* probably simply an age group. *Elders,* officials who are also older. *Humility.* See 3.8; 4.7–11. *God . . . humble.* Prov 3.34. **5.6–11** A final promise of vindication. **5.6** On *exalting* the humble, see Lk 14.11; 18.14; Phil 2.8. **5.7** *Anxiety.* See Mt 6.25–34. **5.8–9** Resisting the *devil,* God's enemy, points to the larger struggle between good and evil within which the Christians are to understand their suffering. **5.10** Four parallel verbs reinforce the expectation *that he may exalt you* (v. 6). **5.11** See 4.11c. **5.12–14** Final exhortation and greetings. **5.12** *Through Silvanus.* Silvanus is the letter bearer, not the author's secretary; see Acts 15.22 ("Silas"); 1 Thess 1.1; 2 Thess 1.1. *Encourage.* See 2.11 (where the same word is translated *urge*) and 5.1 (where it is translated *exhort*). *Stand fast* in God's grace (see 1.13). This exhortation closes the body of the Letter. **5.13** *Babylon,* the author's name for Rome (see Rev 17.5, 18). *Mark.* See Acts 12.12–17. **5.14** The *kiss of love* (see Rom 16.16) is familial, i.e., for members of the household of God (4.17). The farewell mentions *peace,* a concluding wish that reflects the conflict situation addressed by the Letter; see 1.2; 3.11.

The Second Letter of

PETER

THE SECOND LETTER of Peter is presented as Peter's testament, i.e., an account of Peter's teaching as he wished it to be remembered after his death (1.12–15). If Peter himself wrote it, he must have done so shortly before his martyrdom in Rome in 64/65 CE. Most scholars, however, now believe it was written after Peter's death by a writer following a literary convention of the time that allowed an author to attribute a "testament" to a great figure of the past. 2 Peter may well have been sent from the church of Rome and therefore attributed to the apostle who had for a time played a role in the leadership of that church. By writing in Peter's name, the author was able to restate and defend Peter's teaching in a situation in which opponents were criticizing the apostolic message. He also expressed the normative value of the apostolic teaching for the period after the death of the apostles.

Date

2 PETER HAS OFTEN BEEN CONSIDERED the latest book in the New Testament (even as late as 150 CE), but the basis for this view is weak. The best clue to the date of 2 Peter lies in 3.3–4. These verses seem to reflect a time when the early Christian expectation that Christ would come in glory within the lifetime of the first Christian generation had been disappointed. Because the problem this posed for Christian hope was soon surmounted, these verses seem to date 2 Peter around 80–90 CE.

Opponents

2 PETER DEFENDS PETER'S TEACHING against critics who probably wanted to free the Christian message from features that were embarrassing to the church in a pagan environment. Jewish-Christian moral strictness made life difficult for Christians in a more permissive pagan society, so the opponents argued that Christians were free from moral constraints. The Christian hope that Christ would come to judge the world and to establish a new world of righteousness was also alien to pagan views, so the opponents argued that the idea of a coming judgment was simply mistaken. This skepticism reinforced their moral libertinism. In reply, 2 Peter insists that the Christian hope is essential to the gospel and provides a motive for righteous living.

Purpose

2 PETER FACES THE PROBLEMS of Christianity's twin transition from a Jewish to a pagan context and from the apostolic to the postapostolic age. 2 Peter insists on the ethical demand and the future hope of the gospel, maintaining these typically Jewish aspects of early Christian teaching, while also (esp. in 1.3–11) contextualizing them by translating them from Jewish into more typically Hellenistic cultural terms.

Form and Structure

2 PETER IS A TESTAMENT in the form of a letter. Four passages in which Peter foresees the future and provides for his teaching to be remembered reflect the Jewish testament genre (1.3–11, 12–15; 2.1–3a; 3.1–4). Attached to these are passages defending Peter's teaching against the opponents (1.16–19, 20–21; 2.3b–10a; 3.5–10) and two passages contrasting the evil ways of the opponents (2.10b–22) with the righteous conduct expected of the readers (3.11–16).

Relationship to Jude

PARTS OF 2 PETER (esp. 2.1–18; 3.1–3) are closely related to the Letter of Jude. Most scholars now agree that the author of 2 Peter was dependent on Jude's Letter, from which he adapted material for his own purpose. [RICHARD J. BAUCKHAM]

Salutation

1 Simeon[a] Peter, a servant[b] and apostle of Jesus Christ,

To those who have received a faith as precious as ours through the righteousness of our God and Savior Jesus Christ:[c]

2 May grace and peace be yours in abundance in the knowledge of God and of Jesus our Lord.

The Christian's Call and Election

3 His divine power has given us everything needed for life and godliness, through the knowledge of him who called us by[d] his own glory and goodness. 4 Thus he has given us, through these things, his precious and very great promises, so that through them you may escape from the corruption that is in the world because of lust, and may become participants of the divine nature. 5 For this very reason, you must make every effort to support your faith with goodness, and goodness with knowledge,

6 and knowledge with self-control, and self-control with endurance, and endurance with godliness, 7 and godliness with mutual[e] affection, and mutual[e] affection with love. 8 For if these things are yours and are increasing among you, they keep you from being ineffective and unfruitful in the knowledge of our Lord Jesus Christ. 9 For anyone who lacks these things is short-sighted and blind, and is forgetful of the cleansing of past sins. 10 Therefore, brothers and sisters,[f] be all the more eager to confirm your call and election, for if you do this, you will never stumble. 11 For in this way, entry into the eternal kingdom of our Lord and Savior Jesus Christ will be richly provided for you.

12 Therefore I intend to keep on reminding you of these things, though you know them already and are established in the truth that has come to you. 13 I think it right, as long as I am

a Other ancient authorities read *Simon* b Gk *slave* c Or *of our God and the Savior Jesus Christ* d Other ancient authorities read *through* e Gk *brotherly* f Gk *brothers*

1.1–2 The opening address and greeting are characteristic of early Christian letters. 1.3–11 A summary of Peter's teaching as it is to be remembered after his death, stressing both God's grace and the need for moral effort if Christians are to attain final salvation. 1.4 To *become participants of the divine nature* does not mean to share God's essence but to receive "godlike" immortality. 1.5–7 In this "ladder" of virtues, each virtue is the means of producing the next (this sense of the Greek is lost in translation). All the virtues grow out of *faith,* and all culminate in *love.* 1.12–15 Peter's teaching will be his permanent bequest to the church.

in this body,[a] to refresh your memory, [14]since I know that my death[b] will come soon, as indeed our Lord Jesus Christ has made clear to me. [15]And I will make every effort so that after my departure you may be able at any time to recall these things.

Eyewitnesses of Christ's Glory

16 For we did not follow cleverly devised myths when we made known to you the power and coming of our Lord Jesus Christ, but we had been eyewitnesses of his majesty. [17]For he received honor and glory from God the Father when that voice was conveyed to him by the Majestic Glory, saying, "This is my Son, my Beloved,[c] with whom I am well pleased." [18]We ourselves heard this voice come from heaven, while we were with him on the holy mountain.

19 So we have the prophetic message more fully confirmed. You will do well to be attentive to this as to a lamp shining in a dark place, until the day dawns and the morning star rises in your hearts. [20]First of all you must understand this, that no prophecy of scripture is a matter of one's own interpretation, [21]because no prophecy ever came by human will, but men and women moved by the Holy Spirit spoke from God.[d]

False Prophets and Their Punishment

2 But false prophets also arose among the people, just as there will be false teachers among you, who will secretly bring in destructive opinions. They will even deny the Master who bought them—bringing swift destruction on themselves. [2]Even so, many will follow their licentious ways, and because of these teachers[e] the way of truth will be maligned. [3]And in their greed they will exploit you with deceptive words. Their condemnation, pronounced against them long ago, has not been idle, and their destruction is not asleep.

4 For if God did not spare the angels when they sinned, but cast them into hell[f] and committed them to chains[g] of deepest darkness to be kept until the judgment; [5]and if he did not spare the ancient world, even though he saved Noah, a herald of righteousness, with seven others, when he brought a flood on a world of the ungodly; [6]and if by turning the cities of Sodom and Gomorrah to ashes he condemned them to extinction[h] and made them an example of what is coming to the ungodly;[i] [7]and if he rescued Lot, a righteous man greatly distressed by the licentiousness of the lawless [8](for that righteous man, living among them day after day, was tormented in his righteous soul by their lawless deeds that he saw and heard), [9]then the Lord knows how to rescue the godly from trial, and to keep the unrighteous under punishment until the day of judgment [10]—especially those who indulge their flesh in depraved lust, and who despise authority.

Bold and willful, they are not afraid to slander the glorious ones,[j] [11]whereas angels, though greater in might and power, do not bring against them a slanderous judgment from the Lord.[k] [12]These people, however, are

---

a Gk tent   b Gk the putting off of my tent   c Other ancient authorities read my beloved Son   d Other ancient authorities read but moved by the Holy Spirit saints of God spoke   e Gk because of them   f Gk Tartaros   g Other ancient authorities read pits   h Other ancient authorities lack to extinction   i Other ancient authorities read an example to those who were to be ungodly   j Or angels; Gk glories   k Other ancient authorities read before the Lord; others lack the phrase

---

1.16–21 This section replies to the opponents' charges that the apostles' prediction of Christ's future coming was their own invention (vv. 16–19) and that ot prophecies of it did not come from God (vv. 20–21). **1.16–18** At the transfiguration (Mt 17.1–8), the apostles saw Jesus appointed by God as the Messiah who will come to judge and rule the world (Ps 2.6–9). **1.19** The prophetic message, or prophecy in general. The morning star, Christ at his coming in glory (Num 24.17; Rev 22.16). **1.20** One's own interpretation, probably not interpretation of scripture by its readers, but the prophets' interpretation of their visions. **1.21** See Jer 20.9; 23.16–32; Am 3.8.
2.1–3a Peter's prediction of the arrival of false teachers after his death. **2.1** The false teachers probably deny Christ by flouting his moral authority (as in Titus 1.16; Jude 4). **2.3b–10a** A reply to the opponents'

claim that the expected judgment of the world is not going to happen. Examples of God's judgment in the past (see Jude 6–7) are cited, along with examples of righteous people spared from judgment (see Wis 10.4–9). The judgments are warnings for the wicked; Noah and Lot are models for the righteous in a wicked world. **2.4** Angels, the "sons of God" of Gen 6.1–4, as interpreted in Jewish literature. **2.5** Noah is a herald of righteousness because, according to tradition, he preached repentance before the flood. **2.6–8** See Gen 18.16–19.29. **2.7** For Lot as a righteous man, see Gen 18.23–25; Wis 10.6; 19.17. **2.10b–22** Denunciation of the opponents. **2.10b–11** See Jude 8–9, but here the glorious ones are the powers of evil, for whom the opponents fail to show a healthy fear. **2.12** Probably meaning that when the powers of evil are destroyed (see text note a on p. 2070), these people who now

like irrational animals, mere creatures of instinct, born to be caught and killed. They slander what they do not understand, and when those creatures are destroyed,[a] they also will be destroyed, [13]suffering[b] the penalty for doing wrong. They count it a pleasure to revel in the daytime. They are blots and blemishes, reveling in their dissipation[c] while they feast with you. [14]They have eyes full of adultery, insatiable for sin. They entice unsteady souls. They have hearts trained in greed. Accursed children! [15]They have left the straight road and have gone astray, following the road of Balaam son of Bosor,[d] who loved the wages of doing wrong, [16]but was rebuked for his own transgression; a speechless donkey spoke with a human voice and restrained the prophet's madness.

17 These are waterless springs and mists driven by a storm; for them the deepest darkness has been reserved. [18]For they speak bombastic nonsense, and with licentious desires of the flesh they entice people who have just[e] escaped from those who live in error. [19]They promise them freedom, but they themselves are slaves of corruption; for people are slaves to whatever masters them. [20]For if, after they have escaped the defilements of the world through the knowledge of our Lord and Savior Jesus Christ, they are again entangled in them and overpowered, the last state has become worse for them than the first. [21]For it would have been better for them never to have known the way of righteousness than, after knowing it, to turn back from the holy commandment that was passed on to them. [22]It has happened to them according to the true proverb,

"The dog turns back to its own vomit,"
and,
    "The sow is washed only to wallow in the
        mud."

The Promise of the Lord's Coming

3 This is now, beloved, the second letter I am writing to you; in them I am trying to arouse your sincere intention by reminding you [2]that you should remember the words spoken in the past by the holy prophets, and the commandment of the Lord and Savior spoken through your apostles. [3]First of all you must understand this, that in the last days scoffers will come, scoffing and indulging their own lusts [4]and saying, "Where is the promise of his coming? For ever since our ancestors died,[f] all things continue as they were from the beginning of creation!" [5]They deliberately ignore this fact, that by the word of God heavens existed long ago and an earth was formed out of water and by means of water, [6]through which the world of that time was deluged with water and perished. [7]But by the same word the present heavens and earth have been reserved for fire, being kept until the day of judgment and destruction of the godless.

8 But do not ignore this one fact, beloved, that with the Lord one day is like a thousand years, and a thousand years are like one day. [9]The Lord is not slow about his promise, as some think of slowness, but is patient with

---

a Gk *in their destruction*   b Other ancient authorities read *receiving*   c Other ancient authorities read *love-feasts*   d Other ancient authorities read *Beor*   e Other ancient authorities read *actually*   f Gk *our fathers fell asleep*

---

scoff at them will perish with them. **2.13** *Their dissipation,* lit. "their deceits" (Greek *apatais*), which means deceitful pleasures and is also a pun on "love feasts" (Greek *agapais;* see Jude 12). The opponents are turning the church's fellowship meals into mere shams. **2.15–16** See Num 22.21–35; Jude 11. **2.17** See Jude 12–13. **2.19** The *freedom* the opponents promise is liberation from fear of divine judgment and so from moral constraint, but as slaves to sin they cannot give freedom from sin (see Rom 6.15–23; 8.21; 1 Pet 2.16). **2.20** See Mt 12.43–45. **2.22** The first quotation is Prov 26.11; the second is an ancient oriental proverb.

3.1–4 A second prediction of the coming of the false teachers. **3.2** *Your apostles,* those who founded the readers' churches. **3.3** *Scoffers,* people who treat God's revelation with contempt (see Ps 1.1; Prov 1.22; Isa 28.14; Jude 18). **3.4** *Our ancestors,* probably the first Christian generation (though some interpreters take

them to be the Israelites of the past). The *scoffers* say that the apostles' *promise* of Christ's coming in glory set a time limit (within the lifetime of the first Christian generation, see Mk 9.1; 13.30) that has now expired. But they also express a rationalistic assumption about the world: nothing has changed since *the beginning of creation,* i.e., divine interventions in history do not happen. **3.5–7** A reply to the assumption made at the end of v. 4. **3.5** On creation *out of water,* see Gen 1.2, 6–10. **3.6** *Through which,* through the word of God and through water (the flood; see Gen 7.11). **3.7** Jewish traditions spoke of two universal judgments, one by water (in the past), the other by *fire* (in the future). Fire is a common biblical image of judgment. **3.8–10** A reply to the *charge (v. 4) that* the expectation of the Lord's coming has been disproved by the *delay.* **3.8** Ps 90.4, to which this verse alludes, was used in Jewish literature to deal with the problem of apparent delay in the fulfill-

you,[a] not wanting any to perish, but all to come to repentance. [10]But the day of the Lord will come like a thief, and then the heavens will pass away with a loud noise, and the elements will be dissolved with fire, and the earth and everything that is done on it will be disclosed.[b]

11 Since all these things are to be dissolved in this way, what sort of persons ought you to be in leading lives of holiness and godliness, [12]waiting for and hastening[c] the coming of the day of God, because of which the heavens will be set ablaze and dissolved, and the elements will melt with fire? [13]But, in accordance with his promise, we wait for new heavens and a new earth, where righteousness is at home.

Final Exhortation and Doxology

14 Therefore, beloved, while you are waiting for these things, strive to be found by him at peace, without spot or blemish; [15]and regard the patience of our Lord as salvation. So also our beloved brother Paul wrote to you according to the wisdom given him, [16]speaking of this as he does in all his letters. There are some things in them hard to understand, which the ignorant and unstable twist to their own destruction, as they do the other scriptures. [17]You therefore, beloved, since you are forewarned, beware that you are not carried away with the error of the lawless and lose your own stability. [18]But grow in the grace and knowledge of our Lord and Savior Jesus Christ. To him be the glory both now and to the day of eternity. Amen.[d]

---

a Other ancient authorities read *on your account* **b** Other ancient authorities read *will be burned up* **c** Or *earnestly desiring* **d** Other ancient authorities lack *Amen*

---

ment of God's promises. **3.10** *The day of the Lord,* a common biblical expression for the time of God's final judgment. For its coming *like a thief,* see Mt 24.43–44; 1 Thess 5.2. For imagery of it, see Isa 34.4; Mk 13.25; Rev 6.13–14. The wicked and their deeds *will be disclosed* to God's judicial scrutiny. **3.11–16** Just as the opponents, who scoff at the prospect of divine judgment, live wickedly, so the readers, who hope for the new world of righteousness, should live righteously. **3.12** As God defers the judgment to give time for repentance (v. 9), so God may *hasten* it (see Sir 36.10) if people repent. **3.13** For *new heavens and a new earth,* see Isa 65.17; 66.22; Rev 21.1. Probably a renewal of this creation (not its replacement by another) is meant (as in Rom 8.21): the fire will purge it of evil, so that *righteousness* (personified) can at last find a *home* in it. **3.15** God's *patience* is *salvation* because delaying the judgment gives opportunity for repentance (see v. 9). *Paul* also treated the hope of the Lord's coming as a motive for righteous living. The reference is too general to identify which Pauline Letters had been written to the churches addressed here. **3.16** *Ignorant,* lit. "uninstructed." Paul's difficult sayings are open to misinterpretation only by those who have not gained adequate Christian understanding. Either the opponents claimed Paul's teaching on freedom from the law (see, e.g., Rom 4.15; 5.20; 8.1–2; 1 Cor 6.12; 2 Cor 3.17) as support for their own view of freedom (see note on 2.19), or they held that his expectation of the Lord's coming soon (see, e.g., Rom 13.11–12; 16.20; Phil 4.5; 1 Thess 4.15) had been disproved (see note on 3.4). The reference to Paul's Letters alongside *the other scriptures* shows that they were already being treated as scripture, i.e., read in Christian worship along with the OT.

The First Letter of

JOHN

THOUGH IT IS GENERALLY REFERRED TO as a Letter, 1 John does not have the standard opening and closing formulas of a letter. It seems instead to be a kind of essay or homily written to deal with a specific problem.

Author and Relation to Gospel of John

THE LANGUAGE, STYLE, AND IDEAS of 1 John are clearly very similar to those of the Gospel According to John. Therefore, its author was long believed to be identical with the author of the Gospel, who was held to be the apostle John, the son of Zebedee. Though this identification of the Gospel's author is no longer certain (see Introduction to the Gospel of John), it remains possible that the same author wrote both books. Differences in writing style and ideas have, however, led many to conclude that another author wrote 1 John. This person may be the elder who wrote 2 and 3 John, since 1 and 2 John are very similar in style and seem to address the same historical situation. At many points, 1 John seems to quote the words of the Fourth Gospel, or at least the tradition on which that Gospel is based. Thus it is likely that 1 John comes from the same early Christian community or "school" as the Gospel According to John, but from a later point in its history. The author may be speaking for a group who guarded the community's traditions (1.1–5).

Date and Place

IF 1 JOHN WAS COMPOSED after the Gospel, it was probably written no earlier than around 100 CE, though an exact date cannot be determined. According to traditions dating from the second century, 1 John was written in Ephesus. Other places have been suggested, but no better evidence exists for them than for Ephesus.

Historical Background

FIRST JOHN SPEAKS OF CERTAIN PEOPLE who "went out from us," whom it calls antichrists and liars who deny that Jesus is the Christ or that "Jesus Christ has come in the flesh" (2.18–27; 4.1–3). Such language suggests that 1 John was written to oppose a movement that departed from the community's traditional beliefs about Jesus (2.24). We do not know exactly what these opponents believed and taught, though they probably claimed to be speaking under the influence of the Holy Spirit (4.1), perhaps believing that statements such as John 14.25–26; 16.12–13 were being fulfilled in them. Most scholars hold that the movement was a form of Docetism, the belief that Jesus Christ was a spiritual being who only "appeared" (Greek *dokeo*) to be human. The opponents of 1 John may have denied that the human Jesus was to be identified with the divine, spiritual Christ or that Jesus' death had value for salvation.

Message

BY CONTRAST, 1 John urges its Christian readers to stay with what they have heard "from the beginning" (1.1). This means believing in the identity of the physical, human Jesus with the divine Son of God and in the saving value of his death. It also means keeping the commandment to love one another, an area in which the author probably considered the opponents lacking. 1 John repeatedly insists that one cannot truly believe in Jesus Christ without truly and selflessly loving other believers. It is this insistence that "God is love" (4.8) that has kept people interested in 1 John long after the circumstances in which it was written have passed into obscurity. [DAVID K. RENSBERGER, revised by HAROLD W. ATTRIDGE]

The Word of Life

1 We declare to you what was from the beginning, what we have heard, what we have seen with our eyes, what we have looked at and touched with our hands, concerning the word of life— [2]this life was revealed, and we have seen it and testify to it, and declare to you the eternal life that was with the Father and was revealed to us— [3]we declare to you what we have seen and heard so that you also may have fellowship with us; and truly our fellowship is with the Father and with his Son Jesus Christ. [4]We are writing these things so that our[a] joy may be complete.

God Is Light

5 This is the message we have heard from him and proclaim to you, that God is light and in him there is no darkness at all. [6]If we say that we have fellowship with him while we are walking in darkness, we lie and do not do what is true; [7]but if we walk in the light as he himself is in the light, we have fellowship with one another, and the blood of Jesus his Son cleanses us from all sin. [8]If we say that we have no sin, we deceive ourselves, and the truth is not in us. [9]If we confess our sins, he who is

a Other ancient authorities read *your*

1.1–4 The prologue resembles Jn 1.1–18, on which it is probably based. The author uses this familiar material to establish some important themes. One is Jesus Christ's real humanity. Another is the admonition to be faithful to the tradition that the author represents, with its testimony about what has been revealed in Jesus. See also Introduction. **1.1** *What was from the beginning.* See Jn 1.1, but here the phrase means not only the eternal Word, but also the *word of life*, the Christian proclamation that the author regards as having been embodied in Jesus and handed on since his time. See also 1 Jn 2.7, 13–14, 24; 3.11. *Looked at and touched.* The language emphasizes the physical reality of what the tradition proclaims. Cf. Jn 19.35; 20.27. **1.2** *Revealed.* See 3.5, 8. Revelation is a key theme of the Gospel According to John. See Jn 1.18 as well as the various ways in which Jesus is revealed or made known (cf. Jn 1.31; 2.11). In the Gospel revelation takes place primarily through the event of the cross. See Jn 3.14–15. *Eternal life.* See 2.25; 3.14–15; 5.11–13, 20; Jn 3.15–16, 36; 5.24; 6.40, 47; 10.28; 11.25–26; 17.2–3;

20.31. **1.3** 1 John stresses that *Jesus* is *Christ* and God's *Son* (see Introduction; 2.22; 3.23; 4.15; 5.1, 5; also Jn 20.31). *Fellowship* evokes the intimate relationship between God, Jesus, and believers promised by the gospel. Cf. Jn 14.23; 17.21. **1.4** *We are writing.* See 2.1, 12–14, 21, 26; 5.13. *That our joy may be complete.* See Jn 3.29; 15.11; 16.24; 17.13; 2 Jn 12. **1.5–2.11** A unit marked by *light* and *darkness* at both ends and containing six quotations from the author's opponents (*if we say*, 1.6, 8, 10, on sin; *whoever says*, 2.4, 6, 9, on obedience and love). **1.5** *Message.* See 3.11. *God is light.* Cf. 4.8. On *light* and *darkness*, see Jn 1.4–5; 8.12; 9.4–5; 12.46. **1.6–7** *Walking in darkness, walk in the light.* See Jn 3.19–21; 8.12; 11.9–10; 12.35–36. **1.6** See 2.4. **1.7** On imitating Christ (or God), see 2.6; 3.3, 16; 4.11 (also Jn 13.15, 34; 15.10, 12). On Jesus' *blood*, see 5.6–8; Jn 19.34. **1.8–2.2** 1 John maintains the possibility of sinlessness (3.4–10; 5.18) at least as an ideal but recognizes the reality of human sin and expresses the confidence that God forgives sin through Jesus (see also v. 7; 5.16–17). For the notion of Jesus' sinlessness, cf. Heb

faithful and just will forgive us our sins and cleanse us from all unrighteousness. [10]If we say that we have not sinned, we make him a liar, and his word is not in us.

Christ Our Advocate

2 My little children, I am writing these things to you so that you may not sin. But if anyone does sin, we have an advocate with the Father, Jesus Christ the righteous; [2]and he is the atoning sacrifice for our sins, and not for ours only but also for the sins of the whole world.

3 Now by this we may be sure that we know him, if we obey his commandments. [4]Whoever says, "I have come to know him," but does not obey his commandments, is a liar, and in such a person the truth does not exist; [5]but whoever obeys his word, truly in this person the love of God has reached perfection. By this we may be sure that we are in him: [6]whoever says, "I abide in him," ought to walk just as he walked.

A New Commandment

7 Beloved, I am writing you no new commandment, but an old commandment that you have had from the beginning; the old commandment is the word that you have heard. [8]Yet I am writing you a new commandment that is true in him and in you, because[a] the darkness is passing away and the true light is already shining. [9]Whoever says, "I am in the light," while hating a brother or sister,[b] is still in the darkness. [10]Whoever loves a brother or sister[c] lives in the light, and in such a person[d] there is no cause for stumbling. [11]But whoever hates another believer[e] is in the darkness, walks in the darkness, and does not know the way to go, because the darkness has brought on blindness.

[12] I am writing to you, little children,
     because your sins are forgiven on
        account of his name.
[13] I am writing to you, fathers,
     because you know him who is from the
        beginning.
I am writing to you, young people,
     because you have conquered the evil
        one.
[14] I write to you, children,
     because you know the Father.
I write to you, fathers,
     because you know him who is from the
        beginning.
I write to you, young people,
     because you are strong
     and the word of God abides in you,
        and you have overcome the evil one.

15 Do not love the world or the things in the world. The love of the Father is not in those who love the world; [16]for all that is in the world—the desire of the flesh, the desire of the eyes, the pride in riches—comes not from the Father but from the world. [17]And the world

---

a Or that   b Gk hating a brother   c Gk loves a brother
d Or in it   e Gk hates a brother

4.15. **1.8** The *truth* is identical to God's word (see v. 10; see also 2.4, 7; Jn 17.17). **1.9** *Confess.* Admitting one's sinfulness is a condition for forgiveness. It is unlikely that a formal penitential ritual was yet in place. *Just,* rendered *righteous* in 2.1, 29; 3.7. **2.1** *Advocate,* used for the Holy Spirit in Jn 14.16, 26; 15.26; 16.7. On Christ as advocate, see Rom 8.34; Heb 7.25; 9.24. **2.2** An *atoning sacrifice* cleanses from sin (4.10; see also Lev 16.16, 30; Rom 3.25; Heb 9.14). *Sins of the whole world.* See Jn 1.29. **2.3** *Know him.* See 4.8. *Commandments,* in particular the commandment of love. See vv. 7–8; 3.22–24; 4.21; 5.2–3; Jn 13.34; 14.15, 21; 15.10, 12–17. **2.4** *Liar.* See 1.6; 2.22; 4.20; also 1.10; 5.10. **2.5** *Love of God,* love for God or love from God. *Perfection.* See 4.12, 17. The emphasis on the language of "perfection" may respond to concerns of the opponents. The author makes perfection contingent on love. For another treatment of the term, cf. Heb 5.9; 7.28; 10.14. **2.6** *Abide in him.* On mutual abiding among God, Jesus, and Christians, see 2.24, 27–28; 3.6, 9, 15–17, 24; 4.13–16; 5.20; Jn 6.56; 10.38; 14.10–11,

17, 20, 23; 15.1–10; 17.21–23, 26. **2.7** *New commandment, old commandment.* What is "new" on the lips of Jesus is now fixed tradition. See Jn 13.34; 2 Jn 5. *Beginning . . . heard.* See 1.1; 2.24; 3.11. **2.8** *True light.* See Jn 1.5, 9. **2.9–11** *Love* and *hate* are not just feelings, but deeds (3.15–18; 4.20). *Brother or sister,* a fellow Christian. **2.11** *Walks in the darkness.* See note on 1.6–7.

  2.12–14 The author writes to build on the readers' strengths. Note the careful, rhythmic structure. **2.12** *Little children,* the readers as a whole (see vv. 1, 18). **2.13** *Fathers* and *young people* may mean particular groups. *From the beginning.* See note on 1.1. *Conquered,* rendered *overcome* in v. 14 (see also 4.4; 5.4–5; Jn 16.33; Rev 2.7, 11). *Evil one,* i.e., the devil (see note on 3.12). **2.14** *Abides in you.* See note on 2.6. *Overcome.* See note on 2.13. **2.15–17** 1 John aligns the world with the devil and against God (4.4–6; 5.4–5, 19) more than other NT writings, even John (cf. Jn 1.10; 3.16–17; 6.51; 8.12; 12.31; 14.30–31; 15.18–19; 16.8–11; 17.13–18). **2.16** *Flesh* is not sexuality, but human self-seeking; see Gal 5.14–17, 24; Eph 2.3; 1 Pet

and its desire[a] are passing away, but those who do the will of God live forever.

Warning against Antichrists

18 Children, it is the last hour! As you have heard that antichrist is coming, so now many antichrists have come. From this we know that it is the last hour. [19]They went out from us, but they did not belong to us; for if they had belonged to us, they would have remained with us. But by going out they made it plain that none of them belongs to us. [20]But you have been anointed by the Holy One, and all of you have knowledge.[b] [21]I write to you, not because you do not know the truth, but because you know it, and you know that no lie comes from the truth. [22]Who is the liar but the one who denies that Jesus is the Christ?[c] This is the antichrist, the one who denies the Father and the Son. [23]No one who denies the Son has the Father; everyone who confesses the Son has the Father also. [24]Let what you heard from the beginning abide in you. If what you heard from the beginning abides in you, then you will abide in the Son and in the Father. [25]And this is what he has promised us,[d] eternal life.

26 I write these things to you concerning those who would deceive you. [27]As for you, the anointing that you received from him abides in you, and so you do not need anyone to teach you. But as his anointing teaches you about all things, and is true and is not a lie, and just as it has taught you, abide in him.[e]

28 And now, little children, abide in him, so that when he is revealed we may have confidence and not be put to shame before him at his coming.

Children of God

29 If you know that he is righteous, you may be sure that everyone who does right has been

3 born of him. [1]See what love the Father has given us, that we should be called children of God; and that is what we are. The reason the world does not know us is that it did not know him. [2]Beloved, we are God's children now; what we will be has not yet been revealed. What we do know is this: when he[e] is revealed, we will be like him, for we will see him as he is. [3]And all who have this hope in him purify themselves, just as he is pure.

4 Everyone who commits sin is guilty of lawlessness; sin is lawlessness. [5]You know that he was revealed to take away sins, and in him there is no sin. [6]No one who abides in him sins; no one who sins has either seen him or known him. [7]Little children, let no one deceive you. Every-

---

a Or the desire for it b Other ancient authorities read you know all things c Or the Messiah d Other ancient authorities read you e Or it

---

2.11. *Desire of the eyes,* perhaps what attracts the senses. *Riches.* See 3.17. **2.17** *Passing away.* See v. 8. Paul expresses the same sense that the times are dramatically changing. See 1 Cor 7.31. *Live,* or "abide." **2.18–27** The opponents and their "deceitful" ideas about Christ. Note references to anointing near the beginning and end (vv. 20, 27). **2.18** Many early Christians believed that they lived in *the last hour* and expected an enemy of God (2 Thess 2.3–12) or false messiahs (Mk 13.5–6, 21–22) before the end. 1 John applies such ideas about an enemy from outside Christianity, an *antichrist* ("counter-Messiah"; only in 1 Jn 2.18, 22; 4.3; 2 Jn 7), to the *many* opponents within. **2.19** *They,* the author's opponents; *us,* the community, led by the author, with which the opponents broke fellowship. **2.20** *Anointed* here and *anointing* in v. 27 probably refer to the Holy Spirit (see 2 Cor 1.21–22; Isa 61.1 may be in mind), who *teaches . . . all things* (v. 27; Jn 14.26). *Holy One,* probably God, but perhaps Jesus. **2.21** *Know the truth.* See Jn 8.32; 2 Jn 1. **2.22** The opponents perhaps *denied* that the human *Jesus* was identical with the divine *Christ,* God's *Son;* see 4.2–3, 15; 5.5–12; 2 Jn 7. **2.23** *Confesses.* See 4.2–3, 15; Jn 9.22; 12.42. *Has the Father.* See 2 Jn 9. Response to Jesus determines one's relationship to God in the Gospel of John also; see Jn 5.23; 14.9; 15.23. **2.24** *From the beginning.* See note on 1.1.

Abide in you. See note on 2.6. **2.25** *Eternal life.* See 1.2. **2.26** *Deceive.* See 3.7; 2 Jn 7. **2.27** *Anointing, teaches . . . all things.* See note on 2.20.

   2.28–3.10 The focus shifts from the opponents to the readers with an emphasis on revelation. When Jesus comes and is revealed, those who abide in him will also be revealed; indeed, because he was already revealed to destroy sin, God's children are already revealed by their love. See 1.2; 2.28; 3.2, 5, 8, 10. **2.28–29** At some point the referent of *he* and *him* shifts from Jesus to God. **2.28** *Confidence.* See note on 4.17. *Shame . . . at his coming* envisions a last judgment as depicted in Mt 25.31–46. **2.29** Both God and Jesus are called *righteous* (1.9; 2.1; 3.7); on *doing right,* see note on 3.10. *Born of him.* See 3.9–10; 4.7; 5.1, 18; Jn 1.12–13; 3.3–8. **3.1** *Children of God.* See 3.10; Jn 1.12–13. *Know.* See 4.7; Jn 8.19; 14.7; 15.21; 16.3. **3.2** *Like him,* probably like Jesus; see note on 4.17. *See.* See 3.6; Jn 14.19; 16.16; 17.24; for notions of eschatological transformation, see also 2 Cor 3.18. **3.3** On imitating Jesus, see note on 1.7; see also the imitation of God in Lev 11.45; 19.2; 20.26. *Pure* here means free from sin, the topic of 3.4–10. **3.5** *He,* Jesus. *Take away sins.* See 2.2; 4.10; Jn 1.29. *No sin.* See 2 Cor 5.21; Heb 4.15. **3.6–10** The author here insists that *no one who abides in him sins;* see also 5.18; but cf. 1.8–2.2; 5.16–17. Perhaps 1 John's

one who does what is right is righteous, just as he is righteous. [8]Everyone who commits sin is a child of the devil; for the devil has been sinning from the beginning. The Son of God was revealed for this purpose, to destroy the works of the devil. [9]Those who have been born of God do not sin, because God's seed abides in them;[a] they cannot sin, because they have been born of God. [10]The children of God and the children of the devil are revealed in this way: all who do not do what is right are not from God, nor are those who do not love their brothers and sisters.[b]

Love One Another

11 For this is the message you have heard from the beginning, that we should love one another. [12]We must not be like Cain who was from the evil one and murdered his brother. And why did he murder him? Because his own deeds were evil and his brother's righteous. [13]Do not be astonished, brothers and sisters,[c] that the world hates you. [14]We know that we have passed from death to life because we love one another. Whoever does not love abides in death. [15]All who hate a brother or sister[b] are murderers, and you know that murderers do not have eternal life abiding in them. [16]We know love by this, that he laid down his life for us—and we ought to lay down our lives for one another. [17]How does God's love abide in anyone who has the world's goods and sees a brother or sister[d] in need and yet refuses help?

18 Little children, let us love, not in word or speech, but in truth and action. [19]And by this we will know that we are from the truth and will reassure our hearts before him [20]whenever our hearts condemn us; for God is greater than our hearts, and he knows everything. [21]Beloved, if our hearts do not condemn us, we have boldness before God; [22]and we receive from him whatever we ask, because we obey his commandments and do what pleases him.

23 And this is his commandment, that we should believe in the name of his Son Jesus Christ and love one another, just as he has commanded us. [24]All who obey his commandments abide in him, and he abides in them. And by this we know that he abides in us, by the Spirit that he has given us.

Testing the Spirits

4 Beloved, do not believe every spirit, but test the spirits to see whether they are from God; for many false prophets have gone out into the world. [2]By this you know the Spirit of God: every spirit that confesses that Jesus Christ has come in the flesh is from God, [3]and every spirit that does not confess Jesus[e] is not from God. And this is the spirit of the antichrist, of which you have heard that it is coming; and now it is already in the world. [4]Little children, you are

---

a Or *because the children of God abide in him*   *b* Gk *his brother*
c Gk *brothers*   *d* Gk *brother*   *e* Other ancient authorities read
does away with Jesus (Gk *dissolves Jesus*)

---

opponents claimed sinlessness in principle, while 1 John insists on seeking it in practice and warns here against persisting in sin. See also note on 2.6. **3.6** *Known him.* See 2.3–4; 4.7–8; also Jn 14.7–9, 17. **3.8** *Child of the devil.* See Jn 8.44. **3.9** *Seed,* perhaps the Spirit (see 2.27; 3.24; 4.13; Jn 3.5–8; 14.16–17). **3.10** The intent is probably to identify *doing what is right* with *loving one's brothers and sisters,* the subject of the next section. *From God.* See note on 4.1–6. **3.11–17** Love and giving up one's life are contrasted with hatred and taking life. **3.11** *Message.* See 1.5. *From the beginning.* See note on 1.1. *Love one another.* See 2.10; 3.18, 23; 4.7–12; 4.20–5.2; Jn 13.34–35; 15.12–17; 2 Jn 5. **3.12** Some ancient Jewish traditions held that the father of *Cain* (Gen 4.1–16) was the devil. *The evil one.* See 2.13–14; 3.8, 10; 5.18–19; Jn 8.44. On *evil* and *righteous deeds,* see 2.29; 3.7, 10; Jn 3.19–21. **3.13** On the world's *hatred,* see Jn 15.18–19; 17.14. **3.14** *Passed from death to life.* See Jn 5.24. *Whoever . . . death.* See 2.9, 11. **3.15** *Murderers.* See v. 12; Mt 5.21–22; Rom 1.29–32; Rev 21.8; 22.14–15. **3.16** See 4.9; Jn 15.12–13. On imitating Jesus, see note on 1.7. **3.17** See Jas 2.15–16. Language about love becomes concrete in the admonition to aid those *in need. God's*

love. See note on 2.5. *Abide.* See note on 2.6. *Goods.* The same Greek word is translated *riches* in 2.16. *Refuses help,* lit. "closes the heart." **3.18–24** Deeds of love give assurance of a relationship with God; see 4.17–18. **3.19–20** The author probably means to reassure readers that, despite awareness of sin, God knows that they are of the truth because of their acts of love. **3.21** *Boldness,* better "frankness of speech," a quality of the prayer of God's people. Cf. Heb 4.16. **3.22** *Whatever we ask.* See 5.14–15; Jn 14.13–14; 15.7, 16; 16.23–27; Mt 7.7–8; Mk 11.24. *Do what pleases him.* See Jn 8.29. **3.23** *His Son Jesus Christ.* See 2.22. *Love one another.* See note on 3.11. **3.24** See 4.13–16. *Abide.* See note on 2.6. *Spirit.* See Jn 14.15–17, 25–26; 16.7–15.

4.1–6 These verses treat the opponents and their ideas about Jesus, with much attention to what is from God and what is from the world (see 2.16; 3.9–10; 4.7; 5.1, 4, 19; Jn 1.13; 7.17; 8.23, 42, 47; 15.19; 17.14–16; 18.36; 3 Jn 11). **4.1** *Test the spirits,* i.e., test people who claim to speak under the influence of God's Spirit (see 3.24) but may be *false prophets;* see also Deut 13.1–5; 18.20–22; Mt 7.15–23; 1 Cor 12.3. **4.2–3** On the *antichrist* and not confessing that Jesus Christ *has come in*

from God, and have conquered them; for the one who is in you is greater than the one who is in the world. [5]They are from the world; therefore what they say is from the world, and the world listens to them. [6]We are from God. Whoever knows God listens to us, and whoever is not from God does not listen to us. From this we know the spirit of truth and the spirit of error.

God Is Love

7 Beloved, let us love one another, because love is from God; everyone who loves is born of God and knows God. [8]Whoever does not love does not know God, for God is love. [9]God's love was revealed among us in this way: God sent his only Son into the world so that we might live through him. [10]In this is love, not that we loved God but that he loved us and sent his Son to be the atoning sacrifice for our sins. [11]Beloved, since God loved us so much, we also ought to love one another. [12]No one has ever seen God; if we love one another, God lives in us, and his love is perfected in us.

13 By this we know that we abide in him and he in us, because he has given us of his Spirit. [14]And we have seen and do testify that the Father has sent his Son as the Savior of the world. [15]God abides in those who confess that Jesus is the Son of God, and they abide in God. [16]So we have known and believe the love that God has for us.

God is love, and those who abide in love abide in God, and God abides in them. [17]Love has been perfected among us in this: that we may have boldness on the day of judgment, because as he is, so are we in this world. [18]There is no fear in love, but perfect love casts out fear; for fear has to do with punishment, and whoever fears has not reached perfection in love. [19]We love[a] because he first loved us. [20]Those who say, "I love God," and hate their brothers or sisters,[b] are liars; for those who do not love a brother or sister[c] whom they have seen, cannot love God whom they have not seen. [21]The commandment we have from him is this: those who love God must love their brothers and sisters[b] also.

Faith Conquers the World

5 Everyone who believes that Jesus is the Christ[d] has been born of God, and everyone who loves the parent loves the child. [2]By this we know that we love the children of God, when we love God and obey his commandments. [3]For the love of God is this, that we obey his commandments. And his commandments are not burdensome, [4]for whatever is born of God conquers the world. And this is the victory that conquers the world, our faith. [5]Who is it that conquers the world but the one who believes that Jesus is the Son of God?

Testimony concerning the Son of God

6 This is the one who came by water and blood, Jesus Christ, not with the water only but with the water and the blood. And the Spirit is the one that testifies, for the Spirit is the truth. [7]There are three that testify:[e] [8]the

---

a Other ancient authorities add *him*; others add *God*
b Gk *brothers* c Gk *brother* d Or *the Messiah* e A few other authorities read (with variations) [7]*There are three that testify in heaven, the Father, the Word, and the Holy Spirit, and these three are one.* [8]*And there are three that testify on earth:*

---

the flesh, see 2 Jn 7; see also note on 1 Jn 2.18. **4.4** *Conquered.* See note on 2.13. *One who is in the world.* See 5.19; Jn 14.30. **4.6** *Knows God.* See note on 3.6. *Listens to us.* See Jn 8.42–47; 10.25–27; 18.37. *Spirit of truth,* a term used only here and in Jn 14.17; 15.26; 16.13 in the NT (see also 1 Jn 5.6), but also found in ancient Jewish writings. *Spirit of error,* or spirit of "deception." See Mt 24.11, 24; Mk 13.5–6, 21–22; 2 Thess 2.11; 1 Tim 4.1; Rev 12.9. **4.7–18** God's love for us and our love for one another. **4.7** *Born of God and knows God.* See 2.3, 29; 3.6–10. **4.9** See 3.16; also Jn 3.16. **4.10** *Atoning sacrifice for our sins.* See note on 2.2. **4.11** On imitating God, see note on 1.7. **4.12** *No one has ever seen God.* See Jn 1.18; 3.13; 6.46; 3 Jn 11. *God lives in us.* See note on 2.6. *His love is perfected.* See 2.5; 4.17–18. **4.13–16** A summary of everything since 3.23. **4.14** *Seen and . . . testify.* See 1.1–2. *Savior of the world.* See Jn 3.17; 4.42; 12.47. **4.15** See 2.22–24; 3.23–24; 5.5, 10, 20. **4.16** *For us,* or "in us" or "among us." *God is love.* This phrase, and the following language of "abiding" summarizes the core of the Johannine message. **4.17** *Boldness,* rendered *confidence* in 2.28. Cf. also 3.21. *He,* i.e., Jesus; see 2.6; 3.2–3, 7, 16. **4.18** *Fear,* i.e., of judgment. **4.19–5.5** Our love for God and one another is linked with right belief in Jesus by means of God's commandment (see 3.23). **4.19** *We love,* or "Let us love." **4.20** See 1.6; 2.4, 9; also 3.15–17. *Whom they have not seen.* See 4.12. **4.21** See Mk 12.29–31. **5.1** This verse looks back to 4.21 but also forward to 5.5. *Believes that Jesus is the Christ* (see also *believes . . . Son of God,* v. 5). See Jn 20.31; also 1 Jn 2.22–23; 4.2–3, 15. *Born of God.* See note on 2.29. **5.3** *Love . . . commandments.* See Jn 14.15, 21–24, 31; 15.10; 2 Jn 6; also 1 Jn 2.3–5. **5.4** *Conquers the world,* as Jesus did (Jn 16.33); see also Jn 2.13–14; 4.4. **5.6–12** God testifies to Jesus the Son; see also Jn 5.31–40; 8.17–18; 15.26–27. **5.6** *Water only* may refer to Jesus' baptism (Jn 1.31–34) and *blood* to his crucifixion (see Jn 19.34–35). *The Spirit is the truth.* See note on 4.6. **5.7–8** Only a very

Spirit and the water and the blood, and these three agree. [9]If we receive human testimony, the testimony of God is greater; for this is the testimony of God that he has testified to his Son. [10]Those who believe in the Son of God have the testimony in their hearts. Those who do not believe in God[b] have made him a liar by not believing in the testimony that God has given concerning his Son. [11]And this is the testimony: God gave us eternal life, and this life is in his Son. [12]Whoever has the Son has life; whoever does not have the Son of God does not have life.

Epilogue

13 I write these things to you who believe in the name of the Son of God, so that you may know that you have eternal life.

14 And this is the boldness we have in him, that if we ask anything according to his will, he hears us. [15]And if we know that he hears us in whatever we ask, we know that we have obtained the requests made of him. [16]If you see your brother or sister[c] committing what is not a mortal sin, you will ask, and God[d] will give life to such a one—to those whose sin is not mortal. There is sin that is mortal; I do not say that you should pray about that. [17]All wrongdoing is sin, but there is sin that is not mortal.

18 We know that those who are born of God do not sin, but the one who was born of God protects them, and the evil one does not touch them. [19]We know that we are God's children, and that the whole world lies under the power of the evil one. [20]And we know that the Son of God has come and has given us understanding so that we may know him who is true;[e] and we are in him who is true, in his Son Jesus Christ. He is the true God and eternal life.

21 Little children, keep yourselves from idols.[f]

---

b Other ancient authorities read *in the Son*   c Gk *your brother*
d Gk *he*   e Other ancient authorities read *know the true God*
f Other ancient authorities add *Amen*

---

few late manuscripts contain the trinitarian addition (known as the Johannine Comma) to v. 7 (see text note *a*). *Three.* See Deut 19.15. **5.9** On *testimony*, human and divine, see Jn 5.31–40; 8.18. **5.10** See Jn 3.18, 33. *Made him a liar.* See 1.10. **5.11** *Eternal life.* See Jn 3.16; 5.26; 11.25–26; 14.6. **5.12** See 2.23; Jn 3.36; 2 Jn 9.

5.13–21 After a concluding summary similar to Jn 20.31, these verses give a variety of final exhortations. **5.13** *I write.* See note on 1.4. *Believe in the name of the Son.* See 3.23; Jn 1.12; 20.31. **5.14** *In him,* or "toward him." **5.16** *Mortal sin,* one that leads to death; 3.14 may suggest that this sin is failure to love. This is not the same as the sin mentioned in Mk 3.29. On whether or not Christians can *sin,* see note on 3.6–10. *Do not . . . pray.* See also 1 Sam 2.25; Jer 7.16; 11.14; Jn 17.9. **5.18–**

20 Three statements, each introduced by *we know,* contrast those who are of God with the forces of evil. **5.18** *Do not sin.* See 3.8–9; cf. 5.16–17. *The one who was born of God* is probably Jesus, but this could refer to Christians protecting themselves. *Protects them.* See Jn 17.11–12, 15. *Evil one.* See note on 3.12. **5.19** *God's children,* or "from God." See 4.4, 6. *World.* See 2.15–17; 5.4–5. **5.20** *Son of God.* See v. 5. *Know him who is true . . . the true God and eternal life.* This probably means the Father rather than Jesus (see Jn 17.3; but note that Jesus is identified with life in 1 Jn 1.2; Jn 1.3–4; 11.25; 14.6). **5.21** *Idols* are the opposite of the true God and eternal life (v. 20; see Jer 10.9–10; 1 Thess 1.9; see also Acts 14.15; Rom 1.25; 2 Cor 6.16) and so stand for the teaching that 1 John opposes.

The Second Letter of

JOHN

A TRUE LETTER, 2 JOHN contains the usual opening and closing formulas. It is apparently addressed to a Christian congregation, referred to as an "elect lady" (v. 1).

Author and Relation to Other Writings

THE AUTHOR CALLS HIMSELF "the elder" (v. 1), suggesting that he holds a position of some authority within the Christian community concerned. He is presumably the same as the author of 3 John and may have written 1 John also. It is no longer certain that he was the apostle John or even identical with the author of the Fourth Gospel (see Introductions to the Gospel of John and 1 John).

Date and Place

THE SIMILARITIES BETWEEN THE THREE DOCUMENTS suggest that 2 John was probably written at about the same time and place as 1 and 3 John, i.e., around 100 CE, perhaps at Ephesus.

Historical Background and Message

LIKE 1 JOHN, 2 John seems to have been written during a conflict with people who denied that the human Jesus was identical with the divine Christ. Though it insists on the importance of loving one another, it calls on its readers to avoid these opponents and even to refuse them the hospitality usually shown to Christian travelers. [DAVID K. RENSBERGER, revised by HAROLD W. ATTRIDGE]

Salutation

1 The elder to the elect lady and her children, whom I love in the truth, and not only I but also all who know the truth, 2because of the truth that abides in us and will be with us forever:

3 Grace, mercy, and peace will be with us from God the Father and from*a* Jesus Christ, the Father's Son, in truth and love.

Truth and Love

4 I was overjoyed to find some of your children walking in the truth, just as we have been commanded by the Father. 5But now, dear lady, I ask you, not as though I were writing you a new commandment, but one we have had from the beginning, let us love one another. 6And this is love, that we walk according to his commandments; this is the commandment just as you have heard it from the beginning—you must walk in it.

7 Many deceivers have gone out into the world, those who do not confess that Jesus Christ has come in the flesh; any such person is the deceiver and the antichrist! 8Be on your guard, so that you do not lose what we*b* have worked for, but may receive a full reward. 9Everyone who does not abide in the teaching of Christ, but goes beyond it, does not have God; whoever abides in the teaching has both the Father and the Son. 10Do not receive into the house or welcome anyone who comes to you and does not bring this teaching; 11for to welcome is to participate in the evil deeds of such a person.

Final Greetings

12 Although I have much to write to you, I would rather not use paper and ink; instead I hope to come to you and talk with you face to face, so that our joy may be complete.

13 The children of your elect sister send you their greetings.*c*

---

a Other ancient authorities add *the Lord*   *b* Other ancient authorities read *you*   *c* Other ancient authorities add *Amen*

1–3 An opening similar to other NT Letters; see, e.g., 2 Cor 1.1–2 and esp. 1 Tim 1.1–2; 2 Tim 1.1–2. **1** *Elect lady*, perhaps an individual church leader, but more likely a metaphor for a congregation, whose members are *her children;* see v. 13. *Truth* is important in the Gospel and Letters of John. Here it probably relates to the controversy over false teaching (see Introduction). *Loving in the truth.* See 1 Jn 3.18; 3 Jn 1. *Knowing the truth.* See Jn 8.32; 1 Jn 2.21. **2** *The truth that abides . . . forever.* See Jn 14.16–17; 1 Jn 2.27. **4–11** The body of the Letter focuses on truth and love. **4** *Walking in the truth.* See 3 Jn 3–4; see also note on v. 6. **5** On the *new commandment* to *love one another,* which has really been a commandment *from the beginning,* see Jn 13.34–35; 15.12–17; 1 Jn 2.7–11; 3.11, 23. **6** See 1 Jn 5.2–3. *Walk.* See also 1 Jn 1.6–7; 2.6, 11. *Commandments.* See Jn 15.10.

7 For a comparable critique of the opponents and their views, see 1 Jn 2.18–27; 4.1–3. *Has come,* lit. "is coming." *Antichrist.* See note on 1 Jn 2.18. **8** *What we have worked for.* See Jn 6.27–29. *We,* perhaps the au-thor and other church leaders, or it may include the readers, as elsewhere in 2 John. *Reward,* or "payment." The notion of a final recompense for good work is common. See Mt 5.12; Mk 9.41; Lk 6.23; 1 Cor 3.8. **9** *Abide,* typical Johannine language, frequent in 1 John (see note on 1 Jn 2.6). Cf. Jn 14.10; 15.10. *The teaching of Christ,* i.e., the doctrine of Christ *coming in the flesh* (v. 7; see also 1 Jn 2.22–27; 4.15). On having *both the Father and the Son,* see 1 Jn 2.23; 5.12. **10–11** Hospitality was essential to traveling missionaries and teachers in the early churches (see, e.g., 3 Jn 5–8; also Rom 12.13; 15.23–24; 16.1–2; Heb 13.2; *Didache* 11.1; 12.1). By forbidding it to the opponents, the author hopes to hinder the spread of their teaching (see also Rom 16.17; 2 Thess 3.6). In 3 Jn 9–10, the author complains of similar tactics being used against him! *Evil deeds.* See Jn 3.19–20; 7.7; 1 Jn 3.12. **12–13** Concluding greetings, again similar to other NT Letters. See esp. 1 Pet 5.13; 3 Jn 15. **12** See 3 Jn 13–14. *So that our joy may be complete.* See 1 Jn 1.4; also Jn 3.29; 15.11; 16.24; 17.13. **13** *Elect sister.* See note on v. 1.

The Third Letter of
JOHN

LIKE 2 JOHN, 3 JOHN IS A GENUINE LETTER. Its addressee, Gaius, is otherwise unknown. "The elder," as the author of 3 John calls himself (v. 1), is presumably the same as the author of 2 John (see Introductions to the Gospel of John and 1 John). Whatever his relationship to the author of the Gospel and of 1 John, he evidently held a position of some authority within the Christian community concerned.

Date and Place

THE SIMILARITIES BETWEEN 3 John and 1 and 2 John suggest that the three documents were probably written at about the same time and place, i.e., around 100 CE, perhaps at Ephesus.

Historical Background and Message

UNLIKE 1 AND 2 JOHN, 3 John contains no discussion of doctrine or love. Instead, it praises Gaius for his hospitality and criticizes someone named Diotrephes for opposing the elder. It has been suggested that Diotrephes was a leader of the movement confronted by 1 and 2 John or a church leader seeking either to establish his own authority or to keep his church free from controversies. A roughly contemporary parallel appears in the *Didache,* a book of church order from the late first or early second century. That text urges hospitality toward wandering preachers (*Didache* 11.1–4) but requires such teachers to be tested and urges that they be sent off after a two-day stay (11.5). The *Didache* also urges its recipients to elect bishops and deacons (15.10). Diotrephes may have been such a bishop who refused more than minimal hospitality to wandering teachers. [DAVID K. RENSBERGER, revised by HAROLD W. ATTRIDGE]

Salutation

1 The elder to the beloved Gaius, whom I love in truth.

Gaius Commended for His Hospitality

2 Beloved, I pray that all may go well with you and that you may be in good health, just as it is well with your soul. [3] I was overjoyed when some of the friends[a] arrived and testified to your faithfulness to the truth, namely how you walk in the truth. [4] I have no greater joy than this, to hear that my children are walking in the truth.

5 Beloved, you do faithfully whatever you do for the friends,[a] even though they are strangers to you; [6] they have testified to your love before the church. You will do well to send them on in a manner worthy of God; [7] for they began their journey for the sake of Christ,[b] accepting no support from non-believers.[c] [8] Therefore we ought to support such people, so that we may become co-workers with the truth.

Diotrephes and Demetrius

9 I have written something to the church; but Diotrephes, who likes to put himself first, does not acknowledge our authority. [10] So if I come, I will call attention to what he is doing in spreading false charges against us. And not content with those charges, he refuses to welcome the friends,[a] and even prevents those who want to do so and expels them from the church.

11 Beloved, do not imitate what is evil but imitate what is good. Whoever does good is from God; whoever does evil has not seen God. [12] Everyone has testified favorably about Demetrius, and so has the truth itself. We also testify for him,[d] and you know that our testimony is true.

Final Greetings

13 I have much to write to you, but I would rather not write with pen and ink; [14] instead I hope to see you soon, and we will talk together face to face.

15 Peace to you. The friends send you their greetings. Greet the friends there, each by name.

---

a Gk brothers b Gk for the sake of the name c Gk the Gentiles
d Gk lacks for him

1–2 An opening typical of Greek personal letters. *Gaius*, a common Roman name borne by three other men in the NT (Acts 19.29; 20.4; Rom 16.23; 1 Cor 1.14). *Whom I love in truth.* See 2 Jn 1. **3–8** Some Christian workers are commended to the hospitality of Gaius. **3** *Your faithfulness to the truth*, lit. "your truth." *Walk in the truth.* See 2 Jn 4. **5–8** On the importance of hospitality in the early churches, see note on 2 Jn 10–11. **6** *Send them on*, i.e., with provisions (see Titus 3.13). **8** *Co-workers.* Cf. 2 Jn 11.

9–12 A dispute between church leaders. **9–10** *Diotrephes* (see Introduction) uses something like the elder's own tactics (2 Jn 10–11) against him. *Likes to put himself first.* This vague description may allude to the role of Diotrephes as a local bishop, an office that came to prominence in the late first or early second century. For evidence of an emerging hierarchy, see 1 Tim 3.1–7 and the letters of Ignatius, bishop of Antioch, from the early second century. In those letters the position of a singular bishop who heads a local Christian community is clear. *Acknowledge our authority*, or just "welcome us" (cf. *welcome the friends*, v. 10). **11** *Whoever does good is from God.* See 1 Jn 2.29; 3.10. *Seen God.* See 1 Jn 3.6; 4.12; also Jn 1.18; 6.46. **12** The identity of *Demetrius* is unknown; he may have delivered this Letter. The author commends him to Gaius's hospitality and support (see vv. 5–8). *Our testimony is true.* See Jn 5.31–33; 19.35; 21.24. **13–15** Closing greetings typical of NT Letters; see esp. 1 Cor 16.19–20; Phil 4.21–22; Titus 3.15. **13–14** See 2 Jn 12.

The Letter of

JUDE

THIS LETTER IS ATTRIBUTED to Jude (Greek Judas), one of the brothers of Jesus (see Mk 6.3). He is known to have been a prominent leader and traveling missionary in the early Jewish-Christian movement in Palestine (see 1 Cor 9.5). The authenticity of the attribution to Jude has often been doubted, but recent work demonstrates that it is entirely plausible. This Letter may therefore be one of the few NT writings to derive directly from Palestinian Jewish Christianity. We do not know to which churches it was originally written.

Purpose and Opponents

THE LETTER'S PURPOSE is to warn the readers about the danger posed by a form of teaching that is being propagated in their churches and to advise them on how to respond. The proponents of this teaching claim to be inspired prophets whose visionary revelations exempt them and all truly spiritual people (i.e., their followers) from any form of moral authority (v. 8). They claim that the grace of God in Christ liberates them to do as they please (v. 4) and apparently demonstrate this freedom especially by sexual indulgence (v. 7). In response, Jude insists that faith in the Christian gospel is inseparable from moral obedience to Christ. The opponents are a serious danger to his readers, because they encourage deliberate immorality that puts their salvation at risk. Such outright rejection of God's moral authority can only incur judgment when Christ comes as judge. But Jude's purpose is not only to warn of the danger (vv. 4–19). It is also to urge his readers "to contend for the faith" (v. 3) by positively living out the gospel in faith, hope, and love (vv. 20–21). His advice on how to deal with the opponents and their followers (vv. 22–23) combines a realistic sense of the danger they pose to his readers with a pastoral concern for their salvation.

Use of the OT and Extracanonical Literature

JUDE BASES MUCH OF HIS ARGUMENT on OT allusions and employs current Jewish methods of scriptural interpretation. He also refers to Jewish works that are not in the OT canon, especially *1 Enoch* (see vv. 6, 14–15) and an apocryphal story about the burial of Moses (see v. 9) that he may have found in the (now lost) ending of the *Testament of Moses*. Such apocryphal literature was widely read and valued in Judaism at that time. [RICHARD J. BAUCKHAM]

Salutation

1 Jude,[a] a servant[b] of Jesus Christ and brother of James,

To those who are called, who are beloved[c] in[d] God the Father and kept safe for[d] Jesus Christ:

2 May mercy, peace, and love be yours in abundance.

Occasion of the Letter

3 Beloved, while eagerly preparing to write to you about the salvation we share, I find it necessary to write and appeal to you to contend for the faith that was once for all entrusted to the saints. 4 For certain intruders have stolen in among you, people who long ago were designated for this condemnation as ungodly, who pervert the grace of our God into licentiousness and deny our only Master and Lord, Jesus Christ.[e]

Judgment on False Teachers

5 Now I desire to remind you, though you are fully informed, that the Lord, who once for all saved[f] a people out of the land of Egypt, afterward destroyed those who did not believe. 6 And the angels who did not keep their own position, but left their proper dwelling, he has kept in eternal chains in deepest darkness for the judgment of the great day. 7 Likewise, Sodom and Gomorrah and the surrounding cities, which, in the same manner as they, indulged in sexual immorality and pursued unnatural lust,[g] serve as an example by undergoing a punishment of eternal fire.

8 Yet in the same way these dreamers also defile the flesh, reject authority, and slander the glorious ones.[h] 9 But when the archangel Michael contended with the devil and disputed about the body of Moses, he did not dare to bring a condemnation of slander[i] against him, but said, "The Lord rebuke you!" 10 But these people slander whatever they do not understand, and they are destroyed by those things that, like irrational animals, they know by instinct. 11 Woe to them! For they go the way of Cain, and abandon themselves to Balaam's error for the sake of gain, and perish in Korah's rebellion. 12 These are blemishes[j] on your love-feasts, while they feast with you without fear, feeding themselves.[k] They are waterless clouds

---

a Gk Judas   b Gk slave   c Other ancient authorities read sanctified   d Or by   e Or the only Master and our Lord Jesus Christ   f Other ancient authorities read though you were once for all fully informed, that Jesus (or Joshua) who saved   g Gk went after other flesh   h Or angels; Gk glories   i Or condemnation for blasphemy   j Or reefs   k Or without fear. They are shepherds who care only for themselves

---

1–2 The opening address and greeting are characteristic of early Christian letters. 1 Jude. See Mk 6.3. James must be the Lord's brother (see Gal 1.19), leader of the Jerusalem church and so well known as to need no identification (see Acts 15.13; Jas 1.1). 3–4 The theme of the Letter is introduced in two parts: an appeal (v. 3) and a reference to the situation that makes the appeal necessary (v. 4). 3 The faith that was once for all entrusted to the saints, the gospel as the readers received it from the apostles who founded their churches. Paul makes similar references to the gospel as it was first preached to his readers; see Rom 16.17; 2 Cor 11.4; Gal 1.9. 4 This condemnation, the prophecies of judgment (vv. 5–19), esp. Enoch's (vv. 14–15). The opponents pervert the grace of our God by understanding Christian freedom as freedom to do as they like. They deny Christ's moral authority by practicing and teaching immorality.

5–19 Jude indicates the character and fate of the opponents by citing a series of OT examples of God's judgment on the wicked (vv. 5–13) and two prophecies regarding the ungodly (vv. 14–19). By identifying the opponents as these ungodly people who are to be judged at the Lord's coming, Jude shows how dangerous they are to the churches. 5 A whole generation of faithless Israelites died in the wilderness (Num 14.1–35; 26.64–65). 6 The angels who . . . left their proper dwelling. In the story of the "sons of God" (Gen 6.1–4), as interpreted in 1 Enoch 6–19, the angels left heaven to mate with women. 7 The Sodomites attempted sexual relations with angels (Gen 19.4–11). 8 Dreamers, an unusual term referring to the visions the opponents claimed as authorizing their immoral behavior. Glorious ones, a common term for angels. Because the angels were seen as guardians of the moral order of creation, the opponents who claimed freedom from this order disparaged them. 9 In an apocryphal story about the burial of Moses, Michael and the devil engage in a legal dispute. The devil accuses Moses of murder. Michael knows this charge is slanderous, but he does not presume (dare) to condemn the devil for slander on his own authority. Instead, he refers the matter to the authority of the divine judge (the Lord). The implication of v. 9 is to contrast Michael's behavior with that of the opponents, who claim to be exempt from all moral authority (see v. 8) and on their own authority reject all moral charges against them. 11 These OT examples are of people responsible for leading others into sin. Cain (see Gen 4.1–16; 1 Jn 3.12), in Jewish tradition, was the first heretic; the prophet Balaam gave the advice that led Israel into apostasy (Num 25.1–4; 31.16); Korah led a rebellion against Moses (Num 16.1–35). 12 Blemishes. Reefs (see text note j) is preferable: the opponents are a hidden

carried along by the winds; autumn trees without fruit, twice dead, uprooted; 13wild waves of the sea, casting up the foam of their own shame; wandering stars, for whom the deepest darkness has been reserved forever.

14 It was also about these that Enoch, in the seventh generation from Adam, prophesied, saying, "See, the Lord is coming*a* with ten thousands of his holy ones, 15to execute judgment on all, and to convict everyone of all the deeds of ungodliness that they have committed in such an ungodly way, and of all the harsh things that ungodly sinners have spoken against him." 16These are grumblers and malcontents; they indulge their own lusts; they are bombastic in speech, flattering people to their own advantage.

Warnings and Exhortations

17 But you, beloved, must remember the predictions of the apostles of our Lord Jesus Christ; 18for they said to you, "In the last time there will be scoffers, indulging their own un-godly lusts." 19It is these worldly people, devoid of the Spirit, who are causing divisions. 20But you, beloved, build yourselves up on your most holy faith; pray in the Holy Spirit; 21keep yourselves in the love of God; look forward to the mercy of our Lord Jesus Christ that leads to*b* eternal life. 22And have mercy on some who are wavering; 23save others by snatching them out of the fire; and have mercy on still others with fear, hating even the tunic defiled by their bodies.*c*

Benediction

24 Now to him who is able to keep you from falling, and to make you stand without blemish in the presence of his glory with rejoicing, 25to the only God our Savior, through Jesus Christ our Lord, be glory, majesty, power, and authority, before all time and now and forever. Amen.

---

a Gk *came*   *b* Gk *Christ to*   *c* Gk *by the flesh.* The Greek text of verses 22-23 is uncertain at several points

---

danger to the churches, especially at the fellowship meals (*love-feasts*) where they do their teaching. *Feeding themselves.* The text note (*k* on p. 2084) gives the right sense, which echoes Ezek 34.2. *Clouds,* a metaphor from Prov 25.14. **13** *Waves,* a metaphor from Isa 57.20. *Wandering stars* mislead those who are guided by them. **14–15** The prophecy of Enoch (see Gen 5.18–24) is from *1 Enoch* 1.9. **19** The charge *devoid of the Spirit* is probably directed to the opponents' claim that the Spirit makes them superior to ordinary morality.

20–23 This section explains how the readers are to respond to the appeal made in v. 3, indicating the ways in which they can resist the danger from false teaching (vv. 20–21) and the ways in which they should seek to reclaim the false teachers and their followers (vv. 22–23). The text of these two verses varies considerably in the Greek manuscripts. **23** *Fire,* of divine judgment (see Am 4.11; Zech 3.2). *Hating even the tunic defiled by their bodies* implies avoiding the danger of personal contact with those who indulge in sins of the flesh. **24–25** A doxology concludes the Letter (as in Rom 16.25–27; 2 Pet 3.18).

THE REVELATION
TO JOHN
(APOCALYPSE)

THE REVELATION TO JOHN WAS WRITTEN by a person named John (1.1, 4, 9; 22.8), an anglicized version of a common ancient Hebrew name often transliterated Johanan. Early Christian writers assumed that the author of Revelation had also written the Gospel and Letters of John and identified him with John the son of Zebedee, one of the twelve apostles. Both of these assumptions are problematic. The author of Revelation regards the twelve apostles as authoritative figures of the past (21.14) and identifies himself simply as a servant of God (1.1) and a brother who shares the sufferings of those to whom he addresses his book (1.9). On the basis of both literary style and theological emphases it appears unlikely that he wrote either the Gospel or the Letters of John. Although modern critical scholars have generally abandoned the assumption of common authorship for the compositions that make up the Johannine corpus (the Gospel According to John, the three Letters of John, the Revelation to John), the traditional association of these five compositions with the name John has encouraged the view that all five were produced by various members of a "Johannine community" behind which stood the shadowy figure of John the apostle.

Although the specific identity of the author is unknown, Revelation provides some important clues about his general identity. The frequent allusions to the OT (particularly Ezekiel and Daniel) suggest his Jewish origin. The Semitic features of his Greek style indicate that he was a native of Palestine who emigrated to Asia Minor, perhaps in the wake of the first Jewish revolt against Rome (66–73 CE), when many were forced to flee for their lives. By calling his composition a prophetic book (1.3; 22.7, 10, 18, 19), he clearly implies that he is a prophet. His familiarity with the circumstances of the seven Christian communities he addresses further suggests that he was probably a well-known itinerant Christian prophet (22.9).

Date

MANY EARLY CHRISTIAN WRITERS thought that Revelation had been written toward the end of Domitian's reign (81–96 CE), but a few later writers thought that John had written a generation earlier, during the persecution that occurred in 64 under Nero (54–68 CE). Evidence supporting both dates can be found in the book. In favor of the earlier date, 11.1–3 suggests that the Jewish temple in Jerusalem (destroyed by the Romans in 70) was still standing when the book was written. Further, the code name of the beast in 13.18 is 666, widely thought to symbolize the name Nero Caesar. Other data, however, suggest a date late in the first century. For example, there are several allusions (13.3; 17.9–11) to the legend of Nero's return, which circulated throughout the eastern Mediterranean during the two decades following his suicide in 68. Further, Revelation frequently uses "Babylon" as a code name for Rome (14.8; 16.19; 17.5, 18; 18.2, 10, 21), but the evidence suggests that Jews used this code name only *after* the Romans destroyed Jerusalem in 70. In the light of conflicting evidence for the early and late date of Revelation, it seems likely that the book was actually composed and assembled in stages over many years and was only completed in its present form toward the end of the first or the early second century CE. Though certainty is not possible, the first edition of the book probably consisted of 1.4–11; 4.1–22.5, to which 1.1–3; 1.12–3.22; 22.6–21 were added in a second edition.

Occasion

THE DATE ASSIGNED TO REVELATION has usually been closely connected by both ancient and modern scholars with the situation of persecution reflected in the book (1.9; 2.10; 12.17). This persecution may have involved the execution of several Christians (2.13; 6.9–11; 13.15; 17.6; 18.24; 20.4; see also 11.7–10). The persecution under Nero in 64 CE, however, only affected Christians in and around Rome. The view that Domitian instigated an official persecution of Christians in Asia Minor has been widely held by ancient and modern scholars, though it has become clear that no historical evidence confirms it. It appears that the persecution of Christians in Asia Minor was not the result of an official Roman policy but rather the result of random outbreaks of hostility between Christians and their pagan and Jewish neighbors. Roman governors were sometimes drawn, though not always willingly, into these conflicts (see Acts 19.23–41). Christian authors such as Eusebius of Caesarea transformed random instances of persecution into an official persecution fomented by Domitian. In the last analysis, it is difficult to determine whether the widespread and apparently systematic persecution reflected in this book represents what actually happened or what the author expected would happen.

Genre

REVELATION BELONGS TO THE LITERARY GENRE given the modern label "apocalypse," widely attested in early Judaism and early Christianity. The name of this genre is based on 1.1, where the Greek word *apokalypsis* ("revelation") designates the content of the book as a "revelation of Jesus Christ, which God gave him to show his servants what must soon take place." An apocalypse, then, is typically regarded as a first-person narrative in which the author (normally using the pen name of some famous ancient biblical figure such as Adam, Abraham, or Enoch) relates one or more revelatory visions about the future, the heavenly world, or both. Jewish apocalypses often reflect a sharp distinction between the present evil age and the imminent future age of blessing. The conflict between a righteous minority (Israel or a righteous remnant within Israel) and a wicked majority (hostile foreign powers or a hostile group within Israel) is understood as representing a clash between God and Satan. After a period of intense conflict and great suffering, God, sometimes acting through a messianic agent, will decisively intervene in history to vindicate and reward God's people and punish or eliminate their earthly oppressors. Many Jewish apocalypses use a great deal of symbolism, often quite bizarre (e.g., Dan 7.2–8), and Revelation is no exception. One stock figure of Jewish apocalypses also found in Revelation is the "interpreting angel," a heavenly being who explains the meaning of visions to the seer (1.1; 17.1–18; 21.9–22.5). The only other book-length apocalypse in the Bible is Daniel. [DAVID E. AUNE]

Introduction and Salutation

1 The revelation of Jesus Christ, which God gave him to show his servants*ᵃ* what must soon take place; he made*ᵇ* it known by sending his angel to his servant*ᶜ* John, ²who testified to the word of God and to the testimony of Jesus Christ, even to all that he saw.

3 Blessed is the one who reads aloud the words of the prophecy, and blessed are those who hear and who keep what is written in it; for the time is near.

4 John to the seven churches that are in Asia:

Grace to you and peace from him who is and who was and who is to come, and from the seven spirits who are before his throne, ⁵and from Jesus Christ, the faithful witness, the firstborn of the dead, and the ruler of the kings of the earth.

To him who loves us and freed*ᵈ* us from our sins by his blood, ⁶and made*ᵇ* us to be a king-

a Gk slaves   *b* Gk and he made   *c* Gk slave   *d* Other ancient authorities read washed

1.1–2 Following ancient literary conventions, the first sentence functions as a title presenting the essential contents of the composition. **1.1** *Revelation of Jesus Christ* indicates that *God* himself is the immediate source of John's revelatory visions. The insistence that the events predicted in John's visions *must soon take place* frames the book (1.3; 22.6, 10). The interpreting *angel* who mediates revelation (a stock figure in early Jewish and early Christian apocalypses) is mentioned again only in 22.6–9, 16, though two other angelic guides appear in 17.1–18; 21.9–22.5. **1.3** *Blessed* introduces the first of seven beatitudes (14.13; 16.15; 19.9; 20.6; 22.7, 14). The fact that a designated person *reads*

aloud John's book means that it is intended for use in Christian worship (see Col 4.16; 1 Thess 5.27). On the book as *prophecy,* see Introduction. Exhortations that the hearers are to *keep,* or obey (see also 22.7, 9), are largely restricted to the introductory and concluding sections of the book (2.1–3.22; 14.12; 16.15; 22.6–21), providing a hint that those sections are part of the final edition of the book. *The time is near,* i.e., the time when Christ will return to save and to judge. **1.4–5a** After the introductory three verses Revelation takes on the features of a typical early Christian letter, designating the sender and receiver and including a salutation (see also 22.21); the formal features of this episto-

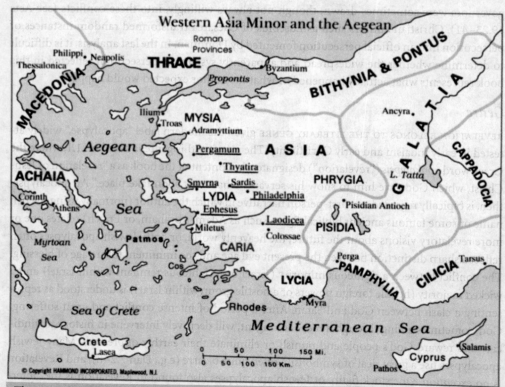

The seven churches addressed in the book of Revelation were in the cities underlined on the map, all in the Roman province of Asia (Rev 1.4).

dom, priests serving[a] his God and Father, to him be glory and dominion forever and ever. Amen.

7 Look! He is coming with the clouds;
    every eye will see him,
    even those who pierced him;
    and on his account all the tribes of the
        earth will wail.
So it is to be. Amen.

8 "I am the Alpha and the Omega," says the Lord God, who is and who was and who is to come, the Almighty.

A Vision of Christ

9 I, John, your brother who share with you in Jesus the persecution and the kingdom and the patient endurance, was on the island called Patmos because of the word of God and the testimony of Jesus.[b] 10 I was in the spirit[c] on the Lord's day, and I heard behind me a loud voice

like a trumpet 11 saying, "Write in a book what you see and send it to the seven churches, to Ephesus, to Smyrna, to Pergamum, to Thyatira, to Sardis, to Philadelphia, and to Laodicea."

12 Then I turned to see whose voice it was that spoke to me, and on turning I saw seven golden lampstands, 13 and in the midst of the lampstands I saw one like the Son of Man, clothed with a long robe and with a golden sash across his chest. 14 His head and his hair were white as white wool, white as snow; his eyes were like a flame of fire, 15 his feet were like burnished bronze, refined as in a furnace, and his voice was like the sound of many waters. 16 In his right hand he held seven stars, and from his mouth came a sharp, two-edged sword, and his face was like the sun shining with full force.

_____

a Gk priests to   b Or testimony to Jesus   c Or in the Spirit

lary introduction seem to reflect Pauline influence (see, e.g., 1 Thess 1.1). **1.4** The *seven churches* (listed in v. 11) were located in seven prominent cities in western Anatolia (modern Turkey) in the Roman province of Asia; all were within one hundred miles of Ephesus. *Seven* (used fifty-seven times in Revelation) symbolizes the divine pattern evident in both the universe and history. *Him who is and who was and who is to come,* a threefold divine name that alludes to a widespread Hellenistic Jewish name for God based on Ex 3.14, "the one who is." It differs slightly from a popular Greek formula describing God as "the one who is and who was and who will be" by emphasizing the future visitation of God. See also 1.8; 11.17; 16.5. *Seven spirits,* the seven archangels who stand before God (3.1; 4.5; 5.6; 8.2; see also Tob 12.15; Lk 1.19; *1 Enoch* 20.1–7), not a metaphor for the Holy Spirit based on Isa 11.2–3 (Septuagint, Latin Vulgate). **1.5a** *Faithful witness,* (1.2, 9; 2.13; 6.9; 12.11; 17.6), *firstborn of the dead* (see Col 1.18), *ruler of the kings of the earth* (17.14; 19.16), three titles of Jesus (corresponding to the threefold title for God; see note on 1.4) that describe three essential aspects of his role: the faithful proclamation of the message of God, which led to his execution; the victory signaled by his resurrection; and his future role as universal sovereign, thus combining a theology of glory with a theology of the cross. **1.5b–8** The opening doxology (see Gal 1.5) is unusual in the NT since it is addressed to Christ (the doxology in 5.13 is addressed to both God and Christ) and is followed by two brief oracles, the first emphasizing the imminent return of Christ and the second emphasizing the sovereignty of God. **1.6** *Made us to be a kingdom, priests.* See Ex 19.6. **1.7** *Coming with the clouds,* an allusion to Dan 7.13 applied to Jesus as the coming Son of Man (see 14.14; Mk 8.38; 13.26). People *wail* because they fear the impending eschatological judgment (see Zech 12.10). **1.8** *Alpha, Omega,* the first and last letters

of the Greek alphabet. The title expresses the idea of totality and symbolizes God's sovereignty (21.6; 22.13); it is similar in meaning to *the first and the last* (1.17; 2.8; 22.13) and *the beginning and the end* (21.6; 22.13); see note on 1.17. **1.9–20** John's terrifying vision of the exalted Christ provides an introduction to the seven proclamations that follow. **1.9** On the problem of *persecution* as the situation motivating John to write, see Introduction. *Patmos,* a populated island thirty-seven miles southwest of Ephesus. There is no evidence that it was ever a Roman penal colony, but John may have been banished from his home territory and forced to go there during the reign of the emperor who banished him. **1.10** *I was in the spirit* means that John experienced a vision trance (4.2; 17.3; 21.10; see also Acts 10.10; 11.5; 22.6–7). *Lord's day,* a term used later, and probably also here, for Sunday, the main weekly Christian day of worship (*Didache* 14.1; *Gospel of Peter* 12.50). This usage may derive from the celebration of the Lord's Supper on that day (1 Cor 11.20), the day commemorating Christ's resurrection (Ignatius, *Magnesians* 9.1). **1.12–16** The description of the exalted Christ resembles other epiphanies of divine figures (19.11–16; Dan 10.5–9). **1.12** The *seven golden lampstands,* representing the seven churches (1.20), are menorahs, lights that burn continually before God in the sanctuary (Ex 27.20–21; Lev 24.2–4); in ancient Judaism the menorah was a symbol of Judaism. **1.13** *One like the Son of Man,* an allusion to Dan 7.13 (see also Rev 1.7; 14.14); the Greek text has "one like a son of man," lacking the definite article characteristic of the title "the Son of Man" in the Gospels. **1.14** *Hair . . . white as white wool* characterizes the Ancient of Days (i.e., God) in Dan 7.9 but here is strikingly part of a description of Christ, implicitly equating him with God. **1.16** The *sword* proceeding from Christ's mouth (see also 2.16; 19.15, 21; cf. 2.12) is a metaphor for both the word of God and judgment (see

17 When I saw him, I fell at his feet as though dead. But he placed his right hand on me, saying, "Do not be afraid; I am the first and the last, 18 and the living one. I was dead, and see, I am alive forever and ever; and I have the keys of Death and of Hades. 19 Now write what you have seen, what is, and what is to take place after this. 20 As for the mystery of the seven stars that you saw in my right hand, and the seven golden lampstands: the seven stars are the angels of the seven churches, and the seven lampstands are the seven churches.

The Message to Ephesus

2 "To the angel of the church in Ephesus write: These are the words of him who holds the seven stars in his right hand, who walks among the seven golden lampstands:

2 "I know your works, your toil and your patient endurance. I know that you cannot tolerate evildoers; you have tested those who claim to be apostles but are not, and have found them to be false. 3 I also know that you are enduring patiently and bearing up for the sake of my name, and that you have not grown weary. 4 But I have this against you, that you have abandoned the love you had at first. 5 Remember then from what you have fallen; repent, and do the works you did at first. If not, I will come to you and remove your lampstand from its place, unless you repent. 6 Yet this is to your credit: you hate the works of the Nicolaitans, which I also hate. 7 Let anyone who has an ear listen to what the Spirit is saying to the churches. To everyone who conquers, I will give permission to eat from the tree of life that is in the paradise of God.

The Message to Smyrna

8 "And to the angel of the church in Smyrna write: These are the words of the first and the last, who was dead and came to life:

9 "I know your affliction and your poverty, even though you are rich. I know the slander

Isa 49.2; Wis 18.15–16; 2 Thess 2.8; Heb 4.12). **1.17** *Fell . . . as though dead.* The fright of the seer is a stock motif of epiphanies narrated in vision reports (see Isa 6.5; Ezek 1.28; Dan 8.17; Lk 24.5). *The first and the last,* a divine title derived from Second Isaiah (Isa 41.4; 44.6; 48.12); see note on 1.8. **1.18** *Keys of Death and of Hades,* i.e., the keys to Death and Hades (as to a door); because Christ was dead but is now alive forever, he controls them. In Anatolia, in Hellenistic and Roman times, there was a widespread belief that the Greek underworld goddess Hekate possessed the keys to Hades. **1.19** Some have taken this as a three-part general outline of Revelation: *what you have seen* (1.9–20), *what is* (2.1–3.22), and *what is to take place after this* (4.1–22.5). Since 4.1–22.5 refers to the past and the future, however, one should see this as a logical division of the subject (not the book) into past, present, and future. **1.20** *Angels of the seven churches,* later referred to individually (2.1, 8, 12, 18; 3.1, 7, 14), are the heavenly counterparts of the earthly Christian communities.

2.1–3.22 The messages to the seven churches are not in the form of ancient letters (see 1.4–5a) but rather resemble the edicts and decrees issued by Persian and Greek kings and Roman emperors. Each proclamation consists of eight stereotypical features: (1) destination, (2) the command to write, (3) the archaic "thus says" formula (*these are the words of*), (4) titles of Christ (largely based on the vision in 1.9–20), (5) the "I know" narrative, (6) admonitions and exhortations, (7) the proclamation formula (*let anyone who has an ear listen*), and (8) the victory formula (*whoever conquers* and similar phrases). Moral exhortation, present implicitly if not explicitly in apocalypses, permeates these proclamations. **2.1** *Ephesus,* largest city of the Roman province of Asia, seat of the proconsul, and an important early Christian center (Acts 18.19–28; 19.1; 20.16–17; 1 Cor 15.32; 1 Tim 1.3). **2.2** *Tested* suggests that visiting missionaries were expected to measure up to certain expectations in teaching and behavior (1 Thess 5.21; 1 Jn 4.1–3; *Didache* 11). *Apostles,* a general term for itinerant missionaries (Acts 14.4, 14; Rom 16.7; 2 Cor 8.23; *Didache* 11.3–6) rather than a technical term for the twelve apostles. **2.5** *I will . . . remove your lampstand* (see 1.12, 20), a threat to obliterate the Ephesian church as a Christian community; i.e., a symbolic action carried out in heaven has earthly consequences. **2.6** *Nicolaitans,* an otherwise unknown Christian sect found in Ephesus and Pergamum (see v. 15), possibly identical to the false apostles of v. 2 and with Jezebel and her followers in Thyatira (vv. 20–23), and often thought to be Gnostics (though the evidence is slim). **2.7** The content of all seven proclamations is attributed to *the Spirit,* who speaks through Christ to John, suggesting a prophetic model. *Eat from the tree of life,* a metaphor for salvation or eternal life (Gen 3.22–24; *1 Enoch* 25.4–6; *Testament of Levi* 18.11). Access to the tree was denied to Adam and Eve (Gen 3.24) but will be available to the righteous (Rev 22.2, 14, 19). The Hebrew term for the garden located in Eden, somewhere on earth (Gen 2.8), was translated *paradise* (an Iranian loanword for "garden" or "park") in the Septuagint. Later, paradise came to be regarded as the abode of the righteous dead (2 Esd 7.36; Lk 23.43; *1 Enoch* 60.8) and was thought to be located in heaven (2 Cor 12.2–4; *2 Enoch* 8.1). **2.8** *Smyrna,* a harbor city forty miles north of Ephesus (modern Izmir) and a center of the imperial cult (i.e., the worship of the Roman emperor). *The first and the last.* See 1.17. **2.9** Despite

on the part of those who say that they are Jews and are not, but are a synagogue of Satan. [10]Do not fear what you are about to suffer. Beware, the devil is about to throw some of you into prison so that you may be tested, and for ten days you will have affliction. Be faithful until death, and I will give you the crown of life. [11]Let anyone who has an ear listen to what the Spirit is saying to the churches. Whoever conquers will not be harmed by the second death.

The Message to Pergamum

12 "And to the angel of the church in Pergamum write: These are the words of him who has the sharp two-edged sword:

13 "I know where you are living, where Satan's throne is. Yet you are holding fast to my name, and you did not deny your faith in me[a] even in the days of Antipas my witness, my faithful one, who was killed among you, where Satan lives. [14]But I have a few things against you: you have some there who hold to the teaching of Balaam, who taught Balak to put a stumbling block before the people of Israel, so that they would eat food sacrificed to idols

and practice fornication. [15]So you also have some who hold to the teaching of the Nicolaitans. [16]Repent then. If not, I will come to you soon and make war against them with the sword of my mouth. [17]Let anyone who has an ear listen to what the Spirit is saying to the churches. To everyone who conquers I will give some of the hidden manna, and I will give a white stone, and on the white stone is written a new name that no one knows except the one who receives it.

The Message to Thyatira

18 "And to the angel of the church in Thyatira write: These are the words of the Son of God, who has eyes like a flame of fire, and whose feet are like burnished bronze:

19 "I know your works—your love, faith, service, and patient endurance. I know that your last works are greater than the first. [20]But I have this against you: you tolerate that woman Jezebel, who calls herself a prophet and is teaching and beguiling my servants[b] to practice fornication and to eat food sacrificed

---

a Or *deny my faith*   *b* Gk *slaves*

physical *poverty,* the Smyrnaean Christians are spiritually *rich. Slander* by the Jews refers to their denunciation of Christians before Roman officials (see Acts 18.12–17; *Martyrdom of Polycarp* 12.2–3), an indication of sharp conflict between the two communities. These polemical statements were not originally as anti-Semitic as they sound today. *Synagogue of Satan,* close to "congregation of Belial" in the Dead Sea Scrolls *Thanksgiving Hymns* (1QH 2.22), may refer to Jews who had abandoned their faith but more likely has in view Jews who (like Satan) were "opponents" of Christians; Jn 8.44 refers to the devil as the "father" of the Jews. **2.10** The *devil* (Greek *diabolos,* "slanderer," a synonym for Hebrew "Satan"), working through his earthly henchmen, will throw them into prison. *Ten days* symbolizes a short but indefinite period of time. *Crown of life* (see 1 Cor 9.25; Jas 1.12), an image based on the wreath awarded to winners in ancient competitions and reminiscent of the wreath design found on many Hellenistic tombstones; a metaphor for the reward of eternal life (3.11). **2.11** *Second death* (20.6, 14; 21.8), the eternal punishment of the wicked following physical death. **2.12** *Pergamum,* a city of 180,000, was the seat of government in the Roman province of Asia and a major center of the imperial cult (see note on 2.8). **2.13** *Satan's throne,* an enigmatic phrase that may refer to the proconsul's judgment seat, to Pergamum as a center of the imperial cult, or to the Great Altar of Zeus erected after 230 BCE (ancients often designated altars as thrones). *Antipas,* an otherwise unknown Christian executed or lynched in Pergamum. *Witness,*

from the Greek *martys,* a word that soon took on the connotation of "martyr" (*Martyrdom of Polycarp* 14.2). **2.14** According to postbiblical Jewish literature, the error of *Balaam* (see Num 22–24; 31.16; 2 Pet 2.15–16; Jude 11) involved idolatry and sexual immorality. *Food sacrificed to idols,* sold to the public in pagan temple meat markets, violated the Jewish prohibition of idolatry (Ex 34.15; 4 Macc 5.2) and, because of its connection with pagan worship, was a problem for observant Christians as well (2.20; Acts 15.20, 29; 21.25; 1 Cor 8.1, 4, 7, 10; 10.28). **2.15** *Nicolaitans* (see v. 6) repeat the error of Balaam. **2.17** *Manna,* from the Hebrew for "What is it?" is also called "bread from heaven" (see Ex 16.4; Neh 9.15; Jn 6.31–34) and "food from heaven" (Ps 105.40); here it is a metaphor for participation in eternal life. According to Jewish expectation, the miraculous feeding would be repeated in the last days. *White stone,* an amulet on which is inscribed *a new name,* i.e., the secret name of God or Christ (3.12; 19.12; cf. 7.3), which is a symbol for the permanent protection of the wearer. In the ancient world amulets containing divine names were thought effective in warding off diseases and evil spirits. **2.18** *Thyatira* (modern Akhisar), lay thirty-five miles inland, between Pergamum and Ephesus. **2.20** *Jezebel,* the Canaanite queen of King Ahab of Israel (1 Kings 18–19; 2 Kings 9), who induced Ahab to worship Canaanite deities. John gives this infamous name to an otherwise unknown Christian prophetess whose teachings were, in his view, leading Christians astray. Since the weapons of ancient slander routinely in-

to idols. 21I gave her time to repent, but she refuses to repent of her fornication. 22Beware, I am throwing her on a bed, and those who commit adultery with her I am throwing into great distress, unless they repent of her doings; 23and I will strike her children dead. And all the churches will know that I am the one who searches minds and hearts, and I will give to each of you as your works deserve. 24But to the rest of you in Thyatira, who do not hold this teaching, who have not learned what some call 'the deep things of Satan,' to you I say, I do not lay on you any other burden; 25only hold fast to what you have until I come. 26To everyone who conquers and continues to do my works to the end,

I will give authority over the nations;
27   to rule*a* them with an iron rod,
         as when clay pots are shattered—

28even as I also received authority from my Father. To the one who conquers I will also give the morning star. 29Let anyone who has an ear listen to what the Spirit is saying to the churches.

The Message to Sardis

3 "And to the angel of the church in Sardis write: These are the words of him who has the seven spirits of God and the seven stars:

"I know your works; you have a name of being alive, but you are dead. 2Wake up, and strengthen what remains and is on the point of death, for I have not found your works perfect in the sight of my God. 3Remember then what you received and heard; obey it, and repent. If you do not wake up, I will come like a thief, and you will not know at what hour I will come to you. 4Yet you have still a few per-

sons in Sardis who have not soiled their clothes; they will walk with me, dressed in white, for they are worthy. 5If you conquer, you will be clothed like them in white robes, and I will not blot your name out of the book of life; I will confess your name before my Father and before his angels. 6Let anyone who has an ear listen to what the Spirit is saying to the churches.

The Message to Philadelphia

7 "And to the angel of the church in Philadelphia write:

These are the words of the holy one, the
         true one,
     who has the key of David,
     who opens and no one will shut,
who shuts and no one opens:

8 "I know your works. Look, I have set before you an open door, which no one is able to shut. I know that you have but little power, and yet you have kept my word and have not denied my name. 9I will make those of the synagogue of Satan who say that they are Jews and are not, but are lying—I will make them come and bow down before your feet, and they will learn that I have loved you. 10Because you have kept my word of patient endurance, I will keep you from the hour of trial that is coming on the whole world to test the inhabitants of the earth. 11I am coming soon; hold fast to what you have, so that no one may seize your crown. 12If you conquer, I will make you a pillar in the temple of my God; you will never go out of it. I will write on you the name of my God, and the name of the city of my

---

a Or *to shepherd*

---

cluded charges of immorality, it is difficult to know what the real situation was. **2.23** *Her children,* the followers of the prophetess. **2.24** *The deep things of Satan,* perhaps a sarcastic revision of the prophetess's motto, which probably was "the deep things of God." **2.28** *Morning star* (the bright planet Venus), an epithet of Christ (22.16) and a messianic symbol (Num 24.17; Mt 2.2, 10).

3.1 *Sardis,* the ancient capital of the Lydian kingdom, then of the Seleucid kingdom. *Seven spirits.* See 1.4. **3.3** *I will come like a thief,* a frequent metaphor for the unexpected arrival of Christ (16.15; Mt 24.42–44; Lk 12.39–40; 1 Thess 5.2; 2 Pet 3.10). **3.4** *Soiled clothes* represent evil deeds, while *white* garments symbolize righteousness. **3.5** *Book of life,* a heavenly registry of the names of God's people, a metaphor for salvation and election (13.8; 17.8; 20.12, 15; 21.27; Ex 32.32;

Dan 12.1; Lk 10.20; Phil 4.3). **3.7** *Philadelphia,* a city thirty miles from Sardis. *Key of David,* symbol of messianic power and authority (see Isa 22.22). **3.8** *Open door,* a widely used Christian metaphor for opportunities to evangelize (Acts 14.27; 1 Cor 16.9; 2 Cor 2.12) and for access to salvation (Lk 13.24). **3.9** *Synagogue of Satan.* See 2.9. **3.10** *Hour of trial,* the period of distress and suffering, often called "the great tribulation," prior to God's eschatological triumph (7.14; 13.5–10; Dan 12.1; Mt 24.21; Mk 13.7–20; 1 Cor 7.26; Hermas *Visions* 2.2.7), probably referred to in the Lord's Prayer (Mt 6.13; *Didache* 8.2). **3.11** *I am coming soon.* The imminent return, or Parousia, of Christ is frequently mentioned (1.3; 16.15; 22.12, 20), though its delay was a theological problem in some phases of early Christianity (2 Pet 3.4; Mt 25.1–13). **3.12** *Pillar in the temple* means a permanent place in the heavenly temple, a

from the tribe of Joseph twelve thousand, from the tribe of Benjamin twelve thousand sealed.

The Multitude from Every Nation

9 After this I looked, and there was a great multitude that no one could count, from every nation, from all tribes and peoples and languages, standing before the throne and before the Lamb, robed in white, with palm branches in their hands. 10They cried out in a loud voice, saying,

"Salvation belongs to our God who is
    seated on the throne, and to the
    Lamb!"

11And all the angels stood around the throne and around the elders and the four living creatures, and they fell on their faces before the throne and worshiped God, 12singing,

"Amen! Blessing and glory and wisdom
    and thanksgiving and honor
    and power and might
    be to our God forever and ever! Amen."

13 Then one of the elders addressed me, saying, "Who are these, robed in white, and where have they come from?" 14I said to him, "Sir, you are the one that knows." Then he said

to me, "These are they who have come out of the great ordeal; they have washed their robes and made them white in the blood of the Lamb.

15 For this reason they are before the throne
        of God,
    and worship him day and night within
        his temple,
    and the one who is seated on the
        throne will shelter them.
16 They will hunger no more, and thirst no
        more;
    the sun will not strike them,
    nor any scorching heat;
17 for the Lamb at the center of the throne
        will be their shepherd,
    and he will guide them to springs of
        the water of life,
    and God will wipe away every tear from
        their eyes."

The Seventh Seal and the Golden Censer

8 When the Lamb opened the seventh seal, there was silence in heaven for about half an hour. 2And I saw the seven angels who stand before God, and seven trumpets were given to them.

---

church as the spiritual Israel (see Rom 9.6–7; 11.17–21; Gal 6.16; Jas 1.1). **7.9–17** A heavenly throne-room scene; see note on 4.1–11. The passage may be based in part on symbolism from the Festival of Booths (see Zech 14.16–21). **7.9** A great multitude, a heavenly assembly that may include but is not identical to the 144,000 Israelites mentioned in vv. 4–8; it represents the spiritualized fulfillment of the promise to Abraham (Gen 22.17; 32.12; cf. Rom 9.27). Its members are identified in v. 14 as the martyrs who have gone through the great tribulation. Throne. See note on 4.10. Robed in white. See note on 6.11. Palm branches, symbols of victory (see 1 Macc 13.51; 2 Macc 14.4; Jn 12.13). **7.13** One of the elders, functioning in place of the more typical figure of the interpreting angel (1.1; 17.1–18; 21.9–22.5; see Introduction), provides an explanation of the vision in vv. 14–17. **7.14** The great ordeal. See note on 3.10. Washed . . . white in the blood of the Lamb, paradoxical metaphor referring to the forgiveness of sins through the atoning death of Jesus (see Rom 3.25; 5.9; 1 Cor 10.16; 1 Pet 1.2). **7.15** God . . . will shelter them. God will be present with them or dwell with them (21.3; see Lev 26.11; Ezek 37.27). **7.16** Cessation of hunger, thirst, and intense heat alludes to the Edenic eschatological conditions described in Isa 49.10 (see also Rev 21.4). **7.17** At the center, i.e., of the throne occupied by both God and the Lamb (3.21; 22.1, 3). Shepherd, a stock metaphor for a king (see 2 Sam 7.7; Isa 44.28; Jer 3.15) in the ancient world gen-

erally and a favorite metaphor for Jesus (Mt 15.24; 25.32; Jn 10.2; Heb 13.20; 1 Pet 2.25). Springs of the water of life, lit. "springs of living water" (cf. Isa 49.10); here "living water" can mean either flowing water (as opposed to the still water stored in cisterns) or water imbued with (eternal) life, a metaphor for salvation (21.6; 22.1, 17; see also Jn 4.14; 6.35; 7.37–38). Wipe away every tear indicates the absence of sorrow in the new order (see Isa 25.8).

8.1 A transitional verse. The opening of the seventh seal means that the scroll of 5.1 is now ready to be opened completely; the events narrated in 8.2–22.5 enact the contents of the scroll. After the cosmic destruction caused by the opening of the sixth seal in 6.12–17, the opening of this seal issues in an anticlimactic silence in heaven. Silence precedes divine manifestations (see Job 4.16; Zeph 1.7; Zech 2.13) and is maintained during the incense offering (see Rev 8.3–5). **8.2–9.21** See also 11.15–19. The seven trumpets (like the seven bowls of 15.1–16.21) introduce eschatological divine judgments that are loosely based on the ten Egyptian plagues (Ex 7–12), though they are universal rather than local in effect. Several variant traditions of seven Egyptian plagues have been preserved (Pss 78.44–51; 105.27–36; Am 4.6–11; Wis 11.1–19.9). **8.2–5** Preparatory heavenly throne-room scene; see note on 4.1–11. **8.2** Seven angels. See note on 1.4. Trumpets can signal the inauguration of the end (see Isa 27.13; Joel 2.1; Mt 24.31; 1 Cor 15.52; 1 Thess

3 Another angel with a golden censer came and stood at the altar; he was given a great quantity of incense to offer with the prayers of all the saints on the golden altar that is before the throne. 4And the smoke of the incense, with the prayers of the saints, rose before God from the hand of the angel. 5Then the angel took the censer and filled it with fire from the altar and threw it on the earth; and there were peals of thunder, rumblings, flashes of lightning, and an earthquake.

The Seven Trumpets

6 Now the seven angels who had the seven trumpets made ready to blow them.

7 The first angel blew his trumpet, and there came hail and fire, mixed with blood, and they were hurled to the earth; and a third of the earth was burned up, and a third of the trees were burned up, and all green grass was burned up.

8 The second angel blew his trumpet, and something like a great mountain, burning with fire, was thrown into the sea. 9A third of the sea became blood, a third of the living creatures in the sea died, and a third of the ships were destroyed.

10 The third angel blew his trumpet, and a great star fell from heaven, blazing like a torch, and it fell on a third of the rivers and on the springs of water. 11The name of the star is

Wormwood. A third of the waters became wormwood, and many died from the water, because it was made bitter.

12 The fourth angel blew his trumpet, and a third of the sun was struck, and a third of the moon, and a third of the stars, so that a third of their light was darkened; a third of the day was kept from shining, and likewise the night.

13 Then I looked, and I heard an eagle crying with a loud voice as it flew in midheaven, "Woe, woe, woe to the inhabitants of the earth, at the blasts of the other trumpets that the three angels are about to blow!"

9 And the fifth angel blew his trumpet, and I saw a star that had fallen from heaven to earth, and he was given the key to the shaft of the bottomless pit; 2he opened the shaft of the bottomless pit, and from the shaft rose smoke like the smoke of a great furnace, and the sun and the air were darkened with the smoke from the shaft. 3Then from the smoke came locusts on the earth, and they were given authority like the authority of scorpions of the earth. 4They were told not to damage the grass of the earth or any green growth or any tree, but only those people who do not have the seal of God on their foreheads. 5They were allowed to torture them for five months, but not to kill them, and their torture was like the torture of a scorpion when it stings someone. 6And in those days people will seek death but will not

---

4.16; Didache 16.6). **8.3** The golden altar, the heavenly counterpart of the incense altar located before the holy of holies in the tabernacle and temple (Ex 30.1–10). **8.4** The incense offering, made twice daily in the temple (Lk 1.8–10), lent itself to spiritualization; here it is associated with (but not, as in 5.8, identified with) the prayers of the saints, which, judging by their effect in 8.5, appear to have been prayers for vengeance (see 6.10). **8.5** The throwing of fire from the altar to the earth anticipates the divine judgments that the trumpets will unleash (see Ezek 10.2) and again indicate that events on earth are determined by events in heaven. Peals of thunder. See note on 4.5. **8.7–12** The first four trumpets form a group, as did the first four seals (see note on 6.1–8). **8.7** The hail, fire, and blood that fall to the earth correspond to the thunder, hail, and fire of the seventh plague (Ex 9.22–26) and to the fourth and seventh bowls in 16.8–9, 19–21. The Romans regarded blood raining from the sky as an omen indicating the anger of the gods. The eschatological destruction of a third of various aspects of the cosmos (based on Ezek 5.2, 12) emphasizes that the destruction is partial, not total (8.9, 10, 11, 12; 9.15, 18). **8.9** Sea became blood, an allusion to the Egyptian plague in which the Nile was turned to blood (the first

plague in Ex 7.20–21; the second bowl in Rev 16.3). **8.10–11** There is no counterpart to the third trumpet among the Egyptian plagues. **8.11** Wormwood, a plant noted for bitter taste, though not poisonous effects (see Prov 5.4; Lam 3.15). **8.12** Fourth . . . trumpet. The darkening of the heavenly bodies resembles the darkness of the ninth plague (Ex 10.21) and of the fifth bowl (Rev 16.10). **8.13** Woe, woe, woe. The three woes become literary devices for designating the last three trumpet plagues in 9.1–12, 13–21; 11.14–19 (see 9.12; 11.14); the counterparts of blessings, woes frequently introduce divine penalties (Lk 6.24–26) and are used in judgment speeches (Isa 5.18–23; Mt 23.13–32).

9.1–12 The fifth trumpet plague alludes to the locust plague of Ex 10.4–20 and is modeled after Joel 2.1–11. **9.1** Star, an angelic messenger sent by God to earth (see 20.1). Bottomless pit, the abode of the dead (see Ps 107.26; Rom 10.7) and the place where demons (Lk 8.31; 1 Enoch 18–21) and Satan (Rev 20.1–3) are imprisoned. **9.3** Locusts, an army of demons (based on the locust plague in Joel 2.1–11). **9.4** Grass . . . any tree, vegetation that is typically devastated by locust plagues. People who do not have the seal of God (see 7.2–8) are attacked, but God's people are exempt. **9.5** Five months (see also v. 10), the life span of the lo-

find it; they will long to die, but death will flee from them.

7 In appearance the locusts were like horses equipped for battle. On their heads were what looked like crowns of gold; their faces were like human faces, [8]their hair like women's hair, and their teeth like lions' teeth; [9]they had scales like iron breastplates, and the noise of their wings was like the noise of many chariots with horses rushing into battle. [10]They have tails like scorpions, with stingers, and in their tails is their power to harm people for five months. [11]They have as king over them the angel of the bottomless pit; his name in Hebrew is Abaddon,[a] and in Greek he is called Apollyon.[b]

12 The first woe has passed. There are still two woes to come.

13 Then the sixth angel blew his trumpet, and I heard a voice from the four[c] horns of the golden altar before God, [14]saying to the sixth angel who had the trumpet, "Release the four angels who are bound at the great river Euphrates." [15]So the four angels were released, who had been held ready for the hour, the day, the month, and the year, to kill a third of humankind. [16]The number of the troops of cavalry was two hundred million; I heard their number. [17]And this was how I saw the horses in my vision: the riders wore breastplates the color of fire and of sapphire[d] and of sulfur; the heads of the horses were like lions' heads, and fire and smoke and sulfur came out of their mouths. [18]By these three plagues a third of humankind was killed, by the fire and smoke and sulfur coming out of their mouths. [19]For the power of the horses is in their mouths and in their tails; their tails are like serpents, having heads; and with them they inflict harm.

20 The rest of humankind, who were not killed by these plagues, did not repent of the works of their hands or give up worshiping demons and idols of gold and silver and bronze and stone and wood, which cannot see or hear or walk. [21]And they did not repent of their murders or their sorceries or their fornication or their thefts.

The Angel with the Little Scroll

10 And I saw another mighty angel coming down from heaven, wrapped in a cloud, with a rainbow over his head; his face was like the sun, and his legs like pillars of fire. [2]He held a little scroll open in his hand. Setting his right foot on the sea and his left foot on the land, [3]he gave a great shout, like a lion roaring. And when he shouted, the seven thunders sounded. [4]And when the seven thunders had sounded, I was about to write, but I heard a voice from heaven saying, "Seal up what the seven thunders have said, and do not write it down." [5]Then the angel whom I saw standing on the sea and the land

---

a That is, *Destruction* b That is, *Destroyer* c Other ancient authorities lack *four* d Gk *hyacinth*

---

cust. **9.6** That *people will seek death but will not find it* underlines the horror of this plague. **9.7** *Like horses equipped for battle,* based on Joel 2.4–9. The demonic locust swarm is depicted as a marauding army. *Crowns of gold,* symbols of domination and invincibility. **9.8** *Like women's hair.* Demons are sometimes described as having disheveled hair like that of women (*Testament of Solomon* 13.1; *Apocalypse of Zephaniah* 4.4). **9.11** *Angel of the bottomless pit,* not Satan (12.9; 20.2), but an otherwise unknown evil angelic figure. *Abaddon,* Hebrew for "place of destruction," used in wisdom literature for the realm of the dead (see Job 26.6; Prov 15.11; 27.20), here personified (see also Job 28.22). *Apollyon,* Greek for "destroyer," linked with the name of the god Apollo. **9.12** *The first woe* corresponds to the events narrated in vv. 1–11; see note on 8.13. The *two woes to come* are described in 9.12–21; 11.15–19. **9.13** *The four horns,* the raised corners of the altar, typical of Israelite and Canaanite altars. **9.14** *Release the four angels who are bound.* The bind/release terminology (20.2; Tob 3.17) suggests that these are evil angels who lead demonic armies. *Euphrates,* a Mesopotamian river symbolizing the enemies of Israel (see Isa 7.20; 8.7; Jer 46.10). **9.18** *Fire* and *sulfur* (see also 14.10; 19.20; 20.10), stereotypical means of terrifying divine punishment first mentioned in the Bible in connection with the judgment of Sodom and Gomorrah (see Gen 19.24; Ps 11.6; Ezek 38.22). **9.20** *Did not repent* (see v. 21; 16.9, 11), a theme from the Exodus plague tradition (see, e.g., Ex 7.13, 22; 8.15); actual repentance is not expected. *Demons,* in Jewish thought the supernatural beings represented by *idols* and believed to inhabit them (Deut 32.17; Ps 96.5; 1 Cor 10.19–20).

10.1–11 Two digressions (10.1–11; 11.1–14) delay the sounding of the seventh trumpet. **10.2** The *little scroll* represents divine revelation but is not identical to the sealed scroll of 5.1–14. **10.3** The import of the *seven thunders* is unclear; John apparently understood what the seven thunders said but was forbidden to write it down. **10.4** *Voice from heaven,* probably God or Christ (see 1.11, 19). In Jewish tradition a heavenly voice was called a *bat qol* (lit. "daughter of a voice") and thought to be the revelatory voice of God, as in the heavenly voice at Jesus' baptism (Mt 3.17; Mk 1.11; Lk 3.22; 2 Pet 1.17). The instruction to *seal up* (see Dan

raised his right hand to heaven
6   and swore by him who lives forever
        and ever,
who created heaven and what is in it, the earth
and what is in it, and the sea and what is in it:
"There will be no more delay, [7]but in the days
when the seventh angel is to blow his trumpet,
the mystery of God will be fulfilled, as he announced to his servants[a] the prophets."

8 Then the voice that I had heard from
heaven spoke to me again, saying, "Go, take
the scroll that is open in the hand of the angel
who is standing on the sea and on the land."
[9]So I went to the angel and told him to give me
the little scroll; and he said to me, "Take it, and
eat; it will be bitter to your stomach, but sweet
as honey in your mouth." [10]So I took the little
scroll from the hand of the angel and ate it; it
was sweet as honey in my mouth, but when I
had eaten it, my stomach was made bitter.

11 Then they said to me, "You must prophesy again about many peoples and nations and
languages and kings."

The Two Witnesses

11 Then I was given a measuring rod like
a staff, and I was told, "Come and measure the temple of God and the altar and those
who worship there, [2]but do not measure the
court outside the temple; leave that out, for it
is given over to the nations, and they will
trample over the holy city for forty-two
months. [3]And I will grant my two witnesses
authority to prophesy for one thousand two
hundred sixty days, wearing sackcloth."

4 These are the two olive trees and the two
lampstands that stand before the Lord of the
earth. [5]And if anyone wants to harm them, fire
pours from their mouth and consumes their
foes; anyone who wants to harm them must be
killed in this manner. [6]They have authority to
shut the sky, so that no rain may fall during
the days of their prophesying, and they have
authority over the waters to turn them into
blood, and to strike the earth with every kind
of plague, as often as they desire.

7 When they have finished their testimony,
the beast that comes up from the bottomless
pit will make war on them and conquer them
and kill them, [8]and their dead bodies will lie in
the street of the great city that is prophetically[b]
called Sodom and Egypt, where also their
Lord was crucified. [9]For three and a half days
members of the peoples and tribes and lan-

a Gk slaves   b Or allegorically; Gk spiritually

12.4, 9) means that some divine secrets must not be
disclosed (2 Cor 12.4). **10.5–7** This scene appears to be
modeled after Dan 12.6–7. **10.6** *No more delay* does
not imply a previous postponement, but the imminent end of time and beginning of eschatological
events. **10.7** *Mystery of God* (see Am 3.7), God's eschatological plan, hidden in OT prophetic books (Rom
16.25–26; 1 Cor 2.6–16; Eph 3.9–10; Col 1.26). *His servants the prophets*, a frequent designation of OT prophets (2 Kings 9.7; 17.13; Jer 7.25; Dan 9.6; see Rev 11.18),
which here probably includes Christian prophets as
well. **10.8** *Voice*, that of v. 4. **10.9–10** Eating the scroll, a
symbolic action based on Ezek 2.8–3.3, signifies accepting a prophetic commission. **10.11** *Prophesy again
about* has the negative meaning "prophesy against," i.e.,
prophesy judgment (see Jer 25.30; Ezek 25.2).

11.1–14 A second digression (see note on 10.1–11)
describes two mysterious witnesses and their ministry.
11.1 *Measure*, a metaphor for preservation (Ezek
40.3–42.20; Zech 2.1–5). *Temple of God*, here the temple in Jerusalem, not in heaven (see note on 11.19).
Altar, i.e., the priest's court where the altar stood.
11.2 The trampling or subjugation of Jerusalem by the
nations (i.e., Gentiles) is a common eschatological
motif (see Isa 63.18; 1 Macc 3.45; Lk 21.24; see also
notes on 11.18; 16.14). *Forty-two months*, i.e., 1,260
days (11.3; 12.6), or three and a half years, a metaphorical period of eschatological distress (see Dan 7.25;

12.7). **11.3** *My two witnesses*, prophetic figures, possibly Enoch and Elijah or Moses and Elijah (see Mk 9.4),
represent the valid witness of the church (see Deut
17.6; 19.15; Mt 18.16; 2 Cor 13.1; 1 Tim 5.19; Heb
10.28). *Sackcloth*, often made of dark goat hair (6.12;
Isa 50.3), the traditional Near Eastern costume of
mourning (Joel 1.13; Mt 11.21). **11.4** *Two olive trees*
and *two lampstands* (see Zech 4.3, 14), originally
metaphors for Joshua the priest and Zerubbabel the
royal heir, God's two anointed ones. **11.5** *Fire pours
from their mouth*, often a metaphor for the word of
God in judgment (see Jer 5.14; 2 Esd 13.10, 37–38;
2 Thess 2.8). **11.6** *Authority to shut the sky* is like Elijah's ability to control rain (1 Kings 17.1; 18.1; Lk 4.25;
Jas 5.17). *Authority . . . blood* recalls Moses' actions (Ex
7.14–25). **11.7** *Beast*, the antichrist, a tyrannical ruler
who opposes Christ and Christians (13.1–10; 17.8;
1 Jn 2.18; 4.3). *Bottomless pit*. See note on 9.1. *Kill them*
(adapted from Dan 7.21). Death was frequently the expected fate of faithful prophets (see 2 Chr 24.19; Neh
9.26; Mt 23.34–35; Lk 11.49–51). **11.8** *The great city*,
Jerusalem (see Jer 22.8), which the prophets occasionally called *Sodom* (see Isa 1.10; Jer 23.14; Ezek 16.46),
the paradigmatic wicked city (Gen 18–19; Jer 49.18;
Mt 10.15). *Egypt* symbolized idolatry (Isa 19.1; Ezek
20.7) and slavery (Josh 24.17; Judg 6.8; 2 Esd 14.3).
11.9 *Refuse . . . placed in a tomb*, a further outrage,
since proper burial was thought to be the right of

guages and nations will gaze at their dead bodies and refuse to let them be placed in a tomb; [10]and the inhabitants of the earth will gloat over them and celebrate and exchange presents, because these two prophets had been a torment to the inhabitants of the earth.

11 But after the three and a half days, the breath[a] of life from God entered them, and they stood on their feet, and those who saw them were terrified. [12]Then they[b] heard a loud voice from heaven saying to them, "Come up here!" And they went up to heaven in a cloud while their enemies watched them. [13]At that moment there was a great earthquake, and a tenth of the city fell; seven thousand people were killed in the earthquake, and the rest were terrified and gave glory to the God of heaven.

14 The second woe has passed. The third woe is coming very soon.

The Seventh Trumpet

15 Then the seventh angel blew his trumpet, and there were loud voices in heaven, saying,

"The kingdom of the world has become
    the kingdom of our Lord
and of his Messiah,[c]
and he will reign forever and ever."

16 Then the twenty-four elders who sit on their thrones before God fell on their faces and worshiped God, [17]singing,

"We give you thanks, Lord God Almighty,
    who are and who were,
for you have taken your great power

and begun to reign.
18 The nations raged,
    but your wrath has come,
    and the time for judging the dead,
for rewarding your servants,[d] the
        prophets
    and saints and all who fear your name,
        both small and great,
    and for destroying those who destroy the
        earth."

19 Then God's temple in heaven was opened, and the ark of his covenant was seen within his temple; and there were flashes of lightning, rumblings, peals of thunder, an earthquake, and heavy hail.

The Woman and the Dragon

12 A great portent appeared in heaven: a woman clothed with the sun, with the moon under her feet, and on her head a crown of twelve stars. [2]She was pregnant and was crying out in birth pangs, in the agony of giving birth. [3]Then another portent appeared in heaven: a great red dragon, with seven heads and ten horns, and seven diadems on his heads. [4]His tail swept down a third of the stars of heaven and threw them to the earth. Then the dragon stood before the woman who was about to bear a child, so that he might devour her child as soon as it was born. [5]And she gave

---

a Or the spirit   b Other ancient authorities read I
c Gk Christ   d Gk slaves

---

every deceased person (see 1 Kings 14.11; 21.24; Jer 8.1–2; 14.16; Tob 2.3–10; Mk 12.8). **11.11** *Breath of life from God.* See Gen 2.7. **11.12** *Come up here.* See 4.1. In Jewish and Christian tradition *clouds* serve as divine vehicles (Pss 68.4; 104.7; Isa 19.1; 2 Esd 13.3) and as means of heavenly ascent (Acts 1.9) and descent (Rev 1.7; Dan 7.13; Mt 24.30; 26.64). **11.13** *Gave glory to the God of heaven,* i.e., were converted (16.9; Dan 4.34; 1 Esd 9.8; Acts 13.48). **11.14** *Woe.* See note on 8.13. **11.15–19** The seventh trumpet introduces yet another throne-room scene; see note on 4.1–11. **11.15** *Messiah,* Hebrew for "anointed one," used primarily for the king of Israel (who was installed in office by being anointed with oil); "Christ" means "anointed one" in Greek. See Jn 1.41. **11.18** *The nations raged.* See Ps 46.6; see also notes on 11.2; 16.14. **11.19** *Temple in heaven,* the counterpart to the temple in Jerusalem. *Ark of his covenant,* the heavenly counterpart to the sacred chest, representing the presence of God, placed in the holy of holies of the tabernacle and temple (Ex 25.10–22; 1 Kings 8.1–13; Heb 9.4). *Flashes of lightning,* typical theophanic language; see note on 4.5.
12.1–17 The portent of the woman, the child, and

the dragon is an adaptation of the myth of Apollo's birth understood by the author to point to the birth of Christ. **12.1** *A great portent,* a celestial phenomenon with a deeper symbolic meaning (see v. 3; 15.1). *A woman clothed with the sun,* a cosmic queen (described much like Isis), used as a symbol for both the Israel from whom the Messiah came (v. 5) and the church (vv. 6, 14, 17), widely understood in Catholic thought to symbolize the Blessed Virgin Mary. *Twelve stars,* the zodiac, here probably understood as representing the twelve tribes of Israel. **12.3** *Dragon,* a designation for Satan used nine times in Revelation. The Greek translation of the OT uses the same term for Leviathan, the enemy of God (Job 41.1 [40.25]; Ps 74.14 [73.14]; Isa 27.1). A dragon with *seven heads* (see 13.1; 17.3), a figure in Ugaritic mythology, here symbolizes seven successive rulers (17.10). *Ten horns* (see Dan 7.7, 20, 24), metaphors for power, here represent ten subordinate kings or kingdoms (17.12). **12.4** *Swept down a third of the stars,* a cosmic upheaval serving as a metaphor for hubris, or excessive pride (see Dan 8.10). **12.5** *Male child,* the Davidic Messiah who will *rule all the nations with a rod of iron* (see Ps 2.8–9), i.e., conquer the ene-

birth to a son, a male child, who is to rule[a] all the nations with a rod of iron. But her child was snatched away and taken to God and to his throne; 6and the woman fled into the wilderness, where she has a place prepared by God, so that there she can be nourished for one thousand two hundred sixty days.

Michael Defeats the Dragon

7 And war broke out in heaven; Michael and his angels fought against the dragon. The dragon and his angels fought back, 8but they were defeated, and there was no longer any place for them in heaven. 9The great dragon was thrown down, that ancient serpent, who is called the Devil and Satan, the deceiver of the whole world—he was thrown down to the earth, and his angels were thrown down with him.

10 Then I heard a loud voice in heaven, proclaiming,

"Now have come the salvation and the
        power
    and the kingdom of our God
    and the authority of his Messiah,[b]
for the accuser of our comrades[c] has been
        thrown down,
    who accuses them day and night before
        our God.
11 But they have conquered him by the
        blood of the Lamb
    and by the word of their testimony,
for they did not cling to life even in the
        face of death.
12 Rejoice then, you heavens

and those who dwell in them!
But woe to the earth and the sea,
    for the devil has come down to you
with great wrath,
    because he knows that his time is
        short!"

The Dragon Fights Again on Earth

13 So when the dragon saw that he had been thrown down to the earth, he pursued[d] the woman who had given birth to the male child. 14But the woman was given the two wings of the great eagle, so that she could fly from the serpent into the wilderness, to her place where she is nourished for a time, and times, and half a time. 15Then from his mouth the serpent poured water like a river after the woman, to sweep her away with the flood. 16But the earth came to the help of the woman; it opened its mouth and swallowed the river that the dragon had poured from his mouth. 17Then the dragon was angry with the woman, and went off to make war on the rest of her children, those who keep the commandments of God and hold the testimony of Jesus.

The First Beast

18 Then the dragon[e] took his stand on the sand of the seashore. 1And I saw a beast rising out of the sea, having ten horns and seven heads; and on its horns were ten di-

---

a Or to shepherd   b Gk Christ   c Gk brothers
d Or persecuted   e Gk Then he; other ancient authorities read Then I stood

---

mies of Israel (see note on 11.2). *Snatched away . . . to God.* The exaltation or ascension of Jesus (see Lk 24.51; Acts 2.32–33; 1 Tim 3.16; Heb 8.1; 10.12) is uniquely depicted here as a rescue from Satan (no allusion to the crucifixion is found in this story). **12.6** *Wilderness,* a place of refuge and salvation based on the exodus tradition (see Ps 78.52; Isa 40.3; Jer 31.2). *One thousand two hundred sixty days.* See note on 11.2. **12.7** *War . . . in heaven.* Nowhere else in Jewish or early Christian literature is a heavenly battle depicted, though Jewish apocalyptic literature preserves the tradition of a revolt in heaven (see Is 14.12–21), the inspiration for Milton's *Paradise Lost. Michael,* one of the seven traditional archangels (see note on 1.4; Dan 10.13; 12.1; Jude 9), often presented as the commander of the host of angels (*Apocalypse of Paul* 14) and the intercessor between humans and God. **12.9** *Great dragon . . . thrown down.* This eschatological expulsion of Satan from heaven (see Lk 10.18; Jn 12.31) is based on an ancient Jewish expulsion myth (see Isa 14.12–15; 2 Enoch 29.4–5). *Ancient serpent,* Satan (Gen 3.1–7; 2 Cor 11.3). *Devil.* See note on 2.10.

His angels, i.e., fallen angels or demons. **12.10** "Satan" means *accuser* in Hebrew (Job 1.9–11; Zech 3.1). **12.11** *They have conquered him,* paradoxically, like Jesus (3.21; 5.5), by dying. **12.14** *Two wings of the great eagle.* See Ex 19.4; Deut 32.10–14. *Wilderness.* See note on 12.6. *A time, and times, and half a time* (Dan 7.25; 12.7), i.e., three and a half years (see note on 11.2). **12.16** *Earth . . . swallowed the river.* A personified Earth sometimes swallows the enemies of God (see Ex 15.12; Num 16.32–34). **12.17** *The rest of her children,* Christians whose persecution is orchestrated by Satan (see 13.7).

12.18–13.18 Two beasts that serve the dragon are introduced. **12.18** *The dragon took his stand on the . . . seashore* to await the emergence of the beast. **13.1** *Beast* (see 11.7). John represents both Rome and its emperors as the sea monster Leviathan (Ezek 29.3; 2 Esd 6.47–52; 1 Enoch 60.7–10, 24). It rises out of the *sea* (representing the bottomless pit; see note on 9.1) and is a composite of the four beasts of Dan 7.3–7. *Blasphemous names,* divine titles such as "Lord," "Savior," and "Son of God" claimed by Roman emperors. *Ten horns and seven*

adems, and on its heads were blasphemous names. 2And the beast that I saw was like a leopard, its feet were like a bear's, and its mouth was like a lion's mouth. And the dragon gave it his power and his throne and great authority. 3One of its heads seemed to have received a death-blow, but its mortal wound[a] had been healed. In amazement the whole earth followed the beast. 4They worshiped the dragon, for he had given his authority to the beast, and they worshiped the beast, saying, "Who is like the beast, and who can fight against it?"

5 The beast was given a mouth uttering haughty and blasphemous words, and it was allowed to exercise authority for forty-two months. 6It opened its mouth to utter blasphemies against God, blaspheming his name and his dwelling, that is, those who dwell in heaven. 7Also it was allowed to make war on the saints and to conquer them.[b] It was given authority over every tribe and people and language and nation, 8and all the inhabitants of the earth will worship it, everyone whose name has not been written from the foundation of the world in the book of life of the Lamb that was slaughtered.[c]

9 Let anyone who has an ear listen:

10   If you are to be taken captive,
     into captivity you go;
  if you kill with the sword,
     with the sword you must be killed.
Here is a call for the endurance and faith of the saints.

The Second Beast

11 Then I saw another beast that rose out of the earth; it had two horns like a lamb and it spoke like a dragon. 12It exercises all the authority of the first beast on its behalf, and it makes the earth and its inhabitants worship the first beast, whose mortal wound[d] had been healed. 13It performs great signs, even making fire come down from heaven to earth in the sight of all; 14and by the signs that it is allowed to perform on behalf of the beast, it deceives the inhabitants of earth, telling them to make an image for the beast that had been wounded by the sword[e] and yet lived; 15and it was allowed to give breath[f] to the image of the beast so that the image of the beast could even speak and cause those who would not worship the image of the beast to be killed. 16Also it causes all, both small and great, both rich and poor, both free and slave, to be marked on the right hand or the forehead, 17so that no one can buy or sell who does not have the mark, that is, the name of the beast or the number of its name. 18This calls for wisdom: let anyone with understanding calculate the number of the beast, for it is the number of a person. Its number is six hundred sixty-six.[g]

The Lamb and the 144,000

14 Then I looked, and there was the Lamb, standing on Mount Zion! And with him were one hundred forty-four thousand who had his name and his Father's name written on their foreheads. 2And I heard a

---

a Gk *the plague of its death* *b* Other ancient authorities lack this sentence *c* Or *written in the book of life of the Lamb that was slaughtered from the foundation of the world* *d* Gk *whose plague of its death* *e* Or *that had received the plague of the sword* *f* Or *spirit* *g* Other ancient authorities read *six hundred sixteen*

---

heads. See note on 12.3. **13.2** *The dragon gave it his power,* i.e., Rome and its emperors are agents of Satan (2 Thess 2.9). **13.3** *One of its heads . . . received a death-blow,* the emperor Nero, who committed suicide in 68 CE. *Mortal wound . . . healed* reflects the widespread belief in Nero's return from death. **13.4** *They worshiped the beast.* The imperial cult included worship of the emperors as well as the traditional Greek and Roman gods (see notes on 2.8; 2.12). **13.5** *Forty-two months.* See note on 11.2. **13.7** *Make war on the saints.* See 12.17. **13.8** *Book of life.* See note on 3.5. **13.10** *If you are . . . be killed,* a reformulation of Jer 15.2; 43.11. **13.11** The *beast that rose out of the earth,* later called the *false prophet* (16.13; 19.20; 20.10), representing the priesthood of the imperial cult (see 13.12) as the male monster Behemoth (2 Esd 6.47–52; *1 Enoch* 60.7–10, 24). The beast with *horns like a lamb* is harmless in appearance, but it *spoke like a dragon,* i.e., as an agent of Satan (see note on 12.3).

13.13 *It performs great signs,* a traditional ploy of the antichrist to deceive people (Mk 13.21–23; 2 Thess 2.9–10; *Didache* 16.4). The motif is derived from Deut 13.1–3. **13.14** *An image for the beast,* cultic statues of the Roman emperors (see Dan 3). **13.15** *Give breath to the image.* In ancient magic the animation of images of the god was a means for securing oracles, an important practice of ancient theurgists (Iamblichus, *On the Mysteries* 5.23). *Speak,* i.e., give oracles. **13.16** *Marked,* i.e., branded or tattooed as a mark of ownership and devotion to the beast (tattooing was used to identify slaves in the ancient world); this marking is a counterpart to the sealing of Christians with the name of God (see note on 7.2). **13.18** *The number of the beast,* a code name based on the numeric value of letters. *Six hundred sixty-six,* perhaps the numeric value of the name Nero Caesar in Hebrew.

14.1–20 Three loosely connected visions dealing

voice from heaven like the sound of many waters and like the sound of loud thunder; the voice I heard was like the sound of harpists playing on their harps, ³and they sing a new song before the throne and before the four living creatures and before the elders. No one could learn that song except the one hundred forty-four thousand who have been redeemed from the earth. ⁴It is these who have not defiled themselves with women, for they are virgins; these follow the Lamb wherever he goes. They have been redeemed from humankind as first fruits for God and the Lamb, ⁵and in their mouth no lie was found; they are blameless.

The Messages of the Three Angels

6 Then I saw another angel flying in midheaven, with an eternal gospel to proclaim to those who live ᵃ on the earth—to every nation and tribe and language and people. ⁷He said in a loud voice, "Fear God and give him glory, for the hour of his judgment has come; and worship him who made heaven and earth, the sea and the springs of water."

8 Then another angel, a second, followed, saying, "Fallen, fallen is Babylon the great! She has made all nations drink of the wine of the wrath of her fornication."

9 Then another angel, a third, followed them, crying with a loud voice, "Those who worship the beast and its image, and receive a mark on their foreheads or on their hands,

¹⁰they will also drink the wine of God's wrath, poured unmixed into the cup of his anger, and they will be tormented with fire and sulfur in the presence of the holy angels and in the presence of the Lamb. ¹¹And the smoke of their torment goes up forever and ever. There is no rest day or night for those who worship the beast and its image and for anyone who receives the mark of its name."

12 Here is a call for the endurance of the saints, those who keep the commandments of God and hold fast to the faith of ᵇ Jesus.

13 And I heard a voice from heaven saying, "Write this: Blessed are the dead who from now on die in the Lord." "Yes," says the Spirit, "they will rest from their labors, for their deeds follow them."

Reaping the Earth's Harvest

14 Then I looked, and there was a white cloud, and seated on the cloud was one like the Son of Man, with a golden crown on his head, and a sharp sickle in his hand! ¹⁵Another angel came out of the temple, calling with a loud voice to the one who sat on the cloud, "Use your sickle and reap, for the hour to reap has come, because the harvest of the earth is fully ripe." ¹⁶So the one who sat on the cloud swung his sickle over the earth, and the earth was reaped.

---

a Gk sit　b Or to their faith in

---

with eschatological judgment and salvation. **14.1–5** A victory vision of the Lamb and the 144,000. **14.1** *Mount Zion*, i.e., Jerusalem as the center of God's eschatological action (Ps 2.6; Isa 24.23; 40.9–11; 2 Esd 13.35–40; Heb 12.22–24). *One hundred forty-four thousand.* See note on 7.4. **14.2–3** Preparatory heavenly throne-room scene; see note on 4.1–11. **14.3** *A new song.* See note on 5.9. *No one could learn that song.* Knowledge of heavenly realities is often said to be reserved only for the pure. **14.4** *Virgins*, males who are chaste, though not necessarily sexually inexperienced; ritual impurity was widely thought to follow sexual intercourse (Lev 15.18), and celibacy was a ritual requirement for holy warriors (Deut 23.9–14; 1 Sam 21.5–6). *Follow the Lamb*, a metaphor for discipleship and martyrdom (see Mt 19.28; Lk 9.57–58; Jn 12.26). The word translated *first fruits* actually means "servants devoted to God" and has nothing to do with first fruits as a sacrificial harvest metaphor. Here the term is applied to martyrs as sacrificial victims (cf. Jer 2.3; Rom 16.5; 1 Cor 15.20, 23). **14.6–13** The second vision consists of three angelic messages. **14.6** *An eternal gospel*, not the saving message of Jesus' death and resurrection, but the message referred to in v. 7. **14.7** The eternal message is the ne-

cessity of repentance in light of the imminent judgment (see also Deut 10.12–15; Acts 14.15–17). **14.8** *Babylon the great,* code name for Rome (see Introduction; 17.1–5, 18; 1 Pet 5.13); Rome's future fall is announced as if past (see 16.19; 17.5, 16–18; 18.2). *The wine of the wrath* of God, a metaphor derived from Jer 25.15–17; 51.7 (repeated in Rev 14.10; 17.2; 18.3). **14.9** *Mark.* See note on 13.16. **14.10** Wine *unmixed* with water was considered extremely potent and was a metaphor for severe judgment (see Ps 75.8; Jer 25.15). **14.13** *Blessed.* See note on 1.3. **14.14–20** A vision of the gathering of the righteous (vv. 14–16) and the judgment of the wicked (vv. 17–20) based on the grain and grape harvests of Joel 3.13. **14.14** The *white cloud* (see note on 11.12) functions as a throne and is also associated with the figure of *the Son of Man* (Dan 7.13; see notes on 1.7; 1.13), a common title for Jesus in the Gospels; he gathers the elect in Mk 13.26–27. The author appears unaware of the extensive Son of Man tradition in the Gospels. **14.15** The grain *harvest* symbolizes judgment (Hos 6.11; Mt 13.30, 39) or, as here, the gathering of the elect (Lk 10.2; Jn 4.35–38), an eschatological event based on the hope of the regathering of the twelve

17 Then another angel came out of the temple in heaven, and he too had a sharp sickle. 18 Then another angel came out from the altar, the angel who has authority over fire, and he called with a loud voice to him who had the sharp sickle, "Use your sharp sickle and gather the clusters of the vine of the earth, for its grapes are ripe." 19 So the angel swung his sickle over the earth and gathered the vintage of the earth, and he threw it into the great wine press of the wrath of God. 20 And the wine press was trodden outside the city, and blood flowed from the wine press, as high as a horse's bridle, for a distance of about two hundred miles. *a*

The Angels with the Seven Last Plagues

15 Then I saw another portent in heaven, great and amazing: seven angels with seven plagues, which are the last, for with them the wrath of God is ended.

2 And I saw what appeared to be a sea of glass mixed with fire, and those who had conquered the beast and its image and the number of its name, standing beside the sea of glass with harps of God in their hands. 3 And they sing the song of Moses, the servant *b* of God, and the song of the Lamb:

"Great and amazing are your deeds,
    Lord God the Almighty!
Just and true are your ways,
    King of the nations! *c*
4 Lord, who will not fear
    and glorify your name?
For you alone are holy.
    All nations will come
    and worship before you,
for your judgments have been revealed."

5 After this I looked, and the temple of the tent *d* of witness in heaven was opened, 6 and out of the temple came the seven angels with the seven plagues, robed in pure bright linen, *e* with golden sashes across their chests. 7 Then one of the four living creatures gave the seven angels seven golden bowls full of the wrath of God, who lives forever and ever; 8 and the temple was filled with smoke from the glory of God and from his power, and no one could enter the temple until the seven plagues of the seven angels were ended.

The Bowls of God's Wrath

16 Then I heard a loud voice from the temple telling the seven angels, "Go and pour out on the earth the seven bowls of the wrath of God."

2 So the first angel went and poured his bowl on the earth, and a foul and painful sore came on those who had the mark of the beast and who worshiped its image.

3 The second angel poured his bowl into the sea, and it became like the blood of a corpse, and every living thing in the sea died.

4 The third angel poured his bowl into the rivers and the springs of water, and they became blood. 5 And I heard the angel of the waters say,

"You are just, O Holy One, who are and were,
    for you have judged these things;
6 because they shed the blood of saints and prophets,
    you have given them blood to drink.
    It is what they deserve!"
7 And I heard the altar respond,
"Yes, O Lord God, the Almighty,
    your judgments are true and just!"

8 The fourth angel poured his bowl on the sun, and it was allowed to scorch people with fire; 9 they were scorched by the fierce heat, but

a Gk one thousand six hundred stadia   *b* Gk slave   *c* Other ancient authorities read *the ages*   *d* Or *tabernacle*   *e* Other ancient authorities read *stone*

tribes of Israel. **14.18** *The angel who has authority over fire.* In Jewish tradition various angels *superintend* particular aspects of the world, including wind *(7.1),* water *(16.5; 1 Enoch* 66.2), and the bottomless pit *(9.11);* see also *1 Enoch* 60.11–22. **14.19** *Wine press,* another metaphor for divine judgment (see 19.15; Isa 63.1–3; Lam 1.15).

15.1–16.21 The last seven plagues; see note on 8.2–9.21. **15.2–8** Preparatory heavenly throne-room scene (see note on 4.1–11). **15.2** *A sea of glass,* i.e., a sea so smooth that it appears glasslike; see note on 4.6. *Harps of God.* See note on 5.8. **15.3** *Song of Moses.* See Ex 15.1–18; Deut 32.1–47. **15.5** *The tent of witness,* i.e., the heavenly tabernacle (Heb 8.2; 9.11), which was considered the model for the earthly tabernacle (see Ex 25.9, 40; 26.30; 27.8). **15.7** *Seven golden bowls,* cultic utensils used for libations (Ex 27.3; 38.3; Num 4.14). **15.8** In the OT, a cloud of *smoke* can represent the presence or *glory* of God (see Ex 24.16; Lev 16.2; 1 Kings 8.10–11; Isa 6.4). **16.2** *A foul and painful sore,* reminiscent of the sixth plague of Ex 9.8–12. **16.3** See the first plague of Ex 7.14–25 (see also Pss 78.44; 105.29). **16.5** *Angel of the waters.* See note on 14.18. *You are just, O Holy One,* a doxology emphasizing God's just dis-

they cursed the name of God, who had authority over these plagues, and they did not repent and give him glory.

10 The fifth angel poured his bowl on the throne of the beast, and its kingdom was plunged into darkness; people gnawed their tongues in agony, [11]and cursed the God of heaven because of their pains and sores, and they did not repent of their deeds.

12 The sixth angel poured his bowl on the great river Euphrates, and its water was dried up in order to prepare the way for the kings from the east. [13]And I saw three foul spirits like frogs coming from the mouth of the dragon, from the mouth of the beast, and from the mouth of the false prophet. [14]These are demonic spirits, performing signs, who go abroad to the kings of the whole world, to assemble them for battle on the great day of God the Almighty. [15]("See, I am coming like a thief! Blessed is the one who stays awake and is clothed,[a] not going about naked and exposed to shame.") [16]And they assembled them at the place that in Hebrew is called Harmagedon.

17 The seventh angel poured his bowl into the air, and a loud voice came out of the temple from the throne, saying, "It is done!" [18]And there came flashes of lightning, rumblings, peals of thunder, and a violent earthquake, such as had not occurred since people were upon the earth, so violent was that earthquake. [19]The great city was split into three parts, and the cities of the nations fell. God remembered great Babylon and gave her the wine-cup of the fury of his wrath. [20]And every island fled away, and no mountains were to be found; [21]and huge hailstones, each weighing about a hundred pounds,[b] dropped from heaven on people, until they cursed God for the plague of the hail, so fearful was that plague.

The Great Whore and the Beast

17 Then one of the seven angels who had the seven bowls came and said to me, "Come, I will show you the judgment of the great whore who is seated on many waters, [2]with whom the kings of the earth have committed fornication, and with the wine of whose fornication the inhabitants of the earth have become drunk." [3]So he carried me away in the spirit[c] into a wilderness, and I saw a woman sitting on a scarlet beast that was full of blasphemous names, and it had seven heads and ten horns. [4]The woman was clothed in purple and scarlet, and adorned with gold and jewels and pearls, holding in her hand a golden cup full of abominations and the impurities of her fornication; [5]and on her forehead was written a name, a mystery: "Babylon the great, mother of whores and of earth's abominations." [6]And I saw that the woman was drunk with the blood of the saints and the blood of the witnesses to Jesus.

---

a Gk and keeps his robes b Gk weighing about a talent
c Or in the Spirit

---

pensation of judgment (see Neh 9.33; Dan 9.14; Tob 3.2). **16.9** *They did not repent,* a motif from the Exodus plagues tradition; see note on 9.20. **16.10** *The throne of the beast,* the center of imperial power in Rome (13.2). **16.12** *Euphrates,* the natural boundary between the rival powers of Parthia and Rome (see note on 9.14). *Its water was dried up.* In antiquity the Euphrates never dried up; this miracle is the antithesis of the crossing of the Red Sea (Ex 14). *Kings from the east,* the Parthians and their subordinate kingdoms. **16.13** *False prophet,* the beast from the land under a new alias (13.11–18). **16.14** *To assemble them for battle.* The tumult and assault of the Gentiles against Israel is a common eschatological motif (see Ezek 38–39; Zech 12.1–9; see also notes on 11.2; 11.18). *The great day of God.* See note on 6.17. **16.15** *I am coming like a thief!* An isolated saying inserted by the author; see note on 3.3. *Blessed.* See note on 1.3. **16.16** *They,* the three demonic spirits. *Harmagedon,* Hebrew term probably meaning "mountain(s) of Megiddo," a city in a valley in central Palestine that was the site of important ancient battles because of its strategic position (see Judg 5.19; 2 Kings 23.29–30). **16.17** *It is done.* The wrath of God has ended (15.1), yet the end is not yet (see 21.6). **16.19** *The great city,* Babylon, i.e., Rome. *God remembered great Babylon.* Divine justice is often linked with divine remembrance (see Jer 14.10; Hos 7.2; 8.13); the destruction of Babylon is described in 17.1–18.24. **16.20** *No mountains were to be found,* a motif found in OT theophany and judgment scenes (see Ps 97.5; Isa 40.4; Ezek 38.20).

17.1–18 A vision of Rome as the great whore. **17.1** *The great whore.* The metaphor of the prostitute is often used in the OT for godless cities (see Isa 1.21; 23.16–17; Nah 3.4). *Seated on many waters* aptly describes the location of historical Babylon (Jer 51.13), just as historical Rome was located on the Tiber. **17.3** *He carried me away in the spirit,* a vision trance in which the seer is transported to a remote place in the world; see note on 1.10. *Scarlet beast,* the Roman Empire. *Full of blasphemous names* with *seven heads and ten horns,* identical to the beast from the sea (13.1). **17.4** *Clothed in . . . pearls,* i.e., dressed like a wealthy courtesan (see 18.16). **17.5** *On her forehead was written a name* suggests the lowest form of prostitute, a tattooed slave. **17.6** *The saints,* the many Christian martyrs.

Alternate Ways of Counting the Roman Emperors Signified in Rev 17.10–11

	A	B	C	D	E	F	G	H
Julius Caesar (101–44 BCE)	1	1						1
Augustus (31 BCE–14 CE)	2	2	1	1				2
Tiberius (14–37 CE)	3	3	2	2				–
Gaius (37–41)	4	4	3	3	1			–
Claudius (41–54)	5	5	4	4	2			3
Nero (54–68)	6	6	5	5	3	1		–
Galba (June 68–January 69)	7	–	6	–	4	2	1	
Otho (69)	8	–	7	–	5	3	2	
Vitellius (69)		–	8	–	6	4	3	
Vespasian (69–79)	7		6		7	5	4	4
Titus (79–81)	8		7		8	6	5	5
Domitian (81–96)			8			7 (8)	6	6
[Neronic Antichrist]								7 (8)
Nerva (96–98)							7 (8)	

Column A begins with Julius Caesar, following a traditional way of counting the emperors (see Dio Chrysostom, *Discourses* 34.7; Josephus, *Antiquities* 18.32; *Sibylline Oracles* 5.12–51).

Column B modifies the sequence of Column A by omitting the three short–lived emperors of 68–69 CE

Column C reflects another traditional way of counting the emperors and begins with Augustus, the first actually to receive that title (see Virgil, *Aeneid* 6.789–97; Tacitus, *Annals* 1.1).

Column D modifies the sequence of Column C by omitting the three short–lived emperors of 68–69.

Column E reflects the judgment of some modern scholars that the enumeration begins with Gaius, infamous for his treatment of Jews.

Column F reflects the judgment of other modern scholars that the enumeration begins with Gaius, infamous for his treatment of Jews.

Column G represents the scheme of Victorinus of Pettau in his *Commentary on the Apocalypse* (17.9–11).

Column H shows the first five emperors deified by the Roman senate, followed by Domitian, who claimed divinity while living. The list concludes with a mythical, Nero-like adversary of God derived from legends about Nero's return from death (see *Sibylline Oracles* 4.138–39; 5.108–10, 214–27).

When I saw her, I was greatly amazed. [7]But the angel said to me, "Why are you so amazed? I will tell you the mystery of the woman, and of the beast with seven heads and ten horns that carries her. [8]The beast that you saw was, and is not, and is about to ascend from the bottomless pit and go to destruction. And the inhabitants of the earth, whose names have not been written in the book of life from the foundation of the world, will be amazed when they see the beast, because it was and is not and is to come.

[9] "This calls for a mind that has wisdom: the seven heads are seven mountains on which the woman is seated; also, they are seven kings, [10]of whom five have fallen, one is living, and the other has not yet come; and when he comes, he must remain only a little while. [11]As for the beast that was and is not, it is an eighth but it belongs to the seven, and it goes to destruction. [12]And the ten horns that you saw are ten kings who have not yet received a kingdom, but they are to receive authority as kings for one hour, together with the beast. [13]These are united in yielding their power and authority to the beast; [14]they will make war on the Lamb, and the Lamb will conquer them, for he is Lord of lords and King of kings, and those with him are called and chosen and faithful."

[15] And he said to me, "The waters that you saw, where the whore is seated, are peoples and multitudes and nations and languages. [16]And the ten horns that you saw, they and the beast will hate the whore; they will make her desolate and naked; they will devour her flesh and burn her up with fire. [17]For God has put it into their hearts to carry out his purpose by agreeing to give their kingdom to the beast, until the words of God will be fulfilled. [18]The woman you saw is the great city that rules over the kings of the earth."

The Fall of Babylon

18 After this I saw another angel coming down from heaven, having great authority; and the earth was made bright with his splendor. [2]He called out with a mighty voice,

"Fallen, fallen is Babylon the great!
    It has become a dwelling place of
        demons,
a haunt of every foul spirit,
    a haunt of every foul bird,
    a haunt of every foul and hateful
        beast. [a]
[3] For all the nations have drunk [b]
    of the wine of the wrath of her
        fornication,
and the kings of the earth have
        committed fornication with her,
and the merchants of the earth have
        grown rich from the power [c] of
        her luxury."

[4] Then I heard another voice from heaven saying,

"Come out of her, my people,
    so that you do not take part in her sins,
and so that you do not share in her
        plagues;
[5] for her sins are heaped high as heaven,

---

[a] Other ancient authorities lack the words *a haunt of every foul beast* and attach the words *and hateful* to the previous line so as to read *a haunt of every foul and hateful bird*   [b] Other ancient authorities read *She has made all nations drink*   [c] Or *resources*

17.8 *Ascend from the bottomless pit.* See 11.7. *It was and is not and is to come,* a parody of the divine title "who is and who was and who is to come" (see note on 1.4). *Is not,* here "has died." **17.9** *Seven mountains.* That Rome was located on seven hills was first popularized by Varro (116–27 BCE). *Seven kings,* either seven actual emperors (either Julius Caesar or Augustus could be counted as the first) or a symbol for a complete series. **17.11** *An eighth,* the returned Nero (see note on 13.3). **17.12** *Ten kings,* subordinate kings on the eastern borders of the empire. *One hour,* an extremely limited period (18.10, 17, 19). **17.14** *War on the Lamb,* the final end-time battle; see 16.12–16; 19.17–21. *Lord of lords and King of kings,* a title of Persian origin (Ezra 7.12) usually reserved for God (see Dan 4.37; 1 Tim 6.15; 1 Enoch 9.4). **17.15** *Waters* (see 17.1), often a symbol for threatening armies (see Isa 8.6–8; Jer 47.2). **17.16** *They will make her desolate and naked.* The returned Nero, with Parthian allies, will destroy Rome (see 16.19). *Devour her flesh,* an allusion to the fate of Jezebel (1 Kings 21.23–24).

18.1–19.10 Reactions to the fall of Babylon. **18.2** *Fallen, fallen is Babylon the great,* a phrase from Isa 21.9 used here to introduce a prophetic taunt anticipating Rome's fall (see also Isa 23–24; Jer 50–51; Ezek 26–27). *A haunt . . . beast,* i.e., a devastated ruin (see Jer 51.37). **18.3** *Fornication,* metaphor for political and religious subservience to Rome. *Merchants . . . have grown rich.* Wealthy Romans bought expensive products from everywhere (see vv. 11–13). Though Rome is implicitly condemned for economic exploitation, the criticism is softer than one might expect. **18.4** *Come out of her,* a prophetic summons to flight (see Isa 48.20–22; Jer 50.8–10; 51.6–10), probably carrying with it the connotation of not participating in the corrupt practices characteristic of pagan society. **18.5** *Sins . . . high as*

and God has remembered her
    iniquities.
6 Render to her as she herself has rendered,
    and repay her double for her deeds;
    mix a double draught for her in the
        cup she mixed.
7 As she glorified herself and lived
        luxuriously,
    so give her a like measure of torment
        and grief.
Since in her heart she says,
  'I rule as a queen;
I am no widow,
  and I will never see grief,'
8 therefore her plagues will come in a
        single day—
    pestilence and mourning and
        famine—
and she will be burned with fire;
    for mighty is the Lord God who judges
        her."

9 And the kings of the earth, who committed fornication and lived in luxury with her, will weep and wail over her when they see the smoke of her burning; 10they will stand far off, in fear of her torment, and say,

"Alas, alas, the great city,
  Babylon, the mighty city!
For in one hour your judgment has
    come."

11 And the merchants of the earth weep and mourn for her, since no one buys their cargo anymore, 12cargo of gold, silver, jewels and pearls, fine linen, purple, silk and scarlet, all kinds of scented wood, all articles of ivory, all articles of costly wood, bronze, iron, and marble, 13cinnamon, spice, incense, myrrh, frankincense, wine, olive oil, choice flour and wheat, cattle and sheep, horses and chariots, slaves—and human lives.*a*
14   "The fruit for which your soul longed
    has gone from you,
  and all your dainties and your splendor

are lost to you,
  never to be found again!"
15The merchants of these wares, who gained wealth from her, will stand far off, in fear of her torment, weeping and mourning aloud,
16   "Alas, alas, the great city,
    clothed in fine linen,
in purple and scarlet,
    adorned with gold,
with jewels, and with pearls!
17 For in one hour all this wealth has been
        laid waste!"

And all shipmasters and seafarers, sailors and all whose trade is on the sea, stood far off 18and cried out as they saw the smoke of her burning,
  "What city was like the great city?"
19And they threw dust on their heads, as they wept and mourned, crying out,
  "Alas, alas, the great city,
    where all who had ships at sea
    grew rich by her wealth!
For in one hour she has been laid waste."

20 Rejoice over her, O heaven, you saints and apostles and prophets! For God has given judgment for you against her.

21 Then a mighty angel took up a stone like a great millstone and threw it into the sea, saying,
  "With such violence Babylon the great
    city
  will be thrown down,
  and will be found no more;
22   and the sound of harpists and minstrels
    and of flutists and trumpeters
  will be heard in you no more;
  and an artisan of any trade
  will be found in you no more;
  and the sound of the millstone
  will be heard in you no more;
23   and the light of a lamp

---

a Or *chariots, and human bodies and souls*

---

heaven. See Jer 51.9. *God has remembered.* See note on 16.19. **18.6** *Render . . . for her deeds* alludes to Jer 50.29; 16.18. **18.7** *I rule as a queen.* The fatal pride of Rome is personalized in this brief hubristic soliloquy. **18.9–20** Three dirges adapted from Ezek 27: of kings (vv. 9–10), merchants (vv. 11–17a), and mariners (vv. 17b–20), an effective poetic way of underscoring the judgment of Babylon/Rome. **18.11** *The merchants . . . weep . . . for her,* ostensibly for her, but actually for themselves; Rome was the hub of a complex economic system that imported products from China, India, Africa,

and northern Europe. **18.12–13** The list of twenty-nine trade goods alludes to Ezek 16.9–13; 27.5–24. **18.16** *Purple and scarlet,* colors symbolic of royalty and evil. See note on 17.4. **18.18** *What city was like the great city?* The question is based on Ezek 27.32. **18.19** *Threw dust on their heads,* an act of mourning or sorrow (see Josh 7.6; Job 2.12; Lam 2.10). **18.20** *God has given . . . against her.* The martyrs' prayer of 6.10 is finally answered. **18.21** The *millstone* thrown into the sea symbolizes Rome's downfall (a symbolic prophetic action adapted from Jer 51.63–64).

will shine in you no more;
and the voice of bridegroom and bride
  will be heard in you no more;
for your merchants were the magnates of
    the earth,
  and all nations were deceived by your
    sorcery.
24 And in you[a] was found the blood of
    prophets and of saints,
  and of all who have been slaughtered
    on earth."

The Rejoicing in Heaven

19 After this I heard what seemed to be
the loud voice of a great multitude in
heaven, saying,
  "Hallelujah!
Salvation and glory and power to our
    God,
2   for his judgments are true and just;
  he has judged the great whore
  who corrupted the earth with her
    fornication,
  and he has avenged on her the blood of
    his servants."[b]
3 Once more they said,
  "Hallelujah!
  The smoke goes up from her forever and
    ever."
4 And the twenty-four elders and the four living creatures fell down and worshiped God
who is seated on the throne, saying,
  "Amen. Hallelujah!"
5 And from the throne came a voice saying,
  "Praise our God,
  all you his servants,[b]
  and all who fear him,
    small and great."
6 Then I heard what seemed to be the voice of a
great multitude, like the sound of many waters

and like the sound of mighty thunderpeals,
crying out,
  "Hallelujah!
  For the Lord our God
    the Almighty reigns.
7 Let us rejoice and exult
    and give him the glory,
  for the marriage of the Lamb has come,
    and his bride has made herself ready;
8   to her it has been granted to be clothed
    with fine linen, bright and pure"—
for the fine linen is the righteous deeds of the
saints.

9 And the angel said[c] to me, "Write this:
Blessed are those who are invited to the marriage supper of the Lamb." And he said to me,
"These are true words of God." 10 Then I fell
down at his feet to worship him, but he said to
me, "You must not do that! I am a fellow servant[d] with you and your comrades[e] who hold
the testimony of Jesus.[f] Worship God! For the
testimony of Jesus[f] is the spirit of prophecy."

The Rider on the White Horse

11 Then I saw heaven opened, and there was a
white horse! Its rider is called Faithful and
True, and in righteousness he judges and
makes war. 12 His eyes are like a flame of fire,
and on his head are many diadems; and he has
a name inscribed that no one knows but himself. 13 He is clothed in a robe dipped in[g] blood,
and his name is called The Word of God.
14 And the armies of heaven, wearing fine
linen, white and pure, were following him on
white horses. 15 From his mouth comes a sharp
sword with which to strike down the nations,
and he will rule[h] them with a rod of iron; he

a Gk her b Gk slaves c Gk he said d Gk slave
e Gk brothers f Or to Jesus g Other ancient authorities read
sprinkled with h Or will shepherd

19.1–10 A heavenly throne-room scene (see note on
4.1–11) reflects on Rome's fall (vv. 1–5) and anticipates the marriage of the Lamb (vv. 6–10). 19.1–6 Hallelujah, a Hebrew term meaning "praise Yah(weh)" (Ps
135.3), occurs in the NT only in these verses, though it
has become a familiar term in Jewish and Christian
liturgy. 19.6 A great multitude. See note on 7.9.
19.7 Marriage of the Lamb, metaphor for the union of
Christ as bridegroom and the church as bride (see 21.2,
9; 22.17; 2 Cor 11.2; Eph 5.25–33); for Israel as the
bride of God, see Isa 54.5; Hos 2.19–20. 19.9 Blessed.
See note on 1.3. 19.10 The spirit of prophecy. The
prophetic spirit is identified with the testimony about
Jesus, which is the essence of prophecy. 19.11–21.8 The
judgment of God's adversaries. 19.11–20.3 Christ

rides forth as a Divine Warrior (in continuity with the
widespread image of God in the OT as the Divine Warrior), leading the heavenly armies against God's adversaries (cf. 1.12–16). 19.11 Then I saw heaven opened,
stereotypical introduction to revelatory visions (see
Ezek 1.1; Mt 3.16; Jn 1.51; Acts 7.56; 10.11). The
white horse symbolizes victory. Rider, the Messiah.
19.13 Robe dipped in blood, the garment of a warrior
stained with the blood of his enemies (see Isa 63.1–6)
and perhaps also an oblique reference to his atoning
death (see 1.5; 7.14). The Word of God, a rare designation for Jesus (see Jn 1.1; 1 Jn 1.1; cf. Wis 18.15–16).
19.14 The armies of heaven, angelic hosts; a common
Hebrew name for God is "Lord of hosts," referring to
angelic armies under his command. 19.15 A sharp

will tread the wine press of the fury of the wrath of God the Almighty. 16On his robe and on his thigh he has a name inscribed, "King of kings and Lord of lords."

The Beast and Its Armies Defeated

17 Then I saw an angel standing in the sun, and with a loud voice he called to all the birds that fly in midheaven, "Come, gather for the great supper of God, 18to eat the flesh of kings, the flesh of captains, the flesh of the mighty, the flesh of horses and their riders—flesh of all, both free and slave, both small and great." 19Then I saw the beast and the kings of the earth with their armies gathered to make war against the rider on the horse and against his army. 20And the beast was captured, and with it the false prophet who had performed in its presence the signs by which he deceived those who had received the mark of the beast and those who worshiped its image. These two were thrown alive into the lake of fire that burns with sulfur. 21And the rest were killed by the sword of the rider on the horse, the sword that came from his mouth; and all the birds were gorged with their flesh.

The Thousand Years

20 Then I saw an angel coming down from heaven, holding in his hand the key to the bottomless pit and a great chain. 2He seized the dragon, that ancient serpent, who is the Devil and Satan, and bound him for a thousand years, 3and threw him into the pit,

and locked and sealed it over him, so that he would deceive the nations no more, until the thousand years were ended. After that he must be let out for a little while.

4 Then I saw thrones, and those seated on them were given authority to judge. I also saw the souls of those who had been beheaded for their testimony to Jesus[a] and for the word of God. They had not worshiped the beast or its image and had not received its mark on their foreheads or their hands. They came to life and reigned with Christ a thousand years. 5(The rest of the dead did not come to life until the thousand years were ended.) This is the first resurrection. 6Blessed and holy are those who share in the first resurrection. Over these the second death has no power, but they will be priests of God and of Christ, and they will reign with him a thousand years.

Satan's Doom

7 When the thousand years are ended, Satan will be released from his prison 8and will come out to deceive the nations at the four corners of the earth, Gog and Magog, in order to gather them for battle; they are as numerous as the sands of the sea. 9They marched up over the breadth of the earth and surrounded the camp of the saints and the beloved city. And fire came down from heaven[b] and con-

---

a Or for the testimony of Jesus   b Other ancient authorities read from God, out of heaven, or out of heaven from God

---

sword. See note on 1.16. He will rule . . . iron. See note on 12.5. Wine press. See note on 14.19. **19.16** King . . . lords. See note on 17.14. **19.17** Come, gather for the great supper of God, an invitation to birds (parodying ancient cultic dinner invitations) not to attend the messianic banquet (Isa 25.6–8; 55.1–2; Mt 8.11; Lk 13.29; 1 Enoch 62.14), but, in a reversal of that image, to eat the remains of the slaughtered enemies of God. **19.19** Beast, kings of the earth. See 16.12–14. **19.20** Lake of fire (20.10, 14–15; 21.8), a place of eternal punishment, located not in the underworld but in the presence of the Lamb (14.10), and elsewhere called Gehenna (see text note a to Mt 18.9). **20.2** Dragon. See 12.3. Ancient serpent, Devil, Satan. See 12.9, 10. The reference to a thousand years, i.e., the millennium, is unparalleled in Jewish eschatology. **20.4–6** During Satan's imprisonment the Christian martyrs are raised to life for a thousand-year reign with Christ. **20.4** Those seated on them were given authority to judge. The seated figures are not specified; the saints are sometimes associated with God in judgment (see Dan 7.9; Mt 19.28; 1 Cor 6.2). Those over whom they exercise judgment also remain unspecified. Those who had been beheaded, martyrs of rel-

atively high social status (more painful forms of execution were reserved for the lower classes). Not worshiped the beast or its image. See 13.11–18. Its mark. See 13.16. **20.5** The rest of the dead, all but the martyrs; in the author's mind they have a privileged position in God's plan. The first resurrection, restricted to Christian martyrs, is not mentioned elsewhere in the NT. **20.6** Blessed. See note on 1.3. Second death. See note on 2.11. **20.7–10** The release and second defeat of Satan are unparalleled in Jewish eschatology. **20.8** Gog and Magog, names for a hostile northern king and his nation (Ezek 38–39) that came to symbolize all of Israel's enemies; rabbinic sources refer to the final war as "the war of Gog and Magog" (see, e.g., Babylonian Talmud Berakot 7b; Sanhedrin 97b). Gather them for battle. See also 16.12–16; 19.19. As the sands of the sea, a metaphor for an enormous, terrifying army (see Josh 11.4; Judg 7.12). **20.9** Marched up. In the biblical idiom one always goes up, never down, to Jerusalem (Isa 2.3; Jer 31.6; Mic 4.2). The camp of the saints implies that the saints constitute an encamped army. The beloved city, Jerusalem (see Pss 78.68; 87.2; Sir 24.11). Fire came down from heaven, the divine destruction of the hostile forces (see Ezek 39.6).

sumed them. 10And the devil who had deceived them was thrown into the lake of fire and sulfur, where the beast and the false prophet were, and they will be tormented day and night forever and ever.

The Dead Are Judged

11 Then I saw a great white throne and the one who sat on it; the earth and the heaven fled from his presence, and no place was found for them. 12And I saw the dead, great and small, standing before the throne, and books were opened. Also another book was opened, the book of life. And the dead were judged according to their works, as recorded in the books. 13And the sea gave up the dead that were in it, Death and Hades gave up the dead that were in them, and all were judged according to what they had done. 14Then Death and Hades were thrown into the lake of fire. This is the second death, the lake of fire; 15and anyone whose name was not found written in the book of life was thrown into the lake of fire.

The New Heaven and the New Earth

21 Then I saw a new heaven and a new earth; for the first heaven and the first earth had passed away, and the sea was no more. 2And I saw the holy city, the new Jerusalem, coming down out of heaven from God, prepared as a bride adorned for her husband. 3And I heard a loud voice from the throne saying,

"See, the home*a* of God is among
     mortals.
He will dwell*b* with them;
they will be his peoples,*c*
and God himself will be with them;*d*

4 he will wipe every tear from their eyes.

Death will be no more;
mourning and crying and pain will be no
     more,
for the first things have passed away."

5 And the one who was seated on the throne said, "See, I am making all things new." Also he said, "Write this, for these words are trustworthy and true." 6Then he said to me, "It is done! I am the Alpha and the Omega, the beginning and the end. To the thirsty I will give water as a gift from the spring of the water of life. 7Those who conquer will inherit these things, and I will be their God and they will be my children. 8But as for the cowardly, the faithless,*e* the polluted, the murderers, the fornicators, the sorcerers, the idolaters, and all liars, their place will be in the lake that burns with fire and sulfur, which is the second death."

Vision of the New Jerusalem

9 Then one of the seven angels who had the seven bowls full of the seven last plagues came and said to me, "Come, I will show you the bride, the wife of the Lamb." 10And in the spirit*f* he carried me away to a great, high mountain and showed me the holy city Jerusalem coming down out of heaven from God. 11It has the glory of God and a radiance like a very rare jewel, like jasper, clear as crystal. 12It has a great, high wall with twelve gates, and at the gates twelve angels, and on the gates are inscribed the names of the twelve tribes of the Israelites; 13on the east three gates, on the north three gates, on the south three gates, and on the west three gates. 14And the wall of the city has

---

a Gk *the tabernacle*   *b* Gk *will tabernacle*   *c* Other ancient authorities read *people*   *d* Other ancient authorities add *and be their God*   *e* Or *the unbelieving*   *f* Or *in the Spirit*

20.10 *The lake of fire and sulfur.* See notes on 9.18; 19.20. **20.11–15** The final judgment embraces the rest of the dead (cf. 20.4–6). **20.11** *A great white throne,* the judgment seat of God. *The earth and the heaven fled from his presence,* a metaphor for the awesome theophanic majesty of God (taken literally in 21.1). **20.12** *Books were opened* (Dan 7.10). The plural suggests two sets of books, one for the righteous, the other for the wicked. *Book of life.* See note on 3.5. **20.13** *The sea,* one of the two abodes of the dead; *Death and Hades* were the abode under the earth. **20.14** *Second death.* See note on 2.11.

21.1–8 A new heaven and earth replace their earlier counterparts. **21.1** *A new heaven and a new earth,* an allusion to Isa 65.17; 66.22 (see also *Jubilees* 1.29; 4.26; *1 Enoch* 91.16); for Judaism the renewal of creation

constitutes the final eschatological event. **21.2** *The new Jerusalem.* Belief in a heavenly counterpart to the earthly Jerusalem was common in early Judaism and early Christianity (see Gal 4.26; Phil 3.20; Heb 11.10, 14–16). **21.3–8** Preparatory heavenly throne-room scene (see note on 4.1–11). **21.3** *The home . . . mortals,* an allusion to Ezek 37.26. **21.4** *Wipe every tear.* See note on 7.17. **21.5** *I am making all things new.* See Isa 43.19; cf. 2 Cor 5.17. **21.6** *I am . . . Omega* (spoken by God). See note on 1.8. *Water of life.* See note on 7.17. **21.7** *Those who conquer,* those faithful unto death (see 2.7, 11, 17, 26; 3.5, 12, 21). *I will be . . . my children.* The covenant relationship is often defined using the metaphor of adoption (see 2 Sam 7.14; Pss 2.7; 89.26–27; Jer 3.19; *Jubilees* 1.24). **21.8** *Second death.* See note on 2.11.

twelve foundations, and on them are the twelve names of the twelve apostles of the Lamb.

15 The angel[a] who talked to me had a measuring rod of gold to measure the city and its gates and walls. [16]The city lies foursquare, its length the same as its width; and he measured the city with his rod, fifteen hundred miles;[b] its length and width and height are equal. [17]He also measured its wall, one hundred forty-four cubits[c] by human measurement, which the angel was using. [18]The wall is built of jasper, while the city is pure gold, clear as glass. [19]The foundations of the wall of the city are adorned with every jewel; the first was jasper, the second sapphire, the third agate, the fourth emerald, [20]the fifth onyx, the sixth carnelian, the seventh chrysolite, the eighth beryl, the ninth topaz, the tenth chrysoprase, the eleventh jacinth, the twelfth amethyst. [21]And the twelve gates are twelve pearls, each of the gates is a single pearl, and the street of the city is pure gold, transparent as glass.

22 I saw no temple in the city, for its temple is the Lord God the Almighty and the Lamb. [23]And the city has no need of sun or moon to shine on it, for the glory of God is its light, and its lamp is the Lamb. [24]The nations will walk by its light, and the kings of the earth will bring their glory into it. [25]Its gates will never be shut by day—and there will be no night there. [26]People will bring into it the glory and the honor of the nations. [27]But nothing unclean will enter it, nor anyone who practices abomination or falsehood, but only those who are written in the Lamb's book of life.

The River of Life

22 Then the angel[d] showed me the river of the water of life, bright as crystal, flowing from the throne of God and of the Lamb [2]through the middle of the street of the city. On either side of the river is the tree of life[e] with its twelve kinds of fruit, producing its fruit each month; and the leaves of the tree are for the healing of the nations. [3]Nothing accursed will be found there any more. But the throne of God and of the Lamb will be in it, and his servants[f] will worship him; [4]they will see his face, and his name will be on their foreheads. [5]And there will be no more night; they need no light of lamp or sun, for the Lord God will be their light, and they will reign forever and ever.

6 And he said to me, "These words are trustworthy and true, for the Lord, the God of the spirits of the prophets, has sent his angel to show his servants[f] what must soon take place."

7 "See, I am coming soon! Blessed is the one who keeps the words of the prophecy of this book."

Epilogue and Benediction

8 I, John, am the one who heard and saw these things. And when I heard and saw them, I fell down to worship at the feet of the angel who showed them to me; [9]but he said to me, "You must not do that! I am a fellow servant[g] with you and your comrades[h] the prophets, and with those who keep the words of this book. Worship God!"

10 And he said to me, "Do not seal up the words of the prophecy of this book, for the time is near. [11]Let the evildoer still do evil, and the filthy still be filthy, and the righteous still do right, and the holy still be holy."

---

a Gk He   *b* Gk twelve thousand stadia   *c* That is, almost seventy-five yards   *d* Gk he   *e* Or the Lamb. [2]In the middle of the street of the city, and on either side of the river, is the tree of life   *f* Gk slaves   *g* Gk slave   *h* Gk brothers

---

21.9–22.7 The final vision: the new Jerusalem. **21.9** *Wife of the Lamb.* See note on 19.7. **21.10** *In the spirit . . . mountain.* See notes on 1.10; 17.3; see also Ezek 40.2. **21.15** The *measuring rod* is to reveal structure and size to the reader; see note on 11.1. **21.16** *The city lies foursquare,* i.e., it forms a gigantic cube; the square shape dominates the eschatological temple in Ezek 40–48 and the Dead Sea Scrolls *Temple Scroll* (11Q19). **21.18–21** On the use of precious stones in the construction of the future temple, a metaphor for magnificence and luxury, see Isa 54.11–12; Tob 13.16–17. **21.23** *The glory of God is its light.* See Isa 60.19–20. **21.27** *Nothing unclean will enter it.* It is like a sanctuary in that nothing profane is allowed in. In the Dead Sea Scrolls and the OT, the sanctity of the temple was sometimes extended to the city (see Isa 52.1). *The Lamb's book of life.* See note on 3.5. **22.1** *The river of the water of life.* See Ezek 47.1–12; Zech 14.8. **22.2** *The tree of life,* a collective noun meaning "trees" (see Ezek 47.7–12; cf. Gen 2.9). *Twelve kinds of fruit* suggests the miraculous fruitfulness of the new world (Ezek 47.12; cf. *1 Enoch* 10.19). *The tree.* The author reverts to a single tree of life (see note on 2.7). *Healing of the nations,* i.e., their conversion. **22.4** *They will see his face.* According to OT tradition, no one can see God (see Ex 33.20; Deut 4.12; see also Jn 1.18; 6.46; 1 Jn 4.12). *His name will be on their foreheads.* See note on 7.3. **22.6** *The spirits of the prophets,* the individual spirits of all the prophets (see 1 Cor 14.32). *His angel.* See note on 1.1. **22.7** *I am coming soon.* See note on 3.11. *Blessed.* See note on 1.3. **22.8–21** Epilogue and benediction. **22.10** *Do not seal up . . . this book.* Jewish apocalypses sometimes contain

12 "See, I am coming soon; my reward is with me, to repay according to everyone's work. [13] I am the Alpha and the Omega, the first and the last, the beginning and the end."

14 Blessed are those who wash their robes,[a] so that they will have the right to the tree of life and may enter the city by the gates. [15] Outside are the dogs and sorcerers and fornicators and murderers and idolaters, and everyone who loves and practices falsehood.

16 "It is I, Jesus, who sent my angel to you with this testimony for the churches. I am the root and the descendant of David, the bright morning star."

17   The Spirit and the bride say, "Come."
And let everyone who hears say, "Come."
And let everyone who is thirsty come.

Let anyone who wishes take the water of
life as a gift.

18 I warn everyone who hears the words of the prophecy of this book: if anyone adds to them, God will add to that person the plagues described in this book; [19] if anyone takes away from the words of the book of this prophecy, God will take away that person's share in the tree of life and in the holy city, which are described in this book.

20 The one who testifies to these things says, "Surely I am coming soon."
Amen. Come, Lord Jesus!

21 The grace of the Lord Jesus be with all the saints. Amen.[b]

---

a Other ancient authorities read *do his commandments*
b Other ancient authorities lack *all*; others lack *the saints*; others lack *Amen*

---

a command to seal the book until the end (see Dan 12.4, 9). **22.13** *I am . . . Omega* (spoken by Christ). See note on 1.8. **22.14** *Blessed.* See note on 1.3. *Who wash their robes.* See note on 7.14. *The tree of life.* See note on 2.7. *Enter the city by the gates,* enter as a citizen, not a thief (see Jn 10.1). **22.15** *Outside.* See note on 21.27.

22.16 *My angel.* See note on 1.1. *Root and the descendant of David.* See note on 5.5. *Bright morning star.* See note on 2.28. **22.17** *Water of life.* See note on 7.17. **22.19** *Tree of life.* See note on 2.7. *Holy city,* the new Jerusalem (21.9–27). **22.21** Revelation ends like a letter (see, e.g., 1 Thess 5.28); see note on 1.4–5a.

The purpose of this table is to help readers study the early church's use and interpretation of the Jewish scriptures. It does not include every possible reference, but only direct quotations and clear allusions to specific passages. The chapter and verse numbering is that of the NRSV.

In using the table, it is important to bear in mind that the NT authors, writing in Greek, generally quoted from the ancient Greek translation of the Hebrew scriptures (known as the Septuagint), whereas the NRSV OT is translated directly from the Hebrew and Aramaic texts. Also, ancient Jewish and Christian interpreters, including the NT authors, were less concerned with the original sense of the Hebrew scriptures than with finding useful and appropriate applications of them in their own situations. For these reasons, there are often differences in wording or meaning between an OT passage and a NT quotation of it.

JEWISH SCRIPTURES (OT)	NEW TESTAMENT	JEWISH SCRIPTURES (OT)	NEW TESTAMENT
Genesis		**Genesis** (cont.)	
1.26	Jas 3.9	25.23	Rom 9.12
1.27	Mt. 19.4; Mk 10.6	26.3–4	Acts 3.25; Gal 3.8, 16
2.2	Heb 4.4	28.12	Jn 1.51
2.7	1 Cor 15.45	28.13–14	Acts 3.25; Gal 3.8
2.24	Mt 19.5; Mk 10.7–8;	47.31	Heb 11.21
	1 Cor 6.16; Eph 5.31		
3.17–18	Heb 6.8	**Exodus**	
5.24	Heb 11.5	1.8	Acts 7.18
12.1	Acts 7.3	2.11–15	Acts 7.23–29
12.3	Acts 3.25; Gal 3.8	2.14	Acts 7.35
12.7	Gal 3.16	3.5–10	Acts 7.32–34
13.15	Gal 3.16	3.6	Mt 22.32; Mk 12.26;
14.17–20	Heb 7.1–2		Lk 20.37; Acts 3.13
15.5	Rom 4.18; Heb 11.12	3.12	Acts 7.7
15.6	Rom 4.3, 9, 22; Gal 3.6;	3.15	Mt 22.32; Mk 12.26;
	Jas 2.23		Lk 20.37; Acts 3.13; 7.32
15.13–14	Acts 7.6–7	9.16	Rom 9.17
17.5	Rom 4.17	12.46	Jn 19.36
17.7	Gal 3.16	13.2	Lk 2.23
17.8	Acts 7.5; Gal 3.16	16.4	Jn 6.31
18.10	Rom 9.9	16.18	2 Cor 8.15
18.18	Acts 3.25; Gal 3.8	19.5–6	1 Pet 2.9
21.10	Gal 4.30	19.12–13	Heb 12.20
21.12	Rom 9.7; Heb 11.18	20.12–16	Mt. 19.18–19; Mk 10.19;
22.9	Jas 2.21		Lk 18.20
22.16–17	Heb 6.13–14	20.12	Mt 15.4; Mk 7.10; Eph
22.17	Heb 11.12		6.2–3
22.18	Acts 3.25; Gal 3.8, 16	20.13–15, 17	Rom 13.9

Based on the appendix to *Old Testament Quotations in the New Testament*, 3d ed., edited by Robert G. Bratcher. London, New York, and Stuttgart: United Bible Societies, 1987. Used with permission of United Bible Societies.

Quotations of the Jewish Scriptures in the New Testament

JEWISH SCRIPTURES (OT)	NEW TESTAMENT	JEWISH SCRIPTURES (OT)	NEW TESTAMENT
Exodus (*cont.*)		**Deuteronomy** (*cont.*)	
20.13–14	Jas 2.11	5.17–18	Jas 2.11
20.13	Mt 5.21	5.17	Mt 5.21
20.14	Mt 5.27	5.18	Mt 5.27
20.17	Rom 7.7	5.21	Rom 7.7
21.17	Mt 15.4; Mk 7.10	6.4–5	Mk 12.29–30; 12.32–33
21.24	Mt 5.38	6.5	Mt 22.37; Lk 10.27
22.28	Acts 23.5	6.13	Mt 4.10; Lk 4.8
24.8	Heb 9.20	6.16	Mt 4.7; Lk 4.12
25.40	Heb 8.5	8.3	Mt 4.4; Lk 4.4
32.1, 23	Acts 7.40	9.19	Heb 12.21
32.6	1 Cor 10.7	17.6	Heb 10.28
33.19	Rom 9.15	17.7	1 Cor 5.13
34.30	2 Cor 3.7	18.15–19	Acts 3.22–23
34.33, 35	2 Cor 3.13	18.15	Acts 7.37
34.34	2 Cor 3.16	19.15	Mt 18.16; Jn 8.17; 2 Cor 13.1; 1 Tim 5.19
Leviticus		19.19	1 Cor 5.13
11.44–45	1 Pet 1.16	19.21	Mt 5.38
12.6–8	Lk 2.24	21.23	Gal 3.13
16.27	Heb 13.11	22.21, 24	1 Cor 5.13
18.5	Rom 10.5; Gal 3.12	24.1	Mt 5.31; 19.7; Mk 10.4
19.2	1 Pet 1.16	24.7	1 Cor 5.13
19.12	Mt 5.33	25.4	1 Cor 9.9; 1 Tim 5.18
19.18	Mt 5.43; 19.19; 22.39; Mk 12.31, 33; Lk 10.27; Rom 13.9; Gal 5.14; Jas 2.8	25.5	Mt 22.24; Mk 12.19; Lk 20.28
24.20	Mt 5.38	27.26	Gal 3.10
26.12	2 Cor 6.16	29.4	Rom 11.8
		29.18	Heb 12.15
Numbers		30.12–14	Rom 10.6–8
9.12	Jn 19.36	31.6, 8	Heb 13.5
12.7	Heb 3.2, 5	32.17	1 Cor 10.20
27.17	Mt 9.36; Mk 6.34	32.21	Rom 10.19; 1 Cor 10.22
30.2	Mt 5.33	32.35	Rom 12.19; Heb 10.30
		32.36	Heb 10.30
		32.43	Rom 15.10; Heb 1.6
Deuteronomy			
4.24	Heb 12.29	**Joshua**	
4.35	Mk 12.32	1.5	Heb 13.5
5.16–20	Mt 19.18–19; Mk 10.19; Lk 18.20		
		1 Samuel	
5.16	Mt 15.4; Mk 7.10; Eph 6.2–3	2.1	Lk 1.46–47
		2.26	Lk 2.52
5.17–19, 21	Rom 13.9	13.14	Acts 13.22

Quotations of the Jewish Scriptures in the New Testament

JEWISH SCRIPTURES (OT)	NEW TESTAMENT	JEWISH SCRIPTURES (OT)	NEW TESTAMENT
2 Samuel		**Psalms** *(cont.)*	
7.8, 14	2 Cor 6.18	22.18	Mt 27.35; Mk 15.24; Lk 23.34; Jn 19.24
7.12–13	Acts 2.30	22.22	Heb 2.12
7.14	Heb 1.5	24.1	1 Cor 10.26
22.50	Rom 15.9	31.5	Lk 23.46
		32.1–2	Rom 4.7–8
1 Kings		34.8	1 Pet 2.3
19.10, 14	Rom 11.3	34.12–16	1 Pet 3.10–12
19.18	Rom 11.4	34.20	Jn 19.36
22.17	Mt 9.36; Mk 6.34	36.1	Rom 3.18
		35.19	Jn 15.25
2 Kings		37.11	Mt 5.5
1.10, 12	Lk 9.54	40.6–8	Heb 10.5–9
		41.9	Jn 13.18
2 Chronicles		44.22	Rom 8.36
18.16	Mt 9.36; Mk 6.34	45.6–7	Heb 1.8–9
		48.2	Mt 5.35
Nehemiah		51.4	Rom 3.4
9.15	Jn 6.31	68.18	Eph 4.8
		69.4	Jn 15.25
Job		69.9	Jn 2.17; Rom 15.3
5.13	1 Cor 3.19	69.21	Mt 27.48; Mk 15.36; Jn 19.28–29
41.11	Rom 11.35	69.22–23	Rom 11.9–10
		69.25	Acts 1.20
Psalms		78.2	Mt 13.35
2.1–2	Acts 4.25–26	78.24	Jn 6.31
2.7	Mk 1.11; Lk 3.22; Acts 13.33; Heb 1.5; 5.5	82.6	Jn 10.34
2.8–9	Rev 2.26–27	90.4	2 Pet 3.8
4.4	Eph 4.26	91.11–12	Mt 4.6; Lk 4.10–11
5.9	Rom 3.13	94.11	1 Cor 3.20
8.2	Mt 21.26	94.14	Rom 11.2
8.4–6	Heb 2.6–8	95.7–11	Heb 3.7–11
8.6	1 Cor 15.27; Eph 1.22	95.11	Heb 3.18; 4.3, 5, 10
10.7	Rom 3.14	102.25–27	Heb 1.10–12
14.1–3	Rom 3.10–12	103.8	Jas 5.11
16.8–11	Acts 2.25–28	103.17	Lk 1.50
16.10	Acts 2.31; 13.35	104.4	Heb 1.7
18.49	Rom 15.9	109.8	Acts 1.20
19.4	Rom 10.18	110.1	Mt 22.44; 26.64; Mk 12.36; 14.62; 16.19; Lk 20.42–43; 22.69; Acts 2.34–35; 1 Cor 15.25;
22.1	Mt 27.46; Mk 15.34		
22.7	Mt 27.39; Mk 15.29; Lk 23.35		
22.8	Mt 27.43		

JEWISH SCRIPTURES (OT)	NEW TESTAMENT	JEWISH SCRIPTURES (OT)	NEW TESTAMENT
Psalms (cont.)		**Isaiah** (cont.)	
110.1 (cont.)	Eph 1.20; Col 3.1; Heb 1.3, 13; 8.1; 10.12–13; 12.2	11.4	2 Thess 2.8
		11.5	Eph 6.14
		11.10	Rom 15.12
110.4	Heb 5.6; 7.17, 21	14.13, 15	Mt 11.23; Lk 10.15
112.9	2 Cor 9.9	22.13	1 Cor 15.32
116.10	2 Cor 4.13	22.22	Rev 3.7
117.1	Rom 15.11	24.17	Lk 21.35
118.6	Heb 13.6	25.7	1 Cor 15.54
118.22–23	Mt 21.42; Mk 12.10–11; Lk 20.17	28.11–12	1 Cor 14.21
		28.16	Rom 9.33; 10.11; 1 Pet 2.6
118.22	Acts 4.11; 1 Pet 2.7		
118.25–26	Mt 21.9; Mk 11.9; Jn 12.13	29.10	Rom 11.8
118.26	Mt 23.39; Lk 13.35; 19.38	29.13	Mt 15.8–9; Mk 7.6–7; Col 2.22
132.11	Acts 2.30		
135.14	Heb 10.30	29.14	1 Cor 1.19
140.3	Rom 3.13	29.16	Rom 9.20
143.2	Rom 3.20	35.3	Heb 12.12
		35.5–6	Mt 11.5; Lk 7.22
Proverbs		40.3–5	Lk 3.4–6
3.4	2 Cor 8.21	40.3	Mt 3.3; Mk 1.3; Jn 1.23
3.11–12	Heb 12.5–6	40.6–8	1 Pet 1.24–25
3.12	Rev 3.19	40.13	Rom 11.34; 1 Cor 2.16
3.34	Jas 4.6; 1 Pet 5.5	41.8	Jas 2.23
4.26	Heb 12.13	42.1–4	Mt 12.18–21
10.12	1 Pet 4.8	42.1	Mt 3.17; 17.5; Mk 1.11; Lk 3.22; 9.35; 2 Pet 1.17
11.31	1 Pet 4.18		
22.9	2 Cor 9.7	43.20–21	1 Pet 2.9
25.21–22	Rom 12.20	45.9	Rom 9.20
26.11	2 Pet 2.22	45.23	Rom 14.11; Phil 2.10–11
		49.1	Gal 1.15
Isaiah		49.6	Acts 13.47
1.9	Rom 9.29	49.8	2 Cor 6.2
5.1–2	Mt 21.33; Mk 12.1	52.5	Rom 2.24
6.3	Rev 4.8	52.7	Rom 10.15; Eph 6.15
6.9–10	Mk 4.12; Acts 28.26–27	52.11	2 Cor 6.17
6.9	Mt 13.14–15; Lk 8.10	52.15	Rom 15.21
6.10	Jn 12.40	53.1	Jn 12.38; Rom 10.16
7.14	Mt 1.23	53.4–6	1 Pet 2.24–25
8.12–13	1 Pet 3.14–15	53.4	Mt 8.17
8.14	Rom 9.33; 1 Pet 2.8	53.7–8	Acts 8.32–33
8.17–18	Heb 2.13	53.9	1 Pet 2.22
9.1–2	Mt 4.15–16	53.12	Lk 22.37; Heb 9.28; 1 Pet 2.24
10.22–23	Rom 9.27–28		

Quotations of the Jewish Scriptures in the New Testament

JEWISH SCRIPTURES (OT)	NEW TESTAMENT	JEWISH SCRIPTURES (OT)	NEW TESTAMENT
Isaiah *(cont.)*		**Daniel** *(cont.)*	
54.1	Gal 4.27	7.25	Rev 12.14
54.13	Jn 6.45	11.31	Mt 24.15; Mk 13.14
55.3	Acts 13.34	11.36	2 Thess 2.4
56.7	Mt 21.13; Mk 11.17; Lk 19.46	12.7	Rev 12.14
		12.11	Mt 24.15; Mk 13.14
57.19	Eph 2.17		
59.7–8	Rom 3.15–17	**Hosea**	
59.17	Eph 6.14, 17; 1 Thess 5.8	1.10	Rom 9.26
59.20–21	Rom 11.26–27	2.23	Rom 9.25; 1 Pet 2.10
61.1–2	Lk 4.18–19	6.6	Mt 9.13; 12.7
61.1	Mt 11.5; Lk 7.22	10.8	Lk 23.30; Rev 6.16
64.4	1 Cor 2.9	11.1	Mt 2.15
65.1–2	Rom 10.20–21	13.14	1 Cor 15.55
65.17	2 Pet 3.13; Rev 21.2		
66.1–2	Acts 7.49–50	**Joel**	
66.1	Mt 5.34–35	2.28–32	Acts 2.17–21
66.15	2 Thess 1.8	2.32	Rom 10.13
66.24	Mk 9.48		
		Amos	
Jeremiah		5.25–27	Acts 7.42–43
1.5	Gal 1.15–16	9.11–12	Acts 15.16–18
5.21	Mk 8.18		
7.11	Mt 21.13; Mk 11.17; Lk 19.46	**Jonah**	
		1.17	Mt 12.40
9.24	1 Cor 1.31; 2 Cor 10.17		
18.6	Rom 9.21	**Micah**	
22.5	Mt 23.38; Lk 13.35	5.2	Mt 2.6; Jn 7.42
31.15	Mt 2.18	7.6	Mt 10.35–36; Lk 12.53
31.31–34	Heb 8.8–12		
31.33–34	Rom 11.27; Heb 10.16–17		
		Nahum	
Ezekiel		1.15	Eph 6.15
12.2	Mk 8.18		
34.5	Mt 9.36; Mk 6.34	**Habakkuk**	
37.27	2 Cor 6.16	1.5	Acts 13.41
		2.3–4	Heb 10.37–38
Daniel		2.4	Rom 1.17; Gal 3.11
5.23	Rev 9.20		
7.2–7	Rev 13.1–2	**Haggai**	
7.13	Mt 24.30; 26.64; Mk 13.26; 14.62; Lk 21.27; Rev 1.7	2.6	Heb 12.26
		Zechariah	
7.21	Rev 13.7	8.16	Eph 4.25

Quotations of the Jewish Scriptures in the New Testament

JEWISH SCRIPTURES (OT)	NEW TESTAMENT	JEWISH SCRIPTURES (OT)	NEW TESTAMENT
Zechariah *(cont.)*		**Malachi**	
9.9	Mt 21.5; Jn 12.15	1.2–3	Rom 9.13
10.2	Mt 9.36; Mk 6.34	3.1	Mt 11.10; Mk 1.2;
11.12–13	Mt 27.9–10		Lk 1.76; 7.27
11.12	Mt 26.15	4.5–6	Mt 17.10–11;
12.10	Jn 19.37; Rev 1.7		Mk 9.11–12;
13.7	Mt 26.31; Mk 14.27		Lk 1.17

Index to Color Maps

This index lists geographical names found in the color maps at the back of the book. The numbers of the map(s) on which the name appears is listed first, followed by the key, or grid reference (a letter-figure combination that refers to the letters and figures at the margins of the map). Places whose names have changed over time are identified by a "see also" reference. For example, the entry for Azotus indicates it can be found on Map 11 in location B-5, and on Map 13 in location A-5, and readers are referred to Ashdod, its alternate name.

Abel, 4, C-2; *see also* Abel-beth-maacah

Abel-beth-maacah, 5, 7, C-1

Abel-meholah, 5, C-3

Abila (in Abilene), 13, D-1

Abila (in Decapolis), 11, D-2; 13, 18, D-3

Abilene, 13, D-1

Abydos (in Egypt), 2, B-4; 6, C-4

Abydos (in Greece), 6, B-1

Acco, 1, 3, 5, 7, 9, 18, B-2; 4, B-3; *see also* Ptolemais

Acco (region), 9, B-2

Accrabah, 9, C-4

Achaia, 12, D-3; 17, C-2

Achshaph, 3, B-3

Achzib, 3, 7, 9, 18, B-2

Achzib (region), 9, B-2

Adam, 3, C-4

Adasa, 11, C-4

Adida, 11, B-4

Adora, 11, B-5

Adoraim, 5, 7, B-5

Adramyttium, 17, D-2

Adria, Sea of, 12, C-2; 17, B-1

Adullam, 3, 5, 7, 9, 11, B-5

Aegean Sea, 6, B-1; 10, A-2; 12, D-3; 17, C-2

Aenon, 13, C-4

Africa, 12, C-3

Agade, 2, E-3

Agrigentum, 17, A-2

Agrippias, 13, A-6

Agrippina, 13, C-3

Ahlab, 3, C-2

Ai, 3, 9, 18, C-4

Aiath, 7, C-4

Aijalon, 3, 5, 7, B-4

Aijalon River, 1, B-4

Ain Feshka, 18, C-5

Ain Ghazzal, 18, D-4

Ain Karim, 18, B-5

Akhetaton (Tell el-Amarna), 2, B-4

Akkad, 2, E-3

Akrabattene, 11, C-6

Akrabbim, Ascent of, 5, B-6

Alaca Huyuk, 2, C-1

Alalakh, 2, C-2

Alashiya (Kittim), 2, B-2; *see also* Cyprus

Albis River, 12, C-1

Aleppo, 6, D-2

Alexandria (in Egypt), 10, A-3; 12, E-3; 17, E-4

Alexandria Arion (Herat), 10, E-2

Alexandria Harmozia, 10, D-3

Alexandria Arachosiorum, 10, E-3

Alexandria Eschata, 10, F-2

Alexandrium, 11, 13, C-4

Alpes, 12, B-2

Alps (mountains), 12, C-2

Amalek (people), 4, B-5

Amasia, 17, F-1

Amathus, 11, C-3; 13, C-4

Amisus, 17, F-1

Amman, 1, 18, D-4; *see also* Rabbah

Ammon, 1, 3, 5, 7, D-4; 4, 9, C-4; 6, C-3

Amon, Temple of, 8, 10, A-3

Amphipolis, 17, C-1

Anat, 6, D-2; 8, C-2

Anathoth, 7, 9, C-4

Ancyra, 6, C-1; 8, B-1; 10, B-2; 12, E-2; 17, E-1

Ankuwa, 2, C-1

Anthedon, 11, A-5

Antioch (in Pisidia), 17, E-2

Antioch (in Syria), 12, E-3; 17, F-2

Antipatris, 13, 18, B-4; *see also* Aphek (in Ephraim)

Antonia, Fortress (in Jerusalem), 16, B-4

Aphairema, 11, C-4; *see also* Ephraim

Aphek (in Asher), 3, B-2

Aphek (in Ephraim), 3, 5, 7, 18, B-4

Aphek (in Geshur), 5, 7, C-2

Apollonia (in E. Macedonia), 17, C-1

Apollonia (in W. Macedonia), 17, B-1

Apollonia (in Palestine), 9, 11, 13, B-4

Apollonia (in Thrace), 8, B-1

Appius, Forum of, 17, A-1

Aqueduct (in Jerusalem), 16, A-5, B-6

Aquileia, 12, C-2

Aquitania, 12, B-2

Ar, 5, 7, C-5

Arabah (rift valley), 1, 5, C-6; 4, B-5

Arabia, 10, C-3; 12, F-4

Arabian Sea, 10, E-4

Arabs (Aribi, people), 6, D-3; 8, C-3

Arachosia, 8, F-2; 10, F-3

Arad, 3, C-5; 4, B-4; 5, 7, B-5; 11, C-6; 18, B-6

Arad-EB, 18, B-6

Aral Sea, 8, 10, E-1

Aram (Syria), 5, 7, D-1

Aram-Damascus, 4, C-2–D-2

Arameans (people), 3, D-1

Aram-zobah, 4, D-1
Araq el-Emir, 18, D-4
Ararat (Urartu), 6, D-1
Ararat, Mount, 2, 6, E-1
Araxes River, 2, 6, E-1; 8, D-1
Arbela (in Assyria), 2, 6, E-2; 8, D-2; 10, C-2
Arbela (in Decapolis), 13, D-3
Arbela (in Galilee), 11, C-2
Archelais, 13, C-5
Areopolis, 13, D-6
Argob, 4, C-3
Aria, 8, F-2; 10, E-2
Aribi (Arabs, people), 6, D-3
Arimathea, 13, B-4
Armenia, 10, C-2; 12, F-2
Arnon River, 1, 3, 5, 7, 9, C-5; 11, D-5; 13, C-6
Aroer (in Moab), 3, 5, 7, C-5; 4, C-4; 18, D-5
Arpad, 6, D-2
Artaxata, 12, F-2
Arvad, 2, 6, 8, C-2; 4, C-1
Arzawa, 2, B-1
Ascalon, 11, 13, A-5; *see also* Ashkelon
Asdudu, 7, A-5
Ashdod, 3, 4, B-4; 5, 7, A-4; 9, 18, A-5; *see also* Azotus
Ashdod (region), 9, A-5
Asher (tribe), 3, B-2
Ashkelon, 3, B-5; 5, 7, 9, 18, A-5; 4, B-4; *see also* Acalon
Ashtaroth, 3, D-3; 4, C-3; 5, 7, D-2
Asia, 12, D-3; 17, D-2
Asia Minor, 10, B-2
Asochis, 13, C-3
Asphaltitis, Lake, 13, C-5–C-6; *see also* Dead Sea; Salt Sea
Asshur, 2, D-2, 6, E-2; 8, C-2
Assos, 17, D-2
Assuwa, 2, B-1
Assyria, 2, 6, D-2; 8, C-2
Assyrian Empire, 6, C-3–E-2; 7, B-4–C-2
Astacus, 6, B-1
Ataroth, 5, 7, C-5
Athens, 6, A-1; 8, 10, A-2; 12, D-3; 17, C-2
Atlantic Ocean, 12, A-1
Atlit, 18, B-2
Attalia, 17, E-2
Augusta Treverorum, 12, C-1
Avaris, 2, B-3
Azekah, 7, 9, 18, B-5
Azotus, 11, B-5; 13, A-5; *see also* Ashdod

Bab edh-Drah, 18, C-6
Babylon, 2, 6, E-3; 8, D-2; 10, C-3
Babylonia,
Bablonian Empire, New, 8, C-2
Bactra, 8, F-2; 10, E-2
Bactria, 8, F-2; 10, E-2
Baetica, 12, A-2
Bashan, 1, 3, 5, D-2
Batanea, 13, C-2
Beas (Hyphasis) River, 10, F-3
Beeroth, 9, B-4
Beer-sheba (Beersheba), 1, B-6; 2, C-3; 3, B-5; 4, B-4; 5, 7, 11, 18, B-6; *see also* Bersabe
Behistun, 8, D-2
Belgica, 12, B-1
Bene-berak, 7, B-4
Beneventum, 17, A-1
Benjamin (tribe), 3, C-4
Beroea, 17, C-1
Berothai, 4, C-2
Bersabe, 13, B-6; *see also* Beer-sheba
Berytus, 4, C-2
Besor River, 1, 5, 7, A-6; 3, B-5
Beth Alpha, 18, C-3
Beth-anath, 3, C-2
Bethany, 13, C-5
Betharamphtha (Livias, Julias), 13, C-5
Bethbasi, 11, C-5
Beth-dagon, 7, 11, B-4
Bethel, 1, 3, C-4; 4, 5, 7, B-4; 11, 18, C-4
Bethesda (Bethzatha), Pool of (in Jerusalem), 16, B-4
Beth-ezel, 7, B-5
Beth-gilgal, 9, C-4
Beth-haccherem, 9, B-5
Beth-horon, 4, B-4; 11, B-4
Bethlehem, 1, 5, 7, 9, 13, B-5; 18, C-5
Beth-pelet, 9, B-6
Beth-rehob, 4, C-2
Bethsaida-Julias, 13, C-2
Beth-shan, 1, 3, 4, 5, 7, 9, 18, C-3; *see also* Scythopolis
Beth Shearim, 18, B-3
Beth-shemesh (in Issachar), 3, C-2
Beth-shemesh (in Judah), 3, 4, B-4; 5, 7, 18, B-5
Bethsura, 13, B-5
Beth-yerah, 9, 18, C-2
Beth-zacharias, 11, B-5
Bethzatha (Bethesda), Pool of (in Jerusalem), 16, B-4

Beth-zur, 3, 5, 7, 18, B-5; 11, C-5
Beycesultan, 2, B-1
Bezer, 3, D-4
Bithynia, 10, B-1; 12, E-2; 17, E-1
Black Sea, 8, 10, B-1; 12, E-2; 17, E-1–E-2
Borsippa, 6, E-3
Bosporus Kingdom, 12, E-2
Bosra, 18, D-3
Bozrah, 4, C-5
Britannia, 12, B-1
Bubastis, 6, C-3
Bucephala, 10, F-2
Burdigala, 12, B-2
Byblos, *see* Gebal
Byzantium, 8, B-1; 12, D-2; 17, D-1
Cabul, 4, B-3; 5, B-2
Cadasa, 11, C-1; 13, C-2; *see also* Kedesh
Caesarea (in Mauretania), 12, B-3
Caesarea (in Palestine), 1, 13, 18, B-3; 17, F-4
Caesarea Augusta, 12, B-2
Caesarea Mazaca, 17, F-2
Caesarea Philippi, 13, C-2; *see also* Paneas
Caiaphas, House of (in Jerusalem), 16, B-6
Calah, 2, D-2; 6, E-2
Caleb (tribe), 3, B-5
Callirrhoe, 13, C-5
Cana, 13, C-2
Capernaum, 13, 18, C-2
Capharsaba, 11, B-4
Capharsalama, 11, C-4
Caphtor, 2, A-2; *see also* Crete
Capitolias, 13, D-3
Cappadocia, 12, E-2; 17, F-2
Caralis, 12, C-2
Carchemish, 2, 8, C-2; 6, D-2
Caria, 17, D-2
Carmania, 8, 10, E-3
Carmel, Mount, 1, 4, 13, B-3; 5, 7, 9, 11, B-2
Carmel Caves, 18, B-2
Carnaim, 11, D-2; *see also* Karnaim
Carpathians (mountains), 12, D-1
Carthage, 12, C-3
Caspian Gates, 10, D-2
Caspian Sea, 2, 6, 12, F-1; 8, 10, D-1
Caucasus (mountains), 8, D-1; 10, C-1; 12, F-2

Cauda (island), 17, C-3
Cedron, 11, B-4
Cenchreae, 17, C-2
Central (Tyropoeon) Valley (in Jerusalem), 14, B-3; 15, D-3
Chaldeans (people), 6, E-3
Charachmoba, 11, D-6; 13, C-6
Chersonesus, 8, B-1
Chinnereth, 5, 7, C-2
Chinnereth, Sea of, 1, 3, C-3; 5, 7, C-2; see also Galilee, Sea of
Chios (island), 6, B-1; 17, D-2
Chorasmia, 8, F-1
Chorasmii (people), 10, D-1
Chorazin, 13, 18, C-2
Cilicia, 6, C-2; 8, B-2; 12, E-3; 17, F-2
Cilician Gates, 10, B-2
Cimmerians (people), 6, C-1
Cirta, 12, B-3
Cnidus, 17, D-2
Cnossus, 2, A-2; 17, D-3
Colchis, 12, F-2
Colossae, 17, D-2
Comana, 17, F-1
Commagene, 12, E-2
Cophen River, 10, F-2
Corcyra, 17, B-2
Corduba, 12, A-2
Corinth, 6, A-1; 12, D-3; 17, C-2
Corsica (island), 12, B-2
Cos (island), 17, D-2
Creta, 12, D-3; see also Crete
Crete, 6, B-2; 8, 10, A-2; 17, C-3; see also Caphtor
Crocodilion, 13, B-3
Croton, 17, B-2
Ctesiphon, 12, F-3
Cush (Ethiopia), 10, B-4
Cuthah, 2, E-3; 6, E-2
Cyprus, 6, C-2; 8, 10, B-2; 12, E-3; 17, F-3; see also Alashiya, Kittim
Cyprus (in Palestine), 13, C-5
Cyrenaica, 10, A-3; 12, D-4; 17, C-4; see also Libya
Cyrene, 6, 8, 10, A-2; 12, D-3; 17, C-4
Cyropolis, 8, F-1
Cyrus River, 2, 6, E-1; 8, D-1
Cyzicus, 6, B-1
Dacia, 12, D-2
Dalmatia (Illyricum), 17, B-1
Damascus, 1, 3, 5, 7, 9, 13, 18, D-1; 2, C-3; 4, 6, 8, C-2; 10, B-2; 17, F-3
Damascus (region), 9, C-1–D-1
Damghan, 8, E-2

Dan, 1, 3, 4, C-2; 5, 7, 18, C-1; see also Laish
Dan (tribe), 3, C-2, B-4
Danube (Ister) River, 8, B-1; 10, A-1; 12, C-1, D-2
Dead Sea, 1, C-5; 18, C-6; see also Asphaltitis, Lake; Salt Sea
Debir (Khirbet Rabud?), 3, 5, 7, B-5; 18, B-6
Decapolis, 13, C-3–D-3
Dedan, 2, C-4; 6, D-4; 8, C-3
Derbe, 17, E-2
Dibon, 3, 5, 7, C-5; 18, D-5
Dilmun, 2, F-4
Dimašqi (Aram), 7, D-1
Dion, 11, D-2; 13, D-3
Diyala River, 2, 6, E-2
Dok, 11, C-4
Dor (Dora), 1, 3, 4, 5, 7, 9, 11, 13, 18, B-3; 2, C-3
Dor (region), 9, B-3
Dorylaeum, 17, E-2
Dothan, 1, 18, C-3; 3, 5, 7, B-3
Drangiana, 8, E-2-F-2
Dumah, 2, 6, D-3; 8, C-3
Dūr-belharran-šadua, 7, B-2
Dur Sharrukin, 6, E-2
Du'ru, 7, B-3
Dyrrhachium, 17, B-1
Eastern (Lower) Sea, 6, F -3; see also Persian Gulf
Ebal, Mount, 1, 3, 13, C-4; 5, 7, C-3; 9, B-4
Ebla, 2, C-2
Ecbatana, 2, 6, E-2; 10, C-2
Ecdippa, 13, B-2; see also Achzib
Edom, 3, C-6; 4, C-5; 5, 7, C-6; 6, C-3
Edrei, 3, 4, C-3; 5,11, D-3
Eglon (possibly Tell 'Aitun or Tell el-Hesi), 3, B-5; 18, A-5–B-5
Egypt, 6, B-3; 7, A-6; 10, A-3; 12, 17, E-4
Egypt, Brook of (river), 3, A-6
Egyptian Empire, 2, B-3
Egypt, Kingdom of, 8, B-3
Egypt, Lower, 2, B-3
Egypt, River of, 4, A-5
Ekron, 3, 5, 7, B-4; 11, B-5
Elah River, 1, B-5
Elam, 2, 6, F-3; 8, D-3; see also Susiana
Elasa, 11, C-4
Elath, 8, B-3
Elbe (Albis) River, 12, C-1
Elealeh, 7, C-4

Elephantine, 8, B-4; see also Syene
Eltekeh, 6, C-3; 7, B-4
Emerita Augusta, 12, A-2
Emmaus (Nicopolis), 11, B-4; 13, B-5
Emmaus (near Jerusalem), 13, B-5
Enclosure Wall (in Jerusalem), 16, B-5
Engaddi, 13, C-6
En-gedi, 5, 9, 11, 18, C-5
En-rimmon, 9, B-5
En-rogel (spring in Jerusalem), 14, B-3; 15, D-3
Ephesus, 8, B-2; 10, A-2; 12, D-3; 17, D-2
Ephraim, 13, C-5
Ephraim (tribe), 3, B-4
Ephron, 11, D-3
Epirus, 10, A-2; 17, B-2
Erech, 2, 6, E-3; 8, D-3
Eridu, 2, E-3
Erythraean Sea, 8, F-4
Esdraelon, Plain of, 1, 11, C-3; 5, B-3–C-3; 13, B-3
Eshnunna, 2, E-2
Essene Gate (in Jerusalem), 16, A-6
Etam, 5, B-5
Ethiopia, 8, 10, B-4
Euboea (island), 6, A-1
Euphrates River, 2, 6, D-2; 8, 10, C-2
Ezion-geber, 4, B-6
Fair Havens, 17, C-3
Farah (river), 1, C-4
Gaba, 11, C-2
Gabae, 8, D-2
Gad (tribe), 3, C-4
Gadara (Umm Geis in Decapolis), 11, 18, D-3; 13, C-3
Gadara (in Perea), 13, C-4
Galaaditis (people), 11, D-3
Galatia, 12, E-3; 17, E-1–E-2
Gal'aza, 7, C-3
Galilee, 5, 9, B-2-C-2; 11, 13, C-2
Galilee, Lower, 1, C-3
Galilee, Sea of, 1, 18, C-2; 13, C-3; see also Chinnereth, Sea of
Galilee, Upper, 1, C-2
Gamala, 11, D-2
Gath (Gittaim), 3, 5, 7, B-4
Gath (Tell es-Safi?), 3, 7, 18, B-5; 4, B-4
Gath-hepher, 3, C-3

Gaugamela, 10, C-2

Gaul, 12, B-1

Gaulanitis, 11, D-2; 13, C-2–D-2

Gaza, 1, 3, 5, 7, 9, 11, 18, A-5; 2, C-3; 4, B-4; 8, 10, B-3; 13, A-6; 17, F-4

Gaza Strip, 18, A-5

Gazara, 11, B-4; *see also* Gezer

Geba, 5, 7, 9, C-4

Gebal, 2, 8, C-2; 4, C-1

Gedor, 11, D-4

Gedrosia, 8, F-3; 10, E-3

Gennath Gate (in Jerusalem), 16, B-5

Gennesaret, Lake, 9, C-2; 11, D-2; *see also* Galilee, Sea of

Gentiles, Court of the (in Jerusalem), 16, B-5

Gerar, 3, B-5; 4, B-4; 5, 7, A-5

Gerar River, 1, 9, A-5

Gerasa, 9, 11, D-3; 13, D-4

Gerizim, Mount, 1, 3, 11, C-4; 5, 7, 9, 13, B-4

Germania, 12, C-1

Gerrha, 8, D-3

Geshur, 4, C-3

Gethsemane (in Jerusalem), 16, C-4

Gezer, 3, 4, 5, 7, 9, 18, B-4; *see also* Gazara

Gibbethon, 5, 7, B-4

Gibeah, 4, 7, B-4; 18, C-5

Gibeon, 3, C-4; 5, 7, 9, B-4; 18, B-5

Gihon (spring in Jerusalem), 14, B-2; 15, D-3; 16, C-5

Gilboa, Mount, 1, 4, 5, C-3

Gilead, 1, 5, 7, C-4–D-3; 3, D-3; 9, C-3–D-3

Gilgal (Khirbet el-Mefjir?), 3, 5, 7, 18, C-4

Ginae, 13, C-3

Gischala, 13, C-2

Golan, 3, C-3

Golan Heights, 18, D-2

Golden Gate (in Jerusalem), 16, C-5

Gomer (people, Cimmerians), 6, D-1

Gophna, 11, C-4; 13, B-5

Gordion, 6, C-1; 8, B-1; 10, B-2

Gozan, 6, D-2

Granicus, 10, A-2

Great Sea, The, 1, A-4; 2, 3, 5, 7, 9, 11, A-3; 4, A-3–B-3; *see also* Mediterranean Sea; Upper Sea

Greece, 8, A-2

Greek City States, 6, A-1–B-1

Gutium, 2, E-2

Habor River, 6, D-2

Hadid (Adida), 9, 11, B-4

Haleb, 2, C-2

Halicarnassus, 10, A-2

Halys River, 2, C-1; 8, B-2; 17, E-1

Hamath, 2, 6, 8, C-2; 4, D-1

Hammath, 5, C-2

Hananel, Tower of (in Jerusalem), 15, D-2

Hannathon, 3, C-3

Haran, 2, 6, D-2; 8, C-2

Hasmonean Palace (in Jerusalem), 16, B-5

Hatti (Hittite) Empire, 2, C-2

Hattusas, 2, C-1

Hauran, 1, D-2-D-3; 9, D-3

Haurina, 7, D-2

Havvoth-jair, 3, 5, C-3

Hazar-enan, 4, D-1

Hazor, 2, 4, C-3; 3, 5, 7, 9, 11, 18, C-2

Hebron, 1, 3, 5, 7, 9, B-5; 2, C-3; 4, B-4; 11, C-5; 13, B-6

Hebrus River, 17, D-1

Hecatompylus, 10, D-2

Heliopolis (in Egypt), 17, E-4; *see also* On

Helkath, 3, B-3

Hellas, 10, A-2

Hepher, 3, 4, B-3

Heraclea, 17, E-1

Heracleopolis, 2, B-4; 6, B-3

Herat (Alexandria Arion), 10, E-2

Hermes River, 2, B-1

Hermon, Mount, 1, 3, 5, 9, 11, 13, D-1; 4, C-2; 7, C-1–D-1

Hermopolis, 2, B-4; 6, B-3

Herod, Kingdom of, 12, E-3

Herod, Palace of (in Jerusalem), 16, A-5

Herodium, 13, 18, C-5

Herod's Family Tomb (in Jerusalem), 16, A-5

Heshbon, 3, 11, D-4; 4, 5, 7, 9, C-4; 18, D-5

Hezekiah's Aqueduct (in Jerusalem), 15, D-3

Hezekiah's Tunnel (in Jerusalem), 16, C-6

Hindu Kush (mountains), 10, F-2

Hinnom Valley (in Jerusalem), 14, A-3; 15, C-3; 16, A-6

Hippicus (tower in Jerusalem), 16, A-5

Hippodrome (in Jerusalem), 16, B-5

Hippos, 11, D-2; 13, C-3; 18, C-2

Hispania, 12, A-2

Hittite Empire, 2, C-1

Hivites (people), 3, D-1

Holdah (Huldah) Gates (in Jerusalem), 16, C-5

Horites (Hurrians), 2, D-1

Hormah, 3, B-5

Hula, Lake (Lake Semechonitis), 1, C-2

Huldah Gates (in Jerusalem), 16, C-5

Hurrians, 2, D-1

Hyphasis River, 10, F-3

Hyrcania, 8, E-2; 11, 13, C-5

Iberia, 12, F-2

Ibleam, 3, 5, 7, C-3

Iconium, 8, B-2; 17, E-2

Idumea, 1, 9, 11, 13, B-6

Ijon, 5, 7, C-1

Illium, 10, A-2

Illyria, 10, A-1

Illyricum, 12, C-2; 17, B-1

India, 10, F-3

Indus River, 10, F-3

Isin, 2, E-3

Israel, 4, 5, B-3–C-3

Israel, Pool of (in Jerusalem), 16, C-4

Issachar (tribe), 3, C-3

Issus, 10, B-2

Ister River, 8, 10, A-1; 12, D-2

Italy, 12, C-2; 17, A-1

Ituraea, 13, D-1

Izalla, 8, C-2

Izbet Serta, 18, B-4

Jabbok River, 1, 3, D-4; 5, 7, 13, C-4; 11, D-3

Jabesh-gilead, 3, 5, 7, C-3

Jabneel, 5, 7, B-4

Jabneh (Jamnia), 11, B-4

Jahaz, 5, 7, D-5

Jamnia, 9, 11, B-4; 13, A-5

Jarmo, 2, E-2

Jaxartes River, 8, F-1; 10, E-1

Jazer, 3, 5, 7, C-4

Jebel Yusha', 1, D-4

Jebus, 3, C-4; *see also* Jerusalem

Jerash, 18, D-3

Jericho, 1, 3, 4, 5, 7, 9, 11, C-4; 2, C-3; 13, C-5; (New Testament period), 18, C-5; (Old Testament period), 18, C-4

Jerusalem, 1, B-5; 2, 6, 6-3; 3, 4, 5, 7, B-4; 8, 10, B-3; 11, C-5; 12, E-3; 17, F-4; plans of city, 14, 15, 16; *see also* Jebus

Jesua, 9, B-6

Jezreel, 3, 4, 7, C-3; 5, B-3

Jezreel, Valley of, 1, C-3

Joppa, 1, 3, 4, 5, 7, 9, 11, 13, 18, B-4; 2, C-3; 17, F-4

Jordan, 18, D-4

Jordan River, 1, 3, 13, C-4; 4, 5, 7, 9, 11, 18, C-3

Jotbah, 7, B-2

Judah, 4, B-4; 5, 7, 9, B-5; 6, C-3; 8, B-3

Judah (tribe), 3, B-5

Judah, Wilderness of, 3, B-5; 5, C-5

Judea, 1, 13, B-5; 11, C-5; 17, F-4

Judea, Wilderness of, 1, C-5

Julias, Livias (Betharamphtha), 13, C-5

Kadesh, 2, C-2; 4, D-1; *see also* Cadasa

Kadesh-barnea, 2, C-3; 4, B-5

Kafr Bir'im, 18, C-2

Kanah, 3, C-2

Kanah River, 1, 5, 7, B-4

Kanish, 2, 6, C-1

Karabel (mountain), 2, A-1

Karnaim, 5, 7, 9, D-2; *see also* Carnaim

Kashka, 2, C-1

Kassites (people), 2, E-3

Kedar, 2, C-3–D-3; 6, D-2

Kedesh, 3, 4, 5, 7, 9, C-2; *see also* Cadasa

Keilah; 9, B-5

Khirbet el-Kerak, 18, C-6

Khirbet el-Mefjir (Gilgal?), 18, C-4

Khirbet el-Mishash, 18, B-6

Khirbet el-Tannur, 18, D-6

Khirbet Irbid, 18, C-2

Khirbet Iskander, 18, D-5

Khirbet Rabud (Debir?), 18, B-5

Kidron Valley (in Jerusalem), 14, B-3; 15, D-3; 16, C-6

Kir, *see* Kir-haresheth

Kir-haresheth, 1, 5, 7, C-6; 3, C-5; 4, C-4; *see also* Khirbet el-Kerak

Kir-heres, *see* Kirhareseth

Kiriath-jearim, 9, B-4

Kishon River, 1, 3, 5, 7, B-3

Kittaim, 9, B-4

Kittim (Cyprus), 2, B-2–C-2

Kizzuwatna, 2, C-2

Kue, 8, C-2

Lachish, 3, 5, 7, 9, 18; B-5; 4, B-4

Lagash, 2, E-3

Laish, 3, C-2; *see also* Dan

Laodicea, 17, D-2

Larisa, 17, C-2

Larsa, 6, E-3

Lasea, 17, C-3

Lebanon, 18, C-1

Lebanon, Mount, 1, 3, 4, 13, C-1

Lebo-hamath, 4, C-1

Lehun, 18, D-6

Lejun, 18, D-6

Leontes River, 1, 5, 7, 11, 13, C-1

Leptis Magna, 12, C-3

Lesbos (island), 6, B-1; 17, D-2

Libnah, 3, B-5

Libya, 8, A-2; 10, A-3; *see also* Cyrenaica

Libyan Desert, 2, A-4; 6, A-B, 3-4; 8, 10, A-3

Libyans (people), 6, A-3–B-3

Livias, Julias (Betharamphtha), 13, C-5

Lod, 5, 7, 9, B-4; *see also* Lydda

Lower City (in Jerusalem), 16, B-5

Lower Sea, 2, F-4; 6, F-3; *see also* Persian Gulf

Lugdunensis, 12, B-1

Lugdunum, 12, B-2

Lukka, 2, B-2

Lusitania, 12, A-2

Lutetia, 12, B-1

Lycaonia, 17, E-2

Lycia, 8, B-2; 12, D-3; 17, E-2

Lydda, 11, B-4; 13, B-5; *see also* Lod

Lydia, 6, B-1; 17, D-2

Lydia, Kingdom of, 8, B-2

Lystra, 17, E-2

Maacah, 4, C-2–C-3

Macedonia, 8, 10, A-1; 12, D-2; 17, C-1

Machaerus, 11, D-5; 13, C-5

Madaba, 18, D-5; *see also* Medeba

Madai, 6, E-2

Maeander River, 2, B-1; 8, B-2

Magdala, 13, C-2

Magidu, 7, B-3–C-2

Mahanaim, 3, 5, 7, C-4; 4, C-3

Maka, 8, F-3; *see also* Gedrosia

Malataya, 2, D-1

Malatha, 13, B-6

Malta (island), 17, A-3

Mamre, 18, B-5

Manasseh (tribe), 3, C-3

Maracanda (Samarkand), 10, F-2

Marathon, 8, A-1

Mare Internum, 12, B-3–D-3; *see also* Great Sea; Mediterranean Sea; Upper Sea

Mareshah, 5, 7, 9, 18, B-5; *see also* Marisa

Margiana, 8, F-2

Margus, 8, E-2

Mari, 2, D-2

Mariamne (tower in Jerusalem), 16, A-5

Marisa, 11, 13, B-5; *see also* Mareshah

Masada, 11, 13, 18, C-6

Massagetae (people), 10, E-1

Mauretania, 12, A-3-B-3

Medeba, 3, 5, 7, 9, C-5; 4, C-4; 11, 13, D-5; *see also* Madaba

Media, 2, F-2; 8, D-2; 10, C-2

Median Empire, 8, D-2

Mediterranean Sea, 2, A-2–B-2; 8, 10, A-2; 13, 18, A-3; 17, B-3–E-3; *see also* Great Sea; Mare Internum; Upper Sea

Megiddo, 1, 3, 4, 5, 7, 18, B-3; 2, C-3; 8, B-2

Meiron, 18, C-2

Melita (Malta, island), 17, A-3

Melitene, 6, D-1; 8, C-2

Memphis, 2, 6, 8, 10, B-3; 12, E-4

Merom, 3, 5, C-2

Meron, Mount, 1, C-2

Mersin, 2, C-2

Mesembria, 17, D-1

Meshech, 6, B-1

Messana, 17, A-2

Mezad Hashavyahu, 18, A-4

Michmash, 11, C-4

Michmethath, 3, C-4

Midian, 2, C-3-C-4

Miletus, 6, B-1; 8, B-2; 17, D-2

Millo (in Jerusalem), 14, B-2

Minni, 6, E-2

Minoan-Mycenaean Domain, 2, A-2

Mittani, 2, D-2

Mitylene, 17, D-2

Mizpah (Tell en-Nasbeh?), 5, 7, 9, 18, B-4; 11, C-4

Moab, 1, D-6; 3, C-5; 4, C-4; 5, C-6; 6, C-3; 7, 9, C-5–D-5

Moab, Plains of, 1, D-5

Modein, 11, B-4

Moesia, 12, D-2; 17, C-1

Moladah, 9, B-6

Moreh, Hill of, 1, C-3

Moresheth-gath, 7, B-5

Moschi (people), 8, C-1

Mycenaean-Minoan Domain, 2, A-2

Myra, 17, E-3

Mysia, 17, D-1

Nabatea, 12, E-3; 13, C-6–D-5

Nabateans (people), 9, B-6–C-6; 11, C-6; 17, F-4

Nabratein, 18, C-2

Nahariyeh, 7, 18, B-2

Nain, 13, C-3

Nairi, 6, D-1

Naphtali (tribe), 3, C-2

Narbata (Narbatah), 9, 11, 13, B-3

Narbo, 12, B-2

Narbonensis, 12, B-2

Nazareth, 1, 13, 18, C-3

Neapolis (in Macedonia), 17, C-1

Neballat, 9, B-4

Nebo, 9, B-5

Nebo, Mount, 1, D-5; 3, D-4; 5, 7, C-5; 18, D-5

Negeb, 1, A-6–B-6; 3, B-6; 5, 7, A-6

Nehemiah's Wall (in Jerusalem), 15, D-2

Netophah, 9, B-5

Nicaea, 10, F-2; 17, D-1

Nicomedia, 17, E-1

Nicopolis (in Achaia), 17, C-2

Nicopolis (in Palestine), 13, B-5; see also Emmaus

Nile River, 2, 8, B-4; 6, C-3; 10, B-3; 12, E-4

Nimrud, 6, E-2; see also Calah

Nineveh, 2, 5, D-2; 8, C-2

Nippur, 2, 6, E-3; 8, D-3

Nisibis, 6, D-2; 8, C-2

No, see Thebes

Nob, 7, B-4

Noth, 2, B-3; see also Memphis

Noricum, 12, C-2

North Wall, First and Second (in Jerusalem), 16, B-4, B-5

Numeira, 18, C-6

Nuzi, 2, E-2

Olbia, 10, B-1

Olives, Mount of, 1, C-5; (in Jerusalem), 16, D-4

On, 2, B-3; 6, C-3; see also Heliopolis

Ono, 9, B-4

Ophel (hill in Jerusalem), 14, B-2

Opis, 8, D-2

Ortona, 17, A-1

Ostia, 17, A-1

Oxus River, 8, F-1; 10, E-2

Paddan-aram, 2, D-2

Paestum, 17, A-1

Palace (in Jerusalem), 14, B-2

Pamphylia, 12, E-3; 17, E-2

Paneas, 11, D-1; 13, C-2; see also Caesarea Philippi

Paneas (region), 13, C-1

Pannonia, 12, C-2

Panticapaeum, 10, B-1

Paphlagonia, 17, E-1

Paphos, 17, E-3

Parsa, 8, D-3; see also Persepolis

Parthia, 8, E-2; 10, D-2

Parthian Empire, 12, F-3

Pasargadae, 8, E-3

Patara, 17, D-3

Pattala, 10, F-3

Pella (in Macedonia), 10, A-1

Pella (in Palestine), 9, 11, 13, 18, C-3

Pelusium, 6, C-3; 8, 10, B-3; 17, E-4

Penuel, 5, 7, C-4

Perea, 13, C-4; 17, E-2

Pergamum, 12, 17, D-2

Persepolis, 8, E-3; 10, D-3

Persian Gulf, 2, F-4; 8, 10, D-3; see also Lower Sea

Persis, 8, E-3; 10, D-3

Pessinus, 17, E-2

Pharathon, 11, C-4

Pharpar River, 1, D-1

Phasael (tower in Jerusalem), 16, A-5

Phasaelis, 13, C-4

Phaselis, 6, B-2

Phasis, 8, C-1

Philadelphia, 11, D-4; see also Amman; Rabbah

Philistia, 4, B-4; 5, 7, A-5; 11, A-5–B-4

Philistia, Plain of, 1, B-5

Philistines (people), 3, A-5

Philoteria, 11, C-2

Phoenicia, 1, 4, 5, 13, B-2–C-1; 6, C-2; 7, B-1–C-1; 11, C-1–C-2

Phoenix, 17, C-3

Phrygia, 6, B-1; 17, E-2

Pisidia, 17, E-2

Polemon, Kingdom of, 17, F-1

Pontus, 12, E-2; 17, E-1

Prophthasia, 10, E-3

Propontis, 17, D-1

Pteria, 8, B-1

Ptolemais, 11, 13, B-2; see also Acco

Punon, 4, C-5

Pura, 8, F-3; 10, E-3

Puteoli, 17, A-1

Qarnini, 7, C-2

Qarqar, 6, C-2

Qumran, 11, 13, 18, C-5

Rabbah, 1, 3, 5, 7, 9, D-4; 4, C-4; see also Amman; Philadelphia

Rabbah-Amman, 18, D-4

Raetia, 12, C-2

Ragaba, 11, D-3

Ramah, 5, 7, B-4; 9, C-4

Ramathaim, 11, C-4

Ramath-mizpeh, 3, D-4

Ramet Rahel, 18, C-5

Ramoth-gilead, 3, 5, 7, 18, D-3; 4, C-3

Raphana, 13, D-2

Raphia, 1, 9, A-6; 4, B-4; 5, 7, A-5; 6, C-3

Red Sea, 2, 6, 8, C-4; 10, B-4; 12, E-4

Rehob, 3, C-2

Reuben (tribe), 3, C-5

Rha River, 12, F-1

Rhagae, 8, 10, D-2

Rhegium, 17, A-2

Rhine River, 12, C-1

Rhodes (island), 2, 6, 8, B-2; 17, D-3

Riblah, 8, C-2

Rimmon, 7, C-4

Rome, 12, C-2; 17, A-1

Royal Portico (in Jerusalem), 16, B-4

Rubicon River, 12, C-2

Rumah, 5, B-2

Sais, 6, 8, B-3

Saka (Scythians, people), 8, 10, F-1

Salamis, 17, F-3

Salecah, 4, D-3

Salim, 13, C-4

Salmone, Cape, 17, D-3

Salonae, 12, C-2

Salt Sea, 3, 5, 7, 9, 11, C-5; 4, C-4; see also Dead Sea

Samaga, 11, D-4

Samal, 6, D-2

Samaria, 1, B-4; 5, 7, 9, B-3; 6, 11, C-3; see also Sebaste

Samaria (region), 1, B-3–C-3; 11, C-3; 13, B-4

Samarkand (Maraeanda), 10, F-2
Samerina, 7, B-4–C-3
Samos (island), 6, E-1; 17, D-2
Samothrace (island), 17, C-1
Sangarius River, 2, B-1; 17, E-1
Sardinia (island), 12, B-2
Sardis, 6, B-1; 8, B-2; 10, A-2; 17, D-2
Sarepta, 13, C-1; *see also* Zarephath
Sarmatia, 12, D-1–E-1
Scythians (people), 8, D-1; 9, B-1, F-1
Scythopolis, 11, 13, C-3; *see also* Beth-shan
Sebaste, 13, 18, B-4; *see also* Samaria
Second Quarter (in Jerusalem), 16, B-4
Sela, 4, C-5; 6, C-3
Seleucia, 11, D-2; 17, F-2
Semechonitis, Lake (Lake Hula), 1, C-2
Sepphoris, 11, 18, C-2; 13, C-3
Serpent's Pool (in Jerusalem), 16, A-6
Sevan, Lake, 6, E-1
Shaalbim, 3, B-4
Sharon, Plain of, 1, 3, 5, 9, 11, B-3; 13, B-4
Sharuhen (Tell el-Far'ah), 3, B-5; 5, 7, A-5; 18, A-6
Shechem, 1, 3, 5, 7, 9, 18, C-4; 2, C-3; 4, B-3
Shephelah, 1, B-5
Shiloh, 1, 3, 5, 7, 9, 18, C-4
Shimron, 3, C-3
Shittim, 5, 7, C-4
Shunem, 5, 7, C-3
Shushan (Susa), 6, E-3
Sibmah, 7, C-4
Sichem, 11, C-4
Sicilia (island), 12, C-3
Sicily, 17, A-2
Sidon, 1, 3, 5, 7, 9, 13, 18, C-1; 2, C-3; 4, 6, C-2; 10, B-2; 17, F-3
Sidonians (people), 3, B-1-B-2
Siloam, Pool of (in Jerusalem), 15, D-3; 16, B-6
Simeon (tribe), 3, B-5
Sinai, 2, C-3; 4, A-6
Sinope, 8, C-1; 10, B-1; 12, E-2; 17, F-1
Sippar, 2, E-3; 6, E-2; 8, C-2
Siut, 6, B-4
Siwa, Oasis of, 6, B-3; *see also* Amon, Temple of

Smyrna, 17, D-2
Socoh (in Sharon), 5, B-3
Socoh (in Judah), 5, B-5
Sogdiana, 8, F-1; 10, E-2
Solomon's Portico (in Jerusalem), 16, C-5
Sorek River, 1, B-5; 3, B-4
Sparta, 6, A-1; 8, 10, A-2; 17, C-2
Strato's Tower, 9, 11, B-3
Subterranean Passage (in Jerusalem), 16, B-5
Succoth (Tell Deir 'Alla?), 3, 5, 7, 18, C-4; 4, C-3
Sumer, 2, E-3
Susa, 2, F-3; 6, E-3; 8, D-3; 10, C-3
Susiana, 8, D-3; 10, C-3–D-3; *see also* Elam
Sychar, 13, C-4
Syene, 6, C-4; 8, 10, B-4
Syracuse, 12, C-3; 17, A-2
Syria, 5, 18, D-1; 6, D-2; 10, B-2; 12, E-3; 13, C-1–D-1; 17, F-3
Taanach, 3, 4, 5, 7, B-3; 18, C-3
Tabgha, 18, C-2
Tabor, Mount, 1, 3, 5, 7, 13, C-3; 11, C-2
Tadmor, 2, 6, D-2; 8, C-2
Tamar, 3, 5, 7, C-6; 4, B-5
Tanis, 6, C-3
Tappuah, 3, C-4
Tarentum, 12, C-2; 17, B-1
Tarraco, 12, B-2
Tarraconensis, 12, A-2–B-2
Tarsus, 6, C-2; 8, 10, B-2; 12, E-3; 17, F-2
Tatta, Lake, 17, E-2
Taurus (mountains), 2, 6, C-2
Tavium, 17, F-1
Taxila, 10, F-2
Tekoa, 5, 7, 9, B-5; 11, C-5
Tekoa Gate (in Jerusalem), 16, B-6
Teleilat el-Ghassul, 18, C-5
Tell Abu Hawam, 18, B-2
Tell Abu Matar, 18, B-6
Tell 'Aitun (Eglon?), 18, B-5
Tell Anafa, 18, C-1
Tell Azur, 1, C-4
Tell Beit Mirsim, 18, B-5
Tell Brak, 2, D-2
Tell Deir 'Alla (Suecoth?), 18, C-4
Tell el-'Aijul, 18, A-5
Tell el-Amarna (Akhetaton), 2, B-4

Tell el-'Areini, 18, A-5
Tell el-Far'ah (Sharuhen), 18, A-6
Tell el-Far'ah (Tirzah), 18, C-3
Tell el-Hesi (Eglon?), 18, B-5
Tell el-Qasileh, 18, B-4
Tell en-Nasbeh (Mizpah?), 18, B-4
Tell en-Nejileh, 18, B-5
Tell esh-Shari'ah, 18, B-6
Tell es-Safi (Gath?), 18, D-5
Tell es-Saidiyeh (Zarethan?), 18, C-3
Tell Halaf, 2, D-2
Tell Jemmeh, 18, A-6
Tell Mor, 18, A-5
Tell Zeror, 18, B-3
Tel Miqne (Ekron), 18, B-5
Tel Shikmona, 18, B-2
Tema, 2, 6, C-4; 8, C-3
Temple (in Jerusalem), 14, B-2; 15, D-2; 16, B-5
Temple, Pinnacle of the (in Jerusalem), 16, B-5
Tepe Gawra, 2, D-2
Tepe Giyan, 2, F-2
Thapsacus, 8, C-2; 10, B-2
Theater (in Jerusalem), 16, B-5
Thebes (in Egypt), 6, C-4; 8, 10, B-3; 12, E-4
Thessalonica, 12, D-2; 17, C-1
Thrace, 8, A-1–B-1; 10, A-1; 12, D-2; 17, C-1–D-1
Three Taverns, 17, A-1
Tiberias, 13, C-3; 18, C-2
Thyatira, 17, D-2
Tigris River, 2, D-2; 6, E-2; 8, 10, C-2
Til Barsib, 6, D-2
Timnah, 7, 18, B-5; 11, C-4
Tingis, 12, A-3
Tirzah (Tell el-Far'ah), 3, 5, 7, 18, C-3
Tishbe, 5, C-3
Tob, 4, C-3
Tobiads (people), 11, C-4–D-4
Tombs (in Jerusalem), 16, B-5, D-5
Tower's Pool (in Jerusalem), 16, A-5
Trapezus, 8, C-1; 10, C-2; 12, E-2
Troas, 17, D-2
Troy, 2, A-1
Tubal, 6, C-1–D-1
Turushpa, 6, E-1
Tuz, Lake, 2, B-1; 6, C-1
Tyana, 17, F-2

Tyre, 3, 4, 8, B-2; 2, C-3; 5, 7, 9, 13, 18, B-1; 6, C-2; 10, B-3; 11, C-1; 17, F-3

Tyre, Ladder of, 11, B-1; 13, B-2

Tyre of Tobiah, 9, D-4

Tyre (region), 9, C-1

Tyropoeon Valley (in Jerusalem), 14, B-2–B-3; 16, B-5–B-6

Tyrrhenian Sea, 17, A-2

Tyrus, 11, D-4

Ugarit, 2, C-2

Ulai River, 8, D-3

Ulatha, 13, C-2

Umm Geis (Gadara), 18, D-3

Upper City (in Jerusalem), 16, B-5

Upper Sea, 2, B-3; 6, A-2–B-2; see also Great Sea; Mediterranean Sea; Western Sea

Ur, 2, 6, E-3; 8, D-3

Urartu, 2, D-1; 6, D-1–E-1; 8, C-1

Urmia, Lake, 2, 6, E-2; 8, D-2

Van, Lake, 2, E-1; 6, D-1; 8, C-2

Volga (Rha) River, 12, F-1

Wadi el-Mughara, 18, B-3

Wadi el-Murabba'at Caves, 18, C-5

Water Gate (in Jerusalem), 16, C-6

West Bank, 18, C-4

Western Hill (in Jerusalem), 14, A-2

Western (Upper) Sea, 6, B-2; see also Great Sea; Mediterranean Sea

Xanthus, 8, B-2

Yahud (Judah), 9, B-5

Yarmuk River, 1, 5, 7, 13, C-3; 9, B-5; 11, D-2

Yazd, 8, E-3

Yiron, 3, C-2

Yusha', Jebel, 1, D-4

Zadrakarta, 8, E-2

Zagros Mountains, 2, E-2

Zanoah, 9, B-5

Zarephath, 18, C-1; see also Sarepta

Zarethan (Tell es-Saidiyeh?), 18, C-3; see also Zarethan alternate site, 18, C-4

Zebulun (tribe), 3, C-3

Zedad, 4, D-1

Zemaraim, 5, C-4

Zered River, 1, 3, 5, 7, C-6; 11, D-6

Zeredah, 5, B-4

Zerqā River, 1, D-4; see also Jabbok River

Ziklag, 3, 5, 7, 9, B-5; 4, B-4

Ziph (in Judah), 3, C-5; 5, 7, B-5

Ziph (in Negeb), 5, B-6

Zoan (Avaris), 2, B-3

Zoar, 3, 5, 7, 18, C-6

Zoara, 11, C-6

Zorah, 3, 5, B-4

NOTES

NOTES

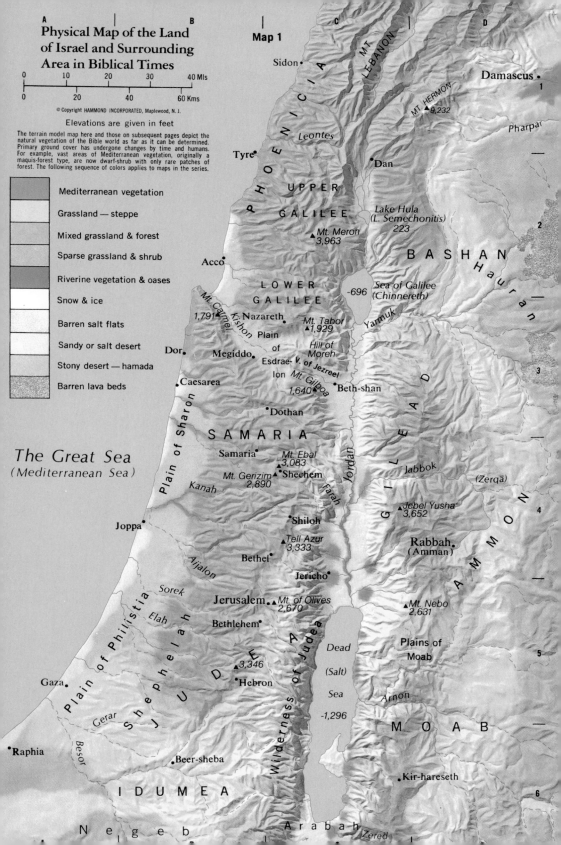

Physical Map of the Land of Israel and Surrounding Area in Biblical Times

Map 1

A · B · C · D

40 Mls
60 Kms

© Copyright HAMMOND INCORPORATED, Maplewood, N.J.

Elevations are given in feet

The terrain model map here and those on subsequent pages depict the natural vegetation of the Bible world as far as it can be determined. Primary ground cover has undergone changes by time and humans. For example, vast areas of Mediterranean vegetation, originally a maquis-forest type, are now dwarf-shrub with only rare patches of forest. The following sequence of colors applies to maps in the series.

- Mediterranean vegetation
- Grassland — steppe
- Mixed grassland & forest
- Sparse grassland & shrub
- Riverine vegetation & oases
- Snow & ice
- Barren salt flats
- Sandy or salt desert
- Stony desert — hamada
- Barren lava beds

The Great Sea
(Mediterranean Sea)

Sidon

Damascus

P H O E N I C I A

Leontes

MT. LEBANON

MT. HERMON
▲ 9,232

Pharpar

Tyre

Dan

UPPER GALILEE

Lake Hula
(L. Semechonitis)
223

B A S H A N

Hauran

Acco

Mt. Meron
▲ 3,963

LOWER GALILEE

-696   Sea of Galilee
(Chinnereth)

Mt. Carmel
1,791

Kishon

Nazareth

Mt. Tabor
▲ 1,929

Plain of Esdrae-lon

Hill of Moreh
V. of Jezreel

Yarmuk

Dor

Megiddo

Mt. Gilboa
1,640

Beth-shan

Caesarea

Dothan

G I L E A D

Jordan

Plain of Sharon

S A M A R I A

Samaria

Mt. Ebal
▲ 3,083

Mt. Gerizim
2,890

Shechem

Jabbok

(Zerqā)

Kanah

Farah

Jebel Yusha'
▲ 3,652

Joppa

Shiloh

Tell Azur
▲ 3,333

A M M O N

Rabbah
(Amman)

Aijalon

Bethel

Sorek

Jericho

Jerusalem   ▲ Mt. of Olives
2,670

Mt. Nebo
▲ 2,631

Bethlehem

Dead
(Salt)
Sea
-1,296

Plains of Moab

Gaza

Elah

Shephelah

▲ 3,346

Hebron

J U D E A

Wilderness of Judea

Arnon

Gerar

M O A B

Besor

Raphia

Beer-sheba

Kir-hareseth

I D U M E A

N e g e b

A r a b a h

Zered

Map 2

Caspian Sea

Black Sea

Mediterranean Sea
(Great or Upper Sea)

Persian Gulf
(Lower Sea)

The Ancient World
in the Late Bronze Age

Areas of influence of major
powers about 1350 B.C.E.

250 Mls   400 Kms
0   50   100   150   200
0   100   200   300

MEDIA

GUTIUM

ZAGROS MOUNTAINS

ELAM

Susa

Ecbatana

Tepe Giyan

URARTU

L. Urmia

L. Van

Mt. Ararat

Cyrus

Araxes

KASHKA

HURRIANS
(HORITES)

Tell
Leilan   Tepe
Gawra
Tell Brak   Nineveh   Arbela
Calah   Asshur
Nuzi

ASSYRIA

Eshnunna
Akkad
Agade?   Sippar
Cuthah   Babylon   Nippur
BABYLONIA
Sumer   Isin
Erech   Lagash
Ur   Eridu

KASSITES

Diyala

Tigris

Euphrates

MITANNI
Haran
Paddan-   Tell
aram   Halaf

HITTITE
EMPIRE
(HATTI)

ASSUWA

Ankuwa
Kanish
Hattusas
Alaca Huyuk
Halys
Sangarius

Hermos
Karabel
Maeander
Beycesultan
ARZAWA
LUKKA
Troy

TAURUS MTS.
Mersin

WIZUWATNA

MINOAN-MYCENAEAN DOMAIN

CAPHTOR
(Crete)
Cnossus

Rhodes

ALASHIYA-
KHITTIM
(Cyprus)

Ugarit   Arvad
Gebal
Sidon   Damascus
Tyre   Hazor
Dor   Shechem
Megiddo   Jericho
Joppa   Jerusalem
Gaza   Hebron
Beer-sheba
Kadesh-barnea

Carchemish
Alalakh   Haleb
Ebla
Hamath
Kadesh

KEDAR

Tadmor   Mari

Dumah

Tema

MIDIAN

Sinai

EGYPTIAN
EMPIRE

Avaris
(Zoan)   On
Lower
Egypt   Memphis
(Noph)
Heracleopolis
Hermopolis
Akhetaton
(Tell el-Amarna)
Nile

Libyan
Desert

Red
Sea

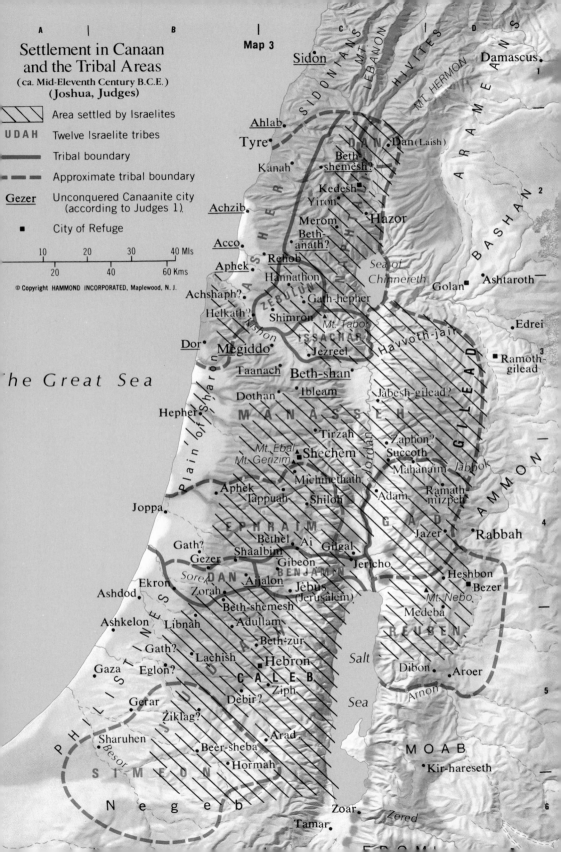

Settlement in Canaan and the Tribal Areas
(ca. Mid-Eleventh Century B.C.E.)
(Joshua, Judges)

Map 3

/////	Area settled by Israelites
UDAH	Twelve Israelite tribes
——	Tribal boundary
– – –	Approximate tribal boundary
Gezer	Unconquered Canaanite city (according to Judges 1)
■	City of Refuge

10   20   30   40 Mls
20   40   60 Kms

© Copyright HAMMOND INCORPORATED, Maplewood, N.J.

Sidon
Damascus
Ahlab
Tyre
Dan (Laish)
Kanah
Beth-shemesh?
Kedesh
Yiron
Achzib
Merom
Beth-anath?
Hazor
Acco
Rehob
Aphek
Hannathon
Gath-hepher
Golan
Ashtaroth
Achshaph?
Helkath?
Shimron
Edrei
Dor
Megiddo
Jezreel
Havvoth-jair
Ramoth-gilead
Taanach
Beth-shan
The Great Sea
Dothan
Ibleam
Jabesh-gilead?
Hepher
Tirzah
Zaphon?
Succoth
Mt. Ebal
Mt. Gerizim
Shechem
Mahanaim
Aphek
Michmethath
Ramath-mizpeh
Joppa
Tappuah
Shiloh
Adam
Jazer
Rabbah
Bethel
Ai
Gilgal
Gath?
Shaalbim
Gibeon
Jericho
Gezer
Ajalon
Jebus (Jerusalem)
Heshbon
Bezer
Ekron
Zorah
Mt. Nebo
Ashdod
Beth-shemesh
Medeba
Ashkelon
Adullam
Libnah
Beth-zur
Gath?
Lachish
Hebron
Dibon
Aroer
Gaza
Eglon?
Ziph
Gerar
Debir?
Ziklag?
Salt Sea
Arnon
Sharuhen
Arad
Beer-sheba
Hormah
MOAB
Kir-hareseth
Zoar
Tamar
Zered

SIDONIANS
MT. LEBANON
MT. HERMON
HIVITES
ARAMEANS
ASHER
NAPHTALI
BASHAN
Sea of Chinnereth
ZEBULUN
ISSACHAR
Mt. Tabor
Kishon
Plain of Sharon
MANASSEH
Jordan
GILEAD
AMMON
EPHRAIM
GAD
DAN
Sorek
BENJAMIN
REUBEN
JUDAH
CALEB
SIMEON
PHILISTINES
Besor
Negeb
EDOM

A   B   C   D
1
2
3
4
5
6

The Empire of David and Solomon

(ca. 1000-924 B.C.E.)

Map 4

Boundary of the empire at its greatest extent

Territory conquered by David

□ **Fortified places of Solomon**

⚒ **Copper mining centers**

Scale:
0 10 25 50 75 Mls
0 20 40 60 80 100 120 Kms

© Copyright HAMMOND INCORPORATED, Maplewood, N.J.

The Great Sea
(Mediterranean Sea)

Hamath
Arvad
Kadesh
Zedad
Hazar
Lebo-hamath
ZOBAH
ARAM —
Gebal
Berothai
Berytus
BETH-REHOB
ARAM —
DAMASCUS
Sidon
Damascus
MT. HERMON
Tyre
Abel
Dan
Kedesh
DAMASCUS
Hazor
MAACAH
Acco
ARGOB
Cabul
Ashtaroth
Mt. Carmel
GESHUR
Dor
TOB
Edrei
Megiddo
Jezreel
Taanach
Mt. Gilboa
Beth-shan
Ramoth-gilead
Salecah
Hepher
Jordan
Shechem
Succoth
Mahanaim
Joppa
ISRAEL
Baalath?
Gezer
Beth-horon
Rabbah
Ashdod
Gibeah
Bethel
AMMON
Ashkelon
Beth-shemesh
Gath?
Jerusalem
Jericho
Heshbon
Gaza
Lachish
Hebron
Medeba
Ziklag?
Salt
Raphia
Gerar
Arad
Sea
Aroer
Beer-sheba
JUDAH
PHILISTIA
MOAB
Kir-hareseth
Tamar
AMALEK
Bozrah
Kadesh-barnea
Punon
EDOM
Sela
Arabah
River of Egypt
Ezion-geber?
Sinai

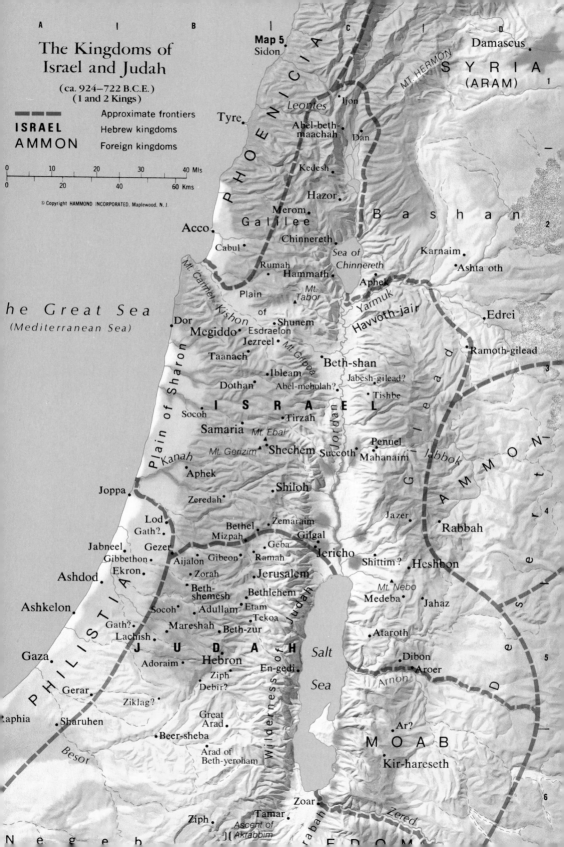

The Kingdoms of Israel and Judah

(ca. 924–722 B.C.E.)
(1 and 2 Kings)

ISRAEL — — — Approximate frontiers
ISRAEL Hebrew kingdoms
AMMON Foreign kingdoms

0   10   20   30   40 Mls
0   20   40   60 Kms

© Copyright HAMMOND INCORPORATED, Maplewood, N.J.

Map 5

A   **B**   **C**   **D**

Damascus

SYRIA
(ARAM)

MT. HERMON

PHOENICIA

Sidon

Leontes   Ijon

Tyre

Abel-beth-maachah

Dan

Kedesh

Hazor

Merom

Galilee

Bashan

Acco

Cabul   Chinnereth

Karnaim

Ashta·oth

Rumah

Hammath   Sea of Chinnereth

Aphek

The Great Sea
(Mediterranean Sea)

Mt. Carmel   Kishon   Plain   Mt. Tabor

Yarmuk

Havvoth-jair

Edrei

Dor

of

Shunem

Megiddo   Esdraelon

Jezreel

Mt. Gilboa

Beth-shan

Ramoth-gilead

Taanach

Jabesh-gilead?

Ibleam

Dothan   Abel-meholah?

Tishbe

I S R A E L

Socoh

Tirzah

Jordan

Gilead

Plain of Sharon

Samaria   Mt. Ebal

Penuel

Jabbok

Kanah   Mt. Gerizim   Shechem   Succoth

Mahanaim

Aphek

A M M O N

Joppa

Shiloh

Zeredah

Jazer

Bethel   Zemaraim

Lod   Mizpah   Gilgal

Rabbah

Gath?

Geba

Jabneel   Gezer   Gibeon   Ramah   Jericho

Shittim?   Heshbon

Gibbethon   Aijalon   Zorah   **Jerusalem**

Ekron

Ashdod   Beth-shemesh   Bethlehem   Mt. Nebo

PHILISTIA   Socoh   Adullam   Etam   Tekoa   Medeba   Jahaz

Ashkelon   Mareshah   Beth-zur

Gath?

Gaza   Lachish   **J U D A H**   Ataroth

Adoraim   Hebron   Salt   Dibon

Gerar   Ziph   En-gedi   Aroer

·aphia   Sharuhen   Debir?   Sea   Arnon

Ziklag?

Great Arad   **M O A B**

Beer-sheba

Arad of Beth-yeroham   Ar?

Kir-haresheth

Zoar

Ziph   Tamar

Ascent of Akrabbim   Zered

N e g e b   Arabah   **EDOM**

Map 6

The Assyrian Empire

Assyrian empire—ca. 824 B.C.E.
Assyrian empire—ca. 640 B.C.E.
Cyrene Greek colonies underlined in red

0 50 100 150 200 250 300 350 Mls

Caspian Sea

Lower (Eastern) Sea

L. Sevan

Cyrus

Araxes

Mt. Ararat

URARTU
(ARARAT)

L. Urmia

Manni

Ecbatana

MADAI

ELAM

Susa
(Shushan)

Diyala

BABYLONIA

Nippur
Erech

Larsa

Ur

CHALDEANS

Turushpa

L. Van

A S S Y R I A

Dur-Sharrukin

Nineveh

Arbela

Calah
(Nimrud)

Asshur

Tigris

Sippar
Cuthah
Babylon
Borsippa

Anat

Euphrates

E M P I R E

CIMMERIANS (GOMER)

Gordion

Ancyra

PHRYGIA

L. Tuz

MESHECH

Sardis

LYDIA

TUBAL

Kanish

TAURUS MTS.

CILICIA

Tarsus

Melitene

Nisibis

Gozan

Habor

Haran

Samal

Carchemish

Til Barsib

Arpad
Aleppo

Qarqar
Hamath

Tadmor

Dumah

Tema

Dedan

A R I B I
(A R A B S)

K E D A R

S Y R I A

Damascus

ARAM

Sidon
Tyre

PHOENICIA

Arvad

Cyprus

Samaria
Eltekeh
Jerusalem
Raphia

AMMON

trib. to MOAB
Assyria
EDOM

Sela

JUDAH

Astacus
Cyzicus

Abydos

GREEK

Chios

Samos

Miletus

Phaselis

Rhodes

Corinth
Athens

Sparta

Lesbos

Euboea

C I T Y   S T A T E S

Aegean
Sea

Crete

Upper (Western) Sea

Pelusium
Tanis
Sais
Bubastis
On
Memphis
Heracleopolis

EGYPT

to Assyria 671-651 B.C.E.

Hermopolis

Siut

Abydos

Thebes

Nile

Red Sea

L I B Y A N S

Oasis of Siwa

Cyrene

L i b y a n   D e s e r t

Judah After the Fall of Israel

(722–586 B.C.E.)
(2 Kings)

- — — Approximate frontiers
- **AMMON** Independent kingdoms
- DU'RU Assyrian provinces

0 10   30   40 Mls
0   20   40   60 Kms

© Copyright MCMLXXVIII HAMMOND INCORPORATED, Maplewood, N.J.

A | B C | D

Map 7

Damascus

Sidon

Leontes

Ijon

MT HERMON

DIMAŠQI
(ARAM)

1

Tyre
(free city)

Abel-beth-
maachah

Dan

E M P I R E

Achzib

Nahariyeh
Acco

Kedesh

Hazor

QARNINI

Karnaim

Ashtaroth

HAURINA

2

DUR-BELHARRAN-SADUA

Chinnereth

Jotbah

Sea of
Chinnereth

Aphek

G. Yarmuk

Mt. Carmel-Kishon

Mt.
Tabor

Shunem

GAL-AZA

e Great Sea
(Mediterranean Sea)

Dor

Megiddo

MAGIDU

Jezreel

Taanach

Beth-shan

Ramoth-gilead

3

DU'RU

Ibleam

Dothan

Jabesh-gilead?

Tirzah

Jordan

Samaria

Mt. Ebal

Shechem

Mt.
Gerizim

Succoth

Penuel

Mahanaim

Gilead

Jabbok

Kanah

Aphek

SAMERINA

Shiloh

AMMON

Joppa

Bene-berak

Jazer

Rabbah

4

Beth-dagon

Lod

Gath?

Rimmon

Bethel

Aiath

Geba

Gilgal

Jericho

Shittim?

Elealeh
Heshbon

Eltekah?

Jabneel

Gezer

Mizpah

Gibeon

Ramah

Gibeah

Anathoth

Sibmah

ASDUDU

Gibbe-
thon

Aijalon

Jerusalem

Nob

Mt. Nebo

Ashdod

Ekron

Timnah

Beth-
shemesh

Bethlehem

Medeba

Jahaz

Ashkelon

Azekah

Adullam

Tekoa

Moresheth-
gath

Mareshah

Beth-zur

Ataroth

Gath?

Lachish

Salt

Dibon

5

Gaza

Adoraim

Hebron

En-gedi

Aroer

Arnon

Bethel-ezel

Ziph

Sea

Gerar

Debir?

MOAB

...phia

Sharuhen

Ziklag?

Great
Arad

Ar?

J U D A H

Beer-sheba

Arad of
Beth-yeroham?

Kir-hareseth
(Kir, Kir-heres)

6

Besor

N e g e b

Tamar

Zoar

Zered

EDOM

Great Empires of the Sixth Century B.C.E.

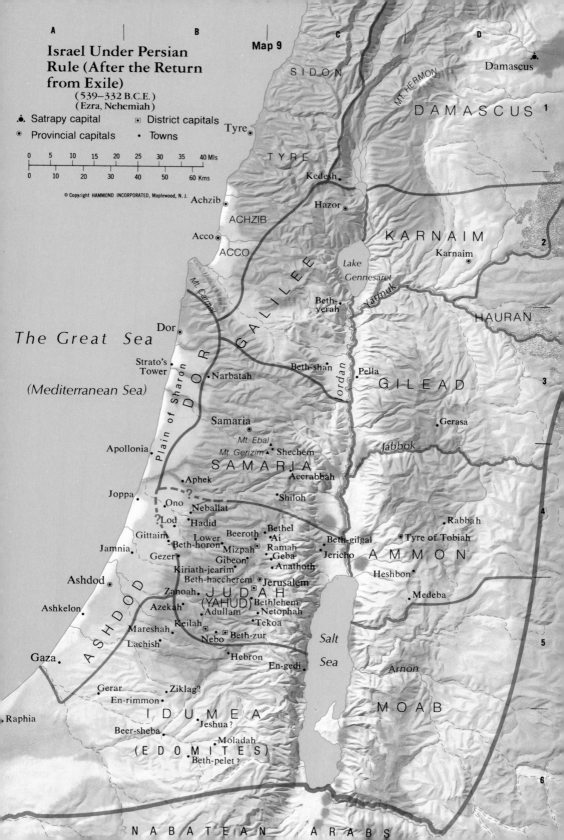

Israel Under Persian Rule (After the Return from Exile)

(539–332 B.C.E.)
(Ezra, Nehemiah)

Map 9

- 🔺 Satrapy capital
- ◉ Provincial capitals
- ▣ District capitals
- • Towns

0 5 10 15 20 25 30 35 40 Mis
0 10 20 30 40 50 60 Kms

© Copyright HAMMOND INCORPORATED, Maplewood, N.J.

A   B   C   D

1

2

3

4

5

6

The Great Sea

(Mediterranean Sea)

SIDON

Damascus

MT. HERMON

DAMASCUS

TYRE

Tyre

Kedesh

Hazor

ACHZIB

Achzib

KARNAIM

Karnaim

Acco

ACCO

GALILEE

Lake Gennesaret

Yarmuk

Beth-yerah

HAURAN

Dor

DOR

Plain of Sharon

Mt. Carmel

Strato's Tower

Narbatah

Beth-shan

Pella

Jordan

GILEAD

Gerasa

Jabbok

Samaria

Mt. Ebal

Mt. Gerizim   Shechem

SAMARIA

Apollonia

Accrabbah

Aphek

Shiloh

Joppa

Ono

?

Neballat

Lod

Hadid

?

Rabbah

Gittaim

Lower Beth-horon

Beeroth

Bethel

Ai

Beth-gilgal

Tyre of Tobiah

Jamnia

Gezer

Mizpah

Ramah

Geba

Jericho

AMMON

Gibeon

Anathoth

Heshbon

Kiriath-jearim

Beth-haccherem

Jerusalem

Zanoah

JUDAH

(YAHUD)

Bethlehem

Medeba

Ashdod

Azekah

Adullam

Netophah

Ashkelon

Keilah

Tekoa

ASHDOD

Mareshah

Nebo

Beth-zur

Salt Sea

Lachish

Gaza

Hebron

En-gedi

Arnon

MOAB

Gerar

Ziklag?

En-rimmon

IDUMEA

Jeshua?

Raphia

Beer-sheba

Moladah?

(EDOMITES)

Beth-pelet?

NABATEAN ARABS

The Empire of Alexander

Limits of Alexander's empire 323 B.C.E.

Allied states and client kingdoms dependent on Alexander

CYPRUS Allied states and client kingdoms dependent on Alexander

—— Alexander's route   • Cities founded by Alexander

- - - - Nearchus' voyage

✕ Major battles

Map 10

Probable ancient coastline

Places and regions

SCYTHIANS (SAKA)
MASSAGETAE
Jaxartes
Alexandria Eschata
Maracanda Samarkand
SOGDIANA
Bactra
BACTRIA
HINDU KUSH
Taxila
Nicaea
Bucephala
Hyphasis (Beas)
Ophian
Aornos
Indus
Oxus
ARIA
Alexandria Arion
Herat
Alexandria Arachostorum
ARACHOSIA
Alexandria Prophthasia
Pattala
CHORASMII
Aral Sea
PARTHIA
Hecatompylus
Alexandria
GEDROSIA
Pura
Caspian Sea
Caspian Gates
Rhagae
MEDIA
Ecbatana
Arbela
Gaugamela
Tigris
SUSIANA
Susa
BABYLONIA
Babylon
Persepolis
PERSIS
CARMANIA
Alexandria
Harmozia
Persian Gulf
Arabian Sea
CAUCASUS
ARMENIA
Euphrates
Thapsacus
Alexander died at Babylon in June 323 B.C.E.
ARABIA
Red Sea

SCYTHIANS
Olbia
Panticapaeum
Sinope
Black Sea
Trapezus
Ancyra
BITHYNIA
Gordion
ASIA MINOR
Sardis
Cilician Gates
Tarsus
Issus
Damascus
Sidon
Tyre
CYPRUS
Jerusalem
Gaza
Pelusium
Memphis
Alexandria
EGYPT
Nile
Thebes
Syene
ETHIOPIA (CUSH)
MACEDONIA
Pella
THRACE
Ister
Danube
HELLAS
Athens
Sparta
Aegean Sea
Ilium
Ephesus
Halicarnassus
Crete
Mediterranean Sea
Cyrene
CYRENAICA
LIBYA
Oracle of Amon
Libyan Desert

Dates along route
334
333
332
331
330
329
328
327
326
325
324
323
330–29
325–24
331–24
336

Scale
0 100 200 300 400 500
0   200   400   600   800

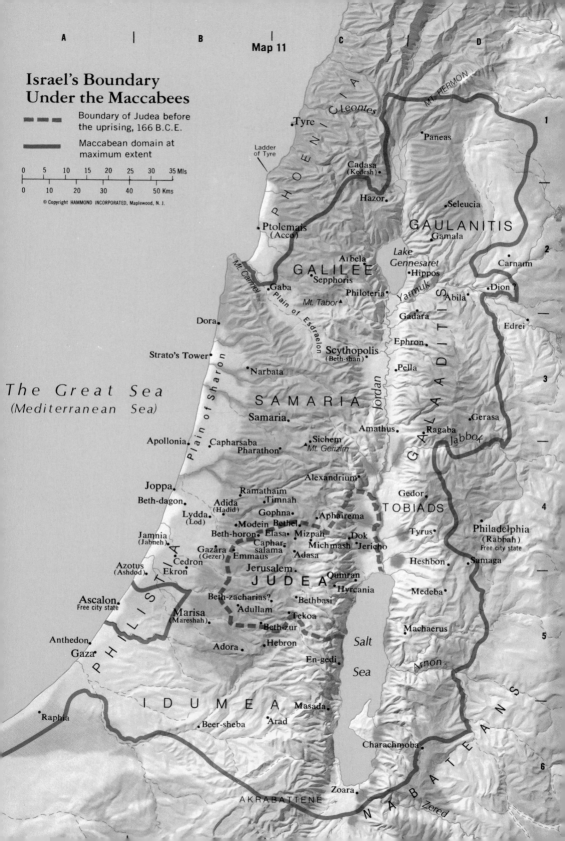

Map 11

Israel's Boundary Under the Maccabees

- - - - Boundary of Judea before the uprising, 166 B.C.E.

──── Maccabean domain at maximum extent

0   5   10   15   20   25   30   35 Mls
0   10   20   30   40   50 Kms

© Copyright HAMMOND INCORPORATED, Maplewood, N.J.

The Great Sea
(Mediterranean Sea)

PHOENICIA

Orontes

Tyre

Ladder of Tyre

Cadasa (Kedesh)

Hazor

Ptolemais (Acco)

MT. HERMON

Paneas

Seleucia

GAULANITIS

Gamala

Carnaim

Mt. Carmel

Gaba

Arbela

Lake Gennesaret

Hippos

Dion ?

Sepphoris

Philoteria

Edrei

GALILEE

Mt. Tabor

Plain of Esdraelon

Yarmuk

Gadara

Abila

Dora

Ephron

Strato's Tower

Scythopolis (Beth-shan)

Pella

Narbata

SAMARIA

Jordan

Amathus

Ragaba

Gerasa

GALAADITIS

Samaria

Plain of Sharon

Apollonia

Capharsaba

Sichem

Mt. Gerizim

Jabbok

Pharathon

Joppa

Alexandrium

Gedor

TOBIADS

Beth-dagon

Ramathaim

Timnah

Aphairema

Tyrus

Philadelphia (Rabbah) Free city state

Adida (Hadid)

Gophna

Lydda (Lod)

Bethel

Modein

Beth-horon

Elasa

Mizpah

Michmash

Dok

Jericho

Heshbon

Sumaga

Jamnia (Jabneh)

Caphar-salama

Gazara (Gezer)

Emmaus

Adasa

Jerusalem

Qumran

Hyrcania

Medeba

Azotus (Ashdod)

Cedron

Ekron

JUDEA

Ascalon Free city state

Beth-zacharias?

Bethbasi

Adullam

Tekoa

Machaerus

Marisa (Mareshah)

Beth-zur

Salt Sea

Anthedon

Adora

Hebron

En-gedi

Arnon

Gaza

PHILISTIA

IDUMEA

Masada

Raphia

Beer-sheba

Arad

Charachmoba

NABATEANS

AKRABATTENE

Zoara

Zered

A   B   C   D

Map 12

The Roman World

Limits of direct Roman rule
or political influence at the
birth of Jesus

Provincial or state boundaries

SYRIA   Roman provinces

LYCIA   Client kingdoms or states

Copyright HAMMOND INCORPORATED Maplewood, N.J.

0   100   200   300   400   500 Mls.
0   200   400   600   800 Kms.

Atlantic

Ocean

Britannia

Gaul

LUGDUNENSIS

AQUITANIA

BELGICA

NARBONENSIS

Lutetia

Burdigala

Lugdunum

Narbo

Augusta
Treverorum

Rhine

Albis (Elbe)

Lost by Rome
in 9 C.E.

Germania

Magna

Sarmatia

Rha (Volga)

Caspian
Sea

CAUCASUS

Iberia

Colchis

Albania

Artaxata

ARMENIA

PARTHIAN

EMPIRE

Ctesiphon

Arabia

Red Sea

Nile

Thebes

EGYPT

Memphis

Alexandria

NABATEA

KDM. OF
HEROD

Jerusalem

SYRIA

Antioch

Tarsus

COMMAGENE

CILICIA

CAPPADOCIA

GALATIA

PAMPHYLIA

LYCIA

ASIA

Ephesus

Pergamum

Ancyra

BITHYNIA & PONTUS

Sinope

Trapezus

BOSPORUS
KDM.

Black Sea

THRACE

Byzantium

MACEDONIA

Thessalonica

MOESIA

Salonae

ILLYRICUM

PANNONIA

NORICUM

RAETIA

ALPES

Aquileia

Dacia

CARPATHIANS

Ister (Danube)

Danube

Rubicon

ITALY

Rome

Tarentum

CORSICA

AND

SARDINIA

Caralis

Tingis

MAURETANIA

NUMIDIA

Cirta

Caesarea

Carthage

AFRICA

Leptis Magna

CYRENAICA

Cyrene

CRETA

ACHAIA

Corinth

Athens

Aegean
Sea

Sea of Adria

SICILIA

Syracuse

Mare

Internum

(Mediterranean Sea)

TARRACONENSIS

Hispania

LUSITANIA

BAETICA

Emerita Augusta

Corduba

Tarraco

Caesarea
Augusta

Mare

Sea of Adria

CYPRUS

Caesarea

Map 13

Judea, Samaria, and Surrounding Areas in New Testament Times

Political boundaries 6-44 C.E.
▫ Cities of the Decapolis
⚔ Fortresses

0   10   20   30   40 Mls
0   20   40   60 Kms

© Copyright HAMMOND INCORPORATED, Maplewood, N.J.

Mediterranean

Sea

ABILENE
• Abila

Iturea

• Sidon

P **H** **O** **E** **N** **I** **C** **I** **A**

MT. LEBANON

S **Y** **R** **I** **A**

Damascus ▫

• Sarepta

Leontes

Paneas

MT. HERMON

Tyre •

• Caesarea Philippi
  (Paneas)

Ladder of Tyre

Ulatha

• Ecdippa

Cadasa •

Trachonitis

• Gischala

Batanea

Ptolemais •

G **a** **u** **l** **a** **n** **i** **t** **i** **s**

Chorazin •

• Bethsaida-Julias

Raphana ▫

GALILEE

Capernaum •

Cana •   Magdala •

Sea of Galilee

Mt. Carmel

• Asochis

Tiberias •

▫ Hippos

▫ Dion?

Sepphoris •

Nazareth •

Mt. Tabor ▲

Yarmuk

Abila ▫

Plain of Esdraelon

Nain •
Agrippina •

▫ Gadara

• Capitolias

Dora •

Crocodilion •

• Arbela

Caesarea •

Scythopolis ▫

D **E** **C** **A** **P** **O** **L** **I** **S**

• Narbata

Ginae •

▫ Pella

Salim •
Aenon •

• Gerasa

S **A** **M** **A** **R** **I** **A**

Jordan

Sebaste •
(Samaria)

Mt. Ebal ▲

• Amathus

Apollonia •

Mt. Gerizim ▲ • Sychar

Jabbok

• Antipatris

Alexandrium ⚔

Joppa •

Phasaelis •

• Gadara

• Arimathea?

Ephraim •

P **E** **R** **E** **A**

Lydda •

Gophna •

Archelais •

▫ Philadelphia

Jamnia •

Jericho •

Betharamphtha
(Livias, Julias)

Emmaus?
(Nicopolis)

Emmaus? •

Cyprus ⚔

• Esbus

Azotus •

Jerusalem •   • Bethany

Qumran •

• Medeba

Bethlehem •

Hyrcania ⚔

Ascalon •

⚔ Herodium

Lake Asphaltitis

Callirrhoe •

Agrippias •

Marisa •

• Bethsura

(Dead Sea)

⚔ Machaerus

Gaza •

Hebron •

J **U** **D** **E** **A**

Arnon

I **D** **U** **M** **E** **A**

Engaddi •

N **A** **B** **A** **T** **E** **A**

Raphia •

Masada •

• Areopolis

Bersabe •

Malatha ⚔

• Charachmoba

A   B   C   D

1   2   3   4   5   6

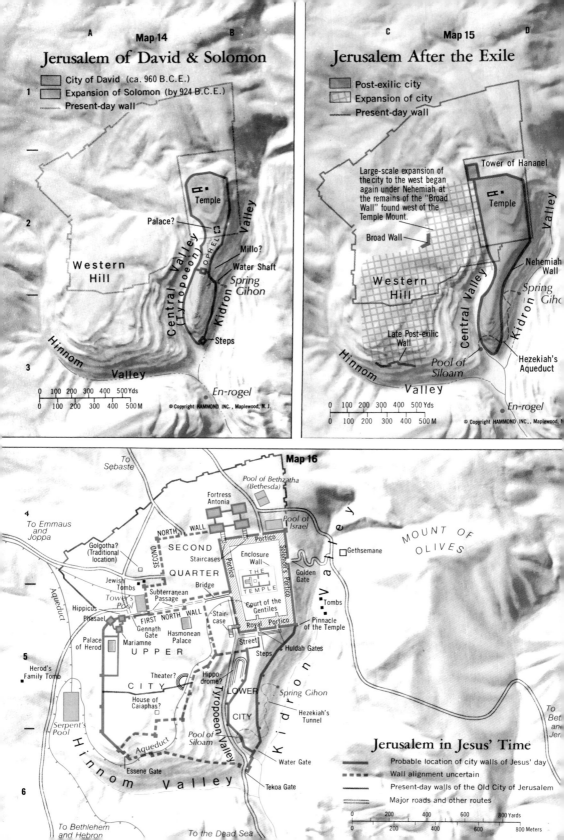

Map 14
Jerusalem of David & Solomon

- City of David (ca. 960 B.C.E.)
- Expansion of Solomon (by 924 B.C.E.)
- Present-day wall

Temple
Palace?
Millo?
Water Shaft
Spring Gihon
OPHEL
Central Valley (Tyropoeon)
Kidron Valley
Valley
Western Hill
Hinnom Valley
Steps
En-rogel

0 100 200 300 400 500 Yds
0 100 200 300 400 500 M
© Copyright HAMMOND INC., Maplewood, N.J.

Map 15
Jerusalem After the Exile

- Post-exilic city
- Expansion of city
- Present-day wall

Large-scale expansion of the city to the west began again under Nehemiah at the remains of the "Broad Wall" found west of the Temple Mount.

Tower of Hananel
Temple
Broad Wall
Nehemiah Wall
Western Hill
Central Valley
Spring Gihon
Kidron
Late Post-exilic Wall
Hinnom Valley
Pool of Siloam
Hezekiah's Aqueduct
En-rogel

0 100 200 300 400 500 Yds
0 100 200 300 400 500 M
© Copyright HAMMOND INC., Maplewood, N.

Map 16
Jerusalem in Jesus' Time

To Sebaste
Pool of Bethzatha (Bethesda)
Fortress Antonia
Pool of Israel
To Emmaus and Joppa
Golgotha? (Traditional location)
NORTH WALL
SECOND
Staircases
Portico
Enclosure Wall
Solomon's Portico
MOUNT OF OLIVES
Gethsemane
SECOND QUARTER
Jewish Tombs
THE TEMPLE
Golden Gate
Valley
Tower's Pool
Subterranean Passage
Bridge
Court of the Gentiles
Tombs
Hippicus
Phasael
FIRST NORTH WALL
Staircase
Royal Portico
Pinnacle of the Temple
Gennath Gate
Hasmonean Palace
Street
Huldah Gates
Palace of Herod
Mariamne
UPPER CITY
Steps
Herod's Family Tomb
Theater?
Hippodrome?
LOWER CITY
Spring Gihon
Kidron
Aqueduct
House of Caiaphas?
Hezekiah's Tunnel
Serpent's Pool
Tyropoeon Valley
Pool of Siloam
Aqueduct
Water Gate
To Bethany and Jericho
Essene Gate
Hinnom Valley
Tekoa Gate
To Bethlehem and Hebron
To the Dead Sea

- Probable location of city walls of Jesus' day
- Wall alignment uncertain
- Present-day walls of the Old City of Jerusalem
- Major roads and other routes

0 200 400 600 800 Yards
0 200 400 600 800 Meters

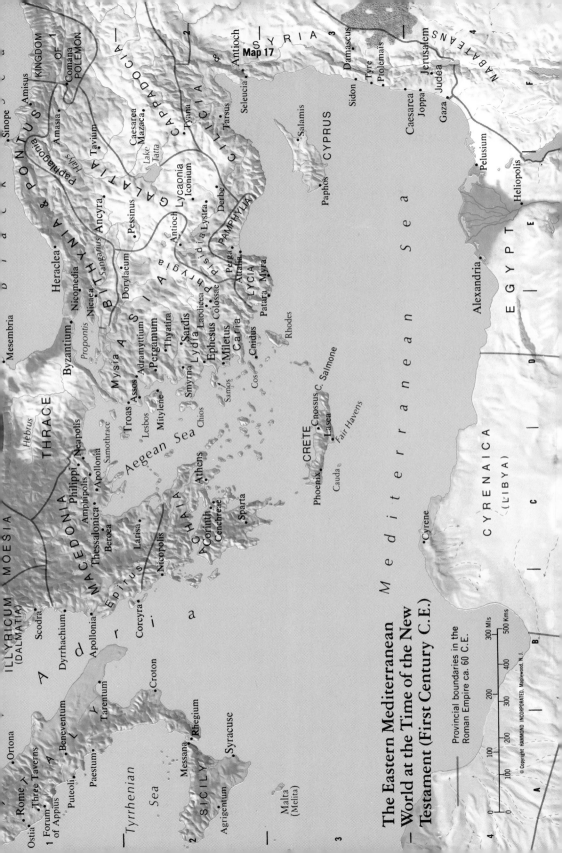

Map 17

The Eastern Mediterranean World at the Time of the New Testament (First Century C.E.)

Provincial boundaries in the
Roman Empire ca. 60 C.E.

300 Mls
500 Kms

© Copyright HAMMOND INCORPORATED, Maplewood, N.J.

Archaeological Sites
in Israel and Jordan

Map 18

■ Principal excavated sites
T, Tel, Tell: city site or mound
Kh, Khirbet: ruin

0 5 10 15 20 25 MIs
0 10 20 30 40 Kms

© Copyright by HAMMOND INC., Maplewood, N.J.

LEBANON

SYRIA

GOLAN HEIGHTS

Mediterranean Sea

ISRAEL

WEST BANK

JORDAN

GAZA STRIP

Dead Sea

Sidon
Zarephath
Tyre
Dan
Baniyas (Caesarea Philippi)
T. Anafa
Damascus
Gush Halab
Kafr Bir'im
Hazor
Meiron
Nabratein
Achzib
Nahariyeh
Acco
Chorazin
Gamala
Tabgha
Capernaum
Kh. Irbid
Sea of Galilee
Kursi
T. Shikmona
T. Abu Hawam
Tiberias
Carmel Caves
Sepphoris
Hippos
Atlit
Beth-yerah
Wadi el-Mughara
Beth Shearim
Nazareth
Jokneam
Abila
Umm Qeis (Gadara)
Dor
Megiddo
Bosra
Caesarea
Taanach
Beth Alpha
Ramoth-gilead
T. Zeror
Beth-shan
Pella
T. el-Hayyat
Dothan
T. el-Far'ah (N) (Tirzah)
T. es-Saidiyeh (Zarethan ?)
Jerash
T. Mikhal
Samaria (Sebaste)
Mt. Ebal
T. Deir 'Alla (Succoth ?)
Aphek (Antipatris)
Shechem
T. el-Qasileh
Mt. Gerizim
Izbet Sarta
Zarethan ?
Joppa
Shiloh
Ain Ghazzal
Bethel
Ai
Kh. el-Mefjir (Gilgal ?)
Rabbah-Amman
Mezad Hashavyahu
T. en-Nasbeh (Mizpah ?)
Araq el-Emir
T. Mor
Gezer
Gibeon
Jericho O.T.
Jericho N.T.
Ashdod Yam
Tel Miqne (Ekron)
Heshbon
Timnah
Jerusalem
Teleilat el-Ghassul
Mt. Nebo
Ashdod
Beth-shemesh
'Ain Karim
Ramet Rahel
Qumran
Madaba
Ashkelon
Azekah
Bethlehem
'Ain Feshka
T. es-Safi (Gath ?)
Herodium
T. el-'Areini
Mareshah
Beth-zur
Kh. Iskander
Lachish
Wadi el-Murabba'at Caves
T. el-Hesi (Eglon ?)
Mamre
Dibon
Gaza
T. en-Nejileh
T. 'Aitun (Eglon ?)
'Aroer
T. el-'Ajjul
T. Beit Mirsim
Kh. Rabud (Debir ?)
Lehun
T. Jemmeh
T. Halif
En-gedi
T. esh-Shari'ah
T. el-Far'ah (S) (Sharuhen)
T. Abu Matar
Beersheba
Arad-EB
Masada
Bab edh-Drah
Lejjun
Kh. el-Mishash
Arad
Kh. el-Kerak
Khalasa
Kuraub
Zoar
Numeira
Kh. et-Tannur